A Hebrew and English Lexicon of the Old Testament

A

HEBREW AND ENGLISH LEXICON

OF THE

OLD TESTAMENT

A

HEBREW AND ENGLISH LEXICON

OF THE

OLD TESTAMENT

WITH AN APPENDIX CONTAINING THE BIBLICAL ARAMAIC

BASED ON THE LEXICON OF

WILLIAM GESENIUS

AS TRANSLATED BY

EDWARD ROBINSON

LATE PROFESSOR IN THE UNION THEOLOGICAL SEMINARY, NEW YORK

Edited with constant reference to the Thesaurus of Gesenius as completed by E Rödiger, and with authorized use of the latest German editions of Gesenius's Handwörterbuch über das Alte Testament

BY

FRANCIS BROWN, D.D , D.LITT.

DAVENPORT PROFESSOR OF HEBREW AND THE COGNATE LANGUAGES IN THE UNION THEOLOGICAL SEMINARY

WITH THE CO-OPERATION OF

S. R. DRIVER, D.D., LITT.D

REGIUS PROFESSOR OF HEBREW, AND CANON OF CHRIST CHURCH, OXFORD

AND

CHARLES A BRIGGS, D.D , D.LITT.

EDWARD ROBINSON PROFESSOR OF BIBLICAL THEOLOGY IN THE UNION THEOLOGICAL SEMINARY

OXFORD

AT THE CLARENDON PRESS

OXFORD
UNIVERSITY PRESS
AMEN HOUSE, E C 4
London Edinburgh Glasgow New York
Toronto Melbourne Capetown Bombay
Calcutta Madras
HUMPHREY MILFORD
PUBLISHER TO THE
UNIVERSITY

IMPRESSION OF 1939
FIRST EDITION 1906
PRINTED IN GREAT BRITAIN

PREFACE

THE need of a new Hebrew and English Lexicon of the Old Testament has been so long felt that no elaborate explanation of the appearance of the present work seems called for. Wilhelm Gesenius, the father of modern Hebrew Lexicography, died in 1842. His *Lexicon Manuale Hebraicum et Chaldaicum in V.T. Libros*, representing a much riper stage of his lexicographical work than his earlier Hebrew dictionaries, was published in 1833, and the corresponding issue of his *Hebräisches und Chaldäisches Handwörterbuch über das Alte Testament*, upon which the later German editions more or less directly depend, appeared in 1834. The *Thesaurus philologicus Criticus Linguae Hebraeae et Chaldaeae Veteris Testamenti*, begun by Gesenius some years earlier, and not completed at his death, was substantially finished by Roediger in 1853, although the concluding part, containing Indices, Additions, and Corrections, was not published until 1858. The results of Gesenius's most advanced work were promptly put before English-speaking students. In 1824 appeared Gibbs's translation of the *Neues Hebräisch-deutsches Handwörterbuch*, issued by Gesenius in 1815, and in 1836 Edward Robinson published his translation of the Latin work of 1833. This broad-minded, sound, and faithful scholar added to the successive editions of the book in its English form the newest materials and conclusions in the field of Hebrew word-study, receiving large and valuable contributions in manuscript from Gesenius himself, and, after the latter's death, carefully incorporating into his translation the substance of the *Thesaurus*, as its fasciculi appeared.

But the last revision of Robinson's Gesenius was made in 1854, and Robinson died in 1863. The last English edition of Gesenius, prepared by Tregelles, and likewise including additions from the *Thesaurus*, dates as far back as 1859. In the meantime Semitic studies have been pursued on all hands with energy and success. The language and text of the Old Testament have been subjected to a minute and searching inquiry before unknown. The languages cognate with Hebrew have claimed the attention of specialists in nearly all civilized countries. Wide fields of research have been opened, the very existence of which was a surprise, and have invited explorers. Arabic, ancient and modern, Ethiopic, with its allied dialects, Aramaic, in its various literatures and localities, have all yielded new treasures; while the discovery and decipherment of inscriptions from Babylonia and Assyria, Phoenicia, Northern Africa, Southern Arabia, and other old abodes of Semitic peoples, have contributed to a far more comprehensive and accurate knowledge of the Hebrew vocabulary in its sources and its usage than was possible forty or fifty years ago. In Germany an attempt has been made to keep pace with advancing knowledge by frequent editions of the *Handwörterbuch*, as well as by the brilliant and suggestive, though unequal,

Wörterbuch of Siegfried and Stade (in 1892-3), but in England and America there has not been heretofore even so much as a serious attempt.

The present Editors consider themselves fortunate in thus having the opportunity afforded by an evident demand. Arrangements have been made whereby the rights connected with 'Robinson's Gesenius' are carried over to the present work, and exclusive authority to use the most recent German editions has been secured[1]. They have felt, however, that the task which they had undertaken could not be rightly discharged by merely adding new knowledge to the old, or by substituting more recent opinions for others grown obsolete, or by any other form of superficial revision. At an early stage of the work they reached the conviction that their first and perhaps chief duty was to make a fresh and, as far as possible, exhaustive study of the Old Testament materials, determine the actual uses of words by detailed examination of every passage, comparing, at the same time, their employment in the related languages, and thus fix their proper meanings in Hebrew.

In the matter of etymologies they have endeavoured to carry out the method of sound philology, making it their aim to exclude arbitrary and fanciful conjectures, and in cases of uncertainty to afford the student the means of judging of the materials on which a decision depends. They could not have been satisfied to pursue the course chosen by Professors Siegfried and Stade in excluding the etymological feature almost entirely from their lexicon. This method deprives the student of all knowledge as to the extra-Biblical history and relationship of his words, and of the stimulus to study the cognate languages, and lessens his opportunity of growing familiar with the modes of word-formation. It greatly simplifies, of course, the task of the lexicographer. The Editors acknowledge, at once, that their labours would have ended much sooner if they had not included the etymology of words, and they are sensible of the exposure to criticism at a thousand points which results from their undertaking to do so. They have cheerfully assumed this burden, and are ready to accept this criticism, from which they hope to learn much. Here, if anywhere, it is certain that results must, in many cases, long remain provisional. They have preferred to make what contribution they could to the final settlement of these difficult questions. For like reasons they have been unwilling to follow Buhl in excluding the explanation of the meaning of proper names, hazardous as such explanations often are.

[1] The eleventh German edition appeared in 1890, the year before the First Part of the present Lexicon was issued, under the editorship of Professors Muhlau and Volck, of Dorpat, who had prepared the eighth, ninth, and tenth also. The twelfth edition, in 1895, marked an era in the history of this useful dictionary, for with it began the careful editorship of Professor Frants Buhl, of Copenhagen, then at Leipzig, who issued the thirteenth edition, also, in 1899, and, after a very thorough revision, the fourteenth in 1905. None of these editions had the exact scope of the present work, and none of them absolved the Editors in any degree from personal investigation of the entire material. The Editors have, however, derived much benefit from the German work, and especially from the contributions to it of Professor Buhl and his co-labourers, Professors Socin and Zimmern. Unfortunately the present Lexicon—with the exception of the Appendix—was almost entirely in type when the fourteenth edition appeared, and adequate use of its new material, especially its extensive references to current philological literature must be reserved for a later opportunity.

That the Editors have made use of the *Thesaurus* of Gesenius on every page, with increasing admiration for the tireless diligence, philological insight, and strong good sense of this great Lexicographer, and recognition of Robinson's wisdom in allowing him to speak directly to English students by the admirable translation and editorship of the *Lexicon Manuale*, need not be further emphasized. They have also made free reference to Gesenius's Hebrew Grammar, in the successive editions prepared by Professor Kautzsch, follower of Gesenius at Halle, and, since 1898, to the excellent English translation of this book made by Messrs. Collins and Cowley, which appeared in that year. The grammars of Ewald, Olshausen, Bottcher, Stade, August Muller, and Konig, the *Syntax* of A B. Davidson, and other grammatical works have been cited as occasion required. Noldeke's contributions to Hebrew Lexicography and Grammar have been constantly used, with the works of Lagarde and Barth on the formation of nouns, of Gerber on denominative verbs, and many which cannot be catalogued here. All the critical commentaries, and a great number and variety of textual, topographical, and geographical works, with monographs and articles bearing on every possible aspect of Old Testament language, have been examined.

The published materials for the study of the languages cognate with Hebrew have reached such proportions as to tax even the most industrious in any extended comparison of kindred words. For the Arabic, constant use has been made of the dictionaries of Lane, Freytag, Dozy, Wahrmund, the Beirût Fathers, and others besides. The Editors have found themselves sharing with peculiar keenness in the unavailing regret of scholars that Mr. Lane's magnificent plan of complete Arabic lexicography was not destined to be realized. Frankel's *Aramäische Fremdworter im Arabischen* has been constantly used. For the vast and increasing storehouse of Assyrian—as yet most imperfectly explored—the dictionaries of Delitzsch, and, as far as the times of its appearance allowed, Muss-Arnolt have been employed, as well as Meissner's *Supplement*, and many special vocabularies. Paul Haupt, Bezold, Guyard, Strassmaier, Zimmern, Jensen, Winckler, Scheil, Sayce, King, Johns, R. F. Harper, and many writers in the *Zeitschrift fur Assyriologie*, the *Beiträge zur Assyriologie und Semitischen Sprachwissenschaft*, and other publications, have been laid under contribution. A place of honour must here be given to Eberhard Schrader, the founder of Assyriology in Germany, whose fruitful work has been prematurely cut short by impaired health, and the *Keilinschriftliche Bibliothek* begun by him is mentioned here many times. Winckler is of course recognized as the chief editor of the inscriptions from Tel el-Amarna. For Syriac, the *Thesaurus* of R. Payne Smith and the *Lexicon* of Brockelmann have been always at hand, with Castell accessible in case of need. Constant reference has been made to Noldeke's *Syrische Grammatik* (now, fortunately, translated), as well as his older works, the *Neu-Syrische Grammatik*, and the priceless *Mandäische Grammatik*. Duval and Nestle also have been laid under contribution. The Aramaic of the Targums and other Jewish-Aramaic documents, as well as the post-Biblical Hebrew have been examined in the dictionaries of Buxtorf, J. Levy, Jastrow, and Dalman, the collections of Bacher, the grammars of Strack, Marti, and Dalman, the editions of Lagarde,

Berliner, and Merx, as well as the older publications. The Christian Aramaic of Palestine has been studied in the treatment of Schwally and Schulthess. In the Aramaic Appendix frequent references have been made not only to the grammars of Kautzsch and Dalman, but also to Krauss's *Griechische u. Lateinische Lehnworter im Talmud*, and especially to the independent and valuable pamphlets of Scheftelowitz; *Arisches im Alten Testament* I and II. The Hebrew text of Ecclesiasticus has been used in the primary editions of Schechter, of Neubauer and Cowley, of Schechter and Taylor, of E. N. Adler, G. Margoliouth, I. Lévi and Gaster, as well as in the more compact editions of Strack and Lévi, and the admirable *facsimile* issued by the Clarendon Press. Dillmann has been the main authority for Ethiopic, with resort, from time to time, to Prätorius and Charles. North-Semitic inscriptions have yielded their material through the *Corpus Inscriptionum Semiticarum*, the *Répertoire d'Épigraphie Sémitique*, the collections of de Vogüé, Euting, and others, and, especially in recent years, by the aid of the Handbooks of Lidzbarski and G. A. Cooke, and the Glossary of S. A. Cook. The important Aramaic texts from Egypt, of the fifth century B. C. which have been just published by Cowley and Sayce, have also been utilized for the Aramaic Lexicon The lexical matter of Southern Arabia has been gathered from the *Corpus*, from the inscriptions published by Osiander, M. Levy, Halévy, Mordtmann, D H. Muller (including the discoveries of Langer), Glaser, and others. Egyptian parallels have been adduced mainly from Wiedemann, Bondi, Erman, Steindorff and Spiegelberg, with occasional reference to Lepsius, Brugsch and Ebers. In all these departments, where active work is going on, fugitive materials have of course been found in many places, often scattered and sometimes remote.

It has been the purpose to recognize good textual emendations, but not to swell the list by conjectures which appeared to lack a sound basis. There is still much to do in textual criticism, and much which has been done since the printing of this Lexicon began would receive recognition if extensive revision were now possible. Among the critical discussion of the Hebrew texts which have been frequently used are those of Geiger, Graetz, Wellhausen (*Samuel*, *Minor Prophets*), Perles, Oort, Cornill (*Ezekiel*, *Jeremiah*), Beer (*Job*), Driver (*Samuel*), Burney (*Kings*), the several Parts of the Polychrome Bible, the Notes by translators in Kautzsch's *Altes Testament*, as well as those found in the Commentaries (especially the two recently completed series published under the editorship of Nowack and Marti, respectively, and the Old Testament volumes of the International Critical Commentary, edited by Professors Briggs and Driver), and in many periodicals.

As to the arrangement of the work, the Editors decided at an early stage of their preparations to follow the *Thesaurus*, and the principal dictionaries of other Semitic languages, in classifying words according to their stems, and not to adopt the purely alphabetical order which has been common in Hebrew dictionaries. The relation of Semitic derivatives to the stems is such as to make this method of grouping them an obvious demand from the scientific point of view. It is true that practical objections to it may be offered, but these do not appear convincing. One is that it compels the Editor to seem to decide, by placing each word under a given stem, some questions of etymology

which in his own mind are still open. The number of such cases, however, is comparatively small, and the uncertainty can always be expressed by a word of caution. And even if the objection were much more important it would be better to assume the burden of it, in order to give students of Hebrew, from the outset, the immense advantage of familiarity with the structure and formative laws of the Hebrew vocabulary in their daily work. Another objection incidental to this arrangement is thought to be the increased difficulty of reference. This difficulty will diminish rapidly as students advance in knowledge, and by the practice of setting words formed by prefix or affix—or otherwise hard for the beginner to trace—a second time in their alphabetical place, with cross-references, it is hoped to do away with the difficulty almost entirely.

The Aramaic of the Bible has been separated from the Hebrew, and placed by itself at the end of the book, as a separate and subordinate element of the language of the Old Testament. This is a change from that older practice which, since it was adopted here, has been made also by Siegfried and Stade, and by Buhl, and which the Editors believe will commend itself on grounds of evident propriety.

The question of adding an English-Hebrew Index has been carefully considered. With reluctance it has been decided, for practical reasons, not to do so. The original limits proposed for the Lexicon have already been far exceeded, and the additional time, space, and cost which an Index would require have presented a barrier which the Editors could not see their way to remove.

The work of preparing the Lexicon has been divided as follows:—The articles written by Professor Driver include all pronouns, prepositions, adverbs, conjunctions, interjections, and other particles, together with some nouns whose principal use (with or without a preposition) is adverbial, also some entire stems of which only one derivative is used adverbially: e g. I בדד, בלה (not בְּלִיַּעַל), יחד, I. כלל, מאם, רגע; but in the case of יוֹמָם, נֶגֶד, סָבִיב, I. עֵבֶר, מַעַל and עַל (sub עלה), עִם, עַתָּה, יַעַן (sub ענה), among others, Professor Driver's responsibility does not go beyond the particular words. Under פָּנֶה he is responsible for the treatment of פְּנֵי with prepositions prefixed. He has prepared a few other articles, as well; e.g. אֱלִיל, II. בדד, הֶבֶל, ישה, תּוּשִׁיָּה, תָּמִיד, מחר, מְעַט, תהו. In addition to articles for which he is exclusively responsible, he has read all the proofs, and made many suggestions.

The following articles have been prepared by Professor Briggs[1]; they are in the main terms important to Old Testament Religion, Theology, and Psychology, and words related to these:—

אֲבַדּוֹן, אח, I. אהל, אוב, II. אוה, I אול, I. און, אור, אל, אֱלֹהִים, אֱלוֹהַּ, II. אלה, I. אמן, אפד, II. ארן, ארר, אִשָּׁה, אשם, אשר (but not אֲשֶׁר); באש, בֶּגֶד, I. בַּד, בוש, בחר, I. בטח, בין (not [בַּיִן], בין), בכר, בְּלִיַּעַל, בָּמָה, בעל, בקש, I ברא, בְּרִית, ברך, I. בַּר, ברר,

[1] Except where words are pointed, or special restrictions made, it is generally to be understood that Professor Briggs is responsible for all words belonging to the stem whose letters are given. Proper names, and much of the etymological material, especially in the last two-thirds of the book, form a standing exception, nor is Professor Briggs responsible for any part of the Biblical Aramaic

בשר, בתל, גאה, I. גאל, גָּבַהּ, גבר, גדל, גלה, גָּמַל (not גָּמֵל), גער; דבר, דין; הוה (incl. יהוה); זבח, I זור, זנה, I זנח, זעם, זרק, חגג, חום, I. חזה, חטא, חיה, חכם, III חלל, II. חלם, I חנן (not חִנָּם), I. חסד, חסה, חפץ, חקק, חרה, I. חרם, I. חרף, חשב, חשך, טהר, טוב, טמא, I יאל, ידה, יטב, יכח, יסר, יעד, יצר, ירא, ירה, ישע, ישר, כבד, כהן, כסה, כסל, כעס, I. כפר, כרוב, כרע, כרת; לאך, לבב, לין, למד, I. מאס, מות, I מחה, מִנְחָה, מעל, מַצָּה, מַצּוֹת, מרה, משח, I משל, נאם, נבא, נדב, נדר, I. נחל, נחם, נסה, I נסך, נפש, I נצח, נצל, I נצר, נקה, נקם; סוד, סֶלָה, סלח, עבד, עוד, II עוה, III עול, עזז, עלה (not עַל, מַעַל), עלם, עמל, III ענה, ערל; I. פאר, פדה, פלא, פלל, I. פסח, פשע; צבא, צדק, צוה; קדש, קהל, I. קטר, II. קִינָה, קנא, I. קנה, קסם, I. קצף, רהב, רוח, רוע, I רחם, I. רעע, רצה, רשע, שטן, שאול, שבת, שגג, שגה, שַׁדַּי, I. שָׁוְא, שוע, שחה, שיר, שָׁכַן, שָׁלֵם, שפט, שקר, שרת, תמם, תעב, תעה.

Professor Brown is responsible for all articles and parts of articles not included in the above statements, as well as for the arrangement of the book and the general editorial oversight.

The work has consumed a much longer time than was anticipated at the outset Twenty-three years have passed since it was undertaken, and nearly fifteen since the issue of the First Part, in June, 1891 Several causes have prevented an earlier completion of it. Not only have the Editors been engaged in the active duties of their professorships, to which they were obliged to subordinate even so important a work as this, but they have more than once encountered serious interruptions from unforeseen circumstances of a personal nature. But, above all, the task itself has proved a greater one than they supposed it to be. The field has been large, the questions have been many, and often difficult, the consideration of usage, involved, as it is, with that of textual change and of fresh proposals in exegesis, has required an enormous amount of time; the study of etymologies is involved with masses of new material, rapidly increasing and as yet imperfectly published and digested; the critical discussion of the many related topics is of great extent and scattered through many books and periodicals. Even tentative conclusions can be reached often only through a careful weighing of facts yielded by prolonged investigation. And so the process has gone on year after year. The Editors are quite aware that the patience of purchasers has been put to a severe test. They would be glad to think that they may find in the result a partial compensation.

They know, indeed, that this result is far from perfect. Their most earnest care has not been able to exclude errors, the First Part, in particular, was printed under unfavourable conditions, and the years since the earlier Parts were issued have brought new knowledge at many points It was not possible, nor would it have been just to owners of these Parts, to make considerable changes in the plates Such changes have been limited, almost wholly, to obvious misprints, and occasional errors in citation A selected, and restricted, list of some of the more important '*Addenda et Corrigenda*' is appended to the volume. The Editors venture to hope that in the future they may be able to utilize the additional material which is now in their hands.

A list of abbreviations was issued with Part I. This has been now revised and enlarged, and it is hoped that by its aid the abbreviations made necessary by the fullness of reference, on the one hand, and the requirements of space, on the other, will be quite intelligible.

Thanks are due to many scholars who have shown an interest in the work, and have contributed to its value by their suggestions. Prominent among these are Professor Hermann L. Strack, D.D., of Berlin; Professor George F. Moore, D.D., of Harvard University; and, for the Biblical Aramaic, Stanley A. Cook, Esq., of Cambridge, who has kindly read the proofs of the Aramaic Appendix, and made various additions and improvements. Dr. Eberhard Nestle, of Maulbronn, Professors Theodor Nöldeke, of Strassburg, Henry Preserved Smith, D.D., of Amherst, Mass., Thomas Kelly Cheyne, D.D., of Oxford, Richard J. H. Gottheil, Ph.D., of Columbia University, New York, A. F. Kirkpatrick, D.D., and William Emery Barnes, D.D., of Cambridge, T. W. Davies, of the University College of North Wales, and Max Margolis, of the University of California, as well as Mr. H. W. Sheppard, of Bromley, Kent, and others, have laid the Editors under obligation by sending important comments, or lists of corrections. Any further communications which may advance the cause of Hebrew scholarship, and promote a more thorough comprehension of the Old Testament Scriptures by supplying material for a possible future edition of the Lexicon, will be cordially welcomed.

It is impossible to bring this Preface to a close without especial reference to the relations between the Editors and their Publishers, in America and in England. The new Hebrew Lexicon owes its origin to Messrs. Houghton, Mifflin and Company, of Boston, Mass., holders of the copyright of 'Robinson's Gesenius,' and long its publishers. The present editors were authorized by them to undertake the work as a revision of that book. The late Mr. Henry O. Houghton, senior member of the firm, gave the project his especial attention, devoting much time to personal conference with the American editors, and making a visit to Oxford for a discussion of the matter with Professor Driver, and with the Delegates of the Clarendon Press, whose co-operation he secured. It is a matter of deep regret that his life was not spared to see the completion of an enterprise in which he took so sympathetic an interest. We desire to record our appreciation of that interest, and of the considerate patience with which he—and the other members of this publishing-house both before and since his death—have met the delays in finishing the work.

We are under similar obligations to the Delegates of the Clarendon Press. Since assuming a share in this enterprise they have shown unfailing regard for it as a serious contribution to Hebrew learning. The Editors have many courtesies to acknowledge from successive Secretaries of the Clarendon Press, the late Master of Pembroke, Professor Bartholomew Price, D.D., P. Lyttleton Gell, Esq., and C. Cannan, Esq.

We desire to express our thanks to the printers, to whose painstaking care in the composition—made complicated and difficult by the great variety of type, including half a dozen founts of foreign characters—in the correcting and in the press-work, the excellent appearance of the page is due; to Horace Hart, M.A.,

under whose direction they have worked; and not least to J. C. Pembrey, M.A., chief Oriental proof-reader, whose sharp eye little escapes, and whose personal enthusiasm is always concentrated upon the book in hand.

The merits of the work—if it have them—are dependent to a large degree on the hearty co-operation of all these, whose service we gratefully acknowledge.

In thus sending out into the world a book to which have gone many years of life and much persistent effort, our most earnest wish is that it shall be of real use to students, as a key with which they may unlock for themselves the rich treasure-house of the Old Testament.

THE EDITORS.

March, 1906.

ABBREVIATIONS

A = Alexandrine MS. of Septuagint.
ABA = Abhandlungen d. Berliner Akademie d. Wissenschaften.
abs. = absolute.
abstr. = abstract.
Abulf = Abulfeda.
Ac = Academy (London).
acc. = accusative (direct obj. etc.).
acc. cogn. = acc. of cognate meaning with verb.
acc. pers. = acc. of person.
acc. rei = acc. of thing.
acc. to = according to.
act. = active.
adj. = adjective.
adv. = adverb.
AE = Aben Ezra.
AGG = Abhandlungen d. Göttinger Gesellsch. d. Wissenschaften.
AGI = Assyrian & English Glossary, Johns Hopkins University.
AJPh = American Journal of Philology.
AJSL = American Journal of Semitic Languages.
Ak. = Akkadian.
al. = *et aliter*, and elsewhere; also *et alii*, and others.
Albr = K. Albrecht.
alttest(am). = alttestamentliche(r,s).
alw. = always.
Am = Amos.
Am.J.Sem.Lang. = AJSL, q. v.
AmRV = American RV.
Andr = Andreas. Andr^{M} = *Id.*, in Marti's Aram.Grammatik.
Aq = Aquila.
AR = Andover Review.
Ar. = Arabic.
Aram. = Aramaic, Aramaism.
Arch. = Archaeology.
ARSK = A. R. S. Kennedy.
As. = Assyrian.
Asrb. = Assurbanipal.
Asrn. = Assurnaṣirpal.
A.T. = Altes Testament.
Ath. = Athenaeum (London).
Av. = Avesta, Avestan.
AV = Authorized Version.
AW = Abu 'l Walid.
A&W = Abel & Winckler, Keilschrifttexte, Glossary.
ÄZ = Ägyptische Zeitschrift.

B = Vatican MS. of Septuagint.
Ba = J. Barth. Ba$^{\text{Erkl. d. Jes.}}$ = *Id.*, Erklärung des Jesaias; Ba^{ES} = *Id.*, Etymologische Studien; Ba^{NB} = *Id.*, Nominalbildung.
Bä = K. C. Bähr.
Bab. = Babylonian.
Bacher = W. Bacher. Bacher$^{\text{Terminol.}}$ = *Id.*, Älteste Terminologie der jüdischen Schriftauslegung.
Bachm = J. Bachmann.
Bäd = K. Bädeker. Bäd$^{\text{Eg.}}$ = Bädeker's Egypt; Bäd$^{\text{Pal.}}$ = Bädeker's Palestine.
Bae = F. Baethgen. Bae$^{\text{Rel.}}$, or Bae$^{\text{Sem. Rel.}}$ = Beiträge zur Semitischen Religionsgeschichte.
Baen = B. Baentsch.
Bähr = K. C. Bähr. Bähr$^{\text{Symb.}}$ = Bähr, Symbolik des Mosaischen Cultus.
BAL = C. Bezold, Babylonisch-Assyrische Literatur.
B.Aram. = Biblical Aramaic.
BarHeb(r) = Bar Hebraeus.
BAS = Beiträge zur Assyriologie u. Semit. Sprachwissenschaft, edd. Dl. & Hpt.
Bau(d) = W. von Baudissin. Bau^{Rel} = *Id.*, Studien zur Semitischen Religionsgeschichte; Bau$^{\text{Priest.}}$ = *Id.*, Geschichte des Alttestamentlichen Priesterthums.
Bd. = Bäd, q. v.
BD = Baer & Delitzsch, Heb. Text.
Be = E. Bertheau.
beg. = beginning.
Behrm = G. Behrmann.
Belsh. = Belshazzar.
Benn = W. H. Bennett.
Benz = J. Benzinger. Benz$^{\text{Arch.}}$ = *Id.*, Hebräische Archaeologie.
Berggren = J. Berggren, Guide Français-Arabe Vulgaire.
Berliner$^{\text{T.Onk.}}$ = A. Berliner, Targum of Onkelos.
Berthol = A. Bertholet.
BeRy = Bertheau's Comm., ed. by Ryssel.
Bev = A. A. Bevan.
Bez = C. Bezold.
BH = Biblical Hebrew.

Bi = G. Bickell.
Bl = F. Bleek.
Bla = J. S. Black.
Bloch$^{\text{(Gl.)}}$ = A. Bloch, Phönizisches Glossar.
Bmg = A. J. Baumgartner.
Bo = S. Bochart. Bo$^{\text{Hieroz.}}$ = *Id.*, Hierozoicon.
Bö = F. Böttcher. Bö^{I}, or Bö$^{\text{I, II}}$ = *Id.*, Lehrbuch d. Hebr. Sprache; Bö$^{\text{Ä. or NÄ.}}$ = *Id.*, Ährenlese, or Neue Ährenlese; Bö$^{\text{Inf.}}$ = *Id.*, De Inferis; Bö$^{\text{Prob.}}$ = *Id.*, Proben alttest. Schrifterklärung.
Bondi = J. H. Bondi, Hebr. Lehnwörter in Hieroglyphischen . . . . Texten.
BOR = Babylonian & Oriental Record.
Br = C. A. Briggs. Br$^{\text{Gen. Intr.}}$ = *Id.*, General Introduction to the Study of Holy Scripture; Br$^{\text{Hex.}}$ = *Id.*, Higher Criticism of the Hexateuch; Br^{MP} = *Id.*, Messianic Prophecy.
Braun$^{\text{de Vest. Sacerd.}}$ = J. Braunius, Vestitus Sacerdotum Hebraeorum.
Brd = C. Bredenkamp.
Brock = C. Brockelmann, esp. *Id.*, Lexicon Syriacum.
Bu = K. Budde. Bu^{RS} = *Id.*, Richter u. Samuel; Bu$^{\text{Urg.}}$ = *Id.*, Die biblische Urgeschichte.
Buhl = Frants Buhl, esp. as editor of eds.$^{12\text{-}14}$ of Gesenius's Handwörterbuch über das A. T.; Buhl$^{\text{G(eogr.)}}$ = *Id.*, Geographie des Alten Palästina; Buhl$^{\text{Edom.}}$ = *Id.*, Geschichte der Edomiter.
Bur = C. F. Burney.
Burckh = J. L. Burckhardt, esp. *Id.*, Travels in Syria, etc.
Bux = J. Buxtorf.
Bz = C. Bezold.

c. = *circa*, about; also *cum* with.
Ca = C. P. Caspari.
Calv = John Calvin.
Cappad. = Cappadocia.
Castell = Edward Castell.
Castle = Castell.

caus. = causative.
Cels$^{Hierob.}$ = O. Celsius, Hierobotanicon.
cf. = *confer*, compare.
1 Ch, 2 Ch = 1 & 2 Chronicles.
Champoll = J. F. Champollion.
Che = T. K. Cheyne. Che^{Founders} = *Id.*, Founders of Old Testament Criticism; Che$^{(Heb.) Hpt}$ = *Id.*, Isaiah, in Hpt.'s Sacred Books of the O. T. ('Polychrome Bible'), Eng. Trans., and Heb. Text; Che$^{Intr. Is.}$ = *Id.*, Introduction to Isaiah; Che^{OP} = *Id.*, Origin and Religious Contents of the Psalter.
ChGn = G. Smith's Chald. Genesis, Germ. ed.
Chron = Chronicles; also Chronicon (*e.g.*, Euseb$^{Chron.}$).
Chr-Pal. = Christian-Palestinian Aramaic.
ChWB = J. Levy, Chaldäisches Wörterbuch.
Cilic. = Cilician (Aramaic).
CIS = Corpus Inscript. Semiticarum.
ClGann = Clermont-Ganneau.
Co = C. H. Cornill.
coll. = collective.
Comm. = Commentary, Commentaries, Commentators.
comp. = compare, compares, comparative.
concr. = concrete.
conj. = conjecture(s); also conjunction.
consec. = consecutive.
constr. = construction.
contr. = contract, contracted.
Cook = Stanley A. Cook.
Cooke = G. A. Cooke.
COT = The Cuneiform Inscr. & the Old Test. (Eng. Trans. of KAT², by O. H. Whitehouse).
Cowley = A. E. Cowley.
cp. = compare.
cpd. = compound, compounded.
CR = Comptes Rendus.
cstr. = construct.
Ct = Canticles = Song of Solomon.
Cuche = *Id.*, Dictionnaire Arabe-Français.

D = Deuteronomist in Dt., in other books Deuteronomic author or redactor.
D (in BAram. Appendix) = G. Dalman, usu. *Id.*, Aramäisches-Neuhebräisches Wörterbuch; D§ = *Id.*, Grammatik des Jüdisch-Aramäischen (2nd ed., 1905).
Da = A. B. Davidson. Da$^{Synt.}$ = *Id.*, Hebrew Syntax.
Dalm = G. Dalman. Dalm^{WB} = *Id.*, Aramäisches-Neuhebräisches Wörterbuch.
Dan. = Daniel.
DB = Dictionary of the Bible, ed. J. Hastings.
De = Franz Delitzsch. De$^{Compl. Var.}$ = *Id.*, Complutensische Varianten zum alttestamentlichen Texte; De$^{HL und Koheleth}$ = *Id.*, Comm. über das Hohelied und Koheleth.
del. = *dele*, strike out (also *delet*, *delent*).
Derenb = (usu.) H. Derenbourg; sts. J. Derenbourg; Derenb^{Études} = *Id.*, Études sur l'Épigraphie du Yémen.
DeW = W. M. L. De Wette.
DHM = D. H. Müller. DHM^{BS} = *Id.*, Burgen u. Schlösser Süd-Arabiens; DHM$^{Epigr. Denkm. (Ar., or aus Abess.)}$ = *Id.*, Epigraphische Denkmäler, or Epigr. Denkm. aus Arabien, or Epigr. Denkm. aus Abessinien; DHM$^{Hofmus.}$ = *Id.*, Inschriften des Hofmuseums; DHM$^{Sendsch.}$ = *Id.*, Inschriften von Sendschirli; DHM$^{Stud.}$ = *Id.*, Südarabische Studien; DHM^{SMB} = *Id.*, Sab. Alterthümer in d. Kön. Museen zu Berlin.
Di = A. Dillmann.
Dict.Bib. = Smith, Dictionary of the Bible.
Dietr = F. E. C. Dietrich, esp. *Id.*, Abhandlungen für semit. Wortforschung.
Diod = Diodorus Siculus.
Dioscor = Dioscorides; Dioscor$^{De Mater. Med.}$ = *Id.*, De Materia Medica.
div. = *divinum, divinitatis*.
Dl = Friedrich Delitzsch. Dl§ = *Id.*, Assyrian Grammar; Dl^{H} = *Id.*, Hebrew & Assyrian; Dl^{HWB} = *Id.*, Assyrisches Handwörterbuch; Dl^{K} = *Id.*, Sprache d. Kossäer; Dl^{L} = *Id.*, Assyrische Lesestücke; Dl$^{Pa(r)}$ = *Id.*, Wo lag das Paradies? Dl$^{Pr(ol)}$ = *Id.*, Prolegomena; Dl^{S} = *Id.*, Assyrische Studien; Dl^{W} = *Id.*, Assyrisches Wörterbuch.
DLZ = Deutsche Literatur-Zeitung.
Dn = Daniel.
Door = A. van Doorninck.
Doughty$^{Arab. Des.}$ = C. M. Doughty, Travels in Arabia Deserta.
Dozy = R. Dozy, (usu.) Suppl. aux Dict. Arabes.
DPV = Deutscher Palästina-Verein.
Dr = S. R. Driver. Dr§ = *Id.*, Hebrew Tenses; Dr$^{Intr.}$ = *Id.*, Introduction to Literature of O. T.; Dr$^{Psalt.}$ = *Id.*, Psalter; Dr^{Sm}, or ^{Sam} = *Id.*, Text of Samuel.
Dr-Wh = Driver and White, Leviticus (Hpt.).
Dt = Deuteronomy.
Du = B. Duhm.
dub. = dubious, doubtful.
Dvd = David.
DWAk = Denkschriften der Wiener Akademie d. Wiss.
Dy = J. Dyserinck.
E = Elohist.
Eb = G. Ebers. Eb^{AgM} = *Id.*, Aegypten u. d. Bücher Mosis; Eb^{GS} = *Id.*, Durch Gosen zum Sinai.
EB(i) = Encyclopaedia Biblica, edd. Black and Cheyne.
Ec = Ecclesiastes.
Ecclus = Ecclesiasticus; Ecclus, Oxford ed., = Heb. Fragments of Ecclesiasticus, edd. Neubauer and Cowley.
Eg. = Egyptian.
elsewh. = elsewhere.
EMey = Eduard Meyer, EMey^{Entstehung} = *Id.*, Entstehung des Judenthums, = *Id.*, Entstehung J., etc.
Enc.Brit. = Encyclopaedia Brittanica, 9th ed.
Ency(cl).Bib. = EB(i), q. v.
Eng.Tr(ans). = English Translation.
Ephr. = Ephraimitic source.
Ephr(em) = Ephrem Syrus.
Esar. = Esarhaddon.
Esdr. = Esdras.
esp. = especially.
Est = Esther.
E.T. = Eng. Trans.
Eth. = Ethiopic.
Eut = J. Euting. Eut^{K} = *Id.*, Sammlung Karthag. Inschriften; Eut^{Nab} = *Id.*, Nabatäische Inschriften; Eut$^{Sin.}$ = *Id.*, Sinaitische Inschriften.
E.V. = English Version(s).
Ew = H. Ewald. Ew§ = *Id.*, Heb. Gram.; Ew$^{G(esch.)}$ = *Id.*, Geschichte d. Volkes Israel; Ew^{H} = *Id.*, History of Isr. (Eng. Trans. of Ew$^{G(esch.)}$); Ew^{JBW}, or Ew$^{Jahrb.}$ = *Id.*, Jahrb. d. bibl. Wissenschaft; Ew^{BTh} = *Id.*, Biblische Theologie; Ew^{Ant} = *Id.*, Antiquities.
Ex = Exodus.
exc. = except.
exil. = exile.
Ez = Ezekiel.
Ezr = Ezra.

f., *f.* = feminine.
f, or ff = and following.

F.B. = F. Brown.
fem. = feminine, *feminae*.
FFP = Flora and Fauna of Palestine (Survey).
Fi = Frederick Field, esp. *Id.*, Origenis Hexaplorum quae supersunt.
fig. = figurative.
fin. = finite, finitivum.
FJB = F. J. Bliss.
Fl = H. L. Fleischer. Fl$^{\text{Kl. Schr.}}$ *Id.*, Kleine Schriften.
Flora = Post, Flora of Syria.
fr. = from.
Fr = S. Frensdorff. Fr^{MM} = *Id.*, Massora Magna.
Frä = S. Fränkel, and (usu.) *Id.*, Aramäische Fremdwörter im Arabischen.
Frankenb(erg) = W. Frankenberg. Frankenb^{Spr} = *Id.*, Comm. Sprüche (ed. Nowack).
Frey = G. W. Freytag, Lex. Arab.; Frey$^{\text{Prov. Ar.}}$, or $^{\text{Prov.}}$ = *Id.*, Arabum Proverbia.
fs. = feminine singular.
Fü = J. Fürst.

𝔊 = Greek Version of the LXX. 𝔊L = LXX of Lucian (Lag).
GACooke = (usu.) G. A. Cooke, North Semitic Inscriptions; = GACooke$^{\text{Inscr.}}$
Gal. = Galilee.
Gann = Clermont-Ganneau.
GASm = George Adam Smith. GA Sm$^{\text{G(eogr.)}}$ = *Id.*, Historical Geography of the Holy Land.
Gei = A. Geiger. Gei$^{\text{Urschr.}}$ = *Id.*, Urschrift u. Übersetzungen der Bibel; Gei $^{\text{Nachgel. Schr.}}$ = *Id.*, Nachgelassene Schriften.
gent. = *gentis*, of a people, *gentilicium*.
geogr. = geography.
Gerber $^{\text{(Verb. Denom.)}}$ = W. T. Gerber, Verba Denominativa.
Ges = W. Gesenius. Ges$^{\text{§}}$ = *Id.*, Heb. Gram. ed. by Kautzsch; Ges^{Lbg} = *Id.*, Lehrgebäude d. Heb. Sprache.
Gesch. = Geschichte.
Gf = K. H. Graf.
GFM = G. F. Moore.
GGA = Göttingsche Gelehrte Anzeigen.
GGAbh. = Gött. Gel. Abhandlungen.
GGN = Gött. Nachrichten.
Gie = F. Giesebrecht.
Gi(nsb) = C. D. Ginsburg.
Gl(as) = E. Glaser; Gl^{MSI} = *Id.*, Mittheilungen über Sab. Inschriften; Gl^{Skizze} = *Id.*, Skizze der Geschichte u. Geographie Arabiens.
Gloss., gl. = glossary, rarely = a gloss.
Gn = Genesis.
Gr = H. Grätz.
Gray = G. B. Gray. Gray$^{\text{Prop. N.}}$ = *Id.*, Hebrew Proper Names.
Gu = H. Guthe, rarely Stan. Guyard. Gu$^{\text{§}}$ = Guyard, Notes de lexicogr. assyrienne.
Guérin = V. Guérin, Description géographique de la Palestine.
Guidi = Ignazio Guidi; Guidi$^{\text{Della Sede}}$ = *Id.*, Della Sede Primitiva dei Popoli Semitici.
Gunk = H. Gunkel. Gunk$^{\text{Schöpf.}}$ = *Id.*, Schöpfung u. Chaos.
Guy = Stan. Guyard.

𝔥 = Hebrew (Consonantal Text).
H = Code of Holiness.
Haev = Haevernick.
Hal = J. Halévy. Hal^{M} = *Id.*, Mélanges; Hal^{DR} = *Id.*, Documents Religieux; Hal^{MA} = *Id.*, Mission Archéol. dans le Yémen; Hal^{ÉS}, or $^{\text{Et. Sab.}}$ = *Id.*, Études Sabéennes.
Ḫamm = Ḫammurabi, esp. *Id.*, Code of Laws.
Hartm$^{\text{Plurilit.-bildungen}}$ = M. Hartmann, Pluriliteralbildungen in den semitischen Sprachen.
Hast = James Hastings. Hast(ings)^{DB}, or $^{\text{Dict. Bib.}}$ = Dictionary of the Bible, ed. James Hastings.
Hb = Habakkuk.
Hbr = Hebraica.
HDerenb = H. Derenbourg.
Heb. = Hebrew.
He(ngst) = E. Hengstenberg.
Herod(ot.) = Herodotus.
Hex = Hexateuch.
Hg = Haggai.
Hi = F. Hitzig.
Hilg = A. Hilgenfeld.
Hilpr = H. V. Hilprecht.
Hirz = L. Hirzel.
Ho = Hosea.
Hoffm = G. Hoffmann.
Hollenb = W. A. Hollenberg.
Holz = H. Holzinger.
Hom = F. Hommel. Hom^{AA}, or $^{\text{A. u. A}}$, or ^{Aufsätze} = *Id.*, Aufsätze u. Abhandlungen; Hom^{Chr}, or $^{\text{Chrest(om.)}}$, or $^{\text{Südar. Chrest.}}$ = *Id.*, Südarabische Chrestomathie; Hom^{NS} = *Id.*, Namen der Säugethiere.
Houb = C. F. Houbigant.
HP = Holmes & Parsons, Septuagint.
HPS = H. P. Smith.
Hpt = Paul Haupt. Hpt^{C} = *Id.*, Akkadische Sprache; Hpt^{D} = *Id.*, Über einen Dialekt der Sumerischen Sprache [GGN. 1880, Nr. 17]; Hpt^{E} = *Id.*, E. vowel; Hpt^{F} = *Id.*, Sumer. Familiengesetze; Hpt^{L} = *Id.*, Beiträge z. Ass. Lautlehre; Hpt^{N} = *Id.*, Nimrodepos; Hpt$^{\text{Prol. As. Gr.}}$ = *Id.*, Prolegomena to an Assyrian Grammar; Hpt^{S} = *Id.*, Sintfluthbericht; Hpt^{T} = *Id.*, ASKT, Akkad. & Sum. Keilschrifttexte; Hpt, or ^{Hpt} (Che^{Hpt}, &c.) usu. = Sacred Books of the O.T, ed. Hpt (Polychrome Bible).
HSch = H. Schultz.
Hultsch = F. Hultsch, Griechische u. Römische Metrologie.
Hup = H. Hupfeld. Hup^{Ri}, Hup^{RiNow}, Hup-Now = *Id.*, Psalmen, edd. Riehm, Nowack.

Idiot. = Idioticon.
Impf. = Imperfect.
Imv. = Imperative.
ind. = indirect.
indef. = indefinite.
Inf. = Infinitive.
infr., *infr.* = *infra*, below.
Inschr. = Inschrift, Inschriften.
inscr. = inscription(s); Inscr. of Carpentr. = Inscription of Carpentras.
intr(ans). = intransitive.
i.q. = *id quod*, i. e. the same with.
Is = Isaiah.

J = Jehovist.
JA = Journ. of the Royal Asiatic Society.
Jacob = G. Jacob. Jacob$^{\text{Ar(ab.) Dichter}}$ = *Id.*, Studien in Arab. Dichtern; *Id.*$^{\text{Bed. Leben}}$ = *Id.*, Leben der vorislamischen Beduinen.
J. Aram. = Jewish-Aramaic (Jüdisch-Aramäisch).
JAs = Journal Asiatique.
Jastr = Marcus Jastrow, Dict. of Targumim, Talmud, etc.; also Morris Jastrow, Jr.; Jastr$^{\text{Rel. Bab.}}$ = M. Jastrow, Jr., Religion of Babylonia and Assyria.
J$^{\text{AT. im Licht d. AO}}$ = A. Jeremias, Das Alte Testament im Licht des Alten Orients.
Jb = Job.
JBL = Journal of Biblical Literature.
JBTh = Jahrbücher f. deutsche Theologie.
JDMich = J. D. Michaelis.
Je = Jeremiah.
Jen = P. Jensen. Jen$^{\text{Cosmol.}}$ = *Id.*, Cosmologie der Babylonier.
Jer = Jerome; also Jerusalem.
Jerem = A. Jeremias.
Jerus. = Jerusalem.
Jes = Jesaias.
JHC = Johns Hopkins Univ. Circulars.

JHMich = J. H. Michaelis.
JLZ = Jenaer Lit.-Zeitung.
Jo = Joel.
Jon = Jonah.
Jos = Joshua.
Jos^{Ant}, Jos^{BJ} = Fl. Josephus, Antiquities, or Bell. Jud.
Joseph = Fl. Josephus (sts.).
JosKi = Joseph Kimchi.
JPh(il). = Journal of Philology (Engl.).
JPTh = Jahrbücher für Prot. Theol.
JQ = Jewish Quarterly.
Jr = A. Jeremias, Leben nach dem Tode.
JThS = Journal of Theological Studies.
Ju = Judges.
Jud. = Judæa, Judæan.
Jüd. Zeitschr. = Monatsschrift für Gesch. u. Wiss. des Judenthums.
juss. = jussive.

K = E. Kautzsch (in B. Aram. Appendix). K§ = *Id.*, Gramm. d. bibl. Aram.; K$^{Aram.}$ = *Id.*, Aramaismen im A.T.
1K, 2K = 1 & 2 Kings.
Ḳam. = al-Ḳamus (Arab. Dict.), by al-Fīrūzābādī.
KAT^{2} = E. Schrader, Keilinschr. u. d. Alte Testament. KAT^{3} = *Id.*, 3rd ed. by H. Winckler and H. Zimmern.
Kau = E. Kautzsch; Kau§ = *Id.*, Gram. d. bibl. Aram.; Kau$^{Aram(aismen) (im AT)}$ = K$^{Aram.}$; Kau^{AT} = Die Heiligen Schriften d. Alten Testaments, ed. Kau.; Kau^{MN} = *Id.*, Mittheilungen u. Nachrichten d. DPV, 1904; ^{Kau} (So^{Kau}, etc.) = Kau^{AT}.
Kay = W. Kay.
KB = E. Schrader, Keilinschriftl. Bibliothek.
Ke = C. F. Keil.
Kenn = B. Kennicott.
Kennedy = (usu.) A. R. S. Kennedy.
KG = E. Schrader, Die Keilinschr. und die Geschichtsforschung.
kg. = king.
Kgs. = Kings.
Ki = David Kimchi (Qamchi).
Kiep(ert) = H. Kiepert.
Kirkp = A. F. Kirkpatrick.
Kit = R. Kittel. Kit^{Di} = Di, Jesaia, ed. Kit; Kit$^{Gesch. (or Hist.)}$ = Kit, Geschichte der Hebräer (or Eng. Trans.).
Kit-Di = Kit^{Di} = Dillmann's Comm. (Isaiah), ed. by Kit.
Klo = A. Klostermann. Kl^{S} = Die Bücher Sam. u. d. Könige.
Kmp = A. Kamphausen.
Kn = A. Knobel.
Knudtzon$^{Ass. Gebete}$ = J. A. Knudtzon, Assyrische Gebete an den Sonnengott.
Kö = E. König. Kö$^{i, ii, iii}$ = *Id.*, Heb. Gram.; Kö$^{Synt.}$ = Kö^{iii}; Kö§ = *Id.*, Heb. Gram.; Kö$^{Einl.}$ = *Id.*, Einleitung in d. A.T.
Köh = A. Köhler.
Kohut-Memorial = Studies in Memory of A. Kohut; Kohut-Studies = *id.*
Kosters^{Herstel} = W. H. Kosters, Het Herstel van Israël in het Perzische Tijdvak.
Kp = A. F. Kirkpatrick.
Krae = R. Kraetzschmar.
Krauss = S. Krauss, esp. *Id.*, Griechische und Lateinische Lehnwörter im Talmud, etc.
Kremer = A. Kremer. Kremer$^{Beitr.}$ = *Id.*, Beiträge.
Krochm = A. Krochmal.
KSGW = Königl. Sächs. Ak. d. Wiss.
Kt = Kᵉthibh.
Kue = A. Kuenen. Kue$^{Ges. Abh.}$ = *Id.*, Gesammelte Abhandlungen.

La = Lamentations.
Lag = P. de Lagarde. Lag$^{Agathang.}$ = *Id.*, Agathangelus; Lag$^{Arm. Stud.}$, or ^{AS} = *Id.*, Armenische Studien; Lag^{BN} = *Id.*, Bildung d. Nomina; Lag^{M}, or $^{Mitth.}$ = *Id.*, Mittheilungen; Lag$^{Novi Psalt. spec.}$ = *Id.*, Novi Psalterii Specim.; Lag$^{Onom.}$ = *Id.*, Onomastica Sacra; Lag^{Or} = *Id.*, Orientalia; Lag$^{Pers. Stud.}$ = *Id.*, Persische Studien; Lag^{Se} = *Id.*, Semitica; Lag^{Sy}, or $^{Sym(m.)}$ = *Id.*, Symmicta.
Landberg = C. Landberg. Landberg$^{Prov.}$ = *Id.*, Proverbes et Dictons.
Lane = E. W. Lane; usu. *Id.*, Arabic Dictionary. Lane$^{(Mod.) Egypt.}$ = *Id.*, Modern Egyptians.
Lay = A. H. Layard.
l.c. = *in loco citato.*
LCB = Litterarisches Centralblatt.
Ldzb = M. Lidzbarski; usu. *Id.*, Nordsemitische Inschriften.
Len = F. Lenormant. Len^{Beginnings} = *Id.*, Beginnings of History (Eng. Trans. of Origines de l'Histoire, I). Len$^{Or(ig.)}$ = *Id.*, Les Origines de l'Histoire.
(v.)Leng = C. von Lengerke.
Levy = Jacob Levy.
Lewy$^{(Sem.) Fremdw(örter)}$ = H. Lewy, Semitische Fremdwörter im Griechischen.
Liḥy. = Liḥyanian (language).
Lindberg$^{Vergl. Sem. Gram.}$ = Lindberg, Vergleichende semitische Grammatik.
Linn = C. Linnaeus (Carl von Linné).
Littm = Enno Littmann.
Lo = R. Lowth.
loc. = local, locality.
Loft = W. K. Loftus, esp. Loft^{CS} = *Id.*, Chaldaea and Susiana.
LOPh = Literaturblatt für Orientalische Philologie.
Löw = J. Löw, Aramäische Pflanzennamen.
Lu = Martin Luther.
Luz(z) = S. D. Luzzatto.
Lv = Leviticus.
Lyon = D. G. Lyon.
Lzb = M. Lidzbarski (v. Ldzb.). Lzb$^{Eph(em).}$ = *Id.*, Ephemeris für semitische Epigraphik.

M, M§ = (in BAram. Appendix) K. Marti, Gram. d. bibl. Aram.
m., *m.* = masculine.
M-A = W. Muss-Arnolt. M-A^{CD} = *Id.*, Compendious Assyr. Dict.
Mal = Malachi.
Mand. = Mandean.
Marquart = J. Marquart. Marquart *Id.*, ^{Fundamente} = *Id.*, Fundamente israelitischer u. jüdischer Geschichte.
Marti = K. Marti.
Mas(s) = Masora.
MBAk = Monatsbericht d. Berliner Akad. d. Wissenschaften.
MDPV = Mittheilungen d. Deutschen Palästina-Vereins.
Me = A. Merx.
Meier^{WurzelWB} = E. Meier, Hebräisches Wurzelwörterbuch.
Meinh = J. Meinhold.
Meissn = B. Meissner. Meissn$^{Suppl.}$ = *Id.*, Supplement zum Assyr. Wörterb.
Mem. = Survey of W. Palestine, Memoirs.
metaph. = metaphor, metaphorically.
Mey = E. Meyer. Mey$^{E. Jud.}$, or ^{Entstehung}, or $^{Ent. J.}$, or $^{Entstehung d. Jud.}$, or $^{Judenth(um)}$ = *Id.*, Die Entstehung des Judenthums.
MGWJ = Monatsschr., q. v.
MI = Mesha-Inscription.
Mi = Micah.
Mich = J. D. Michaelis.
Min. = Minaean.
Mish(n). = Mishna.
mng. = meaning.
Mo = F. E. Movers.
Monatsschr. = Monatsschrift für Geschichte u. Wissen. d. Judenthums.
Mordt(m) = J. H. Mordtmann. Mordtm$^{Him. Inschr.}$ = *Id.*, Himjarische Inschriften.
mpl. = masculine plural.

ms. = masculine singular.
MT = Massoretic Text.
Müll = A. Müller.
Muss-Arn = W. Muss-Arnolt.
MV$^{11(10,9,8)}$ = Gesenius, Handwörterbuch über das A.T, edd. F. Muhlau & W. Volck.
MVAG, or MVG = Mittheilungen d. Vorderasiatischen Gesellschaft.

n. = *nomen*, noun.
Na = Nahum.
Nab. = Nabataean.
Nag = C. W. E. Nagelsbach.
Nasar = Lexid. cod. Nasaraef, ed. M. Norberg
NBab. = New Babylonian.
Nbr = A. Neubauer.
Ne = Nehemiah (rarely = E Nestle).
Neb = Nebuchadnezzar.
Nes = E Nestle. Nes^{S} = *Id*, Syriac Gram., Nes^{Eg} = Eigennamen; Nes^{Marg} = *Id*, Marginalien u. Materialien.
NH = New (Late) Hebrew.
NHWB = Levy, Neuhebr. Wörterb
NKZ = Neue kirchliche Zeitschrift
No = T. Noldeke. No^{S} = *Id.*, Syrische Grammatik; No$^{\text{Beitr(äge)}}$, or ^{BSW} = *Id.*, Beitrage z. semitischen Sprachwissenschaft; No^{M} = *Id*, Mandaische Grammatik, No^{NS} = *Id*, Neu-Syrische Grammatik, No^{Untersuch} = *Id*, Untersuchungen zur Kritik des A.T; No$^{\text{Zur Gram. d class Ar}}$ = *Id*, Zur Grammatik des classischen Arab. (in Denkschriften der Wiener Akademie, 1896).
no. = number.
nom. = *nomen*, noun.
nom. coll = *nom. collectivum*, collective noun.
nom. unit = *nom. unitatis*, noun of singular or individual meaning.
Nor = E. Norris, Assyrian Dictionary.
Norberg$^{\text{Lexid.}}$ = Nasar, q v.
Norzi = J. S. ben Abraham Norzi.
Now = W. Nowack. Now$^{\text{Arch.}}$ = *Id*, Hebräische Archaologie.
n pr = *nomen proprium*, proper name
n pr.loc = *n. pr. loci*, proper name of place.
Nu = Numbers.

Ob = Obadiah.
obj. = object
OBaktr. = Old Baktrian.
Oehl = Oehler.
oft. = often.
OH = Old Hebrew (Inscriptions).
OIran. = Old Iranian.

Ol = J. Olshausen. Ol^{l} = *Id.*, Heb. Gram.
OLZ = Orientalische Literaturzeitung.
Onk = Targum of Onkelos
Oort = H. Oort.
op. cit. = *in opere citato.*
OP(ers.) = Old Persian. OP also (in Che^{OP}) = Origin of Psalter.
opp. = opposite, as opposed to, or contrasted with.
Opp(ert) = Jules Oppert.
Or(elli) = C. von Orelli.
Os = E Osiander.
OT = Old Testament
Öt = S. Öttli.

P = Priests' Code or Narrative
Pal(est). = Palestine, Palestinian, etc.
Pal(m). = Palmyrene.
PAOS = Proceedings of the American Oriental Society
Pap = Papyrus.
part. = particle.
pass. = passive
PB = Proceedings of Soc. of Bib Archaeol.
Pe = J. J S. Perowne.
PEF = Pal. Explor. Fund, usu. *Id*, Quart. Statem'nt. PEF ^{Mem} = Mem, q.v
Pei = F E. Peiser
Perles = F. Perles. Perles$^{\text{(Anal)}}$ = *Id*, Analekten.
pers = person, *personae*
Pers. = Persian.
PESoc = American Palestine Explor Society.
Pf. = Perfect.
Ph = Phenician.
Phi = F. Philippi.
Pietschm = R. Pietschmann (also Pietschm$^{\text{Phön(iz.)}}$, or $^{\text{Gesch. Ph}}$) = (usu) *Id*, Geschichte Phoniziens.
Pinsk = S. Pinsker
pl = plural.
Plin^{HN} = Pliny, Hist. Nat.
POS = Proceedings Am. Orient Soc.
Post = G E Post Post^{Flora} = *Id*, Flora of Syria.
postB = post-Biblical.
postex = post-exilic.
post-pos. = post-positive.
Pr = Proverbs
Pra(t) = F. Pratorius. Pra$^{\text{Amh Spr}}$ *Id*, Amharische Sprache, Pra(t)$^{\text{Neue Beiträge}}$ = *Id*, Neue Beitrage zur Erklarung der Himjarischen Inschriften.
PRE = Herzog's Prot. Real-Encycl
Presb Rev. = Presbyterian Review (New York)
Prol = Prolegomena.
PS = R Payne Smith, Thesaurus Syriacus
Ps = Psalms, Psalmen
Ps-J = Targum of Pseudo-Jonathan.
ψ = Psalm

pt(cp). = participle.
Ptol = Ptolemy (usu. Claudius Ptolemy).
punct = punctuation.

Qor = Qoran.
Qr = Q^{e}rê.
qu = question
q v. = *quod vide.*
qy. = query.

R = Redactor (e.g. in Hexateuch) R^{D} = Deuteronomic redactor
1 R, 2 R, 3 R, 4 R, 5 R = Cuneiform Inscr of Western Asia (H Rawlinson).
RA = Revue Archéologique.
Ra = Rashi.
rd = read.
rdg = reading.
Rd'A = Revue d'Assyriologie.
Re = E. Renan.
Reckend = S. Reckendorf.
refl = reflexive.
RÉJ = Revue des Études Juives.
Rel = H Reland.
RÉS = Répertoire d'Épigraphie Sémitique.
Rev.Bib = Revue Biblique.
Ri = E Riehm Ri^{HWB} = Handworterb d. bibl. Alterth.
Ro = E. Rodiger
Rob = E Robinson. Rob^{BR} = *Id*, Biblical Researches.
Rob-Ges. = Gesenius, Hebrew and English Lexicon, translated by E. Robinson.
Roo = T Roorda.
Rosenm = E. F. C. Rosenmüller.
Rothst = W. Rothstein.
RP$^{\text{2(1)}}$ = Records of Past, 2nd (1st) Series
RS = W. Robertson Smith. RS ^{OTJC} = *Id*, Old Testament in Jewish Church, RS ^{Proph} = *Id.*, Prophets of Israel; RS^{K} = *Id.*, Kinship & Marriage in Early Arabia; RS^{Sem} = *Id*, Religion of Semites.
RTr = Recueil de Travaux.
Ru = Ruth.
RV = Revised Version
RVm = Revised Version margin.
RWB = Bibl. Realwörterbuch, ed. Winer.
Ry = V. Ryssel.

𝔖 = Syriac Version 𝔖^{Jerus} = Chr-Pal. Evang (Lagarde).
1 S, 2 S = 1 & 2 Samuel
Saad = Arabic Version of Saadya.
Sab = Sabean.
SabDenkm = Sabäische Denkmaler, edd Mordtmann & Müller.
SAC = Stanley A. Cook; esp. *Id.*, Aramaic Glossary.
Sam. = Samaria, Samaritan (rarely = Samuel).
Sarg = Sargon.

SahoSpr = Saho Sprache.
SASm = S. A. Smith.
Say = A H Sayce Say^{Monuments} = *Id*, Higher Criticism and the Monuments, Say$^{\text{Rel Bab.}}$ = *Id*, Religion of Babylonia.
SB = SBAk.
SBAk = Sitzungsbericht d Berl Akademie der Wissenschaften
S-C$^{\text{Pap.}}$ = A. H Sayce and A E Cowley, Aram Papyri
Sch = F. W Schultz
Scheft = Scheftelowitz, usu. = Scheft, Arisches im A T, Scheft^{MGWJ} = *Id*, Monatsschrift für Gesch u Wiss d Jud (1903), also pub separately (Scheft^{II})
Schenkel^{BL} = D. Schenkel, Bibel-Lexicon.
Schl(ottm) = C. Schlottmann
Schr = E. Schrader.
Schrod, Schroed = P Schroder, esp *Id*, Phönizische Sprache.
Schu = A. Schultens
Schu = E Schurer, Gesch des judischen Volkes im Zeitalter Jesu Christi
Schulth = F. Schulthess Schulth$^{\text{Hom Wurz.}}$ = *Id*, Homonymische Wurzeln im Syrischen; Schulth^{Lex} = *Id.*, Lexicon d. Chr. Pal Aramaischen
Schw = F. Schwally. Schw(ally)^{Idiot} = *Id.*, Idioticon d Chr. Pal.
Seetzen^{Reise} = Seetzen, Reisen durch Syrien.
seld. = seldom, rare.
Sen = Sennacherib.
Sendsch. = Sendschirli (Zinjirli)
sf. = suffix, *or* with suffix.
sg. = singular.
Shlm = Shalmaneser II
SI = Siloam Inscription.
si vera l. = *si vera lectio*
Siegf = C. Siegfried.
sim = simile.
SK = Studien u. Kritiken.
Skr = Sanskrit
Sm = R. Smend (rarely = Samuel) Sm$^{\text{Rel Gesch.}}$ = Smend, Alttestamentliche Religionsgeschichte, Sm^{Listen} = *Id*, Listen der Bucher Esra u Nehemia.
So(c) = A Socin.
Spi = W. Spitta Spi^{t} = Gram d arab. Vulg Dial
Spieg = F. Spiegel, Spieg^{APK} = *Id*, Altpersische Keilinschriften
Spiegelb = W Spiegelberg
Spr = Sprache, or Sprüche
sq = followed by
SS = C. Siegfried u B Stade, Hebräisches Worterbuch
st = *status*, state, stative
St = H Steiner

Sta = B Stade, Sta^{t} = *Id*, Heb. Gram, Sta$^{\text{G(esch)}}$ = *Id*, Geschichte des Volkes Israel
Steind = G Steindorff
Steuern = C Steuernagel
Str = H L. Strack Str^{t} = *Id*, Gram d bibl Aram
Strassm = foll
Strm = J Strassmaier Strm^{AV} = *Id*, Alphabet Verzeichniss
sts = sometimes
Stu = G Studer
Stud Bib. = Studia Biblica
subst = substantive
Sum(er) = Sumerian
supr, *supr* = *supra*, above
Surenh = W Surenhusius, Mishna
Survey, Survey^{WP} = Survey of Western Palestine (PEF), Survey^{EP} = *Id* of Eastern Palestine
Symm = Symmachus
Syr. = Syriac

𝔗 = Targum
t (following a number) = times
TA = Tel el-Amarna, also Taj-al-'Arûs (Arab Dict).
Talm = Talmud
Tariff = Palmyrene Tariff Inscription
TB, TBA = Transactions of the Society of Biblical Archaeology
TelAm = TA, q v
Tg = Targum Tg^{Jer} = Targum of Jerusalem, etc
Th(e) = O Thenius
Theod = Theodotion.
Theophr = Theophrastus; Theophr$^{\text{Hist Plant.}}$ = *Id*, Historia de Plantis
Thes = W Gesenius, Thesaurus Linguae Hebraeae
Thes^{Add} = *Id*, Additions by E Rodiger
ThT = Theologisch Tijdschrift.
ThLB = Theol Literaturblatt.
ThLZ = Theol. Literaturzeitung.
Tiele = C. P. Tiele.
Tiph. = Tiphel (rare conjugation)
To = Tobler.
TP = Tiglath-Pileser.
Tpg. = Topography
Tr = Transactions.
tr = translate (translated, translation); rarely = transitive.
trans(it) = transitive.
Tristr = H. B Tristram Tristr^{NHB} = *Id.*, Natural History of the Bible, Tristr^{FFP} = *Id.*, Fauna and Flora of Palestine (Survey, Memoirs)
TSBA = TB, q v.
TSWt = Theol Studien aus Württemberg.
TTijdschr = ThT, q v.
Tu = F. Tuch.
txt = text.
txt err. = textual error.

Univ Pa Exp. = Bab Exped. of the Univ. of Pennsylvania.
usu = usual, usually

𝔙 = Vulgate.
v = verse, v. = *vide*, see.
van d. H. = E van der Hooght, Heb text of O.T.
var = variant reading
VB = Variorum Bible
vb. = verb.
vdVelde = C. W M. van de Velde, esp. *Id.*, Reis door Syrie en Palestina, E T., Narrative of a Journey through Syria and Palestine, vdVelde$^{\text{Mem(oir)}}$ = *Id*, Memoir to accompany Map of Holy Land constructed by C. W. M. van de Velde.
vid. = *vide*, see.
vir = *viri*, of a man
Vog = C. J. M. de Vogüé, Syrie Centrale Vog^{Palm} = *Id.*
Vogelst^{Landwirthsch} = H Vogelstein, Landwirthschaft in Palästina zur Zeit der Mišnâh
VOJ = Vienna Oriental Journal (= Wiener Zeitschrift für die Kunde des Morgenlandes).
Vrss = Old Versions
Vulg Ar. = Vulgar Arabic
Vullers = J. A. Vullers, Lexicon Persico-Latinum

W = W. Wright. W^{AG} = *Id.*, Arabic Gram, W^{SG}, or ^{CG} = *Id*, Comp. Semit. Gram
Wahrm = A. Wahrmund, esp. *Id*, Arab. Handworterbuch.
WAW = W. Aldis Wright.
wd = word, also would.
We = J. Wellhausen We$^{\text{Bl Einl.}}$ = *Id.*, Bleek's Einleitung in d A.T.; We$^{\text{Comp.}}$ = *Id.*, Composition des Hexateuchs; We$^{\text{de gent}}$ = *Id*, De gentibus et familiis Iudaeis, We$^{\text{Held. (or. Arab. Heidenthum)}}$ = *Id.*, Reste Arabischen Heidenthums (= We$^{\text{Skizzen iv, 2nd ed.}}$), We$^{\text{Hist.}}$ = *Id.*, History of Israel (trans by Black), We^{Prol} = *Id*, Prolegomena zur Geschichte Israels, We^{Skizzen} = *Id.*, Skizzen und Vorarbeiten
Weissb = F H. Weissbach
Wetzst = J. G. Wetzstein
wi = with, construed with
Wied = A. Wiedemann. Wied^{Samml} *Id*, Sammlung Altägyptische Wörter.
Wild(eb) = G. Wildeboer
Wilkinson$^{\text{(Anc.) Egypt.}}$ = J. G. Wilkinson, Ancient Egyptians.
WisdLt = Wisdom Literature.
Wkl = H. Winckler.

WMM = W. Max Muller WMM As. u Eur(op.), or Asien = *Id.*, Asien u Europa.
Wr = C. H. H. Wright
Wü = A. Wünsche.
WZKM = VOJ, q v

Xen(oph) = Xenophon.

Z = Zeitschrift
ZA = Zeitschr für Assyriologie
ZAW = Z f alttest. Wissenschaft.
Zc = Zechariah
Zehnpf = R. Zehnpfund.
ZEthnol. = Zeitschrift fur Ethnologie.
Zim = H. Zimmern. Zim^{BP} = *Id.*, Babylonische Busspsalmen.
Zinj. = Inscriptions of Zinjirli (N. Syria).
ZK = Z für Keilschriftforschung
ZKM = Z f. Kunde d. Morgenlandes.
ZKW, or ZKWL = Z f kirchl Wiss und kirchl Leben.
ZLuth.Th = Z. für Lutherische Theologie
ZMG = Z d deutsch Morgenland Gesellschaft.
Zö = O. Zöckler.
Zp = Zephaniah.
ZPV = Z. d. deutsch. Pal.-Vereins
ZVolkerpsych. = Z. fur Volkerpsychologie
ZWTh, or ZWiss.Th. = Z für Wissenschaftliche Theologie.

< over a letter, indicates the accented (tone-)syllable
† prefixed, or added, or both, indicates 'All passages cited'
> indicates that the preceding is to be preferred to the following.
< indicates that the following is to be preferred to the preceding
‖ parallel, of words (synonymous or contrasted), also of passages, sometimes = 'see parallel,' or 'so also in parallel'
= equivalent, equals
+ plus, denotes often that other passages, etc, might be cited. So also where the forms of verbs, nouns, and adjectives are illustrated by citations, near the beginning of articles; while 'etc.' in such connexions commonly indicates that other forms of the word occur, which it has not been thought worth while to cite.

[ ] indicates that the form, etc, enclosed, is not actually found, or that the Hebrew offers no positive proof, *e.g.* n [m] denotes that the noun is presumably masculine, though the gender is not clearly exhibited in Hebrew
√ = root *or* stem.
′ = sign of abbreviation (in Hebrew words).
א׳ often = אֱלֹהִים, Elohim
וגו׳ = וְגוֹמֵר = *et caetera* (in Hebrew quotations)
י׳ = Yahweh.
‸ beneath a Hebrew word represents any accent that occasions vowel change.

Note Scripture citations in small superior letters and figures, following n m. or n.f, refer to some passage where the gender is exhibited Small inferior figures following Hebrew words, names of conjugations, etc, denote the (approximate) number of occurrences of such words, conjugations, etc.

א

א, *Âleph*, first letter; in post B Heb. = numeral 1 (and so in marg. of printed MT); א̈ = 1000; no evidence of this usage in OT times.

אָב v. II. אבה.

אבב (*fresh, bright*, As *abâbu* Dl^{W}, AGl)

†**[אֵב]** **n. [m.] freshness, fresh green** (Lag$^{BN\ 207}$ Inf. *ibb;* thence concr., cf. Ar. أَبٌّ; above stem & mng. better than √אנב (spring) cf. As. *inbu*, fruit, Aram. אנבה (q. v.) Dl$^{HA\ 65,\ Pr\ 114}$) עֹדֶנּוּ בְאִבּוֹ *while yet in its freshness* (i.e. אָחוּ, reed) Jb 8^{12}; concr, pl *green shoots* באבי הַנַּחַל Ct 6^{11} (‖ הַפָּרְחָה הַגֶּפֶן הֵנֵצוּ הָרִמֹּנִים:).

†**אָבִיב** **n.m.**$^{Lv\ 2,14}$ **coll.** (Lag$^{BN\ 207}$ Inf) **1. fresh, young ears** of barley Ex 9^{31}; indef. Lv 2^{14} מנחת בכורים ליהוה א׳ קָלוּי בָּאֵשׁ **2.** חֹדֶשׁ הָאָבִיב month of ear-forming, or of growing green, **Abib**, month of Exodus & passover, Ex 13^{4} 23^{15} 34$^{18\ 18}$ (JE), Dt 16$^{1\ 1}$ (1st month = c. April = הַחֹדֶשׁ הָר׳, הָרִאשׁוֹן (q v) in P, v Di Ex 12^{2}, = postexilic נִיסָן q v)

אֲבַגִּיל v. אֲבִיגַיִל sub II אבה

†**אֲבַגְתָא** **n. pr. m.** (Pers. cf בִּגְתָא) eunuch of Ahasuerus Est 1^{10}.

†**אָבַד** **vb. perish** (MI אבד, As *abâtu* Dl$^{W\ 184}$ Aram. אֲבַד, ﺑﻜﺪ) —**Qal** *Pf.* א׳ Nu 21^{30}+; אָבְדוּ ψ 10^{16}+ (+ Ez 6^{3} 𝔊 Co) etc, *Impf.* יֹאבַד Jb 3^{3} Je 4^{9}, יֹאבֵד Jb 20^{7} + 2 t; 3 fs תֹּאבַד Dt 22^{3} + 4 t; תֹּאבֵד Jb 8^{13} + 3 t.; יֹאבְדוּ Ju 5^{31} + 3 t., יֹאבֵדוּ Jb 4^{9}+, 3 fpl תֹּאבדון Dt 4^{26} וַתֹּאבַדְנָה 1 S 9^{3}; +; נֹאבֵד Jn 1^{6} 3^{9}; נֹאבְדָה Jon 1^{14} etc; *Inf abs.* אָבֹד Dt 4^{26} + 2 t.; cstr. אֲבֹד Dt 7^{20} Pr 11^{10}; אֲבָדְךָ Dt 28^{20}, אָבְדֶךָ Dt 28^{22}; אֲבָדְכֶם Jos 23^{13}, אָבְדָם Ob^{12} Pr 28^{28}; *Pt.* אוֹבֵד Dt 26^{5} + 7 t; cstr. אֹבַד Dt 32^{28} (bef. עֵץ v. Di Bö$^{§\ 578}$); etc **1.** *perish, die*, of individuals (mostly late) Nu 17^{27} (‖ גוע & מות (v^{28})), (also Dt 26^{5}? cf infr) Jon 1$^{6.14}$ Jb 31^{19} cf 29^{13} Pr 31^{6} Est 4$^{14\ 16\ 16}$ Mi 4^{9} Je 40^{15} cf Is 57^{1} Pr 11^{10} 28^{28} Ec 7^{15} ψ 119^{92}; emphasis on mortality Jb 4^{20} ψ 146^{4} Ec 9^{6}; Saul & Jonath., under fig of weapons 2 S 1^{27}; lion Jb 4^{11}, caravan Jb 6^{18} (cf Di), cf. מִן־הָאָרֶץ א׳ חָסִיד Mi 7^{2}, וא׳ מֶלֶךְ מֵעַזָּה Zc 9^{5}, *perish, be exterminated* (judgment for sin), of Israel Lv 26^{38} Dt 8$^{19\ 19\ 20}$ 28$^{20\ 22}$ 30$^{18.18}$ Je 27$^{10\ 15}$ cf 6^{21}, Ob^{12} cf ψ 80^{17} Is 27^{13}; other nations Dt 7^{20} Je 10^{15} 51^{18} ψ 2^{12} 10^{16} 83^{18} cf. 9^{4} Am 1^{8} Is 41^{11} 60^{12} cf. Jon 3^{9} v also Ex 10^{7} Nu 21$^{29.30}$ (JE) Je 48^{46}; house of Ahab 2 K 9^{8}, wicked in general Ju 5^{31} Jb 4^{9} cf v^{7}, ψ 37^{20} 49^{11} 68^{3} (‖ sim. of melting wax), 73^{27} 92^{10}; also Pr 19^{9} 21^{18}; לָנֶצַח א׳ Jb 20^{7}, cf. דֶּרֶךְ רְשָׁעִים א׳ ψ 1^{6}; sq מֵעַל הָאָרֶץ (of annihilation of Isr.) Dt 4$^{26\ 26}$ 11^{17} Jos 23$^{13\ 16}$ (D), sq מִתּוֹךְ הַקָּהָל (of Korah's company) Nu 16^{33} (JE); *perish, be ruined, destroyed*, of inanimate things, e.g. land Je 9^{11} (‖ נִצְּתָה כַמִּדְבָּר) cf. 48^{8}; harvest Jo 1^{11}, Jonah's gourd Jon 4^{10}; riches Je 48^{36} Ec 5^{13}, vessel ψ 31^{13}; houses Am 3^{15} (so oft. As. Dl^{W}), city Ez 26^{17} (but del. 𝔊 Co); cf. bamôth Ez 6^{3} 𝔊 Co; heavens & earth ψ 102^{27} **2.** fig *perish, vanish*, subj. memory Jb 18^{17} ψ 9^{7}; name ψ 41^{6} (i e be forgotten); vigour Jb 30^{2}, wisdom Is 29^{14}, cf אֹבַד עֵצוֹת Dt 32^{28}; אֱמוּנָה Je 7^{28} (‖ נִכְרְתָה); חָזוֹן Ez 12^{22}; יוֹם Jb 3^{3} (i e be blotted out), לֵב Je 4^{9} (i e courage fail); תִּקְוָה ψ 9^{19} Pr 10^{28} 11^{7} Ez 19^{5} 37^{11} Jb 8^{13}; so תַּאֲוָה ψ 112^{10} (i e. comes to naught); תּוֹחֶלֶת Pr 11^{7}, sq מִן + agent La 3^{18}; תּוֹרָה + עֵצָה sq מִן + persons negligent Je 18^{18} Ez 7^{26}, cf Je 49^{7}; esp. א׳ מָנוֹס מִן־ (i.e. they could not escape) Am 2^{14} Je 25^{35} Jb 11^{20} ψ 142^{5}. **3.** *be lost, strayed*, asses 1 S 9$^{3\ 20}$; sheep Je 50^{6} Ez 34$^{4\ 16}$ ψ 119^{176} (fig of erring men); perh. Dt 26^{5}.

Pi. caus. of Qal.—*Pf.* אִבַּד 2 K 21^{3} + 2 t.;

sf. וְאִבֶּדְךָ Co Ez 28^{16} cf. infr.; אִבַּדְתִּי Je 15^{7}; וְאִבַּדְתִּי Ez 6^{3} (𝔊 Co וְאֻבְּדוּ) etc.; *Impf.* יְאַבֵּד Ec 9^{18}; וַיְאַבֵּד Ec 7^{7} Zp 2^{13}; 1 s. sf. וָאַבֶּדְךָ Ez 28^{16} (for וָאֲאַבּ׳ Ew^{§72c} Ol^{§79a} Kö I^{338} Ges$^{§68 fn}$; but Co 3 ms.; v. also Co 38^{14}); תְּאַבְּדוּן Dt 12^{2} etc.; *Inf. abs.* אַבֵּד Dt 12^{2}+3 t.; *cstr. id.* Ez 22^{27}+etc.; *Pt.* מְאַבְּדִים Je 23^{1}. **1.** *cause to perish, destroy, kill*, obj. pers. (mostly late) 2 K 11^{1} Est 3^{9} 4^{7} 8^{5} 9^{24}; ‖ הרג 9$^{6.12}$; ‖ הרג + השמיד 3^{13} 7^{4} 8^{11}; ‖ המם 9^{24}; cf. ψ 119^{95}; obj. נְפָשׁוֹת Ez 22^{27} (del. 𝔊 Co); in judgment, subj. י׳ ψ 5^{7}; cf. Pr 1^{32}; sq. מִתּוֹךְ Ez 28^{16}; obj. a people 2 K 13^{7} 2 K 19^{18}=Is 37^{19}; Jb 12^{23}; in judgment Dt 11^{4} Je 12^{17} 15^{7} Zp 2^{13} ψ 9^{6} cf. 21^{11}; obj. inanimate things esp. idols, bamôth etc., Nu. 33$^{52.52}$ (J) Dt 12$^{2.2}$ 2 K 21^{3} Ez 6^{3} (but cf. 𝔊 Co supr.); bars of Zion La 2^{9} (‖ שִׁבַּר). **2.** fig. *cause to vanish, blot out, do away with* names of idols Dt 12^{3}; voice of Babylon Je 51^{55}; memory of dead Is 26^{14}; substance Pr 29^{3}; understanding Ec 7^{7}; good (טוֹבָה q.v.) Ec 9^{18}. **3.** *cause to stray, lose;* obj. Isr. under fig. of flock Je 23^{1} (‖ הֵפִיץ); abs. Ec 3^{6} (‖ בִּקֵּשׁ).

Hiph. *Pf.* וְהֶאֱבִיד Nu 24^{19}; הֶאֱבַדְתָּ Jb 14^{19} etc.; *Impf.* אֹבִידָה Je 46^{8} (Ges$^{§68,2 R.1}$). *Inf. cstr.* הַאֲבִיד 2 K 10^{19}+etc.; *Pt.* מַאֲבִיד Dt 8^{20}. **1.** *destroy, put to death*, in judgment, (subj. י׳) obj. pers. Lv 23^{30} (sq. מִקֶּרֶב עַמָּהּ; ‖ כָּרַת v^{29}); Je 49^{38} (sq. מִשָּׁם); Ob^{8} (sq. מֵאֱדוֹם); obj. nation, Ammon Ez 25^{7} (sq. מִן־הארצות ‖ כָּרַת), cf. v^{16}; Canaanites Dt 8^{20} (sq. מִפְּנֵיכֶם); Canaan = Philistines Zp 2^{5} (‖ כָּרַת); esp. Isr. Dt 28$^{51.63}$ (‖ הִשְׁמִיד), cf. Js 7^{7}; also abs. Je 18^{7} (‖ לִנְתוֹשׁ וְלִנְתוֹץ) = 1^{10} (+ וְלַהֲרוֹס) = 31^{28} (+ וּלְהָרֵעַ); animals Ez 32^{13} (sq. מֵעַל מַיִם רַבִּים); cf. Dt 7^{10}; ψ 143^{12} (‖ הִצְמִית); (human subj.), obj. servants of Baal 2 K 10^{19}, obj. nation Dt 9^{3}, cf. Nu 24^{19} (E; sq. מֵעִיר); 2 K 24^{2}; cf. Je 46^{8}; obj. inanimate, chariots Mi 5^{9}; idols Ez 30^{13} (del. BCo). **2.** fig., obj. name of kings Dt 7^{24} (sq. מִתַּחַת הַשָּׁמָיִם); hope Jb 14^{19}; voice of mirth etc. Je 25^{10} (cf. 51^{55} **Pi.** supr.)

† אֹבֵד **n.[m.]** destruction, עֲדֵי א׳ Nu 24$^{20.24}$ (JE; on form with abstract sense v. Ba$^{NB 149}$).

† אֲבֵדָה **n.f.** a lost thing—abs. exc. Dt 22^{3} cstr. אֲבֵדַת—Ex 22^{8}; with מָצָא Lv 5$^{22.23}$; with מָצָא + אָבַד Dt 22^{3};—(אבדה) Pr 27^{20} Kt cf. אֲבַדּוֹ infr.)

אֲבַדֹּה, אֲבַדּוֹ cf. אבדון infr.

† אָבְדָן, & אָבְדַן (cstr.) **n.[m.]** destruction (Syr. ܐܒܕܢܐ) Est 9^{5} (מַכַּת־חֶרֶב וְהֶרֶג וְא׳), 8^{6}; (on form v. BeRy; Ol$^{§215 b.1}$ Ba$^{NB 49, 487}$).

† אֲבַדּוֹן **n.f.**$^{†Pr 27,20}$ abstr. nearly = **n.pr.** (place of) **Destruction, Ruin, 'Abaddôn** (cf. 𝔊 ܐܒܕܘܢ Jb 28^{22} etc.)—אֲבַדּוֹן Jb 26^{6} (+4 t.); abbrev. אבדה Kt אֲבַדּוֹ Qr †Pr 27^{20}.—Place of ruin in She'ôl for lost or ruined dead, as development of earlier distinction of condition in She'ôl (v. שְׁאוֹל). Only in WisdLt; Jb 31^{12}; ‖ שאול Jb 26^{6} Pr 15^{11} 27^{20}; ‖ מות Jb 28^{22}; ‖ קבר ψ 88^{12}.

† I. אָבָה **vb. be willing, consent** (cf. As. *abûtu, command*, Dl^{W}, Eth. አበየ: *refuse*, Ar. أَبَى, id., Nejd *be willing* So$^{De Jes 3, p. 26; LCB 1880, 817}$)—**Qal** (c. לֹא, אַל exc. Is 1^{19} Jb 39^{9}; in Hex. rare & only JED, incl. Lv 26^{21}); *Pf.* אָבָה Ex 10^{27}+ אָבוּ Ju 19^{25}+7 t.; אָבוּא Is 28^{12} (Sta$^{§31 R.2}$; Kö$^{I.414}$); *Impf.* יֹאבֶה Dt 29^{19}+2 t.; 2 ms. juss. תֹּבֵא Pr 1^{10} (Sta$^{§143 e1 fn}$; Kö$^{I.576 f}$) etc.; *Pt.* אֹבִים Ez 3^{7};—*be willing*, sq. Inf. with לְ Ex 10^{27}+29 t.; without לְ Dt 2^{30}+8 t.; subj. י׳ Dt 10^{10} 23^{6} 29^{19} Jos 24^{10} 2 K 8^{19} 13^{23} 24^{4} 2 Ch 21^{7}; human subj. Gn 24$^{5.8}$ Ju 19^{10} 2 S 2^{21} 13^{25} 14$^{29.29}$ 23$^{16.17}$=1 Ch 11$^{18.19}$ 1 Ch 19^{19}; in bad sense Ex 10^{27} Dt 2^{30} 25^{7} Ju. 19^{25} 20^{13} 2 S 13$^{14.16}$; esp. of perverse Isr. Lv 26^{21} Dt 1^{26} 1 S 15^{9} Is 28^{12} 30^{9} 42^{24} Ez 3$^{7.7}$ 20^{8}; subj. animal, רֵים Jb 39^{9}; abs. (no Inf.) 2 S 12^{17} 1 K 20^{8} 22^{50}; cf. Pr 6^{35}, of jealous man; bad sense Ju 11^{17} Is 30^{15}; good sense 1 S 22^{17} 26^{23} 31^{4}=1 Ch 10^{4} 2 S 6^{10} Pr 1^{10}; + vb. fin. Is 1^{19} (אם תאבו וּשְׁמַעְתֶּם); *consent, yield to*, sq. לוֹ Dt 13^{9} (good sense); sq. לִי ψ 81^{12}; sq. לַעֲצָתִי Pr 1^{30}; sq. acc. תּוֹכַחְתִּי v^{25} (all in bad sense).

† אֶבְיוֹן **adj. in want, needy, poor,**—so, alw. abs., Dt 15^{4}+40 t.; אֶבְיֹנְךָ Ex 23^{6} Dt 15^{11}; אֶבְיוֹנִים Am 4^{1}+14 t.; אֶבְיוֹנֵי (אֶבְיֹנֵי) Ex 23^{11} Is 29^{19}; אֶבְיוֹנֶיהָ ψ 132^{15}—(Hex. only JED; mostly poet., 23 t. ψ) *needy*, chiefly *poor* (in material things); as adj. Dt 15$^{7.7.9}$; 24^{14} ψ 109^{16} (both ‖ עָנִי); elsewhere subst.; ψ 49^{3} (‖ עָשִׁיר); Dt 15$^{4.11}$; subj. to oppression & abuse Am 2^{6} 5^{12} (both ‖ צַדִּיק) 4^{1} 8^{6} (all ‖ דַּל) Is 32^{7}; Am 8^{4} Ez 16^{49} 18^{12} 22^{29} ψ 37^{14} Jb 24$^{4.14}$ Pr 30^{14}—cf. ψ 109^{16} supr.—(all ‖ עָנִי) Je 5^{28} (‖ יָתוֹם) 2^{34}; cared for by good Jb 29^{16} 30^{25} (‖ קְשֵׁה־יוֹם) 31^{19} ψ 112^{9} Est 9^{22}; Pr 14^{31} (‖ דַּל) 31^{20} Je 22^{16} (‖ עָנִי); care of them enjoined, negatively Ex 23^{6};—cf. Dt 24^{14} supr.—positively Ex 23^{11} Dt 15^{11} Pr 31^{9} (both ‖ עָנִי)—cf. Dt 15$^{7.7.9}$ supr.—ψ 82^{4} (‖ דַּל); cared for by God Je 20^{13} ψ 107^{41} 132^{15} Jb 5^{15}; 1 S 2^{8}=ψ 113^{7} Is 14^{30} (all ‖ דַּל) ψ 35^{10} 140^{13} (both ‖ עָנִי), cf. Davidic king ψ 72^{12} (‖ עָנִי)=v^{4} (‖ בְּנֵי אֶבְ׳ *id.*), v$^{13.13}$ (‖ דַּל); *needing help*, deliverance from trouble, esp. as delivered by God ψ 9^{19} 12^{6} 40^{18}=70^{6} 74^{21} 86^{1} 109^{22} Is 29^{19} 41^{17} (all ‖ עָנִי) Is 25^{4} (‖ דַּל) ψ 69^{34} 109^{31}.

† אֲבִיּוֹנָה **n.f. caper-berry** (as stimulating

desire) Ec 12^{5} (v. GFM $^{JBL\ 1891,\ 55\ ff.}$; so 𝔊 𝔙, Mish. אביונות, cf. NHWB; v. also 𝔖; i.e. *capparis spinosa*, cf. Ri^{HWB}; so Thes, Ew De, etc.; but Wetzst in De (Germ. ed. 1875) proposes אֶבְיוֹנָה (as fem. of אביון) *the poor soul* in sense=נַפְשׁוֹ הָאֶבְיוֹנָה cf. Symm 𝔖, where double translation).

†**אֵבֶה** n.[m.] reed, papyrus (etymology uncertain;=Ar. أَبَاءٌ, As. *abu* Dl^{W}, AGl) אֳנִיּוֹת אֵבֶה Jb 9^{26} (craft made of reeds, light & swift, Heliod. $^{Aethiop.\ X,\ 460}$)=כְּלֵי־גֹמֶא Is 18^{2}.

II. **אבה** (perh. at least formally justified as stem of אָב (cstr. אֲבִי), so Thes (cf. infr.), but existence & mng. wholly dub.; as real √ Ba $^{ZMG\ 1887,\ 609\ ff.}$ Ol$^{§\ 123\ c}$; acc. to Dl$^{W\ p.\ 22}$ אבה As. *abû*=*decide*, אָב=*he who decides;* Thes (so RobGes Nö$^{ZMG\ xl,\ 737}$ & cf. Sta$^{§\ 186}$ al.) makes אָב nom. prim. bilit., imitating infant's speech cf. πάππας, *pappa, papa* (cf. Ew$^{§\ 106\ a}$); also As. *bab* Jen$^{ZA\ 1886,\ 404}$).

אָב $_{1191}$ **n.m. father** (Ph. אב, As. *abu*, Ar. أَبٌ, Sab. אב CIS$^{iv,\ 1.\ 37\ l.\ 2}$ al., Eth. አብ: Aram. אַבָּא, ܐܒܐ)—abs. אָב Gn 44^{19}+47 t.; cstr. אֲבִי Gn 17$^{4.5}$ (cf. in אַבְרָהָם *ib.* & elsewh. in n.pr. On Hal's prop. אָבֵר v. אברהם); אָבִי (cf. Ge$^{§§\ 90,\ 3b,\ 96}$) Gn 4^{20} +; sf. אָבִי Gn 19^{34}+(MI אבי); אָבִיךָ Gn 12^{1}+; אָבִיו Gn 2^{24}+; אָבִיהוּ Ju 14^{10}+6 t.; pl. אָבוֹת Ex 12^{3}+; cstr. אֲבוֹת Ex 6^{25}+7 t.; sf. אֲבֹתַי, אֲבוֹתַי (אֲבוֹתָי) Gn 47^{9}+15 t.; אֲבוֹתֵיהֶם 1 Ch 4^{38}+32 t. (late); אֲבוֹתָם Ex 4^{5}+106 t. etc.;—**1.** *father of individual* Gn 2^{24} (+אֵם) 11$^{28.29.29}$ 19$^{31.32.33}$, +oft. (mostly JED); of father as commanding Gn 50^{16} (J) Je 35$^{6\ f}$ Pr 6^{20} (cf. Gn 18^{19} J 28$^{1-5}$ P 1 S 17^{20} 1 K 2^{1}); instructing מוסר Pr 1^{8} 4^{1} (cf. Dt 8^{5}); specif. as begetter, *genitor* Pr 23^{22} Zc 13$^{3.3}$ (+אֵם) Is 45^{10}; cf. Gn 49^{4} (J) Lv 18$^{7.8.11}$ (P); rebuking Gn 37^{10}; loving Gn 37^{4} 44^{20} (JE; cf. 22^{2} 25^{28} 37^{3} 2 S 14^{1}); pitying ψ 103^{13} (in sim. cf. 2 S 18^{5}); blessing Gn 27^{41} (JE cf. 27^{4} also 28^{1} P+); as glad Pr 10^{1} 15^{20} cf. 29^{3}; grieving Gn 37^{35} (JE; cf. 2 S 12^{22} 19$^{1.2\ f}$) etc. Also as obj. of honour, obedience, love Ex 20^{12} (E)=Dt 5^{16}; Ex 21$^{15.17}$ (E) Dt 21$^{18.19}$ Gn 28^{7} (P) 1 K 19^{20} (all+אֵם), 50$^{1.5}$ (J) Mal 1^{6} etc. Hence metaph. of *intimate connection* Jb 17^{14} *to corruption I cry, My father art thou* (‖ אִמִּי וַאֲחֹתִי לָרִמָּה). **2.** of God as *father of his people* (v. RS$^{Sem\ 42}$), who constituted, controls, guides and lovingly watches over it: Dt 32^{6} Je 3$^{4.19}$ 31^{9} Is 63$^{16.16}$ 64^{7} Mal 1^{6} 2^{10} (cf. Ex 4^{22} 19^{4} (JE) Dt 32^{11} Ho 11^{1}); cf. Je 2^{27} (of idolatr. Isr.) אֹמְרִים לָעֵץ אָבִי אַתָּה וְלָאֶבֶן אַתְּ ילדתני; esp. God as *father of Davidic line* 2 S 7^{14} ψ 89^{27}; *f. of needy* (late) ψ 68^{6} (cf. 103^{13}) (in n.pr., *f. of individ.*, cf. infr.) **3.** *head of household*, family or clan; בֵּית אָבִי as abode Gn 38$^{11.11}$ Lv 22^{13}+;=family Gn 24^{40} (‖ מִשְׁפַּחְתִּי) 41^{51} 46^{31} + cf. Nu 18$^{1.2}$ Jos 2$^{12.18}$ 6^{25}; esp. techn. of divisions of Isr. בֵּית אָב לְמִשְׁפָּחוֹת Nu 3$^{30.35}$=a father's house, i.e. a family or clan; more oft. pl. (אבותיו, אבותם) בֵּית אָבוֹת=fathers' houses=families, clans (cf. Di on Ex 6^{14}) Ex 6^{14} 12^{3} Nu 1$^{2,\ 18\ ff}$ (oft. in Nu) Jos 14^{1} 19^{51} 21$^{1.1}$ 22$^{14.14}$ (always P in Hex.); also 1 Ch 5$^{13.15}$+oft. in Ch; cf. רָאשֵׁי אבות הלוים (=ר׳ בית א׳) Ex 6^{25} cf. 1 K 8^{1} 1 Ch 6^{4} 7^{11}+oft. Ch Ezr Ne. **4.** *ancestor* (**a**) of individual; grandfather (instead of precise term) Gn 28^{13} 32^{10} (J; where used by Jacob of Abr. & then of Isaac); greatgr. 1 K 15^{13}; great-greatgr. 1 K 15^{11} etc.; oft. pl. (=*fathers, forefathers*) Gn 15^{15} 46^{34} (JE) 1 K 19^{4} 21$^{3.4}$ 2 K 19^{12} 20^{17}+; particularly שכב עם אבותיו 1 K 1^{21} 2^{10} 11^{21} 22^{40}+; joined with ויקבר עם אב׳ 1 K 14^{31} 15^{24} 22^{51} 2 K 8^{24} 15^{38} cf. v^{7}, 16^{20} + (all of kings of Judah); intens., אֲבֹתֶיךָ וַאֲבוֹת אֲבֹתֶיךָ Ex 10^{6} cf. Dn 11^{24}; (**b**) of people Gn 10^{21} (J) 17$^{4.5}$ (P) 19$^{37.38}$ (J) 36$^{9.43}$ (P) Dt 26^{5} Is 51^{2} 43^{27} (where אביך הראשון *thy first father*, v. Che) cf. also Ez 16$^{3.45}$+ oft.; pl. Ex 3$^{13.15.16}$ (E) Dt 1^{8} Jos 1^{6} Ju 2^{1} 1 S 12^{6}+; 1 S 12$^{15\ ad\ fin}$ rd. וּבְמַלְכְּכֶם 𝔊 We Dr. **5.** *originator* or *patron* of a class, profession, or art Gn 4$^{20.21}$. **6.** fig. of *producer, generator* Jb 38^{28} הֲיֵשׁ לַמָּטָר אָב ‖ מִי הוֹלִיד אֶגְלֵי־טָל). **7.** fig. of *benevolence* & protection Jb 29^{16} אָב אָנֹכִי לָאֶבְיוֹנִים, cf. 31^{18}; of Eliakim Is 22^{21}; perh. also of gracious Mess. king אֲבִי עַד Is 9^{5} *everlasting father* (Ge Ew De Che Brd Di)—others *divider of spoil* (Abarb Hi Kn Kue Br^{MP}). **8.** term of *respect & honour* (*Abbas, Pater, Papa, Pope*); appl. to master 2 K 5^{13}; priest Ju 17^{10} 18^{19}; prophet 2 K 2$^{12.12}$ 6^{21} 13$^{14.14}$ cf. 8^{9}; counsellor Gn 45^{8} (E; cf. δευτέρου πατρός 𝔊 add. Est 3^{13}; τῷ πατρί 1 Mac 11^{32}); king 1 S 24^{12}; artificer 2 Ch 2^{12} 4^{16}. **9.** specif., *ruler, chief* (late) 1 Ch 2$^{24.42.42}$ etc. (cf. Ew$^{§\ 273\ b}$).

†**אֲבִי־עַלְבוֹן** n.pr.m. a hero of David 2 S 23^{31} rd. אֲבִיאֵל so 𝔊 1 Ch 11^{32}, cf. Dr^{S} (We^{S} אבי־בעל (v. sub אביאל)); otherwise Klo^{S}.

†**אֲבִיאֵל** n.pr.m. (*Ēl is (my) father*, cf. אביהו & Ph. אבבעל (*fem.*), also אביבעל; & אבנבעל *our father* etc.; Abi-ba'al KAT$^{2\ 355}$; v. RS$^{Sem\ 45}$. Nö$^{ZMG\ 1888,\ 480}$ makes אבי here, & in אביהו etc., cstr. but this seems unlikely; cf. also אליאב etc.; views differ much as to these n.pr. and uniform interpr. is impossible. Cf. in gen. Ol$^{§\ 277\ f}$). **1.** Saul's grandfather 1 S 9^{1} 14^{51}. **2.** =foregoing, 1 Ch 11^{32}.

†אֲבִיאָסָף **n.pr.m.** (*my father has gathered*) son (descendant) of Korah Ex 6^{24}, Sam. אביסף, so אֶבְיָסָף 1 Ch $6^{8.22}$ 9^{19} (cf. Nes[Eg 185]).

†אֲבִיגַיִל **n.pr.f.** (*my father is joy* (?) orig. אבגל ? (אֲבִגַל ?) cf. MT infr. & Nö[ZMG 1883, 537 Anm2]). **1.** wife of Nabal, then of David 1 S $25^{14.23.39.40.42}$ 27^{3} 30^{5} 2 S 2^{2} 1 Ch 3^{1}; = אֲבִגַיִל 1 S $25^{3.36}$ אֲבוּגַיִל v[18], אֲבִיגַל v[32], אֲבִגַיִל 2 S 3^{3}. **2.** sister of David 1 Ch $2^{16.17}$ = אֲבִיגַל 2 S 17^{25}.

†אֲבִידָן **n.pr.m.** (*my father is judge*) a prince of Benj. Nu 1^{11} 2^{22} $7^{60.65}$ 10^{24}.

†אֲבִידָע **n.pr.m.** (*my father took knowledge*) a son of Midian Gn 25^{4} 1 Ch 1^{33}. Cf. Sab. אבידע, Hal[MA 192, 202], also ידעאב, DHM[ZMG '83, 399].

†אֲבִיָּהוּ **n.pr.m. & f.** (*Yah(u) is (my) father*)—so †2 Ch $13^{20.21}$ = אֲבִיָּם †1 K 14^{31} $15^{1.7.7.8}$ (𝔊 'Αβιου, 'Αβια); = אֲבִי †2 K 18^{2} (𝔊 'Αβου, 'Αβουθ); = אֲבִיָּה 1 S 8^{2} + 22 t.—**1.** king of Judah, son & successor of Rehoboam 1 K 14^{31} $15^{1.7.7.8}$ 1 Ch 3^{10} 2 Ch $11^{20.22}$ 12^{16} $13^{1.2.3.4.15.17.19.20.21.22.23}$. **2.** 2nd son of Samuel 1 S 8^{2} 1 Ch 6^{13}. **3.** son of Jerob. I 1 K 14^{1}. **4.** son of Becher, a Benjamite 1 Ch 7^{8}. **5.** head of a priestly house 1 Ch 24^{10}. **6.** *id.* Ne 10^{8} $12^{4.17}$. **7.** wife of Hezron 1 Ch 2^{24}. **8.** mother of Hezekiah 2 K 18^{2} 2 Ch 29^{1}.

אֲבִיהוּא **n.pr.m.** (*he is father*) a son of Aaron Ex 6^{23} $24^{1.9}$ 28^{1} Lv 10^{1} + 7 t.

†אֲבִיהוּד **n.pr.m.** (*my father is majesty*, cf. עַמִּיהוּד, הוֹד) son of Bela, a Benjamite 1 Ch 8^{3}.

†אֲבִיחַיִל **n.pr.m.** & **f.** (*my father is might*, Sab. אבחיל Hal[MA 234])—prob. = אֲבִיהַיִל 2 Ch 11^{18}, אֲבִיהָיִל 1 Ch 2^{29} — **1.** a Levite Nu 3^{35}. **2.** a Gadite 1 Ch 5^{14}. **3.** father of Esther Est 2^{15} 9^{29}. **4.** wife of Abishur 1 Ch 2^{29}. **5.** wife of Rehoboam 2 Ch 11^{18}.

†אֲבִיטוּב **n.pr.m.** (*my father is goodness*) son of Shaharaim, a Benjamite 1 Ch 8^{11}.

†אֲבִיטַל **n.pr.f.** (*my father is (the) dew*) a wife of David 2 S 3^{4} 1 Ch 3^{3}.

†אֲבִימָאֵל **n.pr.m.** (*a father is Ēl;* South-Arab. name) son of Joktan Gn 10^{28} 1 Ch 1^{22}. Cf. Sab. אבמעתתר, *Abmi 'Aṯtar* a father is *'Aṯtar* ([עשתר] v. עַשְׁתֹּרֶת) Hal[M 86], DHM[ZMG 1883, 18].

אֲבִימֶלֶךְ **n.pr.m.** (*Melek* (= Malik, Molech) *is father*)—אֲבִימֶּלֶךְ Gn 20^{18} + —**1.** king of Gerar Gn $20^{2.3.4}$ +, $21^{22.25.26}$ +, $26^{1.8}$ + (24 t. Gn). †**2.** king of Gath ψ 34^{1} err. for אָכִישׁ, cf. 1 S $21^{11 f}$;—a better known Philist. name substituted for a less known (Hup[3]). > Others (Thes Ol De MV) think a *title* of Philist. kings, cf. Pharaoh. **3.** son of Gideon Ju 8^{31} $9^{1.3.4}$ +, 10^{1} (40 t. Ju), 2 S 11^{21}. †**4.** priest, son of Abiathar 1 Ch 18^{16} err. for אֲחִימֶלֶךְ q.v. (Sab. also **n.pr.f.** Osiander[ZMG 1865, 209]).

†אֲבִינָדָב **n.pr.m.** (*my father is noble*) **1.** a man of Gibeah in whose house the ark tarried 1 S 7^{1} 2 S $6^{3.3.4}$ 1 Ch 13^{7}. **2.** a son of Jesse 1 S 16^{8} 17^{13}; 1 K 4^{11} (? perh. otherwise unknown; Klo prop. אֲבִינֵר בְּ). **3.** a son of Saul 1 S 31^{2} 1 Ch 8^{33} 9^{39} 10^{2}.

†אֲבִינֹעַם **n.pr.m.** (*my father is delight*) father of Barak Ju $4^{6.12}$ $5^{1.12}$.

אֲבִינֵר **n.pr.m.** (*my father is Nêr*, or *is a lamp* cf. 2 S 21^{17}; acc. to Lag[BN 75] = אֲבֶן (= בֵּן) + נֵר = son of Ner; cf. 𝔊 'Αβεννηρ)—so only 1 S 14^{50}, elsewh. אַבְנֵר—cousin of Saul, and captain of his host 1 S $14^{50.51}$ $17^{55.55.55}$ + 52 t. 1 & 2 S + 1 K $2^{5.32}$ 1 Ch 26^{28} 27^{21}.

†אֲבִיעֶזֶר **n.pr.m.** (*my father is help*)— = אִיעֶזֶר Nu 26^{30}—**1.** a Manassite, called 'son' of Gilead Nu 26^{30} (cf. Di) Jos 17^{2} Ju 6^{34} 8^{2}; and son of Gil.'s sister 1 Ch 7^{18}. **2.** a Benjamite, a warrior of David 2 S 23^{27} 1 Ch 11^{28} 27^{12}.

†אֲבִי הָעֶזְרִי **adj.gent.** Abiezrite Ju $6^{11.24}$ 8^{32} = אִיעֶזְרִי Nu 26^{30}.

†אֲבִירָם **n.pr.m.** ((*the*) *Exalted One is* (*my*) *father* (v. Bae[Rel 156]) cf. As. *Aburamu* (?) KAT[2 479] cf. Dl[La, p. 91, 1.225]). **1.** a Reubenite, son of Eliab Nu $16^{1.12.24.25.27.27}$ 26^{9} Dt 11^{6} ψ 106^{17}. **2.** son of Hiel the Bethelite 1 K 16^{34}. Cf. also following.

אַבְרָם **n.pr.m.** (*id.*, Thes al. *exalted father*) **Abram** Gn $11^{26.27}$ + 57 t. Gn (to 17^{5}) + 1 Ch 1^{27} Ne 9^{7}; = אַבְרָהָם **Abraham** Gn $17^{5.9.15}$ + 172 t. OT. (אברהם connected Gn 17^{5} by word-play with הם of המון; really = אברם — רהם = רום which however is not found in Heb.—cf. Di > Hal RÉJ[1887, 177 f] who prop. אַבִּר הָם גּוֹיִם cf. Gn 49^{24} with Is 41^{21}; so that אַבִּר הָם *chief of multitude* is the new name of Gn 17^{5} (הָם) (√המה).

†אֲבִישַׁג **n.pr.f.** (*my father is a wanderer* (שׁגג ?)) a handmaid of David 1 K $1^{3.15}$ $2^{17.21.22}$.

†אֲבִישׁוּעַ **n.pr.m.** (*my father is rescue*, or *is opulence* (cf. שׁוּעַ *rich* Jb 34^{19}; also שׁוּעַ Jb 36^{19}? but v. שׁוע); Lag[BN 75] thinks fr. אֲבֶן (= בֵּן) + שׁוּעַ cf. 𝔊 'Αβεσσουε 1 Ch 8^{4}) **1.** a son of Phinehas 1 Ch $5^{30.31}$ 6^{35} Ezr 7^{5}. **2.** a Benjamite, son of Bela 1 Ch 8^{4}.

†אֲבִישׁוּר **n.pr.m.** (*my father is a wall*, Sab. אבשור Hal[MA 148], cf. As. *Abudûru* Dl[Pr 202]) son of Shammai 1 Ch $2^{28.29}$.

אֲבִישַׁי n.pr.m. (*my father is Jesse;* Lag$^{BN 75}$ thinks fr. אָבְןָ (=בֶּן) + ישי cf. 𝔊 Ἀβεσσα[ι] 1 S 26^{6}) —'א 1 S $26^{6.6}$ + 17 t. 1 & 2 S = אַבְשַׁי 2 S 10^{10} + 5 t. 1 Ch.—grandson of Jesse; son of Zeruiah & brother of Joab 1 S $26^{6.6.7.8.9}$ 2 S $2^{18.24}$ + 20^{6} (where rd. יואב 𝔖 Th We Dr) + 12 t. 2 S + 20^{7} (where insert אבישי 𝔊 We Dr) + 5 t. 1 Ch.

אֲבִישָׁלוֹם n.pr.m. (*my father is peace;* acc. to Lag$^{BN 75}$ = אָבְןָ (בֶּן) + שָׁלֹם, cf. 𝔊 Ἀβεσσαλωμ) —'א † 1 K $15^{2.10}$ = אַבְשָׁלוֹם 2 S 3^{3} +, 2 Ch $11^{20.21}$, אַבְשָׁלֹם 2 S 13^{14} + — **1.** Rehob.'s father-in-law † 1 K $15^{2.10}$ 2 Ch $11^{20.21}$. **2.** 3rd son of Dvd 2 S 3^{3} 13^{1} + 90 t. 2 S (insert 2 S 13^{27} 𝔊 Th We cf. Dr; del. v^{38} Dr cf. We), + † 1 K 1^{6} $2^{7.28}$ 1 Ch 3^{2} ψ 3^{1}.

אֶבְיָתָר n.pr.m. (*the Great One is father* (?) so Bä$^{Rel. 156}$, cf. Sab. ותר) a priest, son of Ahimelech 1 S $22^{20.21.22}$ $23^{6.9}$ $30^{7.7}$ 2 S 8^{17} (rd. אב׳ בן־אחמלך so 𝔖 We Dr) + 22 t. 2 S 1 K 1 Ch.

אבוגיל Kt 2 S 25^{18} v. אֲבִיגַיִל sub II. אבה.

†**אֲבוֹי interj.** exclam. of pain, **Oh!** Pr 23^{29} (|| אוֹי *woe!*). Prob. akin to Syr. ܐܒܘܝ *alas ...!* PS^{53} (AW Ges less prob. as a subst. *need* from אָבָה, cf. אֶבְיוֹן).

אבח (Dl$^{BD Ez. x, Pr 75}$ comp. As. [*abâḫu*], *torment*, but dub.)

[אִבְחָה] n.f. cstr. אִבְחַת חֶרֶב Ez 21^{20}; Dl, as above, *slaughter;* but prob. error for טבחת (v. טבח) Ges Co; 𝔊 σφάγια ῥομφαίας, cf. 𝔗.

אֲבַטִּיחִים v. בטח.

אָבִי v. ביה.

אֲבִי v. אֲבִיָּהוּ sub II. אבה.

אֲבִי הָעֶזְרִי v. אֲבִיעֶזֶר sub II. אבה.

אֲבִיָּה v. אֲבִיָּהוּ sub II. אבה.

אֲבִיהַיִל v. אֲבִיחַיִל sub II. אבה.

אֶבְיוֹן, אֲבִיּוֹנָה v. I. אָבָה.

אֲבִיָּם v. אֲבִיָּהוּ sub II. אבה.

אֶבְיָסָף v. אֲבִיאָסָף sub II. אבה.

†**[אָבַךְ] vb. turn** (?) (cf. As. *abâku* Dl^{W} = הָפַךְ; Thes MV al. compare כוך) **Hithp.** וַיִּתְאַבְּכוּ Is 9^{17}, *roll, roll up*, as volume of smoke (of Isr. under fig. of thickets of forest) v. De & cf. הִתְהַפֵּךְ Ju 7^{3}.

†I. **אָבַל$_{39}$ vb. mourn** (As. [*abâlu*] v. Dl^{W}) —**Qal** *Pf.* אָבַל Is 24^{7} + 2 t. etc. *Impf.* 3 fs. תֶּאֱבַל Ho 4^{3} + 3 t.—*mourn, lament* (poet. & higher style); abs., human subj. Jo 1^{9} Am 8^{8} 9^{5} Is 19^{8} (|| אנה) cf. Jb 14^{22} (subj. נַפְשׁוֹ); sq. על Ho 10^{5}; more oft. fig., inanim. subj., gates Is 3^{26}; land 24^{4} 33^{9} Ho 4^{3} Jo 1^{10} Je 4^{28} (sq. על) 12^{4} 23^{10} cf. 12^{11} (sq. על), יְהוּדָה 14^{2}; pastures Am 1^{2}. **Hithp.** —*Pf.* הִתְאַבֵּל 1 S 15^{35}; *Impf.* יִתְאַבָּל Ez $7^{12.27}$; וַיִּתְאַבֵּל Gn 37^{34} + 3 t. etc.; *Imv.* fs. הִתְאַבְּלִי 2 S 14^{2}; *Pt.* מִתְאַבֵּל 1 S 16^{1} + 2 t. etc.;—mourn (mostly prose) esp. for dead, sq. על Gn 37^{34} 2 S 13^{37} 14^{2} 19^{2} (|| בכה) 2 Ch 35^{24}, cf. also Is 66^{10} (over Jerusalem); abs. 1 Ch 7^{22}; cf. 2 S 14^{2} *play the mourner* (where indic. by dress); over unworthy Saul sq. אֶל 1 S 15^{35} 16^{1}; over sin sq. על Ezr 10^{6} cf. (abs.) Ne 8^{9}; judgment of י׳ Ex 33^{4} abs. (indic. by dress), Nu 14^{39} Ez 7^{27} (del. B Co); sq. כִּי 1 S 6^{19}; calamity Ne 1^{4} Ez 7^{12} cf. Dn 10^{2}. **Hiph.** *Pf.* הֶאֱבַלְתִּי Ez 31^{15}; *Impf.* וַיַּאֲבֶל־ La 2^{8}; —*cause to mourn;* Ez 31^{15} abs. MT, but A B Co obj. תהום sq. על, *caused the deep to mourn over;* La 2^{8} obj. wall etc.; (both these fig., cf. Qal).

†**אֵבֶל n.m.** $^{Gn 50, 11}$ mourning—abs. Gn 50^{10} + 17 t.; cstr. 27^{41} + 3 t.; אֶבְלֵךְ Is 60^{20}; אֶבְלָם Je 31^{13}—for dead, cstr. Gn 27^{41} Dt 34^{8} (||בְּכִי) so א׳ יָחִיד sim. for grievous mourning Am 8^{10}, *id.* metaph. Je 6^{26} (|| מִסְפַּד תַּמְרוּרִים); Gn $50^{11.11}$ Je 16^{7} cf. 2 S 19^{3} עשה א׳ Ez 24^{17} (v. Co) sq. לְ Gn 50^{10} (v. also II. אָבֵל ad fin.); for calamity, Est 4^{3} 9^{22} (|| יָגוֹן); contr. יוֹם טוֹב) Jb 30^{31} (|| קוֹל בֹּכִים) Is 60^{20} 61^{3} (where appar. = mourning garb, sq. מַעֲטֵה תְהִלָּה, v. also Bi Che on txt.; || רוּחַ כֵּהָה; contr. שֶׁמֶן שָׂשׂוֹן); Je 31^{13} (|| שׂשׂוֹן), La 5^{15} (|| מָחוֹל), Am 5^{16} (|| מִסְפֵּד); cf. א׳ כִּבְנוֹת יַעֲנָה Mi 1^{8}; = time, period of mourning 2 S 11^{7}; בֵּית א׳ Ec 7^{2} (|| ב׳ מִשְׁתֶּה, v^{4} (|| ב׳ שִׂמְחָה); בִּגְדֵי א׳ garments of mourning 2 S 14^{2}.

אָבֵל מִצְרַיִם v. אָבֵל מ׳ sub II. אבל.

†I. **אָבֵל adj.** mourning—'א Gn 37^{35} Est 6^{12}; cstr. אֲבֵל־ ψ 35^{14}; אֲבֵלִים Jb 29^{25} Is 61^{2} etc.; —for dead Gn 37^{35}, calamity Est 6^{12}, cf. fig. La 1^{4} (pred., inanim. subj.), elsewhere as subst. *mourner;* sg. ψ 35^{14} (cstr.) for dead (|| קדר); pl. Jb 29^{25} abs.; for calamity Is 57^{18} $61^{2.3}$ (where mourners for Zion, or of Zion, v. Di).

II. **אבל** (perh. أَبَلَ *grow green*, cf. ܬܒܠܐ *grass;* Lag$^{BN 45}$ prop. أَبَلَ *withstand*, hence אָבֵל as withstanding scorching sun (protected by trees, springs, etc.), hence also (Lag) إِبِلٌ *camel*).

†II. **אָבֵל n.f. 1.** meadow (?) 1 S 6^{18} MT but rd. אֶבֶן cf. v$^{14.15}$ 𝔊 𝔖 We Dr. **2. n.pr.loc.** city in N. Isr. 2 S 20^{18}, near Beth Maacah v^{14}=

אָבֵל בֵּית מַעֲכָה v ^{13} (so also v ^{14} Ew Th We Klo Dr), 1 K 15^{20} 2 K 15^{29}; = א׳ מַיִם 2 Ch 16^{4} (= Abil el Kamh, *wheat-meadow* NW. of Dan & S of Mutulleh Rob$^{BR\,III,372}$). **3.** אָבֵל הַשִּׁטִּים **n.pr loc.** (= *acacia-meadow*) in lowlands of Moab Nu 33^{49}, = שִׁטִּים Nu 25^{1} Mi 6^{5} (= Tel Kefrein (?) Tristr & Merrill$^{PEFSoc\ 4th\ Statement,\ 86}$) **4.** אָבֵל כְּרָמִים **n.pr.loc.** (= *vineyard-meadow*) in Ammon Ju 11^{33} (v. Euseb. Ἀβελαμπελων) **5.** אָבֵל מְחוֹלָה **n.pr.loc.** (= *dance-meadow*) Ju 7^{22} 1 K 4^{12}, Elisha's birthplace 19^{16} (v. Euseb Ἀβελμαελαι) **6.** אָבֵל מִצְרַיִם **n.pr.loc.** (= *meadow of Egypt*, i e fertile as Egypt ?) E of Jordan Gn 50^{11} (where interpr as if אֵבֶל מ׳, so 𝔊 𝔙, v. Di)

†**אֲבָל** **adv.** **1.** in older Heb with an asseverative force, **verily, of a truth** Gn 42^{21} 2 S 14^{5} 1 K 1^{43} 2 K 4^{14}, with a slight advers force, **nay, but** Gn 17^{19} (P) **2.** in late Heb as a decided adversative, **howbeit, but** Dn $10^{7\ 21}$ Ezr 10^{13} 2 Ch 1^{4} 19^{3} 33^{17} (cf Ar بَلْ *of a truth*, sometimes, from the context, *nay rather* Qor $2^{82\ 94\ 110\ 129\ 149\ 165\ 261}$ 3^{143} 4^{52} etc)

III. **אבל** (cf Ar آبِل *able to manage camels*, fr إبل, coll, Sab. אבל *camel* DHM$^{ZMG\ 1883,\ 329}$)

†**אוֹבִיל** **n.pr.m.** (? *camel-driver*), overseer of David's camels 1 Ch 27^{30}

אָבַל, אוּבָל v. יבל

אֶבֶן $_{274}$ **n.f.** $^{Gn\ 29,2}$ (**m.** $^{1\ S\ 17,40\ ?}$) **stone** (As *abnu*, = the sharp, projecting ? v Dl$^{W,\ Pr\ 107}$, Ph אבן; Aram אֶבֶן, ܐܒܢܳܐ, Eth. እብን: Sab [ם]אבנ DHM $^{ZMG\ 1883,\ 311}$)—א׳ abs Gn 28^{22}+, אָבֶן 11^{3}+, cstr 49^{24}+, sf אַבְנוֹ 2 K 3^{25}, אֲבָנִים Gn 31^{46}+, etc, —a *stone* (large or small) **1.** in natural state, used as pillow Gn $28^{11\ 18}$ (E), seat Ex 17^{12} (E), cover of well Gn $29^{2\ 3\ 3\ 8\ 10}$ (J); causing one to stumble Is 8^{14}, marring good ground 2 K $3^{19\ 25}$, hand-missile Ex 21^{18} (JE) Nu $35^{17\ 23}$ (P) 2 S $16^{6\ 13}$, esp in judicial stoning, with vb רָגַם Lv $20^{2\ 27}$ 24^{23} Nu 14^{10} $15^{35\ 36}$ Jos $7^{25\,a}$ (all P), so also Dt 21^{21} 2 Ch 24^{21} Ez 16^{40} 23^{47}; cf. 1 K 12^{18} = 2 Ch 10^{18}, with vb סָקַל Dt 13^{11} 17^{5} $22^{21\ 24}$ 1 K 21^{13}, also Jos $7^{25\,b}$ (JE or D); sling-stones Ju 20^{16} 1 S $17^{40\ 49\ 49\ 50}$ 2 Ch 26^{14}; hurled by engines 2 Ch 26^{15}, set up for inscribing law Dt $27^{2\ 4\ 8}$ Jos 8^{32} (all D), as memorial Jos $4^{3\ 5\ 6\ 7\ 8\ 9\ 20\ 21}$ (JED) 1 S 7^{12}, as sacred pillar (מַצֵּבָה) Gn 28^{18} 35^{14} (anointed with oil), 28^{22} (= ביתאל) cf. (רֹעֶה) א׳ יִשְׂרָאֵל Gn 49^{24} (v Di), as witness 31^{45} cf. Jos $24^{26\ 27}$ (all JE); pl gathered into heap (גַּל) over dead, Jos 7^{26} (v Di) 8^{29} cf $10^{18.27}$ (JE) 2 S 18^{17}, גַּל on which meal was eaten, in a compact Gn $31^{46\ 46}$ (JE), built into altar Ex 20^{25} Dt $27^{5\ 6}$ (JED) Jos 8^{31} 1 K $18^{31.32.38}$, cf. 2 K 23^{15} 𝔊 Klo (for הבמה), of figured stone (forbidden) א׳ מַשְׂכִּית Lv 26^{1} (H); א׳ גדולה where ark rested 1 S $6^{14.15}$ also v ^{18} (MT אבל q v), (v. for other noteworthy stones **9.** infr.) **2.** *stone, as material*, of tablets Ex 24^{12} 31^{18} 34^{1} (pl.) v $^{4.4}$ (JE) Dt 4^{13} 5^{19} $9^{9\ 10\ 11}$ $10^{1\ 3}$; of vessels, hence prob. Ex 7^{19} (P, א׳ = vessels of stone ‖ עצים) v. Di; idols (‖ עץ) Dt 4^{28} $28^{36.64}$ 29^{16} 2 K 19^{18} = Is 37^{19}; also Je 3^{9} Ez 20^{32}; pavement 2 K 16^{17}; edifice 1 K 6^{7} cf. Gn 11^{3}, also 2 S 5^{11} 2 K 12^{13} 1 Ch 22^{15}, oft pl of (worked) stones Lv $14^{40.42\ 42.43\ 45}$ (P, in wall of house) 2 K 22^{6}+, cf of city-wall Ne 3^{35}, of (ruined) city 1 K 15^{22} Ne 3^{34}; tomb Is 14^{19}, אַבְנֵי יְקָרוֹת (costly building-stones) 1 K 5^{31} $7^{9\ 10\ 11}$ (v. also sub **3**); אַבְנֵי־שַׁיִשׁ = *marble* (v 𝔊) 1 Ch 29^{2}, אַבְנֵי גָזִית = *hewn stones* 1 K 5^{31} 1 Ch 22^{2} Ez 40^{42} (for altar-tables),—cf א׳ מַחְצֵב, גָּזִית 2 K 12^{13} 22^{6} 2 Ch 34^{11}, foundation-stone, corner-stone Is 28^{16} Je 51^{26} Jb 38^{6} ψ 118^{22}, cap-stone, completing the building, הָא׳ הָרֹאשָׁה Zc 4^{7} (but v. ראש פִּנָּה ψ 118^{22} as above), Zc 3^{9} *upon one stone seven eyes*, prob refers to this cap- or head-stone; the eyes are symbol of God's watchfulness; perhaps explaining cup-stones found in Orient, v. Guthe $^{ZPV\ 1890,\ 129}$, *stone-cutters* חָרָשֵׁי א׳ 2 S 5^{11} 1 Ch 22^{15}; חֹצְבֵי הָא׳ 2 K 12^{13} cf 1 Ch 22^{2} **3.** *precious stone*, gen with modifying word א׳ יְקָרָה coll. 2 S 12^{30} 1 K 10^{2}+oft (v. **2**), א׳ הַשֹּׁהַם Gn 2^{12} (J) cf Ex 25^{7} 28^{9} $35^{9\ 27}$ 39^{6} (P) 1 Ch 29^{2}, א׳ מִלֻּאִים Ex 25^{7} $35^{9\ 27}$ cf 1 Ch 29^{2}, א׳ סַפִּיר Ez 1^{26} 10^{1}; אַבְנֵי פוּךְ וְרִקְמָה, *ib* א׳ חֵפֶץ, אַבְנֵי אֶקְדָּח Is 54^{12}, 1 Ch 29^{2}, א׳ חֵן Pr 17^{8}, on אַבְנֵי אֵשׁ (*stones of fire*) Ez $28^{14\ 16}$ as precious stones = As *aban išâti* (?) v Dl$^{Pa\ 118}$ & $^{W\ 40}$, but Sm al *thunderbolts*; also without distinctive modifier Ex 25^{7} 35^{9}; חָרַשׁ א׳ engraver in stone Ex 28^{11} cf. 31^{5} 35^{33} (P) †**4.** *stones containing metal*, = *ore*, Dt 8^{9} (v. Di) Jb 28^{2} cf. v ^{3}. †**5.** *a weight*, as orig stone (v Pr 27^{3} cf Eng weight *stone* = 14 lb) אַבְנֵי־כִיס Pr 16^{11} (cf. As. Dl$^{W\,38}$); א׳ הַמֶּלֶךְ 2 S 14^{26} (i.e. acc to royal standard, cf COT $^{Gn\ 23,16}$), א׳ וָא׳ Dt 25^{13} Pr $20^{10\ 23}$ (i e. different weights, for dishonest use), כִּיס אַבְנֵי מִרְמָה Mi 6^{11}, just weights אַבְנֵי־צֶדֶק Lv 19^{36}; א׳ שְׁלֵמָה Pr 11^{1}; hence also heavy mass of metal (lead) Zc 5^{8} †**6.** *plummet* Is 34^{11} (*stones of devastation*, or *emptiness*, cf on sense 2 K 21^{13} Am $7^{7\ 8}$), also made of metal הָא׳ הַבְּדִיל Zc 4^{10} (conversely plummet fr. *plumbum*). †**7.** objects like stones; partic. *hail*, explicitly, אַבְנֵי הַבָּרָד Jos 10^{11} cf. Is 30^{30}, א׳ אֶלְגָּבִישׁ Ez $13^{11.13}$ 38^{22}; but also אֲבָנִים

גְּדֹלוֹת Jos 10[11] (E) (cf. As. Dl[W 88]); lime-stones אַבְנֵי־גִר Is 27[9]. **8.** in sim. (mostly poet.) of sinking in water Ex 15[5] = Ne 9[11]; *motionlessness* Ex 15[16]; strength Jb 6[12]; firmness 41[16]; solidity (of ice) 38[30]; in prose, of commonness 1 K 10[27] 2 Ch 1[15]; also metaph. of one in fear 1 S 25[37] (i.e. *petrified* with terror, cf. Ex 15[16] supr.); לֵב הָא׳ = perverse, hard heart Ez 11[19] 36[26]; אַבְנֵי־נֵזֶר Zc 9[16] (of ransomed Isr.)—א׳ personif. Hb 2[11] cf. v[19]; cf. Ez 13[11] (v. **7** supr.) †**9.** In topogr. terms (nearly = n.pr.); אֶבֶן בֹּהַן Jo 15[6] 18[17]; הָא׳ הָעֵזֶר 1 S 5[1] cf. 7[12], also 4[1] (We Dr); הָאֶזֶל 1 S 20[19], rd. הָאַרְגָּב הַלָּאז v. 𝔊 here & v[41] (We Dr Klo); א׳ הַזֹּחֶלֶת 1 K 1[9] (where We[Skizzen III, 171] comp. Ar. *Zuhal* = Saturn).

†[אֹבֶן] **n.[m.]** wheel, disc.—*Du.* הָאָבְנָיִם— **1.** potter's *wheel* Je 18[3] (two discs revolving one above the other; name from likeness to mill-stones; v. AW[18]). **2.** עַל־הָא׳ Ex 1[16] prob. = *sella parturientis*, = δίφροι λοχειαῖοι *bearing-stool, midwife's stool* (fr. likeness to potter's wheel; on custom of labor upon stool v. Ploss[Das Weib, 2nd ed. ii, 35, 179 etc.] & Cesnola Coll. fr. Cyprus, Metrop. Mus., N. York, No. 614, terra cotta fig. fr. 4th or 5th cent. B.C.; Descriptive Atlas of Cesn. Coll.[I, pl. lxvi. No. 435]; cf. W. H. W[ard][PESoc. 2nd Statement 1873, p. 76]).

אבנה Kt 2 K 5[12] v. אֲמָנָה.

אַבְנֵט v. בנט.

אַבְנֵר v. אֲבִינֵר sub II. אָבָה.

†[אָבַס] **vb.** feed, fatten (Mish. *id.*; ? As. [*abâsu*] Dl[W 46]) **Qal** *Pt. pass. fattened,* אָבוּס of ox Pr 15[17]; אֲבוּסִים of fowl 1 K 5[3].

†אֵבוּס **n.m.**[Pr 14,4] crib (= *feeding-trough*, on form v. Ges[§ 84 a 12. R.]) of ass Is 1[3] (cstr.); oxen Pr 14[4] (abs.); אִם־יָלִין עַל־אֲבוּסֶךָ Jb 39[9] (of wild-ox).

†[מַאֲבוּס] **n.[m.]** granary (= *place of fodder;* ? As. *bît abûsâti* Dl[W 46]) pl. sf. מַאֲבֻסֶיהָ Je 50[26].

אֲבַעְבֻּעֹת v. בוע.

אבץ (meaning unknown).

†[אֶבֶץ] **n.pr.loc.** city in Issachar, אֶבֶץ Jos 19[20].

†אִבְצָן **n.pr.m.** judge of Isr. Ju 12[8.10] (Lag[GN 1891, 19] (אֶ)בֶן צָן), 𝔊 Ἀβεσσαν, 𝔖 ܐܒܨܢ).

אבק (Ar. أَبَقَ *run away* (cf. Lag[BN 51])).

†אָבָק **n.m.**[Ez 26,10] dust—א׳ Dt 28[24] + 3 t.; cstr. אֲבַק Na 1[3]; sf. אֲבָקָם Ez 26[10]—*dust* (? fleeing, flying; syn. עָפָר = oft. dust lying on or composing ground) Ex 9[9] Ez 26[10] Dt 28[24] (|| עָפָר) Is 5[24] (|| מֹץ) 29[5] (|| מֹץ); fig. of clouds under Yahweh's feet Na 1[3].

†[אֲבָקָה] *or* [אַבְקָה] **n.f.** prob. coll., cstr. אַבְקַת רוֹכֵל Ct 3[6] **powders** *of merchant* = scent-powders. (On formation cf. Lag[BN 81].)

†[אָבַק] **vb. denom. Niph.** wrestle (= *get dusty*, cf. κόνις, κονίω, v. also Str[Pirke Aboth, 1, 4] מִתְאַבֵּק בַּעֲפַר רַגְלֵיהֶם = *sit at their feet;* others, e.g. Di, comp. חבק). וַיֵּאָבֵק עִם Gn 32[25]; *Inf.* sf. בְּהֵאָבְקוֹ עִם v[26].

אבר (cf. As. *abâru, be firm, strong* Dl[W]).

†אֵבֶר **n.[m.]** pinions (fr. strength, poet. & fig., pl. in sense) as of dove ψ 55[7]; eagle Is 40[31]; אֶרֶךְ הָא׳ of king of Babyl. under fig. of eagle Ez 17[3] (|| גְּדוֹל הַכְּנָפַיִם) of broad, overshadowing wings).

†אֶבְרָה **n.f.** pinion (nom. unit., poet.) of ostrich Jb 39[13]; אֶבְרָתוֹ of eagle, sim. for י׳ Dt 32[11]; metaph. of י׳ ψ 91[4]; אֶבְרוֹתֶיהָ of dove ψ 68[14]; (all || כנף).

†[אָבַר] **vb. denom. Hiph.** fly (= *move pinions*); of hawk יַאֲבֶר־נֵץ Jb 39[29].

†[אָבִיר] **adj.** strong; alw. = subst. *the Strong*, old name for God (poet.); only cstr. in אֲבִיר יַעֲקֹב Gn 49[24] & thence ψ 132[2.5] Is 49[26] 60[16]; א׳ יִשְׂרָאֵל Is 1[24] (cf. Che crit. n.)—Ba[NB 61] assigns this cstr. to אַבִּיר.

†אַבִּיר **adj.** mighty, valiant—א׳ Jb 34[20] + Is 10[13] Kt (Qr כַּבִּיר); cstr. *id.* 1 S 21[8]; pl. אַבִּירִים Jb 24[22] +;—*mighty* (alw. = subst. & poet. exc. 1 S 21[8]). **1.** men Ju 5[22] Jb 24[22] (= *violent*) 34[20] Je 46[15] 1 S 21[8] (rd. א׳ הָרָצִים Gr Dr, cf. 22[17]; but Lag[Probebibel] אֲבִיל הָעֲיָרִים v. *Id.*[BN 45]; Klo גִּבּוֹר), La 1[15]; אַבִּירֵי לֵב *stout of heart* Is 46[12] (= *obstinate*) ψ 76[6]. **2.** angels ψ 78[25] (cf. 103[20]). **3.** animals; bull, sim. of king of Assyr. Is 10[13] (rd. כְּאַבִּיר & v. Di); elsewh. pl.; metaph. for enemies אַבִּירֵי בָשָׁן ψ 22[13] (|| פרים); for princes ψ 68[31]; for Edomites Is 34[7]; hence even as sacrif. ψ 50[13] (|| עתודים); of horses Je 8[16] 47[3] 50[11].

אַבְרָהָם v. אַבְרָם sub II. אבה.

†אַבְרֵךְ proclaimed before Joseph Gn 41[43] (mng. dub.; many Egypt. deriv. proposed; e.g. *a-bor-k*, Copt. = *prostrate thyself!* Benfey[Verh. d. äg. Spr. z. Sem. 302 f]; *âprek*, = *head bowed!* Chabas[RA I], —but *â* = ע, v. also Wiedemann[Altäg. Wörter 1883, 8]; *ap-rex-u, head of the wise,* Harkavy[Berl. äg. Zeitschr. 1869];

àb-rek, rejoice thou! Cook[Speaker's Comm. Gn. ad loc. and p. 482]; Lepage Renouf[PSBA Nov. 1888, 5 f] *àb(u)-rek, thy command is our desire,* i.e. we are at thy service; Say[Rel. Bab. 183] As. *abrikku* = Ak. *abrik, vizier* (unpub. tabl.), v. already Dl[W; L 134 c., l. 11.12] who cp. As. *abarakku* = title, perh. *grand vizier;* against Dl, v. COT & Nö[ZMG 1886, 734]).

אַבְשַׁי, אֲבִרָם v. אֲבִירָם, אֲבִישַׁי sub II. אבה.

אַבְשָׁלֹם, אַבְשָׁלוֹם v. אֲבִישָׁלוֹם sub II. אבה.

אגא (cf. Ar. أَجَأَ, *flee* Frey).

†**אָגֵא** **n.pr.m.** (*fugitive?*) father of a hero of David 2 S 23[11] (ins. also 1 Ch 11[13] Dr[Sm]).

†**אֲגַג**, (אֲגָג Nu 24[7]) **n.pr.m.** (*violent?* As. *agâgu* Dl[W]) king of Amalek 1 S 15[8.9.20.32.32.32.33], also Nu 24[7] (E), as symbol of might; (Is א׳ then title? v. Di).

†**אֲגָגִי** **adj.gent.** of Haman (=Amalekite? so Jew. trad. & cf. Jos.[Ant. xi. 6.5]) Est 3[1.10] 8[3.5] 9[24].

אגד (*bind,* so Talm. אֲגַד, Aram. אֲגַד).

†**אֲגֻדָּה** **n.f.** band (Mishn. אֲגוּדָּה cf. NHWB). **1.** pl. cstr. אֲגֻדּוֹת מוֹטָה *bands, thongs* (fastening ox-bow) metaph. of fetters of slavery Is 58[6]. **2.** אֲגֻדַּת אֵזוֹב *bunch* of hyssop Ex 12[22]. **3.** א׳ abs. *band* of men (cf. חֶבֶל. Eng. *band*) 2 S 2[25]. **4.** אֲגֻדָּתוֹ *vault* of the heavens (as fitted together, constructed, cf. Ar. إِجَادٌ) Am 9[6].

†**אֱגוֹז** **n.**[**m.**] nuts (coll.) (NH *id.,* אַמְגּוּזָא, Ar. جَوْزٌ, Eth. ገውዝ: Aram. ܓܘܙܐ, אֱגוֹזָא; cf. Pers. گوز, whence prob. אֱגוֹז as loan-word) Ct 6[11].

אגל (Hoffm[Hiob. 86] comp. Ar. اجل *restrict,* Eth. አንለ: *a certain one* (name *withheld*), etc.)

אֵגֶל **n.**[**m.**] usually trans. drop, אֶגְלֵי־טָל *dew-drops* Jb 38[28] (‖ מָטָר) so Vrss De Di; Hoffm 'Rückstände,' 'Ansammlungen,' i.e. **collections, stores, reserve-supply.**

†**אֶגְלַיִם** **n.pr.loc.** town in Moab Is 15[8]; (meaning?); ? cf. Αἰγαλειμ (Euseb.) 9 m. S. of Areopolis; v. Lag[Onom. 228, 98; ed. 2, p. 244].

אגם (*troubled, sad,* As. *agâmu* Dl[W] cf. Ar. أَجَمَ *loathe;* also أَجَمَةٌ *marshy jungle;* v. עגם).

†**אֲגַם** **n.**[**m.**] troubled pool (Aram. *id.,* ܐܓܡܐ, As. *agammu* Dl[W])—א׳ abs. Is 35[7]; cstr. 41[18] + 2 t.; אֲגַמִּים Ex 8[1] + 2 t.; אַגְמֵי Is 14[23]; אַגְמֵיהֶם Ex 7[19]—**1.** *troubled* or *muddy* (gloomy) *pools* or *marshes,* pl. אַגְמֵי מַיִם Is 14[23]. **2.** any *pool, pond,* sg. אֲגַם מַיִם Is 41[18] ψ 107[35] 114[8]; pl. without מַיִם Ex 7[19] 8[1] (P) Is 42[15]. **3.** *swamp-reed, rush* (= אַגְמוֹן) Je 51[32].

†[**אָגֵם**] **adj. sad** (cf. Mish.) אַגְמֵי־נָפֶשׁ Is 19[10].

†**אַגְמוֹן, אַגְמֹן** **n.**[**m.**] **rush, bulrush. 1.** used as cord or line Jb 40[26] (of twisted rushes, or spun of rush-fibre, cf. Di ad loc.); as fuel 41[12]; sim. of bending head Is 58[5]. **2.** metaph. of the lowly, insignif. (‖ כִּפָּה) Is 9[13] 19[15].

אגן (prob. *circular, round,* cf. Ar. أُجْنَةٌ *ball of cheek* & v. Talm. אוֹגֶן *curved rim of a vessel*).

†[**אַגָּן**] **n.**[**m.**] **bowl, basin** (Talm. אוֹגָן, Aram. אַגָּנָא, ܐܓܢܐ; Ar. إِجَّانَةٌ, *vessel* in which clothes are washed; As. (pl.) *aganâtē* Dl[W]). **1.** *basins* used in ritual אַגָּנֹת Ex 24[6] (E). **2.** אַגַּן הַסַּהַר, sim. of curves of body Ct 7[3]. **3.** metaph. of family of Eliakim. כְּלֵי הָאַגָּנוֹת=*basin-vessels* Is 22[24] (=bowl-shaped vessels Che) opp. כְּלֵי הַנְּבָלִים; both ‖ כְּלֵי הַקָּטָן.

אגף (As. stem of *agappu, wing,* cf. Dl[W]).

†[**אֲגַף**] **n.**[**m.**] **band, army** (loan-word, orig. *wing* of army; As. *agappu,* Aram. אגף, *wing.* Others, fr. נגף, Sta[§ 256 b])—All Ez. & all *pl.* (or *du.?*) אֲגַפֶּיךָ Ez 38[9] 39[4]; אֲגַפָּיו 12[14] + 3 t.; אֲגַפֶּיהָ 38[6] (all c. כָּל־ exc. 38[22])—*bands, armies* of king of Judah Ez 12[14] 17[21]; *hordes* (RV) of Gog 38[9.22] 39[4]; specif. of גֹּמֶר 38[6]; of תּוֹגַרְמָה *ib.*

†I. [**אָגַר**] **vb. gather** (food)—only **Qal**—*Pf.* אָגְרָה, of ant Pr 6[8] (obj. מַאֲכָל); *Impf.* 2 ms. תֶּאֱגֹר of Isr. Dt 28[39] (obj.=grapes, not expr.); *Pt.* אֹגֵר בַּקַּיִץ subst. *one who gathers* (abs.) Pr. 10[5].

II. **אגר** (*pay, hire,* Ar. أَجَرَ, Aram. אֲגַר, ܐܓܪ, As. *agâru* Dl[W], Palm. אגר Reck[ZMG 1888, 396]).

†**אָגוּר** **n.pr.m.** (perh. *hireling,* Ar. أَجِيرٌ, Aram. אֲגִירָא, ܐܓܝܪܐ v. PS, As. *agîru,* cf. Hpt[BAS I. 124]; others *gatherer,* fr. 1. אגר) son of יָקֶה, an author of proverbs Pr 30[1].

†[**אֲגוֹרָה**] **n.f. payment,** אֲגוֹרַת כֶּסֶף 1 S 2[36].

†**אִגֶּרֶת** **n.f. letter, letter-missive** (late, prob. loan-word, As. *egirtu* Dl[W])—abs. Ne 2[8] + 2 t.; cstr. Est 9[29]; pl. אִגְּרוֹת abs. 2 Ch 30[1] + 3 t.; cstr. Ne 2[9]; אִגְּרֹתֵיהֶם Ne 6[17]—*letter,* esp. royal letter 2 Ch 30[1.6] Ne 2[7.8.9]; but also others Ne 6[5.17.19] Es 9[26.29] (‖ סֵפֶר vv[20.30]; other syn. נִשְׁתְּוָן, מִכְתָּב q.v.)

אֲגַרְטָל v. גרטל.

אֶגְרֹף v. גרף.

אֵד, אוֹדוֹת, אֹדוֹת v. אוד.

†[**אָדַב**] **vb. grieve; Hiph.** *Inf.* לַאֲדִיב (= לְהַאֲדִיב Ges$^{§53.3.R7}$) *to cause to grieve* 1 S 2^{33}. (But Dr prop. לְהָדִיב fr. דוב q.v.)

†**אַדְבְּאֵל** **n.pr.m.** 3rd son of Ishmael (cf. Ar. أَدَّبَ *invite, discipline*?) Gn 25^{13} 1 Ch 1^{29} (As. *Idiba'il* etc., name of north. Ar. tribe Dl$^{Pa\,301}$; cf. Minæan ארבל DHM in MV).

אדד (? cf. Ar. أَدٌّ *strength*).

†**אִדּוֹ** **n.pr.m.** a chief Israelite Ezr 8$^{17.17}$.

אֲדַד **n.pr.m.** v. הדד.

אֲדַלְיָא **n.pr.m.** 5th son of Haman Est 9^{8} (Pers.?).

I. **אדם** (cf. As. [*adâmu*] *make, produce* (?) Dl$^{W\,\&\,Pr\,104}$).

אָדָם $_{560}$ **n.m.** $^{Gn\,1,27}$ **man, mankind** (Ph. אדם, Sab. *id.*, CIS$^{iv.\,1,\,1.\,4}$ al.; cf. As. *admu, young* (of bird) Dl^{W}, but Nö$^{ZMG\,1886,722}$ identif. with Ar. أَنَامٌ coll. *creatures*)—Sg. abs. exc. cstr. Pr 6^{12} cf. Thes; (א׳(הָ) בְּנֵי oft. = pl. of א׳ Gn 11^{5} + 39t., cf. בְּנוֹת הָא׳ Gn 6$^{2.4}$)—**1.** *a man* (= Ger. *Mensch*) = human being Gn 2$^{5.7.7.8.15.16.18}$ +, 16^{12} (27t. J) Lv 5^{4} (|| נֶפֶשׁ) 13$^{2.9}$ (19t. P) Ne 2^{10} Is 13^{12} (|| אֱנוֹשׁ); הָא׳ הַגָּדוֹל Jos 14^{15} (E); א׳ בְּלִיַּעַל Pr 6^{12} (|| אִישׁ אָוֶן cf. 1 S 25^{25} & v. בליעל); = any one Lv 1^{2} Nu 9$^{6.7}$ Jb 20^{29} 27^{13} Pr 15^{20} 21$^{16.20}$ 24^{30} Ec 7^{20} + oft. WisdLt, Je 2^{6} 4^{25} Ne 2^{12}, cf. נֶפֶשׁ א׳ Nu 19$^{11.13}$ +; seld. *man* opp. woman Gn 2$^{22.22.23.25}$ 3$^{8.12.17.20.21}$ Ec 7^{28}. **2.** coll. *man, mankind* Gn 1^{26} 9$^{5.6.6.6}$ + (P 28t.) 6$^{1.5.6.7}$ (JE 24t.) Dt 4^{32} (D 6t.) (on 2 S 7^{19} cf. 1 Ch 17^{17} v. Dr^{Sm}); distinctly = men + women Gn 1^{27} 5^{1} Nu 5^{6}; given as name Gn 5^{2}; but = warriors Is 22^{6} רֶכֶב א׳ (|| פרשים); || beasts (41t.) בְּהֵמָה Gn 6^{7} 7^{23} (J?) Ex 8$^{13.14}$ 9$^{9.10}$ (P) 9$^{19.22.25}$ 12^{12} 13$^{2.13.15}$ (all J) +; late proph. Je 21^{6} 31^{27} 50^{3} 51^{62} Ez 14$^{13.17.19.21}$ 25^{13} 29$^{8.11}$ 32^{13} (del. Co) 36^{11} Jon 3^{8} Zp 1^{3} Hg 1^{11} Zc 2^{8} 8^{10}; || בָּקָר Ez 4^{15}; || צֹאן, חֲמֹרִים, ב׳ Nu 31^{28}; || *id.* + מִכָּל־הַבְּהֵמָה v^{30} cf. Jon 3^{7}; || חַיָּה Gn 9^{5} (P) cf. Ez 1$^{5.8.10.26}$, & descript. of כְּרוּבִים Ez 10$^{8.14.21}$ cf. 41^{19}; || trees Dt 20^{19} (rd. הָאָדָם v. Di); opp. God 1 S 15^{29} 16$^{7.7}$ Is 31^{3} Ez 28$^{2.9}$ 1 Ch 21^{13} 29^{1} 2 Ch 6^{18} Mal 3^{8} cf. Ex 33^{20} Dt 5^{21}; so בֶּן־א׳ Nu 23^{19} (|| אִישׁ) Ez 2$^{1.3.6.8}$ (87t. Ez, alw. addressed to proph.); בְּנֵי הָא׳ 1 S 26^{19}; made in God's image Gn 1$^{26.27}$ 9^{6} cf. Ec 7^{29}; as feeble, earthly, mortal Nu 16$^{29.29}$ Ps 82^{7} 144$^{3.4}$ Jb 5^{7} 14$^{1.10}$ cf. 25^{6} (בֶּן־א׳) Ec 12^{5}; as sinful 1 K 8^{46} 2 Ch 6^{36} Je 10^{14} cf. Nu 5^{6} Jb 31^{33} Ho 6^{7}; of men in general, other men (opp. to particular ones) Ju 16^{17} (cf. אַחַד הָא׳ v$^{7.11}$) 18$^{7.28}$ ψ 73^{5} Je 32^{20} +; || אִישׁ Is 2$^{9.11.17}$ 5^{15} cf. Ez 23^{42} (del. Co Vrss); בְּנֵי א׳ 2 S 7^{14} (|| אֲנָשִׁים) Pr 8^{4} (|| אִישִׁים); ψ 49^{3} 62^{10} (both || בְּנֵי אִישׁ) = men of low opp. men of high degree—so oft. Ph. and = *vassal* Sab. DHM$^{ZMG\,1875,\,680\,cf.\,686}$; נֶפֶשׁ א׳ coll. Nu 31$^{35.40.46}$ 1 Ch 5^{21} Ez 27^{13}. †**3. n.pr.m. Adam,** first man (without art., cf. שָׂטָן 1 Ch 21^{1} over ag. הַשּׂ׳ Jb 1^{6} etc.) Gn 4^{25} (J) 5$^{1.3.4.5}$ (P) 1 Ch 1^{1}. (Gn 2^{20} 3$^{17.21}$ rd. לְא׳ v. Di.) †**4. n. pr.loc.** city in Jordan valley (as *built*?) Jos 3^{16}.

אֲדָמָה $_{224}$ **n.f. ground, land** (as *tilled*, Ger. *bebaut*? Dl$^{Pr\,105}$, but Fleisch. (Merx$^{Archiv\,I,\,236f}$) comp. Ar. أَدَمَةٌ, *skin*, as smoothly covering & close-fitting; √דם cf. Ar. دَمَّ *smear* (spread over surface); cf. also Nö$^{ZMG\,1886,\,737}$)—א׳ Gn 1^{25} +; cstr. אַדְמַת Gn 47^{20} +; *sf.* אַדְמָתִי Jb 31^{38} + 2 t. etc.; *pl.* אֲדָמוֹת ψ 49^{12}—**1.** *ground* (as tilled, yielding sustenance) Gn 2$^{5.9}$ 3$^{17.23}$ 4$^{2.3.12}$ 5^{29} 8^{21} 19^{25} 47^{23} Ex 34^{26} (all J); Ex 23^{19} (E) Dt 7^{13} 11^{17} 26$^{2.10.15}$ 28$^{4.11.18.33.42.51}$ 30^{9} 2 S 9^{10} Is 1^{7} 28^{24} 30$^{23.23.24}$ Je 7^{20} 14^{4} 25^{33} Hg 1^{11} Mal 3^{11} ψ 83^{11} 105^{35} Pr 12^{11} 28^{19} 1 Ch 27^{26} Ne 10$^{36.38}$ cf. fig. Jb 5^{6} (|| עפר); personif. 31^{38} Jo 1^{10}; also אִישׁ הָא׳ Gn 9^{20} (J) *tiller, husbandman;* meton. אֹהֵב א׳ 2 Ch 26^{10} i.e. *lover of husbandry* (or do these point to earlier meaning *tillage*? cf. Dl$^{Pr\,105}$) אִישׁ עֹבֵד א׳ Zc 13^{5}. †**2.** *piece of ground,* landed property Gn 47$^{18.19.19.19.20.22.22.23.26}$ (all J) ψ 49^{12} (pl.) †**3.** *earth* as material substance; of wh. man is made Gn 2^{7} (עָפָר מִן־הָא׳); so animals v^{19} (מִן־הָא׳); altar Ex 20^{24}; earthen vessels חַרְשֵׂי א׳ Is 45^{9}; on head, sign of woe 1 S 4^{12} 2 S 1^{2} 15^{32}; of contrition Ne 9^{1} (cf. עָפָר, אֵפֶר); מַעֲבֵה הָא׳ 1 K 7^{46} cf. 2 Ch 4^{17} (*firmness of earth,* firm earth, clay-ground, for casting-moulds; or *clay-moulds* (Be)? or is this *n.pr.*? Klo prop. בִּמְעָרַה הָאֲדֻמָּה *in the red cave*); mule-loads of 2 K 5^{17}; in it lie the dead מִיְּשֵׁנֵי אַדְמַת־עָפָר Dn 12^{2} cf. Gn 3$^{19.23}$ ψ 146^{4}. **4.** *ground* as earth's visible surface; רֶמֶשׂ הָא׳ Gn 1^{25} 6^{20} (both P) Ho 2^{20} cf. Gn 7^{8} 9^{2} (J?) Lv 20^{25} (P) Dt 4^{18} Ez 38^{20}; also Gn 4^{10} (J) Is 24^{21} Am 3^{5} Zp 1$^{2.3}$; as wet with dew 2 S 17^{12}; rain 1 K 17^{14} 18^{1}; cf. personif. פָּצְתָה הָא׳ אֶת־פִּיהָ Nu 16^{30} (P) (|| ארץ v^{32}), vid. v^{31}; of partic. place, spot א׳ קֹדֶשׁ Ex 3^{5} esp. as abode of man Gn 4^{11} Ex 10^{6} Dt 4$^{10.40}$ 12^{1} 1 S 20^{31} 2 S 14^{7}; oft. פְּנֵי הָא׳ Gn 2^{6} 4^{14} 6$^{1.7}$ 7$^{4.23}$ 8$^{8.13}$ Ex 32^{12} 33^{16} Nu 12^{3} Dt 6^{15} 7^{6} (all J, D) 1 S 20^{15} + 9 t. **5.** *land, territory, country* (= ארץ) Gn 47^{19} (J) Lv 20^{24} (J?—|| ארץ) cstr. bef. n.pr. א׳ מִצְרַיִם Gn 47$^{20.26}$; א׳ יְהוּדָה Is 19^{17}; א׳ יִשְׂרָאֵל Ez 11^{17} + 16 t. Ez; esp. of land as promised or given by

ʼ to his people=Canaan Gn 28^{15} Ex 20^{12} Nu 11^{12} 32^{11} (all J?) Dt 5^{16}+16t Dt, Jos; 1 K $8^{34.40}$ +, Je 16^{15} 24^{10} 25^{5} 35^{15} Ez 28^{25} 2 Ch $6^{25.31}$ 7^{20} 33^{8}, cf also Dt 12^{19} 21^{23} 29^{27} 2 K 17^{23} Is 6^{11} 7^{16} 14^{1}+, Ez $34^{13.27}$+, Ne 9^{25} (א׳ שמנה),—in all c 41t, +Jo 2^{21} (personif), א׳ הַקֹּדֶשׁ Zc 2^{16} (cf sub **4** supr); hence also as Yahweh's land Dt 32^{43} Is 14^{2} Zc 9^{16} 2 Ch 7^{20} †**6.** whole *earth*, inhabited earth (seld; cf also פני הא׳ sub **4** supr) Gn 12^{3} 28^{14} (both J cf אֶרֶץ 18^{18} 22^{18} 26^{4}) Dt 14^{2} Am 3^{2} Is 24^{21} †**7. n.pr.loc.** city in Naphtali (as *built* cf אָדָם **4**?=*ed-Dâmeh*?) W of L Gennes Jos 19^{36} v. Di

†**אַדְמָה n.pr.loc.** city in Vale of Siddim Gn 10^{19} $14^{2.8}$ Dt 29^{22} Ho 11^{8}

אֲדָמִי הַנֶּקֶב n.pr.loc. pass in Naphtali, Jos 19^{33} v נקב

II. **אדם** (אֲדַם, אֹדֶם tawny, Eth. **አደመ**: (only in derivatives), As. *adâmu*? Dl^{W}, cf. Lag$^{BN\ 28}$)

†[**אָדַם, אָדֵם**] **vb. be red** (on format cf Lag$^{BN\ 83\ cf\ 120}$)—**Qal** *Pf* 3 pl אָדְמוּ *ruddy*, of Nazirites La 4^{7}; **Pu.** *Pt* *reddened*, *dyed red*, מְאָדָּם Na 2^{4} (of shield), מְאָדָּמִים of rams' skins Ex 25^{5} 26^{14} $35^{7.23}$ 36^{19} 39^{34} (all P) **Hithp.** *Impf* *redden, grow* or *look red*, יִתְאַדָּם Pr 23^{31} (of wine); **Hiph.** *Impf.* *emit (show) redness* (cf Lag$^{BN\ 120}$) יַאְדִּימוּ כַתּוֹלָע Is 1^{18} (of sins) i e be glaring, flagrant (cf also v ^{15})

†**אָדֹם adj. red**—א׳ Is 63^{2} Zc 1^{8}+Gn $25^{30.30}$, v infr, אָדוֹם Ct 5^{10}, f. אֲדֻמָּה Nu 19^{2}, pl אֲדֻמִּים 2 K 3^{22}+2t,—*ruddy, red*, of man Ct 5^{10}, horse Zc $1^{8.8}$ (‖ שָׂרֹק cf As Dl$^{W\ 87}$) 6^{2} (‖ שָׁחֹר), heifer Nu 19^{2}, water 2 K 3^{22} (א׳ כַּדָּם), cf as subst. *red, redness* on garment Is 63^{2}, הָאָדֹם = *the (red) lentils* Gn $25^{30.30}$, but rd הָאֹדֶם v infr, cf. also מַעֲלֵה

†**אֹדֶם n.[f.]** carnelian (fr. *redness*, 𝔊 σάρδιον, on format cf Lag$^{BN\ 144}$) Ex 28^{17} 39^{10} (P) Ez 28^{13}

†**אדם n.[m.]** name of a condiment (Ar. إِدَامٌ v. Anderson in Di, cf As. *adumatu*? Dl^{W}) הָא׳ Gn $25^{30.30}$ (J; so rd. for הָאָ׳ MT, v. Di).

אֱדוֹם (†אֱדֹם Ez 25^{11}) **n.pr.m. 1. Edom** (name of a god? v Sta$^{G\ 1\ 121}$ RS$^{Sem\ 43}$, vid *n.pr* עבדאדם, but Bae$^{Rel\ 10}$ thinks dial var. of אָדָם, בני אדום = בני אָדָם) = Esau, elder son of Isaac Gn 25^{30} (J) (where etym = *red*, cf v^{25} (E?) & sub אַדְמוֹנִי) $36^{1.8.19}$ (P). **2.** coll. (**m.** but **f.** Mal 1^{4}) *Edomites, Idumeans* as descend of Esau Gn $36^{9.43}$ (P); also 1 S 14^{47}+31t.+2 S 8^{13} (for MT ארם; 𝔊𝔖, v 1 Ch 18^{12} ψ 60^{2}, We Dr), perh also v^{12} (𝔊𝔖 1 Ch 18^{11}; MT ארם but v We Dr), also 2 Ch 20^{2} (v Be); א׳=king of Edom Nu $20^{18.20.21}$; poet בני א׳ ψ 137^{7} בַּת א׳ La $4^{21.22}$. **3.** *land of Edom, Idumaea* (*f.* Ez 32^{29} 35^{15} and 36^{5}) S & SE of Pal. Gn $36^{32.43}$+32t. (incl שדה א׳ Gn 32^{4}, ארץ א׳ Gn $36^{16.17.21.31}$ Nu 20^{23} 21^{4} 33^{37} +),—uncertain whether **2** or **3** are Ex 15^{15} Nu 20^{14} 24^{18}+9t (chiefly in מֶלֶךְ א׳ etc.)

†**אֲדֹמִי adj. gent. Edomite** Dt 23^{8} 1 S 21^{8} $22^{9.18.22}$ 1 K 11^{14} ψ 52^{2}, אֲדוֹמִים 2 Ch 25^{14} 28^{17}, so 2 K 16^{6} (Qr, Kt ארומים, v ארם); אֲדֹמִיִּם 1 K 11^{17}, *f* אֲדֹמִיֹּת 1 K 11^{1}

†**אֲדַמְדָּם adj. reddish** (cf. As *ada(m)mumu*? Dl^{W}) of leprous sores Lv 13^{42} (־דָּם) v^{49} (־דָּם), *f.* אֲדַמְדֶּמֶת v$^{24.43}$, ־דֶּמֶת v^{19}, *f pl* אֲדַמְדַּמֹּת 14^{37}

†**אַדְמוֹנִי adj. red, ruddy**, of Esau as newborn babe Gn 25^{25} (whence name Edom acc. to E? cf Di); of youth 1 S 16^{12} 17^{42} (אַדְמֹנִי).

אֲדֻמִּים n.pr.loc. v מַעֲלֵה sub עלה.

†**אַדְמָתָא n pr m.** a prince of Persia & Media Est 1^{14} (cf. Pers. *admâta, unrestrained*).

אדן (mng. disputed; (1) cf As [*adannu*] *firm, strong*, adv *adanniš, strongly, exceedingly* Dl^{W} > (2) Fu (*a*) *make firm, fasten* (cf. عدن) whence אֶדֶן, (*b*) *determine, command, rule*, whence אָדוֹן, (3) Thes Add, MV al. (*a*) intr. *be under, low, inferior* (cf דון, دان), whence אֶדֶן, (*b*) tr *put under command, rule over* (cf דין) whence אָדוֹן; v also (4) Lag$^{M\ 1.102}$, אָדוֹן fr ادى).

[**אֶדֶן**]$_{57}$ **n.m.** $^{Ex\ 26,19}$ **base, pedestal**—אֶדֶן Ex 38^{7}; pl אֲדָנִים Ex 26^{19}+; cstr אַדְנֵי Ct 5^{15}+, etc. **1.** *pedestals* of fine gold, on wh pillars of marble were set Ct 5^{15}. **2.** *pedestals* of the earth on wh its pillars were placed Jb 38^{6} (‖ corner-stone) **3.** (metal) *pedestals, bases*, or *sockets* in wh. tenons of planks & pillars of tabernacle were set up, two for each plank & one for each pillar Ex $26^{19.19.19}$+52t in Ex 26 27 35–40 Nu 3 4 (all P), cf 𝔊 Sm Co for אַרְצוֹ Ez 41^{22}, of altar.

אָדוֹן n.m. $^{Mal\ 3.1}$ **lord** (Ph אדן)—א׳ ψ 12^{5}+ cstr אֲדוֹן Jos 3^{11}+; pl אֲדֹנִים Is 26^{13}+; cstr אֲדֹנֵי Dt 10^{17}+, sf אֲדֹנֵינוּ 1 S 25^{14}+ etc; (אֲדֹנִי, אֲדֹנָי, אֲדֹנָי are variations of Mass. pointing to distinguish divine reference fr human. Pl, with few exc. an intens pl of rank, word takes sf as pl in all other pers, so doubtless here. Orig. reading prob in all cases אֲדֹנִי (v. Dalman Der Gottesname Adonaj, Lag$^{BN\ 188}$ makes אֲדֹנָי an Aram. format); אֲדֹנִי now found in J 51t; in E

†Gn 31^{35} 32^{19} 42^{10} Ex 21^{5}; in P †Gn 23$^{6.11.15}$ Nu 36$^{2.2}$; often S & K; in Chr only in sources, 1 Ch 21$^{3.3.3.23}$ (=2 S 24$^{3.22}$) 2 Ch 2$^{13.14}$; Is & Je only in hist. parts Is 36$^{8.9.12}$ Je 37^{20} 38^{9}; elsewh. †Dn 1^{10} 10$^{16.17.19}$ 12^{8} Zc 1^{9} 4$^{4.5.13}$ 6^{4} ψ 110^{1} Ju 4^{18} 6^{13} Ru 2^{13}; בִּי אֲדֹנִי †Ex 4$^{10.13}$ Jos 7^{8} (J) Ju 6^{15} 13^{8} is referred to God, but בִּי אֲדֹנִי †Gn 43^{20} 44^{18} Nu 12^{11} (J) 1 S 1^{26} 25^{24} 1 K 3$^{17.26}$ ref. to human superiors. There is uncertainty as to אֲדֹנָי Gn 18^{3} 19^{18}; אֲדֹנַי 19^{2})—†**1.** sg. *lord, master* (1) ref. to men: (*a*) supt. of household, or of affairs Gn 45$^{8.9}$ (E)=ψ 105^{21}; (*b*) master ψ 12^{5}; (*c*) king Je 22^{18} 34^{5}; (2) ref. to God, הָאָדֹן יהוה *the Lord Yahweh* (v. יהוה) Ex 23^{17} 34^{23} (Cov't codes); אֲדוֹן כָּל־הָאָרֶץ *Lord of the whole earth* Jos 3$^{11.13}$ (J) ψ 97^{5} Zc 4^{14} 6^{5} Mi 4^{13}; הָא׳ י׳ צְבָאוֹת, earlier Is 1^{24} 3^{1} 10^{33} 19^{4} (אֲדֹנָי Is 10^{16} in common MT; not Massora, doubtless scrib. error); הָא׳ Mal 3^{1}; אָדוֹן ψ 114^{7}. **2.** pl. *lords, kings* Dt 10^{17}=ψ 136^{3}; Is 26^{13}; elsewh. intens. pl. of rank, *lord, master*, (1) ref. to men: (*a*) *proprietor* of hill Samaria †1 K 16^{24}; (*b*) *master* Gn 40^{7} (E) Ex 21$^{4.4.6.8.32}$ (Cov't code) Gn 24^{9}+ (J, 11 t.) Dt 23^{16} Ju 19$^{11.12}$+13 t. S & K; Jb 3^{19} ψ 123^{2} Pr 25^{13} 27^{18} 30^{10} Is 24^{2} Am 4^{1} Zp 1^{9} Mal 1$^{6.6}$; (*c*) *husband* Ju 19$^{26.27}$ ψ 45^{12}; (*d*) *prophet* 2 K 2$^{3.5.16}$; (*e*) *governor* Ne 3^{5}; (*f*) *prince* Gn 42$^{10.30.33}$ (E) 44^{8} (J) 1 S 29^{10}; (*g*) *king* Gn 40^{1} (E) Ju 3^{25}+40 t. S & K; Ch only in sources 1 Ch 12^{19} cf. 1 S 29^{4}; 2 Ch 13^{6} 18^{16}=1 K 22^{17}; Is 19^{4} 22^{18} 36^{12} 37$^{4.6}$ Je 27^{4}; (2) ref. to God Mal 1^{6}; אֲדֹנֵי הָאֲדֹנִים *Lord of lords* Dt 10^{17}=ψ 136^{3}; אֲדֹנֵינוּ ψ 135^{5} 147^{5} Ne 8^{10}; י׳ אֲדֹנֵינוּ ψ 8$^{2.10}$ Ne 10^{30}; אֲדֹנַיִךְ י׳ Is 51^{22} (prob.=*thy husband, Yahweh*); אֲדֹנָיו Ho 12^{15} (possibly error for אֲדֹנָי). **3.** sf. 1 s. אֲדֹנִי (אֲדֹנִי) (1) ref. to men: *my lord, my master*, (*a*) *master* Ex 21^{5} (Cov't code) Gn 24^{12}+, 44^{5} (J, 20 t.) 1 S 30$^{13.15}$ 2 K 5$^{3.20.22}$ 6^{15}; (*b*) *husband* Gn 18^{12} (J); (*c*) *prophet* 1 K 18$^{7.13}$ 2 K 2^{19} 4$^{16.28}$ 6^{5} 8^{5}; (*d*) *prince* Gn 42^{10} (E), 23$^{6.11.15}$ (P), 43^{20} 44^{18}+, 47^{18}, + (J, 12 t.); Ju 4^{18}; (*e*) *king* 1 S 22^{12}+ (S & K 75 t.); (*f*) *father* Gn 31^{35} (E); (*g*) *Moses* Ex 32^{22} Nu 11^{28} 12^{11} 32$^{26.27}$ (J); 36$^{2.2}$ (P); (*h*) *priest* 1 S 1$^{15.26.26}$; (*i*) *theophanic angel* Jos 5^{14} Ju 6^{13}; (*j*) *captain* 2 S 11^{11}; (*k*) general recognition of superiority Gn 24^{18} 32^{5}+; 33^{8}+; 44^{7}+ (J, 13 t.), Ru 2^{13} 1 S 25^{24}+ (15 t.); (2) ref. to God: אֲדֹנָי **a.** *my Lord* Gn 20^{4} (? E) Ex 15^{17} (Sam. יהוה) elsewhere in Hex, J; Gn 18$^{3(?).27.30.31.32}$ 19$^{2.18(?)}$ Ex 4$^{10.13}$ 5^{22} 34^{9} Nu 14^{17} Jos 7^{8}; also Ju 6^{15} 13^{8}; not S; 1 K 22^{6} 2 K 19^{23}; not Chron. exc. memorials Ezr 10^{3} (ref. to Ezra) Ne 1^{11} 4^{8}; WisdLt only Jb 28^{28} (doubtless scrib. error for יהוה of many MSS.); not Ho; Is 37^{24} 38$^{14.16}$ (hist. part); exil. Is 49^{14} (cf. 51^{22}); Mi 1^{2} ψ 16^{2}+ (47 t., chiefly this sense, exc. sub **b.**; cf. אֱלֹהַי וַאדֹנָי *my Lord and my God* ψ 35^{23}; (writers that use אֱלֹהִים seld. use אֲדֹנָי); **b.** *Adonay* **n.pr.** of God, parallel with *Yahweh*, substit. for it oft. by scrib. error, & eventually supplanting it. In earlier Is 3^{17}+ (19 t. seeming to belong here), Am 7$^{7.8}$ 9^{1} Ez 18$^{25.29}$ 33$^{17.20}$ 21^{14} (prob. אֲדֹנָי י׳ as in usual phrase); Zc 9^{4} Mal 1$^{12.14}$ La 1^{14}+ (14 t.) ψ 2^{4} 37^{13} 78^{65} 90^{17} (יהוה?) 110^{5} (Dalman puts most of these sub (*a*);—many cases are doubtful); 1 K 3$^{10.15}$ (Mass. אדני for יהוה cf. Dalm. 2 K 7^{6}; Dalm. rightly questions; he rds. יהוה). The phrases אֲדֹנָי אֱלֹהַי ψ 38^{16} 86^{12}, *Adonay my God*; אֲדֹנָי הָאֱלֹהִים Dn 9^{3}, א׳ אֱלֹהֵינוּ 9$^{9.15}$, א׳ הָאֵל Dn 9^{4} favour taking א׳ Dn 1^{2} 9$^{7.8}$ (יהוה?) v$^{16.17.19.19.19}$ as the divine name. **4.** אֲדֹנָי יהוה (*a*) *my Lord Yahweh* (v. יהוה) Gn 15$^{2.8}$ (JE) Jos 7^{7} (J, 𝔊 om. י׳) Dt 3^{24} 9^{26} Ju 6^{22} 16^{28} 2 S^{7} (6 t.) 1 K 2^{26} 8^{53}; prob. Am 3$^{7.8}$ 7$^{2.4.5}$ 9^{8} Je 1^{6} 4^{10} 14^{13} 32$^{17.25}$ Ez 4^{14} 8^{1} 9^{8} 11^{13} 20^{49} 37^{3} (יָדַע כִּי אֲנִי א׳ י׳) 13^{9} 23^{49} 24^{24} 28^{24}; 29^{16} inappropriate in mouth of God; del. אֲדֹנָי (Co) or rd. י׳ אֱלֹהֵיכֶם (Dalm.); Mi 1^{2} Zp 1^{7} Ob ^{1} Zc 9^{14} ψ 71$^{5.16}$ 73^{28}; (*b*) appar. **n.pr.** *Adonay Yahweh* Is 25^{8} Je 44^{26}; exil. Is 40^{10}+ (10 t., but 61$^{1.11}$ rd. יהוה, 𝔊); (*c*) uncertain whether (*a*) or (*b*) in proph. formula אָמַר א׳ י׳ Is 7^{7} 28^{16} 30^{15} 49^{22} 51^{4} 65^{13} Je 7^{20} Am 1^{8} 3^{11} 5^{3} 7^{6} Ob ^{1} Ez (131 t.); נְאֻם א׳ י׳ Is 56^{8} Je 2^{22} Am 3^{13} 4^{5} 8$^{3.9.11}$ Ez (80 t.); דְּבַר־א׳ י׳ Ez 6^{3} 25^{3} 36^{4}; כֹּה הִרְאַנִי א׳ י׳ Am 4^{2} 6^{8}; נִשְׁבַּע א׳ י׳ Am 7$^{1.4}$ 8^{1}. **5.** יהוה אֲדֹנָי *Yahweh my Lord* ψ 68^{21} 109^{21} 140^{8} 141^{8} Hb 3^{9}. **6.** אֲדֹנָי יהוה צְבָאוֹת (*a*) *my Lord Yahweh Ṣ.* (v. צבאות) ψ 69^{7} Am 9^{5} Is 10^{23} 22$^{5.12}$ 28^{22} cf. י׳ אֱלֹהֵי הַצְּבָאוֹת א׳, *Yahweh, the God of Hosts my Lord* Am 5^{16}; (*b*) a divine name, *Adonay, Yahweh Ṣ.* Je 46$^{10.10}$ 50^{25}; (*c*) uncertain are כֹּה אָמַר א׳ י׳ צ׳ Is 10^{24} 22$^{14.15}$; נְאֻם א׳ י׳ צ׳ Is 3^{15} Je 2^{19} 49^{5} 50^{31}.

†אַדָּן **n.pr.loc.** in Babylonia Ezr 2^{59} (v. כְּרוּב n.pr.)

†אַדּוֹן *id.* Ne 7^{61}.

†אֲדֹנִי־בֶזֶק **n.pr.m.** (or title) king of Can. city Bezek Ju 1^{7}; without Maqq. v$^{5.6}$.

†אֲדֹנִי־צֶדֶק **n.pr.m.** Canaan. king of Jerusalem Jos 10$^{1.3}$ (*Lord of righteousness; my Lord is righteous*, or *my Lord is Ṣidiq*—divine name—cf. אֲדֹנִיָּהוּ, מַלְכִּי צֶדֶק, Ph. אדנבעל etc.)

אֲדֹנִיָּהוּ (אֲדֹנִיָּה) **n.pr.m.** (*my Lord is Yahweh*, cf. Ph. אדנשמש, אדנבעל, ארנאשמן etc., in As. *Aduniba'al* Schr$^{KB\ II.\ 172}$) **1.** fourth son of David 1 K 1^{8}+11 t., 2^{13}+5 t. (=אֲדֹנִיָּה 2 S 3^{4} 1 K 1$^{5.7.18}$ 2^{28} 1 Ch 3^{2}). **2.** a Levite †2 Ch 17^{8}. **3.** a chief of the people †Ne 10^{17} (=אֲדֹנִיקָם 7^{18} Ezr 2^{13} cf. 8^{13}).

†אֲדֹנִיקָם **n.pr.m.** (*my Lord has arisen*) head of a family Ezr 2[13] 8[13] Ne 7[18] (אֲדֹנִיָּהוּ Ne 10[17]).

†אֲדֹנִירָם **n.pr.m.** (*my Lord is exalted*) official of Solom. 1 K 4[6] 5[28]; so also 2 S 20[24] 1 K 12[18] 𝔊 We Dr[Sm].

†אֲדֹרָם (contr. or corrupt, cf. foregoing) same official, under David 2 S 20[24], & Rehob. 1 K 12[18] (=הֲדֹרָם 2 Ch 10[18]).

†[אָדַר] **vb.** (poet.) **wide, great,** (thence) **high, noble** (? As. *adâru* Dl[W])—**Niph.** *Pt. majestic, glorious,* of ׳י, נֶאְדָּר Ex 15[11]; cstr. נֶאְדָּרִי v[6] (v. Di); **Hiph.** *Impf.* יַאְדִּיר *make glorious* the teaching Is 42[21] (׳י subj.)

†אֶדֶר **n.**[m.] **1. glory, magnificence** (As. *aduru, adiru*) ironic. of price of shepherd (symbol.) Zc 11[13]. **2. mantle, cloak** (as *wide*) Mi 2[8] (∥ שַׂלְמָה), but rd. אדרת (ת lost bef. foll. ת), so WRS[Proph 427].

†אֲדוֹרַיִם **n.pr.loc.** (*two hills?*) city in Judah 2 Ch 11[9] (cf. Ἀδωρα, Δωρα, Jos.[Ant. viii. 10. 1, xiv. 5. 3]); now *Dûra*, W. of Hebron, Rob.[BR II, 215].

†אַדָּר **n.pr.m.** (*noble?*). **1.** son of Bela, grandson of Benjm. 1 Ch 8[3] (perh. error—cf. Be—for אַרְדְּ *q.v.* Nu 26[40] Gn 46[21]). **2.** city in Judah Jos 15[3] (אַדָּרָה); =חֲצַר אַדָּר (*q.v.*) Nu 34[4].

†אַדִּיר **adj.** majestic—׳א ψ 8[2]+; **f.** אַדֶּרֶת Ez 17[8]? (v. infr.) etc.—**1. majestic** (wide, lofty) of waters of sea Ex 15[10] ψ 93[4]; a ship Is 33[21]; a tree Ez 17[23]; a vine Ez 17[8] (גֶּפֶן אַדֶּרֶת, so Fü; or ׳א n. abstr. v. sub אַדֶּרֶת infr.); also fig. of kings ψ 136[18]; nations Ez 32[18]; gods 1 S 4[8]; of ׳י ψ 93[4] 76[5]; of name of ׳י ψ 8[2.10]. **2.** subst. *majestic one,* of nobles, chieftains, etc., Ju 5[13.25] Na 2[6] 3[18] Je 14[3] 25[34] (אַדִּירֵי הַצֹּאן fig. so) [35.36] 30[21] Zc 11[2] 2 Ch 23[20] Ne 3[5] 10[30]; of ׳י Is 10[34] 33[21]; of servants of ׳י ψ 16[3] (=priests? cf. 1 Ch 24[5] & v. Che).

†אַדֶּרֶת **n.f.** glory, cloak—׳א abs. Jos 7[24]; אַדֶּרֶת Ez 17[8]; cstr. Gn 25[25]+4t.; אַדַּרְתּוֹ 1 K 19[13] +3t.; אַדַּרְתָּם Zc 11[3]—**1.** *glory, magnificence,* of vine Ez 17[8] (so Thes MV, but < *adj. f.* fr. אַדִּיר q.v.), of shepherds Zc 11[3] (or *sub* **2**). **2.** *mantle, cloak* (wide garment) of hair שֵׂעָר Gn 25[25] Zc 13[4] (as proph. mantle, so perh. 11[3] of shepherds=false proph.) cf. of Elijah 1 K 19[13.19] 2 K 2[8.13.14]; but אַדֶּרֶת שִׁנְעָר טוֹבָה (fine mantle of Shinar=Babylonian mantle—doubtless costly) Jos 7[21.24] (J) & (late) ׳א alone Jon 3[6].

†אֲדָר **n.pr.**[m.] 12th (Babylonian) month=Feb.–Mar. (late Heb. loan-word, =Bab. *A(d)-daru* v. Dl[W p. 188, cf. Al3 93], meaning dub. perh. *adâru*, be darkened, *eclipsed*, but v. Dl[W p. 190]) Est 3[7.13] 8[12] 9[1.15.17.19.21]; cf. Palm. Nab. אדר Vog[8] Eut[Nab 24].

†אַדְרַמֶּלֶךְ **n.pr.m.** (*Adar is prince*, As. *Adar-malik* (?) v. KAT[2 284], cf. ABK[140]; or *A. is Counsellor, Decider*, cf. Dl[K 52 f]; otherwise Sayce [Rel. Bab. 7]; on Bab. god *Adar* v. Schr[KGGW 1880, 19 f] Dl[K 52 f], but Sayce[Rel. Bab. 151 f]; Jen[Ko 457 f] al. rd. As. name *Ninib;* on Carth. יתנאדר v. Bae[Rel. 54]) **1.** a god of Sepharvaim 2 K 17[31]. **2.** parricidal son of Sennacherib 2 K 19[37] Is 37[38].

אֲדֹרָם v. אדנירם sub אדון.

אֲדַרְכּוֹן v. דרכמון.

אֶדְרְעִי v. דרע.

אדשׁ only *Inf. abs.* אָדוֹשׁ v. דושׁ.

אהב[216] **vb. love**—**Qal** *Pf.* אָהֵב Gn 27[9]+7t.; אָהַב Gn 27[14]; אָהַב Gn 37[3]+3t.; אֲהֵבְךָ Dt 15[16]; 3 fs. אָהֲבָה Ct 1[7]+, etc.; *Impf.* יֶאֱהַב (־הָב) Pr 3[12] +; 1 s. אֹהַב Pr 8[17] (cf. Ew[§ 192 d] Ges[§ 68. 1]); וָאֹהַב Mal 1[2]; וָאֹהֲבֵהוּ Ho 11[1]; אֹהֲבֵם Ho 14[5]; וָאֹהֲבֵם ψ 119[167]; 2 mpl. תֶּאֱהָבוּ Pr 1[22] (cf. Kö[I p. 394] Ges[§ 63 R 2]); תֶּאֱהָבוּ Zc 8[17]; תֶּאֱהָבוּן ψ 4[3]; *Imv.* אֱהַב־ Ho 3[1]; אֱהָבֶהָ Pr 4[6]; אֶהֱבוּ ψ 31[24] Am 5[15]; אֱהָבוּ Zc 8[19]; *Inf. cstr.* אֱהֹב Ec 3[8]; אַהֲבָה Dt 10[12]+; אַהֲבַת Mi 6[8]+ etc.; cf. also sub **n.** אהבה infr.; *Pt.* אֹהֵב (אוֹהֵב) Dt 10[18]+26t.; f. cstr. אֲהֻבַת Ho 3[1] is prob. *active* cf. Ba[NB 174 ff]; sf. אֹהֲבִי Is 41[8] etc.; f. אֹהֶבֶת Gn 25[28]; אֹהֲבַתִּי Ho 10[11] etc.; *Pt. pass.* אָהוּב Ne 13[26]; אֲהוּבָה Dt 21[15.15.16].—*love* (mostly c. acc., sq. לְ+obj. Lv 19[18.34] 2 Ch 19[2] (late), sq. בְּ Ec 5[9]; abs. Ec 3[8] & v. infr.), (affection both pure & impure, divine & human);—**1.** human love to human object; abs., opp. hate שָׂנֵא Ec 3[8]; of love to son Gn 22[2] 25[28] 37[3.4] 44[20] (JE) Pr 13[24]; so also 2 S 13[21] 𝔊 Ew Th We, cf. Dr, of Dvd's loving Amnon; never to parent, but mother-in-law Ru 4[15]; of man's love to woman; wife Gn 24[67] 29[20.30] (cf. v[18])[32] (JE), also Dt 21[15.15.16] Ju 14[16] 1 S 1[5] 2 Ch 11[21] Est 2[17] Ho 3[1] Ec 9[9]; but also Gn 34[3] (J) Ju 16[4.15] 2 S 13[1.4.15] (where of carnal desire) 1 K 11[1] cf. v[2] Ho 3[1]; אֹ׳ רֵעַ *loving a paramour*, v. Ba[NB 176]; woman's love to man 1 S 18[20] (so v[28] MT, but rd. וְכִי כָל־יִשְׂרָאֵל אֹהֵב אתו 𝔊 We Dr) Ct 1[3.4.7] 3[1.2.3.4] (5t. subj. נַפְשִׁי); cf. also fig. of adulterous Judah Je 2[25] Is 57[8] Ez 16[37]; of love of slave to master Ex 21[5] (JE) Dt 15[16]; inferior to superior 1 S 18[22] cf. v[16]; love to neighbour Lv 19[18] (וְאָהַבְתָּ לְרֵעֲךָ כָּמוֹךָ), partic. to stranger

Lv 19^{34} (both P), Dt 10$^{18.19}$; love of friend to friend 1 S 16^{21} 18$^{1.3}$ 20$^{17.17}$ Jb 19^{19} Pr 17^{1} cf. 2 S 19$^{7.7}$ 2 Ch 19^{2}; v. also Pr 9^{8} 16^{13} cf. 15^{12}; v. esp. *Pt.* infr. **2.** less oft. of appetite, obj. food, Gn 27$^{4.9.14}$ (JE); drink Ho 3^{1} Pr 21^{17}; husbandry 2 Ch 26^{10}; cf. fig. of Ephraim Ho 10^{11} sq. inf.; length of life ψ 34^{13}; of cupidity Ho 9^{1} Is 1^{23} Ec 5$^{9.9}$; of love of sleep Pr 20^{13} cf. fig. of sluggish watchmen (sq. inf.) Is 56^{10}; also c. obj. abstr. wisdom (personif.), knowledge, righteousness, etc. Pr 4^{6} 8$^{17.21}$ 12^{1} 22^{11} 29^{3} Am 5^{15} Mi 6^{8} (inf. ‖ infinitives) Zc 8^{19}, cf. Pr. 19^{8} קֹנֶה לֵּב אֹהֵב נַפְשׁוֹ; obj. folly, evil, etc., Mi 3^{2} 4^{3} ψ 11^{5} 52$^{5.6}$ 109^{17} Pr 1^{22} 8^{36} 17$^{19.19}$, cf. 18^{21} Zc 8^{17}, cf. א׳ כֵּן Am 4^{5} Je 5^{3}, sq. Inf. Ho 12^{8} Je 14^{10}, esp. of idolatry Ho 4^{18} (where del. הֵבוּ cf. Kö $^{I, p. 395}$) Je 8^{2}. **3.** love to God Ex 20^{6} (JE) elsewhere Hex only Dt 5^{10} 6^{5} 7^{9} + 9 t. Dt + Jos 22^{5} 23^{11}; also Ju 5^{31} 1 K 3^{3} Ne 1^{5} Dn 9^{4}; esp. in (late) ψ 31^{24} 116^{1} 145^{20}, but usually sq. name, law, etc. of י׳ ψ 5^{12} 26^{8} 40^{17} 69^{37} 70^{5} 97^{10} 119^{47} + 11 t. ψ 119; cf. Is 56^{6}; cf. also of love to Jerusalem Is 66^{10} ψ 122^{6}. **4.** esp. *Pt.* אֹהֵב =(*a*) *lover,* La 1^{2} (fig. of Jerus.); (*b*) *friend* Hiram of David 1 K 5^{15}, cf. Je 20$^{4.6}$ Est 5$^{10.14}$ 6^{13} ψ 38^{12} (‖רֵעַ) so 88^{19}, & Pr 14^{20}; also 18^{24} 27^{6}; Abr. of God Is 41^{8} 2 Ch 20^{7}. **5.** of divine love (*a*) to individual men Dt 4^{37} 2 S 12^{24} Pr 3^{12} 15^{9} ψ 146^{8} Ne 13^{26}; (*b*) to people Israel, etc. Dt 7$^{8.13}$ 23^{6} Ho 3^{1} 9^{15} 11^{1} 14^{5} 1 K 10^{9} 2 Ch 2^{10} 9^{8} Is 43^{4} 48^{14} Je 31^{3} Mal 1$^{2.2.2}$ ψ 47^{5}; to Jerusalem ψ 78^{68} 87^{2}; (*c*) to righteousness, etc. ψ 11^{7} 33^{5} 37^{28} 45^{8} 99^{4} Is 61^{8} Mal 2^{11}. †**Niph.** *Pt.* pl. הַנֶּאֱהָבִים 2 S 1^{23} *lovely, loveable* of Saul & Jonath. (‖הַנְּעִימִם). †**Pi.** *Pt.* pl. sf. מְאַהֲבַי (־בָי) Ho 2^{7} + 3 t.; מְאַהֲבַיִךְ (־בָיִךְ) Je 22^{20} + 6 t.; מְאַהֲבֶיהָ Ho 2^{9} + 4 t. **1.** *friends* Zc 13^{6}; **2.** *lovers* in fig. of adulter. Isr. Ho 2$^{7.9.12.14.15}$ Ez 23$^{5.9}$; Judah Je 22$^{20.22}$ 30^{14} La 1^{19} Ez 16$^{33.36.37}$ 23^{22}.

†[אַ֫הַב]† **n.[m.]** love only pl. אֲהָבִים, *loves, amours;* bad sense Ho 8^{9}, but אַיֶּלֶת א׳ loving hind Pr 5^{19} (fig. of wife ‖ יַעֲלַת חֵן).

†[אֹ֫הַב]† **n.[m.]** id. = loved object, sf. אֹהֲבָם Ho 9^{10} (= בֹּשֶׁת = בַּעַל v. Hi Now) i.e. the idol worshipped; pl. = *amours* (carnal sense) Pr 7^{18}.

† אַהֲבָה **n.f. love** (= Inf. of אהב q.v.)—abs. א׳ Pr 10^{12} + 18 t.; cstr. אַהֲבַת Je 2^{2} + 3 t.; sf. אַהֲבָתִי ψ 109$^{4.5}$; אַהֲבָתְךָ 2 S 1^{26}; אַהֲבָתוֹ Is 63^{9} Zp 3^{17}; אַהֲבָתָהּ Pr 5^{19}; אַהֲבָתָם Ec 9^{6}—*love,* esp. WisdLt & late. **1.** human (to human obj.) abs. Ec 9$^{1.6}$ (both ‖ שִׂנְאָה) so Pr 10^{12} 15^{17} cf. 27^{5}; v. also 17^{9}; of man toward man ψ 109$^{4.5}$; love for one's self (נַפְשׁוֹ) 1 S 20^{17}; between man & woman Ct 2$^{4.5}$ 5^{8} 8$^{6.7.7}$; Pr 5^{19} cf. also 2 S 1^{26} (א׳ נָשִׁים); personif. Ct. 2^{7} 3^{5} 7^{7} 8^{4}; cf. fig. use 3^{10}; of mere sexual desire 2 S 13^{15}; fig. of Jerusalem's love to י׳ Je 2^{2} (א׳ כְּלוּלֹתָיִךְ), & of love of adulter. Jerus. v^{33}. **2.** God's love to his people Ho 11^{4} (עֲבֹתוֹת א׳) Je 31^{3} Is 63^{9} Zp 3^{17}.

אהד (= אחד? v. Thes.)

†אֹ֫הַד† **n.pr.m.** son of Simeon Gn 46^{10} Ex 6^{15}.

†אֵהוּד† **n.pr.m.** **1.** a Benjamite, son of Gera, deliverer of Isr. fr. Moab Ju 3$^{15.16.20.20.21.23.26}$ 4^{1}. **2.** a Benjamite, son of Bilhan (= foregoing?) 1 Ch 7^{10}.

†אֲהָהּ† (אָהּ, ܐܘܗ) **interj. alas!** Ju 11^{35} 2 K 3^{10} 6$^{5.15}$; with לְ Jo 1^{15} אֲהָהּ לַיּוֹם *alas for the day! for* etc. In the combination אֲהָהּ אֲדֹנָי יֱהוִֹה Jos 7^{7} Ju 6^{22} Je 1^{6} 4^{10} 14^{13} 32^{17} Ez 4^{14} 9^{8} 11^{13} 21^{5}.

†אַהֲוָא† **n.pr.loc.** town or district in Babylonia, by which a stream is designated Ezr 8$^{15.31}$, also the stream v^{21} (הנהר א׳), v^{31} (נְהַר א׳).

†אֱהִי† Ho. 13$^{10.14.14}$ **adv. where?** = אֵי, אַיֵּה. So 𝔊 𝔖 𝔙 𝔗 AW in Ho 13^{10}, & 𝔊 𝔖 (cf. 1 Cor 15^{55}) AW in Ho 13^{14}. Taken by many of the older interpreters, and even by Ges in 13^{14}, as 1 s. impf. apoc. of היה *I would be:* but this is less suited to the context, and the jussive form is an objection, being unusual with the 1 ps.

I. **אהל** (*settle down* (?), Ar. أَهَلَ *be inhabited,* cf. As. *âlu, settlement, city, ma'âlu, ma'âltu, bed;* Dl^{W} & $^{Pr 106}$).

אֹ֫הֶל $_{343}$ **n.m.** $^{Gn 13,3}$ tent (cf. As. *âlu,* supr., Ar. أَهْل, *fellow-dwellers, family,* Sab. אהל DHM^{ZMG} $^{1883, 341}$ al., also in n.pr. Sab. & Ph. v. אהליאב)—abs. א׳ Gn 4^{20} +; cstr. *id.* Ex 28^{43} +; אֹהֱלָה (ה loc.) Gn 18^{6} +; sf. אָהֳלִי Jb 29^{4} +; אָהָלְךָ ψ 61^{5}; אָהֳלֹה אָהֳלָה Gn 9^{21} + 3 t. (v. Dr$^{Sm\ xxxv}$); pl. אֹהָלִים Gn 13^{5} + (Ges $^{§ 23.3}$); בָּאֳהָלִים Ju 8^{11} +; cstr. אָהֳלֵי Nu 16^{26} +; sf. אֹהָלַי Je 4^{20}; אֹהָלֶיךָ Nu 24^{5} +; אָהֳלֵיכֶם Jos 22^{8} +, etc.—**1.** *tent* of nomad Ct 1^{5} Je 6^{3} 49^{29}; יֹשֵׁב א׳ *dweller in tents* Gn 4^{20} 25^{27} (J); אָהֳלֵי מִקְנֶה *tents of cattle* 2 Ch 14^{14}; of soldier 1 Sa 17^{54} cf. Dr, Je 37^{10}; 1 K 8^{66} לְאֹהָלֶיךָ, ישראל, exclam., *to thy tents, Israel!* 1 K 12$^{16.16}$ cf. 2 Ch 10^{16} 2 S 20^{1} (but cf. Dr, 1 S 17^{54}); of pleasure-tent on house-top 2 S 16^{22} (= bridal-tent, bridal pavilion, cf. חֻפָּה ψ 19^{5} Jo 2^{16} v. RS $^{Kinship\ 168}$). **2.** *dwelling, habitation;* ψ 91^{10} לְאֹהָלֶךָ א׳ *home* (lit. *to thy tents,* pl.) Ju 19^{9} (after הלך); בֵּיתִי *habitation of my house* ψ 132^{3} cf. Dn 11^{45};

א׳ דוד *habitat* or *palace* of David where throne erected Is 16[5], א׳ בַּת צִיּוֹן *h of daughter of Zion* (=Jerusalem) La 2[4]; אָהֳלֵי יַעֲקֹב Je 30[18] Mal 2[12] א׳ רְשָׁעִים, (מִשְׁכָּן ‖) א׳ יְהוּדָה Zc 12[7] (‖ בית דוד); *h. of wicked* Jb 8[22], cf א׳ רֶשַׁע ψ 84[11], א׳ יְשָׁרִים Pr 14[11]; א׳ שֹׁחַד Jb 15[34]; א׳ צַדִּיקִים ψ 118[15], א׳ אדום=Edom itself, ψ 83[7] cf. א׳ קֵדָר ψ 120[5] א׳ כּוּשָׁן Hb 3[7] **3.** *the sacred tent* used in worship of God, הָאֹהֶל *the tent*, א׳ מוֹעֵד *tent of meeting* of God with his people (tent of congregation or assembly Ges MV al) Acc to E Moses so called the tent which he used to pitch without the camp, afar off, into which he used to enter, & where God spake with him face to face, Ex 33[7−11] Nu 12[5.10] Dt 31[14.15], J seems to have same conception of an א׳ מ׳ outside the camp, Nu 11[24.26], D has no allusion to such a tent, P mentions it 131 t as א׳ מ׳, 19 t as הָאֹהֶל (cf. Ez 41[1]) & א׳ הָעֵדוּת, *tent of the testimony* Nu 9[15] 17[22.23] 18[2] (as containing ark & tables of the testimony) cf. 2 Ch 24[6]; this tent sometimes confounded with the משכן but distinguished in מִשְׁכַּן א׳מ׳ Ex 39[32] 40[2.6.29], cf. 1 Ch 6[17]; אֶת־הַמִּשְׁכָּן וְאֶת־אָהֳלוֹ, הַמִּשְׁכָּן וְהָאֹהֶל Nu 3[25], Ex 35[11]; tent was of three layers of skins, goatskins, ramskins, & *tachash* skins, each layer of eleven pieces stretched in form of a tent, covering & protecting the מִשְׁכָּן, wh was in form of parallelopip (Ex 26) An אֹהֶל מוֹעֵד was at Shilo 1 S 2[22] (om 𝔊; v. Dr) cf ψ 78[60], called א׳ יוֹסֵף v[67] The Mosaic א׳ מ׳ was later at Gibeon 2 Ch 1[3.6.13], courses of ministry arranged for service at א׳ מ׳ 1 Ch 6[17] 23[32] cf 1 Ch 9[19] (הָא׳), v[21.23] (בית הָא׳); David erected an אהל for ark on Mt Zion 2 S 6[17] 1 Ch 15[1] 16[1] 2 Ch 1[4]; Joab fled for refuge to א׳ יהוה 1 K 2[28−30], sacred oil brought fr. הָא׳ 1 K 1[39], the א׳ מוֹעֵד was taken up into temple 1 K 8[4]=2 Ch 5[5], י׳ had not previously dwelt in a בַּיִת, but had gone מאהל אל־אֹהֶל *fr tent to tent*, fr one to another, 1 Ch 17[5], cf 2 S 7[6], א׳ יהוה (‖ הַר קָדְשׁ & בַּיִת) is refuge & dwelling-place of righteous, ψ 15[1] 27[5.6] 61[5] (cf. ψ 90[1])

†[אָהַל] **vb.denom.** tent, move tent fr place to place (cf As *â'ilu*(?) Dl[W No.4 & AGl]) וַיֶּאֱהַל Gn 13[12.18] (J), cf. יֹשֵׁב אֹהֶל (v. אהל); **Pi.** *Impf.* יַהֵל (contr for יְאַהֵל) *pitch one's tent* like nomad Is 13[20].

†אָהֳלָה **n.pr.f.** Ohŏla (for אָהֳלָהּ *she who has a tent, tent-woman*, i e worshipper at tent-shrine, v. Sm) of Samaria, adulteress with Assyria Ez 23[4.4.5.36.44]

†אָהֳלִיאָב **n.pr m.** Ohŏliab (*Father's tent*, cf. Ph אהלמלך, אהלבעל; Sab. אהלאל, אהלעתתר) chief assistant of Bezalel in construction of tabernacle, etc Ex 31[6] 35[34] 36[1.2] 38[23].

†אָהֳלִיבָה **n.pr.f.** Ohŏliba (=אָהֳלִיבָהּ *tent in her*=(in meaning) אָהֳלָה cf Sm) of Jerusalem as adulterous wife of י׳ Ez 23[4.4.11.22.36.44].

†אָהֳלִיבָמָה **n.pr.** Ohŏlibama (*tent of the high place*) **1. f.** wife of Esau Gn 36[2.5.14.18.25] **2. m.** an Edomite chief Gn 36[41] 1 Ch 1[52].

†II [אָהַל] **vb.Hiph.** be clear, shine, Impf 3 ms יַאֲהִיל (subj moon יָרֵחַ) Jb 25[5] (‖ זַכּוּ subj. כוכבים, cf also יָהֵל, (=יָהֵל v[4]) fr הלל, (by text. error?) cf Di so 𝔊 > =I. אֹהֶל Ko[I. 373], after Ki).

†III [אהל] **n.[m.]** odorif tree, aloe (?) (? loan-word from Skr *aguru, agaru*, dial *aghil*, cf Wilson[Skr Dict.]; M. Muller in Pusey Dn 2d ed p 647 f, *aloexylon agallochum* (cf. Sigismund Aromata, Leipz. 1884, p. 38 f, MV cite Kondracki Beitr z. Kenntn d. Aloe, Durpat 1874 & Baer[Reden III, 293 f]); others *aloe succotrina* (Schenkel[BL], cf. Di ad Nu 24[6]); Wetzst in De[Ct 2d ed 167] brings under I אהל, he proposes *cardamum*, Ar أُهَيْل fr. أَهْل = *little tents*, from three-cornered shape of capsules) **1.** pl. אֲהָלִים trees planted by י׳ Nu 24[6] (‖ ארזים) perh error for אילים cf Di **2.** *aloes*, as sweet-smelling; perfume for bed, אֲהָלִים Pr 7[17] (‖ מֹר, קִנָּמוֹן); for garments אֲהָלוֹת ψ 45[9] (‖ מֹר, קציעות), of bride, under fig of odorif tree Ct 4[14] (‖ מֹר, כָּל־רָאשֵׁי בְשָׂמִים)

אַהֲרֹן[346] **n.pr.m.** Aaron, elder brother of Moses Ex 7[7]; the priest Ex 31[10]+, mentioned Ex 4[14] 15[20] 17[10] 24[1] 28[29]+(115 t. Ex), Lv 8[12.23]+ (80 t Lv), Nu 20[24 f] 33[39]+(101 t Nu); 1 Ch 5[29] +, Mi 6[4] (only here in proph) ψ 77[21] 105[26]; called הַכֹּהֵן Ex 31[10] 35[19] 39[41] Lv 7[34]+, v. ψ 99[6] מֹשֶׁה וא׳ בְּכֹהֲנָיו, also בֶּן־א׳ הַכֹּהֵן Ex 38[21] Nu 3[32]+(all P) called קְדוֹשׁ יהוה ψ 106[16]; oft named with his sons Lv 2[3.10] 6[2]+, בני א׳ in strict sense Ex 28[1.4.40]+oft.; בני א׳ הַכֹּהֲנִים Lv 1[5]+ Nu 3[3] 10[8] Jos 21[19] 1 Ch 6[42], of temple-priests in gen'l, as descendants of A., 2 Ch 26[18] 29[21] 31[19] 35[14.14], v. also 13[9.10] & cf. הַכֹּהֵן בֶּן־א׳ Ne 10[39]; so בית א׳ ψ 115[10.12] 118[3] 135[19]; אַהֲרֹן alone (=בית א׳) 1 Ch 12[28] cf. 27[17].

אוֹ[320] (أَوْ, ܐܘ, אוֹ), **conj.** or (whether *aut* or *vel*) **1.** Gn 24[49] 31[43] Ex 4[11] Ct 2[9] Lv 13[24] Nu 5[30]+oft (esp in *laws*), sometimes implying a preference, nearly=*or rather* Gn 24[55] יָמִים אוֹ עָשׂוֹר a few days *or* ten Ju 18[19] 1 S 29[3]

Prefixed to the first as well as to the second alternative (rare) *either* (*whether*)...*or* Lv 5^{1} $13^{48.51}$;=*or, if not* Ez 21^{15} (si vera l.) Ke Mal 2^{17} Jb 16^{3} 22^{11}. **2.** introducing a sentence, esp. a particular case under a general principle, *or* =*or if* Ex 21^{31} אוֹ־בֵן יִגָּח וגו׳ *or if* he gore a son, etc. v^{36} Lv $4^{23.28}$ (v. Di) $5^{21.22}$ 25^{49b} Nu 5^{14} 2 S 18^{13} *or if* I had dealt falsely against his life, then, etc., Ez $14^{17.19}$ *or if* I send, etc. **3.** *if perchance*, 1 S 20^{10} *if perchance* thy father answer thee with something hard, Lv 26^{41}. **4.** once, with the juss. (as in Ar. with the subjunct. v. Dr[§175])=*except:* Is 27^{5} I would burn them together, אוֹ יַחֲזֵק בְּמָעֻזִּי *or else* let him take hold (=*except* he take hold) of my stronghold, etc.

†**אוּאֵל** **n.pr.m.** a Judæan (*will of God*, cf. II. אוה; or contr. fr. אֲבוּאֵל cf. אִיעֶזֶר?) Ezr 10^{34}.

אוב (meaning? Thes comp. Ar. آبَ *return*, أَيَّابٌ *water-carrier;* but cf. Lag[BN 90]). MV comp. אבב (with conjectural sense) to get meaning *have a hollow sound*. Deriv. and signif. totally uncertain).

אוֹב **n.m.** [Jb 32,19] skin-bottle, necromancer, etc.—abs. א׳ Lv 20^{27}+8 t.; pl. אֹבוֹת Lv 19^{31}+7 t.—**1.** *skin-bottle*, only pl. אֹבוֹת חֲדָשִׁים *new (wine-) skins* Jb 32^{19}. **2.** *necromancer*, in phr. אוֹב אוֹ יִדְּעֹנִי *necrom. or wizard* Lv 20^{27} (H; usually tr. 'a man also or woman that hath a familiar spirit or that is a wizard' RV; but better *a man or a woman, if there should be among them, a necromancer or wizard;* no suff. reason for exceptional use of phrase here); א׳ וְיִדְּעֹנִי Dt 18^{11} 2 Ch 33^{6}=2 K 21^{6} (where וידענים א׳); הָאֹבוֹת וְהַיִּדְּעֹנִים Lv 19^{31} 20^{6} (H) 1 S $28^{3.9}$ 2 K 23^{24} Is 8^{19} (where repres. as chirping & muttering, in practice of their art of seeking dead for instruction, prob. ventriloquism, & so 𝔊) 19^{3}. **3.** **ghost**, Is 29^{4} וְהָיָה כְּאוֹב מֵאֶרֶץ קוֹלֵךְ וּמֵעָפָר אִמְרָתֵךְ תְּצַפְצֵף *and thy voice shall be as a ghost fr. the ground and fr. the dust thy speech shall chirp* (so Ge MV Ew De Che al., but chirping might be of necromancer, as 8^{19}). **4.** *necromancy* אֵשֶׁת בַּעֲלַת־אוֹב *a woman who was mistress of necromancy* 1 S $28^{7.7}$; (> RS[JPh xiv, 127 f] makes אוֹב primarily a subterranean spirit, and signif. **2** only an abbrev. of בעלת א׳ etc.); קסם בָּאוֹב *divine by necromancy* 1 S 28^{8}, which seems to be interpr. of 1 Ch 10^{13} שאל בא׳ *inquire by necromancy*. (In these three exx. אוֹב is usually interpreted as ghost or familiar spirit conceived as dwelling in necromancer; but this apparently not the ancient conception.)

†**אֹבֹת** **n.pr.loc.** (*water-skins*) station of Isr. in wildern. Nu 21^{10} 34^{43}; not yet determ., prob. on eastern skirts of Idumæa not far from Moab; acc. to Wetzst in De[Gt 168] *Wêba*, وَيْبَة, in the Arabah, but identif. not prob.; cf. Di on Nu 21^{10}.

אוד (*be curved, bent*, also trans. *burden, oppress*, cf. Ar. آدَ).

†**אוּד** **n.m.** brand, fire-brand (orig. perh. bent stick used to stir fire) א׳ מֻצָּל מִשְּׂרֵפָה Am 4^{11}=א׳ מֻ׳ מֵאֵשׁ Zc 3^{2}, pl. זַנְבוֹת הָאוּדִים הָעֲשֵׁנִים Is 7^{4}, *stumps of smoking firebrands*.

†[**אוֹדָה**] **n.f.** cause (perh. orig. *circumstance*, cf. Sab. אוד *enclosing wall*)—only pl. אֹדֹת Gn 21^{11}+; אוֹדֹת Nu 12^{1}+; (8 t.+2 S 13^{16} vid. infra); אוֹדֹתַי Jos 14^{6}; אוֹדֹתֶיךָ ib.;—*cause*, alw. with עַל, & cstr., exc. Je 3^{8}, where sq. אֲשֶׁר; עַל־א׳ *because of* Gn $21^{11.25}$ Ex 18^{8} Nu 12^{1} 13^{24} Ju 6^{7} Je 3^{8};=*concerning* (*on occasion of*) Gn 26^{32} Jos $14^{6.6}$; in 2 S 13^{16} rd., for אל־אודות, אַל אָחִי כִּי 𝔊L It. We Dr.

†**אֵיד** **n.m.** [Jb 18,12] distress, calamity (under wh. one bends, cf. Ar. آدٌ *burdening*)—א׳ Jb 21^{30}+; cstr. *id.* Jb 31^{23}+; אֵידִי 2 S 22^{19}=ψ 18^{19} etc.;—*distress, calamity* (poet. chiefly WisdLt & late); Pr 17^{5} 27^{10}. **1.** national calam. of Isr. (apostate) Je 18^{17} Ez 35^{5} Ob [13.13.13]; of Egypt Je 46^{21}; Moab 48^{16}; Edom (א׳ עֵשָׂו) 49^{8}; Hazor v^{32}. **2.** of righteous sufferer 2 S 22^{19}=ψ 18^{19} cf. א׳ אֵל i.e. *from* God Jb 31^{23} & אָרְחוֹת אֵידָם 30^{12} *their calamitous paths* (sf. ref. to bereavement, pain, etc.) **3.** oft. of wicked Jb 18^{12} 21^{17} 31^{3} Pr $1^{26.27}$ (wisd. mocks at; ‖ פַּחַד) 6^{15} 24^{22}; also יוֹם א׳ Dt 32^{35} Jb 21^{30} (cf. supr. 2 S 22^{19}=ψ 18^{19} Pr 27^{10} Je 18^{17} 46^{21} Ob [13.13.13] where ‖ יוֹם צָרָה יוֹם אֲבָד $v^{12.14}$, cf. יוֹם יהוה v^{15}).

†**אֵד** **n.m.** mist (deriv. dub.; Ar. آدَ=*be strong;* إِيَادٌ that which affords protection, shade; otherwise Dl[W 125]) Gn 2^{6}; אֵדוֹ Jb 36^{27}.

I. **אוה** **1.** Ar. أَوَى *betake oneself* to a place for dwelling, etc.; **2.** id., *be tenderly inclined*.

†I. **אִי** **n.m.** [Is 20,6] (†**f.** [Is 23,2]) coast, region (contr. fr. אֱוִי so Ol[§152b]; place whither one betakes oneself for resting, etc., orig. fr. mariner's standpoint)—אִי abs. Is 20^{6}+; cstr. Je 47^{4}; (Jb 22^{30} v. sub IV. אִי cf. Di) pl. אִיִּים ψ 72^{10}+; אִיִּן Ez 26^{18} (Co איים) אִיֵּי Gn 10^{5}+;—*coast, border, region* (mostly late), of Philistia & Phenicia with adjacent country Is 20^{6} $23^{2.6}$; so of Caph-

tor (=Crete) Je 47^{4}, מַלְכֵי הָאִי אֲשֶׁר בְּעֵבֶר הַיָּם Je 25^{22}; elswh. pl, coasts of Chittim Je 2^{10} Ez 27^{6}, of Elishah v^{7}, different countries (on or in sea) v$^{3.15.35}$ 26$^{15.18.18}$ (last del. Co cf. 𝔊) cf 39^{6}, so also איי הַגּוֹיִם Gn 10^{5} (P); partic איי הַיָּם= *coast-lands & islands* Is 11^{11} 24^{15}, ‖ הָאָרֶץ Est 10^{1}, v. (without הַיָּם) Dn 11^{18}, & ψ 72^{10}, so oft Is^{2} incl. inhabitants, 41$^{1.5}$ 42$^{4.10}$ (איים וישביהם) ‖ (הַיָּם וּמְלֹאוֹ) v^{12} 49^{1} 51^{5} 59^{18} 60^{9} 66^{19} cf Je 31^{10} ψ 97^{1}, Zp 2^{11} (איי הַגּוֹיִם), *islands*, distinctly (taken up by ׳י as little things) Is 40^{15}, *coasts, banks*, i e habitable lands Is 42^{15} (‖ נְהָרוֹת)

†**אִיתָמָר n.pr.m.** ((*is*) *land of palms*? Thes) youngest (4th) son of Aaron Ex 6^{23} 28^{1} 38^{21} Lv 10$^{6.12.16}$ Nu 3$^{2.4}$ 4$^{28.33}$ 7^{8} 26^{60} (all P) 1 Ch 5^{29} 24$^{1.2.3.4.4.5.6}$ Ezr 8^{2}.

†[**אָוָה**] **vb. incline, desire** (cf Stem **2**) **Pi.** *Pf* אִוָּה ψ 132^{13}, אִוְּתָה Mi 7^{1}+, etc, *Impf* 3 fs. תְּאַוֶּה Dt 12^{20}+4 t—*desire* subj usually נֶפֶשׁ, obj fruit Mi 7^{1} (in metaph); flesh (to eat) 1 S 2^{16}, cf Dt 12^{20} (sq inf. לֶאֱכֹל בָּשָׂר), food & drink Dt 14^{26}, of king desiring rule, וּמָלַכְתָּ בכל אֲשֶׁר־תְּאַוֶּה נַפְשֶׁךָ 2 S 3^{21} 1 K 11^{37}, obj *evil* (רָע) Pr 21^{10}, once obj ׳י Is 26^{9} נַפְשִׁי אִוִּיתִךָ בַּלַּיְלָה, of God וְנַפְשׁוֹ אִוְּתָה וַיָּעַשׂ Jb 23^{13}, as desiring Zion for dwelling-place (late, only cases without נפשׁ) ψ 132$^{13.14}$, **Hithp.** *Pf* הִתְאַוָּה Pr 21^{26}, התאויתי Je 17^{16}, הִתְאַוּוּ Nu 11^{4}, והתאויתם Nu 34^{10}, *Impf* יתאוה Ec 6^{2}, וַיִּתְאַוֶּה 2 S 23^{15}, apoc ויתאו ψ 45^{12}, וַיִּתְאָו 1 Ch 11^{17}, etc—*Pt* fs מִתְאַוָּה Pr 13^{4}, mpl מִתְאַוִּים Am 5^{18} Nu 11^{34}—*desire, long for, lust after*, of bodily appetites; for dainty food Nu 11^{4} (E, sq acc cogn)=ψ 106^{14}, Nu 11^{34} (E), sq ל Pr 23$^{3.6}$ cf Ec 6^{2} (sq acc), v also Pr 13^{4} (abs, subj נַפְשׁוֹ), abs of extreme thirst 2 S 23^{15}=1 Ch 11^{17}, of king desiring the beauty (יֳפִי) of princess ψ 45^{12} (sq acc), of covetous man Pr 21^{26} (sq acc. cogn), obj בית רעך Dt 5^{18} (‖ חמד), sq inf Pr 24^{1} (of desiring evil companionship); obj יוֹם ׳י Am 5^{18} (acc, of presumptuous, reckless longing) cf Je 17^{16} (Nu 34$^{7.8}$ for תְּתָאוּ—Pi of תאה—Di prop תִּתְאַוּ, & queries whether this & הִתְאַוִּיתֶם v^{10} are not fr אוה,=*desire for yourselves*.)

[**אַו**] **n.m.** cstr אַו, Kt Pr 31^{4} **desire**, so Thes MV, but < Qr אֵי q v

†[**אַוָּה**] **n.f. desire**—cstr אַוַּת Dt 12^{15}+5 t., sf אַוָּתִי Ho 10^{10}—*desire, will*, usually sq נַפְשׁ, of natural human desire (morally indiff.), for meat Dt 12$^{15.20.21}$, of longing for sanctuary 18^{6}, of royal good pleasure 1 S 23^{20}, without נַפְשׁ, of wild-ass Je 2^{24}, of divine will Ho 10^{10}

†**אֱוִי n.pr.m.** (*desire*?) one of five chiefs of Midian Nu 31^{8} Jos 13^{21}.

†[**מַאֲוַי**] **n.[m.] desire pl. cstr** מַאֲוַיֵּי רָשָׁע ψ 140^{9}.

†**תַּאֲוָה n f. desire**—abs. Gn 3^{6}+, cstr תַּאֲוַת ψ 10^{3}+etc,—*desire, wish* Pr 13$^{12.19}$ 18^{1}, of physical appetite, longing for dainty food מַאֲכַל ת׳ Jb 33^{20}, distinctly good sense ψ 10^{17} 38^{10} Pr 11^{23} 19^{22} (? cf infr) Is 26^{8} (לְשִׁמְךָ וּלְזִכְרְךָ ת׳־נָפֶשׁ); bad sense, *lust, appetite, covetousness* ψ 10^{3} (ת׳ נַפְשׁוֹ) 112^{10}, Pr 21$^{25.26}$ (as acc cogn.), particularly of longing for dainties of Egypt Nu 11^{4} ψ 106^{14} (both acc cogn) 78^{30} & in **n.pr.** given to place where it occurred קברות הַתַּאֲוָה (q v.) Nu 11$^{34.35}$ 33$^{16.17}$ Dt 9^{22}. **2.** *thing desired*, in good sense Pr 10^{24}, bad sense ψ 78^{29} so ת׳ לִבּוֹ ψ 21^{3}, *thing desirable* (to senses) Gn 3^{6} (ת׳ לְעֵינַיִם), perhaps also Pr 19^{22} *the ornament of a man is his kindness* (Ra Ki, etc but cf. supr.)

†II [**אָוָה**] **vb. sign, mark, describe with a mark** (so Ges (who compares תאה, תוה) Di$^{Pr\ 110\ (not\ W)}$) only **Hithp.** *Pf* הִתְאַוִּיתֶם לָכֶם *mark you out, measure*, Nu 34^{10} (P), so Vrss (cf תְּתָאוּ לָכֶם v$^{7.8}$, v however Di, & sub I אוה)

אוֹת n.m. $_{79}$ $^{Ex\ 4.8}$ (**f.** $^{Jos\ 24\ 17}$) **sign** (Ar آيَة, pl آيٌ, Aram אָתָא, אָת)—א׳ Gn 4^{15}+, cstr 9^{12}+; pl אוֹתוֹת Ex 4^{9}+etc—**1** *sign, pledge, token* Gn 4^{15} (J); אוֹת אֱמֶת *true token* Jos 2^{12} (J), of blood of passover Ex 12^{13} (P), אוֹת לְטוֹבָה *token for good* ψ 86^{17}; *pledges, assurances* of travellers Jb 21^{29}. **2.** *signs, omens* promised by prophets as pledges of certain predicted events 1 S 10$^{7.9}$ +v^{1} where א׳ ins 𝔊 𝔙, vid. We Dr, esp. phr זֶה הָאוֹת ל Ex 3^{12} 1 S 2^{34} 14^{10} 2 K 19^{29} Je 44^{29} Is 7$^{11.14}$, prob also Is 44^{25} (of false proph.). **3.** *sign, symbol* of prophets Is 8^{18} cf. Ez 4^{3}. **4.** *signs, miracles*, as pledges or attestations of divine presence & interposition Ex 4$^{8.8.9}$ (J) 7^{3} (P) 8^{19} (J) ψ 74^{9} 2 K 19^{29} 20$^{8.9}$=Is 37^{30} 38$^{7.22}$; c עָשָׂה Ex 4$^{17.30}$ Nu 14$^{11.22}$ Jos 24^{17} (all JE) Dt 11^{3} Ju 6^{17}, c צִוָּה Ex 4^{28} (J); c שִׁית 10^{1} (J); c שִׂים Ex 10^{2} (J) ψ 78^{43} Is 66^{19}, הָאוֹת וְהַמּוֹפֵת (v. מוֹפֵת) Dt 13^{3} cf 28^{46} Is 20^{3}; א׳ אוֹ מ׳ Dt 13^{2}, נָתַן אוֹתוֹת וּמוֹפְתִים Dt 4^{34} 7^{19} 26^{8} 29^{2} Je 32^{21}, c נָתַן Dt 6^{22} Ne 9^{10}, c שִׂים Je 32^{20} ψ 105^{27}; c שָׁלַח Dt 34^{11} ψ 135^{9} **5.** *signs, memorials*, stones fr Jordan Jos 4^{6} (J), metal of censers Nu 17^{3} (P); Aaron's rod Nu 17^{25} (P); א׳ עוֹלָם Is 55^{13} prob also Ez 14^{8} (‖ מָשָׁל); signs on hands, etc,

Ex $13^{9.16}$ (J)=Dt 6^{8} 11^{18}, prob. belong here; also memorial pillar in Egypt Is 19^{20}. **6.** *sign, pledge* of covenant, א׳ הַבְּרִית (v. ברית) *e.g.* rainbow, of Noachian covenant Gn $9^{12.13.17}$ (P); circumcision, of Abrahamic covenant Gn 17^{11} (P); the sabbath Ex $31^{13.17}$ (P); Ez $20^{12.20}$. **7.** *ensigns, standards* Nu 2^{2} (P) ψ 74^{4}. **8.** *signs, tokens* of changes of weather & times Gn 1^{14} (P; of heavenly luminaries) אותות הַשָּׁמַיִם Je 10^{2} (changes of the heavens as omens to frighten the nations) cf. ψ 65^{9}.

†אוּזַי **n.pr.m.** a Judæan, Ne 3^{25}.

†אוֹי **interj.** (onomatop.; cf. وَىْ, أَوْهِ) woe! an impassioned expression of grief and despair: usually with dative אוֹי לִי Is 6^{5} *woe to me! for I am undone*, so 24^{16} Je 10^{19} 15^{10}; אוֹי־נָא לִי *woe* to us! 1 S $4^{7.8}$ Je 4^{13} 6^{4}; אוֹי לָנוּ Je 4^{31} 45^{3}; אוֹי־נָא לָנוּ La 5^{16}. With the 2nd or 3rd ps. often implying a denunciation; אוֹי־לְךָ מוֹאָב Nu 21^{29} (=Je 48^{46}) Je 13^{27} Ez 16^{23} repeated אוֹי אוֹי לָךְ; Is 3^{9} אוֹי לְנַפְשָׁם v^{11} Ho 7^{13} 9^{12} (‖ שֹׁד לָהֶם). With a voc. (or implicit accus.) Ez $24^{6.9}$ אוֹי עִיר הַדָּמִים; absol. Nu 24^{23}. Used as a subst. Pr 23^{29} לְמִי אוֹי ‖ לְמִי אֲבוֹי.

†אוֹיָה = אוֹי ψ 120^{5} אוֹיָה לִי.

III. אוה (*to cry* אוֹי, *howl* cf. Ar. آوَى, *to cry* آيَ to be assumed prob. as source of two foll. words).

†II. [אִי] **n.m.** jackal (*howler*, for *אִוְי v. Ba$^{NB\,188}$, cf. Ar. اِبْنُ آوَى, whence خَنْفَرِى)—pl. אִיִּים, Is 13^{22} 34^{14} Je 50^{39} (inhabitant of desert, ruin).

†I. אַיָּה **n.f.** hawk, falcon, kite (perh. fr. cry; cf. Ar. يُؤْيُؤ, a kind of hawk) Lv 11^{14} Dt 14^{13} generic, cf. לְמִינָהּ & Di; Jb 28^{7} (keen-sighted).

†II. אַיָּה **n.pr.m.** (*falcon*) **1.** a Horite Gn 36^{24} 1 Ch 1^{40}. **2.** father of Rizpah 2 S 3^{7} $21^{8.10.11}$.

†אֱוִיל מְרֹדַךְ **n.pr.m.** (Bab. *Avêl* (Amêl) *Marduk, man of Merodach*) son & successor of Nebuchadnezzar, king of Babylon, B.C. 562–60, 2 K 25^{27} (v. COT)=Je 52^{31}.

I. אול (*be foolish*, cf. יאל, & Ar. آلَ *grow thick* (of fluids)).

אֱוִיל $_{26}$ **adj.** foolish—א׳ Jb 5^{2}+; *pl.* אֱוִילִים ψ 107^{17}+, etc.;—*foolish*, Pr 29^{9} (א׳ אִישׁ) Ho 9^{7} (pred. of prophet); cf. Is 35^{8}, elsewhere **n.m. fool (always morally bad), who despises wisdom** & discipline Pr 1^{7} 15^{5}; mocks at guilt 14^{9}; is quarrelsome 20^{3}; licentious 7^{22}; it is folly & useless to instruct him 16^{22} 27^{22} (19 t. Pr); cf. also Je 4^{22} Jb $5^{2.3}$ Is 19^{11} ψ 107^{17}.

†אֱוִלִי **adj.** id. Zc 11^{15}.

אִוֶּלֶת $_{25}$ **n.f.** folly.—abs. Pr 12^{23}+; cstr. 14^{8}+; sf. אִוַּלְתִּי ψ 38^{6}, etc.;—*folly*, special product of כְּסִילִים (v. כָּסַל) Pr 12^{23}+ (12 t.); c. פְּתָאִים Pr 14^{18}; c. אֱוִילִים only 16^{22} 27^{22} for alliteration. It is bound up in mind of boy, to be removed only by rod of discipline Pr 22^{15}; א׳ personif. tears down house built by חַכְמוֹת נָשִׁים Pr 14^{1}; it is contrasted with תְּבוּנָה Pr 14^{29} 15^{21}.

II. איל, אול (*be in front of, precede, lead*; v. Thes Nö$^{MBA\,1880,\,774;\ SBA\,1882,\,1175}$, who comp. Ar. أَوَّلُ for آلَ, Targ. אוולא; cf. Sab. אול DHM $^{Epigr.\,Denkm.\,33.\,34}$; v. on the other hand Lag$^{Or\,ii.\,p.\,3;\ M\,i.\,p.\,100}$ & sub I. אלה infr.)

†I. [אוּל] **n.[m.]** body, belly; sf. אוּלָם (in contempt) ψ 73^{4} (lit. *their front, prominent part*).

†II. [אוּל] **n.[m.]** leading man, noble; pl. cstr. אוּלֵי הָאָרֶץ 2 K 24^{15} Kt (Qr אֵילֵי v. III. [אַיִל]).

†I. אוּלָם **n.m.** $^{1\,K\,7,8}$ porch (cf. אֵילָם)—א׳ abs. 1 K 6^{3}+; אֻלָם Ez $40^{48.49}$; cstr. אוּלָם 1 K 7^{6}+; אֵלָם Ez 40^{7}+ (marg. אֻלָם 1 K $7^{7.12.21}$); pl. cstr. אֻלַמֵּי Ez 41^{15} (Co sg. c. sf.; in Ez Co rds. everywhere אילם vid. אֵילָם infr.)—*porch* (only K Ch Ez & Jo). **1.** in Solomon's temple 1 K 7^{19} 2 Ch 29^{7}, א׳ v^{17}; 8^{12} (altar in front of); א׳ יהוה 15^{8} (id.), cf. בֵּין הָאוּלָם וּבֵין הַמִּזְבֵּחַ Ez 8^{16} & Jo 2^{17}; א׳ הַהֵיכָל 1 K 7^{21}; א׳ הַבַּיִת v^{12}; תַּבְנִית הָא׳ 1 Ch 28^{11}. **2.** in Sol.'s palace 1 K $7^{6.8}$; א׳ הָעַמּוּדִים 1 K 7^{6} cf. v^{6}; א׳ הַמִּשְׁפָּט = א׳ הַכִּסֵּא 7^{7} v^{7}. **3.** in temple of Ezek.'s vision, partic. א׳ הַשַּׁעַר Ez $40^{7.8}$ (del. Co vid. 𝔊 𝔖 𝔙) $^{9.9.15.39.40}$ 44^{3} $46^{2.8}$; א׳ הַבַּיִת 40^{48} cf. v$^{48.49}$ $41^{25.26}$; אֻלַמֵּי הֶחָצֵר Ez 41^{25} Co sg. v. אֵילָם ואילמו החיצון.—(III. אוּלָם, adv., v. p. 19.)

II. אוּלָם **n.pr.m.** only geneal. **1.** 1 Ch $7^{16.17}$. **2.** 1 Ch $8^{39.40}$.

I. אַיִל $_{156}$ **n.m.** $^{Gn\,22,13}$ ram (as leader of flock, NHeb. & Aram. *id.*, As. *ailu* Dl^{W}, Ph. איל,=אַיִל rather than אַיִל, cf. CIS$^{i.\,p.\,231}$)—אַיִל (אָיִל) Gn 15^{9} +; cstr. אֵיל Ex 29^{22}+; pl. אֵילִים (אֵלִם, אֵילִם) Gn 32^{15}+; cstr. אֵילֵי Gn 31^{38} Is 60^{7}.—*ram*, **1.** used as food Gn 31^{38} (E) Dt 32^{14} (cf. ram of sacrifice, infr. e.g. Ex 29^{32} cf. Lv 8^{31}); as yielding wool 2 K 3^{4}; as tribute 2 Ch 17^{11}; as merchandise Ez 27^{21}; as gift Gn 32^{15} (E); in sim. of leaping, skipping ψ 114^{4} (הֶהָרִים רָקְדוּ כְא׳) v^{6}; in Dn.'s vision, ram with two horns symbol. kings of Media and Persia Dn $8^{3.4.6.7.7.7.7.20}$; fig. of rich and powerful in Isr. Ez 34^{17}. **2.** slain

in ceremony of ratification of covenant betw. ׳י & Abr. Gn 15^{9} (J), in Abr's sacrif Gn 22$^{13.13}$ (E), Balaam's sacrif Nu 23^{1} + 5 t. Nu 23 (JE), so in ritual (P), (*a*) in consecration ceremony of Aaron & his sons Ex 29^{1} + 15 t. Ex 29 (א׳ מִלֻּאִים v^{22} cf v$^{26.27.31}$) Lv 8^{2} + 8 t. Lv 8 (א׳ הַמִּלֻּאִים v$^{22.29}$ א׳ הָעֹלָה v^{18}); (*b*) in guilt-offering (אָשָׁם) Lv 5$^{15.16.18.25}$ 19$^{21.22}$ cf Ezr 10^{19} & א׳ הַכִּפֻּרִים Nu 5^{8}, (*c*) burnt-offering (עלה) Lv 9^{2} & Nu 15$^{6.11}$ & Ez 46$^{4.5.6.7.11}$, on day of atonement Lv 16$^{3.5}$, Pentecost 23^{18}; (*d*) peace-offering (שְׁלָמִים) Lv 9$^{4.18.19}$, beginning of month Nu 28$^{11.12.14}$ cf 29$^{2.3}$, passover v$^{19.20}$ cf Ez 45$^{23.24}$, day of firstfruits v$^{27.28}$, in 7th month 29^{8} + 18 t. Nu 29, (*e*) in law of Nazarite Nu 6$^{14.17.19}$, (*f*) in consecration of altar of tabernacle Nu 7^{15} + 25 t Nu^{7}, cf consecr of Ezek's temple-altar Ez 43$^{23.25}$, (*g*) more generally 1 S 15^{22} Is 1^{11} Mi 6^{7} Jb 42^{8} ψ 66^{15}, also Is 34^{6} 60^{7}, at bringing ark to Jerus 1 Ch 15^{26}, other occasions 29^{21} 2 Ch 13^{9} 29$^{21.22.32}$ Ezr 8^{35}, cf fig Je 51^{40} Ez 39^{18}. **3** עֹרֹת אֵילִם מְאָדָּמִים *rams' skins dyed red*, of covering of tabernacle Ex 25^{5} 26^{14} 35$^{7.23}$ 36^{19} cf 39^{34} (all P).

II **אַיִל n.[m.] projecting pillar** or **pilaster**—א׳ abs 1 K 6^{31} (but v infr) cstr *id.* Ez 40^{14} (but del Co) ^{16} (Co better אֵילָיו), איל 41^{3}, אל 40^{48}, pl אילים 40^{14}+, אלים 40^{10}, sf אילו Kt 40^{9} + 7 t.; אלו Kt 40^{29} + 2 t Qr (in all) אֵלָיו, אילָיו, אֵלֵיהֶמָּה 40^{16},—*pilaster* or projection in wall at each side of entrance (cf Bo$^{Proben\ 302,\ NA\ 927}$), in Sol's temple 1 K 6^{31} (Bo$^{NA\ 925}$ rds אֵלָם), in Ezek's temple Ez 40$^{9.10}$ + 14 t Ez 40 41 + 40^{14a} Ew Hi Co אֵלָם cf. 𝔊B, 40^{38} rd אֵלָם so Sm Co cf 𝔊, 40^{14b} Co del א׳

†III [אַיִל?] **n.m. leader, chief** (=ram, as leader of flock? cf Di Ex 15^{15} Ol$^{\S 142f}$ Lag$^{BN\ 170}$ & v. Ez 34^{17})—cstr איל Ez 31^{11}, pl cstr. אילי Ex 15^{15} Ez 17^{13} + 2 K 24^{15} Qr (Kt אולי v אול); אֵלִי Ez 32^{21} (del Co, v 𝔊)—*leader, chief* א׳ מוֹאָב Ex 15^{15}, א׳ הָאָרֶץ Ez 17^{13} 2 K 24^{15} Qr, א׳ גּוֹיִם Ez 31^{11} (אֵלִים Jb 41^{17} v sub אלה; perh אֵלֵיהֶם Ez 31^{14} but cf infr IV איל & also אל Note 1)

†IV [אַיִל?] **n.m. terebinth** (prob. as prominent, lofty tree, v Di Gn 12^{6} 14^{6})—cstr. איל only n pr. איל פָּארָן vid infr; pl אילים Is 1^{29}; אלים Is 57^{5} cstr אֵילֵי Is 61^{3}, sf. אֵלֵיהֶם Ez 31^{14} (> del Co vid 𝔅𝔄)—*terebinth* (cf. אֵלָה), as marking idol-shrines Is 1^{29} 57^{5} (so Che Di etc > *gods*), fig of ransomed ones of Zion אֵילֵי הַצֶּדֶק, perh. of haughty ones Ez 31^{14}.

†**אֵיל פָּארָן n.pr.loc.** (*terebinth* (or *palm*? v. Di) *of Paran*) town & harbour at head of Ælanitic Gulf Gn 14^{6} (v Di);=אֵילָה 36^{41}; אֵילַת Dt 2^{8} 2 K 14^{22} 16^{6}, אֵילוֹת 1 K 9^{26} 2 K 16^{6}; close to Ezion Geber (v עֶצְיוֹן גֶּבֶר)

†[אֵילִים], alw. **אֵלִם n.pr.loc.** (=place of *terebinths* or other great trees, v. Di Gn 14^{6} & Ex 15^{27} (12 fountains & 70 palms)) 2nd station of Isr in desert after passing sea Ex 16^{1} Nu 33$^{9.10}$, אֵילִמָה Ex 15^{27} Nu 33^{9}, prob = Wady Gharandel cf Rob$^{BR\ I\ 100,\ 105}$

†I **אֵלָה n.f. terebinth** (=אֵילָה (?) v. IV איל > Sta$^{Gesch\ 456}$ wh derives fr אל=*divine*; but cf *ib* on lack of clear distinction betw. אלה, אלון & (אַלּוֹן)—Gn 35^{4} + 15 t. + אילה Gn 49^{21} (for MT אַיָּלָה v infr)—*terebinth*=*Pistacia terebinthus*, Linn, a deciduous tree with pinnate leaves & red berries, occasional in Palestine; grows to great age, always of single tree, near Shechem Gn 35^{4} (E) cf †אַלָּה Jos 24^{26} (E, rd אֵלָה ?), Ophrah Ju 6$^{11.19}$, in Jabesh 1 Ch 10^{12}; tree in which Absalom was caught 2 S 18$^{9.9.10.14}$; v also 1 K 13^{14}, expressly of idol-shrine Ho 4^{13} (‖ אַלּוֹן, לבנה) Ez 6^{13}, as fading, withering, sim of Judah Is 1^{30}, as hewn down, sim. *id* 6^{13} (‖ אַלּוֹן); fig of Naphtali אֵילָה שְׁלֻחָה Gn 49^{21} (𝔊 Ew Ol Di > MT אַיָּלָה *hind* q v.) ***a slender terebinth***, v. Di & cf II. אֵלָה, in topogr designat. עֵמֶק הָא׳ 1 S 17$^{2.19}$ 21^{10} (v. עמק)

†II **אֵלָה n.pr.m.** (*terebinth*, cf Gn 49^{21} sub I אלה) **1.** a chief of Edom Gn 36^{41} = 1 Ch 1^{52} (= אילת **n.pr.loc.**? v Di) **2.** son of Baasha; reigned two years in Isr. 1 K 16$^{6.8.13.14}$. **3.** father of Hoshea who was last king of Isr. 2 K 15^{30} 17^{1} 18$^{1.9}$. **4.** a son of Caleb 1 Ch 4$^{15.15}$. **5.** a son of Uzzi 1 Ch 9^{8}

†I **אֵלוֹן n.[f.] terebinth** (=אֵלָה)—א׳ cstr. Gn 12^{6} + 4 t; pl cstr אֵלוֹנֵי Gn 13^{18} + 3 t.—*terebinth* (or other tall tree, cf infr. on 1 S 10^{3} Ju 4^{6}), marking shrine, & hence used in topogr. designations; א׳ מוֹרֶה (*teacher's terebinth*) Gn 12^{6} (v Di) so Dt 11^{30}; א׳ מְעוֹנְנִים (*conjurors' tereb.*) Ju 9^{37}, distinguished by owner or ruler א׳ מַמְרֵא Gn 13^{18} 14^{13} 18^{1}, by neighbouring town (בצענים) Ju 4^{11}, cf א׳ בְּצַעֲנַנִּים Jos 19^{33} (edd. אַלּוֹן, but v Norzi Baer Di), א׳ מֻצָּב אֲשֶׁר בִּשְׁכֶם Ju 9^{6} (cf אלה Gn 35^{4}), א׳ תָּבוֹר 1 S 10^{3} rd. א׳ דְּבוֹרָה (& cf אַלּוֹן בָּכוּת Gn 35^{8}, & תֹּמֶר דְּבוֹרָה Ju 4^{4}) cf Ew$^{Gesch.\ III\ 31}$ Th Di Gn 35^{8} (v. also sub אַלּוֹן).

†II. אֵלוֹן n.pr.m. (=*id* cf. אֵלָה n.pr.) **1.** a son of Zebulun Gn 46^{14} Nu 26^{26} **2.** אילן Gn 26^{34}; אֵילֹן 36^{2} a Hittite, father-in-law of Esau. **3.** אילן Ju $12^{11\ 12}$ a judge of Isr., of tribe of Zeb. **4. n.pr.loc.** אילון Jos 19^{43} a town of Dan; so 1 K 4^{9} (where rd. א׳ ובית ח׳ Th Klo).

†אֵלֹנִי **adj.gent.** of אלון **1.** (as n coll) Nu 26^{26}.

†אֵילַת **n.pr.loc.** (*lofty tree*(*s* coll ?) i e. palms? cf. Di Gn 14^{6}) town & harbour, N E arm of Red Sea, hence called Ælanitic Gulf (=Gulf of Akaba, fr. neighbouring fortress) Dt 2^{8} 2 K 14^{22} $16^{6.6}$ (perh later designat. for fuller איל פארן q.v.) = 𝔊 Αἰλων, Αἰλαθ, Gr Αἰλανα, etc; = אֵלָה (? Gn 36^{41} v Di), אילות infr

†אֵילוֹת **n.pr.loc. id** (*grove of lofty trees* (palms?)) 1 K 9^{26} 2 K 16^{6} 2 Ch 8^{17} 26^{2} (cf. אילת, איל פָּארָן)

[אֵילָם] **n.m.** porch (=אוּלָם, q v, only Ez, where Co always for אולם, cf. 𝔊 αἰλαμ, Bo[NA 929] makes אילם *vestibule*, אולם *porch*)—אֵילָם rd for אילים Ez 40^{37} (so Sm Co); sf. אילמו Kt Ez $40^{22.22}$ + 4t. (Qr אֵילַמָּיו) + 41^{15} Co (for MT אַלְמֵי), אלמו Kt Ez 40^{21} + 6 t (Qr אֵלַמָּיו).—Co all sg:—pl. אלמות Ez 40^{16} (Co sg) v^{30} (del Co cf MSS of 𝔖, B etc., also Ew Hi Sm)—*porch*, of Ezek.'s temple Ez $40^{16.21}$ + 13 t

†אַיָּל **n.[m.]** (**f.** ψ 42^{2}) hart, stag, deer (Aram. *id.*, ܐܝܠܐ, Ar إِيَّلٌ, As *ailu* Dl[W], but dub, v. Hpt[BAS I 170], Eth ሀየል: = *leader*? cf. אַיִל)—א׳ abs Dt 12^{15} + 6 t; pl אַיָּלִים Ct 2^{9} + 3 t,—*hart, stag*, allowed as food Dt $12^{15.22}$ 15^{22} (all ‖ צבי), 14^{5} (‖ צְבִי, יַחְמוּר etc), eaten in Sol's household 1 K 5^{3} (‖ as Dt 14^{5}); sim of leaping Is 35^{6}, id עֹפֶר הָא׳ Ct $2^{9.17}$ 8^{14} (all ‖ צבי), as in search of pasture, sim of princes of Judah La 1^{6}, as longing for water, sim of longing for י׳ ψ 42^{2}.

†אַיָּלָה **n.f.** hind, doe—א׳ abs Gn 49^{21} (but rd אֵילָה v. infr.); אַיֶּלֶת Je 14^{5}, cstr אַיֶּלֶת ψ 22^{1} Pr 5^{19}; pl. אַיָּלוֹת ψ 29^{9} + 4 t.; cstr. אַיְלוֹת Ct 2^{7} 3^{5}—*hind, doe*, as calving Jb 39^{1} (‖ חלל א׳ לֶדֶת יַעֲלֵי) cf ψ 29^{9} (קול י׳ יחולל א׳ (סֶלַע; in adjuration Ct 2^{7} 3^{5}; in sim. בצבאות או באי׳ השדה מְשַׁוֶּה רַגְלַי ψ 18^{34} = 2 S 22^{34} cf וַיָּשֶׂם ר׳ כָּא׳ Hb 3^{19} i e surefooted, secure, cf. ‖ ψ 18^{34} ועל בָּמֹתַי יַעֲמִידֵנִי 2 S 22^{34}, so Hb 3^{19} but vb יַדְרִכֵנִי; metaph. of Naphtali Gn 49^{21} א׳ שְׁלֻחָה, but rd. אֵילָה, cf sub

I אֵלָה; in name of a melody ψ 22^{1} עַל־אַיֶּלֶת הַשַּׁחַר cf. De, & for hind as fig. of dawn *Yom* [29 a].

†אַיָּלוֹן **n.pr.loc.** (*Deer*-field) **Aijalon**—א׳ Jos 10^{12} + 8 t, אַיָּלֹנָה 1 S 14^{31}—**1.** city in Dan Jos 19^{42} 21^{24} (Levit. city) Ju 1^{35}; 1 S 14^{31} doubtless same; so 1 Ch 6^{54} (where Dan om); app. later in Benj 1 Ch 8^{13} 2 Ch 11^{10} 28^{18} (v Be); עֵמֶק אַיָּלוֹן Jos 10^{12} almost certainly named from same; = Epiph.'Ιαλω, mod *Jâlo* Rob[BR II 253], Survey[III 19]. **2.** city in Zebulun Ju 12^{12}

†I [אוּלַי] **n pr.fl. Ulai, Eulaeus** (As. *Ulâi*, cf Dl[Pa 329] Gr Εὐλαιος) only אוּלָי, river of Elam Dn $8^{2.16}$, = (at least in lower part) mod. *Karûn* (old *Pasitigris*) v. Dl[Pa 177 189.329], in upper part perh also = mod. *Kerkhah* (= Choaspes), which was formerly connected with Karûn not far from Susa (Loftus [Trav & Researches, 423 ff] Schaff-Herz. [III 2178, art *Shushan*])

II. אוּלַי and (Gn 24^{39}) אֻלַי **adv.** (perh. from לא & או, לֵי = לוּ, as in לולא, = *or not?*) **1.** peradventure, perhaps, usually expressing a hope, as Gn 16^{2} Nu $22^{6.11}$ 23^{3} 1 S 6^{5} Je 20^{10}; but also a fear or doubt, as Gn 27^{12} Jb 1^{5}, sq לא Gn $24^{5.39}$; in mockery Is 47^{12} Je 51^{8} **2.** followed by another clause ἀσυνδέτως, it expresses virtually the protasis = *if peradventure* Gn $18^{24.28}$ (cf. $v^{29\text{-}32}$) Ho 8^{7} the blade shall yield no meal; אולי יַעֲשֶׂה זָרִים יִבְלָעֻהוּ *if perchance* it yield, strangers shall swallow it up **3.** in Nu 22^{33} לוּלֵי (q.v.) must be read; *unless* she had turned aside from me, surely, etc

I & II אוּלָם **n.m. & n.pr.m.** v. sub II. אול

†III. אוּלָם and (Jb 17^{10}, perhaps for sake of assonance with following (כֻּלָּם אֻלָּם **adv.** but, **but indeed, a strong adversative** Jb 2^{5} 5^{8} 13^{3} (where 𝔊 excellently οὐ μὴν δὲ ἀλλά). More usually with ו, ואולם Gn 28^{19} (cf. Ju 18^{29}) 48^{19} *howbeit* his younger brother shall be greater than he, Ex 9^{16} *but in very deed*, Nu 14^{21} (cf. 1 S 20^{3} 25^{34}) 1 K 20^{23} Mic 3^{8} Jb 1^{11} 11^{5} 12^{7} 13^{4} 14^{18} 17^{10} 33^{1}

I און (cf. Ar. آن (med. ى) *be fatigued, tired*. أَيْن *weariness, sorrow, trouble*).

אָוֶן **n.m.** [Jb 5 6] trouble, sorrow, wickedness—abs Nu 23^{21} +, sf אוני Gn 35^{18} etc.; *pl* אונים Ho 9^{4}—**1.** *trouble, sorrow* בן־אוני *son of my trouble* or *sorrow* Gn 35^{18} (E); לא הביט אָוֶן בְּיַעֲקֹב Nu 23^{21} (song of Balaam), *he doth not behold trouble in Jacob* (‖ he doth not see misery—

עָמָל—in Isr.); oft. ‖ עָמָל, ψ 7^{15} (הִנֵּה יְחַבֶּל־אָוֶן *lo he travaileth with trouble* ‖ וְהָרָה עָמָל וְיָלַד שָׁקֶר, *yea he hath conceived misery & brought forth a lie*), prob. thence Jb 15^{35} (הָרֹה עָמָל וְיָלֹד אָוֶן)= Is 59^{4}; cf. עָמָל וָאָוֶן ψ 10^{7} 55^{11} 90^{10} Jb 4^{8} 5^{6} Is 10^{1} (v. עָמָל); also זוֹרֵעַ עַוְלָה יִקְצָר־אָוֶן Pr 22^{8} *the sower of iniquity shall reap trouble;* in this sense elsewh. only Dt 26^{14} Pr 12^{21} Je 4^{15} Hb 3^{7} Am 5^{5}, pl. intens. לֶחֶם אוֹנִים *bread of trouble, sorrow, or mourning* Ho 9^{4}. **2.** *idolatry* Ho 12^{12} Is 41^{29}; אָוֶן וּתְרָפִים הַפְצַר *stubbornness is idolatry & (the use of) teraphim* 1 S 15^{23} (poet. source); בֵּית אָוֶן Ho 4^{15} (for בֵּית אֵל because Bethel, house of God, is given over to idolatry) so also 5^{8} 10^{5} cf. בָּמוֹת א׳ Ho 10^{8}; בִּקְעַת א׳ Am 1^{5} (Baalbek); בַּחוּרֵי א׳ rd. אוֹן, אֹן=On, Heliopolis Ez 30^{17};—abstr. for concr.=*idols* Is 66^{3}. **3.** *trouble of iniquity, wickedness*, מְתֵי אָוֶן Jb 22^{15}; אַנְשֵׁי א׳ 34^{36}=*men of trouble, troublers, wicked men;* cf. אִישׁ א׳ Pr 6^{12} Is 55^{7}; פֹּעֲלֵי אָוֶן *workers of trouble, evil-doers, workers of iniquity* Jb 31^{3} 34$^{8.22}$ ψ 5^{6} +(16 t. chiefly late ψ) Pr 10^{29} 21^{15} Is 31^{2} Ho 6^{8}; מַחְשְׁבוֹת אָוֶן *thoughts of trouble, wicked imaginations* Pr 6^{18} Is 59^{7} Je 4^{14}; oft. of words & thoughts Jb 11^{11}+(5 t.) ψ 36^{5}+(9 t.) Pr 17^{4} 19^{28} 30^{20} Is 29^{20} 32^{6} 58^{9} 59^{6} Ez 11^{2} Mi 2^{1} Hb 1^{3} Zc 10^{2}; לֹא אוּכַל אָוֶן וַעֲצָרָה Is 1^{13} *I cannot bear iniquity with the solemn meeting* (RV & most mod.; AV *it is iniquity, even the solemn meeting*).

†תְּאֻנִים **n.[m.]** **toil** Ez 24^{12} ת׳ הֶלְאָת *she hath wearied* (me or herself) *with toil* (but Co del. as dittogr. cf. 𝔊).

II. **און** (cf. Ar. آنَ (med. و) *be at rest, at ease, enjoy life of plenty;* آيِنٌ *one enjoying a life of ease, freedom from toil & trouble*).

†I. **אוֹן** **n.m. vigour, wealth**—abs. Ho 12^{9}, sf. אוֹנִי Gn 49^{3} + etc.; pl. אוֹנִים ψ 78^{51} +. **1.** *manly vigour* בְּאוֹנוֹ שָׂרָה אֶת־אֱלֹהִים Ho 12^{4} (of Jacob); רֵאשִׁית אוֹן *beginning of manly vigour* Gn 49^{3} (of Reuben, first-born of Jacob); Dt 21^{17} ψ 105^{36} (first-born of Egyptians), so 78^{51}, רֵאשִׁית אוֹנִים where א׳ is assim. to מִצְרָיִם, or intens. pl. **2.** *strength* of man Jb 18$^{7.12}$; behemoth Jb 40^{16}; pl. intens. מֵרֹב אוֹנִים Is 40^{26} *because of the abundance of great strength* (of God); of man אֵין אוֹנִים Is 40^{29} *one not having strength;* תּוֹחֶלֶת אוֹנִים Pr 11^{7} *hope in strength* (not *the hope of iniquity* RV, or *of unjust men* AV). **3.** *wealth* Jb 20^{10} Ho 12^{9} מָצָאתִי א׳ לִי (‖ עָשַׁרְתִּי).

†II. **אוֹן** **n.pr.m.** (*vigour*) a chief of tribe of Reuben Nu 16^{1}.

אוֹנוֹ **n.pr.loc.** (*vigorous*, for אונן) city in Benjamin Ezr 2^{33} Ne 7^{37} 11^{35} 1 Ch 8^{12}; valley of same name Ne 6^{2}; prob. *Kefr 'Anâ*, NW. of Lydda, Survey$^{II, 251}$.

†**אוֹנָם** **n.pr.m.** (*vigorous*). **1.** chief of Horites Gn 36^{23} 1 Ch 1^{40}. **2.** chief of tribe of Judah 1 Ch 2$^{26.28}$.

†**אוֹנָן** **n.pr.m.** (*vigorous*) son of Judah Gn 38$^{4.8.9}$ 46$^{12.12}$ Nu 26$^{19.19}$ 1 Ch 2^{3}.

אוֹן **n.pr.loc.** v. אֹן.

אוניות 2 Ch 8^{18} Kt v. אֳנִי sub **אנה**.

†**אוּפָז** (**n.pr.loc.** unknown & dub.) whence came gold, זָהָב מֵא׳ Je 10^{9}; כֶּתֶם א׳ Dn 10^{5}; so Thes 1 K 10^{18} זָהָב מוּפָז (מֵא׳=מוּפָז); but 𝔊 *δόκιμος*, & 2 Ch 9^{17} טָהוֹר, whence MV Klo make מוּפָז Hoph. Pt. fr. פזז q.v. Klo rds. אוֹפִיר (q.v.) for אוּפָז Je 10^{9} Dn 10^{5}, in view of כֶּתֶם אוֹפִיר Is 13^{12}.

אוֹפִיר **n.pr. Ophir**—א׳ 1 K 10^{11} +; אוֹפִירָה 9^{28} +; אוֹפִר †Gn 10^{29}; אֹפִיר †1 K 10^{11}—**1. n.pr.m.** 11th son of Joktan Gn 10^{29} (J)=1 Ch 1^{23}; 𝔊 *Οὐφειρ, Ὠφειρ*, name of an Arabian tribe, vid. Gn 10^{30} & Di. **2. n.pr.loc.** (land or city S. or SE. fr. Palestine, exact position unknown, cf. infr.; 𝔊 *Σωφηρα, Σωφειρα, Σουφειρ*, etc.; Jb 28^{16} *Ὠφειρ* AC, cf. 1 K 22^{49} A *Ὠφειρδε*, B om.) place whither Sol.'s ships went fr. Ezion Geber, bringing thence gold 1 K 9^{28}—cf. 22^{49}—2 Ch 8^{18}; gold, almug-(sandal-?) wood & gems 10$^{11.11}$, cf. 2 Ch 9^{10}; prob. 1 K 10^{22} ref. to same ships; they came once in three years with gold, silver, ivory, apes & peacocks (all fr. Ophir?); 2 Ch 9^{21} makes these ships go to Tarshish (but on Tarshish-ships, i.e. large, sea-going vessels, merchantmen, v. 1 K 22^{49} & sub תַּרְשִׁישׁ). **3.** characteristic of fine gold (poet. & late) זְהַב א׳ 1 Ch 29^{4}; כֶּתֶם א׳ Is 13^{12} Jb 28^{16} ψ 45^{10}. **4.** hence for fine gold itself Jb 22^{24} (‖ בֶּצֶר).—(If **2**=**1**, then southern, prob. south-eastern, Arabia (cf. Di Gn 10^{29}) furnished the gold; and other articles, which point farther E. (e.g. to India, toward which the words קוֹפִים *apes* & תֻּכִּיִּים *peacocks* seem to lead), were either brought to Ophir by traders, & so found there by Sol.'s men, or were found elsewhere by the latter, whose cruise may have taken them beyond Ophir, the name of Ophir alone, as source of gold-supply, being preserved. If (less likely) **1** & **2** are not the same, the only data for determining loc. of **2** are the articles brought, & one may look toward India, Ceylon or other islands, or even lower Africa. Particular theories have as yet no adequate support; e.g. (*a*) old city *Supara*, or *Uppara*, in the region of Goa, Malabar coast

(cf. 𝔊 supr. **2**, but also **1**; form with ב said on Copt. authority to denote India, v. Jablonskii Opusc ed te Water i. 337, cf also Jos$^{Ant. viii 6. 4}$, in that case its use by 𝔊 may indicate a theory of the location of Ophir); (*b*) peninsula *Malacca*, (*c*) island *Sumatra;* (*d*) *Sofâla*, with city Zimbabye (SE Africa); (*e*) west coast of Arabia (where gold & silver formerly found), etc. On these & other theories, v. Di Gn 10^{29} Ri^{HWB}, Herzog, Smith$^{Dict. Bib}$; cf Glaser$^{Skizze ii. 357 ff.}$)

†[**אוּץ**] **vb. press, be pressed, make haste**—**Qal** *Pf.* אָץ Jos 10^{13} 17^{15}; אַצְתִּי Je 17^{16} *Pt* אָץ Pr 19^{2}+3t. Pr; אָצִים Ex 5^{13},—**1.** *press, hasten* (trans. but obj. not expr) Ex 5^{13} (E) **2.** (intr.) *be pressed, confined, narrow* Jos 17^{15} כִּי אָץ לְךָ הַר־אֶפְרָיִם. **3.** *hasten, make haste*, sq. לְ + Inf. Jos 10^{13} לֹא אָץ לָבוֹא (J, of sun), Pr 28^{20} לֹא א׳ מֵרֹעֶה; sq. מִן Je 17^{16} א׳ לְהַעֲשִׁיר, sq. בְּ (of particular in wh. one hastens) Pr 19^{2} (בְּרַגְלַיִם), 29^{20} (בִּדְבָרָיו); cf also Pr 21^{5} וְכָל־אָץ אַךְ לְמַחְסוֹר. **Hiph.** *Impf.* וַיָּאִיצוּ Gn 19^{15}, תָּאִיצוּ Is 22^{4}—*hasten* (tr) sq בְּ Gn 19^{15} (J); sq לְ + Inf אַל־תָּא׳ לְנַחֲמֵנִי Is 22^{4} (May be Qal Impf, & vb ע׳י)

[**אוֹר**]$_{43}$ **vb. be or become light** (cf Ar أَوْرَ *enkindle*, Aram. (Nasar) ܢܘܪ Aph *illumine*, & deriv. in As.)—**Qal** *Pf.* אוֹר Gn 44^{3}+; אֹרוּ 1 S 14^{29}; *Impf.* 3 fpl וַתָּאֹרְנָה 1 S 14^{27} Qr; *Pt* אוֹר Pr 4^{18} (Ges$^{§ 72 R 1}$), *Imv.* fs אוֹרִי Is 60^{1} Pr 4^{18},—*become light, shine* of sun (esp in early morn) Gn 44^{3}(J) 1 S 29^{10} Pr 4^{18} Is 60^{1}, of eyes (owing to refreshment) 1 S $14^{27 (Qr) 29}$ **Niph.** *Impf.* וַיֵּאֹר 2 S 2^{32}, *Inf.* לֵאוֹר Jb 33^{30}; *Pt.* נָאוֹר ψ 76^{5}—become *lighted up* of day-break 2 S 2^{32}, by light of life, revival Jb 33^{30}; by light of glory, enveloped in light ψ 76^{5}. **Hiph.** *Pf.* והאיר Ex 25^{37}, etc; *Impf.* יָאִיר Jb 41^{24}+, יָאֵר Nu 6^{25}+, וַיָּאֶר ψ 118^{27}+, etc; *Imv* הָאֵר ψ 80^{20}+, הָאִירָה ψ 31^{17}+; *Inf.* הָאִיר Gn 1^{15}+, *Pt.* מֵאִיר Pr 29^{13}; מְאִירַת ψ 19^{9}; מְאִירוֹת Is 27^{11}—**1.** *give light*, of sun, moon & stars Gn $1^{15.17}$(P), of moon Is 60^{19}, of pillar of fire (sq. לְ) Ex 13^{21} 14^{20} (both JE) ψ 105^{39} Ne $9^{12.19}$; of sacred lamp Ex 25^{37} Nu 8^{2} (both P), fig of the words of God ψ 119^{130} **2.** *light up, cause to shine, shine*, sq. acc. האירו בְרָקִים תֵּבֵל *lightnings lighted up the world* ψ 77^{19} 97^{4}; abs הָאָרֶץ האירה מכבדו Ez 43^{2}; *the earth shined with his glory* (of theophany), of leviathan, which makes path shine behind him Jb 41^{24}; לַיְלָה כַּיּוֹם יָאִיר *night shineth as day* ψ 139^{12} **3.** *light* a lamp ψ 18^{29}; wood Is 27^{11}, altar(-fire) Mal 1^{10} **4.** *lighten*, of the eyes, הָאִיר עֵינַיִם, subj י׳, his law, etc. Pr 29^{13} ψ 13^{4} 19^{9} Ezr 9^{8} **5.** *make shine*, of face of God יָאֵר י׳ פָּנָיו אֵלֶיךָ *Yahweh make his face shine upon thee* Nu 6^{25} (priest's blessing), reappearing ψ 31^{17} (sq. עַל־), 67^{2} (sq אֶת־), $80^{4.8.20}$; 119^{135} (sq בְּ), Dn 9^{17} cf ψ 4^{7}; without פָּנִים (sq לְ) ψ 118^{27}, once, of face of man, Ec 8^{1} חָכְמַת אָדָם תָּאִיר פָּנָיו *the wisdom of a man lighteth up his face*

אוֹר$_{121}$ **n.m** $^{Gn 1.3}$(**f.** $^{Jb 36.32}$ $^{Je 13.16}$) **light** (As. *urru* = *ûru* Dl^{W})—abs Gn 1^{3}+; cstr Ju 16^{2}+, sf אוֹרִי ψ 27^{1}, etc, *pl.* אוֹרִים ψ 136^{7},—**1.** *light* as diffused in nature, light of day Gn $1^{3.4.5}$ (P) Jb 3^{9} 38^{19}+. **2.** *morning light, dawn*, אוֹר הַבֹּקֶר light of the morn Ju 16^{2} 1 S 14^{36} $25^{34.36}$ 2 S 17^{22} 2 K 7^{9} Mi 2^{1}, א׳ בֹּקֶר 2 S 23^{4} (poem of David); עַד־הָא׳ Ju 19^{26} (cf. עַד־הַבֹּקֶר v^{25}); לָאוֹר Jb 24^{14}; מִן־הָאוֹר עַד מַחֲצִית הַיּוֹם *fr. dawn till mid-day*, Ne 8^{3} cf Pr 4^{18}. **3.** *light* of the heavenly luminaries, א׳ הַחַמָּה ‖ א׳ הַלְּבָנָה, *moonlight & sunlight* Is 30^{26}, כוכבי אור *stars of light* ψ 148^{3}, מאורי אור *luminaries of light* Ez 32^{8}, אוֹרִים = מְאוֹרִים ψ 136^{7}, so עֲלֵי־אוֹר *in sunshine* Is 18^{4}; the sun itself Jb 31^{26} **4.** *daylight* אוֹר רְשָׁעִים *light of the wicked* Jb 38^{15} (their work-day being the night), יוֹם אוֹר *a day of light* Am 8^{9} (= a clear, sunshiny day) **5.** *lightning* Jb 36^{32} $37^{3.11.15}$ cf Hb 3^{11}. **6.** *light* of lamp Pr 13^{9} Je 25^{10}, of crocodile's hot breath Jb 41^{10} **7.** *light of life* א׳ חַיִּים Jb 33^{30} ψ 56^{14}; cf אוֹר Jb $3^{16.20}$. **8.** *light of prosperity* Jb 22^{28} 30^{26} ψ 97^{11} La 3^{2} **9.** *light of instruction* נר מצוה ותוֹרה אור Pr 6^{23} *the commandment is a lamp and instruction a light*, so the Messian servant is אוֹר גּוֹיִם Is 42^{6} 49^{6}, cf א׳ עַמִּים Is 51^{4}, the advent of Mess is shining of great light Is 9^{1}. **10.** *light* of face אוֹר פָּנִים = bright, cheerful face (of men) Jb 29^{24}; betokening king's favour Pr 16^{15} (cf א׳ עֵינַיִם ψ 38^{11}); of God = his shining, enlightening, favouring face ψ 4^{7} 44^{4} 89^{16}. **11.** Yahweh is א׳ יִשְׂרָאֵל Is 10^{17}, as source of enlightenment & prosperity, light & salvation ψ 27^{1}, light to guide Mi 7^{8} cf ψ 43^{3}, everlasting light of Zion, instead of sun & moon Is $60^{19.20}$, house of Jacob is to walk in his light Is 2^{5}.

†I **אוֹרָה** **n.f. light** (late, Mish *id*, cf Aram אוּרְתָא *evening-light, moon-light, star-light*, etc.) **1.** *light* (opp חֲשֵׁכָה) ψ 139^{12}. **2.** *light* of joy & happiness Es 8^{16}; pl intens אוֹרוֹת *light* of life Is 26^{19} (light that quickens dead bodies as dew the plants Ew Hi De Che Di RVm; vid Br$^{MP 303}$ cf אוֹר חַיִּים, but Ki Ges MV Bo RV transl. *herbs*)

†II [**אוֹרָה**] **n.f. herb** (so Mish., Ges cf נֵצֶן, Ar انوار = *lights & flowers*, & Sam דֶּשֶׁא = יאר of Gn $1^{11.12}$) only *pl* אורות *herbs* 2 K 4^{39} (cf Is 26^{19} supr sub I אוֹרָה).

†I. אוּר **n.m. flame.** לְכוּ בְּאוּר אֶשְׁכֶם *walk in the flame of your fire* Is 50^{11}, & so fire itself, whose light & flame were seen 44^{16} 47^{14}—exil. Is. + 31^{9} & Ez 5^{2} (Co אִישׁ).

†אֻרִים **n.** [**m.**] **pl. region of light, East** Is 24^{15} (so Ges MV Ew De Di RV; Lo Hi Kn Che rd. איים = *coasts*, so Cdd. 𝔊;—𝔊 mostly om. 𝔙 *in doctrina*, thinking of *Urim*, vid. Br[MP 297]).

†אוּרִים **n.m. Urim** (pl. intens., mostly c. art. *the Urim*, and mostly joined with תֻּמִּים q.v.) תֻּמֶּיךָ וְאוּרֶיךָ לְאִישׁ חֲסִידֶךָ Dt 33^{8} *thy Thummim and thy Urim has the man of thy favour*, i.e. the Levite tested at Massah & Meribah; הָאוּרִים וְהַתֻּמִּים were put into the חֹשֶׁן הַמִּשְׁפָּט of the high priest Ex 28^{30} Lv 8^{8} (P); this חֹשֶׁן (q.v.) was a little bag or pouch worn on breast of high priest, to hold the *Urim & Thummim;* the name ח׳ הַמִּשְׁפָּט was given because of decisions made by that which was within it; thus, Eleazar was to inquire of ׳י for Joshua בְּמִשְׁפַּט הָאוּרִים Nu 27^{21} (P); Saul prayed הָבָה אוּרִים, opp. הבה תֻמִּים, 1 S 14^{41} 𝔊, so We Dr (MT om. former, and rds. תָּמִים in latter); ׳י did not answer Saul בָּאוּרִים, or by dreams or prophets 1 S 28^{6}; postex. Jews reserved difficult questions until there stood up a priest לְאוּרִים וּלְתֻמִּים Ezr 2^{63} Ne 7^{65} (here alone without art.) These passages give little information; 𝔊 δήλωσις καὶ ἀλήθεια, 𝔙 *doctrina et veritas*, Sym φωτισμοὶ καὶ τελεώτητες; Jos[Ant. iii. 8. 9] thinks of the twelve gems of face of bag as giving decision by shining; Philo[Vit. Mos. iii] thinks of two small images (א׳ & ת׳), prob. embroidered in the cloth of the bag, like oracle-images of Egypt (Diod[i. 48. 75] Aelian[Var. Hist. 14, 34]); Ew[Gesch. iii, 309; Antiq. 295], of two stones of different colours for sacred lot, on this v. Dr 1 S 14^{41} where 𝔊 אוּרִים & תֻּמִּים as obj. of give, δος = הָבָה; cf. הַפִּילוּ v^{42}, וַיִּלָּכֵד v^{41} (used of taking by lot 10^{20} Is $7^{14.16}$); v. also We & RS[OTJC Lect x. N 4]; Bähr[Symbolik], of one thing within bag, a sacred pledge to high priest of the enlightenment & perfection he would receive fr. ׳י when called to make sacred decisions; Ka[Ex 544] sees the sacred pledge in the twelve sacred gems themselves, that stimulate priest to self-sacrifice & perfect sanctification.

†II. אוּר **n.pr.m.** (*flame*) father of one of David's heroes 1 Ch 11^{35} (III. אוּר n.pr.loc. v. infr.)

†אוּרִי **n.pr.m.** (*fiery*, or contr. for אוּרִיָּה) **1.** prince of Judah Ex 31^{2} 35^{30} 38^{22} 1 Ch 2^{20} 2 Ch 1^{5}; **2.** a porter Ezr 10^{24}; **3.** father of an officer of Solomon 1 K 4^{19}.

†אוּרִיאֵל **n.pr.m.** (*flame of Ēl* or *my light is Ēl*, v. אֵל sub אלה; cf. Ph. ארמלך in As. *Urumilki* (Sen[Taylor Cylind. ii. 50], cf. COT[2 K 18, 13])) **1.** chief of Levit. line of Kohath, in time of David 1 Ch 6^{9} $15^{5.11}$. **2.** maternal grandfather of Abijah 2 Ch 13^{2}.

אוּרִיָּה **n.pr.m.** (*flame of Yah* or *my light is Yah* v. יָהּ). **1.** Hittite husband of Bathsheba 2 S $11^{3 f}$ 23^{39}. **2.** priest in reign of Ahaz Is 8^{2} 2 K $16^{10 f}$. **3.** priest in time of Nehemiah Ezr 8^{33} Ne $3^{4.21}$ 8^{4}.

†אוּרִיָּהוּ **n.pr.m.** (*flame of Yahweh* or *my light is Yahweh* v. יהוה) a prophet slain by Jehoiakim Je 26^{20}.

†יָאִיר **n.pr.m.** (*he enlightens*, or *one giving light*). **1.** son of Manasseh Nu $32^{41.41}$ Dt $3^{14.14}$ Jos 13^{30} 1 K 4^{13} 1 Ch $2^{22.23}$. **2.** a judge in Gilead Ju $10^{3.4.5}$. **3.** father of Mordecai Est 2^{5}.

†יָאִירִי **adj.gent.** Jairite 2 S 20^{26}.

†מָאוֹר **n.m. luminary**—abs. Gn 1^{16}+; cstr. מְאוֹר Pr 15^{30}+; pl. מְאוֹרֹת Gn 1^{15}; מְאֹרֹת $v^{14.16}$; cstr. מְאוֹרֵי Ez 32^{8}—*light, light-bearer, luminary, lamp*, of sun & moon Gn $1^{14.15.16.16.16}$ (P) Ez 32^{8}; moon ψ 74^{16}; מְנֹרַת הַמָּאוֹר *the lamp-stand of the luminary* or *light* (where הַמּ׳ is sum of seven sacred lamps on golden lamp-stand) Ex $35^{14.14.28}$ 39^{37} Nu $4^{9.16}$, cf. Ex 25^{6} 27^{20} 35^{8} Lv 24^{2} (all P); מְאוֹר־עֵינַיִם יְשַׂמַּח־לֵב Pr 15^{30} *the luminary of the eyes* (= the eyes as a lamp) *gives the light of joy to the heart;* מְאוֹר פָּנֶיךָ ψ 90^{8} *the luminary of thy face* (thy face as a lamp) in the light of which the secrets are exposed.

†[מְאוּרָה] **n.f. light-hole**—only cstr. מְאוּרַת — = den of great viper Is 11^{8}, cf. מָאוֹר Mish. *Ohaloth* 13^{1} (others *eye-ball* 𝔗 Ew De Di).

†III. אוּר **n.pr.loc. Ur** (Bab. *Uru;* seat of moon-god worship; hence Eupolemos in Euseb[Praep. Ev. ix. 17] says Καμαρίνη ἥν τινας λέγειν πόλιν Οὐρίην), ancient city in Southern Babylonia; OT alw. אוּר כַּשְׂדִּים, i.e. Ur of the Kasdim (Chaldeans) v. כַּשְׂדִּים sub כשׂד; home of Terah, Abram's father, & A.'s point of departure for Mesopotamia & Canaan Gn 11^{28} 15^{7} (both J), & hence Ne 9^{7}; also Gn 11^{31} (P);—mod. *Muqayyar*, south of Euphrates, c. 150 miles SE. of Babylon; v. KG[94 f] Dl[Pa 226 f] COT on Gn 11^{28}.

אֻוֵרוֹת v. אֻרְיָה sub I. ארה.

אֲוַרְנָה v. אֲרַוְנָה.

†[אוּת] **vb.** only **Niph.** *Impf.* **consent, agree** (cf. Rab. נֵיאוֹת Niph. Pt. esp. *enjoying* NHWB[48]) sq. לְ Gn 34^{22} יֵאֹתוּ לָנוּ; v^{15} נֵאוֹת לָכֶם;

וַיֵּאֹתוּ הַכֹּהֲנִים 2 K 12^{9} sq. Inf. ;נֵאוֹתָה לָהֶם v^{23} לְבִלְתִּי קְחַת־כֶּסֶף.

אוֹת v II. אוה.

אָז **adv.** (cf. إِذْ, إِذَا, Eth አሜ · also BAram אֱדַיִן, prop. a subst = *time* see מֵאָז) **at that time, then, whether expressing duration, or inception (= thereupon). 1.** strictly temporal. **a.** of past time:—without a verb Gn 12^{6} 13^{7} Jos 14^{11} 2 S 23^{14}; with a pf. Gn 4^{26} Ex 4^{26} Jos 10^{33} Ju 8^{3} 13^{21} Je 22^{15} אָז טוֹב לוֹ *then* was it well to him (cf. v^{16} Ho 2^{9}); more usually (esp when = *thereupon*) with an impf (v. Dr ^{§27}) Ex 15^{1} Nu 21^{17} Jos 8^{30} 10^{12} 22^{1} 1 K 3^{16} 8^{1} 9^{11} (v. $Dr^{Intr\ 192}$) al **b.** of fut time (usually where some emph is intended), with impf. Is $35^{5.6}$ 60^{5} Mi 3^{4}, rather differently Lv 26^{41} 1 S 20^{12}; rarely with pf 2 S $5^{24\ b}$ (*will have* gone forth) Is 33^{23}· with an accompanying logical force, implying the fulfilment of a condition, *then* = *if* or *when this has been done* (with the impf) Gn 24^{41} Ex $12^{44.48}$ Dt 29^{19} Jos 1^{8} 1 S 6^{3} Is $58^{8.9}$ Je 11^{15} Hi Ke ψ 19^{14} 51^{21} Pr 3^{23} Jb 11^{15} 13^{20} 22^{26}. **c.** in poetry אָז is sometimes used to throw emphasis on a particular feature of the description Gn 49^{4} Ex 15^{15} Ju $5^{8\ 11\ 13\ 19.22}$ Is 33^{23} 41^{1} Hb 1^{11} ψ 2^{5} 96^{12}. **d.** it points back with emphasis to an inf with בְּ 2 S 5^{24a} ψ $126^{2.2}$ Jb 28^{27} 33^{16}; to בַּיּוֹם הַהוּא (anomalously) 1 Ch 16^{7}. **2.** expressing logical sequence strictly. in the apod —after אִם (rare) for sake of special emphasis Is 58^{14} Pr 2^{5} Jb 9^{31}, = *in that case*, after לוּ or לוּלֵא 2 S 2^{27} hadst thou not spoken, כִּי אָז surely *then* had the people, etc 19^{7} ψ 119^{92}; after אַחֲלֵי 2 K 5^{3} ψ 119^{6}, after a suppressed protasis 2 K 13^{19} Jb 3^{13} יָשַׁנְתִּי אָז יָנוּחַ לִי I had slept, *then* were there rest for me, Jos 22^{31} (strangely) = *now, as things are;* Ec 2^{15} = *that being so* (122 t, besides מֵאָז and מִן־אָז. Seldom used except where some special emphasis is desired 'Then' of AV RV more commonly represents וְ, esp. in the apodosis.)

†**מֵאָז** (cf. مُنْذُ), once (Je 44^{18}) מִן־אָז, lit. *from that time*. used (*a*) absol, as adv = in *time past, of old,* whether of a nearer 2 S 15^{34} Is 16^{13}, or of a remoter past Is 44^{8} 45^{21} $48^{3.5.7.8}$ ψ 93^{2} Pr 8^{22}, (*b*) with foll. gen. or relat clause, as prep. or conj = *from time of, since* With subst. Ru 2^{7} מֵאָז הַבֹּקֶר *from time of* morning ψ 76^{8}; with infin. Ex 4^{10} מֵאָז דַּבֶּרְךָ *since* thy speaking unto thy servant; with finite vb. Gn 39^{5} Ex 5^{23} וּמֵאָז בָּאתִי וגו׳ and *since* I came unto Pharaoh, etc. 9^{24} Jos 14^{10} Is 14^{8} Je 44^{18}.

†**אֲזַי** = אָז (prob a dialectic form; cf. Aram אֱדַיִן) **then, in that case** ψ $124^{3.4.5}$, in apod after לוּלֵי: cf. אָז ψ 119^{92}.

†**אֶזְבַּי** **n.pr.m.** father of one of David's men 1 Ch 11^{37} (where הָאַרְבִּי = בֶּן־אֶזְבָּי 2 S 23^{35}).

†**אֵזוֹב** **n.m.** $^{1\ K\ 5,13}$ **hyssop** (Mish אזוב, Aram. ܙܘܦܐ, Ar. زُوفَا Frey, Eth አዛብ: 𝔊 ὕσσωπος, herb of purging qualities, but perh. not precise botanical term, v. Di Lv $14^{4\ ff}$, v also Low ^{93}) —א׳ abs. Ex 12^{22} + 4 t.; אזב Lv 14^{4} + 4 t,— *hyssop*, little plant (contr. אֶרֶז *cedar*) 1 K 5^{13}, הָא׳ אֲשֶׁר יֹצֵא בַּקִּיר; Ex 12^{22} (J) אֲגֻדַּת א׳ a bunch of h. for sprinkling blood on doorposts; without אגדת, used in cleansing from leprosy Lv $14^{4.6.49.51.52}$; burnt with red heifer Nu 19^{6}; used in cleansing with ashes of red heifer v^{18} (all P); cf ψ 51^{9} תְּחַטְּאֵנִי בְאֵ׳ וְאֶטְהָר

אַזְכָּרָה v. זכר.

†**אָזַל** **vb.** go (mostly poet) (𝔗 *id*, BAram. אֲזַל, Syr. ܐܙܰܠ)—**Qal** *Pf.* אָזַל 1 S 9^{7}, 3 fs אָזְלַת (poet.) Dt 32^{36}, אָזְלוּ Jb 14^{11}, *Impf* 2 fs תֵּזְלִי (for תֵּאזְלִי) Je 2^{36}, *Pt.* אֹזֵל Pr 20^{14}—*go away* Pr 20^{14}; *go about* Je 2^{36} מַה־תֵּזְלִי מְאֹד לְשַׁנּוֹת אֶת־דַּרְכֵּךְ, *be gone, exhausted, used up* Dt 32^{36} (subj יָד *strength*), sq מִן 1 S 9^{7} הַלֶּחֶם אָזַל מִכֵּלֵינוּ, Jb 14^{11} אָזְלוּ מַיִם מִנִּי־יָם, **Pu.** *Pt* מְאוּזָּל Ez 27^{19} (RV *yarn*, cf. Aram עזל *spin* but) rd מֵאוּזָל, v sub אוּזָל infr, so 𝔊 𝔖 Hi Sm Co.

†[אָזֵל] only הָאָזֶל 1 S 20^{19} rd. הַלָּז(א) q v.

†**אוּזָל** **n.pr.m.** (Sam איזל, 𝔊 Αἰζήλ) 6th son of Joktan Gn 10^{27} 1 Ch 1^{21} = **n.pr.loc.** Ez 27^{19}, rd מֵאוּזָל 𝔊 𝔖 Hi Sm Co, old capital of Yemen, later *San'â*, cf. Di Gn 10^{27}

I **אזן** (*pointed, sharp*? cf. Eth ምእዝን: *edge, corner, peak, pinnacle;* v also As. Dl^{W}, & אָזֵן infr)

אֹזֶן $_{188}$ **n.f.** $^{Ex\ 29\ 20}$ **ear** (Ar أُذُن, Aram. ܐܶܕ݂ܢܳܐ, אוּדְנָא, As *uznu*, Eth እዝን:)—abs. 2 S 22^{45} +; cstr Ex 29^{20} +, sf אָזְנִי 1 S 20^{2} +, etc; du. אָזְנַיִם (נַ֫יִם) Dt 29^{3} +, cstr אָזְנֵי Gn 23^{10} +; sf אָזְנַי (נַ֫י) Nu 14^{28} +, (never with article) —**1.** *ear*, as part of body, of human being, as bearing earring Gn 35^{4} Ex $32^{2.3}$ (all JE) Ez 16^{12}; pierced by a master Ex 21^{6} (E) Dt 15^{17}; touched with blood in consecration (תְּנוּךְ א׳ *tip of ear*) Lv $8^{23.24}$ $14^{14\ 17\ 25.28}$, cut off by enemy Ez 23^{25} (of אָהֳלִיבָה q v.), ear of dog Pr 26^{17} מַחֲזִיק בְּאָזְנֵי־כָלֶב; of sheep Am 3^{12} (fragment rescued from lion). **2.** especially as *organ of hearing*, **a.** of man Dt 29^{3} 2 S 22^{45} = ψ 18^{45}, Jb 42^{5} Is 30^{21}; implanted (נטע)

by 'י ψ 94[9], of idols (do not hear) ψ 115[6] 135[17]; שָׁמַע בא' 2 S 7[22] + 8t., esp 'בְּא after vb of saying = *in the ears, in the hearing of* Gn 20[8] (E) 23[10 13.16] (P) 44[18] 50[4] (J) Dt 5[1] 31[11 28.30] + 44 t , cf Is 5[9] (vb om); after noun of utterance, sound 1 S 15[14] Jb 13[17] 15[21], cf 'א after verbal noun Ez 24[26] (לְהַ-ְמָעוּת א') cf. Is 11[3], הַטֵּה א' incline the ear = give attention ψ 45[11] Pr 22[17] + 9t , sq לְ ψ 49[5] + 4 t., so הקשיב א' Is 32[3]; Pr 2[2] (sq לְ), הָבִיא א' לְ' Pr 23[2]; as receiving words א' תקח Jb 4[12] cf Je 9[19], as tingling (צלל) at dreadful news 1 S 3[11] 2 K 21[12] Je 19[3], as hearing with satisfaction, triumph ψ 92[12] תשמַעְנָה אָזְנָי (|| וַתַּבֵּט עיני ב') but Che del ; as *intelligent* (involving mental process) שָׁמְעָה א' וַתָּבֶן לָהּ Jb 13[1]; א' מלין תבחן Jb 12[11] cf 34[3], as unsatisfied Ec 1[8] לֹא תִמָּלֵא א' מִשְּׁמֹעַ, as seeking (בקש) knowledge Pr 18[15]; as hearing & blessing Jb 29[11], cf. א' שֹׁמַעַת Pr 20[12] 25[12] *a hearing* (responsive, obedient) *ear*, cf. Pr 15[31] Is 43[8], opp *stopping the ears* (wilful ignorance) אֹטֵם א' מִן- Pr 21[13] cf Is 33[15], also of adder in simile of wicked ψ 58[5] כמו פתן חרש יַאְטֵם אָזְנוֹ; מסיר א' מִן- Pr 28[9] so עֲרֵלָה א' *their ear is uncircumcised* Je 6[10], הכביד א' Zc 7[11] cf. Is 48[8] Je 5[21] Ez 12[2], cf also Is 42[20] **b.** of Yahweh, 'בא' י after vb of utterance Nu 11[18] (J) 14[28] (P) 1 S 8[21] Ez 8[18], after עָלָה 2 K 19[28] = Is 37[29], after בּוֹא ψ 18[7] cf 2 S 22[7] where vb om., so also (after noun without vb) Nu 11[1] (J) 'בא' י 1 Ch 28[8] nearly = in presence of; incline the ear הַטֵּה א' 2 K 19[16] = Is 37[17] Dn 9[18] ψ 86[1], sq. לְ ψ 17[6] 88[3] 116[2]; sq אֶל- ψ 31[3] 71[2] 102[3], הקשיב א' ψ 10[17]; א' קַשֻּׁבוֹת לְ 2 Ch 6[40] 7[15] cf. ψ 130[2], *id* sq אֶל- Ne 1[6 11]; vb om א' אֶל- ψ 34[16], cf Is 59[1] לֹא כָבְדָה א'; אַל-תַּעְלֵם א' לְ' La 3[56] **3.** †גָּלָה א' *open ears of, reveal to,* subj man 1 S 20[2 12 13] 22[8.8.17] Ru 4[4], subj. 'י 1 S 9[15] 2 S 7[27] 1 Ch 17[25]; ג' א' לַמּוּסָר Jb 36[10], cf. v[15], כָּרִיתָ א' ψ 40[7], יָעִיר לִי א' לִשְׁמֹעַ Is 50[4]; פָּתַח-לִי א' Is 50[5], cf וא' חרשים תִּפָּתַחְנָה Is 35[5]; opp judicial deafness Mi 7[16] Is 6[10]

I. †[אָזַן] [42] **vb denom. Hiph. give ear, listen, hear,** almost wholly poet —*Pf.* הֶאֱזִין Dt 1[45], וְהַאֲזִין consec ψ 77[2] (v. De Ko[I p. 390]); וְהַאֲזַנְתָּ Ex 15[26], הֶאֱזִינוּ Is 64[3] + , *Impf* יַאֲזִין Jb 9[16] + , אָזִין (for אַאֲזִין) Jb 32[11], etc.; *Imv* ms הַאֲזִינָה Nu 23[18] + ; fs הַאֲזִינִי Is 1[2], fpl. הַאֲזֵנָּה Gn 4[23] Is 32[9], etc ; *Pt* מזין (for מַאֲזִין, v. Ko[I 391]) Pr 17[4],—**1.** *hear,* perceive by the ear, abs Is 64[3] (|| שמע) ψ 135[17]; *give ear, listen,* abs (of mts personif.) Dt 32[1], cf Is 1[2] (of earth, personif); cf men Ju 5[3] ψ 49[2] Is 28[23] Jo 1[2] (all || שמע) Ho 5[1] (|| שמע, הקשיב) Is 8[9]; sq acc. rei Gn 4[23] Jb 33[1] Is 1[10] 32[9] (all || שמע) 42[23] (|| שמע, הקשיב); Jb 37[14] (|| התבונן); ψ 78[1] sq על (rei) Pr 17[4] (|| הקשיב), sq עַד (rei) Jb 32[11] (|| הוחלתי); *hearken* to, = be obedient to, abs. Je 13[15] (|| שמע) 2 Ch 24[19] Ne 9[30]; c acc rei Jb 9[16]; לְ (rei) Jb 34[16] (|| שמע) Ex 15[26], sq. לְ pers. Jb 34[2] (|| שמע); sq עָדַי pers Nu 23[18]; sq. אֶל- pers Is 51[4]. **2.** *of God, listening* (*with favour*) to prayer, etc , abs ψ 80[2] 84[9] (|| שמע), sq אֶל- pers ψ 77[2] Dt 1[45] (|| שמע); c acc rei ψ 5[2] (|| בין) 17[1] (|| שמע, הקשיב), ψ 55[2] (|| הקשיב v[3]) 86[6] (|| *id*), 140[7] 141[1], sq. אל- (rei) ψ 39[13] 143[1] (both || שמע); sq לְ (rei) ψ 54[4] (|| שמע)

†[אָזֵן] **n.[m.] coll. implements, tools** (fr. sharpness? Aram אֲזִין, ازمَ weapons אֲזֵנֶךָ Dt 23[14] (Cold אוניך 𝔊 𝔅 אזר cf. Di)

†אָזְנִי **n pr m.** a son of Gad Nu 26[16] (*my hearing,* or *my ear*? Gn 46[16] אֶצְבֹּן q.v)

†אָזְנִי **adj.gent.** fr. same, הָאָזְנִי Nu 26[16].

†אֲזַנְיָהוּ **n pr.m.** (*Yahweh hath heard*) father of Jeshua, a Levite Ne 10[10].

†אַזְנוֹת תָּבוֹר **n.pr.loc.** (*peaks* of Tabor? pl.) Jos 19[34] place in Naphtali cf. Di

†יַאֲזַנְיָהוּ **n pr.m.** (*Yahweh heareth*)—so 2 K 25[23] Ez 8[11], יַאֲזַנְיָה Je 35[3] Ez 11[1]; contr. יְזַנְיָהוּ(ו) Je 40[8], יְזַנְיָה(ו) Je 42[1]—**1.** a Judæan 2 K 25[23] Je 40[8] **2.** an elder of Isr , son of Shaphan Ez 8[11]. **3.** son of Jeremiah Je 35[3] **4** a leading Judæan, son of Azur Ez 11[1]. **5.** a leading Judæan Je 42[1] (= עֲזַרְיָה 43[2])

II †[אָזַן] **vb.** only **Pi.** *Pf* **weigh, test, prove** (cf. Ar وَزَنَ *weigh,* also Ar & Aram. deriv), ואזן (conj) Ec 12[9] (|| חקר, תקן).

†[מֹאזֵן] **n.[m.]du. balances, scales** (Ar مِيزَانٌ, Aram (Nasar) ܡܘܙܢܐ)—מֹאזְנַיִם Is 40[15] + 4 t ; cstr מֹאזְנֵי Lv 19[36] + 9 t —*balances,* for weighing money Je 32[10] וָאֶשְׁקֹל הַכֶּסֶף בְּמ'; hair Ez 5[1] (מ' מִשְׁקָל), שַׁחַק מ' Is 40[15] *dust of bal.*, sim of insignif of nations bef. 'י , fig , calamity Jb 6[2], men ψ 62[10], hills Is 40[12] (שָׁקַל בַּפֶּלֶס הָרִים וּגְבָעוֹת בְּמ'); א' צֶדֶק Lv 19[36] (|| אַבְנֵי-צ', אֵיפַת צ', הִין צ'), Ez 45[10] (|| אֵיפַת-צ', בַּת-צ') cf Pr 16[11] (פֶּלֶס וּמ' מִשְׁפָּט), fig Jb 31[6] יִשְׁקְלֵנִי בְמ' צֶדֶק , opp. מ' מִרְמָה Pr 11[1] (|| אֶבֶן שְׁלֵמָה); 20[23]

(לְהַקְטִין אֵיפָה וּלְהַגְדִּיל שֶׁקֶל ‖) Am 8^{5} (אֶבֶן וָאָבֶן ‖) Ho 12^{8}; מ׳ רֶשַׁע Mi 6^{11} (‖ אַבְנֵי מִרְמָה).

†אֻזֵּן שֶׁאֱרָה **n.pr.loc.** (*portion*—weighed & measured—*of She'ĕra*, Blau$^{ZMG\ 1873,\ 296}$), place built by ׳שׁ, daughter of Ephraim 1 Ch 7^{24}.

אֲזִקִּים v. זקק.

†[אָזַר] **vb. gird, encompass, equip** (Talm. *id.*, Ar. أَزَرَ, Aram. in deriv. Lag$^{BN\ 177\ der.\ fr.}$ وَزَرَ). **Qal** *Pf.* אָזְרוּ 1 S 2^{4}; *Impf.* sf. יַאַזְרֵנִי Jb 30^{18}; 2 ms. תֶּאְזוֹר Je 1^{17}; *Imv.* אֱזָר־נָא Jb 38^{3} 40^{7}; *Pt. pass.* אָזוּר 2 K 1^{8};—*gird, gird on*, sq. acc. rei *loins* חֲלָצֶיךָ Jb 38^{3} 40^{7}, מָתְנֶיךָ Je 1^{17}; pass., subj. אֵזוֹר, וְאֵזוֹר עוֹר אָזוּר בְּמָתְנָיו 2 K 1^{8}; cf. act. c. acc. pers. Jb 30^{18} כְּפִי כֻתָּנְתִּי יַאַזְרֵנִי, subj. לְבוּשִׁי v. Di; fig. 1 S 2^{4} אָזְרוּ חָיִל. **Niph.** *Pt.* נֶאְזָר fig. ψ 65^{7} of God (נ׳ בִּגְבוּרָה) *girded with might*. **Pi.** *Impf.* 2 ms. sf. וַתְּאַזְּרֵנִי ψ 18^{40} 30^{12}; וַתַּזְרֵנִי 2 S 22^{40} (Ges$^{§\ 68\ R2}$); *Pt.* sf. הַמְאַזְּרֵנִי ψ 18^{33}; cstr. מְאַזְּרֵי Is 50^{11} but cf. infr.—*gird*, c. 2 acc. (pers. & rei) fig., ψ 18^{40} = 2 S 22^{40} ψ 18^{33} (חָיִל); ψ 30^{12} (שִׂמְחָה); acc. rei om. Is 45^{5}; acc. pers. om. מְאַזְּרֵי זִיקוֹת Is 50^{12}; but rd. rather מְאִירֵי cf. 27^{11} (𝔖 Kn Brd Di). **Hithp.** *Pf.* הִתְאַזָּר ψ 93^{1}; *Imv.* הִתְאַזְּרוּ Is 8$^{9.9}$—*gird oneself*, for war Is 8$^{9.9}$; with עֹז ψ 93^{1} (subj. ׳י).

†אֵזוֹר **n.m.** $^{Is\ 5,\ 27}$ **waistcloth** (NH *id.*, Ar. إِزَارٌ, cf. RS$^{JQ\ Jan.\ 1892,\ 289\ ff.}$)—׳א abs. Jb 12^{18} + 8 t.; cstr. 2 K 1^{8} + 4 t.;—of skin 2 K 1^{8} (prophet.); of linen Je 13^{1} (v. Che) cf. v$^{2.4.6.7.7.10.11}$ (symbol. of Isr. & Jud. cleaving to ׳י); of Assyrian warriors' waistcloth, '*girdle of loins*' Is 5^{27}; in wall-images of Chaldeans, חֲגוֹרֵי א׳ בְּמָתְנֵיהֶם Ez 23^{15} (cf. 2 K 1^{18} v. sub אָזַר) so fig. of Yahweh's power over kings וַיֶּאְסֹר אֵזוֹר בְּמָתְנֵיהֶם Jb 12^{18} (׳א = fetter, cf. Di; but acc. to RS$^{l.c.}$ ref. to slaves' garment); metaph. of righteousness & faithfulness Is 11$^{5.5}$ (א׳ חֲלָצָיו, א׳ מָתְנָיו).

אֶזְרוֹעַ v. זרע.

אֶזְרָח v. זרח.

אָח v. I. אחה.

I. אָח, אַחְאָב, אֶחָב, אֲחַבָּן etc. v. אחה.

II. אָח v. II. אחה.

†III. אָהּ **interj.** (onomatop.) **ah! alas!** Ez 6^{11} 21^{20}.

†אַחֲלַי ψ 119^{5} and אַחֲלֵי 2 K 5^{3} (perh. from אָח III. and לִי = Aram. לְוַי = לוּ: the varying punctuation is due doubtless to the word being treated by the punctuators as a subst. = *wish*, with suff. & in c. st., '*my wish* is that,' etc.; cf. Ki on ψ 119 תַּחֲנוּנַי וּבַקָּשׁוֹתַי), **ah that!** (𝔊 ὄφελον).

[אָחַד] **vb.** v. יחד or חדד (Co Ez 21^{21}).

אֶחָד $_{972}$ **adj.num. one** (Ph. אחד, Sab. *id.*, cf. DHM$^{ZMG\ 1876,\ 707}$, Ar. أَحَدٌ, Eth. አሐዱ: Aram. חַד, ܚܰܕ; on As. *edu*, *aḫadu*, cf. Dl$^{W\ No.\ 139}$)—abs. ׳א Gn 1^{5} + cstr. אַחַד Gn 21^{15} +; so even bef. prep. 1 S 9^{3} al. v. Dr; f. abs. אַחַת Gn 2^{21} +; אֶחָת Gn 11^{1} +; cstr. אַחַת Dt 13^{13} +; pl. m. אֲחָדִים Gn 11^{1} + 4 t.; חַד Ez 33^{30} del. Co cf. 𝔊;—**1.** *one* Gn 1^{9} 27$^{38.45}$ Ex 12^{49} Jos 23^{10} 1 S 1^{24} 2 S 12^{3} +, Zc 14^{9} Mal 2^{10} Jb 31^{15} +, so also (emph.) 2 S 17^{3} for MT אֲשֶׁר 𝔊 We Dr; *one or two* לֹא לְיוֹם אֶחָד וְלֹא לִשְׁנַיִם Ezr 10^{13}; as subst. sq. מִן Gn 2^{21} Lv 4$^{2.13}$ Is 34^{16} +; הָא׳ Gn 19^{9} 42$^{13.32}$ 2 K 6$^{3.5}$ +; *one and the same* Gn 40^{5} Jb 31^{15}; pl. דְּבָרִים אֲחָדִים †Gn 11^{1} cf. Ez 37^{17} (abs.), but v. Co; = *few, a few* יָמִים א׳ †Gn 27^{44} 29^{20} Dn 11^{20}; כְּאִישׁ אֶחָד *as one man, together* Ju 20^{8} 1 S 11^{7}; also כְּאֶחָד late = Aram. כַּחֲדָא †Ezr 2^{64} (= Ne 7^{66}) 3^{9} 6^{20} Ec 11^{6}; v. esp. Is 65^{25} (‖ earlier יַחְדָּו 11$^{6.7}$). **2.** = *each, every* Ex 36^{30} Nu 7$^{3.85}$ 28^{21} 1 K 4^{7} 2 K 15^{20} +; also repeated, distrib. sense Nu 7^{11} 13^{2} 17^{21} Jos 3^{12} 4$^{2.4}$. **3.** = *a certain* 1 S 1^{1} 2 S 18^{10} 2 K 4^{1} Est 3^{8} + cf. 2 S 17^{9} v. Dr 1 S 1^{1}; hence **4.** = indef. art. 1 S 6^{7} 24^{15} 26^{20} (but del. 𝔊 We Dr) 1 K 19$^{4.5}$ +. **5.** *only* 1 K 4^{19}; & (fem.) *once* 2 K 6^{10} ψ 62^{12} 89^{36} (*once for all*); אַחַת לְשָׁלוֹשׁ שָׁנִים 2 Ch 9^{21}, א׳ בַּשָּׁנָה Lv 16^{34} cf. Jb 40^{5}, פַּעַם אֶחָת Jos 6$^{3.11}$ cf. v^{14}, בְּאַחַת Nu 10^{4} Jb 33^{14}; *at once* בְּאֶחָת Pr 28^{18} cf. וְאִנָּקְמָה נְקַם־אַחַת Ju 16^{28}. **6.** *one . . . another, the one . . . the other* א׳ . . . א׳ Ex 17^{12} 18$^{3.4}$ Am 4^{7} 2 S 12^{1} Je 24^{2} 2 Ch 3^{17} Ne 4^{11} +; 2 S 14^{6} rd. הָאֶחָד אֶת־אָחִיו for האחד את־האחד 𝔊 We Dr; *one after another, one by one*, לְאַחַד אֶחָד Is 27^{12} cf. Ec 7^{27}. **7.** as ordinal, *first* (mostly P & late) Gn 1^{5} (P) 2^{11} (J) Ex 39^{10} (P); Ez 10^{14} esp. of first day of month Ex 40^{2} (P) Ezr 3^{6} 10$^{16.17}$ Ne 8^{2} Hg 1^{1}; *first year*, שְׁנַת אַחַת 2 Ch 36^{22} Ezr 1^{1} Dn 1^{21} 9$^{1.2}$ 11^{1} abs. Jb 42^{14}; cf. *first* (day, יוֹם om.) Gn 8$^{5.13}$ בְּאֶחָד לַחֹדֶשׁ; so Ex 40^{17} Lv 23^{24} Nu 1$^{1.18}$ 29^{1} 33^{38} (all P) Dt 1^{3} 2 Ch 29^{17} Ezr 7$^{9.9}$ Ez 26^{1} 29^{17} 31^{1} 32^{1} 45^{18}. **8.** in combin., **a.** אַחַד עָשָׂר *eleven* (cf. עַשְׁתֵּי עָשָׂר) Gn 32^{23} 37^{9} (JE) Dt 1^{2}; so אַחַת־עֶשְׂרֵה Jos 15^{51} (P) 2 K 23^{36} 24^{18} 2 Ch 36$^{5.11}$ Je 52^{1} (precedes noun, exc. Jos 15^{51}); as ordinal, *eleventh* אַחַת עֶשְׂרֵה שָׁנָה Ez 30^{20} 31^{1} cf. 1 K 6^{38} 2 K 9^{29}; **b.** with other numerals, as

cardinal אֶחָד וְאַרְבָּעִים אֶלֶף וַחֲמֵשׁ מֵאוֹת Nu 1^{41} cf $2^{16.28}$ $31^{34.39}$ (all P; 'א precedes other numeral), but אַרְבָּעִים וְאַחַת שָׁנָה ('א following) 1 K 14^{21} 15^{10} 2 K 14^{23} 2 Ch 12^{13} cf 2 K 22^{1} = 2 Ch 34^{1}, 2 K 24^{18} = Je 52^{1} = 2 Ch 36^{11}; Jos 12^{24} (D) Is 30^{17} Ezr 2^{26} = Ne 7^{30} cf. v^{37}, Dn 10^{13}, as ordinal בְּאַחַת וְשֵׁשׁ מֵאוֹת שָׁנָה Gn 8^{13} (P) Ex 12^{18} (P), 1 Ch 24^{17} 25^{28} 2 Ch 16^{13} ('א preceding), but 1 K 16^{23} Hg 2^{1} ('א following)

†אֵחוּד **n.pr.m.** (*union* fr אחד?) a Benjamite 1 Ch 8^{6} = אֵחִי Gn 46^{21}

†חַד **adj.** = אֶחָד Ez 33^{30} del Co, cf 𝔊

אחה (stem assumed for אָח, which however perh bilit & prim so Thes Rob Ges al, Dl^{HA 59} prop *surround, protect;* Dl^{W} comp *aḫu, side* Zehnpfund^{BAS I 510} prop *belong together*, cf Schult. Thes. De Goeje in RS^{Sem 256 N} suggests connection with *ḥayy, family, clan*)

I **אָח** $_{630}$ **n.m. brother** (Ph אח, Ar أَخٌ (cstr أَخُو etc), Sab אח (sf אחיהו) CIS^{iv 1, 17 and 24} al, Eth እኅው: As *aḫu* cf Dl^{W}, Aram אַח, ܐܚܳܐ, Palm, Nab sf אחוהי, אחיה),—abs אָח Gn 24^{29} + (Ez 18^{10} del Co cf 𝔊 𝔖 𝔙; Ew Sm אַךְ, Dl Ba^{Ez x} defends as = *one* cf As *aḫu*) never c art, cstr אֲחִי Gn 10^{21}+, sf אָחִי Gn 4^{9}+, אָחִיךָ Gn 4^{9}+, אָחִיו Gn 4^{2}+, אָחִיהוּ Je 34^{9} + 3t etc, pl אַחִים Gn 13^{8}+, so rd Ho 13^{15} v De^{Compl Var 23} cf sub אָחוּ, cstr אֲחֵי Nu 27^{10}+; sf אַחַי Gn 19^{7}+, אֶחָי 1 S 20^{29} + (but 1 S 30^{23} 𝔊 We אַחֲרֵי for אֶחָי את), אַחֶיךָ Gn 37^{13}+, אֶחָיו Gn 44^{14}+ etc **1.** *brother*, born of same mother (& father) Gn $4^{2.8.9\,10\,11}$ $27^{6.11}$ 44^{20} 49^{5}, cf 28^{2} $29^{10\,10}$ + Ex 4^{14} + oft, also of half-brother Gn $20^{5\,13\,16}$ (on parentage cf v^{12}) $37^{2.4.5}$ +, 2 S $13^{4\,7\,8}$ + **2.** indef = relative, Lot, of Abr Gn 13^{8} $14^{12\,14\,16}$; Jacob, of Laban $29^{12\,15}$ (nephew), hence of kinship in wider sense, member of same tribe Nu 16^{10} $18^{2.6}$ 2 S 19^{13}, of same people Ex $2^{11\,11}$ 4^{18} Dt 15^{12} Ju 14^{3} Is 66^{20} Ne $5^{1.5.8}$ vid esp Lv 19^{17} cf. v^{18} (extended to incl sojourner גֵּר v^{34}), of Israel & Judah 2 S 19^{42}, Isr & Edom Nu 20^{14}, cf of Ishmael Gn 16^{12} 25^{18}, of friend 2 S 1^{26} 1 K 9^{13} $20^{32.33}$, of allies בְּרִית א' Am 1^{9} **3.** fig of resemblance Jb 30^{29} אָח הָיִיתִי לְתַנִּים ‖ רֵעַ לִבְנוֹת יַעֲנָה i e by reason of his crying, cf Di, Pr 18^{9} מִתְרַפֶּה בִמְלַאכְתּוֹ אָח הוּא לְבַעַל מַשְׁחִית. **4.** in phr *one another* אִישׁ אָחִיו Gn 9^{5} Jo 2^{8} Zc 7^{10}, אִישׁ אָחִיו Gn 13^{11} + 25t + Ex 32^{27} (where also same phr c רֵעֵהוּ & קְרֹבוֹ—v these words—& also אִישׁ, אַחֵר), for development of idiom cf Dt 15^{2} Is 19^{2} Je $34^{14\,(cf\,15)\,17}$ Ez 38^{21} Hg 2^{22}, usually of men; of faces of golden cherubim Ex 25^{20} 37^{9}, of scales of crocodile Jb 41^{9} (אָח *firepot* v. sub II. אחח.)

אַחְאָב $_{91}$ **n.pr.m.** Ahab (*father's brother*, = אחיאב No^{ZMG 1886, 172}, Ἀχίαβος was a nephew of Herod, cf like name in Syr., given *ob maximum cum patre suo similitudinem*, Bar Hebræus in Euseb^{Chron II 23} cf LCB^{1879, 1339} In many cases, however, the mng of n pr. comp with אח is dub, & perfect consistency, especially in comparison with cpds of אָב, seems impossible, cf rem sub אביאל, and further We^{Skizzen, III 1f}, Dl^{Pr cap. vi})—אַחְאָב 1 K 16^{28}+, וְכאחב Je 29^{22}— **1.** son of Omri, king of Isr. 1 K $16^{28.29}$ $18^{1.2.3}$ $20^{2\,13\,14}$ + 41 t 1 K, 27 t 2 K, 14 t. 2 Ch, Mi 6^{16} †**2.** false prophet, time of Jerem. Je $29^{21.22}$.

אֶחְאָב v אַחְאָב

†**אַחְבָּן** **n.pr m** (*brother of an intelligent one*) son of Abishur, of Judah 1 Ch 2^{29}.

†**אֲחוּמַי** **n pr.m.** descendant of Judah 1 Ch 4^{2}.

†**אֲחִיאָם** **n.pr.m.** one of David's heroes 2 S 23^{33} 1 Ch 11^{35}

†**אֲחִיָּה, אֲחִיָּהוּ** (always, exc where other form noted), **אֲחִי** **n.pr m** (*brother of Yah(u)*, cf Ph חמלך *brother of Milk*, & esp אחתמלך *sister of Milk*, where אחת must be cstr since מלך is a male deity, cf Carth חתמלקרת Euting^{214}) **1.** a priest 1 S $14^{3\,18}$ **2.** a scribe 1 K 4^{3} **3** a prophet 1 K $11^{29.30}$ 12^{15} $14^{2\,4}$ 2 Ch 9^{29}, 1 K $14^{4.5.6\,18}$ 2 Ch 10^{15} (last five אֲחִיָּהוּ) **4.** father of king Baasha 1 K $15^{27\,29.33}$ 21^{22} 2 K 9^{9} **5.** grandson of Hezron 1 Ch 2^{25}, or perh **n pr.f.,** mother of preceding four, cf. Be. **6.** son of Ehud, of Benj 1 Ch 8^{7} = אֲחוֹחַ v^{4}. **7.** one of Dvd's heroes 1 Ch 11^{36} **8.** a Levite, Dvd's time 1 Ch 26^{20} **9.** a chief man under Nehem. Ne 10^{27} **10.** a Gadite 1 Ch 5^{15} (אֲחִי) **11.** a man of Asher 1 Ch 7^{34} (*id*)

†**אֲחִיהוּד** **n.pr.m.** prince of Asher Nu 34^{27}, (*brother of majesty*, cf הוד, אביהוד, v. also אֲחִיחֻד)

†**אַחְיוֹ** **n.pr.m.** (= אחיון, i e *fraternal*). **1.** a son of Aminadab, brother of Uzzah 2 S $6^{3.4}$ (𝔊 אֶחָיו, We אחיו, but v Dr) 1 Ch 13^{7} (𝔊 אֶחָיו). **2.** a Benjamite 1 Ch 8^{14}, but rd אֶחָיו 𝔊 Be **3.** a Benjamite 1 Ch 8^{31} = 9^{37} (> 𝔊 אֶחָיו)

†**אֲחִיחֻד** **n.pr.m.** (prob = אחיהוד q.v) son of Ehud, a Benjamite 1 Ch 8^{7}

†**אֲחִיטוּב** **n.pr.m.** (*my brother is goodness*) **1.** grandson of Eli 1 S 14^{3} 1 Ch $5^{33.34.37\,38}$, father

of Ahimelech 1 S $22^{9.20}$ (אֲחִטוּב) $v^{11.12}$ (on identity of pers. v. Be 1 Ch 5^{33}). **2.** father of Zadok 2 S 8^{17} (= 1 Ch 18^{16}), but We rds. Ahim. son of Ahitub; 1 Ch 5^{37} Ezr 7^{2}; grandfather of Zadok 1 Ch 9^{11} Ne 11^{11} (on all cf. We l.c.)

†**אֲחִילוּד**† **n.pr.m.** (acc. to Thes = אֲחִי יָלוּד *child's brother* (?)) **1.** father of Jehoshaphat, David's chronicler 2 S 8^{16} 20^{24} 1 K 4^{3} 1 Ch 18^{15}. **2.** father of Baana, officer of Solomon 1 K 4^{12}.

†**אֲחִימוֹת**† **n.pr.m.** (*my brother is death*) a Levite 1 Ch 6^{10} (cf. מַחַת 1 Ch 6^{20} 2 Ch 29^{12}).

†**אֲחִימֶלֶךְ**† **n.pr.m.** (*brother of Melek*, Ph. חמלך, חמלכת; v. also אחיהו supr.) **1.** priest in Saul's (Dvd's) time 1 S $21^{2.2.3.9}$ $22^{14.16}$ (אֲחִימָ֫לֶךְ) 1 Ch 24^{31} ψ 52^{2} (title); son of Ahitub 1 S 22 $^{9.11 (cf. 12).20}$; father of Abiathar 1 S 23^{6} 30^{7}; so also 2 S 8^{17} 𝔖 Ew We Th Dr; where MT אחימ׳ בֶּן־אביתר; whence *id.* wrongly 1 Ch 24^{6}, cf. v^{4} (אֲחִ׳ מִבְּנֵי אִיתָמָר) & 18^{16} (where rd. אֲחִ׳ for אֲבִ׳). **2.** a Hittite 1 S 26^{6}.

†**אֲחִימַן**† **n.pr.m.** (*my brother is a gift?* so Thes; cf. Ar. مَنّ) **1.** a son of Anak Nu 13^{22} Ju 1^{10}; אֲחִימָן Jos 15^{14}. **2.** a Levite, אֲחִימָן, 1 Ch 9^{17}.

†**אֲחִימַעַץ**† **n.pr.m.** (*my brother is wrath*) **1.** son of Zadok 2 S $15^{27.36}$ $17^{17.20}$ $18^{19.22.23.27.28.29}$ 1 Ch 5^{34} (אֲחִימָ֑עַץ) v^{35} 6^{38}; perh. also 1 K 4^{15} (son-in-law of Sol.) **2.** אֲחִימָ֫עַץ, father-in-law of Saul 1 S 14^{50}.

†**אַחְיָן**† **n.pr.m.** (*fraternal*, Aram. ܐܚܝܢ) a Manassite 1 Ch 7^{19}.

†**אֲחִינָדָב**† **n.pr.m.** (*my brother is noble*) an officer of Solomon 1 K 4^{14}.

†**אֲחִינֹעַם**† **n.pr.f.** (*my brother is delight*) **1.** wife of Saul 1 S 14^{50} (daughter of Ahimaaz). **2.** Jezreelitess, wife of David 1 S 25^{43} 27^{3} 30^{5} 2 S 2^{2} 3^{2} 1 Ch 3^{1}.

†**אֲחִיסָמָךְ**† **n.pr.m.** (*my brother has supported*) father of Oholiab, a workman on tabern. Ex 31^{6} 35^{34} 38^{23}.

†**אֲחִיעֶזֶר**† **n.pr.m.** (*my brother is help*, cf. As. *Aḫulê'te, my brother is strength*, $Dl^{Pr\ 202}$) **1.** a chief of Dan Nu 1^{12} 2^{25} $7^{66.71}$ 10^{25}. **2.** one of David's heroes 1 Ch 12^{3}.

†**אֲחִיקָם**† **n.pr.m.** (*my brother has arisen*) son of Shaphan, Josiah's time 2 K $22^{12.14}$ 2 Ch 34^{20}; protector of Jerem. Je 26^{24}; father of Gedaliah 2 K 25^{22} Je 39^{14} $40^{5.6.7.9.11.14.16}$ $41^{1.2.6.10.16.18}$ 43^{6}.

†**אֲחִירָם** **n.pr.m.** (*brother of* (*the*) *lofty* = Ph. חרם v. חִירָם; cf. אֲבִירָם) son of Benj. Nu 26^{38} (prob. = אחרח 1 Ch 8^{1} v. Be) (cf. אֵחִי וְרֹאשׁ Gn 46^{21}).

†**חִירָם** **n.pr.m.** Hiram (Ph. חרם; abbr. fr. foregoing)—ח׳ 2 S 5^{11} + 18 t. 1 K + Kt 1 Ch 14^{1} 2 Ch 4^{11} 9^{10} (all Qr חוּרָם); חִירוֹם 1 K $5^{24.32}$ 7^{40}; also חוּרָם 1 Ch 8^{5} + 9 t. Ch.—**1.** king of Tyre, contemp. of David & Solomon 2 S 5^{11} 1 K $5^{15.15.16.21.22.24.25.25.26.32}$ $9^{11.11.12.14.27}$ $10^{11.22}$ 1 Ch 14^{1} 2 Ch $2^{2.10.11}$ $8^{2.18}$ $9^{10.21}$. **2.** an artificer of Tyre, sent by Hiram the king 1 K $7^{13.40.40.45}$ 2 Ch 2^{12} $4^{11.11.16}$. **3.** a Benjamite 1 Ch 8^{5}.

†**אֲחִירָמִי**† **adj.gent.** הָא׳ as n.coll. Nu 26^{38}.

†**אֲחִירַע**† **n.pr.m.** (*my brother is evil*) a chief of Naphtali Nu 1^{15} 2^{29} $7^{78.83}$ 10^{27}.

†**אֲחִישָׁחַר**† **n.pr.m.** (*brother of* (*the*) *dawn*, As. *Aḫšêri* $Dl^{Pr\ 202}$) a Benjamite 1 Ch 7^{10}.

†**אֲחִישָׁר**† **n.pr.m.** (*my brother has sung*) over Solomon's household 1 K 4^{6}.

†**אֲחִיתֹפֶל**† **n.pr.m.** (*my brother is folly?*) David's trusted & traitorous counsellor 2 S 15 $^{12.31.31.34}$ $16^{15.20.21.23.23}$ $17^{1.6.7.14.14.15}$ 21^{23} 23^{34} 1 Ch $27^{33.34}$.

†**אַחֲוָה**† **n.f.** brotherhood הָא׳ Zc 11^{14} (between Judah & Israel).

† **חִיאֵל** **n.pr.m.** (prob. (אֲ)חִיאֵל *brother of Ēl*, 𝔊 Ἀχειήλ; cf. חירם & Ph. חמלך, etc.; v. $Bae^{Rel\ 156}$) a Bethelite, rebuilder of Jericho 1 K 16^{34}.

אָחוֹת $_{114}$ **n.f.** sister (Ph. אחת, Aram. אֲחָת, ܚܳܬܳܐ, Ar. أُخْتٌ, As. *aḫâtu*, Dl^{W}, Eth. እኅት: Sab. in n.pr. אחתאמהו $Os^{ZMG\ 1865,\ 273}$) — abs. א׳ 2 S 13^{1} + (never with art.); cstr. אֲחוֹת Gn 4^{22}+; sf. אֲחֹתִי (אֲחוֹתִי) Gn 12^{13}+, etc.; *pl.* sf. אַחְיֹתַי (Qr אַחְיוֹתַי) Jos 2^{13}; אֲחוֹתַיִךְ Ez 16^{51} (Qr; Kt אחותך) + 2 t. (Co all אחיו׳); אַחְיוֹתֵךְ Ez 16^{52} (Co ־תיך); אֲחוֹתֵךְ Ez 16^{52} (must be pl., but del. Co); אַחְיֹתָיו Jb 42^{11}; אֲחוֹתֵיכֶם Ho 2^{3}; אַחְיֹתֵיהֶם 1 Ch 2^{16} Jb 1^{4} — **1.** *sister* Gn 4^{22} $12^{13.19}$; $20^{2.5.12}$ (same father, diff. mother) so Lv 18^{11} cf. Ez 22^{11}; Gn $24^{30.30}$ +, Ex $2^{4.7}$; Lv 18^{9} (either parent same) so Dt 27^{22} Nu 6^{7} 2 S $13^{1.2.4}$ +, Ct $8^{8.8}$; called upon, in mourning for dead Je 22^{18}; = near relative Gn $24^{59.60}$ (or because Laban prominent? so Di); woman of same nationality Nu 25^{18} cf. Ho 2^{3}. **2.** = beloved Ct $4^{9.10.12}$ $5^{1.2}$ (4 t. ‖ כַּלָּה *bride*; phr. orig. implying that marriage with half-sister — of same father—was allowed? cf. $Nö^{ZMG\ 1886,\ 150}$, & Gn 20^{12}). **3.** symbol. of Judah, Samaria,

Sodom & Jerusalem Je 3[7.8.10] Ez 16[45.52.52 (del Co)] +, 23[4.11]+ **4.** fig of intimate connection אמר לַחָכְמָה אֲחֹתִי אָתְּ .. קָרָאתִי Jb 17[14], אמֹר לַחָכְמָה אֲחֹתִי אָתְּ Pr 7[4] †**5.** *another,* אִשָּׁה אֶל־אֲחֹתָהּ, of curtains of tabern Ex 26[3.3.6], loops v[5], tenons v[17], of wings of living creatures, Ezek 's vision Ez 1[9.23] 3[13]; not of persons, but vid רעות

†**אָחוּ n. m.** [Jb 8.11] **coll reeds, rushes** (Aram אָחוּא, orig. Egypt, cf demot *aχu* fr *aχa be green,* v Ebers[AG & BB Mos. 338], Wied[Sammlung 16]) Gn 41[2.18] (E) Jb 8[11], also Ho 13[15] where rd אֲחִים pl. for אַחְוִים (cf AV), or fr a parall form [אָחָה], v De[Compl Var 23 f].

חוה v אַחֲוָה

†**אָחַז** [68] **vb. grasp, take hold, take possession** (Ar أَخَذَ, Sab. אחד Sab Denkm [39], Aram אֲחַד, أحد, As *aḫazu,* Eth አኀዘ:)—**Qal** *Pf* אָחַז Ex 15[14]+, אָחֲזָה Jb 23[11] Is 33[14], sf אֲחָזַנִי 2 S 1[9], 1 s sf אֲחַזְתִּיו Ct 3[4], etc, *Impf* יֹאחֵז Jb 17[9]+, וַיֹּאחֶז 2 S 6[6], 3 fs תֹּאחֵז Dt 32[41], וַתֹּאחֶז Ru 3[15], וַתֹּחֶז 2 S 20[9], וָאֹחֵז Ju 20[6], יֹאחֵזוּן Is 13[8], *sf* יֹאחֲזֵמוֹ Ex 15[15]; יֹאחֲזוּךְ Je 13[21], etc,—+ as פ׳ gutt וַיֶּאֱחֹז Ju 16[3] 1 K 6[10], 2 ms תֶּאֱחֹז Ec 7[18], *Inf* אֱחֹז 1 K 6[6], אֱחֹז 1 Ch 13[9]+3 t, *Imv* אֱחֹז Ex 4[4] 2 S 2[21], אֶחֱזִי Ru 3[15], אֶחֱזוּ Ct 2[15], אֶחֱזוּ Ne 7[3], *Pt act* אֹחֵז 2 Ch 25[5], *pass* אָחוּז Est 1[6], etc,—*grasp, take hold of,* sq בְּ Gn 25[26] Ex 4[4] (both J) Ju 16[3] 20[6] (=וַיַּחֲזֵק בְּ 19[29]) 2 S 4[10] 6[6] 20[9] 1 K 1[51] Ru 3[15.15]; 1 K 6[6] of beams having hold in a wall, (cf בית אֲבָנִים יֶחֱזֶה Jb 8[17]; Hoffm rds יֹאחֵז=יֶחֱזֶה), also Ct 7[9] of taking hold of branches, in metaph., poet fig, of God's seizing man in wrath Jb 16[12], taking hold graciously ψ 73[23]; taking hold of judgment Dt 32[41], subj man בַּאֲשֻׁרוֹ אָחֲזָה רַגְלִי Jb 23[11] (דַּרְכּוֹ שָׁמַרְתִּי ‖) cf also 17[9]), of taking hold of folly Ec 2[3] cf. 7[18], subj הַשַּׁחַר Jb 38[13], לֶאֱחֹז בְּכַנְפוֹת הָאָרֶץ, also sq acc Ju 1[6] 12[6] 16[21] 2 S 2[21] Is 5[29] Ct 2[15] 3[4] 1 Ch 13[9] 2 Ch 25[5] ψ 56[1] 137[9], cf 1 K 6[10] (cf v[6] supr), subj וַיֹּא׳ אֶת־הַיָּצוּעַ, הַבַּיִת בַּעֲצֵי אֲרָזִים, of a snare catching the heel, in metaph Jb 18[9], fig, subj God ψ 77[5], God's hand 139[10], subj pain, sorrow, fear, etc Ex 15[14.15] 2 S 1[9] Jb 21[6] 30[16] ψ 48[7] 119[53] Is 21[3] 33[14] Je 13[21] 49[24], subj man, obj fear, etc Jb 18[20] Is 13[8], obj דֶּרֶךְ *take one's way* Jb 17[9] יֹאחֵז צַדִּיק דַּרְכּוֹ AV RV *hold on his way* (cf 23[11] supr, & As *sabâtu urḫu,* e g V R[1.74]),—abs Ne 7[3] of barring gates, pt pass *caught* Ec 9[12], *fastened, held* Est 1[6], *taken* (by lot) 1 Ch 24[6.6.6] (on text v Ot), *taken out* of a number Nu 31[30.47]; pt. act of same form אֲחֻזֵי חֶרֶב Ct 3[8] cf Thes Ba[NB 175] & Eth. pt, similarly Aram אָחִיד, e g 𝔗 Am 2[5], أحيد e g 𝔖 Ju 8[10] 1 Ch 5[18], & Ez 41[6.6] (but v. Co) **Niph.** *Pf* 3 pl נֹאחֲזוּ Jos 22[9], ונא׳ (cons) Nu 32[30]; *Impf.* וַיֵּאָחֲזוּ Gn 47[27], *Imv* הֵאָחֲזוּ Gn 34[10] Jos 22[19], *Pt* נֶאֱחָז Gn 22[13], נֶאֱחָזִים Ec 9[12],—*be caught* Gn 22[13] Ec 9[12], elsewhere *have possessions* Gn 34[10] 47[27] Nu 32[30] Jos 22[9.19] (P) **Pi.** *Pt* מְאַחֵז Jb 26[9] c acc *enclose, overlay* (so As Dl[W p 294], cf Aram أحد, *shut*) **Hoph.** *Pt* pl מָאֳחָזִים 2 Ch 9[18] *fastened to* sq לְ.

אָחָז n.pr.m. (*he hath grasped,* abbrev for יְהוֹאָחָז (q v) cf As *Ia-u-ḫa-zi* (i e. Ahaz) COT on 2 K 16[9]) **1.** king of Judah, son of Jotham, father of Hezekiah 2 K 15[38] 16[1.2.5.7.8]+ 13 t 2 K, Is 1[1] 7[1.3.10.12] 14[28] 38[8], 1 Ch 3[13] 2 Ch 27[9] +8 t 2 Ch, Ho 1[1] Mi 1[1] **2.** son of Micah, & great-grandson of Jonathan 1 Ch 8[35.36] 9[42] (+9[41] cf. 𝔊L 𝔙)

†**אֲחֻזָּה** [66] **n.f.** possession—א׳ Gn 47[11]+ 11 t, cstr אֲחֻזַּת Gn 17[8]+21 t.; sf אֲחֻזָּתְךָ ψ 2[8], —*possession,* P & late, of landed property Gn 47[11] Lv 14[34] 25[10.13.24.27.28.33 (houses) 41.45.46] Nu 27[4] 32[5.22.29] 35[8] Dt 32[49] Jos 21[12.39] Ez 44[28] 45[5.6.7.7.8] 46[18.18.18] 48[20.21.22.22] 1 Ch 7[28] 9[2] 2 Ch 11[14] 31[1] Ne 11[3]; c אֶרֶץ, א׳ אֲחֻזָּה = *land possessed, one's own land* Gn 36[43] Lv 14[34] 25[21] Nu 35[28] Jos 22[4.9.19.19], cf אֲחֻזַּת הָאָרֶץ Lv 27[24], c שָׂדֶה, שׂ׳ אֲחֻזָּה Lv 27[16.22.28], cf v[21], c עִיר, ע׳ אֲחֻזָּה Lv 25[32.33], נַחֲלָה, אֲחֻזַּת נַחֲלָה = *possession by right of inheritance* Nu 27[7] 32[32], & א׳ בְּנַחֲלָה, נַחֲלַת א׳ 35[2] cf Ez 46[16] (but Co as Nu 27[7] so B), אֲחֻזַּת קֶבֶר Gn 23[4.9.20] 49[30] 50[13]; א׳ עוֹלָם Gn 17[8] 48[4] Lv 25[34], in promise to Davidic king וַאֲחֻזָּתְךָ אַפְסֵי־אָרֶץ ψ 2[8] (נַחֲלָה ‖), fig of י׳ as portion of Levit priests Ez 44[28] (נַחֲלָה ‖)

אֲחַזְיָה, אֲחַזְיָהוּ, אַחְזַי n.pr.m. (*Yah(u) hath grasped,* 𝔊 'Οχοζ(ε)ιας 1 K 22[52] etc, cf Lag[BN 53]) **1.** king of Isr., son of Ahab 1 K 22[40.50.52] 2 K 1[18] 2 Ch 20[37] (אֲחַזְיָהוּ), +2 K 1[2] 2 Ch 20[35] (אֲחַזְיָה) **2.** king of Judah, son of Joram 2 K 8[24.25] 9[21] 10[13] 11[1] 12[19] 13[1] 14[13] 1 Ch 3[11] 22[1]+15 t 2 K 1 Ch (all אֲחַזְיָהוּ), 2 K 9[16.23.27.29] 11[2] (אֲחַזְיָה) **3.** אַחְזַי a priest Ne 11[13] (for which יַחְזֵרָה 1 Ch 9[12] v Sm[Listen, Taf. I])

†**אֲחֻזָּם n.pr.m.** (*possessor*) a man of Judah 1 Ch 4[6].

†**אֲחֻזַּת n.pr.m.** (*possession*) friend of Abimelech Gn 26[26]

I **אחח** (*cry, howl,* onomat, cf Ar أَخّ)

†**[אֹחַ] n.[m.]** jackal (As *aḫû* Dl[W]) pl אֹחִים Is 13[21] וּמָלְאוּ בָתֵּיהֶם א׳ (צִיִּים ‖)

II **אחח**?

†II. **אָח n.f** fire-pot, brasier (Ar. أَجّ, in

Thes, is an error) alw. c. art. Je 36^{22} הָאָ׳ לְפָנָיו מְבֹעָרֶת *the brasier before him was burning*; v^{23} הָאֵשׁ אֲשֶׁר אֶל־הָאָ׳; v^{23} הָאֵשׁ אֲשֶׁר עַל־הָאָ׳ (I. אָח, *brother* v. sub אחה; III. אָח interj., p. 25).

†**אֲחוֹחַ** **n.pr.m.** a Benjamite 1 Ch 8^{4} (perh. corruption of אחיה v^{7} q. v.)

†**אֲחוֹחִי** (אֲחֹחִי) **adj.gent.** 2 S 23^{9} (where for בֶּן־אָ׳ rd. הָאָ׳ We Dr; ref. unknown: Klo prop. (בֶּן אִישׁ חַיִ(ל) cf. v^{20}) v^{28} = 1 Ch $11^{12.29}$ 27^{4}.

אֲחִי **n.pr.m.** a son of Benjamin Gn 46^{21} (P) (perh. corruption of אֲחִירָם Nu 26^{38} (P); so also אַחְרַח 1 Ch 8^{1} cf. אַחֵר 7^{12} & comm.)

אחל (existence & meaning dub.)

†**אַחְלַי** **n.pr.** (Dl[Pr 210] trans. *O! would that!* (cf. אַחֲלַי sub III. אָח supr. p. 25) & comp. interjectional Bab. name *Aḫulapia, O! that I at last!* Zim[BP 116]; cf. Ol[§ 277]; otherwise Hal[JAS 7, x. 360]) **1. f.** daughter of Sheshan 1 Ch 2^{31}; so Be Öt al. in view of v^{34}. **2. m.** father of one of David's mighty men (not in 2 S 23) 1 Ch 11^{41}.

אַחְלָב v. חלב.

†**אַחְלָמָה** **n.f.** perh. amethyst (etym. dub.; sub חלם Thes q.v.; Hal[JAs 7, x. 426] fr. חלם *être fort, solide;* Di Kn comp. Talm. חַלָּמִית, *malva* & think of green malachite; Dl[HA 36 N] der. fr. Aram. land *Aḫlamû*), *amethyst* acc. to 𝔊𝔙 Josephus; v. also Lag[GGA 1884, 285], but cf. Di; one of the gems on the ephod Ex 28^{19} 39^{12}.

אֲחַסְבַּי **n.pr.m.** father of Eliphelet, one of David's heroes 2 S 23^{34}. (Meaning dub.; 1 Ch 11^{35} has אוּר:, sq. חֵפֶר:; txt. prob. corrupt.)

†**אחר** **vb.** **to remain behind, delay, tarry** (Ar. أَخَّرَ *to put off*, also *to remain behind;* Aram. Pa. אַחַר, Aph. ܐܘܚܪ, Shaph. ܫܘܚܪ, Sab. אחר Osiander[ZMG 1865, 197]; אהחר DHM[Epigr. Denkm. 34]). †**Qal** once only Gn 32^{5} וָאֵחַר (contr. fr. וָאֶאֱחַר cf. אֹהֵב Pr 8^{17}) *and I have tarried* until now. †**Pi.** *Pf.* אֵחַר Gn 34^{19}; אֶחֱרוּ Ju 5^{28}; *Impf.* יְאַחֵר, תְּאַחֵר (3 t. תְּאַחַר) etc. Gn 24^{56} + 9 t.; *Pt.* (־רֵי) מְאַחֲרִים 3 t. **1.** intensive, *delay, tarry*, abs. Ju 5^{28} (‖ בֹּשֵׁשׁ לָבוֹא) Is 46^{13} and my salvation לֹא תְאַחֵר Hb 2^{3} ψ 40^{18} = 70^{6} Dn 9^{19}; with לְ & inf. Gn 34^{19}.—Pr 23^{30} מְאַחֲרִים עַל־הַיָּיִן *those tarrying* over the wine, Is 5^{11} מְאַחֲרֵי בַנֶּשֶׁף, ψ 127^{2} מְאַחֲרֵי שֶׁבֶת ‖ מַשְׁכִּימֵי קוּם). **2.** causat. of Qal, *cause one to delay, hinder* Gn 24^{56}; *keep back* (= *bring late*) Ex 22^{28}; with לְ & inf. *delay to . . .* Dt 23^{22} quoted Ec 5^{3}: ellipt. Dt 7^{10} *he delayeth* (it, the recompense) not to his enemy. —2 S 20^{5} Qr וַיּוֹחֶר is taken by Ol[§ 241 a] as Qal (cf. וַתֹּחֶז v^{9} from אָחַז), by Sta[§ 498 c] Kö[I. 307] Ges[§ 68 2 Rem] as Hiph. (lit. *shewed, exhibited delay*): on the Kt (וַיִּיחֶר ?) v. Dr[Sm].

I. **אַחֵר** **adj.** **another** (prop. *one coming behind*), f. אַחֶרֶת (with dag. f. implic.); pl. אֲחֵרִים (as if from sg. אָחֵר), once Jb 31^{10} אֲחֵרִין, אֲחֵרוֹת (= Ar. آخَرُ, Sab. אאחר, As. *aḫru* future, fpl. as subst. *aḫrat ûmê* future of days) Gn 4^{25} זֶרַע אַחֵר *another* seed 8^{10} שִׁבְעַת יָמִים אֲחֵרִים *even other* days Ex 22^{4} בִּשְׂדֵה אַחֵר in the field of *another* + oft.; אִישׁ אַחֵר *another* man (husband) Gn 29^{19} Dt 24^{2} Je 3^{1}; חָצֵר הָאַחֶרֶת 1 K 7^{8} *the other* court, v. חָצֵר; הַחוֹמָה א׳ 2 Ch 32^{5} the *other* wall, v. חוֹמָה. Appended to a n. pr. for distinction Ezr 2^{31} = Ne 7^{34} (see v^{7} = Ne v^{12}) Ne 7^{33} (prob. here txt. err., v. Be Ry[18]: not in Ezr 2^{29}). Often with the collat. sense of *different*, as בְּגָדִים א׳ *other* garments Lv 6^{4} 1 S 28^{8} Ez 42^{14} 44^{19}; עָפָר, אֲבָנִים Lv 14^{42}; רוּחַ Nu 14^{24}; וְנֶהְפַּכְתָּ לְאִישׁ א׳ 1 S 10^{6}; לֵב v^{9} Ez 11^{19} (𝔊 Hi Sm); שֵׁם Is 65^{15} (cf. 62^{2} חָדָשׁ); with that of *strange, alien*, as אִישׁ א׳ Dt $20^{5.6.7}$ 28^{30} (so אַחֵר, אֲחֵרִים alone ψ 109^{8} Jb $31^{8.10}$ Is 65^{22} Je 6^{12} 8^{10} al.); עַם Dt 28^{32}; אֶרֶץ 29^{27} Je 22^{26}; אִשָּׁה Ju 11^{2}; לָשׁוֹן Is 28^{11} (‖ בְּלַעֲגֵי שָׂפָה); esp. in the phrase אֱלֹהִים אֲחֵרִים *other gods* (63 t.) Ex 20^{3} (= Dt 5^{7}) 23^{13} (both JE) Jos $24^{2.16}$ (E) 1 S 26^{19} Ho 3^{1}, & particularly in Dt (6^{14} 8^{19} + 15 t.) & Deut. writers, as Jos 23^{16} Ju $2^{12.17.19}$ Je (18 t.) & compiler of Kings; אֵל אַחֵר once Ex 34^{14} (JE). So אַחֵר alone Is 42^{8} ψ 16^{4}. † Of time, *following, next* (rare) בַּשָּׁנָה הָאָ׳ Gn 17^{21} (P) in the *next* year; 2 K 6^{29} בַּיּוֹם הָאָ׳; דּוֹר א׳ Joel 1^{3} ψ 109^{13} poet. *the next* generation (Ju 2^{10} in prose = *another* generation).

אַחַר prop. subst. *the hinder* or *following part* (cf. the pl.) **1. adv. a.** of place, behind, twice Gn 22^{13} (many MSS. Sam. 𝔊 𝔖 Ol Ew read אֶחָד v. Di) ψ 68^{26}. **b.** of time, **afterwards** Gn 10^{18} 18^{5} 24^{55} 30^{21} Ju 19^{5} +; וְאַחַר in laws of P, as Lv $14^{8.19}$ 15^{28} 22^{7} Nu 5^{26} al. **2. prep. a.** of place, behind, after Ex 3^{1} 11^{5} 2 K 11^{6} Ct 2^{9} Is 57^{8}: הָלַךְ אַחַר *to go after, follow* Gn 37^{17} 2 K 13^{2} 23^{3} Is 65^{2} Ez 13^{3} Jb 31^{7}; הָיָה אַחַר 1 S 12^{14}; מֵאַחַר *from after* † 2 S 7^{8} ψ 78^{71} Is 59^{13}. **b.** of time, after Gn 9^{28} Lv 25^{15} al; אַחַר הַדְּבָרִים הָאֵלֶּה *after* these things † Gn 15^{1} 22^{1} 39^{7} 40^{1} 1 K 17^{17} 21^{1} Ezr 7^{1} Est 2^{1} 3^{1}; אַחַר כֵּן † Lv 14^{36} Dt 21^{13} 1 S 10^{5}; אַחַר זֶה (late) 2 Ch 32^{9}; sq. inf. † Nu 6^{19} Je 40^{1} 1 Ch 2^{24} Jb 21^{3}; עַד אַחַר *till after* † Ne 13^{19}. **c.** Ne 5^{15} strangely: Ew RV *besides;* but text prob. corrupt, v. Be Ry. **3.** †**conj.** אַחַר אֲשֶׁר

after that Ez 40^{1}; and without אשר Lv 14^{43} Je 41^{16} Jb 42^{7}. As prep & conj the pl אַחֲרֵי is much more freq., which in any case must be used before suffixes **Plur.** only cstr. אַחֲרֵי with sf. אַחֲרַי, אַחֲרֶיךָ, etc **1. subst.** hinder part †2 S 2^{23} בְּאַחֲרֵי הַחֲנִית with the *hinder end* of the spear **2. prep. a.** of place, **behind, after** Gn 18^{10} והוא אַחֲרָיו and it *behind* him Dt 11^{30} Ju 5^{14} 1 S 14^{13} 21^{10}, Ho 5^{8} אַחֲרֶיךָ Behind thee! (sc Look *or* The foe is), with a vb as הבים to look Gn 19^{17} 1 S 24^{9}, הניע ראש to shake the head 2 K 19^{21} (=Is 37^{22}), esp verbs expressing or implying motion, as בָּא to enter in (v Dr 2 S 20^{14}), פָּנָה, מלא, הָלַךְ, הָיָה, דָּלַק, דָּבַק, בער, הִשְׁלִיךְ, רָדַף (see these words) **b.** of time, **after** Gn 9^{9} זַרְעֲכֶם אַחֲרֵיכֶם your seed *after* you; similarly 17$^{7-10.19}$ 35^{12} 48^{4} Ex 28^{43} Nu 25^{13} all P (also Dt 1^{8} 4^{37} 10^{15} 1 S 24^{22} 2 S 7^{12} ||), & with בָּנָיו Gn 18^{19} J (+ ביתו) Ex 29^{29} P Lv 25^{46} H Dt 4^{40} 12$^{25.28}$ Je 32$^{18.39}$ 1 Ch 28^{8} Pr 20^{7}, דורותינו Jos 22^{27}, ביתו Jb 21^{21}, Ex 10^{14} Ju 10^{3} etc, with inf Gn 5^{4} אַחֲרֵי הולידו *after his begetting* Sheth, 13^{14} 14^{17} 18^{12} 25^{11} + oft, אַחֲרֵי־כֵן *afterwards* Gn 6^{4} (אחרי כן אשר = *afterwards, when*, cf 2 Ch 35^{20}) 15^{14} 23^{19} 25^{26} 32^{21} 41^{31} 45^{15} etc; ויהי אחרי־כן as a formula of transition chiefly in 2 S (2^{1} 8^{1} || 10^{1} || 13^{1} 21^{18} ||) cf 1 S 24^{6} Ju 16^{4} 2 K 6^{24} 2 Ch 20^{1} 24^{4}†, in late Heb אַחֲרֵי זאת †Jb 42^{16} Ezr 9^{10} 2 Ch 21^{18} (+ כָּל־) 35^{20} (do), cf Aram. אַחֲרֵי דְנָה Dn 2$^{29.45}$, and בָּאתַר דְּנָה Dn 7$^{6.7}$ —The local (metaph) and temporal senses blend ψ 49^{14} ואחריהם בפיהם ירצו & *after* them (i e following, imitating them) men applaud their speech, cf Jb 21^{33}. **3. conj.** אַחֲרֵי אֲשֶׁר **after that,** with the finite vb Dt 24^{4} Jos 7^{8} 9^{16} 23^{1} 24^{20} +, without אשר †Lv 25^{48} 1 S 5^{9}†. (The most common constr of אחרי is as a prep with the inf cstr) Jos 2^{7} אַחֲרֵי כַּאֲשֶׁר יָצְאוּ must be an error, either for אחרי אשר or for כאשר alone (notice אחריהם twice in the same verse); 2 S 24^{10} rd. אַחֲרֵי סָפַר vid Dr **4.** with other preps —**a.** מֵאַחֲרֵי 57, 1 Ch 17^{7} מִן־אַחֲרֵי (|| 2 S 7^{8} מֵאַחַר), (α) *from behind* Gn 19^{26} 2 S 2^{23}, *from after* i e. *from following after*, usually with שוב or סור 1 S 24^{2} 2 S 2$^{22.26.30}$ 11^{15}, oft with God as obj as Nu 14^{43} 32^{15} Dt 7^{4} Jos 22$^{16.18.23.29}$ 1 S 15^{11} +, with other vbs of motion, as עָלָה 1 S 14^{46} 2 S 20^{2}, נַעֲלָה 2 S 2^{27}, לָקַח Am 7^{15} 1 Ch 17^{7}, זָנָה Ho 1^{2}; pregn Is 30^{21} thy ears shall hear a word מֵאַחֲרֶיךָ *coming from behind* thee, Je 9^{21} (sc נָפַל, see v^{a}) 1 S 13^{7} 𝔊L We Dr חָרְדוּ מֵאַחֲרָיו (β) denoting *position* (מִן = *off, on the side of*, see מִן) *behind* Ex 14$^{19.19}$ Jos 8$^{2.4.14}$ 1 K 10^{19} Ne 4^{7} (מֵאַחֲרֵי לְ) 2 Ch 13^{13b} (γ) of time (rare) †Dt 29^{21} Ec 10^{14}, מֵאַחֲרֵי כֵן †2 S 3^{28} 15^{1} 2 Ch 32^{23} **b.** †אֶל־אַחֲרֵי 2 S 5^{23} 2 K 9^{18} סב אֶל־אַחֲרַי v^{19} Zc 6^{6} **c.** †עַל־אַחֲרֵי Ez 41^{15} *beside, at the back of.*

†אַחֲרַי **adj.** Pr 28^{23} (si vera l.) אָדָם אַחֲרַי a man **that turneth backwards** (cf. Je 7^{24}) so Jos Ki De Ol$^{p\ 429}$ (doubtfully) Now Sta^{§301b} acc. to Ew^{§220a} Hi an abnormal adv = *afterwards*, Lag^{Pr} conj בְּאָרְחוֹ cf 𝔊 ὁδοὺς

אָחוֹר 41 **subst.** (Arab. أُخُر) **the hinder side, back part,** in the sg, mostly in adverbial phrases —**a.** as accus, in poetry *backwards* 23 t. (=prose אֲחֹרַנִּית) with vbs such as נָפַל *fall* Gn 49^{17}, נָסוֹג *be turned* 2 S 1^{22} (|| רֵיקָם תָּשׁוּב), שוב ψ 9^{4} 56^{10} +, נָסוֹג 35^{4} 40^{15} + (of enemies repulsed), 44^{19} Is 50^{5} (from obedience to God), נָזוֹר Is 1^{4}, השיב 44^{25} ψ 44^{11}, הִכָּה 78^{66}; *behind* (opp קדם) ψ 139^{5} Jb 23^{8}, in the phrase פָּנִים ואחור in front and *behind* †1 Ch 19^{10} (altered from מִפָּ׳ וּמֵאָ׳ in 2 S v infr) 2 Ch 13^{14} Ez 2^{10}. **b.** בְּאָחוֹר †Pr 29^{11}, וְחָכָם בְּאָחוֹר יְשַׁבְּחֶנָּה Ges Hi but a wise man stilleth it (רוּחוֹ anger) *backwards* (sc when it would break forth), De *in the background*, sc of his heart (|| כָּל־רוּחוֹ יוֹצִיא כסיל) **c.** לְאָחוֹר (α) as **a.** †ψ 114$^{3.5}$ Je 7^{24}, (β) of time, *hereafter* (cf לְפָנִים = before) †Is 41^{23} 42^{23}. **d.** מֵאָחוֹר *behind* (מִן = on the side of) †2 S 10^{9} Is 9^{11} ופלשתים מאָ׳ מִפָּנִים וּמ׳ in front and *behind*, and the Philistines *behind* (= on the West), opp. אֲרָם מִקֶּדֶם †**Plur.** cstr אַחֲרֵי **hinder part** (of the tabernacle) Ex 26^{12}, (of a man or animal) 33^{23} 1 K 7^{25} (=2 Ch 4^{4}) Ez 8^{16}.

†אֲחֹרַנִּית **adv.** (prop an adj. fem, cf קדרנית Sta^{§367}) **backwards** (=poet אָחוֹר) Gn 9$^{23.23}$ 1 S 4^{18} 1 K 18^{37} 2 K 20$^{10.11}$ Is 38^{8}.

אַחֲרוֹן 51 **f.** אַחֲרוֹנָה, pl אַחֲרֹנִים (also אַחֲרוֹנִים), **adj.** from אַחַר, **coming after** or **behind** (as a compar or superl, acc. to the context), hence **a.** of place, *behind, hindermost* Gn 33$^{2.2}$, הַיָּם הָאַחֲרוֹן *the hinder* (=the Western) sea (i.e the Mediterranean opp. הַיָּם הַקַּדְמוֹנִי the front sea =the Dead Sea, the Semites, in defining the quarters of the heavens, turning naturally to the East, cf קֶדֶם of the East, תֵּימָן, יָמִין of the South, above s v אָחוֹר **d.** and As *mat aharru* 'the Western land,' of Phoenicia & Palestine) †Dt 11^{24} 34^{2} Jo 2^{20} Zc 14^{8}; Jb 18^{20} poet אַחֲרֹנִים Ew Hi Di De *the dwellers in the West* (opp. קַדְמוֹנִים) More commonly **b.** of time, *latter* or *last* (acc. to context) Ex 4^{8} Dt 24^{3} 2 S 19^{12} Is 8^{23}, of God Is 44^{6} (|| רִאשׁוֹן) 48^{12} (do) cf 41^{4}; in genl *subsequent* (vaguely), יוֹם אַ׳ = time *to come* †Is 30^{8} Pr 31^{25} (but Ne 8^{18} הַיּוֹם הָאַ׳ = *the last* day), (הַ)דּוֹר (הָ)אַ׳ *the following* generation †Dt 29^{21} ψ 48^{14} 78$^{4.6}$ 102^{19}, (הָ)אַחֲרֹנִים

they that come after Jb 18^{20} (Ges Schl) Ec 1^{11} 4^{16}, but Is 41^{4} *the last*, Jb 19^{25} וְאַחֲרוֹן עַל־עָפָר יָקוּם and as *one coming after* (me) (and so able to establish my innocence when I am dead) will he (גֹּאֲלִי my Vindicator) arise upon the dust.—The *fem.* is used adverbially (cf. רִאשֹׁנָה)=*afterwards* or *at the last* (acc. to context): (α) absol. †Dan 11^{29}; (β) בָּאַחֲרוֹנָה (opp. בָּרִאשֹׁנָה) †Dt 13^{10} 17^{7} 1 S 29^{2} 2 S 2^{26} 1 K 17^{13} Dn 8^{3}; (γ) לָאַ׳ †Nu 2^{31} (P) Ec 1^{11}.

אַחֲרִית $_{61}$ **n.f. after-part, end;—a.** of place, only ψ 139^{9} (late) א׳ יָם. **b.** of time, *latter part* or actual *close* (acc. to context), opp. רֵאשִׁית; —of year Dt 11^{12}; of a man's life Nu 23^{10} Pr 5^{11} Jb 8^{7} 42^{12}; of a people's existence Nu 24^{20}; =*final lot* Dt $32^{20.29}$ Je 12^{4} 31^{17} ψ 73^{17}; *a future*, i.e. a happy close of life, suggesting sometimes the idea of a posterity, promised to the righteous Pr 23^{18} (|| תִּקְוָה *hope*) 24^{14} Je 29^{11} (לָתֵת לָכֶם א׳ וְתִקְוָה), withheld from the wicked Pr 24^{20} (|| נֵר יִדְעָךְ׃ : v. infr.); the *end* or ultimate *issue* of a course of action Je 5^{31} Pr 14^{12} 23^{32} (of wine, i.e. of indulgence in it) 25^{8} Is 46^{10} (absol., but implicitly of a phase of history) 47^{7} (of the conduct described v^{6b-7a}) Dn 12^{8} Ec 7^{8}; of a prediction = the *event* Is 41^{22}. בְּאַחֲרִית הַיָּמִים *in the end of the days*, a prophetic phrase denoting the final period of the history so far as the speaker's perspective reaches; the sense thus varies with the context, but it often=the ideal or Messianic future; †Gn 49^{1} (of the period of Israel's possession of Canaan) Nu 24^{14} Dt 4^{30} (of the period of Israel's return to God after adversity) 31^{29} (of the period of Israel's rebellion) Ho 3^{5} Is 2^{2} (=Mi 4^{1}) Je 23^{20} (v. Graf)=30^{24} 48^{47} 49^{39} Ez 38^{16} (of the period of Gog's attack upon restored Israel) Dn 2^{28} (Aram.) 10^{14} (of the age of Antiochus Epiphanes): cf. בְּאַ׳ הַשָּׁנִים Ez 38^{8}. **c.** א׳ הַגּוֹיִם Je 50^{12} the *last*, *hindermost* of the nations (of Babylon), opp. ראשית הגוים Am 6^{1} (Israel) cf. Nu 24^{20} (Amalek) chief of the nations. **d.** concr. *posterity* (extension of usage noted above in Pr 24^{20}) ψ $37^{37.38}$ (*possibly* not more than 'a future' here) 109^{13} (|| בְּדוֹר אַחֵר יִמַּח שְׁמָם) Am 4^{2} 9^{1} Ez $23^{25.25}$ (acc. to others, in these four passages, *remnant*, *residue*) Dn 11^{4}.

†II. **אַחַר n.pr.m.** 1 Ch 7^{12} (ident. & meaning quite dub.; Be thinks=אַחֵר **adj.** *another*, to avoid naming Dan (cf. Gn 46^{23} Nu 26^{42}) on account of the narrative Ju 17 f. Öt identifies with שֻׁחִים 8^{8}).

†**אַחְרַח n.pr.m.** a son of Benjamin 1 Ch 8^{1} (perh. corruption of אֲחִירָם Nu 26^{38}, cf. also אֵחִי).

†**אֲחַרְחֵל n.pr.m.** app. a descendant of Judah 1 Ch 4^{8} (deriv. & mng. dub.)

†**אֲחַשְׁדַּרְפְּנִים n.m.pl. satraps** (Pers. *Khshatrapâvan*, *protectors of the realm*, v. Spieg $^{APK\ 215}$ = ἐξατράπης, σατράπης, cf. Lag $^{G.\ Abh.\ 68,\ 14;\ Sem.\ i.\ 42\ f}$, who rds. אֲחַשְׁדַּרְפָּן)—א׳ Est 8^{9} 9^{3}; cstr. אֲחַשְׁדַּרְפְּנֵי 3^{11} Ezr 8^{36}.

אֲחַשְׁוֵרוֹשׁ n.pr.m. Ahasuerus = Xerxes (Pers. *Khshayârshâ*=*mighty*+*eye* or *man*, vid. Spiegel $^{l.c.\ 216}$; in Aram. חשיארש, CIS $^{II.\ i.\ 122}$ [B.C. 481]) king of Pers. Ezr 4^{6} Est $1^{1.1.2.9.10}$ + 18 t. Est + Est 10^{1} Qr (Kt אחשרש); אֲחַשְׁוֵרֹשׁ Est 1^{16} 2^{21} 3^{12} $8^{7.10}$; also Dn 9^{1} where made father of 'Darius the Mede,' cf. Meinh.

†**אֲחַשְׁתָּרִי n.pr.m.** but in form *adj. gent.* (cf. Be) הָאֲחַ׳ 1 Ch 4^{6} (perh. Pers. = *belonging to the realm*, *royal*, vid. infr.)

†[**אֲחַשְׁתְּרָן**] **adj.** (?) royal (fr. Pers. *Khshatra*, *lordship*, *realm*, vid. Spiegel $^{l.c.\ 215}$) pl. הָאֲחַשְׁתְּרָנִים agreeing with הָרֶכֶשׁ Est $8^{10.14}$.

אַחַת v. אֶחָד.

אַט v. אטט.

אטד (mng. dub.; perh. cf. Ar. وطد *make firm*, *strong*, cf. Thes MV).

†**אָטָד n.m.** $^{Ju\ 9,\ 15}$ bramble, buck-thorn (cf. Che ψ 58^{10}) (*rhamnus*, Ar. أَطَد, As. *etidu* v. Dl $^{W.\ No.\ 153}$, Aram אַטְדָּא, ܐܛܕܐ cf. Löw $^{No.\ 15}$) contr. עֵצִים Ju $9^{14.15.15}$ (personif., in fable); ψ 58^{10} as fuel (in fig., cf. Che); בְּגֹרֶן הָאָ׳, n.loc., Gn $50^{10.11}$ (v. גֹּרֶן & אבל מצרים).

אטט Arab. أَطَّ *to emit a moaning or creaking sound* (cf. AW $^{Lex.\ 36}$ Ges $^{Jes.\ i.\ 604\ f}$ Lane $^{i.\ 66}$).

†[**אִטִּי** Ol. ^{412}] **n.m. mutterer**, pl. אִטִּים Is 19^{3} *mutterers* (|| אֹבוֹת, יִדְּעֹנִים) i.e. either ventriloquists or whisperers of charms (cf. 8^{19} 29^{4}).

†**אַט subst. gentleness**, used only adverbially:—**a.** as adverb. accus. 1 K 21^{27} וַיְהַלֵּךְ אַט׃ and he (Ahab) went about *softly* (sc. in penitence); **b.** with לְ of norm or state (as in לָבֶטַח, v. לְ) 2 S 18^{5} לְאַט־לִי לַנַּעַר (deal) *gently* for me with the young man, Is 8^{6} the waters of Shiloah הַהֹלְכִים לְאַט that go *gently*; with pretonic qameṣ Jb 15^{11} דָּבָר לָאַט עִמָּךְ׃ a word (spoken) *gently* with thee; with sf. Gn 33^{14} and I אֶתְנַהֲלָה לְאִטִּי will lead on *gently* (lit. *according to my gentleness*).

†[**אָטַם**] **vb. shut, shut up** (Mish. אטם, cf.

אֹטֶם stoppage, Aram אֲטַם, Ar. أُطُمٌ *contract, stop,* أُطُمٌ *fortress,* As. *aṭamu,* in list of headgear, etc. = *turban?* Dl$^{W. No 155}$) —**Qal** *Pt act* אטם Pr 17^{28} + 2 t.; *pass* אֲטֻמִים 1 K 6^{4}, אֲטֻמוֹת Ez 40^{16} + 2 t ;—*shut, stop,* obj lips Pr 17^{28}, ears 21^{13} Is 33^{15}, pass = *closed* (i e *narrowed, narrowing,* cf 𝔖 in Co) חַלּוֹנוֹת א׳ Ez 40^{16} $41^{16.26}$, cf חַלּוֹנֵי שְׁקֻפִים אֲטֻמִים 1 K 6^{4} **Hiph.** *Impf* i q Qal יַאְטֵם ψ 58^{5} (juss with sense of indic , cf Dr$^{§173 obs.}$) of adder, stopping ears, sim of wicked.

†אֵטוּן **n [m.]** thread, yarn (etym unknown, on form v Ges$^{§84a\ 12\ R.}$ Talm אֲטוּנָא, אֵטוּנָא, *cord, rope,* so 𝔗) cstr. א׳ מִצְרָיִם Pr 7^{16}.

†[אָטַר] **vb. shut up, close, bind** (Ar أَطَرَ *bend, curve,* إِطَارٌ *what surrounds, encloses*) **Qal** *Impf.* 3 fs תֶּאְטַר ψ 69^{16} (אַל תּ׳ עָלַי בְּאֵר פִּיהָ)

†אָטֵר **n.pr.m.** (*binder?*) a chief of Jews Ezr $2^{16.42}$ Ne $7^{21.45}$ 10^{18}.

†אִטֵּר **adj shut up, bound** (NH אטר, *lame*) אִישׁ א׳ יַד־יְמִינוֹ Ju 3^{15} 20^{16} *a man bound, restricted, as to his right hand,* i e *left-handed*

[אַי] (أَنَّى, ܐܝܟ: in Syr in cpds as ܠܡܢ *how?* W$^{SG\ 120-2}$; cf As *aiu, who? what?*) †**1. interrog. adv. where? a.** so with sf אַיֶּכָּה [a verbal form, v Sta$^{§365\ b\ 3}$] Gn 3^{9}, אַיּוֹ Ex 2^{20}, poet. *where is he?* = he is nowhere Jb 14^{10} 20^{7} (Je 37^{19} rd Qr אַיֵּה); אַיָּם Na 3^{17} (in indirect qu.) and the place thereof is not known, אַיָּם *where they are* Idiomatically, with the sf anticipating the noun to which it refers (Ew^{§309c}, cf Dr$^{Sm\ 1.21,14}$) 2 K 19^{13} אַיּוֹ מֶלֶךְ־חֲמָת *where is he,* the king of Hamath? (|| Is 37^{13} אַיֵּה) Is 19^{12} Mi 7^{10}. When used alone, or with other adverbs (v infr), it is contracted to אֵי Gn 4^{9} Dt 32^{37} 1 S 26^{16} Pr 31^{4} Qr. (The more usual form is אַיֵּה) **b.** strengthened by the enclitic זֶה (v זֶה, 4) אֵי־זֶה$_{15}$ *where, then?* (never of a *person*, exc. Est 7^{5} (late), & only once 1 K 22^{24} [but v 2 Ch 18^{23}] with a *verb*) Is 50^{1} 66^{1} Je 6^{16}, in indirect qu 1 S 9^{18}, in the phrase . . . אֵי־זֶה הַדֶּרֶךְ *where is the way (that)* . ? †1 K 13^{12} 2 K 3^{8} 2 Ch 18^{23} Jb $38^{19.24}$. **2.** prefixed to other adverbs or prons, א׳ imparts to them an interrog force thus **a.** אֵי־זֶה *which* (of two or more)? only Ec 2^{3} 11^{6} (late), in indirect qu **b.** †אֵי־מִזֶּה *whence?* (מִזֶּה = *hence,* v sub זֶה) Gn 16^{8} אֵי־מִזֶּה בָאת 1 S 30^{13} 2 S $1^{3.13}$ Jb 2^{2}; in indirect qu Ju 13^{6} 1 S 25^{11}, with subst annexed 2 S 15^{2} אֵי־מִזֶּה עִיר אַתָּה lit *whence,* as regards city, art thou? Jon 1^{8}. **c** †אֵי־לָזֹאת Je 5^{7} *upon what ground?* (𝔙 super quo?) *how?* With other adverbs, א׳ coalesces into one word, v אֵיפֹה, אֵיכָכָה, אֵיכָה.

†אַיֵּה$_{45}$ (lengthened from א׳, cf. הֵן & הִנֵּה) **interr. adv. Where?** Gn 18^{9} 19^{5} 22^{7}; the most gen term expressing this idea, used of both persons & things (but never with a *verb* [contrast אֵיפֹה]); oft. in poet or elevated style, where the answer *nowhere* is expected, Is 33^{18} 36^{19} 51^{13} Je 2^{28} (cf Dt 32^{37} א׳) 17^{15} 37^{19}, Jb 15^{23} he wandereth abroad for bread אַיֵּה (saying) *Where is it?* 21^{28} Zc 1^{5} (אַיֵּה־הֵם); in the (iron.) phrase *where is thy (their) God?* †ψ $42^{4.11}$ 79^{10} 115^{2} (אַיֵּה־נָא) Jo 2^{17}, rhetorically, of an earnest inquiry Je $2^{6.8}$ Job 35^{10}, or longing Is $63^{11.15}$ Ju 6^{13}.

†אֵיךְ$_{59}$ (Aram אֵיךְ, ܐܝܟ [pron. *ăch*]) **adv. 1. interrog. How?** Gn 26^{9} 2 S $1^{5.14}$ 1 K 12^{6} Is 20^{6} al ; oft with impf (esp. in 1 ps) in an expostulation Gn 39^{9} $44^{8.34}$ Jos 9^{7} 2 S 2^{22} 12^{18} ψ 137^{4}, Is 48^{11} for *how* should it be profaned? (ו)אֵיךְ תֹּאמַר *how canst* or *dost* thou (do you) say. ? Ju 16^{15} Is 19^{11} Je 2^{23} (cf 8^{8} אֵיכָה) 48^{14} ψ 11^{1}, in an indirect sentence 2 K 17^{28} Je 36^{17} Ru 3^{18} **2. as an exclam. How!** whether of lamentation 2 S 1^{19} Je 2^{21} 9^{18} Mi 2^{4}, or of satisfaction Is $14^{4.12}$ Je 48^{39} 51^{41} Ob^{5} al ; with intensive force = *how gladly!* Je 3^{19}, *how terribly!* 9^{6} (but others render here 'for how [else] should I do'? etc)

†אֵיכָה (from א׳ and כֹּה = כָה, cf. As *ekiam*) **adv. 1. interrog. In what manner?** τίνι τρόπῳ; (rather more definite than אֵיךְ = πῶς,) Dt 1^{12} 7^{17} 12^{30} 18^{21} 32^{30} Ju 20^{3} (indirect sentence) 2 K 6^{15} Je 8^{8} ψ 73^{11}. **2. exclam. How!** (slightly more emph than אֵיךְ) Is 1^{21} Je 48^{17} La 1^{1} 2^{1} $4^{1.2}$. **3. Where?** (prob. north-Isr., cf. Aram. אֵיכָא, ܐܝܟܐ *where?* Cf. Dr$^{Intr\ 178.421}$) only 2 K 6^{13} Kt Ct $1^{7.7}$,—each time in an indirect sentence.

†אֵיכוֹ 2 K 6^{13} Qr **where?** v. אֵיכָה **3.**

†אֵיכָכָה (Ct) אֵיכָכָה (Est) (from א׳ & כָּכָה *thus*) **How?** only Ct $5^{3.3}$ Est $8^{6.6}$

I. [אַיִן] **adv.** (from א׳, As *aina, ainu,* Arab أَيْنَ *where?* مِنْ أَيْنَ *whence?*) only in the compound מֵאַיִן$_{17}$ **whence?** Gn 29^{4} 42^{7} (syn. אֵי־מִזֶּה e g. Gn 16^{8} 1 S 30^{13}) Ju 17^{9} 19^{17} Jb 1^{7} (2^{2} אֵי־מִזֶּה); used in a rhet or poet style (where אֵי־מִזֶּה would be too prosaic) Nu 11^{13} מֵאַיִן לִי בָּשָׂר *whence* have I flesh etc.? 2 K 6^{27} Je 30^{7} Alas! for that day is great, מֵאַיִן כָּמֹהוּ *whence* is its like? (see also II אַיִן ad fin.) Na 3^{7} ψ 121^{1} Jb $28^{12.20}$, in an indirect sentence Jos 2^{4} (cf. אֵי־מִזֶּה 1 S 25^{11})

אָ֫ן adv. (contracted fr. I. [אַיִן]) **where? or whither?** 1 S 10^{14} (cf. 27^{10} 𝔖 𝔗, v. sub אֶל ad fin.); only besides in †מֵאָן *whence?* 2 K 5^{25} Kt (Qr מֵאַיִן); †עַד־אָן of time *to what point? how long?* Jb 8^{2}. With ה *locale:* אָ֫נָה (*a*) *whither?* Gn 16^{8} 32^{18} 2 S 2^{1} 13^{13} 2 K 6^{6} Is 10^{3} ψ $139^{7.7}$ + 9 t.; in indirect sentence Jos 2^{5} Ne 2^{16}; (*b*) = *where?* †Ru 2^{19}; (*c*) in the phrase אָ֫נָה וָאָ֫נָה *any whither* †1 K $2^{36.42}$ 2 K 5^{25}; (*d*) of time, עַד־אָ֫נָה *how long?* †Ex 16^{28} Nu $14^{11.11}$ (c. לֹא) Jos 18^{3} Je 47^{6} (sq. לֹא) Hb 1^{2} ψ $13^{2.2.3.3}$ 62^{4} Jb 18^{2} 19^{2} (less common than the syn. עַד מָתַי).

†**אֵיפֹה** (from אֵי & פֹּה *here*) **adv. 1. where?** Gn 37^{16} 1 S 19^{22} 2 S 9^{4} Is 49^{21} Je 3^{2} Jb 4^{7} 38^{4} Ru 2^{19}; in indirect sentence Je 36^{19} (less common than אַיֵּה, used of *persons* [contrast אֵי־זֶה] and with a verb [contrast אַיֵּה]). **2. of what kind?** (*qualis?*) only Ju 8^{18}.

†III. **אִי interj.** (so in Rabb., v. De^Koh 197^ Wr^Eccl 490^) **alas!** (late) Ec 4^{10} אִי לוֹ (written in MT as one word) *alas* for him (Ew^§ 309 c^), the one, who falleth, etc. (i.e. who falleth alone) 10^{16}.

†IV. **אִי adv. not** (frequently in Rabb., as אִי אֶפְשָׁר *impossible;* and in Eth. the ordinary negative; cf. Ph. אי CIS^I. 3,5^, and in איבל^165,18; 167,11^; As. *ai*) Jb 22^{30} אִי־נָקִי *the non-innocent.*

†**אִי כָבוֹד** (1 S 4^{21}), **אִי־כָבוֹד** (1 S 14^{3}) **n.pr.m.** (*inglorious*), son of Phinehas (explained 1 S 4^{21} by גָּלָה כָבוֹד מִיִּשְׂרָאֵל *glory is gone into exile from Israel*).

אִיזֶבֶל n.pr.f. (sense uncertain, CIS^I. 158^ there occurs the n.pr.f. בעלאזבל *Baal exalts?* or *is husband to?* [v. זָבַל], of which אִיזֶבֶל is conjectured by DHM to be an intentional alteration, made for the purpose of avoiding the name Baal. If so, א׳ perhaps suggested to the Hebrew ear the idea of *un-exalted* or *un-husbanded*), queen of Ahab, daughter of Ethbaal, king of Tyre 1 K 16^{31} $18^{4.13.19}$ $19^{1.2}$ 21^{5}+; 2 K 9^{7}+.

I. **אִי n.m.** *isle, coast,* v. I. אָוָה.

II. **אַ֫יִן** *nought,* v. p. 34.

אִיעֶזֶר v. אֲבִיעֶזֶר.

אִיתָמָר v. I. אָוָה.

[אָיַב]$_{283}$ **vb. be hostile to** (As. *aibu* (v. Dl^W^), *enemy* = אֹיֵב)—**Qal** *Pf.* †וְאָיַבְתִּי Ex 23^{22}; *Pt.* אֹיֵב (אוֹיֵב) Ex 15^{6}+; sf. אֹיְבִי (אוֹיְבִי) 2 S 22^{18} = ψ 18^{18}+; f. sf. אֹיַבְתִּי Mi $7^{8.10}$; אֹיִבְךָ Ex 23^{4}+, etc.; pl. אוֹיְבִים ψ 68^{24} 127^{5}; אֹיְבִים ψ 139^{22}, etc.;—*be hostile to, treat as enemy* Ex 23^{22} (E, Cov't code) וְאָיַבְתִּי אֶת־אֹיְבֶיךָ וְצַרְתִּי אֶת־צֹרְרֶיךָ (subj. י׳); elsewhere *Pt.* 1 S 18^{29} וַיְהִי שָׁאוּל אֹיֵב אֶת־דָּוִד; usually as subst. & mostly sf.; *enemy,* of personal foe Ex 23^{4} (E ‖ שֹׂנֵא v^5^) Nu 35^{23} (P) 1 S 19^{17} (cf. 18^{29}) $24^{5.20}$ 2 S 4^{8} 1 K 21^{20} Jb 27^{7} ψ 54^{9} 55^{13} (‖ מְשַׂנֵּא; opp. מְיֻדָּע, אַלּוּף v^14^) Mi 2^{8} Pr 16^{7} 24^{17}+; in sim. Je 30^{14} (מַכַּת אוֹיֵב); of public national enemy, sg. Ju $16^{23.24}$; coll. Ex $15^{6.9}$ Dt 33^{27} Na 3^{11} 2 Ch 6^{24}+; personif. Mi $7^{8.10}$; more oft. pl. Ex 23^{22} (E) Lv 26^{7f} (H) Nu 10^{9} (P) Dt 1^{42} 6^{19} Je 15^{9} $34^{20.21}$+; of enemies of God, as protector of his people Nu 10^{35} (J) Ju 5^{31} 1 S 30^{26} 2 S 18^{19} ψ 66^{3} $68^{1.22}$ Na $1^{2.8}$ Is 66^{6}+; as morally supreme Jb 13^{24} 33^{10} ψ 37^{20} $92^{10.10}$+; of God as enemy of rebellious people Is 63^{10}, in sim. La $2^{4.5}$.

†**אֵיבָה n.f.** enmity—א׳ Gn 3^{15} + 2 t.; cstr. אֵיבַת Ez 25^{15} 35^{5}—*enmity,* personal hostility, betw. men Nu $35^{21.22}$ (P), betw. serpent & woman Gn 3^{15} (J), betw. peoples אֵיבַת עוֹלָם Ez 25^{15} 35^{5}.

אִיּוֹב n.pr.m. Job (meaning unknown; Thes √איב; *obj. of enmity,* cf. for pass. sense יִלּוֹד; Ew comp. Ar. أَوَّابٌ *he who turns* (to God); but cf. Di on 1^{1}; all dub. cf. Lag^BN 90^) Jb $1^{1.5.5.5.8.9.14}$ + 48 t. Jb; Ez $14^{14.20}$.

אִיד, אֵד v. אוד.

אַיֵּה v. III. אוה, sub אֵי.

אַיֵּה v. אֵי. **אִיִּים** v. III. אוה.

אֵיךְ, אֵיכָה, אֵיכָכָה v. *ib.*

אַיִל, אַיָּל, אַיָּלָה, אֵילוֹן, אֵילָם, אֵילִם, אֵילַת, אֱיָלוּת etc. v. אול.

†**אֱיָל n.m. help** (loan-word from Aram. ܐܝܠܐ *help,* so Lag^Or II. 7, BN 175^, Nö^ZMG 1886, 526^) only in sim. כְּגֶבֶר אֵין א׳ ψ 88^{5}.

†**[אֱיָלוּת] n.f.** id. sf. אֱיָלוּתִי ψ 22^{20} *my help* (‖ יהוה).

אים (cf. 𝔗, Talm. אַיֵּם *terrify* Lag^BN 28^).

†**אָיֹם adj. terrible, dreadful**—*terrible,* of Chaldeans אָיֹם וְנוֹרָא הוּא Hb 1^{7}; of dignified woman, *awe-inspiring* אֲיֻמָּה כַּנִּדְגָּלוֹת Ct $6^{4.10}$.

†**אֵימָה**$_{17}$ **n.f. terror, dread** (Talm. *id.,* cf. As. *imtu,* Dl^W^)—א׳ Gn 15^{12}+; אֵימָ֫תָה Ex 15^{16} (cf. Ges^§ 90, 2 R. b^); cstr. אֵימַת Pr 20^{2}; sf. אֵימָתִי Ex 23^{27}; אֵמָתִי Jb 33^{7}, etc.; pl. אֵימִים Je 50^{38}; אֵמִים

Jb 20^{25}, אימות ψ 55^{5}; sf. אֵמֶיךָ ψ 88^{16},—*terror, dread* (mostly poet.), inspired by ׳י Ex 15^{16} (song ‖ פַּחַד E) 23^{27} (E) Dt 32^{25} Jb 9^{34} 13^{21} cf 33^{7}, 20^{25} ψ 88^{16} (‖ חֲרוֹנִים, בעותים v^{17}), cf Gn 15^{12} אֵימָה חֲשֵׁכָה גדולה; occasioned by enemies Jos 2^{9} Is 33^{18} Ezr 3^{3}; by king Pr 20^{2}, cf ψ 55^{5} אימות מָוֶת (‖ יִרְאָה ‖ רַעַד, פַּלָּצוּת v^{6}), pred. of snorting of a war-horse Jb 39^{20}, of teeth of crocodile Jb 41^{6}, pl. fig = idols (i e dreadful, shocking things) Je 50^{38} (‖ פסלים)

†אֵימִים **n.pr m.pl.** Emim (*terrors*) ancient inhab. of Moab Gn 14^{5} (הָאֵימִים), Dt 2^{10} (הָאֵמ׳), v^{11} (אֵמ׳)

I [אַיִן], מֵאַיִן *whence?* v. sub אַי.

II **אַיִן, אָיִן** cstr אֵין **subst.** prop **nothing, nought** (Moab אן, As *ênu*) **1.** †Is 40^{23} הַנּוֹתֵן רוֹזְנִים לְאָיִן who bringeth princes *to nothing*, †כְּאַיִן *as nothing*, ib 40^{17} 41$^{11.12}$ Hg 2^{3} ψ 39^{6}, *almost* (‖ כמעט) ψ 73^{2}, †מֵאַיִן *of nothing* Is 41^{24}. **2.** cstr אֵין, very freq as **particle of negation, is not, are not, was not, were not,** etc (corresp to the affirm. יֵשׁ q v. Similar in usage, though not etym akin, are لَيْسَ, לית, ܠܰܝܬ, ʾalbo), prop. 'there is *nought of*' sq a subst or a pron. suffix (אֵינֶנִּי [*verbal* form, Ges$^{\S 100.5\ 152,1c}$], אֵינְךָ, אֵינֵךְ, אֵינֶנּוּ, אֵינֶנָּה, אֵינְכֶם, אֵינָם, also ψ 59^{14} אֵינֵמוֹ, 73^{5} אֵינֵימוֹ). twice abnormally, in late Heb, a nom אֵין אֲנַחְנוּ, אֵין אֲנִי Ne 4^{17} (so sts לית, ܠܰܝܬ, No$^{M\ p\ 296}$), once, incorrectly, אֵת Hg 2^{17} **a.** denying existence absolutely Is 44^{6} 47^{10} אֵין רֹאֵנִי *there is none* that seeth me, lit. *nought of* one seeing me! אֵין עוֹד *there is none* else Dt 4^{39} 1 K 8^{60} Is 45$^{5.6.18.22}$ **b** more commonly, in a limited sense, *there is none here* or *at hand* Ex 2^{12} and he saw כִּי־אֵין אִישׁ that *there was no* man (sc there), Nu 21^{5}, Gn 5^{24} וְאֵינֶנּוּ and he *was not* (of Enoch's disappearance from earth) 42^{13} one (*cas pend* as oft), *he is not*, v^{36}, oft = *is* (or *has*) *vanished* Gn 37^{30} 1 K 20^{40} Is 17^{14} ψ 37^{10} 103^{16} Jb 8^{22} 24^{24} 27^{19} **c.** with the sense determined by a predic following. Gn 37^{29} Joseph *was not in the pit*, 41^{39} + oft, Ex 5^{10} אֵינֶנִּי נֹתֵן לָכֶם תֶּבֶן *I am not giving* you straw, and so often with particip where duration has to be expressed Gn 39^{23} Dt 21^{18} Is 1^{15} Je 7^{16}, or intention Gn 20^{7} אִם אֵינְךָ מֵשִׁיב דַּע . . . if thou *art not restoring* her, know, 43^{5} Ex 8^{17} 33^{15} (idiomatically, after אִם; v. Dr$^{\S 137}$) Ju 12^{3}. Foll once pleon by יֵשׁ ψ 135^{17} Treated as a *mere* part. of negation, אין may vary its position in the sentence, the subst. which should strictly stand in the genitive being not only separated from it by a little word, as Gn 37^{24}, אין לו Ex 22^{1}, אֵין שָׁם Ex 12^{30}, אֵין גַּם ψ 14^{3}, etc., but even for emphasis *prefixed* to it, as Gn 19^{31} 40^{8} וּפֹתֵר אֵין אֹתוֹ 41^{15} Ex 5^{16} Ju 13^{9} 14^{6} 16^{15} 19^{1} (so MI^{24}) if however it be thus brought to the end of a sentence, or be disconnected with what follows, it stands in the absol. form, as Gn 2^{5} וְאָדָם אַיִן לַעֲבֹד הָאֲדָמָה and man *there was none* to till the ground, Lv 26^{37} וְרֹדֵף אָיִן, Nu 20^{5} 2 K 19^{3} Ho 13^{4} Mi 7^{2}. **d.** sometimes the subj has to be supplied from the context: thus (*a*) †1 S 9^{4} and they passed through the land of Shaalim וָאַיִן *and they* (the asses) *were not* (lit *and nought!*), esp after vbs. of *waiting* or *seeking* Is 59^{11} ψ 69^{21} Jb 3^{9}, Is 41^{17} Ez 7^{25} Pr 14^{6}, 13^{4}, 20^{4} (*β*) †Ex 17^{7} is ׳י in the midst of us אִם־אָיִן *or not?* Nu 13^{20} (*γ*) †Ju 4^{20} וְאָמַרְתְּ אָיִן: then thou shalt say, *There is not*, 1 K 18^{10} 1 S 10^{14} (*δ*) Gn 30^{1} give me children, וְאִם־אַיִן *and if not*, I die, Ex 32^{32} Ju 9$^{15.20}$ 2 S 17^{6} (v Dr) 2 K 2^{10} Jb 33^{33} **e.** with subj. not expressed, once (late), Dn 8^{5} וְאֵין נוֹגֵעַ בָּאָרֶץ and (it) *was not touching* the earth. **f.** once, Jb 35^{15} with the finite vb, but rd here כִּי אֵין בֹּקֵד (the usage of لَيْسَ, cited by De, does not justify the anomaly in Heb) Je 38^{5} the impf. may be due to the fact that no ptcp. of יָכֹל was in use, and a relat. must be tacitly supplied. 'The king *is not* (one that) can do aught against you' On Ex 3^{2} see Ges$^{\S 152,2R\ 6}$, Ew$^{\S 169d}$. **3.** אֵין לְ׳, with subst, or pron, *there is* (*was*) *not to* . . = . . *have, has, had,* etc *not* Gn 11^{30} אֵין לָהּ וָלָד *she had no* child, Nu 27^{9} וְאִם־אֵין לוֹ בַּת and if *he have no* daughter + oft, with a ptcp. Dt 22^{27} Je 14^{16} 30^{17} 49^{5} 50^{32} ψ 142^{5} La 1$^{2.9.17}$, Ex 22^{2} אִם־אֵין לוֹ if he *have nought*, Dn 9^{26} וְאֵין לוֹ and *have nought* (or *none*). **4.** in circumst clauses (Dr$^{\S 164}$) —(*a*) Ex 21^{11} she shall go out free אֵין כָּסֶף *without money*, 22^{9} אֵין רֹאֶה *none seeing it*, Nu 11^{6} Is 47^{1} Je 2^{32} Ho 3^{4} 7^{11} ψ 32^{9} 88^{5} + (*b*) Dt 32^{4} a God of faithfulness וְאֵין עָוֶל *and no iniquity*, i e. *without iniquity*, Je 5^{21} Jo 1^{6} ψ 104^{25}. (*c*) very oft, in such phrases as וְאֵין מַחֲרִיד *with none to affright* Lv 26^{6} (12 t), וְאֵין מְכַבֶּה Is 1^{31} al, וְאֵין מַצִּיל 5^{29} ψ 7^{3}, etc (Dr$^{\S 159}$) **5.** with inf and לְ׳, *it is not to*. · i e (*a*) like οὐκ ἔστιν, *it is not possible to* . (cf sub יֵשׁ and לֹא), but hardly exc in late Heb, 2 Ch 20^{6} וְאֵין עִמְּךָ לְהִתְיַצֵּב *it is not possible to* stand (in conflict) with thee, 22^{9} Ezr 9^{15} Ec 3^{14} Est 4^{2}. Once without לְ, ψ 40^{6} אֵין עֲרֹךְ אֵלֶיךָ οὐκ ἔστι παραβάλλειν σοι. (*β*) *there is no need to* . . . 1 Ch 23^{26} וְגַם לַלְוִיִּם אֵין־לָשֵׂאת for the Levites also *there was no need* to bear 2 Ch 5^{11} 35^{15} (v. Dr$^{\S 202\ 1}$). **6.** with

prefixes:—**a.** † בְּאֵין prop *in defect of*—(*a*) *for want of, without*—Pr 5^{23} HE will die בְּאֵין מוּסָר *for lack of* instruction, 11^{14} בְּאֵין תַּחְבֻּלוֹת *without* guidance, 14^{4} 15^{22} 26^{20} 29^{18} Is 57^{1} Ez 38^{11}; cf. בְּלֹא. (*β*) of time = *when there was* (*were*) *not* Pr 8$^{24.24}$. **b.** † כְּאֵין Is 59^{10} כְּאֵין עֵינַיִם poet. for כַּאֲשֶׁר אֵין לוֹ עֵינַיִם (cf Ew$^{\S 286 g}$ Ges$^{\S 152.1 h}$) **c.** † לְאֵין (*a*) for לַאֲשֶׁר אֵין לוֹ Is 40^{29}, in late prose 2 Ch 14^{10} Ne 8^{10}. (*β*) *in the condition of not*... (לְ of state, v. sub לְ) = *without* or *so that not*... (peculiar to Ch), 1 Ch 22^{4} cedar trees לְאֵין מִסְפָּר *without* number, 2 Ch 14^{12} and there fell of the Cushites לְאֵין־לָהֶם מִחְיָה *so that they had none* remaining alive, 20^{25} לְאֵין מַשָּׂא *so that there was no* carrying away, 21^{18} Ezr 9^{14}. (*γ*) עַד־לְאֵין (see עַד לְ), 2 Ch 36^{16} *until there was no* remedy (cf.... עַד אֵין ψ 40^{13} Jb 5^{9}) **d.** מֵאֵין (*a*) (מִן causal) *from lack of*... Is 50^{2} Je 7^{32} 19^{11}. (*β*) (מִן negative, v. מִן) prop *away from there being no*... (with אֵין pleon, cf מִבְּלִי, and מִבְּלִי אֵין), i e. *so that not*, *without*, mostly epexegetical of some term expressing desolation: Is 5^{9} Surely many houses shall be desolate מֵאֵין יוֹשֵׁב *without* inhabitant, 6^{11} + oft. Je & Zp; Is 6^{11} מֵאֵין אָדָם, Je 32^{43} מֵאֵין אָדָם וּבְהֵמָה 33$^{10.12}$ Ez 33^{28}; La 3^{49} Once sq. inf. Mal 2^{13} *so that there is no* regarding more (*γ*) in Je 10$^{6.7}$ מֵאֵין כָּמוֹךָ is supposed by some to = a strengthened אֵין, *even none, none at all*, but it is difficult to justify this expl. logically; and it is preferable to point מֵאַיִן כָּמוֹךָ *whence* is any like thee? cf. 30^{7}. (So Hi: v. Dr$^{\text{Hbr II 34-7}}$.)

† אִין 1 S 21^{9}... וְאִין יֶשׁ prob. irreg. for אֵין (so Ki Ges Ew$^{\S 213 e. 286 h}$ Ol^{840} Sta$^{\S 194 c}$) with יֶשׁ pleon. (as ψ 135^{17}); > dialect = Aram. لَيْ, אִין *num?* (De, but v. Dr^{Sm} *ad loc.*)

† אֵיפָה, אֵפָה $_{85}$ **n.f.** ephah (etym. dub, 𝔊 οἰφι etc., cf Copt. ὀιπι, Thes Lag $^{\text{Or II 2}}$ & cit) —א׳ Nu 5^{15} +; אֵפָה Ex 16^{36} +; cstr. אֵיפַת Lv 19^{36} +;—*ephah*, a grain-measure. **1.** a certain quantity of wheat, barley, etc = ten omers (עֹמֶר) Ex 16^{36} (cf in measure of offerings Lv 5^{11} 6^{13} Nu 5^{15} 28^{5}, all עֲשִׂירִית הָא׳, = $\frac{1}{10}$ chomer (חֹמֶר) Ez 45^{11} (= bath, בַּת, liqu meas *q.v.*) cf Is 5^{10}; chiefly of offerings, v supr. & 1 S 1^{24} Ez 45$^{13.13.24.24.24}$ 46$^{5.5.7.7.7.11.11.11.14}$, cf Ju 6^{19}, but also of food 1 S 17^{17} cf. Ru 2^{17} & Is 5^{10} supr. **2.** receptacle or measure, holding an ephah, in proph vision Zc 5$^{6.7.8.9.10}$, just measure אֵיפַת־צֶדֶק Lv 19^{36} (‖ הִין צ׳, אַבְנֵי־צ׳, מֹאזְנֵי־צ׳) cf Ez 45$^{10.11}$, אֵיפָה שְׁלֵמָה וָצֶ׳ Dt 25^{15} (‖ אֶבֶן שְׁ׳ וָצֶ׳); of unjust measure אֵיפָה וְאֵיפָה Dt 25^{14} Pr 20^{10}, הַקְטִין א׳ Am 8^{5}, אֵיפַת רָזוֹן Mi 6^{10}. (On the actual size of ephah, cf. בַּת).

אֵיפֹה v. sub אֵ׳.

אוש, איש (Stem assumed in Thes for איש; existence & mng. somewhat dub Thes (Add) & most derive איש fr [אנשׁ] √אנש (q. v.) In favour are pl אֲנָשִׁים, fem אִשָּׁה = [אִנְשָׁה], lack of proven √איש, & lack of clear parallels for איש in cogn. lang. Against the deriv of איש fr *inš* is the vocalization (י—, and that fully written, not —), maintained even with suff, the (rare) pl אִישִׁים, the impossibility of deriving איש & אִשָּׁה from same √ (אִשָּׁה fr أنث), the existence of אֱנוֹשׁ as parallel form, and the (exceptional) parallel Aram איש (Inscr. of Carpentras), also Ar. إِيسَانٌ (cf Frey) ‖ إِنْسٌ, MI, SI, Ph. אש are not decisive; Sab. has both אסם & אנסם; the former app = איש, the latter אֱנוֹשׁ; but on former cf. DHM$^{\text{ZK 1884 360}}$ & Sab Denkm^{37}. On the whole, probability seems to favour √איש; Thes gave mng. *be strong*, Dl $^{\text{HA 9 Pr 161}}$ comp As *išanu, strong* (cf Dl$^{\text{W p 244}}$), & n pr. יְהוֹאָשׁ; cf. also Prat$^{\text{LOPh Feb 1884}}$; otherwise DHM$^{\text{l.c. \& ZMG 1883, 330}}$ & esp No$^{\text{ZMG 1886, 739}}$ Lag $^{\text{BN 68}}$; cf. also Wetzst in De$^{\text{Psalmen, ed. 4 p 888}}$ al. v. also אנשׁ, אֱנוֹשׁ)

אִישׁ $_{2166}$ **n.m.** man (= *vir*) (MI, SI, Ph. אש, perh also Sab אסם cf. Prat$^{\text{l.c.}}$, but DHM$^{\text{ZMG 1883, 330}}$)—א׳ abs. Gn 2^{23} +; cstr. Gn 25^{27} +; sf. אִישִׁי Gn 29^{32} +, etc; pl אִישִׁים ψ 141^{4} + 2 t. (Ph. אשם); usually אֲנָשִׁים Gn 12^{20} +, fr. √אנש q v.; cstr. אַנְשֵׁי Ju 6^{27} +, sf. אֲנָשַׁי 1 S 23^{12} etc;—*man*, opp. woman Gn 2$^{23.24}$ Lv 20^{27} Nu 5^{6} Dt 17^{2f} Jos 6^{21} 8^{25} Je 40^{7}, emph on sexual distinction & relation Gn 19^{8} 24^{16} 38^{25} Ex 22^{15} Lv 15^{16} (שִׁכְבַת זֶרַע) v^{18} (וְאִשָּׁה אֲשֶׁר יִשְׁכַּב אִישׁ אֹתָהּ שִׁ׳־ז׳) 20^{10f} Nu 5^{13f} Dt 22^{22f} Is 4^{1} +; thence = *husband*, esp. c sf. Gn 3$^{6.16}$ 16^{3} 29$^{32.34}$ Lv 21^{7} Nu 30^{7f} Dt 28^{56} Ju 13^{6f} Ru 1^{3f} 1 S 25^{19} Je 29^{6} Ez 16^{45} +, fig of ′ה as husb of Isr. אִישִׁי Ho 2^{18} (opp. בַּעְלִי); *man* as procreator, father Ec 6^{3}; of *male child* Gn 4^{1} cf זֶרַע אֲנָשִׁים 1 S 1^{11}, *man*, opp. beast Ex 11^{7} Lv 20^{15} (cf. אָדָם); cf fig ψ 22^{7} but also of male of animals Gn 7$^{2.2}$ (אִישׁ וְאִשְׁתּוֹ); *man*, opp. God Gn 32^{29} Nu 23^{19} לֹא אִישׁ אֵל וִיכַזֵּב ‖ וּבֶן־אָדָם וְיִתְנֶחָם); Jb 9^{32} 32^{13} Ho 11^{9} cf Is 31^{8} Jb 12^{10} (רוּחַ כָּל־בְּשַׂר־אִישׁ), hence in phrases to denote ordinary, customary, common שֵׁבֶט אֲנָשִׁים 2 S 7^{14} (‖ נִגְעֵי בְנֵי אָדָם); לֶחֶם אֲנָשִׁים Ez 24$^{17.22}$ (cf. Is 8^{1}); אַמַּת־אִישׁ Dt 3^{11}, but also contr. אָדָם ψ 49^{3} 62^{10}, *man*, as valiant 1 S 4$^{9.9}$ (וִהְיוּ לַאֲנָשִׁים) so 1 K 2^{2} cf 1 S 26^{15}, so אִישׁ חַיִל 31^{12} 2 S 24^{9} 1 K 1^{42} +; also אִישׁ מִלְחָמָה Nu 31^{49} Dt 2$^{14.16}$ Jos 5$^{4.6}$ +; even of ′ה

Ex 15³ יהוה איש מלחמה; oft. prefixed to other nouns in app. א׳ שַׂר וְשֹׁפֵט Gn 42^{30.33}, א׳ אָדוֹן Ex 2¹⁴, א׳ כֹּהֵן Lv 21⁹, א׳ סָרִים Je 38⁷, partic. bef adj gent איש מצרי Gn 39¹ Ex 2^{11.19} cf Gn 37²⁸ 38^{1.2} 39¹⁴ 1 S 17¹² 30^{11.13}+; a *man* as resident in, or belonging to a place or people Nu 25⁶ Ju 10¹+(so Ph), usually pl אַנְשֵׁי יִשְׂרָאֵל 1 S 7¹¹ 31^{7.7} cf. Jos 7^{4.5}+, also sg coll Dt 27¹⁴ Jos 9^{6.7} Ju 20¹¹ 1 S 11⁸ (v Dr)+, 2 S 10^{6.8} (א׳ טוֹב), (so MI 10.13), *men*=retainers, followers, soldiers 1 S 18²⁷ 23^{3.5} 24³ 25¹³+ cf Dt 33⁸ sg coll v Di, איש אלהים *man of God*=proph. Dt 33¹ Jos 14⁶ 1 S 9^{6.7} 1 K 12^{22}+(v. אלהים), in phrase sq abstr איש חַיִל, א׳ הַדָּמִים v supr, א׳ שֵׂיבָה Dt 32²⁵, א׳ מִלְחָמָה 2 S 16⁷ cf v 8, א׳ הַבְּלִיַּעַל 2 S 16⁷, א׳ מָוֶת 1 K 2²⁶, א׳ חָמָס ψ 140¹² Pr 3³¹+, sq word of occupation, etc א׳ שָׂדֶה Gn 25²⁷, א׳ הָאֲדָמָה Gn 9²⁰ (cf Zc 13⁵), א׳ הַבֵּנַיִם *champion* 1 S 17⁴ (cf. Dr) v²³, א׳ בשׂרה 2 S 18²⁰, איש עֲצָתוֹ *his counsellor* Is 40¹³, cf איש חֶרְמִי 1 K 20⁴², א׳ רֵעִים Pr 18²⁴, oft distrib=*each, every* Gn 9⁵ 10⁵ 40^{5.5} Ex 12³+, incl. women Jb 42¹¹ 1 Ch 16³ וַיְחַלֵּק לְכָל־אִישׁ יִשְׂרָאֵל מֵאִישׁ וְעַד אִשָּׁה לְאִישׁ כִּכַּר־לֶחֶם, of inanim things 1 K 7^{30.36}, also איש איש Ex 36⁴ Nu 4^{19.49} Ez 14^{4.7}+, *any one* Ex 34^{3.3.24}+; also איש איש Lv 15² 22^{4.18}+; of gods 2 K 18³³=Is 36¹⁸, *one another* איש והרגו ...איש אֶת־אָחִיו וְאִישׁ אֶת־רֵעֵהוּ וְאִישׁ אֶת־קְרֹבוֹ Ex 32²⁷, אָחִיו Dt 1¹⁶ Mi 7² (v אָח), איש...רֵעֵהוּ Gn 11³⁷+ (v רֵעַ) of inanimate things Gn 15¹⁰

†**אִישׁ־בֹּשֶׁת** **n pr.m. Ishbosheth** (for איש בַּעַל *man of Baal* v בַּעַל, בשת & Di *Baal* MBAk June 1881) **1.** son of Saul, & king of Isr, with David as rival 2 S 2^{8.10.12.15} 3^{8.14.15} 4^{5.8.8.12}, also v^{1.2} 𝔊 Dr cf We,= אֶשְׁבַּעַל 1 Ch 8³³ 9³⁹, cf also **2.** 2 S 23⁸, where rd אישבשת for ישב בשבת so 𝔊 We Dr, one of Dvd's heroes, v. יָשָׁבְעָם 1 Ch 11¹¹ 27²

†**אִישְׁהוֹד** **n.pr m.** (*man of majesty*) a man of Manasseh 1 Ch 7¹⁸

†**אִישׁוֹן** **n.[m.]** pupil of eye (cf Dl^{HA 9} Prat LOPb Feb 1884, but also Ar إِنْسَانُ العَيْن, & No ZMG 1886, 739)—א׳ all cstr—א׳ עַיִן Dt 32¹⁰ Pr 7², א׳ בַּת־עַיִן ψ 17⁸ (in all, sim of preciousness), =*middle, midst* of night בְּא׳ לַיְלָה וַאֲפֵלָה Pr 7⁹, בְּא׳ חשֶׁךְ 20²⁰ Kt i e *in deep darkness* (Qr בֶּאֱשׁוּן v Now)

אִשַׁי v יִשַׁי.

איתון Ez 40¹⁵ Qr v אתיון sub אתה

אִיתִיאֵל, אִיתַי v את *with*

אִיתָמָר v א׳ sub I אוה

אֵיתָן, אֵתָן v יתן

---

†**אַךְ**₁₅₉ **adv.** (perh from the same demonstr. root found also in כִּי, כֹּה, כֵּן) **1 surely. 2.** with a restrictive force, emphasizing what follows **a.** in contrast to what precedes, **howbeit, b.** in contrast with other ideas generally, **only** **1.** asseverative, often introducing with emphasis the expression of a truth (or supposed truth) newly perceived, esp. in colloquial language, *surely, no doubt* (*doch wohl*); Gn 26⁹ אַךְ הִנֵּה אִשְׁתְּךָ הִוא *of a surety*, lo, she is thy wife! 29¹⁴ 44²⁸ Ju 3²⁴ 20³⁹ 1 S 16⁶ *surely* the anointed of ׳׳ is before him! 25²¹ Je 5⁴ ψ 58¹² 73^{1.13}, but also in other cases, though rarely, Is 34^{14.15} Zp 3⁷ ψ 23⁶ 139¹¹ 140¹⁴ Jb 16⁷ 18²¹, & rather singularly Ex 12¹⁶ 31¹³ Lv 23^{27.39} (all P) **2.** restrictive. **a.** in contrast to what precedes, *howbeit, yet, but* Gn 9⁴ *howbeit*, flesh with the life thereof . ye shall not eat, 20¹² Ex 21²¹ Lv 21²³ 27²⁶ Nu 18^{15.17} 2 S 3¹³, Je 10²⁴ correct me, אַךְ בְּמִשְׁפָּט *but* with judgment, Jb 2⁶ 13¹⁵, sts with an advers force, as Is 14¹⁵ 43²⁴; before an imper. (minimizing the request), Gn 23¹³ *only*, if thou wilt, I pray thee, hear me! 27¹³ Ju 10¹⁵ 1 S 18¹⁷ 1 K 17¹³ al So 1 S 8⁹ אַךְ כִּי (v כִּי, and cf πλὴν ὅτι). **b.** in contrast to other ideas generally:—(*a*) Gn 7²³ 18³² אַךְ הַפַּעַם *only* this once (so Ex 10¹⁷ al) 34¹⁵ Ex 12¹⁶ (note accents), 1 S 18⁸ וְעוֹד לוֹ אַךְ הַמְּלוּכָה and there yet remains for him *only* the kingdom, 21⁵ Isa 45¹⁴ אַךְ בָּךְ אֵל *only* in thee is God! ψ 62² etc Jb 14²², ψ 37⁸ fret not thyself אַךְ לְהָרֵעַ (which leadeth) *only* to do evil, Pr 11²⁴ he that withholdeth more than is meet אַךְ לְמַחְסוֹר (tendeth) *only* to penury, 14²³ 21⁵ 22¹⁶, (β) attaching itself closely to the foll word (usually an adj, rarely a verb), *only*, i e. *exclusively, altogether, utterly* Dt 16¹⁵ and thou shalt be אַךְ שָׂמֵחַ *altogether* rejoicing, 28²⁹ (cf. v³³ רַק) Isa 16⁷ אַךְ נְכָאִים *utterly* stricken, 19¹¹ Je 16¹⁹ *nought but* lies, 32³⁰ Ho 12¹² Jb 19¹³ אַךְ זָרוּ are *wholly* estranged (with play on אַכְזָר *cruel*) **c.** as an adv. of time (with inf abs), twice Gn 27³⁰ אַךְ יָצֹא יָצָא יַעֲקֹב ... וְעֵשָׂו בָּא *only just* (or *scarcely*) had Jacob gone out, ... and (=when) Esau came in, Ju 7¹⁹—וְאַךְ thrice: Gn 9⁵ *and only* (second limitation of v³), Nu 22²⁰ *but only*, Jos 22¹⁹ *but howbeit*

Note—In some passages the affirmative and restrictive senses agree equally with the context, and authorities read the Hebrew differently Thus *only*=*nought but, altogether*, is adopted by Ges Ew Hi De in ψ 23⁶ 62¹⁰ 73^{1.13}, by Ew Hi De in 39^{6.7} (Che *surely*); by Ges Ew De in 39¹² (but Hi Che *surely*), by Ew Hi in 73¹⁸ (De Che *surely*); by Ges Hi De in 139¹¹ (Ew *doch*) Isa 45¹⁴ Ges Ew Hi Di *only*, but De Che *of a truth*.

†אַכַּד **n.pr.loc.** Akkad Gn 10[10] וַתְּהִי רֵאשִׁית מַמְלַכְתּוֹ בָּבֶל וְאֶרֶךְ וְא׳ וְכַלְנֵה בְּאֶרֶץ שִׁנְעָר׃; name of a city in Northern (?) Babylonia; = Bab. *Akkadi*, mostly name of land or district, but also of city, v. Hilpr. Freibrief Neb. I. col. ii, l. 50; location uncertain; on possible identif. or confusion with *Agade* (*Agate*, *Agane*?), city of Sargon I, cf. Dl Pa 198 & K 19 f. COT Gn 10[10] Tiele Gesch. i. 76 f.

אַכְזָב, אַכְזִיב v. כזב.

אַכְזָר, אַכְזָרִי, אַכְזְרִיּוּת v. כזר.

אָכִישׁ **n.pr.m.** king of Gath 1 S 21[11.12.13.15] + 15 t. 1 S 27–29 + 1 K 2[39.40] (perh. cf. ܟܐܒܐ "*anger*").

אָכַל 806 **vb.** eat (Ar. أَكَلَ, As. *akâlu* Dl W, Aram. אֲכַל, ܐܟܠ)—**Qal** *Pf.* אָכַל Ex 34[28]+; אָכְלָה Nu 21[28]+, etc. *Impf.* יֹאכַל Gn 49[27]+; וַיֹּאכַל Gn 25[34]+; וַיֹּאכַל Gn 3[6]+; יֹאכַל Lv 21[22]+; אֹכַל Gn 24[33]+; וָאֹכַל 27[33]; וָאֹכַל Is 44[19]; וַתֹּאכַל Gn 3[12.13]; 3 pl. יֹאכְלוּ Gn 32[33]+; יֹאכֵלוּ Dt 18[18]+; etc. (for יֹכְלוּ Ez 42[5] rd. יאצלו, יוצלו 𝔊 Ew Co); sf. יֹאכְלֻנוּ Lv 7[6]+; תֹּאכַלְכֶם Is 33[11], etc., prob. also תְּאָכְלֵהוּ Jb 20[26], either as secondary form fr. תא׳ (Ew § 253 Di) or text. error (Ges § 68.1) >Pi., Thes Kö I. 389; or Po'el, Ki De MV; *Imv.* אֱכוֹל 1 K 18[41]+, etc.; *Inf. abs.* אָכוֹל Gn 2[16]+; cstr. אֲכֹל Nu 26[10]+ 2 t.; לֶאֱכֹל Gn 24[33]+; לְאָכְלָה Je 12[9]; *Pt.* אֹכֵל (אוֹכֵל) Gn 39[6]+, אֹכֶלֶת Ex 24[17]+, etc.—**1.** *eat*, human subject Gn 3[11.18] + oft.; mostly c. acc. Ex 16[35]+; also sq. מִן־ (*eat of*,—some of,—or *from*) Ex 34[15] Ru 2[14]+; sq. בְּ (*eat of* or *at*) Ex 12[43 f]; abs. Dt 2[6]+; as act of worship Gn 31[54] (cf. 46[1]) Ex 18[12] 24[11] 34[15] Dt 12[7.18] 14[23.26]+; cf. of priests Ex 29[32] Lv 10[13]+; cf. אָכַל אֶל־הֶהָרִים Ez 18[6.11.15] 22[9]+33[25] עַל־הֶהָרִים Co עַל־הַדָּם; (but RS Rel. Sem. i. 324 N would emend first 4 by last); *eat up*, finish eating Gn 43[2] (c. כלה) 1 K 13[23]+; אָכַל לֶחֶם = take a meal Gn 43[25] Ex 2[20] 1 S 20[24] Je 41[1]+; so א׳ alone Gn 43[16] 1 S 20[5]+; א׳ לֶחֶם = *eat, get food* Gn 3[19] 2 K 4[8]+; Am 7[12] (i.e. spend one's life) cf. Ec 5[16]; לֹא א׳ ל׳ i.e. *fast* 1 S 28[20] 30[12] Ezr 10[6] cf. Dn 10[3]; fig. א׳ אֶת־בְּשָׂרוֹ Ec 4[5] (i.e. waste away); eat words Je 15[16] (i.e. eagerly receive); of adultery, Pr 30[20] אָכְלָה וּמָחֲתָה פִיהָ וְאָמְרָה לֹא־פָעַלְתִּי אָוֶן׃; eat (taste) good fortune, א׳ בַּטּוֹבָה Jb 21[25]; לְפִי אָכְלוֹ *according to his eating*, i.e. acc. to his needs in eating Ex 12[4] 16[16.18] also v[21]; cf. Jb 20[21] & sub אָכְלָה; אָכֹל הַפְּרִי 2 K 19[29] Am 9[14], of peaceful enjoyment of results of labour; fig. of receiving consequences of action, good or bad Pr 1[31] 18[21] Ho 10[13] cf. וַיֹּאכַל גַּם־אָכוֹל אֶת־כַּסְפֵּנוּ Gn 31[15] i.e. he has reaped all the benefit, cf. Ho 7[9]; fig. of mourner, אֵפֶר כַּלֶּחֶם אָכָלְתִּי ψ 102[10] (cf. 80[6] Hiph., & As. *akâl al âkul, bikîtum kurmatî* = food I ate not, weeping (was) my refreshment Hpt ASKT 166 f. Obv. l. 21, 22 Zim BP 34, 42); of gods, partaking of sacrifices Dt 32[38]; fig. = destroy Dt 7[16] (cf. Nu 14[9]); cf. Je 10[25] 30[16] 50[7] Ho 7[7]. **2.** of beasts, birds, etc., *eat, devour;* Gn 37[20.33] 40[17.19] 1 K 13[28] 14[11] 16[4] 21[23.24] Ho 2[14]+; specif. of locusts Jo 1[4] 2[25] 2 Ch 7[13] cf. Am 4[9]; moth Jb 13[28]; flies ψ 78[45]; worms Dt 28[39]; also Ez 19[3.6] (of Isr. under fig. of lion), cf. Je 50[7.17] 51[34]; also Ho 13[8] (of י׳ under fig. of lion), Ez 22[25] (נֶפֶשׁ אָכָלוּ, of false proph. under fig. of lion). **3.** fig. of fire, *devour, consume* Lv 6[3] (sq. 2 acc. *consume offering* to *ashes*) Na 3[13] Is 5[24] (in sim.), partic. of fire fr. י׳ Lv 10[2] 16[25] Ju 9[15 f] 1 K 18[38] 2 K 1[10.12.14] 2 Ch 7[1]; cf. Am. 1[4.7.10.12.14] 2[2.5] 5[6]+; Dt 5[22] of fire at Sinai; of י׳ as fire (in judgment) Dt 4[24] כִּי י׳ אֱלֹהֶיךָ אֵשׁ אֹכְלָה הוּא; cf. Dt 9[3] Is 10[17] (בער||) 30[27.30] 33[14] (||מוֹקְדֵי עוֹלָם). **4.** of sword, *devour, slay* Dt 32[42] 2 S 2[26] 11[25] 18[8] Ho 11[6] Je 2[30] 12[12]; cf. of devastation of land Is 1[7] Je 8[16]. **5.** in genl. *devour, consume, destroy* (inanim. subj.) of drought Gn 31[40]; of pestilence Ez 7[15]; of forest 2 S 18[8]; cf. Lv 26[38] וְאָכְלָה אֶתְכֶם אֶרֶץ אֹיְבֵיכֶם; of הַבֹּשֶׁת Je 3[24] (v. בֹּשֶׁת). **6.** fig. of oppression, *devour* the poor, etc. Pr 30[14] Hb 3[14] cf. ψ 14[4]; of bitter enmity לֶאֱכֹל אֶת־בְּשָׂרִי ψ 27[2]. (cf. Jb 19[22]). †**Niph.** *Pf.* וְנֶאֱכַל cons. Ex 22[5] *Impf.* יֵאָכֵל Gn 6[21]+; וַיֵּאָכֵל Nu 12[12], etc.; *Inf. abs.* הֵאָכֹל Lv 7[18] 19[7]; *Pt.* f. נֶאֱכֶלֶת Lv 11[47];—**1.** *be eaten* by man Ex 12[46] 13[3.7] 21[28] 29[34] Lv 6[9.16.19.23] 7[6.15.16.16.18] 11[41] 19[6.7.23] 22[30] 28[17] Ez 45[21]; of custom, usage Gn 6[21] Ex 12[16] Dt 12[22] Jb 6[6]; of permission to eat Lv 7[19] 11[13.34.47.47] 17[13]; c. neg. *be uneatable* Je 24[2.3.8] 29[17]. **2.** *be devoured* by fire, *consumed* Zp 1[18] 3[8] Zc 9[4] Ez 23[25]. **3.** *be wasted, destroyed,* of flesh Nu 12[12] Je 30[16]. **Pu.** *Pf.* אֻכְּלוּ *be consumed* with fire Ne 2[3.13] cf. Na 1[10] (fig.); so *Pt.* אֻכָּל (= מְאֻכָּל Ew § 169 d) Ex 3[2]; by sword Is 1[20] תְּאֻכְּלוּ. †**Hiph.** *Pf.* 2 ms. sf. הֶאֱכַלְתָּם ψ 80[6], וְהַאֲכַלְתִּי Is 49[26]; sf. וְהַאֲכַלְתִּיךָ cons. Is 58[14]; הֶאֱכַלְתִּיךְ Ez 16[19]; וְהַאֲכַלְתִּים cons. Je 19[9]; *Impf.* sf. יַאֲכִלֵנוּ Nu 11[4.18], etc.; 2 ms. js. תַּאֲכֵל; 1 s. אוֹכִיל Ho 11[4]; *Imv.* הַאֲכִילֵהוּ Pr 25[21], etc.; *Inf.* לְהָכִיל Ez 21[33] (but Co להחל, q.v.); *Pt.* מַאֲכִיל Je 23[15], etc.;—**1.** *cause to eat, feed with,* sq. 2 acc. subj. mostly י׳; Ex 16[32] Dt 8[3.16] Ez 3[2] Je 19[9]; abs. Ho 11[4]; cf. Nu 11[4.18]; fig. Je 9[14] 23[15] Is 49[26] 58[14] Ez 16[19]; also ψ 80[6] הֶאֱכַלְתָּם לֶחֶם

דִּמְעָה (cf. 102^{10} Qal supr); sq acc. pers. + מִן ψ 81^{17}, but also subj man Pr 25^{21}; 1 K 22^{27} 2 Ch 18^{26} וְהַאֲכִלֻהוּ לֶחֶם לַחַץ of prison fare; sq acc pers only 2 Ch 28^{15}, cf. Ez 2^{8} **2.** *cause to devour*, obj sword Ez 21^{33} (but on text vid Co)

אֹכֶל 40 **n.m.** Gn 41,36 food (Ar أُكْل, Aram אוּכְלָא, ܐܘܟܠܐ, As *akalu* Dl^{W}, Eth. ኣክል:)—א׳ abs Gn 41^{35} +, cstr Gn $41^{35.48}$, sf אָכְלְךָ Lv 25^{37}, אָכְלוֹ Mal 1^{12}, etc;—Hex mostly JED, not Ez —*food, food-supply*, esp cereals of store in Egypt Gn $41^{35.36}$ + 12 t Gn 41–44, 47^{24} cf 14^{11} (JE), also Lv 11^{34} 25^{37} (P) Dt $2^{6.28}$ (D); נֶשֶׁךְ א׳ *usury of food* Dt 23^{20} (D) (‖ נ׳ כֶּסֶף, etc); לְעֵת הָאֹכֶל *at meal-time* Ru 2^{14}, †poet. 17 t,—*food* ψ 107^{18}, of offerings Mal 1^{12}, partic. food Jb 12^{11} (as tasted), 36^{31} (as given by God) so ψ 145^{15}, א׳ לְהָשִׁיב נֶפֶשׁ La 1^{11} cf v^{19}, esp cereals Pr 13^{23} Jo 1^{16} Hb 3^{17}, but also flesh ψ $78^{18.30}$, of food (prey) of wild animals ψ 104^{21} (‖ טרף) ^{27}, of prey of eagles Jb 9^{26} 39^{29}, ravens 38^{41}.

†אָכְלָה 17 **n f** food, eating (with some verbal force, cf Dr$^{JPh\ xi\ 217}$) only P, & Ez, always לְאָכְלָה, **1.** esp in phr like לָכֶם יִהְיֶה לְא׳ Gn 1^{29} 6^{21} 9^{3} Lv 11^{39}, so 25^{6} וְהָיְתָה שַׁבַּת הָאָרֶץ לָכֶם לְאָכְלָה, cf נָתַן לְא׳ Gn 1^{30} Ex 16^{15} **2.** *devouring*, by wild beasts, only fig. of ravaged people Ez 29^{5} $34^{5.8.10}$ 39^{4}, cf 35^{12} **3.** *consuming*, in fire Ez $15^{4.6}$, of fire-sacrifice of children 23^{37}, fig of judgment of י׳ Ez 21^{37}, (cf. also inf of אָכַל).

וְאֻכָל Pr 30^{1} rd. וָאֵכֶל & v. כלה.

†אֲכִילָה **n.f.** an eating, a meal 1 K 19^{8} (on form v Ba$^{NB\ 136}$)

†מַאֲכָל 30 **n m** Ju 14,14 (f. Hb 1^{16}) food—מ׳ Gn 2^{9} + 21 t, cstr מַאֲכַל Gn 40^{7} + 3 t; sf מַאַכָלְךָ Ez 4^{10}, מַאֲכָלוֹ, Hb 1^{16}; מַאֲכָלָהּ Pr 6^{8}, מַאֲכַלְכֶם Dn 1^{10}—*food*, in genl Gn 6^{21} 1 K 10^{5} = 2 Ch 9^{4} Hg 2^{12}, opp drink Ezr 3^{7} 2 Ch 11^{11} Dn 1^{10}, מַאֲכַל תַּאֲוָה Jb 33^{20}, fig of peoples as fishes, food for Chaldeans Hb 1^{16}, appl. to fruit Gn 2^{9} 3^{6} (of tree טוֹב לְמ׳) cf עֵץ מ׳ Lv 19^{23} Dt 20^{20} Ne 9^{25} Ez $47^{12.12}$, appl to דָּגָן Is 62^{8}, appl. to honey Ju 14^{14}, to flour 1 Ch 12^{41} where appos. קֶמַח, to food of ants Pr 6^{8} (‖ לֶחֶם), to baker's work Gn 40^{17} cf Ez 4^{10}, appl to carcasses, as food for beasts & birds of prey Dt 28^{26} ψ 79^{2} cf. 44^{12} (צֹאן מ׳, sim of suffering people) Je 7^{33} 16^{4} 19^{7} 34^{20} ψ 74^{14}.

†מַאֲכֶלֶת **n.f** knife (as *cutting* instrum, or instrument for dividing, making small, cf S[iegfr] $^{ThLZ\ Nov\ 17\ 83}$) Ju 19^{29}, מַאֲכָלֶת Gn $22^{6.10}$, pl מַאֲכָלוֹת Pr 30^{14}.

†מַאֲכֹלֶת **n.f.** fuel est, only מַא׳ אֵשׁ Is $9^{4.18}$.

†מַכֹּלֶת **n.f.** food-stuff, consisting in חִטִּים, 1 K 5^{25} (on form v Bo^{§415} Sta$^{§112\ a.2}$)

†אָכֵן (perh. from אַךְ, cf Aram דָּךְ & דִּכֵן) **adv.** with strong asseverative force **a.** surely, truly, esp at beginning of a speech (stronger & more decided than אַךְ) Gn 28^{16} Ex 2^{14} 1 S 15^{32} Is 40^{7} 45^{15} Je $3^{23.23}$ 4^{10} 8^{8}. In 1 K 11^{2} אָכֵן stands unusually, and פֶּן (cf 𝔊 𝔖 𝔗) should prob be read (so Klo) **b.** emphasizing a contrast, *but indeed, but in fact*, esp. after אָמַרְתִּי *I said* or *thought*, expressing the reality, in opp to what had been wrongly imagined, Is 49^{4b} (opp to v^{4a}) 53^{4} (opp. to v$^{3\ end}$) Je 3^{20} (opp to the expectation v^{19b}) Zp 3^{7b} ψ 31^{23b} (opp to v^{23a}) 66^{19} 82^{7} (opp to v^{6}) Jb 32^{8} (opp to v^{7})

†אָכַף **vb.** press, urge (Mish *id*, Aram ܐܟܦ *be urgent*, cf ܐܘܟܦܐ, Ar إِكَافٌ *saddle*),—**Qal** *Pf* Pr 16^{26} נֶפֶשׁ עָמֵל עָמְלָה לּוֹ ‖ א׳ עָלָיו פִּיהוּ) i e his hunger impels him to work

†[אֶכֶף] **n m.** pressure, sf אַכְפִּי Jb 33^{7} (𝔊 al. rd. כַּפִּי cf 13^{21}, but cf Di)

אכר (Ar أَكَرَ *dig, till* the ground)

†אִכָּר **n.m.** Jo 1 11 ploughman, husbandman (Ar أَكَّارٌ, Aram. ܐܟܪܐ, אִיכָּרָא, cf Mish) א׳ sg abs Je 51^{23} (+ צִמְדּוֹ) Am 5^{16}, pl. אִכָּרִים Je 14^{4} 31^{24} (‖ וְנָסְעוּ בַּעֵדֶר) 2 Ch 26^{10} (‖ כֹּרְמִים) Jo 1^{11} (‖ *id.*), אִכָּרֵיכֶם Is 61^{5} (‖ *id.*)

אַכְשָׁף v. כשף.

I אַל (= أَلْ, Ar article, preserved perh. in following words derived by Hebrews from (or through) Arabic-speaking tribes, cf Eng. *algebra, Alhambra, alkali, alcohol, alcove*, etc)

†אֶלְגָּבִישׁ **n.[m.]** hail (= Ar ٱلْجِبْس *gypsum*; cf. sub גבש) אַבְנֵי א׳ Ez $13^{11.13}$ 38^{22}.

†אַלְגּוּמִים **n.[m.] pl.** a tree (foreign & obscure) alw with עֲצֵי, perh **sandal-wood** —2 Ch 2^{7} עֲצֵי אֲרָזִים בְּרוֹשִׁים וא׳ (fr Lebanon), עֲצֵי אַ׳ 2 Ch 9^{10} (‖ אֶבֶן יְקָרָה, both fr. Ophir), cf v^{11}, vid foll.

†אַלְמֻגִּים **n.[m.]pl.** *id.* עֲצֵי אַלְמֻגִּים 1 K $10^{11.12}$ (fr Ophir), ע׳ הָא׳ 1 K 10^{12}

†אַלְמוֹדָד **n.pr.** of South-Arab people (but prob rd אֵל (Sab, *god*) for אַל, cf. Di Gn 10^{26}, & Glas$^{Sk\ ii\ 290}$ *God is loved* (?)) Gn 10^{26} 1 Ch 1^{20}.

†אַלְקוּם band of soldiers (=Ar. القَوْمُ, *people;* so E. Castle, Thes etc., cf. Che$^{Job\ \&\ Sol.\ 175}$; >text. error for אֱלֹהִים Hi cf. Now) Pr 30^{31}.

†אֶלְתּוֹלַד **n.pr.loc.** (cf. תּוֹלָד sub ילד) city in southern Judah Jos 15^{30} 19^{4}; cf. also תּוֹלָד (q.v.) 1 Ch 4^{29}.

II. אַל **adv. of negation** (so Ph. e.g. CIS i.$^{3.4.5.8}$, BAram., Sab. (DHM$^{ZMG\ 1875,\ 596}$), and in the Eth. አልቦ: *albo, is not*), denying however, not objectively as a fact (like לֹא, οὐ), but subjectively as a wish (like μή), expressing therefore a *deprecation* or *prohibition:* **a.** (*a*) with a verb, which is then always an impf. (never an imperative), by preference in the cohort. or jussive mood, where this is in use, and may be of any person or number; Gn 15^{1} and often אַל־תִּירָא *fear not!* 22^{12} אַל־תִּשְׁלַח יָדְךָ *put not forth* thy hand, 37^{27} וְיָדֵנוּ אַל־תְּהִי־בוֹ and *let not* our hand *be* upon him, 21^{16} אַל־אֶרְאֶה *let me not* look upon the death of the lad! ψ 25^{2} אַל־אֵבוֹשָׁה *let* me *not be* ashamed; with 1 pl. (rare) 2 S 13^{25} Je 18^{18} Jon 1^{14}. In an imprecation: Gn 49^{4} אַל־תּוֹתַר have not thou the excellency! ψ 109^{12} Jb $3^{4.6}$. Sometimes strengthened by נָא: Gn 13^{8} 18^{3} al. (*b*) without a verb, (α) 2 S 1^{21} *let* (there be) *not* dew & *not* rain upon you! Is 62^{6} ψ 83^{1}. (β) used absol., in deprecation Gn 19^{18} 2 S 13^{16} (v. sub אוֹדֹת) 2 K 3^{13} 4^{16} 6^{27} (v. RVm: but possibly to be expl. by Dr$^{§\ 152\ iii}$; so Th Ke: hardly as Ew$^{§\ 358\ b}$) Ru 1^{13} אַל בְּנֹתַי *Nay,* my daughters, cf. Ju 19^{23}; (γ) after a preceding imper. Am 5^{14} Jo 2^{13} Pr 8^{10}, a juss. 27^{2}, an inf. abs. 27^{2}. (*c*) in poetry אַל sometimes expresses vividly the emotion or sympathy of the poet (v. Dr$^{§\ 56-8}$); Is 2^{9} וְאַל־תִּשָּׂא לָהֶם and *forgive* them *not!* (with a touch of passion), ψ 41^{3} Pr 3^{25} Jb 5^{22}; ψ 34^{6} (but 𝔊 𝔖 Ew Che here rd. וּפְנֵיכֶם, prob. rightly); 50^{3a} may our God come וְאַל־יֶחֱרַשׁ and *not be* silent! (the psalmist identifying himself with a spectator of the scene v$^{2.3b-c}$) 121^{3} (contrast v^{4} לֹא) Je 46^{6}+. **b.** once Pr 12^{28} joined closely to a subst. (cf. לֹא **2** *b*) to express with emph. its negation: In the way of righteousness is life, and in the pathway thereof אַל־מָוֶת there is *no-death!* i.e. *immortality.* **c.** once Jb 24^{25} used poet. as a subst., And bring my words לְאַל to *nought!* —N.B. 1 S 27^{10} אַל־פְּשַׁטְתֶּם הַיּוֹם with the pf. is against all analogy; and either אֶל־מִי (with 𝔊 𝔙), or better אָן *whither?* (with 𝔖 𝔗: v. 1 S 10^{14}) must be read.

אֶל (nearly always followed by Makkeph), poet. אֱלֵי (cf. עֲדֵי, עֲלֵי), but only in Job (+3^{22} 5^{26} 15^{22} 29^{19}), with suff. אֵלַי, אֵלֶיךָ, אֵלַיִךְ, etc. אֵלֵינוּ, אֲלֵיכֶם & (5 t.) אֲלֵכֶם, אֲלֵיהֶם & אֲלֵהֶם (both very often), once אֵלֵימוֹ ψ 2^{5}, אֲלֵיהֶן, once אֲלֵהֶן Ex 1^{19} (As. *ili*, Ar. إِلَى), **prep.** denoting **motion to or direction towards** (whether physical or mental). **1.** of motion *to* or *unto* a person or place Gn $2^{19.22}$ 3^{19} 8^{9} 14^{22} 16^{9} etc., after every kind of verb expressing motion (בּוֹא, הָלַךְ, יָצָא, etc.) So with נָתַן *to give* (though לְ is here more common) Gn 21^{14} 35^{4} Dt 13^{2}+; מָכַר *to sell* 37^{36}, etc. Metaph. Je 2^{19} וְלֹא פַחְדָּתִי אֵלַיִךְ and that my fear (cometh) not *unto* thee (cf. Jb 31^{23}).—Peculiarly Gn 6^{16} אֶל אַמָּה *unto* the length of a cubit, etc. And metaph. in the phrase אֶל־(אֱלֵי־)גִּיל *unto* exultation +Ho 9^{11} Jb 3^{22}. Once, exceptionally (si vera l.)=*even:* Jb 5^{5} וְאֶל־מִצִּנִּים יִקָּחֵהוּ and *even* out of thorns he taketh it. Sometimes pregnant, as Is 66^{17} Je 41^{7} זָנָה אֶל commit whoredom (by going) *to* Nu 25^{1} Ez $16^{26.28.29}$; דָּרַשׁ אֶל seek (by resorting) *to* one (sc. for oracles) Dt 18^{11} Is 8^{19} 11^{10}+; חִבֵּר אֶל join together (& come) *unto* Gn 14^{3}; הִשְׁכִּים אֶל rise early (and go) *to* 19^{27}; 24^{11} הִבְרִיךְ אֶל made to kneel down *at;* 47^{18} תַּם אֶל i.e. has been made over *to;* פָּחַד אֶל to come in fear *to* Hos 3^{5} Mi 7^{17}. Opp. is מִן, as מִן־הַקָּצֶה אֶל־הַקָּצֶה from end *to* end Ex 26^{28}; מִפֶּה אֶל־פֶּה Ezr 9^{11} (syn. 2 K 21^{16} פֶּה לָפֶה). And of time (rare) מֵעֵת אֶל־עֵת +1 Ch 9^{25}; מִיּוֹם אֶל־יוֹם +Nu 30^{15} (P) 1 Ch 16^{23} (in the ‖ ψ 96^{2} מִיּוֹם לְיוֹם).

2. Where the limit is actually entered, *into,* Gn 6^{18} and thou shalt enter *into* the ark 7^{1} 19^{3} 41^{21} 42^{17}; & so after verbs of throwing, casting, putting 37^{22} (הִשְׁלִיךְ) 39^{20} וַיִּתְּנֵהוּ אֶל־בֵּית הַסֹּהַר put him *into* the prison house, Ex 28^{30} (Lv 8^{8}) Dt 23^{25}; so after קָבַר to bury Gn 23^{19} 25^{9} 49^{29}; שָׂחַט to squeeze 40^{11}; מָחָה to blot out Nu 5^{23}, etc.; metaph. Gn 6^{6} was pained *into* or *unto* his heart, שָׂם אֶל־לֵב, הֵשִׁיב to place, bring *into* (=lay *to*) heart Dt 4^{39} 2 S 19^{20} al. In connexion with a number or multitude *into* which something enters, *in among:* 1 S 10^{22} behold he had hid himself אֶל־הַכֵּלִים *in among* the baggage, Je 4^{3} sow not אֶל־קֹצִים *in among* thorns.

3. Of direction *towards* anything: (*a*) of physical acts or states, as Gn 30^{40} נָתַן פְּנֵי הַצֹּאן אֶל, 39^{7} נָשָׂא עֵינָיו אֶל, Ex 25^{20}, Nu 6^{26} נָשָׂא פָּנָיו אֶל (2 K 9^{32} differently), 24^{1} שִׁית פָּנָיו אֶל, Jos 8^{18} ψ 28^{2} 1 K $8^{29.30}$ (to pray *towards*) v^{38}; pregn. חָרַד אֶל

to tremble (turning) *to* Gn 42^{28}, תָּמַהּ אֶל to wonder (turning) *towards* Gn 43^{33} Is 13^{8}, פָּחַד אל Je 36^{16}· without a vb פָּנִים אֶל־פָּנִים face *to* face Gn 32^{31}+; פה אֶל־פֶּה Nu 12^{8}, כי־איננו אלי Gn 31^{5} the face of Laban, that he is not *toward* me, עיני י׳ אֶל־פ׳ the eyes of ’‘ are *towards* ψ 34^{16} (cf. 33^{18}) (*b*) with words such as אָמַר to say *to* Gn 3^{1}+oft., דִּבֶּר 8^{15}+oft., קָרָא 19^{5}, הִתְפַּלֵּל 20^{17} etc, שָׁמַע to hearken *to* 16^{11}, הִלֵּל to praise *to* 12^{15} (cf Ez 13^{19} חִלֵּל אֶל to profane *to*), הזכיר 40^{14}. (*c*) with words expressing the direction of the mind, as קִוָּה *to wait* ψ 27^{14}+, יִחֵל *to hope* Is 51^{5}, נָשָׂא נפשׁ אֶל to lift up the soul (i.e. set the desire) *towards* Dt 24^{15} ψ 25^{1}, שִׁית, שָׂם לב אל to set the heart (mind) *to* Ex 9^{21} al, לָמַד אֶל to accustom oneself *to* Je 10^{2}, חָרֵד אֶל to shew fear *towards* 2 K 4^{13}, Gn 43^{33}; Dt 28^{32} and thy eyes כָּלוֹת אֲלֵיהֶם failing (with longing) *towards* them, La 4^{17}, Is 63^{15} 2 S 3^{8} 1 K 14^{13} ψ 40^{6}, alone, as predic, *directed* or *disposed towards*, Gn 3^{16} 4^{7} 2 K 6^{11} who of ours *is towards* (i e favours) the king of Syria? Ho 3^{3} וְגַם־אֲנִי אֵלָיִךְ: Ez 36^{9} Hg 2^{17} Je 15^{1} (אין נַפְשִׁי אֶל)

4. Where the motion or direction implied appears from the context to be of a hostile character, אל = *against* · Gn 4^{8} וַיָּקָם ק׳ אֶל־הבל and Cain rose up *against* Abel (so 1 S 24^{8}) 22^{12} Ex 14^{5} Nu 32^{14}, with נִקְבַּץ Jos 10^{6}, הָלַךְ Ju 1^{10} 20^{30}, with בָּא of calamity, etc, coming *to* or *upon* any one Gn 42^{21} Ju 9^{57} 1 S 2^{34} 1 K 14^{10}+, Is 2^{4} 3^{8} their tongue and doings are אֶל־י׳ 32^{6} (לְדַבֵּר אל) Ho 7^{15} (cf Na 1^{9}) 12^{5} וַיָּשַׂר אֶל־מַלְאָךְ and he strove *against* the angel. Here also belongs in partic the phrase הִנְנִי אֶל... Behold I am *against* (thee, you, etc) †Na 2^{14} 3^{5} Je 21^{13} (23$^{30-32}$ (על) 50^{31} 51^{25} Ez 13$^{8.20}$ 21^{8} 29^{10} 30^{22} 34^{10} 35^{3} 38^{3} 39^{1} (5^{8} 26^{3} 28^{22} 29^{3} על: on 36^{9} v supr)

5. *Unto* sometimes acquires from the context the sense of *in addition to*, as Lv 18^{18} thou shalt not take אִשָּׁה אֶל אֲחֹתָהּ a woman *to, in addition to*, her sister, Jos 13^{22} (‖ Nu 31^{8} על), 1 S 14^{34} to eat אֶל־הַדָּם *together with* the blood (v^{32} & generally על); 1 K 10^{7} הוסיף אל (generally על), Je 25^{26}, Ez 7^{26} שְׁמוּעָה אֶל שְׁמוּעָה (‖ על), 44^{7}, La 3^{41} let us lift up לְבָבֵנוּ אֶל־כַּפַּיִם our hearts *together with* the hands (cf إِلَى, Qor 4^{2}, W$^{AG\ II}$ ^{161} c)

6. Metaph *in regard to, concerning, on account of* thus הִתְאַבֵּל to mourn *concerning* 1 S 15^{35}, הִנָּחֵם to repent *as regards* 2 S 24^{16}; דָּרַשׁ to inquire 1 K 14^{5}, הִתְפַּלֵּל to pray *with regard to* 1 S 1^{27} 2 K 19^{20}, צָעַק to cry 2 K 8^{3} (v^{5} על), נעצב be pained 1 S 20^{34}, נִחַם to comfort 2 S 10^{2}, more gen 1 K 16^{11} 21^{22}, אֶל־נֶפֶשׁ *on account of, for the sake of*, one's life 1 K 19^{3} 2 K 7^{7} (Gn 19^{17} על) (על is more common in this sense) And specially with verbs of saying, narrating, telling, etc *with regard to*, as אָמַר Gn 20^{2} Is 29^{22} 37$^{21.33}$+, דבר 2 S 7^{19} Je 40^{16b}, ספר ψ 2^{7} 69^{27}, צִוָּה Is 23^{11}, שָׁמַע Ez 19^{4}; הַשְּׁמוּעָה אֶל the report *regarding* 1 S 4^{19}. (Not freq, exc in the case of אָמַר)

7. Of rule or standard, *according to* (rare): אֶל־פִּי ... *according to* the command of, Jos 15^{13} 17^{4} 21^{3} (generally עַל־פִּי); אֶל־נָכוֹן *according to* what is fixed = of a certainty †1 S 23^{23} 26^{4} (v Dr) perh ψ 5^{1}; 80^{1} (45^{1} על)

8. Expressing presence at a spot, *against, at, by*, not merely after verbs expressing or implying motion (cf **1**, Gn 24^{11}), as Jos 11^{5} and they came and encamped together אֶל־מֵי מרום *at* the waters of Merom, 1 S 5^{4} cut off (and fallen) *on to* the threshold, 2 S 2^{23} al. and smote him אֶל־הַחֹמֶשׁ *in* or *on* the belly, Dt 33^{28} Ex 29^{12} Lv 4^{7}, but also in other cases, as Jos 5^{3} and he circumcised the Israelites אֶל *against, at* the hill of the foreskins, 22^{11} have built an altar אל גלילות הַיַּרְדֵּן *by* the districts of Jordan, Ju 12^{6} 2 S 3^{27}, 14^{30} & 18^{4} אֶל־יַד *at* the side of (elsewhere עַל יַד, לְיַד), 1 K 13^{20} as they were sitting אֶל־הַשֻּׁלְחָן *at* the table, 2 K 11^{14} אֶל־הַמֶּלֶךְ *by* the king, Je 41^{12} and found him *by* the great waters, etc, 46^{10} אֶל־נְהַר פְּרָת *by* the Euphrates, Ez 3^{15} 11^{11} 17^{8} 31^{7} 40^{18} 43^{3} 47^{7} 48^{12}.

9. Prefixed to other preps it combines with them the idea of *motion* or *direction to* · thus סב אֶל־אַחֲרַי 2 S 5^{23} 2 K 9$^{18.19}$ אֶל־אַחֲרַי turn *to* behind me, Zc 6^{6} (where אל is pleon, prob due to clerical error, note יצא אל before & after); אֶל־בֵּין *in between* Ez 31$^{10.14}$, אל־בינות similarly Ez 10^{2}, אֶל־מִבֵּית ל׳ *to* (the part) *within* (v sub בַּיִת), *in within* Lv 16^{15}, 2 K 11^{15}‖ have her forth *in within* the ranks, אֶל־מוּל v מוּל; אֶל־מִנֶּגֶב ל׳ *unto* the south of Jos 15^{3}, אֶל־מִחוּץ ל׳ *to* the outside of Lv 4$^{12.21}$+, אֶל־נֹכַח *to* the front of Nu 19^{4}, אֶל־תַּחַת Ju 6^{19} 1 K 8^{6} al (v sub תַּחַת)

Note 1 —In Gn 20^{13} אֶל־כָּל־הַמָּקוֹם אֲשֶׁר נָבוֹא שָׁמָּה אמרי־לי וג׳, Nu 33^{54} אֶל־אֲשֶׁר וג׳; Pr 17^{8} (cf. Dt 16^{6}), אֶל— appears to be used by a species of attraction, the idea of motion involved in the relative clause influencing illogically the beginning of the sentence and causing אֶל to be used instead of ב In Ez 31^{14} אֲלֵיהֶם, as pointed, can only be from אַיִל III

or IV (q. v.); if the word be taken as the pron. with suff. (Hi Ke), אֲלֵיהֶם must be read.

Note 2.—There is a tendency in Hebrew, esp. manifest in S K Je Ez, to use אֶל in the sense of עַל; sometimes אֶל being used exceptionally in a phrase or construction which regularly, and in acc. with analogy, has עַל; sometimes, the two preps. interchanging, apparently without discrimination, in the same or parallel sentences. Thus (*a*) Jos 5^{14} וַיִּפֹּל אֶל־פָּנָיו; 1 S 13^{13} הֵקִים י׳ אֶת־מַמְלַכְתְּךָ אֶל־יִשְׂרָאֵל; 14^{34} (v. sub **5**); 17^{3} עֹמְדִים אֶל־הָהָר (contr. עַל Dt 11^{29}); 19^{16} 2 S 6^{3} 20^{23} (contr. 8^{16}) 1 K 13^{29} 18^{46} (contr. 2 K 3^{15} עַל) Je 35^{15} Ez 7^{18}. (*b*) Ju 6^{37} and upon (עַל) all the earth let there be dryness, v^{39} let there be dryness *on* (אֶל) the fleece; 1 S 14^{10} come up עָלֵינוּ, v^{12} come up אֵלֵינוּ; 16^{23*16}; 16^{13} & 18^{10} צָלַח אֶל, 10^{6} al. צָלַח עַל; 25^{17} evil is determined אֶל־אֲדֹנֵינוּ וְעַל כָּל־בֵּיתוֹ; v^{25}; 27^{10}; 2 S 2^{9} וַיַּמְלִכֵהוּ אֶל ... וְאֶל ... וְעַל ... וְעַל ... וְעַל; 3^{29} יָחֻלוּ עַל ... וְאֶל ...; 2 K $8^{3.5}$; $9^{6.3}$; Je 19^{15}; 25^{2}; 26^{15} ye lay innocent blood עֲלֵיכֶם וְאֶל־הָעִיר הַזֹּאת; 27^{19} 28^{8} 33^{14} 34^{7} 36^{31} $37^{13.14}$ Ez $18^{6.11.15}$ 21^{12} etc. ψ 79^{6} (Je 10^{25} עַל twice). It is prob. that this interchange, at least in many cases, is not original, but due to transcribers.

Conversely, though not with the same frequency, עַל occurs where analogy would lead us to expect אֶל, or even in juxtaposition with אֶל, as 1 S 1^{10} הִתְפַּלֵּל עַל to pray *to* (v^{26} אֶל); v^{13}; 25^{25} אֶל ... עַל; 1 K 20^{43} וַיֵּלֶךְ עַל־בֵּיתוֹ (21^{4} אֶל); Is 22^{15} Je 11^{2} 23^{35} 31^{12}. Cf. Dr$^{Sm\ i.\ 13,13;\ ii.\ 8,7;\ 15,4}$.

†אֶלְיְהוֹעֵינַי **n.pr.m.** (*unto* י׳ *are mine eyes*) **1.** a Korahite 1 Ch 26^{3}. **2.** a returning exile Ezr 8^{4}.

†אֶלְיוֹעֵינַי **n.pr.m.** (*id.*) **1.** a descendant of David 1 Ch $3^{23.24}$. **2.** a Simeonite אֶלְיוֹעֵנַי 1 Ch 4^{36}. **3.** a Benjamite (*id.*) 7^{8}. **4.** priests in time of Ezra (*a*) Ezr 10^{22}; (*b*) 10^{27} (אֶלְיוֹעֵנַי); (*c*) Ne 12^{41}.

†I. אֵל **pr. pl. m.** & **f.** = the more usual אֵלֶּה, *these* 1 Ch 20^{8}; with art. הָאֵל Gn $19^{8.25}$ $26^{3.4}$ Lv 18^{27} Dt 4^{42} 7^{22} 19^{11}. (Merely an orthogr. variation of אֵלֶּה, and doubtless pronounced similarly; the kindred dialects have in genl. a dissyllabic form: v. sub אֵלֶּה. Written similarly in Ph., e.g. CIS 3^{22} 14^{5} 93^{3} (האל), but ZMG $^{1875,\ 240}$ (Neo-Punic) אלא; in Plaut. Poen. v. 1. 9 transliterated *ily;* Schroed.$^{Ph.\ Gr.\ p.\ 81,\ 160,\ 286\ ff}$.)

אֵלֶּה (أُولَى, أُلَى; ኢሉ: ኢላ: Rabb. אֵלּוּ, Aram. אִלֵּין, & compd. with ܗܳܠܶܝܢ and ܠ in ܗܳܠܶܝܢ, ܐܶܠܶܝܢ, ܐܶܠܶܝܢ) **pr. pl. m.** & **f. these,** in usage the pl. of זֶה. **a.** Gn 2^{4} & oft.: in appos. to a subst. with a pron. suff. (always *without* the art.) Ex 9^{14} (rd. with Hi. אֵלֶּה בְּךָ for אֶל־לִבְּךָ) 10^{1} אֹתֹתַי אֵלֶּה *these* my signs, 11^{8} Dt 11^{18} 1 K 8^{59} 10^{8} 22^{23} 2 K 1^{13} Je 31^{21} Ezr 2^{65} Ne 6^{14}; in the genit. 2 K 6^{20} Is 47^{9} Dt 18^{12} ψ 15^{5}; and after כל Gn 14^{3} + oft. Standing alone in a neuter sense, *these things* (rare in best prose, & not very common in poetry), with עָשָׂה Dt 18^{12} 22^{5} 25^{16} 2 S $23^{17.22}$ ψ 15^{5} +; with other vbs. Ezr 9^{1} Is 44^{21} 47^{7} Je 13^{22} Ho 14^{10} ψ 42^{5} 50^{21} 107^{43} Jb 8^{2}; with אֶת־ Nu 15^{13} Is 48^{14}; with כָּל־ Ju 13^{23} Is 66^{2} +; v. also some of the cases with preps. sub **d.** אלה may point indifferently to what follows, Gn 6^{9} 10^{1} $25^{7.12.13}$ ψ 42^{5}; or to what has preceded, Gn 9^{19} $10^{20.31.32}$ 25^{4} Lv 21^{14} 22^{22} ψ 15^{5}; = *such as these* (τοιαῦτα), ψ 73^{12} Jb 18^{21}. **b.** repeated, אלה ... ואלה, *these ... those* Dt 27^{13} Jos 8^{22} Is 49^{12} (3 t.) ψ 20^{8} +. **c.** with the art. (but only after a subst. determined likewise by the art.) הָאֵלֶּה Gn 15^{1} + oft. **d.** with preps.: בְּאֵלֶּה Lv 25^{54} 26^{23} 1 K 22^{11} (7 t.), †1 S 16^{10} בָּאֵלֶּה 17^{39}; לָאֵלֶּה Lv 11^{24} (4 t.), 1 K 22^{17} (5 t.); מֵאֵלֶּה Gn 9^{19} (16 t.); עַד אֵלֶּה Lv 26^{18}; עַל־אֵלֶּה *on account of these things* Is 57^{6} 64^{11} Je 5^{9} al.; כְּאֵלֶּה †Jb 16^{2} Je 10^{16} = 51^{19}, כָּאֵלֶּה †Gn 27^{46} Lv 10^{19} (things like these, so Is 66^{8} Je 18^{13}) Nu 28^{24} P (cf. Ez 45^{25}) 2 K 25^{17} = Je 52^{22}, כְּמוֹ־אֵלֶּה †Jb 12^{3}.

II. אֵל *god,* אֶלְדָּעָה, אֶלְדָּד etc. v. I. אלה.

†אֵלָא **n.pr.m.** father of an officer of Solomon 1 K 4^{18} (= II. אֵלָה *terebinth?*).

I. אלה (assumed as √ of אֵל, אֱלֹהִים (אֱלוֹהַּ), *god, God,* but question intricate, & conclusions dub. It is uncertain whether אֵל & אֱלֹהִים are from the same √. Following are the chief theories: **1. a.** Thes makes אֵל & אֱלֹהִים distinct, and both really primitive, but associates אֵל in treatment with אֵל *strong, Pt.* of √ אול; *strong,* acc. to Thes, being derived from mng. *be in front of;* (different order in Lex. Man., RobGes); **b.** אֵל & אֱלֹהִים distinct; former fr. אול *strong;* latter pl. of אֱלוֹהַּ from √[אלה] = أَلِهَ (وَلِهَ) *go to and fro* in perplexity or fear, hence אֱלוֹהַּ *fear & object of fear,* reverence, *revered one;* أَلِهَ إِلَى = פחד אל *trepide confugere ad* Ho 3^{5}; פחד = אלהים Gn 31^{42} = מוֹרָא Is 8^{13}

(poet. Moses || צור & אֱלֹהֵי קֶדֶם) 2 S 22^{32} 23^{3} (poet. David || צור) and in the combinations אל עליון (5 t; vid. עליון) & אל שדי (10 t, vid. שַׁדַּי).

†7. אֵל *strength, power* (on connection with I. אֵלָה cf. Di Gn 1^{1} 31^{29}) in יֶשׁ־לְאֵל יָדִי *it is according to the power of my hand* = it is in my power, etc. Gn 31^{29} (E; sq. לְ + Inf), בהיות לאל יָדְךָ Pr 3^{27} (sq id), יֶשׁ־לְאֵל יָדָם Mi 2^{1} (abs), neg. וְאֵין לְאֵל יָדֶךָ Dt 28^{32} (abs.) = *thou shalt be powerless*, so Ne 5^{5}.

אֱלֹהַּ $_{57}$ so Dt 32^{17}; לֶאֱלֹהַּ Dn 11^{38} (vid. BD) sf. לֶאֱלֹהוֹ Hb 1^{11}; elsewhere אֱלוֹהַּ **n.m. god, God** (Sam *id*, Aram. אֱלָהּ, ܐܠܗܐ, Ar إِلٰهٌ, Sab אלה DHM$^{l.c.}$,—אֱלֹהַּ as found in Heb prob. a sg formed by inference fr. pl אֱלֹהִים: cf Nes$^{l.c.}$)—**1.** *a heathen god*, late usage; כָּל־אֱלוֹהַּ 2 Ch 32^{15} Dn 11^{37}; זו כחו לאלהו *whose power is his god* Hb 1^{11} 2 K 17^{31} (but Qr אֱלֹהֵי), אשר הביא אֱלוֹהַּ בְּיָדוֹ *who doth bring God in his hand* Jb 12^{6} (Ew Di RVm, etc.) **2. God**, used in ancient poems Dt 32$^{15.17}$ ψ 18^{32}, and on their basis an archaism in later poetry Jb 3^{4} + (41 t. Jb), ψ 50^{22} 114^{7} 139^{19} Pr 30^{5} Is 44^{8} Hb 3^{3} Ne 9^{17} (citing Ex 34^{6} where אל is used)

אֱלֹהִים $_{2570}$ **n.m.pl.** (**f.** 1 K 11^{33}; on number of occurrences of אֱלֹהִים, אֱלוֹהַּ, אל cf. also Nes$^{l.c.}$) **1.** *pl.* in number. †**a.** *rulers, judges*, either as divine representatives at sacred places or as reflecting divine majesty and power האלהים Ex 21^{6} (Onk 𝔖, but τὸ κριτήριον τοῦ Θεοῦ 𝔊) 22$^{7.8}$; אלהים 22$^{8.27}$ (𝔗 Ra AE Ew RVm, but *gods*, 𝔊 Josephus Philo AV; *God*, Di RV, all Covt. code of E) cf. 1 S 2^{25} v. Dr, Ju 5^{8} (Ew, but *gods* 𝔊, *God* 𝔖 BarHeb.; יהוה 𝔅 Be) ψ 82$^{1.6}$ (De Ew Pe; but *angels* Bl Hup) 138^{1} (𝔖 𝔗 Rab Ki De, but *angels* 𝔊 Calv; *God*, Ew; *gods*, Hup Pe Che). †**b.** *divine ones*, superhuman beings including God and angels ψ 8^{6} (De Che Br; but *angels* 𝔊 𝔖 𝔗 Ew, *God*, RV and most moderns) Gn 1^{27} (if with Philo 𝔗 Jer De Che we interpret נעשה as God's consultation with angels; cf. Jb 38^{7}) †**c. angels** ψ 97^{7} (𝔊 𝔖 Calv, but *gods*, Hup De Pe Che), cf. בני (ה)אלהים = (*the*) *sons of God*, or *sons of gods* = angels Jb 1^{6} 2^{1} 38^{7} Gn 6$^{2.4}$ (J; so 𝔊 Bks of Enoch & Jubilees Philo Jude v^{6} 2 Pet 2^{4} Jos $^{Ant. i. 3. 1}$, most ancient fathers and modern critics; against usage are *sons of princes, mighty men*, Onk and Rab; *sons of God*, the pious, Theod Chrys Jer Augustine Luther Calv Hengst; 𝔊L rd. οἱ υἱοὶ τοῦ Θεοῦ), cf. בני אלים **d.** *gods* האלהים Ex 18^{11} 22^{19} (E) 1 S 4^{8} 2 Ch 2^{4} ψ 86^{8}; אלהי האלהים the *God of gods*, supreme God Dt 10^{17} ψ 136^{2}; אלהים Ex 32$^{1.23}$ (JE) Ju 9^{13}; אלהים אחרים *other gods* Ex 20^{3} 23^{13} Jos 24$^{2.16}$ (E) Dt 31$^{18.20}$ (JE) 5^{7} + (17 t in D, not P) Ju 2$^{12.17.19}$ 10^{13} 1 S 8^{8} 26^{19} 1 K 9$^{6.9}$ (= 2 Ch 7$^{19.22}$) 11$^{4.10}$ 14^{9} 2 K 5^{17} 17$^{35.37.38}$ 22^{17} (= 2 Ch 34^{25}) 2 Ch 28^{25} Je 1^{16} + (18 t. Je) Ho 3^{1}; אלהי (ה)נכר *foreign gods* Gn 35$^{2.4}$ Jos 24$^{20.23}$ (E) Dt 31^{16} (JE) Ju 10^{16} 1 S 7^{3} 2 Ch 33^{15} Je 5^{19}, א׳ נחור Gn 31^{53} (E), א׳ מצרים Ex 12^{12} (P) Je 43$^{12.13}$, א׳ האמרי Jos 24^{15} (E) Ju 6^{10}, א׳ ארם etc Ju 10^{6}, אלהים מעשה ידי Dt 4^{28}, א׳ הגוים *gods of the nations* 2 K 18^{33} 19^{12} Dt 29^{17} 2 Ch 32$^{17.19}$ Is 36^{18} 37^{12}, א׳ העמים Dt 6^{14} 13^{8} Ju 2^{12} ψ 96^{5} 1 Ch 5^{25} 16^{26} 2 Ch 32$^{13.14}$, א׳ כסף Ex 20^{23} (E), א׳ זהב Ex 20^{23} (E) 32^{31} (JE), א׳ מַסֵּכָה Ex 34^{17} (J) Lv 19^{4} (H)

2. *Pl. intensive* **a.** *god or goddess*, always with sf. 1 S 5^{7} (Dagon), Ju 11^{24} (Chemosh), 1 K 18^{24} (Baal), Ju 9^{27} Dn 1$^{2.2}$; or cstr לעשתרת א׳ צדנים לכמוש א׳ מואב to Ashtoreth goddess of the Zidonians, Chemosh god of Moab, etc. 1 K 11^{33}, א׳ הארץ god of the land 2 K 17$^{26.26.27}$, and so the Syrians suppose that Yahweh is a mountain-god and not a god of valleys 1 K 20^{28} **b.** *godlike one* Ex 4^{16} (J; Moses in relation to Aaron), Ex 7^{1} (P, in relation to Pharaoh), 1 S 28^{13} (the shade of Samuel), ψ 45^{7} (the Messianic king, *O God*, 𝔊 𝔖 Jer, most scholars ancient and modern, but *thy throne is God's* = God's throne AE Ki Thes Ew Hup, cf 1 Ch 28^{5}). **c.** works of God, or things specially belonging to him (vid. אל **5**) הר אלהים ψ 68^{16}, Ez 28$^{14.16}$; איש אלהים Jb 1^{16}, גן (ה)אלהים Ez 28^{13} 31$^{8.9}$. **d. God** (vid. **3** & **4**)

3. הָאֱלֹהִים *the* (*true*) *God*, י׳ הוא האלהים *Yahweh is* (*the*) *God* Dt 4$^{35.39}$ 7^{9} 1 K 8^{60} 18$^{39.39}$ 2 Ch 33^{13}; הוא האלהים Is 45^{18}, י׳ האלהים Jos 22^{34} (P?) 1 K 18$^{21.24}$ 2 Ch 32^{16}; אתה הוא האלהים 2 S 7^{28} 1 K 18^{37} 2 K 19^{15} 1 Ch 17^{26} Is 37^{16} Ne 9^{7}; האלהים as subj or obj is used in E 33 t, Chr 38 t, Ec 31 t, Jon 5 t, elsewhere Gn 5$^{22.24}$ 6$^{9.11}$ (sources of P) 17^{18} (P) Jos 22^{34} (P?) Gn 44^{16} (J) Dt 4$^{35.39}$ 7^{9} Ju 6$^{36.39}$ 7^{14} 10^{14} 16^{28} 21^{2} 1 S 10$^{3.7}$ 14^{36} 2 S 2^{27} 6^{7} 7^{28} 12^{16} 1 K 8^{60} 18$^{21.24.24.37.39.39}$ 19^{15} (Ephr) Jb 2^{10} Je 11^{12} Is 37^{16} 45^{18} ψ 108^{14} Dn 1$^{9.17}$; הא׳ אשר Ne 8^{6}; י׳ הא׳ הגדול 1 S 6^{20}; י׳ הא׳ הקדוש בירושלם Ezr 1^{3}, אדני האלהים Dn 9^{3}; in many phrases, as איש האלהים *the man of God*, acting under divine authority and influence: = (*a*) *angel* Ju 13$^{6.8}$, (*b*) *prophet* (the term coming into use in the Northern kingdom in the age of Elijah 1 S 9$^{9.10}$, cf. איש הָרוּחַ Hos 9^{7}). of *Moses* Dt 33^{1} Jos 14^{6} (E) 1 Ch 23^{14} 2 Ch 30^{16} Ezr 3^{2} ψ 90^{1};

of *Samuel* 1 S 9$^{6-10}$, of *David* 2 Ch 8^{14} Ne 12$^{24.36}$, *Shemaiah* 1 K 12^{22} (= 2 Ch 11^{2}), *Elijah*, *Elisha*, and others of their time 1 K 13$^{1-31}$ 17$^{18-24}$ 20^{28} 2 K 1$^{9-13}$ 4$^{7-42}$ 5$^{8-20}$ 6$^{6-15}$ 7$^{2-9}$ 8$^{2-11}$ 13^{19} 23$^{16-17}$ (Ephr) 2 Ch 25$^{7.9}$, unnamed prophet 1 S 2^{27}, *Hanan* Je 35^{4}, a later title of prophet was עֶבֶד האלהים *the servant of God*, used of Moses 1 Ch 6^{34} 2 Ch 24^{9} Ne 10^{30} Dn 9^{11} בית האלהים *the house of God*, Ju 18^{31}, esp. late, Chr (52 t.) Ec 4^{17} Dn 1^{2}, בית י׳ והא׳ 1 Ch 22^{1}, ארון (ברית) האלהים *the ark (of the covenant) of God* Ju 20^{27} 1 S 4–5 14, 2 S 6–7 15 (23 t) 1 Ch 13 15 16, 2 Ch 1^{4} (13 t), מטה האלהים *the rod of God* Ex 4^{20} 17^{9} (E), הר האלהים *the mount of God* (Horeb) Ex 3^{1} 4^{27} 18^{5} 24^{13} (E) 1 K 19^{8} (Ephr); מלאך האלהים *the (theophanic) angel of God* Gn 31^{11} Ex 14^{19} (E) Ju 6^{20} 13$^{6.9}$ 2 S 14$^{17.20}$ 19^{28}, in other combinations Ex 18^{16} Nu 23^{27} (E) Ju 20^{2} 1 S 4^{8} 5^{11} 10^{5} 2 S 16^{23} 1 K 12^{22} 1 Ch 21^{7} + (14 t) ψ 87^{3} Ec 9^{1}

4. אֱלֹהִים = *God* י׳ אלהים אֱמֶת = *Yahweh is God in truth* Je 10^{10} **a** אלהים (as subj obj. direct or indirect) is used by P (50 t in story of creation and deluge, elsewhere 28 t) by E (91 t), J chiefly in poetic sources Gn 3$^{1.3.5.5}$ 9^{27} 39^{9} Dt 32$^{17.39}$, by D (11 t) Ju (21 t) S (50 t) K (29 t) Chr (45 t); in ψ 42–86 (180 t often by editorial change for an original יהוה), elsewhere ψ 3^{3} 5^{11} 7$^{11.12}$ 9^{18} 10$^{4.13}$ 14$^{1.2.5}$ 25^{22} 36$^{2.8}$ 77^{14} 100^{3} 108$^{2.6.8.12.12}$ 149^{9} Jb 5^{8} 20^{29} 28^{23} 32^{2} 34^{9} (& in Prologue 6 t) Pr 2^{5} 3^{4} 25^{2} Ec (7 t) Hos (5 t) Am 4^{11} (כמהפכת אלהים את סדם *as God overthrew Sodom* = Je 50^{40} = Is 13^{19}) Zc 8^{23} 12^{8} Mi 3^{7} (but אליהם 𝔊 𝔖) Is 35^{4} Is^{2} (9 t) Je 10^{10} Ez (13 t) Mal (5 t) Jon (4 t), the phrase היה ל׳ לאלהים Gn 28^{21} (E^{R}) 17$^{7.8}$ Ex 6^{7} 29^{45} Lv 11^{45} 22^{33} 25^{38} 26$^{12.45}$ Nu 15^{41} (P) Dt 26^{17} 29^{12} 2 S 7^{24} (= 1 Ch 17^{22}) Zc 8^{8} Je (6 t) Ez (6 t), אלהים צדיק *righteous God* ψ 7^{10}; א׳ קדשים *holy God* Jos 24^{19} (E), א׳ חיים *living God* Dt 5^{23} 1 S 17$^{26.36}$ Je 10^{10} 23^{36}, א׳ חי 2 K 19$^{4.16}$ (= Is 37$^{4.17}$) For the phrases א׳ צבאות, יהוה א׳, י׳ א׳ צבאות, י׳ אלהי צבאות, א׳ צבאות, יה א׳, אל א׳, א׳ י׳, אדני & צבאות vid אדני, יהוה, יה, צבאות **b** cstr אלהי (*a*) *with persons* אלהי אַבְרָהָם = *God of Abraham*, a phrase of J, Gn 26^{24} 28^{13} 31^{53}, elsewhere ψ 47^{10} 1 K 18^{36} 1 Ch 29^{18} 2 Ch 30^{6}, א׳ אדני אברהם Gn 24$^{12.27.42.48}$ (J), אלהי אב *father's God* (various sf & names), a phrase of E, Gn 31$^{5.29.42}$ 46^{3} 50^{17} Ex 3$^{6.13.15.16}$ 15^{2} 18^{4} Jos 18^{3}, elsewhere Gn 32^{10} 43^{23} (J) Ex 4^{5} (J ?) Dt (8 t) Ju 2^{12} 2 K 21^{22} Chr (31 t) Dn 11^{37}, אלהי ישראל *Israel's God*, phrase of E, Gn 33^{20} Ex 5^{1} 24^{10} 32^{27} Jos 8^{30} 14^{14} 22^{16} 24$^{2.23}$, elsewhere Ex 34^{23} Jos 7$^{13.19.20}$ (JE) Nu 16^{9} Jos 9$^{18.19}$ 22^{24} 10$^{40.42}$ 13$^{14.33}$ (R vid. Di Jos 7^{13}) Ju 4^{6} 5$^{3.5}$ 6^{8} 11$^{21.23}$ 21^{3} 1 S 1^{17} + (20 t) K (26 t) Chr (45 t) ψ 41^{14} 106^{48} (doxol) 59^{6} 69^{7} Is 17^{6} 21$^{10.17}$ 29^{23} Is^{2} 24^{15} 37$^{16.21}$ Is^{2} 41^{17} + (6 t) Je 35^{17} + (48 t), Ez 8^{4} + (7 t) Zp 2^{9} Mal 2^{16} Ru 2^{12}, א׳ מערכות ישראל *God of the battle array of Israel* 1 S 17^{45}, א׳ יַעֲקֹב 2 S 23^{1} (poet.) ψ 20^{2} 46$^{8.12}$ 75^{10} 76^{7} 81$^{2.5}$ 84^{9} 94^{7} Is 2^{3} (= Mi 4^{2}), א׳ העבריים *God of the Hebrews* Ex 3^{18} 5^{3} 7^{16} 9$^{1.13}$ (JE), it is used with other proper names, Nahor Gn 31^{53} (E), Shem Gn 9^{26} (J), David 2 K 20^{5} 2 Ch 21^{12} 34^{3} Is 38^{5}, Hezekiah 2 Ch 32^{17}, Elijah 2 K 2^{14}, א׳ אדני המלך *the God of my lord the king* 1 K 1^{36}. (*β*) *with nouns of attributes or relationships*, א׳ קֶדֶם *ancient God* Dt 33^{27}, א׳ עולם *everlasting God* Is 40^{28}, א׳ אֱמֶת *true God* 2 Ch 15^{3}, א׳ אָמֵן Is 65^{16} (vid אָמֵן), א׳ משפט Is 30^{18} Mal 2^{17}, א׳ מרום Mi 6^{6}, א׳ כָּל בָּשָׂר *God of all flesh* Je 32^{27}, cf א׳ הרוחות לכל בשר Nu 16^{22} 27^{16} (P), א׳ השמים *God of heaven* Gn 24^{7} (J^{R}) 2 Ch 36^{23} Ezr 1^{2} Ne 1$^{4.5}$ 2$^{4.20}$, cf י׳ א׳ השמים וא׳ כל הארץ Is 54^{5}, א׳ הארץ Gn 24^{3} (J^{R}), א׳ מקרב *a God at hand* opp א׳ מֵרָחֹק Je 23^{23}, א׳ יִשְׁעִי, א׳ ישועתי *God of my salvation* ψ 18^{47} (= 2 S 22^{47}) 24^{5} 25^{5} 27^{9} 65^{6} 79^{9} 85^{5} Is 17^{10} Mi 7^{7} Hb 3^{18} 1 Ch 16^{35}, א׳ ישועתי ψ 88^{2}, א׳ תשועתי ψ 51^{16}, א׳ צדקי *God of my righteousness* ψ 4^{2}, א׳ חַסְדִּי ψ 59$^{11.18}$; א׳ צורי *God who is my rock* 2 S 22^{3} (cf ψ 18^{3}), א׳ מָעֻזִּי *God who is my stronghold* ψ 43^{2}; א׳ תהלתי *God who is my praise* ψ 109^{1} **c.** *with sf.* in P (22 t incl phr ויראת מאלהיך) Lv 19$^{14.32}$ 25$^{17.36.43}$ (H) Ex 8^{21} Jos 24^{27} (E) Dt 32^{17} (poet) Jos 9^{23} (JE) Dt 10^{21} 31^{17} Ju 10^{10} 16$^{23.24}$ 1 S 10^{19} 2 S 10^{12} 22^{32} + (4 t poet) 1 K 12^{28} 20^{23} 2 K 19^{10} Chr (83 t) ψ (62 t) Pr 2^{17} 30^{9} Ru 1$^{15.16.16}$ Is 1^{10} 7^{13} 8$^{19.21}$ Is^{2} (29 t) Je 5$^{4.5}$ 23^{36} 51^{5} Ez 34^{31} Dn (5 t) Ho (12 t) Am 2^{8} 4^{12} Jo 1$^{13.13.16}$ 2^{17} Mi 6^{8} 7^{7} Jon 1$^{5.6}$ Zp 3^{2} Na 1^{14} Zc 9^{7} 12^{5}, אלהים with sf. is also used with יהוה several hundred times (vid יהוה)

†אֶלְדָּד **n.pr.m.** (*God has loved*, cf Sab ודדאל DHM$^{ZMG\ 1883\ 15}$, v also יְדִידְיָה) one of the elders Nu 11$^{26.27}$, prob = אֱלִידָד Nu 34^{21} where called a prince of Benjamin — On n pr with אל cf those with אָב & אָח, & esp. No^{1c}, v. p. 42, & (Sab) DHM$^{Epigr\ Denkm\ 84}$

†אֶלְדָּעָה **n.pr.m.** (*God has called*? cf دعا Ar.) son of Midian Gn 25^{4} 1 Ch 1^{33}

†אֶלְזָבָד **n.pr.m.** (*God has given*, cf. Θεόδωρος, זְבַדְיָה, זַבְדִּיאֵל) **a.** one of David's band of Gadites 1 Ch 12^{12} **b.** a Korahite 1 Ch 26^{7}

†אֶלְחָנָן **n.pr.m.** (*God has been gracious*,

cf Ph. בעלחנן ,אלחנן, in As. *Ba'alḫanunu* COT Gn 10^{18}) two of David's chiefs 2 S 21^{19} = 1 Ch 20^{5}; 2 S 23^{24} = 1 Ch 11^{26}.

†אֱלִיאָב **n.pr.m.** (*God is father*, cf אֲבִיאֵל) **a.** prince of Zebulon Nu 1^{9} 2^{7} 7$^{24.29}$ 10^{16} **b.** prince of Reuben Nu 16$^{1.12}$ 26$^{8.9}$ Dt 11^{6} **c.** brother of David 1 S 16^{6} 17$^{13.28.28}$ 1 Ch 2^{13} 2 Ch 11^{18} (cf אֱלִיהוּ 1 Ch 27^{18}). **d.** a Kohathite 1 Ch 6^{12} = אֱלִיאֵל v^{19} cf אֱלִיהוּ 1 S 1^{1} **e.** a Gadite 1 Ch 12^{9}. **f.** Levite singer 1 Ch 15$^{18.20}$ 16^{5}

†אֱלִיאֵל **n.pr.m.** (*Ēl is God*, or *my God is God*) only Ch. **a.** two or three of David's chiefs 1 Ch 11$^{46.47}$ 12^{11}. **b.** chief of Manasseh 1 Ch 5^{24}. **c.** two chiefs of Benjamin 1 Ch 8$^{20.22}$. **d.** chief of the Hebronites 1 Ch 15$^{9.11}$ **e.** a chief Kohathite 1 Ch 6^{19} = אֱלִיאָב v^{12} cf אֱלִיהוּ 1 S 1^{1}. **f.** a Levite 2 Ch 31^{13}.

†אֱלִיאָתָה **n.pr.m.** (*God has come*) a Hemanite 1 Ch 25^{4} = אֱלִיָּתָה 1 Ch 25^{27}

אֱלִידָד v. אֶלְדָּד supr.

†אֶלְיָדָע **n.pr.m.** (*God knows*, cf דעואל, Sab. אלידע Hal^{209}) **a.** son of David 2 S 5^{16} 1 Ch 3^{8} = בעלידע 1 Ch 14^{7} which perh rd here, cf Dr^{Sm} **b.** father of an adversary of Solomon 1 K 11^{23}. **c.** chief of Benjamin 2 Ch 17^{17}

אֵלִיָּה 2 K 1^{3} + 4 t., אֵלִיָּהוּ 1 K 17^{1} + 62 t, **n.pr.m.** (*Yah(u) is God*, cf. יואל) **a.** Elijah, the great prophet of the reign of Ahab 1 K 17^{1} + 65 t. K; 2 Ch 21^{12} Mal 3^{23} **b.** Benjamite 1 Ch 8^{27}; **c.** a priest of Ezra's time Ezr 10^{21}, **c.** a son of Elam Ezr 10^{26}.

†אֱלִיהוּ Jb 32^{4} + 3 t.; אֱלִיהוּא Jb 32^{2} + 6 t.; **n.pr.m.** (*He is (my) God*) **a.** the young friend of Job Jb 32$^{2.4.5.6}$ 34^{1} 35^{1} 36^{1}. **b.** an Ephraimite, Samuel's great-grandfather 1 S 1^{1} cf אֱלִיאָב 1 Ch 6^{12}, אֱלִיאֵל v^{19}. **c.** chief of Manasseh 1 Ch 12^{20}. **d.** a Korahite 1 Ch 26^{7} **e.** one of the brethren of David 1 Ch 27^{18} (cf. אֱלִיאָב 1 S 16^{6}).

†אֶלְיַחְבָּא **n.pr.m.** (*God hides*) one of David's chiefs 2 S 23^{32} 1 Ch 11^{33}

†אֱלִיחֹרֶף **n.pr.m.** (*Autumn God?* cf Jb 29^{4}) one of Solomon's scribes 1 K 4^{3}.

†אֱלִימֶלֶךְ (& -מָלֶךְ Ru 2^{1}) **n.pr.m.** (*God is king*, cf. מַלְכִּיאֵל) husband of Naomi Ru 1$^{2.3}$ 2^{3} 4$^{3.9}$.

†אֶלְיָסָף **n.pr.m.** (*God has added*) **a.** chief of Gad Nu 1^{14} 2^{14} 7$^{42.47}$ 10^{20}. **b.** chief of Gershon Nu 3^{24}

†אֱלִיעֶזֶר (-עָזֶר Gn 15^{2} +) **n.pr.m.** (*God is help*, cf Ex 18^{4}; v. also אֶלְעָזָר infr., עֲזַרְאֵל, Ph. עזרבעל, בעלעזר, אשמנעזר) **a.** Abraham's steward (אֱלִיעָזֶר), a Damascene Gn 15^{2}. **b.** a son of Moses Ex 18^{4} 1 Ch 23$^{15.17.17}$. **c.** Benjamite 1 Ch 7^{8} **d.** several priests 1 Ch 15^{24} 1 Ch 26^{25} Ez 10^{18}. **e.** Reubenite 1 Ch 27^{16} **f.** prophet in time of Jehoshaphat 2 Ch 20^{37}. **g.** Levite chief Ez 8^{16} 10^{23}. **h.** son of Harim Ezr 10^{31}.

†אֱלִיעָם **n.pr.m.** (*God is kinsman*; Ph אלעם) **a.** father of Bathsheba 2 S 11^{3}; cf עַמִּיאֵל 1 Ch 3^{5} **b.** one of David's heroes 2 S 23^{34} (acc. to some = **a**).

†אֱלִיפַז **n.pr.m.** (*God is fine gold?*) **a.** son of Esau Gn 36$^{4.10.11.12.12.15.16}$ 1 Ch 1$^{35.36}$. **b.** friend of Job Jb 2^{11} 4^{1} 15^{1} 22^{1} 42$^{7.9}$.

†אֱלִיפָל **n.pr m.** (*God has judged*) one of David's heroes 1 Ch 11^{35} (but v. אליפלט 2 S 23^{34})

†אֱלִיפְלֵהוּ **n.pr.m.** (*may God distinguish him*) one of the doorkeepers 1 Ch 15$^{18.21}$

†אֱלִיפֶלֶט (-פָּלֶט 2 S 5^{16} +) **n.pr.m.** (*God is deliverance*, cf. פַּלְטִיאֵל) **a.** son of David 2 S 5^{16} 1 Ch 3$^{6.8}$ 14^{7}, = אֶלְפָּלֶט 1 Ch 14^{5} **b.** one of David's heroes 2 S 23^{34} (cf also אֱלִיפַל 1 Ch 11^{35}). **c.** a Benjamite 1 Ch 8^{39}. **d.** one of the line of Adonikam Ezr 8^{13} **e.** of the line of Hashum Ezr 10^{33}

†אֱלִיצוּר **n.pr.m.** (צוּר *Rock is God*, cf Dt 32^{4}, v. also צוּרִיאֵל) chief of Reuben Nu 1^{5} 2^{10} 7$^{30.35}$ 10^{18}.

†אֱלִיצָפָן **n.pr m.** (*God has protected*, cf. Ph. צפנבעל) **a.** chief of the Kohathites Nu 3^{30} 1 Ch 15^{8} 2 Ch 29^{13}, = אֶלְצָפָן Ex 6^{22} Lv 10^{4}. **b.** chief of Zebulun Nu 34^{25}.

†אֱלִיקָא **n.pr.m.** (not in 𝔊, 1 Ch 11^{27} Dr) one of David's heroes 2 S 23^{25}

†אֶלְיָקִים **n.pr.m.** (*God sets up*, cf. Sab יקמאל, הקמאל Hal^{615}) **a.** Hezekiah's prefect of the palace 2 K 18$^{18.26.37}$ 19^{2} Is 22^{20} 36$^{3.11.22}$ 37^{2}. **b.** son of Josiah, made king by Pharaoh 2 K 23^{34} 2 Ch 36^{4}, = יְהוֹיָקִים 2 K 24^{1} Je 1^{3} 1 Ch 3^{15}. **c.** a priest Ne 12^{41}.

†אֱלִישֶׁבַע **n pr.f.** (*God is an oath*, by which one swears, cf. Is 19^{18} Am 8^{14} Zp 1^{5}) wife of Aaron Ex 6^{23}; = Ἐλισαβεθ 𝔊, cf Lu 1^{7}.

†אֱלִישׁוּעַ **n.pr.m.** (*God is salvation*, cf. אֱלִישָׁע infr.; or *is opulence*, cf. אֲבִישׁוּעַ) son of David 2 S 5[15] 1 Ch 14[5].

†אֶלְיָשִׁיב **n.pr.m.** (*God restores*, cf. Nes [Eg 194] & Sab. תובאל DHM[ZMG 1883, 16]) **a.** a descendant of David 1 Ch 3[24]. **b.** priest of David's time 1 Ch 24[12]. **c.** high priest of Nehemiah's time Ezr 10[6] Ne 3[1.20.21.21] 12[10.10.12.23] 13[4.7.28]. **d.** a singer Ezr 10[24]. **e.** one of the line of Zattu Ezr 10[27]. **f.** one of the line of Bani Ezr 10[36].

†אֱלִישָׁמָע (*God has heard*, cf. יִשְׁמָעֵאל, & Sab. אלסמע, יסמעאל Hal[187, 193]) **a.** chief of Ephraim Nu 1[10] 2[18] 7[48.53] 10[22] 1 Ch 7[26]. **b.** son of David 2 S 5[16] 1 Ch 3[6.8] 14[7]. **c.** scribe of Jehoiakim Je 36[12.20.21]. **d.** one of the royal seed 2 K 25[25] Je 41[1]. **e.** a man of Judah 1 Ch 2[41]. **f.** a priest 2 Ch 17[8].

אֱלִישָׁע **n.pr.m.** (*God is salvation*, cf. אֱלִישׁוּעַ, Sab. יתעאל DHM[ZMG 1883, 15]) the prophet Elisha, the successor of Elijah 1 K 19[16] + 57 t. all K; Ἐλισα, Ἐλισαιε 𝔊; Ἐλισαιος Lu 4[27].

†אֱלִישָׁפָט **n.pr.m.** (*God has judged*, Ph. שפטבעל, בעלשפט) a captain in the time of Jehoiada 2 Ch 23[1].

אֱלִיָּתָה v. אֱלִיאָתָה.

אֶלְמוֹדָד v. sub I. אֵל.

†אֶלְנַעַם **n.pr.m.** (*God is pleasantness*) father of two of David's heroes 1 Ch 11[46] (not in S).

†אֶלְנָתָן (*God has given*, cf. נְתַנְאֵל, & As. *Ilu-iddin* Dl[Pr 207], Ph. בעליתן, יתנבעל, Palm. קסנתן, והבאל, עתנתן, והבלת Vog[Pal 30 & p. 31 f], Nab. אלוהב, והבאל Eut[Nab 12, 1], Sab. DHM[ZMG 1883, 15. 361. 388] CIS[iv. 1. 1.2.6], Theodore, Diodate). **a.** the grandfather of Jehoiakim 2 K 24[8]; cf. Je 26[22] 36[12.25](?). **b.** Levites of the time of Ezra Ezr 8[16.16.16].

†אֶלְעָד **n.pr.m.** (*God has testified*) an Ephraimite 1 Ch 7[21].

†אֶלְעָדָה **n.pr.m.** (*God has adorned*, cf. עֲדִיאֵל) an Ephraimite 1 Ch 7[20].

†אֶלְעוּזַי **n.pr.m.** (*God is my strength* = אֶלְעֻזִּי, cf. עֻזִּיאֵל, Sab. אלעת (אלעז) DHM[ZMG 1883, 15]) one of the heroes of David 1 Ch 12[5].

אֶלְעָזָר **n.pr.m.** (*God has helped*, cf. אֱלִיעֶזֶר supr.) **a.** Eleazar the priest Ex 6[23] + (50 t. in Hex) Ju 20[28] 1 Ch 5[29.30] 6[35] 9[20] 24[1.2.3.4.4.5.6] Ezr 7. **b.** son of Abinadab 1 S 7[1]. **c.** one of David's heroes 2 S 23[9] 1 Ch 11[12]; ins. also 1 Ch 27[4] cf. Dr[Sm 280]. **d.** a Levite 1 Ch 23[21.22] 24[28]. **e.** priest of the time of Ezra Ezr 8[33] Ne 12[42]. **f.** one of the line of Parosh Ezr 10[25].

†אֶלְעָלֵא, אֶלְעָלֵה ‖ **n.pr.loc.** (*God doth ascend*?) of a village in the tribe of Reuben, near Heshbon, in ruins, *el Âl* (vid. Rb[BR ii. 278]) Nu 32[3.37] Is 15[4] 16[9] Je 48[34].

†אֶלְעָשָׂה **n.pr.m.** (*God has made*, cf. עֲשָׂהאֵל, יַעֲשִׂיאֵל etc.) **a.** descendant of Judah 1 Ch 2[39.40]. **b.** a Benjamite 1 Ch 8[37] 9[43]. **c.** of the line of Pashur Ezr 10[22]. **d.** son of Shaphan Je 29[3].

אֶלְפָּלֶט v. אֱלִיפֶלֶט.

†אֶלְפַּעַל **n.pr.m.** (*God of doing*? cf. Ph. פעלאבסת) a Benjamite 1 Ch 8[11.12.18].

אֶלְצָפָן v. אֱלִיצָפָן.

אֶלְקָנָה **n.pr.m.** (*God has created*, or *taken possession*) **a.** father of Samuel 1 S 1–2 (8 t.) 1 Ch 6[12.19]. **b.** son of Korah Ex 6[24]. **c.** a ruler in Jerusalem in the time of Ahaz 2 Ch 28[7]. **d.** one of David's warriors 1 Ch 12[6]. **e.** several Levites (*a*) 1 Ch 6[8.10.21] (*β*) v[11.20] (*γ*) 9[16] (*δ*) 15[23].

†II. אָלָה **vb. swear, curse** (cf. I. אלה? so Thes Lag[Or ii. 3])—**Qal** *Pf.* 1 K 8[31] (= 2 Ch 6[22] all Vrss Th Bö Bä Kp reading וְאָלָה); אָלִית Ju 17[2]; *Inf. abs.* אָלֹה Ho 4[2]; אָלוֹת Ho 10[4]. **1.** *swear, take oath* before God 1 K 8[31] (= 2 Ch 6[22]); in covenants Ho 4[2] 10[4] (falsely). **2.** *curse* Ju 17[2]. **Hiph.** *Impf.* וַיֹּאֶל 1 S 14[24]; *Inf.* לְהַאֲלֹתוֹ 1 K 8[31] = 2 Ch 6[22] *adjure, put under oath.*

†אָלָה **n.f.** oath Gn 26[28] +; sf. אָלָתִי, אָלָתוֹ Gn 24[41] + (4 t.); pl. אָלוֹת Dt 29[20] + (4 t.) **1.** *oath* in testimony Lv 5[1] Nu 5[21.21] (P) Pr 29[24]; בא באלה *come into an oath* Ne 10[30]; הביא באלה *bring into an oath* Ez 17[13]; נשא אלה 1 K 8[31] (= 2 Ch 6[22]). **2.** *oath* of covenant Gn 24[41.41] 26[28] (J) Dt 29[11.13]; בזה אלה *despise an oath* Ez 16[59] 17[16.18.19]. **3.** *curse* (*a*) from God Nu 5[23] (P) Dt 29[18.19.20] 30[7] 2 Ch 34[24] Is 24[6] Je 23[10] Dn 9[11] Zc 5[3]; (*b*) from men Jb 31[30] ψ 10[7] 59[13]. **4.** *execration* in the phrase היה לאלה *become an execration* Nu 5[27] (P) Je 29[18] 42[18] 44[12].

†תַּאֲלָה, sf. תַּאֲלָתְךָ, **n.f.** curse La 3[65].

†III. [אָלָה] **vb. wail** (Aram. אֱלָא, אֲלָא) only **Qal** *Imv.* fs. אֱלִי Jo 1[8] (v. אַלְלַי).

†אַלְיָה **n.f.** fat tail of sheep, still accounted a delicacy in the East; (Mish. *id.* 𝔗,

אֲלִיתָה, אַלִיתָא, etc.; Ar أَلْيَة, cf. Fl.[TWB i. 418a]) Ex 29[22] Lv 3[9] 7[3] 8[25] (all ‖ חֵלֶב); 9[19], prob. also 1 S 9[24] for הֶעָלֶיהָ v Gei Dr (cf Tristram Nat. Hist Bib. ch. vi Ri[HWB Schafe] Smith[Dict. Bib. sheep]).

†אִלּוּ **conj.** (oft. in Mishnah; Aram אִילּוּ, ܐܠܘ, ܐܠܘ: from אִין, ܐܢ, and לוּ) if, though, only in late Heb, Ec 6[6] Est 7[4]

I אֱלוּל **n.pr.** of 6th month, Aug—Sept Ne 6[15] (Mish. id, Pal. אלול Vog[79], As *Ululu* COT Ne 1[1], Ar أَيْلُول, Aram ܐܝܠܘܠ)

†אָלוּשׁ **n.pr.loc.** a station of Israel in the wilderness Nu 33[13.14].

†[אָלַח] **vb.** only **Niph.** **be corrupt** morally; *tainted* (Che ψ 14[3]) (cf. Ar أَلِخَ viii *be confused* (of a thing), of milk, *turn sour*) *Pf* 3 pl נֶאֱלָחוּ ψ 14[3] 53[4]; *Pt* נֶאֱלָח *a corrupt man* Jb 15[16].

אֱלֵי Gn 24[39] v אוּלַי.

†אֱלִישָׁה **n.pr.loc.** as *son of Javan* Gn 10[4] 1 Ch 1[7]; אִיֵּי א׳ Ez 27[7] (*Aeolis* Josephus Jer Kn; H. Derenbourg[Mélanges Graux. 235 f (Eng trans. Hbr Oct. 1887 7)], *Hellas* 𝔗[Jon] etc., Len[Orig ii 2. 34 f]; *Italy*, with *Sicily*, cf. מדינת איטַלְיָא 𝔗 Ezek, Di Gn 10[4]; *Carthage*=Elissa, Sta[De Populo Javan, 8 f], E Meyer Gesch i § 282; decision difficult; last view very attractive)

I. [אלל] (*to be weak* or *insufficient*, assumed in Thes as root of אֱלִיל (as also of אַל): cf Ar أَلَّ *to fail* in a thing).

†II. אֱלוּל Je 14[14] Kt, 1 q אֱלִיל, q v.

†אֱלִיל **n.m.** (etym uncertain. most prob akin to Syr. ܐܠܝܠܐ *weak, feeble, poor*, perh also in usage [cf **b**] felt to suggest אַל *not;* cf Che on Is 2[8]) *insufficiency, worthlessness* **a.** Zc 11[17] רֹעִי הָאֱלִיל the shepherd of *worthlessness*=the worthless shepherd, Jb 13[4] רֹפְאֵי אֱלִל *worthless* physicians (‖ טֹפְלֵי־שֶׁקֶר), Je 14[14] Qr concr. *a thing of nought* (uttered by prophets), but here קֶסֶם אֱלִיל a *worthless* divin. (‖ חֲזוֹן שֶׁקֶר, תַּרְמִית לִבָּם) should perh be read (cf. Gf). **b** esp pl אֱלִילִים concr *worthless gods, idols* (cf. הֲבָלִים) (*possibly* orig. an indep. word=*gods*, cf. Sab. אלאלת, & v No[SBAk 1882 p. 1191], but even if so, associated by the prophets with idea of worthlessness, & used by them in iron contrast with אֱלֹהִים, אֵלִים) Lv 19[4] (not to be *made*) 26[1] (both H), Is 2[8.18.20.20] (of silver & gold), 10[10] מַמְלְכוֹת הָאֱלִיל (coll.) kingdoms of *idolatrous worthlessness*, v[11] 19[1.3] (of Egypt) 31[7.7] Ez 30[13] (Egypt), Hb 2[18] א׳ אִלְּמִים *dumb* idols, ψ 96[5] (=1 Ch 16[26]) all the gods of the nations are א׳ *vain, worthless gods* 97[7].

II. אלל (✓assumed for following words)

†אַלָּה **n.f.** oak (cf אַלּוֹן, but 𝔊 here τερέμινθος) only Jos 24[26] *the oak which is in the sanctuary of* י׳, rd. however perh אֵלָה, *terebinth* (v. I. אֵלָה)

†אַלּוֹן **n.m.**[Gn 35. 8] oak (𝔊 βάλανος, δρῦς, etc) —א׳ abs. Gn 35[8]+; cstr. *ib*, pl אַלּוֹנִים Am 2[9] Ez 27[6], cstr אַלּוֹנֵי Is 2[13] Zc 11[12],—as marking grave of Deborah, Rebekah's nurse Gn 35[8] (E), whence called *oak of weeping*, א׳ בָּכוּת *ib.* (v. Di *ad loc*, & sub אלון p 18); elsewhere only in prophets, as marking illicit shrines Ho 4[13] (‖ לִבְנֶה, אֵלָה), as felled Is 6[13] (in sim.; ‖ אֵלָה); as furnishing material for making idols Is 44[14] (‖ אֹרֶן, תִּרְזָה, אֹרֶן); as sim for strength (חסן) Am 2[9]; also אַלּוֹנֵי הַבָּשָׁן Is 2[13] (as lofty & majestic), cf. Ez 27[6] (as strong, for making oars); Zc 11[2], metaph of prominent men

†אַלּוֹן **n.pr.m.** (*oak*) a Simeonite 1 Ch 4[37] (on Jos 19[33] v. אלון p. 18)

†אַלַּמֶּלֶךְ **n.pr.loc.** in Asher (=אַלַּת מֶלֶךְ so Thes MV) Jos 19[26] (Baer אַלְמ׳)

†אַלְלַי **interj.** (prob onomatop. cf. أَلَّ, אֵלָה, ܐܠܠܝ *to wail*, ኦሎ: *woe!* Di[715]) alas! woe! sq לִי *to me* Mi 7[1] Jb 10[15].

†[אָלַם] **vb.** bind (perh. cf. As. [*alāmu*], *almattu, fortress* Dl in Zim[BP 114] & in BD Ezek.[xi], Ar أَلِمَ *be in pain*, Aram. ܐܠܡ *retain* anger) **Niph.** (*be bound*=) **be dumb**, *Pf.* 3 fs. נֶאֱלָמָה Is 53[7], וְנֶאֱלַמְתָּ Ez 3[26], etc; *Impf.* 2 ms תֵּאָלֵם Ez 24[27], 3 fpl. תֵּאָלַמְנָה ψ 31[19].—**1.** *be dumb*, i e silent ψ 39[3] (‖ הֶחֱשֵׁיתִי, כ׳ דוּמִיָּה), cf v[10] (‖ לֹא אֶפְתַּח־פִּי); sim of sheep Is 53[7] (‖ *id*); *be dumb*, i e. unable to speak Ez 3[26] (result of וּלְשׁוֹנְךָ אַדְבִּיק אֶל־חִכֶּךָ) cf. 24[27] ... יִפָּתַח פִּיךָ; 33[22] וְתְדַבֵּר וְלֹא תֵאָלֵם עוֹד, וַיִּפָּתַח פִּי וְלֹא נֶאֱלַמְתִּי עוֹד; also Dn 10[15] (cf. v[16]); *be made dumb* subj. שִׂפְתֵי שָׁקֶר *lying lips* ψ 31[19] (‖ יִדְּמוּ לִשְׁאוֹל v[18])

Pi. *Pt bind* Gn 37[7] (E) מְאַלְּמִים אֲלֻמִּים *binding sheaves.*

†[אֲלֻמָּה] **n.f. sheaf,** in Joseph's dream Gn 37[7 7 7 7] (E) sq sf אֲלֻמָּתִי, pl אֲלֻמִּים, אֲלֻמֹּתֵיכֶם, also ψ 126[6] אֲלֻמֹּתָיו (in fig of ret fr captivity)

†אֵלֶם **n.[m.] silence,** ψ 56[1] (title) vid Ol De, in name of melody עַל־יוֹנַת אֵלֶם רְחֹקִים, also ψ 58[2] (=adv *in silence*?) but rd אֵל(י)ם Ol De Che, etc

†אִלֵּם **adj. dumb,** unable to speak, Ex 4[11] מִי שָׂם פֶּה לָאָדָם אוֹ מִי יָשׂוּם אִלֵּם, Is 56[10] כְּלָבִים אִלְּמִים fig of false proph, of idols אֱלִילִים א׳ Hb 2[8], as subst Pr 31[8] ψ 38[14] Is 35[6]

אֻלָם v אוּלָם p 19

אֵלָם v אֵילָם sub II אול

†אַלְמָן **adj forsaken,** of Israel Je 51[5] (sq מֵאֱלֹהִים)

†אַלְמֹן **n.[m.] widowhood,** fig of Babylon Is 47[9] (|| שְׁכוֹל, cf v[9], vid. Ba[NB 59])

†אַלְמָנָה **n f widow** (Mish *id*, As *almattu* Dl in Zim[BP 114])—א׳ Gn 38[11]+, no cstr, pl אַלְמָנוֹת Ex 22[23]+, pl sf אַלְמְנוֹתָיו Jb 27[15], etc—*widow* 1 K 17[20], אִשָּׁה אַ׳ 2 S 14[5] (|| וַיָּמָת אִישִׁי) 1 K 7[14] 11[26] 17[9 10], Gn 38[11] (J, living in father's house) cf Lv 22[13] (H, || גְּרוּשָׁה); 21[14] (H), where widow forbidden as wife of h p, like חֲלָלָה, גְּרוּשָׁה, זֹנָה cf Ez 44[22 22.22] (*id* of all priests, exc widow of priest), Nu 30[10] (P; of widow's vow, || גְּרוּשָׁה), נְשֵׁיכֶם אַלְמָנוֹת = ye shall be slain Ex 22[23] (|| בְּנֵיכֶם יְתֹמִים) cf ψ 109[9] Je 15[8] 18[21] Ez 22[25], also La 5[3] (sim), of those snatched away by pestilence אַלְמְנוֹתָיו לֹא תִבְכֶּינָה Jb 27[15], by sword, *id*, ψ 78[64], 𝔊 We rd אַלְמְנוֹת חַיּוּת 2 S 20[3] (v אַלְמָנוּת infr) of imprisoned concubines; fig of Jerusalem La 1[1]; Babylon Is 47[8], esp widow as helpless, exposed to oppression & harsh treatment (oft || יָתוֹם, & גֵּר); Is 1[23] 10[2] Jb 22[9] 24[3] 31[16] ψ 94[6] Mal 3[5], harshness forbidden, & care for them enjoined Ex 22[21] (E) Dt 14[29] 16[11 14] 24[17 19.20 21] 26[12 13] 27[19] Is 1[17] Je 7[6] 22[3] Zc 7[10], cf Jb 29[13], under esp. care of God Dt 10[18] Je 49[11] Pr 15[25] ψ 68[6] 146[9], once of severity of judgment in not sparing widow Is 9[16] (אַל׳ Is 13[22] vid sub אַרְמוֹן, Ez 19[7] vid *ib* & also sub מעך)

†[אַלְמָנוּת] **n.f. widowhood** (Mish *id*, Ph אלמת) sf בִּגְדֵי אַלְמְנוּתָהּ *her widow's garments* Gn 38[14 19]; cstr. אַלְמְנוּת חַיּוּת 2 S 20[3] (of David's imprisoned concubines; but text impossible, 𝔊 We אַלְמָנוֹת חַיּוֹת, cf Dr; Klo thinks gloss); fig of Jerusalem Is 54[4] אַלְמְנוּתַיִךְ.

†אַלְמֹנִי **adj. some one, a certain** (name *unspoken*), מְקוֹם פְּלֹנִי א׳ 1 S 21[3] 2 K 6[8]; פ׳ א׳ alone, of person, = *such-an-one, so-and-so* Ru 4[1].

†אֶלָּסָר **n.pr.loc. Ellasar** Gn 14[1 9] (= Bab. *Larsa*, mod *Senkereh*, c. 28 miles NE. from Ur; cf Loft[CS 240 f] Dl[Pa 223 f] Tiele[Gesch 1 86], COT[ad loc])

†I [אָלַף] **vb. learn** (Ar أَلِفَ *keep, cleave to, become familiar with,* Aram אֲלַף, ܝܠܦ, *learn,* ܐܠܦ, Pa *teach*) **Qal** *Impf.* 2 ms תֶּאֱלַף אֹרְחֹתָו Pr 22[25], **Pi. teach,** sq. acc וִיאַלֶּפְךָ Jb 15[5] (subj עֲוֹנְךָ), so *Pt* מַלְּפֵנוּ (for מְאַלְּ׳ Sta[§ 111, 3] Ko[I 383] Ge[§ 68 k], cf Ew[§ 73 b]) Jb 35[11], sq 2 acc אֲאַלֶּפְךָ חָכְמָה Jb 33[33]

†I. [אֶלֶף] **n.m.** [ψ 8, 8], only pl **cattle** (Ph אלף, As *alpu*, COT[Gloss])—אֲלָפִים Pr 14[4] Is 30[24] used in tillage; subject to man ψ 8[8] (|| צֹנֶה), their increase שְׁגַר אֲלָפֶיךָ a blessing Dt 7[13] 28[4 18.51] (|| all עַשְׁתְּרֹת צֹאנֶךָ)

1. אַלּוּף **adj. tame**—א׳ abs Mi 7[5]+; cstr. Pr 2[17]+, sf אַלּוּפִי ψ 55[14], pl. אַלֻּפִים Je 13[21], sf אַלּוּפֵינוּ ψ 144[14], etc.,—**1.** *tame, docile,* כֶּבֶשׂ אַלּוּף *a docile* (gentle) *lamb* Je 11[19]. **2. n m** *friend, intimate* ψ 55[14] (|| מְיֻדָּע) Mi 7[5] (|| רֵעַ) Pr 16[28] 17[9] Je 13[21]; of a woman's husband א׳ נְעוּרֶיהָ Pr 2[17], fig of ׳י as husband of Judah, *id*, Je 3[4]. **3.** 1 q 1 אֶלֶף, אַלּוּפֵינוּ מְסֻבָּלִים ψ 144[14] (i e. cows)

II אֶלֶף **n.m.** [Ju 6 15] **thousand** (אלף MI, SI, Sab DHM[ZMG 1875, 615]; Ar أَلْف, Aram. ܐܠܦ, אַלְפָּא, אֲלַף)—א׳ (אָ׳) Gn 20[16]+, sf אַלְפִּי + Ju 6[15]; du אַלְפַּיִם Nu 4[36]+; pl. אֲלָפִים Ex 18[21]+, cstr. אַלְפֵי Ex 32[28]+, אֲלָפֶיךָ Dt 7[13]+2 t, אֲלָפָיו Qr 1 S 18[7]+2 t (Kt ־פו)—*a thousand.* **1.** numeral **a.** used with noun alone, mostly before noun Nu 35[4] Jos 7[3] Ne 3[13] 1 Ch 18[4]+, after noun (late) 1 Ch 12[35]+6 t. Ch Ezr Ne; א׳ בָּאַמָּה Nu 35[5.5.5 5] Ez 47[3] (del Co), the noun always pl when preceding, sometimes when following, 1 S 25[2] 1 K 3[4] 2 K 18[23] = Is 36[8] 2 Ch 30[24] ψ 90[4] Jb 42[12] Ec 6[6], elsewh sg. אִישׁ Ju 9[49] 15[15 16] Jos 7[3]+, אַמָּה Nu 35[4]+ (so SI), דּוֹר Dt 7[9]+, cf. 1 Ch 18[4] 19[6] 2 K 15[19] Jb 42[12] Ct 4[4] Is 7[23], noun sometimes coll, א׳ pl cstr. Mi 6[7] ψ 119[72] Gn 24[60], noun not

expr. (or not fully) Gn 20[16] Nu 31[5.6]+; distrib אָלֶף . . . אָלֶף Nu 31[4]; multipl Dt 1[11] א׳ פְּעָמִים; indef. for great no (pl) Ex 20[6] 34[7] Dt 5[10] Je 32[18], (sg) Dt 32[30] Ec 6[6]+ **b.** א׳ + other num usually precedes it Ex 38[26] + oft; but foll. רִבּוֹא Ezr 2[64] + 2 t., it follows also smaller no. Nu 3[50] 1 K 5[12] (so SI); the noun foll. in sg. Ex 28[25] + 8 t.; pl 2 S 8[4] + 2 t.; noun precedes, in pl (late) Dn 12[12] + 2 t.; noun not expr Ex 38[28] + oft. **c.** א׳ × other no always foll. Ex 12[37]+; usual order is *no* × א׳ + *additional no* (if any) + *noun* (if expr.) Nu 31[52] Ju 20[35] cf. Ex 12[37] 2 K 3[4.4]+; less oft *noun* + *no*. × א׳ Nu 31[33] 1 K 8[63]+; (other combin v Ex 38[26] Nu 26[51] 31[32] Ex 48[30] 1 Ch 29[7] etc.), א׳ usually sg. Nu 11[21]+; exc after units, where pl. abs Nu 1[46] Ju 20[34]+ (so MI); seld. pl cstr Ex 32[28] Ju 4[10] Jb 1[3.3]; (noun mostly sg when foll Ju 4[10] 1 K 12[21]+, yet pl. Jos 4[13] 1 S 13[5]+; when preceding it is pl. 1 Ch 5[21]+, or coll. Nu 31[33] 1 S 25[2] 1 K 8[63] 2 Ch 7[5]+), אֶלֶף אֲלָפִים 1 Ch 21[5] 22[14] 2 Ch 14[8]; אלפי שִׁנְאָן ψ 68[18], cf. שִׁנְאָן; בְּהַרְרֵי אָלֶף ψ 50[10], rd אל cf ψ 36[7], Ol Bi Che; yet v. Hup De—*Note.* 10,000 = עֲשֶׂרֶת אֲלָפִים etc. Ju 1[4] 3[29] 1 K 5[28] 1 Ch 29[7]+; less oft. רִבּוֹ, רְבָבָה etc. q v. **2.** *a thousand*, a company of 1000 men, as united under one superior, or leader, hence שַׂר א׳ (שָׂרֵי) Ex 18[21.25] cf Nu 31[14]+; cf. רָאשֵׁי א׳ יִשְׂרָאֵל Nu 1[16] 10[4] Jos 22[21.30] & v infr, cf. also 1 S 29[2], esp *family*, etc Ju 6[15] 1 S 10[19] (|| שֵׁבֶט & cf מִשְׁפָּחַת v[21]); cf. Mi 5[2],—Nu 10[36] (רִבְבוֹת אַלְפֵי יִשְׂרָאֵל) 31[5] Jos 22[14] 1 S 23[23] apparently shew transit. to this technical use

III. **אֶ֫לֶף n.pr.loc.** city in Benj, הָא׳ Jos 18[28]; perh *Lifta* NW fr. Jerus. Survey[iii 18] (cf. II אֶלֶף **2** for prob. meaning).

II. **אַלּוּף n.m.** [1 Ch 1, 51] **chief, chiliarch** (denom. fr. II אֶלֶף v. Di Gn 36[15])—א׳ abs Gn 36[15]+; pl. cstr. אַלּוּפֵי (אַלֻּפֵי) Ex 15[15]+, sf אַלּוּפֵיהֶם Gn 36[19.30]—*chief* (tribal) of Edom Gn 36[15(8 t.)] + 38 t Gn 36 (P), Ex 15[15] (E) 1 Ch 1[51(4 t.)] + 9 t; of Judah Zc 12[5.6]; so אַלֻּף 9[7] (in sim.)

†[**אָלַץ**] **vb. Pi. urge** (Aram. אֲלַץ, Sam. ‭ࠀࠋࠑ‬) 3 fs. וַתְּאַלְצֵהוּ Ju 16[16] (|| הֵצִיקָה לוֹ בִדְבָרֶיהָ).

אַלְקוּם v I. **אַל**.

†**אֶלְקֹשִׁי adj gent.** c art Nahum the **Elkoshite** Na 1[1] (perhaps = *from Elkosh*, but locality unknown; identified by Jer[Comm] with a village *Elcesi* in Galilee; cf also Capernaum (= כְּפַר נַחוּם ?); others (improbably) with an Elkosh on E. bank of Tigris, near Mosul).

†**אֶלְתְּקֵה, אֶלְתְּקֵא n.pr.loc.** Levitical city in the tribe of Dan, between Ekron & Timna, As *Altaku* (COT) Jos 19[44] 21[23].

†**אֶלְתְּקֹן n.pr.loc.** a city in the tribe of Judah north of Hebron Jos 15[59]

אִם conj. (= Aram אִן *if* [and in אֶלָּא, אִלָּא = אִן לָא *if not, except*], Ar. إِنْ *if* [and in إِلَّا = إِنْ لَا *if not, except*], Eth ኤመ: (*ĕmma*) *if* = אִם + מָה (إِنْ + مَا) [and in አላ: (*allâ*) *if not, but*], As. *umma*; also in Ar أَمْ ʼAn *ʼi*' = أَمْ, cf. הַאִם: v. No[M p. 208, ZMG 1886, p. 739], WAG i § 367 e)

1. hypoth. part. if **a.** *construction* (v. more fully Dr[§ 136-138, 143] Friedrich[Die Hebr Condit sätze 1884]): (1) with **impf.** (continued by pff. & waw consec., apod usually begins with pf & waw consec. or bare impf., or, if necess., with imper. or juss) (*a*) of *future* time. Gn 18[26] אִם־אֶמְצָא if I shall find 50 righteous in Sodom, וְנָשָׂאתִי I will pardon, etc., 24[8] 32[9] Dt 19[8 f.] 1 K 1[52 b] 6[12] ψ 89[31-33], Gn 42[37] Ju 13[16] 1 K 1[52 a] ψ 132[12]. (*b*) of *past* time (rare, but classical) Gn 31[8] אִם יֹאמַר *if ever* he said . וְיָלְדוּ *then* they *used to* bear, etc., Ex 40[37], & in the protestations Jb 31[7 13.16.25] etc (alternating with pff., v. infr, & with jussives in apod) (*c*) assuming a purely imaginary case (with impf in both clauses, like the double opt. in Greek), *if, though:* Gn 13[16] so that אִם־יוּכַל *if* a man *were* able to number the stars, thy seed also יִמָּנֶה *might* be numbered, Nu 22[18] Is 1[18] אִם־יִהְיוּ ח׳ כַּשָּׁנִים יַלְבִּינוּ *though* your sins *were* as scarlet, they *should* become white as snow, Am 9[2-4] אִם־יַחְתְּרוּ *though* they *were* to dig into Sheôl, from thence תִּקָּחֵם *would* my hand fetch them, ψ 27[3] 139[8]+. (2) with **pt.** (expressing either a present process, or an approaching future: apod as 1 *a*) Gn 24[42.49] Ju 6[36] 9[15] 11[9] אִם מְשִׁיבִים אַתֶּם if ye are going to bring me back . וְנָתַן י׳ then י׳ will, etc., similarly with יֵשׁ or אֵין Gn 44[26] Ex 22[2] 1 S 20[8] 23[23], & with no explicit copula Dt 22[2] 25[2] Lv 1[3.14], etc. (3) with **perf.** (*a*) of *fut.* or *pres* time (continued by pff. & waw consec.: apod. as 1 *a*) Gn 43[9] אִם־לֹא הֲבִיאֹתִיו אֵלֶיךָ וְהִצַּגְתִּיו לְפָנֶיךָ if I do not bring him back (si eum non reduxero) and set him before thee, I will be guilty for ever, 47[6] *if* thou *knowest* that there are men of worth among them וְשַׂמְתָּם then make them, etc., Ju 16[17] 2 S 15[33] 2 K 7[4] ψ 41[7] 94[18] Jb 7[4] 9[30 f] 10[14] אִם חָטָאתִי וּשְׁמַרְתָּנִי if I sin, thou watchest me On אִם־נָא Gn 18[3] al. v. נָא. (*b*) of *past* time, whether (*α*) in actual fact, or (*β*) in an assumed case (the pf. is here continued by the *impf.* and waw consec., apod. begins as

before) (*a*) Ju $9^{16.19}$ אם . . . עֲשִׂיתֶם *if ye have done* honestly וַתַּמְלִיכוּ *and have made* Abimelech king . ., 1 S 26^{19}; esp. in protestations, as ψ 7^{4} אם עָשִׂיתִי זאת *if I have* done this . , let the enemy pursue my soul, etc Je 33^{25f} Jb $31^{5f.9}$, etc (*b*) Nu 5^{27} *if she have* defiled herself וַתִּמָּעַל *and been* faithless, וּבָאוּ *then shall* they come, etc, 15^{24} $35^{22.24}$. (*c*) with bare pf. in apod, in sense of *If . . had* , only Dt 32^{30} אם־לא כי *were it not that* , ψ 73^{15}. (לוּ is more usual in such cases) (4) with **inf.** once (si vera l) Jb 9^{27} אם אָמְרִי = if I say (lit if (there is) my saying)—Note that the vb. following אם is often strengthened by the inf abs, as Ex 15^{26} 19^{5} 21^{5} $22^{3.12.16.22}$ Ju 11^{30} 14^{12} 16^{11} etc; cf Dr[§ml 29 6].

b *Special uses:* (1) repeated אם . . . אם *whether . . or* (sive . sive) Ex 19^{13} Dt 18^{3} 2 S 15^{21}; similarly אם . . . ואם Gn 31^{52} Je 42^{6} Ez 2^{5} Ec 11^{3} 12^{14} (cf ܐܶܢ . ܐܶܢ , ܐܰܘ . ܐܰܘ PS[2:0], إِنْ . . وَإِنْ & إِمَّا . . وَإِمَّا)

(2) After an oath (expressed, or merely implied) אם (the formula of imprecation being omitted) becomes an emph negative, and אם־לא an emph affirmative · 2 S 11^{11} by thy life אם־אֶעֱשֶׂה אֶת־הַדָּבָר הַזֶּה (may God bring all manner of evil upon me) *if* I do this thing!= *surely I will not* do this thing! (cf the full phrases in 1 S 3^{17} 2 K 6^{31}) Gn 14^{23} 42^{15} Nu 14^{23} 1 S 3^{14} 19^{6} 2 K 2^{2} 3^{14} & oft, Is 22^{14} ψ 89^{36} 95^{11} Jb 6^{28}, אם־לא Nu 14^{28} Jos 14^{9} 1 K 20^{23} 2 K 9^{26} Is 5^{9} 14^{24} Je 15^{11} 49^{20} Jb 1^{11} + esp. Ez, after a neg. clause, emphasizing a contrasted idea, Gn 24^{38} (where the expl by Aram אִלָּא is not supported by Heb usage), cf Je 22^{6} Repeated, אם . . . ואם 2 S 20^{20} 2 K 3^{14} Is 62^{8} Je 38^{16}, Ez 14^{16} In adjurations (with 2nd or 3rd ps) = *that not* Gn 21^{23} 26^{29} 31^{50} 1 S 24^{22} 1 K 1^{51} Ct 2^{7} 3^{5} + Of past or present time. 1 S 25^{34} as יהוה liveth (I say) that, unless thou hadst hastened , כי אם נוֹתַר that *surely there had not been* left . ! 17^{55} as thy soul liveth אם־יָדַעְתִּי *if* I know it! 1 K 17^{12} 18^{10}—both אם־יֵשׁ (כי here merely introduces the fact sworn to, & need not be translated, so 2 S 3^{35} v כי), ψ 121^{2} אם־לא (after a neg clause. cf supr. Gn 24^{38}). Cf Sti[§90]

(3) Part of wishing, *if but* . . ! *oh that* . ! (rare) ψ 81^{9} *If thou wouldest* hearken to me! 95^{7} 139^{19} Pr 24^{11} Cf Ex 32^{32}. With an imv (si vera l) Jb 34^{16} ואם־בִּינָה, and with an anacoluthon, Gn 23^{13} (P) אם־אַתָּה לוּ שְׁמָעֵנִי *if* thou!—oh that thou wouldst hear me!

(4) Nearly = *when*—with the pf (*a*) of past, Gn 38^{9} Nu 21^{9} וְהָיָה אם־נָשַׁךְ . . . וְרָאָה and it used to be, *if* or *when* a serpent had bitten a man, that he would look, etc, Ju 6^{3} ψ 78^{34} (v. Dr[§136 & Obs.]); Am 7^{2}. (*b*) of pres. or fut, Is 4^{4} אם רָחַץ *when* the Lord shall have washed, 24^{13} 28^{25}, cf Nu 36^{4} (with the impf)

c. Compounded with other particles—(*a*) בלתי אם *except if, except*, †Gn 47^{18} Ju 7^{14} Am $3^{3.4}$. (*β*) הֲלוֹא אם †2 K 20^{19} (for which Is 39^{7} has simply כי), perh *Is it not* (good), *if* ? (De Di) (*γ*) כִּי־אם, q v. (*δ*) עַד אם †Gn $24^{19.33}$ Is 30^{17} Ru 2^{21}, & עַד אֲשֶׁר אם †Gn 28^{15} Nu 32^{17} Is 6^{11}, *until*, prop *until if* or *when* (*ε*) רַק אם *if only* (v sub רַק). אם־לא in Ez 3^{6b} is very difficult. The Vrss render *If I had sent*, etc, implying לוּ for אם־לא (for Ew's אִלּוּ = אם־לא, q v, is precarious) Ges Hi Co 'but (אם־לא after a neg, cf supr Gn 24^{38} ψ 131^{2}) unto *them* (Isr.) have I sent thee *they* can understand thee' (but *understand* is a dub rendering of שָׁמַע אֶל)

2. Interrog.part. a. in direct qu (*a*) alone (not freq and usually = *Num?* expecting the answer *No*, esp in a rhet style): Gn 38^{17} 1 K 1^{27}, Ju 5^{8} מָגֵן אם־יֵרָאֶה וָרֹמַח *was* there a shield to be seen or a spear ? Is 29^{16}, and repeated Am 3^{6} Je 48^{27} Jb 6^{12}. (*b*) more freq in disjunctive interrogation (*α*) הֲ . . . אם, expressing a real alternative Jos 5^{13} הֲלָנוּ אַתָּה אם־לְצָרֵינוּ *art* thou for us, or for our enemies? Ju 9^{2} 1 K $22^{6.15}$. more oft. expressing a merely formal alternative, esp in poetry (a rhetorical *Num?*) Gn 37^{8} Nu $11^{12.22}$ Ju 11^{25b} 2 S 19^{36} Is 10^{15} 66^{8} Je 3^{5} Hb 3^{8} ψ 77^{10} 78^{20} Jb 4^{17} $6^{5.6}$ $10^{4.5}$ 11^{7} etc (*β*) הֲ . . . ואם (rarer than הֲ . . . אם, but similar in use) 2 S 24^{13} (a real alt), Is 49^{24} 50^{2} Je 5^{9} (v^{29} אם) 14^{22} Jo 1^{2} 4^{4} Jb 8^{3} 11^{2} 21^{4} 22^{3} 34^{17} $40^{8f.}$ (formal), Gn 17^{17} P (with an anacol) shall a child ? ואם־שָׂרָה הֲבַת־תִּשְׁעִים שָׁנָה תֵּלֵד *or* Sarah,—shall she that is 90 years old bear? Pr 27^{24} (ואם after neg clause). **b.** in oblique interrogation, *if, whether* · (*a*) alone, after verbs of seeing, inquiring, etc. 2 K 1^{2} Je 5^{1} 30^{6} Mal 3^{10} ψ 139^{24} Ct 7^{13} La 1^{12} Ezr 2^{59}, once מי יודע אם *who knoweth if* ? i e (like *haud scio an*) *perhaps* Est 4^{14} (older syn מי יודע alone see 2 S 12^{22} Jo 2^{14} Jon 3^{9}) (*b*) disjunctively הֲ . . . אם Gn 27^{21} Nu 13^{18-20}, so אם . . . ואם Jos 24^{15}. **c.** compounded with הֲ, הַאִם †Nu 17^{28} הַאִם תַּמְנוּ לִגְוֹעַ prob an emph *Num? Shall we ever* have finished dying? Jb 6^{13} difficult perh *Is it* that my help is not in me? (a forcible means of expressing that that which might be thought impossible is nevertheless the case), Hi as an aposiop, If my help is not in me (am I still to wait)? (The view that הַאִם = הֲלֹא *nonne?* is inconsistent with the fact that אם in a question has regularly the force of *Num?*)

אֵם v. אמם.

אָמָה, אַמָּה v אמם

אמה (assumed as √ of foll, which however prob. bilit. cf. Sta§^{188}, vid also Lag$^{BN\ 82}$)

†**אָמָה** **n.f. maid, handmaid** (Ph אמת, Ar. أَمَة, Sab. אמת in n pr Sab.Denkm ^{20}, Aram ܐܡܬܐ, As. *amtu* Zim$^{BP\ 67}$)—א׳ abs Gn 21^{10}+, sf. אֲמָתִי Gn 30^{3}+, etc; pl abs אֲמָהֹת Gn 31^{33} 2 S 6^{22}, cstr. אַמְהוֹת 2 S 6^{20}; אַמְהֹתַי Jb 19^{5} etc —*maid, handmaid.* **1.** lit. *maidservant* (= שִׁפְחָה q v., wh. however sometimes more servile, rarely P in Hex) Gn 30^{3} 31^{33} (‖ שִׁפְחָה 29$^{24.29}$ P 30^{4f} J etc) Ex 2^{5} (all E); 2 S 6$^{20.22}$ Jb 19^{15} Na 2^{8} (sf refers to mistress, exc. Jb 19^{15} cf 2 S 6$^{20.22}$); in legisl. (‖ עֶבֶד) Ex 20$^{10\ 17}$ 21$^{20.26.27\ 32}$ (all E) Lv 25$^{6.44.44}$ (H) Dt 5$^{14\ 14\ 18}$ 12$^{12\ 18}$ 15$^{17\,(cf\ v\ 12)}$ 16$^{11\ 14}$, cf also Jb 31^{13} Ezr 2^{65} Ne 7^{67}, applied to *concubine* (sf. of master) Gn 20^{17} 21^{12} Ex 23^{12} (all E) Ju 9^{18} 19^{19}; also Gn 21$^{10\ 10\ 13}$ (16^{1f} P שִׁפְחָה q.v.) Ex 21^{7} (all E), vid. on this Sta $^{Gesch\ I\ p\ 380}$ **2.** fig. in address, אֲמָתְךָ etc., referring to speaker, in token of humility; Ru 3$^{9.9}$ (‖ שפחה 2^{13}) 1 S 1^{16} (‖ *id* v^{18}) 25$^{24.24.25.28.31.41}$ (‖ *id* v^{27}) 2 S 14$^{15\ 16}$ (‖ *id.* v$^{6.7\ 12\ 15.17\ 19}$), 20^{17}; 1 K 1$^{13\ 17}$ 3^{20}, in addressing God (never שפחה) 1 S 1$^{11\ 11\ 11}$, cf. בֶּן־א׳ ψ 86^{16} 116^{16}

†I **אָמוֹן** **n pr.** **Amon,** an Egyptian god Na 3^{8} Je 46^{25}, comp. by Greeks with Zeus (Herod $^{II\ 42}$, Diod.$^{I.\ 13}$), Ἀμμῶν. He was originally the local deity of Thebes (=נא, called נֹא אָמוֹן Na 3^{8}, cf. א׳ מִנֹּא Je 46^{25}), but subsequently became the supreme god of the Egyptian Pantheon, the successor of the sun-god *Ra* and so-called *Amon Ra* He was the secret god, who hid himself and was difficult to find (Amon= concealment, hidden); v Rawl $^{Hist.\ Anc\ Egypt,\ I\ 322}$ Ebers Ri^{HWB}. (II. III אָמוֹן v p 54)

†**אָמִי** **n.pr.m.** Ezr 2^{57} = III. אָמוֹן Ne 7^{59}.

†[**אָמַל**] **vb. be weak, languish** (cf Ar أَمَلَ *hope, expect*) **Qal** *Pt.* pass f. מָה אֲמֻלָה לִבָּתֵךְ *how weak is thy heart!* Ez 16^{30} (but < Co אֲמַלֵּא, מַה־לִּי וּלְבְרִיתֵךְ), **Pu'l.** *Pf* אֻמְלַל Jo 1^{10}+, אֻמְלְלָה Is 33^{9}+; אֻמְלָלוּ Je 14^{2} etc.;—*be* or *grow feeble, languish*, of loss of fertility (woman) 1 S 2^{5} Je 15^{9}; of fisherman whose trade fails Is 19^{8} (‖ אבל, אנה); in genl of inhab. of smitten land Ho 4^{3} (‖ תֶּאֱבַל הָאָרֶץ); Is 24^{4} cf infr. usually subj inanim, personif.; שַׁדְמוֹת חֶשְׁבּוֹן Is 16^{8}, cf. Na 1$^{4.4}$; תבל Is 24^{4} (‖ אבל, נבל), אֶרֶץ 33^{9} (‖ אבל); subj גֶּפֶן Is 24^{7} (‖ אָבַל תירוש); יִצְהָר Jo 1^{10} (‖ שדד, אבל, הוביש; kindred subj.), אֻמְלָלָה Je 14^{2} (‖ שְׁעָרִים), תְּאֵנָה v^{12} (‖ הַגֶּפֶן הוֹבִישָׁה), cf La 2^{8} וַיַּאֲבֶל־חֵל וְחוֹמָה יַחְדָּו אֻמְלָלוּ (יְהוּדָה).

†[**אֲמֵלָל**] **adj. feeble** (Mish. *id*, on formation cf Ew§$^{157\,b}$ Sta§^{232}), הַיְּהוּדִים הָאֲמֵלָלִים Ne 3^{34}.

†**אֻמְלַל** **adj. id.** (Ew^{ib} Sta§^{230}), א׳ אָנִי ψ 6^{3} (‖ נִבְהֲלוּ עֲצָמָי)

I **אמם** (perh *be wide, roomy*, As [*amāmu*] whence *ummu, womb, mother*=אם cf Dl$^{Pr\ 109}$, but אם n prim acc. to Thes Sta§$^{189\,b}$ Lag$^{BN\ 22}$)

אֵם $_{221}$ **n.f. mother** (Ph אם, Ar أُمّ, إِمّ, Eth እም, Sab אם (only in n.pr cf e g Bae$^{Rel\ 118}$) As *ummu* COT^{Gloss}, Aram אִם, אִימָּא, ܐܡܐ)—א׳ abs Gn 32^{12}+, cstr. Gn 3^{20}+; sf אִמִּי Gn 20^{12} +etc, †pl only sf אִמֹּתֵנוּ La 5^{3}, אִמֹּתָם Je 16^{3} La 2$^{12.12}$,—**1.** lit (human) *mother*, as parent Gn 20^{12} 32^{12} 44^{20} Ex 2^{8} ψ 51^{7} 113^{9} (opp עֲקָרָה) Je 15$^{8.10}$ 20^{14} 22^{26} 50^{12} 1 Ch 4^{9} Ct 6^{9} 8^{5}+, hence of Eve אֵם כָּל־חָי Gn 3^{20}, poet of birth, יָצָא מִבֶּטֶן אֵם Jb 1^{21} Ec 5^{14}, יָצָא מֵרֶחֶם אֵם Nu 12^{12} cf ψ 139^{13} (Je 20^{18} &) ψ 71^{6} מִמְּעֵי אִמִּי גּוֹזִי (subj. י׳, cf. נחה 22^{10}, > גֹּזִי= *my benefactor* fr birth Thes Ew Hup Pe), also מִבֶּטֶן אֵם=fr. earliest existence Ju 16^{17} Jb 31^{18} ψ 22^{11}, so וַתְּהִי אִמִּי קִבְרִי Je 20^{17}, מִמְּעֵי אִם Is 49^{1}, as giving suck Ct 8^{1} (שְׁדֵי אִם) ψ 22^{10} cf 131^{2} (v Ex 2^{9} cf v^{8}); as exercising authority Gn 21^{21} 24^{28} 27$^{11\ 13\ 14}$ Ju 17^{2f} Ru 1^{8} Ct 3^{4} 8^{2} etc., esp of queen-mother as possessing dignity & influence 1 K 1^{11} 2$^{13.19.20}$ 2 Ch 22^{3} Ct 3^{11} Pr 31^{1}, cf. names of mothers of kings of Judah 1 K 14$^{21.31}$ 15$^{2\ 10\ 13}$+, as shewing love & care 1 S 2^{19} 1 K 3^{27} 17^{23} 2 K 4^{30} Is 66^{13} (sim of י׳'s comforting his people, cf also Gn 27^{45}); as beloved & lamented 1 K 19^{20} (‖ אָב) Gn 24^{67} ψ 35^{14}, בֶּן־אִמּוֹ=*own* (uterine) *brother* Gn 43^{29}, & ‖ אָח Gn 27^{29} Dt 13^{7} Ju 8^{19} ψ 50^{20} 69^{9} Ct 1^{6} cf 8^{1}; so בַּת־אִמּוֹ Lv 18^{9} 20^{17} Dt 27^{22} (‖ בַּת־אָבִיו) Gn 20^{12}, oft with אָב, as *parentes* Je 16^{3} Zc 13$^{3.3}$ Is 8^{4}, as rightfully claiming honour, authority, etc, cf supr, Gn 28^{7} (P) cf 37^{10} (E) Ju 14^{2f}, so in precept Pr 1^{8} 6^{20} 10^{1} 15^{20} etc. cf. Ez 22^{7}, laws enjoining these Ex 20^{12}=Dt 5^{16} Lv 19^{3} cf. Dt 22^{15}, laws prohib. contrary Ex 21$^{15\ 17}$ (E) Lv 20$^{9.9}$ (H) Dt 21$^{18\ 19}$ 27^{16}; laws as to mourning for Lv 21$^{2\ 11}$ (H) Nu 6^{7} (P) cf. Je 16^{7} Ez 44^{25}; left for wife Gn 2^{24}, for mother-in-law Ru 2^{24}, for husband Dt 21^{13} (law for captive women), cf. Dt 33^{9} (of devoted service of Levites); loving, caring for children Pr 4^{3} (on the opposite cf ψ 27^{10}), loved, cared for Jos 2^{13} cf. v^{18} 6^{23}

1 S 22^{3} 1 K 19^{20} cf. 2 S 19^{38}. †**2.** fig. of Deborah as caring for her people אֵם בְּיִשְׂרָאֵל Ju 5^{7} (cf. אָב Is 22^{21} Jb 29^{16}); so of a city 2 S 20^{19} ('stock, race, community' RS$^{K 28}$ cf.$^{Proph. iv. n 8}$); of Israel Ho 2$^{4.7}$ 4^{5} cf. 10^{14}; of Judah Is 50$^{1.1}$; of Hittite as mother of Jerusalem אָבִיךְ הָאֱמֹרִי וְאִמֵּךְ חִתִּית Ez 16$^{3.45}$ cf. v$^{44.45}$; also 19$^{2.10}$ & vid. 23^{2}. †**3.** of animals, *dam* Ex 22^{29} (of ox & sheep) Lv 22^{27} (of bullock, sheep, or goat); Ex 23^{19}=34^{26} =Dt 14^{21} (of kid); *mother-bird* Dt 22$^{6.6.7}$; fig. Jb 17^{14} לַשַּׁחַת קָרָאתִי אָבִי אָתָּה אִמִּי וַאֲחֹתִי לָרִמָּה׃. †**4.** =*point of departure* or *division* אֵם הַדֶּרֶךְ Ez 21^{26} (‖ רֹאשׁ שְׁנֵי הַדְּרָכִים).

†I. **אַמָּה** **n.f.** only **mother-city,** metropolis (cf. אֵם 2 S 20^{19} & Ph.); in phrase מֶתֶג הָאַמָּה *authority of mother-city* 2 S 8^{1}; v. מֶתֶג; cf. Dr.

II. **אַמָּה** $_{246}$ **n.f. ell, cubit** (SI אמה; so Sab. DHM$^{ZMG 1865, 613}$; Aram. ܐܡܬܐ, אַמָּא; As. *ammatu* Nor^{280}; Eth. እመት: etym. dub.; Thes al. *mater brachii*, i.e. length of fore-arm; others der. fr. √אמם, أَمَّ *precede*, be in front, & hence fore-arm cf. Di Is 6^{4}; Dl$^{Pr 109}$ MV der. immediately from √אמם be wide (v. supr.), אַמָּה= *distance*, & hence a particular distance, *ell, cubit*)—א׳ abs. Gn 6^{16}+; cstr. אַמַּת Dt 3^{11} Je 51^{13}; *du.* אַמָּתַיִם Ex 25^{10}+; *pl.* אַמּוֹת Ex 26^{16}+;— **1.** *cubit*, so אַמַּת־אִישׁ i.e. ordinary cubit, Dt 3^{11} (cf. Is 8^{1}); in Ez 40^{5} 43^{13} is a cubit one handbreadth longer, cf. 2 Ch 3^{3} א׳ בַּמִּדָּה הָרִאשׁוֹנָה; absol. length dub., cf. Smith$^{Dict. Bib., art. Weights and Measures}$; Lepsius$^{Längenmaasse der Alten, SBAk 1883, 1195 f.}$ identif. with Egyptian, longer cubit ·525 m., shorter ·450 m.; v. also *Id.*$^{Bab.-Assyr. Längenmaasse 1877; MBAk 1877, 741}$ Oppert$^{GGA 1878, 1053; Rev. d'Assyr. i. 124}$ (also on the Bab. 'half-cubit'=·270 m. Hpt$^{AJPh 1888, 419}$ Hom$^{Semiten i. 501}$); on א׳ אַצִּילָה Ez 41^{8} cf. Sm & Co (Co del.); חֲמֵשׁ אמות קָנִים Ez 42^{16} Kt, rd. מֵאוֹת so Qr Co; chiefly in Ex 25–27. 36–38 (56 t.) 1 K 6. 7 (45 t.) 2 Ch 3. 4 (21 t.) Ez 40–43 (86 t.); *a* (one) *cubit*=אַמָּה Gn 6^{16} Ex 25$^{10.23}$+; הָאַמָּה Ez 43^{14}; א׳ אַחַת Ez 40$^{12.12.42.42.42}$ 42^{4} 43^{14}; *two cubits*= אַמָּתַיִם Ex 25$^{10.17.23}$ 30^{2} 37$^{1.6.10.25}$ Nu 11^{31}; שְׁתַּיִם אַמּוֹת Ez 40^{9} 41$^{3.22}$ 43^{14}; c. num. 1–10 א׳ mostly follows num. in pl. Ex 26^{16} 27$^{1.1.1}$ 1 K 6^{10} Ez 40$^{5.7.9}$+; c. num. 11–1000+, it mostly foll. num. in sing. Gn 6$^{15.15.15}$ Ex 27$^{12.13}$ 38$^{13.14.15}$ Nu 35^{4} Jos 3^{4} 1 K 6$^{2.2.3}$ 7$^{15.15}$ Je 52$^{21.22}$ Ez 40$^{49.49}$+; seld. foll. in pl. Ez 40^{11} (del. Co) v^{27} (Co sg.) 42^{2}; so also חָמֵשׁ וְעֶשְׂרִים אַמּוֹת Ez 40$^{13.29}$ but עֶשְׂרִים וְחָמֵשׁ אַמָּה Ez 40$^{25.30.33.36}$; (late) also in pl. precedes all num. 2 Ch 3$^{3.3.4.8.8}$+; 6^{13} Ez 42^{2}; also oft. בָּאַמָּה foll. all num. Ex 26$^{2.2.8.8}$ 27$^{9.18}$ 36$^{9.9.15.15.21}$ Nu 35$^{5.5.5.5}$ 1 K 6$^{6.6.6}$ 7$^{23.23.23}$ 2 Ch 4$^{2.2.2}$ Ez 40^{21} 47^{3} Zc 5$^{2.2}$+, cf. לְאַמּוֹת חָמֵשׁ 2 Ch 3^{11}; oft. א׳ וָחֵצִי Ex 25$^{10.10.10.17.17}$+, also א׳ וַחֲצִי הָא׳ Ex 26^{16} 36^{21} 1 K 7$^{31.32.35}$ etc.; cf. שֵׁשׁ אַמּוֹת וָזָרֶת 1 S 17^{4}; sq. בַּמִּדָּה *in measurement* Jos 3^{4} 2 Ch 3^{3}. **2.** †*measure*, full measure, limit, only אַמַּת בִּצְעֵךְ *the measure of thy gain-making* Je 51^{13} (‖ קִצֵּךְ).

†III. [**אַמָּה**] **n.f.** (etym. & mng. dub.; Thes *foundation* (cf. Talm. AW), fr. אֵם in metaph. sense, cf. MV; De on Is 6^{4} der. similarly, but makes *support* of *superliminaria* (cf. 𝔊 𝔖 𝔙); Ew Di der. fr. √אמם=أَمَّ *precede*, whence إِمَامٌ *front;* Dl$^{Pr 110}$ tr. *holder* fr. √אמם *be wide*, hence *contain, hold*) only אַמּוֹת הַסִּפִּים Is 6^{4}.

†IV. **אַמָּה** **n.pr.loc.** hill near Gibeon, גִּבְעַת־אַמָּה 2 S 2^{24}.

[†**אֻמָּה**] **n.f. tribe, people** (Ar. أُمَّةٌ; As. *ummatu* cf. Jen$^{Kosmol. 336}$, Aram. ܐܘܡܬܐ, אוּמְּא) only pl. אֻמּוֹת Nu 25^{15}; אֻמִּים ψ 117^{1}; sf. אֻמֹּתָם Gn 25^{16};—of tribes of Ishmaelites Gn 25^{16}; of Midian (‖ בֵּית־אָב) Nu 25^{15}; ‖ גּוֹיִם ψ 117^{1}.

†**אֲמָם** **n.pr.loc.** in southern Judah Jos 15^{26} (𝔊^{L} Ἀμαμ, so A, but B Σην).

†I. [**אָמַן**] **vb. confirm, support** (cf. Ar. أَمِنَ, etc., v. infr.; Sab. אמן in deriv. & n.pr. cf. CIS$^{iv. 1, 10}$ DHM$^{ZMG 1885, 598}$; Aram. אֲמַן, ܐܡܢ in Haph. Eth. አምነ: As. in deriv.)—only **Qal** *Pt.* אֹמֵן;—**1.** as vb. *support, nourish* 2 K 10$^{1.5}$ Est 2^{7}. **2.** as subst. *foster-father* Nu 11^{12} (J) Is 49^{23}. **3.** אֹמֶנֶת *foster-mother, nurse* Ru 4^{16} 2 S 4^{4}. **4.** אֹמְנוֹת *pillars, supporters of the door* 2 K 18^{16}. *Pt. pass.* **a.** הָאֱמֻנִים *those brought up* (in scarlet) La 4^{5}. **b.** אֱמוּנִים intrans. *faithful* (as firm, stable) as subst. m. *faithful ones* ψ 12^{2} (> 𝔊 𝔖 al. *faithfulness*) 2 S 20^{19} (cf. Ar. أَمُنَ *be faithful*, أَمِنَ *trust in*, أَمِنَ *be secure*); ψ 31^{24} *faithful ones* י׳ *keepeth*, אֱמוּנִים נֹצֵר י׳; but א׳ is here taken by 𝔊 Ri De Che as n. abstr. v. אֵמֻן. **Niph.** נֶאֱמַן Pr 11^{13}+(6 t.); *Impf.* יֵאָמֵן, יֵאָמֵן 1 K 8^{26}+(9 t.); *Pt.* נֶאֱמָן Pr 25^{13}+(16 t.) נֶאֱמָנָה Is 1^{21}+(4 t.); נֶאֱמֶנֶת ψ 89^{29}; נֶאֱמָנִים Pr 27^{6}+(9 t.); נֶאֱמָנוֹת Dt 28^{59}. **1.** *carried by a nurse* Is 60^{4}. **2.** *made firm, sure, lasting:* place Is 22$^{23.25}$; name 1 Ch 17^{24}; waters Is 33^{16} Je 15^{18}; an event Ho 5^{9}; sickness Dt 28^{59}; mercy Is 55^{3}. **3.** *confirmed, established, sure:* kingdom 2 S 7^{16}; house, dynasty 1 S 2^{35} 25^{28} 1 K 11^{38} 1 Ch 17^{23}; prophet Samuel 1 S 3^{20}; cf.

word-play אם לא תַאֲמִינוּ לֹא תֵאָמֵנוּ = *if ye believe not* (have not firm confidence) *ye will not be confirmed* Is 7^{9}; הַאֲמִינוּ בי׳ וְתֵאָמֵנוּ = *believe in Yahweh and ye will be confirmed* 2 Ch 20^{20}. **4.** *verified, confirmed:* words of God 1 K 8^{26} 2 Ch 1^{9} 6^{17}; his precepts ψ 111^{7}; testimonies ψ 19^{8} 93^{5}; covenant ψ 89^{29}; words of men Gn 42^{20} (E). **5.** *reliable, faithful, trusty:* persons 1 S 2^{35} 22^{14} Jb 12^{20} ψ 89^{38} 101^{6} Pr 25^{13} Is 8^{2} Ne 13^{13}; a city Is 1^{21}; האל הנאמן *the faithful God* Dt 7^{9} cf. Is 49^{7}; נֶאֱמַן רוּחַ *faithful in spirit* (disposition) Pr 11^{13}; לְבָבוֹ נֶאֱמָן *his heart faithful* Ne 9^{8}; עֵד אֱמֶת וְנֶאֱמָן *true and faithful witness* Je 42^{5}; נאמנים פצעי אוהב *faithful the wounds of a loving one* Pr 27^{6}; c. אֵת ψ 78^{8}; עם Ho 12^{1}; בְּ of thing ψ 78^{37}; בְּכָל־בֵּיתִי *in all my house* (of Moses) Nu 12^{7} (E). **Hiph.** הֶאֱמִין Gn 45^{26} + (18 t.); *Impf.* יַאֲמִין, יַאֲמִן Jb 15^{31} + (30 t.); *Imv.* הַאֲמִינוּ 2 Ch 20^{20} + (2 t.); *Pt.* מַאֲמִין Dt 1^{32} Jos 25^{16}. **1.** *stand firm* Jb 39^{24} (c. neg. of the horse when the trumpet sounds Di De MV RVm; but *neither believeth* RV, *hardly trusts* Da). **2.** *trust, believe:* (*a*) abs. Ex 4^{31} (J) Is 7^{9} 28^{16} Hb 1^{5} ψ 116^{10} Jb 29^{24}; (*b*) with לְ of person, *trust to, believe* Gn 45^{26} (E) Ex 4$^{1.8}$ (J) Je 40^{14} 2 Ch 32^{15}; with God Dt 9^{23} Is 43^{10}; לְ of thing Ex 4$^{8.9}$ (J) ψ 106^{24} 1 K 10^{7} 2 Ch 9^{6} Is 53^{1} Pr 14^{15}; (*c*) with בְּ of person, *trust in, believe in* Ex 19^{9} (J) 1 S 27^{12} 2 Ch 20^{20} Jb 4^{18} 15^{15} Pr 26^{25} Je 12^{6} Mi 7^{5}; the usual construction with God Gn 15^{6} (E) Ex 14^{31} Nu 14^{11} (J) 20^{12} (P) Dt 1^{32} 2 K 17^{14} 2 Ch 20^{20} ψ 78^{22} Jon 3^{5}; with בְּ of thing Dt 28^{66} Jb 15^{31} 24^{22} 39^{12} ψ 78^{32} 106^{12} 119^{66}; (*d*) with כִּי *trust or believe that* Ex 4^{5} (J) Jb 9^{16} La 4^{12}; (*e*) so with infin. Jb 15^{22} ψ 27^{13}; also *trust* to do a thing, almost = *allow*, Ju 11^{20}.

†אֹמֶן **n.[m.] faithfulness;** אֱמוּנָה אֹמֶן *perfect faithfulness* (faithfulness, faithfulness) Is 25^{1}.

†אָמֵן **adv. verily, truly** Dt 27$^{15-26}$ (12 t.) 1 K 1^{36} Ne 5^{13} Je 11^{5} 28^{6} & doxologies 1 Ch 16^{36} (= ψ 106^{48}); אָמֵן (וְ)אָמֵן Nu 5^{22} (P) Ne 8^{6}, & in the doxologies ψ 41^{14} 72^{19} 89^{53} 106^{48}. ἀμήν = *Amen:* אֱלֹהֵי אָמֵן Is 65$^{16.16}$ *God of Amen* De Che RVm; cf. Rev 3^{14}, or *God of faithfulness, God of truth* (RV) (perh. rd. אֹמֶן Che Di).

†אָמָּן (*ommān*) **n.m. master-workman, artist** Ct 7^{2} (Mish. Talm. אוּמָן, אוּמָנוּת *handiwork*, Syr. ܐܘܡܢܐ 𝔖 Ex 28^{11}, where = Heb. חָרָשׁ & is likewise used of gems; Nab. אמנא Yog^{94}, As. *mar ummâni*, Lyon$^{Sargontexte\ 65}$, cf. Zim$^{BP\ 12}$; cf. II. אָמוֹן).

†אֵמֻן **n.[m.] trusting, faithfulness** (on format. cf. Ges$^{§84a\ R.12}$). **1.** בָּנִים לֹא אֵמֻן בָּם *children in whom there is no trusting* Dt 32^{20} (poet.) **2.** אֱמוּנִים pl. abst. *faithfulness;* צִיר א׳ *messenger of faithfulness*, trusty messenger Pr 13^{17}; עֵד א׳ *faithful witness* Pr 14^{5}; cf. אִישׁ א׳ Pr 20^{6}; שֹׁמֵר א׳ *keeping faithfulness* Is 26^{2}, perh. also ψ 31^{24} נצר א׳ v. I. [אָמַן].

†אֱמוּנָה **n.f. firmness, steadfastness, fidelity** Ex 17^{12} + 46 t.; אֱמוּנוֹת Pr 28^{20}. **1.** lit. *firmness, steadiness:* Ex 17^{12} וַיְהִי יָדָיו א׳ *his hands were steadiness* (i. e. steady). **2.** *steadfastness*, אֱמוּנַת עִתֶּיךָ *steadfastness of thy times* Is 33^{6}. **3.** *faithfulness, trust:* **a.** *of human conduct* ψ 37^{3} Pr 12^{22} Je 5^{3} 7^{28} 9^{2} 2 K 12^{16}; in office 2 K 22^{7} 2 Ch 19^{9} 31^{12} 34^{12}; בֶּאֱמוּנָה (על) *in trust* (over) 1 Ch 9$^{22.26.31}$ 2 Ch 31$^{15.18}$; דֶּרֶךְ א׳ ψ 119^{30}; אִישׁ אֱמוּנוֹת *man of great faithfulness* Pr 28^{20}; associated with צֶדֶק in human character יָפִיחַ א׳ יַגִּיד צֶדֶק *who breatheth out faithfulness sheweth forth righteousness* Pr 12^{17}; cf. 1 S 26^{23} Is 59^{4} Je 5^{1}; צַדִּיק בֶּאֱמוּנָתוֹ יִחְיֶה *a righteous man by his faithfulness liveth* Hb 2^{4} (> *faith* Luth AV RV). **b.** *as a divine attribute* ψ 88^{12} 89$^{2.3.6.9}$ Is 25^{1} Ho 2^{22} La 3^{23}; אֵל אֱמוּנָה Dt 32^{4}; his faithfulness is shewn in his works ψ 33^{4}; commands ψ 119^{86}; in affliction ψ 119^{75}; in his oath to David ψ 89^{50}; it reacheth unto the skies ψ 36^{6}; unto all generations ψ 100^{5} 119^{90}; he will not belie it ψ 89^{34}. It is אֱמוּנָה אֹמֶן Is 25^{1}; cf. אֱמוּנָה מְאֹד ψ 119^{138}. It is closely associated with the divine חֶסֶד *mercy* ψ 89^{25} 92^{3} 98^{3} Ho 2^{22}; with the divine צְדָקָה, צֶדֶק ψ 96^{13} 143^{1} Is 11^{5}; & salvation ψ 40^{11}.

†אָמְנָה **n.f. bringing up, nourishment,** Est 2^{20}.

†אָמְנָה **adv.** (fr. אֹמֶן by affix ָה) **verily, truly, indeed** Gn 20^{12} (E) Jos 7^{20} (JE).

†אֲמָנָה **n.f. faith, support. 1.** אֲנַחְנוּ כֹּרְתִים אֲמָנָה *we are plighting faith* (make a sure covenant AV RV) Ne 10^{1}. **2.** א׳ עַל הַמ׳ *support, fixed provision*, for the singers Ne 11^{23}.

†אֲמָנָה **n.pr.fl. 1.** a river (*constant?* cf. Is 33^{16}) flowing down from Antilebanon into the plain of Damascus 2 K 5^{12} (Qr; אֲבָנָה Kt), the Gr. *Chrysorrhoas*, mod. Ar. *Nahr Baradâ*. **2.** the region from which it flows Ct 4^{8}.

†אָמְנָם **adv.** (fr. אֹמֶן by aff. ָם) **verily, truly, indeed,** always in interrog. Gn 18^{13} (J), elsewh. הַאֻמְנָם Nu 22^{37} (E) 1 K 8^{27} 2 Ch 6^{18} ψ 58^{2}.

†אֻמְנָם **adv.** (= אָמְנָם) **verily, truly, in**

asseverations 2 K 19^{17} (=Is 37^{18}) Jb 19$^{4.5}$ 34^{12} 36^{4} Ru 3^{12}, also ironical Jb 9^{2} 12^{2}.

†אֱמֶת **n.f. firmness, faithfulness, truth** (contr. for אֱמֶנֶת, fr. אָמֵן) Gn 24^{48} + 106 t.; sf. אֲמִתּוֹ, אֲמִתְּךָ ψ 91^{4} + 18 t. **1.** *reliability, sureness:* דֶּרֶךְ אֱמֶת *sure way* Gn 24^{48} (J); שֶׂכֶר אמת *sure reward* Pr 11^{18}; אות אמת *sure token* Jos 2^{12} (J); זֶרַע אמת Je 2^{21}. **2.** *stability, continuance:* שָׁלוֹם וֶאֱמֶת *peace and stability* Is 39^{8} (=2 K 20^{19}) Est 9^{30} Je 33^{6} Zc 8^{19}, cf. שלום אמת Je 14^{13}. **3.** *faithfulness, reliableness:* (*a*) *of men* אִישׁ אֱמֶת *faithful man* Ne 7^{2}; אנשי אמת Ex 18^{21} (E); הָלַךְ בֶּאֱמֶת *walk in faithfulness, faithfully* 1 K 2^{4} 3^{6} 2 K 20^{3} Is 38^{3} cf. 1 S 12^{24}; of י׳ בַּאֲמִתֶּךָ ψ 25^{5} 26^{3} 86^{11}; עיר האמת Zc 8^{3}; of men ψ 45^{5} 51^{8} 2 Ch 31^{20} 32^{1} Pr 29^{14} Is 10^{20} 42^{3} 48^{1}; בא׳ ובתמים Ju 9$^{16.19}$ Jos 24^{14}; חֶסֶד וֶאֱ׳ *mercy and faithfulness* Pr 3^{3} 14^{22} 16^{6} 20^{28} Ho 4^{1}, & the phrase עשׂה חסד ואמת Gn 24^{49} 47^{29} Jos 2^{14} (J) 2 S 15^{20}. (*b*) *an attribute of God* ψ 54^{7} 71^{22} Is 38$^{18.19}$ 61^{8}; נתן אמת Mi 7^{20}; עשׂה אמת Ez 18^{9} Ne 9^{33}; עשׂה חסד ואמת Gn 32^{11} (J) 2 S 2^{6}; רב חסד ואמת *abundant in mercy and faithfulness* Ex 34^{6} (J) ψ 86^{15}; these attributes are also associated ψ 40$^{11.12}$ 61^{8} 115^{1} 138^{2} Is 16^{5} Gn 24^{27} (J); they are messengers of God to men ψ 57^{4} 85^{11} 89^{15} cf. ψ 43^{3}; כל ארחות י׳ חסד ואמת ψ 25^{10}; the faithfulness of God endureth for ever ψ 117^{2}; he keepeth it for ever ψ 146^{6}; it reacheth unto the skies ψ 57^{11} 108^{5}; it is shield & buckler ψ 91^{4}; he is אל אמת ψ 31^{6} = אלהי אמת 2 Ch 15^{3}; אֱמֶת is also associated with the divine ישר ψ 111^{8}; צֶדֶק ψ 85^{12}; צְדָקָה Zc 8^{8}; מִשְׁפָּט ψ 111^{7} Je 4^{2}; & salvation ψ 69^{14}. **4.** truth (*a*) *as spoken:* דבר אמת *speak truth* 1 K 22^{16} 2 Ch 18^{15} Je 9^{4} Zc 8^{16} ψ 15^{2}; דִּבְרֵי א׳ Ec 12^{10}; אֱמֶת הַדָּבָר *the thing is true* Dt 22^{20} 1 K 10^{6} 2 Ch 9^{5} Dn 10^{1}; אמת נכון הדבר *the thing is certainly true* Dt 13^{15} 17^{4}; אמרים אמת = אִמְרֵי אֱמֶת Pr 22^{21}; הנה אמת Pr 8^{7}; הגיד א׳ Dn 11^{2}, אֲמִתֶּךָ ψ 30^{10}; שׂפת אמת Pr 12^{19}; אֱמֶת *it is true* Is 43^{9}; האמת אתכם *whether truth* is with you Gn 42^{16} (E) cf. Is 59$^{14.15}$. (*b*) *of testimony and judgment* עֵד אֱמֶת *true witness* Pr 14^{25}; עד אמת ונאמן Je 42^{5}; משפט אמת Ez 18^{8} Zc 7^{9}; שְׁפַט אמת Zc 8^{16}. (*c*) *of divine instruction* כְּתָב אֱמֶת Dn 10^{21}; תורת אמת Mal 2^{6} cf. Ne 9^{13}; תורתך אמת ψ 119^{142}; דבר י׳ בְּפִיךָ אמת 1 K 17^{24} cf. 2 S 7^{28}; משפטי י׳ אמת ψ 19^{10}; ראש דברך אמת ψ 119^{160}; מצותיך אמת ψ 119^{151}. (*d*) *truth* as a body of ethical or religious knowledge Dn 8^{12}; להשׂכיל באמתך Dn 9^{13}. **5. adv.** *in truth, truly* ψ 132^{11}; יהוה אלהים אמת *Yahweh is God in truth, truly* Je 10^{10}; elsewhere בֶּאֱמֶת Ju 9^{15} ψ 145^{18} Je 26^{15} 28^{9} 32^{41}.

†II. אָמוֹן **n.m. artificer, architect, master-workman,** as firm and sure in his workmanship: וָאֶהְיֶה אֶצְלוֹ אָמוֹן *I was at his side architect, master-workman* (𝔊 𝔖 𝔙 Ges Ew De MV RV, >*foster-son* AE Ki AV) Pr 8^{30}; יֶתֶר הָאָמוֹן *rest of the master-workmen* Je 52^{15} (Hi Gf De RVm, but *rest of the multitude* Ges MV RV et al., אמון = המון)—I. אָמוֹן v. supr. p. 51.

†III. אָמוֹן **n.pr.m.** (*master-workman*) (*a*) king of Judah 2 K 18$^{19.23.24.25}$ 1 Ch 3^{14} 2 Ch 33$^{20.21.22.23.25}$ Je 1^{2} 25^{3}; (*b*) captain of a city 1 K 22^{26} 2 Ch 18^{25}; (*c*) one of the line of Solomon's servants Ne 7^{59} = אָמִי Ezr 2^{57}.

†אַמְנוֹן **n.pr.m.** (*faithful*) **1.** eldest son of David 2 S 3^{2} 13$^{1-39}$; = אֲמִינוֹן 2 S 13^{20}; = אַמְנֹן 1 Ch 3^{1}. **2.** a son of Shimon 1 Ch 4^{20}.

אֲמִינוֹן dimin., so Ew § 167 a cf. W I. § 269, or txt. err.; cf. Dr 2 S 13^{20}, v. אַמְנוֹן.

†אֲמִתַּי **n.pr.m.** (*true*, fr. אֱמֶת by adj. affix ־ַי) father of the prophet Jonah 2 K 14^{25} Jon 1^{1}.

†הֵימָן **n.pr.m. Heman** (*faithful*, cf. Aram. מְהֵימַן, ܡܗܝܡܢ) a wise man with whom Solomon is compared 1 K 5^{11}, where app. son of Mahol (Klo *sons of the dance*); named with 3 others, one being Ethan the Ezrahite; 1 Ch 2^{6} a Heman is named with same 3 + 1 other, & all called sons of Zerah of Judah; Heman appears ψ 88^{1} also as the Ezrahite (v. sub זרח), cf. Ethan supr.; in other passages Heman is a Levite; specif. Kohathite, son of Joel, called *the singer* (הַמְשׁוֹרֵר) 1 Ch 6^{18} (∥ Asaph v^{24}, Ethan v^{29}); Heman, Asaph & Ethan named as the singers (הַמְשֹׁרְרִים) 1 Ch 15$^{17.19}$; cf. Heman & Jeduthun 16$^{41.42}$ (∥ Asaph v^{37}); Heman, Asaph & Jeduthun 25^{6} 2 Ch 5^{12} 35^{15}; elsewhere בְּנֵי אָסָף וְהֵימָן וידותון 1 Ch 25^{1} cf. v$^{4.4.5.5}$; בְּנֵי הֵימָן 2 Ch 29^{14} (∥ בְּנֵי ידותון);—25^{5} Heman is called חֹזֵה הַמֶּלֶךְ בְּדִבְרֵי הָאֱלֹהִים (cf. Asaph 2 Ch 29^{30}, Jeduthun 2 Ch 35^{15}).—On question of identity of Heman in these various connections, v. Thes Comm.

†מְהוּמָן **n.pr.m.** a eunuch of Ahasuerus (*id.*; but 𝔊 Ἀμαν) Est 1^{10}.

II. [אָמֵן] v. יָמַן.

†[אָמֵץ] **vb. be stout, strong, bold, alert** (acc. to Lag $^{BN\ 28\ f.}$ fr. earlier אָמֹץ cf. אֹמֶץ)—**Qal** *Pf.* 3 pl. אָמְצוּ 2 S 22^{18} + 2 t.; *Impf.* יֶאֱמָץ Gn 25^{23}; וַיֶּאֶמְצוּ 2 Ch 13^{18}; *Imv.* אֱמַץ Jos 1^{7} 1 Ch

28^{20}; אֱמָץ Jos 1^{6}; אֱמָ֑ץ Dt 31^{7} + 3 t.; אִמְצוּ Dt 31^{6} + 2 t.—**1.** *be strong*, of a people Gn 25^{23} (J); of personal enemies 2 S 22^{18} = ψ 18^{18}; ψ 142^{7} (all sq. מִן of compar.); also (without מן) *prevail* 2 Ch 13^{18}. **2.** *Imv. be bold* (alw. ‖ חֲזַק, חִזְקוּ) Dt 31$^{7.23}$ Jos 1$^{6.7.18}$; (‖ id. + אַל־תִּירְאוּ וְאַל־תַּעַרְצוּ) Dt 31^{6}; ‖ id. + אַל־תַּעֲרֹץ וְאַל תֵּחָת) Jos 1^{9}; (‖ id. + אַל תִּירְאוּ וְאַל תֵּחָתּוּ) Jos 10^{25} 1 Ch 22^{13} 28^{20} 2 Ch 32^{7}. **Pi.** *Pf.* אִמֵּץ Dt 2^{30} etc.; *Impf.* יְאַמֵּץ Am 2^{14} etc.; וַיְאַמֶּץ־לוֹ Is 44^{14} 3 fs. sf. 3 ms. תְּאַמְּצֶנּוּ ψ 89^{22}; 1 s. sf. אֲאַמִּצְכֶם Jb 16^{5} etc.; *Imv.* אַמֵּץ Na 2^{2}; אַמְּצוּ Is 35^{3}; אַמְּצֵהוּ Dt 3^{28}; *Inf.* sf. אַמְּצוֹ Pr 8^{28}; *Pt.* מְאַמֶּץ־ Pr 24^{5};—**1.** *make firm, strengthen*, sq. acc., of giving clouds their place Pr 8^{28} (subj. י׳); of repairing temple 2 Ch 24^{13}; of physical vigour Pr 31^{17} חָגְרָה בְעוֹז מָתְנֶיהָ וַתְּא׳ זְרוֹעֹתֶיהָ׃ (subj. אֵשֶׁת חַיִל); of strength for war אַ׳ כֹּחַ Na 2^{2} (‖ חַזֵּק מָתְנַיִם) Am 2^{14} (subj. חָזָק); cf. Pr 24^{5}; of royal power 2 Ch 11^{17} (‖ חִזֵּק); cf. אַ׳ בִּרְכַּיִם כֹּשְׁלוֹת Is 35^{3}; אַ׳ ב׳ כֹּרְעוֹת Jb 4^{4} (both ‖ חַזְּקוּ יָדַיִם רָפוֹת) fig. of encouragement; so א׳ alone Dt 3^{28} (‖ חַזֵּק) Jb 16^{5} (‖ חשׂך q.v.); ψ 89^{22} (subj. זְרוֹעַ י׳); of support Is 41^{10} (subj. י׳; ‖ עזר, תמך;—De Che sub **2**). **2.** *assure, secure* for one's self, alw. sq. לְ + sf.; of carpenter appropr. tree Is 44^{14}; cf. of י׳ appropriating Isr. under fig. of bough ψ 80^{16}; under fig. of chosen man v^{18}. **3.** sq. לֵבָב *harden, make obstinate* Dt 2^{30} (subj. י׳; ‖ הִקְשָׁה רוּחוֹ) Dt 15^{7} (of unkind man); 2 Ch 36^{13} (of king Zedekiah, ‖ הִקְשָׁה אֶת־עָרְפּוֹ). **Hithp.** *Pf.* הִתְאַמֵּץ 1 K 12^{18} = 2 Ch 10^{18}; *Impf.* וַיִּתְאַמְּצוּ 2 Ch 13^{7}; *Pt.* מִתְאַמֶּצֶת Ru 1^{18}; **1.** *strengthen oneself*, of conspirators 2 Ch 13^{7} (sq. עַל). **2.** *confirm oneself* in a purpose, *be determined* Ru 1^{18} (sq. לְ + Inf.) **3.** *make oneself alert*, make haste 1 K 12^{18} = 2 Ch 10^{18} (sq. לְ + Inf.) **Hiph.** *Impf. Juss. exhibit strength, be strong* חִזְקוּ ויא׳ לִבְּךָ, וְיַאֲמֵץ ψ 27^{14}, so also 31^{25}.

†**אֹמֶץ** **n.[m.]** **strength**, fig. טְהָר־יָדַיִם יֹסִיף אֹמֶץ Jb 17^{9} *the clean of hands increaseth strength.*

†**אַמְצָה** **n.f. strength**, fig. Zc 12^{5}, but sense difficult, cf. Wr$^{\text{Zech. p. 585}}$; Sta$^{\text{ZAW 1881, 34}}$ prop. אֶמְצְאָה לְיוֹשְׁבֵי (after 𝔊 𝔗) *may I be sufficient for.*

†**אָמוֹץ** **n.pr.m.** father of Isaiah (= following) Is 1^{1} 2^{1} 13^{1} 20^{2}; 37$^{2.21}$ 38^{1} = 2 K 19$^{2.20}$ 20^{1}; 2 Ch 26^{22} 32$^{20.32}$.

†[**אָמֹץ**] **adj. strong**, only pl. אֲמֻצִּים of horses Zc 6$^{3.7}$ (in v^{7} perh. rd. אֲדֻמִּים, cf. v^{2}, & Hi; see another view in Lag$^{\text{BN 29}}$).

†**אַמִּיץ** (**אַמִּץ**) **adj. mighty**—א׳ abs. 2 S 15^{12} + 2 t.; cstr. Jb 9^{4} + 2 t.—*mighty*, of Absalom's conspiracy 2 S 15^{12}; elsewh. of persons; as subst., instrum. of י׳ (i.e. Assyrians) Is 28^{2} (‖ חָזָק); א׳ לִבּוֹ = valiant, conqueror Am 2^{16}; of י׳, חֲכַם לֵבָב וְא׳ כֹּחַ Jb 9^{4}; cf. א׳ כֹּחַ v^{19} (v. Di & RV), א׳ כֹּחַ Is 40^{26} (‖ רֹב אוֹנִים).

†**אַמְצִי** **n.pr.m.** **1.** a Levite 1 Ch 6^{31}. **2.** man of priestly line Ne 11^{12} (not in ‖ 1 Ch 9^{12}).

אֲמַצְיָה, **אֲמַצְיָהוּ** **n.pr.m.** (י׳ *has been mighty*). **1.** king of Jud., son of Joash, father of Azariah; אֲמַצְיָהוּ 2 K 14$^{1.9}$ + 8 t. 2 K 14; 15^{3} 1 Ch 3^{12}; 2 Ch 24^{27} 25^{1} + 15 t. 2 Ch 24; 26$^{1.4}$; אֲמַצְיָה 2 K 12^{22} 13^{12} 14^{8} 15^{1}. **2.** אֲמַצְיָה, a Simeonite 1 Ch 4^{34}. **3.** *id.*, a Levite 1 Ch 6^{30}. **4.** priest of Bethel, under Jerob. II, Am 7$^{10.12.14}$.

†[**מַאֲמָץ**] **n.[m.] power, strength, force**, pl. cstr. מַאֲמַצֵּי־כֹחַ Jb 36^{19}.

אָמַר $_{5287}$ **vb. utter, say** (MI Ph. אמר, Aram. אֲמַר, Eth. አመረ: I. 2 *shew, declare*, Ar. أَمَرَ *command;* perh. √ אמר orig. = *be or make prominent*, hence Hithp. infr., אָמִיר; Sab. אמר *lofty*, epith. of king JHMordtm$^{\text{ZMG 1876, 37}}$; cf. Dl$^{\text{Pr 28}}$ who thinks orig. mng. *hell, sichtbar sein*, whence As. *amâru, see, & shew, declare, say*)—**Qal** *Pf.* א׳ Gn 3^{1} +, etc.; *Impf.* יֹאמַר Gn 31^{8} +; וַיֹּאמֶר Gn 1^{3} +; וַיֹּאמַר Gn 14^{19} +; in Jb alw. וַיֹּאמַר Jb 3^{2} +; 3 fs. תֹּאמַר Gn 21^{12} +; תֹּאמֵר Pr 1^{21}; 1 s. אֹמַר Gn 22^{2} +; אוֹמְרָה ψ 42^{10}; וָאֹמַר Gn 20^{13} +; וָאוֹמַר Ne 2$^{7.17.20}$; 3 m. pl. יֹאמְרוּ Ex 4^{1} + etc.; sf. יֹמְרוּךָ ψ 139^{20}; 2 mpl. תֹּמְרוּ 2 S 19^{14} (cf. Kö$^{\text{I. p. 385}}$); *Imv.* אֱמֹר (אֱמָר־) Gn 45^{17} +, etc.; *Inf. abs.* אָמוֹר Ex 21^{5} +; cstr. אֱמֹר Ez 25^{8} +; (הֶ)אֱמֹר Jb 34^{18} but rd. הַאֹמֵר 𝔊 𝔙 Di, or better הָאָמֹר *Inf. abs.* c. ה interrog. cf. Ew$^{\text{§ 328 d}}$; sf. אָמְרִי Jos 6^{10} +; אֱמָרְכֶם Je 23^{38}; אֱמָרְכֶם Mal 1^{7} +; לֵאמֹר Gn 1^{22} +, etc.; *Pt. act.* אֹמֵר Gn 32^{10} +, etc.; *pass.* הֶאָמוּר Mi 2^{7}, but this grammatically indefensible, rd. הֶאָמוֹר, *Inf. abs.* c. ה interrog., v. Dr$^{\text{Expositor, April, 1887, 263}}$.

1. *Say* (subj. God Gn 3^{3} + or man 32^{5}, serpent 3^{1}, ass Nu 22^{28}, horse יֹאמַר הֶאָח Jb 39^{25} etc.; inanimate things, personif. Jb 28^{14} cf. v^{22} etc.; so in allegory or fable Ju 9^{8} 2 K 14^{9} etc.; esp. in narrat., וַיֹּאמֶר etc., Gn 4^{6} + very oft.): mostly sq. thing said, either subst. Je 14^{17} (c. cl. app.) Dt 27$^{16f.}$ Ju 12^{6}; pronoun Gn 44^{16} 2 K 20^{14} +; or (usually) clause Gn 1^{3} 3^{1} 37^{20}

+ oft. (*orat. recta*); with adv. *thus, so* Gn 32^{5} Nu 20^{14} 1 K 20$^{3.5}$ + oft.; esp. כֹּה אָמַר י׳ Ex 5^{1} 7^{17} 8$^{1.20}$ 1 Ch 17^{4} + oft.; the person addressed usu. introduced by אֶל Gn 3^{1} 15^{7} 22^{7} Lv 21^{1} 2 S 3^{7} 1 K 12$^{5.23}$, or לְ Gn 3^{13} 4^{15} 1 S 20^{2} 2 S 2^{21} 1 K 14^{2} + oft.; rarer combinations are, א׳ בְּאָזְנֵי Is 49^{20} (cf. 5^{9} & vid. דבר); א׳ לִפְנֵי Ez 28^{9}; א׳ לְעֵינֵי Dt 31^{7} Jos 10^{12} Je 28^{11}; א׳ בְּ Jo 2^{17} ψ 126^{2}, where בְּ local; in all cases usually sq. dir. obj. of words said, Ex 19^{25} being very singular; Gn 4^{8} the object-clause has probably fallen out, cf. Vrss Di; = *mention, name, designate* Gn 22$^{2.3}$ 43$^{27.29}$ Ex 32^{13} Nu 14^{40} 1 S 10^{16} 16^{3} 2 S 6^{22} Ne 6^{19}; cf. ψ 139^{20} יֹמְרוּךָ לִמְזִמָּה *speak of thee for falsehood* (but many, as Hup Pe Dy Che, rd. יַמְרוּךָ); = *tell, declare, proclaim* (sq. dir. obj. only) ψ 40^{11} Ez 13^{7}; in reply to question = *answer* Ex 12^{27} Jos 4^{7} 1 K 9^{9} Je 5^{19} 22^{9}. The obj. spoken of may be referred to by אֶל 2 K 19^{32} Je 22^{18} 27^{19}, or לְ Gn 20^{13} אִמְרִי לִי say *of* me, etc. Dt 33^{9} Ju 9^{54} Is 5^{20} ψ 3^{3} 71^{10}, very rarely by a simple accus. Is 3^{10} (where rd. prob. for אִמְרוּ, אַשְׁרֵי), except after אֲשֶׁר where the words used follow (cf. אֲשֶׁר **4 d**) Gn 3^{17} Nu 10^{29} 14^{31} Dt 28^{68} Ju 7^{4} 1 S 9$^{17.23b}$ 1 K 8^{29} La 4^{20}; cf. Nu 21^{16} 2 K 17^{12} 21^{4}, & (two extreme cases) Is 8^{12} La 2^{15} (v. Dr$^{Sm\ 1.24.5}$); הֶאָמוֹר Mi 2^{7} rd. inf. abs. c. ה interrog. הֶאָמוֹר (v. supr.) *shall one say? shall it be said?* After another vb. of saying, introducing thing said: Dt 21^{7} 25^{9} 27^{15} Ct 2^{10} +, even after אמר Gn 22^{7} Lv 21^{1} Je 34^{2} Est 7^{5} +; esp. inf. לֵאמֹר, after דבר Gn 8^{15}, צוה 2^{16}, ענה 44^{16}, ברך 1^{22}, נשׁבע 24^{7}, נדר 28^{20}, etc.; after אמר 2 S 3^{18} 1 K 12^{23} Ru 4^{4} 1 Ch 21^{18} +; after שׁלח 2 Ch 35^{21}, שׁוב Gn 32^{7}; cf. also Gn 28^{6} Ex 5^{13} 9^{5} 13^{8} 17^{4} Nu 11^{20} Dt 1^{28} 13^{7} Ju 8^{15} 1 S 23^{2} 1 K 13^{3} Je 32^{3} 37^{9} +; also when subj. of לֵאמֹר differs from that of preceding clause Gn 31^{1} 38$^{13.24}$ etc.; after שמע Is 37^{9} = 2 K 19^{9}.

2. *Say in the heart* (= think) א׳ בלבב Dt 8^{17} cf. 1 K 12^{26} ψ 10$^{6.11.13}$ 14^{1} 35^{25} Is 14^{13} 47$^{8.10}$ 49^{21} Ec 2$^{1.15}$ 3$^{17.18}$; א׳ אֶל־לִבּוֹ א׳ לִלְבָבָם Ho 7^{2}; Gn 8^{21} *said unto his heart* (to himself), subj. י׳, cf. 1 S 27^{1}; אָמְרָה נַפְשִׁי La 3^{24}; thence א׳ alone Gn 20^{11} 26^{9} Nu 24^{11} Ru 4^{4} 1 S 20^{26} 2 S 5^{6} 12^{22} 2 K 5^{11}; sq. cl. with כִּי Ju 15^{2}; in particular = *desire* מַה־תֹּאמַר נַפְשְׁךָ 1 S 20^{4} cf. Est 2^{13}; sq. inf. = *purpose*, Ex 2^{14} *thinkest thou to kill me, as thou killedst the Egyptian?* Jos 22^{33} 1 S 30^{6} 1 K 5^{19} 2 Ch 28$^{10.13}$; *expect* 2 S 21^{16} *he expected to slay David* 2 Ch 13^{8} 32^{1}.

3. *Promise* (sq. inf.) 1 Ch 27^{23} 2 Ch 21^{7} Est 4^{7}; (*id.* + לְ of pers.) 2 K 8^{19} Ne 9^{15}; (sq. acc. of dir. obj. + לְ of pers. + inf. of purpose) Ne 9^{23}.

4. *Command* (esp. late) sq. אֶל־ of person addressed, Nu 15^{38} 1 Ch 21^{18}; sq. לְ Jos 11^{9} 2 S 16^{11} 2 K 4^{24} Jb 9^{7} ψ 106^{34} (v. sub אֲשֶׁר **8 e**); sq. inf. 1 S 24^{11} 1 Ch 21^{17} 2 Ch 1^{18} 29$^{27.30}$ 31^{11} 35^{21} Est 1^{17} 4$^{13.15}$ 6^{1} 9^{14}; sq. inf. + לְ of pers. 2 Ch 14^{3} 29^{21} 31^{4} Est 1^{10}; sq. acc. dir. obj. 2 Ch 29^{24} *the king commanded the burnt-offering and the sin-offering*, cf. 1 K 5^{20} Est 2^{15}; sq. cl. with אשׁר = *that* Ne 13^{19}; *id.* + לְ of pers. v^{22}; sq. cl. with כִּי Jb 36^{10}; abs. 1 S 16^{16} (rd. however prob. יאמרו for יאמר, cf. Dr); also ψ 105$^{31.34}$ 107^{25} 1 Ch 14^{12} 2 Ch 24^{8} Ne 13$^{9.19}$ (all sq. vb. consec.); *command by letter* א׳ עִם־הַסֵּפֶר Est 9^{25} (sq. impf.); *appoint, assign* לֶחֶם א׳ לוֹ 1 K 11^{18} = *threaten* sq. inf. Dt 9^{25} ψ 106^{23}.

†**Niph.** *Pf.* נֶאֱמַר Dn 8^{26}; *Impf.* יֵאָמֵר Gn 22^{14} +; יֵאָמֶר לוֹ Is 4^{3}; יֵאָמַר Gn 10^{9} +; וַיֵּאָמַר Jos 2^{2}; *be said, told* Gn 10^{9} 22^{14} ψ 87^{5} Je 4^{11} 16^{14} (all abs., indef. subj., of current saying); so *said* in a book Nu 21^{14}; *be related, told*, of vision Dn 8^{26}; *said, told* to (sq. לְ ind. obj.) Jos 2^{2} Ho 2$^{1.1}$ Zp 3^{16}; either so, or *told concerning* Nu 23^{23}; Ez 13^{12} (אֶל־); יֵאָמֵר לָכֶם = *ye shall be called* (it shall be said to you) Is 61^{6} (‖ תִּקָּרְאוּ), cf. 4^{3} 19^{18} 32^{5} (‖ יִקָּרֵא לְ) 62$^{4.4}$; hence *be called*, of Tophet לֹא־יֵאָמֵר עוֹד הַתֹּפֶת Je 7^{32}; subj. שֵׁם Gn 32^{29}; Jb 34^{31} כִּי אֶל־אֵל הֶאָמַר, Rabb. (cf. AV) treat הֶאָמַר as Niph. Inf. for לְהֵאָמֵר, but against grammar; the form as it stands is Qal Pf., אֶל־אֵל being prefixed to the interrog. for emphasis (cf. Je 22^{15} 23^{26} Ne 13^{27}), v. Dr$^{§ 9}$ Di al.; Hoffm., however, reads הֶאָמֹר inf. abs. = imv. 'so must one speak (it be spoken) to God.' †**Hiph.** *Pf. avow, avouch* Dt 26^{17} אֶת־י׳ הֶאֱמַרְתָּ הַיּוֹם לִהְיוֹת לְךָ לֵאלֹהִים; v^{18} וי׳ הֶאֱמִירְךָ היום להיות לו לְעָם (*lit. cause to declare*, i.e. through agency of Moses; on this & other interpr. vid. Di). †**Hithp.** *Impf.* יִתְאַמְּרוּ ψ 94^{4} subj. כָּל־פֹּעֲלֵי אָוֶן *act proudly, boast* (‖ יַבִּיעוּ יְדַבְּרוּ עָתָק); prob. also 2 mpl. תִּתְיַמָּרוּ Is 61^{6} (in good sense, sq. בְּ of thing gloried in) 𝔖 𝔙 𝔗 & cf. 𝔊; Ges$^{Comm.}$ so De Che Kö$^{i.\ 457\ f.}$ (fr. [ימר] *exchange* Thes Hi Kn Ew Di; but vid. ימר, מור).

†אֹמֶר **n.m.** $^{ψ\ 77.9}$ **utterance, speech, word,** only poet., & Jos 24^{27} exalted style;—abs. א׳ Jb 22^{28} + 5 t.; sf. אִמְרוֹ Jb 20^{29}; *Pl.* abs. אֲמָרִים Pr 19^{7} 22^{21}; cstr. אִמְרֵי Nu 24^{4} +; אֲמָרָיו Jb 22^{22}; אִמְרֵיכֶם Jb 32^{14} Is 41^{26} (on deriv. fr. אָמַר cf. Di

Jb 15^{33}) etc.;—**1.** *utterance, word,* esp. pl. Jb. 6^{26} (הָגִיג ‖) $32^{12.14}$ (מִלִּין ‖) 33^{3} 34^{37}; ψ 5^{2} (הֲגִיג ‖), 141^{6} (on this v. cf Che); Pr 2^{1} (מִצְוָה ‖), v^{16} $4^{10.20}$ (דָּבָר ‖), 7^{1} (מִצְוָה ‖), v^{5} 19^{7} Is 41^{26}; words of God Nu $24^{4.16}$ cf. Jos 24^{27} Jb 6^{10} 22^{22} ψ 107^{11}; fig. of day ψ 19^{3} (sing); cf v^{4} (דְּבָרִים ‖) but vid. Che on v.; of wisdom (personif) Pr 1^{21} (קוֹל ‖), oft. in phrase אִמְרֵי־פִי Dt 32^{1} ψ 19^{15} (הֶגְיוֹן ‖); 54^{4} (תְּפִלָּה ‖); 78^{1} (תּוֹרָה ‖), Pr 4^{5} 5^{7} 7^{24} 8^{8}; cf. Jb 8^{2} Pr $6^{2.2}$; of ׳י Jb 23^{12} (מִצְוַת שְׂפָתָיו ‖), ψ 138^{4}, Ho 6^{5} (of Yahweh's words as weapon; in phrases אִמְרֵי־יֹשֶׁר Jb 6^{25}; א׳ בִינָה Pr 1^{2}; א׳ נֹעַם Pr 15^{26} 16^{24}; השיב אֲמָרִים אֱמֶת 22^{21}, cf. א׳ אֱמֶת, 22^{21} א׳ דָעַת 19^{27} 23^{12} v^{21} *return answer;* תָּשִׁיב אֲמָרֶיהָ לָהּ Ju 5^{29} *she returneth* (i.e *repeateth*) *her words to herself;* חָשַׂךְ א׳ *spare* (i.e refrain fr) *words* Pr 17^{27}. **2.** sg. *promise* ψ 77^{9}, *appointment, decree* Jb 20^{29}, *command* ψ 68^{12} (but v. Che); *plan, purpose* Jb 22^{28} א׳־גְּזַר; Hb 3^{9} Thes *sworn are the rods of appointment* (i.e the chastisements decreed), but passage dub, v Comm.,—Gn 49^{21} rd. אֲמִרִי cf. אָמִיר, vid Di.

[אִמְרָה] **n.f. utterance, speech, word** (poet, mostly sg coll, cf. pl vb ψ 119^{103}, but here rd. prob. pl n. cf 𝔊 Ol Hi De Che)—cstr אִמְרַת Is 5^{24}+, אִמְרָתִי Gn 4^{23}+etc., *Pl.* abs אִמְרוֹת ψ 12^{7}; cstr. אִמְרוֹת ib,—*utterance, speech* Gn 4^{23} (song of Lamech, ‖ קוֹל) so Is 28^{23} 32^{9}, Dt 32^{2} (לֶקַח ‖), ψ 17^{6} Is $29^{4.4}$ (‖ also דבר), esp *saying(s), word(s)* of ׳י (command & promise) Dt 33^{9} (בְּרִית ‖), Is 5^{24} (תּוֹרָה ‖) 2 S 22^{31} = ψ 18^{31} ψ 12^{7} 105^{19} (דָּבָר ‖); esp ψ $119^{11.38.41}$ + 16 t; 138^{2} 147^{15} (דָּבָר ‖), Pr 30^{5}

†[אֶמְרָה] **n.f.** id, only אֶמְרָתוֹ אֲשֶׁר צִוָּה La 2^{17}.

†אוֹמָר **n.pr.m.** grandson of Esau (*eloquent?*) Gn $36^{11.15}$ 1 Ch 1^{36}.

†אָמִיר **n.m. top, summit,** of tree Is 17^{6}, of mt. v^{9} (? so Ew Kn De Di; Lag Che Brd Or foll 𝔊 & rd. הָאֱמֹרִי); *Pl.* cstr אֲמִרֵי Gn 49^{21} (so rd. for אִמְרֵי, Ew Di al, cf. also 1 אֵלָה p. 18)

†אִמֵּר **n.pr.m.** **1.** a priest assigned to Dvd's time 1 Ch 24^{14} perh = **2.** ancestor of priest 1 Ch 9^{12} cf. Ne 11^{13} Ezr 2^{37} 10^{20} Ne 7^{40} **3.** priest in Jerem's time Je 20^{1} **4.** father of Zadok Ne 3^{29} **5. n.pr loc.** (?) Ezr 2^{59} = Ne 7^{61}.

אֱמֹרִי **n.pr.m.coll.** (construed as pl. Dt 3^{9} + 5 t.) **Amorites** (perh. = *mountain-dwellers*, cf Nu 13^{29} Dt $1^{7.19f}$ etc & Di Gn 10^{16} al)—alw. c art, exc. Nu 21^{29} Ez 16^{45} **1.** called son of Canaan Gn 10^{16} (J) 1 Ch 1^{14} = **2.** a chief people dispossessed by Hebrews; (*a*) living E. of Jordan Nu $21^{13.13.25}$ + 9 t. Nu + Jos 24^{8} (all E), cf. Jos 2^{10} 9^{10} (JE) Dt 1^{4} $3^{2.9}$ + 7 t. D, also Ju $10^{8.11}$ $11^{19.21.22.23}$ 1 K 4^{19} ψ 135^{11} 136^{19} (Sihon their king Nu 21^{1}+; Sihon & Og Dt 3^{8}+); (*b*) living W. of Jordan Jos $10^{5.6}$ $24^{12.15.18}$ (all E), cf. 7^{7} (JE); 5^{1} 10^{12} (both D; cf. also 13^{4}, q del Di) Ju $1^{34.35.36}$ 6^{10} 1 K 21^{26} 2 K 21^{11} cf. 1 S 7^{14} 2 S 21^{2}; (*c*) living in south Dt $1^{7.19.20.27.44}$, cf. Gn 14^{7} (W of Dead Sea); (*d*) in gen = ancient inhabitants of Canaan Gn 15^{16} (J or R) 48^{22} (E) Am $2^{9.10}$; (*e*) named in list of Canaanitish peoples, to be dispossessed by Isr Ex $3^{8.17}$ 13^{5} 33^{2} 34^{11} Jos 3^{10} 9^{1} (all J); Dt 7^{1} 20^{17} Jos 11^{3} 12^{8} (all D); Ex 23^{23} Nu 13^{29} Jos 24^{11} (all E), Ju 3^{5} 1 K 9^{20} 2 Ch 8^{7} Ezr 9^{1} Ne 9^{8}, cf Ez $16^{3.45}$; (on these lists cf. Bu Urgesch 344 ff & We JBTh xxi. 602) **3. adj.gent.** sg Gn 14^{13} Dt 2^{24}.

†אִמְרִי **n.pr.m.** **1.** a man of Judah 1 Ch 9^{4}; cf **2.** Ne 3^{2} (= *tall?* or *eloquent?*).

אֲמַרְיָה, אֲמַרְיָהוּ **n.pr.m.** (*Yah(u) hath promised*, cf. Palm. אמרשמשא, Sab יתעאמר) long form only 1 Ch 24^{23} 2 Ch 19^{11} 31^{15}. **1.** a Levite 1 Ch 23^{19} 24^{23} (in Dvd's time), cf. 1 Ch $5^{33.33}$ 6^{37} Ezr 7^{3}, vid also **2.** 1 Ch $5^{37.37}$, also **3.** Ezr 10^{42} **4.** chief priest under Jehosh. 2 Ch 19^{11}. **5.** Levite under Hezekiah 2 Ch 31^{15}. **6.** son of Hezekiah & great-grandfather of Zephaniah Zp 1^{1} **7.** a priest Ne 10^{4} $12^{2.13}$. **8.** a man of Judah Ne 11^{4}

†[מַאֲמָר] **n.m.** Est 9. 32 **word, command** (late; Mish *id.*) cstr. מַאֲמַר Est 1^{15} 2^{20} 9^{32}.

†אַמְרָפֶל **n.pr.m.** king of Shinar Gn $14^{1.9}$ (prob. = חמרבי, *Ḥammurabi* of Babylon, who reigned c 2100 B C, cf. Schr SBA 1887, xxxi (June 23) COT ii 296 f. Dl in De Gen 1887 Excursus)

†אֶמֶשׁ **adv. yesterday** (etym dub, MV after Fl De on Jb 30^{3} cf. Sta § 256 e der fr. √משה = Ar. مسا, whence مَسَآءٌ, *evening;* v. also in Thes, & cf As *mušu, night* COT Gloss, Eth. ትማልም: but also Ar أَمْسِ = As *amšatu, yesterday*) = *last night* Gn 19^{34} $31^{29.42}$ (אָמֶשׁ); = recently 2 K 9^{26} —Jb 30^{3} א׳ שׁוֹאָה is difficult & uncertain Thes MV al. *darkness, gloom* of waste-ness, so RV, but dub, cf. Di; G Hoffm. rds אֵם שׁ׳ = *the mother of* (*all*) *the ruined* (said of the desert)

אֲמִתַּי, אֱמֶת v. אמן

אַמְתַּחַת v מתח

אָן **adv.** v. sub אַי

†אֹן (Gn 41^{45} 46^{20}) אוֹן (Gn 41^{50} Ez 30^{17}) **n. pr.loc. On** (Egypt *Ân* cf Eb$^{GS 74}$ Wied$^{Sammlg 146}$, perh = As *Unu*, Steindorff$^{BAS I 610}$, contr Dl$^{Pa 318}$) city in lower Egypt, prob on border of land of Goshen, residence of 'Potiphera, priest of On,' father-in-law of Joseph Gn 41$^{45.50}$ 46^{20}, also Ez 30^{17} (where MT אָוֶן), it was celebrated for worship of sun-god Ra, & hence called also *sun-city*, בית שמש Je 43^{13}, 𝔊 Ἡλίου πόλις, mod *Matarîye*, on E bank of Nile, c 7 miles E of N fr Cairo & 18 fr Memphis,—cf. Eb$^{GS 75. 507 f}$ & map Wied$^{1 c}$

אֹן *sorrow*, v אָוֶן

†אָנָּא **interj.** (from אָהּ and נָא, q v) a strong part of entreaty, **ah, now! I** (or **we**) **beseech thee!** oft sq an imper; Gn 50^{17} (to Joseph) אָנָּא שָׂא נָא וגו׳ *Ah, now!* forgive, we pray, etc, Ex 32^{31} (to God), elsewhere always sq ׳' or אֲדֹנָי ψ 118$^{25.25}$ Ne 1$^{5.11}$ Dn 9^{4}. Written אָנָּה 2 K 20^{3} (= Is 38^{3}) Jon 1^{14} 4^{2} ψ 116$^{4.16}$.

אנב (perh *spring, leap*, so Dl$^{HA 65. Pr 114}$, inferred fr As *annabu, hare*, ag this No$^{ZMG 1886, 731}$)

†אַרְנֶבֶת **n.f. hare** (Ar أَرْنَب, Syr ܐܪܢܒܐ, As *annabu*, as *springer*?) eating of it forbidden Lv 11^{6} (P) Dt 14^{7}.

אָנָה, אָנָה v. sub אַי

I †[אָנָה] **vb. mourn**—**Qal** *Pf* 3 pl וְאָנוּ cons Is 3^{26} 19^{8} (‖ אָבַל q v)

†אֲנִיָּה **n.f. mourning**; Is 29^{2} La 2^{5} (both times in combin תַּאֲנִיָּה וַאֲנִיָּה).

†תַּאֲנִיָּה **n.f.** id *ib*

†אֲנִיעָם **n.pr.m.** (*lament of people*) 1 Ch 7^{19} a man of Manasseh

II אנה (√ whence foll nouns, cf. As *ûnu, unûtu, vessel, utensil*, v Dl in Zim$^{BP 115}$ Hpt in KAT$^{2 Gloss}$, Ar إِنَاءٌ)

†אֳנִי **n.m.**$^{1 K 10 11}$ & **f**$^{v 22}$ **coll. ships, fleet**—abs. 1 K 9^{26}+, cstr. 10^{11}+,—of Sol. 1 K 9$^{26.27}$, called אֳ׳ תַרְשִׁישׁ (i e large, sea-going vessels, such as sail to Tarshish) 10$^{22.22}$, אֳ׳ חִירָם 10$^{11.22}$, propelled by oars אֳ׳־שַׁיִט Is 33^{21}.

†אֳנִיָּה **n.f. unit. a ship**—abs Jon 1^{3}+3t, *Pl* abs אֳנִיּוֹת Dt 28^{68}+, אוֹנִיּוֹת 2 Ch 8^{18}, cstr = abs. 1 K 22^{49}+, etc,—*a ship* Pr 30^{19} Gn 49^{13} Dt 28^{68} Ju 5^{17} (where, however, cf Bu$^{RB Richter u Sam p. 16}$ on text) 1 K 22$^{49.50}$ Is 43^{14} 2 Ch 8^{18} 20$^{36.37}$ Jon 1$^{4.5}$ ψ 104^{26} 107^{23} Dn 11^{40}, אֳ׳ הַיָּם Ez 27^{9}, propelled by oars Ez 27^{29}; esp אֳ׳ תַרְשִׁישׁ (cf. אֳנִי) 1 K 22^{49} 2 Ch 9^{21} (cf. 1 K 10^{22} supr sub אֳנִי) ψ 48^{8} Is 2^{16} 23$^{1.14}$ 60^{9} Ez 27^{25}; late of ship going to Tarshish 2 Ch 9^{21} 20^{36} Jon 1^{3}, *merchant-ship*, אֳ׳ סוחר Pr 31^{14}, אֳ׳ אֵבֶה *swift ships* Jb 9^{26} (cf. אבה), *seamen* אַנְשֵׁי־אֳנִיּוֹת 1 K 9^{27}

†III [אָנָה] **vb. be opportune, meet, encounter opportunely** (Ar أَنَى *the right time is come*, or *it is come to the right time*, or *to maturity*, or *is opportune*) **Pi.** *Pf* אִנָּה Ex 21^{13} *cause* (or *allow*) *to meet* in הָאֱלֹהִים אִ׳ בְּיָדוֹ (obj om), i e without any purpose of the man to whom sf ref **Pu.** *be allowed to meet, be sent*, *Impf.* יְאֻנֶּה Pr 12^{21} (c לְ), 3 fs. תְאֻנֶּה ψ 91^{10} (c. אֶל), subj *evil* **Hithp.** *cause oneself to meet, seek occasion* (= seek a quarrel with) sq. לְ 2 K 5^{7}.

†[תַּאֲנָה] **n.f. occasion, time of copulation**, sf. תַּאֲנָתָהּ i e of wild ass Je 2^{24}.

†תֹּאֲנָה **n f. opportunity**, i.e. ground of quarrel; of Samson, sq. מִן Ju 14^{4}

אָנָּה v אָנָּא

אנו Je 42^{6} Kt v after אֲנִי

†[אָנַח] **vb.** only **Niph. sigh, groan**, mostly poet & late (Aram. אֲנַח, ܐܢܚ Ethp cf As [*anâḫu*], *inḫu, sigh* Zim$^{BP 12.30}$)—*Pf.* 3 fs. נֶאֶנְחָה La 1^{8} Jo 1^{18}, 3 pl נֶאֶנְחוּ Is 24^{7}, *Impf* יֵאָנַח Pr 29^{2} etc, *Imv* הֵאָנַח Ez 21^{11}, *Pt* נֶאֱנָח Ez 21^{12}; נֶאֱנָחָה La 1^{21} etc,—**1.** *sigh*, in token of grief Is 24^{7} Pr 29^{2} La 1^{4} (‖ נוגות) v^{21} Ez 21$^{11.11}$, of Jerus La 1^{8}, mostly abs but sq עַל־ Ez 9^{4} (‖ נאנק); sq עַל־ & אֶל־ 21^{12} **2.** in physical distress La 1^{11} (‖ בִּקֵּשׁ לֶחֶם), Ex 2^{23} sq מִן *by reason of* (‖ זָעַק) **3.** *groan* of cattle (בְּהֵמָה) Jo 1^{18}

†אֲנָחָה **n f. sighing, groaning** (poet & late),—*abs* ψ 31^{11}+, *sf.* אַנְחָתִי Jb 3^{4}+; אַנְחָתָהּ Is 21^{2} (sf with Raphe), *Pl. sf.* אַנְחֹתַי La 1^{22},—*sighing, groaning*, in distress, physical or mental Jb 3^{24} (‖ שַׁאֲגָה), 23^{2} (‖ שִׂיחַ), ψ 6^{7}, 38^{10} (‖ תַּאֲוָה), Is 21^{2}, La 1^{22}, ‖ יָגוֹן ψ 31^{11} Is 35^{10} 51^{11} Je 45^{3}, קוֹל אֲ׳ ψ 102^{6}.

אֲנַחְנוּ **pron. 1 pl. we** v infr.

†אֲנָחֲרַת **n.pr.loc.** city in Naphtali Jos 19^{19} Kn (cf Di) comp *en-Na'ûra*, on E. side of Jebel Dahi, little Hermon; cf. Rob$^{BR III 339}$.

אֲנִי, אָנִי **pron. 1 s. comm. I** (أَنَا, אֲנָא,

III. **אנשׁ** (*soft, delicate*, cf. Ar. أَنُثَ, *id.*, v. Lag$^{BN 68}$ Dl$^{Pr 160}$, also sub I. אנשׁ; but cf. Nö$^{ZMG 1886, 739}$ who der. this mng. fr. *feminine*).

אִשָּׁה$_{775}$ **n.f. woman, wife, female** (Ar. أُنْثَى, Sab. אנתת etc. DHM$^{ZK 1884, 300}$, Aram. אִתְּתָא, אִתְּתָא, אִנְתְּתָא, ܐܢܬܬܐ, Palm. Nab. אנתתא, Eth. አንስት: Ph. אשת, As. *aššatu* COT^{Gloss})—א׳ abs. Gn 2^{23}+; cstr. אֵשֶׁת Gn 11^{29}+ (appar. abs. Dt 21^{11} 1 S 28^{7} ψ 58^{9} but cf. Bö^{§728} Ges$^{§130.5}$); sf. אִשְׁתִּי Gn 20^{11}+; אִשְׁתְּךָ Gn 12^{18}+ (אֶשְׁתְּךָ ψ 128^{3}), etc.; *Pl.* †אִשֹּׁת Ez 23^{44} (Co לעשׂות); נָשִׁים Gn 4^{19}+; cstr. נְשֵׁי Gn 4^{23}+; sf. נָשַׁי Gn 30^{26} 1 K 20^{7}; נְשֵׁיכֶם Ex 22^{23}+, etc.;—**1.** *woman* Gn $3^{1.2}$ 12^{11}+; opp. man $2^{22.23}$ Ex 35^{29} 36^{6} Dt $7^{2.5}$; 22^{22} 1 S 21^{5}+; א׳ emphat. *a genuine* (or ideal) *woman* Ec 7^{28} (‖ ארם); sim. of men as feeble, timid Je 50^{37} 51^{30}; note esp. הַטַּף בַּנָּשִׁים *the children among the women, female children* Nu 31^{18} (P); as conceiving Ex 2^{2} Lv 12^{2} 2 S 11^{5}+; travailing Je 13^{21}; bearing children Ju 13^{24} 1 K 3^{18}; cf. Jb 14^{1} 15^{14} 25^{4}+, etc.; suckling Is 49^{15}; אֹרַח כַּנָּשִׁים Gn 18^{11}; דֶּרֶךְ נָשִׁים 31^{35}; with adj., or app., א׳מֵינֶקֶת *nursing woman, nurse* Ex 2^{7}; א׳ זוֹנָה *harlot* Jos 2^{1} 6^{22} Ju 11^{1} 16^{1} 1 K 3^{16} Pr 6^{26} Je 3^{3} Ez 16^{30} 23^{44}; so א׳ זָרָה Pr 2^{16} 7^{5}; cf. also Ez 23^{44} supr.; א׳ מְנָאָפֶת *adulteress* Pr 30^{20} (cf. אֵשֶׁת אִישׁ 6^{26}), אֵשֶׁת זְנוּנִים Ho 1^{2}; נָשִׁים נָכְרִיּוֹת *foreign women* 1 K $11^{1.8}$ Ezr $10^{2.10.11.14.17.18.44}$ Ne $13^{26.27}$ (cf. v^{23}); א׳ חֲכָמָה *wise woman*, one known as clever, shrewd 2 S 14^{2} 20^{16}, etc.; also א׳ פִּילֶגֶשׁ *concubine* Ju $19^{1.27}$: א׳ אַלְמָנָה *widow* 2 S 14^{5} 1 K 11^{26} $17^{9.10}$; א׳ נְבִיאָה *prophetess* Ju 4^{4}; also cstr. bef. noun of quality א׳ חַיִל Pr 6^{24}; אֵשֶׁת רָע 11^{16}; א׳ חֵן 9^{13}; א׳ כְּסִילוּת 12^{4} 31^{10} Ru 3^{11}; א׳ מִדְיָנִים Pr 21^{9} 25^{24} 27^{15}; א׳ מ׳ וָכָעַס 21^{19}.

2. *Wife* (woman belonging to a man, usually cstr. or sf.) Gn $2^{24.25}$ $3^{8.17}$ $4^{1.17}$+ oft.; of one betrothed (ארשׂ) Dt 20^{7} 28^{30}; בַּעַל (הָ)אִשָּׁה Ex $21^{3.22}$; אִישׁ הָאִשָּׁה Ju 20^{4}; לְאִשָּׁה *to wife* Gn 2^{22} 12^{19} 16^{3} 34^{21}+ oft. (after נָתַן, לָקַח husband or father subj.); *for wife* (after הָיְתָה, woman subj.) Gn 20^{12} Nu $36^{3.6.6.11.12}$ Dt $22^{19.29}$+; for unfaithful wife cf. **1**; cstr. in phr. אֵשֶׁת חֵיקֶךָ Dt 13^{7} cf. 28^{54}; א׳ נְעוּרֶיךָ Pr 5^{18} Mal $2^{14.15}$; א׳ בְּרִיתֶךָ v^{14}; אֵשֶׁת אָב = step-mother Lv $18^{8.11}$ 20^{11}.

3. *Female* of animals Gn $7^{2.2}$; v. also sub **4.**

†**4.** With distrib. & recipr. sense, א׳ מֵאֵת רְעוּתָהּ *each woman from her neighbour* Ex 11^{2} (E); cf. Ru $1^{8.9}$ Je 9^{19}; *each one*, of birds of prey Is 34^{15} cf. v^{16} (del. Bi Che); of cows (fig. of heartless women of Isr.) Am 4^{3}; of sheep (fig. of Isr.) Zc 11^{9}; & of inanimate things (P, & late) א׳ אֶל אֲחֹתָהּ Ex $26^{3.3.5.6.17}$ (P) Ez 1^{9} (del. Co) v^{23} 3^{13}.

אנת (the root of the pron. 2 pers. in Shemitic: أَنْتَ, አንተ: *anta*; f. أَنْتِ, አንቲ: *anti*; BAram. Kt אַנְתָּה (m.), ℑ אַנְתְּ & אַתְּ (both m. & f.); Syr. ܐܢܬ, f. ܐܢܬܝ, the *n* being written but not pronounced; As. *atta*, f. *atti-e* Dl^{§55a}, the *nt* being merged in the double *t*; Heb. similarly. Pl. أَنْتُمْ, አንትሙ: f. أَنْتُنَّ, አንትን: Aram. אַנְתּוּן, ܐܢܬܘܢ, f. אַתִּין, ܐܢܬܝܢ; As. *attunu*).

אַתָּה, אַתָּה (so regularly; but 26–7 t., with different disj. accents, אָתָּה: v. Fr$^{MM 228}$; Sta^{§178a} (rd. 8 for 18)) **pron. 2 s.m. thou** (for *anta*, v. supr.; cf. נָתַתָּ for נָתַנְתָּ) Gn $3^{11.19}$+ oft. Written אַתְּ †1 S 24^{19} ψ 6^{4} Jb 1^{10} Ec 7^{22} Ne 9^{6}. Appended to a vb. for emph., Ex $18^{19.19}$ 1 S 17^{56} שְׁאַל אַתָּה inquire *thou*, 20^{8} 22^{18} Is 43^{26} סַפֵּר אַתָּה. Added for the purpose of strengthening a gen. or accus. sf. 1 K 21^{19} Pr 22^{19} (Ges$^{§135.2}$).

אתי, i.e. אַתִּי, the older & more original form of אַתְּ *thou* (fem.), preserved, prob. dialectically, 7 t. in Kt, Ju 17^{2} 1 K 14^{2} 2 K $4^{16.23}$ 8^{1} Je 4^{30} Ez 36^{13}. (V. supr. As in Syr., the י may not have been fully sounded: the Massorites direct אַתְּ to be everywhere read.)

אַתְּ, אָתְּ pron. 2 s.f. thou (fem.) (shortened from אַתִּי (q.v.); in Syr. the two genders are written differently, ܐܢܬ, ܐܢܬܝ, but, the ܝ not being sounded, are pronounced alike: in ℑ both are written אַתְּ or אַנְתְּ) Gn $12^{11.13}$ 24^{23}+ oft. Thrice Nu 11^{15} Dt 5^{24} Ez 28^{14} used as a masc. (as in Aram. of ℑ); but prob. אַתָּה (v. sub אַתָּה) should be here read.

אַתֶּם pron. 2 m.pl. you (masc.) (for *antem*, v. supr.) Gn 9^{7} 26^{27} 29^{4}+ oft. With הָ, הַאַתֶּם †Ju 6^{31}; following the vb. for emph. Ju 15^{12} Je 34^{15}; construed inaccurately with a fem. Ez 13^{20}.

†**אַתֵּן** Ez 34^{31} (many edd. אַתֶּן), אַתֵּנָה Gn 31^{6} Ez $13^{11.20}$ (edd. אַתֶּנָה) 34^{17} **pron. 2 f.pl. you** (fem.)

I. **אסה** (perh. cf. Ar. أَسَا *heal*, Aram. אַסָּא, ܐܣܐ).

אָסָא n.pr.m. (perh. *healer*) king of Judah, son of Abijam and father of Jehoshaphat 1 K $15^{8.9.11}$ + 24 t. 1 K 15.16.22; 1 Ch 3^{10} 9^{16} 2 Ch 13^{23} + 28 t. 2 Ch 14–21; Je 41^{9}.

II. **אסה** (cf. Ar. أَسِيَ be sorrowful, distressed).

†אָכוֹן **n.m. mischief, evil, harm,** alw abs without art Gn 42$^{4.38}$ (as subj. of קרא), 44^{29} (קרה), Ex 21$^{22.23}$ (היה)

אָכוּךְ v סוך

אסם (*gather, store,* Aram ܐܰܣܶܡ)

†[אָסָם] **n m.** Pr 3.10 *storehouse* (Aram אסנא, id, ܐܣܡܐ *store, supply*) pl sf אֲסָמֶיךָ Dt 28^{8} Pr 3^{10}

†אַסְנָה **n pr.m.** (Aram. אַסְנָא *thorn-bush*?) head of a family of Nethinim Ezr 2^{50} (om Ne 7^{52}).

†אָסְנַת **n.pr.f.** wife of Joseph (𝔊 Ἀσεννέθ, 𝔊L Ἀσσενὲθ, Egyptian, = *belonging to* (goddess) *Neith* (Thes), Cook Speaker's Comm i 479 prop either *As-Neit, favourite of Neith,* or < *Isis-Neit*) Gn 41$^{45.50}$ 46^{20}

אָסַף vb. gather, remove (As *asâpu,* Dl Pr 40)—**Qal** *Pf* אָסַף Gn 30^{23}+, אָסַפְתָּ ψ 85^{4}, etc, *Impf* יֶאֱסֹף 2 K 5^{3}, יַאַסְפֵנִי ψ 27^{10}, etc, also וַיֹּסֶף 2 S 6^{1}, 2 ms תֹּסֵף ψ 104^{29}, 1 s אֹסְפָה Mi 4^{6}, so prob (sf) אֹסִפְךָ 1 S 15^{6} (rd אֹסִפְךָ) v. Ko$^{i\ 382}$ Dr^{Sm}, *Imv* אֱסֹף Nu 21^{16} + אֶסְפָה Nu 11^{16}, 2 fs. אִסְפִּי Je 10^{17}, אִסְפוּ ψ 50^{5}+, *Inf abs* אָסֹף Je 8^{13}+ (Hiph, fr סוף acc. to Ba$^{NB\ 73}$); *cstr* אֱסֹף 2 K 5^{7}+, אָסְפְּךָ Ex 23^{16}, אָסְפְּכֶם Lv 23^{39}, *Pt act* אֹסֵף Nu 19^{10}, אֹסִפְךָ 2 K 22^{20} 2 Ch 34^{28} (pointed אֹסִפְךָ i e Hiph, cf Ko$^{i\ c}$), אֹסְפָם ψ 39^{7}, *pass* pl cstr אֲסֻפֵי Ez 34^{29},—**1.** *gather, collect* (*a*) persons Gn 29^{22} 42^{17} (sq אֶל־) Ex 3^{16} 4^{29} Nu 11$^{16.24}$ 21^{16} Jos 2^{18} (sq אֶל־+ ־ה loc) 24^{1} (sq ־ה loc, all these JE), 1 S 5$^{8.11}$ 2 K 23^{1} (sq אֶל־) Jos 2^{16} Is 11^{12} Zp 3^{8} Hb 2^{5} Ez 11^{17} (all ‖ קִבֵּץ) +, collect men, people, armies, etc, for fighting Nu 21^{23} (E) Ju 11^{20} 1 S 17^{1} 2 S 10^{17} 12^{29}+; cf. Zc 14^{2} (sq עַל־ *against*), (*b*) once obj. beasts Je 12^{9}, (*c*) things, esp fruits of earth Ex 23$^{10.16}$ (Cov't code) Lv 25$^{3.20.39}$ (H) Dt 11^{14} 16^{13} 28^{38} Is 17^{5} Je 40$^{10.12}$ Jb 39^{12} ψ 39^{7}, cf. Ru 2^{7} (‖ לִקֵּט *glean*), the quails Nu 11$^{32.32}$, food in gen. (מַאֲכָל) Gn 6^{21} (sq אֶל־), eggs Is 10^{14}, money 2 K 22^{4} 2 Ch 24^{11}, ashes of red heifer Nu 19$^{9.10}$; chariots 1 K 10^{26} 2 Ch 1^{14}, etc, of fisherman (בְּמִכְמַרְתּוֹ, in metaph) Hb 1^{15}, of collecting wind Pr 30^{4} מִי אָ׳־רוּחַ בְּחָפְנָיו **2.** *gather* an individual into company of others (*a*) obj pers esp. *gather to one's fathers* 2 K 22^{20} (עַל־אֲבֹתֶיךָ) = 2 Ch 34^{28} (אֶל־, both ‖ Niph of same vb q. v), hence also (*b*) *bring,* obj pers 1 S 14^{52} (on form here v Dr) 2 S 11^{27} (both sq אֶל־), association, responsibility, protection being implied; also of stray ox or sheep Dt 22^{2} (sq אֶל־תּוֹךְ), hence also (*c*) *take up, care for,* subj י׳ ψ 27^{10} (cf. perh Is 40^{11} קִבֵּץ), (*d*) *draw up* the feet upon the bed (אֶל־) Gn 49^{33} **3.** *bring up the rear of* Is 58^{8} כְּבוֹד י׳ יַאַסְפֶךָ i e be thy rear-guard (‖ הָלַךְ לְפָנֶיךָ צִדְקֶךָ)—52^{12} has Pi מְאַסִּפְכֶם q v. †**4.** *gather and take away, remove, withdraw* 1 S 14^{19} (obj hand), Je 10^{17} (bundle, sq. מִן), leprosy 2 K 5^{11} (v צרע), cf also אָ׳ מִצָּרַעַת, remove (set free) a man from leprosy v$^{3.6.7}$, Gn 30^{23} Is 4^{1} (reproach), ψ 85^{4} (wrath, ‖ הֵשִׁיב), Je 16^{5} (peace, sq מִן), Jo 2^{10} 4^{15} (light), ψ 26^{9} (נֶפֶשׁ) so Ju 18^{25}, ψ 104^{29} (רוּחַ) v. also Jb 34^{14} (sq אֶל־), hence *destroy* 1 S 15^{6} obj pers); pass אֲסֻפֵי רָעָב *destroyed with hunger* Ez 34^{29}, also *Inf abs* Je 8^{13} Zp 1^{2} (joined with הָסֵף fr. סוּף, v Ko$^{i\ 445}$; considered Hiph Inf abs by Ba$^{NB\ 73}$ v supr) **Niph.** *Pf* נֶאֱסַף Nu 27^{13}+ נֶאֶסְפָה Je 48^{33} etc, *Impf* יֵאָסֵף Ex 9^{19}+, וַיֵּאָסֵף Gn 25^{8}+, יֵאָסֵפוּן ψ 104^{22} etc, *Imv* הֵאָסֵף Dt 32^{50}, הֵאָסְפִי Je 47^{6}, הֵאָסְפוּ Gn 49^{1}+, *Inf abs* הֵאָסֵף 2 S 17^{11} (on form cf Ba$^{NB\ 74}$), *cstr.* הֵאָסֵף Gn 29^{7} Nu 12^{15}, *Pt* נֶאֱסָף Gn 49^{29}, נֶאֱסָפִים 1 S 13^{11} Is 13^{14}, נֶאֱסָפִים Is 57^{1},—**1.** *assemble, be gathered,* reflex (*a*) subj. men Gn 49^{1} (‖ קבץ v^{2}), Is 43^{9} (‖ קבץ), 2 Ch 30^{3} (sq לְ) v^{13} (sq acc loc), Ezr 3^{1} 9^{4} Ne 8$^{1.13}$ (all sq. אֶל־) 9^{1} 12^{28}; earlier mostly of assembling for war Gn 34^{30} (sq עַל־), Jos 10^{5} Ju 6^{33} 9^{6} 10^{17} (‖ נצעק), 20^{11} (sq אֶל־) v^{14} (sq. ־ה loc.), 1 S 13^{11} (sq. acc loc) +, (*b*) subj flocks, etc. Gn 29^{3} (pass, sq שָׁמָּה) v$^{7.8}$ (all J), fish Nu 11^{22} (cf Hb 1^{15} Qal), (*c*) inanim subj herbs Pr 27^{25}; water 2 S 14^{14} (in sim), bones for burial Je 8^{2} cf. 25^{33} (bodies of slain) v also Ez 29^{5} (‖ קבץ which Co rds קבר), appar. = *compose, arrange* for burial **2.** pass of Qal **2,** (*a*) *be gathered to one's fathers* נֶאֱ׳ אֶל־אֲבוֹתָיו Ju 2^{10}, elsewh *to one's people* אֶל־עַמָּיו (all P) Gn 25$^{8.17}$ 35^{29} (‖ וַיִּגְוַע וַיָּמָת) 49$^{29.33}$ (‖ גוע), Nu 20$^{24.26}$ (‖ מות) 27$^{13.13}$ 31^{2} Dt 32$^{50.50}$ (both ‖ מות), also אֶל־קִבְרֹתֶיךָ 2 K 22^{20} = 2 Ch 34^{28} (both ‖ Qal q v), hence also (*b*) *be brought in* (into association with others, etc) Nu 12$^{14.15}$ (E) of Miriam, after leprosy, also refl *betake oneself,* of Moses 11^{30} (E), cf. 2 S 17^{13} (both sq. אֶל־), even with inanim subj Je 47^{6} הֵאָסְפִי אֶל־תַּעְרֵךְ (addressed to sword); of man & beast *brought home* (sq ־ה loc) for protection Ex 9^{19}.

3. Pass of Qal **4,** *be taken away, removed, perish,* of men Is 57^{11} (‖ אבד), fish Ho 4^{3}, *gladness* Is 16^{10} Je 48^{33} (sq מִן), also reflex, *withdraw itself,* of moon Is 60^{20} (‖ בוא שמש) †**Pi.** *Pt* מְאַסֵּף Nu 10^{25}+, מְאַסְּפָיו Is 62^{9} (so BD v

Kö$^{I.201}$); מְאַסִּפְכֶם Is 52^{12};—**1.** *gather* harvest Is 62^{9} (‖קִבֵּץ); bodies for burial Je 9^{21}. **2.** *take in, receive into* (sq. בַּיְתָה) Ju 19$^{15.18}$. **3.** as subst. *rearguard, rearward* Nu 10^{25} (P) Jos 6$^{9.13}$ (both E); fig. of God Is 52^{12}. †**Pu.** *Pf.* וְאֻסַּף (cons.) Is 33^{4} Zc 14^{14} etc.; *Pt.* מְאֻסָּף Ez 38^{12}—*be gathered*, of men Is 24^{22} Ho 10^{10} (sq. עַל *against*), Ez 38^{12}; booty Is 33^{4}; wealth Zc 14^{14}. †**Hithp.** *Inf.* הִתְאַסֵּף Dt 33^{5} *gather themselves.*

†**אֹסֶף** **n.m.**$^{Is\,32,\,10}$ **gathering** (on formation cf. Ba$^{NB\,109}$) of summer fruit אָסְפֵּי־קַיִץ Mi 7^{1}; cf. abs. אֹסֶף Is 32^{10}; א׳ הֶחָסִיל *gathering of the locust*, i.e. as the locust devours, destroys Is 33^{4}.

אָסָף **n.pr.m.** (*gatherer*, cf. Ph. n.pr.f. אספת) †**1.** father of יוֹאָח the recorder 2 K 18$^{18.37}$=Is 36$^{3.22}$. **2.** one of David's chief musicians, a Levite, son of Berechiah 1 Ch 6$^{24.24}$ (‖ הֵימָן v^{18}, אֵיתָן v^{29} vid. these names); 15^{17} (‖ Heman & Ethan, all called) הַמְשֹׁרְרִים v^{19}; v. also 16$^{5.5.7}$ cf. v^{37} (‖ Heman & Jeduthun v$^{41.42}$); 25^{9}, named with Heman & Jeduthun also 25^{6} 2 Ch 5^{12} 35^{15}; ψ 50. 73–83 are ascribed to Asaph; cf. also בִּימֵי דָוִיד וְאָסָף Ne 12^{46}; he is called also הַחֹזֶה 2 Ch 29^{30}, cf. אָסָף הַנִּבָּא עַל־יְדֵי־הַמֶּלֶךְ 1 Ch 25^{2}; repeated mention is made also of *sons of Asaph* בְּנֵי־אָסָף, sons, descendants, and pupils, or those who sang and played after his manner 1 Ch 25^{1} (‖ Heman & Jeduthun) v$^{2.2}$; called הַמְשֹׁרְרִים 2 Ch 35^{15} Ezr 2^{41} Ne 7^{44} 11^{22}, cf. Ezr 3^{10}; performing service of purification, Hezekiah's time 2 Ch 29^{13}; one of them prophesying 2 Ch 20^{14};—1 Ch 26^{1} for בְּנֵי אָסָף rd. בְּנֵי אֶבְיָסָף, cf. 9^{19}; on זַכּוּר ,זִבְדִּי Ne 11^{17}, זַכּוּר 12^{35}, called בֶּן־אָסָף, v. these names. †**3.** keeper of king's park Ne 2^{8}.

†**אָסִיף** **n.[m.]** **ingathering, harvest** (on formation cf. Lag$^{BN\,173}$ Ba$^{NB\,136}$) חַג הָאָסִיף Ex 34^{22} (J); ח׳ הָאָסִף Ex 23^{16} (E)—both Cov't codes.

†[**אָסֹף**] **n.[m.]** what is gathered, **store**, hence בֵּית הָאֲסֻפִּים *store-house*, near south gate of temple 1 Ch 26^{15} (cf. 2 Ch 25^{24}); v^{17} הָא׳ alone in same sense; cf. אֲסֻפֵּי הַשְּׁעָרִים Ne 12^{25}.

†**אֲסֵפָה** **n.f.verbal.** **a collecting, gathering**; אֻסְּפוּ א׳ אַסִּיר Is 24^{22} *they are collected, as a collecting captives* unto a pit (dungeon); or *they are gathered with a gathering* (as) *captives*, cf. 22^{18}; but perh. rd. אֹסֶף הָאַסִּיר (cstr.); v. Weir Che.

†[**אֲסֻפָּה**] **n.f.** **collection** (cf. Ph. אספת *assembly*) only בַּעֲלֵי אֲסֻפּוֹת Ec 12^{11} (דִּבְרֵי חֲכָמִים) compared to driven nails; *members of* learned *assemblies* Thes MV al.; so postB. Heb. NHWB $^{I.127}$; but Hitz-Now al. refer to the wise utterances, called *lords* (possessors) *of collection* because of their well-connected grouping.

†[**אֲסַפְסֻף**] **n.[m.]** **collection, rabble,** only הָאסַפְסֻף Nu 11^{4} of the camp-followers attending Hebrews at the Exodus.

†**אַסְפָּתָא** **n.pr.m.** 3rd son of Haman Est 9^{7} (Pers. *aspadâta*, ab equo sacro datus acc. to Thes Add^{71}, after Pott & Benfey).

†[**אָסַר**] **vb.** **tie, bind, imprison** (Ar. أَسَرَ, As. *asâru*, cf. COT^{Gloss}, Aram. אֲסַר, ܐܣܰܪ, Eth. አሰረ: ሖሠረ:)—**Qal** *Pf.* sf. אֲסָרָם Jb 36^{13}; 3 fs. אָסְרָה Nu 30^{5}+, etc.; *Impf.* יֶאְסֹר 1 K 20^{14}; וַיֶּאְסֹר Gn 42^{24}; וַיֶּאְסֹר Gn 46^{29}+; pl. sf. יַאַסְרֻנִי Ju 16^{7} etc.; *Imv.* אֱסֹר 1 K 18^{44} 2 K 9^{21}; אִסְרוּ Je 46^{4} ψ 118^{27}; *Inf. abs.* אָסֹר Ju 15^{13}; אָסוֹר 16^{11}; *cstr.* לֶאְסֹר Nu 30^{3}+; לֶאֱסוֹר Ju 15^{10}; לְאָסְרְךָ 15^{12}; אָסְרָם Ho 10^{10}; *Pt. act.* cstr. אֹסְרִי Gn 49^{11}; *pass.* אָסוּר Gn 40^{3}+; pl. אֲסוּרִים 39^{20}+; also Ju 16$^{21.25}$ Qr (Kt אסירים); הָסוּרִים Ec 4^{14} (cf. Now); אֲסֻרוֹת 2 S 3^{34}; cstr. אסורי Gn 39^{20} Kt (Qr אֲסִירֵי);—**1.** *tie, bind*, for security, foal to vine (sq. לְ) Gn 49^{11} (blessing of Jacob); horses and asses 2 K 7$^{10.10}$; ψ 118^{27} is dub. De *bind the festal victim with cords;* Che *bind the procession with branches*, etc. **2.** *tie, harness*, kine to (בְּ) cart 1 S 6$^{7.10}$; so (metaph.) Ho 10^{10} *harness them to* (לְ) *their two iniquities* (but Jer Ew Now make א׳ here=יסר *chastise*, cf. אֶסֳּרֵם v^{a}); also sq. acc. *chariot* Gn 46^{29} (J) Ex 14^{6} (E) 2 K 9^{21}; abs. 1 K 18^{44} 2 K 9^{21}; even of making ready chargers א׳ הַסּוּסִים Je 46^{4} (‖ עֲלוּ הַפָּרָשִׁים). **3.** *bind*, with cords, fetters, etc., as prisoner, Simeon Gn 42^{24} (E), Samson Ju 15$^{10.12.13.13.13}$ 16$^{5.7.8.11.11.12}$; א׳ בַּנְחֻשְׁתַּיִם 2 K 25^{7} = 2 Ch 36^{6}=Je 39^{7} 52^{11}; also 2 Ch 33^{11}; cf. (without עָצַר ‖ א׳ בֵּית כֶּלֶא) (בְּנ׳) 2 K 17^{4}, 23^{33}; cf. of divine chastisement Jb 36^{13} & v. also Ez 3^{25} ψ 149^{8}; fig. of absolute authority ψ 105^{22}; esp. *Pt. pass.* 2 S 3^{34} *thy hands were not bound* (‖ *and thy feet not put in fetters*); א׳ בָּאזִקִּים Je 40^{1} cf. א׳ בְּזִקִּים Jb 36^{8} (prob. fig. ‖ חַבְלֵי־עֹנִי); metaph. of king held captive by a woman's tresses Ct 7^{6}; perh. = *imprisoned* (whether bound or not) Gn 39^{20} 40$^{3.5}$ (all JE); as subst. pl. *prisoners* Gn 39^{20} (Kt, v. supr.); so (late) as distressed, & obj. of divine compassion Is 49^{9} 61^{1} ψ 146^{7}; בֵּית האסורים *prison* Ju 16$^{21.25}$; cf. Ec 4^{14}. **4.** *gird* (rare & late) א׳ אֵזוֹר בְּמָתְנֵיהֶם Jb 12^{18} (אֵזוֹר=slaves' waistcloth, RS p. 25 supr.; Hoffm rds. וַיֶּאְסֹר for וַיַּסַּר); חַרְבוֹ אֲסוּרִים עַל־מָתְנָיו

Ne 4[12] · **5.** sq מִלְחָמָה *begin the battle, make the attack* (cf Germ. *mit jemandem anbinden*) 1 K 20[14] 2 Ch 13[3] **6.** fig. of obligation of oath or vow (only Nu 30, P) א׳ עַל־נֶפֶשׁ, usually sq acc cogn אִסָּר, אֱסָר Nu 30[3.5.5.6.8.9 11 12], without אִסָּר etc, v[7 10]; cf v[4] אסר א׳ (עַל־נפשׁ om.) **Niph.** pass of Qal **3**, *be bound, imprisoned, Impf* (juss) יֵאָסֵר Gn 42[19] (E), 2 ms תֵּאָסֵר Ju 16[6 10.13] (of Samson); *Imv* הֵאָסְרוּ Gn 42[16] (E) **Pu.** *Pf. be taken prisoner* אֻסָּרוּ Is 22[3], אֻסְּרוּ *ib*

†**אֵסוּר n.m.** [Ju 15 14] **band, bond** (Aram אֱסוּר, ܐܣܘܪܐ, on the form v Ges[§84a12 R]) אֱסוּרָיו, of Samson Ju 15[14], אֲסוּרִים Ec 7[26] of hands of evil woman, בֵּית הָאֵסוּר = prison Je 37[15]

†**אָסִיר n.m.** [Gn 39 20] **bondman, prisoner** (Ar. اسير, Aram ܐܣܝܪܐ, MI אסר)—א׳ abs ψ 79[11] 102[21], pl אֲסִירִים Gn 39[22] +, cf Ju 16[21 25] Kt, cstr אֲסִירֵי ψ 107[10] +, Gn 39[20] Qr, אֲסִירָיו ψ 69[34] +, etc,—*prisoner* Gn 39[20 22] (J), elsewhere only poetic; Is 14[17], as having rest in grave from task-master Jb 3[18], esp as obj of divine compassion ψ 68[7] (‖ יְחִידִ), 69[34] (‖ אֶבְיוֹנִים), אֶנְקַת א׳, 79[11] 102[21] (both ‖ בְּנֵי תְמוּתָה), 107[10] א׳ עֳנִי וּבַרְזֶל (‖ יֹשְׁבֵי חשֶׁךְ וְצַלְמָוֶת); cf. א׳ אָרֶץ La 3[34]; specif of liberated exiles of Isr Zc 9[11], called *captives of hope* א׳ הַתִּקְוָה v[12]

†**אַסִּיר n.[m.]** mostly coll **prisoners** (acc. to Ol[§185a] corruption of אָסִיר, cf Lag[BN 110]) taken in battle Is 10[4] (Lag[Symm i 105, GGA 1884, 279] rds חַת אֹסִיר etc, *Osiris is broken*, but cf. Che[crit n.]), 24[22] (sim of judgment upon kings of earth), 42[7] (‖ יֹשְׁבֵי חֹשֶׁךְ, ref to exiled Isr, but v also Hi Che Di), 1 Ch 3[17] בְּנֵי יְכָנְיָה אַסִּר prob = *sons of Jeconiah the captive* (yet note omission of art) so Be Zo Ot al.; 𝔊 𝔙 trans as n pr

†**אַסִּיר n.pr.m.** son of Korah Ex 6[24] 1 Ch 6[7], called son of Ebiasaph v[8.22].

†**אֱסָר n.m.** [Nu 30. 8] **bond, binding obligation** (cf. BAram אֱסָר, Syr. ܐܣܪܐ, so forms with suff. infr v. Ba[NB 62] cf Sta[§208a]; but perh Aram loan-word v Lag[BN 174])—א׳ abs. Nu 30[3] +; cstr v[13], sf אֱסָרָהּ v[5], pl sf אֱסָרֶיהָ v[6.15], אֱסָרֶיהָ v[8]—only Nu 30 (P), *binding obligation* of oath or vow, mostly acc. cogn with אָסַר (q v.), Nu 30[3.4.5.5.6.8 11 12]; אֱסָר נַפְשָׁהּ v[13], שְׁבֻעַת אִסָּר *binding oath* v[14]

†**מָסֹרֶת n f** cstr מ׳ הַבְּרִית *bond of the covenant* Ez 20[37] (= מַאֲסֹרֶת, text dub cf. Lag [GN 1882, 158 f M 61], Co rds מוּסָר, i e מוּסָר v. sub יסר; so 𝔖)

†[**מוֹסֵר**] **n.m.** [Is 28. 22] **band, bond**, poet & late (= מַאֲסֹר; Eth ሞሰር: Syr ܡܘܣܪܐ, cf As *mêsiru, sheathing, plating*, e g Lyon [Sargontexte, p 16, l 65 & p. 80])—cstr. מוֹסֵר Jb 12[18] (so Di Hoffm al for מוּסַר); pl מוֹסֵרוֹת Je 5[5] 27[2]; cstr. מֹסְרוֹת Jb 39[5], מוֹסְרֵי Is 52[2]; sf. מוֹסֵרָי ψ 116[16]; מוֹסְרוֹתַיִךְ Je 30[8]; מוֹסְרֵיכֶם Is 28[22], מוֹסְרוֹתֵימוֹ ψ 2[3] etc;—*bands* acc. after פִּתַּח Jb 39[5] restraining-bands of wild ass; ψ 116[16] bonds of distress; Is 52[2] מ׳ צַוָּארֵךְ bonds of captivity of Zion, vb. Hithp; cf also Jb 12[18] מוּסַר מְלָכִים פִּתֵּחַ (so rd., v supr & AV RV), Di understands bonds imposed by kings; Hoffm girdles of kings, & rds. וַיֶּאְסֹר in ‖, for וַיֶּאְסֹר; more oft. acc. after נִתַּק ψ 2[3] bonds imposed by י׳ & his anointed, cf. Je 5[5] & 2[20] (𝔊 𝔙, v. Comm.); of Yahweh's breaking bonds of Isr. Je 30[8] Na 1[13] (last four ‖ שָׁבַר עֹל), bonds of oppressed ψ 107[14], יֶחֶזְקוּ מ׳ Is 28[22], i.e. bonds imposed by Assyria; cf. Je 27[2] (‖ מֹט) lit, symbol of rule of Nebuchadrezzar

†**מוֹסֵרָה n.pr.loc.** station of Isr. in wilderness, where Aaron died (this was Mt Hor acc to Nu 20[22 f] 33[37 f]) Dt 10[6], locality unknown Another form is

†**מֹסֵרוֹת n.pr.loc.** *id*, Nu 33[30.31]

†**אֵסַר־חַדֹּן n.pr.m. Esarhaddon** (As. *Ašur-aḫ-iddina, Ashur hath given a brother*) king of Assyria B C 681–668, son & successor of Sennacherib Is 37[38] = 2 K 19[37] (van d H אַסַר־חַדֹּן); Ezr 4[2], cf COT

אֶסְתֵּר n pr f. Esther (Pers *stâra*, **star**)—daughter of Abihail, cousin and adopted daughter of Mordecai, of tribe of Benjamin; made queen in Vashti's place by Ahasuerus, her Jewish name הֲדַסָּה q.v. Est 2[7 8 10 11 15 15.16.17] + 47 t. Est

I **אַף** v. sub אנף

II. **אַף conj.** denoting addition, esp. of something greater, **also, yea** (so Ph. Aram ܐܦ, אַף, אוּף; cf ڤ) **1.** very rare in plain prose (in which גַּם is more usual)· Gn 40[16]* (*with pron, as rather often) I *also* in my dream, Nu 16[14] Dt 2[11* 20*] 2 S 20[14] (v Dr) 2 K 2[14]* Est 5[12], more freq. in poetry, esp as introducing emphatically a new thought Dt 33[3.20.28] 1 S 2[7] ψ 16[6.7 9] 18[49] 65[14] they shout for joy, *yea*, they sing! 68[8.17] 74[16] 89[28]* 93[1] Pr 22[19]* 23[28]* +, or in more elevated prose style, Lv 26[16* 24* 28* 41*], and 25 t in the impassioned rhetoric of Is[2] (40[24]–48[15]), e g 40[24] 41[10.26] 42[13] 43[7 19] 46[11] *yea*, I have spoken, I will *also* bring it to pass, I have

purposed, I will *also* do it! 48[12.15]. Implying something surprising or unexpected, *even, indeed* Jb 14[3] 15[4*]. ואף *and also* Lv 26[39.40.42.44] Dt 15[17] Hb 2[15] ψ 68[19] 1 Ch 8[32*] = 9[38*] 2 Ch 12[5*] Ne 2[18] 13[15]; *and even* Jb 19[4] וְאַף־אָמְנָם שָׁגִיתִי *and even* indeed (if) I have erred . . . With הֲ, הַאַף *indeed* . . . ? *really* . . . ? † Gn 18[13.23] wilt thou *indeed* sweep away the righteous with the wicked? v[24] Am 2[11] Jb 34[17] 40[8]. In contrast to a preceding thought (expressed or implied) *but, nay* (*imo*) ψ 44[10] 58[3]; cf. Ju 5[29*].

2. (Equally in prose and poetry) with ref to a preceding sentence, *yea, à fortiori, the more so* (= *how much more!* after an affirm clause; = *how much less!* after a neg. one): †2 S 4[10f] when one told me, Saul is dead . I took hold of him and slew him...אַף כִּי־אֲנָשִׁים רְשָׁעִים הָרְגוּ וגו׳ *à fortiori, how much more* (should I do so), when wicked men have slain a righteous person, etc.! Ez 14[21] (Ew Hi) 15[5] Pr 21[27] (in all these passages כִּי = *when*) Jb 4[19]. So ואף †1 S 23[3] 2 K 5[13] . . . וְאַף כִּי־אָמַר אֵלֶיךָ *and the more* (= *and how much rather*), when he hath said to thee, etc More commonly in this sense strengthened by כִּי (q. v), v infr.

אַף כִּי **1.** *furthermore* †Ez 23[40] Hb 2[5] (Ges *quin imo, quin etiam*). **2.** in a qu., *indeed* (is it) *that* . . . ? †Gn 3[1] אַף כִּי־אָמַר אֱלֹהִים *indeed, that* God has said ? i e. has God *really* said . . ? (cf. הַאַף above). **3.** with ref to a preceding sentence (which is often introduced by הֵן or הנה), *yea, that* . . . ! i.e *how much more* (or *less*)! †Pr. 11[31] lo, the righteous is recompensed in the earth אַף כִּי רָשָׁע וחוטא *'tis indeed that* (= how much more) the wicked and the sinner! 15[11] 17[7] 19[7.10] Jb 9[14] 15[16] 25[6] 1 S 14[30] 1 K 8[27] (= 2 Ch 6[18]) lo, the heavens . . cannot contain thee אַף כִּי הַבַּיִת הַזֶּה *'tis indeed that* this house (cannot do so), i.e. *how much less* this house! 2 Ch 32[15]. So ואף כי †Dt 31[27] 1 S 21[6] (perh., but v. RS[Sem i 436] Dr[Sm 293]) 2 S 16[11]. (In Jb 35[14] (Hi De) Ne 9[18] אַף כִּי is simply = *yea, when* . .)

אפד (existence & mng. dub Thes MV al identify with אָפַד *gird on*, but this denom. v. infr; Lag[BN 178 GN 1890, p 15] prop. وفد, *come as ambassador*, as √ of אפוד).

אֵפוֹד (28 t.) & **אֵפֹד** (20 t.) **n.m.**[Ex 28,7] ephod (Eth. አፌድ: cf Aram. ܦܕܐ‎ *id* (on mng v Lag[l c]), perh also As *pid, pitlu* Zim[BP 39], on form v. Ges [§84a12.R.] but Lag[l c] comp وفاد, & thinks אפוד shortened from חֵשֶׁב הָא׳ '*robe of approach*' to God)—א׳ abs Ex 25[7] +, cstr. 1 S 2[18] +,—**1.** *ephod*, priestly garment, shoulder-cape or mantle, **a.** as worn by ordinary priest made of white stuff (בַּד) 1 S 22[18], נֹשֵׂא א׳ cf. **2**; so Samuel as a temple-servant 2[8]; חָגוּר א׳ *girt with an eph*; so David when dancing before ark 2 S 6[14] (*id.*) 1 Ch 15[27] ועל דויד א׳. **b.** as prescribed in P for high priest, more costly, woven of gold, blue, purple, scarlet, & linen (?שֵׁשׁ) threads, provided with shoulder-pieces & breast-piece of like material, ornamented with gems and gold, Ex 25[7] 28[4.6.12.15] 29[5] 35[9.27] 39[2.7] + 17 t Ex 28, 39, also Lv 8[7], cf. prob. 1 S 2[28] (נשׂא א׳) 14[3] 21[10] (v sub **2**), חֵשֶׁב הָא׳ Ex 28[27.28] 29[5] 39[20.21] Lv 8[7]; מְעִיל הָא׳ 29[5] 39[22] (cf Lv 8[7]); with vb נָתַן אֶת־הָא׳ עַל־ *put the ephod on* Aaron Lv 8[7]. **2.** *ephod used in consulting* י׳ 1 S 23[6] א׳ borne in hand (rd. יָרַד וְהָא׳ בְּיָדוֹ 𝔊 We Dr) v[9] 30[7.7] (all c הגישׁ) + 14[18] (הגישׁ) & v[18], in both rd. הָא׳ for ארון & v[18] also נשׂא 𝔊 Klo Dr, **a.** acc. to Thes MV Di Ex 28[6] al. properly sub **1 b**; consultation of י׳ in that case by Urim & Thummim in the breast-piece attached to the ephod (cf Ex 28[28-30] & v. אוּרִים); if so, in view of נשׂא 1 S 2[28] 14[3.18] (cf supr), not used elsewhere = *wear* exc. 22[18], & of 23[6], the word might be used by meton. for the breast-piece itself, **b.** others, e g Sta[Gesch i 466, 471] Bu[RS 116] al., think of an image representing י׳; cf. following. **3. a.** *ephod of gold* made by Gideon Ju 8[27] for a local sanctuary, by which Isr. was ensnared; = **2 b** acc. to 𝔖 Thes ('sine controversia') Stu al. + Sta Bu l c.; orig = gold *sheathing* of an image (cf. etymol supr. & Is 30[22] sub אֲפֻדָּה); MV Be Ko[Hauptprobleme 69] think of garment, as sub **1** v. supr. **b.** made (material not given) for a private, local sanctuary Ju 17[5] 18[14.17.18.20] (|| פֶּסֶל, תְּרָפִים, מַסֵּכָה in all, for 𝔊 gives מַסֵּכָה v[20], om. 𝔖), cf. Ho 3[4] Isr. shall abide without king, prince, sacrifice, pillar, ephod or teraphim; acc. to Thes al + Sta Bu l.c = **2 b**; Stu Be Ry al. regard as sub **1**, in view of distinction from פסל, מסכה & תרפים it seems more likely that this is not an image, but some means of consulting deity, perh in imitation of Urim & Thummim

†**אֵפֹד** **n.pr m.** father of a chief of Manasseh Nu 34[23].

†[**אָפַד**] **vb.denom.** gird on ephod, **Qal** *Pf.* וְאָפַדְתָּ לוֹ בְּחֵשֶׁב הָאֵפֹד Ex 29[5] *and thou shalt gird the ephod upon him with the cunningly-wrought band of the ephod*; so *Impf.* וַיֶּאְפֹּד לוֹ בּוֹ (|| חגר) Lv 8[7].

†**אֲפֻדָּה** **n.f.** ephod (= אֵפוֹד, for which it

supplies cstr. & sf forms) **1.** of high-priest's ephod, cf אפוד **1 b**, only חֵשֶׁב אֲפֻדָּתוֹ Ex 28[8] 39[5] the *cunningly-wrought band of his ephod* **2.** of sheathing of idol-images, אֲפֻדַּת מַסֵּכַת זְהָבֶךָ Is 30[22] (‖ צִפּוּי פְּסִילֵי כַסְפֶּךָ) cf אפוד **3 a**

†[אַפֶּדֶן] **n [m.]** palace (Syr. ܐܦܕܢܐ, both from Pers *apadâna*, cf Spiegel [Altpers. Keilschr 128], but this = *treasury, armoury*, M Schultze [ZMG 1885. 491]) אָהֳלֵי אַפַּדְנוֹ Dn 11[45], of the 'king of the north,' i.e Antiochus Epiphanes

†**אָפָה** **vb. bake** (As *êpû*, Zim [BP 43] Aram אֲפָא, ܐܦܐ)—**Qal** *Pf* 'א Gn 19[3], אָפִיתִי Is 44[19], וְאָפוּ consec Lv 26[26] etc ; *Impf* 3 fs. sf. וַתֹּפֵהוּ 1 S 28[24], יֹאפוּ Ez 46[20], תֹּאפוּ Ex 16[23], *Imv* אֵפוּ Ex 16[23], *Pt* אֹפֶה Gn 40[1]+, אֹפֵהֶם Ho 7[6]; pl אֹפִים Gn 40[16]+, אֹפוֹת 1 S 8[13], etc —*bake*, obj לֶחֶם Lv 26[26] (H) Is 44[15 19] (cf Je 37[21]), מַצּוֹת Gn 19[3] (J) 1 S 28[24], עֻגֹת מַצּוֹת Ex 12[39] (J), חַלּוֹת Lv 24[5] (H), מִנְחָה Ez 46[20], מָן Ex 16[23.23] (P; — c. 2nd obj of material Ex 12[39] בָּצֵק, Lv 24[5] סֹלֶת, 1 S 28[24] קֶמַח) *Pt* alw as subst. *baker* Gn 40 [1 2.5 16 17 20.22] 41[10] (all E) Ho 7[4.6], Je 37[21] מִחוּץ הָא׳ *out of the bakers' street*, also 1 S 8[13] (‖ טַבָּחוֹת, רַקָּחוֹת; only here fem) Nowhere as a menial office, not even 1 S 8[13] where despotic power & growth of court emphasized. **Niph.** *Impf.* 3 fs תֵּאָפֶה Lv 6[10] 7[9], 3 fpl. תֵּאָפֶינָה Lv 23[17],— pass of **Qal** *be baked, baken* of לֶחֶם Lv 23[17], מִנְחָה 7[9] cf 6[10]

†[מַאֲפֶה] **n.[m.]** thing baked, cstr. מִנְחַת מַאֲפֵה תַנּוּר Lv 2[4]

†**אֵפוֹ** (Jb 17[15] 19[6 23] 24[25]), elsewh **אֵפוֹא** (cf. רבו and רבוא), **enclitic part. then** (prob from פוֹ, a part with a demonstr force, cf פֹּה, פוֹ *here*, with א prefixed In the Targs פוֹן is used somewhat similarly, e g Gn 26[10] Nu 11[29] Is 1[9] 48[18 19]),—used **1** in connexion with interrogatory pronouns or adverbs (like ἄρα, ποτε, *tandem*) מִי אֵפוֹא Gn 27[33] who, *then*, ? v[37] וּלְכָה אֵפוֹא מָה אֶעֱשֶׂה and for thee, *then*, what shall I do, my son? Ex 33[16] וּבַמֶּה יִוָּדַע אֵפוֹא and wherein shall it be known, *then* ...? אַיֵּה אֵפוֹא where, then? Ju 9[38] Is 19[12] Jb 17[15], Ho 13[10] אֱהִי מַלְכְּךָ אֵפוֹא, Is 22[1] מַה־לָּךְ אֵפוֹא what is there to thee, *pray* ? **2.** in a command or wish: 2 K 10[10] דְּעוּ אֵפוֹא know, *then*, (in apod.) Pr 6[3] Jb 19[6], Jb 19[23] מִי־יִתֵּן אֵפוֹ וְיִכָּתְבוּן מִלַּי would, *then*, that my words were written! **3.** after אִם, Gn 43[11] אִם־כֵּן אֵפוֹא זֹאת עֲשׂוּ if it be so, *then*, do this, Jb 9[24] if not *then*, who is it? 24[25].

†אֲפִיחַ **n.pr.m.** an ancestor of Saul 1 S 9[1] (etymology & meaning dubious)

אפל (Ar أَفَلَ *disappear depart, set* (of the sun))

†אֹפֶל **n.m.** [Jb 3.6] **darkness, gloom** (only poet.) —'א alw abs —**1.** *darkness*, of night ψ 91[6] (opp צָהֳרַיִם), deep in the earth, אֶבֶן א׳ Jb 28[3] (‖ צַלְמָוֶת, חֹשֶׁךְ), *darkness, gloom* of underworld Jb 10[22.22] (‖ צַלְמָוֶת, אֶרֶץ חֹשֶׁךְ, א׳ עֵיפָתָה), personif Jb 3[6] *that night—let darkness take it* יִקָּחֵהוּ א׳, fig of spiritual darkness Is 29[18] (‖ חֹשֶׁךְ), of secrecy, treachery ψ 11[2] **2.** esp fig of *calamity* Jb 23[17] (‖ חשך q v), 30[26] (opp אוֹר)

†אָפֵל **adj.** gloomy, of day of 'י Am 5[20] (‖ חֹשֶׁךְ, opp נֹגַהּ) cf אֲפֵלָה

†אֲפֵלָה **n.f** darkness, gloominess, calamity—'א Ex 10[22]+, אֲפֵלָתְךָ Is 58[10]; pl אֲפֵלוֹת Is 59[9]—**1.** *darkness* Dt 28[29] Pr 7[9] (‖ אִישׁוֹן לַיְלָה), of supernatural darkness in Egypt Ex 10[22]; of day of 'י (cf Am 5[20] sub אָפֵל) Jo 2[2] Zp 1[15] (both ‖ חשֶׁךְ, עָנָן, עֲרָפֶל) sim. of wickedness Je 23[12] Pr 4[19] **2.** fig. of *calamity* Is 8[22] (‖ חֲשֵׁכָה), 58[10] (‖ חֹשֶׁךְ, opp צהרים), 59[9] (‖ *id*, opp נגהות)

†[אָפִיל] **adj.** (darkened, concealed, thence) **late,** of crops,—אֲפִילֹת Ex 9[32] of wheat & spelt.

†מַאֲפֵל **n.[m.]** darkness, Jos 24[7] (E) וַיָּשֶׂם מ׳ בֵּינֵיכֶם וגו׳, between Hebrews & Egyptians.

†מַאְפֵּלְיָה **n.f.** deep darkness (= מַאְפֵל יָהּ acc to Thes MV cf. Ct 8[6] שַׁלְהֶבֶתְיָה; but Ew [§ 165 b] & on Je 2[31] rds. מַאְפֵּלִיָּה, fem of [מאפלי], der fr Hiph Pt ; cf Sta [§ 302 b] מַאְפֵּלְיָה; Jager [BAS 471] thinks this יָה an enclitic part. of emphasis, & comp As.)—only אֶרֶץ מ׳ Je 2[31] fig. of 'י in dealing with his people (‖ מִדְבָּר)

אֹפֶל v sub פלל

אפן (meaning dub, perh turn, cf פנה).

†אוֹפַן, אֹפַן **n.m.** [Ez 1.20] **wheel.**—abs אוֹפָן 1 K 7[32]+, אוֹפָן Ez 1[16]+; cstr אוֹפַן 1 K 7[33] Is 28[27]; אֹפַן Ex 14[25], pl. אוֹפַנִּים 1 K 7[32]+, cstr. אוֹפַנֵּי 1 K 7[30], אוֹפַנֵּיהֶם Ez 10[12], etc.—**a.** *wheel* of chariot (מֶרְכָּבָה) Ex 14[25] 1 K 7[33] Na 3[2], of (threshing) cart (עֲגָלָה) Is 28[27] cf. Pr 20[26] (as instr of punishment) **b.** wheels in Ezek's vision Ez 1[15 16 16 19 19.20.20.21 (del Co) 21] 3[13] 10[6 9.9.9 9 10 10 12 12 12 13 16.16 19] 11[22] **c.** wheels of the ten bases beneath the lavers in Sol.'s temple 1 K 7[30.32.32.32.33].

†[אֹ֫פֶן] **n.[m.]** **circumstance, condition** (perh. lit. *turning*) only du. (or pl.) sf. עַל־אָפְנָיו = *in* (right) *circumstances* Pr 25[11] (cf. Str ad loc., also Orelli[Syn. d. Zeit u. Ewigkeit 38 f.]).

†אָפ֫וּנָה ψ 88[16] (ἅπ. λεγ. Dl[Pr 135 f.] comp. As. *appuna(ma)* adv. = *ma'diš, very, very much*, but dub.; Thes MV form fr. √פון, & comp. Ar. أَفَنَ *diminuit, mente diminuit* (Frey.), hence *be confused, helpless*, cf. 𝔊 ἐξηπορήθην; 𝔙 *conturbatus sum;* others emend אָפ֫וּגָה fr. פוג q.v. A vb. however is not needed for parallelism).

†אָפֵס (cf. פָּסַס) **vb. cease, fail, come to an end**: only **Qal** *Pf.* 3 ms.; Gn 47[15.16] (of money, כֶּסֶף), Is 16[4] (extortioner: ‖ תַּם, כָּלָה), 29[20] (terrible one: ‖ כָּלָה, נִכְרַת), ψ 77[9] (חַסְדּוֹ: ‖ גָּמַר).

†אֶ֫פֶס, אָ֑פֶס **n.m.** prop. *ceasing*, hence **1. end, extremity**, only in the poet. phrase אַפְסֵי אָ֑רֶץ (ψ 59[14] (א׳ הארץ) *ends, extreme limits*, of the earth, used esp. hyperbolically: Dt 33[17] 1 S 2[10] Mi 5[3] Je 16[19] ψ 2[8] 59[14] 72[8] (= Zc 9[10]); + כָּל־ Is 45[22] 52[10 b] (= ψ 98[3 b]) ψ 22[28] 67[8] Pr 30[4].

2. **Expressing non-existence**: **a.** as subst. (mostly a rare poet. syn. of אַיִן): Is 34[12] and all his princes יִהְיוּ אָ֑פֶס shall become *nought*, 41[29]; 41[12] יִהְיוּ כְאַיִן וּכְאֶ֫פֶס; 40[17] מֵאֶ֫פֶס וָתֹהוּ (‖ כְּאַיִן) as made of *nought* and worthlessness are they accounted by him, 41[24] (rd. פָּעָלְכֶם מֵאָ֑פֶס, ‖ מֵאַיִן, v. אָ֫פַע); 52[4] and Asshur oppressed him בְּאֶ֫פֶס *for nought*. **b.** as part. of negation, prop. *cessation of...*! (cf. אֵין... *nought of...*), very rare in prose (2 S 9[3]), chiefly a poet. syn. of אַיִן: Is 5[8] עַד אֶ֫פֶס מָקוֹם till there is *an end of* place = till there is *no* place (cf. עַד אֵין ψ 40[13]), Am 6[10] (cf. אָ֑יִן Ju 4[20]), Dt 32[36] (hence, in prose, 2 K 14[26]), Is 45[6] (cf. אין 43[11]) v[14] 46[9] 54[15]; אֲנִי וְאַפְסִי עוֹד Zp 2[15] Is 47[8.10] is prob. to be rendered, 'I am, and *there is none* besides' (so Ges Ew Di etc.), the י being 'paragogic' as in זוּלָתִי etc. (Ges[§ 90. 3 a] Ew[§ 211 b]), cf. וְאֵין עוֹד Is 45[5.6.18.21]; but acc. to De the י is sf. of 1 s. 'I am, and *I am nought* besides' (i.e. and I am nought besides my all-sufficient self).—בְּאֶ֫פֶס (like בְּאֵין, q.v.) *without:* Pr 14[28] 26[20] Jb 7[6] Dn 8[25]. **c.** as adv. of limitation: (*a*) *only:* †Nu 22[35] (cf. אַךְ v[20]) 23[13]. (*b*) אֶ֫פֶס כִּי *save that, howbeit* (qualifying a preceding statement): †Nu 13[28] Dt 15[4] Ju 4[9] Am 9[8] (+ 1 S 1[5] 𝔊 We Sta Dr). So אֶ֫פֶס alone †2 S 12[14] (the foll. כִּי signifying *because*).

†[אֹ֫פֶס] **n.[m.]** only in the **du.** אָפְסַ֫יִם (not אַ; v. Baer), lit. **the two extremities**, i.e. either *the soles* of the feet (so AW Ges; cf. Aram. פִּיסְתָּא, ܦܣܬܐ), or *the ankles* (so 𝔖 𝔗 𝔙, & most): only Ez 47[3] מֵי א׳ water of (i.e. reaching to) the *soles* (or *ankles*); cf. v[4] מֵי מָתְנָיִם water reaching to the loins.

†אֶ֫פֶס דַּמִּים **n.pr.loc.** in Judah, c. 16 miles SW. of Jerusalem, called in 1 Ch 11[13] פַּס דַּמִּים, (meaning unknown; Lag[BN 78] on basis of MSS. of 𝔊 would read ספר מים *edge* or *brink* (ܣܦܐ) *of water;* but such a pronounced Aramaism is not probable), only 1 S 17[1].

†[אֶ֫פַע] מֵאָ֑פַע Is 41[24] txt. err. for מֵאֶ֫פֶס v. אפס; so 𝔙 𝔗 Saad Thes Ew Di al.

אֶפְעֶה v. sub פעה.

†[אָפַף] **vb. surround, encompass** (As. *apâpu* Zim[BP 59])—**Qal** *Pf.* אָֽפְפוּ ψ 40[13]; אֲפָפוּנִי ψ 18[5] +;—*encompass* (poet.) lit. Jon 2[6] (subj. מַ֫יִם); fig., subj. evils & misfortunes רָעוֹת ψ 40[13] (sq. עָלַי); מִשְׁבְּרֵי מוֹת 2 S 22[5], cf. חֶבְלֵי מ׳ ψ 18[5], also 116[3].

†[אָפַק] **vb. hold, be strong** (so Thes wh. comp. Ar. أَفَقَ *excel* = *multum valuit;* MV comp. also فاق)—only **Hithp.** *Pf.* 3 pl. הִתְאַפָּ֑קוּ Is 63[15]; *Impf.* וַיִּתְאַפַּק Gn 43[31] Est 5[10]; 2 ms. תִּתְאַפַּק Is 64[11]; אֶתְאַפָּק Is 42[14]; וָאֶתְאַפַּק 1 S 13[12]—**1.** *force, compel oneself* 1 S 13[12]. **2.** *restrain oneself, refrain* Gn 43[31] 45[1] Is 42[14] Est 5[10]; of י׳ Is 64[11]; of Yahweh's compassion Is 63[15], הֲמוֹן מֵעֶיךָ וְרַחֲמֶיךָ אֵלַי הִתְאַפָּ֑קוּ (almost passive).

†[אָפִיק] **n.m.** [2 S 22, 16] **channel** (as holding, confining waters; poet.)—cstr. אֲפִיק Jb 6[15]; pl. אֲפִיקִים Ez 6[3] +; אֲפִקִים Ez 32[6]; cstr. אֲפִיקֵי Jo 1[20] +; sf. אֲפִיקֶיךָ Ez 35[8]; אֲפִיקָיו Is 8[7]—*channel* = *stream-bed, ravine, wady* א׳ מַ֫יִם ψ 42[2] Jo 1[20] cf. 4[18] Ct 5[12]; also ψ 18[16], but better א׳ יָם 2 S 22[16]; א׳ נְחָלִים Jb 6[15]; of river-bed Is 8[7]; so also (without defining word) Ez 31[12] 32[6] 34[13] ψ 126[4]; ‖ גַּיְא Ez 6[3] 35[8] 36[4.6]; fig. of bones of hippopotamus (as hollow) א׳ נְחֻשָׁה Jb 40[18]; of furrows betw. scales of crocodile א׳ מָגִנִּים 41[7]. —מְזִיחַ אֲפִיקִים Jb 12[21] is dub.; Thes MV Di al. say *girdle of* the *strong* (אָפִיק = *firm, forceful*, or—Di—*capable, powerful*); ‖ נְדִיבִים.

†אֲפֵק, אֲפִיק (Ju 1[31]) **n.pr.loc. Aphek** (perh. *enclosure*, or *fortress*). **1.** city near Jezreel (As. *Apku*, cf. Dl[Pa 287]) Jos 12[18] 1 S 29[1] (אֲפֵקָה, so) 1 K 20[26.30] cf. 2 K 13[17]. **2.** city in tribe of Asher Jos 19[30] Ju 1[31] (אֲפִיק). **3.** city NE. of

Beirût, mod. Afqa Jos 13⁴ אֲפֵקָה v. Di. **4.** place near Mizpah 1 S 4¹ (cf. 7¹²)

†אֲפֵקָה **n.pr.loc.** (mng perh *id*) one of a group of cities including Hebron Jos 15⁵³

I אפר (cf perh عَفَرَ leap, أَفِرَ be agile, v אבק)

†אֵפֶר **n.[m.] ashes** (as *light, flying?*)—א׳ abs. Gn 18²⁷+; cstr Nu 19⁹ ¹⁰—*ashes* of red heifer, used in purifications Nu 19⁹ ¹⁰, on head, as sign of humiliation 2 S 13¹⁹, contrition Dn 9³ (‖ צוֹם, שַׂק), Jon 3⁶ (‖ שַׂק) cf Jb 42⁶ (עָפָר וא׳), Is 58⁵ (‖ שַׂק); mourning Est 4¹ ³ (‖ שַׂק) cf Jb 2⁸ (ישב בתוך הא׳), Je 6²⁶ (‖ שַׂק), Ez 27³⁰ (‖ עפר), in sim *scattereth hoarfrost* כָּא׳ ψ 147¹⁶, but also as filthy, loathsome כעפר וא׳ Jb 30¹⁹ (Di sim. of mourning, grief), as worthless, משלי א׳ Jb 13¹² *proverbs of ashes*, fig of worthlessness Is 44²⁰, insignificance עפר וא׳ Gn 18²⁷; ignominy Ez 28¹⁸ Mal 3²¹, distress & sorrow א׳ כַּלֶּחֶם אָכָלְתִּי ψ 102¹⁰ (so As cf Zim^BP 47) cf La 3¹⁶ Is 61³ (פאר תַּחַת אֵפֶר)

II. אפר (*enclose, envelope*, As *apâru, attire* Dl^Pr 64, Thes comp Ar غَفَرَ, *cover*, MV comp Aram ܡܥܦܪܐ, מעפרא, *mantle, turban*, but connection of √ פ׳ ע(غ) with אפר is dub.)

†אֲפֵר **n.[m.] covering, bandage** (As *ipru, covering* Zim^BP 95, *êpartu, garment*, Id.^1b & Dl^Pr 64) א׳ עַל־עֵינָיו 1 K 20³⁸ cf v⁴¹.

אפרח v. פרח

†אַפִּרְיוֹן **n.[m.] sedan, litter, palanquin** (so NH, origin dub; no plausible Shemitic etymol, perh. (so RS in Yule ^Gloss. of Anglo-Indian Words, 502) Skr. *paryaṅka, litter-bed, 'palankeen,'* perh (if poem be late) Gr. φορεῖον,—𝔊 has φορεῖον, 𝔙 *ferculum*, 𝔖 ܦܘܪܝܐ, 𝔗 פוריא) Ct 3⁹ א׳ עָשָׂה לוֹ הַמֶּלֶךְ שְׁלֹמֹה

אֶפְרַיִם **n.pr.m. Ephraim** (Gn 41⁵² connected with הִפְרָה, Hiph of פרה, cf פרא Hiph Ho 13¹⁵) **1.** 2nd son of Joseph Gn 41⁵² 46²⁰, reckoned among sons of Jacob, blessed by him, and given preference over Manasseh 48^1.5 13 14 17 17 (cf. v¹⁹) v^20.20 50²³ Nu 1¹⁰ 1 Ch 7^20.22 **2.** בְּנֵי אֶפְרַיִם (=descendants, tribe of E.) Nu 1³² 2^18.18 24 7⁴⁸ 10²² 26^35.37 Jos 16⁵ ⁹ (boundaries of territory), 17⁸ 1 Ch 9³ 12³¹ 27^10 14 20 2 Ch 28¹², less oft. מַטֵּה א׳ Nu 1³³ 13⁸ Jos 21⁵ 1 Ch 6⁵¹; מַטֵּה בְנֵי־א׳ Nu 34²⁴ Jos 16⁸ cf 14⁴, שבט א׳ ψ 78⁶⁷ (‖ אהל יוסף), בית א׳ Ju 10⁹, also א׳ alone, tribe *Ephraim* Nu 26²⁸ Dt 33¹⁷ Jos 16¹⁰+oft; אֶרֶץ א׳ וּמְנַשֶּׁה Jos 17¹⁷ cf Ju 12¹⁵ 2 Ch 30¹⁰ esp

3. הַר־אֶפְרַיִם *the mountain-country of Ephraim*, a ridge stretching from N. to S through territory assigned to Ephr., with fruitful land on both slopes, esp. the western (cf. Di Jos 16¹) Jos 17¹⁵ 19⁵⁰ 20⁷ Ju 2⁹ 3²⁷ 4⁵+26 t **4.** by Ho & Is (rarely later) אֶפְרַיִם=kingdom of northern Israel (from Ephr as largest & strongest tribe in it) Ho 4¹⁷ 5^3.3.5 (‖ יִשְׂרָאֵל) v^11 12+30 t Ho, Is 7^2.5.8.9 17+9 t Is; also Je 7¹⁵ 31^9.18.20 Ez 37¹⁶ (del. Co) v¹⁹ ψ 78⁹ 2 Ch 25⁷ ¹⁰ cf. 30¹ ψ 60⁹ =108⁹, עָרֵי א׳ 2 Ch 17² cf 34⁶, שׂדה א׳ Ob ¹⁹; hence א׳ alone in loc. sense 2 Ch 31¹, also Ho 5⁹, where *fem.* (& perh Is 7²) †**5.** יַעַר אֶפְרַיִם 2 S 18⁶, E. of Jordan, 𝔊L Klo rd יַעַר מַחֲנַיִם, cf 17^24.27 †**6.** name of a city near Baal-hazor 2 S 13²³ (='Εφραΐμ John 11⁵⁴ & 1 Macc 11³⁴? Klo comp 𝔊L Γοφραιμ & עפרון, Qr עֶפְרַיִן 2 Ch 13¹⁹; so previously Bo Th Ke cf Dr). †**7.** שַׁעַר אֶפְרַיִם a chief gate of Jerusalem 2 K 14¹³ 2 Ch 25²³ Ne 8¹⁶ 12³⁹, perh. at NW. angle, near Holy Sepulchre, cf Schick-Guthe^ZPV 1885.

אפרתה v אפרת

†אֶפְרָתָה **n.pr.** (v Sta^§ 308 d 1, 342 d 2, Morgenl. Forsch 216)—might in several cases, e g Gn 35¹⁶, be אפרת+ה loc, but v. Ru 4¹¹;—**1. n.pr.loc.** place near Bethel, where Rachel died & was buried Gn 35^16 19 48⁷ (אֶפְרָת only Gn 48⁷ where ה perh. dropped on acc of ה following (Ol); in last two passages הוא בית לחם is a gloss, v. Di; cf 1 S 10²) **2.** *id*, a name of Bethlehem Mi 5¹ Ru 4¹¹, cf perh כָּלֵב אפרתה 1 Ch 2²⁴ (𝔊 ἦλθεν Χαλὲβ εἰς 'Εφράθα) **3.** *id* ψ 132⁶, perh. applied to district where Kirjath Jearim lay, on the border of Judah & Benjamin, cf De Che. **4. n pr.f.** אֶפְרָת name given to wife of Caleb 1 Ch 2¹⁹=אפרתה v⁵⁰ 4⁴.

†אֶפְרָתִי **adj.gent. Ephrathite. 1.** Ephraimite, cf אֶפְרָתָה **1.** Ju 12⁵ 1 S 1¹ (of ancestor of Elkanah) 1 K 11²⁶ (of Jerob) **2.** from א׳ **2**; אֶפְרָתִים 1 S 17¹² (of Jesse); pl א׳ מבית לֶחֶם מבית לחם Ru 1²

אפת (meaning dub √ whence Ar إِفْتٌ *calamity*, & also *wonder, portent*, acc to Thes Ar. √=أَيِفَ *suffer evil*)

†מוֹפֵת **n.m.**^Dt 29,2 **wonder, sign, portent** (=מאפת)—מופת Ex 7⁹+14 t; מוֹפְתֵכֶם Ez 12¹¹; מוֹפְתִי; מוֹפְתִים Dt 4³⁴+4 t; מֹפְתִים Dt 6²²+9 t; Ex 7³ 11⁹, מוֹפְתָיו ψ 78⁴³, מֹפְתָיו 1 Ch 16¹² ψ 105⁵ —**1.** *wonder*, as special display of God's power Ex 7³ 11⁹ ψ 105⁵ 1 Ch 16¹² Jo 3³, by Moses and Aaron Ex 4²¹ 11¹⁰ cf 7⁹ (in mouth of

Pharaoh), by false proph. Dt 13$^{2.3}$ (‖אות); usually ‖ אות Dt 4^{34} 6^{22} 7^{19} 26^{8} 29^{2} 34^{11} ψ 78^{43} 105^{27} 135^{9} Je 32$^{20.21}$ Ne 9^{10}; applied to effect of Yahweh's curse Dt 28^{46} (‖אות); to one protected by ′י ψ 71^{7}. **2.** *sign* or *token* of future event (cf. אוֹת) 1 K 13$^{3.3.5}$ 2 Ch 32$^{24.31}$; symbolic act Is 20^{3} (‖אות); as such the term is applied to persons Is 8^{18} (‖אות) Ez 12$^{6.11}$ 24$^{24.27}$; cf. אַנְשֵׁי מ׳ Zc 3^{8} *men who serve as a symbol or sign.*—Vb used, of divine act, is נתן Ex 7^{9} etc., שׂים Je 32^{20}; שׂים also of entrusting to human power Ex 4^{21}, cf. דִּבֶּר 1 K 13^{3}; of human agency עשׂה Ex 4^{21} 11^{10}, נתן 1 K 13$^{3.5}$.

†אֶצְבּוֹן **n.pr.m. 1.** אֶצְבֹּן a son of Gad (Sam אצבעון, 𝔊 Θασοβαν) Gn 46^{16} = אָזְנִי Nu 26^{16} (𝔊 Ἀζενι, Ἀζαν), this shorter form less probable **2.** אֶצְבּוֹן a grandson of Benjamin 1 Ch 7^{7} (𝔊 Ἀσεβων, Ἐσσεβων).

אֶצְבַּע v. II. צבע.

[אצל] prob. i.q. وَصَلَ *to join* (cf. on the א W^{8071}).

I. אֵ֫צֶל$_{61}$ **subst.** conjunction, proximity, with sf. אֶצְלִי, אֶצְלוֹ etc; only used as a **prep. a.** (as an implicit accus.) in proximity to (as though وَصْل Lag$^{BN\ 68}$), **beside**. Gn 39$^{10.15}$ 41^{3} and stood אצל הַפָּרוֹת *beside* the kine, 1 S 5^{2} אצל דָּגוֹן *beside* Dagon, 1 K 13$^{24.25}$ 21^{1} Pr 8^{30} Ez 1$^{15.19}$ 33^{30} 39^{15}; oft. in phrase (מ׳ ו׳) אצל הַמִּזְבֵּחַ Lv 1^{16} 6^{3} Dt 16^{21} 1 K 2^{29} Am 2^{8}+, of a locality (cf. II. את **2**) Dt 11^{30} *beside* the terebinths of Moreh, 1 K 1^{9} 4^{12} Je 41^{17}. After a vb of motion (late) Dn 8$^{7.17}$; cf 2 Ch 28^{15b}. **b.** with מִן, מֵאֵצֶל *from proximity to, from beside* (cf. מאת, מעם) †1 S 20^{41} (read with 𝔊 מֵאֵצֶל הָאַרְגָּב *from beside* the mound); Ez 40^{7} *contiguous to, beside* (מן **3 c**); with suff. 1 S 17^{30} וַיִּסֹּב מאֶצְלוֹ and he turned about *from beside him,* 1 K 3^{20} 20^{36} Ez 10^{16}.

†[אָצַל] **vb. denom.** lay aside, reserve, withdraw, withhold—**Qal** *Pf.* אָצַלְתָּ Gn 27^{36}, אָצַלְתִּי Ec 2^{10}, וְאָצַלְתִּי cons Nu 11^{17};—*reserve,* לִי בְּרָכָה Gn 27^{36}, (*withdraw*), *set apart* מִן־הָרוּחַ Nu 11^{17}; *withhold* מהם Ec 2^{10}. **Niph.** *Pf* נֶאֱצַל Ez 42^{6} *be withdrawn,* i e *shortened* or *narrowed.* **Hiph.** *Impf* וַיָּאצֶל Nu 11^{25} (Ko$^{I\ 390}$) = Qal Nu 11^{17}.

†II. אֵ֫צֶל in **n.pr.[m.]** בֵּית־הָאֵצֶל Mi 1^{11}, acc. to Hi Ew Ca Ke = אָצַל Zc 14^{5}, but dub; cf. II אָצַל infr.

†I. אָצֵל, in pause אָצָ֑ל (Ges$^{§29.4c}$) **n.pr.m.** (perh. *noble,* cf אָצִיל **2**) a descendant of Jonathan 1 Ch 8$^{37.38}$ = 9$^{43.44}$

II. [אָצַל], in pause אָצָל Zc 14^{5}, acc. to 𝔊 𝔗 Thes Ew al., **n.pr.loc.** near Jerusalem; but no site found, & identification with בֵּית־הָאֵצֶל uncertain; hence Symm 𝔅 Koh Wi make subst, אֶל־אָצַל = *very near, hard by* (אָצַל being the supposed abs. form of I אֵצֶל, cf. Ol^{§167b}).

†[אָצִיל] **n.[m.]** side, corner, chief—pl. cstr. אֲצִילֵי Ex 24^{11}; sf אֲצִילֶיהָ Is 41^{9},—**1.** *sides* (borders) of earth Is 41^{9} (‖קְצוֹת), cf ירכתי א׳ Je 6^{22} etc. **2.** fig *nobles* (perh. as *sides, supports,* cf. sub פִּנּוֹת; so Ew Di: but perh = أَصِيل *noble*—from أَصُلَ *be rooted,* أَصْل *root,* met. *origin, stock*—prop. a man having a (known) origin, sprung from an ancient and famous stock, so Ges, cf Lag$^{BN\ 68}$) Ex 24^{11}

†[אַצִּיל] **n.[f.]** joining, joint (cf ܐܨܝܠܐ *elbow*)—pl cstr [י׳]אַצִּילֵי יד Ez 13^{18} (on יד cf Sm Co),—*joint* of hand, i e *elbow* Ez 13^{18}, אַצִּילוֹת יָדֶיךָ Je 38^{12} *arm-joints*—: אַצִּילָה Ez 41^{8} is obscure; perh א׳ is here a technical architectural term *to the joining* (cf. Sm Ke).

†אֲצַלְיָ֫הוּ **n.pr.m.** (*Yahweh hath reserved,* or *set apart*) father of Shaphan the scribe 2 K 22^{3} 2 Ch 34^{8}

אצם (meaning dub, cf. Ar. أَصِمَ *be angry*)

†אֹ֫צֶם **n.pr.m. 1** elder brother of David 1 Ch 2^{15}. **2.** a descendant of Judah 1 Ch 2^{25}

אֶצְעָדָה v צעד

†[אָצַר] **vb.** lay up, store up (Mish. *id*, Aram אֲצַר, ܐܨܰܪ, Ar أَصَرَ *confine, restrict*)—**Qal** *Pf* 3 pl אָֽצְרוּ 2 K 20^{17} Is 39^{6}, *Pt* הָאוֹצְרִים Am 3^{10},—*store up* treasure 2 K 20^{17} = Is 39^{6}, obj. חָמָס וָשֹׁד Am 3^{10}, i e. treasure gained by violence and robbery. **Niph.** *Impf.* יֵאָצֵר be stored up, of the merchandise of Tyre Is 23^{18}. **Hiph.** *Impf.* וָאוֹצְרָה (cf Ko$^{I.391}$) (*denom.* from אוצר) Ne 13^{13} *and I appointed treasurer,* sq acc. pers. +עַל־אוֹצָרוֹת.

†אֵ֫צֶר **n pr.m.** (*treasure,* or *covenant* Ar. إِصْر) a chief of the Horites Gn 36$^{21.27.30}$ 1 Ch 1$^{38.42}$

†אוֹצָר **n.m.**$^{Pr\ 15.16}$ treasure, store, treasury, storehouse (so Aram., also ܐܘܨܪܐ)—אוֹצָר Pr 15^{16}+, cstr. אוֹצַר Jos 6^{19}+; sf. אוֹצָרוֹ Dt 28^{12}+2 t; pl אוֹצָרוֹת Jo 1^{17}+; אֹצְרוֹת Pr 21^{6}+;

cstr אוצרות Mi 6[10]+, אצרות Jb 38[22]+; pl. sf. אוֹצְרֹתָי Dt 32[34] Is 39[4], אֹצְרֹתָי Dt 32[34], אוֹצְרוֹתֶיךָ Je 17[3], אוֹצְרֹתָם Is 30[6]; אצרתיהם Pr 8[21], etc.—**1.** *treasure(s)*, gen pl (gold, silver, costly utensils, etc), Jos 6[19.24] Is 2[7] 30[6] 45[3] (א׳ חֹשֶׁךְ, i e. concealed, hoarded) Ho 13[15] Je 15[13] 17[3] 20[5] 48[7] 49[4] 51[13] 1 K 14[26.26] 2 K 24[13.13], perh also Is 39[2.4] = 2 K 20[13.15]; wealth Pr 15[16] 21[6.20], gathered for temple-building (sg) א׳ בית י׳ 1 Ch 29[8], א׳ הַמְּלָאכָה Ezr 2[69] = Ne 7[70], also v[69] (cf 1 Ch 26[27]) **2.** *store*, supply of food, drink, etc, 2 Ch 11[11] 1 Ch 27[27.28]; fig א׳ רֶשַׁע Mi 6[10] Pr 10[2], יראת י׳ היא אוצרו Is 33[6]. **3.** בית אוצר **a.** *treasure-house* Ne 10[39] cf Dn 1[2], **b.** *storehouse*, *magazine* Mal 3[10]; & without בית **a.** *treasure-house* or *chamber*, *treasury* 1 K 7[51] 15[18.18] 2 K 12[19] 14[14] 16[8] 18[15] Je 38[11] 50[37] (?) 1 Ch 9[26] 26[20.20.22.24.26] 28[12.12] 2 Ch 5[1] 16[2] (?) 32[27] cf Ez 28[4], **b.** *storehouse* Jo 1[17] Pr 8[21] 1 Ch 27[25.25] Ne 13[12.13], **c.** *magazine* of weapons, fig of Yahweh's *armoury* Je 50[25]; **d.** *storehouses* of God for rain, snow, hail, wind, sea Dt 28[12] Jb 38[22.22] Je 10[13] 51[16] ψ 135[7] 33[7].

אֶקְדָּח v קדח

†אַקּוֹ **n.m. wild goat** (?) only Dt 14[5] in list of clean animals אַיָּל וּצְבִי וְיַחְמוּר וְאַקּוֹ וְדִישֹׁן וּתְאוֹ וָזָמֶר (𝔊 ὄρυξ, 𝔖 𝔗 *ibex*, cf Bo[Hieroz. i 900 f], Thes sub אנק cf MV, with ref to Ar عناق *goat*, Thes comp also Talm אִיקָּא, but NHWB MV refer this to *aiḳ*)

אר v אוֹר, for Am 8[8] v. יְאֹר.

†אֲרָא **n.pr.m.** (meaning unknown, Thes conject = אֲרִי *lion*) a descendant of Asher 1 Ch 7[38].

אַרְאֵל, אֲרִאֵלִי, v. אֲרִיאֵל sub I ארה.

† אָרַב **vb. lie in wait** (Ar أَرِبَ *be crafty*, also أَرَّبَ *tie* (a knot) Frey)—**Qal** *Pf* וְאָרַב consec Dt 19[11] Ju 21[20], אָרָבְתִּי Jb 31[9], אָרְבוּ ψ 59[4] La 4[19], *Impf.* יֶאֱרֹב ψ 10[9.9], יֶאֱרֹבוּ Pr 1[18] Mi 7[2]; וַיֶּאֶרְבוּ Ju 9[34] 16[2], נֶאֶרְבָה Pr 1[11]; *Imv.* אֱרֹב Ju 9[32], *Inf* אֱרָב־ Pr 12[6], *Pt.* ארב Jos 8[2] + 11 t, אֹרֵב Jos 8[12] + 4 t, אֹרְבִים Jos 8[4] + 2 t.,—*lie in wait* (with hostile purpose), abs Ju 9[32.43] + 21[20] Jb 31[9] ψ 10[9] Pr 7[12] 23[28] 1 S 22[8.13] La 3[10] (of bear, cf. ψ 10[9]), c inf of purpose ψ 10[9], c. acc א׳ דָּם Pr 12[6], c. עַל, and pers against whom Dt 19[11] Ju 9[34]; usually c. לְ Mi 7[2] Ju 16[2] ψ 59[4] Pr 1[11.18] 24[15] La 4[19] cf. Jos 8[2.4.14], *Pt* as subst. = *liers-in-wait* (pl) Ju 20[29], usually sg. coll *ambush* Jos 8[2.12.14.19.21] Ju 16[9.12] 20[33.36.37.37.38] Ezr 8[31]; pl of this sing = ambuscades Je 51[12]; sg. = *place of lying-in-wait*, *ambush* (loc sense) Jos 8[7]

Pi. *Pt.* pl. *liers-in-wait* i q. **Qal** *Pt.* מְאָרְבִים Ju 9[25] (c לְ), 2 Ch 20[22] (c עַל) ? **Hiph.** *Impf.* וַיָּרֶב בנחל (for וַיֶּאֱרֹב) 1 S 15[5] (cf. Dr Ko[i 390], Ges-Kau [68 2] queries) but txt. dub; cf Ol[§ 257 b], & Klo, who prop. ויעבר בנחל

†[אֹרֶב] אֶרֶב **n [m.]**—**1.** *a lying-in-wait* Jb 38[40] **2.** *covert*, *lair* 37[8] (|| מְעוֹנֹת)

†אֲרָב **n.pr.loc.** city near Hebron Jos 15[52] (𝔊 Ἐρεμ, 𝔊L Ἐρεβ; acc to Onomast. Ἐρεμινθα Lag[On 254 2nd ed 260] Ereb Id[119, 2nd ed 152], a village *Heromith* in Daroma; cf Di Survey[iii 311])

†אַרְבִּי **adj gent.** הָא׳ 2 S 23[35] (but cf Dr).

†[אֹרֶב] **n.[m.] ambuscade** only fig—**a.** בְּקִרְבּוֹ יָשִׂים אָרְבּוֹ Je 9[7] i e he planneth treachery. **b.** אָרְבָּם *their intrigue* Ho 7[6] cf Now[p. 126].

†[אָרְבָּה] **n.f. artifice**, pl cstr אָרְבּוֹת יָדָיו Is 25[11] (lit *tricks of his hands*)

†אֲרֻבָּה **n.f. lattice, window, sluice** (Mish. *id*)—א׳ Ho 13[3]; pl אֲרֻבּוֹת 2 K 7[2]+, cstr *id.* Mal 3[10], אֲרֻבֹּת Gn 7[11] 8[2]; אֲרֻבֹּתֵיהֶם Is 60[8],—*lattice*, latticed opening, where smoke escaped Ho 13[3]; openings of dove-cote Is 60[8], metaph. of eyes Ec 12[3] (as latticed by lashes? Hi Now, only here of opening to look through); elsewhere of sluices in sky, opened by י׳, through which rain pours destructively, א׳ הַשָּׁמַיִם Gn 7[11] 8[2], cf Is 24[18] (א׳ מִמָּרוֹם); but also fertilizing 2 K 7[2.19] (א׳ בשמים); fig of blessing Mal 3[10] (א׳ השמים)

†אֲרֻבּוֹת **n.pr.loc.** (= אֲרָב? cf Klo ad loc) 1 K 4[10] בָּאֲרֻבּוֹת

†מַאֲרָב **n.m ambush**—מַאֲרָב Jos 8[9] + 2 t., מָאֳרָב Ju 9[35]; cstr מַאֲרַב ψ 10[8];—**1. a.** *ambush*, place of lying-in-wait Jos 8[9] Ju 9[35], **b.** *lurking-place* ψ 10[8] (|| מסתרים) **2.** *liers-in-wait* 2 Ch 13[13.13] (cf ארב *Pt*)

אַרְבֵּאל cf בֵּית אַרְבֵּאל, sub בית.

אַרְבֶּה v sub רבה

אַרְבַּע, אַרְבָּעָה, אַרְבַּעַת, אַרְבָּעִים etc v. רבע

†[אָרַג] **vb. weave** (Mish. *id* cf. Ph. ארג *weaver*)—**Qal** *Impf* 2 fs תַּאַרְגִי Ju 16[13], 3 mpl. יֶאֱרֹגוּ Is 59[5], *Pt* אֹרֵג Ex 28[32] + 4 t.; pl. ארגים Is 19[9] + 5 t, ארגות 2 K 23[7],—*weave* cloth, etc. Is 19[9] (in Egypt) 2 K 23[7], Samson's locks Ju 16[13]; metaph weave spider's web = intrigue Is 59[5]; most often Pt. used as subst = *weaver* Is 38[12];

work of the weaver מעשה א׳ Ex 28^{32} $39^{22.27}$ cf. 35^{35}; weavers' beam (pl.) מְנוֹר א׳ 1 S 17^{7} 2 S 21^{19} 1 Ch 11^{23} 20^{5} (sim. of huge spear-shaft)—cf. also sub יַעֲרֵי ארגים.

†אֶ֫רֶג n.[m.] loom (v. GFM $^{PОS\ Oct.\ 1889}$)—אֶרֶג Ju 16^{14} hand-loom to which Samson's hair was fastened, plucked up by him (א׳ obj. of וַיִּסַּע; del. הַיְתַד as gloss, cf. GFM supr.); Jb 7^{6} יָמַי קַלּוּ מִנִּי אָ֑רֶג *my days are swifter than a loom.*

אַרְגֹּב v. רגב.

אַרְגָּז v. רגז.

†**אַרְגְּוָן** n.[m.] purple (of Aram. form, cf. Heb. infr.; perh. txt. err.)=*purple thread* 2 Ch 2^{6} (+ כַּרְמִיל וּתְכֵ֫לֶת), cf. 2^{13} 3^{14} sub אַרְגָּמָן.

†**אַרְגָּמָן** n.[m.] **purple, red-purple,** i. e. **purple thread & cloth** (As. *argamannu* COT Ex 25^{4}, Ar. أُرْجُوَانٌ, Aram. ܐܪܓܘܢܐ, cf. אַרְגְּוָן supr.; etym. dub.; possibly Skr. *râgaman*, adj. *red, reddish*, fr. *râga*, red colour, so Benary cf. Thes Add^{111} RobGes; vid. MV; Thes earlier, fr. רגם; but prob. loan-word, cf. also Lag $^{BN\,205}$; Pers. ارغوان is also cited by PS)—form alw. as above—**1.** *purple thread*, cf. esp. Ex 35^{25} 39^{3} Est 1^{6}; **a.** mostly Ex (P) with ref. to the hangings of tabernacle, the ephod, etc.; seld. alone; c. תְּכֵ֫לֶת, *violet* (q.v.), תּוֹלַ֫עַת שָׁנִי, שֵׁשׁ (מָשְׁזָר), (also עִזִּים) Ex 25^{4} $26^{1.31.36}$ 27^{16} $35^{6.25.35}$ $36^{8.35.37}$ $38^{18.23}$ 39^{24} (on text v. Di) v^{29}; with these + זָהָב $28^{5.6.8.15}$ $39^{2.3.5.8}$; om. שֵׁשׁ מ׳ 28^{33} 39^{1}; also of temple-hangings, with תְּכֵ֫לֶת, בּוּץ & כַּרְמִיל, 2 Ch 3^{14} cf. 2^{13} (v. also 2^{6} v. sub אַרְגְּוָן). **b.** as indicating wealth & luxury of Tyre, c. שֵׁשׁ, רִקְמָה, תְּכֵ֫לֶת Ez 27^{7}; c. רִקְמָה & בּוּץ v^{16} (as articles of commerce); also in Persia, c. בּוּץ Est 1^{6}. **2.** *purple cloth*, chiefly of garments, בֶּגֶד א׳ Nu 4^{13} Ju 8^{26}; שֵׁשׁ וְא׳ לְבוּשָׁהּ Pr 31^{22}; וְתַכְרִיךְ בּוּץ וְא׳ Est 8^{15}, תְּכֵ֫לֶת וְא׳ לְבוּשָׁם Je 10^{9}; also מֶרְכָּבוֹ א׳ Ct 3^{10}; in simile, of woman's hair Ct 7^{6}.

†**אַרְדְּ** n.pr.m. Gn 46^{21} son of Benjamin, but Nu 26^{40} *grand*son of Benjamin = אַדָּר 1 Ch 8^{3}.

†**אַרְדִּי** adj.gent. c. art. as n.pr.coll., מִשְׁפַּ׳ הָאַרְדִּי Nu 26^{40}.

†**אֲרוֹד** n.pr.m. son of Gad Nu 26^{17} = אֲרוֹדִי Gn 46^{16}.

†**אֲרוֹדִי** adj.gent. c. art. as n.pr.coll., מִשְׁפַּ׳ הָא׳ Nu 26^{17}; without art. as n.pr. = אֲרוֹד Gn 46^{16}.

†**אַרְדּוֹן** n.pr.m. son of Caleb, of tribe of Judah 1 Ch 2^{18}.

†**אַרְוַד** n.pr.loc. city of Phenicia (As. *Aruada*, etc. v. COT Gn 10^{18} Dl$^{Pa\,281}$; 𝔊 Ἀράδιοι; mod. *Ruâd*) on an island near main land, northward fr. Tripolis, mentioned with Sidon Ez $27^{8\,cf.\,11}$.

†**אַרְוָדִי** adj.gent. c. art. as n.coll. (As. *Arudai*, etc. COT^{Gloss}) mentioned among Canaanites, הָאַרְוָדִי Gn 10^{18} = 1 Ch 1^{16}.

†**אֲרִידַי** n.pr.m. a son of Haman Est 9^{9} (Pers., perh. = *haridayas, delight of Hari*, v. Add Thes^{72}; but text very uncertain; cf. diff. tradition as to the names in 𝔊).

†**אֲרִידָתָא** n.pr.m. a son of Haman Est 9^{8} (Pers., perh. = *Hari-dâta, given by Hari*, v. *ib.*, but 𝔊 Φαραδαθα).

† I. [**אָרָה**] vb. **pluck, gather** (Eth. አረየ:)—**Qal** *Pf.* 1 s. אָרִיתִי Ct 5^{1}; 3 pl. sf. וְאָרוּהָ ψ 80^{13} *pluck* (grapes from) vine ψ 80^{13}, myrrh Ct 5^{1}.

†**אֲרִי** n.m.$^{Pr\,28,\,15}$ **lion** (As. *aria*, Eth. አርዊ: *wild beast*, cf. also אַרְיֵה infr.)—אֲרִי Am 3^{12} + 13 t. + 2 S 23^{20} Qr (Kt אריה), La 3^{10} (id.) + ψ 22^{17} (כָּאֲרִי for wh. rd. כָּרוּ = כארו cf. De Pe Che crit. note); pl. אֲרָיִים 1 K 10^{20}; אֲרָיוֹת (also m.) Zp 3^{3} + 16 t. (f. Je 51^{38}? but cf. Ju 14^{5});—*lion*, lit. in narrative Ju 14^{5} 1 S $17^{34.36.37}$ 2 S 23^{20} = 1 Ch 11^{22} 2 K $17^{25.26}$ Pr 22^{13} 26^{13} Ct 4^{8} cf. Am 3^{12} 5^{19}; *lion-images* 1 K $7^{29.29.36}$ $10^{19.20}$ = 2 Ch $9^{18.19}$; in comparison Nu 23^{24} 24^{9} Ju 14^{18} Is 38^{13} Je 51^{38} 2 S 1^{23} Ez 22^{5} La 3^{10}; metaph. Na 2^{12} Zp 3^{3} Je 50^{17} Ez $19^{2.6}$ Pr 28^{15}. For כארי ψ 22^{17} rd. כארו, cf. above. Cf. also אַרְיֵה.

†[**אֻרְיָה**] n.f. **manger, crib** (Aram. אוּרְיָא, ܐܘܪܝܐ, Ar. آرِيٌّ *stall*, etc., As. *urû* Dl$^{BAS\,I.\,211}$)—*Pl.* אֻרָוֺת 2 Ch 32^{28} (Aram. form for אֻרְיוֹת; cf. Lag$^{BN\,172}$); cstr. אֻרְוֺת 1 K 5^{6}, אֻרְיוֹת 2 Ch 9^{25};—*crib* of horses 1 K 5^{6} (app. in enumeration of horses themselves, Eng. *head*, or *span*, cf. also 2 Ch 9^{25} with 1 K 10^{26}; so Th MV, but txt. here dub. cf. Klo), hence 2 Ch 9^{25}; of any animals (כל־בהמה) 2 Ch 32^{28} (on לְאֻ׳ v. Add.).

†**אַרְיֵה** n.m.$^{Am\,3,\,8}$ **lion** (𝔗 *id.* Syr. ܐܪܝܐ, cf. also אֲרִי supr.)—only sg. as above Am 3^{4} + 44 t. + 2 S 23^{20} Kt (Qr אֲרִי) La 3^{10} (id.);—*lion*, lit. in narrative Ju $14^{8.8.9}$ 2 S 23^{20} 1 K $13^{24.24.25.26.28}$ (c. עמדים txt. err. acc. to Klo)^{28} $20^{36.36}$ cf. Is 11^{7} 35^{9} 65^{25}; in simile Gn 49^{9} 2 S 17^{10} ψ 7^{3} 10^{9} 17^{12} 22^{14} Is 21^{8} 31^{4} Je 2^{30} 12^{8} 49^{19} 50^{44} La 3^{10} (Kt) Ez 1^{10} 10^{14} 1 Ch 12^{8} Ho 11^{10} Jo 1^{6} Mi 5^{7}, cf. Am $3^{4.8}$ Ec 9^{4}; metaph. Gn 49^{9} Dt 33^{22} Jb 4^{10} ψ 22^{22} Is 15^{9} Je 4^{7} 5^{6} Na $2^{12.12.13}$.

†אֲרִיֵה **n.pr.m.** so appar. 2 K 15^{25} an officer of Pekahiah, but c. art הָאַרְיֵה, & on text with possible corruption & dittography v Klo

†אֲרִיאֵל **1. n.pr.f.** (prob, v Ew) **Ariel** (*lioness of Ēl*) name applied to Jerusalem Is $29^{1.2.2.7}$ (so Ges Ew Che Di al, 𝔗 De Brd Or al say *hearth of Ēl*, cf אֲרִיאֵל). **2. n.pr.m** a chief man among returning exiles Ezr 8^{16} **3.** אֲרִיאֵל מוֹאָב 2 S 23^{20} = אֲרִיאֵל מ׳ 1 Ch 11^{22} taken by 𝔊 RV Dr^{Sm} al as **n.pr.m.**, rd *two sons of Ariel of Moab*, RS$^{Sem\ i\ 469}$ comp אראל MI ^{12}, *altar-hearth* (so Sm & So, and Dr$^{Sm\ xci}$, v sub אֲרִיאֵל) and transl א׳ מוֹאָב *altar-hearths of Moab* **4.** Ez 43^{15} & Qr $v^{15\ 16}$ vid sub אֲרִיאֵל.

†אַרְאֵלִי **n.pr.m** (app n gent. from foregoing, but 𝔊 Nu 26^{17} Ἀριηλ (Gn 46^{16} Ἀροηλεις, Ἀροηδις, Ἀπηδεις) = foregoing) a son of Gad Gn 46^{16} Nu 26^{17}, also **adj.gent.** c art. as n pr. coll Nu 26^{17} מִשְׁפַּחַת הָאַרְאֵלִי 𝔊 Ἀριηλι

†[אֶרְאֵל] **n.[m.]** (form & meaning dub. v. infr)—only in אֶרְאֶלָּם Is 33^{7}, Ges אֶרְאֶלָּם *heroes;* cf Thes Kn Che, Hi אַרְאֵלָם, cf. De, who der from אֲרִיאֵל, lit = *lion of God*, coll c sf, & transl *their heroes*, n gent fr. אֲרִיאֵל = Zion Nbr $^{Athen\ 1880,\ p\ 400}$ cf Say$^{ib\ 468}$, Ew אֶרְאֶל = אֶרְעֶל *trembling*, cf Di Brd prop הֵילִילוּ 'cry pitifully' 𝔖 𝔗 al rd some form of ראה, 𝔊 ירא. Wholly uncertain

II. ארה (*burn*, cf Ar أَرِىَ, whence إِرَةٌ *hearth;* Ew^{§163g} al v. infr)

†אֲרִיאֵל **n.[m.] hearth, altar-hearth** (𝔊 Ἀριηλ, fr ארה with ל aff acc. to Ew^{§163g} Ol^{§220} Sm Ez 43^{15} Di Is 29^{1} al, but this formation very rare & here dub; 𝔗 Hi De Brd Or Is 29^{1} der fr ארי+אל = *hearth of Ēl*, v also RS $^{Sem\ i\ 469}$, who thinks of pillar-altars, cf אראל דודה MI^{12} v Sm & So, and Dr$^{Sm\ xci}$)—אראיל Kt Ez $43^{15\ 16}$, (Qr אֲרִיאֵל), = הַרְאֵל v^{15} (Vrss Co אריאל), all c art, —of altar-hearth in Ezekiel's temple

†[אֲרוּמָה] **n.pr.loc.** home of Abimelek (Thes Add sub ארם) Ju 9^{41} בָּארוּמָה, prob = רוּמָה 2 K 23^{36}, cf Jer Lag$^{Onomast.\ 146\ 2nd\ ed\ 178}$. It must have lain near Shechem; identified by MV al with *El 'Ormah*, 2 hours SE from Shechem (van de Velde$^{Reisen\ ii\ 268}$), but this place not otherwise known, cf Survey$^{ii\ 387}$.

†אֲרַוְנָה **n.pr.m. Araunah**, a Jebusite—א׳ 2 S $24^{20.20.21\ 22.23}$ (but rd עֶבֶד אֲדֹנִי cf We Dr) $v^{23.24}$; Kt גֹּרֶן האורנה v^{16} (Qr הָאֲרַוְנָה) c. art. but cf Dr, Kt ג׳ ארניה v^{18} (Qr אֲרַוְנָה); = אָרְנָן (q v) 1 Ch $21^{15\ f}$, 𝔊 in S & Ch Ὀρνα

ארז (cf Ar أَرَزَ *be firm*, also *withdraw, retreat*)

†אֶ֫רֶז **n m.** $^{Ez\ 17.23}$ **cedar**;—**f.** Ez 17^{22} א׳ הָרָמָה, but del. הרמה 𝔊 Co,—(Ar. أَرْزٌ *pine-tree*, etc; Eth. አርዝ: Syr ܐܪܙܐ)—א׳ abs Lv 14^{4} + 19 t., אָ֑רֶז Jb 40^{17} + 6 t, pl אֲרָזִים Is 9^{9} + 35 t, cstr. אַרְזֵי Is 2^{13} + 5 t, sf אַרְזֶיךָ Je 22^{17} Zc 11^{1}; אֲרָזָיו Is 37^{24} = 2 K 19^{23},—**1.** *cedar-tree*, (*a*) as *growing* Nu 24^{6} ψ 148^{9} Is 41^{19} 44^{14} cf Ez 31^{8}, esp as growing on Lebanon 1 K 5^{13}, 2 K 14^{9} = 2 Ch 25^{18} (both in fable of Jehoash); oft אַרְזֵי (הַ)לְּבָנוֹן Ju 9^{15} Is 2^{13} 14^{8} ψ $29^{5.5}$ (fig) 104^{16}, cf. 1 K 5^{20} 2 K 19^{23} = Is 37^{24} ψ 92^{13} Ct 5^{15} Ez 27^{5} (sg coll) Zc $11^{1\ 2}$ (fig), Ct 1^{17} Ezr 3^{7} Je 22^{23} (fig) Ez 17^{3} (fig), (*b*) esp in sim, of outward power, stateliness & majesty ψ 80^{11} (א׳ אֵל) cf. Ez 31^{3} (personif, but v. Co on text), Am 2^{9}, of individuals Je 22^{7} ψ 92^{13} Ez $17^{22.23}$, cf. other exx. of fig use, supr; sim of straightness & strength Jb 40^{17} (tail of hippopotamus) **2.** *cedar-timber, cedar-wood* for building, עֲצֵי אֲרָזִים 1 S 5^{11} 1 K $5^{22.24}$ 6^{10} 9^{11} 1 Ch 14^{1} $22^{4.4}$ 2 Ch 2^{7} Ezr 3^{7}, without עֵץ 2 S $7^{2\ 7}$ 1 K $6^{9\ 15\ 16\ 18.18.20.36}$ $7^{2.2.3.7\ 11\ 12}$ 10^{27} 1 Ch $17^{1\ 6}$ 2 Ch 1^{15} 2^{3} 9^{27} & Ct 8^{9} Is 9^{9} Je $22^{14.15}$ (cf also Is 44^{14} 1 K 5^{20} Ez 27^{5} Ezr 3^{7} supr) **3.** *cedar-wood* used in purifications, c. עֵץ Lv $14^{4.6.49.51.52}$ Nu 19^{6} (all P)

†אַרְזָה **n f coll. cedar-panels, cedar-work** Zp 2^{14}

†[אָרוּז] **adj. firm, strong** (cf Ar أَرَزَ supr) אֲרֻזִים Ez 27^{24}

†מֵרוֹז **n.pr.loc.** Meroz, in northern Palestine Ju 5^{23} (expl as = مَأْرِزٌ, מֵאֶרֶז, *retreat* by Thes MV al)

†אָרַח **vb. wander, journey, go** (Ph ארח in מארח, prob = מֵאֹרַח cf. Eth መርሐ: *lead, conduct*, v No$^{ZMG\ 1886\ 472}$, epithet of god Eshmun, Sab ארח DHM$^{Epigr\ Denkm\ p\ 70}$, Aram. אוֹרַח, ܐܪܚ *traveller*)—**Qal** *Pf* וְאָרַח consec. Jb 34^{8}, *Pt.* ארח Ju 19^{17} +, pl ארחים Je 9^{1};—**1.** *journey, go*, c. עִם fig of association, companionship Jb 34^{8} וא׳ לְחֶבְרָה עִם־פֹּעֲלֵי אָוֶן וְלָלֶכֶת עִם־אַנְשֵׁי־רֶשַׁע: (cf. also הלך ψ 1^{1}) **2.** *Pt wandering, wayfaring, journeying*, הָאִישׁ הָאֹרֵחַ Ju 19^{17}, as subst. *wanderer, wayfarer, traveller* ארח 2 S 12^{4} (‖הֵלֶךְ), Je 14^{8} (‖גֵּר, in sim of י׳), מְלוֹן אֹרְחִים *wayfarers' lodging-place* Je 9^{1}.

†**אֹ֫רַח n.m.** $^{Jb\ 6,18}$ (**f.** $^{Pr\ 15,19}$) **way, path** (As. *urḫu* COT^{Gloss}, Aram. אֹרַח, ܐܘܪܚܐ)—א׳ abs. ψ 19^{6}+; cstr. Pr 4^{18}+; sf. אָרְחִי Jb 19^{8} ψ 139^{3} etc.; pl. abs. אֳרָחוֹת Ju 5$^{6.6}$; cstr. אָרְחוֹת Jb 8^{13} +; sf. אָרְחֹתָי Jb 13^{27} 33^{11}; אָרְחוֹתָם Jo 2^{7} Pr 9^{15}; אָרְחֹתֵיהֶם Pr 2^{15}; also אֹרְחֹתָיו Is 2^{3}+; אֹרְחֹתֶיךָ ψ 119^{15}+ etc.;—*way, path* (in Heb. mostly poet.) **1.** lit. Ju 5$^{6.6}$ song of Deb. (alone = *highways*, opp. א׳ עֲקַלְקַלּוֹת *crooked (by-)paths*; cf. also הֹלְכֵי נְתִיבוֹת *ib.*); Is 33^{8} עֹבֵר א׳ = *wayfarer* (‖ מְסִלּוֹת), v. also Gn 49^{17} (blessing of Jacob) (‖ דֶּרֶךְ) & הַמְיַשְּׁרִים אָרְחוֹתָם *those who make straight their ways* (‖ עֹבְרֵי דֶרֶךְ) Pr 9^{15}, בּוֹא א׳ *go* (tread) *a path* Is 41^{3}; of course of locusts Jo 2^{7} לֹא יְעַבְּטוּן א׳ *they confuse not their paths* (‖ דְּרָכִים); א׳ יַמִּים *paths of the seas* ψ 8^{9}; רוּץ אֹרַח *run along a path*, fig. of sun ψ 19^{6}. **2.** fig. *path, way*, of course & fortunes of life Jb 8^{13} 13^{27} = 33^{11} 19^{8} (‖ נְתִיבוֹת) ψ 139^{3} (‖ דֶּרֶךְ) 142^{4} (‖ נְתִיבָה) Pr 3^{6} (‖ דֶּרֶךְ) 4^{18} 15^{19} (both ‖ *id.*) Is 26^{7} (‖ מַעְגָּל) so א׳ מִישׁוֹר דֶּרֶךְ אָרְחֹתֶיךָ Is 3^{12}; *plain* or *even path* ψ 27^{11}; in two cases with a special ref. (1) אֹרַח כַּנָּשִׁים Gn 18^{11} (J) of menstruation; (2) אֹרַח לֹא אָשׁוּב אֶהֱלֹךְ *a path* (*which*) *I shall not return, I am going* Jb 16^{22} i.e. to *Sh^{e}ôl*, cf. As. name of lower world *irṣit lâ târat, land without return*, v. Jr^{10,65}. **3.** fig. *way*, of mode of living, or of character Jb 34^{11} (‖ פֹּעַל) ψ 119^{9}. Specif.: **a.** *ways of* י׳, his mode of action ψ 25^{10}; **b.** of man's righteousness, called *ways of* י׳ ψ 25^{4} (‖ דְּרָכִים) 44^{19} 119^{15} (‖ פִּקּוּדִים) Is 2^{3} = Mi 4^{2} (‖ דְּרָכִים) cf. א׳ מִשְׁפָּטֶיךָ Is 26^{8}; also *way of justice, uprightness*, etc. א׳ מִשְׁפָּט Pr 2^{8} (‖ דֶּרֶךְ) 17^{23} Is 40^{14} (‖ דֶּרֶךְ), א׳ יֹשֶׁר Pr 2^{13} (‖ *id.*), א׳ צְדָקָה 8^{20} (‖ נְתִיבוֹת), 12^{28} (‖ דֶּרֶךְ נְתִיבָה); so אֹרַח alone Is 30^{11} (‖ דֶּרֶךְ) Pr 15^{10}; note esp. אֹרַח חַיִּים, *path of life*, in righteousness & enjoyment of God ψ 16^{11} Pr 2^{19} 5^{6} 15^{24} (opp. שְׁאוֹל), also א׳ לְחַיִּים 10^{17} (on these cf. Str Pr 14^{32}); **c.** of wickedness, א׳ פָּרִיץ *way, path of the violent* ψ 17^{4}, cf. also Pr 22^{25}; א׳ רְשָׁעִים Pr 4^{14} (‖ דֶּרֶךְ), א׳ בֹּצֵעַ 1^{19}; sq. abstr. א׳ שָׁקֶר ψ 119^{104}, so v^{128} (‖ פִּקּוּדִים), also c. adj. א׳ רָע ψ 119^{101} cf. Pr 2^{15} (עִקְּשִׁים *crooked*) called הָא׳ עוֹלָם Jb 22^{15}; note also א׳ אֵידָם *their destructive ways*, i.e. ways that cause destruction Jb 30^{12} (cf. 19^{12}). **4.** by meton. *traveller, wayfarer* Jb 31^{32} (cf. הֵלֶךְ 2 S 12^{4}) & in pl. *caravans* 6$^{18.19}$; but rd. perh. לָאֹרֵחַ 31^{32}, אֹרְחוֹת 6$^{18.19}$.

†**אָרַח n.pr.m.** (*traveller?*) **1.** a man of Asher 1 Ch 7^{39}. **2.** head of a family of returning exiles Ezr 2^{5} = Ne 7^{10}; perh. = אָרַח Ne 6^{18}.

†**אֲרֻחָה n.f. meal, allowance** (of food) abs. Je 40^{5}; cstr. אֲרֻחַת יָרָק Pr 15^{17} *a portion of herbs*, i.e. a slender meal; elsewh. of allowance given to captive king Jehoiachin, א׳ תָּמִיד *a continual allowance* 2 K 25^{30} = Je 52^{34}; אֲרֻחָתוֹ *ib.* = *id.*

†[**אֹרְחָה**] **n.f. travelling company, caravan** (strictly *Pt.* of אָרַח), cstr. אֹרְחַת Gn 37^{25}; pl. cstr. אֹרְחוֹת Is 21^{13}; cf. also sub אֹרַח, **4.**

אֲרִיאֵל, אֲרִיאֵל etc., v. I. & II. ארה.

†**אַרְיוֹךְ n.pr.m.** king of Ellasar Gn 14$^{1.9}$, ally of Chedorlaomer in his western foray (prob. = *Rim-Aku*, Elamite king of Larsa = Ellasar; cf. COT$^{ii.\ 297\ f.}$).

†[**אָרַךְ, אָרֵךְ**] **vb. be long**, almost alw. of time (As. *arâku* COT^{Gloss}, Aram. אֲרַךְ, ܐܪܟ)—**Qal** *Pf.* אָרְכוּ Gn 26^{8}; *Impf.* יַאַרְכוּ Ez 12^{22}; 3 fpl. וַתֶּאֱרַכְנָה Ez 31^{5} (del. B Co)—*be long*, subj. הַיָּמִים (i.e. a long time passed Gn 26^{8} (J); cf. As. *urriku ûmî, days grew long*, Creation Tablet^{a} v. COT Gn 1^{1}); of delayed fulfilment of prophecy Ez 12^{22}; subj. פֹּארֹת Ez 31^{5} (but cf. supr.) **Hiph.** *Pf.* הֶאֱרִיךְ Pr 19^{11}; וְהַאֲרַכְתָּ Dt 22^{7}, etc.; *Impf.* יַאֲרִיךְ Dt 17^{20}+; יַאֲרִיכוּ Dt 25^{15}; יַאֲרִכוּן Ex 20^{12} cf. Dt 5^{16} 6^{2}; תַּאֲרִיכֻן Dt 4^{26} 30^{18}, etc.; *Imv.* fs. הַאֲרִיכִי Is 54^{2}: *Inf.* cstr. הַאֲרִיךְ Nu 9$^{19.22}$; *Pt.* מַאֲרִיךְ Ec 7^{15} 8^{12};—**1.** trans. *prolong*, (*a*) obj. יָמִים (i.e. live long) Dt 4$^{26.40}$ 5^{30} 11^{9} 17^{20} 22^{7} 30^{18} 32^{47} Jos 24^{31} = Ju 2^{7} (c. אַחֲרֵי = *survive*), Pr 28^{16} Is 53^{10} Ec 8^{13}; also (late) without ימים Ec 7^{15} 8^{12}; (*b*) *id.* 1 K 3^{14} י׳ subj. וְהַאֲרַכְתִּי אֶת־יָמֶיךָ *I will prolong thy days*; (*c*) *postpone* anger Is 48^{9} cf. Pr 19^{11} (i.e. shew oneself slow to anger); v. also Jb 6^{11} אַאֲרִיךְ נַפְשִׁי i.e. be patient; (*d*) lit. (but in fig.) *make long* furrows (c. לְ) ψ 129^{3}; tent-cords Is 54^{2}; tongue 57^{4} (stretch out in mockery). **2.** intrans. *grow long, continue long* (i.e. *display* length or continuance), subj. יָמִים Ex 20^{12} = Dt 5^{16} 6^{2} 25^{15}; *tarry long* Nu 9$^{19.22}$ (subj. הֶעָנָן), *last* (continue) *long*, subj. כֵּן Pr 28^{2}; *be long* (lit.) of staves of ark 1 K 8^{8} 2 Ch 5^{9}.

אֹ֫רֶךְ $_{94}$ **n.[m.] length**—only sg., א׳ abs. Ex 27^{1}+; cstr. Gn 6^{15}+; אָרְכּוֹ Ex 25^{10}+; אָרְכָּם 2 Ch 3^{11}; אָרְכָּן Ez 42^{11}, etc.—**a.** *length* of ark Gn 6^{15} (P), of land of Canaan 13^{17} (J); most oft. of ark & other measurements in tabernacle & temple Ex 25$^{10.17}$ 26$^{2.8}$ 27$^{1.9}$+ (22 t. Ex, P), 1 K 6$^{2.3.20}$+ (13 t. K & Ch), Ez 40$^{7.11.18}$+ (41 t. Ez), etc. **b.** of time א׳ יָמִים Dt 30^{20} Jb 12^{12} ψ 21^{5} 23^{6} 91^{16} 93^{5} Pr 3$^{2.16}$ La 5^{20}. **c.** א׳ אַפַּיִם *forbearance, self-restraint*, Pr 25^{15},—(Ez 31^{7} 𝔊 𝔖 Co rd. רֹב for אֹרֶךְ, cf. v^{5} where Co del. vb. ארך; 41^{22} rd. prob. ארנו 𝔊 Sm, or ארניו Co = *base*.)

†[אָרֵךְ] **adj.** long—only cstr אֶרֶךְ Ex 34^{6} + 14 t —א׳ הָאֵבֶר *long of pinion* Ez 17^{3} (‖ גדול הַכְּנָפַיִם) of eagle, in metaph ; elsewhere always of feelings, as subst Ec 7^{8} א׳ רוּחַ *the patient of spirit* (opp גְּבַהּ ר׳); א׳ אַפַּיִם *one slow to anger* Pr 14^{29} (opp קְצַר־רוּחַ),so 15^{18}(opp איש חמה), 16^{32} (‖ מֹשֵׁל ברוחו); more oft of י׳, א׳ אַפַּיִם, Ex 34^{6} רַחוּם וְחַנּוּן א׳ אַפַּיִם וְרַב־חֶסֶד וֶאֱמֶת cf Nu 14^{18} Ne 9^{17} ψ 86^{15} 103^{8} 145^{8}, so+ וְנִחָם עַל־הָרָעָה Jo 2^{13} cf Jon 4^{2} (where אֵל), א׳ אַפַּיִם וּגְדָל כֹּחַ Na 1^{3}, לְאֶרֶךְ אַפְּךָ only Je 15^{15}, א׳ appar noun; rd אֶרֶךְ? cf Pr 25^{15}.

†[אָרֹךְ] **adj.** long—only fs abs אֲרֻכָּה,—**a** of time, א׳ מִלְחָמָה *long war* 2 S 3^{1}, of the exile Je 29^{28}, **b.** fig of God's wisdom א׳ מֵאֶרֶץ מִדָּהּ Jb 11^{9} (‖ רְחָבָה מִנִּי־יָם)

†אֲרוּכָה **n f.** healing of a wound, restoration (properly the new flesh that grows at the wounded spot, Ar أَرِيكَةٌ, Fl $^{JPh\ xiii\ 114-6}$, so Fl De on Is 58^{8}, v also Di)—א׳ 2 Ch 24^{13} Ne 4^{1}, אֲרֻכָה Je 30^{17} 33^{6}, cstr אֲרֻכַת Je 8^{22}, אֲרֻכָתְךָ Is 58^{8},—always fig **a.** *healing, restoration* of Israel Is 58^{8}, here c. vb צָמַח, elsewhere c עָלָה, Je 8^{22} (‖ רָפָא), c עָלָה Hiph , subj י׳, 30^{17} 33^{6} (‖ *id*) **b.** *restoration* of walls of temple 2 Ch 24^{13}, of walls of Jerusalem (cf. Fl supr.) Ne 4^{1} (both c עלה)

†אֶרֶךְ **n pr loc.** city in Babylonia (Bab *Urûk* v Dl infr) on left bank of Euphrates, c 40 miles NW fr Ur (אור) toward Babylon, mod *Warka*, cf Loftus$^{CS\ 162f.}$ Dl$^{Pa\ 221\ f.}$

†אַרְכִּי **adj.gent.** (deriv unknown) applied to חוּשַׁי 2 S 15^{32} 16^{16} $17^{5.14}$ 1 Ch 27^{33}; with art =n coll גְּבוּל הָא׳ Jos 16^{2} (not far fr Bethel)

אֲרָם ^{149} **n.pr.m. Aram** (As *Aramu*, etc., v Dl$^{Pa\ 257}$, Thes al prop √אָרַם=רוּם but cf. No as below)—**1** 5th son of Shem Gn $10^{22.23}$ 1 Ch 1^{17} **2.** grandson of Nahor Gn 22^{21}. **3.** 1 Ch 2^{23} **4.** a descendant of Asher 1 Ch 7^{34}.—Elsewhere only of Aramæan people & land (=**1** supr), **f.**$^{2\ 8\ 8,5}$ **m.**$^{2\ 8\ 10,14}$ **a.** people, sg. coll.=*the Aramæans*, a leading branch of the Shemitic stock inhabiting Mesopotamia & northern Syria, in many tribes & settlements; 2 S $8^{5.5.6}$+ 1 K $20^{20.21}$ + 1 Ch $19^{10\ 12}$+(64 t S K Ch) Am 9^{7} Is $7^{2.4.5.8}$ 9^{11} 17^{3} Je 35^{11}, so Ez 16^{57} 27^{16}, but Co in both אדום, עַם אֲרָם Am 1^{5}, of particular divisions of Aram, א׳ בֵּית רְחוֹב 2 S 10^{6}, א׳ צוֹבָא 2 S $10^{6.8}$ ψ 60^{2} (title), א׳ דַּמֶּשֶׂק 2 S 8^{6} cf 1 Ch 18^{5}, even א׳ נַהֲרַיִם ψ 60^{2} (title); (note that As never gives name *Aramu* to people W. of Euphrates, but *Chatti* instead, with other particular names, COT Gn 10^{22}, also Dl$^{1\ c}$), on 2 S $8^{12\ 13}$ 1 Ch 18^{11} v אֱדוֹם **b.** less often clearly of land, Aram Nu 23^{7} 2 S 15^{8}+ 2 Ch 20^{2} (rd however here אדום Thes Add al.), שְׂדֵה א׳ Ho 12^{13}, also of particular divisions of the territory א׳ נַהֲרַיִם *'Mesopotamia,'* i e prob. land between Euphrates & Chaboras, so Di after Kiep, Gn 24^{10} Dt 23^{5} Ju 3^{8} (cf ψ 60^{2} supr), cf פַּדַּן א׳ *Paddan-Aram* Gn 25^{20} 31^{18} 33^{18} $35^{9.26}$ 46^{15}, פַּדֶּנָה א׳ $28^{2.5.6.7}$ v פדן; א׳ דַּמֶּשֶׂק 2 S 8^{6} cf. 1 Ch 18^{6} **c.** often indeterminate, esp in מֶלֶךְ א׳ etc , perh primarily land but often including people so Ju 2^{11} 10^{6} (אֱלֹהֵי א׳) 1 K 10^{29}+ 2 Ch 1^{17}+(41 t K & Ch) Is 7^{1}.—(Cf esp No$^{Schenkel\ BL,\ ZMG\ 1871,\ 113\ \ Hermes\ v\ 3,\ 443\ f.}$ Dl$^{Pa\ 257}$.)

†אֲרַמִּי **adj.gent.** Aramæan, c. art הָא׳ Gn $25^{20.20}$ 28^{5} $31^{20.24}$ 2 K 5^{20}, of Israel א׳ אֹבֵד Dt 26^{5}, pl אֲרַמִּים 2 K $8^{28\ 29}$ (‖ אֲרָם) 9^{15} (‖ *id*); הָרַמִּים (=הָא׳) 2 Ch 22^{5} (‖ *id*), פִּילַגְשׁוֹ הָאֲרַמִּיָּה 1 Ch 7^{14} *his Aramæan concubine* —(ארומים Kt 2 K 16^{6} rd rather Qr אֲדוֹמִים)

†אֲרָמִית **adv.** only of language in **Aramaic** 2 K 18^{26}=Is 36^{11} Ezr $4^{7\ 7}$ Dn 2^{4}.

ארם (√ of following, cf רום?)

†אַרְמוֹן $^{18\ 32,\ 14}$ **n.m.** citadel—א׳ abs Je 30^{18} +, cstr Is 25^{2}, pl אַרְמְנוֹת abs Am $3^{9.9}$, cstr 1^{4}+, אַרְמְנוֹתֵינוּ Mi 5^{4}+, etc —*citadel, castle, palace*, not used before royal period, mostly in prophets, esp common in Am & Je, citadel as securely barred (in sim) Pr 18^{19}, א׳ בֵּית הַמֶּלֶךְ i e the *citadel, stronghold* 1 K 16^{18}, cf 2 K 15^{25}; usually more general, of *castles, palaces*, prominent buildings, esp used in speaking of conquest, because the fine buildings would be esp. object of attack & plunder, palaces of Isr Am 6^{8}, of Jerusalem Is 32^{14} (sg coll.) La $2^{5.7}$ 2 Ch 36^{19} ψ $48^{4\ 14}$ 122^{7} cf Ho 8^{14} Mi 5^{4} Am 2^{5} Je 17^{27}; of Samaria Am $3^{10\ 11}$, also Je 6^{5} 9^{20} belonging to Benhadad (i e Aram) Am 1^{4} Je 49^{27}; of Tyre Is 23^{13} Am 1^{10}, of Babylon Is 25^{2} (sg coll.), cf. 13^{22} where rd אַרְמְנוֹתָיו for אלמנותיו so 𝔊 𝔗 𝔙 Che Di (‖ הֵיכָלִים); cf Ez 19^{7} acc to 𝔗 al., but v rather מעון, Dl$^{BD\ xi}$ defends MT in Ez 19^{7} & comp. As. *almattu, fortress*); of Edom Is 34^{13}, of Gaza Am 1^{7}, of Rabbah 1^{14}, of Bozrah 1^{12}, of Kerioth 2^{2}, of Ashdod 3^{9}, of Egypt 3^{9}

†אַרְמֹנִי **n.pr m.** a son of Saul (*palatinus*) 2 S 21^{8}.

I ארן (cf. Ar. أَرِنَ *alacer, lætus fuit;* possible √ of following)

†אֲרָן **n.pr.m.** a descendant of Esau (? Aram. ܐܪܢܐ *wild-goat*) Gn 36[28] = 1 Ch 1[42] (v. also דִּישָׁן).

†I. **אֹרֶן n.**[**m.**] **fir or cedar** (As. *êrinu* COT[Gloss], Mish. pl. ארנים) Is 44[14] (|| תִּרְזָה, אֶרֶז, עֲצֵי יַעַר, אַלּוֹן).

†II. **אֹרֶן n.pr.m.** (*fir-tree*) a descendant of Judah 1 Ch 2[25].

†ארנבן **n.pr.loc.** whence wine, so Co Ez 27[19] for MT וְדָן וְיָוָן; cf. As. *wine of Aranabanim*.

†אַרְנָן **n.pr.m.** a descendant of David 1 Ch 3[21].

†אָרְנָן **n.pr.m.** a Jebusite, whose threshing-floor was bought by David to erect an altar 1 Ch 21[15.18.20.20.21.21.22.23.24.25.28], & acc. to 2 Ch 3[1] became site of temple; called אֲרַוְנָה 2 S 24[16 f.] q.v.

†אַרְנוֹן, אַרְנֹן **n.pr.fl. Arnon**, wady & stream in Moab (MI ארנן, Thes Add Rob Ges MV der. fr. רנן, i.e. *the rushing, roaring* stream)—אַרְנוֹן Nu 21[13.13] + 12 t., אַרְנֹן Nu 21[14] + 10 t.—called boundary between Moab & Amorites Nu 21[13] Ju 11[18.22] cf. גְּבוּל אַרְנֹן Nu 22[36]; oft. נַחַל אַרְנֹן Dt 2[24.36] 3[8.12.16] 4[48] 2 K 10[33]; נ׳ אַרְנוֹן Jos 12[1.2] 13[9.16]; הַנְּחָלִים אַרְנוֹן Nu 21[14], i.e. the stream-ravines that unite to form Arnon, cf. Di; also בָּמוֹת אַרְנֹן *heights of Arnon* Nu 21[28]; מעברות אַרְנוֹן *fords of Arnon* Is 16[2]; elsewh. Nu 21[13.24.26] Ju 11[13.18.26]; syn. of Moab Je 48[20]; (cf. Tristr[Moab 125 f.]; mod. *Môjib*.)

II. **ארן** (√assumed for foll. word, cf. Sta §208 c; Dl[Pr 125] argues for √ארה (so Thes), on ground of an As. *êrû*, synon. of *êrênu*).

אֲרוֹן, c. art. **הָאָרוֹן, הָאָרֹן** 203 **n.m.**[Ex 35.12] (**f.** 1 S 4, 17; 2 Ch 8, 11) **chest, ark** (Ph. ארן, *sarcophagus*, As. *êrênu* (& *êrû*) *chest* Zim[BP 6, 22], Ar. إِرَانٌ, *chest*, so Aram. ܐܪܘܢܐ, also Nab. ארנא, Vog[p. 102], Ph.; Mish. also pl. ארונות)—only sg.; abs. †אָרוֹן 2 K 12[10] = 2 Ch 24[8]; c. art. הָאָרוֹן Dt 10[2] + alw. exc. Ex Lv Nu where הָאָרֹן (Ex 25[14.14] + 13 t. Ex, Lv 16[2] Nu 3[31] 10[35]); cstr. אֲרוֹן Ex 25[10] +, †אֲרֹן Ex 30[6] Nu 4[5] 7[89];—†**1.** *chest*, for money-offerings 2 K 12[10.11] 2 Ch 24[8.10.11.11]. †**2.** *sarcophagus, mummy-case* of Joseph Gn 50[26] (E). **3.** *chest, ark* in tabernacle & temple, containing tables of law, with cherubim above, the esp. seat of י׳ among his people, only Hex (71 t.) S (61 t.) K (12 t.) & Ch (48 t.) + Ju 20[27] Je 3[16] ψ 132[8]; used alone & in various combinations (cf. Seyring[ZAW 1891, 114 f.]). **a.** indef. אֲרוֹן עֲצֵי שִׁטִּים *an ark of shittim-wood* Ex 25[10] Dt 10[3] cf. v[1]. **b.** def. הָא׳ Ex 25[14] + 54 t. (Hex P, exc. Jos JE; S K Ch). **c.** א׳ יהוה Jos 4[11] + 32 t. Jos (JED) S K Ch. **d.** א׳ הָאֱלֹהִים 1 S 3[3] 4[11] + 1 S 4[13] + 32 t. S Ch (but 1 S 14[18.18] rd. הָאֵפוֹד ⅏ We Dr), cf. א׳ אֱלֹהֵינוּ †1 Ch 13[3]. **e.** א׳ אלהי יִשְׂרָאֵל 1 S 5[7] + 6 t. S, term used only by Philistines; א׳ יהוה אלהי יִשְׂרָאֵל †1 Ch 15[12.14]; א׳ יהוה אֱלֹהֵיכֶם †Jos 4[5] (JE); א׳ יהוה אֲדוֹן כָּל־הָאָרֶץ †Jos 3[13] †1 K 2[26]; אֲדֹנָי יהוה (JED) cf. א׳ [הברית] ארון כל־הארץ v[11], where הברית (c. art.) is prob. interpol., v. Di; only once & late the long phrase א׳ האלהים יהוה יֹשֵׁב הַכְּרוּבִים אֲשֶׁר נִקְרָא־שֵׁם 1 Ch 13[6]. **f.** in combination with בְּרִית, largely D & under D's influence; ארון הַבְּרִית *ark of the covenant* †Jos 3[6.6.8] 4[9] 6[6] (all JED); א׳ בְּרִית יהוה Nu 10[33] 14[44] (both J) Dt 10[8] 31[9.25] Jos 4[7.18] 6[8] 8[33] Je 3[16] + 17 t. S K Ch; once longer א׳ בְּרִית י׳ צְבָאוֹת יֹשֵׁב הַכְּרֻבִים †1 S 4[4]; also א׳ בְּרִית הָאֱלֹהִים †Ju 20[27] 1 S 4[4] 2 S 15[24] 1 Ch 16[6]; & א׳ בְּרִית י׳ אלהיכם Dt 31[26] Jos 3[3]. **g.** אֲרוֹן הָעֵדוּת *ark of the testimony*, only in P, corresponding to א׳ בְּרִית (cf. Di on Ex 25[16]), Ex 25[22] + 8 t. Ex, †Nu 4[5] 7[84] Jos 4[16]. **h.** †א׳ הַקֹּדֶשׁ 2 Ch 35[3]. **i.** א׳ עֻזֶּךָ *the ark of thy strength* 2 Ch 6[41] ψ 132[8].—(Cf. also tables given by Seyring[l.c.] & his theory as to earliest designation of ark.)

אַרְנֶבֶת v. אנב.

ארניה v. אֲרַוְנָה.

†**אַרְפָּד n.pr.loc.** city in northern Syria (As. *Arpadda* Dl[Pa 275])—א׳ Is 10[9] elsewh. אַרְפָּד; c. 15 miles N. of Aleppo, mod. *Tel Erfâd*; in OT only as conquered by Assyria, alw. named with Hamath, etc. 2 K 18[34] 19[13] = Is 36[19] 37[13] (on ⅏ Ῥαφέθ = Ἀρφάθ cf. Lag[BN 78]), also Is 10[9] Je 49[23]; (cf. Nö[ZMG 1871, 258] Kiep[ib. 655].)

†**אַרְפַּכְשַׁד n.pr.m.** 3rd son of Shem א׳ Gn 10[22.24] 11[12.13] 1 Ch 1[17.18.24]; אַרְפַּכְשָׁד Gn 11[10.11]; doubtless a geogr. name (deriv. & mng. dub., Thes der. fr. أُرْفَةٌ *boundary* (stem أَرَفَ *define, limit*), cf. also Eth. አርፍት: *wall*, + כשׂד = כֶּשֶׂד, i.e. *Chaldean*; so Schr[COT Gn 10.22] who identifies with *Babylonia* (cf. Gn 11[12 f.] & אור כַּשְׂדִּים v[28.31]); v. another interpr. Dl[Pa 255]; acc. to most = *Arrapachitis* on Upper Zab, NE. fr. Nineveh, As. *Arbaḫa*, Armen. *Albak* Lag[Armen. Stud. 55 & reff.] so Bo MV, Di Gn 10[22] Lag[Sy 1. 54] Nö[ZMG 1882, 182]; but As. *Arbaḫa* is unfavourable to this).

אֶרֶץ 2407 **n.f.**[Gn 10, 11] & (seld.) **m.**[Gn 13, 16] **earth, land** (Ph. MI ארץ, As. *irṣitu* COT[Gloss], Ar. أَرْضٌ, Sab. ארץ e.g. Os[9] DHM[ZMG 1875, 594, 614; Sem. Sprachf. 12], cf. Prä[BAS i. 374 n.], Aram. אֲרַע, ܐܪܥܐ)—א׳ abs.

Gn 1^{24}+; cstr. 2^{11}+; אֶ֫רֶץ 1^{10}+; c. art. always הָאָ֫רֶץ 1^{11}+; c. ־ָה loc. אַ֫רְצָה 11^{31}+, (this form also poet. = אֶ֫רֶץ Jb 34^{13}+); sf. אַרְצִי 20^{15}+; אַרְצְךָ (אַרְצֶ֑ךָ) 12^{1}+, etc.; pl. אֲרָצוֹת Je 28^{8}+65 t.; cstr. אַרְצוֹת Ez 39^{27}+6 t.; sf. אַרְצֹתָם Gn 10^{5}+2 t.;—**1. a.** *earth*, whole earth (opp. to a part) Gn 18$^{18.25}$ 22^{18}(= הָאֲדָמָה 12^{3}) Je 25$^{26.29.30}$ 26^{6} Is 37$^{16.20}$ = 2 K 19$^{15.19}$ Zc 4$^{10.14}$+. **b.** *earth*, opp. to heaven, sky Gn 1^{2} Ex 20^{4} Dt 5^{8} 30^{19} Ju 5^{4} La 2^{1} Is 37^{16} = 2 K 19^{15} ψ 146^{6} 1 Ch 21^{16} 29^{11} 2 Ch 2^{11} +; as permanent Ec 1^{4}; built on foundations, or pillars 1 S 2^{8} ψ 104^{5} Jb 38^{4} Is 48^{13} 51$^{13.16}$ cf. also Is 24^{18} ψ 82^{5}; firm, so that its shaking is something terrible, & token of terrible power 1 S 14^{4} 2 S 22^{8} = ψ 18^{8} Jb 9^{6} cf. ψ 46^{2} & v^{6}; so also Am 8^{8} Is 2$^{19.21}$ 24$^{18.19.20}$ ψ 60^{4} 77^{19} 99^{1} 114^{7}; as hung on nothing Jb 26^{7}; with waters under it Ex 20^{4} = Dt 5^{8} cf. Gn 7^{11}; personified, esp. as addressed, called to witness, etc. Dt 32^{1} Je 6^{19} 22^{29} Is 1^{2} Mi 1^{2} Jb 16^{18}. **c.** *earth* = inhabitants of earth Gn 6^{11} 11^{1} 1 K 2^{2} 10^{24} ψ 33^{8} 66^{4}+ cf. תֵּבֵל א׳ Pr 8^{31} Jb 37^{12}. **2.** *land* = **a.** country, territory, א׳ שִׁנְעָר Gn 10^{10}, א׳ מִצְרַיִם 21^{21}; cf. also 10^{11} 11$^{28.31}$ 13^{10} 47$^{6.27}$ 50^{8} Is 7^{18} 23$^{1.13}$ 27^{13} ψ 78^{12} Je 25^{20} 1 Ch 1^{43}; personif. Is 62^{4} Ec 10$^{16.17}$. **b.** district, region Gn 19^{28} 22^{2} Jos 11^{3} ψ 42^{7}. **c.** tribal territory Dt 34^{2} Ju 21^{21} 1 S 9$^{4.16}$ 13^{7} 1 K 15^{20} Is 8^{23}; and still smaller territories 1 S 9$^{4.5}$. **d.** piece of ground Gn 23^{15}. **e.** specif. *land* of Canaan, or Israel Gn 11^{31} 12$^{1.5.6.7}$ 31^{3} Ex 14^{34} Dt 17^{14} 18^{9} 2 K 5$^{2.4}$+; esp. obj. of יָרַשׁ *possess* Dt 3^{20}+oft. Dt ψ al.; so after נָחַל Jos 19^{49}+; נָתַן Dt 1^{21}+. **f.** = inhabitants of land Lv 19^{29} Ez 14^{13}+cf. Dt 24^{4} Zc 12^{12} etc. **g.** used even of *Sheʼôl* Jb 10$^{21.22}$ (cf. As. *irṣit la târat, land without return*, in Descent of Ishtar, v. Jr$^{10.65}$); v. also ψ 139^{15} Is 44^{23}. **3. a.** *ground*, surface of ground = אֲדָמָה q.v. Gn 1$^{26.30}$ 18^{2} 33^{3} 38^{9} Ex 4^{3} 16^{4} Ru 2^{10} 1 S 5^{4}+very oft. in S. **b.** *soil*, as productive = אֲדָמָה Gn 1$^{11.12}$ Lv 19^{9} 25^{9} 26^{4} cf. Nu 14$^{7.8}$ Is 36^{7} = 2 K 18^{32} ψ 72$^{6.16}$ 107$^{34.35}$ Ezr 9^{12} Ne 9^{25}. **4.** אֶ֫רֶץ in phrases: **a.** *people of the land* עַם־הָא׳ of non-Israelites Gn 23$^{7.12.13}$ (P) Nu 14^{9}(JE); as well as Isr. Lv 20^{4}(H) 2 K 15^{5} 16^{15} 21$^{24.24}$; esp. common people, opp. officials, princes Lv 4^{27}(P) Ez 7^{27} 2 K 11$^{18.19}$. †**b.** in measurements of distance, כִּבְרַת הָא׳ *the space* or *distance of country* (v. כברה) Gn 35^{16}, so כִּבְרַת א׳ *some distance* Gn 48^{7} 2 K 5^{19}. **c.** אֶרֶץ הַמִּישׁוֹר *the country of the plain, level* or *plain country* Dt 4^{43} Je 48^{21}; א׳ מִישׁוֹר fig. ψ 143^{10} (but rd. אֹרַח 𝔖 Bi Gr Che, cf. ψ 27^{11}). **d.** א׳ חַיִּים *land of the living* ψ 27^{13}; א׳ הַחַיִּים ψ 142^{6}. **e.** קְצֵה הָא׳ *end(s) of the earth* Is 42^{10} 43^{6} (‖ רָחוֹק) ψ 135^{7} Pr 17^{24}, so אַפְסֵי א׳ Pr 30^{4}+; קְצוֹת הָא׳ Is 40^{28} 41$^{5.9}$. **5.** pl. אֲרָצוֹת is almost wholly late, Je 16^{15}+6 t. Je; 23 t. Ez; Is 36^{20} 37^{11} = 2 K 18^{35} 19^{11} (Is 37^{18} rd. הַגּוֹיִם v. Che Di & cf. 2 K 19^{17}); 22 t. Chr; Dn 9^{7} 11$^{40.42}$; ψ 105^{44} 106^{27} 107^{3} 116^{9}; besides these only P Gn 10$^{5.20.31}$ Lv 26$^{36.39}$, exc. Gn 26$^{3.4}$ (J^{R}) 41^{54} (JE); it denotes *lands, countries*, often in contrast to Canaan, *lands of the nations*, etc., v. esp. abs. Ez 20^{32} 22^{4}; = the various petty divisions of Canaan afterward united under Israel's control Gn 26$^{3.4}$, cf. 1 Ch 13^{2} אַרְצוֹת יִשְׂרָאֵל, 2 Ch 11^{23} אַרְצוֹת יְהוּדָה.

†אַרְצָא **n.pr.m.** chamberlain of Zimri 1 K 16^{9}.

[אָרַר] **vb.** curse (As. *arâru* Zim$^{BP\ 68}$; on relation of mngs. *bind* & *curse* in As. v. Dl$^{Pr\ 101}$) —**Qal** *Pf.* אָרוֹתִיהָ, וְאָרוֹתִי Mal 2^{2}; *Impf.* 2 ms. תָּאֹר Ex 22^{27} Nu 22$^{6.12}$; אָאֹר Gn 12^{3}; *Imv.* אָ֫רָה־ Nu 22^{6} 23^{7}; אֹרוּ, אוֹרוּ & *Inf. abs.* אָרוֹר all Ju 5^{23}; *Pt.* אֹרְרֵי Jb 3^{8}; אֹרְרֶיךָ Gn 27^{29} Nu 24^{9}; אָרוּר Gn 3^{14} + 36 t. etc.;—*curse* ‖ בֵּרֵךְ *bless*, chiefly in poetic & legal sources of JED & later imitations: Gn 12^{3} 27^{29} (J) Nu 22$^{6.12}$ 23^{7} 24^{9} (E) Ex 22^{27} (E) Mal 2^{2}; אֹרוּ אָרוֹר יֹשְׁבֶיהָ = *curse for ever her inhabitants* Ju 5^{23}; אֹרְרֵי יוֹם *cursers of the day* (magicians whose imprecations made days unlucky) Jb 3^{8}. *Pt. pass.* אָרוּר, chiefly as exclamation, ‖ בָּרוּךְ Gn 3$^{14.17}$ 4^{11} 9^{25} 27^{29} 49^{7} Nu 22^{12} 24^{9} (E, poet.) Dt 27$^{15-26}$ Ju 21^{18} 1 S 14$^{24.28}$ 26^{19} Je 11^{3} 17^{5} 20$^{14.15}$ 48$^{10.10}$ Mal 1^{14}; אֲרוּרִים הַשֹּׁגִים מִמִּצְוֹתֶיךָ *cursed be those who wander from thy commands* ψ 119^{21} (𝔊 𝔖 Jer De Ri), הָאֲרוּרָה הַזֹּאת *this cursed woman* 2 K 9^{34}. †**Niph.** *Pt.* נֵאָרִים *cursed* Mal 3^{9}. †**Pi.** 3 ms. sf. אֵרְרָהּ *curse, lay under a curse* Gn 5^{29} (J); *Pt.* הַמַּיִם הַמְאָרֲרִים *the curse-bringing waters* Nu 5$^{18-27}$ (P 6 t. waters destroying the perjured adulteress drinking them). †**Hoph.** *Impf.* יוּאַר *be cursed* Nu 22^{6} (E).

†מְאֵרָה **n.f.** a curse Dt 28^{20} Mal 2^{2} 3^{9}; cstr. מְאֵרַת Pr 3^{33}; pl. מְאֵרוֹת Pr 28^{27}.

אֲרָרִי v. הֲרָרִי.

†אֲרָרַט **n.pr.terr.** Ararat (As. *Urarṭu* COT^{Gloss}, cf. Lag$^{Armen.\ Stud.\ §\ 100}$)—א׳ Je 51^{27}; אֲרָרָט Gn 8^{4}+3 t.—a district in Eastern Armenia between the river Araxes & lakes Van & Oroomiah, cf. KGF; to this prob. ref. in 2 K 19^{37} = Is 37^{38} אֶרֶץ א׳; also Gn 8^{4} הָרֵי א׳, where the ark rested; used perhaps with wider ref. Je 51^{27} (‖ מַמְלְכוֹת א׳, מִנִּי, אַשְׁכְּנַז).

†[אָרַשׂ]† **vb.** betroth (Mish. ארס, Ph. ארש

in n.pr., Lag[Sem i. 60] connects with Ar. أَرْشٌ *a fine*, lit. *pay the price*, & so gain the right of possession; cf. Aram. אָרִים *one who farms land*, As. *mirsu*, *tribute*, Zehnpf[BAS i 518])—only **Pi. Pu.**, **Pi.** *Pf.* 3 ms. אֵרַשׂ Dt 20[7]; אֵרַשְׂתִּי 2 S 3[14]; sf אֵרַשְׂתִּיךְ Ho 2[21.21.22], *Impf.* 2 ms. תְּאָרֵשׂ Dt 28[30],—*betroth* (subj. man) obj. woman, אִשָּׁה Dt 20[7] 28[30], sq. בְּ of price paid to father & לְ of husband 2 S 3[14], בְּ of gift to bride & לְ of husband Ho 2[21.22], where fig. of Yahweh's covenant mercy to Israel. **Pu.** *Pf.* 3 fs. אֹרָשָׂה *be betrothed*, c. לֹא, subj. בתולה Ex 22[15] Dt 22[28] (נער בתולה), *Pt* f מְאֹרָשָׂה Dt 22[23], where affirmed of נער בתולה (sq. לְ of husband) v[25.27] (in both subj הַנַּעֲרָ)

ארשׁ (*to desire, request*, As. *êrêšu* Dl[Pr 60])

†**אֲרֶשֶׁת** **n.f.** desire, request (As. *êrištu* Dl[l c]) only cstr א׳ שְׂפָתָיו ψ 21[3] (||תַּאֲוַת לִבּוֹ) request granted by י׳.

ארת v. אוֹרָה.

†**אַרְתַּחְשַׁשְׁתָּא** **n.pr.m.** **Artaxerxes** (Pers. *Artakhshatrâ*, Spieg[APK 68 207] 𝔊 Ἀρταξέρξης, cf. BeRy on Ezr 4[23] 7[1f.] Ne 1[1]) א׳ Ezr 4[7] v. BD[102], אַרְתַּחְשַׁשְׂתְּא Ezr 4[7], אַרְתַּחְשַׁסְתְּא Ezr 7[1.11] 8[1] Ne 2[1] 5[14] 13[6]; *Artaxerxes I*, or *Longimanus*, son & successor of Xerxes, reigned B.C. 465–424.

†**אֲשַׂרְאֵל** **n.pr.m.** a descendant of Judah 1 Ch 4[16] (the latter element in this & foll may be אל *God*, but mng. of former part dub. Thes comp. אסר bind, *quem Deus obligavit* sc. *voto*).

†**אֲשַׂרְאֵלָה** **n.pr.m.** a son of Asaph 1 Ch 25[2] cf. יְשַׂרְאֵלָה v[14].

†**אַשְׂרִיאֵל** **n.pr.m.** a Manassite (Thes *votum Dei*, cf supr) Nu 26[31] Jos 17[2] 1 Ch 7[14]

†**אַשְׂרִאֵלִי** **adj.gent.** הָא׳ as n coll Nu 26[31]

אֵשׁ 377 **n f.**[Ex 9, 23] (**m.**[Je 48, 45, ψ 104, 4]; **f. & m.**[Je 20, 9, Jb 20, 26]) **fire** (As. *išatu* COT[Gloss], Syr. ܐܫܬܐ, Eth እሳት: deriv fr. II אנשׁ, أَنِسَ, sociable, friendly element (MV Wetzst in De[Psalmen, ed. 4 p. 889] Lag[BN 68] cf. انسة, مانوسة), improb esp in view of As; daghesh prob secondary; cf also Sta[§ 189 b])—א׳ abs. Ex 9[24] +, cstr. Lv 6[2] + (seld.); †sf אִשִּׁי Dt 4[36] Jb 18[5]; אֶשְׁכֶם Is 50[11]; אִשָּׁם Is 66[24];—**1.** *fire*, of conflagration, e g in briers, endangering or destroying crops תֵצֵא אֵשׁ וּמָצְאָה קֹצִים Ex 22[5] cf 3[2] הַסְּנֶה בֹּעֵר בָּאֵשׁ (both E), more often of deliberate destruction by fire, esp שָׂרַף בָּאֵשׁ (בְּ c qam. preton) obj. golden calf Ex 32[20] (J), other idols Dt 7[5.25], Asherim 12[3], chariots Jos 11[6.9] 2 K 23[11], house Ju 12[1] 14[15], tower 9[52], city-gates Ne 1[3] 2[3.13.17], city Jos 6[24] Ju 18[27] cf. Is 1[7] +; also שִׁלַּח אֵשׁ בְּ Am 1[4.7.10] +; שִׁלַּח אֶת־הָעִיר בָּאֵשׁ †Ju 1[8] 20[48] cf. 2 K 8[12]; הִצִּית אֶת־הָעִיר בָּאֵשׁ Jos 8[8.19] Je 17[27] +, cf. Ju 9[49] 2 S 14[30.31] (of field, cf. Ex 22[5] supr) **2.** of supernatural fire, attending theophany Ex 3[2] 19[18] (both JE) Dt 4[11.12.15.33.36] +, specif. עַמּוּד (הָ)אֵשׁ Ex 13[21.22] 14[24] (all JE) Ne 9[12.19] cf Dt 1[33] (v מַרְאֵה־אֵשׁ Nu 9[15.16] P), of destructive fire from י׳ Nu 11[1.2.3] (J) 26[10] (P) Lv 10[2] (P), cf א׳ אֹכֶלֶת in sim of Yahweh's glory Ex 24[17] (E) Dt 4[24] 9[3], v also 1 K 18[24.38] 2 K 1[10.10.12.12.14] Jb 1[16] (perh. lightning intended), cf. further of lightning Ex 9[23.24] (JE) ψ 18[13.14] 148[8] etc. **3.** fire for cooking, roasting, parching, etc צְלִי אֵשׁ *roasted at a fire* Ex 12[8.9] (P) cf Lv 2[14] 2 Ch 35[13] Is 44[16.19], of tinder for lighting fire Gn 22[6.7] (E); of fire for melting (gold for the idolatrous calf) Ex 32[24], for refining Je 6[29], where rd with Qr מֵאֵשׁ תַּם עֹפָרֶת; cf Mal 3[2] (sim. of purifying work of messenger of cov't). **4.** esp of altar-fire Lv 1[7.7] 6[2.3.5.6] +, in offering incense Lv 10[1], also אֵשׁ זָרָה *strange fire*, i e. an incense not commanded, offered presumptuously 10[1] Nu 3[4] 26[61]; fire from י׳ consuming sacrifice (cf. **2**) Lv 9[24] 2 Ch 7[1.3], of fire in child-sacrifice (usually הֶעֱבִיר בֵּן בָּאֵשׁ (לְ)) 2 K 16[3] 21[6] cf 17[17] 23[10] 2 Ch 33[6], also שָׂרַף בָּא׳ 2 K 17[31], בִּעֵר בָּא׳ 2 Ch 28[3]. **5.** fig. of Yahweh's anger ψ 89[47] (sim.) cf. Na 1[6] La 2[4] אֵשׁ־עֶבְרָתִי Ez 21[36] 22[31] 38[19], אֵשׁ־קִנְאָתִי Ez 36[5]; v. also Is 66[15] ψ 79[5] 89[47] etc., of word of י׳ Je 23[29]; fig. of outbursting emotion ψ 39[4], of flagrant wickedness Is 9[17], etc. **6.** in various combinations, לַפִּיד אֵשׁ Gn 15[17] (J) *a torch of fire* (cf Di), לַבַּת־אֵשׁ Ex 3[2] *flame of fire*, לַהַב אֵשׁ Jo 2[5], לַפִּידֵי אֵשׁ (in sim) Dn 10[6] cf. Zc 12[6], לַהֲבוֹת אֵשׁ ψ 29[7] לַהֲבֵי אֵשׁ Is 66[15] cf. לֶהָבוֹת א׳ ψ 105[32], נֹגַהּ א׳ לֶהָבָה Is 4[5] cf Ho 7[6], שְׁבִיב אִשּׁוֹ *spark of his fire* Jb 18[5] cf כִּידוֹדֵי אֵשׁ 41[11]; תַּנּוּר אֵשׁ ψ 21[10] *oven of fire*, כִּיּוֹר אֵשׁ Zc 12[6], אוּר אֵשׁ *light of fire* ψ 78[14]; אֵשׁ לֹהֵט *flaming fire* ψ 104[4], לְשׁוֹן אֵשׁ Is 5[24] *tongue of fire*, גַּחֲלֵי אֵשׁ Ez 1[13] *coals of fire*, so 10[2], cf רִשְׁפֵּי אֵשׁ Ct 8[6], on אַבְנֵי אֵשׁ Ez 28[14.16] v. אבן, אֵשׁ דָּת Dt 33[2], lit. *fire of a law*, or *fire was a law*, but דָּת *law* is Pers. & late, rd. perh. אֵשׁ [לַפִּ]דת cf Ex 20[18] or אֵשׁ [יֹקֶ]דֶת cf. Is 65[5].

†[**אִשָּׁה**] **n.f.** id. Je 6[29] Kt אשתם(מ) i.e. *from their fire*, but Qr מֵאֵשׁ תַּם, v sub אֵשׁ.

אִשֶּׁה **n.m.** [Jos 13, 14] **an offering made by fire** (> Wetzst in De[Psalmen, ed. 4, 889] der. fr. √II. אנשׁ.

means to friendly relations betw. God & man, cf Lag$^{BN 190}$) Ex 29^{18}+32 t, cstr. אשה Lv 1^{9}+14 t, pl cstr אִשֵּׁי Lv 4^{35}+15 t; sf אִשַּׁי Nu 28^{2}, אִשָּׁיו Lv 6^{10}; used chiefly of offerings of animals, but also of the מנחה Lv 2^{11}, and of the sacred bread and frankincense Lv 24$^{7.9}$ which was placed on the table as a memorial, and finally went to the priests The word is used in Dt 18^{1} Jos 13^{14} (D) 1 S 2^{28}, elsewhere in P Lv 6^{10} 10^{15} 22^{22} Nu 28$^{2.3}$, esp in phrases אשי יהוה Lv 2^{3}+11 t, אִשֵּׁה רֵיחַ נִיחֹחַ ליהוה Lv 1^{9}+14 t, אשה ריח ניחח אשה ליהוה Ex 29^{18}+6 t, אשה לריח ניחח Lv 3^{16} Nu 18^{17}, ליהוה ריח ניחח Lv 23^{13}, אִשֶּׁה ליהוה (הוא) אשה Ex 29^{25} Lv 2^{16}; acc after verbs of offering Ex 30^{20}+14 t, אִשֶּׁה קָרְבַּן אִשֶּׁה ליהוה Lv 22^{27} Nu 15^{25} עֹלָה ליהוה Nu 28^{19},

†אִשׁ 2 S 14^{19} Mi 6^{10}, softer form for the usual יֵשׁ (q v), *there is are* (Cf Aram אִתַי, Ar أَيْسَ, and on the softening of *ye, yi* to *'i*, see Ew$^{§ 53c}$ Ol$^{p 425}$ No$^{§ 40c}$)

†אַשְׁבֵּל n.pr.m. (=אשבאל? so Thes, more likely אֶשְׁבַּעַל) 2nd son of Benjamin Gn 46^{21} (𝔊 'Ασβηλ) Nu 26^{38} (𝔊 'Ασυβηρ) 1 Ch 8^{1} (𝔊 B Σαβα, A & 𝔊L 'Ασβηλ).

†אַשְׁבֵּלִי adj.gent. הָא׳ as n coll Nu 26^{38}

†אֶשְׁבָּן n.pr.m. a chief of Edom Gn 36^{26} 1 Ch 1^{41} (etym dub, 𝔊 'Ασβαν, 'Εσεβαν, 'Ασεβων)

אַשְׁבֵּעַ v שׁבע.

אֶשְׁבַּעַל v אִישׁ־בֹּשֶׁת

אשד (√of following, cf. prob As. *išdu, foundation*)

†אֶשֶׁד n.[m.] **foundation, bottom, lower part** (slope) (As *išdu* cf Lotz$^{TP 186}$; >others fr. אָשַׁד, سد *pour*, Sab אסד=מסקי (משקה) DHM$^{ZMG 1883, 8}$, whence *fall, slope*, cf Di Nu 21^{15}) א׳ הַנְּחָלִים *the bottom of the ravines* Nu 21^{15}.

†[אֲשֵׁדָה] n f. **foundation,** (mountain-) **slope** (cf supr)—only pl abs. אֲשֵׁדוֹת Jos 10^{40} 12^{8}, cstr אַשְׁדּוֹת Jos 12^{3} 13^{20}, אַשְׁדֹּת Dt 3^{17} 4^{49}—*mountain-slopes* Jos 10^{40} ההר והנגב והשפלה והא׳; 12^{8} (‖ id + מדבר), elsewhere defined תַּחַת א׳ הַפִּסְגָּה Dt 3^{17} 4^{49} Jos 12^{3} cf 13^{20}

†אַשְׁדּוֹד n.pr.loc. **Ashdod** (As *Asdudu*, COT^{Gloss} Dl$^{Pa 289}$, Thes MV der. fr. √שׁדד q v) a powerful city of the Philistines on Mediterr Sea, W. from Jerusalem, modern *Esdûd*, Jos 11^{22} 15$^{46.47}$ (where assigned to Judah) 1 S 5$^{5.6}$ (but del. Dr cf 𝔊) 6^{17} Am 1^{8} 3^{9} Zp 2^{4} Zc 9^{6} Is 20^{1} Je 25^{20} 2 Ch 26^{6}, c. ה — loc 1 S 5^{1} Is 20^{1}, אַנְשֵׁי א׳ 1 S 5^{7}; appar.=territory of Ashdod 2 Ch 26^{6} וַיִּבְנֶה עָרִים בְּאַשְׁדּוֹד (Cf Survey$^{J. 442}$.)

†אַשְׁדּוֹדִי adj.gent. **Ashdodite,** הָא׳ n sg coll Jos 13^{3}, usually pl (הָ)אַשְׁדּוֹדִים 1 S 5$^{3.6}$ Ne 4^{1}, and as adj f נָשִׁים אשדודיות Ne 13^{23} Kt (Qr אַשְׁדֳּדִיּוֹת)

†אַשְׁדּוֹדִית adv. **in the language of Ashdod,** i.e of Philistines Ne 13^{24} מְדַבֵּר א׳

אשה (*support,* √whence following).

†[אָשְׁיָה] n f. (support) **buttress** (Ar آسِيَة *column, support,* AW No$^{M 113}$, 𝔗 אֻשְּׁא, pl אֻשַּׁיָּתָא, אוּשְׁוָתָא) only pl sf *buttresses* of city of Babylon Je 50^{15} אשויתיה Kt, אָשְׁיוֹתֶיהָ Qr (‖ חוֹמוֹתֶיהָ)

יֹאשִׁיָּהוּ, יֹאשִׁיָּה n.pr.m. (י׳ *supporteth*) **1** יֹאשִׁיָּהוּ king of Judah, son of Amon 1 K 13^{2} 2 K 21$^{24.26}$ + 11 t K, +19 t Ch, +17 t Je + Zp 1^{1}, also יֹאוֹשִׁיָּהוּ Je 27^{1} **2.** יֹאשִׁיָּה a returned exile Zc 6^{10}

אִשָּׁה v sub III אנשׁ.

אֱשׁוּן Qr Pr 20^{20} v. אִישׁוֹן sub אישׁ.

אַשּׁוּר n.pr.gent. & terr. **Asshur, Assyria** (As *Aššur*, land & city Dl$^{Pa 252}$ COT on Gn 2^{14}, Pers *Athura*, Syr. ܐܬܘܪ, on the connection with name of god *Ašur*, & with √אשׁר=ישׁר *good, gracious*, cf COT$^{l c}$; v. also Jen$^{ZA. 1886, 1 f.}$ Schr$^{ib 209 f.}$ No$^{ib 268 f}$) **1.** *Asshur* as person, 2nd son of Shem Gn 10^{22} (P, in table of nations) 1 Ch 1^{17} **2.** *people of Asshur* (oft as invading army & even world-power) Nu 24$^{22.24}$ (poem of Balaam) Ho 12^{2} 14^{4} Is 10^{5} 14^{25} 19$^{23.23.24.25}$ 23^{13} 30^{31} 31^{8} 52^{4} La 5^{6} Ez 23^{5} 27^{23} 32^{22} (here fem) Zc 10^{11}; ψ 83^{9} perh. rd. נשׁוּר, cf 2 S 2^{9} sub אֲשׁוּרִי, or (if ψ 83 be late) regard אַשּׁוּר (like עֲמָלֵק *ib.*) as used because of ancient significance, sts. personified as one Is 10^{5} Ez 31^{3} (but del Co q v), cf also Mi 5$^{4.5}$ Zp 2^{13}; מַחֲנֵה א׳ 2 K 19^{35}=Is 37^{36}, בְּנֵי א׳ Ez 16^{28} 23$^{7.9.12.23}$ **3.** *land of Assyria* Gn 2^{14} 10^{11} Ho 5^{13} 7^{11} 8^{9} 9^{3} 10^{6} Is 11$^{11.16}$ 19^{23} Je 2$^{18.36}$ Mi 7^{12} Zc 10^{10}, אַשּׁוּרָה Gn 25^{18} Is 19^{23} 2 K 15^{29} 17$^{6.23}$ 18^{11}, אֶרֶץ אַשּׁוּר Is 7^{18} 27^{13} Ho 11^{11} Mi 5^{5} **4.** esp מֶלֶךְ אַשּׁוּר Is 8^{4} 10^{12} 20$^{1.4.6}$ (prob. gloss Is 7$^{17.20}$ 8^{7}) 2 K 15^{19}+41 t 2 K, 14 t Is 36–38, 1 Ch 5^{6} (אַשֻּׁר)+13 t Ch; also Je 50$^{17.18}$ Na 3^{18} Ezr 4^{2}, (only Ezr 6^{22} of Persian or any king not strictly Assyrian), note also הַמֶּלֶךְ א׳ Is 36$^{8.16}$ (א׳ perh. gloss, cf Di who holds same view as to 2 K 18$^{23.31}$), מַלְכֵי א׳ 2 K 19$^{11.17}$=Is 37$^{11.18}$ 2 Ch 28^{16} 30^{6} Ne 9^{32}.

†אַשּׁוּרִם n.pr.gent.pl. an ° Arab tribe

traced back to Abraham & Keturah Gn 25³ cf Di.

†אַשּׁוּרִי adj.gent. הָא׳ as n coll. 2 S 2⁹, but rd. perh. הַגְּשׁוּרִי q v., cf also We Dr; Koh Klo al. rd. הָאָשֵׁרִי & comp Ju 1³².

אַשְׁחוּר v. שחר

†אֲשִׁימָא n.pr.[m.] a god of Hamath 2 K 17³⁰, otherwise wholly unknown.

†[אֶשֶׁךְ] n.[m.] testicle (Syr. ܐܫܟܐ, Eth. አሥክ: etym. unknown) only מְרוֹחַ אָשֶׁךְ Lv 21²⁰.

†אֶשְׁכּוֹל (אֶשְׁכֹּל Ct 7⁸) n.m. [Nu 13, 23] cluster (Eth. አስካል: Ar. إِثْكَال, Aram. איתכלא; etym dub; Thes MV sub √שׁכל, but no suitable meaning proven; Sta [§ 258, 300] der fr. √אשך c afformat. ל)—א׳ abs. Nu 13²⁴+, cstr. v²³+; pl. אֶשְׁכֹּלוֹת Ct 7⁸; cstr. אַשְׁכְּלֹת Dt 32³², אֶשְׁכְּלוֹת Ct 7⁹, sf. אַשְׁכְּלֹתֶיהָ Gn 40¹⁰,—**1.** *cluster* of grapes, א׳ עֲנָבִים Nu 13²³ cf v²⁴, vid. also Gn 40¹⁰ הבשילו א׳ עֲנָבִים *its clusters ripened grapes;* hence fig. of deeds of enemies of Israel, *clusters of gall have they* Dt 32³² (‖ עִנְּבֵי רוֹשׁ), fig. of Isr. Is 65⁸ יִמָּצֵא הַתִּירוֹשׁ בָּא׳; Mi 7¹ אֵין אֶשְׁכּוֹל לֶאֱכוֹל fig. of desolation of Israel under Yahweh's judgment, Ct 7⁸ in sim שָׁדַיִךְ כְּאֶשְׁכְּלוֹת הַגֶּפֶן cf v⁸ (where Thes MV think of clusters of dates, v. תָּמָר *palm-tree, ib*) **2.** *cluster* of henna-flowers, א׳ הַכֹּפֶר (v. כפר), metaph of the beloved one Ct 1¹⁴. (Cf Grunwald [Israel. Letterbode, Amst., xi. 148 f])

†אֶשְׁכֹּל n.pr. **1. m.** an Amorite, brother of Mamre, dwelling in neighbourhood of Hebron Gn 14¹³·²⁴. **2.** in combination נַחַל אֶשְׁכֹּל Nu 13²³ Dt 1²⁴, נ׳ אֶשְׁכּוֹל Nu 13²⁴ 32⁹;—*valley of Eshcol,* = *valley of a cluster,* region of Hebron (cf. 13²²); in 13²⁴ der fr א׳ *cluster,* q v.; see however Di *ad loc.*

אַשְׁכְּנַז n.pr.m. **1.** a descendant of Japhet Gn 10³ = 1 Ch 1⁶; = **2.** a northern people Je 51²⁷ מַמְלְכוֹת אֲרָרַט מִנִּי וְאַשְׁכְּנָז (perh. a people of Bithynia, = *Ascan(ians)* + *az* ending of Armen patronymics, v. esp Len [Or ii 358 f], also Lag [Ges. Abhandl. 254 f.] Di Gn 10³; but v Lag [Armen. Stud 143])

אֶשְׁכָּר v. II שכר

אשל (*be firm, firmly rooted,* cf. Ar. أَثَلَ *be firm*).

†אֵשֶׁל n.m. *tamarisk-tree* (Ar. أَثْل, Sab. אתל Sab. Denkm.⁸⁵ cf. DHM [BS ii 956], on an Aram אתלא v. Low [No. 38]; cf. Tristr [FFP 250]) planted by Abraham Gn 21³³ (J); in 1 S 22⁶ Saul is dwelling בַּגִּבְעָה תַּחַת־הָאֵשֶׁל בָּרָמָה; 31¹³ Saul and his sons are buried תַּחַת־הָא׳; it was perh a sacred tree, marking shrine

†אשם, אָשֵׁם vb. offend, be guilty (Ar. أَثِمَ, *id*, أَثَّمَ, *reum judicavit,* أَثَام, إِثْم, *fault, guilt, mulct,* cf Eth. ኣሰመ:)—אָשַׁם Lv 5¹⁹ Nu 5⁷; אָשֵׁם Hb 1¹¹ + 7 t; אָשְׁמָה Nu 5⁶, אָשֵׁמָה Pr 30¹⁰, אָשַׁמְתְּ Ez 22⁴; אָשֵׁמוּ Lv 4¹³; *Impf.* יֶאְשַׁם Ho 4¹⁵ + 13 t, *Inf. abs* אָשֹׁם Lv 5¹⁹, אָשׁוֹם Ez 25¹²,—**1.** *commit an offence, a trespass, do a wrong,* or *an injury,* with לְ: אָשֹׁם אָשַׁם לַיהוה *he hath done a great wrong to Yahweh* (in violating the commands) Lv 5¹⁹ (P), וְנָתַן לַאֲשֶׁר אָשַׁם לוֹ *and he shall give it* (restitution) *to him to whom he did wrong* Nu 5⁷ (P), cf. 2 Ch 19¹⁰ ¹⁰, וַיֶּאְשְׁמוּ אָשׁוֹם *and they committed lasting wrong* (irreparable wrong, the Edomites against Judah) Ez 25¹². **2.** *be* or *become guilty* Ju 21²² Je 50⁷ Ho 4¹⁵ Hb 1¹¹, in offences requiring sin-offering Lv 4¹³·²²·²⁷ (P), of trespass-offering Lv 5²·³·¹⁷ ²³ Nu 5⁶ (P), with לְ *guilty of* Lv 5⁴·⁵ (P), with בְּ *in* or *through* Ez 22⁴ Ho 13¹. **3.** *be held guilty, bear punishment* ψ 34²²·²³ Pr 30¹⁰ Is 24⁶ Je 2³ Ho 5¹⁵ 10² 14¹ Zc 11⁵ Ez 6⁶ (but cf. שָׁמֵם). **Niph.** נֶאְשְׁמוּ *suffer punishment* Jo 1¹⁸ **Hiph.** *Impf.* sf הַאֲשִׁימֵם *declare them guilty* ψ 5¹¹.

†אָשֵׁם adj. guilty, א׳ abs. 2 S 14¹³, pl. אֲשֵׁמִים אֲל־אָחִינוּ Gn 42²¹ (E), *guilty,* and so bound to offer a trespass-offering Ezr 10¹⁹; but rd prob וַאֲשָׁמָם, so Kue [Chronol v h. Perzische Tijdvak, 1890 43].

אָשָׁם n.m. offence, guilt—א׳ Gn 26¹⁰ + 37 t., sf. אֲשָׁמוֹ Nu 5⁷ + 7 t;—**1.** *offence, trespass, fault* ψ 68²² (*guiltiness* RV) **2.** *guilt* Gn 26¹⁰ (J) Pr 14⁹ Je 51⁵ **3.** *compensation,* לְהָשִׁיב הָאָשָׁם אֵלָיו *to whom to return the compensation* (or satisfaction for injury) Nu 5⁷·⁸ (P, *restitution for guilt* RV). **4.** *trespass-offering* (AV, but *guilt-offering* RV) used only in Lv 5, 6¹⁰ 7, 14, 19²¹ ²² Nu 5, 6¹² 18⁹ (P), & Ez 40³⁹ 42¹³ 44²⁹ 46²⁰, cf Ezr 10¹⁹. This offering seems to have been confined to offences against God or man that could be estimated and so covered by compensation. The ordinary trespass-offering was a ram, together with restitution and a penalty of a fifth of its value. The trespass-offerings of the leper and Nazirite were he-lambs Lv 14 Nu 6¹², if the person who suffered wrong or his kinsmen were not living the fine went to the priests. The victims were offered, the blood and fat pieces going to the altar, the skin and flesh to the priests. There seems to have been no applica-

tion of the blood to the horns of the altar (the chief ceremony of the sin-offering) because the guilt was not expiated at the altar but by compensation to the wronged person or his representative. A part of the blood of the leper's trespass-offering was applied to his person to consecrate him (as in the case of the ram of consecration to consecrate the priests Lv 8^{23}) The trespass-offering is unknown to JED and the older Hebrew literature. However, the Philistines send an אשם of golden mice and tumours 1 S 6$^{3.4.8.17}$, and an אשם of money was given to the priests 2 K 12^{17}, but these are entirely different from the trespass-offering of P The Messianic servant offers himself as an אשם in compensation for the sins of the people, interposing for them as their substitute Is 53^{10} (incorrectly, *sin-offering* AV RV) See further Oehler$^{OT\ Theol\ §137}$ Di Lv 5^{14}

†אַשְׁמָה **n.f. wrong-doing, guiltiness** (properly *Inf* cf אַהֲבָה, יִרְאָה)—א׳ Lv 22^{16} + 5 t, cstr אַשְׁמַת Ezr 10^{10} + 3 t., sf. אַשְׁמָתוֹ Lv 5^{24} + 6 t, pl. אַשְׁמוֹת 2 Ch 28^{10}, sf. אַשְׁמוֹתַי ψ 69^{6},—**1.** *doing wrong, committing a trespass or offence* 2 Ch 24^{18} 28$^{10.13\ 13\ 13}$ (‖ חטאת v^{13}) 32^{23} Ezr 9$^{6\ 7\ 13.15}$ (‖ עָוֹן v^{13}) ψ 69^{6} (‖ אִוֶּלֶת), מכל אֲשֶׁר יַעֲשֶׂה לְאַשְׁמָה בָהּ *of all that one may do wrong therein* Lv 5^{26} (P, ‖ לַחֲטֹא בָהֵנָּה v^{22}). **2.** *becoming guilty* 1 Ch 21^{3} Ezr 10$^{10\ 19}$; יֶחֱטָא לְאַשְׁמַת הָעָם *sin to the becoming guilty of the people* (so that the people incur guilt) Lv 4^{3}, אַשְׁמַת שֹׁמְרוֹן *guilt of Samaria* (their idols) Am 8^{14} **3.** *bringing a trespass-offering*, בְּיוֹם אַשְׁמָתוֹ *in the day of his bringing his trespass-offering* Lv 5^{24}; עֲוֹן אַשְׁמָה *iniquity requiring a trespass-offering* Lv 22^{16}.

אַשְׁמוּרָה (־מֹרֶת, ־מֻרוֹת) v. שמר

אַשְׁמַנִּים v שמן

אשן (√assumed for foll., perh *be hard, firm*, cf Aram אֻשְׁנָא, אֻשִּׁינָא, something *firm*)

†אֶשְׁנָה **n pr.loc.** (*the firm*?) name of two cities in Judah **1.** Jos 15^{33}. **2.** v^{43}

אֶשְׁנָב v. שנב

אֶשְׁעָן v. שען

†[אַשָּׁף] **n.m. conjurer, necromancer** (prob Bab. loan-word, As *ašipu* COT^{Gloss} cf Dl$^{Pr\ 141}$, Aram אָשַׁף, ܐܫܘܦܐ, v also As. *šiptu, conjuration*) only pl אַשָּׁפִים Dn 1^{20} (‖ חַרְטֻמִּים), 2^{2} (‖ ח׳, מְכַשְּׁפִים, כַּשְׂדִּים)

אשף (√of dub meaning, whence foll)

†אַשְׁפָּה **n.f. quiver** for arrows (As. *išpatu* Dl$^{K\ 29}$) א׳ lit. as part of warlike equipment Jb 39^{23} Is 22^{6}, fig in sim of sons of one's youth as arrows (weapons which the father may wield) ψ 127^{5} אַשְׁרֵי הַגֶּבֶר אֲשֶׁר מִלֵּא אֶת־אַשְׁפָּתוֹ מֵהֶם *the happiness of the man that hath filled his quiver with them!* of Yahweh's quiver, in metaph of prophet as arrow of י׳ Is 49^{2} וַיְשִׂימֵנִי לְחֵץ בָּרוּר בְּאַשְׁפָּתוֹ הִסְתִּירָנִי *and he made me into a polished arrow, in his quiver he hid me;* also of quiver in which י׳ has his arrows of chastisement, בְּנֵי אַשְׁפָּתוֹ, i e *his arrows* La 3^{13} (‖ חִץ v^{12}).

†אַשְׁפְּנַז **n pr.m.** the רַב־סָרִיסִים, chief of eunuchs, of Nebuchadrezzar Dn 1^{3} (meaning unknown)

†אֶשְׁפָּר 2 S 6^{19} = 1 Ch 16^{3}, 𝔊 2 S 6^{19} Aq. Symm *cake* or *roll*, other Verss ancient & mod have various conjectures, but actual etym & mng unknown; v. Lag$^{GGA\ 1884,\ No.\ 7\ 282=M\ i.\ 214}$ Dr^{Sm}

אַשְׁפֹּתוֹת, אַשְׁפֹּת v שפת

†אַשְׁקְלוֹן **n.pr.loc.** a city of the Philistines (As *Isqaluna* COT^{Gloss} Dl$^{Pa\ 290}$, Ph adj gent cf. infr) Ju 1^{18} 14^{19} 1 S 6^{17} 2 S 1^{20} Je 25^{20} 47$^{5\ 7}$ Am 1^{8} Zp 2$^{4\ 7}$ Zc 9$^{5.5}$, on the Medit Sea, S of W. fr. Jerusalem, mod *'Asqalân*, Survey$^{III\ 237\ f.}$ (with plan); cf. also ZPV$^{II.\ 164\ f}$

†אֶשְׁקְלוֹנִי **adj.gent.** c. art as subst הָא׳ Jos 13^{3} (Ph אשקלני).

†[אָשַׁר] **vb. go straight, go on, advance** (As. *ašâru* Zim$^{BP\ 11}$; Ar Aram in deriv)—**Qal** *Imv* אִשְׁרוּ Pr 9^{6} אִשְׁרוּ בְּדֶרֶךְ בִּינָה *go straight on in the way of understanding* **Pi.** *Pf* אִשְּׁרוּ Mal 3^{12} Gn 30^{13}, *Impf* תְּאַשֵּׁר Pr 4^{14} + 4 t; *Imv.* אַשֵּׁר Pr 23^{19}, *Pt* pl מְאַשְּׁרִים Mal 3^{15} + 2 t,—**1.** intensive *go straight on, advance* Pr 4^{14} **2.** causative *lead on* Pr 23^{19} Is 3^{12} 9^{15}. **3.** *set right, righten* Is 1^{17} **4.** *pronounce happy, call blessed* Gn 30^{13} (J) Jb 29^{11} ψ 72^{17} Pr 31^{28} Ct 6^{9} Mal 3$^{12\ 15}$ **Pu.** *Impf* יְאֻשַּׁר ψ 41^{3}, *Pt* מְאֻשָּׁר Pr 3^{18} Is 9^{15}. **1.** *be led on* Is 9^{15} **2.** *be made happy, blessed* ψ 41^{3} Pr 3^{18}

†[אֶשֶׁר, or אֹשֶׁר, cf. Lag$^{BN\ 143}$] **n.[m.]** only *Pl* cstr אַשְׁרֵי **happiness, blessedness of** 1 K 10^{8} + 32 t & c.sf., v infr., abstr intens exclam *O the happiness, blessedness of*, אַשְׁרֵי אֲנָשֶׁיךָ אַשְׁרֵי עֲבָדֶיךָ אֵלֶּה *happy thy men, happy these thy servants* 1 K 10^{8} (= 2 Ch 9^{7}), אַשְׁרֵי אֱנוֹשׁ יוֹכִחֶנּוּ אֱלוֹהַּ *blessed the man whom Eloah correcteth* Jb

5^{17}; אַשְׁרֵי תְמִימֵי דָרֶךְ *blessed the perfect in way* ψ 119^{1}; אַשְׁרֵי בָנָיו אַחֲרָיו *blessed his children after him* Pr 20^{7}; elsewhere cstr. with אָדָם ψ 32^{2} 84$^{6.13}$ Pr 3^{13} 8^{34} 28^{14}; with הַגֶּבֶר ψ 34^{9} 40^{5} 94^{12} 127^{5}; (הָ)אִישׁ ψ 1^{1} 112^{1}; אֱנוֹשׁ Is 56^{2}; הַגּוֹי ψ 33^{12}; הָעָם ψ 89^{16} 144$^{15.15}$; before ptcp. ψ 2^{12} 32^{1} 41^{2} 84^{5} 106^{3} 119^{2} 128^{1} Is 30^{18} Dn 12^{12}; before verbal clauses without relative ψ 65^{5} Pr 8^{32}; with שֶׁ ψ 137$^{8.9}$ 146^{5}; with sf. אַשְׁרֶיךָ (for אֲשָׁרֶיךָ) *O thy happiness!* Dt 33^{29} ψ 128^{2}; אַשְׁרֵיךְ Ec 10^{17}; אַשְׁרֵיכֶם Is 32^{20}; אַשְׁרָיו Pr 14^{21} 16^{20}; אַשְׁרֵהוּ Pr 29^{18} (on these forms v. Ges[§93, R. 1, E]).

†[אֹשֶׁר] **n.[m.]** happiness, only sf. בְּאָשְׁרִי *in my happiness* Gn 30^{13} (J).

†[אַשּׁוּר, אֲשֻׁר] **n.f.** [ψ 44, 19] **step, going** (cf. Ar. أَثَرٌ, إِثْرٌ, Eth. **አሠር:** *footstep*) only sf. אֲשֻׁרוֹ Jb 23^{11} Pr 14^{15}; אֲשֻׁרַי ψ 17^{5}; אֲשֻׁרָי ψ 40^{3} 73^{2}; אֲשֻׁרֵנוּ ψ 44^{19}; אֲשֻׁרָיו ψ 37^{31}, all poet. & fig. of mode of life, etc.

†[אַשֻּׁר] **n.f.** [Jb 31, 7] **step, going,** same usage, אַשֻּׁרִי Jb 31^{7}; אַשֻּׁרֵנוּ ψ 17^{11}.

†אָשֵׁר **n.pr.m.** **Asher** (*happy one, Felix,* cf. Ph. אשרשלח, which however may contain (god) Asshur or Osiris, cf. Bae[Rel 161]). **1.** son of Jacob and Zilpah Gn 30^{13} 35^{26} 46^{17} Ex 1^{4} Nu 26^{46} 1 Ch 2^{2}. **2.** *the tribe* Gn 49^{20} Nu 1^{13} Dt 27^{13} 33$^{24.24}$ Jos 17$^{10.11}$ 19^{34} Ju 1^{31} 5^{17} 6^{35} 7^{23} 1 K 4^{16} 1 Ch 12^{36} 2 Ch 30^{11} Ez 48$^{2.3.34}$; בְּנֵי אָשֵׁר Nu 1^{40} 2^{27} 7^{72} 10^{26} 26$^{44.47}$ 34^{27} Jos 19$^{24.31}$ 1 Ch 7$^{30.40}$; מַטֵּה אָשֵׁר Nu 1^{41} 2^{27} 13^{13} Jos 21$^{6.30}$ 1 Ch 6$^{47.59}$. **3. n.pr.loc.** city E. of Shechem Jos 17^{7}.

†אָשֵׁרִי **adj.gent.** c. art. הָא׳ as n.coll. Ju 1^{32}.

†אֲשֻׁרִים, in בַּת א׳ Ez 27^{6} (rd. בִּתְאַשֻּׁרִים *with box-wood* Bo Hi MV Co al., cf. foll.)

†תְּאַשּׁוּר **n.f. box-tree** (on form cf. Sta[§ 267]) Is 41^{19} 60^{13} Ez 27^{6} (cf. supr.) a small evergreen tree about 20 feet high, growing on Lebanon, Bo Tristr[Nat. Hist. Bib. 339], so 𝔙 𝔗 RV. (Others *sherbîn,* a species of cedar distinguished by the smallness of its cones and the upward direction of its branches, cf. Thes RobGes.)

†אֲשֵׁרָה, אֲשֵׁירָה 2 K 17^{16} **n.pr.f.** **Ashera** (As. n.pr.f. *Aš-ra-tu,* c. sign for deity, in Canaanitish n.pr. *Abad-Ašratum, servant of A.* Schr[ZA 1888. 363], cf. Wkl & Abel[Thontafelfund v. El Amarna ii. No. 77, l. 9], & Sayce[RP2. ii. 67, iii. 71]; on deriv. cf. As. *aširat,* adj. fem. *gracious,* COT[Gloss]):—usually with the art.: prob. **a.** a Canaanitish goddess of fortune & happiness; having prophets 1 K 18^{19}, an image 15^{13} = 2 Ch 15^{16} 2 K 21^{7}, sacred vessels 2 K 23^{4}, houses v^{7}. **b.** a symbol of this goddess, a *sacred tree* or *pole* set up near an altar 1 K 16^{33} 2 K 13^{6} 17^{16} 18^{4} 21^{3} 23$^{6.15}$; prohibited Dt 16^{21}; burnt by Gideon Ju 6$^{25.26.28.30}$. *Pl.* אֲשֵׁרוֹת **a.** the goddess Ju 3^{7} (prob. error for עַשְׁתָּרֹת 𝔙). **b.** *sacred trees* or *poles* 2 Ch 19^{3} 33^{3}; elsewhere אֲשֵׁרִים *id.* Is 27^{9} + 12 t.; sf. Mi 5^{14} + 5 t.;—Ex 34^{13} (J) Dt 7^{5} 12^{3} Is 17^{8} 27^{9} Je 17^{20} Mi 5^{13} 1 K 14$^{15.23}$ 2 K 17^{10} 23^{14} 2 Ch 14^{2} 17^{6} 24^{18} 31^{1} 33^{19} 34$^{3.4.7}$.—(Cf. also Sta[ZAW 1881, 344 f.] RS[Sem. i. 171 f., 175 n.] We[H 235], who think א׳ only the sacred pole.)

אֲשֶׁר **part. of relation** (Moab. *id.;* origin dub.: **1.** acc. to Tsepreghi[Diss. Lugd. p. 171] Mühlau[Bö. Lb. ii. 79 n.] Sta[Morg. Forsch. 1875, 188; Lb. § 167] Hommel[ZMG 1878, 708 ff.] Müll[§ 153] Sayce[Hbr. ii. 51] Lag[M. i. 255] & esp. Kraetzschmar[Hbr. vi. 298 ff], orig. a subst. 'place' = أَثَرٌ *footstep, mark,* **አሠር:** (do.), אֲתַר, ܐܬܪ *place,* As. *ašru,* used (v. Kraetz.) both as a subst. 'there, where,' and as a relative of place 'where': in Heb. this development has advanced further, and it has become a relative sign generally. The chief objection to this explanation is that it would isolate Heb. from the other Semitic languages, in which pronouns are formed regularly from *demonstrative* roots (cf. also Nö[ZMG 1886, 738]). **2.** according to Phi[St. C. 73] Sperling[Nota Rel. im Hebr. 1876, 15–22] for אֲשֶׁל, developed from the relative שׁ (q.v.) by (1) the prefixing of either a merely prosthetic א, or, better, a pronominal א (giving rise to אש, the form of the relative in Ph.), and (2) the addition of the demonstr. root ל [found also in אֵל, אֵלֶּה, הַלָּזֶה (q.v.), اَلَّذِى *he who,* **እለ:** *who* (pl.)]: the main objection to this explanation is the change of ל to ר, which is hardly rendered probable by the comp. of Syr. ܗܘܪܐ by side of Targ. הִלְכָּא. **1** seems preferable, the primitive root having acquired different significations in the different Semitic languages, and having been weakened in Heb. to a mere particle of relation). A **sign of relation,** bringing the clause introduced by it into relation with an antecedent clause. As a rule אֲשֶׁר is a mere **connecting link,** and requires to be supplemented (see the grammars) by a pron. affix, or other word, such as שָׁם, defining the nature of the relation more precisely: e.g. Gn 1^{11} אֲשֶׁר זַרְעוֹ־בוֹ lit. *as to which,* its seed is in it = in which is its seed, ψ 1^{4} like the chaff אֲשֶׁר־תִּדְּפֶנּוּ רוּחַ *as to which,* the wind drives it = which the wind drives, etc.; & so אֲשֶׁר...שָׁם = *where,* אֲשֶׁר...מִשָּׁם = *whence,* Gn 2^{11} 3^{23} 20^{13} etc. Sometimes also (v. infr.) the relation

expressed by it is specifically temporal, local, causal, etc. More particularly **1.** it includes its pronominal antecedent, whether in the nom. or obl. cases, as Nu 22[6] וַאֲשֶׁר תָּאֹר יוּאָר and *he whom* thou cursest is cursed, Ex 4[12] and I will teach thee אֲשֶׁר תְּדַבֵּר *that which* thou shalt say; and with particles or prepositions, as אֵת אֲשֶׁר (acc. to the context) *him who…, those who…, that which…*; לַאֲשֶׁר to *him who…* Gn 43[16], to *those who…* 47[24], to *that which* 27[8]; מֵאֲשֶׁר Ju 16[30] 2 S 18[18] *than those* whom; Lv 27[24] לַאֲשֶׁר קָנָהוּ מֵאִתּוֹ *to him* from whom he bought it, Nu 5[7]; Is 24[2] כַּאֲשֶׁר נֹשֶׁא בוֹ *like him* against whom there is a creditor. **2.** instances of אֲשֶׁר followed by a pron. affix, or by מִשָּׁם, שָׁמָּה, שָׁם, are so common that the exx. cited above will be sufficient. Very rarely there occurs the anomalous constr. עִם אֲשֶׁר Gn 31[32] for אֲשֶׁר עִמּוֹ (see Gn 44[9]), בַּאֲשֶׁר Is 47[12] for לַאֲשֶׁר, אֲשֶׁר בָּהֶם for אֲשֶׁר…לָהֶם Ez 23[40]: ψ 119[49] see under על אשר. It is followed by the pron. in the *nomin.*, in the foll. cases:—(*a*) immediately, mostly before an adj. or ptcp., Gn 9[3] all moving things אֲשֶׁר הוּא־חַי which are living, Lv 11[26] Nu 9[13] 14[8.27] 35[31] Dt 20[20] 1 S 10[19] (v. Dr) 2 K 25[19] (‖ Je 52[25] היה) Je 27[9] Ez 43[19] Hg 1[9] Ru 4[15] Ne 2[18] Ec 7[26]; before a vb. 2 K 22[13] (omitted 2 Ch 34[21]). (*b*) in a *negative* sentence, at the end: Gn 7[2] 17[12] Nu 17[5] Dt 17[15] אֲשֶׁר לֹא אָחִיךָ הוּא who is not thy brother, 20[15] Ju 19[12] 1 K 8[41] ‖ 9[20] ‖. N.B. ψ 16[3] אֲשֶׁר בָּאָרֶץ הֵמָּה is an unparalleled expression for 'who are in the land'; rd. 'אֲשֶׁר בָּאָרֶץ הֵמָּה אַדִּירֵי וג 'the saints that are in the land, they (המה) are the nobles, in whom,' etc. **3.** sometimes (though rarely) the defining adjunct is a pron. of 1 or 2 ps. as well as of 3 ps. In such cases it is strictly to be rendered *I who…, thou who*, etc.; Ho 14[4] אֲשֶׁר־בְּךָ יְרֻחַם יָתוֹם *thou by whom* the fatherless is compassionated! Je 31[32] *I, whose* covenant they brake, 32[19] Is 49[23] Jb 37[17f.] *thou whose* garments are warm…, canst thou? etc., ψ 71[19.20] 144[12] *we whose* sons, etc., 139[15] my frame was not hidden from thee, אֲשֶׁר־עֻשֵּׂיתִי בַסֵּתֶר—*I who* was wrought in secret (=*though I* was wrought in secret), Ex 14[13] for *ye who* have seen the Egyptians to-day,—ye shall not see them again for ever! (cf. ψ 41[9]). **4.** the defining pron. adjunct is *dispensed with*—**a.** when אֲשֶׁר represents the simple subj. of a sentence, or the direct obj. of a vb.: so constantly, as Gn 2[1] the work אֲשֶׁר עָשָׂה *which* he made, 3[3] the tree אֲשֶׁר בְּתוֹךְ הַגָּן *which* is in the midst of the garden, etc. **b.** after words denoting time, place, or manner, so that אֲשֶׁר then becomes equivalent to *when, where, why*: (*α*) Gn 6[4] אַחֲרֵי כֵן אֲשֶׁר afterwards, *when*, etc. (cf. 2 Ch 35[20]) 45[6] there are still 5 years אֲשֶׁר אֵין חָרִישׁ *when* there shall be no plowing, Jos 14[10] 1 K 22[25]; after יוֹם or הַיּוֹם Dt 4[10] Ju 4[14] 1 S 24[5] (v. Dr) 2 S 19[25] Je 20[14] al.; similarly Gn 40[13]. (*β*) Gn 35[13] בַּמָּקוֹם אֲשֶׁר דִּבֶּר אִתּוֹ in the place *where* he spake with him, v[14] 39[20] Nu 13[27] 22[26] Dt 1[31] in the desert which thou sawest, *where* (accents Ke Di), 8[15] 1 K 8[9] (unless לוּחוֹת הַבְּרִית has here fallen out: v. 𝔊 & Dt 9[9]) Is 55[11] 64[10] ψ 84[4]. So (*γ*) in אֶל אֲשֶׁר *to* (the place) *which* (or *whither*) Ex 32[34] Ru 1[16]; אֶל־כָּל־אֲשֶׁר *to* every (place) *whither* Jos 1[16] Pr 17[8]; בַּאֲשֶׁר *in* (the place) *where* †Ju 5[27] 17[8.9] 1 S 23[13] 2 K 8[1] Ru 1[16.17] Jb 39[30], once only with שָׁם Gn 21[17]; בְּכֹל אֲשֶׁר *wheresoever* Jos 1[7.9] Ju 2[15] 1 S 14[47] 18[5] 2 S 7[7] 2 K 18[7]; מֵאֲשֶׁר *from* (the place) *where*=*whencesoever* †Ex 5[11] Ru 2[9]; עַל־אֲשֶׁר *to* (the place) *whither* (or *which*) 2 S 15[20] 1 K 18[12]; עַל־כָּל־אֲשֶׁר Je 1[7]. (*δ*) …זֶה הַדָּבָר אֲשֶׁר this is the reason *that* or *why*… Jos 5[4] 1 K 11[27]. **c.** more extreme instances Lv 14[22.30.31] Nu 6[21], Dt 7[19] (wherewith), 28[20] 1 S 2[32] (wherein), 1 K 2[26] Ju 8[15] (about whom), Is 8[12] (where יאמר would be foll. normally by לוֹ), 31[6] turn ye to (him as to) whom they have deeply rebelled, 47[15] Zp 3[11] Ec 3[9], 1 K 14[19] (=how). **d.** it is dispensed with only in appearance after (אָמַרְתִּי וג׳) אֲשֶׁר אָמַר followed by the words used, its place being really taken by a pron. in the speech which follows, as Gn 3[17] the tree *as to which* I commanded thee saying, Thou shalt not eat *from it*, Ex 22[8] Dt 28[68] Ju 7[4] (זֶה) 8[15] (where the noun repeated takes the place of the pron., cf. Dt 9[2]) 1 S 9[17] (זֶה) [23] +; cf. 2 S 11[16] 2 K 17[12] 21[4]. **5.** אֲשֶׁר sts. in poet.=*one who, a man who* (*men who*), ὅστις, οἵτινες, ψ 24[4] 55[20] 95[4.5] Jb 4[19] 5[5] 9[5] (Hi) 15[17]. **6.** אֲשֶׁר occas. receives its closer definition by a subst. *following* it, in other words, its logical antecedent is inserted in the rel. clause: (*a*) in the phrase peculiar to Je., אֲשֶׁר הָיָה דְבַר י׳ אֶל יר׳ that which came (of) the word of י׳ to Je. †14[1] 46[1] 47[1] 49[34] (cf. Ew §334); (*b*) Ex 25[9] Nu 33[4] 1 S 25[30] 2 K 8[12] 12[6] לְכֹל אֲשֶׁר־יִמָּצֵא שָׁם בָּדֶק׃ Ez 12[25]; cf. the Eth. usage Di §201; (*c*) (antec. *repeated*) Gn 49[30]=50[13], 1 S 25[39] (י׳ repeated), Is 54[9] (prob.) *as to which* I sware that, etc., Am 5[1] which I take up over you (as) a dirge. **7.** אֲשֶׁר לִ׳ *that* (*belongs, belong,*

belonged) to, is used **a.** either alone or preceded by כָּל־ to express (*all*) *that* (*belongs*) *to*, as Gn 14^{23} מִכָּל־אֲשֶׁר־לָךְ of all that is *thine*, 31^{1} מֵאֲשֶׁר לְאָבִינוּ of *that which was* our father'*s*, 32^{24} & sent over אֶת־אֲשֶׁר־לוֹ *that which he had*, + oft. **b.** as a circumlocution of the genitive, as Gn 29^{9} עִם־הַצֹּאן אֲשֶׁר לְאָבִיהָ with the sheep *that were* her father'*s*, 40^{5} 47^{4} Lv 9^{8} Ju 6^{11} 1 S 25^{7} הָרֹעִים אֲשֶׁר־לָךְ, 2 S 14^{31} אֶת־הַחֶלְקָה אֲשֶׁר־לִי, 23^{8} 1 K $1^{8.33}$ עַל הַפִּרְדָּה אֲשֶׁר־לִי upon mine own mule, v^{49} 4^{2} 2 K 11^{10} 16^{13} Ru 2^{21}; and esp. in the case of a compound expression depending on a single genit., as Gn 23^{9} 40^{5} 41^{43} מִרְכֶּבֶת הַמִּשְׁנֶה אֲשֶׁר־לוֹ the chariot of the second rank *which he had*, Ex 38^{30} Ju 3^{20} 6^{25} 1 S 17^{40} 21^{8} אַבִּיר הָרֹעִים אֲשֶׁר לְשָׁאוּל the mightiest of *Saul's herdmen*, 24^{5} אֶת־כְּנַף־הַמְּעִיל אֲשֶׁר־לְשָׁאוּל, 2 S 2^{8} Saul's captain of the host, 1 K 10^{28} 15^{20} 22^{31} Je 52^{17} Ru 4^{3}. **c.** with names of places (esp. such as do not readily admit the st. cstr.) Ju 18^{28} 19^{14} הַגִּבְעָה אֲשֶׁר לְבִנְיָמִין Gibeah (the hill) of Benjamin, 20^{4} 1 S 17^{1} 1 K 15^{27} 16^{15} 17^{9} 19^{3} 2 K 14^{11}. Comp. שֶׁל (q.v.) which in Rabb., like the Aram. -דִּיל, ܕܝܠ-, is in habitual use as a mark of the genitive.—N.B. In Aram. also דִּי, ܕ, without לְ, expresses the gen. relation, as מִלְּתָא דִי־מַלְכָּא, lit. the word, *that of* the king = the word of the king. The few apparent cases of a similar use of אשר are, however, too foreign to the general usage of the language to be regarded otherwise than as due to textual error: 1 S 13^{8} read אֲשֶׁר אָמַר (or שָׂם Ex 19^{5}) שְׁמוּאֵל (𝔊 εἶπε); 1 K 11^{25} supply אֶת עָשָׂה (𝔊 ἣν ἐποίησεν); 2 K 25^{10} supply אֶת *with* (as ‖ Je 52^{14}); 2 Ch 34^{22} read וַאֲשֶׁר אָמַר הַמֶּלֶךְ (cf. 𝔊) and those whom the king appointed (abbreviated from 2 K 22^{14}); cf. Ew § 292 a, b with note.

3. אֲשֶׁר becomes, like Aram. דִּי, ܕ, a **conj.** approximating in usage to כִּי: thus **a.** = *quod*, ὅτι, *that*, subordinating an entire sentence to a verb of knowing, remembering, etc. (*α*) with אֶת Dt 9^{7} forget not אֵת אֲשֶׁר הִקְצַפְתָּ *the fact that* (= *how*) thou provokedst, etc., 29^{15} Jos 2^{10} 1 S $24^{11.19}$ 2 S 11^{20} know ye not אֵת אֲשֶׁר־יֹרוּ *how* they shoot from off the wall? 2 K 8^{12} Is 38^{3} + oft. As subj. (rare) 1 K 14^{19} 2 K 14^{15} 20^{20}. Of time (peculiarly) †2 S 14^{15} עַתָּה אֲשֶׁר now (is it) *that*... Zc 8^{20} (prob.) yet (shall it be) *that*... v^{23}; cf. כִּמְעַט שֶׁ Ct 3^{4}. (*β*) without אֶת (not very common, כִּי being usually employed): after יָדַע Ex 11^{7} Ez 20^{26} (very strange in Ez: v. Hi) Jb 9^{5} (Ew De Di) Ec 8^{12}, רָאָה, Dt 1^{31} (RV) 1 S 18^{15}, הִתְוַדָּה to confess Lv 5^{5} 26^{40b}, הִשְׁבִּיעַ 1 K 22^{16} (caused to swear *that*...); after a noun Is 38^{7} הָאוֹת אֲשֶׁר the sign *that*... (‖ 2 K 20^{9} כִּי): with growing frequency in late Hebrew, 2 Ch 2^{7}, and esp. Ne Est: Ne $2^{5.10}$ 7^{65} (= Ezr 2^{63}) $8^{14.15}$ 10^{31} $13^{1.19.22}$ Est 1^{19} 2^{10} 3^{4} 4^{11} 6^{2} 8^{11} Ec 3^{22} (מֵאֲשֶׁר) 5^{4} 7^{18} (with טוֹב: contrast Ru 2^{22}) v$^{22.29}$ $8^{12.14}$ 9^{1} Dn $1^{8.8}$. (*γ*) prefixed to a *direct* citation, like כִּי q.v. (= ὅτι *recitativum*) (rare) 1 S 15^{20} 2 S 1^{4} 2^{4} (v. Dr) ψ 10^{6} (prob.), Ne 4^{6}. **b.** it is resolvable into *so that*: Gn 11^{7} אֲשֶׁר לֹא יִשְׁמְעוּ *so that* they understand not, etc., 13^{16} 22^{14} אֲשֶׁר יֵאָמֵר so that it is said, Ex 20^{26} Dt $4^{10.40}$ אֲשֶׁר יִיטַב לְךָ 6^{3} $28^{27.51}$ 1 K $3^{12.13}$ 2 K 9^{37} Mal 3^{19}. **c.** it has a causal force, *forasmuch as, in that, since*: Gn 30^{18} 31^{49} and Mizpah, אֲשֶׁר אָמַר *for that* he said, $34^{13.27}$ 42^{21} we are guilty, אֲשֶׁר רָאִינוּ *we who* saw (or, *in that* we saw), Nu 20^{13} Meribah, *because* they strove there, Dt 3^{24} Jos $4^{7.23}$ 22^{31} Ju 9^{17} 1 S 2^{23} 15^{15} 20^{42} go in peace, אֲשֶׁר נִשְׁבַּעְנוּ *forasmuch as* we have sworn, 25^{26} *thou whom* (= or, *seeing that*) י׳ hath withholden, 2 S 2^{5} blessed are ye of י׳, אֲשֶׁר עֲשִׂיתֶם, *who* (οἵτινες) have done (or *in that ye* have done), 1 K 3^{19} 15^{5} 2 K 12^{3} 17^{4} 23^{26} Je 16^{13} Ec $8^{11.12}$ (Hi De Now). Here also belongs its use in אֲשֶׁר לָמָּה *since why*...? (= *lest*) Dn 1^{10}: v. sub לָמָּה. On אֲשֶׁר עַל כֵּן *forasmuch as* Jb 34^{27} v. sub כִּי עַל כֵּן. **d.** it expresses a *condition* (rare & peculiar): Lv 4^{22} אֲשֶׁר נָשִׂיא יֶחֱטָא in (case) that = *when* (or *if*) a ruler sinneth (v$^{3.13.27}$ אִם), Nu 5^{29} (explained differently by Ew § 334 a), Dt 11^{27} and the blessing אֲשֶׁר תִּשְׁמְעוּ *if* ye hearken (v^{28} אִם), 18^{22} Ges, Jos 4^{21}... אֲשֶׁר יִשְׁאָלוּן *when* they ask..., then... (v^{6} כִּי), Is 31^{4}. In 1 K 8^{33} (‖ 2 Ch 6^{24} כִּי, cf. K v$^{35.37}$) אֲשֶׁר may be rendered indifferently *because* or *when*. Once, similarly, אֵת אֲשֶׁר 1 K 8^{31} (‖ אִם). **e.** perh. (exceptionally) = כַּאֲשֶׁר, *as*, Je 33^{22} Is 54^{9} (sq. כֵּן; but כֵּן q.v. sts. stands without כאשר, & אשר may in these passages connect with what precedes); acc. to some also Je 48^{8} ψ 106^{34} (in a connexion where כַּאֲשֶׁר would be more usual: אֲשֶׁר may however be the obj. of אָמַר). In 1 S 16^{7} אֲשֶׁר יִרְאֶה הָאָדָם rd. כַּאֲשֶׁר, v. Dr. **f.** combined with preps., אֲשֶׁר converts them into conjunctions: see below, מֵאֲשֶׁר, כַּאֲשֶׁר, בַּאֲשֶׁר. On its use similarly with לְמַעַן, יַעַן, עַל דְּבַר, בַּעֲבוּר, מִבְּלִי, (אַחֲרֵי) אַחַר, תַּחַת, מִפְּנֵי, עֵקֶב, עַל, עַד, כְּפִי, see these words.—הַאֲשֶׁר, with ה *interrog.*, occurs once, 2 K 6^{22}.

Note 1. אֲשֶׁר being a connecting link, without any perfectly corresponding equivalent in Engl., its force is not unfreq. capable of being

represented in more than one way. See e.g. 2 S 2[5] (above **8 c**), Is 28[12] unto *whom* he said, or *for that* he said tó *them*.

Note 2. The opinion that אֲשֶׁר has an asseverative force (like כִּי, q.v.), or introduces the apodosis, is not prob., being both alien to its general usage & not required by the passages alleged. Render Is 8[20] either 'Surely acc. to this word will those speak *who* have no dawn,' or '... will they speak *when* (cf. supr. **8 d** Dt 11[27] Jos 4[21]) they have no dawn.'

בַּאֲשֶׁר 19 **a.** *in* (that) *which* ... Is 56[4] 65[12] 66[4] (supr. **1**); Ec 3[9] *in* (that, in) *which* (**4 c**); Is 47[12] (v. **2**). **b. adv.** *in* (the place) *where*: supr. **4 b** (γ). **c. conj.** *in that, inasmuch as*, †Gn 39[9.23] Ec 7[2] 8[4]; cf. بِـ. **d.** †Jon 1[8] בַּאֲשֶׁר לְמִי *on account of* whom? (בַּאֲשֶׁר לְ *on account of*, framed on model of Aram. בְּדִיל: v. sub שֶׁל).

כַּאֲשֶׁר v. sub כְּ.

מֵאֲשֶׁר 17 **a.** *from* (or *than*) *that which* (*him, them*, etc., *that*...) Gn 31[1] Ex 29[27.27] Nu 6[11] (see Lv 4[26]) Jos 10[11] Ju 16[30] Is 47[13]+; *than that*... †Ec 3[22]; לְבַד מֵאֲשֶׁר †Est 4[11]. **b. adv.** *from* (the place) *where*: supr. **4 a** (β). **c. conj.** *from* (the fact) *that* ..., *since* †Is 43[4].

†[אשׁשׁ] (cf. أَشَّ *found, establish*) **Hithpo.** וְהִתְאֹשָׁשׁוּ Is 46[8] (der. fr. above by 𝔗 Jer Hi Kn De MV, *shew yourselves firm*, but) rd. perh. הִתְבֹּשְׁשׁוּ Lag Che, v. בּוֹשׁ (Thes expl. as denom. from אִישׁ; on other views cf. Di).

†אֲשִׁישָׁה **n.f.** (pressed) **raisin-cake**—א׳ 2 S 6[19] 1 Ch 16[3] distributed, with other viands, to people; esp. as stimulating, pl. אֲשִׁישׁוֹת Ct 2[5]; more explicitly אֲשִׁישֵׁי עֲנָבִים Ho 3[1] used in sacrificial feasts (cf. RS[OTJC Lect. xi. n. 7]); אֲשִׁישֵׁי קִיר חֲרֶשֶׂת Is 16[7], i.e. the raisin-cakes which were an article of trade at Qir-hareseth (taken by Thes al. = *foundations*, i.e. foundations exposed by ruin, from [אָשִׁישׁ] with such a meaning).

אֶשֶׁת v. אִשָּׁה sub III. אנשׁ.

†אֶשְׁתָּאוֹל Jos 15[33] + 2 t., אֶשְׁתָּאֹל Ju 13[25] + 3 t. **n.pr.loc.** (in form like the inf. of the Arab. VIII. conj. from שָׁאַל: so אֶשְׁתְּמֹעַ from שָׁמַע. Perh. Arabic-speaking tribes may have settled in parts of S. of Judah) city of Danites in the שְׁפֵלָה of Judah, named with צָרְעָה Jos 15[33] 19[41] Ju 13[25] 16[31] 18[2.8.11]; perh. mod. *'Eshûʿa* Survey[iii. 25] Guerin[Pal. ii. 13 f. 382].

†אֶשְׁתָּאֻלִי **adj.gent.** c. art. הָאֶ׳ as n.coll. 1 Ch 2[53].

†אֶשְׁתּוֹן **n.pr.m.** a man of Judah (perh. fr. אֶשֶׁת = *effeminate* or *uxorious*) 1 Ch 4[11.12].

†אֶשְׁתְּמֹעַ Jos 21[14], אֶשְׁתְּמוֹעַ 1 S 30[28] 1 Ch 4[17.19] 6[42], אֶשְׁתְּמֹה Jos 15[50] **n.pr.loc.** Levitical city in mountain-country of Judah, south of Hebron, mod. *Semûʿa* v. Rob[BR i. 464, ii. 204] Survey[iii. 403] Bd[Pal. 153]; 1 Ch 4[17.19] it appears as **n.pr.m.** of a man of Judah. (On the form, cf. sub אֶשְׁתָּאוֹל.)

I. אֵת, with makk. אֶת־, with suff. אֹתִי; אֹתְךָ, אֹתְכָה †Nu 22[33], אֹתָךְ, אֹתָכָה †Ex 29[35], fem. אֹתָךְ; אֹתוֹ etc.; 2 pl. אֶתְכֶם, once אוֹתְכֶם Jos 23[15]; 3 mpl. regularly אֹתָם, rarely אֶתְהֶם †Gn 32[1] Ex 18[20] Nu 21[3] Ez 34[12] 1 Ch 6[50], once אוֹתְהֶם Ez 23[45]; 3 fpl., on the contrary, regularly אֶתְהֶן (13 t.), once אֹתָן Ez 16[54] (also אוֹתְהֶן Ez 23[47], אֹתְהֵנָּה Ex 35[26], אוֹתָנָה Ez 34[21]); forms with *cholem* also oft. written *plene*:—the **mark of the accusative**, prefixed as a rule only to nouns that are *definite* (Moab. *id.*, Ph. אית i.e. אִיַת (Schröd[p. 213 f.]); Aram. יָת freq. in 𝔗; Syr. ܝܳܬ very rare as mark of accus. (for which ܠ is preferred), but used often in the sense of *substance* οὐσία, also in that of *self*, e.g. ܒܝܳܬܶܗ *per se, reapse*, ܠܝܳܬܶܗ *sibi ipsi*, PS[1640 f.], Sam. ࠀࠉࠕ; Ar. إِيَّا, only used with sf., when it is desired to emphasize the pronoun, e.g. Qor 1[4] W[AG i. § 189]. [Eth. uses ኪያ: *kīyā* similarly, Di[§ 150 a]; but it is dub. if this is etymologically akin.] The primitive form will have been *'iwyath*, orig. a subst. with foll. gen., Ol[p. 432]; whether ultim. a parallel development with אוֹת *sign* from √אוה is uncertain: Ol W[AG i. § 188] Lag[M i. 226] affirm, Nö[ZMG 1886, 738] doubts. In Heb. the ground-form is אוֹת; the forms with *ē, e* being abbreviated. In postB Heb., used in combination with another prep.: thus בְּאוֹתוֹ הַיּוֹם = Bibl. בַּיּוֹם הַהוּא, בְּאוֹתָהּ הַשָּׁעָה; or as a nomin., e.g. אוֹתוֹ הָאִישׁ = Bibl. הָאִישׁ הַהוּא).

1. As mark of the accus. prefixed to substs. defined either by the art. (or כֹּל), or by a genitive or pron. affix, or in virtue of being proper names: **a.** with transitive verbs, Gn 1[1.16.29.30] 2[11] 4[1.2] 9[3] (אֶת־כֹּל) etc. Similarly אֶת־מִי *whom* (in particular), Jos 24[15] 1 S 12[3] 28[11] Is 6[8] al. (but never אֶת־מָה); also with זֶה Gn 29[33] 44[29] 1 S 21[16] 1 K 22[27]+, זֹאת Gn 29[27] 2 S 13[17]+, אֵלֶּה Gn 46[18] Lv 11[13] Is 49[21]+. So pretty uniformly in prose; but in poetry את is commonly dispensed with. By the use of את with the pron. affix, a pron. can at once, if required, be placed in a position of emphasis; let the order of words from this point of view be care-

fully noticed in the foll. passages: Gn 7[1] 24[14] 37[4] Lv 10[17] 11[33] Nu 22[33] *thee* I had slain, and *her* I had kept alive, Dt 4[14] 6[13.23] 13[5] Ju 14[3] אֹתָהּ קַח לִי take for me *her*, 1 S 14[35] 15[1] 18[17] 21[10] אִם־אֹתָהּ תִּקַּח־לְךָ קָח if thou wilt take *that*, take it, 1 K 1[35] 14[9] Is 43[22] 57[11] Je 9[2]. So הַאוֹתִי †Je 5[22] 7[19]. It also sometimes enables the reflexive sense to be expressed (elsewhere נַפְשָׁם) Je 7[19] Ez 34[2]. Rarely with a subst. which is undefined (Ew[§277 d 2] Ges[§117. 1 R. 2]), as Ex 21[28] Nu 21[9] Lv 20[14] 1 S 24[6] (but v. Dr) 2 S 4[11] 18[18] 23[21]; or which, though definite, is without the art., Gn 21[30] 2 S 15[16] Lv 26[5] 1 S 9[3] (so Nu 16[15]) Is 33[19] 41[7] Ez 43[10] (for further exx. v. Ew *l.c.*) **b.** with a *passive* verb (Ges[§121.1] Ew[§295 b]) conceived as expressing neutrally the action in question, and construed accordingly with an *accus.* of that which is its real object: exx. occur with tolerable frequency from Gn 4[18] (J) וַיִּקָּרֵא אֶת־שְׁמוֹ חֲנוֹךְ and there was called (= one called) his name Enoch, 17[5] (P), 21[5] (E), 27[42] 2 S 21[11] 1 K 18[13] Ho 10[6] etc., to Je 35[18] 38[4] 50[20] Ez 16[4.5] Est 2[13] (cf. Dr[JPh xi. 227 f.]): also with pass. vbs. of filling (Ew[§281 b]), as Ex 1[7]+. **c.** with *neuter* verbs or expressions, esp. such as involve the idea of *regarding*, or *treating*, appy. by a constr. *κατὰ σύνεσιν* (rare), Jo 22[17] 2 S 11[25] Ne 9[32] (cf. 1 S 20[13] Dr). Once after אַיִן, Hg 2[17] אֵין אֶתְכֶם אֵלַי. **d.** poet. (si vera l.), after an abstr. noun used with a verbal force, †Hb 3[13] (Am 4[11] Is 13[19] Je 50[40] מַהְפֵּכָה exerts a verbal force, like the Arab. *nom. verbi* [v. W[AG i. §196, 48]]; and Nu 10[2] Ez 17[9] לְמַשְּׂאוֹת, לְמַסַּע are Aramaizing infinitives: cf. Ew[§238 a]).

2. את marks an accus. in other relations than that of direct obj. to a verb: **a.** with verbs of motion (very rare) Nu 13[17] Dt 1[19] 2[7] (to 'walk the wilderness'); denoting the goal Ju 19[18] Ez 21[25] (Ew[§281 d, n., 282 a 1]). **b.** denoting time (duration), also very rare: Ex 13[7] Lv 25[22] Dt 9[25]. **c.** expressing the accus. of limitation (rare): Gn 17[11.14] 1 K 15[23].

3. Chiefly in an inferior or later style, אֵת (or וְאֵת) is used irregularly, partly (*a*), as it would seem, to give greater definiteness (so esp. וְאֵת) at the mention of a new subject (when it may sometimes be rendered *as regards*), or through the influence of a neighbouring verb (a cstr. *κατὰ σύνεσιν*), or by an anacoluthon, partly (*β*) as resuming loosely some other prep. Thus (*a*) Ex 1[14] Nu 3[26.46] 5[10] (with הָיָה: so Ez 35[10]) Nu 18[21b] Dt 11[2] (anacol.), 14[13] Jos 17[11] Ju 20[44.46] (contr. v[25.35]) 1 S 17[34] (v. Dr) 26[16] 2 S 21[22] 2 K 6[5] Is 53[8] (prob.), 57[12] Je 23[33] (but rd. rather with 𝔊 𝔙 אַתֶּם הַמַּשָּׂא) 27[8] 36[22] 38[16] Kt, 45[4b] Ez 16[22] 17[21] 20[16] 29[4b] 43[7] (𝔊 Co prefix הֲרָאִיתָ) 44[3] Zc 8[17] Ec 4[3] Dn 9[13] Ne 9[19.34] 1 Ch 2[9] 2 Ch 31[17]. In 1 S 30[23] Hg 2[5] prob. some such word as *remember* is to be understood. (*β*) Je 38[9] Ez 14[22b] 37[19b] Zc 12[10]; סָבִיב אֵת 1 K 6[5] Ez 43[17] strangely (in 1 K 𝔊 om. the clause: so Sta[ZAW 1883, 135]).—In 1 K 11[1] וְ is merely *and also, and especially* (v. וְ); v[25] is corrupt (rd. with 𝔊 וְזֹאת הָרָעָה אֲשֶׁר עָשָׂה הֲדַד); Ez 47[17.18.19] rd. similarly for זֹאת, וְאֵת: see v[20].—For some particulars as to the use of את, see A. M. Wilson[Hbr. vi. 139 ff. 212 ff.] (who, however, confuses it sts. with II. אֵת). For denoting the pron. obj. of a vb., את with suff. preponderates relatively much above the verbal affix in P, as compared with JE Dt Ju S K (v. Giesebrecht[ZAW 1881, 258 f.]),—partly, probably, on account of the greater distinctness and precision which P loves.

II. **אֵת**, **prep. with**—with makk. אֶת־, with suff. אִתִּי, אִתְּךָ, אִתְּכֶם etc. (also, however, אוֹתְךָ, אוֹתוֹ, and similarly מֵאוֹתְךָ, מֵאוֹתוֹ etc.), first in Jos 10[25] 14[12], next 2 S 24[24]; then repeatedly (but not exclusively) 1 K 20–2 K 8, & in Je Ez, e.g. 1 K 20[25] (but v[23] אִתָּם) 22[7.8.24] (beside מֵאִתִּי) 2 K 1[15] 3[11.12.26] 6[16] (beside מֵאִתּוֹ) 8[8] Je 2[35] 10[5] 16[8] 19[10] 20[11] Ez 2[6] 10[17] 23[23] 37[26] (v. infr. **1 d**; also Is 59[21], contr. Gn 17[4]: on שָׁכַב אִתָּהּ Gn 34[2] al., v. sub שָׁכַב, & cf. Dr[Sm ii. 13, 14]) prep. denoting **proximity** (syn. עִם; Ph. את, e.g. CIS[i. 3. 8] לא יכן לם משכב את רפאם let there not be for them a resting-place *with* the shades; As. *itti* (perh. akin to *ittu* 'side,' Dl[Pr 115] Hpt KAT[2.498]; but cf. Nö[ZMG '86, 738 f.]). Not found as yet in the other cogn. languages: but cf. Eth. **እንተ**: *'enta*, towards, which supports the view that אֵת is for *'int* [cf. תַּחַת, תַּחְתִּי], perh. from √אנת *to meet* Ol[p. 431] Prät[ZMG '73, 643], Lag[M i. 226]).

1. Of companionship, *together with*: Gn 6[13] behold, I destroy them אֶת־הָאָרֶץ *together with* the earth, 11[31] 12[4]+oft., esp. with *verbs of* dwelling, abiding, going, etc., as Ju 1[3] 14[11] 19[4], & in the phrase הָעָם אֲשֶׁר אִתּוֹ Ju 4[13] 7[1] 9[33.48] 1 S 14[20] 30[4] etc.; thou, and thy sons . . . אִתָּךְ *with thee* Gn 6[18]; similarly (3rd pers.) 7[7.13] 8[18] 9[8] al. (charact. of P: Dr[Intr 124]); הִתְהַלֵּךְ אֶת־הָאֱלֹהִים to walk *with* God, i.e. to have him as a companion (sc. by adopting a course of life pleasing to him) Gn 5[22.24] 6[9] (cf. הִתְהַלֵּךְ אֵת lit. 1 S 25[15]); —*by the side of, like* Is 45[9], *equally with* Lv 26[39], *in common with* Je 23[28b] (cf. עִם **1 e, f**). Hence, in partic.—**a.** *with* for the purpose of help: Nu 14[9] וי׳ אִתָּנוּ, Jos 14[12] (אוֹתִי, as Je 20[11]) Ju 1[19] 2 K 6[16] 9[32] מִי אִתִּי מִי who is *on my side*, who?

כי אתך אני Is 43^{5} Je 1$^{18.19}$+, Is 63^{1} ψ 12^{5} our lips are *with us, on our side*, in the phrase נָשָׂא (הָיְתָה) יַד פ׳ את 2 S 14^{19} 2 K 15^{19} Je 26^{24}, נשׂא את to bear *together with*, i.e. to assist Ex 18^{22} Nu 11^{17}. Exceptionally, =*with the help of* Gn 4^{1} for I have gotten a man אֶת־י׳ *with the help of* י׳ (cf. עם 1 S 14^{45}) 49^{25} (where, however, the parallelism, & 𝔊 𝔖 Sam. favour ואל שַׁדַּי for ואת שַׁדַּי) Mi 3^{8}, cf Est 9^{29} **b.** *beside* (Germ *neben*) Gn 39^{6} לֹא יָדַע אתו מאומה he knew not *with* him, *beside* him, aught (i.e Joseph managed everything), v^{8} Ex 20^{23} לֹא תַעֲשׂוּן אִתִּי ye shall not make (aught) *beside* me **c.** *beside*= *in the presence of* (rare) Gn 20^{16b} and *before* all thou shalt be righted, Is 30^{8} Mi 6^{1} In this sense אֶת־פני פ׳ is more freq, v. sub פָּנִים **d.** of intercourse of different kinds *with* another, e.g. after verbs of making a covenant or contract, or (less often) of speaking or dealing: (α) Gn 9^{9} 15^{18} 17^{4} (Ez 16^{60} Is 59^{21} אות-) Jos 10^{4} 1 K 3^{1} etc; cf 1 S 2^{13} (but here הַכֹּהֵן מאת־ is prob to be read with 𝔊 𝔖 𝔗 Kc We etc., cf Dt 18^{3}) (β) Gn 17^{3} 42^{30} דִּבֶּר אִתָּנוּ קָשׁוֹת, 1 K 8^{15} ψ 109^{2}, & esp in Je and Ez (as Je 1^{16} 4^{12} [52^{9} אִתּוֹ] 5^{5} 12^{1}; Ez 2^{1} 3$^{22.24.27}$ 14^{4} 44^{5}—all אות-), Gn 24^{49} to perform kindness את (עם is here more genl), 2 S 16^{17} זֶה חַסְדְּךָ אֶת־רֵעֶךָ, Ru 2^{20} Zc 7^{9}, Ju 11^{27} וְאַתָּה עֹשֶׂה אתי רָעָה, Dt 1^{30} 10^{21} 1 S 12^{7b}, (אות-) Je 21^{2} 33^{9} Ez 7^{27} 16^{59} 22^{14} 23$^{25.29}$ 39^{24}; abs Ez 17^{17} 20^{44} ψ 109^{21} Zp 3^{19}, (γ) in a pregn. sense, (in dealing) *with*, i.e *towards* (rare): Is 66^{14} ψ 67^{2} יָאֵר פָּנָיו אִתָּנוּ make his face to shine *with* (=toward) us (varied from אֶל Nu 6^{25}) Dt 28^{8}, faithful *with* ψ 78^{8} (cf v^{37} נָכוֹן עם), Ez 2^{6} (אוֹתָךְ); Ju 16^{15} ולבך אין אתי (δ) often with verbs of fighting, striving, contending, as Gn 14$^{2.8.9}$ Nu 20^{13} Is 45^{9a} 50^{8} ψ 35^{1} Pr 23^{11}; with בָּא בְמִשְׁפָּט ψ 143^{2} (Is 3^{14} al עם).

2. Of localities, esp. in the phrase אֲשֶׁר את describing a site Ju 3^{19} 4^{11} אֲשֶׁר אֶת־קֶדֶשׁ which is *near* Kedesh, 1 K 9^{26} 2 K 9^{27} (cf עם **2**, which is commoner in this sense); Ez 43^{8}; Ex 33^{21} הנה מָקוֹם אתי Perh, anomalously, 1 S 7^{16} *at* or *by* all those places (but v. Dr), in 2 S 15^{23} עַל־פְּנֵי דֶרֶךְ את־המדבר, את=*towards* is against anal: rd with 𝔊L עַל־פָּנָיו דֶּרֶךְ הַזַּיִת אֲשֶׁר בַּמִּדְבָּר, 1 K 9^{25} אתו *beside* it (sc. the altar), but עָלָיו 13^{1} etc. would be idiomatic, & for אתו אֲשֶׁר Klo proposes plausibly אֶת־אִשּׁוֹ (v. Ex 30^{20})

3. את פ׳ denotes specially, **a.** in one's possession or keeping Gn 27^{15} 30^{29} thou knowest ... את אשר הָיָה מקנך אתי how thy cattle fared *with* me, v^{33} Lv 5^{23} 19^{13} Dt 15^{3} Ju 17^{2} 1 S 9^{7} מָה אִתָּנוּ=what *have we?* 25^{29} Is 49^{4} my right is *with* Jehovah (contr. 40^{27}), Je 8^{8} ψ 38^{11} the light of mine eyes also אין אתי i.e is gone from me, Pr 3^{28} 8^{18}; in his power, Je 10^{5} היטיב אין אוֹתָם is not *in their power*, perh ψ 12^{5}. A dream, or the word of י׳, is said to be את *with* a prophet, 2 K 3^{12} Je 23^{28} 27^{18}. Metaph. of a mental quality, Pr 11^{2} 13^{10}. **b.** in one's knowledge or memory: Is 59^{12} פְּשָׁעֵינוּ אִתָּנוּ our transgressions are *with us*, i.e present to our minds (ועולתינו יְדַעֲנוּם ||), Jb 12^{3} אֶת־מִי־אֵין כמו־אלה *with* whom are not (i e who *knoweth* not? τίς οὐ σύνοιδε;) things like these? 14^{5} אִתָּךְ i e. known to thee, Pr 2^{1} Gn 40^{14} Je 12^{3} (Ew Gf *towards* thee, as **1 d** γ) So אִם־יֵשׁ אֶת־נַפְשְׁכֶם Gn 23^{8} [2 K 9^{15} נ׳ alone], אֶת־לְבָבְךָ 2 K 10^{15} Comp. עם **4 b**, which is more frequent in this sense.

4. מֵאֵת (מֵאִתִּי, etc.; also מֵאוֹת-, v p. 85) *from proximity with* (like Gk. παρά with a genit., Fr *de chez*, in Syr Arab مِنْ عِنْدَ, ܡܢ ܠܘܬ, correspond Synon. מעם; see below) coupled almost always with *persons* (contrast מעם, **a**). Thus **a.** with קָנָה to buy Gn 25^{10}+oft. (cf. 17^{27}); לָקַח Gn 42^{24} Ex 25^{2} Lv 25^{36} Nu 17^{17}+oft., נָשָׂא ψ 24^{5}, שִׁלַּח, as Gn 8^{8} וַיְשַׁלַּח אֶת־הַיּוֹנָה מאתו and he sent forth the dove *from with him* 26^{27}; הָלַךְ Gn 26^{31} 1 K 18^{12} 20^{36} Je 9^{1}, of a wife deserting her husband Ju 19^{2} וַתֵּלֶךְ מאתו, Je 3^{1} (cf. Is 57^{8}); with sim. words Gn 38^{1} Dt 2^{8} 1 K 11^{23} Je 2^{37} (v Ex 5^{20}), Is 54^{10} ψ 66^{20}; with שָׁאַל Ju 1^{14} 1 K 2^{16} ψ 27^{4}+, דָּרַשׁ 1 K 22^{7} al., שָׁמַע 1 S 2^{23}.—מאת פני פ׳ Gn 27^{30} 43^{34} Ex 10^{11} Jb 2^{7}, Lv 10^{4} (הַקֹּדֶשׁ), 2 K 16^{14} (הַבַּיִת). Hence **b.** of rights or dues, handed over *from*, given *on the part of*, any one. Gn 47^{22} חק מאת פַּרְעֹה; oft. in P, as Gn 23^{20} Ex 27^{21} a perpetual due מֵאֵת בני יִשְׂרָאֵל *from*, or *on the part of*, the children of Israel, Lv 7^{34b} 24^{8} Nu 3^{9} 7^{84}+, Dt 18^{3} 1 S 2^{13} (𝔊, etc; v **1 d**) 2 S 15^{3} וְשֹׁמֵעַ אֵין־לְךָ מאת הַמֶּלֶךְ but there is none to hear thee *deputed of* the king, 1 K 5^{14}. **c.** expressing origination: 1 K 1^{27} אם מאת אֲדֹנִי הַמֶּלֶךְ נהיה. Esp. מאת י׳—of a concrete object proceeding *from* him: Gn 19^{24} (brimstone), Nu 11^{31} (a wind), 16^{35} (fire), 1 S 16^{14} (evil spirit), Is 38^{7} (a sign), Je 51^{53} (wasters), Mi 5^{6} (dew); of wrath Zc 7^{12} (cf. Nu 17^{11}), teaching Is 51^{4}, the word of prophecy Je 7^{1} (so 11^{1} 18^{1}+oft in Je) 37^{17} Ez 33^{30}; with 'have I (we) heard' Is 21^{10} 28^{22} Je 49^{14} (=Ob^{1}), of an event, or phase of history Jos 11^{20} מאת י׳ הָיְתָה *it came of* י׳ to ..., 1 K 12^{24} Hb 2^{13} ψ 118^{23} מאת י׳ הָיְתָה זֹּאת (𝔊 παρὰ Κυρίου) Ezr 9^{8} Ne 6^{16}; of trouble (רָעָה) 2 K 6^{33} Mi 1^{12} (יָרַד), of a good or evil lot, having its

source in י׳ Je 13[25] Is 54[17] ψ 109[20], cf Jb 2[10], ψ 22[26] מֵאִתְּךָ תְהִלָּתִי *from thee* cometh my praise (thou art the source of it), Is 44[24] Qr מֵאִתִּי *of myself* (cf. ἀπ' ἐμαυτοῦ John 5[30], Kt is מי אתי who was with me?), 54[15] אֶפֶס מֵאוֹתִי not *at my instance* (cf. לא מִמֶּנִּי 30[1], לא מִמֶּנִּי Ho 8[4]). **d.** of a place † 1 K 6[33] (corrupt: rd. with 𝔊 𝔖 𝔙 [partly] מְזוּזוֹת רְבֻעוֹת, & cf. Ez 41[21]).

Note. את expresses closer association than עם: hence while מֵעִם sts. denotes hardly more than *from the surroundings* or *belongings of*, מאת expresses *from close proximity to* Thus Saul asks, מִי הָלַךְ מֵעִמָּנוּ who has gone *from* (those) *about* us? but Jacob, speaking of the loss of Joseph, says, Gn 44[28] וַיֵּצֵא הָאֶחָד מֵאִתִּי and the one is gone *from with* me מֵאֵת is accordingly preferred to מעם in the sense of origination or authorship; מאת is not usual in the sense of מעם **c**, nor מעם in the sense of מאת **b.**

†אֶתְבַּעַל **n.pr.m.** Ethbaal (*with Baal*, i e. living under B.'s favour; Ἰθόβαλος, Εἰθώβαλος Jos[Ant viii. 13, 1 2 c. Ap. 1, 18], on later king of like name, in As. *Tuba'lu*, v. COT Gn 10[15]) king of Sidon, father of Jezebel 1 K 16[31]

†אִתַּי **n.pr.m.** (perh from את *with* = *companionable*)—**1.** one of David's captains, a native of Gath 2 S 15[19.21 22.22] 18[2.5 12] **2.** one of David's 30 mighty men, a Benjamite 2 S 23[29] (in 1 Ch 11[31] אִיתַי).

†איתיאל **1.** Pr 30[1] נְאֻם הַגֶּבֶר לְאִיתִיאֵל לְאִיתִיאֵל וְאֻכָל׃, in MT. **n.pr m.** (prob *with me is God* · v. Ol[§ 88 c]) usually taken as name of a son or pupil of Agur, but most moderns read לָאִיתִי אֵל לָאִיתִי אֵל וָאֵכֶל׃ *I have wearied myself* (v. לָאָה), *O God, I have wearied myself, O God, and am consumed.* **2.** a Benjamite Ne 11[7].

III. את v אתת.

אַתָּה, אַתְּ, אַתִּי, אַתָּה v. sub אנת

†אָתָה **vb.** come (in Heb. only poet) (Ar أَتَى, Sab. אתו DHM[ZMG 1875, 597, 1883, 343], Aram. אֲתָא, ܐܬܐ)—**Qal** *Pf.* 'א Dt 33[2], אָתָא Is 21[12] v. Ges [§ 75 R. 22]; 1 pl אָתָנוּ Je 3[22], *Impf.* יֶאֱתֶה Jb 37[22] Pr 1[27], וַיֵּתֵא Dt 33[21] (= וַיֶּאֱתֶה cf Di Ko[i 577]), וַיֵּאת Is 41[25], sf. יְאָתָיו וַיֶּאֱתָיֵנִי Jb 3[25], 3 fs תאתה Mi 4[8]; 3 mpl. יֶאֱתָיוּ Jb 16[22] + 2 t; וַיֶּאֱתָיוּן Is 41[5]; *Imv.* mpl. אֵתָיוּ Is 21[12] + 2 t.; *Pt.* fpl. אתיות Is 41[23] + 2 t;—*come*, of men Dt 33[21] ψ 68[32] Is 41[25] 56[12] *Imv.* = *come now*, with hostile purpose Jb 30[14], of men unto י׳ Je 3[22] (sq. לְ) cf. Is 21[12], of י׳ Dt 33[2]; of ends of earth, etc, personif. Is 41[5]; of time, morning Is 21[12], years Jb 16[22]; of weather Jb 37[22], of beasts, to devour Is 56[9] (sq inf.), of calamity Pr 1[27] Jb 3[25] *come upon*, c. sf, of dominion Mi 4[8] (sq. עַד). *Pt.* pl. fem as subst *things to come*, future things Is 41[23] 44[7] 45[11] **Hiph.** *bring*, *Imv* הֵתָיוּ מַיִם Is 21[14] *bring water* (on form, for הֵאתִיוּ cf Di Ew[§ 141 a] Ges[§ 68. 2 R. 1]), Je 12[9] *bring beasts*, to devour

†אִיתוֹן Qr, יאתון Kt, **n.m.** entrance, הָיאתון Ez 40[15]; Co rds אתון; cf Sm Ol[§ 215 d].

אִתַּי, אִתִּי, אִיתִיאֵל v sub II את.

†אֵתָם **n.pr.loc.** (perh = Egypt. *Chetem*, cf. Ebers[GS 521 f] but 𝔊 Ὀθομ, Ὀθωμ, cf. Lag[BN 84]) Ex 13[20] in Egypt, place on edge of desert, so Nu 33[6.7]; מִדְבַּר אֵתָם Nu 33[8].

אַתֶּם v sub אנת.

אתמול v sub תמל

אתן (mng? Thes comps. Ar. أَتَنَ *take short steps*, but this appy only by-form of أَتَلَ)

†אָתוֹן **n.f.** [Gn 45, 23] she-ass (Ar. أَتَانٌ, Aram אֲתָנָא, ܐܬܢܐ, As *atânu*)—אָתוֹן Nu 22[23] + 10 t.; אתנך Nu 22[30.32]; אתנו Gn 49[11] + 2 t.; pl abs. אתנת Gn 12[16] + 2 t, אֲתֹנֹת Ju 5[10] + 12 t., אתונות Jb 1[3] 42[12],—she-ass, as dam Gn 49[11] Zc 9[9], as property (constituting wealth) Gn 12[16] 32[16] Jb 1[3.14] 42[12] cf 1 Ch 27[30], so of the asses of Kish 8 t. 1 S 9[3.3.5.20] 10[2.2 14 16]; as beasts of burden Gn 45[23], for riding Ju 5[10] Nu 22[21 22] 2 K 4[22.24], of Balaam's ass 14 t. Nu 22[21 22.23.23.23.25.27 27 28.29.30.30.32.33].

אֶתְנָה, אַתֵּן v. sub אנת.

אֶתְנָה v. תנה

†אֶתְנִי **n.pr.m.** an ancestor of Asaph 1 Ch 6[26] apparently identical with יְאָתְרַי v[6].

אֶתְנַן v II. תנן.

†[אתוק] **n.m.** gallery, porch (deriv. uncertain) Ez 41[15] Kt ואתוקיהא, Qr וְאַתִּיקֶיהָא, Co (q.v) וקירותיה

†אַתִּיק **n m.** *id* Ez 42[3.3]; pl אַתִּיקִים Ez 42[5], 41[15] Qr, v. אתוק Kt; v[16] הָאַתִּיקִים (Co del.)

†אֲתָרִים **n.pr.loc.** only Nu 21[1] דֶּרֶךְ הָא׳; so 𝔊, perh. (Di) name of a caravan-route, cf. أَثَرٌ *vestige, footprint*, others (after 𝔗 𝔖) transl *way of the spies* (cf. 13[22]); but הָאֲתָרִים for הַתָּרִים is highly improbable, and a locality would hardly receive its designation from the spies.

אתת (? √of following, meaning dubious Lag $^{M\ II.\ 254}$ proposes √אנה, whence he derives also Ar تَانٌ a tool used in tillage)

†III [אֵת] **n.[m.]** a cutting instrument of iron, usually transl **ploughshare**—sg sf. אתו 1 S 13^{20}; pl אתים 1 S 13^{21}, אתים Is 2^{4}=Mi 4^{3}, sf. אתיכם Jo 4^{10}, acc to Klo al also 2 K 6^{5} אֶת־הַבַּרְזֶל, i.e. *the axe of iron*

ב

ב, ב, *Bêth*, 2nd letter, post B Heb = numeral 2 (and so in margin of printed MT), ב = *2000*, no evidence of this usage in OT times.

I **ב, prep.** in (Moab ב, Syr ܒ, Ar. بِ, Eth **በ.**) before tone-syllables in certain cases (Ges $^{§\,102.\,2}$) בָּ, with suff בִּי, בְּךָ (Ex 7^{29} 2 S 22^{30} ψ 141^{8} בכה), in pause and fem בָּךְ; בוֹ (once, Je 17^{24} Kt בה), בָּהּ, בָּנוּ, בָּכֶם, [בָּכֶן], בָּהֶם, בָּם [also בָּהֵמָּה †Ex 30^{4} 36^{1} Hb 1^{16}], בָּהֶן †1 S 31^{7} Is 38^{16} Ez 42^{14} [15 times בָּהֵן (Fr $^{MM\ 235}$), and thrice, Lv 5^{22} Nu 13^{19} Je 5^{17}, בָּהֵנָּה] Prep denoting properly *in*, Gk. *ἐν*, but applied in many derived and fig significations The senses expressed by ב are grouped by the Rabbis in three classes, בית הַכְּלִי *Beth vasculi*, בית הַדִּיבּוּק וְהַנְּגִיעָה *Beth coniunctionis et viciniae*, בית הָעֵזֶר *Beth auxilii;* and the same arrangement may be followed here, though the limits between the three classes are not clearly defined, and they sometimes overlap one another

I. *In* · **1.** strictly, of position *in* a place (which often is expressed more precisely by בקרב, בתוך), as בַּבַּיִת *in* the house, בָּעִיר *in* the city, בַּדּוּד *in* the pot, בָּאָרֶץ *in* the land, etc constantly Heb idiom also says בָּהָר *in* the mountain Ex 24^{18} etc, even in cases where we could hardly avoid saying *on*, as 1 K 11^{7} 19^{11} so בחרב Dt 1^{16} al, בראש הָהָר Ex 24^{17} ψ 72^{16} Preceded by a verb of motion (esp. עָבַר) ב = *through*, as Gn 12^{6} and Abram passed through בָּאָרֶץ *in* the land = passed through it, 13^{17} 2 S 24^{2} +, *in* (= *through*) a gate, Is 62^{10} Je 17^{19} Mi 2^{13}. Fig to speak בְּאָזְנֵי *in* the ears of ; to be good (*or* evil, etc) בְּעֵינֵי *in* the eyes of , **2.** of presence in the midst of a multitude, *among*, Ex 14^{28} there was not left בָּהֶם *among* them even one, Lv 26^{36} 2 S 15^{31} Ahitophel בַּקֹּשְׁרִים is *among* the conspirators, 2 K 18^{5} בכל מַלְכֵי יהודה So בְּךָ *in* thee (of Israel, coll) Dt 7^{14} $15^{4.7}$ 18^{10} 23^{11} 28^{64} (diff. from עִמְּךָ *beside* thee Lv 25^{35}).—Spec. **a.** of an individ, implying eminency among: Jos 14^{15} Je 46^{18} Tabor *among* the mountains, 49^{15} Pr 30^{30} Ct 1^{8} הַיָּפָה בַּנָּשִׁים the fair one (= the fairest) *among* women, La 1^{1} cf Luke 1^{42} On 1 S 17^{12} v Dr **b.** hence with some verbs, when the action refers to only a part of the object, as הִכָּה בְּ to smite *among*... i.e to smite some of... (diff from הִכָּה with accus.); הָרַג בְּ ψ 78^{31}, נָשָׂא בְ to bear *in*, i e. to share in bearing, Nu 11^{17} al, בָּנָה בְּ to build *in* or *at* Zc 6^{15} Ne 4^{4}; עָשָׂה בְ Ex 5^{9}, עָמַל בְּ to labour *on* Jon 4^{10}; אָכַל בְּ, שָׁתָה בְ to eat or drink *of* Ju 13^{16} Pr 9^{5}; חָלַק בְּ to give a share *in* Jb 39^{17}. **c.** specifying the parts of which a whole consists (esp. in P) Gn 7^{21} 8^{17} $9^{10.16}$ 17^{23} Ex 12^{19} Nu $31^{11.28}$ Ho 4^{3}. **3.** with ref to the limits enclosing a space, *within* Ex 20^{10} בשעריך *within* thy gates, Is 56^{5} בחומתי *within* my walls **4.** often pregn with verbs of motion, when the movement *to* a place results in rest *in* it, *into* · after בּוֹא Gn 19^{8} Is 19^{23}, נָתַן Gn 27^{17}; שָׁלַח *to send* Lv 16^{22}; *in among* Jos $23^{7.12}$ 1 K 11^{2}.—Ho 12^{7} (an extreme case) שוּב בְּ to return (and rest) *in* thy God, 1 S 16^{3} (unless לַזֶּבַח should be read, as v^{7}) — עַיִן בְּעַיִן (with) eye (looking) *into* eye †Nu 14^{14} Is 52^{8}; פָּנִים בְּפָנִים †Dt 5^{4}; עיני פ׳ ב the eyes of... are *upon*, both in favourable (Dt 11^{12} ψ 101^{6}) and hostile (Am 9^{8} Jb 7^{8}) sense **5.** applied to *time*, as Gn 1^{1} בראשית *in* the beginning, 2^{2} בַּיּוֹם הַשְּׁבִיעִי *on* the seventh day, Ju 10^{8} בַּשָּׁנָה הַהִיא *in* that year; & constantly. **6.** of a state or condition, whether material or mental, *in* which an action takes place: so oft, בשלום *in* peace Gn 15^{15}, בַּצָּרָה *in* distress ψ 91^{15}; הָלַךְ בְּתֻמּוֹ to walk *in* his integrity; Ex 5^{19} בְּרָע *in* evil case **7.** ב introduces the *predicate*, denoting it as that *in* which the subj. consists, or *in* which it shews itself (the *Beth essentiae*,—common in Arabic, esp. with a ptcp or adj and in a negative sentence: Qor 2^{79} وَمَا ٱللّٰهُ بِغَافِلٍ and God (appears) not *as* one remiss, 2^{7} وَمَا هُمْ بِمُؤْمِنِينَ and they are not believers [comp. French *en—en honnête homme*], v. W $^{AG\ II\ §56\ a}$): viz. **a.** a primary pred, Ex 18^{4} the God of my fathers בְּעֶזְרִי was my help, ψ 146^{5} Ho 13^{9} (rd כִּי מִי בְעֶזְרֶךָ: with 𝔊 𝔖 Che al.); ψ 68^{5} בְּיָהּ שְׁמוֹ his name consists in Yah, Jb 23^{13} 37^{10} With the pred in the pl (as *pl. maj.*) ψ 118^{7} י׳ בְּעֹזְרָי J is my

great helper, 54^{6} (v. Che), Ju 11^{35}. **b.** a secondary pred., Ex 6^{3} and I appeared unto them באל שדי *as* God Almighty, Nu 26^{53} בנחלה *as* an inheritance, 34^{2} Ez 46^{16} 47^{14} Dt 10^{22} 26^{14} I have not put away therefrom בטמא *as* one unclean = while unclean, 28^{62} Is 40^{10} בחזק יבוא he cometh *as* a strong one, ψ 35^{2} (where v. De) and rise up *as* my help, v^{16}, 39^{7} 55^{19} Pr 3^{26} Jb 36^{32}(De). **c.** a pred. as accus., Is 48^{10} I have refined thee ולא בכסף but not *as though* silver, Ez 20^{41}; Nu 18^{26} 36^{2} Jos $13^{6.7}$ 23^{4} Ez 45^{1} $47^{22.23}$ (rd. יפלו) 48^{29} (v. 𝔊 Co) all בנחלה (cf. **b**), ψ 78^{55} & allotted it בחבל נחלה *as* a line of inheritance (i.e. as a measured inheritance). Is 26^{4} כי ביה יהוה צור עולמים י׳ is different—for *in* Yah there is a rock of ages (cf. Qor $4^{7.47}$ there is sufficiency *in* God as a patron). **d.** in comparisons, ψ 37^{20} consume away בעשן *in the form of, as,* smoke 78^{33} 102^{4} Jb 34^{36} 36^{14}.

II. Denoting proximity—**1.** *at, by* (not very common): 1 S 29^{1} בעין *by* the spring; Ez $10^{15.20}$ בנהר כבר *by* the river Chebar (1^{3} על). **2.** *on:* Gn 8^{20} Nu 23^{2} במזבח *on* the altar; Ju 8^{21} *on* the necks of the camels; 1 K 2^{5} al. במתניו *on* his loins; Is 59^{17} a helmet בראשו *on* his head. **3.** often with verbs of *touching, approaching, taking hold of, cleaving,* etc., as תפש, תמך, פגע, קרב, נגש, נגע, חשק, דבק, אחז (see these words). **4.** with words expressing or implying an act of hostility—**a.** *against:* Gn 16^{12} ידו בכל ויד כל בו his hand *against* all, and the hand of all *against* him; היתה יד פ׳ ב Dt 13^{10} 1 S 5^{9} 18^{17} + oft. Hence after verbs (q.v.) of *fighting* (ריב, נלחם), *going up* to invade (עלה), *being angry* (חרה אף, אנף, התעבר), *sinning* or *acting treacherously* (מרד, בגד, חטא), (כחש, כזב, שקר, פשע, מעל, מרה), *testifying* (ענה, העיד), *mocking* (התל, הליץ), *feeling loathing* (קוץ), *rebuking* (גער: prop. to protest loudly), *speaking* (דבר: Nu 12^{8b}), etc., & even (an extreme case) Ho 7^{14} יסורו בי they turn aside (so as to be) *against* me. In a weaker sense משתין בקיר mingens *ad* parietem 1 S 25^{22} al. **b.** *down to, upon* (*super* with accus.), esp. in such phrases as דמיו בו Lv 20^{9} al. his blood be *upon* him; דמו בראשו his blood be *upon* his head Jos 2^{19}; שוב (השיב י׳) בראשו Ju 8^{57} (רעה), 1 K 2^{33} (דם), v^{44} (רעה), ψ 7^{17} (עמלו); נתן דרך פ׳ בראשו 1 K 8^{32} & oft. in Ez, as 9^{10} 11^{21}.

III. 1. *With*—**a.** of accompaniment: Nu 20^{20} בעם כבד *with* much people, Jos 22^{8} Ju 11^{34} 1 K 10^{2} 2 K 5^{9} Je 41^{15}; Ex 21^{22} and he shall give בפללים *with arbitrators* (arbitrators being employed), Is 8^{16} בלמדי: *with* my disciples, i.e. having them present; Ex $8^{1.13}$ Je 11^{19} עץ בלחמו a tree *with* its sap; 1 K 19^{19} והוא בשנים העשר and he *with* the 12th. **b.** often of what one takes or brings with one: Gn 32^{11} במקלי *with* my staff I passed over Jordan, Ju 11^{34} 15^{1} 1 S 1^{24} Is 7^{24}; Mi 6^{6} al. קדם ב׳ to go to meet *with;* בא ב׳ to come *with* Lv 16^{3} ψ 66^{13} 71^{16}. (In Arabic this usage is developed more fully than in Hebrew, and أتى ب lit. *to come with,* ذهب ب lit. *to go away with,* are used idiomatically in the sense of *to bring,* and *to take away* respectively: W$^{AG\ II.\ §56b}$.) Hence באין, בלא, בבלי, באפס = *without.* **c.** of concomitant (or surrounding) conditions, as בחפזון *with* (or *in*) haste; בצדק *with* (or *in*) righteousness; בשגגה *in* error; בתרועה ובקול שופר 2 S 6^{15}; often in such phrases as בצדקתך ψ 31^{2} *in* thy righteousness; בחסדך *in* thy mercy Ex 15^{13};—באשרי *with* my happiness! = happy am I Gn 30^{13}; ψ 29^{4} the voice of י׳ is בכח *with* power = is powerful; Ex 32^{12} ברעה *with* evil purpose; ψ 73^{8} ברע *in* wickedness; 90^{10} בגבורת *with* strength. **2.** of the instrument or means: as **a.** בחרב *with* the sword Ex 5^{3} etc.; ברגלים *with* the feet Is 28^{3}; . . . ביד *by* the hand of . . . (v. sub יד); to stone באבן or באבנים *with* stones Lv 20^{2} Nu 14^{10} etc.; שתה ב׳ to drink *with* a cup Gn 44^{5} Am 6^{6} (cf. in Aram. Dn 5^{2}); to cry בגרון *with* the throat Is 58^{1}; to burn באש *in* or *with* fire (oft.); to slay or to perish ברעב *through* hunger or בדבר *through* pestilence Ex 16^{3} Je 21^{9} + oft. (cf. Jb 27^{15} במות יקברו); to save *with* or *by* Ju 7^{7} 1 S 14^{6}. **b.** idiom., with certain verbs, as שחק ב׳ to play *with* Jb 40^{29}; עבד ב׳ to labour *with* a person (as with an instrument), i.e. to use him as a slave Ex 1^{14} Je 22^{13} 27^{7} al.; עשה ב׳ Je 18^{23} Ne 9^{24} Dn 11^{7} Est 1^{15} 2^{11} 3^{11} 6^{6}; & perh. דבר ב׳ (of God) to speak *with* one Nu $12^{2.8a}$ al. (v. Ew$^{§217\ f.\ (3)}$; Dr$^{Sm\ II.\ 23.2}$). Further התנבא ביהוה, בבעל to prophesy *with* or *by* י׳ or Baal, י׳ or Baal being the inspirer; דרש, שאל ב׳ to inquire or ask *by means of* a god (or oracle). **c.** ביהוה *through* י׳ (= by His aid) in many connexions, as ψ 18^{30} 44^{6} $56^{5.11}$ 60^{14} Is 26^{13} 45^{25} Ho 1^{7} Zc 10^{12}; with pass. verbs Dt 33^{29} Is 45^{17} (to be saved): and even of the immediate cause Nu 36^{2} to be commanded ביהוה *by* י׳, Gn 9^{6} באדם *by* man shall his blood be shed (both unusual), Ho 14^{4}. **d.** allied is the use of ב׳ in such phrases as

to bless, swear, speak, prophesy, etc., בְּשֵׁם *in* the name of ... (i.e. the name being used or appealed to in the act) Dt 6^{13} Je 11^{21}, etc. (so to swear ביהוה *by* ׳י Jos 2^{12} etc., בִּימִינוֹ Is 62^{8}; to bless בְּךָ *with thee* Gn 48^{20}, to swear *with me* ψ 102^{9}, i.e. using my name in oath, Je 29^{22}); almost = in the authority and power of 1 S 17^{45} 25^{5} 1 K 21^{8} Mi 4^{5} Zc 10^{12} ψ 20^{6} 44^{6} 89^{25}. **e.** בַּמֶּה or בַּמָּה *by means of what? how?* Gn 15^{8} Ju 6^{15} $16^{5.6.10}$ 1 K 22^{21} Mal 2^{17}. בְּזֹאת *by means of this* Gn $42^{15.33}$ Ex 7^{17} Nu 16^{28}; *with this* = *on this condition* Gn $34^{15.22}$ 1 S 11^{2} Is 27^{9}. **3.** of cost or price (the *Beth pretii*), the price, whether given or received, being treated as the instrumental means by which the act is accomplished, *with, for, at the cost of:* thus regularly **a.** with שָׂכַר *hire* Gn 30^{16}, פָּדָה *redeem* Ex 34^{20}, אֵרַשׂ *betroth* 2 S 3^{14}, קָנָה *buy* 2 S 24^{24}; 1 K 2^{23} בְּנַפְשׁוֹ *at the cost of* his life hath A. spoken this word, 2 S 23^{17} who went בְּנַפְשׁוֹתָם *at peril of* their lives, Pr 7^{23} La 5^{9} Jos 6^{26} בִּבְכֹרוֹ יְיַסְּדֶנָּה *at the price of* his firstborn shall he lay its foundations, 1 Ch 12^{19} בְּרָאשֵׁינוּ *to the jeopardy of* our heads he will fall away, etc. **b.** with מָכַר *sell* Dt 21^{14}; עָבַד *serve* Gn $29^{18.20}$ Ho 12^{13}; הֵמִיר *exchange* Lv 27^{10} Ho 4^{7} their glory I will exchange *for* ignominy, ψ 106^{20}; נָתַן בְּנֶשֶׁךְ to give *for* interest Lv 25^{37} ψ 15^{5}; in other connexions Gn 23^{9} $47^{16f.}$ Is 45^{13} La 1^{11} Ct $8^{7.11}$; Dt 19^{21} נֶפֶשׁ בְּנֶפֶשׁ עַיִן בְּעַיִן life *for* life, eye *for* eye; Is 2^{22} בַּמֶּה נֶחְשָׁב הוּא *at what* is he to be accounted? 7^{23} a thousand vines בְּאֶלֶף כָּסֶף *at* a thousand (shekels of) silver.—Hence (perhaps) the idiom. usages שָׁנָה בְשָׁנָה year *for* year, one year like another, annually Dt 15^{20} al.; יוֹם בְּיוֹם (late), כְּיוֹם בְּיוֹם + 1 S 18^{10}; כְּפַעַם בְּפַעַם (v. פַּעַם, יוֹם); חֹדֶשׁ בְּחֹדֶשׁ + 1 Ch 27^{1}. **4.** rather peculiarly, in certain cases where the object of an action may be treated as the *instrument* by which it is accomplished: as הֵנִיעַ בְּרֹאשׁ to shake *with* the head Je 18^{6} Jb 16^{4} (as well as הֵנִיעַ רֹאשׁ ψ 22^{8}); to open *with* the mouth Jb 16^{10}, *with* the lips ψ 22^{8}; to gnash *with* the teeth Jb 16^{9} (to gnash the teeth ψ 35^{16}); to wink *with* the eye Pr 6^{13} (to wink the eye, *ib.* 10^{10}); נָתַן בְּקוֹל to utter *with* the voice ψ 46^{7} 68^{34} Je 12^{8} (but נָתַן קוֹל is more common); to stretch out *with* the hand La 1^{17}; הֵרִים בַּמַּטֶּה (unusual) Ex 7^{20}. So קָרָא בְּשֵׁם to call *with* the name—in diff. senses, acc. to the context, viz. to *proclaim* Ex 33^{19} 34^{5} Is 44^{5} ψ 49^{12}; to *invoke* Gn 4^{26} 12^{8} 1 K 18^{24-26} Is 12^{4}; to *name honourably* Is 43^{1} 45^{3}. Cf. Ew § 282 d Ges § 119. 3 b R. WAG II. § 56 b β De Jb 31. 12; Pr 20. 30. **5.** with a causal force, *through, on account of:* Gn 18^{28} הֲתַשְׁחִית בַּחֲמִשָּׁה wilt thou destroy *on account of* five the whole city? Lv 26^{39} Nu 16^{26} Dt $9^{4.5}$ 24^{16} אִישׁ בְּחֶטְאוֹ יוּמָתוּ׃ they shall be put to death, each *because of* his own sin (cf. Je 31^{30} Ez 3^{18}, v. 18^{17}) 2 S 3^{27} 14^{7} (cf. Jon 1^{14}) Is 7^{4} (‖ מִן) 28^{7} (‖ מִן) 50^{1} 53^{5} 57^{17} Je 51^{46} ψ $5^{8.11}$ 6^{8} (‖ מִן) 31^{10} 32^{3} 42^{10} 90^{9} 94^{23}. So in בִּגְלַל, בַּאֲשֶׁר (v. גָּלָל, אֲשֶׁר), & (sts.) in בִּדְבַר *at, through,* the word of.... **6.** of the material *with* which a work is wrought, both absol. עָשָׂה בַּזָּהָב to work *with* gold Ex 31^{4} 1 K 7^{14}; and to make a thing *with* (in our idiom, *of*) gold Ex 38^{8} Ez 7^{20} 1 K 15^{22} (בָּנָה). Without a verb Lv 13^{52} 2 Ch 9^{18}. **7.** *with* for *although, in spite of* (cf. Germ. *bei* alle dem): Lv 26^{27} Nu 14^{11} בְּכֹל הָאֹתוֹת *in spite of* all the signs that I have wrought, Dt 1^{32} Is 47^{9} ψ 27^{3}; esp. in the phrase בְּכָל־זֹאת *for* all this Is 5^{25} $9^{11.16.20}$ 10^{4} ψ 78^{32} al. (Cf. in Ar. بِمَا Qor 9^{25}.) **8.** of a standard of measurement or computation, *with, by:* Ex 12^{4} בְּמִכְסַת נְפָשֹׁת *by* the computation of souls; Lv 5^{25} al. בְּעֶרְכְּךָ *by* thy reckoning; Ez 4^{10}; בְּמִסְפָּר *by* number Dt 25^{2}+; ... בְּמִסְפַּר *by* the number of ... Lv $25^{15.50}$ Nu 1^{2}, etc.; בְּשֶׁקֶל הַקֹּדֶשׁ Ex 30^{13} al. (in P); בָּאַמָּה often (v. אַמָּה); Dt 3^{11} בְּאַמַּת אִישׁ *by* the cubit of a man; 2 S 14^{26} בְּאֶבֶן הַמֶּלֶךְ. Of a model, Gn 1^{26} בְּצַלְמֵנוּ *in* our image, $5^{1.3}$ Ex 25^{40}; בְּדַרְכְּךָ *with* the way (= in the manner) of ... Is $10^{24.26}$ Am 4^{10}.

IV. בְּ is used also with certain classes of verbs, though the explanation of its use may be sometimes doubtful: viz. **a.** with verbs of *taking refuge, trusting, relying,* as בָּטַח, הֶאֱמִין, נִשְׁעַן, חָסָה. **b.** with verbs of *ruling, governing, restraining,* as מָלַךְ, מָשַׁל, נָגַשׂ, עָצַר, רָדָה, שָׁלַט. **c.** with verbs of *rejoicing, feeling pleasure* or *satisfaction,* etc., as גִּיל, עָלַץ, שׂוּשׂ, שָׂמַח, חָפֵץ, רָצָה, שָׂבַע (but with this verb מִן is more common). [Prob. a case of **III. 5.**] **d.** with verbs expressive of sensible perception, to denote the pleasurable or attentive exercise of the faculty concerned, as שָׁמַע בְּ to listen *to*, הִבִּיט, רָאָה, חָזָה בְּ, to look *upon*, הֵרִיחַ בְּ to smell *at* (see these words). **e.** occasionally also with verbs of *speaking, thinking, mentioning, knowing,* to denote the object of the action, as דִּבֶּר בְּ to speak *about* Dt 6^{7} ψ 87^{3} al. (v. sub דִּבֶּר); הִלֵּל בְּ, הָגָה, שִׂיחַ ψ 44^{9} 63^{7} 69^{13}; יָדַע Je 38^{24}; זָכַר once Je 3^{16}, הִזְכִּיר oft.; ψ 71^{6} בְּךָ תְהִלָּתִי *of* thee is my praise.

V. Followed by an inf. c., בְּ forms a periphrasis for the gerund, though in English it is commonly to be rendered by a verb and

conj., viz.:—**1.** as a *temporal* conj., as Gn 2^{4} בְּהִבָּֽרְאָם *in* their *being created=when* they *were* created, 4^{8} בִּהְיוֹתָם *in* their *being* (=*when* they *were*) in the field; and constantly. Sometimes it has in appearance the force of *after that*, as Gn 33^{18} Ex 3^{12} 13^{17}; but as a rule this is really due to the action denoted by the inf. being treated as extending over a period *within* which the action of the principal verb takes place: so esp. in the phrase בְּצֵאת יִשְׂרָאֵל מִמִּצְרַיִם, even of events at the close of the 40 years, Dt 4^{45} 23^{5} Jos 5^{4}, the whole period being treated as that in which Egypt was left (comp. 2 K 2^{1}, where the time included is future). Cases, however, occur in which this explanation will hardly apply, as Dt 27$^{4.12}$. **2.** as a *causal* conj. (cf. above **III. 5**), as Gn 19^{16} בְּחֶמְלַת י׳ עָלָיו *through* J.'s having compassion upon him, Ex 16^{7} 33^{16} 34^{29} Dt 1^{27} בְּשִׂנְאַת י׳ אֹתָנוּ *through* J.'s hating us, etc. (9^{28} similarly מִן), 1 K 18^{18} (=*in that* ye have ...) Ez 9^{8} 43^{8} 44^{7} 2 Ch 28^{6}. **3.** as a *concessive* conj., *when=though:* Is 1^{15} ψ 46^{3} בְּהָמִיר אָרֶץ *though* the earth do change.

Note.—Ex 10^{12} בָּאַרְבֶּה can only be rendered '*with* the locusts,' the locusts being conceived as implicit in Moses' uplifted hand: but prob. לָאַרְבֶּה should be read. Thrice in late Heb. בְּ is used peculiarly: 1 Ch 7^{23} for *with* misfortune was it in his house (בְּרָעָה chosen for the purpose of explaining בְּרִיעָה); 9^{33} עֲלֵיהֶם בַּמְּלָאכָה it devolved upon them *with* the work; Ezr 3^{3} for *with* terror (was it) upon them from the peoples of the countries (the sentence without a verb as oft. in Chr.: Dr $^{\text{Intr. 504 f.}}$): cf. 8^{34}. Comp. Ew$^{\S 295 f.}$

†**בְּמוֹ** poet. for בְּ (v. sub מוֹ: cf. Sab. בם, DHM$^{\text{ZMG 1883, 344}}$) Is 25^{10} Qr (<Kt בְּמֵי) 43^{2} 44$^{16.19}$ ψ 11^{2} Jb 9^{30} Kt (>Qr בְּמֵי) 16$^{4.5}$ 19^{16} 37^{8}.

II. **בְּ**, perh. abbrev. in **n.pr.** for בֵּית, בֶּן־ q.v.

בָּאָה v. sub בּוֹא.

†[**בָּאַר**] **vb.** only **Pi. make distinct, plain** (so NH, Aram.; Lag$^{\text{BN 88}}$ prop. for Qal בָּאַר, בְּאֵר, cf. deriv. infr.; Thes & most comp. Ar. بَأَرَ *dig a pit* or *well*, but this prob. denom. v. Lag$^{\text{l.c.}}$)—**Pi.** *Pf.* 3 ms. בֵּאֵר Dt 1^{5}, *Imv.* בָּאֵר Hb 2^{2}; *Inf. abs.* בַּאֵר Dt 27^{8} (cf. Bö$^{\S 393, 4}$)—*make distinct, plain,* of letters on tablets Hb 2^{2} כְּתֹב חָזוֹן וּבָאֵר עַל־הַלֻּחוֹת לְמַעַן יָרוּץ קוֹרֵא בוֹ, i.e. so that one may run past and (still) read; or, so that one may read swiftly; on stones Dt 27^{8} וְכָתַבְתָּ עַל־הָאֲבָנִים .... בַּאֵר הֵיטֵב *and thou shalt write upon the* [whitewashed] *stones* all the words of this law, *doing it plainly and well;* fig. *explain, expound* Dt 1^{5} הוֹאִיל מֹשֶׁה בֵּאֵר הַתּוֹרָה *Moses began* (and) *expounded the law.*

†**בְּאֵר** **n.f.** $^{\text{Gn 26, 21}}$ **well, pit,** mostly Hex, Gn 23 t. Ex 1 t. Nu 5 t., 37 t. in all; Ar. بِئْرٌ, Aram. בְּאֵרָא, בֵּירָא, בֵּיר, ܒܺܐܪܳܐ, Sab. באר DHM$^{\text{ZMG. 1875, 608}}$, As. *bêru*, Lyon$^{\text{Sargon 61}}$ (connexion with above √ not clear; Lag$^{\text{l.c.}}$ *spring* of water, as *coming to light, appearing;* possible, although meaning in use rather *well*, than *spring;* v. however, Gn 16^{14} cf. v^{7} 26^{19} Nu 21^{17})—בּ׳ abs. Gn 21^{30}+; cstr. 21^{19}+; sf. בְּאֵרֶךָ Pr 5^{15}; Pl. abs. בְּאֵרֹת Gn 26^{15}; cstr. id. 26^{18}; cf. בֶּאֱרֹת בֶּאֱרֹת חֵמָר Gn 14^{10};—**1.** *a well*, often as made by digging (חָפַר) Gn 21$^{25.30}$ (E), 26$^{15.18.19.21.22.32}$ (all J), also poet. Nu 21^{18} (+ כרה) vid. also v$^{16.17}$ (where the well addressed, in song, עֲלִי בְאֵר); also c. כרה in prose Gn 26^{25}; also with no ref. to its origin Gn 16^{14} (J; ‖ עַיִן v^{7}), 29^{2} Ex 2^{15} (J) Nu 20^{17} 21^{22} (E) 2 S 17$^{18.21}$; בְּאֵר (ה)מַּיִם Gn 21^{19} (E) 24^{11} (J; ‖ עַיִן vv$^{13.16.43.45}$); (cf. also 21^{25} 26^{18} supr. & esp. v^{19} בְּאֵר מַיִם חַיִּים); water taken from it by drawing (שָׁאַב) Gn 24$^{11.20}$; flocks watered from it (הִשְׁקָה) 29$^{2.3.8.10}$ (cf. esp. Ex 2^{16} *they drew,* דלה, and filled the troughs); also שְׁתֵה מַיִם....מִתּוֹךְ בְּאֵרֶךָ Pr 5^{15} (‖ בּוֹר); the opening called פִּי הַבְּאֵר Gn 29$^{2.3.3.8.10}$; cf. פְּנֵי הַבּ׳ 2 S 17^{19} (rd. prob. פִּי so Sam. 𝔗 𝔖 𝔙, cf. Dr); fig. of fresh delights of woman beloved Ct 4^{15} מַעְיַן גַּנִּים בְּאֵר מַיִם חַיִּים וְנֹזְלִים מִן־לְבָנוֹן. **2.** *pit* (=בּוֹר); *pits of bitumen* Gn 14^{10} (cf. supr.); ψ 55^{24} בְּאֵר שַׁחַת *pit of* (*the*) *grave;* cf. 69^{16} וְאַל־תֶּאְטַר עָלַי בְּאֵר פִּיהָ *and let not* (*the*) *pit shut its mouth over me* (‖מְצוּלָה); fig. of strange woman בְּאֵר צָרָה *a narrow pit,* out of which rescue is difficult Pr 23^{27} (‖ שׁוּחָה עֲמֻקָּה). **3.** as **n.pr.loc.** **a.** c. ה ָ loc. בְּאֵרָה a station of Isr. in desert Nu 21^{16}, possibly= בְּאֵר אֵילִים Is 15^{8}. **b.** same form Ju 9^{21}, acc. to Euseb. Lag$^{\text{Onom. 238, 2nd ed. 250}}$ 8 miles north of Eleutheropolis; cf. Rob$^{\text{BR I. 452}}$ who comp. *el-Bîreh*, near Beth-shemesh.

בְּאֵר אֵילִים v. בְּאֵר **3. a.**

†**בְּאֵר לַחַי רֹאִי** **n.pr.loc.** (lit. *well* of the *living One that seeth me*) Gn 16^{14} (where explan., from story of Hagar) 24^{62} 25^{11} (all J); perh. name of ancient shrine or holy place, cf. Sta$^{\text{ZAW ii. 347}}$ & Di Gn 16^{14}; W. of Kadesh, cf. Jer sub Barad, Lag$^{\text{Onom. 101, 2nd ed. 135}}$, v. Rowlands in Williams$^{\text{Holy City, 489}}$ Trumbull$^{\text{Kadesh-Barnea 64}}$.

†בְּאֵר שֶׁבַע **n.pr.loc.** **Beersheba** (*well of seven*, explained Gn 21$^{30.31}$ as place of *swearing by seven* lambs, or, *well of oath*, v. שְׁבֻעָה; cf. same meaning otherwise derived 26^{33})—בְּאֵר שֶׁבַע Gn 26^{33} + 13 t., בְּאֵר־שֶׁבַע, Jos 19^{2}; בְּאֵר שָׁבַע Gn 21^{14} + 18 t.; בְּאֵרָה שֶׁבַע (ה‍ָ— loc.) Gn 46^{1}—south from Hebron, acc. to Onom. c. 20 miles Lag$^{Onom. 103, 234, 2nd\ ed. 138, 248}$; mod. *Bîr-es-Seba*, 12 h. fr. Hebron Rob$^{BR\ i.\ 204\ f.}$ Survey$^{iii.\ 394}$ Gn 21$^{14.31.32.33}$ 22$^{19.19}$ 26$^{23.33}$ 28^{10} 46$^{1.5}$ Jos 15^{28} 19^{2} Ju 20^{1} 1 S 3^{20} 8^{2} 2 S 17^{11} 24^{7} 1 K 19^{3} 2 K 12^{2} 23^{8} Am 5^{5} 1 Ch 4^{28} 2 Ch 19^{4} 24^{1} Ne 11$^{27.30}$; in phrase מִדָּן וְעַד־ב׳ *from Dan to Beersheba* (i.e. all the territory of Israel, v. דָּן) Am 8^{14} Ju 20^{1} 1 S 3^{20} 2 S 3^{10} 17^{11} 24$^{2.15}$ 1 K 5^{5}, & (only Ch) מִבְּאֵר שֶׁבַע וְעַד־דָּן *from Beersheba to Dan* 1 Ch 21^{2} 2 Ch 30^{5}.

†בְּאֵרָא **n.pr.m.** a man of Asher 1 Ch 7^{37}.

†בְּאֵרָה **n.pr.m.** a Reubenite 1 Ch 5^{6}.

†בְּאֵרוֹת **n.pr.loc.** (but only 2 S 4^{2} acc. to Masorah, v. BD$^{Ezr\ 2,\ 25}$ elsewh. בְּאֵרֹת), city of the Gibeonites Jos 9^{17}; assigned to Benjamin 2 S 4^{2} Jos 18^{25}; cf. also Ezr 2^{25} Ne 7^{29}; mod. *el-Bîreh* Rob$^{BR\ i.\ 452}$ Bd$^{Pal\ 214}$ Survey$^{iii.\ 88}$.

†בְּאֵרֹתִי **adj.gent.** always c. art. 2 S 4$^{2.5.9}$, 23^{37} = הַבֵּרֹתִי 1 Ch 11^{39}; pl. הַבְּאֵרֹתִים 2 S 4^{3}.

†בְּאֵרֹת בְּנֵי־יַעֲקָן **n.pr.loc.** Dt 10^{6} (cf. Nu 33$^{31.32}$, where בני יעקן), a station of Isr. in desert, prob. in country of Horites, cf. Di.

†בְּאֵרִי **n.pr.m.** (*my well*). **1.** a Hittite, Esau's father-in-law Gn 26^{34}. **2.** Hosea's father Ho 1^{1}.

†[באר] **n.m.** $^{Je\ 2,\ 13}$ **cistern, pit, well** (for בְּאֵר cf. בּוֹר)—sg. Kt באר 2 S 23$^{15.16.20}$ (Qr בֹּר); appar. *well* v$^{15.16}$ (rd. perh. בְּאֵר), *pit* v^{20}; pl. Je 2^{13} *me they have forsaken, the fountain of living water,* לַחְצֹב לָהֶם בֹּארוֹת בֹּארֹת נִשְׁבָּרִים, *to hew out for themselves cisterns, broken cisterns*, etc.

†בּוֹר **n.m.** $^{Gn\ 37,\ 20}$ **pit, cistern, well** (= בְּאֵר, MI בר, Ar. نُورَة *hole* or *hollow* for cooking, As. *bûrtum* Dl$^{Pr\ 182}$, *bûru* Lotz$^{TP\ 169}$)—ב׳ abs. Gn 37^{22} +; בֹּר Ex 21^{33} (2 S 23^{20} Qr, v. באר supr.); cstr. בּוֹר 2 K 10^{14} + (2 S 23$^{15.16}$ Qr, v. באר supr.); בֹּרָה (ה‍ָ— loc.) Gn 37^{24}; sf. בּוֹרוֹ Is 36^{16} = בֹּרוֹ 2 K 18^{31}; בּוֹרֶךָ Pr 5^{15}; pl. בֹּרוֹת Gn 37^{20} + 3 t.; בֹּרֹת Dt 6^{11}:—**1.** *cistern*, containing water, made by digging (חצב) Dt 6^{11} 2 Ch 26^{10} Ne 9^{25}; also (without ref. to origin) Pr 5^{15} (‖ בְּאֵר) Lv 11^{36} (‖ מַעְיָן), 1 S 19^{22} Is 36^{16} = 2 K 18^{31}. **2.** later appar. *well* (= בְּאֵר) 1 Ch 11$^{17.18}$ = Qr 2 S 23$^{15.16}$ (yet now no well at Bethlehem Rob$^{BR\ i.\ 470,\ 473}$ cf. also Survey$^{iii.\ 28}$ Guérin$^{Judée\ i.\ 130}$), cf. Ec 12^{6} & Je 6^{7} Kt כְּהָקִיר בּוֹר מֵימֶיהָ *as a well casteth out its water* (Qr בַּיִר); but הקיר perh. *keep cool, fresh* 𝔊 𝔙 Hi Gf. **3.** *pit* Ex 21^{33} (vb. פתח), v^{33} (כרה), cf. v^{34}; cf. fig. ψ 7^{16} of wickedness (‖ שַׁחַת; vb. חפר, כרה); 1 S 13^{6} as hiding-place; 2 S 23^{20} (Qr) = 1 Ch 11^{22} 2 K 10^{14} בּוֹר בֵּית עֵקֶד; of pit into wh. Joseph was cast Gn 37$^{20.22.24}$ (וְהַבּוֹר רֵק אֵין בּוֹ מָיִם) v$^{28.29.29}$ (JE), cf. further Je 41$^{7.9}$; fig. of Sarah as mother of Israel מַקֶּבֶת ב׳ Is 51^{1}; fig. of calamity ψ 40^{3} בּוֹר שָׁאוֹן; cf. ψ 88^{7} ב׳ תַּחְתִּיּוֹת. **4.** *dungeon* (pit with no water in it Je 38^{6} Zc 9^{11} cf. Gn 37^{24} supr.) Gn 40^{15} 41^{14} (E). Is 24^{22} Je 38$^{6.6}$ (ב׳ אֵין מַיִם) v$^{7.9.10.11.13}$; also בֵּית הַבּוֹר *prison* Ex 12^{29} Je 37^{16}; fig. of exile Zc 9^{11} (מִבּוֹר אֵין מַיִם בּוֹ); cf. also La 3$^{53.55}$. **5.** (poet. & late; never c. art.) *pit of the grave* Pr 28^{17}; so אַבְנֵי ב׳ *stones of the pit* Is 14^{19} (of sepulchre, walled with stones) & of Sh^{e}ʾôl ψ 30^{4} (‖ שאול); יַרְכְּתֵי ב׳ *loins of (the) pit*, i.e. remotest pit Is 14^{15} (‖ שאול) Ez 32^{23} esp. in phrase יוֹרְדֵי בוֹר *those going down to (the) pit* ψ 28^{1} 143^{7} Is 38^{18} Ez 26^{20} 32$^{25.29.30}$; also, (‖ שאול), ψ 88^{5} Pr 1^{12}; further Ez 26^{20} 32$^{18.24}$ (all ‖ אֶרֶץ תַּחְתִּיּוֹת), 31$^{14.16}$ (both ‖ אֶרֶץ תַּחְתִּית; v^{14} ‖ also מָוֶת, v^{16} שְׁאוֹל).

†בּוֹר הַסִּרָה **n.pr.loc.** 2 S 3^{26} (*cistern of Sirah*, Thes *cist. declinationis*, MV *of the pot*, v. סיר).

†בּוֹר עָשָׁן (so rd. for ordinary כּוּר ע׳, v. BD$^{Gn,\ p.\ vi.}$ 𝔊 𝔖) **n.pr.loc.** 1 S 30^{30} (*smoking pit*), in S.W. of Judah; elsewhere עָשָׁן q. v.

בַּיִר Qr Je 6^{7} v. בּוֹר.

†בֵּרִי **n.pr.m.** a descendant of Asher 1 Ch 7^{36} (perh. = בְּאֵרִי).

†בֵּרוֹתָה **n.pr.loc.** near Hamath Ez 47^{16} (contr. fr. בְּאֵרוֹתָה?), cf. foll.;—hardly = Berytus (Beirût) with wh. form of name might agree v. Steph. Byzant. al. in Movers$^{Phen.\ ii.\ 1.\ 110\ n.}$; perh. *Bereitān* near Baalbek, v. Furrer$^{ZPV\ viii.\ 34}$.

†בֵּרֹתַי **n.pr.loc.** belonging to Hadadezer of Zoba 2 S 8^{8}; perh. = foregoing.

†בֵּרֹתִי **adj.gent.** 1 Ch 11^{39} v. הַבְּאֵרֹתִי supr.

†בָּאַשׁ **vb. have a bad smell, stink** (Ar. بَئِسَ *be evil*, Aram. בְּאֵשׁ, ܒܐܫ *be evil*, As. *bîšu* Lotz$^{TP\ 78}$)—**Qal** *Pf.* וּבָאַשׁ consec. Ex 7^{18}; *Impf.* וַתִּבְאַשׁ v^{21}, וַיִּבְאַשׁ ־אַשׁ 16^{20}; 3 fs. תִּבְאַשׁ Is 50^{2}; Ex 8^{10};—*stink*, of Nile, on account of dead fish Ex 7$^{18.21}$ (E); of land of Egypt, owing to dead frogs 8^{10} (J); of manna kept over 16^{20} (P? or

R) וַיָּרֶם תולעים וַיִּבְאַשׁ *and it grew foul* (rotten, decayed) *with worms, and stank,* Is 50^2 תִּבְאַשׁ דגתם מאין מים וְתָמֹת בַּצָּמָא *their fish stink for lack of water,* etc. (𝔊 Lo Di rd. תִּיבַשׁ, *dry up* and die, which suits ∥, but not the usage of יָבֵשׁ). **Niph.** *Pf.* נבאשׁ 1 S 13^4; נִבְאֲשׁוּ 2 S 10^6; נִבְאַשְׁתָּ 2 S 16^{21},—only fig. *make oneself odious, become odious* (cf Eng. *be in bad odour*), sq. את *with=towards,* נבאשת אֶת־אָבִיךָ 2 S 16^{21} *thou hast become odious with thy father;* also sq ב (rather strangely) 1 S 13^4 *Isr made themselves odious to the Philistines;* 2 S 10^6 Ammonites to David. **Hiph.** *Pf.* הבאיש Ex 16^{24} 1 S 27^{12}; הבאישׁוּ ψ 38^6; הבאשתם Ex 5^{21}; *Impf* יַבְאִישׁ Pr 13^5 Ec 10^1; *Inf. abs* הבאש 1 S 27^{12}, *cstr. sf.* לְהַבְאִישֵׁנִי Gn 34^{30};—**1.** *emit a stinking odour* Ex 16^{24} of manna (cf. Qal v^{20}); ψ 38^6 הִבְאִישׁוּ נָמַקּוּ חַבּוּרֹתָי *my wounds have grown stinking, they have festered* (of chastisement for sin); 1 S 17^{12} fig. of David הַבְאֵשׁ הבאיש בעמו *he hath become utterly abhorred among his people* **2.** *cause to stink,* זְבוּבֵי מָוֶת יַבְאִישׁ יַבִּיעַ שֶׁמֶן רוֹקֵחַ *dead flies cause to stink* (and) *to ferment the oil of a perfumer;* usually fig. הבאשתם אֶת־רֵיחֵנוּ Ex 5^{21} (J), i.e. ye have made us odious, sq בְּעֵינֵי, cf. (c. acc pers) Gn 34^{30} sq. ב, also without obj Pr 13^5 *a wicked man makes odious and shameful* (De Now Str, Be Ew Hi Zo *acts odiously and shamefully*). **Hithp.** *Pf* הִתְבָּאֲשׁוּ 1 Ch 19^6 *they had made themselves odious* (=Niph in ∥ 2 S 10^6), sq עִם

†**באשׁ n.m.** stench—ב׳ cstr. Am 4^{10}, sf בָּאְשׁוֹ Jo 2^{20}; בָּאְשָׁם Is 34^3,—ב׳ מַחֲנֵיכֶם, i e. *stench* of corpses Am 4^{10}, also Is 34^3; cf. Jo 2^{20} of locusts (תַּעַל צַחֲנָתוֹ ∥ עָלָה ב׳).

†**בָּאְשָׁה n.f.** (stinking things) **stinking** or **noxious weeds,** Jb 31^{40} תַּחַת חִטָּה יֵצֵא חוֹחַ וְתַחַת־שְׂעֹרָה בָאְשָׁה *instead of wheat may there spring forth bramble, and instead of barley stinking weeds* (cf. As *bišu* Zehnpfund$^{BAS\,1\,633}$).

†**בְּאֻשִׁים n.[m.]pl. stinking** or **worthless** things, **wild grapes** (NH n. unit באושה) (perh. adj. om. עֲנָבִים cf Di) Is 5$^{2.4}$ of Yahweh's vineyard, 𝔙 *labruscae* (v. further De)

†**[בָּבָה] n.f.** only בָּבַת עֵינוֹ Zc 2^{12} *the apple of his eye* (Aram. ܒܒܬܐ, ܒܒܐ; בָּבָא *gate* 𝔗 Est 5^{14}, Thes sub נבב to which Ges gives sense *perforate,* hence *opening of eye;* but cf. Ar. نونو *pupil* of eye, perh.=ܒܒܐ Dozy^{49} *babe, baby, bébé* (imitating infant's prattle) i e. child of the eye; v. Hi St, Fl in ChWB$^{1\,419\,b}$; cf אִישׁוֹן?)

†**בֵּבַי n.pr.m.** a chief of returning exiles בֵּבָי Ne 10^{16}; בני בבי Ezr 8^{11}; בֶּן־בֵּבָי Ezr 8^{11}; בְּנֵי בֵבָי Ezr 2^{11} 10^{28} Ne 7^{16}.

בָּבֶל$_{262}$ **n.pr.loc. Babel, Babylon** (in As written *Bab-ilu, gate of god* Dl$^{Pa\,212}$, cf on other hand Jen$^{Kosmol\,495}$)—c ־ָה loc. בָּבֶ֫לָה Ez 12^{13}+, בָּבֶ֑לָה 2 K 20^{17}+once מִבָּבֶ֫לָה Je 27^{16},—the ancient capital of Babylonia, mod *Hillah,* situated on Euphrates, in long. c 44° 30′ E., and lat. c 32° 50′ N.; Gn 10^{10} 11^9 (where name connected with בלל *confuse, confound*), both J, not elsewh. in Hex, 2 K 17^{24}+31 t 2 K, 18 t Chr; Est 2^6; late ψ 87^4 137$^{1.8}$; Is$^{2.3}$, viz. 13$^{1\,19}$ 14$^{4.22}$ 21^9 39$^{1.3.6.7}$ 43^{14} 47^1 48$^{14.20}$, Mi 4^{10} (but here prob. not orig, cf RS$^{Proph.\,vii.\,n\,5}$ & reff) Zc 2^{11} 6^{10} Dn 1^1 Ez 12^{13} +19 t Ez, Je 20$^{4.4.5.6}$+165 t Je,—note esp. אֶרֶץ ב׳ Je 50^{28}, also of land & people=realm, partic. in מֶלֶךְ ב׳ 2 K 20^{12} of Merodach Baladan; v^{18} 24$^{1\,7\,11\,12\,12}$+oft. of Nebuchadrezzar; 2 K 25^{27}=Je 52^{31} cf v^{34} of Evil-Merodach; Ne 13^6 of Artaxerxes, the city personif. as בַּת בָּבֶל Is 47^1 Je 50^{42} (See Dl$^{Pa\,212}$ COT Gn 11^9 KG^{96})

בַּג Ez 25^7 rd בַּז v בזז

†**[בָּגַד] vb. act or deal treacherously**—**Qal** *Pf* בָּגְדָה Je 3^{20}+14 t; *Impf.* יִבְגֹּד Mal 2^{15}+5 t; נבגד Mal 2^{10}, *Inf abs* בָּגוֹד Is 48^8 Je 5^{11}; *cstr* בגד Is 33^1, בגדו Ex 21^8, *Pt.* בגד Pr 22^{12}+11 t, בוגד Is 33^1+10 t,—*act* or *deal treacherously, faithlessly, deceitfully,* in the marriage relation, in matters of property or right, in covenants, in word and in general conduct. **a.** *abs* 1 S 14^{33} Jb 6^{15} ψ 78^{57} Is 24^{16} 33^{11} 48^8 Mal 2^{11}. Cf. phrases אחי בגדו כמו נחל *my brethren have dealt deceitfully as a brook* Jb 6^{15}, בֹּגְדִים בָּגָדוּ וּבֶגֶד בוגדים בָּגָדוּ *the treacherous have dealt treacherously, yea in treachery have the treacherous dealt treacherously* Is 24^{16} (striking alliteration); בֹּגְדֵי אָוֶן *treacherous in wickedness* ψ 59^6. **b.** with ב Ex 21^8 (E), Ju 9^{23} Is 33^{11} Je 3^{20} 5^{11} 12^6 La 1^2 Ho 5^7 6^7 Mal 2$^{10\,14\,15.16}$ **c.** c acc. ψ 73^{15}. **d.** c. מִן pregnant, בָּגְדָה אִשָּׁה מֵרֵעָהּ *acteth treacherously* (*in departing*) *from her friend* Je 3^{20}. The ptcp. is used Pr 2^{22}+8 t., ψ 25^3 59^6 119^{158} Is 21^2 24$^{16\,16}$ 33^1 Je 3$^{8\,11}$ 9^1 Hb 1^{13} 2^5; בגדי בֶגֶד *dealers treacherously in treachery* (very treacherously) Je 12^1.

†I. **בֶּ֫גֶד n.[m.] treachery,** Is 24^{16} Je 12^1.

†**בגדות pl.abst.** אַנְשֵׁי בֹּגְדוֹת *men of treachery* Zp 3^4.

†**[בָּגוֹד] adj. treacherous,** f בָּגוֹדָה (on form cf. Ew$^{\S\,152\,b}$ No$^{\S\,107}$) Je 3$^{7\,10}$.

II. **בֶּ֫גֶד n.m.** (except Lv 6^{20} עָלֶיהָ, but Sam. עליו,

cf Di in *loco* Ko$^{i\ 182}$) **garment, covering**—Gn 28^{2}+36 t, *sf* בגדו Ez 9^{3}+(14 t without *dag lene* Ges$^{Lgb.\ 94}$), pl בְּגָדִים Lv 6^{4}+32 t., cstr בגדי Gn 27^{15}+39 t, sf. בְּגָדֶיךָ 1 K 22^{20}+81 t, בגדתיך ψ 45^{9},—**1.** *garment, clothing, raiment, robe* of any kind, from the filthy clothing of the leper to the holy robes of the high priest, the simplest covering of the poor as well as the costly raiment of the rich and noble, used throughout Heb Lit Gn 24^{53} (J), 28^{20} (E; 14 t JE), Ex 28^{2}+(P 90 t.), Dt 24^{17} Ju 8^{26}+4 t, 1 S 19^{13}+10 t, 1 K 1^{1}+23 t, 2 Ch 18^{9}+(Chr 9 t), Est $4^{1.4}$ Jb 13^{28} 22^{6} 37^{17} ψ 22^{19} 45^{9} 102^{27} 109^{19} Pr 6^{27} 20^{16} 25^{20} 27^{13} Ec 9^{8} Is^{2} 24^{16} 36^{22} 37^{1} Is^{3} 50^{9}+10 t, Je 12^{1}+3 t, Ez 16^{16}+13 t, Jo 2^{13} Am 2^{8} Hg 2^{12} Zc $3^{3.4.5}$ 14^{14}, מלא בגדו *his lap-ful* 2 K 4^{39} **2.** *covering, wrapping,* of furniture of tabernacle Nu 4^{6-13} (6 t), *coverlet* of a bed 1 S 19^{13}.

†בֵּגְוַי **n.pr.m.** (cf Skr *bhagavân, happy?*) **1.** a companion of Zerubbabel Ezr 2^{2}=Ne 7^{7}; perh = head of a family of returning exiles Ezr 2^{14} (בגוַי)=Ne 7^{19}, cf. Ezr 8^{14}. **2.** a chief of the people in Nehemiah's time Ne 10^{17}, cf. Sm$^{Listen\ 13}$.

בגלל v גלל.

†בִּגְתָא **n.pr.m.** (Pers. cf אֲבַגְתָא) a eunuch of Ahasuerus Est 1^{10}.

†בִּגְתָן **n.pr.m.** (Pers *bagadâna, gift of God?*) a eunuch of Ahasuerus Est 2^{21}=בִּגְתָנָא 6^{2}.

בִּגְתָנָא v. foregoing

†I. בַּד, בַּד **n.[m.]** **white linen** (deriv. unknown) pl בַּדִּים—אֵפוֹד בָּד 1 S 2^{18} (Samuel), 22^{18} (priests of Nob), 2 S 6^{14}=1 Ch 15^{27} (David). in P as material of diff priestly vestments Ex 28^{42} 39^{28} Lv $6^{3.3}$ $16^{4.4.4.4.23.32}$. *Pl* (ה)לבוש (ה)בַּדִּים clad in (the) *linen garments,* of angel Ez $9^{2.3.11}$ $10^{2.6.7}$ Dn 10^{5} $12^{6.7}$.

II, III בַּד v sub I, II. בדד

†בָּדָא **vb. devise, invent** (bad sense) (Mish *id*, Aram בְּדָא, ܒܕܐ *invent; cf* Ar. بَدَأَ *begin, make a beginning*)—**Qal** *Pf* בָּדָא 1 K 12^{33}; *Pt. sf.* בּוֹדָאם (instead of בּוֹרְאָם) Ne 6^{8}—Jeroboam *devised* a feast in 8th month 1 K 12^{33}, *invent* accusation Ne 6^{8}.

†I [בָּדַד] **vb. be separate, isolated** (Ar بَدَّ *cause to withdraw,* II *separate, disunite,* Gn 11^{8} Saad., IV *divide into parts;* X *go alone, act independently*), only *Pt* בּוֹדֵד Is 14^{31} (of straggler in army), Ho 8^{9} פֶּרֶא בּוֹדֵד לוֹ a wild-ass (sim of Ephr.) *going alone* for itself (i e wilfully: v. sub ל), ψ 102^{8} (of bird sitting solitarily)

II. בַּד, בַּד **n.m. separation,** concr **part** (بَدّ, بِدّ *portion*)—sf (always with ל) לְבַדִּי, לְבַדּוֹ etc, 3 f pl †Gn 21^{28} לְבַדְּהֶן, v^{29} לְבַדָּנָה;—**1.** with ל, only in sg, לְבַד prop. *in a state of* (v. sub ל) *separation, alone, by itself* (Fr *à part*) **a.** Ex 26^{9} (=36^{16}) five curtains לְבַד *by themselves,* and six curtains לְבַד *by themselves,* Ju 7^{5} him shalt thou set לְבַד *apart,* Zc 12^{12-14}. **b.** with sf (89 t.) to express the idea of *by oneself, alone* (prop. *in his, thy, my separation*), Gn 2^{18} it is not good for man to be לְבַדּוֹ *alone,* 21^{28} and A set the seven lambs לְבַדְּהֶן *by themselves* (lit in their separation), 32^{17} 43^{32} 2 S 10^{8} Is 5^{8}, Gn 42^{38} הוּא לְבַדּוֹ he *alone,* Ex 18^{14} אַתָּה לְבַדֶּךָ thou *alone,* Nu 11^{14} אָנֹכִי לְבַדִּי I *alone,* 1 K $19^{10.14}$; Dt 8^{3} not upon bread *alone,* 29^{13} 2 S 13^{32} 18^{24} Is 44^{24} 49^{21} 63^{3}+; after an oblique case, as a dat Ex 22^{19} Ju 3^{20} ψ 51^{6} לְךָ לְבַדְּךָ against thee *alone* have I sinned; a genit 71^{16} I will make mention of צִדְקָתְךָ לְבַדֶּךָ׃ the righteousness of thee *alone.* **c.** as adv of limitation, †Is 26^{13} *only* through thee do we celebrate thy name, Ec 7^{29} **d.** followed by מִן it becomes a prep, *apart from, besides,* Ex 12^{37} Nu 29^{39} Dt 3^{5} 18^{8}(rd. מִמְּכָרָיו with 𝔊 𝔖 𝔗 Aq Ew Di) Ju 8^{26} 20^{15} al (15 t.), once, Ezr 1^{6}, with עַל instead of מִן **e.** מִלְּבַד$_{33}$ (prob. inverted for לְבַד מִן *besides*) (chiefly P and late) Gn 26^{1} 46^{26} Lv 9^{17} 23^{38} (4 t.) Nu 5^{8} 6^{21} 17^{14}+12 t Nu 28–29, Dt 28^{69} Jos 22^{29} 1 K 10^{13} 1 Ch 3^{9} 2 Ch 9^{12} 17^{19} 31^{16} Ezr 2^{65}=Ne 7^{67} Dn 11^{4}. With sf †Dt 4^{35} אֵין עוֹד מִלְּבַדּוֹ there is none else *besides* him (cf מִבַּלְעָדַי Is 45^{21})

†**2.** concr *part* Ex 30^{34} (P) בַּד בְּבַד יִהְיֶה *part* for (i e like; cf ב **III. 3.** end) *part* shall it be.

†**3.** בַּדִּים *parts,* spec. *extended from something,* i e (*a*) of a body, *members, limbs* Jb 18^{13} (of man), 41^{4} (of crocodile); (*b*) of a vine, *rods* or *shoots* Ez 17^{6} 19^{14}; (*c*) of *poles* or *staves* used for carrying the ark Ex $25^{13.14.15}$ 35^{12} $37^{4.5}$ 39^{35} 40^{20} Nu 4^{6} 1 K $8^{7.8.8}$ (=2 Ch $5^{8.9.9}$), or table of shewbread Ex $25^{27.28}$ 35^{13} $37^{14.15}$ Nu 4^{8}, or altar of B. O. Ex $27^{6.6.7.7}$ 35^{16} $38^{5.6.7}$ 39^{39} Nu 4^{14}, or altar of incense Ex $30^{4.5}$ 35^{15} $37^{27.28}$ Nu 4^{11}; (*d*) more gen. *bars* (of fortress) Ho 11^{6}, (of a gate) Jb 17^{16} fig. בַּדֵּי שְׁאֹל (v Is 38^{10})

†בָּדָד **n.[m.] isolation, separation.** Is 27^{10} עִיר בְּצוּרָה בָּדָד the fenced city is *isolation,* i e. is solitary (subst for adj: Dr$^{\S 189\ 2}$); more usu. as adv accus, to signify *alone,* Dt 32^{12}, esp. with vbs of dwelling, Lv 13^{46} בָּדָד יֵשֵׁב he shall dwell *alone* (lit *in isolation*), Je 15^{17} La 1^{1} 3^{28}: fig. of freedom from attack, security Dt 33^{28}

(of Isr.), Je 49[31] (Kedar); so לְבָדָד Nu 23[9] (Isr.) Mi 7[14] ψ 4[9] for thou לְבָדָד לָבֶטַח תּוֹשִׁיבֵנִי makest me dwell *solitarily*, in safety (v. Dt 33[28]).

II. בדד (prob. i.q. בָּדָא q.v. *talk idly*).

†III. [בַּד] **n.m.** only *Pl.* בַּדִּים. **a.** *empty, idle talk* (Ph. CIS [3,6] listen not to ברנם = Heb. בַּדֵּיהֶם; cf. ܒܕܝܐ *vain talk*), esp. with collat. idea of imaginary pretensions or claims: Jb 11[3] בַּדֶּיךָ מְתִים יַחֲרִישׁוּ thy *idle talk* brings men to silence (‖וַתִּלְעַג), Is 16[6] (of Moab) לֹא כֵן בַּדָּיו his *boastings* are not right (unfounded), hence Je 48[30]. **b.** concr. *empty talkers, praters* (cf. NH בַּדָּאָה, Syr. ܒܕܘܝܐ, *liar*), of false prophets, Is 44[25] Je 50[36].

†בֵּדַד **n.pr.m.** father of an Edom. ruler (הֲדַד) Gn 36[35] = 1 Ch 1[46].

בְּדֵי v. דַּי.

†בֵּדְיָה **n.pr.m.** (= עֲבַדְיָה *servant of* י׳? 𝔊 Βαραια, 𝔊L Βαδαια) an Israelite Ezr 10[35].

[בָּדַל] **vb. be divided, separate** (Ar. بَدَلَ *change, substitute*, Mish. בָּדַל *divide*, Syr. ܒܕܠ Ithp. Ethp.)—**Hiph.** *divide, separate; Pf.* הִבְדִּיל Nu 16[9] Dt 10[8]; sf. וְהִבְדִּילוֹ consec. Dt 29[20]; 3 fs. וְהִבְדִּילָה Ex 26[33]; וְהִבְדַּלְתָּ Nu 8[14]; הִבְדִּילוּ Ez 22[26], etc.; *Impf.* יַבְדִּיל Lv 1[17]+; וַיַּבְדֵּל Gn 1[4.7] 1 Ch 25[1]; sf. יַבְדִּילַנִי Is 56[3]; וָאַבְדִּל Lv 20[26]; וָאַבְדִּילָה Ezr 8[24], etc.; *Inf. abs.* הַבְדֵּל Is 56[3]; *cstr.* לְהַבְדִּיל Gn 1[14]+; *Pt.* מַבְדִּיל Gn 1[6]; מַבְדִּילִים Is 59[2];—**1.** *divide, separate,* subj. God Gn 1[4] sq. בֵּין ... וּבֵין *between light and darkness,* cf. v[7]; subj. heavenly bodies v[14.18]; subj. firmament sq. בֵּין ... לְ Gn 1[6] (all in P's source); Ex 26[33] of the פָּרֹכֶת in tab., sq. בֵּין ... וּבֵין ... לָכֶם; of iniquities, separating men from God Is 59[2] בֵּין ... לְבֵין. **2.** *separate, set apart,* sq. מִן, of י׳, setting off Isr. from other peoples Lv 20[24] (H) Nu 16[9] (P); Lv 20[26] sq. also לִהְיוֹת לִי; cf. 1 K 8[53] הִבְדַּ׳ לְךָ לְנַחֲלָה *separate them to thyself as an inheritance;* of Moses, setting apart Levites, sq. מִתּוֹךְ Nu 8[14]; of separating an individual from the people, i.e. excluding him Dt 29[20], sq. also לְרָעָה; sq. מֵעַל Is 56[3.3], i.e. excluding him; cf. also Ne 13[3] sq. מִן; of setting apart (forbidding) beasts as unclean לָכֶם לְטַמֵּא Lv 20[25]; of setting apart the tribe of Levi לָשֵׂאת וגו׳ Dt 10[8] (subj. י׳); cf. also (hum. subj.) 1 Ch 25[1], sq. לַעֲבֹדָה, 2 Ch 25[10] sq. Inf.; similarly Ezr 8[24]; even sq. ptcp. Ez 39[14] they shall set apart men עֹבְרִים, i.e. *to pass through,* or, *men that shall pass through* (RV); so of setting apart cities, acc. Dt 4[41] cf. 19[2.7]. **3.** *make a distinction* between clean and unclean, holy and profane, sq. בֵּין ... וּבֵין Lv 20[25] (H); 10[10] 11[47] (both P); sq. בֵּין ... לְ Ez 22[26] 42[20]. **4.** *divide into parts* Lv 1[17] 5[8] (P), prohibited in case of fowls offered in sacrifice. **Niph.** *Pf.* נִבְדְּלוּ 1 Ch 12[8] Ezr 9[1]; *Impf.* יִבָּדֵל Ezr 10[8]; וַיִּבָּדֵל 1 Ch 23[13]; וַיִּבָּדְלוּ Ezr 10[16] Ne 9[2]; *Imv.* הִבָּדְלוּ Nu 16[21] Ezr 10[11]; *Pt.* נִבְדָּל Ezr 6[21] Ne 10[29]. **1.** (reflex. of **Hiph. 2**) **a.** *separate oneself* from people of the land, heathen, and their practices, also from non-Jewish wives, sq. מִן Ezr 6[21] 9[1] 10[11] Ne 9[2]; abs. in same sense Ezr 10[16] (cf. Sta [G. II. 190 & 179 n.] Wl [Pharisäer u. Sadd. 76]). **b.** *withdraw from* (Moses & Aaron from Israel) Nu 16[21] (P), sq. מִתּוֹךְ. **c.** *separate oneself* unto (אֶל) David 1 Ch 12[8]. **d.** Ne 10[29] combines **a.** & **c.** *separate oneself* מֵעַמֵּי הָאֲרָצוֹת אֶל־תּוֹרַת הָאֱלֹהִים. **2.** pass., *be separated.* **a.** *be excluded* from the people, sq. מִן Ezr 10[8]. **b.** *be set apart,* of Aaron, sq. לְהַקְדִּישׁוֹ 1 Ch 23[13].—On הבדיל, & distinction fr. הפריד v. Dr [JPh. xi. 219].

†[בָּדָל] **n.[m.]** piece, severed piece, cstr. בְּדַל־אֹזֶן Am 3[12].

†[מִבְדָּלָה] **n.f.** separate place, הַמִּבְדָּלוֹת Jos 16[9] (appos. הֶעָרִים); but rd. prob. הַמֻּבְדָּלוֹת **Hoph.** *Pt.* fr. בדל, or הַנִּבְדָּלוֹת **Niph.** *Pt.*, cf. Di.

†בְּדִיל **n.[m.]** alloy, tin, dross (orig. *that which is separated* from precious metal; cf. Plin. [Hist. Nat. xxiv. 16, xxxiii. 9])—ב׳ abs. Nu 31[22] + 4 t.; Pl. sf. בְּדִילָיִךְ Is 1[25];—**1.** *alloy,* Is 1[25] fig. of evil of Jerusalem, which י׳ will remove (הָסִיר; ‖ סִגַיִךְ). **2.** *tin* (*plumbum album*) Nu 31[22] (P; + עֹפֶרֶת, בַּרְזֶל, נְחֹשֶׁת, כֶּסֶף, זָהָב); fig. of Isr. Ez 22[18] (+ עוֹפֶרֶת, בַּרְזֶל, נְחֹשֶׁת); in simile v[20] (+ id. + כֶּסֶף); as article of commerce brought to Tyre from Tarshish Ez 27[12] (+ בַּרְזֶל, כֶּסֶף, עוֹפֶרֶת). **3.** *plummet,* הָאֶבֶן הַבְּדִיל (appos.) Zc 4[10].

†בְּדֹלַח **n.[m.]** prob. **bdellium** (𝔖 ܒܕܘܠܚܐ; 𝔗 בְּדוּלְחָא; etym. dub.; Lag [Ges. Abh. 20] prop. Skr. *udûkhala*) c. art. הַבְּ׳, apparently therefore well known; one of the products of the land Havilah Gn 2[12]; used in simile of colour of manna וְעֵינוֹ כְּעֵין הַבְּדֹלַח Nu 11[7].—Meaning somewhat uncertain; 𝔊 Gn 2[12] ἄνθραξ, Nu 11[7] κρύσταλλος; Saad. AW Ki Bo al. *pearls,* cf. Lag [Or. II. 44]; Jos [Ant. III. 1. 6] Aq Theod Symm 𝔙 most *bdellium,*

an odoriferous transparent gum, of yellowish colour. (Cf Smith Dict Bible Sigismund Aromata 18)

†**בְּדָן** **n pr.m.** (=עַבְדֹּן ?) **1.** a judge of Israel 1 S 12[11], but rd prob בָּרָק, so 𝔊 𝔖 We, cf Dr (v Ju 4[6 f]) **2.** a Manassite 1 Ch 7[17]

בדק (*penetrate, split?* cf Aram. בְּדַק, ܒܕܩ, *explore;* but these perh denom cf Lag GN 1882, 400).

†**בֶּ֫דֶק** **n.m.** 2 K 12. 6 **fissure, rent, breach** (Aram בידקא, ܒܶܕܩܳܐ (Nasar))—ב׳ abs 2 K 12[6], cstr *ib* + 6 t; sf בדקך Ez 27[9.27],—in a building, temple ב׳ הַבַּיִת 2 K 12[6.7.8.9] 22[5], cf 12[13] (ב׳ בית י׳), v[6] abs, alw c חזק *repair*, cf מַחֲזִיקֵי ב׳ *repairers of thy fissures* Ez 27[9.27] (of Tyre).

†[**בָּדַק**] **vb denom.** mend, repair, only **Qal** *Inf. cstr* לבדוק וּלְחַזֵּק הַבָּיִת 2 Ch 34[10]

†**בִּדְקַר** **n pr.m** Isr. officer 2 K 9[25] (v בן).

בהה (cf Ar بَهِيَ *be empty;* on a possible connexion in As cf. Hpt BAS i 18)

†**בֹּ֫הוּ** **n.[m.]** emptiness (on form v Ges § 84 a, 1 b Sta § 95, 198 a, on usage cf Lag Or ii 60 f) alw. c תהו q v,—תֹּהוּ וָבֹהוּ Gn 1[2] of primæval earth, Je 4[23] of earth under judgment of י׳, קַו־תֹהוּ וְאַבְנֵי בֹהוּ Is 34[11], *the line of wasteness and the stones of emptiness,* i e plummets, employed, not as usual for building, but for destroying walls, cf Di & v. sub אבן **6.**

†**בַּ֫הַט** **n.[m.]** a costly stone, perh porphyry (cf Egypt *behiti, behet, behat* Brugsch Dict v 436 Dumichen Gesch 167 f. Wendel Altäg Bau- u Edelsteine (1888) 77 f.; 𝔊 has σμαραγδίτης). Est 1[6] עַל רִצְפַת בַּ׳־וָשֵׁשׁ וְדַר וְסֹחָרֶת *upon a pavement of porphyry and marble,* etc

†[**בָּהַל**] **vb.** (NH id Pt pass בהול *disquieted,* Pi *disquiet,* 𝔗 Pa. בַּהֵיל *hasten, be precipitate,* also *dismay* but ܒܗܠ is *be quiet*)—**Niph.** *Pf* נִבְהַל 1 S 28[21], נִבְהֲלָה ψ 6[4], נִבְהַלְתִּי Is 21[3], וְנִבְהַלְתִּי consec Jb 21[6], נִבְהֲלוּ Gn 45[3] +, etc, *Impf* יִבָּהֵל Ju 20[41], 2 ms תִּבָּהֵל Ec 8[3]; יִבָּהֵלוּן ψ 104[29], etc, *Pt* נִבְהָל ψ 30[8]; נִבְהָל Pr 28[22], f נִבְהָלָה Zp 1[18],—**1.** *be disturbed, dismayed, terrified,* Gn 45[3] (E) Ju 20[41] 1 S 28[21] 2 S 4[1] (‖ וַיִּרְפּוּ יָדָיו, cf Ez 7[27] supr.), of bones of sufferer ψ 6[3] (‖ cf infr. v[4]), of hands of dismayed people Ez 7[27], esp. at chastisements & judgments of י׳ Ex 15[15] (song, in E) ψ 6[4] (subj נֶפֶשׁ, ‖ cf supr v[3]) v[11] (‖ בושׁ) 30[8] cf 104[29], 83[18] (‖ בושׁ) 90[7] Is 13[8] 21[3] (sq מִן of occasion of fear) Jb 23[15] (*id*) Je 51[32] Ez 26[18] (del 𝔊 Co), Jb 4[5] (‖ לאה), cf. also 21[6] as adj *terrible* Zp 1[18] כָּלָה אַךְ־נִבְהָלָה. **2.** *be in haste, hasty* (late, cf. Aram above) Ec 8[3] אַל־תִּבָּ׳ מִפָּנָיו תֵּלֵךְ *be not hasty (to) go from him;* Pr 28[22] נִבְהָל לַהוֹן *hastening after riches* **Pi.** *Impf* וַיְבַהֵל Est 2[9], sf. יְבַהֲלֻהוּ Dn 11[44], וִיבַהֲלֵךְ Jb 22[10], יְבַהֲלֵמוֹ ψ 2[5], 2 ms תְּבַהֲלֵם ψ 83[16], אַל־תְּבַהֵל Ec 5[1] 7[9]; *Inf.* sf. לְבַהֲלֵנִי 2 Ch 35[21], ־ם 32[18]; *Part* מבלהים Kt, מְבַהֲלִים Qr Ezr 4[4] (BeRy pref Kt, v בלה);—**1** *dismay, terrify,* sq sf 2 Ch 32[18] (‖ ירא), Dn 11[44] Jb 22[10] (subj פַּחַד), ψ 2[5] (subj י׳) 83[16] (‖ רדף, subj י׳), cf. also Ezr 4[4] (v. sub בלה) **2.** *hasten, make haste, act hastily* (late), 2 Ch 35[21] ואלהים אָמַר לְבַהֲלֵנִי *God hath given command to speed me* (RVm); sq inf. *make haste* Est 2[9], of hasty speech Ec 5[1] אַל־תְּבַ׳ (וְלִבְּךָ אַל־יְמַהֵר לְהוֹצִיא דָבָר ‖) עַל־פִּיךָ; of anger Ec 7[9] אַל־תְּבַ׳ בְּרוּחֲךָ לִכְעוֹס **Pu.** *Pt* pl. מְבֹהָלִים Est 8[14], cf מבהלת Qr Pr 20[21] (so rd. with Vrss Now Str; AV RV), Kt מבחלת v. בחל;—*hastened* Est 8[14] of royal posts (‖ דְּחוּפִים), *hastily gained* נַחֲלָה מְבֹ׳ Pr 20[21]. **Hiph.** *Pf* sf הִבְהִילֻנִי Jb 23[16], *Impf* sf. וַיַּבְהִלֻהוּ 2 Ch 26[20], 3 mpl. וַיַּבְהִלוּ Est 6[14],—**1.** *dismay, terrify,* sq. sf Jb 23[16] (subj שַׁדַּי ‖ הֵרַךְ לִבִּי). **2.** (late) *hasten, hurry* (trans), 2 Ch 26[20] וַיַּבְהִלוּהוּ מִשָּׁם *and they hurried him thence* (‖ נדחף), *make haste,* sq. inf Est 6[14] וַיַּבְ׳ לְהָבִיא *and they made haste to bring* Haman

†**בֶּהָלָה** **n.f. dismay, sudden terror or ruin** (cf As *bêltu, terror,* Dl Pr 32)—ב׳ abs. Lv 26[16] + 2 t, pl וּבֶהָלוֹת Je 15[8],—*sudden terror* Lv 26[16] והפקדתי עליכם ב׳ (appositives follow), cf. Je 15[8], Is 65[23] לֹא יֵלְדוּ לַבֶּהָלָה, ψ 78[33] וַיְכַל־בַּהֶבֶל יְמֵיהֶם וּשְׁנוֹתָם בַּבֶּהָלָה *and he ended their days in a breath, and their years in sudden terror*

בהם (Ar بهم, iv *shut,* x. *impeded in speech, tongue-tied,* Eth ብህመ: *be dumb*).

בְּהֵמָה [187] **n.f. beast, animal, cattle** (Ar بَهِيمَة)—ב׳ Gn 1[24] + 137 t, cstr. בֶּהֱמַת Nu 3[41.41] + 10 t, sf בהמתך Lv 19[19] + 4 t; בְּהֶמְתְּךָ Ex 20[10] + 4 t, בהמתו Gn 36[6] Pr 12[10]; pl. abs. בהמות Dt 32[24] + 6 t + ψ 73[22] (v infr), cstr בַּהֲמוֹת ψ 8[8] + 5 t;—*beast,* & coll *beasts* (Gn 8[1] + very oft.) **1.** of living creatures other than man (אָדָם) Gn 8[1] Ex 8[13.14] 9[9.10.22] 22[18] Lv 18[23.23] (where ב׳ is male, so 20[16]) Dt 27[21] ψ 36[7] etc; מֵאָדָם וְעַד ב׳ (ב׳ including all the larger animals) Ex 9[25] 12[12] ψ 135[8] Je 50[3] etc; as inferior to man Jb 18[3] ψ 49[13.21], so also Ec 3[18.19.19.21], opp also birds & reptiles Gn 6[7] 7[23] 8[17] cf Ez 44[31] etc; also to

fishes 1 K 5^{13} Jb 12^{7} cf v^{8}, ψ 8^{9} Zp 1^{3} **2.** opp. also to wild beasts חַיַּת הָאָרֶץ, ח׳ הַשָּׂדֶה Gn 1$^{24.25.26}$ 2^{20} 3^{14} 7$^{14.21}$ 9^{10} ψ 50^{10} 148^{10} Is 46^{1} etc.; esp. therefore *cattle*, as owned and used by man, Gn 47^{18} (מִקְנֵה הַבּ׳) Ex 20^{10} = Dt 5^{14}, Lv 19^{19} 26^{22} Nu 3$^{41.41.45.45}$ Dt 2^{35} 11^{15} Jon 4^{11} Zc 2^{8} 8^{10} 14^{15} Ezr 1$^{4.6}$ Ne 9^{37} 10^{37} etc.; in one (late) passage of animal for riding (horse? mule?) Ne 2$^{12.12.14}$ **3.** rarely of *wild beasts*, esp. carnivora, בּ׳ יַעַר Mi 5^{7}; בּ׳ הָאָרֶץ Dt 28^{26} Is 18$^{6.6}$ Je 7^{33} 15^{3} 16^{4} 19^{7} 34^{20}; בּ׳ הַשָּׂדֶה 1 S 17^{44}; alone, Pr 30^{30}; שֶׁן־בְּהֵמוֹת Dt 32^{24}; שֹׁד בּ׳ Hb 2^{17}—On בהמות ψ 73^{22} cf. infr

†**בְּהֵמוֹת** **n.m.** behemoth, i e **hippopotamus** (appar. pl. intens of foreg.; acc to Di Jb 40^{15} cf. De Is 30^{6} fr an (assumed) Egyptian *p-ehemau, ox of the water*) Jb 40^{15} (on identity, cf. further Bo$^{\text{Hieroz. III. 705}}$), prob. also ψ 73^{22} בְּהֵמוֹת הָיִיתִי עִמָּךְ *a behemoth was I with (toward) thee* (so Hi De; Che *beasts*); acc. to De Or also in בַּהֲמוֹת Is 30^{6} *the burden of the behemoth of the south* (supposed to be a designation of Egypt, but this unlikely, cf. Che Di, rd. therefore) rather *beasts of the south*, viz. of Judah.

בהן (cf. Ar. بَهَمَ IV *shut, cover* (v foregoing) whence also בֹּהֶן = إِبْهَام; as closing and covering the hand, cf. Lane).

†**בֹּהֶן** **n.**[**f.**] (cf. Sta$^{§ 310 e}$) c. יָד thumb, c. רֶגֶל **great toe** (Ar. إِبْهَام, & (vulg) بُهَام, تَامِم)—בּ׳ only cstr Ex 29$^{20.20}$ + 12 t., pl cstr בהנות Ju 1$^{6.7}$ (fr. sg. [בֹּהֶן] as alw. Cod. Sam for MT בֹּהֶן),—*thumb* (יָדָם) בּ׳ יָדוֹ, & *great toe* (רַגְלָם) בּ׳ רַגְלוֹ (always named together) Ex 29$^{20.20}$ Lv 8$^{23.23.24.24}$ 14$^{14.14.17.17.25.25.28.28}$; בהנות י׳ ור׳ Ju 1$^{6.7}$.

†**בֹּהַן** **n.pr.m.** (*closing, covering?*) אֶבֶן בּ׳ בֶּן־ראובן Jos 15^{6} 18^{17}, a mark of division between Judah & Benjamin

בהק (NH בָּהַק *shine*, Aram. בְּהַק, ܒܗܩ, Aph. *id.*; hence בַּהֲקִיתָא, ܒܘܗܩܐ, an eruption, v sq)

†**בֹּהַק** **n.m.** a harmless eruption on the skin (NH *id.*, Aram בּוּהֲקָא, Ar. بَهَق) Lv 13^{39}

בהר (NH Hiph. *be bright, shine*; cf. Aram בְּהַר, ܒܗܪ (not Pe.) & deriv., Eth. በሀረ: Ar. بَهَرَ *surpass*, esp in brightness, *shine brightly*)

†**בַּהֶרֶת** **n f.** **brightness, bright spot,** of eruption on skin (NH *id*, Aram. בַּהֲרָא)—בּ׳ abs Lv 13^{2} + 7 t; בַּהָרֶת Lv 14^{56}; pl abs בֶּהָרוֹת Lv 13$^{38.39}$;—*bright spot* (sore, scar, etc), clean or unclean Lv 14^{56}, following a burn (from fire) Lv 13$^{24.25.26.28}$, possible beginning of leprosy Lv 13$^{2.4.19.23}$, but possibly a (passing) eruption מִסְפַּחַת v^{6}, or due to a boil שְׁחִין v$^{19.23}$;—due to בֹּהַק (q v) Lv 13$^{38.39}$

†**בָּהִיר** **adj.** **bright, brilliant,** of light; only Jb 37^{21} לֹא רָאוּ אוֹר בּ׳ הוּא בַּשְּׁחָקִים.

בּוֹא $_{2569}$ **vb.** **come in, come, go in, go** (As. *bâ'u* Hpt$^{\text{KAT 499}}$, Eth ቦአ: Ar. بَاتَ *return*)—**Qal** *Pf* בָּא Gn 6^{13} +; 3 fs בָּאָה Gn 15^{17} +; sf. בָּאַתְנוּ ψ 44^{18}; 2 ms בָּאתָ Jos 13^{1} +, בָּאתָה 2 S 3^{7}; 2 fs בָּאת Gn 16^{8} Ru 2^{12}, וּבָאתְ consec. Ru 3^{4} 2 S 14^{3} Mi 4^{10}, 3 pl בָּאוּ Gn 7^{9} +; 1 pl בָּאנוּ Gn 32^{7} + (בָּנוּ 1 S 25^{8}), etc, *Impf* יָבוֹא Gn 32^{9} +, יָבֹא Gn 49^{10} +, 3 fs תָּבוֹא Gn 41^{50} +; sf. תבואתך Jb 22^{21} (but text dub. v. Ko$^{\text{I. 644}}$), 2 ms תָּבוֹא Gn 15^{15} +, 2 fs. תָּבוֹאִי Ru 3^{17} +, 1 s אָבוֹא Gn 33^{14} +; cohort. אָבֹאָה Ju 15^{1}, אָבוֹאָה Gn 29^{21} +, וַתָּבֹאתִי 1 S 25^{34} (Qr וַתָּבֹאת, but text prob wrong, v Ko$^{\text{I. 647}}$ Dr, rd. וַתָּבֹאִי); 3 pl m. יָבוֹאוּ Gn 6^{20} +, also (by text err) בֹּאוּ Je 27^{18} cf Ko$^{\text{I. 645}}$, יְבֹאוּן ψ 95^{11}; sf. יבאוני ψ 119^{77}, וִיבֹאֻנִי v^{41}; 3 f pl תָּבֹאןָ Gn 30^{38}, תְּבוֹאנָה 1 S 10^{7} +; תבאינה 1 S 10^{7} ψ 45^{16}, etc., *Imv.* בּוֹא, בֹּא Gn 7^{1} +, בֹּאָה 1 S 20^{21} 1 K 13^{7}, בֹּאִי, בּוֹאִי 2 S 13^{11} +; mpl בֹּאוּ Gn 45^{17} +, *Inf.* בּוֹא, בֹּא Gn 39^{16} +; sf. בּוֹאִי, בֹּאִי Gn 48^{5} +, בּוֹאֲךָ 1 S 29^{6} +, בֹּאֲכָה Gn 10^{19} +, etc, בֹּאָם Gn 34^{5} +, בֹּאָן Gn 30^{38} cf Ez 42^{12} (where Co for בְּבוֹאָן reads לבוא להנה); *Pt.* בָּא Gn 33^{1} +, f בָּאָה Gn 29^{6} +, הַבָּאָה Gn 18^{21} + (accent wrong Ew$^{§ 331 b N}$), pl בָּאִים Gn 18^{11} +, cstr. בָּאֵי Gn 23^{10} +; f abs בָּאוֹת Gn 41^{29}; (see further on forms Ko$^{\text{I. 643 f.}}$),—**1.** *come in*, sq. אֶל Gn 6^{18} 7$^{9.13}$, sq. בְּ Gn 19^{8} & so (subj. רוּחַ) Ez 2^{2} 37^{10}, sq לְ Est 6^{4}, sq ה— loc. Gn 12^{11} 41^{57} Nu 14^{24}, sq acc (בית) Ju 18^{18} 2 K 11^{19} cf. ψ 100^{4} (שְׁעָרָיו), & בָּאֵי שַׁעַר עִירוֹ Gn 23$^{10.18}$; even of lifeless things 2 K 18^{21}, וּבָא בְכַפּוֹ (of broken reed) = pierce, of food and drink (sq. אֶל) Dn 10^{3} cf Gn 41^{21} (fat kine when eaten by lean kine); v also (sq. בְּ) Nu 5$^{22.24.27}$; abs. Gn 7^{16} 24^{31} 1 K 1^{42} 14^{6} cf 2 K 11$^{5.9}$ = 2 Ch 23$^{4.8}$ +; more partic. **a.** opp. יָצָא, *go out and come in* (Sab. תאם או בהאם Hal^{152}) Jos 6^{1} 2 K 11^{8} = 2 Ch 23^{7}; esp. in sense of going about one's affairs (including all one's undertakings) Dt 28$^{6.19}$ Zc 8^{10} ψ 121^{8}; *id.* + ישב 2 K 19^{27}; also sq לִפְנֵי הָעָם etc. = act as ruler (judge) of, Nu 27^{17} 2 Ch 1^{10} cf. 1 K 3^{7}; of leading an army 1 S 18$^{13.16}$ cf. also Jos 14^{11}; v. further Dt 31^{2} 1 S 29^{6} & sub **c.** infr. **b.** of taking part in worship of congregation Dt 23$^{2.3.3.4.4}$ + (sq. בְּ); or entering into tabernacle for priestly service Ex 28$^{29.35}$ Lv 16^{23} (all sq.

אֶל־), Ex 28^{30} (sq לִבְנֵי יהוה), Lv 16^{17} (sq inf) + **c.** of entering on official duty 2 K 11^{9} = 2 Ch 23^{8} 1 Ch 27^{1} (all opp יצא) **d.** of bride coming into her husband's house Jos 15^{18} = Ju 1^{14} **e.** of entering a woman's tent or apartment (with implication *coire cum femina*, cf Ar. [illegible], NH בִּיאָה *coitio*, on origin of this use of word cf. RS K 90 167 291) Ju 15^{1} אֶל־אִשְׁתִּי הֶחָדְרָה, 16^{1} Gn 6^{4} 16^{2} 30^{3} $38^{8.9}$ 39^{14} Dt 22^{13} 2 S 12^{24} 16^{21} 20^{3} Ez $23^{44.44.44}$ Pr 6^{29} (all sq אֶל־), sq עַל־ Gn 19^{31} Dt 25^{5} יָבֹא עָלֶיהָ וּלְקָחָהּ לוֹ לְאִשָּׁה, cf בָּאֶיהָ Pr 2^{19},—subj rarely woman Gn 19^{34} 2 S 11^{4}. **f** of associating with (sq בְּ) Jos $23^{7.12}$ cf Gn 49^{6} בְּסֹדָם אַל תָּבֹא נַפְשִׁי (בִּקְהָלָם ‖ אַל־תֵּחַד) **g.** of entering into specific relations, בּוֹא (בְּרִית, אָלָה v) בּ׳ בִּבְרִית, בּ׳ בְּאָלָה; בְּדָמִים *come into blood-guiltiness*, became guilty of murder 1 S 25^{26}. **h.** of burial, בּ׳ אֶל־קֶבֶר 1 K 13^{22} 14^{13} cf תָּבוֹא אֶל־אֲבוֹתֶיךָ Gn 15^{15} (‖ תִּקָּבֵר) **i.** of sun, *set* (go in, enter, cf As *êrib šamši* COT Gn 19^{23}, opp יצא *go forth, rise*) Gn $15^{12.17}$ 28^{11} Ex 17^{12} 22^{25} Lv 22^{7} Dt 16^{6} 23^{12} $24^{13.15}$ Jos 8^{29} $10^{13.27}$ Ju 19^{14} Ec 1^{5} 2 S 2^{24} 3^{35} 1 K 22^{36} 18^{34}, so also fig. Je 15^{9} of calamity בָּאָה שִׁמְשָׁהּ בְּעוֹד יוֹמָם (‖ אֻמְלְלָה יֹלֶדֶת הַשִּׁבְעָה etc), cf Is 60^{20}, Mi 3^{6} וּבָ׳ הַשֶּׁמֶשׁ עַל־הַנְּבִיאִים of ignorance and confusion **j.** of harvest, *come in* = be gathered Lv 25^{22} (cf תְּבוּאָה), so of revenue (*income*) 1 K 10^{14} = 2 Ch 9^{13} (sq לְ pers),—opp יצא *be expended* **k.** in other phrases וַתָּבֹא הָעִיר בַּמָּצוֹר 2 K 24^{10} + *and the city came into siege*, cf ψ 105^{18} בַּרְזֶל בָּאָה נַפְשׁוֹ *his soul came into iron* (v AV RVm, Che *felt iron chains*, cf Ew Ol Hup Pe, 𝔗 Hi De al *iron came upon his soul*); בָּא בַיָּמִים *come into* (*the*) *days*, = advanced in age Gn 24^{1} Jos 13^{1} 23^{1} (all ‖ זָקֵן), on 1 S 17^{12} v. Dr. **2.** *come* (approach, arrive) opp הָלַךְ Gn 16^{8} 1 S 20^{21} (cf v^{22}) Ne 6^{17} Ec $5^{14.15}$ (of birth opp death), sq אֶל־ pers vel rei Gn 14^{7} 37^{23}, sq עַל־ Ex 18^{23} 2 Ch 20^{24} (*come up upon*, almost = *ascend*), cf also Lv 21^{11} Nu 6^{6}, sq לְ 1 S 9^{12} 2 Ch 29^{17}, sq עַד Nu 13^{22} Ju 15^{14} 2 S 16^{5}, cf. בָּאוּ בָנִים עַד־מַשְׁבֵּר 2 K 19^{3} = Is 37^{3} *children have come to the birth*, sq. אֶל + עַד 2 K 9^{20} בָּא עַד אֲלֵיהֶם, sq. ־ָה loc. Ju 11^{16} 2 K 6^{4}, sq acc 1 S 4^{12} 2 K 8^{7} Je 32^{24}, cf also La 1^{4} בָּאֵי מוֹעֵד *those coming to an appointed feast*, abs Gn 45^{16} *Joseph's brethren are come*, & oft, also of lifeless things, ark of י׳ 1 S 4^{6}, wind Jb 1^{19}, so כַּסְפְּכֶם בָּא אֵלָי Gn 43^{23} *your money came unto me* = I received your money, *our inheritance has fallen to us* Nu 32^{19} (c אֶל־), so 1 S 9^{16} *its cry is come unto me*, cf Gn 18^{21} Ex 3^{9} La 1^{22}, of time, oft. of imminent future, esp in phr הִנֵּה יָמִים בָּאִים Is 39^{6} = 2 K 20^{17} Je 7^{32} 9^{24} 16^{14} 19^{6}, cf also 1 S 26^{10} Ez 7^{7} +, of day of י׳ Jo 2^{1} 3^{4} Zc 14^{1} Mal $3^{2.19.23}$, also ptcp as adj הַיָּמִים הַבָּאִים Ec 2^{16} cf Je 47^{4}, as subst הַבָּאוֹת Is 41^{22} *things to come*, future things; & הַבָּאִים alone = adv. *in* (*days*) *to come* Is 27^{6}, partic **a.** *come with*, i.e come, bringing, sq בְּ ψ 66^{13} אָבוֹא בֵיתְךָ בְעוֹלוֹת, אָבוֹא בִּגְבֻרוֹת אֲדֹנָי י׳ ψ 71^{16} (‖ אַזְכִּיר צִדְקָתְךָ) so Lv 16^{3} & perh. Pr 18^{6}—cf בְּ **III. 1 b.** **b.** *come upon, fall* or *light upon*, of enemy, *attack*, sq עַל־ Gn 34^{27} 1 S 11^{12} cf Gn 32^{9} (sq אֶל־); sq sf Jb 15^{21}, so also 20^{22} Ez 32^{11}, of calamity, etc Pr 10^{24} 28^{22} ψ 44^{18} (all c sf.); sq. לְ Jb 3^{25} (‖ אתה c sf) Is 47^{9} (‖ בוא על), of blessing, sq. עַל־ Jos 23^{15}, sq. sf Jb 22^{21} (cf Di) ψ $119^{41.77}$. **c** *come to pass*, of signs, wonders, predictions, etc Dt 13^{3} Jos 23^{14} 1 S 9^{6} (בֹּא יָבֹא) Is 42^{9} Je 28^{9} Pr 13^{12} Jb 6^{8} +. **d.** Gn 6^{13} קֵץ כָּל־בָּשָׂר בָּא לְפָנַי perh *has presented itself before me* (v Kn), cf La 1^{22} supr & 2 Ch 7^{11} (where בוא for usual עלה); but perh. (cf. Di) *has come to pass before me*, i e. in my mind it is already a fact. **e.**† in phr עַד־בּוֹאֲךָ עַזָּה Ju 6^{4} cf 11^{33} 1 S 17^{52} 2 S 5^{25} 1 K 18^{46} (עַד־בֹּאֲכָה) *until thou comest to* = as far as, so also בֹּאֲךָ (בֹּאֲכָה) alone, = as far as, or in the direction of, Gn $10^{19.19.30}$ 13^{10} 25^{18} 1 S 27^{8} (all sq ־ָה loc) 1 S 15^{7}; so לְבוֹא חֲמָת Nu 13^{21} 34^{8} Ez 48^{1}, cf Ez 47^{15} (in a different connexion לָבוֹא אפרתה Gn 35^{16} 48^{7}), עד לבוא ח׳ Jos 13^{5} Ju 3^{3} 1 Ch 13^{5}, cf 5^{9} 2 Ch 26^{8} Ez 47^{20}, מלבוא ח׳ Am 6^{14} 1 K 8^{65} 2 K 14^{25} 2 Ch 7^{8}, of Isaac בָּא מִבּוֹא בְּאֵר לַחַי רֹאִי Gn 24^{62} (but text dub) **f.** *attain to* עַד הַשְּׁלֹשָׁה לֹא בָא 2 S 23^{19} = 1 Ch 11^{21} **g.** *be enumerated* הַבָּאִים בְּשֵׁמוֹת, lit. *those coming with names* 1 Ch 4^{38} **3.** *go*, i e *walk, associate with* (עם) ψ 26^{4}, so c את Pr 22^{24} (cf. הלך את 13^{20} & התהלך את Gn $5^{22.24}$ 6^{9}) **4.** *go* (cf הלך) from speaker, but with limit of motion given Is 22^{15} לֶךְ־בֹּא אֶל־, so Ez $3^{4.11}$, Gn 45^{17} וּלְכוּ־בֹאוּ, לֵךְ וּבָאתָ־לְּךָ אֶרֶץ יְהוּדָה 1 S 22^{5}, אַרְצָה כְנָעַן Is 47^{5} Jon 1^{3} אֳנִיָּה בָּאָה תַרְשִׁישׁ *a ship going to Tarshish; go to war* יָבֹאוּ לַמִּלְחָמָה Nu 32^{6} **Hiph.** *Pf* הביא Gn 4^{4} +, sf הביאני Dt 9^{4} +, etc, 2 ms הבאת Is 43^{23}, הבאת Gn 20^{9} +, etc; sf הֲבֵאתָנוּ Nu 16^{14}, הֲבִיאֹתַנִי 2 S 7^{18} 1 Ch 17^{16}, הֲבֵאתָנוּ ψ 66^{11}, 1 s הבאתי Gn 31^{39} +, והבאותי Je 25^{13} Kt (Qr והבאתי), sf וַהֲבִיאוֹתִיךָ Ez 38^{16} +, הֲבֵאתִיהָ Is 37^{26}, etc., 3 pl הביאו Gn 43^{2} +, sf הביאוהו 2 Ch 28^{27} etc, 2 mpl הֲבֵאתֶם Nu 20^{4} +, וַהֲבִיאֹתֶם 1 S 16^{17}, 1 pl sf הֲבִיאֹנֻם Nu 32^{17}; *Impf* יָבִיא (יָבֵא) Lv 4^{32} +, וַיָּבֵא Gn 2^{19} +, sf וַיְבִיאֵנִי Ez 40^{17}, etc;

2 ms. תָּבִיא Jb 14[3], sf תְּבִיאֵהוּ Je 13[1], וַתְּבִיאֵם Ne 9[23], תְּבִאֵמוֹ Ex 15[17], אָבִיא Ex 11[1] + (אָבִי 1 K 21[29] Mi 1[15]), etc.; *Imv.* הָבֵא Gn 43[16] Ex 4[6], הָבִיא 1 S 20[40], הָבִיאָה Gn 27[7] +; fs הָבִיאִי 2 S 13[10] +, etc.; *Inf abs.* הָבֵא Hg 1[6]; *cstr* הָבִיא Gn 18[19] +; *Pt* מֵבִיא Ex 10[4] +, מֵבִי 1 K 21[21] + 3 t, מְבִיאֲךָ Dt 8[7]; pl מְבִיאִים (מְבָאִים) 1 K 10[25] +; cstr מְבִאֵי Je 17[26], מְבִיאֶיהָ Dn 11[6];—**1.** *cause to come in, bring in* (conduct, lead, obj. persons and animals), sq אֶל־ Gn 6[19] Ct 2[4] 3[4]; sq. בְּ Lv 26[41] ψ 66[11]; sq. לְ Ju 19[21] 1 S 9[22]; sq לִפְנֵי Est 1[11.17]; sq ־ָה loc Gn 24[67] 46[7], sq ־ָה + אֶל־ Gn 19[10]; sq acc. (חֶדֶר) Ct 1[4] 2 K 9[2], also *bring, carry in* (lifeless things), sq אֶל־ Nu 31[54] Mal 3[10]; sq בּ Je 17[21], *send*, of sending (shooting) arrows (fig.) La 3[13], cf. Lv 26[36]; of sending breath (רוּחַ) into dry bones Ez 37[5] (Co עַל), sq. ל Ne 13[12]; sq. ־ָה loc Ex 26[33] 2 K 20[20] וַיָּבֵא אֶת־הַמַּיִם הָעִירָה; sq acc (חֶדֶר) 2 S 13[10]; also 2 Ch 15[18] (בית), abs. 2 S 6[17], partic. **a.** opp הוֹצִיא (*bring out*) Dt 9[28] (sq אֶל־); esp. in combination with הוֹצִיא *lead out and in* (to and from battle) Nu 27[17] 1 Ch 11[2] **b.** *bring in* women as wives for sons (sq מִן הַחוּץ) Ju 12[9] (opp. שִׁלַּח הַחוּצָה). **c.** *bring into judgment* ואתי תָּבִיא בְמִשְׁפָּט עִמָּךְ Jb 14[3] cf Ec 11[9] 12[14] **d.** *cause* sun *to go down* Am 8[9] (symbol of judgment) **e.** of harvest, *bring in, gather* 2 S 9[10] Hg 1[6] (opp. זרע) cf Ne 13[15]. **f.** *put* staves into (בְּ) rings Ex 25[14] 37[5] 38[7] cf. 26[11] Lv 14[42], hand into (בּ) bosom Ex 4[6.6]; girdle into (בְּ) water Je 13[1]. **g.** other phrases, הֵבִיאוּ צַוָּרָם בַּעֲבֹדַת אֲדֹנֵיהֶם Ne 3[5] *put their necks to the work*, etc.; fig. הביאו את־צואריכם בְּעֹל Je 27[12]; הָבִיאָה לַמּוּסָר לִבֶּךָ Pr 23[12] *apply to instruction thy heart;* וְנָבִא לְבַב חָכְמָה ψ 90[12] *that we may gain a heart of wisdom.* **2.** *cause to come, bring, bring near*, etc. (animate obj.), sq אל־ Gn 2[19.22] 43[9] Lv 24[11] Nu 5[15]; oft. of bringing Isr. to Canaan Ex 6[8] 23[23] +, cf. Is 14[2] 56[7] Ne 1[9]; abs. Dt 4[38] 6[23], sq לְ Gn 39[14.17], sq ־ָה loc Ez 12[13], sq. הֲלֹם Ju 18[3], & עַד־הֲלֹם (fig of Yahweh's prospering care) 2 S 7[18] = 1 Ch 17[16], abs Gn 46[32], also with lifeless obj., Gn 27[10] (sq לְ), so 2 Ch 36[7]; Gn 31[39] (sq. אֶל־), sq acc 2 K 12[5] 2 Ch 36[18] Dn 1[2.2], sq. ־ָה loc. Ex 26[33] Je 20[5]; sq. לפני 2 Ch 24[14]; of ravens bringing food 1 K 17[6] (sq לְ); of bringing presents Gn 43[26] 1 S 9[7] 10[27] (all sq לְ), cf 1 S 17[18]; esp offerings, sq ל Gn 4[3] Nu 15[25] Ne 10[35.37] (לְבֵית), etc; Lv 2[2] sq. אֶל־ of priest, abs. Gn 4[4] Lv 4[32] 23[14.15] Mal 1[13.13] 2 Ch 31[5], cf also Ex 35[21.22.23.24.24.27.29] (sq לְ *for*) so 36[3] +, of time, *cause a day to come* La 1[21], *cause cry to come* (עַל־) Jb 34[28], = *carry* והבי׳ בָנַיִךְ בְּחֹצֶן Is 49[22] (עַל־כָּתֵף || נשׂא), *carry God in* (בְּ) *the hand* Jb 12[6] (cf. אֱלוֹהַּ p. 43), *allow to come*, almost = *invite* Est 5[12] (sq. אֶל־) cf v[10], partic. **a.** sq עַל־ *bring against*, or *upon*, bring enemies against Je 25[9] cf. Ez 23[22], obj sword Lv 26[25] Ez 5[17] 11[8] 14[17] 33[2]; plague Ex 11[1]; curse or calamity Gn 27[12] Dt 29[26] 1 K 9[9] = 2 Ch 7[22] Jb 42[11] cf Je 25[13] 36[31] 44[2] 49[8.37] Ez 14[22], sin Gn 20[9] 26[10] Ex 32[21], cf. also sq. אֶל־ Je 32[42] 49[36] **b.** *bring to pass* 2 K 19[25] = Is 37[26] cf. 1 Ch 4[10] ψ 78[29]. **c.** *bring, bring forward, bring on the scene* Mi 1[15] Zc 3[8] **d.** *bring* for a purpose, sq inf. ψ 78[71] מֵאַחַר עָלוֹת הביאו לרעות בְּיַעֲקֹב עַמּוֹ. **e.** *bring, procure* בנפשנו נָבִיא לַחְמֵנוּ La 5[9] †**Hoph.** *Pf.* הוּבָא Lv 10[18] +; 3 fs הֻבָאת Gn 33[11] (v. infr), 2 ms. הֻבָאתָה Ez 40[4], 3 pl הוּבְאוּ Gn 43[18]; *Impf.* יוּבָא Lv 6[23] +, יוּבָאוּ Je 27[22], *Pt* מוּבָא 2 K 12[10] +, pl מוּבָאִים Gn 43[18] Ez 30[11] + 23[42] (Co מרבדים), מוּבָאוֹת ψ 45[15];—**a.** *be brought in* (of pers. and things), abs Gn 43[18]; sq בית *into a house* Gn 43[18], temple 2 K 12[5.10.14.17] 22[4] 2 Ch 34[9.14]. **b.** *be brought*, sq ל Gn 33[11] (but 𝔊 rd Hiph. *I have brought*), ψ 45[15]; sq אֶל־ *unto* Lv 6[23] 10[18] 13[2.9] 14[2], cf Ez 23[42] (but v Co VB); sq הֵנָּה Ez 40[4]; sq בָּבֶלָה Je 27[22], sq inf. Lv 16[27] Ez 30[11], sq מִן Je 10[9]. **c.** *be introduced, put*, sq בְּ, staves into rings Ex 27[7], vessel into water Lv 11[32].

†[בָּאָה] **n.f.** entrance, entry, בְּבָאָה Ez 8[5], i.e. of temple (but del B Co)

†מָבוֹא **n.m.** [Je 38.14] entrance, a coming in, entering;—מ׳ abs. Je 38[14] + 3 t. + Ez 42[9] Kt (Qr מֵבִיא wrong, cf Co); cstr. מְבוֹא Dt 11[30] + 12 t.; sf מבואו ψ 104[19] + 2 t., מבאו ψ 50[1], מבואך 2 S 3[25] Kt (Qr מוֹבָאֶךָ inexplicable cf. Dr); pl cstr. מבואי Ez 26[10], מְבוֹאֹת Ez 27[3], —**1.** *entrance* i e place or way of entrance, into a city Ju 1[24.25] 1 Ch 4[39] Pr 8[3] (מ׳ פְּתָחִים), into buildings 2 K 11[16] 16[18] 1 Ch 9[19] (שׁמרי הַמָּבוֹא), 2 Ch 23[13.15] Je 38[14] Ez 42[9] 46[19]; v. also מבואת ים *entrance of (the) sea, gate of the sea*, of situation of Tyre Ez 27[3]. **2.** *entering*, act of entrance, by violence, in storm of city Ez 26[10]; *coming in* or together, making a crowd, כִּמְבוֹא עָם Ez 33[31] sim. of eagerness to hear Yahweh's word, in phrase אֶת־מוֹצָאֲךָ וְאֶת־מבואך 2 S 3[25] *thy going out and thy coming in; mode of entering temple*, or *the people who enter* Ez 44[5], particularly of *sunset* מְבוֹא הַשֶּׁמֶשׁ ψ 104[19]; = *west* Dt 11[30], Jos 1[4] 23[4] הַיָּם הַגָּדוֹל מְבוֹא

הַשֶּׁמֶשׁ = Mediterranean, Zc 8^{7} אֶרֶץ מְבוֹא הַשֶּׁמֶשׁ (‖ אֶרֶץ מִזְרָח), Mal 1^{11} ψ 50^{1} 113^{3} *sunset = west*, opp. sunrise = east, in phr *from E. to W*, i e over the whole earth, everywhere on earth.

†[מוֹבָא] **n.[m.] in-coming, entrance,** מוֹבָאֶךָ Qr 2 S 3^{25}, cf Kt sub מבוא, וּמוֹבָאָיו Ez 43^{11} *and its entrances* (‖ וּמוֹצָאָיו), del. B Co. In both, ungramm. form for assonance with מוצא

†תְּבוּאָה **n.f.** *proventus*, **product, revenue** —ת׳ abs. ψ 107^{37} + 3 t., cstr תְּבוּאַת Lv 23^{39} + 11 t; sf. תבואתי Jb 31^{12} Pr 8^{19}; תְּבוּאָתְךָ Dt 14^{28} + 2 t, תבואתֶךָ Pr 3^{9}, תְּבוּאָתוֹ Lv 19^{25} + Ez 48^{18} Qr (Kt תבואתה), תְּבוּאָתָה Je 2^{3}; תְּבוּאָתָהּ Ex 23^{10} + 7 t + Ez 48^{18} Kt (so Co), תבואתנו Lv 25^{20}, pl תבואת Lv 25^{15} + 4 t.; תְּבוּאוֹת Pr 14^{4} 16^{8}, תבואתיכם Je 12^{13},—**1.** *product, yield*, usually of earth (= crops, etc) ת׳ הָאָרֶץ Ex 23^{10} Lv 19^{25} 23^{39} $25^{3.7}$ (used as food for man & beast, cf v^{22}) Jos 5^{12}, cf Ne 9^{37} Lv $25^{15.16}$, also Ez 48^{18}, in Gn 47^{24} בַּת׳ must = *of the crops* (ב partitive, cf ב **I. 2. b**, 𝔊 del ב), ת׳ שָׂדֶה 2 K 8^{6} 2 Ch 31^{5}, ת׳ כֶּרֶם Dt 22^{9} cf ψ 107^{37}, לֶחֶם ת׳ הָאֲדָמָה Is 30^{23}, ת׳ יֶקֶב & ת׳ גֹּרֶן Nu 18^{30}, ת׳ זֶרַע Dt 14^{22}, ת׳ דָּגָן 2 Ch 32^{28}, as property of husbandmen, or people Lv 25^{20} Dt 14^{28} 16^{15} 26^{12} Pr 3^{9}, crops as determined by season, ת׳ שֶׁמֶשׁ Dt 33^{14} (‖ גֶּרֶשׁ יְרָחִים), *yield* of a year שָׁנָה Lv $25^{12.22}$, cf. v^{21} עָשָׂה ת׳, subj שָׁנָה. **2. a.** *income, revenue*, in general Jb 31^{12} (almost = possessions) Pr 10^{16} 14^{4} 15^{6} 16^{8} Ec 5^{9} cf. Is 23^{3} (revenue of Tyre from trade with Egypt in bread stuffs) **b.** fig *gain* of wisdom ת׳ חָכְמָה Pr 3^{14} 8^{19}, *product of lips* (ת׳ שפתיו) Pr 18^{20}, i e. results of his speech (‖ פְּרִי פִי־אִישׁ); of Isr. as Yahweh's product Je 2^{3}, of Israel's wickedness Je 12^{13}

†I [בּוּז] **vb. despise** (NH *id.*) — **Qal** *Pf* 3 ms בָּז Zc 4^{10} (cf Kö $^{1.439}$); 3 pl בָּזוּ Pr 1^{7}, *Impf* יָבוּז Pr 23^{9}, 3 fs. וַתָּבָז Pr 30^{17}, 2 ms. תָּבוּז (juss) Pr 23^{22}, pl יָבוּזוּ Pr 6^{30} Ct 8^{7}, Ct 8^{1}, *Inf abs* בוז Ct 8^{7}; *Pt.* Pr 11^{12} + 2 t.,—*despise, shew despite toward* (WisdLt & poet.) c acc Pr 1^{7}, c Inf + ל Pr 30^{17}; elsewh. sq ל + noun, Pr 6^{30} 11^{12} 13^{13} 14^{21} $23^{9.22}$ Ct $8^{1.7}$ Zc 4^{10}

†II בּוּז **n.m.** $^{Pr\,18.3}$ **contempt**—ב׳ abs Gn 38^{23} + 9 t, cstr Jb 31^{34},—(WisdLt & poet, exc Gn 38^{23} J) **1.** *contempt* springing from pride and wickedness Jb 31^{34} ψ $123^{3.4}$ (‖ לַעַג), joined in one adverb. phr with נאוה ψ 31^{19} בְּגַ׳ וָב׳; springing from prosperity and ease Jb 12^{5}; = object of contempt Gn 38^{23} Pr 12^{8}, ‖ חֶרְפָּה ψ 119^{22} Pr 18^{3} **2.** judicial, poured out (שפך) by God, in judgment Jb 12^{21} = ψ 107^{40}

†בּוּזָה **n.f.** contempt Ne 3^{36} הָיִינוּ ב׳ *we have become* (an object of) *contempt*

†III בּוּז **n.pr.m.** (cf. As n.pr loc *Bâzu* Dl $^{Pa\,307,\ ZK\,1885,\ 93\,f}$) **1.** 2nd son of Nahor, Abraham's brother Gn 22^{21} J, = tribe named with דְּדָן & תֵימָא Je 25^{23}. **2.** a Gadite 1 Ch 5^{14}.

†I. בּוּזִי **adj.gent** (= בעזי fr. בֹּעַז acc. to J Derenbourg $^{RÉJ\,i\,6}$) of Elihu's father Jb $32^{2.6}$.

†II. בּוּזִי **n.pr m** father of Ezekiel Ez 1^{3}

†בַּוַּי **n.pr.m.** a Jew of Nehem's time Ne 3^{18} = בִּנּוּי v^{24} which prob. rd also v^{18} (𝔊 Βεδει, Βενει, Βεζερ), cf. further Sm $^{Listen\,12}$

†בּוּךְ **vb. perplex, confuse** (? Ar. بَاكَ *stir up* (water of spring) then *be disturbed, confused*, cf. As *bâku, lead captive*, orig *lead astray*? COT Ezr 4^{2})—only **Niph.** *Pf* 3 fs נָבֹוכָה Est 3^{15}; 3 mpl נָבֹכוּ Jo 1^{18}; *Pt* pl נְבֻכִים Ex 14^{3};—*be confused, in confusion* (of a city) Est 3^{15}, = wander aimlessly (of Isr) Ex 14^{3}, so of cattle Jo 1^{18} (Merx prop. בָּכוּ, after 𝔊 ἔκλαυσαν, but בכה not elsewhere of cattle)

†מְבוּכָה **n.f. confusion, confounding,** Is 22^{5} יוֹם מְהוּמָה וּמְבוּסָה וּמְבוּכָה *a day of consternation and down-treading and confusion;* Mi 7^{4} עַתָּה תִהְיֶה מְבוּכָתָם *now shall be their confusion.*

†I. בּוּל **n.[m.] Bul,** 8th month = *Marcheswan*, As. *Araḫ samna*, 1 K 6^{38} בְּיֶרַח בּוּל הוּא הַחֹדֶשׁ הַשְּׁמִינִי, (Canaanitish; Ph ירח בל, a Palm. god is בול (in n pr. עבדבול, Vog^{93} זבדבול etc.) & ירחבול (Vog^{93}, moon-god), which DHM $^{Ber\ Wien\ Ak.\ cviii,\ 977}$ connects with Heb בּוּל; Bae $^{Rel\,87\,f}$ (q.v) thinks = בעל, cf. Thes $^{p\,860}$)

II. בּוּל **n.m.** *product, produce*, v. יבל.

בּוּנָה **n.pr.m.** v בין.

בּוּנִי **n.pr.m.** v בנה.

†[בּוּס] **vb. tread down, trample**—**Qal** *Impf* יָבוּס ψ 60^{14} = 108^{14}, 3 *fs* תָּבוּס Pr 27^{7}, אָבוּס Is 63^{6}, *sf* 3 s אֲבוּסֶנּוּ Is 14^{25}; 1 *pl.* נָבוּס ψ 44^{6};—*tread down, trample* (of warriors), no obj. expr Zc 10^{5}, *id*, fig. c. acc (subj. י׳, as warrior) Is 14^{25} cf ψ 60^{14} = 108^{14} Is 63^{6}; (subj men, with God's help) ψ 44^{6}, fig = *reject, loathe* Pr 27^{7}. **Pol.** *Pf* בּוֹסְסוּ Is 63^{18}, בֹּסְסוּ Je 12^{10}—*tread down*, in bad sense, subj enemies of י׳, obj acc. Je 12^{10} (in metaph), = *desecrate* (obj מקדש) Is 63^{18} **Hithpol.** *Pt f.* מִתְבּוֹסֶסֶת

Ez 16$^{6.22}$—of the blind movements of infant's limbs, *kick out* (this way and that), fig. of Jerusalem. **Hoph.** *Pt.* מוּבָס Is 14^{19}—pass. *trodden down* Is 14^{19}, of corpse, sim. of king of Babylon

†יְבוּס **n.pr.loc.** **Jebus**, name of Jerusalem acc. to Ju 19^{10} יְבוּס הִיא ירוּשָׁלָם, cf. also v^{11}; 1 Ch 11^{4} יְרוּשָׁלַם הִיא יְבוּס, cf. v^{5}

†יְבוּסִי, יְבֻסִי **1. adj.gent.** **Jebusite, Jebusites**, sg. אורנה הַיְבֻסִי 2 S 24$^{16.18}$ cf. 1 Ch 21$^{15.18.28}$ 2 Ch 3^{1}; as subst *a Jebusite* Zc 9^{7}; usually c. art. הַיְ׳ coll. *the Jebusites*, in hist. statement Gn 10^{16} (J) = 1 Ch 1^{14} Nu 13^{29} (E) Jos 9^{1} 11^{3} 12^{8} 24^{11} (all D) Ju 3^{5} Ne 9^{8}, all in list of Canaanitish peoples; so also 1 K 9^{20} = 2 Ch 8^{7}, where remnant of these peoples referred to; also Ezr 9^{1}, which seems to shew that this list had become a standing expression for early inhabitants; cf. further in promises (JED) Gn 15^{21} Ex 3$^{8.17}$ 13^{5} 23^{23} 33^{2} 34^{11} Dt 7^{1} 20^{17} Jos 3^{10}; specif. defined as inhabitants of Jebus-Jerusalem Jos 15$^{63.63}$ (J) Ju 1$^{21.21}$ 2 S 5$^{6.8}$ (on which cf. Dr) 1 Ch 11^{4} (called also יוֹשֵׁב הָאָרֶץ 2 S 5^{6} & יֹשְׁבֵי הָאָרֶץ 1 Ch 11^{4}), v. also עִיר הַיְבוּסִי הַזֹּאת Ju 19^{11}; whence **2.** *Jerusalem*, Hex only P, Jos 15^{8} גֵּי בֶן־הִנֹּם אֶל־כֶּתֶף היבוסי מִנֶּגֶב היא יְרוּשָׁלָם, cf. 18^{16}, 18^{28} וְהַיְבוּסִי היא יְרוּשָׁלַם—Cf כנען.

†מְבוּסָה **n.f.** **down-treading, subjugation,** גּוֹי קַו־קָו וּמְבוּסָה Is 18$^{2.7}$ *a nation of might and of down-treading* (Che *all-subduing*); יוֹם מְהוּמָה וּמְ׳ וּמְבוּכָה Is 22^{5}, cf. מְבוּכָה sub בוך

†[תְּבוּסָה] **n.f.** **down-treading = ruin, downfall,** cstr. תְּבוּסַת אחזיהו 2 Ch 22^{7} *the downfall of Ahaziah.*

בוע (assumed as √ of foll., cf Lag$^{BN 10}$, but √ perh. בעבע, acc. to Sta$^{§ 257}$ a quadrilit. Ar. بَغَّ, *efferbuit et commotus fuit* (sanguis), بُغْبُغ *puteus cujus aqua haurienti propinqua*).

†אֲבַעְבֻּעֹת **n.f pl.** **blisters, boils** (𝔗 אֲבַעְבּוּעָן; cf. 𝔗 בֻּעְבַּע, NH בַּעְבּוּעַ בּוּעָה, Syr ܐܒܥܒܘܥܐ) Ex 9^{9} שְׁחִין פֹּרֵחַ אֲבַעְבֻּעֹת, cf v^{10}

בוץ so Thes, better **ביץ** (cf Ar. بَاضَ *surpass in whiteness*, بَيَاض *whiteness*).

†[בֵּיצָה] **n.f.** $^{Is\ 10.14}$ **egg** (NH *id*, Ar بَيْضَة, Aram. בֵּיעֲתָא, ܒܝܥܬܐ)—only *Pl* בֵּיצִים Dt 22$^{6.6}$ Is 10^{14}; cstr. בֵּיצֵי Is 59^{5}; sf. בֵּיצֶיהָ Jb 39^{14}, בֵּיצֵיהֶם Is 59^{5},—*eggs* Is 10^{14} (of small bird צפור) Dt 22$^{6.6}$, cf Is 10^{14} (in simil), (of ostrich רננים) Jb 39^{14}; (of great viper צפעוני) Is 59$^{5.5}$ (metaph.)

†בּוּץ, בֻּץ **n.[m.]** **byssus** (late), (Ph. בץ, Aram. בוּץ, ܒܘܨܐ; √ dub.; Birch, Wilkinson $^{Egyptians\ ii.\ 156\ f.}$ fr Egypt. *hbos, clothe;* v. Say Herodot$^{ii\ 86}$, Thes fr. √ בוץ, but No$^{ZMG\ 1876,\ 650}$, Armen., acc. to Lag$^{Sem.\ i.\ 72\ al}$) **a fine white Egyptian linen, and cloth made of it,** מִשְׁפְּחוֹת בֵּית־עֲבֹדַת הַבֻּץ 1 Ch 4^{21} *families of the house of byssus-working;* cf. 2 Ch 2^{13}, מְכֻרְבָּל בִּמְעִיל בּוּץ 1 Ch 15^{27} *clothed in a robe of byssus* (but rd rather as ‖ 2 S 6^{14} מְכַרְכֵּר בְּכָל־עֹז *was dancing with all his might*), cf. תַּכְרִיךְ בּ׳ Est 8^{15}, מְלֻבָּשִׁים בּוּץ 2 Ch 5^{12}, חַבְלֵי בוּץ Est 1^{6}; 2 Ch 3^{14} material of פָּרֹכֶת, article of trade Ez 27^{16} (del. 𝔊 Co) Cf also שֵׁשׁ.

בוק (=בקק)

†בּוּקָה **n.f.** **emptiness,** Na 2^{11} בּוּקָה וּמְבוּקָה וּמְבֻלָּקָה *emptiness and void and waste.*

†מְבוּקָה **n.f.** *id*, Na 2^{11} v. supr.

I בּוֹר, *cistern,* v sub באר.

II בּוֹר, *cleanness,* v. בֹּר sub ברר.

†**בור** **vb.** **Qal** *Inf cstr.* לָבוּר Ec 9^{1} (c. acc.), **prob.** (si vera l) **make clear, clear up, explain** (VB, so sts, in NH, ברר q.v.) but rd. perh. וְלִבִּי רָאָה 𝔊 𝔖 Bi, or לָתוּר Gr, cf 1^{13} 2^{3} 7^{25}.

בושׁ $_{109}$ **vb.** **be ashamed** (Sab מהבאם בוס; =*evil-doer* DHM$^{ZMG\ 1883,\ 375}$, ‖ Aram. בְּהַת, Syr. ܒܗܬ, Ar. بَاتَ, بَثَّ mean *disperse*)—**Qal** *Pf.* Je 48^{39}; בֹּשׁ Je 48^{13}; בּוֹשָׁה Je 15^{9}; בֹּשְׁתִּי Je 31^{19} + 25 t., *Impf.* יֵבוֹשׁ Is 29^{22} + 57 t, *Inf.* abs בּוֹשׁ Je 6^{15} 8^{12}; *Imv.* בּוֹשִׁי Is 23^{4} Ez 16^{52}, בּוֹשׁוּ Ez 36^{32}; *Pt.* pl. בּוֹשִׁים Ez 32^{30},—**1.** abs. *feel shame* Je 6^{15} + 16 t, Is 19^{9} 23^{4} 37^{27} Is^{2} 45^{16} + 14 t., Ez 16^{63} Mi 7^{16} Jo 2$^{26.27}$ 2 K 19^{26} Ez 9^{6} Jb 6^{20} ψ 6^{11} (+ 27 t., chiefly in late Psalms). **2.** sq מִן, *be ashamed of,* i e *disconcerted, disappointed by reason of* Je 2$^{36.36}$ 12^{13} 48^{13} Is 1^{29} 20^{5} Ez 32^{30} 36^{32}. **3.** with obj בֹּשְׁתִּי לִשְׁאוֹל *I am ashamed to ask* Ez 8^{22}; לֹא תֵבשׁוּ תַּהְכְּרוּ לִי *ye are not ashamed to deal hardly with me* (impf.subj) Jb 19^{3}. בוש often ‖ נכלם & חפר, בֹּשׁוּ וְהָכְלְמוּ *they are ashamed and confounded* Je 14^{3}, 22^{22} Is^{2} 41^{11} 45$^{16.17}$ Ez 16^{52} 36^{32} ψ 35^{4} 69^{7} Ez 9^{6}; וּבֹשׁוּ הַחֹזִים וְחָפְרוּ הַקֹּסְמִים *and the seers shall be ashamed and the diviners confounded* Mi 3^{7}, cf Je 15^{9} Jb 6^{20} ψ 35^{26} 40^{15} 70^{3} 71^{24}; יֵבוֹשׁ מְקוֹרוֹ Ho 13^{15} (rd. יִיבַשׁ *be dry*); עַד־בּוֹשׁ + Ju 3^{25} 2 K 2^{17} 8^{11}. **Polel** *Pf.* בֹּשֵׁשׁ *delay* (in shame), בֹּשֵׁשׁ משֶׁה לָרֶדֶת *Moses delayed to descend* Ex 32^{1} (J), מַדּוּעַ בֹּשֵׁשׁ רִכְבּוֹ לָבוֹא *why delay his chariots to come?* Ju 5^{28}. **Hiph. 1.** הֱבִישׁוֹתָ ψ 44^{8}; הֱבִישֹׁתָה ψ 53^{6}; *Impf.* 2 ms. sf תְּבִישֵׁנִי ψ 119$^{31.116}$; תָּבִישׁוּ ψ 14^{6}; *put to shame, Pt* מֵבִישׁ Pr 10^{5} 14^{35}

19^{26} 29^{15}, *one causing shame* or *acting shamefully*, || עֶבֶד מַשְׂכִּיל יִמְשֹׁל בְּבֵן מֵבִישׁ , מַשְׂכִּיל *a servant acting wisely will rule over a son causing shame* Pr 17^2, אֵשֶׁת חַיִל || מְבִישָׁה Pr 12^4 **2.** הוביש 2 S 19^6 Je 2^{26} 6^{15} Jo $1^{10.12}$, הביש Je 10^{14} +7 t, Ho 2^7 Jo $1^{12.17}$ Is 30^5 (but הבאיש Kt), הבשו Je $8^{9.12}$, *Imv.* הֹבִישׁוּ Jo 1^{11} (all the forms in Joel derived √יבשׁ by ancient versions and some moderns, vid Ew §122 e Ges §72 6) **a.** *put to shame* 2 S 19^6 **b.** *act shamefully* Ho 2^7. **c.** *to be put to shame* Je 2^{26} 6^{15} 46^{24} $48^{1.20}$ $50^{2.2}$ Jo $1^{10.12.17}$ (?). **d.** *be ashamed* Je $8^{9.12}$ Jo $1^{11.12}$ (?) Is 30^5 (Qr), c מִן Je 10^{14} = 51^{17} **Hithp.** *Impf* יִתְבֹּשָׁשׁוּ *ashamed before one another* Gn 2^{25} (J)

†בּוּשָׁה **n.f.** shame ψ 89^{46} Mi 7^{10} Ob v^{10} Ez 7^{18}.

†בָּשְׁנָה **n.f.** shame (בשן Ew §163 f) Ho 10^6

†בֹּשֶׁת **n.f.** shame Jb 8^{22} + 20 t, sf בָּשְׁתִּי ψ 69^{20} + 7 t **1** *shame* 1 S $20^{30.30}$ ψ 40^{16} 69^{20} 70^4 Is $30^{3.5}$ 61^7 Je 2^{26} 3^{25} 20^{18} Hb 2^{10} Zp $3^{5.19}$, לָבַשׁ בֹּשֶׁת *clothe with shame* Jb 8^{22} ψ 35^{26} 132^{18}, || עטה בשת ψ 109^{29}, בֹּשֶׁת (ה)פָּנִים *shame* (or *confusion*) *of face* 2 Ch 32^{21} Ezr 9^7 Dn $9^{7.8}$, cf ψ 44^{16} Je 7^{19}, בשת עלוּמַיִךְ *shame of thy youth* Is 54^4, עֶרְיָה־בֹשֶׁת *nakedness* (*that is*) *shame* Mi 1^{11} cf ψ 45^5, בֹּשֶׁת עֶרְוַת אמך 1 S 20^{30} **2.** *shameful thing*, substituted for בַּעַל (q v) by later editors, Ho 9^{10} Je 3^{24}, מזבחות לַבֹּשֶׁת Je 11^{13}, cf. יְרֻבֶּשֶׁת 2 S 11^{21} = יְרֻבַּעַל Ju 6^{32}, אִישׁ־בֹּשֶׁת 2 S 2^8 = אֶשְׁבַּעַל 1 Ch 8^{33}.

†[מְבוּשׁ] **n.[m.]** pl sf. מְבֻשָׁיו, **his privates,** that excite shame, *pudenda*, Dt 25^{11}.

בַּז v sub בזז

†[בָּזָא] **vb. divide, cut through** (? cf Aram. בְּזַע, ܒܙܥ *cleave*)—**Qal** *Pf* בָּזְאוּ נהרים Is $18^{2.7}$ whose land *rivers cut through* (of Cush)

†בָּזָה **vb. despise** (Pal בָּזָא, cf ܒܙܐ *raise the head loftily and disdainfully*)—**Qal** *Pf* Nu 15^{31} +; בָּזִיתָ 2 S 12^9, sf. בְּזִתָנִי 2 S 12^{10}, etc., *Impf* וַיִּבֶז Gn 25^{34} Est 3^6, sf. וַיִּבְזֵהוּ 1 S 17^{42}; 3 fs וַתִּבֶז 2 S 6^{16} 1 Ch 15^{29}, 2 ms תִּבְזֶה ψ 51^{19} 73^{20}, וַיִּבְזוּ Ne 2^{19}, וַיִּבְזֻהוּ 1 S 10^{27}, *Inf. cstr* בזה Is 49^7 (Di Ew §150 b); *Pt act* בוזה Pr 15^{20} 19^{16}, בוזהו Pr 14^2, בֹּזִים 2 Ch 36^{16}, בוזי Mal 1^6, sf בֹּזַי 1 S 2^{30}, *pass* בָּזוּי Je 49^{15} +; f בזויה Ec 9^{16},—*despise, regard with contempt*, sq acc rei, birthright Gn 25^{34} (J); words of י׳ Nu 15^{31} (P, not elsewh in Hex), 2 S 12^9 cf 2 Ch 36^{16}, name of י׳ Mal $1^{6.6}$ (cf infr), oath (אָלָה) Ez 16^{59} $17^{16.18.19}$, holy things Ez 22^8; one's own ways Pr 19^{16} (i e is careless of them, lives recklessly, opp שֹׁמֵר נַפְשׁוֹ, cf נצר דרכו 16^{17}); distress of the distressed ψ 22^{25} (||שִׁקֵּץ, subj י׳), prayer, subj id ψ 102^{18}, broken & contrite heart ψ 51^{19} (c. לֹא), cf on other hand 73^{20}, sq acc pers. Saul 1 S 10^{27}, David 17^{42} cf. Pr 15^{20}, י׳ 1 S 2^{30} 2 S 12^{10} Pr 14^2, his prisoners ψ 69^{34} (subj י׳), sq לְ, וַתִּבֶז לוֹ בְּלִבָּהּ 2 S 6^{16} = 1 Ch 15^{29}, 2 K 19^{21} = Is 37^{22}; sq עַל pers. Ne 2^{19}; sq Inf וַיִּבֶז בְּעֵינָיו לִשְׁלֹחַ יָד Est 3^6, note esp בזה נפש Is 49^7 *a despising of soul*, i e *one despised from the soul, thoroughly despised*, on other views v Che Di *Pt* pass *despised*, of pers cstr בזוי עם *despised of people* (|| חֶרְפַּת אָדָם) ψ 22^7, cf בָּזוּי בָּאָדָם Je 49^{15} also Ob v^2, of wisdom Ec 9^{16}. **Niph.** *Pt.* נבזה ψ 15^4 +, **f.** נִבְזָה 1 S 15^9 (so rd for נמבזה cf We Dr), pl נבזים Mal 2^9,—**1.** *despised* ψ 15^4 119^{141} Is $53^{3.3}$ Je 22^{28} **2.** *vile, worthless* 1 S 15^9 **3.** *despicable, contemptible* Mal 1^7 said of table of י׳, cf v^{12} 2^9, Dn 11^{21} as subst. of Antiochus Epiph. **Hiph.** *Inf* לְהַבְזוֹת בַּעְלֵיהֶן Est 1^{17} *so as to cause to despise their lords* (cause their lords to be despised)

†בִּזָּיוֹן **n.[m.]** contempt Est 1^{18} (ב׳ וָקָצֶף).

בִּזָּה v sub בזז

†בָּזַז **vb. spoil, plunder** (Ar بَزَّ, Aram ܒܙ; Amhar. ብዘበዘ: perh Eth ቤዘወ: *rescue* Pra BAS I 33)—**Qal** *Pf* 3 ms וּבָזַז (consec) Ez 29^{19}, 3 pl בָּזְזוּ Nu 31^{53} + 7 t, בָּזוּ Nu 31^9, sf וּבְזָזוּם consec. Je 20^5, 1 pl בָּזַזְנוּ Dt 2^{35}, בַּזּוֹנוּ 3^7; *Impf* 2 ms תָּבֹז Dt 20^{14}, pl יָבֹזּוּ Is 10^2 + 2 t, וַיָּבֹזּוּ Gn 34^{27} + 4 t, sf יָבֹזּוּם Zp 2^9, 2 mpl תָּבֹזּוּ Jos 8^2, 1 pl. cohort נָבֹזָּה 1 S 14^{36} (cf Ges §67 R. 11); *Imv.* בֹּזּוּ Na $2^{10.10}$, *Inf cstr* בֹּז Is 10^6 + 3 t.; בֹּזֹּ Est 3^{13} 8^{11}; *Pt. act* pl בֹּזְזִים Is 42^{24} 2 Ch 20^{25}, sf. בֹּזְזַיִךְ Je 30^{16}, בֹּזְזֵינוּ Is 17^{14}, בֹּזְזֵיהֶם Ez 39^{10}; *pass* בָּזוּז Is 42^{22},—*spoil* = take as spoil, c acc rei Nu 31^9 Dt 2^{35} (c לְ & refl suff.) Je 20^5 Ez 26^{12} Na 2^{10} ψ 109^{11}, oftener c acc cogn, בַּז Nu 31^{32} Is 10^6 (|| שָׁלַל שָׁלָל, as oft) 33^{23} Ez 29^{19} $38^{12.13}$; בִּזָּה 2 Ch 25^{13}, שָׁלָל Dt 3^7 20^{14} (both sq לְ c refl suff) 2 Ch $20^{25.25}$ 28^8 Est 3^{13} 8^{11}; שלל & בהמה Jos $8^{2.27}$ 11^{14} (all sq לְ c refl suff), obj. pers. carried off (cf בַּז) Gn 34^{29} (MT, but cf Ol); *plunder, despoil*, c. acc pers. robbed Is 10^2 11^{14} 17^{14} (שסה) 42^{22} (|| id) Zp 2^9 Je 30^{16} Ez $39^{10.10}$; c. בָּהֶם (pers) 1 S 14^{36}, c acc. of place plundered Gn 34^{27} 2 K 7^{16} 2 Ch 14^{13}, *abs* Nu 31^{53} Is 42^{24}. †**Niph.** *Pf.* וְנָבֹזּוּ consec Am 3^{11}; *Impf* 2 ms תִּבּוֹז Is 24^3; *Inf abs.* הִבּוֹז Is 24^3—*be spoiled, plundered,*

subj. ארמנות Am 3[11]; הארץ Is 24[3]; הִבּוֹז תִּבּוֹז (|| הִבּוֹק תִּבּוֹק). †**Pu.** *Pf.* וּבֻזְּזוּ consec. Je 50[37]—*be taken as spoil*, subj. אוצרת.

†**בַּז n.[m.] spoiling, robbery; spoil, booty**—בַּז abs. Nu 14[3]+; so also Ez 25[7] Qr (Kt בג meaningless); בָּז Je 2[14]+; but הַבָּז Nu 31[32] v. d. H; sf. בִּזָּהּ Ex 29[19];—**1.** *spoiling, robbery*, לָבַז i.e. to be plundered, despoiled Ez 7[21] (of temple || שָׁלָל) 23[46]. **2.** *spoil, booty, plunder* Is 10[6] 33[23] Ez 29[19] 38[12.13] (all acc. cogn. || שָׁלָל); cf. Nu 31[32] Je 15[13] 17[3]; in phr. הָיָה לָבַז Je 49[32] (of camels) Ez 36[4] cf. v[5]; also of human beings Nu 14[3.31] Dt 1[39] Je 2[14] (all היה לב׳) + 2 K 21[14] (|| מְשִׁסָּה) Is 42[22] (|| *id.*) Je 2[14], cf. 30[16] (|| מְשִׁסָּה); also Ez 25[7] Qr, 26[5] (היה לב׳; both in personif.); fig. of Isr. as sheep Ez 34[8.22] (both היה לב׳) v[28] היה בז (no לְ). On Is 8[1.3] מַהֵר שָׁלָל חָשׁ בַּז v. מהר.

†**בִּזָּה n.f. spoil, booty (late)**—בִּזָּה 2 Ch 14[13]+ 9 t.;—*spoil, prey*, of things 2 Ch 28[14] Est 9[10.15.16], cf. 2 Ch 14[13] 25[13] Dn 11[24] (|| שָׁלָל & רכוש); n. verb., *spoiling*, בַּבִּ׳ Ezr 9[7] Dn 11[33], cf. also לְבִ׳ Ne 3[36].

בִּזָּיוֹן v. sub בזה.

†**בִּזְיוֹתְיָה n.pr.loc.** acc. to MT place near Beersheba Jos 15[28]; but rd. prob. וּבְנוֹתֶיהָ 𝔊 *and her daughters* (villages, cf. בת sub בן) v. Ne 11[27] (We[Sm 215] Hollenb[Alex. Übers. Jos. 14] Di al.)

בזק (Aram. בְּזַק, ܒܙܩ *scatter*; Ar. بَزَقَ *rise* (of sun) is prob. erroneous v. Lane[199]).

†**בָּזָק n.[m.] lightning flash?** Ez 1[14] Hi Co del.; verse om. in old MSS. of 𝔊; sense uncertain, possibly error for ברק.

†**בֶּזֶק n.pr.loc.** 1 S 11[8] (בְּבָזֶק) rendezvous of Israel under Saul and Sam.; Ju 1[4.5] home of Adoni-bezek; on loc. cf. Euseb. Lag[Onom. 105, 2nd ed. 139]; see also Stu. Ju 1[4]; 17th (mile-)stone fr. Neapolis toward Scythopolis; mod. *Ḫirbet Ibzîḳ*, 14 Eng. m. fr. Nâblus, Survey[II. 231].

†**[בָּזַר] vb. scatter** (Ar. بَذَرَ, Aram. בְּדַר)—**Qal** *Impf.* Dn 11[24] בִּזָּה וְשָׁלָל וּרְכוּשׁ לָהֶם יִבְזוֹר *plunder and spoil and possessions he will scatter among them* (subj. Antiochus Epiph.) **Pi.** *Pf.* בִּזַּר, *id.*, ψ 68[31], but rd. *Imv.* בַּזֵּר (בַּזֵּר) (𝔊 𝔖 𝔙 so most; De follows MT), subj. ref. to י׳, obj. עַמִּים.

†**בִּזְּתָא n.pr.m.** a eunuch of Ahasuerus, Est 1[10] (Thes comp. Pers. *beste, ligatus* sc. *membro*, e.g. *spado*, cf. Vullers[Dict. Pers.] sub بَسْتَه).

† **I. [בָּחַל] vb. feel loathing** (cf. Syr. ܒܚܠ (so in lexx.) *nauseated* (yet v. Gei[Urschrift. 270]); NSyr. ܒܚܠ *envy* cf. Stoddard[Gram. 12, 87])—**Qal** *Pf.* 3 fs. Zc 11[8] וַתִּקְצַר נַפְשִׁי בָּהֶם וְגַם נַפְשָׁם בָּחֲלָה בִי *felt a loathing* against me.

†**II. [בָּחַל] vb.** (Ar. بَخِلَ *be avaricious*); only **Pu.** *Pt.* נַחֲלָה מְבֹחֶלֶת an inheritance *gotten by greed* Pr 20[21] Kt; < Qr Vrss נ׳ מְבֹהֶלֶת, v. בהל.

†**[בָּחַן] vb. examine, try** (cf. Aram. בְּחַן, Syr. ܒܚܢ, *try, examine;* Ar. محن I. VIII. *test*, cf. W[SG 65])—**Qal** *Pf.* sf. בְּחָנַנִי Jb 23[10], בָּחַנְתָּ ψ 17[3]+ 7 t.; *Impf.* יִבְחָן ψ 11[5]+5 t.; *Imv.* sf. בְּחָנֵנִי ψ 26[2] +2 t.; *Inf.* בְּחֹן Zc 13[9]; *Pt.* בֹּחֵן Je 11[20]+5 t. (|| נסה, צרף);—**1.** *examine, scrutinize, try* ψ 11[5] 139[23] Jb 7[18]; עַפְעַפָּיו יִבְחֲנוּ בְּנֵי אָדָם *His eyelids try the children of men* (search them through and through) ψ 11[4]. **2.** *prove, test, try.* **a.** with the metaphor of gold Jb 23[10]; וּבְחַנְתִּים כִּבְחֹן אֶת־הַזָּהָב *and I will try them as one tries gold* Zc 13[9]. **b.** without metaphor, of God testing persons ψ 26[2] 66[10] 81[8] Je 9[6]; their ways Je 6[27]; the לֵב ψ 17[3] Je 12[3] Pr 17[3] 1 Ch 29[17]; reins Je 17[10]; heart and reins ψ 7[10] Je 11[20] (=20[12]). **c.** of man testing or tempting God ψ 95[9] Mal 3[10.15]. **d.** the ear trying words Jb 12[11]=34[3]. **Niph.** *Impf.* יִבָּחֵן Jb 34[36] Gn 42[15.16], *to be tried, proved.* **Pu.** בֹּחַן Ez 21[18] *the trial has been made* (𝔊 𝔖 𝔙 Ges MV Ew Ke, but noun בֹּחַן MT Symm Haev.; rd. בְּחֵן *with grace, favour*, Hi Co).

†**בֹּחַן n.[m.] testing**, Is 28[16] אֶבֶן בֹּחַן *a tested, tried stone*, i.e. approved for use as a foundation-stone. On Ez 21[18] MT v. foreg. *ad fin.*

†**בַּחַן n.[m.] watch-tower**, Is 32[14].

†**[בַּחוּן]** sf. בַּחוּנָיו (dag. f. implic. Qr; בחיניו Kt) Is 23[13] *their siege-towers.*

†**בָּחוֹן n.[m.] assayer**, one who tries metals Je 6[27] (Ges[§ 84. 3] Ew[§ 152 b]).

בחיניו Is 23[13] Kt; v. [בחון] supr.

†**בָּחַר vb. choose** (cf. Aram. בְּחַר, Syr. ܒܚܰܪ || בחן, As. *bêru* (√באר₃) Dl[Pr 76])—**Qal** *Pf.* בָּחַר Dt 7[6]+66 t.; יִבְחַר Is 41[24]+60 t.; אֶבְחַר Jb 29[25] (Baer); *Imv.* בְּחַר Ex 17[9]+5 t.; *Inf. abs.* בָּחוֹר 1 S 2[28] Is 7[15.16]; *Inf. cstr.* sf. בָּחֳרִי Ez 20[5]; *Pt.* בֹּחֵר 1 S 20[30] Zc 3[2]; *pass.* בָּחוּר Ex 14[7]+18 t.;—**1.** with בְּ, **a.** *divine choice*, of Abraham Ne 9[7]; Israel Dt 7[7] Is 44[1] Ez 20[5]; to become his people Dt 7[6] 14[2]; Jeshurun Is 44[2]; the seed of the patriarchs Dt 4[37] 10[15]; Levites Dt 18[5] 21[5] 1 Ch 15[2] 2 Ch 29[11]; Aaron ψ 105[26]; Judah 1 Ch 28[4] not Ephraim ψ 78[67]; Levi and Judah Je 33[24]; the king Dt 17[15], especially David 1 S 10[24] 16[8.9.10]

2 S 6^{21} 1 K 8^{16} (= 2 Ch 6^{6}) 1 Ch $28^{4.5}$ 29^{1} 2 Ch 6^{6} ψ 78^{70}, others Nu 16^{5} 17^{20} (P) Hg 2^{23}, place of sacrifice Dt 12^{18} 14^{25} $16^{7.15}$ 17^{8} 2 Ch 7^{12}; the city 1 K $8^{16.44}$ (= 2 Ch $6^{5.34}$) 11^{32}; Jerusalem 2 Ch 6^{6} Is 14^{1} Zc 1^{17} 2^{16} 3^{2}, Zion ψ 132^{13}; delusions Is 66^{4}. **b.** *man's choice*, of ways Pr 3^{31} Is 66^{3}, good things Is $7^{15.16}$; life Dt 30^{19}, gods Ju 10^{14} Is 41^{24}, God's pleasure Is 56^{4} 65^{12} 66^{4}. **2.** with אֲשֶׁר (alone, for אשר בחר ב׳). **a.** *divine choice*, of Israel Is 41^{8} יַעֲקֹב אֲשֶׁר בְּחַרְתִּיךָ, 43^{10}; the people 1 K 3^{8} ψ 33^{12}; men Nu 16^{7} (P) ψ 65^{5}; king 2 S 16^{18} 1 K 11^{34}, place of sacrifice Dt $12^{14.26}$ 15^{20} 17^{10} 31^{11} (D) Jos 9^{27} (P), especially לָשׂוּם שְׁמוֹ שָׁם Dt $12^{5.21}$ 14^{24}, לְשַׁכֵּן שְׁמוֹ שָׁם Dt 12^{11} 14^{23} $16^{2.6.11}$ Ne 1^{9}, the city 1 K 8^{48} (= 2 Ch 6^{38}), לשום שמי שם 1 K 11^{36} 14^{21} (= 2 Ch 12^{13}); Jerusalem 1 K 11^{13} 2 K 21^{7} (= 2 Ch 33^{7}) 23^{27}, fast Is $58^{5.6}$, way ψ 25^{12}. **b.** *man's choice*, place to dwell in Dt 23^{17}; gardens Is 1^{29}, king 1 S 12^{13}, wives Gn 6^{2} (J), what to do 2 S 15^{15}. **3.** with acc. & לְ, *choose some one or something for* **a.** *divine choice*, of Levi 1 S 2^{28}, Jacob ψ $135^{4.5}$, inheritance ψ 47^{5}. **b.** *human choice*, persons Ex 17^{9} Jos $24^{15.22}$ (E) 1 S 8^{18} 13^{12} 2 S 24^{12} (= 1 Ch 21^{10}), things Gn 13^{11} (J) 1 S 17^{40} 1 K $18^{23.25}$ Jb 34^{4} **4.** with acc. and מִן, *choose, select from* 2 S 10^{9} (= 1 Ch 19^{10}) **5.** acc **a.** *divine choice*, temple 2 Ch 7^{16}, Judah ψ 78^{68}, servant Is 41^{9} 49^{7} **b.** *man's choice*, persons Ex 18^{25} (E) Ju 5^{8} Jos 8^{3} (J) 2 S 17^{1}; things Jb 7^{15} 9^{14} 15^{5} 29^{25} 34^{33} $119^{30.173}$ Pr 1^{29} Is 40^{20}. **6.** with עַל, כי על זה בחרת מעני *for this thou hast chosen rather than affliction* Jb 36^{21}, with acc and עַל pregn כל אשר תבחר עלי *all that thou choosest* (to lay) *upon me* 2 S 19^{39} **7.** with לְ of acc 1 S 20^{30} (many MSS have בְּ, but 𝔊 We Dr read חָבֵר *companion*) The ptcp בָּחוּר *chosen*, of a ruler ψ 89^{20}, warrior Je 49^{19} (= 50^{44}), as cedars Ct 5^{15}; coll. רכב בחור *chosen chariots* Ex 14^{7} (E), אִישׁ בחור *chosen men, warriors* Ju $20^{15.16.34}$ 1 S 24^{3} 2 Ch $13^{3.17}$, for wh. בָּחוּר alone 1 K 12^{21} = 2 Ch 11^{1}, 2 Ch 25^{5}; בחורי ישׂראל 1 S 26^{2} ψ 78^{31}, 2 S 10^{9} בחורי בישראל (‖ 1 Ch 19^{10} בחור בישראל, doubtless the true reading, as 2 S 6^{1}) **8.** *test, try* (Aram = בחן) בְּחַרְתִּיךָ בְּכוּר עֹנִי Is 48^{10} *I have tested thee in the furnace of affliction* 𝔖 𝔗 Ges Hi Ew De Che Dr, but *chosen* 𝔙 Rab Calv AV **Niph.** נִבְחַר Je 8^{3}, *Pt* נִבְחָר Pr 8^{10} + 5 t;—*to be chosen.* **a.** abs. *chosen, choice* Pr $8^{10.19}$ 10^{20} **b.** cstr. ונבחר מִן מות מחיים *death will be chosen rather than life* Je 8^{3}; *choicer than* Pr 16^{16} 22^{1}, נבחר ליהוה מזבח *choicer* (more acceptable) *to Yahweh* than peace-offering Pr 21^{3} **Pu.** יְבֻחַר *chosen, selected* Ec 9^{4} (יְחֻבַּר Qr).

†בָּחוּר **n.m.** young man Is 62^{5} + 7 t; pl. בַּחוּרִים (intensive with dag f. implic) Pr 20^{29} + 13 t., cstr. בַּחוּרֵי Ez 23^{6} + 4 t., sf. בַּחוּרַי etc La 1^{15} + 16 t,—*young man* (choice, in the prime of manhood) 1 S 9^{2} Ec 11^{9} Is 62^{5}, coll. *young men* Je 15^{8}, בָּחוּר וּבְתוּלָה *young men and virgins* Dt 32^{25} 2 Ch 36^{17} Je 51^{22} Ez 9^{6}; usually pl. Ju 14^{10} Ru 3^{10} 1 S 8^{16} 2 K 8^{12} 2 Ch 36^{17} Pr 20^{29} Is 9^{17} 31^{8} 40^{30} Je 6^{11} 9^{20} 11^{22} 18^{21} 48^{15} 49^{26} 50^{3} 51^{3} La 1^{15} $5^{13.14}$ Ez $33^{6.12.23}$ 30^{17} Jo 3^{1} Am 2^{11} 4^{10}, ‖ בתולות ψ 78^{63} 148^{12} Is 23^{4} Je 31^{13} La 1^{18} 2^{21} Am 8^{13} Zc 9^{17}.

†[בְּחוּרִים] **n.f.abstr.pl.** youth, pl sf. בְּחֻרָיו Nu 11^{28} (J; Onk 𝔖 Ges De Di; 𝔊 בחיריו Sam 𝔙 Lu Ke), בחורותיך Ec 11^{9}, בְּחוּרֹתֶיךָ Ec 12^{1}.

†[בָּחִיר] **n.m.** chosen, cstr. בחיר 2 S 21^{6} (but We Dr בְּהַר י׳), sf. בְּחִירָיו 1 Ch 16^{13} ψ 89^{4} $105^{6.43}$ $106^{5.23}$ Is^{3} 42^{1} 43^{20} 45^{4} $65^{9.15.22}$; always the *chosen* or *elect* of Yahweh.

†בַּחֻרִים **n pr.loc.** (*young men's village*) of a small town of Benjamin beyond the Mt. of Olives on the way to Jericho (cf. Rob [BR i 433]; Kasteren [ZPV 1890, 100 ff.]) 2 S 3^{16} 16^{5} 17^{18} 19^{17} 1 K 2^{8} (= עַלְמוֹן acc to 𝔗 [Jon] Schwarz Marti-Schick [ZPV iii 8 f.])

†יִבְחָר **n.pr.m.** (*He* (*Êl* or י׳) *chooses*) son of David 2 S 5^{15} 1 Ch 3^{6} 14^{5}

†[מִבְחָר] **n.[m.]** (**f.** Ez 24^{5}) choicest, best, cstr מבחר Dt 12^{11} + 10 t, sf מִבְחָרָיו Dn 11^{15}, vows Dt 12^{11}, valleys Is 22^{7}, fir trees Is 37^{24}; cedars Je 22^{7}, bones Ez 24^{4}; sepulchres Gn 23^{6} (P); of the flock Ez 24^{5}, of the Assyrians Ez 23^{7}, captains Ex 15^{4} (E poet), young men Je 48^{15}, מבחר וטוב לבנן Ez 31^{16} (del. וטוב 𝔊 Co), עַם מִבְחָרָיו Dn 11^{15} = *his choice troops*

†מִבְחוֹר **n.[m.]** choice, in the phrases עיר מבחור *choice city* 2 K 3^{19}, מבחור בְּרֹשָׁיו *choice fir trees* 2 K 19^{23} = מִבְחַר ברושיו Is 37^{24} (prob. scribal error in both cases for מבחר).

†מִבְחָר **n.pr.m.** (*choice*) one of David's warriors 1 Ch 11^{38}.

†בַּחֲרוּמִי **adj.gent.** Baharumite 1 Ch 11^{33} = בַּרְחֻמִי 2 S 23^{31}. Prob בַּחֻרִמִי Dr

†[בָּטָא, בָּטָה] **vb.** **speak rashly, thoughtlessly** (NH *id*, בטי)—**Qal** *Pt.* בּוֹטֶה Pr 12^{18} *one that babbleth* (opp לְשׁוֹן חֲכָמִים) **Pi.** *Impf* יְבַטֵּא בשבועה Lv 5^{4} *speak rashly, unadvisedly*, so וַיְבַטֵּא בִּשְׂפָתָיו (of Moses) ψ 106^{33}; *Inf* לְבַטֵּא בִּשְׂפָתַיִם Lv 5^{4} (P).

†מִבְטָא n.[m.] **rash utterance**, מִבְטָא שְׂפָתֶיהָ Nu 30[7.9].

†I. **בָּטַח** vb. **trust** (cf. Ar. بَطَحَ *to throw one down upon his face* Thes, اِنْبَطَحَ *lie extended on the ground, 'se reposer sur quelqu'un'* Fl MV)—**Qal** *Pf.* בָּטַח ψ 28[7] + 35 t.; *Impf.* יִבְטַח Jb 40[23] + 27 t.; *Imv.* בְּטַח ψ 37[3] + 8 t.; *Inf. abs.* בָּטוֹחַ Is 59[4], *cstr.* בְּטֹחַ ψ 118[8] + 2 t.; *Pt.* בֹּטֵחַ ψ 21[8] + 35 t.; pass. בָּטוּחַ ψ 112[7] Is 26[3]. **I.** *trust.* **1.** abs. Is 12[2]. **2.** with cogn. acc. מה הבטחון הזה אשר בטחת *what is this trust that thou dost trust?* 2 K 18[19] = Is 36[4]. **3.** with בְּ *trust in*—**a.** *God* 2 K 18[5] 19[10] 1 Ch 5[20] ψ 9[11] 21[8] 22[5.6] 25[2] 26[1] 28[7] 32[10] 37[3] 40[4] 55[24] 56[5.12] 62[9] 84[13] 91[2] 112[7] 115[9.10.11] 125[1] 143[8] Pr 16[20] 29[25] Is 26[3.4] 37[10] Je 17[7] 39[18] Zp 3[2]. **b.** *persons* Ju 9[26] ψ 41[10] 118[8.9] 146[3] Pr 31[11] Je 17[5] 46[25] Mi 7[5]. **c.** *things* Dt 28[52] Jb 39[11] ψ 27[3] 44[7] 52[9] 62[11] 115[8] 135[18] Pr 11[28] 28[26] Is 30[12] 42[17] 47[10] Je 5[17] 7[14] 12[5] 13[25] 48[7] 49[4] Ez 16[15] Ho 10[13] Am 6[1]. **d.** in the name of God ψ 33[21] Is 50[10]; mercy of God ψ 13[6] 52[10]; word of God ψ 119[42]; salvation of God ψ 78[22]. **4.** with עַל, *trust* or *rely upon*—**a.** *God* ψ 31[15] 37[5] Pr 28[25] Je 49[11]. **b.** *persons* 2 K 18[20.21.24] = Is 36[5.6.9], Je 9[3]. **c.** *things* 2 K 18[21] = Is 36[6] 2 Ch 32[10], ψ 49[7] Is 31[1] 59[4] Ez 33[13] Hb 2[18]. **5.** with אֶל *trust to*—**a.** *God* 2 K 18[22] (= Is 36[7]) ψ 4[6] 31[7] 56[4] 86[2] Pr 3[5]. **b.** *persons* Ju 20[36]. **c.** *things* Je 7[4] (= על דבר 7[8]). **II.** *be confident* Jb 6[20] 40[23] Pr 14[16]; צַדִּיקִים כִּכְפִיר יִבְטָח *the righteous are bold as a lion* Pr 28[1]; *secure* Jb 11[18] Pr 11[15]; עַם בֹּטֵחַ *a people secure* Ju 18[7.10.27]; בָּנוֹת בֹּטְחוֹת *careless daughters,* (*women*) Is 32[9] cf. v[10.11]. **Hiph.** *Pf.* הִבְטַחְתָּ Je 28[15]; *Impf.* יַבְטַח Is 36[15] + 2 t.; *Pt.* מַבְטִיחִי ψ 22[10]; *cause to trust, make secure,* abs. ψ 22[10]; with עַל Je 28[15] 29[31]; with אֶל 2 K 18[30] = Is 36[15].

†I. בֶּטַח n.[m.] **security**—Gn 34[25] + 41 t.; הַשְׁקֵט וָבֶטַח Is 32[17] *quietness and security* = בְּהַשְׁקֵט וּבְבִטְחָה Is 30[15] (but prob. both infs.) elsewhere always adverb;—*securely,* ישב לבטח Lv 25[18.19] 26[5] Ju 18[7] 1 K 5[5] ψ 4[9] Pr 3[29] Is 47[8] Je 32[37] 49[31] Ez 28[26] 34[25.28] 38[8.11.14] 39[6.26] Zp 2[15] Zc 14[11]; ישב בטח Dt 12[10] 1 S 12[11]; שכן לבטח Dt 33[12] ψ 16[9] Je 23[6] 33[16]; שכן בטח Dt 33[28] Pr 1[33]; (היה) לבטח Jb 24[23] Ez 34[27]; היה בטח Ju 8[11]; שכב לבטח Pr 3[23]; הלך בטח Pr 10[9]; הלך לבטח Jb 11[18] Ho 2[20]; רבץ לבטח Is 14[30]; נחה לבטח ψ 78[53]; עבר בטח Mi 2[8]; כּוּשׁ בטח *Cush* (dwelling) *securely* Ez 30[9] (pregnant construction, del. בטח Co); וַיָּבֹאוּ עַל הָעִיר בֶּטַח *and they came upon the city* (dwelling) *securely* Gn 34[25] (J).

†בִּטְחָה n.f. **trusting** Is 30[15] (prob. *inf. f.* = בֶּטַח Is 32[17]).

†בִּטָּחוֹן n.m. **trust** 2 K 18[19] = Is 36[4]; *hope* Ec 9[4].

†בַּטֻּחוֹת n.f.pl. **security, safety** Jb 12[6].

†מִבְטָח n.[m.] **confidence** Ez 29[16]—cstr. מִבְטַח Pr 14[26] + 2 t.; sf. מִבְטַחִי Jb 31[24] + 6 t. (dag. implicit); מִבְטֶחָם Je 48[13]; מִבְטֶחָה Pr 21[22]; pl. מִבְטַחִים Is 32[18]; מִבְטַחַיִךְ Je 2[37];—**1.** *the act* of confiding Pr 21[22] 22[19] 25[19]. **2.** *the object* of confidence Jb 8[14] 18[14] 31[24] ψ 40[5] 65[6] 71[5] Je 2[37] 17[7] 48[13] Ez 29[16]. **3.** the state of confidence, *security* Pr 14[26] Is 32[18].

†II. בֶּטַח n.pr.loc. city of Hadadezer king of Zobah 2 S 8[8] (but read rather טִבְחַת so 1 Ch 18[8]; 𝔊 Sm Μασβακ, 𝔊L Ματεβακ; 𝔊 Ch Μεταβηχας, 𝔊L ταβααθ; cf. also We Dr).

II. **בטח** (√assumed for following).

†אֲבַטִּחִים n.[m.]pl. **water-melons** (Mish. אבטיח, Sam. [Samaritan]; cf. Löw[No. 207]; Ar. بِطِّيخ etc.; perh. loan-word in Heb. cf. Sta[§ 258]; mod. Egypt. *baṭṭich, biṭṭich* cf. reff. in Di Nu 11[5]; on formation cf. Lag[BN 10], who comp. Eth. *aqṭala*)—Egyptian fruit, הָא׳ Nu 11[5] (‖ הַקִּשֻּׁאִים, הֶחָצִיר, הַבְּצָלִים, הַשּׁוּמִים); 𝔊 τοὺς πέπονας.

†[**בָּטֵל**] vb. **cease** (NH בָּטֵל, Ar. بَطَلَ, Eth. በጥለ: both *be futile, vain,* but As. *baṭâlu, cease* Lotz[TP 68], so Aram. בְּטֵיל, [Syriac])—**Qal** *Pf.* וּבָטְלוּ consec. Ec 12[3] *and* the grinders *cease.*

I. **בטן** (meaning dub.; √of following).

†I. בֶּטֶן n.f.[Nu 5, 25] **belly, body, womb** (Ar. بَطْنٌ—'ב)—abs. Ju 13[7] +; בָּטֶן v[5] +; cstr. בֶּטֶן ψ 139[13] +; sf. בִּטְנִי Jb 3[10] +; בִּטְנְךָ Dt 7[13] +; בִּטְנֵךְ Gn 25[23]; בִּטְנוֹ Jb 15[2] +, etc.;—**1. a.** *belly, abdomen,* of man Ju 3[21.22]; of woman Nu 5[21.22.27]; as beautiful in form Ct 7[3]; as seat of hunger Pr 13[25]; as eating Ez 3[3] (‖ מֵעִים); cf. Pr 18[20] (fig.); as seat of passion, avarice, etc. Jb 20[20.23]; in fig. of God's casting riches out of extortioner's belly Jb 20[15] (‖ יְרִשֶׁנּוּ), cf. also ψ 17[14]; fig. of innermost part of a man = *inmost soul* Pr 18[8] = 26[22], 20[27.30] (all חַדְרֵי ב׳); as seat of intell. faculties (= Eng. *breast* or *bosom*) 22[18] (cf. מֵעִים ψ 40[9]) Jb 15[2.35] 32[18], רוּחַ בִּטְנִי v[19]; as trembling at theophany Hb 3[16]. **b.** belly of hippopotamus Jb 40[16]. **c.** בֶּטֶן שְׁאוֹל Jon 2[3] (Jonah's prayer: ‖ מְצוּלָה בִּלְבַב יַמִּים). **2.** *body,* opp. soul ψ 31[10]

(opp נֶפֶשׁ), also 44[26] (opp יד;—on this cf Zim[BP 71]) **3.** *womb* Gn 25[23.24] 38[27] (all J) Ho 12[4] Jb 10[19] (|| רֶחֶם v[18]) Ec 11[5] Jb 31[15] הֲלֹא בַבֶּטֶן עֹשֵׂנִי עָשָׂהוּ *did not he that made me in the womb make him* (|| וַיְכֻנֶנּוּ בָּרֶחֶם אֶחָד), cf ψ 139[13] תְּסֻכֵּנִי בְּבֶטֶן, & Je 1[5], esp פְּרִי ב׳ i e. offspring Gn 30[2] (E) ψ 127[3] Is 13[18], Pr 31[2] בַּר בִּטְנִי=*my son* (|| ברי) cf בֶּן־בִּטְנָהּ Is 49[15], of birth יָצָא מִבֶּטֶן Jb 1[21] 3[11] Ec 5[14], בטן alone=*birth* Ho 9[11] (|| לֵדָה, הֵרָיוֹן), cf fig. מִבֶּטֶן מִי יָצָא הַקָּרַח Jb 38[29] *out of whose womb came the ice?* cf לֹא סָגַר דַּלְתֵי בִטְנִי Jb 3[10] i e *of my* (mother's) *womb*; גֹּחִי מִבָּטֶן *take, draw out of the womb,* subj י׳ (i e cause to be born) ψ 22[10], פְּרִי בֶטֶן used also of father Mi 6[7], cf. ψ 132[11] (David as ancestor of Messian king), Jb 19[17] בְּנֵי בִטְנִי *sons of my body,* of doubtful interpr., perh.= *sons of my (mother's) womb,* cf 3[10] (Ges De), i e my brothers or *men of my clan* RS[K 33 f], others *my sons* (Ew), *my grandsons* (Di), also in addressing Isr as a whole (masc sf) Dt 7[13] 28[4 11 18.53] 30[9], cf. מַחֲמַדֵּי בִטְנָם Ho 9[16] *beloved ones of their womb;* מִן־הַבֶּטֶן (מִבֶּטֶן)=*from birth* Ju 13[5 7] ψ 58[4] 71[6], cf also Is 44[2.24] 46[3] (|| רָחַם) 48[8] 49[1 5], מִבֶּטֶן אִמִּי *id.* Ju 16[17] Jb 31[18] ψ 22[11] (|| רָחֶם) **4.** architectural word of some rounded projection connected with the two pillars Jachin & Boaz 1 K 7[20] (Klo rds. הבית)

† II בֶּ֫טֶן **n.pr.loc.** city in Asher Jos 19[25] (=*depression, basin, valley?* cf. Ar. بَطْن, Lane[220 col 3]) = Βατναι, called Βεθβετεν cf. Lag Onom 236, 2nd ed 249, 𝔊 Βαιθοκ, 𝔊L Βετελ.

II **בטן** (assumed as √ of following, mng. unknown)

† **בָּטְנִים** **n.[m.]pl. pistachio,** an oval nut (cf As *butnu* COT[Gloss] & Schr[MBAk 1881, 419], Aram בוטנא, ܒܛܡܐ, Ar. بُطْم; on Punic βουτνουμ Blau[ZMG 1873 527]) =*pistacia terebinthus* Rob[BR i 208, ii. 222], Post[PEF Oct 1888, 218, No 214 f., Tr Vict. Inst xxii 271 etc] (*pist. vera* Low[No 44]), Gn 43[11] one of the articles carried from Canaan to Egypt by sons of Jacob as present to Joseph, still a delicacy in Egypt and Syria, cf Wetzst in Low[p 420].

† **בְּטֹנִים** **n.pr.loc.** city of Gad, E of Jordan Jos 13[26], mod *Batne,* W. of *Es-Salt* (v.d Velde[Memoir 296])=Βοτνια cf. Lag[Onom. 234, 2nd ed 247]

† [**בִּי, בָּיַי**] **vb entreat** (Ar بَيَّ *come as suppliant, entreat,* still current in the Hauran· v Wetzst in De[Jb 34, 36]), of which (prob) אָבִי Jb 34[36] is 1 s impf (used dialectically)· אָבִי יִבָּחֵן אִיּוֹב *would that* (lit *I entreat that*) Job were tried!

† **בִּי** **part. of entreaty,** craving permission to address a superior, always foll by אֲדֹנִי (or אֲדֹנָי), and always (exc. Jos 7[8]) at the beginning of a speech, **I pray, excuse me**—(not improb. from √ביי; so that בִּי אֲדֹנִי will be literally *a supplication of* (i e *to*) *my lord!* cf Wetzst l c, who compares the Ar دَخْل سَيِّدِي lit. *a prayer to my lord!* a standing formula=*Pray, excuse me,* used exactly as בִּי אֲדֹנִי Acc to others contr from בְּעִי, from בָּעָה *to ask,* and so lit *a petition!* cf Aram בְּבָעוּ, ܒܒܥܘ (e g. Gn 19[18] 𝔗, Nu 12[13] 𝔖), but ע is not often elided in Heb)—Gn 44[18] בִּי אֲדֹנִי יְדַבֶּר־נָא *I pray,* my lord, let thy servant speak, etc.; so Nu 12[11] Ju 6[13] 1 S 1[26] 1 K 3[17 26], and foll by a pl subj Gn 43[20] בִּי א׳ יָרֹד יָרַדְנוּ *Oh,* my lord, we came down, etc; בִּי אֲדֹנָי (to God) Ex 4[10 13] Jos 7[8] Ju 6[15] 13[8] (𝔊 in Pent and Jos δέομαι, δεόμεθα in other books absurdly ἐν ἐμοί)

† **בִּין** **vb. discern** (No[ZMG 1883 532 f], Ar بَانَ *become separated, be distinct,* IV *speak perspicuously,* Eth ለበወ: I 2 *consider, perceive,* Aram. ܐܒܝܢ *make to understand,* cf. Sab בין (*the*) *wise,* as epith, Mordt[ZMG 1876 37])—**Qal** *Pf* בִּין Dn 10[1]; בִּינֹתִי ψ 139[2], בִּנֹתָה Dn 9[2], *Impf* יָבִין ψ 19[13] + 25 t, וַיָּבֶן Je 9[11] + 2 t.; וָאָבִין 1 S 3[8] + 2 t., אָבִינָה ψ 73[17] + 4 t, יָבִינוּ Pr 28[5] + 12 t; *Imv* בִּין Dn 9[23], בִּינָה ψ 5[2], בִּינוּ Dt 32[7] + 2 t, *Inf* abs בִּין Pr 23[1], *Pt* בָּנִים Je 49[7],—**1.** *perceive* (with the senses) —**a.** *eyes,* acc Pr 7[7], with ל Jb 9[11] 14[21] 23[8] Pr 14[15] **b.** *ears,* acc Pr 29[19], with ל Jb 13[1]. **c.** *touch,* acc ψ 58[10] **d** *taste,* acc Jb 6[30] **2.** *understand, know* (with mind) —**a.** abs Jb 18[2] 38[20] 42[3] ψ 49[21] 82[5] Pr 24[12] Is 6[9 10] 44[18] Dn 12[10] Ho 4[14] 14[10], שמעתי ולא אבין *I heard but I could not understand* Dn 12[8]. **b.** acc Jb 15[9] 23[5] 36[29] Pr 2[5.9] 20[24] 28[5] ψ 19[13] 92[7] Je 9[11]; יבין משפט Jb 32[9] Pr 28[5], יבין דעת Pr 29[7]. **c.** with כִּי 1 S 3[8] 2 S 12[19] Is 43[10] **d.** with inf & ל, יבין לָדַעַת Is 32[4]. **3.** *observe, mark, give heed to, distinguish, consider* (with attention).—**a.** acc. Dt 32[7] ψ 5[2] 50[22] 94[7 8] Pr 23[1] 21[29] (Qr) Dn 9[2] 10[1]. **b.** with לְ, ψ 73[17] 139[2] Dt 32[29] **c.** with בְּ, Ezr 8[15] Ne 13[7] Dn 9[23] **d.** with אֶל, ψ 28[5]. **e.** with עַל, Dn 11[30.37] **4.** *have discernment, insight, understanding* Je 49[7] **Niph.** נְבוּנֹתִי Is 10[13], *Pt* נָבוֹן Gn 41[33] + 15 t., pl. נְבוֹנִים Je 4[22], elsewhere נבנים Dt 1[13] Is 5[22] (Baer) Ec 9[11], נְבֹנָיו Is 29[14], *be intelligent, discreet, discerning, have understanding* 1 S 16[18] Pr 1[5] 10[13] 14[6] 16[21] 17[28] 19[25] Ec 9[11] Is 3[3] 5[21] 10[13] 29[14] Je 4[22] Ho 14[10], לֵב נָבוֹן intelligent mind Pr 14[33] 15[14] 18[15], נָבוֹן וְחָכָם Gn 41[33.39],

חכם ונבון Dt 4^{6} 1 K 3^{12}; חכמים ונבנים Dt 1^{13}. **Po.** יְבוֹנְנֵהוּ *he attentively considereth him* Dt 32^{10}. **Hiph.** *Pf.* הֵבִין Jb 28^{23} + 5 t.; *Impf.* יָבִין Is 28^{9} + 4 t.; וַיָּבֶן 2 Ch 11^{23} Dn 9^{22}; *Inf.* הָבִין ψ 32^{9} + 9 t.; *Imv.* הָבֵן Dn 8^{16} + 12 t.; *Pt.* מֵבִין Pr 28^{7} + 26 t.;—**1.** *understand:*—**a.** abs. Is 29^{16} 40^{21} 56^{11} 1 K 3^{11} ψ 32^{9} Dn 8^{17} 10^{12}. **b.** acc. 1 Ch 28^{9} Jb 28^{23} Pr 1$^{2.6}$ 8^{5} 14^{8} Is 28^{19} Dn 8^{23} Mi 4^{12}; מֵבִין one with understanding Pr 8^{9} 17$^{10.24}$ 28$^{2.7.11}$; מְבִינֵי מַדָּע Dn 1^{4}; able to understand (i.e. old enough) Ne 8^{3} 10^{29}, cf. 8^{2} (sq. לִשְׁמֹעַ). **2.** give heed to, attend to, observe, discern, abs. Is 57^{1} 2 Ch 11^{23} Dn 8^{5}; c. בְּ Ne 8^{12} Dn 9^{23} 10^{11}; מֵבִין בְּ skilled in 2 Ch 26^{5} 34^{12}; c. אֶל ψ 33^{15}; בין טוב לרע 1 K 3^{9}. **3.** *give understanding, make understand, teach:*—**a.** abs. Dn 8^{27} 9^{22}. **b.** with acc. pers. ψ 119$^{34.73.125.130.144.169}$ Jb 32^{8} Ne 8$^{7.9}$ Is 40^{14}. **c.** with לְ pers. 2 Ch 35^{3} Dn 11^{33}; with לְ pers. & acc. rei Jb 6^{24} Dn 8^{16}. **d.** בְּ rei Ne 8^{8}, + acc. pers. Dn 1^{17}. **e.** double acc. Is 28^{9} ψ 119^{27} Dn 10^{14}; מֵבִין *teacher* 1 Ch 15^{22} 25$^{7.8}$ 27^{32} Ezr 8^{16}. **Hithp.** *Pf.* הִתְבּוֹנַן Is 1^{3} + 6 t.; *Impf.* אֶתְבּוֹנָן Jb 23^{15} + 3 t.; אֶתְבֹּנָן Jb 32^{12} + 5 t.; יִתְבּוֹנָנוּ ψ 107^{43} + 2 t.; יִתְבּוֹנָנוּ Is 14^{16} 43^{18}. **1.** *shew oneself attentive, consider diligently:*—**a.** abs. Jb 11^{11} 23^{15} Is 1^{3} Je 2^{10} 9^{16}. **b.** acc. Jb 37^{14} ψ 107^{43} 119^{95} Is 43^{18} 52^{15}. **c.** with אֶל 1 K 3^{21} Is 14^{16}. **d.** with עַל Jb 31^{1} ψ 37^{10}. **e.** with עד Jb 32^{12} 38^{18}. **f.** with בְּ Jb 30^{20} Je 23^{20} (= 30^{24}). **2.** *get understanding, understand* Jb 26^{14} ψ 119^{104}. **3.** *shew oneself to have understanding* ψ 119^{100}.

†בּוּנָה† **n.pr.m.** (*intelligence* = Palm. n.pr. בונא Vog$^{No. 3}$) a man of Judah 1 Ch 2^{25}.

[בַּיִן] **subst.** prop. **interval, space between** (בֵּינַיִן *id.*)—cstr. בֵּין, once Is 44^{4} (Baer) בֵּן, בֵּינִי, בֵּינְךָ, בֵּינֶךָ (בֵּינָיו Jos 3^{4} 8^{11} Qr) בֵּינוֹ +; with pl. sf. in pl. form בֵּינֵינוּ (בֵּינֵנוּ), etc.; also בֵּינוֹת +Ez 10$^{2.2.6.6.7.7}$ (+ 1^{13} 𝔊 Hi Ew etc. for דְּמוּת), בֵּינוֹתֵינוּ +Gn 26^{28} Jos 22^{34} Ju 11^{10}, בֵּינוֹתָם +Gn 42^{23} 2 S 21^{7} Je 25^{16}; dual בֵּנַיִם (v. infr.);—**1.** always (exc. dual) as **prep. in the interval of, between** (so Aram. בֵּין, & pl. בֵּינֵי, ܒܝܢܬ, ܒܝܢܝ; በበይናቲ፡), as Gn 15^{17} בֵּין הַגְּזָרִים *between* the pieces, Ex 13^{9} al. בֵּין עֵינֶיךָ *between* thy eyes (v. עַיִן), Is 22^{11} al. *between* the two walls (v. חוֹמָה), Jb 24^{11} 30^{7} 40^{30} part him *between* merchants; rather more gen. *among* Ho 13^{15} Ct 2$^{2.3}$ Ez 19^{2} 31^{3} Jb 34^{37}; less exactly *within* Pr 26^{13} a lion is בֵּין הָרְחֹבוֹת *within* the broad places (cf. 23^{13} בְּתוֹךְ): once with a sing. (unusual) Dn 8^{16} בֵּין אוּלָי *between* the Ulai, i.e. between its banks.

When the space separating two distinct objects is to be indicated, this is done **a.** most commonly by repeating בין, as Gn 13^{3} בֵּין בֵּית־אֵל וּבֵין הָעַי lit. *in the interval of* Bethel, and *in the interval of* ʿAi, i.e. *between* Bethel *and* ʿAi, 16^{14} 17^{7} 31$^{50.51}$ + oft. **b.** more rarely by בֵּין ... לְ, Gn 1^{6} dividing בֵּין מַיִם לָמָיִם lit. *in the interval of* waters *with reference to* waters, i.e. *between* the waters *and* the waters, Lv 20^{25} 27^{33} Dt 17$^{8.8.8}$ 2 S 19^{36} 1 K 3^{9} Ez 41^{18} 42^{20} 44$^{23.23}$ Jon 4^{11} Mal 3$^{18.18}$ 2 Ch 14^{10}. **c.** by בֵּין ... וּלְ +Jo 2^{17}. **d.** by בֵּין ... לְבֵין +Is 59^{2}. בֵּין is used not only of actual locality, but also with verbs of dividing (fig.) Gn 1^{14} Lv 10^{10}, and of judging, knowing, teaching, etc., if the idea of *distinguishing* be involved, as Gn 16^{5} 2 S 19^{36} הַאֵדַע בֵּין טוֹב לְרָע can I discern *between* good and evil? 1 K 3^{9} Jon 4^{11}; Gn 31^{49} (watch *between*), Ju 11^{10} (hear), Jos 22^{27} (witness), Is 2^{4} and he shall judge (arbitrate) *between* the nations, 5^{3}; Lv 27^{33}; Ez 44^{23}; Mal 3^{18}; 2 Ch 14^{10} (see RV); and in other metaph. applications, as of a covenant or sign *between* two contracting parties, Gn 9$^{12.15}$ Ex 31^{13} +; or an oath Gn 26^{28} 2 S 21^{7}; enmity or strife Gn 3^{15} 13^{7} Dt 25^{1} Pr 6^{19}; peace 1 K 5^{26}; good-will Pr 14^{9}.—It is used of *time* in the phrase of P בֵּין הָעַרְבַּיִם (v. sub עֶרֶב), & Ne 5^{18} בֵּין עֲשֶׂרֶת יָמִים *during the interval of* ten days, i.e. every ten days (unusual).

With other prepositions:—**a.** †אֶל־בֵּין, after a verb implying motion, *in between, in among* Ez 31$^{10.14}$. So אֶל־בֵּינוֹת לְ †ib. 10^{2}. **b.** †בְּבֵין Is 44^{4} *in the midst of, amongst* (𝔊 Ew Di Che כְּבֵין מַיִם חָצִיר). **c.** †עַל־בֵּין nearly as אֶל־בֵּין Ez 19^{11}. **d.** †מִבֵּין *from between:* Gn 49^{10} nor the ruler's staff מִבֵּין רַגְלָיו *from between* his feet (where, as the king sits in state, he holds it), Ex 25^{22} *from between* the cherubim (so Nu 7^{89}), Ho 2^{4} Zc 6^{1} 9^{7}; Dt 28^{57} the after-birth הַיּוֹצֵת מִבֵּין רַגְלֶיהָ that cometh forth *from between* her feet, i.e. from her womb (cf. Il. 19. 10 πεσεῖν μετὰ ποσσὶ γυναικός). Repeated 2 K 16^{14} to specify the two objects *from between* which a thing is moved. Ez 47^{18} is difficult and uncertain: v. Comm. Less precisely *from the midst of:* Nu 17^{2} מִבֵּין הַשְּׂרֵפָה *out of the midst of* the burning, ψ 104^{12} מִבֵּין עֳפָאיִם *from amongst* the branches they utter their song, Je 48^{45} and a flame מִבֵּין סִיחוֹן *from the midst of* Sihon (Sihon representing his people: but expression is singular; rd. perh. מִבֵּית ס׳, cf. Nu 21^{28} מִקִּרְיַת ס׳: ‖ in both passages מֵחֶשְׁבּוֹן), Ez 37^{21}. **e.** †מִבֵּינוֹת לְ *from between* Ez 10$^{2.6.6.7}$.

various purposes:—(1) בית הַמֶּלֶךְ=*palace* 1 K 9$^{1.10}$ 10^{12}+, etc.; בית מַמְלָכָה Am 7^{13} cf. sub **2** infr.; ב׳ הַמַּלְכוּת Est 5^{1} cf 2^{16}; ב׳ לְמַלְכוּתוֹ 2 Ch 1^{18}, (2) בית הַסֹּהַר=*the prison* Gn 39$^{20.20.21.22.22.23}$ 40$^{3.5}$; cf. ב׳ מִשְׁמַרְכֶם Gn 42^{19}; ב׳ מִשְׁמֶרֶת 2 S 20^{3}; ב׳ הָאֲסוּרִים Ju 16$^{21.25}$; ב׳ הָאֲסִירִים Je 37^{15}; הָאֵסוּר Ec 4^{14}; ב׳ הַכֶּלֶא 1 K 22^{27} 2 K 17^{4} 2 Ch 18^{26} Je 37$^{15.18}$ cf Is 42^{7}; ב׳ כֶּלֶא 2 K 25^{27}, ב׳ הַמַּהְפֶּכֶת 2 Ch 16^{10}; ב׳ הַכְּלִיא Je 37^{4} 52^{31}; בָּתֵּי כְלָאִים Is 42^{22}, (3) בית הַפְּקֻדֹּת Je 52^{31}; ב׳ הַפְּקֻדּוֹת Je 37^{16}; בית־הַבּוֹר הַנָּשִׁים *house of the women, harem* Est 2$^{9.11.13.14}$; (4) ב׳ מִשְׁתֵּה הַיַּיִן Est 7^{8}, ב׳ הַיַּיִן Ct 2^{4}; cf. בָּתֵּי מָשׂוֹשׂ Is 32^{13}, (5) בית הַחֹרֶף Am 3^{15} Je 36^{22}; ב׳ הַקַּיִץ Am 3^{15}, (6) בית נְכֹתֹה & בית כֵּלָיו 2 K 20^{13}= Is 39^{2}; (7) בית הַגָּן *garden-h.* (or n pr ? cf p. 111) 2 K 9^{27}; (8) בית־עֵקֶד *binding-h.* (or n pr. ?) 2 K 10$^{12.14}$, (9) בית עֲבָדִים *h. of slaves* (where slaves live), only fig. of Egypt Ex 13$^{3.14}$ 20^{2} Dt 5^{6} 6^{12} 7^{8} 8^{14} 13$^{6.11}$ Jos 24^{17} Ju 6^{8} Mi 6^{4} Je 34^{13},—on ב׳ הַחָפְשִׁית 2 K 15^{5}=2 Ch 26^{21} cf. חפשית; esp. (10) בית י׳= *temple* 1 K 7$^{12.40.45.51}$ & very oft.; also (mostly late) בית הָאֱלֹהִים 1 Ch 9$^{11.13.26}$+ oft.; but also of earlier tent of worship Ju 18^{31}; v. also ב׳ הָאֹהֶל 1 Ch 9^{23}; cf. ב׳ אלהים of local shrine 17^{5}; & also in mouth of Jacob, as explanation of name of Bethel Gn 28^{17} (cf. v^{19}), & as name of stone, or *Maççeba* v^{22} (all E); also ב׳ י׳ of earlier tent of worship Ju 19^{18} 1 S 1$^{7.24}$ 2 S 12^{20} (cf. further הֵיכַל הַבַּיִת ,(יהוה ,אֱלֹהִים), ב׳ הָאוֹצָר Mal 3^{10}; cf. 1 K 6^{3}, & ב׳ alone in same sense, esp. 1 K 6 cf. 2 Ch 1^{18} 2$^{3.11}$+; v. 1 Ch 28^{2} ב׳ מְנוּחָה לַאֲרוֹן בְּרִית־י׳ ב׳ קֹדֶשׁ 29^{3}; also בית הַקֹּדֶשׁ וְלַהֲדֹם רַגְלֵי אֱלֹהֵינוּ ב׳ קָדְשֵׁנוּ וְתִפְאַרְתֵּנוּ Is 64^{10}; הַקֳּדָשִׁים 2 Ch 3$^{8.10}$; בית מִקְדָּשָׁם 2 Ch 6^{2}; בית זָבַח 2 Ch 7^{12}; בית־זְבֻל 2 Ch 36^{17}; ב׳ תְּפִלָּה Is 56$^{7.7}$; ב׳ תִּפְאַרְתִּי 60^{7}; also of heathen temples ב׳ בַּעַל־בְּרִית Ju 9^{4}; ב׳־דָגוֹן 1 S 5^{5}; ב׳ עַשְׁתָּרוֹת 1 S 31^{10}; ב׳ רִמּוֹן 2 K 5$^{18.18.18}$; ב׳ הַבַּעַל 2 K 10$^{21.21.23.25.26.27}$ 11^{18}, ב׳ עֲצַבֵּיהֶם 1 S 31^{9} (but rd. rather את־עצביהם as in ‖ 1 Ch 10^{9} so 𝔊 We Dr), בית בָּמוֹת 1 K 12^{31} (cf MI בת במת), v. also 13^{32} 2 K 17$^{29.32}$; בית אוֹצַר אֱלֹהָיו Dn 1^{2}, etc; made of woven material 2 K 23^{7}; אֲשֶׁר הַנָּשִׁים אֹרְגוֹת שָׁם בָּתִּים לָאֲשֵׁרָה perh =*tent-shrines* but txt dub. 𝔊 χεττιιν (כתנות ?); 𝔊L στολάς; cf. Ew$^{H iii 718}$ & Klo; (ζ) of portion of larger building (late), so pl. בָּתָּיו 1 Ch 28^{11} i e of the temple (‖ גַּנְזַכָּיו, עֲלִיֹּתָיו, חֲדָרָיו); cf ב׳ הַכַּפֹּרֶת *ib.*; ב׳ הַמְבַשְּׁלִים Ez 46^{24}. **b.** as shelter or abode of animals 1 S 6$^{7.10}$ cf. Ex 9^{19}; בית עַכָּבִישׁ Jb 8^{14} *spider's web* (cf בָּנָה בֵיתוֹ כָּעָשׁ 27^{18}); of wild ass Jb 39^{6} שַׂמְתִּי עֲרָבָה בֵּיתוֹ, צִפּוֹר מָצְאָה בַיִת ψ 84^{4} (‖ קֵן); חֲסִידָה בְּרוֹשִׁים בֵּיתָהּ ψ 104^{17} (cf. ‖ & Che); Pr 30^{26} (of the שְׁפַנִּים 'conies') **c.** fig of human bodies בָּתֵּי־חֹמֶר Jb 4^{19} *houses of clay*, cf. in phr. שֹׁמְרֵי הַבַּיִת Ec 12^{3} *keepers of the house*, i. e the arms; v further בית מְגוּרַי ψ 119^{54}. **d.** of Sh^{e}ôl, שְׁאוֹל בֵּיתִי Jb 17^{13}, cf בית מוֹעֵד לְכָל־חָי 30^{23} (‖ מָוֶת); בית עוֹלָמוֹ Ec 12^{5} (perh =tomb, v De). **e.** of abode of light & darkness Jb 38^{20}. **f.** of land of Ephraim as ב׳ יהוה Ho 8^{1} 9^{15} (cf אֶרֶץ י׳ 9^{3}) **2.** *place*, of Jerusalem בית קִבְרוֹת אֲבֹתַי Ne 2^{3} (‖ עִיר v^{5}), cf also n.pr. cpd with בית, infr, & בית מַמְלָכָה Am 7^{13} (pred. of Bethel); בית נתיבות Pr 8^{2} i e. where paths meet RV, ב׳ אֲבָנִים Jb 8^{17}, on both these v. בית sub [בין] בַּיִן p. 108. † **3.** *receptacle*, תְּעָלָה כְּבֵית סָאתַיִם 1 K 18^{32} *a trench like a receptacle of two seahs*; בָּתֵּי נֶפֶשׁ Is 3^{20} i.e. vials of perfume; esp. בָּתִּים לְבַדִּים Ex 25^{27} *holders for the staves*, i e. rings, טַבַּעַת *ib*; so 37$^{14.27}$ 38^{5}; cf. בָּתִּים לבריחם 26^{29} 36^{34} *holders for the bars* (all P, & all expl. by טבעת); בית־לָהּ סָבִיב Ez 1^{27} (si vera l) *its* [cstr. as ψ 58^{5}] *house* (=enclosing cage) *was round about* (del BHiCo). **4.** of house as containing a family, hence in phr of slaves belonging to household יְלִידֵי בֵיתוֹ Gn 14^{14} cf. 17^{12} (opp. מִקְנַת־כֶּסֶף) v^{13} (all ‖ *id*), fig. of Israel Je 2^{14} (‖ עֶבֶד); cf. בֶּן־בֵּיתִי Gn 15^{3}; בְנֵי־בַיִת הָיָה לִי Ec 2^{7} (as token of wealth & prosperity), also of one's sister מוֹלֶדֶת בַּיִת Lv 18^{9} (‖ מ׳ חוּץ cf. infr); כָּל־הַנֶּפֶשׁ לְבֵית־יַעֲקֹב Gn 46^{27}. Hence **5.** *household, family* (592 t.) **a.** ordinary sense, those belonging to the same household Gn 7^{1} 12$^{1.17}$+, Dt 6^{22} 11^{6}+; Hex mostly JD; E Gn 35^{2} 42^{33} 50^{22} cf. Ex 1^{21} infr.; P Gn 36^{6} Ex 1^{1} 12^{4} Lv 16$^{6.11.17}$ Nu 16^{32} 18^{31} Jos 22^{15}; even where expressly said to inhabit *tents* Nu 16^{32} Dt 11^{6} אֶת־בָּתֵּיהֶם וְאֶת־אָהֳלֵיהֶם; specif זְקַן־ב׳ Gn 24^{2} cf. 50^{7} (of rank & dignity in household); of a family of handicraftsmen מִשְׁפְּחוֹת בֵּית־עֲבֹדַת הַבֻּץ 1 Ch 4^{21} (v. בוץ); also, with fig. of house clearly in mind מִשְׁקֹלֶת ב׳ 2 K 21^{13}; מַפְתֵּחַ ב׳ Is 22^{22} **b.** family of descendants, descendants as organized body Gn 18^{19} (J ‖ בָּנִים)+, & so c. יִבְנֶה ב׳ אחיו (q. v) בָּנָה Dt 25^{9} cf. Ru 4^{11} &, subj י׳, בָּנָה ב׳ לְ 2 S 7^{27}=1 Ch 17$^{10.25}$, also 1 S 2^{35} 1 K 11^{38} (both ב׳ נֶאֱמָן), so וַיַּעַשׂ לָהֶם בָּתִּים Ex 1^{21}; also pl. עשׂה ב׳ לְ 2 S 7^{11} 1 K 2^{24}; עָשָׂה ב׳ נֶאֱמָן לְ 1 S 25^{28}; cf esp. c n pr, e g **c.** בית שָׁאוּל† 2 S 3$^{1.1.6.6.8.10}$ 9$^{1.2.3.9}$ 16^{5} (משפחת ב׳ שׁ׳), v^{8} 19^{18} (cf 21^{1} where rd. וְאֶל־ בֵּיתֹה דָמִים, so 𝔊 We Dr) 1 Ch 12^{29}; בית דָוִד† 2 S 3$^{1.6}$ 7^{26}=1 Ch 17^{24} (cf. context in both), 1 K 12^{19}

= 2 Ch 10^{19}, v$^{20.26}$ 13^{2} 14^{8} 2 K 17^{21} Is 7$^{2.13}$ 22^{22} Je 21^{12} Zc 12$^{7.8.10.12}$ (משפחת ב׳ ד׳) 2 Ch 21^{7} ψ 122^{5}, ב׳ יָרָבְעָם† 1 K 13^{34} 14$^{10.10.13.14}$ 15^{29} 16^{3} 21^{22} 2 K 9^{9} 13^{6}; ב׳ אַחְאָב† 2 K 8$^{18.27.27.27}$ (of Ahaziah חֲתַן ב׳ א׳), 9$^{7.8.9}$ 10$^{10.11}$ 21^{13} Mi 6^{16} 2 Ch 21$^{6.13}$ 22$^{3.4.7.8}$, etc **d.** esp of Hebrew people & subdivisions. (α) בית יִשְׂחָק† Am 7^{16}; (β) ב׳ עֵשָׂו† Ob$^{18.18}$, (γ) בית† יַעֲקֹב Gn 46^{27} (P) Ex 19^{3} (E) Am 3^{13} 9^{8} Mi 2^{7} 3^{9} Ob$^{17.18}$ Is 8^{17} 10^{20} 14^{1} 29^{22} 46^{3} 48^{1} 58^{1} Je 2^{4} 5^{20} ψ 114^{1}, also זֶרַע ב׳ יעקב Ez 20^{5} (del. Co), most frequently (δ) בית ישׂראל (Vrss & var. sometimes בני v בן) †Hex Ex 16^{31} 40^{38} Lv 10^{6} Nu 20^{29} (all P) Lv 17$^{3.8.10}$ 22^{18} (H) Jos 21^{43} (D)†; 1 S 7^{2} + 8 t. S K; Ho 1$^{4.6}$ 5^{1} 6^{10} 12^{1}, Am 5^{1} + 7 t Am, †Mi 1^{5} 3$^{1.9}$ Is 5^{7} 14^{2}, also 46^{3} 63^{7} Zc 8^{13}†, but esp Je 2$^{4.26}$ + 17 t Je, Ez 3$^{1.4.5.7.7.17}$ + 75 t Ez; also זֶרַע ב׳ יִשְׂרָאֵל Je 23^{8} Ez 44^{22} (Co del ב׳), שְׁנֵי בָתֵּי† ישׂראל Is 8^{14}, בית ישׂראל ויהודה Ez 9^{9} + 25^{8} Co, further בית מרי *rebellious house* (of Isr.) Ez 2$^{5.6}$ 3$^{9.26.27}$ 12$^{2.3}$, & ב׳ הַמֶּרִי Ez 2^{8} 12$^{2.9.25}$ 17^{12} 24^{3} [+ 44^{6} Co], (ε) בית יְהוּדָה 2 S 2$^{4.7.10.11}$ 1 K 12^{21} = 2 Ch 11^{1}, 2 K 19^{30} = Is 37^{31}, Is 22^{21} Ho 1^{7} 5$^{12.14}$ Zp 2^{7} Zc 8$^{13.15.19}$ 10$^{3.6}$ 12^{4}, & esp Je 3^{18} + 9 t Je; Ez 4^{6} + 4 t. Ez + 9^{9} supr; also ב׳ יְהוּדָה וּבִנְיָמִן† 1 K 12^{23}, ב׳ מֶלֶךְ יְהוּדָה† Je 21^{11} 22^{6}, (ζ) ב׳ יוֹסֵף† Gn 50^{8} Jos 17^{17} 18^{5} (all JE) Ju 1$^{22.23.35}$ 2 S 19^{21} 1 K 11^{28} Am 5^{6} Ob^{18} Zc 10^{6}, (η) ב׳ אֶפְרַיִם† Ju 10^{9}, (θ) ב׳ בִּנְיָמִן 2 S 3^{19} cf 1 K 12^{23} supr; (ι) ב׳ יִשָּׂשכָר† 1 K 15^{27}; (κ) ב׳ לֵוִי† Ex 2^{1} (E) Nu 17^{23} (P) Zc 12^{13} (משפחת ב׳ ל׳), ψ 135^{20}, & (λ) ב׳ אַהֲרֹן ψ 115$^{10.12}$ 118^{3} 135^{19}. **e.** technically, yet with some looseness of usage, בית אָב *father's house*, of family or clan, pl בית אָבוֹת *father-houses, families* (e g Nu 1^{2}) (79 t; only P & Chr) Ex 6^{14} 12^{3} Nu 1$^{2.4.18}$ + 41 t Nu; Jos 22$^{14.14}$ 1 Ch 4^{38} 5^{13} + 25 t Ch, Ezr 2^{59} 10^{16} Ne 7^{61} 10^{35}, = tribe Nu 17$^{17.17.18.21}$, = main division of tribe Nu 3$^{20.24}$ +, cf 34$^{14.14}$ etc, further sub-division Ex 12^{3} 1 Ch 7$^{2.7}$ +; cf. esp. 1 Ch 23^{11} *Jeush and Beriah had not many sons, therefore they became* לבית אָב לִפְקֻדָּה אֶחָת (cf ראשׁי אבות, sub אב) **6.** house, including *household affairs*, persons, property, etc וַיַּפְקִדֵהוּ עַל־בֵּיתוֹ Gn 39^{4} cf ^{5}, v בביתו, אֲשֶׁר עַל־בֵּיתוֹ Gn 44$^{1.4}$, hence אשׁר על הבית as title of governor of the palace (Ew$^{\S III 269}$) Is 22^{15} 36^{3} cf 1 K 4^{6} 2 K 15^{5}, in Israel 1 K 16^{9} 18^{3} 2 K 10^{5}. further 2 S 17^{23} 2 K 20^{1} = Is 38^{1}, hence of personal property 1 K 13^{8} אִם־תִּתֶּן־לִי אֶת־חֲצִי בֵיתְךָ; family and property (everything on which one depends) Jb 8^{15}. **7.** בַּיְתָה, בָּיְתָה, lit. *housewards*, hence metaph *inwards*, †Ex 28^{26} = 39^{19} (sc of the ephod), 1 K 7^{25} = 2 Ch 4^{4} (sc of the circle of oxen supporting the molten sea); 2 S 5^{9} מִן־הַמִּלּוֹא וָבָיְתָה from the Millo and *inward*, Ez 44^{17}. **8.** מִבַּיִת **a.** adv. *on the inside* (of a building, chest, etc. opp מחוץ) †Gn 6^{14} Ex 25^{11} = 37^{2} Lv 14^{41} 1 K 6$^{15.16}$ 7^{9} 2 K 6^{30} (of a person's clothes), Ez 7^{15}, so with ה *loc* מִבַּיְתָה† 1 K 6^{15} **b.** מִבֵּית לְ† (cstr Ges$^{\S 130.1n}$) prep. *within* (opp מחוץ ל), מבית לַפָּרֹכֶת *within* the veil Ex 26^{33} Lv 16$^{2.12}$ Nu 18^{7} לְכָל־דְּבַר הַמִּזְבֵּחַ וּלְמִבֵּית לַפָּרֹכֶת for everything of the altar, and for (that) *within* the veil, 1 K 7$^{8.31}$ (rd לַכְּתֵפֹת; see VB & Sta$^{ZAW 1883, 165}$), אֶל־מִבֵּית לְ (after a verb of motion) *in within* Lv 16^{15} 2 K 11^{15} = 2 Ch 23^{14}

Note — בית perh occurs abbrev. into ב in n pr בְּעֶשְׁתְּרָה q v. so Thes al.; cf. also Aram בית = בא in like usage Lag$^{Armen Stud \S 339}$ Se i 51, GGA 1884, 276.

†בַּיִת c art הַבַּיִת Is 15^{2} acc. to Ew Brd Di al **n.pr.loc.** but abbrev; perh for בית דבלתים Je 48^{22} (so Ew al) or בית בָּמוֹת cf. MI^{27} (cf De Di), others (Ges De Che Or) take הַבּ׳ here = *the house*, i e temple or shrine

†בֵּית אָוֶן **n.pr.loc.** (*house of iniquity or idolatry*? hardly likely unless as alteration of orig בית און, *house of wealth* or *strength*) eastward from Bethel Jos 7^{2} 18^{12} 1 S 14^{23}, 1 S 13^{5} בית־א׳ (on Ho 4^{15} 5^{8} 10^{5} v. בֵּיתאל infr.); site unknown.

בֵּיתאֵל$_{71}$ **n.pr.loc. Bethel** (so read, not בית־אל as Jos 7^{2} + acc to v d H; cf Baer Gn 12^{8}, *house of God*, or *house of Ēl*)—**1.** ancient place and seat of worship in Ephraim on border of Benjamin, identif. with *Luz* (former name) Gn 28^{19} 35^{6} Jos 18^{13} Ju 1^{23}; appar distinguished from Luz Jos 16^{2} (yet cf. Di), name connected with vision of Jacob when journeying to Paddan-Aram (JE) Gn 28^{19} 35^{7} (where אֵל בֵּיתאל, but 𝔊 𝔖 𝔙 Ol del אל, Di maintains); cf Ho 12^{5}, when journeying *from* P.-A 35^{15} (P), name appar given first to a stone (Gn 28^{18} 35^{14}) cf We$^{Skizzen III 70}$, הַר בֵּיתאל 1 S 13^{2}; later important place of worship 1 S 10^{3} עֹלֶה אֶל־הָאֱלֹהִים בֵּיתאל; abode of prophet 1 K 13^{11} 2 K 2^{3}; Jeroboam set up one of the golden calves at Bethel 1 K 12^{29f} cf also 13^{1f} 2 K 10^{29} 23^{15} Je 48^{13} v further 2 K 17^{28}, 2 K 23^{15} Th prop on internal grounds, בית אֵל *house of nothingness*, or ב׳ אָלָה *house of execration*, ב׳ אָלָה also Renan$^{Hist I.i 186}$, in proph Am 3^{14} 4^{4} 5$^{5.5.6}$ 7$^{10.13}$ Ho 10^{15}, note esp. Am 5^{5} בֵּיתאֵל יִהְיֶה לְאָוֶן, &

בֵּית אָוֶן (*house of iniquity*) as substit. for ביתאל Ho 4^{15} 5^{8} 10^{5} (עֶגְלוֹת בית און);—mod. *Beitîn* Rob[BR i. 448 f.] Guérin[Judée iii. 14–27] cf. Bd[Pal 215] Survey[ii. 305]. **2.** place in south country of Judah, not far from Beersheba & Ziklag 1 S 30^{27} cf. We Dr; =MT כסיל Jos 15^{30} (txt. err.; 𝔊 Βαιθηλ); also בְּתוּל Jos 19^{4}, בְּתוּאֵל 1 Ch 4^{30}.

†בֵּית הָאֱלִי **adj.gent.** c. art. the Bethelite 1 K 16^{34}.

†בֵּית הָאֵצֶל **n.pr.loc.** in Judah Mi 1^{11}; dub., cf. sub אצל, p. 69.

†בֵּית אַרְבֵאל **n.pr.loc.** Ho 10^{14}, perh. *Arbel* near Pella (E. of Jordan) Jer Euseb. in Lag[Onom. 88, 2nd ed. 123; 214, 2nd ed. 236], cf. Now *ad loc.*; but in Galilee Rob[BR ii. 399], mod. *Irbid*, cf. Furrer[ZPV ii. 1879, 57 f.]; Bd[Pal 257].

†בֵּית בַּעַל מְעוֹן **n.pr.loc.** Jos 13^{17}, =בַּעַל מְעוֹן Nu 32^{38} Ez 25^{9} 1 Ch 5^{8} (MI בעל מען & בת בעל מען)=בֵּית מְעוֹן Je 48^{23} = בְּעֹן Nu 32^{3} (rd. prob. מְעֹן; cf. Dr[Sm lxviii.]); city assigned to Reuben Jos 13^{17} Nu $32^{3.38}$ 1 Ch 5^{8}; possessed by Moab Je 48^{23} Ez 25^{9};—mod. *Ma'în* Tristr[Moab 303 f.] Schick[ZPV ii. 1879, 5] Survey[EP i. 176] Bd[Pal 192].

בֵּית בִּרְאִי **n.pr.loc.** v. בית לבאות infr.

†בֵּית בָּרָה **n.pr.loc.** in combin. עַד בּ׳ בּ׳ וְאֶת־הַיַּרְדֵּן Ju $7^{24.24}$ (? = בֵּית עֲבָרָה *place of ford*).

†בֵּית גָּדֵר **n.pr.loc.** in Judah (*place of a wall*) 1 Ch 2^{51} (as n.pr.m.) 𝔊 Βαιθγαιδων 𝔊L Βηθγεδδωρ; = גֶּדֶר Jos 12^{13}?, cf. הַגְּדֵרִי 1 Ch 27^{28}, etc.

†בֵּית הַגִּלְגָּל **n.pr.loc.** Ne 12^{29}; cf. גִּלְגָּל.

†בֵּית גָּמוּל **n.pr.loc.** in Moab Je 48^{23} (*place of recompense*)—mod. *Umm ej-Jemâl*? Bd[Pal 203], 5 hours S. from Boṣra.

†בֵּית הַגָּן **n.pr.loc.**? 𝔊 Βαιθαν (Βαιαγαν), 𝔊L Βαιθωρων, 2 K 9^{27}; mod. *Jenîn*? v. גַּן, sub גנן, and עֵין גַּנִּים; cf. Sta[Gesch i. 542].

†בֵּית דִּבְלָתַיִם **n.pr.loc.** in Moab Je 48^{22} =עַלְמֹן דִּבְלָתָיְמָה Nu $33^{46.47}$ (MI בת דבלתן) v. ד׳.

†בֵּית־דָּגוֹן Jos 15^{41}, בֵּית דָּגֹן 19^{27} **n.pr.loc.** **1.** in Judah (*house*, i.e. *temple of Dagon;* As. *Bit-Daganna* COT[Jos 15, 41, & i. p. 281]) Jos 15^{41} (𝔊 Βαγαδιηλ, but 𝔊L Βηθδαγων)—name appears in mod. *Beit Dejân*, SE. of Jaffa, but loc. unsuitable, cf. Rob[BR ii. 232]. **2.** in Asher Jos 19^{27} (𝔊 Βαιθεγενεθ, but 𝔊L Βηθδαγων) perh.=*Beit Dejen*, near Akko, cf. Di.

†בֵּית הָרָם **n.pr.loc.** in Gad Jos 13^{27} = בֵּית הָרָן Nu 32^{36}, mod. *Beit Harrân*, 1 hour E. of Jordan, opp. Jericho, Tristr[Moab 348]; name *Tell er-Ram(eh)* Merrill[PE Soc. iv. 1877] Schick[ZPV 1879, 3, 246] (cf. Lag[Onom. 103, 16, 2nd ed. 137] al.)

בֵּית הָרָם v. בֵּית הָרָן.

†בֵּית חָגְלָה **n.pr.loc.** (*place of partridge*) in Benjamin, on border of Judah Jos 15^{6}; בֵּית־ח׳ $18^{19.21}$, mod. *'Ain Ḥajla* (or *Qaṣr Ḥajla* cf. Rob & Di Gn 50^{11}) Rob[BR i. 544] Bd[Pal 172].

†בֵּית חוֹרֹן **n.pr.loc.** Jos $10^{10.11}$, also בּ׳ חֹרֹן, בּ׳ חוֹרוֹן, & in Ch בּ׳ חֹרוֹן, two cities in Ephraim, lower & upper B.H. (*place of a hole* or *hollow* (?) חוּר, perh. fr. a wady betw. the two, or near by; cf. also מַעֲלֵה Jos 10^{10}, מוֹרַד v^{11} 1 Macc $3^{16.24}$) 1 Ch 7^{24} אֶת־בֵּית־חוֹרוֹן הַתַּחְתּוֹן וְאֶת־הָעֶלְיוֹן; further, **a.** בּ׳ ח׳ עֶלְיוֹן Jos 16^{5}; בּ׳ ח׳ הָעֶלְיוֹן 2 Ch 8^{5}. **b.** 1 hour W. from **a.** בּ׳ ח׳ תַּחְתּוֹן Jos 16^{3} 18^{13} 1 K 9^{17}; בּ׳ ח׳ הַתַּחְתּוֹן 2 Ch 8^{5}; also Jos $10^{10.11}$ 18^{14}; prob. also 21^{22} 1 S 13^{18} 1 Ch 6^{53} 2 Ch 25^{13};—mod. *Beit 'Ûr el-fôqa & et-taḥta* Rob[BR ii. 250 f.] Bd[Pal 21] Survey[iii. 86];—cf. הַחֹרֹנִי **adj.gent.** Ne $2^{10.19}$ 13^{28}, only of Sanballat; also du. חֹרֹנַיִם Jos $10^{10.11}$ 𝔊 & 2 S 13^{34} 𝔊 We Dr.

†בֵּית חָנָן **n.pr.loc.** in Dan (Judah? Philistine territory) 1 K 4^{9} (where rd. וּב׳ ח׳ v. sub ii. אֵלוֹן p. 19);—mod. *Beit Ḥanûn* cf. Rob[BR ii. 33].

†בֵּית הַיְשִׁימוֹת **n.pr.loc.** E. of Jordan (*place of the desert*, ישׁם) in Moab Ez 25^{9}; בּ׳ הַיְשִׁמֹת Nu 33^{49} Jos 12^{3}; given to Reuben בּ׳ הַיְשִׁמוֹת Jos 13^{20};—perh. mod. *es-Suweime*, De Saulcy[Voyage i. 315 f.], cf. Merrill[PE Soc. iv. 1877] Bd[Pal 172] Survey[EP i. 156].

†בֵּית כָּר **n.pr.loc.** (*place of a lamb*) appar. belonging to Philistines 1 S 7^{11}.

†בֵּית הַכֶּרֶם **n.pr.loc.** in Judah (*vineyard place*) Je 6^{1}, בּ׳ הַכָּרֶם Ne 3^{14}; on location cf. Schick[ZPV iii. 83 f.], but v. editorial remarks *ib.*, & Bd[Pal 136].

†בֵּית לְבָאוֹת **n.pr.loc.** in Simeon (*place of lionesses*?) Jos 19^{6}=בּ׳ בִּרְאִי (perh. text. err.) 1 Ch 4^{31};=לְבָאוֹת (in Judah) Jos 15^{32}.

בֵּית לֶחֶם 41 **n.pr.loc.** **1.** in Judah (*place of bread* (*food*), mod. Ar. بَيْت لَحْم, *place of meat*), 2 hours south of Jerusalem; birth-place of David;—בֵּית לָחֶם Ru 1^{19}+11 t.; בּ׳־לָחֶם 1 S 20^{6} + 9 t.; בֵּית לֶחֶם Ju 12^{8} + 11 t. + Gn 35^{19} 48^{7}, where הוא בית לחם is a gloss, v. אֶפְרָתָה, p. 68; בּ׳־לָחֶם 1 S 17^{15} + 3 t.;—as cstr. בּ׳ לֶחֶם יְהוּדָה Ju $17^{7.8.9}$ $19^{1.2.18.18}$ Ru $1^{1.2}$ 1 S 17^{12}; treated as n.pr.m. 1 Ch $2^{51.54}$ 4^{4}; *men of Bethlehem*

אַנְשֵׁי בּ׳ Ne 7^{26} = בְּנֵי ב׳ Ezr 2^{21};—on אֶפְרָתָה as name of Bethlehem, & confusion arising from gloss Gn 35^{19} 48^{7}, v p. 68,—mod *Beit Lahm*, 5 m S of Jerus Rob$^{BR\ I.\ 471}$ Bd$^{Pal\ 123}$ Survey$^{III\ 28\ 83}$ Guérin$^{Judée\ I\ 120\text{-}206}$. **2.** בֵּית לֶחֶם in Zeb. Jos 19^{15}, perh. also Ju $12^{8\ 10}$, = *Beit Lahm*, 7 m NW. of Nazareth Rob$^{BR\ III.\ 113}$ Survey$^{I.\ 301}$.

†בֵּית הַלַּחְמִי **adj.gent.** the Bethlehemite 1 S 16^{18} 17^{51} 2 S 21^{19}, so read prob. also in ‖ 1 Ch 20^{5} for MT אֶת לַחְמִי cf. Be Th Ew$^{H\ III\ 70}$ We$^{H\ 206}$ Kue Dr^{Sm}, ב׳־הַלּ׳ 1 S 16^{1}.

†בֵּית לְעַפְרָה **n.pr loc.** appar in Philistine territory Mi 1^{10}; site unknown, & txt. dub

בֵּית מִלּוֹא v. מִלּוֹא sub מלא.

בֵּית מְעוֹן v בֵּית בַּעַל מְעוֹן supr

†בֵּית מַעֲכָה **n.pr.loc** so only אָבֵלָה וּב׳ מ׳ 2 S 20^{14}, where rd as in v^{15} and in אָבֵל ב׳ מ׳ 1 K 15^{20} 2 K 15^{29} *Abel of Beth Maacah*; c. ה loc, אָבֵלָה בּ׳ הַמַּעֲכָה 2 S 20^{15}; cf. sub II. אָבֵל

†בֵּית הַמֶּרְחָק possibly **n.pr.loc.** house or settlement on bank of Kidron 2 S 15^{17} (RV *Beth-merhak*, cf MV RVm *Far House*; Ew The Ke Sta *the last house* of the city)

†בֵּית מַרְכָּבוֹת **n.pr.loc.** in Simeon (*place of chariots*) 1 Ch 4^{31} = ב׳־הַמַּרְכָּבֹת Jos 19^{5}, site unknown

†בֵּית נִמְרָה **n.pr.loc.** E. of Jordan, in Gad (*place of leopard*) Nu 32^{36} = Jos 13^{27}, 𝔊 Ναμραμ, Βαιθαναβρα, etc, v. also Lag$^{Onom.\ Sacr\ 232,\ 2nd\ ed\ 246}$;—mod *Tel Nimrîn* Survey$^{EP\ I\ 387}$ Bd$^{Pal\ 179}$, cf also מֵי נִמְרִים Is 15^{6}, & Rob$^{BR\ I\ 551}$.

†בֵּית עֶדֶן **n.pr loc.** Am 1^{5} Aramaean city, or land = *Paradisus* (Ptol$^{Geogr\ v\ 14}$), mod *Jusieh* (cf. Rob$^{BR\ III\ 556}$)? or cuneif. *Bit-Adini*, in Mesopot cf Schr$^{KG\ 199}$ Dl$^{Pa\ 263\ f.}$, COT 2 K 19^{12} & v. sub עֶדֶן; otherwise St, & Hoffm$^{ZAW\ III\ 1883,\ 97}$.

†בֵּית־עַזְמָוֶת **n.pr.loc.** near Jerusalem Ne 7^{28} = עַזְמָוֶת Ezr 2^{24} & עַזְמָוֶת Ne 12^{29}, cf 1 Ch 12^{3} (where n pr m),—mod. *El-Hizmeh* c 5 m. NNE of Jerus acc to Ritter$^{Geogr\ xvi\ 519}$ Survey$^{III\ 9}$.

†בֵּית הָעֵמֶק **n.pr.loc.** on border of Asher (*valley-house*) Jos 19^{27} Survey$^{I\ 145}$ comp *'Amka*, 7 m NE of Akko (but v. Rob$^{BR\ III\ 103,\ 108}$)

†בֵּית־עֲנוֹת **n.pr.loc.** in Judah (perh = *temple of 'Anât* Bae$^{Rel\ 53}$ Hal$^{JAs.\ 7\ xiii\ 1879\ p\ 208}$, cf foll) Jos 15^{59};—mod *Beit 'Anûn* Rob$^{BR\ III.\ 280\ f}$ Guérin$^{Judée\ III\ 151\ f.}$ Survey$^{III\ 351}$ But 𝔊L Βηθαρωθ, cf. mod. *Bittîr*, c 2½ hours SW fr. Jerus. Bd$^{Pal\ 271}$.

†בֵּית־עֲנָת **n.pr.loc.** in Naphtali (*temple of 'Anât* Nes$^{Eg\ 114}$ Bae$^{Rel\ 53}$ Mey$^{ZMG\ 1877,\ 718}$) Jos 19^{38} Ju 1^{33}, בֵּית ע׳ v^{33},—perh. mod. *Ain-Ata* v. d. Velde$^{Narr\ I\ 170}$, 6 m W of Kedesh (name *'Anata* Guérin$^{Gal\ II\ 374}$, *'Ainîtha*, Survey$^{I\ 200}$).

†בֵּית־עֵקֶד הָרֹעִים perh **n.pr.loc.** (*binding-house of the shepherds*) 2 K 10^{12}, cf v^{14} בּוֹר ב׳־ע׳; *Bethacath* Jer Lag$^{Onom.\ 107\ 17\ 2nd\ ed\ 141}$;—mod *Beit Kâd* near Mt Gilboa (*Fuku'a*) acc. to Survey$^{II\ 83}$, but cf. בַּיִת **1.** p. 109

†בֵּית הָעֲרָבָה **n.pr.loc.** (*place of the depression*) reckoned to Judah Jos $15^{6.61}$, to Benjamin 18^{22} = הָעֲרָבָתָה 18^{18}, הָעֲרָבָה v^{18}; cf. also **adj.gent** הָעַרְבָתִי 2 S 23^{31} (perh. rd. בֵּית־הָע׳ Klo cf Dr) = 1 Ch 11^{32},—site unknown.

†בֵּית פֶּלֶט **n.pr.loc.** (*place of escape*) in south of Judah Jos 15^{27} Ne 11^{26}, cf. **adj.gent.** הַפַּלְטִי 2 S 23^{26}, & so rd. also 1 Ch 11^{27} 27^{10} (Be).

†בֵּית פְּעוֹר **n.pr.loc.** (= ב׳ בַּעַל פ׳, cf. sub בעל) E of Jordan Dt 3^{29}, in land of Amorites 4^{46} cf Jos 13^{20} (where assigned to Reuben), in land of Moab Dt 34^{6} On site cf. Di Nu 23^{28} Lag$^{Onom\ 232,\ 2nd\ ed\ 246}$ Cond$^{Heth\ \&\ Moab\ 142\ f.}$ PEF$^{1882,\ 85\ f.}$ Tristr$^{Moab\ 303}$.

†בֵּית פַּצֵּץ **n.pr.loc.** in Issachar (*place of dispersion*) Jos 19^{21}; site unknown.

†בֵּית־צוּר **n.pr.loc.** in Judah (*house of rock*) Jos 15^{58} 2 Ch 11^{7} Ne 3^{16}; as n pr.m. 1 Ch 2^{45};—mod *Beit Ṣûr*, c 12 m S fr. Jerusalem Rob$^{BR\ III\ 276\ f.}$ Survey$^{III\ 311}$ Bd$^{Pal\ 138}$ (*Burj Ṣûr*)

†בֵּית־רְחוֹב **n.pr.loc.** (*place of street, or market*?) near Dan on road to Hamath Ju 18^{28} 2 S 10^{6} (where אֲרַם בֵּית־רְחוֹב) = רְחֹב Nu 13^{21}, cf. אֲרַם צוֹבָא וּרְחוֹב 2 S 10^{8},—loc dub. (cf. Rob$^{III\ 371\ f.}$).

†בֵּית רָפָא **n pr.loc.**? in Judah; as **n.pr.m.** 1 Ch 4^{12}.

†בֵּית שְׁאָן **n.pr.loc.** in Manasseh, W. of Jordan (*place of quiet*) 1 K $4^{12\ 12}$; בֵּית־שְׁאָן Jos $17^{11\ 16}$ Ju 1^{27} 1 Ch 7^{29}; = בֵּית שַׁן 1 S $31^{10\ 12}$; בֵּית־שַׁן 2 S 21^{12},—mod *Beisân* (Scythopolis), NH בֵּישָׁן Rob$^{BR\ III\ 329}$ Bd$^{Pal\ 224}$ Survey$^{I.\ 101\ f.}$

†בֵּית הַשִּׁטָּה **n.pr.loc.** (*place of the acacia*) Ju 7^{22} (on site cf Rob$^{BR\ II\ 356}$)

†בֵּית שֶׁמֶשׁ **n.pr.loc.** (*sun-temple*)—ב׳ ש׳ Jos 19^{22} + 8 t.; ב־ש׳ Jos 15^{10} + 6 t., ב׳ שָׁמֶשׁ Jos 19^{38} + 4 t,—**1.** city in SW Judah Jos 15^{10} 1 S $6^{9\ 12\ 12\ 13\ 15\ 19.20}$ 1 K 4^{9} 2 K 14^{13} = 2 Ch 25^{23} 2 Ch

28^{18}; distinguished from other places of same name as בֵּית שֶׁ׳ אֲשֶׁר לִיהוּדָה 2 K 14^{11} = 2 Ch 25^{21}; assigned to Levites Jos 21^{16} = 1 Ch 6^{44};—ruin at mod. *'Ain Shems* Rob $^{BR\ II\ 223\ f.}$ Bd $^{Pal\ 163}$ Survey $^{III\ 35,\ 60}$. **2.** city in Naphtali Jos 19^{38} Ju 1$^{33.33}$. **3.** city in Issachar Jos 19^{22}; possibly *'Ain esh-Shemsîyeh*, Jordan valley, S. of Beisân (Beth Shean) Survey $^{II\ 231}$ **4.** = On-Heliopolis, in Egypt Je 43^{13} Rob $^{BR\ I\ 25}$ Eb $^{GS\ 505\ f.}$ Dl $^{Pa\ 318\ f.}$

†בֵּית־הַשִּׁמְשִׁי **adj.gent.** of foregoing **1.** c. art. 1 S 6$^{14.18}$.

†בֵּית־תַּפּוּחַ **n.pr.loc.** in Judah (*place of apples*) Jos 15^{53};—mod. *Taffûh* Rob $^{BR\ II\ 71}$ Bd $^{Pal\ 154}$ Survey $^{III\ 310,\ 379}$

†בִּיתָן **n.[m.]** **house, palace**—abs. הַבִּיתָן Est 7$^{7.8}$ (גִּנַּת הַבּ׳); cstr. בִּיתַן Est 1^{5} (גִּנַּת בּ׳ הַמֶּלֶךְ), all *garden of* ב׳; acc. to Dieulafoy $^{REJ\ 1888,\ cclxxvii.}$ *throne-room*, syn of *apadâna* in mng, but cf. אַפֶּדֶן

בית **prep.** between, v. [בַּיִן] sub בין

†בָּכָא **n.[m.]** **balsam-tree** (v. Ar. بُكًا Dozy $^{ZMG\ 1869,\ 188}$ but Low $^{No.\ 47}$, acc to TA like جرجير, an *eruca*, cf Lane s v, perh cf بَكَأَ *give little milk*, of camel, i e. *drop, drip*); pl בְּכָאִים 2 S 5$^{23.24}$ = 1 Ch 14$^{14.15}$; sg in עֵמֶק הַבָּכָא ψ 84^{7} *balsam-vale*, cf. De Che

†בָּכָה $_{114}$ **vb. weep, bewail** (Ar بَكَى, Aram. בְּכָא, ܒܟܐ, As *bakû* Zim $^{BP\ 23,\ 56}$, Eth በከየ:)—**Qal** *Pf.* בּ׳ Gn 43^{14} Ho 12^{5}, וּבָכְתָה consec. Dt 21^{13}; בָּכִיתִי Jb 30^{25}, etc; *Impf.* וַיֵּבְךְּ Gn 37^{35} + 16 t. (וַיֵּבְךְ Gn 27^{38} etc); 3 fs. תבכה 1 S 1^{10} + 2 t.; וַתִּבְכֶּה 1 S 1^{7}, וַתֵּבְךְּ Gn 21^{16} (where 𝔊 masc cf. Di) + 4 t; 2 ms. תִּבְכֶּה Is 30^{19} Ez 24^{16}, וַתִּבְכֶּה 2 K 22^{19}, וַתֵּבְךְּ 2 S 12^{21} 2 Ch 34^{27}; 2 fs תִּבְכִּי 1 S 1^{8}; אֶבְכֶּה Ju 11^{37} + 4 t; וָאֶבְכֶּה 2 S 12^{22} + 2 t.; יִבְכּוּ Lv 10^{6} + 3 t.; יִבְכָּיוּן Jb 31^{38} Is 33^{7}; 3 fpl. תִּבְכֶּינָה Jb 27^{15} ψ 78^{64}, וַתִּב׳ Ru 1$^{9.14}$, etc; *Imv.* pl. בְּכוּ Je 22^{10} Jo 1^{5}; בְּכֶינָה 2 S 1^{24}; *Inf. abs* בָּכוֹ Is 30^{19} + 3 t. + Mi 1^{10} (where rd. בְּעַכּוֹ, v עכו); בָּכֹה 1 S 1^{10} + 3 t.; *cstr.* לִבְכּוֹת Gn 43^{30} + 3 t.; לִבְכֹּתָהּ Gn 23^{2}, *Pt* בֹּכֶה (בּוֹכֶה) Ex 2^{6} + 6 t.; fs. בֹּכִיָּה La 1^{16}; pl. בֹּכִים (בּוֹ׳) Ezr 3^{12} +, etc,—**1.** *weep* (in grief, humiliation, or joy), abs. Gn 42^{24} 43$^{30.30}$ Ex 2^{6} Nu 11$^{4.10}$ 14^{1} 1 S 1$^{7.8.10}$ 11^{5} 30$^{4.4}$ 2 S 1^{12} 3^{16} 13^{36} 15$^{30.30}$ 19$^{1.2}$ 2 K 8$^{11.12}$ Is 30$^{19.19}$ Je 41^{6} 50^{4} Ez 24$^{16.23}$ La 1^{2} Zc 7^{3} Jo 1^{5} 2^{17} ψ 78^{64} 126^{6} cf. 69^{11} (but on text v Che) Jb 27^{15} Ec 3^{4} (opp. *laugh* שחק) Ezr 10^{1} Ne 8^{9} Est 8^{3}; once c. inanim subj. Jb 31^{38} תְּלָמֶיהָ יִבְ׳ *its furrows weep*, on Ne 1^{4} יָשַׁבְתִּי וָאֶבְכֶּה cf As. *attašab abakî*, Flood $^{130\ ed.\ Dl}$ Gu ^{§77} Hpt $^{BAS\ I\ 145}$; of loud weeping נָשָׂא הַקּוֹל וַיֵּבְ׳ Gn 21^{16} 27^{38} 29^{11} Ju 2^{4} 21^{2} 1 S 11^{4} 24^{17} 2 S 3^{32} 13^{36} Jb 2^{12} Ru 1$^{9.14}$, cf בּ׳ בְּאָזְנֵי י׳ Nu 11^{18}, also Jb 30^{31}. **2.** c acc cogn בְּכִי Ju 21^{2} 2 S 13^{36} 2 K 20^{3} = Is 38^{3}, cf בִּבְכִי Is 16^{9}, מִבְּכִי Je 48^{32}, & בּ׳ הַרְבֵּה בֶכֶה Ezr 10^{1}, sq. קוֹל גָּדוֹל 2 S 15^{23}, cf. בּ׳ בקול גדול Ezr 3^{12}; *weep bitterly* מַר יִבְ׳ Is 33^{7}, also c inf. abs. *weep intensely, grievously* 1 S 1^{10} Je 22^{10} La 1^{2}, cf. Is 30^{19} & Mi 1^{10} (but on text v. supr) **3.** sq עַל *weep upon*, i e embrace and weep, עַל־צַוָּארָיו Gn 45^{14} 46^{29} cf. 45^{15} 50^{1}; also בּ׳ עַל־פָּנָיו 2 K 13^{14}; v. further Gn 33^{4} 45^{14} & וַיִּבְכּוּ אִישׁ אֶת־רֵעֵהוּ 1 S 20^{41}; also sq עַל *weep over, for* Ju 11$^{37.38}$ 2 S 3^{34} La 1^{16}, sq אֶל־ 2 S 1^{24} 3^{32} Ez 27^{31}; sq לְ Je 22^{10} 48^{32} Jb 30^{25}; sq מפני *because of* Je 13^{17}, sq. temporal clause (of occasion of weeping) Gn 50^{17} ψ 137^{1} Ne 8^{9}. **4.** sq. acc. *bewail* Gn 23^{2} 37^{35} 50^{3} Lv 10^{6} Nu 20^{29} Dt 21^{13} 34^{8} Je 8^{23}, cf. Is 16^{9}. **5.** sq. עַל in sense of burden annoy with weeping Nu 11^{13} Ju 14$^{16.17}$ cf לִפְנֵי Nu 11^{20}. **6.** בּ׳ לִפְנֵי י׳ of penitent weeping Ju 20^{23} (cf. Be; v. also 21^{2}) Dt 1^{45} 2 K 22^{19} 2 Ch 34^{27}, cf. also Nu 25^{6}; joined with fasting Ju 20^{26} 2 S 12$^{21.22}$ cf. Ezr 10^{1}; so of weeping in anxious entreaty Ho 4^{5}; on pt. as n pr. Ju 2$^{1.5}$ v בֹּכִים infr. **Pi.** *Pt* fs מְבַכָּה *lament* Je 31^{25} sq עַל; *bewail*, pl מְבַכּוֹת sq. acc Ez 8^{14}.

†בֶּכֶה **n.[m.]** *a weeping*, only Ezr 10^{1} בכו העם הַרבה ב׳

†בְּכִי **n m.** $^{Ju\ 21,\ 2}$ **weeping**—בְּכִי Ju 21^{2} + 20 t. (also cstr Dt 34^{8}, etc); בִּבְכִי Gn 45^{2}; בֶּכִי Is 15^{2} + 6 t; sf בִּכְיִי ψ 6^{9},—*weeping* ψ 30^{6} Is 15$^{2.5}$, as acc cogn (c בכה) Ju 21^{2} 2 S 13^{36} 2 K 20^{3} = Is 38^{3} cf. Is 16^{9} (בבכי) Je 48^{32} (מבכי), audible קוֹל בּ׳ ψ 6^{9} Is 65^{19} Ezr 3^{13} cf. Je 3^{21} 31^{15} Is 15^{3} (יילִיל ירד בבכי v. Je 9^{17}); so also Gn 45^{2} (ויתן את־קלו בב׳) & Je 48^{5} (בבכי יעלה בכי i.e. the sound of it shall ascend)—but text here suspicious, cf. Is 15^{5}; as disfiguring Jb 16^{16}; ‖ words of mourning Est 4^{3} (מִסְפֵּד, צוֹם, אֵבֶל), Je 31^{9} (תחנונים cf 3^{21}), 9^{10} 31^{15} (נְהִי), cf. בכי אבל משה Dt 34^{8} & Di *ad loc.*; contrition (humiliation) Jo 2^{12} (צוֹם, מִסְפֵּד), Is 22^{12} (קרחה, מספד, חגור שק), cf Mal 2^{13} (דמעה, אנקה); of bitter weeping Is 22^{4} אֲמָרֵר בַּבֶּכִי, cf Je 31^{15} (& Is 33^{7}), בכי יעזר Is 16^{9} Je 48^{32} i e. Ya'zer in Moab, cf יעזר n pr; ψ 102^{10} (שקוי בב׳ מסכתי) cf 42^{4} 80^{6} & Bab *dîmtu maštîtî, tears (were) my drink* Zim $^{BP\ 34,\ 42}$) Trop, of trickling streams (נהרות) in mines—hindrance to miners Jb 28^{11}

†בָּכוּת **n.f. weeping** Only in אַלּוֹן בָּכוּת Gn 35^{8} i.e *mourning oak*, cf אַלּוֹן, p 47

†[בְּכִית] **n.f.** weeping Gn 50^{4} יְמֵי בכיתו, i e. the appointed time of mourning for him

†בֹּכִים **n.pr loc** near Bethel, אֶל־הַבֹּכִים Ju 2^{1}, בֹּכִים v^{5} (cf v^{4}), 𝔊 2^{1} τὸν Κλαυθμῶνα καὶ ἐπὶ Βαιθηλ; v^{5} Κλαυθμῶνες i e. בְּכִים (𝔊L Κλαυθμών),—on poss. connex. with אַלּוֹן בָּכוּת Gn 35^{8} cf Stu & We Bleek's Einl ed 4 183, Comp Hex 1889, 216; but perh. rd. ביתאל instead of בכים in v^{1}, cf. We Bu RS 20.

†[בָּכַר] **vb.** (NH בכר, Aram בְּכַר, ܒܟܰܪ, cf Ar بَكَرَ *rise early, do anything early*, بِكْر, *virgin, woman having her first child*, Eth በኵር: *primogenitus*, As *bukru, first-born*, Dl $^{\S 65, 6}$)—**Pi** *Impf* יְבַכֵּר Ez 47^{12}, *Inf* לְבַכֵּר Dt 21^{16},—**1.** *bear early, new fruit* Ez 47^{12}. **2.** *make* or *constitute as first-born* Dt 21^{16} (den. of בכור) **Pu.** *Impf* יְבֻכַּר Lv 27^{26} *born* or *made a firstling*. **Hiph.** *Pt f* מַבְכִּירָה Je 4^{31} *one bearing her first child*

בְּכוֹר, בְּכֹר$_{122}$ **n.m. first-born**—Gn 35^{23} + 78 t; בְּכֹר Gn 25^{13} + 14 t, sf בְּכֹרִי Gn 49^{3} + 14 t, בְּכוֹרוֹ Gn 38^{6} + 3 t, pl cstr. בְּכוֹרֵי Ne 10^{37} + 2 t, בְּכוֹרֵיהֶם ψ 136^{10}, pl f. בְּכֹרוֹת Gn 4^{4} Ne 10^{37}, בכרת Dt $12^{6\,17}$ 14^{23},—**1.** *men and women* **a.** *individuals* Gn 25^{13} + 69 t **b.** coll Nu $3^{46.50}$ 8^{16} 18^{15} **c** pl Ne 10^{37} ψ 135^{8} 136^{10} **d.** כל בכור Ex 11^{5} $12^{12\,29}$ $13^{2\,13.15.15}$ 22^{28} 34^{2} Nu $3^{12\,12\,12\,13.40\,42.43.45}$ $8^{17\,17\,18}$ 33^{4} ψ 78^{51} 105^{36} **2.** *animals* **a** *individuals* Lv 27^{26} Nu 18^{17} Dt $15^{19\,19}$ 33^{17}. **b.** coll. בכור בהמה Ex 11^{5} 12^{29} 13^{15} Nu 3^{41} 18^{15}, כל הבכור Dt 15^{19} **c.** pl בכרות Gn 4^{4} Dt $12^{6\,17}$ 14^{23} Ne 10^{37} **3.** *figurative*, n. of relation בכור מות *first-born of death* Jb 18^{13} (deadly disease), בְּכוֹרֵי דַלִּים *first-born of the poor* (the poorest) Is 14^{30}, Israel is the first-born of Yahweh among the nations Ex 4^{22} cf Je 31^{9}, and the seed of David among dynasties ψ 89^{28}

†בֶּכֶר **n pr.m.** (*young camel*, Ar. بَكْر, As. *bakru* Asrb Annals ix 65)—**1.** son of Ephraim Nu 26^{35} = בֶּרֶד 1 Ch 7^{20} **2.** son of Benjamin Gn 46^{21} 1 Ch $7^{6.8}$ (בֶּכֶר)

†בַּכְרִי **adj.gent.** c art as n. coll Nu 26^{35}

†בֹּכְרוּ **n.pr.m.** a Benjamite (on form cf. גַּשְׁמוּ, מַלּוּךְ, & Ol $^{\S 107\text{ ad fin}}$, on Nab n.pr. in ו v. Eut Nab 24 25, etc & No ib 73 ff.) 1 Ch 8^{38} = 9^{44}.

†בִּכְרִי **n.pr.m.** (*youthful*)—**1.** a Benjamite 2 S $20^{1\,2.6.7\,10\,13.21\,22}$, only in phr. שֶׁבַע בֶּן־בִּכְרִי **2.** perh **adj.gent.** pl c art הַבִּכְרִים 2 S 20^{14} *the Bichrites* (i e family of Sheba'), MT הַבֵּרִים, cf 𝔊 ἐν Χαρρει = ב(כרי), so Klo Dr

†בִּכְרָה **n.f.** young camel, dromedary (Ar بَكْرَة *young she-camel*) Je 2^{23}; pl cstr בִּכְרֵי Is 60^{6}.

†בְּכֹרָה **n.f.** right of first-born Gn $25^{31.34}$ (J) Dt 21^{17} 1 Ch $5^{1.2}$, sf בְּכֹרָתִי Gn 27^{36} (JE), בְּכֹרָתְךָ Gn 25^{31} (J), בכרתו Gn 25^{33} 43^{33} (J) 1 Ch 5^{1}.

†בְּכוֹרַת **n.pr.m.** (*first-born*) Benjamite 1 S 9^{1}

†בְּכִירָה **n.f.** first-born, always of women Gn $19^{31\,33.34.37}$ 29^{26} (JE) 1 S 14^{49}.

†בִּכּוּרָה **n f** first ripe fig, early fig (regarded as a delicacy) (Low ^{391}; cf Ar. بَاكُورَة, Span *albacora*, Moorish *bokkôre*) Mi 7^{1} Ho 9^{10}, sf בִּכּוּרָתָהּ = בכורה (rd בִּכּוּרָה Di), Is 28^{4}; pl. בִּכֻּרוֹת Je 24^{2}

†בִּכּוּרִים **n.m.** first-fruits—Lv 2^{14} 23^{17} Nu 28^{26} (P) 2 K 4^{42} Ne 3^{12} 13^{31}, בִּכֻּרִים Lv 23^{20} (P); cstr בכורי Ex $23^{16\,19}$ (E) $34^{22.26}$ (J) Nu 13^{20} (E) 18^{13} (P) Ne $10^{36.36}$ Ez 44^{30}, sf בִּכּוּרֶיךָ Lv 2^{14};—the first of grain and fruit that ripened and was gathered and offered to God according to the ritual, לֶחֶם הַבִּכּוּרִים bread made of the new grain offered at Pentecost Lv 23^{20}, יום הבכורים *day* of the first-fruits (Pentecost) Nu 28^{26}.

בַּל v sub בלה

בַּל, בְּלַאֲשֶׁר v sub בעל, p. 128.

†בַּלְאֲדָן **n.pr.m.** (=Bab. *abal-iddina, he hath given a son* COT 2 K 20^{12}) father of מְרֹדַךְ בַּלְאֲדָן king of Babylon (v sub מְרֹדַךְ) 2 K 20^{12} = Is 39^{1}, name prob abbreviated by omission of name of god (v *ib Merodach-baladan* = *Marduk-abal-iddina, Marduk hath given a son;* cf *Esarhaddon*, v. אֵסַר־חַדֹּן p 64)

†[בָּלַג] **vb.** gleam, smile (Ar بَلَجَ)—only **Hiph.** *Impf* 1 s c ו subord וְאַבְלִיגָה Jb 9^{27} + 2 t, *Pt* מַבְלִיג Am 5^{9},—**1.** *shew a smile, look cheerful* ψ 39^{14} Jb 9^{27} 10^{20}. **2.** *cause to burst* or *flash* המב׳ שׁד על־עָז Am 5^{9} (cf Ew St).

†בִּלְגָּה **n.pr.m.** (*cheerfulness*)—**1.** priest of 15th course (David's time) 1 Ch 24^{14} **2.** priest that went up with Zerubbabel Ne $12^{5.18}$.

†בִּלְגַּי **n.pr.m.** (*id*) priest with Neh Ne 10^{9}.

†[מַבְלִיגִית] **n.f.** smiling, cheerfulness, source of brightening—מַבְלִיגִיתִי עֲלֵי יָגוֹן Je 8^{18} *a source of brightening to me in sorrow;* but text dub. cf. VB Che.

† בִּלְדַּד **n.pr.m.** (𝔊 Βαλδαδ; No$^{ZMG\ 1886,\ 479}$ *Bel has loved*, cf אֶלְדָּד; Dl$^{Pa\ 208,\ ZK\ II\ 177}$ comp. cuneif *Bir-Dadda*, cf Hpt$^{Hbr\ 1885,\ 224}$) 2nd friend of Job (ב׳ הַשּׁוּחִי (הַשֻּׁחִי)) Jb 2^{11} 8^{1} 18^{1} 25^{1} 42^{9}.

† בָּלָה **n.pr.loc.** in Simeon Jos 19^{3}.

† [בָּלָה] **vb.** become old and worn out (Ar. بَلِيَ, Aram בְּלִי, ܒܠܐ, Eth ቦለየ: *id*)—**Qal** *Pf.* בָּלְתָה Dt 8^{4}, בָּלוּ 29^{4}+, *Impf* יִבְלֶה Jb 13^{28} etc.; *Inf* c. sf בְּלֹתִי Gn 18^{12};—*wear out* (intr), esp. of garments Dt 8^{4} 29$^{4.4}$, all c. מֵעַל pregn *wear out* (and fall) *from upon*.. (hence Ne 9^{21}), Jos 9^{13}; fig. of the heavens (with sim. of garment) Is 50^{9} ψ 102^{27} כַּבֶּגֶד יִבְלוּ, the earth Is 51^{6} כַּבֶּגֶד תִּבְלֶה; the bones (through suffering) ψ 32^{3}, afflicted man Jb 13^{28} והוא כרקב יִבְלֶה || כְּבֶגֶד), of an aged and decrepit woman Gn 18^{12} (J) אַחֲרֵי בְלֹתִי after *I am worn out*. **Pi.** caus of Qal. **a.** *wear out* (trans), fig La 3^{4} בִּלָּה בְשָׂרִי וְעוֹרִי, ψ 49^{15} and their form לְבַלּוֹת שְׁאוֹל is for She'ôl *to consume away* (others rd לִבְלוֹת is for *wasting away* [Dr^{§204}], connecting שׁ׳ with foll), 1 Ch 17^{9} לְבַלֹּתוֹ *to wear* it (Isr) *out* (altered fr. לְעַנּוֹתוֹ 2 S 7^{10}), cf Dn 7^{25} Aram. **b.** *wear out by use, use to the full*, Is 65^{22} and the work of their hands יְבַלּוּ they shall *use to the full, enjoy*, Jb 21^{13} they *wear out* their days in prosperity (Qr here יְכַלּוּ *complete*, which perh is the true reading in both passages, cf Ex 5^{13} Jb 36^{11})—On בַּלֹּתִי ψ 92^{11}, v. sub בָּלַל

† [בָּלֶה] **adj.** worn out; f בָּלָה Ez 23^{43} (of a woman, cf. Gn 18^{12} supr), pl בָּלִים Jos 9^{4} (sacks), v^{4} (wine-skins), בָּלוֹת v^{5} (sandals), v^{5} (garments).

† [בְּלוֹא] **n.[m.] worn out things, rags** (Syr. ܒܠܘܐ *id*) pl cstr בְּלוֹיֵ Je 38$^{11.11}$, בלואי v^{12}

† [תַּבְלִית] **n.f. destruction**. c. sf Is 10^{25} וְאַפִּי עַל־תַּבְלִיתָם and mine anger for *their destruction*

בַּל$_{69}$ **adv.** not (Ph. *id*. e.g CIS$^{I\ 165,\ 15}$ בל יכן לכהן shall *not* be for the priest, $^{3.3}$ בל עתי = before my time) a poet. syn of לֹא, of comparatively rare occurrence, Ho 7^{2} 9^{16} (Qr) Is 14^{21} 35^{9} 43^{17} Pr 9^{13} 14^{7} 19^{23} 22^{29} 23$^{7.35.35}$ 24^{23} 1 Ch 16^{30} (=ψ 96^{10}), only besides, except in the passages cited, in other Psalms · often repeated in the same context, as Is 26$^{10.10.11.14.14.18.18}$ 33$^{20.20.21.23.23.24}$ 44$^{8.9.9.9}$ ψ 10$^{4.6.11.15.18}$ 16$^{2.4.4.8}$ 17$^{3.3.5}$ 21$^{3.8.12}$; also used oft with תִּמּוֹט, יִמּוֹט, אֶמּוֹט ψ 10^{6} 16^{8} 21^{8} 30^{7} 46^{6} 93^{1} 96^{10} 104^{5} Pr 10^{30} 12^{3} Jb 41^{15}.

In Is 40^{24} it is prob that it acquires from the context the sense of *hardly*. yea, *hardly* are they planted, yea, *hardly* are they sown.., when he even bloweth upon them, and they wither; cf. לֹא 2 K 20^{4} Joined anomalously with an infin, ψ 32^{9} בַּל קְרוֹב אֵלֶיךָ (else) there is *not* coming nigh thee (i e. else they will not approach thee).

† בְּלִי **subst.** wearing out (ܒܠܐ, بِلًى *wearing out* of a garment), hence **1.** fig *destruction* Is 38^{17} שַׁחַת בְּלִי pit of destruction (of She'ôl). **2.** *defect, failure*, hence **adv. of negation** (cf אֶפֶס), chiefly poet for לֹא, אין:—**a.** with finite vb rare and only once in prose, Gn 31^{20} (E) עַל־בְּלִי הגיד לו because he told him not, Is 14^{6} 32^{10} Ho 8^{7} 9^{16} (Kt) Jb 41^{18} **b.** used to negative an adj or ptcp 2 S 1^{21} בְּלִי מָשִׁיחַ *not* anointed, ψ 19^{4} Ho 7^{8}: more freq, esp. in Job, joined with a subst in sense of *without*, Jb 8^{11} will the reed-grass grow בלי־מַיִם *without* water? 24^{10} they go about naked בלי לבוש *without* clothing, 31^{39} 33^{9} 34^{6} 38^{2} words בלי־דעת *without* knowledge, 39^{16} 42^{3} ψ 59^{5} בְּלִי־עָוֹן ירוצון *without* (my) iniquity they run (against me), cf. v^{4} לֹא, 63^{2} a dry land בְּלִי מָיִם *without* water, Is 28^{8}; Jb 30^{8} בני בלי־שם children of (men of) *no* name

With preps. **a.** † בִּבְלִי, in בבלי דַעַת Dt 4^{42} 19^{4} Jos 20$^{3.5}$ D (=*unawares* · all in D's law of homicide), *without knowledge* Jb 35^{16} 36^{12}. **b.** † לִבְלִי *in a state of* (v. sub לְ) *no*..., i e. *without*, Is 5^{14} לבלי־חק *regardless of, without* measure, Jb 38^{41} 41^{25} that is made לבלי־חת (to be) *in a state of no* fear, i e. to be fear*less*. **c.** † מִבְּלִי (α) *from want of*, followed by a subst. or infin, מִן expressing *causation*, Dt 9^{28} מבלי יְכֹלֶת י׳ on account of Jehovah's *not* being able (in Nu 14^{16} מִבִּלְתִּי), 28^{55} (Ew^{238d}, but also RS$^{JPh\ xvi.72}$), Is 5^{13} *for want of* knowledge, Ho 4^{6} Ez 34^{5} La 1^{4} מבלי בָּאֵי מועד *for lack of* comers to the stated feast. Followed by a pleon. אַיִן in the phrase הֲמִבְּלִי אֵין... is it *on account of* there being *no*...? (lit is it *from the deficiency of no*...? cf. ܡܢ ܡܛܠ ܕܠܐ in Syr.; PS^{528}), Ex 14^{11} 2 K 1$^{3.6.16}$. (β) *so that there is no*... (lit. *away from* there being *no*.., מִן expressing *negation*, and בלי being pleon., as in מֵאֵין, v sub אַיִן **6 d** β), Je 2^{15} its cities are burnt מבלי יושב *so that there is no* inhabitant, 9$^{9.11}$ Ez 14^{15} Zp 3^{6}. Once as a conj מבלי אֲשֶׁר, with pleon לֹא, *so that not*... Ec 3^{11}. In Job מִבְּלִי is used more freely=

without, the connexion with a preceding verb being no longer distinctly felt · 4^{20} *without* any heeding, they perish for ever, $6^{6}\ 24^{7.8}$, prob. also $4^{11}\ 31^{19}$ (though here the sense (*a*) would be admissible) (γ) in Jb 18^{15} מִן ,תִּשְׁכּוֹן בְּאָהֳלוֹ מִבְּלִי־לוֹ is prob *partitive* (so Hi): there shall dwell in his tent *what is naught* of his: Ew $^{\S 323a}$ De less probably *even naught*, cf sub אַיִן **6 d** γ, Ges 'terror (supplied from v^{14}) shall dwell in his tent *so that it is no more* his' **d.** †עַד־בְּלִי *till* there be *no* ψ 72^{7} Mal 3^{10}

†בְּלִימָה n.[m.] nothingness (from בְּלִי & מָה, lit. *not-aught*) Jb 26^{7} who hangeth the earth on בּ׳

†בְּלִיַּעַל $_{27}$ **n.[m.]** worthlessness (cpd בְּלִי *not, without* and יַעַל *worth, use, profit*)—בּ׳ Dt 13^{14} + 20 t; בְּלִיַּעַל ψ 101^{3} + 5 t,—the quality of *being useless, good for nothing* **1.** abstr. אִישׁ (ה)בליעל, אַנְשֵׁי הבליעל, *worthless, good-for-nothing, base fellows* 1 S 25^{25} 2 S $16^{7}\ 20^{1}$ 1 K 21^{13} Pr 16^{27}, =בֶּן־בּ׳ 1 S 25^{17}, בְּנֵי בּ׳ Dt 13^{14} Ju $19^{22}\ 20^{13}$ 1 S $2^{12}\ 10^{27}$ 1 K $21^{10.13}$ 2 Ch 13^{7}; בַּת בּ׳ 1 S 1^{16} (drunken woman), עֵד בּ׳ *base witness* Pr 19^{28}, דְּבַר בּ׳ *base, wicked thing* ψ 41^{9} (yet cf **3** infr.), 101^{3} (add prob also 1 S 29^{10}, so 𝔊 We Dr), דָּבָר...בּ׳ (elliptical and in apposition) Dt 15^{9} **2.** concr elliptical of אִישׁ בּ׳ 2 S 23^{6} Jb 34^{18}, כָּל־אִישׁ רַע וּבְלִיַּעַל 1 S 30^{22}, אָדָם בְּלִיַּעַל Pr 6^{12}. **3.** *ruin, destruction:* so ψ 41^{9} acc. to De Che al., but v. supr, יֹעֵץ בּ׳ *counsellor of ruin* Na 1^{11}, בּ׳ alone *a man of ruin, destroyer* Na 2^{1}; נַחֲלֵי בּ׳ *floods of destruction* (‖ שְׁאוֹל) 2 S 22^{5}=ψ 18^{5}.

†בִּלְעֲדֵי (perh. from בַּל and עֲדֵי, עַד *unto;* Syr ܒܠܥܕ=ἄνευ, χωρίς, Nab בלעד *except*, Eut $^{Nab\,3\,9}$)—sf בִּלְעָדַי (3 t), בִּלְעָדֶיךָ (4 t), בִּלְעָדָיו (once)—prop *not unto*, hence **apart from, except, without** · **a.** Jb 34^{32} בִּלְעֲדֵי אֶחֱזֶה *except, apart from* (what) I see myself, do thou instruct me. With sf Gn 41^{44} בִּלְעָדֶיךָ *apart from* thee, *without* thee, no one shall lift up the head, Is 45^{6} for there is none בִּלְעָדָי *except* me. Also with sf, as a particle of deprecation, Gn 14^{24} בִּלְעָדַי *not to me!* i e I claim nothing, (in our idiom) *not at all!* 41^{16} **b.** with מִן, מִבַּלְעֲדֵי (so ܡܢ ܒܠܥܕ *without*) (*a*) *apart from*, esp with the collat idea of without the knowledge and consent, Nu 5^{20} 2 K 18^{25} (=Is 36^{10}) am I now come up *apart from, without* י׳ against this place to destroy it? Je 44^{19} (cf בִּלְעָדֶיךָ Gn 41^{44}) (β) *apart from, besides, except*, Jos 22^{19} 2 S 22^{32a} (=ψ 18^{32a}) for who is God *except* י׳? v^{32b}; similarly Is 43^{11} ואין מִבַּלְעָדַי מושיע, $44^{6.8}\ 45^{21}$.

[בְּלָה] **subst.** (from בָּלָה, of the form דֶּלֶת Ol $^{\S 146b}$) prop *failure*, hence used as **particle of negation, not, except** (cf אֶפֶס, בְּלִי), twice with sf. (v. infr), elsewhere always בִּלְתִּי (with binding vowel ִי, as mark of cstr state Sta $^{\S 343}$ Ges $^{\S 90\,3}$), (Ph בלת *only:* Tabnith-Inscr ^{5}) —**†1. adv.** not, with an adj. 1 S 20^{26} בִּלְתִּי טָהוֹר *not* clean, with a subst. Is 14^{6} מַכַּת בלתי סָרָה a stroke of *non*-cessation, i.e. a never-ceasing stroke, with a finite vb. (si vera l.) Ez 13^{3} (RVm but v Dr $^{\S 41\,Obs}$). **†2.** after a preceding negation, *not*=**except** (syn זוּלָתִי), Gn 21^{26} I have not heard בלתי הַיּוֹם *except* to-day, Ex 22^{19} he that sacrificeth בלתי לי׳ *except* unto י׳, Nu 32^{12} Jos 11^{19} so בלתי אם Gn 47^{18} Ju 7^{14} (cf. כי אם Gn 28^{17} Ne 2^{2}) With sf (attached to the ground-form בלת) בלתי *except* me †Ho 13^{4}, בִּלְתֶּךָ *except* thee †1 S 2^{2} **†3. conj.** (likewise after a neg, expressed or implied) Gn 43^{3} בִּלְתִּי אֲחִיכֶם אתכם *except* your brother (be) with you, v^{5} Nu 11^{6} our soul is dry, there is nothing at all, *save that* our eyes are toward the manna, Is 10^{4} (and where will ye leave your glory?) *save that* they bow down under the prisoners, and fall under the slain! i e. (iron.) their only refuge will be among the corpses of a battle-field. So בִּלְתִּי אם Am $3^{3.4}$.—Dn 11^{18}, where no neg precedes, it is difficult to extract a sense consistent with the gen. usage of בִּלְתִּי· Ges *besides that* his reproach he will return unto him, Ew *only, nothing but*, Hi *certainly*, Drechsler (on Is 10^{4}) *nay, even* (cf. RV)

4. With preps **a.** לְבִלְתִּי $_{84}$ *so as not ..., in order not...* (negation of לְ sq inf), usually sq inf. cstr, as Gn 4^{15} gave a sign to Cain לְבִלְתִּי הַכּוֹת־אֹתוֹ *in order* that any finding him should *not* smite him, $19^{21}\ 38^{9}$ Ex $8^{18.25}\ 9^{17}$ Lv $18^{30}\ 20^{4}\ 26^{15}$ Dt $8^{11}\ 17^{12}$ the man that doeth presumptuously לְבִלְתִּי שְׁמֹעַ *so as not* to hearken etc (cf Je $16^{12}\ 17^{23}\ 18^{10}\ 42^{13}$ Dn 9^{11}) v^{20} Ju 2^{23} +. לבלתי הוֹעִיל *in order not to* profit (the result represented forcibly as the design, cf sub לְמַעַן) Is 44^{10} Je 7^{8}, after vbs. of commanding Gn 3^{11} which I commanded thee לְבִלְתִּי אֲכָל־מִמֶּנּוּ *not to* eat thereof, 2 K 17^{15} Je $35^{8f.14}$ Ru 2^{9}, swearing Dt 4^{21} Jos 5^{6} Ju 21^{7} Ez 20^{15}, agreeing 2 K 12^{9}, interceding Je 36^{25} Once לְבִלְתִּי לְ 2 K 23^{10} (cf לְמַעַן לְ Ez 21^{20}, בַּעֲבוּר לְ 1 Ch 19^{3}).

Twice as conj. with the impf., Ex 20[20] 2 S 14[14] (cf. בַּעֲבוּר, & מִן Dt 33[11]). In Je 23[14] 27[18] sq. perf., which is inconsistent with the nature of a final conj.: rd. either יָבֹאוּ ,יָשׁוּבוּ, or שׁוּב ,בּוֹא (cf. Dr [§41 Obs.]). On Ez 13[3] v. supr. †**b.** מִבִּלְתִּי *an account of not*... (negation of מִן sq. inf.): sq. inf. Nu 14[16] מִבִּלְתִּי יְכֹלֶת י׳; a verbal noun Ez 16[28] מִבִּלְתִּי שָׂבְעָתֵךְ. †**c.** עַד־בִּלְתִּי *until not*..., sq. a perf. (Ges; RS [JPh xvi, 72]), or an inf. (Ew [§238 d]), in the phrase עַד־בִּלְתִּי הִשְׁאִיר־לוֹ (לָהֶם) שָׂרִיד *until* one left him (them) *not* a remnant, Nu 21[35] Dt 3[3] Jos 8[22] 10[33] 11[8] 2 K 10[11].—Jb 14[12] עַד־בִּלְתִּי שָׁמַיִם *till* there be *no* heaven (cf. עַד־בְּלִי ψ 72[7]).

†[**בָּלַהּ**] **vb. trouble** (Aram. ܒܠܗ, cf. Ar. بَلِهَ *be weak in intellect*; v. also בהל)—only **Pi.** *Pt.* מְבַלֲהִים אותם לִבְנוֹת Kt (Qr מְבַהֲלִים needless) Ezr 4[4] *troubled them in building.*

†**בַּלָּהָה n.f. terror, dreadful event, calamity, destruction**—בַּלָּהָה Is 17[14]; pl. בַּלָּהוֹת Jb 18[11] + 7 t.; cstr. בַּלְהוֹת Jb 24[17];—**1.** only pl. *terrors* Jb 18[11] 27[20] 30[15]; מֶלֶךְ בּ׳ Jb 18[14] = death, cf. בּ׳ צַלְמָוֶת Jb 24[17]. **2.** *calamity* Is 17[14], pl. ψ 73[19]; *calamity, destruction* Ez 26[21] 27[36] 28[19].

†**I. בִּלְהָה n.pr.f.** (etym. dub.) handmaid of Rachel, concubine of Jacob Gn 29[29] 30[3.4.5.7] 35[22.25] (sons Dan & Naphtali) 37[2] (prob. gloss, Ol) 46[25] 1 Ch 7[13].

†**II. בִּלְהָה n.pr.loc.** a city of Simeon 1 Ch 4[29], prob. = בַּעֲלָה Jos 15[29], בָּלָה 19[3] cf. Di; site dub.

†**בִּלְהָן n.pr.m. 1.** descendant of Esau Gn 36[27] = 1 Ch 1[42]. **2.** a Benjamite 1 Ch 7[10.10].

בְּלוֹא v. sub בלה.

†**בֵּלְטְשַׁאצַּר n.pr.m.** Dn 1[7], בֵּלְטְאשַׁצַּר Dn 10[1] (prob. = Bab. *balâṭsu-uṣur, protect his life!* COT Dn 1[7] Dl in BD [Dn. p. ix]; Hoffm [ZA 1887, 56] conj. בלט ש[ר] אצר *Balaṭ* (= god Saturn?) *protect the king!*—Dn 4[5] conn. with *Bel*, but name then inexplicable), name given to Daniel by Neb.

בְּלִי, בְּלִימָה, בְּלִיַּעַל v. sub בלה.

†**I. בָּלַל vb. mingle, mix, confuse, confound** (Ar. بَلَّ *moisten* (with water), cf. بَلَل *moisture*, As. *balâlu*, Dl [Pr 70]; cf. Ph. בלל name of a sacrifice, & NH בִּלְבֵּל; Aram. בַּלְבֵּל, ܒܠܒܠ)—**Qal** *Pf.* בָּלַל Gn 11[9], בַּלּוֹתִי ψ 92[11] (but cf. infr.); *Impf.* 1 pl. נָבְלָה = נָבֹלָּה Gn 11[7], cf. Kö [i. 335]; *Pt.* pass. בָּלוּל Ex 29[40] + 3 t., בְּלוּלָה Lv 2[5] + 28 t., בְּלוּלֹת Ex 29[2] + 4 t.;—**1.** *mingle, confuse* (obj. שָׂפָה = speech, language, q.v.) Gn 11[7.9] (J). **2.** *mix* (cakes or flour, etc. always with oil) term. techn. sacrif., only P (H Lv 23[13]), cf. Di on Lv 2[4]; usually as סֹלֶת בּ׳ בַּשֶּׁמֶן, מנחה Ex 29[40] Lv 2[5] 14[10.21] 23[13] Nu 7[13.19.25.31.37.43.49.55.61.67.73.79] Nu 8[8] 15[4.6.9] 28[5.9.12.12.13.20.28] 29[3.9.14], מנחה בּ׳ בשׁ׳ Lv 7[10] (opp. חֲרֵבָה) 9[4], חַלּוֹת מַצּוֹת בּ׳ בשׁ׳ Ex 29[2] Lv 7[12.12], i.e. made by mixing with oil; סלת חלות מצות בּ׳ בשׁ׳ ,סלת Lv 2[4], Nu 6[15], i.e. fine flour (in the form) of cakes so made. בַּלֹּתִי בְּשֶׁמֶן רַעֲנָן ψ 92[11] *I shall be* (*am*) *anointed with fresh oil* AV RV; vb. not elsewhere in this sense; 𝔊 𝔙 Hup Che rd. בַּלֹּתִי fr. בלה, inf. cstr. sf., abstr. for concrete, *my wasting* = *my wasting strength*, of declining age; Israel under figure of old man; this however is not favoured by context. The passage is therefore doubtful. **Hithpo.** *Impf.* אפרים בעמים הוא י׳ יִתְבּוֹלָל Ho 7[8]; *Ephraim, among the peoples doth he mix himself;* but Ew Now derive here fr. בלל = בלה (or נבל) *waste away*, cf. Hiph. **Hiph.** *Impf.* וַנָּבֶל Is 64[5] *and we faded away*, but rd. perh. וַנִּבֹּל fr. נבל cf. Di (De, less probably, derives from בלל —cf. Ew Now Ho 7[8]—or נבל = בול).

†**בְּלִיל n.m.** [Is 30, 24] **fodder** (Aram. ܒܠܝܠܐ; cf. Ar. بُلَّة *moisture of fresh pasture*)—בְּלִיל Is 30[24]; sf. בְּלִילוֹ Jb 6[5] 24[6]—*fodder* (strictly, *mixed fodder, farrago*) Jb 6[5]; as growing in field 24[6] cf. Is 30[24].

†**II. [בָּלַל] vb. denom. to give provender**—**Qal** *Impf.* וַיָּבָל Ju 19[21] Qr (Kt ויבול) sq. לְ *give provender to* the asses.

†**שַׁבְּלוּל n.m. snail** (Shaph. form, *causing moisture*, from notion of moisture or fluid in בלל);—name due to slimy trail ψ 58[9], שַׁבְּלוּל תֶּמֶס יַהֲלֹךְ.

†**תֶּבֶל n.[m.] confusion,** violation of nature, or the divine order—Lv 18[23] 20[12] (H) cf. Di on 18[15].

†**תְּבַלֻּל n.[m.] confusion, obscurity** (on form cf. Ar. conj. v. Inf. Sta [§267]) Lv 21[20] (H) ת׳ בעינו i.e. defective sight? cf. Di. (|| שֶׁבֶר, מְרוֹחַ אָשֶׁךְ, דַּק, גִּבֵּן, etc.)

†[**בָּלַם**] **vb. curb, hold in** (NH *id.*, Aram. בְּלַם, ܒܠܡ)—**Qal** *Inf.* לִבְלוֹם ψ 32[9], cf. Che.

בלס (cf. Eth. **በለስ:** *fig*, Ar. بَلَس a kind of *fig*, cf. Lag [M. i. 59 f. 68 f.]; hence following).

†[**בָּלַס**] **vb. denom.** gather figs, tend fig-trees, sycamores (𝔊 *κνίζων*, 𝔙 *vellicans*, prob. properly to *nip* the sycamore fruit to fit it for eating, v. Tristr [Nat. Hist. Bib. 399] Bo [ii. cap. 39, p. 383 f.]; Theodoret ap. Fi [Hexapl. ad loc.] Theophrast [iv. 2])—**Qal** *Pt.* בּוֹלֵס, Am 7[14] ב׳ שִׁקְמִים.

†**בָּלַע** **vb.** swallow down, swallow up, engulf (idea of quickness, suddenness) (NH *id.*, Ar. بَلَعَ *swallow*, Eth. **በልዐ:** *eat*, Aram. בְּלַע, ܒܠܥ; As. *bêlû*, Pi. *destroy* Zim [BP 27])—**Qal** *Pf.* בָּלַע Jb 20[15], sf. בְּלָעַנִי Je 51[34] (Qr, cf. 𝔊 Kt -נוּ); 3 fs. בָּלְעָה Nu 16[30]; 3 pl. sf. בְּלָעוּנוּ ψ 124[3]; *Impf.* יִבְלָע Jb 20[18], וַיִּבְלַע Ex 7[12], sf. יִבְלָעֶנָּה Is 28[4]; 3 fs. וַתִּבְלַע Nu 16[32] + 2 t.; sf. תִּבְלָעֵנִי ψ 69[16], תִּבְלָעֵנוּ Nu 16[34], וַתִּבְלָעֵם Dt 11[6], תִּבְלָעֵמוֹ Ex 15[12]; 3 mpl. sf. יִבְלָעֻהוּ Ho 8[7]; 3 fpl. וַתִּבְלַעְנָה Gn 41[7], וַתִּבְלַעְןָ Gn 41[24]; 1 pl. sf. נִבְלָעֵם Pr 1[12]; *Inf.* לִבְלֹעַ Jon 2[1]; sf. בִּלְעִי Jb 7[19];—**1.** *swallow down*, c. acc. Jb 7[19] Is 28[4], subj. דָּג Jon 2[1]; subj. שִׁבֳּלִים Gn 41[7.24]; מַטֶּה Ex 7[12]. **2.** *swallow up, engulf*, subj. אֶרֶץ Ex 15[12] Nu 16[30.32.34] 26[10] Dt 11[6] ψ 106[17]; fig. of greed Jb 20[15] (obj. חַיִל; opp. קיא *vomit*); of violence, extortion Pr 1[12] (כִּשְׁאוֹל); of devastation by enemy Ho 8[7] Je 51[34] ψ 124[3]; overwhelming by calamity ψ 69[16] (subj. מצולה); of full enjoyment, profit Jb 20[18] (no obj.) **Niph.** *Pf.* נִבְלַע Ho 8[8], נִבְלְעוּ Is 28[7];—*swallowed up*, i.e. devastated Ho 8[8]; engulfed by wine (yet cf. **Pi.** Is 3[12]) Is 28[7] (שָׁגוּ בַשֵּׁכָר ‖ נ׳ מִן־הַיַּיִן). **Pi.** *Pf.* בִּלַּע Is 25[8] + 3 t.; וּבִלַּע consec. Is 25[7]; 3 pl. בִּלֵּעוּ Is 3[12]; 1 pl. בִּלָּעְנוּ La 2[16], sf. בִּלַּעֲנוּהוּ ψ 35[25]; *Impf.* יְבַלַּע־ Pr 19[28], sf. 3 ms. יְבַלְּעֶנּוּ Jb 8[18] Pr 21[20]; יְבַלְּעֵם ψ 21[10]; 3 fs. sf. 3 ms. תְּבַלְּעֶנּוּ Ec 10[12]; 2 ms. תְּבַלַּע 2 S 20[19], sf. וַתְּבַלְּעֵנִי Jb 10[8]; 1 s. אֲבַלַּע 2 S 20[20], אֲבַלֵּעַ Is 19[3]; *Imv.* בַּלַּע ψ 55[10]; *Inf.* בַּלַּע Nu 4[20] Hb 1[13], בַּלֵּעַ La 2[8], sf. בַּלְּעוֹ Jb 2[3]; *Pt.* sf. מְבַלְּעָיִךְ Is 49[19];—**1.** *swallow* Nu 4[20] (כְּבַלַּע *as a swallowing* = for an instant); elsewhere **2.** *swallow up, engulf*, usually c. acc., **a.** fig. of destruction, ruin, Is 3[12] (obj. דֶּרֶךְ); (Ba from a √ II. בלע *confound*, cf. Di; v. also 9[15] 19[3] 28[7] ψ 55[10] 107[27]); subj. י׳ La 2[2.5.5.8] Jb 2[3] 10[8] ψ 21[10] (‖ אכל), Is 19[3] (obj. עֵצָה), i.e. *confuse, confound;* so ψ 55[10] בַּלַּע אֲדֹנָי פַּלַּג לְשׁוֹנָם *confuse, Lord, divide their speech* (cf. בלל Gn 11[7.9] & v. De Che); subj. wicked men, enemies ψ 35[25] Is 49[19] cf. La 2[16] (abs.) Hb 1[13]; obj. reflex. in sense Ec 10[12]; = annihilate Is 25[7.8]; **b.** lit. = *destroy* 2 S 20[19.20] (‖ הִשְׁחִית); indef. subj. Jb 8[18] יב׳ ממקמו; **c.** fig. for greedily (seize, adopt) practise Pr 19[28], for extravagance, squandering Pr 21[20]. **Pu.** *Impf.* יְבֻלַּע 2 S 17[16], יְבֻלָּע Jb 37[20]; *Pt.* מְבֻלָּעִים Is 9[15];—*be swallowed up*, i.e. destroyed Jb 37[20]; cf. פֶּן־יְבֻלַּע לַמֶּלֶךְ 2 S 17[16] (impers.); ruined Is 9[15] (yet cf. sub **Pi.**) **Hithp.** *Impf.* 3 fs. תִּתְבַּלָּע ψ 107[27] (subj. חכמה) their wisdom is all gone, 'they are at their wit's end' (cf. sub **Pi.**)

†I. **בֶּלַע** **n.[m.]** swallowing, devouring, thing swallowed. **1.** *swallowing = destruction,* דִּבְרֵי־בָלַע ψ 52[6] *devouring words* (‖ לְשׁוֹן מִרְמָה). **2.** *thing swallowed* בִּלְעוֹ, Je 51[44] וְהֹצֵאתִי את־ב׳ מִפִּיו *and I will bring forth that which he hath swallowed out of his mouth.*

†II. **בֶּלַע** **n.pr.m.** **1.** בֶּלַע Gn 36[32] = 1 Ch 1[43]; בָּלַע Gn 36[33] = 1 Ch 1[44] a king of Edom, בעור ב׳ בן (cf. בִּלְעָם & Di Gn 36[32]). **2.** בֶּלַע 1st son of Benjamin Gn 46[21] Nu 26[38.40] 1 Ch 7[6.7] 8[1.3] (בָּלַע). **3.** בֶּלַע a Reubenite 1 Ch 5[8].

†**בַּלְעִי** **adj.gent.** of **2,** הַבּ׳ n. coll. Nu 26[38].

†III. **בֶּלַע** **n.pr.loc.** city = צֹעַר q. v. Gn 14[2.8].

בִּלְעֲדֵי v. sub בלה.

I. **בִּלְעָם** **n.pr.m.** Balaam (acc. to Sta [§ 293] = בלע + ם; Nbr [Stud. Bib. i, 226] prop. בל = בעל + (god) עם), son of בְּעוֹר, prophet fr. פְּתוֹר (q.v.):—Nu 22[5.7.8.9] + 47 t. Nu 22–24 (all JE) 31[8.16] (P) Dt 23[5.6] (D) (cf. R[D] Jos 13[22]) Jos 24[9.10] (E) Mi 6[5] Ne 13[2].

†II. **בִּלְעָם** **n.pr.loc.** town in Manasseh 1 Ch 6[55]; A Ιβλααμ, 𝔊L Ιεβλααμ = יִבְלְעָם (q.v.) Jos 17[11] + 2 t.; mod. *Bel'ame*, 6 hours N. of Nâblus, Bd [Pal 228], so Survey [ii. 47].

†[**בָּלַק**] **vb.** waste, lay waste (As. *balâḳu*, Pi. *destroy*, Lyon [Sargon 61]; cf. Ar. بَلُّوقَةٌ *a desert*)—**Po.** *Pt.* without מ, sf. בּוֹלְקָהּ Is 24[1] (‖ בּוֹקֵק, subj. י׳, obj. הארץ);—on form (which might also be Qal Pt.) cf. Ol [§ 254] Lag [GN 1882, 403]; also בקק Po. Je 51[2], and intensive use of Inf. abs. Niph. Is 24[3]; further Pu. (i.e. intens.) Pt. Na 2[11] (this however perhaps largely influenced by assonance). **Pu.** *Pt.* מְבֻלָּקָה Na 2[11] (בּוּקָה וּמְבוּקָה ומב׳), *devastated*, or as subst. *a devastated city.*

בָּלָק **n.pr.m.** (*devastator*) king of Moab,

ב׳ בֶּן צִפּוֹר Nu 22[2.4.7] + 37 t. Nu 22–24 (all JE) + Jos 24[9] (E) Ju 11[25] Mi 6[5].

בלשאצר, בֵּלְאשַׁצַּר, בֵּלְשַׁאצַּר v. בֵּל sub בעל.

† בִּלְשָׁן n.pr.m. (=*inquirer*? NH & Aram. בלש; cf. sub בן) an Israelite who returned with Zerubbabel Ezr 2[2] = Ne 7[7].

[בֵּלֶת], בִּלְתִּי v. sub בלה.

† בָּמָה[104] **n.f. high place** (√appar. בום on account of firm ‒; cf. As. *bâmâtê* Zim[BP 48], Moab. במת MI[3.27])—Je 48[35] + 18 t.; הַבָּמָתָה 1 S 9[13]; pl. בָּמוֹת Nu 21[19] + 62 t.; cstr. בָּמֳתֵי Jb 9[8] Is 14[14] Am 4[13]; בָּמֳותֵי Dt 32[13] Is 58[14] Mi 1[3] (Ew §211d Ges §87.5 archaic fem. cstr. with retracted accent before monosyl. in poetry, *bâmŏ-thê* not *bŏm*); sf. בָּמֹתַי 2 S 22[34] + 3 t.; בָּמוֹתֵי ψ 18[34] + 10 t.; —**1.** *high place, mountain:* בָּמוֹת יָעַר *forest mountains* Mi 3[12] = Je 26[18]; במות עולם *ancient mountains* Ez 36[2]; במות ארנן Nu 21[28] (E poet.) **2.** *high places, battle-fields,* the chief places of the land giving possession, victory, dominion: על במותיך *on thy high places* (Gilboa, the battle-field) 2 S 1[19.25] (in v[19] 𝔊 has a doublet מֵתֶיךָ *thy dead*, v. We Dr). **a.** *of Israel:* רכב על במתי ארץ *ride upon the high places of the land* Dt 32[13] & Is 58[14] cf. Dt 33[29] ψ 18[34] = 2 S 22[34], Hb 3[19]. **b.** *of God:* דרך על במתי ארץ *tread upon the high places of the earth* Am 4[13] cf. Mi 1[3]; במתי ים Jb 9[8]; עלה על במתי עב (aspiration of the king of Babylon) Is 14[14]. **3.** *high places,* as places of worship, at first on hills and mountains, later on artificial mounds or platforms, under green trees, and in cities; still later for the chapels erected thereon, and once apparently for a portable sanctuary (decked with diverse colours) Ez 16[16]. The ancient worship of Israel was conducted on these high places. In the times of Samuel and David they ascended to them, descended from them, and offered sacrifices on them, 1 S 9[12-25] 10[5.13] (הבמה for הביתה We Dr). The custom continued in the reign of Solomon, but Gibeon was הבמה הגדולה 1 K 3[2-4] cf. 1 Ch 16[39] 21[29] 2 Ch 1[3.13]. High places of Baal were also used Nu 22[41] (E) Je 19[5] 32[35]; of Moab Is 15[2] 16[12] Je 48[35] (cf. MI[27]); these must be demolished Nu 33[52] (J). Solomon built במות (platforms or chapels) to Chemosh and Milkom on the Mt. of Evil Counsel opposite Jerusalem 1 K 11[7]: Jeroboam made temples on the ancient high places of Dan and Bethel 1 K 12[31.32] 2 Ch 11[15]; they are called במות און Ho 10[8], במות ישחק Am 7[9]: the kings of Israel built במות and בתי הבמות in all their cities 2 K 17[9], and the people worshipped there 2 K 17[11]; these were also used by the mixed population after the exile of Israel 2 K 17[29.32.32]: these various idolatrous high places were first destroyed by Josiah 1 K 13[2.32.33] 2 K 23[5-20] 2 Ch 34[3]. The worship of Yahweh on high places continued in Judah until the exile 1 K 22[44] 2 K 15[35]; the sanctity code predicts that Yahweh will destroy them Lv 26[30]; they were regarded as the reason for the rejection of Shiloh ψ 78[58]. The compiler of Kings, writing from the point of view of the Deut. code, complains רַק הַבָּמוֹת לֹא סָרוּ 2 K 12[4] 14[4] 15[4.35] cf. 2 Ch 15[17] 20[33], and praises the few pious kings who destroyed them. **a.** Rehoboam built במות with מצבות & אשרים on every high hill and under every green tree 1 K 14[23]. **b.** Asa did not remove the high places 1 K 15[14] (2 Ch 14[2.4] is incorrect unless במות בעל). **c.** Jehoshaphat in his reform on the basis of the covenant code did not remove them 1 K 22[44] (עוֹד הֵסִיר אֶת־הַבָּמוֹת 2 Ch 17[6] is doubtless incorrect, possibly rd. מצבות); Jehoram, his son, made high places in the cities of Judah 2 Ch 21[11] (𝔊 𝔙; not *mountains* 𝔖); and Ahaz sacrificed on high places on the hills and under every green tree and in every city of Judah 2 K 16[4] 2 Ch 28[4.25]; cf. Mi 1[5] (rd. חטאת? so 𝔊 𝔖 𝔗 Che al.; yet cf. JBL[1890, 73 f.]) **d.** Hezekiah removed them 2 K 18[4.22] 2 Ch 31[1] 32[12] Is 36[7]; but Manasseh rebuilt them 2 K 21[3] 2 Ch 33[3.19], and the people continued to sacrifice thereon to Yahweh 2 Ch 33[17]. **e.** Josiah, in his reform, based on the Deut. code, defiled them and brake them down from Geba to Beersheba 2 K 23[5.8.9]; but subsequently there were במות התפת in the valley of Ben Hinnom Je 7[31], and במות throughout Judah Je 17[3] cf. Ez 6[3.6] 20[29] (questioned by Ew & Co). **4.** *funereal mound*(?) Ez 43[7] (Thes, but *in their high places* AV RV; *in their death* 𝔗 Theod Ew Hi RVm), Is 53[9] (Lowth Ew Bö Rodwell Orelli; but *in his death* AV RV, or *martyr death* De Che Br).

† בָּמוֹת **n.pr.loc.** (*high place* or *great high place*) place in Moab Nu 21[19.20] = בָּמוֹת בַּעַל Nu 22[41] Jos 13[17] possibly on Mt. *'Attarûs* cf. Di.

† בִּמְהָל **n.pr.m.** (=בֶּן־מ׳ *son of circumcision*? cf. sub בן) descendant of Asher 1 Ch 7[33].

בָּמוֹ v. sub בְּ, p. 91.

בָּמוֹת v. sub במה.

בֵּן[4870] **n.m. son** (MI Ph. בן; so Sab. CIS[iv. No. 2], cf. בני DHM[Sem. Sprachforsch. 6]; Ar. إِبْنٌ; As. *bin(u)*, Lyon[Sargon 9, l. 57]; esp. in *bin-bin, grandson* COT[Gloss], cf. Dl infr.; Aram. בַּר, ܒܪ, pl. בְּנִין, ܒܢܝܢ; cf. Palm., esp. Vog[No. 21. 31. 36 & al.]; possibly orig. con-

nected with בנה *build*, so Thes, cf. As. *bânu, begetter* (Dl$^{Pr\ 104}$ & cf. Ba$^{ZMG\ 1887,\ 638\ ff.}$); but all traces of this √ lost in Heb. form; √ perh. orig. bilit. (בֶּן, בְּן) * בֵּן v. Sta^{§183})—abs. בֵּ׳ Gn 4^{25}+; בֶּן־ Ez 18^{10}; cstr. בֶּן Gn 49$^{22.22}$; בֶּן־ Gn 5^{32}+; בֶּן Est 2^{5} Ne 6^{18}, & c. prefix Gn 17^{17} Nu 8^{25} 1 Ch 27^{23} 2 Ch 25^{5} 31$^{16.17}$; בְּנוֹ Nu 23^{18} 24$^{3.15}$; בְּנִי Gn 49^{11}; בִּן Dt 25^{2}; בִּן־ Ex 33^{11}+32 t. (29 t. in combination בִּן־נוּן (יהושע (הושע, ישוע); sf. בְּנִי Gn 21^{10}+; בִּנְךָ Ex 20^{10}+; לְבִנֵךְ Dt 7^{3} 1 K 11^{13}; בְּנֵךְ Gn 30^{14}+; בְּנוֹ Gn 4^{17}+; בְּנָהּ Gn 21^{10}+; pl. בָּנִים Gn 3^{16}+; cstr. בְּנֵי Gn 6^{2}+; sf. בָּנַי Gn 31^{43}+; בָּנֵינוּ Jos 22^{25}+; בְּנֵיכֶם Ex 3^{22}+, etc.;—**1.** *son*, male child, born of a woman Gn 4^{25} 16$^{11.15}$ 17^{19} cf. v^{16} 18$^{10.14}$ 19$^{37.38}$+ oft., cf. בֶּן־בִּטְנִי Is 49^{15}; begotten by a man Gn 5$^{4\ f.\ 28}$ 6^{10} 11$^{11\ f.}$+ oft.; ‖ בַּת (בָּנוֹת) *daughter* Gn 5$^{4.7.10\ f.}$ 11$^{11.13.15\ f.}$ Ex 20^{10} Dt 5^{14} 16$^{11.14}$ 1 S 30$^{3.6}$ Jb 1^{2} 42^{13}+; of son as desired Gn 30^{2} (cf. 15^{2} 16^{2} 17^{17} 18$^{10\ f.}$ 1 S 1$^{5\text{-}11}$) 2 K 4$^{14.28}$ ψ 127^{3}+; rejoiced in Gn 30^{6}+; beloved Ex 21^{5} 2 S 19$^{1.3.5}$ 1 K 3^{26}; cared for Dt 1^{31}; spared Mal 3^{17}; disciplined & trained Dt 8^{5} Pr 3^{12} 13^{24} 19^{18} 29^{17}; owing reverence, obedience, etc. to parents Pr 6^{20} 10^{1} 13^{1}; בִּנְךָ בְּכֹרְךָ *thy first-born son* Gn 27^{32}; הַבֵּן הַבְּכֹר Dt 21^{15} cf. 1 S 8^{2}; בְּנָהּ הַגָּדֹל *her elder son* Gn 27$^{15.42}$; 27^{1} בְּנוֹ הַגָּדֹל; בְּנָהּ הַקָּטָן *her younger son* Gn 27$^{15.42}$. In partic. **a.** בֶּן־אִמּוֹ *son of his mother*, i.e. own (uterine) brother Gn 43^{29}, cf. 27^{29} Ju 8^{19} ψ 50^{20} 69^{9}, & v. אֵם. בְּנֵי אָבִיךָ *sons of thy father*=brethren Gn 49^{8} (poet.) †**b.** בְּנֵי דֹדֵיהֶן=*cousins* Nu 36^{11}. **c.** בְּנִי *my son*, as term of kindliness or endearment, used by Eli to Samuel 1 S 3$^{6.16}$ cf. 4^{16} 24^{17} 26$^{17.21.25}$, v. also Pr 1$^{8.10}$ 2^{1}+; cf. בִּנְךָ, used by Benhadad of himself to Elisha 2 K 8^{9}; by Ahaz to Tiglath-pileser 16^{7}; esp. to express intimate and gracious relation with God: י׳ calls Israel בְּנִי בְכֹרִי Ex 4^{22} cf. v^{23} Ho 11^{1}, v. also ψ 80^{16} (but cf. Che); בָּנִים אַתֶּם ליהוה אלהיכם Dt 14^{1}; בְּנֵי אֵל־חָי Ho 2^{1}; cf. further ψ 82^{6} (‖ אלהים) עֶלְיוֹן; Dt 32^{5} (pl.) v^{20} (pl.) Is 1$^{2.4}$ 30$^{1.9}$ Je 3$^{14.22}$ 4^{22} 31^{20}; of future Davidic king 2 S 7^{14}=1 Ch 17^{13} cf. ψ 2^{7}; expressly referred to Solomon 1 Ch 22^{10} 28^{6}; also of children (offered in fire) Ez 16^{21}. **d.** בְּנֵי האלהים applied to supernatural beings Gn 6$^{2.4}$ Jb 1^{6} 2^{1}; בְּנֵי אלהים Jb 38^{7}; בְּנֵי אֵלִים ψ 29^{1} (on which cf. Che's note) 89^{7}. **e.** בֶּן־אָדָם *son of man*, cf. בְּנֵי א׳, v. אָדָם; בְּנֵי אִישׁ† ψ 4^{3} & (‖ בני אדם) 49^{3} 62^{10}. †**f.** בֶּן־בִּנְךָ=*thy grandson* Ex 10^{2} Dt 6^{2} Ju 8^{22} cf. Je 27^{7}; also pl. Ex 34^{7} Dt 4$^{9.25}$ Ju 12^{14} 2 K 17^{41} 2 Ch 8^{40} Jb 42^{16} ψ 128^{6} Pr 13^{22} 17^{6} Ez 37^{25}; also בֵּן alone with similar reference Gn 29^{5} (Laban son of Nahor); Laban calls his daughters' children his own sons Gn 31$^{28.43}$ cf. 32^{1}; so of Naomi Ru 4^{17}; בְּנֵי רִבֵּעִים 2 K 10^{30} *sons of the fourth generation*, and, in general, descendants Jos 22$^{24.25.27}$+; v. also sub **i.** infr. **g.** constantly, as more precise designation, added to personal name כָּלֵב בֶּן־יְפֻנֶּה Nu 14^{30} 32^{12} 34^{19}+; יְהוֹשֻׁעַ בִּן־נוּן Nu 11^{28} 14^{30} 32$^{12.28}$ 34^{17}+; יָרָבְעָם בֶּן־נְבָט 1 K 12$^{2.15}$+, etc.; also without personal name (often with implication of contempt) בֶּן־קִישׁ 1 S 10^{11}; בֶּן־יִשַׁי 1 S 20$^{27.30.31}$ 22$^{7.8.9.13}$ 25^{10} 2 S 20^{1}; בְּנֵי צְרוּיָה 2 S 16^{10}; בֶּן־רְמַלְיָהוּ Is 7$^{4.5.9}$ 8^{6}; בֶּן־טָבְאַל Is 7^{6}; cf. also בְּנֵי לֵוִי Nu 16$^{7.8}$. **h.** designated as בֶּן־זְקֻנִים i.e. born in old age of father Gn 37^{3}; opp. בְּנֵי הַנְּעוּרִים *sons of one's youth* ψ 127^{4}; also בֶּן־בֵּיתִי *one born in my house* Gn 15^{3} (i.e. slave) so בְּנֵי בַיִת Ec 2^{7}. **i.** in various combinations: (*a*) as expression of contumely, בֶּן־נַעֲוַת הַמַּרְדּוּת 1 S 20^{30}; בֶּן־הַמְרַצֵּחַ הַזֶּה 2 K 6^{32} *this son of a murderer*; cf. בְּנֵי־נָבָל Jb 30^{8}; בְּנֵי בְלִי־שֵׁם *ib.*; בְּנֵי עֹנְנָה Is 57^{3} (‖ זֶרַע מְנָאֵף); cf. בֶּן־אִשָּׁה אַחֶרֶת Ju 11^{2} (cf. v^{1}); (*β*) as term of respect, dignity, בֶּן־חוֹרִים *son of nobles* Ec 10^{17} (in Aram.=*free born*); בֶּן־חֲכָמִים Is 19^{11}; בֶּן־מַלְכֵי־קֶדֶם *ib.*; cf. בֶּן־מֶלֶךְ ψ 72^{1} (‖ מֶלֶךְ); בֶּן־אֲמָתֶךָ ψ 86^{16} in addressing י׳ (‖ עַבְדְּךָ) & בְּנֵי־עֲבָדֶיךָ ψ 102^{29}; of noble appearance בְּנֵי הַמֶּלֶךְ Ju 8^{18}. **j.** oft. pl. with name of ancestor, people, land, or city, to denote descendants, inhabitants, membership in a nation or family, etc.: (*a*) e.g. בְּנֵי־עֵבֶר Gn 10^{21}; בְּנֵי־חֵת Gn 23$^{3.5.7.10.}$ $^{10.11.16.18.20}$ 25^{10} 49^{32} (all P); בְּנֵי־שֵׁת Nu 24^{17} v. sub (שֵׁת **8**); בְּנֵי־חֲמוֹר Gn 33^{19} Jos 24^{32}; בְּנֵי עֵשָׂו Gn 36$^{5.15.19}$ Dt 2$^{4.8.12.22.29}$; בְּנֵי שֵׂעִיר Gn 36$^{20.21}$; בֶּן־(בני)הִנֹּם Jos 15^{8}+ (cf. sub גַּיְא); בְּנֵי לוֹט Dt 2$^{9.19}$ ψ 83^{9}; בְּנֵי־יוֹסֵף (lit. Gn 46^{27} 48^{8} 1 Ch 5^{1}) Nu 1^{32} 26$^{28.37}$ 34^{23} 36^{5} (מַטֵּה ב׳ י׳)+6 t. Jos, cf. ψ 77^{16}; even בְּנֵי חֲצִי שֵׁבֶט מְנַשֶּׁה 1 Ch 5^{23}; בְּנֵי דָוִד (lit. 2 S 8^{18}=1 Ch 18^{17}, 1 Ch 3$^{1.9}$) 2 Ch 13^{8} 23^{3} 32^{33}; בְּנֵי אָסָף 2 Ch 29^{13} Ezr 2^{41} 3^{8}+ (v. אָסָף); בְּנֵי קֹרַח in titles of ψ 42–49, 84, 85, 87, 88; esp. (*β*) בְּנֵי־עַמּוֹן (standing designation of people of Ammon) Gn 19^{38}+ 81 t. (cf. עַמּוֹן & Nö$^{ZMG\ 1886,\ 171}$ Dr$^{Sm\ 66}$); בְּנֵי יַעֲקֹב (lit. Gn 34$^{7.13.25.27}$ 35$^{5.22.26}$ 49^{2}) 2 K 17^{34} ψ 105^{6} Mal 3^{6} cf. ψ 77^{16}; & chiefly (*γ*) בְּנֵי יִשְׂרָאֵל (lit. Gn 42^{5} 45^{21} 46^{5} Ex 1^{1}) Ex 1^{7}+613 t., incl. Hex 427 (of which 328 P, 49 E, 25 J, 25 D), Ju 61, S K Ch 73 (23 in ref. to ancient history, 10 in opp. to Judah); so also Vrss & var. sometimes for בֵּית יִשׂ׳, e.g. Jos 21^{43}+ v. Di, Ez 3^{1}+ v. Co; also the reverse Ez 2^{3} al.; note esp. עַם ב׳ יִשְׂרָאֵל Ex 1^{9}; עֲדַת בְּנֵי יִשְׂרָאֵל Ex 3^{10} 7^{4}; עַמִּי ב׳ יִשְׂרָאֵל Ex 16$^{1.2.9.10}$ 17^{1} Lv 16^{5} 19^{2} Nu 1$^{2.53}$ 8$^{9.20}$ 13^{26} 15$^{25.26}$

17^{6} 19^{9} 25^{6} 26^{2} 31^{12} (all P), דּוֹרוֹת ב׳ יִשׂ׳ Ju 3^{2}, כָּל־ב׳ יִשׂ׳ וְכָל־הָעָם 20^{26}, ב׳ יִשׂ׳ וּבְנֵי הַלֵּוִי Ne 10^{40}, also (δ) בְּנֵי יְהוּדָה (lit Gn 46^{12} 26^{19} 1 Ch 2$^{3\,10}$ 4^{1}) Nu 1^{26} + 18 t. Nu Jos, Ju 1$^{8.9\,16}$ (so rd. also v$^{21.21}$ cf Jos 15^{63} & v. sub בנימן) 2 S 1^{18} 1 Ch 4^{27} + 8 t Chr, Je 7^{30} + 4 t Je; Ho 2^{2} Jo 4$^{6.8.19}$ Ob^{12} (not in K, of Judah or of any other tribe, except 1 K 12^{21}) incl. מַטֵּה בְּנֵי יְהוּדָה Jos 15$^{1.20.21}$ בְּנֵי לֵוִי 21^{1} 1 Ch 6^{50}; for usage with other tribes of Isr., v. the articles;—but note (ε) בני לוי† (lit Gn 46^{11} Ex 6^{16} Nu 3^{17} 1 Ch 5^{27} 6^{1} cf. 23^{6}) Ex 32^{28} Nu 3^{15} 16$^{7.8}$ 18^{21} Jos 21^{10} (as including sons of Aaron etc), כָּל־אָחִיךָ ב׳ ל׳ Ex 32^{26}; כָּל־בְּנֵי לֵוִי Nu 16^{10}; הַכֹּהֲנִים ב׳ ל׳ Dt 21^{5} 31^{9} cf 1 K 12^{31} & Mal 3^{3}; 1 Ch 23$^{24.27}$ 24^{20} Ezr 8^{15} (distinguished from priests) Ne 12^{23} Ez 40^{46} (including בְּנֵי צָדוֹק the priests); also מַחֲנוֹת ב׳ ל׳ 1 Ch 9^{18}, בְּנֵי הַלֵּוִי 1 Ch 12^{27} Ne 10^{40}; בְּנֵי הַלְוִיִּם 1 Ch 15^{15} 24^{30} (cf also לְוִי), (ζ) בְּנֵי אַהֲרֹן (lit. Ex 28$^{1.40}$ 1 Ch 5^{29} 24^{1}; oft. Aaron and his sons lit. Ex 27^{21} 28$^{1\,4}$ +) Lv 3$^{5.8.13}$ 6$^{7\,11}$ 7$^{10.33}$ Jos 21^{10} 1 Ch 6$^{35.39.42}$ 15^{4} (+ Levites) 24$^{1.31}$ Ne 12^{47}; also בני א׳ הַכֹּהֲנִים Lv 1$^{5.8\,11}$ 2^{2} 3^{2} Nu 3^{3} 10^{8} & Jos 21^{19} 2 Ch 31^{19} cf 26^{18} 29^{21} 35$^{14\,14}$; בני אַהֲרֹן הַכֹּהֵן Lv 1^{7} Jos 21^{4} (as subdivision of Levites) v^{13} cf. Lv 7^{34}, אֶת־כֹּהֲנֵי יהוה אֶת־בְּנֵי אַהֲרֹן 2 Ch 13^{9} cf. v^{10}; once in sing הַכֹּהֵן בֶּן־אַהֲרֹן וְהַלְוִיִּם Ne 10^{39}; v. also sub אַהֲרֹן, (η) בני צָדוֹק† Ez 40^{46}, 44^{15} הכהנים הלוים בני צדוק; הַכֹּהֲנִים הַמְקֻדָּשׁ 48^{11} מבני צדוק (𝔊 Sm Co join מ of מבני to preceding word, making pl.), (θ) בני with names of peoples, lands, and cities, בני כֻשִׁיִּים Am 9^{7}; בני מִצְרַיִם Ez 16^{26}; בְּנֵי אַשּׁוּר Ez 16^{28} 23$^{7\,9\,12.23}$; ב׳ בָּבֶל Ez ב׳ אֶרֶץ הַבְּרִית Ez 30^{5} (Co del ארץ), 23$^{15.17\,23}$; ב׳ ירושלם Jo 4^{6}; ב׳ צִיּוֹן Jo 2^{23} La 4^{2} ψ 149^{2} (cf. Zc 9^{13}) Vid. further (ι) בני עַמְּךָ Lv 19^{18} cf 20^{17} Nu 22^{5} Ju 14$^{16\,17}$ Ez 3^{11} 33$^{2\,12\,17\,30}$ 37^{18} Dn 12^{1}; בְּנֵי פָרִיצֵי עַמְּךָ Dn 11^{14}, (κ) קֶבֶר בני הָעָם 2 K 23^{6} 2 Ch 35$^{5\,7\,12}$; קִבְרֵי בני הָעָם Je 26^{23}, (λ) בני־קֶדֶם Gn 29^{1} Ju 7^{12} 8^{10} 1 K 5^{10} Jb 1^{3} Is 11^{14} Je 49^{28} Ez 25$^{4\,10}$, †(μ) בְּנֵי הַמְּדִינָה Ezr 2^{1} = Ne 7^{6}, (ν) of bulls, בני בָשָׁן Dt 32^{14} (song) cf. Klo$^{SK\,1872\,254}$ Di **2.** *children* (male and female) Gn 3^{16} 21^{7} Ex 21^{5} 22^{23}; hence בְּנֵי מְנַשֶּׁה הַזְּכָרִים Jos 17^{2} *male children*, בֵּן זָכָר Je 20^{15}. **3.** *youth, young men* (pl) Pr 7^{7} Ct 2^{3}. **4.** *the young* of animals Lv 22^{28} (שׁוֹר אוֹ שֶׂה) cf. Dt 22$^{6.7}$ 1 S 6$^{7\,10}$ Zc 9^{9} Jb 4^{11} 28^{8} 39$^{4\,16}$,—בֶּן־בָּקָר etc v sub **7 b** infr. **5.** of plant-shoots בֵּן פֹּרָת Gn 49$^{22.22}$; also בֵּן ψ 80^{16}† (‖ כַּנָּה; see Che trans & crit. n.) **6.** fig. of lifeless things, בני רֶשֶׁף *sparks* Jb 5^{7}; *stars* עַיִשׁ בני עַל־בָּנֶיהָ Jb 38^{32}; *arrows* בֶּן־קָשֶׁת Jb 41^{20}, בני אַשְׁפָּתוֹ La 3^{13}; cf בֶּן־גָּרְנִי i.e. *corn of my threshing-floor* Is 21^{10}. **7. a.** *member* of a guild, order or class, †בְּנֵי הַנְּבִיאִים i.e. those belonging to the prophetic order 1 K 20^{35} 2 K 2$^{3.5.7\,15}$ 4$^{1\,38.38}$ 5^{22} 6^{1} 9^{1} (Hoffm RS$^{Proph.\,85.\,384,\,K\,15f}$; Zehnpfund$^{BAS\,I.\,344}$ comp. As. *mâr šipri* (*šiprâtum*), *son of a messenger* = *messenger*, and explains from the son's succeeding to father's calling) & בֶּן־נָבִיא Am 7^{14}; prob. also בני הַכֹּהֲנִים† 1 Ch 9^{30} Ezr 2^{61} 10^{18}, בְּנֵי הַשֹּׁעֲרִים† Ezr 2^{42}; cf. בני הַגְּדוּד 2 Ch 25^{13} *men of the troop*, v Palm בני שירתא *men of the caravan* Vog$^{No.\,4\,a1}$; also בני הַגּוֹלָה = *exiles* †Ezr 4^{1} 6$^{19.20}$ 8^{35} 10$^{7\,16}$ (v גולה sub גלה); further, in בֶּן־נֵכָר = *foreigner* (only P, poet, & late) †Gn 17$^{12\,27}$ Ex 12^{43} Lv 22^{25} Ez 44$^{9.9}$; ב׳־הַנּ׳ †Is 56^{3}; בְּנֵי־נֵכָר † 2 S 22$^{45.46}$ = ψ 18$^{45.46}$ Ne 9^{2} Is 60^{10} 61^{5} 62^{8} Ez 44^{7} ψ 144$^{7\,11}$, בני־הַנּ׳ Is 56^{6}; also בְּנֵי הַתּוֹשָׁבִים הַגָּרִים עִמָּכֶם Lv 25$^{4.5}$. **b.** of animals, בֶּן־בָּקָר *son of* (*the*) *herd*, i.e young one of the herd, בָּקָר וּבְנֵי בָקָר 1 S 14^{32} cf עֵגֶל בֶּן־בָּקָר Lv 9^{2} (P); then, in general, one of the herd. fit for food Gn 18$^{7\,8}$ (J), for sacrifice Nu 15$^{8.9}$ (P), בֶּן־הַבּ׳ only Lv 12^{6} (P), esp. פַּר בֶּן־בָּקָר Ex 29^{1} Lv 4$^{3.14}$ 16^{3} 23^{18} Nu 7^{15} + 16 t Nu (all P) + 2 Ch 13^{9} Ez 43$^{19\,23.25}$ 45^{18} 46^{6}; פָּרִים בני בָקָר Nu 28$^{11\,19.27}$ 29$^{13\,17}$ (P); also בְּנֵי אֲתֹנוֹ Gn 49^{11} (poem, J, ‖ עִירֹה), בני־צֹאן ψ 114$^{4.6}$; בֶּן־רְאֵמִים ψ 29^{6}, בני הָרַמָּכִים Est 8^{10}; בני (הַ)יּוֹנָה Lv 1^{14} + 7 t. Lv + Nu 6^{10} cf. בֶּן־יוֹנָה Lv 12^{6} (all P); בְּנֵי־נֶשֶׁר Pr 30^{17}, בני ערב ψ 147^{9} **8.** ב׳ as n relat. followed by word of quality, characteristic, etc. esp †(α) בֶּן־(בני)חַיִל = *mighty man* 1 S 14^{52} 18^{17} 2 S 2^{7} 13^{28} 17$^{10\,10}$ 1 K 1^{52} + 7 t. Ch; אֲנָשִׁים בני ח׳ Ju 18^{2} 2 K 2^{16}, אֶלֶף איש מבני הֶחָיִל Ju 21^{10}; †(β) בני עַוְלָה *wicked men* 2 S 3^{34} 7^{10} 1 Ch 17^{9} Ho 10^{9}; בֶּן־ע׳ ψ 89^{23} (for בליעל v בני בליעל); †(γ) בְּנֵי מֶרִי *rebels* Nu 17^{25} (cf. בית); †(δ) בְּנֵי הַתַּעֲרֻבוֹת *sons of pledges* = hostages 2 K 14^{14} = 2 Ch 25^{24}; †(ε) בני מָוֶת i.e. those deserving of death 1 S 26^{16}; so בן־מות 2 S 12^{5}; בני תְמוּתָה *appointed* or *exposed to death* ψ 79^{11} 102^{21}, cf. †(ζ) בֶּן הַכּוֹת one worthy of smiting Dt 25^{2}; †(η) בְּנֵי עֹנִי Pr 31^{5}; †(θ) בני חֲלוֹף Pr 31^{8}; †(ι) בְּנֵי שָׁאוֹן Je 48^{45} = *tumultuous ones;* so also (= שאת) בְּנֵי שֵׁת Nu 24^{17} cf. RV Di al, †(κ) בני הַיִּצְהָר Zc 4^{14} i.e. anointed ones, †(λ) בֶּן־מֶשֶׁק Gn 15^{2} *son of possession*, i.e heir; †(μ) הילל בֶּן־שָׁחַר Is 14^{12} *son of dawn;* †(ν) of animals בני שָׁחַץ i.e. proud beasts Jb 28^{8} 41^{26}; (ξ) of Jonah's gourd בִּן־לַיְלָה Jon 4$^{10\,10}$; †(ο) of a fertile hill קֶרֶן בֶּן־שָׁמֶן Is 5^{1}. **9.** n relat. of age: **a.** of men, וַיְהִי נֹחַ בֶּן־חֲמֵשׁ מֵאוֹת שָׁנָה Gn 5^{32} cf. 7^{6} + 71 t P, Gn 50^{26} Jos 14$^{7\,10}$ 24^{29} (all E); Nu 32^{11} (J), Dt 31^{2}, also Ju 2^{8} 1 S 4^{15} 2 S 4^{4} 19$^{33.36}$ 1 Ch 2^{21}

2 3[3.21.27] 27[3] 2 Ch 24[14] 25[5] 31[16 17] Ezr 3[8] Is 65[20.20] Je 52[1], + 41 t S K Ch of kings at accession, note esp (incl in above) the phrase מִבֶּן עֶשְׂרִים שָׁנָה וָמָ֑עְלָה Ex 30[14] 38[26] Nu 1[3] + 21 t Nu 1–3 + 26[2 4] 32[11] 1 Ch 23[24 27] 2 Ch 25[5] Ezr 3[8], cf. Lv 27[7] Nu 8[24] 26[62] 1 Ch 23[3] & without מעלה Nu 8[25] 18[16], also מִבֶּן עשרים שנה ועד בֶּן־ששים שָׁנָה Lv 27[3] cf v[5 6], מבן שלשים שנה ומעלה ועד בן־חמשים שנה Nu 4[3.3] + 12 t. Nu 4, מבן שלוש שנים וּלְמַ֑עְלָה 2 Ch 31[16] cf. v[17], & למבן עשרים שנה וּלְמַטָּה 1 Ch 27[23] **b.** of animals, (Hex all P, incl H) בֶּן־שָׁנָה Ex 12[5] 29[38] Lv 9[3] 23[18 19] Nu 7[17] + 28 t. Nu 7, 28, 29, also Mi 6[6], בֶּן־שְׁנָתוֹ Lv 12[6] 23[12] Nu 6[12 14] + 12 t Nu 7; also Ez 46[13].

Note—בן appears perh abbrev as ב in a few cpd n pr, v בדקר (=בן־דקר?), בְּמַהְל, בלשׁן, בשׁלם, ברשׁע, בַּעֲנָה, בְּעָלִים (so MV after Schol Hamâsa[3] ed Freytag, Ro[de libr hist. interpr Arab 20 21]; but this is very uncertain, cf Ol[† 227 b, p. 613]) —On Lag's explan of אבי in some n pr as for אבן=בן cf Lag[BN 75] & v אבינר p 4, etc., but this is dub

†בֶּן **n pr.m.** a Levite 1 Ch 15[18], but del 𝔊 Be Ot cf. v[20]

†בֶּן־אֲבִינָדָב **n.pr.m.** (?) (*son of Abinadab*) an officer of Solomon 1 K 4[11], but cf אבינדב p 4

†בֶּן־אוֹנִ֑י **n.pr.m.** (*son of my sorrow*) Rachel's name for Benjamin (cf infr) Gn 35[18].

†בֶּן־גֶּ֫בֶר **n.pr.m.** (*son of a man*, or *of Geber*) an officer of Solomon 1 K 4[13]

†בֶּן־דֶּ֫קֶר **n pr.m.** (?) (*son of Deker*) an officer of Solomon 1 K 4[9]

†בֶּן־הֲדַד **n.pr.m.** (appar *son of (god) Hadad*=Aram ܒܪ ܗܕܕ, 𝔊 ܒܪ ܗܕܕ PS cf. Bae[Rel 68], also Bab *Bin-addu-natan* etc, Pinches[PB Feb 1883, 71], As *Bir-Dadda* COT 1 K 20[1] Hpt[Hbr 1885, 224], but cf 𝔊 υἱὸς Ἄδερ, & Dl[ZK II 1885 161 f], v. also Schr[KG 375 ff 538 f]) name for king of Aram Je 49[27]; in partic,—**1.** time of Asa & Baasha 1 K 15[18.20] = 2 Ch 16[2 4] **2.** son of **1.** (cf 1 K 20[34]) As *Dad-idri* COT (*Bir-idri* Dl[l.c.]) 1 K 20[1.3.5 9 10.16 17 20.26 30.32.33.33] 2 K 6[24] 8[7 9] **3.** son of Hazael 2 K 13[3.24.25] cf. Am 1[4] —Vid הדד

†בֶּן־זוֹחֵת **n.pr.m.** one of tribe of Judah, 1 Ch 4[20] וּבְנֵי יִשְׁעִי זוחת וּבֶן־זוחת.

†בֶּן־חוּר **n.pr.m.** (*son of Chur*) an officer of Solomon 1 K 4[8]

†בְּנוֹ 1 Ch 24[26 27] as **n pr.m.** in AV RV, but render the sons of Jaaziah *his son*, & the sons of Merari by Jaaziah *his son*, cf. VB & Be Ot

†בֶּן־חַ֫יִל **n.pr.m.** (*son (man) of might*) a prince of Jehoshaphat 2 Ch 17[7]

†בֶּן־חָנָן **n.pr.m.** one of tribe of Judah 1 Ch 4[20]

†בֶּן־חֶ֫סֶד **n.pr.m.** (*son of mercy*) an officer of Solomon 1 K 4[10]

†בֶּן־עַמִּי **n.pr.m.** (*son of my people*) son of Lot by his younger daughter, and ancestor of the Ammonites (בני־עמון v. עמון) Gn 19[38]

†בְּנֵי־בְרַק **n.pr.loc.** city of Dan (in As *Banai-barka* COT Jos 19[45]) Jos 19[45],—mod *Ibn Abrak*, or *Ibrak*, c 1¼ hour S. of E. from Jaffa, Scholz[Reise 256] Di, cf. Map Bd[Pal] & Survey II 251

†בְּנֵי יַעֲקָן **n.pr.loc.** a station of Israel in wilderness Nu 33[31.32] (= בארות בני יעקן Dt 10[6] q v, p 92, cf also יַעֲקָן 1 Ch 1[42] = עֲקָן Gn 36[27], & Di Nu 33[31])

בִּנְיָמִן Gn 35[18] +, usually בִּנְיָמִן **n pr.m.** [166] (*son of (the) right hand*)—**1.** youngest son of Jacob, so called by him, but by Rachel, the mother, who died at Benjamin's birth, called בן־אוני (q v) Gn 35[18], own brother of Joseph Gn 35[24] 42[4] 43[29] 45[12], cf 42[36] 45[15.34] +; name of tribe of Benjamin Nu 1[11] Dt 27[12] 33[12] Ju 5[14] + 23 t Ju; 32 t. S K Chr, Ho 5[8] Ez 48[23] Ob [19] ψ 68[28] 80[3], בני בנימן (lit Gn 46[21]) of tribe Nu 1[36] 2[22] 7[60] 26[38.41] Jos 18[20.28] Ju 20[3 14 15.18.21 23.24.28 30 31.32 36 48] 21[13.20 23] 2 S 2[25] 4[2] 23[29] 1 Ch 8[40] 9[3.7] 11[31] 12[2 17 30] Ne 11[4 7.31] Je 6[1], Ju 1[21 21] (but בני יהודה in ‖ Jos 15[63] cf Bu[RS 7]), explicitly מַטֵּה בִנְיָמִן Nu 1[37] 2[22] 13[9] 34[21] Jos 21[4] 1 Ch 6[45] cf Jos 21[17]; מַטֵּה בני ב׳ Nu 10[24] Jos 18[11 21] 1 Ch 6[50], שֵׁבֶט ב׳ 1 S 10[20.21] 1 K 12[21], observe also כָּל־שבטי ב׳ Ju 20[12] cf 1 S 9[21], איש בנימן Ju 20[41] 1 S 4[12] cf. איש ימיני 1 S 9[1], אֶרֶץ בנימן Ju 21[21] 1 S 9[16] 2 S 21[14] Je 1[1] 17[26] 32[44] 33[13] 37[12] cf 32[8], גבול ב׳ 1 S 10[2] Ez 48[22] (del Co) v[24], בית בנימן 2 S 3[19], בית יְהוּדָה וּב׳ 1 K 12[23] 2 Ch 11[1], in name of a temple-gate שַׁעַר ב׳ הָעֶלְיוֹן Je 20[2] cf 37[13] 38[7] Ez 48[32] Zc 14[10] †**2** a son of Bilhan and great-grandson of Benjamin **1.** 1 Ch 7[10] †**3.** a Jew of Ezra's time Ezr 10[32] cf Ne 3[23] 12[34] —בנימן בני פרץ 1 Ch 9[4] Kt rd with Qr בְּנֵי מִן־בני פ׳.

†בֶּן־יְמִינִי **adj.gent.** from בִּנְיָמִן **1.** 1 S 9[21] ψ 7[1], בֶּן־הַיְמִינִי Ju 3[15] 2 S 16[11] 19[17] 1 K 2[8], pl. בני ימיני 1 S 22[7] Ju 19[16]; לִבְנֵי ימיני 1 Ch 27[12] (Qr לבן ימיני), = יְמִינִי (q.v) 1 S 9[4] +

†בְּנִינוּ **n.pr.m.** (*our son?* Ol §277b, p 613) a Levite Ne 10^{14}.

I בַּת$_{887}$ **n.f.** daughter (=*בִּנְתּ fr. בן, Ph. בת, MI בנת pl. *maidens*, As. *bintu* Winckler Sargon, Gloss., Ar. بِنْتٌ; Sab בנת, בת DHM ZMG 1883, 391 CIS IV 1, No. 6. 21; Aram. ܒܪܬܐ)—ב׳ abs. Ex 1^{16} +; cstr. Gn 11^{29} +, sf בתי Dt 22^{16} +; בִּתְּךָ Gn 29^{18}+; בתנו Gn 34^{17} etc., pl בָּנוֹת Gn 5^{4}+, cstr בנות Gn 6^{2}+, sf בנֹתַי Gn 31^{26}+; בנֹתֶיךָ Gn 19^{12}+; בנֹתָם Gn 34^{21}, בנותיהם Dt 12^{31}+, etc.,—**1.** *daughter*, female child, born of a woman Gn 30^{21} 34^{1} Ex $1^{16.22}$ 21^{4} Lv 12^{6} Ho 1^{6} cf. Gn 20^{12} Lv 18^{9} Dt 27^{22}+, begotten by a man Gn $5^{4.7\ 10}$ $11^{11\ 13\ 15}$ cf. Gn 11^{29} 19^{8} 20^{12} 28^{8} Lv 19^{9} Dt 27^{22}+; oft. ‖ בן *son* Gn $5^{4.7}$+ (v בן); cf. in allegory of Jehoash 2 K 14^{9} = 2 Ch 25^{18}, note esp בנות הָאָדָם i.e. human women Gn $6^{2.4}$, בִּתְּךָ הַקְּטַנָּה *thy younger daughter* Gn 29^{18} (cf. הַצְּעִירָה v^{26} opp. הַבְּכִירָה); בתי הַגְּדוֹלָה *my eldest daughter* 1 S 18^{17}, בַּת־(הַ)מֶּלֶךְ=*princess* 2 Ch 22^{11} 2 K 9^{34} Dn 11^{6} cf. 2 S 13^{18} Je 41^{10} 43^{6} ψ 45^{10}, cf as term of praise בַּת־נָדִיב Ct 7^{2}; in partic. †**a.** girl called בתנו by father and brothers Gn 34^{17} cf בתכם v^{8} †**b.** of adopted daughter Est $2^{7\ 15}$ †**c.** used in speaking to daughter-in-law Ru $1^{11\ 12\ 13}$ $2^{2.8.22}$ $3^{1\ 16.18}$. †**d.** בַּת־אָבִיו=*sister* Ez 22^{11} (appos אחותו), also *half-sister* Gn 20^{12} בַּת־אָבִי אַךְ לֹא בַּת־אמי, cf. Lv 18^{9} & v^{11} בַּת־אֵשֶׁת אָבִיךָ, 20^{17} †**e.** בַּת־דֹּדוֹ = *cousin* Est 2^{7} †**f.** used in kindly address, בתי Ru $3^{10.11}$ (Boaz to Ruth), cf ψ 45^{11}; בְּנוֹתַי in mouth of י׳ Is 43^{6} (‖ בָּנַי) †**g.** בנות בָּנָיו = *granddaughters* Gn 46^{7} (P) cf. Lv 18^{10} & v^{17} (H), note also Gn 37^{35}, where בנותיו must include other than actual daughters. **h.** רבקה בַּת־בתואל (as more precise designation) Gn 25^{20} cf. $24^{23.24\ 47\ 47}$ also $26^{34\ 34}$ 29^{10}+, note esp. †בַּת־פַּרְעֹה (without personal name) Ex $2^{5\ 7.8.9.10}$ cf 1 K 3^{1} 7^{8} 9^{24} 11^{1} 2 Ch 8^{11}; בַּת־אִישׁ כְּנַעֲנִי וּשְׁמוֹ שׁוּעַ Gn 38^{2} cf. v^{12} (but cf 1 Ch 2^{3} sub בַּת־שׁוּעַ **n.pr.f.** infr) †**i.** oft pl. as designation of women of a particular city, land, or people. בנות צִיּוֹן Is $3^{16\ 17}$ 4^{4} Ct 3^{11} cf Is 49^{22} 60^{4} La 3^{51}, בנות יְרוּשָׁלָםִ Ct 1^{5} 2^{7} $3^{5\ 10}$ $5^{8.16}$ 8^{4}; בנות־שילו Ju $21^{21\ 21}$; בנות רַבָּה Je 49^{3}, observe transitional phrase בנות אַנְשֵׁי הָעִיר Gn 24^{13}, further בנות כְּנָעַן Gn $28^{1\ 6.8}$ 36^{2} (all P) cf ב׳ הַכְּנַעֲנִי Gn $24^{3\ 37}$ (J); בנות הָאָרֶץ Gn 27^{46} 34^{1} (both P), בנות מואב Nu 25^{1} Is 16^{2} cf. Nu 21^{29}, ב׳ חֵת Gn $27^{46.46}$ (P), ב׳ פלשתים Ju $14^{1\ 2}$ 2 S 1^{20} ‖ ב׳ הָעֲרֵלִים v^{20} (poet); ב׳ יִשְׂרָאֵל Ju 11^{40} 1 S 1^{24} (poet), ב׳ יהודה ψ 48^{12} 97^{8}, ב׳ מְנַשֶּׁה Jos 17^{6}, ב׳ דָן 2 Ch 2^{13}, cf. בַּת־לֵוִי Ex 2^{1} i.e. a woman of tribe of Levi, also ב׳ אַחֶיךָ Ju 14^{3}; ב׳ עַמְּךָ Ez 13^{17}—בַּת־צִיּוֹן etc. v. sub **3** infr. †**2.** *young women, women* Gn 30^{13} (J) Pr 31^{29} Ct 2^{2} 6^{9}; בָּנוֹת בֹּטְחוֹת Is 32^{9}, also בַּת הַנָּשִׁים Dn 11^{17}. †**3.** with name of city, land, or people, poet personif of that city or inhabitants, etc בַּת־צִיּוֹן Is 1^{8} 10^{32} 16^{1} 62^{11} Mi 1^{13} $4^{8\ 10\ 13}$ Je 4^{31} $6^{2.23}$ Zp 3^{14} Zc 2^{14} 9^{9} ψ 9^{15} La 1^{6} $2^{1.4}$ 4^{22}, even זִקְנֵי בת־ציון La 2^{10}, חוֹמַת ב׳ צ׳ v$^{8.18}$, also שְׁבִיָּה ב׳־צ׳ Is 52^{2}, בתולת ב׳־צ׳ 2 K 19^{21}=Is 37^{22} La 2^{13}, ב׳ יְרוּשָׁלָםִ 2 K 19^{21}=Is 37^{22} Mi 4^{8} Zp 3^{14} Zc 9^{9} La $2^{13\ 15}$, cf. בַּת־פוּצַי Zp 3^{10} *daughter of my dispersed ones*, בַּת־צֹר ψ 45^{13}, ב׳ בָּבֶל Je 50^{42} 51^{33} ψ 137^{8}, בתולת ב׳ בָּבֶל Is 47^{1}, v further Zc 2^{11}; also of Tarshish Is 23^{10}, Sidon v^{12} (+ בתולת), Dibon Je 48^{18} (+ יושבת), Gallim Is 10^{30}, בַּת־יְהוּדָה La 1^{15}, cf. מבצרי בַּת יְהוּדָה 2^{2}; בַּת־עַמִּי *daughter of my people* Is 22^{4} Je 4^{11} $6^{14.26}$ $8^{11\ 19.21\ 22.23}$ 9^{6} La 3^{48} $4^{3.6\ 10}$, בתולת ב׳ ע׳ Je 14^{17}; בַּת־מִצְרָיִם Je 46^{24}, also 46^{11} (+ בתולת), v^{19} (+ יֹשֶׁבֶת); ב׳ אֱדוֹם La $4^{21\ 22}$, ב׳ כַּשְׂדִּים Is $47^{1\ 5}$, note הַבַּת הַשּׁוֹבֵבָה Je 31^{22} (‖ v^{21} בתולת ישראל) 49^{4} (=Ammon), on בַּת־אֲשֻׁרִים Ez 27^{6} v. sub אֲשֻׁרִים p. 81; less often in pl בנות הַגּוֹיִם Ez 32^{16}; ב׳ גּ׳ אַדִּרִם v^{18} (these perh sub **1 i**); בנות פְּלִשְׁתִּים Ez 16^{27} (in allegory), cf. also of Sodom, Samaria, Syria etc v$^{44.46.46.48.53\ 55\ 55.57\ 57}$ 23^{2}. **4.** pl =*villages*, after name of city, וּבְחֶשְׁבּוֹן וּבְכָל־בְּנֹתֶיהָ Nu 21^{25} cf. v^{32} 32^{42} (E) Jos $15^{45\ 47\ 47}$ (JE?) + v^{28} 𝔊 Di, 17^{11} (6 t.) v^{16} (J) = Ju $1^{27\ 27\ 27\ 27}$ $11^{26.26}$ Je 49^{2} + 17 t Ch + 6 t. Ne $11^{25.31}$ On 1 Ch 18^{1} & its variation from ‖ 2 S 8^{1} vid. We Dr **5.** in phrases denoting character, quality, etc, בַּת־אֵל נֵכָר *daughter of a strange god*, i e idolatrous (woman or people) Mal 2^{11}, בַּת־גְּדוּד *daughter of a troop*, i.e war-like city Mi 4^{14}; בנות הַשִּׁיר Ec 12^{4} *the daughters of song*, i.e. songs, melodious notes, בַּת־בְּלִיַּעַל 1 S 1^{16} v. בְּלִיַּעַל sub בלה. †**6.** בַּת יַעֲנָה=*ostrich* Lv 11^{16}=Dt 14^{15}; pl בנות יַעֲנָה Jb 30^{29} Mi 1^{8} Is 13^{21} 34^{13} 43^{20} Je 50^{39} (v. יָעֵן); בַּת־עַיִן *pupil of the eye* La 2^{18} cf. Eth ወለተ፡ ዐይን፡ v also אִישׁוֹן. †**7.** fig. לַעֲלוּקָה שְׁתֵּי בָנוֹת Pr 30^{15} *two daughters* (i e She'ôl & the barren womb, cf. Comm.) †**8.** of vine=*branch* בָּנוֹת צָעֲדָה עֲלֵי־שׁוּר Gn 49^{22} cf Di & v. sub בֵּן. †**9.** as n relat. (all P), of age of woman בַּת־תִּשְׁעִים שָׁנָה Gn 17^{17}; of ewe-lamb בַּת־שְׁנָתָהּ Lv 14^{10} Nu 6^{14}; of she-goat id Nu 15^{27}. Cf בן **9.**—II בַּת v. sub בתת p. 144

†בַּת־רַבִּים **n pr.loc.** (*daughter of multitudes*) appellation of populous city of Heshbon, or of its gate, Ct 7^{5} (‖ חֶשְׁבּוֹן).

†בַּת־שֶׁ֫בַע **n.pr.f.** (*daughter of oath?* cf. אֱלִישֶׁ֫בַע) wife of Uriah 2 S 11^{3} ψ 50^{2}; afterwards of David, & mother of Solomon 12^{24} 1 K 1$^{11.15.16.31}$ 2$^{13.18.19}$; בַּת־שָׁ֫בַע 1 K 1^{28}; cf. also foll.

†בַּת־שׁ֫וּעַ **n.pr.f.** (?) (*daughter of opulence?*)—**1.** wife of David, mother of Solomon, etc. 1 Ch 3^{5} = בַּת־שֶׁ֫בַע q.v.; We Klo בַּת־שֶׁ֫בַע cf. Be; but prob. text. error v. Dr on 2 S 11^{3}. **2.** wife of Judah 1 Ch 2^{3} ב״ש׳ הַכְּנַעֲנִית, RV *Bath-shua* but in ‖ Gn 38$^{2.12}$ not a n.pr. (cf. v^{2}).

†בִּתְיָה **n.pr.f.** (= בַּת יָהּ i.e. *worshipper of Yah?* cf. Ph. n.pr.f. בתבעל) 1 Ch 4^{18} wife of Mered of Judah, called בַּת־פַּרְעֹה.

בָּנָה $_{373}$ **vb.** build (MI, Nab. Eut$^{No.1}$ בנה, Ph. בן, Ar. بَنَى, As. *banû* COT$^{Gloss.}$ cf. Ba$^{ZMG\ 1887,\ 640}$, Sab. בני CIS$^{iv.\ 1,\ No.\ 56}$, Aram. בְּנָא, ܒܢܐ, Palm. בנא Vog$^{No.\ 31}$)—**Qal** *Pf.* ב׳ Dt 20^{5}+, בָּֽנְתָה Pr 9^{1} 14^{1}, בָּנִיתָ Dt 6^{10}, בָּנִ֫יתָה 1 K 9^{3}; וּבָנִ֫יתָ consec. Dt 20^{20}+; בָּנִית Ez 16^{25}; בָּנִיתִי 1 K 8^{13}+; pl. בָּנוּ Gn 11^{5}+, etc.; *Impf.* יִבְנֶה Dt 25^{9}+; juss. וַיִּבֶן Ezr 1^{3}, וַיִּבְנֶה Jos 19^{50} + 2 t., וַיִּ֫בֶן Gn 2^{22}+; sf. יִבְנֵ֫הוּ Jb 20^{19}; 3 fs. וַתִּ֫בֶן 1 Ch 7^{24} Zc 9^{3}; אֶבְנֶה 2 S 7^{27}+; pl. יִבְנוּ Is 65^{22}+, etc.; *Imv.* בְּנֵה Nu 23^{1}+; pl. בְּנוּ Nu 32^{24}+; *Inf. abs.* בָּנֹה 1 K 8^{13}; cstr. בְּנוֹת 1 Ch 6^{17}+, etc.; *Pt. act.* בֹּנֶה (בּוֹנֶה) Gn 4^{17}+; cstr. בֹּנֵה ψ 147^{2}; pl. בֹּנִים (בּוֹנִים) Ezr 4^{1}+; cstr. בֹּנֵי 1 K 5$^{32.32}$, etc.; *pass.* בָּנוּי Ct 4^{4} Ju 6^{28}; f. בְּנוּיָה ψ 122^{3}; pl. בְּנוּיִם Ne 7^{4};—*build,* **1.** (lit.) **a.** c. acc. (α) of city (Hex only JE) Gn 4^{17} 10^{11} 11$^{4.5}$ (+ tower) v^{8} (all J & his sources); Ex 1^{11} Nu 32^{24} Jos 24^{13} (all E) Ju 1^{26} 18^{28} + 22 t. K Ch + Je 32^{31} ψ 122^{3} (pt. pass.) cf. Hb 2^{12}; of village (חָצֵר) Ne 12^{29}; v. also sub *rebuild,* **i.** infr.; (β) house Gn 33^{17} (J), elsewhere in Hex only Dt 6^{10} 8^{12} 20^{25} 22^{8} 28^{30}; also 2 S 5^{11} 1 K 22^{39} 1 Ch 14^{1} 2 Ch 2^{2} Pr 24^{27} Am 5^{11} Zp 1^{13} Is 65^{21} Je 35$^{7.9}$ cf. Zc 5^{11}; as sign of security Ez 28^{26} cf. 11^{3}; of luxury Ec 2^{4} cf. Je 22^{14}; of permanent residence 1 K 2^{36} Je 29$^{5.28}$; esp. of temple 1 K 3^{1} 5^{32} 6^{2} + oft. S K Chr; fig. of wisdom's house Pr 9^{1}; esp. build temple ליהוה etc. 2 S 7$^{5.7}$ 1 K 6^{1} (= began to build) + 13 t. Chr + Is 66^{1}; לְשֵׁם י׳ etc. 2 S 7^{13} 1 K 5^{17} + 8 t. K, 13 t. Ch; לְךָ לְשִׁמְךָ 2 Ch 20^{8}; לִהְיוֹת שְׁמִי שָׁם 1 K 8^{16} 2 Ch 6^{5}; לָשׂוּם שְׁמִי שָׁם 1 K 9^{3}; obj. chambers, or stories 1 K 6$^{5.10}$, court 6^{36} Ho 8^{14} perh. of idol-temples; cf. 1 K 16^{32}; ψ 78^{69} of Yahweh's building his sanctuary, 147^{2} Jerusalem, ψ 127^{1} a house; also Am 9^{6} his chambers in the heavens; of Sol.'s palace 1 K 7$^{1.2}$ 9$^{1.10}$+; (γ) of a fortress 2 Ch 17^{12} 27^{4} cf. of Tyre Zc 9^{3} (מָצוֹר); (δ) of wall 1 K 3^{1} Is 60^{10} Ez 13^{10} 2 Ch 33^{14} (cf. 27^{3}) Ne 4^{4} 6^{1}+; (ε) gate 2 K 15^{35} = 2 Ch 27^{3}; (ζ) tower Is 5^{2} 2 Ch 26$^{9.10}$ 27^{4} cf. fig. Ct 8^{9} & pt. pass. Ct 4^{4} (in sim.); †(η) siege-works against (עַל־) a city Dt 20^{20} (מָצוֹר), Ec 9^{14} (מְצוֹדִים), 2 K 25^{1} = Je 52^{4} Ez 4^{2} (all דָּיֵק), & so (without עַל־) Ez 17^{17} 21^{27}; cf. בנה עָלַי, abs. La 3^{5} (in fig.); (θ) altar Gn 22^{9} 35^{7} Ex 17^{15} 20^{25} 24^{4} Nu 23$^{1.14.29}$ (all E), Gn 26^{25} Ex 32^{5} (both J), Jos 22^{11} + 6 t. Jos 22 (all P) Ju 6^{28} (pt. pass.) 21^{4} + 6 t. K Ch; oft. sq. ליהוה etc. Gn 8^{20} 12$^{7.8}$ 13^{18} (all J), Dt 27$^{5.6}$ Jos 8^{30} (E) Ju 6$^{24.26}$ + 8 t. S K Ch; †(ι) high places (בָּמָה) 1 K 11^{7} 14^{23} 2 K 17^{9} 21^{3} 23^{13} 2 Ch 33$^{3.19}$ Je 7^{31} 19^{5} 32^{35}; cf. גַּב Ez 16$^{24.31}$ (both ‖ רָמָה) & רָמָה v^{25}; †(κ) צִיּוּן Ez 39^{15}; also †(λ) גִּדְרֹת צֹאן Nu 32^{16} (E); †(μ) מֵיסַךְ הַשַּׁבָּת 2 K 16^{18}. †**b.** c. acc. of material Ex 20^{25} (E) 1 K 6^{36} 18^{32} 15^{22} = 2 Ch 16^{6} Ez 27^{5}; c. בְּ of material 1 K 6$^{15.16}$ 15^{17} 2 Ch 16^{6}; cf. †**c.** וַיִּבֶן אֶת־הַצֵּלָע לְאִשָּׁה Gn 2^{22} *and he* (Yahweh) *fashioned the rib into a woman.* †**d.** abs. 2 S 5^{9} 1 K 6^{16} Is 9^{9} Je 1^{10} 18^{9} 22^{13} 31^{28} Is 65^{22} + 12 t. Chr + Mal 1^{4} Ec 3^{3} (opp. פרץ); also **e.** Pt. act. = *builder* 1 K 5$^{32.32}$ + 6 t. Chr + Ez 27^{4} ψ 118^{22} 127^{1}. †**f.** c. indef. obj. 1 K 9^{19} = 2 Ch 8^{6}. †**g.** וַיִּבֶן אֶת־הָהָר = *and he built* on *the hill* 1 K 16^{24}. †**h.** sq. בְּ *build at* Zc 6^{15} Ne 4^{11} (cf. בְּ **I 2 b**, p. 88). †**i.** = *rebuild* Jos 6^{26} 1 K 16^{34} Am 9^{14} Is 45^{13} ψ 69^{36} Ne 2^{5} Dn 9^{25} all of city; cf. phrase בנה חָרְבוֹת עוֹלָם Is 58^{12} 61^{4} & Ez 36^{36} Mal 1^{4} Jb 3^{14}; of walls Mi 7^{11} 2 Ch 32^{5} Ne 2^{17} 3$^{33.35.38}$ 6^{6} ψ 51^{20} (act. of י׳); of gate Ne 3$^{1.13.14.15}$; temple Zc 6$^{12.13}$ Ezr 1^{3}; altar 2 Ch 33^{16} (Qr וַיִּבֶן so Bö < Kt ויכן, fr. כון, so Öt), Ezr 3^{2}; high places 2 K 21^{3} = 2 Ch 33^{3}; in some of these apparently an idea of merely repairing; so, sts. with added notion of enlarging etc., city Nu 32$^{34.37.38}$ (E) Jos 19^{50} (P) Ju 21^{23} 2 K 14^{22} = 2 Ch 26^{2}, 1 Ch 11^{8} 2 Ch 8^{2} 11^{6} cf. Mi 3^{10}; Millo 1 K 9^{24} 11^{27}; cf. house Jb 20^{19}. **2.** fig. **a.** *build a house* (בית) = perpetuate and establish a family; subj. Leah & Rachel Ru 4^{11}; subj. a brother Dt 25^{9}; subj. י׳ (promise to David) 1 S 2^{35} 2 S 7^{27} 1 K 11^{38} 1 Ch 17^{10} and 17^{25}; (to Solomon) 1 K 11^{38}; cf. further סֻכַּת דָּוִיד Am 9^{11} (*rebuild, restore*); = cause a household to flourish Pr 14^{1} cf. opp. 27^{18}; also of establishing David's throne ψ 89^{5}. **b.** build up Israel (after exile) subj. י׳ Je 24^{6} 31^{4} 33^{7} 42^{10} cf. 45^{4} & ψ 28^{5}; obj. Zion ψ 102^{17}. †**Niph.** *Pf.* נִבְנָה 1 K 3^{2} 6^{7}, נִבְנְתָה Nu 13^{22} Ne 7^{1}, וְנִבְנְתָה consec. Je 30^{18} + 2 t.; 2 fs. וְנִבְנֵית consec. Je 31^{4}; 3 pl. נִבְנוּ Mal 3^{15}; וְנִבְנוּ consec. Je 12^{16} Ez 36^{33}; *Impf.* יִבָּנֶה Jb 12^{14} + 4 t.; 3 fs. תִּבָּנֶה Nu 21^{27}+

3 t.; 2 ms. תִּבָּנֶה Jb 22^{23}, אִבָּנֶה Gn 16^{2}, וְאִבָּנֶה Gn 30^{3}; 3 fpl תִּבָּנֶינָה Ez 36^{10}; 2 fpl. תִּבָּנֶינָה Is 44^{26}; *Inf* לְהִבָּנוֹת Hg 1^{2} Zc 8^{9}, בהבָּנֹתוֹ 1 K $6^{7.7}$; *Pt.* נִבְנֶה 1 Ch 22^{19};—**1. a.** *be built*, (lit.) of city Nu 13^{22}; of temple 1 K 3^{2} (לְשֵׁם י׳) 1 K $6^{7.7.7}$ (c acc. mater); Pt.=*to be built* (gerundive) 1 Ch 22^{19}. **b.** *be rebuilt:* of city of Sihon Nu 21^{27} cf. Is 25^{2} 44^{26}, of wall of Jerusalem Ne 7^{1}, of Jerusalem Je 30^{18} $31^{4.38}$ Is 44^{28} cf. Dn 9^{25} תָּשׁוּב ונבנְתָה, & Ez 26^{14} (c. עוֹד), of ruinous places (הֶחֳרָבוֹת) Ez $36^{10.33}$, of a devoted city Dt 13^{17} (c עוד), of temple Hg 1^{2} Zc 1^{16} 8^{9}, indef. subj Jb 12^{14}. **2. a.** (fig) of restored exiles, = *established* Je 12^{16}, of prosperous wicked Mal 3^{15}, of repentant offender Jb 22^{23}. **b.** *established*, made permanent, subj חֶסֶד ψ 89^{3} (c עוֹלָם), subj בַּיִת Pr 24^{3} (by wisdom). **c.** of childless wife, by means of concubine אִבָּנֶה מִמֶּנָּה Gn 16^{2} 30^{3} *I shall be built up*, i.e become the mother of a family, *from* or *through her*, cf. **Qal 2 a.**

בּוּנִי v. בָּנִי infr

†בּוּנִּי **n.pr.m. 1.** head of a family that returned with Zerubbabel Ne 7^{15} (=בָּנִי || Ezr 2^{10} & perh. Ezr 10^{34} cf Sm$^{\text{Listen 14}}$, but BeRy prop here בְּנוּי). **2.** a Levite of Ezra's time Ezr 8^{33} Ne 10^{10} (prob.=בָּנִי 8^{7}, בָּנִי 9^{4}) 12^{8} cf 3^{24} (בִּוַּי, text err. v^{18}) v. BeRy; also Ezr 2^{40}=Ne 7^{43} לבני rd. perh. לְבִנֻּי cf. Sm$^{\text{Listen 18}}$ but BeRy otherwise; cf. further Gr$^{\text{Gesch. II 2, 389}}$ **3.** Israelites of Ezra's time, **a.** Ezr 10^{30}; **b.** Ezr 10^{38}.

†בָּנִי **n.pr.m. 1.** one of David's heroes 2 S 23^{36} בָּנִי הַגָּדִי (|| 1 Ch 11^{38} has בֶּן־הַגְּרִי, but v. Dr^{Sm}) **2.** Levites, **a.** 1 Ch 6^{31}; **b.** Ne 3^{17} cf. 8^{7} (=בנוי 10^{10}) $9^{4.4}$ (repeated prob. by error, cf BeRy) v^{5} 10^{14} 11^{22}. On Ezr 2^{40}=Ne 7^{43} cf Gr$^{\text{Gesch II 2 389}}$; he reads קדמיאל בני for קדמיאל לבני, taking בני as n.pr., as 3 Ezr 5^{26} Καδμιηλου καὶ Βαννου **3.** a man of Judah 1 Ch 9^{4} (מן) בָּנִי Qr (> Kt בנימן). **4.** Ezr 2^{10} rd בנוי cf ||Ne 7^{15}. **5.** heads of families of Isr **a.** Ezr 10^{29}, **b.** Ne 10^{15}, **c.** Ezr 10^{34} but perh. rd. בנוי or בִּנּוּי cf. supr. **6.** an Israelite Ezr 10^{38}.—(בני as n.pr. Palm Vog$^{\text{No 34}}$)

†בֻּנִּי **n.pr.m. 1.** Levites, **a.** Ne 9^{4}, but rd. perh בנוי cf BeRy & vid. 10^{10} 12^{8} Ezr 8^{33}; **b.** (בן) בוני Ne 11^{15}, but rd perh מן בני etc cf BeRy. **2.** a chief of people Ne 10^{16}, perh repetit of בָּנִי v^{15} cf BeRy.

†בִּנְיָה **n.f. structure, building** Ez 41^{13}, cf also בִּנְיָן

†בְּנָיָה, בְּנָיָהוּ **n.pr.m.** (*Yah hath built up*, cf. יבנאל, Sab. בנאל DHM$^{\text{ZMG 1883, 15}}$)—**1.** one of David's captains and heroes, son of Jehoiada, בניהו 2 S 8^{18} $23^{20.22}$ 1 K $1^{8.10.26.32.36.38.44}$ $2^{25.29.30.30.34.35.46}$ 4^{4} 1 Ch 11^{24} 18^{17} $27^{5.6}$ cf v^{34} (v. Be), =בניה 2 S 20^{23} 1 Ch 11^{22}. **2.** one of David's thirty, בניהו 2 S 23^{30}=בניה 1 Ch 11^{31} 27^{14} **3.** a Simeonite, בניה 1 Ch 4^{36}. **4.** Levites, **a.** בניהו 1 Ch $15^{18.20.24}$; **b.** (id.) 2 Ch 31^{13}; **c.** בניה 2 Ch 20^{14} **5.** Israelites, בניה, **a.** Ezr 10^{25}; **b.** v^{30}, **c.** v^{35}, **d.** v^{43}, **e.** Ez 11^{13}=בניהו v^{1}

†בִּנְיָן **n.m.** structure (loan-word = [illegible] acc to Lag$^{\text{BN 205}}$) applied **a.** to enclosing wall of Ezekiel's temple Ez 40^{5}, **b.** to rear-building of same $41^{12.12.15}$, but rd prob בִּנְיָה q v.; so Sm Co; **c.** appar to whole temple $42^{1.10}$ (Co rds. הבית), cf v^{5} (del Co);—Sm refers v^{1} to enclosing wall, vid **a.**

†יַבְנְאֵל **n.pr.loc.** (*Ēl causeth to build*, cf יַבְנֶה, בניהו)—**1.** town in Judah Jos 15^{11} (𝔊L Ἰαβνηλ)=יַבְנֶה (q v.) 2 Ch 26^{6};=Gk *Iamnia*, mod. Yebna Bd$^{\text{Pal 161}}$ **2.** town in Naphtali Jos 19^{33}

†יַבְנֶה **n.pr loc.** (*he causeth to build*) a Philistine city 2 Ch 26^{6} 𝔊L Ἰαβνη (B Ἀβεννηρ) cf Ἰεμναθ 𝔊L Jos 15^{46} (A Ἰεμναι); = יַבְנְאֵל **1**, q v

†I. יִבְנְיָה **n.pr.m.** (*Yah buildeth up*, cf בניהו) a Benjamite 1 Ch 9^{8a} 𝔊 Βαναιαμ, 𝔊L Ἰεβναα.

†II יִבְנִיָּה **n pr.m.** (*id*, al יִבְנְיָה but v. Baer's n) a Benjamite 1 Ch 9^{8b} 𝔊 Βαναια, but 𝔊L Ἰεχονιου

†[מִבְנֶה] **n.m.** structure, cstr כְּמִבְנֵה־עִיר Ez 40^{2} *like the structure of a city.*

†מְבֻנַּי **n.pr.m.** one of David's heroes 2 S 23^{27} rd prob סבכי || 1 Ch 11^{29} cf. Dr^{Sm}

†תַּבְנִית **n.f. construction, pattern, figure**—ת׳ abs. 1 Ch 28^{19}, cstr. Ex $25^{9.9}$ + 14 t. + Ez 8^{10} (del. Co); תַּבְנִיתוֹ 2 K 16^{10}, תַּבְנִיתָם Ex 25^{40},—**1.** app. originally *construction, structure*, yet only P & late. תַּבְנִית מִזְבַּח י׳ Jos 22^{28}; cf ψ 144^{12} in sim. בנותינו כָּזָוִיּוֹת מְחֻטָּבִים ת׳ היכל *carved acc to the construction of a palace, palace-fashion* **2.** *pattern*, acc to which anything is to be constructed (P & late), of tabernacle Ex 25^{9}, utensils of tab $v^{9.40}$, an altar 2 K 16^{10} תַּבְנִיתוֹ לְכָל־מַעֲשֵׂהוּ (disting fr. דמות), temple 1 Ch 28^{11} cf. v^{12}; chariot, i e. cherubim 1 Ch 28^{18}, מַלְאֲכוֹת הַתּ׳ 1 Ch 28^{19} i e objects of which the pattern is given **3.** *figure, image*, Hex only D, of idols in form of animals Dt $4^{16.17.17.18.18}$; elsewhere late Is 44^{13} Ez 8^{10} (del. B Co) ψ 106^{20}; cf. ת׳ יָד Ez 8^{3} 10^{8} i e. something like a hand.

בנט (assumed as √ of אבנט, Thes Sta[1 2-7])

†אַבְנֵט **n.[m.]** **girdle**—א' abs Ex 28⁴+, אַבְנֵטְךָ Is 22²¹, cstr Ex 39²⁹, אַבְנֵטִים Ex 28⁴⁰,—*girdle*, of high priest Ex 28^{4 39} 39²⁹ Lv 8⁷ 16⁴, of priests Ex 28⁴⁰ 29⁹ Lv 8¹³ (all P), of high official Is 22²¹ —Josephus[III 7 2] ἀβανήθ, cf further Lag[Ges Abh 30]

בָּנִים v sub [בין]

†**בְּנִינוּ** **n.pr.m** a descendant of Jonathan 1 Ch 8³⁷ 9⁴³

†**בְּסוֹדְיָה** **n pr m.** (*in the secret of Yah*) Israelite in Nehemiah's time Ne 3⁶

†**בֵּסַי** **n.pr m.** head of a family of Nethinim, בני־בסי Ne 7⁵² = ב׳־בֵסָי Ezr 2⁴⁹

בסר (*be too early*, Ar بَسَرَ, cf Aram בסירה *half-ripe*)

†**בֹּסֶר** **n.m.**[Is 18, 5] **unripe or sour grapes coll** (NH *id*, Aram בּוּסְרָא, ܒܘܣܪܐ, Ar بُسْر *unripe dates*)—בֹּסֶר Is 18⁵ + 3 t, בסרו Jb 15³³,—*unripe grapes* Is 18⁵ Jb 15³³, *sour g* Je 31^{29.30} Ez 18²

בעד (Ar بَعُدَ, بَعِدَ, *be remote, distant*, Qor 9⁴², بَعِيدٌ *distant*, Eth በዐደ: *to change*, ψ 33 title, ብዑድ: *different, distinct*, ባዕድ: *another*)

בַּעַד[118] **subst.** prop **separation**, with a gen, *in separation from*, in usage a **prep. away from, behind, about, on behalf of** (Ar بَعْدُ, of time, *after*)—abs. †Ct 4^{1.3} 6⁷, elsewhere cstr בְּעַד, with sf בַּעֲדִי Ex 8²⁴+, בַּעֲדֵנִי + ψ 139¹¹, בַּעַדְךָ Gn 20⁷+, בַּעֲדוֹ etc., 1 pl בַּעֲדֵנוּ, †Am 9¹⁰ בַּעֲדֵינוּ 1 S 7⁸+; בַּעֲדָם Lv 9⁷+, בַּעַדְכֶם, בַּעֲדֵינוּ,—**1.** lit **a.** with vbs of falling, letting down, leaning forward so as to look out, *through* (lit. *away from*) a window, etc.. Jos 2¹⁵ and she let him down by a cord בעד הַחַלּוֹן *away from* the window, i e *out through* it, 1 S 19¹² 2 S 20²¹ 2 K 1² and A fell בעד הַשְּׂבָכָה *out through* the lattice, Gn 26⁸ Ju 5²⁸ *out through* the window נשקפה she *looked forth* (lit *leant forward*), 2 S 6¹⁶+, pregn Jb 22¹³ will he judge בעד עֲרָפֶל (looking) *out through* the thick clouds? Conversely Jo 2⁹ *in through* the windows they come (the locusts) as a thief **b.** idiom with vbs of *shutting*, esp. סָגַר בעד to shut *behind* or *upon*—whether oneself, Ju 9⁵¹ and they entered the tower וַיִּסְגְּרוּ בַּעֲדָם and shut (the doors) *upon* themselves (sc from the inside), 2 K 4^{4.5.33} Is 26²⁰, or another, Gn 7¹⁶ וַיִּסְגֹּר י׳ בַּעֲדוֹ and י׳ shut *behind* or *upon* him (sc from the outside), i e shut him in, Ju 3²³ (the sf. in בַּעֲדוֹ referring to Eglon), 2 K 4²¹ (but N.B. persons leaving a room shut the door אַחֲרֵי themselves Gn 19⁶ 2 S 13^{17 18}) see also Ju 3²² 1 S 1⁶ סָגַר י׳ בעד רַחְמָהּ (cf Gn 20¹⁸ עָצַר בְּעַד רֶחֶם), Jb 9⁷ חָתַם בעד to seal *up*, 1¹⁰ 3²³ שׂוּךְ (הסך) בעד to make a hedge *about*, La 3⁷ גָּדַר בעד to fence *about*. Somewhat peculiarly Am 9¹⁰ (who say,) Evil will not draw near, or come in front בַּעֲדֵינוּ *so as to be about us* (but Gr עָדֵינוּ *unto* us), Jo 2⁸ (of the locusts) בעד הַשֶּׁלַח יִפֹּלוּ (prob) *in among* the weapons they throw themselves (i e they pass about and between them without being injured or having their course impeded), 1 S 4¹⁸ and Eli fell backward בעד יַד הַשַּׁעַר, i e (si vera l.) *about* the side of the gate but text dub, v Dr Without a vb Jon 2⁷ the earth, בְּרִיחֶיהָ בַעֲדִי her bars were *upon* me (or *about* me) for ever, ψ 139¹¹ night shall be the light *about* me, ψ 3⁴ thou מָגֵן בַּעֲדִי art a shield *about* me Hence **c.** after a vb. of protecting, †Zc 12⁸ in that day יָגֵן י׳ בעד יושב ירושלם will י׳ give protection *about*, etc. **2.** metaph *on behalf of* (ὑπέρ), very freq after הִתְפַּלֵּל Gn 20⁷ Nu 21⁷ 1 S 7⁵ ψ 72¹⁵+; also with other vbs of entreating Ex 8²⁴ 1 S 7⁹, or consulting (דָּרַשׁ) Is 8¹⁹ 2 K 22¹³ Je 21², with כפר *atone* Ex 32³⁰ Lv 9⁷ 16^{6 11}+, עָשָׂה (=offer) †Ez 45²²: see also 2 S 10¹² 12¹⁶ Is 37⁴ Je 7¹⁶ 11¹⁴ Ez 22³⁰ Pr 20¹⁶ 27¹³ ψ 138⁸ Jb 2⁴ עור בעד עור (v. עור), 6²² Almost = *for the sake of, on account of* Pr 6²⁶ Je 11¹⁴ (but 𝔊 𝔖 𝔙 𝔗 and many MSS. בְּעֵת רָעָתָם, cf v¹² 15¹¹). Is 32¹⁴ hill and watchtower הָיָה בעד מְעָרוֹת are come to be *on behalf of* (i e. take the place of, serve as) caves for ever · but use is singular, and בעד is prob only dittogr from מערות in מער (so Gr) —With מִן, מִבַּעַד לְ׳ (cf מִתַּחַת לְ׳, מִמַּעַל לְ׳). †Ct 4^{1.3} 6⁷ thine eyes are doves מִבַּעַד לְצַמָּתֵךְ *from behind* thy veil Cf. on בַּעַד Gratz[Monatsschrift, 1879 49 ff.]

†[**בָּעָה**] **vb. inquire, cause to swell** or **boil up** (NH *id*, Ar بَغَى *seek, suppurate, swell*, Aram בְּעָא, ܒܥܐ *seek*)—**Qal** *Impf.* 3 fs תִּבְעֶה Is 64¹; 2 mpl. תִּבְעָיוּן Is 21¹², *Imv* בְּעָיוּ Is 21¹²,—**1.** of rising desire, *seek, inquire*, abs, of inquiring of prophet Is 21^{12 12}. **2.** *cause to boil up*, מַיִם תִּבְ־אֵשׁ Is 64¹ (but gloss Che). **Niph.** *Pf* נִבְעוּ Ob⁶ *searched out* (‖ נחפשו), *Pt.* נִבְעֶה Is 30¹³ *swelling, swelling out* (of decaying wall, Dr *swelling, enlarging*, of crack in wall).

בעז (*quick*? cf Ar بَغْز *swiftness* (of horse))

†**בֹּעַז** **n.pr.m.** (*quickness*?)—**1.** kinsman of Naomi, who married Ruth Ru 2^{1.3 4.5.8.11}

$^{14.15.19.23}$ $3^{2.7}$ $4^{1.1.5.8.9.13}$, also $v^{21.21}$ 1 Ch $2^{11.12}$ (𝔊 Βοος, Βοοζ). **2.** name of the left hand of two pillars set up before temple (cf. also יָכִין sub כון) 1 K 7^{21} = 2 Ch 3^{17}; (mng. obscure; MT appar. ref. to **1**, cf. 𝔗 2 Ch 3^{17}; Thes supposes name of architect or donor; Ew perh. sons of Solomon, etc.; rd. possibly בְּעֹז *in strength*, 𝔊 2 Ch 3^{17} ἰσχύς; Th thinks יכין בעז a sentence, one word being engraved on each pillar, *he* (God) *establisheth in strength;* against him, however, Ke Be; Öt thinks an exclamation, *in strength!* expressing satisfaction of architect; Klo prop. for בעז, בַּעַל עֹז (cf. B 1 K 7^{21} Βαλαζ)).

†[**בָּעַט**] **vb. kick** (so NH, Aram. בְּעַט, ܒܥܛ)—**Qal** *Impf.* וַיִּבְעַט Dt 32^{15}; 2 mpl. תִּבְעֲטוּ 1 Sa 2^{29};—*kick* (only fig. of refractory Israel) Dt 32^{15} (abs.); *kick at* (c. בְּ) 1 S 2^{29}.

בְּעִי Jb 30^{24} v. עִי.

†**בָּעַל** **vb. marry, rule over** (cf. Ar. بَعَلَ = *own, possess*, esp. a wife or concubine; Eth. በዐለ: *to be rich*, As. *bâlu, rule* COT ^{Gloss}, Aram. בְּעַל *take possession of wife or concubine*)—**Qal** *Pf.* Mal 2^{11} + 6 t.; *Impf.* יִבְעַל Is $62^{5.5}$; *Pt.* sf. בֹּעֲלַיִךְ Is 54^{5}; pass. f. בְּעוּלָה Is 54^{1} + 3 t.;—**1.** *marry* Gn 20^{3} (E) Dt 21^{13} 22^{22} 24^{1} Is $54^{1.5}$ $62^{4.5.5}$ Mal 2^{11}; sq. בְּ Je 3^{14} 31^{32} *be lord (husband) over.* **2.** *rule over* 1 Ch 4^{22} (sq. לְ) Is 26^{13}. **Niph.** *Impf.* תִּבָּעֵל Pr 30^{23} Is 62^{4} *be married.*

†I. **בַּעַל**$_{166}$ **n.m. owner, lord** (Ph. בעל; Palm. *id. husband* Vog^{62} cf. Bae $^{Rel\ 72\ ff.}$; As. *bêlu* $^{l.\ c.}$ Dl $^{Gram.\ Gloss.}$; Ar. بَعْل *husband* etc., v. esp. Nö $^{ZMG\ 1886,\ 174}$, Sab. בעל CIS $^{iv.\ 1,\ 2}$)—Gn 20^{3} + 92 t.; sf. בַּעְלִי Ho 2^{18}; בַּעְלָהּ Dt 24^{4} + 5 t.; pl. בְּעָלִים Ju 2^{11} + 17 t.; cstr. בַּעֲלֵי Gn 14^{13} + 27 t.; sf. בְּעָלָיו Ex 21^{29} + 14 t.; בְּעָלֶיהָ Jb 31^{39} + 2 t.; בַּעְלֵיהֶן Est $1^{17.20}$;—I. **1.** *owner* (oft. pl. c. sf. in sg. mng.): of ox Ex $21^{28.29.29}$ $22^{10.11.13.14}$ (E); ב׳ הבור of pit Ex $21^{34.36}$ (E), of house Ex 22^{7} (E) Ju $19^{22.23}$, debt Dt 15^{2}, the land Jb 31^{39}, the ass Is 1^{3}, goods Ec 5^{10}, riches Ec 5^{12}; ב׳ טוב one to whom good is due Pr 3^{27}, gain Pr 1^{19}; ב׳ שׂכל one having understanding Pr 16^{22}; ב׳ השחד receiver of the gift Pr 17^{8}. **2.** *husband* Gn 20^{3} Ex $21^{3.22}$ (E) Dt 22^{22} 24^{4} 2 S 11^{26} Jo 1^{8} Pr 12^{4} $31^{11.23.28}$ Est $1^{17.20}$; בַּעְלִי Ho 2^{18} (*my Baal*, reference to the divine name used in the northern kingdom, here for the first time forbidden). **3.** *citizens, inhabitants:* בַּעֲלֵי of Jericho Jos 24^{11} (E), of the high places of Arnon Nu 21^{28} (E), of Shechem Ju 9^{2} + 12 t., of the tower of Shechem Ju $9^{46.47}$, of the city Ju 9^{51}, of Gibeah Ju 20^{5}, of Keilah 1 S $23^{11.12}$, of Jabesh 2 S 21^{12}. **4.** *rulers, lords:* בַּעֲלֵי גוֹיִם Is 16^{8}. **5.** *n. of relation:* **a.** בַּעַל: ב׳ החלמות dreamer Gn 37^{19} (E); ב׳ דברים whosoever hath cases, complaints Ex 24^{14} (E); ב׳ שׂער an hairy man 2 K 1^{8}; ב׳ חמה wrathful Na 1^{2} Pr 29^{22}; ב׳ אף one given to anger Pr 22^{24}; ב׳ החכמה one having wisdom Ec 7^{12}; ב׳ משחית destroyer Pr 18^{9}; ב׳ כנף winged thing, bird Pr 1^{17} Ec 10^{20}; ב׳ נפשׁ one given to appetite Pr 23^{2}; ב׳ מזמות mischievous person Pr 24^{8}; ב׳ הלשׁון charmer Ec 10^{11}; ב׳ רשׁע one given to wickedness Ec 8^{8}; ב׳ פיפיות double-edged Is 41^{15}; ב׳ משׁפט adversary Is 50^{8}; ב׳ פקדת captain of the ward Je 37^{13}; ב׳ הקרנים two-horned Dn $8^{6.20}$. **b.** בַּעֲלֵי: ב׳ בְּרִית confederates Gn 14^{13}; ב׳ חצים archers Gn 49^{23} (poet.); ב׳ הפרשׁים horsemen 2 S 1^{6}; ב׳ שׁבועה conspirators Ne 6^{18}; ב׳ אספות members of assemblies; or well-grouped sayings; or collectors (of wise sentences) Ec 12^{11}.—On 2 S 6^{2} v. II. בַּעֲלָה. (בַּעַל in Hex not J or P; בעל Lv 21^{4} 𝔊 ἐξάπινα = כבלע Nu 4^{20}: Di בְּאֵבֶל). Esp. II. *lord*, specif. as divine name, †**Baal.** **1.** *without article:* בעל במות Nu 22^{41} (poet. Balaam); בַּעַל פעור Nu $25^{3.5}$ (E) Dt 4^{3} (vid. below). This divine name is not used elsewhere in Hex. It probably originated from the sense of divine ownership, rather than sovereignty (RS $^{Sem\ 92}$). It seems to have been used in Northern Israel = אדון in the South. It was the special name of the God of the Canaanites, Philistines, etc., = Babylonian בֵּל, cf. Schr $^{SK\ 1874,\ 335\ ff.}$ In later times scribes substituted בֹּשֶׁת, in n.pr. (אשׁבעל = אשׁבשׁת, ירבעל = ירבשׁת, vid. בֹּשֶׁת, Gei $^{ZMG\ 1862,\ 728\ ff.}$), & also in the text for בעל Ho 9^{10} Je 11^{13} (hence ἡ βάαλ Je 2^{23} 7^{9} $11^{13.17}$ 19^{5} Ho 2^{10} 13^{1} +, Rom 11^{4}, see Di $^{Baal\ mit\ d.\ weib.\ Artikel,\ MBA\ 1881,\ June\ 16}$ Dr 2 S 4^{4}). **2.** c. *art.*: הַבַּעַל Ju 2^{13} $6^{25.28.30.31.32}$ 1 K $16^{31.32.32}$ $18^{19.21.22.25.26.26.40}$ 19^{18} 22^{54} 2 K 3^{2} $10^{18.19.19.20.21.21.21.22.23.23.23.25.26.27.27.28}$ $11^{18.18}$ 17^{16} 21^{3} $23^{4.5}$ 2 Ch $23^{17.17}$ Je 2^{8} 7^{9} $11^{13.17}$ 12^{16} $19^{5.5}$ $28^{13.27}$ $32^{29.35}$ Ho 2^{10} 13^{1} Zp 1^{4}. **3.** הַבְּעָלִים *emphatic pl.* (cf. האלהים, האדונים) *the great lord, the sovereign owner* Ju 2^{11} 3^{7} 8^{33} $10^{6.10}$ 1 S 7^{4} 12^{10} 1 K 18^{18} 2 Ch 17^{3} 24^{7} 28^{2} 33^{3} 34^{4} Je 2^{23} 9^{13} Ho $2^{15.19}$ 11^{2} (or local special Ba'als, vid. Dr $^{Sm.\ p.\ 50}$; pillars of Baal MV). **4.** c. *attrib.*: בַּעַל בְּרִית *Lord of covenant* Ju 8^{33} 9^{4} (cf. אל ברית 9^{46}; Nö $^{ZMG\ 1888,\ 478}$); ב׳ זְבוּב *Lord of flies* 2 K $1^{2.3.6.16}$, Philistine god, 𝔊 Βααλ μυῖαν (Beelzebub, Mt 12^{24}) cf. Bae $^{Rel\ 25}$.

†II. **בַּעַל** **1. n.pr.loc.** city in the tribe of Simeon 1 Ch 4^{33} = בַּעֲלַת בְּאֵר. **2. n.pr.m. a.** a Reubenite 1 Ch 5^{5}; **b.** a Gibeonite 1 Ch 8^{30} 9^{36}.

†בַּעַל גָּד n.pr.loc. Jos 11[17] 12[7] 13[5] (D), where Baal was worshipped as Gad, god of fortune, a city in the בקעה of Lebanon, under Mt. Hermon, either mod *Bânıâs*, Gk. Paneas, NT Caesarea Philippi, where a grotto of Pan took the place of the ancient worship of Gad, Rob[BR iii. 410] Tristr[Tpg 271], or *Ḥâsbêyâ* Bd[Pal 297] Di, possibly = בעל חרמון cf Thes Rob[BR iii 409]

†בַּעַל הָמוֹן n pr.loc (*possessor of abundance*, or is 'ב here n pr. divin ?) Ct 8[11].

†בַּעַל חָנָן n.pr.m. (*Baal is gracious*, cf Ph חנבעל & (in As) *Baalḫanunu*) **1.** king of Edom Gn 36[38.39] 1 Ch 1[49 50] **2.** a Gederite 1 Ch 27[28].

†בַּעַל חָצוֹר n.pr.loc. (*possessor of a court*, or 'ב n pr divin ?) city on the border of Ephraim and Benjamin 2 S 13[23], prob = חצור Ne 11[33], ? mod *Tell 'Asûr* (with ע) Rob[BR ii 264] doubtfully, cf Survey[ii. 298] (after de Saulcy)

†בַּעַל חֶרְמוֹן n.pr.loc Ju 3[3] 1 Ch 5[23], a city so named as seat of the worship of Baal. 'The crest of Hermon is strewn with ruins and the foundations of a circular temple of large hewn stones,' Tristr[Tpg], cf on sacredness, Euseb. Lag[Onom 217] possibly = בעל גד q v.

†בַּעַל מְעוֹן n.pr loc. Nu 32[38] 1 Ch 5[8] Ez 25[9] = בית בעל מעון Jos 13[17] (cf MI[30]) = *Ma'în* Tristr[Moab 316] Bd[Pal 192] Survey[EP 176].

†בַּעַל פְּעוֹר n.pr.m. Nu 25[3.5] Dt 4[3.3] ψ 106[28] Ho 9[10], *Baal of Peor* (VB) i e worshipped at פעור q v, or *Baal-P* (whence *Peor* as n pr loc), cf Di Nu 25[3] Baud[Stud ii. 233] Bae[Rel 14. 210]

†בַּעַל פְּרָצִים n.pr.loc (*possessor of breaches*, or *Baal of Perasim* ?) where David defeated Philist 2 S 5[20.20] 1 Ch 14[11 11], site unknown

†בַּעַל צְפוֹן n.pr.loc. Ex 14[2.9] Nu 33[7], near Red Sea in Egypt, prob Mt *'Atâka*, Eb[GS 524]

†בַּעַל שָׁלִשָׁה n.pr.loc. 2 K 4[42], place in Ephraim near Gilgal, = Βαιθσαρισαθ Lag[Onom 289 2nd ed 250] c 15 m fr Diospolis ('ב ? n pr divin)

†בַּעַל תָּמָר n pr.loc. (*possessor of palms*, or *Baal of Tamar* ?) Ju 20[33], near Gibeah

†I [בַּעֲלָה] n.f. **1** *mistress*, בַּעֲלַת הַבַּיִת mistress of the house 1 K 17[17] **2** n rel ב' אוב necromancer 1 S 28[7 7], ב' כשפים sorceress, Na 3[4]

†II בַּעֲלָה n.pr.loc. Jos 15[9 10 11 29] 1 Ch 13[6] = קִרְיַת בַּעַל Jos 15[60] 18[14] (*city of Baal*, from a high place of Baal there) = בַּעֲלֵי יְהוּדָה 2 S 6[2] (We Dr read בעל; י added by dittogr; so-called as seat of Baal-worship in Judah, in distinct. fr like places elsewhere) = קִרְיַת יְעָרִים Jos 9[17] v 15[9] 1 Ch 13[6], a city of Judah, ? *Kirjat el 'Enab* Rob[BR ii. 11] Tristr[Tpg].

†בַּעֲלַת n.pr.loc. Jos 19[44] 1 K 9[18] 2 Ch 8[6], a city of Dan, possibly *Bel'aîn* Survey[ii 296]

†בְּעָלוֹת n.pr.loc. pl Jos 15[24] 1 K 4[16], a city in the south of Judah, possibly the same as II. בעל.

†בַּעֲלַת בְּאֵר n.pr.loc. (*mistress of a well*) = *Ramath Negeb* Jos 19[8], a city of Simeon = II. בַּעַל, mod. *Kurnub* acc to Tristr[Tpg] but dub.

†בְּעֶלְיָדָע n.pr.m. (*Baal knows*) son of David 1 Ch 14[7], the original name changed to אלידע 2 S 5[16] (cf We Dr)

†בְּעַלְיָה n.pr.m. (*Yah is lord*) one of David's heroes 1 Ch 12[5]

†בֵּל n pr.m. a chief Babylonian deity (Bab. *Bêlu* = בַּעַל, *lord*, *Bêl* regarded as older form than בַּעַל by Hpt[Hbr i 178, BAS i 17]) = Merodach (cf מרדך), tutelary god of Babylon (to be distinguished from older *Bêlu*, one of ancient Babylonian triad) Je 50[2] (|| מְרֹדַךְ) 51[44], Is 46[1] (|| נבו)—both writers of Babylonian period;—on Bel v COT Gn 11[4] Ju 2[11], Say[Rel Bab 108, 110] Jen Kosmologie 24, 134 307 391

†בֵּלְאשַׁצַּר n.pr.m. (*Bêl-šar-uṣur*, *Bel*, *protect the king* COT Dn 5[1]) Dn 8[1], represented as king of Babylon, successor, and appar son of Nebuchadrezzar (5[1 2 11] etc); in cuneif inscr known only as prince, son of Nabonidus (last Shemitic king of Babylon), v COT l.c.

†בַּעֲלִיס n.pr.m. (Gr[Monatsschrift, 1885, 471] rds. בַּעְלִים, = בן־עלים *son of delight* ? cf. sub ב) king of Ammonites Je 40[14] (Codd & Jos[Ant. x. 9, 3] rd בעלים).

†בְּעֹן v בית בעל מעון sub בית

†בַּעֲנָא n.pr.m (בן־עָנָה? *son of distress*)— **1.** name of two officers of Solomon, **a.** 1 K 4[12], **b.** v[16]. **2.** father (ancestor) of an Israelite of Nehemiah's time Ne 3[4] cf foll

†בַּעֲנָה n.pr.m (id)—**1.** a Benjamite, one of the murderers of Ishbosheth 2 S 4[2.5.6 9] **2.** father of one of David's heroes 2 S 23[29] = 1 Ch 11[30] **3.** head of a family of returning exiles Ezr 2[2] = Ne 7[7], perh also = בַּעֲנָא Ne 3[4] **4.** a chief of the people Ne 10[28].

†I [בָּעַר] vb burn, consume (ܐ בער *burn*, ܒܥܪ *seek out, collect, glean*; this apparently

earlier mng.)—**Qal** *Pf.* 3 fs. בָּֽעֲרָה Nu 11^{3} + 2 t., וּבָֽעֲרָה consec. Is 10^{17} + 3 t., בָּֽעֲרוּ Ju 15^{14} + 2 t. + 2 S 22^{13} (but cf. De on ψ 18), וּבָֽעֲרוּ consec. Is 1^{31}; *Impf.* יִבְעַר Ex 3^{3} ψ 2^{12}, etc.; *Pt.* בֹּעֵר Ex 3^{2} + 6 t., בֹּעֵרָה Is 34^{9}, בוֹעֵרָה Ho 7^{4}, בֹּעֵרָה Is 30^{33}, בֹּעֶרֶת Je 20^{9}, בֹּעֲרוֹת Ez 1^{13};—*burn*, **1.** (intr.) specif. *begin to burn, be kindled* ψ 18^{8} sq. מִן (subj. גֶּחָלִים)=2 S 22^{9} (in v^{13} text. error cf. supr.), ψ 106^{18} (subj. אֵשׁ); fig. ψ 2^{12} (subj. אַפּוֹ) cf. Je 44^{6} (subj. חֵמָה); Is 30^{33} (c. בְּ, subj. נִשְׁמַת י׳), ψ 39^{4} (subj. אֵשׁ fig. of grief, distress) cf. Je 20^{9}. **2.** *be burning, burn*, Ju 15^{14} (subj. פִּשְׁתִּים, c. בָּאֵשׁ), Ex 3^{2} (הסנה, c. בָּאֵשׁ), v^{3} (subj. *id.*); Dt 4^{11} 5^{20} 9^{15} (all subj. הר, c. בָּאֵשׁ), cf. Is 34^{9} (זֶפֶת בערה), fig. of destruction Is 1^{31} (subj. חָסֹן & פֹּעֲלוֹ); of torch לַפִּיד Is 62^{1}; of oven תַּנּוּר Ho 7$^{4.6}$ (i.e. heated by fire within it). **3.** trans. *burn, consume* (subj. אש, להבה etc., sq. בְּ) Nu 11$^{1.3}$ (אשׁ י׳), Jb 1^{16} (אשׁ אלהים); in simile Ez 1^{13} (גחלי אש י׳), ψ 83^{15} (only here trans. c. acc.; should תבער be pointed as Pi.?); fig. (subj. wrath of י׳) Is 42^{25} cf. La 2^{3} (subj. fire = fiery trial) Is 43^{2}. **4.** act. but abs., fig., subj. wrath of י׳ Je 4^{4} 7^{20} 21^{12} ψ 89^{47} cf. Is 10^{17} ψ 79^{5} Is 30^{27} (שֵׁם י׳ . . . בֹּעֵר אַפּוֹ) Mal 3^{19} (היום בא); of human anger Est 1^{12}; subj. wickedness Is 9^{17}. **Pi.** *Pf.* בִּעֵר 1 K 22^{47} 2 K 23^{24}, וּבִעֵר consec. Lv 6^{5}, בִּעַרְתָּ 2 Ch 19^{3}, וּבִעַרְתָּ Dt 13^{6} + 9 t. in Dt; וּבִעֲרוּ cons. Ez 39$^{9.9}$ (9^{a} del. Co after Vrss), etc.; *Impf.* יְבַעֵר 1 K 14^{10}; 2 ms. תְּבַעֵר Dt 21^{9}, יְבַעֲרוּ Ez 39^{10}; 2 mpl. תְּבַעֲרוּ Ex 35^{3}, וּנְבַעֲרָה subord. Ju 20^{13}; *Pt.* מְבַעֲרִים Je 7^{18};—**1.** *kindle*, lit. c. acc. אֵשׁ Ex 35^{3} Je 7^{18} cf. Ez 39^{9} (v. supr.) v^{10}; fig. of י׳ sending destruction Ez 21^{4} cf. of human schemes Is 50^{11}; *light*, obj. lamps in temple 2 Ch 4^{20} cf. 13^{11}. **2.** *burn*, lit. c. acc. עֵצִים Lv 6^{5}, גָּלָל *dung* 1 K 14^{10}; abs. Is 44^{15} cf. 40^{16} Ne 10^{35}. **3.** fig. *consume*, utterly remove, partic. of evil and guilt, c. acc., esp. in Deuteronomic phrase (מישראל) ובערת הרע מקרבך Dt 13^{6} 17$^{7.12}$ 19$^{13.19}$ 21^{21} cf. v^{9} 22$^{21.22.24}$ 24^{7}, v. also Ju 20^{13}; further, 1 K 22^{47} 2 K 23^{24} 2 Ch 19^{3}; also of devoted (tabooed) things Dt 26$^{13.14}$; of persons (*exterminate*) 2 S 4^{11}; sq. אחרי pregn. 1 K 14^{10} 21^{21}; = devour, devastate, greedily enjoy the fruits of, Is 3^{14}; abs. היה לְבָעֵר *be for destruction, be destroyed* Nu 24^{22} Is 5^{5} 6^{13}; cf. רוּחַ בָּעֵר Is 4^{4}. **Pu.** *Pt.* מְבֹעֶרֶת Je 36^{22};—*burn* (i.e. be supplied with fire), of fire-jar, הָאָח. **Hiph.** *Pf.* וְהִבְעַרְתִּי Na 2^{14}; *Impf.* וַיַּבְעֵר Ju 15^{5} 2 Ch 28^{3}, וַיַּבְעֶר־ Ju 15^{5}; תַּבְעִיר Ez 5^{2}; *Pt.* מַבְעִיר 1 K 16^{3}, מַבְעֵר Ex 22^{5};—**1.** *kindle* (c. acc. cogn.) Ex 22^{5}, cf. Ju 15^{5} ויב׳ אשׁ בלפידים *caused fire to burn among the brands.* **2.** *burn up*, c. acc. Ju 15^{5} 2 Ch 28^{3} (sacrifice of children בָּאֵשׁ) Ez 5^{2} (בָּאוּר but cf. Co) Na 2^{14} (בעשׁן). **3.** *consume=destroy* (cf. Pi.) 1 K 16^{3} (sq. אַחֲרֵי).

†בְּעֵרָה **n.f.** burning, only הַבּ׳ as acc. cogn. with הִבְעִיר Ex 22^{5}.

†תַּבְעֵרָה **n.pr.loc.** in the wilderness (*burning*, cf. Nu 11^{3}) Nu 11^{3} Dt 9^{22}.

†[בְּעִיר] **n.m.**$^{Ex\ 22,4}$ **beasts, cattle, coll.** (NH *id.*, Aram. *id.*, ܒܥܝܪܐ, Eth. ብዑራዊ: etc., Sab. בער DHM$^{ZMG\ 1876,\ 674;\ 1883,\ 329}$; Ar. بَعِيرٌ of *camel*; also *ass*, etc., cf. Lane^{227a}; connexion with above √ obscure)—sf. בְּעִירֹה Ex 22^{4}, בְּעִירֵנוּ Nu 20^{4}, בְּעִירְכֶם Gn 45^{17}, בְּעִירָם Nu 20^{8} + 2 t.;—*beasts* of burden Gn 45^{17} (i.e. asses 44$^{3.13}$); elsewhere general, *cattle* Ex 22^{4} Nu 20$^{4.8.11}$ ψ 78^{48}.

†II. [בָּעַר] **vb.denom.** be brutish—**Qal** *Impf.* יִבְעֲרוּ Je 10^{8} (‖ יכסלו) *be stupid, dull-hearted, unreceptive*; cf. Pt. pl. בֹּעֲרִים ψ 94^{8} (‖ כסילים); of *inhuman, cruel, barbarous* men Ez 21^{36}. **Niph.** *Pf.* נִבְעַר Je 10^{14} 51^{17}, נִבְעֲרוּ Je 10^{21}; *Pt.* נִבְעָרָה Is 19^{11};—*brutish, stupid* Is 19^{11} (עצה, ‖ אויל); *dull-hearted*, ignorant of God Je 10$^{14.21}$ 51^{17}. **Pi.** *Pf.* וּבִעֵר consec. Ex 22^{4} *feed, graze* (בשׂדה אחר). **Hiph.** *Impf.* יַבְעֶר־ Ex 22^{4} *cause to be grazed over*, sq. שׂדה.

†בַּעַר **n.m.** brutishness (only poet.)—abs. ב׳ ψ 49^{11} + 3 t., בָּעַר Pr 12^{1};—in combination, אִישׁ־ב׳ *brutish man* ψ 92^{7} (‖ כְּסִיל); elsewhere ב׳ alone in same sense (concrete) ψ 49^{11} (‖ *id.*), & as pred.=adj., ψ 73^{22} Pr 12^{1} 30^{2}.

†בַּעֲרָא **n.pr.f.** wife of a Benjamite 1 Ch 8^{8}.

†בְּעוֹר **n.pr.m.** (*a burning*; 𝔗 *torch*)—**1.** father of Balaam Nu 22^{5} 31^{8} Dt 23^{5} Jos 13^{22} 24^{9} Mi 6^{5}; בְּעֹר Nu 24$^{3.15}$ (בנו ב׳). **2.** father of בֶּלַע, a king of Edom Gn 36^{32} = 1 Ch 1^{43}.

†בַּעֲשֵׂיָה **n.pr.m.** (?=מַעֲשֵׂיָה; so Thes; cf. Dr$^{Sm.\ lxviii}$) a Levite 1 Ch 6^{25};—cf. מַעֲשֵׂיָה(וּ) sub עשׂה.

בַּעְשָׁא **n.pr.m.** a king of Israel 1 K 15$^{16.17.19}$ + 18 t. 1 K 15–16 + 21^{22} 2 K 9^{9} 2 Ch 16$^{1.3.5.6}$ Je 41^{9}.

†בְּעֶשְׁתְּרָה **n.pr.loc.** (? = בֵּית עשתרה = *house of Ashtoreth*, cf. sub בית) a Levitical city in Manasseh Jos 21^{27}; = עַשְׁתָּרֹת 1 Ch 6^{56}

†[בָּעַת] **vb.** fall upon, startle, terrify (Ar. بَغَتَ *come* or *happen suddenly*, NH בָּעַת

Hiph *startle*; so Aram בעת Pa ܒܥܬ Aph)—**Niph.** (late prose) *Pf.* נִבְעַת 1 Ch 21^{30}, נִבְעַתְּ Est 7^{6}, נִבְעַתִּי Dn 8^{17},—*be terrified*, abs. Dn 8^{17}, c מפני 1 Ch 21^{30} Est 7^{6} **Pi.** (mostly poet.) *Pf* 3 fs sf בִּעֲתַתְנִי Is 21^{4}, וּבִעֲתַתּוּ 1 S 16^{14}, 3 pl sf. בִּעֲתֻהוּ Jb 18^{11}, *Impf* 3 fs תְּבַעֵת Jb 13^{11}, sf תְּבַעֲתַנִּי Jb 9^{34} 13^{21}, תְבַעֶתְךָ Jb 33^{7}, 2 ms sf תְּבַעֲתַנִּי Jb 7^{14}, 3 mpl sf יְבַעֲתֻנִי ψ 18^{5} = יְבַעֲתֻנִי 2 S 22^{5}, יְבַעֲתֻהוּ Jb 3^{5} 15^{24},—**1.** *fall upon* 1 S 16^{14} ^{15} (only here in prose), *overwhelm* Jb 3^{5} (cf לקח v^{6}) 9^{34} 13^{11} (|| פחד נפל על) v^{21} (cf ||) 15^{24} (|| תקף) 18^{11} (|| הפיץ) 33^{7} (|| כבד על) Is 21^{4}, *assail* ψ 18^{5} = 2 S 22^{5} **2.** *terrify* Jb 7^{14} (|| חתת)

†בְּעָתָה **n.f. terror, dismay** Je 8^{15} = 14^{19}.

†[בְּעוּתִים] **n.m.pl. terrors, alarms,** occasioned by God בִּעוּתֵי אֱלוֹהַּ Jb 6^{4} (|| חִצֵּי שַׁדַּי); בִּעוּתֶיךָ ψ 88^{17} (|| חֲרוֹנֶיךָ)

בצין v בץ

†בֵּצַי **n pr.m.** Ne 10^{19} one of the chiefs of the people, Ezr 2^{17} Ne 7^{23} בְּנֵי ב׳ i e a family

בצל (*strip, strip off*, Eth በጸለ: I 2; Ar بَصَلَ, appar denom)

†[בָּצָל] **n.m. onion** (NH בָּצָל or בְּצָל, Ar بَصَل, Eth በጸል: Aram בוּצְלָא, ܒܨܠܐ)—בְּצָלִים Nu 11^{5} (אֶת הַקִּשֻּׁאִים וְאֵת הָאֲבַטִּחִים וְאֶת־הֶחָצִיר וְאֶת־הַבּ׳ וְאֶת־הַשּׁוּמִים).

†בְּצַלְאֵל **n.pr.m.** (*in the shadow* (*protection*) *of Êl*, cf cuneif *Ṣil-Bêl*, a king of Gaza, COT Jos 11^{22})—**1.** a skilled artisan of tribe of Judah Ex 31^{2} 35^{30} 36^{1} ^{2} 37^{1} 38^{22} (all P) 1 Ch 2^{20} 2 Ch 1^{5} **2.** an Israelite Ezr 10^{30}.

†בַּצְלוּת **n.pr.m.** (*stripping*)—head of Isr fam at return from exile; בְּנֵי־ב׳ Ezr 2^{52} = Ne 7^{54} Kt, בַּצְלִית Ne 7^{54} Qr.

†[בָּצַע] **vb. cut off, break off, gain by violence** (so NH, Ar بَضَعَ, Eth በፀዐ: Aram בְּצַע)—**Qal** *Impf* יִבְצַע Jb 27^{8}, יְבַצְּעוּן Jo 2^{8}, *Imv* sf בְּצַעַם בראש Am 9^{1}, *Inf.* בְּצֹעַ Ez 22^{27}, *Pt* בּוֹצֵעַ Pr 15^{27} Je 6^{13}, בֹּצֵעַ ψ 10^{3} + 3 t,—*cut off*, *break off* (c acc capitals of pillars) Am 9^{1} (but Lag$^{Prov\ v.\ vi}$ בְּזַעַם = בְּצַעַם Hb 3^{12} *in wrath*), so fig. Jb 27^{8} *when Eloah cutteth off, draweth out, his soul*, obj om. *their course*, i.e stop Jo 2^{8} (cf Hi-St), usually *gain by violence* or in gen. *wrongfully* Ez 22^{27}, *Pt* abs ψ 10^{3} = *greedy getter, robber*, & c acc cogn בֶּצַע Pr 1^{19} 15^{27} Je 6^{13} 8^{10} Hb 2^{9} **Pi** *Pf* בִּצַּע La 2^{17}, *Impf* יְבַצַּע Is 10^{12}, sf. יְבַצְּעֵנִי Is 38^{12} Jb 6^{9}; 2 fs. וַתְּבַצְּעִי Ez 22^{12}, 3 fpl. תְּבַצַּעְנָה Zc 4^{9},—*cut off*, (*dis*)*sever* (i e from life) Jb 6^{9} cf. Is 10^{19} (מִדַּלָּה), = *finish, complete* Is 10^{12} Zc 4^{9}; *accomplish* (= carry out, fulfil) La 2^{17} (obj אמרתו), *violently make gain of*, obj pers. Ez 22^{12} (instr. בעשק).

†בֶּצַע **n.m. gain made by violence, unjust gain, profit**—בֶּצַע Gn 37^{26} + 7 t (cstr. Ju 5^{19} +), בָּצַע Ex 18^{21} + 7 t; sf. בִּצְעֶךָ Je 22^{17}, בִּצְעֵךְ Je 51^{13} Ez 22^{13}; בִּצְעוֹ Is 56^{11} 57^{17}; בִּצְעָם Ez 33^{31} Mi 4^{13},—*gain made by violence* (nearly = plunder) Ju 5^{19} Mi 4^{13}, more generally, *unjust gain* Ex 18^{21} 1 S 8^{3} ψ 119^{36} Pr 28^{16} Is 33^{15} 56^{11} 57^{17} Je 22^{17} 51^{13} Ez 22^{13} 33^{31}, as acc cogn. c. בָּצַע Pr 1^{19} 15^{27} Je 6^{13} 8^{10} Ez 22^{27} Hb 2^{9}, *profit* (with selfish suggestion) מַה־בּ׳ Gn 37^{26} Mal 3^{14} cf. ψ 30^{10} Jb 22^{3}.

†בְּצַעֲנַנִּים, בצענים, perh **n.pr.loc.** in Naphtali אֵלוֹן בּ׳ Jos 19^{33} Ju 4^{11} Cf. צעננים

בצץ (?cf Ar. نَضَّ *be* نَضٌّ, i e. *one soft, tender, impressible* in body, etc)

†בֹּץ **n.[m.] mire** Je 38^{22}.

†בִּצָּה **n f. swamp,** Jb 8^{11} as place where rushes grow, cf. 40^{21}, בִּצֹּאתָו (Co וּבִצּוֹתָיו) pl. sf. Ez 47^{11} (|| וּגְבָאָיו)

†בּוֹצֵץ **n.pr.loc.** a rock by Michmash 1 S 14^{4},—Βωσης Lag$^{Onom\ 238,\ 2nd\ ed\ 250}$

†בָּצֵק **vb. swell**—**Qal** *Pf.* 3 fs. בָּצֵקָה Dt 8^{4}, 3 pl. בָּצֵקוּ Ne 9^{21};—*swell*, or *receive swellings, blisters*, of foot, Di Dt 8^{4}, Ry Ne 9^{21}.

†בָּצֵק **n.[m.] dough**—בָּצֵק Ex 12^{39} + 4 t., sf בְּצֵקוֹ Ex 12^{34},—*dough*, not fermented Ex 12$^{34.39}$ (E), no restriction 2 S 13^{8} Ho 7^{4} Je 7^{18}.

†בָּצְקַת **n.pr.loc.** (?cf Ar نَضْقَة an elevated region covered with volcanic stones) city of Judah toward Philistines, בָּצְקַת Jos 15^{39}, בָּצְקַת 2 K 22^{1} (home of Josiah's mother)

†[בָּצַר] **vb. cut off, make inaccessible** (esp by fortifying), **enclose** (NH id, Aram בְּצַר, ܒܨܪ (Pa. *diminish, subtract*), perh cf Ar نَصْرٌ *side, edge*, بَصْرٌ, etc, *rough stone*, أَرْضٌ بَصِرَةٌ *land in wh are sharp stones* (cf Lane))—**Qal** *Impf.* יִבְצֹר ψ 76^{13}, 2 ms. תִבְצֹר Lv 25^{5} Dt 24^{21}, וַיִּבְצְרוּ Ju 9^{27}, תִבְצְרוּ Lv 25^{11}, *Pt* act בּוֹצֵר Je 6^{9}, בֹּצְרִים Je 49^{9} Ob^{5}, pass m בָּצוּר Zc 11^{2} Kt (Qr בָּצִיר). f בְּצוּרָה Is 2^{15} + 3 t + Ez 21^{25} v infr; pl f. בְּצוּרוֹת Ez 36^{35}, בְּצֻרוֹת Nu 13^{28} + 14 t, בְּצֻרֹת Dt 1^{28} Ne 9^{25}, בְּצֻרֹת Dt 3^{5} 9^{1},—*cut off*, grape-clusters, עֲנָבִים Lv 25^{5}, cf v^{11} (obj נְזִיר), Dt 24^{21} Ju 9^{27} (obj.

in both, כרם); hence Pt. act. *grape-gathering, -gatherer* Je 6^{9} 49^{9} Ob^{5}; fig. *cut off* (= take away) ψ 76^{13} (obj. רוח נגידים); most often Pt. pass. *cut off, made inaccessible*, De Is 2^{15} = *fortified*, always f.; generally adj. c. עיר, ערים; Nu 13^{28} Dt 1^{28} 3^{5} 9^{1} Jos 14^{12} 2 S 20^{6} 2 K 18^{13} = Is 36^{1} 2 K 19^{25} = Is 37^{26} 2 Ch 17^{2} 19^{5} 32^{1} 33^{14} Ne 9^{25} Is 25^{2} 27^{10} Ez 36^{35} Ho 8^{14} Zp 1^{16}, rarely c. חומה Dt 28^{52} Is 2^{15} Je 15^{20}, יער הב׳ Zc 11^{2} (rd. Kt); once, subst. of *secrets, mysteries* (= unattainable things) Je 33^{3},—ב׳ Ez 21^{25} 𝔊 Sm Co בתוֹכָהּ, doubtless right **Niph.** *Impf* יִבָּצֵר *be withheld* Gn 11^{6} (מֵהֶם), Jb 42^{2} (מִמְּךָ) **Pi.** *Impf.* 3 fs תְּבַצֵּר Je 51^{53} *fortify*, so *Inf* לְבַצֵּר Is 22^{10}.

†I. [בֶּ֫צֶר] **n.[m.] precious ore** (AW^{105} Thes), > **gold, ring-gold** Hoffm$^{ZA\ 1887,\ 48\ f.\ Hiob\ 70}$ (AW Thes *ore* as *that broken off*, Hoffm comp Ar. نَطْر *ring*, Heb בִּצְרָה *enclosure*, Talm בצרא *finger-measure*, etc.; a √II. בצר must then be assumed, = نطر)—בֶּצֶר Jb 22^{24} (|| אוֹפִיר q v); בִּצְרֶיךָ v^{25} (|| כֶּסֶף) possibly also בִּצְרֵי כָסֶף ψ 68^{31} for MT בְּרַצֵּי׳, cf Che$^{crit.\ n}$ Ne$^{JBL,\ 1891,\ 151}$.

†II. בֶּ֫צֶר (*fortress*)—**1. n.pr.loc.** city in Reuben (MI בצר) Dt 4^{43} Jos 20^{8} 1 Ch 6^{63}. **2. n.pr.m.** a descendant of Asher 1 Ch 7^{37}

†I. בָּצְרָה **n.f.** enclosure, i e. (sheep-)fold, צאן ב׳ Mi 2^{12}.

†II. בָּצְרָה **n.pr.loc.** **1.** city of Edom (*fortress*; (v. Palm n pr loc. בצרא Vog$^{No\ 22}$ 𝔊 Βο-σ(σ)ορρα; cf. Βοσορ; Lag$^{Onom\ Sacr\ 102,\ 232,\ 2nd\ ed\ 137,\ 247}$ = Βοστρα) Gn 36^{33} = 1 Ch 1^{44} Is 34^{6} 63^{1} (in both || אדום (ארץ)) Je 49$^{13.22}$ Am 1^{12}. **2.** of Moab Je 48^{24}, prob. = II. בצר **1**;—on Mi 2^{12} cf. foregoing.

†בִּצָּרוֹן **n.[m.]** stronghold, לב׳ Zc 9^{12}.

†בַּצֹּ֫רֶת **n.f.** dearth (cf. foll.), שְׁנַת ב׳ Je 17^{8}.

†בַּצָּרָה **n.f.** dearth, destitution (i e *diminution*, cf. ܒܘܨܪܐ PS^{572}, v also vb. בצר 𝔗 Pr 14^{28} *people reduced*)—*dearth* (= בצרת) עתות ב׳ ψ 9^{10} 10^{1}, pl בַּצָּרוֹת Je 14^{1}.

†בָּצִיר **n.m.**$^{Lv\ 26.5}$ **vintage** (cf בָּצַר)—בָּצִיר Lv 26^{5} + 4 t. + Zc 11^{2} Qr (but rd. בצור Kt), cstr. בציר Ju 8^{2}, sf בצירך Je 48^{32};—*vintage*, lit. Lv 26$^{5.5}$ Ju 8^{2} Is 32^{10} Je 48^{32}, in simile Is 24^{13} Mi 7^{1}; Zc 11^{2} rd בצור (Kt) and cf. sub בָּצַר

†מִבְצָר **n.m.**$^{Is\ 17.3}$ **fortification**—מִבְצָר Nu 32^{17} + 18 t; cstr. מבצר Jos 19^{29} + 2 t.; pl מבצרים Nu 13^{19} Dn 11^{24}; מִבְצָרוֹת Dn 11^{15}, מבצרי La 2^{2} Dn 11^{39}; sf. מִבְצָרֶיךָ Ho 10^{14} + 2 t.; מִבְצָרַיִךְ Na 3^{12}; מִבְצָרֶיהָ v^{14} Je 48^{18}; מבצריו ψ 89^{41} La 2^{5}, מִבְצָרֶיהָ Is 34^{13}; מִבְצְרֵיהֶם 2 K 8^{12};—*fortification*, esp. in phrase (הַמ׳) (עָרֵי) מ׳ עיר = *fortified city* Nu 32$^{17.36}$ Jos 10^{20} 19$^{29.35}$ 1 S 6^{18} 2 K 3^{19} 10^{2} 17^{9} 18^{8} Je 4^{5} 5^{17} 8^{14} 34^{7} ψ 108^{11} (עיר מ׳ = עיר מָצוֹר ψ 60^{11}), 2 Ch 17^{19} Dn 11^{15} (מ׳ in this connexion sing. exc. Je 5^{17} & Dn 11^{15} (מבצרות)); Je 1^{18} fig of prophet, so without עיר Je 6^{27}, *fortress, stronghold*, lit without עיר etc. Nu 13^{19} 2 K 8^{12} Je 48^{18} Is 17^{3} 25^{12} (מ׳ משגב חומתיך) 34^{13} (|| ארמנת), La 2$^{2.5}$ (|| *id*) ψ 89^{41} Ho 10^{14} Am 5^{9} Mi 5^{10} Na 3$^{12.14}$ Hb 1^{10} Dn 11$^{24.39}$, sq n pr. מ׳ צר 2 S 24^{7} (cf. Jos 19^{29} עיר מ׳ צר).

בַּקְבּוּק, בַּקְבֻּק v. sub בקק

†בַּקְבַּקַּר **n pr.m.** (form strange, mng dub.) a Levite 1 Ch 9^{15}.

בַּקְבֻּקְיָה v. sub בקק

בקה

(*test, prove*, cf. Aram. בְּקָא).

†בֻּקִּיָּ֫הוּ **n.pr.m.** (*proved of* י׳) Levite, son of Heman 1 Ch 25^{4}, son of Asaph (?) v^{13}.

†בֻּקִּי **n.pr.m.** (*id*)—**1.** a Danite chief Nu 34^{22} **2.** a descendant of Aaron 1 Ch 5$^{31.31}$ 6^{31} Ezr 7^{4}.

†בָּקַע **vb. cleave, break open or through** (NH *id*, MI^{15} מבקע השחרת *from break of dawn*; Aram. בְּקַע; cf. Eth በቅዐ: *profit, be useful*, orig. *findere, aperire*, Di)—**Qal** *Pf.* בָּקַע ψ 78^{13}, בָּקְעָה Is 34^{15}, בָּקַעְתָּ Ne 9^{11} ψ 74^{15}, וּבָקַעְתָּ Ez 29^{7}; *Impf* וַיִּבְקַע Ju 15^{19} Is 48^{21}, וַיִּבְקְעוּ 2 S 23^{16} = 1 Ch 11^{18}, וַיְבַקְּעוּהָ 2 Ch 21^{17}, *Imv.* וּבְקָעֵהוּ Ex 14^{16}; *Inf. cstr.* sf בִּקְעָם Am 1^{13} 2 Ch 32^{1}; *Pt. act.* בּוֹקֵעַ Is 63^{12} Ec 10^{9}, בֹּקֵעַ ψ 141^{7};—**1.** *cleave, cleave open*, sq. acc, Ju 15^{19} *God cleft open the hollow* (הַמַּכְתֵּשׁ), and water came out, cf. Is 48^{21} (obj צור), also ψ 74^{15} *bring forth by cleaving*, obj. מַעְיָן וָנַחַל, all three of divine operation; *cleave* or *rip open* pregnant women Am 1^{13}, of a broken staff, tearing the shoulder Ez 29^{7} (but rd. כַּף *hand* for כָּתֵף, 𝔊 𝔙 Sm(?) Co); *cleave* wood Ec 10^{9} (|| מַסִּיעַ אֲבָנִים), of ploughing (furrowing) the earth ψ 141^{7} (|| פֹּלֵחַ; in sim), esp. of *dividing* the sea, Ex 14^{16} (P) Ne 9^{11} ψ 78^{13}, cf. Is 63^{12}, obj מַיִם,—in all these subj י׳ exc. Ex 14^{16} where he commands Moses; of *hatching out* (a brood, but no obj. expr.) Is 34^{15}, subj. קִפּוֹז *arrow-snake*. **2.** *break through* or *into*, sq ב 2 S 23^{16} = 1 Ch 11^{18}; sq. acc 2 Ch 21^{17} וַיַּעֲלוּ ביהודה וַיְבַקְּעוּהָ; also 32^{1}, obj suff. ref to cities, ויאמר לְבִקְעָם אליו *and he thought to break into them* and so bring them *unto himself*.

Niph. *Pf.* נִבְקַע Jb 26^{8} Zc 14^{4} (וְ consec.); נִבְקְעוּ Gn 7^{11} Is 35^{6}, נִבְקָ֑עוּ 2 Ch 25^{11} Pr 3^{20}; *Impf.* יִבָּקַע Is 58^{8}, יִבָּקֵעַ Jb 32^{19}; 3 fs. תִּבָּקַע Is 59^{5}, וַתִּבָּקַע Nu 16^{31}+3 t.; *Inf.* cstr. לְהִבָּקַע Ez 30^{16};—**1.** *be cleft, rent open*, subj. the ground, הָאֲדָמָה Nu 16^{31} (J), הָאָרֶץ 1 K 1^{40} (hyperb.); mountain Zc 14^{4}; *burst open*, of men hurled from rock 2 Ch 25^{12}; of cloud beneath its weight of water Jb 26^{8}; hyperb. of belly full of words seeking a vent, Jb 32^{19} *like new wine-skins it will burst open;* so of the water-receptacles (מעינות) of the great deep, at the flood Gn 7^{11}; of the water-masses themselves, תהומות Pr 3^{20}, מים ונחלים Is 35^{6}; also of the Red Sea, וַיִּבָּקְעוּ המים Ex 14^{21}; of light breaking forth Is 58^{8} (fig.); of serpent's egg *hatching out* as a viper Is 59^{5} הַזּוּרֶה תִּבָּקַע אֶפְעֶה. **2.** *be broken into*, of city captured by breaches in walls 2 K 25^{4}=Je 52^{7}, Ez 30^{16}. **Pi.** *Pf.* בִּקַּע 2 K 15^{16} Jb 28^{10}, וּבִקַּעְתִּי Ez 13^{13}, בִּקֵּ֑עוּ Is 59^{5}; *Impf.* יְבַקַּע ψ 78^{15}, וַיְבַקַּע Gn 22^{3}; 3 fs. תְּבַקַּע Ez 13^{11}, תְּבַקְּעֵם Ho 13^{8}; 2 ms. תְּבַקַּע־ Hb 3^{9}, תְּבַקֵּעַ 2 K 8^{12}; 2 fpl. וַתְּבַקַּעְנָה 2 K 2^{24};—*cleave, cut to pieces*, or *rend open* (oft. more complete or more violent than Qal), sq. acc., of cleaving wood Gn 22^{3} i.e. cut it up for burning, so 1 S 6^{14}; of ripping open pregnant women 2 K 8^{12} 15^{16}; of tearing in pieces children 2 K 2^{24}; cf. also Ho 13^{8} (fig.); of cleaving open rocks, to bring forth water ψ 78^{15} (subj. God); of cutting mining-shafts Jb 28^{10} בַּצּוּרוֹת יְאֹרִים בִּ׳; נְהָרוֹת תְּבַקַּע־אָרֶץ Hb 3^{9} *into rivers thou cleavest* (*the*) *earth; break through* or *down* (a wall, but no obj. expr.), Ez 13^{11} וּבִקַּעְתִּי רוּחַ סְעָרוֹת תְּבַקֵּעַ (but Co תִּבָּקַע), cf. v^{13} רוּחַ סְעָרוֹת בַּחֲמָתִי; of *hatching* eggs Is 59^{5} בֵּיצֵי צִפְעוֹנִי בִּקֵּ֑עוּ (fig.) **Pu.** *Impf.* יְבֻקָּ֑עוּ Ho 14^{1}; *Pt.* מְבֻקָּעָה Ez 26^{10}, מְבֻקָּעִים Jos 9^{4};—*be ripped open*, of women Ho 14^{1} (vb. of masc. form); *rent*, of old wine-skins Jos 9^{4}; *broken into*, of a city in whose walls a breach has been made Ez 26^{10}. **Hiph.** *Impf.* 1 pl. sf. וְנַבְקִעֶנָּה Is 7^{6}; *Inf. cstr.* לְהַבְקִיעַ 2 K 3^{26};—*break into*, sq. sf. ref. to Judah, Is 7^{6} ונב׳ אֵלֵינוּ *let us break into it*, lay it open, and so bring it *unto ourselves* (cf. Qal 2 Ch 32^{1}); *break through* (abs.) with sword, שְׁלֹף חֶרֶב לְהַבְקִיעַ אֶל־מֶלֶךְ אֱדוֹם 2 K 3^{26}. **Hoph.** *Pf.* 3 fs. הָבְקְעָה הָעִיר Je 39^{2} *the city was broken into*, entrance was made by a breach. **Hithp.** *Pf.* הִתְבַּקָּעוּ Jos 9^{13}, *Impf.* יִתְבַּקָּ֑עוּ Mi 1^{4};—*burst* (*themselves*) *open*, of wine-skins Jos 9^{13}; *cleave asunder*, of valleys Mi 1^{4}.

†בֶּ֫קַע **n.[m.]** fraction, half, i.e. half-shekel, a weight; בֶּקַע מִשְׁקָלוֹ Gn 24^{22}, cf. Hesychius in Lag Ges. Abh. 199, l. 18 βακαίον [Lag βέκαον] μέτρον τι; v. also בֶּקַע Ex 38^{26} (=מַחֲצִית הַשָּׁקֶל).

†בִּקְעָה **n.f.** **valley** (cleft), **plain**—abs. ב׳ Gn 11^{2}+8 t.; cstr. בִּקְעַת Dt 34^{3}+7 t.; pl. בְּקָעוֹת Is 41^{18} ψ 104^{8}; בִּקְעֹת Dt 11^{11};—**1.** *valley* (opp. הַר mountain) Dt 8^{7} 11^{11} cf. Is 41^{18}; also 63^{14} כַּבְּהֵמָה בַּבִּקְעָה תֵרֵד; in creation-poem ψ 104^{8} יַעֲלוּ הָרִים יֵרְדוּ בְקָעוֹת. **2.** *plain* (sts. valley-plain, broad valley) Gn 11^{2}; also Ez 3$^{22.23}$ 8^{4} 37$^{1.2}$ (עַל־פְּנֵי הַבִּ׳) as level, opp. הָרְכָסִים Is 40^{4} (|| מִישׁוֹר); elsewhere cstr., mostly with n.pr. Dt 34^{3} בִּ׳ יְרֵחוֹ (appos. הַכִּכָּר), בִּ׳ מִצְפֶּה Jos 11^{8}, בִּ׳ הַלְּבָנוֹן 11^{17} 12^{7}, בִּ׳ מְגִדּוֹ 2 Ch 35^{22} cf. Zc 12^{11}, בִּ׳ אוֹנוֹ Ne 6^{2}; בִּ׳־אָוֶן Am 1^{5} *plain of idolatry*=Baalbek (Damascus, acc. to Wetzst in De Jes 3, 702; 𝔊 πέδιον Ὢν).

†[בָּקִיעַ, בְּקִיעַ] **n.[m.]** **fissure, breach,** Am 6^{11} בְּקִעִים, into which the small house is to be smitten (|| רְסִיסִים); בְּקִיעֵי עִיר־דָּוִד Is 22^{9}.

†I. [בָּקַק] **vb. be luxuriant** (Ar. بَقَّ *be profuse, abundant* (v. esp. Conjj. I. IV, Lane))—**Qal** *Pt.* בּוֹקֵק *luxuriant* Ho 10^{1} (fig. of Isr. as vine).

†II. [בָּקַק] **vb. empty** (cf. probably Ar. بَقَّ *make a gurgling noise*, of a mug dipped in water, or emptied of water)—**Qal** *Pf.* וּבַקֹּתִי Je 19^{7}, בְּקָקוּם Na 2^{3}; *Pt.* בּוֹקֵק Is 24^{1}, בֹּקְקִים Na 2^{3}; *empty, lay waste* land, acc., Is 24^{1} Na 2^{3}, also abs. v^{3}; fig. *make void* (obj. עֵצָה) Je 19^{7}. **Niph.** *Pf.* וְנָבְקָה (cf. Ges §67. R. 11) Is 19^{3}; *Impf.* 3 fs. תִּבּוֹק Is 24^{3}; *Inf. abs.* הִבּוֹק Is 24^{3};—*be emptied* (laid waste) Is 24^{3} הִבּוֹק תִּבּוֹק, of land (|| תִּבּוֹז); fig. of spirit, courage Is 19^{3}. **Po.** *Impf.* יְבֹקְקוּ Je 51^{2} *empty out* (devastate) land.

†בַּקְבֻּק **n.[m.]** **flask** (from gurgling sound of emptying, cf. Ar. بَقْبَقَةٌ *gurgling sound;* also Syr. [illegible], *cantharus*, etc.)—abs. בַּקְבֻּק Je 19^{10}; cstr. *id.* 1 K 14^{3} Je 19^{1}.

†בַּקְבּוּק **n.pr.m.** head of a family of Nethinim; בני־ב׳ Ezr 2^{51} Ne 7^{53}.

†בַּקְבֻּקְיָה **n.pr.m.** a Levite Ne 11^{17} 12$^{9.25}$.

†יַבֹּק **n.pr.fl.** (√ prob. בקק; so Thes after Simonis, Sam. Di) מַעֲבַר (ה)יבק Gn 32^{23} (where perhaps connected with יאבק = אבק); נַחַל יַבֹּ׳ Dt 2^{37}, יַבֹּ׳ הַנַּחַל Dt 3^{16} Jos 12^{2}, יַבֹּק Nu 21^{24} (|| אַרְנוֹן, cf. Dt 3^{16} Jos 12^{2}), הַיַּבֹּק Ju 11$^{13.22}$ (in both, || ארנון); it empties into Jordan from East, in latitude of Shechem; called (southern)

boundary of Ammon Dt 3^{16}, and (northern) of Amorites Jos 12^{2}; but some confusion (Di Nu 21^{24} Dt 2^{37});—mod. *Wady Zerqa*, Bd$^{Pal\ 181}$.

†[בָּקַר] **vb. inquire, seek** (NH *id.*, Aram. בְּקַר, ܒܩܰܪ; also Eth **በቀበ:** in deriv.; orig. *divide, discern*, cf. Ar. بَقَرَ *slit, rip, split*)—only **Pi.** *Pf* 1 s sf. וּבִקַּרְתִּים consec Ez 34^{11}, *Impf* יְבַקֵּר Lv 13^{36} 27^{33}, אֲבַקֵּר Ez 34^{12}; *Inf cstr.* לְבַקֵּר 2 K 16^{15} + 2 t;—*seek, look for*, sq. לְ Lv 13^{36}; *seek* (to distinguish) sq. בֵּין־טוֹב לָרַע Lv. 27^{33}; *seek* (in order to care for) sq. acc. צאן Ez 34^{11} (‖ דרש) v^{12}, fig. of ׳י seeking his people, *contemplate*, sq. בְּ ψ 27^{4} (‖ חָזָה בְ); *consider, reflect*, abs. Pr 20^{25} אַחַר נְדָרִים i.e. whether the vows were wise, or should be kept (cf Str ad loc. & reff); cf. perh 2 K 16^{15} *consider* (what shall be done with the old altar); *look at* Klo, (so לְבַקֵּר 1 K 3^{21} for 2nd בַּבֹּקֶר), AV RV *to inquire by*, 𝔖 *for praying*; perh. denoting some religious service to be performed by king himself, cf. esp. RS$^{Sem\ i\ 467}$.

בָּקָר 182 **n.m.** $^{1\ K\ 5,3\ +}$ (**f.** $^{Gn\ 33,13,\ Jb\ 1,14\ cf\ Dt\ 32,14\ 2\ S\ 17,29}$) **cattle, herd, ox** (Ar. بَقَرٌ, Aram. בַּקְרָא, ܒܩܪܳܐ, בַּקרתָא (cf. also Hom$^{NS\ 222\ ff.}$); name from *ploughing*, so Thes Lag$^{BN\ 61}$ al)—abs. ב׳ Gn 12^{16} +; cstr בְּקַר Nu 7^{88}, sf. בְּקָרְךָ Gn 45^{10} +, בְּקָרֶךָ Ex 20^{24} Je 5^{17}; בְּקָרוֹ 1 S 11^{7} 2 S 12^{4}; בְּקַרְכֶם Dt 12^{6}, בְּקָרָם Je 3^{24} +, pl בְּקָרִים Am 6^{12} (al. rd. בַּבָּקָר יָם) 2 Ch 4^{3} (but rd פְּקָעִים v ‖ 1 K 7^{24} infr); sf. בְּקָרֵינוּ Ne 10^{37}; rd בקריכם for בחוריכם 1 S 8^{16} 𝔊 We Dr;—**1.** mostly coll. **a.** *cattle*, generic (never pl in form) Gn 12^{6} 13^{5} 20^{14} 21^{27} 24^{35} Lv 1^{2} Dt 8^{13} 1 S 11^{5} Ho 5^{6} Jo 1^{18} 1 Ch 27$^{29.29}$ + oft. (frequently ‖ צֹאן); as grazing, 1 Ch 27^{29} +; in sim כַּב׳ Jb 40^{15} Is 11^{7} 65^{25}; as lowing (קוֹל הַב׳) 1 S 15^{14}; מִקְנֵה בָקָר *possession of* (i.e property in) cattle Gn 6^{14} 47^{17} (both J); עֶדְרֵי ב׳ Jo 1^{18} *herds of cattle*; esp. בֶּן־בָּקָר *son of cattle* (i.e. belonging to the בקר), to denote a single ox, calf, etc.; as used for food Gn 18^{7} cf. v^{8} (J),—in these prob. = *calf* (v. also 1 S 14^{32} בָּקָר וּבְנֵי בָקָר), usually for sacrifice (Hex only P) Nu 15$^{8.9}$; בֶּן־הַב׳ Lv 1^{5}; appos עֶגְלַת בָּקָר cf עֵגֶל †Lv 9^{2},—cf †Dt 21^{3} 1 S 16^{2} Is 7^{21},—mostly appos. פַּר Ex 29^{1} + 27 t.; also pl. †פָּרִים בְּנֵי בקר Nu 28$^{11.19.27}$ 29$^{13.17}$ (on all these cf. בֵּן), also indef. *cattle, oxen*, of a number not specified Nu 7$^{87.88}$ (in both enumerated as פָּרִים); 22^{40} 1 S 14^{32} 15^{21} 1 K 1^{9} 7$^{29.29}$ (here of graven work) 8^{5} 1 Ch 12^{40} 2 Ch 5^{6} 18^{2} Is 22^{13} ψ 66^{15}; also as beasts of burden †1 Ch 12^{40}. **b.** a particular *herd* of cattle Gn 18^{7} (J); cf pl בְּקָרֵינוּ, *our herds*, only Ne 10^{37}.

2. more individually, *head of cattle*,—yet alw. of more than one (Hex mostly P; pl. only Am 6^{12} + 2 Ch 4^{3} v. supr.); of two Nu 7^{17} + 11 t. Nu 7; †cf also צֶמֶד ב׳ *yoke* (pair) *of oxen* 1 S 11^{7} cf. v^{7}, 1 K 19^{21} cf v^{21} (ploughing, cf. v^{19}); also 2 S 6^{6} = 1 Ch 13^{9} (drawing a cart, cf. Nu 7$^{3.6}$ 1 S 6^{7f}), 2 S 24^{22} = 1 Ch 21^{23}, 2 S 24$^{22.24}$ 1 K 19^{20} Am 6^{12} (pl.), 500 *yoke of oxen* Jb 1^{3} cf. v^{14}; 1000 *yoke* 42^{12}; further, of four Nu 7^{7}; five Ex 21^{37} (תַּחַת הַשּׁוֹר); seven 2 Ch 29^{22} (‖ פָּרִים v^{21}); eight Nu 7^{8}, ten 1 K 5^{3}; twelve Nu 7^{3} (singly called שׁוֹר) cf v^{6}, of the twelve brazen bulls beneath the sea in Sol.'s temple 1 K 7$^{25.44}$ = 2 Ch 4$^{4.15}$ cf. 2 K 16^{17} 2 Ch 4^{3} (דמות בקרים) v^{3} (but rd. in both פְּקָעִים, as ‖ 1 K 7^{24} cf. Be Ot) v^{4} Je 52^{20}, of twenty 1 K 5^{3}; seventy 2 Ch 29^{32}; hundreds or thousands 1 K 8^{63} = 2 Ch 7^{5}, 2 Ch 15^{11} 29^{33} 35$^{7.8.9}$ (cf v^{12}), & Nu 31$^{33.38.44}$ +. Note חֶמְאַת בָּקָר Dt 32^{14} (poem), שְׁפוֹת ב׳ 2 S 17^{29}, כְּלִי הַב׳ 2 S 24^{22} 1 K 19^{21}, מַלְמַד הַב׳ Ju 3^{31}, צְפוּעֵי הַב׳ Ez. 4^{15} (opp גֶּלְלֵי הָאָדָם).

†בּוֹקֵר **n.m denom. herdsman** Am 7^{14}; of Amos himself, cf. אֲשֶׁר־הָיָה בַנֹּקְדִים 1^{1}.

בֹּקֶר 214 **n.m.** $^{Ex\ 10,13}$ **morning** (NH *id.*; from *split, penetrate*, as the dawn the darkness, light through cloud-rifts, etc.)—ב׳ Gn 1^{5} + (alw. abs.), pl. בְּקָרִים Jb 7^{18} + 4 t,—**1.** *morning* (of point of time, time at which, never during which, Eng *morning* = forenoon) —**a.** of end of night (opp. לַיְלָה) Ex 10^{13} (J) Lv 6^{2} (P) Ju 19^{25} Ru 3$^{13.13}$ Is 21^{12} cf 1 S 19^{11} (‖ מחר, opp. לילה); opp לילות ψ 92^{3}; also (opp לון) Ex 23^{18} 34^{25} (both JE) Lv 19^{13} (H) Dt 16^{4}; opp. צלמות Am 5^{8}, cf further Gn 40^{6} 41^{8} (both E) Ex 12^{22} 34$^{2.2}$ (both JE) 1 S 3^{15} +. †**b.** implying the coming of dawn, and even daylight Gn 29^{25} (E) 44^{3} (J) 1 K 3^{21} (but Klo here for 2nd בַּבֹּקֶר, rds לְבַקֵּר *by looking at* it v. בָּקַר) Jb 24^{17} 38^{12} (‖ שַׁחַר), לִפְנוֹת הַב׳ Ex 14^{27} (JE) *at the turn of the morning*, so Ju 19^{26} (‖ בַּעֲלוֹת הַשַּׁחַר v^{25}; sq. עַד־הָאוֹר, as something later, v^{26}); vid Ru 3^{14} (‖ בטרום יכיר איש את רעהו *before men could recognise each other*), cf. כּוֹכְבֵי בֹקֶר Jb 38^{7} *stars of morning*, but also **c.** אוֹר vb. Gn 44^{3} (J), הבקר אור, c אוֹר noun, באור הבקר Mi 2^{1}, & esp עד אור הבקר Ju 16^{2} (opp. לילה) so 1 S 14^{36}, also 1 S 25$^{22.34.36}$ 2 S 17^{22} 2 K 7^{9}; cf. 1 S 29^{10} (‖ וְאוֹר לָכֶם). †**c.** of coming of sunrise Ju 9^{33} 2 S 23$^{4.4}$ 2 K 3^{22} cf. מוֹצָאֵי ב׳ וערב ψ 65^{9} i.e. places of sunrise and sunset (‖ קְצוֹת i e *ends* of earth) **d.** of beginning of day, מֵאָז הַב׳ וְעַד־עַתָּה Ru 2^{7} (cf v^{14}) vid. 2 S 24^{15} (but

del We Dr), time of prayer, & praise ψ $5^{4\,4}$ (v. Hu) 59^{17} 88^{14} 92^{3}, ‖צהרים *noon* 1 K 18^{26} Je 20^{16}; of three hours of prayer, ערב ובקר וצהרים ψ 55^{18} (cf Dn $6^{10.13}$), cf also c. עֶרֶב infr. **e.** opp. ערב Gn 49^{27} (poem in J) Ex $16^{7.8.12\,13}$ Lv 6^{13} Nu 9^{21} (all P) Dt $28^{67\,67}$ 2 S 11^{14} 1 K 17^{6} Is 17^{14} Zp 3^{3} Ez $24^{18\,18}$ 33^{22} Dn 8^{26} ψ 30^{6} $90^{5.6}$ Ec 11^{6} 1 Ch 16^{40} 2 Ch 2^{3} 13^{11} 31^{3} Ezr 3^{3} Est 2^{14}, opp. בין הערבים Ex $29^{39.41}$ Nu $28^{4.8}$ (all P), esp מִן־הבקר עד־הערב = *all day* Ex 18^{13} & (without art) v^{14} (both E); מבקר לָעֶרֶב Jb 4^{20} = between morning and evening, also מֵעֶרֶב עַד־בֹּקֶר = *all night*, Ex 27^{21} (P) Lv 24^{3} (H) Nu 9^{21} & בָּעֶרֶב עַד־ב׳ Nu 9^{15} (both P), note also the formula וַיְהִי ערב ויהי בקר *and evening came and then morning* Gn $1^{5\,8\,13\,19\,23.31}$ (all P), i e the day ended with evening, and the night with morning; peculiar is Dn 8^{14} of om. of daily sacrif עַד עֶרֶב בֹּקֶר אַלְפַּיִם וּשְׁלֹשׁ מֵאוֹת, *until 2300 evening-mornings*, prob = 2300 half-days (Ew Hi Meinh Bev Dr $^{Intr\ 464}$, cf v^{26} & $3\frac{1}{2}$ times (years) 7^{25} $12^{11\,17}$) **f.** oft (above & elsewh) c prep (+art exc Jb 7^{18}), *in the morning*, בַּבֹּקֶר Gn 19^{27} + 110 t, cf. also בהיֹת הַבּ׳ Ex 19^{16}; *in* (or *at*) *the morning*, לַבּ׳ Am 4^{4} + 7 t.; *for* (*against* or *by*) *the morning*, לַבּ׳ Ex 34^{2} cf ψ 130^{6} (cf Che crit n); nearly = *until* (עַד־) Ex 34^{25} Dt 16^{4} Zp 3^{3}, further בַּבּ׳ בַּבּ׳ *morning by morning, every morning* † Ex 16^{21} 30^{7} 36^{3} Lv 6^{5} (all P) 2 S 13^{4} 1 Ch 23^{30} 2 Ch 13^{11} Is 28^{19} 50^{4} Ez $46^{13\,14\,15}$ Zp 3^{5}, also לַבּ׳ לַבּ׳, same sense, † 1 Ch 9^{27}, † pl לַבְּקָרִים *every m.* afresh ψ 73^{14} Is 33^{2} cf La 3^{23}, alm = *continually* ψ 101^{8} (cf Je 21^{12}), v לַבְּקָרִים † Jb 7^{18} (‖ לִרְגָעִים *every moment*), also without prep or art. *in the morning* Ho 7^{6} cf ψ $5^{4\,4}$ ψ 55^{18}, **d.** supr, & sub **2.** **g.** fig of bright joy after night of distress (poet) Jb 11^{17}, cf ψ 30^{6} 46^{6} (לִפְנוֹת ב׳) 49^{15} 59^{17} 90^{14} 143^{8}. **h** in phrases, הִשְׁכִּים בַּבּ׳ (וַיַּשְׁכֵּם etc) *he rose early in the morning* † Gn 19^{27} 20^{8} 21^{14} 22^{3} 26^{31} 28^{18} 32^{1} Ex 8^{16} 9^{13} 24^{4} 34^{4} Nu 14^{40} Jos 3^{1} 6^{12} 7^{16} 8^{10} (all JE) Ju 6^{28} $19^{5\,8}$ 1 S 1^{19} 5^{4} cf 15^{12}, 17^{20} $29^{10\,10}$ cf. v^{11}, 2 K 3^{22} 19^{35} = Is 37^{36}, 2 Ch 20^{20} Jb 1^{5} Pr 27^{14} Is 5^{11}; ויקם (ויקומו etc) בַּבּ׳ † Gn 24^{54} Nu $22^{13\,21}$ (all JE) Ju 19^{27} 20^{19} 2 S 24^{11} 1 K 3^{21}; אַשְׁמֹרֶת הַבּ׳ *morning watch* † Ex 14^{24} 1 S 11^{11}. **2.** *morrow, next day* (cf. Germ *Morgen, morgen*) without art. Ex $16^{19.20}$ Lv 7^{15} 22^{30} (opp הַיּוֹם הַהוּא) Nu 16^{5} (‖ מָחָר $v^{7\,16}$) cf. Ex $12^{10\,10}$ Nu 9^{12}, with art. Ex $16^{23.24}$ 29^{34}, לַבּ׳ Ex 34^{25} Nu 22^{41} Zp 3^{3}, בַּבּ׳ 1 S 9^{19} (opp הַיּוֹם *to-day*) cf. 20^{35}, *to-morrow morning* הַבּ׳ Ju 6^{31} (Stu), בַּבּ׳ Ex 7^{15} Jos 7^{14} Est 5^{14}, definitely בַּבּ׳ מִמָּחֳרָת 1 S 5^{4}, מֵהַבּ׳ 2 S 2^{27}, adverb. use in this sense (without prep or art) Ex 16^{7} Nu 16^{5}.

† [בַּקָּרָה] **n.f verbal.** a seeking, כְּבַקָּרַת רֹעֶה עֶדְרוֹ Ez 34^{12} *like a shepherd's seeking his flock*

† בִּקֹּרֶת **n.f. punishment** after examination (**inquisition**) Lv 19^{20}, (*scourging* 𝔅 AV after Jewish trad Kerith ^{11a} Sifra Saad. AE Ki cf Malbim ^{Sifra} Jastrow $^{Dict\ 165}$)

† [בִּקֵּשׁ] $_{224}$ **vb. seek** (Ph. בקש)—**Pi.** *Pf* בִּקֵּשׁ Dt 13^{11} + 15 t; בִּקְשָׁה Ec 7^{28} Est 2^{15}, sf בִּקַּשְׁתֶּם Ho 2^{9}; בִּקַּשְׁתִּיו Ct $3^{1\,2}$ cf 5^{6}; בִּקְשׁוּ Ezr 2^{62} + 12 t; sf בִּקְשֻׁנִי Is 65^{1} + 2 t; *Impf.* יְבַקֵּשׁ Jos 22^{23} + 37 t, יְבַקֶּשׁ־ Pr 15^{14} + 2 t., אֲבַקְשָׁה ψ 122^{9} + 3 t., sf יְבַקְשֶׁנּוּ 1 S 23^{14} + 7 t, יְבַקְשׁוּ 1 S 16^{16} + 23 t; *Imv* בַּקֵּשׁ 1 S 9^{3} + 3 t; בַּקְּשׁוּ 1 S 28^{7} + 8 t., *Inf* לְבַקֵּשׁ 1 S 10^{2} + 29 t; *Pt* מְבַקֵּשׁ Gn 37^{15} + 23 t; pl. מְבַקְשִׁים Ex 10^{11} + 38 t.;—**1.** *seek to find*: **a.** abs Ju 6^{29} 2 K 2^{17} Je 5^{1} Ez 34^{6} Ec 3^{6} 8^{17} (yet v. Ew) **b.** acc. Gn $37^{15\,16}$ Jos 2^{22} (J) Ju 4^{22} 14^{4} 1 S 9^{3} $10^{2\,14.21}$ 16^{16} 1 S $23^{14.25}$ 24^{3} 26^{2} $27^{1\,4}$ + 26^{20} obj *a flea*, but rd נַפְשִׁי 𝔊 Th We Kirkp Klo Dr, 2 S $17^{3\,20}$ 1 K 1^{3} 2^{40} 18^{10} 2 K 2^{16} 6^{19} 1 Ch 4^{39} 2 Ch 22^{9} Ezr 2^{62} (= Ne 7^{64}) Ne 12^{27} $37^{25.36}$ 119^{176} Pr 2^{4} 21^{6} 23^{35} 7^{28} Ct $3^{1\,1\,2.2}$ 5^{6} 6^{1} Is $41^{12\,17}$ Je $2^{24.33}$ La 1^{11} Ez 7^{25} 22^{30} $34^{4\,16}$ Ho 2^{9} Na 3^{11} Zc 11^{16} Mal 2^{15} **c.** with לְ Jb 10^{6}. **d.** acc rei לְ pers Ju 18^{1} 1 S 13^{14} 28^{7} 1 K 1^{2} Ru 3^{1} Est 2^{2} ψ 122^{9} Is 40^{20} La 1^{19} Na 3^{7}. **2.** *seek to secure*: **a.** acc. the priesthood Nu 16^{10} (P); David for king 2 S 3^{17}; in battle 2 S 5^{17} (= 1 Ch 14^{8}); ψ 27^{4} Je 45^{5} (cf. v^{5}), בקש נפש *seek to take one's life* Ex 4^{19} (J) 1 S 20^{1} $22^{23.23}$ 23^{15} 25^{29} 2 S 4^{8} 16^{11} 1 K $19^{10\,14}$ ψ 35^{4} 38^{13} 40^{15} 54^{5} 63^{10} 70^{3} 86^{14} Pr 29^{10} Je 4^{30} 11^{21} $19^{7\,9}$ 21^{7} 22^{25} $34^{20\,21}$ 38^{16} $44^{30.30}$ 46^{26} 49^{37}. **b.** *aim at, practise* בקש רעה *seek hurt* of Nu 35^{23} (P) 1 S 24^{10} 25^{26} (אֶל) 1 K 20^{7} ψ $71^{13.24}$ Est 9^{2}; ב׳ כזב ψ 4^{3} cf. Pr 17^{11}, שבר Pr 17^{19}, רצון Pr 11^{27}, טובה Ne 2^{10}, אמונה Je 5^{1}, צדק, ענוה Zp $2^{3.3}$ שלום ψ 34^{15}, חכמה Pr 14^{6} Ec 7^{25}, בינה Dn 8^{15}, דעת Pr 15^{14} 18^{15}, תורה Mal 2^{7}, אהבה Pr 17^{9}, תאוה 18^{1} (לְ of dir. obj), חשבנות Ec 7^{29} **c.** *Inf* Ex 4^{24} (J) Je 26^{21}. **d.** לְ & *Inf* Gn 43^{30} Ex 2^{15} 10^{11} (JE) Dt 13^{11} 1 S 14^{4} $19^{2\,10}$ 23^{10} 2 S 20^{19} 21^{2} 1 K $11^{22.40}$ Est 2^{21} 3^{6} 6^{2} ψ 37^{22} Ec 12^{10} Zc 6^{7} 12^{9}. **3.** *seek the face* **a.** *of rulers* 1 K 10^{24} (= 2 Ch 9^{23}) Pr 29^{26}. **b.** *of God* (from resorting to sacred places) Ho 5^{15} 1 Ch 16^{11} (= ψ 105^{4}) 2 Ch 7^{14} 2 S 21^{1} ψ 24^{6} $27^{8.8}$, without פְּנֵי **c.** יהוה Dt 4^{29} Zp 1^{6} 2^{3} Ho 3^{5} 5^{6} Ex 33^{7} (J) 1 Ch 16^{10} (= ψ 105^{3}) 2 Ch 11^{16} 20^{4} Is 51^{1} Pr 28^{5} Zc $8^{21\,22}$ Je 50^{4}; אלהים 2 S 12^{16}, cf. Ez 8^{22} Is 45^{19} 65^{1} 2 Ch $15^{4\,15}$ Ho 7^{10} Je 29^{13} Mal 3^{1} ψ 40^{17} 70^{5} 69^{7} Dn 9^{3}; דבר י׳

Am 8^{12}; שמך ψ 83^{17}. **d.** sq. *Inf.* c. לְ, of resort to wizards, but obj. not expr. Lv 19^{31} (H). **4.** *desire, demand:* **a.** acc. 1 Ch 21^{3}. **b.** acc. rei מִן pers. Ez 7^{26} Dn 1^{20}. **5. a.** *require, exact,* acc. rei מִיַּד pers Is 1^{12}; מִן pers. Ne 5^{12}, acc. rei v^{18} **b.** *exact equivalent* or *penalty* for, acc rei, מִיַּד pers. Gn 31^{39} 43^{9} (JE) 1 S 20^{16} 2 S 4^{11} Ez 3$^{18.20}$ 33^{8}, cf. דרשׁ, no obj. expr. Jos 22^{23} (P) **6.** (late) *ask, request,* acc. rei Est 2^{15}; עַל rei Ne 2^{4}; עַל rei מִן pers. Est 7^{7} Ezr 8^{23}; עַל rei מלפני pers Est 4^{8}; acc rei מִן pers. Dn 1^{8} (obj. cl c אשׁר), ψ 104^{21}, מִן pers. 2 Ch 20^{4}. **Pu.** *Impf* יְבֻקַּשׁ Je 50^{20}, ויב׳ Est 2^{23}, תְּבֻקְשִׁי Ez 26^{21} *be sought*

†[בַּקָּשָׁה] **n.m.** request, entreaty, בַּקָּשָׁתִי Est 5$^{7.8}$ 7^{3}, בַּקָּשָׁתֵךְ; Est 5^{3} 9^{12}, בַּקָּשָׁתוֹ Ezr 7^{6}.

†I. בַּר **n.m.** son (Aram. בַּר, Syr. ܒܪ) only in late Heb. of Pr 31$^{2.2}$ (both cstr.), v^{2} sf. בְּרִי, נשׁקו בר ψ 2^{12} *kiss the son,* 𝔖 Modern Vrss Ges De Pe et al; *receive instruction* 𝔗; δράξασθε παιδείας 𝔊; *apprehendite disciplinam* 𝔙 Ew; *kiss purely, do sincere homage* Aq Sym Jer Br $^{MP 136}$; emend. Lag (מוֹסֵרוֹ) נַשְּׁקוּ מוסרו *put on his bonds* (cf. v^{3}) so Kmp Che $^{OP 351}$.

II. בַּר corn, III בַּר pure, בָּר, I. II. בר v. ברר.

†I. בָּרָא $_{53}$ **vb.** shape, create (cf Ar بَرَى, *form, fashion by cutting, shape out, pare a reed for writing, a stick for an arrow,* but also بَرَأَ, *create;* Ph. הברא CIS $^{1.347}$ *incisor, a trade involving cutting,* As. *barû, make, create,* COT ^{Gloss} & Hpt KAT$^{2 Gloss 1}$ but dub, Sab ברא *found, build,* DHM $^{ZMG 1883, 413}$, synon. בנה; Ba $^{ZA 1888, 58}$, comp As. *banû, create, beget,* with change of liquid; Aram. בְּרָא, ܒܪܐ, *create*)—**Qal** *Pf.* Gn 1^{1} + 19 t; *Impf.* יִבְרָא Gn 1$^{21.27}$ Nu 16^{30}; *Inf.* ברא Gn 5^{1}; *Imv.* בְּרָא ψ 51^{12}; *Pt.* בורא Is 42^{5} + 10 t., sf בֹּרַאֲךָ Is 43^{1}; בּוֹרְאֶיךָ Ec 12^{1};—*shape, fashion, create,* always of divine activity, with acc. rei, seldom except in P and Is^{2}. **1.** obj. heaven and earth Gn 1^{1} 2^{3} (P) Is 45$^{18.18}$, mankind Gn 1$^{27.27.27}$ 5$^{1.2}$ (P) 6^{7} (J) Dt 4^{32} ψ 89^{48} Is 45^{12}; the host of heaven Is 40^{26}; heavens Is 42^{5}, ends of the earth Is 40^{28}; north and south ψ 89^{13}; wind Am 4^{13}; the תנינים Gn 1^{21} (P). **2.** the individual man Mal 2^{10} (|| father) Ec 12^{1}; the smith and the waster Is 54$^{16.16}$, Israel as a nation Is 43^{15}; Jacob Is 43^{1}; the seed of Israel Is 43^{7}. **3.** new conditions and circumstances: righteousness and salvation Is 45^{8}; darkness and evil Is 45^{7}; fruit of the lips Is 57^{19}; a new thing חֲדָשָׁה (a woman encompassing a man) Je 31^{22}, בְּרִיאָה (swallowing up the Korahites) Nu 16^{30} (J); cloud and flame over Zion Is 4^{5}. **4.** of transformations: a clean heart ψ 51^{12} (|| חָדָשׁ); new heaven and earth Is 65^{17} (in place of old), transformation of nature Is 41^{20}, with double acc. בורא ירושלם גילה *transform Jerusalem into rejoicing* Is 65^{18} **Niph.** *Pf.* 2 fs. נִבְרֵאת Ez 21^{35}; 3 pl. נבראו Ex 34^{10} + 2 t, *Impf.* יִבָּרֵאוּן ψ 104^{30}, *Inf* sf. הִבָּרְאֲךָ Ez 28^{13}, הִבָּֽרַאֲךָ Ez 28^{15}, הִבָּֽרְאָם Gn 2^{4} 5^{2}; *Pt.* נִבְרָא ψ 102^{19},—*Pass* **1.** *be created:* heaven and earth Gn 2^{4} (P), creatures ψ 104^{30}; mankind Gn 5^{2} (P); heavens ψ 148^{5}. **2.** with reference to birth: במקום אשׁר נבראת *in the place where thou wast created* (i.e. native land) Ez 21^{35}; יום הבראך *day when thou wast created* (king of Tyre) Ez 28$^{13.15}$ (cf היום ילדתיך ψ 2^{7}); עַם נִבְרָא ψ 102^{19} (|| עַם נולָד ψ 22^{32}). **3.** of something new, astonishing: miracles Ex 34^{10} (J); new things, חדשׁות Is 48^{6}. **Pi.** *Pf.* בֵּרֵאתָ Jos 17^{15}; ובראתו Jos 17^{18}; *Inf* abs. בָּרֵא Ez 21$^{24.24}$ 23^{47},—**1.** *cut down,* a forest Jos 17$^{15.18}$ (J), וּבָרֵא אותהן בְּחַרְבוֹתָם Ez 23^{47}. **2.** *cut out:* יָד hand, as an index Ez 21$^{24.24}$.

†בְּרִיאָה **n.f.** a creation, thing created, as preternatural, unparalleled, acc cogn. אִם־בּ׳ יִבְרָא י׳ Nu 16^{30}, cf. בָּרָא **Qal 3, Niph. 3.**

†בְּרָאיָה **n.pr.m.** (י׳ *hath created*) a Benjamite 1 Ch 8^{21}.

†II. [בָּרָא] **vb.** be fat (Ar. بَرِئَ *be free of a thing, sound, healthy,* v מרא)—**Hiph.** *Inf.* לְהַבְרִיאֲכֶם 1 S 2^{29} *to make yourselves fat*

†בָּרִיא **adj.** fat—ψ 73^{4} Ju 3^{17}; pl בְּרִיאִים 1 K 5^{3}, cstr. בריאי Dn 1^{15}, f בְּרִיאָה Hb 1^{16} + 2 t + Ez 34^{20} בְּרִיָּה; Hi Ol$^{§ 171a}$ בריאה > בְּרִיָּה, pl בריאות Gn 41^{5} + 3 t., בריאת Gn 41$^{2.4}$,—*fat,* cattle בקר Gn 41$^{2.4.5.7.18.20}$ (E) 1 K 5^{3}; sheep Ez 34$^{3.20}$ Zc 11^{16}; food Hb 1^{16}; איש ב׳ *fat man* Ju 3^{17}, בריאי בשר Dn 1^{15}, ב׳ אולם *their body fat* ψ 73^{4}.

בְּרֹאדַךְ בַּלְאֲדָן **n.pr.m.** v. sub מְרֹדַךְ.

בְּרָאִי v. בית בראי sub בית

בַּרְבֻּרִים v sub ברר.

ברד (cf. Ar بَرَدَ *be* or *become cold*).

†בָּרָד **n.m.** $^{Ex 9,18}$ hail (Ar. بَرَدٌ, Aram. בַּרְדָּא, ܒܪܕܐ; also Sab ברדם, *cold* DHM $^{ZMG 1875, 607}$)—בָּרָד Ex 9^{18} + 28 t,—*hail,* c. המטיר י׳ Ex 9$^{18.23}$, c. נתן י׳ 9^{23}, also Ex 9$^{19.22.24.25.25.26}$ 10$^{5.12.15}$; || קֹלֹת *thunder* Ex 9$^{23.28.29.33}$, || קלת & מָטָר Ex 9^{34}, || אשׁ lightning 9^{24}; all JE, Egypt plague; cf. ψ 78$^{47.48}$ 105^{32}; another great hailstorm Jos 10^{11} (E), where אַבְנֵי הַבּ׳, further, in theoph. ψ 18^{13} (|| גחלי־אשׁ) 2 S 22^{13} om. by error; del. however

in ψ 18^{14} cf De Che etc., אוצרות ב׳ Jb 38^{22}, ψ 148^{8} אש וב׳ שלג וקיטור, ירקון וב׳ Hg 2^{17}; in sim Is 28^{2} זרם ב׳ שער; fig Is 28^{17} 30^{30} (אבן ב׳) —fig of judgment of י׳

†[בָּרַד] **vb.denom.** hail, וּבָרַד בְּרֶדֶת הַיָּעַר consec Is 32^{19} *it shall hail.*

†[בָּרֹד] **adj.** spotted, marked (as if sprinkled with hail? so Ki cf Lag$^{BN 29}$, Syr ܒܪܘܕܐ, i e *grandinatus, grêlé*, PS), mpl. of sheep & goats עֲקֻדִּים נְקֻדִּים וּבְרֻדִּים Gn 31$^{10.12}$, horses Zc 6$^{3.6}$.

†בֶּרֶד **1. n.pr.loc** בֶּרֶד Gn 16^{14} near Kadesh. **2. n.pr.m.** בֶּרֶד an Ephraimite 1 Ch 7^{20}

†I בָּרָה **vb. eat** (As *barû* & deriv. Zim$^{BP 31}$)—**Qal** *Pf* 2 S 12^{17}, *Impf* אברה 2 S 13$^{6.10}$ *eat bread* (1 S 17^{8} ברו־לכם scribal error for בחרו לכם 1 K 18^{25} Dr$^{Sm 107}$). **Pi.** *Inf* לִבְרוֹת La 4^{10} *for devouring.* **Hiph.** *Impf* תַּבְרֵנִי 2 S 13^{5}, *Inf* לְהַבְרוֹת 2 S 3^{35} *cause to eat bread*

†בִּרְיָה **n.f.** food 2 S 13$^{5.7.10}$, Ez 34^{20} v בָּרִיא

†[בָּרוּת] **n.f** food, בְּבָרוּתִי ψ 69^{22} *in* (or *as*) *my food*

II ברה (cf As *barû, bind*, whence *birîtu, fetter* Zim$^{BP 59 n2}$, & *treaty, covenant* Dl$^{K 7}$)

בְּרִית $_{285}$ **n.f. covenant** (|| Aram קְיָם, *διαθήκη, constitutio*)—ב׳ Gn 9^{13} + 199 t., sf. בריתי Gn 6^{18} + 50 t., בריתך Dt 33^{9}, בְּרִיתֶךָ ψ 44^{18} + 11 t., בריתכם Is 28^{18}, בריתך Ez 16^{61}; בריתו Ex 2^{24} + 18 t., —*pact, compact, covenant* **I.** *between men* **1.** *treaty, alliance, league* Abraham and Amorites Gn 14^{13}, Edom and its allies Ob^{7}, with Philistines Gn 21$^{27.32}$ (E) 26^{28} (J), Jacob and Laban Gn 31^{44} (J); Joshua and Gibeonites Jos 9$^{6.7.11.15.16}$ (J), Israel and Canaanites Ex 23^{32} 34$^{12.15}$ (JE) Dt 7^{2} Ju 2^{2}; Ammonites and Jabesh 1 S 11^{1}, Solomon and Hiram 1 K 5^{26}, Ahab and Benhadad 1 K 20^{34}, Syria and Israel 1 K 15^{19} = 2 Ch 16^{3}, Nebuchadnezzar and Zedekiah Ez 17$^{13-19}$, nations against Israel ψ 83^{6}, nations with Egypt Ez 30^{5}; Ephraim and Assyria Ho 12^{2}, Judah and Israel Ez 16^{61}; Judah and Tyre Am 1^{9}; Assyria and Judah Is 33^{8}; נגיד ברית *a prince in league* (with him) Dn 11^{22} (so He Ew, Hi Meinh Bev ref to h p. Onias III, & translate *prince of cov't*, cf AV RV), fig., with death Is 28$^{15.18}$; with stones of the field Jb 5^{23}. **2.** *constitution, ordinance*, between monarch and subjects David and Abner 2 S 3$^{12.13.21}$; David and the elders of Israel 2 S 5^{3} = 1 Ch 11^{3}; Zedekiah and his people Je 34$^{8-18}$, hostile prince and Israelites Dn 9^{27}. **3.** *agreement, pledge*. Jehoiada and captains 2 K 11^{4} = 2 Ch 23^{1}; with oneself Jb 31^{1}, with Leviathan to be a servant Jb 40^{28}, between man and man Ho 10^{4} cf. בעל ברית Ju 8^{33} 9^{4} = אל ברית Ju 9^{46}. **4.** *alliance* of friendship between David and Jonathan 1 S 18^{3} 20^{8} 23^{18} cf. ψ 55^{21} **5.** *alliance* of marriage Pr 2^{17} Mal 2^{14}.—In all cases כרת ברית is the technical phrase for making covenant except Je 34^{10} באו בברית; Dn 9^{27} הגביר ברית ל. Various preps are used, most oft. ל Ex 23^{32}+, but also עם Gn 26^{28}+, את 2 S 3^{12}+, בין 2 Ch 16^{3}. **II.** *between God and man* **1.** *alliance* of friendship (|| סוד) ψ 25^{14}. **2.** *covenant*, as a divine constitution or ordinance with signs or pledges (vid אות) **a.** *with Noah* Gn 9$^{9-17}$ (P) Is 54^{10} Je 33$^{20.25}$, a divine promise that there would be no other deluge **b.** *with Abraham, Isaac and Jacob* Gn 15^{18} (J) 17$^{2-21}$ Ex 2^{24} 6$^{4.5}$ Lv 26^{42} (P) 2 K 13^{23} 1 Ch 16^{15} = ψ 105$^{8.10}$, Ne 9^{8} Je 34^{18}, a promise to multiply their seed, give them the land of Canaan, and make them a blessing to the nations **c.** *with Israel at Sinai* = Horeb, with a covenant sacrifice Ex 19^{5} 24$^{7.8}$ (E) 34$^{10.27.28}$ (J) 31^{16} Lv 2^{13} (P) 24^{8} 26$^{9.15.25.44.45}$ (H) Dt 4^{13}, renewed in plains of Moab Dt 28^{69}; with blessings and curses Dt 29^{20}, frequently referred to in other books 2 Ch 34^{32} ψ 25^{10} 44^{18} 50$^{5.16}$ 74^{20} 78$^{10.37}$ 103^{18} 106^{45} 111$^{5.9}$ Is 56$^{4.6}$ Je 11$^{2.3.6.8.10}$ 14^{21} 22^{9} 31^{32} Ez 16$^{8.59.60}$ 44^{7} Dn 9^{4} 11$^{28.30.32}$ Ho 6^{7} 8^{1} Zc 9^{11} 11^{10}; a divine constitution given to Israel with promises on condition of obedience and penalties for disobedience, in the form of tables of the covenant Dt 9$^{9.11.15}$, inscribed with the ten words, placed in ארון ברית (י׳) the ark of the covenant Nu 10^{33} + 40 t. (vid ארון, in 1 S 4$^{3.4.4.5}$ om ברית after ארון 𝔊 We Dr), set forth in דברי הברית *words of the covenant* Ex 34^{28} (J) Dt 28^{69} 29^{8} 2 K 23^{3} (= 2 Ch 34^{31}) Je 11$^{2-8}$, written in ספר הברית *the book of the covenant* Ex 24^{7} (E, cf 34^{27} J) 2 K 23$^{2.21}$ (cf 2 Ch 34^{30}) **d.** *with Phinehas* Nu 25$^{12.13}$ (P), a constitution, establishing an everlasting priesthood in his line, cf ברית הכהנים Ne 13^{29} & ברית הלוי Mal 2$^{4.8}$ **e.** *with Joshua and Israel* Jos 24^{25} (E), an ordinance or constitutional agreement to serve Yahweh only. **f.** *with David* ψ 89$^{4.29.34.39}$ 132^{12} Je 33^{21} (cf. 2 S 7 = 1 Ch 17); a divine promise to the seed of David of an everlasting kingdom, the relation of sonship, and the superintendence of the temple (cf ψ 2) **g.** *Jehoiada and the people* 2 K 11^{17} = 2 Ch 23^{3}, a constitutional agreement to be the people of Yahweh. **h.** *Hezekiah and the people* 2 Ch 29^{10}, a constitutional agreement to reform the worship. **i.** *Josiah and the people* 2 K 23^{3}, a constitutional agreement to obey the book of the covenant. **j.** *Ezra and the people*

Ezr 10^{3}, a constitutional agreement to put away foreign wives and observe the Law. **k.** *the prophetic covenant*, a divine promise through a series of prophets to establish a new constitution ברית חדשה Je 31^{31}, with new institutions and precepts Is 42^{6} 49^{8} 55^{3} 59^{21} 61^{8} Je 31$^{31\ 33}$ 32^{40} 50^{5} Ez 16$^{60.62}$ 20^{37} 34^{25} 37^{26} Ho 2^{20}. In Is^{2} the Messianic servant is ברית עם Is 42^{6} 49^{8}, cf מלאך הברית Mal 3^{1}. **III.** Phrases **1** *covenant making*: כרת ברית Gn 15^{18} Ex 34$^{10\ 27}$ (J) Jos 24^{25} (E) Dt 5$^{2.3}$ 28^{69} 29$^{13.24}$ 1 K 5^{26} 2 K 11^{17} 17$^{35.38}$ 23^{3} 2 Ch 21^{7} 23$^{3\ 16}$ 29^{10} 34^{30} Ezr 10^{3} Ne 9^{8} ψ 50^{5} 89^{4} Is 55^{3} 61^{8} Je 11^{10} 31$^{31.32.33}$ 32^{40} 34^{13} Ez 34^{25} 37^{26} Hos 2^{20}; הקים ברית *establish a covenant* Gn 6^{18} 9$^{9\ 11\ 17}$ 17$^{7\ 19.21}$ Ex 6^{4} (P) Ez 16$^{60.62}$, but *confirm covenant* Lv 26^{9} (?, H) Dt 8^{18}; נתן ברית Gn 17^{2} Nu 25^{12} (P), שם ברית 2 S 23^{5} (poet.); עבר בברית Dt 29^{11}; בא בברית 2 Ch 15^{12} Ez 16^{8}; צוה ברית ψ 111^{9}; נשא ברית על פי ψ 50^{16}. (Cf. further on these Dr$^{\text{J Ph xi 1882, 210 ff}}$) **2.** *covenant keeping:* on the part of man שמר ברית 1 K 11^{11} Ne 1^{5} 9^{32} ψ 78^{10} 103^{18} 132^{12} Dn 9^{4}, נצר ברית Dt 33^{9} ψ 25^{10}, מחזיקים בברית Is 56$^{4\ 6}$, on the part of God זכר ברית Gn 9$^{15\ 16}$ Ex 2^{24} 6^{5} (all P), Lv 26$^{42.42.42}$ (H; on sf. cf. Di Ges$^{\S 128, 1 R b}$) v^{45} (H) ψ 105^{8} 106^{45} 111^{5} 1 Ch 16^{15} Ez 16^{60}. Thus we have נאמנת ψ 89^{29}; ברית עולם Gn 9^{16} 17$^{7\ 13\ 18\ 19}$ Ex 31^{16} Lv 24^{8} Nu 18^{19} 25^{13} (P) 2 S 23^{5} (poet.) 1 Ch 16^{17} (=ψ 105^{10}) Is 24^{5} 55^{3} 61^{8} Je 32^{40} 50^{5} Ez 16^{60} 37^{26}; ברית מלח Lv 2^{13} 2 Ch 13^{5} 21^{7} (a cov't with sacrificial meal and salt; on cov't. with salt in Arabia cf We$^{\text{Skizzen iii 124}}$), ברית שלום Nu 25^{12} (P) Is 54^{10} Ez 34^{25} 37^{26}, הברית והחסד Dt 7$^{9\ 12}$ 1 K 8^{23} (=2 Ch 6^{14}) Ne 1^{5} 9^{32} Dn 9^{4}; ברית קדש Dn 11$^{28.30}$; מסרת הברית Ez 20^{37} **3.** *covenant violation:* עבר ברית Dt 17^{2} Jos 7$^{11\ 15}$ 23^{16} (D) Ju 2^{20} 2 K 18^{12} Ho 6^{7} 8^{1}; הפר ברית Gn 17^{14} Lv 26$^{15.44}$ (H) Dt 31$^{16.20}$ (J) Ju 2^{1} Is 24$^{5.5}$ Je 11^{10} 14^{21} 31^{32} 33$^{20.21}$ Ez 16^{59} 17$^{18\ 19}$ 44^{7} Zc 11^{10}, עזב ברית 1 K 19$^{10\ 14}$ Je 22^{9} Dn 11^{30}; מאס ברית 2 K 17^{15}, נאר ברית ψ 89^{39}; חלל ברית ψ 89^{34} Mal 2^{10}; שקר בברית ψ 44^{18}; שכח ברית Dt 4$^{23.31}$ Je 50^{5}

. ברוש, ברות v. sub ברשׁ

בָּרוּת v. sub I. ברה.

בְּרוֹתָה, ברתי v. sub באר

ברז (? cf Aram ברח *bore, pierce*, or Ar بَرَزَ, *appear*)

† **ברזות** **n.pr.f.** (?) descend. of Asher (perh. ברזא *foramen*, Thes, or بَرْزَةٌ woman whose beauties are *apparent*) 1 Ch 7^{31} Kt (Qr בִּרְזָיִת)

† **בַּרְזֶל** **n.m.**$^{\text{Dt 19 5}}$ iron (c. ל afform; fr. *piercing*? NH *id.*, Aram. *id.*, פַּרְזְלָא, فُولَاذ, Ph. ברזל, As *parzillu* COT^{Gloss}, (Ar فِرْزِل *fetter* is loan-word))—alw. abs ב׳ Gn 4^{22} + 74 t (בַּרְזֶל Gn 4^{22} etc);—**1.** *iron*, lit: **a.** iron-ore, stone containing iron, Dt 8^{9} Jb 28^{2}; **b.** as raw material (to be worked) Gn 4^{22} 1 Ch 22$^{3.14\ 16}$ 29$^{2.2\ 7}$ 2 Ch 2$^{6.13}$ 24^{12} Is 44^{12}, **c.** as article of commerce Ez 27$^{12\ 19}$, **d.** as material of furniture, utensils, implements, etc, עֶרֶשׂ ב׳ Dt 3^{11}, רֶכֶב ב׳ Jos 17$^{16.18}$ Ju 1^{19} 4$^{3\ 13}$, כְּלֵי ב׳ Jos 6$^{19\ 24}$ cf 1 K 6^{7} Nu 35^{16}, עֵט־ב׳ Jb 19^{24} & fig. Je 17^{1}, חֲרִצֵי הַבּ׳ 2 S 12^{31} = 1 Ch 20^{3}, מַגְזְרוֹת הַבּ׳ 2 S 12^{31} *cutting instr of iron*, vid. Am 1^{3}, כַּבְלֵי ב׳ ψ 149^{8} (‖ זקים), קִיר ב׳ Jb 20^{24}, קַרְנֵי ב׳ 1 K 22^{11} = 2 Ch 18^{10}, נֵשֶׁק ב׳ & מַחֲבַת ב׳ Ez 4^{3}, בְּרִיחֵי ב׳, i e of Babylon, ag Cyrus Is 45^{2}; cf 1 S 17^{7} & Is 60$^{17\ 17}$ (fig) **2.** *tool* of iron Dt 27^{5} Jos 8^{31} Pr 27$^{17\ 17}$ Ec 10^{10} Is 10^{34} (metaph); head of an axe Dt 19^{5} 2 K 6$^{5\ 6}$, so *weapon* 2 S 23^{7} Jb 41^{19}; cf also Nu 31^{22} Jos 22^{8} where iron as spoil of war **3.** *iron* in fig of unwatered earth Dt 28^{23}; of Egyptian bondage, כּוּר הַבּ׳ Dt 4^{20} 1 K 8^{51} Je 11^{4}, of oppression עֹל ב׳ Dt 28^{48} Je 28^{14} cf. v^{13}, of strength קֶרֶן ב׳ Mi 4^{13}, cf ב׳ מִנְעָלֶיךָ Dt 33^{25} & Je 15$^{12\ 12}$, of prophet, firm through Yahweh's might, עַמּוּד ב׳ Je 1^{18}, of distress, בְּרִיחֵי ב׳ ψ 107^{16} cf v^{10} of judgments of ׳ה, & 105^{18}, שֵׁבֶט ב׳ ψ 2^{9}; of evil-doers, Je 6^{28} Ez 22$^{18.20}$, simile of scorching sky Lv 26^{19}, מְטִיל ב׳ of bones of hippopotamus Jb 40^{18}, גִּיד ב׳ of obstinate neck of Isr. Is 48^{4}.

† **בַּרְזִלַּי** **n.pr.m.** (*man of iron*)—**1.** a Gileadite 2 S 17^{27} 19$^{32\ 33.35.40}$ 1 K 2^{7}, בַּרְזִלָּי 2 S 19^{34}; Ezr 2^{61} = Ne 7^{63} בני בַרְזִלַּי אֲשֶׁר לָקַח מבנות בַּרְזִלַּי הַגִּלְעָדִי וַיִּקָּרֵא עַל־שְׁמָם, where 2nd Barzillai = above, & former is **2** a priest Ezr 2^{61} = Ne 7^{63}, who adopted name בַּרְזִלַּי. **3.** 2 S 21^{8} a Meholathite.

† **בָּרַח** **vb** go through, flee (cf. Germ *durchgehen*) (Ar بَرِحَ *go away, withdraw, flee*) —**Qal** *Pf* בָּרַח Gn 31^{22} + 9 t, בָּרְחוּ Jb 9^{25}, בָּרָחוּ Is 22^{3}, *Impf.* יברח Jb 20^{24}, יִבְרָח Jb 27^{22} Ne 6^{11}, וַיִּבְרַח Gn 31^{21} + 13 t., 3 fs. וַתִּבְרַח Gn 16^{6}, אֶבְרָח ψ 139^{7}, יברחו Je 52^{7}, וַיִּברחו 2 S 4^{3} + 4 t., נִבְרָחָה 2 S 15^{14}, *Imv* בְּרַח Gn 27^{43} + 3 t., בִּרְחוּ Is 48^{20}, *Inf. abs* בָּרֹחַ Jb 27^{22}; *cstr.* ברח 1 S 23^{6} + 3 t, ברוח Jon 1^{3}, sf. בָּרְחִי 1 K 2^{7}, בָּרְחֲךָ Gn 31^{1}, בָּרְחוֹ Gn 35^{7} + 2 t.,—**1.** *go* or *pass through*, of bar, וַיַּעַשׂ אֶת־הַבְּרִיחַ...לִבְרֹחַ Ex 36^{33} (P) **2.** *flee* Gn 31$^{20\ 21\ 22}$ (E) Ex 14^{5} (J) Ju 9^{21} 1 S 19$^{12\ 18}$ 22^{17} 2 S 13$^{34\ 37\ 38}$ (del. Dr cf. We) 15^{14} Is 22^{3} Je 4^{29} 26^{21} 39^{4} 52^{7} Ne 6^{11}, fig of days fleeing away

Jb 9^{25}; of man, like a shadow Jb 14^{2}; c מִן *flee from* a place 1 S 20^{1} 2 S 19^{10} (+ מֵעַל pers) Is 48^{20}, a weapon Jb 20^{24}, a person, c. מֵאֵת 1 K 11^{23}, usually c מִפְּנֵי Gn 16$^{6.8}$ 31^{27} 35^{17} Ex 2^{15} (all JE) Ju 11^{3} 2 S 21^{11} 1 K 2^{7} 12^{2} = 2 Ch 10^{2} ψ 3^{1} 57^{1} (titles) 139^{7} Jon 1^{10}, מִיַּד ׳י fig. Jb 27^{22}, *flee to*, c acc place 1 S 27^{4} 1 K 11^{40} Ho 12^{13}, c place & לְ Ne 13^{10}, c place & ־ָה loc Jon 1^{3} 4^{2} 2 S 4^{3}, c place & אֶל־ Nu 24^{11} Am 7^{12}, c אֶל־ & pers 1 S 23^{6} Gn 27^{43} (J) 1 K 2^{39} 1 K 11^{40}, אַחֲרֵי & pers 1 S 22^{20}, *flee*, sq inf 1 K 11^{17} Dn 10^{7} **3.** flee=*hasten, come quickly* Ct 8^{14} **Hiph.** *Pf* הִבְרִיחוּ 1 Ch 8^{13}, *Impf* יַבְרִיחַ Pr 19^{26}, sf יַבְרִיחֶנּוּ Jb 41^{20}, וָאַבְרִיחֵהוּ Ne 13^{28}, וַיַּבְרִיחוּ 1 Ch 12^{15}, *Pt* מַבְרִיחַ Ex 26^{28},—**1.** *pass through*, lit Ex 26^{28} (P) cf **Qal** **2.** *cause to flee, put to flight*, animal Jb 41^{20}, men 1 Ch 8^{13} 12^{16}; *drive away* Pr 19^{16} Ne 13^{28} (sq מֵעָלַי)

† I [בָּרִחַ] **adj. fleeing** (=* בָּרִיחַ): נָחָשׁ בָּרִחַ Jb 26^{13} of eclipse-dragon, לִוְיָתָן נָחָשׁ בָּרִחַ Is 27^{1} (prob fig of Assyrians); as subst. בָּרִיחִים Is 43^{14} *as fugitives* (for other views cf Comm), so prob also Is 15^{5} בריחיה, v בְּרִיחַ

† II בָּרִיחַ **n.pr.m.** son of Shemaiah 1 Ch 3^{22}

† בְּרִיחַ **n m** bar (cf As *burûḫu, spear-shaft, spear*, COT^{Gloss})—בְּרִיחַ Dt 3^{5} + 11 t. (cstr Am 1^{5} etc), בריחו Ex 35^{11} 39^{33} Kt (Qr both ־יחָיו needless), pl בְּרִיחִם Ex 26^{26} + 8 t, בריחים 2 Ch 14^{6}, בְּרִיחֵי Ex 36^{31} + 3 t., בְּרִיחַיִךְ Na 3^{13}, בְּרִיחָיו Ex 40^{18} + 7 t (+ Qr Ex 35^{11} 39^{33}), בְּרִיחֶיהָ Je 51^{30} La 2^{9}, בְּרִחֶיהָ Jon 2^{7}, בְּרִיחֶהָ Is 15^{5} but cf infr,—**1. a.** *bar*, of wood, joining boards of tabern Ex 26$^{26.27\ 27\ 28.29\ 29}$ 35^{11} 36$^{31\ 32.32.33.34\ 34}$ 40^{18} Nu 3^{36} 4^{31} (all P) **b.** *bar*(*s*) of city-gates Dt 3^{5} Ju 16^{3} 1 S 23^{7} 2 Ch 8^{5} 14^{6}; *id.* of gates of Jerusalem La 2^{9}, also (‖ מנעולים) Ne 3$^{3\ 6\ 13\ 14\ 15}$ cf ψ 147^{13}, cf. Am 1^{5} Na 3^{13} Je 49^{31} Ez 38^{11} Je 51^{30}; bars of city-gates, ב׳ נחשת 1 K 4^{13}, ב׳ ברזל Is 45^{2} (of Babylon, broken bef Cyrus); בְּרִיחֶהָ Is 15^{5} rd prob c 𝔗 Di al בָּר׳ v בָּרִחַ; yet cf. Che's crit n **2.** fig ב׳ בַּרְזֶל of distress, etc ψ 107^{16}, of fortress, ב׳ אַרְמוֹן in simile Pr 18^{19}, fig ב׳ of earth (pictured as house out of which Jonah is shut) Jon 2^{7}. (Older usage *sg.* of bar of door or gate, i e the great bar across the gate, so Dt 3^{5} Ju 16^{3} Am 1^{5} 1 S 23^{7} 1 K 4^{13} Je 49^{31} Pr 18^{9} Jb 38^{10} 2 Ch 8^{5} Ez 38^{11} Later *pl.* Is 45^{2} La 2^{9} 2 Ch 14^{6} Ne 3$^{3\ 6\ 13\ 14\ 15}$ ψ 147^{13}, but also Na 3^{13})

† [מִבְרָח] **n.m.** (flight) fugitive—Ez 17^{21} מברחו Kt coll, מִבְרָחָיו Qr, Co rds Qr, but del. as gloss; 𝔗 𝔖 Ew Sm rd. מִבְחָרָיו

בַּרְחֻמִי 2 S 23^{31} = בַּחֲרוּמִי 1 Ch 11^{33}, rd prob. בַּחֲרֻמִי v. sub בחר & cf. Dr.

בֵּרִי **n.pr.m.** v sub באר p 92

בְּרִי Jb 37^{11} v. רִי sub רוה.

[בָּרִי], בִּרְיָה v. בָּרִיא sub II ברא

בֵּרִים 2 S 20^{14} obscure, many after 𝔙 rd. בַּחֻרִים, Klo prefers הַבְּכָרִים after 𝔊 & so Dr.

בְּרִית v sub II. ברה, v. also אֵל **3,** בַּעַל **4.**

בֹּרִית v sub ברר.

† [בָּרַךְ]$_{329}$ **vb. kneel, bless** (NH *id.*, Ar. بَرَكَ, Eth **በረከ:** Aram ברך, ܒܪܟ (*praise*), Palm esp in בריך שמו לעלמא Vog$^{Palm\ 74\ ff\ cf\ 94\ 144}$)—**Qal** *Impf* יִבְרַךְ 2 Ch 6^{13}, נִבְרְכָה ψ 95^{6}; בָּרוּךְ (v. **Pi.**), *Pt. pass* בָּרוּךְ Gn 9^{26} + 70 t,—**1.** *kneel down* (so Ar Syr Eth) וַיִּבְרַךְ עַל־בִּרְכָּיו *and he kneeled upon his knees* 2 Ch 6^{13}, נִבְרְכָה לִפְנֵי ׳י *let us kneel before Yahweh* ψ 95^{6} **2.** *bless* (only pt pass) **a** *of God.* בָּרוּךְ ׳י *blessed be* (or *is*) ׳י Ex 18^{10} (E) Gn 9^{26} 24^{27} (J) Ru 4^{14} 1 S 25$^{32.39}$ 2 S 18^{28} 1 K 1^{48} 5^{21} 8$^{15.56}$ 10^{9} 1 Ch 16^{36} 29^{10} 2 Ch 2^{11} 6^{4} 9^{8} Ezr 7^{27} ψ 28^{6} 31^{22} 41^{14} 72^{18} 89^{53} 106^{48} 119^{12} 124^{6} 135^{21} 144^{1} Zc 11^{5}, ב׳ אלהים ψ 66^{20} 68^{36}, ב׳ אדני ψ 68^{20} (prob. for an original יהוה), ב׳ אל עליון Gn 14^{20} (E), ב׳ צורי 2 S 22^{47} (= ψ 18^{47}), ב׳ כבוד ׳י Ez 3^{12}, ב׳ שם כבודו ψ 72^{19} **b.** *of men* Gn 27^{33} (J) Nu 22^{12} (E) Dt 7^{14} 28$^{3.6}$ 33$^{20.24}$ 1 S 25^{33} 26^{25} Ju 17^{2} 1 K 2^{45} ψ 118^{26} Is 19^{25} Je 17^{7} 20^{14}; מברכך ברוך *blessed be the one blessing thee* Gn 27^{29} Nu 24^{9} (E), ב׳ ליהוה Ru 2$^{19.20}$ 3^{10} 1 S 15^{13} 23^{21} 2 S 2^{5} ψ 115^{15}, ב׳ לאל עליון Gn 14^{19}, ברוך ׳י Gn 24^{31} 26^{29} (J), ברוכי ׳י Is 65^{23}. **c.** *things*· בָּרוּךְ פרי בטנך *blessed be the fruit of thy womb* Dt 28^{4} cf. Dt 28^{5} 1 S 25^{33} Pr 5^{18}. **Niph.** *Pf* נִבְרְכוּ Gn 12^{3} 18^{18} 28^{14} (J) *bless oneself* (cf **Hithp.**) **Pi.**$_{233}$ *Pf* בֵּרַךְ Gn 24^{1} + 29 t, בֵּרֵךְ ψ 10^{3} Nu 23^{20}; בֵּרְכוּ 2 Ch 20^{26}, וּבֵרְכוּ Jb 1^{5}, sf בֵּרְכוֹ, בֵּרְכַנִי, etc, Gn 27^{27} + 5 t., בֵּרַכְךָ Dt 2^{7} + 9 t; *Impf* יְבָרֵךְ, וַיְבָרֶךְ etc, Gn 28^{3} + 52 t.; אֲבָרְכָה Gn 12^{3} + 2 t.; pl יְבָרְכוּ Gn 24^{60} + 11 t, sf יְבָרֶכְךָ Gn 27^{10} + 21 t; יְבָרֲכֵךְ Gn 49^{25} + 2 t; יְבָרְכֵהוּ Gn 14^{19} + 16 t, יְבָרֲכֵם Gn 48^{20} + 6 t, אֲבָרֶכְכָה Gn 27^{7}, תְּבָרְכַנִי Gn 27$^{19.31}$, יְבָרֲכֶנְהוּ ψ 72^{15}; יְבָרְכוּכָה ψ 145^{10}; *Imv* בָּרֵךְ Dt 33^{11} + 29 t, *Inf* cstr בָּרֵךְ Gn 22^{17} + 24 t, *Inf* abs בָּרוֹךְ Jos 24^{10} (Ki, cf. Ko$^{i\ 191}$, Ew$^{§\ 240\ b.\ 2}$ Ol Sta), *Pt* מְבָרֵךְ Pr 27^{14} + 4 t.,—**1.** *bless God*, adore with

bended knees: acc. ברך י׳ Gn 24^{48} (J) Dt 8^{10} Ju 5$^{2.9}$ 1 Ch 29$^{10.20}$ 2 Ch 20^{26} 31^{8} Ne 9^{5} ψ 16^{7} 26^{12} 34^{2} 63^{5} 103$^{20.21.22}$ 115^{18} 134$^{1.2}$ 135$^{19.20}$ 145$^{2.10}$; ברכי נפשי את י׳ ψ 103$^{1.2.22}$ 104$^{1.35}$; ברך שם *bless the name of Yahweh* Ne 9^{5} ψ 96^{2} 100^{4} 145$^{1.21}$; ברך אלהים Jos 22^{33} ψ 66^{8} 68^{27} (doubtless for an original יהוה), with לְ 1 Ch 29^{20}; מְבָרֵךְ אָוֶן Is 66^{3} (of idolatrous worship). **2.** *God blesses* **a.** *men:* abs. Nu 23^{20} (E) ψ 109^{28}; with acc. Gn 32$^{27.30}$ 48^{16} Ex 20^{24} Nu 24^{1} Jos 24^{10} (E) Gn 12$^{2.3}$ 22^{17} 24$^{1.35}$ 26^{12} 30$^{27.30}$ 39^{5} 49^{25} Jos 17^{14} (J) Gn 1$^{22.28}$ 5^{2} 9^{1} 17$^{16.20}$ 25^{11} 26$^{3.24}$ 28^{3} 35^{9} 48^{3} Nu 6$^{24.27}$ (P) Dt 1^{11} 2^{7} 7^{13} 12^{7} 14$^{24.29}$ 15$^{4.6.10.14.18}$ 16$^{10.15}$ 23^{21} 24$^{13.19}$ 26^{15} 28^{8} 30^{16} Ju 13^{24} 2 S 6$^{11.12}$ 7^{29} 1 Ch 4^{10} 13^{14} 17^{27} 26^{5} 2 Ch 31^{10} Ne 8^{6} Ru 2^{4} Jb 42^{12} ψ 5^{13} 28^{9} 29^{11} 45^{3} 67$^{2.7.8}$ 107^{38} 115$^{12.13}$ 128^{5} 134^{3} 147^{13} Pr 3^{33} Is 19^{25} 51^{2} 61^{9} Je 31^{23} Hg 2^{19}. **b.** *things:* sabbath Gn 2^{3} Ex 20^{11} (P); field Gn 27^{27} (E); bread Ex 23^{25} (E); work Dt 28^{12} Jb 1^{10} cf. Dt 33^{11} ψ 65^{11} 132^{15}. **3.** *men bless men:* priests & kings בשם י׳ Dt 10^{8} 21^{5} 2 S 6^{18} 1 Ch 16^{2} 23^{13} ψ 129^{8}; Melchizedek Abraham Gn 14^{19}; Moses Dt 33^{1} Ex 12^{32} 39^{43}; Joshua Jos 14^{13} 22$^{6.7}$; priests Lv 9$^{22.23}$ Nu 6^{23} Dt 27^{12} Jos 8^{33} 2 Ch 30^{27} ψ 118^{26}; Solomon 1 K 8$^{14.55}$ (=2 Ch 6^{3}); David 2 S 6^{20} (=1 Ch 16^{43}) 19^{40}; Eli 1 S 2^{20}; Balaam Nu 22^{6} 23$^{11.20.25}$ 24^{10}; fathers, esp. on death-bed Gn 27^{4} + 12 t. Gn 27 (all JE) 28$^{1.6}$ (P) 32^{1} (E) 48^{9} (P) 48$^{15.20}$ 49^{28} (J) 2 S 13^{25}; in consecrating a sacrifice 1 S 9^{13}. **4.** *salute, greet,* with an invocation of blessing (stronger than שלום): בך יברך ישׂראל *with thee will Israel bless* Gn 48^{20} (E). **a.** *in meeting* Gn 47^{7} (P) 2 K 4^{29} 10^{15} 1 S 13^{10}. **b.** *in departing* Gn 24^{60} (J) 47^{10} (P) 1 K 8^{66}. **c.** *by messengers* 1 S 25^{14} 2 S 8^{10} 1 Ch 18^{10}. **d.** *in gratitude* Jb 31^{20} Pr 30^{11} Ne 11^{2}. **e.** *morning salutation* Pr 27^{14}. **f.** *congratulations* for prosperity Gn 12^{3} (J) 27^{29} Nu 24^{9} (E) 1 K 1^{47} ψ 49^{19} 62^{5}. **g.** *in homage* 2 S 14^{22} ψ 72^{15}. **h.** *in friendliness* 2 S 21^{3}. **5.** *bless,* with the antithetical meaning *curse* (Thes) from the greeting in departing, saying adieu to, taking leave of; but rather a blessing over-done and so really a curse as in vulgar English as well as in the Shemitic cognates: 1 K 21$^{10.13}$ Jb 1$^{5.11}$ 2$^{5.9}$ ψ 10^{3}. **Pu.** *Impf.* יְבֹרַךְ 2 S 7^{29} + 3 t.; תְּבֹרַךְ Ju 5^{24} Pr 20^{21}; *Pt.* מְבֹרָךְ Nu 22^{6} + 3 t.; f. מְבֹרֶכֶת Dt 33^{13}; מְבֹרָכָיו ψ 37^{22};—**1.** pass. *to be blessed, adored:* שם י׳ Jb 1^{21} ψ 113^{2}. **2.** *prospered by God:* **a.** persons 2 S 7^{29} 1 Ch 17^{27} ψ 37^{22} 112^{2} 128^{4} Pr 20^{21}. **b.** things Dt 33^{13}. **3.** *have prosperity invoked,* by Balaam Nu 22^{6}. **4.** *in gratitude* Pr 22^{9} Ju 5^{24}. **Hiph.** וַיַּבְרֵךְ הַגְּמַלִּים *and he made his camels kneel* Gn 24^{11} (J). **Hithp.** הִתְבָּרֵךְ Dt 29^{18} + 3 t.; *Impf.* יִתְבָּרֵךְ Is 65^{16} ψ 72^{17}; *Pt.* מִתְבָּרֵךְ Is 65^{16};—*bless oneself,* congratulate oneself בלבבו in his heart Dt 29^{18}; בזרעך with or by (cf. בְּ III. **2. d**) thy seed (invoke for oneself the blessing of the seed of Abraham) Gn 22^{18} 26^{4} (J); by the Messianic king ψ 72^{17}; באלהי אמן Is 65^{16}; by י׳ Je 4^{2}.

†בֶּ֫רֶךְ **n.f.** $^{Is. 45, 23}$ knee (As. *birku* COT^{Gloss}; Eth. ብርክ: Aram. בְּרַךְ, ܒܘܪܟܐ) Is 45^{23}; du. בִּרְכַּיִם Jb 3^{12} + 10 t.; sf. בִּרְכַּי etc. Gn 30^{3} + 11 t.;—*knee, knees:* מים ברכים water reaching to the knees Ez 47^{4}; וַתְּנִיעֵנִי על ברכי Dn 10^{10}; יַכְּכָה בשחין רע על הברכים Dt 28^{35}; כרע על ברכים *kneel on knees* in worship 1 K 8^{54} Ezr 9^{5} cf. Is 45^{23} 1 K 19^{18} 2 Ch 6^{13}, in entreaty 2 K 1^{13}, to drink of a fountain Ju 7$^{5.6}$; שׂם פניו בין ברכיו *put his face between his knees* in prayer 1 K 18^{42}; על ברכים *upon the knees,* Gn 30^{3} (E; on תֵּלֵד עַל ב׳ v. Ploss $^{Das\ Weib\ Aufl.\ 2.\ ii.\ 180\ ff.}$ Sta $^{ZAW\ 1886,\ 143\ ff.}$) 50^{23} (E) Jb 3^{12} Ju 16^{19} 2 K 4^{20} Is 66^{12}; הוציא מעם ברכים Gn 48^{12} (E); knees as seat of strength, weak from terror Jb 4^{4} Is 35^{3} Ez 7^{17} 21^{12} Na 2^{11}; or fasting ψ 109^{24}.

†I. בְּרָכָה **n.f.** blessing (Ar. بَرَكَة; Eth. በረከት: Aram. בִּרְכָּא, ܒܘܪܟܬܐ; NH as Heb.)—ב׳ Gn 12^{2} + 39 t.; cstr. בִּרְכַּת Gn 28^{4} + 9 t.; sf. בִּרְכָתִי Gn 49^{28} + 7 t.; pl. בְּרָכוֹת ψ 21^{7} + 4 t.; cstr. בִּרְכוֹת, בִּרְכֹת Gn 49^{25} + 5 t.; sf. בִּרְכוֹתֵיכֶם Mal 2^{2};—**1.** *blessing:* **a.** *of parent* Gn 27$^{12-41}$ 49^{28} (JE), of Moses Dt 33^{1}. **b.** *of God* Ex 32^{29} (E) Lv 25^{21} (P) Dt 11$^{26.27.29}$ 23^{6} (=Ne 13^{2}) 28$^{2.8}$ 30$^{1.19}$ Jos 8^{34} (D) 2 S 7^{29} ψ 3^{9} 21^{4} 133^{3} Is 44^{3} Ez 34^{26} 44^{30} Jo 2^{14} Mal 3^{10}; ברכת יהוה Gn 39^{5} (J) Dt 12^{15} 16^{17} 33^{23} ψ 129^{8} Pr 10^{22}; ברכה מאת י׳ ψ 24^{5}; ברכת אברהם Gn 28^{4} (P), the blessing given to Abraham. **c.** *of the people,* in recognition of good men ψ 109^{17} Pr 10^{6} 11^{26} 24^{25} 28^{20}. **d.** *of a poor man,* in recognition of benefits Jb 29^{13}. **2.** *source of blessing:* Abraham Gn 12^{2} (J); Israel Is 19^{24} Ez 34^{26} Zc 8^{13}; seed of the righteous ψ 37^{26}; the king ψ 21^{7}; memory of the righteous Pr 10^{7}; new wine Is 65^{8}. **3.** *blessing, prosperity:* בברכת ישרים *by the prosperity of the upright* (the city is exalted) Pr 11^{11}; גם ברכות יעטה מורה *yea, the early rain covereth with blessings* ψ 84^{7} cf. Gn 49$^{25.26}$; וארותי את ברכותיכם *and I will curse your prosperity* Mal 2^{2}. **4.** *blessing, praise of God* Ne 9^{5}. **5.** *a gift, present* Gn 33^{11} (E) Jos 15^{19} (J) Ju 1^{15} 1 S 25^{27} 30^{26} 2 K 5^{15}; נֶפֶשׁ בְּרָכָה *a liberal person* Pr 11^{25} (cf. Syr. ܒܘܪܟܬܐ, Eth. በረከት:). **6.** *treaty of peace* 2 K 18^{31} = Is 36^{16}.

†II. בְּרָכָה **1. n.pr.loc.** valley in wilderness by Tekoa 2 Ch 20$^{26.26}$; mod. *Bereikût* cf. Be & reff. **2. n.pr.m.** one of David's band 1 Ch 12^{3}.

†בָּרוּךְ **n.pr.m.** (*blessed*) **1.** friend and amanuensis of Jeremiah Je $32^{12.13.16}$ 36^{4-32} $43^{3.6}$ $45^{1.2}$. **2** a priest, son of Zabbai (Zaccai) Ne 3^{20} 10^{7} **3.** son of Colhozeh, of the tribe of Judah Ne 11^{5}.

†בְּרֵכָה **n.f.** pool, pond (הברכה SI[5], Ar بِرْكَة, Sab ברכת Sab Denkm[73], Aram בְּרֵיכְתָא)—ב׳ 2 S $2^{13.13}$ 4^{12} 2 K 18^{17} (= Is 36^{2}) 20^{20} Ne 3^{16} Is 7^{3} $22^{9.11}$; cstr בְּרֵכַת 2 S 2^{13} 1 K 22^{38} Ne 2^{14} 3^{15} Na 2^{9}, pl ברכות Ec 2^{6} Ct 7^{5}

†בָּרַכְאֵל **n.pr.m.** (*Ēl doth bless*, cf Ph ברכבעל, Palm בלברך Vog[117], Bab *Barīki-ili* Opp JAs 1887 Nov.-Dec 536 f.) father of Elihu Jb $32^{2.6}$

†יְבֶרֶכְיָהוּ **n pr.m.** (=יְבָרְכְיָהוּ s *Yah blesseth* Ges § 27.3) father of a Zechariah in Isaiah's time Is 8^{2}, usually in abbreviated form as foll בֶּרֶכְיָה, **1.** son of Zerubbabel 1 Ch 3^{20} **2.** a Levite guard of the ark 1 Ch 9^{16} 15^{23} **3.** father of Meshullam, one of Nehemiah's chiefs Ne $3^{4.30}$ 6^{18}. **4.** father of the prophet Zechariah Zc 1^{1}=בְּרֶכְיָהוּ v[7], בֶּרֶכְיָהוּ also **5.** father of Asaph 1 Ch 6^{24} 15^{17} **6.** Ephraimite chief 2 Ch 28^{12}.

בֶּרֶכְיָה, בֶּרֶכְיָהוּ v יְבֶרֶכְיָהוּ supra

ברם (cf Ar بَرَمَ *twist a rope of two strands*)

†בְּרֹמִים **n.[m.]** variegated cloth (Ar بَرِيمٌ *rope* (or fabric) *of two strands* or *colours*, cf As *birmu*, a kind of clothing COT[Gloss], *burmu*, *iris*, Zim[BP 82], on *burūmu* cf Jen[Kosmol 6 ff]) ובגנזי ברמים Ez 27^{24}.

בַּרְנֵעַ cf קדש ב׳.

†בֶּרַע **n.pr.m.** king of Sodom Gn 14^{2} (√ unknown, 𝔊 Βαλλα)

†בְּרִיעָה **n.pr.m.** **1.** a son of Asher Gn $46^{17.17}$ Nu $26^{44.45}$ 1 Ch $7^{30.31}$ **2.** son of Ephraim 1 Ch 7^{23} (where expl as if fr בְּרָעָה) **3.** a Benjamite ברעה 1 Ch 8^{13}, בריעה 1 Ch 8^{16}. **4.** a Levite 1 Ch $23^{10.11}$

†בְּרִיעִי **adj gent.** c art. as n coll. משפחת הַבְּ׳ Nu 26^{44}.

†בָּרַק **vb. flash**, of lightning (Ar بَرَقَ *gleam, flash, lighten*, As *barāku* Zim[BP 76], Aram בְּרַק, ܒܪܰܩ, Eth በረቀ: Sab. ברק Hal[152] cf DHM ZMG 1875. 607)—**Qal** *Pf* בָּרַק so rd. after 𝔊 L 2 S 22^{15} & also in ∥ ψ 18^{15} (cf Klo Che crit n), *Imv* בְּרוֹק ψ 144^{6},—all c acc cogn בָּרָק, בְּרָקִים,—*flash*, trans *flash lightning*, subj ׳ה

†בָּרָק **n.m.** Ez 1.13 **lightning** (chiefly in poetry) (Ar. بَرْق, As *birku* COT[Gloss], Zim[BP 76. 82] Aram בְּרַק, ܒܰܪܩܳܐ)—abs ב׳ Jb 20^{25} + 7 t + 2 S 22^{15} (cf. infr.), cstr בְּרַק Dt 32^{41} + 2 t., pl בְּרָקִים Ex 19^{16} + 7 t, בְּרָקָיו ψ 97^{4},—*lightning*, **1.** lit. mostly pl = *lightnings, lightning-flashes* Ex 19^{16} ψ 18^{15} (in theoph., on 2 S 22^{15} v. infr) 77^{19} 97^{4} 135^{7} Jb 38^{35} Je 10^{13} 51^{16}; so in sim. of swift brightness Na 2^{5}, sg. only ψ 144^{6} 2 S 22^{15} (where however rd. בְּרָקִים בָּרָק cf. בָּרַק—so 𝔊L Klo Che, cf his crit n ψ 18^{15}), Ez 1^{13} (in vision), and in sim of brightness Dn 10^{6}, swift destruction Zc 9^{14} **2.** fig. (always sing) of flashing arrow-head Jb 20^{25}, cf ב׳ חרב Dt 32^{41}, ב׳ חנית Na 3^{3} Hb 3^{11}, cf *glitter* of weapon Ez $21^{15.20.33}$.

†בָּרָק **n.pr m.** (*lightning-flash*, cf. Pun *Barcas*, surname of Hamilcar, cf Nepos Hamilcar 1 1; Sab ברקם DHM ZMG, 1875, 602, Palm ברק Vog Palm 76) son of Abinoam, & leader of Israel Ju $4^{6.8.9.10.12.14.14.15.16.22}$ $5^{1.12.15}$.

בְּרַק cf בני ברק

†בָּרֶקֶת **n f.** a precious stone, **emerald**, acc to 𝔊 𝔙 Josephus, (from *flashing, sparkling;* Lag[Rel Jur Eccl 2] comp. Skr *marakata*, Gk μάραγδος, ζμάραγδος) Ex 28^{17} 39^{10} (both P)

†בָּרְקַת **n.f.** id, Ez 28^{13}, cf. Ges § 80 R 2 Pinsk Etal 73

†בַּרְקוֹס **n pr.m.** (√ & mng unknown; Bab *Barkūsu* Dl[Pr 212]) head of a family of Nethinim, בני־ב׳ Ezr 2^{53}=Ne 7^{55}

†בַּרְקָנִים **n.m.pl.** briers (so Vrss Ki al, also Stu q v, Be, √unknown, cf ∥קוֹצִים; >J D. Michaelis, Thes al *threshing-sledges*, furnished with sharp (*glittering*) stones) Ju 8^{7} ודשתי אֶת־בְּשַׂרְכֶם את־קוֹצֵי הַמִּדְבָּר וְאֶת־הַבּ׳ (so d also דוש) *and I will thresh your flesh together with the thorns of the wilderness and the briers;* v[16] וַיִּקַּח אֶת־זִקְנֵי הָעִיר וְאֶת־קוֹצֵי הַמִּדְבָּר וְאֶת הַבּ׳ וַיֹּדַע בָּהֶם את אַנְשֵׁי סֻכּוֹת (rd וַיָּדָשׁ for וַיֹּדַע 𝔊 Bu[RS 114]; cf Stu Be) *and he took the thorns of the wilderness and the briers and threshed*, etc

†[בָּרַר] **vb. purify, select** (cf. As. *barāru*, *be shining*, in deriv. Zim[BP 46 73] Belser[BAS II 104]; Ar بَرَّ *pious, kind, true;* بَرَّ *he was pious, good, virtuous, honest*)—**Qal** *Pf.* בָּרוֹתִי Ez 20^{38}, *Inf* sf לְבָרָם Ec 3^{18}, Ges § 67 R 3, cf. לָבוּר 9^{1} (si vera l) as metaplastic form, but on text vid בור supra p 101; *Pt* pass m בָּרוּר Jb 33^{3} + 4 t, f בְּרוּרָה Ne 5^{18} Zp 3^{9};—**1.** *purge out, purify* · וּבָרוֹתִי

מִכֶּם הַמֹּרְדִים *and I will purge out from among you the rebels* Ez 20[38]; שָׂפָה ברוּרָה *a purified lip* Zp 3[9]; בָּרוּר מִלֵּלוּ *utter in a pure, sincere manner* Jb 33[3]. **2.** *choose, select*, only *Pt.* and in Chronicler: chosen, valiant men 1 Ch 7[40]; porters 1 Ch 9[22]; musicians 1 Ch 16[41]; sheep Ne 5[18]. **3.** *cleanse, make shining, polish*, pt. pass. חֵץ בָּרוּר *polished arrow* Is 49[2] (cf De & Je 51[11] infr.) **4.** *test, prove* Ec 3[18] לְבָרָם הָאֱלֹהִים *that God may prove them* (RV);—on 9[1] v. בּוּר. **Niph.** הִבָּרוּ Is 52[11], *Pt.* נָבָר 2 S 22[27] (=ψ 18[27]);—*purify oneself* **a.** ceremonially, the bearers of the sacred vessels Is 52[11]. **b.** morally 2 S 22[27]=ψ 18[27] **Pi.** *Inf.* לְבָרֵר Dn 11[35] *purify* (‖ לִצְרוֹף, לְלַבֵּן). **Hiph. 1.** *Inf* לְהָבַר Je 4[11] *purify, cleanse.* **2.** *Imv.* הָבֵרוּ הַחִצִּים Je 51[11] *polish arrows* (vid **3** above). **Hithp. 1.** *Impf.* יִתְבָּרְרוּ Dn 12[10] *purify oneself.* **2.** תִּתְבָּרָר ψ 18[27]=תִּתָּבָר 2 S 22[27] *shew oneself pure, just, kind.*

†II. בַּר **adj.** pure, clean, Jb 11[4] ψ 24[4]; בָּר Pr 14[4]; pl. cstr. בָּרֵי ψ 73[1]; f. בָּרָה ψ 19[9] Ct 6[9.10],—**1.** *pure, clear:* בר לבב *pure in heart* ψ 24[4]; ברי לבב ψ 73[1]; a pure damsel Ct 6[9.10], man Jb 11[4], commands of God ψ 19[9]. **2.** *clean* אבוס בָּר *crib is clean* Pr 14[4]. **3.** perh. adv נַשְּׁקוּ־בַר *kiss purely*, of *sincere* homage ψ 2[12] but cf. I בַּר, p. 135.

†III. בַּר **n.m. grain, corn** (cf Ar بُرّ *wheat, grain of wheat*), ψ 72[16] Am 5[11] 8[5.6], בָּר Gn 41[35.49] 42[3.25] 45[23] (E) ψ 65[14] Pr 11[26] Je 23[28] Jo 2[24].

†I. בֹּר **n.m. lye, potash,** alkali used in smelting metals Is 1[25] (see בֹּרִית)

†II. בֹּר **n.m. cleanness, pureness** · בֹר יָדַי *cleanness of my hands* 2 S 22[21] (=ψ 18[21]) ψ 18[25] (=בֹּרִי *my cleanness* 2 S 22[25]); בֹּר כַּפָּי Jb 9[30] 22[30].

†בֹּרִית **n.f. lye, alkali, potash, soap,** used in washing Je 2[22] Mal 3[2].

†בָּר **n.m. field** (BAram בָּרָא, Syr ܒܪܐ, Ar. بَرّ *open country, land*)—יִרְבּוּ בַבָּר *they grow up in the open field* Jb 39[4] (Aram. usage)

†בַּרְבֻּרִים **n.m.pl.** birds fattened for table of Solomon 1 K 5[3], *capons* Ki, *geese* (from their pure white feathers) 𝔗[Jer] Thes, *swans* Ew, *guinea-hens* Th, *fowls* Tristr AV RV (ברברי= ינשוף water-birds Lv 11[17] 𝔗[Sam])

ברשׁ (√ of foll., meaning unknown).

†ברוש **n.m.**[Ho 14.9] cypress or fir (As. *burâšu* COT[Gloss], Aram. ברותא, ܒܪܘܬܐ cf. בְּרוֹת infr, v. also Gr. βράθυ, Lat *bratum, cypress, juniper* (PS), in favour of *cypress*, also 𝔊𝔖 & so Thes; in favour of *fir* or *pine*, 𝔙 Rob in RobGes (because cypress not now indigenous on Lebanon), cf also RS[Proph iv n. 20] who lays stress on Ph. n pr.loc. אי בשם(=איברושים)=Gr. Πιτυοῦσαι i.e. *isle of firs*,—v. further Schroed[Phön Spr. 99] Low[No 59] & *Brathu* as name of Hermon Philo Bybl. in Euseb[Praep. Evang i 10])—ברוש Ho 14[9]+4 t; בְּרוֹשִׁים 2 S 6[5]+11 t., ברשים Na 2[4], ברושיו Is 37[24], ברשיו 2 K 19[23];—**1.** (lit) a noble tree, usually ‖ ארז (exc. 2 S 6[5] 1 K 6[34] 2 Ch 3[5] ψ 104[17] Is 55[13] Ho 14[9] Na 2[4]), as standing and growing Is 14[8] 37[24] = 2 K 19[23], Is 41[19] 55[13] 60[13] (‖ הָדָר) (ארז=כבוד לבנון ‖) ψ 104[17] **2.** sim. of luxuriance, stateliness Ez 31[8], productiveness Ho 14[9] (Now thinks *cypress*), fig. for spear-shafts Na 2[4] Hi-St, but 𝔊 𝔖 פרשים; fig for mighty men Zc 11[2]. **3.** as material (always pl.), for building temple (עצי ב׳) 1 K 5[22.24] 6[34] cf 9[11] 2 Ch 2[7], עֵץ ב׳ (sing.) 2 Ch 3[5] (cf. Baer's n); צלעות ב׳ 1 K 6[15]; for ships (no עץ) Ez 27[5],—בְּכֹל עצי ברושים 2 S 6[5] appar.=*with all musical instruments made of fir*, but ‖ 1 Ch 13[8] בְּכָל־עֹז וּבשירים & so here 𝔊 We Dr

†[בְּרוֹת] **n.m.** id. (Aramaic (prob North-Palest) form of same) only pl. ברותים ‖ אֲרָזִים Ct 1[17]; ref. to arbour of trees as their home, cf אֶרֶז

†בִּרְשַׁע **n.pr.m.** (√ & meaning unknown) king of Gomorrha Gn 14[2].

בְּרֹתָה, ברתי, בֵּרֹתַי v. sub בארות, p. 92.

בשׂם

(*have a sweet odour*, cf. Aram. בסים, ܒܣܡ *be sweet, pleasant*, Pa. ܒܣܡ *to delight*, בְּסִימָא, *sweet;* Palm בשימא (משחא) Vog[JAs 1868, Août Sept. 153 I 12, 155 I 16, 18, 20 etc] *spiced (oil)*, cf. Reckendorf[ZMG 1888, 403], As *bašâmu*, Pa *make fine, beautiful* COT[Gloss])

בְּשָׂם, [בָּשָׂם] v בֹּשֶׂם

†בֶּשֶׂם **n.m.** [1 K 10. 10] **spice, balsam, balsam-tree** (Ar بَشَام, Aram בּוּסְמָא, ܒܣܡܐ, Gk. βάλσαμον, cf. Low[5-])—ב׳ Is 3[24]+, בֹּשֶׂם Ex 30[23] v. infr., בְּשָׂמִי Ct 5[1] (as if fr בָּשָׂם); pl. בְּשָׂמִים Ex 25[6]+18 t., בְּשָׂמָיו Ct 4[16],—**1.** *spice, perfume, sweet odour* Is 3[24]; קִנְּמָן־בֶּשֶׂם Ex 30[23] (ב׳ perh. so pointed to distinguish it from) קנה־בשם v[23],—with this cf Aram קני בוסמא, ܩܢܝ ܒܣܡܐ,—*spices* as costly, token of wealth 2 K 20[13] = Is 39[2] cf 2 Ch 32[27]; royal gifts 1 K 10[2.10.25]=2 Ch 9[1.19.24], cf sg 1 K 10[10]=2 Ch 9[9]; as article of commerce Ez 27[22], burnt at burial 2 Ch 16[14];

appointed for ingredient of the anointing oil Ex 25^{6} 35^{8} cf v^{28} (all P), cf. 1 Ch 9^{30} (Palm v supr), stored in temple 1 Ch 9^{29}, used for purifying the women of Ahasuerus Est 2^{12}; elsewhere only Ct 4$^{10.14}$ *spices*, v^{16} *balsam-juice*, gathered Ct 5^{1}; *balsam-tree* הָרֵי ב׳ Ct 8^{14}; *beds of balsam* עֲרֻגַת ב׳ Ct 6^{2}, cf עֲרוּגַת ב׳ Ct 5^{13} sim of lover's cheeks

†בָּשְׂמַת **n.pr.f.** (*perfume?*)—**1.** Hittite woman, a wife of Esau Gn 26^{34} (P), called daughter of Ishmael, and sister of Nebaioth Gn 36^{3} (but due prob to R, this daughter of Ishmael is מָחֲלַת in 28^{9} P), v also 36$^{4.10.13.17}$ (all P) (Sam has מחלת throughout Gn 36) **2.** daughter of Solomon, wife of Ahimaaz 1 K 4^{15}

†יִבְשָׂם **n pr.m.** a descendant of Issachar 1 Ch 7^{2}

†מִבְשָׂם **n.pr.m.** **1** a son of Ishmael Gn 25^{13} = 1 Ch 1^{29} **2.** a descendant of Simeon 1 Ch 4^{25}

†[בָּשַׂר] **vb. bear tidings** (√*rub, smooth the face*, cf Ar بَشَرَ *remove the face or surface of a thing*, cf Ar بَشِرَ *be glad, joyful*, بَشَّرَهُ بِمَوْلُودٍ *he rejoiced him with the message of the birth of a son*, Eth በሠረ: *bring a joyful message*, so As *bussuru* (Pa) Dl$^{Pr 170}$, Sab תבשר DHM^{MV}, also בשר n pr dei, بشير DHM$^{ZMG 1883 358}$, CIS$^{iv 1, 41 1 3}$)—**Pi.** *Pf* בִּשַּׂר Je 20^{15} + 2 t; *Impf* תְּבַשֵּׂר 2 S 18^{20} + 4 t, אֲבַשְּׂרָה 2 S 18^{19}, *Imv* בַּשְּׂרוּ 1 Ch 16^{23} = ψ 96^{2}, *Inf* לְבַשֵּׂר 1 S 31^{9} + 2 t; *Pt.* מְבַשֵּׂר Is 41^{27} + 6 t., f מְבַשֶּׂרֶת Is 40$^{9.9}$, pl. מְבַשְּׂרוֹת ψ 68^{12},—**1.** *gladden with good tidings* birth of a son Je 20^{15}, victory 1 S 31^{9} 2 S 1^{20} 1 Ch 10^{9} ψ 68^{12}, היה כמבשר בעיניו *he was in his eyes as a bearer of good tidings* 2 S 4^{10} **2.** *bear tidings* 2 S 18$^{19.20.20.26}$; even of evil 1 S 4^{17}, and so with acc בשר טוב 1 K 1^{42}. **3.** *herald as glad tidings* the salvation of God, *preach* (chiefly exilic usage) the advent of י׳ in salvation Na 2^{1} Is 40$^{9.9}$ 41^{27} 52$^{7.7}$, the praises of Yahweh 60^{6}, His righteousness in the great congregation ψ 40^{10}, His salvation daily ψ 96^{2} = 1 Ch 16^{23}, the Messianic servant preaches good tidings to the meek Is 61^{1}. **Hithp.** *Impf.* יִתְבַּשֵּׂר 2 S 18^{31} *receive good tidings* (so Kirkp Klo, cf Ar تَبَشَّرَ iv x, otherwise AV)

בָּשָׂר$_{266}$ **n.m. flesh** (cf Ar بَشَرٌ *skin*, Syr. ܒܣܪܐ, As *bišru*, *blood-relation*, Dl$^{As Stud 1 143, cf. Pr 170}$, Sab בשר תורם *flesh of bulls*)—Gn 2^{21} + 126 t; cstr בְּשַׂר Gn 17^{11} + 40 t; sf. בְּשָׂרִי etc ψ 16^{9} + 96 t., pl. בְּשָׂרִים Pr 14^{30},—**1.** *of the body* **a.** *of animals* Gn 41$^{2-19}$ Ex 21^{28} 22^{30} Nu 12^{12} (E) Nu 11$^{4.33}$ (JE) Gn 9^{4} + (P 30 t) Dt 12^{15} + (D 9 t.) Ju 6$^{19-21}$ 1 S 2$^{13.15}$ 1 K 17^{6} 19^{21} Jb 31^{31} 41^{15} ψ 50^{13} Pr 23^{20} Is 22^{13} 44$^{16.19}$ 65^{4} 66^{17} Je 7^{21} 11^{15} Ez 4^{14} + 6 t. Dn 10^{3} Ho 8^{13} Mi 3^{3} Hg 2^{12} Zc 11$^{9.16}$. **b** *of men* Gn 40^{19} (E) 2^{21} Ex 4^{7} (J) Lv 12^{3} 13^{2} + 16 t 26^{29} (P) Dt 28$^{53.55}$ 32^{42} Ju 8^{7} 1 S 17^{44} 1 K 4^{34} 5$^{10.14}$ 6^{30} 9^{36} Jb 2^{5} 4^{15} 6^{12} 7^{5} 10^{11} 13^{14} 19$^{20.22}$ 21^{6} 33$^{21.25}$ ψ 27^{2} 38$^{4.8}$ 79^{2} 102^{6} 109^{24} Pr 4^{22} 5^{11} Is 9^{19} 17^{4} 49^{26} Je 19^{9} La 3^{4} Ez 32^{5} 37$^{6.8}$ 39$^{17.18}$ Dn 1^{15} Zc 14^{12}. The flesh of the body is contrasted with stone Ez 11^{19} 36^{26} **2.** *flesh for the body itself* (esp in P) על בשר אדם לא ייסך *upon the body of man it shall not be poured* Ex 30^{32} (P), מכנסי בד ילבש על בשרו *linen drawers shall he put on his body* Lv 6^{3} 16^{4} (P); וישם שק על בשרו 1 K 21^{27}, ורחץ את בשרו *and he shall bathe his body* Lv 14^{9} 15$^{13.16}$ 16$^{24.26.28}$ 17^{16} 22^{6} Nu 19$^{7.8}$ (P), שרט לנפש לא תתנו בבשרכם *ye shall not put any cutting for any one in your body* Lv 19^{28} cf Lv 21^{5} (P), והעבירו תער על כל בשרם *and they shall pass a razor over all their body* Nu 8^{7} (P) Ec uses בשר only in this sense 2^{3} 4^{5} 5^{5} 11^{10} 12^{12}; elsewhere this usage only in poetry, the body antith to נפש Jb 14^{22} Is 10^{18} ψ 63^{2}; לב ψ 16^{9} 84^{3} Pr 14^{30} (only here emphatic pl = *entire body* Bö^{§695}, *Leiblichkeit* De); מִבְּשָׂרִי *apart from my body*, in disembodied state Jb 19^{26}, סמר מפחדך בשרי *my body trembleth for fear of thee* ψ 119^{120}. **3.** *male organ of generation* (euphemism). בְּשַׂר עָרְלַתְכֶם Gn 17$^{11.14.23.24.25}$ (P); בשר ערוה Ex 28^{42} (P), but בשׂר Gn 17^{14} Lv 15$^{2-19}$ (P) Ez 16^{26} 23^{20} 44$^{7.9}$. **4.** *flesh for kindred, blood-relations* עצם מעצמי ובשר מבשרי *bone of my bone and flesh of my flesh* Gn 2^{23} (J). והיו לבשׂר אחד *and they shall become one flesh* Gn 2^{24} (J), עצמי ובשרי Gn 29^{14} (J) Ju 9^{2} 2 S 5^{1} 19$^{13.14}$ 1 Ch 11^{1}, בשׂר with sf in same sense Gn 37^{27} (J) Ne 5^{5} Is 58^{7}, for which שְׁאֵר בשרו *near of kin*, man or woman Lv 18^{6} 25^{49} (both H; 25^{49} ‖ מִשְׁפָּחָה, cf RS$_{K}$ ^{149}) **5.** *man over against God as frail* or *erring* Gn 6^{3} (J) ψ 56^{5} 78^{39}, eyes of flesh Jb 10^{4}, arm of flesh 2 Ch 32^{8} Je 17^{5}, horses are flesh not spirit Is 31^{3}. **6.** the phrase כָּל־בָּשָׂר **a.** *all living beings* Gn 6$^{17.19}$ 7^{21} 9$^{11.15.16.17}$ Lv 17^{14} Nu 18^{15} (P) Jb 34^{15} ψ 136^{25}. **b.** *animals* Gn 7$^{15.16}$ 8^{17} (P) **c.** *mankind* Gn 6$^{12.13}$ Nu 16^{22} 27^{16} (P) Dt 5^{23} ψ 65^{3} 145^{21} Is 40$^{5.6}$ 49^{26} 66$^{16.23.24}$ Je 12^{12} 25^{31} 32^{27} 45^{5} Ez 21$^{4.9.10}$ Jo 3^{1} Zc 2^{17}, cf כל בשר איש Jb 12^{10}.

†בְּשׂרָה **n.f. tidings** (cf. Ar. بِشَارَةٌ v Ba$^{NB 61}$; Sab. בשרן DHM$^{ZMG 1876, 672}$), 2 S 4^{10} + 3 t; בְּשׂוֹרָה 2 S 18$^{25.27}$—**1.** *good tidings* 1 K

7^{9}. **2.** *tidings, news* 2 S $18^{20.25}$; with טובה 2 S 18^{27}. **3.** *reward for good tidings* 2 S 4^{10} 18^{22}.

†בְּשׂוֹר **n.pr.** of brook in Philistine territory; alw. נַחַל הַבְּשׂוֹר 1 S $30^{9.10.21}$; 𝔊 Βοσορ (v^{21} Βεανα, but 𝔊L Βοσορ); mod. *Wady Razze* (Gaza) acc. to Guérin $^{Judée\ ii.\ 213}$;—it empties into sea SW of Gaza. (Connexion with above √dub.)

†בָּשַׁל **vb.** boil, seethe (intr.), grow ripe (Aram. בְּשֵׁל, ܒܫܠ *ripen*, Nas. ܒܫܠ *boil*, NSyr. ܒܫܠ *be boiled, cooked*, cf. As. *bašâlu* (*bašlu*, *cooked*) Zim $^{BP\ 76}$)—**Qal** *Pf.* בָּשַׁל Jo 4^{13}, בָּשְׁלוּ Ez 24^{5};—*boil, cook* (intr.) Ez 24^{5}; *grow ripe* (of קָצִיר) Jo 4^{13};—**Pi.** *Pf.* 3 ms. sf. בִּשְּׁלָם 1 K 19^{21}; וּבִשַּׁלְתָּ Ex 29^{31} Dt 16^{7}, בִּשְּׁלוּ La 4^{10} + 2 t., וּבִשְּׁלוּ consec. Zc 14^{21}; *Impf.* 3 fs. וַתְּבַשֵּׁל 2 S 13^{8}; 2 ms. תְּבַשֵּׁל Ex 23^{19} + 2 t., יְבַשְּׁלוּ, וַיְבַשְּׁלוּ Ez $46^{20.24}$, 2 Ch 35^{13}, תְּבַשְּׁלוּ Ex 16^{23}, וַנְּבַשֵּׁל 2 K 6^{29}; *Imv.* בַּשֵּׁל 2 K 4^{38}, בַּשְּׁלוּ Lv 8^{31}, בַּשֵּׁלוּ Ex 16^{23}; *Inf.* בַּשֵּׁל 1 S 2^{13}; *Pt.* מְבַשְּׁלִים Ez 46^{24};—**1.** *boil* (tr.) obj. om. Nu 11^{8}, בָּשָׂר 1 S 2^{13}; גְּדִי Ex 23^{19} 34^{26} Dt 14^{21}; נזיד 2 K 4^{38}; of offerings, obj. הקדשים 2 Ch 35^{13}; obj. אשם Ez 46^{20}, זבח Ez 46^{24} (no obj.) v^{24}, cf. Zc 14^{21} (no obj.); Ex $16^{23.23}$ opp. אפה *bake*. **2.** *cook* (general), obj. בשר 1 K 19^{21} Ex 29^{31} Lv 8^{31} (both P); obj. בֵּן 2 K 6^{29} cf. יֶלֶד La 4^{10}; hence also of הפסח Dt 16^{7} (cf. Di; ‖ Ex $12^{8.9}$ has צְלִי אֵשׁ opp. (מְבֻשָּׁל בַּמָּיִם) 2 Ch 35^{13} (בָּאֵשׁ), cakes (הלבבות) 2 S 13^{8}. **Pu.** *Pf.* 3 fs. בֻּשָּׁלָה Lv 6^{21}; *Impf.* 3 fs. תְּבֻשַּׁל־ Lv 6^{21}; *Pt.* מְבֻשָּׁל Ex 12^{9} 1 S 2^{15};—*be boiled, sodden,* במים Ex 12^{9} cf. Lv $6^{21.21}$ (all P) 1 S 2^{15}. **Hiph.** *Pf.* הִבְשִׁילוּ *ripened, brought to ripeness* Gn 40^{10} (a vine, its grape-clusters).

†בָּשֵׁל **adj.** cooked, boiled (As. *bašlu*, *ripe* COT ^{Gloss})—Ex 12^{9} בָּשֵׁל מְבֻשָּׁל במים; f. בְּשֵׁלָה Nu 6^{19}, (both P).

†מְבַשְּׁלוֹת **n.f.pl.** cooking-places Ez 46^{23} (cf. בֵּית הַמְבַשְּׁלִים v^{24}).

†בִּשְׁלָם **n.pr.m.** (= בֶּן־שָׁלֹם *son of peace*? cf. sub בן) a Persian officer in Canaan Ezr 4^{7}.

בשן (√of foll. = *smooth, soft*? cf. Ar. بَثْنَةٌ, بِثْنَةٌ *soft and smooth ground*).

בָּשָׁן 60 **n.pr.terr.m.** $^{Dt\ 3,\ 3}$ (*smooth* (& fertile) land) Bashan, first mentioned as kingdom of Og, E. of Jordan, stretching from stream Jabboḳ (thus including northern Gilead) northward to Hermon, between Gennesaret (W) and mts of Hauran (E); cf. Di Nu 21^{33} Wetzst $^{Hauran\ 82}$; later a type of fertility;—usually c. art. הַבּ׳ Nu $21^{33.33}$ 32^{33} Dt 1^{4} + 30 t. Dt Jos; 1 K $4^{13.19}$ 2 K 10^{33} 1 Ch $5^{11.12.16.23}$ $6^{47.56}$ Ne 9^{22} ψ 68^{23} 135^{11} 136^{20} Je 22^{20} 50^{19} (‖ הַכַּרְמֶל), Mi 7^{14} (‖ *id.*), Na 1^{4} (‖ *id.*; personif., subj. of אֻמְלַל), Is 33^{9} (‖ *id.*; personif. subj. of נֹעֵר); הַר־בָּשָׁן (i.e. range of Hauran) ψ $68^{16.16}$ (called הַר־אלהים,—from a sanctuary there?—& הַר־גַּבְנֻנִּים *many-peaked mt.*); of stately trees אַלּוֹנֵי הַבּ׳ Is 2^{13} (still seen on western slope of mts. of Hauran, Wetzst $^{Hauran\ 88}$); אַלּוֹנֵי ב׳ Zc 11^{2} (fig. of prominent men); אַלּוֹנִים מִבּ׳ Ez 27^{6}; of bulls אַבִּירֵי ב׳ ψ 22^{13} (‖ פָּרִים, fig.); so בְּנֵי־ב׳ Dt 32^{14} (+ כָּרִים וְאֵילִים) also עַתּוּדִים, cf. בָּקָר & צֹאן v^{a}; vid. בֵּן **1. j.** (ν)); appar. more general is מְרִיאֵי ב׳ Ez 39^{18} (ref. to אֵילִים כָּרִים וְעַתּוּדִים פָּרִים . . . כֻּלָּם); once of kine (fem., fig. of luxurious and haughty women of Samaria) Am 4^{1} פָּרוֹת הַבּ׳.

†נִבְשָׁן **n.pr.loc.** in south. Judah הַנּ׳ Jos 15^{62}.

בָּשְׁנָה v. sub בוש.

†[בשס] **vb. Po.** *Inf.* sf. בּוֹשַׁסְכֶם Am 5^{11} prob. *your trampling* (by dissim. fr. בּוּס) sq. עַל.

בֹּשֶׁת v. sub בוש.

I. בַּת *daughter* v. sub בן.

II. בַּת *bath* (a measure), בַּתָּה v. sub בתת.

†I. בְּתוּאֵל **n.pr.m.** (? = מְתוּאֵל *man of God*) Gn $22^{22.23}$ $24^{15.24.47.50}$ (J) son of Nahor, neph. of Abr., living in Aram-Naharaim, in city of Nahor; 25^{20} $28^{2.5}$ (P) Aramaean of Paddan-Aram.

†II. בְּתוּאֵל **n.pr.loc.** in Simeon 1 Ch 4^{30} = בְּתוּל Jos 19^{4}; כְּסִיל 15^{30}; בֵּיתְאֵל 1 S 30^{27} (v. p. 111 supr.); yet cf. Lag $^{BN\ 64}$; site unknown.

בְּתוּל v. II. בְּתוּאֵל.

בִּתְיָה v. בַּת sub בן, p. 124.

בָּתִּים v. בית.

בתל (cf. Ar. بَتَلَ *sever, separate*).

†בְּתוּלָה 50 **n.f.** virgin (cf. Ar. بَتُولٌ, بَتِيلٌ, As. *batultu* (also *batûlu* of young man) 5 R 42^{56} v. Jer $^{ZA\ 1886,\ 399}$; NH בְּתוּלָא, ܒܬܘܠܬܐ)—Gn 24^{16} + 19 t.; cstr. בְּתוּלַת Dt 22^{19} + 12 t.; pl. בְּתוּלוֹת Est 2^{2} + 7 t.; בְּתֻלוֹת Zc 9^{17}; בְּתוּלֹת Ex 22^{16} + 2 t.; בְּתֻלֹת La 5^{11}; sf. בְּתוּלֹתָיו ψ 78^{63} + 3 t.;—one living apart in her father's house as *a virgin* Gn 24^{16} (J) Ex 22^{15} (E) Lv $21^{3.14}$ (P) Dt 22^{19} Ju 19^{24} 2 S 13^{2} Jb 31^{1} Is 62^{5} Je 2^{32} 31^{13} Jo 1^{8}; נערה בתולה *a virgin damsel* Dt $22^{23.28}$ Ju 21^{12} 1 K 1^{2} Est 2^{3}; בחור ובתולה Dt 32^{25} 2 Ch

36[17] Je 51[22] Ez 9[6], personification of nations בתולת ישראל Je 18[13] 31[4.21] Am 5[2]; ב׳ בת ציון 2 K 19[21] (= Is 37[22]; on double st. cstr v Ges § 130.5 Phi St Cstr 63) La 2[13], ב׳ בת עמי Je 14[17], ב׳ בת יהודה La 1[15]; ב׳ בת צידון Is 23[12], ב׳ בת בבל Is 47[1], ב׳ בת מצרים Je 46[11], pl. *virgins* Ex 22[16] 2 S 13[18] Est 2[2 17 19] ψ 45[15] 78[63] La 1[4] 2[10] 5[11] Ez 44[22] Am 8[13]; בחורים ובתולות ψ 148[12] Is 23[4] Zc 9[17] La 1[18] 2[21].

†בתולים **n.f. virginity,** pl. abs intens. Dt 22[14 17 20], cstr. בְּתוּלֵי Dt 22[15 17], all concrete, *tokens of virginity;* abstr, sf בתולי Ju 11[37], בתוּלֶיהָ Lv 21[13] Ju 11[38] Ez 23[3], בתוליהן Ez 23[3]

†[בָּתַק] **vb.** cut, cut off, cut down (As *batâku*, COT Gloss Zim BP 104 n, cf. also Ar. بَتَكَ *secuit, amputavit*)—only **Pi.** *Pf* consec וּבִתְּקוּךְ בחרבותם Ez 16[40] *and they shall cut thee to pieces with their swords*

†[בָּתַר] **vb.** cut in two (Ar بَتَرَ *cut off prematurely; extirpate by cutting*)—**Qal** *Pf* בָּתַר Gn 15[10], **Pi.** *Impf* וַיְבַתֵּר Gn 15[10] *id*

†[בֶּתֶר] **n.m.** Gn 15 10 **part, piece** **1.** בתרו Gn 15[10], pl. sf בְּתָרָיו Je 34[18], בתרי הָעֵגֶל Je 34[19], always of halves of animals cut in two in making covenants **2.** הָרֵי בָתֶר Ct 2[17] *mountains of cutting*, i e *cleft mountains* 𝔊 Thes al; or *of separation* (between us) Ew al., acc to We Prol. 415 Eng Tr 391 ב׳ = *malobathron.*—*Bether* as n pr AV RV

†בִּתְרוֹן prob **n.pr.terr.** (*cleft, ravine*) E of Jordan, כָּל־הַב׳ 2 S 2[29]

בתת (? *cut off, sever*, cf Ar بَتَّ, *secuit, resecuit, abrupit*)

†II בַּת **n.m.** Ez 45. 14 (**f.** Is 5. 10) **bath** (Thes al. fr above √ in sense of *define, measure;* cf. τέμνω, Lag Or. ii 10 f makes = בדת, = בד + fem ת, cf Syr. ܒܬ, instrument for pressing olives; cf. Epiphan. βάδος = ἐλαιοτριβεῖον, & βάδος also Hesych Jos Ant viii 2 9 but ed. Niese βάτους, βάτος)—ב׳ abs Is 5[10] + 6 t.; (בַּת Ez 45[11]) cstr. Ez 45[10]; pl בַּתִּים 2 Ch 2[9] + 3 t;—a liquid measure = אֵיפָה of dry measure, each being $\frac{1}{10}$ חֹמֶר (q v) Ez 45[11 11 14 14], also Is 5[10] 1 K 7[26.38] 2 Ch 2[9] 4[5] + Ez 45[14 14] (4 t in this v, Co del *a* & *d*). Ez 45[10] בַּת־צֶדֶק *a righteous* (right, accurate, full) *bath* (‖ אֵיפַת־צֶדֶק) The actual size of bath (= ephah) is appar. c 40 litres (= Attic *metretes* cf Jos Ant. viii 2. 9; = 39 39 lit cf. Boeckh Metrol Untersuch 259 f, v also J. Brandis Münz- Mass- u. Gewichtswesen 29 f. Smith Dict Bible, art. Weights & Measures Ri HWB 934 f) —I. בַּת v. sub בן

†[בַּתָּה] **n f. precipice, steep** (as *cut off, abrupt*)—בְּנַחֲלֵי הַבַּתּוֹת Is 7[19] *in the ravines of the precipices*

†בָּתָה **n.f. end, destruction** (for בָּתָה, perh. on account of difference of meaning, perh. fr. analogy of כָּלָה with like sense, cf Di)—וַאֲשִׁיתֵהוּ בָתָה Is 5[6] *and I will make it* (the vineyard) *a destruction*, a waste, or (Che) *make an end of it*

ג

ג, ג, *Gîmel*, third letter; in postB Heb. = numeral 3 (and so margin of printed MT); ג = 3000; no evidence of this usage in OT times

גא v sub גאה

†גָּאָה **vb. rise up** (Aram. Pe. (𝔗 1 S 2[3]) & oft Ethp אִתְגָּאִי, ܐܬܓܐܝ *be boastful, proud*, cf also NH)—**Qal** *Pf* ג׳ Ex 15[1 21], גָּאוּ Ez 47[5], *Impf.* יגאה Jb 8[11] 10[16], *Inf.* abs. גָּאֹה Ex 15[1.21],—**1.** *rise up*, of waters Ez 47[5]. **2.** *grow up*, of plants Jb 8[11] **3.** *be lifted up, exalted*, of head Jb 10[16], of י׳ in triumph Ex 15[1 21]

†גֵּא **adj.** proud, scribal error for גֵּאֶה Is 16[6] (as in Je 48[29])

†גֵּאֶה **adj.** proud, Jb 40[11 12] Is 2[12] Je 48[29], pl. גֵּאִים ψ 94[2] 140[6] Pr 15[25] 16[19]; cstr. גֵּאֵי ψ 123[4] Qr גאי יונים (> Kt גאייונים), yet cf. De al.

†גַּאֲוָה **n.f.** pride, Pr 8[13].

†גַּאֲוָה **n.f. majesty, pride** (cf. Syr ܓܐܘܬܐ)—Jb 41[7] + 6 t., cstr. גַּאֲוַת Pr 29[23] + 2 t., sf גַּאֲוָתִי Is 13[3] + 8 t.,—**1.** *rising up, swelling* of the sea ψ 46[4]. **2.** *majesty*, of Israel Dt 33[29], Moab Is 16[6] = Je 48[29], scales of crocodile Jb 41[7], of God Dt 33[26] ψ 68[35] **3.** *pride, haughtiness* ψ 10[2] 31[19.24] 36[12] 73[6] Pr 14[3] 29[23] Is 9[8] 13[11] 25[11], עַלִּיזֵי גאותי *my proudly exulting ones* Is 13[3] cf Zp 3[11].

†גָּאוֹן **n.m.** Ho 5. 5 **exaltation**— Jb 40[10] + 5 t., cstr. גְּאוֹן Lv 26[19] + 31 t.; sf. גאונך etc Ex 15[7] + 9 t.; pl sf גְּאוֹנַיִךְ Ez 16[56],—**1.** *exaltation, majesty, excellence*, **a.** of nations, their wealth, power, magnificence of buildings, e.g. Egypt Ez 32[12], Chaldeans Is 13[11 19] 14[11], Philistines Zc 9[6], Assyria Zc 10[11], Jacob ψ 47[5] Am

6^{8} 8^{7} Na 2^{3}, Israel Ho 5^{5} 7^{10} (prob appellation of 'י), Na 2^{3}, Judah Je 13^{9}, Jerusalem v^{9} Ez 16^{56}, גְּאוֹן עֻזָּהּ *pride of her strength* Ez 30$^{6.18}$ 33^{28}; גאון עזים Ez 7^{24} (but 𝔊 Ew Hi Co rd. עזם); גאון עזכם Lv 26^{19} Ez 24^{21}; the fruit of land of Judah will become לגאון ולתפארת *majestic and beautiful* Is 4^{2}, גאון כל צבי *the majesty of all the splendour* (of Tyre) Is 23^{9}, Zion is to become גאון עולם *an everlasting excellency* Is 60^{15}. **b.** of God Ex 15^{7} Is 24^{14} Mi 5^{3}; הֲדַר גאנו Is 2$^{10.19.21}$; יַרְעֵם בקול גאונו Jb 37^{4}, עֲדֵה נָא גָאוֹן וָגֹבַהּ Jb 40^{10} **c.** גאון הירדן *majesty of the Jordan*, referring to the green and shady banks, clothed with willows, tamarisks, and cane, in which the lions made their covert Je 49^{19} 50^{44} Zc 11^{3}, and therefore dangerous Je 12^{5} (Ew thinks of the *swelling* of its agitated waters), גאון גַּלֶּיךָ *majesty of thy waves* Jb 38^{11} **2.** *pride* (bad sense) Jb 35^{12} ψ 59^{13} Pr 8^{13} 16^{18} Ez 7^{20} 16^{49} Zp 2^{10}; of Moab Is 16$^{6.6}$ = Je 48$^{29.29}$

†גֵּאוּת **n.f.** majesty, ψ 93^{1} + 7 t.,—**1.** *lifting up* גאות עָשָׁן *column of smoke* Is 9^{17}; גאות הַיָּם *swelling of the sea* ψ 89^{10}. **2.** *majesty* of God ψ 93^{1} Is 26^{10}; גֵּאוּת עָשָׂה *he hath done majestically* Is 12^{5}; עֲטֶרֶת גאות *crown of majesty* Is 28$^{1.3}$ (Samaria, on a round hill majestically commanding the country) **3.** *pride* דִּבְּרוּ בגאות *they speak proudly* ψ 17^{10}; so for גאות 74^{20} Bi Che

†גְּאוּאֵל **n.pr.m.** (*majesty of Ēl*) the spy of the tribe of Gad Nu 13^{15}.

†[גַּאֲיוֹן] **adj.** proud, גאיונים ψ 123^{4} (Kt cf Baer's note, yet rd. prob גַּאֲיוֹנִים, but Qr better, גאי יונים *proudest oppressors*, v. גֵּאָה)

גאיונים v. foregoing, and also גאה

גֵּוָה **n.f.** pride (contr. for גַּאֲוָה Ew §62 b, 73 b cf. Aram Dn 4^{34} & 𝔗)—**1.** *pride* Jb 33^{17} Je 13^{17}. **2.** *lifting up* Jb 22^{29} an exclamation, *up!* Ew Di De al.; but *pride* Hi Dr § 154 n (ed. 3).

גֵּאָיוֹת v. גַּיְא

†I. גָּאַל **vb. redeem, act as kinsman** (NH, Niph. *be redeemed*; also גואל, גְּאֻלָּה (גאולה))—**Qal** *Pf* 'גָּ, etc Is 44^{23} + 14 t; *Impf* יִגְאַל, etc Lv 25^{33} + 18 t; *Imv.* גְּאַל, etc. Ru 4^{6} + 3 t; *Inf.* abs גָּאֹל Lv 27^{13} + 2 t; cstr לִגְאוֹל Ru 4^{4} + 2 t; sf. לְגָאָלֵךְ Ru 3^{13}, *Pt.* גאל Lv 25^{26} + 24 t, גואל Is 59^{20} ψ 103^{4}; sf גֹּאַלְךָ Is 48^{17}, גֹּאֲלֵךְ Is 54^{8} (sf 19 t.); pass. pl. גְּאוּלִים, etc. Is 35^{9} + 4 t,—**1.** *act as kinsman, do the part of next of kin* (chiefly in D H P Ru), גֹּאֵל *kinsman* Lv 25^{25} (H) Nu 5^{8} 35^{12} (P) Ru 2^{20} 3$^{9.12}$ 4$^{1.3.6.8.14}$ 1 K 16^{11}. **a.** in taking a kinsman's widow אם יגאלך טוב יגאל ואם לא יחפץ לגאלך וגאלתיך *if he will do thee the kinsman's part* (raise up children by the widow) *well, let him do the kinsman's part, but if he is not pleased to do thee the kinsman's part then I will do thee the kinsman's part* Ru 3^{13}; **b.** in redeeming from bondage Lv 25$^{48.49}$ (H); **c.** in redeeming a field Lv 25$^{26.33}$ (H) Ru 4$^{4.6}$, **d.** claim as kinsman Jb 3^{5}; **e.** גֹּאֵל הַדָּם *the avenger of blood* Nu 35$^{19.21.24.25.27.27}$ Jos 20$^{3.5}$(?, not in 𝔊) v^{9}(P) Dt 19$^{6.12}$ (D) 2 S 14^{11}. **2.** *redeem*, by payment of value assessed, of consecrated things, by the original owner Lv 27$^{13.15.19.20.31}$ (P). **3.** *redeem*, with God as subj implying personal relationship, chiefly in poetry —**a.** individuals, from death ψ 103^{4} La 3^{58} Ho 13^{14}, מכל רע Gn 48^{16} (E poetry), נפשׁ ψ 69^{19} 72^{14}, orphans Pr 23^{11} Je 50^{34}, ריבה ריבי וגאלני ψ 119^{154}, גֹּאֲלִי Jb 19^{25}, צורי וגֹאֲלִי ψ 19^{15} **b.** Israel, from Egyptian bondage Ex 6^{6} (P?) 15^{13} (song) ψ 74^{2} 77^{16} 78^{35}, מיד אויב ψ 106^{10}. **c.** from exile (chiefly Is^{2}, the vb. not in Is^{1}) Is 43^{1} 44$^{22.23}$ 48^{20} 52^{9} 63^{9} Mi 4^{10}, מיד ψ 107^{2} Je 31^{11}; Yahweh is גאל Is 41^{14} 43^{14} 44$^{6.24}$ 47^{4} 48^{17} 49$^{7.26}$ 54$^{5.8}$ 59^{20} 60^{16} 63^{16}; and the people גאולים Is 35^{9} 51^{10} 62^{12} 63^{4} (cf גאולי infr.), ψ 107^{2} **Niph.** *Pf* נִגְאַל Lv 25^{49}; *Impf.* יִגָּאֵל Lv 25^{30} + 5 t; תִּגָּאֵלוּ Is 52^{3},—**1.** refl. *redeem oneself* Lv 25^{49} (H) **2.** pass. *be redeemed*, **a.** field Lv 25^{30} (H), slave Lv 25^{54} (H), **b.** consecrated things Lv 27$^{20.27.28.33}$ (P), **c.** Jerusalem by Yahweh Is 52^{3}.

†גְּאוּלַי Is 63^{4}, in שְׁנַת גְּ', **n.abstr.** *redemption*, acc. to 𝔊 𝔖 𝔙 Ges Hi De MV Che Di RVm, then either pl. abstr. sf. *year of (my) redemption* (so most), or abstr form. in י—, after Syr. analogy, Lag Symm. ii. 101 f Sem i. 19 68. BN 192 (𝔊 om. *my*), but < Pt pass pl. sf *my ransomed (released) ones* Ew Br Brd AV RV cf. sub גאל supra

†גְּאֻלָּה **n.f.** kin(?), redemption—Lv 25^{24} + 5 t, cstr גְּאֻלַּת Lv 25^{32}, sf. גְּאֻלָּתִי Ru 4^{6}, גְּאֻלָּתֶךָ Ez 11^{15}, גְּאֻלָּתוֹ Lv 25^{26} + 4 t; —**1.** *kin*, אַנְשֵׁי גְאֻלָּתֶךָ *men of thy kindred* Ez 11^{15}, RV Thes Hi al, but 𝔊 𝔖 Ew Co א' גלותך *thy fellow-exiles* **2.** *redemption*, of field Lv 25^{24} (H) Ru 4^{7} **3.** *right of redemption* Lv 25$^{29.31.32.48}$ (H) Ru 4^{6} Je 32^{8} = משׁפט הגאלה Je 32^{7}. **4.** *price of redemption* Lv 25$^{26.51.52}$ (H).

†יִגְאָל **n.pr.m.** (*He redeems*)—**1.** one of the spies Nu 13^{7} **2.** one of David's heroes 2 S 23^{36}. **3.** descendant of Zerubbabel 1 Ch 3^{22}.

†II [גָּאַל] **vb.** defile, late (cf גָּעַל)—**Niph.** *Pf* 3 mpl נְגֹאֲלוּ Is 59^{3} La 4^{14}, on form v. Ges^{§51,2}, Kö$^{i\,263}$, *Pt* נְגֹאָלָה Zp 3^{1},—*be defiled,* hands with blood בַּדָּם, Is 59^{3} cf La 4^{14}, pt as subst *defiled, polluted one* Zp 3^{1} of Jerusalem (‖ מֹרְאָה, appos. הָעִיר הַיּוֹנָה) **Pi.** *Pf* 1 pl. sf גֵּאַלְנוּךָ Mal 1^{7} *pollute, desecrate,* obj. י׳ (desecrated in his altar) **Pu.** *Impf* וַיְגֹאֲלוּ מִן־הַכְּהֻנָּה Ezr 2^{62} = Ne 7^{64} cstr pregn. *and they were desecrated out of the priesthood,* i e deposed, as desecrated ones, *Pt* מְגֹאָל of bread laid on Yahweh's altar Mal 1^{7}, of Yahweh's altar (table, שֻׁלְחָן) v^{12} **Hiph.** *Pf* 1 s אֶגְאָלְתִּי Is 63^{3} (on Aram form v Kö$^{i\,27}$ Ges$^{§53\,R.\,6}$ but) rd perh. גֵּאַלְתִּי *Pi*, v GFM$^{ThLZ\,1887\,292}$ cf also Ges$^{l\,c\,n}$ Ol$^{§255\,b}$ Sta$^{§159\,b\,3}$,—*I have polluted,* i.e. *stained, all my raiment* **Hithp.** *Impf* יִתְגָּאַל Dn 1^{8}, יִתְגָּאַל v^{8},—*defile himself*

†[גֹּאַל] **n.[m.]** defiling, defilement, גָּאֳלֵי הַכְּהֻנָּה Ne 13^{29}

גַּב back, etc, v. sub גבב

[גֵּב], גֵּבִים v גוב p 155.

I [גֵּב] *locust,* v. sub גבה

II [גֵּב] pit, III [גֵּב] *beam,* v. sub גוב

גֹּב, גּוֹב **n.pr.loc.** v. sub גבב

גבא (cf Ar جَبَى, جَبَأَ *restrain* or *withhold oneself,* perh. = جَبَا *collect* (water in a cistern, also tribute), so Lane جَبَى I. ad fin, Fl NHWB$^{i\,431}$, v. also NH גְּבִי, גָּבָה, Aram. גְּבָא, ܓܒܐ *collect* debts, taxes, etc)

†גֶּבֶא **n.m.** $^{Ez\,47\,11}$ cistern, pool (cf Ar. مِيم מִגְבָּא جَابِيَة *watering-trough*)—**1.** *cistern* Is 30^{14} **2.** *pool, marsh* גְּבָאָיו Ez 47^{11} (‖ בִּצֹּאתָו)

גבב (prob *be curved, convex, elevated,* Aram גְּבִבָא *hill, be* or *make hollow, dig,* Ar جَبَّ *cut off* or *out,* جُبّ, Aram גֻּב, Eth ገብ: As *gubbu,*—all = *cistern,* cf e g As. *gubbâni ša mê, cisterns of water,* Asrb$^{Annals\,Col\,viii\,102}$, KB$^{ii\,220}$, v n pr גֹּב infr)

†גַּב **n.m.** $^{?cf\,Ez\,43,13}$ (**f** $^{Ez\,1,18}$) anything convex, curved, gibbous, e g back, chiefly late,—abs גַּב Ez 16^{24}, cstr גַּב Ez 43^{13} (rd גֹּבַהּ 𝔊 Ew Sm Co); sf. גַּבִּי ψ 129^{3}, גַּבֵּךְ Ez 16$^{31.39}$, pl cstr. גַּבֹּת Lv 14^{9}, גַּבֵּי Jb 13^{12} 15^{26}, sf גַּבֵּיהֶם 1 K 7^{33}, גַּבֵּהֶם Ez 10^{12}, גַּבֵּיהֶן Ez 1^{18}, גַּבֹּתָם Ez 1^{18},—**1.** *back,* of man (fig of Isr) ψ 129^{3}, appar. of cherubim Ez 10^{12}, but Hi Sm emend v. so that גַּב׳ ref to wheels, *rim* v **6** infr **2.** *mound,* for illicit worship Ez 16$^{24.31.39}$ (all ‖ רמה); 𝔊 𝔙 *lupanar, brothel,* after analogy of *fornix,* but this without sufficient proof, & needless. **3.** *boss,* or convex projection, of shield Jb 15^{26} (fig) *he runneth against him . . . with the stout bosses of his shields* (i e. wicked against י׳), so ظهر in Ar in similar phrase, cf also Ar جَوْبٌ, *shield,* also French *bouclier* fr *boucle* **4.** *bulwarks, breastworks,* fig for arguments לְגַבֵּי־חֹמֶר גַּבֵּיכֶם Jb 13^{12} *breastworks of clay are your breastworks* **5.** *brow,* only גַּבֹּת עֵינָיו Lv 14^{9} *his eyebrows* **6.** *rim* of wheel, *felloe* 1 K 7^{33} Ez 1$^{18.18}$; so perh 10^{12} v. **1** supr —Ez 43^{13}, *elevation,* i e basement of altar, Da after MT, but v גֹּבַהּ, cf supr

†גֹּב 2 S 21^{18}, גּוֹב v^{19} **n.pr.loc.** (cf Aram. גֻּבָּא *den,* and ܓܘܒܐ, Ar. جُبّ, Eth. ገብ: As *gubbu, well, cistern,* v גבב)—field of battle with Philistines 2 S 21^{18} = גֶּזֶר in ‖ 1 Ch 20^{4} (so here Th Ew, cf Jos 10^{33}), but = גַּת 𝔊𝔖 2 S 21^{18} (𝔊L Γαζεθ); 2 S 21^{19} (om ‖ 1 Ch 20^{5}), 𝔊 Ρομ, Ροβ; Klo *Gath,* in v^{16} We Dr (q. v) rd בְּנֹב for בְּגֹב; site of Gob (si vera l) unknown

†גַּבַּי סַלָּי appar. **n.pr.m.** (cf Aram ܓܒܝܐ, Talm גַּבַּי, *tax-gatherer*) a Benjamite Ne 11^{8}, but text dub cf 1 Ch 9^{8} & Sm$^{Listen\,7}$

†גִּבְּתוֹן **n.pr.loc.** (*mound, height,* cf 𝔗 גִּבְתָּא *ridge*) Philistine city 1 K 15$^{27.27}$ 16$^{15.17}$, assigned to Dan Jos 19^{44}, and to Levites 21^{23} site unknown, cf Lag$^{Onom\,246,\,2nd\,ed.\,255}$.

גבה (*collect,* Ar جَبَا (= جَبَأَ?, cf גבא supr), NH גְּבִי, גָּבָה, Aram גְּבָא, ܓܒܐ, ‖ form גבא q v)

†I [גֵּב] **n.[m.]** locust (name from *swarm, collection,* Eth ገብእ: cf also Eth አንበጣ: *locust* √ = Ar نَبَغَ *scaturivit, manavit*), only pl גֵּבִים Is 33^{4} (in sim. of leaping) —גֵּב II, III, v. sub גוב

†גּוֹב **n.[m.]** locusts, Na 3^{17}, cf גֹּבַי

†גֹּבַי, גּוֹבַי **n.m.** $^{Am\,7\,1\,cf\,v\,2}$ **coll.** locusts (*swarm, multitude,* Aram. גּוֹבָא, pl גּוֹבָאי; on format. v Ol$^{§216\,d}$), גֹּבַי symbol of Yahweh's judgment on Isr Am 7^{1}; in sim. of disappearance of Assyrian leaders at destruction of Nineveh גּוֹב גּוֹבַי Na 3^{17} (*locust-*) *swarm of locusts* (‖ אַרְבֶּה); but del. גּוֹב as dittogr We al.

†גָּבַהּ **vb.** be high, exalted (NH *id* (Hiph), Aram גְּבַהּ, cf. Ar. جَبْهَة *forehead,* جَبَهٌ *prominence of forehead;* compare perhaps also As. *gabâni, heights* (?) Lotz$^{TP\,133}$)—**Qal** *Pf.* גָּ׳ 2 Ch 26^{16} + 5 t.; גָּבְהָא Ez 31^{5} (א = ה); גָּבַהַתְּ Ez

31^{10}, גָּבְהוּ Jb 35^{5} + 3 t.; *Impf* יִגְבַּהּ Pr 18^{12} + 5 t.; sf. יִגְבְּהוּ Ez 31^{14}, יִגְבָּהוּ Jb 36^{7}, תִּגְבְּהוּ Je 13^{15}, תִּגְבְּהֶינָה Ez 16^{50}, *Inf.* כִּגְבֹהַּ ψ 103^{11}, לְגָבְהָה Zp 3^{11};—**1.** *be high, lofty, tall*, e g. tree Ez 19^{11} 31$^{5.10.14}$, heavens Jb 35^{5} Is 55^{9} ψ 103^{11}, man 1 S 10^{23}. **2.** *be exalted*, of man in dignity and honour Jb 36^{7}, of servant of Yahweh Is 52^{13}, God Is 5^{16}, God's ways Is 55^{9}. **3.** *lofty* גָּבַהּ לִבּוֹ:—**a.** in a good sense, *encouraged* in the ways of Yahweh 2 Ch 17^{6}; **b.** elsewhere in a bad sense, *be haughty* ψ 131^{1} Pr 18^{12} 2 Ch 26^{16} 32^{25} Ez 28$^{2.5.17}$, and so without לב Is 3^{16} Je 13^{15} Ez 16^{50} Zp 3^{11}. **Hiph.** *Pf.* הִגְבַּהְתִּי Ez 17^{24}; *Impf.* יַגְבִּיהַּ Jb 39^{27} Je 49^{16} Ob^{4}; וַיַּגְבִּיהֶהָ 2 Ch 33^{14}; יַגְבִּיהוּ Jb 5^{7}, *Inf* הַגְבֵּהַּ Is 7^{11} Ez 21^{31}; *Pt* מַגְבִּיהַּ Pr 17^{19} ψ 113^{5},—*make high, exalt*, e g. trees Ez 17^{24}, wall 2 Ch 33^{14}, gate Pr 17^{19}, nest Je 49^{16} Ob^{4}, dwelling ψ 103^{5}, a request Is 7^{11}, the lowly Ez 21^{31}; יַגְבִּיהוּ עוּף *make their flight high, soar aloft* Jb 5^{7}, without עוּף Jb 39^{27}.

†גָּבֹהַּ **adj. high, exalted**—1 S 9^{2} + 15 t; גָּבֹהַּ ψ 138^{6}; cstr. גְּבַהּ 1 S 16^{7}, גְּבַהּ (Ew^{§213d}) ψ 101^{5} + 3 t.; pl. גְּבֹהִים Ec 5^{7} + 5 t; f. גְּבֹהָה Dt 3^{5} + 6 t.; pl. גְּבֹהוֹת Dn 8^{3} + 2 t.; גבהת Dt 28^{52},—**1.** *high, lofty, tall*, e g tree Ez 17^{24}, tower Is 2^{15} Zp 1^{16}, mountain Gn 7^{19} ψ 104^{18} Is 40^{9} 57^{7} Ez 17^{22} 40^{2}; cf. phrases על כל גבעה גבהה *upon every high hill* 1 K 14^{23} 2 K 17^{10} Je 2^{20}; על גבעות הגבהות Je 17^{2}; עַל־כָּל־הַר גָּבֹהַּ Is 30^{25} Je 3^{6}, man 1 S 9^{2}; tree גְּבַהּ קוֹמָה Ez 31^{3}, horns Dn 8^{3}; walls Dt 3^{5} 28^{52}; gallows Est 5^{14} 7^{9}; gate Je 51^{58}, altar Ez 41^{22}; high things Jb 41^{26} Ec 12^{5} **2.** *exalted in station* Ez 21^{31}, כִּי גָבֹהַּ מֵעַל גָּבֹהַּ שֹׁמֵר וּגְבֹהִים עֲלֵיהֶם *for high one above high one is watching, & the Most High over them* Ec 5^{7} so Ew Zö al., but Vrss De Now al *higher* (earthly), potentates *over them*. **3.** *haughty* ψ 138^{6} Is 5^{15} 10^{33} 1 S 2^{3}, גְּבַהּ־עֵינַיִם ψ 101^{5}; גְ׳ לֵב Pr 16^{5}, גְ׳ רוּחַ Ec 7^{8}. **4.** **n.[m.]** *loftiness*, גְּבֹהַּ קוֹמָתוֹ 1 S 16^{7}, cf. גָּדוֹל **10**, p. 153.

†גֹּבַהּ **n.m.** height—Jb 22^{12} + 9 t; sf. גָּבְהוֹ 1 S 17^{4} + 5 t; pl. cstr גָּבְהֵי Jb 11^{8};—**1.** *height*, of buildings and trees Ez 1^{18} 19^{11} 31$^{10.14}$ 40^{42} 41^{8} 2 Ch 3^{4} Am 2^{9}, prob. also Ez 43^{13} (of altar), so 𝔊 Ew Co for MT גַּב (q. v.), of man 1 S 17^{4}, heaven Jb 11^{8} 22^{12} (גבה cstr. SI^{6} of rock). **2.** *exaltation, grandeur* Jb 40^{10} **3.** *haughtiness*, Je 48^{29}; גְ׳ אַף ψ 10^{4}; גְ׳־לִבּוֹ 2 Ch 32^{26}, גְ׳ רוּחַ Pr 16^{18}.

†גַּבְהוּת **n.f.** haughtiness, Is 2$^{11.17}$

†יָגְבְּהָה **n.pr** (*exalted*? Ol $^{§277 k.4}$) place in the tribe of Gad Nu 32^{35} Ju 8^{11};—*Ḫirbet-Aǧbêhât*, NW. fr. ʿAmmân, Bd $^{Pal 189}$.

(ה)גבול Jos 15^{47} Kt; rd הַגָּדוֹל Vrss. Codd. cf. v^{12}.

גבח (only in foll. derivatives found in P, cf. also NH גִּבֵּחַ, *giant*)

†גִּבֵּחַ **adj. having a bald forehead,** גִּ׳ הוּא Lv 13^{41} (P ‖ קֵרֵחַ הוּא v^{40})

†גַּבַּחַת **n.f.** bald forehead (NH *id*, Aram. ܓܒܚܬܐ), only Lv 13—abs. Lv 13^{42} (P, asson. בְקָרַחַת אוֹ בְגַבַּחַת), גַּבַּחְתּוֹ v$^{42.43}$ (both P & ‖ קָרַחְתּוֹ), in all, as place of appearance of an eruption; v^{55} (P; ‖ id) = *in its front*, i.e front of garment.

גַּבִּי v sub גבה

גַּבַּי, גַּבֵּי סַלָּי v sub גבב

גבים **n.pr.loc.** v sub גב

גבל (acc to Thes orig *twist, wind*, whence not only מִגְבָּלֹת, גַּבְלֻת, but also גְּבוּל (*cord* and then) *boundary*, as determined by measuring cord, or line, whence vb. denom. גָּבַל *bound, border*, q v. infr; NH גָּבַל, Aram גְּבַל mean *mix, knead*; Ar. جَبَلَ, Syr. ܓܒܠ = *create, fashion*; MV assume meaning *massive*, whence Ar جَبَل *mountain* (cf. As *gablu* HA^{48}), and גבול as originally earth-wall, etc, serving as boundary; this explains גַּבְלֻת etc. less well)

גְּבוּל$_{240}$ **n.m.** $^{Nu 34, 3}$ **border, boundary, territory** (NH *id*, Punic *gubulim* (pl, Plaut $^{Poen. I. 9}$)—גְּבוּל Gn 10^{19} + 168 t. + Jos 15^{47} Kt (but rd Qr גָּדוֹל), גְּבֻל Nu 21^{13} + 9 t.; (both, in abs. & cstr, e g abs Nu 22^{36} 34^{6}, cstr Gn 10^{19} 2 S 21^{5}); sf. גְּבוּלִי 1 Ch 4^{10}, גְּבוּלְךָ Ex 7^{27}, גְּבֻלְךָ Ex 23^{31} + 3 t, etc., pl. (8 t.) only sf גְּבוּלַיִךְ Je 15^{13} 17^{3}, etc,—**1.** *border, boundary*, **a.** of a land or people Canaanites Gn 10^{19} (J), Edom Nu 20^{23} Jos 15$^{1.21}$ (all P) cf. Ob^{7}, Amorites Nu 21^{13} (E) Jos 13^{4} (D) cf 12^{5} (D) Ju 1^{36}, Moab Nu 21$^{13.15}$ 22^{36} (E) 33^{44} (P) Dt 2^{18} Ju 11$^{18.18}$ 2 K 3^{21} Is 15^{8}, Ammon Nu 21^{24} (E) Dt 3^{16} Jos 12^{2} 13^{10} (all D) Am 1^{3}, Bashan Jos 12^{4} (D), Egypt 1 K 5^{1} = 2 Ch 9^{26}, Is 19^{19}, esp of promised land Ex 23^{31} 34^{24} (JE) Nu 34^{3} + 13 t. Nu 34 (all P) Dt 11^{24} 12^{20} 16^{4} Jos 1^{4} (D), cf. Ez 45^{1} + 10 t. Ez 45–48; also of Israel 2 K 14^{25} Am 6^{2} Mal 1^{5}. **b.** *boundary* of smaller divisions, e g. Geshurites Dt 3^{14} Jos 12^{5} 13^{11} (all D), cf Jos 16$^{2.3}$ (J) 19^{12} (P); esp of tribes of Israel Dt 3$^{16.17}$ Jos 13^{30} (all D) 13^{16} + 60 t. Jos 13–19 (P);—15^{47} rd. גדול v. supr.; Jos 22^{25} (P) & 17^{8} 18^{11} 24^{30} (JE), cf. 1 Ch 6$^{39.51}$

2 Ch 11[13] Ez 48[1] + 15 t Ez 48 (incl v[22 22] q del Co),—in 1 S 13[18] rd for הַגֶּבַע, גבול 𝔊 We Dr †c. *boundary* of territory belonging to an individual,—of field, piece of ground, etc Gn 23[17] (P) Dt 19[14] 27[17], Jos 24[30] (E) = Ju 2[9] 1 Ch 4[10] Pr 15[25] 22[28] 23[10] Ho 5[10] †d *border* of stream Nu 22[36] †e *limit* to waters of deep ψ 104[9] cf Je 5[22] †f. a concrete object marking limit, (α) *barrier* in Ezekiel's temple Ez 40[12] (del 𝔊 𝔖 Co) v[12], (β) *border* of altar Ez 43[13 17 20], (γ) *surrounding wall* of restored Zion Is 54[12] (so 𝔊 Ew Kn Che; De Brd *territory*, Di undecided) †2 *territory* (enclosed within boundary), **a.** of land or people Gn 47[21] (J) Ex 7[27] (P) 10[4 14] (‖ארץ) v[19] 13[7] (all J), Nu 20[16 17 21] 21[22] (E, ‖ארץ) = Ju 11[20], Nu 21[23] (E) Dt 2[4] 19[3] (ג׳ אַרְצְךָ) v[8] 28[40] Jos 18[5 5] (E) Ju 11[22] 19[29] 2 S 21[5] 1 K 1[3] 2 K 10[32] 1 Ch 21[12] (‖ארץ) ψ 105[31] (= ארץ in ‖ Ez 8[16 17]) v[33] 147[14] Je 31[17] Ez 11[10 11] Jo 4[6] Zp 2[8] **b.** *territory* of a city (or *limit* of such territory) Nu 35[26 27] Jos 13[26] Ju 1[18.18.18] Ez 47[16 16 17 17] (del 𝔊 Co) 48[1] Am 6[2] †c. *territory* about Ezekiel's temple Ez 43[12] †d. pl in like sense (only use of pl), of land Mi 5[5] Is 60[18] (‖ארץ) Je 15[13] 17[3], of city 1 S 5[6] 2 K 15[16] 18[8], so Ez 27[4] of Tyre. †e. fig *territory* (region) *of darkness* Jb 38[20]; *territory of wickedness* Mal 1[4] (of Edom); *territory of his holiness* ψ 78[54] (of Canaan)

†[גְּבוּלָה] **n.f.** border, boundary—sf. גְּבֻלָתוֹ Is 28[25], *Pl* abs גְּבֻלֹת Nu 32[33], גְּבֻלוֹת Jb 24[2], cstr גְּבוּלוֹת ψ 74[17], גְּבוּלֹת Is 10[13], גְּבֻלֹת Dt 32[8], sf גְּבוּלֹתֶיהָ Jos 18[20] 19[49], גְּבֻלֹתֶיהָ Nu 34[2 12],—1. *border, boundary* of the earth (poet) ψ 74[17], of peoples Is 10[13] Dt 32[8] (poem); of land of Canaan Nu 34[2.12] (P) Jos 19[49] (JE), of a tribe Jos 18[20] (P), of territory about cities Nu 32[33] (P?), of a piece of ground Jb 24[2], of barley-field Is 28[25]

†גַּבְלֻת **n f. twisting**—שַׁרְשֹׁת גַּבְלֻת Ex 28[22], שַׁרְשְׁרֹת ג׳ 39[15] (both P), *cords of twisting*, i e. (well or tightly) twisted cords.

†מִגְבָּלֹת **n f.pl. the twisted, i.e cords,** Ex 28[14] cf Di (appos שַׁרְשְׁרֹת זָהָב ‖ שׁ׳ הָעֲבֹתֹת)

†גָּבַל **vb.denom. bound, border**—**Qal** *Pf* גָּבְלוּ Dt 19[14], *Impf.* 3 ms יִגְבּוֹל Jos 18[20], 3 fs תִּגְבָּל־ Zc 9[2],—*bound, border*, c acc. Jos 18[20] (P), c ב *border upon, adjoin* Zc 9[2], trans *set bounds* Dt 19[14] (c acc cogn) **Hiph.** *Pf* 2 ms *set bounds for*, c acc וְהִגְבַּלְתָּ Ex 19[12], *Imv. id.* הַגְבֵּל v[23] (both JE), + *Pt* מַגְבִּיל Ez 47[18] 𝔊 𝔖 𝔙 Co

†גְּבַל **n.pr.loc.** maritime city on the Phenician coast Ez 27[9], (Ph גבל = Byblus (Sm Di Jos 13[5]), in As *Gubli* COT[Gloss]); mod *Jebeil* Bd[Pal 358], v also Furrer[ZPV viii 30]

†גִּבְלִי **adj.gent.** of foregoing, c art. = n coll. Jos 13[5] והארץ הַגִּבְלִי, but rd גְּבוּל הַגּ׳, cf Di. 1 K 5[32] הַגִּבְלִים (but prob. txt. err; Th rds. וַיַּגְבִּלוּם *and they bordered them, made a border for them* (the stones), 𝔊 ἔβαλον, cf also Klo).

†גְּבָל **n.pr loc** (= Ar جبال, Γεβαληνη) mountainous region S. of Dead Sea, 𝔗 Seir, cf. Jos[Ant ii 1 2 ix 9 1], ψ 83[8] גְּבָל ועמון ועמלק,—mod. *Jibâl*, Seetzen[ii 357] Burckh[Travels 401] Rob[BR ii 154].

גבן (prob. *be curved, contracted, coagulated,* Syr Pa ܓܒܢ *coagulate,* Ar. جَبُنَ is *be timid,* perh from *shrinking, cowering*)

†גִּבֵּן **adj. crook-backed, hump-backed** (cf Aram גִּבִּין *id.*, NH גַּבְּן *highlander;* also NH גַּבִּין, Aram. גְּבִינָא, ܓܒܝܢܐ, all = *brow* (*eye-brow*, etc.), cf Ar جَبِين *side of forehead*), Lv 21[20]

†גְּבִינָה **n.f. curd, or cheese** (NH *id*, Ar جُبْن, Eth ግብት: Aram גְּבִנָא, ܓܒܢܐ, cf ܓܒܬܐ)—וְכַגְּבִינָה תַּקְפִּיאֵנִי Jb 10[10] (‖ חָלָב)

†[גַּבְנֹן] **n.[m.] peak, rounded summit,** pl גַּבְנֻנִּים ψ 68[16] הַר־אֱלֹהִים הַר־בָּשָׁן הַר־ג׳ הַר־בָּשָׁן; הָרִים ג׳ v[17] (appos, Thes Dr[§ 188] al; others adj *many-peaked*) Cf. Wetzst[Batan Glebelgeb., 1884]

גבע (*convex, projecting, high,* cf Aram Pa גַּבַּע *swell, swell up*, גְּבִיעַ *hump-backed*, גִּבְעֲתָא *hill,* v. also 1. גִּבְעָה infr)

†גֶּבַע **n.pr.loc.**—ג׳ abs Jos 21[17] +, cstr. Ju 20[10] +, גָּבַע Jos 18[24] +,—Levitical city, in Benjamin Jos 21[17] = 1 Ch 6[45] Jos 18[24] cf. 1 Ch 8[6], 1 K 15[22] Ne 11[31], also 1 S 13[16] & Ju 20[10.33] MT, in all three rd גבעה (גבעת), cf. context,—northernmost city in kingdom of Judah 2 K 23[8] *from Geba to Beersheba*, cf. Zc 14[10], situated S of pass of *Michmash* Is 10[29] 1 S 14[5] cf. 1 S 13[3]; mentioned also 2 Ch 16[6] Ezr 2[26] Ne 7[30] 12[29]; in 1 S 13[18] 𝔊 We Dr id הַגֶּבַע for MT גבול q v.; (2 S 5[25] rd גבעון with 𝔊 and 1 Ch 14[16]).—Mod *Jeba'* Rob[BR i 440f] Bd[Pal 120]

†גִּבְעָא **n.pr.m.** a son of Caleb 1 Ch 2[49]

†1. גִּבְעָה **n.f.** hill—abs. גִּבְעָה 2 S 2[25] + 13 t + Ez 6[13] (del. Co q v) 1 S 7[1] 2 S 6[3.4] (cf. Dr), cstr גִּבְעַת Jos 5[3] + 8 t + 1 S 10[5] (cf Dr), sf. גִּבְעָתִי Ez 34[26] (but del Co), גִּבְעָתָהּ Is 31[4]; pl abs. גְּבָעוֹת Dt 12[2] + 35 t., cstr גִּבְעוֹת Dt 33[15]

ψ 18[26] (= 2 S 22[26] גִּבּוֹר but 𝔊 𝔖 rd גבר); pl גְּבָרִים Je 41[16] + 10 t;—man as strong, disting. fr women, children, and non-combatants whom he is to defend, chiefly poetic Ex 10[11] Nu 24[3.15] (E) Ex 12[37] Jos 7[14.17.18] (J) Dt 22[5.5] Ju 5[30] 2 S 23[1] 1 Ch 23[3] 24[4] 26[12] Jb 3[3] + 14 t. Jb, ψ 18[26] + 8 t ψ; Pr 6[34] + 7 t. Pr, Is 22[17] Je 17[5] + 8 t Je; La 3[1.27.35.39] Dn 8[15] Mi 2[2] Hb 2[5] Zc 13[7], also 1 S 10[21] 𝔊 We Dr; = *each* (of locusts) Jo 2[8], cf אִישׁ.

†11 **גֶּבֶר n.pr.m.** an official of Solomon 1 K 4[19] (cf בֶּן־גֶּבֶר v[13], p. 122 supr.)

†**גִּבָּר n.pr.** (Aram *id* = *hero*) Ezr 2[20] prob. = גִּבְעוֹן Ne 7[25]

גִּבּוֹר 159 **adj.** strong, mighty (cf Ar جَبَّارٌ *one who magnifies himself, behaves proudly, a tyrant, who is bold, audacious*)—Gn 10[9] + 58 t; גִּבֹּר Gn 10[8] + 2 t, גִּבֹּרִם 1 S 17[51], pl גִּבּוֹרִים Je 46[9] + 27 t, גִּבֹּרִים Jos 10[2] + 21 t., cstr גִּבּוֹרֵי 1 Ch 11[27] + 29 t, גִּבֹּרֵי 1 Ch 9[26] + 4 t; sf גִּבּוֹרֶיךָ Ho 10[13] + (var sfs 11 t),—**1. adj.** גִּבּוֹר בַּבְּהֵמָה *mightiest among beasts* Pr 30[30], אִישׁ גִּבּוֹר 1 S 14[52], גִּבּוֹר בָּאָרֶץ ψ 112[2], גִּבֹּר צַיִד *mighty in hunting* Gn 10[9] (J), מֶלֶךְ גִּבּוֹר Dn 11[3], אֵל גִּבּוֹר the Messiah Is 9[5], attribute of God especially as fighting for his people ψ 24[8.8] Dt 10[17] Ne 9[32] Is 10[21] Je 32[18] (cf. Ar. الْجَبَّارُ) **2. n.m.** *strong, valiant man* Jos 10[2] (E) Gn 6[4] 10[8] (J) Ju 5[13.23] 1 S 2[4] + 16 t 1 K 1[8.10] 2 K 24[16] 1 Ch 1[10] + 11 t Ezr 7[28] Jb 16[14] ψ 19[6] 33[16] 45[4] 52[3] 78[65] 89[20] 120[4] 127[4] Pr 16[32] 21[22] Ct 3[7.7] 4[4] Ec 9[11] Is 3[2] 13[3] 21[17] 42[13] 49[24.25] Je 5[16] + 17 t Ez 32[12] + 5 t Ho 10[13] Jo 2[7] 4[9.10.11] Am 2[14.16] Ob[9] Na 2[4] Zp 1[14] 3[17] Zc 9[13] 10[5.7]; cf phrases גִּבּוֹר חַיִל *mighty man of valour* Ju 6[12] 11[1] 1 S 9[1] 16[18] 1 K 11[28] 2 K 5[1] (וְהָאִישׁ הָיָה גִּבּוֹר חַיִל מְצֹרָע so 𝔊 al, but 𝔊L *ὁ ἄνθρωπος ἦν λεπρός*, cf also Klo's dub emend), 1 Ch 12[28] 28[1] 2 Ch 13[3] 17[16.17] 25[6] 32[21], אִישׁ גִּבּוֹר חַיִל Ru 2[1], גִּבּוֹרֵי הַחַיִל Jos 1[14] (D) 6[2] 10[7] (JE) 2 K 15[20] 24[14], אִישׁ גִּבּוֹרֵי הַחַיִל Jos 8[3], גִּבֹּרֵי חַיִל 1 Ch 5[24] + 14 t. Ne 11[14], גִּבּוֹרֵי חֲיָלִים 1 Ch 7[5.7.11.40], גִּבּוֹרֵי הַחֲיָלִים 1 Ch 11[26], גִּבֹּרֵי כֹחַ ψ 103[20], גִּבּוֹרֵי מִלְחָמָה 2 Ch 13[3], גִּבֹּרֵי הַשְּׁעָרִים 1 Ch 9[26]; בֵּית הַגִּבֹּרִים Ne 3[16], (הַ)צָּבָא הַגִּבּוֹרִים 2 S 10[7] 1 Ch 19[8], רָאשֵׁי הַגִּבֹּרִים 1 Ch 11[10], גִּבּוֹרִים לִשְׁתּוֹת *valiant to drink* Is 5[22]

†**גְּבוּרָה** 61 **n.f. strength, might**—Ex 32[18] + 16 t, cstr גְּבוּרַת ψ 147[10], sf גְּבוּרָתוֹ + (sfs. 32 t.), pl. גְּבוּרוֹת Jb 41[4] + 3 t, גְּבֻרוֹת ψ 71[16], גְּבוּרֹתֶיךָ Dt 3[24] + (sfs 6 t),—**1.** *strength*, of horse Jb 39[19] ψ 147[10], crocodile Jb 41[4], sun Ju 5[31], body of man ψ 90[10] Ec 9[16] 10[17] **2.** *might, valour*, of warriors Ju 8[21] Pr 8[14] Is 3[25] 28[6] 30[15] Je 9[22] 23[10] 49[35] 51[30] Ez 32[29.30] Mi 3[8] 7[16], קוֹל עֲנוֹת גְּבוּרָה *noise of shouting in warlike strength* Ex 32[18] (E); עֵצָה וּגְבוּרָה 2 K 18[20] Is 11[2] 36[5], cf. phrases of compiler of Kings כָּל גְּבוּרָתוֹ 1 K 15[23] 2 K 10[34] 20[20]; אֲשֶׁר עָשָׂה וּגְבוּרָתוֹ 1 K 16[5.27] 22[46] 2 K 13[8.12] 14[15.28], cf also מַלְכוּתוֹ וּגְבוּרָתוֹ 1 Ch 29[30], תָּקְפּוֹ וּגְבוּרָתוֹ Est 10[2] **3.** *might* of God Jb 26[14] ψ 21[14] 54[3] 65[7] 66[7] 71[18] 80[3] 89[14] 106[8] 145[11] Is 33[13] Je 10[6] 16[21]; cf phrases כֹּחַ וּגְבוּרָה 1 Ch 29[12] 2 Ch 20[6], חָכְמָה וּג׳ Jb 12[13], מִשְׁפָּט וּג׳ Mi 3[8], הַגְּדֻלָּה וְהַג׳ 1 Ch 29[11], גְּבוּרוֹת *mighty deeds* of God Dt 3[24] ψ 20[7] 71[16] 106[2] 145[4.12] 150[2] Is 63[15]

†**גְּבִיר n.m. lord,** Gn 27[29.37]

†**גְּבִירָה n.f. 1. lady, queen,** 1 K 11[19]; **2 queen-mother,** 1 K 15[13] = 2 Ch 15[16]; וַיְסִרֶהָ מִגְּ׳ *he removed her from* (the position of) *queen-mother*, cf 2 K 10[13] Je 13[18] 29[2]

†**גְּבֶרֶת n.f. 1.** *lady, queen,* Is 47[5.7]. **2.** *mistress* of servants, sf גְּבִרְתִּי Gn 16[8], גְּבִרְתֵּךְ Gn 16[9], גְּבִרְתָּהּ Gn 16[4] 2 K 5[3] ψ 123[2] Pr 30[23]; (pl גְּבָרוֹת *women* MI[16])

†**גַּבְרִיאֵל n.pr.m** (*man of Ēl*) an archangel Dn 8[16] 9[21] (cf Lu 1[19])

גבשׁ (*be firm, massive,* cf As *gabâšu, be thick, massive,* Zim[BP 76], & deriv., cf also Aram גַּבֵּשׁ Pa. *heap up,* & גַּבְשׁוּשִׁית *height, hill*)

†**גָּבִישׁ n.m. crystal** (cf. אֶלְגָּבִישׁ *hail*—on relation of meanings cf. Gk. κρύσταλλος, & Eth. usage of አብን: በረድ: Di[Lex Aeth. 759]—Ar. جِبْسٌ *gypsum,* As *gibšu, mass, abundance,* COT[Gloss])—רָאמוֹת וְגָבִישׁ Jb 28[18] *coral and crystal*

†**מַגְבִּישׁ n.pr.m** Ezr 2[30] בְּנֵי מ׳ 𝔊 Μαγεβως, etc., a family of returning exiles, om ‖ Ne 7[33], but 𝔊A א Μαγεβως, etc, 𝔊L Μαγβεις; cf. Sm Listen 16

גבתון v. sub גבב.

†**גָּג n.m.** roof, top (NH *id.*, Di comp Eth. ገግ: ገግ: *vinculum* (ferreum), *jugo simil collare ferreum,* √dub., Thes prop גנג, perh גנג (=גנן) *cover* Bo[§292] Sta[§189a] MV)—גָּג Jos 2[6] + 9 t. + 1 S 9[26] Kt (Qr גָּגָה), גָּגָה Jos 2[8] 1 S 9[26] Qr (Kt גג), cstr Ju 9[51] + 2 t. + Ez 40[13] (del Co v. infr); sf. גַּגֶּךָ Dt 22[8], גַּגּוֹ Ex 30[3] + 2 t. + Ez 40[13] (del Co v. infr.); pl. גַּגּוֹת Is 37[27] + 5 t, sf גַּגֹּתֶיהָ Is 15[3], גַּגּוֹתֵיהֶם Je 32[29], Je 19[13],—**1.** *roof* (of house) Dt 22[8] Jos 2[6.6.8] 16[27] 1 S 9[25.26] 2 S 11[2.2] 16[22] 2 K 19[26] = Is 37[27], Ne 8[16] ψ 102[8] 129[6] Pr 21[9] 25[24] Is 15[3] 22[1] Je 48[38], as places of idolatrous worship (esp of heavenly bodies) Je 19[13] 32[29] Zp 1[5], so הַגָּג עֲלִיַּת אָחָז 2 K

23^{12}, roof of tower Ju 9^{51}, over gate 2 S 18^{24}, of chamber Ez $40^{13.13}$ (but 𝔊 Co קִיר). **2.** top of altar of incense, in tabern. Ex 30^{3} 37^{26} (both P).

גַּד, גָּד, גְּדָגֹּד, גֻּדְגֹּדָה v. sub נדד.

†[גָּדַד] **vb.** **penetrate, cut** (NH *id.*, *cut, cut out*, Aram. גְּדַד, ܓܕ, Ar. جَدَّ *cut, cut off;* Eth. ገደደ: in deriv.)—**Qal** *Impf.* ψ 94^{21} יָגוֹדּוּ עַל־נֶפֶשׁ צַדִּיק *they attack* (penetrate, make inroads upon) *the life of a righteous man* (Ol prop. יָגוּרוּ cf. 56^{7} 59^{4} where, however, Che יגורו; si vera l., perh. denom. fr. גְּדוּד cf. Ho 6^{9} & infr.; cf. also גוד & Kö $^{I. 356}$). **Hithpo.** *Impf.* יִתְגֹּדַד Je 16^{6}; 2 fs. תִּתְגֹּדְדִי Mi 4^{14}, תִּתְגּוֹדָדִי Je 47^{5}; pl. וַיִּתְגֹּדְדוּ 1 K 18^{28}, יִתְגּוֹדָדוּ Je 5^{7} + Ho 7^{14} v. infr., תִּתְגֹּדְדוּ Dt 14^{1}; *Pt.* pl. מִתְגֹּדְדִים Je 41^{5};—**1.** *cut oneself*, as religious (heathen) practice 1 K 18^{28}; practised also by men of Shechem, etc. in worship of ׳י (late) Je 41^{5}; for the dead, forbidden Dt 14^{1} לֹא תִתְגֹּדְדוּ וְלֹא תָשִׂימוּ קָרְחָה בֵּין עֵינֵיכֶם לָמֵת, Je 16^{6}; cf. 47^{5} (subject Philistia personified); also for MT יִתְגּוֹרָרוּ Ho 7^{14} Codd, *they cut themselves*, 𝔊 Gr Che RVm, or perh. (cf. גּוּר) sub. **2.** *gather in troops,* or *bands; go in troops* or *throngs, throng;* (denominative fr. גְּדוּד q.v.) cf. תִּתְגֹּדְדִי בַת־גְּדוּד Mi 4^{14} (addressed to Jerusalem); Je 5^{7} וּבֵית זוֹנָה יִתְג׳ *and to a harlot's house they throng.*

I. גְּדוּד **n.m.**$^{Gn 49,19}$ band, troop (as *making inroads;* others, as a *division, detachment* (as severed), but this usually later in Heb.)—ג׳ abs. 1 S 30^{8} + 19 t.; cstr. 2 Ch 25^{9}; pl. גְּדוּדִים 2 S 4^{2} + 2 t.; cstr. גְּדוּדֵי 2 K 6^{23} + 6 t.; sf. גְּדוּדָיו Jb 19^{12} 25^{3};—**1.** *marauding band* (making *incursions, inroads,* cf. גדד) 1 S $30^{8.15.15.23}$ cf. 1 Ch 12^{22}, also 2 Ch 22^{1} 1 K 11^{24} 2 K 5^{2} 6^{23} $13^{20.21}$ $24^{2.2.2.2}$ cf. 2 S 22^{30} = ψ 18^{30}, & Gn 49^{19} (v. גַּד 30^{11}) Ho 6^{9} 7^{1} Je 18^{22}; שָׂרֵי גְדוּדִים 2 S 4^{2}, cf. וַיִּקָּחֻם בְּרָאשֵׁי הַגְּדוּד 1 Ch 12^{19}; fig. of God's attacking forces, his chastisements Jb 19^{12} (cf. 25^{3} infr.) **2.** *troop,* of divisions of army of Isr. (late) גְּדוּדֵי צְבָא מִלְחָמָה 1 Ch 7^{4}, cf. 2 Ch 26^{11}; *band of Israel,* i.e. troop of mercenaries hired from Isr. by Amaziah 2 Ch $25^{9.10}$; בְּנֵי הַגְּדוּד i.e. *soldiers of the band* 2 Ch 25^{13}; of army in general כְּמֶלֶךְ בַּגְּדוּד Jb 29^{25}, in sim.; also Mi 4^{14} בַּת־גְּדוּד of Zion. **3.** *foray, raid* 2 S 3^{22}.

†II. [גְּדוּד, or גְּדוּדָה] **n.[m.** or **f.]** **furrow, cutting**—**1.** *furrow,* pl. defect. גְּדוּדֶהָ ψ 65^{11} (‖ תְּלָמֶיהָ). **2.** pl. גְּדֻדֹת, *cuttings* upon hands, cf. גדד Hithpo. **2,** sign of mourning Je 48^{37} (‖ שַׂק).

†I. גַּד **n.m.** **coriander** (NH גִּיד, Aram. גִּידָא; connexion with above √ dub.; v. further Löw$^{No. 155}$)—זֶרַע גַּד Ex 16^{31} Nu 11^{7}, sim. of manna.

†II. [גַּד] **1. n.[m.]** **fortune, good fortune** (Ar. جَدّ *id.*, Aram. גַּדָּא, ܓܕܐ)—Gn 30^{11} בגד Kt, i.e. בְּגָד (בָּא גָד Qr), 𝔊 ἐν τύχῃ, *by* or *with good fortune.* **2. n.pr.m.** **god of fortune** (Ar. جَدّ We$^{Skizzen iii. 171}$; גד named often in Ph. & Aram. inscript., & found in Ph. & Aram. n.pr., Bae $^{Rel 76 f.}$ Nö$^{ZMG 1888, 479}$; v. esp. Siegf$^{JPTh 1875, 356 ff.}$)—c. לְ + art. לַגַּד Is 65^{11} cf. Che.

III. גָּד n.pr.m. (*fortunatus*? perh. der. fr. foreg. divine name Siegf$^{JPTh 1875, 364}$ Sta$^{Gesch. i. 148}$; but v. also Bae$^{Rel 159 f.}$)—גָּד Gn 35^{26} +, as well as גָּד Gn 30^{11} +;—**1.** son of Jacob and Zilpah; **a.** strictly as personal name Gn 30^{11} 35^{26} 46^{16} Ex 1^{4} cf. Gn 49^{19} 1 Ch 2^{2}. **b.** as name of tribe Nu 1^{14} Dt 27^{13} $33^{20.20}$ Jos 18^{7} Ez $48^{27.28}$; cf. אֶרֶץ גָּד 1 S 13^{7} v. also Je 49^{1}, שַׁעַר גָּד Ez 48^{34}, on הַנַּחַל הַגָּד 2 S 24^{5} cf. We Dr; explicitly מַטֵּה גָד Nu 1^{25} 2^{14} 13^{15} Jos 13^{24} 20^{8} $21^{7.36}$ 1 Ch $6^{48.65}$; once, צְבָא מַטֵּה בְנֵי־גָד Nu 10^{20}; בְּנֵי גָד (MI^{10} אש גד) Nu 1^{24} + 12 t. Nu; Jos 4^{12} + 14 t. Jos; 1 Ch 5^{11} 12^{14}. †**2.** a prophet in David's time, called הַנָּבִיא 1 S 22^{5}, but הַנָּבִיא חֹזֵה דָוִד 2 S 24^{11} & חֹזֵה דָוִיד ‖ 1 Ch 21^{9}, הַחֹזֶה 1 Ch 29^{29} & חֹזֵה־הַמֶּלֶךְ 2 Ch 29^{25}.

†I. גָּדִי **adj.gent.** of גָּד **1,** **Gadite** 2 S 23^{36} (so perh. also ‖ 1 Ch 11^{38} where MT הַגְּרִי q.v.; cf. Th Be Dr); elsewhere as n.pr. coll.: so 1 Ch 5^{18} (only here without art., rd. perh. גָּד so 𝔊), Dt $3^{12.16}$ 4^{43} 29^{7} Jos 1^{12} 12^{6} 13^{8} 22^{1} 2 K 10^{33} 1 Ch 5^{26} $12^{8.37}$ 26^{32}.

†II. גָּדִי **n.pr.m.** father of Menahem 2 K $15^{14.17}$ (cf. גדו (גדי?) n.pr.m. Eut$^{Nab No. 25}$; Palm. גדיא n.pr.m. Vog$^{No. 32}$).

גַּדָּה in חֲצַר ג׳ v. sub חצר.

†גַּדִּי **n.pr.m.** (*my fortune*) a man of Manasseh Nu 13^{11}.

†גַּדִּיאֵל **n.pr.m.** (*Ēl is my fortune*) a man of Zebulun Nu 13^{10}.

גִּדְגָּד, in הֹר הַגִּ׳ v. following & sub הֹר.

†גֻּדְגֹּדָה c. art. הַגֻּדְגֹּדָה **n.pr.loc.** (mng. dub.) station of Israel in wilderness Dt $10^{7.7}$ (in ‖ Nu 33^{32} הֹר הַגִּדְגָּד v. sub הֹר).

†מְגִדּוֹ and (Zc 12^{11}) מְגִדּוֹן **n.pr.loc.** (connexion with above √ not clear; 𝔊 Μαγεδδω, Μεκεδω, Μαγεδω, etc.; 𝔙 Mageddo; As. *Magadû, Magidû,* COT^{Gloss} Dl$^{Pa 287}$) old Canaanitish city,

assigned to Manasseh 1 K 4^{12} 9^{15} 2 K 9^{27} $23^{29.30}$; מֵי מ׳ מֶלֶךְ מ׳ Jos 12^{21}; יֹשְׁבֵי מ׳ Jos 17^{11} = Ju 1^{27}; מֵי מ׳ Ju 5^{19}; בִּקְעַת מ׳ Zc 12^{11} 2 Ch 35^{22};—mod. *Lejjûn* (= *Legio*) Rob $^{BR\,ii.\,329\,f.\,364}$ Bd$^{Pal\,229}$.

גדה (*cut, cut* or *tear away?*).

† [גָּדָה] **n.f.** bank of river (cf. Ar. جُدَّةٌ, جِدَّةٌ *id.*, Aram. גִּידָא, *wall*), גְּדוֹתָיו Jos 3^{15} 4^{18} 1 Ch 12^{16} Qr (Kt גדיתיו) Is 8^{7}.

[גדיה] only pl. sf. Is 8^{7} Kt, v. foregoing.

† גְּדִי **n.m.**$^{Gn\,27.9}$ **kid** (NH *id.*, Ar. جَدْيٌ, Ph. גדא, Aram. גַּדְיָא, ܓܰܕܝܳܐ; cf. As. *gadû, gadiia*, Meissner$^{ZA\,iv.\,1889,\,286}$ Zehnpfund$^{BAS\,i.\,505}$)—גְּדִי־ Gn 38^{17} + 12 t. (abs. Gn 38^{23} +, & (generally) cstr. Gn 38^{17} +); pl. גְּדָיִים 1 S 10^{3}, cstr. גְּדָיֵי Gn $27^{9.16}$;—*kid*, almost always ג׳ עִזִּים Gn $27^{9.16}$ $38^{17.20}$ Ju 6^{19} $13^{15.19}$ 15^{1} 1 S 16^{20}; abs. Ex 23^{19} 34^{26} Dt 14^{21} (all לא תבשל ג׳ בחלב אמו), & c. art. הַגּ׳ Gn 38^{23} Ju 14^{6}; abs. pl. 1 S 10^{3};—cf. also עֵין גֶּדִי.

† [גְּדִיָּה] **n.f.** only pl. **kids** sf. גְּדִיֹּתַיִךְ Ct 1^{8} (‖ הצאן).

† גָּדַל$_{115}$ **vb. grow up, become great** (Aram. גְּדַל (Ithpe.), ܓܕܰܠ *twist, twine*, Ar. جَدَلَ *twist a cord, make firm, strong, become strong*, so NH)—**Qal** *Pf.* ג׳ etc. Gn 38^{14} + 14 t.; sf. גְּדֵלַנִי Jb 31^{18}; *Impf.* יִגְדַּל etc. ψ 35^{27} + 34 t.;—**1.** *grow up*, **a.** child Gn $21^{8.20}$ 25^{27} $38^{11.14}$ Ex $2^{10.11}$ (JE) Ju 11^{2} 13^{24} Ru 1^{13} 1 S 2^{21} 3^{19} 1 K $12^{8.10}$ (= 2 Ch $10^{8.10}$) 2 K 4^{18}; גְּדֵלַנִי כְאָב *he grew up to me as to a father* Jb 31^{18}; **b.** lamb 2 S 12^{3}. **2.** *become great*, **a.** in extent, wealthy Gn $26^{13.13}$ 41^{40} (JE) Je 5^{27}; **b.** in value, גָּדְלָה נַפְשְׁךָ בְּעֵינַי, בְּעֵינֵי י׳ *prized by* 1 S $26^{24.24}$; **c.** in intensity, grief Jb 2^{13}, mourning Zc 12^{11}, punishment La 4^{6}, trespass Ez 9^{6}; **d.** in sound, loud cry Gn 19^{13} (J); **e.** in importance, of a king Ec 2^{9} 1 K 10^{23} (= 2 Ch 9^{22}) Dn $8^{9.10}$ (under fig. of horn), chief Gn 24^{35} 48^{19} (J), Messiah Mi 5^{3}, Jerusalem Ez 16^{7}; **f.** of God 2 S 7^{22} ψ 104^{1}, his works ψ 92^{6}, his power Nu 14^{17} (J). **3.** *to be magnified*, **a.** house of David Zc 12^{7}; **b.** Yahweh ψ 35^{27} 40^{17} 70^{5} Mal 1^{5}, his name 2 S 7^{26} (= 1 Ch 17^{24}). **Pi.** *Pf.* גִּדַּל Jos 4^{14} Est 3^{1}; גִּדֵּל Is 49^{21}; גִּדְּלָה Is 51^{18}, etc.; *Impf.* יְגַדֵּל Is 44^{14} + 8 t.; *Imv.* גַּדְּלוּ ψ 34^{4}; *Inf.* גַּדֵּל Nu 6^{5} + 3 t.; *Pt.* מְגַדְּלִים 2 K 10^{6} (מְגַדְּלוֹת Ct 5^{13} 𝔊 𝔙 Hi Bö De);—**1.** *cause to grow*, e.g. hair Nu 6^{5} (P), plants Jon 4^{10} Is 44^{14} Ez 31^{4} Ct 5^{13}; *bring up children* 2 K 10^{6} Is 1^{2} 23^{4} 49^{21} 51^{18} Dn 1^{5} Ho 9^{12}. **2.** *make great, powerful* Gn 12^{2} (J) Jos 3^{7} 4^{14} (D) 1 K $1^{37.47}$ 1 Ch $29^{12.25}$ 2 Ch 1^{1} Est 3^{1} 5^{11} 10^{2}. **3.** *magnify*, **a.** man Jb 7^{17}; **b.** God ψ 34^{4} 69^{31}. **Pu.** *Pt.* pl. מְגֻדָּלִים *brought up* ψ 144^{12}. **Hiph.** *Pf.* הִגְדִּיל ψ 41^{10} +, etc.; *Impf.* יַגְדִּיל Is 42^{21} Dn 8^{25}, etc.; *Inf.* הַגְדִּיל 1 Ch 22^{5} Am 8^{5}; *Pt.* מַגְדִּיל ψ 18^{51} (= מִגְדּוֹל in ‖ 2 S 22^{51}); pl. מַגְדִּילִים ψ 35^{26};—**1.** *make great*, e.g. shekel Am 8^{5}, pile for fire Ez 24^{9}, joy Is 9^{2}, counsel Is 28^{29}, wisdom Ec 1^{16}, works Ec 2^{4}, house of Yahweh 1 Ch 22^{5}; the heel ψ 41^{10} either *lifted high* (Ges), or (cf. De Now) *gave me insidiously a great fall*; cf. ג׳ פִּיךָ Ob ^{12} i.e. utter proud words (v. רחב Hiph.) **2.** *magnify*, salvation ψ 18^{51}, mercy Gn 19^{19} (J), teaching Is 42^{21}, the word of Yahweh ψ 138^{2}. **3.** *do great things* הִגְדִּיל לַעֲשׂוֹת, **a.** in a good sense, of God ψ $126^{2.3}$ Jo 2^{21}, also pregn. without Inf. 1 S 12^{24}. **b.** in bad sense, of 'the northern one' Jo 2^{20}, also pregn. without Inf. La 1^{9} Zp $2^{8.10}$ Dn $8^{4.8.11.25}$; with עַל, of enemies ψ 35^{26} 38^{17} 55^{13} Jb 19^{5} Je $48^{26.42}$; Ez 35^{13} of speaking ג׳ עָלַי בְּפִיכֶם. **c.** also, with Inf. implied, wept greatly 1 S 20^{41}. **Hithp.** *Pf.* וְהִתְגַּדִּלְתִּי Ez 38^{23} *I will magnify myself*, shew myself great and powerful (of God); *Impf.* יִתְגַּדֵּל, with עַל in a bad sense, *magnify oneself against* Is 10^{15} Dn 11^{36}; יִתְגַּדָּל Dn 11^{37}.

† גָּדֵל **pt.m.** or **adj.verbal. becoming great, growing up**, Gn 26^{13} (J) 1 S 2^{26} (cf. Dr) 2 Ch 17^{12}; also **great**, pl. cstr. גִּדְלֵי בָשָׂר Ez 16^{26} *great of flesh*.

† גֹּדֶל **n.m. greatness**—Dt 32^{3} + 5 t.; sf. גָּדְלוֹ Dt 5^{21} + 5 t.; גֻּדְלוֹ ψ 150^{11};—**1.** *greatness, magnitude*, tree Ez 31^{7}, arm of God ψ 79^{11}, mercy of God Nu 14^{19}. **2.** *magnificence*, **a.** king Ez $31^{2.18}$; **b.** God Dt 3^{24} 5^{21} 9^{26} 11^{2} 32^{3} ψ 150^{2}. **3.** in a bad sense, גֹּדֶל לֵבָב = *pride, insolence of heart* Is 9^{8} 10^{12}.

† גְּדִלִים **n.[m.]pl. twisted threads** (NH גְּדִיל, Bab. *gidlu, cord* on which onions were strung, *a string* of onions, Zehnpfund$^{BAS\,i.\,511}$; Aram. גְּדִילָא, ܓܕܝܠܐ *thread, cord, rope*, also *plaited locks*, ܓܕܘܠܐ *id.*)—**1.** *tassels* Dt 22^{12} on border of garment (‖ צִיצִת Nu $15^{38.39}$). **2.** *festoons*, on capitals of columns 1 K 7^{17}.

גָּדוֹל$_{522}$ **adj. great**—ג׳ Gn 4^{13} + 279 t.; גָּדֹל Dt 26^{8} + 22 t.; cstr. גְּדוֹל Ez $17^{3.7}$, גְּדָל Ex 15^{16} Je 32^{19}, גְּדָל־ Pr 19^{19}, גְּדָוֹל־ ψ 145^{8} Na 1^{3}; sf. גְּדוֹלָם Je 6^{13} + 2 t.; pl. גְּדֹלִים Ex 7^{4} + 11 t., גְּדֹלִים Gn 12^{17} + 22 t.; cstr. גְּדֹלֵי 2 K 10^{6}; sf. גְּדֹלָיו 2 K 10^{11} Jon 3^{7}; גְּדוֹלֶיהָ Na 3^{10}; f. גְּדוֹלָה Nu 22^{18} + 96 t.; גְּדֹלָה Gn 15^{12} + 31 t.; pl. גְּדוֹלֹת Ne 9^{26} 12^{31}, גְּדֹלוֹת

Dt 27^{2} + 30 t., גְּדֹלֹת Nu 13^{33} + 7 t.;—*great*, **1.** *in magnitude and extent*, e.g sea Nu 34^{6}, river Gn 15^{18}, wilderness Dt 1^{19}, rain 1 K 18^{45}, mountain Zc 4^{7}, city Gn 10^{12}, house Je 52^{13}, altar Jos 22^{10}, throne 2 Ch 9^{17}, sea-monsters Gn 1^{21}, fish Jon 2^{1}, eagle Ez 17^{3}, terebinth 2 S 18^{9}, substance Gn 15^{14}, wealth Dn 11^{2}, victory 1 S 19^{5}; 1 S 19^{22} בּוֹר הַגָּדוֹל rd. בְּ׳ הַגֹּרֶן acc to 𝔊 We Dr. **2.** *in number*, e g nation Gn 12^{2}, congregation Je 31^{8}, camp 1 Ch 12^{22}, army Ez 17^{17}, sacrifice 2 K 10^{19}, slaughter Dt 28^{59} 1 S 4^{17}. **3.** *in intensity*, fear Dt 4^{34}, weeping Is 38^{3}, power כֹּחַ Ex 32^{11}, joy Jon 4^{6}, anger Dt 29^{23}, indignation Je 21^{5}, sin Gn 20^{9}, iniquity Gn 4^{13}, evil Gn 39^{9}, trespass Ez 9^{7}. **4.** *in sound, loud* voice Gn 39^{14}, cry Ex 11^{6}, shout Jos 6^{5} **5.** *in age*, elder, eldest, son Gn 27^{1}, daughter Gn 29^{16}, brother Gn 10^{21}, sister Ez 16^{46}. **6.** *in importance*, **a.** *things* †(הַ)דָּבָר (הַ)גָּדֹל *an important thing* or *affair* Ex 18^{22} Dt 4^{32} 1 S 12^{16} 2 K 5^{13} 8^{13}; יום יהוה Je 30^{7} Ho 2^{2} Jo 2^{11} 3^{4} Zp 1^{14} Mal 3^{23}. **b.** *of men, great, distinguished*, Moses Ex 11^{3}, David 2 S 5^{10}, Job Jb 1^{3}, Mordecai Est 9^{4}, kings Ec 9^{14} Je 27^{7}; esp. of king of Assyr. הַמֶּלֶךְ הַגָּדוֹל 2 K 18$^{19.28}$ = Is 36$^{4.13}$, = As. *šarru rabbu, šarru dannu*, e g. KB I ^{94,11}; הַכֹּהֵן הַגָּדוֹל *the h p* Lv 21^{10} + 20 t; (הָ)אִישׁ גָּדוֹל 1 S 25^{2} 2 S 19^{33} 2 K 5^{1}; אִשָּׁה גְדוֹלָה 2 K 4^{8}; †גָּדוֹל *a great man* 2 S 3^{38} Mi 7^{3}; לֹא תֶהְדַּר פְּנֵי גָדוֹל *thou shalt not honour* (favour) *the person of a great man* (opp. דָּל) Lv 19^{15} (H); †(הַ)גְּדוֹלִים *the great* 2 S 7^{9} = 1 Ch 17^{8} Ne 11^{14} (vid. infr.) Pr 18^{16} 25^{6} Je 5^{5} (2 K 10^{11} 𝔊L ἀγχιστεύοντας, Klo גֹּאֲלָיו); further גדלי הָעִיר כָּל־ 2 K 10^{6}; (כָּל־)גְּדֹלָיו 2 K 10^{11}; Jon 3^{7}; גְּדוֹלֶיהָ Na 3^{10}. **c.** †*of God, himself* 2 Ch 2^{4} Ne 4^{8} 8^{6} ψ 86^{10} 99^{2} 135^{5} 147^{5} Is 12^{6} Je 10^{6}; (הָ)אֵל (הַ)גָּדוֹל Dt 7^{21} 10^{17} Ne 1^{5} 9^{32} ψ 77^{14} 95^{3} Je 32^{18} Dn 9^{4}; גדול מכל האלהים Ex 18^{11}, גדול ומהלל מאד 1 Ch 16^{25} ψ 48^{2} 96^{4} 145^{3}, מלך גדול ψ 47^{3} 95^{3} Mal 1^{14}, †*his works* Dt 11^{7} Ju 2^{7} ψ 111^{2}, †*glory* ψ 21^{6} 138^{5}, †*name* Jos 7^{9} 1 S 12^{22} 1 K 8^{42} 2 Ch 6^{32} ψ 76^{2} 99^{3} Je 10^{6} 44^{26} Ez 36^{23} Mal 1$^{11.11}$, *mercy* 1 K 3^{6} 2 Ch 1^{8} ψ 57^{11} 86^{13} 108^{5}, *goodness* Ne 9^{25}, *compassion* Is 54^{7}. **7.** in phrases †עוֹד הַיּוֹם גָּדוֹל *it is yet high day* (Fr. *grand jour*, Germ. *hoch am Tage*, the day is at its height) Gn 29^{7}; †כַּקָּטֹן כַּגָּדֹל (or reverse) *as well small as great* Dt 1^{17} 1 Ch 25^{8} 26^{13} 2 Ch 31^{15}; †(לְ)מִקָּטֹן וְעַד גָּדוֹל (or reverse) *from small to great* Gn 19^{11} 1 S 5^{9} 30$^{2.19}$ 2 K 23^{2} 25^{26} 2 Ch 15^{13} 34^{30} Est 1$^{5.20}$ Je 6^{13} 8^{10} 31^{34} 42$^{1.8}$ 44^{12} Jon 3^{5}. **8.** cstr. גְּדֹל (הַ)כְּנָפַיִם *great* of wings Ez 17$^{3.7}$, so of anger Pr 19^{19} (Qr), usually of God, in power Na 1^{3}, counsel Je 32^{19}, mercy ψ 145^{8} **9.** as subst. concr. †עשׂה גדלות *do great things*, of God's great acts of redemption and judgment Dt 10^{21} Jb 5^{9} 9^{10} 37^{5} ψ 71^{19} 106^{21}, of the miracles of Elisha 2 K 8^{4}; of things *too great* and so presumptuous, haughty תבקשׁ גְ׳ Je 45^{5}; מדברת גְ׳ ψ 12^{4}; לא הִלַּכְתִּי בִּגְ׳ ψ 131^{1} (cf. BAram. Dn 7$^{8.11.20}$; also Rev 13^{5}). **10.** †as subst neut. *greatness* of arm Ex 15^{16}, cf. גֹּבַהּ **4.**

†גְּדוּלָּה **n.f.** greatness—2 S 7^{21} + 3 t., גְּדֻלָּה 1 Ch 29^{11}; cstr. גְּדֻלַּת Est 10^{2}, sf. גְּדוּלָּתוֹ Est 1^{4}, גְּדֻלָּתוֹ ψ 145^{3}; גְּדֻלָּתִי ψ 71^{21}; גְּדוּלָּתְךָ ψ 145^{6}, pl. intens גְּדֻלּוֹת 1 Ch 17$^{19.21}$,—chiefly late Heb. **a.** of Psalmist ψ 71^{21}, Mordecai Est 6^{3} 10^{2}, king Est 1^{4}, **b.** *of God's greatness*, as an attribute 1 Ch 29^{11} ψ 145$^{3.6}$, or of his acts 2 S 7^{21} (cf. Dr) v^{23} = 1 Ch 17$^{19.19.21}$.

†הַגְּדוֹלִים **n.pr.m.** father of Zabdiel Ne 11^{14} (RV & so most; but 𝔊 RVm al. *the great*).

†גִּדֵּל **n pr.m.** (*very great*)—**1.** head of one of the families of Nethinim Ezr 2^{47} Ne 7^{49}. **2.** head of one of the families of Solomon's servants Ezr 2^{56} Ne 7^{58}.

†גְּדַלְיָה **n.pr.m.** (*Yah is great*)—**1.** governor of Judea appointed by Nebuchadnezzar Je 40$^{5.8}$ 41^{16}. **2.** son of Amariah, a son of Hezekiah Zp 1^{1} **3.** priest of the sons of Jeshua Ezr 10^{18}

גְּדַלְיָהוּ **n.pr.m.** (*Yah(u) is great*) — **1.** governor of Judea = גדליה 2 K 25$^{22-25}$ Je 39^{14} 40$^{6-16}$ 41$^{1-18}$ 43^{6} (24 t) **2.** son of Pashur, one of the chiefs of Jerusalem in the time of Jeremiah Je 38^{1}. **3.** one of the sons of Jeduthun, in the time of David 1 Ch 25$^{3.9}$.

†גִּדַּלְתִּי **n.pr.m.** (*I magnify (God)*) son of Heman 1 Ch 25^{4} (cf on this remarkable list of names Ew $^{§ 274 b}$ We RS$^{OTJC 422, 2nd ed. 143}$) v^{29}.

†יִגְדַּלְיָהוּ **n.pr.m.** (*Yah(u) is great*) a prophet of the age of Josiah Je 35^{4}.

†מִגְדָּל **n.m.** tower, Gn 11^{4} + 11 t; cstr. מִגְדַּל Ju 8^{17} + 21 t., pl. מִגְדָּלִים 2 Ch 26^{9} + 6 t; מִגְדָּלֶיהָ ψ 48^{13} Ez 26^{4}; pl.f. מִגְדָּלוֹת 2 Ch 32^{5} + 2 t; cstr מגדלות Ct 5^{13}(1); sf. מִגְדְּלֹתַיִךְ Ez 26^{9} 27^{11},—**1.** *tower* Gn 11$^{4.5}$ Ju 8^{9} 9$^{51.51.52.52}$ 2 K 9^{17} 17^{9} 18^{8} 1 Ch 27^{25} 2 Ch 14^{6} 26$^{9.10.15}$ 27^{4} 32^{5} Ne 3$^{25.26.27}$ Is 2^{15} 30^{25} 33^{18} Ez 26$^{4.9}$ 27^{11} ψ 48^{13}, watch-tower in vineyard Is 5^{2}; fig. of God as refuge ψ 61^{4} Pr 18^{10}; beautiful neck like tower of David

Ct 4^{4}, an ivory tower 7^{5}, breasts 8^{10} (Cf MI^{22} מגדלתה, Sab (more precisely Lihyân) מגדלנהן; Eut, v. DHM$^{\text{Epigr Denkm. 4, 1 5}}$) Special towers mentioned on Lebanon Ct 7^{5}, Penuel Ju 8^{17}, Shechem Ju $9^{46.47.49}$; and at Jerusalem, the tower of David Ct 4^{4} (the arsenal), מֵאָה Ne 3^{1}, חֲנַנְאֵל Ne 3^{1} 12^{39} Je 31^{38} Zc 14^{10}, תַּנּוּרִים Ne 3^{11} 12^{38} (tower of the furnaces) **2.** *elevated stage, pulpit* of wood Ne 8^{4} **3.** *raised bed* ‖ עֲרוּגָה Ct 5^{13}, but 𝔊 𝔙 Hi Bo De rightly rd. מְגַדְּלוֹת

†מִגְדַּל־אֵל **n.pr.** (*tower of God*) stronghold in Naphtali Jos 19^{38} prob = Μαγδαλά Matt 15^{39} = *Mejdel* in the plain of Gennesareth Rob $^{\text{BR iii. 298}}$ Bd$^{\text{Pal 257}}$

†מִגְדַּל־גָּד **n.pr.** (*tower of Gad*) stronghold in Judah Jos 15^{37},—cf *Magdala*, Lag$^{\text{Onom 139 12, 2nd ed 171}}$, possibly *Mejdel*, eastward of Askalon, Guérin$^{\text{Judée ii 130 f.}}$ cf Bd$^{\text{Pal 162}}$

†מִגְדַּל־עֵדֶר **n pr.** (*flock-tower*) shepherd's watch-tower near Bethlehem Gn 35^{21} Mi 4^{8}

†מִגְדּוֹל **n.m. tower,** 2 S 22^{51} Qr (Kt מגדיל = ψ 18^{51} מַגְדִּל)

†מִגְדֹּל **n.pr.** (מגדול only Je 46^{14}) fortified city on the NE border of Egypt Ex 14^{2} Nu 33^{7} Je 44^{1} 46^{14} Ez 29^{10} 30^{6}; Copt *meschtôl* (Champoll L'Egypte sous les Pharaons ii 79), Egyptian *makθel* Eb$^{\text{GS 522}}$

†גָּדַע **vb. hew, hew down or off** (NH id (rare), Aram גדע Ithp; Ar. جَدَعَ *cut off* hand or other member, *mutilate*)—**Qal** *Pf* גָּדַע La 2^{3}, וְגָדַעְתִּי 1 S 2^{31}, *Impf* וָאֶגְדַּע Zc $11^{10.14}$, *Pt* pass גְּדוּעָה Is 15^{2} (so many edd but) Baer גְּרוּעָה; cf infr, גְּדֻעִים Is 10^{33};—*hew, cut in two,* a staff Zc $11^{10.14}$, metaph *hew off,* an arm 1 S 2^{31}, horns La 2^{3}, *hew down,* trees Is 10^{33}; if in Is 15^{2} then = *shave off* (object זָקָן, beard), but no other indication of this meaning, and true MT גְּרוּעָה, cf Baer's note & Je 48^{37}, v. גרע **Niph.** *Pf* נִגְדַּע Ju 21^{6}, נִגְדַּע Je 50^{23}, 3 fs נִגְדְּעָה Je 48^{25}, וְנִגְדְּעָה consec Is 22^{25}, 2 ms נִגְדַּעְתָּ Is 14^{12}, 3 pl. וְנִגְדְּעוּ consec Ez 6^{6} Am 3^{14},—*be hewn off,* of altar-horns Am 3^{14}, of idols Ez 6^{6} (‖ נִשְׁבַּר); of severance of a tribe from nation Ju 21^{6}, fig of king of Babylon Is 14^{12}, of Babylon as hammer Je 50^{23} (‖ נִשְׁבַּר), of a minister, under fig. of secure peg or pin Is 22^{25}, of horn of Moab Je 48^{25} (‖ נִשְׁבַּר) **Pi.** *Pf* גִּדַּע 2 Ch 34^{7}, גִּדַּעְ 2 Ch 34^{4} ψ 107^{16}, וַיְגַדַּע 2 Ch 14^{2}, אֲגַדֵּעַ ψ 75^{11} Is 45^{2}, וַיְגַדְּעוּ 2 Ch 31^{1}; 3 mpl תְּגַדֵּעוּן Dt 7^{5} 12^{3},—*hew off, down, in two* (cf. Qal) of *Asherîm* Dt 7^{5} 2 Ch 14^{2} 31^{1}, of idols Dt 12^{3} (פסילים) 2 Ch $34^{4.7}$ (חַמָּנִים), fig. horns of wicked ψ 75^{11}, bars of iron (i e of Babylon's gates) Is 45^{2}, cf. ψ 107^{16} †**Pu.** *Pf.* גֻּדְּעוּ Is 9^{9} *hew down* (of trees)

גִּדְעוֹן **n.pr.m.** judge of Israel Ju $6^{11.13.19}$ + 36 t. Ju 6–8,—called also יְרֻבַּעַל (q v) Ju 6^{32} 7^{1} etc, & יְרֻבֶּשֶׁת (q v) 2 S 11^{21}

†גִּדְעֹנִי **n.pr.m.** a Benjamite Nu 1^{11} 2^{22} $7^{60.65}$, גדעוני 10^{24} (always אֲבִידָן בֶּן־ג׳).

†גִּדְעֹם **n.pr loc.** marking limit of pursuit of Benjamites by rest of Israel Ju 20^{45}

†[גָּדַף] **vb.** only **Pi. revile, blaspheme** (NH גָּדַף *cut, wound,* then (esp Pi) *revile,* Ar جَدَفَ *cut, cut off,* ii. *deny a favour, be ungrateful,* etc, Aram Pa. גַּדֵּף, ܓܕܦ, *revile*)—*Pf* 2 ms וְגִדַּפְתָּ 2 K 19^{22} = Is 37^{23}, 3 pl. גִּדְּפוּ 2 K 19^{6} = Is 37^{6}; *Pt.* מְגַדֵּף Nu 15^{30} ψ 44^{17};—**1.** *revile,* between man and man, (abs) קוֹל מְחָרֵף וּמְגַדֵּף ψ 44^{17} *the voice of* (him that) *reproacheth and revileth* **2.** *blaspheme,* sq acc. י׳ Nu 15^{30} (P), 2 K 19^{22} = Is 37^{23} (‖ חרף, obj אֶת־מִי, ref. to י׳ as above); Ez 20^{27}, 2 acc. הַדְּבָרִים ... אֲשֶׁר ג׳ נַעֲרֵי מֶלֶךְ אַשּׁוּר אֹתִי 2 K 19^{6} = Is 37^{6} *the words* with *which the servants of the king of Assyria blaspheme me*

†גְּדוּפָה **n.f. taunt,** only Ez 5^{15} וְהָיְתָה חֶרְפָּה וּג׳ מוּסָר וּמְשַׁמָּה לַגּוֹיִם *and she shall become a reproach and a taunt, an admonition and an astonishment, to the nations*

†גִּדּוּפִים **n.m.pl. revilings, reviling words**—ג׳ Is 43^{28}, cstr. גִּדּוּפֵי Zp 2^{8}, sf גִּדֻּפֹתָם Is 51^{7} between men, Is 43^{28} (‖ חֵרֶם); 51^{7} Zp 2^{8} (both ‖ חֶרְפָּה)

גָּדַר **vb. wall up or off, build a wall** (denom ? NH id, Ar جَدَرَ and v. גָּדֵר infr)—**Qal** *Pf* גָּדַר Jb 19^{8} + 2 t, וְגָדַרְתִּי Ho 2^{8} Am 9^{11}; *Impf* 2 mpl וַתִּגְדְּרוּ Ez 13^{5}; *Pt.* גֹּדֵר Is 58^{12} Ez 22^{30}, pl גֹּדְרִים 2 K 12^{13} 22^{6},—*wall up, shut off,* lit only *Pt*, abs = *masons* (wall-builders) 2 K 12^{13} 22^{6}; also Is 58^{12} (obj פֶּרֶץ), fig of Yahweh's dealings with men, obj אֹרַח Jb 19^{8}, דֶּרֶךְ La 3^{9}, cf Ho 2^{8} (acc cogn גָּדֵר), in all = obstructing path of life, cf also La 3^{7} (c בַּעֲדִי), of restoring fallen booth of David Am 9^{11} (obj. פרצים); of repairing fortunes of Israel, a work neglected by prophets Ez 13^{5}, and by all in power 22^{30} (both c. acc. cogn.)

†גָּדֵר **n.m.** $^{\text{Ez 42,7}}$ **wall** (NH גָּדֵר, Aram. גְּדֵירָא, גַּדְרָא, Ar. جَدْرٌ, جِدَارٌ, and more commonly جِدَارٌ *enclosing-wall* cf. Heb גָּדוֹר infr.)

—abs. גָּדֵר Nu 22$^{24.24}$ + 5 t. + ψ 62^{4} (rd. גדרה cf infr.) + Ez 13^{5} (Co גדרת cf infr.); cstr. גְּדֶר Pr 24^{31} Ez 42^{10} (Co del), sf גדרו Is 5^{5}, גְּדֵרָהּ Ho 2^{8} (cf. Baer, note); pl sf. גְּדֵרֶיךָ Mi 7^{11}, גְּדֵרֶיהָ ψ 80^{13};—*wall, fence*, bordering a road Nu 2$^{24.24}$ cf. Ec 10^{8}, connected with Ezekiel's temple Ez 42^{7}, city wall Mi 7^{11} cf. Ezr 9^{9}; fig of Yahweh's vineyard Is 5^{5} ψ 80^{13}; of fortunes of Israel Ez 22^{30}; so also Ez 13^{5} (Co גְּדֶרֶת cf. גדרה); of hindrance in path of Israel (fig. as woman) Ho 2^{8}, of man beset by enemies ψ 62^{4} (ג׳ הַדְּחוּיָה, but rd גדרה ד׳ Ol De etc.)

†גֶּדֶר **n.pr.loc.** Canaanitish city Jos 12^{13}. Γαδερ A & 𝔊L also Euseb Lag $^{Onom\ 244\ 2nd\ ed.\ 254}$ = בית גָּדֵר ? Lag $^{BN\ 76}$; cf. גדרי infr.; possibly = בית גָּדֵר 1 Ch 2^{51} (v. p 111)

†I. גְּדֵרָה, גְּדֶרֶת **n.f.** wall—גְּדֵרָה 1 Ch 4^{23} + ψ 62^{4} (MT גָּדֵר q.v.), גְּדֶרֶת Ez 13^{5} (Co, cf. 𝔊, MT גָּדֵר) 42^{12} (del Co); pl גְּדֵרוֹת Na 3^{17} + 2 t, גדרֹת Nu 32^{24}, cstr גִּדְרוֹת Nu 32^{36} + 2 t, גדרת Nu 32^{16}; sf. גְּדֵרֹתָיו ψ 89^{41};—*wall, hedge* 1 Ch 4^{23} (or is this n pr loc ? cf Ot) Na 3^{17} (where grasshoppers alight), Je 49^{3}; wall, connected with Ezekiel's temple Ez 42^{12} (del Co), defences ψ 89^{41}, elsewhere ג׳ צאן *sheep-folds* Nu 32$^{16.36}$ 1 S 24^{4} Zp 2^{6} cf. Nu 32^{24}, Ez 13^{5} Co גְּדֶרֶת after 𝔊; ψ 62^{4} MT גדר הדחויה, rd. גדרה ד׳ cf. גָּדֵר.

†גְּדֵרָתִי **adj.gent.** of II. גְּדֵרָה, הַגְּדֵרָתִי 1 Ch 12^{4}.

†II. גְּדֵרָה **n.pr.loc.** a city of Judah הַגְּדֵרָה Jos 15^{36}; 𝔊 Γαδηρα, 𝔊L Γαδιρα; ? cf Γεδουρ Lag $^{Onom\ 245,\ 2nd\ ed\ 254}$.

†גְּדֵרוֹת **n.pr.loc.** in Judah Jos 15^{41}; הַגּ׳ 2 Ch 28^{18}.

†גְּדֵרֹתַיִם **n.pr.loc.** in Judah Jos 15^{36}; perh. del, so 𝔊; whole number too large, cf Di

†גְּדֵרִי **adj.gent.** of גֶּדֶר (q v) so Lag $^{BN\ 77}$, cf. MV al; others גְּדֵרָה; but 𝔊 Γεδωρειτης, 𝔊L Γεδδωριτης;—הַגְּדֵרִי 1 Ch 27^{28}.

†גְּדוֹר, גְּדֹר **n.pr.** (Ar. جِدَارٌ *wall*),—**1. n.pr.loc.** city of Judah גְּדוֹר Jos 15^{58}, also as n.pr.m., under fig of genealogy גְּדֹר son of Penuel 1 Ch 4^{4}, גְּדוֹר son of Yered 1 Ch 4^{18}; also הַגְּדוֹר 1 Ch 12^{7} v. d H.; הַגְּדוֹר Baer, cf. his note **2. n.pr.loc.** גְּדֹר 1 Ch 4^{39}, but read Gerar, acc to 𝔊 Ew Hi Be al. **3. n.pr.m.** גְּדוֹר 1 Ch 8^{31} 9^{37} a Benjamite, of Gibeon.

I. גדשׁ (NH גָּדַשׁ, Aram. גְּדַשׁ, *heap up;* cf. also Ar. كَدَسَ)

†I. גָּדִישׁ **n.m.** $^{Jb\ 5.\ 26}$ heap, stack (NH id, Aram id)—גָּדִישׁ Ex 22^{5} + 3 t;—*stack* of sheaves Ex 22^{5} Ju 15^{5} (‖ קָמָה in both) Jb 5^{26}.

II גדשׁ (= جدث*, exact mng. unknown).

†II גָּדִישׁ **n.[m.]** tomb (Ar جَدَثٌ id) Jb 21^{32}; Dr $^{§178,\ ed\ 3,\ p\ 229}$ suggests reading גָּדֵשׁ.

†גֵּה Ez 47^{13}, rd זֶה 𝔊 𝔗 𝔙 & all moderns

†[גָּהָה] **vb.** depart, i.e. be cured, healed (subj. wound) (cf. Aram ܓܗܐ *be freed* (from guilt, pain, disease, etc.), Aph *set free*, also *become free*) ולא־יגהה מכם מָזוֹר Ho 5^{13}.

†גֵּהָה **n.f.** healing, cure—גֵּהָה Pr 17^{22} לב שָׂמֵחַ יֵיטִב ג׳ cf. Now.

†[גָּהַר] **vb.** bend, crouch (so Vrss)—**Qal** *Impf* וַיִּגְהַר 1 K 18^{42} sq. אַרְצָה Elijah, with face between knees, 2 K 4$^{34.35}$ Elisha, over dead boy, sq עליו (‖ וישכב v ^{34}, cf. שׁכב)

גַּו, גֵּו v. sub גוה.

גּוֹב, גּוֹבַי v. sub גבה

†[גּוּב] **vb.** dig (cf. Ar جَابَ *pierce, bore, hollow out*)—**Qal** *Pt.* גֹּבִים *diggers* or *ploughmen* 2 K 25^{12} Kt; but cf Qr יֹגְבִים as Je 52^{16} (v. יגב), and v. גב infr.

†II. [גֵּב] **n.[m.]** pit, ditch, trench (Ar. جَوْبَةٌ *hollow, depression*, Syr. ܓܘܒܐ *cistern*)—only pl. גֵּבִים Je 14^{3}, in 2 K 3^{16} גבים גבים, i.e *full of ditches;* further, *cisterns* (acc. to Klo 2 K 25^{12}) Je 39^{10} ויגבים (rd וגבים); cf also ‖ 2 K 25^{12} (ולגבים Kt, וּלְיֹגְבִים Qr) = Je 52^{16} (וּלְיֹגְבִים; both c. כרמים); Klo prop to emend these, so as to rd. in all וַיִּתֵּן לָהֶם כְּרָמִים וגבים *and gave to them vineyards and cisterns;* another view in Th, cf further גוב, יגב.—I גב v. sub גבה.

†גֵּבִים **n.pr.loc.** (*trenches*) N fr. Jerusalem, c. art הַגּ׳ Is 10^{31}; site unknown.

†III [גֵּב] **n.[m.]** beam, rafter? (Thes sub גוב, but mng & √ dub.), גֵּבִים 1 K 6^{9}; but Lag $^{Armen\ Stud\ §499\ M\ I\ 212,\ BN\ 155}$ rds גְּבָרִים (Pers. گنبد, Armen. γμβεθ) *vaulted roofs.*

†גּוֹג **n.pr.m.** (√unknown)—**1.** 1 Ch 5^{4} a Reubenite **2.** *Gog of the land of Magog, prince of Rosh, Meshek, and Tubal,* גוג אֶרֶץ הַמָּגוֹג נשׂיא רֹאשׁ מֶשֶׁךְ וְתֻבָל Ez 38$^{2.3}$ (om. אֶ׳ מגוג) 39^{1} (om. id.) cf 38$^{14.16}$ (del 𝔊 𝔖 Co) v^{18} 39$^{11.11.11.11}$ (גיא הֲמוֹן ג׳) v^{15} (id.), cf. As *Gâgu*, chief of a mountain tribe N. of Assyria Dl $^{Pa\ 247}$ COT on Ez 38^{2}

†בֵּיגוֹג **n pr.terr.** (=*land of Gog?* cf Dl Pa 246 Len Or i.1. 465)—Ez 38² 39⁶, in Gn 10² = 1 Ch 1⁵ a son of Japhet, בני יֶפֶת גמר וּמָגוֹג וּמָדַי וְיָוָן וְתֻבָל וּמֶשֶׁךְ ותירס, = Scythians? cf Jos Ant 1 6 1, Lag Ges. Abh 158 refers name to mountainous region between Cappadocia and Media; cf Di Gn 10², Kiep MBAk Feb 1859, 207 (N & E Armenia), Len (SE Armenia), v esp Len Or ii. 1 412-476.

†[גּוּד] **vb. invade, attack** (cf גדד, whence גְּדוּד etc actually derived by Ki Bö Ko i. 374 q v.; SS, perh better, denom fr גדוד)—**Qal** *Impf* יָגֻד Gn 49¹⁹, יְגוּ־נֶנּוּ v¹⁹, יְגוּדֶנּוּ Hb 3¹⁶, יגודו ψ 94²¹ Kt (v גדד),—*attack* Gn 49¹⁹, allit c גָּד n pr. & גדוד: גָּד גְּדוּד יְגוּדֶנּוּ והוא יָגֻד עָקֵב *Gad, a troop shall troop upon him, but he shall troop upon the heel* (i e pursue them in their retreat) VB, Hb 3¹⁶ לַעֲלוֹת לְעַם יְגוּדֶנּוּ cf VB & Comm

I גֵּוָה v sub גאה.

גוה (*project, be convex?*)

†[גֵּו] **n.[m.] back**—only sf גֵּוְךָ 1 K 14⁹, גֵּוֵּךְ Ez 23³⁵, גֵּוָם Ne 9²⁶,—alw השליך אַחֲרֵי ג׳ *cast behind the back*, i.e put out of mind, ignore, reject ׳י 1 K 14⁹ Ez 23³⁵, and his law Ne 9²⁶

†I גֵּו **n.[m.] back**—גו abs. unused, cstr. Pr 10¹³ + 2 t, sf גוי Is 50⁶, גוך Is 38¹⁷, גֵּוֵךְ 51²³,—*back*, as beaten, lashed Pr 10¹³ 19²⁹ 26³ cf. Is 50⁶, in phr. השליך אַחֲרֵי ג׳ (as גֵּו) Is 38¹⁷, of Yahweh's casting sins of penitent behind his back, putting them out of mind, as trodden upon Is 51²³, fig of extreme humiliation.

†II גֵּו **n.[m.] midst**, Aramaism (cf Aram גַּוָּא, גו *middle*, NH גו *midst, interior*, جوّ *id.*, *belly*, Ar. جَوٌّ *midst*) Jb 30⁵ מִן־גֵּו יְגֹרָשׁוּ *from the midst* (of men) *they are driven*, Rosenmüller al comp Cicero Off iii 8: *e medio pelluntur*

†II גֵּוָה **n f back**—(so also Di Hoffm SS; 𝔊 Thes De AV RV *body*=גְּוִיָּה, cf Ba ZMG 1887 606) Jb 20²⁵ וַיֵּצֵא מִגֵּוָה *it comes out from the back* (of arrow which has struck a fugitive, and is then extracted, Hoffm rds. מִגֵּוָה)—I. גֵּוָה sub גאה.

†גְּוִיָּה **n.f. body, corpse**—abs.׳ג Na 3³, cstr גְּוִיַּת Ju 14⁸ + 2 t, sf. גְּוִיָּתִי 1 S 31¹⁰ Dn 10⁶, גְּוִיָּתֵנוּ Gn 47¹⁸, גְּוִיָּתָם Na 3³, pl abs. גְּוִיּוֹת ψ 110⁶; sf. גְּוִיֹּתֵנוּ Ne 9³⁷, גויתיהם Ez 1²³, גְּוִיֹּתֵיהֶנָה v¹¹,—**1.** living human *body* Gn 47¹⁸ (sg., of many persons) cf pl. Ne 9³⁷, of man in Daniel's vision Dn 10⁶ (body apart from extremities); also of the living creatures in Ezek.'s vision Ez 1¹¹ ²³ **2.** *dead body, corpse, carcass:* **a.** of man 1 S 31¹⁰ (so orig in ‖ 1 Ch 10¹⁰ v We⁸ᵐ cf Dr) v¹² ¹² (sg of several persons), ψ 110⁶; coll. Na 3³·³, **b.** of lion Ju 14⁸ ⁹.

גּוֹי ₅₆₁ **n.m.** Gn 12, 2 **nation, people** (NH *id. Gentiles*, Ph גו *community*, جَوٌّ, Sab גו *id*, DHM ZMG 1883, 348)—׳ג Gn 12² + 121 t, sf 1 s. גּוֹיִי Zp 2⁹, גּוֹיֵךְ ψ 106⁵, גּוֹיֵךְ Kt Ez 36¹³ ¹⁴ ¹⁵ (Qr wrongly גּוֹיַיִךְ cf. Co, who del v¹⁵), pl גּוֹיִם Gn 10⁵ + 410 t. + Qr Gn 25²³ ψ 79¹⁰ (Kt גיים) + 6 t. Ez (var. emend. Co), cstr. גּוֹיֵי Gn 18¹⁸ + 8 t, גּוֹיֵ 2 Ch 32¹³ Ezr 6²¹ (cf. Baer's notes); sf גּוֹיֵהֶם Gn 10⁵ ²⁰·³¹·³²,—**1.** *nation, people* Gn 10⁵·²⁰·³¹·³²·³² (all P) +; Is 2⁴ ⁴ = Mi 4²·³·³, †Jb 12²³ ²³ 34²⁹†; Pr 14³⁴, כל גּוֹיֵי הָאָרֶץ Gn 18¹⁸ 22¹⁸ 26⁴ (all J) Dt 28¹ **a.** specif of descendants of Abraham, גוי גָּדוֹל Gn 12² cf 18¹⁸ (both J), הֲמוֹן גּוֹיִם 17⁶, גּוֹיִם 17⁴ ⁵ (all P), of Sarah גּוֹיִם 17¹⁶ (P), of Ishmael גוי 21¹³, גּוֹי גָּדוֹל v¹⁸ (both E), גּוֹי גָּדוֹל 17²⁰ (P), of Jacob גּוֹי וּקְהַל גוים Gn 35¹¹ (P), גּוֹי גָּדוֹל 46³ (E), of Ephraim מְלֹא הַגּ׳ 48¹⁹ (J); of Moses גּוֹי גָּדוֹל Ex 32¹⁰ (J) cf Nu 14¹² (J) Dt 9¹⁴; of Jacob and Esau as *two nations* Gn 25²³ (J). **b.** definitely of Israel Ex 19⁶ (גּ׳ קָדוֹשׁ) 33¹³ (both JE), Dt 4⁶ (הַגּוֹי הַגָּדוֹל הַזֶּה, said by heathen cf. v⁷ ⁸) v also v³⁴, 26⁵ cf ψ 33¹², ψ 83⁵ (said by enemies) Je 31³⁶ 33²⁴ Ez 37²²; in narrative Jos 3¹⁷ 4¹ 5⁸ (JE), v⁶ (D), 10¹³ (poet, no art.); of Israel and Judah as *two nations* Ez 35¹⁰ (said by heathen) 37²², of Judah Is 26² ¹⁵ ¹⁵ cf. 58² 60²² Mi 4⁷, once *my people* Zp 2⁹ (‖עם); *thy people* ψ 106⁵ (i.e of ׳י), cf also Ez 36¹³ ¹⁴ (rd Kt), esp of Israel and (or) Judah as sinful, rebellious Dt 32²⁸ Ju 2²⁰ Is 1⁴ 10⁶ Je 5⁹·²⁹ 7²⁸ 9⁸ 12¹⁷ Ez 2³ (del 𝔊 Co) Hg 2¹⁴ Mal 3⁹.—Note. This definite ref to Israel and (or) Judah is comparatively rare; in Hex not P (yet v Gn 17⁴·⁵·⁶ ¹⁶ 35¹¹ P); seldom in exil & post-exil proph, not Chr—**c.** usually of non-Heb peoples Ex 9²⁴ 34¹⁰ (JE) Lv 25⁴⁴ (H) Nu 14¹⁵ (J) Dt 15⁶ ⁶ 1 K 5¹¹ 1 Ch 14¹⁷ 16²⁰ Is 11¹⁰ ¹² + oft; opp Israel as ׳עם י 2 S 7²³ 1 Ch 17²¹·²¹ etc, v. עם, cf. also Nu 23⁹, note esp. גְּלִיל הַגּוֹיִם Is 8²³ *circle or district of the nations* (v. גָּלִיל), also חֲרֹשֶׁת הַגּ׳ Ju 4² ¹³ ¹⁶ *Charosheth of the nations*, & מֶלֶךְ גּוֹיִם לְגִלְגָּל Jos 12²³ *king of nations* (peoples, tribes) belonging *to Gilgal* (𝔊 Di *to the district*, i e. 'Galilee'), esp of these peoples as heathen: idolatrous Lv 8²⁴·²⁸ (P) 20²³ (H) 1 K 14²⁴ 2 K 17⁸ ¹¹ ¹⁵·²⁶·²⁹ ²⁹ 2 Ch 28³ 32¹³ +, Ezr 6²¹ Ez 5⁶ +, hostile Gn 15¹⁴ (J) Lv 26³³·³⁸·⁴⁵ (H) Dt 4²⁷ 9⁴ ⁵ 18⁹ 1 Ch 16³⁵ Je 5¹⁵ Ez 4¹³ + oft Je Ez, etc.; in simile Ez 20³² 25⁸, sometimes ‖ עם ψ 33¹⁰ ¹² Is 11¹⁰ Je 6¹⁸, v. also Is 2²⁴ comp. with Mi 4¹³. **2.** fig of swarm of locusts Jo 1⁶; of all species of beasts Zp 2¹⁴ **3.** גּוֹיִם Gn 14¹⁹ prob mutilated n pr v. infr.

†I. [גּוּז] **vb. pass over, away** (Ar. جَازَ

pass by, over; Aram. גזז *cross,* جَازَ *pass away, fail*)—**Qal** *Pf.* גָּז ψ 90[10]; *Impf.* וַיָּגָז Nu 11[31]; —*pass away,* of the life of the aged, ψ 90[10] גָּז חִישׁ; trans. *bring over,* subj. wind, obj. quails fr. sea, Nu 11[31] (rd. perh. Hiph. וַיָּגֶז cf. Kö[i.442] Di).

†גּוֹזָן **n.pr.loc.** (As. *Guzana* COT 2 K 17[6] Dl[Pa 184]) city and district of Mesopotamia, on or near the middle course of the Euphrates, through which the river *Chabur* (חָבוֹר) flowed; thither some of the exiled Israelites were brought [by Sargon, B.C. 722–21]: גּוֹזָן 2 K 19[12] = Is 37[12]; חָבוֹר נְהַר גּוֹזָן 2 K 17[6] 18[11]; וְחָבוֹר וְהָרָא וּנְהַר גּוֹזָן 1 Ch 5[26] where *Chabur* is separated entirely from the *river of Gozan* (v. חבור).

גוח v. גיח.

גוֹי v. sub גוה.

גְּוִיָּה v. sub גוה.

†גּוֹיִם **n.pr.gent.** Gn 14[1.9], in phr. תִּדְעָל מֶלֶךְ גּוֹיִם *Tid'al king of Goim;* prob. a Babylonian (Elamitic, etc.) name corrupted; H. Rawlinson prop. *Gutî,* a people NE. of Babylonia, COT on Gn 14[1]; also KGF[258 al.]; cf. also Dl[Pa 293 f.]

גול v. גיל.

†גּוֹלָן **n.pr.loc.** (? connected with √גול, Ar. جَالَ *go about, around;* جَوْلٌ *circuit;* cf. Ph. גול n.pr. insul.; also גְּלִילָה, גָּלִיל) city of Manasseh in Bashan, named as a city of refuge Dt 4[43] cf. Jos 20[8] 21[27] both Qr (Kt גלון); given to sons of Gershom son of Levi acc. to 1 Ch 6[56]; Euseb. knew it as a very large village Γαυλὼν ἢ Γωλάν Lag[Onom. 242, 2nd ed. 253]; district of same name *ib.,* Josephus[Ant. viii. 2, 3 etc.] Gaulanitis, mod. Jaulân Rob[BR ii. 432] Bd[Pal 270] Schumacher[ZPV 1886 = Jaulân 1888], acc. to most, name applied first to city, thence to district, but perh. otherwise if above deriv. be correct.

גּוּן (mng. dub., cf. perh. Aram. גַּוֵּן *tinge,* ܓܘܢ, ܓܘܢܐ; Ar. جَوْنٌ *reddish black,* cf. Hommel[Säugethiere 64]).

†גּוּנִי **n.pr.m.** **1.** a Naphtalite Gn 46[24] Nu 26[48] 1 Ch 7[13]. **2.** 1 Ch 5[15] a Gadite.

†גּוּנִי **adj.gent.** of foregoing **1**; c. art. as n. coll. הַגּוּנִי Nu 26[48]; also of individ. 2 S 23[32] acc. to 𝔊L (Ιεσσαι ὁ Γουνι) Klo Dr; rd. יִשַׁי הַגּוּנִי; also 1 Ch 11[34] where rd. *id.* for השם הגזוני (𝔊L Εἰρασαι ὁ Γουνι).

†גָּוַע **vb. expire, perish, die** (cf. Ar. جَاعَ *be empty, hungry*)—**Qal** *Pf.* גָּוַע Nu 20[29] Jos 22[20], גָּוְעוּ La 1[19], גָּוַעְנוּ Nu 17[27] 20[3]; *Impf.* יִגְוַע Jb 34[15], יִגְוָע Gn 6[17], יִגְוְעוּ Jb 36[12], יִגְוָעוּ Zc 13[8], יִגְוָעוּן ψ 104[29] etc.; *Inf.* cstr. גְּוַע Nu 20[3], גְּוֹעַ Nu 17[28]; *Pt.* גֹּוֵעַ ψ 88[16];—*expire* and die, only P & poet.; ג׳ וימת Gn 25[8.17] 35[29] (all P); ‖ מות Jb 3[11] 14[10] cf. Nu 17[28] (P); ‖ אבד Nu 17[27] *we expire, we perish* (P); ‖ עָנִי ψ 88[16] (progressive parall.) *distressed and about to die;* ‖ יאסף אל אבותיו Gn 49[33]; ‖ על־עפר ישׁוב Jb 34[15] cf. ψ 104[29]; ‖ יִכָּרֵתוּ Zc 13[8]; abs., both prose and (esp.) poetry Nu 20[3.3.29] Jos 22[20] Gn 6[17] 7[21] (all P) Jb 10[18] 13[19] 27[5] 36[12] La 1[19]; Jb 29[18] עִם־קִנִּי אגוע *with my nest shall I die,* i.e. in full possession of what is mine, cf. Di.

†[גּוּף] **vb. shut, close** (NH *id.,* v. NHWB[i. 314, 352])—**Hiph.** *Impf.* juss. יָגִיפוּ Ne 7[3] *close* (doors, דלתות).

†[גּוּפָה] **n.f. body, corpse** (late; NH גּוּף, Aram. גּוּפָא; Ar. جِيفَةٌ)—cstr. sg. גּוּפַת 1 Ch 10[12]; cstr. pl. גּוּפֹת 1 Ch 10[12], cf. Be (‖ 1 S 31[12] has גְּוִיָּה).

†I. גּוּר **vb. sojourn** (cf. Ar. جَارَ *turn aside, tarry,* v. esp. III. IV. VIII. X; Aram. ܓܘܪ, Eth. in der.)—**Qal** *Pf.* גָּר Gn 35[27] + 3 t., וְגָר consec. Is 11[6]; גַּרְתָּה Gn 21[23]; גַּרְתִּי Gn 32[5] ψ 120[5]; גָּרוּ Ex 6[4]; *Impf.* יָגוּר Ex 12[48] + 12 t., וַיָּגָר Gn 20[1] + 2 t.; sf. יְגֻרְךָ ψ 5[5]; 3 fs. וַתָּגָר 2 K 8[2]; 2 fs. תָּגוּרִי 2 K 8[1]; cohort. אָגוּרָה ψ 61[5], יָגוּרוּ Is 16[4]; *Imv.* גּוּר Gn 26[3], גּוּרִי 2 K 8[1]; *Inf. cstr.* גּוּר Gn 12[10] + 17 t.; *Pt.* גָּר Dt 18[6] Ju 17[7] + 17 t.; f. cstr. גָּרַת Ex 3[22]; pl. גָּרִים Lv 25[6] + 8 t.; cstr. גָּרֵי Jb 19[15];—**1.** *sojourn,* dwell for a (definite or indef.) time, dwell as a new-comer (cf. גֵּר) without original rights, v. esp. Gn 19[9] (J) Dt 18[6] & cf. Ju 17[7.8.9] 19[1]; also Gn 12[10] 20[1] 21[23.34] 32[5] 47[4] (all JE); of patriarchs in Canaan Gn 26[3] (J) 35[27] Ex 6[4] (both P) cf. ψ 105[12] = 1 Ch 16[19], Ju 19[16] 2 S 4[3] 2 K 8[1.1.2] (seven years) Is 16[4] Ru 1[1] Ezr 1[4] (in exile); cf. further Ex 3[22] (E) גָּרַת בֵּיתָהּ of a woman in another's house as lodger or guest (v. Di), גָּרֵי בֵיתִי Jb 19[15]; so (poet.) of worshipper in Yahweh's house ψ 15[1] 61[5] cf. Is 33[14.14]; fig. of evil לֹא יְגֻרְךָ רָע ψ 5[5] *evil cannot be a guest of thine* (Che; sq. acc., as in Ar. جاوره III); particularly of the גֵּר (q.v.) in Israel Ex 12[48.49] Lv 16[29] (all P) 17[8.10.12.13] 18[26] 19[33.34] 20[2] 25[6.45] (all H) Nu 9[14] 15[14.15.16.26.29] 19[10] Jos 20[9] (all P) Ez 14[7] 47[22.23]; of Ephraim and Manasseh sojourning with Judah and Benjamin 2 Ch 15[9]; of Rechabites sojourning in Judah Je 35[7]; of Israelites sojourning in Egypt Dt 26[5] Is 52[4] ψ 105[23]; so of Judah, to escape from

under Babylonian power Je $42^{15.17.22}$ 43^{2} $44^{8.12.14.28}$ **2.** *abide*, nearly or quite=*dwell* Je 43^{5} cf. La 4^{15}, Je $49^{18.33}$ 50^{40}, also Jb 28^{4}; of wolf dwelling with lamb Is 11^{6}, *stay* (inactive) Ju 5^{17},—in Is 5^{17} rd perh, for גָּרִים, גְּדָיִים or כָּרִים cf 𝔊 Lo Ew Di & Che crit n (> Stu גרים). **Hithpol.** *Pt* מתגורר 1 K 17^{20} *seek hospitality with*, sq עם (cf Ar x), יִתְגּוֹרָרוּ Ho 7^{14} is dub (cf II גור), AE Ki Ties Wu AV RV *they assemble themselves*, but txt prob err, v נדד

†1. גּוּר n pr.loc. (*sojourning, dwelling*) 2 K 9^{27} מַעֲלֵה־גוּר אשר את־יבלעם, otherwise unknown.

†גּוּר־בַּעַל **n.pr.loc.** (*dwelling* or *Gûr of Baal*) 2 Ch 26^{7} הָעַרְבִיִּים הַיֹּשְׁבִים בְּגוּר־בָּעַל.

גֵּר **n.m.** ^{Ez 12.48} sojourner (Ar جَارٌ, Eth. ጎር: ጎር: Aram. ܓܝܘܪܐ, גִּיּוֹר, *proselyte*, גַּיֵּר *proselytize*, Ph גר in n pr, & pl גרם)—גֵּר Gn 15^{13} + 74 t, sf. גֵּרְךָ Ex 20^{10} + 4 t, גֵּרוֹ Dt 1^{16}; pl גֵּרִים Ex 22^{20} + 9 t, גֵּירִים 2 Ch 2^{16},—**1.** *sojourner*, temporary dweller, new-comer (no inherited rights), cf Ex 12^{19} Lv 24^{16} Nu 15^{30} Jos 8^{33} (opp *homeborn*); of Abraham at Hebron Gn 23^{4} (P, ‖ תּוֹשָׁב), Moses in desert Ex 2^{22} (J) 18^{3} (E, here explan of name Gershom, Moses' son), as claiming hospitality Jb 31^{32}, perh in above cases, and certainly in general, with technical sense, fig. of Yahweh Je 14^{8}, of Israel in Egypt Gn 15^{13} Ex 22^{20} 23^{9} (all JE) Lv 19^{34} (H) Dt 10^{19} 23^{8}, גרים with Yahweh Lv 25^{23} (H) 1 Ch 29^{15} ψ 39^{13} (in all ‖ תושׁב) cf. 119^{19}. **2.** usually of גֵּרִים in Israel 2 S 1^{13} (Amalekite) cf Jos $8^{33.35}$ (E) 20^{9} (P) Is 14^{1}, dwellers in Israel with certain conceded, not inherited rights (cf RS ^{OTJC 434, 2nd ed 342 n} ^{K 42} ^{Sem 75 f.} Sta ^{Gesch I 400}) The גר is to share in Sabbath rest Ex 20^{10} 23^{12} (both JE) Dt 5^{14}, otherwise he is to have like obligations with Israel Ex $12^{19.48.49}$ Lv 16^{29} (all P) Lv $17^{8.10.12.13.15}$ 18^{26} 20^{2} 22^{18} $24^{16.22}$ (all H) Nu $9^{14.14}$ $15^{14.15.15.16.26.29.30}$ 19^{10} 35^{15} (all P) Ez 14^{7}; similar rights Dt 1^{16} Ez $47^{22.23}$, and like privileges Dt $16^{11.14}$ 26^{11} 29^{10} 31^{12} cf 2 Ch 30^{25}, very rarely any distinction made, in obligation Lv $25^{47.47.47}$ (H), in permissible food Dt 14^{21}, in future success Dt 28^{43}, kindness to גר frequently enjoined. Lv 19^{10} (‖ עָנִי), 23^{22} (‖ *id*) 19^{34} (all H); Dt $10^{18.19}$ 14^{29} $24^{19.20.21}$ $26^{12.13}$ (all ‖ יָתוֹם וְאַלְמָנָה), oppression prohibited Lv 19^{33} (H) Dt 24^{14}, Ex 22^{20} 23^{9} (JE) Dt 24^{17} 27^{19} Je 7^{6} 22^{3} Zc 7^{10} (these eight ‖ יָתוֹם וְאַלְמָנָה), obj of care to י׳ ψ 146^{9} (‖ *id*.), charge that גר has been oppressed Ez 22^{7} Mal 3^{5} (both ‖ *id*), also Ez 22^{29} (‖ עני ואביון), ψ 94^{6}, cf also command that a poor brother be treated like גֵּר, i.e. kindly, Lv 25^{35} (H) Latest conception somewhat different גר 1 Ch 22^{2} 2 Ch 2^{16} (הַגֵּירִים) gathered for hard service; yet cf. 2 Ch 30^{25}. (Oft. c. verb cogn Ex $12^{48.49}$ Lv 16^{29} $17^{8.10.12.13}$ 18^{26} 19^{33} 20^{2} Nu 9^{14} $15^{14.15.16.26.29}$ 19^{10} Jos 20^{9} Ez $47^{22.23}$; oft ‖ תּוֹשָׁב Gn 23^{4} Lv $25^{23.35.47}$ 1 Ch 29^{15} ψ 39^{13})

†גֵּרוּת **n.f. lodging(-place)**—וישבו בגרות כִּמוֹהָם אשר אצל בית לחם Je 41^{17}, *inn, khan*? so Ew Gf, Hi al גִּדְּרוֹת *folds*, after Joseph Aq.

†יָגוּר **n.pr.loc.** a southern city of Judah, toward Edom Jos 15^{21}.

†[מָגוּר] **n.[m.] sojourning-place, dwelling-place, sojourning**—sf. מגוּרָם ψ 55^{16}; pl cstr מגורי Gn 37^{1}, sf מְגוּרַי Gn 47^{9}, מְגוּרָי ψ 119^{54}, מְגֻרֶיךָ Gn 17^{8} 28^{4}, מגוּריו Jb 18^{19}, מְגוּרֵיהֶם Gn 36^{7} + 2 t, מְגֻרֵיהֶם Ex 6^{4},—*dwelling-place* ψ 55^{16} Jb 18^{19},—*sojourning(-place)*, always pl, אֶרֶץ מ׳ Gn 17^{8} 28^{4} 36^{7} 37^{1} Ex 6^{4} (Hex always P) Ez 20^{38}; *sojourning* (pl)=life-time, שני מ׳ Gn 47^{9} ימי מ׳ Gn 47^{9}; cf בית מ׳ ψ 119^{54}.

†מְגוּרָה **n.f. store-house, granary** Hg 2^{19}.

†מַמְּגֻרוֹת **n.f.pl.** *id*, Jo 1^{17} (‖ אֹצָרוֹת; but 𝔊 ληνοί, Me נחות)

†II [גּוּר] **vb. stir up strife, quarrel** (cf גרה)—so Ew Che Di RVm (Is 54^{15}), **gather together** Ges De Br cf. 𝔗 𝔙, so AV RV,—**Qal.** *Pf* גָּר Is 54^{15}, *Impf* יָגוּר v^{15}, יָגוּרוּ ψ 56^{7} 59^{4} 140^{3} (on all cf infr); *Inf* abs גּוֹר Is 54^{15},—**1.** *stir up strife*, abs גּוֹר יָגוּר Is 54^{15}; cf ψ 56^{7} (but AE Che rd יָגוֹדּוּ *attack*, v. גדד); sq. עַל ψ 59^{4} (but Che *id*; cf ψ 94^{21}, wh however Ol would emend by 56^{7} 59^{4}), sq. acc. מִלְחָמוֹת ψ 140^{3} (Hup Che rd יְגָרוּ Pi. Impf of גרה) **2.** *quarrel*, sq אֵת־ *with* Is 54^{15} Here also **Hithpol.** *Impf* Ho 7^{14} יִתְגּוֹרָרוּ (cf I גור), acc to Ew, *they excite themselves*, but unlikely, v נדד

†[גּוּר] **n.[m.] whelp** (as *quarrelsome*? or onomatop? perhaps=As *gîru* Zehnpfund ^{BAS I 504}) of lion—גּוּרֵי אֲרָיוֹת Je 51^{38} (‖ כְּפִרִים) sim of Babylonians; cf גֹּרֹתָיו Na 2^{13} (‖ *id* v^{14}) fig. of Assyrians

†II גּוּר **n.m.** ^{Ez 19.3.5} **whelp, young**—cstr. גּוּר(אַרְיֵה) Gn 49^{9} + 2 t; sf. גּוּרֶיהָ Ez 19^{2}, גֻּרֶיהָ Ez $19^{3.5}$, גּוּרֵיהֶן La 4^{3},—**1.** lion's *whelps*, fig of Judah Gn 49^{9}, of Dan Dt 33^{22}, of Assyrian (prince?) Na 2^{12}; fig. of Israelites Ez $19^{2.3.5}$ (‖ כפיר) **2.** young of jackals (תַּנִּין) La 4^{3}.

†III. [גּוּר] **vb. dread** (cf יָגֹר)—**Qal** *Impf* וַיָּגָר Nu 22^{3} 1 S 18^{15}, 2 ms תָּגוּר Dt 18^{22}, אָגוּר

Dt 32^{27}; pl. יָגוּרוּ ψ 33^{8} Jb 41^{17} + Ho 10^{5}, תָּגוּרוּ Dt 1^{17}; *Imv.* גּוּרוּ ψ 22^{24} Jb 19^{29};—**1.** *be afraid* of, sq. מִפְּנֵי Nu 22^{3} Dt 1^{17} 1 S 18^{15}, גּוּרוּ לָכֶם מִפְּנֵי Jb 19^{29}; c. מִן 41^{17} Dt 18^{22}; c. acc. Dt 32^{27} (poet.) Ho 10^{5} rd. prob. ינודו *lament* (|| אבל, used c. לְ *e.g.* Na 3^{7} Je 15^{5} al.; cf. Che). **2.** *stand in awe* of, sq. מִן ψ 22^{24} 33^{8} (|| יָרֵא).

†מָגוֹר **n.m.** fear, terror—abs. מ׳ ψ 31^{14} + 6 t. + Je 20^{3} cf. infr.; pl. sf. מְגוּרַי La 2^{22};—*fear, terror* Is 31^{9}; = cause of terror Je 20^{4}; elsewhere in phrase, coined by Jerem., מ׳ מִסָּבִיב *terror on every side* Je 6^{25} 20^{3} (where as n.pr.), v^{10} 46^{5} 49^{29} ψ 31^{14} La 2^{22} (מְגוּרַי מִסּ׳).

†[מְגוֹרָה] **n.f.** fear, terror—cstr. מְגֹרַת Pr 10^{24}; pl. sf. מְגוּרוֹתַי ψ 34^{5}, מְגוּרֹתָם Is 66^{4} (on these forms with ו cf. Ges § 27.3. R.1, & 85.48);—*terror* (= thing dreaded) ψ 34^{5} Pr 10^{24} Is 66^{4}.

[גּוֹרֶן] Je 2^{25} גורנך Kt v. גָּרוֹן.

גושׁ (*be hard*, cf. Ar. جَسَأَ *be hard*, of hands, from toil).

†גּוּשׁ **n.[m.]** clod, lump (NH *id.*, Aram. גּוּשְׁה; cf. Ar. جُسْءٌ etc., *rough ground*, also *ice*)—וְגִישׁ עָפָר Jb 7^{5}, Qr וְגוּשׁ ע׳.

גֵּז v. sub גזז.

†גִּזְבָּר **n.m.** treasurer (loan-word; NH *id.*; cf. BAram. [גִּזְבַּר], pl. גְּדָבְרַיָּא; Syr. ܓܝܙܒܪܐ, also ܓܙܒܪܐ, Pers. گنجور, cf. Lag Ges. Abh. 27 f., Arm. Stud. § 454), Ezr 1^{8}.

†[גָּזָה] **vb.** cut, (cut off, sever), √of גָּזִית (cf. Talm. גְּזָא *cut off*); hence perh. **Qal** *Pt. act.* sf. גֹּזִי ψ 71^{6} thou art *he that severed me* from my mother's womb (De Che; 𝔊 σκεπαστής, De prop. ἐκσπαστής, v. 𝔊 ψ 22^{10}; 𝔙 *protector* cf. 𝔊, Thes Ew Hup Pe *benefactor*, cf. Ar. جَزَا *requite*, Jerus. Syr. ܓܙܐ, Talm. גְּזָא *id.*);—txt. and mng. dub.; || ψ 22^{10} has גֹּחִי; v. Che crit. n. and OP 476; Du עֻזִּי.

†גָּזִית **n.f.** a cutting, hewing—גָּזִית Ex 20^{25} + 10 t., always abs.;—*hewing*, אַבְנֵי ג׳ = *hewn stones* (building-stones) 1 K 5^{31} 1 Ch 22^{2} Ez 40^{42} (for tables), cf. אֲבָנִים יְקָרוֹת כְּמִדּוֹת ג׳ 1 K 7$^{9.11}$ (but Klo del. as gloss, cf. 𝔊); also without אבני = *hewn stones* Ex 20^{25} (altar) Am 5^{11} (בָּתֵּי ג׳) Is 9^{9} (opp. לְבֵנִים); טוּרֵי ג׳ 1 K 6^{36}, טוּרִים ג׳ 7^{12}; also La 3^{9} גָּדַר דְּרָכַי בְּג׳.

גִּזָּה v. sub גזז.

†גִּזוֹנִי **adj.gent.** 1 Ch 11^{34} הַשֵּׁם הַגִּזוֹנִי, but rd. יָשֵׁן הַגּוּנִי (𝔊L Εἱρασαι ὁ Γουνι) cf. גּוּנִי.

†[גָּזַז] **vb.** shear (NH *id.*, Aram. גְּזַז, ܓܙ; Ar. جَزَّ, As. deriv.)—**Qal** *Impf.* וַיָּגָז Jb 1^{20}; 2 ms. תָּגֹז Dt 15^{19}; *Imv.* 2 fs. גָּזִּי Je 7^{29}, גֹּזִּי Mi 1^{16}; *Inf.* cstr. גְּזֹז Gn 31^{19} (E) 1 S 25^{2}, גֹּז Gn 38^{13} (J); *Pt.* גֹּזֵז 1 S 25^{4}; pl. גֹּזְזִים 1 S 25^{7} + 2 t.; cstr. גֹּזְזֵי Gn 38^{12}; sf. גֹּזְזַי 1 S 25^{11}, גֹּזְזֶיהָ Is 53^{7};—*shear* sheep (obj. צֹאן) Gn 31^{19} 38^{13} Dt 15^{19} 1 S 25$^{2.4}$; cf. *Pt. shearer* (c. צאן) Gn 38^{12}, also גֹּזְזֶיהָ (i.e. רָחֵל) Is 53^{7}; abs. = *sheep-shearer*, 1 S 25$^{7.11}$ 2 S 13$^{23.24}$; obj. man's head (ראשׁ) Jb 1^{20}; of a woman's (fig. of Israel) Mi 1^{16} (no obj.; || קרחי), (fig. of Jerusalem) Je 7^{29} (obj. נֵזֶר q.v.) **Niph.** נָגֹזּוּ *be cut off* (= destroyed) of Assyrians Na 1^{12}.

†גֵּז **n.[m.]** shearing, mowing (As. *gizzu* Zehnpfund BAS i. 530, Aram. גִּזָּא, ܓܙܬܐ *fleece*)—גֵּז ψ 72^{6}, also cstr. Dt 18^{4} Jb 31^{20}; pl. cstr. גִּזֵּי Am 7^{1};—*shearing* = thing sheared off, *wool, fleece* ג׳ צֹאן Dt 18^{4}, ג׳ כְּבָשַׂי Jb 31^{20}; *mowing* Am 7^{1} (ג׳ הַמֶּלֶךְ cf. RS Sem. i. 228); = land to be mown ψ 72^{6} (but *shearing* in both, acc. to Hoffm ZAW 1883, 116 ff. SS).

†גִּזָּה **n.f.** fleece—(Ar. جِزَّةٌ, Aram. ܓܙܬܐ) גִּזָּה Ju 6^{37} + 5 t.; cstr. גִּזַּת Ju 6^{37};—*fleece*, ג׳ צֶמֶר Ju 6^{37}; abs. Ju 6$^{37.38.38.39.39.40}$.

†גָּזֵז **n.pr.m.** son of עֵיפָה, concub. of Caleb 1 Ch 2$^{46.46}$; v^{b} says that חָרָן son of עיפה (and Caleb?) begat Gazez.

גָּזִית v. sub גזה.

†I. גָּזַל **vb.** tear away, seize, rob (NH *id.*, Ph. גזל Niph., Aram. גְּזַל, ܓܙܠ & (Nas.) ܓܙܠ; Ar. جَزَلَ *cut off*)—**Qal** *Pf.* גָּזַל Jb 20^{19} Ez 18^{18}, גָּזַל Lv 5^{23} + 2 t., גָּזַלְתִּי ψ 69^{5} etc.; *Impf.* יִגְזֹל Ez 18^{7}, וַיִּגְזֹל 2 S 23^{21} 1 Ch 11^{23} etc.; *Inf.* גְּזֹל Is 10^{2}; *Pt.* act. גּוֹזֵל Pr 28^{24}; sf. גֹּזְלוֹ ψ 35^{10}; pl. cstr. גֹּזְלֵי Mi 3^{2}; pass. גָּזוּל Dt 28^{29} + 4 t.;—*tear away, rob*, c. obj. rei (movable), flock (עֵדֶר) Jb 24^{2}, ass Dt 28^{31}, women Ju 21^{23} cf. Gn 31^{31} (E), tear away orphan child from breast Jb 24^{9} יתום מִשֹּׁד, snatch a spear from enemy's hand 2 S 23^{21} = 1 Ch 11^{23}; fig. of drying up snow-water Jb 24^{19}; (obj. stationary) *take violent possession of*, well of water Gn 21^{25} (E), house Jb 20^{19}, fields Mi 2^{2}; (hyperb.) the skin Mi 3^{2}; c. acc. cogn. = *seize, plunder*, obj. גְּזֵלָה Lv 5^{23} (P) Ez 18$^{7.12.16}$, גֵּזֶל Ez 18^{18} 22^{29}; indef. ψ 69^{5}; fig., obj. מִשְׁפָּט Is 10^{2}; c. obj. pers. robbed ψ 35^{10} Pr 22^{22} 28^{24}, prob. also Ju 9^{25} cf. Lv 19^{13} (H; abs.); cf. also pass. Dt 28^{29} (|| עָשׁוּק); הציל גָּזוּל מיד עושק Je 21^{12} cf. 22^{3}; Mal 1^{13} גָּזוּל (|| פִּסֵּחַ *lame* and חולה *sick*), prob. that rescued

after seizure by wild beasts, therefore mutilated †**Niph.** *Pf* 3 fs ונגזלה, subj *sleep* Pr 4[16] (|| לא יִשְׁנוּ).

†גָּזֵל **n.[m.] robbery**—abs גָּזֵל Lv 5^{21} + 3 t. + Ez 18^{18} cf infr, cstr. גְּזֶל Ec 5^{7} Ez 18^{18} (but cf infr),—*robbery* Lv 5^{21} (P) ψ 62^{11} (|| עשֶׁק) Is 61^{8}, = *thing plundered*, taken as plunder, as acc cogn. Ez 22^{29} (גָּזְלוּ גָּזֵל); fig גֵּזֶל מִשְׁפָּט = wresting of justice (cf Is 10^{2}) Ec 5^{7} —Ez 18^{18} has גֵּזֶל אָח, but 𝔊 Co del אח; rd. then גָּזֵל —Cf Lag[BN 172].

†גְּזֵלָה **n.f. plunder, spoil**—גזלה Lv 5^{23} + 3 t.; cstr גְּזֵלַת Is 3^{14}, גזלות Ez 18^{12};—*thing seized, spoil* Lv 5^{23} (P) Ez 33^{15}, גְּזֵלַת הֶעָנִי Is 3^{14}, as acc cogn Ez $18^{7.12.16}$

II גזל (✓ of foll, mng dub; acc to Fl NHWB i 433 onomatop., cf جَزَلَ Frey *crassa vox, vox columbi*, v also Fra[114])

†גּוֹזָל **n m.** [Dt 32, 11] **young of birds** (Syr. ܙܘܠܐ, cf Ar جَوْزَل)—ותר וגוזל: Gn 15^{9} pigeon, גּוֹזָלָיו Dt 32^{11} eaglet (suff ref to נֶשֶׁר)

גזם (*cut off*, NH *id*, Eth ገዘመ: cf Ar جَزَمَ [= Aram. ܓܙܡ], or possibly جَذَمَ [= Aram. ܓܕܡ])

†גָּזָם **n m.** [Am 4, 9] **locusts** (coll)—abs גָּזָם Jo 1^{4} 2^{25} Am 4^{9},—always as devouring, devastating, Jo 1^{4} (|| אַרְבֶּה, יֶלֶק, חָסִיל), 2^{25} (|| *id*); Am 4^{9} alone *your gardens and your vineyards, and your fig-trees and your olive-trees* יֹאכַל הַגָּזָם.

†גַּזָּם **n.pr.m.** head of a family of returned exiles בני ג׳ Ezr 2^{48} = Ne 7^{51}

גזע (✓ of foll, cf Ar جَزَعَ *cut off*, & Eth. ገዘዐ. *saw in two*).

†[גֶּזַע] **n m** [Jb 14, 8] **stock, stem** (NH *id*, cf Syr ܓܙܥܐ *stem, trunk*)—cstr גֶּזַע Is 11^{1}, sf גִּזְעוֹ Jb 14^{8}, גִּזְעָם Is 40^{24},—*stock, stem* of a tree Jb 14^{8} (|| שֹׁרֶשׁ); fig ג׳ יִשַׁי '*stem of Jesse*' Is 11^{1} (|| שָׁרָשׁ), שֹׁרֵשׁ בָּאָרֶץ ג׳ Is 40^{24} (|| זרע, נטע).

†גָּזַר **vb. cut, divide** (Ar جَزَرَ, NH גָּזַר *cut, determine, circumcise*, Eth ገዘረ: Aram גְּזַר, ܓܙܰܪ)—**Qal** *Pf* גָּזַר Hb 3^{17}, *Impf* וַיִּגְזֹר Is 9^{19}; 2 ms תִּגְזַר Jb 22^{28}, וַיִּגְזָר־ 2 K 6^{4}, *Pt.* act גֹּזֵר ψ 136^{13},—**1.** *divide, cut in two*, sq. acc 1 K 3^{25} (ג׳ לִשְׁנַיִם) cf v^{26} (obj not expressed) **2.** *divide* the Red Sea (acc) ψ 136^{13} sq לִגְזָרִים **3.** *cut down* הָעֵצִים 2 K 6^{4} **4.** *cut off* (piece of meat to eat, but obj not expr || אכל) Is 9^{19} **5.** *cut off*, i e *destroy, exterminate* Hb 3^{17} (c acc.; indef subj), sq. מִן loc. **6.** *decree* (Aramaism, cf. B Aram) Jb 22^{28} c. acc **Niph.** *Pf* נִגְזַר 2 Ch 26^{21} Est 2^{1}, נִגְזַרְתִּי La 3^{54}, נִגְזָרוּ ψ 88^{6}, נִגְזָרְנוּ Ez 37^{11} Is 53^{8},—**1.** *be cut off*, separated, excluded from (מִן) temple 2 Ch 26^{21}, from (מִן) Yahweh's hand ψ 88^{6} (of the slain), from (מִן) the land of the living Is 53^{8} (of the suffering servant of י׳) **2.** *be cut off* = *destroyed* La 3^{54} Ez 37^{11} **3** *be decreed*, Est 2^{1} sq עַל *against* (cf **Qal 6**)

†I [גֶּזֶר] **n.[m.] part**, only pl. הַגְּזָרִים Gn 15^{17} of halves of animals, גְּזָרִים ψ 136^{13} of divided portions of Red Sea.

†II גֶּזֶר **n.pr.loc.** (*portion*) Levitical city on border of Ephraim Jos 10^{33} 12^{12} 21^{21} 1 K 9^{16} 1 Ch 6^{52} 7^{28} 20^{4}; גָּזֶר Jos $16^{3.10}$ Ju $1^{29.29}$ cf. 2 S 5^{25} 1 K $9^{15.17}$; c ־ָה loc. גָּזְרָה 1 Ch 14^{16};—cuneiform *Gazri*, Bez [Tell el Amarna Tabl BM 148], mod Tell-Jezer, c 18 m N of W fr Jerus, S of the Jaffa road, Gann in PEF [1873, 78 f., 1875, 74 f.] cf Bd [Pal 17]

†גִּזְרִי **adj.gent.** 2 S 27^{8} Qr (Kt והגרזי) cf Dr

†גְּזֵרָה **n.f. separation**—אֶל־אֶרֶץ גְּזֵרָה Lv 16^{22} (P) *unto a land of separation*, of the goat for Azazel, *solitary land* RV, 'cut off,' i e. *whence it would not readily find its way back* VB.

†גִּזְרָה **n f. cutting, separation**—גִּזְרָה Ez 41^{12} + 6 t; sf גִּזְרָתָם La 4^{7},—**1.** *cutting*, i e *polishing* (AV RV or *carving*, i e beauty of form, shape, cf. VB) סַפִּיר גִּזְרָתָם La 4^{7}, their *polishing* (or *beauty of form*) was as *sapphire*. **2.** *separation*, הַגִּזְרָה Ez $41^{12.13.14.15}$ $42^{1.10.13}$, separate place AV RV cf Da, i e yard, or space adjoining temple on three sides

†[מַגְזֵרָה] **n.f. cutting instrument, axe**—2 S 12^{31} of David's treatment of captives, וַיָּשֶׂם בַּמְּגֵרָה . . . וּבְמַגְזְרוֹת הַבַּרְזֶל.

גחזי v. sub גיא

גחי v [גוח, גיח]

גחל (prob = *kindle, burn*)

†גַּחֶלֶת **n.f** [Ez 1, 13] **coal** (cf As *guhlu*, a shining precious stone? COT [Gloss] Zim [BP 40])—abs גַּחֶלֶת Is 47^{14}; sf גַּחַלְתִּי 2 S 14^{7}, pl גֶּחָלִים ψ 18^{9} + 6 t., cstr גַּחֲלֵי Lv 16^{12} + 5 t + ψ 18^{14} (del 𝔊 De Che), sf גֶּחָלָיו Is 44^{19}, גֶּחָלֶיהָ Ez 24^{11}, —*coal*, pl ג׳ אֵשׁ *coals of fire* Lv 16^{12} (P), 2 S 22^{13} = ψ 18^{13} [also ψ 18^{14} cf. supr] Ez 10^{2} (in vision), cf. 2 S 22^{9} = ψ 18^{9} Jb 41^{13}, also Pr 6^{28} Is 44^{19}, in simile (of strife) Pr 26^{21} (opp. פֶּחָם *black coal*); Ez 1^{13} גַּחֲלֵי אֵשׁ (of the living creatures),

fig. of hope in posterity 2 S 14^{7}, of divine judgment, ג׳ רתם *coals of broom-plant* ψ 120^{4}, cf. 140^{11}, also (negat) Is 47^{14} Ez 24^{11}; of kindness to enemy Pr 25^{22}.

גחם (? cf Ar جَحَمَ *kindle*, جَحِمَ, جَحُمَ *burn*).

† **גַּחַם** **n.pr.m.** (*flame*?) Gn 22^{24} a son of Nahor, brother of Abraham, by ראוּמָה his concubine.

גחן (cf Aram. גְּחַן, Nasar. ܓܚܢ (Syr. ܓܚܢ PS) *curve, bend*).

† **גָּחוֹן** **n.m.** belly, of reptiles (cf. perh. As. *giḫinnu, cord* (from twisting?) Zim$^{BP\ 104}$)—גְּחֹנְךָ Gn 3^{14} (J) of the serpent, cf. גָּחוֹן Lv 11^{42} (P).

גחר (? cf. Ar جَحَرَ *retire, retreat*, etc)

† **גַּחַר** **n.pr.m.** head of a family of returned exiles Ezr 2^{47} בני־ג׳=Ne 7^{49} בְּנֵי־גָחַר.

† **גַּיְא** **n m.** $^{Is\ 40.4}$ (**f.** $^{Zc\ 14.4}$) valley—abs. גַּיְא Nu 21^{20}+8 t + 1 S 17^{52} (cf. infr.), גָּיְא 1 Ch 4^{39}, גֵּיא Zc 14^{4}, גֶּיא Is 40^{4}, גֵּי Dt 34^{6}+2 t; cstr. גֵּיא Is 22^{1}+21 t, גֵּי Jos 15^{8}+13 t.; pl. abs גֵּאָיוֹת Ez 31^{12} $36^{4.6}$+7^{16} 32^{5} (del. Co)+6^{3} 2 K 2^{16} Qr (so Co Ez 6^{3}, Kt גיאות), sf גֵּיאֹתֶיךָ Ez 35^{8};—*valley* Jos 8^{11} (E) Mi 1^{6} 1 S 17^{3} 2 K 2^{16} (opp. הַר) Is 40^{4} (opp. הַר, גִּבְעָה), Ez 6^{3} 35^{8} $36^{4.6}$ (in all c. הרים, גבעות, אפיקים), 31^{12} (opp. הַר), cf. 7^{16} (del. B Co) 32^{5}; specif., valley in Moab, a station of Isr Nu 21^{20} (E); over against Beth-Peor Dt 3^{29} 4^{46} 34^{6}, a valley near גְּדוֹר 1 Ch 4^{39}; ג׳ חִזָּיוֹן Is $22^{1.5}$ near Jerus; ג׳ שְׁמָנִים Is $28^{1.4}$ *valley of fatness*, fertility, the valley surrounding Samaria; שַׁעַר הַגַּ׳ 2 Ch 26^{9} Ne $2^{13.15}$ 3^{13}, apocalyptic valley Zc 14^{4}, made by cleaving Mt. of Olives, cf ג׳ הרים v$^{5.5}$, valley of slaughter ג׳ ההרגה, a future name of valley of Hinnom Je 7^{32} 19^{6} 1 S 17^{52} (גַּיְא) 𝔊 rds גַּת cf. We Dr; Je 2^{23} of valley of Hinnom, v. infr.; fig. ψ 23^{4} ג׳ צלמות cf צלמות, Ez 39^{11} ג׳ הָעֹבְרִים, Co הָעֲבָרִים n pr. cf. infr., elsewhere in combination with n pr.:—**a.** ג׳ יִפְתַּח־אֵל Jos $19^{14.27}$ perh = *Jotapata* Jos$^{BJ\ III\ 7\ 7}$, Rabbin נופתחא Reland$^{Pal\ 816}$;—*Tell Jefât* Rob$^{BR\ III.\ 107}$. Guérin$^{Gal\ I.\ 476\ f.}$ cf. Bd$^{Pal\ 243}$. **b.** ג׳ הַצְּבֹעִים 1 S 13^{18}. **c.** ג׳־הַמֶּלַח 2 K 14^{7} (Kt; Qr om. art) 1 Ch 18^{12} 2 Ch 25^{11}=ג׳־מֶלַח 2 S 8^{13} ψ 60^{2} (title); S of Dead Sea, in or bordering on Edom, *el-Ghôr* Rob$^{BR\ II.\ 109}$. **d.** ג׳ הַחֲרָשִׁים 1 Ch 4^{14} Ne 11^{35}, appar. near Lod & Ono, NW of Jerus., not far from the sea. **e.** ג׳ צְפַתָה לְמָרֵשָׁה 2 Ch 14^{9} (? rd. צָפֹנָה, 𝔊 κατὰ βορρᾶν, *to the north of M.*) prob. near the great plain of Judah, W. of Jerus, toward the sea; ג׳ הָעֹבְרִים Ez 39^{11}, E of Dead Sea (Hi Sm), Co rds. ג׳ הָעֲבָרִים. **f.** name to be changed to ג׳ הֲמוֹן־גּוֹג Ez $39^{11.15}$. Most frequently **g.** גֵּי הִנֹּם Jos 15^{8} 18^{16} Ne 11^{30}, גֵּי בֶן־הִנֹּם Jos 15^{8} 18^{16} 2 K 23^{10} Qr (Kt (גי בני ה׳) 2 Ch 28^{3} 33^{6} Je $7^{31.32}$ $19^{2.6}$ 32^{35}; valley SW. & S. of Jerus. (Rob$^{BR\ II\ 273\ f.}$), where incense was burned, and children were offered in sacrifice to 'Molech.' Others identify with the Tyropœon valley, cf RS$^{Sem.\ I\ 353}$; vid further הִנֹּם, תֹּפֶת.

† **גֵּיחֲזִי, גֵּחֲזִי** **n.pr.m.** (*valley of vision*?) servant of Elisha, גֵּיחֲזִי 2 K $4^{12.14.25.27.29.36}$ $5^{20.21}$, גחזי 2 K 4^{31} 5^{25} $8^{4.5}$.

גִּיד (√ of foll; mng dub; ? cf As *gîdu, bind, fetter*, Jäger$^{BAS\ I\ 469\ f.}$)

† **גִּיד** **n.m.**$^{Gn\ 32.33}$ sinew (NH *id*, Aram גִּידָא, ܓܝܕܐ, cf Ar جِيد *neck*)—cstr גִּיד Gn $32^{33.33}$ Is 48^{4}; pl. גִּידִים Jb 10^{11} Ez 37^{6}, גִּדִים Ez 37^{8}; cstr גִּידֵי Jb 40^{17},—*sinew*, in general of human body, ‖ בשר, עור, עצמות, Jb 10^{11} cf. Ez $37^{6.8}$; of thigh Gn 32^{33} (of beast) v^{33}, iron sinew, fig of obstinacy, Is 48^{4} וג׳ בַּרְזֶל עָרְפֶּךָ וּמִצְחֲךָ נְחוּשָׁה; of hippopot, ג׳ פחדו, i e. of his loins, Jb 40^{17}

† [גּוּחַ, גִּיחַ] **vb.** burst forth (cf Nö$^{ZMG\ 1883,\ 536}$, NH *id.*, Aram *id*, and جاح; Eth. ገሐ: *break forth*, of light, etc.)—**Qal** *Impf.* יָגִיחַ Jb 40^{23}, 2 ms. וַתָּגַח Ez 32^{2}, *Imv.* fs. גֹּחִי Mi 4^{10}, *Inf.* sf. (ב)גיחו Jb 38^{8}; *Pt* sf. גֹּחִי ψ 22^{10} (but cf. infr),—**1.** intrans. *burst forth*, of dashing river (a very Jordan) Jb 40^{23}, of sea fig. as babe from womb Jb 38^{8}, cf. **2.** trans. **a.** *draw forth* from womb (subj י׳) ψ 22^{10} (where rd גֹּחִי pt. fr גחה, or regard גֹּחִי as metapl., as if fr גחח*? v. De & Che$^{crit.\ note}$) cf. ψ 71^{6}; also **b.** *thrust forth, bring forth*, fig of travail, applied to Jerusalem in distress Mi 4^{10} (cf Sta$^{§\ 399\ b}$ Kö$^{I\ 505}$); burst forth with rivers (fig of Pharaoh under image of תַּנִּים) Ez 32^{2}, but for בנהרותיך (*rivers*) rd. prob. בנחרותיך Jb 41^{12} (*nostrils*), i e. snort with thy nostrils, so Ew Co; on fig. then cf. Jb 41^{11-13}.

† **גִּיחַ** **n.pr.loc.** (fr. *a spring*?) near Gibeon in Benjamin 2 S 2^{24}.

† **גִּיחוֹן** **n.pr.fl** (*a bursting forth*)—**1.** one of the rivers of Eden Gn 2^{13} (on theories of identity v Comm, also Smith$^{Dict.\ Bible}$ Schaff-Herzog$^{Art.\ Eden}$ Spurrell$^{Text\ of\ Gen.\ ad\ loc}$ Ri^{HWB}). **2.** spring of water near Jerusalem: גחון 1 K $1^{33.38.45}$, מֵימֵי גִיחוֹן בַּנַּחַל 2 Ch 32^{30}, לְגִיחוֹן בַּנַּחַל 2 Ch 33^{14};—there are two main theories as to locality: **a.** W. of Jerusalem, connected with *Birket Mamilla*, and aqueduct into city Rob$^{BR\ I.\ 329,\ 345\ ff.}$

Survey[Jerusalem] al ; **b.** E of Jerusalem = Fountain of the Virgin, Furrer[Schenkel BL II 463] Bd[Pal 101], or Siloah water-system Guthe[ZPV. v. 1882 378 ff]

גֵּיחֲזִי v sub גַּיְא

† [**גִּיל**] **vb. rejoice** (No[ZMG 1883, 337], cf Ar جَالَ *go round* or *about, be excited* to levity, etc)—**Qal** *Pf.* גַּלְתִּי Is 65[19], *Impf* יָגִיל, תָּגִיל ψ 21[2] + 4 t (ψ 21[2] Kt יגיל, Qr יָגֶל with retracted tone), יָגֵל, תָּגֵל, ψ 13[6] + 11 t, וַיָּגֶל ψ 16[9], אָגִילָה, נָגִילָה ψ 9[15] + 5 t, יָגִילוּ ψ 13[5] + 5 t, יגילון ψ 89[17], תָּגֵלְנָה ψ 48[12] + 2 t., יָגוֹל Pr 23[24], *Imv* גִּילוּ ψ 2[11] + 4 t, גִּילִי Is 49[13] + 2 t ,—**1.** *rejoice,* **a** abs ψ 13[6] 51[10] Zc 9[9], ‖ שמח ψ 14[7] 16[9] 32[11] 48[12] 53[7] 96[11] 97[1.8] Pr 23[24.25] 1 Ch 16[31] Hb 1[15], ‖ שׂושׂ, שׂישׂ Is 35[1] 65[18] **b** c בְּ ψ 149[2] Pr 2[14] 24[17] Is 9[2], בירושלם Is 65[19] 66[10]; בישׁועתך ψ 9[15] 13[6] 21[2], ביהוה ψ 35[9] Is 41[16] Zc 10[7], באלהים Is 61[10] Hb 3[18], בשם י׳ ψ 89[17], בקדושׁ ישׂראל Is 29[19], גיל ושׂמח ב׳ ψ 31[8] 118[24] Ct 1[4] Is 25[9] Jo 2[23], גילי ושׂמחי כי Jo 2[21] **c.** with עַל Zp 3[17] Besides persons the subj is לב ψ 13[6] Pr 24[17] Zc 10[7], נפשׁ ψ 35[9] Is 61[10], כבוד (=נפשׁ) ψ 16[9], ארץ 1 Ch 16[31] ψ 96[11] 97[1] Is 49[13], ערבה Is 35[1.2] **2** *tremble* (cf Ar وَجِلَ) ψ 2[11] ‖ עבד (Thes Ew Hi Che, but 𝔊 Hu De Pe AV RV *rejoice*), Ho 10[5] ‖ אבל (Thes and most mod., but AV RV that *rejoiced* over it), possibly error for חיל Ew Gr Che

† I **גִּיל** **n.[m.] rejoicing**—Jb 3[22] + 6 t, גּוֹל Pr 23[24], sf גִּילִי ψ 43[4],—*rejoicing* ψ 65[13] Pr 23[24], ‖ שׂמחה ψ 45[16] Is 16[10] Je 48[33] Jo 1[16], שִׂמְחַת גִּילִי ψ 43[4], שׂמח אל גיל *glad unto rejoicing* Ho 9[1] Jb 3[22]

† II [**גִּיל**] **n.[m.] circle, age,** מן הילדים אשׁר כגִלְכֶם *of the youths which are of your age* Dn 1[10] (cf Ar جِيل, Sam. גיל = Heb דור = γενεά, Talm. בן גילו *one born at the same time, a contemporary*).

† **גִּילָה** **n f. rejoicing** Is 65[18], גילת ורנן Is 35[2] (nom verbal for Inf abs. cf De Di, cstr before ו Ges[§ 130 2], but rd prob גִּילָה (הַגִּילָה), read Is 9[2] for הַגּוֹי לא by Krochm Che RS Di

† **גִּלֹה** **n.pr loc** city in mountains of Judah Jos 15[51] 2 S 15[12], (on √ cf Dr 2 S 15[12])

† **גִּילֹנִי** **adj gent.** 2 S 15[12], 23[34] = 1 Ch 11[36], where also rd הַגִּ׳ (for MT הַפְּלֹנִי)

גִּינַת v sub גנן

גִּיר (*boil, boil up*? cf Aram גִּיר *wave*, NH *id foam*, Ar. جَيَّارٌ *quicklime*, also *heat in chest from rage or hunger* (Lane); *admodum aestuans* acc to Fl NHWB[I 435 b], but cf infr.)

† **גִּר** **n.[m.] chalk, lime** (perh Aram. loan-word cf Fra[8], Aram (also B Aram) גִּיר, ܓܺܝܪܳܐ; Ar جِيرٌ is loan-wd Fra[l c])—כאבני גר מְנֻפָּצוֹת Is 27[9].

† [**גִּיר**] **n.m.** 2 Ch 2[16] v גֵּר sub I. גור

† **גִּישׁ** Jb 7[5] Kt, v. גוּשׁ.

† **גֵּישָׁן** **n.pr.m.** a descendant of Judah through Caleb 1 Ch 2[47].

גַּל, גֵּל, גֻּל v. sub גלל

גלב (= *shear, shave,* As [*galâbu*] Hpt[SFG], Aram גְּלַב *id*, גַּלְּבָא *razor,* cf. ܓܠܒܐ 2 S 20[8] v PS)

† [**גַּלָּב**] **n.[m.] barber** (Ph גלב CIS[I, 257 ff])—תַּעַר הַגַּלָּבִים Ez 5[1]

† **גִּלְבֹּעַ** **n.pr.loc. Gilboa'** (derivation unknown), mountain-ridge at S.E. end of plain of Jezreel, where Saul & Jonathan were killed; usually c art. הַר הַגִּ׳ 1 S 31[1.8] 2 S 1[6], הָרֵי בַגִּלְבֹּעַ 2 S 1[21] (David's lament), בַּגִּ׳ alone 1 S 28[4] 2 S 21[12], without art. הַר גִּלְבֹּעַ 1 Ch 10[1.8] (‖ 1 S 31[1.8] supr),—mod. *Jebel Fukû'a* Bd[Pal 244]

גַּלְגַּל, גִּלְגָּל, גֻּלְגֹּלֶת v sub גלל

גלד (√ of foll. mng dub perh cf. Eth. ገለደ: *obducere, inducere ;* Ar. جَلَدَ *scourge*).

† [**גֶּלֶד**] **n.m. skin** (Ar جِلْدٌ, Aram. גִּלְדָּא, ܓܶܠܕܳܐ) of man Jb 16[15] שַׂק תָּפַרְתִּי עֲלֵי גִלְדִּי.

גָּלָה [189] **vb. uncover, remove** (NH *id*, cf. Ar جَلَا *be* or *become clear, uncovered, display, reveal, declare, go forth, emigrate,* cf Eth ገለወ: *obducere, velare,* & II ገለየ: in deriv. (rare) Di[1141]; Aram גְּלָא, ܓܠܳܐ *reveal*)—**Qal**[51] *Pf* גָּ׳ etc 1 S 4[21] + (18 t in all); *Impf* יִגְלֶה 1 S 20[2] + 5 t, וַיִּגֶל 2 K 17[23] + 3 t., also juss. יִגֶל Jb 20[28] 36[15], 3 mpl יִגְלוּ Am 6[7], *Imv.* ms גְּלֵה Ez 12[3]; *Inf abs* גָּלֹה Am 5[5] + 2 t, *cstr* גְּלוֹת Ju 18[30] Je 1[3], *Pt* גֹּלֶה 2 K 24[14], גֹּלָה 1 S 22[8] + 3 t., f גּוֹלָה Is 49[21], *pass* גָּלוּי Est 3[14] + 2 t, cstr גְּלוּי Nu 24[4 16];—**1.** גָּלָה אֹזֶן *uncover the ear* of one, i e. *reveal* to him 1 S 9[15] 20[2 12 13] 22[8.8 17] 2 S 7[27] 1 Ch 17[25] Ru 4[4] Jb 33[16] 36[10 15], גְּלוּי עֵינַיִם *uncovered of eyes,* having the eyes open Nu 24[4 16], גָּלָה סוֹד *reveal a secret* Am 3[7] Pr 20[19], הגלוי *the revealed* opp הֶחָתוּם Je 32[11], גָּלוּי לְ *disclosed, published* Est 3[14] 8[13] **2.** intr *remove, depart,* גלה משׂושׂ

יגל הארץ *the mirth of the land is departed* Is 24^{11}; יבול ביתו *the increase of his house shall depart* Jb 20^{28}; גלה חציר Pr 27^{25}. **3.** *go into exile* Ju 18^{30} 2 K 17^{23} 25^{21} Is 5^{13} Je 1^{3} 52^{27} Ez 12^{3} 39^{23} Am 1^{5} 5^{5} 6^{7} $7^{11.17}$ Mi 1^{16} La 1^{3}, גלה כבוד 1 S $4^{21.22}$ Ho 10^{5}; pt. גֹּלָה *an exile* 2 S 15^{19} 2 K 24^{14} Is 49^{21} Am 6^{7}. **Niph.** *Pf* נִגְלָה 1 S 3^{21}+9 t., נִגְלְתָה Is 53^{1}, נִגְלֵיתִי 1 S 2^{27}, נגלו Gn 35^{7}+2 t., נגלינו 1 S 14^{8}, *Impf* תִּגָּלֶה, יִגָּלֶה 1 S 3^{7}+4 t., תגל Is 47^{3}, יִגָּלוּ 2 S 22^{16}+2 t; *Imv.* הִגָּלוּ Is 49^{9}, *Inf.* abs. נִגְלֹה 1 S 2^{27}, cstr נגלות 2 S 6^{20}, הִגָּלוֹת 2 S 6^{20}+2 t.; *Pt.* pl נגלת Dt 29^{28};—**1.** refl **a.** *uncover oneself* (one's nakedness) 2 S 6^{20} **b.** *discover* or *shew oneself* Is 49^{9}, אֶל 1 S $14^{8.11}$. **c.** *reveal himself* (of God), אֶל Gn 35^{7} (E) 1 S 2^{27} 3^{21}, באזני Is 22^{14} **2.** pass **a.** *be uncovered* (one's nakedness), ערוה Ex 20^{26} (E) Is 47^{3} Ez 16^{36} 23^{29}, שולים Je 13^{22}. **b.** *be disclosed, discovered*, foundations 2 S 22^{16} (=ψ 18^{16}) Ez 13^{14}; gates of death Jb 38^{17}, עון Ho 7^{1}, פשע Ez 21^{29}, רעה Pr 26^{26} Ez 16^{57}. **c.** *be revealed* כבוד י׳ Is 40^{5}, זרוע י׳ Is 53^{1}, דבר י׳ 1 S 3^{7}, צדקה Is 56^{1}; with לְ Is 23^{1} Dn 10^{1}, הַנִּגְלֹת *the things revealed* Dt 29^{28}. **3.** *be removed*, דורי נִסַּע ונגלה מִנִּי *my habitation is plucked up and removed from me* Is 38^{12}. **Pi.**$_{56}$ *Pf* גִּלָּה Lv 20^{11}, גִּלִּית Is 57^{8}, גִּלֵּיתִי Je 33^{6}, *Impf.* יְגַלֶּה Dt 23^{1}, תְּגַל Pr 25^{9}; *Imv.* גַּל ψ 119^{18}, גַּלִּי Is 47^{2}, *Inf.* גַּלּוֹת Lv 18^{6}; *Pt* מְגַלֶּה Jb 12^{22},—**1.** *uncover*, **a.** *nakedness* (oft=*contract marriage*, RSLag$^{GN\ 1882,\ 408,\ JPh\ ix\ 94}$) Lv 18^{6-19} 20^{11-21} (H 23 t) Ez 22^{10}; cf כנף אביו Dt 23^{1} 27^{20}; of *exposure*, as a reproach, Ez 16^{37} 23^{10}, cf. נבלת Ho 2^{12}, שולים Na 3^{5}, *immodesty* Ez 23^{18}, מקור דמיה Lv 20^{18} (H), תזנותיה Ez 23^{18}; ג׳ alone Is 57^{8} (all subj. fem) **b.** in gen. feet Ru $3^{4.7}$, leg Is 47^{2}, vail v^{2} (i e. *remove it*) cf 22^{8}, פני לבושו Jb 41^{5}, eyes Nu 22^{31} (E) ψ 119^{18} (open them so as to see) **2.** *disclose, discover, lay bare*, secret places Je 49^{10}, deep places Jb 12^{22}, foundations Mi 1^{6}, blood Is 26^{21}, iniquity Jb 20^{27}, secret Pr 11^{13} 25^{9}, a wanderer (betray) Is 16^{3}. **3.** *make known, shew, reveal*, ריב אֶל *make known a cause unto* Je 11^{20} 20^{12}; with לְ Jb 33^{6}; גלה צדקתו לעיני *shew his righteousness in the eyes of* ψ 98^{2}; with על. על חטאת, על עון *make known concerning*, iniquity, sin La 2^{14} 4^{22}. **Pu.** *Pf.* גֻּלְּתָה *be uncovered* Na 2^{8}, *Pt.* תוכחת מְגֻלָּה *open rebuke* Pr 27^{5}. **Hiph.**$_{39}$ *Pf.* הגלה 2 K 17^{11}+, הגלה 2 K 24^{14}, הֶגְלָם 1 Ch 8^{7}, הֶגְלָם Je 20^{4}, *Impf* וַיֶּגֶל 2 K 17^{6}+3 t., sf וַיַּגְלֵם, וַיַּגְלֶהָ 2 K 16^{9}, וַיַּגְלֵם 2 K 15^{29}, 1 Ch 5^{26}, יַגְלוּם 1 Ch 8^{6}. *Inf.* הַגְלוֹת 1 Ch 5^{41}+5 t., בְּגַלּוֹתוֹ Je 27^{20},—*carry away into exile, take into exile* 2 K 15^{29} 16^{9} $17^{6.11.26.27.28.33}$ 18^{11} $24^{14.15}$ 25^{11} 1 Ch $5^{6.26.41}$ $8^{6.7}$ 2 Ch 36^{20} Ezr 2^{1} Ne 7^{6} Est 2^{6} Je 20^{4} 22^{12} 24^{1} 27^{20} $29^{1.4.7.14}$ 39^{9} 43^{3} $52^{15.28.29.30}$ La 4^{22} Ez 39^{28} Am 1^{6} 5^{27}. **Hoph.** *Pf.* הָגְלָה Est 2^{6}, f. הָגְלְתָה Est 2^{6}, הָגְלוּ 1 Ch 9^{1} Je 40^{7}, הָגְלַת Je $13^{19.19}$ (Ges $^{§\ 75\ R\ 1}$), *Pt.* pass. מֻגְלִים Je 40^{1} *carried into exile* **Hithp. 1.** *Impf* וַיִּתְגַּל *was uncovered* (naked) Gn 9^{21}. **2.** *Inf* בהתגלות לבו *that his heart may reveal itself* Pr 18^{2}

† גּוֹלָה$_{42}$ **n.f. exiles, exile**—(cf. Ar جَالٍ *one emigrating*, جَالِيَةٌ *a company of exiles*)—Je 28^{6}+38 t., גֹּלָה Is 49^{21} 1 Ch 5^{22} Est 2^{6} Na 3^{10},—**1.** coll *exiles*, Est 2^{6} Je 29^{1} Ez 1^{1} $3^{11.15}$ $11^{24.25}$ Na 3^{10}; קהל הגולה Ezr 10^{8} כל־הגולה Je 28^{6} $29^{4.20.31}$, **2.** abstract, *exile*, Ezr 6^{21} 9^{4} 10^{6} Zc 6^{10}, הלך בגולה *go into exile* Je 48^{11} 49^{3} Ez 12^{11} 25^{3} Am 1^{15}, יצא בג׳ Je 29^{16} 48^{7} Zc 14^{2}, הוליך גולה *carry into exile* 2 K 24^{15}, הביא ג׳ 2 K 24^{16}, הוציא ג׳ Ez 12^{4}, העלה ג׳ Ezr 1^{11}, כלי גולה *equipment for exile* Je 46^{19} Ez $12^{3.4.7}$, עד הגלה *until the exile* 1 Ch 5^{22}; בני הגולה *exiles* Ezr 4^{1} $6^{19.20}$ 8^{35} $10^{7.16}$, שבי הגולה *captivity of the exile* Ezr 2^{1} Ne 7^{6}.

† גָּלוּת **n.f. exile**—Is 20^{4}+9 t, גָּלֻת Ob$^{20.20}$; sf. גָּלוּתִי Is 45^{13}, גָּלוּתֵנוּ Ez 33^{21} 40^{1} (Qames unchangeable),—**1.** abs *exile*, 2 K 25^{27} Je 52^{31} Ez 1^{2} 33^{21} 40^{1} Am $1^{6.9}$ Ob$^{20.20}$ **2.** coll. *exiles*, גלות כוש Is 20^{4}, גלות יהודה Je 24^{5} 28^{4} 29^{22} 40^{1}, גלותי ישלח *he shall let my exiles* (*Yahweh's*) *go free* Is 45^{13}, vid. Lag$^{Arm\ Stud\ §\ 445}$

† גִּלָּיוֹן **n m. table, tablet** (Talm גליון, the empty margin of page or roll, vid Lag$^{GN\ 1881\ 403,\ cf.\ BN\ 199}$)—קַח־לְךָ גִּלָּיוֹן גָּדוֹל וּכתב עָלָיו *take thee a great tablet and write upon it* Is 8^{1}; pl הַגִּלְיֹנִים *tablets of polished metal, mirrors* Is 3^{23} 𝔗 𝔚 Ges Che Di De; but *transparent garments, gauzes*, 𝔊 Ew (cf Ar. جَلْوَةٌ *fine garment*)

† גָּלְיַת **n.pr.m.** (*conspicuous?* On ending ת cf. Dr 1 S 17^{4} & No in Eut$^{Nab\ 73}$) (גָּלְיָת 1 Ch 20^{5}) Philistine giant slain by David 1 S $17^{4.23}$ 21^{10} 22^{10}, but acc to 2 S 21^{19} slain by Elhanan of Bethlehem (בית הַלַּחְמִי; acc. to 1 Ch 20^{5} Elhanan slew לַחְמִי brother of Goliath).

† יָגְלִי **n.pr.m.** (*led into exile?*) chief of tribe of Dan Nu 34^{22}

גִּלֹה **n.pr.loc.** v. sub גיל

גֻּלָּה v sub גלל

†[גָּלַח] **vb. be bald** (Ar. جَلِحَ); **Pi. shave, shave off** (so NH, Aram.)—*Pf.* וְגִלַּח consec. Lv 14⁹ + 2 t.; sf. וְגִלְּחוֹ consec. 2 S 14²⁶; 3 fs. וְגִלְּחָה consec. Dt 21¹²; *Impf.* יְגַלַּח Lv 14⁹ Is 7²⁰, יְגַלָּח Lv 13³³ + 2 t., וַיְגַלַּח Gn 41¹⁴ 2 S 10⁴; sf. (3 ms.) וַיְגַלְּחֵנוּ, וַיְגַלְּחֵם 1 Ch 19⁴; 3 fs. וַתְּגַלַּח Ju 16¹⁹; 3 mpl. יְגַלֵּחוּ Lv 21⁵ Ez 44²⁰; *Inf.* sf. of subj. גַּלְּחוֹ 2 S 14²⁶;—**1.** *shave*, obj. the head, ראשׁ Nu 6^9.9.18 (P) Dt 21¹² (hair as containing impurity, cf. RS^Sem i. 407), 2 S 14^26.26 cf. 26 Ez 44²⁰; Lv 13³³ (P), obj. הַנֶּתֶק; obj. persons 1 Ch 19⁴. **2.** *shave off*, the hair שֵׂעָר Lv 14^8.9.9 (P) cf. Ju 16¹⁹; the beard זָקָן Lv 21⁵ (H) 2 S 10⁴. **3.** fig. of devastation by Assyrians Is 7²⁰ (obj. שְׂעַר הָרַגְלָיִם, הָרֹאשׁ and הַזָּקָן). **4.** intrans. *he shaved* (himself) Gn 41¹⁴ (E). **Pu.** *Pf.* גֻּלָּח Ju 16²², גֻּלַּחְתִּי Ju 16¹⁷; *Pt.* cstr. מְגֻלְּחֵי Je 41⁵;—*be shaven*, subj. pers. (of Samson) Ju 16^17.22; מְגֻלְּחֵי זָקָן Je 41⁵. **Hithp.** *Pf.* וְהִתְגַּלָּח consec. Lv 13³³; *Inf.* sf. הִתְגַּלְּחוֹ Nu 6¹⁹;—*shave oneself* Lv 13³³; c. acc. אֶת־נִזְרוֹ Nu 6¹⁹ (both P).

I. גלל (جَلَّ *be great in rank* or *dignity* (often of God)).

†1. [גָּלָל] **n.[m.] account,** only in cstr. st. with בְּ, בִּגְלַל *on account of, for the sake of* (جَلَلٌ *a great and momentous matter;* مِنْ جَلَلِكَ on thy *account;* cf. מִן בִּגְלַל דְּ *because that* in Palestinian 𝔗, as ψ 4⁹, and ܒܓܠܠ in Jerus. Syriac PS⁷³¹) Gn 39⁵ ׳י blessed the house of the Egyptian בִּגְלַל יוֹסֵף *on account of* Joseph, Dt 15¹⁰ 18¹² 1 K 14¹⁶ Je 11¹⁷ 15⁴; with sf. בִּגְלָלֶךְ Gn 30²⁷; בִּגְלָלְךָ 12¹³; בִּגְלַלְכֶם Dt 1³⁷ Mi 3¹².

†II. [גָּלַל] **vb. roll, roll away** (NH *id.*, & deriv.; Aram. Pa. גַּלֵּל, Palp. גַּלְגֵּל *roll*, Ithpalp. reflex., & deriv.; cf. ܓܠ Ethp., Ethpalp. (v. PS), ܓܠܓܠܐ *rota*, ܓܠܠܐ *fluctus*, etc.)—**Qal** *Pf.* 1 s. גַּלּוֹתִי Jos 5⁹, וְגָלֲלוּ consec. Gn 29^3.8; *Imv.* גֹּל ψ 22⁹ (MT De; but 𝔊 Bi Che rd. גַּל 3 ms. pf., so AV RVm) Pr 16³, גּוֹל ψ 37⁵, גַּל 119²² (but rd. גֹּל Ew Hi Ri Gr Che), גֹּלּוּ Jos 10¹⁸ 1 S 14³³; *Pt.* גֹּלֵל Pr 26²⁷;—*roll* a stone Pr 26²⁷; *roll away* stone from upon (מֵעַל) the mouth of a well Gn 29^3.8; *roll* stones unto (אֶל) the mouth of a cave Jos 10¹⁸; stone unto (אֶל) Saul, at which to slay beasts 1 S 14³³; fig. reproach from upon (מֵעַל) the people Jos 5⁹ (subj. ׳י), cf. ψ 119²² (sq. מֵעַל); but also גּוֹל עַל־׳י דַּרְכֶּךָ ψ 37⁵, cf. 22⁹ Pr 16³ (both sq. אֶל־). **Niph.** *Pf.* וְנָגֹלּוּ consec. Is 34⁴; *Impf.* וְיִגַּל (juss.) Am 5²⁴;—*roll, roll up* or *along* (intrans.), וְנָגֹלּוּ כַסֵּפֶר הַשָּׁמָיִם Is 34⁴ *and the heavens shall roll up like a book;* יִגַּל כַּמַּיִם מִשְׁפָּט Am 5²⁴ *let judgment roll along* (flow down) *as the waters.* **Pilp.** *Pf.* וְגִלְגַּלְתִּיךָ consec. Je 51²⁵ *and I will roll thee down from* (מִן) the rocks (subj. ׳י; obj. Babylon under fig. of mt.) **Pō'al** *Pt.* שִׂמְלָה מְגוֹלָלָה בְדָמִים Is 9⁴ *garment rolled* (dabbled, rolled over and over) *in blood.* **Hithpo.** *Inf.* לְהִתְגֹּלֵל Gn 43¹⁸; *Pt.* מִתְגֹּלֵל 2 S 20¹²; *roll oneself over and over,* וַעֲמָשָׂא מִתְג׳ בַּדָּם 2 S 20¹² *now Amasa was wallowing in his blood;* fig. Gn 43¹⁸ לְהִתְג׳ עָלֵינוּ *to roll himself upon us,* i.e. assail us with overwhelming force (‖ וּלְהִתְנַפֵּל עָלֵינוּ). **Hithpalp.** *Pf.* הִתְגַּלְגָּלוּ Jb 30¹⁴ (abs.; ‖ כְּפֶרֶץ רָחָב יֶאֱתָיוּ) cf. Hithpo. Gn 43⁸. **Hiph.** *Impf.* וַיָּגֶל Gn 29¹⁰;—*roll away* stone from upon (מֵעַל) mouth of well; as **Qal** (which it really is, Impf. in *i*, acc. to Ba^ZMG 1888, 178).

†גַּל **n.m.** ^Gn 31, 48 **heap, wave, billow** (as *rolled together, rolling, rolling up*), also **spring,** MT Ct 4¹² cf. **3** infr.—abs. גַּל Jb 8¹⁷ + 5 t. (incl. הַגַּל Gn 31⁴⁸ +); גָּל Gn 31⁴⁶; הַגָּל Gn 31⁴⁶; לְגַל Is. 25²; cstr. גַּל־ Jos 7²⁶ + 2 t. + Gn 31^47.48 q.v. infr.; pl. גַּלִּים 2 K 19²⁵ + 6 t.; cstr. גַּלֵּי־ Is 48¹⁸; sf. גַּלָּיו ψ 89¹⁰ + 6 t.; גַּלֵּיהֶם ψ 65⁸ + 2 t.;—**1.** *heap* of stones, **a.** ג׳ אבנים raised (הקים) over dead body Jos 7²⁶ 8²⁹; cf. 2 S 18¹⁷ (c. הִצִּיב). **b.** גַּל alone Jb 8¹⁷ (roots wrapped about it). **c.** *heap* or *pile* made (עשׂה) for use in ratifying compact of Jacob with Laban Gn 31^46.46.48.51.52.52.52 cf. also גִּלְעָד **n.pr.** **d.** *heap* of ruins Is 25²; elsewhere pl. Ho 12¹² 2 K 19²⁵ = Is 37²⁶ Jb 15²⁸ Jer. 9¹⁰ 51³⁷. **2.** *waves* (*rollers*) poet., only pl., waves of sea Je 5²² 31³⁵ Is 51¹⁵ Jb 38¹¹ ψ 65⁸ 89¹⁰ 107^25.29; cf. also in simile Ez 26³ Is 48¹⁸ (גַּלֵּי־הַיָּם); fig. of chastisements from ׳י ψ 42⁸ (‖ מִשְׁבָּרִים) Jon 2³ (‖ id.); of army of Babylon's conqueror Je 51^42.55; cf. Ze 10¹¹ (VB; but Bev ^JPh xviii. 88 prop. גְּבָלִים cf. Ez 27⁹). **3.** *spring,* Ct 4¹² גַּן נָעוּל אֲחֹתִי כַלָּה גַּל נָעוּל מַעְיָן חָתוּם *a garden barred (is) my sister, bride, a spring barred, a fountain sealed;* but גַּן for גַּל 𝔊 𝔖 𝔙.

†גַּלִּים **n.pr.loc.** (*heaps*);—place N. of Jerus. 1 S 25⁴⁴; personified as בַּת־ג׳ Is 10³⁰.

†גַּלְעֵד **n.pr.loc.** (*witness-pile*) name of pile of stones erected by Jacob and his company (Kit Gesch 129; by Laban We Di) Gn 31^47.48 (v. גַּל **1 c**) appar. intended to explain גִּלְעָד q v; Di conj. also (as name of altar) Jos 22^34 (cf 𝔖).

†[גֵּל] **n.[m.] dung** (*ball* of dung, Ar. جَلَّة etc., dung of camels etc, cf. Aram. גַּלְלָא; on form v. Ew § 255 b Ol § 150, 163)—sf. גֶּלְלוֹ Jb 20^7, pl cstr. גֶּלְלֵי (צֵאת) הָאָדָם Ez 4^12.15;—human dung used as fuel Ez 4^12.15 ג׳ (צֵאת) הָאָדָם; perh. also Jb 20^7, but cf Di, who thinks no ref to fuel, & De who thinks of cattle-dung, (v. on Ar. word Wetzst in De)—See also II. גָּלָל.

גֻּלָּה, גֹּל v גֻּלָּה.

†גֻּלָּה **n.f.** basin, bowl—ג׳ Zc 4^3 + v^2 cf. infr.; cstr. גֻּלַּת Ec 12^6, pl. abs גֻּלֹּת Jos 15^19.19 + 2 t.; ־וֹת 2 Ch 4^12, cstr גֻּלֹּת (־וֹת) 1 K 7^41 (הַגּ׳ Th, so ‖ 2 Ch 4^12 cf Be), v^41 + 3 t.;—**1.** *basin* (*pool, well*?) ג׳ מַיִם Jos 15^19 = Ju 1^15; om. מ׳ Jos 15^19.19 = Ju 1^15.15 (prob. old **n pr.loc.**, cf Di) **2.** *bowl*, **a.** of lamp, i.e. oil-receptacle Zc 4^3, also v^2, where MT גֻּלָּהּ as if fr. [גֹּל]; rd גֻּלָּה Brd Ges § 91.1, R. 2; (> Hi-St Bö § 734 b De on ψ 27^5 Sta § 347 e, who think גֻּלָּה=גֻּלָּתָהּ);—so also Ec 12^6 גֻּלַּת הַזָּהָב **b.** of bowl- or globe-shaped portion of capitals of the two pillars in temple 1 K 7^41.41.42 = 2 Ch 4^12.12.13.

†II. גָּלָל **n.[m.]** dung (Ar. جَلَّة), הַגּ׳ 1 K 14^10.—See also [גֵּל]

†III. גָּלָל **n.pr.m.** of two Levites;—**1.** 1 Ch 9^15. **2.** 1 Ch 9^16 Ne 11^17.

†גִּלֲלַי **n.pr.m.** a Levitical musician Ne 12^36.

†I. [גָּלִיל] **adj. turning, folding** (=revolving), pl גְּלִילִים of leaves of doors 1 K 6^34.34.

†II. גָּלִיל **n.m. cylinder, rod, circuit, district**;—**1.** *cylinder, rod*, only pl. cstr גְּלִילֵי כֶסֶף Est 1^6 of support of rich hangings (‖ עַמּוּדֵי שֵׁשׁ); & גְּלִילֵי זָהָב מְמֻלָּאִים בַּתַּרְשִׁישׁ Ct 5^14, sim of (? fingers of) hands: *cylinders of gold set with topaz* **2.** *circuit, district*, on northern border of Israel, in Naphtali (v. infr.), population largely heathen (NH *id.* Aram. גְּלִילָא, ܓܠܝܠܐ)—גְּלִיל הַגּוֹיִם Is 8^23, elsewhere=**n.pr.loc.** always c. art Jos 20^7 21^32 1 Ch 6^61 all קֶדֶשׁ בַּגּ׳; אֶרֶץ הַגּ׳ 1 K 9^11, so also 𝔊 Jos 12^23 (cf Di) for גִּלְגָּל q. v.—See also גְּלִילָה *ad fin.*

†גְּלִילָה **n.f. circuit, boundary, territory**—ג׳ Ez 47^8 2 K 15^29; pl. cstr. גְּלִילוֹת Jos 13^2 22^10.11 Jo 4^4;—belonging to a people כָּל־גְּלִילוֹת הַפְּלִשְׁתִּים Jos 13^2 cf. Jo 4^4 (כֹּל ג׳ פְּלָשֶׁת); so ג׳ הַיַּרְדֵּן Jos 22^10.11 acc to some, but v. foll.; abs. Ez 47^8 הַגּ׳ הַקַּדְמוֹנָה, as **n.pr.loc.** 2 K 15^29 *Galilee*, 𝔊 Γαλιλαια (‖ כֹּל אֶרֶץ נַפְתָּלִי) cf. II גָּלִיל.

†גְּלִילוֹת **n.pr.loc.** (strictly pl of foreg; prob.=*circles* of stones, 𝔅 *tumuli*, cf. Di) **1.** Jos 18^17 (cf. הַגִּלְגָּל 15^7), place on border between Benj. & Judah. **2.** locality described as follows: **a.** אֶל־ג׳ הַיַּרְדֵּן אֲשֶׁר בְּאֶרֶץ כְּנָעַן Jos 22^10 *unto Geliloth* (= *the circles*) *of Jordan which is in the land of Canaan*, (𝔊 Γαλγαλα, 𝔊L Γαλιλωθ). **b.** אֶל־מוּל אֶרֶץ כְּנַעַן אֶל־גְּלִילוֹת הַיַּרְדֵּן אֶל־עֵבֶר בְּנֵי יִשְׂרָאֵל v^11 *in front of the land of Canaan, in Geliloth of Jordan, beyond the sons of Israel* (𝔊 Γαλααδ, 𝔊L om) v. Di; yet cf. Dr Intr 108 n. Others render ג׳ here *circuit of Jordan*=כִּכַּר הַיַּרְדֵּן; *districts* VB, cf גְּלִילָה.

†[גִּלּוּל] **n.m.** Je 50, 27 only pl. **idols** (=*logs, blocks*, shapeless things Ges Baud Rel i. 95; Ew *doll-images* > *dungy things* Sm Ez 6^4 SS after Rabb)—גִּלּוּלִים Ez 22^3 + 3 t + Ez 30^13 (del B Co); גִּלֻּלִים 1 K 15^12 + 2 t; cstr. גִּלּוּלֵי Ez 8^10 + 6 t; גִּלּוּלַיִךְ Ez 22^4, גִּלּוּלָיו 2 K 21^11 + 4 t., גִּלּוּלֶיהָ Je 50^2, ־יכֶם — Lv 26^30 + 7 t.; ־יכֶן — Ez 23^49; ־יהֶם — Ez 6^9 + 14 t. + Ez 6^5 (del BA al Co); ־יהֶן — Ez 23^37,—*idols* (39 t Ez);—1 K 15^12 2 K 17^12 21^21 Ez 6^5 (del Co) v^6 6^13.13 14^4.5 18^6.15 20^16.24.39 23^37.39.49 33^25 44^10.12; ‖ שִׁקּוּצִים Dt 29^16 2 K 23^24 (‖ also תְּרָפִים), Ez 20^7.18 (both c vb טמא) v^8 37^23, cf. also 8^10 (שֶׁקֶץ, but שקוצים appar. 𝔊𝔖𝔗 & so Co); ‖ תּוֹעֵבָה Ez 14^6 2 K 21^11, cf Ez 18^12 16^36 (גִּלּוּלֵי תוֹעֲבוֹתַיִךְ), & 1 K 21^26 (where vb תָּעַב); ‖ טֻמְאוֹת Ez 36^25; ‖ מִכְשׁוֹל עָוֹן Ez 14^3.4.7; ‖ עֲצַבִּים Je 50^2; ‖ חַמָּן Ez 6^4.6 Lv 26^30 (cf. infr); ‖ אֱלִילִים Ez 30^13 (Co אֵילִים, cf. also supr), ‖ תְּרָפִים 2 K 23^24 (supr); in phr. טמא בגל׳ etc Ez 20^7.18.31 22^3.4 23^7.30 36^18 (del Co), הִתְחַלֵּל בְּגִל׳ Ez 20^39;—note especially the expression וְנָתַתִּי פִּגְרֵיכֶם עַל־פִּגְרֵי גִּלּוּלֵיכֶם Lv 26^30 *and I will lay your carcases upon the carcases of your idols.*

†גַּלְגַּל **n.m.** Ec 12.6 **wheel, whirl, whirlwind** (on format cf. Ba NB 204)—abs. ג׳ Ez 10^2 + 7 t, גִּלְגַּל ψ 83^14, pl. c. sf. גַּלְגִּלָּיו Is 5^28 Je 47^3,—**1.** *wheel*, **a.** of war-chariot Is 5^28 Je 47^3, also coll Ez 23^24 26^10; perh. also in Ezekiel's vision Ez 10^2.6.13 (cf. *wheelwork*) but cf. infr. **b.** for drawing water Ec 12^6. **2. a.** *whirl* (of dust or

chaff) ψ 83^{14} Is 17^{13}, sim. of foes put to flight by God. **b.** perh. *whirling* of wheels Ez $10^{2.6.13}$ Sm RV, but cf. supr. **c.** *whirlwind* ψ 77^{19}.

†I. [גַּלְגַּל] **n.[m.]** wheel (on format. cf. Ba$^{NB\ 204}$) of cart, גִּלְגַּל עֶגְלָתוֹ Is 28^{28}.

†II. גִּלְגָּל **n.pr.loc.** (= (sacred) *circle* of stones; cf. Di on Jos 5^{9}, where word-play on *roll away, off*)—c.art.exc. Jos 5^{9} 12^{23};—**1.** place E. of Jericho, where Isr. lay encamped Jos $4^{19.20}$ $5^{9.10}$ 9^{6} $10^{7.9}$ 14^{6} cf. also Mi 6^{5} & Ju 3^{19} הַפְּסִילִים אֲשֶׁר אֶת־הַגּ׳; ? mod. *Tell Jeljul* Bd$^{Pal\ 169}$; perh. also the place where sacrifices were offered 1 S 10^{8} $11^{14.15.15}$ $13^{4.7.8.12.15}$ (in v^{15} ins. also c. other words, Dr cf. We) $15^{12.21.33}$; place of illicit sacrifice Ho 4^{15} 9^{15} 12^{12} Am 4^{4} $5^{5.5}$, named also Ju 2^{1} 1 S 7^{16} 2 S $19^{16.41}$; ? = בֵּית הַגִּלְגָּל Ne 12^{29}. **2.** place on border between Judah & Benjamin Jos 15^{17} (= גְּלִילוֹת 18^{17} cf. Di). **3.** place in N. Isr., dwelling of prophets 2 K 2^{1} 4^{38}, mod. *Jiljilie* S. from Nâbulus, SW. from *Seilûn* (Shiloh) cf. Di Ri$^{HWB\ 518}$. **4.** place in N. Isr. near Mt. Gerizim and Mt. Ebal Dt 11^{30}, identif. with **3** by Ke Ri $^{HWB\ 518}$ Schenkel^{BL} SS; but cf. Di. **5.** in phr. מֶלֶךְ גּוֹיִם לְגִלְגָּל Jos 12^{23}, in list of Canaanitish kings; prob. name of a (northern) district cf. Di (B βασιλέα Γεεὶ τῆς Γαλιλαίας—but 𝔊L & Codd. Γοειμ τῆς Γελγελ); Di comp. Is. 8^{23}.

†גֻּלְגֹּלֶת **n.f.** skull, head, poll (person) (on format. cf. Ba$^{NB\ 205}$; Aram. גּוּלְגַּלְתָּא)—abs. ג׳ 2 K 9^{35} + 3 t.; sf. גֻּלְגָּלְתּוֹ Ju 9^{53} 1 Ch 10^{10}; pl. sf. גֻּלְגְּלֹתָם Nu 1^{2} + 5 t.;—**1.** *skull*, as broken by a stone Ju 9^{53}; as severed from body 2 K 9^{35} 1 Ch 10^{10}. **2.** *head, poll* (in counting, taxing, etc.; only P and late) עֹמֶר לַגּ׳ Ex 16^{16} *an omer for every man;* cf. 38^{26} Nu $1^{2.18.20.22}$ 3^{47} 1 Ch $23^{3.24}$.

†מְגִלָּה **n.f.** roll (writing, book; late)—מ׳ Je 36^{28} + 16 t.; cstr. מְגִלַּת־ ψ 40^{8} + 3 t.;—*roll* of writing, book מְגִלַּת־סֵפֶר Je $36^{2.4}$ Ez 2^{9} ψ 40^{8}; מ׳ alone Je 36 $^{6.14.14.20.21.23.25.27.28.28.29.32}$ Ez $3^{1.2.3}$ Ze $5^{1.2}$.

†[גָּלַם] **vb. wrap up, fold, fold together** (NH *id.*, Aram. in deriv.)—**Qal** *Impf.* וַיִּגְלֹם 2 K 2^{8} וַיִּקַּח אֵלִיָּהוּ אֶת־אַדַּרְתּוֹ וַיִּגְלֹם.

†[גְּלוֹם] **n.[m.]** wrapping, garment (Aram. גְּלִימָא, ܓܠܝܡܐ = Pers. گلیم acc. to Fl ChWB$^{i.\ 143}$ SFrä$^{LOPh.\ i.\ (1883\text{-}4)\ 410}$), בִּגְלוֹמֵי תְכֵלֶת Ez 27^{24}.

†[גֹּלֶם] **n.[m.]** embryo (NH גּוֹלֶם, Aram. גּוֹלְמָא, *unfinished vessel*), גָּלְמִי רָאוּ עֵינֶיךָ ψ 139^{16} *mine imperfect substance* (RV) *did thine eyes see.*

†גַּלְמוּד **adj. hard, barren** (NH *id. lonely* NHWB; Ar. جَلْمَد *rock*, جَلْمَدَة *stony* (of land); Aram. גַּלְמוּדָה cf. Ba$^{NB\ 208}$)—ג׳ Jb 3^{7} + 2 t. Jb; f. גַּלְמוּדָה Is 49^{21};—*hard, barren, unproductive,* mostly fig.: Jb 15^{34} of company of wicked men, where prob. a subst. v. De Di; Jb 30^{3} *through want and famine* (they are) *stiff* (*lifeless;* RV *gaunt*); of exiled Zion as bereaved and barren woman Is 49^{21}; so of night of Job's birth Jb 3^{7}.

†[גָּלַע] **vb. expose, lay bare** (NH Pi. *disclose, make known;* cf. Ar. جَلَعَ (Frey) **a.** *exuit* (vestem), *removit* (praeputium); جُلُوعٌ *nuda fuit* (femina); **b.** جَلِعَ *patuit* (os) *labiis non tegentibus dentes; impudica fuit* (mulier); comp. also Syr. ܓܠܥ *circumcise* (in Lexx.); Eth. ገለፀ: *cortex, crusta, testa;* Gr $^{Monatsschr.\ 1884,\ 24\ f.}$; Schult Thes De Pr 17^{14} Fl in De, Now Str & most der. Heb. mng. from Ar. **b**; *shew the teeth,* then *snarl, quarrel* (cf. Ar. conj. III), but v. Gr$^{l.\ c.}$)—only **Hithp.** *Pf.* הִתְגַּלָּע Pr 17^{14}; *Impf.* יִתְגַּלָּע Pr 18^{1} 20^{3};—**disclose oneself, break out,** Pr 17^{14} subj. רִיב; *break* or *burst out* in contention, strife Pr. 20^{3} subj. כָּל־אֱוִיל; similarly 18^{1} (sq. בְּ *against;* Gr$^{l.\ c.}$ prop. יִלָּעֵג or יִלָּעִיג).

גִּלְעָד v. sub II. גלל.

†גִּלְעָד **n.pr.loc.** of mountain-range or hill-country, land & city, E. of Jordan (cf. Ar. جَلْعَدٌ *durus, fortis* Frey, so Thes; Hi $^{Gesch.\ Isr.\ 26}$ comp. same √ used of *camel* (جَلْعَادٌ *camelus robustus ac firmus,* cf. Hom$^{NS\ 144}$), whence *camel hump,* orig. name of mt.)—ג׳ Gn 37^{25} + 79 t. (mostly as **n.pr.m.** and in combin. with other **n.pr. loc.** cf. infr.); הַגּ׳ Gn 31^{21} + 50 t. (so usually as name of mt. and land); גִּלְעָדָה Nu 32^{39} 1 Ch 27^{21}; הַגִּלְעָדָה 2 S 24^{6};—*Gilead,* used of territory between the Arnon and the Jabboḳ, mod. *Belḳa;* also of that between the Jabboḳ and the Jarmuk, mod. *Jebel Ajlûn;* also of the entire E.-Jordan land occupied by Israel, including both the parts just named (cf. Di Gn 31^{54} Stu Ju 10^{4}; Bd$^{Pal\ 178}$; also L. Oliphant$^{Land\ of\ Gilead,\ 1880}$);—**1.** territory S. of Jabboḳ, **a.** אֶרֶץ הַגּ׳ Nu 32^{29} (P), אֶרֶץ ג׳ v^{1} (JE), both connected with Reuben and Gad; so אֶרֶץ ג׳ חֲצִי הַר הַגּ׳ Dt 3^{12}; also 1 Ch 5^{9} (of Reuben); 1 K 4^{19} (of Sihon and Og); cf. אֶרֶץ גָּד וְג׳ 1 S 13^{7}; further, **b.** הַגּ׳ alone, Ju 10^{17} (or possibly here name of city ?), 11^{29} (prob.);

†גמזו **n.pr.loc** (cf Syr ܓܡܙܐ (Lexx) *sycamore;* Ar جُمَّيز is loan-wd. Fra^{140}, cf As n pr loc *Gamuzanu* Pinches$^{Abr\ July, 1886\ 222}$), city of Judah toward Philistines 2 Ch 28^{18}, mod *Jimzu*, E from Lydda Rob$^{BR\ ii\ 249}$ Bd$^{Pal\ 21}$.

†גָּמַל **vb. 1. deal fully or adequately with, deal out to. 2. wean. 3. ripen** (As *gamâlu, deal with, benefit*, e g VR 35^{19}, NH גָּמַל, Aram גְּמַל; v. Palm n pr אגמלא Vog$^{No\ 124}$, Nab. n pr f גמלת Vog$^{Nab\ sub\ No.\ 7}$, perh orig *complete, accomplish*, cogn גמר;—Ar جَمَلَ is *collect*, جَمُلَ *be beautiful, goodly*)—**Qal** *Pf.* ψ 13^{6}+, *Impf* יגמל Nu 17^{23}+, *Imv* גְּמֹל ψ 119^{17}, *Inf* גְּמֹלְךָ, גְּמֹלָהּ 1 S 1^{23}; *Pt* גֹּמֵל Pr 11^{17}+; pass גָּמוּל Is 11^{8}, גָּמֻל ψ 131^{22},—**1. a.** *deal out to, do to*, c 2 acc גְּמָלַתְהוּ טוֹב וְלֹא רָע *she doeth him good and not evil* Pr 31^{12}, כי אַתָּה גְּמַלְתַּנִי הַטּוֹבָה וַאֲנִי גְּמַלְתִּיךָ הָרָעָה *for thou hast done unto me the good but I have done unto thee the evil* 1 S 24^{18}; *do* evil (ה)רע *unto* Gn 50$^{15.17}$ Pr 3^{30}, c לְ pers Is 3^{9}; *do good unto*, 2 acc. Is 63$^{7.7}$; cf. also גֹּמֵל נַפְשׁוֹ איש חסד Pr 11^{17} **b.** with עַל pers *deal bountifully with* ψ 13^{6} 116^{7} 119^{17} 142^{8}, c acc pers *reward* 2 S 22^{21} (=ψ 18^{21}), perh. also לָמָּה יגמלני הַגְּמוּלָה הַזֹּאת *why should he reward me with this reward?* 2 S 19^{37}. **c** *recompense, repay, requite*, in a bad sense, with 2 acc ψ 7^{5}, with לְ pers Dt 32^{6} ψ 137^{8}, with עַל pers 2 Ch 20^{11} ψ 103^{10} Jo 4^{4}. **2.** *wean a child* (complete his nursing) 1 S 1$^{23.23.24}$ 1 K 11^{20} Ho 1^{8}; גָּמוּל *weaned child* ψ 131^{22} Is 11^{8}; גְּמוּלֵי מֵחָלָב *weaned from milk* Is 28^{9}. **3.** trans. *ripen, bear ripe* (almonds) Nu 17^{23}; intrans *become ripe* (grapes) Is 18^{5} **Niph.** *Impf.* וַיִּגָּמַל, יִגָּמֵל 1 S 1^{22}, Gn 21^{8}, *Inf* הִגָּמֵל Gn 21^{8},—*be weaned.*

†גְּמוּל **n.m. dealing, recompence, benefit**—ג׳ ψ 94^{2}+11 t, sf גְּמֻלְךָ Ob^{15}, etc.; pl. sf גְּמוּלָיו ψ 103^{2},—**1.** גְּמוּל יָדַיִם *dealing of the hands* Ju 9^{16} Pr 12^{14} (יָשׁוּב לְ) Is 3^{11} (יעשׂה לְ) **2.** *dealing*, hence (from context) *equivalent of dealing, recompence*. c suff Ob^{15} גמלך ישוב בראשך, Jo 4$^{4.7}$ (השיב), so with לְ ψ 28^{4}, השיב לְ שלם 137^{8} Pr 19^{17}; absolutely שלם (השיב) גמול לְ Is 59$^{18.18}$ 66^{6} Je 51^{6} La 3^{64}, עַל Jo 4^{4} ψ 94^{2}, Is 35^{4} ג׳ אֵל אלהים *the recompence of God* **3.** *benefit*. ψ 103^{2} תשכחי כל גמוליו, כגמול עליו *according to the benefit* (done) *unto him* 2 Ch 32^{25}

†גָּמוּל **n.pr.m.** (*weaned*) a chief of the Levites 1 Ch 24^{17} Vid also בית גָּמוּל (Je 48^{23})

†גְּמוּלָה **n.f.** $^{2\ S\ 19,\ 37}$ **dealing, recompence**—ג׳ 2 S 19^{37} cf גָּמַל; pl גְּמוּלוֹת *dealings* Is 59^{18}; Je 51^{56} אֵל גְּמֻלוֹת *God of recompence.*

†[תַּגְמוּל] **n.m. benefit**—pl c Aram. sf. כָּל־תַּגְמוּלוֹהִי עָלָי *all his benefits unto me* ψ 116^{12}

†גַּמְלִיאֵל **n.pr.m.** (*reward of God*) a prince of Manasseh Nu 1^{10} 2^{20} 7$^{54.59}$ 10^{23}, cf Mishn. גמליאל, Palm Vog$^{No\ 124}$, 𝔊 Γαμαλιήλ Acts 5^{34}

†גָּמָל **n.m.** Gn 24^{10}+9 t., **f. & m.** Gn 32^{16} (cf. infr), **camel** (NH *id* Ar جَمَلٌ (جُمْلٌ), Eth. ገመል: As *gammalu* COT^{Gloss} Aram. גַּמְלָא, ܓܡܠܐ; Palm Tariff pl גמלין Reckendorf$^{ZMG\ 1888,\ 401}$; √גמל but mng of √dub.; Bo$^{Hieroz\ i.\ 73}$ der. fr. גמל *requite*, so Lag$^{BN\ 20,\ 49}$ (camel as μνησίκακος), v. also conject in MV, Dl in Hpt$^{F\ 70}$ Hpt$^{BAS\ i.\ 171}$, A. v. Kremer$^{Semit\ Culturentlehn.,\ 2}$, Hom$^{NS\ 144\ ff}$)—abs גָּמָל Gn 24^{64}+7 t., pl גְּמַלִּים Gn 12^{16}+30 t.; cstr. גְּמַלֵּי Gn 24^{10}; *sf* גְּמַלֶּיךָ Gn 24^{14}+3 t; גְּמַלָּיו Gn 24^{20}, גְּמַלֵּיהֶם Gn 37^{25}+6 t;—*camel*, **1.** as property (in Hex only J) Gn 12^{16} (‖ אתנות) 24$^{10.35}$ (‖ חמורים etc) 30^{43} (‖ *id*) 32^{8} (‖ בקר ,צאן) Ex 9^{3} (Egyptian ‖ סוסים ,חמורים ,בקר ,צאן, etc) Ju 6^{5} 7^{12} 1 S 15^{3} (‖ חמור etc.) 27^{9} 1 Ch 5^{21} 27^{30} (all ‖ *id*) 2 Ch 14^{14} (‖ צאן) Ezr 2^{67} (‖ סוסים ,פרדים, חמורים) = Ne 7^{68} Jb 1^{3} (‖ אתנות ,בקר ,צאן) cf. v^{17} 42^{12} (‖*id.*) Je 49^{29} (‖ צאן) v^{32} Zc 14^{15} (‖ סוס, חמור ,פרד) [4 t. ‖ סוס and other words, Ex 9^{3} (Egyptians), Zc 14^{15} (enemies of Israel), Ezr 2^{67} = Ne 7^{68} (returned exiles)] **2.** as beasts of burden Gn 24^{10} cf. v$^{11.14.19.20.22.30.31.32.32.44.45.46}$ 37^{25} (all J), 1 K 10^{2} 2 K 8^{9} 1 Ch 12^{41} 2 Ch 9^{1} Is 30^{6} (עַל־דַּבֶּשֶׁת ג׳), Is 60^{6} (‖ בכרי מדין) **3.** for riding Gn 24$^{61.63.64}$ (all J), 31$^{17.34}$ (both E) 1 S 30^{17}, cf also Ju 8$^{21.26}$, and particularly Is 21^{7} רֶכֶב גמל; a riding-company of camels i e a troop of camels with riders, נוה גמלים an abode for camels, in prediction against Ammon Ez 25^{5}, (‖ מִרְבַּץ צאן) **4.** forbidden as food Lv 11^{4} (P) Dt 14^{7}.

†גְּמַלִּי **n.pr.m.** a Danite Nu 13^{12}

גמם (Ar جَمَّ *become much* or *abundant*, جَمٌّ *abundance, much*, جُمَّةٌ *collection* (of water), *company* (of people)).

גַּם $_{768}$ **adv.** denoting *addition*, **also, moreover, yea** (Moab. *id*. prob. akin to √جَمّ; cf.

جَمًّا (accus.) *in a mass, altogether*)—**1.** *also, moreover*, emphasizing sts. the thought of an entire sentence, but more usually the word immediately following, as Gn 3^{6} וַתִּתֵּן גַּם לְאִישָׁהּ and gave *also* to her husband, v^{27} and take *also* of the tree of life, 7^{3} 19^{21} 24^{19} 26^{21} 29^{27} 30^{15} 32^{21}(...גַּם הִנֵּה: so Est 7^{9}) 48^{11} Ex 8^{28} 12^{32b} Dt 1^{37} 1 S 28^{20} 2 S 11^{12} 2 K 9^{27} Is 7^{13}+. Often before pronouns, Gn 4^{4} וְהֶבֶל הֵבִיא גַם הוּא and Abel, *he* also brought, 20^{5} וְהִיא־גַם־הִוא (so only here) and she herself *also*, v^{6} 27^{31} וַיַּעַשׂ גַּם הוּא, 30^{3} Dt 3^{20} Ju 3^{31} 6^{35} 9^{19} 1 S 19$^{20\text{-}24}$ Je 12^{6} 48^{26} etc. (cf. MI ^{6} ויאמר גם הא): esp. in genealogies of J (Bu $^{Urg.\ 220}$) Gn 4$^{22.26}$ 10^{21} 19^{38} 22$^{20.24}$ cf. Ju 8^{31}. גַּם sq. pron. also begins a sentence with emph. in an elevated style, *thou* (*they*) *also*, Is 14^{10} Je 12$^{6.6}$ 48^{7} Ez 16^{52} Na 3$^{11.11}$. After a pron. in an oblique case (Ges$^{§\ 135.2}$) Gn 27^{34} 1 S 19^{23} 2 S 17^{5} Je 25^{14} 27^{7}+. וְגַם *and also* (more often than גַּם alone attaching a sentence) Gn 6^{4} 14^{16} 15^{14} 17^{16} 20^{12} 24$^{14.46}$ 30^{6} 37^{7} 38^{24} 42^{28} Ex 2^{19} 3^{9} 4^{14} Jos 7^{11} (5 t.) 1 S 4^{17} 1 K 21^{19}+oft.; with a negative=*neither* Ex 5^{2} 34^{3} al.—גַּם ... גַּם (like *et ... et*) *both ... and* Gn 44^{16} 47$^{3.19}$ Nu 18^{3} Je 51^{12} ψ 49^{3}+: גַּם ... וְגַם Gn 24^{25} Ju 8^{22} Ec 9^{6}: with a negative *neither ... nor* Nu 23^{25} 1 S 20^{27} 1 K 3^{26}, and (3 t.) Gn 43^{8} Ex 4^{10} 1 S 28^{6}. So (but seldom) גַּם ... וְגַם Gn 24^{44} Ex 10$^{25f.}$ 1 S 2^{26} 12^{14} 26^{25}: with neg. 1 S 21^{9}.—N.B. In poetry independence and emphasis is sts. given by גַּם to a new idea, where in English we should be satisfied with *and*: ψ 107^{5} 137^{1} Jb 24^{19} Ct 7^{14} La 4^{15}. **2.** with stress on a particular word, *even*, Ex 4^{9} Nu 22^{33} גַּם אוֹתְךָ *even* thee I had slain, and kept her alive, 2 S 17^{10} Je 2^{33} ψ 132^{12} Pr 14^{13} *even* in laughter the heart is sorrowful, v^{20} 17^{28} 20^{11} Ru 2^{15} Ne 3^{35}; and so often after כִּי, Dt 12^{31} for *even* their sons they burn in the fire to their gods, 1 S 22^{17} Is 26^{12} Je 6^{11} 12^{6} 14^{5} Ho 9^{12} כִּי־גַם־אוֹי לָהֶם for *even* woe is it to them when I depart from them; הֲגַם †Gn 16^{13} 1 S 10$^{11.12}$=19^{24} 1 K 17^{20} ψ 78^{20} Jb 41^{1} Est 7^{8}. Other cases:—1 S 24^{12} גַּם רְאֵה גַּם רְאֵה see, *yea* see! (but Hup$^{Qu.\ Job\ vi.}$: cf. infr.) ψ 118^{11}; Jb 2^{10} גַּם אֶת־הַטּוֹב נְקַבֵּל shall we receive *good* (emph.) from God and not evil? 21^{7}; interposed once between a subst. and adj. Gn 20^{4} gentemne *etiam* justam interficies? emphasizing כֹּל, Dt 28^{61} Ju 9^{49b} 1 S 22^{7} גַּם־לְכֻלְּכֶם to *all* (emph.) of you will he give ...? 2 S 19^{31} גַּם אֶת־הַכֹּל יִקָּח *yea*, the whole let him take! Is 26^{12}; אֶחָד 2 S 17^{12b} and we will not leave ...גַּם אֶחָד *even* one (similarly v^{13b}), ψ 14^{3} (=53^{4}) אֵין גַּם אֶחָד; an inf. or cogn. accus. attached to a verb, †Gn 31^{15} 46^{4} Nu 11^{15} 16^{13} 1 S 1^{6}. גַּם שְׁנֵיהֶם lit. *even both* i.e. the one as well as the other (Germ. *alle beide*) is said idiomatically, †Gn 27^{45} (שְׁנֵיכֶם), Dt 22^{22} 23^{19} 1 S 25^{43} (שְׁתֵּיהֶן), Pr 17^{15} 20$^{10.12}$ Ru 1^{5}. **3.** introducing a climax, *yea*, esp. in a rhetorical style, Gn 27^{33} Dt 23$^{3.4}$ Ju 5$^{4.4}$ Is 13^{3} 14^{8} 43^{13} *yea*, from to-day I am the same, 44^{12} גַּם רָעֵב *yea*, he is hungry, and has no strength, 47^{3} 48$^{8.8.8}$ 57^{7} Je 46^{16} 48^{2} 51^{44} Ho 7^{9} ψ 41^{10} 84^{7} 139^{12}; Is 66^{8} כִּי־חָלָה גַּם־יָלְדָה צִיּוֹן אֶת־בָּנֶיהָ, Je 5^{28} 12^{2} Ez 24^{5} Jb 21^{7} Ct 8^{1}: emphasizing an extreme, or aggravated, case, *yea, even*, Is 49^{15} *yea*, these may forget, Je 8^{17} *yea*, the stork knoweth, etc., Is 23^{12} גַּם שָׁם *even* there no rest shall be for thee (so ψ 139^{10}), 49^{25} 57^{6} Je 23^{11b} Mal 3^{15} ψ 84^{4}. **4.** expressing *correspondence*, esp. in the matter of *retribution* (the גַּם *correlativum*), so frequently גַּם אֲנִי, גַּם אָנֹכִי I *also* (on my part):—Gn 20^{6} I *also* [as well as thyself] know that thou hast done this innocently, Jos 24^{18} Ju 2^{21} 1 S 1^{28} (cf. Dr) 28^{22} גַּם אַתָּה thou *also* (as I have done v^{21}), 2 S 12^{13} ׳י *also* [responding to thy confession] hath removed thy sin, 2 K 2$^{3.5}$ Is 31^{2} 66$^{3\text{-}4}$ (גם ... גם, emphasizing the action of both parties), Je 2^{36} 4^{12} now will I *also* [in correspondence with their deeds] speak judgments with them, 7^{11} 51^{49} (גם...גם), Ez 5$^{8.11}$ 16^{43} (וְגַם=therefore *also*), 23^{35} Ho 4^{6} because thou hast forgotten the direction of thy God, I *also* (on my part) will forget thy children, ψ 52^{7} (thou lovest evil, etc.) גַּם אֵל יִתָּצְךָ God *also* (on his part) will pluck thee up, 71^{22} 133^{1} Pr 1^{26} Jb 7^{11} 12^{3} 16^{4}; so וְגַם Ju 2^{3} Am 4$^{6.7}$ Mi 6^{13} Mal 2^{9}. In the apodosis (uncommon): Gn 13^{16} if a man could number the dust of the earth, גַּם זַרְעֲךָ יִמָּנֶה thy seed *also* should be numbered, Je 31$^{36.37}$ 33$^{21.26}$ Zc 8^{6}. The correspondence is sometimes of the nature of a climax: Gn 27^{33} 30^{8} I have wrestled, גַּם יָכֹלְתִּי (cf. 1 K 22^{22} וְגַם תּוּכָל, Je 50^{24}), Is 66^{8}. **5.** connecting two ideas which express (or imply) a contradiction, גַּם acquires sts. an adversative force (cf. אַף **1** end), *yet, but, though*: ψ 95^{9} they tried me, *but also* (Che) saw my work (viz. of judgment), 129^{2} Je 6^{15}=8^{12} Ez 20^{23} Ec 4$^{8.16}$ 5^{18} Ne 6^{1}. So וְגַם Ez 16^{28} 20^{15} Ec 3^{13} 6^{7} Ne 5^{8}. **6.** גַּם כִּי (with impf.) *yea, when* La 3^{8}, *even when* Pr 22^{6}; *yea though* (stating an imagined case) Is 1^{15} Ho 8^{10} 9^{16} ψ 23^{4} (so גַּם אִם Ec 8^{17}); *also* (is it) *that* Ru 2^{21} (v. כִּי **1 d**). כִּי גַם=*for even* (v. supr. **2**); = *though even, although* (conceding a fact) Ec 4^{14} (v. De) 8^{12}.

†[מְגַמָּה] **n.f.** Hb 1^{9} (of the Chaldaeans) מְגַמַּת פְּנֵיהֶם קָדִימָה, of uncertain meaning: Ges the *assembling* of their faces is (directed) for-

wards; Ew De Ke *eagerness*, comparing (questionably) גָּמָא *swallow* Jb 39[24], and جَامَ (Freyt.) *seek* (whence St prop. מְגַמַּת). Text prob. erron.

גמץ (√ of foll., Aram. גְּמַץ *dig* (perh. denom.)).

†**גּוּמָּץ** n.m. pit (Aram. loan-wd., cf. גּוּמְצָא, ܓܘܡܨܐ; NH גּוּמָּצָא cf. Ba[NB 66, Anm. 1]), Ec 10[8] חֹפֵר ג׳ בּוֹ יִפּוֹל *he that diggeth a pit shall fall into it;* so also Pr 26[27] 𝔗 𝔖 where 𝔊 כֹּרֶה שַׁחַת.

†**גָּמַר** vb. end, come to an end, complete (only ψ) (NH *id. complete;* As *gamâru* Lotz[TP. Register] & deriv. COT[Gloss] al.; Aram. גְּמַר, ܓܡܰܪ; Eth. ገመረ: (II); cf. also Ar. جَمَرَ *collect, assemble*)—**Qal** *Pf.* ג׳ ψ 12[2] 77[9]; *Impf.* יִגְמֹר ψ 138[8]; יִגְמָר ψ 7[10]; *Pt.* גֹּמֵר ψ 57[3];—**1.** *come to an end, be no more* ψ 7[10] 12[2] (‖ [פָּסַס]); 77[9] (‖ אָפֵס). **2.** trans. *bring to an end, complete,* אֵל גֹּמֵר עָלָי ψ 57[3] God that *completeth, accomplisheth, for me* (𝔊 Gr Bi נמל, & so Che doubtfully), י׳ יִגְמֹר בַּעֲדִי 138[8].

†**גֹּמֶר** n.pr. **1. m. a.** son of Japhet Gn 10[2.3] = 1 Ch 1[5.6]; Ez 38[6]; Lag[Onom. Sacr. 2, 95, 2nd ed. 367, v. BN 77] prop. גמרים for גמדים Ez 27[11] q.v.; he identif. גֹּמֶר with Cappadocia (cf. 𝔗 Ez 27[11], Kiep[Lb. d. alt. Geogr. 91]) = Armen. *Gamir* -χ (with pl. ending) v. also Lag[Arm. Stud. 32 § 448]; cf. further As. *Gimirrai*, Schr[KG 157 ff.] Dl[Pa 245 f.] also Len[Or. ii. 1, 332 ff.] **2. f.** wife of Hosea, Ho 1[3].

†**גְּמַרְיָהוּ**, **גְּמַרְיָה** n.pr.m. (*י׳ hath accomplished*)—**1.** גמריהו son of Shaphan Je 36[10.11.12.25]. **2.** גמריה son of Hilkiah Je 29[3].

גַּן, **גַּנָּה** v. sub גנן.

†[**גָּנַב**] vb. steal (NH *id.*, Aram. גְּנַב, ܓܢܰܒ; Ar. جَنَبَ is *hurt the side*, or *put aside*, den. fr. جَنْبٌ *side*)—**Qal** *Pf.* 3 fs. sf. גְּנָבַתּוּ Jb 21[18] 27[20], גְּנַבְתֶּם Gn 31[32]; 2 ms. גָּנַבְתָּ Gn 31[30]; 1 s. וְגָנַבְתִּי consec. Pr 30[9]; גָּנְבוּ Jos 7[11] 2 S 21[12]; sf. גְּנָבוּךָ 2 S 19[42]; *Impf.* יִגְנֹב־ Ex 21[37], יִגְנוֹב Pr 6[30], וַיִּגְנֹב Gn 31[20]; 3 fs. וַתִּגְנֹב Gn 31[19] + 2 t.; 2 ms. תִּגְנֹב Ex 20[15] Dt 5[17], וַתִּגְנֹב Gn 31[26.27], יִגְנְבוּ Ob[5], תִּגְנֹבוּ Lv 19[11], נִגְנֹב Gn 44[8]; *Inf. abs.* גָּנֹב Ex 22[11] + 2 t.; *Pt.* גֹּנֵב Ex 21[16] + 2 t., גָּנוּב Gn 30[33]; f. cstr. גְּנֻבְתִי Gn 31[39.39]; pl. גְּנוּבִים Pr 9[17]; in Hexateuch always JED, exc. Lv 19[11] (H);—*steal* c. acc. rei Gn 31[19.30.32] 44[8] Ex 21[37] 2 S 21[12] cf. pass. Gn 30[33] 31[39] Pr 9[17]; c. obj. pers. Ex 21[16] Dt 24[7] 2 S 19[42]; = *take by stealth* (for good purpose) 2 K 11[2] = 2 Ch 22[11]; abs. Ex 20[15] = Dt 5[17], Lv 19[11] Jos 7[11] Pr 6[30] 30[9] Ob[5] Zc 5[3], cf. *Inf. abs.* Ho 4[2] Je 7[9] & (c. Niph.) Ex 22[11]; גנב לֵב = *deceive* Gn 31[20.26] cf. Di; ג׳ אֹתִי Gn 31[27] *id.*; of sudden sweeping off by storm, in simile Jb 21[18]; fig. of destruction of wicked 27[20]. **Niph.** *be stolen*, subj. rei גָּנֹב יִגָּנֵב Ex 22[11]. **Pi.** *steal away* (trans.) וַיְגַנֵּב אבשלום את־לֵב 2 S 15[6]; מְגַנְּבֵי דְבָרַי Je 23[30]. **Pu.** *be stolen away* subj. pers. גֻּנֹּב גֻּנַּבְתִּי Gn 40[15]; subj. rei וְגֻנַּב consec. Ex 22[6]; *be brought by stealth* Jb 4[12] יְגֻנָּב. **Hithp.** *go by stealth, steal away* יִתְגַּנֵּב 2 S 19[4], וַיִּתְגַּנֵּב 2 S 19[4]. (Syr. ܐܶܬܓܢܶܒ ܢܰܦܫܶܗ *steal* oneself *away;* so ܠܗ Gn 31[27].)

†**גְּנֵבָה** n.f. thing stolen (on format. cf. Ba[NB 161, 166])—גְּנֵבָה Ex 22[3] (an animal); בִּגְנֵבָתוֹ Ex 22[2], בְּ׳ pret. cf. Di.

†**גַּנָּב** n.m. [Ex 22, 1] thief—גַּנָּב Ex 22[1] + 12 t.; גַּנָּבִים Is 1[23] + 3 t.—*thief* that breaks in Ex 22[1.6.7] (JE); by window Jo 2[9] (in simile); *thief* as one who steals Is 1[23] ψ 50[18] Pr 6[30] 29[24] Je 2[26] 48[27] Ho 7[1] (‖ גְּדוּד) Zc 5[4]; coming by night Je 49[9] cf. Jb 24[14] (in simile), Ob[5] (‖ שׁוֹדְדֵי לַיְלָה); Jb 30[5]; stealer of men (slave-dealer) Dt 24[7].

†**גְּנֻבַת** n.pr.m. (cf. Palm. גנבא Vog[No. 137]) son of Hadad the Edomite 1 K 11[20.20] (on the ת, cf. Dr[§ 181 N]).

גנז (*cover up, hide*, cf. NH *hide*, Ar. جَنَزَ *cover up*, Aram. גְּנַז Ithpa, ܐܶܬܓܢܶܙ Ethp. *be hidden*, Eth. ገነዘ: *enwrap*).

†[**גְּנָזִים**] n.[m.] pl. **1.** chests(?); **2.** treasury —only pl. cstr. גִּנְזֵי;—**1.** perh. *chests* of variegated cloth ג׳ בְּרֹמִים Ez 27[24] so Thes AV RV; Sm Co al. *cloths, carpets*, Ew *Taschen*. **2.** *treasury* (NH גִּנְזָ, Aram. גִּנְזָא, גִּנְזִין, BAram. cstr. pl. גִּנְזֵי; Pers. loan-word from گنج *treasure*? cf. Vullers[ii. 1032] Lag[Ges. Abh. 27]); גִּנְזֵי הַמֶּלֶךְ Est 3[9] 4[7].

†[**גַּנְזַךְ**] n.[m.] treasury (NH גנזכה *treasure;* loan-wd. fr. or through Pers. cf. supr. & Lag[Ges. Abh. 28]), וְגַנְזַכָּיו 1 Ch 28[11]. 𝔊 τῶν ζακχὼ αὐτοῦ; but 𝔊L τῶν ἀποθηκῶν αὐτοῦ.

†[**גָּנַן**] vb. cover, surround, defend (Ar. جَنَّ, Aram. אַגֵּן (Aph.), Palm. אגן Vog[Palm. 132 ff.]) —**Qal** *Pf.* וְגַנּוֹתִי Is 37[35] + 3 t.; *Inf. abs.* גָּנוֹן Is 31[5] (c. Hiph. q.v.)—*defend*, subj. always י׳; obj. the city Jerusalem c. על Is 37[35] 38[6] = 2 K 20[6]; 2 K 19[34] c. אֶל־ (‖ הוֹשִׁיעַ). **Hiph.** *Impf.* —or **Qal** acc. to Ba[ZMG 1889, 178], who comp. Ar. يَجِنُّ—יָגֵן Is 31[5] + 2 t.—*defend* (= Qal), Jeru-

salem Is 31^{5} יגן . . . גָּנוֹן c. על (‖ הִצִּיל); obj. Yahweh's people Zc 9^{15} c. על, 12^{8} c. בְּעַד.

† **גַּן n.m.** $^{Ct\,4,12}$ & (Gn 2^{15}) **f. enclosure, garden** (NH *id.*, גִּנָּה, Ar. جَنَّةٌ, Eth. ገነት: As. *ginû* COT^{Gloss}, also *gannatu* Dl$^{Pr\,84}$; Aram. גִּנְתָּא, גִּנָּא, ܓܢܬܐ; Ph. [צ]פר אנגן אם צץ CIS$^{1,165,11\,\&\,p.\,232\,f.}$ *birds of enclosure* (domestic fowls) *or of wing*)—abs. גַּן Gn 2^{8}+3 t.; cstr. id. Gn 2^{15}+19 t.; c. art. הַגָּן Gn 2^{9}+9 t., but כַּגַּן La 2^{6}; *sf.* גַּנִּי Ct 4^{16} 5^{1}, גַּנּוֹ Ct 4^{16} 6^{2}; *Pl.* גַּנִּים Ct 4^{15}+2 t.—*garden* as enclosure La 2^{6} (simile); הַיּוֹשֶׁבֶת בַּגַּנִּים Ct 8^{13}; cf. Ct 4^{12} (fig. of bride גַּן נָעוּל); *g. of herbs* (יָרָק) Dt 11^{10} 1 K 21^{2}; fig. of bride, *g. of plants, fruits, and spices* Ct 4$^{16.16}$ 5^{1} 6$^{2.2}$ cf. מַעְיַן גנים Ct 4^{15}; *g. of (king's) house* 2 K 21^{18} = גַּן־עֻזָּא 2 K 21$^{18.26}$; גַּן הַמֶּלֶךְ 2 K 25^{4} Je 39^{4} 52^{7} Ne 3^{15}, cf. בֵּית הַגָּן 2 K 9^{27} (at Jezreel? but this perhaps **n.pr.loc.** v. sub בית p. 111); most often of garden (orchard?) in Eden (Hex only Gn & only J) Gn 2$^{8.9.10.16}$ 3$^{1.2.3.8.8.10}$, called גַּן־עֵדֶן Gn 2^{15} 3$^{23.24}$ Ez 36^{35} Jo 2^{3}, cf. גן־י׳ Gn 13^{10} Is 51^{3} (both in simile); גן־אלהים Ez 28^{13} (עֵדֶן גן־אל׳), 31$^{8.8.9}$ (‖ עֵדֶן); in last three the trees of the garden are comp. with Assyrian under fig. of cedar of Lebanon.

† **גַּנָּה n.f.** garden (cf. foregoing)—גַּנָּה Is 1^{30} 61^{11}; cstr. גַּנַּת Ct 6^{11}+3 t.; sf. גַּנָּתוֹ Jb 8^{16}; pl. גַּנּת Nu 24^{6}, גַּנּוֹת Ec 2^{5}+6 t.; sf. גַּנּוֹתֵיכֶם Am 4^{9}; *garden, orchard,* Am 4^{9} (‖ כְּרָם, תְּאֵנָה, זַיִת), 9^{14} (fruit-garden; ‖ כֶּרֶם), Je 29$^{5.28}$ Ec 2^{5} (‖ פַּרְדֵּס), גִּנַּת אֱגוֹז Ct 6^{11} nut-garden; cf. גִּנַּת־בִּיתַן Est 1^{5} 7$^{7.8}$; in simile, of prosperous Isr. Nu 24^{6} (poem in JE; ג׳ עֲלֵי נָהָר), of chastised Isr. Is 1^{30} (ג׳ אשר מים אין לָהּ), of Yahweh's blessing Is 61^{11}; in Jb 8^{16} עַל־גַּנּוֹ in fig. of prosperity of wicked, as a luxuriant plant; gardens as places of idolatrous worship Is 1^{29} (‖ אֵילִים), 65^{3} (‖ לְבֵנִים), 66^{17} (i.e. groves).

† **גִּינַת n.pr.m.** father of Tibni 1 K 16$^{21.22}$.

† **גִּנְּתוֹי** Ne 12^{4} = following.

† **גִּנְּתוֹן n.pr.m.** a priest among the returned exiles Ne 10^{7} 12^{16} cf. foregoing.

† **מָגֵן n.m.** $^{1\,K\,14,27}$, & **f.** $^{1\,K\,10,17}$, **shield** (Ar. مِجَنٌّ, Aram. מְגִנָּא, ܡܓܢܐ)—מָגֵן Gn 15^{1}+33 t. (also cstr. Dt 33^{29} Na 2^{4}); sf. מָגִנִּי ψ 7^{11}+5 t.; מָגִנֵּנוּ ψ 33^{20}+3 t.; מָגִנָּם ψ 115$^{9.10.11}$; pl. מָגִנִּים 1 K 10^{17}+6 t.; מָגִנּוֹת 2 Ch 23^{9}; cstr. מָגִנֵּי 1 K 14^{26}+4 t.; sf. מָגִנָּיו Jb 15^{26}; מָגִנֶּיהָ Ho 4^{18};—*shield, buckler,* carried by warrior for defence Ju 5^{8} 2 S 1$^{21.21}$ 2 K 19^{32} = Is 37^{33}, 1 Ch 5^{18} 14^{7} 17^{17} 23^{9} 26^{14} 32^{5} Ne 4^{10} ψ 76^{4} Je 46$^{3.9}$ Ez 23^{24} 38$^{4.5}$ 39^{9} Na 2^{4} Is 22^{6} cf. 21^{5} (anoint the shield, to make it slippery), so also ψ 35^{2} (where י׳ fig. as warrior); אִישׁ מָגֵן = armed man Pr 6^{11} 24^{34}; laid up for show, or as treasure 1 K 10$^{17.17}$ 14$^{26.27}$ (= 2 Ch 9$^{16.16}$ 12$^{9.10}$) 2 Ch 32^{27} cf. Ct 4^{4} Ez 27^{10}; of scales of crocodile (leviathan) אֲפִיקֵי מָגִנִּים Jb 41^{7}; fig. of wicked's defence against judgments of י׳, עֲבִי גַּבֵּי מָגִנָּיו Jb 15^{26}; fig. of king ψ 89^{19} (cf. Che); fig. of rulers of Ephraim Ho 4^{18}; fig. of rulers of earth ψ 47^{10}; fig. (very often) of י׳, as defence of his servants, ψ 3^{4} 7^{11} (rd. מָגִנִּי עֲלֵי אל׳ cf. Che crit. note) 18$^{3.31.36}$ (= 2 S 22$^{3.31.36}$) 28^{7} 33^{20} 59^{12} 84$^{10.12}$ 115$^{9.10.11}$ 119^{114} 144^{2} Pr 2^{7} 30^{5}, and v. esp. Gn 15^{1} (E).

† **[מְגִנָּה] n.f. covering,** מְגִנַּת־לֵב La 3^{65} *covering of heart,* i.e. a hard shell about the heart = *obstinacy,* so Ges (cf. Qor 6^{25} وَجَعَلْنَا عَلَى قُلُوبِهِمْ أَكِنَّةً) RV; or, *covering of the understanding, blindness of heart,* so Ew Ke Näg Che.

† **[מָגַן] vb.** only **Pi. deliver up, deliver** (denom. fr. מָגֵן; on connex. of meanings cf. סָגַר)—*Pf.* מִגֵּן Gn 14^{20}; *Impf.* 3 fs. sf. תְּמַגְּנֶךָּ Pr 4^{9} אֲמַגֶּנְךָ Ho 11^{8};—*deliver up* to adversary Gn 14^{20} Ho 11^{8} + Is 64^{6} 𝔊 𝔖 𝔗 Ew Che al. וַתְּמַגְּנֵנוּ for MT וַתְּמוּגֵנוּ; also *deliver, give,* c. acc. & sf. of indirect obj. Pr 4^{9}.

† **גָּעָה vb. low** (of cattle) (NH *id.*, Aram. גְּעָא, ܓܥܐ)—יִגְעֶה־שּׁוֹר Jb 6^{5}; הָלְכוּ וְגָעוֹ 1 S 6^{12}.

† **[גֹּעָה] n.pr.loc.** close to Jerusalem גֹּעָתָה Je 31^{39};—site unknown.

† **[גָּעַל] vb. abhor, loathe** (NH געל Nithpa. *be fouled,* Hiph. *rinse out* with hot water; גְּעִילָה *rejection;* Aram. געל Ithpe. *be fouled, soiled*)—**Qal** *Pf.* 3 fs. גָּעֲלָה Lv 26^{43} Je 14^{19}, וְגָעֲלָה cons. Lv 26^{30}; גְּעַלְתִּים Lv 26^{44}; גָּעֲלוּ Ez 16^{45}; *Impf.* 3 fs. תִּגְעַל Lv 26$^{11.15}$; *Pt.* f. גֹּעֶלֶת Ez 16^{45};—*abhor, loathe,* (usually c. acc.), Yahweh, his people Lv 26$^{11.30.44}$ (H) Je 14^{19} (c. בְּ); the people, Yahweh's statutes, Lv 26$^{15.43}$ (H); Ez 16$^{45.45}$ women their husbands (fig., in proph. ag. Jerusalem). **Niph.** נִגְעַל מָגֵן גִּבּוֹרִים 2 S 1^{21} *the shield of heroes was defiled* RVm VB Kirkp. but < *is rejected, cast away* (*with loathing*) Dr, cf. Klo; 𝔊 προσωχθίσθη. **Hiph.** *Impf.* שׁוֹרוֹ עִבַּר וְלֹא יַגְעִל Jb 21^{10}; *and doth not cause,* or *allow,* (the cow) *to reject as loathesome* Ra De, cf. Di^{1}; Di^{2}, however, of bull, *cast away* (semen), or *shew aversion.*

†גֹּ֫עַל n.m. loathing, בגֹעַל נַפְשֵׁךְ Ez 16[5].

†גַּ֫עַל n.pr.m. appar a Canaanite, son of עֶבֶד (but cf VB) Ju 9[26.28.30.31.35.36.37.39.41]

†גָּעַר vb. rebuke (Aram גער, ܓܥܪ, id, Eth ገዐረ: *cry out*, Sab ינער n pr., Sab Denkm p. 29.30)—Is 17[13], גָּעֲרָה ψ 9[6] + 2 t, etc, *Impf* ינער Zc 3[2] + 3 t, תגערו Ru 2[16]; *Imv* גְּעַר ψ 68[31]; *Inf* מִגְּעָר Is 54[9], *Pt.* גּוֹעֵר Na 1[4], גֹּעֵר Mal 2[3],—c ב except ψ 9[6] 68[31] 119[21] Mal 2[3] where acc,—**1.** *rebuke*, father his son Gn 37[10] (E), reapers Ruth Ru 2[16], priest Jeremiah Je 29[27]. **2.** of God rebuking nations ψ 9[6] Is 17[13], proud ψ 119[21], Satan Zc 3[2.2], חית קנה ψ 68[31], בָּאֹכֵל (the devouring swarm of locusts, restraining them) Mal 3[11], the sea drying it up ψ 106[9] Na 1[4], Zion Is 54[9], הַזֶּרַע the *seed* (prevent the usual harvest) Mal 2[3] (𝔊 Aq 𝔙 הַזְּרֹעַ, *the arm*, viz, of priests, that they may not extend it to bless).

†גְּעָרָה n.f. rebuke—Pr 13[1] + 2 t, גַּעֲרַת Ec 7[5] + 5 t, sf גַּעֲרָתְךָ ψ 18[16] + (sfs 6 t),—**1.** of man Pr 13[1.8] 17[10] Ec 7[5] Is 30[17.17] **2.** of God Jb 26[11] ψ 18[16] (=2 S 22[16]) 76[7] 80[17] 104[7] Is 50[2] 51[20] 66[15].

†מִגְעֶ֫רֶת n f. rebuke Dt 28[20].

†[גָּעַשׁ] vb shake, quake (NH *id*)—**Qal** *Impf* וַתִּגְעַשׁ ψ 18[8a] = 2 S 22[8a] Kt (Qr Hithp),—*quake* of earth at theoph., ψ 18[8] = 2 S 22[8] (rd Kt, ‖ רעש) **Pu.** *Impf. be shaken up, convulsed* יְגֹעֲשׁוּ־עָם Jb 34[20] *a people are convulsed* **Hithp.** *shake back and forth, toss* or *reel to and fro* וַיִּתְגָּעַשׁ Qr 2 S 22[8a] (< Kt **Qal**); יִתְגָּעֲשׁוּ Je 46[7], וַיִּתְגָּעֲשׁוּ ψ 18[8b] + 2 t;—of mountains ψ 18[8b] = 2 S 22[8b], of waves of sea, Je 5[22], of waters of Nile Je 46[7] (cf v[8]) **Hithpo.** *Pf* וְהִתְגֹּעֲשׁוּ consec Je 25[16], *Impf* יִתְגֹּעֲשׁוּ Je 46[8], *id.* of waters of Nile Je 46[8], of drunken men, *reel to and fro*, Je 25[16] (fig of nations confounded by י׳)

†[גַּ֫עַשׁ] n.pr loc. הַר־גָּ֑עַשׁ Jos 24[30] Ju 2[9] mt. in Ephraim, S of (חֶרֶס) תִּמְנַת־סֶרַח q v., נַחֲלֵי גָעַשׁ 2 S 23[30] = 1 Ch 11[32] of ravines thereon, or near by.

†גַּעְתָּם n.pr m. a chief of Edom, son of Eliphaz Gn 36[11.16] 1 Ch 1[36].

גַּף v sub גפף

גפן (✓of following, meaning ?).

†גֶּ֫פֶן n.f. [Ju 9 13+] (m. only Ho 10[1], perh. infl of יִשְׂרָאֵל, 2 K 4[39]) vine (NH *id*, Ar. جَفْنٌ (Yemen), As *gapnu*, cf. Zehnpfund[BAS i. 652], Aram גּוּפְנָא, גֻּפְנָא, ܓܦܬܐ, pl ܓܘܦܢܐ)—נ׳ Gn 40[9] + 38 t. (also cstr, as Nu 6[4] Dt 32[32] Is 16[8.9]), גָּ֑פֶן Ju 9[12] + 2 t, *sf.* גַּפְנִי Jo 1[7], גַּפְנְךָ Je 5[17], גַּפְנוֹ 1 K 5[5] + 3 t., גַּפְנָהּ Ho 2[14], גַּפְנָם Dt 32[32] + 2 t, pl גְּפָנִים Ct 2[13] Hb 3[17]—*vine* (always grape-bearing exc. 2 K 4[39]) Gn 40[9.10] (in dream) 49[11] Nu 20[5] Dt 8[8] Ju 9[12.13] (in allegory) 1 K 5[5] 2 K 18[31] = Is 36[16], ψ 78[47] 105[33] Ct 2[13] 6[11] 7[13] Is 7[23] 24[7] 32[12] Je 5[17] 8[13] Ho 2[14] Jo 1[7.12] 2[22] Mi 4[4] Hb 3[17] Hg 2[19] Zc 2[10] 8[12] Mal 3[11]; גֶּפֶן שָׂדֶה a vine bearing poisonous gourds 2 K 4[39]; גֶּפֶן הַיַּיִן Nu 6[4] (cf. Gn 40[10] Ju 9[13]) Ju 13[14], אֶשְׁכְּלוֹת הַגֶּפֶן Ct 8[9]; עֵץ הַגֶּפֶן Ez 15[2.6]; in simile of stars fading away at Yahweh's judgment Is 34[4]; in simile of wicked losing early promise Jb 15[33], in simile of wife ψ 128[3]; fig of Israel ψ 80[9.15] Ez 17[6.6.7.8] Ho 10[1] cf Ez 19[10], Je 2[21] 6[9], also Ho 14[8]; fig. of Israel as easily destroyed Ez 15[2.6], fig. of godless enemies of Israel Dt 32[32] cf. Di; גֶּפֶן שִׂבְמָה fig for prosperity of Moab Is 16[8.9] Je 48[32]—On the vine in Syria cf Anderlind[ZPV 1888, 160 ff]

גפף (✓of foll, cf Syr. ܓܦܦ in deriv., ܓܦܝܦܐ *curved, convex;* also Ar. جَفْجَفٌ both *hilly country* and *depression*, Frey)

†[גַּף] n.m. body, self, height, elevation (cf NH (גּוּף) — sg sf. גַּפּוֹ Ex 21[3.3.4]; pl. cstr גַּפֵּי Pr 9[3],—**1.** *body, self*, only in phr יָבֹא (יֵצֵא) בְּגַפּוֹ *he shall come in (go out) by himself* (with his body) Ex 21[3.3.4], in law of slave (cf. Di). **2.** *height, elevation* עַל־גַּפֵּי מְרֹמֵי קָרֶת Pr 9[3]

†גֹּ֫פֶר n.[m] gopher, only in עֲצֵי־גֹפֶר Gn 6[14] (P), wood of which the ark was made (word dub; Thes comp כֹּפֶר & so Rob Ges (hence '*pitch-wood*, resinous wood'), cf. Di; Lag Semitica i 64, Symmict ii. 93, BN 217 ff thinks word not original, but inferred from גפרית, and substituted here for גפרית by copyist, or editor Cf. following).

†גָּפְרִית n.f. brimstone (Aram גּוּפְרִיתָא, also כִּבְרִיתָא, כּוּבְרִיתָא, ܟܒܪܝܬܐ, ܟܘܒܪܝܬܐ, Ar. كِبْرِيت (certainly foreign wd.); der. from (כָּפַר), גפר by Thes RobGes, cf. Di Gn 6[14]; i.e *pitch*, and then other combustibles, esp *sulphur;* Lag[l. c.] thinks fr. Bactr. *vohûkereti*)—גָּפְרִית Gn 19[24] + 6 t—*brimstone*, after הִמְטִיר Gn 19[24] (J), fig of judgment ψ 11[6] Ez 38[22] (in all ‖ אֵשׁ etc), cf also Jb 18[15] Is 34[9], & Dt 29[22]; נַחַל נ׳ simile for the destroying breath of י׳ Is 30[33].

גר v. sub I. גור.

גֵּר v. sub גיר.

†גֵּרָא n.pr.m. (Ph גרא) son of Benjamin Gn 46[21] (lacking Nu 26[38-40]); son of Bela', & grandson of Benj, acc to 1 Ch 8[3,5] cf. v[7]; designation of a Benjamite family or clan; hence Ehud called בֶּן־גֵּרָא Ju 3[15], & so Shimei, 2 S 16[5] 19[17,19] 1 K 2[8].

גרב (√ of foll.; Ar. جَرِبَ, Aram. ܓܪܒ (*have the scab* etc.), are appar. denom.)

†גָּרָב **n.[m.]** itch, scab (Ar. جَرَبٌ, Aram. גַּרְבָא, ܓܰܪܒܳܐ, As. *garabu* Dl § 162)—גָּרָב Lv 21[20] 22[22] Dt 28[27].

†גָּרֵב **1. n.pr.m.** (cf Palm. n.pr m גריבא Vog[141]) one of David's heroes 2 S 23[38] = 1 Ch 11[40]. **2. n.pr.loc.** (cf. Sab n pr loc גרבם Hal No. 379, 382) only in גִּבְעַת גָּרֵב Je 31[39] *hill of Gareb*, appar. close to Jerusalem on the SW. cf. Gf; v. also Hi Che.

גַּרְגַּר, גַּרְגְּרוֹת v. sub גרר.

†גִּרְגָּשִׁי **adj.gent.** only הַגּ׳ as n.pr.coll, 'begotten' by Canaan Gn 10[16] = 1 Ch 1[14]; in list of Canaanitish peoples displaced by Isr.; territ. unknown; Gn 15[21] Dt 7[1] Jos 3[10] 24[11] Ne 9[8]; cf. Gn 10[16] 1 Ch 1[14] supr. (Hex only JED).

†[גָּרַד] **vb. scrape, scratch** (NH *id.*, Aram. גְּרַד, ܓܪܰܕ & Ph. מגרדם *flesh-scrapers* CIS 338.4; cf. also Ar. جَرَدَ *peel* or *strip off* bark, *shave* hair fr. a hide etc)—**Hithp.** *Inf.* לְהִתְגָּרֵד *scrape one's self* Jb 2[8].

†[גָּרָה] **vb.** only **Pi. stir up strife, Hithp. engage in strife** (cf. NH Pi. *stir up, excite*, against (ב) Hithp; Aram. Pa גָּרֵא ܓܰܪܺܝ; esp As. *garû*, Qal *attack, be at war with, garû, girû, enemy*, etc. Asrb Annals iv 49, 50 (KB ii. 190) also SASmith Asrb. i ii. Gloss.; Ar. جَرَى is *run*, esp. of water, *flow*, etc)—**Pi.** *Impf.* 3 ms. יְגָרֶה Pr 15[18] 28[25] 29[22], all c. obj. מָדוֹן *excite, stir up, strife*—On גֵּרָה Dt 14[8] v I גֵּרָה sub גרר. **Hithp.** *Pf* 2 fs. הִתְגָּרִית Je 50[24], *Impf.* 3 ms. יִתְגָּרֶה Dn 11[25], וְיִתְגָּרוּ v[10]; 2 ms. תִּתְגָּרֶה 2 K 14[10] 2 Ch 25[19]; juss. apoc. תִּתְגָּר Dt 2[9,19], 3 mpl. יִתְגָּרוּ Pr 28[4] Dn 11[10], cf Dn 11[10] Kt., v. supr.; 2 mpl. תִּתְגָּרוּ Dt 2[5] (juss.); *Imv.* ms. הִתְגָּר Dt 2[24];—**1.** *excite oneself* against (בְּ pers.), *engage in strife* with, lit. Dt 2[5,19], 2 K 14[10] = 2 Ch 25[19] (sq בְּרָעָה,—רעה personif as challenged opponent), also + acc of manner, מִלְחָמָה Dt 2[9,24]; fig. וְשֹׁמְרֵי תוֹרָה יִתְגָּרוּ בָם Pr 28[4] *while they that keep the law are at strife with them*, i.e. with those that forsake it. **2.** abs., *excite oneself* (against foe), *wage war*, only Dn 11: יִתְגָּרוּ וְאָסְפוּ הֲמוֹן חֲיָלִים רַבִּים v[10] *they shall wage war*, etc.; וְיָשֹׁב וְיִתְגָּרוּ עַד־מָעֻזֹּה v[10] *and he shall return and war, even to his stronghold;* v[25] sq. לַמִּלְחָמָה + בְּחַיִל גָּדוֹל (instr.)

†גָּרוֹן **n.m.** ψ 69, 4 **neck, throat** (connexion with above √dub., Thes RobGes (cf. MV) from גרה in (assumed) sense of גרר of a *dragging, scraping* sound; cf. מְגֵרָה; yet √perh. גרן q.v.; Ar. جِرَانٌ (sub جَرَنَ Frey Lane) *front part of neck* of camel, etc)—ג׳ Is 3[16] 58[1]; sf. גְּרוֹנִי ψ 69[4], גְּרוֹנֵךְ Ez 16[11] + Je 2[25] Qr (Kt גורנך), גְּרוֹנָם ψ 115[7] 149[6], גְּרֹנָם ψ 5[10],—*throat;* **1.** of the visible exterior (front) of throat, *neck* נְטוּוֹת ג׳ Is 3[16] *outstretched of neck* (= with outstretched neck); וְרָבִיד עַל־גְּרוֹנֵךְ Ez 41[19] *and a chain upon thy neck.* **2.** *throat*, as capable of thirst Je 2[25]; as organ of speech קְרָא בְגָרוֹן Is 58[1] (‖ הָרֵם קוֹלֶךָ), לֹא יֶהְגּוּ בִּג׳ ψ 115[7]; also רוֹמְמוֹת אֵל בִּגְרוֹנָם ψ 149[6] *high songs to God (be) in their throat*, cf. נִחַר גְּרוֹנִי ψ 69[4] *my throat is parched* (‖ יָגַעְתִּי בְקָרְאִי); so also קֶבֶר־פָּתוּחַ גְּרֹנָם ψ 5[10] *their throat is an opened sepulchre.*

†[תִּגְרָה] **n.f. contention, strife, hostility** (cf Aram. תִּגְרָא, oft 𝔗, v Thes; תִּגְרָה NHWB & Fl in ChWB ii 561)—only cstr sg. מִתִּגְרַת יָדְךָ ψ 39[11] *from* (i e *through*) *the hostility of thy hand I am consumed.*

I. גֵּרָה, II. גֵּרָה v. sub גרר.

גרות v. sub I. גור.

†[גָּרַז] **vb.** cut, cut off (Ar. جَرَزَ *cut, cut off, exterminate*)—**Niph.** *Pf.* נִגְרַזְתִּי ψ 31[23] = destroyed out of Yahweh's sight.

†גַּרְזֶן **n.m.** Is 10, 15 **axe** (*pick, pick-axe*, 3 t. in SI; on format. cf Sta 294 a Ges § 85, xi. 54)—Dt 19[5] 20[19] Is 10[15] 1 K 6[7] (Co conj. also Ez 31[11]).

†גִּרְזִי Kt, גִּזְרִי (q v) Qr **adj.gent.** 1 S 27[8].

†גְּרִזִּים **n.pr.loc.** mt. in N. Israel, S of Sichem (Nabulus), opp. *Ebal* (עֵיבָל), which was on N; only הַר ג׳ Dt 11[29] 27[12] Jos 8[33] Ju 9[7]; mod. *Jebel et-Tôr* Rob BR ii. 274 ff Bd Pal 220, 222.

גרטל (possibly quadrilit √, whence foll c. א prosthet Cf. however infr)

†[אֲגַרְטָל] **n.m.** a kind of vessel, **basin or basket** (?; others *basket-like, basket-shaped*

vessel); only pl. cstr. א׳ כֶּסֶף, & אֲגַרְטְלֵי זָהָב, both Ezr 1⁹, denoting vessels from temple at Jerus. restored by Cyrus. (Etym. & mng. dub. cf. supr.; A 𝔊L Codd. 𝔊 ψυκτῆρες, *wine-coolers;* B om.; now commonly compared with Aram. קַרְטָלִיתָא Levy NHWB iv. 376, ܩܪܛܠܐ, Ar. قِرْطَالَة, قِرْطَالَة, supposed to be loan-word fr. Hellenist. Gk. κάρταλος, κάρταλλος (e.g. 𝔊 2 K 10⁷, Heb. דּוּדִים), all = *basket, fruit-basket,* etc., *canistrum* (so MV BeRy SS); but κάρταλλος itself is possibly a Pers. or Shemit. loan-word; cf. esp. Frä 77 f.; further conject. in Thes BeRy.)

גרל (cf. Ar. جَرَلٌ, pl. أَجْرَالٌ *stones,* or *stony place* planted with trees; جَرْوَلٌ *stony;* جَرْوَلٌ, جُرَوَلٌ *stony ground, stones;* hence foll., because stones were used in casting lots; cf. Gk. ψῆφος *pebble, vote;* κύαμος *bean, lot*).

גּוֹרָל 77 **n.m.** Lv 16. 8 & (†Jos 21¹⁰, but v. infr.) **f.** lot, (NH *id.* & denom. Hiph. הִגְרִיל *cast lots*) —abs. ג׳ Jos 16¹ + 51 t.; cstr. גּוֹרַל Jos 18¹¹ + 2 t., גֹּרַל Nu 36³; sf. גּוֹרָלִי ψ 16⁵, גֹּרָלִי Ju 1³, גּוֹרָלְךָ Pr 1¹⁴, גֹּרָלְךָ Dn 12¹³, גּוֹרָלֶךָ Ju 1³, גּוֹרָלֵךְ Je 13²⁵ Is 57⁶, גּוֹרָלוֹ 1 Ch 26¹⁴, גּוֹרָלָם Jos 18¹¹ + 2 t.; pl. גּוֹרָלוֹת Jon 1⁷ + 8 t., גֹּרָלוֹת Lv 16⁸;—*a lot* cast for the decision of questions Pr 18¹⁸, designation of persons, etc., for service or punishment, assignment of property, etc.; prob. stones put into the bosom-fold of a garment, Pr 16³³ (בַּחֵיק יוּטַל אֶת־הַגּ׳), or into a vessel, and shaken until one springs out (יָצָא, עָלָה, or—late—נָפַל); this was regarded originally as divine decision (cf. on Urim & Thummim p. 22, supr.); for the agent, the usual verbs are נָתַן, יָרָה, הִשְׁלִיךְ, and הִפִּיל. Particularly:—**1.** *lot* for dividing land, esp. that which Joshua cast at Shiloh לִפְנֵי י׳ Jos 18⁶ (יָרָה) v⁸·¹⁰ (both הִשְׁלִיךְ; all three sq. לְ of pers. for whom; all JE); cf. 19⁵¹ (P); so of lot coming up, or forth, עָלָה Jos 18¹¹ (cstr.; P), also sq. לְ pers. 19¹⁰ (P), & foll. c. יָצָא 16¹ (JE), Nu 33⁵⁴ Jos 19¹·¹⁷·²⁴·³²·⁴⁰ 21⁴ (all P); *be divided by lot* יֵחָלֵק בְּג׳ Nu 26⁵⁵, or *according to lot* עַל־פִּי הַגּ׳ תֵּחָלֵק v⁵⁶; *apportion by lot* הִתְנַחֲלוּ נָחַל בְּג׳, 34¹³, נָתַן בְּג׳ 33⁵⁴ Jos 19⁵¹; *give by lot* בְּג׳ Nu 36² נָתַן בַּגּ׳ Jos 21⁸ (all P) 1 Ch 6⁵⁰; *have by lot* הָיָה לְ׳ בַּגּ׳ Jos 21⁴, & (היה om.) v⁵·⁶ (all P) cf. 1 Ch 6⁴⁶·⁴⁸; also Jos 21¹⁰ (P; הַגּ׳ רִאשֹׁנָה, only here f.; 𝔊—not 𝔊L—om. ראישנה, & so) ‖ 1 Ch 6³⁹; cf. further Is 34¹⁷ (הִפִּיל לְ). **2.** *lot* for assigning to service, duty or punishment, **a.** concerning the goats on day of atonement, Lv 16⁸ (נָתַן עַל) v⁸·⁸ (sq. לְ); cf. v⁹·¹⁰ (עָלָה עַל; all P). **b.** assigning priests to their courses, singers, musicians & porters to their duties, by lot חָלַק בְּג׳ 1 Ch 24⁵; הִפִּיל ג׳ v³¹ 25⁸ 26¹³ (sq. לְ of position) v¹⁴; of lot coming forth (יָצָא לְ pers.) 24⁷ (cf. v⁷ ¹⁸) 25⁹ (cf. v⁹⁻³¹) 26¹⁴ cf. וַיֵּצֵא גּוֹרָלוֹ v¹⁴. **c.** *cast lots* for dwelling in Jerus. (הִפִּיל ג׳) Ne 11¹ (sq. inf.) **d.** for supplying wood for altar-fire Ne 10³⁵ (הִפִּיל עַל); here belongs prob. also **e.** Ju 20⁹ עָלֶיהָ בְּג׳, ref. to v¹⁰ (determining who shall go up, and who supply provision) 𝔊 ἀναβησόμεθα ἐπ' αὐτὴν ἐν κλήρῳ so Stu (insert perh. נעלה), cf. AV RV, Bu RS 151 (who rds. נַפִּילָה בְּג׳); > 𝔖 Be Ke who ref. ג׳ here to division of land of captured city. **f.** to determine guilty persons Jon 1⁷·⁷ (both הִפִּיל) v¹⁷ (נָפַל עַל); so appar. Ez 24⁶ of inhab. of Jerus. under fig. of flesh in pot לֹא־נָפַל עָלֶיהָ ג׳ *no lot is fallen over it,* i.e. no discrimination is made, destruction is to include the whole city; (cf. also Jos 7¹⁴ ff. 1 S 14⁴¹ ff. where divine agency in detection is prominent but word גּוֹרָל not used). **g.** in allotting slaves Jo 4³ אֶל־עַמִּי יַדּוּ ג׳; Na 3¹⁰ (יַדּוּ עַל); so Ob¹¹ וְעַל־יְרוּשָׁלַםִ יַדּוּ ג׳, —all c. vb. ידד q.v. **h.** in distributing plundered garments ψ 22¹⁹ (הִפִּיל עַל). **i.** to determine favourable day for a scheme, הִפִּיל Est 3⁷ (לִפְנֵי הָמָן) 9²⁴ (sq. inf.; v. also פּוּר). **3.** *thing assigned, apportioned, allotted* esp. of land assigned by lot, *allotment* Jos 15¹ 17¹ 21³⁸ (all P), 17¹⁴·¹⁷ = *portion, share* (‖נַחֲלָה; JE); cf. גֹּרַל נַחֲלָתֵנוּ Nu 36³ (P), גּוֹרַל נַחֲלָתָם Jos 14² (P; but perh. rd. abs. גּוֹרָל cf. Di); also גְּבוּל גּוֹרָלָם 18¹¹ (P) *the boundary of their allotment;* עָרֵי גּוֹרָלָם 21²⁰ (P); v. further Ju 1³·³; so prob. Mi 2⁵ הִשְׁלִיךְ חֶבֶל בְּג׳ (Hi Che; cf. also Ew); ψ 125³, land, exposed to oppressive exaction; also fig. of י׳ as portion, allotment of his people ψ 16⁵ (so Che, & on תָּמִיד for תּוֹמִיךְ cf. his crit. n.; v. also Ew; otherwise De al.;—‖מְנָת חֶלְקִי); on the other hand, of idols Is 57⁶ (‖חֵלֶק); also עֲמֹד לְג׳ Dn 12¹³, of *allotted portion, share,* in the Messianic consummation; more generally, one's *portion, lot, fortune* גּוֹרָלְךָ תַּפִּיל בְּתוֹכֵנוּ Pr 1¹⁴ *cast thy fortune into the midst of us, in with us* (‖כִּיס אֶחָד יִהְיֶה לְכֻלָּנוּ). **4.** *portion = recompence, retribution* Is 17¹⁴ (‖חֵלֶק), Je 13²⁵ (‖ מְנָת מִדַּיִךְ), both implying divine agency.

†[גָּרָל] **adj.** גְּרָל־חֵמָה Pr 19¹⁹ Kt; < Qr גְּדָל־ cf Vrss, AV RV Now Str al

I. [גָּרַם] **vb. lay aside, leave, save** (NH גָּרַם is *shorten, occasion, bring about, to pass,* Aram. גְּרַם Pa. *occasion, bring about,* جرم *abscidit, decrevit,* cf. also Ar. جَرَمَ *cut off* (fruit), *shear* (sheep);—on connexion of ideas v. Fl NHWB¹·⁴³⁷) **Qal** *Pf* 3 pl לֹא גָרְמוּ לַבֹּקֶר Zp 3³ *they have left nothing for the morrow,* in fig. of cruel judges (dub.. al. fr. II. [גָּרַם], v Kau^AT Dr).

†גֶּרֶם **n.[m.] bone, strength, self** (?) (Ar. جِرْمٌ *body,* Aram גַּרְמָא, ܓܪܡܐ *bone, self*)—abs. גָּרֶם Gn 49¹⁴ + 2 t; cstr גֶּרֶם 2 K 9¹³, sf גְּרָמָיו Jb 40¹⁸;—**1.** *bone* Pr 17²² (coll) 25¹⁵; of behemoth (hippopot.) Jb 40¹⁸ (‖ עצם q.v) **2.** *strength* Gn 49¹⁴ חֲמֹר גָּרֶם *strong ass* (lit. *bony,* so VB) **3.** *self* (cf. עצם), 2 K 9¹³ גֶּרֶם הַמַּעֲלוֹת so Ges Ew Ke, but text dub., v conjectures in Klo.

†II. [גָּרַם] **vb. denom. break bones, break,** —**Pi.** *Impf.* וְעַצְמֹתֵיהֶם יְגָרֵם Nu 24⁸ (JE); but also וְאֶת־חֲרָשֶׂיהָ תְּגָרֵמִי Ez 23³⁴ (yet on txt. v. Co)

†גַּרְמִי **adj. gent.** c. art 1 Ch 4¹⁹.

גרן (√of foll; ? cf. Ar. جَرَنَ, *become accustomed, worn smooth* (of skin, garment, etc), also *grind grain vehemently;* vid. further جَرِينٌ *what one has ground,* of grain; & *place in which dates are dried* = مَجْرَنٌ)

†גֹּרֶן **n.m. threshing-floor** (cf further vulg. Ar جُرْنٌ *stone basin, trough, mortar,* etc. Dozy Lane, v. Mohît^243 b.7)—גֹּרֶן Gn 50¹⁰ + 27 t. (cstr e.g. Gn 50^10.11 2 S 6⁶); גָּרְנָה Mi 4¹², sf. גָּרְנִי Is 21¹⁰; גָּרְנְךָ Dt 15¹⁴ 16¹³; pl. הַגֳּרָנוֹת 1 S 23¹, הַגֳּרָנוֹת Jo 2²⁴; cstr. גָּרְנוֹת Ho 9¹—**threshing-floor,** (on form v Rob^BR I 550 cf Fl NHWB¹ ⁴³⁷) Gn 50^10.11 (גֹ׳ האטד) Nu 18²⁷ (דָּגָן מִן־הגֹ׳) Dt 15¹⁴ 16¹³ Ju 6³⁷ Ru 3² (הוא זֹרֶה גֹ׳ הַשְּׂעֹרִים) v^3.6 14 2 S 6⁶ 24^16 18.21 24 1 Ch 13⁹ 21^15 18.21.22.28 2 Ch 3¹ Ho 9¹ (גֹ׳ דָּגָן) v² Mi 4¹² Jb 39¹² cf. Di; תְּרוּמַת גֹ׳ Nu 15²⁰; תְּבוּאַת גֹ׳ Nu 18³⁰, of these, three may be n.pr loc.:—גֹּרֶן הָאָטָד Gn 50^10 11; גֹּרֶן נָכוֹן 2 S 6⁶ (cf. We Dr) = גֹּרֶן כִּידֹן 1 Ch 13⁹; place of storing corn, etc. 1 S 23¹ 2 K 6²⁷ Jo 2²⁴; open place at city-gate גֹּרֶן פֶּתַח שַׁעַר שֹׁמְרוֹן 1 K 22¹⁰ = 2 Ch 18⁹, where kings of Isr & Jud sat (but this peculiar & text dub.; 𝔊 (in K) ἔνοπλοι; We om.; 𝔖 Th Be בְּרָדִים, agreeing with בְּגָדִים preceding; yet this elsewh. in Heb. only of animals); in simile of daughter of Babylon, Je 51³³ (trodden smooth) cf. fig. of Israel בֶּן־גָּרְנִי (‖ מְדֻשָׁתִי) Is 21¹⁰; ....מֹץ מִגֹּ׳ Ho 13³.

גָּרוֹן, גָּרֹן v. sub נרה.

גָּרַס **vb.** v. sub גרש

†[גָּרַע] **vb. diminish, restrain, withdraw** (NH *id.,* Aram גְּרַע, ܓܪܥ *shave head,* etc.; cf. جَرِعَ *swallow*)—**Qal** *Impf.* יִגְרַע Jb 36⁷, יִגָּרַע Ex 21¹⁰; 2 ms. תגרע Dt 13¹ + 3 t; אֶגְרַע Ez 5¹¹ (but cf *infr*), וָאֶגְרַע Ez 16²⁷, תגרעו Ex 5⁸ + 2 t; *Inf.* לִגְרֹעַ Ec 3¹⁴; *Pt.* גְּרוּעָה Is 15² (so Baer; v.d.H. גְּדוּעָה v. גדע), גְּרֻעָה Je 48³⁷;—**1.** *diminish,* usually sq. מִן Ex 5^8 19 (the tale of bricks), Dt 4² 13¹ (in both, word of י׳, opp הוסיף) cf. Ec 3¹⁴, and also Je 26² (c. acc), c acc. also Ex 21¹⁰ (food etc) cf. Ez 16²⁷, *Pt. pass. diminished, clipped,* of beard, Je 48³⁷ and Is 15² (so Baer, rightly, cf. his note and v. גדע) **2.** *restrain* Jb 15⁴ (c acc. שִׂיחָה meditation, devotion), Jb 15⁸ (c. acc. חָכְמָה, sq אֵלֶיךָ, i e *unto, for thyself,* monopolize; De Di Da render *draw unto thyself,* appropriate, Schult. comp Ar. *swallow,* cf. Ew *saugst zu dir ein Weisheit*). **3.** *withdraw* Jb 36⁷ (obj. עַיִן, *eye,* sq מִן); Ez 5¹¹ absol. (si vera l.), Co reads אֶתְגָּרֶה, for אֶגְרַע, on intern. grounds, others: *withdraw* (thy needs) Sm (cf. 16²⁷); *withdraw* (mine eye) Ges Ke. **Niph.** *Pf* ונגרע consec Lv 27¹⁸, וְנִגְרְעָה Nu 36³, *Impf.* יִגָּרַע Nu 27⁴ 36⁴, יִגָּרֵעַ Nu 36³, 1 pl. נִגָּרַע Nu 9⁷; *Pt.* נגרע Ex 5¹¹,—**1.** *be withdrawn* c. מִן Nu 36^3.3.4 (inheritance, נחלה); Nu 27⁴ a name out of a family; Ex 5¹¹ (מֵעֲבֹדַתְכֶם דָּבָר); impers. Lv 27¹⁸ (*abatement shall be made*). **2.** *be restrained* sq inf Nu 9⁷. **Pi.** *Impf.* יְגָרַע Jb 36²⁷ *withdraw* = *draw up* c. acc נִטְפֵי־מָיִם cf Di (on other hand, De al. *draw down, let down*).

†[מִגְרָעָה] **n.f. recess, rebatement** (RV), i. e **ledge,** only pl., נָתַן מִגְרָעוֹת לַבַּיִת 1 K 6⁶.

†[גָּרַף] **vb. sweep away** (orig. *shovel* or *scoop up, away,* cf. NH *id,* Ar. جَرَفَ; Aram גְּרַף, ܓܪܦ, Eth in deriv)—גְּרָפָם (נַחַל קִישׁוֹן) Ju 5²¹.

†[אֶגְרֹף] **n.[m.] fist** (𝔊 πυγμή, so 𝔙; but 𝔗 *club, staff* (?), & so SS, cf. esp. Ex 21¹⁸;—NH אֶגְרוֹף)—וְהִכָּה אִישׁ אֶת־רֵעֵהוּ בְּאֶבֶן אוֹ בְאֶגְרֹף Ex 21¹⁸, (cstr) לְהַכּוֹת בְּאֶגְרֹף רֶשַׁע Is 58⁴.

†[מֶגְרָפָה] **n.f. shovel** (NH *id;* Aram. מַגְרוֹפִיתָא, Ar مِجْرَفَة (v. Lane)) only pl. מֶגְרְפֹתֵיהֶם Jo 1¹⁷ (Thes *clods,* after Jewish interpreters, so AV RV, cf however Me^Joel 100 f; 𝔊 Me ארותיהם *their cribs,* of cattle; mng. of clause dubious).

†[גָּרַר] **vb. drag, drag away** (NH *id*, Ar. جَرَّ, Aram גְּרַר, ܓܪܰ; As. *garâru, run*, Zim$^{BP\ 102}$, etc)—**Qal** *Impf* sf יְגֹרֵהוּ Hb 1^{15}, יגורם Pr 21^{7}—*drag away*, fishes in net, fig Hb 1^{15} (Chaldeans, their opponents); violence, the wicked Pr 21^{7}. **Niph.** (rd. **Qal**? Sam יָגוּר, cf Di) *Impf* יִגָּר Lv 11^{7} c acc. cogn גֵּרָה לֹא־יִגָּר=(the) *cud he cheweth not*, cf also Dt 14^{8} Sam 𝔊 (Di). **Po'al** *Pt* (denom, so NH Qal & Niph) מְגֹרָרוֹת בַּמְּגֵרָה 1 K 7^{9} *sawn with the saw.* **Hithpo.** סַעַר מִתְגּוֹרֵר Je 30^{23} *a* (sweeping) *roaring whirlwind* (‖ 23^{19} has מִתְחוֹלֵל) On יתגוררו Ho 7^{14}, v I גּוּר, גדד.

†I. גֵּרָה **n.f. cud** (Ar جِرَّة, so called fr sound of rumination?)—גֵּרָה Lv 11^{3}+10t—*cud*, only in legislation of clean and unclean animals, and almost always c (·ָה, ·ַת, ·ִי) מַעֲלָה Lv 11$^{3.4.4.5.6.26}$ (P) Dt 14$^{6.6.7}$, ג׳ יִגָּר (cf גרר Niph.) Lv 11^{7}, Dt 14^{8} has גֵּרָה without vb, but read there as Lv 11^{7} (so Sam 𝔊 Di)

†II גֵּרָה **n f.** a weight, 20th part of shekel, **gerah** (As *girû*, Zehnpfund$^{BAS\ I\ 506}$)—גֵּרָה Ex 30^{13}+4t—Only in definition of שֶׁקֶל, c num. עשרים Ex 30^{13} Lv 27^{25} Nu 3^{47} 18^{16} Ez 45^{12}

†[גַּרְגַּר] **n.m. berry** (NH *id*), גַּרְגְּרִים בראשׁ אָמִיר Is 17^{6}

†גַּרְגְּרוֹת **n f pl. neck** (on format cf. Ba$^{NB\ 204}$)—גַּרְגְּרֹתֶךָ Pr 1^{9} 3^{22}, גַּרְגְּרוֹתֶךָ Pr 3^{3}, 6^{21}—always in fig., instruction of parents an ornament, a chain *upon neck* Pr 1^{9}, *bind them upon thy neck* 6^{21}, so of mercy & truth 3^{3}, cf. v^{22}

†מְגֵרָה **n.f. saw** (NH *id*, perh. from its harsh *dragging* sound)—מגרה 2 S 12^{31a} + 2t, pl מגרות 1 Ch 20^{3} (<מְגוּרוֹת 2 S 12^{31b})—*saw*, used in cutting stone מְגֹרָרוֹת בַּמְּגֵרָה 1 K 7^{9}, used in torture (or as tools for enforced labour) of captives 2 S 12^{31a} 1 Ch 20^{3a}.

†גְּרָר **n.pr loc.** south of Gaza, usually identif with mod. *Umm Jerâr* Bd$^{Pal\ 159}$ Guérin$^{Judée\ ii\ 257\ ff}$; but *Wady Jerūr* W of *'Ain Kadīs* acc. to Trumbull$^{Kadesh\ Barnea\ 61\ ff.}$ cf Guthe$^{ZPV\ viii\ 1885,\ 215}$, Gn 20^{2} 26$^{6.20.26}$ 2 Ch 14$^{12.13}$; גְּרָרָה Gn 10^{19} 26^{1}, נַחַל גְּרָר Gn 26^{17}; וַיָּגָר בִּגְרָר Gn 20^{1}.

גרשׁ (Ar جَرَشَ *bray, pound, grind coarse*, Aram גְּרַס (rare) *crush*, ܓܪܺܝܣ *crushed*, ܓܪܰܣ *crush, destroy*, cf following)

†[גָּרַס] **vb be crushed** (Aram. ܓܪܰܣ [*be crushed*,] *perish*)—**Qal** *Pf* 3 fs גָּרְסָה ψ 119^{20} fig ג׳ נַפְשִׁי לְ *my soul is crushed* (i e. perisheth: cf. Syr) with longing *for* (cf כָּלָה לְ). **Hiph.** *Impf* וַיַּגְרֵס בֶּחָצָץ שִׁנָּי La 3^{16} *and he hath crushed my teeth with gravel*, fig. of divine chastisement.

†גֶּרֶשׂ **n.[m.] a crushing**, but only concrete of that which is crushed, *groats, grits* (cf Ar. جَرِيش, NH גריסים, Aram (rare) גְּרִישָׂא, גְּרוֹסְיָא, ܓܪܺܝܣܳܐ)—אָבִיב קָלוּי בָּאֵשׁ גֶּרֶשׂ כַּרְמֶל Lv 2^{14} *young ears parched with fire, groats* (&) *fresh fruit* (v Sifra ad loc); (מְגֹרָשָׂה (ומשׂטנה Lv 2^{16}.

†[גָּרַשׁ] **vb. drive out, cast out** (NH *id*, Aram גְּרַשׁ Pa Ithp. of divorce, MI^{19} (ויגרשה)—**Qal** *Impf.* וַיִּגְרְשׁוּ Is 57^{20}, *Inf* sf מִגְרָשָׁהּ Ez 36^{5} infr.; *Pt act* גֹּרֵשׁ Ex 34^{11}; *pass* f. גְּרוּשָׁה Lv 21^{7}+4t,—*cast out, thrust out*, י׳, the Amorites Ex 34^{11} (JE, c מִפְּנֵי); waters, mire and dirt רֶפֶשׁ וָטִיט Is 57^{20}; pass. only of divorced woman Lv 21^{7} (sq מֵאִישָׁהּ; elsewh with אַלְמָנָה *widow*), v^{14} 22^{13} (all H), Nu 30^{10} (P) Ez 44^{22}. On מִגְרָשָׁהּ Ez 36^{5} as Aram *Inf.* cf. Ges$^{§ 45.1\ c}$ Ko$^{I\ 166}$; Co del, on intern. grounds, cf. 𝔊. **Niph.** *Pf.* נִגְרַשׁ Is 57^{20}; 3 fs וְנִגְרְשָׁה consec. Am. 8^{8}, נִגְרַשְׁתִּי Jon 2^{5},—*be driven* away, sq מִנֶּגֶד עֵינֶיךָ, i e. from the presence of Yahweh Jon 2^{5}; *be driven, tossed*, as the Nile Am 8^{8}, of the sea Is 57^{20} rel cl, אֲשֶׁר om., *like the sea that is tossed* **Pi.** *Pf* 3 fs. וגרשה consec. Ex 23^{28}, גֵּרַשְׁתָּ Gn 4^{14}, sf 3 mpl וְגֵרַשְׁתָּם consec. Ex 23^{31}; וְגֵרַשְׁתִּי Ex 33^{2}, sf גֵּרַשְׁתִּיהוּ Ez 31^{11} (so 𝔗 𝔙, not 𝔊; cf. Co's conj), וְגֵרַשְׁתִּיו consec Nu 22^{11}; 3 pl. sf גֵּרְשׁוּנִי 1 S 26^{19}; *Impf* יְגָרֵשׁ Ex 11^{1}, וַיְגָרֶשׁ Gn 3^{24}+6 t., sf. וַיְגָרְשֵׁהוּ ψ 34^{1}, יְגָרְשֵׁם Ex 6^{1}, 2 ms תְּגָרֵשׁ ψ 80^{9}, וַתְּגָרֵשׁ Jos 24^{12}; אֲגָרֵשׁ Ju 2^{3}, וָאֲגָרֵשׁ Ju 6^{9}; sf. 3 ms. וַיְגָרְשׁוּ Ex 23$^{29.30}$ Nu 22^{6}; אֲגָרְשֵׁם Ho 9^{15}; וַיְגָרְשׁוּ Ju 11^{2}; וַיְגָרְשׁוּם Zp 2^{4}, יְגָרְשׁוּהָ Ex 2^{17}, 2 mpl תְּגָרְשׁוּן Mi 2^{9}, וַתְּגָרְשׁוּנִי Ju 11^{7}; *Inf.* cstr. לְגָרֵשׁ 1 Ch 17^{21}+ ‖ 2 S 7^{23} Gei We Dr, for MT לְאַרְצֶךָ; לְגָרְשֵׁנוּ 2 Ch 20^{11}; abs. *id* Ex 11^{1}, *Imv.* גָּרֵשׁ Gn 21^{10} Pr 22^{10},—*drive out, away*, Hex all JE, incl. poem Dt 33, (י׳ subj), Adam fr. garden Gn 3^{24} cf Cain Gn 4^{14} (sq. מִן loc, & so 21 t.), David (men subj) 1 S 26^{19}, id. (Abimelech subj) ψ 34^{1} (title), Hagar (Abr. subj.) Gn 21^{10} cf scorner, Pr 22^{10} daughters of Reuel (subj. shepherds) Ex 2^{17}, Moses and Aaron fr. Pharaoh's presence (indef subj) Ex 10^{11}; Gaal etc. (subj Zebul) Ju 9^{41} (sq מִן c. Inf.), Jephthah (Gil. subj) Ju 11$^{2.7}$, Abiathar (subj. Sol.) 1 K 2^{27} (sq מִן c. Inf) wicked fr temple (י׳ subj.) Ho 9^{15}; women fr. houses (nobles subj.) Mi 2^{9}; oft. of Canaanites

(hornet subj.) Ex 23^{28} Jos 24^{12} cf. Ex 23^{31} (Israel subj.); also (י׳ subj.; cf. MI^{19}) Ex 23$^{29.30}$ 33^{2} Dt 33^{27} Jos 24^{18} Ju 2^{3} 6^{9} ψ 78^{55} 80^{9} 1 Ch 17^{21}; of Israel from Egypt (subj. Pharaoh) Ex 6^{1} 11$^{1.1}$; from land of Moab (subj. Balak) Nu 22$^{6.11}$; Judah from Canaan (subj. Moab & Ammon) 2 Ch 20^{11}; Egypt from her land (י׳ subj.) Ez 31^{11} (but cf. text, supr.); Ashdod (indef. subj.) Zp 2^{4}. †**Pu.** *Pf.* גֹּרְשׁוּ subj. Israelites Ex 12^{39}; *Impf.* יְגֹרָשׁוּ subj. despised and miserable outcasts Jb 30^{5} both sq. מִן loc.

†[גֶּ֫רֶשׁ] **n.[m.]** **thing thrust or put forth, yield**; cstr. גֶּרֶשׁ יְרָחִים Dt 33^{14} *yield, produce* of moons ‖ תְּבוּאֹת שָׁ֑מֶשׁ; i.e. produce in its seasons, cf. Di.

†[גְּרוּשָׁה] **n.f.** **expulsion, violence.** Only pl. sf. גְּרֻשֹׁתֵיכֶם Ez 45^{9} *your acts of expulsion* (cf. Ew Da; *'Raubereien'* Sm Co).

†גֵּרְשֹׁם **n.pr.m.** **1.** son of Moses & Ṣipporah Ex 2^{22} (expl. as if fr. גור) = 18^{3}; גֵּרְשׁוֹם 1 Ch 23$^{15.16}$ 26^{24}; so also גֵּרְשֹׁם Ju 18^{30} MT בֶּן־מְנַ֫שֶּׁה cf. VB. **2.** a son of Levi גֵּרְשֹׁם 1 Ch 6$^{1.28}$ 15^{7} (cf. גֵּרְשׁוֹן); גֵּרְשׁוֹם 1 Ch 6$^{2.5.47.56}$. **3.** a son of Phinehas Ezr 8^{2}.

†גֵּרְשׁוֹן **n.pr.m.** son of Levi (= גרשׁם 1 Ch 6$^{1.28}$ 15^{7} גרשׁום 1 Ch 6$^{2.5.47.56}$) Gn 46^{11} Ex 6$^{16.17}$ Nu 3$^{17.18.21.25}$ 4$^{22.38.41}$ 7^{7} 10^{17} 26^{57} Jos 21$^{6.27}$ 1 Ch 5^{27} 23^{6} (particularly in expression *sons of Gershon*, i.e. family, descendants of Gershon Nu 3^{25} 4$^{22.38.41}$ 7^{7} 10^{17} Jos 21$^{6.27}$; cf. *sons of Gershom* 1 Ch 6$^{47.56}$ 15^{7}).

†גֵּרְשֻׁנִּי **adj.gent.** c. art. as subst. collect. Nu 3$^{21.23.24}$ 4$^{24.27.28}$ 26^{57} Jos 21^{33} 1 Ch 23^{7} 26^{21} 2 Ch 29^{12}; c. art. as adj. sing. m. 1 Ch 26^{21} 29^{8}.

מִגְרָשׁ **n.m.**$^{Nu\ 35,2}$ **common, common-land, open land** (perhaps orig. *pasture-land*, as place of [cattle] *driving*)—abs. מ׳ Ez 45^{2} + 2 t. + Ez 48^{15} (Co מגרשׁה); cstr. מִגְרַשׁ Lv 25^{34} 2 Ch 31^{19}; (on מִגְרָשֶׁהָ Ez 36^{5} cf. גרשׁ); elsewh. pl., abs. מִגְרֹשׁוֹת Ez 27^{28} (Baer); Co מרעשׁת assumed fr. רָעַשׁ, cf. 𝔊; cstr. מִגְרְשֵׁי Nu 35^{4} + 2 t.; sf. מִגְרָשֶׁיהָ Jos 21$^{13.13}$ + 42 t.; מִגְרָשָׁהּ Jos 21^{11} + 46 t. in Jos 21 (generally ‸ or ˙ but also ˛ v^{21}); מִגְרְשֵׁיהֶם Nu 35^{3} + 4 t.; מִגְרְשֵׁיהֶן Nu 35^{7} + 8 t.—*common-land*, usually pl., and usually as attached to a city or town, esp. as surrounding Levitical cities Nu 35$^{2.3.4.5.7}$ Jos 14^{4} 21^{2} + 55 t. Jos 21 (all P; in Codd. & old Vrss. are two vv. Jos 21, betw. v$^{35.36}$, with מ׳ 4 t.; om. Mass., Edd., Baer, but cf. Theile, & Di ad loc.); 1 Ch 6^{40} + 40 t. 1 Ch 6; 13^{2} 2 Ch 11^{14}; so also שְׂדֵה מ׳ Lv 25^{34} (H), שְׂדֵי מ׳ 2 Ch 31^{19}; lands surrounding the holy city Ez 48$^{15.17}$; *open land* or *space* about the temple Ez 45^{2}; only 1 Ch 5^{16} כָּל־מִגְרְשֵׁי שָׁרוֹן of (pasture-)lands in a district, cf. שׁרון.—Ez 27^{28} מגרשׁות, if true text, = open country about Tyre (opp. sea, cf. context), but v. Da & cf. supr.

גֵּרֹתִיו v. גּוּר sub II. גור.

גשׁם (√of foll.; cf. Ar. جَسُمَ *be bulky, massive*, جِسْمٌ *body*, Syr. ܓܘܫܡܐ *id.*)

†I. גֶּ֫שֶׁם **n.pr.m.** an opponent of Nehemiah Ne 2^{19} 6^{1} (in both called הָעַרְבִי); v^{2}; also גַּשְׁמוּ 6^{6}; ו as in Nab. n.pr. cf. Nö in Eut$^{Nab\ 73}$.

†II. גֶּ֫שֶׁם **n.m.**$^{Gn\ 7,12}$ **rain, shower** (NH *id.*, conn. wi. above √ dub.)—abs. ג׳ Gn 7^{12} +; גָּ֑שֶׁם 1 K 18^{41} +; cstr. גֶּשֶׁם Jb 37$^{6.6}$ +; pl. גְּשָׁמִים Ezr 10$^{9.13}$; cstr. גִּשְׁמֵי Ez 34^{26}; sf. גִּשְׁמֵיכֶם Lv 26^{4}; גִּשְׁמֵיהֶם ψ 105^{32};—*rain, shower* Gn 7^{12} 8^{2} (both J) Lv 26^{4} (H) Ho 6^{3} Am 4^{7} Je 5^{24} 14^{4} Is 44^{14} 55^{10} Ez 1^{28} Jo 2^{23} (‖ מַלְקוֹשׁ, מוֹרֶה); 1 K 17$^{7.14}$ 18^{45} (ג׳ גדול) 2 K 3^{17} Pr 25$^{14.23}$ Ec 11^{3} Ct 2^{11} ψ 105^{32}, וּמֵהַגּ׳ Ezr 10^{9} *and because of the rains*, cf. v^{13}; קוֹל הֲמוֹן הַגּ׳ 1 K 18^{41} cf. v^{44} Zc 14^{17} Ec 12^{2}; גֶּשֶׁם מָטָר וְג׳ מִטְרוֹת עֻזּוֹ Jb 37^{6}; מְטַר־גֶּשֶׁם Zc 10^{1}; cf. ג׳ נְדָבוֹת ψ 68^{10}; fig. of blessing Ez 34^{26}, ג׳ בְּרָכָה v^{26}; of destruction ג׳ שֹׁטֵף Ez 13$^{11.13}$ cf. 38^{22}.

†[גשׁם] **vb.denom.** (cf. NH Qal Pt. pass. & Hoph.)—**Pu.** *Pf.* 3 fs. גֻּשְּׁמָה Ez 22^{24} *be rained upon* (גְּשֻׁמָה Baer, but v. Ke Sm). **Hiph.** *cause* or *send rain*, *Pt.* מַגְשִׁמִים Je 14^{22}.

†[גֹּ֫שֶׁם] **n.[m.]** גָּשְׁמָהּ Ez 22^{24} (or גֻּשְּׁמָה from גֶּשֶׁם ?) acc. to punct.; but cf. sub גשׁם **vb.**

גַּשְׁמוּ **n.pr.**, v. I. גֶּשֶׁם.

†גֹּ֫שֶׁן **n.pr.loc.** (on etym. cf. Di Gn 45^{10})—**1.** district in Egypt E. of lower Nile, v. Eb $^{GB\ 500\ ff.}$; Naville$^{Goshen,\ 1887}$, who rds. hierogl. *Kesem*, but cf. Groff$^{JAs\ xiv.\ 527}$ (𝔊 Γεσεμ (Ἀραβιας))—אֶרֶץ גֹּשֶׁן Gn 45^{10} (JE) 46^{34} 47$^{1.4.6.27}$ 50^{8} Ex 8^{18} 9^{26} (all J); אַרְצָה גֹּשֶׁן Gn 46^{28} (J); גֹּשְׁנָה v$^{28.29}$ (both J), in both 𝔊 καθ' Ἡρώων πόλιν cf. Di. (P has land רעמסס 47^{11} etc., cf. Di Gn 45^{10}). **2.** ארץ הַגֹּשֶׁן Jos 11^{16} (D), אֶרֶץ גֹּשֶׁן Jos 10^{41} (D), גֹּשֶׁן Jos 15^{51} (P) (𝔊 in all Γοσομ) a city named with חלן & גִּלֹה cf. Di.—not clearly located, but on southern border of Judah.

†גִּשְׁפָּא **n.pr.m.** named after ציחא as an officer of Nethinim Ne 11^{21}; v. om. B; 𝔊L & Codd. Γεσφα; name not elsewhere in OT, not even ‖ 1 Ch 9; possibly corrupted from חֲשׂוּפָא

Ne 7[46] (following צִחָא, in ‖ Ezr 2[43] חֲשׂוּפָא, צִיחָא), 𝔊 Ἀσφα (B, Codd Ασειφα, etc.), cf BeRy.

גשר (√ of foll Cf As *gašâru, strengthen, make firm* Lotz [TP Register], Ar. جَسَرَ *be bold*, also *arch a bridge*, cf جِسْرٌ, جَسْرٌ *bridge*, NH גֶּשֶׁר *id*, Aram. גִּישְׁרָא, ܓܶܫܪܳܐ, ܓܶܫܪܳܐ)

†**גְּשׁוּר** **n.pr.m.** (*bridge? or land of bridges?* cf Wetzst [Hauran, 82]) **1** of people, = הַגְּשׁוּרִי Jos 13[13] cf 1 Ch 2[23] **2.** of land מֶלֶךְ גְּשׁוּר 2 S 3[3] 13[37] cf v[38] (but text in disorder cf 𝔊 We Dr) 14[32] 15[8] בְּנֵי גּ׳ בַּאֲרָם 1 Ch 3[2], גְּשׁוּרָה 2 S 14[23]; a territory E of the upper Jordan, exact limits unknown, acc to Guthe [ZPV xii 1889, 232 f] between Gilead and Hermon, in *Jaulân;* acc. to Furrer [ib. xiii. 1890, 198] = the *Ledjah*, district E of Jaulân, with town *Jisre;* against him Guthe [ib 285 f.]

†**גְּשׁוּרִי** **adj.gent.** = subst הַגּ׳; **1.** people dwelling in Geshûr (supr.) Dt 3[14] Jos 12[5] 13[11.13] **2.** a tribe of, or near, the Philistines Jos 13[2], also 1 S 27[8], but del 𝔊 (not 𝔊L) cf. We Dr; rd possibly אַשּׁוּרִי Hom [Aufsätze i (1892), 9], 2 S 2[9] rd. הגּ׳ for האשורי

†[**גָּשַׁשׁ**] **vb. feel with the hand, feel, stroke** (NH *id*, Ar. جَسَّ, Aram. גַּשֵּׁשׁ Pa, ܓܫܫ; Eth ገሠሠ: or ገሠሠ: *stroke, touch*)—**Pi.** *Impf.* 1 pl coh נְגַשְׁשָׁה Is 59[10], נְגַשֵּׁשָׁה *ib.*, *grope, grope for* cf Che

גַּת wine-press. **גַּת** **n.pr.** **גִּתִּי** **adj.gent.** **גִּתַּיִם** **n pr.loc.** **גִּתִּית** **adj.** v. sub ינן

†**גֶּתֶר** **n.pr.m.** (√unknown) a son of Aram Gn 10[23] = 1 Ch 1[17].

ד

ד, ד׳, *Dāleth*, fourth letter; in modern Heb = numeral 4, ד = 4000; no evidence of this usage in OT times

†[**דָּאַב**] **vb. become faint, languish** (NH *id*. Hiph, cf Ar دَأَبَ *toil, weary oneself*, v. also דְּאָבָה, דְּאָבוֹן & cf. דוב)—**Qal** *Pf* 3 fs דָּאֲבָה ψ 88[10] (subj עַיִן); *Inf* לְדַאֲבָה Je 31[12] לֹא יוסיפוּ לד׳ (subj ransomed Israel),—Je 31[25] has נֶפֶשׁ דְּאֵבָה, of hunger (‖ נֶפֶשׁ עֲיֵפָה), where adj or pt. seems needed, Hi Gf דְּאֵבָה or דֹּאֲבָה (the punctuators had, acc. to them, the Aram participle in mind); Thes. makes relative clause

†**דְּאָבָה** **n.f. faintness, failure of mental energy, dismay** Jb 41[14] וּלְפָנָיו תָּדוּץ דְּאָבָה *and before him* (i e the crocodile) *danceth dismay.*

†[**דְּאָבוֹן**] **n.[m.] faintness, languishing,** cstr. וְכִלְיוֹן עֵינַיִם וְדַאֲבוֹן נָפֶשׁ Dt 28[65] (cf Lv 26[16] & Syr ܕܘܳܒܳܐ ܕܢܰܦܫܳܐ v דוב)

†**דָּאַג** **vb. be anxious, concerned, fear** (Talm דאג *id*, דְּאִיג)—**Qal** *Pf* 3 ms. וְדָאַג consec 1 S 9[5] 10[2], 2 fs דָּאַגְתְּ Is 57[11]; *Impf* 3 ms יִדְאָג Je 17[8], אֶדְאַג ψ 38[19], *Pt.* דֹּאֵג Je 38[19], דֹּאֲגִים Je 42[16],—**1.** *be anxious, concerned,* with reference to, in behalf of, c לְ 1 S 9[5] 10[2]; *id* c מִן Je 42[16] (famine personif); sq. מֵחַטָּאתִי ψ 38[19], *be anxious*, abs. Je 17[8] (‖ יִרָא) **2.** **fear, dread,** sq acc. of pers. feared Is 57[11] (‖ יָרֵא) Je 38[19] (where also sq cl with פֶּן)

†**דֹּאֵג** **n.pr.m.** an Edomite, servant of Saul 1 S 21[8] 22[9.18.18.22] (v[18.18.22] Kt דויג cf. Dr) דּוֹאֵג ψ 52[2] (title)

†**דְּאָגָה** **n.f. anxiety, anxious care**—דְּאָגָה Jos 22[24] + 5 t, *anxiety* for = for fear of, c. מִן Jos 22[24]; *anxiety* Pr 12[25] (where c verb. masc cf Now), Je 49[23] בַּיָּם ד׳; *anxious care* Ez 4[16] 12[19] (in both ‖ שִׁמָּמוֹן), 12[18] (‖ רַעַשׁ and רָגְזָה).

דָּאג *fish*, cf דָּג sub דגה

†[**דָּאָה**] **vb. fly swiftly, dart through the air** (cf. perhaps Ar. دَأْدَأَ *run vehemently* (of camel))—**Qal** *Impf.* יִדְאֶה Dt 28[49] + 2 t; וַיֵּדֶא ψ 18[11] (> ‖ 2 S 22[11] וַיֵּרָא); *fly swiftly, dart,* of eagle Dt 28[49], in simile of swift army; of Chaldaeans comp with eagle, in judgment against Moab & Edom Je 48[40] 49[22] (in both ‖ פרש כנפיו); of י׳ in theoph. ψ 18[11] (cf. 2 S 22[11]) (וַיִּרְכַּב עַל־כְּרוּב וַיָּעֹף ‖ וַיֵּדֶא עַל־כַּנְפֵי רוּחַ)

†**דָּאָה** **n.f.** a bird of prey, possibly **kite** (𝔙 Saad. Bo [Hieroz. ii. 191] Di Lv 11[14]; Aram דַּיְתָא, ܕܰܝܬܳܐ, NH דַּיָּה of diff. birds of prey; name prob. fr. flying, swooping), Lv 11[14] forbidden as food; cf. also Dt 14[13] וְהָרָאָה ואת־הָאַיָּה וְהַדַּיָּה, where for הראה rd הַדָּאָה & del. הַדַּיָּה, so Sam 𝔊, cf. Di *l c*

†[**דַּיָּה**] **n.f. id.**—frequenting ruins, cf. Di *l.c.*; דַּיּוֹת Is 34[15] (on הַדַּיָּה Dt 14[13] cf. foregoing).

דאר **n.pr.** v. sub II דור

דֹּב, דּוֹב v. דבב.

דבא (? √ of foll.; existence & mng. dub.)

†[דֹּבֶא] **n.[m.]** perh. **rest**, but sense very doubtful (? Ar. دَبَا *rest*, Ḳamus; 𝔊 𝔖 𝔗 Onk *strength*, reading perh. רבאך cf. Sam. רביך, vid. Di) וּכְיָמֶיךָ דָּבְאֶךָ׃ Dt 33^{25}.

†[דָּבַב] **vb. move gently, glide, glide over** (NH דָּבַב *flow slowly, drop*; Ar. دَبَّ *walk leisurely, gently*, دَابَّة *any animal that walks or creeps*, cf. דֹּב; As. *dabâbu, plot, plan*, COT Gloss, cf. דִּבָּה)—only **Qal** *Pt.* דּוֹבֵב שִׂפְתֵי יְשֵׁנִים Ct 7^{10}, of wine *gliding over the lips of sleepers;* (ד׳ שְׂפָתַי וְשִׁנָּי i.e. *my lips and teeth* 𝔊 𝔖 Aq Gei Urschrift 405).

†דֹּב **n.m.** Pr 28,15, **f.** 2 K 2,24 (sold.) **bear** (from soft or gliding motion, NH *id.*, Eth. ድብ: As. *dabû*(?) Dl $^{8\,55}$; Aram. דּוּבָּא, ܕܒܳܐ; Ar. دُبّ, دُبَّة, is however a loan-word cf. Hom NS 301 f.);—abs. דֹּב Am 5^{19} + 5 t.; דּוֹב 1 S 17^{34} + 2 t.; pl. דֻּבִּים 2 K 2^{24} Is 59^{11};—*bear*, female 2 K 2^{24} 2 S 17^{8} Pr 17^{12} Ho 13^{8} cf. Is 11^{7}; undetermined 1 S $17^{34.36.37}$ Am 5^{19} Pr 28^{15} Is 59^{11} La 3^{10} (on art. 1 S 17^{34} Am 5^{19} cf. RS Sem. i. 119 n.)

†דִּבָּה **n.f. whispering, defamation, evil report** (? as that which glides stealthily)—abs. ד׳ Nu 14^{36} Pr 10^{18}; cstr. דִּבַּת Je 20^{10} + 4 t.; sf. דִּבָּתְךָ Pr 25^{10} דִּבָּתָם Gn 37^{2};—**1.** *whispering* ψ 31^{14} Je 20^{10} (Hi Hup De Gf VB; yet cf. Che ψ). **2.** *defamation* Pr 10^{18} (c. הוציא). **3.** *evil report*, specif. a (true) report of evil doing Gn 37^{2} (P) וַיָּבֵא אֶת־דִּבָּתָם רָעָה; cf. also Pr 25^{10} & Ez 36^{3} וַתֵּעָלוּ עַל־שְׂפַת לָשׁוֹן וְדִבַּת־עָם, unfavourable report of spies Nu 13^{32} $14^{36.37}$ (all P & all c. הוֹצִיא; adj. רעה only 14^{37}).

†דִּבְיוֹנִים **n.[m.]** so Qr; = דב יונים *dove's dung*(?) 2 K 6^{25} for Kt חרייונים; 𝔊 κόπρου περιστερῶν (Klo gives conject. emend.)

דבל (Ar. دَبَلَ *collect*, also *make into lumps, gobbets* (Lane); Eth. & cogn. in deriv.)

†דְּבֵלָה **n.f. lump of pressed figs, pressed (fig-) cake** (NH דְּבֵילָה, Aram. *id.*, ܕܒܠܬܐ, = Greek παλάθη; Ar. دُبْلَة *lump, large gobbet* or *mouthful;* cf. As. *dublu, foundation*, & Heb. synon. אֲשִׁישָׁה Dl HA 58)—דְּבֵלָה 1 S 30^{12}; cstr. דְּבֶלֶת 2 K 20^{7} = Is 38^{21}; pl. דְּבֵלִים 1 S 25^{18} 1 Ch 12^{40};—used as food 1 S 25^{18} 30^{12} 1 Ch 12^{40}; דְּבֶלֶת תְּאֵנִים, as application to boil, or eruption 2 K 20^{7} = Is 38^{21}.

†[דִּבְלָה] **n.pr.loc.** only c. ה loc. דִּבְלָתָה Ez 6^{14} but rd. רִבְלָתָה JDMich Hi Sm Co Da.

†[דִּבְלַיִם] **n.pr.m.** father of Gomer wife of Hosea דִּבְלָיִם Ho 1^{3}.

דִּבְלָתַיִם in **n.pr.loc.** v. עלמן ד׳, בית ד׳ (possibly fr. √ דבל in sense of *collect, assemble*, Eth. ተደበለ: III. 3 *se colligere*, ምድባል: *coetus, chorus, conventus, concilium*)—Je 48^{22}; דִּבְלָתָיְמָה Nu $33^{46.47}$.

†דָּבַק, דָּבֵק **vb. cling, cleave, keep close** (NH *id.*, Ar. دَبِقَ, Aram. דְּבַק, דְּבֵק, ܕܒܶܩ, ܕܒܰܩ)—**Qal** *Pf.* דָּבַק 1 K 11^{2} + 2 t.; וְדָבַק consec. Gn 2^{24}; דָּבֵק 2 K 3^{3}; 3 fs. דָּבְקָה Ru 1^{14} + 5 t.; דָּבֵקָה Job 29^{10}; 1 s. דָּבַקְתִּי ψ 119^{31}; 3 pl. דָּבְקוּ 2 S 20^{2}; וְדָבְקוּ consec. Dt 28^{60}; דָּבֵקוּ Jb 41^{15}; וּדְבַקְתֶּם consec. Jos 23^{12}; *Impf.* יִדְבַּק Dt 13^{18} + 3 t.; 3 fs. תִּדְבַּק 2 K 5^{27} ψ 137^{6}; וַתִּדְבַּק Gn 34^{3} + 2 t.; sf. תִּדְבָּקַנִי Gn 19^{19}; 2 ms. תִּדְבָּק Dt 10^{20} Ez 29^{4} (del. B Co); 2 fs. תִּדְבָּקִין Ru $2^{8.21}$; 3 pl. יִדְבְּקוּ Nu $36^{7.9}$; 2 mpl. תִּדְבָּקוּ Jos 23^{8}; תִּדְבָּקוּן Dt 13^{5}; *Inf. cstr.* וּלְדָבְקָה־בוֹ Dt 11^{22} + 2 t.;—in Hexateuch only JD, except Nu $36^{7.9}$ (P);—**1.** *cling, cleave to*, **a.** lit. sq. בְּ Jb 19^{20} (bone to skin), so sq. לְ ψ 102^{6}; sq. אֶל 2 S 23^{10} (hand to sword; accidentally om. with other words 1 Ch 11^{12} cf. Dr 2 S 23^{11}), Je 13^{11} (girdle to loins), La 4^{4} (tongue to roof of mouth, in thirst), so sq. לְ Jb 29^{10} ψ 137^{6} (as a judgment); so also in metaph. ψ 44^{26} דָּבְקָה לָאָרֶץ בִּטְנֵנוּ *our belly cleaveth to the earth* (|| שָׁחָה לֶעָפָר נַפְשֵׁנוּ), 119^{25} דָּבְקָה לֶעָפָר נַפְשִׁי; fish to scales of crocodile (fig. of Pharaoh), sq. בְּ Ez 29^{4} (but cf. supr.); abs. (recipr.) of folds of crocodile's belly Jb 41^{15}; further of the חֵרֶם remaining in (*sticking to*) the hand sq. בְּ Dt 13^{18}; so of spot, stain Jb 31^{7}. **b.** so also of abiding on the land of one's tribe Nu $36^{7.9}$ (sq. בְּ). **c.** = *remain with, close to* sq. עִם Ru $2^{8.21}$ sq. בְּ v ^{23}. **2.** *cling, cleave to*, **a.** fig. of loyalty, affection etc., sts. with idea of physical proximity retained, sq. בְּ Gn 2^{24} (J; man to wife) cf. 34^{3} (J) 1 K 11^{2} Jos 23^{12} (D); further Ru 1^{14} (Ruth to Naomi); 2 S 20^{2} (people to king); esp. (sq. בְּ) of cleaving to י׳ Dt 11^{22} (הָלַךְ בְּכָל־דְּרָכָיו, אָהֵב ||) 30^{20} (אָהֵב ||, שָׁמַע בְּקֹלוֹ), Jos 22^{5} (|| אָהֵב, הָלַךְ וגו׳, שָׁמַר מִצְוֹתָיו); cf. further Dt 10^{20} 13^{5} Jos 23^{8} (all D), 2 K 18^{6}; ψ 63^{9} (sq. אַחֲרֵי) & ψ 119^{31} דָּבַקְתִּי בְעֵדְוֹתֶיךָ; so **b.** of the opposite בְּחַטֹּאות יָרָבְעָם ... דָּבֵק 2 K 3^{3}; **c.** subj. disease, calamity, sq. בְּ pers. Dt 28^{60} 2 K

5^{27}; sq. אַחֲרֵי Je 42^{16}; sq. acc. Gn 19^{19} (J); subj. sin ψ 101^{3} (sq. בְּ pers.) **Pu.** *Impf.* 3 mpl. יְדֻבָּקוּ pass. of Hiph. **1** sq. בְּ, of crocodile's scales, *they are joined together* Jb 41^{9} (‖ יִתְלַכְּדוּ); abs. of earth-clods Jb 38^{38}. **Hiph.** *Pf.* 3 fs. sf. הִדְבִּיקַתְהוּ Ju 20^{42}; 3 pl. sf. הִדְבִּיקֻהוּ 2 S 1^{6}; 1 s. הִדְבַּקְתִּי Je 13^{11}; וְהִדְבַּקְתִּי Ez 29^{4}; *Impf.* juss. יַדְבֵּק Dt 28^{21}; וַיַּדְבֵּק Gn 31^{23}; אַדְבִּיק Ez 3^{26}; וַיַּדְבִּיקוּ Ju 18^{22} 20^{45}; וַיַּדְבְּקוּ 1 S 14^{22} + 2 t. (cf. Ges § 53 R 4 Kö I. 210). **1.** *cause to cling* or *cleave* to, sq. acc. + אֶל, lit. וּלְשׁוֹנְךָ אַדְבִּיק אֶל־חִכֶּךָ Ez 3^{26}; v. also 29^{4} (sq. acc. + בְּ; lit., but in metaph.); fig. of causing to cleave to י׳ Je 13^{11} (sq. acc. + אֶל); cf. further Dt 28^{21} (subj. י׳, sq. acc. of disease + בְּ). **2.** *pursue closely*, sq. אַחֲרֵי Ju 20^{45} 1 S 14^{22} 1 Ch 10^{2} = 1 S 31^{2} (sq. acc.); so also 2 S 1^{6} (sq. acc.) **3.** *overtake*, sq. acc. Gn 31^{23} (E), Ju 18^{22}; cf. 20^{42} (subj. הַמִּלְחָמָה). **Hoph.** *Pt.* וּלְשׁוֹנִי מֻדְבָּק מַלְקוֹחָי ψ 22^{16} *and my tongue is made to cleave (to) my gums;* cf. sub **Qal 1.**

†דָּבֵק **adj. clinging, cleaving** (to), ד׳ abs. וְיֵשׁ אֹהֵב דָּבֵק מֵאָח Pr 18^{24}; דְּבֵקָה לְ 2 Ch 3^{12} (of cherub's wing); of cleaving to הַדְּבֵקִים בְּ י׳ Dt 4^{4}.

†דֶּבֶק **n.m.** Is 41, 7 **joining, soldering, appendage**—**1.** ד׳ *joining, soldering* Is 41^{7}. **2.** pl. הַדְּבָקִים *appendages* of breastplate (?) 1 K 22^{34} = 2 Ch 18^{33} בֵּין הַד׳ וּבֵין הַשִּׁרְיָן. (The Be al. cf. VB: the jointed *attachment* or *appendage* to the rigid breast-armour, which covered the abdomen; > Klo prop. appendage of helmet; Thes suggests armpits, lit. *joints* (cf. מַרְפְּקֵי יָד Je 38^{12} 𝔗); Ew the soft muscles etc. *connecting* the chest with the bottom of the back.)

[דָּבַר] 1142 **vb. speak** (original mng. dub.; *range in order* Thes is conjectural and not comprehensive enough; *treiben* MV does not explain Ar. or Heb. usage, but only Aram. A mng. *go away*, sustained by Ar. دَبَرَ بِهِ *go away with it*, would best explain the four branches of usage:—(1) Ar. دَبَرَ *depart, perish,* IV. *retreat*, fig. *retrograde, decline;* دَبْرٌ *passing away, death;* As. *dabâru*, Pi. *drive away*, Bez Orient. Diplom. Vocab., *Dibbara*, pest-god, Hpt. in KAT 2.500, דֶּבֶר *pestilence.* (2) Ar. دَبَرَ *follow behind*, in time, place, or station; دَبْرٌ *part behind*, دُبُرٌ *back*, דְּבִיר *hindmost chamber of temple.* (3) Syr. ܕܒܰܪ *lead, guide*, cattle, sheep, government, *take* a wife, = Aram. דְּבַר; Syr. ܕܳܒܽܘܪܳܐ, Aram. דַּבָּר *leader;* Syr. ܕܽܘܒܳܪܳܐ, Aram. דֻּבְרָא *guidance;* Syr. ܕܰܒܪܳܐ, Aram. דַּבְרָא, Heb. דֹּבֶר; Syr. ܡܰܕܒܪܳܐ, Aram. מַדְבְּרָא, Heb. מִדְבָּר *pasture, wilderness;* Ar. دَبْرٌ, Syr. ܕܰܒܽܘܪܬܳܐ, Aram. דַּבַּרְתָּא, Heb. דְּבוֹרָה *swarm of bees*, may be in this line, as led by their queen, so Thes. (4) Ar. دَبَّرَ *consider the end* or *issue* (of an affair), *relate* (a story or tradition); دَبَّرَ فِي *consider,* دَبَّرَ عَلَى *plan against;* Ph. דבר *speak;* Heb. דִּבֶּר etc. Syn. of אָמַר *say*, as Aram. מַלֵּל with אֲמַר; Gk. λαλεῖν, λέγειν; Lat. *loqui, dicere;* Germ. *reden, sagen*)—†**Qal** 41 only inf. (once ?) & pt.: *Inf.* sf. בְּדָבְרֶךָ (by attraction to בְּשָׁפְטֶךָ for usual Piel) ψ 51^{6}; *Pt.* דֹּבֵר Ex 6^{29} + 30 t.; pl. דֹּבְרִים Nu 36^{5} ψ 109^{20}; cstr. דֹּבְרֵי ψ 5^{7} + 3 t.; f. דֹּבְרוֹת Nu 27^{7} ψ 31^{19}; pass. דָּבֻר Pr 25^{11};—*speak,* abs. Nu 27^{7} 32^{27} 36^{5} (P) ψ 51^{6} (?); דָּבָר דָּבֻר *word spoken* Pr 25^{11}; with acc. rei דֹּבֵר דָּבָר *speaking a word* Jb 2^{13}; אמת ψ 15^{2}, תמים Am 5^{10}, (מ)ישרים Pr 16^{13} Is 33^{15}, צדק Is 45^{19}, שלום Est 10^{3} ψ 28^{3}, שקר(ים) ψ 63^{12} 101^{7} Je 40^{16}, כזב ψ 5^{7} 58^{4}, רע ψ 109^{20}, נבלה Is 9^{16}, הַוַּת נפשו Mi 7^{3}; with אֶל of *person, unto* Gn 16^{13} (J) Ex 6^{29} (P) Je 38^{20} 40^{16} Dn 10^{11} Jon 3^{2}; בְּאָזְנֵי *in the ears of* Dt 5^{1} Je 28^{7}; עַל *concerning, about* ψ 31^{19} 109^{20} Je 32^{42} (sometimes rendered *against*, but dub.); עִם *with* ψ 28^{3}; הַמַּלְאָךְ הַדֹּבֵר בִּי *the angel that spake with me* (as a prophet, an instrument of communicating with Israel) Zc $1^{9.13.14}$ $2^{2.7}$ $4^{1.4.5}$ $5^{5.10}$ 6^{4} (vid. prep. בְּ **III. 2** Ew § 217 f. (3)). †**Niph.** 4 *Pf.* נִדְבְּרוּ Mal 3^{16}, נִדְבְּרוּ ψ 119^{23}, נִדְבַּרְנוּ Mal 3^{13}; *Pt.* הַנִּדְבָּרִים Ez 33^{30}; reciprocal sense, *speak with one another, talk*, abs. Mal 3^{16}; with בְּ, *against* ψ 119^{23} Ez 33^{30}; with עַל, *concerning, about* Mal 3^{13} (RV *against*, vid. Ew § 217 i.) **Pi.** 1089 *Pf.* דִּבֶּר Gn 12^{4} +, דִּבַּר Gn 21^{1} + (on דִּבֶּר Ex 12^{25} Dt 26^{19} v. Bö § 1021 d (1) Kö I. 188); *Impf.* יְדַבֵּר Gn 44^{7} +, יְדַבֶּר־ Gn 44^{18} +; תְּדַבְּרוּן Gn 32^{20}, תְּדַבֵּרוּן ψ 58^{2}; *Imv.* דַּבֵּר Gn 24^{33} +, דַּבֶּר־ Ex 11^{2} +; *Inf.* דַּבֵּר Gn 24^{50} +, דַּבֶּר־ Is 59^{13} +; *Pt.* מְדַבֵּר Gn 27^{6} +; f. מְדַבֶּרֶת 1 S 1^{13} +;—(הַדִּבֵּר) Je 5^{13}, inf. Ki 48, prob. Ol § 182 e Kö § 23 (5), perhaps MV; but more prob. a noun, as Ges § 52 (2), Anm. 3 Ew § 156 a, dub. pf. as Sta § 222; בְּיוֹם דִּבֶּר Ex 6^{28} Nu 3^{1} Dt 4^{15}; תְּחִלַּת דִּבֶּר־ Ho 1^{2}, inf. Ki 48 Bö § 987 (7) Kö § 23 (5); but more prob. pf., as Ges § 52 (2), Anm. 3);—*speak*, **1.** abs. Dt 18^{17} + (throughout the literature) usu. with לֵאמֹר, less freq. וַיֹּאמֶר: 2 K 18^{28} +, cf. the phrases †אני (י׳) דברתי Ez 5^{13} + 18 t. Ez; †כי י׳ דבר Is 1^{2} 21^{17} 22^{25} 24^{3} 25^{8} Je 13^{15} Jo 4^{8} Ob 18; †כי פי י׳ דבר Is 1^{20} 40^{5} 58^{14} Mi 4^{4}; †פי ידבר ψ 49^{4}; †(י)דבר פיו ψ 66^{14} 145^{21}; †השכם ודבר Je 7^{13} 25^{3} 35^{14}; †עוד זה מדבר Jb $1^{16.17.18}$. **2.** with acc. rei, very frequently, ד׳ את הדברים האלה Ex 20^{1} Dt 5^{19} +; לָמָּה תְּדַבֵּר עוֹד דְּבָרֶיךָ *why speakest thou any more of thy affairs?* 2 S 19^{30}; עַד אִם־דִּבַּרְתִּי דְּבָרָי *until I*

have told my errand Gn 24[33]; seld. sq. דָּבָר indef, as ד׳ דָּבָר Is 58[13] *speak a* (mere, empty) *word;* so prob. also ד׳ דְּבָרִים Ho 10[4]; with other nouns, e.g. דבר קשות *spake rough words* Gn 42[7.30] (E); ד׳ גבהה *proud words* 1 S 2[3], טבות *friendly words* Je 12[6]; טוב 1 S 19[4] 1 K 22[13] Est 7[9]; שקר Is 59[3]+, כזב Dn 11[27], אמת Je 9[4]+, שוא ψ 12[3]+; דבר שיר *utter, sing a song* Ju 5[12], משל 1 K 5[12]; יְהוּדִית *the Jewish language* Ne 13[24]; †סרה *rebellion* Dt 13[6] Je 28[16] 29[32]. **3.** *with persons* **a.** rarely acc. יָכְלוּ דַּבְּרוֹ לְשָׁלֹם *they could* [*not*] *speak unto him peaceably* Gn 37[4] (J; but Ew § 283 a *about him*); וַיְדַבֵּר...אֹתָם Nu 26[3] (P, but text corrupt vid. Di; no satisfactory explanation yet given, possibly rd. אִתָּם vid. **d**) **b.** most frequently with אֶל throughout the literature: Gn 8[15]+, cf phrases וַיְדַבֵּר י׳ אֶל מֹשֶׁה לֵאמֹר Ex 6[10] + 87 t. P, but †וידבר י׳ אל משה לך Ex 32[7] 33[1] (JE); דבר אל בני אהרן Lv 6[18] + 8 t. (P), דבר אל בני ישראל Ex 6[9]+38 t. (P); elsewhere, Ex 19[6] (E) Dt 1[3] 4[45] (D); ד׳ אל (כל) העדה Ex 12[3] Lv 19[2] Nu 16[24.26] (P); ד׳ אל לב *speak unto one's heart* Gn 24[45], i. e. to oneself, cf. also ד׳ על לבה 1 S 1[13], v. **5** infr; אל is used inexactly for על 1 S 3[12] 1 K 16[12] Is 16[13] Je 27[13] 30[4] 33[14] 36[7.31] 40[2] 50[1] 51[12.62] where it is rendered *concerning* or *against* **c** with לְ, *speak to* 1 K 2[19] Ez 32[21] Dn 2[4]; ליהוה *speak, sing to Yahweh* words of a song Jos 10[12] (D) 2 S 22[1] (= ψ 18[1] title); in D, דבר ל *promise to,* in phrases †כאשר דבר(י׳) ל Dt 1[11.21] 6[3] 9[3] 10[9] 11[25] 12[20] 15[6] 18[2] 26[18] 27[3] 29[12] Jos 13[14.33] 22[4] 23[5.10] (all D); אשר דבר ל Dt 9[28] 1 K 8[24.25.26] (= 2 Ch 6[15.16.17])—דבר ל Gn 24[7] 28[15] 49[28] Ex 32[34] (J) Jos 9[21] (P) Ju 14[7] 2 S 23[3] Is 30[10] Zc 9[10] usu. rendered *speak to,* but oft rather *promise to.* הֲיֵשׁ לְדַבֶּר־לָךְ אֶל־הַמֶּלֶךְ *is it possible to speak for thee unto the king?* 2 K 4[13] (by attraction to לַעֲשׂוֹת לָךְ). **d.** with †אֶת *speak with* Gn 17[3.22.23] 21[2] 23[8] 34[6.8] 35[13.15] Ex 25[22] 31[18] 34[29.33.34.35] Nu 3[1] 7[89] Jos 22[15.21] (all P) Gn 35[14] 41[9] 42[7] 45[15] Jos 17[14] (all E) Dt 5[21]; sources of S K Ch 2 S 3[27] 7[7] = 1 Ch 17[6] 1 K 8[15] = 2 Ch 6[4] 1 K 22[24] = 2 Ch 18[23] 2 Ch 10[10] (= אל 1 K 12[10]) Je 5[5] 7[22] 9[7] 35[2] 38[25] Ez 2[1] 3[22.24.27] 14[4] 20[3] 44[5] Dn 1[19] Zc 8[16], cf phrases †דבר חד את אחד *speak one with another* Ez 33[30]; †דבר משפטים אתו *speak judgments with,* usu. = *give judgment against,* (not Je 12[1]), Je 1[16] 4[12] 12[1] 39[5] 52[9] (= 2 K 25[6]), דבר טבות את *speak kindly with* 2 K 25[28] = Je 52[32]. **e.** c †עם *speak with,* (not P), Gn 29[9] 31[24.29] Ex 19[9] 20[19.19.22] 33[9] Nu 11[17] 22[19] Jos 24[27] (all JE) Dt 5[4] 9[10] Ju 6[17] 1 S 9[25] (𝔊 Th We Dr וַיִּרְבְּדוּ לְ *spread a couch for*) 17[23] 2 S 13[22] 1 K 1[14.22] 2 K 6[33] 18[26] 2 Ch 9[1] (= אֶל 1 K 10[2]) Ne 9[13] Est 6[14] Je 32[4] Dn 8[18] 9[22] 10[11.15.17.19] Ho 12[5], דִּבַּרְתִּי אֲנִי עִם לִבִּי *I spake, communed with my heart* Ec 1[16]. **f.** †לפני *before, in the presence of* Ex 6[12] Nu 36[1] (P) Ju 11[11] 1 K 3[22] Est 8[3]. **4.** with בְּ. **a.** *instrumental,* דבר בְּ *speak with, by,* or *by means of a person* (vid supr **Qal** ad fin) Nu 12[2.2.6.8] (E) 2 S 23[2] (cf. Dr), 1 K 22[28] = 2 Ch 18[27], Hb 2[1], †דבר בשם *speak in the name of* Ex 5[23] (J) Dt 18[19.20.20.22] 1 Ch 21[19] Je 20[9] 26[16] 29[23] 44[16] Dn 9[6] Zc 13[3], †ביד *by the hand of* Nu 17[5] 27[23] Jos 20[2] (P) 1 S 28[17] 1 K 8[53] + 13 t K, 2 Ch 10[15] (= 1 K 12[15]) Is 20[2] Je 37[2] 50[1] Ez 38[17] **b.** *local* (fig), בְּאָזְנֵי *in the ears of* Gn 20[8] (E) Ex 11[2] Dt 32[44] (J) Gn 23[16] Nu 14[28] Jos 20[4] (P) Dt 31[28.30] Ju 9[2.3] 1 S 8[21] 11[4] 25[24] 2 S 3[19.19] Je 26[15] Pr 23[9], †דבר בלב *speak in the heart* Ec 2[15]. **c.** *of the object, speak of, about* (prep ב **IV. e** Ew § 217 f (2)) Dt 6[7] 11[19] 1 S 19[3.4] ψ 119[46] 122[8]; *propose for* (a wife) 1 S 25[39] (cf Ct 8[8]). **d.** *of hostility, against* (Ew § 217 f. (1)) Nu 12[1.8] 21[5.7] (E) Jb 19[18] ψ 50[20] 78[19] **e.** *of price,* בנפשו *at the cost of his life* 1 K 2[23] (vid. ב **III. 3**) **5.** with †עַל, of the object *concerning* or *about which* one speaks Gn 18[19] Nu 10[29] (J) Jos 23[14] (D) Ju 9[3] 1 S 25[30] 1 K 2[4.27] 5[13.13] 14[2], 22[23] (= 2 Ch 18[22]), 2 K 10[10], 19[21] = Is 37[22], 1 Ch 22[11] 2 Ch 23[3] Je 1[16] 18[7.8.9] 42[19]. It may have this sense in most if not all of the following, where RV renders 1 K 2[18.19] Est 7[9] Je 18[20] *for;* 2 Ch 32[16] Ne 6[12] Je 11[17] 16[10] 25[13] 26[13.19] 35[17] Ez 36[5] Dn 9[12] 11[36] Ho 7[13] Am 3[1] *against,* and 1 K 9[5] 2 K 22[19] Je 10[1] 19[15] *unto* (על is used for אל *unto* 2 Ch 32[19] Je 6[10] 25[2] 26[2] Ho 12[11]); cf the phrase †דבר על לב *speak upon the heart, speak kindly, comfort* Gn 34[3] 50[21] (E) Ju 19[3] Ru 2[13], 1 S 1[13] (seemingly from context על for אל, *to her heart, to herself,* vid. Dr), 2 S 19[8] 2 Ch 30[22] 32[6] Is 40[2] Ho 2[16]. **6.** with infin. †דבר לעשות *promise to do* Ex 32[14] (J) Dt 1[14] Ez 6[10] Jon 3[10], †דבר לתת *promise to give* Dt 19[8]; †דבר למחות *threaten to blot out* 2 K 14[27], cf. †דבר להזהיר i.e so as to warn Ez 3[18] 33[8].

Note—וַתָּקָם וַתְּדַבֵּר אֶת־כָּל־זֶרַע הַמַּמְלָכָה 2 Ch 22[10] 𝔊 ἀπώλεσε, 𝔙 *interfecit,* scribal error for וַתְּאַבֵּד 2 K 11[1]. Other explanations. *plot against, waylay* (Ar. دَبَرَ) Thes MV; *pronounce sentence,* ellipt. וַתְּדַבֵּר מִשְׁפָּטִים Ges [Hdw] Rob; but cf. VB.—†**Pu.** *Impf* בַּיּוֹם שֶׁיְּדֻבַּר־בָּהּ *in the day when she may be spoken for* Ct 8[8] (vid. **Pi. 4 c**), *Pt.* נִכְבָּדוֹת מְדֻבָּר בָּךְ *glorious things are being spoken in thee* (RV Pe MV[a] *of thee*) ψ 87[3] †**Hithp.** *Pt.* מִתְדַּבֵּר = מִדַּבֵּר with acc. מִדַּבֵּר הַדָּבָר הַזֶּה *speaking this word* 2 S 14[13];

שָׁמַע (אֶת הַקּוֹל) מְדַבֵּר אֵלָיו *heard* (*the voice*, or) *one speaking unto* Nu 7^{89} (P) Ez 2^{2} 43^{6} (Di Nu 7^{89} would rd. מְדַבֵּר after 𝔊, the meaning not appreciably different from Piel, the Hithp difficult to reconcile with אֶל) † **Hiph** *Impf* וַיַּדְבֵּר עַמִּים תַּחְתָּי ψ 18^{48} (2 S 22^{48} has ומוריד for rare וַיַּדְבֵּר), יַדְבֵּר עַמִּים תַּחְתֵּינוּ 47^{4}, either (cf. Aram דְּבַר) *leads* subject (so Ges *coegit*, De Now), or (cf Ar أَدْبَرَ *turn the back, retreat*) *puts to flight*, fig for *subdues* (so Hi)

דָּבָר$_{1439}$ **n.m** speech, word—Gn 18^{14} + 446 t, cstr. דְּבַר Gn 12^{17} + 361 t, sf דְּבָרִי Nu 11^{23} + (sfs. 66 t), sg. in all 875 t, pl דְּבָרִים Ex 4^{10} + 182 t, cstr דִּבְרֵי Gn 24^{30} + 253 t, sf דְּבָרָיו Gn 37^{8} (sfs. 127 t), pl in all 564 t.,—**I.** sg *speech, discourse, saying, word*, as the sum of that which is spoken **1.** *of men*, **a.** נְבוֹן דָּבָר *discreet in speech* 1 S 16^{18}, ד׳ שְׂפָתַיִם *speech of lips* ψ 59^{13}, *mere talk* Is 36^{5} (= 2 K 18^{20}) Pr 14^{23} (cf ψ 17^{4} speech of God's lips), דָּבָר מַר *bitter speech* ψ 64^{4}, ד׳ כָּזָב *lying speech* Pr 30^{8}, טוֹב דְּבָרְךָ *thy saying is good* 1 S 9^{10}, וּדְבַר אַבְנֵר הָיָה עִם *and the speech of Abner had been with* the elders of Israel 2 S 3^{17} (cf 1 K 1^{7}), † אמר הדבר הזה *say this saying* Je 23^{38} 31^{23} cf 13^{12} 14^{17} (of God), 1 S 8^{10} (דברי י׳) **b.** *word of command*, ד׳ (הַ)מֶּלֶךְ 1 Ch $21^{4.6}$ Est 1^{12} + 6 t. Est, Ec 8^{4} cf 2 Ch 30^{6} 31^{5} Dn $9^{23.25}$, † ד׳ מַלְכוּת *royal edict* Est 1^{19}, עשׂה כדבר *do according to the command of* Gn 44^{2} 47^{30} Ex $8^{9.27}$ 12^{35} 32^{28} (J) Lv 10^{7} (P) Ju 11^{10} Ezr 10^{5} Ne $5^{12.13}$, cf. 2 S 17^{6} (word of counsel), 1 K 3^{12} (request), 1 K 17^{13} (proposal; on these mngs v infr) **c.** *message, report, tidings*, וַיִּשְׁמַע הָעָם אֶת־הַדָּבָר הָרָע הַזֶּה *and the people heard this evil report* Ex 33^{4} (JE) cf 1 K 20^{12}, אמת (היה) הדבר *the report was true* 1 K 10^{6} = 2 Ch 9^{5}, עַד בּוֹא דָבָר מֵעִמָּכֶם *until word come from you* 2 S 15^{28}; וינע הדבר אל מלך נינוה Jon 3^{6}, † השׁיב דָּבָר *return* or *bring word, report* Gn 37^{14} Nu 13^{26} 22^{8} (J) Dt $1^{22.25}$ Jos 14^{7} 22^{32} (D) 1 K 2^{30} 20^{9} 2 K $22^{9.20}$ (= 2 Ch $34^{16.28}$), but *answer* 1 S 17^{30} 2 S 3^{11} 24^{13} (= 1 Ch 21^{12}), 1 K $12^{6.9}$ (= 2 Ch $10^{6.9}$), 12^{16} Ne 2^{20} Pr 18^{13} 27^{11} Is 41^{28} Ez 9^{11} (Dr Sm p 190 explains the phrase as *turn back with a word*), cf. ענה (לא) דבר *answer something* or *nothing* 1 K 18^{21} 2 K 18^{36} ψ 119^{42} Is 36^{21} Je 44^{20} vid **IV. 6**; השׁיב דברים *return words* Ex 19^{8} (E) Pr 24^{26} vid **III. 1.** **d.** *advice, counsel*, בדבר בלעם *by advice of Balaam* Nu 31^{16} (P), cf Ju 20^{7} 2 S 19^{44} Est 5^{5}. **e** *request*, אמתו of *his maid*, עבדו of *his servant* 2 S $14^{15.22}$. **f.** *promise*, לא יחל דברו *he shall not break his word* Nu 30^{3} (P), cf הקים דבר *perform a promise* Ne 5^{13}, vid also **2 b** **g.** *charge, complaint*, אם אמת היה הדבר הזה *if this charge be true* Dt 22^{20} cf 13^{15} 17^{4}, שׂים דבר בְּ 1 S 22^{15}, שׂים עלילות דברים ל Dt $22^{14.17}$ **h.** *decision, sentence*, דְּבַר הַמִּשְׁפָּט *the sentence of judgment* Dt 17^{9} cf. v $^{10.11}$ **i** *theme, story*, רָחַשׁ לִבִּי דָּבָר טוֹב my heart swells with a *good theme* ψ 45^{2}; דבר גְּבוּרוֹת *the story of his great might* Jb 41^{4}. **2.** *word of God*, as a divine communication in the form of commandments, prophecy, and words of help to his people, used 394 times. This word is communicated in several ways: **a.** ויהי דבר י׳ אל *then the word of Yahweh came unto* 1 S 15^{10} 2 S 7^{4} (cf אלהים 1 Ch 17^{3}), 1 K 6^{11} 13^{20} 16^{1} $17^{2.8}$ $21^{17.28}$ 2 Ch 11^{2} (cf האלהים 1 K 12^{22}); cf. 1 Ch 22^{8} (על by confusion), Is 38^{4} Je 1^{4} + 20 t. Je, Ez 3^{16} + 41 t Ez, Jon 1^{1} 3^{1} Hg 2^{20} Zc 4^{8} 6^{9} $7^{4.8}$ 8^{1} (without אל) v ^{18}, † היה ד׳ י׳ אל Gn 15^{1} 2 Ch 12^{7} Je 25^{3} + 4 t Je, Ez 1^{3} + 7 t. Ez, Dn 9^{2} Zc $1^{1.7}$ 7^{1}; † הנה ד׳ י׳ אל Gn 15^{4} 1 K 19^{9}, † ד׳ י׳ היה אל 2 S 24^{11} 1 K 16^{7} 18^{1} 2 K 20^{4} Ez 24^{20}; † היה ד׳ י׳ ביד Hg 1^{1} $2^{1.10}$, † ויהי ד׳ י׳ ביד Hg 1^{3}, † ד׳ י׳ אשׁר היה אל Ho 1^{1} Jo 1^{1} Mi 1^{1} Zp 1^{1}, † אשׁר היה ד׳ י׳ אליו 1 K 18^{31} Je 1^{2}, † אשׁר היה ד׳ י׳ אל יר׳ Je 14^{1} 46^{1} 47^{1} 49^{34} (vid. אשׁר **6 a**); הדבר אשׁר היה אל Je 7^{1} + 11 t. Je; † את ד׳ י׳ 2 K 3^{12} Je 23^{28} 27^{18}; cf אֵלַי דָּבָר יְגֻנָּב *unto me a word was brought by stealth* Jb 4^{12}, cf. וטרם יִגָּלֶה אליו דבר י׳ *and the word of Yahweh was not yet revealed unto him* 1 S 3^{7} Yahweh also sends his word שׁלח ψ 107^{20} 147^{18} Is 9^{7} Je 42^{5} (cf. pl. Zc 7^{12}) and makes it an object of vision ראה Je 2^{31} 38^{21} (cf pl. Ez 11^{25}), חזה Is 2^{1}, it is also commanded צוה Ex $16^{16.32}$ 35^{4} Lv 8^{5} 9^{6} 17^{2} Nu 30^{2} 36^{6} (P) Dt 4^{2} 13^{1} 15^{15} Jos 1^{13} 4^{10} (D) 1 Ch 16^{15} (= ψ 105^{8}) Ne 1^{8} Je 7^{23}, cf הדברים אשׁר צוה Ex 35^{1} Lv 8^{36} (P) Ex 19^{7} (E) Dt 6^{6}. **b.** Yahweh confirms his word of promise Dt 9^{5} 1 S 1^{23} (where read דְּבָרְךָ *thy word* acc. to 𝔊 𝔖 & Dr), 1 K 2^{4} 6^{12} 8^{20} Je 29^{10} 33^{14}, and his word of warning 1 K 12^{15} Dn 9^{12}, his word stands for ever Is 40^{8}, it is settled for ever in heaven ψ 119^{89}, he remembers his *holy word* דבר קדשׁו ψ 105^{42} (cf. דברי קָדְשׁוֹ Je 23^{9}), he himself Jo 2^{11}, the angels ψ 103^{20}, and forces of nature ψ 148^{8} עשׂה דברו do his word of command; by his word the heavens were made ψ 33^{6}; it is near his people, in their mouth and heart Dt 30^{14}, a lamp to their feet ψ 119^{105}. **II.** *saying, utterance, sentence*, as a section of a discourse.—**1.** *of men*, **a.** דָּבָר בעתו *a word in due season* Pr 15^{23} cf. Jb 4^{2} Pr 12^{25}, commonly in plural, † דברי (הַ)שִּׁיר(ה) *words of the song* (i e its lines of poetry) Dt 31^{30} 32^{44} ψ 18^{1} (= 2 S 22^{1}) 137^{3}, הלל בדברי דויד *to sing praises with the words of David* (his psalms) 2 Ch 29^{30}, דברי חֲכָמִים *sentences of the wise* Pr 1^{6} 22^{17} Ec

9^{17} 12^{11}; these sayings are commonly *written*, cf. דברי האגרת *words of the letter* Est 9^{26}; דִּבְרֵי הדברים עתיקים *the records are ancient* 1 Ch 4^{22}, (ה)ספר Is 29$^{11.18}$ Je 29^{1}. **b.** *title of writings:* דִּבְרֵי קֹהֶלֶת Ec 1^{1}, ד׳ אגור Pr 30^{1}, ד׳ למואל Pr 31^{1}, ד׳ ירמיהו Je 1^{1}, so Am 1^{1} Ne 1^{1}, cf. in appended phrase or clause, Je 51^{64}, ד׳ איוב Jb 31^{40}. **c.** in Ch *name of a work*. ד׳ החזים 2 Ch 33$^{18.19}$, על ד׳ 2 Ch 12^{15}, בד׳ יהוא 2 Ch 20^{34}, בד׳ שמעיה על 1 Ch 29^{29} 2 Ch 9^{29}, על ד׳ נתן 1 Ch 29^{29}, שמואל ד׳ גד 1 Ch 29^{29}. (It is not certain whether writings of prophets or histories about them are referred to; in the latter case they are *acts*, **IV. 2**, vid Dr$^{Intr\ 497}$) **2.** *of God:* עֲשֶׂרֶת הַדְּבָרִים *the ten words* (sentences in the tables) Ex 34^{28} (JE) Dt 4^{13} 10^{4}, referred to as הדברים Ex 34^{1} (JE) Dt 4$^{10.36}$ 5^{19} 9^{10} 10^{2}; of commands of covenant code Ex 24$^{3.4.8}$ cf. 34^{27} (JE); of Deuteronomic code Dt 17^{19} (+ 16 t D) 2 K 22^{11} 23$^{3-24}$ (cf. 2 Ch 34$^{19-31}$) Je 11$^{2-8}$ 34^{18}; the law-book of Joshua Jos 24^{26} (E); of the code of Ezra Ezr 7^{11} 9^{4} Ne 8$^{9.13}$; the words of Yahweh written by Jeremiah Je 25^{13} 36$^{4-32}$ 51^{61}; the words of the book of Daniel Dn 12$^{4.9}$; commands in general 1 S 15^{11} ψ 50^{17} 119$^{57.130.139}$; promises 2 S 7^{28} Ne 9^{8}, cf. 1 Ch 25^{5} 2 Ch 36^{16}. **III.** *a word, words* —**1.** *of men:* שָׂפָה אֶחָת וּדְבָרִים אֲחָדִים *one lip, and one and the same words* Gn 11^{1} (J); אֵין אֹמֶר וְאֵין דְּבָרִים *no speech and no words* ψ 19^{4}; אִישׁ דְּבָרִים *man of words*, ready in speech, Ex 4^{10} (J), רב דברים *multitude of words* Jb 11^{2} Pr 10^{19} Ec 5^{2}, קְחוּ עִמָּכֶם דְּבָרִים *take with you words* Ho 14^{3}; דבר(י) (ה)שקר *lying word(s)* Ex 5^{9} 23^{7} (E) Pr 13^{5} 29^{12} Is 59^{13} Je 7$^{4.8}$; דִּבְרֵי רוּחַ *words of wind*, vain words Jb 16^{3}; וּמַה־שֵּׁמֶץ דָּבָר נִשְׁמַע־בּוֹ *and what a whisper of a word we hear of him!* Jb 26^{14}. **2.** *of God* It is difficult to determine how many of the following should come under **II. 2.** The pl. for *words of God* is relatively seldom: Gn 20^{8} Ex 19^{6} Nu 12^{6} Jos 3^{9} (E) Ex 4$^{28.30}$ Nu 11^{24} (J) Dt 18^{19} Jos 23^{14} (D) 1 S 3^{18} 8^{10} 15^{1} 2 Ch 11^{4} Jb 42^{7} Pr 30^{6} Is 31^{2} Dn 10^{11} Am 8^{11} Mi 2^{7}, apart from Je 3^{12} + 30 t. Je, Ez 2^{7} + 4 t. Ez, Zc 1^{6} + 4 t Zc. **IV** *matter, affair*, thing about which one speaks:—**1.** *business, occupation:* דְּבַר הַמֶּלֶךְ *king's business* 1 S 21^{9}; לְכָל־דְּבַר *for every matter of* 1 Ch 26^{32} 27^{1} 2 Ch 19^{11}, לְכֹל־דְּבָרֶיךָ *for all thine affairs* 1 Ch 28^{21}; דבר המזבח Nu 18^{7}, דָּבָר אֵין־לָהֶם עִם *they had no dealings with* Ju 18$^{7.28}$, †דְּבַר־יוֹם בְּיוֹמוֹ *the task or portion of a day in its day, daily duty or due* Ex 5$^{13.19}$ (E) 16^{4} (J) Lv 23^{37} (P) 1 K 8^{59} 2 K 25^{30} 1 Ch 16^{37} 2 Ch 8^{13} (ביום) v^{14} 31^{16} Ezr 3^{4} Ne 11^{23} 12^{47} Je 52^{34} Dn 1^{5}; †דבר שנה בשנה 1 K 10^{25} 2 Ch 9^{24}. **2.** pl *acts* cstr דברי 1 K 11$^{41.41}$ 1 Ch 29^{29} 2 Ch 12^{15} 16^{11}; †דְּבָרָיו *his acts* 2 Ch 13^{22} 35^{27}; especially in phrases, וְיֶתֶר דִּבְרֵי . . עַל־סֵפֶר דִּבְרֵי הַיָּמִים *and the rest of the acts of. . in the book of the chronicles* (*daily record of events*) *of* 1 K 14^{29} + 32 t. K., וְיֶתֶר דִּבְרֵי 2 Ch 13^{22} + 8 t Ch, שְׁאָר דברי 2 Ch 9^{29} וְיֶתֶר דְּבָרָיו 2 Ch 28^{26} are referred to various sources, cf. also במספר דברי הימים 1 Ch 27^{24}, בדברי דויד 1 Ch 23^{27}, על־דברי מלכי ישׂראל 2 Ch 33^{18}: דברים טובים *good deeds* 2 Ch 12^{12} 19^{3}, דברי עֲוֹנֹת *acts of iniquity* ψ 65^{4} (De, *Fälle von Missethaten*), דִּבְרֵי־רָע *evil deeds* Je 5^{28}. It is used of God, only in כל דבריו ד׳ נִפְלְאֹתֶיךָ ψ 105^{27}, ד׳ אֹתוֹתָיו Jb 33^{13}, לא יענה ψ 145^{5} **3.** *matter, affair*· דבר אוריה *affair of Uriah* 1 K 15^{5}, שֹׁרֶשׁ דבר *root of the matter* Jb 19^{28}, מה היה הדבר *how went the matter?* 1 S 4^{16} 2 S 1^{4} cf Ru 3^{18}, סבב את פני הדבר *change the face of the matter* 2 S 14^{20}, דִּבְרֵי הָאֲתֹנוֹת *the matter of the asses* 1 S 10^{2}; זה דבר הרצח *this is the case of the slayer* Dt 19^{4}, לְכָל־דְּבָרָיו 1 K 6^{38} *as to all its particulars.* **4.** *events, things*· in the phrase, †אחר הדברים האלה *after these things* (events in time) Gn 15^{1} 22^{1} 40^{1} (E) 39^{7} (J) 1 K 17^{17} 21^{1} Ezr 7^{1} Est 2^{1} 3^{1}, †אחרי הדברים האלה Gn 48^{1} Jos 24^{29} (E) Gn 22^{20} (J) 2 Ch 32^{1}. **5.** *cause, case* for judicial investigation: כִּי־יִהְיֶה לָהֶם דָּבָר *if they have a case* Ex 18^{16} cf. 18^{22} 22^{8}; בעל דברים *one having a case* Ex 24^{14}, cf בדבר משפט 2 Ch 19^{6}; דְּבָרֶיךָ טוֹבִים וּנְכֹחִים *pleas, good and right* 2 S 15^{3} cf. Jos 20^{4}. **6.** *something, anything* (indefinite): עשה דבר *do a thing* Gn 22^{16} + (frequent); עשׂה דברים Is 42^{16} + (less frequent), היפלא מי׳ דבר Gn 18^{14} cf. Je 32$^{17.27}$; לא...דבר *nothing* 1 K 5^{7} 10^{3} Is 39^{2} Je 42^{4} + (frequent), אין דבר Ex 5^{11} (E) Nu 20^{19} 1 S 20^{21}; לא דבר מ׳ *nothing of* Ex 9^{4} (J) Jos 8^{35} 11^{15} 21^{45} 23^{14} (D); כל דבר *anything* Nu 31^{23} Dt 23^{20} +; דָּבָר־מָה 1 K 14^{13} +, ד׳ טוב ψ 141^{4} +, דבר רע *whatsoever* Nu 23^{3} (E); עֶרְוַת דבר Dt 23^{15} *nakedness of a thing*, i e. unclean or unseemly thing (indecency in camp); so of a wife 24^{1}. **7.** *way, manner:* זֶה דְּבַר הַשְּׁמִטָּה *this is the manner of the release* Dt 15^{2} (cf. SI^{1}), כֵּן דְּבַר הַמֶּלֶךְ *so was the way of the king* Est 1^{13}; כדבר הזה *after this manner, thus* †Gn 18^{25} 32^{20} 44^{7} (JE) 2 S 15^{6} Ezr 10^{5} Ne 5$^{12.13}$ with (עשׂה), 1 S 9^{21} 2 S 14^{3} 17^{6} (דבר), 1 S 17$^{27.30}$ Is 8^{20} (אמר), Ne 6$^{4.5}$ (שלח), Ne 6^{4} (השיב) cf. 1 S 17^{30}, 2 K 7^{19} (היה); (peculiar to D, כדבר הרע הזה *such a wicked deed as this* Dt 13^{12} 19^{20}, כדבר הגדול הזה Dt 4^{32}); כדברים האלה עשה *thus and thus did he* Gn 39^{19}

(J) 1 S 2^{23} (but usually the pl. = *these words*). **8.** *reason, cause* זה הדבר 1 K 9^{15}, זה דבר־הַמַּס אשר *this is the reason why* Jos 5^{4} (D) 1 K 11^{27}, so 1 S 17^{29} AV RV, *was it not but a word?* Th Ke RVm VP Dr, . . . עַל דְּבַר *because of, for the sake of* Gn 20$^{11.18}$ (E) 12^{17} 43^{18} Ex 8^{8} (J) Nu 17^{14} (P) ψ 45^{5} 79^{9}, עַל דִּבְרֵי Je 14^{1}, עַל־דִּבְרֵיכֶם *for your sakes* Dt 4^{21}, עַל דְּבַר אֲשֶׁר Dt 22$^{24.24}$ 23^{5} 2 S 13^{22}

דֶּ֫בֶר$_{49}$ **n.m. pestilence** (cf Ar دَبْرٌ, إِدْبَارٌ, *departure, death*)—Ex 9^{3}+, דָּ֑בֶר Hb 3^{5}; sf דְּבָרֶיךָ Ho 13^{14},—**1.** *plague, pestilence*, in general Ex 5^{3} 9^{15} Nu 14^{12} (J) Lv 26^{25} (H) Dt 28^{21}, 2 S 24$^{13.15}$ (+ v^{15} * 𝔊 We Di) = 1 Ch 21$^{12.14}$, 1 K 8^{37} = 2 Ch 6^{28}, 2 Ch 7^{13} 20^{9} ψ 91$^{3.6}$ Je 14^{12} + 16 t. Je, Ez 5^{12} + 11 t Ez, Ho 13^{14} Am 4^{10} Hb 3^{5} Rd וּבַדֶּבֶר, or the like, 1 S 4^{8}, for MT בַּמִּדְבָּר, We Klo Dr. †**2.** *cattle-plague, murrain* Ex 9^{3} (J) = ψ 78^{50}.

†[**דֹּ֫בֶר**] **n.[m.] pasture** (cf. Aram. דַּבְרָא, Syr ܕܒܪܐ)—sf כְּעֵדֶר בְּתוֹךְ הַדָּבְרוֹ *as a flock in the midst of its pasture* Mi 2^{12} (art with sf, cf Ges § 127. 4 b, who attaches ו as conj to foll word), וְרָעוּ כְבָשִׂים כְּדָבְרָם *and lambs shall feed as (in) their pasture* Is 5^{17}.

†**דֹּבְרוֹת** **n.f.pl. floats, rafts** 1 K 5^{23}

†[**דִּבְרָה**] **n.f. cause, reason, manner**—cstr עַל דִּבְרַת *because of, for the sake of* Ec 3^{18} 7^{14} 8^{2}, עַל־דִּבְרָתִי מַלְכִּי־צֶדֶק *after the order, or manner, of Melchizedek* ψ 110^{4} (י ancient genit. ending, to soften transition in poetry, Ges § 90 (3) a), sf דִּבְרָתִי *my cause, suit* Jb 5^{8}

†I **דְּבוֹרָה** **n.f. bee** (cf. Ar دَبْرٌ, *swarm of bees*, Aram דַּבַּרְתָּא, Syr. ܕܒܘܪܬܐ) Is 7^{18}; pl דְּבֹרִים Dt 1^{44} Ju 14^{8} ψ 118^{12}. Rd also דְּבֹרוֹ *its bees* 1 S 14^{26} for MT דְּבַשׁ cf 𝔊 We Dr.

†II **דְּבוֹרָה** **n.pr.f.** (*bee*)—**1.** the nurse of Rebekah Gn 35^{8} **2.** the prophetess Ju 4$^{4.5.9.10.14}$ 5$^{1.7.12.15}$.

†**דָּבְרַת** **n.pr.loc.** Levitical city in Issachar, the present *Debûrîye* at the foot of Mt. Tabor (Rob BR iii 210 Bd Pal 249) Jos 19^{12} (הַדָּבְרַת) 21^{28} 1 Ch 6^{57}

†I **דְּבִיר** **n.m.** (cf. Ar. دُبُرٌ *back*, دُبْرٌ *part behind*) *hindmost chamber, innermost room of the temple of Solomon* = קֹדֶשׁ הַקֳּדָשִׁים *holy of holies, most holy place*, the place of the ark and the cherubic images, the throne-room of Yahweh 1 K 6$^{5.16.19.20.21.22.23.31}$ 7^{49} (= 2 Ch 4^{20}) 8$^{6.8}$ (= 2 Ch 5$^{7.9}$) 2 Ch 3^{16} ψ 28^{2} Prob. rd. דְּבִיר 2 K 10^{25} also, for MT עִיר, so Klo after 𝔊L (It is translated *oracle* in AV RV after Aq Sym χρηματιστήριον, 𝔙 *oraculum*, on the incorrect theory that it was derived from דבר *speak*)

†II. **דְּבִיר** **1. n.pr.m.** king of Eglon Jos 10^{3}. **2. n.pr.loc. a.** דְּבִ֫רָה c. ה ָ loc, N border Judah Jos 15^{7} (*westward* Hup ψ 28^{2}) **b.** לִדְבִר town of the Gadites Jos 13^{26}, perh *Lôdebâr* 2 S 9^{4} vid לֹא דְבָר Di MV. **c.** דְּבִיר Ju 1$^{11.11}$ 1 Ch 6^{43}, דְּבִ֫רָה Jos 10$^{38.39}$, elsewhere דְּבִר Jos 15^{15}+, a royal city of Canaanites anciently called קִרְיַת סֵפֶר Jos 15^{15} Ju 1^{11}, קִרְיַת סַנָּה Jos 15^{49}, on the mountains of Judah, in region of Hebron Jos 11^{21} 15^{49}, assigned to the Aaronite priests Jos 21^{15} as a city of refuge 1 Ch 6^{43}; mod. *Dhoherîye*, 5 hours SW. fr. Hebron, acc to Kn, so Survey iii 402, other conject in Di Jos 10^{39} Ri HWB 265

†**דַּבֵּר** **n [m.] speaking** (so Ew § 156) Je 5^{13} וְהַדִּבֵּר אֵין בָּהֶם, acc. to Hi Gf Ki (less prob) vb with art for relat (vid [דָּבַר] **Pi.**): but rd. rather הַדָּבָר, *and the word is not in them*

†[**דָּבְרָה**] **n.f word**—יִשָּׂא מִדַּבְּרֹתֶיךָ *he receiveth of thy words* Dt 33^{3} (poem)

†**דִּבְרִי** **n.pr m.** a Danite Lv 24^{11}

†I [**מִדְבָּר**] **n.m.** mouth, as organ of speech,—מִדְבָּרֵךְ נָאוֶה *thy mouth is lovely* Ct 4^{3} ‖ שִׂפְתוֹתַיִךְ, 𝔊 λαλιά, Jer *eloquium*

II **מִדְבָּר**$_{270}$ **n.m wilderness**—Dt 32^{10} +; c ה loc מִדְבָּ֫רָה Jos 18^{12} + 15 t, cstr Ex 15^{22}+, מִדְבַּ֫רָה 1 K 19^{15}; sf מִדְבָּרָהּ Is 51^{3},—**1.** tracts of land, used for the pasturage of flocks and herds, דָּשְׁאוּ נְאוֹת מִדְבָּר *the pastures of the wilderness put forth green grass* Jo 2^{22}, יִרְעֲפוּ נ׳ מ׳ *the pastures of the wilderness drop* (fertility) ψ 65^{13}; יָבְשׁוּ נ׳ מ׳ *are dried up* Je 23^{10}, cf Je 9^{9} Jo 1$^{19.20}$. **2.** *uninhabited land*, מִדְבָּר לֹא־אָדָם בּוֹ *wilderness in which is no man* Jb 38^{26}; the abode of pelicans ψ 102^{7}, wild asses Jb 24^{5} Je 2^{24}; jackals Mal 1^{3}, ostriches Lam 4^{3}; מִי־יִתְּנֵנִי בַמִּדְבָּר מְלוֹן אֹרְחִים וְאֶעֶזְבָה אֶת־עַמִּי *O that I had in the wilderness a lodging place of wayfarers, that I might leave my people* Je 9^{1}; טוֹב שֶׁבֶת בְּאֶרֶץ מִדְבָּר *better to dwell in a desert land*, than with a contentious woman Pr 21^{19}, בְּאֶרֶץ מִדְבָּר וּבְתֹהוּ יְלֵל יְשִׁמֹן *in a desert land, and in a waste howling wilderness* Dt 32^{10} **3.** *large tracts* of such land bearing various names, in certain districts of which there might be towns and cities. יִשְׂאוּ מִדְבָּר וְעָרָיו חֲצֵרִים תֵּשֵׁב קֵדָר *let the wilderness and its cities lift up* (their voice), *the villages that Kedar doth inhabit* Is 42^{11} There were six cities in the wilderness of Judah Jos 15$^{61.62}$, הַמִּדְבָּר usually = wilderness of the wanderings

Gn 14⁶ Nu 14[16.29.32.33.35] +, or the great Arabian desert Ju 11²²+; but may also refer to any other Ct 3⁶ 8⁵. Special tracts—(a) of the wilderness of the wanderings were מ׳ שׁור Ex 15²², סין Ex 16¹+, סיני Ex 19¹+, פארן Nu 13²⁶+, צן Nu 20¹+, קדשׁ ψ 29⁸, אתם Nu 33⁸; (b) in W. Pal. מ׳ יהודה Ju 1¹⁶ ψ 63¹ cf. Jos 15⁶¹, מעון 1 S 23[24.25], זיף 1 S 23¹⁵ 26², באר שׁבע Gn 21¹⁴, עין גדי 1 S 24², תקוע 2 Ch 20²⁰, ירואל 2 Ch 20¹⁶, גבעון 2 S 2²⁴; (c) in East. Palestine מואב Dt 2⁸, אדום 2 K 3⁸, קדמות Dt 2²⁶. **4.** fig וְשַׂמְתִּיהָ כַמִּדְבָּר וְשַׁתִּהָ כְּאֶרֶץ צִיָּה *and (lest I) make her as a wilderness and set her like a dry land* Ho 2⁵; הַמִדְבָּר הָיִיתִי לְיִשְׂרָאֵל *have I been a wilderness to Israel?* Je 2³¹.

דבשׁ (√ of foll; cf Ar. دبس ix. *become black* or *brown*, of a colour between black and red; vid. deriv.; so Fl v. infr.; yet vb in this mng. perh denom. fr دِبْس i e. having the colour of *dibs*).

†**דְּבַשׁ** 54 **n.m.** [18 14. 29] honey (named from colour acc. to Fl NHWB[I 430], Ar. دُبْس (دِبْس), دِبْس) *date-honey;* NH דבשׁ, Aram דובשׁא, ܕܒܫܐ, *honey* both of fruits and of bees; cf also As *dišpu* COT[Gloss] Zim[BP 84] Dl[Pr 70])—abs ד׳ Gn 43¹¹+33 t.; דְּבָשׁ Ex 3⁸+18 t.; sf. דִּבְשִׁי Ct 5¹, —*honey*, product of bees, used as food Ju 14[8.9.18] (in lion's carcass), found in (clefts of) rock Dt 32¹³ (ד׳ מִסֶּלַע, in song, JE), ψ 81¹⁷ (מצור ד׳); in forest, on ground 1 S 14²⁵ (על־פני השׂדה) v²⁶ (הֵלֶךְ ד׳); but read rather הָלַךְ דְּבֹרוֹ *its bees had departed*, We Dr after 𝔊) v[29.43]; transported in jar or bottle בַּקְבֻּק ד׳ 1 K 14³; contrib. to priests and Levites 2 Ch 31⁵, ‖ חֶמְאָה 2 S 17²⁹ Is 7[15.22] (in last two the being limited to such food is apparently token of destitution); kept in store Je 41⁸, a choice gift Gn 43¹¹ (J), article of trade Ez 27¹⁷ (in these two perh. = *grape syrup*, mod. *dibs*, cf Di Gn 43¹¹ v. Rob[BR II 81]), forbidden as burnt offering Lv 2¹¹ (‖ שְׂאֹר), *honey comb* = יַעְרַת הַד׳ 1 S 14²⁷ (cf יַעְרִי Ct 5¹); also צוּף ד׳ Pr 16²⁴ (cf נפת צופים ψ 19¹¹); most often in phrase describing abundance in land of Canaan אֶרֶץ זָבַת חָלָב וּד׳ Ex 3[8.17] 13⁵ 33³ (all JE) Lv 20²⁴ (H) Nu 13²⁷ 14⁸ 16[13.14] (all JE) Dt 6³ 11⁹ 26[9.15] 27³ 31²⁰ (all D) Jos 5⁶ (D) Je 11⁵ 32²² Ez 20[6.15]; cf. Dt 8⁸ 2 K 18³² (of land of captivity, words of the Rabshak); v also Ez 16[13.19] Jb 20¹⁷ נַחֲלֵי ד׳ וְחֶמְאָה; *honey*, used to illustrate moral teachings Pr 24¹³ (‖ נֹפֶת), 25[16.27] (danger of surfeit), sim. of sweetness of taste Ez 3³ (the roll), cf כְּצַפִּיחִת בִּד׳ Ex 16³¹ (P, description of manna); of sweetness of the law ψ 19¹¹ (‖ נֹפֶת צוּפִים) cf. 119¹⁰³; (of pleasant words Pr 16²⁴ cf. supr.); sweetness of lips ד׳ וְחָלָב Ct 4¹¹; fig. of love דִּבְשִׁי Ct 5¹ (‖ חֲלָבִי, יֵינִי, יַעְרִי).

†[**דַּבֶּשֶׁת**] **1. n.f.** hump (of camel) (etymol.?) cstr Is 30⁶ עַל־דַּבֶּשֶׁת גְּמַלִּים. **2. n.pr.loc.** on border of Zebulun Jos 19¹¹ דַּבָּשֶׁת.

†**ידבשׁ** **n.pr.m.** a son of Etam? 1 Ch 4³, MT has ואלה אֲבִי עֵיטָם יִזְרְעֶאל ... וְיִדְבָּשׁ 𝔊 οὗτοι υἱοὶ Αἰτάν, cf 𝔙; = ואלה בני ע׳ cf Be Ot (< אלה בני אבי ע׳, as some MSS) On real significance of names cf. עֵיטָם.

†[**דָּגָה**] **vb. multiply, increase** (intr), —**Qal** *Impf* 3 mpl. וְיִדְגּוּ לָרֹב בְּקֶרֶב הָאָרֶץ Gn 48¹⁶ (E).

†**דָּג** **n.m.** [Jon 2.1] **fish** (NH *id*)—דָּג Jon 2[1.1.11]+ Ne 13¹⁶ Qr (Kt דָּאג), דָּגִים 1 K 5¹³+6 t.; דְּגֵי Gn 9²+7 t.;—*fish* of sea Jon 2[1.1.11] (in v¹ ד׳ גָּדוֹל); Ne 13¹⁶ דָּג Kt דָּאג article of Tyrian trade, only here coll, rd perh דָּגָה; or regard as late usage, cf converse דָּגָה of individual Jon 2²);—elsewhere always pl.· as subj of Solomon's utterance 1 K 5¹³; fish-spear צִלְצַל דגים Jb 40³¹; most often דְּגֵי הַיָּם Gn 9² (P), ψ 8⁹ Ho 4³ Zp 1³ Ez 38²⁰ Jb 12⁸ (in all opp to beasts & birds, & appar. used with them, + רֶמֶשׂ Ez. cf. vb. רמשׂ Gn, for animal creation in general; also Hb 1¹⁴ cf. infr.); Nu 11²² (JE) of fish (with beasts) as food (cf. Gn 9^{2f}) in simile of men ensnared, like fish taken in net (מְצוֹדָה) Ec 9¹² cf Hb 1¹⁴ (דגי הַיָּם), 4 t שַׁעַר הַדָּגִים *fish-gate* 2 Ch 33¹⁴ Zp 1¹⁰ Ne 3³ 12³⁹ (on situation cf שַׁעַר).

†**דָּגָה** **n f. fish** (NH *id*)—דָּגָה Nu 11⁵+5 t; cstr דְּגַת Gn 1²⁶+4 t + Ez 29^{4b} (del. B Co); sf. דְּגָתוֹ Ez 47¹⁰ 𝔊 𝔙 Co; (MT דגתם), דְּגָתָם Is 50² ψ 105²⁹+Ez 47¹⁰ MT cf. supr.—*fish*, almost always coll, fish of sea דְּגַת הַיָּם Gn 1[26.28] (P) Ez 47¹⁰ (in sim.), in Nile (יְאֹר) Ex 7[18.21] (E) cf. ψ 105²⁹, דְּגַת יְאֹרֶיךָ Ez 29[4.4] (cf. supr.) v⁵; in sea and rivers Is 50² Ez 47[9.10]; food in Egypt Nu 11⁵ (JE); image of fish forbidden in worship, as of beasts and birds Dt 4¹⁸ (on sacredness of fish, and use in sacrifice cf. Selden[De Diis Syris, II 3]; RS[Sem I 274]); of single fish only Jon 2² (2[1.1.11] דָּג) by late usage, cf. conversely דָּג=דָּאג coll. Ne 13¹⁶.

†[**דּוּג, דִּיג**] **vb. denom. fish for, catch**—**Qal** *Pf.* 3 mpl. sf. ודיגום consec. Je 16¹⁶ (but as **Qal** dub Ges[§ 73 2], Sta[§ 160 b. 2] regards as **Hiph.** (abbrev.), No[ZMG 1883, 540] conj **Pi.**)

†[דַּיָּג] **n.m.** Ez 47, 10 **fisher, fisherman**, only pl. דַּיָּגִים Is 19[8], דַּיָּגִים Qr Je 16[16] (Kt דוגים), דַּוָּגִים Ez 47[10] & Kt Je 16[16].

†דּוּגָה **n.f. fishing, fishery**, only in וְנִשָּׂא בְּסִירוֹת דּוּגָה Am 4[2] (‖ בְּצִנּוֹת) of י׳, metaph. for dragging Isr. captive (cf. for practice referred to, in case of fish, Ez 29[4] & Jb 40[26] scornful summons to do it with crocodile, if possible! v. Herod ii. 70 on mode of capturing crocodiles).

†דָּגוֹן **n.pr.m.** 13, 4 god & idol of Philistines (cf. As. *Dagan, Dakan(nu)*, name perh. non-Shemitic COT Ju 16[23] Dl Pa 139 Sayce Rel. Bab. 188 f. but v. Jen infr.)—god of Ashdod, exc. Ju 16[23] (Gaza) & 1 Ch 10[10] (but cf. infr.);—דגון אֱלֹהֵיהֶם Ju 16[23] cf. דגון אֱלֹהֵינוּ 1 S 5[7], בֵּית ד׳ 1 S 5[2.5] 1 Ch 10[10] (here hardly orig. cf. ‖ 1 S 31[10] & We Dr); כֹּהֲנֵי ד׳ 1 S 5[5], מִפְתַּן ד׳ v[5]; as name of image (אֶל) ד׳ v[2.3.4], דגון נֹפֵל v[3.4], רַק ד׳ נִשְׁאַר עָלָיו v[4] (but sense difficult; We prop. דָּגוֹ *only his fish*, i.e. fishy part, *was left upon him*, v. also Dr;—but was Dagon a fish-god? Cf. works cited above & Scholz Götzendienst 238 ff., Baud in PRE² iii. 460 ff., esp. Jen Kosmol. 449 ff.). Vid. בֵּית דָּגוֹן p. 111.

†[דָּגַל] **vb. look, behold** (As. *dagâlu*, Lotz TP 131; Thes RobGes MV SS De make דָּגוּל a denom. fr. דֶּגֶל = *lifted up like a banner*, or *furnished with a banner*, i.e. *exalted, distinguished*, AV RV *chiefest*);—*Pt. pass.* דָּגוּל מֵרְבָבָה Ct 5[10] *looked at, conspicuous*, acc. to Dl HA 40.

†[דֶּגֶל] **n.m.** Nu 10, 14 **standard, banner** (As. *diglu* Dl HA 40 Pr 58; cf. also Di Nu 2[2]); cstr. דֶּגֶל Nu 2[3] + 7 t.; sf. דִּגְלוֹ Nu 1[52] + 2 t.; pl. sf. דִּגְלֵיהֶם Nu 2[17.31.34];—*standard*, partic. of separate tribes of Isr. ד׳ מחנה יהודה etc. Nu 2[3.10.18.25] 10[14.18.22.25]; cf. also 1[52] 2[2] (‖ אֹתֹת) v[17.31.34] (all P); fig. Ct 2[4] ודגלו עלי אהבה.

†[דָּגַל] **vb. denom. carry**, or **set up standard, banner**—**Qal** *Impf.* 1 pl. נִדְגֹּל ψ 20[6] (Gr Che נָגִיל; Bi נְגַדֵּל, after 𝔊 𝔖; Now נְגַדֵּל; poss. נִגְדֹּל?) *set up standard* in battle, cf. Dl Pr 61. **Niph.** *Pt.* fpl. נִדְגָּלוֹת Ct 6[4.10] *bannered, supplied with standards*, pt. as subst., of *bannered hosts*, cf. De.

דגן (√of foll. mng. dub.; NH דָּגַן Pa. *heap up* etc. seems to be denom.; Ol § 215 b. 4 der. דָּגָן fr. דָּגָה, cf. MV; We Skizzen iii. 170 inclines to regard דָּגָן as der. fr. n.pr. divin. דגן (cf. דָּגוֹן), as *cereal* fr. *Ceres*).

†דָּגָן **n.m. corn, grain** (of cereals) (NH *id.*, Sam. ࠃࠂࠍ v. Thes.; cf. Ph. ארצת דגן)—דָּגָן Gn 27[28] + 29 t.; cstr. דְּגַן ψ 78[24]; sf. דְּגָנִי Ho 2[11], דְּגָנְךָ Dt 7[13] 12[17] 14[23] 18[4], דְּגָנֶךָ Dt 11[14], דְּגָנֵךְ Is 62[8], דְּגָנָם ψ 4[8] 65[10]—*corn*, c. תִּירוֹשׁ *must*, q.v., Gn 27[28.37] (both J) ψ 4[8] Is 62[8] Ho 2[11] 7[14] 9[1] Zc 9[17]; cf. also Nu 18[27] (P; here, for תירושׁ, מְלֵאָה מִן־הַיֶּקֶב), La 2[12] (where יַיִן), Ho 14[8] (where יַיִן & גֶּפֶן לְבָנוֹן); ארץ דגן ותירושׁ of land of Canaan Dt 33[28]; of land of captiv. (words of the Rabshak) 2 K 18[32] = Is 36[17] (other products, also, named in both); usually c. תירושׁ & יצהר Nu 18[12] Dt 7[13] 11[14] 12[17] 14[23] 18[4] 28[51] 2 Ch 31[5] (+ דבשׁ) 32[28] Ne 5[11] 10[40] 13[5.12] Je 31[12] Ho 2[10.24] Jo 1[10] 2[19] Hg 1[11]; also Jo 1[17] Me; (cf. 2 K 18[32] Is 36[17] supr.); alone, rare and late Ne 5[2.3.10] ψ 65[10] Ez 36[29]; דְּגַן־שָׁמַיִם ψ 78[24];—of the above the following refer to firstfruits offered to the priests Nu 18[12] (cf. v[27]) Dt 18[4] 2 Ch 31[5]; to tithe Dt 12[17] 14[23] Ne 13[5.12]; to both generally Ne 10[40]; to loaning on usury Ne 5[10.11].

†[דָּגַר] **vb. gather together as a brood** (cf. Aram. דְּגַר *heap together;* so دَجَرَ Nasar.)—**Qal** *Pf.* 3 ms. דָּגַר Je 17[11]; 3 fs. דָּגְרָה Is 34[15]—*gather together* into its shadow Is 34[15] (of קִפּוֹז, q.v.), דָּגַר וְלֹא יָלָד Je 17[11] (of partridge; sim. of one getting riches unjustly).

†[דַּד] **n.m.** Pr 5, 19 **breast**, better **teat, nipple** (τιτθοί Aq Pr 5[19] Symm Ez 23[3.21]; NH & Aram. דַּד; primit. caressing word; acc. to Fl in NHWB i. 439)—Du. cstr. דַּדֵּי Ez 23[3.8] (both del. 𝔊 𝔖 Co); sf. דַּדַּיִךְ Ez 23[21] (rd. בתוליך 𝔖 Co); דַּדֶּיהָ Pr 5[19];—of breasts of woman Pr 5[19] (Hi Bi rd. דֹּדֶיהָ *her love* cf. 7[18]); of Samaria & Jerusalem under fig. of young women Ez 23[3] (דַּדֵּי בְּתוּלֵיהֶן) cf. v[8]; דַּדַּיִךְ v[21]; but prob. del. ד׳ in Ez cf. supr. & Gei Urschrift 397.—Vid. also שַׁד sub שׁדה.

דֹּד, דּוֹדָה v. sub דוד.

†[דָּדָה] **vb.** [move slowly] (NH Pi. דִּדָּה *lead slowly*, Hithp. הִדַּדָּה; Aram. דַּדִּי, אִידַּדִּי; Ar. دَادَأ is *run quickly* (of a camel): on form, cf. Kö i. 587; SS der. fr. ראה cf. Sta § 112 a, 150 a, 129 b, 581 d)—**Pi.** *Impf.* 1 s. sf. אֲדַדֵּם (so read for MT אֶדַּדֵּם Dy Bi & Che, cf. his crit. note) *lead slowly* (in procession) ψ 42[5]. **Hithp.** *Impf.* 1 s. אֶדַּדֶּה Is 38[15]; also sf. אֶדַּדֵּם ψ 42[5] MT but cf. supr.;—*walk deliberately*, at ease (De Che Di), or as in procession (Ew), Is 38[15] (cf. Che Di VB).

דדי Kt v. דּוֹדוֹ sub דוד.

†דְּדָן **n.pr.loc. & gent.**;—ד׳ Gn 10[7] + 8 t.

+ Ez 27^{20} (but v. infr.) c. ה loc דְּדָ֫נָה Ez 25^{13} cf. Ges [§ 90. 2 ad fin.];—**1.** under fig. of son of רַעְמָה and grandson of כּוּשׁ (v. these arts.) Gn 10^{7} (brother of שְׁבָא) = 1 Ch 1^{9} Ez 27^{20}; cf. בְּנֵי ד׳ v[15] (but rd. here perh. רדן 𝔊 *viol* Ῥοδίων, cf. Sta [De Pop. Javan. 11], also 𝔖 ܪܘܕܢ, Co; v sub דְּדָנִים infr.) cf. also Ez 38^{13}, שְׁבָא וּד׳; also Je 25^{23}, south-Arabian tribe on Persian Gulf, = Sab. בנו דדן acc to DHM [ZMG 1876, 122, Sab Denkm. 28] (dubit. Mordt); but in NW. of Arabian peninsula, Glaser [Skizze ii. 391 ff]; perhaps orig. further south cf. Di Gn 10^{7} **2.** as son of יָקְשָׁן, father of אַשּׁוּרִם etc., Gn $25^{3.3}$ (here also brother of שְׁבָא) = 1 Ch 1^{32}; Je 49^{8} יֹשְׁבֵי ד׳ This is appar. a northern branch of **1**, cf Di Gn 25^{3}.—On דדן in MI [31.31] cf Sm & So [MI p. 29] No [LCB Jan 8, 1887] Cl Gann [JAs. Jan 1887 107].

דְּדָן v. דְּדָ֫נָה.

†[דְּדָנִי] **adj gent.** only pl as subst. אֹרְחוֹת דְּדָנִים Is 21^{13}

†דֹּדָנִים **n.pr.gent.pl.** Gn 10^{4}; but = רוֹדָנִים 1 Ch 1^{7}; rd. here רֹדָנִים, so 𝔊 Sam Di Sta [De Pop. Javan. 11]; cf. Ez 27^{15} supr. sub דְּדָן

†[דָּהַם] **vb. astonish, astound** (Ar دَهِمَ, دَهَمَ)—**Niph.** *Pt.* כְּאִישׁ נִדְהָם Je 14^{9} *like a man astounded* (‖ כְּגִבּוֹר לֹא יוּכַל לְהוֹשִׁיעַ); 𝔊 ὑπνῶν = נִרְדָּם.

†[דָּהַר] **vb. rush, dash,** of horse (onomat.? perh. cf. Ar. دَهَرَ *befall, fall upon, overcome, conquer*)—**Qal** *Pt.* סוּס דֹּהֵר Na 3^{2}.

†[דַּהֲרָה] **n.f. rushing, dashing,** of riders —*Pl.* cstr. דַּהֲרוֹת דַּהֲרוֹת אַבִּירָיו Ju 5^{22}, repetition for intensity, *furious dashing.*

†תִּדְהָר **n.[m.]** name of a tree, prob elm (Syr. ܕܕܪܐ (or ܕܪܕܪܐ PS) Lag [BN 130] Low [71]; Ar دَرْدَار Lane [864] Dozy [i. 432] (also *ash,* v. Dozy [ib.]); so Symm & 𝔙 Is 41^{19}; cf. Di, where also other views, e g. *plane-tree* (Rabb. Che), or *pine,*—√dub; Ges Is 41^{19} Thes der from דהר *endure* inferred from Ar. دَهْرٌ *time,* but this questionable; perh a loan-word), בְּרוֹשׁ תִּדְהָר וּתְאַשּׁוּר יַחְדָּו Is 41^{19} = 60^{13}.

†[דּוּב] **vb. pine away** (cf דאב, דאבון)—**Hiph.** *Pt.* f. pl. מְדִיבֹת נֶפֶשׁ Lv 26^{16} (diseases) *causing to pine away the soul* (life), cf. Di; in 1 S 2^{33} read prob *Inf.* לְהָדִיב אֶת נַפְשְׁךָ (for MT לַאֲדִיב) so Dr; trans. *to cause thy* (al. *his*) *soul to pine away* (cf. VB)

דוב *bear,* v. sub דבב

דּוּג, דַּוָּג, דּוּגָה v. sub דנה.

דוד (√assumed for foll, wh however perh. primitive caressing word, Fl NHWB [i. 439] *swing, rock, dandle, fondle, love;* > Thes Dietr [Sem. Wortforsch 227] MV, who connect with דוד (cf. infr.) cf. Syr. ܕܘܕ *disturb*)

†דּוֹד **n.m.** [Ct 1, 2] **beloved, love** (pl.), **uncle** (NH *id*, Syr. ܕܕܐ, ܕܕܝܐ, As. *dâdu* Dl [HA 19])—abs דּוֹד Ct $5^{9.9}$; cstr. דּוֹד 1 S 10^{14} + 3 t; דֹּד Lv 10^{4} Est 2^{15}; sf. דּוֹדִי Is 5^{1} (but cf. infr) + 26 t. all Ct, דֹּדִי Je 32^{8} + 2 t; דֹּדְךָ Je 32^{7}; דּוֹדֵךְ Ct $5^{9.9}$ + 2 t, דּוֹדוֹ Am 6^{10} 1 S 10^{16}, דֹּדוֹ Lv 20^{20} + 4 t, דּוֹדָהּ Ct 8^{5}; pl דּוֹדִים Ct 5^{1}; דֹּדִים Pr 7^{18} Ez 16^{8} 23^{17}; pl. sf דֹּדַי Ct 7^{13}, דֹּדֶיךָ Ct $1^{2.4}$; דֹּדַיִךְ Ct $4^{10.10}$; דֹּדֵיהֶן Nu 36^{11}.—**1.** most often *loved one, beloved* (lover, betrothed) Ct $1^{13.14.16}$ $2^{3.8.9.10.16.17}$ 4^{16} $5^{2.4.5.6.6.8.9.9.10.16}$ $6^{1.1.2.3.3}$ $7^{10.11.12.14}$ $8^{5.14}$; *beloved one, friend,* שִׁירַת דּוֹדִי Is 5^{1} (where Lo Che שׁ׳ דּוֹדִים *love-song,* v **3** infr) **2.** specif. *uncle,* Lv 10^{4} (father's brother, *patruus;* Syr. = also *avunculus*) Nu 36^{11} 1 S 14^{50} 2 K 24^{17} Lv 20^{20} $25^{49.49}$ 1 S $10^{14.15.16}$ Est $2^{7.15}$ Je $32^{7.8.9.12}$; perhaps also 1 Ch 27^{32} Jonathan, David's דּוֹד, so AV RV, = kinsman (?, so St RVm) Am 6^{10}. **3.** pl. abstr. *love* Pr 7^{18} Ct $1^{2.4}$ $4^{10.10}$ 5^{1} (5^{1} al concr *beloved ones,* so AV RV, 𝔊 ἀδελφοί), so עֵת דֹּדִים Ez 16^{8}; מִשְׁכַּב דֹּדִים Ez 23^{17}

†[דּוֹדָה] **n.f. aunt**—only *sf.* דֹּדָתְךָ Lv 18^{14} father's brother's wife, דֹּדָתוֹ Lv 20^{20} Ex 6^{20} father's sister [cf. Nu 26^{59}]

†דּוֹדוֹ **n.pr.m.** (*his beloved,* cf. דּוֹדָוָהוּ, or comp דּוֹדָה n pr divin. MI [12], cf. דָּוִד infra)—**1.** man of tribe of Issachar Ju 10^{1}. **2.** דֹּדַי Kt 2 S 23^{9} (= דּוֹדַי 1 Ch 27^{4}), דּוֹדוֹ Qr = דּוֹדוֹ 1 Ch 11^{12} **3.** father of אֶלְחָנָן 2 S 23^{24} דּוֹדוֹ = 1 Ch 11^{26}.

†דּוֹדַי **n.pr.m.** = דּוֹדוֹ (q.v.) 1 Ch 27^{4} (cf. דדי 2 S 23^{9} Kt).

†דּוֹדָוָהוּ **n.pr.m.** (< 𝔊 τοῦ Ὠδεια, 𝔊L Δουδιου, i e דּוֹדִיָהוּ, *beloved of* י׳, cf. Nes [Eg 70]) father of Eliezer 2 Ch 20^{37}.

דָּוִד, דָּוִיד [1066] **n.pr.m. David,** son of יִשַׁי, king of Israel, whose dynasty remained on the throne of Jerusalem till the Babylonian exile (cf. 2 S 7^{11-15} etc) (*beloved one*? cf. Ba [NB 189], acc. to Sayce [Mod Rev 1884, 158 ff. Rel. Bab 53, 56 f.] orig. *Dodo,* title of sun-god worshipped in Isr. cf. דודה n.divin. among E. Jordan Israelites MI [12])—דָּוִד alw. Ru Sa Ki (exc 1 K 3^{14} $11^{4.36}$) ψ Pr Ec Is Je; also 1 Ch 13^{6} Ez 34^{24} $37^{24.25}$ (c. 790 t); דָּוִיד alw. Zc Ch (exc. 1 Ch 13^{6}) Ezr Ne; also

Am 6^{5} (where gloss acc to Peters [Hbr Apr 1886 p 175]) 9^{11} Ho 3^{5} Ez 34^{23} 1 K 3^{14} 11$^{4.36}$ Ct 4^{4} (c. 276 t), —first named 1 S 16^{13}, cf. also Ru 4$^{17.22}$ 2 S 1^{1}+, 1 K 1^{1}+, 2^{1}+, etc (v. supra); in titles of ψ 3–9, 11–32, 34–41, 51–65, 68–70, 86, 101, 103, 108–110, 122, 124, 131, 133, 138–145 (73 in all); also in ψ 18^{51} (= 2 S 22^{51}) 72^{20} 89$^{36.50}$ 122^{5} 132$^{1.11.17}$, ד׳ עבדי (י׳ speaks) 2 S 3^{18} 7$^{5.8}$ = 1 Ch 17$^{4.7}$ cf v^{26} = 1 Ch 17^{24}, also 1 K 8$^{24.25.26.66}$ = 2 Ch 6$^{15.16.17.42}$, 1 K 11$^{13.32.34.36.38}$ 14^{8} 2 K 8^{19} 19^{34} = Is 37^{35}, 2 K 20^{6}; cf further ψ 18^{1} 36^{1} (both titles cf supr) 78^{70} 89$^{4.21}$ 132^{10} 144^{10} Je 33$^{21.22.26}$, so also as represented in coming (Messianic) ruler Ez 34$^{23.24}$ 37$^{24.25}$, cf Ho 3^{5} Je 30^{9} (עֶבֶד י׳). Phrases are **a.** עיר ד׳ (acc to Sayce [Mod Bcr 1.c] orig *city of god Dod[o]*) = stronghold or citadel of Zion, 2 S 5$^{7.9}$ = 1 Ch 11$^{5.7}$, 2 S 6$^{10.12.16}$ = 1 Ch 13^{13} 15$^{1.29}$, cf Is 22^{9}, esp of burial of kings 1 K 2^{10} 3^{1}, 8^{1} = 2 Ch 5^{2}, 1 K 9^{24} = 2 Ch 8^{11}, 1 K 11^{27} v^{43} = 2 Ch 9^{31}, 1 K 14^{31} 15^{8} = 2 Ch 12^{16} 13^{23}, 1 K 15^{24} = 2 Ch 16^{14}, 1 K 22^{50} = 2 Ch 21^{1}, 2 K 8^{24} = 2 Ch 21^{20}, 2 K 9^{28} 12^{22} = 2 Ch 24^{25}, 2 K 14^{20} 15^{7}, v^{38} = 2 Ch 27^{9}, 2 K 16^{20}, burial of Jehoiada 2 Ch 24^{16}, further 2 Ch 32$^{5.30}$ 33^{14} Ne 12^{37}, cf also קִרְיַת חָנָה ד׳ Is 29^{1}. **b.** בית ד׳ 2 S 3$^{1.6}$+ (cf בית **5 c**) **c.** אהל ד׳ Is 16^{5} (cf. אֹהֶל **2**) **d.** סֻכַּת ד׳ Am 9^{11} (cf סֻכָּה sub סכך) **e.** כסא ד׳ 2 S 3^{10} cf 1 K 1^{37} 2$^{12.24.45}$ Is 9^{6} Je 17^{25} 22$^{2.30}$ 29^{16} 36^{30} cf 13^{13} 22^{4}, (cf. also כסא) **f.** קברי ד׳ Ne 3^{16} cf 2 Ch 32^{33} (קִבְרֵי בני־ד׳) (cf קֶבֶר) **g.** מִגְדַּל ד׳ Ct 4^{4} **h.** כלי־שיר ד׳ איש האלהים Ne 12^{36} **i.** אֱלֹהֵי ד׳ 2 K 20^{5}+ (cf אֱלֹהִים **4 b**). **j.** חַסְדֵי ד׳ 2 Ch 6^{42} Is 55^{3} (cf 2 S 7^{15} 1 K 3^{6} ψ 89^{50} 2 Ch 1^{8} etc) —(On txt. note the foll —דָּוִד 1 S 30^{26a} del 𝔊 𝔙 We Dr, 2 S 3^{5} rd. prob name of a former husband of Eglah We Dr, 2 S 13^{39} rd רוּחַ We$^{p. 223}$ Dr, 2 S 19^{44} rd. בְּכוֹר (for בדוד) 𝔊 The We Dr, insert דָּוִד 2 S 9^{11} 15^{32} & 24^{15} 𝔊 We Dr, in 1 Ch 18^{12} ψ 60^{1} אבשי & יואב are less orig than דָּוִד 2 S 8^{13} We Dr)

†[דּוּדַי] **n.m.** [Gn 30, 14] **mandrake** (as love-producing, cf. Di Gn 30^{14})—pl דּוּדָאִים (cf Ew [186 e] Sta [§§ 301 122]) Gn 30^{14} Ct 7^{14}, cstr. דּוּדָאֵי Gn 30^{14} + 3 t, —*mandrakes*, as exciting sexual desire, and favouring procreation Gn 30$^{14.14.15.15.16}$ (J), also Ct 7^{14} where odour referred to. On דּוּדָאֵי Je 24^{1} *vessels, baskets*, v דוד

†דּוּד **n.m.** [Je 24, 2] **pot, jar** (Aram דּוּדָא, ܕܘܕܐ, perh. cf Syr ܕܳܕ *disturb*, from the idea of boiling) —abs. דּוּד 1 S 2^{14} + 4 t, pl דּוּדִים 2 K 10^{7}, דְּוָדִים 2 Ch 35^{13}, pl cstr דּוּדָאֵי Je 24^{1}—**a.** *pot, kettle* for cooking (בשׁל) 1 S 2^{14} (|| כִּיּוֹר, קַלַּחַת, פָּרוּר), 2 Ch 35^{13} (vb בשׁל, || סִירוֹת, צֵלָחוֹת), cf. Jb 41^{12}; **b.** receptacle for carrying, all Vrss *basket*, 2 K 10^{7} (heads of king's sons), Je 24$^{2.2}$ (figs) cf דּוּדָאֵי Je 24^{1}, as if fr. a II [דּוּדַי], ψ 81^{7} (clay or bricks, || סֵבֶל)

†[דָּוָה] **vb. be ill, unwell** (NH ד׳ *sorrowful, miserable*, not in physical sense, cf. Ar [دَاءَ] دَوِيَ *be ill*; Eth ደወየ: As perh. deriv. *di'û, illness* Zim[BP 96.97]; Aram דְּוֵי, דְּוָא, ܕܘܐ, ܕܘܳܐ *be sad*)—**Qal** *Inf. cstr* כִּימֵי נִדַּת דְּוֹתָהּ ... אִשָּׁה Lv 12^{2}.

†דְּוַי **n.[m.] illness**, עֶרֶשׂ דְּוָי ψ 41^{4} *bed of languishing* (Che); sg. cstr. (Ew De Di) הֵמָּה כִּדְוֵי לַחְמִי Jb 6^{7} *they* (i e my sufferings) *are like disease* (VB *loathsomeness*) *in my meat*, cf. Di; but txt dub

†דָּוֶה **adj. faint, unwell**—דָּוֶה La 5^{17}, f דָּוָה Lv 15^{33} + 3 t, **1.** *faint*, La 1^{13} (|| שֹׁמֵמָה) 5^{17}. **2.** *unwell, menstruous* Lv 15^{33} 20^{18}, Is 30^{22} דָּוָה perh = כלי דָוָה De.

†[מַדְוֶה] **n.m.** [Dt 7, 15] **sickness**—cstr sg. מַדְוֵה מצרים Dt 28^{60} (rd מַדְוֵי pl., as 7^{15}?); cstr. pl מַדְוֵי מצרים Dt 7^{15} (both || חֳלִי).

†[דַּוָּי] **adj. faint** (on form cf Ba[NB 487])—דַּוָּי Is 1^{5} + 2 t—*faint*, always of heart Is 1^{5} (|| לָחֳלִי) fig of condition of people), Je 8^{18} La 1^{22} of sorrow and distress.

†דְּיוֹ **n.m. ink** (NH *id*, Aram דְּיוּתָא, ܕܝܘܬܐ; Ar دَوَاةٌ *inkbottle, inkhorn*; Ges-Dietr Fl NHWB[i 41] der fr √דוה in assumed sense of *slowly flowing*, Fl comp. Ar. دِوَايَةٌ دُوَايَةٌ *thin skin on surface of milk*, cf. also Ol[§ 173 g]), וַאֲנִי כֹּתֵב עַל־הַסֵּפֶר בַּדְּיוֹ Je 36^{18}, cf Lag[Ges Abh 216] —On erasible quality of Hebrew ink cf. RS [OTJC, 400 f ed 2, 71], v. further L. Low[Graphische Requisiten etc. bei den Juden, 1870, I 145 ff]

†[דִּיחַ, הֵדִיחַ] **vb. rinse, cleanse away by rinsing, washing** (NH Hiph., Aram. Aph. *id*; cf As *dâḫu* Dl[Pr 177])—**Hiph.** *Pf* sf. הדיחנו Kt Je 51^{34} Qr הֱדִיחָנִי but rd. הִדִּיחַנִי fr. נדח (Hi, cf 50^{17}), *Impf* 3 ms יָדִיחַ Is 4^{4}; 3 mpl. יָדִיחוּ 2 Ch 4^{6} + Ez 40^{38} (Co conj הַקְּרָבִים);—**1.** *rinse*, victims to be offered in sacrifice Ez 40^{38}, so 2 Ch 4^{6} (cf. supr) **2.** fig *cleanse* by washing Is 4^{4}, of removing guilt

דויג Kt v דאג sub דאג

†[דּוּךְ] **vb. pound, beat** (in mortar) (NH & Aram *id*, Ar دَاكَ; cf. also As. *dâku, kill*

COT[Glos])—**Qal** *Pf* 3 pl דָּכוּ בַּמְּדֹכָה (milra') Nu 11[8] (|| טָחֲנוּ בָרֵחַיִם).

†מְדֹכָה **n.f.** mortar, Nu 11[8].

†דּוּכִיפַת **n.f.** an unclean bird, perh. hoopoe, 𝔊 𝔙 Saad al. (cf Di Kn Lv 11[19]) Lv 11[19] Dt 14[18].

דום (NH דום *spread slander*, perh. orig *whisper*, cf דמם, דממה)

†I. דּוּמָה **n.f.** silence;—ד׳=שְׁאוֹל ψ 94[17], יֹרְדֵי ד׳ ψ 115[17], also Is 21[11] מַשָּׂא דּוּמָה *oracle of silence*, i.e. of concealment, hidden meaning, acc. to Ew Di, but v II ד׳, **3.**

†II. דּוּמָה **n.pr. 1. m.** son of Ishmael Gn 25[14]=1 Ch 1[30], cf. prob. *Dumath al-Jandal* in Northern Arabia in *Jôf* v Burckhardt[Travels in Syria 662 f] Di, also Ges[Comm] on Is 21[11], Glaser[Skizze ii 392. 440]. **2.** city in mountains of Judah Jos 15[52], comp. Δοῦμα in the Daroma, 17 miles fr. Eleutheropolis Lag[Onom 250, 2nd ed 258], = mod *Daume*, SW. fr. Hebron van de Velde[Memoir 308] Guérin[Judée iii. 359 ff] cf. Di **3.** name of Edom with mystic mng Is 21[11] *Duma=silence* of death, desolation, De Che al. (JDMich Ges Hi think **3=1**; 𝔊 has Ἰδουμαία; Jer interpr as *part* of Idumea; still another view sub I. דּוּמָה)

†דּוּמִיָּה, דֻּמִיָּה (ψ 65[2]) **n.f. silence, still waiting, repose**—ψ 39[3] *silence;* 62[2] *still waiting, resignation* (Dr[§189 2]; but rd. prob., as v[6], דֻּמִּי, Bi Gr Che); 65[2] *id.* (but Ew Che Ba al לְךָ דֻּמִיָּה *is meet?* fr. I. דָּמָה, 𝔊 πρέπει, v. Che); 22[3] *repose* (fr. grief and tears Je 14[17])

†דּוּמָם **n.[m.]** silence Hb 2[19] אֶבֶן ד׳ *stone of silence=dumb stone;* **adv. in silence, silently,** Is 47[5] La 3[26] (? rd. here וְדָמָם fr. דמם).

דּוּמֶשֶׂק 2 K 16[10] cf. דַּמֶּשֶׂק.

[דון] **vb.** dub.; only in יָדוֹן Gn 6[3], v דין.

†[דּוֹן] **n.[m.]** dub.; Qr Jb 19[29] שַׁדּוּן; v. דִּין **n.**

†[דּוּץ] **vb. spring, leap, dance** (Aram. דּוּץ *be joyous*, ܘ..., *leap, dance, be joyous;* Ar. داص med. ى, *decline, slip* or *move about, glide to and fro;* Dl[Pr 65.66] comp. As. *dâṣu, withdraw, retreat,* but cf No[ZMG 1886, 730])—**Qal** *Impf* 3 fs. תָּדוּץ דְּאָבָה Jb 41[14] before him *danceth dismay*

דוק (? √ of foll; mng dub. cf. Sm Ez 4[2] Lag[Ges. Abhandl 36])

†דָּיֵק **n.m. bulwark, siege-wall**—דָּיֵק 2 K 25[1] + 5 t.—בָּנָה ד׳ עָלֶיהָ סָבִיב 2 K 25[1] = Je 52[4], cf. Ez 4[2] 17[17] 21[27] (all || שָׁפַךְ סֹלְלָה), נָתַן ד׳ עַל Ez 26[8] (|| *id*)

דּוּר vb. 1. heap up, pile. 2. dwell (orig *move in a circle, go about, surround,* cf Ar. دَارَ; دَارٌ *house,* esp as group of buildings about a court, As *dûru, wall, fortress,* COT[Glos], thence (denom Fl NHWB[i 440]) *dwell* Aram. דּוּר, [Syriac] (pt & Pa), hence in Heb cf Giesebr[ZAW i 304] Fl[l c] Che[OP 479]; Eth ደር: *generation* (=דּוֹר· prob. loan-word); acc. to Hpt KAT[2 Gloss. i] As. [*darû, endure*], *dârû, everlasting* (cf Bez[Orient Diplom.])=Ar دَهْرٌ *long time, age*)—**Qal** in *Inf.* מִדּוּר בְּאָהֳלֵי־רֶשַׁע ψ 84[11] *than to dwell in tents of wickedness. Imv* (or *Inf abs.* irreg for דּוּר), cf || (לְקַח) דּוּר הָעֲצָמִים Ez 24[5] *heap up*—In Gn 6[3] some rd. *Impf.* 3 ms יָדוּר *shall dwell,* for יָדוֹן, v. דין

†דּוּר **n.[m.] circle, ball—1.** *circle* וְחַנִּיתִי כַדּוּר עָלָיִךְ Is 29[3] (>𝔊 Brd כְּדָוִד) **2.** *ball* צָנוֹף יִצְנָפְךָ צְנֵפָה כַּדּוּר Is 22[18] (so most; but Bo[NA ii. 134] De Or Jastr[PAOS 1888, xcv ff.] regard noun as כַּדּוּר, *ball,* as Talm, cf also MV SS s v.; vid. כדר) [**3.** *heap, pile* Ez 24[5] Thes Ke MV cf. מְדוּרָה v[9], but v supr. sub דּוּר **vb.**]

†I. דּוֹר, דֹּר **n.m.** [Dt 32, 5] **period, generation, dwelling** (cf. sub **vb.** supr., also NH דּוֹר, Aram. (incl. B Aram) דָּר, [Syriac], *age, generation;* Ar دَوْرٌ *gyrus, orbis, periodus;* Sab דר, *one time, once,* דרם דרם *each once* in a year DHM in MV)—abs. דּוֹר Gn 7[1]+68 t.; דֹּר Ex 3[15]+36 t.; cstr. דּוֹר Dt 32[20] + 7 t., דֹּר Ex 3[15], sf דּוֹרִי Is 38[12], דּוֹרוֹ Is 53[8], pl דּוֹרִים ψ 72[5]+2 t., דֹּרוֹת abs Jb 42[16] Is 41[4], cstr. Ju 3[2], דּוֹרוֹת cstr Is 51[9], דֹּרֹת Gn 9[12], sf דֹּרֹתָיו Gn 6[9] Lv 25[30], דֹּרֹתֵינוּ Jos 22[27], v[28], דֹּרֹתֵיכֶם Gn 17[12] + 27 t, דֹּרֹתָם Gn 17[7] + 10 t;—**1.** *period, age, generation,* mostly poet: **a.** of duration in the past, *former age(s)* דּוֹרוֹת עוֹלָמִים Is 51[9] (|| יְמֵי קֶדֶם); שְׁנוֹת דֹּר וָדֹר Dt 32[7] (song, || יְמוֹת עוֹלָם), בְּדֹר וָדֹר ψ 90[1] (cf v[2]), מוֹסְדֵי דוֹר־וָדוֹר Is 58[12] (|| חָרְבוֹת עוֹלָם), שֹׁמְמוֹת דּוֹר וָדוֹר 61[4] (|| *id.*) **b.** usually of duration to come, *future age(s)*, לְדֹר דֹּר Ex 3[15] (E, || לְעֹלָם) cf Pr 27[24] Kt (Qr לְדוֹר וָדוֹר; || *id*), מִדֹּר דֹּר Ex 17[16] (E),=מִדּוֹר לְדוֹר Is 34[10], לְדֹר וָדֹר ψ 10[6] 33[11] (|| לְעוֹלָם) 49[12] 79[13] 85[6] 102[13] 119[90] 135[13] 146[10] Jo 4[20] (all || *id*); ψ 89[2] (|| עוֹלָם) 89[5] (|| עַד־עוֹלָם) 106[31] (|| *id.*) Is 34[17] (|| *id*); ψ 77[9] (|| לָנֶצַח); עַד־דֹּר וָדֹר ψ 100[5] (|| לְעוֹלָם) בְּכָל־דֹּר Is 13[20] (|| לָנֶצַח) Je 50[39] (|| *id*), שְׁנוֹתָיו כְּמוֹ דֹר וָדֹר ψ 61[7] cf שְׁנֵי דּוֹר וָדוֹר Jo 2[2] (|| הָעוֹלָם); דֹּר וָדֹר ψ 45[18] (|| לְעוֹלָם וָעֶד) cf. Est 9[28]; as modifying phrase מְשׂוֹשׂ דּוֹר וָדוֹר Is 60[15] (|| גְּאוֹן עוֹלָם); further דּוֹר דּוֹרִים ψ 72[5]; יְשׁוּעָתִי לְדוֹר דּוֹרִים

Is 51[8] (‖ לעולם) **c.** apparently including both past and future בדור דורים שנותיך ψ 102[25], בכל דור ודר ψ 145[13], לדור ודור La 5[19]. **2.** of men living at a particular time (period, age), *generation*, as transitory דור הלך ודור בא Ec 1[4] specific **a.** in the present, and (or) the past Gn 7[1] (J) Ex 1[6] (P) Nu 32[13] (JE) Dt 1[35] 2[14] Ju 2[10 10] Is 53[8] (cf. Che crit n.) Je 2[31]; also ψ 95[10] Jb 8[8] Is 41[4]. **b.** Ju 3[2] (present & future); cf. pl. דרתיו Gn 6[9] (i.e. his own gen. and those immediately contiguous, before and after). **c.** esp of a future generation Gn 15[16] (JE), with numeral, cf Dt 23[3 4 9], also Dt 29[21] ψ 48[14] 71[18] 78[4.6] 102[19] 109[13] Jo 1[3] cf ψ 22[31.32] (Che crit n.), of a succession of generations דור לדור ישבח מעשיך ψ 145[4], בכל־דור ודור Est 9[28], usually pl לדרת עולם Gn 9[12] (P), with num לאלף דור ψ 105[8] (‖ עולם) = 1 Ch 16[15] (‖ לעולם); Dt 7[9], v further, of posterity, ארבעה דרות Jb 42[16], usually pl c sf Gn 17[7 9 12] Ex 12[14.17 42] 16[32.33] 27[21] 29[42] 30[8 10.21 31] 31[13 16] 40[15] Lv 3[17] 6[11] 7[36] 10[9] (all P), 17[7] 21[17] 22[3] 23[14 21.31 41.43] 24[3] 25[30] (all H); Nu 9[10] 10[8] 15[14 15.21.23.38] 18[23] 35[29] Jos 22[27 28] (all P) **3.** generation characterized by quality or condition, *class* of men: דור עקש *crooked generation* Dt 32[5] (song) cf. v[20] ψ 78[8.8] Je 7[29], of diff classes of wicked, Pr 30[11 12 13 14] cf ψ 12[8]; of the righteous, as a class ψ 14[5] 24[6] 73[15] (דור בניך) 112[2] (cf 22[31] MT, but < Che joins לדור to v[32] cf supr. sub **2 c**); so also דור אבותיו i e the dead ψ 49[20] (so most; yet v. infr sub **4**) **4.** *dwelling-place, habitation* Is 38[12] cf. דור vb, so Saad Ki Ges De Che RVm (Ew *life* ‖ חיי), so also ψ 49[20] De Witt, cf Che[OP 479].

†II דאר, דור **n.pr.loc.** (Ph דאר; cuneif *Du'ru* KG[121] COT on Jos 17[11]) city in Manasseh, on Mediterr, S of Carmel (9 Roman miles N of Caesarea, cf Lag[Onom 115, 2nd ed 149]), דור Jos 12[23], דאר וב׳ Ju 1[27] 1 Ch 7[29] = דור ובנותיה Jos 17[11], נפת דור Jos 12[23] = נפת דאר 1 K 4[11], נפות דור Jos 11[2] (cf נפה); mod. *Ṭanṭura* (*Tortura*) Wilson[Lands of Bible ii 249] van de Velde[Narrat 1 333] Bd[Pal 238] cf Di Jos 11[2] On (דור) עין־דר v sub עין

†מדורה **n.f.** pile (of wood, etc) מ׳ Ez 24[9], מדרתה אש ועצים הרבה Is 30[33] = *pyre* (so Ges Hi De Che Brd, Ew Di *its circuit, compass*)

†דוש, דיש **vb. tread, thresh** (Ar دَاسَ, As *dâšu*, Impf 1 s. *adîš* Dl[Pr 191] COT[Gloss] Hom[NS 391], cf NH דוש, Aram *id*, ܕܳܫ; v further No[ZMG 1883, 536])—**Qal** *Pf* דש 1 Ch 21[20], ודשתי Ju 8[7]; *Impf* וידש so rd for וידע Ju 8[16] cf. Be Door Bu Vrss, 2 ms תדוש Is 41[15] Hb 3[12], 3 ms. sf. ידושנו Is 28[28], 3 fs sf. תדושה Jb 39[15]; *Imv.* fs דושי Mi 4[13]; *Inf. cstr* לדש 2 K 13[7], לדוש Ho 10[11], sf דושם Am 1[13]; דישו Dt 25[4]; *abs* אדוש Is 28[28] as if fr. אדש cf Kö[i 444]; yet אדש nowhere else & form very possibly textual error, cf Ol[§ 245 k]; *Pt* f. דשא Je 50[11],—*tread on, trample on*, c. acc. Jb 39[15] (beast on eggs, ‖ זור); *thresh*, lit c. acc חטים 1 Ch 21[20] Je 50[11], לחם (*i e.* its material) Is 28[28] (in sim), abs 2 K 13[7] (in sim), Ho 10[11] (metaph. of Ephraim as heifer), *tread* or *thresh* Ju 8[7] *with* (את = *together with*, cf Stu, Ew[§ 284 c] takes as acc, & vb as abbrev. Hiph) *thorns*, קוצים and ברקנים q v.; and also in Ju 8[16] (rd וידש cf. supr.) sq בהם, *with them*, ref to קוצים and ברקנים; fig. of devastation of land Am 1[3] (Gilead), destruction of peoples Hb 3[12] (גוים); espec. Mi 4[13] (abs), where full metaph.; hyperbol of Israel Is 41[15] c acc הרים —**Niph.** *be trampled down*, Pf ונדוש consec Is 25[10] fig., subj Moab; *Inf.* הדוש *ib* (simile, subj. מתבן *straw-heap*, on form cf. Ol[§ 193 a] Ba[NB 156])—**Hoph.** *be threshed, Impf* יודש Is 28[27] (subj קצח).

†דיש **n.m. threshing,** i.e. the process of threshing, Lv 26[5] (H) והשיג לכם ד׳ את־בציר

†[מדשה] **n.f. that which is threshed**, sf מדשתי Is 21[10] (‖ בן־גרני) fig. in address to Israel by prophet.

†I דישן **n.[m.]** a clean animal, 𝔊 πύγαργος cf. 𝔙; hence AV RV & most **pygarg**, a kind of antelope or gazelle, cf Di Lv 11[22]; perh rather **mountain-goat**, Hom[NS 391] cf. Eth. Vrs; only Dt 14[5]—(Hom[l.c.] der. fr. √דוש with kindred meaning of *spring, leap* & comp. As. *daššu*; so already Dl[S1 64])

†II. דישון **n.pr.m. 1.** a son of Seir דשון Gn 36[21] = דישון 1 Ch 1[38]; **2.** a son of Anah & grandson of Seir דשן Gn 36[25] cf. v[30] so also v[26] (for דישן q v.) = דישון 1 Ch 1[41.41.42], cf. also foll.

†דישן **n.pr.m.** a son of Seir דישן Gn 36[21] (𝔊 Ῥισών; so v[28.30] cf Di) 1 Ch 1[38]; (v[42] rd. דישון q.v) Gn 36[26] (rd. דישון 𝔊 𝔖 𝔙 Ol Di) v[30] דישן Gn 36[28].

דחה **vb. push, thrust** (NH *id*, Aram דחי, דחא, ܕܚܐ; cf also Ar. دَحَا, *spread, extend*, also *throw, propel*)—**Qal** *Pf.* 2 ms. sf דחיתני ψ 118[13], *Inf cstr.* לדחות ψ 140[5]; *abs.* דחה ψ 118[13]; *Pt. act.* דחה ψ 35[5] (rd דחם 𝔊 De Che); *pass* f. הדחויה ψ 62[4],—*push*, דחה דחה *push*

violently fig. c. acc. ψ 118[13] sq. cl. of purpose לִנְפֹּל, cf. לִדְחוֹת פעמי ψ 140[5] (Che *trip up my feet*), & ψ 35[5] (transp. דחה with רדפם v[6] and rd. דֹּחָם 𝔊; cf. יְהִי־דרכם חשך וַחֲלַקְלַקֹּת v[a], and Je 23[12]); *pushed in* (Che), in sim., pt. pass., said of גָּדֵר *wall* ψ 62[4] (|| קיר נטוי). **Niph.** *Impf.* יִדָּחֶה Pr 14[32]; (3 mpl. יִדַּחוּ Je 23[12] is fr. דחח, if rightly pointed; נִדְחֵי Is 11[12] 56[8] ψ 147[2], v. sub נדח);—*be thrust* or *cast down*, fig. of wicked Pr 14[32], cf. ψ 35[6] supr. **Pu.** *Pf.* 3 *pl.* דֹּחוּ ψ 36[13] *they are thrust down* (|| לא יכלו קום & נפלו).

†[דְּחִי] **n.[m.]** stumbling, הִצַּלְתָּ . . . רַגְלַי מִדֶּחִי ψ 56[14] = 116[8].

†מִדְחֶה **n.m.** means or occasion of stumbling, Pr 26[28] פֶּה־חָלָק יַעֲשֶׂה מ׳ || לְשׁוֹן־שֶׁקֶר יִשְׂנָא דַכָּיו).

[דָּחַח] **vb.** only **Niph.** *Impf.* 3 mpl. יִדַּחוּ (Kö[i. 377]) Je 23[12] *they shall be thrust down*, fig., of wicked; rd. perh. יִדָּחוּ, fr. דחה q. v.

דחן (√ of following; perh. cf. Ar. دَخَنَ *smoke arose*, hence *become dusky, dingy, inclining to black*).

†דֹּחַן **n.m.** millet (NH דּוֹחַן, Aram. דּוּחִינָא), Ez 4[9] in the series חִטִּין וּשְׂעֹרִים וּפוֹל וַעֲדָשִׁים וְד׳ וְכֻסְּמִים ד׳ v. Löw[72].

†[דָּחַף] **vb.** drive, hasten (late) (NH *id.*, Aram. דְּחַף)—**Qal** *Pt. pass.* pl. דְּחוּפִים of runners Est 3[15] 8[14] (|| מְבֹהָלִים). **Niph.** *Pf. hasten one's self, hurry* נִדְחַף לָצֵאת Est 6[12]; נִדְחַף אֶל־ 2 Ch 26[20] (|| בהל).

†[מַדְחֵפָה] **n.f.** thrust, ψ 140[12] יְצוּדֶנּוּ לְמַדְחֵפֹת (*evil*) *shall hunt him with thrust upon thrust* (Che, cf. De).

†[דָּחַק] **vb.** thrust, crowd, oppress (NH *id.*, Ar. دَحَقَ *drive away, remove*, Aram. דְּחַק, ܕܚܩ)—**Qal** *Impf.* יִדְחָקוּן *thrust, crowd*, of locusts in swarm Jo 2[8]; *Pt. act.* pl. sf. לֹחֲצֵיהֶם וְדֹחֲקֵיהֶם Ju 2[18] (because of) *them that maltreated and oppressed them.*

†דַּי **subst.** sufficiency, enough (NH, but not known in other cogn. languages)—cstr. דֵּי, with sf. (v. infr.) דַּיֶּךָּ, דַּיָּם:—**1.** absol. thrice only Mal 3[10] I will pour you out a blessing עַד־בְּלִי־דָי until there is not *sufficiency*, i.e. until my abundance can be exhausted, or, as this can never be, for ever (cf. ψ 72[7]), Est 1[18] וּכְדַי בִּזָּיוֹן וָקָצֶף and (there will be) *as enough* (i.e. in plenty) contempt and wrath, 2 Ch 30[3] לְמַדַּי = לְמַה־דַּי for what was *sufficient*. With a gen. of the person or thing *for* which anything suffices: Ex 36[5] מִדֵּי הָעֲבֹדָה (more) than *enough for* the work, Lv 5[7] and if his hand do not reach (if he do not command) דֵּי שֶׂה *enough for* (i.e. to buy) a lamb, 12[8] 25[28] דֵּי הָשִׁיב לוֹ *enough for* recovering it, Dt 15[8] דֵּי מַחְסֹרוֹ *enough for* his need, Is 40[16.16]. With suff. Pr 25[16] אֱכֹל דַּיֶּךָּ eat *that which is sufficient for* thee; דַּיָּם Ex 36[7] Je 49[9] Ob v[5]. Once with gen. of the thing which is sufficient, Pr 27[27] דֵּי חֲלֵב עִזִּים *enough of* goats' milk.

2. Combined with בְּ, כְּ, and esp. מִן (דֵּי) דַּי has a tendency to form compound prepositions, used idiomatically in certain applications:— **a.** בְּדֵי (α) *for* (the בְּ *pretii*) *what suffices for:* Na 2[13] the lion tare in pieces בְּדֵי גֹרוֹתָיו *for the need of* his whelps (|| לְלִבְאֹתָיו; but ? כְּדֵי, v. **b**); iron. Hb 2[13] Je 51[58] the peoples labour בְּדֵי־אֵשׁ *for* fire (only to satisfy the fire), and the nations weary themselves בְּדֵי־רִיק *for* what is empty. (β) *in the abundance of*, i.e. *as often as* Job 39[25] בְּדֵי שׁוֹפָר *in the abundance of* the trumpet, i.e. as often as the trumpet sounds (מִדֵּי elsewhere in this sense). **b.** כְּדֵי *according to the sufficiency*, or *abundance, of* Lv 25[26] and find כְּדֵי גְאֻלָּתוֹ *acc. to the sufficiency of* his redemption, i.e. *as much as* it demands, Dt 25[2] Ne 5[8] כְּדֵי בָנוּ (*st. c.* before בְּ: Ges[§ 130, 1]) 'quantum in nobis erat,' after our ability, Ju 6[5] they came כְּדֵי אַרְבֶּה לָרֹב *acc. to the abundance of* the locust in multitude (for which כְּאַרְבֶּה לָרֹב would ordinarily be said: cf. 7[12]). **c.** מִדֵּי *out of the abundance of*, hence *as often as*;—(α) sq. inf. 1 S 1[7] מִדֵּי עֲלֹתָהּ = *as often as* she went up, 18[30] 1 K 14[28] (= 2 Ch 12[11]) 2 K 4[8] Is 28[19] מִדֵּי עָבְרוֹ *as often as* it passeth over, Je 31[20]; (β) sq. subst., Je 48[27] מִדֵּי דְבָרֶיךָ בּוֹ *as often as* thy words (are) of him; and in the idiom. phrases מִדֵּי שָׁנָה בְּשָׁנָה = *yearly* (a combination of מִדֵּי שָׁנָה and שָׁנָה בְשָׁנָה: v. sub שָׁנָה) 1 S 7[16] (v. Dr) Zc 14[16] 2 Ch 24[5]; and מִדֵּי חֹדֶשׁ בְּחָדְשׁוֹ Is 66[23] *as often as* month (comes) in its month (i.e. in its own time: חֹדֶשׁ made more precise by the add. of בְּחָדְשׁוֹ; cf. the phrase דְּבַר יוֹם בְּיוֹמוֹ): so מִדֵּי שַׁבָּת בְּשַׁבַּתּוֹ *ib.*; (γ) as conj., with the finite verb (אֲשֶׁר being understood: cf. בַּעֲבוּר etc.), Je 20[8] מִדֵּי אֲדַבֵּר *as often as* I speak.

†דִּי זָהָב **n.pr.loc.** appar. on border of Moab Dt 1[1] (𝔊 Καταχρύσεα).

†דִּיבֹן, דִּיבוֹן **n.pr.loc.**—**1.** city in Moab (MI[21.28] דיבן, cf ib[1] adj gent הדיבני)—דיבן Nu 21[30] 32[3.34] (built up or at by Gad) Is 15[2], in territory of Gad, hence דִּיבֹן גָּד Nu 33[45.46] (cf on these vv. & 32[34] MI[10 f.]), also דיבון Jos 13[9.17] Je 48[22], יֹשֶׁבֶת בַּת דִּיבוֹן Je 48[18];=דימון Is 15[9], vid also מֵי דִימוֹן v[9]=Arnon, cf Che & Hpt ZA 1887, 268,—mod *Dîbân*, north of Arnon, cf Seetzen Reisen i 409 Tristr Land of Moab 132 ff Bd Pal 103 **2.** דיבן Ne 11[25] place in Judah, toward south =דימונה Jos 15[22], cf Hpt l c, conject. by Kn Ke (cf Di) to be *Tell ed Dheib* (van de Velde Mem 252) called also Ehdeib (Rob BR ii 102)

דַּיָג דיג v. sub דגה

דַּיָּה v sub דאה

דיר v sub דוה

†דִּימוֹן **n.pr.loc.**=דיבון **1,** q v

†דִּימוֹנָה **n pr.loc.**=דיבון **2,** q v

†דִּין **vb.** judge (cf Ar دَانَ intrans *to be obedient, submissive,* trans *requite, compensate, rule, govern,* دِينٌ *obedience, abasement, recompense,* دَيَّانٌ *requiter, governor,* مَدِينَةٌ *city,* As *dânu*, Impf *idin, judge* Asrb Ann x 120 Dl HA 49, Aram דִּין, ܕܳܢ *judge, exercise judgment, punish,* דַּיָּנָא, ܕܰܝܳܢܳܐ *judge,* דִּינָא, ܕܺܝܢܳܐ *judgment,* ܡܕܺܝܢ݈ܬܳܐ *city,*—on √ע״י v. No ZMG 1883 533), syn שָׁפַט—**Qal** *Pf* דָּן Je 22[16], etc ; *Impf* יָדִין Gn 49[16] + 9 t, יָדוֹן Gn 6[3] cf. infr, etc, *Imv* דִּין Pr 31[9] Jb 35[14], דִּינוּ Je 21[12], *Inf.* לָדִין ψ 50[4] + 2 t, *Pt* דָּן Gn 15[14] Je 30[13];—**1.** *act as judge, minister judgment,* of God יָדִין עַמּוֹ Dt 32[36] (poet = ψ 135[14]) ψ 50[4], דין עמים ψ 7[9] 96[10] Is 3[13], יָדִין לְאֻמִּים בְּמֵישָׁרִים ψ 9[9], Messianic king ψ 72[2] **2.** *plead the cause,* **a.** of men, usu c. acc cogn, אֵין־דָּן דִּינֵךְ *there is none to plead thy cause* Je 30[13]; ד׳ דין יתום *plead cause of orphan* Je 5[28]; ד׳ דין עני ואביון Je 22[16], also, acc cogn om., Pr 31[9] **b.** of God, דָּנַנִּי אֱלֹהִים *God has pled my cause* Gn 30[6] (E) **3.** *execute judgment, vindicate,* in battle against enemies, דָּן יָדִין עַמּוֹ *Dan will judge* (vindicate as a warrior) *his people* (v. Di) Gn 49[16] (poet), the Messianic king בגוים ψ 110[6], God, בִּגְבוּרָתְךָ תְדִינֵנִי *in thy might judge me* (vindicate me) ψ 54[3] **4.** *execute judgment, requite,* of man, דִּינוּ לַבֹּקֶר מִשְׁפָּט *execute judgment every morning* Je 21[12], of God, upon Egypt Gn 15[14] (E), עמים by means of powers of nature Jb 36[31], אפסי ארץ 1 S 2[10] (poet) **5.** *govern,* אַתָּה תָּדִין אֶת־בֵּיתִי *thou shalt govern my house* Zc 3[7]. **6.** לֹא־יוּכַל לָדִין עִם *he cannot contend with* one mightier than he Ec 6[10]. **Niph.** *Pt* וַיְהִי כָל־הָעָם נָדוֹן בְּכָל־שִׁבְטֵי יִשְׂרָאֵל *and all the people were at strife throughout all the tribes of Israel* 2 S 19[10] (reciprocal, cf. Dr)

Note—לֹא־יָדוֹן רוּחִי בָאָדָם לְעֹלָם Gn 6[3] is difficult. (1) 𝔊𝔙𝔖 Onk rd ידור or (Kue) ילון *abide in, dwell,*—*My spirit will not abide in man for ever,* this best suits the context, but ידור, as Aramaism, is dub. (2) Kn De Schr RVm render *rule in,* supported by Zc 3[7] only (3) Thes Ew Di render *be humbled in,* sustained by Ar. usage, but not by Heb (4) *strive with* of AV RV (cf. **6** supr.) is hardly justified.

†דִּין **n.[m.]** judgment—Dt 17[8] + 16 t ; sf דִּינִי ψ 9[5], דִּינֵךְ Je 30[13],—**1.** כסא דין *throne of judgment* Pr 20[8], משמים השמעת דין *from heaven thou didst cause judgment to be heard* ψ 76[9]. **2.** *cause, plea,* בין דין לדין *between plea and plea* Dt 17[8]; דין דין *plead a cause* Je 5[28] 22[16] 30[13], עשה דין *maintain the cause* ψ 9[5] 140[13], ידע דין *consider the cause* Pr 29[7], דין לפניו *the cause is before him* Jb 35[14], שנה דין *change the cause* Pr 31[5], לְהַטּוֹת מִדִּין דַּלִּים Is 10[2]; דין יתום Je 5[28]; דין כל בני חֲלוֹף Pr 31[8]. **3.** *judgment, condemnation,* דין רשע *judgment of the wicked* Jb 36[17], דין ומשפט *judgment and justice* v[17]. **4.** *strife,* דין וקלון Pr 22[10] (*legal strife, law-suit* Str). **5.** *government,* דת ודין *law and government* Est 1[13].

Note—לְמַעַן תֵּדְעוּן שַׁדִּין Jb 19[29] is variously explained. (1) AV RV *that ye may know there is a judgment* follow Aq Symm Theod, so De Da, in interpreting ש relative + דין *judgment,* but ש is unknown to the dialect of Job and דין is used only in Elihu section. (2) 𝔊 rds. ὕλη, or ἰσχύς (i e. שַׁדַּי (cf. 29[5] 𝔊)? or שׁד?), & Qr שַׁדּוּן, indicating ancient uncertainty and a corrupt text (3) Ew Di rd שַׁדַּי *the Almighty,* which accords with usage of Job. (4) Siegf כי שֵׁדָיו (doubtfully)

†דִּינָה **n.pr.f.** daughter of Jacob Gn 30[21] 34[1.3.5.13.25.26] 46[15]

†דָּן **n.pr.m.** (*judge*)—**1.** son of Jacob and Bilhah Gn 30[6] 35[25] Ex 1[4] Jos 19[47] Ju 18[29] 1 Ch 2[2] **2.** the tribe of Dan, מַטֵּה דָן Ex 31[6] 35[34] 38[23] Lv 24[11] Nu 1[39] 13[12] Jos 21[5.23] (all P), בְּנֵי דָן Gn 46[23] Nu 1[38] 2[25] 7[66] 10[25] 26[42] 34[22] Jos 19[40.47.47.48] (all P) Ju 1[34] 18[2.16.22.23.25.26.30], מַחֲנֵה דָן Nu 2[25.31] (P)—on Ju 13[25] 18[12] v. מַחֲנֶה, מִשְׁפַּחַת דָּן Nu 26[42] (P), דָּן alone in poetry Gn 49[16.17] Dt 33[22.22] Ju 5[17], elsewhere Nu 1[12] (P) Dt 27[13] 1 Ch 27[22] 2 Ch 2[13] Ez 48[1.2.32] **3.** a city on northern frontier of

Israel at one of the sources of the Jordan, originally לַיִשׁ Ju 18[29] (cf v[7]); = לֶשֶׁם Jos 19[47]; captured by a colony of Danites; named Dan, and made a sacred place with rites of worship that lasted until the exile (Ju 18[30]); = *Tell el Kâḍî*, Rob[BR iii 351 358] Bd[Pal 265]. This place is frequently referred to: Gn 14[14] Dt 34[1] 1 K 12[29.30] 15[20] 2 K 10[29] 2 Ch 16[4] Je 4[15] 8[16] Am 8[14]; rd. also וּבְדָן for וְכֵן 2 S 20[18] 𝔊 Ew We cf. Dr; and v. the phrase מִדָּן וְעַד־בְּאֵר שָׁבַע Ju 20[1] 1 S 3[20] 2 S 3[10] 17[11] 24[2.15] 1 K 5[5], given by Chr מִבְּאֵר שֶׁבַע וְעַד־דָּן 1 Ch 21[2] 2 Ch 30[5]. (Ez 27[19] v. ודן)

Note — דָּנָה יַעַן 2 S 24[6]. As no such place is known, the text is usually regarded as corrupt, and, 𝔊 being uncertain, is variously changed (1) דָּנָה יַעַר *to Dan in the wood*, Thes after 𝔙 *silvestria*. (2) דָּנָה ועיון (וַיָּסֹבּוּ) *to Dan and Ijon* Klo (cf. 1 K 15[20]). (3) דָּן וּמִדָּן (סָבְבוּ) We Dr cf. 𝔊.

†דָּנִי **adj.gent.** alw c art as n pr. coll. מִשְׁפַּחַת הַדָּנִי 1 Ch 12[35]; שֵׁבֶט הַדָּנִי Ju 18[1.30], Ju 13[2] 18[11].

†דַּיָּן **n.m.** judge 1 S 24[16], cstr. דַּיַּן ψ 68[6].

דָּנִאֵל, later דָּנִיֵּאל **n.pr m.** (cf. Ew[§ 45 d]; *El is my judge;* on a possible connexion with Zend *dânu, wise*, or *wisdom* cf Che[OP 107], v. Palm. דנאל Vog[93])—**1.** son of David 1 Ch 3[1], דָּנִיֵּאל, but dub cf Che[OP 108], 𝔊 Δαμνιηλ, 𝔊L & Codd. Δαλουια; ‖ 2 S 3[3] כִלְאָב, 𝔊 Δαλουια, Klo[Sm] prop. דִּדְיָה, & in Ch דִּדְיָאֵל, but grounds precarious. **2.** דָּנִיֵּאל, priest of the line of Ithamar Ezr 8[2] Ne 10[7] **3.** דָּנִאֵל a great sage Ez 28[3]; classed with Noah and Job as models of righteousness Ez 14[14.20]; perh. the same as **4.** דָּנִיֵּאל, one of the noble young men taken into captivity by Nebuchadrezzar acc. to Dn 1[1-6], the hero of the book of Daniel, Dn 1[6] + 22 t. (also frequently in Aramaic section)

†I. מָדוֹן **n.m.**[Pr 22, 10] strife, contention—ψ 80[7] + 9 t.; pl מְדָיָנִים Pr 18[18], מִדְיָנִים Pr 18[19] + 7 t.; contracted into מְדָנִים Pr 6[19] 10[12], מִדְּיָנִים Pr 6[14]; cstr. מִדְיְנֵי Pr 19[13] **1.** *strife, contention*, alm. wholly Pr:—Pr 18[19] 23[29] 26[20]; also 17[14] (‖ רִיב), 22[10] (‖ דִּין וְקָלוֹן); מ׳ יִשָּׂא Hb 1[3] *contention ariseth* (‖ רִיב); שִׁלַּח מ׳ *let loose strife* Pr 6[14] 16[28]; יְגָרֶה מ׳ *he stirreth up strife* 15[18] 28[25] 29[22], note esp אִישׁ מִדְיָנִים 26[21] = *a contentious, quarrelsome man;* oftener אֵשֶׁת מ׳ = *a contentious woman* 21[9] 25[24] 27[15], cf. אשת מ׳ וָכָעַס 21[19] **2.** *object of contention* ψ 80[7], cf. אִישׁ מָדוֹן Je 15[10] (‖ אִישׁ רִיב)—On מָדוֹן 2 S 21[20] Qr, v. I. מִדָּה sub מדד.

†II. מָדוֹן **n.pr.loc.** a royal city of the Canaanites Jos 11[1] 12[19], 𝔊 Μαρρων, Μαδων, Λαμορων; = *Madîn*, close to *Ḥattîn*, Survey[i 365], dub.; a village *Maron* lies 2 hours WSW fr. Kedesh, van de Velde[Mem 146], cf Di

†מְדָן **n.pr.m.** son of Abraham and Keturah Gn 25[2] 1 Ch 1[32]

מִדְיָן **n.pr.m.** **1.** son of Abraham and Keturah Gn 25[2.4] (J) 1 Ch 1[32.33]. **2.** an Arabian tribe Gn 36[35] (= 1 Ch 1[46]) Nu 31[3.3.7.8.8.9] (P) Ju 6–9 (31 t); having a כֹּהֵן (as chieftain?) Ex 2[16] 3[1] 18[1] (E); זקנים Nu 22[4.7] (JE), נשׂיא(ים) Nu 25[18] (P) Jos 13[21] (P), שׂרים Ju 7[25] 8[3], מלכים Nu 31[8.8] Ju 8[5 12 26]; בִּכְרֵי מִדְיָן *dromedaries of Midian* Is 60[6]; יוֹם מִדְיָן *day of Midian* Is 9[3] (the victory over Midian Ju 7–8) cf 10[26] ψ 83[10]. **3.** אֶרֶץ מִדְיָן *the land of Midian* Ex 2[15] (E) Hb 3[7], מִדְיָן Ex 4[19] (J) Nu 25[15] (P) 1 K 11[18], land on Ælanitic gulf (where Arab geographers still place town مدين) Cf. on Midian, Glaser[Skizze ii. 447 ff.], Hom Aufsätze i (1892), 4 f.

†מִדְיָנִי **adj.gent.** Midianite—Nu 10[29] (J), f. מִדְיָנִית Nu 25[6 14 15] (P); pl. מִדְיָנִים Gn 37[28] (JE) Nu 25[17] 31[2] (P), מְדָנִים Gn 37[36] (E)

מְדִינָה **n f** province (an Aramaic word, cf. Syr. ܡܕܝܢܬܐ, Ar مَدِينَةٌ *city*)—Est 1[1] + 28 t; pl מְדִינוֹת 1 K 20[14] + 23 t.;—a district of an empire, **1.** districts of realm of Ahab with שרים over them 1 K 20[14 15 17 19] **2.** of the Babylonian empire: Ez 19[8], Dn 8[2] (of Elam); שָׂרָתִי בַּמְּדִינוֹת *princess among the provinces* La 1[1] (of Judea) **3.** of the Persian empire Est 1[1] + oft.; one of which was Palestine, Ne 1[3], the returning exiles, בְּנֵי הַמְּדִינָה *children of the province* Ezr 2[1] Ne 7[6], having רָאשֵׁי הַמְּדִינָה Ne 11[3]. **4.** provinces in general Ec 2[8] 5[7]; בְּמִשְׁמַנֵּי מדינה *in the fat places of the province* Dn 11[24] (fertile regions, prob. Egypt; other trans. vid. in Bev.)

†יָדוֹן **n.pr.m.** a Meronothite, one of the builders of the walls of Jerusalem Ne 3[7]

†דִּיפַת **n.pr.m.** a son of Gomer son of Japhet 1 Ch 1[6], but rd prob. רִיפַת (q. v.); 𝔊 Ἐρειφαθ, Ῥιφαθ, 𝔊L Ῥιφαθ, ‖ Gn 10[3] רִיפַת 𝔊 Ῥιφαθ, Ἐριφαθ

דָּיֵק v sub דוק.

דַּיִשׁ, דִּישׁ, דִּישׁוֹן, דִּישָׁן v. דושׁ

†[דָּכָא] **vb. crush**, poet. (As. *dakû, crush*, Muss-Arnolt[Hbr Oct. 1890, 66]) not in **Qal**;—**Niph.**

Pt. נִדְכָּאִים Is 57[15];—*crushed*, fig. = *contrite ones*. **Pi.** *Pf.* דִּכָּא ψ 143[3]; 2 ms. דִּכֵּאתָ ψ 89[11]; *Impf.* וִידַכֵּא ψ 72[4]; 2 ms. תְּדַכֵּא Pr 22[22] (juss.); יְדַכְּאוּ ψ 94[5], תְּדַכְּאוּ Is 3[15]; sf. וִידַכְּאֵנִי Jb 6[9], יְדַכְּאוּם Jb 4[19]; 2 mpl. וּתְדַכְּאוּנַנִי Jb 19[2] (so Baer, v. his ed. p. 44, cf. Norzi); *Inf.* לְדַכֵּא La 3[34]; *sf.* דַּכְּאוֹ Is 53[10];—*crush*, (fig.) c. acc. one's life to the earth ψ 143[3], Egypt ψ 89[11] (cf. De Che; י׳ subj.), servant of Yahweh Is 53[10] (י׳ subj.), Jb 6[9] וְיֹאֵל אֱלוֹהַּ וִיד׳; oppressor ψ 72[4], God's people ψ 94[5] (‖יְעַנּוּ), Is 3[15], cf. Pr 22[22] illegally in tribunal, La 3[34] ד׳ תחת רגליו (in all human oppressor subj.); *crush me* בְּמִלִּים Jb 19[2] (Job's friends, subj.; ‖ תּוֹגְיוּן נַפְשִׁי); never lit., not even Jb 4[19] (יְדַכְּאוּם, with indef. subj.), for suff. ref. not to בָּתֵּי־חֹמֶר, but rather to שֹׁכְנֵי, i.e. men inhabiting the clay houses, bodies, cf. Di. **Pu.** *Pf.* דֻּכְּאוּ Je 44[10]; *Impf.* יְדֻכָּא Jb 22[9]; *Pt.* מְדֻכָּא Is 53[5], מְדֻכָּאִים Is 19[10];—*crushed*, broken in pieces, shattered Jb 22[9] c. obj. fem. זרועות; Is 19[10] subj. שָׁתוֹת (here metaphor. for nobles); fig. of servant of י׳ Is 53[5]; made humble, contrite Je 44[10]. **Hithp.** *Impf.* יִדַּכְּאוּ Jb 5[4], יִדַּכָּאוּ Jb 34[25];—*must let themselves be crushed*, i.e. maltreated Jb 5[4] (in court בשער, cf. **Pi.** Pr 22[22]); *are crushed* Jb 34[25] (the mighty, by God).

†I. **דַּכָּא** **adj.** contrite (crushed)—דַּכָּא Is 57[15]; דַּכְּאֵי ψ 34[19]—*contrite* Is 57[15] (‖ שְׁפַל־רוּחַ); ד׳ רוּחַ ψ 34[19] (‖ נִשְׁבְּרֵי־לֵב).

†II. **דַּכָּא** **n.[m.]** dust (as pulverized), תָּשֵׁב אֱנוֹשׁ עַד־דַּכָּא ψ 90[3] (on form cf. Ba[NB 143]).

†[**דָּכָה**] **vb.id.** (only ψ);—**Qal** dub.; ודכה (יָשֹׁחַ) ψ 10[10] Kt is rd. as **Qal** *Pf.* וְדָכָה consec. by RobGes Ol De al., i.e. *and he is crushed*, or *and he croucheth* (Qr יִדְכֶּה *Impf.* so AV RV *he croucheth*); others rd. וְדָכָה יָשֹׁחַ (adj. intrans. or passive) *and crushed he sinketh down*, cf. VB Che; possible wd. be יִדְּכֶה Niph. (‖ יָשֹׁחַ and ונפל). **Niph.** *Pf.* וְנִדְכֵּיתִי ψ 38[9]; *Pt.* נִדְכֶּה ψ 51[19];—*be crushed, broken*, of physical distress ψ 38[9] (‖ נְפוּגוֹתִי); *be contrite* (לֵב נִדְכֶּה) ψ 51[19] (‖ נִשְׁבָּר). **Pi.** *Pf.* דִּכִּיתָ ψ 51[10]; sf. דִּכִּיתָנוּ ψ 44[20]; *crush down*, of divine wrath; c. acc. ψ 44[20], and *crush to pieces*, obj. ref. to עצמות, in metaph. ψ 51[10].—דָּכוֹ Nu 11[8] v. דוך.

†[**דֳּכִי**] **n.[m.]** (crushing), crashing, dashing, sf. ישאו נהרות דָּכְיָם ψ 93[3] of ocean (waves).

דכך (√of foll.; cf. Ar. دَكَّ, Aram. דְּכַךְ, NH in deriv.; v. also דכא, דכה).

†**דַּךְ** **adj.** crushed, oppressed—דַּךְ ψ 74[21], דָּךְ ψ 9[10] 10[18]; pl. sf. דַּכָּיו Pr 26[28] (Baer; edd. al. דַּכָּיו)—poet.; always fig., *oppressed, distressed* ψ 9[10], 10[18] (‖ יתום) 74[21] (‖ עָנִי and אביון); Pr 26[28] דַּכָּיו = *those crushed by it* (a lying tongue).

†**דַּכָּה** **n.f.** crushing, פְּצוּעַ־דַּכָּה Dt 23[2] *one wounded by crushing* (viz. of testicles).

דַּל, **דָּל** **n.** *door*, v. sub דלה.

דַּל **adj.** v. sub דלל.

†[**דָּלַג**] **vb.** leap (NH *spring over, skip* (a verse), omit)—**Qal** *Pt.* דּוֹלֵג Zp 1[9] *leap*, c. art. *one leaping* עַל־הַמִּפְתָּן; 𝔊 1 S 5[5] ὑπερβαίνοντες ὑπερβαίνουσιν = דָּלֹג יִדְלְגוּ cf. Dr. **Pi.** *Impf.* יְדַלֵּג Is 35[6]; אֲדַלֶּג־ ψ 18[30] = 2 S 22[30]; *Pt.* מְדַלֵּג Ct 2[8];—*leap, leap over* c. acc. שׁוּר ψ 18[30] = 2 S 22[30]; abs. *leap as the stag*, יְד׳ כָּאַיָּל פִּסֵּחַ Is 35[6]; sq. עַל of locality Ct 2[8] (‖ מְקַפֵּץ).

†**דָּלָה** **vb.** draw (water) (NH *id.*, Aram. דְּלָא, دَلَا; Ar. دَلَا *pull up* bucket; II, IV *let down*; V *hang down*; cf. دَلْوٌ *bucket*; Eth. ደለወ: *weigh*; As. *dalû, draw water*, cf. Dl[§ 108] C Adler PAOS Oct. 1888, xcix.; also *dilûtu, bucket*, Id[lb.], *dalâni* COT[Gloss])—**Qal** *Pf.* דָּלָה Ex 2[19]; *Impf.* 3 ms. sf. יִדְלֶנָּה Pr 20[5]; דַּלְיוּ Pr 26[7] v. infr.; 3 f. pl. וַתִּדְלֶנָה Ex 2[16]; *Inf. abs.* דָּלֹה Ex 2[19];—*draw* (water, but no obj. expr.) Ex 2[6.19.19]; fig. of drawing counsel (עֵצָה) out of heart, c. acc. (sf.) Pr 20[5].—דַּלְיוּ Pr 26[7] is difficult; rd. perh. 3 m. pl. דָּלְיוּ intrans., a lame man's legs *hang down* (helpless) so Ew Sta[§ 413 a]; other views in De Now. **Pi.** *Pf.* 2 ms. sf. דִּלִּיתָנִי ψ 30[2] fig. (cf. Pa. in Syr.) subj. י׳ *thou hast drawn me up* (out of Sheʾôl, cf. v[4]).

†[**דַּל**] **n.[m.]** door (Ph. דל) only fig.: cstr. דַּל שְׂפָתָי ψ 141[3].

†[**דֶּלֶה**] **n.f.** door, only Qr דְּלָתֶךָ (Kt דלתיך) Is 26[20] fig., door of chamber in which people (personified) hides (cf. also דֶּלֶת du.)

†**דְּלִי** **n.[m.]** bucket, כְּמַר מִדְּלִי *like a drop* (hanging) *from a bucket* Is 40[15]; Du. sf. יזל מים מִדָּלְיָו Nu 24[7] cf. Di (on form dolyāw cf. Ew [§ 180 a & Anm. 3], also Sta[§ 52 a]); fig. of Israel's prosperity.

†[**דָּלִיּוֹת**] pl. of [**דָּלִית**] **n.f.** branch, bough, metaph. of Israel under figure of olive tree דָּלִיּוֹתָיו Je 11[16] Ez 17[6.7] (figure of vine); v[23]

(under figure of cedar); 31$^{7.9.12}$ of Asshur as a cedar, דָּלִיּוֹתָיו Ez 19^{11} Isr. as a vine (cf. Low^{65}).

†**דֶּ֫לֶת n.f.** (? **m.**$^{Ne\,13.19}$) **door** (NH *id.*; As *daltu(m)* Strm$^{AV\,1843}$ Schr$^{COT\,Gloss}$, Ph. pl. דלהת CIS$^{1\,7.3}$;—acc to Ba$^{ZMG\,1887,\,607}$ fr. √ידל, As. *edilu, to bolt, bar*)—דָּ֫לֶת (always abs, and c art exc. Ct 8^{9} + Ez 41^{24} but here Co art.) Gn 19^{10} + 18 t.; דָּ֫לֶת Gn 19^{9} Ju 19^{22}; *sf* דַּלְתּוֹ 2 K 12^{10}; Du. דְּלָתַיִם (cf Sta^{§187a}) Dt 3^{5} + 9 t., דְּלָתָ֑יִם Jb 38^{10}; cstr. דַּלְתֵי Jos 2^{19} + 6 t. + Ez 26^{2} Co; *sf.* דְּלָתַי Jb 31^{32}, דְּלָתֶיךָ Zc 11^{1} + Is 26^{20} Kt (cf דְּלָת n f), דְּלָתֶיהָ Jos 6^{26} 1 K 16^{34}, pl דְּלָתוֹת Je 36^{23} + 10 t, cstr. דַּלְתוֹת Ju 3^{23} + 19 t + Ez 26^{2} (Co דלתי); *sf.* דַּלְתֹתַי Pr 8^{34}, דַּלְתוֹתָיו 2 Ch 3^{7} 4^{22}; דלתתיו Ne 3$^{1.3.6.13.14.15}$, דלתותיהם 2 Ch 4^{9}, **1.** *door* of house (disting fr. door-way, cf. 1 K 6^{31} פֶּתַח Gn 19^{6}) Gn 19$^{9.10}$ Ex 21^{6} (all JE) Dt 15^{17} Jos 2^{19} (JE) Ju 11^{31} 19$^{22.27}$ 1 S 21^{14} (דלתות השער) 2 K 4$^{4.5}$ 6$^{32.32}$ Is 57^{8} Jb 31^{32}, so fig of wisdom's house Pr 8^{34} לִשְׁקֹד עַל־דַּלְתֹתַי, partic *doors* of house of 'י 1 S 3^{15} (היכל 'י v^{3}), temple 1 K 6$^{34.34.34}$ 7^{50} 2 K 18^{16} 1 Ch 22^{3} 2 Ch 3^{7} 4^{22} 28^{24} 29^{3} Ne 6^{10} Mal 1^{10}; so of Ezek.'s temple, Ez 41$^{23.24.24.24.24.24.25}$ **2.** *door* of room Ju 3$^{23.24.25}$ 2 S 13$^{17.18}$ 2 K 4^{33} 9$^{3.10}$, esp. *doors* of דביר or ק' קדשים 1 K 6$^{31.32}$ 7^{50} 2 Ch 4^{22} cf. also Ez 41^{23}, also of court עֲזָרָה 2 Ch 4$^{9.9}$, and of porch אוּלָם 2 Ch 29^{7}. **3.** *gates of city* Dt 3^{5} Jos 6^{26} (cf 1 K 16^{34}) Ju 16^{3} 1 S 23^{7} 2 Ch 8^{5} 14^{6} Ne 3$^{1.3.6.13.14.15}$ 6^{1} 7^{1} ('ד then generally distinct fr. שַׁעַר, wh. denotes the whole structure of gate, incl posts, open space, etc., while 'ד is swinging door), 7^{3} 13^{19} (where also sense narrower than ‖ שער) Is 45^{1} (‖ שערים) cf v^{2} and ψ 107^{16}, Je 49^{31} Ez 38^{11}. **4.** in other senses (mostly fig.) door (prob. *lid*) of chest 2 K 12^{10}, aperture of womb Jb 3^{10} (ד' בטני), jaws of crocodile Jb 41^{6} (ד' פניו), lips of man Ec 12^{4}; doors enclosing and shutting off sea Jb 38$^{8.10}$; doors of heaven through wh comes rain ψ 78^{23} (cf אֲרֻבֹּת הַשּׁ' Gn 7^{11}), of column of MS. (from shape) Je 36^{23}; fig of easily accessible woman, Ct 8^{9}; in simile Pr 26^{14}, of Jerus as gate of people Ez 26^{2}, of Lebanon Zc 11^{1}.

†**דְּלָיָה, דְּלָיָהוּ n.pr.m.** (*Yah(u) hath drawn*)—**1.** דְּלָיָהוּ, **a.** a priest, contemp David, 1 Ch 24^{18}. **b.** a prince of Judah, contemp Jerem Je 36$^{12.25}$. **2.** דְּלָיָה, **a.** head of a family contemp. with Zerubb. Ezr 2^{60} = Ne 7^{62}. **b** descendant of Zerubb 1 Ch 3^{24} **c.** father of contemp. of Neh. Ne 6^{10}.

†[**דָּלַח**] **vb. make turbid** (As *dalâḫu, disturb*, Zim$^{BP\,81}$ also in deriv; Pal ℭ דְּלַח fig. *be anxious, fear*, كدر? *turbavit, conturbavit*) —**Qal** *Impf.* 2 ms, וַתִּדְלַח Ez 32^{2}, 3 fs sf תִּדְלָחֵם Ez 32^{13} + v^{13} (Co תרפשם);—*stir up, trouble, make turbid* (always with *feet*) sq מים Ez 32^{2} (‖ תרפס,—ס Baer, and not ש), so 32$^{13a.b}$ (but v^{13b} Co rds תרפש (cf v^{2}) for תדלחם)

†[**דָּלַל**] **vb. hang, be low, languish** (NH Hiph. *thin, thin out* vines, etc; As. *dalâlu, be weak, humble* Zim$^{BP\,74.97}$; Ar. دَلَّ *direct, guide*, دُلَّ *be directed, guided*; دَلْدَلَ *put in motion, commotion*; تَدَلْدَلَ *be in motion, hang, dangle*, also دَلّ *amorous, coquettish, gesture* or *behaviour* of women)—**Qal** *Pf.* דַּלֹּתִי ψ 116^{6}, דַּלּוֹתִי 142^{7}, 1 pl. דַּלּוֹנוּ ψ 79^{8}, דָּֽלֲלוּ Is 19^{6}, דַּלּוּ Is 38^{14} Jb 28^{4} (on דַּלְיוּ Pr 26^{7} cf דָּלָה),—*hang, 'depend,'* Jb 28^{4} (of one descending a miner's shaft ‖ נָעוּ), *be low*, of streams Is 19^{6} (‖ חָרְבוּ); *be low, brought low*, metaph of distress ψ 79^{8} 116^{6} 142^{7}, *languish*, of eyes, *look languishingly* (Che) Is 38^{14} —**Niph.** *Impf.* יִדַּל Is 17^{4}, וַיִּדַּל Ju 6^{6},—*be brought low, laid low* Ju 6^{6} fig. of Israel; Is 17^{4} of glory of Jacob.

†**דַּל adj low, weak, poor, thin** (especially common in Wisd lit. and poet)—דַּל Lv 14^{21} + 8 t, דָּל Ex 23^{3} + 17 t + דָּֽל ψ 82^{3}; דַּלִּים Am 2^{7} + 17 t; דַּלּוֹת Gn 41^{19},—*weak, thin*, of kine Gn 41^{19} (E), of Amnon 2 S 13^{4}; *weak*, of family of Saul 2 S 3^{1} (opp חָזָק) cf Ju 6^{15}; *reduced, poor* (opp. rich) Lv 14^{21} (P) Ru 3^{10} (opp. עָשִׁיר) Je 5^{4} (opp. to הגדולים, v^{5}) Pr 28^{15} Zp 3^{12} (עַם עָנִי וָדָ֑ל), mostly subst., *a poor* (man), *the poor* Ex 23^{3} (JE); opp. to עָשִׁיר Ex 30^{15} (P) Pr 10^{15} 22^{16} 28^{11}, opp הוֹן Pr 19^{4}, ‖ אביון 1 S 2^{8} Jb 5^{16} ψ 72^{13} 82^{4} 113^{7} Pr 14^{31} Is 14^{30} 25^{4} Am 4^{1} 8^{6}; cf. also Jb 20$^{10.19}$ Pr 22^{9} Je 39^{10}; *reduced, weak, helpless* (‖ עני) Jb 34^{28} ψ 82^{3} (‖ also יתום), Pr 22^{22} Is 10^{2} 11^{4} 26^{6} Am 2^{7}; ‖ אלמנה Jb 31^{16}; opp. שׁוֹעַ Jb 34^{19},—cf also ψ 41^{2} Pr 19^{17} 21^{13} 28$^{3.8}$ 29$^{7.14}$.

†I. **דַּלָּה n.f.** coll, **hair, thrum** (both from hanging down)—דַּלָּה Is 38^{12}, cstr. דַּלַּת Ct 7^{6},—*hair*, ד' ראשך Ct 7^{6}; *thrum* (threads of warp hanging in loom) in sim. of premature death מִדַּלָּה יְבַצְּעֵנִי Is 38^{12}.

†II [**דַּלָּה**] **n.f. the poor**—cstr. דַּלַּת Je 40^{7} + 2 t, pl דַּלּוֹת Je 52$^{15.16}$;—*the poor* (coll, weak, helpless ones) Je 40^{7} 2 K 24^{14} 25^{12} (in ‖ Je 52^{16}, as also v^{15}, MT has strangely the pl.)

†דְּלִילָה **n.pr.f.** **Delila**, Philistine woman, mistress of Samson Ju $16^{4.6.10.12.13.18}$.

†דִּלְעָן **n.pr.loc.** a city of Judah, Jos 15^{38}.

†[דָּלַף] **vb. drop, drip** (WisdLt.) (NH *id.* (זלף more common), דֶּלֶף *trough*, etc., Aram. דְּלַף, ܕܠܰܦ, *drip*)—**Qal** *Pf.* 3 fs. אֶל־אֱלוֹהַּ דָּלְפָה עֵינִי Jb 16^{20} i.e. weeps (*drops* in tears); דָּלְפָה נַפְשִׁי מִתּוּגָה ψ 119^{28} i.e. weeps (itself away Che cf. De); *Impf.* בְּשִׁפְלוּת יָדַיִם יִדְלֹף הַבָּיִת׃ Ec 10^{18} *the house drips*, i.e. leaks, because cracks are not mended.

†דֶּלֶף **n.m. a dropping** (of rain, cf. Wetzst $^{ZPV\ xiv.\ 1891,5}$), fig. דֶּלֶף טֹרֵד מִדְיְנֵי אִשָּׁה Pr 19^{13} etc.; ד׳ טוֹרֵד בְּיוֹם סַגְרִיר וְאֵשֶׁת מִדְוָנִים נִשְׁתָּוָה׃ Pr 27^{15}.

†דַּלְפוֹן **n.pr.m.** a son of Haman, Est 9^{7}.

†[דָּלַק] **vb. burn** (intrans.), **hotly pursue** (NH *id.*, Aram. דְּלַק, ܕܠܰܩ all intrans. *burn, kindle;* Hiph., Aph. transitive)—**Qal** *Pf.* 2 ms. דָּלַקְתָּ Gn 31^{36}; 3 mpl. וְדָלְקוּ consec. Ob^{18}; sf. דְּלָקֻנִי La 4^{19}; *Impf.* יִדְלַק ψ 10^{2}; *Inf. cstr.* דְּלֹק 1 S 17^{53}; *Pt. act.* pl. דֹּלְקִים ψ 7^{14} Pr 26^{23};—**1.** *burn,* וְדָלְקוּ בָהֶם Ob^{18} (fig. of Isr. ravaging among Edomites, ‖ וַאֲכָלוּם; on construction c. בְּ cf. 2 K 17^{25}); also in חִצָּיו לְדֹלְקִים יִפְעָל ψ 7^{14} *his arrows he maketh burning ones* (subj. God) RV De Che al.; & שְׂפָתַיִם דֹּלְקִים Pr 26^{23} *burning* (*fervent*) *lips* (opp. לֵב רָע). **2.** *hotly pursue* Gn 31^{36} (E; sq. אַחֲרֵי) 1 S 17^{53} (sq. id.); ψ 10^{2} La 4^{19} (both sq. acc.) **Hiph.** *Impf.* sf. יַדְלִיקֵם Is 5^{11}; *Imv.* הַדְלֵק Ez 24^{10};—*inflame,* c. acc., subj. wine Is 5^{11}; *kindle* obj. הָאֵשׁ Ez 24^{10}.

†דַּלֶּקֶת **n.f. inflammation,** Dt 28^{22}.

דֶּלֶת v. sub דלה.

†דָּם $_{360}$ **n.m.** $^{Gn\ 9,6}$ **blood** (NH *id.*, Ar. دَمٌ, Eth. ደም: As. *damu* Nor^{239} Zim$^{BP\ 72,76}$; Aram. דַּם, דְּמָא, ܕܡܳܐ, (ܕܡܐ)—abs. ד׳ Gn 37^{22} + 154 t.; cstr. דַּם Gn 9^{6} + 62 t.; sf. דָּמִי 1 S 26^{20} + 3 t.; דָּמְךָ 2 S 1^{16} (Qr; Kt דמיך) + 4 t.; דָּמֵךְ Ez 16^{22} + 3 t.; דָּמוֹ Gn 9^{4} + 30 t.; דָּמָהּ Lv $4^{30.30}$ + 11 t.; דִּמְכֶם Gn 9^{5}; דָּמָם Lv 16^{27} + 11 t.; pl. דָּמִים Ex 4^{25} + 35 t.; cstr. דְּמֵי Gn 4^{10} + 18 t.; sf. דָּמֶיךָ 2 S 1^{16} Kt (Qr דָּמְךָ); דָּמַיִךְ Ez $16^{6.6.6.9}$; דָּמָיו Lv 20^{9} + 3 t.; דָּמֶיהָ Lv 12^{7} + 2 t.; דְּמֵיהֶם Lv 20^{11} + 5 t.;—**1.** *blood* of man or animal, = the life (נֶפֶשׁ) Gn 9^{4} (P) Dt 12^{23} Lv $17^{14.14}$ (H); cf. נֶפֶשׁ הַבָּשָׂר בַּדָּם הִוא v^{11} (H) & דִּמְכֶם לְנַפְשֹׁתֵיכֶם Gn 9^{5} (P); see also ψ 72^{14} וְיֵיקַר דָּמָם בְּעֵינָיו; hence blood of animals not to be eaten Lv 3^{17} $7^{26.27}$ (all P) $17^{10.10.12.12.14}$ 19^{26} (all H) Dt $12^{16.23}$ 15^{23} 1 S $14^{32.33.34}$ Ez 33^{25} (cf. RS$^{K\ 310}$), but to be poured out & covered with dust Lv 17^{13} (cf. RS$^{Sem.\ i.\ 216\ f.}$). **2.** usually blood become visible, **a.** as from a wound ד׳ הַמַּכָּה 1 K 22^{35} (cf. חֲתַן דָּמִים Ex $4^{25.26}$ v. infr. **h**); licked by dogs 1 K $21^{19.19}$ 22^{38} Ez 32^{6}; from the nose Pr 30^{33}; bloody issue of a woman Lv 15^{19} cf. v^{25}; pl. דְּמֵי טָהֳרָה $12^{4.5}$, & מְקֹר דָּמֶיהָ v^{7} (all P) 20^{18} (H); blood in which child welters Ez $16^{6.6.22}$ + v^{6} (del. AB𝔊 Co al.); of goat Gn 37^{31} (JE); of slain bird Lv $14^{6.51.52}$. **b.** oft. obj. of שָׁפַךְ *spill, shed* Gn 9^{6} (P) 37^{22} (E) Nu 35^{33} (P) Lv 17^{4} (H) Dt 21^{7} 1 S 25^{31} 1 K 18^{28} 2 K 21^{16} 24^{4} 1 Ch 22^{8} Ez 16^{38} $22^{4.6.9.12.27}$ 23^{45} 33^{25} 36^{18} (del. B Co) Pr 1^{16}; also ψ 79^{3} שָׁפְכוּ דָמָם כַּמַּיִם; שֹׁפֵךְ דָּם *a blood-shedder* Ez 18^{10}; עִיר שֹׁפֶכֶת דָּם Ez 22^{3} cf. v^{4} (also 1 K 2^{31} Je $22^{3.17}$ 1 Ch 22^{8} 28^{3} Pr 6^{17} La 4^{13}); less oft. subj. of pass. נִשְׁפַּךְ, שָׁפוּךְ, etc. Gn 9^{6} Nu 35^{33} (both P) Dt 19^{10} Zp 1^{17} ψ 79^{10}. **c.** דַּם חָלָל Dt 32^{42} (song) *blood of slain;* ד׳ חֲלָלִים 2 S 1^{22} so Nu 23^{24} (JE), obj. of שָׁתָה, of Isr. under fig. of lion; cf. also Ez $39^{17.18.19}$, & 2 S 23^{17} = 1 Ch 11^{19} (דַּם הָאֲנָשִׁים hyperbol. for imperilled life); as food of young eagles Jb 39^{30}. **d.** oft. of *innocent blood,* i.e. blood shed with injustice & cruelty, דָּם נָקִי Dt $21^{8.9}$ 1 S 19^{5} 2 K 21^{16} 24^{4} ψ 94^{21} 106^{38} cf. v^{38} Pr 6^{17} Is 59^{7} Je 7^{6} 22^{3} (also 26^{15}); דָּם נָקִיא Jo 4^{19} Jon 1^{14}; also in cstr. דַּם נָקִי Dt 19^{10}; cf. 27^{25} לְהַכּוֹת נֶפֶשׁ דַּם נָקִי; ד׳ נ׳ Dt 19^{13} Je 22^{17} 2 K 24^{4}; דַּם הַנָּקִי Je 19^{4}; דַּם נְקִיִּים Je 2^{34}; further דַּם נַפְשׁוֹת אֶבְיוֹנִים נְקִיִּים La 4^{13}; דַּם צַדִּיקִים 1 K 2^{31}; in ψ 30^{10} דְּמֵי חִנָּם *my death* (‖ רִדְתִּי אֶל־שַׁחַת). **e.** *avenger of blood* גֹּאֵל הַדָּם Nu $35^{19.21.24.25.27.27}$ (all P); Dt $19^{6.12}$ Jos $20^{3.5.9}$ 2 S 14^{11}. **f.** pl. דָּמִים of abundance, blood in quantity, hence sts. of blood shed by rude violence, and of blood-stains;—Gn $4^{10.11}$ (J) as crying from the ground for vengeance (cf. RS$^{Sem.\ i.\ 397}$), comp. also 2 S 3^{28} 16^{8} 2 K $9^{26.26}$; Is 1^{15} 9^{4} 26^{21} Ez $16^{6.6.6.9.36}$ (on txt. of v^{6} vid. supr.) Zc 9^{7} 2 Ch 24^{25}; דְּמֵי אָדָם Hb $2^{8.17}$, and in other connexions; but interchangeably with sg. 2 S 3^{27} 20^{12} 2 K 9^{33} Is $34^{3.6.6.7}$ Ez 21^{37} 22^{13} (pl. Co) $24^{8.8}$ al.; v. esp. אֶרֶץ אַל־תְּכַסִּי דָמִי Jb 16^{18}; דְּמֵי ירושלם *blood-stains of Jerusalem* Is 4^{4}; = slaughter, sg. Gn 37^{26} (J) Je 48^{10} Ez 5^{17} 28^{23} 38^{22} (‖ דֶּבֶר) (‖ id.); דַּם־עֲבָדָיו Dt 32^{43} (song: cf. ψ 79^{10}); pl. דְּמֵי עֲבָדַי 2 K $9^{7.7}$; דְּמֵי יִזְרְעֶאל Ho 1^{4} *bloodshed at Jezreel;* cf. דָּמִים בְּדָמִים נָגָעוּ Ho 4^{2}; דְּמֵי מִלְחָמָה 1 K $2^{5.5}$; in Ez 9^{9} וַתִּמָּלֵא הָאָרֶץ דָּמִים (Baer) rd. חָמָס for דָּמִים v. d. H

Vrss Co Comm.; אָרַב לְדָם *lie in wait for blood* Pr 1^{11} cf v^{18} 12^{6} Mi 7^{2}, דָּמִים of a *plan of murder* Is 33^{15} (obj. of שׁמע); מִשְׁפַּט דָּמִים Ez 7^{23} *bloody crime*, as symbol of oppression, violence Mi 3^{10} (‖ עַוְלָה), Hb 2^{12} (‖ id) **g.** דָּמִים = *guilt of bloodshed, blood-guiltiness* Ex 22^{1}, then more generally, *mortal sin* (RS$^{OTJC\ 417,\ 2nd\ ed\ 441}$, cf. Ez 18^{13}) ψ 51^{16} (cf Ho 12^{15}); also בוא בְדָמִים 1 S 25$^{26.33}$. **h.** pl. also in phrases: חֲתַן דָּמִים *bloody bridegroom* Ex 4$^{25.26}$, also those denoting character, chiefly poet., אִישׁ דָּמִים *bloody man* (sanguinary) 2 S 16^{8} ψ 5^{7} אִישׁ הַדָּמִים 2 S 16^{7}, אַנְשֵׁי דָמִים, ψ 26^{9} 55^{24} 59^{3} 139^{19} Pr 29^{10}; ואל־בית הַדָּמִים *bloody house* 2 S 21^{1} but rd. with 𝔊 We Dr ואל ביתה דמים, *& on his house is blood*; עִיר דָּמִים Na 3^{1}; עִיר הַדָּמִים Ez 22^{2} 24^{6} + v^{9} (del. B Co). **i.** דָּמָיו בּוֹ *his blood is in (upon) him*, he is responsible for his own death Lv 20^{9} cf v$^{11.12.13.16.27}$ (all H), Ez 18^{13} (+ יִהְיֶה); דָּמוֹ בוֹ Ez 33^{5}, דָּמוֹ בְרֹאשׁוֹ Jos 2$^{19.19}$; so with שָׁבוּ 1 K 2^{33}, יִהְיֶה v^{37} Ez 33^{4}, דָּמְךָ עַל רֹאשֶׁךָ 2 S 1^{16}, and הֵשִׁיב י׳ אֶת־דָּמוֹ עַל־רֹאשׁוֹ 1 K 2^{32}, also לֹא תָשִׂים דָּמִים בְּבֵיתֶךָ Dt 22^{8}; and דָּמָם לָשׂוּם עַל אֲבִימֶלֶךְ Ju 9^{24}; נָתַן דָּם עַל (אל) Je 26^{15} Jon 1^{14}; וְהָיָה עָלֶיךָ דָּמִים Dt 19^{10}, v. 2 S 21^{1} supr.; also sg. Ez 22^{4} בְּדָמֵךְ אָשַׁמְתְּ, and as subj of יֵחָשֵׁב לְ *shall be imputed to* Lv 17^{4} (H); אין לו דָּמִים Ex 22^{1} cf. v^{2} (both JE) & (sg.) Nu 35^{27} (P) **j.** of judicial process in case of bloodshed דָּבָר לֹא תַעֲמֹד לְמִשְׁפָּט בֵּין־דָּם לְדָם Dt 17^{8} cf 2 Ch 19^{10}, עַל־דַּם רֵעֶךָ Lv 19^{16} (H) **k.** in phrase *require blood at the hand of*, exact vengeance (for it) from, דָּמוֹ נדרשׁ Gn 9^{5}, דָּרַשׁ דָּמוֹ מִיַּד Ez 33^{6} Gn 42^{22} (E); abs. דורשׁ דמים ψ 9^{13}; אֲבַקֵּשׁ אֶת־דָּמוֹ מִיֶּדְכֶם 2 S 4^{11} cf Ez 3$^{18.20}$ 33^{8}, פָּקַד ד׳ עַל־ Ho 1^{4}, ונקיתי ד׳ Jo 4^{21}; Ez 35$^{6.6.6.6}$; cf. on the other hand אַל־יִפֹּל דָּמִי אַרְצָה מִנֶּגֶד פְּנֵי י׳ 1 S 26^{20} i.e. let it not be unavenged. **l.** of blood as defiling a land Nu 35^{33} (P) cf. ψ 106^{38} (pl בדמים), עֲקֻבָּה מִדָּם Ho 6^{8} of a city *foot-printed* (VB) *with blood*; defiling hands Is 1^{15} 59^{3} La 4^{14} cf Ez 23$^{37.45}$; further, of blood as oppressing one who has shed it עָשֻׁק בְּדַם נָפֶשׁ Pr 28^{17}. **m.** atonement for blood-guilt is expressed by וְנִכַּפֵּר לָהֶם הַדָּם Dt 21^{8} (on form of vb. cf Ges$^{§55.9}$ & Di). **n.** blood (-shedding) as connected with divine wrath וְשָׁפַכְתִּי חֲמָתִי עָלֶיהָ בְּדָם Ez 14^{19}; דַּם חֵמָה וְקִנְאָה Ez 16^{38}; v further אַשְׁכִּיר חִצַּי מִדָּם Dt 32^{42}, cf. Je 46^{10}; cf. also of human vengeance by divine help יִרְחַץ בְּדַם הָרָשָׁע ψ 58^{11}; תִּמְחַץ רַגְלְךָ בְּדָם 68^{24}; note further Is 49^{26} Ez 39^{19} (in both fig. of being drunk with blood); then of simple human vengeance וְהוֹרַדְתָּ אֶת־שֵׂיבָתוֹ בְּדָם שְׁאוֹל 1 K 2^{9}. **o.** of water turned into blood (sg.) in Egypt, by divine power Ex 4^{9} (J) 7$^{17.20}$ (JE) v$^{19.19.21}$ (P) ψ 78^{44} 105^{29}, cf Is 15^{9} & Ez 32^{6}; further, of appearance of blood in sky Jo 3^{3}, & of colour of moon v^{4}, specifically of red colour of water אֲדֻמִּים כַּדָּם 2 K 3^{22} cf v^{23} **3.** blood used with religious significance, **a.** blood of passover-lamb Ex 12$^{7.13.13}$ (all P) v$^{22.22.23}$ (all JE), note also דַּם הַבְּרִית, i.e. blood by which a covenant was ratified Ex 24^{8} (JE) Zc 9^{11} **b.** blood used in ritual, Lv 17^{11} הַדָּם הוּא בַּנֶּפֶשׁ יְכַפֵּר (H); cf. 2 Ch 29^{24}, also Ez 44$^{7.15}$ (both ‖ חֵלֶב), further Lv 1^{5} Is 1^{11} ψ 50^{13}, thrown on altar, vb זָרַק usually c עַל Ex 24^{6} (JE) 29$^{16.20}$ Lv 1$^{5.11}$ 3$^{2.8.13}$ 7$^{2.14}$ 8$^{19.24}$ 9$^{12.18}$ (all P) 17^{6} (H) Nu 18^{17} (P) Ez 43^{18} 2 K 16$^{13.15.15}$ 2 Ch 29$^{22.22.22}$ cf. 30^{16}; sprinkled, vb הִזָּה Lv 5^{9} 16^{19} (both P), sprinkled toward tent of meeting (vb הִזָּה) Nu 19^{4} (P); brought into tent of meeting Lv 4$^{5.16}$ 6^{23} cf. 10^{18} (all P); sprinkled toward the holy of holies (vb הִזָּה) Lv 4$^{6.6.17}$ 16$^{14.14}$ (all P); brought within the veil on day of atonement Lv 16$^{15.15.16}$ (cf v^{14}) v^{27} (all P); thrown on people Ex 24^{8} (JE, זָרַק), sprinkled on priests (הִזָּה) Ex 29^{21} Lv 8^{30} (both P), on garment (in sanctuary, הִזָּה) Lv 6^{20} (P), applied with finger to horns of altar Ex 29^{12} Lv 4$^{7.18.25.30.34}$ 8^{15} 9$^{9.9.9}$ 16$^{18.18}$ (all P; cf also Ez 45^{19}) Ez 43^{20}, applied to tip of right ear of priest Ex 29^{20} Lv 8$^{23.24}$ (all P, also Lv 14$^{14.25}$ P); poured out at base of altar (שָׁפַךְ אֶל־) Ex 29^{12} Lv 4$^{7.18.25.30.34}$ (all P); cf. with מָצָה (Niph) Lv 1^{15} 5^{9}, with יָצַק 8^{15} (all P), half of blood put in basons Ex 24^{6} (JE); blood poured out on altar Dt 12$^{27.27}$; blood of red heifer burned Nu 19^{5} (P), vid. further such terms as דַּם זבחי Ex 23^{18} 34^{25} (both JE) (cf. Dt 12^{27} 2 K 16^{15}); דַּם הַשְּׁלָמִים Lv 7^{33} (P; cf. v^{14}); דַּם חַטַּאת הַכִּפֻּרִים Ex 30^{10} (P) cf Ez 45^{19}; דַּם הָאָשָׁם Lv 14$^{14.17.25.28}$; (v. זֶבַח, שֶׁלֶם, חַטָּאת, אָשָׁם), דַּם־חֲזִיר, *swine's blood*, as heathen offering Is 66^{3}; cf נִסְכֵּיהֶם מִדָּם ψ 16^{4} (v. Che) **4.** fig of wine דַּם־עֲנָבִים Gn 49^{11} (blessing of Jacob ‖ יַיִן); cf. Dt 32^{14} (song) דַּם עֵנָב תִּשְׁתֶּה־חָמֶר—בְּדָמְךָ Ez 19^{10} prob. text. error cf VB, Da prop. ברוּמָה *in her height*

†I דָּמָה vb **be like, resemble** (NH *id*, Aram. דְּמֵי, דְּמָא, ܕܡܐ; cf. דמין, ܕܡܝܐ *price*, Nab דמי *id* (No in Eut$^{Nab.\ Inscr\ p\ 35}$); also ܕܡܘܬܐ, and ܕܡܘܬܐ *likeness* (whence Ar دُمْيَة *image, effigy*, as loan-wd. Fra^{272}) cf דְּמוּת)—**Qal** *Pf.* 3 ms ד׳ Ez 31^{8} ψ 144^{4}; 3 fs דָּמְתָה Ct 7^{8}, 2 ms.

דָּמִיתָ Ez 31$^{2.18}$, 1 s דָּמִיתִי ψ 102^{7}, 3 pl דָּמוּ Ez 31^{8}, 1 pl דָּמִינוּ Is 1^{9}, *Impf* 3 ms יִדְמֶה ψ 89^{7}, 1 pl ונדמה consec Is 46^{5}, *Imv* ms דמה Ct 2^{17} 8^{14}, *Pt* דּוֹמֶה Ct 2^{9},—*be like, resemble*, of external appearance, sq לְ, Ct 7^{8} 2$^{9.17}$ 8^{14}, sq אֶל־ Ez 31$^{8.8.18}$ (all of tree, fig of Pharaoh), of condition or quality sq לְ Is 1^{9} ψ 102^{7} 144^{4}, so מי...ידמה ליהוה ψ 89^{7}, also abs Is 46^{5}, sq אל Ez 31^{2} **Pi.** *Pf* דִּמָּה 2 S 21^{5}, דִּמִּיתָ ψ 50^{21}, דמו דמיתי Nu 33^{56}, Is 14^{24}, sf דמיתיך Ct 1^{9}, 2 S 21^{5}, *Impf* יְדַמֶּה Is 10^{7}, 2 fs תְּדַמִּי Est 4^{13} (juss), אֲדַמֶּה La 2^{13} Ho 12^{11}, 2 mpl תְּדַמְּיוּן Is 40^{18}, sf תדמיוני Is 40^{25} 46^{5},—*liken, compare, imagine, think, devise*,—**1.** *liken*, i.e. *consider to be like, compare*, causat of **Qal**, sq לְ of external appearance Ct 1^{9}, of quality or condition Is 46^{5} (obj י׳) La 2^{13}, sq אֶל of external appearance Is 40$^{18.25}$ (both obj God in ref. to idols), abs *use comparisons* or *similitudes* (parables, symbols, etc.) Ho 12^{11} (subj י׳) **2.** *imagine, form an idea, devise* 2 S 21^{5} (on context cf Dr); *think, intend*, sq Inf Nu 33^{56} (J or H) Ju 20^{5} Est 4^{13}, abs Is 10^{7} cf 14^{24}, *think that*, sq obj cl (Impf without conj) ψ 50^{21}, *think of*, sq acc. ψ 48^{10} **Hithp** *make oneself* or *become like*, *Impf* אֶדַּמֶּה לְעֶלְיוֹן Is 14^{14} *I will make myself like the Most High* (on form cf Ges §54.2).

†**דְּמוּת** **n.f** **likeness, similitude** (mostly late) (acc to Lag$^{BN 12, 147 ff}$ mispunct. for דמות fr. דְּמָוָה, acc to We$^{Prol\ 413,\ Eng\ Tr\ 389}$ an Aram loan-word, but v Di Gn 5^{1}, Dr$^{JPh\ xi\ 216}$ Che$^{OP\ 474}$)—abs ד׳ Is 40^{18} + 3 t, cstr ד׳ Gn 5^{1} + 16 t, sf דמותו Gn 5^{3}, דמותנו 1^{26},—**1.** *likeness, similitude*, of external appearance, chiefly in Ezek. Ez 1^{5} (*likeness*, i.e. something that appeared like) so v^{26} 8^{2} דמות כמראה (אש) (cf Co), 10^{1} כְּמַרְאֵה ד׳ כסא; cf also Dn 10^{16} כדמות בני אָדָם i.e. *one like the sons of man*, *similitude, resemblance* Ez 1$^{5.10.16.22.26}$ 10$^{10.21.22}$, דְּמוּת כְּמַרְאֵה אָדָם 1^{26}, מַרְאֵה ד׳ כְּבוֹד י׳ v^{28}, also 2 K 16^{10} (pattern of altar), 2 Ch 4^{3} (images of oxen), of son in likeness of father Gn 5^{3} (P), so also of man in likeness of God Gn 1^{26} (‖ צֶלֶם) 5^{1} (both P); cf. Is 40^{18} *what* ד׳ *will ye compare to him* (אל) ‖ דִּמָּה q.v. **2.** adverbially, *in likeness of, like as* Is 13^{4} cf Ez 23^{15} & כד׳ ψ 58^{5}—Ez 1^{13} rd. וּבֵינוֹת, v בין and J P Peters$^{JBL\ 1892.\ 40.42}$ On דְּמוּת אֶחָד Ez 1^{16} 10^{10} (apparently masc) cf Thes & Sm who trans *the likeness of one had they all four*, Co rds אחת.

†**[דִּמְיוֹן]** **n.[m.]** **likeness**, דִּמְיֹנוֹ כְּאַרְיֵה ψ 17^{12} *his likeness is as a lion*, i.e. he is like a lion.

†II **[דָּמָה]** **vb. cease, cause to cease, cut off, destroy**—**Qal** *Perf* 1 s. דָּמִיתִי Je 6^{2}, וְדָמִיתִי consec. Ho 4^{5}, *Impf* 3 fs תִּדְמֶה La 3^{49}; 3 fpl juss. תִּדְמֶינָה Je 14^{17},—**1.** intr. *cease* Je 14^{17} (eyes from weeping) La 3^{49} (*id*) **2.** *cause to cease, cut off, destroy*, c acc Israel (under fig of בַּת־צִיּוֹן) Je 6^{2}, (under fig of אִמֶּךָ) Ho 4^{5}. **Niph.** *Pf* נִדְמָה Is 15^{1} +, 3 fs נִדְמְתָה Je 47^{5}, 2 ms נִדְמֵיתָה Ob^{5}, נִדְמֵיתָ Ez 32^{2}, 1 s נִדְמֵיתִי Is 6^{5}, 3 pl. נִדְמוּ Ho 4^{6} +, *Inf abs.* נִדְמֹה Ho 10^{15}; *Pt* נִדְמֶה Ho 10^{7}, *be cut off, destroyed, ruined*, of a city Is 15^{1} (‖ שֻׁדַּד) Je 47^{5}; of people Ho 4^{6} Zp 1^{11} Ob^{5}, of king Ho 10$^{7.15.15}$ cf. Ez 32^{2}; of beasts ψ 49$^{13.21}$; *be ruined, undone*, prophet at sight of Yahweh Is 6^{5}.

†**דֳּמִי** **n.[m.] cessation, pause, quiet, rest**, ד׳ Is 62^{6} + 2 t., cstr דמי Is 38^{10} (but v. infr.), —**1.** *quiet*, in phr אַל־ד׳ לָכֶם Is 62^{6} *keep not quiet* (let there be *no quiet to you*); in prayer to God אַל־ד׳ לָךְ ψ 83^{2} *keep not quiet* (inactive; ‖ שקט, חרש), cf וְאַל־תִּתְּנוּ ד׳ לוֹ Is 62^{7} *and give no rest to him* (י׳) **2.** in phr. בִּדְמִי יָמַי, appar. *quiet, peacefulness, even tenour*, of my days (so De Or SS), others, as Hi Ew Che Di, *pause, resting-time*, i.e. *noon-day* (cf. 𝔖𝔙, & *height* 𝔊), fig of middle life, but usage dub., Klo$^{SK\ 1884,\ 157}$ *cessation, pause*, of natural end of life, Hezekiah's natural expectation, in contrast with the speedy death implied in v^{b}; but parallelism of v^{11a} is ag. this; Brd emends בְּרֹם after 𝔊; Klo$^{l.c.}$ suggests בתם or כתם as poss., though not necessary,—but view stated first is on the whole best

†I. **[דָּמַם]** **vb. be or grow dumb, silent, still** (NH *id*; Eth in II. አደመመ: *stupefy*; III, 1 & 2 ተደመ: ተደመመ: *be astounded, stupefied*)—**Qal** *Pf* דַּמּוּ Jb 30^{27}, דַּמּוּ ψ 35^{15}, *Impf* ידם Am 5^{13} + 2 t, וַיִּדֹּם Lv 10^{3} Jos 10^{13}, 3 fs. תדם La 2^{18}, 2 fs תדמי Je 48^{2} (so Ki Ol & Ko^{327} q.v, others Niph.), וָאֶדֹּם Jb 31^{34}; יִדְּמוּ Ex 15^{16} + 3 t, 1 pl cohort. נִדְּמָה Je 8^{14} (so Thes Ol Bo Ko^{327} q v; others Niph);—**1.** *be silent* ψ 4^{5} 30^{13} 35^{15} (prob., cf. De Che), Ez 24^{17} Lv 10^{3} (P) Am 5^{13}, in grief La 2^{10} 3^{28} **2.** *be still* (opp to both speech and motion) Jb 31^{34}; = perish Je 8^{14} 48^{2} ψ 31^{18} (ד׳ לשאול); c לְ *be silent to* i.e. be resigned to ψ 37^{7} 62^{6}, sq. לְמוֹ עֲצָתִי Jb 29^{21} (‖ לִי שָׁמְעוּ); *be still*, motionless, stand still Jos 10$^{12.13}$ (of sun ‖ עמד); 1 S 14^{9} (men), Je 47^{6} (of sword ‖ הֵרָגְעִי); so also of bowels, as seat of mental excitement Jb 30^{27};

La 2[18] אַל־תִּדֹּם בַּת־עֵינֵךְ, i.e. cease not to weep (הוֹרִידִי כַנַּחַל דִּמְעָה ||). **3.** *be struck dumb, astounded,* in amazement and fear Ex 15[16] (כאבן) Is 23[2] (but cf. II. דמם). **Niph.** *Pf.* 3 pl. וְנָדַמּוּ consec. Je 25[37]; *Impf.* יִדַּמּוּ Je 49[26] 50[30], יִדָּמּוּ 1 S 2[9]; 2 mpl. תִּדַּמּוּ Je 51[6]—*be made silent,* i.e. destroyed; the wicked 1 S 2[9] (בַּחֹשֶׁךְ), cf. Je 51[6]; men of war Je 49[26] 50[30]; dwellings Je 25[37]. **Po.** *Pf.* 1 s. שִׁוִּיתִי וְדוֹמַמְתִּי נַפְשִׁי ψ 131[2] '*composed and quieted my soul*' Che (as a weaned child). **Hiph.** *Pf.* 3 ms. sf. הֲדִמָּנוּ *he* (God) *hath silenced us* (= caused to perish) Je 8[14].

†דְּמָמָה **n.f.** (silence) **whisper** (on format. cf. Ba[NB 87])—וְאַחַר הָאֵשׁ קוֹל דְּמָמָה דַקָּה 1 K 19[12]; דְּמָמָה וָקוֹל אֶשְׁמָע Jb 4[16] *a whisper* and a voice, i.e. an articulate whisper (cf. Di); יָקֵם סְעָרָה לִדְמָמָה ψ 107[29] *he settleth storm into whisper.*

†דֻּמָה **n.f.** one silenced, brought to silence (?; destroyed?) מִי כְצוֹר כְּדֻמָה בְּתוֹךְ הַיָּם Ez 27[32] (form pecul. & sense dub.: Baer כְּדֻמָּה; Co כְּבֻדָה fr. כָּבֵד adj., cf. 23[41] ψ 45[14]) AV *What city is like Tyrus, like the destroyed* (as though for מְדֻמָּה cf. ההללה 26[1]; but Pi. Pu. not elsewh.) *in the midst of the sea?* RV *like her that is brought to silence.*—Dl[Baer Ezech p. xi. & Pr 64] der., hesitantly, fr. II. דמם.

†II. [דָּמַם] **vb. wail** (?; cf. As. *damâmu, groan, wail, lament,* Dl[Baer's Ezech xi; Pr 64])—only **Qal** *Imv.* דֹּמּוּ יֹשְׁבֵי אִי Is 23[2] *wail, ye coast dwellers* (cf. Dl[l.c.]), || הֵילִילוּ יֹשְׁבֵי אִי v[1], & הֵילִילוּ v[6]; most, however, assign this to I. דמם q.v. (**3**).

דמן (√of foll., mng. dub.; Ar. دَمَنَ, *prepare, improve, manure land,* appar. denom.)

†דֹּמֶן **n.m. dung** (Ar. دِمْنٌ) always in this form and always of corpses, lying on ground as offal 2 K 9[37] Je 8[2] 9[21] 16[4] 25[33] ψ 83[11].

†דִּמְנָה **n.pr.loc.** Levitical city in Zebulun Jos 21[35] (but rd. perh. רִמֹּנָה +; cf. 1 Ch 6[62] Jos 19[13], and v. Di).

†מַדְמֵן **n.pr.loc.** in Moab Je 48[2] (on text, however, cf. Che Is 25[10]).

†I. מַדְמֵנָה **n.f. dung-place, dung-pit,** במי מ׳ Is 25[10] (Qr בְּמוֹ מ׳).

†II. מַדְמֵנָה **n.pr.loc.** in Benjamin, N. of Jerusalem Is 10[31].

†מַדְמַנָּה **1. n.pr.loc.** city of southern Judah Jos 15[31]; loc. dub., Onom. Μηδεβηνα = Μηνοεις near Gaza Lag[Onom. 279, 2nd ed. 276]; cf. *Minyay* S. of Gaza Rob[BR i. 602]; on other proposed identif. cf. Di. **2. n.pr.m.** descendant of Caleb 1 Ch 2[49].

†[דָּמַע] **vb. weep** (NH *id.,* Ar. دَمَعَ & دَمِعَ; Aram. דְּמַע, ܕܡܰܥ: As. in deriv., v. infr.), **Qal** *Impf.* 3 fs., and *Inf. abs.,* וְדָמֹעַ תִּדְמַע וְתֵרַד עֵינִי דִּמְעָה Je 13[17].

†[דֶּמַע] **n.[m.]** (weeping, trickling) **juice,** i.e. wine or (&) oil (cf. foll.) דִּמְעֲךָ Ex 22[28] (מְלֵאָתְךָ ||), cf. Di; Ar. دَمْعَةُ الكَرْمِ = *wine.*

†דִּמְעָה **n.f.** coll. **tears** (chiefly poet. and late; freq. in Je. and contemp.) (Ar. دَمْعٌ; As. *dimu, dimtu* Hpt[KAT 2 Gloss i.] Zim[BP 23, 95]; Aram. דִּמְעָא, ܕܶܡܥܬܳܐ; NH דִּמְעָה, דֶּמַע)—abs. ד׳ ψ 80[6] + 10 t.; cstr. דִּמְעַת Ec 4[1]; *sf.* דִּמְעָתִי ψ 6[7] + 4 t.; דִּמְעָתֶךָ 2 K 20[5] = Is 38[5] + Ez 24[16] (del. 𝔊 Co); דִּמְעָתָהּ La 1[2]; pl. דְּמָעוֹת ψ 80[6] La 2[11]—*tears* ψ 6[7] Ec 4[1] La 1[2] 2[11]; esp. in Je. in phrase תֵּרֵד עֵינִי ד׳ etc. Je 9[17] 13[17] 14[17], cf. La 2[18]; Je 8[23] וְעֵינִי מְקוֹר ד׳; אֲרַיָּוֶךְ דִּמְעָתִי of weeping over, in behalf of one Is 16[9]; as appealing to God's compassion 2 K 20[5] = Is 38[5] ψ 39[13]; ψ 56[9] שִׂימָה ד׳ בְנֹאדֶךָ (cf. Che); v. also ψ 116[8] Je 31[16] Is 25[8]; opp. רִנָּה ψ 126[5]; of hypocritical tears Mal 2[13]; fig. tears as food ψ 42[4] (דִּמְעָתִי לחם); לחם ד׳ 80[6]; as drink 80[6], cf. Babyl. *dimtu maštîti, tears (were) my drink* (Zim[BP 42]; || *bikîtum kurmatî, weeping (was) my sustenance*).—Ez 24[16] וְלֹא תָבוֹא דִּמְעָתֶךָ del. 𝔊 Co cf. v[23].

†דַּמֶּשֶׂק **n.pr.loc. Damascus** (As. *Dimašḳi, Dimasḳi,* Dl[Pa 280] Schr[COT Gn 15, 2 & ABK 323] Jäger[BAS ii. 281 f.]; Ar. دِمَشْقُ, دَمَشْقُ; Aram. 𝔗 Onk, etc. דמשק, Ps-Jon דרמשק; ܕܰܪܡܣܘܩ)—דַּמֶּשֶׂק 1 K 11[24] + 28 t.; דַּמָּשֶׂק Gn 14[15] + 8 t.; דַּרְמֶשֶׂק 1 Ch 18[5] + 3 t. Ch; דַּרְמָשֶׂק 2 Ch 24[23] 28[5]; דּוּמֶשֶׂק 2 K 16[10]; דְּמֶשֶׁק Am 3[12] v. foll., Vrss. דַּמֶּשֶׂק;—ancient Aramaean city, situated lat. 33° 30′ N., long. 36° 15′ E., in plain E. of Hermon & SE. of Anti-Lebanon; on the *Nahr Baradâ* (Gk. Chrysorrhoas); mod. *Dimishḳ* & *Esh-Sham,* Rob[BR iii. 440 ff.] Bd[Pal 307]; *Damascus* Gn 14[15] Am 5[27] 1 K 11[24.24] 2 K 14[28] Ct 7[5]; so also prob. Gn 15[2] (perh. gloss cf. Di), (Am 3[12] v. foll.); a trading-centre Ez 27[18]; as capital & residence of king of Aram 1 K 15[18] = 2 Ch 16[2], cf. 1 K 20[34] 2 K 16[9.10.10.11.11.12] 2 Ch 28[5] Is 7[8.8] 8[4] 10[9] (cf. Peters[Hbr. April 1885, 242]) 17[1.1.3] Je 49[23.24.27]; including also surrounding territory Ez 47[16.17] cf. v[18] 48[1], v. מִדְבַּר ד׳ 1 K 19[15]; נַהֲרוֹת ד׳ 2 K 5[12]; = kingdom Am 1[3.5] cf. Zc 9[1];

once (late) מֶלֶךְ ד׳ 2 Ch 24[23], note also אֲרַם ד׳ 2 S 8[5.6] = 1 Ch 18[5.6], further אֱלֹהֵי ד׳ 2 Ch 28[23] (‖ אֱלֹהֵי מַלְכֵי אֲרָם).

†דְּמֶשֶׁק n.[m.]? Am 3[12] וּבִד׳ עָרֶשׂ; punct & mng dub all ancient Vrss דַּמֶּשֶׂק, and so Pusey Hoffm ZAW iii 102 ('in Damascus on a couch') al, yet this hardly suitable in context; Thes Hi Ew Baur Ke Gunning RV al follow MT, & render *damask, silk*, etc (Ar دِمَقْسٌ, connex with city דַּמֶּשֶׂק (Ar دِمَشْقُ) disputed; acc to Fra 40.288 Ar دِمَقْسٌ is by metath from مِدَقْسٌ, & this a loan-word from Syr ܡܛܟܣܐ, & this from Gk. μέταξα (Old Lat *metaxa*)).

דָּן v. sub דין

דָּנִאֵל v sub דין

דנג (√of foll, mng. unknown).

†דּוֹנַג n.m. wax, דּוֹנַג Mi 1[4] + 2 t, ψ דּוֹנָג 22[15] —always in simile, of melting, at theophany hills melt like wax ψ 97[5]; like wax before fire Mi 1[4], wicked perish as wax melteth before fire ψ 68[3], heart melteth like wax ψ 22[15] (simile of fear, despair) On ד׳ in ψ 118[12] cf Bae Che crit n

†דַּנָּה n.pr.loc. a city of Judah 'in the hill country,' named just before *Kiryath Sanna* = *Debîr* (= *K. Sepher*), Jos 15[49] 𝔊 Ρεννα

†דִּנְהָבָה n.pr.loc. capital city of king Bela in Edom Gn 36[32] = 1 Ch 1[43], identif with *Tennib* (perh = *Thenib*, near the edge of the Belka, ENE. from Heshbon, described by Tristr Moab 222) by Neubauer Acad. 1891, 260 cf Tomkins ib 284

דָּנִיֵּאל v דָּנִאֵל sub דין

דֵּעַ, דֵּעָה v sub ידע

דְּעוּאֵל (רְעוּאֵל) v sub ידע, רעה.

†[דָּעַךְ] vb go out, be extinguished (poet & esp Wisd lit) (Aram דְּעֵיךְ, ܕܥܟ)—**Qal** *Pf* 3 mpl דָּעֲכוּ Is 43[17], *Impf* יִדְעַךְ Pr 20[20], יִדְעָךְ Jb 18[5] + 4 t,—*go out, be extinguished*, of lamp, always fig, lamp of wicked (i e prosperity) אוֹר רְשָׁעִים Jb 18[5], נֵר ר׳ Jb 18[6] 21[17] Pr 13[9] 20[20] 24[20], of hostile armies Is 43[17] (‖ כָּבוּ). **Niph.** *Pf* 3 pl. נִדְעֲכוּ *be made extinct, dried up*, Jb 6[17] (of brooks) **Pu.** *Pf* 3 pl דֹּעֲכוּ of assailants, *be extinguished, quenched* כְּאֵשׁ קוֹצִים ψ 118[12], but rd perh בָּעֲרוּ with 𝔊 Bae & Che, v Che crit n

דַּעַת v sub ידע

דפה (√of foll., mng. unknown; NH דּוֹפִי is *blemish, fault*).

†[דֳּפִי] n.[m.] blemish, fault בְּבֶן־אִמְּךָ תִּתֶּן־דֹּפִי׃ ψ 50[20] *against thy mother's son thou dost allege a fault* (‖ בְּאָחִיךָ תְדַבֵּר)

†[דָּפַק] vb. beat, knock (Ar. دَفَقَ *pour out*, also *drive* (beasts))—**Qal** *Perf* 3 mpl sf. וּדְפָקוּם consec Gn 33[13], but rd 1 s sf. וּדְפַקְתִּים 𝔊 𝔖 Sam Di *beat* (in driving, drive severely or cruelly), *Pt* דּוֹפֵק Ct 5[2] abs. *knocking* (at door) **Hithp.** *Pt* מִתְדַּפְּקִים עַל־הַדָּלֶת Ju 19[22] *beat violently* (beat themselves tired) against the door

†דָּפְקָה n.pr.loc. first station of Isr after מִדְבַּר סִין Nu 33[12.13] 𝔊 Ραφακα; situation unknown, cf views in Di (On an interpret of name from a stone or metal *Mafkat*, *Ta-Mafkat* = *Mafkat*-district, v. Eb GS 148 f. 552 ff)

דַּק, דֹּק v sub דקק.

דקל (√ of foll cf دَقَلٌ a kind of *palm*, NH דֶּקֶל, *date-tree, palm*, Aram. דִּיקְלָא, ܕܩܠܐ)

†דִּקְלָה n.pr.m.(loc.) a son of Joktan, i.e an Arabian territory or people Gn 10[27] = 1 Ch 1[21], unknown, cf Di Gn 10[27].

†[דָּקַק] vb. crush, pulverise, thresh, be fine (Ar. دَقَّ *be or become thin, minute*; Eth ደቀቀ: As *dakâku* Pa. *break in pieces* COT Gloss; Ph. דק *id*, Aram דְּקַק Pa *id*, ܕܩ)—**Qal** *Pf* 3 ms דַּק Dt 9[21], דָּק Ex 32[20], *Impf* 3 ms. sf יְדֻקֶּנּוּ Is 28[28], 2 ms. תָּדֹק Is 41[15];—**1.** *crush* (trans) sq. acc. לֶחֶם *bread-stuff, corn* Is 28[28], of threshing ‖ דּוּשׁ Is 41[15] (fig of pulverizing mts) **2.** only Pf; *be fine*, of state to wh. Moses reduced the golden calf by grinding וָאֶלֹּת אֹתוֹ טָחוֹן עַד אֲשֶׁר־דַּק Ex 32[20], וַיִּטְחַן עַד אֲשֶׁר־דָּק הֵיטֵב Dt 9[21] **Hiph.** *Pf* הֵדַק לְעָפָר 2 K 23[15] 2 Ch 34[4], 2 fs וַהֲדִקּוֹת consec Mi 4[13], *Impf* וַיָּדֶק 2 K 23[6] 2 Ch 15[16], 1 s. sf אַדִּקֵּם 2 S 22[43] (but אֲרִיקֵם ‖ ψ 18[43]), *Inf abs* הָדֵק Ex 30[36], *cstr* לְהָדֵק 2 Ch 34[7] (form anomalous cf Ew § 238 d Ol § 258 b Be; rd. perh לְהָדֵק Ki, or לָדֹק [v כַּדֹּק Is 40[15]] cf Ot),—*make dust of, pulverize* וַיָּדֶק לְעָפָר 2 K 23[6] (i.e the Ashera), ‖ 2 Ch 34[4.7] (כִּתַּת לְהָדֵק); so of the *bamah* הֵדַק לְעָפָר 2 K 23[15], of the מִפְלֶצֶת 2 Ch 15[16], fig. Mi 4[13] (obj עַמִּים רַבִּים), Ex 30[36] (P) has וְשָׁחַקְתָּ מִמֶּנָּה הָדֵק *and thou shalt beat some of it fine*

(i e the incense); 2 S 22[43] rd. אֲרִיקֵם (|| ψ 18[43]) for אֲדִקֵּם. **Hoph.** *Impf* יוּדַק Is 28[28] *be crushed*, subj. לֶחֶם *bread corn* (cf. supr. **Qal**); —on sense cf. Che Di

†**דַּק adj. thin, small, fine**—abs. m. ד׳ Ex 16[14] + 4 t.; דָּק Lv 13[30], f. דַּקָּה Lv 16[12] 1 K 19[12], pl f. abs. דַּקּוֹת Gn 41[6] + 2 t.; cstr דַּקֹּת 41[24]; cstr דַּקּוֹת ד׳ בָּשָׂר Gn 41[3], דקת v[4],—**1.** *thin*, of kine 41[3] cf. v[4] (Sam has in both דַּקּוֹת cf. MT v[19 20.27]), of ears of corn v[6 7 23.24] (all E), *thin, shrunk, withered*, of man Lv 21[20] (H). **2.** *small, fine*, of the manna דַּק מְחֻסְפָּס דַּק כַּכְּפֹר Ex 16[14]; of incense Lv 16[12], hair 13[30] (all P); of dust אָבָק דַּק Is 29[5]; in sim. of isles in hand of ׳י, אִיִּים כַּדַּק יִטּוֹל Is 40[15] (דַּק = subst. *fine thing, fine dust*), once of a low whisper קוֹל דְּמָמָה דַקָּה 1 K 19[12].

†**דֹּק n.[m.] veil, curtain** (as thin), הַנּוֹטֶה כַדֹּק שָׁמַיִם Is 40[22] *he who spreadeth out, like a veil, the heavens.*

†[**דָּקַר**] **vb. pierce, pierce through** (NH *id*, Aram. דְּקַר, ܕܩܪ)—**Qal** *Pf* 3 *pl.* דָּקָרוּ Zc 12[10], *sf.* וּדְקָרֻנִי consec 1 S 31[4], וּדְקָרֻהוּ consec. Zc 13[3]; *Impf.* וַיִּדְקֹר Nu 25[8], וַיְדָקְרֵהוּ Ju 9[54]— *pierce, run through* (always c. acc) · as retributive act, Israelite and Midianit woman Nu 25[8]; false prophet Zc 13[3], but also as speedy death Ju 9[54] (Abimelech); 1 S 31[4a] (Saul) = 1 Ch 10[4], also 1 S 31[4b] (but del. Be We after 1 Ch 10[4] & so ⲄL 1 S 31[4b]), see also Zc 12[10] (cf John 19[37]). **Niph.** *Impf.* יִדָּקֵר *be pierced through*, slain Is 13[15] (in conquest of Bab. by Medes) **Pu.** *Pt.* pl. מְדֻקָּרִים *pierced, riddled*, (i.e. desperately wounded) warriors, Je 37[10], slain Je 51[4] (|| חללים), by hunger La 4[9] (|| חַלְלֵי רָעָב).

†**דֶּקֶר n.pr.m.** (*piercing*, i.e *sharp weapon?* Talm. *pick, mattock*) 1 K 4[9] בֶּן־דֶּקֶר cf. sub. בן

†[**מַדְקֵרָה**] **n.f. piercing, stab, thrust**, only *pl. cstr.* כְּמַדְקְרוֹת חָרֶב Pr 12[18] *like thrusts of a sword*, sim. of rash speaking.

דַּר v דרר.

דר v. דור.

דרא (√of foll cf. Ar. دَرَأَ *repel*)

†**דֵּרָאוֹן n.m. aversion, abhorrence**, abs ד׳ Is 66[24] *object of abhorrence*; cstr. דראון עולם *everlasting abhorrence* Dn 12[2] (on form cf. Lag[BN 200, 202]).

דרב (√of foll cf Ar دَرِبَ *become accustomed, trained*, دَرَّبَ *train*, cf Fl NHWB[1 444]; also Eth. ደረበ፡ (quadrilit) *jaculando infigere*, etc; or, since דָּרְבָן Aram. in form, & 1 S 13[21] perh. secondary, possibly regard as Aram loan-word & connect with Ar ذَرِبَ *be sharp, penetrating* (GFM, note of Apr 1892))

†**דָּרְבָן n.[m.] goad** (NH *id*), לְהַצִּיב הַדָּרְבָן 1 S 13[21] (on form cf Ol[§ 215 b 3] al Dr)

[**דָּרְבֹנָה**] **n.[f.] goad**, only abs pl, in sim. דִּבְרֵי חֲכָמִים כַּדָּרְבֹנוֹת Ec 12[11] (cf De[Koh 434]).

דרג (√of foll cf Ar دَرَجَ *go on foot, step by step, walk*, دَرَّجَ *rise in grade, rank;* NH דרג Hiph. *raise, make high*, Eth ደረገ፡ is *be connected*, Aram ܕܪܓ (verb denom. acc to PS), also As. *darâgu, be high, lift*, Lyon[Sargontexte 80], *durgu, daragu, path, way* (of steep mountain paths) COT[Gloss] (cf also דרך), Ar دَرَجَة *a step, stair*, Aram. דַּרְגָּא, ܕܪܓܐ, ܕܪܓܬܐ, *id*)

†**מַדְרֵגָה n.f steep place steep**,—מ׳ Ct 2[14] (|| סֶלַע), pl הַמַּדְרֵגוֹת Ez 38[20] (|| ההרים and חומה)

†**דַּרְדַּע n pr.m.** (etym. dub.; possibly = דַּרְדַּר, belonging then sub דרר, cf. Thes Add[83]) —only 1 K 5[11] *Ethan the Ezrahite, and Heman, and Calcol, and Darda, the sons of Mahol* (types of wise men, but Solomon wiser than they), = דָּרַע 1 Ch 2[6], where rd. דַּרְדַּע with ⲤⲦ & Codd

דַּרְדַּר v דרר

דְּרוֹם, דְּרוֹר v. דרר.

†**דָּרְיָוֶשׁ n.pr.m. Darius** (Old Pers *Dârayava'ush* cf Spieg[APK 81])—**1.** Darius Hystaspis, 522–485 Ezr 4[5] Hg 1[1 15] 2[10] Zc 1[1 7] 7[1]. **2.** Darius Codomannus, 336–332 Ne 12[22]. **3.** 'Darius the Mede,' Dn 9[1] 11[1], cf Bev[Dan p 19].

דָּרְיוֹשׁ Ezr 10[16] v. דרשׁ

†**דָּרַךְ vb. tread, march** (Aram דְּרַךְ, ܕܪܟ, NH Hiph *lead, conduct;* Ar IV. ادرك *reach, overtake;* Eth ደረከ፡ *be rough, severe* (from *calcavit*, Di); መድረክ፡ *threshold, vestibule*)—**Qal** *Pf* 3 ms דָּרַךְ Nu 24[17] + 6 t.; 3 fs דָּרְכָה Jos 14[9]; 2 ms דָּרַכְתָּ Hb 3[15], 1 s. דָּרַכְתִּי Is 63[3] Zc 9[13], pl דָּרְכוּ Jb 22[15] + 3 t.; *Impf.* 3 ms יִדְרֹךְ Mi 5[4] + 6 t + ידרך Je 51[3] (כתיב ולא קרי); 3 fs תִּדְרֹךְ Dt 11[24] Jos 1[3]; 2 ms תִּדְרֹךְ Dt 33[29] + 2 t.; 2 fs. תִּדְרְכִי Ju 5[21], 1 s. sf. ואדרכם Is 63[3], 3 mpl. יִדְרְכוּ 1 S 5[5], יִדְרְכוּן ψ 11[2], וַיִּדְרְכוּ Ju 9[27]; 2 mpl. תִּדְרְכוּ Dt 11[25]; *Pt.* act. דֹּרֵךְ Am 4[13] + 5 t; דֹּרֵךְ Jb 9[8], דֹּרְכִים Je 25[30] Ne 13[15]; דֹּרְכֵי Je 46[9] + 5 t.;

pass f דְּרוּכָה Is 21^{15}, דְּרֻכוֹת 5^{28},—**1.** *tread, march, march forth,* abs, תדרכי נַפְשִׁי עֹז Ju 5^{21}, cf דָּרַךְ כּוֹכָב מִיַּעֲקֹב Nu 24^{17} (poem) *a star hath marched forth from Jacob.* **2.** *tread upon* (land), sq ב Dt 1^{36} 11^{25} (subj pers.), Jos 14^{9} (subj רֶגֶל) cf Dt 11^{24} = Jos 1^{3} (subj. כַּף רַגְלְכֶם), tread in a path, sq ב Is 59^{8} (fig. of mode of life), tread in (on) the sea, sq ב Hb 3^{15} (but txt. dub cf VB), of an invader ידרך בארמנותינו Mi 5^{4} (|| יָבוֹא בְאַרְצֵנוּ); יד׳ בגבולנו v^{5} (|| *id*), sq על 1 S 5^{5} (עַל־מִפְתַּן דָּגוֹן); ψ 91^{13} (עַל־שַׁחַל וָפֶתֶן), esp (poet) עַל־בָּמֳתֵי אָרֶץ Mi 1^{3}, of י׳, so Am 4^{13}, & (עַל־בָּמֳתֵי יָם) Jb 9^{8}, of Isr treading on heights of enemies, i e subduing them Dt 33^{29}. Once sq acc (אֲשֶׁר ref אֹרַח) Jb 22^{15}. In technical senses **3.** *tread* wine- (or oil-) press, sq acc יְקָבִים Jb 24^{11} (|| יַצְהִירוּ), נתות Ne 13^{15}, sq acc. of thing pressed ד׳ עֲנָבִים Am 9^{13}, also of product תדרך־זית . . . והירוש יַיִן בַּיְקָבִים לֹא יִדְרֹךְ Mi 6^{15}, הַדֹּרֵךְ Is 16^{10}, sq גַּת Is 63^{2} (in sim); abs. Je 25^{30} (sim) 48^{33}, fig of judgment Is 63^{3} sq acc. פּוּרָה *winepress,* subj י׳, cf. v^{3} ואדרכם באפי (|| רמס), i e *tread them down,* so גַּת דָּרַךְ אֲדֹנָי לִבְתוּלַת בַּת־יְהוּדָה La 1^{15}. **4.** *tread* (i e bend) the bow, sq acc קֶשֶׁת Je 51^{3} (אֶל־יִדְרֹךְ יִדְרֹךְ הַדֹּרֵךְ קַשְׁתּוֹ), fig of assaults of wicked ψ 11^{2} 37^{14}, of judgments of י׳ ψ 7^{13} La 2^{4} 3^{12}; also fig of Judah as bow in hand of י׳, כִּי דָרַכְתִּי לִי יְהוּדָה Zc 9^{13} (|| קֶשֶׁת מִלֵּאתִי אֶפְרַיִם); twice in like mng c obj חִצּוֹ *arrow* ψ 58^{8} (but on txt cf Che$^{crit\ n}$) 64^{4}, דֹּרְכֵי קֶשֶׁת = *bow-benders, archers* Je 50$^{14.29}$ 1 Ch 5^{18} 8^{40} 2 Ch 14^{7}, קֶשֶׁת דְּרוּכָה *bent bow* Is 21^{15}, קַשְּׁתֹתָיו דְּרֻכוֹת 5^{28}. **Hiph.** *Pf.* וְהִדְרִיךְ Is 11^{15}, sf הִדְרִיכָהּ Je 51^{33} (where many Inf cstr) cf. RS$^{J\ Ph\ xvi\ (1888)\ 72}$, 1 s sf. הִדְרַכְתִּיךָ Pr 4^{11}; 3 pl sf הִדְרִיכֻהוּ Ju 20^{43}, הִדְרִיכוּהוּ Jb 28^{8}; *Impf.* יַדְרֵךְ ψ 25^{9}, sf יַדְרִכֵנִי Hb 3^{19}; וַיַּדְרִיכֵם ψ 107^{7}; 1 s sf אַדְרִיכֵם Is 42^{16}, וַיַּדְרְכוּ Je 9^{2} (cf Ges$^{§53,\ 3.\ R\ 4}$), *Imv* ms sf הַדְרִיכֵנִי ψ 25^{5} 119^{35}, *Inf cstr* v supr, *Pt* sf. מַדְרִיכְךָ Is 48^{17},—**1.** *tread, tread down,* of treading down enemy in battle Ju 20^{43}, of treading a path Jb 28^{8}, levelling threshing-floor Je 51^{33} (all sq sf). **2.** *tread* (bend) the bow (= **Qal 4**), only fig וַיַּדְרְכוּ אֶת־לְשׁוֹנָם קַשְׁתָּם שֶׁקֶר Je 9^{2} *and they have bent their tongue as their bow in falsehood* **3.** causat., *cause to tread* or *march, lead,* returning exiles Is 11^{15} (subj י׳, no obj expressed), cf. וַיַּדְרִיכֵם בְּדֶרֶךְ יְשָׁרָה ψ 107^{7} *and he led them in a straight way,* v also Is 42^{16} (|| הוליך), with a moral application הדרכתיך בְּמַעְגְּלֵי־יֹשֶׁר Pr 4^{11}, cf ψ 119^{35} הַדְרִיכֵנִי בנתיב מִצְוֹתֶיךָ *lead me in the path of thy commandments;* ψ 25^{5} בַּאֲמִתֶּךָ (|| לַמְּדֵנִי) cf. v^{9} (במשפט || ילמד דרכו), Is 48^{17} בְּדֶרֶךְ תֵּלֵךְ (|| מְלַמֶּדְךָ לְהוֹעִיל); once of giving security & triumph עַל־בָּמוֹתַי יַדְרִכֵנִי Hb 3^{19} *upon mine heights he maketh me tread* (cf. **Qal 2**)

דֶּרֶךְ ^{706} **n.m.** $^{Dt\ 17\ 16}$ & (less often) **f.** $^{Ex\ 18,\ 20}$ **way, road, distance, journey, manner**—abs. ד׳ Gn 38^{16} +; דָּ֑רֶךְ v^{21} +, cstr דֶּרֶךְ 3^{24}, sf. דַּרְכִּי 24^{42} + 4 t + 2 S 22^{33}, דַּרְכּוֹ, דַּרְכְּךָ Ho 10^{13} 1 K 19^{15}; דַּרְכּוֹ Gn 6^{12} +; דַּרְכֶּךָ ψ 5^{9} + 9 t, דַּרְכֵּךְ Je 2^{23} + 8 t.; דַּרְכְּכֶם 1 S 1^{18} Jb 28^{23}, דַּרְכֵּנוּ Ju 18^{5} + 2 t., דַּרְכָּהּ Gn 19^{2} + 3 t, דַּרְכָּם 1 K 2^{4} +, du דְּרָכַיִם Pr 28$^{6.18}$, pl דרכים Dt 28^{7} + 6 t., cstr. דַּרְכֵי Pr 3^{17} + 24 t; sf דְּרָכַי Jb 13^{15} + 17 t, דְּרָכָ֑י ψ 95^{10} + 4 t, דְּרָכֶיךָ Dt 28^{29} + 16 t., דְּרָכֶךָ Ex 33^{13} + 2 t.; דְּרָכַיִךְ Je 3^{13} + 4 t, דְּרָכַיִךְ Ez 7^{3} + 3 t; דְּרָכָיו Dt 10^{12} +; דְּרָכֶיהָ Pr 3^{17} + 3 t, דְּרָכֵינוּ La 3^{40} Zc 1^{6}; דַּרְכֵיכֶם Lv 26^{22} + 17 t.; דַּרְכֵיהֶם Je 16^{17} + 5 t, דַּרְכֵיהֶן Ez 16^{47};—**1.** *way, road, path* Gn 35^{3} (E) 38$^{16.21}$ (both J) 48^{7} (P), 49^{17} (J, poem) Lv 26^{22} (H, only here in Lv) Nu 22$^{22.23.23.23.31.34}$ (all JE) Dt 6^{7} 22$^{4.6}$ 23^{5} 24^{9} 25$^{17.18}$ Jos 3^{4} (D) Ru 1^{7} 1 S 4^{13} (on text cf Dr) 15^{2} 24^{4} 2 S 16^{13} 1 K 13$^{9.10.10.12.17.24.24.25.26.28}$ 18$^{6.6.7}$ 20^{38} 2 K 2^{23} 3^{8} 6^{19} 7^{15}, 19$^{28.33}$ = Is 37$^{29.34}$, Ho 6^{9} 13^{7} Is 43$^{16.19}$ 49$^{9.11}$ 51^{10} 57$^{14.14}$ Je 6^{25} La 1^{4} Ez 21$^{24.25}$ 42$^{11.12}$ Jo 2^{7}, Ezr 8$^{22.31}$ Jb 12^{24} ψ 107^{40} 110^{7} Pr 7^{8} 8^{2} 26^{13} Ec 10^{3} 12^{5}, cstr. *way of* (oft = to, toward) ד׳ עֵץ הַחַיִּים Gn 3^{24} (J) ד׳ שׁוּר 16^{7} (J) ד׳ אֶרֶץ פְּלִשְׁתִּים Ex 13^{17} (E) ד׳ הַבָּשָׁן Nu 21^{33} (JE), cf. Dt 1$^{2.19}$ 3^{1} Jos 2^{7} (JE) 12^{3} 1 S 6$^{9.12}$ 13$^{17.18.18}$ 17^{52} 2 K 3^{20} Is 15^{5} Je 2$^{18.18}$ 50^{5} Ez 47^{15} 48^{1}; ד׳ הַמִּדְבָּר (of different ways) Ex 13^{18} (E) Jos 8^{15} (JE) Ju 20^{42}, cf Dt 2^{8} 2 S 2^{24} 2 K 3^{8}, ד׳ הַזַּיִת אֲשֶׁר אֶת־הַמִּדְבָּר 2 S 15^{23} is corrupt; rd ד׳ בַּמִּדְבָּר 𝔊L Dr cf. We: *the way of the olive-tree which,* etc; ד׳ הָעֲרָבָה Dt 2^{8} and (with diff reference) 2 S 4^{7} 2 K 25^{4} = Je 52^{7}, Je 39^{4}; ד׳ הַכִּכָּר 2 S 18^{23}; ד׳ יַם־סוּף Nu 14^{25} 21^{4} (JE) Dt 1^{40} 2^{1}, oft of gateway, as ד׳ הַשַּׁעַר 2 S 15^{2} cf 2 K 11^{19} 25^{4} = Je 52^{7}, Ez 9^{2} 43^{4} 44$^{1.4}$ 46$^{9.9.9.9.9}$ 47^{2}; ד׳ ד׳ גַּן־הַמֶּלֶךְ 2 K 9^{27}, ד׳ בֵּית הַגָּן 44^{3} 46$^{2.8}$ ד׳ אוּלָם הַשַּׁעַר Je 39^{4}; ד׳ הַיָּם Is 8^{23} (cf Comm & Schumacher $^{Jaulân\ 63\ and\ PEF\ Apr\ 1889,\ 78}$); ד׳ מְבוֹא הַסּוּסִים 2 K 11^{16}, sq ־ָה loc Gn 35^{19} (E), 38^{14} (J) 48^{7} (P, rd. אפרתה Ol), ד׳ הַמֶּלֶךְ נֵלֵךְ Nu 20^{17} 21^{22} (both JE; Ar. درب السلطان) of diff highroads, cf Seetzen $^{I.\ 61,\ 132,\ II\ 336}$ Rob $^{BR\ III\ 141}$ Di; = מְסִלָּה 20^{19}) i e the *highway,* used by king with his army; cf. || בַּדֶּרֶךְ בַּדֶּרֶךְ Dt 2^{27} i e. straight (or steadily) along the way; in particular of path, way, in

which God moves † בַּיָּם דַּרְכֶּךָ ψ 77^{20} (|| וּשְׁבִילְךָ); בְּסוּפָה וּבִשְׂעָרָה דַּרְכּוֹ Na 1^{3}; cf. בַּמִּדְבָּר פַּנּוּ ד׳ י׳ Is 40^{3} (|| יַשְּׁרוּ בָּעֲרָבָה מסלה לאלהינו); also Mal 3^{1}, comp. Is 43$^{16.19}$ (way made by י׳) & 51^{10}, path of lightning Jb 28^{26} 38^{25}; of light 38$^{19.24}$, of camel (בִּכְרָה) Je 2^{23}, of locusts Jo 2^{7} (pl.); v. further the four wonderful things Pr 30^{19} *the way of an eagle in the air, the way of a serpent upon a rock, the way of a ship in the heart of the sea*, and *the way of a man with a maid* (i.e. no trace is left in any case), cf. also v^{20} כֵּן דֶּרֶךְ אִשָּׁה מְנָאָפֶת; figure of death אָנֹכִי הוֹלֵךְ הַיּוֹם בְּדֶרֶךְ כָּל־הָאָרֶץ Jos 23^{14} *I am going to-day in the way of all the earth* (D), so also 1 K 2^{2} (cf. Gn 19^{31} **4 a**) **2.** *journey* Gn 24$^{21.40.42.56}$ (all J) Nu 9$^{10.13}$ (P) Jos 9$^{11.13}$ (both JE) 1 K 18^{27}, 19^{7} רַב מִמְּךָ הַד׳, Ju 17^{8} לַעֲשׂוֹת ד׳, ד׳ בְּאֵר שֶׁבַע Am 8^{14} (*journey of—to—Beersheba* cf. Hi St; but txt. dub., 𝔊 ὁ θεός, cf Gunning; Hoffm ZAW 1883, 123 prop. דֹּדְךָ, We בארך cf Bu ThLz 1892, 62); דֶּרֶךְ חֹל 1 S 21^{6} *a common* (not sacred) *journey;* esp c. temp. modif. ד׳ שְׁלֹשֶׁת יָמִים Gn 30^{36} (J) Ex 3^{18} 5^{3} 8^{23} Nu 10$^{33.33}$ (all JE), 33^{8} (P) cf. also Gn 31^{23} (E) Nu 11$^{31.31}$ (JE), 1 K 19^{4}, 2 K 3^{9}; *go one's way* † הָלַךְ לְדַרְכּוֹ Gn 19^{2} (J), 32^{2} (E), 33^{16} (J), Nu 24^{25} Jos 2^{16} (both JE), Ju 18^{26} 19^{27} 1 S 1^{18} 26^{25} 30^{2} 1 K 1^{49} Je 28^{11}, vid הלך; also † הָפַךְ לד׳ 1 S 25^{12}, & (fig.) † פָּנָה לְד׳ Is 53^{6} (so 56^{11} **5** infr.); of זוֹנָה, fig of Israel, וַתְּפַזְּרִי אֶת־דְּרָכַיִךְ לַזָּרִים Je 3^{13} **3.** of *direction*, almost or quite=*toward*, 1 K 8$^{44.48}$=2 Ch 6$^{34.38}$ *pray toward the city*, etc., 18^{43} *look toward the sea;* esp in Ezek. of looking, going, etc. ד׳ צָפוֹנָה Ez 8$^{5.5}$ cf. 21^{2} 40^{6}, cstr. ד׳ הַקָּדִים Ez 40^{10} (del. 𝔊 Hi Co) v^{22} 43^{1}, ד׳ הַצָּפוֹן v^{20} cf ד׳ הַדָּרוֹם v$^{24.24}$, ד׳ הַיָּם, 41^{12}, ד׳ הֶחָצֵר 42^{7} etc. (c. 28 t. Ez), (v also מִדֶּרֶךְ Ez 9^{2} cf. 43^{2} 44^{3}; on ד׳ אַמָּה אֶחָת Ez 42^{4} v. VB Co Da) cf. לֹא־יִפְנֶה דֶּרֶךְ כְּרָמִים Jb 24^{18}. †**4.** *way, manner:* **a.** *usage* ד׳ כָּל־הָאָרֶץ Gn 19^{31} (J cf. also Jos 23^{14} 1 K 2^{2} supr.) **b.** =customary experience, or condition ד׳ נָשִׁים Gn 31^{35} (E). **c.** ד׳ מִצְרַיִם Am 4^{10} *the manner of Egypt*, i.e. as was done in Egypt, Is 10$^{24.26}$. **d.** *habit* of animals, ants Pr 6^{6} (pl.) †**5.** fig. of course of life, or action, undertakings, etc. לֹא תַצְלִיחַ אֶת־דְּרָכֶיךָ Dt 28^{29} cf. Jos 1^{8} (D) 1 S 18^{14} 2 S 22^{33}=ψ 18^{33}; Jb 3^{23} 8^{19} 17^{9} 22^{28} 24^{23} 31^{4} 34^{21} ψ 10^{5} 35^{6} 37$^{5.7.23}$ 91^{11} 102^{24} 119^{37} 128^{1} 139^{3} 146^{9} Pr 2^{8} 3$^{6.23}$ 11^{5} 20^{24} 29^{27} 31^{3}; Is 40^{27} 45^{13} 48^{15} 55$^{8.9}$ Je 2^{36} 10^{23} 12^{1} 23^{12} La 3$^{9.11}$ Ho 2^{8} 9^{8} 10^{13} Am 2^{7} (ד׳ עֲנָוִים); thrice (Ch) in summary of a king's life, of Abijah וּדְרָכָיו וּדְבָרָיו 2 Ch 13^{22}; of Jotham וְכָל־מִלְחֲמֹתָיו וּדְרָכָיו 2 Ch 27^{7}; of Ahaz ד׳ אֹרְחֹתֶיךָ 2 Ch 28^{26}; וְכָל־דְּרָכָיו הָרִאשֹׁנִים וְהָאַחֲרוֹנִים Is 3^{12} cf. also Is 30^{11} and 57^{18}, =gain Is 56^{11}, pleasure, etc. Is 58^{13}. †**6. a.** of moral action and character הִשְׁחִית כָּל־בָּשָׂר אֶת־דַּרְכּוֹ עַל־הָאָרֶץ Gn 6^{12} (P), cf. Je 3^{21}; יִשְׁמְרוּ אֶת־דַּרְכָּם 1 K 2^{4} 8^{25}=2 Ch 6^{16}; cf v^{39}=2 Ch 6^{30}; הֵכִין דְּרָכָיו לִפְנֵי י׳ 2 Ch 27^{6}; ψ 5^{9} 39^{2} 49^{14} 50^{23} 119$^{5.26.59.168}$ Pr 4^{26} 5$^{8.21}$ 10^{9} 14$^{2.8.12}$ 16$^{2.7.9.17.25}$ 19$^{3.16}$ 21$^{2.29}$ Je 2^{33} 6^{27} 7$^{3.5}$ 16^{17} 17^{10} 18$^{11.15}$ 26^{13} 32$^{19.19}$ La 3^{40} Ez 7$^{3.8.9.27}$ 14$^{22.23}$ 18$^{25.29.30}$ 24^{14} 28^{15} 33$^{17.20}$ 36^{19} Hg 1$^{5.7}$ Zc 1^{6}; דַּרְכֵי לִבְּךָ Ec 11^{9} cf Is 57^{17} (& Je 32^{39} **c.** infr.) **b.** of duty (commanded by י׳, etc.) הַד׳ יֵלְכוּ בָהּ Ex 18^{20} (E) cf. 32^{8} (JE) Dt 9$^{12.16}$ 13^{6} 31^{29} Ju 2^{17} Jb 31^{7} ψ 25$^{8.12}$ 32^{8} 119^{1} 143^{8} Pr 21^{16} 22^{6} 23^{19} Is 30^{21} 48^{17} Je 7^{23} Mal 2^{8}; so, too, of wisdom דְּרָכֶיהָ דַּרְכֵי־נֹעַם Pr 3^{17}, ד׳ חָכְמָה 4^{11} 8^{32} cf. 23^{26}, ד׳ בִּינָה 9^{6} cf. Is 40^{14}. †**c.** specif. in good sense ד׳ הַטּוֹבָה וְהַיְשָׁרָה 1 S 12^{23} 1 K 8^{36}=2 Ch 6^{27}, cf. Pr 16^{31} Je 6^{16}, תֹּם דְּרָכֶיךָ Jb 4^{6} cf. 22^{3} Pr 13^{6}; דְּרָכָיו (i.e. of light) Jb 24^{13} (|| נְתִיבֹתָיו); ד׳ צַדִּיקִים ψ 1^{6}, ד׳ טוֹבִים Pr 2^{20}, יִשְׁרֵי־דָרֶךְ ψ 37^{14}, תְּמִימֵי דָרֶךְ Pr 11^{20} ψ 119^{1}; ד׳ תָּמִים ψ 101$^{2.6}$, ד׳ אֱמוּנָה ψ 119^{30}, ד׳ שָׁלוֹם Is 59^{8}; ד׳ עוֹלָם ψ 139^{24}, ד׳ חַיִּים Pr 6^{23}, cf. 12^{28} Je 21^{8} (opp ד׳ המות v. infr.), without modifier 1 S 8$^{3.5}$ Jb 13^{15} 23^{10}, לֵב אֶחָד וְד׳ אֶחָד Je 32^{39}; cf also **a.** supr.; esp. cstr before names of good kings 1 K 22^{43} 2 K 22^{2} 2 Ch 11^{17} 20^{32} 21$^{12.12}$ (pl.) so 34^{2}; cf. דַּרְכֵי דָוִיד הָרִאשֹׁנִים 2 Ch 17^{3} *the first ways of David*, also דַּרְכֵי עַמִּי Je 12^{16}. †**d.** oftener in bad sense דַּרְכָּם הַקָּשָׁה Ju 2^{19}, דַּרְכּוֹ הָרָעָה 1 K 13^{33}, ד׳ רַע Pr 2^{12} 8^{13} 28^{10}; cf 2 K 17^{13} 2 Ch 7^{14} Je 18^{11} 23^{22} 25^{5} 26^{3} 35^{15} 36$^{2.7}$ Ez 3$^{18.19}$ 13^{22} 20^{44} 33^{11} Jon 3$^{8.10}$ Zc 1^{4}; ד׳ לֹא טוֹב ψ 36^{5} Pr 16^{29} Is 65^{2}, דַּרְכֵּךְ זִמָּה Ez 16^{27}; cf. with completed metaph. ד׳ לֹא סְלוּלָה Je 18^{15}; further ד׳ שֶׁקֶר ψ 119^{29}, ד׳ עֹצֶב ψ 139^{24}, ד׳ פִּשְׁעָם ψ 107^{17}; דַּרְכֵי־חֹשֶׁךְ Pr 2^{13}, דַּרְכֵי מָוֶת Pr 14^{12}=16^{25}; דרך המות Je 21^{8}, cf supr. **c**, ד׳ עָצֵל Pr 15^{19} (cf. 6^{6}); ד׳ חַטָּאִים ψ 1^{1} cf v^{6} Pr 1^{15} 3^{31} 4^{19} (ד׳ רְשָׁעִים), 12^{15} (ד׳ אויל), 13^{15} (ד׳ בגדים), also 15^{9} 21^{8} Is 55^{7}; ד׳ עִקֵּשׁ Pr 22^{5}, cf. עִקֵּשׁ דְּרָכַיִם Pr 28^{6} cf v^{18}, further, without modifier, Ho 4^{9} 12^{3} Pr 7^{25} 14^{14} Is 53^{6} 66^{3} Je 2^{23} (of idolatry רְאִי דַרְכֵּךְ בַּגַּיְא) v^{33} 4^{11} (cf. Hi Gf) v^{18} 15^{7} 22^{1} Ez 16$^{47.47.61}$ 18^{23} 20^{43} 23$^{13.31}$ 33$^{8.9.9.11}$ 36$^{17.17.31.32}$ cf. also sub **a.** supr.; לָתֵת דַּרְכּוֹ בראשו 1 K 8^{32} *to place his way upon his head*, i.e. requite it on him=2 Ch 6^{23}, cf. Ez 7^{4} 9^{10} 11^{21} 16^{43} 22^{31}; פְּרִי דַרְכָּם Pr 1^{31}, esp. cstr before names of bad kings ד׳ יָרָבְעָם 1 K 15^{34} (cf v^{26}) 16$^{2.19.26}$ 22^{53} cf. v$^{53.53}$; also ד׳ מַלְכֵי יִשְׂרָאֵל 2 K 8^{18} 16^{3} 2 Ch 21$^{6.13}$ 28^{2} (pl.); דַּרְכֵי בֵּית אַחְאָב

2 K 8[27] = 2 Ch 22[3] (of Ahaziah, grandson of Ahab), ד׳ הָעָם הַזֶּה Is 8[11], ד׳ הַגּוים Je 10[2], ד׳ אֲבוֹתֵיכֶם Ez 20[30] cf 2 K 21[21] †e. way of ׳י. (a) = his creative activity Jb 26[14]; applied in concrete sense to behemoth (hippopotamus) הוּא רֵאשִׁית דַּרְכֵי־אֵל Jb 40[19] (hyperb); cf. of wisdom רֵאשִׁית דַּרְכּוֹ Pr 8[22]; (b) = his moral administration, Ex 33[13] (pl; JE); Dt 32[4] 2 S 22[31] = ψ 18[31] Jb 21[31] 36[23], אלהים בַּקֹּדֶשׁ דַּרְכֶּךָ ψ 77[14] (מי אל גָּדוֹל כאלהים ‖), ψ 85[14] 103[7] 138[5] 145[17], Pr 10[29] Is 55[8.9] Je 5[4.5] Ez 18[25.25.29.29] 33[17.20] Ho 14[10] (c) = his commandments וְשָׁמְרוּ ד׳ י׳ לַעֲשׂוֹת צְדָקָה וּמִשְׁפָּט Gn 18[19] (J), כָּל־הַדֶּרֶךְ אֲשֶׁר צִוָּה י׳ Dt 5[30] cf (pl.) 8[6] 10[12] 11[22.28] 19[9] 26[17] 28[9] 30[16] Jos 22[5] (D) Ju 2[22] 2 S 22[22] = ψ 18[22], 1 K 2[3] 3[14] 8[58] 11[33.38] 2 K 21[22] 2 Ch 6[31] Jb 21[14] 23[11] 34[27] ψ 25[4.9] 27[11] 37[34] 51[15] 67[3] 81[14] 86[11] 95[10] 119[3] Is 2[3] = Mi 4[2], Is 42[24] 58[2] 63[17] 64[4] Zc 3[7] Mal 2[9]; cf וַיִּגְבַּהּ לִבּוֹ בְּדַרְכֵי י׳ 2 Ch 17[6], v also ד׳ עֵדְוֹתֶיךָ ψ 119[14], ד׳ פִּקּוּדֶיךָ v[27], ד׳ חֻקֶּיךָ v[32], ד׳ מִצְוֹתֶיךָ v[33].

†[מִדְרָךְ] **n [m.] treading- or stepping-place,** place for the foot to tread on, only cstr מִדְרַךְ כַּף־רָגֶל Dt 2[5] *a treading-place for the sole of a foot* (cf. 11[24] = Jos 1[3])

†[אֲדַרְכוֹן, דַּרְכְּמוֹן] (א prosthet) **n.[m.]** unit (appar. of weight, certainly) of value, rare & late, perh **drachma,** others **daric,** v infr:—only pl דַּרְכְּמוֹנִים of gold Ezr 2[69] (‖ מָנִים of silver) = Ne 7[70] (‖ *id*); so דַּרְכְּמֹנִים Ne 7[69.71], also אֲדַרְכֹנִים of gold money 1 Ch 29[7] (‖ כִּכָּרִים ,כ׳ also in same v. of silver, brass & iron), of weight (or worth) of gold utensils Ezr 8[27].—Weight of Gk. δραχμή = 4.32 grammes (= 66.5 Eng gr), value of silver dr = c 9¾ *d* Eng, value of gold dr (½ stater) = c 9*s* 5*d* Eng, cf Hultsch[Gr u Röm Metrol (1882) 224, 227, 230-250, & Tab. xiv xvi]—(If ד׳ = *drachma,* then perhaps edit insertion in Ne Ezr (regarded as loan-word in both Gk & Heb fr some Asiatic source by Ew[GGA 1855 1302 ff, 1856 794; Gesch 1 274 H. L 189] cf. Sm[Listen 18, N 24], but on Gk deriv cf Lex. Lidd. & Sc, also Brandis[Münz Mass-u Gewichtssystem 68 f.] Hultsch[l c 131]), cf Ph pl דרכמנם ,דרכנם = *drachmæ* acc. to Re[RA 1888, 7] Berger[Mém. Soc Ling de Paris, 1889 3o5] Hoffm[AGG xxxvi Mai 1889 8] Acc to view commonly current hitherto ד׳ = *daric,* Gk δαρεικός, cf Syr ܕܪܝܩܘܢ, Pers gold coin = c. Eng sovereign (weight = c 2 drachm) Brandis[l c 62, 244 ff] Hultsch[l c 466] Schr in Ri[HWB Art Darike] Erman[ZPV ii, 75] Hoffm[ZA 1887, 49 ff] (Hoffm[l c] abandons), cf Ryle Ezr 2[69])

דַּרְמֶשֶׂק v דַּמֶּשֶׂק

†דרע (acc. to Thes connected with Aram. דְּרָע ,אֶדְרָע *arm,* Heb זרוע, whence foll in sense *strong,* of fortified city; this, however, is dub.)

†אֶדְרֶעִי **n.pr.loc.** a chief city of Bashan אדרעי Jos 19[37], אֶדְרֶעִי Nu 21[33] = Dt 3[1], Dt 3[10]; בְּעַשְׁתָּרֹת בְּאֶדְרֶעִי Dt 1[4]; בעשתרות ובאדרעי Jos 12[4] 13[12] cf 13[31],—on identity of all these cf. Di Dt 3[10], modern *Der'ât,* 7½ hours WNW. of Bosra, Euseb. 'Αδραά (Lag[Onom 213, 86, 2nd ed 235]) cf. Di Nu 21[33] Wetzst[Hauran 47, 77 123] Bd[Pal 201].

דָּרַע 1 Ch 2[6] v. דרדע.

דרק (√ of foll mng dub; Ar. دَرِقَ = *walk rapidly, hasten,* دَرَقَة *shield*)

†דַּרְקוֹן **n.pr.m.** head of a family of Nethinim, who went up with Zerubbabel, בני־ד׳ Ezr 2[56] = Ne 7[58].

דרר (√ of foll words: Ar. دَرَّ,—**1.** *stream, flow abundantly* (of milk, tears, rain, etc.), cf. I דרור **2.** *be abundant, luxuriant* (of herbage), cf. دَرْدَار a kind of tree, now *elm* (Lane), & דַּרְדַּר **3** *run vehemently, easily* (of horse), cf دَرِير *swift* horse, or other beast, & II דרור **4.** *give light, shine* (of lamp), cf. كَوْكَبٌ دُرِّيٌّ *shining star,* دُرِّيّ *glistening* or *shining* of sword, دُرّ *pearls* (coll) & דַּר; hence prob דָּרוֹם)

†דַּר **n.[m] pearl? mother of pearl?** (Ar دُرّ *pearls,* دُرَّة *a pearl*) Est 1[6].

†I. דְּרוֹר **n.[m.] a flowing; free run, liberty,—1.** מָר־דְּרוֹר Ex 30[23] (P) i.e *myrrh of flowing,* fine-flowing m cf מר & Di. **2. c.** קרא וּקְרָאתֶם דְּרוֹר בָּאָרֶץ לְכָל־יֹשְׁבֶיהָ *proclaim liberty,* Lv 25[10] (H) in Jubilee year, cf Is 61[1] (‖ פְּקַח־קוֹחַ); Je 34[8.15.17] all ref to liberty of Sabbatical year; v[17] (iron.) *lo! I proclaim to you liberty unto the sword, unto pestilence & unto famine,* i e liberty to be destroyed by sword, pestilence and famine, (a judgment of Yahweh), שְׁנַת־הַד׳ Ez 46[17] i.e year of Jubilee (cf Lv 25[10]).

†II. דְּרוֹר **n.f.** ψ 84, 4 **swallow** ψ 84[4] (‖ צִפּוֹר), Che (q v.) makes simile of quiet, peace, security, and supplies ellipsis; in simile, Pr 26[2] כַּצִּפּוֹר לָנוּד כַּדְּרוֹר לָעוּף (of groundless curse, which does not alight, i e is not fulfilled)

†דָּרוֹם **n.m. south** (poet. & late) (on formation cf Ol[§ 216 a] Sta[§ 296])—דָּרוֹם Jb 37[17] + 14 t + Ez 40[27b 28b] (del 𝔊 Co in v[27b], AB 𝔅 Co in v[28b]—*south,* Ez 42[18] (over against קָדִים, צָפוֹן,

יָם), 12 t. more in Ezek. (of wh. Co del. 2, cf. supr.) 21[2] (=תֵּימָנָה and נֶגֶב); דֶּרֶךְ הַדּ׳ *toward south* 40[24.24.27], rd. also דֶּרֶךְ הַדּ׳ 42[10] for ד׳ הַקָּדִים 𝔊 Ke Co; שַׁעַר הַדּ׳ *south gate* 40[[27].28.[28]] cf. Co supr., 40[44] (opp. צפון; also קדים), v[45] (opp צפון) 42[12]=לַדּ׳ 41[11] (opp. צפון), לִשְׁכוֹת הד׳ 42[13] (opp צפון). Elsewhere only Dt 33[23] (‖ יָם), Jb 37[17]; Ec 1[6] 11[3] (both opp צפון).

† **דַּרְדַּר n.[m.] thistles** (coll.) (Ar. دردار, still current in Pal., Low[p. 100]; Eth ደንደር:) קוֹץ וְדַרְדַּר Gn 3[18] (J) Ho 10[8] symbol of wildness, desert

† **דָּרַשׁ** [163] **vb. resort to, seek** (cf. Ar. دَرَسَ *rub over, efface* (a site), *tread* (wheat), fig. *read repeatedly, study,* ... *beat* (a path), *discuss,* Pa *practise in;* NH *search out* (a meaning), *expound*)—**Qal** *Pf.* 1 Ch 10[14]; *Impf* יִדְרֹשׁ ψ 10[4]+, אֶדְרְשָׁה 1 S 28[7], נִדְרְשָׁה 1 K 22[7]+, יִדְרְשׁוּן Is 55[2]; *Imv* דְּרֹשׁ 1 K 22[5]+, *Inf* abs דָּרוֹשׁ Lv 10[16] Dt 23[22], cstr. דרשׁ Dt 22[2]+ לִדְרֹשׁ Ez 14[7], לדריוֹשׁ (scribal error for לִדְרוֹשׁ Ew[§ 238 a] Ol[§ 245 f]) Ezr 10[16]; *Pt.* דֹּרֵשׁ Dt 11[12]+10 t, דּוֹרֵשׁ 1 Ch 28[9]+3 t.; pass. דְּרוּשִׁים ψ 111[2], דְּרוּשָׁה Is 62[12], syn. בקשׁ;—**1.** (*tread* a place,) *resort to, frequent,* with religious obj, c. acc. loc. Am 5[5] 2 Ch 1[5], לְ loc. Dt 12[5] **2.** *seek, consult, inquire of:* **a.** acc. י׳, אֱלֹהִים Gn 25[22] (J) Ex 18[15] (E) 1 S 9[9] 1 K 22[8] 2 K 3[11] 8[8] 22[13.18] 1 Ch 15[13] 21[30] 2 Ch 18[7] 34[21] ψ 24[6] 78[34] Je 21[2] 37[7] Ez 20[1.3]; *the ark of God* 1 Ch 13[3]; *word of Yahweh* 1 K 22[5] (=2 Ch 18[4]) cf. 1 K 14[5], with בְּ Yahweh 1 Ch 10[14] 2 Ch 34[26] Ez 14[7]; his word 2 K 1[16]; with אֶל, אֶל־אֵל Jb 5[8], their God Is 8[19], Messianic king Is 11[10]; מֵעַל־סֵפֶר י׳ *out of the book of* י׳ Is 34[16] (in gloss, acc. to Che[JQ Jan. 1892, 332]), c. מֵאוֹת of a נָבִיא לי׳ 1 K 22[7] (=2 Ch 18[6]) cf (supr) v[8] 2 K 3[11] and 1 K 14[5] (מֵעִמְּךָ) **b.** *heathen gods* and *necromancers,* הַדֹּרֵשׁ *the inquirer* Ez 14[10], with בְּ, בְּבַעַל זְבוּב 2 K 1[2.3.6.16], בָּאוֹב 1 Ch 10[13], בְּבַעֲלַת אוֹב 1 S 28[7], with אֶל, אֶל־הָאֹבוֹת Is 8[19], אֶל־הַמֵּתִים Dt 18[11], אֶל־הָאֱלִילִים Is 19[3] **3.** *seek deity in prayer and worship:* **a.** *the true God* (cf בקשׁ **3**) דָּרַשׁ י׳ Dt 4[29] Ho 10[12] Am 5[4.6] Is 9[12] 31[1] 55[6] 58[2] 65[10] Je 10[21] 29[13] Zp 1[6] La 3[25] 1 Ch 16[11] (=ψ 105[4]) 28[9] 2 Ch 12[14] 14[3.6] 15[2.12] 16[12] 22[9] 26[5] ψ 9[11] 22[27] 34[5.11] 119[2.10]; דרשׁ (ה)אלהים 2 Ch 19[3] 26[5] 30[19] ψ 14[2] (= 53[3]) 69[33], אֲדֹנָי ד׳ ψ 77[3], with לְ, only in Chronicler, ליהוה 1 Ch 22[19] 2 Ch 15[13] 20[3] Ezr 6[21], לאלהים 2 Ch 17[4] 31[21] 34[3] Ezr 4[2]; Dr[Intr 503] finds in Chr weakened mng, *revere.* **b.** *seek heathen deities,* c. acc Je 8[2] 2 Ch 25[15.20]; with לְ, Dt 12[30] 2 Ch 17[3]. **4. a.** *seek,* with idea of demanding, *require* (בקשׁ is *seek,* simply), with acc. lost sheep Dt 22[2] Ez 34[6.8.11]; goat Lv 10[16.16] (P); with אחר, after green fodder Jb 39[8]. **b.** *inquire, investigate* (a matter), abs. Ju 6[29] Dt 13[15] 17[4.9] 19[18]; with acc. כָּל־לְבָבוֹת דּוֹרֵשׁ י׳ *all hearts Yahweh searches* 1 Ch 28[9], לִדְרֹשׁ הַמּוֹפֵת *to inquire into the wonder* 2 Ch 32[31]; with לְ, *to inquire about* 2 S 11[3] Jb 10[6], sq. עַל pers + inf. 2 Ch 24[6] *apply to the Levites to bring,* etc, cf. 31[9] (עַל both pers. and rei) **5.** *ask for, require, demand,* c acc. rei Ez 20[40]; + מִן pers Dt 23[22] Mi 6[8]; *exact,* oft. with collat. idea of *avenging,* מֵעִם Dt 18[19], so with מִיַּד Ez 34[10], דָּרַשׁ דָּם מִיַּד Gn 9[5] (P) Ez 33[6], acc only, דרשׁ דמים ψ 9[13], ד׳ רִשְׁעוֹ 10[15]; abs. v[4.13] 2 Ch 24[22] **6.** *seek with application, study, follow, practise,* abs by wisdom Ec 1[13]; with acc ד׳ מִשְׁפָּט *study* or *practise justice* Is 1[17] 16[5], ד׳ מַעֲשֵׂי י׳ ψ 111[2], טוֹב ואל־רע Am 5[14], commands of God ψ 119[45.94.155] 1 Ch 28[8], the law Ezr 7[10], † ד׳ שָׁלוֹם *seek* or *study the peace, welfare* of any one Dt 23[7] Je 29[7] Ezr 9[12], לשלום Je 38[4], ד׳ טוב Est 10[3], ד׳ רעה Pr 11[27] ψ 38[13] (cf. בקשׁ **2**, where this use is more common) **7.** *seek with care, care for,* ארץ אשׁר יהוה אלהיך דרשׁ אתה *land which Yahweh thy God careth for* Dt 11[12], אַל־יִדְרְשֵׁהוּ אֱלוֹהַּ *let not Eloah care for it* Jb 3[4]; אוֹתָךְ לֹא יְד׳ Je 30[14], דָּרְשָׁה צֶמֶר Pr 31[13], with לְ Je 30[17], אין דורשׁ לְנַפְשִׁי *no one careth for me* ψ 142[5], but in both these לְ perh belongs to אֵין, cf. ‖ אֵין לִי מַכִּיר ψ 142[5], also La 4[4] etc.; דְּרוּשָׁה *cared for* (of Jerus.) Is 62[12] **Niph.** *Pf* נִדְרָשׁ Gn 42[22], נִדְרַשְׁתִּי Is 65[1], נִדְרָשׁוּ 1 Ch 26[31], *Impf* אִדָּרֵשׁ Ez 14[3] 20[3.31.31] 36[37]; *Inf* abs הִדָּרֹשׁ Ez 14[3] (for ההדרשׁ);—**1.** *let oneself be inquired of, consulted,* only of God Ez 14[3.3] 20[3.31.31] 36[37] Is 65[1]. **2.** *be sought out* 1 Ch 26[31]. **3.** *be required,* of blood (cf. **Qal 5**) Gn 42[22] (E)

Note—וְדָרְשׁוּ מֵחָרְבוֹתֵיהֶם *and beg out of their desolate places* ψ 109[10] (Ki al. *wedŏrŭšu,* vid. Baer), many MSS rd וְגֹרְשׁוּ, so most interpr., 𝔊 Hup Bi Che rd. גֹּרְשׁוּ *be driven from.*

† **[מִדְרָשׁ] n.[m.] study, exposition, midrash,** only cstr. מִדְרַשׁ (late; common in NH, in sense of *imaginative exposition* or *didactic story*)—מִדְרַשׁ סֵפֶר הַמְּלָכִים *midrash of the book of Kings* 2 Ch 24[27]; מִדְרַשׁ הַנָּבִיא עִדּוֹ *midrash of the prophet Iddo* 2 Ch 13[22]. These were prob. of a didactic character, cf Dr[Intr 497]

† **[דָּשָׁא] vb. sprout, shoot, grow green** (As *dašû* Pi *make abundant* Lyon[Sargontexte 77]; cf. also sub דֶּשֶׁא, whence, acc. to others, vb. denom)—**Qal** *Pf* דָּשְׁאוּ Jo 2[22] (subj נְאוֹת מִדְבָּר)

Hiph *Impf* 3 fs תַּדְשֵׁא (juss) Gn 1^{11} *cause to sprout* or *shoot forth* דֶּשֶׁא—תַּדְשֵׁא הָאָרֶץ דֶּשֶׁא Je 50^{11} v sub דוש

† דֶּשֶׁא **n.m.** $^{Is 15. 6}$ **grass** (NH *id*, As *dišu*, *herb*, Lyon$^{Sargontexte 69}$, Sab דתא *fresh shoots* DHM$^{ZMG 1875, 607}$ = *springtime* CIS$^{iv p. 11}$, Aram דִּתְאָה, דִּתְאָא (cf Lag$^{BN 130}$))—ד׳ abs. Gn 1^{11} + 13 t —acc cogn. תַּדְשֵׁא Gn 1^{11}, cf v^{12} (in both, produced by earth); springing out of earth 2 S 23^{4}, of a second crop of grass Pr 27^{25} (opp חָצִיר), caused to spring forth by God לְהַצְמִיחַ מֹצָא דֶשֶׁא Jb 38^{27}, refreshed by rain Dt 32^{2}, נְאוֹת ד׳ ψ 23^{2}, as food of wild ass Jb 6^{5}, as failing (withered) Is 15^{6}, lacking for animals Je 14^{5}, וִירַק דֶּשֶׁא sim of weakness 2 K 19^{26} (‖ עֵשֶׂב שָׂדֶה) = Is 37^{27}, of transitoriness (withering) ψ 37^{2} (יֶרֶק ד׳), of growth and prosperity, Is 66^{14}.

† דָּשֵׁן **vb** be fat, grow fat (Ar دَسِمَ, whence also دَسَمٌ *grease, fat*, NH דשן *make fat*, cf. NH דשן *fat*)—**Qal** *Pf* 3 ms וְדָשֵׁן consec Dt 31^{20}(JE) fig. of Isr's prosperity. **Pi.** *Pf* דִּשַּׁנְתָּ ψ 23^{5}, וְדִשְּׁנוּ consec Nu 4^{13}, *Impf* יְדַשְּׁנֶה־סֶּלָה ψ 20^{4} volunt (cf. Ges$^{§ 48. 3}$ De, but perh rd sf נָּה-, נְהָ- v Ki Ges$^{1 c}$); 3 fs תְּדֻשַּׁן Pr 15^{30}, *Inf* לְדַשְּׁנוֹ Ex 27^{3}—causat *make fat* ד׳ בשמן ראשי i e anoint, symbol of festivity and joy ψ 23^{5}, ד׳ עֶצֶם Pr 15^{30} of bodily effect of good news, ד׳ עולה *find* a burnt-offering *fat* = acceptable ψ 20^{4}, elsewhere *denom* fr. דֶּשֶׁן (fat ashes),—*take away, clear away the fat ashes* (acc of altar cleared) Nu 4^{13} (P), so סירות לְדַשְּׁנוֹ Ex 27^{3} (P) **Pu.** *Impf.* יְדֻשָּׁן Pr 28^{25} Is 34^{7}, 3 fs תְּדֻשָּׁן Pr 11^{25} 13^{4}—pass. of causat. Pi *be made fat*, of dust saturated מֵחֵלֶב Is 34^{7}, fig of prosperity of the liberal Pr 11^{25}, the diligent 13^{4}, the trustful 28^{25} **Hothp.** *Pf* 3 *fs* הֻדַּשְּׁנָה (cf Ol$^{§ 271}$ Ges$^{§ 54. 7}$) Is 34^{6}, of Yahweh's sword—*it hath fattened itself* מֵחֵלֶב (‖ מָלְאָה דָם)

† דֶּשֶׁן **n.m** **fatness, fat ashes**—abs ד׳ ψ 63^{6} + 8 t, הַדֶּשֶׁן Lv 1^{16} + 3 t, cstr. דֶּשֶׁן ψ 36^{9}; sf דִּשְׁנִי Ju 9^{9}—**1.** *fatness*, abundance, luxuriance, oil, Ju 9^{9} (of olive tree); abundance, fertility ψ 63^{6} (in simile ‖ חֵלֶב), 65^{12}, of food and drink, Jb 36^{16} Je 31^{14}, passing over into fig of spiritual blessing ψ 36^{9} (ד׳ ביתך), Is 55^{2} **2.** *fat ashes*, i e ashes of victims, mixed with the fat Lv 1^{16} 4$^{12. 12}$ 6$^{3. 4}$ (all P) Je 31^{40} 1 Ki 13$^{3. 5}$

† דָּשֵׁן **adj. fat,** דָּשֵׁן Is 30^{23} (‖ שָׁמֵן), of לֶחֶם as product of ground, fig of righteous as trees דְּשֵׁנִים ψ 92^{15} (‖ רעננים) fat, full of oil (?) or sap (Che, cf דֶּשֶׁן Ju 9^{9}), as subst *vigorous, stalwart ones* (opp יוֹרְדֵי עָפָר cf. Che) ψ 22^{30} דִּשְׁנֵי אֶרֶץ (Brull שׁוֹכְנֵי, Renan$^{Hist III 134}$ יֹשְׁבֵי).

† דָּת **n.f.** $^{Est 3, 13}$ **decree, law, usage,** only in Persian period (B Aram NH *id*, Syr. ܕܳܬ or ܕܳܬܳܐ, Pers loan-w., Old Pers *dâta, law*, Spieg$^{APK 225}$)—ד׳ abs. Est 1^{8} + 9 t, cstr דַּת Est 2^{12}, דָּת 9^{13}, sf דָּתוֹ Est 2^{8} + 4 t, pl cstr. דָּתֵי Ezr 8^{36} + 2 t.; sf דָּתֵיהֶם Est 3^{8},—**1.** *decree, edict, commission* of Pers king Ezr 8^{36} (word elsewhere only in Est) Est 2^{8} (‖ דְּבַר הַמֶּלֶךְ), 4^{3} (‖ *id*) 8^{17} (‖ *id*) 9^{1} (‖ *id*, c. עשה *execute*) cf also 9^{13}, c. vb נִתַּן 3$^{14. 15}$ 8$^{13. 14}$ 9^{14}, written כְּתָב־הַדָּת 4^{8}(cf 3^{14} 8^{13}) **2.** *law*, permanently valid and applicable, וְיִכָּתֵב בְּדָתֵי פָרַס־וּמָדַי וְלֹא יַעֲבוֹר Est 1^{19} cf v^{15} 4$^{11. 16}$, יֹדְעֵי דָּת וָדִין 1^{13} *those that understood law and judgment;* דָּתֵי הַמֶּלֶךְ 3^{8}, of laws of the Jews in Persia 3^{8}; even of rules for drinking at a feast 1^{8}; for purifying of women 2^{12}.—The distinction between **1** & **2** is not absolute. The king's will was law, and the royal edict (דְּבַר מַלְכוּת) concerning Vashti was reckoned among the laws (דָּתֵי) of the Persians & Medes (1^{19})—In Dt 33^{2} MT אֵשׁ דָּת לָמוֹ *fire was a law for them* is corrupt, many emend proposed, cf Di, Di suggests אֵשׁ [לַפִּ]דת *fire of flames*, flaming fire, cf הַלַּפִּידִם Ex 20^{18} (but לַפֶּדֶת pl in ־ת not in OT unless as n pr), or (better), אֵשׁ [יֹקֶ]דֶת *a burning fire*, cf. Is 65^{5} (diff sense)

† דָּתָן **n.pr.m.** (cf As *Datana* Shlm$^{Obelisk 1 161}$) a Reubenite, son of Eliab Nu 16$^{1. 12. 24. 25. 27. 27}$ 26$^{9. 9}$ Dt 11^{6} ψ 106^{17}

† דֹּתָן **n.pr.loc.** (𝔊 Δωθαειμ)—in N Israel, north of Samaria, דֹּתָיְנָה Gn 37^{17} 2 K 6^{13}, דֹּתַיְנָה Gn 37^{17} cf. Di, mod *Tel Dotân*, Bd$^{Pal 228}$

ה

ה, *Hē*, fifth letter, = numeral 5 in postB. Heb; no evidence of this usage in OT times

הַ, הָ, הֶ, ה (on the use of these different forms, see the Grammars: e g Ges$^{§ 35}$), **definite article, the** (so Moab. Ph (Schrod$^{§ 62-4}$), Lihyan (NW. Arabia) *ha* (DHM$^{Epigr Denkm 4 13. 64 ff.}$); not As Aram or Eth Arab ال, of which,

before dentals, sibilants, and liquids, the *l* is written but not pronounced, thus اَلشَّمْسُ pron. *'ash-shamsu*=Heb. הַשֶּׁמֶשׁ)—in gen. the use of the art. in Heb. is analogous to its use in Greek or German: but naturally there are applications peculiar to Hebrew (comp. with what follows Ges^{§126} Ew^{§277}):—**1.** joined with *substantives:* **a.** to mark a definite concrete object, as Gn 1^{1} *the* heavens and *the* earth, הַמֶּלֶךְ the king, etc. Never, however (as in Greek e.g. ὁ Πλάτων), before true proper names, though it is used with certain terms, chiefly geographical, of which the orig. appellative sense has not been lost, as הַבַּעַל 'Baal,' lit. 'the lord,' in pl. הַבְּעָלִים i.e. the various local Baals, הַשָּׂטָן *the* Adversary Jb 1$^{6\,ff.}$ (as a pr. n. שָׂטָן, 'Satan,' only 1 Ch 21^{1}); הַלְּבָנוֹן (but not הַחֶרְמוֹן), הַיַּרְדֵּן (but not הָאַרְנֹן), הַכַּרְמֶל, הַשָּׁרוֹן the Sharon, הַשְּׁפֵלָה the (Judaean) lowland, הַכִּכָּר, הַמִּישׁוֹר the (Moabite) table-land, הָעֲרָבָה, הָעַי ''Ai,' הַגִּבְעָה 'Gibeah,' Ju 20$^{5\,ff.}$, הַגָּלִיל 'Galilee,' הַגִּלְגָּל, הַגִּלְבֹּעַ, הַבָּשָׁן, הַיְשִׁימוֹן, הָרָמָה, הַמִּצְפָּה, הַשִּׁטִּים, הַגִּלְעָד (oft.), הָעֹפֶל, הַפִּסְגָּה. **b.** with an adjective to denote one who exhibits a quality κατ' ἐξοχήν, i.e. to express the compar. or superl. degree: so oft., as Gn 1^{16} המאור הגדל the *greater* light, המאור הקטן the *lesser* light, 27^{1} בנו הגדול=his *elder* son, 48^{14} הצעיר the *younger*, 42^{13} הַקָּטֹן the little one, i.e. the *youngest* (of Joseph's brethren), Lv 21^{10} הַגָּדוֹל מֵאֶחָיו the *chiefest* of his brethren, Nu 35^{25}+ הכהן הגדול the *chief* priest, הצעיר ב׳ the *least* among Ju 6^{15}, הצעירה מן the *least* of 1 S 9^{21}, הַיָּפָה ב׳ the *fairest* among Ct 1^{8}, 2 K 10^{3} Pr 30^{30}, cf. Jos 14^{15}. **c.** with nouns which are not definite in themselves, but *acquire their definition from the context, or from the manner in which they are introduced:* thus (*a*) in the standing phrases הַיּוֹם *to-day*, Gn 4^{14} 21^{26}+oft.; הַלַּיְלָה *to-night*, Gn 19^{5} 30^{15}+, once 1 S 15^{16} *last night;* so הַשָּׁנָה *this* year, 2 K 19^{29} Jer 28^{16}; הַפַּעַם *this* time, Gn 18^{32}+. (β) הַנָּהָר *the* river (κατ' ἐξοχήν), i.e. the Euphrates; Ex 2^{15} *the well*, the well viz. of the district, Jos 8^{11} *the* valley, 1 S 17^{3}; 1 S 19^{10} *the* wall, v^{13} *the* bed, 20^{21} הַנַּעַר *the* lad (whom Jonathan would naturally take with him), v^{34} *the* table. Hence occas. where a suffix would define the noun more precisely, as הַחֲמוֹר 2 S 19^{27}+ =*my* ass, Ju 3^{20} 1 S 1^{9} הַכִּסֵּא=*his* seat, Ju 4^{15} 1 K 22^{35} 2 K 10^{15}+ הַמֶּרְכָּבָה, 1 S 18^{10} 20^{33} הַחֲנִית. **d.** it is a peculiarity of Hebrew thought to conceive an object as defined by its being *taken for a particular purpose*, and thus by a kind of prolepsis to prefix the art. to the noun denoting it: 1 S 10^{1} and Samuel took אֶת־פַּךְ הַשֶּׁמֶן lit. *the* cruse of oil, not, however, a cruse which had been defined previously, but one rendered definite by *being now taken;* in English idiom '*a* cruse of oil,' v^{25} בַּסֵּפֶר lit. in *the* scroll or book, the one, viz. taken for the purpose, i.e. in *a* scroll (so Ex 17^{14} Nu 5^{23} Jb 19^{23}), 21^{10} בַּשִּׂמְלָה, Ju 4^{18} וַתְּכַסֵּהוּ בַּשְּׂמִיכָה, v^{19} 7^{13} הָאֹהֶל *a tent*, 8^{25} 9^{48} אֶת־הַקַּרְדֻּמּוֹת *hatchets*, 20^{16} every one able to sling בָּאֶבֶן אֶל־הַשַּׂעֲרָה with *a* stone at *a* hair, 1 S 6^{8} בָּאַרְגַּז (unless indeed the אַרְגַּז was an understood appendage in every cart), Nu 11^{27} הַנַּעַר *a* young man, 13^{23} בַּמּוֹט on *a* pole, Jos 2^{15} בַּחֶבֶל with *a* cord, 2 S 17^{17} השפחה *a* girl (cf. Dr$^{1\,S\,1.\,4;\,19.\,13}$). Sts. it is uncertain whether an art. is to be referred to **c** or **d**: e.g. 1 S 2^{13} *his* prong or *a* prong, 2 S 18^{9} *his* mule or *a* mule, etc. **e.** with nouns that denote *objects or classes of objects that are known to all*, as הַמַּיִם, הַזָּהָב, הַצֹּאן; Gn 13^{2} Abram was very rich בַּמִּקְנֶה בַּכֶּסֶף וּבַזָּהָב, Ex 31^{4} לַעֲשׂוֹת בַּזָּהָב וּבַכֶּסֶף, Dt 14^{26} and thou shalt lay out the money בַּבָּקָר וּבַצֹּאן וּבַיַּיִן וּבַשֵּׁכָר, 2 K 9^{30} וַתָּשֶׂם בַּפּוּךְ עֵינֶיהָ, in French 'elle mit *du* fard à ses yeux.' It is, however, remarkable that this usage depends mostly on the punctuation, הַלֶּחֶם, הַיַּיִן, הַכֶּסֶף etc. (except as applied to denote *definite* quantities of gold, wine, etc., as Jos 6^{24}) being far less common than כֶּסֶף, יַיִן etc., but לַכֶּסֶף, בַּכֶּסֶף etc. being much more freq. than לְכֶסֶף, בְּכֶסֶף etc.: for instances in which the art. forms part of the consonantal text, see Gn 6^{20} 7^{8}+ העוף and הבהמה, Dt 8^{3} הַלֶּחֶם, 1 K 5$^{8.13}$ Is 28^{7} הַיַּיִן and הַשֵּׁכָר, 60^{17} Ez 15$^{4.7}$ הָאֵשׁ, Hb 2^{5} Pr 20^{1} ψ 65^{14} הַצֹּאן, Ct 1^{11} Ec 7^{12}. Cf. below, **h.** **f.** in *comparisons*, the object compared being, as a rule, not an individual as such, but one exhibiting the characteristics of a class: Is 1^{18} כַּשָּׁנִים, כַּתּוֹלָע like scarlet, like crimson (both meant generally), 5^{24} כַּפֶּסֶק יִהְיֶה, v^{28} כַּצֹּר and כַּסּוּפָה, 10^{14} כַּקֵּן, 13^{8} כַּיּוֹלֵדָה (as always with this word, e.g. 42^{14} ψ 48^{7}), 11^{7} כַּבָּקָר; + oft. (The usage is not, however, quite uniform, at least acc. to the punctuation: there occurs e.g. כְּקַשׁ Jb 41^{21} Is 47^{14}; כְּאַרְיֵה ψ 7^{3} al.: and we find both כַּלָּבִיא Is 5^{29} and כְּלָבִיא Ho 13^{8}; כָּאֲרִי Is 38^{13} and כַּאֲרִי Nu 24^{9}; כַּגִּבּוֹר Is 42^{13} and כְּגִבּוֹר Jb 16^{14}; etc.) Similarly Gn 19^{28} כְּקִיטֹר הַכִּבְשָׁן as the smoke of *a* furnace, Nu 11$^{8.12}$ כַּאֲשֶׁר יִשָּׂא הָאֹמֵן אֶת־הַיֹּנֵק, Dt 28^{29} (הָעִוֵּר), Ju 8$^{18\,b}$ כְּתֹאַר בְּנֵי הַמֶּלֶךְ, 14^{6} כְּשַׁסַּע הַגְּדִי like (a lion's) rending

a kid, 16^{9} 1 K 14^{15} Zc 12^{10} כְּמִסְפֵּד עַל הַיָּחִיד as mourning over *an* only child, 13^{9}+ Where, however, the standard of comparison is not the class in general, but only a particular part of it, defined by a special epithet (whether adj or verb), the art. is naturally omitted thus כַּמֹּץ like chaff (in general) Is 41^{15}, but כְּמֹץ עֹבֵר like chaff passing away 29^{5}, כַּצֵּל Jb 14^{2}, but כְּצֵל נָטוּי ψ 102^{12}, כַּקַּשׁ Is 40^{24}, but כְּקַשׁ נִדָּף 41^{2}, כָּאַיָּל Is 35^{6}, but כְּאַיָּל תַּעֲרֹג עַל וגו׳ like *a hind* (*that*) *longeth for streams of water* ψ 42^{2}, כָּאֵשׁ Is 9^{17}, but כְּאֵשׁ תִּבְעַר יַעַר like *fire* (*that*) *kindleth a wood* ψ 83^{15}, כֶּעָשָׁן Is 51^{6}, but כְּעָשָׁן מֵאֲרֻבָּה like *smoke from a chimney* Ho 13^{3} so Is 62^{1b} Jb 9^{26} 11^{16} כְּמַיִם עָבָרוּ like *waters* (*that*) *have passed by*, etc, Dt 32^{2a} כַּטַּל, כַּמָּטָר, but v^{2b} כִּשְׂעִירִם עֲלֵי־דֶשֶׁא כִּרְבִיבִים עֲלֵי־עֵשֶׂב Where the art is found, although a rel clause follows (as ψ 1^{4} 49^{13} Is 61^{10}), this is prob to be regarded not as *limiting* the class of object compared, but as *describing* it **g.** prefixed to *generic* nouns (in the singular) it designates the *class*, i e it imparts to the noun a *collective* force, as Ex 1^{22} כָּל־הַבֵּן all (lit the whole of) *the sons*, כָּל־הַבַּת all *the daughters*, Lv 17$^{8\,10}$ מִן־הַגֵּר of *the strangers*, who sojourn in their midst, Nu 21^{7} הַנָּחָשׁ *the serpents;* Gn 14^{13} Ez 24^{26} 33^{21} הַפָּלִיט those who escaped, Jos 6^{7}+ הֶחָלוּץ, v 9^{13} הַמְאַסֵּף; 8^{19} הָאֹרֵב, 1 S 13^{17}
הָ ד הַמַּשְׁחִית, Mi 2^{13}, Is 6^{4} הַקּוֹרֵא the choir of criers, 1 S 24^{14} הַקַּדְמֹנִי the ancients, Ec 7^{26} אֶת־הָאִשָּׁה woman, and oft with gentile names, as הַיְבוּסִי the Jebusites, הַכְּרֵתִי וְהַפְּלֵתִי 2 S 8^{18} al, הַדָּנִי Ju 18^{1} etc, הַלֵּוִי the Levites, Nu 3^{20} 18^{23} Mal 2^{8} ψ 135^{20}+ **h.** with nouns denoting abstract ideas, esp the names of moral qualities (cf Gk ἡ δικη, Fr la justice), chiefly in two cases—(*a*) where the art is recognizable in the consonantal text, exceptionally, when some emphasis or definiteness is intended, as Dt 7^{9} שֹׁמֵר הַבְּרִית וְהַחֶסֶד, 2 S 2^{6} הַחֶסֶד הַזֶּה 1 K 3^{6}, אֶת הַחֶסֶד וְהָרַחֲמִים Je 16^{5} (contr Zc 7^{9}), הַצֶּדֶק †Is 1^{26} 61^{3} Ec 3^{16}, הַצְּדָקָה †Is 32$^{17\,17}$ (contrast v^{16}) Dn 9^{7} (emph); הָאֱמֶת הַדַּעַת Ho 4^{6}, Gn 32^{11} (sq אֲשֶׁר), Is 59^{15} (contrast v^{14}) Zc 8$^{3\,19}$, הָאֱמוּנָה †Is 11^{5b} (contr v^{a}) Je 7^{28}, הַחָכְמָה Jb 28$^{12\,20}$, הַחַיִּים Gn 2^{9}+, הָאַהֲבָה †Ct 2^{7} 3^{5} 8$^{4\,7}$, הָרֶשַׁע Is 25^{8} Ru 1^{17}+, הַמָּוֶת Je 7$^{4\,8}$ 23^{26}, הַשֶּׁקֶר †ψ 125^{3} Ec 3^{16}, הָרִשְׁעָה †Zc 5^{8}, הַחֹשֶׁךְ Is 60^{2} Ec 2^{13}, see also Dt 30$^{15\,19}$ (Je 21^{8}), 1 K 7^{14} Je 32^{19} Mal 2^{5} הַחַיִּים וְהַשָּׁלוֹם, ψ 123^{4} 130^{4} Dn 9^{9} 1 Ch 29^{11} 2 Ch 1^{12} Pr 31^{30} Ec 2$^{13.17}$ 7$^{12\,19}$ 10^{6} 11^{10}: but in all such cases אֱמֶת, צֶדֶק, חֶסֶד, etc are far more common (β) where the art. depends on the punctuation, after preps, esp בְּ, but with much irregularity, as בַּחֶסֶד Is 16^{5} Pr 20^{28} (but בח׳ Ho 2^{21} Pr 16^{6}), בַּצֶּדֶק Pr 25^{5} (elsewhere always בצ׳ בִּצְדָקָה also always); בֶּאֱמֶת and בֶּאֱמוּנָה always, בַּשֶּׁקֶר †Is 28^{15} (but ‖ כָּזָב, not הַכָּזָב) Je 5^{31} 13^{25} 20^{6} 23^{14} (בְּשֶׁקֶר †Je 3^{10} 29^{9}); בַּשָּׁלוֹם †ψ 29^{11} Jb 15^{21} (elsewhere בשלום); Zc 12^{4} to smite בַּשִּׁגָּעוֹן וּבַעִוָּרוֹן (but Dt 28^{28} בשגעון ובעורון), cf Gn 19^{11} Dt 28^{28}, to enter with one בַּמִּשְׁפָּט Jb 9^{32} 22^{4} (but במשפט ψ 143^{2}), contrast also Pr 18^{5} with 24^{23}, לַמִּשְׁפָּט Is 59^{11} ψ 9^{8} (but למ׳ Is 5^{7} ψ 122^{5}), Pr 2^{2} 7^{4} לַחָכְמָה (but never הַחכמה in Pr 1–9, or indeed in the whole book), Pr 2^{3} 7^{4} לַבִּינָה, Jb 39^{17} בַּבִּינָה (but never הַבִּינָה); Pr 2$^{2.3}$ לַתְּבוּנָה (but הַתְּבוּנָה only 1 K 7^{14} emph); to perish בַּצָּמָא Ju 15^{18}+; Is 29^{21} בַּתֹּהוּ, 32^{19} בַּשִּׁפְלָה תִּשְׁפַּל הָעִיר Germ in *die* Niedrigkeit sinkt die Stadt, 45^{16} together they go בַּכְּלִמָּה (in die Schmach), 46^{2} בַּשְּׁבִי into captivity, 47^{5} בֹּאִי בַחֹשֶׁךְ (so always: never בחשך). The living language may have used the art more readily after a prep, where it did not lengthen the word by an entire syll., still the disparity of usage between *a* and β makes it not improb that the art in β is in many cases not original but due to the punctuators **i.** to mark the *vocative* 1 S 17^{55} חֵי־נַפְשְׁךָ הַמֶּלֶךְ as thy soul liveth, *O* king, I do not know, v^{58} בֶּן מִי אַתָּה הַנַּעַר Whose son art thou, *lad?* 2 S 14^{4} Help, *O* king! 1 K 18^{26} הַבַּעַל עֲנֵנוּ, 2 K 9^{5} אֵלֶיךָ הַשָּׂר, Is 42^{18} הַחֵרְשִׁים שְׁמָעוּ, Je 2^{31} הַדּוֹר אַתֶּם רְאוּ וגו׳, Ez 37^{4} הָעֲצָמוֹת הַיְבֵשׁוֹת *O* dry bones, Mal 3^{9} הַגּוֹי כֻּלּוֹ (Dr § 198 Obs. 2)

N B. In poetry, the article is frequently dispensed with before words which would naturally take it in prose thus ψ 2$^{2.8\,10}$ & oft. אֶרֶץ; 8^{9} 18^{10} 33^{6} + שָׁמַיִם; (rarely in prose, Gn 1^{8} 2^{4} 1 K 8^{35}), 21^{2} 45$^{14\,16}$ 61^{7} al מֶלֶךְ, 66^{6} 72^{8}+ יָם, 59$^{7\,15}$ עִיר, Ju 5^{2} ψ 18^{44} עָם etc, ψ 9$^{6\,17}$ & oft. רָשָׁע, Is 1$^{2.6.21}$ 3$^{10\,11}$ 11$^{6.7\,8}$

2. With *adjectives, participles,* and *demonstrative pronouns* (זה, הם, המה, היא, הוא, אלה, זאת): viz. **a.** (so regularly) when the subst qualified by these words *is defined by it likewise,* as המלך הגדול = ὁ βασιλεὺς ὁ μέγας, Gn 2^{12} הָאָרֶץ הַהִוא, 20^{1} הַדָּבָר הַזֶּה, Jos 2^{3} האנשים הבאים אליך = οἱ ἄνδρες οἱ ἐλθόντες πρὸς σέ, Gn 13^{5} 16^{13} 24^{65} 32^{21} Ju 6^{28} Is 65$^{3.4.5}$ 66^{24} ψ 31^{9} So also with adjj & ptcpp, if the subst be defined by a sf (as Dt 4^{37} בְּכֹחוֹ הַגָּדֹל, 1 S 8^{14}

וִיתִיכֶם הַטֹּבוֹת); and with a pron., if it be defined by a gen. (as Dt 29[20] 1 S 14[29] 15[14] 2 K 6[32] בֶּן־הַמְרַצֵּחַ הַזֶּה *this* son of a murderer), but not if it be defined by a sf, as Ex 10[1] אֹתֹתַי אֵלֶּה (not אֹתֹתַי הָאֵלֶּה), Jos 2[14] דְּבָרֵנוּ זֶה *this* our word (not ד׳ הַזֶּה). v. Dr[§ 209 Obs] Similarly when the art. with the ptcp has a *resumptive* force, ψ 33[15] (v[14] he looketh forth from the place, &c.), הַיֹּצֵר יַחַד לִבָּם *he that formeth*, etc, 19[11] הַנֶּחֱמָדִים מִזָּהָב *which* (v[10b]) *are more desirable* than gold, 49[7] ([6b] the iniquity of my aggressors surroundeth me), הַבֹּטְחִים *who trust* in their riches, etc., Gn 49[21] Is 46[6] 51[20] Jb 6[16] + (v. Dr[§ 135. 7]). **b.** (rare) when the subst qualified by the adj. or ptcp. was felt to be sufficiently definite for its own art. to be dispensed with, as sts. with the word *day* Gn 1[31] יוֹם הַשִּׁשִּׁי, 2[3] יוֹם הַשְּׁבִיעִי, Ex 12[15. 16] 20[10] (= Dt 5[14]) Lv 19[6] 22[27]: so with מָבוֹא *entrance* Je 38[14], שַׁעַר Zc 14[10], חָצֵר *court* 1 K 7[8. 12] Ez 40[28] al.; also in certain phrases (peculiar to P) where the subst. is defined by כל, as Gn 1[21] כָּל־נֶפֶשׁ הַחַיָּה *all* living souls, v[28] כָּל־חַיָּה הָרֹמֶשֶׂת all living things *that creep*, etc, 7[21] 9[10] Lv 11[10. 46]; further in isolated cases, hardly reducible to rule, Lv 24[10] 1 S 12[23] דֶּרֶךְ הַטּוֹבָה, 16[23] רוּחַ הָרָעָה, 2 S 12[4] לְאִישׁ הֶעָשִׁיר Je 6[20] 17[2] Zc 4[7] ψ 104[18] Ezr 10[9] חֹדֶשׁ הַתְּשִׁיעִי (quite exceptional in OT) (With prons. this use is so rare that, where it occurs, it is dub if the text be sound. 1 S 17[12. 17] Je 40[3] Kt Mi 7[11]). And with the ptcp. · 1 S 25[10] רַבּוּ עֲבָדִים הַמִּתְפָּרְצִים many are the slaves who break away etc, Is 7[20] Je 27[3] 46[16] = 50[16] חֶרֶב הַיּוֹנָה the oppressing sword, Ez 2[3] (but 𝔊 Co om. הגוים), 14[22] 32[22. 24] ψ 62[4] Pr 26[18] Ju 21[19] (very anomal., rd. prob. לַמְסִלָּה) This usage is somewhat more freq. in the later parts of OT; and in postB. Heb it is very general (e g. יֵצֶר הָרָע the evil inclination): v. further Dr[§ 209]. **c.** with the ptcp, where the ptcp. with the art. forms really the *subject*: Gn 2[11] הוּא הַסֹּבֵב not 'it was encompassing,' but 'it is *that which encompassed*,' 45[12] פִּי הַמְדַבֵּר my mouth is *that which* speaketh, Dt 3[21] עֵינֶיךָ הָרֹאֹת thine eyes were *those which saw*, 4[3] 8[18] ὅτι οὗτός ἐστιν ὁ διδούς σοί, Is 14[27] 66[9] (v. Dr[§ 135. 7]).

3. The article is prefixed exceptionally—mostly in the latest Hebrew—with the force of a relative to the *verb*. †Jos 10[24] הֶהָלְכוּא אִתּוֹ *that* went with him, Ez 26[17], הָעִיר הַהֻלָּלָה, 1 Ch 26[28] וְכֹל הַהִקְדִּישׁ שְׁמוּאֵל and all *that* Samuel had dedicated, 29[8. 17] 2 Ch 1[4] בְּהֵכִין in (the place) *that* he had prepared, 29[36] Ezr 8[25] 10[14. 17]. Acc. to the punctuation, it occurs similarly elsewhere, as Gn 18[21] הַבָּאָה (so 46[27] Jb 2[11]), 21[3] הַנּוֹלַד־לוֹ, 1 K 11[9] & Dn 8[1] הַנִּרְאָה, Is 51[10] הַשָּׂמָה, 56[3] הַנִּלְוָה, Ru 1[22] 2[6] 4[3] (all הַשָּׁבָה) · but in all these passages, the change of a point, or even sts. of an accent, would restore the normal participial construction (as הַנּוֹלָד לוֹ, הַבָּאָה, cf Gn 48[6], הַנִּרְאֶה), which is, no doubt, what was intended by the orig. writers, and is recognised elsewhere by the Massorah, e.g. Gn 12[7] 35[1] הַנִּרְאֶה, 46[26] & Ru 4[11] הַבָּאָה (cf. Ew[§ 331 b] Ges[138. 3 b]) Once, still more anomalously, before a prep. 1 S 9[24] וְהֶעָלֶיהָ (as though καὶ τὸ ἐπ' αὐτῆς). but rd prob וְהָאַלְיָה *and the fat tail*, v Dr. (In Arab. اَلْ also occurs, though very rarely, as a relative: W[AG 1 § 345 b, CO 117]) —On the anomalous use of the art. with a word in the *st. c*, v Gramm, as Ew[§ 290 d], Ges[§ 127 R. 4], also Dr[§ 190-1].

הֲ, הַ, הָ, הֶ (on the different forms, see Ges[§ 100. 4]: on Dt 32[6], v. הַל, p 210), **interrog. part.** (B Aram. and 𝔗 הֲ, Arab. أ), prefixed, as a rule, to the first word of a sentence (or clause). **1.** in *direct* questions: **a.** as a simple interrogative, where the answer expected is uncertain, Ex 2[7] הַאֵלֵךְ *shall I go* and call thee a nurse? 1 S 23[11] הֲיַסְגִּרֻנִי *will* the men of Keilah deliver me into his hand? הֲיֵרֵד שָׁאוּל *will* Saul come down? Jb 1[8]; and frequently **b.** often in questions, expressed in a tone of surprise, or put rhetorically, to which a *negative* answer is expected (= Lat. *num?*). Gn 4[9] הֲשֹׁמֵר אָחִי אָנֹכִי *Am* I my brother's keeper? 18[17] *shall* I hide from Abraham that which I am about to do? 30[2] 50[19] Nu 11[22a] Dt 4[33] . . . הֲשָׁמַע עָם *Did* a people ever hear the voice of God speaking out of the midst of the fire, . . and live? 20[19] (rd. with 𝔊𝔗𝔖𝔙 Ew Ke Di etc הָאָדָם for הָאָדָם), 2 S 7[5] הַאַתָּה תִּבְנֶה־לִּי בַיִת (altered in 1 Ch 17[4] to the neg. לֹא אַתָּה תִּבְנֶה וג׳), 2 K 6[22] . . . הַאֲשֶׁר שָׁבִיתָ those whom thou hast taken captive with thy sword and with thy bow, wilt thou smite? Is 28[24] 36[12a] 57[6] 58[5] Je 15[12] 16[20] Am 5[25] ψ 50[13] Jb 8[11] 15[7. 8. 11] 38[12. 16. 17. 22] etc, before an inf. absol. (Ew[§ 328 a]) Je 7[9] Jb 40[2] and prob Mi 2[7] (rd הֶאָמוּר: see p 55). After a protasis, הֲ . . . הִנֵּה Nu 22[38] 2 K 7[2. 19] Je 32[27] Ez 17[10]; after הֵן Je 3[1] Hg 2[12]: cf. after אוּלַי Gn 24[5], after אִם Jb 14[14] אִם יָמוּת גֶּבֶר הֲיִחְיֶה if a man dieth, shall he live? Occasionally, one or more words precede הֲ (in the same clause)

for special emphasis · 2 S 7[7] Jb 34[31] כִּי אֶל־אֵל הֶאָמַר for *to God* did one ever say.. ? Ne 13[27], Je 22[15] (הֲלֹא), cf 23[26] **c.** it is used in questions which, by seeming to make doubtful what cannot be denied, have the force of an impassioned or indignant affirmation Gn 27[36] ('dubitantis speciem prae se fert Esavus, ut eo acerbius affirmet,' Maurer, cited by Ges), 1 S 2[27] הנגלה נגליתי וג׳ *Did I reveal* myself to the house of thy father, when they were in Egypt? etc (i e. of course I did, although thy sons, by their actions, appear to belie it), 1 K 16[31] (expressing astonishment), 21[19] הֲרָצַחְתָּ וְגַם־יָרָשְׁתָּ *Hast thou* slain, and also taken possession? Je 31[20] Jb 20[4] 41[1] (cf Hi), also Gn 16[13], and the phrases הֲרְאִיתֶם *do ye see?* 1 S 10[24] 2 K 6[32]; הֲרָאִיתָ *dost thou see?* 1 K 20[13] Ez 8[12 15 17] al **d.** in disjunctive questions, the first question being introduced usually by הֲ, the second by אם or (more rarely) ואם see exx under אם **2** (p 50) The disjunctive question may express a real alternative (as Jos 5[13]), or (as esp. in poetry) the same thought may be repeated in a different form, in two parallel clauses (e g. Is 10[15]) in the latter case, the answer *No* is usually expected (v p 50) Only very rarely is the second question introduced by הֲ Ju 14[15] (where, however, הֲלֹם ought no doubt to be read, with MSS, 𝔗 Be al, for הֲלֹא), or אוֹ Ju 18[19] Jb 16[3] 38[28.31]

2. In *indirect* interrogation, *whether* (Germ *ob* ?)—**a.** singly, after verbs of *seeing* Gn 8[8] לראות הֲ to see *whether*, 18[21] Ex 4[18] Ct 6[11], *telling* Gn 43[6], *trying* Dt 13[4], *knowing* Ju 3[4] Ec 3[21] (rd הַעֹלָה and הַיֹּרֶדֶת: v De or Wr *ad loc*) **b.** disjunctively,—usually הֲ...אם, Nu 13[18end 19a] (and see the land)...הַטּוֹבָה הִיא אִם רָעָה *whether* it be good *or* bad, v[19 b.20.20]; הֲ...אם לא Gn 24[21] 27[21] 37[32] Ex 16[4] that I may try it (the people) הֲיֵלֵךְ בְּתוֹרָתִי אִם לֹא *whether* it will walk in my law or not, Nu 11[23] Dt 8[2] Ju 2[22], הֲ...הֲ Nu 13[19] (by side of הֲ...אם), הֲ...אוֹ Ec 2[19] 11[6]

It is prefixed to other particles, as הַאִם, הֲלֹא, הֲכִי, הֲגַם, הַאַף · see אַף, אִם, etc.

†**הֲלְ** Dt 32[6] הַלְ יְהוָה תִּגְמְלוּ־זֹאת (so V.d.H and other edd) The reading here became early a subject of dispute, and MSS and edd. vary accordingly Some follow the school of Nehardea, and read הַלְ יְהוָֹה, others (so Norzi) follow the school of Sora, and read הֲ לַיהוָֹה, others (so Hahn) have הֲלַיהוָֹה. Were הַלְ original, it would be an interrog part.=Ar هَلْ, for which elsewhere הֲ is always found. The other punctuations would also each be highly irregular. The true reading is undoubtedly הַ לַיהוָֹה (הֲלַיהוָֹה) Cf De Rossi [Var Lect ad loc.], and on the possible origin of the anomaly, Gei [Jüd Ztschr 1864-65, p 89 f.]

†**הָא** **interj** (Aram. הָא, Dn 2[43] הא (q v.), ܗܳܐ, Arab هَا) **lo, behold**! Gn 47[23] Ez 16[43]

†**הֶאָח** **interj.** (onomatop) expressing **joy, Aha!** always introduced by אָמַר, Is 44[16] he says, *Aha*, I am warm, I have seen the fire. Of satisfaction over the misfortune of an enemy or rival, ψ 35[21 25] let them not say in their heart האח נפשנו *Aha*, so would we have it! (*lit* our desire!) 40[16] (=70[4]), Ez 25[3] 26[2] 36[2]. Metaph, of the neighing of a war horse in the battle, Jb 39[25]

הָאֲרָרִי 2 S 23[33b] v הָרָרִי

הַב v יהב

הַבְהָבִים v. sub יהב

I **הֶבֶל** [73] **n.m. vapour, breath** (NH *id.*, Syr ܗܰܒܠܳܐ *id*) fig **vanity** (so NH, Syr ܗܒܳܠܳܐ)—הָבֶל Ec 1[2]+, cstr הֲבֵל +Ec 1[2.2] 12[8], sf. הֶבְלִי etc Ec 6[12] 7[15] 9[9], pl. הֲבָלִים Je 10[8]+, cstr. הַבְלֵי Je 8[19]+, sf. הַבְלֵיהֶם Dt 32[21]+;—**1.** lit Is 57[13] all of them (the idols) יִשָּׂא־רוּחַ יִקַּח הָבֶל a *breath* (𝔙 aura) will carry away, Pr 21[6] the getting of treasures by a lying tongue is הבל נִדָּף a *vapour* driven away Elsewhere always **2.** fig. of what is evanescent, unsubstantial, worthless, **vanity**, as of idols Je 10[15]=51[18] 16[19] הֶבֶל וְאֵין בָּם מוֹעִיל (‖שֶׁקֶר), heathen observances 10[3], and in phr הָלַךְ אַחֲרֵי הַהֶבֶל 2[5] 2 K 17[15]; Pr 13[11] הוֹן מֵהֶבֶל wealth (gotten) *out of vanity* (i e not by solid toil, opp קֹבֵץ עַל יָד) is minished (but 𝔊 𝔙 Ew מְבֹהָל, v. 20[21] Qr), 31[30] שֶׁקֶר הַחֵן והבל הַיֹּפִי, La 4[17] אֶל עֶזְרָתֵנוּ הָבֶל to our *vain* (Dr [§ 193 n.]) help; of life Jb 7[16] וַיְכַל בַּהֶבֶל יְמֵיהֶם ψ 78[33] consumed כִּי הבל יָמָי: their days *as* (ב **I, d**) *vanity*, man ψ 39[6 12] 62[10] הֶבֶל בְּנֵי אָדָם...הֵמָּה מֵהֶבֶל יָחַד: they are altogether (made) *of vanity*, 94[11] 144[4], esp in Ec (31 t + הֲבֵל הֲבָלִים 1[2.2] 12[8]) of the fruitlessness of all human enterprise and endeavour, 1[2] הַכֹּל הבל, v[14] הַכֹּל הֶבֶל וּרְעוּת רוּחַ all was *vanity* and the pursuit of wind, 2[1 14 15] etc, 6[4] (of an abortion) בַּהֶבֶל בָּא i.e into a lifeless existence, v[11] יֵשׁ דְּבָרִים הַרְבֵּה מַרְבִּים הָבֶל (of discussions lead-

ing to no result), note also the phrases יְמֵי הֶבֶל (הֶבְלְךָ, הֶבְלוֹ) יְמֵי חַיֵּי ה׳ 6^{12} 9^{9}; Jb 7^{16} 9^{9}; Jb 27^{12} (v. הָבַל), Is 49^{4} לְתֹהוּ וְהֶבֶל for nought and *vanity* have I spent my strength; as adv. accus. *vainly, to no purpose* Is 30^{7} הֶבֶל וָרִיק יַעְזֹרוּ, ψ 39^{7} אַךְ הֶבֶל יֶהֱמָיוּן they disquiet themselves *to no purpose*, Jb 9^{29}: הֶבֶל אִיגָע 35^{16}, with נִחֵם to comfort 21^{34} Zc 10^{2}. *Pl.* †הֲבָלִים of false gods, Dt 32^{21} כִּעֲסוּנִי בְּהַבְלֵיהֶם (‖ בְּלֹא־אֵל) 1 K $16^{13.26}$ Je 8^{19} הַבְלֵי נֵכָר (‖ בִּפְסִלֵיהֶם), 10^{8} 14^{22} הַבְלֵי הַגּוֹיִם, ψ 31^{7} הַשֹּׁמְרִים הַבְלֵי־שָׁוְא empty *vanities* Jon 2^{9}; in more general sense Ec $1^{2.2}$ 12^{8} הֲבֵל הֲבָלִים, 5^{6}.

†הָבַל **vb. denom.** act emptily, become vain—**Qal** Je 2^{5} = 2 K 17^{15} they went after vanity וַיֶּהְבָּלוּ and *became vain*, ψ 62^{11} וּבְגָזֵל אַל־תֶּהְבָּלוּ do not *become vain* (i.e. be demoralized) by robbery; with cogn. acc. Jb 27^{12} לָמָּה זֶּה הֶבֶל תֶּהְבָּלוּ why do ye *become vain* with vanity (i.e. shew yourselves utterly vain)? **Hiph.** *cause to become vain* Je 23^{16} (of false prophets) מַהְבִּלִים הֵמָּה אֶתְכֶם i.e. fill you with vain hopes.

†II. הֶבֶל, הָבֶל **n.pr.m.** (perh. i.q. As. *ablu*, son, COT[Gloss]; cf. also We[Skizzen iii. 70]: der. from I. הֶבֶל not prob.) second son of Adam Gn $4^{2.2.4.4.8.8.9.25}$.

†[הָבְנִי] **n.[m.]** ebony (so Symm 𝔙 Ki & moderns; otherwise 𝔊 𝔖; Egypt. *heben*, Lieblein[ÄZ 1886, 13] cf. Pinsker[Einleitung 89]; Gk. *ἔβενος*, Lat. *hebenum*)—only pl. הָבְנִים Ez 27^{15} Qr (Kt הובנים) קַרְנוֹת שֵׁן והבנים; it was brought fr. India, & (finer) fr. Ethiopia, cf. Sm & reff.

†[הָבַר] **vb.**? **divide** (so most, but dub.; Ar. هَبَرَ *cut into large pieces, cut up*, is perh. denom. fr. هَبْرَةٌ *a 'chunk'* of meat; comparison of Ar. خَبَرَ *be acquainted with, skilled in* (AW Kn Di) is also doubtful; if correct, then rd. חבר; but cf. infr.)—**Qal** *Pf.* 3 pl. הברו Is 47^{13} Kt, *Pt.* הֹבְרֵי Qr; הֹבְרוּ שָׁמַיִם הַחֹזִים בַּכּוֹכָבִים *they that divide the heavens, that gaze at the stars* (Kt would be rel. cl. without אֲשֶׁר; ה׳ then refers to the distinguishing of signs of zodiac, or other astrological division of sky, cf. Che; on zodiac in Babylon v. Jen[Kosmologie 57 ff.]; & on planets & constellations Id[ib. 95 ff.] Epping & Strm[Astronomisches aus Bab. 109 ff.];—but text prob. corrupt; GFM (June, 1892) suggests חֹקְרֵי (cf. חקר את־הארץ Ju 18^{2}).

†הֵגָא **n.pr.m.** eunuch of Ahasuerus (prob. Pers.; cf. Ἡγίας, courtier of Xerxes, Ctesias Pers 24; also Herodot[ix. 33]; Roed. in Thes Add) Est 2^{3}; = הֵגַי $2^{8.15}$, הֵגֶא 2^{8}.

הגג (*murmur*, then *muse*; cf. Ar. هَجَّ *burn, blaze* (of fire), *make a murmuring noise* in burning; PS gives Syr. ܗܓܓ *phantasma vidit, somniavit*; Ethpe. & esp. Ethpa. *mente concepit, imaginatus est*; cf. also הָגָה).

†[הָגִיג] **n.m. murmuring** (Che), **whisper, musing** (on form cf. Ba[NB 136])—only sf. הֲגִיגִי **1.** ψ 5^{2} בִּינָה ה׳ *understand my murmuring* (whispering, faint utterance), addressed to י׳. **2.** ψ 39^{4} בַּהֲגִיגִי *in my musing* i.e. while I was musing.

הַגִּדְגָּדָה v. sub גדד p. 151.

†I. הָגָה **vb. moan, growl, utter, speak, muse** (only poet.) (onomatop.; NH הָגָה *muse, speak, spell* a word, so Aram. הֲגָא; ܗܓܐ *muse*, esp. Ethpa.; Ar. هَجَا *satirize, insult, scold*, also *spell* (borrowed mng.))—**Qal** *Perf.* 2 ms. וְהָגִיתָ consec. Jos 1^{8}; 1 s. הָגִיתִי ψ 143^{5}, וְהָגִיתִי consec. ψ 77^{13}; *Impf.* יֶהְגֶּה Jb 27^{4} + 8 t.; 3 fs. תֶּהְגֶּה ψ 35^{28} + 2 t., אֶהְגֶּה ψ 63^{7} Is 38^{14}, יֶהְגּוּ ψ 2^{1} + 2 t., תֶּהְגּוּ Is 16^{7}; נֶהְגֶּה Is 59^{11}; *Inf. abs.* הָגוֹ Is 59^{11};—**1.** of inarticulate sounds: **a.** *growl*, of lion growling over prey, sq. עַל Is 31^{4}. **b.** *groan, moan*, in distress (like dove), abs., Is 38^{14} 59^{11} (הָגוֹ נֶהְגֶּה); *sigh for* (לְ) in sorrow, mourning, *moan for* Is 16^{7} (‖ יְיֵלִיל לְ), so also Je 48^{31}. **2.** *utter*, sq. acc. rei, ψ 38^{13}; subj. לָשׁוֹן Jb 27^{4} (‖ דִּבֶּר) ψ 35^{28} 71^{24} Is 59^{3}; subj. פֶּה ψ 37^{30} Pr 8^{7}—cf. also sub **Po.** infr.; *speak* (abs.) ψ 115^{7} (בְּ instr.) **3. a.** (*soliloquize*) *meditate, muse*, c. בְּ rei, Jos 1^{8} ψ 1^{2} 63^{7} 77^{13} 143^{5}; c. acc. Is 33^{18}, subj. לֵב. **b.** *imagine, devise*, c. acc. ψ 2^{1} Pr 24^{2} (subj. לֵב); c. Inf. Pr 15^{28} (subj. *id.*) **Po.** *Inf. abs.* only הֹרוֹ וְהֹגוֹ מִלֵּב דִּבְרֵי־שָׁקֶר Is 59^{13} *a conceiving and an uttering, out of the heart, lying words* (‖ דַּבֶּר עֹשֶׁק וְסָרָה);—on form cf. Kö[i. 555]; but rd. rather הָרוֹ וְהָגוֹ **Qal** *Inf. abs.* cf. Di; Ba[NB 77] retains MT & expl. as Qal Inf. pass. **Hiph.** *Pt.* pl. הַמְצַפְצְפִים וְהַמַּהְגִּים Is 8^{19} *those that make chirpings and mutterings*, of necromancers and wizards.

†הֶגֶה **n.m.** [Jb 37, 2] **a rumbling, growling, moaning**:—ה׳ abs. Ez 2^{10} + 2 t.;—**1.** *a rumbling, growling sound* וְה׳ מִפִּיו יֵצֵא Jb 37^{2} of thunder, as sound going forth from God's mouth. **2.** *a moaning* קִנִים וָה׳ וָהִי Ez 2^{10} *lamentations and moaning and woe.*

3. *a sigh* or *moan*, as transient, כִּלִּינוּ שָׁנֵינוּ כְמוֹ־הֶגֶה ψ 90⁹ *we bring our years to an end as a sigh*, i e *a fleeting sound* (cf. RVm VB)

† **הָגוּת n.f. meditation, musing,** only cstr. (with firm ־ָ cf. Sta § 304 e) פִּי יְדַבֵּר חָכְמוֹת וה׳ לִבִּי תבונות ψ 49⁴ *my mouth shall speak wisdom, and the musing of my heart* shall be *understanding*

† **הִגָּיוֹן n.m. resounding music, meditation, musing,**—ה׳ abs ψ 9¹⁷ 92⁴, cstr. הגיון ψ 19¹⁵, sf. הֶגְיוֹנָם La 3⁶²,—**1** *resounding music*, עֲלֵי הִגָּיוֹן בכנור ψ 92⁴ *with sounding music upon the lyre* (Che), cf ה׳ סֶלָה ψ 9¹⁷ (a musical direction, v סלה) **2.** *meditation, musing* אמרי־פי והגיון לבי ψ 19¹⁵ *the words of my mouth and the meditation of my heart*, also in bad sense = *plotting* שִׂפְתֵי קָמַי וְהֶגְיוֹנָם עָלַי La 3⁶² *the lips of those rising against me, and their imagining against me* (‖ מַחְשְׁבֹתָם v⁶¹, cf I הָגָה **3 b**)

†II **הָגָה vb. remove** (Thes comp יגה)—**Qal** *Pf* הָגָה Is 27⁸ (Di rds הָגָה), *Inf abs* הָגוֹ Pr 25⁴·⁵,—הָגוֹ סִיגִים מִכָּסֶף Pr 25⁴ *remove* (lit *a removing*) *dross from silver*, as sim of following הָגוֹ רָשָׁע לִפְנֵי מֶלֶךְ Pr 25⁵ *remove (the) wicked before a king*, הָגָה בְּרוּחוֹ הַקָּשָׁה Is 27⁸, acc to Di (v supr) *he* (׳י) *hath removed her* (i e sent into exile, his people under fig of faithless wife) *by his harsh wind*, so transl also Ew Che (*he scared her away*) Brd RV VB, De follows MT, regards as ellipt rel. cl, and renders by ptcp, 'sichtend (i.e *sifting, winnowing*) heftigen Hauches,' but conjectures הָגֹה (Inf abs.)

הַגִּי, הָגֵא **n.pr.m.** v. הגא

הגן (NH הָגַן, Aram הֲגֵן *be suitable, fit, worthy* on orig mng cf Fl in NHWB, s v)

† [**הָגִין**] **adj. appropriate, suitable?** (cf. NH Aram, supr) — הַגִּדְרָה הֲגִינָה Ez 42¹² *the corresponding* (?) *wall*, Ke; otherwise Vrss (𝔊 καλάμου, 𝔙 *separatum*, etc.); Thes connects הגין with preceding דֶּרֶךְ, '*aptus, idoneus* (de via),' AV RV 'the way *directly* before the wall,' in neither connexion does it give good sense, and the text is doubtless wrong cf. Sm Da; Co conj. החצר החיצונה *the outer court*

הגר (√of foll, ? cf Ar هَجَرَ *forsake, retire*; هِجْرَة *emigration, Hegira*)

† **הָגָר n.pr.f. Hagar,** Sarah's Egyptian maid, mother of Ishmael, Gn 16¹·³·⁸ (all J), v³·¹⁵·¹⁵·¹⁶ 25¹² (all P), 21⁹·¹⁴·¹⁷·¹⁷ (all E)

† **הַגְרִי 1. n.pr.gent.** only pl הַגְרִים ψ 83⁷; הַהַגְרִאִים 1 Ch 5¹⁰, הַהַגְרִיאִים 1 Ch 5¹⁹·²⁰; a tribe (Aramaean? Arabian?) with which the E Jordan Israelites waged successful war; v dub conj as to identity in Glas Skizze ii 407. **2. adj.gent.** of an officer of David יָזִיז הַהַגְרִי 1 Ch 27³¹. **3. n.pr.m.** father of one of David's warriors בֶּן־הַגְרִי 1 Ch 11³⁸ (but ‖ 2 S 23³⁶ בָּנִי הַגָּדִי, so here Ot, cf Be Th^Sm Dr^Sm)

הַגְרִאִים, הַגְרִיאִים v foregoing.

הַד v sub הדד

הדד (perh *make a loud noise*, so Ar هَدَّ (of a falling building, rain, the sea, a braying camel), هَدَّة *crash* (of a falling wall, etc), هَادَّة *thunder*)

הֵידָד n.m. Is 16, 9 **shout, shouting, cheer** (of a multitude, on formation compare Ol § 181 a Sta § 218 b),—ה׳ only abs, Is 16⁹ + 6 t. Is & Je,—**1.** *shouting* in harvest Is 16¹⁰, Je 48³³·³³·³³ where לֹא יִדְרֹךְ הֵידָד הֵידָד לֹא הֵידָד, i.e the shouting is no vineyard-shouting, but that of the foe, cf. infr; comp 25³⁰ ׳י *shall utter* (עָנָה) *a shout like the* (*grape-*) *treaders* (sq אֶל כָּל־יֹשְׁבֵי הָאָרֶץ) Hence also **2.** *shout* of the foe Is 16⁹ (נָפַל עַל), Je 51¹⁴ (וְעָנוּ עָלַיִךְ הֵידָד); cf 25³⁰ 48³³ supr.

† **הֵד n.[m.]** id., only Ez 7⁷ הֵד הָרִים (*joyous*) *shout on mountains* (opp מְהוּמָה *noise of battle*).

† **הֲדַד n.pr.m. Hadad** (𝔊 Ἀδερ but v הדר Aram n pr.div DHM Altsem Inschr von Sendschirli 56, and n pr עבדהדד Scholz Götzendienst 245, הדדנדנאח Eut SBAk 1887, 410 cf Bae Rel 68 & sub בֶּן־הֲדַד p. 122, also *Adda*, etc., in cpd n pr. Bez Tell el-Amarna BM 106, *Hadad, Adad, Addu* is known as an Aram. deity, weather- or storm-god, cf. Bae Rel 67 68, perh. = *thunderer* Dl ZK 1885, 166 Bae l.c, cf. רמון, on Hadad in Arabia cf We Skizzen iii 51; Sab. הדד Hal²⁷, as **n.pr.div.** Heb. only in cpd **n.pr.m.**, v infr) —**1.** name of kings of Edom, **a.** Gn 36³⁵ = 1 Ch 1⁴⁶, Gn 36³⁶ = 1 Ch 1⁴⁷ (הֲדָד); **b.** 1 Ch 1⁴⁷ (‖ Gn 36³⁹ הֲדַר), v⁵¹ (הֲדָד) **2.** an Edomite (הָאֲדֹמִי ה׳) 1 K 11¹⁴·¹⁷·¹⁹·²¹·²¹·²⁵ (הֲדַד), = אֲדַד v¹⁷

† **הֲדַדְעֶזֶר n.pr.m. Hadadezor** (so Aram inscr. הדדעזר Eut SBAk 1885, 679 cf Bae Rel 67; 𝔊 throughout (erroneously) Ἀδρα(α)ζαρ;—*Hadad is help(er)*, cf COT 1 K 20¹ & Ph אשמנעזר); king of צוֹבָה (q.v), son of רחב, defeated by David 2 S 8³·⁵·¹⁰·¹² v⁷·⁸·⁹·¹⁰ הֲדַדְעֶזֶר (= הֲדַרְעֶזֶר q v. 10¹⁶·¹⁶·¹⁹ 1 Ch 18³·⁵·⁷·⁸·¹⁰·¹⁰ 19¹⁶·¹⁹, all erron, v. inscr. supr, & cf Bae l.c Dr on 2 S 8³ 10¹⁶), also 1 K 11²³

†הֲדַדְרִמּוֹן n.pr.divin. (or n.pr.loc. der. fr n.pr.divin.), Hadadrimmon (=n.pr. divin. Hadad (cf supr) + n.pr.divin. Rimmon, Rammân, v. רִמּוֹן, cf. COT Zc 12[11] Dl ZK 1885, 175 & on question of nom loc. or divin Brd[Zc] Baud[Stud i 293 f.] Hi-St[Zc] Ri[HWB] RS[Sem i. 392])—in simile of mourning in Jerusalem כְּמִסְפַּד הֲדַדְרִמּוֹן בְּבִקְעַת מְגִדּוֹן Zc 12[11]; on ה׳ for ההרמונה Am 4[3], v. הרמון; & cf. Hi-St Gunning.

†הָדָה vb. stretch out the hand (cf Ar. هَدَى lead, guide, Aram. Pa. ܗܰܕܺܝ) Is 11[8] יָדוֹ הָדָה, sq. עַל, the weaned child shall stretch out his hand upon.

†[יַהְדַּי] n.pr.m. one of the family of Caleb (acc. to Thes = יהדיה, י׳ leads cf Ol[§ 277 h. p. 621], but dub.) יַהְדָּי 1 Ch 2[47] (Baer, al. יָהְדַי)

הדה v הוד.

†הֹדּוּ n.pr.loc. India (Old Pers Hiñd'u Spieg[Altpers. Keilinschr 246] Skr. Sindhu, sea, great river, v reff. in Ro[Thes Add 83], Yule[Anglo-Indian Glossary, 329 ff]; cf. in Ar. هِنْدٌ, Aram ܗܶܢܕܽܘ, etc) only מֵהֹדּוּ וְעַד־כּוּשׁ (הַמֶּלֶךְ) Est 1[1] 8[9] (𝔊 in both ἀπὸ τῆς Ἰνδικῆς)

†הֲדוֹרָם n pr.m. 1. Arabian tribe, called son of Joktan Gn 10[27] (cf Di) = 1 Ch 1[21], Glas ii. 435 comp Dauram near Ṣan'â in Yemen (Sab. הדרום CIS[iv 1. p. 1]; 𝔊 Ὀδορρα Gn 10[27], 𝔊L Οδορραμ, 1 Ch 1[21] 𝔊B om, 𝔊L Αδωραμ). 2. son of Tou (תֹּעוּ) king of Hamath 1 Ch 18[10] (𝔊 Ἰδουρααμ, 𝔊L Αδωραμ); so rd. prob in ‖ 2 S 8[10], for יוֹרָם, cf. 𝔊 Ἰεδδουραν, v We Dr).—הֲדֹרָם v. p 214.

†הִדַּי n.pr.m. one of David's heroes 2 S 23[30] = חוּרַי 1 Ch 11[32].

†[הָדַךְ] vb. cast or tread down (Ar هَدَكَ tear down (a building), synon. of هَدَمَ)—Qal Imv הֲדֹךְ רְשָׁעִים Jb 40[12] cast or tread down wicked men.

הדם (√ of foll., cf Ar هَدَمَ overthrow, overturn, cast down)

†הֲדֹם n.m. stool, footstool, always joined with רַגְלַיִם, only in poet and late writings, (properly something cast down, low)—ה׳ abs. ψ 110[1] (or cstr. bef לְ, cf. Ges[§ 130. 1]), cstr. La 2[1] + 4 t.:—footstool, never lit., usually of י׳ Is 66[1] הַשָּׁמַיִם כִּסְאִי וְהָאָרֶץ ה׳ רַגְלָי; elsewh. with ref. to sanctuary ה׳ רַגְלָיו (cf מְקוֹם רַגְלַי Is 60[13]) La 2[1], or perhaps of ark (as place on which God rests) בֵּית מְנוּחָה לַאֲרוֹן בְּרִית־י׳ וְלַה׳ רַגְלֵי אֱלֹהֵינוּ ψ 99[5] 132[7], 1 Ch 28[2], of conquest of enemies of Messianic king by Yahweh's agency אָשִׁית אֹיְבֶיךָ הֲדֹם לְרַגְלֶיךָ ψ 110[1].

†הֲדַס n.m.[Is 55. 13] myrtle (-tree), only late (NH, Aram. id; Ar هَدَس (in the dialect of Yemen), also آس, Aram. אָסָא, ܐܳܣܳܐ, cf. Löw[No 25])—abs. ה׳ Is 41[19] Ne 8[15], הֲדַס Is 55[13]; pl. הַהֲדַסִּים Zc 1[8] + 2 t. (on form cf Ges[§ 93. R. 4])—Is 41[19] (אֶרֶז, שִׁטָּה, עֵץ שֶׁמֶן, ברוש, תדהר, תאשור ‖), Is 55[13] (ברוש ‖, opp הַסִּרְפַּד), עֲלֵי הֲדַס Ne 8[15] (עֲלֵי־זַיִת, ע׳ עֵץ־שֶׁמֶן, ע׳ תְמָרִים, ע׳ עֵץ עָבֹת ‖); pl Zc 1[8 10 11].

†הֲדַסָּה n.pr.f. Jewish name of Esther (= myrtle, on form cf. Sta[§ 109 a]) Est 2[7] (cf אֶסְתֵּר)

†[הָדַף] vb thrust, push, drive (הֲדַף in 𝔗, Ar هَدَفَ is ingressus ad aliquem fuit, propinquus fuit, also of time prope accessit)—Qal Pf. 3 ms. sf. הֲדָפוֹ Nu 35[22] Je 46[15], 1 s sf וַהֲדַפְתִּיךָ consec Is 22[19]; Impf 3 ms יהדף Pr 10[3], sf 3 ms יֶהְדָּפֶנּוּ Nu 35[20]; sf. 3 mpl יֶהְדֳּפֵם Jos 23[5]; 3 mpl. sf יֶהְדָּפֻהוּ Jb 18[18], 2 mpl תֶּהְדֹּפוּ Ez 34[21], Inf הֲדֹף Dt 6[19] 9[4], sf. הָדְפָה 2 K 4[27];—1. thrust, push, subj. man, sq. acc Nu 35[20. 22] (here fatally); subj cattle, fig. of men, Ez 34[21] (instr בְּכָתֵף ‖ נָגַח); push away 2 K 4[27] (Gehazi, the Shunammite); thrust away (fr. oneself) fig = reject, הַוַּת רְשָׁעִים Pr 10[3] (subj י׳). 2. thrust out, drive out, sq מִן of place whence & acc. pers., of י׳ driving out enemies of Isr. fr Canaan Dt 6[19] 9[4] Jos 23[5]; cf. also indef. subj. יֶהְדְּפֻהוּ מֵאוֹר אֶל־חֹשֶׁךְ Jb 18[18] (וּמִתֵּבֵל יְנִדֻּהוּ ‖), & Je 46[15] (where no pl whence) Hence 3. = depose Is 22[19] of י׳ deposing Shebna (sq מִן of station).

†[הָדַר] vb. swell (?), honour, adorn, (NH הדר adorn; Aram. הֲדַר, ܗܕܰܪ Pa. adorn, honour; perh. all denom; cf. Palm. n.pr.f הדירת ornata, honorata Vog[No 65], Ar. هَدَرَ be of no account, but also ferbuit (vinum) & اهْدَرَ inflatus, tumens (venter))—Qal Pf 2 ms. וְהָדַרְתָּ Lv 19[32], Impf. 2 ms. תֶּהְדַּר Ex 23[3] Lv 19[15]; Pt pass הָדוּר Is 63[1], pl הֲדוּרִים Is 45[2] (poss הררים 𝔊 ὄρη, cf. Di, but v. הר) —1. swell, only pt. pass. pl. Is 45[2] (si vera l.) in neuter sense, of hills, swelling places, swells of land (made level before Cyrus). 2. honour, pay honour to, sq. acc, in good sense וְהָדַרְתָּ פְּנֵי זָקֵן Lv 19[32] (H) and thou shalt honour the face of an old

man (‖ מִפְּנֵי שֵׂיבָה תָּקוּם); in bad sense (of partiality, favouritism) לֹא תֶהְדַּר פְּנֵי גָדוֹל Lv 19^{15} (H) (‖ לֹא תִשָּׂא פְנֵי־דָל); cf. וְדָל לֹא תֶהְדַּר בְּרִיבוֹ Ex 23^{3} (JE; either rd. גָּדֹל for ודל, — ו not needed at beginning of v.,—so Kn SS al., yet 𝔊 πένητα;—or suppose balancing cl., as Lv 19^{15}, to have fallen out, cf. Di). **3.** *adorn*, only pt. pass. *adorned, made splendid* הָדוּר בִּלְבוּשׁוֹ Is 63^{1}. **Niph.** *Pf.* נֶהְדָּרוּ La 5^{12} *were* (not) *honoured*, subj. פְּנֵי זְקֵנִים. **Hithp.** *Impf.* juss. 2 ms. תִּתְהַדַּר Pr 25^{6} *honour oneself*, i.e. *claim honour*.

†הֶדֶר **n.** [m.] **ornament, adornment, splendour,** only cstr. ה׳ מַלְכוּת Dn 11^{20} *splendour of (the) kingdom*, cf. AV RV, i.e. Judaea, or perh. Jerusalem acc. to Leng Hi Meinh; but rather *royal splendour*, cf. Gr, & esp. Bev who reads נֹגֵשׂ מַעֲבִיר ה׳ (for 𝔐 מעביר נוגש), i. e. *an exactor who shall cause the royal splendour to pass away*.

†הָדָר **n.m.** ^{ψ149,9} **ornament, splendour, honour** (chiefly poet.)—abs. ה׳ Dt 33^{17} + 12 t.; cstr. הֲדַר Is 2^{10} + 7 t.; sf. הֲדָרִי Mi 2^{9} (but cf. infr.) Ez 16^{14}; הֲדָרְךָ ψ 45^{5} 90^{16}; הֲדָרֶךָ ψ 45^{4}; הֲדָרֵךְ Ez 27^{10}; הֲדָרָהּ Is 5^{14} La 1^{6}; pl. cstr. הַדְרֵי ψ 110^{3} (but rd. prob. הררי so Symm Jer edd.; Ol Hup Gr Bi Che);—**1.** *ornament* Pr 20^{29} (grey hair, for old men; ‖ תִּפְאֶרֶת), Ez 16^{14} (fig. of ornaments of Jerus. as bride of י׳); פְּרִי עֵץ הָדָר Lv 23^{40} (H) i.e. *fruit of goodly* (ornamental, beautiful) *trees*, so AV RV & most, or *goodly tree-fruit*, 𝔊 καρπὸν ξύλου ὡραῖον, so Di;—here would come also בהדרי קדש ψ 110^{3}, ref. to sacred, festal garments, acc. to Thes al. cf. RVm; but read prob. *on the holy mountains*, vid. supr. **2.** *splendour, majesty* Dt 33^{17} of Ephraim under figure of a noble bull (cf. Di); of Jerusalem Is 5^{14} cf. La 1^{6}; of Carmel Is 35^{2} (‖ כָּבוֹד); of *majesty & dignity* conferred by י׳ on man ψ 8^{6} (‖ כָּבוֹד), on king 21^{6} (‖ *id.*, הוֹד), cf. 45^{4} (‖ הוד) & v^{5} (but txt. perh. erron. Che[crit. n.]); denied of suffering servant of י׳ Is 53^{2} (‖ תֹּאַר); of *dignity* of good & capable woman (אֵשֶׁת חַיִל) Pr 31^{25} (‖ עֹז); of *splendour* due to warlike equipment Ez 27^{10}; especially of *majesty* of י׳ 1 Ch 16^{27} = ψ 96^{6}, cf. Jb 40^{10} ψ 111^{3} (all ‖ הוֹד); also ψ 104^{1} (‖ *id.*, under fig. of garment); further ψ 29^{4} (‖ כֹּחַ), 90^{16} (‖ פֹּעַל); in combination הֲדַר כְּבוֹד הוֹדֶךָ ψ 145^{5}; כְּבוֹד ה׳ v^{12}; הֲדַר גְּאֹנוֹ Is $2^{10.19.21}$. **3.** *honour, glory* ψ 149^{9} for saints of י׳; cf. Mi 2^{9} of י׳'s glory as possession of his people, lost by exile & slavery: but perh. txt. err.; Hoffm ZAW [1882. 103] prop. הַדְּרוֹר, fr. their children ye take *freedom* (yet מֵעַל then hardly suitable).

†[הֲדָרָה] **n.f. adornment, glory**—only cstr. הַדְרַת;—**1.** ה׳־קֹדֶשׁ *holy adornment* (Che[ψ]), always in connexion with public worship of י׳ 1 Ch 16^{29} 2 Ch 20^{21} ψ 29^{2} 96^{9}. **2.** ה׳־מֶלֶךְ *the glory of a king*, fig. of רָב־עָם, Pr 14^{28}.

†הֲדַר **n.pr.m.** a king in Edom (Aram. form) Gn 36^{39} = הֲדַד (q. v.) 1 Ch 1^{50} (so here Codd., 𝔖 Sam. no doubt rightly, cf. Di).

†הֲדֹרָם **n.pr.m.** an official of Rehoboam 2 Ch 10^{18} (𝔊 Ἀδωνειραμ) = אֲדֹרָם 1 K 12^{18} (𝔊 Ἀραμ, Ἀδωνιραμ), & אֲדֹנִירָם, q.v.—הֲדוֹרָם v. p. 213.

†הֲדַרְעֶזֶר **n.pr.m.** a king of Aram (צוֹבָה) defeated by David 2 S $10^{16.16.19}$ = 1 Ch $19^{16.19}$; also 1 Ch $18^{3.5.8.9.10}$ & הֲדַדְעֶזֶר $v^{7.10}$; all erron. for הֲדַדְעֶזֶר (q.v.), although 𝔊 throughout Ἀδρααζαρ.

†הָהּ **interj.** expressing woe, **alas!** Ez 30^{2} howl ye הָהּ לַיּוֹם *alas* for the day! AV *Woe* worth the day! (cf. אֲהָהּ לַיּוֹם Joel 1^{15}.)

†הוֹ **interj.** i.q. the more usual הוֹי (q.v.) **Ah!** Am 5^{16} of mourners וּבְכָל־חוּצוֹת יֹאמְרוּ הוֹ־הוֹ.

הִוא Je 29^{23} Kt, v. הוא.

הוּא **m.** הִיא **f.** (pl. m. הֵמָּה, הֵם; fem. הֵנָּה, הֵן [the latter only with prefixes]; see these words), **pron. of the 3rd ps. sing., he, she,** used also (in both genders) for the neuter **it**, Lat. *is, ea, id.* (The א is not orthographic merely, but radical, being written on Moab. and Ph. inscriptions, though dropped in some of the later dialects. [In Heb. only Je 29^{23} Kt, and in the pr. n. אֱלִיהוּ.] Moab. (MI[6.27]) and Ph. (often) הא; Aram. of Zinjirli הא, once הו (DHM [Inschr. von Sendschirli 55]); 𝔗 הוּא, הִיא, Syr. ܗܘ, ܗܝ; Ar. هُوَ, هِيَ (for *hū'a, hī'a*, W[SG 104]); Eth. ውእቱ: ይእቲ: *we'ĕtū, ye'ĕtī*; perh. also As. *šû, šî, himself, herself*, suff. *šu, ši*, cf. demonstr. *šuatu, šiati* (v. Kraetzschmar [BAS. i. 383] & reff., W[SG 98, 105] Dl[§ 55 b, 57]). In the Pent., הוא is of common gender, the fem. form היא occurring only 11 times, viz. Gn 14^{2} 20^{5} 38^{25} (v. Mass. here), Lv 11^{39} $13^{10.21}$ 16^{31} 20^{17} 21^{9} Nu $5^{13.14}$. The punctuators, however, sought to assimilate the usage of the Pent. to that of the rest of the OT, and accordingly wherever הוא was construed as a fem. pointed it הִוא (as a *Qrê perpetuum*). Outside the Pent. the same Qrê occurs 1 K 17^{15} Is 30^{33} Jb

31^{11a}—prob. for the sake of removing gramm. anomalies: five instances of the converse change, viz of היא to be read as הוא, occur for a similar reason, 1 K 17^{15} (וַתֹּאכַל הוא־וָהיא to be read as וַתֹּאכַל היא־וָהוּא, on account of the fem verb) ψ 73^{16} Jb 31^{11b} (כי הוא זמה והיא עָוֹן פלילים to be read as כי היא זמה והוא עון פלילים), Ec 5^{8} 1 Ch 29^{16}. The origin of the peculiarity in the Pent. is uncertain It can hardly be a real archaism: for the fact that Arab., Aram, & Eth. have distinct forms for masc. & fem. shews that both must have formed part of the original Semitic stock, and consequently of Hebrew as well, from its earliest existence as an independent language Nor is the peculiarity confined to the Pent · in the MS. of the Later Prophets, of A D 916, now at S. Petersburg, published in facsimile by Strack (1876), the fem occurs written הוא (see the passages cited in the *Adnotationes Criticae*, p 026). In Ph. both masc. and fem are alike written הא (CIS i. 1^{9} מלך צדק הא, l^{13} מלאכת הא, 3^{10} ארם הא, l^{11} ממלכת הא, 93^{2} 94^{2}), though naturally this would be *read* as *hu'* or *hi'* as occasion required. Hence, as 𝔊 shews that in the older Heb. MSS. the *scriptio plena* was not yet generally introduced, it is prob. that originally הא was written for both genders in Hebrew likewise, and that the epicene הוא in the Pent. originated at a comparatively late epoch in the transmission of the text—perh. in connexion with the assumption, which is partly borne out by facts (cf. De ZKWL 1880, pp 393-399), that in the older language fem. forms were more sparingly used than subsequently.)

In usage הוא (f היא; pl הֵ֫מָּה, הם, הֵ֫נָּה · v הֵ֫מָּה) is **1.** an emph **he (she, it, they)**, sometimes equivalent to **himself (herself, itself, themselves)**, or (esp. with the art) **that (those)** **a.** Gn 3^{15} הוא ישופך ראש *he* (𝔊 *αὐτὸς*) shall bruise thee as to the head (opp. to the foll אתה *thou*), v^{20} for *she* (and no one else) was the mother of all living (so oft. in causal sentences, where some emph on the subject is desirable, as Ju 14^{3} ψ 24^{2} 25^{15} 33^{9} 91^{3} 103^{14} 148^{5} Jb 5^{18} 11^{11} 28^{24} Je 5^{5} 34^{7b} Ho 6^{1} 11^{10}: Dr $^{\S 14,18}$), 4^{20} Adah bare Jabal הוא היה אבי ישב אהלים *he* (*ἐκεῖνος*) was the father of tent-dwellers, v^{21} 10^{8} *he* began to be a mighty one in the earth, 20^{5} (*αὐτός*), Ju 13^{6} Is 32^{7} 33^{22} 2 K $14^{7.22.25}$; Ho 10^{2} *he*—the unseen observer of their thoughts and deeds (Che), 13^{15b} (*he*, the foe figured by the E. wind). (For its use thus in circ clauses v. Dr $^{\S 157, 160, 168, 169}$.) And where the predic. is a subst or ptcp., Gn 2^{11} . . . הוא הַסֹּבֵב *that* is the one which encompasseth etc, $v^{13.14}$ 10^{12} *that* is the great city So in the explanatory notices, Gn 14^{3} הוא יָם הַמֶּלַח *that* is the salt sea, v^{8} הוא־צֹעַר *that* is Zoar, 36^{1} + oft. **b.** pointing back to the subj and contrasting it with something else: Gn 4^{4} הבל גם־הוא Abel, *he* also . . . v^{26} 10^{21} 20^{5} וְהִיא־גַם־הוא and she, *herself* also said, Ex 1^{10} + oft. **c.** appended alone to a *verb* (more rarely, but always with intentional emphasis), Ex 4^{14} I know כי דבר ידבר הוא that *he* can speak, v^{16} 1 S 22^{18} ויפגע הוא בכהנים and *he* (though none else would do it) smote the priests, 23^{22} for one hath told me, עָרוֹם יַעְרִם הוא *He* can deal subtilly, Ez 12^{12} (peculiarly), cf Dr $^{\S 160 n}$: very rarely indeed to a noun Nu 18^{23} הַלֵּוִי הוא, Is 7^{14} י׳ הוא, Est 9^{1} (הֵמָּה) being probably all the exx. in the OT **d.** Gn 13^{1} and Abram came up out of Egypt, הוא וְאִשְׁתּוֹ *himself* and his wife, and all that he had, 14^{15} הוא וַעֲבָדָיו *he* and his servants, 19^{30}; so very oft. **e.** *prefixed* to a noun (very rare, and mostly late), Ex 12^{42b} Ez 3^{8} & 33^{8} הוא רָשָׁע to pr names Ex 6^{27} הוא משה ואהרן, 1 Ch 26^{26} *that* Shelomoth, 27^{6} 2 Ch 28^{22} 32^{12} (diff from 2 K 18^{22}), v^{30} 33^{23} Ezr 7^{6} cf הם Ne 10^{38} (comp. in Syr. ܗܘ, No $^{\S 227}$). cf ψ 87^{5} 1 S 20^{29}.

2. It resumes the subj with emph.. **a.** when the predic is a *verb* (esp. if it be separated from its subject by an intervening clause), Gn 15^{4} but one that shall come forth out of thine own bowels, הוא יִירָשֶׁךָ *he* shall be thy heir, 3^{12} the woman whom thou gavest to be with me, הוא נתנה לי *she* gave to me, 24^{7} 44^{17} etc. Ju 7^{4} 2 S 14^{19} (throwing stress on יוֹאָב) 1 Ch 11^{20} Is 33^{15-16} 34^{16} 38^{19} 47^{10} 59^{16} 63^{5} Ho 7^{8}, oft. in Pr, as $10^{18.22.24}$ 11^{28} 13^{13} 19^{21} 22^{9} 24^{12}, 1 S 1^{13} (v. Dr), ψ 68^{36}. **b.** when the predic. is a *noun*, Gn 2^{14} and the fourth river, הוא פְרָת *it* was the Euphrates, v^{19} 9^{18} 15^{2} 42^{6} ויוסף הוא הַשַּׁלִּיט and Joseph, *he* was the ruler etc.: in sentences of the type י׳ הוא הָאֱלֹהִים, י׳ הוא הַנִּלְחָם לָכֶם, י׳ הוא נַחֲלָתוֹ, Dt 3^{22} 4^{35} 7^{9} 10^{9} Jos $13^{14.33}$ Is 9^{14} 33^{6} Ho 11^{5} (in these cases, to avoid stiffness, it is convenient often to drop the pron in translating, as 'And the fourth river *was* the Euphrates' the pronoun, however, though it then corresponds to the substantive verb in English, does not really *express* it, the copula, as the exx. shew, being in fact understood Sts in AV the pron is retained for emphasis, as Dt. *ll cc*) So **c.** after אֲשֶׁר in an *affirmative* sentence, Gn 9^{3} all creeping things אֲשֶׁר הוא־חַי which are living, Lv 11^{39} Nu 9^{13} 14^{8} 35^{31} אֲשֶׁר הוא רָשָׁע לָמוּת who is guilty of death, Dt 20^{20} 1 S 10^{19} Hg 1^{9} al (On **2**, cf. Dr $^{\S 199, \text{ with Obs.}}$)

3. Where, however, the pron *follows* the

pred, its position gives it the minimum of emphasis, and it expresses (or resumes) the subject as unobtrusively as possible: thus **a.** Gn 12[18] why didst thou not tell me כי אשתך הוא that she was thy wife? 20[13] 21[13] כי זרעך הוא for he is thy seed, 31[20] because he told him not כי ברח הוא, 37[3] + oft (the opp. order rare and emph: Gn 24[65] Dt 4[6] 30[20] Jos 10[2] 1 K 2[22] 3[4] 21[2] Ho 2[4] ψ 45[12]) **b.** resuming the subj, Gn 31[16] all the wealth which God hath taken etc, לנו הוא ולבנינו *it is* ours and our children's, v[43] and all that thou seest, לי הוא *it is* mine (or, omitting the pronoun, as not required in our idiom, simply) *is* mine, 41[25] חלום פרעה אחד הוא the dream of Pharaoh *is* one, 48[5] (לי הם), Ex 3[5] for the place whereon thou standest, אַדְמַת קֹדֶשׁ הוּא *it* is holy ground, Nu 13[32] 21[26] Dt 1[17] Jos 5[15] 6[19] Jb 3[19] + oft, Gn 23[15] מַה־הוּא ארץ, so ψ 39[5] Is 41[22] (הֵנָּה), אַתֶּם .... הֵמָּה (unusual) Zp 2[12] (In all such cases the predicate is not referred directly to the subject, but, the subject being made a casus pendens, it is resumed by the pron, and the pred thus referred to it indirectly. By this means the sentence is lightened and relieved, esp if the subject consist of many words. in Gn 31[16] for instance, the direct form of predicate כי לָנוּ וּלְבָנֵינוּ כָּל־הָעֹשֶׁר אֲשֶׁר הִצִּיל אֱלֹהִים מֵאָבִינוּ would have been heavy and inelegant.) So **c.** after אֲשֶׁר in a *negative* sentence, Gn 7[2] 17[12] אֲשֶׁר לֹא מִזַּרְעֲךָ הוּא which is not of thy seed, Nu 17[5] Dt 17[15] 1 K 8[41] (cf הֵמָּה **3 c**) **d.** peculiarly, as the subject of לא, Je 5[12] לוא הוא *He* is not, and as embracing its predicate in itself, Is 18[2,7] a nation terrible מִן־הוּא (=מאשר הוא) from (the time that) *it was*, Na 2[9] מימי היא from the days that (*st c* Ges[§130.4]) *it was*, 2 K 7[7] they left the camp כַּאֲשֶׁר היא as *it was* (cf כַּאֲשֶׁר הֵמָּה v[10]) (On **3**, cf Dr[§198, with Obs])

4. It *anticipates* (as it seems) the subject viz. **a** (rare) Ct 6[9] אַחַת היא יוֹנָתִי תַמָּתִי one is *she*, my dove my perfect one, Lv 25[11] Ez 11[15] 21[16], La 1[18] צַדִּיק הוּא י׳ (oft so in NH), Ec 6[10] ונוֹדָע אֲשֶׁר הוּא אָדָם and that which he, even man, is, is known (De Now), cf 1 S 6[19] מִקְרֶה הוּא הָיָה לָנוּ an accident is *it*, (that) hath befallen us (Cf הֵמָּה **4 a.**) **b.** after pronouns—(*a*) 2 S 7[28] אתה אַתָּה הוּא הָאֱלֹהִים Thou art *he*—God, ψ 44[5] אתה הוא מלכי thou art *he*—my king, Is 37[16] 43[25] (אנכי), 51[9 10 12] 52[6] Je 14[22] 29[23] Kt +, cf Je 49[12] ואתה הוא נָקֹה תִנָּקֶה and art thou he (that) shall be unpunished? (with change of pers κατὰ σύνεσιν, cf Ju 13[11] 1 Ch 21[17] Ez 38[17]) So Ew[§297 b] Mull[§499] But others, as Ges[Thes] Roo[§463] De[Is 37 16, ψ 44,5], treat הוא as emphasizing the pronoun, 'Thou, he, art God' i e. Thou and none else art God, '*Thou* (emph.) art my king' (*β*) מי הוא, sq a ptcp or subst. Gn 27[33] ψ 24[10] מי הוא זֶה מֶלֶךְ הַכָּבוֹד who is he, then—the king of glory? (acc. to others, as before, '*Who* (emph.), then, is the king of glory?'); sq. a verb Is 50[9] מי הוא יַרְשִׁיעֵנִי who is he (that) will condemn me? (al. '*Who* (emph) will condemn me?') Jb 4[7] 13[19] 17[3] 41[2] Je 30[21] (so with הֵנָּה Gn 21[29], הֵמָּה Zc 1[9] 4[5]) (*γ*) זֶה־הוּא † 1 Ch 22[1] Ec 1[17] (freq in NH, where the two words coalesce into one זְהוּ) On the analogous אֵלֶּה הֵם ..., v. הֵמָּה **4 b** (*γ*) (Cf Dr[§200, 201].)

5. As an emph predicate, of God, 'I am He,' i e I am He Who *is* (opp. to unreal gods, named in context, or to transitory world), the Unseen, yet Omni-present, and Self-consistent, Ruler of the world, † Dt 32[39] אֲנִי אֲנִי הוּא I, I am *he*, and beside me there is no God, Is 41[4] (v Che) 43[10 13] even from to-day I am *he*, 46[4] 48[12] ψ 102[28] (v Che) thou art *he*, and thy years have no end (𝔊 usu. ἐγώ εἰμι. in ψ σὺ δὲ ὁ αὐτὸς εἶ). So also, acc to many, Jb 3[19], but is הוא a *mere* predicate of identity? v. rather **3 b.**

6. In a neuter sense, *that, it* (of an action, occurrence, matter, etc.)—**a.** Jos 2[21] כְּדִבְרֵיכֶם כֶּן־הוּא acc to your words, so be *it;* Gn 42[14] הוא אשר דברתי *that* is what I said, Ex 16[23] Lv 10[3] 2 K 9[36], Jb 8[19] הן הוא משוש דרכו lo *that* (what has just been described) is the joy of his way, 13[16] 15[9] 31[28] Pr 7[23] Ec 2[1] 3[22] 9[9] Est 9[1b], similarly the fem היא, Ju 14[4] they knew not כי מי׳ היא that *it* was from י׳, Nu 14[41] Jos 10[13] Is 14[24] ψ 77[10] חַלּוֹתִי היא *it* (this perplexity) is my sickness, Jb 9[22] Pr 18[13] Je 22[16] 2 Ch 25[20] Ec 3[13], ref to זאת Am 7[6] ψ 118[23] Jb 5[27], זה Ec 2[24] (Where there is a predicate, the gender of this usually regulates the choice of *m.* or *f.*: hence הוא Gn 34[14] Ex 8[15] Nu 15[25] (Ec 5[5]) Dt 4[6] +) **b** affirming the presence or existence of something (rare) 2 K 18[36] = Is 36[21] כי מִצְוַת הַמֶּלֶךְ היא for *it was* the king's command, saying etc, 1 S 20[33] (text dub.), Je 50[15.25] 51[6 11] Mi 2[3], perh. Jb 32[8]

7. With the art הַהוּא, הַהִיא, הַהֵמָּה, הָהֵם, הָהֵנָּה: so regularly when joined to a subst. defined itself by the art: Gn 2[12] הָאָרֶץ הַהוּא *that* land, 19[35] ובלילה ההוא and in *that* night, 21[22] בָּעֵת הַהוּא at *that* time, Dt 1[19] המדבר הגדול והנורא ההוא Only four times does there occur the anomalous construction בַּלַּיְלָה הוּא Gn 19[33] 30[16] 32[23] 1 S 19[10].

† [הָוָא] vb fall (Ar هَوَى *id* e.g. of a

star Qor 53^{1})—**Qal** *Imv.* Jb 37^{6} for he saith to the snow הֱוֵא־אָרֶץ *Fall* earthwards (an Arabizing usage).

הובנים v. [הָבְנִי].

הוד (√of foll.; De Jb 39^{20} comp. Bed. هَوِيدٌ *crash, roar, resonance;* 'weithin hallende Selbstverkündigung' Id. ψ 8^{6}; but هَادَ ordinarily means *be gentle, quiet,* esp. in speech).

†I. **הוֹד** **n.m.** $^{Jb\ 37.22}$ **splendour, majesty, vigour** (chiefly poet.) (NH *id.*)—ה׳ abs. Jb 37^{22} + 8 t. (הַה׳ 1 Ch 29^{11}); cstr. Is 30^{30} + 3 t.; sf. הוֹדִי Dn 10^{8}; הוֹדְךָ Nu 27^{20} + 2 t.; הוֹדֶךָ Pr 5^{9} ψ 145^{4}; הוֹדוֹ Ho 14^{7} + 3 t.; הֹדֹה Je 22^{18};—**1.** *splendour, majesty,* of king הוֹדְךָ וַהֲדָרֶךָ ψ 45^{4}; גָּדוֹל כְּבוֹדוֹ ‖ י׳ הוֹד וְהָדָר תְּשַׁוֶּה עָלָיו ψ 21^{6}, subj. (בִּישׁוּעָתֶךָ); foretold of the צֶמַח Zc 6^{13} וְהוּא־יִשָּׂא הוֹד וְיָשַׁב וּמָשַׁל עַל־כִּסְאוֹ; cf. וַיִּתֵּן עָלָיו הוֹד מַלְכוּת 1 Ch 29^{25} (י׳ confers on Sol.); וְלֹא נָתְנוּ עָלָיו ה׳ מַלְכוּת Dn 11^{21} (of usurper); v. also וְהוֹי הֹדֹה Je 22^{18} in lament for king. Hence also **2.** divine *splendour, majesty,* light & glory which God wears as king: הוֹד וְהָדָר לָבָשְׁתָּ ψ 104^{1} (7 t. joined with הָדָר); cf. Jb 40^{10} where י׳ addresses Job in irony; עַל־אֱלוֹהַּ נוֹרָא הוֹד Jb 37^{22}; ה׳ וְהָדָר לְפָנָיו ψ 96^{6} = 1 Ch 16^{27}; also הַגְּדֻלָּה וְהַגְּבוּרָה וְהַתִּפְאֶרֶת וְהַנֵּצַח וְהַה׳ 1 Ch 29^{11}; see further כִּסָּה שָׁמַיִם הוֹדוֹ Hb 3^{3} (‖ וּתְהִלָּתוֹ מָלְאָה הָאָרֶץ); מָה־אַדִּיר שִׁמְךָ ‖ אֲשֶׁר־תְּנָה הוֹדְךָ עַל־הַשָּׁמָיִם ψ 8^{2} (בְּכָל־הָאָרֶץ); also הוֹדוֹ עַל־אֶרֶץ וְשָׁמָיִם ψ 148^{13} (‖ נִשְׂגָּב שְׁמוֹ לְבַדּוֹ); הֲדַר כְּבוֹד הוֹדֶךָ 145^{5}; of Yahweh's actions הוֹד וְהָדָר פָּעֳלוֹ 111^{3}; of his voice וְהִשְׁמִיעַ י׳ אֶת־הוֹד קוֹלוֹ Is 30^{30}. **3. a.** *splendour* of Israel under divine blessing וִיהִי כַזַּיִת הוֹדוֹ Ho 14^{7}. **b.** *majesty, dignity, authority* of Moses Nu 27^{20} (P; only here in Hex) וְנָתַתָּה מֵהוֹדְךָ עָלָיו. Also, **c.** manly *vigour* פֶּן־תִּתֵּן לַאֲחֵרִים הוֹדֶךָ Pr 5^{9}, in warning against licentiousness; as displayed in outward appearance וְהוֹדִי נֶהְפַּךְ עָלַי לְמַשְׁחִית Dn 10^{8} (‖ כֹּחַ). **4.** of a horse, *majesty, majestic force* הוֹד נַחְרוֹ אֵימָה Jb 39^{20} *the majesty of his snorting* (*majestic snorting,* VB) *is a terror;* also in sim. of Yahweh's dealings with Judah, וְשָׂם אוֹתָם כְּסוּס הוֹדוֹ בַּמִּלְחָמָה Zc 10^{3} *and he will make them like the horse of his majesty in battle.*

†II. **הוֹד** **n.pr.m.** (*splendour, vigour*)—a man of Asher 1 Ch 7^{37}.

†**הודוה** Kt, הוֹדְיָה Qr, **n.pr.m.** only in בְּנֵי לְה׳ Ne 7^{43} of a Levitical family; = הוֹדַוְיָה Ezr 2^{40} q.v. sub ידה.

†**הוֹדִיָּה** **n.pr.m.** (*my splendour is Yah*)—**1.** a man of Judah 1 Ch 4^{19}. **2.** Levites **a.** Ne 8^{7} 9^{5} 10^{11}; **b.** Ne 10^{14}. **3.** a chief of the people Ne 10^{19}.

†**הוֹדְיָה** Qr Ne 7^{43} v. הודוה supr.

†**הוֹדַוְיָה, הוֹדַוְיָהוּ, הודיוהו** **n.pr.m.** v. sub ידה.

†[**הָוָה**] **vb.** become (Ar. هَوَى *to fall* (v. הָוָא), also *to gape* or *yawn,* and *to desire* (cf. הַוָּה): cf. Fl$^{De\ Jb\ 6.2}$; Aram. הֲוָא, ܗܘܐ the usual word for *to be* (prob. orig. *to fall out, accidit,* hence *come to pass, come to be,* γίγνεσθαι), Mish. *id.* very common) a rare syn. of הָיָה q.v.:—**Qal** *Impf.* apoc. יְהוּא Ec 11^{3} (for יְהִי with א *otiosum;* Ges$^{§75\ R\ 13\ c}$ Kön$^{p.\ 597\ f.}$; but Gr. plausibly הוּא); *Imv.* ms. הֱוֵה Gn 27^{29}, fs. הֱוִי Is 16^{4}, *Pt.* הוֶֹה Ec 2^{22} Ne 6^{6}:—Gn 27^{29} הֱוֵה גְבִיר לְאַחֶיךָ *become* lord to thy brethren, Is 16^{4} (perh. in imit. of Moab. dialect) הֱוִי סֵתֶר לָמוֹ *become* thou (Zion) a defence to them, Ec 2^{22} 11^{3} Ne 6^{6}.

†**הַוָּה** **n.f. 1. desire; 2. chasm,** fig. **destruction** (cf. هَوًى *desire,* هَوَاءٌ *atmosphere, emptiness,* هَاوِيَةٌ *a deep pit, hell* (cf. sub הָוָה)); Aram. ܗܘܬܐ *gulf, chasm* (Lu 16^{26} (𝔖)) cstr. הַוַּת Mi 7^{3} +, sf. הַוָּתִי Jb 6^{2} +, pl. הַוּוֹת ψ 5^{10} +;—**1.** *desire* (in bad sense) Mi 7^{3} דֹּבֵר הַוַּת נַפְשׁוֹ speaketh *the desire of* his soul, Pr 10^{3} הַוַּת רְשָׁעִים, 11^{6} ה׳ בֹּגְדִים, ψ 52^{9} יָעֹז בְּהַוָּתוֹ became strong through his (evil) *desire* (but read rather with 𝔖𝔗 Lag Gr Bi Che Now בְּהוֹנוֹ ‖ בְּעָשְׁרוֹ). **2.** *engulfing ruin, destruction* Jb 6^{2} Qr 30^{13} (cf. Baer's note) הַוָּתִי of Job's great calamity; pl. (intens.) הַוּוֹת, esp. as wrought, or meditated, by one against another, ψ 5^{10} קִרְבָּם הַוּוֹת their inward part is *engulfing ruin* (Che), 38^{13} דִּבְּרוּ הַוּוֹת, 52^{4} ה׳ תַּחְשֹׁב לְשׁוֹנֶךָ (cf. Pr 17^{4} לְשׁוֹן הַוֹּת), 55^{12} ה׳ בְּקִרְבָּהּ, 57^{2} עַד יַעֲבֹר ה׳ till *the storm of ruin* (Che) pass by, 91^{3} דֶּבֶר ה׳ *destructive* pestilence, 94^{20} כִּסֵּא ה׳ the seat (tribunal) of destruction (i.e. which ruins the innocent by injustice), Pr 19^{13} a foolish son is הַוֹּת לְאָבִיו, Jb 6^{30} (cf. v^{2} supr.)

הַיָּה **n.f. destruction,** sf. הַיָּתִי Jb 6^{2} Kt, i.q. הַוָּתִי (Qr), and prob. an error for it: v. הַוָּה **2.**

†**הוֹה** **n.f. ruin, disaster** (cf. sub הַוָּה) Ez 7^{26} הֹוָה עַל הוָֹה תָּבוֹא *disaster* shall come upon *disaster,* Is 47^{11} וְתִפֹּל עָלַיִךְ הֹוָה *disaster* shall fall upon thee (‖ שֹׁאָה, רָעָה).

יהוה $_{c.\ 6823}$ i.e. **יַהְוֶה** **n.pr.dei Yahweh,** the proper name of the God of Israel—(**1.** MT יְהוָֹה $_{6518}$ (Qr אֲדֹנָי), or יֱהוִֹה $_{305}$ (Qr אֱלֹהִים), in

the combinations אדני יהוה & יהוה אדני (vid אֲדֹנָי), and with prep מיהוָֹה, לַיהוָֹה, בַּיהוָֹה (Qr מֵאדֹנָי, לַאדֹנָי, בַּאדֹנָי), do not give the original form 𝔊 and other Vrss follow the Qr On the basis of Ex 20[7] Lv 24[11] יהוה was regarded as a *nomen ineffabile* (vid Philo[de Vita Mosis iii 519 529]), called by the Jews הַשֵּׁם and by the Samaritans שִׁימא. The pronunciation *Jehovah* was unknown until 1520, when it was introduced by Galatinus, but it was contested by Le Mercier, J Drusius, and L Capellus, as against grammatical and historical propriety (cf Bo[i 88]) The traditional Ἰαβέ of Theodoret and Epiphanius, the יְהוֹ־, יהו־ of compound n pr and the contracted form יָהּ, all favour יַהְוֶה (cf יַהֲלֹמוּן ψ 74[6], תַּהֲרוּ Is 33[11]), v. Lag[Sym i 14] Baudissin[Studien i 179 ff], Dr[Stud Bib. i 1 ff] For *Jeve* v Sta[ZAW 1881, 346] De[ib 1882, 173 f & Gn Excurs. ii] **2.** on liter of interpret v Nes[Eg 67] Dr[l c].—Many recent scholars explain יַהְוֶה as Hiph of הוה (=היה) *the one bringing into being, life-giver* (cf. חַוָּה Gn 3[20]) Schr HSch, *giver of existence, creator*, Kue Tiele; *he who brings to pass* (so already Le Clerc), *performer of his promises*, Lag, Nes[Eg 88] (but Nes[Eg 91] inclines to Qal as RS[Brit & For Ev Rev] v infr); or from הוה *he who causes to fall*, rain or lightning RS[OTJC ed 1 423; om ed 2, 245], cf We[Skizzen iii 175], '*Faller*,' destroying foes, Sta[G i 429] (dubiously) But most take it as Qal of הוה (= היה), *the one who is*: i.e *the absolute and unchangeable one*, Ri, *the existing, ever-living*, as self-consistent and unchangeable, Di, or *the one ever coming into manifestation* as the God of redemption, De Oehl, cf also RS[Brit & For Ev Rev 1876], *he will be* it, i e all that his servants look for (cf Ew[infr]), *he will approve himself* (*give evidence of being, assert his being* Dr[l c 17]))

I. יהוה is not used by E in Gn, but is given Ex 3[12 15] as the name of the God who revealed Himself to Moses at Horeb, and is explained thus אהיה עִמָּךְ *I shall be with thee* (v[12]), which is then implied in אהיה אֲשֶׁר אֶהְיֶה *I shall be the one who will be* it v[14a] (i e. with thee v[12]) and then compressed into אהיה v[14b] (i e. with thee v[12]), which then is given in the nominal form יהוה *He who will be* it v[15] (i e. with thee v[12]) Cf Ew[BTh ii 337 338] RS[l c, Proph 385 ff.] Other interpretations are. *I am he who I am*, i e it is no concern of yours (Le Clerc Lag[Psalt. Hieron 156]), *I am*, (this is my name), *inasmuch as I am* (כִּי=אֲשֶׁר, AE JDMich We[JD Th xxi, 540 = Comp. Hex 72]), Di al *I am who I am*, he who is essentially unnameable, inexplicable.—E uses יהוה sparingly by the side of אלהים and האלהים in his subsequent narrative. The Ephraimitic writers in Ju S K use it in similar proportions P abstains from the use of יהוה until he gives an account of its revelation to Moses Ex 6[3], but subsequently uses it freely He gives no explanation of its meaning. He represents that אל שַׁדַּי was the God of the patriarchs J uses יהוה from the beginning of his narrative, possibly explaining it, Gn 21[33] by אל עולם, the evergreen tamarisk being a symbol of the ever-living God, cf. De Gn 21[33]. Elsewhere יהוה is the common divine name in pre-exilic writers, but in post-exilic writers gradually falls into disuse, and is supplanted by אלהים and ארני In Job it is used 31 t. in prose parts, and 12[9] (a proverb), not elsewhere in the poem Chr apart from his sources prefers אלהים and האלהים Dn uses יהוה only in chap 9 (7 t.), Ec not at all. In the Elohistic group of ψ 42–83 it is used 39 t (see אלהים). It occurs as the name of Israel's God MI[18] It is doubtful whether it was used by other branches of the Shemitic family, cf. COT Gn 2[4b] Dl[Pa 158 ff] Di[Stud Bib i. 7 ff.]

II. 1. יהוה is used with אלהים and suffixes, especially in D, **a.** with אֱלֹהֶיךָ in the Ten Words Ex 20[2–12] (5 t) = Dt 5[6–16], in the law of worship of JE, Ex 23[19] 34[24.26], in D 234 t; Jos 1[9 17] 9[9 24] (D[2]), elsewhere Gn 27[20] Ex 15[26] (JE), Ju 6[26], S & K 20 t. 1 Ch 11[2] 22[11 12] 2 Ch 9[8.8] 16[7] Is 7[11] 37[4.4] 41[13] 43[3] 51[15] 55[5] Je 40[2] +(3 t) Ho 12[10] 13[4] 14[2] Am 9[15] ψ 81[11]. **b.** with אֱלֹהֵיכֶם in D 46 t.; D[2] 28 t, H 15 t., P 15 t., elsewhere Ex 23[25] (E), 8[24] 10[8.16 17] (JE); Ju 6[10] 1 S 12[12 14] 2 K 17[39] 23[21] 1 Ch 22[18] +(10 t Chr) ψ 76[12] Je 13[16]+(5 t) Ez 20[5.7 19.20] Jo 2[13]+(6 t) Zc 6[15]. **c.** with אֱלֹהֵינוּ in D 23 t; in D[2] 5 t., Ex 8[6] (JE) Ex 3[18] 5[3] 8[22.23] 10[25.26] (E) Ju 11[24] 1 S 7[8] 1 K 8[57 59.61 65] 2 K 18[22] 19[19] = Is 36[7] 37[20], 1 Ch 13[2]+(15 t. Chr) Mi 4[5] 7[17] Is 26[13] Je 3[22]+(17 t) ψ 20[8] 90[17] (?; Baer אֲדֹנָי) 94[23] 99[5.8.9 9] 105[7] 106[47] 113[5] 122[9] 123[2] Dn 9[10 13 14]. **d.** c אֱלֹהֵיהֶם Ex 10[7] (J) Ex 29[46.46] Lv 26[44] (P) Ju 3[7] 8[34] 1 S 12[9] 1 K 9[9] 2 K 17[7 9 14 16 19] 18[12] 2 Ch 31[6] 33[17] 34[33] Ne 9[3.3.4] Je 3[21] 22[9] 30[9] 43[11] 50[4] Ez 28[26] 34[30] 39[22.28] Ho 1[7] 3[5] 7[10] Zp 2[7] Hag 1[12 12] Zc 9[16] 10[6]. **e** with אֱלֹהָיו Nu 23[21] (E) Ex 32[11] (J) Lv 4[22] (P) Dt 17[19] 18[7] 1 S 30[6] 1 K 5[17] 11[4] 15[3.4] 2 K 5[11] 16[2] 2 Ch 1[1]+13 t. Chr; Mi 5[3] Je 7[28] ψ 33[12] 144[15] 146[5] Jon 2[2]. **f.** with אֱלֹהַי Nu 22[18] (JE) Dt 4[5] 18[16] 26[14] Jos 14[8 9] 2 S 24[24] 1 K 3[7] 5[18 19]

8^{28} 17$^{20.21}$ 1 Ch 21^{17} 22^{7} 2 Ch 2^{3} 6^{19} Ezr 7^{28} 9^{5} ψ 7$^{2.4}$ 13^{4} 18^{29} 30$^{3\,13}$ 35^{24} 40^{6} 104^{1} 109^{26} Is 25^{1} Je 31^{18} Dn 9$^{4.20}$ Jon 2^{7} Hab 1^{12} Zc 11^{4} 13^{9} 14^{5}. **g.** with אֱלֹהַיִךְ Is 60^{9} Je 2$^{17\,19}$ 3^{13} Mi 7^{10} Zp 3^{17}. **h.** with אלהים, probably always due to later editors, or to a Qr which has crept into the text Gn 2^{4b}—3^{23} (J, 20 t. either אלהים inserted by R^{P} as Di De; or יהוה inserted by J in an older source); Ex 9^{30} (J, but not in 𝔊 Sam.; Sam אדני יהוה; possibly MT from earlier Qr, & Sam from later Qr); 2 S 7$^{22.25}$ (𝔊 אדני יהוה and 1 Ch 17$^{20-23}$ only יהוה); 1 Ch 17$^{16\,17}$ (but 2 S 7$^{18\,19}$ אדני יהוה) 1 Ch 28^{20} 29^{1} 2 Ch 1^{9} 6$^{41.41.42}$ 26^{18} (but in the original ψ 132^{8} stood יהוה (so 𝔖), or else no divine name), ψ 72^{18} (the late doxology) 84^{12} (but it makes the line too long); Jon 4^{6}. For the combinations with other divine names see those names. **2.** the phrase †אֲנִי יהוה is noteworthy:—**a.** after אמר either alone Ex 6$^{2.29}$ (P) or before relative and other clauses: Gn 28^{13} (J) 15^{7} (R) Ex 6^{6} (P) with אלהיכם Ju 6^{10} Ez 20^{5}. **b.** after ידע כי (α) Ex 7^{17} 8^{18} 10^{2} (J), Ex 7^{5} 14$^{4\,18}$ (P), 1 K 20$^{13.28}$ Je 24^{7} Ez 6^{7} + 48 t. Ez; (β) with אלהיכם Ex 6^{7} 16^{12} Dt 29^{5} (P) Ez 20^{20} Jo 4^{17}; (γ) with אלהיהם Ex 29^{46} (P) Ez 28^{26} 34^{30} 39$^{22.28}$, (δ) before relative and other clauses Is 45^{3} 49$^{23.26}$ 60^{16} Ez 7^{9} 17^{24} 21^{10} 22^{22} 35^{12} 36^{36}, (ε) with various forms of קדש Ex 31^{13} (P) Ez 20^{12} 37^{28} 39^{7}; (ζ) with דברתי Ez 5^{13} 17^{21}, cf. יֵדְעוּ אשר אני י׳ Ez 20^{26}. **c.** after כי in various combinations Lv 11$^{44.45}$ Nu 35^{34} (P), Lv 20$^{7\,26}$ 21$^{8\,15.23}$ 22^{16} 24^{22} 25^{17} 26$^{1.44}$ (all H), Ex 15^{26} (R) Is 41^{13} 43^{3} 61^{8} Je 9^{23} Ez 12^{25} 21^{4} Zc 10^{6} Mal 3^{6} **d.** emphatic Ex 6^{8} 12^{12} Lv 26$^{2.45}$ Nu 3$^{13.41\,45}$ (all P), Lv 18$^{5.6.21}$ 19$^{12\,14\,16\,18.28.30.32.37}$ 21^{12} 22$^{2.3.8.30.31.33}$ (all H) Is 43^{15}, with אלהיהם Ex 29^{46}; with אלהיך Is 48^{17}, with אלהיכם Lv 23^{43} 25$^{38.55}$ Nu 10^{10} 15$^{41.41}$ (P) Lv 18$^{2.4.30}$ 19$^{2.3.4\,10.25.31.34\,36}$ 20^{24} 23^{22} 26^{13} (all H) Ez 20$^{7\,19}$ Jo 2^{27}; with מְקַדֵּשׁ Lv 20^{8} 22$^{9.32}$ (H), with דברתי Nu 14^{35} (P) Ez 5^{15} + (11 t. Ez); with clauses Is 27^{3} 41$^{4\,17}$ 42$^{6.8}$ 45$^{5.6.7\,8\,18.19.21}$ 60^{22} Je 17^{10} 32^{27} Ez 14$^{4.7\,9}$ 34^{24}, †אָנֹכִי יהוה is used in the Ten Words Ex 20$^{2.5}$ = Dt 5$^{6\,9}$ cited ψ 81^{11} Ho 12^{10} 13^{4}; elsewhere only Ex 4^{11} (J) Is 43^{11} 44^{24} 51^{15}. **3.** יהוה is also used with several predicates, to form sacred names of holy places of Yahweh יהוה יראה Gn 22^{14} (J), יהוה נסי Ex 17^{15} (E) יהוה שלום Ju 6^{24} יהוה צדקנו Je 33^{16} (cf. 23^{6} where it is applied to the Messiah); יהוה שָׁמָּה Ez 48^{35}—On combinations such as הַר י׳, י׳ צְבָאוֹת etc., v. הַר, צָבָא, etc

Note—Bonk$^{\text{ZAW 1891, 126 ff}}$ seems to shew that as prefix, in comp. n pr, יְהוֹ is the oldest and the latest form and that יוֹ is intermediate, belonging to the earlier post-exilic period until the time of Chr, occasional copyists' mistakes being taken into the account

†יָהּ$_{\text{τ 50}}$ **n.pr.dei** contr. fr. יהוה, first appears in early poems; Ex 15^{2} עָזִּי וְזִמְרָת יָהּ *My strength and song is Yah* (cited Is 12^{2} ψ 118^{14}), cf. the poetic extract יָד עַל כֵּס יָהּ = *hand to the throne of Yah* Ex 17^{16} (E), the song of Hezekiah Is 38^{11} (repeated by dittography), (אֵשׁ) להבת יה (so read in preference to the MT שַׁלְהֶבֶתְיָה) = *flame of fire from Yah* Ct 8^{6}; ביה יהוה Is 26^{4} (יהוה sustained by Aq and the rhythmical movement, unless it be a mistake for שמו, cf ψ 68^{5}), יה אלהים ψ 68^{19}. Elsewhere יָהּ is used only in late ψ, especially in the Hallels, in the phrase הַלְלוּ־יָהּ *praise ye Yah* ψ 104^{35} 105^{45} 106$^{1\,48}$ 111^{1} 112^{1} 113$^{1\,9}$ 115^{18} 116^{19} 117^{2} 135$^{1\,3.21}$ 146$^{1\,10}$ 147$^{1.20}$ 148$^{1\,14}$ 149$^{1\,9}$ 150$^{1\,6}$, cf. also יהלל יה 102^{19} יהללו יה 115^{17} תהלל יה ψ 150^{6} (v. הלל), in var other phrases ψ 77^{12} 89^{9} 94$^{7\,12}$ 115^{18} 118$^{5.5\,17\,18\,19}$ 122^{4} 130^{3} 135^{4}

יהוא **n pr.m.** (prob contr. fr. יהווא = י׳ *is He*, cf יֵשׁוּעַ and reff, cuneif. *Ia-u-a* COT 1 K 16^{23} 2 K 9^{2} (further Schr$^{\text{MBAW 1880, 277, ZA III 3}}$ Hpt$^{\text{BAS I 296 329}}$ Jager$^{\text{ib 468}}$), cf also אֱלִיהוּ)—**1.** king of Israel who overthrew the dynasty of Omri (𝔊 Εἰου, A oft Ἰηου, 𝔊^{L} Ἰου) 1 K 19$^{16.17\,17}$ 2 K 9^{2} + 36 t 2 K 9 & 10 + 12^{2} 13^{1} 14^{8} 15^{12}; 2 Ch 22$^{7\,8.9}$ 25^{17} Ho 1^{4}. †**2.** prophet of N. Israel in time of Baasha & Jehoshaphat (𝔊 Εἰου, A Εἰηου 𝔊^{L} Ἰου in K, 𝔊 Ἰου, Ἰησου, A 𝔊^{L} Ἰηου in Ch) 1 K 16$^{1\,7\,12}$ 2 Ch 19^{2} 20^{34}. †**3.** one of David's heroes 1 Ch 12^{3} (𝔊 Ἰηουλ, 𝔊^{L} Ἰηουδ) †**4.** a Judaite 1 Ch 2$^{38.38}$ (𝔊 Ἰησους, A 𝔊^{L} Ἰηου). †**5.** a Simeonite prince 1 Ch 4^{35} (𝔊 οὗτος i e (י)הוא), A 𝔊^{L} Ἰηου).

†**יְהוֹאָחָז, יוֹאָחָז** **n.pr.m.** (י׳ *hath grasped;* 𝔊 Ἰωαχας, & Ἰωαχαζ; cf also אֲחַזְיָהוּ, & cuneif. *Ia-u-ḫa-zi* for Ahaz, v אָחָז, and cf. further Jager$^{\text{BAS I 467 f}}$)—**1.** יְהוֹאָחָז king of Judah, son of Josiah 2 K 23$^{30.31\,34}$ 2 Ch 36^{1}, = יוֹאָחָז v$^{2\,4}$ (appar = יוֹחָנָן 1 Ch 3^{15}). **2.** יְהוֹאָחָז king of Isr, son of Jehu 2 K 10^{35} 13$^{1.4\,7.8.9\,10.22\,25.25}$ 14$^{8\,17}$ 2 Ch 25$^{17\,25}$ = יוֹאָחָז 2 K 14^{1}. **3.** יְהוֹאָחָז king of Judah, son of Jehoram of Judah 2 Ch 21^{17} 25^{23} = אֲחַזְיָהוּ (אֲחַזְיָה) **2,** q.v. **4.** יוֹאָחָז father of יוֹאָח Josiah's chronicler 2 Ch 34^{8}.

†**יְהוֹאָשׁ, יוֹאָשׁ** **n.pr.m.** 𝔊 Ἰωας (י׳ *is strong,* cf. אישׁ, or *hath bestowed,* cf Ar. آسَ bestow, Ph יאשׁ n pr f., Sab. אלאום Hal^{150}, אוסאל Hal^{144}, יאוסאל Hal^{192}, cf. DHM$^{\text{ZMG 1883, 15}}$);—**1.** יְהוֹ׳ king

of Judah, son of Ahaziah (Jehoahaz **3**) 2 K $12^{1.2.3.5.7.8.19}$ 14^{13},=יוֹאָשׁ 2 K 11^{2} $12^{20.21}$ $13^{1.10}$ $14^{1.3.17.23}$ 1 Ch 3^{11} 2 Ch 22^{11} $24^{2.4.22.24}$ $25^{23.25}$,= יֹאָשׁ 2 Ch 24^{1}. **2.** 'יהו king of Israel, son of Jehoahaz **2**, 2 K $13^{10.25}$ $14^{8.9.11.13.15.16.17}$=יוֹאָשׁ 2 K $13^{9.12.13.13.14.25}$ $14^{1.23.27}$ 2 Ch $25^{17.18.21.23.25}$ Ho 1^{1} Am 1^{1}. **3.** 'יו father of Gideon (Jerubbaal) Ju $6^{11.29.30.31}$ 7^{14} $8^{13.29.32.32}$. **4.** 'יו a prince of Ahab's house, called בֶּן־הַמֶּלֶךְ 1 K 22^{26}=2 Ch 18^{25} **5** 'יו one of David's heroes 1 Ch 12^{3} (𝔊 Ἰωα, Ἰωας, A Ἰωρας) **6.** יוֹאָשׁ a Judaite prince 1 Ch 4^{22} (𝔊 Ἰωαδα, Ἰωας)

†**יְהוֹזָבָד, יוֹזָבָד** n.pr.m. 𝔊 usu Ἰωζαβαδ ('י *hath bestowed;* cf Palm נבוזבד Vog ^{73}, v. also זְבַדְיָהוּ, זבדיאל)—**1.** יְהוֹזָבָד servant & murderer of Joash of Judah 2 K 12^{22} (𝔊 Ἰεζεβουθ) =2 Ch 24^{26} (𝔊 Ζωζαβεδ, Ἰωζαβεδ, Ἰωζαβεθ) **2.** יוֹזָבָד three of David's mighty men, **a.** 1 Ch 12^{5}, **b.** v^{21}, **c.** v^{21} (𝔊 Ἰωζαβειθ, Ἰωζαβειδ) **3.** יְהוֹזָבָד a Benjamite chief 2 Ch 17^{18} **4.** priests & Levites, **a.** יְהוֹזָבָד 1 Ch 26^{4}, **b.** יוֹזָבָד 2 Ch 31^{13} (𝔊 Ἐζαβαθ, Ἰωαζαβαθ, 𝔊L Ἰωαζαβαδ), **c.** 35^{9} (𝔊 Ἰωζαβαδ, 𝔊L as foreg), **d.** Ezr 8^{33}, **e.** Ezr 10^{22}, **f.** Ezr 10^{23}, **g.** Ne 8^{7}, **h.** Ne 11^{16}, (**d. f. g.** & **h.** perh the same man)

†**יְהוֹחָנָן, יוֹחָנָן** n.pr.m. 𝔊 mostly Ἰωαναν, Ἰωναν ('י *hath been gracious*, cf אֶלְחָנָן, חֲנַנְאֵל & reff, also Ph יחנבעל בעליחן)—**1. a.** 'יְהו a priest Ne 12^{13}, **b.** high priest Ezr 10^{6}=יוֹחָנָן Ne $12^{22.23}$ appar =יוֹנָתָן Ne $12^{11.11}$ (𝔊 Ἰωναθαν) **2.** 'יהו Levite Ne 12^{42}. **3.** 'יהו son of Tobiah Ne 6^{18} (𝔊 Codd. Ἰωναθαν) **4.** 'יְהו porter in David's time 1 Ch 26^{3} (𝔊 Ἰωνας, 𝔊L Ἰωναθαν) **5.** 'יהו a Judaite captain 2 Ch 17^{15} appar also 23^{1} **6.** 'יהו an Ephraimite 2 Ch 28^{12}. **7.** 'יהו an Israelite, Ezra's time Ezr 10^{28} **8.** 'יו (& so all foll) a Jewish captain, after fall of Jerus 2 K 25^{23} Je $40^{8.13.15.16}$ $41^{11.13.14.15.16}$ $42^{1.8}$ $43^{2.4.5}$ **9.** eldest son of king Josiah 1 Ch 3^{15} 𝔊L Ἰωαχας (appar =יְהוֹאָחָז 2 K 23^{30}+) **10.** a post-exilic prince of the line of David 1 Ch 3^{24}. **11.** father of Azariah, priest in Sol's time 1 Ch $5^{35.36}$ **12.** two of David's mighty men: **a.** a Benjamite 1 Ch 12^{4}, **b.** a Gadite 1 Ch 12^{12} **13.** a returning exile Ezr 8^{12}

†**יְהוֹיָדָע, יוֹיָדָע** n pr m. ('י *knoweth;* cf. יְדַעְיָה, אֶלְיָדָע & reff, בְּעֶלְיָדָע)—**1.** 'יְהו; 𝔊 usu. Ἰωδαε, A sts. Ἰωιαδαε (2 S 23^{20}+), 𝔊L Ἰωαδ (2 S 20^{23} Ἰωαδδαι), father of Benaiah (David's time), in combin. בְּנָיָהוּ בֶּן־יְהו' 2 S 8^{18} 20^{23} $23^{20.22}$ 1 K $1^{8.26.32.36.38.44}$ $2^{25.29.34.35.46}$ 4^{4} 1 Ch $11^{22.24}$ 18^{17} 27^{5}; יְהוֹיָדָע בֶּן־בְּנָיָהוּ 1 Ch 27^{34} is prob erron inversion of the usual order, 'יְהו alone only 1 Ch 12^{28} (where called הַנָּגִיד לְאַהֲרֹן). **2.** 'יהו, 𝔊 usu Ἰωδαε A sts Ἰωιαδαε etc., (chief) priest at Jerus in time of Joash 2 K $11^{4.9.9.15.17}$ $12^{3.8.10}$ 2 Ch 22^{11} $23^{1.8.8.9.11.14.16.18}$ $24^{2.3.6.12.14.14.15.17.20.22.25}$ Je 29^{26}. **3.** יוֹיָדָע a builder at wall of Jerus., with Nehemiah, Ne 3^{6} (𝔊 Ἰωειμα, Ἰωειδα, Ἰωδαε, etc) **4.** 'יו son of h. p. Eliashib Ne $12^{10.11.22}$ 13^{28} (𝔊 Ἰωδα, Ἰωδαε, Ἰωιαδα).

†**יְהוֹיָכִין, יְהוֹיָכִן, יוֹיָכִין** n.pr.m. ('י *appointeth*) last king but one of Judah, son of Jehoiakim (𝔊 Ἰωακειμ; in K, 𝔊L Ἰωακειν; 𝔊 in Je (usu.) & Ch Ἰεχονίας); יְהוֹיָכִין 2 K $24^{6.8.12.15}$ $25^{27.27}$ 2 Ch $36^{8.9}$ Je 52^{31}=יְהוֹיָכִן ^{31b},=יוֹיָכִין Ez 1^{2}; =יכוניה Je 27^{20}, =יְכָנְיָה 28^{4} 29^{2} 1 Ch $3^{16.17}$ Est 2^{6}; =יְכָנְיָהוּ Je 24^{1}=כָּנְיָהוּ Je $22^{24.28}$ 37^{1}.

יְהוֹיָקִים, יוֹיָקִים, יוֹקִים n.pr.m. 𝔊 Ἰωακειμ ('י *raiseth up*, cf אֶלְיָקִים & reff, also יָקִים, יְקַמְיָה)—**1.** 'יְהו one of the last kings of Judah, son of Josiah 2 K $23^{34.35.36}$ $24^{1.5.6.19}$ 1 Ch $3^{15.16}$ 2 Ch $36^{4.5.8}$ Je 1^{3} $22^{18.24}$ 24^{1}+19 t. Je, Dn $1^{1.2}$, name changed fr orig אֶלְיָקִים 2 K 23^{34}=2 Ch 36^{4} †**2.** יוֹיָקִים priest, son of Jeshua Ne $12^{10.10.12.26}$ †**3.** יוֹקִים a Judaite 1 Ch 4^{22}.

†**יְהוֹיָרִיב, יוֹיָרִיב** n pr.m. 𝔊 Ἰωιαρειβ, Ἰωαρειβ, Ἰωαρειμ, etc. ('י *pleadeth*, or *contendeth*) —**1.** name of a priestly family 'יְהו 1 Ch 9^{10} 24^{7},='יו Ne 11^{10} $12^{6.19}$. **2.** teacher in Ezra's time Ezr 8^{16} **3.** a Judaite Ne 11^{5}.

†**יְהוּכַל, יוּכַל** n.pr.m. 𝔊 Ἰωαχαλ (Codd. have ζ, χ, ς, for λ) (prob. contr. fr. יהויוכל, 'י *is able*) a courtier of king Zedekiah, 'יהו Je 37^{3}='יו 38^{1}.

†**יְהוֹנָדָב, יוֹנָדָב** n.pr m. ('י *is noble*, or *is liberal*, or *hath impelled*, cf. נְדַבְיָה)—**1.** 'יְהו son of Rechab & chief of the Rechabites (𝔊 Ἰωναδαβ) 2 K $10^{15.15.23}$ Je $35^{6.14.16.18}$,='יו Je $35^{6.10.19}$. **2.** 'יְהו nephew of David (𝔊 Ἰωναδαβ, Ἰωναδαμ; 𝔊L Ἰωναθαν) 2 S 13^{5},='יו 2 S $13^{3.3.32.35}$; (appar. called Jonathan 2 S 21^{21} 1 Ch 20^{7}, cf. יְהוֹנָתָן **3.**)

יְהוֹנָתָן, יוֹנָתָן n pr.m. 𝔊 Ἰωναθαν throughout, with occasional var. ('י *hath given;* cf אֶלְנָתָן, נְתַנְיָהוּ, נְתַנְאֵל, & reff, Temanite רמננתן Hal $^{REJ\ 1884,\ ix\ 7f}$ Nbr $^{Stud\ Bib\ i\ 211}$, Sab והבאום Hal ^{10})—**1** 'יהו son of Saul 1 S $14^{6.8}$ 18^{1}+40t 1 S, 2 S 1^{4}+18t 2 S, 1 Ch $8^{33.34}$ $9^{39.40}$,='יו 1 S $13^{2.3}$+27 t 1 S, 1 Ch 10^{2}. †**2.** 'יְהו son of Abiathar 2 S $15^{27.36}$ $17^{17.20}$;='יו 1 K $1^{42.43}$. †**3.** 'יְהו nephew of David 2 S 21^{21}=1 Ch 20^{7}; appar called Jonadab 2 S $13^{3ff.}$ where 𝔊L Ἰωναθαν, cf.

יהונדב **2.** †**4.** יְהוֹ׳; דּוֹד of David, i.e. his uncle? 1 Ch 27^{32}. †**5.** יְהוֹ׳ one of David's heroes 2 S 23^{32} (cf. Dr) = יוֹנָתָן 1 Ch 11^{34}. †**6.** יְהוֹ׳ one of David's treasurers 1 Ch 27^{25}. †**7.** יְהוֹ׳ a scribe Je 37$^{15.20}$ 38^{26}. †**8.** Levites **a.** יְהוֹ׳ 2 Ch 17^{8}; **b.** יוֹ׳ Ne 12^{35}. †**9.** יְהוֹ׳ a priest Ne 12^{18}. †**10.** יְהוֹ׳ priest to the tribe of Dan, son of Gershom Ju 18^{30}. †**11.** יוֹ׳ a Judaite captain, after fall of Jerus. Je 40^{8}. †**12.** יוֹ׳ a Judaite 1 Ch 2$^{32.33}$. †**13.** יוֹ׳ father of Ebed Ezr 8^{6}. †**14.** יוֹ׳ son of Asahel Ezr 10^{15}. †**15.** יוֹ׳ a priest Ne 12^{14}. †**16.** יוֹ׳ son of Joiada Ne 12$^{11.11}$ appar. = יְהוֹחָנָן **2.**

†יְהוֹעַדָּה **n.pr.m.** (mng. dub.; Thes י׳ *hath adorned* (as Heb. עדה Hiph.; vb. of *Pa.* form); MV י׳ *is equipment*, cf. Ar. عُدَّةٌ; possibly י׳ *hath carried off spoil*, or *hath deposed* (𝔗 עדא Pe Pa Aph; cf. Haph. Dn 2^{21}); or perh. י׳ *hath numbered* Ar. عَدَّ)—a descendant of Saul 1 Ch 8$^{36.36}$ (𝔊 Ἰαδα, A Ἰωιαδα, 𝔊L Ἰωδα) = יַעְרָה 9$^{42.42}$ (for יְעַדָּה? cf. Be; 𝔊 Ἰαδα, 𝔊L Ἰωδα).

יהועדין 2 K 14^{2} Kt v. foll.

†יְהוֹעַדָּן **n.pr.f.** (? du. (cf. Kt 2 K 14^{2}) or f.pl. of יהועדה, (עדה as noun) Aram. form; Klo 2 K 14^{2} cf. עַד־אָנָה יהוה ψ 13^{2}; comp. Bab. n.pr. *Aḫulapia*, v. אַחְלַי p. 29 supr.) mother of Amaziah, king of Judah 2 K 14^{2} Qr (Kt יהועדין, 𝔊 Ἰωαδειμ, A Ἰωαδειν), 2 Ch 25^{1} (𝔊 Ἰωνaa, A Ἰωαδεν, 𝔊L Ἰωαδειν).

†יְהוֹצָדָק, יוֹצָדָק **n.pr.m.** (י׳ *is righteous*; cf. צִדְקִיָּהוּ Sab. צדקאל Hal^{193}) father of Joshua the high-priest, יְהוֹ׳ Hg 1$^{1.12.14}$ 2$^{2.4}$ Zc 6^{11} 1 Ch 5$^{40.41}$; = יוֹ׳ Ezr 3$^{2.8}$ 5^{2} 10^{18} Ne 12^{26} (𝔊 Ἰωσαδακ, Ἰωσεδεκ).

†יְהוֹרָם, יוֹרָם, יֹרָם **n.pr.m.** (י׳ *is exalted*; cf. מַלְכִּירָם; further, Ph. רמבעל, בעלרם; Sab. אלרם DHM ZMG 1876, 686)—**1.** יְהוֹ׳ (𝔊 Ἰωραμ) king of Judah, son of Jehoshaphat 1 K 22^{51} 2 K 1^{17} 8$^{16.25.29}$ 12^{19} 2 Ch 21$^{1.3.4.5.9.16}$ 22$^{1.6.11}$; = יוֹ׳ 2 K 8$^{21.23.24}$ 11^{2} 1 Ch 3^{11}. **2.** יְהוֹ׳ (𝔊 Ἰωραμ) king of Israel son of Ahab 2 K 1^{17} 3$^{1.6}$ 9$^{15.17.21.21.22.23}$ 2 Ch 22$^{5.6.7}$; = יוֹ׳ 2 K 8$^{16.25.28.28.29.29}$ 9$^{14.14.16.16.29}$ 2 Ch 22$^{5.7}$. **3.** יְהוֹ׳ priest in time of Jehoshaphat 2 Ch 17^{8} (𝔊 Ἰωραμ, Ἰωραν). **4.** יוֹ׳ son of Tou, king of Hamath 2 S 8^{10} (𝔊 Ἰεδδουραν) prob. err. for הֲדוֹרָם ‖ 1 Ch 18^{10}. **5.** יֹרָם a Levite 1 Ch 26^{25} (𝔊 Ἰωραμ).

†יְהוֹשֶׁבַע, יְהוֹשַׁבְעַת **n.pr.f.** (י׳ *is an oath*; cf. אֱלִישֶׁבַע)—daughter of Joram of Judah, & wife of Jehoiada the priest; יְהוֹשֶׁבַע 2 K 11^{2} (𝔊 Ἰωσαβεε, Ἰωσαβεθ); = יְהוֹשַׁבְעַת 2 Ch 22$^{11.11}$ (𝔊 Ἰωσαβεε).

יְהוֹשַׁבְעַת v. foregoing.

יְהוֹשֻׁעַ, יְהוֹשׁוּעַ, and (later) יֵשׁוּעַ, **n.pr.m.** (& **loc.**, v. **9** infr.) (י׳ *is salvation*, or י׳ *is opulence*, cf. אֱלִישׁוּעַ, אֱלִישָׁע, אֲבִישׁוּעַ, & Nes SK 1892, 573 f.; in any case it came to be associated with ישׁע, cf. Mat 1^{21}; on יֵשׁוּעַ v. esp. Frä VOJ iv, 1890, 332 f. Müll SK 1893, 177 f. who cite analog. for change of וֹ to later ◌ֻ, & Nes l.c.)—**1.** Moses' successor, son of Nun, (𝔊 Ἰησοῦς) יְהוֹשׁוּעַ Dt 3^{21} Ju 2^{7}; = יְהוֹשֻׁעַ Ex 17$^{9.10.13.14}$ 24^{13} 32^{17} 33^{11} Nu 11^{28} 13^{16} 14$^{6.30.38}$ 26^{65} 27$^{18.22}$ 32$^{12.28}$ 34^{17} Dt 1^{38} 3^{28} 31$^{3.7.14.14.23}$ 34^{9} Jos 1^{1} + 167 t. Jos; Ju 1^{1} 2$^{6.7.8.21.23}$ 1 K 16^{34} 1 Ch 7^{27}; = יֵשׁוּעַ Ne 8^{17} (𝔊 Ἰησοῦς); acc. to P, name changed by Moses fr. הוֹשֵׁעַ q.v. Nu 13$^{8.16}$ (𝔊 Αὐση) Dt 32^{44} (𝔊 Ἰησοῦς). †**2.** יְהוֹשֻׁעַ a Bethshemite 1 S 6$^{14.18}$ (𝔊 Ὡσηε, A Ἰησοῦς, 𝔊L Ἰωσηε). †**3.** h.p. after the restoration, son of Jehozadak יְהוֹשֻׁעַ (𝔊 Ἰησοῦς) Hg 1$^{1.12.14}$ 2$^{2.4}$ Zc 3$^{1.3.6.8.9}$ 6^{11}; = יֵשׁוּעַ (𝔊 Ἰησοῦς) Ezr 2^{2} 3$^{2.8}$ 4^{3} 5^{2} 10^{18} Ne 7^{7} 12$^{1.7.10.26}$. †**4.** יְהוֹשֻׁעַ governor of Jerusalem under Josiah 2 K 23^{8} (𝔊 Ἰησοῦς, 𝔊L Ἰωσηε). †**5.** יֵשׁוּעַ (𝔊 Ἰησοῦς) head of one of the classes of priests 1 Ch 24^{11}, possibly also Ezr 2^{36} = Ne 7^{39}. †**6.** יֵשׁוּעַ (𝔊 Ἰησοῦς, etc.), a Levitical family-name of frequent occurrence: **a.** Ezr 2^{40} 3^{9} = Ne 7^{43} 8^{7} 9$^{4.5}$ 10^{10} 12^{8}. **b.** 2 Ch 31^{15} Ezr 8^{33} Ne 12^{24}. †**7.** יֵשׁוּעַ (𝔊 *id.*), father of a builder at the wall Ne 3^{19}, perh. = †**8.** a Judaite family-name (𝔊 *id.*), Ezr 2^{6} = Ne 7^{11} (cf. Sm Listen 12). †**9. n.pr.loc.** in south of Judah Ne 11^{26} בְּיֵשׁוּעַ (𝔊 ἐν Ἰησοῦ, 𝔊L ἐν Σουα).

†[יְהוֹשָׁמָע] only abbrev. (or txt. err.) הוֹשָׁמָע **n.pr.m.** (י׳ *hath heard*, cf. אֱלִישָׁמָע & reff.)—a descendant of the royal house of Judah 1 Ch 3^{18} (𝔊 Ὡσαμω(θ), 𝔊L Ωσαμα).

יְהוֹשָׁפָט, יוֹשָׁפָט **n.pr.m.** 𝔊 Ἰωσαφαθ, Ἰωσαφατ (י׳ *hath judged*, cf. שְׁפַטְיָהוּ, אֱלִישָׁפָט & reff.)—**1.** יְהוֹ׳ (so all exc. **5.** & **6**) king of Judah, son of Asa 1 K 15^{24} 22^{2} + 21 t. 1 K; 2 K 1^{17} 3$^{1.7.11.12.12.14}$ 8$^{16.16}$ 12^{19} 1 Ch 3^{10} 2 Ch 17^{1} + 40 t. 2 Ch. †**2.** father of Jehu king of Israel 2 K 9$^{2.14}$. †**3.** chronicler under David & Solomon, son of Ahilud 2 S 8^{16} 1 K 4^{3} 1 Ch 18^{15}; also 2 S 20^{24} (𝔊L Σαφαν). †**4.** one of Sol.'s 12 officers who provided victuals for the royal household 1 K 4^{17} (𝔊L Ἰωασαφατ). †**5.** יוֹ׳ one of David's heroes 1 Ch 11^{43}. †**6.** יוֹ׳ a priest & trumpeter in David's time 1 Ch 15^{24}. †**7.** in **n.pr.loc.** עֵמֶק יְהוֹשָׁפָט Jo 4$^{2.12}$, symbolical name

of a valley near Jerusalem, place of ultimate judgment

יוֹאָב n pr m (׳י *is father*, cf. אֲבִיָּהוּ, אֱלִיאָב, אֲבִיאֵל & reff)—**1.** David's sister's son & captain of his host (𝔊 Ἰωαβ) 1 S 26^{6} 2 S 2^{13} + 100 t 2 S (also 2 S 20^{6} for MT אֲבִישַׁי cf. 𝔖 We Dr), 1 K 1^{7} + 14 t. 1 K, 1 Ch 2^{16} + 22 t 1 Ch; ψ 60^{2}. †**2.** a descendant of Judah 1 Ch 4^{14} (but 𝔊B 𝔊L Ἰωβαβ). †**3.** a family-name after the exile Ezr 2^{6} = Ne 7^{11} (𝔊 Ἰωβαβ, Ἰωαβ) Ezr 8^{9} (𝔊 Ἰωαβ).

†**יוֹאָח n.pr.m.** (׳י *is brother*, cf. אֲחִיָּהוּ & reff)—**1.** son of Asaph the chronicler in Hezekiah's time 2 K 18$^{18.26.37}$ (𝔊 Ἰωας, 𝔊L Ἰωαχ), = Is 36$^{3\ 11\ 22}$ (𝔊 Ἰωαχ) **2.** Levites **a.** son of Zimmah 1 Ch 6^{6}, **b.** id 2 Ch 29$^{12\ 12}$ (𝔊 Ἰωα, Ἰωαχ(α) Ἰωδααθ) **3.** son of Joahaz the chronicler in Josiah's time 2 Ch 34^{8} (𝔊 Ἰωαχ, Ἰωας) **4.** a Levite, son of Obed-edom 1 Ch 26^{4} (𝔊 Ἰωαθ, Ἰωαα, Ἰωαδ)

יוֹאָחָז v. יְהוֹאָחָז.

†**יוֹאֵל n.pr.m.** 𝔊 Ἰωηλ (usu. interpr. as ׳י *is God*, cf. אֵלִיָּהוּ, but Ph. . . . יאל CIS$^{1\ 1321\ 4}$ & in יאלפעל (Louvre) appar. n pr. dei, perh = *Iolaos*, CIS$^{1\ p\ 163}$ & reff; v also Nes$^{Es\ 86}$ RS$^{K\ 301}$, Nes *strong-willed*, cf. ויל, ואל Sin. Inscr وائل, v ואלו Eut$^{Sin\ Inschr\ No.5+oft}$, yet cf. Dr$^{Stud\ Bib.\ i.\ 5\ n}$, W in RS$^{1\ c}$ prop connex with Ar *Wâil* in n pr trib Bakr Wâil (√ وَأَلَ *take refuge*) cf. RS$^{K\ 194}$)—**1.** Samuel's first-born 1 S 8^{2}, 1 Ch 6^{13}, ins also v^{13} after 𝔊L Ἰωηλ (cf Dr 1 S 8^{2}) **2.** a Simeonite prince 1 Ch 4^{35}. **3.** a Reubenite 1 Ch 5$^{4.8}$. **4.** a Gadite chief 1 Ch 5^{12}. **5.** a chief man of Issachar 1 Ch 7^{3}. **6.** one of David's heroes 1 Ch 11^{38} **7.** a chief of Manasseh 1 Ch 27^{20} **8.** a Jew of Ezra's time Ezr 10^{43}. **9.** a Benjamite Ne 11^{9}. **10.** the prophet, son of Pethuel Jo 1^{1} **11.** Levites **a.** 1 Ch 6^{21}, **b.** 2 Ch 29^{12}, **c.** 1 Ch 15$^{7\ 11\ 17}$, perh. = **d.** 1 Ch 23^{8} 26^{22}

יוֹאָשׁ v יְהוֹאָשׁ

יוֹזָבָד v יְהוֹזָבָד.

†**יוֹזָכָר n.pr.m.** (׳י *hath remembered*, cf זְכַרְיָהוּ; Sab ידכראל Hal^{187})—servant & murderer of Joash king of Judah 2 K 12^{22} (𝔊 Ἰεζειχαρ, A 𝔊L Ἰωζαχαρ), = זָבָד 2 Ch 24^{26} (𝔊 Ζαβελ, Ζαβεθ, Ζαβαθ)

יוֹחָנָן v. יְהוֹחָנָן.

יוֹיָדָע v. יְהוֹיָדָע.

יוֹיָכִין v. יְהוֹיָכִין.

יוֹיָקִים v. יְהוֹיָקִים.

יוֹיָרִיב v יְהוֹיָרִיב.

†**יוֹכֶבֶד n.pr.f.** 𝔊 Ἰωχαβεδ (׳י *is glory;* cf. Ph כבדמלקרת) daughter of Levi, wife of Amram and mother of Moses Ex 6^{20} Nu 26^{59} (both P)

יוּכַל v. יְהוּכַל.

יוֹנָדָב v. יְהוֹנָדָב

יוֹנָתָן v יְהוֹנָתָן

†**יוֹעֵד n.pr.m.** 𝔊 Ἰωαδ (׳י *is a witness*) a Benjamite Ne 11^{7}.

†**יוֹעֶזֶר n.pr.m.** (׳י *is a help;* cf. עֲזַרְיָהוּ, עֲזַרְאֵל, עֲזִיאֵל, אֱלִיעֶזֶר & reff) one of David's mighty men 1 Ch 12^{7} (𝔊 Ἰωζαρα, Ἰωζααρ, 𝔊L Ἰεζρααρ).

†**יוֹעָשׁ n.pr.m.** 𝔊 Ἰωας (׳י *hath aided* (?; cf. Ar. غَاثَ), comp Sab אלעוה DHM in MV)—**1.** a Benjamite, son of Becher 1 Ch 7^{8}. **2.** an officer under David 1 Ch 27^{28}.

יוֹצָדָק v יְהוֹצָדָק.

יוֹקִים v יְהוֹיָקִים.

יוֹרָם v. יְהוֹרָם.

יוֹשָׁפָט v יְהוֹשָׁפָט

†**יוֹתָם n.pr.m.** (׳י *is perfect*)—**1.** king of Judah, son of Azariah (𝔊 Ἰωαθαμ, Ἰωαθαν, Ἰωναθαν) 2 K 15$^{5.7\ 30.32.36.38}$ 16^{1} 1 Ch 3^{12} 5^{17} 2 Ch 26$^{21\ 23}$ 27$^{1\ 6.7\ 9}$ Is 1^{1} 7^{1} Ho 1^{1} Mi 1^{1}. **2.** youngest son of Jerubbaal (Gideon) Ju 9$^{5.7\ 21.57}$ (𝔊 ut supr., Codd. Ἰωθαμ, Ἰωαθαμ). **3.** a descendant of Caleb 1 Ch 2^{47} (𝔊 Ἰωαθαμ).

יֵשׁוּעַ v יְהוֹשֻׁעַ

†**הוֹהָם n.pr.m.** Canaanitish king of Hebron Jos 10^{3}.

הוֹי$_{81}$ interj. (onomatop.; cf. ܘܘܝ = הו הו Am 5^{16} 𝔖, = הידד Je 51^{14} 𝔖; also Mod. Aram. *ú hú, ú hú* (in a lament), So$^{Urmia\text{-}Dial.\ 102.4}$)—expressing usually dissatisfaction and pain, **Ah, Alas, Ha** (not distinctly *Woe!* which is אוֹי) used in lamentations, 1 K 13^{30} and they mourned over him (saying) הוֹי אָחִי *Ah*, my brother! Je 22^{18} הוֹי אָחִי וְהוֹי אָחוֹת . . . הוֹי אָדוֹן וְהוֹי הֹדֹה, 34^{5} וְהוֹי אָדוֹן יִסְפְּדוּ לָךְ (cf הו־הו Am 5^{16}) hence Is 1^{4} הוֹי גּוֹי חֹטֵא *Ah!* sinful nation, v^{24} *Ah!* I will ease me of my adversaries; esp

preparatory to a declaration of judgment, Is 10^{5} הוֹי אַשּׁוּר שֵׁבֶט אַפִּי, 17^{12} 28^{1}, oft. sq. a ptcp. *Ah!* those that . . , 5$^{8\ 11\ 18}$ 29^{15} 31^{1} 45$^{9\ 10}$ Je 22^{13} Am 5^{18} 6^{1} Hb 2$^{6\ 9.12\ 15\ 19}$ Zc 11^{17}+ (more sympathetic than אוֹי לְ). sq. כי Je 30^{7}, אֶל 48^{1}, עַל 50^{27} Ez 13^{3}, לְ 13^{18}. Sts hardly more than an exclam. arousing attention *Ha!* (though perh with a touch of sympathy or pity) Is 18^{1} 55^{1} Zc 2$^{10\ 10.11}$ Je 47^{6}

†[**הוּם, הִים**] **vb. murmur, roar, discomfit** (Ar هَامَ (med ى) is *rush about madly* (lit., or in passion, love, &c), fig. *be distracted*, on ✓ הים v. Hi$^{\psi 55.3}$ No$^{ZMG\ 1883,\ 540}$)—**Qal** *Pf.* 3 ms. sf. וְהָמָם consec Dt 7^{23} וה׳ מְהוּמָה גְדֹלָה (י׳ subj) *and he shall discomfit them* (*with*) *a great discomfiture* (acc to Di הָמַם ו is fr. הָמַם, here pointed as ע״ו because of מְהוּמָה; but v. Ko$^{i.\ 486}$ & reff.); here, acc to No$^{l\ c}$, belongs *Impf.* 1 s cohort אָהִימָה (i. e ✓ע״י) ψ 55^{3} *am driven about* (Hi De), or *distracted*. **Niph.** *Impf.* 3 fs וַתֵּהֹם 1 S 4^{5} + 2 t. (on form cf. Ges$^{\S 72\ R\ 5}$), *be in a stir*, of a city Ru 1^{19} (sq. עַל *over*, *on account of*), 1 K 1^{45}, of ground *re-echoing* shout 1 S 4^{5}. **Hiph.** *Impf.* 1 s אָהִימָה ψ 55^{3} *shew disquietude* (so most, cf supr.), but Ol Che וְאֶהֱמָיָה (77^{4}); Lag$^{Proph.\ Chald.\ xlviii\ 2,\ BN\ 27}$ אֶהֱמֶה (v^{18}), 3 fpl. תְּהִימֶנָה (תְּהֱמֶינָה ?) Mi 2^{12} *they* (i.e. fold & pasture) *shall murmur* with men.

†**מְהוּמָה** **n.f. tumult, confusion, disquietude, discomfiture**—abs. מ׳ Dt 7^{23} + 7 t.; cstr מְהוּמַת 1 S 5^{11} Ez 22^{5}, pl. abs מְהוּמֹת 2 Ch 15^{5}, מְהוּמֹת Am 3^{9},—**1.** *tumult, confusion* Am 3^{9} (‖ עֲשׁוּקִים *oppression*), *disturbance, turmoil* (opp peace) 2 Ch 15^{5} (‖vb. המם v^{6}), cf. Ez 22^{5}, *disquietude* (of mind) Pr 15^{16}; esp *tumult & confusion, panic*, as due to divine judgment מְהוּמַת־י׳ Zc 14^{13} cf. Ez 7^{7}; also 1 S 5^{9} and מְהוּמַת מָוֶת v^{11} **2.** *discomfiture* (due to י׳) in war 1 S 14^{20} (cf v$^{15.22}$); Dt 7^{23} (acc. cogn. c. הום q.v.), 28^{20} (‖ מְאֵרָה, מִגְעֶרֶת), cf. יוֹם מ׳ Is 22^{5} (‖ מְבוּסָה, מְבוּכָה) *a day of discomfiture & down-treading & confusion*.

הוֹמָם **n.pr.** v. sub המם.

†[**הוּן**] **vb. be easy** (Ar هَانَ *be light, easy*, cf. هَيْنٌ, هَوْنٌ (v אוֹן), Aram NH הוּן *gentleness*, ܗܘܢܐ, ܗܘܢ is *mind, sense*, vid. conject. on development of mngs. Fl ChWB$^{i.\ 423}$)—only **Hiph.** *Impf.* וַתָּהִינוּ sq Inf. Dt 1^{41} *regard as easy* to go up, or *make light* of going up, so Thes Kn Ke Di RVm (construct. as Nu 14^{44} וַיַּעְפִּלוּ לַעֲלוֹת, though ‖ to this in Dt is v^{43}).

†**הוֹן** **n.m.**$^{Pr\ 8\ 18}$, **wealth, sufficiency** (poet, almost wholly WisdLt, especially Pr; cf. 1. אוֹן p 20 supr.)—abs הוֹן Pr 1^{13} + 15 t. + Ez 27$^{12\ 18}$ (where 𝔊 𝔖 Co הוֹנֵךְ); cstr Pr 6^{31} + 3 t, sf. הוֹנֶךָ Pr 3^{9}; הונך Ez 27^{27} + v$^{12\ 18}$ Co; הונו Pr 28^{8}; pl. sf. הוֹנַיִךְ Ez 27^{33}—**1.** *wealth* ψ 112^{3} (‖ עֹשֶׁר) Pr 8^{18} (‖ *id*) 1^{13} (‖ שָׁלָל) cf. הוֹן עָשִׁיר Pr 10^{15} (opp דַּלִּים), 18^{11}; Pr 3^{9} (‖ ראשית כָּל־תְּבוּאָתֶךָ) הוֹן ביתו Pr 6^{31} Ct 8^{7}, בַּיִת וָהוֹן Pr 19^{14}, see 19^{4} (opp. דָּל) 28^{8} (opp. דַּלִּים); also ψ 119^{14} Pr 11^{4} 12^{27} 13$^{7\ 11}$ 24^{4} 28^{22} (opp. חֶסֶר) 29^{3}, Ez 27$^{12.18.27.33}$. **2.** with בְּ + מָכַר *pretii*, = *high value*, or *price* תִּמְכֹּר עַמְּךָ בְלֹא הוֹן ψ 44^{13}—i.e. cheaply, = 'for no price at all' (‖ מחיר). **3.** *sufficiency, enough!* in exclam. Pr 30$^{15.16}$ (so also 𝔊𝔗, Aq Sym Theod ἀρκεῖ)

†[**הוֹר**], assumed by Thes al as ancient form for הַר *mountain*, to explain הוֹרַי Gn 49^{26}, rd הוֹרֵי־עַד, but better הַרְרֵי־עַד *everlasting mountains*, v. הַר sub הרר

הוֹשָׁמָע **n.pr.m.** = יְהוֹ׳ v. יהוה sub היה.

הוֹשֵׁעַ v. sub ישע

הוֹשַׁעְיָה v sub ישע.

†[**הוּת**] **vb. shout at,** si vera l. (Ar هَوَّتَ c. على *shout at, threaten*, dialect. for هَيَّتَ, cf. De ψ 62^{4} who comp Damascene هَوَّتَ عَلَى فُلَانٍ *rush upon one* with cries and raised fist, cf further Wetzst in De, so MV SS. Thes al assign to [התת], *attack*, txt dub)—only **Po.** *Impf* תְּהוֹתְתוּ עַל־אִישׁ ψ 62^{4}; but Hup Che rd. תְּהוֹלְלוּ *be frantic* against, cf. 102^{9}.

הוֹתִיר **n.pr.m.** v יתר.

†[**הָזָה**] **vb. dream, rave** (Ar هَذَى *talk deliriously*, Syr. ܗܕܐ, in Lexx., *id.*, cf. also Vrss, v esp. Bo$^{Hieroz.\ ii.\ 56,\ p\ 680,\ ed.\ Rosenm\ vol.\ i.\ 782}$); —only **Qal** *Pt. act.* pl. הֹזִים Is 56^{10} לֹא יוּכְלוּ לִנְבֹּחַ ה׳ שֹׁכְבִים of dogs, metaph of false prophets.

†**הִי** (?) **n.[m.] lamentation, wailing**, only Ez 2^{10} וְכָתוּב אֵלֶיהָ קִנִים וָהֶגֶה וָהִי *and written in it were lamentations and mourning and wailing* (𝔊 οὐαί, *woe!* Ew$^{\S 101\ c}$ comp. אִי, cf III. אִי p. 33 supr.; acc. to Thes Sta$^{\S 125\ b}$ al נְהִי = הִי, נ being dropped; Ol$^{\S 77\ c\ 144\ c}$ would emend נהי & so Co; v. נהי sub נהה Text very dubious)

הִיא v הוא

הֵידָד v sub הדד

הִידוֹת v. sub ידה

הָיָה 3570 **vb.** **fall out, come to pass, become, be** (SI ^{16} היה, ib^{3} הית, parallel form of הוה, Ar هَوِىَ, Aram הֲוָא, ܗܘܐ; v. הָוָה supr)—**Qal** *Pf.* 3 ms הָיָה Gn 3^{1}+, וְהָיָה consec. Gn 4^{14}+; 3 fs הָיְתָה Gn 1^{2}+, הָיָתָה Is 14^{24}+3 t; וְהָיְתָה consec. Gn 9^{13}+; והית 2 K 9^{37} Kt (Qr וְהָיְתָה), 2 ms הָיִיתָ Dt 5^{15}+; 1 s הָיִיתִי Gn 31^{40}, 3 pl הָיוּ Gn 6^{4}+; 2 mpl הֱיִיתֶם Ex 22^{20}+, והייתם consec Gn 3^{5}+, 1 pl הָיִינוּ Is 1^{9}+; etc, *Impf* 3 ms יהיה Gn 1^{29}+, juss. יְהִי Gn 1^{3}+, יֶהִי Ez 16^{15}, ויהי Gn 1^{5}+; וַיְהִי Gn 1^{3}+, יְהִי ψ 33^{9} Ez 16^{19}, 3 fs. תִּהְיֶה Gn 21^{30}+, 1 s. אֶהְיֶה Ex 3^{12}+; וָאֶהְיֶה 2 S 7^{6}+9 t.; וָאֱהִי Ju 18^{4}+12 t; 3 mpl. יהיו Gn 6^{19}+, 3 fpl. תהיינה Is 16^{2}+19 t, וַתִּהְיֶינָה, ותהינה Gn 41^{36}+11 t, ותהינה Je 18^{21} 48^{6}, וַתִּהְיֶינָה 2 S 20^{3}+6 t; וַתִּהְיֶיןָ Gn 26^{35} 1 S 25^{43}; 1 Ch 7^{15}; 2 mpl תהיו Gn 34^{15}+, תהיון Ex 22^{20}; 1 pl נהיה Gn 38^{23}+; וַנִּהְיֶה 2 S 11^{23} Je 44^{17}, ונהי Nu 13^{33} Is 64^{5}, etc.; *Imv.* ms הֱיֵה Ex 18^{19}+; fs הֲיִי Gn 24^{60}, mpl. הֱיוּ Ex 19^{15} Nu 16^{16}, והיו 1 S 4^{9}+6 t, *Inf abs* הָיוֹ Gn 18^{18}+3 t.; הָיֹה 1 K 13^{32} Ez 1^{3}, *cstr.* הֱיוֹת Gn 2^{18}+, so rd prob also for הָיֵה Ez 21^{15} cf. Sm Ko^{1} p. 600 f. (Co em היה־לה to הָהֵל *shine, glitter*), with pref בהיות Ex 5^{13}+, בהית Ex 19^{16}+; להיות Gn 10^{8}+, להית Ex 23^{1}+, sf הֱיוֹתִי Jon 4^{2}, היותך Ju $18^{19\,19}$; להיתך Dt 26^{19}, etc, *Pt* f הוֹיָה Ex 9^{3}.

I. 1. a. *Fall out, happen* מֶה־הָיָה הַדָּבָר 1 S 4^{16} *how has the matter fallen out,* (*gone, turned out*)? so 2 S 1^{4}, מֶה־הָיָה לוֹ Ex $32^{1\,23}$ (both JE) *what has happened to him?* cf. 1 S 10^{12}, מִקְרֶה הוּא הָיָה לָנוּ 1 S 6^{9} *a chance it is that has befallen us,* also וַיְהִי־לוֹ כֵּן 2 K 7^{20} *and so it happened to him,* cf וַיְהִי־כֵן infr. **b.** *occur, take place, come about, come to pass*—מַגֵּפָה גדולה הָיְתָה בָעָם 1 S 4^{17} *a great slaughter has taken place among the people,* cf. 2 S 17^{9}; וַתְּהִי הַמִּלְחָמָה בְּיַעַר אפרים 2 S 18^{6} *and the battle took place in the wood of Ephraim* (on אפרים cf. Klo Dr), Jos 22^{17} (P, of plague); תהי נָא אָלָה Gn 26^{28} (J) *let an oath take place* (be taken) so Ju 21^{5}; cf. 2 K 17^{7} (si vera l), Ez 16^{34}, esp. late, 2 Ch 29^{36} 32^{31} Ec $1^{9\,10}$ 3^{22} 8^{7} 10^{14} etc; oft of fulfilment of prediction, command, expectation, etc:—כֵּן הָיָה Gn 41^{13} (E) *so it came to pass,* וַיְהִי־כֵן 2 S 13^{25}, Ju 6^{38} 2 K 15^{12} Is 29^{5}, & esp. וַיְהִי־כֵן Gn $1^{7\,9\,11\,15.24\,30}$ (all P)+, יהי כִדְבָרֶךָ Gn 30^{34} *let it be as thou sayest,* Zc 6^{15}, v also לֹא תָקוּם ולא יהיה Is 7^{7} *it shall not arise* (be realized) *& shall not come* about, 14^{24}, (so oft בוא q.v **2 c**, p 98 supr) **2.** esp & very oft., *come about, come to pass* sq. substantive (subj) cl almost alw.+ modifying (usu temporal) cl or phr.: **a** (1) וַיְהִי *and it came to pass* that, most often (c. 292 t.) foll by (*a*) Impf. consec: *α* with Inf. c כְּ temp. Gn 12^{14} 19^{17} (both J)+75 t+Est 3^{4} Qr (Hex chiefly J,—so alw. Gn,—& JE, P only Ex 16^{10}, D only Dt 5^{20} 31^{24} Jos 5^{1} 9^{1}, 27 t. in K),—somewhat diff is 2 K 7^{18}, *β.* with Inf c. ב Gn 4^{8} 11^{2} (both J)+29 t.+Est 3^{4} Kt (in Hex 10 t JE, 3 t. P, Gn 19^{29} Ex 34^{29} Nu 17^{7}; not in D), *γ* with ב sq nom temp (בקר, יום, etc.) Gn 21^{22} (E) 26^{32} (J)+45 t. (Hex 14 t. JE; 3 t. P, Ex 6^{28} 16^{13} Nu 7^{1}; not D), *δ* ל temp. 1 S 1^{20} 2 S 13^{23} 1 K 20^{26} 1 Ch 20^{1}; *ε* כ temp Gn 39^{11} 1 S 25^{38}, *ζ* מן temp viz: מאז Gn 39^{5}, מיום 1 S 7^{2} cf 30^{25}, מִיָּמִים Ju 11^{4} 15^{1}, מקץ Gn 4^{3} 8^{6}+6 t, מקצה Jos 3^{2} 2 K 8^{3} Ez 3^{16}, esp. מִמָּחֳרָת Gn 19^{34} Ex 18^{13}+11 t; *η.* כַּאֲשֶׁר temp. Gn 12^{11} (J) 20^{13} (E)+31 t (Hex 13 t. JE, Dt 2^{16}, not P), characteristic of Neh's memoirs, †Ne 3^{33} $4^{1\,6.9}$ $6^{1\,16}$ 7^{1} 13^{19}; *θ.* with כִּי temp. Gn 6^{1} (J) Ex 3^{21} (E)+14 t+Ju 16^{25} Kt, *ι* אַחֲרֵי temp. Gn 22^{20} (J)+13 t., אַחַר Gn 39^{7} Jb 42^{7}, אַחֲרֵי־כֵן Ju 16^{14}+6 t; *κ* sq עַד temp. 1 S 14^{19} (on which cf Dr), comp. עַד־כֹּה ועד־כֹּה 1 K 18^{45}; *λ.* with combinations, as ב c nom. temp + ב Inf. Gn 34^{25} Ex 19^{16} 1 S 25^{37}, ב Inf + כְּ Inf Jos 3^{14}, double prep. כְּמִשְׁלֹשׁ חֳדָשִׁים Gn 38^{24}, מקצה + מִיָּמִים + id. 23^{1}, אַחֲרֵי אֲשֶׁר Jos 9^{16}; *μ.* other unusual constructions under this head are: those where temporal idea is expr. by a circumst. cl. Is 22^{7} 1 K 13^{20} 2 K 8^{21} (Dr § 165, & Obs.) = 2 Ch 21^{9}, those with indef כל 1 S 10^{11} 2 S 2^{23} 15^{2}, or with pt = rel cl. 1 S 11^{1} (on all v. Dr § 78 n & 8 m); quite unique is 1 K 16^{31}, with הֲנָקֵל לֶכְתּוֹ וגו׳ in place of temp. cl (*b*) וַיְהִי sts. sq. simple Pf, with a negative Gn 39^{10} (c. כְּ Inf.), Ex 13^{17} (c ב Inf) 2 K 12^{7} 17^{25} (both c בְּ temp); & without neg, Gn 8^{13} (P) 14^{1}+, usu. c. ב temp. (38 t.), Hex chiefly P; rarely c. other prep & adv as above, note esp. מִדֵּי sq Inf 1 S 18^{30} 2 Ch 12^{11}; sts the subj. of foll. Pf precedes it c. ו, as Gn 22^{1} 41^{1} 1 S 18^{19} 30^{1} 2 K 2^{9} 4^{40}+, note esp. 2 S 17^{27} where several subj & also several objects precede the Pf (cf Dr), in these cases the temporal modifier is occasionally a circumst cl 2 S 13^{30} 1 K 8^{10} 2 K 19^{37} = Is 37^{38}, rarely subj. precedes Pf without ו 1 K 11^{4} 21^{1}, comp subj preceding Pt without ו Ne 4^{10}, in 2 Ch 8^{1} the obj. (with ו) precedes what is appar. the principal vb. (*c*) וַיְהִי sq וְהִנֵּה Gn 24^{15} (J, טֶרֶם in temp

cl.), 29^{25} (E), 38^{27} (J, both בּ temp.) v^{29} (כְּ Pt.), 1 S 13^{10} (כְּ Inf.); also 2 S 1^{2} 13^{36} 15^{32} (circumst. cl.) 2 K 2^{11} (*id.*), 3^{20}, 13^{21} (circumst. cl.). (*d*) rarely וַיְהִי (in this sense) sq other constructions: אָז יִתֵּן 1 K 9^{10} (c. מקצה), Impf. frequentat. 14^{28} (c. מִדֵּי־בֹא), 2 K 4^{8} (c. מִדֵּי עָבְרוֹ) Je 36^{23} (c כְּ Inf); Pf. consec. frequentat. 2 Ch 24^{11} (c. בְּ temp.). (2) rarely also Pf. c וְ conj. וְהָיָה (cf Dr§ 133) sq. Impf. consec. as subj. cl. 1 S 1^{12} (c. several circumst. cl.), 10^{9} (c. כְּ Inf) 2 K 3^{15} (*id*), 1 S 17^{48} (c. כִּי), Je 37^{11} (c. בְּ Inf.), Am 7^{2} (c. אם temp.); also Je 3^{9} (appar. c מִן causat, but obscure); 1 S 13^{22} (c. בְּ temp.) is foll. by וְלֹא & Pf. as well as Impf. consec. **b.** less oft. וְהָיָה Pf. consec *and it shall come to pass*, or frequentat., *came to pass* (repeatedly, etc.) usu. (*a*) sq. simple Impf (c 100 t.)· *a.* c. בּ temp. Dt 21^{16} 25^{19} + 37 t., (esp. בַּיּוֹם הַהוּא Ho 2$^{18.23}$ Is 7$^{18.21.23}$ + 21 t.), *β.* c בְּ loc. Ez 47^{23} Zc 13^{8} cf. also Ho 2^{1} (בִּמְקוֹם אֲשֶׁר, but perh = *instead of*, cf. VB); *γ.* c indef. rel. cl, or its equiv. (כֹּל indef., etc), cf Dr§ 121, Obs. 1. Gn 4^{14} Nu 17^{20} Dt 12^{11} 18^{19} Jos 7$^{14.15}$ Ju 7^{4} 1 S 2^{36} 17^{25} 2 S 15^{35} 1 K 19^{17} 20^{6} Is 4^{3} 24^{18} Na 3^{7} Je 27^{8} 42^{4} Ez 47^{9} Zc 14^{17} Jo 3^{5}; *δ.* c. כַּאֲשֶׁר Nu 33^{56} Dt 28^{63} Jos 23^{15} Ju 7^{17} Is 29^{8} Je 31^{28} Zc 8^{13}, *ε* less often with other modif. phr.: כְּ Inf. Ex 33$^{8.9}$ (both frequentat), Jos 3^{13} 8^{8} Je 25^{12} 51^{63}; בּ Inf. Gn 9^{14} (P) 2 K 4^{10} Ez 44^{17}, אם condit. Dt 20^{11} (+ v^{11} Dr§ 118 n), also Jos 22^{18}, where the arrangement is peculiar, & the condit. is expressed without אם (cf Dr§ 155); לְ temp Dt 23^{12}; מִקֵּץ Is 23^{17}; טֶרֶם Is 65^{24}; מִדֵּי חֹדֶשׁ בְּחָדְשׁוֹ Is 66^{23}, etc. (*b*) וְהָיָה sq. Pf consec. (c 85 t)· *a.* most often + cl. c. כִּי temp Gn 12^{12} 46^{33} (both J) Ex 1^{10} (E) Dt 11^{29} Is 8^{21} + 25 t.; *β* c. אם Ex 4$^{8.9}$ Nu 15^{24}; Dt 11^{13} + 14 t.; also Gn 38^{9} Nu 21^{9} (both frequentat.); *γ.* c. בּ temp Gn 30^{41} (frequentat) 47^{24} (but cf. Ol Di) Ex 16^{5} + 11 t; *δ.* c. indef. rel. cl. or equivalent (Dr§ 121 Obs. 1)· Gn 24^{14} Nu 10^{32} (Dr§ 118 n) 21^{18} Dt 21^{3} Ju 11^{31} 19^{30} Zc 14^{16}; *ε.* occas. with other modif. phr: כַּאֲשֶׁר Gn 27^{40} +; כְּ Inf Gn 44^{31} +; בּ Inf. Ex 33^{22} +; מִקֵּץ 2 S 14^{26}; עֵקֶב causat. Dt 7^{12}; also (*c*) sq. וְלֹא + simple Impf. Ex 3^{21} (c. כִּי temp) (*d*) וְהָיָה sq *Imv.* (very rare) Dt 6^{10} (c. כִּי temp), 1 S 10^{7} (c כִּי), cf. 29^{10}, cf. Pf. consec. in command 1 S 3^{9} (c. אם). (*e*) וְהָיָה sq. simple Pf. (also very rare) Dt 8^{19} (c. אם). (*f*) וְהָיָה sq. cl without vb.: Gn 24^{43} Jos 2^{19} 1 K 18^{24} (all c. indef rel. modifier, or equiv., v. (*a*) *γ*, (*b*) *δ*, supr) (*g*) וְהָיָה (וְ conj) sq. Impf. consec. v. **a.** (*e*) supr.

II. *Come into being, become:*—**1. a.** abs, in lively narrative, *arise, appear, come* וַתְּהִי צְעָקָה גְדֹלָה Ex 12^{30} (J) *and there arose a great cry* in Egypt, וַיְהִי־קוֹל Ez 1^{25} (del. Co cf. Da), 37^{7} (del. קוֹל 𝔊 Co), כִּי הָיְתָה הָרְוָחָה Ex 8^{11} (J) Pharaoh saw *that respite had come*, Mi 7^{4} *now shall come their confusion* (‖ בוא); also of concrete objects וְהָיְתָה הַקֶּשֶׁת בֶּעָנָן Gn 9^{16} (P) *and the bow shall appear in the clouds* (‖ ונראתה), וְרִמָּה לֹא הָיְתָה בּוֹ Ex 16^{24} (P) *and worms did not appear in it;* of condition or action begun & continuing, as: famine Gn 12^{10} 26^{1} (all J), 41^{54} (E), Ru 1^{1} 2 S 21^{1} 2 K 6^{25}; strife Gn 13$^{7.8}$ (J), Hb 1^{3} (‖ מָדוֹן יִשָּׂא), oft. of action of the elements, as the coming of hail Ex 9$^{18.24.26}$ (all J), thunder & lightning, etc, Ex 19^{16} (E), rain 1 K 18^{45}, storm Jon 1^{4}; esp of creative fiats יְהִי אוֹר וַיְהִי אוֹר Gn 1^{3} *let light appear, and light appeared*, cf v$^{5.8.13.19.23.31}$ (all P), also *arise, come on the stage* or *scene*, וְאַחֲרָיו הָיָה שַׁמְגַּר Ju 3^{31} *and after him arose Shamgar* (= וַיָּקָם 10^{1}); further וַעֲלָטָה הָיָה Gn 15^{17} (JE) *and darkness came on;* הַבֹּקֶר הָיָה Ex 10^{13} (J) *the morning came*, 19^{16} (E), וַיְהִי הַיּוֹם † 1 S 1^{4} *and the day came*, when (v. Dr), 14^{1} 2 K 4$^{8.11.18}$ Jb 1$^{6.13}$ 2^{1}. **b.** sq prep: בְּ, וְיָדֵנוּ אַל־תְּהִי־בוֹ Gn 37^{27} (J) *but our hand, let it not come upon him*, of hand of י׳ 1 S 5^{9} 7^{13} 12^{15} + (all in hostile sense), וַיְהִי בִּרְכַּת י׳ בְּכָל־אֲשֶׁר יֶשׁ־לוֹ Gn 39^{5} (J) *and the blessing of* י׳ *came into* (on) *all that he had;* but also of plague Ex 12^{13} (P), sq עַל, וּמֵי הַמַּבּוּל הָיוּ עַל־הָאָרֶץ Gn 7^{10} (J) *that the waters of the flood came upon the earth*, עָלַי הָיוּ כֻלָּנָה Gn 42^{36} (E) Gn 9^{2} (P) *fear shall come upon*, cf. 35^{5} (P) 2 Ch 14^{13} 17^{10} 20^{29} +; of wrath Jos 22^{20} 1 K 3^{27}; so of Saul's evil spirit fr God 1 S 16$^{16.23}$ 19^{9} (אֶל); but sq עַל also in good sense וַתְּהִי עָלָיו רוּחַ י׳ conferring strength & efficiency Ju 3^{10} 11^{29} (צלח = היה Ju 14^{6} + oft.), cf. Nu 24^{2} (JE) of prophetic power; (on וַתְּהִי עָלָיו יַד י׳ 2 K 3^{15} Ez 3^{22} and the like, vid. יָד); יַד אֱלֹהֵינוּ הָיְתָה עָלֵינוּ Ezr 8^{31}, so ψ 80^{18}; even וַתְּהִי עַל־רֹאשׁ דָּוִד 2 S 12^{30} *and it* (the crown, עֲטֶרֶת) *came* (i e. was put, set) *on David's head*, with a diff. mng. וַנִּהְיֶה עֲלֵיהֶם עַד־פֶּתַח הַשָּׁעַר 2 S 11^{23} *and we were* close *upon them even to the gateway* (cf. We Dr); *come, go, follow* (sq. אַחֲרֵי) i e. take the side of, adhere to, Ex 23^{2} (JE) 1 S 12^{14} 2 S 2^{10} 1 K 12^{20} 16^{21}, sq. לְ, of blessings Gn 49^{26} (poem); of judgment, punishment Je 40^{3}, esp. ויהי דבר . . . אֶל *and the word of . . . came unto*· word of Samuel 1 S 4^{1}, usually word of God (or י׳) Gn 15^{1} 1 S 15^{10} +; con-

stantly in prophets: Ho 1^{1} Mi 1^{1} etc.; esp. Je & Ez: Je 1$^{4.11.13}$ 2^{1} 13^{8}+; Ez 3^{16} 6^{1} 7^{1} 11$^{14.17.21.26}$ 12$^{1.8}$+; so also abs. הָיָה הַמַּשָּׂא הַזֶּה Is 14^{28} in the death-year of king Ahaz *came this utterance;* also sq. מִן; מַלְכֵי עַמִּים מִמֶּנָּה יִהְיוּ Gn 17^{16} (P), וְהָיָה אַדִּירוֹ 35^{11} (P), וּקְהַל גּוֹיִם יִהְיֶה מִמֶּךָּ הַכֹּל הָיָה מִן־הֶעָפָר ;(מִקִּרְבּוֹ יֵצֵא ‖) Je 30^{21} מִמֶּנּוּ וְהַכֹּל שָׁב אֶל הֶעָפָר Ec 3^{20} *all came from the dust, & all return unto the dust;* וַיְהִי קֶצֶף גָּדוֹל מֵאֵת י׳ צְבָאוֹת Zc 7^{12}. **2.** *become:* **a.** sq. pred. noun (to be viewed as implicit accus. Dr$^{§161.3 n.}$, according to the Arab. usage W$^{AG ii. §41.44.74}$): הִוא הָיְתָה אֵם כָּל־חָי Gn 3^{20} (J) *it was she that became the mother of all living;* וַיְהִי הֶבֶל רֹעֵה צֹאן וְקַיִן הָיָה עֹבֵד אֲדָמָה 4^{2} (J) *and Abel became a shepherd of flocks, while Cain became a tiller of ground;* 2 S 8^{14} Mi 2^{11}+oft. **b.** sq. pred. adj. Gn 38^{7} Ex 36^{13}+; cf. Gn 37^{20} *let us see what his dream will become* (turn out to be, signify); **c.** *become like* (כְּ), וִהְיִיתֶם כֵּאלֹהִים Gn 3^{5} *and ye shall become like gods* cf. v^{22}, Nu 11^{1} (JE), Ho 2^{1} 7^{11} Is 9^{18} 1 K 7^{8} Zc 9^{7}+; cf. Gn 15^{5} *so* (כֹּה) *shall thy seed become;* specif. of likeness in punishment Is 1^{9} 1 S 17^{36}+; also with כְּ repeated וְהָיָה כָעָם כַּכֹּהֵן Ho 4^{9} *and the people shall become like the priest* (lit., and the like of the people shall become the like of the priest), so esp. Is 24^{2} (6 pairs of words as above); וְהָיָה כַצַּדִּיק כָּרָשָׁע Gn 18^{25} (J), v. כְּ. **b+c** Gn 27^{23} *his hands had become like the hands of Esau his brother, hairy.* **d.** sq. pred.+לְ pers. וּתְהִי אִשָּׁה לְבֶן־אֲדֹנֶיךָ Gn 24^{51} (J) *and let her become wife to the son of thy lord,* 1 S 16^{21} 1 K 11^{25} ψ 89^{42} 1 Ch 18^{6}+; = *be instituted, established,* וְהָיְתָה לָהֶם חָק־עוֹלָם Ex 30^{21} (P) *and it shall be established for them as a perpetual ordinance* (cf. **f** infr.). **e.** sq. לְ pred.: וַיְהִי הָאָדָם לְנֶפֶשׁ חַיָּה Gn 2^{7} (J) *and the man became a living soul;* וְהָיָה לְאַרְבָּעָה רָאשִׁים Gn 2^{10} (J) *and it became four heads;* גַּם־הוּא יִהְיֶה־לְּעָם Gn 48^{19} (J) *he too shall become a people;* וִהְיוּ לַאֲנָשִׁים 1 S 4^{9} *and become* (shew yourselves to be) *men* (‖ הִתְחַזְּקוּ; cf. with double לְ, **f** infr.); Zp 1^{13} Ez 17^{6} 47^{12} Jb 16^{8}; וַיְהִי לְמַס עֹבֵד; וְהָיָה י׳ לְמֶלֶךְ עַל־כָּל־הָאָרֶץ Zc 14^{9}; +Gn 49^{15} Jos 16^{10}; so oft.; also in sense of *turn into,* be changed so as to become, וַיְהִי לְנָחָשׁ Ex 4^{3} *and it became a serpent,* v^{4} 7^{10} Is 1^{22} Dt 26^{5}+; fig. וַיְהִי לָמָיִם Jos 7^{5} *and it* (their heart) *turned to water,* so וְהוּא הָיָה לְאָבֶן 1 S 25^{37}; or, *serve as* וְהָיוּ לִמְאוֹרֹת Gn 1^{15} (P) *and they shall become* (fulfil the function of, serve as) *luminaries,* cf. v^{14}; וְהָיְתָה לְאוֹת בְּרִית Gn 9^{13} 17^{11} (both P). **f.** oft. c. לְ pred.+לְ pers.: וַתְּהִי לָהֶם הַלְּבֵנָה לְאָבֶן Gn 11^{3} (J) *and the bricks became* (served as) *stone for them;* וַתְּהִי לִי לְאִשָּׁה Gn 20^{12} (E) cf. 24^{67} (J)+, . . . וַתִּהְיֶינָה מַחְלָה וְתִרְצָה . . . לִבְנֵי דֹדֵיהֶן לְנָשִׁים Nu 36^{11}; וְהָיָה לְךָ וְלָהֶם לְאָכְלָה 6^{21} (P), Ex 2^{10} 15^{2} Ju 8^{27}; וְהָיָה י׳ לִי לֵאלֹהִים Gn 28^{21} (E); אֲנִי אֶהְיֶה לּוֹ לְאָב וְהוּא יִהְיֶה־לִּי לְבֵן 1 Ch 17^{3}+; = *shew or prove oneself as* הֱיֵה־לִי לְבֶן־חַיִל 1 S 18^{17} *shew thyself for me a valiant man* (cf. 1 S 4^{9} **e** supr.); = *be instituted, established* (cf. **e** supr.) וְהָיְתָה לְאַהֲרֹן וּלְבָנָיו לְחָק־עוֹלָם Ex 29^{28} *and it shall be instituted for Aaron and his sons as a perpetual ordinance;* cf. v^{9} Lv 10^{15}; וְהָיְתָה לִהְיֹת לָהֶם מָשְׁחָתָם לִכְהֻנַּת עוֹלָם לְדֹרֹתָם Ex 40^{15} (all P). **g.** with עַל and לְ 1 S 22^{2} וַיְהִי עֲלֵיהֶם לְשָׂר *and he became over them prince.* **h.** sts. c. לְ pers. only = *become the property of, come into the possession of* וַיְהִי־לוֹ צֹאן־וּבָקָר וגו׳ Gn 12^{16} (J), *and he came to have flocks and herds* etc., 26^{14} 30^{43}; לֹא לוֹ יִהְיֶה הַזָּרַע Gn 38^{9} *not his should the seed become;* וְהָיָה לַי׳ Ju 11^{31} *it shall become Yahweh's;* Dt 10^{9} Jos 13^{20} 1 K 10^{26} 11^{3}+oft.; so of a woman, as wife תְּהִי־נָא לְךָ Ju 15^{2} *pray let her become thine,* cf. also וַתְּהִי אֵשֶׁת שִׁמְשׁוֹן לְמֵרֵעֵהוּ 14^{20}, Ho 3^{3} Ru 1^{13} Lv 21^{3} Dt 24^{2} Je 3^{1} Ez 16^{8} (and also+לְאִשָּׁה, לְנָשִׁים v. **f** supr.)

III. *Be* (often with subordinate idea of becoming);—**1.** *exist, be in existence* (i.e. orig. *have come into existence*), כָּל־הַיָּמִים אֲשֶׁר הָיָה 1 S 1^{28} *all the days which he shall have been* (lived, = חַי Gn 5^{5} etc., cf. Dr^{Sm}), Jb 3^{16}, Is 23^{13}; oft. c. בְּ loc. וְכֹל שִׂיחַ הַשָּׂדֶה טֶרֶם יִהְיֶה בָאָרֶץ Gn 2^{5} (J) *and there was not yet in the earth any shrub of the field;* וּבְאֵלֶּה לֹא הָיָה אִישׁ וגו׳ Nu 26^{64} (P) *and among them there was not a man to be found,* etc.; also וְלֹא הָיָה כַּיּוֹם הַהוּא לְפָנָיו וְאַחֲרָיו Jos 10^{14} (JE) *& there hath not been a day like that before it nor since,* cf. 2 S 14^{25} 1 K 18^{5} 21^{25} 23^{25} Ne 13^{26}+; somewhat weaker, in the freq. introductory clause וַיְהִי אִישׁ *now there was a man* Ju 13^{2} 1 S 1^{1} 9^{1} Nu 9^{6} (P), Jb 1^{1}+; on אֶהְיֶה אֲשֶׁר אֶהְיֶה Ex 3^{14} v. יהוה. **2.** *abide, remain, continue* (with word of place or time) וַיְהִי מֹשֶׁה בָּהָר Ex 24^{18} *and Moses remained in the mount* forty days, etc., so 34^{28} (both JE), Ju 17$^{4.12}$ 1 S 6^{1} 1 K 11^{20} 2 K 11^{3}=2 Ch 22^{12}+; also Lv 22^{27} 25^{28} (both H), etc.; sq. עַד temp. *remain until* Dt 22^{2} 1 K 11^{40} 2 K 15^{5} 2 Ch 5^{9} 26^{21} Dn 1^{21} etc.; cf. הוּא יִהְיֶה לְעוֹלָם Ec 3^{14}; so also of space

sq. עַד *extend unto, as far as*, Jos 19^{10}: of net beneath altar, Ex 27^{5} *shall reach as far as* (עד) *the middle of the altar.* **3.** with word of locality, *be in* or *at a place, be situated, stand, lie;* בִּהְיוֹתָם בַּשָּׂדֶה Gn 4^{8} (J) *when they were in the field,* הַמָּקוֹם אֲשֶׁר־הָיָה שָׁם אָהֳלֹה בַּתְּחִלָּה 13^{3} (J) *the place where his tent had stood at first;* וְהָאָרֶץ תִּהְיֶה לִפְנֵיכֶם 34^{10} *and the land, it lieth before you;* cf. Jos 19^{1} Ju $7^{1.8}$ Mi $5^{6.7}$; sq. עַל *be, be found or situated upon* Is 30^{25} *and there shall be upon every high mountain* etc., *streams, water-courses;* Ez 37^{27} *and my dwelling-place shall be over them;* fig. of guilt וְהָיָה עָלֶיךָ דָּמִים Dt 19^{10} *and blood* (-guilt) *be upon thee.* **4.** as copula, joining subj. & pred.:—**a.** sq. pred. adj. וַיִּהְיוּ שְׁנֵיהֶם עֲרוּמִּים Gn 2^{25}, וְהַנָּחָשׁ הָיָה עָרוּם 3^{1}, וַיְהִי יוֹסֵף יְפֵה־תֹאַר 34^{25}, בִּהְיוֹתָם כֹּאֲבִים 39^{6}; Dt 23^{15} Jos 19^{9} Ju 11^{1} Jb $1^{1.3b}$ 2 Ch 7^{21}. **b.** sq. pred. noun Gn 1^{2} 9^{18} 25^{3} 36^{14} 40^{13} 1 S $17^{34.42}$ 2 S 8^{10} 20^{25} 1 K 10^{6} 2 K 3^{4} $5^{1.1}$ 1 Ch 9^{20} 11^{20} 18^{10} 26^{10} 2 Ch 13^{7}; כִּי לֹא־הָיָה מֶלֶךְ יִשְׂרָאֵל 2 Ch 18^{32} (כִּי־לֹא־מֶלֶךְ ישראל הוא ‖ 1 K 22^{33})+; oft. of age: וַיְהִי אַבְרָם בֶּן־תִּשְׁעִים שָׁנָה וְתֵשַׁע שָׁנִים Gn 17^{1} (P) 2 K 8^{17} 14^{2} $15^{2.33}$ 18^{2} 2 Ch 21^{20} 27^{8}+; sq. pred. Inf. abs. (very anomal.) וְהַמַּיִם הָיוּ הָלוֹךְ וְחָסוֹר Gn 8^{5};=*amount to, come to,* in enum. of days of life, number of people, amounts of money, etc.: Gn $5^{4.5.8.11.14}$ 9^{29} 11^{32} 23^{1}+; Ex 38^{24} Nu 1^{46}, etc. **c.** sq. adv. & adverbial phr.: לֹא־טוֹב הֱיוֹת הָאָדָם לְבַדּוֹ Gn 2^{18} (J) *it is not good that the man be alone;* חָדַל לִהְיוֹת לְשָׂרָה אֹרַח כַּנָּשִׁים 18^{11} (J). **d.** sq. prep.: (*a*) *be with, accompany* c. עִם, subj. most oft. י׳ or אלהים with added idea of protection, aid Gn 26^{3} 31^{3} 39^{10} 48^{21} Jos 1^{5} 6^{27} Ju 1^{19} 2^{18} 1 S 3^{19} 18^{12} 20^{13} 1 K 1^{37} 1 Ch 11^{13} 2 Ch 17^{3}; sq. עִמָּדִי Gn 28^{20} 31^{5} 35^{3}; sq. עִם, human subj., of accompaniment וְהָיָה הַכֹּהֵן בֶּן־אַהֲרֹן עִם־הַלְוִיִּם Ne 10^{39}; 1 Ch 11^{12}, rd. also in ‖ 2 S 23^{9} (Th We Dr);= *be on the side of* 1 K 1^{8}; c. עִם also=*be near* וּמַלְאַךְ י׳ הָיָה עִם־גֹּרֶן האורנה 2 S 24^{16} (cf. Dr); also 2 S 13^{20} implying sexual intercourse, so Gn 39^{10} (perh. gloss, cf. Di); peculiar uses with עִם are: וּדְבַר־אַבְנֵר הָיָה עִם־זִקְנֵי יִשְׂרָאֵל 2 S 3^{17} *and the speech of A. had been with the elders of Isr.*, cf. 1 K 1^{7}; וַיְהִי עִם־לְבַב דָּוִד אָבִי לִבְנוֹת 1 K 8^{17} *and it was with* (i.e. in) *the heart of David my father to build,* =2 Ch 6^{7} cf. 1 K $8^{18.18}$ 1 Ch 22^{7} 2 Ch $6^{8.8}$ 24^{4}; also 1 K 10^{2}=2 Ch 9^{1}; (*b*) *be with,* sq. אֶת, subj. י׳, אלהים, Gn 21^{20} $39^{2.21}$ but also c. human subj. וּבָנָיו הָיוּ אֶת־מִקְנֵהוּ Gn 34^{5}, cf. 1 S 29^{3}+; (*c*) sq. לְ of possessor כֶּרֶם הָיָה לִידִידִי Is 5^{1} *a vineyard had my beloved,* Gn 30^{30} cf. Ex 20^{3}=Dt 5^{7}, Ju 18^{27} 1 S 9^{2} 1 K 5^{6}+oft. (cf. I. **2 d, f, h**); (*d*) sq. לְ+other prep.: of boundary וַיְהִי לָהֶם Jos 13^{16}, cf. וַיְהִי גְבוּלָם מִמַּחֲנַיִם הַגְּבוּל מֵעֲרוֹעֵר v^{30}; וַיְהִי לָהֶם הַגְּבוּל לִפְאַת צָפוֹנָה מִיַּרְדֵּן 18^{12}, etc.; (*e*) sq. בְּ *be among,* or *of,* Am 1^{1} *who was* one *of the herdsmen,* 1 K 2^{7} *let them be among those eating,* Pr 22^{26} 23^{20}. **5.** periphrastic conjug.: **a.** היה+pt., of continuous state, or condition, sts., esp. late (cf. NH), of habit, c. וַיְהִי also of beginning and continuance (cf. Dr § 135, (5)): pt. act. Gn 39^{22} (J), Ex 3^{1} (E), 1 S 2^{11} 7^{10} 18^{9} (cf. Dr) v$^{14.29}$ 2 S 8^{15}=1 Ch 18^{14}, Dt 28^{29} Is 30^{20} 1 K $5^{1.15.24}$ 2 K 6^{5} 9^{14} 2 Ch 9^{26} Ezr 4^{4} Ne 1^{4} 2^{13} Dn 1^{16}+; Gn 1^{6} (P); הָיָה יָרֵא אֶת־י״י 1 K 18^{3} 2 K 4^{1} 2 Ch 26^{1}; pt. pass. Jos 10^{26} 1 K 13^{24} 22^{35} וְהַמֶּלֶךְ הָיָה מָעֳמָד בַּמֶּרְכָּבָה (הָיָה מַעֲמִיד ‖ 2 Ch 18^{34}), Is 2^{2}=Mi 4^{1}, וְאָהוּב לֵאלֹהָיו ה׳ Ne 5^{18}, ה׳ נַעֲשָׂה Ez 44^{2}, וְהָיָה סָגוּר 13^{26};—on 2 S 13^{32} cf. Dr. **b.** sq. Inf. c. לְ (Dr § 203, 204): וְהָיָה לְבָעֵר Is 5^{5} *and it shall be to burn* (is to be, is destined to be burned) etc.; וַיְהִי הַשֶּׁמֶשׁ לָבוֹא Gn 15^{12} *and the sun was about to set;* וַיְהִי הַשַּׁעַר לִסְגּוֹר Jos 2^{5} *and the gate was about to be shut;* but also וַיְהִי לִדְרֹשׁ אֱלֹהִים 2 Ch 26^{5} (nearly =וַיְהִי+Pt.) †**Niph.** *Pf.* נִהְיָה 1 K 1^{27}+6 t.+ Mi 2^{4} (cf. infr. ad fin.); 3 fs. נִהְיְתָה Ju 19^{30}+ 5 t., נִהְיָתָה Ex 11^{6} Je 48^{19}, וְנִהְיְתָה consec. Ez 39^{8} +21^{12} (del. B Codd𝔊 Co); 2 ms. נִהְיֵיתָ Dt 27^{9}; 1 s. נִהְיֵיתִי Dn 8^{27}; *Pt.* fs. נִהְיָה Pr 13^{19};—**1.** either, *be done, be brought about,* or *occur, come to pass:* in the strong expressions אֲשֶׁר כָּמֹהוּ לֹא נ׳ וְכָמֹהוּ לֹא תֹסִף Ex 11^{6} (J) a cry *such as hath not occurred* (been raised), *and will not be again,* cf. Dt 4^{32} (*be done;* ‖ נִשְׁמַע), & Ju 19^{30} (‖ נִרְאֲתָה);—but simply intrans. Jo 2^{2} Dn 12^{1} & appar. Ez 21^{12} (‖ בָּאָה; on txt., however, v. supr.) 39^{8} (‖ *id.*);—also אֵיכָה נִהְיְתָה הָרָעָה הַזֹּאת Ju 20^{3} *how hath this wickedness been done?* cf. v^{12} Je 5^{30} 48^{19} also Ne 6^{8}; c. לֹא, existence denied לֹא נ׳ Zc 8^{10} (‖ אֵינֶנָּה); in all the above (exc. Jo 2^{2} Dn 12^{1} & Ez 21^{12} 39^{8}) personal agency is clearly implied; it is expressed מֵאֵת אֲדֹנִי הַמֶּלֶךְ נ׳ הַדָּבָר הַזֶּה 1 K 1^{27}, so of divine agency (מֵאִתִּי) 1 K 12^{24}=2 Ch 11^{4}; further *be attained, secured,* of wages Zc 8^{10} (c. לֹא ‖ אֵינֶנָּה); תַּאֲוָה נִהְיָה Pr 13^{19} *a desire come to pass, realized.* **2.** *be done, finished, gone,* only Dn וּשְׁנָתוֹ נִהְיְתָה עָלָיו Dn 2^{1} *and his sleep was finished upon him,* i.e. left him (cf. Aram. Dn 6^{19}); נִהְיֵיתִי 8^{27} *I came to an end, was exhausted* (si vera l., del. 𝔊; ‖ נֶחֱלֵיתִי);

נִהְיָה, in וְנָהָה נְהִי נִהְיָה Mi 2[4], is dub.; *it is done, over, the ruin is come* RobGes Ew Hi Ca Che RVm; ? < om. as dittogr. Sta[ZAW 1886, 122 f.] cf. JBL[1890, 74.77].

†[הַיָּה] **n.f.** only הַיָּתִי Jb 6[2] Kt v. הַוָּה.

†**הֵיךְ** **adv.** *how?* (הֵיךְ, ܐܝܟ, *id.*, in Palest. Aram., as Jb 21[34] 𝔗, Gn 3[9] Dt 1[12] 𝔗 [Ps.-J.], Mat 22[12] 𝔖 [Jerus.] (though usu. these words have the force of *as*), and in הֵיכְדֵין *how, then?* ψ 73[11] + 𝔗; cf. Bevan [Dan. p. 29])—only twice, in late Heb., 1 Ch 13[12] (‖ 2 S 6[9] אֵיךְ), Dan 10[17].

†**הֵיכָל** **n.m.**[Na 2, 7] (on Is 44[28] cf. Che Di) **palace, temple** (v. also NH *id. temple*, Aram. הֵיכְלָא, הֵיכְלָא, ܗܰܝܟܠܳܐ, *palace, temple*, Palm. הכלא *temple* Vog[16]; cf. Ar. هَيْكَل (prob. Aram. loan-wd. acc. to Frä[274]), Eth. ሀይከል: *temple;* As. *ekallu, palace, temple;*—prob. loan-wd. fr. Akk. *e-gal, great house,* cf. Schr[HI 148] COT 2 K 20[18] Hpt[E-vowel 11 f.] Lehmann[Šamaššumukin 126], and on usage Dl[338]; > fr. יכל (וכל) = כול *contain* Ew[§ 162 b] Thes Add[84]; cf. Ol[§ 191 b] Hoffm[AGG xxxvi. Mai 1889, 25] Dl[W]; fr. an orig. יכל Lag[BN 121], but cf. Hom[ZMG 1890, 547]) abs. ה׳ Am 8[3] + 27 t. (הה׳ 1 K 6[17] +); cstr. הֵיכַל Mi 1[2] + 35 t.; sf. הֵיכָלֶךָ ψ 48[10] + 2 t.; הֵיכָלוֹ Je 50[28] + 7 t.; pl. הֵיכָלוֹת Ho 8[14]; cstr. הֵיכְלֵי Is 13[22] + 2 t.; sf. הֵיכְלֵיכֶם Jo 4[5];—never in Hex, rarely in S & pre-exil. prophets; esp. freq. in Ki Ez & late proph., also Chr; occasionally in ψ;—**1.** rather seld. (royal) *palace* (so alm. always in As.); of Ahab 1 K 21[1], of king of Babylon 2 K 20[18] = Is 39[17], 2 Ch 36[7], cf. Dn 1[4], and pl. הֵיכְלֵי עֹנֶג Is 13[22] *luxurious palaces;* at Nineveh וְהַה׳ נָמוֹג Na 2[7]; not clearly defined are הֵיכַל מֶלֶךְ ψ 45[16] and הֵיכְלֵי שֵׁן v[9]; הֵיכָלוֹת Ho 8[14] (in N. Israel); vid. also וְהֵילִילוּ שִׁירוֹת הֵיכָל בַּיּוֹם הַהוּא Am 8[3] *and palace-songs shall be howlings in that day;* cf. also (prob.) of Phœnician palaces Jo 4[5]; quite general הֵיכְלֵי מֶלֶךְ Pr 30[28], & תַּבְנִית הֵיכָל ψ 144[12] (sim. of well-proportioned daughters);—usual term for royal palace in Heb. is בֵּית הַמֶּלֶךְ, v. בית. **2.** of palace of God considered as king, = *house of God* or *of* י׳, *temple* (cf. הה׳ Is 6[1] **e** infr. where proph. sees אדני ישֵׁב עַל־כִּסֵּא): **a.** of early, pre-Solomonic house at Shiloh 1 S 1[9] 3[3] (= בֵּית י׳ 1[7] 3[15]; פֶּתַח אֹהֶל מוֹעֵד הֵיכַל י׳ 2[22] om. 𝔊 We Klo Dr) with doors (דלתות, 3[15]) & a doorpost (מזוזה 1[9]) (cf. 2 S 22[7] = ψ 18[7] **e** infr.). **b.** of Solomon's temple: specif. the *hall* or *nave* of the temple (the holy place, distinguished from the דְּבִיר the inner sanctuary, the Holy of Holies, and with this included in the more general term בֵּית י׳ or הַבַּיִת, 1 K 6[1.2] + oft.) 1 K 6[17] (cf. v[19.20] & v[3]) also v[5.33] 1 K 7[50] = 2 Ch 4[22]; further 2 Ch 4[7.8] Ez 8[16.16] הָאוּלָם עַל־פְּנֵי עַל־פְּנֵי ‖ 1 K 7[21] אֻלָם הַהֵיכָל 1 K 6[3]; הֵיכַל הַבַּיִת 2 Ch 3[17]; הֵיכַל י׳ 2 K 18[16]; also in wide sense (appar. = בֵּית י׳), הֵיכַל י׳ 2 K 23[4] 24[13] (‖ בֵּית י׳), Je 7[4.4.4] (‖ בֵּית י׳ v[2]), 24[1] v. also נִקְמַת הֵיכָלוֹ Je 50[28] 51[11] (both ‖ נִקְמַת י׳); 2 Ch 26[16] 27[2], cf. 29[16] (‖ פְּנִימָה בֵּית י׳); opp. חֲצַר בּ׳ י׳), in all three הֵיכַל י׳. **c.** *hall* or *nave* of Ezek.'s temple, the holy place (v. supr.) (included in הַבַּיִת, the general term embracing the whole group of buildings) Ez 41[1.4.15.21.23.25] (cf. v[20]) 42[8]. **d.** general designation of *2nd temple*, הֵיכַל י׳ Zc 8[9] (‖ בֵּית י׳ צְבָאוֹת); oftener הֵיכַל י׳ Hg 2[15.18] Zc 6[12.13.14.15] Ezr 3[6.10], הֵיכָלוֹ Mal 3[1] ψ 27[4]; (הַ)הֵיכָל Ezr 4[1]; בּוֹנִים הֵיכָל ליהוה אֱלֹהֵי יִשְׂרָאֵל Ne 6[10.10] (‖ בֵּית הָאֱלֹהִים), v[11]; Is 44[28], cf. also 66[6].—הֵיכָל occurs occasionally in ψ, without conclusive evidence, in all cases, to what temple ref. is had; appar. distinguished fr. בֵּית י׳ (as sub **b**) ψ 5[8] (הֵיכַל קָדְשְׁךָ; v. בֵּיתֶךָ v[7]); perhaps also ψ 68[30] (disting. from Holy of Holies by De Che; yet verse obscure); but no distinction evident ψ 79[1] 138[2] Jon 2[5.8] (all הֵיכַל קָדְשֶׁךָ); cf. קְדשׁ הֵיכָלֶךָ ψ 65[5] (‖ בֵּיתֶךָ); as containing the worshipping assembly ψ 48[10]. **e.** of the heavenly temple where י׳ sits enthroned Is 6[1]; his abode in the heavens 2 S 22[7] = ψ 18[7], ψ 11[4] (‖ שָׁמַיִם); cf. זְבֻל קָדְשׁוֹ Is 63[15], (‖ *id.*), 29[9]; אֲדֹנָי מֵהֵיכַל קָדְשׁוֹ Mi 1[2], cf. Hb 2[20] ויהוה בְּהֵיכַל קָדְשׁוֹ.

הֵילֵל Is 14[12] v. sub הלל.

הֵים v. הום.

הֵימָם **n.pr.** v. הוֹמָם sub המם.

הֵימָן **n.pr.** v. אמן.

†**הִין** **n.m.**[Lv 19, 36] **hin,** a liquid measure (𝔊 εἶν (ἶν); 𝔊L ἶν); but χοῦς Lv 19[36]; Gk. ἴνιον, Egypt. measure, = *sextarius,* acc. to Böckh [Metrol. Unters. 244] cf. Brandis [Münz- Mass- & Gewichtswesen 29, 30]; the Heb. hin (6.06 litres) was, however, much larger than the Egypt. hin (0.456 litre), v. Hultsch [Metrol., Tab. xxi. p. 714, & pp. 368, 450 ff.]; v. further Ri[HWB] Smith [Dict. Bib.] E. Meyer [Gesch. i. 228])—abs. הִין Ex 30[24] + 4 t. Ez 45, 46; הַהִין Ex 29[40.40] + 14 t.; cstr. הִין Lv 19[36];—**1.** a measure, used of quantity of water for drinking Ez 4[11]; usually in connexion with offerings: **a.** of oil used with meal-offering Ex 29[40] Nu 15[4.6.9] 28[5]

(all P), Ez 45^{24} $46^{5.6.11.14}$;—usually $\frac{1}{4}$ hin to $\frac{1}{10}$ ephah (of meal-offering); Nu 15^{6} $\frac{1}{3}$; v^{9} $\frac{1}{2}$; in Ez a (whole) hin, exc. 46^{14} $\frac{1}{3}$ hin to $\frac{1}{6}$ ephah. **b.** used in mixing the anointing oil Ex 30^{24}. **c.** of wine as drink-offering Lv 23^{13} (H); elsewh. P, Ex 29^{40} Nu 15^{5} 28^{14} (all $\frac{1}{4}$ hin) 15^{7} 28^{14} (both $\frac{1}{3}$ hin), 15^{10} 28^{14} (both $\frac{1}{2}$ hin; all with $\frac{1}{10}$ to $\frac{3}{10}$ ephah in case of meal-offering). **d.** once of שֵׁכָר as drink-offering Nu 28^{7} (P; $\frac{1}{4}$ hin; cf. Di). **2.** vessel with capacity of hin Lv 19^{36} (H) הִין צֶדֶק *a just hin* (‖ אַבְנֵי־צ׳, מֹאזְנֵי צ׳, אֵיפַת צ׳).—The hin = $\frac{1}{6}$ bath acc. to Joseph. Ant. iii. 8, 3; 9, 4, = 6.06 litres (Hultsch l.c.), v. II. בַּת. On order of words in above passages, note that הִין (רְבִיעִת ה׳) etc.) is usually appos. of liquid measured, & either precedes it Ex 29^{40} Nu 15^{4} 28^{14}, or, more oft., follows it Ex 30^{24} + 10 t.; Nu 28^{7} they are in diff. clauses; in Ex 29^{40} we find בְּשֶׁמֶן ... רֶבַע הַהִין, cf. Nu $15^{6.9}$ 28^{5};—Nu 28^{14} is peculiar: וְנִסְכֵּיהֶם חֲצִי הַהִין יִהְיֶה לַפָּר וּשְׁלִישִׁת הַהִין לָאַיִל וּרְבִיעִת הַהִין לַכֶּבֶשׂ יָיִן (יין only at end).

†[הָכַר] **vb.** only **Qal** or **Hiph.** (Ges § 53 R. 4 Kö I. 251) *Impf.* 2 mpl. תַּהְכְּרוּ in phrase לֹא־תֵבֹשׁוּ תַּהְכְּרוּ־לִי Jb 19^{3}, sense very dubious; Schult Thes De al. (as Hiph.) *ye cause me* (לִ = acc.) *to wonder* (cf. Ar. هَكِرَ); others (as Qal) *ye deal hardly with, wrong me* (so context seems rather to require, v. Ges in Add^{84} RobGes Ew Di Da RV; cf. Ar. حَكَرَ *wrong, detract from*; Codd. rd. תחכרו, which is preferable, if this mng. be adopted; 𝔊 ἐπίκεισθέ μοι, 𝔙 *opprimentes*); conjectures are תַּחְרְפוּ Ol Hiob; תַּחְבְּרוּ אֵלַי Me; Siegf תִּתְחַבְּרוּ.

הַכָּרַת Is 3^{9} v. נכר.

הַל Dt 32^{6} v. sub הֲ p. 210 supr.

הָלְאָה v. sub foll.

†הָלְאָה (i.e. *hā-le'āh*, the final *-āh*, the ה *locale*, being toneless), **adv.** out there, onwards, further (𝔗 הָלְאָ, always with לְ or מְ prefixed; Syr. ܗܠܐ, ܠܗܠ, ܡܢ ܗܠ PS^{1009} *id.*; Ar. هَلَا *forward! on!* Fl Kl. Schr. i. 355)—**a.** of *place* Gn 19^{9} גֶּשׁ־הָלְאָה *approach out there!* i.e. *make way, get back* (𝔊 ἀπόστα ἐκεῖ: 𝔙 *recede illuc*), Nu 17^{2} and the fire זְרֵה־הָלְאָה scatter *yonder*; מֵהָלְאָה לְ *beyond* (lit. *off the yonder side of*; v. מִן **4 c**) Gn 35^{21} Je 22^{19} Am 5^{27} *beyond* Damascus: וָהָלְאָה attached to an indication of place, to mark direction, 1 S 10^{3} and thou shalt pass on מִשָּׁם וָהָלְאָה thence *and onwards*; 20^{22} מִמְּךָ וָהָלְאָה from thee *and onwards* i.e. beyond thee (opp. to מִמְּךָ וָהֵנָּה v^{21}), v^{37} Nu 32^{19} on the side of Jordan *forwards* (opp. to 'on the side of Jordan eastwards'). **b.** of *time*, Lv 22^{27} from the 8th day וָהָלְאָה *and onwards*, Nu 15^{23} 1 S 18^{9} מהיום ההוא והלאה from that day *and onwards*, Ez 39^{22} 43^{27} Is $18^{2.7}$. Hence

†[הָלָא] **vb.denom.** only **Ni. ptcp.** *fem.* Mi 4^{7} הַנַּהֲלָאָה (of sheep) removed far off.

†הַלָּז **pron.comm.** this, a rare synonym of זֶה or הַזֶּה, *this* (Ar. اَلَّذِى (also اَلَّذْ), pl. اَلَّذِينَ, *who, which* (cf. זֶה, which is used also sts. as rel.), formed from اَلْ the def. art., and the pron. ذَا, זֶה, זוּ, with the insertion of the demonstr. element *la*, and thus in fact = הַזֶּה: W AG i. § 347, CG p. 117)—usually with a subst. defined by the art., Ju 6^{20} הַסֶּלַע הַלָּז *this* rock, 1 S 14^{1} מֵעֵבֶר הַלָּז off *this* side-across, 17^{26} אֶת־הַפְּלִשְׁתִּי הַלָּז, (+ 20^{19} 𝔊 Th We Dr τὸ ἐργαβ ἐκεῖνο, i.e. הָאַרְגָּב הַלָּז (or הַלָּאז) *this* mound (*or* cairn), for (האבן האזל) 2 K 23^{17} Zc 2^{8}; with a *fem.*, 2 K 4^{25} הַשּׁוּנַמִּית הַלָּז: without a subst. Dn 8^{16} לְהַלָּז to *this one* (= normal לָזֶה). The fuller form is

†הַלָּזֶה Gn 24^{65} הָאִישׁ הַלָּזֶה, 37^{19} בַּעַל הַחֲלֹמוֹת הַלָּזֶה *this* dreamer (contemptuously). Once also there occurs

†הַלֵּזוּ Ez 36^{35} (*fem.*) הָאָרֶץ הַלֵּזוּ.

הלחות Je 48^{5} Kt v. לוּחִית.

הָלַךְ $_{1545}$ **vb.** go, come, walk (MI ואהלך, לך; SI וילכו; NH הָלַךְ (rare), Aram. הֲלַךְ, הַךְ (also BAram.), oftener הַלֵּיךְ Pa., ܗܰܠܶܟ, Palm. Ithp. אתילכא Vog No. 15, l. 4; As. *alāku* Dl W; also Ar. هَلَكَ *perish*)—**Qal** *Pf.* 3 ms. ה׳ Gn 26^{26}+; הָלְכָה 2 S 8^{6}+; 3 pl. הָלְכוּ Gn 14^{24}+; (הָ)הָלְכוּא Jos 10^{24} (Ges § 23, 3; 138, 3 b Kö I. 414 f.), etc.; *Impf.* rarely **a.** 3 ms. יַהֲלֹךְ Je 9^{3} + 4 t. Jb ψ; וַיַּהֲלֹךְ Jb 14^{20}; 3 fs. תַּהֲלַךְ ψ 73^{9}; וַתִּהֲלַךְ Ex 9^{23} (Ew § 138 b Ges § 69, R. 8 Kö I. 415); 1 s. אֶהֱלֹךְ Jb 16^{22} 23^{8} (cf. MI 14.15); יַהֲלֹכוּ Jb 41^{11}; usually **b.** (629 t.) as if fr. ילך (ולך); vid. **Hiph.** Ges § 69, 2 R. 8 Kö I. 414 ff. Prät ZAW 1882, 310 ff.; cf. also יָלַד etc.) 3 ms. יֵלֵךְ Ex 10^{24}+; יֵלֶךְ Ec 5^{15}+; וַיֵּלֵךְ Jb 27^{21}; וַיֵּלֶךְ Ex 34^{9}+; וַיֵּלֶךְ Gn $12^{4.4}$ + 210 t., וַיֵּלַךְ Gn 24^{61} + 6 t.; 3 fs. תֵּלֵךְ Gn 24^{39} תֵּלֶךְ ψ 97^{3}; וַתֵּלֶךְ Gn 7^{18}+; 2 ms. תֵּלֵךְ etc. Gn 3^{14}+; 2 fs. תֵּלְכִי etc. Ju $4^{8.8}$+;

1 s אֵלֵךְ Ex 3[11]+, ואלך, Ju 19[18]+; וָאֵלֵךְ Jb 19[10]; אֵלְכָה Gn 45[28]+, אילכה Mi 1[8], 3 mpl. ילכו Ex 5[7]+, יֵלֵכוּן ψ 89[31]+2 t; וילכו Gn 9[23] (וילכו also SI[4])+; 3 fpl תֵּלַכְנָה Ju 11[40]+, 2 mpl תלכו Gn 42[38]+; תלכון Dt 6[14], תֵּלֵכוּן Ex 3[21] Is 52[12], 2 fpl. תֵּלַכְנָה Ru 1[11], 1 pl. נֵלֵךְ Ex 8[23]+, וַנֵּלֶךְ Dt 1[19], etc.; *Imv* rarely **a.** הֲלוֹךְ Pr 13[20] (Kt, Qr הֹלֵךְ, cf. De Now), mpl הלכו Je 51[50]; usu **b.** (241 t) ms לֵךְ Gn 26[16]+ (לך also MI[14]), לֶךְ Gn 27[9]+; לְכָה Gn 19[32]+, לֵךְ Nu 23[13] Ju 19[13] 2 Ch 25[17], לֵכָה 1 S 23[27], fs לכי Ju 9[10]+; mpl לכו Gn 37[20]+, fpl לֵכְנָה Ru 1[8], לֵכְןָ Ru 1[12], etc, *Inf abs* הָלוֹךְ Gn 8[3]+, הָלֹךְ Gn 31[30]+, *cstr* rarely **a.** הֲלֹךְ Ex 3[19]+4 t, הֲלָךְ Ec 6[9]; usu. **b** (129 t) לֶכֶת Mi 6[8]+, לֶכֶת Pr 15[21]+2 t; sf לֶכְתִּי 1 K 2[8], לֶכְתָּם 2 S 17[21]+7 t (6 Ez), לֶכְתָּן Ez 1[9 12 17], etc, *Pt* הלך Gn 18[16]+; הולך Gn 15[2]+, f הלכה Je 3[6], הֹלֶכֶת Gn 32[21]+2 t + הֹלַכְתִּי 2 K 4[23], pl הלכים Ex 33[15]+, etc, cstr הלכי Ju 5[6]+3 t, fpl הלכת etc. Ex 2[5]+3 t,—found in all documents of Hex, esp JE (240 t, D 65 t, P 30 t + H 14 t),—**I.** lit **1.** of persons, **a** *go, proceed, move, walk* Gn 22[6.8] Ex 17[5] Am 3[3] Zp 1[17]+oft; of cherubim Ez 10[16] = living creatures 1[9 12 19.20.21 24], opp to sitting (ישב) Dt 6[7] 11[19] (both c בַּדֶּרֶךְ), ‖ running (רוץ) Pr 4[12] Is 40[31], cf also 2 Ch 30[6], distinguished from riding, driving Gn 24[65] (J, sq בַּשָּׂדֶה לקראתנו), Ju 5[10] (עַל־הַדֶּרֶךְ), Is 41[3] (ברגליו), cf Ec 5[1] (sq. אֶל), 10[7] (sq עַל־הָאָרֶץ); on usage with prep v infr, but also ‖ וַיִּרְכַּב 1 K 13[13] 18[45] cf 2 K 9[16]; נְהַג וָלֵךְ v[18] (sq לִקְרָאתוֹ), וַתֵּלֶךְ . וילך רכב הַסּוּס 4[24] *drive and go forward . and she went, and came* **b.** *depart, go away* Gn 18[33] (J), *and ׳י departed,* Gn 34[17] (P) *then we will take our daughter and depart,* cf 1 S 14[3] 15[27] Ex 3[19] (J), 12[29] (P) 2 K 5[25]+, *go, go out* (to a specific duty etc) of Samuel 1 S 7[16], Barak Ju 4[8 9], *go out, forth* (opp שׁוּב) Ru 1[21]+, = *go into exile* (without modifier) 1 Ch 5[41] cf Je 22[10] (הלך of one going into exile; opp. death), v further אֲשֶׁר הָלְכוּ שָׁם Ez 37[21] **c.** less oft where Eng idiom requires or prefers *come,* (approach, arrive), vb in Heb being referred to starting point, mostly c prep (on usage c. prep in gen v infr)—לְכָה אֵלַי 1 S 17[44], so in prayer to ׳י, וּלְכָה לִישֻׁעָתָה לָּנוּ ψ 80[3], also in Yahweh's exhortations to Isr Is 55[1] (לַמַּיִם), v[3] (אֵלַי), *come to, arrive at* a land (ה ָ loc) Gn 29[1], *come unto* (אֶל) a people Ru 2[11], but cf. esp (without prep) Imv followed by another Imv, etc, v infr. **5 f**, & partic cases like Nu 22[6 11 17] 23[7 7] Is 55[11] etc, where actual summons to approach the speaker. **d.** with modifiers: (1) *a* of space traversed. את כָּל־הַמִּדְבָּר Dt 1[19] (cf I. **2**), את כָּל־הַבִּתְרוֹן 2 S 2[29]; esp c. acc דֶּרֶךְ *way,* Gn 35[3] (E) Nu 20[17] (JE) Dt 1[31] 2 S 4[7] 1 K 13[12 12]; Je 52[7] cf וְלֹא תָשׁוּב בַּדֶּרֶךְ אֲשֶׁר הָלָכְתָּ 1 K 13[9]; הֹלֵךְ דֶּרֶךְ = *traveller* Is 35[8]; sq אֳרָחוֹת Ju 5[6] (song), ptcp cstr. הלכי נתיבות v[6] *goers of paths* (wayfarers), c acc. דרך = *journey* Pr 7[19]; *β* c acc. of time Dt 2[14] 2 S 2[32], cf Jos 5[6] 14[10]; also, with combination of ideas of space & time דֶּרֶךְ שְׁלֹשֶׁת יָמִים Ex 3[18] (+ בַּמִּדְבָּר v. infr) cf 5[3] 8[23] 15[22] (all JE), Nu 33[8] (P) 1 K 19[4] (2) c prep.: *a* sq. בּ of space (territory, country, etc) in which בַּמִּדְבָּר Ju 11[16 18], cf. וַיֵּלֶךְ בַּבַּיִת אַחַת הֵנָּה ואחת הנה 2 K 4[35] *and he walked in the house once hither, once thither;* esp + acc of time or distance (cf supr.) Jos 5[6] 14[10] (both D) 1 K 19[4]; בַּיַּבָּשָׁה 2 S 2[29], cf בָעֲרָבָה Ex 14[29] = 15[19] (P?); בתוך הָעֵמֶק Jos 8[13] (JE); sq בּ of way, path בַּדֶּרֶךְ 1 K 18[6.6] בד׳ Nu 21[22] (JE) Jos 24[17] (E) Dt 1[33] 2[27] Ju 18[6] 1 S 28[22], לֹא תָשׁוּב לָלֶכֶת בַּדֶּרֶךְ אֲשֶׁר הָלַכְתָּ בָהּ 1 K 13[17] (הלך of both going & coming); so oft fig, cf infr **II. 3**, *walk in the streets* ברחבת La 4[18], *walk by the way* בד׳ (opp יָשַׁב *sit*) Dt 6[7] 11[19], *β* sq. עַל, *go* or *walk on (by)* עַל־יַד הַיְאֹר Ex 2[5], עַל־הַדֶּרֶךְ 1 S 9[6] (i e *set out, start, upon* cf Dr); cstr sq על Ju 5[10] (3) *go to, unto*· *a* sq acc, in general בְּכֹל אֲשֶׁר תֵּלֵךְ Gn 28[15] (J) *whithersoever thou goest* Jos 1[7 9] (D), cf. 2 S 7[9] 8[6.14] = 1 Ch 17[8] 18[6 13]; more definitely, to a land, with or without ארץ Ju 1[26] 21[21] Je 37[12]; so fig Ho 7[11] *resort to* (acc.) *Asshur* (‖ קרא), to a city 1 S 11[14 15] 23[5] 1 K 2[8] 11[21] 12[1] 14[2.4] 2 K 9[1] 1 Ch 11[4] 2 Ch 8[3] Ezr 8[31]; to a house בית 2 S 13[7 8], house of ׳י ψ 122[1], a field, Gn 27[5] (J, + Inf of purpose), valley of salt 2 Ch 25[11]. *β* sq ה ָ loc., אַרְצָה Gn 11[31] 12[5], פַּדֶּנָה אֲרָם 28[2.5 7] (all P) cf 29[1] (E) Nu 32[39] (JE) 2 S 14[23], of city Gn 18[22] 28[10] (both J) Ju 9[1] 1 S 15[34] 16[13] 19[22] 2 S 15[9] 1 K 3[4] 18[46] 2 Ch 10[1]; of river Euphrates Je 13[4 6.7]; of a wood 1 S 23[16], a mountain Jos 2[16] (JE), cf. also אָנָה הָלְכוּ *whither have they gone* Gn 16[8] 32[18] Jos 2[5] (all JE) cf. Ne 2[16] Ct 6[1] Ju 19[17], שָׁמָּה 1 K 2[42] (but also אָן ה׳ 1 S 10[14]), אָנֶה וָאָנָה Je 40[4] but also שָׁם 1 S 9[6] Je 45[5]; הֵנָּה 2 K 4[35]. *γ*. c. prep.· (*a*) most often sq. אֶל־ *unto,* e.g, *unto the place,* הַמָּקוֹם, Gn 22[3] (E) 30[25] (J),

etc.; of land Gn 22^{2} (E) 24$^{4.10}$ (J) 36^{6} (P) Jos 22^{9} (D), etc.; of city Gn 22^{19} (E) 1 S 9^{10} Jon 3^{3}, etc.; of house Gn 24^{38} (J) Ec 7$^{2.2}$, house of God Ec 4^{17}, of people Ex 19^{10} (E) etc.; in other designations of place, Jos 8^{9} (JE), Ezr 10^{6} Ru 2^{8}, etc.; also sq אֶל = *against*, of military expedition: Ju 1^{10} against Canaanites; a city Ju 9^{1} 1 K 22^{15} = 2 Ch 18$^{5.14}$, also sq. אֶל of individual persons Gn 26$^{1.26}$ (both J), 41^{55} (E) 2 K 6$^{22.23}$ 22^{14} = 2 Ch 34^{22} Je 41^{14}+, once with implic. *coire cum femina* Am 2^{7} (cf בוא **1 e**, p. 98); vid. esp. לַהֲלֹךְ אֶל־אֵל בַּמִּשְׁפָּט Jb 34^{23} of judicial inquiry by God; *come unto* the speaker Nu 22$^{16.37}$ (both JE), unto the one addressed Is 60^{14} (*b*) rarely sq עַל־ *unto* (Je K Ez) c בַּיִת 1 K 20^{43}, שָׂדֶה 1 K 2^{26} (+acc. loc.), cf. עַל־כָּל אֲשֶׁר Je 1^{7}, אֶל־אֲשֶׁר יִהְיֶה שָׁם Ez 1^{12} (of the רוּחַ; cf. עַל־אֲשֶׁר יִהְיֶה שָׁמָּה v^{20}); also וַאֲנִי הוֹלֵךְ עַל אֲשֶׁר־אֲנִי הוֹלֵךְ 2 S 15^{20} = *I am going I know not where* cf Lag$^{Psalt. Hieron 1874, 156 f.}$ Dr^{Sm}; v further Je 3^{6} (sq both אֶל & עַל; on confusion of אֶל and עַל vid these words); sq עַל *against* city 1 K 22^{6}, king 2 Ch 22^{5}. (*c*) sq עַד *as far as, unto*, place עַד־כֹּה Gn 22^{5} (E), cf 1 K 12^{30} (וַיֵּלְכוּ הָעָם לִפְנֵי הָאֶחָד עַד דָּן), 2 K 6^{2} 10^{2b} 7^{15} cf 2 Ch 26^{8}; persons 1 S 9^{9}. (*d*) sq לְ, *to* a land 1 K 10^{13} etc; a city 2 Ch 8^{17}; a mountain 1 Ch 4^{42}; a bamah 2 Ch 1^{3}, cf. לִמְבוֹא גדר 1 Ch 4^{39} & v. infr; also before n pr. of pers Gn 24^{56} (J); further לַמִּלְחָמָה Ez 7^{14}; לְסִבְלֹתֵיכֶם Ex 5^{4} (J) *go to your burdens* cf Is 60^{3}, וְהַתּוֹדָה הַשֵּׁנִית הַהוֹלֶכֶת לְמוֹאל Ne 12^{38} *the second thanksgiving choir, that went the opposite way*; frequently לְדַרְכּוֹ etc, *go (to, on) one's way* Gn 19^{2} (J) 32^{2} (E) Nu 24^{25} Jos 2^{16} (both JE) Ju 18^{26} 1 S 1^{18} 26^{25}+; לְמַסָּעָיו Gn 13^{3} (J); cf. הַהוֹלֵךְ לְמֶרְחֲבֵי־אֶרֶץ Hb 1^{6} *that marcheth through the breadth of the land* (of invader); note esp in sense of *depart to, go away to*, almost = *return to*, וְהָלַכְתָּ לְאֹהָלֶיךָ Dt 16^{7} *and thou shalt go* (back) *to thy tents*, so Ju 19^{9} 20^{8} 1 K 8^{66} 12^{16} = 2 Ch 10^{16}; לְבֵיתוֹ 1 S 10^{26} cf. 14^{8} 23^{18} 1 K 14^{12} 1 Ch 16^{43}; לִמְקוֹמוֹ 1 S 2^{20} (cf. VB Dr) 14^{46}, v. also *go away* or *off to* 1 Ch 4^{42} 2 Ch 8^{17}. (*e*) sq בְּ *into* בַּשָּׂדֶה Nu 22^{23} (of Balaam's ass); esp. in ה׳ בַּשְּׁבִי *go into captivity* Am 9^{4} Na 3^{10} Dt 28^{41} Je 20^{6} 22^{22} 30^{16} La 1^{18} (= ה׳ שְׁבִי v^{5}) cf Ez 30$^{17.18}$ Is 46^{2} 48^{11} ה׳ בַּגּוֹלָה Je 48^{11} Ez 25^{3}, v also ה׳ בַּכְּלִמָּה Is 45^{16}, ה׳ בַּמִּלְחָמָה 1 S 17^{13}, ה׳ בַּקְּרָב 2 S 17^{11} (but v. Dr) (**4**) *go from, depart from*, sq. מִן, e g 1 K 2^{41}, etc, מִשָּׁם Gn 42^{26} (E) 1 K 19^{19}; cf. אָנָה אֵלֵךְ מֵרוּחֶךָ ψ 139^{7}; note esp. וּמַלְאַךְ י׳ הָלַךְ מֵעֵינָיו Ju 6^{21} cf. 1 S 14^{17} (מֵעִמָּנוּ), Ho 9^{6} (מִשֹּׁד, *from destruction*); also sq. מֵאֵת of divorced woman Je 3^{1} (מֵאִתּוֹ), cf also Gn 26^{31} (J), Jos 22^{9} (? P) מֵאֵצֶל 1 K 20^{36}. (**5**) c prep denoting other relations:—*a*. אֵת of accompaniment, ה׳ אִתִּי (on warlike expedition) Gn 14^{24} cf. 2 S 15^{11} Jos 10^{24} Ju 1^{3} (sq. בְּ *into*), 7$^{4.4}$, v. also 1 S 23^{23} 2 S 16^{17}+. *β*. עִם Ju 4$^{8.8.9.9}$ 7^{4} 11^{8} 1 S 30$^{22.22}$ 2 S 19^{26} Nu 22$^{13.14}$ (JE)+ *γ* בְּ *with* (cf. בְּ **III. 1**, p 89), esp. Ex 10^{9}, cf Ho 5^{6} בְּצֹאנָם וּבִבְקָרָם יֵלְכוּ לְבַקֵּשׁ אֶת־י׳, of vain sacrifices, 2 Ch 30^{6} *the runners went with* (בְּ) *letters* *δ* בְּקֶרֶב *in the midst of*, Ex 34^{9} (JE) *ε* לִפְנֵי *in front of, before*, before Cyrus Is 45^{2}, (cf of fire & pestilence, infr **3**); of י׳ going before Isr Ex 13^{21} Nu 14^{14}, cf also Ex 23^{23} 32^{34} & (in mng) 33^{14} (פָּנַי יֵלֵכוּ), v^{15}, Is 52^{12}, with which comp וְה׳ לְפָנֶיךָ צִדְקֶךָ 58^{8}; of other gods Ex 32$^{1.23}$ (all JE); לְנֶגְדֶּךָ Gn 33^{12} (J) *ζ*. c אַחַר *go after, follow*, persons Gn 37^{17} (J) 2 K 7^{15}, אַחֲרֵי Gn 24$^{5.8.39.61}$ (all J), Jos 3^{3} (D), Nu 16^{25} (JE)+; cf also **II. 3 d** (going after false gods, etc); מֵאַחֲרֵיהֶם Ex 14^{19} (J) *η* לְ with sense of dativ. ethic. וַיֵּלֶךְ לוֹ אֶל־אַרְצוֹ Ex 18^{27} (E) *and he gat him* (betook himself) *to his country*, אֵלֶךְ לִי אֶל Ct 4^{6} *I will get me unto*; וְנֵלְכָה־לָּנוּ 1 S 26^{11} *and let us be gone*, cf. v^{12}, Ct 2^{11} (of rain cf infr **3**), Imv. in same construction. לֶךְ־לְךָ אֶל Gn 22^{2} (E) *get thee unto*, לֶךְ־לְךָ מִן Gn 12^{1} לְכוּ לָכֶם לְאָהֳלֵיכֶם Jos 22^{4} (D) also (J), & לְכִי־לָךְ Ct 2$^{10.13}$ *get thee away, come away* *θ* adverbial phrases of manner c prep. (*a*) בְּ, ה׳ בְּשָׁלוֹם *go in peace* Gn 26^{31} (J) 1 S 29^{7} 2 S 3$^{21.22.23}$ 15^{9}, ה׳ בְּכֹחַ הָאֲכִילָה הַהִיא 1 K 19^{8}, ה׳ בְּחֵמָה 2 K 5^{12}, cf. also 1 S 17^{39} Is 52^{12}; וְה׳ בְּסַעֲרוֹת תֵּימָן Zc 9^{14} of י׳, *and he shall go in* (or with) *storms of the south*, בְּ pretii, הַהֹלְכִים בְּנַפְשׁוֹתָם 2 S 23^{17} *who went at risk of their life* (otherwise in ‖ 1 Ch 11^{19}), cf (*b*) אֶל, ה׳ אֶל־נַפְשׁוֹ 1 K 19^{3} *he went for his life* (*c*) לְ, ה׳ לְרַגְלָהּ 1 S 25^{42} *go according to her foot*, i.e. follow, attend her; לֵךְ לְשָׁלוֹם *go to, for* (in) *peace* Ex 4^{18} (E) Ju 18^{6} 1 S 1^{17} 20$^{13.42}$ 2 K 5^{19}, וְהֹלְכִים לְתֻמָּם 2 S 15^{11} *κ*. with adj or noun, agreeing with subj of vb, in acc. (Ges$^{§ 118.5}$), sometimes where Lat & Eng. use an attributive or appositive. *walk barefoot* 2 S 15^{30}, *walk naked and barefoot* Is 20^{3} (c. acc. of duration); וְתֵלַכְנָה נְטוּוֹת גָּרוֹן וגו׳ Is 3^{16}, cf. 1 K 8^{66}, also לֹא תֵלֵךְ רָכִיל בְּעַמֶּיךָ Lv 19^{16} (H) *thou*

shalt not walk as a slanderer among thy people, Je 9³, הלכי רָכִיל הולך רָכִיל Pr 11¹³ 20¹⁹, and even Je 6²⁸ (yet רכיל poss abstr, ה׳ ר׳ *walk in slander*), with adv accus, construed more generally (Ges §118. 5. c, Ew §279 c): *ye shall not walk loftily* (רוֹמָה) Mi 2³, *they shall come bending* (שְׁחוֹחַ) Is 60¹⁴, *and Agag came delicately* (מַעֲדַנֹּת) 1 S 15³², cf also Lv 26²³ (II. **3 b**) Ex 3²¹ 2 S 17¹⁸.

2. Also of animals, in similar meanings and combinations הָלַךְ Na 2¹² *walk about, prowl* (lions, fig of rulers of Assyria), Pr 30²⁹ (vid v³⁰·³¹, of three beasts & a king), *walk, go, move* בִּמְסִלָּה אַחַת ה׳ 1 S 6¹² (of cows bringing ark), horses in Zec's vision Zc 6⁷ וַיְבַקְשׁוּ לָלֶכֶת לְהִתְהַלֵּךְ בָּאָרֶץ, of beasts & birds Je 9⁹, cf 50³ *both man & beast, they are fled, they are gone*; of flocks and herds (מִקְנֶה) יֵלֵךְ עִמָּנוּ Ex 10²⁶ *they shall go with us*, ה׳ מֵהַר אֶל־גִּבְעָה Je 50⁶ *they have gone fr mt. to hill* (Isr under fig of wandering sheep), in 1 S 14²⁶ rd prob הֹלֵךְ for הֵלֶךְ q v; esp. in laws of clean & unclean Lv 11²⁰·²¹ *every swarming winged thing that goeth on* (הַהֹלֵךְ עַל) *all fours*, cf. v²⁷·⁴², also v²⁷ *everything that goeth on its paws*, & v⁴² *everything that goeth on (its) belly*, (all P), so of serpent Gn 3¹⁴ *on thy belly* (עַל־גְּחֹנְךָ) *shalt thou go* (J), cf also Je 46²² קוֹלָהּ כַּנָּחָשׁ יֵלֵךְ; (where appar rel cl, *her voice like the serpent that moves*, i e like the rustling sound of a gliding serpent, cf VB), locusts Jo 2⁷ (אִישׁ בִּדְרָכָיו), v⁸ (גֶּבֶר בִּמְסִלָּתוֹ) **3.** in like manner of inanimate things, as: the ark (הַתֵּבָה) Gn 7¹⁸ (P, sq עַל־פְּנֵי הַמָּיִם), ships 1 K 22⁴⁹ (sq ה ָ loc) = 2 Ch 20³⁶ (sq acc of limit), cf 2 Ch 9²¹ (sq acc) 20³⁷ (אֶל), of אֳנִי־שַׁיִט Is 33²¹ '*galley with oars*' (sq בְּ of place in which), wheels (in Ezekiel's vision) Ez 1¹⁷ ¹⁷ ¹⁹ ²¹ 10¹¹ ¹¹ ¹¹ ¹¹; moon Jb 31²⁶, wind ψ 78³⁹ Ec 1⁶·⁶, of streams (הַנְּחָלִים) = *flow* אֶל־הַיָּם Ec 1⁷; cf. אֶל־מְקוֹם שֶׁהַנְּחָלִים הֹלְכִים שָׁם הֵם שָׁבִים לָלָכֶת v⁷ *unto the place whither the streams flow, thither they flow again*; also אֲפִיקִים, sq מַיִם as accus of that with wh, Jo 4¹⁸ ‖ of hills *flowing* חָלָב, *with milk*, cf. further fig כָּל־בִּרְכַּיִם תֵּלַכְנָה מַּיִם Ez 7¹⁷ 21¹² *all knees shall flow down in water*, i.e be as weak as water, וְהָלַךְ עַל־כָּל־גְּדוֹתָיו נְהָרוֹת Ez 31⁴ (sq. סָבִיב), Is 8⁷ i e *overflow* (‖ עָלָה עַל־כָּל־אֲפִיקָיו) cf. Jos 4¹⁸ (JE), so of water (as SI⁴) Is 8⁶, 1 K 18³⁵ (וַיֵּלְכוּ הַמַּיִם סָבִיב לַמִּזְבֵּחַ), ψ 105⁴¹ (הָלְכוּ בַּצִּיּוֹת נָהָר), *they flowed through dry regions as a river*); (on Inf abs used of waters of flood, Gn 8³·⁵, cf. infr. **4 c** (4), (5)), of the sea הַיָּם הוֹלֵךְ וְסֹעֵר Jon 1¹¹ ¹³ *was going on and being stormy = was growing more and more stormy* (cf infr **4 d**), of wine (יַיִן) Ct 7¹⁰ *that goeth down, for my beloved, smoothly* (simile); also of lightning *go, dart* (בָּרָק) Jb 38³⁵, so אֵשׁ Ex 9²³ (E) וַתִּהֲלַךְ אֵשׁ אָרְצָה *and fire darted to earth* (on form, here & ψ 73⁹ infr., as intens, of rapid motion, cf. Thes Ew §138 b Kö¹ ⁴¹⁵), אֵשׁ לְפָנָיו תֵּלֵךְ ψ 97³, of torches, in fig of violent breathing of crocodile מִפִּיו לַפִּידִים יַהֲלֹכוּ Jb 41¹¹, of sword אַחֲרַיִךְ תֵּלֶךְ חָרֶב Je 48², of arrow בָּרָק Jb 20²⁵ drawn from a wound; of pestilence דֶּבֶר (personified) ψ 91⁶ (בָּאֹפֶל), Hb 3⁵ (לְפָנָיו), of fame שָׁמְעוֹ הוֹלֵךְ בְּכָל־הַמְּדִינוֹת Est 9⁴; of the tongue (bad sense) וּלְשׁוֹנָם תִּהֲלַךְ בָּאָרֶץ ψ 73⁹ (cf Ex 9²³ supr; ‖ שַׁתּוּ בַשָּׁמַיִם פִּיהֶם); of sound of trumpet Ex 19¹⁹ (Pt cf. infra **4 d**), of letters אִגְּרוֹת Ne 6¹⁷ (sq. עַל, unto), of dew (טַל ‖ עֲנַן־בֹּקֶר) sim. of Isr.'s חֶסֶד Ho 6⁴ cf. 13³ *like dew that passeth away*; so of עָנָן Jb 7⁹ כָּלָה עָנָן וַיֵּלַךְ; of rain הַגֶּשֶׁם חָלַף הָלַךְ לוֹ Ct 2¹¹ *the rain is over, it hath taken itself away*; of ark of י׳ (אֲרוֹן י׳) 1 S 6⁸ *depart* (cf also **5 d**); of shadow on dial *go forward* 2 K 20⁹ (opp. שׁוּב ‖ נָטָה, v²⁰ & יָרַד Is 38⁸); *grow*, of wicked under fig. of trees, יֵלְכוּ גַּם־עָשׂוּ פֶרִי Je 12²; cf יֵלְכוּ יוֹנְקוֹתָיו Ho 14³ *his branches shall spread*, said of Isr under fig. of tree, of name (= fame) 2 Ch 26⁸ (sq עַד־לְבוֹא מִצְרַיִם), also of a thing that does not actually move, וְהָלַךְ הַגְּבוּל אֶל Jos 17⁷ *and the boundary went unto* etc, cf 16⁸ (sq. מִן & ה ָ loc),—in 2 K 13²¹ *and it* (the dead body) *went* i e. was let down into the grave, rd וַיֵּלְכוּ for וַיֵּלֶךְ 𝔊L Th Klo, *and they went away*

†**4.** The Inf abs. is often used **a.** as in other vbs, quite independently (Ges §113. 1): הֲגָנֹב . . . . וְהָלֹךְ אַחֲרֵי אֱלֹהִים אֲחֵרִים Je 7⁹ (series of 6 Inf. abs) (are there) stealing, murdering, and adultery and false swearing and incense-burning to the Baal, *and going after other gods* . ? as obj, וְלֹא־אָבוּ בִדְרָכָיו הָלוֹךְ Is 42²⁴ *and they desired not walking in his ways*, as appos of obj, Je 23¹⁴ *I have seen . . . . an abominable thing, committing adultery and walking in lies* (נָאוֹף וְהָלֹךְ בַּשֶּׁקֶר); cf. וַיַּעַשׂ כֵּן הָלֹךְ עָרוֹם וְיָחֵף Is 20² *and he did so, a walking naked and barefoot*, where also two adverb accus modifying the Inf abs (Ges §113. 2). **b.** to intensify meaning of finite form of הָלַךְ (Ges §113. 3). (1)

before finite vb. הָלוֹךְ אֵלֵךְ עִמָּךְ Ju 4^{9} *I will surely go with thee*, cf. Je 37^{9}; הָלֹךְ הָלַכְתָּ Gn 31^{30} concessive, *thou art indeed gone*, הָלוֹךְ הָלְכוּ הָעֵצִים Ju 9^{8} introductory, *the trees went forth on a time* to anoint them a king. (2) after finite vb. וַיֵּלֶךְ הָלוֹךְ 2 S 3^{24} *and he is actually gone!* (a grave imprudence to permit it!), נֵלְכָה הָלוֹךְ לְחַלּוֹת אֶת־פְּנֵי י׳ Zc 8^{21} *let us by all means go to seek the favour of* י׳. **c.** most noteworthy is the joining of the Inf. abs. (1) with a following Inf. abs. denoting a simultaneous action or process, and so emphasizing duration or continuance: *a.* both Infs. preceding the finite vb., הָלוֹךְ וְטָפֹף תֵּלַכְנָה Is 3^{16} *a going and a tripping they go*, i.e. they keep tripping as they go; so הָלוֹךְ וּבָכוֹ יֵלֵכוּ Je 50^{4} *continually weeping they shall go*; *β.* one Inf. before, & one after the fin. vb. הָלוֹךְ יֵלֵךְ וּבָכֹה ψ 126^{6} *continually may one go weeping*; *γ.* elsewhere both after fin. vb. Jos 6^{9} *the rearguard* was *going* (הֹלֵךְ) *after the ark, continually blowing on the trumpets* (הָלוֹךְ וְתָקוֹעַ בַּשּׁוֹפָרוֹת), cf. v^{13} (where הָלוֹךְ cf. infr.; both JE), ... וַיֵּלֶךְ הָלוֹךְ וּבָכוֹ 2 S 3^{16}, of cows הָלְכוּ הָלוֹךְ וְגָעוֹ 1 S 6^{12} *they went continually lowing*, וַיֵּלֶךְ הָלוֹךְ וְאָכֹל Ju 14^{9} *and he went on, eating as he went*; הֹלְכִים הָלוֹךְ וְדַבֵּר 2 K 2^{11} *they were going on, talking as they went*; in הֹלֵךְ הָלֹךְ וּבֹכֶה Je 41^{6}, the pt. בֹּכֶה is peculiar, rd. perh. בָּכֹה, and for הֹלֵךְ rd. הֹלְכִים 𝔊 Hi cf. Gf. (2) with a foll. vb. fin. c. ו consec. (rare): הֹלְכִים הָלוֹךְ וְתָקְעוּ Jos 6^{13} (JE) they were *going along continually blowing* on the trumpets; וַתֵּלֶךְ הָלוֹךְ וְזָעָקָה 2 S 13^{19} *and she went, crying out as she went*; הֹלֵךְ ... הָלוֹךְ וַיְקַלֵּל 2 S 16^{13} he *went along ... cursing as he went*; so 1 S 19^{23} *and he went on, prophesying as he went*, until he came, etc. (3) in cases where vb. fin. is foll. by Inf. abs. + adj. denoting progress, advance: וַיֵּלֶךְ הָלוֹךְ וְקָרֵב 2 S 18^{25} *and he came continually nearer* (nearer & nearer); elsewh. with idea of actual motion lost fr. vb. fin.: וַיֵּלֶךְ הָלוֹךְ וָרָב 1 S 14^{19} *and the tumult kept growing greater and greater*; so וַיֵּלֶךְ דָּוִד הָלוֹךְ וְגָדוֹל 2 S 5^{10} = 1 Ch 11^{9}; cf. Ju 4^{24} *and the hand of the sons of Israel kept growing more and more severe* (וַתֵּלֶךְ ... הָלוֹךְ וְקָשָׁה) *upon Jabin*; note esp. וַיִּגְדַּל הָאִישׁ וַיֵּלֶךְ הָלוֹךְ וְגָדֵל עַד־כִּי־גָדַל מְאֹד Gn 26^{13} (J) *and the man grew great and kept on growing greater and greater until* etc. (גָּדֵל partic. adj.). (4) twice, where vb. fin. is not הלך, but another vb. denoting motion: וַיָּשֻׁבוּ הַמַּיִם ... הָלוֹךְ וָשׁוֹב Gn 8^{3} (J) *and the waters retired continually more and more*; וַיִּסַּע אַבְרָם הָלוֹךְ וְנָסוֹעַ הַנֶּגְבָּה Gn 12^{9} (J) *and Abram journeyed on continually further toward the south country*. (5) quite by itself is Gn 8^{5} (P) וְהַמַּיִם הָיוּ הָלוֹךְ וְחָסוֹר *and the waters, they continually diminished* (were a going and a diminishing; the Infs. abs. being predicate). (6) 13 t. the Inf. abs. = Imv. & is followed by Pf. consec. (chiefly in Je): הָלוֹךְ וְדִבַּרְתָּ 2 S 24^{12} *go and speak*, so Je 35^{2}; ה׳ וְאָמַרְתָּ *go and say*, Is 38^{5} Je 28^{13} 34^{2} 35^{13} 39^{16}; ה׳ וְקָרָאתָ Je 2^{2} 3^{12}; also ה׳ וְרָחַצְתָּ 2 K 5^{10} *go and wash*, ה׳ וְקָנִיתָ Je 13^{1} 19^{1} *go and buy*, ה׳ וְעָמַדְתָּ 17^{19} *go and stand*. **d.** akin to the use of Inf. abs. are some instances of Pt. הֹלֵךְ + adj. (or pt.): וַיֵּלֶךְ הַפְּלִשְׁתִּי הֹלֵךְ וְקָרֵב 1 S 17^{41} *and the Philistine came continually nearer* (cf. 2 S 18^{25} supr.); in other cases as predicate, with same idea of *growing, increasing*: וְדָוִד הֹלֵךְ וְחָזֵק וּבֵית שָׁאוּל הֹלְכִים וְדַלִּים 2 S 3^{1} *and David was growing stronger and stronger, while the house of Saul were growing weaker and weaker*, cf. 2 Ch 17^{12} Est 9^{4} (of individuals), 2 S 15^{12} (of people); + 2 adj. וְהַנַּעַר שְׁמוּאֵל הֹלֵךְ וְגָדֵל וָטוֹב 1 S 2^{26}; cf. (with different order) of wind, Ec 1^{6} *goeth* (הוֹלֵךְ) *toward* the south, and turneth about (סוֹבֵב) unto the north, *the wind turneth about and about continually* (סוֹבֵב סֹבֵב הוֹלֵךְ הָרוּחַ); of sea הַיָּם הוֹלֵךְ וְסֹעֵר Jon 1$^{11.13}$ *the sea was growing more and more stormy*; also וַיְהִי קוֹל הַשֹּׁפָר הוֹלֵךְ וְחָזֵק מְאֹד Ex 19^{19} *and the sound of the trumpet kept growing louder and louder*; & in metaph. אֹרַח צַדִּיקִים כְּאוֹר נֹגַהּ הוֹלֵךְ וָאוֹר עַד־נְכוֹן הַיּוֹם Pr 4^{18} *the path of just men is like a shining light, growing lighter and lighter until the full day*.

5. In combination with other verbal forms: **a.** sq. Inf. of purpose (c. לְ) Gn 25^{22} 31^{19} 37^{25} (all JE) Nu 14^{38} (P) 24^{1} (JE), Ju 8^{1} 9$^{8.9.11.13}$ + oft.; esp. ה׳ לִקְרַאת *go to meet* Jos 9^{11} (JE), 2 S 19^{16} 1 K 18$^{16.16}$ +; sometimes with hostile sense 1 S 23^{28} 1 K 20^{27} 2 K 23^{29}; also ה׳ לָשׁוּב *go to return*, Ex 4^{21} (RV *go back*), cf. also שׁוּב לָלֶכֶת *return again* Ec 1^{7} 5^{14}; ה׳ לָבוֹא *go to come* (*enter*, etc.) Je 41^{17} cf. 2 Ch 26^{8}. **b.** sq. finite vb. *go and do* so and so: Gn 22^{13} 27^{14} Ex 2^{8} 4$^{27.29}$ (all JE), Dt 13$^{7.14}$ 17^{3} 24^{2} Is 2^{3} = Mi 4^{2} Je 11^{12} + oft.; וַיֵּלֶךְ וַיָּשָׁב Ex 4^{18} (E), יֵלֵךְ וְיָשֹׁב Dt 20$^{5.6.7.8}$, וַיֵּלְכוּ וַיָּשׁוּבוּ Ju 21^{23} cf. Ho 2^{9} 5^{15}; ה׳ וַיָּבוֹא *went & came* Nu 13^{26} (P), Ru 2^{3} 1 S 22^{5}

2 S 11^{22} 2 K 4^{25}; notably וַיֵּלֶךְ וַיִּשְׁלַח 2 K 3^{7} *and he went and sent.* **c.** following other verbs: וַיָּקֻמוּ וַיֵּלְכוּ Gn 22^{19} (E) cf. 24^{10} (J) 43^{8} (J) Nu 16^{25} (JE) Ju 4^{9}; נִסְעָה וְנֵלֵכָה Gn 33^{12} (J). **d.** esp. as result of action expr. in preced. vb., such as vb. of sending, etc.: וַיְשַׁלַּח אֶת־אֶחָיו וַיֵּלֵכוּ Gn 45^{24} (E) cf. Jos 1^{16} (D) 1 S 6^{8} Jb 38^{35}; also יִשָּׂאֵהוּ קָדִים וְיֵלַךְ 27^{21} *an east wind shall carry him off, and he shall depart;* וַיְגָרְשֵׁהוּ וַיֵּלַךְ ψ 34^{1} (title). (Cf. *depart* also of inanimate things **3** supr.) **e.** in longer series: וַיֵּלֶךְ וַיִּבְרַח וַיִּמָּלֵט 1 S 19^{12}; וַיִּסַּע וַיֵּלֶךְ וַיָּשָׁב . . . וַיֵּשֶׁב 2 K 19^{36} = Is 37^{37}; cf. Nu 24^{25} (JE); וַיָּקָם וַיֵּלֶךְ וַיָּבֹא Ju 19^{10}; also וַיָּקָם וַיָּבֹא וַיֵּלֶךְ 2 K 10^{12}. **f.** oft. in Imv. foll. by 2nd Imv. or equiv., (1) לֵךְ קַח־לִי Gn 27^{13} (J) *go, bring me* (them), cf. Ho 1^{2}; לְכוּ רְעוּ Gn 29^{7} (J) *go, feed* (them), cf. 37^{14} 42^{19} Ex 4^{19} + (in all c. 57 t.; only JED in Hex); but also (2) weakened to mere introductory word (as also supr. passim: esp. 2 K 3^{7} etc.), *go to,* or *come, do* (*let us do*) so & so; לְכָה נִכְרְתָה בְרִית Gn 31^{44} *come, let us make a compact,* cf. לְכָה נַשְׁקֶה 19^{32} (where subj. fem.); לְכוּ וְנֵלְכָה 1 S 9^{9} *come, and let us go,* so v^{10}, 11^{14} Is 2^{3} = Mi 4^{2}, cf. Zc 6^{7}+; even לֵךְ בֹּא וְאֶשְׁלְחָה 2 K 5^{5} *go to, come, and let me send,* cf. Is 22^{15} 26^{20} Ez 3$^{4.11}$, further Ju 19$^{11.13}$ 1 S 9^{5} 1 K 1^{12} ψ 34^{5}+ (in all c. 49 t.; only JE in Hex). (3) apparently intermediate, and shewing transition fr. (1) to (2) are: לְכוּ סֹרוּ לֶךְ־רֵד Ex 19^{24} 32^{7} cf. Ju 18^{2}; לְכוּ וְהִתְהַלְּכוּ; לֵךְ עֲלֵה מִזֶּה Ex 33^{1}; רְדוּ 1 S 15^{6} בָאָרֶץ Jos 18^{8} & לְכוּ בֹאוּ אַרְצָה Gn 47^{17} cf. 1 S 22^{5} 1 K 1^{13} 2 K 7^{9}; v. further לֵכְנָה שֹׁבְנָה Ru 1^{8} & שֹׁבְנָה לֵכְןָ v^{12}; also 2 S 3^{16} 1 K 19$^{15.20}$ + (in all c. 36 t.)

II. Fig.; the most common uses follow; in most the origin in a literal meaning is evident: †**1.** *pass away, die;* in phrases denoting or implying death (cf. Ar. هَلَكَ *perish*); וְהִנֵּה אָנֹכִי הוֹלֵךְ הַיּוֹם בְּדֶרֶךְ כָּל־הָאָרֶץ Jos 23^{14} (D) *lo, I am going to-day the way of all the earth* cf. 1 K 2^{2}; perh. also Gn 15^{2} (JE) *I pass away childless,* but possibly sub **2** infr.; also 2 S 12^{23} *I am going* (אֲנִי הֹלֵךְ) *to him* 2 S 12^{23}; so of mankind דּוֹר הֹלֵךְ וְדוֹר בָּא Ec 1^{4}; more explicitly, הַכֹּל הוֹלֵךְ אֶל־מָקוֹם אֶחָד הַכֹּל הָיָה מִן הֶעָפָר וְהַכֹּל שָׁב אֶל־הֶעָפָר Ec 3^{20} cf. 6^{6}; also הֹלֵךְ הָאָדָם בִּשְׁאוֹל אֲשֶׁר אַתָּה הֹלֵךְ שָׁמָּה 9^{10}, & אֶל־בֵּית עוֹלָמוֹ 12^{5}; cf. בְּטֶרֶם אֵלֵךְ וְאֵינֶנִּי ψ 39^{14} *before I depart and be not;* so acc. to some 2 Ch 21^{20} but cf. infr. **3 a** (2); once with weaker sense sq. inf., הִנֵּה אָנֹכִי הוֹלֵךְ לָמוּת Gn 25^{32} (J). **2.** *live* ('*walk*'), in general (cf. **Pi. Hithp.**) (usu. poet., with modifying words): כִּי־אֵלֵךְ בְּגֵיא צַלְמָוֶת ψ 23^{4} *though I walk in a valley of deep darkness;* cf. 138^{7} & אֵלֵךְ חֹשֶׁךְ Jb 29^{3}; קֹדֵר אֵלֵךְ ψ 42^{10}; ה׳ חֲשֵׁכִים Is 50^{10}, v. also Ez 3^{14}; perh. also Gn 15^{2} cf. **1** supr.; יֵלְכוּ מֵחַיִל אֶל־חָיִל ψ 84^{8} *they go from strength to strength;* הוֹלֵךְ בַּתֹּם יֵלֶךְ בֶּטַח Pr 10^{9}; esp. **3.** of moral and religious life; יְיַשֶּׁר־לָכֶת Pr 15^{21} *he maketh straight to walk* (walketh straight, upright); partic. **a.** *walk in* (בְּ) *ways* (counsels, statutes, etc.), (1) in good sense: (α) ה׳ בְּדֶרֶךְ תָּמִים ψ 101^{6}, cf. Is 30^{21} Je 6^{16} 1 K 8^{36} = 2 Ch 6^{27}; (β) in (בְּ) ways of י׳, esp. D: Dt 8^{6} (לְיִרְאָה אֹתוֹ ‖) cf. 10^{12}, 11^{22} (לְאַהֲבָה אֶת־י׳ ‖ etc.), 28^{9} (שָׁמַר מִצְוֹת י׳ ‖); v. also 13^{15}+; 1 K 11^{33} (sq. לַעֲשׂוֹת), v^{38} (sq. וְעָשִׂיתָ) 2 K 21^{22} ψ 119^{3} 128^{1}; בְּאֹרְחֹתָיו Is 2^{3} = Mi 4^{2}; further (sq. דֶּרֶךְ) Ju 2^{17}; (γ) †in commandments of י׳ 2 Ch 17^{4}; (δ) in his law(s) (תּוֹרָה) Ex 16$^{4.14}$ (J) 2 K 10^{31} Je 9^{12} 44^{23} (+ בְּחֻקֹּת & בְּעֵדְוֹת), 2 Ch 6^{16} Dn 9^{10}, cf. Ne 10^{30} (of אֱלֹהִים); (ε) †in his ordinances, statutes (חֻקּוֹת) Lv 26^{3} 1 K 6^{12} Je 44$^{10.23}$ (v. supr.), Ez 5$^{6.7}$ 11^{20} 18$^{9.17}$ 20$^{13.16.19.21}$, cf. בְּחֻקּוֹת חַיִּים 33^{15}; also בְּחֻקַּי 1 K 8^{61} Ez 11^{12} 36^{27}; (ζ) †in his judgments (מִשְׁפָּטִים) ψ 89^{31} Ez 37^{24}; (η) †in ordinances of David 1 K 3^{3}, cf. also infr.; (θ) in way(s) of good man 1 S 8$^{3.5}$ 2 Ch 21^{12}, of David 2 Ch 11^{17} 34^{2}, of David & Sol. 17^{3}. (2) in bad sense, (α) in (evil) ways c. בְּ 2 K 21^{21} Ez 16^{47} 23^{31} 2 Ch 22^{3}; cf. also (prob.) 2 Ch 21^{20} וַיֵּלֶךְ בְּלֹא חֶמְדָּה *and he lived undesirably* (cf. 𝔊 𝔙 Kmp Öt); > others *he departed* (died) *unregretted,* so AV RV; (β) sq. acc. 2 K 21^{21} Je 18^{15} (ה׳ נְתִיבוֹת); (γ) c. adverb. acc. הוֹלֵךְ עִקְּשׁוּת פֶּה Pr 6^{12} *one walking in perversity* (falseness) *of mouth* (cf. צְדָקוֹת Is 33^{15}); (δ) in (בְּ) ordinances, statutes (חֻקּוֹת) of bad men Lv 18^{3} 20^{23} (both H) 2 K 17$^{8.19}$ Ez 20^{18} (בְּחוּקֵּי). **b.** *walk with* (עִם, אֶת) i.e. associate, be familiar with: בְּשָׁלוֹם וּבְמִישׁוֹר ה׳ אִתִּי Mal 2^{6} *in peace and uprightness he walked with me* (י׳); הַצְנֵעַ לֶכֶת עִם־אֱלֹהֶיךָ Mi 6^{8}; but also of people at variance with י׳ וַהֲלַכְתֶּם עִמִּי קֶרִי Lv 26^{23} cf. v$^{27.40}$; & of י׳ at variance with people וְהָלַכְתִּי . . . עִמָּכֶם בְּקֶרִי v^{24} cf. v^{28} (all H); with men, אֶת־חֲכָמִים Pr 13^{20}; עִם אַנְשֵׁי רֶשַׁע Jb 34^{8}; cf. *walk with* (עִם) *vanity* Jb 31^{5}. **c.** *walk before* י׳ (לִפְנֵי י׳; c. בֶּאֱמֶת, בְּכָל־לְבָבָם etc.) 1 K 2^{4} 3^{6} 8$^{23.25}$ 9^{4} 2 Ch 6^{16} 7^{17} cf.

ה׳ קְדֹרַנִּית מִפְּנֵי י׳ Mal 3^{14}; *walk before the living* (i.e. walk *aright* before them) Ec 6^{8}. **d.** *walk, go, after* (אַחֲרֵי) (1) י׳ Dt 13^{5} 1 K 14^{8} Je 2^{2} Ho 11^{10}+; (2) other gods, Ju 2^{12} esp. D: Dt 4^{3} 6^{14} 8^{19} 13^{3} 28^{14} Je 2^{23} 7^{6} 8^{2} 11^{10} 16^{11} 25^{6}+; cf. *go & serve other gods* Jos 23^{16} Dt $13^{7.14}$ 17^{3} 29^{17} (cf. 28^{14} supr.); (3) things which do not profit Je 2^{8}; (4) vanity Ho 5^{11} (reading שָׁוְא cf. VB); v. also Am 2^{4}. **e.** *walk* in (1) one's integrity, etc., בְּתֻמִּי ψ 26^{11} cf. 84^{12} Pr 10^{9}, v. also הֹלְכֵי תֹם ψ 15^{2}, תְּמִים ה׳ Pr 2^{7}; (2) bad sense, in (בְּ) sin 1 K $15^{3.26.34}$ $16^{2.26}$ 2 K $13^{6.11}$+ (esp. of wicked kings); (evil) counsel 2 Ch 22^{5} cf. ψ 1^{1}. **f.** (1) לֵב as subj., (α) = *thoughts,* לֹא לִבִּי הָלַךְ 2 K 5^{26} *did not my thoughts go forth;* (β) *evil inclination,* Jb 31^{7}; sq. אַחֲרֵי ... אֶל־לֵב שִׁקּוּצֵיהֶם . . . לִבָּם הֹלֵךְ Ez 11^{21}; 20^{16} אַחֲרֵי גִלּוּלֵיהֶם, 33^{31} אַחֲרֵי בִּצְעָם; (2) נֶפֶשׁ = *desire,* טוֹב מַרְאֵה עֵינַיִם מֵהֲלָךְ־נָפֶשׁ Ec 6^{9} *better is sight of the eyes than outgoing of desire.* **4.** other fig. uses: *depart from* מִפְּנֵי Ho 11^{2} (from prophets as God's messengers; opp. קָרָא); *go into,* הָלְכוּ בַכְּלִמָּה Is 45^{16} *they have gone into confusion* (judgment on idol-makers); etc. †**Niph.** *Pf.* 1 s. כְּצֵל כִּנְטוֹתוֹ נֶהֱלָכְתִּי ψ 109^{23} *like a shadow when it stretches out I am gone* (cf. היה **Niph.**)

†**Pi.** (chiefly poet. & late) *Pf.* הִלַּכְתִּי Jb 30^{28} ψ 131^{1}; הִלָּכְתִּי ψ 38^{7}; 3 pl. הִלְּכוּ Jb 24^{10} La 5^{18}; *Impf.* יְהַלֵּךְ Ez 18^{9}+2 t.; וַיְהַלֵּךְ 1 K 21^{27}; 1 s. אֲהַלֵּךְ ψ 86^{11}+2 t.; 3 mpl. יְהַלֵּכוּ Hb 3^{11}+2 t.; יְהַלֵּכוּן ψ 89^{16}+2 t.; 1 pl. נְהַלֵּךְ ψ 55^{15} Is 59^{9}; *Imv.* הַלֵּךְ Ec 11^{9}; *Pt.* מְהַלֵּךְ Pr 6^{11} ψ 104^{3}; מְהַלְּכִים Ec 4^{15};—**1.** *walk* in or with a throng sq. בְּ loc.: בְּבֵית א׳ נְהַלֵּךְ בְּרָגֶשׁ ψ 55^{15}; *walk, tread on coals* עַל־הַגֶּחָלִים Pr 6^{28}; of idols ψ 115^{7} *they do not walk,* have not the power of walking (cf. יִצְעָדוּ Je 10^{5}); of one *tramping,* formidable, sim. of poverty וּבָא־כִמְהַלֵּךְ רֵאשֶׁךָ Pr 6^{11},—a highwayman acc. to Ges Ew Hi Now, cf. 𝔊; מַחְסֹרְךָ כְּאִישׁ מָגֵן || (cf. also Hithp. 24^{34}); of י׳, *walking* (in majesty), *marching,* עַל־כַּנְפֵי רוּחַ ψ 104^{3} *on the wings of the wind;* of righteousness, personified, צֶדֶק לְפָנָיו יְהַלֵּךְ ψ 85^{14}; of wisdom בְּאֹרַח צְדָקָה אֲהַלֵּךְ Pr 8^{20} *in the path of righteousness do I walk* (stedfastly, unswervingly); of animals, *go about, prowl,* עַל הַר־צִיּוֹן שֶׁהֹשָׁמֵם שׁוּעָלִים הִלְּכוּ בוֹ (Qr שֶׁשָּׁמֵם) La 5^{18}, of ships, in (stately) movement ψ 104^{26}; of springs 104^{10} *between mountains they go (run, flow)*; of arrows Hb 3^{11} *at the light of thine arrows* that go (*fly, shoot;* cf. **Hithp.** ψ 77^{18}). **2.** also of *walking about* = living הַמְהַלְּכִים תַּחַת הַשָּׁמֶשׁ Ec 4^{15}; עָרוֹם הִלְּכוּ בְּלִי לְבוּשׁ Jb 24^{10} *naked they keep going about* (freq.), *without clothing;* so of going about as mourner קֹדֵר הִלַּכְתִּי Jb 30^{28} ψ 38^{7} (cf. **Qal** ψ 42^{10}); בָּאֲפֵלוֹת נְהַלֵּךְ Is 59^{9} *in darkness we walk* (of distress); on the other hand בְּאוֹר פָּנֶיךָ יְהַלֵּכוּן ψ 89^{16} (of blessedness & prosperity). **3.** *depart, go entirely away* (מִן) מִמְּקוֹם קָדוֹשׁ יְהַלֵּכוּ Ec 8^{10} *from the holy place they must depart* (on text cf. VB; || וְיִשְׁתַּכְּחוּ בָעִיר). **4.** fig. of mode of life, action, etc.: of particular path of one's life בְּאֹרַח־זוּ אֲהַלֵּךְ ψ 142^{4}; specif. in good sense וַיְהַלֵּךְ אַט 1 K 21^{27} *and he* (Ahab) *walked softly* (as a penitent); oftener c. בְּ of path in which: בִּדְרָכַי יְהַלֵּכוּ ψ 81^{14} *that in my ways they would walk!* cf. 86^{11} (בַּאֲמִתֶּךָ), Ez 18^{9} (בְּחֻקּוֹתַי) יְהַלֵּךְ; in bad or doubtful sense וְהַלֵּךְ בְּדַרְכֵי לִבְּךָ וּבְמַרְאֵי עֵינֶיךָ Ec 11^{9}; cf. also לֹא הִלַּכְתִּי בִּגְדֹלוֹת ψ 131^{1} *I do not walk (move, tread) among great things* (|| וּבְנִפְלָאוֹת מִמֶּנִּי; fig. of humility, cf. also v^{a}).

†**Hithp.** *Pf.* הִתְהַלֵּךְ Gn 6^{9} 1 S 30^{31}; וְהִתְהַלֵּךְ consec. Ex 21^{19} 1 S 2^{35}; 2 ms. הִתְהַלַּכְתָּ Ez 28^{14} Jb 38^{16}; 1 s. הִתְהַלַּכְתִּי Gn 24^{40}+5 t., etc.; *Impf.* יִתְהַלָּךְ Pr 23^{31} Jb 18^{8} 22^{14}; 1 s. אֶתְהַלֵּךְ ψ 43^{2}+2 t.; וָאֶתְהַלְּכָה ψ 119^{45}; 3 mpl. יִתְהַלְּכוּ 1 S 2^{30}+2 t.; וַיִּתְהַלְּכוּ Ju 21^{24}+3 t.; יִתְהַלָּכוּ 1 S 23^{13}+3 t.; יִתְהַלָּכוּן ψ 12^{9}; 3 fpl. וַתִּתְהַלַּכְנָה Zc 6^{7}, etc.; *Imv.* הִתְהַלֵּךְ Gn 13^{17} 17^{1}; הִתְהַלְּכוּ Jos 18^{8} Zc 6^{7}; *Inf.* (לְ)הִתְהַלֵּךְ ψ 56^{14}+4 t.; sf. הִתְהַלֶּכְךָ Pr 6^{22}; *Pt.* מִתְהַלֵּךְ Gn 3^{8}+7 t.; fs. מִתְהַלֶּכֶת Ez 1^{13}; mpl. מִתְהַלְּכִים 1 S 25^{27};—*walk, walk about, move to and fro:* **1.** lit. **a.** *traverse,* in this direction and that, Gn 13^{17} (J; בָּאָרֶץ) Jos 18^{4} (JE), v^{8} (*id.;* לְכוּ וְהִתְהַ׳ בָאָרֶץ); cf. Jb 1^{7} = 2^{2} (both || שׁוּט) Zc $1^{10.11}$; similarly also 1 Ch 21^{4}; of fiery appearance in Ezek.'s vision מִתְהַ׳ בֵּין הַחַיּוֹת Ez 1^{13}; of horses in Zec.'s vision Zc 6^{7} (לָלֶכֶת לְהִתְ׳ בָּאָרֶץ), v^{7} (לְכוּ הִתְהַלְּכוּ בָא׳), v^{7}; *go in different directions* וַיִּתְהַ׳ מִשָּׁם בְּנֵי יִשְׂרָאֵל . . . . אִישׁ לְשִׁבְטוֹ Ju 21^{24} (|| וַיֵּצְאוּ מִשָּׁם etc.); so of lightning flashes as *arrows* of י׳ ψ 77^{18} *went hither & thither;* of water running off different ways 58^{8} (sim. of vanishing of wicked). **b.** *walk, walk about* הִתְהַלֵּךְ בַּחוּץ עַל־מִשְׁעַנְתּוֹ Ex 21^{19} (JE) i.e. leaning upon his staff; Pr 6^{22} (distinguished fr. שָׁכַב, הֵקִיץ); 2 S 11^{2} (עַל־גַּג בֵּית הַמֶּלֶךְ); וּבְחֵקֶר תְּהוֹם הִתְהַלָּכְתָּ Jb 38^{16} *and in the farthest ground of*

the deep hast thou walked? בתוך אַבְנֵי־אֵשׁ הִתְהַלָּכְתָּ Ez 28^{14}, so also of ׳י, walking on earth, in anthropomorphic conception קול י׳ אלהים מתהלך בַּגָּן Gn 3^{8} (J) *the sound of* ׳י *Elohim walking about in the garden*, of God (*El*) וחוג שָׁמַיִם יִתְהַלָּךְ Jb 22^{14} *and the vault of heaven he walketh*, *walk about in front of* (לפני) Est 2^{11}, *attend*, *follow*, of retainers הַמִּתְהַלְּכִים בְּרַגְלֵי אֲדֹנִי 1 S 25^{27}, *wander*, of Israel מִגּוֹי אֶל־גּוֹי ψ 105^{13} = 1 Ch 16^{20}, *rove about*, of David and his band אֲשֶׁר־הִתְהַלֵּךְ־שָׁם 1 S 30^{31}, וַיִּתְהַלְּכוּ בַּאֲשֶׁר יִתְהַלָּכוּ 23^{13} (on this phr cf Lag Psalt Hieron 1874, 156 f Dr ^{Sm}), *walk about*, *prowl*, of Jehoiachin under fig. of lion, וַיִּתְה׳ Ez 19^{6}, cf also וּבָא־מִתְהַלֵּךְ רֵישֶׁךָ בתוך־אֲרָיוֹת Pr 24^{34} *and thy poverty cometh marching* (cf. **Pi.** 6^{11}), *glide*, *flow* of wine יתה׳ בְּמֵישָׁרִים Pr 23^{31} *glideth down smoothly* (VB; cf. **Qal 3** Ct 7^{10}), note esp the foll., where emphasis lies not on verb, but on an auxiliary word; these cases form the natural transition to the figurative use.—ψ 12^{9} *on every side wicked men are walking;* בְּצֶלֶם יִתְהַלֶּךְ־אִישׁ 39^{7} *in appearance* (*semblance*, lit *image* cf Che $^{crit\ n}$) *walketh a man*, also לָמָּה קֹדֵר אֶתְהַלֵּךְ 43^{2} (cf **Qal** 42^{10}, **Pi.** 38^{7} Jb 30^{28}) **2.** fig *walk about* = *live*, the king before (לפני) his people 1 S 12^{2}, so of Samuel v^{2}, of priest 2^{35} (לפני משיחי), of friendly intercourse with (את) men 1 S 25^{15}, cf כְּרֵעַ כְּאָח־לִי הִתְהַלָּכְתִּי ψ 35^{14}, of man's relation to God: especially sq לִפְנֵי, ה׳ לְפָנַי וֶהְיֵה תָמִים Gn 17^{1} (P) *walk before me* (live constantly in my presence) *and* (*so*) *be perfect*, cf 24^{40} (J), 48^{15} (E), ה׳ לְפָנֶיךָ באמת ובלבב שָׁלֵם 2 K 20^{3} = Is 38^{3}, as token of divine favour יִתְהַלְּכוּ לְפָנַי עַד־עוֹלָם 1 S 2^{30} (v esp Dr, on sense here & elsewh); ψ 116^{9} אֶתְהַלֵּךְ לפני י׳ בְּארצות הַחַיִּים, 56^{14} (בְּאוֹר הַחַיִּים); בשמו יתה׳ Zc 10^{12} *they shall walk in his name;* c אֵת, of Enoch and Noah ה׳ אֶת־הָאֱלֹהִים Gn $5^{22.24}$ 6^{9} (denoting intimacy, fellowship all P), further ה׳ בַּאֲמִתֶּךָ ψ 26^{3} *I have walked in thy faithfulness*, מתה׳ בְּתֻמּוֹ צַדִּיק Pr 20^{7} *he that walketh justly in his* (own) *integrity*, אֶתְה׳ בְּתָם־לְבָבִי בקרב ביתי ψ 101^{2}, cf also ψ 119^{45} *and let me walk in a large place* (untrammelled, undismayed), of the wicked מִתְהַלֵּךְ בַּאֲשָׁמָיו ψ 68^{22} *one going on in his guilty deeds*, בַּחֲשֵׁכָה יתה׳ ψ 82^{5} they *walk in darkness* (|| לֹא יָדְעוּ וְלֹא יָבִינוּ); of their exposure עַל־שְׂבָכָה יִתְה׳ Jb 18^{8} *he walketh on net-work*, (snare, cf שבכה; || שֻׁלַּח בְּרֶשֶׁת בְּרַגְלָיו);

esp of ׳י as accompanying Israel מתה׳ בְּקֶרֶב מַחֲנֶךָ Dt 23^{15} *walk in the midst*, etc, בְּתוֹכְכֶם Lv 26^{12}, 2 S 7^{7} *wherever* (בכל אֲשֶׁר) *I have walked with* (*among* ב) *all* (*the sons of*) *Isr.* = 1 Ch 17^{6}, as inhabiting a tent, on the march, וָאֶהְיֶה מִתְהַלֵּךְ בְּאֹהֶל וּבְמִשְׁכָּן 2 S 7^{6} *and I was walking in a tent and in a tabernacle.*

†**Hiph.** *Pf* 3 ms הוֹלִיךְ (as if from ילך, i e a verb פ״י, cf reff sub **Qal** *Impf* supr) 2 K 24^{15}, sf. הוֹלִיכְךָ Dt 8^{2}, וְהוֹלִיכוּ consec. Pr 16^{29}, etc.; *Impf* יוֹלִיךְ Ec 10^{20}, יוֹלֵךְ Je 32^{5}, juss יוֹלֵךְ Dt 28^{36}, שֶׁיֹּלֵךְ Ec 5^{14}, וַיּוֹלֶךְ Ex 14^{21} 2 K 6^{19} + 2 t., אוֹלִיךְ 1 s וַיֹּלֶךְ La 3^{2}, sf וַיּוֹלִכֵנִי Ez 40^{24} 43^{1} 47^{6} 2 S 13^{13} Ez 32^{14}, cohort. וְאוֹלִיכָה 2 K 6^{19}, וָאוֹלֵךְ Am 2^{10} + 3 t, etc.; *Imv.* הוֹלֵךְ Nu 17^{11}; fs. הֵילִיכִי Ex 2^{9} (Bö $^{II\ 461,\ \S\ 1103}$; but rd prob. הוֹלִיכִי Ol $^{\S\ 256.\ b}$ Ges $^{\S\ 69\ 2.\ R\ 8}$), mpl הַלִיכוּ 2 K 17^{27}, *Inf.* sf לְהוֹלִיכוֹ 2 Ch 36^{6}; *Pt.* מוֹלִיךְ Je 2^{6} + 4 t.; sf. מוֹלִיכְךָ Dt 8^{15}, מוֹלִכֵךְ Je 2^{17}; מוֹלִיכָם Is 63^{12}, fpl. מוֹלִכוֹת Zc 5^{10};—**1.** *lead, bring:* sq. acc. usually of person, **a.** c ב of space or region through which, Dt 8^{15} (Isr. in wilderness) Je 2^{6} ψ 136^{16}, so also Is 48^{21}; בַּדֶּרֶךְ Je 2^{17}; cf Jos 24^{3} (E), Is 63^{13} ψ 106^{9}; also fig. Is 42^{16} *and I will lead* (*the*) *blind in a way* (בְּדֶרֶךְ) *they know not*, **b.** c acc. pers, ב of space + acc of time וָאוֹלֵךְ אֶתְכֶם אַרְבָּעִים שָׁנָה בַּמִּדְבָּר Dt 29^{4}, so Am 2^{10} (sq. Inf of purpose c לְ) **c.** sq. acc. pers + acc. of *way, road*, Dt 8^{2}, cf. דֶּרֶךְ הַדָּרוֹם Ez 40^{24} (acc. of direction) **d.** sq acc pers. + acc. of place or condition to which . . . אֶת־נְשֵׁי הַמֶּלֶךְ הוֹלִיךְ גּוֹלָה 2 K 24^{15} *the women of the king*, etc., *he led into exile* (מִירוּשָׁלַםִ בָּבֶלָה); so also, of exile וְהוֹלַכְתִּיהָ הַמִּדְבָּר Ho 2^{16}; בָּבֶל Je 32^{5}, cf of Yahweh's chastisement, La 3^{2} *me hath he driven and brought*, into *darkness and not into light;* sq acc pers + אֶל: אֶל־גּוֹי etc. Dt 28^{36} (of exile), אֶל־נַחֲלֵי־מַיִם Je 31^{9}, אֶל־הַשַּׁעַר Ez 43^{1}; אֶל־הָעֵדָה Nu 17^{11} (P; implic. obj. being censer), אֶל of pers 2 K 6^{19} Je 52^{26}, עַל in || 2 K 25^{20}; עַל also 1 K 1^{38} וַיֹּלִכוּ אֹתוֹ עַל־גִּיחוֹן (see sub עַל **7 c** β). **e.** sq acc. pers. + ־ָה loc. שֹׁמְרוֹנָה 2 K 6^{19}, בָּבֶלָה 2 Ch 33^{11} 36^{6} (cf. 2 K 24^{15} supr); cf שָׁמָּה 2 K 17^{27} **2.** *lead away* sq acc. pers + appos; מוֹלִיךְ יוֹעֲצִים שׁוֹלָל Jb 12^{17} *he* (׳י) *leadeth away counsellors despoiled* cf. v^{19}; of Yahweh's judgment on the wicked ψ 125^{5} ׳י *will lead them away with* (אֶת) *the workers of iniquity* **3.** *carry, bring*: c obj. help-

less, or inanimate: **a.** + acc loc, Josiah to Jerusalem (יְרוּשָׁלִַם) 2 Ch 35[24] (וַיְבִיאֻהוּ in ‖ 2 K 23[30]), cf Zc 5[10] *whither are these carrying the ephah?* אָנָה אוליך אֶת־חֶרְפָּתִי 2 S 13[13]. **b.** *carry, take, take away,* הילִיכִי אֶת־הַיֶּלֶד Ex 2[9] (E; on form cf supr); also carry away בְּיָדוֹ, in his hand, Ec 5[14], of the spread of a careless speech Ec 10[20] *fowl of the heavens shall carry the voice* (‖ בַּעַל הַכְּנָפַיִם יַגִּיד דָּבָר). **4.** fig., of influence on character: c acc pers + בְּ *into*· Pr 16[29] *and he will lead him into a way* that is *not good* (i e. sinful) **5. a.** *cause to walk, go,* men (i e. עַמִּי יִשְׂרָאֵל) on (עַל) the mountains of Israel Ez 36[12] (‖ וְהָיִיתָ לָהֶם לְנַחֲלָה ,וִירֵשׁוּךָ); cf וָאוֹלֵךְ אֶתְכֶם קוֹמְמִיּוּת Lv 26[13] *and I caused you to walk upright* (fig, opp to being bowed down by a yoke); Is 63[12] *that caused his glorious arm to go at* (לְ) *the right hand of Moses* **b.** *cause to flow, run* Ez 32[14] *and rivers like oil will I cause to flow.* **c.** *cause to depart, retire, go back,* ׳י, the sea, Ex 14[21] (בְּ instr, בְּרוּחַ קָדִים).

†הֵלֶךְ **n.m. traveller** (properly *a going, journey,* whence *wayfarer, traveller*) only הָארֵחַ הַבָּא לוֹ ‖) 2 S 12[4] וַיָּבֹא הֵלֶךְ לְאִישׁ הֶעָשִׁיר, הָאִישׁ הַבָּא לוֹ),—in MT 1 S 14[26] ,הֵלֶךְ דְּבַשׁ ה׳ must be cstr. & = *flowing,* or *dropping* (*of honey*), but rd. rather הָלַךְ 𝔊 The Klo We Dr (& דְּבֹרוֹ for דְּבַשׁ q v, 𝔊 We Dr)

†[הָלִיךְ] **n.[m.]** *step,* only pl. sf בִּרְחֹץ הֲלִיכַי בְּחֵמָה Jb 29[6] *when my steps were bathed in cream* (חֶמְאָה = חֵמָה) hyperb of abundance, wealth.

†[הֲלִיכָה] **n.f. a going, way, travelling-company,** sf. הֲלִיכָתָם Na 2[6] Qr (הלוכתם Kt); elsewh only pl., cstr. הֲלִיכוֹת ψ 68[25], so Pr 31[27] Qr (הילכות Kt), הֲלִכוֹת Hb 3[6], הֲלִיכֹת Jb 6[19]; sf הֲלִיכוֹתֶיךָ ψ 68[25];—**1.** *going, walk,* **a.** Na 2[6] *they shall stumble in their going;* elsewh. pl *goings.* **b.** ψ 68[25.25] of *going, marching, progress of God into the sanctuary* (בַּקֹּדֶשׁ; so Hup Pe Che; Ew Hi De *in holiness*) ref either to solemn processions of worshippers (e g. De) or, perh. better, to the theophanic progress of God himself (e g. Che), also **c.** of goings = *doings* צוֹפִיָּה ה׳ בֵּיתָהּ Pr 31[27] *watching the doings of her household;* of God Hb 3[6] הֲלִכוֹת עוֹלָם לוֹ *ways of eternity* (al. *of old*) *are his.* **2.** *travelling-company, caravan* הֲלִיכֹת שְׁבָא Jb 6[19] (‖ אָרְחוֹת תֵּמָא).

†[מַהֲלָךְ] **n.m.**[Ne 2.6] *walk, journey, going* (late); cstr. מַהֲלַךְ Ez 42[4] + 2 t; sf. מַהֲלָכְךָ Ne 2[6]; pl מַהְלְכִים Zc 3[7],—**1.** *walk* 'of 10 cubits' breadth before the chambers' in Ezekiel's temple Ez 42[4] (cf. Da). **2.** *journey* fr. Bab. to Jerusalem Ne 2[6]; of dimension of Nineveh, *a journey of three days* Jon 3[3] i e diameter or length, cf v[4]; (acc to Herodot[v 53] one day's journey = 150 stadia, = length of Nineveh acc. to Diod[ii 3]). **3.** pl. *goings,* i.e *free access* (VB) Zc 3[7].

†[תַּהֲלוּכָה] **n.f.** procession, only pl. תַּהֲלֻכֹת Ne 12[31] of thanksgiving-processions at dedication of wall

†I. [הָלַל] **vb. shine** (acc to Thes al = II הלל (*splenduit,* from *sonuit acute, clare,* so Thes; these mngs, however, merely assumed), but v. Lag[Or ii 19] & sub foll; cf. Ar. هَلَّ *begin to shine,* هِلَال *new moon,* As *êllu, bright* COT[Gloss])—**Qal** only *Inf.* sf. בְּהִלּוֹ נֵרוֹ עֲלֵי רֹאשִׁי Jb 29[3] *when it,* viz. *his lamp, shone upon my head* (cf Ew[§ 309 c]), fig. of God's favour **Hiph.** *Impf* יָהֵל Jb 31[26], 3 fs. תָּהֶל Jb 41[10], 3 mpl. יָהֵלּוּ Is 13[10],—*flash forth light,* of heavenly bodies, אוֹר = *sun* Jb 31[26] (‖ יָרֵחַ יָקָר הֹלֵךְ); sq. acc. cogn כּוֹכְבֵי הַשָּׁמַיִם וּכְסִילֵיהֶם לֹא יָהֵלּוּ אוֹרָם Is 13[10] (‖ יָרֵחַ לֹא־יַגִּיהַּ אוֹרוֹ & ,חָשַׁךְ הַשֶּׁמֶשׁ), also of crocodile עֲטִישֹׁתָיו תָּהֶל אוֹר Jb 41[10] *his sneezings flash forth light* (shining water-drops)

†הֵילֵל **n.m. appell. shining one,** epith of king of Babylon, אֵיךְ נָפַלְתָּ מִשָּׁמַיִם ה׳ בֶּן־שָׁחַר Is 14[12] *how art thou fallen, shining one, son of dawn!* i e star of the morning. (Cf. As. *muštilil,* epith of (Venus as) morning-star III R 57[60] Opp[JAS 1871, 448] Schr[SK 1874, 337] COT[ad loc.])

†II [הָלַל] **vb. be boastful, Pi. praise** (Ar. هَلَّ *shout,* both in joy & (if conject. of No RS be right, v. cit. infr.) in terror; esp. II. in formula of worship; Syr. Pa ܗܰܠܶܠ *cecinit, laudavit;* cf NH הִלּוּל *praise,* הַלֵּל *id., Hallel* (ψ 113–118), Aram. הִילּוּלָא *marriage-song,* &c.; on As. *alâlu, shout for joy, rejoice* v. Lyon[Sargontexte 66 (Cylinder 1 36)] also Winckler[Sargontexte 134, 1 194, 156, 1 149] KB[ii. 1 36 80. 1 194]; all variations of *cry aloud,* cf No[ZMG 1887, 723] RS[Sem. 411]; perh. orig. *break through,* or *out* (in a cry), cf. We[Skizzen iii. 107 ff., esp. 109], comp also (acc to Prat[BAS i 369 f.]) Eth. ተሀለለ: *implore* (cf. Amhar. Tigr.), & መሀለ: *swear*)—**Qal** *Impf.* 2 mpl. תָּהֹלּוּ ψ 75[5], *Pt* הוֹלְלִים ψ 5[6] + 2 t.,—*be boastful* אַל־תָּהֹלּוּ ψ 75[5] (‖ אַל־

(תָּרִים קַרְנֵ); pt. *boastful ones, boasters* ψ 5^{6} (‖ פֹּעֲלֵי אָוֶן); 73^{3} 75^{5} (both ‖ רְשָׁעִים). **Pi.** *Pf.* הִלֵּל ψ 10^{3}, 1 s. sf. הִלַּלְתִּיךָ ψ 119^{164}; 3 mpl. וְהִלְּלוּ consec. Is 62^{9}, sf. הִלְלוּךָ Is 64^{10}, etc.; *Impf.* יְהַלֶּל־ ψ 63^{6} 102^{19}; sf. יְהַלֶּלְךָ Pr 27^{2}, יְהַלְלֶךָּ Is 38^{18}, וַיְהַלְלוּהָ Pr 31^{28}; 1 s. אֲהַלֵּל ψ 56^{5} + 2 t., cohort. אֲהַלְלָה ψ 69^{31} + 2 t., etc.; *Imv.* fs. הַלְלִי ψ 146^{1} 147^{12}; mpl. הַלְלוּ ψ 104^{35} + 30 t. ψ + Je 20^{13} 31^{7}; sf. הַלְלוּהוּ ψ 22^{24} + 15 t. ψ; *Inf. abs.* הַלֵּל 1 Ch 16^{36}; *cstr.* הַלֵּל 2 S 14^{25} + 16 t. Chr; *Pt.* pl. מְהַלְלִים 1 Ch 23^{5} + 4 t. Ch;—**1.** *praise* man or woman, acc. וַיְהַלְלוּ אֹתָהּ אֶל־פַּרְעֹה Gn 12^{15} (J) *and they praised her to Pharaoh*, cf. Pr 27^{2} 31$^{28.31}$ Ct 6^{9}; וְהַמְהַלְלִים אֶת־הַמֶּלֶךְ 2 Ch 23^{12} *and those praising* (shouting acclamations to) *the king;* v. also לְהַלֵּל מְאֹד 2 S 14^{25} (of Absalom's beauty); in bad sense עֹזְבֵי תוֹרָה יְהַלְלוּ רָשָׁע Pr 28^{4} *deserters of law praise a wicked man.* **2.** usually praise י׳, אֱלֹהִים, etc.: **a.** sq. acc. of heathen god Ju 16^{24}. **b.** obj. י׳ (אֱלֹהִים); ψ 119^{164} (עַל *on account of*), subj. heaven, earth, seas, etc., ψ 69^{35}; תְּחִי נַפְשִׁי וּתְהַלְלֶךָּ ψ 119^{175}; in summons to all creatures to praise 148$^{5.13}$; Is 38^{18} לֹא שְׁאוֹל תּוֹדֶךָּ מָוֶת יְהַלְלֶךָּ (cf. ψ 115^{17}); often of public worship in sanctuary, Is 62^{9} (thanksgiving in sanctuary after harvest), cf. 64^{10} ψ 22^{23} (‖ אֲסַפְּרָה שִׁמְךָ), v^{27} 35^{18} 109^{30} (both ‖ אוֹדְךָ) 107^{32} (‖ יְרוֹמְמוּהוּ) 84^{5}, v. also 146^{2} (‖ אֲזַמְּרָה לֵא׳) 149^{3} (c. בְּ instr.; ‖ יְזַמְּרוּ לוֹ); also obj. שֵׁם י׳ (in some cases of public worship) ψ 74^{21} 148^{5}, Jo 2^{26} (thanksgiving after harvest); ψ 69^{31} שֵׁם־אֱלֹהִים בְּשִׁיר (‖ וַאֲגַדְּלֶנּוּ בְתוֹדָה), 145^{2} (‖ אֲבָרְכֶךָּ); further, ψ 56^{5} בֵּאלֹהִים אֲהַלֵּל דְּבָרוֹ, also v^{11} + v^{11b} ביהוה ונו׳, but cf. Hup Che on 11^{b} as editorial addition; obj. not expressed הַשְׁמִיעוּ הַלְלוּ וְאִמְרוּ הוֹשַׁע י׳ אֶת־עַמְּךָ Je 31^{7}, וְשִׂפְתֵי רְנָנוֹת יְהַלֶּל־פִּי ψ 63^{6}. **c.** use of Imv. deserves special notice: הַלְלוּהוּ ψ 22^{24} (‖ כַּבְּדוּהוּ; of temple-worship cf. v$^{23.25}$); also in summons to angels, sun, moon, etc. (all created things) to praise י׳ 148$^{2.2.3.3.4}$ 150^{1}; of temple-worship 150^{2} (בְּ *on account of*) v^{2} (כְּ), v$^{3.3.4.4.5.5}$ (all c. בְּ instr.); further Je 20^{13} (‖ שִׁירוּ לי׳), הַלְלוּ אֶת־י׳ ψ 117^{1} (addressed to nations, ‖ שַׁבְּחוּהוּ), 148^{7} (created things), הַלְלִי אֱלֹהַיִךְ צִיּוֹן 147^{12} (‖ שַׁבְּחִי יְרוּשָׁלַםִ אֶת־י׳). **d.** note esp.: *praise ye Yah!* הַלְלוּ־יָהּ ψ 135^{3}, liturgical (‖ זַמְּרוּ לִשְׁמוֹ); elsewh. always one word v. Baer$^{ψ\ p.\ 115}$, & alw. at beginning or end of ψ (chiefly late), appar. liturgical; הַלְלוּיָהּ ψ 104^{35} (‖ בָּרְכִי נַפְשִׁי אֶת־י׳), elsewh. הַלְלוּיָהּ: (1) at beginning ψ 106^{1} 111^{1} (both ‖ הודה) 112^{1} 113^{1} (‖ הַלְלוּ & ה׳ אֶת־שֵׁם י׳), 135^{1} (‖ *id.*), 146^{1} (‖ הַלְלִי נַפְשִׁי אֶת־י׳), 147^{1} (sq. זַמְּרָה in cl. with כִּי), 148^{1} (‖ הַלְלוּ אֶת־י׳, הַלְלוּהוּ), 149^{1} (‖ שִׁירוּ לי׳), 150^{1} (‖ הַלְלוּ־אֵל, הַלְלוּהוּ); (2) at end ψ 104^{35} (supr.), 105^{45} 106^{48} 113^{9} 115^{18} (‖ נְבָרֵךְ יָהּ), 116^{19} 117^{2} 135^{21} (‖ בָּרוּךְ י׳) 146^{10} 147^{20} 148^{14} 149^{9} 150^{6} (‖ כֹּל הַנְּשָׁמָה תְּהַלֵּל יָהּ); add to these (not liturgical) כֹּל נְשָׁמָה תְּהַלֵּל יָהּ ψ 102^{19}, יְהַלֶּל־יָהּ 150^{6}, לֹא הַמֵּתִים יְהַלְלוּ־יָהּ 115^{17}. **e.** also sq. ליהוה, in Chr, of technical Levitical function (cf. Lag$^{Or.\ ii.\ 18\ ff.}$, who limits this technical הלל to priests, using חֲצֹצְרוֹת, *for a signal to the people*; v. e.g. Ne 12^{24} cf. v^{27}), 1 Ch 16^{4} (with instrumental music, cf. בִּכְלֵי נְבָלִים וּבְכִנֹּרוֹת & בִּמְצִלְתַּיִם, all v^{5}, and Ne 12^{27}) 23^{30} 25^{3} (all ‖ הוֹדוֹת); exercised (apparently) by both priests and Levites Ezr 3^{11} (‖ הוֹדוֹת) cf. v^{11}; by Levites 2 Ch 20^{19} (בְּקוֹל גָּדוֹל), 29^{30} (בְּדִבְרֵי דָוִיד) in which the people also joined 1 Ch 16^{36}; also 2 Ch 5^{13} (בַּחֲצֹצְרוֹת וּבִמְצִלְתַּיִם וּבִכְלֵי הַשִּׁיר cf. also v^{12}; ‖ הוֹדוֹת), v^{13} (appar. of Levites & priests), מְהַלְלִים לי׳ בִּכְלֵי 1 Ch 23^{5} (Levites) cf. 2 Ch 30^{21} (Levites & priests) (בִּכְלֵי עֹז לי׳); sq. לְשֵׁם תִּפְאַרְתֶּךָ 1 Ch 29^{13} (‖ מוֹדִים; David speaks in name of people); sq. לְהַדְרַת־קֹדֶשׁ 2 Ch 20^{21} (before the army; ‖ מְשֹׁרְרִים לי׳; prob. of Levites, cf. v^{19}). **f.** sq. acc. י׳ Ezr 3^{10} (priests & Levites: עַל־יְדֵי דָוִיד), Ne 5^{13} (people). **g.** other forms, with like technical sense, but abs.: לְהַלֵּל לְהוֹדוֹת בְּמִצְוַת דָּוִיד Ne 12^{24} (Levites) cf. 1 Ch 23^{6} 2 Ch 8^{14} 29^{30} (עַד־לְשִׂמְחָה) 2 Ch 31^{2} (appar. priests & Levites; לְשָׁרֵת וּלְהֹדוֹת ‖ בְּשַׁעֲרֵי מַחֲנוֹת י׳); v. also מוֹדִיעִים לְהַלֵּל 2 Ch 23^{13} (‖ מְשׁוֹרְרִים בִּכְלֵי הַשִּׁיר); בְּהַלֵּל דָּוִיד בְּיָדָם 2 Ch 7^{6} (‖ הודות ליהוה). **3.** appar. *boast, make one's boast* cf. **Qal 2** (sq. בְּ *in, of*), בֵּאלֹהִים ψ 44^{9} (‖ שִׁמְךָ לְעוֹלָם נוֹדֶה); so, acc. to most, in bad sense, ה׳ רָשָׁע עַל־תַּאֲוַת נַפְשׁוֹ ψ 10^{3} *a wicked man boasteth of the desire of his soul,* but Che *praiseth* (י׳) *for* (i.e. in a mercenary spirit). **Pu.** *Pf.* 3 pl. הוּלָּלוּ ψ 78^{63}; *Impf.* יְהֻלַּל־ Pr 12^{8}; *Pt.* מְהֻלָּל 2 S 22^{4} + 6 t.; f. הַהֻלָּלָה Ez 26^{17} (cf. Ol$^{§\ 250\ c}$ Sta$^{§\ 220,\ 617\ b}$; MT, however, accents as Pf., regarding הַ as = relative, v. Sta$^{§\ 176\ c}$ Ges$^{§\ 52.\ 2,\ R.\ 6}$);—*be praised*, **1.** human subj., be *praised, commended* Pr 12^{8} (opp. יִהְיֶה לָבוּז); of maidens, *praised, celebrated* (in song) ψ 78^{63}; pt. (v. supr.) of city, *renowned* Ez 26^{17}. **2.** of י׳, only pt. = gerundive, *to be praised, worthy*

of praise 2 S 22^{4} = ψ 18^{4}, ψ 48^{2} גָּדוֹל י׳ וּמְהֻ׳ מְאֹד 96^{4} = 1 Ch 16^{25}, ψ 145^{3}; so מְהֻ׳ שֵׁם י׳ 113^{3} **Hithpa.** *Impf.* יִתְהַלֵּל 1 K 20^{11} + 5 t; יִתְהַלָּל Pr 20^{14}; 3 fs תִּתְהַלֵּל ψ 34^{3}, תִּתְהַלָּל Pr 31^{30}, 2 ms. תִּתְהַלֵּל ψ 52^{3} Pr 27^{1}, תִּתְהַלָּל Is 41^{16}; 2 fs תִּתְהַלְלִי Je 49^{4}, 3 mpl יִתְהַלְלוּ ψ 64^{11} Is 45^{25}; יִתְהַלָּלוּ ψ 49^{7} Je 4^{2}, *Imv* mpl. הִתְהַלְלוּ 1 Ch 16^{10} ψ 105^{3}; *Inf.* לְהִתְהַלֵּל ψ 106^{5}, *Pt* מִתְהַלֵּל Pr 25^{14} Je 9^{23}; pl. מִתְהַלְלִים ψ 97^{7};—*glory, boast, make one's boast*:—**1.** of self-confident boasting, abs 1 K 20^{11} cf Pr 20^{14}, sq בְּ of ground of boast Je 9$^{22.22.22}$ 49^{4} ψ 49^{7} 52^{3} Pr 25^{14}, אַל־תִּתְהַלֵּל בְּיוֹם מָחָר Pr 27^{1}; of glorying in idols הַמִּתְהַלְלִים בָּאֱלִילִים ψ 97^{7}. **2.** of glorying, making one's boast in (בְּ, on the ground of) י׳: בַּי׳ תִּתְהַלֵּל נַפְשִׁי ψ 34^{3}, cf. Is 45^{25} Je 4^{2} (‖ וְהִתְבָּרְכוּ בוֹ); sq בִּקְדוֹשׁ יִשְׂרָאֵל Is 41^{16}; v. also ψ 105^{3} = 1 Ch 16^{10} sq בְּשֵׁם קָדְשׁוֹ (‖ יִשְׂמַח לֵב מְבַקְשֵׁי י׳), cf further Je 9^{23}, less oft abs. Je 9^{23} ψ 63^{12} 64^{11} & 106^{5} sq. עִם־נַחֲלָתֶךָ *together with thine heritage* (‖ לִשְׂמֹחַ בְּשִׂמְחַת גּוֹיֶךָ) **3.** once, late = pass. *be praised, commended*, of God-fearing woman Pr 31^{30} **Po'el** *Impf.* יְהוֹלֵל Is 44^{25} + 2 t.,—*make into a fool, make fool of*, obj. שֹׁפְטִים Jb 12^{17} (subj י׳ ‖ מוֹלִיךְ יוֹעֲצִים שׁוֹלָל); obj קֹסְמִים Is 44^{25} (subj י׳ ‖ מֵפֵר אֹתוֹת בַּדִּים); obj. חָכָם Ec 7^{7} (subj. הָעֹשֶׁק ‖ וִיאַבֵּד אֶת־לֵב מַתָּנָה) **Po'al** *Pt.* לִשְׂחוֹק אָמַרְתִּי מְהוֹלָל Ec 2^{2} *of laughter I said, It is mad* (folly); מְהוֹלָלַי ψ 102^{9} *those mad against me* (‖ אוֹיְבָי). **Hithpo.** *Impf* וַיִּתְהֹלֵל 1 S 21^{14}, 3 mpl. יִתְהוֹלְלוּ Je 51^{7}, יִתְהוֹלְלוּ Na 2^{5}, הִתְהֹלָלוּ Je 50^{38}, *Imv.* mpl הִתְהֹלְלוּ Je 49^{9}, יִתְהֹלָלוּ Je 25^{16};—*act madly*, or *like a madman*, וַיִּתְהֹלֵל בְּיָדָם 1 S 21^{14} (of David) *and he acted like a madman in their hands*, of idolatrous worship by Chaldeans וּבָאֵימִים יִתְהֹ׳ Je 50^{38}, of nations, as drunken men, fig. of terror at Yahweh's judgments, Je 25^{16} (‖ הִתְגָּעֲשׁוּ) 51^{7}, also of madly driving & jolting chariots Na 2^{5} Je 46^{9}

†הִלֵּל **n.pr.m.** (*he hath praised*, cf NH n pr. הִלֵּל, *Hillel*) father of a judge of Israel Ju 12$^{13.15}$, called הַפִּרְעָתוֹנִי v פִּרְעָתוֹן

†[הִלּוּל] **n.[m.]** (NH *id*) only pl. הִלּוּלִים **rejoicing, praise**· **1.** וַיַּעֲשׂוּ הִלּוּלִים Ju 9^{27} i e a vintage-rejoicing, merry-making, connected with thanksgiving וַיָּבֹאוּ בֵּית אֱלֹהֵיהֶם, etc (i e god Baal-Berith, see v^{4}) **2.** of praise to י׳, קֹדֶשׁ הִ׳ Lv 19^{24} (H) *holiness of praise*, i. e. a consecrated thing in token of thanksgiving for fruit, offered in 4th year (cf. NH).

†[הוֹלֵלָה] **n f.** madness (on txt. v infr.), only pl. הוֹלֵלוֹת, הֹלֵלוֹת, and only Ec. Ec 1^{17} *and I set my heart* (וָאֶתְּנָה לִבִּי) *to know wisdom, and to know madness and folly* (הֹלֵלוֹת וְשִׂכְלוּת), cf וְלָדַעַת רֶשַׁע כֶּסֶל וְהַסִּכְלוּת הוֹלֵלוֹת 7^{25}, i.e to know folly to be madness; possibly rd הוֹלֵלוּת, cf סִכְלוּת & foll., the moral evil of it is specif. recognised in Ec 9^{3} (‖ רָע) 2^{12} (‖ *id*), ה׳

†הוֹלֵלוּת **n.f.** id. (formed unusually from the ptcp, an Aram formation, cf Ba$^{NB 414 f.}$) תְּחִלַּת דִּבְרֵי־פִיהוּ סִכְלוּת וְאַחֲרִית פִּיהוּ הוֹלֵלוּת רָעָה Ec 10^{13} *the beginning of the words of his mouth is folly, and the end of his mouth* (his speech) *is evil madness*

הַלְלוּיָהּ, הַלְלוּ־יָהּ v. הלל **Pi.**

†יְהַלֶּלְאֵל **n.pr.[m.]** (*he shall praise God*, cf מַהֲלַלְאֵל infr),—**1.** a man of Judah 1 Ch 4^{16}. **2.** a Levite 2 Ch 29^{12}.

†[מַהֲלָל] **n.[m.]** praise,—only in וְאִישׁ לְפִי מַהֲלָלוֹ Pr 27^{21} the refining pot for silver, and the furnace for gold, *and a man according to his praise*, i e prob. acc. to the praise of him by others, which tests him; so De Str al; perh however *so let a man be to the mouth of his praise*, i e. *that praises him*,—testing the praise to determine its worth, Thes RobGes; other views are: *according to the measure of his boasting* Ew, i. e. is judged according to his success or failure in that of which he boasts; Hi *according to the thing of which he boasts*

†מַהֲלַלְאֵל **n pr.m.** (*praise of God*, cf. יְהַלֶּלְאֵל supr),—**1.** great-grandson of Seth acc to genealogy of P, Gn 5$^{12.13.15.16.17}$ 1 Ch 1^{2}. **2.** a man of Judah Ne 11^{4}

†תְּהִלָּה **n.f.** praise, song of praise (cf. Ar. تَهْلِيل, the shouting of a sacred formula, Sprenger$^{Muhammad\ III\ 527}$ We$^{Skizzen\ III.\ 107\ ff.\ 114\ 117\ 214}$ No $^{ZMG\ 1887,\ 723}$ RS$^{Sem\ I\ 411}$ Che$^{OP\ 460}$) abs. תְּ׳ Is 60^{18} + 19 t + Je 49^{25} Kt, v infr.; cstr. תְּהִלַּת Je 48^{2} + 2 t, sf. תְּהִלָּתִי Je 17^{14} + 6 t, תְּהִלָּתְךָ Dt 10^{21}, תְּהִלָּתוֹ ψ 9^{15}; תְּהִלָּתֶךָ ψ 48^{11}, תְּהִלָּתֶיךָ ψ 35^{28} + 6 t; Is 42^{10} + 10 t., pl abs תְּהִלֹּת Ex 15^{11}; cstr תְּהִלּוֹת ψ 22^{4} + 3 t,—**1.** *praise, adoration, thanksgiving*, paid to י׳— ψ 48^{11} כְּשִׁמְךָ אֱלֹהִים כֵּן תְּהִלָּתְךָ עַל קַצְוֵי אֶרֶץ *as thy name, O God, so is thy praise to the ends of the earth*, 111^{10} תְּהִלָּתוֹ עֹמֶדֶת

תָּמִיד תְּהִלָּתוֹ בְּפִי ,לְעַד ψ 34^{2} *continually is his praise in my mouth* (אֲבָרְכָה אֶת־י׳ ‖) cf 71^{6}, also תְּהִלָּתֶךָ יִמָּלֵא פִי תְּהִלָּתֶךָ, 71^{8} פִּי יַגִּיד ת׳ 51^{17}, תְּבַעְנָה, וִיבָרֵךְ כָּל־ ‖) 145^{21} ת׳ י׳ יְדַבֶּר פִּי, 119^{171} שְׂפָתַי ת׳ יָשִׁירוּ (בָּשָׂר שֵׁם קָדְשׁוֹ); as sung, *song of praise* הַמְשֹׁרְרִים וְשִׁיר־תְּהִלָּה וְהוֹדוֹת לֵאלֹהִים, 106^{12} תְּהִלָּתוֹ Ne 12^{46}, cf ת׳ לֵאלֹהֵינוּ ψ 40^{4} (appos שִׁיר חָדָשׁ) & Is 42^{10} (appos *id*), also לַיְשָׁרִים נָאוָה ת׳ 33^{1} (רַנְּנוּ צַדִּיקִים בַּי׳ ‖), vid. perh ψ 148^{14} (Che; yet see De VB), note further אֱלֹהֵי תְּהִלָּתִי ψ 109^{1}; יוֹשֵׁב תְּהִלּוֹת יִשְׂרָאֵל ψ 22^{4} *inhabiting the praises of Isr.*, וּמְרוֹמַם עַל־כָּל־בְּרָכָה וּתְהִלָּה Ne 9^{5} *exalted above all blessing and praise;* cf also תְּהִלָּתִי Is 48^{9} (שְׁמִי ‖), & of *praise due to* י׳ Is 42^{8}. **2.** the act of *general, public, praise* (cf also supr. esp ψ 22^{4} 33^{1} 106^{12} Ne 12^{46});—בֹּאוּ שְׁעָרָיו בְּתוֹדָה חֲצֵרֹתָיו בִּת׳ ψ 100^{4} *enter his gates with thanksgiving, his courts with praise,* שִׁירוּ לַי׳ שִׁיר חָדָשׁ תְּהִלָּתוֹ בִּקְהַל חֲסִידִים ψ 149^{1}, cf ψ 22^{26} 65^{2} 66^{2} 147^{1}, before the army הַחֵלּוּ בְּרִנָּה וּתְהִלָּה 2 Ch 20^{22}, in exhortation to the peoples הַשְׁמִיעוּ קוֹל תְּהִלָּתוֹ ψ 66^{8} (בָּרְכוּ עַמִּים אֱלֹהֵינוּ ‖), cf. Is 42^{12}. **3.** *praise-song*, as title, תְּהִלָּה לְדָוִד ψ 145^{1} (so NH תְּהִלִּים ,תִּילִים & סֵפֶר תְּהִלּוֹת, = *Psalms*) **4.** qualities, deeds, etc., of י׳, demanding praise·—נוֹרָא תְהִלֹּת Ex 15^{11} (song), i.e. terrible in attributes that call for praise (נֶאְדָּר בַּקֹּדֶשׁ ‖ & עֹשֵׂה פֶלֶא); oft (both sg. and pl) of Yahweh's deeds c vb סִפֵּר ψ 9^{15} 78^{4} 79^{13} Is 43^{21}, also + שֵׁם י׳ ψ 102^{22}, c. יַשְׁמִיעַ ψ 106^{2} (יְמַלֵּל גְּבוּרוֹת י׳ ‖); חַסְדֵי י׳ + c יֶהְגֶּה ψ 35^{28}, c יְבַשֵּׂרוּ Is 60^{6}; + צִדְקֶךָ, c אַזְכִּיר Is 63^{7}; vid also לְהֹדוֹת לְשֵׁם קָדְשֶׁךָ לְהִשְׁתַּבֵּחַ בִּתְהִלָּתֶךָ ψ 106^{47} = 1 Ch 16^{35} *to give thanks unto thy holy name, to glory in thy praises* (= praiseworthy deeds) **5.** *renown, fame, glory* **a.** of Damascus עִיר תְּהִלָּה Je 49^{25} (on Qr תְּהִלַּת v Hi Ges § 80 2 b); comp perhaps מַעֲטֵה תְהִלָּה Is 61^{3} *mantle of renown* (*renown as a mantle*, cf De VB; > Di *splendid garment;* but Bi Che Du read מַעֲטֵה אֵבֶל and translate ת׳ *praise, song of praise,* cf **1. 2**). **b.** of י׳, כִּסָּה שָׁמַיִם הוֹדוֹ וּת׳ מָלְאָה הָאָרֶץ Hb 3^{3} *his splendour hath covered (the) heavens, and of his renown the earth is full* Also **c.** fig, *praise, renown,* = obj of praise, possessor of renown, used (*a*) of Israel Dt 26^{19} (abs), Je 13^{11} (+ לִי), 33^{9} (+ לִי and לְכֹל גּוֹיֵי הָאָרֶץ)—all ‖ שֵׁם, תִּפְאֶרֶת; v. also Is 61^{11}, & perh ψ 148^{14} (see sub **1** supr.), (*b*) of Jerusalem Is 62^{7}, also Zp 3^{19} ^{20} (both ‖ שֵׁם), all these c. vb הָיָה or שִׂים, cf וְקָרָאת יְשׁוּעָה חוֹמֹתַיִךְ וּשְׁעָרַיִךְ ת׳ Is 60^{18}, (*c*) of Babylon אֵיךְ וַתִּתָּפֵשׂ תְּהִלַּת כָּל־הָאָרֶץ Je 51^{41}, (*d*) of Moab אֵין עוֹד ת׳ מוֹאָב Je 48^{2}; (*e*) of י׳, הוּא תְהִלָּתְךָ וְהוּא אֱלֹהֶיךָ Dt 10^{21}, כִּי תְהִלָּתִי אָתָּה Je 17^{14} (no vb.)

†[הָלַם] **vb. smite, hammer, strike down** (cf Ph מהלם infr. sub מַהֲלֻמוֹת),—**Qal** *Pf.* 3 fs. וְהָלְמָה consec. Ju 5^{26}; 3 pl הָלְמוּ Ju 5^{22} Is 16^{8}, sf הֲלָמוּנִי Pr 23^{35}, *Impf* 3 ms. sf. יֶהֶלְמֵנִי ψ 141^{5}, 3 mpl. יַהַלְמוּן ψ 74^{6}, *Pt act.* הוֹלֵם Is 41^{7} (cf Ges § 29 3 b), *pass* cstr. הֲלוּמֵי Is 28^{1},—*smite* (with hammer), sq acc pers Ju 5^{26} (fatally; ‖ מָחֲקָה, מָחֲצָה); also fig. of correction, discipline ψ 141^{5} (הוֹכִיחַ ‖), of intoxicating wine גֶּפֶן שִׂבְמָה בַּעֲלֵי גוֹיִם הָלְמוּ שְׂרוּקֶּיהָ Is 16^{8} *the vine of Sibma, its choice branches smote down lords of nations* (so Hi De Che Brd Di al, RVm, *lords* subj acc to Ges Ew al. AV RV); also הֲלוּמֵי יָיִן *smitten down by wine* Is 28^{1}; cf further Pr 23^{35}, sq. acc. rei. הוֹלֶם־פָּעַם Is 41^{7} *one striking an anvil, smite down*, or *strike off* ψ 74^{6} (obj. פִּתּוּחִים *carved work*), also abs of horses' hoofs Ju 5^{22}.—On הֲלֹם וַהֲלֹם 1 S 14^{16} v. הֲלֹם.

†הֵלֶם **n pr.m.** a man of Asher 1 Ch 7^{35}.

†הַלְמוּת **n.f. hammer, mallet,** only cstr. הַ׳ עֲמֵלִים Ju 5^{26} *a workman's hammer.*

†יַהֲלֹם **n.[m.]** a precious stone, **jasper?** (so 𝔊 𝔙), or **onyx?** (cf. Di Ex 28^{18}) (appar. fr √ הלם, owing to its hardness, as able to *smite, hammer?*)—mentioned in lists of precious stones Ex 28^{18} 39^{11} Ez 28^{13}.

†מַהֲלֻמוֹת **n f.pl. strokes, blows** (cf. Ph. מהלם *stroke, stamp, impression,* once on a coin מהלם אנדר *coinage of Gader* (Gades), = *percussura,* κόμμα, Ges Mon. pl 40, xv c also p. 307)—Pr 18^{6} (cf Baer) 19^{29}, both times of blows on the body.

†הֲלֹם **adv. of place, hither** (Ar. هَلُمَّ *hither!*)—Ex 3^{5} אַל־תִּקְרַב הֲלֹם approach not *hither*, Ju 18^{3} 20^{7} 1 S 10^{22} 14^{16} and lo, the camp melted away וַיֵּלֶךְ וַהֲלֹם rd with 𝔊 (ἔνθεν καὶ ἔνθεν) Th We Dr הֲלֹם וַהֲלֹם *hither and thither* i e in different directions (cf. הֵנָּה וָהֵנָּה Jos 8^{20}), v$^{36.38}$ Ru 2^{14}; עַד הֲלֹם fig. *hitherto, thus far* (i.e. to this point of dignity and greatness) 2 S 7^{18} (= 1 Ch 17^{16}) ψ 73^{10}, if text be sound, הֲלֹם must mean *thither* (sc. after the persons described v$^{3-9}$), but such sense questionable; rd. prob with Houb La for יָשׁוּב עַמּוֹ הֲלֹם, יְשַׂבְּעֵמוֹ

לֶחֶם satisfies them with bread: cf Che Hup^{Now}. Gn 16^{13}=*here*, but here also text is dub: v Di. Ju 14^{15} rd. הֲלֹם for הלא v הֲ **1** *end*

†הָם n.pr.loc. only in הַזּוּזִים בְּהָם Gn 14^{5}; not otherwise known; Vrss בָּהֶם, Jer$^{Quaest\ in\ libr\ Genes.}$ בחם; Ol conj בַּחֲמַת; Tu Di think perh old name of Rabbath Ammon.

†[הֵם ,√המה] only in מֵהֱמֵהֶם Ez 7^{11} Ew nothing *of their moaning, wailing;* Thes RV *wealth*, cf הָמוֹן **5**, but precarious; form very suspicious; prob dittogr. for preceding מהם, del. B Co

†הַמְּדָתָא n.pr.m. father of Haman (Pers. *mâh, moon* (*mâha, month*, Spieg$^{APK 236}$)+*data, given?* so (written *hamaodata*) Ot; 𝔊 Ἀμαδαθου (alw. Genit.); in Gk perh Μαδάτης [Μαδάρας, Μαδέτης], cf. Xenoph$^{Cyr\ v\ 3\ 41}$ Diod$^{xvii.67}$ Pott$^{ZMG\ 1859,\ 424}$),—הַמְּדָתָא הָאֲגָגִי Est 3$^{1.10}$ 8^{5} 9^{24}, without האגגי 9^{10}.

הֵמָּה and **הֵם** (without appreciable distinction in usage, except prob. in so far as the longer or shorter form was better adapted to the rhythm of particular sentences: on the whole הֵמָּה (alone) is somewhat more freq than הֵם, הָהֵם on the contrary is said regularly, הָהֵמָּה occurring only 12 t, viz Nu 9^{7}(P), Je 14^{15} Zc 14^{15}, and in the phr בַּ(הַ)יָּמִים הָהֵמָּה 2 K 18^{4} Je 3$^{16.18}$ 5^{18} 50^{4} Jo 3^{2} 4^{1} Zc 8^{23} Ne 13^{15}, though בַּיָּמִים הָהֵם is much more common) **pron. 3 pl. masc.** (הֵמָּה used incorrectly for the fem Zc 5^{10} Ru 1^{22} Ct 6^{8}), **fem.** הֵנָּה [NH also הֵן, which occurs however in Bibl Heb. only after a prefix v. infr. **8**], **pr. 3 pl. they** (BAram הִמּוֹ, q v; هُمْ, هُمْ; Eth (one form) እሙንቱ: እማንቱ: *'emūn-tū, 'emān-tū;* cf. also for the dissyl. form, the sf. *-ōmū* [fem. *-ōn*], perh also As suff. *šunu, šina*[*ni*], cf. reff sub הוא) In usage not different in genl from הוּא, היא (which see, under the corresponding headings, for fuller explanations), thus:—

1. a. Gn 6^{4} Ex 5^{7} הֵם יֵלְכוּ let *them* (emph.) go and gather straw, Nu 31^{16} Is 24^{14} Ho 4^{14} 7^{3} etc; after כִּי Je 5^{5} 34^{7}. (For the use in circumst. clauses v Dr$^{§160\ 169}$) **b.** Ju 1^{22} וַיַּעֲלוּ ... גַם הֵם, Dt 2^{11} (אַף הֵם), 3^{20} Jos 9^{4} Ez 30^{17}. **c.** Ex 18^{22} every small matter יִשְׁפְּטוּ־הֵם let them judge *themselves*, v^{26} Je 15^{19} 17^{18} ψ 109^{28}, Est 9^{1} **d.** Gn 33^{6} 44^{3} Jud 6^{5} etc **e** cf Ne 10^{38}

2. a. (Resuming the subj. with emph.) Gn 14^{24} (note accents), Dt 1^{39} ψ 23^{4} 27^{2} (accents), 37^{9} 107^{24} Ez 36^{7} 44^{15}. **b.** Is 30^{7} Ez 27$^{15.17.21}$; cf Is 44^{11}. **c.** Nu 14^{27a} Je 27^{9} Ez 43^{19} אֲשֶׁר הֵם מִזֶּרַע צָדוֹק, Ec 4^{2} Ne 2^{16}

3. a. Gn 3^{7} Ex 5^{8} כִּי נִרְפִּים הֵם for *they* are idle, 14^{3} 15^{23} 29^{33} etc (the opp order rare: Nu 11^{16} Is 61^{9}, cf. De$^{ψ 94,11}$) **b.** Gn 34$^{21.23}$ 41^{26} 48^{5} שְׁנֵי בָנֶיךָ ... לִי הֵם thy two sons ..., they are mine, Ex 32^{16}+oft: Is. 41^{22} הָרִאשֹׁנוֹת מָה הֵנָּה, 49^{21} אֵלֶּה אֵיפֹה הֵם these—where were they? Zp 2^{12} after אַתֶּם, peculiarly (cf Dr$^{§198\ Obs.\ 2}$) **c.** Dt 20^{15} אֲשֶׁר לֹא־מֵעָרֵי הַגּוֹיִם הָאֵלֶּה הֵנָּה, Ju 19^{12} 1 K 9^{20}. **d.** 2 K 7^{10} כַּאֲשֶׁר הֵמָּה (Pr 19^{7} Kt לֹא־הֵמָּה is prob. corrupt v. Comm)

4. a. Pr 30^{24} אַרְבָּעָה הֵם קְטַנֵּי־אָרֶץ four things are *they*, the little ones of the earth, v^{29} (cf before a rel clause v$^{15.18}$ 6^{16}) Ct 6^{8} Is 51^{19} שְׁתַּיִם הֵנָּה קֹרְאֹתַיִךְ, 1 Ch 9^{26} (v. הוא **4 a**) **b.** (β) Gn 21^{29} ... מָה הֵנָּה שֶׁבַע *lit.* What are they—these seven sheep? Zc 1^{9} 4^{5}. (γ) ... אֵלֶּה הֵם +Gn 25^{16} (=1 Ch 1^{31}) Lv 23^{2} Nu 3$^{20.21.27.33}$ 1 S 4^{8} 1 Ch 8^{6} 12^{15} (v. Dr$^{§201.3}$)

6. a. In a neuter sense (rare), Jb 6^{7} הֵמָּה כִּדְוֵי לַחְמִי *they* (i.e. such sufferings as mine) are as loathsomeness in my meat, Je 7^{4} הֵיכַל י׳ הֵמָּה *they* (i e. these buildings) are the temple of י׳; and in the fem., Lv 5^{22} of all that a man doeth to sin בָּהֵנָּה *therein*, 1 Ch 21^{10} מֵהֵנָּה (‖ 2 S 24^{12} מהם); 2 S 12^{8} Jb 23^{14} כָּהֵנָּה things *such as these.*

7. With art. הָהֵם, Gn 6^{4} Ex 2^{11} Nu 14^{38}+oft, הָהֵמָּה 12 t. (v supr), הָהֵנָּה +1 S 17^{28}.

N.B.—Ez 8^{6} Kt מֵהֶם stands for מָה הֵם (so Qr), cf מַזֶּה for מַה־זֶּה Ex 4^{2}, 2 K 9^{18} עַד־הֵם is irreg for עֲדֵיהֶם, 2 S 4^{6} וְהֵנָּה וגו׳ is textual error for וְהִנֵּה שֹׁעֶרֶת הַבַּיִת סֹקֶלֶת חִטִּים וגו׳ v. We Dr (𝔊 & RVm)

8. With preps (in lieu of the normal, and more usual, forms with suffixes לָהֶם, בָּהֶם, מהם etc [כָּהֶם & כָּהֵן, however, each once only, כְּמוֹהֶם thrice: v. כ])—**a.** בָּהֵמָּה +Ex 30^{4} 36^{1} (both P), Hb 1^{16}, כָּהֵמָּה +Je 36^{32}; לָהֵמָּה +Je 14^{16}, מֵהֵמָּה +Je 10^{2} Ec 12^{12}. **b.** כָּהֵם +2 S 24^{3} Yahweh add to the people כָּהֶם וְכָהֶם מֵאָה פְעָמִים *the like of themselves* and *the like of themselves* 100 times, = 1 Ch 21^{3} (but כָּהֶם here only once, cf. Dt 1^{11} כָּכֶם), 2 Ch 9^{11} Ec 9^{12}. **c.** בָּהֵנָּה +Lv 5^{22} (P) Nu 13^{19} (JE) Je 5^{17}: כָּהֵנָּה +Gn 41^{19} 2 S 12^{8} וְאֹסִפָה לְּךָ כָּהֵנָּה וְכָהֵנָּה, Jb 23^{14}: לָהֵנָּה +Ez 1$^{5.23.23}$ 42^{9} Zc 5^{9} מֵהֵנָּה +Lv 4^{2} (P) Is 34^{16} Je 5^{6} Ez 16^{51} 42^{5} ψ 34^{21} 1 Ch 21^{10} (‖ 2 S 24^{12} מהם) **d** בָּהֵן +Gn 19^{29} (P) 30$^{26.37}$ Ex 25^{29} 37^{16} (both P) Lv 10^{1} 11^{21} 14^{40} Nu 10^{3} 16^{7} (all

P) Dt 28^{52} Je 4^{29} 48^{9} 51$^{43.43}$ (כָּהֵן) thrice only, v. p 88), לָהֵן, כָּהֵן +Ez 18^{14} (edd, Baer כָּהֵן), (=*therefore*) +Ru 1$^{13.13}$ (also BAram); מֵהֵן +Ez 16$^{47.52}$ (edd; Baer מהן) (With the exception of כָהֵנָּה, these forms are found mostly in P and writers not earlier than Je; **b** and **d**, however, depend solely on the punctuation)

†[הָמָה] **vb. murmur, growl, roar, be boisterous** (𝔗 הֲמָא, but rare, and perh not genuine Aram, cf Ar هَمْهَمَ *murmur*),—**Qal** *Pf* 3 mpl הָמוּ ψ 46^{7} + 2 t, וְהָמוּ consec Je 5^{22} + 2 t; *Impf* יֶהֱמֶה Je 6^{23} + 3 t, 2 fs תֶּהֱמִי ψ 42^{12} 43^{5}, וַתֶּהֱמִי 42^{6}, אֶהֱמֶה 55^{18}, אהמיה 77^{4}; יֶהֱמוּ 46^{4} + 3 t, וַיֶּהֱמוּ Is 51^{15} Je 31^{35}, יֶהֱמָיוּן ψ 39^{7} + 2 t; 1 pl נֶהֱמֶה Is 59^{11}, *Inf* הֲמוֹת Is 17^{12}; *Pt* הֹמֶה Pr 20^{1} Je 4^{19}; f הוֹמִיָּה 1 K 1^{41}, המיה Pr 7^{11} 9^{13}, הוֹמִיָּה Is 22^{2}, fpl המיות Pr 1^{21}, המות Ez 7^{16} (Co הֹמוֹת cf 𝔊 𝔖),—**1.** *growl* like a dog כַּכֶּלֶב ψ 59$^{7.15}$, subj wicked men; *groan* (in distress, lamentation), like bears כַּדֻּבִּים Is 59^{11} (|| הגה כיונה), of doves (also in sim) Ez 7^{16} cf Da (several, vid supr) **2.** *murmur*, fig of soul (נֶפֶשׁ) in discouragement ψ 42$^{6.12}$ 43^{5}, in prayer 55^{18} 77^{4} (both || אָשִׂיחָה), also subj. מעים, of the *thrill* of deep-felt compassion or sympathy, sq לְ of person pitied, Je 31^{20} (|| רחם ארחמנו), sq עַל, Ct 5^{4}, further כַּכִּנּוֹר, *like the lyre* (*zither*) Is 16^{11}, כַּחֲלִלִים, *like flutes*, subj לב Je 48^{36} (sq לְ) v^{36} (sq. אֶל); cf Je 4^{19} לבי המה־לי **3.** *roar*, of waves, subj גַּלִּים Je 5^{22} 31^{35} Is 51^{15} cf ψ 46^{4}, sim of roar of multitudes Is 17^{12} Je 6^{23} 50^{42}, metaph *id*, Je 51^{55}; *be tumultuous*, of peoples ψ 46^{7} (|| מָטוּ); 83^{3} (|| נָשְׂאוּ ראש) **4** *be in commotion, stir*, of city 1 K 1^{41} Is 22^{2}, so pt fpl as subst. ראש המיות Pr 1^{21} *head of stirring, bustling* streets (|| פתחי שערים); of man, אַךְ־הֶבֶל יֶהֱמָיוּן ψ 39^{7} *surely to no purpose they bustle about* (|| אַךְ־בְּצֶלֶם יתהלך־איש) **5.** *be boisterous, turbulent*, as with wine Zc 9^{15} (but id perh דָּמָם, cf. Fi$^{Hexapl\ II.\ 3.\ 1024}$ Klo$^{Th\ LZ\ 1879,\ 504}$ Sta$^{ZAW\ 1881,\ 18}$); also pt as adj, of שֵׁכָר (by meton) Pr 20^{1}; of shameless woman Pr 7^{11} 9^{13}

†הָמוֹן **n.m** $^{1\ S\ 4.14}$ (**f.** + Jb 31^{34}) **sound, murmur, roar, crowd, abundance**,—abs ה׳ 1 S 4^{14} + 27 t (+ 2 K 25^{11} = אָמוֹן in || Je 52^{15}, v II. אָמוֹן p 54 supr), cstr הֲמוֹן Gn 17^{4} + 30 t + Ez 39$^{11.15}$ (גיא הֲמוֹן גּוֹג), sf הֲמוֹנוֹ Is 5^{13} + 2 t. + Ez 31^{18} Qr + 3 t (Kt המונה), so also Co for n pr. (?) הֲמוֹנָה (q.v) 39^{16}, הֲמוֹנָהּ Is 5^{14} + 6 t + Ez 7$^{12.13}$ 30^{4} (all del. B Co; in 7^{13} also Da), הֲמוֹנָהּ Ez 29^{19}; הֲמוֹנָם Is 31^{4} Ez 7^{11}; pl הֲמֹנִים Jo 4$^{14.14}$; sf. הֲמוֹנֶיהָ Ez 32^{20},—הֲמָנְכֶם Ez 5^{7} v. sub המן infr;—**1.** *sound, murmur, rush, roar*, esp sound made by a crowd of people, *murmur, roar* ψ 65^{8} ה׳ לְאֻמִּים (|| שְׁאוֹן יַמִּים etc.); cf קול ה׳ Is 13^{4} *sound of a roaring* (|| קוֹל שְׁאוֹן), 33^{3} Dn 10^{6}; הֲמוֹן עַמִּים Is 17^{12} (|| שְׁאוֹן לְאֻמִּים) where again compared with הֲמוֹת יַמִּים, also 31^{4} of throng of shepherds (|| קוֹל); of a city ה׳ קריה Jb 39^{7} (|| תְּשֻׁאוֹת נֹגֵשׂ), cf ה׳ עִיר = *noisy city* Is 32^{14}, הֲמוֹנָהּ Is 5^{14}, of *sound* of songs ה׳ שִׁירַיִךְ Ez 26^{13} (|| קוֹל כִּנּוֹרַיִךְ), cf. Am 5^{23} (|| קוֹל זִמְרַת נְבָלֶיךָ); of crying קוֹל ה׳ 1 S 4^{14} (|| קוֹל צְעָקָה), v. further הֲמוֹן מעים fig of sympathy Is 63^{15} (|| רַחֲמִים), cf הָמָה **2**, of rain קוֹל ה׳ הַגֶּשֶׁם 1 K 18^{41}, cf Je 10^{13} = 51^{16};—of *rumbling* of chariot-wheels ה׳ גַּלְגִּלָּיו Je 47^{3} (|| קוֹל שַׁעֲטַת פרסות & רַעַשׁ לרכבו) **2.** *tumult, confusion* (as occasioning a roar) 1 S 14^{19} 2 S 18^{29}. **3.** *crowd, multitude* (esp freq. in Ez Ch)·—**a.** frequently of great army Ju 4^{7} 1 S 14^{16} 1 K 20$^{13.28}$ Is 29$^{5.5}$ 2 Ch 13^{8} 14^{10} 20$^{2.12.15.24}$ 32^{7}; cf. Ez 39^{11}, also 7$^{12.13}$ 30^{4} (cf emend supr); on Je 3^{23} cf VB, v. further גיא הֲמוֹן גוג Ez 39$^{11.15}$; Dn 11^{10} (|| חַיִל גָּדוֹל) $^{11.11.12.13}$ v^{11} (ה׳ חֲיָלִים רַבִּים); also pl Jo 4$^{14.14}$ **b.** of a whole people 2 S 6^{19} Is 5^{13} 16^{14} Ez 7$^{11.14}$ 29^{19} 30$^{10.15}$ 31$^{2.18}$ 32$^{12.12.16.18.20.24.25.26.31.32}$ **c.** of any great throng 2 K 7$^{13.13}$ (so MT 25^{11}, but || Je 52^{15} הָאָמוֹן) ψ 42^{5} Jb 31^{34} (ה׳ רַבָּה) Ez 23^{42}, ה׳ גוים Gn 17$^{4.5}$ (P) cf. Is 29$^{7.8}$; so, under fig of overwhelming mass of waves Je 51^{42}. **4.** *great number, abundance* (late) ה׳ נָשִׁים 2 Ch 11^{23}, of cattle Je 49^{32}; of things: materials for temple-building 1 Ch 29^{16}; tithes & gifts 2 Ch 31^{10}. Hence **5.** *abundance, wealth*, ψ 37^{16} cf Ec 5^{9} (|| כֶּסֶף), Is 60^{5} (ה׳ יָם || חֵיל גוים).

†[הֶמְיָה] **n.f. sound, music, of instruments** הֶמְיַת נְבָלֶיךָ Is 14^{11}.

†הֲמוֹנָה **n.pr.loc.** a city appar. to be founded to commemorate defeat of Gog, וְגַם שֶׁם־עִיר ה׳ Ez 39^{16}, but txt. dub. cf. Da, Co prop. הֲמוֹן v ונמר המונו supr.

המל (√ of foll; cf Ar هَمَلَ *shed tears* (sc the eye), *rain steadily* (sc. the sky)).

†הֲמוּלָה, הֲמֻלָּה **n.f. rain-storm** (?), **rushing or roaring sound** (?): קוֹל הֲמוּלָּה גְדֹלָה Je 11^{16} *sound of a great storm*, of wind fanning flames in tree (in fig. of Yahweh's judgment on Judah), > AV RV Da *tumult*; קוֹל הֲמֻלָּה כְּקוֹל

מַחֲנֶה Ez 1[24] of noise of wings of living creatures in Ezekiel's vision (del. B Co cf. Hi).

†הָמַם **vb. make a noise, move noisily, confuse, discomfit** (cf [הום])—**Qal** *Pf.* וְהָמַם consec. Is 28[28]; sf הֲמָמַנִי Je 51[34] Qr (Kt הֲמָמָנוּ), הֲמָמָם 2 Ch 15[6], 1 s וְהַמֹּתִי Ex 23[27]; *Impf.* וַיָּהָם Ex 14[24] Ju 4[15]; sf וַיְהֻמֵּם Jos 10[10] 1 S 7[10] ψ 18[15] + 2 S 22[15] Kt (doubtless right; Qr וַיָּהֹם); 2 ms sf וּתְהֻמֵּם ψ 144[6], *Inf. sf* לְהֻמָּם Dt 2[15] Est 9[24];—**1.** *move noisily*, trans., drive a wagon in threshing הֹ׳ גִּלְגַּל עֶגְלָתוֹ וּפָרָשָׁיו Is 28[28] (‖דוש). **2.** *confuse, discomfit*, c. acc Ex 14[24] 23[27] Jos 10[10] Ju 4[15] 1 S 7[10] ψ 18[15] = 2 S 22[15] (‖הפיץ), ψ 144[6] (‖*id.*), *discomfit, vex*, 2 Ch 15[6] c acc. & בְּכָל־צָרָה of instr.; c. acc. also Dt 2[15] (sq. עַד תֻּמָּם), Est 9[24] (sq לְאַבְּדָם); prob. also Je 51[34] (‖אָכַל), cf. הום Dt 7[23].

†הוֹמָם **n.pr.m.** son of Seir the Horite 1 Ch 1[39] 𝔊 Αἱμαν 𝔊L Ημαν ;=הֵימָם Gn 36[22].

†[הָמַן] **vb. rage, be turbulent** (? denom fr. המון Thes, after Rabb.; cf Ke RV, AV *multiply;* but very dub)—only **Qal** *Inf.* sf. יַעַן הֲמָנְכֶם מִן־הַגּוֹיִם Ez 5[7] (Sm queries; Ew, after 𝔖 Aq, הֶמְנְכֶם fr. מנה); rd rather, with Bo Co Da, המרותכם (fr. מָרָה) *because ye rebelled.*

הָמָן **n.pr.m. Haman**, favourite of Ahasuerus (etym dub.; acc. to Jen[VOJ 1892, 58 ff] = Elamit n pr.div. *Humban*, or *Humman*)—Est 3[1] + 53 t. in Esther.

המס (√ of foll.; meaning dubious)

†[הֶמֶס] **n.[m.]** only pl. הֲמָסִים **brushwood** (cf. De Che Di RV; some such mng. prob. fr context) כִּקְדֹחַ אֵשׁ הֲמָסִים Is 64[1] *as fire kindleth brushwood* (VB).

המר (√ of foll., cf Ar. هَمَرَ *pour, pour out*).

†[מַהֲמֹרָה] **n.f. flood** (cf. Ar. √), or **watery pit** (prop *place of flowing waters;* cf. Symm βοθύνους, and NH, NHWB[iii. 40])—only pl. מַהֲמֹרוֹת ψ 140[11] (Gr Che מכמרות, *nets*, v. sub כמר, comp. רֶשֶׁת v[6]).

I. [הֵן] **pron. 3 pl. fem.**, oft. in NH, in Bibl Heb. only with prefixes, בָּהֵן, etc. see under הֵמָּה **3 d.**

II. הֵן[100] (הֶן־ †Nu 23[9.24] Jb 8[19.20] 13[1] 26[14] 33[6.12.29] 36[5.22.26], הֶן־ Jb 13[15] 36[30] 41[1]+) **demonstr. adv.** or **interj.** lo! **behold** (on etym. v. הִנֵּה), less widely used than הנה, and in prose mostly confined to calling attention to some fact upon which action is to be taken, or a conclusion based; **a.** Gn 3[22] הֵן הָאָדָם הָיָה *behold*, the man is become as one of us, & now lest, etc., 4[14] *behold*, thou hast driven me forth etc, 11[6] 15[3] 19[34] 27[11] 29[7] 30[34] (nearly=*yea*), Ex 5[5] 6[12.30] Lv 10[18.19] Nu 17[27] Dt 5[21] (in prose only in Pent. (23 t.) and Ez 18[4] in this usage), in poetry, used more freely, but chiefly in Is[2] & Jb,—Nu 23[9.24] (Balaam) Is 23[13] 32[1] 33[7] ψ 51[7.8] 68[34] 78[20] 139[4] Pr 11[31] (stating the premiss to a conclusion introduced by אַף כִּי, q v), 24[12] elsewhere (except in senses **b, c**) only in Is[2] (23 t) & Jb (31 t), as Is 40[15 15] 41[11 24.29] 50[1 2.9.9 11] Jb 4[18] 15[15] 25[5] (in these three passages before אַף or אַף כִּי), 9[11 12] etc. (v supr.). †**b.** as a **hypoth. part.**, propounding a possibility, **if** (so NH BAram, Mand Palm. (ZMG 1888, 404); on the contr Syr ܐܢ, Pal ܐܢ אין, also Palm. (*ib* p 415), Ar. إِنْ, with א), a special application or development of the use **a**: Ex 4[1] והן לא יאמינו לי and *behold* (=and *suppose*) they will not believe me? etc., Lv 25[20] and if (וכי) ye say, What shall we eat the 7th year? הן לא נזרע *behold*, we shall not sow etc (i e *supposing* we do not sow), Is 54[15] Jb 40[23] 2 Ch 7[13.13] (v[13 b] ואם), stating the ground on which a qu. is based, Ex 8[22] (הֲלֹא=ולא), Je 3[1] Hg 2[12] (v הן Aram **b**). †**c. if, whether**, in an indirect question, Je 2[10] ראו הֵן הָיְתָה כָּזֹאת (but Gr הֲנִהְיְתָה); cf. אם **2 b**, and הֵן Aram. **c.**

הִנֵּה, once הִנֶּה־ Gn 19,2, **demonstr. part. lo! behold!** (إِنَّ *certainly, surely*, lit *lo!*), with sf. (the pron being conceived as accus, Ew § 262 e, cf إِنَّ, which takes an accus, whether of a noun or pron. sf) הִנְנִי Gn 6[13] + oft. (also הִנֵּנִי Gn 22[7]), הִנֵּנִי Gn 22[1 11] +, (הִנֶּנִּי Gn 27[18]), †Is 65[1] הִנֵּנִי הִנֵּנִי (but הנה אָנֹכִי is also said Gn 24[13.43] 25[32] 48[21] Ex 4[23] 7[17] +, and, more rarely, הִנֵּה אֲנִי Ez 37[5 12 19.21] 2 Ch 2[3], cf 2 K 10[9] Je 32[27]); הִנְּךָ Gn 20[3] + (†2 K 7[2] הִנְּכָה), הִנָּךְ †ψ 139[8], fem. הִנָּךְ Gn 16[11] + 6 t.; הִנּוֹ †Nu 23[17] Jb 2[6] 1 Ch 11[25], הִנֹּהוּ †Je 18[3] Kt (הִנֵּה הוּא is more usual, as Gn 20[16] 42[27] 1 S 10[22] Je 38[5] Ru 3[2]) · 1 pl. הִנְנוּ †Jos 9[25] 2 S 5[1] Je 3[22] Ezr 9[15], הִנֶּנּוּ †Gn 44[16] 50[18] Nu 14[40], הִנֵּנוּ Jb 38[35]; הִנְּכֶם †Dt 1[10] Je 16[12]; הִנָּם Gn 40[6] + oft. (37 t.)—*lo! behold!* **a.** pointing to persons or things, Gn 12[19] and now הנה אשתך *behold* thy wife! 18[9] הִנֵּה בָאֹהֶל *behold* (she is) in the tent (the suffix, when the noun to which הנה refers has immediately pre-

ceded, being not unfrequently omitted, 16^{14}. cf. Dr$^{§135.6.2}$), 30^{3} 31$^{51\ 51}$ Ex 24^{8} etc With sf of 1 ps, esp in response to a call, indicating the readiness of the person addressed to listen or obey, *Here I am!* (lit *Behold me!*) Gn 22$^{1\ 7\ 11}$ 27$^{1\ 18}$ 31^{11} 37^{13} 46^{2} Ex 3^{4} 1 S 3$^{4.5.6.8\ 16}$ 22^{12} 2 S 1^{7} Is 6^{8}, cf 1 S 12^{3} הנני ענו בי *here I am*, answer against me, 14^{43} (cf. Dr$^{p.202}$), 2 S 15^{26} (in resignation cf Gn 44^{16} 50^{18} Jos 9^{25} Ezr 9^{15}) of God Is 52^{6} 58^{9} 65$^{1\ 1}$ (repeated for emphasis) In the pl הננו Nu 14^{40} Je 3^{22} Jb 38^{35}—Emph הִנְנִי אָנִי Ez 34$^{11\ 20}$, cf 6^{3}. On ...הנני אל, v אל 4, p 40 **b.** introducing clauses involving predication. (*a*) with ref to the past or present, it points generally to some truth either newly asserted, or newly recognised, Gn 1^{29} *behold!* I have given to you all herbs etc. 17^{20} 27^{6} 1 S 14^{33} etc, often one upon which some proposal or suggestion is to be founded, Ex 1^{9} (cf. הן Gn 11^{6}) 1 S 20$^{2\ 5}$ 2 K 5^{20} When the proposal is to be of the nature of an entreaty or request, הנה־נא is often used, instead of the simple הנה Gn 12^{11} 16^{2} 18^{7} 1 K 20^{31} 22^{13} al (v נָא). (*b*) with ref to the future. Here it serves to introduce a solemn or important declaration Ex 32^{34} 34^{10} Is 7^{14}, and is used esp. with the ptcp (the *fut instans*, Dr$^{§135.3}$) in predictions or threats, Gn 20^{3} הנך מת (lit) *behold* thee (accus) about to die, thou art about to die, Ex 4^{23} 7^{17} 9^{3} Dt 31^{17} 1 S 3^{11} 1 K 20^{36} 22^{25} Is 3^{1} 10^{33} 17^{1} 19^{1} 22^{17} 24^{1} + oft, in the phrase הנה ימים באים † 1 S 2^{31} 2 K 20^{17} = Is 39^{6} Am 4^{2} 8^{11} 9^{13} + Je 15 t, very often with the suffix of 1 ps sg, as הנני מביא *Behold*, I bring (lit. *behold me bringing*, or *about to bring*).. Gn 6^{17} Ex 10^{4} & often, esp. in Je; Gn 9^{9} Ex 8^{17} 9^{18} 34^{11} 2 K 22^{20} Is 13^{17} 29^{14} 43^{19} Je 8^{17} 11^{22} (הנני פקד, so 23^{2} +) 16^{16} 20^{4}, etc, anomalously, with change of person, Is 28^{16} הנני יסד (acc. to points) *behold me*, one who *has founded*, 29^{14} הנני יוֹסִף *behold me*, one who *will add* (so 38^{5}), but it is dub whether the ptcp יסד, יוסף should not be read **c.** ...והנה very freq in historical style, esp (but not exclusively) after verbs of *seeing* or *discovering*, making the narrative graphic and vivid, and enabling the reader to enter into the surprise or satisfaction of the speaker or actor concerned Gn 1^{31} and *behold*, it was very good, 6^{12} 8^{13} 15^{12} 18^{2} 37^{29} Ex 2^{6} Dt 9^{13} etc. in the description of a dream Gn 37$^{7\ 9}$ 40$^{9\ 16}$ 41$^{1\ 2.3}$ Is 29^{8}, or of a vision Am 7$^{1.4}$ 8^{1} etc With a ptcp (the context fixing the sense to the past), Gn 24^{30} 37^{15} (both without suffix); Ju 9^{43} 11^{34} 1 K 19$^{5\ 11}$ + **d.** like II הן (**b**), nearly = *if* (rare)· Lv 13$^{5\ 6.7\ 8.9}$ (& elsewhere in this and the next ch) והנה *and behold = and if*, Dt 13^{15} and 17^{4} והנה אמת *and behold* it is true = *and if* it be true, 19^{18} 1 S 20^{12}, cf 1 S 9^{7} 2 S 18^{11} Ho 9^{6}.

I הֵנָּה $_{49}$ **adv.** hither (perh from II. הן, used δεικτικῶς, with ה-*loc*, prop *lo hitherwards!* or perh akin to هُنَا, هَنَّا, هِنَا *here*)—**a.** of *place* (*a*) **hither** Gn 15^{16} יָשׁוּבוּ הֵנָּה, 42^{15} 45^{5} that you have sold me הֵנָּה *hither*, v$^{8\ 13}$ Jos 2^{2} 3^{9} 18^{6} 2 S 1^{10} Is 57^{3} וְאַתֶּם קרבו הֵנָּה, Je 31^{8} 51^{6} +; 1 S 20^{21} מִמְּךָ וָהֵנָּה from thee *and hitherwards*, i e on this side of thee (opp. מִמְּךָ וָהָלְאָה): repeated 2 K 4^{35} אַחַת הֵנָּה וְאַחַת הֵנָּה once *hither* and once *thither* = once *to and fro;* הֵנָּה וָהֵנָּה *hither and thither* i e. in different (or opposite) directions, † Jos 8^{20} 2 K 2$^{8\ 14}$ 1 K 20^{40} strangely וַיְהִי עַבְדְּךָ עשה הֵנָּה וָהֵנָּה *lit.* and thy servant was a *doer of hitherwards and thitherwards*, i.e. was engaged in different directions (Ew$^{§360.c}$ treats ה׳ here as the pron 3 pl fem construed irregularly, cf. עשה אלה but rd. prob. with 𝔊 𝔗 𝔖 𝔙 Th Klo פֹּנֶה *was turning* or *looking* (Ex 2^{12}) for עשה), עַד־הֵנָּה *even hither*, Nu 14^{19} 1 S 7^{12} 2 S 20^{16} קְרַב עַד־הֵנָּה, 2 K 8^{7}, *to this point* (in a book) Je 48^{47} 51^{64} (note of compiler or scribe) (β) *here* (cf שָׁמָּה = *there*) Gn 21^{23} swear to me הֵנָּה *here*, Dn 12^{5} ...הֵנָּה לִ׳ הֵנָּה לִ׳ *on this side* of . *on that side* of ... †**b.** of *time*, in עַד הֵנָּה *hitherto* Gn 15^{16} (with a neg., = not *yet*) 44^{28} Ju 16^{13} ψ 71^{17} & *until now* do I keep declaring thy wonders, 1 Ch 9^{18} 12^{29} *until now* (the point reached in the narrative) In late Heb, contracted to עֲדֶנָּה *hitherto, still* † Ec 4^{2}, עֲדֶן † Ec 4^{3} אֲשֶׁר עֲדֶן לֹא הָיָה = who has not *yet* been (cf Mish עֲדַיִן *hitherto, still*, עֲדַיִן לֹא = *not yet*)

II הֵנָּה **pron. 3 pl. fem. they**. v. הֵמָּה.

הֲנָחָה v. sub נוח

† הִנֹּם **n.pr m.** (deriv & mng dub; acc. to Sim Bo Gf al = *wailing*, Ar. هَنَّ, fr cries of children (v. infr), but this improbable)—only in גֵּי(גיא)(בן־)ה׳, & abbrev. ג׳ ה׳, **n.pr.loc.** of valley S of Jerusalem, (𝔊 φάραγγα Ὀνομ Jos 15$^{8.8}$ Σονναμ 18^{16}; Γαιεννα v^{16}; Γαιβενθομ 2 Ch 28^{3}, 𝔊L φάρ Βενεννομ; γὲ βανὲ Ἐννομ 33^{6}, 𝔊L γῆ Βενεννομ, elsewh usu. φάρ (υἱοῦ) Ἐννομ) —cf. sub גַּיְא,—as mere topographical term גֵּי בֶן־הִנֹּם, boundary between Judah & Benjamin

Jos 15⁸ 18¹⁶; also ג׳ ה׳ 15⁸ 18¹⁶ (all P) cf. Ne 11³⁰; elsewhere alw. ג׳ בֶן־ה׳ (2 K 23¹⁰ Kt has גי בני הנם, Qr & 𝔊 𝔙 sing.), & alw. with ref. to the sacrifice of children by fire, 2 K 23¹⁰ 2 Ch 28³ 33⁶ Je 7³¹·³² 19²·⁶ 32³⁵; on account of this inhuman & idolatrous practice it was abhorred by priest & prophet, & defiled by Josiah; this conception afterward developed, through Is 66²⁴, into Jewish *Gehinnom* (cf. Weber [Synagog Theol 326 ff.] Di [Buch Henoch 131 f.]) & NT γέεννα On locality cf. Rob [BR ii. 273 f] Tobler [Topogr. ii 50 ff] Bd [Pal 108]; mod. name (of lower half of valley, toward SE) *Wady er-Rabâbi*.

†הֵנַע **n.pr.** *loc.* named betw *Sepharvaim* and *Iwwa;* site unknown, yet cf Dl [Pa 279]; 2 K 18³⁴ 19¹³ = Is 37¹³.

הַנָּפָה v sub נוף

†הַס, הָס **interj. hush! keep silence** (prob onomatop.) Ju 3¹⁹ and he said, I have a secret errand unto thee, O king, וַיֹּאמֶר הָס and he said, *Keep silence!* Am 6¹⁰ וְאָמַר הָס (while burying men in a pestilence), 8³ (ellipt.) in every place הִשְׁלִיךְ הָס׃ they cast them (the corpses) forth, (saying) *Hush!* sq מִפְּנֵי ׳י Hb 2²⁰ Zp 1⁷ Zc 2¹⁷. Inflected, as though a verb, *imv. pl* הַסּוּ Ne 8¹¹ (Ges compares Arab هَلُمَّ [=הֲלֹם] *hither!* inflected as an imv., e.g هَلُمُّوا, هَلُمِّي: W [AG i § 368]) Hence as denom †**Hiph.** *impf apoc* וַיַּהַס Nu 13³⁰ and Caleb *stilled* the people

הֲפֻגָה v. sub פוג.

†הָפַךְ **vb. turn, overturn** (NH *id*, Aram. הֲפַךְ, ܗܦܰܟ, Ar. أَفَكَ W [BG 47], As *abâku*, *apâku* Dl [W])—**Qal** *Pf* Lv 13³ + 13 t; וְהָפַךְ consec. 2 K 21¹³ Jb 34²⁵, 3 mpl הָפְכוּ ψ 78⁹, הֲפַכְתֶּם Am 6¹² Je 23³⁶, etc, *Impf* יַהֲפֹךְ La 3³ Je 13²³; וַיַּהֲפֹךְ Gn 19²⁵ + 6 t, וַיַּהֲפָךְ־ 1 S 10⁹; sf וַיַּהַפְכֵהוּ Ju 7¹³; 3 fs. וַתַּהֲפֹךְ 2 Ch 9¹², אהבך Zp 3⁹; וַיַּהַפְכוּ 1 S 25¹² Jb 12¹⁵; *Imv* הֲפֹךְ 1 K 22³⁴ = 2 Ch 18³³; *Inf abs* הָפוֹךְ Pr 12⁷; *cstr.* הֲפֹךְ Gn 19²⁹ 1 Ch 19³; sf. הָפְכִּי Gn 19²¹; הֲפֹכָה 2 S 10³;—on הַפְכְּכֶם (so Baer, q. v) Is 29¹⁶, v. הֶפֶךְ, *Pt. act* הֹפֵךְ Am 5⁸, הַהֹפְכִי ψ 114⁸; pl. הַהֹפְכִים Am 5⁷; *pass* הֲפוּכָה Ho 7⁸ La 4⁶.—**1.** trans **a.** *turn, turn about, turn over,* c. acc e.g turn the back (עֹרֶף) Jos 7⁸ (JE), a dish (צַלַּחַת) עַל־פָּנֶיהָ 2 K 21¹³; the hand, & so the horses of a chariot 1 K 22³⁴ = 2 Ch 18³³, 2 K 9²³, but also (sq. בְּ) of hostility La 3³; turn a cake (pass) Ho 7⁸; of ׳י, אֶל־עַמִּים ה׳ שָׂפָה בְרוּרָה Zp 3⁹ i e. restore speech of a pure kind, sq לֵב אַחֵר, 1 S 10⁹ *another heart,* sq לוֹ, turn a wind (רוּחַ; i.e bring from different quarter) Ex 10¹⁹ (J) **b.** *overturn, overthrow,* sq acc. Sodom, etc., Gn 19²¹·²⁵·²⁹ (J), Dt 29²² Je 20¹⁶ La 4⁶ (cf. מַהְפֵּכַת וגו׳ Am 4¹¹ v. infr, also הֲפֵכָה, [מַהְפֵּכָה]), city of Ammon 2 S 10³ = 1 Ch 19³ (obj. om); mountains Jb 9⁵ 28⁹; throne Hg 2²² (‖ השמיד), chariots v²²; tent (אהל), ה׳ לְמַעְלָה Ju 7¹³, obj. earth (ה׳=*devastate*) Jb 12¹⁵; wicked men Am 4¹¹ הָפַכְתִּי בָכֶם כְּמַהְפֵּכַת אֱלֹהִים אֶת־סְדֹם וְאֶת־עֲמֹרָה) Pr 12⁷ Jb 34²⁵ (obj. om). **c.** *turn=change, transform* (1) sq. acc.=*alter;* a colour (עֵינוֹ) Lv 13⁵⁵ (P), skin Je 13²³, bed (מִשְׁכָּבוֹ v. מ׳; Che *his lying down*) ψ 41⁴ i.e restore to health, (2) *pervert* דִּבְרֵי אֱלֹהִים Je 23³⁶; (3) sq. acc. c. Inf ψ 105²⁵ *he turned their heart to hate his people;* (4) *turn to, into,* sq. two acc Lv 13¹⁰ ψ 114⁸ rock into pool of water; usu sq acc. + לְ, ψ 66⁶ sea into dry land, ψ 78⁴⁴ rivers into blood, cf 105²⁹, Je 31¹³ mourning into joy, so ψ 30¹²; Am 5⁷ justice into wormwood, cf 6¹², 8¹⁰ feasts into mourning; Dt 23⁶ = Ne 13² curse into blessing, Am 5⁸ death-shade into morning. **2.** *intrans.* **a.** *turn, turn back,* Ju 20³⁹·⁴¹ 2 K 5²⁶ ψ 78⁹ 2 Ch 9¹², sq לדרך 1 S 25¹²; **b.** *turn = change, change into,* sq pred adj. ה׳ לָבָן turn white Lv 13³·⁴·¹³·²⁰ (all P) **Niph.** *Pf* נֶהְפַּךְ Ex 7¹⁵ + 10 t, נֶהְפָּךְ Jb 20¹⁴; וְנֶהְפַּךְ consec Lv 13¹⁶; נֶהֶפְכָה La 5²; 3 mpl נהפכו Jb 19¹⁹ + 3 t., נֶהֶפְכוּ 1 S 4¹⁹ Dn 10¹⁶, ונהפכו consec. Ex 7¹⁷ Is 34⁹, etc.; *Impf* יֵהָפֵךְ Is 60⁵ Jo 3⁴, וַיֵּהָפֵךְ Ex 14⁵ Is 63¹⁰, 2 ms. תֵּהָפֵךְ Jb 30²¹ Ez 4⁸, וַיֵּהָפְכוּ Ex 7²⁰; *Inf. abs.* נַהֲפוֹךְ Est 9¹, *Pt.* נֶהְפָּךְ Pr 17²⁰, נֶהְפֶּכֶת Jon 3⁴,—**1.** reflex & intrans **a.** *turn oneself, turn, turn back* (cf **Qal 2 a**) Jos 8²⁰ (JE); *turn aside* ψ 78⁵⁷, *turn* from side to side Ez 4⁸; *pains turned upon* (עַל) *her* 1 S 4¹⁹ (i e. came suddenly upon her) cf Dn 10¹⁶, *turn against* sq בְּ Jb 19¹⁹, *turn to(ward)*, sq. עַל, Is 60⁵ (‖ בּוֹא לְ). **b.** *turn=change* (oneself) sq pred adj Lv 13²⁵ (P); sq pred noun (?), vine turns into degenerate plant Je 2²¹; no pred. expressed Jb 20¹⁴ (cf v^b), of heart turned in compassion Ho 11⁸ (‖ נִכְמְרוּ נִחוּמָי), in sorrow, distress, La 1²⁰; of heart changed, so as to be favourably disposed *toward* (sq. אֶל) Ex 14⁵ (J) = change of mind, sq לְ, of plague spots changing colour Lv 13¹⁶·¹⁷ (P); rod changing to serpent

Ex 7^{15} (P), faces to paleness Je 30^{6}, dance to mourning La 5^{15}; comeliness to corruption Dn 10^{8}, וַיֵּהָפֵךְ לָהֶם לְאוֹיֵב Is 63^{10} Jb 30^{21}. **c.** *be perverse*, only pt. used subst. נֶהְפָּךְ בִּלְשׁוֹנוֹ Pr 17^{20} *he that is perverse with his tongue* **2.** pass., **a** *be turned, turned over to* sq לְ, an inheritance to strangers La 5^{2} **b.** *be reversed* Est 9^{1}. **c.** *be turned, changed*, sq לְ, waters into blood Ex 7$^{17.20}$ (E), Saul into another man 1 S 10^{6}, streams into pitch Is 34^{9}, sun to darkness Jo 3^{4}, stones to chaff Jb 41^{20}, month changed from sorrow to gladness Est 9^{22}, cf ψ 32^{4} where complem om **d.** *be overturned, overthrown*, of city Nineveh Jon 3^{4} **e.** *be upturned*, of subterran work of miners Jb 28^{5} = *there is an upturning.* **Hithp** *Impf* 3 fs תִּתְהַפֵּךְ Jb 38^{14}, *Pt.* מִתְהַפֵּךְ Ju 7^{13} Jb 37^{12}, מִתְהַפֶּכֶת Gn 3^{24},—reflex & intrans **1** *turn this way & that, every way*, of the flaming sword Gn 3^{24} (J), storm-cloud Jb 37^{12}, *turn over & over* Ju 7^{13}, of bread-cake tumbling into the host of Midian **2.** *transform oneself*, Jb 38^{14} of earth under rising dawn. **Hoph.** *Pf* הָהְפַּךְ עָלַי בַּלָּהוֹת Jb 30^{15} *there have been turned upon me terrors* (cf הִתְגַּלְגָּלוּ v^{14}, of foes)

†הֵפֶךְ **n.m.** **the contrary, contrariness, perversity**,—abs ה׳ Ez 16^{34}, הָפֶךְ v^{34}, sf הַפְכְּכֶם Is 29^{16} (v Baer),—**1.** *the contrary, opposite thing* וַיְהִי־בָךְ הֶפֶךְ מִן־הַנָּשִׁים Ez 16^{34} *& there hath occurred in thee the contrary from other women*, v^{34} וַתְּהִי לְהֶפֶךְ *so thou hast become the contrary* **2.** הַפְכְּכֶם Is 29^{16} *Oh, your perversity!*

†הֲפֵכָה **n.f** **overthrow** (cf esp As *abiktu* Dl^{W}), of the cities (of the plain) Gn 19^{29}, cf [מַהְפֵּכָה] and הָפַךְ **1 b**

†הֲפַכְפַּךְ **adj.** **crooked**, הֲפַכְפַּךְ דֶּרֶךְ אִישׁ וָזָר Pr 21^{8} *crooked is the way of a guilty man.*

†[מַהְפֵּכָה] **n f** **overthrow**—always cstr. מַהְפֵּכַת, & always of overthrow of Sodom, Gomorrah etc, exc Is 1^{7} מ׳ זָרִים, where rd. סְדֹם (Ew Che RS $^{Proph\ 345}$ Di al.; also Lag $^{Sem\ i\ 3}$), yet even so prob. gloss, cf Stud $^{JPTh\ 1877.\ 714}$, מ׳ סְדֹם Dt 29^{22} Je 49^{18}, and with force of verbal noun, governing acc, מ׳ אֱלֹהִים אֶת־סְדֹם Is 13^{19} Je 50^{40} Am 4^{11}. Cf. also הֲפֵכָה, הָפַךְ **1 b**,

†מַהְפֶּכֶת **n.f** **stocks or similar instrum** of punishment (compelling *crooked* posture, or *distorting*), mentioned rather late; as punishment for Jeremiah הַמּ׳ אֲשֶׁר בְּשַׁעַר בִּנְיָמִן Je 20^{2} (𝔊 εἰς τὸν καταράκτην κ τ λ), cf אֶל־הַמּ׳ 29^{26} (𝔊 εἰς τὸ ἀπόκλεισμα, ‖ אֶל־הַצִּינֹק, 𝔊 εἰς τὸν καταράκτην, but order of words perhaps reversed in 𝔊), בֵּית הַמַּהְפֶּכֶת 20^{3}; הַמַּהְפֶּכֶת assigned also to Asa's time 2 Ch 16^{10} (𝔊 εἰς φυλακήν, 𝔊L εἰς οἶκον φυλακῆς; cf. Acts 16^{24}, where εἰς τὴν ἐσωτέραν φυλακήν, + εἰς τὸ ξύλον)

†[תַּהְפֻּכָה] **n.f.** **perversity, perverse thing** (only Pr exc. Dt 32^{20})—Pl abs. תַּהְפֻּכוֹת Dt 32^{20} + 8t, cstr id Pr 2^{14},—*perverse things*, particularly utterances Pr 2^{12} 10^{32} 23^{33}, cf. לְשׁוֹן ת׳ 10^{31}, and even אִישׁ ת׳ Pr 16^{28} (‖ נִרְגָּן *slanderer*), but also thoughts, devices Pr 6^{14} 16^{30}, דּוֹר ת׳ Dt 32^{20} = *perverse generation* (‖ לֹא־אֵמֻן בָּם), ת׳ רָע Pr 2^{14} (‖ עֲשׂוֹת רָע).

הֻצַּב Na 2^{8} dub; perhaps txt err, v. נצב

הַצָּלָה v. sub נצל

†הֹצֶן **n.[m.]** deriv & mng. dub, only Ez 23^{24} וּבָאוּ עָלַיִךְ הֹצֶן רֶכֶב וְגַלְגַּל, txt. prob. in error 𝔊 מִצָּפוֹן so Co (cf 26^{7}); 𝔖 𝔗 *with arms*, Hi הָצֵן, Inf Hiph of √צנן, *with rattling;* Ew חֹצֶן (so Codd) *with shoulder* as place of carrying weapon; Bo Sm הָמוֹן *multitude;* Dl $^{Baer's\ Ezech\ xi}$ gains like sense without emend by comparing As *êsin* (-*ši*) *collect, gather*, Flood Tabl $^{ii\ 25\ ff}$, but this very dubious.

הַר v sub הרר

†הֹר **n pr.mont.** **1.** mt on border of Edom, alw הֹר הָהָר, named as stage in Isr's journey to Canaan Nu 20^{22} 21^{4} 33^{47} Dt 32^{50}; as place of Aaron's death Nu 20$^{23.25.27}$ 33$^{38.39.41}$ Dt 32^{50} (all P), = mod. *Jebel Nebi Hârûn* c. 50 miles S of Dead Sea, just S (SW.) of Petra, acc to Rob $^{BR\ ii\ 125.\ 152.\ cf\ 519\ ff}$ Bd $^{Pal\ 1.3}$; disputed by Ew Kn Di, & esp. Trumbull $^{Kadesh\ Barnea\ 128\ ff}$, who thinks of *J Maduraḥ*, NW of Edom **2.** a NE spur of Lebanon Nu 34$^{7.8}$ (P), mod *Jebel Akkar* cf Porter $^{Damascus,\ ed\ 2,\ p\ 333}$ Nbr $^{Géogr\ du\ Talm.\ p\ 9}$ Furrer $^{ZPV\ viii\ 27}$, yet v. Di

†הָרָא **n.pr.loc.** 1 Ch 5^{26} but rd. עָרֵי מָדַי cf. Schr $^{KGF\ 430}$, v ‖ 2 K 17^{6} 18^{11}

הַרְאֵל Ez 43^{15} v אֲרִיאֵל sub II ארה.

†הָרַג **vb** **kill, slay** (NH *id*, ואהרג MI (1 s. Impf consec.), Ar هَرَجَ *fall into war, conflict, disorder, slaughter;* Sab הרג *fight* Os$^{4.1\ 17}$, *kill* Sab Denkm$^{24.2}$)—**Qal** *Pf* 3 ms ה׳ Ju 9^{24} + 4 t, הָרַג 2 S 14^{7} + 2 t, וְהָרַג consec. Is 27^{1}, sf וַהֲרָגַנִי consec 1 S 16^{2} + 2 t, הֲרָגוֹ Gn 4^{25}, etc., *Impf.* יַהֲרֹג ψ 10^{8} + 4 t., יַהֲרָג Jb 5^{2}, וַיַּהֲרֹג Ex 13^{15} + 14 t.; sf. יַהַרְגֵנִי Gn 4^{14}; 1 s. אֶהֱרֹג Am 2^{3}, אֶהֱרֹג Am 9^{1}, cohort וְאַהַרְגָה Gn 27^{41}, sf.

וְאֶהֶרְגֵהוּ 2 S 4^{10} 2 K 10^{9}; 3 mpl. יַהֲרֹגוּ ψ 94^{6} Ez 23^{47}; וַיַּהַרְגוּ Gn 34^{25} + 4 t.; sf יַהַרְגֻנִי Gn 26^{7}, etc; *Imv* הֲרֹג Ju 8^{20}; sf הָרְגֵנִי Nu 11^{15}; pl. הִרְגוּ Nu 25^{5} + 2 t.; הִרְגוּ Nu 31^{17}; *Inf. abs* הָרֹג Nu 11^{15} + 2 t.; הָרוֹג Est 9^{16}; *cstr.* הֲרֹג Ex 2^{15} + 11 t, הֲרוֹג, Ec 3^{3} Est 7^{4}, *sf* הָרְגֵנִי Ex 2^{14}; הָרְגוֹ Ex 5^{21}; תְּהָרְגֵךְ 1 S 24^{11}, הָרְגֶךָ Gn 27^{42} + 2 t; הָרְגוֹ Ex 21^{14}, *Pt. act.* הֹרֵג Gn 4^{15} + 4 t., הֹרֵג Ez 21^{16}; הֹרְגֶךָ Ez 28^{9}; הֹרְגִים Je 4^{31} 2 K 17^{25}; *pass.* הֲרוּגִים Is 10^{4} + 2 t.; הֲרֻגִים Is 14^{19}; cstr. הֲרֻגֵי Je 18^{21}; הֲרוּגָיו Is 27^{7}; הֲרוּגֶיהָ Is 26^{21}; הֲרֻגֶיהָ Pr 7^{26},—**1. a.** *kill, slay*, implying ruthless violence, esp private violence Gn $4^{8.14.15.23.25}$ 12^{12} (all J), 20^{11} (E) 26^{7} $27^{41.42}$ $34^{25.26}$ $37^{20.26}$ (all J), 49^{6} (poem in J), Ex $2^{14.14.15}$ (E), 5^{21} (J) 21^{14} 23^{7} (both JE), Nu 31^{19} (P) Ju $9^{5.18.24.24.56}$ 16^{2} 20^{5} 1 S 16^{2} 22^{21} $24^{11.12.18}$ 2 S 3^{30} $4^{10.11.12}$ 12^{9} 14^{7} 23^{21} 1 K $2^{5.32}$ $18^{12.13.14}$ $19^{1.10.14}$ 2 K 9^{31} 10^{9} 1 Ch 7^{21} 11^{23} 2 Ch $21^{4.13}$ 22^{8} $24^{23.25}$ 25^{3} Ne 4^{5} $6^{10.10}$ Zc 11^{5} ψ 10^{8} 94^{6} (|| רצח); cf Ju $8^{18.19.20.21}$ 9^{54} 1 K 12^{27} Is 14^{20} 2 Ch 22^{1} Ne 9^{26}, so of massacre of Jews planned by Haman Est 3^{13} 7^{4} (both לְהַשְׁמִיד לַהֲרֹג וּלְאַבֵּד), and of slaughter of Jews' enemies in defence and revenge Est 8^{11} (same combin.) $9^{6.10.12.15.16}$ cf. v^{11} (pt. pass. *the slain*). **b.** hence of wholesale slaughter after battle Nu $31^{7.8.8.17.17}$ (all P), Jos 8^{24} 10^{11} (both JE), 13^{22} (P), Ju $7^{25.25}$ 8^{17} 9^{45} 2 S 10^{18} 1 K 9^{16} 11^{24} 2 K 8^{12} 1 Ch 19^{18} 2 Ch $28^{6.7.9}$ 36^{17} Ez $26^{8.11}$, cf. Ju 9^{26}; pt. pass. *the slain* Is 10^{4} 14^{19} cf Ez $23^{10.47}$ 37^{9}, Je 18^{21} (מֻכֵּי־חֶרֶב || הֲרֻגֵי מָוֶת); further Ho 9^{13} Hb 1^{17} Je 4^{31} Ez 21^{16} 28^{9}; also of slaughter in a revolt 2 K 11^{8} = 2 Ch 23^{17}. **2.** of God's slaying in judgment (stern and inscrutable), Gn 20^{4} (E), Ex 4^{23} 13^{15} 22^{23} (all JE), Am 2^{3} 4^{10} $9^{1.4}$ La $2^{4.21}$ 3^{43} ψ 59^{12} $78^{31.34}$ 135^{10} 136^{18} cf. Nu $11^{15.15}$ (JE), 22^{33} (J), Is 14^{30}, 26^{21} (pass. *the slain*, so 27^{7}), Je 15^{3}; fig. הֲרַגְתִּים באמרי־פִי Ho 6^{5} (|| חָצַבְתִּי בַּנְּבִיאִים) **3.** rarely of judicial killing by men (at God's command), Ex 32^{27} (JE), Lv $20^{15.16}$ (H), Nu 25^{5} (JE), Dt $13^{10.10}$ cf. Ez 9^{6} תַּהַרְגוּ לְמַשְׁחִית **4.** of killing beasts, Nu 22^{29} (J; Balaam's ass), Lv 20^{15} cf. supr, Is 22^{13} (oxen; || שָׁחֹט), הַתַּנִּין אֲשֶׁר בַּיָּם Is 27^{1}; also of killing vines, by hail ψ 78^{47}. **5.** of killing by beasts. lions 2 K 17^{25}, viper Jb 20^{16}. **6.** quite general is עֵת לַהֲרוֹג וְעֵת לִרְפּוֹא Ec 3^{3} **7.** *destroy, ruin* לֶאֱוִיל יַהֲרָג־כָּעַשׂ וּפֹתֶה תָּמִית קִנְאָה Jb 5^{2}, מְשׁוּבַת פְּתָיִם תַּהַרְגֵם וְשַׁלְוַת כְּסִילִים תְּאַבְּדֵם Pr 1^{32}; also of those ruined by shameless woman Pr 7^{26}.—Regular construction is c. acc., obj. sometimes om., as La 2^{21}, used abs. Ho 9^{13} Je 4^{31} 15^{3} La 3^{43} Ez 21^{16} Ec 3^{3}; sq. בְּ *slay among*, i.e. some of, 2 K 17^{25} 2 Ch $28^{6.9}$ ψ 78^{31}; sq מִן (part of), + acc., 1 Ch 19^{18}; sq dir. obj. c. לְ †2 S 3^{30} Jb 5^{2} ψ 135^{11} = $136^{19.20}$ (but in last 3 first obj. is acc). **Niph.** *Impf.* **1.** pass of **Qal 1 a,** יֵהָרֵג La 2^{20} *shall priest and prophet be slain in the sanctuary?* **2.** pass. of **Qal 1 b,** 3 fpl. תֵּהָרַגְנָה Ez 26^{6}, also Ez 26^{15} בֵּהָרֵג הֶרֶג (= בְּהֵהָרֵג), but 𝔊 Co בַּהֲרֹג חֶרֶב. **Pu.** *Pf* 3 ms. הֹרַג Is 27^{7} *be slain* (pass of **Qal 1 b**), cf. 1 pl. הֹרַגְנוּ ψ 44^{23} (|| נֶחְשַׁבְנוּ כְּצֹאן טִבְחָה)

†הֶ֫רֶג n.m. Is 30, 25 **slaughter**—הֶ׳ abs Pr 24^{11} + 2 t. + Ez 26^{15} (𝔊 Co חֶרֶב), cstr. Is 27^{7}—of Jews' slaughter of their enemies Est 9^{5} (|| אַבְדָן); מָטִים לַהֶרֶג Pr 24^{11} (|| לְקֻחִים לַמָּוֶת); כְּהֶרֶג הֲרוּגָיו הֹרָג Is 27^{7}, בְּיוֹם הֶרֶג רָב Is 30^{25} (cf בְּיוֹם חֲבֹשׁ י׳ אֶת־שֶׁבֶר עַמּוֹ v.^{26}). Ez 26^{15} rd with 𝔊 Co supr

†הֲרֵגָה n.f. slaughter, only abs in foll combinations, גֵּיא הַ׳ Je 7^{32} 19^{6} new name for גֵּיא בֶן־הִנֹּם; יוֹם הַ׳ Je 12^{3} of the wicked, i.e. day of judgment, צֹאן הַ׳ Zc $11^{4.7}$ i.e. Judah and Israel, slaughtered by their shepherds

†I. הָרָה vb. conceive, become pregnant (As *êrû* cf Dl Pr 21 Muss. Arnolt Hbr Oct. 1890, 67 Jäger BAS i 473),—**Qal** *Pf.* 3 ms. וְהָרָה consec. ψ 7^{15}, 3 fs הָרְתָה Gn $16^{4.5}$, 2 fs וְהָרִית consec. Ju 13^{3}, 1 s. הָרִיתִי Nu 11^{12}, 1 pl. הָרִינוּ Is 26^{18}; *Impf.* וַתַּהַר Gn 4^{1} + 26 t. (וַתַּהַר Gn 16^{4}); 3 fpl וַתַּהֲרֶיןָ Gn 19^{36}, 2 mpl. תַּהֲרוּ Is 33^{11}; *Inf. abs* הָרֹה Jb 15^{35}, הָרוֹ Is 59^{4} cf also v^{13} sub **Po.** infr.; *Pt* f. sf הוֹרָתִי Ct 3^{4}; הוֹרָתָם Ho 2^{7};—**1.** lit *conceive, become pregnant* Gn $16^{4.4.5}$ 19^{36} 25^{21} 38^{18} (all J). 2 S 11^{5} (agency of man expressed by מִן Gn 19^{36}, לְ 38^{18}); usu. in phr וַתַּהַר וַתֵּלֶד Gn $4^{1.17}$ 21^{2} $29^{32.33.34.35}$ $30^{5.7}$ (all J), v$^{17.19.23}$ (all E), $38^{3.4}$ (both J), Ex 2^{2} (E), 1 S 1^{20} 2^{21} 2 K 4^{17} 1 Ch 7^{23} Is 8^{3} Ho $1^{3.6.8}$, prob. also 1 Ch 4^{17} ותהר [ותלד] אֶת־מִרְיָם cf. Be; further Ju 13^{3}, and cf. Moses' question הֶאָנֹכִי הָרִיתִי את כָּל־הָעָם הַזֶּה אִם־אָנֹכִי יְלִדְתִּיהוּ Nu 11^{12} *have I conceived all this people, or have I brought it forth?* Pt. f. || אֵם Ho 2^{7} Ct 3^{4}. **2.** metaph. הָרִינוּ חַלְנוּ כְּמוֹ יָלַדְנוּ רוּחַ Is 26^{18} of anxious and disappointed waiting; תַּהֲרוּ חֲשַׁשׁ תֵּלְדוּ קַשׁ Is 33^{11}, of futile planning, cf. Che; elsewhere of evil, mischief וְהָרָה עָמָל וְיָלַד שָׁקֶר ψ 7^{15} (subj wicked man), cf. Jb 15^{35} Is 59^{4}, so also v^{13}, read הָרוֹ (Inf. abs) cf. Di. **Pu.** *Pf.* 3 ms. הֹרָה גָבֶר Jb 3^{3} *a man hath been conceived* (Bo ii. p. 103 Ba NB 77 regard as **Qal** pass.). **Po.** *Inf. abs*, *conceive, contrive, devise* הֹרוֹ וְהֹגוֹ

הָרוֹ וְהֹגוֹ מִלֵּב דִּבְרֵי שָׁקֶר Is 59^{13}, but rd. rather הָרוֹ וְהָגוֹ **Qal** *Inf. abs.* v. supr. (Ba$^{l.c.}$ expl. MT as **Qal** *Inf. pass.*).—On הוֹרַי Gn 49^{26} v. הור and הַר **1 c.**

†II. הָרָה **adj.f. pregnant**—; abs. ה׳ Gn 16^{11} + 10 t.; cstr. הָרַת Je 20^{17}; pl. cstr. הָרוֹת Am 1^{13}; sf. הָרוֹתֶיהָ 2 K 15^{16}; הָרֹתֵיהֶם 2 K 8^{12};—*pregnant*, as attrib., אִשָּׁה ה׳ Ex 21^{22}; as pred. Gn 38^{24} (לִזְנוּנִים), v^{25} (לְאִישׁ), 1 S 4^{19} 2 S 11^{5} Is 7^{14} (+וְיֹלֶדֶת); in phr. הִנָּךְ הָרָה וְיֹלַדְתְּ Gn 16^{11} (on resemblance to Is 7^{14} cf. Peters$^{Hbr. Apr. 1885, 243; Apr. 1886, 175}$), Ju $13^{5.7}$; = subst. *pregnant women, women with child* Am 1^{13} 2 K 8^{12} 15^{16} Je 31^{8}, and, in sim., Is 26^{17}; once of womb וְרַחְמָהּ הֲרַת עוֹלָם Je 20^{17}.

הֵרָיוֹן v. הֵרוֹן.

†[הָרִיָּה] **adj.f. pregnant,** only pl. as subst. וְהָרִיּוֹתָיו Ho 14^{1} (cf. As. *êriiâtê* Jäger$^{BAS i. 473}$).

†הֵרָיוֹן **n.[m.] conception, pregnancy;**—ה׳ abs. Ho 9^{11} Ru 4^{13}; sf. הֵרֹנֵךְ Gn 3^{16}, either contr., so Ew$^{§ 214 a}$, or erron. for הריונך which stands in Sam. cf. Di;—*conception*, in combin. מִלֵּדָה וּמִבֶּטֶן וּמֵהֵרָיוֹן Ho 9^{11}; וַיִּתֵּן י׳ לָהּ ה׳ וַתֵּלֶד Ru 4^{13}; עִצְּבוֹנֵךְ וְהֵרֹנֵךְ Gn 3^{16} (|| תֵּלְדִי).

†הֲרוֹרִי **adj. gent.** 1 Ch 11^{27} הַהֲרוֹרִי; but read prob. הַחֲרֹדִי (cf. || 2 S 23^{25}) q.v.

†הֹרָם **n.pr.m.** a Canaanitish king ruling in Gezer Jos 10^{33}.

†הָרֻם **n.pr.m.** a Judaite (DHM$^{Epigr. Denkm. 59}$ comp. Sab. n. pr. הרם, הרמה, Ar. n.pr. هِرِم, etc.) 1 Ch 4^{8}.

הָרָם v. בֵּית הָרָם p. 111 supr.

†[הַרְמוֹן] **n.m.** mng. dub.; text perhaps corrupt; only Am 4^{3} וְהִשְׁלַכְתֶּנָה הַהַרְמוֹנָה and *ye shall cast* them (your אחרית, posterity, AE; Hi RV *cast* [yourselves], but read rather with Vrss as pass. וְהֻשְׁלַ׳ *shall be cast*) *into Harmon;* if text be sound, some locality must be meant, though the nature of the allusion is lost (AV, *into the palace*, treats הרמון improb. as=ארמון). 𝔗 𝔖 have *mountain(s) of Armenia* (הַר מוֹנָה), Symm *Armenia*, cf. Lag$^{Ges. Abh. 172}$, Hoffm$^{ZAW iii. 1882, 102}$, of exile; Hi-St for ה׳ rd. הֲדַדְרִמּוֹנָה *to Hadadrimmon*, n.pr.loc. in plain of Jezreel, so Gunning; 𝔊 εἰς τὸ ὄρος τὸ Ῥομμαν, whence Ew ingeniously ההר רמונה and ye shall cast *Rimmonah* (name of idol, supposed fem. of Rimmon 2 K 5^{18}) *to the mountains.*

הַרְמִים v. אַרְמִי p. 74 supr.

†הָרָן **n.pr.m.** (*mountaineer;* i.e. mountain-people (or land)? cf. Di Gn 11^{27});—**1.** son of Teraḥ, brother of Abram and father of Lot Gn $11^{27.27.31}$ (all P), v^{28} (J); also father of Milcah (Nahor's wife) & Iscah v^{29} (J). **2.** a Levite (Gershonite) 1 Ch 23^{9}.—On הָרָן in **n.pr.loc.** v. sub בית הרם, p. 111.

†הָרַס **vb. throw down, break or tear down** (MI הרס; ? Ar. هَرَسَ, *bruise, bray, pound, crush* (grain))—**Qal** *Pf.* הָ׳ La $2^{2.17}$; הָרַס Is 14^{17}; וְהָרַסְתָּ Ju 6^{25} וְהָרַסְתִּי Ez 13^{14} Mi 5^{10}; וְהָרְסוּ Ez 16^{39} $26^{4.12}$ הָרָסוּ 1 K $19^{10.14}$; *Impf.* יַהֲרוֹס Jb 12^{14}; sf. יֶהֶרְסֶךָ Is 22^{19}; וַיֶּהֶרְסֶהָ 1 Ch 20^{1}; יֶהֶרְסֶנָּה Pr 29^{4} יֶהֶרְסֵם ψ 28^{5}; 3 fs. sf. 3 ms. תֶּהֶרְסֶנּוּ Pr 14^{1}; 2 ms. תַּהֲרֹס Ex 15^{7}; אֶהֱרֹס Je 24^{6} 42^{10} אֶהֱרוֹס Mal 1^{4}; 3 mpl. יֶהֶרְסוּ Ex $19^{21.24}$; יֶהֱרָסוּ 2 K 3^{25}; *Imv.* הֲרָס־ ψ 58^{7}; sf. הָרְסָהּ 2 S 11^{25}; *Inf.* הֲרֹס Je 31^{28}, הֲרוֹס Je 1^{10}; *Pt. act.* הֹרֵס Je 45^{4}; *pass.* הָרוּס 1 K 18^{30};—**1.** *throw down, tear down*, c. acc.: altar(s) Ju 6^{25} 1 K 18^{30} $19^{10.14}$; height (גַּב, where idol-altar stood? cf. גַּב sub נבב) Ez 16^{39}; city (cities) Is 14^{17} 2 S 11^{25} 2 K 3^{25} 1 Ch 20^{1} (cf. MI^{27}) Mal 1^{4} (obj. not expr.); wall(s) Ez 13^{14} 26^{12}; house Pr 14^{1} (fig. of foolish woman's action); strongholds (מִבְצָרִים) La 2^{2} Mi 5^{10}; tower(s) Ez 26^{4}; fig. *overthrow* (i.e. *ruin*) land Pr 29^{4} (opp. יַעֲמִיד); obj. men Ex 15^{7} (poem in E) Is 22^{19} (*cast down* Shebna from office); fig., opp. building up, of Yahweh's dealings with men ψ 28^{5}, cf. (without obj.) Je 24^{6} 42^{10}; obj. indef. אשר בָּנִיתִי אֲנִי הֹרֵס Je 45^{4}; abs. Je 1^{10} 31^{28} La 2^{17} Jb 12^{14}. **2.** *break down, break away* ה׳ שִׁנֵּימוֹ בְּפִימוֹ ψ 58^{7} *break away their teeth in their mouth!* fig., addressed to God. **3.** *break through*, intr., sq. אֶל־י׳ Ex 19^{21}; sq. לַעֲלֹת אֶל־י׳ v^{24} (both J). **Niph.** *Pf.* 3 fs. נֶהֶרְסָה Pr 24^{31}; 3 pl. נֶהֶרְסוּ Je 50^{15} Jo 1^{17}; וְנֶהֶרְסוּ consec. Ez 30^{4} 38^{20}; *Impf.* יֵהָרֵס Je 31^{40}; 3 fs. תֵּהָרֵס Pr 11^{11}; יֵהָרֵסוּן ψ 11^{3}; *Pt.* הַנֶּהֱרָסוֹת Ez $36^{35.36}$;—*be thrown* or *torn down;* wall(s) of vineyard Pr 24^{31}, of city Je 50^{15}; cities Ez 36^{35} cf. v^{36}; fig. *ruined* Pr 11^{11} (opp. תָּרוּם); foundations, יְסוֹדֹת Ez 30^{4}; שָׁתוֹת ψ 11^{3}; mountains Ez 38^{20}; storehouses מַמְּגֻרוֹת Jo 1^{17} [v. מ׳]; valley E. of Jerus. לֹא־יִנָּתֵשׁ וְלֹא־יֵהָרֵס Je 31^{40} *it shall not be plucked up nor thrown down,* appar. proverb. expression, implying destruction, removal. **Pi.** *Impf.* 2 ms. sf. תְּהָרְסֵם Ex 23^{24}; *Inf. abs.* הָרֵס Ex 23^{24}; *Pt.* pl. sf. מְהָרְסַיִךְ Is 49^{17};—*overthrow, tear down* הָרֵס תְּהָרְסֵם Ex 23^{24} *thou shalt utterly tear them down* (JE; obj. = idols cf. Di); pt. *destroyers*, of Zion Is 49^{17} (|| מַחֲרִיבַיִךְ).

†הֶ֫רֶס **n.[m.]** overthrow, destruction, only Is 19^{18} one shall be called עִיר הַהֶרֶס *city of destruction*, i. e. (as usually explained) with punning allusion to On-Heliopolis: it shall be called no longer עִיר הַחֶרֶס *city of the sun*, but עיר ההרס *city of destruction*, city whose temples, etc., of the sun have been destroyed; but perh. < 𝔊 πόλις ασεδεκ = עִיר הַצֶּדֶק *city of righteousness*, so Gei$^{\text{Urschrift 79}}$ Brd Di (change intentional? cf. id.); on other views v. id. & De Che.

†[הֲרִיסָה] **n.f.** ruin (concr.);—וַהֲרִסֹתָיו Am 9^{11} *and its ruins* (i.e. of סֻכַּת דָּוִיד) *will I raise up* (‖ פִּרְצֵיהֶן).

†[הֲרִיסוּת] **n.f.** overthrow, destruction, ruin;—אֶרֶץ הֲרִסֻתֵךְ Is 49^{19} *the land of thine overthrow*, i.e. thy ruined land (‖ חָרְבֹתַיִךְ וְשֹׁמְמֹתַיִךְ).

הרר (√of foll.; meaning dubious).

הַר $_{558}$ **n.m.** $^{\text{Gn 7, 19}}$ **mountain, hill, hill-country** (NH *id.*, pl. הָרִים, הֲרָרִים; Ph. הר +CIS$^{\text{I. 3, 17}}$; Sab. sf. הרתהמו DHM$^{\text{ZMG 1876, 673}}$);—ה׳ abs. Jos 17^{18}+; c. art. הָהָר Ex 3^{12}+; c. ה ָ loc. הָ֫רָה Gn 14^{10}, הָהָ֫רָה Gn 12^{8}+12 t.; cstr. הַר Gn 10^{30}+; sf. הַרְרִי ψ 30^{8}, הֲרָרִי Je 17^{3}; הַרְכֶם ψ 11^{1}; הַרְרָם Gn 14^{6}; pl. הָרִים Dt 11^{11}+; c. art. הֶהָרִים Gn 7^{19}+; cstr. הָרֵי Gn 8^{4}+27 t.; הַרְרֵי Dt 33^{15}+8 t. (all poet.); sf. הָרַי Is 14^{25} 49^{11} Zc 14^{5}+Ez 38^{21} (B Co חרדה), הָרָ֑י Is 65^{9}; הָרָיו Ez 35^{8} Mal 1^{3}; הֲרָרֶיהָ Dt 8^{9};—**1.** *mountain, hill* (these often not sharply distinguished, but): **a.** specif. *mountain, high elevation*, oft. in all the literature;—e.g. הַר סִינַי *Mount Sinai* (properly, the Mount of Sinai; so always) +Ex 19$^{11.18.20.23}$ 24^{16} 31^{18} 34$^{2.4.29.32}$ Lv 7^{38} 25^{1} 26^{46} 27^{34} Nu 3^{1} 28^{6} Ne 9^{13} (v. סִינַי); also הָהָר = *id.*, Ex 19^{2}+10 t. Ex 19 (v^{18} rd. הָעָם, so Codd. 𝔊 Di) 20^{18} 24^{4}+6 t. Ex 24; 25^{40} 26^{30} 27^{8} 32$^{1.15.19}$ 34$^{2.3.3.29}$; = הַר חוֹרֵב +Ex 33^{6} (v. חֹרֵב), also אֶל־הַר הָאֱלֹהִים חֹרֵב Ex 3^{1}, עַד הַר הָאֱלֹהִים חֹרֵ֑בָה 1 K 19^{8}; further הָהָר = *id.*, Dt 4$^{11.11}$ 5$^{4.5.19.20}$ 9^{9}+10 t. Dt 9.10, 1 K 19^{11}; = הַר הָאֱלֹהִים Ex 4^{27} 18^{5} 24^{13} (all JE) = הַר יהוה Nu 10^{33} (cf. Di); v. further הֹר הָהָר *Hor the mount* (so always) Nu 20^{22}+10 t. Nu; Dt 32^{50}; = הָהָר Nu 20$^{28.28}$; הַר נְבוֹ Dt 32^{49} 34^{1} = הָהָר 32^{50}; = הַר הָעֲבָרִים הַזֶּה Nu 27^{12} Dt 32^{49}, cf. הָרֵי הָעֲבָרִים (לִפְנֵי נְבוֹ) Nu 33$^{47.48}$; הַר גְּרִזִּים *Mt. Gerizim* +Dt 11^{29} 27^{12} Jos 8^{33}; רֹאשׁ הַר־גְּרִזִּים Ju 9^{7}; הַר עֵיבָל *Mt. Ebal* +Dt 11^{29} 27$^{4.13}$ Jos 8$^{30.33}$; also הַר חֶרְמוֹן *Mt. Hermon* Dt 3^{8} Jos 11^{17} 12$^{1.5}$ 13$^{5.11}$ 1 Ch 5^{23}; cf. Dt 4^{48} הַר שִׂיאֹן הוּא חֶרְמוֹן (v. חֶרְמוֹן), & הַר בַּעַל חֶרְמוֹן (v. *id.*, & בעל חרמון sub בעל); הַר הַלְּבָנוֹן *Mt. Lebanon* Ju 3^{3}, cf. מְרוֹם הָרִים יַרְכְּתֵי לְבָנוֹן 2 K 19^{23} = Is 37^{24} (v. לבנון); הַר הַכַּרְמֶל *Mt. Carmel* 1 K 18$^{19.20}$ 2 K 2^{25} 4^{25} (v. כרמל); הָהָר = *id.*, 4^{27}, appar. also 1^{9}; הַר תָּבוֹר *Mt. Tabor*, Ju 4$^{6.12.14}$, cf. Je 46^{18} תָּבוֹר בֶּהָרִים (opp. כַּרְמֶל בַּיָּם); הַר הַגִּלְבֹּעַ 1 S 31$^{1.8}$ 2 S 1^{6}, also (poet.) הָרֵי בַגִּ׳ v^{21} (cf. Dr); הַר־חֶרֶס Ju 1^{35} (Stu עִר חֶרֶס) cf. חֶרֶס; הַר הַזֵּיתִים Zc 14$^{4.4}$ *Mount of Olives*, (opp. גַּיְא) cf. הָהָר אֲשֶׁר מִקֶּדֶם לָעִיר Ez 11^{23}; also בָּהָר אֲשֶׁר עַל־פְּנֵי יְרוּשָׁלַ͏ִם 1 K 11^{7} (place of Sol.'s idolatry) = הַר־הַמַּשְׁחִית 2 K 23^{13} *mt. of the destroyer* (same combin. in another, fig. sense Je 51^{25}), others der. הַמ׳ here fr. משׁח *anoint*, and render as = *Mt. of Olives* (cited as הר המשחה Talm., Shabb. 56 b), cf. Hoffm$^{\text{ZAW 1882, 175}}$; אַחַד הֶהָרִים in land of Moriah Gn 22^{2}; mts. about Jerus. in gen., יְרוּשָׁלַ͏ִם הָרִים סָבִיב לָהּ ψ 125^{2}; cf. also ψ 121^{1} (‖ יהוה); הָהָר of citadel of Jerus. Is 22^{5}; of temple hill הַר הַבַּיִת Mi 3^{12} = Je 26^{18}; הַר בֵּית־י׳ Is 2^{2} = Mi 4^{1}, 2 Ch 33^{15}; also הֲרָרִי בַּשָּׂדֶה Je 17^{3}; further הַר צִיּוֹן *Mt. Zion* Is 4^{5} 8^{18} 10^{12} 18^{7} 24^{23} 29^{8} 31^{4} 37^{32} Mi 4^{7} La 5^{18} Ob^{17} Jo 3^{5} ψ 48$^{3.12}$ 74^{2} 78^{68} 125^{1} (v. also צִיּוֹן); comp. הַר בֵּית־צִיּוֹן Is 10^{32}, הַר בַּת צ׳ 16^{1}; הַר־י׳ Is 2^{3} = Mi 4^{2}, Is 30^{29} ψ 24^{3}; (*id.* of Horeb Nu 10^{33} JE); הַר־י׳ צְבָאוֹת Zc 8^{3}, הַר הַקֹּדֶשׁ הַר־קָדְשִׁי Zp 3^{11} Ob^{16} Ez 20^{40} Is 11^{9} = 65^{25}, cf. 56^{7} 57^{13} 65^{11} Jo 2^{1} (‖ צִיּוֹן) 4^{17} (‖ *id.*) ψ 2^{6} (‖ *id.*) 3^{5} 15^{1} 43^{3} 48^{2}; v. further הַר־קָדְשִׁי יְרוּשָׁלַ͏ִם Is 66^{20} cf. Dn 9^{16} & הַר הַקֹּדֶשׁ יְרוּשָׁלַ͏ִם Is 27^{13}; also הַר צְבִי־קֹדֶשׁ Dn 11^{45}; הַר־הַקֹּדֶשׁ Je 31^{23}; even הַר קֹדֶשׁ אֱלֹהַי Dn 9^{20}; other designations of temple-hill are הָהָר חָמַד א׳ לְשִׁבְתּוֹ ψ 68^{17}, & הַר מְרוֹם יִשְׂרָאֵל Ez 17^{23} 20^{40} (‖ הַר־קָדְשִׁי); הַר קֹדֶשׁ אֱלֹהִים Ez 28^{14} of the distant abode of God (or gods?) so הַר אֱלֹהִים v^{16} (הַר־אֱלֹהִים ψ 68^{16} is general, *a God's mountain*, i.e. a majestic mt., likewise in simile כְּהַרְרֵי־אֵל מִשְׁפָּטֶיךָ ψ 36^{7});—הַר הָאֱלֹהִים elsewh. of Horeb (Sinai) Ex 4^{27} 18^{5} 24^{13} 1 K 19^{8} (v. supr.). Note partic. †הַר־מוֹעֵד Is 14^{13} *mountain of meeting* or *of assembly*, i.e. the dwelling-place of the gods, acc. to Babylonian conception, here represented as in the far north, v. esp. Che De Di, Dl$^{\text{Pa 117 ff.}}$ COT$^{\text{ad loc.}}$ Jr$^{\text{57 ff.}}$ Jen$^{\text{Kosmologie 23}}$. *Upon the mt.* is עַל־הָהָר cf. וַתֵּבְךְּ עַל־בְּתוּלֶיהָ עַל־הֶהָרִים Ju 11^{38}, & the peculiar phr. וְאֵלְכָה וְיָרַדְתִּי עַל־הֶהָרִים v^{37}; *go up upon* עָלָה אֶל־ Ex 19^{23} 24^{13} 34^{4} (all JE); cf. acc. in הַעַל אֹתָם הֹר הָהָר Nu 20^{25};

speak with one *upon* is דבר בהר Ex 31^{18} 34^{32} Nu 3^{1} (all P), Lv 25^{1} (H), cf *command, give commands, law*, etc , בהר Lv 7^{38} 26^{46} 27^{34} (all P or H), other phrases with ב *upon* (lit. *in*, i e in the midst of a group of mts) Ex 34^{3} בְּכָל (JE) 25^{40} 26^{30} 27^{8} Nu 28^{6} (all P), Is 13^{4}, but בחרב ψ 106^{19} = *at Horeb*, בהר הָהָר Nu 33^{37} *at Mt Hor; go down from the mt* is יָרַד מִן־הָהָר Ex 32$^{1.15}$ (both JE) 34$^{29.29}$ (both P), cf Ju 9^{36} etc **b.** *mountain-range* הַר־בָּשָׁן ψ 68$^{16.16}$ = הַר־אֱלֹהִים v^{16}, = הַר־גַּבְנֻנִּים v^{16}, הָרִים גַּבְנֻנִּים v^{17} (of the Jebel Hauran v בָּשָׁן) **c.** *mountain*, indef., Jb 14^{18} (‖צור), usu pl *mountains*, in general, or *the mountains*, esp in poet & the higher style, oft fig , הָרִים, ההרים, covered by flood Gn 7^{20} cf v^{19} 8^{5}, covered by waters & freed therefrom by word of God (at creation) ψ 104^{6}, a chief work of God (in creation) Am 4^{13} ψ 65^{7} 90^{2} Pr 8^{25} (‖גְּבָעוֹת), weighed by God Is 40^{12}, removed and overturned in anger of God Jb 9^{5} cf ψ 46$^{3.4}$, devastated by God Is 42^{15} (‖גבעות) cf Je 9^{9}, smoking at God's touch ψ 104^{32} 144^{5}, melting at presence of ׳י Ju 5^{5} Mi 1^{4} ψ 97^{5} Is 63^{19} 64^{2}, trembling Is 5^{25} cf Je 4^{24} (‖גְּבָעוֹת), Na 1^{5} (‖*id*), Hb 3^{10}, called to witness Yahweh's dealings with his people Mi 6^{2} (‖הָאֵתָנִים מֹסְדֵי אָרֶץ ‖הַגְּבָעוֹת), cf v^{1} (‖הַגְּבָעוֹת), entreated to cover the guilty Ho 10^{8} (‖גְּבָעוֹת), addressed by ׳י also Ez 6^{3} (‖גְּבָעוֹת, opp אֲפִיקִים, גֵּאָיוֹת), specif, mts of Israel summoned to hear ׳י and addressed by him Ez 36$^{1.1.4.8}$ 37^{22} 38^{8} 39$^{2.4}$, summoned to praise ׳י ψ 148^{9} (‖גְּבָעוֹת) cf Is 44^{23} 49^{13} 55^{12} (‖גְּבָעוֹת), leaping in praise of ׳י ψ 114$^{4.6}$ (both ‖ גְּבָעוֹת), הַרְרֵי־קֶדֶם Dt 33^{15} הַרְרֵי־עַד (‖גבעות עולם), הַרְרֵי־עַד Hb 3^{6} (‖*id*), also ψ 76^{5} (acc to 𝔊 Bi Che; MT has טֶרֶף for עַד), and prob Gn 49^{26} for MT הוֹרַי עַד (‖גבעת עוֹלָם) cf Di **d.** *high mt* הַר גָּבֹהַּ Is 30^{25} (‖גבעה נִשָּׂאָה) cf 40^{9} 57^{7}, הַר גָּבֹהַּ מְאֹד Ez 40^{2}, הַר גָּבֹהַּ וְתָלוּל Ez 17^{22}, pl הֶהָרִים הַגְּבֹהִים Gn 7^{19} ψ 104^{18} (‖סְלָעִים), הה׳ הָרָמִים Is 2^{14} as symbol of strength and pride (‖הַגְּבָעוֹת הַנִּשָּׂאוֹת), cf. ההרים Ez 38^{20} (‖חוֹמָה, מַדְרֵגוֹת) **e.** opp valley or plain Jos 12^{8} (D, opp עֲרָבָה, אֲשֵׁדוֹת, מִדְבָּר, שְׁפֵלָה), cf Dt 1^{7}, also Je 17^{26} (opp שְׁפֵלָה), Gn 19^{17} (J, opp כִּכָּר), oft opp גַּיְא 2 K 2^{16} Ez 31^{12} (fig) 32^{5} (*id*) 35^{8} (‖גְּבָעָה), 36^{4} (‖*id*), Is 40^{4} (‖*id*), opp בִּקְעָה Dt 8^{7} 11^{11} ψ 104^{8}, opp מִדְבָּר La 4^{19} (cf Jos 12^{8} supr), בֵּין הָרִים ψ 104^{10} is ‖ בַנְּחָלִים, see also אֱלֹהֵי הָרִים ׳י ולא־אלהי עֲמָקִים 1 K 20^{28}, cf. v^{23} (opp מִישׁוֹר), note also הַר הָעֵמֶק Jos 13^{19} (P), & גֵּיא־הָרַי, גֵּי־הָרִים Zc 14$^{5.5}$, further מדבר הָרִים ψ 75^{7} *mountainous desert* Vrss & most mod (Baer מִדְבַּר but cf. De); *mountainward* is הָהָרָה Gn 14^{10}. **f.** mts. as hiding-places.—הַמִּנְהָרוֹת אֲשֶׁר בֶּהָרִים Ju 6^{2} *the burrows* (Stanley, VB) *which are in the mts* , cf. ψ 11^{1} Je 16^{16} (‖גִּבְעָה); הָפַךְ מִשֹּׁרֶשׁ הָרִים Jb 28^{9} (of mining), v also Dt 8^{9}. **g.** mts as running-place of gazelles 1 Ch 12^{8}, of leopards הַרְרֵי נְמֵרִים Ct 4^{8}, hunting-ground for partridges 1 S 26^{20}, עוֹף הָרִים ψ 50^{11} cf 11^{1} (fig); wandering-place of lost sheep (fig) Na 3^{18} 1 K 22^{17} Je 50^{6} cf v^{6} (‖גִּבְעָה), Ez 34^{6} (‖כָּל־גִּבְעָה רָמָה) 2 Ch 18^{16} **h.** grazing-places for cattle בְּהֵמוֹת בְּהַרְרֵי־אָלֶף ψ 50^{10} (rd אל for אלף Ol Bi Che), cf יְתוּר הָרִים Jb 39^{8} of pasture of wild ass, also (si vera l) בוּל הָרִים Jb 40^{20}, i e. mts as furnishing food for hippopot ; v further Ct 4^{8} 8^{14} Pr 27^{25} **i.** as place of field and vineyards 2 Ch 26^{10} (opp. שְׁפֵלָה, מִישׁוֹר) Is 7^{25}, v also הַמַּצְמִיחַ הָרִים חָצִיר ψ 147^{8} cf. Hg 1^{11}; fig ψ 72^{3} (‖גְּבָעוֹת), in promise יִטְּפוּ הֶהָרִים עָסִיס וְהַגְּבָעוֹת תֵּלַכְנָה חָלָב Jo 4^{18} cf Am 9^{13}, **j** as kindled into flame (i e their forests, in sim) ψ 83^{15}. **k.** as scene of massacre, (fig) Is 34^{3} *melting with blood*, as place of battle array, *height* 1 S 17$^{3.3}$ **l.** as places of illicit worship Is 65^{7} (‖גְּבָעוֹת) cf Je 3^{6} & appar v^{23} (‖*id.*) so הַר־גָּבֹהַּ וְנִשָּׂא Is 57^{7}, הֶהָרִים הָרָמִים Dt 12^{2} (‖הַגְּבָעוֹת), but Ez 18$^{6.15}$ rd. perh הַדָּם for הרים cf. RS $^{K\,310}$ & Ez 33^{25} **m.** in various combinations צַד הָהָר 1 S 23$^{26.26}$ 2 S 13^{34} *side of the mt.*, צֶלַע הָהָר 16^{13} *id* , מֹץ הָרִים Is 17^{13} *chaff of mts* , זֶרֶם הָרִים Jb 24^{8} *mountain-shower*, צֵל הֶהָרִים Ju 9^{36} *shadow of the mts* ; מִבֵּין שְׁנֵי הָרִים וְהֶהָרִים הָרֵי נְחֹשֶׁת Zc 6^{1}; *top of mt* usu רֹאשׁ הָהָר Nu 14$^{40.44}$ 1 S 26^{13} 2 K 1^{9}, as place for beacon Is 30^{17} (‖גִּבְעָה), (cf הַר־נִשְׁפֶּה 13^{2} & נשׂא־נס הָרִים Is 18^{3}), רֹאשׁ הֶהָרִים Is 2^{2} = Mi 4^{1}, רֹאשׁ הָרִים Is 42^{11} (‖ סֶלַע as dwelling-place) v also ψ 72^{16}, רָאשֵׁי הֶהָרִים Gn 8^{5}, as lurking-places for ambuscade Ju 9$^{25.36}$, places for altars Ez 6^{13} (‖גִּבְעָה רָמָה), for sacrifice Ho 4^{13} (‖הַגְּבָעוֹת), רֹאשׁ הָהָר Jos 15^{8} = *mt -ridge*, cf v^{9} Ju 16^{3}; תּוֹעֲפוֹת הָרִים ψ 95^{4}; *foundations of mts* מוֹסְדֵי הָרִים Dt 32^{22} ψ 18^{8} (‖מוֹסְדוֹת הַשָּׁמַיִם 2 S 22^{8}); cf. לְקִצְבֵי הָרִים יָרַדְתִּי Jon 2^{7} **n** in fig uses: תָּדוּשׁ הָרִים וְתָדֹק וּגְבָעוֹת כַּמֹּץ תָּשִׂים Is 41^{15} fig of Isr.'s overcoming its foes, יִתְנַגְּפוּ רַגְלֵיכֶם עַל־הָרֵי נָשֶׁף Je 13^{16} of encountering hopeless calamities; ההרים Is 54^{10} as less permanent & changeless than Yahweh's kindness (‖גְּבָעוֹת), הַר הַמַּשְׁחִית Je 51^{25} & הַר שְׂרֵפָה v^{25} fig of Babylon **2.** *hill-country, mountain-*

region, **a.** opp. plain, etc :—dwelling-place of Canaanites, הָהָר Nu $13^{17.29}$ (of promised land; opp. יַד־הַיַּרְדֵּן & הַיָּם ,אֶרֶץ הַנֶּגֶב); בָּעֲרָבָה בָּהָר בָּהָר וּבָעֲרָבָה נֶגֶב וּבַשְּׁפֵלָה וּבַנֶּגֶב וּבְחוֹף הַיָּם Dt 1^{7}, בָּהָר כִּנֲּרוֹת וּבַשְּׁפֵלָה וּבְנָפוֹת דּוֹר מִיָּם Jos 11^{2}; וּבַשְּׁפֵלָה וּבָעֲרָבָה וּבָאֲשֵׁדוֹת וּבַמִּדְבָּר וּבַנֶּגֶב 12^{8}; cf 9^{1} 10^{40} Ju 1^{9}, הָהָר indef. (*the hill-country, the mountains*, in gen.) 2 Ch 2^{1} (place for hewing wood) so v^{17}; Ne 8^{15} (place for cutting boughs), etc **b.** of a particular mountain-region, hill-country: הַר הָאֱמֹרִי Dt 1^{7} (cf v^{7}) v^{19} (cf v^{24}), also Jos 10^{6}, cf Amalekites Ju 12^{15}, of Ephraim Jos 17^{15} 19^{50} 20^{7} 21^{21} $24^{30.33}$ Ju 3^{27} 4^{5} 7^{24} 9^{43} 17^{1} + 6 t Ju 17, 1 S 1^{1} 9^{4} 14^{22} 2 S 20^{21} 1 K 4^{8} 12^{25} 2 K 5^{22} 1 Ch 6^{52} 2 Ch 13^{4} 15^{8} 19^{4} Je 4^{15} 31^{6}, Ephraim and Gilead 50^{19} (cf. also הר(ה) Jos $17^{16.18}$ Ju 3^{27}), of Israel Jos $11^{16.21}$, cf. הָרֵי יִשְׂרָאֵל Ez 6^{2} 19^{9} 33^{28} 34^{13} 35^{12}; הַר מְרוֹם יִשְׂרָאֵל Ez 17^{23} 20^{40} (|| הַר־קָדְשִׁי) 34^{14}, עָרֵי הָהָר i.e. in mountain-country Dt 2^{37} (of Ammonites), Je 32^{44} 33^{13}, hill-country of Judah Jos 11^{21} 15^{48} 18^{12} 20^{7} 21^{11} 2 Ch 21^{11} (הָרֵי יהודה) 27^{4}, abode of Jebusites Jos 11^{3}

הַרְרֵי ,הֲרָרֵי ,הֲרָרִם ,הֲרֵי ,הֲרָרֶיהָ v הר

†הֲרָרִי ,הָרָרִי ,הָרְרִי **adj. gent.** (= *mountain-dweller* (Thes)? or deriv fr some unknown **n.pr.loc.**);—used only in defining certain of David's heroes. **1. a.** שַׁמָּה הַהֲרָרִי 2 S 23^{33a} (cf. Dr) = 1 Ch 11^{34b} (where rd prob. שַׁמָּה for שָׁגֵה, 𝔊^L Σαμαια) **b.** שַׁמָּה בֶן־אָגֵא הָרָרִי 2 S 23^{11} (rd perh. הַהֲרָרִי cf. Dr; but 𝔊 ὁ Ἀρουχαῖος, 𝔊^L ὁ Αραχι, i.e. הָאַרְכִּי? cf. Klo). On שַׁמּוֹת הַהֲרוֹרִי 1 Ch 11^{27} (𝔊 ὁ Ἀδι, 𝔊^L ὁ Αρωρι) v. הַחֲרוֹרִי supr p 248 **2.** אֲחִיאָם בֶּן־שָׂכָר הָאֲרָרִי 2 S 23^{33b} (rd prob הַהֲרָרִי = (אֲחִיאָם בֶּן־שָׂכָר הַהֲרָרִי 1 Ch 11^{35}

†הָשֵׁם **n.pr.m.** father of one (or more?) of David's heroes 1 Ch 11^{34}, but rd prob יָשֵׁן 2 S 23^{32} and del בני, cf Dr^{Sm} and v. further sub יָשֵׁן.

הַשְּׁבָעוֹת v. sub שבע.

הָשְׁפּוֹת v אַשְׁפֹּת sub שפת.

הַתּוּךְ v. sub נתך

הִתְחַבְּרוּת v sub חבר

†הֲתָךְ **n.pr.m.** a Persian official at court of Ahasuerus Est $4^{5.6.9.10}$

†[הָתַל] **vb** —only **Pi** deceive, mock, *Impf* וַיְהַתֵּל בָּהֶם 1 K 18^{27} (secondary formation fr תלל Hiph, q v., cf Thes Ol § 257 f. ad fin. Sta § 145 e; otherwise Ko i. 3.2, v further sub תלל).

†הֲתֻלִּים **n.[m.]pl.** mockery.—אִם־לֹא הֲ׳ עִמָּדִי Jb 17^{2} *truly mockery surroundeth me* (De Di Da cf VB)

הֲתַת √of תְּהוֹתְתוּ ψ 62^{4} acc to Thes al, but v הות.

ו

ו, *Wāw*, sixth letter, in modern Heb = numeral 6, no evidence of this usage in OT times.

וּ ,וַ ,וְ **demonstr. adv.** and **conj.** so, then, and (Ph Moab. Aram. ו; Ar. وَ, Eth. ወ: As *u* Dl^W (but between vbs the usu connective is the enclitic *ma* KAT^{2.508}, Dl §§ 82, 160) The use in Heb shews that orig ו was not a merely copulative conj, but that it possessed a *demonstrative* force (cf. Dr § 122), which is often perceptible as such, though in other cases, from its being applied to denote mere juxtaposition or connexion [cf. Gk τε, and Lat *tum* . . . *tum* = 'both . . . and,' both properly demonstratives: As *ma* has also a demonstr. force, Dl § 79], it is less palpable)—ו before shwa' mobile or a labial is vocalized וּ; often before a tone-syll, when the word itself has a disj accent, וָ (as וָמֵתִי: Gn 19^{19}, וָמֵתוּ 33^{13}, וָמֵת 44^{9}, וָחָיָה: Ex 1^{16}; וָיָמָה Jos 15^{46}, וָלֹא 2 S 13^{26}, וָאָרֶץ Is 26^{19}, וָקָמוּ 49^{7}, וָחָתָה: Je 48^{1}; וָרָע ψ 10^{15}); esp when it forms with the preceding word a *pair*, whether of parallel or opposed ideas (as כה וָכֹה Ex 2^{12}, מִי וָמִי 10^{8}, אֶבֶן וָאָבֶן Dt 25^{13}, דֹּר וָדֹר 32^{7} +, תֹהוּ וָבֹהוּ Gn 1^{2}, בְּהֵמָה וָרֶמֶשׂ 1^{24}, וְקַיִץ וָחֹרֶף וְיוֹם וָלַיְלָה 8^{22}, נָע וָנָד 4^{12}, טוֹב וָרָע: 2^{9}, אֲנִי וָאַתָּה 31^{44}, שָׁמַיִם וָאָרֶץ: 14^{19}, קַח וָלֵךְ: 12^{19}, אַתָּה וָהֵם 41^{11}, עִבְרוּ וָשׁוּבוּ Ex 32^{27}, אֲנִי וָהוּא Nu 16^{16}, אֱלֹהִים וָמֶלֶךְ 1 K 21^{13}, נִין וָנֶכֶד Is 14^{22},

עַד וָעֶבֶר 59^{7}, and often: v. more fully Bo § 600); occas also with a conj. accent (as וָחַי לְעֹלָם׃ Gn 3^{22} cf. Lv 18^{5}, וְמַתְנוּ שָׁם 2 K 7^{4}, וָאָרֶץ חֲדָשָׁה Is 65^{17}, Pr 25^{3} עַד וָשֶׁבֶר גָּדוֹל׃ Je 48^{3}, cf 32^{29}) — ו is used very freely and widely in Heb, but also with much delicacy, to express relations and shades of meaning which Western languages would usu indicate by distinct particles But in Heb particles such as אוֹ, אַךְ, אָכֵן, אוּלָם, בַּעֲבוּר, לְמַעַן, לָכֵן, etc, were reserved for cases in which special emph or distinctness was desired their frequent use was felt instinctively to be inconsistent with the lightness and grace of movement which the Hebrew ear loved, and thus in AV, RV, words like *or, then, but, notwithstanding, howbeit, so, thus, therefore, that,* constantly appear, where the Heb has simply ו

1. *And,* connecting both words (v supra), and sentences (Gn 1^{5} ולַחֹשֶׁךְ קָרָא וגו׳) When three, four, or more words follow, the conj may connect them all, as Gn 7^{21} 10^{2} (6 t) 24^{35} (7 t) Jos 7^{24} (10 t) 2 S 17^{28f}. often however it is prefixed only to the last, as Gn 5^{32} 10^{1} Dt 18^{10} etc, occas even it connects only the first two, 1 K 8^{47} Is 1^{13} ψ 45^{9} Jb 42^{9} Remarkably, however, ו as a *mere* conj is, as a rule, not in classical Hebrew attached directly to *verbs* (esp in the perf), the construction with ו consec. (v. **2**) being (as in Moab) preferred: thus יָצָא וַיִּבֶן is said, not יָצָא וּבָנָה. Exceptions in class Heb. are (*a*) sts where *synonyms* are coupled, as Nu 23^{19} אָמַר...ודבר, Dt 2^{30} Ju 5^{26} 1 S 12^{2} Is 1^{2} גדלתי ורוממתי 2^{11} 5^{14} 8^{8} 19^{6} 29^{20}, (*b*) isolated cases, difficult to reduce to rule (perh sts due to text error), as Gn 28^{6} 38^{5} Jud 3^{23} 7^{13} 16^{18} 1 S 1^{12} 3^{13} 4^{19} 5^{7} 10^{9} $17^{38.48}$ 25^{20} al. (in other passages, appar similar, the pf. and ו has a frequent force (v **2**), as Gn 37^{3} Ex 36^{29f} Nu 10^{17f} $21^{15.20}$ 1 S 2^{22} 16^{14} 17^{34f} (v Dr) 27^{9} 2 S 16^{13} 17^{17}, perh also Gen. 15^{6} 21^{25} 34^{5}) In later parts of OT, prob through Aram influence, the pf with simple ו occurs more freq. so esp in Ec, where it is all but universal (e g. $2^{11\ 12\ 13.15}$ etc). With the impf, the simple ו is not so unidiomatic, even in class Heb (cf **3**), v Gen $1^{9.26}$ 9^{27} 17^{2} 22^{17} 27^{29} Ex 23^{8} (freq) 24^{7} Nu 14^{12} Dt 17^{13} $30^{12\ 13}$ Jos 3^{13} 7^{3} Ju 7^{3} 13^{8} Is 5^{29} 14^{10}, oft also in Je Is² Jb ψ, e g. Is 40^{30} 41^{20} (Dr § 116 contrast 28^{13}). Vid more fully Dr § 130-4 Ges § 112 6 Special senses.— **a.** it sts = *and specially,* Gn 3^{16} 1 K 11^{1} many strange women, *and specially* the daughter of Ph, Is 1^{1} Judah *and* (= *and particularly*) Jerusalem, 2^{1} 9^{7} ψ 18^{1}. **b.** *and in particular* ('und zwar'), *and that* (explicative), Gn 4^{4} Ju 7^{22} 1 S 17^{40} וּבַיַּלְקוּט, 28^{3} in Ramah, *and that* in his city (unusual. text suspicious), 2 S 13^{20} ושׁמֵמָה *and that* desolate, Is 57^{11} I have been silent ומעולם *and that* from of old, Is 32^{7} Je 15^{13} Am 3^{11} (si vera l), 4^{10} Zc 9^{9b} Mal 1^{11} ψ 68^{10} Pr 3^{12} La 3^{26} Ec 8^{2} Dn 1^{3} 8^{10} $9^{25\ 27}$ Ne 8^{13} 1 Ch 9^{27} 2 Ch 8^{13} 29^{27} (but 'even' for ו, before ל and inf, e g in Is 44^{28} Je 17^{10} 19^{12}, is wrong, v. Ew § 351 c, Dr § 206) **c.** sts it introduces an idea which so exceeds or adds to what has preceded, that it is nearly equivalent to *also,* 1 S 25^{43} 1 K 2^{22} ask *also* the kingdom for him, unusually Ho 8^{6} כי מישׂראל והוא for of Isr is it *also,* Ec 5^{6} והבלים (v. De) 2 Ch 27^{5} (but v. 𝔊). Or it may be rendered *yea* so esp in the ascending numerations 3–4 Am $1^{3.6.9.11\ 13}$ $2^{1\ 4\ 6}$ Pr $30^{18\ 21\ 29}$, 6–7 Pr 6^{16} Jb 5^{19}, 7–8 Mi 5^{4}—the first number being aggravated, or augmented, by a higher In one idiom וּגְבוּל, occurring in geogr descriptions, it is used peculiarly, seemingly = *at the same time:* † Nu 34^{6} and as for the W border, וְהָיָה לָכֶם הַיָּם הַגָּדוֹל וגבול the great sea shall be to you *also* (Germ 'zugleich') a border, Dt 3^{16} תּוֹךְ הַנַּחַל וגבול the middle of the stream being *at the same time* the border, v^{17} Jos $13^{23.27}$ $15^{12.47}$ (but these, exc Nu 34^{6}, might be cases of **5 c** γ) **d.** it connects *alternative* cases, so that it = *or* Ex $20^{10\ 17}$ 21^{16} he that stealeth a man וּמְכָרוֹ ונמצא בידו and selleth him, *and* (= *or if*) he be found in his hand, v^{17} Lv 21^{14} $22^{23.24}$ Pr 29^{9} (Fl Ew RV. *whether* . *or*) Jb $31^{13.16.26}$, etc **e.** it connects *contrasted* ideas, where in our idiom the contrast would be expressed explicitly by *but;* in such cases prominence is usu given to the contrasted idea by its being placed immed after the conj· Gn 2^{17} *but* of the tree of the knowledge . . . thou shalt not eat, $4^{2.5}$ 6^{8} 17^{21} 31^{10} etc, 1 K 2^{26} 10^{7} $11^{32.34}$ 15^{14} Pr $10^{1.2.3.4}$ + oft, even after לא (where כי or כי אם might be expected), as Gn 42^{10} Ex 21^{18} Lv 26^{45} Dt 11^{11} Ju 19^{12} 1 K 3^{11}. **f.** it introduces a contrasted idea in such a way as to suggest a *question,* esp before a pron, Ju 14^{16} I told it not to my father or my mother, וְלָךְ אַגִּיד and shall I tell it *unto thee?* 2 S 11^{11} Je 25^{29} וְאַתֶּם הִנָּקֵה תִנָּקוּ and shall *ye* be guiltless? 45^{5} Ez 20^{31} 33^{25b} Jon 4^{11}. So the ו consec. and pf (see **2 a**), Ex 5^{5} וְהִשְׁבַּתֶּם *and* will ye make them rest from their burdens? Nu 16^{10} וּבִקַּשְׁתֶּם *and* seek ye the priesthood also? 1 S 25^{11} Is 66^{9} ψ 50^{21} *and* shall I keep

silence? Jb 32^{16} (cf. Dr $^{§119\gamma}$) **g.** attaching a fresh subj. (or obj.) to a clause already grammatically complete, it = *and also*, Gn 2^{9b} Nu $16^{2.18}$ and they stood at the entrance of the tent of meeting, ומשה ואהרן *and* Moses and Aaron (stood also), v^{27} Ex 35^{22} Ju 6^{5}; Gn 1^{16b} 12^{17} 44^{2} 46^{15} Ex 29^{3} Je 32^{29} (cf Dr $^{Sm\ 4\ 6.11,\ \&\ p\ 293}$). when the idea thus attached is subordinate, or not logically embraced in the principal pred., it approximates to the Arab. وَاوُ ٱلْمَعِيَّة or 'waw of association' (foll. by an *accus*. W $^{A\ ii.\ §\ 37}$), Est 4^{16} אֲנִי וְנַעֲרֹתַי אָצוּם I will fast (*sing*) *and* (= with) my maidens, Ex 21^{4} 1 S 25^{42} 29^{10b} (but insert here אַתָּה with 𝔊) 2 S 12^{30} (but read וְבָה, as 1 Ch 20^{2}) 20^{10} Ne 6^{12}; Gn 4^{20} Is 42^{5} Je 19^{1} (but read וְלָקַחְתָּ מִזקני with 𝔊) 2 Ch 2^{3} 13^{11}, cf. Je 22^{7} (אִישׁ וכליו), Jb 41^{12}. Whether Is 48^{16} וְרוּחוֹ belongs here, is dub **h.** ו repeated = *both* . . . *and* (but גַּם . . . גַּם is more usual in this sense), Gn 34^{28} Nu 9^{14} Jos 9^{23} 2 S 5^{8} (txt. dub), Is 16^{5} 38^{15} Je 13^{14} 21^{6} 32^{14} (txt dub) v^{20} 40^{8} ψ 76^{7} Jb 34^{29} Dn 8^{13} Ne 12^{28}. **i.** a repetition of the *same* word with ו interposed expresses (*a*) *diversity* (rare), Dt 25^{13} אֶבֶן וָאָבֶן a weight *and* a weight, i.e different weights (explained by גְּדֹלָה וּקְטַנָּה), v^{14} Pr 20^{23}; ψ 12^{3} בלב וָלֵב with a heart and a heart = with a double heart, 1 Ch 12^{33} בלֹא לֵב וָלֵב; (*b*) *distribution* (exc. in דר וָדֹר Dt 32^{7} Is 13^{20} + oft exclusively a late usage: cf. Dr $^{Intr\ 505}$) †ψ 87^{5} 1 Ch 26^{13} לְשַׁעַר וָשָׁעַר: = for *every* gate, $28^{14.14}$ 2 Ch 8^{14} 34^{13} 35^{15} Ezr 10^{14} זִקְנֵי עִיר וָעִיר elders of *every* city, Ne 13^{24}, Est $1^{8.22.22}$ 2^{12} $3^{4.12.12.12.12}$ $8^{9.9}$, strengthened by כָּל־ 2 Ch 11^{12} בכל עיר ועיר in *every several city*, 19^{5} 28^{25} 31^{19} 32^{28} Est 2^{11} בכל־יום ויום, 3^{14} 4^{3} $8^{11.13.17.17}$ $9^{21.27.28}$ ψ 45^{18} 145^{13} (common in postB. Heb, esp with כל) **j.** it is used in the formulation of proverbs (the *Vav adaequationis*, וָו הַשְׁתָּוָאָה) as Pr 17^{3} $25^{3.20.25}$ cold waters to a thirsty soul *and* good news from a far country (i.e. they are like each other), $26^{3.9.14.20}$ 27^{21} Ec 5^{2} 7^{1} 8^{8} cf 9^{11}; ψ 19^{5} 125^{2} Jb $14^{11f.19}$ (cf in Arab 'every man *and* his cares [*accus*],' 'every thing *and* its price,' i.e. they go together · 'merchants *and* dogs [*accus*] of Seleucia,' i.e. they are like one another v Fl $^{Kl\ Schr\ iii\ 535\ f.}$) More rarely in the opp. order, Jb 5^{7} 12^{11}. But 1 S 12^{15b} cannot be thus explained: rd. with 𝔊 וּבְמַלְכְּכֶם, and v. Dr. **k.** in *circumstantial clauses* ו introduces a statement of the *concomitant conditions* under which the action denoted by the principal verb takes place: in such cases, the relation expressed by ו must often in Engl. be stated explicitly by a conj, as *when, since, seeing, though*, etc, as occasion may require. So very often, as Gn 11^{4} let us build a tower וְרֹאשׁוֹ בַשָּׁמַיִם *and* its top in the heavens (= *with* its top in etc.), 18^{12} shall I have pleasure, וַאדֹנִי זָקֵן *and* my lord is old (= my lord *being* old)? Ju 16^{15} How sayest thou, I love thee, ולבך אין אתי *and* (= *when*) thy heart is not with me? and esp. with a pers. pron, Gn 15^{2} what wilt thou give me וְאָנֹכִי הוֹלֵךְ עֲרִירִי *and* I (= *the case being that* I) am going hence childless? 18^{13} 20^{3} lo, thou wilt die because of the woman thou hast taken והוא בעֻלַת בָּעַל: = *seeing* she is married, 24^{62} והוא ישב = *since* or *for* he was dwelling (different from וַיֵּשֶׁב = *and he proceeded* to dwell), 26^{27} ואתֶּם *seeing* ye hate me, Ju 13^{9} and came to her וְהִיא יוֹשֶׁבֶת = *as* she was sitting, 1 S 18^{23} 1 K 19^{19} + oft. Of a more except type are ψ 72^{12} the afflicted ואין־עוזר לו *and* (= *when*) he has no helper (cf. Jb 29^{12}), 104^{25} ואין מספר, 105^{34} Jb 5^{9}. Vid. more fully Dr $^{§156-60}$ Ges $^{§141.\ R\ 2}$ (The analogous use of the وَاوُ ٱلْحَال is very common in Arabic: W $^{ii\ §183}$.) Introducing an appeal to a fact *confirmatory* of some statement or promise, it almost = *as truly as* (cf Ew ^{§340c}) Ho 12^{6} *and* J. is God of hosts, J. is his name! Jo 4^{20} Am 9^{5-6} Is 51^{15} *and* I [who promise this] am J. thy God, who . . ! Je 29^{23} ψ 89^{38b} (comp in Qor the freq 'And God is . . . . [the mighty, the merciful, etc.]').

2. The ו **consecutive** (formerly called the Waw 'conversive'),—**a.** with the **impf.** (וַ with foll daghesh, before א, וָ), as וַיֹּאמֶר prop. = *and he proceeded* to say, chiefly in contin of a preceding *perfect* tense (so Moab.), **b.** with the **perf.** (וְ,—in 1 & 2 sg., the tone, with certain exceptions [v Dr ^{§110}], being thrown forward to the ultima), as וְיָשַׁבְתָּ prop *so* [*viz* as limited by a verb, or other term, preceding] *hadst thou sat*, chiefly in continuation of a preceding *imperfect* tense, in its various senses of future, jussive, or frequentative. The further analysis of these idioms belongs to the grammar; see on **a** Dr $^{Ch.\ vi}$, Ges ^{§111}, and on **b** Dr $^{Ch.\ viii}$ Ges ^{§112}. Here it must suffice to note—(*a*) ו consec (esp. with the impf) freq couples two verbs in such a manner that the first, indicating the *general* character

of the action, receives its closer definition in the second in such cases, the first may often be represented in Engl by an *adv*, as Gn 26^{18} וַיָּשָׁב וַיַּחְפֹּר and he turned *and* dug = and he dug *again*, so oft.; and similarly with הוֹסִיף Gn 25^{1}, מִהַר 24^{18}, הוֹאִיל Jos 7^{7}, etc, more exceptionally, Gn 30^{27} Est 8^{6}, and (not consec) Gn 47^{6} Jb 23^{3} Ct 2^{3} La 3^{26} (v Ges$^{§120.2a}$, cf. in Syr. Nö$^{§335-6}$ In Arab. the stronger form of the conj فَ here corresponds W$^{II §140}$) (*b*) ו with the impf sts expresses a contrast = *and yet*, Gn 32^{31} I have seen God face to face וַתִּנָּצֵל *and yet* my soul is delivered, Dt 4^{33} 2 S 3^{8} 19^{29} Is 51^{12} ψ 73^{14} 144^{3} Jb 10^{8}+ (cf. Dr ^{§74β}) (*c*) there is a tendency in the later books of the OT to use the pf with simple ו, where the classical language would employ the impf with ו (cf supr **1**), so esp. in Ec, where ו occurs thrice only, 1^{17} 4^{17} (*d*) a double pf with ו consec is sts used, informally but neatly, with a hypoth force, thus (*a*) in past or present time Ex 16^{21} וְחַם הַשֶּׁמֶשׁ וְנָמָס: and the sun used to be warm, and it used to melt = and *if* (or *when*) the sun was warm, it melted, 33^{10} 1 K 18^{10} Je 18$^{4.8}$ וְשָׁב וְנִחַמְתִּי = and *if* it turns, I repent, 20^{9} (v RV); (*β*) in fut time, Gn 44^{22} ועזב אביו ומת and he will leave his father, and he will die = and *if* he leaves his father, he will die, 33^{13} 42^{38} Ex 4^{14} 12^{13} 1 S 16^{2} 19^{3} Ez 33^{3} 39^{15} etc (Dr$^{§147-9}$, Ges$^{§159.2a}$).

3. With a **voluntative** (cohort. or juss) ו expresses an intention, that or so that (an elegancy by which the too frequent use of לְמַעַן or בַּעֲבוּר is avoided): Ex 10^{17} entreat God, וְיָסֵר *so may he* remove (= *that he may* remove) this death, Gn 27^{4} and bring it me וְאֹכֵלָה *so let me* eat (= *that I may* eat), and without the modal form being externally indicated, Ex 14^{1} speak . וְיָשֻׁבוּ *that* they return, v^{15}, and oft Sts even of past time, as 1 K 13^{33} whom he would, he consecrated וִיהִי *that* there might be priests of the high places, 2 K 19^{25} Is 25^{9a} La 1^{19} After a neg, ψ 51^{18} thou desirest not sacrifice, וְאֶתֵּנָה *so* [= in that case] *would I* give it (or, *that I might* give it), 55^{13} וְאֶשָּׂא *so* could I bear it (or, *that I might* bear it), Is 53^{2} RVm Nu 23^{19} Je 5^{28} RV Sts also before an imv, Gn 12^{2} *and be* (= that thou mayest be) a blessing, 2 S 21^{3}+. See more fully Dr$^{§59-65}$, Ges$^{§109.2, 109.2, 110.2}$. (In Arabic فَ with the *subjunctive* is used similarly: W$^{II §15d}$.) A volunt is also sts attached by ו to a preceding volunt. or imv., so as to form a virtually hypothetical sentence, as Gn 42^{18} זאת עשׂו וחיו = *if* you do this, you shall live, 30^{28} 34^{12} Pr 3^{9f} 4$^{4.8}$ Is 55^{2}: v Dr^{§152}.

4. It expresses often an informal inference, or consequence, so, then, esp at the beginning of a speech: Gn 27^{8} ψ 2^{10} and often וְעַתָּה now, *therefore;* וְלָמָּה and וּמַדּוּעַ why, *then?* Gn 29^{25} Nu 12^{8} 16^{3}+, Ex 2^{20} וְאַיּוֹ where, *then*, is he? Gn 34^{21} 1 S 15^{14} 26^{22} וְיַעֲבֹר let, *then*, . come over, 2 S 24^{3} 2 K 4^{41} וּקְחוּ קֶמַח *then* bring meal, Ez 18^{32} So the ו consec and the pf., as Dt 2^{4} ונשמרתם take heed, *therefore*, 4^{15} 7^{9} וְיָדַעְתָּ know, *therefore*, 30^{19} 1 S 6^{5} 1 K 2^{6} Ru 3^{9}, Jos 15^{19} Is 49^{6b} (Dr^{§119δ})

5. ו introduces the *predicate* or *apodosis* viz **a.** ו consec. and the *pf* — in answer to אם or כי constantly, as Ex 19^{5} 23^{22} if thou hearkenest to my voice, וְאָיַבְתִּי *then* am I (= I will be) enemy to thy enemies (v Dr$^{§136-8}$); after the *casus pendens*, Ex 12^{44} every servant that is bought for money, וּמַלְתָּה thou shalt circumcise him, etc Nu 14^{31} 24^{24} 1 S 25^{27} 2 S 14^{10} he that spake unto thee, וַהֲבֵאתוֹ אֵלַי *so hast thou* brought him (= *thou shalt* bring him) unto me, Is 9^{4} 56^{6f}+, Ex 12^{15} 31^{14} Dt 17^{12}+, after various time-determinations, as Gn 3^{5} in the day of your eating from it ונפקחו *then* shall your eyes be opened, Ex 16^{6} עֶרֶב וִידַעְתֶּם at even, *then* shall ye know, v^{7} 32^{34} 2 S 15^{10} 1 K 13^{31} במותי וקברתם אתי when I die, *so* ye shall bury me, etc, + oft., after conjs, as כִּי Gn 29^{15}, יַעַן 1 K 20^{28} Is 3^{16f}, תַּחַת 60^{15}, etc, (v Dr^{§123}) **b.** ו consec and the *impf.* (but much less frequently than the pf), as Gn 30^{30} the little that thou hadst, וַיִּפְרֹץ *it* hath increased, Ex 9^{21} 2 S 4^{10} 1 K 9^{20f} 15^{13}+; after time-determinations, Gn 22^{4} on the third day וַיִּשָּׂא *then* Abraham lifted up his eyes, 19^{15} 27^{34} 37^{18} 1 S 6^{6} 12^{8} Is 6^{1} Ho 11^{1} when Isr was a child, וָאֹהֲבֵהוּ *then* I loved him, +, occas. after conjs., as כַּאֲשֶׁר Ex 16^{34}, יַעַן 1 S 15^{23}, לְמַעַן Is 45^{4}, אם ψ 59^{16} (Dr^{§127}) **c.** in other cases (not 'consecutive')—all more or less uncommon · viz *a* ו closely joined to the impf. Gn 13^{9} if to the left, ואימינה *then* I will take the right (cf 2 S 12^{8}) Ex 12^{3} on the 10th of the month ויקחו *then* let them take, Nu 16^{5} Is 43^{4} Ho 4^{6} 10^{10} ψ 69^{23} Jb 15^{17}, 2 S 22^{41} Pr 23^{24} Kt (Dr^{§125}); *β* separated fr the vb, Ex 8^{22} Lv 7^{16} וּמִמָּחֳרָת וְהַנּוֹתָר יֵאָכֵל and on the morrow, *then* the remainder shall be eaten, Jos 3^{3} 1 K 8^{32} Is 8^{7}

48[7] Jb 14[7] 20[18b] 23[12] 25[5] 32[14]+; γ. without a vb, Gn 40[9] בַּחֲלֹמִי וְהִנֵּה in my dream, *behold*, a vine was before me, v[16] 2 S 23[3f.] Pr 10[25], and the extreme cases 2 S 15[34] thy father's slave, וַאֲנִי מֵאָז I was *that* of old,—but now וַאֲנִי עַבְדֶּךָ *well*, I will be thine, Is 34[12] (si vera l), Jb 4[6b] תִּקְוָתְךָ וְתֹם דְּרָכֶיךָ thy confidence—*it is* the uprightness of thy ways, 36[26] מִסְפַּר שָׁנָיו וְלֹא חֵקֶר Ges. seine Jahre, *da* ist kein Zahlen (cf. Dr[§ 124-5, 158-9])—With **4, 5** comp the Arab ف, W[I § 366 b, 367 e, ii, § 187], Dr[§ 165 end].

†**וְדָן**, appar **n.pr.loc.**, only in וְדָן וְיָוָן Ez 27[19] *Wedān and Yāwān* (cf. VB and reff.) but identif wholly dub, = *Waddân* near Medina acc. to Glas[Skizze ii 428]. 𝔊 om., text prob. corrupt, cf Sta[Javan 11 ff] Da al., Ew Hi rd. דְּדָן, but דְּדָן is in following v., and anticipation improb, cf Sta[l.c.], Co rds (for ודן ויון) וּאַרְנָבָן, on the basis of Bab & As *Aranabanim*, *Arnabani*, n. pr loc, following *Hilbunim* (חֶלְבּוֹן) in lists of places whence wine was brought (cf. יֵין חֶלְבּוֹן v[18], & 𝔊 καὶ οἶνον for וְיוָן; also COT Ez 27[18]).

†**וָהֵב**, appar **n.pr.loc.**, אֶת־וָהֵב בְּסוּפָה Nu 21[14], obj of a vb now lost out of the text (cf. RV & esp Di VB), situation unknown, 𝔊 Ζωοβ, Ζοοβ, so Lag[BN 54] Say[Ac. Oct 22 1892] (זָהָב).

†[**וָו**] **n.[m.]** hook, pin or peg (etym. unknown)—pl abs וָוִים Ex 38[28]; cstr וָוֵי Ex 27[10]+5 t, וָוֵיהֶם Ex 26[32]+5 t.;—only P, in description of tabernacle Ex 26[32.37] 27[10.11.17] 36[36.38] 38[10 11 12 17 19.28], the *hooks* or *pegs* of gold and silver, fastened on, or in, the posts of the tabernacle, to support the various hangings (curtains, screens, etc)

וזר (√of foll, cf. Ar. وَزَرَ *bear a burden*, or وَزِرَ *be guilty*, yet v Fl in De Pr 21[8])

†**וָזָר** **adj.** criminal, guilty הֲפַכְפַּךְ דֶּרֶךְ אִישׁ וָזָר Pr 21[8] *crooked is the way of a guilty man* (si vera l, txt dub.; possible dittogr. in וְזָר זַךְ?)

†**וַיְזָתָא** **n.pr.m.** (perhaps = Pers. n.pr m. *Vahyazdâta* Benfey[Pers Keilinschr (1847) 1[4], 93] cf Spieg[APK 240], who conjectures meaning *given-of-the-Best-One* (vom Besten gegeben)),—a son of Haman Est 9[9]

וָלָד, **וְלָד** v sub ילד

†**וַנְיָה** **n.pr.m.** one of those with strange wives, Ezr 10[36] (text dubious, 𝔊B Οὐιεχωα, א Οὐιερεχω, A Οὐουνια, 𝔊L Οὐανια).

†**וָפְסִי** **n.pr.m.** a man of Naphtali, in נַחְבִּי בֶּן־וָפְסִי Nu 13[14] (text dubious, 𝔊 Ναβει υἱὸς Ἰαβει).

†**וַשְׁנִי** acc. to MT appar **n.pr.m.** son of Samuel, only הַבְּכוֹר וַשְׁנִי וַאֲבִיָּה 1 Ch 6[13], but rd. הַבְּכוֹר יוֹאֵל וְהַשֵּׁנִי אֲבִיָּה cf 𝔊L, and ‖ 1 S 8[2]; v Th[8m] Be[Ch] Di[8m] al

†**וַשְׁתִּי** **n.pr.f.** (= Pers (Zend) *vahista*, *best*, cf. Justi[Hdb. d Zendsprache, 272]) queen of Ahasuerus (Xerxes) king of Persia, Est 1[9 11 12 15 16 17 19] 2[1 4 17]

ז

ז, *Zâyin*, seventh letter; used as numeral 7 in modern Heb., no evidence of this usage in OT times

זאב (√of foll; acc to Fl[Bericht d sächs G d W i. (1846-47) 430 f = Kleinere Schriften iii. 212 f] i.q. Ar. ذَأَبَ *drive away, and despise, drive* or *frighten away*, whence ذِئْبٌ, ذَأْبٌ, זְאֵב wolf, as *driven* or *chased away*; cf Hom[NS 304] MV al)

†I. **זְאֵב** **n.m.**[Is 11, 6] wolf (NH *id.*, Ar. ذِئْبٌ (*jackal* according to Hom[NS 303 ff.], but see RS ZMG 1880, 373 and Doughty[Arab Deserta i 327, ii 144, 145]) Aram. דִּיבָא, דֵּיבָא, As *zību* Dl[S 47]; Eth. ዝእብ: *hyena* Di[1056] (on format. cf. Lag[BN 88]); Ph. in cpd n pr. (זיבקם)—זְאֵב abs. Gn 49[27]+2 t, cstr. Je 5[6], pl. זְאֵבִים Ez 22[27], cstr. זְאֵבֵי Hb 1[8] Zp 3[3],—*wolf*, never in narrative; in predictions of peace in Messian age וְגָר זְאֵב עִם כֶּבֶשׂ Is 11[6] זְאֵב וְטָלֶה יִרְעוּ כְאֶחָד Is 65[25]; in simile, of Benjamin's fierceness בִּ׳ זְאֵב יִטְרָף Gn 49[27]; of fierce horses of Chaldeans חַדּוּ מִזְּאֵבֵי עֶרֶב Hb 1[8] (‖ קַלּוּ מִנְּמֵרִים); of princes of Judah כִּזְאֵבִים טֹרְפֵי טָרֶף Ez 22[27]; metaph. of enemies of Judah Je 5[6] זְאֵב עֲרָבוֹת (‖ אַרְיֵה, נָמֵר); of corrupt and oppressive judges שֹׁפְטֶיהָ זְאֵבֵי עֶרֶב Zp 3[3] (‖ אֲרָיוֹת שֹׁאֲגִים)

†II. **זְאֵב** **n.pr.m.** (*wolf*)—a prince of

Midian, Ju 7^{24.25.25} 8^3 ψ 83^{12}; also in **n.pr.loc.** יֶקֶב־זְאֵב Ju 7^{25} *wine-vat of Zeeb*

זאת pron.f. v. זה

זבב (√of foll; cf Ar. ذَبَّ *go hither and thither* (of a man), ذَبْذَبَ *make to dangle*, or *move to and fro*, of a thing suspended in the air, but in this sense perhaps denom)

† **זְבוּב n.m.** ^{Ec 10.1} **fly** (as *moving to and fro in the air*? cf Fl NHWB^{I 438 b}; NH *id*, As *zumbu*, Dl^{863f}, Ar ذُبَابٌ, Aram דִּיבָּבָא, ܕܶܒܳܐ, ܕܶܒܳܒܳܐ),—lit. only זְבוּבֵי מָוֶת Ec 10^1 i e *dead flies*, so AV RV Hi Now al., >𝔊 De al *death-bringing, deadly flies*; זבוב metaph of Egyptian army Is 7^{18} (‖ דְּבוֹרָה, *bee*, of Assyrian), on בַּעַל זבוב v. בַּעַל II **4**, p 127 supr.

† **זַבַּי n.pr.m.** (Palm זבי Vog^{No 23} (but this perh = *loricatus*, cf زَغْفٌ *lorica*), connex with above √ uncertain)—Jew in Ezra's time Ezr 10^{28}, 𝔊 Ζαβου(θ), cf also Ne 3^{20} Kt (𝔊 Ζαβου etc, but Qr זַכַּי; v זַכַּי Ezr 2^9 = Ne 7^{14})

† [**זָבַד**] **vb. bestow upon, endow with** (Ar زَبَدَ, Aram. זְבַד, ܙܒܰܕ + Gn 30^{20}, ܙܶܒܕܳܐ *dowry*; in Sab n pr, v sub זָבָד infr., also in Palm n pr נבוזבד Vog^{73} and many others (זבידא, זבדא, זבד, זבדעתא, זבדבל = Ζαβδιβηλος, etc) see Euting Sechs Inschr aus Idalien p. 15), זְבָדַנִי אֱלֹהִים אֹתִי זֶבֶד טוֹב Gn 30^{20 a} (E), appar in expl of name Zebulun, cf Thes Di, another expl in v^b, v sub זבל

† **זֶבֶד n.m. endowment, gift**, Gn 30^{20 a} cf foregoing

† **זָבָד n.pr.m.** (*he hath given*, or, *a gift*, cf Sab n pr זבדם Hal^{158} DHM^{ZMG 1883, 15}, זביד DHM Epigr Denkm 50 = زُبَيْد, also NH n pr זביד)—**1.** a descendant of Judah 1 Ch 2^{36.37}. **2** an Ephraimite 1 Ch 7^{21} **3** one of David's valiant men 1 Ch 11^{41} **4.** one of the murderers of Joash of Judah 2 Ch 24^{26} (𝔊 Ζαβελ, Ζαβεθ, Ζαβαθ), called יוֹזָכָר (q.v sub יהוה, הוה) 2 K 12^{22}. **5.** name of three returned exiles who had taken strange wives **a.** Ezr 10^{27}, **b.** v^{33}; **c** v^{43}.

† **זָבוּד n.pr m.** (*bestowed*) an officer of Solomon 1 K 4^5

† **זבוד n.pr m** a returned exile Ezr 8^{14} Kt, Qr זַכּוּר, q v (B om, A Ζαβουδ, i.e זָבוּד, 𝔊L Ζακχουρ)

† **זבידה** Kt, **זְבוּדָה** Qr, **n pr.f.** mother of Jehoiakim 2 K 23^{36} וְזְבִידָה בַּת־פְּדָיָה מִן־רוּמָה, (‖ 2 Ch 36^5 om MT); quite otherwise 𝔊B Ἰελλα, daughter of Ἐδειλ, in A the names are Ειελδαφ & Ειεδδιλα, 𝔊 2 Ch 36^5 Ζε(κ)χωρα & Νηρειου; 𝔊L (K & Ch) Ἀμιταλ & Ἱερεμιου (confusion with Zedekiah's mother 24^{18})

† **זַבְדִּי n.pr.m.** (cf Ar. زُبْدٌ *gift*; ? *gift of* י׳, vid Dr^{Stud Bib i 5 & reff}; perh *my gift*, *gift to me*: cf זַבְדִּיאֵל, in NH n.pr זבדי (זַבְדִּי or זִבְדִּי?); NT Ζεβεδαῖος, e g Mk 1^{19}, 𝔖 ܙܰܒܕܰܝ, *Zebedee*)—**1.** grandfather of Achan, of Judah (𝔊 Ζαμβρ(ε)ι etc, 𝔊L Ζαβδ(ε)ι) Jos 7^1 (app = זִמְרִי 1 Ch 2^6, 𝔊 Ζαμβρ(ε)ι) v^{17 18}. **2.** a Benjamite 1 Ch 8^{19} **3.** an officer of David 1 Ch 27^{27}. **4.** a Levite Ne 11^{17} (om B, A Ζεχρι, 𝔊L Ζεχρει) prob. rd זִכְרִי, as ‖ 1 Ch 9^{15}

† **זַבְדִּיאֵל n.pr.m.** (*my gift is God*)—**1.** father of one of David's officers 1 Ch 27^2. **2** a prominent Hebrew in Nehemiah's time Ne 11^{14}

זְבַדְיָהוּ, זְבַדְיָה n.pr.m (י׳ *hath bestowed*, cf. יְהוֹזָבָד, & reff., also זַבְדִּיאֵל supr)—זְבַדְיָהוּ **1.** Levites, **a.** 1 Ch 26^2, **b.** 2 Ch 17^8 **2.** an officer of Jehoshaphat 2 Ch 19^{11}. זְבַדְיָה **3.** Benjamites, **a.** 1 Ch 8^{15}; **b.** 1 Ch 8^{17}. **4.** one of David's men 1 Ch 12^8 **5.** an officer of David 1 Ch 27^7 **6.** a returning exile Ezr 8^8 **7.** one of priestly house Ezr 10^{20}

זָבַח ^{† 134} **vb. slaughter for sacrifice** (NH *id*, Ph זבח, As *zibû* Dl^{Pr 174} cf Lotz^{TP 174}, Ar ذَبَحَ, Sab. דבח CIS^{iv 1. 2, No 74 i 11, 12}, Aram. דְּבַח, ܕܒܰܚ, Eth ዘብሐ:) **Qal**_{112} *Pf.* י׳ 1 K 8^{63} 13^2, זָבַחְתָּ Ex 20^{24} + 3 t, זָבַחְתִּי Ez 39^{19}, זָבְחוּ Ex 34^{15} Lv 17^5, וּזְבַחְתֶּם Ex 8^{24}, וְזָבַחְנוּ Ex 8^{23}, *Impf.* וַיִּזְבַּח Gn 31^{54} + 14 t; 2 ms sf. תִּזְבָּחֶנּוּ Dt 15^{21}, 2 fs sf וַתִּזְבָּחִים Ez 16^{20}, 1 s אֶזְבַּח ψ 116^{17}, אֶזְבְּחָה ψ 27^6 54^8 Jon 2^{10}, 2 mpl תִּזְבָּחֻהוּ Lv 19^5 + 2 t, תִּזְבָּחוּ Lv 22^{29} + 2 t, 1 pl נִזְבְּחָה Ex 3^{18} +, etc (61 t Impf), *Imv* זְבַח ψ 50^{14}, זִבְחוּ Ex 8^{21} ψ 4^6, *Inf cstr.* זְבֹחַ 1 S 15^{15} + 14 t, לִזְבּוֹחַ 2 Ch 11^{16}, בְּזָבְחוֹ 2 S 15^{12}, *Pt act* זֹבֵחַ Ex 13^{15} + 8 t, זוֹבֵחַ Is 66^3, pl. זֹבְחִים Lv 17^5 + (20 t. Pt.)—**I.** *slaughter for sacrifice* **1.** c. acc. of **a.** kind of sacrifice זבח י׳ Gn 31^{54} +, † פֶּסַח Dt 16^{2.5.6}, † שְׁלָמִים Dt 27^7 Jos 8^{31}, † תּוֹדָה ψ 50^{14. 23}, † עֹלוֹת וּשְׁלָמִים Ex 20^{24} (E) **b.** victims, (*a*) animals † צֹאן וּבָקָר 1 K 8^{63} Nu 22^{40}, † צאן ובקר 2 Ch 18^2, † הַבְּרִיאָה Ez 34^3, † כָּל־פֶּטֶר רֶחֶם Ex 13^{15} (J); † פָּרִים וְאֵילִים 1 Ch 15^{26}, שׁוֹר וָשֶׂה Dt 17^1; (β) mankind † בָּנִים וּבְנוֹת ψ 106^{37} Ez 16^{20}, † זֹבְחֵי אָדָם *sacrificers of mankind* Ho 13^2 (so Ra AE Hi Wü MV, *men that sacrifice* AV RV after Ki, so Pu Ew Ke Now Che SS) **c.** † תּוֹעֲבַת מִצְרַיִם

Ex 8$^{22.22}$ (E), †מִשְׁחָת Mal 1^{14}. **2.** absolute 1 S 1^{3}+oft. **3.** c. לְ of deity, †לְדָגוֹן Ju 16^{23}, †לַשְּׂעִירִם Lv 17^{7} (H), †לַשֵּׁדִים Dt 32^{17} ψ 106^{37}; *other gods* Ex 34^{15} (JE)+; but usually ליהוה Ex 3^{18}+9 t. JE, Lv 17^{5} 19^{5} 22^{29} (all H, not elsewh. in P), Dt 15^{21} 16^{2} 17^{1} 1 S 1^{3}+; †לֵאלֹהֵי אָבִיו Gn 46^{1} (E), לאלהים ψ 50^{14}, †לאדני Mal 1^{14}. **4.** with local prep. בְּ Gn 31^{54} (E)+, עַל Ex 20^{24} (E)+; לפני Lv 9^{4} (P)+, על פני השדה Lv 17^{5}(H). **II.** *slaughter for eating* (connected also with sacrifice, as all eating of flesh among ancient Hebrews was sacrificial, RS$^{Sem. 219}$) 1 S 28^{24} (fat calf for Saul), Ez 34^{3} (fat sheep for shepherds), 2 Ch 18^{2} (sheep and oxen for Jehoshaphat, c. לְ of person); cf. Dt 12^{15} v^{21} (abs.), 1 K 19^{21}. **III.** *slaughter in divine judgment* Ez 39$^{17-19}$ c. acc. זִבְחִי (Gog and Magog as feast for vultures), 1 K 13^{2} 2 K 23^{20} (priests of high-places on their own altars).

†**Pi.**$_{22}$ *Pf.* זִבַּח 2 Ch 33^{22}, זִבְּחוּ ψ 106^{38}, זִבֵּחוּ Ho 12^{12}; *Impf.* יְזַבֵּחַ Hb 1^{16}, יְזַבֵּחוּ Ho 4$^{13.14}$ 11^{2} (7 t. Impf.); *Inf. cstr.* לְזַבֵּחַ 1 K 12^{32}; *Pt.* מְזַבֵּחַ 1 K 3^{3}, pl. מְזַבְּחִים 2 Ch 5^{6}+8 t., מְזַבְּחוֹת 1 K 11^{8};—*sacrifice*, **1.** of the abundant sacrifices made to Yahweh by Solomon 1 K 8^{5} = 2 Ch 5^{6}, and Hezekiah 2 Ch 30^{22}, and prob. intensive; but **2.** elsewhere of sacrifice to other deities, possibly iterative in some cases, but certainly not in all: לַבְּעָלִים Ho 11^{2}, לֵאלֹהֵיהֶן 1 K 11^{8}, לָעֲגָלִים 12^{32}, לְחֶרְמוֹ Hb 1^{16}, לַעֲצַבֵּי כְנָעַן ψ 106^{38}, לֵאלֹהֵי דַרְמֶשֶׂק 2 Ch 28^{23}, לְכָל־הַפְּסִילִים 33^{22}; or in unlawful places עַל־רָאשֵׁי הֶהָרִים Ho 4^{13} cf. v^{14}, בַּגִּלְגָּל 12^{12}, בַּבָּמוֹת 1 K 3$^{2.3}$ 22^{44} 2 K 12^{4} 14^{4} 15$^{4.35}$, 16^{4} = 2 Ch 28^{4}. It is used without direct obj. Ho 4^{14} and oft.; also c. acc. of victim שְׁוָרִים Ho 12^{12} צאן ובקר 1 K 8^{5} = 2 Ch 5^{6}; sons and daughters ψ 106^{38}, זִבְחֵי שְׁלָמִים 2 Ch 30^{22}.

I. זֶבַח$_{162}$ **n.m.**$^{Ju 16, 23}$ **sacrifice**, ז׳ abs. Gn 31^{54}+; cstr. Ex 34^{25}+; זֶבַח Lv 17^{8}+16 t.; sf. זִבְחוֹ Lv 7^{16} Ez 34^{15}, זִבְחֲכֶם Lv 19^{6}; pl. זְבָחִים Gn 46^{1}+; cstr. זִבְחֵי Lv 17^{5}+; sf. 3 mpl. זִבְחֵיהֶם Lv 17^{5}, זִבְחֵימוֹ Dt 32^{38}, זִבְחוֹתָם †Ho 4^{19} etc.;—the common and most ancient sacrifice, whose essential rite was eating the flesh of the victim at a feast in which the god of the clan shared by receiving the blood and fat pieces. In the older literature it is distinguished from מִנְחָה and עֹלָה, in the later literature from חַטָּאת and אָשָׁם. †**I.** general name for all sacrifices eaten at feasts:—**1.** of the God of Israel Gn 46^{1} Ex 10^{25} 18^{12} (E) Ho 3^{4} 6^{6} 9^{4} Am 5^{25} Is 1^{11} 19^{21} Dt 12^{27} 18^{3} 1 S 2$^{13.29}$ 3^{14} 6^{15} 9$^{12.13}$ 15$^{22.22}$ 16$^{3.5.5}$ 2 S 15^{12} 1 K 8^{62} 12^{27} 2 K 5^{17} 16^{15} ψ 40^{7} 50^{8} 51$^{18.19}$ Pr 15^{8} 21$^{3.27}$ Is 43$^{23.24}$ 56^{7} Je 6^{20} 7$^{21.22}$ 17^{26} 33^{18} Ez 40^{42} 44^{11} 1 Ch 29$^{21.21}$ 2 Ch 7$^{1.4.5.12}$ Ne 12^{43} Dn 9^{27} Ec 4^{17}. They should be זִבְחֵי צֶדֶק *sacrifices of righteousness* (offered in righteousness by the righteous) Dt 33^{19} ψ 4^{6} 51^{21}; זִבְחֵי הַבְהָבַי *sacrifices of gifts to me* (י׳) Ho 8^{13}; the temple is בֵּית זָבַח 2 Ch 7^{12}; they should not be ז׳ רִיב *sacrifices of strife*, where strife prevails Pr 17^{1}. **2.** of other deities Ex 34^{15} Nu 25^{2} Dt 32^{38} (JE) Ju 16^{23} 2 K 10$^{19.24}$ Ho 4^{19} Is 57^{7} Ez 20^{28}; these are זִבְחֵי מֵתִים *sacrifices to dead things* (lifeless gods, opp. to י׳ as living) ψ 106^{28}. **II.** there are several kinds of זְבָחִים which are gradually distinguished: †**1.** *the covenant sacrifice*, between Jacob and Laban Gn 31^{54} (E), with God ψ 50^{5} (cf. Ex 24^{5} 1 S 11^{15}). †**2.** *the passover* זֶבַח חַג הַפָּסַח Ex 34^{25} (JE), זבח פסח Ex 12^{27} (J); and prob. also זבחי Ex 23^{18} (JE)=34^{25} (*id.*) †**3.** *annual sacrifice* זֶבַח הַיָּמִים 1 S 1^{21} 2^{19} 20^{6}, cf. ז׳ מִשְׁפָּחָה sacrifice of the clan 1 S 20^{29}. †**4.** *thank offering* ז׳ (הַ)תּוֹדָה Lv 7^{12} 22^{29} ψ 107^{22} 116^{17}, which is given as הַזֶּבַח, זִבְחוֹ, ז׳ קָרְבָּנוֹ Lv 7$^{16.17}$; and as a variety of שְׁלָמִים Lv 7$^{13.15}$; it is implied in זִבְחֵי תְרוּעָה ψ 27^{6}; yet זֶבַח is generic with תּוֹדָה 2 Ch 29$^{31.31}$. **5.** in ritual of H & P זבחים are defined by שלמים (q.v.) Lv 3^{1}+39 t. Lv Nu, 1 S 10^{8} 1 K 8^{63} 2 Ch 30^{22} 33^{16} Pr 7^{14}, but sometimes (rarely) ז׳ alone is used in this sense, with or without suffix, where the meaning is plain from the context: Lv 17$^{5.7.8}$ 19^{6} 23^{37} (H) Nu 15$^{3.5.8}$ Jos 22$^{26.29}$ (all P). These ritual offerings are of three varieties תּוֹדָה, נֶדֶר and נְדָבָה Lv 7$^{12.16}$ (P); in the several lists זבחים are distinguished from תודות Am 4$^{4f.}$ 2 Ch 29^{31}, from נדרים Nu 15^{8} (P) Dt 12$^{6.11}$ Jon 1^{16}, from נדבות Am 4$^{4f.}$ Dt 12^{6} and from the more comprehensive שלמים Nu 15^{8} Jos 22^{27} (P). So also the sacrifice at the institution of the covenant at Horeb Ex 24^{5} (JE) and the sacrifice at the installation of Saul 1 S 11^{15} are defined as †זבחים שלמים. Thus ז׳ seems not only to be used for all these special forms but also to include other festal sacrifices not defined in the codes of law. The ritual was the same for the entire class. They were all sacrifices for feasts in which the flesh of the victim was eaten by the offerers, except so far as the officiating priests had certain choice pieces and the blood and fat pieces went to the altar for God. The sacrifice at the institution of the covenant at Horeb, the Passover victim,

and the ram of consecration, were special, in that there was an application of a portion of the blood to the persons and things which were to be consecrated, Ex 12[22] 24[8] Lv 8[23] †**6.** the slaughter of hostile nations is also a זֶבַח offered by God Himself, in which the vultures devour the flesh of the victims Is 34[6] Je 46[10] Ez 39[17 17 19] Zp 1[7 8] **7.** the verb used with זֶבַח is ordinarily זָבַח but others also are found e.g. †עָשָׂה Nu 6[17] 15[3.5.8] Jos 22[23] (P) 1 K 12[27] 2 K 5[17] 10[24] Je 33[18] (cf. Sab. עסי דבח Hal[148] DHM[ZMG 1885, 374]), †הביא Am 4[4] Dt 12[6 11] Je 17[26], †הגיש Am 5[25], †הקריב Lv 7[11 16] 22[21] (all P), †עָבַד Is 19[21], †נָתַן Ec 4[17], יַעֲלֶה עֹלָה או זבח Lv 17[8] (H), בשל ז׳ Ez 46[24], שָׁחַט אֶת־הָעוֹלָה וְהַזֶּבַח Ez 40[42] cf 44[11]

†II **זֶ֫בַח** **n pr m** a Midianite king Ju 8[5.6.7 10 12 12 15 15 18.21 21] ψ 83[12], 𝔊 Ζεβεε

מִזְבֵּחַ 401 **n.m.**[Jos 22, 10] **altar** (Ar مَذْبَحٌ, *place of slaughter, trench made by torrent*, Sab. מדבחת DHM[Epigr Denkm 24]), מ׳ abs 2 K 18[22] + 223 t, הַמִּזְבֵּחָה Ex 29[13] + 31 t, cstr מִזְבַּח Ex 20[24] + 76 t, sf מִזְבְּחִי Ex 20[26] + 7 t, מִזְבַּחֲךָ 1 K 8[31] + 3 t, מִזְבְּחֶךָ Dt 33[10], מִזְבְּחוֹ Ju 6[31] + 2 t, pl מִזְבְּחוֹת Nu 23[1] + 5 t, מִזְבְּחוֹת 2 K 21[3] + 23 t, sf מִזְבְּחוֹתֶיךָ ψ 84[4], other sfs 21 t.,—**1.** JE narrate that altars were built by Noah after leaving the ark Gn 8[20], by Abraham at Shechem 12[7], Bethel 12[8], Hebron 13[18], mt in land Moriah 22[9], by Isaac at Beersheba 26[25], by Jacob at Shechem 33[20] (yet this perh mistake for מַצֵּבָה, being obj of וַיַּצֶּב־שָׁם, not elsewhere with מִזְבֵּחַ, cf also Di), at Bethel 35[7], by Moses at Rephidim Ex 17[15], Horeb 24[4], by Balak at Bamoth Baal, Pisgah, & Peor Nu 23[1 14 29], by Joshua on Mt Ebal Jos 8[30] the prophetic histories narrate that altars were built by Gideon at Ophra Ju 6[24]; by a man of God at Bethel Ju 21[4], by Samuel at Ramah 1 S 7[17], by Saul after Michmash 1 S 14[35], by David on the threshing floor of Ornan 2 S 24[25] = 1 Ch 21[18], 1 Ch 22[1], that Solomon sacrificed on the altar at Gibeon 1 K 3[4] and built altars in the temple at Jerusalem 1 K 6[20] 8[64], that Jeroboam built an altar at Bethel 1 K 12[32] (which was destroyed by Josiah 2 K 23[15]); and that Elijah repaired an ancient altar on Carmel 1 K 18[30] An altar in Egypt is predicted Is 19[19] All this accords with the law of the Covenant code Ex 20[24-26] which recognises a plurality of altars and prescribes that they shall be built of אֲדָמָה, or of unhewn stones, and without steps So אֲבָנִים Dt 27[6] (JE), אֲבָנִים שְׁלֵמוֹת Jos 8[31], and twelve stones 1 K 18[30.32], cf. Is 27[9] The altar was also a place of refuge Ex 21[14] (JE) 1 K 1[50.51] 2[28] **2.** D prescribes one central altar Dt 12[5 f 27], but no attempt to enforce this principle appears before Hezekiah (2 K 18[4.22]), and Josiah, whose reform is more effectual, 2 K 23[8-20] **3.** P limits sacrifices to the altars of the tabernacle A great altar was built E of the Jordan, but it was according to P only as an עֵד after the pattern of the altar before the Tabernacle Jos 22[10-34] P describes two altars **a.** the מִזְבַּח הָעֹלָה Ex 30[28] 31[9] 35[16] 38[1] 40[6 10 29] Lv 4[7 10.25 25.30.34] = מ׳ הַנְּחֹשֶׁת Ex 38[30] 39[39], made of acacia wood plated with brass, 5 × 5 × 3 cubits in size, with four horns and a network of brass, on which all sacrifices by fire were made Ex 27[1-8] 38[1-7]; **b.** מ׳ מִקְטַר קְטֹרֶת made of acacia wood plated with gold, 1 × 1 × 2 cubits in size, with four horns and a crown of gold Ex 30[1-6] = מ׳ הקטרת Ex 30[27] 31[8] 35[15] 37[25] = מ׳ הזהב Ex 39[38] 40[5.26] Nu 4[11] = מ׳ קְטֹרֶת הַסַּמִּים Lv 4[7], these altars are named elsewhere only in Chr. 1 Ch 6[34] 16[40] 21[29] 2 Ch 1[5.6]. **4.** Solomon made two altars for the temple at Jerusalem. **a.** מ׳ הַנְּחֹשֶׁת for the court 1 K 8[64] (which was laid aside by Ahaz 2 K 16[14 15], who made an altar after the model of one he saw in Damascus 2 K 16[11]), in v[14] הַמִּזְבַּח הַנ׳ (cstr. form c art) is erron, rd prob מִזְבַּח cf Ges § 127 4 a and fin, this altar, according to Chr, measured 20 × 20 × 10 cubits 2 Ch 4[1], this מזבח (ה)נחשת also 7[7] & Ez 9[2], = מ׳ העולה 2 Ch 29[18], repaired by Asa 2 Ch 15[8], **b.** an altar of cedar, plated with gold, in the temple before the דביר 1 K 6[20 22] 7[48], = מ׳ הזהב 2 Ch 4[19], = מ׳ הַקְּטֹרֶת 1 Ch 28[18] 2 Ch 26[16]. **5.** Ezekiel plans two altars for the new temple: **a.** a table of wood 3 × 2 cubits Ez 41[22], **b.** an altar for the court, prob same dimensions as **4 a,** with stairs Ez 43[13-17]. **6.** after the return Jeshua built an altar on the ancient site in the court of the temple Ezr 3[2]. **7.** besides these altars used in the worship of Yahweh, Ahab built an altar to Baal in Samaria 1 K 16[32], Ahaz made an altar on the roof of the upper chamber, and other kings of Judah made altars in the two courts, all of which were destroyed by Josiah 2 K 23[12] **8.** the ancient and most common term for making altars was בָּנָה Gn 35[7] (E) 8[20] (J) Dt 27[5 6] Ex 32[5] (JE) +, implying building material, other vbs are הקים 2 S 24[18] 1 K 16[32] 2 K 21[3] 1 Ch 21[18] 2 Ch 33[3], הכין Ezr 3[3] (sq עַל־מְכוֹנָתוֹ), שׂים Je 11[13], וַיַּצֶּב־ Gn 33[20] (but cf. **1**); Nu 23[4] (E) has עָרַךְ *arrange,*

prepare; עָשָׂה Gn 35^{13} Ex 20^{24} (E) Gn 13^{4} (J) Ju 22^{28} 1 K 12^{33} 18^{26}, this becomes usual in P, Ex 27^{1} 30^{1} 37^{25} 38$^{1.30}$, so 2 Ch 4$^{1.19}$ 7^{7} 28^{24} **9.** the dedication of the altar was חֲנֻכַּת המזבח Nu 7$^{10.11.84.88}$ 2 Ch 7^{9}, it was anointed with oil מָשַׁח Ex 40^{10} Lv 8^{11} Nu 7^{10} (all P) **10.** removal of unlawful altars is expr. by נָתַץ Ex 34^{13} (JE) Dt 7^{5} Ju 2^{2} 6$^{30.31.32}$ 2 K 11^{18} 23$^{12.15}$; נִתַּץ (Pi) Dt 12^{3} 2 Ch 31^{1} 34$^{4.7}$; נָתַץ Ju 6^{28}, הָרַס Ju 6^{25} 1 K 19$^{10.14}$, שִׁבַּר 2 Ch 23^{17}; הסיר 2 K 18^{22}=Is 36^{7}, 2 Ch 14^{2} 30^{14} 32^{12} 33^{15}. **11.** ministry at the altar was מִשְׁמֶרֶת הַמ׳ Nu 18^{5} Ez 40^{46}, cf. Nu 3^{31} (P), מְשָׁרְתֵי מ׳ Jo 1^{13}; עָמַד עַל is said of officiating priest 1 K 13^{1}, עָלָה עַל Ex 20^{26} 1 S 2^{28} 1 K 12^{33} + (cf יָרַד Lv 9^{22}); sacrifices were usually offered עַל־הַמִּזְבֵּחַ Gn 22^{9} Dt 12^{27} +; v. especially the phrases with זָרַק Ex 29$^{16.20}$ + (v. זרק); הקטיר Lv 4^{10} (v. קטר **Hiph.**); הֶעֱלָה Lv 6^{3} + (v עלה **Hiph.**) לְבַעֵר Ne 10^{35}; but בַּמִּזְבֵּחַ Gn 8^{20} (J) Nu 23$^{2.4.14.30}$ (E); one touching the altar is הַנֹּגֵעַ בַּמ׳ Ex 29^{37} (P); לִפְנֵי המ׳ of placing, or standing *before* altar Dt 26^{4} 1 K 8^{22}, as **acc.loc.** הַמִּזְבֵּחָה in phrases esp c הִקְטִיר Ex 29^{13} +, and הֶעֱלָה Lv 14^{20} **12.** the horns of the altar were especially for the application of the blood of the sin-offering in the ritual, sin is represented as graven לְקַרְנוֹת מִזְבְּחוֹתֵיכֶם Je 17^{1}, therefore of blood for cleansing it was said נָתַן עַל קרנות המ׳ † Ex 29^{12} Lv 4$^{7.18.25.30.34}$ 8^{15} 9^{9} 16^{18} (all P) An ancient custom is referred to, ψ 118^{27} אסרו־חַג בַּעֲבֹתִים עַד־קַרְנוֹת המזבח *bind the festal victim with cords, unto the horns of the altar:* Ainsworth paraphrases. 'that is, all the court over, untill you come even to the hornes of the altar, intending hereby many sacrifices,' so De; but Che 'bind the procession with branches, (step on) to the altar-horns,' that is in sacred procession round the altar **13.** the יְסוֹד (q v) is also referred to in the ritual of the sin-offerings in the phrases יָצַק אֶל יסוד Lv 8^{15} 9^{9} & יִמָּצֵה Ex 29^{12} Lv 4$^{7.18.25.30.34}$ (all P) שָׁפַךְ אֶל יסוד אֶל יסוד Lv 5^{9} **14.** the altar was קֹדֶשׁ קָדָשִׁים Ex 29^{37} 40^{10} (P), but repeated sin-offerings were necessary to keep it pure and cleanse it from the pollution of the people in whose midst it was situated This is expressed by חִטֵּא Lv 8^{15} (P) Ez 43^{22}, כִּפֶּר Lv 16$^{20.33}$ (P) Ez 43^{26}; קִדֵּשׁ Ex 29^{44} 40^{10} Lv 8^{15} Nu 7^{1} (P), טִהַר 2 Ch 29^{18}.

זַבַּי v. sub זבב

†זְבִינָא **n.pr.m.** (*bought;* Aram, fr. √זְבַן, *buy*, cf. BAram Dn 2^{8})—name of one who had taken a strange wife Ezr 10^{43}.

†[זָבַל] **vb.** prob **exalt, honour** (As. *zabâlu* COT^{Gloss} and id. on Gn 30^{20} 1 K 8^{13}, cf Dl$^{Pr 62f}$ so De; Ph n pr f בעלאזבל (prob =*Baal has exalted*) cf. אִיזֶבֶל p. 33 supr.; cf Ar زَبَلَ *take up and carry;* > No$^{ZMG\ 1886,\ 729}$, who connects these vbs. with Syr. ܣܒܠ *bear, carry*, cf. Heb סָבַל)—**Qal** *Impf.* יִזְבְּלֵנִי אִישִׁי Gn 30^{20b} (J), *my husband will honour me* (in expl. of name Zebulun (v. infr), on another appar. expl. in v^{a} cf. זבד); > AV al *dwell with me*, cf. Thes RobGes who derive *dwell with* fr an assumed mng *be round* (cf דור); and others (cf MV$^{8.9}$), who derive *dwell* as denom from זְבֻל in sense *dwelling*

†I זְבֻל **n.[m.] elevation, height, lofty abode** (NH זְבוּל *temple*),—בָּנֹה בָנִיתִי בֵּית זְבֻל לָךְ 1 K 8^{13} = 2 Ch 6^{2} (poet; prob from book of Jashar, cf 𝔊 We$^{Comp\ 271}$ Dr$^{Intr\ 182}$; on בֵּית־זְבֻל = As *bît zabal, lofty house* cf. COT 1 K 8^{13} Dl$^{Pr 62f}$); ψ 49^{15} לְבַלּוֹת שְׁאוֹל מִזְּבֻל לוֹ text dub., Ew Hi Ri Now rd. מִזְּבוּל (or מִזְבוּל, Ew) as n. =*dwelling;* Che prop for מִזְּבֻל ל׳ [לְעוֹלָ]ם Che$^{crit\ n}$, זְבֻל קָדְשְׁךָ Is 63^{15} (‖ שָׁמַיִם) *the high abode of thy holiness* (cf Che$^{crit.\ n}$), of the lofty abode of sun and moon: שֶׁמֶשׁ יָרֵחַ עָמַד זְבֻלָה Hb 3^{11}.

†II זְבֻל **n.pr.m.** an officer of Abimelech Ju 9$^{28.30.36.36.38.41}$.

†זְבֻלוּן, זְבוּלֻן **n.pr.m.** Zebulun (on expl. of name given in E and J cf זבד, זבל),—זְבוּלֻן Gn 49^{13} + 25 t, זְבֻלוּן Ju 5^{18} + 17 t; זְבוּלוּן Ju 1^{30},—**1.** sixth son of Jacob and Leah Gn 30^{20} 35^{23} 46^{14} 49^{13} Ex 1^{3} 1 Ch 2^{1} **2.** the tribe of Zebulun Nu 1^{9} Dt 27^{13} 33$^{18.18}$ Ju 1^{30} 4^{10} 5$^{14.18}$ Ez 48^{26} 1 Ch 12$^{34.41}$ 27^{19} 2 Ch 30$^{11.18}$; cf שְׂרֵי ז׳ ψ 68^{28}; שַׁעַר ז׳ Ez 48^{33}, בְּנֵי ז׳ Nu 1^{30} 2^{7} 7^{24} 26^{26} Jos 19$^{10.16}$ Ju 4^{6}, מַטֵּה ז׳ Nu 1^{31} 2^{7} 13^{10}, מַטֵּה בני ז׳ Nu 10^{16} 34^{25}. **3.** territory of the tribe אֶרֶץ ז׳ Ju 12^{12}, אַרְצָה ז׳ Is 8^{23}, גבול ז׳ Ez 48^{27}, also ז׳ alone Jos 19$^{27.34}$ 2 Ch 30^{10}, מַטֵּה ז׳ Jos 21$^{7.34}$ 1 Ch 6$^{48.62}$.

†זְבוּלֹנִי **adj.gent.** Ju 12$^{11.12}$; c. art = n. coll. *the Zebulonites* Nu 26^{27}.

זוג, זיג (appar √of foll, 𝔗 NH זוג, זיג is *be clear, bright, transparent* (ChWB Jastr^{391a}); others (so Thes) derive foll. from √זגג with same meaning, v. infr. & Fl NHWB$^{i.\ 560\ b}$)

†זָג n.[m.] name of some comparatively insignif. product of vine (גֶּפֶן הַיַּיִן), the eating of which was included in prohibition to Nazirite, skin of grape, so Thes (after Onk Mishna Maaser. 5[14], Orla 1[18], cf Sifre ad loc) מֵחַרְצַנִּים וְעַד־זָג לֹא יֹאכֵל Nu 6[4] (NH זג, זוג, so called as transparent? cf Aram זְגוּגִיתָא, ܙܓܘܓܝܬܐ glass, NH זַגָּג glazier (Ar زُجَاج glass, is a loan-wd acc to Fra[64]); cf theory of √in Lag[Ges. Alb 41], Fl[1 c]: but in Heb glass is זְכוּכִית)

זֵד, זָדוֹן v. sub זיד.

זֶה **demonstr. pron.** and **adv.**, fem זֹאת, once זֹאתָה, Jer 26[6] Kt (also זה and זוֹ, q v); comm זוּ (q v.) this, here (the element ז = ذ = ܕ is widely diffused in the Semitic languages, as a demonstr. particle, often acquiring, like Engl *that*, Germ *der, die, das*, the force of a relative Thus **a.** Ph ז *this* (e g קבר ז *this grave*), also sts. זן, f זא, comm אז (v. CIS I 1 1[4.5.6 12] 44[1] 88[2] etc); Aram. of Nineveh, Babylon, Têma, Egypt, זי as mark of the genit [lit *that of*] (CIS II. 1 1, 2, 3, 4, etc, 65, 69–71, 113, 114, 141, 142, etc), זנה *this* (ib. 113[22] 145 C[2]), f זא 113[15] 145 B[6]; Aram. of Zinjirli ז, זן, זנה *this*, זי *which* (DHM[Sendsch 56]), Eth ዝ: *ze, this*, f ዛ: *zā*, ዘ: *za, who* (masc), also (like זי, and די, ד [v. infr]) in common use as a mark of the genitive, **b.** Arab. ذَا *this*, fem ذِي, ذُو (gen ذِي, acc. ذَا, fem ذَاتُ), *possessor of* (lit *that of* , i e one who owns), or in the Tayyite dialect, *who, which*. from ذَا, with هَا *lo!* prefixed, هَاذَا *this*, f هَاذِهِ, with the pron element *-k* affixed, ذَاكَ = *this*: with *'al* (= the art) + a demonstr element *la* prefixed, اَلَّذِي *who, which* (in origin = Heb הַלָּזֶה *this*, q v), Sab דן *this*, f דת, ד *who, which*, f דת (Pra[ZMG 1872, 419], DHM[ZMG 1883 338 f], also [Epigr Denkm 65]), **c.** BAram די *which*, דֵּךְ, דִּכֵּן, דְּנָה (q v) *this*, f דָּא (=זֹאת), דָּךְ, Palm and Nab די *which*, דנה *this*; ד *which*, דין, דיכי *this*, f דָּא, with הא *lo!* prefixed, הָדֵין, הָדָא (Syr ܗܳܢܳܐ, ܗܳܕܶܐ, contr from), ܗܳܕܶܐ, Syr ܕ *who, which*, Sam *who, which*, *this*, f , Mand ד *who, which*, דה *this* (rare), more commonly האזין, האדין (No[Mand § 80, 81]) Alike in Heb and the other dialects, the corresp plur is derived from a different source Heb. אֵלֶּה, Ph אל, Eth *'ellū, 'ellā, these, 'ella, who*, Arab أُولَى, أُولَى, *these*, أُولُو, أُولِي *owners of*, Sab אלן *these*, אל, אלי *who, which*, Aram. אלין, with הא *lo!* prefixed, ܗܳܠܶܝܢ, Sam. , Mand. עלין. Only the Arab. اَلَّذِي forms its own pl اَلَّذِينَ. V further W[SG 107 ff])—**1.** standing alone: **a.** *this one*, sts contemptuously (esp. with זאת), Gn 2[23] לְזֹאת יִקָּרֵא אִשָּׁה כִּי מֵאִישׁ לֻקֳחָה־זֹּאת, 5[29] . . . זֶה יְנַחֲמֵנוּ, 12[12] 38[28] Ex 10[7] עַד מָתַי יִהְיֶה זֶה לָנוּ לְמוֹקֵשׁ, 1 S 10[27] מַה יֹּשִׁעֵנוּ זֶה how shall *this man* save us? 16[8.9] 21[16] that ye have brought אֶת־זֶה *this fellow* to play the madman against me? 25[21] in vain have I kept אֶת־כָּל־אֲשֶׁר לָזֶה all that *this fellow* hath etc 2 S 13[17] אֶת־זֹאת, 1 K 22[27] אֶת־זֶה, Mi 5[4] Is 66[2], as a genit, Gn 29[27 28] 1 K 21[2]; with a *collective* force Lv 11[4.9] (= Dt 14[7 9]), v[21.29] Ju 20[16 17] (כָּל־זֶה), Jb 19[19] (with a *plural* verb). In a purely *neuter* sense (of an act, event, announcement, etc) זאת is most common, as with עשה to do *this* Gn 3[14] 20[5.6] 45[19] and oft, שמעו זאת Am 8[4] Is 47[8] 48[1 16] 51[21] al; Gn 41[39] Ex 17[14] Dt 32[6] Ju 7[14] 21[3] לָמָּה . . . הָיְתָה זֹאת (cf. Jb 1[13] ψ 118[23]) 1 K 11[39] 2 S 7[19] 2 K 3[18]+; אין זאת 1 S 20[2b] cf. Am 2[11], rarely so with את־ +Jos 22[24] Je 9[11] ψ 92[7], as an accus. of limit, *as regards this, in this*, Ez 20[27] 36[37] Jb 19[26] (si vera l), 33[12] *in this* thou art not just; (late) אַחֲרֵי זֹאת +Jb 42[16] Ezr 9[10], א׳ כל־זאת +2 Ch 21[18] 35[20]; pointing forward to a foll. clause, Gn 42[18] 43[11] Nu 8[24] 14[35] Is 56[2] Jb 10[13] etc; Ex 9[16] 1 S 25[31] Is 1[12] מי בִקֵּשׁ זאת מידכם רְמֹס חֲצֵרָי, to one introduced by כי 2 S 19[22] ψ 102[19] 119[50.56] (see also בזאת **6 b** β): but זֶה also sts occurs similarly Ex 13[8] Pr 24[12] Jb 15[17] Ne 2[2] Ec 1[17] 2[15] גם זה הבל (so v[19.21 23]+), 7[18.18]; of a concrete obj, Ex 30[31] 2 K 4[43] מָה אֶתֵּן זֶה לִפְנֵי מֵאָה אִישׁ in late Heb, Ne 13[6] בְּכָל־זֶה during all this, 2 Ch 32[9] אַחַר זֶה, pointing forwards La 5[17 f], to כי ψ 56[10] Je 22[21]. (See also below, **6 g**) **b** repeated זֶה . . . זֶה, *this . that, the one . the other* or (if indefinite) *another*, Gn 29[27] (זאת), Ex 14[20] ולא קָרַב זה אֶל זֶה, 1 K 3[23] 22[20] Is 6[3] 44[5] (3 t), ψ 75[8] זֶה יַשְׁפִּיל וְזֶה יָרִים, Jb 1[16-18] 21[23.25]+.

2. In appos to a subst. **a.** preceding it (rare) Ex 32[1 23] זֶה משֶׁה, Ju 5[5] (=ψ 68[9]) זֶה סִינַי *this* Sinai, Jos 9[12] זֶה לַחְמֵנוּ *this* our bread, 1 K 14[14] 2 K 6[33] Is 23[13] זֶה הָעָם, ψ 34[7] 49[14] 104[25] זה הים גדול וג׳ *this* sea *there* is great and broad, 118[20] Ct 7[8] Ezr 3[12]. (Cf זוּ Hb 1[11].) **b.** following it —(*a*) when the subst. is determined by a pron affix, Gn 24[8] שְׁבֻעָתִי זֹאת, *this* my oath, Dt 5[16] O that לְבָבָם זֶה *this their*

heart (their present temper) might continue always! 21^{20} Jos 2$^{14.20}$ דְּבָרֵנוּ זֶה, Ju 6^{14} go בְּכֹחֲךָ זֶה in *this* thy strength, Dn 10^{17} 2 Ch 24^{18}. (Cf. אֵלֶּה, **a.**) Rarely when it is undetermined, 2 K 1^{2} חֳלִי זֶה (so 8$^{8.9}$), ψ 80^{15}. (β) with the art., הַזֶּה, הַזֹּאת, after a subst. determined also by the art, Gn 7^{1} בַּדּוֹר הַזֶּה, v^{13} הַיּוֹם הַזֶּה, 12^{7} הָאָרֶץ הַזֹּאת, 15^{7} 17$^{21.23}$ Dt 4^{6} הגוי הגדול הזה, and continually Not however after a n pr., except such as are construed with the art., as הַיַּרְדֵּן הַזֶּה Gn 32^{11} Dt 3^{27} 31^{2} Jos 1$^{2\ 11}$ 4^{22}, הַלְּבָנוֹן הַזֶּה Jos 1^{4}, cf. Nu 27^{12}=Dt 32^{49} (2 K 5^{20} הַזֶּה belongs to הָאֲרַמִּי): and hardly ever (2 Ch 1^{10}) after a noun with a pron. affix (Jos 2^{17} מִשְּׁבֻעָתֵךְ הַזֶּה the gender of הזה shews that the text is in error: v. Dr$^{§ 209 Obs.}$)

3. More oft. as pred., as 1 S 24^{17} הֲקוֹלְךָ זֶה, 2 K 3^{23} דָּם זֶה *this* is blood, 9^{37} זֹאת אִיזָבֶל, Ez 5^{5} etc; הַזֹּאת הַזֶּה Is 14^{16}, 23^{7} La 2^{15}; oft at the beginning or close of enumerations (esp. P), descriptions, injunctions, etc., as Gn 5^{1} זה ספר *this* is the book . . ., 9^{12} זאת אות הַבְּרִית, 17^{10} 20^{13} זה חַסְדֵּךְ אֲשֶׁר תַּעֲשִׂי עִמָּדִי, Lv 6$^{2\ 13\ 18}$ 7$^{1\ 11}$ Dt 6^{1} 33^{1} Jos 13^{2} Jb 27^{13} Is 58^{6} etc, . . . זה הדבר אשר Ex 16^{16} 35^{4} Jos 5^{4} Ju 20^{9} 21^{11} Is 27^{22} Je 38^{21}+, cf. . . . זה אשר *this* is what (*or* how) . . . Gn 6^{15} Ex 29^{38} Je 33^{16}, זה לְּךָ הָאוֹת Ex 3^{12} 1 S 2^{34}+; at the end, Lv 7^{37} 11^{46} 13^{59} Nu 5^{21} 7$^{17\ 23}$ etc, Jos 19$^{8\ 16.23}$ etc, Is 14^{26} 16^{13} (זֶה הַדָּבָר אֲשֶׁר . . .), 17^{14} 54^{17} Je 13^{25} ψ 109^{20} Ct 5$^{16\ 16}$ Jb 5^{27}, in the latter case sts. with the force of *such* (i.e. such as has been described), 18^{21} 20^{29} (cf. אֵלֶּה ψ 73^{12}), ψ 24^{6} 48^{15} *such* (=such a one) is God, our God, for ever (Hi De) Zp 2^{15}, cf. Jb 14^{3} אַף־עַל־זֶה upon one *such as this* (v$^{1.2}$) dost thou open thy eyes?

4. It is attached enclitically, almost as an adv, to certain words, esp interrog. pronouns, to impart, in a manner often not reproducible in Engl idiom, directness and force, bringing the question or statement made into close relation with the speaker. (Contrast from this point of view מי זה and מי הוא v. הוא **4 b.**) Thus **a.** אֵי־זֶה$_{15}$ where, *then?* Jb 28^{12} אֵי־זֶה מְקוֹם בִּינָה, v^{20} 38^{19b} (v. other exx. sub אֵי **1 b**, p 32) **b.** מִי־זֶה, †1 S 17$^{55.56}$ בֶּן־מִי־זֶה הָעָלֶם: the son of *whom, here,* is the lad? Je 49^{19} (=50^{44}) וּמִי זֶה רעה אֲשֶׁר וגו׳ and *who* (emph) is the shepherd that etc, La 3^{37} ψ 24^{8} *Who* is the King of glory? (for which in v^{10} the stronger מי הוא זה is said so Je 30^{21} Est 7^{5}), 25^{12}. Elsewhere, the rend *Who* is *this* . . . is admissible: Is 63^{1} Je 46^{7} Jb 38^{2} 42^{3}; cf. מי־זאת Ct 3^{6} 6^{10} 8^{5}. **c.** מַה־זֶּה *how, now?* Gn 27^{20} Ju 18^{24} וּמַה־זֶּה תאמרו אלי and *how, now,* do ye say to me . . .? 1 K 21^{5} 2 K 1^{5}; מַה־זֶּה הָיָה לְבֶן־קִישׁ *what, now?* (τί τοῦτο,) 1 S 10^{11}; עַל־מַה־זֶּה *for what?* Ne 2^{4}: contracted into מַזֶּה Ex 4^{2}. (Cf. Aram מְדִין *why?* ܡܕܝܢ used as a conj *therefore,* e.g 2 S 18^{22} 𝔖, PS^{2013}. both formed similarly) **d.** מַה־זֹּאת in the phrase (עָשִׂית, עֲשִׂיתֶם) מַה־זֹּאת עָשִׂיתָ Gn 3^{13} 12^{18} 26^{10} 29^{25} 42^{28} Ex 14^{11} Ju 2^{2} 15^{11}+. Either *What, now,* hast thou (have ye) done? (Fl De) or *What* is *this* (that) thou hast (ye have) done? (The Arab grammarians dispute on the precise construction of the corresp phrase in Arabic مَا ذَا صَنَعْتَ, De$^{Gen. 3. 13 (ed. 4)}$, and esp. Fl$^{Kl Schr i 356}$ Lane$^{p. 948}$.) **e.** לָמָּה־זֶּה *wherefore, now?* Gn 18^{13} 25^{22} 32^{30} Ex 5^{22} Nu 11^{20}+oft Cf Arab لِمَا ذَا. **f.** הַאַתָּה זֶה †2 S 2^{20} האתה זה עשהאל Art thou Asahel? 1 K 18$^{7\ 17}$, without הֲ Gn 27^{24}; in an indirect question Gn 27^{21} **g.** הנה זה *behold, here* . . . †1 K 19^{5} (in narrative), Is 21^{9} Ct 2$^{8.9}$. Cf. Nu 13^{17} (unusual) עֲלוּ זֶה בַּנֶּגֶב go up *here* in the South. **h.** עַתָּה זֶה, †1 K 17^{24} עַתָּה זֶה יָדַעְתִּי *now* I know that . . ., 2 K 5^{22} *just now.* Also **i.** prefixed to expressions denoting a period of time: Gn 27^{36} he hath supplanted me זֶה פַעֲמַיִם *now* two times (so 43^{10}), 31^{38} *now, already* twenty years, v^{41} (זה־לִּי . . .), 45^{6} Nu 14^{22} *now* ten times, 22$^{28.32}$ זֶה שָׁלֹשׁ רְגָלִים, Dt 8$^{2.4}$ Jos 22^{3} זֶה יָמִים רַבִּים, 2 S 14^{2}+; Zc 7^{3} זֶה כַּמֶּה שָׁנִים *already* how many years! cf. Ru 2^{7}

5. In poetry, as a *relative* pron. (rare but see also זוּ, זוֹ): ψ 74^{2} the hill of Zion זה שכנת בו *wherein* thou dwellest, 78^{54} 104^{8} אֶל־מְקוֹם זה to the place (*st. c* Ges$^{§ 130.3}$) *which* . . . v^{26} Pr 23^{22} Is 25^{9}; =*that which* Jb 15^{17}, *those who* 19^{19} (so once, Ex 13^{8}, even in prose) In some of the passages cited the punctuators, by coupling זה with the preceding subst, and separating it from what follows by a disj accent (as הַר־זֶה), appear not to have recognised its relative sense, but to have construed, '*this* mountain, (which) thy right hand,' etc.

6. With prefixes (in special senses).— **a.** בָּזֶה$_{15}$ *in this* (place), *here,* Gn 38$^{21.22}$ Ex 24^{14} Nu 23^{11} 1 S 1^{26} 9^{11}+; of time, *then,* †Est 2^{13}. Once בָּזֶה 1 S 21^{10} **b.** בזאת (*a*) *with this* = *on these conditions,* Gn 34$^{15.22}$ 1 S 11^{2} Is 27^{9}, = *herewith, thus provided* Lv 16^{3}. (β) *by* or *through this* (esp. with יָדַע), Gn 42$^{15.33}$ Ex 7^{17} Nu 16^{28} Jos 3^{10} ψ 41^{12}, so בְּזֹאת Mal 3^{10}. (γ) *in spite of this,* Lv 26^{27} ψ 27^{3}, for which the

fuller בְּכָל־זאת occurs, Is 5[25] 9[11.16.20] 10[4] ψ 78[32] Je 3[10] Ho 7[10] (δ) בְּזאת *for this cause* (late style) † 1 Ch 27[24] 2 Ch 19[2], *in this matter* 20[17] **c.** כָּזֶה (α) † Gn 41[38] . . . הֲנִמְצָא כָזֶה איש אשר, Is 56[12] 58[5] Je 5[9] גּוֹי אֲשֶׁר כָּזֶה (so v[29] 9[8]) (β) כָּזֶה וְכָזֶה *thus and thus*, † Ju 18[4] 2 S 11[25] 1 K 14[5] **d.** כָּזאת *the like of this = as follows*, † Gn 45[23], כָּזאת *the like of this = things such as these* Ju 13[23] (c השמיע), 15[7] 19[30] לא נראתה כָזאת, 1 S 4[7] (cf Je 2[10] 2 Ch 30[26]), 2 S 14[13] (c חשב), Is 66[8] (c שמע), Ezr 7[27], *= accordingly, to that effect* (c דבר) 2 Ch 34[22], *= in like manner* Ju 8[8], *= thus* (as has been described) 1 K 7[37] 1 Ch 29[14] 2 Ch 31[20] 32[15] כָּזאת וכזאת *thus and thus* † Jos 7[20] 2 S 17[15.15] 2 K 5[4] 9[12] **e.** מִזֶּה *from here, hence* Gn 37[17] 42[15] 50[25] Ex 11[1] 13[3] Dt 9[12] + cft: מִזֶּה . . . מִזֶּה *on one side . on the other side* Ex 17[12] מזה אחד ומזה אחד, 25[19] 26[13] 32[15] מזה ומזה הם כתובים, Nu 22[24] 1 S 14[4] 1 K 10[19.20] Zc 5[3] +, מזה ומזה ל *on one side and on the other side of* Ex 38[15] Jos 8[33] Ez 45[7] 48[21] **f** עַל זה *on this account* (rare), La 5[17] (pointing forwards), Est 6[3] So עַל זאת Am 8[8] Mi 1[8] Je 2[12] (Jb 17[8]) 4[8.28] ψ 32[6], in late prose Ezr 8[23] 9[15] 10[2] Ne 13[14] 2 Ch 16[9.10] 29[9] 32[20] **g.** עִם זֶה *in spite of this* † Ne 5[18] —On אֵי זֶה *which?* אֵי מִזֶּה *whence?* אֵי לָזאת *how?* v sub אֵי **2**, p 32, and on הַלָּז, הַלָּזֶה, הַלֵּזוּ, v p 229

Note —זֶה in 1 S 17[34] (in many edd) is a typographical error (not a Kt) of Jacob b Chayim's Rabbin Bible of 1525 for שֶׂה *sheep*, which has been perpetuated hence in other subseq edd The reading of MSS and of the best ancient edd is שֶׂה (cf. de Rossi[Var Lect ii 161]).

† **זֹה** *this* (f) = זאת (cf זוֹ, in Mish the regular fem of זה)—2 K 6[19] Ez 40[45] Ec 2[2.24] 5[15.18] 7[23] 9[13] (זאת does not occur in Ec), also in the phr כָּזֹה וְכָזֶה (v זה **6 c** β).

† **זוּ** 1 q זה (q v) only Ho 7[16 b] זוּ לַעְגָּם *this* (i e. the falling by the sword, v[a]) is their derision, and (as relat) ψ 132[12] וְעֵדֹתִי זוֹ and my testimony *which* . . (neglecting the accentuation. v De, and cf the remark under זֶה **5**)

† **זוּ** **pron.** (poet), indeclinable **1.** a **demonstr.** Hb 1[11] זוּ כֹחוֹ *this* his strength, ψ 12[8] מִן־הַדּוֹר זוּ (unusual, for הַזֶּה), 62[12] שְׁתַּיִם־זוּ שָׁמָעְתִּי *these* two things &c (but better (Wickes[Poet Acc 64]) שְׁתַּיִם זוּ two things (are there) *which* &c v **2**) **2.** a **relative,** Ex 15[13] עַם־זוּ גָּאָלְתָּ the people *which* thou hast redeemed, v[16] Is 42[24] זוּ חָטָאנוּ לוֹ *against whom* we sinned, 43[21] ψ 9[16] (fem.) בְּרֶשֶׁת־זוּ טָמָנוּ so 31[5], 10[2] 17[9] (with a *plural* antecedent) מִפְּנֵי רְשָׁעִים זוּ שַׁדּוּנִי, 32[8] 68[29] (thou) *who* hast wrought for us! 142[4] 143[8]. To most of these passages the remark made under זה **5** respecting the intention of the punctuators also applies comp. De on ψ 9[16]. (Cf ذُو, used as an indeclin. relat pron. = الَّذِى in the Tayyite dialect· thus أتى عليهم ذو أتى there has come upon them *that which* has come· نحن ذو فعلنا كذا it is we *who* have done this See Schu[Hariri Cons ii. 73], Thes[406], W[AG i 347.a], Lane p 986, Fl[Kl Schr i p 389])

זהב (√ of foll., meaning dubious, cf. Lag[BN 55 Anm])

זָהָב 38.. **n.m.**[Gn 2. 12] **gold** (NH *id*, Ar ذَهَبٌ, Sab דהב e g Os[29] DHM[ZMG 1883. 338], Aram. דְּהַב, ܕܗܒܐ, Palm דהבא Vog[No 23])—ז׳ abs Gn 2[11] + 364 t, cstr Gn 2[12] + 6 t, sf זְהָבִי 1 K 20[7] + 2 t, זְהָבְךָ 1 K 20[3.5] זְהָבְךָ Is 30[22], זְהָבוֹ Is 2[20] 31[7], זְהָבָם Ho 8[4] + 4 t, —*gold,* **1.** = gold-ore, gold in a raw state, Gn 2[11.12] Je 10[9] Pr 17[3] 27[21] Jb 28[1] +; perh. also 1 K 9[28] 10[11] 22[49] etc, cf עַפְרֹת ז׳ Jb 28[6] *gold-dust,* v also Zc 13[9] (sim. of tried people of י׳) and cf Mal 3[3]; likewise Jb 23[10] (sim of Job's purity, as shewn by divine tests); מִצָּפוֹן זָהָב Jb 37[22] is dub; Ew De al *out of the North comes gold,* others, however, *golden light, brightness,* of sun after clouds dispersed by north wind, 𝔊 Rabb Da al, or *golden splendour* of God coming from north Bo[A 76] Hi al; Siegf conj יהוה for זהב **2.** gold as wealth Gn 13[2] (J; + מִקְנֶה, כֶּסֶף) 24[35] (J; + צאן, בָּקָר, כֶּסֶף, עֲבָדִם, שְׁפָחֹת, גְּמַלִּים, חֲמֹרִים) cf Ho 2[8] Is 2[7] Dt 8[13] 17[17] Jb 3[15] 31[24] Zc 14[14] Ezr 1[4.6] +, in gen, as precious נבחר שם מעשר רָב מכסף וּמִזָּהָב חן טוב Pr 22[1] *to be chosen is a name more than great riches, and good favour more than silver and than gold,* Jb 28[17] (of wisdom) *gold and glass do not equal it;* ψ 19[10] (ordinances of י׳) *which are more to be desired than gold,* cf 119[72.127], also metaph of princes and chief men of Zion La 4[1] (cf v[2]) **3.** gold as spoil of war Jos 6[19] (+ כסף, כְּלֵי־נחשת, בַּרְזֶל) so v[24], cf 7[21.24] 22[8] 2 K 7[8] +. **4.** gold as merchandise Ez 27[22] (+ רֹאשׁ כָּל־בֹּשֶׂם, אֶבֶן יְקָרָה), cf also gold from Ophir 1 K 9[28] etc. (v. sub **7** infr) **5** gold as costly gift. to a prophet מלא ביתו כֶּסֶף וז׳ (hypothet), Nu 22[18] 24[13] (both E), brought by queen of Sheba to Solomon 1 K 10[2.10] (both + אֶבֶן יְקָרָה and בְּשָׂמִים) = 2 Ch 9[1.9], as tribute 2 K 23[35.35] (cf v[33], all + כֶּסֶף), as satisfaction for murder 2 S 21[4] (+ כֶּסֶף). **6.** gold as

material: of (nose- or ear-)ring, נֶזֶם Gn 24^{22} Ex 32$^{2.3}$ Ju 8$^{24.26}$ Pr 11^{22} 25^{12} Jb 42^{11}; of chain Gn 41^{42}, shields 2 S 8^{7}, images of emerods 1 S 6$^{4.17}$ and mice v$^{4.11.18}$; תַּפּוּחֵי ז׳ בְּמַשְׂכִּיּוֹת כָּסֶף Pr 25^{11}; גֻּלַּת ז׳ Ec 12^{6}; כְּלֵי־ז׳ Ex 3^{22} 11^{2} 12^{35} 1 S 6^{8} ψ 105^{37} etc.; כְּלֵי־כֶסֶף וּכְלֵי זָהָב Gn 24^{53} as presents to a bride (+בְּגָדִים); so of presents to secure king's favour 2 S 8^{10} (+כְּלֵי נְחֹשֶׁת), and in list of yearly gifts or tribute to Sol. 1 K 10^{25}=2 Ch 9^{24}; as material of idols אֱלֹהֵי כֶסֶף וֵאלֹהֵי ז׳ Ex 20^{23} cf. 32^{31} Ho 8^{4} Is 2^{20} 30^{22} 31^{7} Dt 29^{16} ψ 115^{4} 135^{15}; as plating of idols Dt 7^{25}; especially as material of the furnishings of Solomon's temple, or (oftener) the platings of temple, or parts thereof, or of its furnishings 1 K 6$^{20.21.21.21.22.22.28}$ 7^{48} + 10t. 1 K 6. 7; also 2 Ch 3$^{5.5.6}$ + 14t. 2 Ch 3. 4; cf. 1 Ch 28$^{14.14}$ + 14 t. 1 Ch 28. 29 (David's preparation for temple); v. also 2 K 24^{13} cf. 14^{14} = 2 Ch 25^{24}, 2 K 25^{15}=Je 52^{19} (in accounts of plundering temple etc.); but more often still of furnishing and utensils of tabernacle, insignia of high-priest etc., Ex 25$^{3.11.24}$+97 t. Ex 25–40, Lv 8^{9} Nu 4^{11} 8^{4}; (in case of large objects frequently of plating or sheathing, cf. **12 c** infr.) Note the expressions תְּנוּפַת ז׳ לַיהוה Ex 35^{22} *a wave-offering of gold*, זְהַב הַתְּנוּפָה 38^{24}; also זְהַב הַתְּרוּמָה Nu 31^{52} (all P) cf. Ezr 8^{25}, and (of offering to heathen god) יְכַבֵּד בְּזָהָב Dn 11^{38}. †**7.** gold described by its source, esp. gold from Ophir (cf. Glas$^{Skizze\ ii.\ 357\ ff.\ 368}$) 1 K 9^{28} 10^{11} 22^{49} 1 Ch 29^{4} 2 Ch 8^{18} 9^{10}; so perh. Je 10^{9} (rd. אוֹפִיר for אוּפָז Ew Klo al.); זְהַב שְׁבָא ψ 72^{15}; on ז׳ פַּרְוָיִם 2 Ch 3^{6} v. פרוים; cf. further Gn 2$^{11.12}$. **8.** gold defined by var. adj. and pts.: ז׳ שָׁחוּט *beaten gold* (v. שָׁחַט) 1 K 10$^{16.17}$=2 Ch 9$^{15.15.16}$; ז׳ סָגוּר 1 K 6$^{20.21}$; also 7$^{49.50}$ 10^{21}=2 Ch 4$^{20.22}$ 9^{21} (on mng. v. סָגַר); esp. (but only P & Ch) ז׳ טָהוֹר *pure gold* Ex 25$^{11.17.24}$+21 t. Ex 25. 28. 30. 37. 39 (of equipments of tabernacle and high priest's insignia), 1 Ch 28^{17} 2 Ch 3^{4} 9^{17}; cf. ז׳ טוֹב 2 Ch 3$^{5.8}$; on ז׳ מוּפָז 1 K 10^{18}, AV *best gold*, cf. פָּז, אוּפָז. **9.** ז׳ as measure of weight and value: **a.**=*gold-shekel*, עֲשָׂרָה ז׳ מִשְׁקָלָם Gn 24^{22}; כַּף אַחַת עֲשָׂרָה ז׳ Nu 7^{14}+11 t. Nu 7; אֶלֶף וּשְׁבַע־מֵאוֹת ז׳ Ju 8^{26}, cf. 1 K 10^{16} 2 K 5^{5} 2 Ch 9$^{15.16}$; אַלְפֵי ז׳ וָכָסֶף ψ 119^{72}; comp. further Jos 7^{21}; but also (only Ch) שֶׁקֶל expressed: שִׁקְלֵי ז׳ מִשְׁקַל שֵׁשׁ מֵאוֹת 1 Ch 21^{25} (50 shekels of silver in ‖ 2 S 24^{24}); וּמִשְׁקָל לְמִסְמְרוֹת לִשְׁקָלִים חֲמִשִּׁים ז׳ 2 Ch 3^{9}. **b.** שְׁלֹשֶׁת מָנִים ז׳ 1 K 10^{17} *three minas of gold* (v. מָנֶה). **c.** כִּכַּר ז׳ *talent of gold* 2 S 12^{30} 1 K 9^{14}+ (v. כִּכָּר). **d.** זָהָב דַּרְכְּמוֹנִים שֵׁשׁ־רִבֹּאות וָאֶלֶף Ezr 2^{69} cf. Ne 7$^{69.70.71}$; also וּכְפֹרֵי ז׳ עֶשְׂרִים לַאֲדַרְכֹנִים אָלֶף Ezr 8^{27} (v. דַּרְכְּמוֹן);—with the above should perh. be compared הַזָּלִים ז׳ מִכִּיס Is 46^{6} i.e. the gold used in making the god was the coin carried in the bag. **10.** ז׳=*golden oil*, from colour, Zc 4^{12}. **11.** ז׳ often named with כֶּסֶף, and then, in earlier and sts. in later writings, follows it: בַּכֶּסֶף וּבַזָּהָב Gn 13^{2} (J), cf. 24$^{35.53}$ 44^{8} (all J), Ex 3^{22} 11^{2} 12^{35} Nu 22^{18} 24^{13} (all E), Jos 6$^{19.24}$ (JE), Dt 7^{25} 17^{17} 29^{16} 2 S 8^{11} 21^{4} 1 K 7^{51} 15$^{15.18.19}$ 2 K 7^{8} 16^{8} 18^{14} 20^{13} 23$^{33.35.35}$ Ho 2^{10} 8^{4} Is 2^{7} 60^{9} Je 10^{4} Zp 1^{18} Ez 7^{19} 38^{13} Zc 6^{11} Jo 4^{5}, Pr 22^{1} ψ 105^{37} 115^{4} 135^{15} 2 Ch 1^{15} 5^{1} Ezr 1^{4} 8^{25} Dn 11^{8} Ec 2^{8}+; in later writings ז׳ oft. precedes Ez 28^{4} Zc 14^{14} Mal 3^{3} 1 Ch 18^{10} 22$^{14.16}$ 28$^{15.16}$ 29$^{3.4.5.7}$ 2 Ch 9$^{14.21}$ 24^{14} 25^{24} Ezr 1^{11} ψ 119^{72} Ct 1^{11} Dn 11^{38}+, and so in P, Ex 25^{3} 31^{4} 35$^{5.32}$ Nu 31^{22}; yet also as early as Hb 2^{19} 1 K 10^{22} 2 K 25^{15}. **12.** the chief vbs. used with ז׳ are: **a.** עָשָׂה *make* of (c. 2 acc.) 1 K 7^{48} (cf. v$^{49.49.50.50}$) 10^{16} 12^{28} 14^{26} 2 Ch 4$^{7.8.19}$ 12^{9} 13^{8}, and esp. in P (tabern.) Ex 25$^{11.17.18}$+35 t. Ex 25–39; also sq. בְּ *work in* gold, לַעֲשׂוֹת בַּז׳ וּבַכֶּסֶף וּבַנְּחֹשֶׁת Ex 31^{4} 35^{32}, also (+בַּבַּרְזֶל, etc.), 2 Ch 2$^{6.13}$; **b.** יָצַק (obj. טַבְּעֹת ז׳) Ex 25^{12} 37$^{3.13}$ (all P); **c.** צִפָּה *overlay with* (c. 2 acc.) 1 K 6$^{20.21.21.22.28.30.32.35}$ (v$^{32.35}$ one acc. om.), 10^{18} 2 Ch 3$^{4.10}$ 9^{17}, and esp. P (tabern.) Ex 25$^{11.13.24.28}$+15 t. Ex 26–37; in same sense **d.** וַיְחַפֵּהוּ ז׳ 2 Ch 3^{5} cf. v$^{7.8.9}$, and **e.** תָּפוּשׂ ז׳ וָכֶסֶף Hb 2^{19} *encased in gold and silver;* also **f.** בַּז׳ יְרַקְּעֶנּוּ Is 40^{19}; **g.** רדד Hiph., וַיָּרֶד עַל־הַכְּרוּבִים וְעַל־הַתִּמֹרוֹת אֶת־הַז׳ 1 K 6^{32} *and he spread upon the cherubim and upon the palm-trees the gold;* further **h.** בָּחַן *try*, Zc 13^{9}, cf. **i.** זָקַק Mal 3^{3}.—On דִּי זָהָב, n.pr. v. p. 191; on מֵי זָהָב n.pr. v. sub מַיִם.

†[זָהַם] **vb. be foul, loathsome,** but only **Pi.,** causat. (NH *id.*, *be foul*, Pi. *make foul;* Aram. זְהַם *foul*, ܙܗܡ *make foul, fetid;* Ar. زَهِمَ *stink, be greasy*)—**Pi.** *Pf.* 3 fs. sf. 3 ms. וְזִהֲמַתּוּ חַיָּתוֹ לָחֶם (consec.) Jb 33^{20} *his life maketh it, bread, loathsome* to him (‖ וְנַפְשׁוֹ מַאֲכַל תַּאֲוָה). (On sf. v. Ges$^{§ 131, 2, R. 4}$; Dr$^{§ 81, 14}$: acc. to Siegf the word is hopelessly corrupt.)

† זַהַם **n.pr.m.** (fr. above √?) a son of Rehoboam, 2 Ch 11^{19}.

†I. [זָהַר] **vb. be light, shining** (Ar. زَهَرَ, زَهَرَ *shine*, adj. أَزْهَرُ *bright* (cf. Lag$^{BN\ 120}$); Aram.

זְהַר, زهر; NH in deriv.; v. also sub II. זהר)—**Hiph.** intrans (late) *send out light, shine*, fig of everlasting glory of teachers of righteousness וְהַמַּשְׂכִּלִים יַזְהִרוּ כְּזֹהַר הָרָקִיעַ Dn 12[3] *and they that make wise shall shine like the shining of the firmament* (‖ וּמַצְדִּיקֵי הָרַבִּים כַּכּוֹכָבִים לְעוֹלָם וָעֶד)

†**זֹהַר** **n.[m.]** **shining, brightness** (Ar. زُهْرَة, NH זוהר, cf Aram זִיהֲרָא),—abs Ez 8[2] כְּמַרְאֵה ז׳ *like an appearance of shining* (explained, v[b], as resembling amber, חַשְׁמַל cf. 1[27]); also cstr Dn 12[3] v foregoing.

†II [**זָהַר**] **vb.** only **Hiph.**, **Niph.** (NH Hiph, *admonish*, cf Aram זְהַר (Aph Pa. etc.), زهر (Ar زَهِرَ viii. *take care of, be mindful of* is perh Aram. loan-word, so TA cf. Lane)—Most identify with I זהר = *give light, enlighten, instruct, admonish*, this possible, but not certain, mng *shine* is late in Heb; usual sense as given below is not *enlighten, illumine* mentally, but *warn*, v also construction with two accusatives Ex 18[20]),—**Hiph.** *Pf.* והזהיר consec Ez 33[3]; sf. והזהירה 2 K 6[10], 2 ms הִזְהַרְתָּ Ez 3[19] 33[9], וְהִזְהַרְתָּ Ez 3[17] 33[7], וְהִזְהַרְתָּה Ex 18[20], sf הִזְהַרְתּוֹ Ez 3[18.20.21], וְהִזְהַרְתָּ consec Ez 3[17] 33[7], וְהִזְהַרְתֶּם consec 2 Ch 19[10], *Inf cstr* לְהַזְהִיר Ez 3[18] 33[8],—*instruct, teach, warn* Ex 18[20] (E) *teach them ordinances* (2 acc); 2 K 6[10] the place *which* (אֲשֶׁר) *the man of God told him of* (אָמַר־לוֹ) and *warned him* (sf) *of*, elsewh only Ez Ch, *warn, give a warning to*, alw sq. acc. pers. only: Ez 3[18.19.20] 33[3], *give them* (acc) *a warning from me* (מִמֶּנִּי, ׳י speaks) Ez 3[17] 33[7], *warn the wicked* (רָשָׁע) *from* (away from, מִן) *his way* Ez 3[18] 33[8.9], *warn the righteous* (צַדִּיק) Ez 3[21] sq Inf *in order that the righteous sin not*, cf 2 Ch 19[10] sq acc. pers. + final cl c ו

Niph. *Pf* 3 ms נִזְהַר Ez 3[21] 33[4.5.6], also נִזְהָר v[6] (rd. perh הזהיר, so We Sm Co); *Imv.* הִזָּהֵר Ec 12[12], *Inf cstr.* לְהִזָּהֵר Ec 4[13]; Pt נִזְהָר ψ 19[12],—*be instructed, admonished, warned* (pass of Hiph).—גַּם־עַבְדְּךָ נִזְהָר בָּהֶם ψ 19[12] *yea thy servant, he is instructed* (or *warned*) *by them* (i e lets himself be instructed or warned by the מִשְׁפְּטֵי ׳י v[10]), in Ez distinctly *take warning*, abs Ez 3[21] (cf **Hiph.**) 33[4.5a], so Ec 12[2] and, more generally, אֲשֶׁר לֹא יָדַע לְהִזָּהֵר Ec 4[13] *who knoweth not how to take admonition, be warned, receive warning* Ez 33[6] (of people, c לֹא, i e if no warning be given them), also MT v[5b], but rd perh. Hiph (v. supr.) *but he* (i.e the watchman) *gave warning, he hath delivered his* (*own*) *soul*.

†**זִו** appar. **n.pr.** of 2nd month, = c April–May, named as month of beginning the temple-building; בְּחֹדֶשׁ זִו הוּא הַחֹדֶשׁ הַשֵּׁנִי 1 K 6[1] = בְּיֶרַח זִו v[37], 𝔊B v[1] has simply ἐν μηνὶ τῷ δευτέρῳ, v[37] (in 𝔊 v[4]) ἐν μηνὶ Νεισῶ καὶ τῷ δευτέρῳ μηνί; 𝔊 codd ἐν μηνὶ Ζιου μηνὶ τῷ δευτέρῳ, 𝔊L (only v[37]) ἐν δευτέρῳ μηνί, ἐν μηνὶ Ζιου;—(si vera l comp perh. Aram. זִיו ܙܝܘܐ *brightness, freshness*, so B Aram. Dn 2[31]+; cf 𝔗 יֶרַח זִיו נִיצָנַיָּא *month of brightness of flowers;* As. *zîmu* (*zîvu*), Dl[Pr 152 f.] cf No[ZMG 1886, 732]; Thes al der. זו, זיו (= זהיו) fr זהה in sense *be bright, splendid*, etc., cf Ar. زَهَا *increase, thrive* (of seed-produce), زَهْو *a beautiful and bright*, or *fresh*, plant; Aram זְהָא, adj זָהוֹהָא *haughty, proud;* ܙܗܐ *glory, boast, be magnificent*, yet cf. Ol[§ 174 ad fin])

זוֹ, זוּ, v p 262

†[**זוּב**] **vb.** **flow, gush** (NH *id*, Aram. דּוּב, דִּיב, ܕܘܒ, all used oft in sense **4** infr; Ar. ذَابَ (med و) *melt, dissolve, flow*)—only **Qal** *Impf* יָזוּב Lv 15[25] etc., *Pt.* זָב Je 49[4] f זָבָה Lv 15[19] etc;—**1.** *flow, gush* (poet.), of water from the smitten rock ψ 78[20] (‖ שָׁטַף), 105[41] (‖ הָלַךְ), Is 48[21] (‖ נָזַל) **2.** *Pt.* freq in אֶרֶץ זָבַת חָלָב וּדְבַשׁ, always of promised land, Ex 3[8.17] 13[5] (all J) 33[3] Nu 13[27] 14[8] 16[13.14] (all JE) Dt 6[3] 11[9] 26[9.15] 27[3] 31[20] Jos 5[6] (D) Lv 20[24] (H) Je 11[5] 32[22] Ez 20[6.15] (in last two ins. ארץ 𝔊 Co), זָב עִמְקֵךְ Je 49[4] (fertile valley of Ammon) **3.** fig. *flow away = pine away* (from hunger) La 4[9]. **4.** *flow*, of issue from woman (all P), Lv 15[25] יָזוּב זוֹב דָּמָהּ (v זוֹב), esp *have an issue* (*flux, gleet*), of woman Lv 15[25] and 15[19] (תִּהְיֶה זָבָה), usu. of man, 2 S 3[29] (‖ מְצֹרָע), elsewhere P, Lv 15[2] זָב מִבְּשָׂרוֹ, with cogn acc 15[33], ordinarily *Pt.* זָב *one that has an issue* Lv 15[4.6.7.8.9.11.12.13.32] (all P), 22[4] (H; ‖ צָרוּעַ), also Nu 5[2] (P, ‖ *id*)

†**זוֹב** **n.m.** **issue** (Ar. ذَوْب *fluid, liquid*, NH זוֹב, Aram. דּוּבָא in specif. sense of Heb),—*issue, flux*, alw fr genitals (cf Di Lv 15[2]), only P of man or woman Lv 15[33],—of man Lv 15[2.3.3.3.13.15], of woman Lv 15[19] (דָּם יִהְיֶה זֹבָהּ בִּבְשָׂרָהּ, of monthly period), also v[25.25.26.28.30] (of morbid issue of blood, sts. connected with the other, cf. Mat 9[20] etc)

זוּד v **זיד**.

זוה (√of foll; cf. Ar. زَوَى *put aside* or *away, draw together, contract*).

†[זָוִית] **n.f.** corner (late) (Aram. זָוִיתָא, ܙܘܝܬܐ (oft. for Heb. פִּנָּה, מִקְצוֹעַ), hence, as loan-word (Frä Aram. Fremdw 11. 168) Ar. زَاوِيَة);—Pl. abs זָוִיּוֹת ψ 144[12]; cstr. זָוִיּוֹת Zc 9[15];—וּמָלְאוּ כַּמִּזְרָק כְּזָוִיּוֹת מִזְבֵּחַ Zc 9[15] simil. of warriors streaming with blood, v. Lv 1[5.11] etc.; בְּנוֹתֵינוּ כְּז׳ וגו׳ ψ 144[12] *our daughters like corner* (-pillar)*s*, carved (so Che al., but v. II. חטב) in palace-fashion

†[מָזוּ] **n.m.** garner (on format. cf. Ol § 144 b, 197 b)—only Pl. sf מְזָוֵינוּ מְלֵאִים ψ 144[13] *our garners* are *full* (word inflected as if מְ were radical; cf. Ol l.c.)

I. **זוז** (NH זז *move*, As. *zâzu*, *move*, *rise*, *come forth* cf. COT gloss.; also *be agitated*, *enraged*, V R[64. 1, 1 11])

†I. **זִיז** **n.m.**[ψ 80.14] **coll. moving things** (i.e. beasts) (etym. & exact meaning still rather dub., cf. Che OP 472 and on ψ 50[11]; Thes al √זוז; De ψ 50[11] comp As *zizânu*, coll. *reptiles*, Dl S. 74 f. from a זאוא cf زَعْزَعَ *move to and fro*, *agitate* (cf. זוע); others comp. As. *zâzu*, *abundance* v. II. זוז, so even Di Is 66[11], this hardly suits ψ 80[14]; 𝔗 זִיזָא *worm*),—only cstr. זִיז שָׂדַי ψ 50[11] *the moving things of the field*, as all known to י׳ (|| עוֹף הָרִים), also in v[10] חַיְתוֹ־יָעַר, etc.); fig. of enemies of Isr. ψ 80[14] (|| חֲזִיר מִיַּעַר).

†**זִיזָא** **n.pr.m.**—**1.** a Simeonite 1 Ch 4[37]. **2.** a son of Rehoboam 2 Ch 11[20].

†**זִיזָה** **n.pr.m.** a Levite 1 Ch 23[11], = זִינָא v[10] (rd. prob. זִיזָא, 𝔊 Ζιζα in both).

†**זָזָא** **n.pr.m.** (perh belongs under this √; comp. As. n pr. Zazâ Zim BP 97 cf. Strm AV No 2816) —a descendant of יְרַחְמְאֵל of Judah 1 Ch 2[33].

†**מְזוּזָה** **n.f. door-post, gate-post,** abs מ׳ Ex 21[6] Is 57[8]; cstr. מְזוּזַת 1 S 1[9] Ez 46[2]+ Ez 41[21] (del. 𝔊 Co cf 𝔊 Hi), 45[19 19] (in both מזוזות 𝔊 𝔖 𝔙 Co); sf מְזוּזָתִי Ez 43[8], מְזוּזָתָם v[8]; pl. מְזוּזוֹת 1 K 6[31]+2 t. (+Ez 45[19 19] Co v. supr.), מְזוּזֹת Ex 12[7]+4 t., מְזֻזוֹת Dt 6[9] Ju 16[3],—*door-post, gate-post*, **1.** of dwelling-house Ex 12[7] (P), v[22.23] 21[6] (all JE), Dt 6[9] 11[20] cf. Is 57[8], also מ׳ פְּתָחָי Pr 8[34], מְזוּזָתָם Ez 43[8]; of Sol's house 1 K 7[5]. **2.** of house of י׳ **a.** of the pre-Solomonic sanctuary of י׳ 1 S 1[9]. **b.** of Sol's temple 1 K 6[33], of the דְּבִיר v[31]. **c.** of Ezek's temple Ez 41[21] (del. Co v. supr), 43[8] (מְזוּזָתִי), מ׳ הַבַּיִת Ez 45[19], מ׳ שַׁעַר v[9], cf. 46[2]. **3.** of city-gates Ju 16[3].

†**זִיזָא** **n.pr.m.** an officer of David זִיזָא הַהַגְרִי 1 Ch 27[31].

II **זוז** (*be abundant*, cf. esp As *zâzu*, *abundance*, Dl Pr 67 f. Zim BP 94. 97; only as √of foll., perh. related to I זוז (cf. Thes), but this very dubious).

II **זִיז** **n.[m.] abundance, fulness.** only מִזִּיז כְּבוֹדָהּ Is 66[11] that ye may suck out and be delighted, *from the abundance of her glory* (i e. of Jerusalem) (so Di al.; > Che crit n., and OP 472 f. Brd (cf. Ew '*Euter*'), who comp vulg Ar. *zîza*, *udder* (breast, teat); this suits vb. תָּמֹצּוּ and || תִּינְקוּ וּשְׂבַעְתֶּם מִשֹּׁד, but is dub in Heb, perh. not Shemit, v Dozy i 619 a and reff; also Lag Proph Chald who proposes, plausibly, מִבִּיז, cf. Aram ܒܐܙܐ PS 502, בִּיזָא; Ar. بَزّ *pap*).

†**זוּזִים** **n. pr. gent.** an ancient trans-Jordanic people, dwelling in הָם Gn 14[5]; otherwise unknown; abode appar. in (later) land of Ammon, between Bashan and Moab, commonly supposed = זַמְזֻמִּים q v, in that case perh txt. error in one case or the other, cf No Untersuchungen z Kritik d A. T 162 —(𝔊 ἔθνη ἰσχυρά) —On n pr loc Ziza, زيزا, between Bosra and Lejûn, cf Kn Di ad loc, Tristr Moab 182 ff.

†**זוֹחֵת** **n.pr.m.** a descendant of Judah (etym and mng. unknown) 1 Ch 4[20] (v. also בֶּן־זוֹחֵת), 𝔊 Ζωαν, Ζωαβ, A Ζωχαθ, 𝔊L Ζαωθ.

זָוִית v sub זוה

I **זול** (prob. √of foll, Ar. زَالَ *remove*, *depart*)

†[**זוּלָה**] **n.[f.]** prop. **removal,** only found in the st c as **prep.** and **conj. except, only, save that**—cstr. זוּלַת 2 K 24[14] and (with the obsolete case-ending ־ִי) זוּלָתִי Dt 1[36] 4[12] Jos 11[13] 1 K 3[18] 12[20] ψ 18[32]; with sf. זוּלָתִי Ho 13[4] Is 45[5.21], זוּלָתְךָ, זוּלָתֶךָ 2 S 7[22] = 1 Ch 17[20] Is 26[13] 64[3] Ru 4[4], זוּלָתָהּ 1 S 21[10];—**1. prep.** *except, besides*, lit. *with removal of*...(syn. מִבַּלְעֲדֵי ψ 18[32] Is 45[21]; בִּלְתִּי Ho 13[4]; and cf. Dt 1[36] with Nu 32[12]), Dt 1[36] זוּלָתִי כָּלֵב *with the exception of* Caleb, 1 S 21[10] אֵין אַחֶרֶת זוּלָתָהּ there is none other *except* it, 1 K 12[20] 2 K 24[14] Ru 4[4]: oft. in such phrases as, There is no God (or, Who is God?) *except* me (or thee), 2 S 7[22] ψ 18[32] Ho 13[4] Is 45[5.21] 64[3]. Always after a neg. or qu., exc Is 26[13] אֲדֹנִים זוּלָתְךָ lords *other than* thou. Connected inexactly with what precedes,

ז׳ acquires the force of *only*, Dt 4[12] ye saw no form זוּלָתִי קוֹל *save* a voice = (there was) *only* a voice, 1 K 3[18] **2.** conj Jos 11[13] *except that* he burnt Hazor alone

†II [זוּל] **vb. lavish** (cf Aram זוּל, *be cheap, of little value, lightly esteem*, similarly זלל q v)—**Qal** *Pt* הַזָּלִים זָהָב מִכִּיס Is 46[6] (‖כֶּסֶף בַּקָּנֶה יִשְׁקֹלוּ).

†[זון] **vb. feed** (NH BAram *id*, Syr ܙܳܢ, Sam ...),—**Hoph** *Pt* סוּסִים מוּזָנִים Je 5[8] (Kt, i e. מוּזָנִים, Qr מְיֻזָּנִים from יזן q v) *well-fed horses*, fig of adulterers, Dl [Pr 73 f.] comp As. *zanânu, be full* (i e of sexual desire)

†מָזוֹן **n.m.** food, sustenance (so Talm BAram Syr)—מָזוֹן בַּר וָלֶחֶם וּמָזוֹן Gn 45[23] (Di מ׳ rather an Aram word, perh later gloss for orig צֵדָה v[21] 42[25]), הַמָּזוֹן לָרֹב 2 Ch 11[23].

זֹנָה v זנה

†זוע **vb.** tremble, quake (Aram. (incl BAram) *id*, ܙܳܥ, cf also Ar زَاعَ *impel*, زَعْزَعَ *move, agitate, shake* (on these v No [ZMG 1886, 725]), As. *zû, storm-wind* (= Aram זוֹעָא) Zim [BP 94]),—**Qal** (late) *Pf* 3 ms זָע Est 5[9], *Impf.* 3 mpl c rel. שֶׁיָּזֻעוּ Ec 12[3],—*tremble, quake*, in presence of powerful superior Est 5[9] (sq מִמֶּנּוּ), said of שֹׁמְרֵי הַבַּיִת in descr of infirm old man Ec 12[3] **Pilp.** *Pt* sf מְזַעְזְעֶיךָ Hb 2[7], causat and intens they that shall *violently shake thee*, fig of foes of Babylon, instruments of Yahweh's judgment

†זְוָעָה, and, by transpos, זַעֲוָה (Di Dt 28[25] cf Sta [§ 122 a]) **n.f. a trembling**, i.e **object of trembling, terror** זְוָעָה Is 28[19], also Kt Je 15[4] + 4 t, זַעֲוָה Dt 28[25] Ez 23[46] (also Qr Je 15[4] + 4 t),—*object of trembling, terror, fright*, וְהָיִיתָ לְזַעֲוָה Dt 28[25] *and thou shalt become a terror* to all (לְכֹל) the kingdoms of the earth, וּנְתַתִּים לְז׳ וגו׳ Je 15[4] 29[18], 34[17] (‖ לְאָלָה וּלְשַׁמָּה וְלִשְׁרֵקָה וּלְחֶרְפָּה), also וּנְתַתִּים לְז׳ וגו׳ 24[9] (‖ לְחֶרְפָּה וּלְמָשָׁל לִשְׁנִינָה וְלִקְלָלָה), Ez 23[46] 2 Ch 29[8]

†זִיעַ **n pr.m.** a Gadite, 1 Ch 5[13], 𝔊 Ζουε, Ζεα

†זַעֲוָן **n.pr m.** a Horite Gn 36[27] = 1 Ch 1[42]

†I [זוּר] **vb.** be a stranger (Ar زَارَ (med و) *incline toward, repair to, visit*, II. *honour as visitor or guest*, IX *decline, turn aside*, زَائِر *visitor*, Aram זוּר, oft = Heb סוּר *turn aside, turn aside to visit*)—**Qal** *Pf* 3 pl. זָרוּ ψ 58[4] (Ko [i 443]), זֹרוּ ψ 78[30] Jb 19[13], *Pt* זָר Ex 30[33] + 27 t, f. זָרָה Ex 30[9] + 7 t, mpl. זָרִים Ho 5[7] + 30 t, fpl. זָרוֹת Pr 22[14] 23[33], sf זָרַיִךְ Is 29[5], **1.** Pf. *become estranged* ψ 58[4], c מִן *from* Jb 19[13] ψ 78[30]. **2.** Pt as adj *strange*, or as noun *stranger* **a.** to the family, of another household, אִישׁ זָר Dt 25[5], elsewhere זָר 1 K 3[18] Jb 19[15] Pr 6[1] 11[15] 20[16] 27[13]; זָרִים ψ 109[11] Pr 5[10 17]; בָּנִים זָרִים, children of another household than God's Ho 5[7], especially of another family than priests' אִישׁ זָר Lv 22[12] (H) Nu 17[5] (P); זָר Lv 22[10 13] (H) Ex 29[33] 30[33] Nu 3[10.38] 18[7] (P); not belonging to the tribe of Levi, Nu 1[51] 18[4] (P) **b.** to the person, *another* Jb 19[27] Pr 14[10] 27[2], (אִשָּׁה) זָרָה *strange woman, harlot* Pr 2[16] 5[3 20] 7[5] 22[14] 23[33] **c.** to the land, *foreign*, זָרִים *foreigners* (as such usu enemies) Ho 7[9] 8[7] Is 1[7] 25[2 5] 29[5] 61[5] Je 5[19] 30[8] 51[2.51] La 5[2] Ez 7[21] 11[9] 16[32] 28[7 10] 30[12] 31[12] Jo 4[17] Ob [11] Jb 15[19] ψ 54[5], אֵל זָר *foreign god* ψ 44[21] 81[10] = זָר Is 43[12], so זָרִים Dt 32[16] and (in fig) Je 2[25] 3[13], מַיִם זָרִים *foreign waters* 2 K 19[24] Je 18[14], זְמֹרַת זָר Is 17[10] *vine-slip of a stranger*, כְּמוֹ־זָר נֶחְשָׁבוּ Ho 8[12] *they are regarded as foreign*, מַעֲשֵׂהוּ זָר Is 28[21] *his work is foreign* (as if dealing with enemies) **d** *strange* to the law, קְטֹרֶת זָרָה *strange incense* Ex 30[9] (P), אֵשׁ זָרָה *strange fire* Lv 10[1] Nu 3[4] 26[61] (P) **Niph.** *Pf* נָזֹרוּ Is 1[4] Ez 14[5], *be estranged* Is 1[4], pregn, sq אָחוֹר (cf RV); מֵעַל Ez 14[5]. **Hoph.** *Pt* מוּזָר *estranged* ψ 69[9].

†II [זִיר, זוּר] **vb.** be loathsome, Bö [§ 1142] (Ar ذَارَ *fastidivit, abhorruit*, As *zâru, resist*, *Impf izîru*, Dl [Pr 65] Schr [COT Gloss])—only 3 fs זָרָה Jb 19[17] רוּחִי זָרָה לְאִשְׁתִּי *my breath is loathsome to my wife* (וְחַנֹּתִי ל׳ in ‖ cl), > most, who derive fr I זור, *become strange* and so *repugnant*.

†זָרָא **n.[f.]** loathsome thing, עַד אֲשֶׁר יֵצֵא מֵאַפְּכֶם וְהָיָה לָכֶם לְזָרָא Nu 11[20] (JE) *and it* (the flesh) *become to you a loathsome thing* (𝔊 εἰς χολέραν, 𝔙 *in nauseam*), prob err for זָרָה (Sam)

†III [זוּר] **vb. press down and out** (Aram זוּר *press together*, Syr. ܙܳܪ, ܙܰܪ *compress*; cf Ar زَرَّ *twist* the lip of a beast)—**Qal** *Pf* 3 pl זֹרוּ Is 1[6] (pass, > √זרר, Ar زَرَّ *draw forcibly together* Ol [§ 235 c, 245 l] Ko [i 333]), *Impf.* 3 ms וַיָּזַר Ju 6[38], 3 fs sf. תְּזוּרֶהָ Jb 39[15]; *Pt. pass* f. זוּרֶה (= זוּרָה Ges [§ 80, 2 d]) Is 59[5], —*press* (twist or

wring) *out* a fleece Ju 6^{38}; *not pressed out*, of sore (fig. of continued disaster) Is 1^{6}; *press under foot* an egg, Jb 39^{15} (‖ דּוּשׁ), Is 59^{5} (pass.)

†זֵר **n.m. circlet, border** (orig. *that which presses, binds*, cf. also Aram. ܙܪܐ *bracelet*, זֵירָא *wreath, crown*, NH זִיר *id.*, זִירָה *ring, wrestler's ring;* others fr. a √זרר)—זֵר זָהָב Ex $25^{11.24.25}$ 30^{3} $37^{2.11.12.26}$; זֵרוֹ Ex 30^{4} 37^{27} (all P).

†זַרְזִיר **adj. girded, girt** (cf. Ba [NB 206])—only cstr. Pr 30^{31} זַרְזִיר מָתְנַיִם אוֹ־תַיִשׁ *that which is girt in the loins*, etc., named with lion, he-goat, and king, as stately in motion. Perh. = *greyhound* Ew Bö De al., or *war-horse* Bo Ges Hi al.; Vrss. *cock*, Talm. *raven*, v. De Now (NH זַרְזִיר *starling* (*war-horse* only in interpr. of Pr 30^{31}), Aram. ܙܪܙܝܪܐ; Lexx. also ܙܘܙܝܪܐ *starling*, in Ar. زُرْزُور, perh. loan-wd. Others der. fr. a √זרר, v. supr.)

†מָזוֹר **n.[m.] wound** (as needing to have its matter *pressed out*)—fig. of injury to, or sufferings of, Isr. and Judah: מְזוֹר Ho 5^{13} also Je 30^{13} (Gf Che RVm; but accents Ew Ges Gie AV RV *for pressing*, i.e. binding up); מְזוֹרוֹ Ho 5^{13} (cf. III. זור Is 1^{6}).—מָזוֹר Ob ^{7} v. sub מזר.

†זָזָא v. sub זוז.

†[זָחַח] **vb. remove, displace** (Ar. زَحَّ *push, thrust away;* comp. also Aram. זְחַח, ܙܚ *move, move away* (intrans.))—**Niph.** *Impf.* וְלֹא יִזַּח הַחֹשֶׁן מֵעַל הָאֵפוֹד Ex 28^{28} *and that the breast-piece be not displaced* etc., 39^{21} (both P).

†I. [זָחַל] **vb. shrink back, crawl away** (Aram. זְחַל *crawl* (also *drop, drip*, of water: so NH זָחַל), זָחִיל *worm;* Syr. ܙܚܠܐ *locust* (as *crawling*); Ar. زَحَلَ *withdraw, retire to a distance* (v. Lane, Wetzst in De [Hiob 2, 428]), and Sab. זחל *withdraw, humble oneself* DHM [ZMG 1875, 610]) —**Qal** only *Pt.* pl. cstr. זֹחֲלֵי Dt 32^{24} Mi 7^{17};—*crawl*, of reptiles (pt.) זֹחֲלֵי עָפָר Dt 32^{24} i.e. serpents (as poisonous), instruments of Yahweh's judgment on Isr.; ז׳ ארץ Mi 7^{17} *id.* (as crawling into the earth to hide), sim. of nations in fear of י׳.

†זֹחֶלֶת **n.f.** mng. dub.; perh. **crawling thing, serpent** (We [Skizzen iii. 171] cites Ar. *Zuḥal* = *Saturn*, in connex. with 1 K 1^{9}; cf. Lane & Wetzst in De [Hiob 2, 428] on view that Zuḥal = *he who withdraws*, because of planet Saturn's remoteness)—only c. art., in design. loc. עִם אֶבֶן הַזֹּחֶלֶת 1 K 1^{9} (cf. אֶבֶן ad fin.)

†II. [זָחַל] **vb. fear, be afraid** (Aram. דְּחַל, ܕܚܠ; cf. Ar. ذَحْل *rancour, malevolence;* Nö [ZMG. 1886, 741])—only **Qal** *Pf.* 1 s. זָחַלְתִּי Jb 32^{6} *therefore I feared* (‖ וָאִירָא); > most, who derive fr. I. זחל = *shrink away* in fear, *hold back* (RV), cf. ℭ אִסְתְּפֵיתִי Fl ChWB [ii. 571].

†[זוּד, זִיד] **vb. boil up, seethe, act proudly, presumptuously, rebelliously** (NH Hiph. הזיד as Heb.; Aram. of Zinjirli זד *presumptuous*, DHM [Sendsch. 56]; Ar. زَادَ (med. ى) *increase, exceed, exaggerate*, e.g. in talk; also Sab. n.pr. זיד (زَيْد) DHM [Epigr. Denkm. 44] זידאל Id [ib. 52] (on distinct. betw. זוד and זיד in Sab. v. Sab.Denkm.[64]); perh. also Sab. מזודן *great one, prince*, e.g. Sab.Denkm.[89])—**Qal** *Pf.* 3 fs. זָדָה Je 50^{29}; 3 pl. זָדוּ Ex 18^{11};—of Egyptians, בַּדָּבָר אֲשֶׁר זָדוּ עֲלֵיהֶם Ex 18^{11} (E) *in the matter* as to *which they acted presumptuously against them;* of Babylon, אֶל־י׳ זָדָה Je 50^{29} *against* י׳ *hath she acted presumptuously.* **Hiph.** *Pf.* 3 pl. הֵזִידוּ Ne 9^{10} + 2 t.; *Impf.* 3 ms. יָזִיד Dt 18^{20}, יָזִד Ex 21^{14}; וַיָּזֶד Gn 25^{29}; 3 mpl. יְזִידוּן Dt 17^{13}; 2 mpl. וַתָּזִדוּ Dt 1^{43}; **1.** *boil, seethe*, trans., וַיָּזֶד יַעֲקֹב נָזִיד Gn 25^{29} *and Jacob boiled pottage.* **2.** *act presumptuously, insolently*, Ex 21^{14} (JE) כִּי יָזִד אִישׁ עַל־רֵעֵהוּ לְהָרְגוֹ בְעָרְמָה *when a man acteth presumptuously against his neighbour to slay him;* usually against י׳; sq. vb. fin. Dt 1^{43} *and ye acted presumptuously and went up;* sq. inf. 18^{20} the prophet who *shall presume to speak* a word in my name; also abs. 17^{13}; elsewh. only Ne; of Egyptians 9^{10} sq. עַל (= **Qal** Ex 18^{11}); abs. v^{16} (‖ וַיַּקְשׁוּ אֶת־עָרְפָּם וְלֹא שָׁמְעוּ וגו׳); v^{29} (‖ וְלֹא שָׁמְעוּ וגו׳).

†זֵד **adj. insolent, presumptuous:**—ז׳ Pr 21^{24}; pl. זֵדִים Je 43^{2} + 11 t.;—alw. masc., and alw. of opposition to י׳, wickedness; with qualified noun expressed, only הָאֲנָשִׁים הַזֵּדִים Je 43^{2}, of opponents of Jerem.; elsewh. used substantively, as term. techn. for godless, rebellious men; once sg. זֵד יָהִיר לֵץ שְׁמוֹ Pr 21^{24} *a haughty insolent one, scorner is his name* (‖ עֹשֶׂה בְּעֶבְרַת זָדוֹן); usu. pl. Is 13^{11} (גְּאוֹן ז׳; ‖ גַּאֲוַת עָרִיצִים); Mal 3^{13} (‖ עֹשֵׂי רִשְׁעָה), v^{19} (‖ עֹשֵׂה רִשְׁעָה); and in ψ 86^{14} (‖ עָרִיצִים), 119^{21} (‖ הַשֹּׁגִים מִמִּצְוֺתֶיךָ), v$^{51.69.78.85.122}$; so prob. also ψ 19^{14} גַּם מִזֵּדִים חֲשֹׂךְ עַבְדֶּךָ *also from presumptuous men hold back thy servant* (Ew Ol Hup Che RVm); > *presumptuous sins* De al. (AV RV).

†**זָדוֹן** **n.m.** Pr 11, 2 **insolence, presumptuousness** (on format. cf. Lag BN 204, Anm.), abs. ׳ז Dt 17^{12} + 7 t.; cstr. זְדוֹן Je 49^{16} Ob^{3}; sf. זְדֹנְךָ 1 S 17^{28};—**1.** *insolence, presumption* toward men; affirmed of David by Eliab 1 S 17^{28} (‖ רֹעַ לְבָבֶךָ); usu. **2.** of presumptuous godlessness (cf. זֵד ,זוד), exhibited in disobedience to priest or judge Dt 17^{12}; in false prediction 18^{22}; in gen. Pr 11^{2} (opp. צְנוּעִים), 13^{10}; עֶבְרַת ז׳ Pr 21^{24} (cf. זֵד); ז׳ לִבֶּךָ Je 49^{16} (=Ob^{3}) *presumption of thine heart;* of Babylon personif. under fig. of ׳ז Je $50^{31.32}$; dub. is פָּרַח הַזָּ׳ Ez 7^{10} *insolence hath blossomed* (preceded by צָץ הַמַּטֶּה) i.e. either of Isr. as demanding punishment, or of Babylon as instr. of punishment.

†[**זֵידוֹן**] **adj.** insolent, raging, only pl. and fig. הַמַּיִם הַזֵּידוֹנִים ψ 124^{5}.

†**נָזִיד** **n.[m.]** thing sodden or boiled, pottage; abs. ׳נ Gn 25^{29} + 4 t.; cstr. נְזִיד Gn 25^{34};—a kind of boiled leguminous food, obj. of וַיָּזֶד Gn 25^{29} (v. זוד **Hiph.**); defined v^{34} as נְזִיד עֲדָשִׁים (v. עדש); obj. of בַּשֵּׁל 2 K 4^{38}; boiled in a סִיר v^{39} cf. v^{40}; mentioned, appar. as a common food, Hg 2^{12}.

זִיז ,**זִיזָא** ,**זִיזָה** v. sub I. זוז.

זִיזָא v. זִיזָה sub I. זוז.

†**זִינָא** **n.pr.m.** 1 Ch 23^{10} = זִיזָה v^{11} q.v.

זִיעַ v. sub זוע.

†**זִיף** **n.pr. 1. n.pr.loc. a.** city S.E. from Hebron, Jos 15^{55} 1 Ch 2^{42} 2 Ch 11^{8}, mod. *Tell Zîf;* Rob BR i. 492, 498 Guérin Judée iii. 159 ff.; מִדְבַּר־ז׳ 1 S $23^{14.15}$ $26^{2.2}$; c. ה loc., זִיפָה 1 S 23^{24}. **b.** city of southern Judah Jos 15^{24}, site unknown. **2. n.pr.m.** a son of יְהַלֶּלְאֵל of Judah 1 Ch 4^{16}, whether related to **n.pr.loc.** supr. does not appear. 𝔊 Ζαφα, Ζιφ(αι). (1 Ch 2^{42} v. supr.)

†[**זִיפִי**] **adj.gent.** of זִיף **1. a**; only mpl. as n.pr.gent. זִפִים 1 S 23^{19} 26^{1}; זִיפִים ψ 54^{2} (title).

†**זִיפָה** **n.pr.m.** a son of יְהַלֶּלְאֵל 1 Ch 4^{16} (זִיף וְזִיפָה) (𝔊 Ζαιρα, Ζ(α)ιφα), cf. זִיף supr.)

זִיקוֹת v. 1. [זֵק].

. **זִיר** v. זור.

†**זַיִת** **n.m.** ψ 52, 10 **olive-tree, olive** (NH *id.;* Aram. ܙܰܝܬܳܐ ,זֵיתָא; Eth. **ዘይት**: Ar. زَيْتُونٌ *olive-tree, olive,* زَيْتٌ *olive-oil;* v. Lag M iii. 215 ff. Hom Aufsätze u. Abh., 1892, 94, 99 ff.; √dub.; Thes and most der. fr. assumed זהה *be bright, fresh, luxuriant* (v. sub זִו) + ת afformat. which is then treated as radical, cf. Sta § 187 a; but this not certain, cf. Ol § 119 b, 142 a; acc. to Lag Armen. Stud. § 1347 ׳ז is Armen. loan-word, v. also Lag M l. c.; BN 219, Anm.);—abs. ׳ז Gn 8^{11}, cstr. זֵית Dt 8^{8} 2 K 18^{32}; sf. זֵיתְךָ Dt 24^{20}, זֵיתֶךָ Ex 23^{11} Dt 28^{40}; pl. זֵיתִים Dt 6^{11}, etc.;—**1.** *olive-tree* Ju $9^{8.9}$ (personif., in Jotham's fable), Ho 14^{7} (sim. of beauty), Jb 15^{33} (as casting off its flowers, sim. of wicked man); in 2 S 15^{23} ins. הַזַּ׳ אֲשֶׁר (before הַמִּדְבָּר, read (בַּמִּ׳) 𝔊L Dr; also pl. of two *olive-trees* Zc $4^{3.11}$; ז׳ רַעֲנָן ψ 52^{10} *fresh,* (thriving) *olive-tree* (sim. of prosperity), so Je 11^{16}; עֲלֵה־ז׳ Gn 8^{11} (J) *olive-branch, sprig,* cf. Ne 8^{15} (here + עֲלֵי עֵץ־שֶׁמֶן, etc.); also pl. שְׁתִלֵי זֵיתִים ψ 128^{3} *olive-shoots* (sim. of children); שִׁבֲּלֵי זֵיתִים Zc 4^{12} *olive-branches* (in Zech.'s vision); זַיִת in representative or coll. sense, = *olive-trees,* groups of growing olive-trees, as property, source of wealth, *olive-yards* Ex 23^{11} (JE; + כֶּרֶם), Ju 15^{5} (+ *id.*); עֵץ־הַזַּיִת Hg 2^{19} (+ הַגֶּפֶן וְהַתְּאֵנָה וְהָרִמּוֹן); also in phr. כִּחֵשׁ מַעֲשֵׂה־זַיִת Hb 3^{17} *the bearing, yield,* of *olive-trees* (‖ שְׁדֵמוֹת לֹא־עָשָׂה אֹכֶל, cf. also תְּאֵנָה and יְבוּל גְּפָנִים v^{a}); specif. זֵית שֶׁמֶן, *oil-yielding olive-trees* Dt 8^{8} cf. 2 K 18^{32}; נֹקֶף ז׳ *striking* or *beating of olive-trees* Is 17^{6} 24^{13} (sim. of desolation at judgment of ׳י), cf. כִּי תַחְבֹּט זֵיתְךָ Dt 24^{20}; rather more often pl.; Am 4^{9} (‖ תְּאֵנִים ,כְּרָמִים ,גַּנּוֹת), 1 S 8^{14} (‖ שָׂדוֹת ,כְּרָמִים), cf. also Dt 6^{11} 28^{40a} Jos 24^{13} 2 K 5^{26} 1 Ch 27^{28} Ne 5^{11} 9^{25}. **2.** of fruit of olive-tree, *olives:* Dt 28^{40b} (c. שֶׁמֶן); תִּדְרֹךְ זַיִת Mi 6^{15} (‖ שֶׁמֶן); also שֶׁמֶן זַיִת *olive-oil* Ex 27^{20} 30^{24} (P) Lv 24^{2} (H). **3.** in designations of place: מַעֲלֵה הַזֵּיתִים 2 S 15^{30} *the ascent of the olive-trees* (𝔊 ἐν τῇ ἀναβάσει τῶν ἐλαιῶν = Mount of Olives); הַר־הַזֵּיתִים Zc $14^{4.4}$ (𝔊 τὸ ὄρος τῶν ἐλαιῶν); the well-known hill E. of Jerus. (NT usu. as Zc 14^{4} 𝔊, e.g. Mk 13^{3}; cf. also הָהָר 1 K 11^{7} Ez 11^{23} Ne 8^{15}; 𝔗 טוּר זֵיתַיָּא 2 K 23^{13} cf. 2 S 15^{30} Zc 14^{4} etc.; 𝔗 Ct 8^{5} טוּר מִשְׁחָא, and so Talm. etc.)

†**זֵיתָן** **n.pr.m.** (? *olive-tree*)—a Benjamite 1 Ch 7^{10}, 𝔊 Ζαιθαν, 𝔊L Ζηθα.

†**זֵתָם** **n.pr.m.** (sub זית in Thes, = foregoing)—a Levite (Gershonite) 1 Ch 23^{8}, appar. son of לַעְדָּן and brother of יְחִיאֵל and יוֹאֵל; 26^{22} appar. grandson of לַעְדָּן, and son of יְחִיאֵלִי (expressly called brother of יוֹאֵל); 𝔊 Ζεθομ, Ζοθομ, 𝔊L Ζηθαν.

זָךְ, זַךְ, v. sub זכך.

†[**זָכָה**] **vb. be clear, clean, pure,** alw. in moral sense (As. *zakû* Zim^{BP}, Aram. דְּכָא, ܙܟܐ, ܕܟܐ; cf. Ar. ذَكَا *be bright* (of a fire), *pungent* (of an odour); *be acute, quick of mind*)—**Qal** *Impf.* 3 ms. יִזְכֶּה Jb 15^{14} 25^{4}; 2 ms. תִּזְכֶּה ψ 51^{6}; 1 s. interrog. הַאֶזְכֶּה Mi 6^{11};—**1.** *be clean, pure,* of man, in the sight of God, Jb 15^{14} 25^{4} (in both ‖ יצדק; cf. also זַכּוּ 15^{15} 25^{5}). **2.** *be clear, be justified* = be regarded as just, righteous, of God, ψ 51^{6} (‖ תצדק), Mi 6^{11} **Pi.** *Pf.* 1 s. זכיתי ψ 73^{13} Pr 20^{9}, *Impf.* יְזַכֶּה־ ψ 119^{9}:—*make* or *keep clean, pure,* obj לְבָבִי ψ 73^{13} (‖ אֶרְחַץ כַּפָּי), obj. לִבִּי Pr 20^{9} (‖ טָהַרְתִּי); obj. אֶת־אָרְחוֹ ψ 119^{9}. **Hithp.** *Imv.* m pl. הִזַּכּוּ Is 1^{16} *make yourselves clean* (‖ רַחֲצוּ);—on form cf. Ges$^{§ 54\ 2.\ b,\ Rem}$ Ko$^{Lgb.\ i,\ 345,\ 834}$ Sta$^{§ 129\ d}$

זְכוֹכִית v. sub זכך.

†[**זָכַךְ**] **vb. be bright, clean, pure** (kindred with foregoing Only La Jb)—**Qal** *Pf* only 3 mpl. זַכּוּ,—**1.** *be bright, shining,* fig of splendour of nobles זַכּוּ נְזִירֶיהָ מִשֶּׁלֶג La 4^{7} (‖ צַחוּ מֵחָלָב). **2.** *be clean, pure* in God's sight, of heavens Jb 15^{15}, of stars 25^{5} (‖ יַאֲהִיל of moon; cf. also יִזְכֶּה 15^{14} 25^{4}) **Hiph.** *cleanse,* only *Pf.* 1 s. וַהֲזִכּוֹתִי בְּבֹר כַּפָּי Jb 9^{30}, fig. of making morally spotless (‖ הִתְרָחַצְתִּי)

† **זַךְ adj. pure, clean,** abs זַךְ Jb 8^{6} + 5 t.; זָךְ Ex 27^{20} Lv 24^{2}; f זַכָּה Ex 30^{34} + 2 t.;—**1.** lit, *pure,* i e unmixed, free from foreign substances, of olive oil Ex 27^{20} Lv 24^{2}, of frankincense Ex 30^{34} Lv 24^{7} (all P and H) **2.** fig, *pure, clean, righteous* (only Jb Pr)—of man Jb 8^{6} (‖ יָשָׁר), 33^{9} (+ בְּלִי פָשַׁע, ‖ חַף); as subst = *the pure, righteous* וְזַךְ יָשָׁר פָּעֳלוֹ Pr 21^{8} (opp וָזָר q.v); of mode of life כָּל־דַּרְכֵי־אִישׁ זַךְ בְּעֵינָיו Pr 16^{2}; of mode of action (פָּעֳלוֹ) 20^{11} (‖ יָשָׁר); of doctrine (לִקְחִי) Jb 11^{4} (‖ בַר הָיִיתִי); of prayer 16^{17} (‖ לֹא חָמָס בְּכַפָּי).

†**זְכוֹכִית n.[f.] glass** (𝔗 זכוכיתא, but v. Fra^{64}); as precious (‖ זָהָב), yet of less value than wisdom Jb 28^{17}. (Baer as above; זְכוּכִית van d H, al)

†**זַכַּי n.pr.m.** head of a family of returned exiles, זַכַּי Ezr 2^{9} (𝔊 Ζακχου, 𝔊L Ζακχαιου) = Ne 7^{14} (𝔊 Ζαθου, A Ζακχουρ, 𝔊L Ζακχαιου); perh. = זַבַּי Ne 3^{20} Qr (Kt זכי q.v, 𝔊 Ζαβ(ρ)ου, 𝔊L Ραββαι).

†**זָכַר**† **vb. remember** (As. *zikâru, name, mention,* cf. n. *zikru,* Hpt in KAT$^{2\ Gloss.\ i}$ Lyon^{Sarg}; Zinj. זכר, Ar. ذَكَرَ, Aram דְּכַר, ܕܟܪ, Palm. דכרנא *monument,* Vog$^{No\ 36\ b}$, דכיר *memorial,* Vog$^{No.\ 63}$, Sab. in n pr יזכראל DHM$^{Epigr\ Denkm.\ 43}$, but Eth ሐከረ:) —**Qal** *Pf* 3 ms ז׳ Gn 40^{23} +, 3 fs. זָכְרָה La 1$^{7.9}$; 2 ms. וְזָכַרְתָּ Dt 5^{15} +; sf. זְכַרְתַּנִי Gn 40^{14} cf. 1 S 1^{11}, זְכַרְתָּם ψ 88^{6}, 2 fs. זָכַרְתְּ Is 47^{7} 57^{11} cf 17^{10} + Ez 16$^{22.43}$ Qr (both Kt זכרתי), וְזָכַרְתְּ consec Ez 16^{61}; 3 pl. זָכְרוּ Ju 8^{34} +, etc., *Impf* 3 ms יִזְכֹּר Ho 8^{13} +; וַיִּזְכֹּר Gn 8^{1} +; sf. וַיִּזְכְּרֶהָ 1 S 1^{19}, 2 fs. יִזְכְּרֵי 2 S 14^{11} Pr 31^{7}; תִזְכְּרִי Is 54^{4} + 2 t.; 1 s אֶזְכֹּר Lv 26$^{42.42}$ Is 43^{25} (ψ 77^{12} Qr v. infra), אֶזְכָּר־ Je 31^{34}, וָאֶזְכֹּר Ex 6^{5}, sf 2 ms. אֶזְכָּרְךָ ψ 42^{7}, sf. 2 fs אֶזְכְּרֵכִי ψ 137^{6} (v Ges$^{§ 58.\ 3.\ R.\ 1}$ Sta$^{§§ 336\ a.\ 2,\ 634\ a.\ 2}$), etc; *Imv* ms. זְכֹר Ex 32^{13} +, זְכָר־ ψ 25^{7} +; זָכְרָה Ne 6^{14} +; sf. זָכְרֵנִי Ju 16^{28} + 2 t, mpl. זִכְרוּ Is 46^{9} +, זָכְרוּ Ne 4^{8}; *Inf. abs* זָכוֹר Ex 13^{3} +, זָכֹר Je 31^{20} +; *cstr* לִזְכֹּר Gn 9^{16} Ez 23^{19}, etc.; sf. בְּזָכְרֵנוּ ψ 137^{1}; *Pt* act pl cstr. וּלְזֹכְרֵי ψ 103^{18}, זָכוּר ψ 103^{14} v. infr. —**I.** human subj. **1.** *remember, recall, call to mind,* usu as affecting present feeling, thought, or action: **a.** *remember* past experiences (acc) Gn 42^{9} (E), 2 K 9^{25} (acc. pers. agent); sq cl. with מִי Jb 4^{7}; things formerly known (acc) Je 17^{2}; sq cl with כִּי Ju 9^{2}, with implied regret, longing Nu 11^{5} (JE), ψ 42^{5} 137^{1} La 1^{7} cf ψ 77^{7}, neg. 137^{5} (‖ שכח v^{5}); so (sq בְּ) Je 3^{16} (‖ עלה על לב and פקד). **b.** *recall* past distress, etc.; obj not expressed, La 3^{20} (זכור זכר), Jb 11^{16} (שכח in ‖ cl), neg, sq. acc. Is 54^{4} (‖ שכח), Pr 31^{7} (‖ *id.*). **c.** *remember* sins, (1) to repent of them Dt 9^{7} (+ אל־תשכח, sq. cl. with את־אשר), elsewh. only Ezek., usu c. acc. Ez 16^{61} (+ ונכלמת), v^{63} (obj not expressed), 20^{43} 36^{31}, (2) to renew and repeat them Ez 23^{19}, neg v^{27}. **d.** esp. *remember* the dealings of י׳, expressed in great variety of terms in acc, Dt 7^{18} 8^{2} 24^{9} 32^{7} (‖ בין), Is 46^{9} 63^{11} ψ 77^{12} Qr (Kt Hiph. q.v.) v^{12} 105^{5} 143^{5} (‖ הגיתי, אשוחח) 1 Ch 16^{12}; negatively, Is 43^{18} (‖ אַל תִּתְבֹּנְנוּ), Ez 16$^{22.43}$ ψ 78^{42} 106^{7} Ne 9^{17} (‖ וַיְמָאֲנוּ לִשְׁמֹעַ), obj cl. with כִּי esp. D, Dt 5^{15} 15^{15} 16^{12} 24$^{18.22}$ ψ 78^{35} **2.** *remember* persons (human subj), **a.** to their advantage:—sq. acc. Gn 40^{14} (E), v^{23} (E; neg, ‖ שכח), 1 S 25^{31}. **b.** to make use of them (acc) Na 2^{6}. **c.** their acts (acc.), to their advantage 2 Ch 24^{22}, to their disadvantage 2 S 19^{20} (neg), to take vengeance Dt 25^{17} **d.** *remember* human obligations, acc. rei: בְּרִית אַחִים Am 1^{9}; cf. perh. Est 2^{1} (acc pers. and also of deed); neg. Ec 9^{15} (acc. pers.), ψ 109^{16} (sq. עשות חסד). **3.** *remember* י׳: **a.** *call* him *to mind*

2 S 14^{11} (i e recall a specific command of his). **b.** *recall*, and (esp) *keep* ׳י *in mind* Dt 8^{18} Je 51^{50} Is 64^{4} (‖ עשה צדק), Ez 6^{9} Zc 10^{9} Jo 2^{8} ψ 42^{7} 63^{7} (‖ אהגה), 77^{4} Ne 4^{8}, negatively Ju 8^{34} Is 17^{10} (opp שכח), 57^{11} (‖ לא שַׂמְתְּ על־לבך); cf also ז׳ את־בוראֶיךָ Ec 12^{1}, and (no obj expressed) ψ 22^{28} (+ וישובו אל י׳), remember ׳י's name ψ 119^{55} **4.** *remember* **a.** words of Moses Jos 1^{13} (D) Mal 3^{22}, ׳י's instructions through prophet Is 44^{21} 46^{8} (‖ השיבו על לב), also Mi 6^{5} (sq. cl. with מה) **b.** commandments of ׳י (so as to do them) Nu 15^{39} (P, or H), v^{40} (P, + ועשיתם), ψ 103^{18} (+ לעשותם), 119^{52} (משפטים), his covenant 1 Ch 16^{15}. **5.** *think of* or *on*, *call to mind* something present or future.—sq acc, issue of conduct Is 47^{7}, La 1^{9} (end of Jerusalem), fight with crocodile Jb 40^{32}, obj a general truth, prosperity of wicked Jb 21^{6} (obj not expr), (fleeting) days of life Ec 5^{19}; (coming) days of darkness, 11^{8}, a duty Jb 36^{24} (sq cl with כי) **6.** *remember* a day, to observe, commemorate it —day of Exodus Ex 13^{3} (J) Dt 16^{3}, sabbath Ex 20^{8} (E, ‖ שמר Dt 5^{12}) **7.** *remember*, with implied *mention of*, obj ׳י Je 20^{9} (‖ דבר בשמו), מַשָּׂא י׳ 23^{36}

II Subj ׳י (אלהים) **1.** *remember* persons. **a.** individuals, with kindness, granting requests, protecting, delivering etc, c. acc pers, Gn 30^{22} (E), 1 S 1^{11} (opp. שכח), v^{19}, Ju 16^{28} (sq וחזקני), Je 15^{15} (‖ פָּקְדֵנִי), ψ 106^{4} (‖ *id*), Jb 14^{13} (+ תשית לי חק), also Gn 8^{1} (P), 19^{29} (P), neg ψ 88^{6} (‖ מידך נגזרו), sq ל pers ψ 25^{7} (yet cf Che), sq acc rei + ל pers (dat commod) Ne 5^{19} 13$^{14.22.31}$ **b** individuals, to punish, sq ל pers Ne 6^{14} 13^{29} **c.** his servants, people, the afflicted, (graciously) sq ל Ex 32^{13} (JE), Dt 9^{27} ψ 136^{23}, sq acc. ψ 9^{13} (opp שכח), 74^{2} 115^{12} (sq יְבָרֵךְ), cf Je 31^{20} (זכור זכר) **d** his land Lv 26^{42} (H), and neg La 2^{1} (his footstool) **e.** mankind ψ 8^{5} (‖ פקד) **2 a.** *remember* the distress of his servants, La 3^{19} (sq cl with מה), 5^{1} (‖ הַבִּיטָה וראה) **b.** their devotion, acc, ψ 20^{4} Je 2^{2} (+ ל pers), ψ 132^{1} (+ *id*), sq cl with את אשר 2 K 20^{3} = Is 38^{3} **c.** their intercession Je 18^{20} (sq inf c sf) **3. a.** *remember* his own covenant (with them), acc, Gn 9$^{15.16}$ Ex 2^{24} 6^{5} (all P), Lv 26$^{42.42}$ (H, as also) v^{45} (+ ל pers), Je 14^{21} (+ אַל־תָּפֵר), Ez 16^{60} ψ 105^{8}, cf v^{42} (obj דבר קָדְשׁוֹ), and 119^{49} Ne 1^{8}, ψ 106^{45} (+ ל pers), 111^{5} **b.** his mercy, etc, acc, ψ 25^{6} 98^{3} 2 Ch 6^{42}, also Hb 3^{2}. **c.** extenuating circumstances, sq cl with כִּי, Jb 7^{7} 10^{9} ψ 78^{39} 103^{14} (זָכוּר *be-thinketh him*, Che, cf. De Ko$^{i\ 20.14}$ Ba$^{NB\ 179}$), also ψ 89^{48} (sq אני + epex. cl. with מה). **4.** *remember* sins, idolatries etc, sq acc, Ho 7^{2} 8^{13} (‖ פקד), 9^{9} (‖ *id*), Je 14^{10} (‖ *id.*), neg Je 44^{21} (‖ עלה על לבו), Is 43^{25} 64^{8} ψ 25^{7} 79^{8} (+ ל pers); sq ל Je 31^{34}, also (obj. reproach) ψ 74$^{18.22}$ 89^{51}, and (obj day of Jerusalem) ψ 137^{7} (+ לבני אֱדוֹם, i e against them) **Niph.** *Pf.* 2 mpl consec וְנִזְכַּרְתֶּם Nu 10^{9}, *Impf* 3 ms יִזָּכֵר Je 11^{19}+, 3 fs. תִּזָּכֵר Ez 25^{10}, (תִּזָּכֵר) Ex 34^{19} rd תִּזָּכָר v הַזָּכָר); 2 fs תִּזָּכְרִי Is 23^{16} Ez 21^{37}, 3 mpl. יִזָּכְרוּ Ho 2^{19}+; 3 fpl. תִּזָּכַרְנָה Is 65^{17}+; תִּזָּכַרְןָ Ez 3^{20}, *Inf cstr* sf הִזָּכֶרְכֶם Ez 21^{29} (om 𝔊 Co), *Pt* pl נִזְכָּרִים Est 9^{28}—**1.** *be brought to remembrance, remembered, thought of,* usu. c neg—**a.** in general, subj Baalim Ho 2^{19} (+ בִּשְׁמָם), cf Zc 13^{2} (‖ אכרית); former heaven and earth Is 65^{17} (‖ עלה על לב), (wicked) dead Jb 24^{20} (‖ ישכחהו v^{a}), coral (not to be thought of [others, *be mentioned*] in comparison with wisdom) Jb 28^{18}, of *attention paid* to Tyre under fig. of harlot Is 23^{16} (opp. נשכחה). **b.** *brought to* ׳י's *remembrance*, subj the people, (1) with gracious result Nu 10^{9} (P, לפני י׳, ‖ ונושעתם), (2) for judgment Ez 21^{29} (om. 𝔊 Co) **c.** *be remembered* by ׳י, neg. of deeds, as affecting ׳י's judgment, (1) righteous Ez 3^{20} 18^{24} 33^{13} (sq ל of advantage, acc. to Co); (2) wicked 18^{22} (sq ל, om A B 𝔅 etc, Co) 33^{16} (sq. ל) **d.** *be remembered* אֶל־י׳ ψ 109^{14} (‖ אַל־תִּמָּח) **2.** neg *be not remembered* = no longer exist, of name of Israel, as nation Je 11^{19} (‖ נכרת), ψ 83^{5} (‖ נַכְחִידֵם מִגּוֹי), of Ammonites Ez 21^{37} 25^{10}. **3** *be remembered*, of particular days, in order to be observed, commemorated, Est 9^{28} (sq וְנַעֲשִׂים *observe, celebrate*). **Hiph.** *Pf.* 3 ms. הִזְכִּיר Is 49^{1}, 2 ms sf 1 s וְהִזְכַּרְתַּנִי consec Gn 40^{14}; *Impf* 3 ms יַזְכִּיר Is 19^{17}; 1 s אַזְכִּיר Ex 20^{24}+, etc, *Imv* ms sf 1 s הַזְכִּירֵנִי Is 43^{26}, mpl הַזְכִּירוּ Is 12^{4} Je 4^{16}, *Inf cstr* (לְ)הַזְכִּיר 2 S 18^{18}+; sf 3 ms. כְּהַזְכִּירוֹ 1 S 4^{18}, sf 2 mpl. הַזְכַּרְכֶם Ez 21^{29} (cf Sta^{§245} Ko$^{i\ 29.11}$), *Pt* מַזְכִּיר Gn 41^{9}+, etc; fs מַזְכֶּרֶת Nu 5^{15},—**1.** *cause to remember, remind*, c acc pers Is 43^{26} **2.** *cause to be remembered, keep in remembrance*, c. acc rei, a person's name 2 S 18^{18} ψ 45^{18}, of ׳י, causing his name to be remembered, by some token, Ex 20^{24} (JE) **3.** *mention*, **a.** sq acc. pers Gn 40^{14} (E, sq אֶל־ pers.), ׳י, = *call upon* Is 62^{6}, name of ׳י 26^{13} 49^{1} (‖ קראני), name of other gods, neg, Ex 23^{13} (JE, ‖ יִשָּׁמַע); sq. בשם Am 6^{10}, cf. ψ 20^{8} (De Che al. *boast of, praise*, 𝔊

μεγαλυνθησόμεθα, whence Hup Bae prop. נַגְבִּיר (= *we display strength*), neg Jos 23^{7} (D; ‖ ולא תשביעו), so באלהי ישראל Is 48^{1} (‖ הַנִּשְׁבָּעִים בשם) **b.** sq acc. rei: faults Gn 41^{9} (E), the ark 1 S 4^{18}, land of Judah Is 19^{17}, Rahab (= Egypt) ψ 87^{4}, works of י׳ ψ 77^{12} (Kt, Qr Qal q.v.), his righteousness ψ 71^{16}, lovingkindness, Is 63^{7}; human love Ct 1^{4}; also in technical sense, apparently = *accuse* before God, alw. sq עָוֹן, 1 K 17^{18} Nu 5^{15} (P) Ez 21^{28} v^{29} (sq. בְּהִגָּלוֹת פִּשְׁעֵיכֶם), 29^{16}. **c.** sq cl, with כי Is 12^{4}; no conjunction Je 4^{16} (ל indir obj., ‖ הַשְׁמִיעוּ) **d.** abs. *commemorate, praise* 1 Ch 16^{4} (לְהַז׳, appar. Levitical function, sq. ולהודות ולהלל ליהוה), so perh also לְהַזְכִּיר in titles ψ 38^{1} 70^{1} (others sub **5**). **4.** *record*, only pt. מַזְכִּיר as subst (title of public officer) = *recorder* 2 S 8^{16} 20^{24} 1 K 4^{3} 2 K 18$^{18.37}$ = Is 36$^{3.22}$, 1 Ch 18^{15} 2 Ch 34^{8}. **5.** of sacrifice, *make a memorial*, i e offer an אַזְכָּרָה q.v.; sq לְבֹנָה Is 66^{3} — JPPeters$^{JBL, 1893, xii, 58}$ rds. אַזְכָּרָה ψ 42^{5} (v **Qal I. 1**), 'let me make my *azkara*, and pour out libation for (עָלַי) my life'

†I. [זֵכֶר] **n.pr.m.** only זֶכֶר 1 Ch 8^{31} (𝔊 Ζαχουρ) = זְכַרְיָה 9^{37} q.v (cf Ph. n pr. זכר)

II. זֵכֶר **n.m.** Ex 17^{14}, vid following.

†זֵכֶר **n.m.**$^{\psi 9,7}$ **remembrance, memorial** (cf Hpt$^{Hbr\ 1885,\ 230}$)—ז׳ abs ψ 111^{4}, cstr Dt 25^{19}+, זֵכֶר cstr Ex 17^{14} van d. H, sf זכרי Ex 3^{15}, זִכְרְךָ Is 26^{8}+, זִכְרֶךָ ψ 6^{6}, זִכְרוֹ Ho 12^{6}+, זִכְרָם Dt 32^{26}+:—**1.** *remembrance, memory*. **a.** of persons or people, blotted out by their destruction, Ex 17^{14} (E; c מחה) = Dt 25^{19}, Dt 32^{26} (השבית) ψ 34^{17} 109^{15} (both הכרית), ψ 9^{7} (אבד), Jb 18^{17} (אבד; ‖ שם), Is 26^{14} (אבד), cf. on other hand ז׳ עולם as portion of righteous. **b.** of י׳ ψ 6^{6} 102^{13} (‖ אַתָּה = יהוה) **c.** of י׳'s character and works ψ 30^{5} 97^{12} 111^{4}. **d.** *remembrance* of particular days, i e their observance Est 9^{28} (יְמֵי הַפּוּרִים) **2.** *memorial*, by which one is remembered: **a.** nearly = שֵׁם, ז׳ צַדִּיק לִבְרָכָה Pr 10^{7} (‖ שֵׁם), cf. also Ec 9^{5} (c. נשכח), esp. of י׳ Ex 3^{15} (E), Ho 12^{6} Is 26^{8} ψ 135^{13} (all ‖ שֵׁם) **b.** = renown (of Israel) Ho 14^{8} (cf VB).

†זָכָר **n.m. & adj. male** (As *zikaru, zikru*, COT^{Gloss} Lyon$^{Manual,\ Gloss}$, Ar ذَكَر, Aram דְּכַר, ܕܟܪܐ; Sab. ד[כ]רם DHM$^{ZMG\ 1876,\ 675}$; relation to above √ obscure; male as *mentioned, talked of*, Lane$^{969\,f}$; fr. assumed orig. sense *be sharp* (traces of this in Arab v Lane), Bo$^{Prob\ 207}$ Fl in ChWB$^{i,\ 422}$, cf Ar. ذَكَر *male organ*; Schwally ZAW$^{1891,\ 176\,ff}$ fr. זָכַר = *call upon* in worship; hence *male* as *competent to worship*)—alw abs. ז׳ Gn 1^{27}+, pl. (ה)זְכָרִים Ex 13^{12}+, vid. also [זָכוּר].—**I.** subst *male*, offspring of men and animals Ex 13$^{12.15}$ (pl, both JE), opp נְקֵבָה Dt 4^{16}; specif **1.** of men **a.** in phr אשר לא יָדְעָה אִישׁ לְמִשְׁכַּב זָכָר Ju 21^{12} (Bu$^{RS\ 153}$ Dr$^{Intr\ 161}$), cf. v^{11}, Nu 31$^{17.18.35}$ (all 3 P), צַלְמֵי זָכָר Ez 16^{17} **b.** alone = *man* Je 30^{6} (ראו אם־ילד זָכָר, ‖ גֶּבֶר); usu coll, *men, male persons* (of all ages) Ju 21^{11} 1 K 11$^{15.16}$, Gn 34^{25} Lv 6$^{11.22}$ 7^{6} Nu 1$^{2.20.22}$ 3$^{28.34.39}$ 18^{10} 26^{62} 31$^{7.17}$ (all P); pl. (ה)זכרים 2 Ch 31^{16} Ezr 8$^{3.4.5.6.7.8.9.10.11.12.13.14}$, so also Jos 5^{4} (‖ כל־העם, and כל־אנשי המלחמה), 17^{2} (gloss? cf Dr $^{Intr\ 104}$); esp. of individ, in connex. with circumcision Gn 17$^{10.12.14.23}$ 34$^{15.22.24}$ Ex 12^{48} (all P), of male child Lv 12^{2} (P) Is 66^{7}; opp נְקֵבָה Gn 1^{27} 5^{2} Lv 12^{7} (child) 15^{33} 27$^{3.5.6.7}$ Nu 5^{3} (all P; cf. Sab. אנתים פאו ד(כ)רם DHM$^{l.c.}$), opp אִשָּׁה in command ag sodomy Lv 18^{22} 20^{13} (both H) **2.** of animals, esp for sacrifice Ex 34^{19} (JE, rd הַזָּכָר for MT תִּזָּכָר), Ex 12^{5} Lv 1$^{3.10}$ 4^{23} (all P) 22^{19} (H), Mal 1^{14}, opp. נְקֵבָה Gn 6^{19} 7$^{3.9.16}$ Lv 3$^{1.6}$ (all P). **II.** adj. sg *male* (only human beings) ז׳ בן יֻלַּד־לְךָ Je 20^{15}, כָּל־בכור ז׳ Nu 3$^{40.43}$ (both P).

†[זָכוּר] **n.m. male**, i q זָכָר, but only c sf.;—coll כָּל־זְכוּרְךָ Ex 23^{17} = 34^{23} (both JE), = Dt 16^{16}, of attendance at feasts, כָּל־זְכוּרָהּ (of city refusing terms of peace) Dt 20^{13} commanded to be slain (opp הַנָּשִׁים, הַטַּף, etc., v^{14}).

†זִכְרִי **n.pr.m.** 𝔊 Ζεχρει, Ζαχρι, etc, exc as below:—**1.** a Reubenite 1 Ch 27^{16}. **2.** a Judahite 2 Ch 17^{16}. **3.** Levites. **a.** Ex 6^{21} (P). **b.** 1 Ch 26^{25}. **c.** an Asaphite 1 Ch 9^{15} ‖ Ne 11^{17} where rd. זכרי (for זַבְדִּי, q.v), cf also *infr.* זַכּוּר **3 b.** **4.** a priest Ne 12^{17} (𝔊L Ζαχαριας) **5.** Benjamites. **a** 1 Ch 8^{19}. **b.** v^{23}. **c.** v^{27} **d.** Ne 11^{9}. **6.** father of a captain in Jehoiada's time 2 Ch 23^{1} (𝔊 Ζαχαρια, 𝔊L Ζεχρι) **7.** mighty man of Ephraim 2 Ch 28^{7} (𝔊 Ἐζεχρει, 𝔊L Ζαχαριας).

†זַכּוּר **n.pr.m.** 𝔊 Ζακχυρ, Ζακχουρ, etc —**1.** a Reubenite Nu 13^{4} (P) **2.** a Simeonite 1 Ch 4^{26}. **3.** Levites **a.** 1 Ch 24^{27}. **b.** an Asaphite 1 Ch 25^{2} (Σακχους), v^{10} (Ζαχχουθ), Ne 12^{35} (Ζακχουρ), cf. זכרי supr **3 c** **c** Ne 10^{13} cf. 13^{13}. **4.** companion of Ezra, Ezr 8^{14} Qr (Kt זבוד, cf supr. p. 256 a). **5.** contemp. of Nehemiah, Ne 3^{2}.

†זִכָּרוֹן, זִכָּרֹן **n.m.**$^{Ec 1, 11}$ **memorial, remembrance** (cf. Lg$^{BN 199, 200}$)—abs. זִכָּרוֹן Jos 4^{7}+; זִכָּרֹן Ex 28$^{12.12.29}$; cstr. זִכְרוֹן Ec 1^{11}+2 t.; sf. זִכְרוֹנֵךְ Is 57^{8}; pl. הַזִּכְרֹנוֹת Est 6^{1}; sf. זִכְרֹנֵיכֶם Jb 13^{12};—**1.** *memorial, reminder:* **a.** memorial-day Ex 12^{14} (P). **b.** memorial-usage Ex 13^{9} (JE). **c.** memorial-objects, altar-plates Nu 17^{5} (P); stones in Jordan Jos 4^{7} (JE); crowns in temple Zc 6^{14}; ז׳ in Is 57^{8} is symbol of strange god (Di), or perh. phallus-image, as sign of harlot (Che), cf. >Du (who prop. זָכְרוֹן, from זָכָר). **d.** memorial-record; in a book Ex 17^{14} (E); cf. סֵפֶר זִכָּרוֹן Mal 3^{16}, ס׳ הַזִּכְרֹנוֹת דברי הימים Est 6^{1}; memorial, as proof of citizenship Ne 2^{20} (‖צְדָקָה, חֵלֶק); reminder of Israel, לִפְנֵי י׳, of כֶּסֶף הַכִּפֻּרִים Ex 30^{16}; spoils of war Nu 31^{54}; inscribed stones of ephod Ex 28$^{12.29}$, called אַבְנֵי ז׳ v^{12}= 39^{7}; blowing of trumpets Nu 10^{10} (foregoing all P), cf. זִכְרוֹן תְּרוּעָה Lv 23^{24} (H; where, however, no לִפְנֵי י׳, v. Di); מִנְחַת (ה)זכרון Nu 5$^{15.18}$ (P); *memorial-sentence, apophthegm* Jb 13^{12}. **2.** *remembrance* Ec 1^{11} (cstr. before prep. Ges$^{§130, 1}$), v^{11} 2^{16}.

†זְכַרְיָהוּ, oftener זְכַרְיָה **n.pr.m.** (Sab. ידכראל DHM$^{Epigr. Denkm. 43}$) 𝔊 Ζαχαρια(ς), etc.:—**1.** זכריהו, king of Isr., son of Jerob. II, 2 K 15^{8} = זכריה 14^{29} 15^{11}. **2.** זכריהו, father of Hezekiah's mother 2 Ch 29^{1} = זכריה 2 K 18^{2}. **3.** זכריהו, contemporary of Isaiah Is 8^{2}. **4.** זכריהו, a Reubenite 1 Ch 5^{7}. **5.** זכריה, a Benjamite 1 Ch 9^{37} (𝔊 Ζαχαρια, A Ζαχχουρ 𝔊L Ζεχρει) = זֶכֶר 1 Ch 8^{31} (v. I. [זָכַר]). **6.** זכריהו, a Manassite 1 Ch 27^{21} (𝔊 Ζαβδειου, 𝔊L Ζαχαριου). **7.** זכריהו, a son of Jehoshaphat 2 Ch 21^{2}. **8.** זכריה, a captain of Jehosh. 2 Ch 17^{7}. **9.** זכריהו, teacher of Uzziah 2 Ch 26^{5}. **10.** Levites, זכריהו: **a.** 1 Ch 15^{18} = זכריה v^{20}, 16^{5}. **b.** 1 Ch 24^{25}. **c.** 1 Ch 26$^{2.14}$. **d.** 1 Ch 26^{11}. **e.** 2 Ch 20^{14}. **f.** 2 Ch 29^{13} (𝔊 Ἀζαριας, A Ζαχαριας, so 𝔊L). זכריה: **g.** 1 Ch 9^{21}. **h.** 2 Ch 34^{12}. **i.** an Asaphite Ne 12^{35}. **11.** priests, זכריהו: **a.** 1 Ch 15^{24}. **b.** 2 Ch 35^{8}. זכריה: **c.** 2 Ch 24^{20} (𝔊 Ἀζαριαν; 𝔊L Ζαχαριαν; prob. referred to Matt 23^{35}, where appar. confusion with **f**). **d.** Ne 11^{12}. **e.** Ne 12^{41}. **f.** the well-known prophet Zc 1$^{1.7}$ 7$^{1.8}$ Ne 12^{16} [cf. Aram. Ezr 5^{1} 6^{14}]. **12.** returned exiles, זכריה: **a.** Ezr 8^{3} and perh. v^{16}, cf. Ne 8^{4}. **b.** Ezr 8^{11} (𝔊 Ἀζαριας, A Ζαχαριας, so 𝔊L). **c.** Ezr 10^{26}. **d.** a man of Judah Ne 11^{4}. **e.** *id.* Ne 11^{5} (𝔊 Θηζεια, א Θηδεια, A Ζαχαριου, so 𝔊L).

†אַזְכָּרָה **n.f.** memorial-offering, only P (an Aram. inf. form; cf. Ba$^{NB 90}$ Sta^{§244})—abs. א׳ Lv 24^{7}; sf. אַזְכָּרָתָהּ Lv 2^{2}+5 t.;—used of the frankincense burned for the shew-bread והיתה ללחם לאז׳ אִשֶּׁה לי׳ Lv 24^{7}; elsewh. alw. after הקטיר, only c. sf., referring to מִנְחָה Lv 2$^{2.9.16}$ 6^{8} Nu 5^{26}; of the meal used as חַטָּאת by the very poor Lv 5^{12}; alw. connected with אִשֶּׁה, exc. Lv 6^{8} Nu 5^{26}.

מַזְכִּיר **n.m.** recorder, v. זָכַר **Hiph.**

זלא (√ of foll.; meaning unknown).

†יִזְלִיאָה **n.pr.m.** a Benjamite 1 Ch 8^{18} (𝔊 Ζαρεια, A Ἐζλια, 𝔊L Ἰεζελια).

זלג (Ar. زَلَجَ *glide, slip;* of arrow, *skim, slide along;* مِزْلَجٌ a kind of *latch, sliding bolt;* Aram. זְלַג is *pour forth* (tears), *flow down*).

†מַזְלֵג **n.m.** appar. a sacrificial implement, three-pronged fork הַמַּ׳ שְׁלֹשׁ הַשִּׁנַּיִם 1 S 2^{13}, cf. v^{14} (v. Dr$^{Sm. pp. 23, 291}$).

†[מִזְלָגָה] **n.[f.]** id., only pl. הַמִּזְלָגֹת Ex 38^{3} Nu 4^{14}; הַמִּזְלָגוֹת 1 Ch 28^{17} 2 Ch 4^{16}; sf. מִזְלְגֹתָיו Ex 27^{3};—a sacrificial implement, belonging to altar in tabernacle, Ex 27^{3} 38^{3} Nu 4^{14} (all P); belonging to temple 1 Ch 28^{17} 2 Ch 4^{16}.

†I. [זָלַל] **vb. shake** (Ar. زَلَّ *slip,* زَلْزَلَ *agitate, shake;* تَزَلْزَلَ *be agitated, quake,* esp. of earth-quake)—**Niph.** *Pf.* נָזֹלּוּ *shake, quake* Is 63^{19} of mts. at י׳'s presence (Ges De Che Di Du; 𝔊 𝔙 as if fr. נזל *flow down*); so 64^{2} (but here prob. not original Che Di Du); read נָזֹלּוּ likewise Ju 5^{5} (𝔊 Thes Stu Be Bla MV SS; MT נָזְלוּ, fr. נזל).

†[זַלְזַל] **n.[m.]** (quivering) **tendrils;**—only pl. *tendrils* of vine הַזַּלְזַלִּים Is 18^{5} (‖הַנְּטִישׁוֹת), in fig. of Yahweh's destroying the Assyrians.

†II. [זָלַל] **vb. 1. be light, worthless, 2. make light of** (As. *zalâlu, be in ruins,* COT^{Gloss} (Asrn$^{Standard Inscr. 15}$), Ar. ذَلَّ = Aram. ܙܠ (rare), ܙܠܝܠ *easy;* but זְלַל, ܙܠ, are more common (all intrans.))—**Qal** only *Pt.* act. זוֹלֵל Dt 21^{20}+2 t.; זוֹלֵלָה La 1^{11}; pl. זוֹלְלִים Pr 28^{7}, cstr. זֹלְלֵי Pr 23^{20}—**1.** *be worthless, insignificant* Je 15^{19} (opp. יָקָר) La 1^{11} (of Jerusalem in distress). **2.** trans. *make light of = be lavish with, squander* (cf. II. זול), esp. of gluttony ז׳ בשׂר Pr 23^{20} (‖ סֹבְאֵי יַיִן), abs. v^{21} Dt 21^{20} (both ‖ סֹבֵא), Pr 28^{7}.

Hiph. *Pf.* sf. הִזִּילוּהָ La 1^{8} causat of **Qal 1** *make light of, despise* (opp. כבד); on form cf. Ges $^{§67, R.8}$ RobGes, MV SS (> assigned to זול by Thes Ko$^{Lgb.I\ 471}$).

†**זֻלּוּת** **n.f.** **worthlessness,** only כְּרֻם זֻלֻּת לִבְנֵי אָדָם [van d. H. זֻלּוּת] ψ 12^{9} cf De & Che$^{crit\ n}$

זלעף (quadrilit. √of foll; v. reff. infr.)

†**זַלְעָפָה** **n.f.** **raging heat** (on format. cf. Ges$^{Lbg\ 863}$ Ol$^{§196\ a.\ 1.2}$)—ז׳ ψ 119^{53}; pl. abs. זִלְעָפוֹת ψ 11^{6}; cstr. זַלְעֲפוֹת La 5^{10};—**1.** of fever heat of famine ז׳ רָעָב La 5^{10} **2.** of burning wind רוּחַ ז׳ ψ 11^{6} (in fig. of י׳'s judgment, with אֵשׁ, גָּפְרִית). **3.** fig of zeal ז׳ אֲחָזַתְנִי ψ 119^{53}.

זלף (√ of foll; Thes comp Aram. זְלַף Pa. *drop, drip;* cf. ܙܠܦ; also NH זִלּוּף *sprinkling,* ܙܠܦܐ *dropping, pouring,* زُلْفَةٌ a *full bowl,* etc)

†**זִלְפָּה** **n.pr.f.** Leah's maid, one of Jacob's wives, mother of Gad and Asher Gn 29^{24} $30^{9.10.12}$ (all J), 35^{26} 37^{2} 46^{18} (all P).

†**זָמַם** **vb.** **consider, purpose, devise** (Aram. זְמַם in der. conjj; cf Ar زَمَّ *speak, talk* (rare); Aram. ܙܡ is *sonuit, resonavit,* the n ܙܡܙܡܐ is *tinnitus, strepitus*) — only **Qal** *Pf.* זָמַם Dt 19^{19}+2 t.; זָמַם La 2^{17}, זָמְמָה Pr 31^{16}; זַמּוֹתָ Pr 30^{32}; זַמֹּתִי Je 4^{28} but also זָמַמְתִּי Zc $8^{14.15}$; זַמֹּתִי ψ 17^{3} either belongs here with irreg accent (v De), or is Inf. after anal of ל״ה e.g. חֲנוֹת cf. 77^{10} (Hi Ri); Che$^{crit.\ n}$ rds זַמֹּתִי; זָמְמוּ ψ 31^{14}; *Impf.* יָזְמוּ Gn 11^{6} (Ges$^{§67,\ R.11}$), on poss. *Inf.* זַמֹּתִי ψ 17^{3} v supr; *Pt.* זֹמֵם ψ 37^{12};—**1.** *consider, fix thought upon,* c. acc. of concrete obj שָׂדֶה Pr 31^{16}. **2.** *purpose, devise*· **a.** esp of Yahweh's purpose in punishment Je 4^{28} (abs), 51^{12} sq. עשה + acc (‖מְזִמָּה), La 2^{17} (sq. אשר) Zc 1^{6} (c כן שַׁבְתִּי כאשר sq. inf), 8^{14} (*id.*); of blessing only זָמַמְתִּי לְהֵיטִיב Zc 8^{15} (opp. v^{14}). **b.** of evil purpose of wicked men אשר יָ׳ לעשׂות Gn 11^{6} Dt 19^{19} (c כאשר + inf), ψ 31^{14} (sq. inf.); abs. Pr 30^{32} (‖נבל), ψ 17^{3} *have I* (i e. if I have) *devised evil* (so De), sq לְ pers. (= *against*) ψ 37^{12}.

†**[זָמָם]** **n.[m.]** **plan, device** (bad sense), only זְמָמוֹ ψ 140^{9} (‖ מַאֲוַיֵּי רָשָׁע).

†I. **זִמָּה** **n.f.** **plan, device, wickedness**—abs. ז׳ Lv 18^{17}+17 t; cstr. זִמַּת Pr 24^{9}+2 t.; sf. זִמָּתֵךְ Ez 16^{58}+3 t; זִמָּתֵכָנָה Ez $23^{48.49}$, pl. זִמּוֹת Is 32^{7}, sf. זִמֹּתַי Jb 17^{11};—**1.** *plan, purpose* Jb 17^{11}; elsewhere always **2.** in bad sense: **a.** *evil device* Is 32^{7} (c. יעץ, sq. לְחַבֵּל); זִמַּת אִוֶּלֶת Pr 24^{9}; cf ψ 26^{10} (‖שֹׁחַד), 119^{150} **b.** *wickedness* in act עָשָׂה ז׳ Ho 6^{9} (where murder in context), Pr 10^{23} 21^{27} cf. Now. Esp. **c.** of unchastity. incest Lv 18^{17} $20^{14.14}$, licentiousness 19^{29} (all H), Ju 20^{6} (‖נְבָלָה), adultery Jb 31^{11}; freq (mostly Ez) metaph. of idolatry of people under fig. of harlotry and adultery Je 13^{27} (זִמַּת זְנוּתֵךְ), Ez 16^{27} (דַּרְכֵּךְ זִמָּה), $v^{43.58}$ (both ‖תועבה), 22^{9} (c. עשׂה), v^{11} (‖תועבה, טמא בזמה), $23^{21.27}$ (‖זְנוּתֵךְ), v^{29} (עֶרְוָה), v^{35} (‖תַּזְנוּתָיִךְ), וְזִמָּתֵךְ וְתַזְנוּתָיִךְ, v^{44} (אֵשֶׁת הַזִּ׳), Co לַעֲשׂוֹת ז׳), $v^{48.48.49}$ (‖חֲטָאֵי גִלּוּלֵיכֶן), 24^{13}. [In Ez $16^{27.43}$ 24^{13} del. Co, chiefly on intern. grounds.]

†II. **זִמָּה** **n.pr.m.** of several Levites (Gershonites)—**1.** 1 Ch 6^{5}. **2.** 1 Ch 6^{27}. **3.** 2 Ch 29^{12}

†**מְזִמָּה** **n.f.** **purpose, discretion, device** (Je and WisdLit), מְזִמָּה Jb 42^{2}+5 t.; הַמְזִמָּתָה Je 11^{15} (but rd. for הַמְ׳ רַבִּים with 𝔊 הַנְּדָרִים); מְזִמָּתוֹ Je 51^{11}; pl. abs. מְזִמּוֹת ψ 37^{7}+7 t.; cstr. id. Je 23^{20} 30^{24}, sf. מְזִמּוֹתָיו ψ 10^{4};—**1.** of י׳'s *purposes* Jb 42^{2}, chiefly in punishment (cf. זָמַם, זִמָּה) Je 23^{20} 30^{24} 51^{11} (‖ v^{12} זמם) **2.** *power of devising, discretion* Pr 1^{4} (‖דַּעַת), 2^{11} (‖תְּבוּנָה), 3^{21} (‖תֻּשִׁיָּה), 5^{2} (‖דַּעַת), דַּעַת מְזִמּוֹת 8^{12}. **3. a.** evil *thoughts* of men ψ 10^{4}, evil *devices* of men Jb 21^{27} (‖מחשבות), ψ 10^{2} 21^{12} (both c חָשַׁב). **b.** *wickedness* in act Je 11^{15} ψ 37^{7} (both c עָשָׂה), 139^{20} לִמְזִמָּה = *wickedly;* — note phrases: אִישׁ מְזִמּוֹת *a man of* (*evil*) *devices* (or *practices*) Pr 12^{2} (opp. טוב) 14^{17}; בַּעַל־מְזִמּוֹת Pr 24^{8} (‖מְחַשֵּׁב לְהָרַע; v. בַּעַל)

†**זַמְזֻמִּים** **n.pr.gent.** said to be a name given to רְפָאִים by the Ammonites who dispossessed them Dt 2^{20} (cf Ar. زَمْزَمَ *talk gibberish*?), 𝔊 Ζοχομμιν, Ζομζομμειν, and Ζομμειν (so 𝔊L); cf. Gn 14^{5} זוּזִים q v. (𝔊 ἔθνη ἰσχυρά)

†**[זָמַן]** **vb.** (Aram. and late) only **Pu.** *Pt.* **be fixed, appointed,** of time (Ar. زَمِنَ *continue,* Aram Pa. זַמֵּן, ܙܡܢ *summon to fixed time* or *place, invite, appoint;* cf זְמַן infr)—עִתִּים מְזֻמָּנִים Ezr 10^{14} Ne 10^{35}; עִ׳ מְזֻמָּנוֹת Ne 13^{31}

†**זְמָן** **n.m.** (late) **appointed time, time** (Ar زَمَن, Eth. ዘመን: BAram. 𝔗 זְמַן, but Syr. ܙܒܢܐ, Mand. זיבנא, Sam ࠆࠁࠍ, Palm. זבנא, cf. Reckendorf$^{ZMG\ 1888,\ 394}$)—sg. זְמָן Ne 2^{6} Ec 3^{1}; sf.

וְכִזְמַנָּם Est 9^{27}, בִּזְמַנֵּיהֶם v^{31} (on Dagh cf Ges § 20 2 c).

†I. [זָמַר] **vb.** only **Pi.** **make music** in praise of God (י׳), only poet. (Ar زَمَرَ *pipe, play* on a reed, Aram. ܙܡܰܪ, זַמַּר and deriv., Eth ዘመረ: in der. conjj., on an orig mng *hum, murmur*, cf Hup ZKM iii (1840) 394 ff iv, 139 ff. Id Psalm. Einl. § 7, 2 De^{4} on ψ 3)—**Pi.** *Impf* 3 ms. sf יְזַמֶּרְךָ ψ 30^{13}; 1 s אֲזַמֵּר Ju 5^{3} 2 S 22^{50}, (וְ)אֲזַמְּרָה ψ 7^{18} + 7 t, אֲזַמֵּ֫רָה ψ 18^{50} + 3 t; sf אֲזַמֶּרְךָּ ψ 57^{10} 108^{4}, אֲזַמֶּרְךָ֫ ψ 131^{1}, 3 mpl. יְזַמְּרוּ ψ 66^{4} 149^{3}; וִיזַמְּרוּ ψ 66^{4}; 1 pl. נְזַמְּרָה ψ 21^{14}, *Imv.* mpl. זַמְּרוּ ψ 9^{12} + 14 t, זַמֵּ֫רוּ ψ $47^{7.7}$; *Inf* לְזַמֵּר ψ 92^{2}, זַמְּרָה ψ 147^{1},—*make music, melody* (only ψψ, exc. Ju 5^{3} Is 12^{5}),—**1.** of *singing* to (ל) God (Yahweh) Ju 5^{3} ψ 27^{6} 101^{1} 104^{33} 105^{2} = 1 Ch 16^{9} (all ‖ שׁיר vb), ψ 9^{12} 30^{5} (both ‖ הוֹדוּ), 47^{7} (לְמַלְכֵּנוּ), 66^{4} 71^{23} (with תְּרַנֵּנָּה שְׂפָתַי), 75^{10} (‖ הִגִּיד), 146^{2} (‖ הלל); sq אֶל־ 59^{18}, to his name לְשֵׁם, ψ 18^{50} = 2 S 22^{50} (‖ אודך), ψ 92^{2} (‖ להדות), 135^{3} (‖ הללויה); sq sf = *sing thee, praise thee in song* ψ 30^{13} 57^{10} 108^{4} 138^{1} (all ‖ אודך), sq acc י׳ Is 12^{5}, אֱלֹהִים ψ 47^{7}, אלהינו 147^{1}, אדני 68^{33} (‖ שירו), sq. שְׁמוֹ 7^{18} (‖ אודה), 9^{3} 61^{9} 66^{4} 68^{5} (‖ שירו), sq כבוד שמו 66^{2}, גבורתך 21^{14} (‖ נשירה), sq acc of the song, מַשְׂכִּיל ψ 47^{8} (v מ׳ sub שׂכל), abs 57^{8} (‖ אשירה), 98^{4} (‖ הָרִיעוּ, פִּצְחוּ, רַנְּנוּ), 108^{2} (‖ אשירה, instrumental accomp. v^{3}, cf. also v^{4} *supr*) $47^{7.7}$. **2.** of playing musical instruments בְּנֵבֶל עָשׂוֹר זַמְּרוּ־לוֹ ψ 33^{2} (‖ הודו לי׳ בכנור), cf. 144^{9} (‖ אשירה), אזמרה לך בכנור 71^{22} (‖ אודך בכלי־נבל); זמרו לי׳ בכנור בכנור וקול זמרה 98^{5}, 147^{7} (‖ ענו לי׳ בתודה), זמרו לא׳ בכנור; יזמרו־לו בתף וכנור 149^{3} (‖ יהללו שמו במחול)

†I. זִמְרָה **n.f. melody, song,** in praise of י׳—abs זמרת י׳ ψ 81^{3} + 2 t; זמרת Ex 15^{2} ψ 118^{14} Is 12^{2}, rd זִמְרָת(י) (v Di^{Ex} SS), cstr זִמְרַת Am 5^{23}, on Gn 43^{11} v infr.,—**1.** of instrumental music זִמְרַת נְבָלֶיךָ Am 5^{23} (‖ הֲמוֹן שִׁירֶיךָ). **2.** of singing י׳ תּוֹדָה וְקוֹל ז׳ Is 51^{3}, as *subject* of song עָזִּי וְזִמְרָת יָהּ (so rd.) Ex 15^{2} Is 12^{2} ψ 118^{14}. **3.** not clearly determined שְׂאוּ־ז׳ וּתְנוּ־תֹף כִּנּוֹר נָעִים עִם־נָ֑בֶל ψ 81^{3}, בכנור וקול ז׳ 98^{5} (cf III זמר ad fin)—On זִמְרַת הארץ Gn 43^{11} v. II זמרה infr.

זִמְרָת v I זִמְרָה

†I [זָמִיר] **n m.**$^{Is 25.5}$ **song** (cf $Ba^{NB 136}$)—cstr. זְמִיר Is 25^{5}, pl abs. זְמִרוֹת Jb 35^{10} + 2 t, cstr זְמִרוֹת 2 S 23^{1},—*song* נְעִים זְמִרוֹת Is 24^{16}, cstr זְמִרוֹת 2 S 23^{1},—*song* זְמִרוֹת יִשְׂרָאֵל 2 S 23^{1} in epith of David, Jb 35^{10} Is 24^{16}, of (hostile) song of triumph זְמִיר עָרִיצִים Is 25^{5} (‖ שְׁאוֹן זָרִים); song in praise of י׳ זְ׳ הָיוּ לִי חֻקֶּיךָ ψ 119^{54}, i e. they are the subject of my song.—On Ct 2^{12} v II זמיר sub II. זמר.

†מִזְמוֹר **n.[m.] melody** (techn. design of psalms, cf Hup Psalm Einl. § 7, 2 De^{4} on ψ 3, Bae Psalmen xiii, ܡܙܡܘܪܐ, مَزَامِيرُ, መዝሙር: loan-wds, all = *Psalm(s)*, on מ׳, in relation to תהלה cf. Lg Or ii 221), always in this form, in 57 ψ-titles—מ׳ alone ψ 98^{1}, מ׳ שִׁיר לְיוֹם הַשַּׁבָּת 92^{1}, מ׳ לְתוֹדָה 100^{1}; usu with pers. name or title; מ׳ לְדָוִד ψ 3^{1} 15^{1} 23^{1} 29^{1} 63^{1} 141^{1} 143^{1}, שִׁיר מ׳ לדוד מ׳ שִׁיר־חֲנֻכַּת הבית 30^{1}, מ׳ לדוד לְהַזְכִּיר 38^{1}, 108^{1}, לַמְנַצֵּחַ מ׳ לדוד 110^{1}, 24^{1} 101^{1} לדוד מ׳ 30^{1}, לַמְנַצֵּחַ . . . מ׳ לדוד 13^{1} 19^{1} 20^{1} 21^{1} 31^{1} 41^{1} 51^{1} 64^{1} 140^{1}, לַמְנַצֵּחַ מ׳ לדוד 4^{1} 5^{1} 6^{1} 8^{1} 9^{1} 12^{1} 22^{1} 39^{1} 62^{1}, למנצח לדוד מ׳ 40^{1} 109^{1} 139^{1}, למנצח לדוד מ׳ שיר 65^{1}, למנצח לדוד מ׳ שיר 68^{1}, also simply לַמְנַצֵּחַ מ׳ שיר ψ 67^{1}, לַמְנַצֵּחַ שיר מ׳ 66^{1}, but also שיר מ׳ לבני קרח ψ 48^{1}, לבני־קרח מ׳ שיר 87^{1}, שיר מ׳ לבני קרח לַמְנַצֵּחַ . . . מַשְׂכִּיל לְהֵימָן הָאֶזְרָחִי 88^{1}, לַמְנַצֵּחַ לבני קרח מ׳ 47^{1} 49^{1} 85^{1}, למנצח . . . לבני־קרח מ׳ 84^{1}, further מ׳ לְאָסָף ψ 50^{1} 73^{1} 79^{1} 82^{1}, שיר מ׳ לאסף לַמְנַצֵּחַ . . . מ׳ לאסף שיר 75^{1} 76^{1}, 83^{1}, לַמְנַצֵּחַ . . . לאסף מ׳ 77^{1} 80^{1}. [Summary—מ׳ in 34 ψψ with לַמְנַצֵּחַ, of wh 23 have לדוד also, 5 לבני קרח also, 4 לְאָסָף, and 2 no n pr., in addit., in 13 ψψ with לדוד, 2 with לבני קרח, 5 with לאסף; in only 3 without either n pr. or title, מ׳ is preceded by שיר 5 t, and foll. by שיר 8 t.]

II [זָמַר] **vb. trim, prune** (NH *id*, relation to √I obscure)—**Qal** *Impf* 2 ms. תִּזְמֹר Lv $25^{3.4}$ of pruning a vineyard (כרם; H). **Niph.** *Impf* יִזָּמֵר Is 5^{6} *be pruned,* subj כרם (‖ יֵעָדֵר)

†II. זָמִיר **n.[m.] trimming, pruning** (cf. $Lg^{BN 173}$)—only עֵת הַזָּמִיר Ct 2^{12} (> others *singing*).—I זמיר v. sub I. זמר supr.

†זְמוֹרָה **n [f.] branch, twig, shoot**—abs. ז׳ Nu 13^{23}, הַזּ׳ Ez 8^{17} 15^{2}, cstr. זְמֹרַת Is 17^{10}; sf זְמֹרֵיהֶם Na 2^{3},—*branch* of grape-vine Nu 13^{23} (JE), Ez 15^{2}; *branch, twig* (Co *Reisigbündel*) used in idolatrous worship הַזּ׳ אֶל־אַפָּם Ez 8^{17} (v. Sm and most), but custom obscure (v Da), and txt. dub., זְמֹרַת זָר (cf Ew § 287 b) Is 17^{10} *twigs* of a strange one (i. e. of a strange god) fig of idolatrous cults adopted by Isr., ז׳ pl in fig. of Israelites Na 2^{3}.

†[מְזַמֵּרָה] **n.f. pruning-knife,** only pl. לְמַזְמֵרוֹת Is 2[4] Mi 4[3] (both ‖ לְאִתִּים); וּמַזְמְרֹתֵיכֶם Jo 4[1] (‖ אִתֵּיכֶם). וְכָרַת הַזַּלְזַלִּים בַּמַּזְמֵרוֹת Is 18[5],

†[מְזַמֶּרֶת] **n.f. snuffers,** as utensil of Sol.'s temple, only pl. abs מְזַמְּרוֹת 2 K 12[14], הַמְזַמְּרוֹת 1 K 7[50] = 2 Ch 4[22], 2 K 25[14] = Je 52[18].

III. **זמר** (√of foll., mng. dub.; DHM in MV[10.963] comp. Ar. ذمار *thing to be protected, thing sacred, inviolable,* Lane[978], Sab. דמר *protect;* Aram. ܙܡܰܪ *wonder at, admire,* ܙܡܺܝܪܳܐ *mirus, admirabilis,* etc.; hence זמרת Gn 43[11] 'die Merkwürdigkeiten des Landes').

†II. **זִמְרָה** **n.f.** of uncertain meaning, perh **choice products** (cf DHM supr), of various fruits, etc. מִזִּמְרַת הארץ Gn 43[11]; 𝔊 οἱ καρποί, so MV Str.; > *music,* or *praise of the land,* fig for produce (√I. זמר) Thes Tu Kn SS.—I. ז׳ v. sub I. זמר; III. ז׳ v. infr.

Uncertain in deriv. are the five foll —

†[זֶמֶר] **n.[m.]** a certain animal allowed as food, most prob some kind of *mountain-sheep* or *-goat* (𝔖 ܕܰܡܪܳܐ) וָזָמֶר Dt 14[5] (AV RV *chamois* but see Tristram[DB 2.s.v.], who points out that this is not a native of any Bible land.)

†I. **זִמְרִי** **n pr.m.** 𝔊 Ζαμβρ(ε)ι—**1.** a Simeonite Nu 25[14] (P) **2.** grandson of Judah 2 Ch 2[6] (app = זַבְדִּי Jos 7[1] q.v.) **3.** king of Isr. before Omri 1 K 16[9 10 12 15 16 18.20] 2 K 9[31]. **4.** a Benjamite 1 Ch 8[36.36] = 9[42.42]

†II. **זִמְרִי** **n.pr.gent.** vel **patr.,** only מַלְכֵי ז׳ Je 25[25] (+ מלכי עילם and מלכי מָדָי); = Σεμβρῖται in Ethiopia (Strabo[xvii. 1 786])? cf. Gf; om. 𝔊; interpol. acc to Kue Gie.

†**זִמְרָן** **n.pr.m.** son of Abraham & Keturah, 𝔊 Ζε(μ)βραν Gn 25[2] and 1 Ch 1[32] (𝔊L here Ζεμραμ). On locality referred to v. Di.

†**זְמִירָה** **n.pr.m.** a Benjamite, 1 Ch 7[8], 𝔊 'Αμαριας; 𝔊A, 𝔊L Ζαμαρια(ς).

†**זַן** **n.[m.]** (late) **kind, sort** (Aram ܙܢܳܐ, זן; √ dub., cf De ψ 144[13])—מִזַּן אֶל זַן ψ 144[13] *from kind to kind,* i e *all sorts, kinds;* pl. זְנִים 2 Ch 16[14] (various) *sorts*

זנב (√of foll, meaning unknown).

†**זָנָב** **n.m.**[Ju 15 4] **tail,** also (fig) **end, stump** (NH id, As. *zibbatu* Hom[NS 308], Eth. ዘነብ: Ar. ذَنَبٌ, Aram. ܕܘܢܒܳܐ, דּוּנְבָּא, דְּנַבָּא)—ז׳ abs Ju 15[4.4] + 5 t.; sf זְנָבוֹ Jb 40[17], pl. זְנָבוֹת Ju 15[4]; cstr. זַנְבוֹת Is 7[4];—**1. a.** *tail* of fox Ju 15[4.4.4], of serpent Ex 4[4] (J), of hippopot. Jb 40[17], **b.** fig of common people, opp. to rulers Is 9[13] 19[15] (in both, ראש וזנב ‖ כִּפָּה ואגמון; Is 9[14] is incorrect gloss); of subject-people (opp ראש) Dt 28[13.44]. **2.** *end, stump* (of firebrand, אוד) in metaph. Is 7[4]

†[זנב] **vb.denom. Pi.** cut off, or smite, the tail, only fig, of hostile attack in war; *Pf.* consec. 2 mpl וְזִנַּבְתֶּם Jos 10[19] (sq אֹתָם), *Impf.* 3 ms. וַיְזַנֵּב בְּךָ כָּל־הַנֶּחֱשָׁלִים Dt 25[18]; in both = *attack* or *smite in the rear.*

†**זָנָה** **vb.** commit fornication, be a harlot (Ar زنى *commit fornication,* Aram ܙܢܳܐ, זנא; cf. Eth. ዘንዘ: *effusio seminis virilis, semen effusum,* Di[1065]; on this and ሖረ: (comp. by Ges al) v Prat[BAS i 32, Anm.])—**Qal** *Pf* ז׳ Dt 31[16], זָנְתָה Gn 38[24] + 3 t., etc; *Impf* תִּזְנֶה (Kt) Ez 23[43], תזנה Lv 19[29] + 4 t; וַתִּזֶן Je 3[8] Ez 23[5], תִזְנִי Ho 3[3], וַתִּזְנִי Je 3[6] (but rd. prob. וַתִּזֶן. וַתִּזְנִי is *not* Aram form of 3 fs, v. Ko[i 540] Kau[§ 47 8 b]) Ez 16[15] + 4 t, וַתִּזְנִים Ez 16[28], יִזְנוּ (Qr) Ez 23[43], וַיִּזְנוּ Ju 8[27] + 4 t, תִּזְנֶינָה Ho 4[13.14]; וַתִּזְנֶינָה Ez 23[3], *Inf. abs.* זָנֹה Ho 1[2]; cstr. לִזְנוֹת Lv 20[5] + 3 t; לִזְנוֹת Lv 20[6], sf. בִּזְנוּתֵךְ Ez 23[30]; *Pt.* זוֹנֶה ψ 73[27] Ez 6[9], זֹנָה Ho 4[15]; pl זֹנִים Lv 17[7] + 3 t, זוֹנָה Dt 23[19] + 25 t; זֹנָה Lv 21[7] + 2 t, זונות Pr 29[3]; זֹנוֹת Ho 4[14] + 4 t —**1.** *be* or *act as a harlot,* abs Gn 38[24] (J), Dt 22[21] (D), Lv 21[9] (H), Ho 4[13.14] Am 7[17], (ה)אשה + זונה Jos 2[1] 6[22] (J), Lv 21[7] (H), Ju 11[1] 16[1] Pr 6[26] Je 3[3] Ez 16[30] 23[44]; זוֹנָה Gn 34[31] 38[15] Jos 6[17 25] (all J), Dt 23[19] Lv 21[14] (H), Pr 7[10] 23[27] Is 23[15 16] Jo 4[3] Mi 1[7.7] Ez 16[31], נָשִׁים זונות 1 K 3[16]; ז(ו)נות 1 K 22[38] Pr 29[3] Ho 3[3] 4[14] Ez 16[33], בית זונה Je 5[7], *commit fornication,* man's act ז׳ אל Nu 25[1] (J); of woman's act Ju 19[2]; of a land given to harlotry Lv 19[29]. **2.** fig *of improper intercourse with foreign nations* (religious reference sometimes involved) ז׳ את Is 23[17]; אחרי Ez 23[30]; אל Ez 16[26.28.29]; וַתִּזֶן אָהֳלָה תַּחְתָּי ז׳ Ez 23[43] Na 3[4]; וַתִּזֶן אָהֳלָה תַּחְתָּי *and Ohola committed fornication* (whilst) *under me* Ez 23[5] (cf Nu 5[19]). **3.** *of intercourse with other deities,* considered as harlotry, sts. involving actual prostitution, ז׳ אחרי Ex 34[15 16] Dt 31[16] (all J), Lv 17[7] 20[5.6] (all H), Ju 2[17] 8[27.33] 1 Ch 5[25] Ez 6[9] 20[30], after אבת, etc. Lv 20[6] (H), one's own heart & eyes Nu 15[39] (H), esp. of Isr., Judah, and Jerus. under fig of lewd woman Ez 16[15]

(abs) v^{16} (על במות), v^{17} (ר׳ ב), 23$^{3.5.19}$ (abs.), Je 3^{1} (c. acc); v$^{6.8}$ (abs); abs. elsewh. Ho 2^{7} 4^{15} Is 57^{3} ψ 106^{39}; as leaving ׳י, sq. מעל Ho 9^{1}; מאחרי 1^{2}, מתחת 4^{12}, sq מן alone ψ 73^{27}; ז(ו)נה Je 2^{20} Ez 16$^{35.41}$, בית זונה Je 5^{7}, לִבָּם הַזּוֹנֶה *their whorish heart* Ez 6^{9}. **4.** זונה of moral defection Is 1^{21}. **Pu.** *Pf* 3 ms אַחֲרַיִךְ לֹא זוּנָּה *fornication was not done* (in going) *after thee* Ez 16^{34} (but del Co) **Hiph.** *Pf* 2 ms הִזְנִיתָ Ho 5^{3}; 3 pl הזנו Ho 4$^{10.18}$ Ex 34^{16}, *Impf* וַיִּזֶן 2 Ch 21^{11}, וַתַּזְנֶה 2 Ch 21^{13}; *Inf. abs* הַזְנֵה Ho 4^{18}; *cstr* הַזְנוֹת 2 Ch 21^{13}; sf. לְהַזְנוֹתָהּ Lv 19^{29} **1.** *cause to commit fornication*. **a.** sexual Lv 19^{29} (H) **b** religious Ex 34^{16} (J), 2 Ch 21$^{11.13.13}$. **2.** *commit fornication*. **a.** sexual Ho 4^{10}. **b.** religious Ho 4$^{18.18}$ 5^{3}.

†**זנונים n.[m.] fornication,** *pl abstr intens* (Ol ^{§215a}, Dl $^{Pr 74}$, der fr √זנן, As *zanânu, fill full*, cf Dl $^{ib 73}$)—׳ז Ho 1^{2}+5 t., cstr זנוני Na 3^{4} +2 t, זְנוּנַיִךְ Ez 23^{29}, זְנוּנֶיהָ Ho 2^{4} Na 3^{4}. **a.** sexual Gn 38^{24} (J) Ho 1$^{2.2}$ **b.** international Na 3$^{4.4}$. **c.** religious 2 K 9^{22} Ez 23$^{11.29}$ Ho 2$^{4.6}$ 4^{12} 5^{4}.

†**זנות n.f.abstr. fornication**;—׳ז Ho 4^{11} 6^{10}; sf. זְנוּתֵךְ Je 13^{27} Ez 23^{27}, זְנוּתָהּ Je 3^{9}, זְנוּתָם Ez 43$^{7.9}$, זנותיך Je 3^{2}, זנותיכם Nu 14^{33} **a.** sexual Ho 4^{11} **b.** international Ez 23^{27}. **c.** religious Nu 14^{33} (J) Je 3$^{2.9}$ 13^{27} Ez 43$^{7.9}$ Ho 6^{10} (where We $^{Kl Proph}$ suggests זְנִיָּת), cf זָנָה **3**

†[**תַּזְנוּת**] **n f.abstr. fornication**;—sf תזנותך Ez 16^{20} (Kt) v^{25} (Kt) v^{29}, תַּזְנֻתֵךְ Ez 16^{26}, תַּזְנוּתָם Ez 23$^{8.17}$, תזנותיך Ez 16$^{15.34.36}$; תַּזְנֻתַיִךְ Ez 16^{22}; תַּזְנוּתַיִךְ Ez 16^{20} (Qr) v^{25} (Qr) v^{33} 23$^{29.35}$, תַּזְנוּתֶיהָ Ez 23$^{7.8.11.14.18.19.43}$ These are all international mingled with religious references.

†I **זָנַח vb. reject, spurn** (perh cf As *zinû, be angry*, esp. of gods Gu ^{§10a} Zim $^{BP 23 ff}$) —**Qal** *Pf* ׳ז Ho 8$^{3.5}$ La 2^{7}, זָנַחְתָּ ψ 44^{10}+2 t; sf זְנַחְתָּנִי ψ 43^{2}, זנחתנו ψ 60$^{3.12}$ 108^{12}, זנחתים Zc 10^{6}, *Impf* יזנח ψ 77^{8} La 3^{31}, תִּזְנַח ψ 44^{24}+2 t,—*reject*, Isr rejects good Ho 8^{3}, Samaria's calf rejects her Ho 8^{5} (others make ׳י subj., We $^{Kl. Proph}$ rds אזנח *I reject*), elsewh God rejects people ψ 43^{2} 60^{3} 77^{8} 88^{15} Zc 10^{6}, ׳ז לָנֶצַח ψ 44^{24} 74^{1}; לעולם La 3^{31}, נַפְשִׁי מִשָּׁלוֹם ψ 44^{10} 60^{12} 108^{12}; ולא תצא בצבאותינו La 3^{17}, king ψ 89^{39}, altar La 2^{7}. **Hiph.** *Pf.* הִזְנִיחַ 2 Ch 29^{19}, sf. הזניחם 2 Ch 11^{14}, 3 pl. האזניחו Is 19^{6}, v II זנח, *Impf.* יַזְנִיחֲךָ 1 Ch 28^{9}, —(late) *reject* (= earlier **Qal**), Jeroboam *rejects* the Levites מכהן לי׳ 2 Ch 11^{14}, Ahaz the sacred vessels 2 Ch 29^{19}, ׳י rejects Solomon 1 Ch 28^{9}.

†II [**זָנַח**] **stink, emit stench** (cf. Ar. زَنِخَ *become rancid*, of oil, etc , Lane),—only **Hiph.** *Pf.* 3 mpl. הֶאֶזְנִיחוּ נְהָרוֹת *rivers stink* Is 19^{6} (rd. הזניחו Ges $^{§53.6}$ Ol ^{§255b} Sta ^{§420a} Ko $^{i 293}$, but Ew ^{§126b} De Di derive from elative אַזְנָח or אֶזְנָח).

זָנוֹחַ n.pr.loc. 1. *Zanu'a*, SE Sorea (Rob $^{BR ii 61}$ Bd $^{Pal 163}$) Jos 15^{34} Ne 3^{13} 11^{30} 1 Ch 4^{18}. **2.** a place in the mts. Jos 15^{56}, possibly *Zânûta*, SW. of Hebron, Guérin $^{Judée iii 200}$ Survey $^{iii 404}$; but Di thinks this is too far south

†[**זָנַק**] **vb.** only **Pi. leap** (NH זנק *cause to spring, spurt*; Aram. ܙܢܩ *throw, shoot*, also *bind*)—*Impf.* 3 ms. יְזַנֵּק מִן־הַבָּשָׁן Dt 33^{22} *he leapeth forth from Bashan* (of Dan under fig. of lion's whelp)

זֵעָה v **זוע**

זַעֲוָה v. זְוָעָה sub **זוע**.

†**זַעֲוָן n.pr.m.** a descendant (branch or tribe) of Seir (𝔊 Ζουκαμ, but Ζαυαν 𝔊L 1 Ch 1^{42}, Sam זועו)—Gn 36^{27} = 1 Ch 1^{42}

†[**זָעַךְ**] **vb. extinguish,** only **Niph.** *be extinguished* יָמַי נִזְעָכוּ Jb 17^{1} (|| רוּחִי חֻבָּלָה). Elsewhere always דעך (q v), and so in cogn. languages. Prob error for נדעכו

†**זָעַם vb. be indignant** (cf Aram (rare) ܙܥܡ *blame*, & n. ܙܘܥܡܐ; Ar. تَزَعَّمَ onomatop., of *roar* of camel, *angry speech*, v. Frey, De on ψ 7^{12})—*Pf.* ׳ז Nu 23^{8}+3 t; זָעַמְתָּה Zc 1^{12}, *Impf.* אֶזְעֹם Nu 23^{8}, 3 pl sf. יִזְעָמוּהוּ Pr 24^{24}, *Imv* זָעֲמָה Nu 23^{7} (for זָעֳמָה Ges $^{§64.(2)}$); *Pt. act* זעם ψ 7^{12}; *pass* cstr זְעוּם Pr 22^{14}; f זְעוּמָה Mi 6^{10};—**1.** *be indignant, have indignation*, of hostile prince על ברית קודש Dn 11^{30}, elsewhere of Yahweh, who is אל זעם ψ 7^{12} (|| שופט), c acc of enemy Is 66^{14}, cities of Judah Zc 1^{12}, people Mal 1^{4}; a man Pr 22^{14}. **2.** *express indignation in speech, denounce, curse* || יִקְּבֻהוּ Pr 24^{24}; || אָרָה־ and קָבָה Nu 23$^{7.8.8}$ (E), אֵיפַת רָזוֹן זְעוּמָה Mi 6^{10} *an ephah of scantiness, denounced*, or *cursed* **Niph** *Pt* pl פָּנִים נִזְעָמִים Pr 25^{23} *face stirred with indignation.*

†**זַעַם n.m.** $^{Is 10.25}$ **indignation**,—׳ז Is 10^{25}+7 t., זַעַם Is 26^{20}+2 t.; sf זַעְמִי Is 10^{5}+3 t, זַעַמְךָ ψ 102^{11}; זַעַמְךָ ψ 38^{4} 69^{25}; זַעְמוֹ Is 13^{5}+3 t,—*indignation* of men Ho 7^{16} Je 15^{17}; elsewh of ׳י Is 26^{20} 30^{27} Na 1^{6} Hb 3^{12} ψ 38^{4} 102^{11} Dn 11^{36}; || חרון אף ψ 69^{25} Zp 3^{8}; || עברה ψ 78^{49} Ez 21^{36} 22^{31}, || קצף Je 10^{10} ψ 102^{11}, || אף Is 10$^{5.25}$ 30^{27};

cf. בזעם אפו La 2^{6}; שפך ז׳ על ψ 69^{25} Ez 21^{36} 22^{31} Zp 3^{8}; כְּלֵי זַעַם Is 13^{5} Je 50^{25}, יום זעם Ez 22^{24}; אחרית הזעם Dn 8^{19}.

†[**זָעַף**] **vb. be out of humour, vexed; be enraged** (Aram. ܙܥܦ *rage against,* זְעַף *to storm,* זַעְפָּא *storm;* cf. Sam ࠆࠏࠐ *blow, breathe*)—**Qal** *Impf.* יִזְעַף Pr 19^{3}, וַיִּזְעַף 2 Ch 26^{19}; *Inf.* זַעְפּוֹ 2 Ch 26^{19}; *Pt.* pl. זֹעֲפִים Gn 40^{6} Dn 1^{10};—**1.** *be out of humour* Gn 40^{6} (E), *dejected,* of face Dn 1^{10}; sq על Pr 19^{3} *fret against* (AV). **2.** *be enraged* (late: cf. Aram. above) 2 Ch 26^{19}, sq עִם v^{19}.

†**זַעַף n.m. storming, raging, rage** (poet. and late)—ז׳ abs 2 Ch 16^{10} 28^{9}, cstr Is 30^{30} + 2 t.; sf. זַעְפּוֹ Jon 1^{15},—**1.** *rage* of king, leading to violence Pr 19^{12} (‖ נַהַם כַּכְּפִיר), 2 Ch 16^{10} (‖ כעס; בו׳ עמו על־זאת), 28^{9}, ז׳ אַף Is 30^{30} *raging* of anger (of י׳); ז׳ י׳ Mi 7^{9}. **2.** *raging* of sea Jon 1^{15}.

†**זָעֵף adj. out of humour, vexed,** only of Ahab 1 K 20^{43} 21^{4} (‖ סַר).

†[**זָעַק**] **vb. cry, cry out, call** (‖ form of צעק q.v.; Ar زعق, Aram. ܙܥܩ)—**Qal** *Pf.* 3 fs זָעֲקָה 2 S 13^{19}; 1 s זָעַקְתִּי ψ 142^{6}; 3 pl זָעֲקוּ Ju 6^{7} + 3 t; וְזָעֲקוּ consec Ju 11^{11} + 2 t; 2 mpl וּזְעַקְתֶּם consec. 1 S 8^{18}, *Impf.* 3 ms יִזְעַק Is 15^{5}; וַיִּזְעַק 1 S 7^{9} + 5 t, etc, *Imv.* זעק Ez 21^{17}; fs. זַעֲקִי Is 14^{31}, cf. Je 48^{20} Kt; זַעֲקוּ Ju 10^{14} + 2 t., וּזְעָקוּ Je 48^{20} Qr; *Inf cstr* מִזְּעֹק 1 S 7^{8}; וְלִזְעֹק 2 S 19^{29}, sf. זַעֲקֵךְ Is 30^{19}; בְּזַעֲקֵךְ Is 57^{13} (Ol § 245 b Ges § 61 1. R1),—**1.** *call,* to one's aid, sq. acc. pers. Ju 12^{2}. **2.** *cry, cry out,* in need: **a.** unto God (י׳), sq. אֶל־ Ju $3^{9.15}$ $6^{6.7}$ 10^{10} 1 S $7^{8.9}$ (+ בעד of intercession), $12^{8.10}$ 15^{11} Mi 3^{4} Je 11^{11} Hb 1^{2} (c. acc. חמס, cf Ho 8^{2} infr.), 2 Ch 20^{9} ψ 22^{6} $107^{13.19}$ 142^{6} Jo 1^{14}; sq אֶל־י׳ + בְּקוֹל גָּדוֹל Ne 9^{4}; קוֹלִי + ψ 142^{2} (‖ התחנן); בְּלִבָּם + Ho 7^{14} (opp. הֵילִיל); sq לְ Ho 8^{2} (+ obj. of words uttered), 1 Ch 5^{20}; sq. sf. Ne 9^{28}; sq. הַשָּׁמַיִם (without divine name) 2 Ch 32^{20} (‖ התפלל); abs, but with implication of cry to י׳ 1 S 8^{18} Is 30^{19}. **b.** unto other gods, sq. אֶל־ Ju 10^{14} Je 11^{12} Jon 1^{5}. **c.** unto king, sq. אֶל־ 2 S 19^{29}. **d.** abs, utterance of horror, anxiety, alarm, distress, sorrow, etc. 1 S 4^{13} 5^{10} 28^{12} (+ בקול גדול), 2 S 13^{19} 19^{5} (+ קול גדול), 1 K 22^{32} = 2 Ch 18^{31}, Is 15^{4} 26^{17} 57^{13} Je 20^{8} (‖ קרא, cf Hb 1^{2} supr), La 3^{8} (‖ אֲשַׁוֵּעַ) Ez 9^{8} 11^{13} 27^{30}, also of cry heard by God Ex 2^{23} (P); sq לְ of that in behalf of, or for which one cries Is 15^{5} Je 48^{31}; so sq. על־ Je 30^{15}; sq. acc cogn. זְעָקָה Est 4^{1}; ‖ הילִיל Je 47^{2}; and esp. Imv. Is 14^{31} Je 25^{34} 48^{20} Ez 21^{17}. **e.** *cry out* against one, sq. על־ Jb 31^{38} *if my land cry out against me* (‖ יִבְכָּיוּן), cf. also (abs, and without prep.) Hb 2^{11} *the stone shall cry out of* (מן) *the wall.* **Niph.** *Pf.* 2 ms נִזְעַקְתָּ Ju 18^{23}, 3 mpl נִזְעֲקוּ Ju 18^{22}, *Impf.* וַיִּזָּעֵק Ju 6^{34} + 2 t; וַיִּזָּעֲקוּ Jos 8^{16},—*be called together, assemble, join* Jos 8^{16} (JE), Ju $18^{22.23}$ 1 S 14^{20}; sq אַחֲרָיו Ju $6^{34.35}$ *assembled after him,* i e joined him as his followers. **Hiph.** *Impf.* וַיַּזְעֵק Ju 4^{10} + 3 t; יַזְעִיקוּ Jb 35^{9}; *Imv.* הַזְעֶק־ 2 S 20^{4}; *Inf cstr.* לְהַזְעִיק 2 S 20^{5};—**1.** *call, call out,* or *together,* for military service, sq. acc Ju $4^{10.13}$ 2 S $20^{4.5}$. **2.** *make a crying* Jb 35^{9} (‖ יְשַׁוֵּעוּ in ‖ cl) **3.** *have proclamation made* ויז׳ ויאמר Jon 3^{7} **4.** *call out to, or at,* sq. acc. וַיַּזְעֵק אֹתִי וַיְדַבֵּר Zc 6^{8} (si vera l; Gr queries וַיָּעַר ?).

†**זְעָקָה n.f. cry, outcry,** abs. ז׳ Je 18^{22} + 5 t; cstr. זַעֲקַת Gn 18^{20} + 3 t.; sf זַעֲקָתִי Jb 16^{18}; זַעֲקָתָם Is 15^{5} + 3 t;—**1.** *outcry,* against, זעקת סדם וגו׳ Gn 18^{20} (J). **2.** *cry of distress,* concerning something זַעֲקַת־שֶׁבֶר Is 15^{5} (obj. of יְעֹעֵרוּ; cf בִּבְכִי in prev. cl), abs. v^{8} (subj. of הִקִּיפָה ‖ יִלְלָה), Je 18^{22} (תִּשָּׁמַע ז׳), 20^{16} 48^{4} 50^{46} Ne 5^{6} 9^{9} (all c. שמע), Je 48^{34} (joined with נתן קול), Jb 16^{18} Est 9^{31} (lamentation), cf. 4^{1} (ז׳ גְּדוֹלָה וּמָרָה, acc cogn c. זעק), specif זעקת־דָּל Pr 21^{13} *cry of poor;* קול ז׳ Is 65^{19} (‖ קול בכי), Je 51^{54} Ez 27^{28}. **3.** *outcry, clamour* זעקת מושל בַּכְּסִילִים Ec 9^{17} (opp. דברי חכמים בְּנַחַת נשמעים)

זער (Ar زَعِرَ *be scanty,* of hair, plumage, etc; Aram. ܙܥܪ, זְעַר *be* or *grow small,* cf. צער).

†**זְעֵיר n.[m] a little** (diminutive form Ol § 180 Lag BN 85)—**1.** of quantity, amount (of instruction) ז׳ שָׁם ז׳ שָׁם Is $28^{10.13}$ (in both ‖ צַו, קַו) **2.** of time, כַּתַּר־לִי ז׳ וַאֲחַוֶּךָּ Jb 36^{2}

†**מִזְעָר n.[m] a little, a trifle, a few. 1.** of time עוֹד מְעַט מִזְעָר Is 10^{25} 29^{17} *yet a trifle, a little* = a very little while. **2.** of number שְׁאָר מעט מזער Is 16^{14} *a remnant, a very few* (opp. לוא כַּבִּיר). In Is^{3} without מעט—. ונשאר אנוש מִזְעָר Is 24^{6}

†[**זִפְרֹן**] **n.pr.loc.** only c ה loc זִפְרֹנָה Nu 34^{9}, place on northern boundary of Canaan;

𝔊 Δεφρωνα, Ἐφρωνα; 𝔊L Ζεφρωνα; site dub., Wetzst [Hauran 88] prop. *Zifrân*, NE. fr. Damascus; Furrer [ZPV viii. 28] Bd [Pal 397] ('perh.') *Zaʿferâne*, between Ḥumṣ and Hamath; Di rejects both.

† זֶפֶת **n.f.** [Is 34, 9] **pitch** (cf. on format. Ol [§ 164 c] Sta [§ 187 a]. Word is Armenian acc. to Lag [Arm. Stud. 1351, BN 219]; on Egypt. deriv. cf. Cook [Speaker's Comm. i. 484]; Ar. زِفْت; acc. to Frä [151], if Shemit., is Aram. loan-wd.; v. also Eth. ዝፍት: Di [1068])—*pitch*:—וַתַּחְמְרָה בַחֵמָר וּבַזָּפֶת Ex 2[3] of ark of bulrushes; Is 34[9a] וְנֶהֶפְכוּ נְחָלֶיהָ לְזֶפֶת וַעֲפָרָהּ לְגָפְרִית, v[9b] והיתה אַרְצָהּ לְזֶפֶת בֹּעֵרָה׃.

† I. [זֵק] **n.[m.]** **missile, spark** (√dub.; cf. NH זִיקִין *fiery arrows*, Aram. זִיקָא *id.*, זִיקוּקָא *id.*+*spark*, ܙܝܩܐ *shooting star, ray of light*, ܙܝܩܬܐ *shooting star*)—only pl. זִקִּים of (fire-?) missiles Pr 26[18] (|| חִצִּים, c. ירה); so זִיקוֹת *sparks, brands* (as leaping, springing forth?) מְאַזְּרֵי ז׳ (v. אזר) Is 50[11] (|| קֹדְחֵי אֵשׁ), בְּעַרְתֶּם ז׳ v[11] (|| אוּר אֶשְׁכֶם).

II. [זֵק], זִקִּים *fetters*, v. sub II. זקק.

זקן (√of foll.; meaning dubious).

† זָקָן **n.m.** [2 S 10, 5+] and **f.** [Is 15, 2+] **chin, beard** (As. *ziḳnu*, Asrb [Annals iv. 29]; Ar. ذَقَن, Aram. דְּקַן, ܕܩܢܐ)—abs. ז׳ Lv 13[30]+; cstr. זְקַן 2 S 20[9]+; sf. זְקָנִי Ezr 9[3]; זְקָנְךָ Lv 19[27] Ez 5[1]; זְקָנוֹ 1 S 21[14]+ 2 t.; זְקַנְכֶם 2 S 10[5] 1 Ch 19[5]; זְקָנָם 2 S 10[4] Lv 21[5]; never pl.—**1.** *chin* (opp. ראשׁ, top of head) Lv 13[29.30] 14[9] (all P), 2 S 20[9] Ez 5[1]; cf. also 1 S 21[14] ψ 133[2] (where however chin as *bearded* may be meant); chin, or lower jaw, of lion and bear 1 S 17[35]. **2.** *beard*, as growing (צמח) 2 S 10[5] = 1 Ch 19[5]; as cut off Is 7[20] (ספה), 15[2] = Je 48[37] (גרע); cf. מְגֻלְּחֵי זָקָן Je 41[5] 2 S 10[4] (גלח); שער ראשי וּזְקָנִי Ezr 9[3]; here belongs פאת זקנ(ך) Lv 19[27] 21[5] (both H; opp. ראשׁ).

† זָקֵן **vb. be** or **become old** (cf., acc. to Thes, Ar. ذَقُون *a she-camel that lets her lower lip hang down*, v. Lane [968]; ذَقْن *decrepit man*)—**Qal** *Pf.* 3 ms. זָקֵן Gn 18[12] + 14 t. (often hard to disting. fr. pred. adj. זָקֵן q. v.); 3 fs. זָקְנָה Pr 23[22]; 2 ms. זָקַנְתָּ 1 S 8[5]; זָקַנְתָּה Jos 13[1]; 1 s. זָקַנְתִּי Jos 23[2] + 3 t.; זָקַנְתִּי Gn 18[13] 27[2]; *Impf.* וַיִּזְקַן 2 Ch 24[15];—*be* (or *become*) *old* Gn 18[12.13] 19[31] 27[1.2] (all J), 1 S 2[22] 4[18] 8[1.5] 12[2] 17[12] 2 S 19[33] 1 K 1[1.15] 2 K 4[14]; also Gn 24[1] (|| בא בימים), so Jos 13[1.1] 23[1.2] (|| here בָּאתִי בימים), 1 Ch 23[1] (|| שְׂבַע ימים), 24[15] (|| *id.*); Pr 23[22] ψ 37[25] (opp. || היה נער); note esp. זָקַנְתִּי מִהְיוֹת לְאִישׁ Ru 1[12] *I am too old to belong to a man* (*husband*). **Hiph.** only *Impf.* 3 ms. יַזְקִין inchoat. *shew age, grow old* = senescere Ew [§ 122 c], cf. Di; of youth Pr 22[6]; of tree-root Jb 14[8].

זָקֵן **adj.** old, abs. ז׳ Gn 19[4] + 30 t. (on distinct. fr. vb. v. supr.); cstr. זְקַן Gn 24[2]; pl. זְקֵנִים Gn 18[11] + 44 t.; זְקֵנוֹת Zc 8[4]; cstr. זִקְנֵי Gn 50[7] + 85 t.; sf. זְקֵנַי La 1[19], זְקֵנֶיךָ Dt 21[2] 32[7], זְקֵנָיו Jos 8[33] + 3 t., זְקֵנֵינוּ Ju 8[14], זְקֵנֵיכֶם Ex 10[9] Jos 9[11], זְקֵנֶיהָ Dt 5[20] + 2 t.;—**1.** *old*, of human beings, as adj. pred. Gn 18[11] (J), Jb 32[4] (מִמֶּנּוּ לְיָמִים ז׳, in compar.), or attrib. אָב זָקֵן Gn 44[20] (J), אִישׁ ז׳ Ju 19[16.17.20.22], מֶלֶךְ ז׳ Ec 4[13]; נָבִיא ז׳ 1 K 13[11.25.29], prob. also ז׳ וּשְׂבַע ימים Gn 35[29] (P), Jb 42[17] and Gn 25[8] (P) acc. to 𝔊 Sam Di; cf. also Ezr 3[12]. **2.** usu. as subst.: **a.** *old man* (or woman), **b.** *elder*; **a.** *old man* Gn 43[27] (J), Lv 19[32] (H), Dt 28[50] 32[7] (|| אָב), 1 S 2[31.32] 28[14] Is 47[6] Jb 12[20] 32[9] Pr 17[6] 20[29] ψ 119[100] Jo 1[2]; *old men and old women* Zc 8[4.4]; cf. זְקַן בֵּיתוֹ Gn 24[2] (J), זִקְנֵי בֵיתוֹ 2 S 12[17]; esp. opp. נַעַר Ex 10[9] (E), Is 3[5] 20[4] Je 51[22] La 2[21] ψ 148[12], and in phr. מִנַּעַר וְעַד זָקֵן Gn 19[4] (J), Jos 6[21] (JE), Est 3[13]; opp. ילדים 1 K 12[6.8.13] = 2 Ch 10[6.8.13]; opp. בַּחוּרִים Je 31[13] Ez 9[6] Jo 3[1], cf. 2 Ch 36[17] (+ יָשֵׁשׁ) and Je 6[11] (+ מְלֵא ימים); opp. עוּל ימים Is 65[20]; opp. יונקי שדים and עוללים Jo 2[16]. **b.** usu. pl. *elders*, as having authority, term techn. (100 t. +); elders of a people, esp. **Israel** Ex 3[16.18] 12[21] (all J), 17[5.6] 18[12] 19[7] 24[1.9.14] Jos 24[1] (all E), Nu 11[16.16] (שֹׁטְרָיו), v[24.25.30] 16[25] Jos 7[6] 8[10] 9[11] (all JE), Dt 5[20] (|| רָאשֵׁי שִׁבְטֵיכֶם), 27[1] 29[9] (|| שֹׁטְרִים), 31[9.28] Jos 8[33] (|| שֹׁטְרֵיכֶם, ראשי שבטיכם), 23[2] (|| שֹׁטְרָיו, שֹׁפְטָיו, רָאשָׁיו, וְשֹׁפְטָיו); cf. also prob. Jos 24[31] = Ju 2[7] (all D); Lv 9[1], cf. זִקְנֵי הָעֵדָה Lv 4[15] († both P), Ju 21[16]; see also 1 S 4[3] 8[4] 15[30] 2 S 3[17] 5[3] = 1 Ch 11[3], 2 S 17[4.15] 1 K 8[1.3] = 2 Ch 5[2.4], also 1 Ch 15[25] 21[16]; cf. Is 3[2] (גִּבּוֹר וְאִישׁ מִלְחָמָה, שׁוֹפֵט וְנָבִיא וְקֹסֵם וְז׳), 9[14] (|| נְשׂוּא־פָנִים), but v. prob. gloss, cf. Ew Che Di Du al.); elders of one tribe (Judah) 1 S 30[26] 2 S 19[12], so of Gilead Ju 11[5.7.8.9.10.11]; after the division of the kingdoms, of N. Isr. זקני הארץ 1 K 20[7] cf. v[8], also 2 K 6[32.32] 10[1] (|| שָׂרִים etc.) cf. v[5]; under Josiah זקני יְהוּדָה 2 K 23[1] = 2 Ch 34[29]; see also ז׳ הארץ Je 26[17], cf. זקני ארץ Pr 31[23], cf. La 1[19] 2[10] 4[16] 5[12.14] (|| שָׂרִים; + שַׁעַר); oft. in Ezek.: Ez 7[26] (|| כהן), of Judah 8[1], of Isr. 8[11.12] 14[1] 20[1.3], also 9[6] (but del. Co). Exil. ז׳ הַגּוֹלָה Je 29[1] (|| הכהנים, הנביאים); post-exil. Ezr 10[8] (|| שׂרים), poss. also Jo 1[14]; elders of ׳י Is 24[23] (cf. Ex 24[1.9]), זִקְנֵי הַכֹּהֲנִים 2 K 19[2] = Is 37[2], so Je 19[1] (|| זקני העם); of other peoples,

Midian Nu 22$^{4.7}$, Moab v^{7} (all E), Egypt ψ 105^{22} (‖ שׂרים); of Gebal Ez 27^{9}; elders of a city, esp. as sitting in the gate to judge Dt 19^{12} 21^{2} (+ שֹׁפְטֶיךָ) v$^{3.4.6.19}$ (+ שַׁעַר־מְקֹמוֹ), v^{20} 22^{15} (+ הַשָּׁעְרָה), v$^{16.17.18}$ 25^{7} (+ הַשַּׁעְרָה), v$^{8.9}$ (all in Dt. code, and only so therein), Ru 4$^{2.4.9.11}$ (cf. שַׁעַר v$^{1.11}$), מוֹשַׁב זְקֵנִים ψ 107^{32} (‖ קְהַל־עָם); Ju 8^{14} (‖ שׂרים), v^{16} 1 S 11^{3} 16^{4} 1 K 21$^{8.11}$ Ezr 10^{14}.

†זֹקֶן **n.[m.]** old age—עֵינֵי ישׂראל כָּבְדוּ מִזֹּקֶן Gn 48^{10} (E).

†זִקְנָה **n.f.** old age—זִקְנָה ψ 71^{9} + 2 t.; cstr. זִקְנַת 1 K 11^{4}; sf. זִקְנָתוֹ 1 K 15^{23}; זִקְנָתָהּ Gn 24^{36};—*old age*, ‖ שֵׂיבָה ψ 71^{18} Is 46^{4}; *in the time of old age* לְעֵת ז׳ 1 K 11^{4} 15^{23} ψ 71^{9}; אַחֲרֵי ז׳ (i.e. after she had become old) Gn 24^{36} (J).

†זְקֻנִים **n.pl.[m.]** old age—בֶּן־ז׳ Gn 37^{3} i.e. a late-born son; יֶלֶד ז׳ Gn 44^{20} *id.*; (ילדה) בֵּן לִזְקֻנָיו Gn 21$^{2.7}$ (all JE).

†[זָקַף] **vb.** (late) **raise up** (NH *id.*; Aram. זְקַף, ܙܩܦ; As. *zakâpu*, Asrb$^{Hunting\ Inscr.\ IR\ 7,\ ix.\ A,\ 3}$; Nö$^{ZMG\ 1886,\ 725}$ suggests Ar. زقف *carry off* (Ḳam.), orig. *lift up*)—only **Qal** *Pt. act.* and only fig. of י׳'s dealing with prostrate men:—וְזוֹקֵף לְכָל־הַכְּפוּפִים ψ 145^{14} (‖ סוֹמֵךְ); זֹקֵף כְּפוּפִים 146^{8} י׳ *raiseth up prostrate ones.*

†I. [זָקַק] **vb. refine, purify** (Aram. זְקַק; perh. kindr. with As. *zaḳiḳu, wind*, Asrb$^{Annals\ vi.\ 64}$ and Aram. ܙܩܐ, זִיקָא *violent wind, violent rain with whirlwind*)—**Qal** *Impf.* 3 mpl. יָזֹקּוּ Jb 28^{1} obj. זָהָב, 36^{27} obj. מָטָר (v. Di). **Pi.** *Pf.* וְזִקַּק consec. Mal 3^{3} (‖ וְטִהַר) fig., of purifying sons of Levi, like gold and silver כַּזָּהָב etc. **Pu.** *Pt.* מְזֻקָּק *refined*, of gold 1 Ch 28^{18}, of silver 1 Ch 29^{4}: ψ 12^{7} (מ׳ שבעתים); of settled wines שְׁמָרִים מְזֻקָּקִים Is 25^{6}.

II. זקק (NH זָקַק *bind, fetter*, Aram. זְקַק *id.*; comp. (perh. fr. idea of *restraint*) Ar. زِقّ, Aram. ܙܩܐ, זִיקָא, זִיקוּקָא, Eth. ዝቅ: all = (wine-)*skin*, etc.; also NH זִיקָה, *obligation*; Aram. ܙܩܘܡܐ *ring*).

†II. [זֵק] **n.[m.]** fetter, only pl. זִקִּים:—*fetters* of captives רֻתְּקוּ בַזִּ׳ Na 3^{10}; בַּזִּ׳ יַעֲבֹרוּ Is 45^{14}; בְּז׳ ψ 149^{8} (c. אסר; ‖ בְּכַבְלֵי בַרְזֶל); fig. בַּזִּ׳ Jb 36^{8} (c. אסר; ‖ חַבְלֵי עֹנִי).

†[אֲזִק] **n.[m.]** id., specif. **manacle**, only pl. *manacles* אָסוּר בָּאזִקִּים Je 40^{1}, and מִן־הָאזִקִּים אֲשֶׁר עַל־יָדְךָ v^{4}.

זָר v. I. זור, זָרָא v. sub II. זור.

זֵר v. III. זור.

†[זָרַב] **vb.** only **Pu.**, meaning dub.; prob. (from context) **be burnt, scorched**—**Pu.** *Impf.* in rel. cl., בְּעֵת יְזֹרְבוּ נִצְמָתוּ Jb 6^{17} (‖ בְּחֻמּוֹ נִדְעֲכוּ מִמְּקוֹמָם), of brooks *scorched* and drying up (‖ form of צָרַב q.v.; so Ew Di De Hoffm Kau AV RV MV; > Thes RobGes who comp. Ar. زَرِبَ *flow away*, cf. NH זְרִיבָה; and Mich Dl$^{Pr\ 36\ f.}$ VBm (*are straitened*) RVm (*shrink*) cf. Aram. ܙܪܒ *compress*, (Ar. زَرَبَ is to *make a wooden enclosure*), As. *zarâbu*, Zim$^{BP\ 32\ n.\ 56,\ 70,\ 96}$).

†זְרֻבָּבֶל **n.pr.m.** (acc. to MV perh. = זְרוּעַ בָּבֶל *begotten* in Babylon, v. also Thes)—grandson of king Jehoiachin, and son of Pedaiah 1 Ch 3$^{19.19}$ (but son of Shealtiel Ezr 3$^{2.8}$ etc., cf. שְׁאַלְתִּיאֵל brother(?) of פְּדָיָה 1 Ch 3^{17}); leader of first returning exiles Ezr 2^{2} = Ne 7^{7}, Ezr 3$^{2.8}$ 4$^{2.3}$ Ne 12$^{1.47}$ Hg 1^{12} 2^{4} Zc 4$^{6.7.9.10}$; called פַּחַת יְהוּדָה Hg 1$^{1.14}$ 2$^{2.21}$, called עַבְדִּי (by י׳) Hg 2^{23}.—𝔊 Ζοροβαβελ.

†זֶרֶד **n.pr.fl.** (√ dub.; on form cf. Lg$^{BN\ 77}$)—נַחַל זָרֶד Dt 2^{13}; נַחַל זֶרֶד Nu 21^{12} (JE), Dt 2$^{13.14}$; identification disputed; Rob$^{BR\ ii.\ 157}$ prop. *Wady-el-Aḥsy* (= נַחַל הָעֲרָבִים Is 15^{7}), between Moab & Edom; < either *Sail Sa'ide* (Kn), chief source of Arnon fr. SE. (Burckh$^{Syrien,\ 635}$), or W. *Kerak* (Ges Ke Di); so also GASm$^{Geog.\ 557}$.

†[זָרָה] **vb. scatter, fan, winnow** (Ar. ذَرَا *cause to fly, scatter* (of wind), *winnow*; Aram. דְּרָא, ܕܪܐ; Eth. ዘረወ:)—**Qal** *Impf.* וַיִּזֶר Ex 32^{20}; 2 ms. תִּזְרֶה Ez 5^{2}; sf. תִּזְרֵם Is 30^{22} 41^{16}; וָאֶזְרֵם Je 15^{7}; *Imv.* זְרֵה Nu 17^{2}; *Inf.* לִזְרוֹת Je 4^{11}; *Pt.* זֹרֶה Ru 3^{2} Is 30^{24};—**1.** *scatter*, the powder into which golden calf was ground Ex 32^{20} (E, obj. not expr.); c. acc. (strange) fire from censers Nu 17^{2} (P); hair (symbol. act) Ez 5^{2}; Is 30^{22}. **2.** *fan, winnow*, obj. גֹּרֶן הַשְּׂעֹרִים Ru 3^{2} Is 30^{24} (where *pt.* has indef. subj.), 41^{16} metaph., obj. mountains and hills, fig. of winnowing; fig. fan, winnow, in purification Je 4^{11} (‖ לְהָבַר); in chastisement Je 15^{7} (ז׳ בְּמִזְרֶה). **Niph.** *Impf.* וַיִּזָּרוּ Ez 36^{19} *be scattered, dispersed*, of Israel; *Inf.* בְּהִזָּרוֹתֵיכֶם Ez 6^{8} *when ye shall be dispersed* (on pl. sf. Ew$^{§\ 259\ b}$, but Co del. י). **Pi.** *Pf.* sf. וְזֵרָם 1 K 14^{15}; זֵרִיתָ ψ 139^{3}, sf. זֵרִיתָנוּ ψ 44^{12}; וְזֵרִיתִי Ez 5^{10} etc.; *Inf.* זָרוֹת Ez 20^{23}

etc ,—**1.** (intens. of Qal) *scatter, disperse*, esp. of peoples, c. acc. (Israel and Judah) 1 K 14[15] Lv 26[33] (H), ψ 44[12] Je 31[10] Ez 5[10 12] 12[14 15] 20[23] 22[15] cf Zc 2[2.4 4] ψ 106[27], bones of Israel Ez 6[5], people of Hazor Je 49[32]; of Elam 49[36]; of Babylon 51[2] (זָרִים = strangers?), Egyptians Ez 29[12] 30[26] + 30[23] (del Co, intern grounds); in general the wicked Pr 20[26], evil 20[8], pt מְזָרִים = subst. *scatterers*, epith of winds Jb 37[9] (cf Qor 51[1]); וזריתי פרש על־פניכם Mal 2[3] *scatter* dung on your faces (token of shame and curse), fig *disperse* knowledge (of lips) Pr 15[7] **2.** *winnow, sift* (cf **Qal 2**) only fig אָרְחִי ורבעי זֵרִיתָ ψ 139[3] *my path and my couch thou siftest* (Che; Ba[ZMG 1887, 607] *measurest, determinest*, whence זֶרֶת, q v) **Pu** *be scattered, Impf* יזרה Jb 18[15], subj גָּפְרִית, sq עַל, *Pt.* f. מְזֹרָה (agreeing with רֶשֶׁת *net*) Pr 1[17].

†מִזְרֶה **n.**[**m**] pitch-fork, with six prongs (=مذراة) used in winnowing, cf Wetzst[ZPV 1891, xiv 2], for winnowing provender זֹרֶה בָרַחַת ובמ׳ Is 30[24], fig. for winnowing, i e chastising the people וָאֶזְרֵם בְּמ׳ Je 15[7]

זַרְזִיף ψ 72[6] v זרף

זַרְזִיר Pr 30[31] v sub III. זור.

†זָרַח **vb. rise, come forth** (NH *id*, As *zarâḫu* Dl[Pr 180], Sab דרח *lofty, majestic* (of king) and in cpd n pr. DHM[ZMG 1875, 605, 1883, 327] Mordt[ZMG 1876, 37])—**Qal** *Pf.* ז׳ Dt 33[2] ψ 112[4], זָרַח Is 60[1], וזרח consec Is 58[10] Ec 1[5], 3 fs. זָרְחָה Ex 22[2] + 3 t, וזרחה consec. Mal 3[20]; *Impf.* יזרח 2 S 23[4] Is 60[2], יִזְרָח Jb 9[7]; וַיִּזְרַח Gn 32[32], 3 fs תזרח ψ 104[22], *Inf. cstr.* זְרֹחַ Ju 9[33] Jo 4[8], *Pt* זורח Ec 1[5],—**1.** *rise*. **a.** (of sun) Ju 9[33] Na 3[7] 2 S 23[4] Jon 4[8] Jb 9[7] ψ 104[22] Ec 1[5 5]; sq על Ex 22[2] (JE), 2 K 3[22], sq לְ Gn 32[32] (J). **b.** fig, sq. לְ, שֶׁמֶשׁ צְדָקָה Mal 3[20], of י׳, וזרח מִשֵּׂעִיר לָמוֹ Dt 33[2], sq עַל, Is 60[2] (‖ כבודו יראה); כבוד י׳ Is 60[1], subj. אור, fig (= happiness, blessedness) Is 58[10] ψ 112[4] (sq לְ). **2.** *come out, appear*, of appearance of leprosy (הַצָּרַעַת) 2 Ch 26[19].

†I [זֶרַח] **n.**[**m.**]**dawning, shining**;—only fig., נֹגַהּ זַרְחֵךְ i e. of Zion, Is 60[3] (‖ אור)

†II. זֶרַח **n pr.m.** (on form cf Lg[BN 77 and Anm]) —**1.** 𝔊 *Ζαρα*, son of Judah and Tamar Gn 38[30] 46[12] (both J), 1 Ch 2[4] (all זָרַח), v[6], as head of a family Nu 26[20] Jos 7[1] (both P), v[18.24] (JE), 22[20] (P) 1 Ch 9[6] (𝔊L *Ζηρα*), Ne 11[24] (cf. Sm[Listen 7]). **2.** Edomites. **a.** 𝔊 *Ζαρε* Gn 36[13.17] (both P) = 1 Ch 1[37]. **b.** 𝔊 *Ζαρα* Gn 36[33] (P) = 1 Ch 1[44] (**b** = **a**?) **3.** 𝔊L *Ζαρα*, Levites· **a.** (var. *Ιααρα*) 1 Ch 6[6]. **b.** (var. *Ζααραι*) 1 Ch 6[26] **4.** head of a Simeonite family, 𝔊 *Ζαρα* Nu 26[13] (P), 1 Ch 4[24] (var. *Ζαρες*) (= צֹחַר 𝔊 *Σααρ* Gn 46[10] Ex 6[15], cf Di Nu 26[13]). **5.** a Cushite, 𝔊 *Ζαρε*, foe of king Asa 2 Ch 14[8].

†זַרְחִי **adj. gent.** alw c art as subst. coll. הַזּ׳ **1.** fr. זֶרַח **1**·—Jos 7[17 17] (JE), Nu 26[20] (P), cf לַזּ׳ 1 Ch 27[11 13] **2** fr זֶרַח **4**—Nu 26[13].

†זְרַחְיָה **n pr.m.** (י׳ *hath risen*, or *shined*; Sab. דרחאל Hal[49])—𝔊 *Ζαραια*·—**1.** priest 1 Ch 5[32.32] 6[36] Ezr 7[4] **2.** head of a family of returned exiles Ezr 8[4] (= **1**?).

†אֶזְרָח **n.m.**[ψ 37, 35] **a native** (*one arising from the soil*, = 'free tribesman' RS[Sem I. 75])—abs א׳ Lv 19[34] + 13 t; cstr. אזרח Ex 12[19] + 2t; —**1.** *a native* Israelite, usu coll, c. art, כָּל־הָא׳ בְּיִשְׂרָאֵל Lv 23[42] (H), cf Nu 15[13] (P); elsewh. opp. גר (q v) —הָא׳ בבני ישׂר׳ Nu 15[29] (P), cf. Ez 47[22]; אֶזְרַח הָאָרֶץ Ex 12[19.48] Nu 9[14] (all P), א׳ מִכֶּם Lv 19[34] v also 17[15] 18[26] 24[16.22] (all H); Ex 12[49] Lv 16[29] Nu 15[30] (all P), Jos 8[33] (D) **2.** *a native* tree, growing in its natural soil א׳ רַעֲנָן ψ 37[35] (fig of prosperous wicked).

†אֶזְרָחִי **adj. gent.** i.e of family of זֶרַח, only in אֵיתָן הָא׳ 1 K 5[11] (𝔊L *Ἰσραηλίτης*), ψ 89[1] (𝔊 *id*), and 88[1] הֵימָן הָא׳, both sons of זֶרַח (1 Ch 2[6]).

†יִזְרָח **adj. gent.** only in שַׁמְהוּת הַיִּ׳ 1 Ch 27[8] 𝔊 *Εσραε*, 𝔊L *Ιεσρα*; rd הַיּוֹרְחִ(י) (= הַזַּרְחִי? cf v[11 13]).

†יִזְרַחְיָה **n.pr.m.** (י׳ *will arise*, or *shine*)—**1.** 𝔊 *Ζαρεια*, A *Ιεζρια*, 𝔊L *Ιεζερια*.—a man of Issachar 1 Ch 7[3.3] **2.** overseer (הַפָּקִיד) of the singers Ne 12[42], 𝔊L al. *Ιεζριας*

†מִזְרָח **n** [**m.**] **place of sunrise, east**—abs. מ׳ Jos 11[3] + 21 t, cstr. מִזְרַח Nu 21[10] + 19t, c. ה loc. מִזְרָחָה Ex 27[13] + 28 t, cstr. מִזְרְחָה Dt 4[41] Jos 12[1] Ju 21[19] (not in Gn Lv Sa Ez etc), —**1.** *sunrise*, always of quarter of the heavens = *east* מ׳ (ה)שמש Nu 21[11] (P), Dt 4[41.47] Jos 1[15] 12[1] 13[5] (all D), 19[12.27 34] (all P), Ju 20[43] 21[19] 2 K 10[33] Is 41[25] 45[6] 59[19], cf. מ׳ שמש לארץ Ju 11[18], ממז׳ שמש ועד־מְבוֹאוֹ ψ 50[1] 113[3] Mal 1[11], more often **2.** without שֶׁמֶשׁ· **a.** *the east* כרחק מ׳ ψ 103[12]. **b.** ממ׳ *from the east* Is 41[2] 43[5] (opp מִמַּעֲרָב), 46[11] Dn 11[44] (+ מִצָּפוֹן); ממ׳

וּמִמַּעֲרָב מִצָּפוֹן וּמִיָּם ψ 107³ **c.** *to* or *toward the place of sunrise, to the east, eastward:* (1) מִזְרָחָה Nu 32¹⁹ (P), Dt 3¹⁷ ²⁷ (יָמָּה וצָפֹנָה וְתֵימָנָה ומ׳), 4⁴⁹ Jos 11⁸ 16¹ (JE), 12¹·³·³ 13⁸ (all D), v²⁷ ³² 16⁵ 18⁷ 20⁸ (all P), 1 Ch 9¹⁸ 26¹⁴, ‖ קֵדְמָה Nu 3³⁸ Jos 19¹³ (both P) Je 31⁴⁰, ‖ נֶגְבָּה, יָמָּה, צָפוֹנָה 1 K 7²⁵, cf Jos 16⁶ (P) 1 Ch 26¹⁷; + קֵדְמָה Ex 27¹³ 38¹³ Nu 2³ 34¹⁵ (all P); מִקֶּדֶם Zc 14⁴ (opp יָמָּה); מ׳ יָמָּה צָפוֹנָה וָנֶגְבָּה (2) מִזְרָח (without ה loc.), 1 Ch 9²⁴, cf. Ne 12³⁷, מ׳ לַמִּזְבֵּחַ 2 Ch 5¹²; (3) לַמִּזְ׳ 1 Ch 5⁹ 7²⁸ (opp לַמַּעֲרָב) 12¹⁶ (so Baer; v¹⁵ van d H; opp. *id*), 26¹⁷ (+ לַנֶּגְבָּה, לַצָּפוֹנָה), Ne 3²⁶, לְמִזְרָחָה 2 Ch 31¹⁴; (4) אֶל־הַמּ׳ Dn 8⁹ (+ אֶל־הַנֶּגֶב, אֶל־הַצֶּבִי); (5) מִיָּם עַד־יָם וּמִצָּפוֹן עַד־מִזְרָח Am 8¹². **d.** (on) *the east side* of, cstr קְצֵה מִזְרַח יְרֵחוֹ Jos 4¹⁹ (P); also c לְ לְמִזְרַח הַגַּיְא 1 Ch 4³⁹, לְמ׳ הַיַּרְדֵּן 6⁶³; c. מִן, מִמִּזְ׳ Jos 11³ (opp מִיָּם) cf. 17¹⁰ (+ מִצָּפוֹן; both JE), also 16⁶ (P) **e.** after a cstr עַל־כָּל־פְּנֵי מ׳ לַגִּלְעָד 1 Ch 5¹⁰; רְחוֹב הַמּ׳ 2 Ch 29⁴; שַׁעַר הַמּ׳ Ne 3²⁹; אֶרֶץ מ׳ Zc 8⁷ (opp. אֶרֶץ מְבוֹא הַשָּׁמֶשׁ).

†[זָרַם] **vb. pour forth in floods, flood away** (As *zarâmu, overwhelm*, VR⁵⁶·⁵⁷ᵉ Dl^Pr 73 & in Zim^BP 119) —**Qal** *Pf.* 2 ms. sf. זְרַמְתָּם ψ 90⁵ *thou floodest them with rain, sweepest them* (men) *away.* **Po.** *Pf.* 3 pl זֹרְמוּ מַיִם עָבוֹת ψ 77¹⁸ the *cloud masses* (Che) *poured forth water.*

†זֶרֶם **n.m.** ^Hb. 3 10 **flood of rain, rain-storm, downpour** (Aram. זַרְמִית *id*)—abs. ז׳ Is 4⁶ + 2 t.; זֶרֶם זֶרֶם Is 32²; cstr. זֶרֶם Jb 24⁸ + 4 t., Is 4⁶ (‖ מָטָר), ז׳ מַיִם Is 28² Hb 3¹⁰; ז׳ הָרִים Jb 24⁸, i e such as falls among mts. cf. Di; ז׳ בָּרָד Is 28²; מַחְסֶה מִזֶּרֶם 25⁴, זֶרֶם קִיר v⁴ i.e. such as dashes against a wall, 32² (‖ רוּחַ), נֶפֶץ וָזֶרֶם וְאֶבֶן בָּרָד 30³⁰.

†זִרְמָה **n.f. issue** (of *semen virile*), in fig. of the paramours of Jerusalem וְזִרְמַת סוּסִים זִרְמָתָם Ez 23²⁰.

†I. זָרַע **vb. sow, scatter seed** (NH *id.*; As. *zarû* TP^Prism vi 15; Ar زَرَعَ; Aram. זְרַע, ܙܪܰܥ; Eth ዘርአ: ዘርዐ: but in Sab. דרא DHM^ZMG 1883, 15 and in n.pr, Id in MV^10, pp 242, 983)—**Qal** *Pf.* 3 ms. זָרַע Ju 6³, 1 s. וְזָרַעְתִּי Je 31²⁷; sf וּזְרַעְתִּיהָ consec. Ho 2²⁵, 3 pl. זָרְעוּ Je 12¹³; 2 mpl. זְרַעְתֶּם Hg 1⁶; וּזְרַעְתֶּם consec. Gn 47²³ + 2 t; *Impf.* יִזְרָע Ec 11⁴; וַיִּזְרַע Gn 26¹²; sf וַיִּזְרָעֶהָ Ju 9⁴⁵; 1 s. אֶזְרָעָה Jb 31⁸; sf. וְאֶזְרָעֵם Zc 10⁹, etc, *Imv.* ms. זְרַע Ec 11⁶; mpl זִרְעוּ Ho 10¹² + 2 t.; *Inf.* לִזְרֹעַ Is 28²⁴, *Pt. act.* זֹרֵעַ Is 55¹⁰ + 3 t; זוֹרֵעַ Pr 22⁸ Je 50¹⁶, etc., *Pt. pass.* זָרֻעַ ψ 97¹¹ (but on text v. infr.), f זְרוּעָה Je 2²,—**1.** lit *sow.* **a.** abs. *sow* (seed), do one's sowing Ju 6³ Gn 26¹² (J), Is 28²⁴ (after ploughing חרש); זִרְעוּ וקצרו ונטעו כרמים Is 37³⁰ = 2 K 19²⁹; ‖ קצר also Mi 6¹⁵ Lv 25¹¹ (H), Ec 11⁴. ‖ אסף Lv 25²⁰ (H); opp אכל Jb 31⁸, זֹרְעֵי עַל־כָּל־מַיִם Is 32²⁰ (on cstr. cf Ges § 130 1); c. אֶת־הַשָּׁנָה הַשְּׁמִינִת Lv 25²²; sq הַרְבֵּה Hg 1⁶ (opp הָבֵא מְעָט) **b.** c. acc. of land אדמה Ex 23¹⁰ (JE; ‖ אסף), Gn 47²³ (J); field (שָׂדֶה) Lv 25³ (‖ אסף), cf. v⁴ ψ 107³⁷, as pt pass אֶרֶץ לֹא זְרוּעָה Je 2² (‖ מִדְבָּר). **c.** c. acc. of seed ז׳ אֶת־זַרְעֲךָ Dt 11¹⁰, cf 22⁹ Je 35⁷ Lv 26¹⁶ (H) Ec 11⁶, sq חִטִּים Je 12¹³ (‖ קצר); cf. also בִּכּוּרֵי מַעֲשֶׂיךָ אֲשֶׁר תִּזְרַע בַּשָּׂדֶה Ex 23¹⁶ (JE). **d.** sq. 2 acc. שָׂדְךָ לֹא תִזְרַע כִּלְאָיִם Lv 19¹⁹ (H), לֹא תִזְרַע כַּרְמְךָ כִּלְאָיִם Dt 22⁹, cf זַרְעֲךָ אֲשֶׁר־תִּזְרַע אֶת־הָאֲדָמָה Is 30²³; also of destroyed city וַיִּזְרָעֶהָ מֶלַח Ju 9⁴⁵ **e.** pt. act as subst. זוֹרֵעַ Je 50¹⁶ (‖ תֹּפֵשׂ מַגָּל בְּעֵת קָצִיר); זֶרַע לַזֹּרֵעַ Is 55¹⁰ (‖ לֶאֱכֹל) **2.** of shrub and tree *producing, yielding seed,* c acc. cogn Gn 1²⁹·²⁹ (P), cf. **Hiph.** **3.** fig.: **a.** of Yahweh's *sowing* (planting) Isr. in the land וּזְרַעְתִּיהָ לִּי בָּאָרֶץ Ho 2²⁵ (We וזרעתיהו, obj. being Jezreel); on the other hand וְאֶזְרָעֵם בָּעַמִּים Zc 10⁹. **b.** c. 2 acc, of Yahweh's fructifying Isr and Judah וזרעתי את־בית ישראל ואת־ב׳ יהודה זֶרַע אדם וזרע בהמה Je 31²⁷. **c.** of moral action, זִרְעוּ לָכֶם לִצְדָקָה Ho 10¹² (‖ קצר); ז׳ צדקה Pr 11¹⁸; אַל־תִּזְרְעוּ אֶל־קֹצִים Je 4³ *sow not in among thorns* (said of a few righteous deeds amid much wickedness); esp of evil-doing כִּי רוּחַ יִזְרָעוּ וְסוּפָתָה יִקְצֹרוּ Ho 8⁷; זֹרְעֵי עָמָל Jb 4⁸ (‖ קצר); זוֹרֵעַ עַוְלָה יִקְצוֹר־אָוֶן Pr 22⁸. **d.** of Israel's practising idolatry וּזְמֹרַת זָר תִּזְרָעֶנּוּ Is 17¹⁰ (2 acc) **e.** הַזֹּרְעִים בְּדִמְעָה בְּרִנָּה יִקְצֹרוּ ψ 126⁵ metaph. of distress followed by joy. **f.** אוֹר זָרֻעַ לַצַּדִּיק ψ 97¹¹ rd prob. זָרַח, Viss Ol Hu Bae Che al.

Niph. **be sown, fructified,** *Pf.* 3 fs וְנִזְרְעָה consec Nu 5²⁸; 2 mpl. וְנִזְרַעְתֶּם consec. Ez 36⁹, *Impf* 3 ms יִזָּרַע Na 1¹⁴; יִזָּרֵעַ Dt 21⁴ Lv 11³⁷; 3 fs תִּזָּרַע Dt 29²²,—**1.** *be sown:* **a.** subj. אֶרֶץ, לֹא תִזָּרַע וְלֹא תַצְמִחַ Dt 29²², cf. (of נַחַל אֵיתָן) לֹא יֵעָבֵד בּוֹ וְלֹא יִזָּ׳ Dt 21⁴; in address to הָרֵי יִשְׂרָאֵל, וְנֶעֱבַדְתֶּם וְנִזְרַעְתֶּם Ez 36⁹. **b.** subj. זֶרַע, זֶרַע זֵרוּעַ אֲשֶׁר יִזָּרֵעַ Lv 11³⁷ (P); fig. לֹא יִזָּ׳ מִשִּׁמְךָ עוֹד Na 1¹⁴ *no more of thy name be sown,* in judgment against Nineveh. **2.** *be fructified, made pregnant*

זָרַע ונזרעָה Nu 5^{28} (P; of woman) **Pu.** *Pf* 3 pl זֹרָעוּ Is 40^{24} of princes and judges under fig of trees (|| נִטָּעוּ, שֹׁרֵשׁ בָּאָרֶץ גּזְעָם) **Hiph.** *Impf.* 3 fs תַּזְרִיעַ Lv 12^{2}, *Pt.* מַזְרִיעַ Gn 1$^{11.12}$,—**1.** *produce seed*, of herb, c acc cogn. Gn 1$^{11.12}$, appar. denom fr. זֶרַע; cf **Qal 2.** **2.** of a woman,=*bear a child* תַּזְרִיעַ וְיָלְדָה זָכָר Lv 12^{2}

†**זֶרַע n.m.** Dt 28, 38 sowing, seed, offspring (NH *id*, Aram זַרְעָא, زَرْعُ, Ph. זרע, Zinj *id*, Ar زَرْعٌ *seed-produce, seed*, Eth **ዘርእ:** As *zêru, cultivated land*, Belser BASII 130, cf Ar. زِرِّيعَةٌ)—abs. ז׳ Gn 47^{23}+, זָרַע Gn 1^{29}+, cstr זֶרַע Is 5^{10}+, זְרַע־ Nu 11^{7}, sf. זַרְעִי 1 S 20^{42} 24^{22}; זַרְעֲךָ Dt 11^{10}+, זַרְעֶךָ Ec 11^{6}+, etc; pl sf. זַרְעֵיכֶם 1 S 8^{15},—**1** lit **a.** a *sowing* לְזֶ׳ הַשָּׂדֶה Gn 47^{24} (J, + אָכְלְכֶם, otherwise Lv 27^{16b}, v infr. **2 c**), לֹא מְקוֹם ז׳ Nu 20^{5} *no place for sowing* (JE; + וּתְאֵנָה וגפן ורמון), cf. שְׂדֵה ז׳ Ez 17^{5} *a field* suitable *for sowing*, hence **b.** *sowing* as regularly recurring at its season Gn 8^{22} (J, || קָצִיר, + קֹר וָחֹם וְקַיִץ וָחֹרֶף ויום וָלַיְלָה), Lv 26^{5} (H, || בָּצִיר, דַיִשׁ, —cf Am 9^{13} infr **2 a**) **2.** *seed* **a.** lit., sown, to raise crops for food, usu corn (wheat, barley, etc) Gn 47$^{19.23}$ (J; cf v^{14f}), Nu 24^{7} (JE), נָתַן ז׳ לַזֹּרֵעַ Is 55^{10} (|| לֶחֶם), Dt 28^{38} (ז׳ רַב), Lv 26^{16} (H, c זָרַע), 27^{16a}, ז׳ חֹמֶר שְׂעֹרִים v^{16b} (both P), cf Is 5^{10} **b.** fig, of idolatry of Judah Is 17^{11} (|| קציר), of fortunes of Zion מֶשֶׁךְ הַזֶּ׳ ψ 126^{6} *the dropping of seed*, i e the proper quantity for sowing (opp אֲלֻמֹּת), Je 35^{7} (c זָרַע, || כֶּרֶם לֹא תִטָּעוּ), cf v^{9} (|| שָׂדֶה, כֶּרֶם), מְטַר ז׳ Is 30^{23} (c זָרַע, || לֶחֶם תְּבוּאַת הָאֲדָמָה); also Dt 11^{10} (c זָרַע), Ec 11^{6} (c *id*), ז׳ זֵרוּעַ Lv 11^{37}, cf. v^{38} (both P), as yielding the crop תְּבוּאַת זַרְעֶךָ Dt 14^{22} *the product of thy seed*, cf **d** infr, וְנִגַּשׁ חוֹרֵשׁ בַּקֹּצֵר וְדֹרֵךְ עֲנָבִים בְּמֹשֵׁךְ הַזֶּ׳ Am 9^{13}, in fig of rapid and plentiful growth in the coming time; ז׳ הָאָרֶץ producing a vine Ez 17^{5}, of growth and prosperity of Isr; הַזֶּ׳ Mal 2^{3}, rd perh הַזְּרֹעַ (cf. VB). **c.** *seed* as product, the manna is comp with ז׳ גַּד, *coriander seed* in Nu 11^{7} (JE), Ex 16^{31} (P), seed of herbs and trees Gn 1$^{11.11.12.12.29.29}$ (all P) Esp **d.** *seed* as *corn-product, corn-crop*, so (although not quite clearly) Dt 22^{9} (c זָרַע, || תְּבוּאַת הַכָּרֶם); pl 1 S 8^{15} (perh better *arable lands*, cf supr As. *zêru*; || כְּרָמִים), ז׳ הָאָרֶץ Lv 27^{30} (|| פְּרִי־עֵץ), otherwise Gn 47^{24}, cf supr. **1 a**), ז׳ שִׁחֹר Is 23^{3} (|| קְצִיר יְאוֹר); הַעוֹד הַזֶּ׳ בַּמְּגוּרָה Hg 2^{19} (|| עֵץ הַזַּיִת, רִמּוֹן, תְּאֵנָה, גֶּפֶן), יָשׁוּב זַרְעֶךָ וְגָרְנְךָ יֶאֱסֹף Jb 39^{12} (of harvest), so perh כְּבֵית סָאתַיִם ז׳ 1 K 18^{32}. **e** זֶרַע הַשָּׁלוֹם הַגֶּפֶן Zc 8^{12}, rd perh. הַזֶּ׳ שָׁלוֹם *the crop is security* (= secure), so 𝔖 Or al., > Ew Hi al. who transl ז׳ הַשָּׁ׳ *the growth of peace*, making הַגֶּפֶן appos —Vbs used c ז׳ in these senses are:—usu זָרַע Gn 1^{11} Lv 26^{16} Je 35^{7}+, ב הִפְרִיחַ Is 17^{11}, נָתַן =*plant, sow* Ez 17^{5}, נָתַן *yield* Is 55^{10}; מָשַׁךְ Am 9^{13} **3.** *seed*=semen virile, וְנִזְרְעָה זָרַע Nu 5^{28}, *and she shall be made pregnant* with *seed*; usu שִׁכְבַת־ז׳, *flow of semen* Lv 22^{4} (H), Lv 15$^{16.32}$ (P; all c תֵּצֵא), 15^{17} (P, c. הָיָה), as *acc. modi* שׁכב אֶת־אִשָּׁה שׁ׳ ז׳ Lv 19^{20} (H), 15^{18} Nu 5^{13} (both P), so also נתן שְׁכָבְתּוֹ לְזֶרַע Lv 18^{20} (ל genitiv); cf ז׳ אָדָם וז׳ בְּהֵמָה Je 31^{27} (as 2nd acc. after זָרַע q v **3 b**) **4.** *seed=offspring* · **a.** rarely of animals, coll Gn 3^{15} 7^{3} (both J) Usu **b.** of mankind, coll =*descendants, posterity; seed of the woman* Gn 3^{15} (J), seed of the patriarchs (esp. Abr.) 12^{17} 13$^{15.16.16}$ 16^{10} 22$^{17.17.18}$ 24^{7} 26$^{3.4.4.4.24}$ 28$^{13.14.14}$ 32^{13} (all J), 15$^{13.18}$ Ex 32$^{13.13}$ 33^{1} (all JE), Gn 21^{12} Jos 24^{3} (both E; in both promised seed of Abr restricted to line of Isaac), Dt 11^{9} 34^{4} Ne 9^{8},=a son as involving posterity Gn 15$^{3.5}$ (JE) cf infr; phr זַרְעָם אַחֲרֵיהֶם Dt 1^{8}, cf 4^{37} 10^{15}, so P, Gn 17$^{7.7.8.9.10.19}$ 35^{12} 48^{4}, זַרְעֲךָ אַחֲךָ Gn 28^{4} (P, cf Nu 18^{19}), v. also infr **c.** **c.** *seed* (= posterity) of other individuals Gn 21^{13} (E; of Ishmael) 24^{60} 48^{19} (both J), Nu 14^{24} (JE), Lv 21^{21} 22$^{3.4}$ (all H), Nu 17^{5} (P), 1 S 20$^{42.42}$ 24^{22} 2 S 4^{8} 1 K 2$^{33.33}$ 11^{39} 2 K 5^{27} Je 29^{32} Ez 43^{19} Jb 5^{25} (|| צֶאֱצָאֶיךָ), 21^{8} (|| *id.*); esp of seed of David as anointed to reign ψ 18^{51}=2 S 22^{51} (|| לִמְשִׁיחוֹ), as sitting on throne Je 33^{21}, cf v$^{22.26}$, ψ 89$^{5.30.37}$, of Jehoiachin Je 22$^{28.30}$, Jehoiakim 36^{31} (cf v^{30}), of child (son) as involving posterity Gn 38$^{8.9.9}$ (of Er's seed by Onan), 48^{11} (all J), cf. 19$^{32.34}$ (J), 2 S 7^{12} Ru 4^{12} Lv 21^{15} (H); phr זַרְעָם אַחֲרֵיהֶם of seed of Noah and his sons Gn 9^{9}, of Aaron Ex 28^{43}, of Phinehas Nu 25^{13} (all P), of David 1 Ch 17^{11}; לְזַרְעוֹ לְדֹרֹתָם Ex 30^{21} (P), cf Lv 21^{17} (H, both of Aaron), v also **b** supr ז׳, of *seed* of righteous, esp ψψ —ψ 25^{13} 37$^{25.26}$ 69^{37} 102^{29} (|| בָּנִים), 112^{2} (|| דּוֹר יְשָׁרִים), cf 22^{31} (on txt. v. Che), of wicked ψ 21^{11} 37^{28}. **d.** specif of a *particular child* (son) ז׳ אַחֵר Gn 4^{25} (J), ז׳ אֲנָשִׁים 1 S 1^{11}, of children Lv 18^{21} 20$^{2.3.4}$ 22^{13} (all H), 1 S 2^{20} (cf. v^{21} בָּנוֹת, בָּנִים), children and grandchildren Gn 46$^{6.7}$ (P) **e.** =*family* Gn 17^{12} (P; cf As *zêr bît abîšu* Asrb Annals iii 10), note esp. *of royal family* ז׳ הַמֶּלֶךְ 1 K 11^{14}, ז׳ הַמַּמְלָכָה 2 K 11^{1}= 2 Ch 22^{10}, ז׳ הַמְּלוּכָה 2 K 25^{25}=Je 41^{1}, Ez 17^{13} Dn 1^{3}, =*pedigree* בֵּית אֲבוֹתָם וְזַרְעָם Ezr 2^{59}= Ne 7^{61}, =one's *nation*, as of same blood Est 10^{3} (|| עַם).—Some vbs. used c. ז׳ in these senses

are:—נָתַן, God subj. Gn 15^{3} Ru 4^{12} (sq. מִן of woman); שִׂים 1 S 2^{20}; c. man as subj. נתן Gn 38^{9}; הֵקִים v^{8}; חִיָּה ז׳, *keep alive*, or *give life to*, of animals Gn 7^{3}; of woman 19$^{32.34}$ (sq. מִן of man). **f.** esp. as name for people of Isr., *seed of Abr.* Is 41^{8} 2 Ch 20^{7} (עַמְּךָ יִשְׂרָאֵל ‖), Je 33^{26} ψ 105^{6} (בְּנֵי יעקב ‖); of Isr. or Jacob 2 K 17^{20} Ne 9^{2} (בני ישראל ‖ v^{1}), Is 43^{5} 45$^{19.25}$ Je 31$^{36.37}$ 33^{26} ψ 22$^{24.24}$ 1 Ch 16^{13} (בני יעקב ‖); so ז׳ בֵּית ישראל Je 23^{8} Ez 44^{22} (𝔖 𝔊 codd. Co del. בית); ז׳ בית יעקב Ez 20^{5}; in Est. ז׳ הַיְּהוּדִים Est 6^{13}; so of Edom (seed of Esau) Je 49^{10}, cf. מִזֶּרַע מָדַי Dn 9^{1}. **g.** *seed* of Isr. (or Jacob, or the people), is used also, by (later) prophets, of *future generations*, in addressing the people:—Dt 28$^{46.59}$ 30$^{6.19}$ 31^{21}, cf. Nu 18^{19} (P; לְזַרְעֲךָ אִתָּךְ ‖ וּלְבָנֶיךָ וְלִבְנֹתֶיךָ), Je 30^{10} = 46^{27} (Jacob and Isr. here = people), ψ 106^{27}; צֶאֱצָא(יך) ‖ Is 44^{3} (Jacob and Jeshurun), 48^{19}, cf. 61^{9}; also Je 7^{15} Is 54^{3} 66^{22} (שִׁמְכֶם ‖); מִפִּי זַרְעֲךָ וּמִפִּי זֶרַע זַרְעֲךָ Is 59^{21}; of Jews (יהודים) Est 9$^{27.28.31}$. **5.** *seed* as marked by moral quality = persons (or community) of such a quality; transition to this through such cases as those of ז׳ בְּרוּכֵי י׳ Is 65^{23} (צֶאֱצָאִים ‖), cf. 61^{9} 65^{9}; ז׳ הַקֹּדֶשׁ Ezr 9^{2} (of Isr.), cf. Is 53^{10}; note, in good sense ז׳ צַדִּיקִים Pr 11^{21} (opp. רַע); ז׳ אֱמֶת Je 2^{21} (שׂוֹרֵק ‖); ז׳ אלהים Mal 2^{15};—ז׳ קֹדֶשׁ Is 6^{13} is a gloss;—in bad sense ז׳ מְרֵעִים Is 1^{4} *community of evil-doers* (גּוֹי־חֹטֵא ‖, עַם כֶּבֶד עָוֹן, בָּנִים מַשְׁחִיתִים), 14^{20}; ז׳ מְנָאֵף 57^{3} (בני עֹנְנָה ‖); ז׳־שָׁקֶר v^{4} (יִלְדֵי־פֶשַׁע ‖).

†זֵרוּעַ **n.[m.] sowing, thing sown** (intensive format. acc. to Ol $^{§ 186 b}$ Sta $^{§ 228}$, yet on this and foll. cf. Ba $^{NB 42, 178 Anm. 4}$)—זֶרַע ז׳ Lv 11^{37} (P), כְּגַנָּה זֵרוּעֶיהָ תַצְמִיחַ Is 61^{11} in sim. of Yahweh's causing righteousness to spring up.

†[זֵרֹעַ] **n.[m.] vegetable** (cf. foregoing; on this and foll. cf. Bev $^{Dn 62, and n. 2}$)—only pl. מִן־הַזֵּרֹעִים Dn 1^{12}.

†[זֵרְעֹן] **n.[m.]** id., only pl. זֵרְעֹנִים Dn 1^{16}.

†יִזְרְעֶאל **1. n.pr.loc.** (*God soweth*; Sab. אלדרא Mordt $^{ZMG 1876, 489}$; v. Lag $^{BN 131}$)—י׳ Jos 15^{56} 2 S 2^{9}+; יִזְרְעָאל 1 S 25^{43} Jos 17^{16}+; יִזְרְעֶאלָה Jos 19^{18}+6 t.: **a.** city in the Negeb of Judah Jos 15^{56} 1 S 25^{43} (home of Ahinoam, one of David's wives), site unknown; cf. n.pr.m. 1 Ch 4^{3}. **b.** city in Issachar Jos 19^{18} on NW. spur of Mt. Gilboa 2 S 4^{4} (cf. 1 S 31$^{1.8}$) 1 K 4^{12} (cf. 1 S 31$^{10.12}$), mod. *Zer'în* (Rob $^{BR ii. 318 ff.}$ Bd $^{Pal 244}$), close to scene of great battle with Philistines 1 S 29^{1} (בְּעַיִן אשר בְּיִז׳, cf. Rob $^{BR ii. 323}$) v^{11}; subject to Ishbosheth 2 S 2^{9} (yet v. infr.), residence of Ahab and Jehoram of Isr. 1 K 18$^{45.46}$ 21^{1} (Naboth) 2 K 8$^{29.29}$ = 2 Ch 22$^{6.6}$, 2 K 9$^{15.15.16.17.30}$ 10^{11} cf. דְּמֵי יִז׳ Ho 1^{4}, and symbolical name of Hosea's son Ho 1^{4} (cf. Che);—in 2 K 10^{1} for שָׂרֵי יִז׳ rd. שָׂרֵי שֹׁמְרוֹן so 𝔊. Used by Hosea as representing Isr., with play on etymol., Ho 2^{24} (cf. וּזְרַעְתִּיהָ לִּי v^{25}), cf. also גָּדוֹל יוֹם יִז׳ v^{2}. Territory immediately about the city is חֵלֶק יִז׳ 2 K 9$^{10.36.37}$; cf. חֵל יִז׳ 1 K 21^{23} (rd. prob. חלק, v. Th Klo after 𝔖 𝔙; the adjacent plain is עֵמֶק יִז׳ (cf. Di Jos 17^{16} Bd $^{Pal 229}$) Jos 17^{16} Ju 6^{33} Ho 1^{5} (perh. also = יִז׳ 2 S 2^{9} supr., ‖ Gilead, Ephr., Benj., etc.) **2. n.pr.m. a.** Hosea's son Ho 1^{4}, cf. **1 b** supr. **b.** Judahite name 1 Ch 4^{3}, cf. **1 a** supr.

†יִזְרְעֵאלִי **m.**, יִזְרְעֵאלִית **f., adj.gent. 1. m.** fr. יִזְרְעֶאל **1 b**; alw. נָבוֹת הַיִּז׳ 1 K 21$^{1.4.6.7.15.16}$ 2 K 9$^{21.25}$. **2. f.** fr. יִזְרְעֶאל **1 a**; alw. אֲחִינֹעַם הַיִּז׳ a wife of David; ending ־ית 1 S 30^{5} 2 S 2^{2} 1 Ch 3^{1}; ending ־ת 1 S 27^{3} 2 S 3^{2} (= 1 Ch 3^{1}).

†[מִזְרָע] **n.[m.] place of sowing, seed-land**, only cstr. כֹּל מִזְרַע יְאוֹר Is 19^{7} (עָרוֹת יְאוֹר ‖); > Du who tr. *seed* (cf. מאכל etc.) on acc. of foll. vb. נִדַּף.

II. זרע (cf. Ar. ذَرَعَ *stretch out, extend*, esp. arm or leg; ذَرْعٌ *power*, ذِرَاعٌ *forearm*).

†זְרֹעַ, זְרוֹעַ **n.f.** $^{Ex 6, 6}$ and (rare) **m.** $^{Is 51, 5, cf. infr.}$ **arm, shoulder, strength** (NH *id.*; As. (Tel el Amarna $^{102, 1. 12, etc.}$) *zurû*, cf. Jastrow $^{JBL, xi, 1892, 123}$; Ar. ذِرَاعٌ; Aram. דְּרָעָא, ܕܪܥܐ; Eth. መዝራዕት:)—abs. זְרוֹעַ Ex 6^{6}+, זְרֹעַ Dt 7^{19}+; cstr. זְרוֹעַ ψ 10^{15}+, זְרֹעַ ψ 89^{11}+; sf. זְרֹעִי Je 27^{5} ψ 89^{2}, זְרֹעִי Is 51^{5} 63^{5}; זְרוֹעֲךָ ψ 71^{18}+, זְרֹעֲךָ 1 S 3^{31}+, etc.; pl. זְרֹעִים Dn 11^{31}; cstr. זְרֹעֵי Gn 49^{24}; sf. זְרֹעַי Is 51^{5}, זְרֹעָיו 2 K 9^{24}; elsewh. fem. form, cstr. זְרוֹעוֹת ψ 37^{17}, זְרֹעוֹת Jb 22^{9}+6 t., זְרֹעֹת Dt 33^{27}; sf. זְרוֹעֹתָי ψ 18^{35}, זְרֹעֹתַי 2 S 22^{35}, etc. (In abs. and cstr. sg. more oft. *plene*, in pl. and c. sf. more oft. *defect.* In three instances where ז׳ is masculine it means a political or military *force* Dn 11$^{15.22.31}$).—**1.** *arm*, **a.** lit., of a man Ju 15^{14} 16^{12} 2 S 1^{10} Is 9^{19} 17^{5} (prob. acc. instr.), Dt 33^{20} Zc 11$^{17.17}$ Ct 8^{6} Dn 10^{6}; Ez 13^{30} (del. Co); ז׳ כֹּחוֹ Is 44^{12} (of a smith, forging); ז׳ חֲשׂוּפָה Ez 4^{7} (of prophet); in fig. of י׳ teaching Ephr. to walk Ho 11^{3}; זְרֹעֵי יָדָיו Gn 49^{24} *arms of his hands*, i.e. arms that by their strength enable him (Joseph)

to draw the bow; וַיַּךְ אֶת־יְהוֹרָם בֵּין זְרֹעָיו 2 K 9^{24}, i.e. his arms seen from behind, *his shoulders*. **b.** *arm* as *seat of* (human) *strength* ψ 18^{35}= 2 S 22^{35}; ז׳ לֹא עֹז Jb 26^{2}, כֹּחַ הַז׳ Dn 11^{6} cf. v^{6}; ז׳ לֹא עֹז Jb 26^{2}; חִזַּקְתִּי ז׳ Ho 7^{15} cf. Ez $30^{24.25}$; also c. שׁבר ψ 10^{15} 37^{17} Je 48^{25} (‖ קֶרֶן), Ez $30^{21.22.24}$ cf. v^{25}; ז׳ רָמָה תִּשָּׁבֵר Jb 38^{15}.—On Mal 2^{3} cf. VB. Esp. **c.** *Yahweh's arm* as instrument of deliverance and judgment (oft. Dt Je Is^{2} ψ):—ז׳ נְטוּיָה Dt 4^{34} 5^{15} 26^{8} Ez $20^{33.34}$ ψ 136^{12}, cf. Dt 7^{19} 11^{2} 1 K 8^{42}=2 Ch 6^{32} (all ‖ יָד חֲזָקָה), Dt 9^{29} 2 K 17^{36}; (of creation) Je 27^{5} 32^{17} (all ‖ כֹּחַ גָּדוֹל); בִּז׳ נְטוּיָה Ex 6^{6} (P, or D's revision; no ‖); זְ׳ חֲזָקָה Je 21^{5} (‖ יָד נְטוּיָה); גְּדֹל זרועך Ex 15^{16} (song), גֹּדֶל ז׳ ψ 79^{11}; זְרוֹעִי תְּאַמְּצֶנּוּ ψ 89^{22} (‖ יָדִי); בִּז׳ ψ 77^{16}; ז׳ ψ 44^{4} (‖ יְמִינְךָ), ז׳ קָדְשׁוֹ ψ 98^{1} (‖ יְמִינוֹ), cf. Is 52^{10}; ז׳ עֻזֶּךָ ψ 89^{11} cf. Is 62^{8} (‖ יְמִינוֹ); לִבְשִׁי־עֹז זְרוֹעַ י׳ Is 51^{9}; לְךָ ז׳ עִם־גְּבוּרָה ψ 89^{14}; ז׳ תִּפְאַרְתּוֹ Is 63^{12}; as support of weak Is 40^{11} (fig. of shepherd), cf. זְרֹעֹת עוֹלָם Dt 33^{27}; נַחַת זְרוֹעוֹ יַרְאֶה Is 30^{30} (of lightning stroke, ‖ השמיע הוד קולו of thunder); also אִם־זְרוֹעַ כָּאֵל לָךְ Jb 40^{9}.

Hence, **2.** *arm*, as symbol of *strength*: **a.** human 1 S $2^{31.31}$ (𝔊 rd. זַרְעֲךָ and זֶרַע, but v. Klo Dr), Ez 22^{6} 31^{17}; וַתְּאַמֵּץ זְרוֹעֹתֶיהָ Pr 31^{17}; בְּשָׂר ז׳ 2 Ch 32^{8}; שָׂם בָּשָׂר זְרֹעוֹ Je 17^{5} (‖ יִבְטַח בָּאָדָם); cf. ψ 44^{4} (‖ חַרְבָּם); איש זרוע Jb 22^{8}; זְרֹעוֹת יְתֹמִים Jb 22^{9} (i.e. strength, resources); זְרֹעַ גְּדוֹלָה Jb 35^{9}; ז׳ רַבִּים ψ 83^{9}; הָיוּ זרוע לִבְנֵי־לוֹט Ez 17^{9} (for pulling up a tree, in metaph.). **b.**=divine strength ψ 71^{18} (‖ גְּבוּרָה), זְרֹעוֹ מֹשְׁלָה לוֹ Is 40^{10} (‖ חָזָק); זְרֹעַי עַמִּים יִשְׁפֹּטוּ 51^{5} [Str thinks masc. to avoid verbal ending נָה, cf. 49^{11}]; and help Is 33^{2} (‖ יְשׁוּעָה) cf. 59^{16} 63^{5}; see also 53^{1}.

3. Pl. *forces*, political and military, c. יַעֲמֹדוּ Dn $11^{15.31}$; v^{22} (see Bev).

4. *Shoulder* of animal sacrificed, belonging to priest Nu 6^{19} (P) Dt 18^{3}.

† אֶזְרוֹעַ **n.f. arm** (=foregoing c. א prosthet.)—*arm* of man כְּתֵפִי מִשִּׁכְמָה תִפּוֹל וְאֶזְרֹעִי מִקָּנָה תִשָּׁבֵר׃ Jb 31^{22}; of י׳ בְּיָד חֲזָקָה וּבְאֶזְרוֹעַ נְטוּיָה Je 32^{21}, cf. זְרוֹעַ **1 c.**

† [זָרַף] **vb.** prob. **drip** (cf. either Ar. ذَرَفَ *shed* tears, or Aram. ܙܪܝܦܐ *imber vehemens*)—**Hiph.** יַזְרִיף rd. in ψ 72^{6} by Hup Bi Che (for זַרְזִיף) sq. אֶרֶץ *cause to drip, irrigate.*

† זַרְזִיף **n.[m.] drop, dripping** (NH *id.*; on form (if genuine) cf. Nö $^{M 85, NS 191}$)—ψ 72^{6} כִּרְבִיבִים ז׳ אָרֶץ as showers, a *dripping* of the earth, but v. foregoing.

† זָרַק **vb. to toss or throw (in a volume), scatter abundantly** (NH *id.*; Aram. זְרַק *id.*, ܙܪܩ *disperse*; As. *zarâḳu* Lotz $^{TP 138}$ Jäger $^{BAS ii. 292 Anm.**}$; cf. also Ar. زَرَقَ *cast at, pierce*, زَرَّاقَةٌ and مِزْرَاقٌ *javelin*=Eth. መዝራቅ፡)—**Qal** *Pf.* ז׳ Ex 24^{6} Lv 17^{6}, sf. זְרָקוֹ Ex 9^{8}, זָֽרְקָה Ho 7^{9} (12 t. Pf.); *Impf.* יִזְרֹק Lv 7^{2} + 16 t.; *Inf.* לִזְרֹק Ez 43^{18}; *Imv.* זְרֹק Ez 10^{2}; *Pt.* זֹרֵק Lv 7^{14}, pl. זֹרְקִים 2 Ch 30^{16}; **1.** *toss* (in handfuls, v. Ex 9^{8}; or from a *bowl*, מִזְרָק; opp. הִזָּה to *sprinkle* with the finger): **a.** cummin Is 28^{25}, dust, sq. עַל 2 Ch 34^{4} Jb 2^{12}, ashes השמימה, heavenward, Ex $9^{8.10}$ (P), coals of fire על העיר Ez 10^{2}. **b.** blood, על (ה)מזבח *throw* (from a bowl) against the altar Ex 24^{6} (JE), Lv 17^{6} (H), Nu 18^{17} (P), 2 K $16^{13.15}$ Ez 43^{18}, esp. in the ritual, על המזבח סביב against the altar round about Ex $29^{16.20}$ Lv $1^{5.11}$ $3^{2.8.13}$ 7^{2} $8^{19.24}$ $9^{12.18}$ (all P); sq. על העם Ex 24^{8} (JE), sq. המזבחה 2 Ch $29^{22.22.22}$; without designation of place Lv 7^{14} (P), 2 Ch 30^{16} 35^{11}. **c.** *water* for purification, sq. עַל, Ez 36^{25}. **2.** intrans. (si vera l.) Ho 7^{9} גַּם שֵׂיבָה זָֽרְקָה בּוֹ grey hairs are *profuse* upon him (? rd. זָֽרְחָה, as in 2 Ch 26^{19}). **Pu.** *Pf.* זֹרַק, of water of purification *poured* over (עַל) one defiled by a corpse Nu $19^{13.20}$ (P).

† מִזְרָק **n.m.** $^{Nu 7, 84}$ **bowl, bason** (prop. vessel for *throwing* or *tossing* a liquid); מ׳ Nu 7^{13} + 13 t., pl. מִזְרָקִים Zc 14^{20}, cstr. מִזְרְקֵי Nu 7^{84} + 2 t., מִזְרָקוֹת Ne 7^{70} + 9 t., מִזְרְקֹת Ex 38^{3} + 2 t., sf. מִזְרְקֹתָיו Ex 27^{3};—**1.** *bowl* for wine Am 6^{6}. **2.** elsewh. for use in ritual of sacrifice: **a.** for use at altar Ex 27^{3} 38^{3} Nu 4^{14} (all P), 1 K $7^{40.45}$ Je 52^{18} Zc 9^{15} 14^{20}. **b.** given by the princes full of flour mingled with oil for a מנחה Nu $7^{13.19.25.31.37.43.49.55.61.67.73.79.84.85}$ (P). **c.** golden basons for use in the temple 1 K 7^{50} 2 K 12^{14} 25^{15} 1 Ch 28^{17} 2 Ch $4^{8.11.22}$ Je 52^{19}. **d.** golden basons for the second temple Ne 7^{70}.

† [זָרַר] **vb.** only **Po. sneeze** (cf. זְרִירוֹ(ה)י 𝔗 Jb 41^{10} for Heb. עֲטִישֹׁתָיו; vb. prob. onomatop.);—וַיְזוֹרֵר הַנַּעַר עַד שֶׁבַע פְּעָמִים 2 K 4^{35}.

† זֶרֶשׁ **n.pr.f.** wife of Haman Est $5^{10.14}$ $6^{13.13}$ (acc. to Opp $^{Esth. 25}$=Pers. *zaris*, Zend *zairis*, *la dorée*, cf. زريشت *aurum ductile*, Vull $^{ii. 128 b}$; Jen $^{VOJ, 1892, 64}$ comp. Elamit. goddess *Kiriša*).

† זֶרֶת **n.f. span** (NH *id.* (𝔗 זַרְתָּא, Syr. ܙܪܬܐ; appar. fr. Heb.), etym. dub.; Thes and most der. fr. √ זרה, vid. Ol $^{§ 146 b}$ but also Sta $^{§ 187 a}$; Ba $^{ZMG 1887, 607}$ prop. √ זרה *measure off, determine*,

cf p 280)—*span*, as standard of measurement, שָׁמַיִם בַּזֶּ׳ תִּכֵּן Is 40^{12}; elsewh. of actual size, *a span*, distance between ends of thumb and little finger of spread hand, = ½ cubit (v. אַמָּה & reff.; cf. Ex 25^{10} with Joseph $^{Ant. iii. 6, 5}$), ז׳ Ex 28$^{16.16}$ 39$^{9.9}$ (all P) Ez 43^{13}, זָ֑רֶת 1 S 17^{4} six cubits and *a span*. Vid. Hultsch $^{Metrol. 1882, 443}$ Benz $^{Archäol 179}$.

† זַתּוּא **n.pr.m.** head of a family of returned exiles Ezr 2^{8} = Ne 7^{13}; cf. also Ezr 10^{27} Ne 10^{15}.

† זֵתָם **n.pr.m.** a Levite 1 Ch 23^{8} 26^{22}.

† זֵתַר **n.pr.m.** an eunuch of Ahasuerus Est 1^{10} (Opp $^{Esth 25}$ comp Pers *zaitar, conqueror*)

ח

ח, *Ḥêth*, 8th letter; = numeral 8 in post BHeb.

[חֹב], חֻבִּי v sub חבב.

†[חָבָא] **vb. withdraw, hide** (not in **Qal**); cf. also חבה (NH *id*; Ar. خَبَأَ, Eth ኀብአ: As. *ḫabû* Dl $^{Pr 175}$, ܬ Ethpa. *hide oneself*)—**Niph.** *Pf.* 3 ms. נֶחְבָּא Ju 9^{5} + 1 S 10^{22} 2 S 17^{9} (both may be *pt*); נַחְבֵּאתָ Gn 31^{27}, וְנֶח׳ consec. 1 S 19^{2}; נֶחְבְּאוּ Jos 10^{27}, נֶחְבָּ֫אוּ Jb 29$^{8.10}$, *Impf.* 2 ms תֵּחָבֵא Jb 5^{21}; *Inf. cstr.* הֵחָבֵא 2 Ch 18^{24} Dn 10^{7}, *Pt* pl. (cf. also *supr*) נֶחְבָּאִים Jos 10^{17}, etc.—*hide oneself* in fear Gn 3^{10} (J), Jos 10$^{16.17.27}$ (all JE), Ju 9^{5} 1 S 19^{2} 2 S 17^{9} Am 9^{3} 2 Ch 18^{24} Dn 10^{7}; from modesty 1 S 10^{22}, cf Jb 29^{8}; also לָמָּה נַחְבֵּאתָ לִבְרֹחַ Gn 31^{27} (E), i.e. why didst thou flee secretly? pass, *be hidden* Jb 29^{10} קוֹל נְגִידִים נֶחְבָּ֫אוּ ‖ וּלְשׁוֹנָם לְחִכָּם דָּבֵקָה, cf also v. 9) i.e in reverence, = *hushed* (so we speak of a *veiled* voice); be hidden for protection בְּשׁוֹט לָשׁוֹן Jb 5^{21}. **Pu.** *Pf.* 3 pl. חֻבָּ֫אוּ *have been hidden* (=are made to hide themselves, Di *ad loc*) Jb 24^{4} **Hiph.** *Pf.* 3 ms. sf. הֶחְבִּיאָ֫נִי Is 49^{2}; 3 fs. הֶחְבְּאָ֫תָה Jos 6^{17}, cf. Ges $^{§ 75. Rem. 21 a}$ Ko $^{i. 624 ff.}$ etc; *Impf.* וַיַּחְבִּיאֵם 1 K 18^{4}; 3 fs. וַתַּחְבִּא 2 K 6^{29}, וָאַחְבִּא 1 K 18^{13},—*hide*, trans., c. acc. Jos 6$^{17.25}$ 1 K 18$^{4.13}$ 2 K 6^{29}, metaph., of divine protection Is 49^{2} בְּצֵל יָדוֹ ה׳. **Hoph.** *Pf be hidden* הָחְבָּ֫אוּ Is 42^{22} (בְּבָתֵּי כְלָאִים), i e. imprisoned. **Hithp.** *Pf* הִתְחַבְּאוּ 1 S 14^{11}; *Impf* יִתְחַבֵּא 1 S 23^{23}; וַיִּתְ׳ Gn 3^{8}; יִתְחַבָּ֑אוּ Jb 38^{30}, וַיִּתְחַבְּאוּ 1 S 13^{6}; *Pt.* מִתְחַבֵּא 2 K 11^{3} + 2 t; מִתְחַבְּאִים 1 S 14^{22} 1 Ch 21^{20};—**1.** *draw back, hide oneself*, usu. c. ב loc.; Gn 3^{8} (J), 1 S 13^{6} 14$^{11.22}$ 23^{23} 2 K 11^{3} 1 Ch 21^{20} 2 Ch 22$^{9.12}$. **2.** *draw together, thicken, harden*, of water becoming ice Jb 38^{30} כָּאֶבֶן מַיִם יִתְחַ׳.

† מַחֲבֵא **n.[m.]** hiding-place, only cstr כְּמַחֲבֵא רוּחַ וְסֵתֶר זָרֶם Is 32^{2} *hiding-place from wind.*

†[מַחֲבֹא] **n.[m.]** id., pl. abs. מִכֹּל הַמַּחֲבֹאִים אֲשֶׁר יִתְחַבֵּא שָׁם 1 S 23^{23}.

†[חָבַב] **vb. love** (NH Pi *id.*; Ar. حَبَّ *be loved*; Eth. ተሐበበ: *amore alicujus incendi* Di; Aram. حَبّ *kindle, be set on fire*, ܚܒܒ, חַבֵּב *love, embrace*, חוּבָּא *bosom*)—**Qal** *Pt* אַף חֹבֵב עַמִּים Dt 33^{3} (Di rds עַמּוֹ, cf. 𝔊)

†[חֹב] **n.[m.]** bosom (Aram) לִטְמוֹן בְּחֻבִּי עֲוֺנִי Jb 31^{33} (cf. חֵיק).

† חֹבָב **n.pr.m.** (cf. Ph n pr. חבב, We $^{Skizzen iii, 171. 217}$ suggests compar. with حُبَاب *serpent*)—son of Reuel, חֹתֵן of Moses (v חתן), Nu 10^{29} (JE), Ju 4^{11}; ins. ח׳ prob. also Ju 1^{16}, v. GFM.

† חֻבָּה **n.pr.m.** a descendant of Asher, 1 Ch 7^{34} (rd. וְחֻבָּה, so Qr; > Kt יְחֻבָּה).

†[חָבָה] **vb.** withdraw, hide, cf. חבא;—**Qal** *Imv* ms. חֲבִי Is 26^{20} (Aram form, Ol $^{§ 235. 3}$ Ew $^{§ 224 c}$ Du, Di rds חֲבִי=חֲבֵה), *withdraw* into privacy (‖ בֹּא בַחֲדָרֶיךָ) **Niph.** *Pf.* וְנֶחְבָּה consec. Je 49^{10}; וְנֶחְבֵּתֶם consec. Jos 2^{16} (JE), *Inf.* לְהֵחָבֵה (as ל״א) 1 K 22^{25} 2 K 7^{12}; *withdraw, hide oneself*, lit Jos 2^{16} (JE), sq. שָׁ֫מָּה; 2 K 7^{12} c. ב loc.; 1 K 22^{25}; of Esau=Edom, *hiding* from judgment of י׳, וְנֶחְבָּה לֹא יוּכָל Je 49^{10}, as pointed, meant no doubt as pf, but constr. then hard; rd rather inf abs. נַחְבֹּה; so Gf Gie al. (v. Ko $^{i. 624}$).

† חֶבְיוֹן **n.[m.]** hiding, hiding-place, or < veil, envelope, only cstr. וְשָׁם ח׳ עֻזֹּה Hb 3^{4} (< 𝔊 𝔖 Hi-St Gr וְשָׂם *and he maketh*, cf ψ 18^{12}).

† חֲבַיָּה **n.pr.m.** head of a priestly family Ezr 2^{61} = Ne 7^{63} (van d. H. Ezr חֳבַיָּה; Ne חֲבַיָּה,

marg. חֲבַיָּה; cf. Baer's note on Ezr 2^{61}; 𝔊 Ezr Λαβεια, 𝔊L Ωδουια, A Οβαια, 𝔊 Ne Εβεια, 𝔊L Αβια, א Αβεια).

חֲבָיָה, חֲבַיָּה v. foregoing.

יַחְבָּה v. חֻבָּה sub חבב.

†**נַחְבִּי** **n.pr.m.** a Naphtalite, one of the Hebrew spies Nu 13^{4} (P).

†[**חָבַט**] **vb.** **beat off, beat out** (NH *id.*, *strike, beat*, Ar. خَبَطَ, Aram. ܚܒܛ, חֲבַט)—**Qal** *Impf.* יַחְבֹּט Is 27^{12}; 3 fs. וַתַּחְבֹּט Ru 2^{17}; 2 ms. תַּחְבֹּט Dt 24^{20}; *Pt.* חֹבֵט Ju 6^{11};—**1.** *beat off*, זַיִתְךָ Dt 24^{20}. **2.** *beat out* (grain), Gideon חֹבֵט חִטִּים בַּגַּת Ju 6^{11}, so Ru 2^{17}, of small quantities;—distinct fr. threshing on open floor, with cattle; fig. of 'י's judgment, and subsequent gathering of Isr. Is 27^{12} (no obj. expr.), so Che Di Du; Ges Hi Kn Brd place sub **1**; VB undecided. **Niph.** *Impf.* יֵחָבֶט Is 28^{27} fennel (קֶצַח) beaten out בַּמַּטֶּה.

חֲבִיָּה, חֲבַיָּה, חֲבִיָּה v. sub חבה.

חֶבְיוֹן v. sub חבה.

†I. [**חָבַל**] **vb.** **bind, pledge** (Ar. حَبَلَ *bind*; cf. Aram. ܚܒܠ, ܚܒܠ *travail*; חֲבַל *pledge* (but rare and dub.); esp. ܚܒܠܐ *cord, field*, חַבְלָא *cord*, ܚܒܠܐ, חֶבְלָא *pain*, esp. of travail; Sab. חבל *border-territory*, or *field*, Sab.Denkm. 48.49; Eth. ሐብል: Zim^BP 93n., comp. As. *naḫbalu*, *rope, snare* (but ḫ = خ))—**Qal** *Pf.* חָבַל Ez 18^{16} *Impf.* יַחְבֹּל Dt 24^{6}; 2 ms. תַּחֲבֹל Dt 24^{17}; תַּחְבֹּל Ez 22^{25} Jb 22^{6}; יַחְבֹּלוּ Jb 24^{3}; Jb 24^{9}; *Imv.* sf. חֲבְלֵהוּ Pr 20^{16} 27^{13}; *Inf. abs.* חָבֹל Ex 22^{25}; *Pt. act.* חֹבֵל Dt 24^{6}, cf. חֹבְלִים Zc $11^{7.14}$ (name of מַקֵּל); *pass.* חֲבֻלִים Am 2^{8};—**1.** *bind*, only in חֹבְלִים, name of one of Zec.'s symbolic staves, Zc $11^{7.14}$ symbol. of fraternity. Esp. **2.** *bind* by taking a pledge of, *hold by a pledge*, sq. acc. pers. Pr 20^{16} 27^{13} Jb 22^{6}; *take* or *hold in pledge*, sq. acc. rei Ex 22^{25}(JE), Dt $24^{6.6.17}$ Jb 24^{3}; sq. acc. cogn. חֲבֹל Ez 18^{16}; עַל־עָנִי יַחְבֹּלוּ Jb 24^{9} prob. pregn. (v. Di) *take pledges* (getting power) *over the poor*; בְּגָדִים חֲבֻלִים Am 2^{8} *garments taken in pledge.* **Niph.** *Impf.* יֵחָבֶל לוֹ Pr 13^{13} *becometh pledged to it* (i.e. pledged to pay the penalty, opp. יְשֻׁלָּם), so Ew Hi De Now Str RV^m VB. > sub II. חָבַל q.v. **Pi.** *Pf.* 3 fs. חִבְּלָה Ct 8^{5}; חִבְּלַתְךָ Ct 8^{5}; *Impf.* יְחַבֶּל־ ψ 7^{15};—*writhe, twist*, hence *travail;* of mother Ct $8^{5.5}$ (c. acc. of child; ‖ יְלָדַתְךָ); metaph. of wicked man ψ 7^{15} יְחַבֶּל־אָוֶן וְהָרָה עָמָל וְיָלַד שָׁקֶר׃.

† I. **חֶבֶל** **n.m.** ^Jos 2,14 **f.** †^Zp 2,6 (but v. infr.) **cord, territory, band**; ח׳ abs. Jos 2^{15} +; cstr. Dt 3^{4} +, חֶבֶל Jos 19^{29}; sf. חַבְלוֹ Jb 18^{10}; pl. חֲבָלִים 2 S 8^{2} + 10 t. + Ez 47^{13} Jb 21^{7} v. infr.; cstr. חַבְלֵי Jos 17^{5} + 5 t.; חֶבְלֵי ψ 116^{3} + 2 t. + ψ 18^{5} (rd. משברי v. infr.); sf. חֲבָלָיִךְ Is 33^{23}; חֲבָלָיו Is 33^{20};—**1.** *cord, rope*, by which men were lowered Jos 2^{15} (JE), Je $38^{6.11.12.13}$, or stones dragged 2 S 17^{13}; of tents Is 33^{20}; tackling of ship v^{23}; for binding Ez 27^{24} Jb 40^{25} Est 1^{6}; symbol of captivity or subjection 1 K $20^{31.32}$; fig. of snare for wicked Jb 18^{10} (‖ מַלְכֻּדְתּוֹ), set by wicked ψ 140^{6} (‖ פַּח); ψ 119^{61} *cords of wicked men have surrounded me;* of wicked held בחבלי חַטָּאתוֹ Pr 5^{22}; ח׳ הַשָּׁוְא Is 5^{18} *cords (ropes) of wickedness* (‖ כַּעֲבוֹת הָעֲגָלָה); of cords of distress (עֳנִי) Jb 36^{8} (‖ זִקִּים); so חֶבְלֵי מָוֶת (prob.) ψ 116^{3}, ψ חֶבְלֵי שְׁאוֹל 18^{6} = 2 S 22^{6} (‖ מוֹקְשֵׁי מָוֶת);—for חבלי מות ψ 18^{5} rd. מִשְׁבְּרֵי, v. 2 S 22^{5} and ‖ נַחֲלֵי בְלִיַּעַל, De Che Bae; to draw בְּחַבְלֵי אָדָם Ho 11^{4} (i.e. *humanely*, kindly); of cord of life חֶבֶל הַכֶּסֶף Ec 12^{6}. **2.** *measuring-cord, line* ח׳ מִדָּה Zc 2^{5}; so ח׳ alone 2 S $8^{2.2.2}$ Am 7^{17} Mi 2^{5} ψ 78^{55}; fig. (of favoured life) ψ 16^{6}; in gen. of one's portion, fortune Jb 21^{17} acc. to 𝔗 Thes Add. Ew Di al., but < v. חֵבֶל. Thence **3.** *measured portion, lot, part, region*, ח׳ נַחֲלָה *inherited portion* Dt 32^{9} 1 Ch 16^{18} = ψ 105^{11}; also ח׳ alone Jos $17^{5.14}$ 19^{9} Ez 47^{13} (חבלים; 𝔙 𝔗 rd. as dual, v. Ew Sm Da al.; Co del. on intern. grounds); of particular regions ח׳ אַרְגֹּב Dt $3^{4.13.14}$ 1 K 4^{13}; ח׳ אַכְזִיב Jos 19^{29} (si vera l., v. WMM^Asien 194); ח׳ הַיָּם Zp 2^{5}; also v^{6}, but היתה ח׳ here dub.; Sta prop. 2 fs. הָיְתָ, and del. ח׳ הים; without הים, v^{7}. **4.** *band, company* of prophets 1 S $10^{5.10}$.—II. חֶבֶל v. sub II. חָבַל.

†**חֵבֶל** **n.m.** ^Is 66,7 (but v. Je 49^{24}) **pain, pang**;—ח׳ abs. Is 66^{7}; elsewh. pl. חֲבָלִים Is 13^{8} + 3 t. + Jb 21^{17} v. infr.; cstr. חֶבְלֵי Ho 13^{13}; sf. חֲבָלֶיהָ Is 26^{17}; חֶבְלֵיהֶם Jb 39^{3} (on sf. v. Ges § 135, 5, R 1);—*pain, pang:* **1.** *pains of travail:* **a.** obj. of תְּשַׁלַּחְנָה Jb 39^{3} meton. for *offspring* (‖ יַלְדֵיהֶן; v. Di; of goats and hinds). **b.** sim. of distress of exiles Is 26^{17}; fig. of anguish of

nations (‖ כַּיּוֹלֵדָה יְחִילוּן) צִירִים וַחֲבָלִים יֹאחֵזוּן Is 13^{8}, also Je 13^{21} 22^{23} 49^{24}; of crisis of redemption Ho 13^{13} (‖ חֶבְלֵי יוֹלֵדָה), of birth of new Isr. Is 66^{7}. **2.** of other than birth-pangs only חבלים Jb 21^{17}; *pains, pangs, sorrows* (so 𝔊 𝔙 Thes,—otherwise Add.—RobGes Hi Da al.; ‖ גֵּר יְרִעֵהוּ, יָבֹא אֵידָם); >others, *portion, fortune*, v. חֶבֶל.

†חֲבֹל **n.[m.]** pledge (as *binding*)—יָשִׁיב ח׳ Ez 18^{12} 33^{15}; as cogn. acc. c. חָבַל Ez 18^{16}.

†[חֲבֹלָה] **n.f. id.** (on format. cf. Lg$^{BN 179}$)—חֲבֹלָתוֹ Ez 18^{7}.

†חִבֵּל **n.[m.]** prob. mast (as *corded* or *roped* in place; denom. fr. חֶבֶל)—only in sim. of drunken man שֹׁכֵב בְּרֹאשׁ ח׳ Pr 23^{34} (opp. שֹׁכֵב בְּלֶב־יָם) i.e. in the lookout-basket at the mast-head, cf. Thes *in carchesio*.—𝔊 𝔙 read חֹבֵל.

†חֹבֵל **n.m.** sailor (denom. fr. חֶבֶל; i.e. *rope*-puller)—חֹבְלֵי הַיָּם Ez 27^{29}; חֹבְלָיִךְ Ez 27$^{8.27.28}$; coll. רַב הַחֹבֵל i.e. the captain Jon 1^{6}.

†חֹבְלִים **n.[m.]pl.** union (lit. *binders*) name of Zec.'s second symbolic staff Zc 11^{7} and c. art. v^{14}. See חֶבֶל **1.**

†[תַּחְבֻּלָה] **n.f.** direction, counsel (prob. orig. of *rope*-pulling, i.e. *steering, directing* a ship, v. חֹבֵל, so Thes; v. De Pr 1^{5});—only pl. and only WisdLt. תַּחְבֻּלוֹת abs. Pr 1^{5} + 3 t.; cstr. Pr 12^{5}; *sf.* תַּחְבּוּלֹתָו Jb 37^{12}—*direction, guidance* (i.e. by God) Jb 37^{12} (of thunder cloud); *counsels* of wicked (רשׁעים) Pr 12^{5} (opp. מַחְשְׁבוֹת צדיקים); gen. *good, wise counsels* Pr 1^{5}; 11^{14} (‖ רֹב יוֹעֵץ), 24^{6} (‖ *id.*); 20^{18} (‖ עֵצָה).

II. חָבַל **vb.** act (ruinously) corruptly (NH *id. wound, injure*; Ar. خَبَلَ *corrupt* or *render unsound* (the mind, a limb, etc.), خَبِلَ *be deranged* (in mind); As. *ḫabâlu, injure*, VR$^{62, 11}$; Aram. , חַבֵּל *corrupt, ruin*; Eth. : *be arrogant, audacious*; Sab. חבל DHM$^{Epigr. Denkm. 48}$; cf. Palm. חבל *mortuus* Vog$^{No. 161}$ and oft.)—**Qal** *Pf.* 1 pl. חָבַלְנוּ Ne 1^{7}; *Impf.* 1 s. אֶחְבֹּל Jb 34^{31}; *Inf. cstr.* (used as *abs.*) Ne 1^{7};—*act corruptly* against, חֲבֹל חבלנו לְ Ne 1^{7}; abs. Jb 34^{31}. **Niph.** *Impf.* יֵחָבֶל לוֹ Pr 13^{13} *shall be ruined* (לְ reflex.), Thes RobGes AV RV, but <I. חָבַל (q.v.) **Pi.** *ruin, destroy*: *Pf.* 3 ms. consec. וְחִבֵּל את מעשׂה ידיך Ec 5^{5}, subj. God. *Impf.* 3 fs. תְּחַבֵּל וְחֶבֶל נִמְרָץ Mi 2^{10} *that destroyeth, even with sore destruction*; but rd. rather תֵּחָבְלוּ ח׳ נ׳ *ye shall be destroyed with* etc., so 𝔊 Roorda Che. *Inf. cstr.* לְחַבֵּל c. acc., the poor Is 32^{7}, the land 13^{5}; abs. 54^{16}; cf. *Pt.* pl. מְחַבְּלִים Ct 2^{15} c. acc. of foxes ruining vineyards. **Pu.** *Pf.* 3 ms. וְחֻבַּל consec. Is 10^{27} of yoke, *be ruined, broken*, si vera l.; RS$^{JPh xiii. 1885, p. 62}$ prop. יחדל, cf. also Che$^{crit. n.}$; and rem. by Di Du; 3 fs. חֻבָּלָה Jb 17^{1} *my spirit is broken* (‖ יָמַי נִזְעָכוּ); *Impf.* 2 mpl. תְּחֻבְּלוּ Mi 2^{10} (emend.: v. supr.)

†II. חֶבֶל **n.m.** destruction—חֶבֶל נִמְרָץ Mi 2^{10}; cf. II. חָבַל **Pi.**

†חֲבַצֶּלֶת **n.f.** meadow-saffron or crocus (*colchicum autumnale*, Linn.) (Syr. , v. Ges$^{Comm. Is 35,1}$ Löw$^{p. 174, No. 128}$; As. *ḫabaṣillatu* VR$^{32, 62}$ is a marsh-plant, reed; cf. Zim$^{BP 59}$ Dl$^{HA 34; Pr 82}$; also Che$^{l.c.}$ and crit. n.);—ח׳ הַשָּׁרוֹן שׁוֹשַׁנַּת הָעֲמָקִים Ct 2^{1} (fig. of Shulamite), וְתָגֵל עֲרָבָה וְתִפְרַח כַּחֲבַצָּלֶת׃ Is 35^{1} (*narcissus* Che$^{Is 35, 1}$ cf. Conder$^{PEF, 1878, 46}$ Tristr$^{NHB 476}$ al.)

†חֲבַצִּנְיָה **n.pr.m.** a Rechabite Je 35^{3}, 𝔊 *Χαβασ(ε)ιν*.

†[חָבַק] **vb.** clasp, embrace (NH *id.*; 𝔗 חַבֵּק; Mand. , NSyr. ; Ar. حَبَقَ II. *collect* one's possessions, etc., Frey)—**Qal** *Inf.* לַחֲבוֹק Ec 3^{5}; *Pt.* חֹבֵק Ec 4^{5}; חֹבֶקֶת 2 K 4^{16};—*embrace*, c. acc. בֵּן 2 K 4^{16}; יָדָיו Ec 4^{5} (said of הַכְּסִיל = fold his arms, i.e. be idle; cf. חִבֻּק); no obj. expr. Ec 3^{5} (‖ **Pi**). **Pi.** *Pf.* חִבְּקוּ Jb 24^{8} La 4^{5}; *Impf.* וַיְחַבֵּק Gn 48^{10}; וַיְחַבֶּק־ Gn 29^{13}; וַיְחַבְּקֵהוּ Gn 33^{4}; 3 fs. sf. תְּחַבְּקֵנִי Ct 2^{6} 8^{3}; 2 ms. וּתְחַבֵּק Pr 5^{20}, sf. תְּחַבְּקֶנָּה Pr 4^{8}; *Inf.* חַבֵּק Ec 3^{5};—*embrace* of pers., no obj. עת לִרְחֹק מֵחַבֵּק Ec 3^{5} (‖ **Qal**); sq. לְ Gn 29^{13} (J), 48^{10} (E); sq. sf. 33^{4} (J), Pr 4^{8} Ct 2^{6} 8^{3}; c. acc. Pr 5^{20}; embrace צוּר for want of shelter Jb 24^{8} (of poor); embrace refuse-heaps אשׁפתות La 4^{5}, i.e. are outcasts.

†חִבֻּק **n.[m.]** a clasping, folding of the hands, only cstr. מְעַט ח׳ יָדַיִם לִשְׁכָּב Pr 6^{10} 24^{33} (cf. חָבַק **Qal**).

†חֲבַקּוּק **n.pr.m.** the prophet Habakkuk Hb 1^{1} 3^{1}; 𝔊 Ἀμβακουμ (As. *ḫambakûku* is name of a plant, Dl$^{HA 36, Pr 84}$, so حبقبق in Yemen (Schweinfurth) v. Hom$^{Aufsätze u. Abh. 1892, 27, 28}$).

†[חָבַר] **vb.** unite (usu. intr.), be joined, tie a magic knot or spell, charm (NH *id.*;

Eth. ሐበረ: yet As [*abâru*], *ubburu*, *bind*, *ban* (of spells), *ébru*, friend, and many deriv., Dl W 51 ff; Aram. ܚܒܪ, חֲבַר and many deriv; cf Ph n חבר *associate*)—**Qal** *Pf* 3 mpl חָבְרוּ Gn 14³, *Pt. act* m. חבר Dt 18¹¹, חוֹבֵר ψ 58⁶, fpl חברת Ex 26³·³ + 2 t + Ez 1⁹ (cf infr), חוֹברות Ez 1¹¹, *Pt pass.* cstr. חֲבוּר Ho 4¹⁷ (yet v infr), —**1.** *unite, be joined*: **a.** of allies, sq אֶל־ loc. Gn 14³, constr praegn = *came as allies unto*, pt. pass fig. חֲבוּר עֲצַבִּים אֶפְרָיִם Ho 4¹⁷ *Ephr. is joined to idols* (but We rds חַבֵּר, v חָבֶר **2 d**, and cf. חֲבֵרָיו Is 44¹¹, חֲבֶרְתְּךָ Mal 2¹⁴) **b.** of one thing reaching to, touching another, wings of Ezek's living creatures sq אֶל־ rei, Ez 1⁹ (del. 𝔊 B Co, but v Sm); cf. אִישׁ ח׳ v¹¹, i e *joining each one* (trans), < 𝔊 𝔖 Co ח׳ אִשָּׁה אֶל־אֲחוֹתָהּ (as v⁹), *united each to the other*; so of curtains of tabernacle, sq אֶל־ rei Ex 26³·³, abs *joined together*, of shoulderpieces of ephod Ex 28⁷ (all P; cf. also **Pu**). **2.** *tie magic knots, charm* (RS JPh xiv 1885 123 thinks mng *charm* is der. fr. *nectere verba*, and comp Ar خَبَرٌ, *narrative*), only c acc. cogn. ח׳ חָבֶר Dt 18¹¹ (in a long series of kindred phrases), specif. of charming serpents ψ 58⁶ (|| מְלַחֲשִׁים). **Pi.** *Pf* 3 ms חִבֵּר Ex 36¹⁰, 2 ms. וְחִבַּרְתָּ Ex 26⁶ + 2 t., *Impf* וַיְחַבֵּר Ex 36¹⁰ + 2 t., sf וַיְחַבְּרֵהוּ 2 Ch 20³⁶, *Inf cstr* לְחַבֵּר Ex 36¹⁸,—**1.** *make an ally of, unite* one with, only וַיְחַבְּרֵהוּ עִמּוֹ 2 Ch 20³⁶ *and he united him with himself*, sq. Inf of purpose. **2.** *unite, join* (trans), only Ex (P), of tabern., obj. the curtains, sq acc. + אֶל־ rei Ex 26⁶ 36¹⁰·¹⁰·¹³, sq acc only 26⁹ 36¹⁶, obj אֶת־הָאֹהֶל *join the tent together*, 26¹¹ 36¹⁸ **Pu** *Pf.* 3 ms חֻבַּר Ex 39⁴, וְחֻבָּר consec. Ex 28⁷ (but v infr), 3 fs שֶׁחֻבְּרָה־ ψ 122³, *Impf.* 3 ms יְחֻבַּר Ec 9⁴ Qr (Kt יבחר v. infr.), sf. הַיְחָבְרְךָ ψ 94²⁰ (Kö¹ ²⁵⁷ f, Ges Ew Bo De al as **Qal**); —**1. a** *be allied with* thee (sf ref. to י׳) ψ 94²⁰; **b.** *be united to* = be one of, מִי אֲשֶׁר יְח׳ אֶל כָּל־ הַחַיִּים *whoever is united to all the living* (Kt יבחר is meaningless) **2.** *be joined together*, of ephod עַל־שְׁנֵי קְצוֹוֹתָו ח׳ Ex 39⁴ *by its two edges was it joined together*, cf. || 28⁷ (where MT ק׳ עַל־ש׳ < 𝔊 Sam which rd. אֶל־שְׁנֵי קְצוֹתָיו וְחֻבָּר), עִיר שֶׁחֻ׳־לָהּ ψ 122³ *joined together for itself*, i e compactly built (of Jerusalem). **Hiph.** *Impf* 1 s אַחְבִּירָה עֲלֵיכֶם בְּמִלִּים Jb 16⁴ *I could make a joining with words* (i e. *join words together* RV VB) *against you* **Hithp.** (late) *Pf.* אֶתְחַבַּר (Ges § 54. 1 a) 2 Ch 20³⁵; *Impf.* יִתְחַבְּרוּ Dn 11⁶; *Inf.* sf. הִתְחַבֶּרְךָ 2 Ch 20³⁷, Aram form הִתְחַבְּרוּת Dn 11²³ (Ges § 54. 2 B 1),—*join oneself* to, *make an alliance* with, sq. עִם pers. 2 Ch 20³⁵·³⁷, sq. אֶל־ pers Dn 11²³; recipr. *league together* (abs.) Dn 11⁶.

†I. חֶבֶר **n.[m.]** **company, association, spell**—abs. חָבֶר Dt 18¹¹ + 2 t, cstr. חֶבֶר Ho 6⁹, pl חֲבָרִים ψ 58⁶, sf. חֲבָרַיִךְ Is 47⁹·¹¹,—**1.** *company, band* of (bad) priests Ho 6⁹. **2.** *association, society* (abstr.), only in בֵּית חָבֶר Pr 21⁹ = 25²⁴ *house of association*, i. e. shared with a contentious woman (*house in common*, v. RVᵐ VB) **3. spell**: **a.** as acc. cogn c חָבַר (q v) Dt 18¹¹ ψ 58⁶. **b.** alone, of Babylonian magic Is 47⁹·¹¹ (v. Len Chald Magic [1878]; Magie u. Wahrsagekunst, 1878; Scholz Götzendienst u. Zauberwesen, 1877, 80 ff Say TBA III 145 ff. and Bel Bab 396 ff 440 ff.).

†II. חֶבֶר, חֵבֶר **n.pr.m. 1.** חֶבֶר (𝔊 Χαβερ) the Kenite, husband of Deborah Ju 4¹¹·¹⁷·¹⁷·²¹ 5²⁴. **2.** a man of Asher חֶבֶר Gn 46¹⁷ (P) 𝔊 Χοβωρ 1 Ch 7³¹·³² 𝔊 Χαβερ 𝔊L Ιεχοβερ, חֵבֶר Nu 26⁴⁵ 𝔊 Χοβερ, on poss identif with *Habiri* of Tel el Amaina v. Jastr JBL 1892, xi 118 ff. 1893, xii 61 ff **3.** חֶבֶר name in Judah 1 Ch 4¹⁸ 𝔊 Αβεισα, 𝔊L Αβερ **4.** חֶבֶר a Benjamite 1 Ch 8¹⁷ 𝔊 Αβαρ, 𝔊L Αβερ

†חֶבְרִי **adj.gent.** of **2** supr, only c art. = n coll מִשְׁפַּחַת הַחֶבְרִי Nu 26⁴⁵ (𝔊 Χοβερ(ε)ι)

†חֶבְרָה **n.f. association, company** (abstr) וְאָרַח לְח׳ עִם פֹּעֲלֵי אָוֶן Jb 34⁸ *and he goeth for company with doers of wickedness* (|| וְלָלֶכֶת עִם־אַנְשֵׁי־רֶשַׁע)

†חָבֵר **adj.** and **n.m.** Ct 8. 13, **united, associate, companion**—ח׳ abs Pr 28²⁴ ψ 119⁶³; sf חֲבֵרוֹ Ec 4¹⁰ (+ 3 t Ez Kt, Qr חֲבֵרָיו, v infr.), pl חֲבֵרִים Ju 20¹¹ Ct 8¹³; cstr חַבְרֵי Is 1²³, sf. חֲבֵרֶךָ ψ 45⁸, חֲבֵרֶיךָ Ct 1⁷; חֲבֵרָיו Is 44¹¹ + 3 t Ez Qr;—**1.** adj *united* כְּאִישׁ אֶחָד חֲבֵרִים Ju 20¹¹ *knit together as one man* (AV RV) **2. n.** *associate, fellow*: **a.** of children (tribes) of Isr. assoc with Judah as head Ez 37¹⁶, id. assoc. with Joseph (Ephr) as head v¹⁶·¹⁹ (in all these rd Qr חֲבֵרָיו). **b.** of like rank ψ 45⁸ **c.** of like calling Ct 1⁷. **d.** *worshippers* (associates, belonging to the society or guild) of idols Is 44¹¹ (v Che; > others *priests*, Geiger Urschr. 121 493 SS, cf חֶבֶר Ho 6⁹, Du rds חֲבָרִים *enchantments*) **e.** in gen. Ct 8¹³. **f.** implying likeness of character Is 1²³ Pr 28²⁴ ψ 119⁶³ **3.** *companion* at a particular time Ec 4¹⁰.

†[חַבֶּ֫רֶת] **n.f. consort,** i.e. wife וְהִיא חֲבֶרְתְּךָ Mal 2^{14} (‖ אֵשֶׁת בְּרִיתֶ֑ךָ)

†חֹבֶ֫רֶת **n.f. a thing that joins or is joined,** only of the *curtain-pieces* of the tabernacle, as *joined together* :—הַח׳ Ex 26^{10} 36^{17}, בַּחֹבָ֑רֶת Ex $26^{4.10}$.

†[חַבָּר] **n.m. associate, partner** in a trade or calling, only יִכְרוּ עָלָיו חַבָּרִים Jb 40^{30} *will partners* (i.e. those engaged in the catch) *make traffic upon it* (the crocodile)?

†חַבּוּרָה, [חַבֻּרָה, חַבֻּרָה] **n.f. stripe, blow;**—abs חַבּ׳ Is 1^{6} + 2 t; sf. חַבֻּרָתִי Gn 4^{23}; חֲבֻרָתוֹ Is 53^{5}, pl. cstr חַבֻּרוֹת Pr 20^{30}, sf. חַבּוּרֹתָ֑י ψ 38^{6}.—*stripe, blow, stroke,* Gn 4^{23} *my blow,* i.e. for *striking me* (J), cf. Ex $21^{25.25}$ (JE), also of injury to land of Judah (under fig. of human body) Is 1^{6} (all ‖ פֶּצַע, v. infr.); of blows (sg. coll.) inflicted on suffering servant of י׳ Is 53^{5}; (pl.) ψ 38^{6}, חַבֻּרוֹת פֶּצַע Pr 20^{30}, i.e. *blows that cut in* (‖ מַכּוֹת)

†[חֲבַרְבֻּרָה] **n.f. stripe, mark,** only pl sf. חֲבַרְבֻּרֹתָיו Je 13^{23} of stripes on a panther (tiger? cf. נָמֵר ;—‖ עוֹרוֹ of a Cushite)

†I. חֶבְרוֹן **n.pr.loc. Hebron** (*association, league*)—ח׳ Gn 13^{18}+; c ה loc חֶבְרוֹנָה Jos 10^{36} + 6t.; חֶבְרֹ֑נָה 2 S 2^{1},—𝔊 Χεβρων; mod *El-Ḫalîl* (v. Rob $^{BR\ i.\ 213\ f.\ ii\ 73\ ff}$ Guérin $^{Judée\ iii.\ 214\ ff}$); ancient city in southern Judah, where (or near which) Abr. built an altar Gn 13^{18}(J), and where was a sanctuary in Dvd.'s time 2 S 15^{7}, cf. לִפְנֵי י׳ בח׳ 2 S 5^{3} = 1 Ch 11^{3}, built 7 yrs. bef. Soan in Egypt acc. to Nu 13^{22b} (JE); under a king Jos $10^{3.5.23}$ (JE) 12^{10}(D); assigned to Caleb Jos $14^{13.14}$(JED) Ju 1^{20} yet v 1 Ch 6^{40} (cf v^{41}); older name קִרְיַת (הָ)אַרְבַּע acc to Jos 14^{15} (JED), cf Gn 23^{2} 35^{27} Jos 15^{54} 20^{7} (all P) Ju 1^{10b}, v. also Jos 15^{13} 21^{11} (both P); called also מַמְרֵא Gn 23^{19} (and 35^{27}, both P); a city of refuge Jos 21^{13}(P) = 1 Ch 6^{42}, עֵמֶק ח׳ Gn 37^{14} (J); named elsewhere Nu 13^{22a} (JE) Jos $10^{36.39}$ 11^{21} (all D) Ju 1^{10a} 16^{3} 2 S 2^{32} 15^{9} 2 Ch 11^{10}; a resort of David, and for 7 yrs. his royal city 1 S 30^{31} 2 S $2^{1.11}$ $3^{2.5.19.20.22.27.32}$ $4^{1.8.12.12}$ $5^{1.3.13}$ 1 K 2^{11} 1 Ch $3^{1.4}$ $11^{1.3}$ $12^{24.39}$ (van d H. $v^{23.38}$) 29^{27}; rd. also perh for תחתו 2 S 3^{12}, 𝔊L εἰς Χεβρων, cf. Dr; seat of Absalom's rebellion 2 S 15^{10}; עָרֵי ח׳ 2 S 2^{3} abode of David's men.

II. חֶבְרוֹן **n.pr.m.** (𝔊 Χεβρων) **1.** grandson of Levi Ex 6^{18} Nu 3^{19} (both P) = 1 Ch 5^{28} = 6^{3}, $23^{12.19}$, cf. 15^{9}. **2.** name in Caleb's family 1 Ch $2^{42.43}$.

†חֶבְרֹנִי, חֶבְרוֹנִי **adj gent.** of II. חֶבְרוֹן **1**:—alw c art. as subst. coll., לַחֶבְרוֹנִי 1 Ch $26^{23.30.31.31}$, מִשְׁפַּחַת הַחֶבְרֹנִי Nu 3^{27} 26^{58}.

†מַחְבֶּ֫רֶת **n.f. thing joined, place of joining,**—abs. מ׳ Ex 26^{4} + 3 t; מַחְבָּ֑רֶת Ex $36^{11.17}$, sf. מַחְבַּרְתּוֹ Ex 28^{27} 39^{20};—**1.** *thing joined,* of curtain-pieces of tabernacle (cf. חֹבֶרֶת), Ex $26^{4.5}$ $36^{11.11.12}$. **2.** *place of joining.* **a.** of the curtains Ex 36^{17}. **b.** of shoulder-pieces of the ephod Ex 28^{27} 39^{20} (all P)

†[מְחַבְּרָה] **n.f. binder, clamp, joint,** only pl abs מְחַבְּרוֹת, of iron, *clamps* or the like, 1 Ch 22^{3}, of wood, *binder,* or *coupling,* 2 Ch 34^{11}.

†חָבוֹר **n.pr.fl.** called נְהַר גּוֹזָן 2 K 17^{6} = 18^{11}, erron. 1 Ch 5^{26} וְח׳ וְהָרָא וּנְהַר גּוֹזָן, 𝔊 (Χ)αβωρ, Gk Χαβωρας, etc., Assyr *Ḫabur,* flowing into Euphrates fr. E (Dl $^{Pa\ 183\ ff}$ KAT$^{2\ 275.\ 614}$ COT$^{i.\ 267}$), v גּוֹזָן.

חֲבֻרָתוֹ v. חַבּוּרָה supr.

†[חָבַשׁ] **vb. bind, bind on, bind up** (NH *id.,* As. *abâšu,* acc to Dl $^{W\ 70.\ Pr\ 174}$; Ar. حَبَسَ *confine, restrict;* yet on As *ḫibšu 'Kopfbinde'* (c. ח), etc., v. Zehnpfund $^{BAS\ i.\ 490.\ 526}$, Aram ܚܒܫ, cf. ܚܒܘܫܝܐ, חֲבוּשְׁיָא *imprisonment,* etc.)—**Qal** *Pf.* 2 ms. וְחָבַשְׁתָּ Ex 29^{9}; 2 mpl. חֲבַשְׁתֶּם Ez 34^{4}, *Impf.* יַחֲבֹשׁ Jb 34^{17}, וַיַּחֲבֹשׁ Gn 22^{3} + 4 t, וַיַּחֲבָשׁ־ 1 K 13^{23}; וְיַחְבֹּשׁ Jb 5^{18}; וְיַחְבְּשֵׁנוּ Ho 6^{1}; 3 fs וַתַּחֲבֹשׁ 2 K 4^{24}; אֶחֱבֹשׁ Ez 34^{16}, cohort. אֶחְבְּשָׁה־ 2 S 19^{27} (but cf. infr.), וָאֶחְבָּשֵׁךְ Ez 16^{10}; וַיַּחְבְּשׁוּ־ 1 K 13^{13}, וַיַּחְבְּשׁוּ 1 K 13^{27}; *Imv* חֲבֹשׁ Jb 40^{13}, חִבְשׁוּ Ez 24^{17}, חִבְשׁוּ 1 K $13^{13.27}$, *Inf. cstr.* חֲבֹשׁ Is 30^{26} 61^{1}; לְחָבְשָׁה Ez 30^{21} (del. Co, cf 𝔊) *Pt act* חֹבֵשׁ Is 3^{7}, *pass.* חָבוּשׁ Jon 2^{6}, חֲבֻשִׁים Ju 19^{10}; חֲבֻשִׁים 2 S 16^{1} Ez 27^{24},—**1.** *bind, bind on.* **a.** headgear, c. acc rei, לְ pers. Ex 29^{9} Lv 8^{13} (both P), c. עַל pers. Ez 24^{17} (P); *pass* of seaweeds clinging about head סוּף חָבוּשׁ לְרֹאשִׁי Jon 2^{6}, c. sf pers. et בְּ rei וָאֶחְבָּשֵׁךְ Ez 16^{10} *and I bound* (or *wound*) *about thee* (i.e thy head, Sm VB) שֵׁשׁ (in metaph. of י׳'s care for Jerus.; ‖ אַנְעִלֵךְ, אַלְבִּישֵׁךְ); fig. of punishment for wicked פְּנֵיהֶם חֲבֹשׁ בַּטָּמוּן Jb 40^{13} *bind their faces in darkness* (‖ טָמְנֵם בֶּעָפָר) v. Di. **b.** pass. prob. *twined, twisted* in חֲבָלִים חֲבֻשִׁים וַאֲרֻזִים Ez 27^{24}, *cords twisted and strong,* v Sm Da. Esp **c.** of equipping a beast for riding; ass, in acc. Gn 22^{3} Nu 22^{21} (both E), 2 S 17^{23} & 19^{27} (where however rd לִי חִבְשָׁה־לִּי, so 𝔊 𝔖 𝔙 Th We Dr),

1 K 2^{40} 13$^{13.13.23.27.27}$ (v^{27b} no dir. obj expressed) 2 K 4^{24}, pass, also of asses, Ju 19^{10} 2 S 16^{1}. **d.** fig. = *restrain, control* (Germ *bändigen*), abs. Jb 34^{17}. **2.** *bind up*, viz a wound, usually in fig, of comforting the distressed, etc, c. sf pers Ho 6^{1} (‖ רָפָא, opp הִכָּה), sq. לְ pers לַחֲבֹשׁ לְנִשְׁבְּרֵי־לֵב Is 61^{1}; cf Ez 34^{4} (sq לַנִּשְׁבֶּרֶת, ‖ רפא, חִזֵּק), v^{16} (sq *id*; ‖ חזק), sq acc rei ביום חֲבֹשׁ י׳ אֶת־שֶׁבֶר עַמּוֹ Is 30^{26} (‖ רָפָא), c acc of Pharaoh's broken arm Ez 30^{21} (several, v supr.; cf. **Pu.**), abs Jb 5^{18}, also Is 3^{7} of repairing fortunes of people (opp הכאיב, ‖ רָפָא = רָפָה) **Pi.** *Pf* חִבֵּשׁ *bind, restrain* מִבְּכִי נהרות Jb 28^{11}, *Pt* מְחַבֵּשׁ *bind up* לְעַצְּבוֹתָם ψ 147^{3} **Pu.** *Pf be bound up* חֻבָּשָׁה Ez 30^{21} (metaph) Pharaoh's broken arm, חֻבָּשׁוּ Is 1^{6} (wounds of land of Judah)

חבת (√ of foll; cf Ar خَبَتَ *be obscure*, iv *be lowly, submissive*, خَبْتٌ *low ground*)

† **חֲבִתִּים** **n.[m.]pl.** (NH *id*)—some kind of **flat cakes, or bread-wafers**, only מַעֲשֵׂה הַח׳ 1 Ch 9^{31}.

† **מַחֲבַת** **n.f. flat plate, pan, or griddle** for baking, only P and late, abs מ׳ Lv 2^{5} + 2 t, מַחֲבַת Lv 7^{9}, cstr מַחֲבַת Ez 4^{3},—**1.** used in preparing the (baken) *mincha*, preceded by עַל־ Lv 2^{5} 6^{14} 7^{9} (all P), cf 1 Ch 23^{29} **2.** מ׳ בַּרְזֶל Ez 4^{3} *a plate of iron*, signifying an iron wall, in prediction of siege of city

חָגָא, חָג v sub חגג

חגב (√ of foll, mng dub, poss. cf Ar حَجَبَ *prevent, intervene, hide*, حِجَابٌ *that which veils, conceals, hides*, Syr ܡܚܓܒܐ *shrine*, hence *locusts* as *concealing* the sky ?)

† I. **חָגָב** **n.m.**$^{Ec 12,5}$ **locust, grasshopper** (NH *id*, cf ﺝ), prob a non-flying species, v Kn in Di$^{Lv 11,22}$, הֶחָגָב allowed as food Lv 11^{22} (P, ‖ אַרְבֶּה, סָלְעָם, חַרְגֹּל), כַּחֲגָבִים Nu 13^{33} (JE, sim of insignificance), so Is 40^{22}, as agent of Yahweh's wrath חָגָב לֶאֱכוֹל הארץ 2 Ch 7^{13}, ויסתבל הֶחָגָב Ec 12^{5} *and the grasshopper shall be a burden*; better *shall drag itself along*, De Hi Now RV^{m}, De thinks ח׳ here fig of the back part of the pelvic cavity (Ar. حَجَبَةٌ is *point of hip-bone*, Bo, cf Lane), and refers to stiffness of aged joints, so Now, but the meaning is dubious, v. other views in Comm

† II. **חָגָב** **n.pr.m.** head of a family of returning exiles Ezr 2^{46} 𝔊 Ἀγαβ (no ‖ in Ne 7 H; but 𝔊L Ne 7^{48} has both Αγαβ and Αγαβα, cf חֲגָבָא)

† **חֲגָבָא** **n.pr.m.** head of a family of returning exiles Ne 7^{48}, 𝔊 Ἀγαβα (cf. also foregoing) prob = following

† **חֲגָבָה** **n.pr.m.** head of a family of returning exiles Ezr 2^{47}, prob = foregoing, 𝔊 Ἀγαβα

† **[חָגַג]** **vb. make pilgrimage, keep a pilgrim-feast** (Ar. حَجَّ *betake oneself to or towards an object of reverence, make a pilgrimage to Mecca*; Sab. חגג *make pilgrimage* Sab Denkm 86 cf 85, Syr ܚܰܓ *celebrate a feast* In Palm חגגו is n pr Vog$^{No 61}$, cf also Ph. n.pr חגי, חגת),—**Qal** *Pf* 2 mpl חַגֹּתֶם Ex 12^{14} + 2 t.; *Impf* 2 ms תָּחֹג Ex 23^{14} Dt 16^{15}, 3 mpl. יָחֹגּוּ ψ 107^{27} (Bö § 1118(2)), וְיָחֹגּוּ Ex 5^{1}, 2 mpl תָּחֹגּוּ Lv 23$^{39.41}$, *sf* תְּחָגֻּהוּ Ex 12^{14}, *Imv.* f חָגִּי Na 2^{1}; *Inf* cstr. חֹג Zc 14^{18} + 2 t, *Pt* חוֹגֵג ψ 42^{5}, pl חֹגְגִים 1 S 30^{16},—**1.** *keep a pilgrim-feast*, abs Ex 5^{1} (JE) cf one proposed by Moses, שָׁלֹשׁ רְגָלִים תָּחֹג לִי *three times shalt thou make pilgrimage unto me* (in the year) Ex 23^{14} (covt code), of pilgrim-feasts in general Na 2^{1}, the Passover Ex 12^{14} (P), elsewh feast of Booths, all celebrated in part by sacred processions and dances, הָמוֹן חוֹגֵג ψ 42^{5} *multitude keeping festival* (led by the Psalmist in procession), חגג חג Lv 23^{39} (H), Nu 29^{12} (P), Na 2^{1} Zc 14$^{16.18.19}$, חגג אתו חג Ex 12^{14} (P), Lv 23^{41} (H); אתו Lv 23^{41} (H), sf Ex 12^{14} (P). **2.** behave as at a חַג 1 S 30^{16} (of the Amalekites when surprised by David i e *enjoying themselves merrily*, Dr; others, *circling in the sacred dance*) **3.** *reel*, in giddiness on the sea ψ 107^{27} (cf חָגָּא Is 19^{17}), this either points to an earlier meaning of √, or better, the ψ being late, means *reel* as from festival excesses (‖ וְיָנוּעוּ כַּשִּׁכּוֹר)

† **חַג** **n.m.**$^{Is 29,1}$ **festival-gathering, feast, pilgrim-feast** (NH *id.*, Aram ܚܰܓܳܐ, חַגָּא; Ar. حَجّ *pilgrimage*, Sab חג DHM$^{Epigr Denkm 31}$, Nö$^{ZMG 1887 719}$, RS$^{Proph Lect. ii n 6}$; > We$^{Skizzen iii 106, 165}$ *sacred dance*)—חַג abs and cstr Ex 10^{9} + 36 t; חָג Nu 28^{17} + 13 t; sf חַגִּי Ex 23^{18}, חַגֶּךָ Dt 16^{14}; חַגָּהּ Ho 2^{13}, חַגֵּנוּ ψ 81^{4}; pl חַגִּים Is 29^{1} + 2 t, sf. חַגַּיִךְ Na 2^{1}, חַגֵּיכֶם Am 5^{21} + 2 t,—**1.** *feast*, esp one observed by a *pilgrimage* (Ex 23$^{14.17}$) **a.** *special feast* to the golden calf Ex 32^{5} (J, where there was a

sacred dance v^{19}), a feast in the 8th month observed by Jeroboam in place of the feast of the 7th month in Judah 1 K 12$^{32.33}$, pilgrim feast proposed by Moses Ex 10^{9} (JE); feast at Shiloh Ju 21^{19}. Elsewhere **b.** apparently always of the three great pilgrim feasts, celebrated by processions and dancing (1) *in general* Is 30^{29} Am 8^{10} Na 2^{1}; חגים ינקפו *let feasts come round* Is 29^{1}, ||עצרות Am 5^{21}; חג י׳ Lv 23^{41}(H); disting fr. the more gen. מועדים (sacred seasons) Ez 45^{17} 46^{11} Ho 9^{5} (יום חג), and fr specif חדשים, שבתות as well, Ho 2^{13}, (2) in particular: unleavened cakes and Passover חג (ה)מצות Ex 23^{15} = 34^{18}(JE), Lv 23^{6}(P), Dt 16^{16} 2 Ch 8^{13} 30$^{13.21}$ 35^{17} Ezr 6^{22}; חג Ex 12^{14}(P); first day of the seven Nu 28^{17}(P); the last day Ex 13^{6} (J); the seven Ez 45$^{21.23}$; חג הפסח Ex 34^{25}, חגי Ex 23^{18} (both JE); בַּכֶּסֶה לְיוֹם חַגֵּנוּ ψ 81^{4} (probably the full moon of Passover); חג הקציר Ex 23^{16} = חג שבעת Ex 34^{22}(JE), cf. Dt 16$^{10.16}$ 2 Ch 8^{13}; חג האס(י)ף Ex 23^{16} = 34^{22} (JE) = חג הסכ(ו)ת Lv 23^{34}(P), Dt 16$^{13.16}$ 31^{10} 2 Ch 8^{13} Ezr 3^{4} Zc 14$^{16.18.19}$; also חג י׳ Lv 23^{39} (H), הֶחָג 1 K 8$^{2.65}$ = 2 Ch 5^{3} 7$^{8.9}$, Ez 45 Ne 8^{14}; חַגֶּךָ (i.e. of people) Dt 16^{14}; 7 days Nu 29^{12}(P), Ne 8^{18}.—Vbs. c. חג are חגג Lv 23$^{39.41}$ (H), Ex 12^{14} Nu 29^{12} (P), Na 2^{1} Zc 14$^{16.18.19}$; שמר Ex 23^{15} = 34^{18}(JE), התקדש Is 30^{29}, but usually עשה Ex 34^{22} (JE), Dt 16$^{10.13}$ 1 K 8^{65} 12$^{32.33}$ 2 Ch 7$^{8.9}$ 30$^{13.21}$ 35^{17} Ezr 3^{4} 6^{22} Ne 8^{18}. **2.** *festival sacrifice* (cf. NH חֲגִיגָה) ψ 118^{27} (see מזבח **12**); Mal 2^{3} (RV after Thes Ke al., but AV Ew Or *feast*)

†חָגָּא **n.[f.]** reeling (Aramaism for חגה Ew §173b, by copyist's err. Di)—וְהָיְתָה...לְמִצְרַיִם לְח׳ Is 19^{17} and the land of Judah *shall become to Egypt a reeling*, i.e. Egypt shall reel in terror at the sight of it (||יִפְחָד, this mng may either be fr. an orig. sense of חגג, or = be excited as at a חָג, cf. חגג **3**).

†חַגַּי **n.pr m.** (*festal*, Ph. חגי, חגת, Palm. חגגו Vog No 61)—the prophet Haggai Hg 1$^{1.3.12.13}$ 2$^{1.10.13.14.20}$ Ezr 5^{1} 6^{14}, 𝔊 Ἀγγαῖος

†חַגִּי **n.pr.m.** (*festal*) **1.** 𝔊 Ἀγγις, son of Gad Gn 46^{16} Nu 26^{15}(both P) **2. adj. gent.** as subst. coll., c. art. Nu 26^{15} (P)

†חַגִּיָּה **n.pr.m.** (*feast of Yah*) a Levite, son of Shimea 1 Ch 6^{15}, 𝔊 Ἀγγια.

†חַגִּית **n.pr.f.** (*festal*) wife of David and mother of Adonijah 2 S 3^{4} 1 K 1$^{5.11}$ 2^{13} 1 Ch 3^{2}, 𝔊 Ἀγγιθ.

חגה (√of foll.; cf. Ar حَجَا *conceal*; حَجًا, حَجًى *place of refuge, protection*).

†[חֲגָוִים] **n.m.pl.** places of concealment, retreats, as abode of dove יוֹנָתִי בְּחַגְוֵי הַסֶּלַע Ct 2^{14} (in metaph.), also, hyperbol., as abode of Edom שֹׁכְנִי בח׳ (ה)סלע Je 49^{16} Ob^{3}.

חגל (√of foll.; Ar حَجَلَ, *hobble, hop*, whence حَجَل *partridge*, cf Syr. ܚܓܠܐ, ܚܓܠܐ, *id*)

†חָגְלָה **n.pr.f.** (=*partridge*, v. supr)—a daughter of Selophchad of Manasseh Nu 26^{33} 27^{1} 36^{11} Jos 17^{3} (all P), 𝔊 Ἐγλα, A Αιγλα(μ). On n pr loc. בית ח׳ v p 111 b

†[חָגַר] **vb.** gird, gird on, gird oneself (NH *id.*, Aram חֲגַר; Ar. حَجَرَ *hinder, restrain*, so Syr. ܚܓܪ; As *agâru, surround*, in deriv., Dl W 105 ff, Sab. מחגרת (cf Ar مَحَاجِر, مَحْجِر *enclosed space, district*, etc), DHM in MV; also n pr. dei and loc. חגר, Sab. Denkm 3.81.93 CIS iv 1, No. 49 etc.)—**Qal** *Pf* 3 fs חָגְרָה Pr 31^{17}, 2 ms וְחָגַרְתָּ Ex 29^{9}, 3 pl חָגְרוּ Is 15^{3} La 2^{10}; וח׳ consec Ez 7^{18} 27^{31}, *Impf.* 3 ms. יַחְגֹּר Lv 16^{4}, וַיַּחְגֹּר Lv 8$^{7.7}$ + 4 t; sf. יַחְגְּרֶהָ ψ 109^{19}, 2 ms תַּחְגֹּר ψ 76^{11} (but on txt. v infr.), 3 mpl יַחְגְּרוּ Ez 44^{18} 2 S 22^{46} (but on txt. of both v. infr.), וַיַּחְגְּרוּ 1 S 25^{13} 1 K 20^{32}; 3 fpl תַּחְגֹּרְנָה ψ 65^{13}; 2 mpl. וַתַּחְגְּרוּ Dt 1^{41}, *Imv* ms. חֲגֹר 2 K 4^{29} 9^{1}, חֲגוֹר ψ 45^{4}, fs חִגְרִי Je 6^{26}; mpl. חִגְרוּ 1 S 25^{13} + 3 t; fpl חֲגֹרְנָה Je 49^{3}, cf חֲגוֹרָה Is 32^{11} (v. infr), *Inf cstr* לַחְגֹּר Is 22^{12}; *Pt. act* חגר 1 K 20^{11} 2 K 3^{21}; *pass* m חָגוּר Ju 18^{11} + 5 t.; f. cstr. חֲגֻרַת Jo 1^{8}, pl. חֲגֻרִים Ex 12^{11} Ju 18^{16}, חֲגֻרִים Dn 10^{5},—**1.** trans., *gird* some one, with girdle, c. 2 acc Ex 29^{9} Lv 8^{13} (both P), pass., *girded* with ephod (acc.) 1 S 2^{18} 2 S 6^{14}; sq. ב Dn 10^{5}, c acc and ב, fig. Pr 31^{17}, חגרה בעוז מתניה Lv 8$^{7.7}$ (P), c. acc מתנים *gird up thy loins*, i.e. make ready to go 2 K 4^{29} 9^{1}, pass. Ex 12^{11} (P); cf. prob also חֲגוֹרָה עַל־חֲלָצַיִם Is 32^{11} *gird upon the loins* (2nd acc. om.), on verb form as Imv. fpl v AE Ki Ew §226a Di Du, > as ms Ol §234a Ges §48.5 Sta §591d Ko §20.12. **2.** *gird on, bind on* (=gird oneself with), a girdle ψ 109^{19} (in sim.), so esp c. acc. שַׂק, שַׂקִּים of mourning Is 15^{3} 22^{12} La 2^{10} Ez 7^{18} 27^{31} 2 S 3^{31} Je 4^{8} 6^{26} 49^{3}; also 1 K 20^{32} (c. acc שק + ב bef. מתנים), pass., sq על bef obj of mourning Jo 1^{8} (sim.), abs (שק om.) Jo 1^{13}(||ספדו); sq. חֶרֶב 1 S 25$^{13.13}$ Dt 1^{41}, ψ 45^{4} ח׳ חרב על יָרֵךְ, so Ju 3^{16}, 1 S 17^{39} (sq acc. + מֵעַל); c. acc. cogn ח׳ חגורה 2 K 3^{21};

abs. 1 K 20^{11}, pass Ju $18^{11\,16\,17}$ 2 S 20^{8b} (where rd. חֶרֶב Klo Dr—not We), 21^{16}, rd perh also חָגֻר for חֲגוֹר 20^{8*}, so Klo Dr **3.** intr *gird oneself*, sq בְּ rei Lv 16^{4} (P), so לֹא יַח׳ בַּיָּזַע *they shall not gird themselves with sweat* (?), but del. 𝔖 Co Sgfr; c acc rei (fig) גִּיל גְּבָעוֹת תַּח׳ ψ 65^{13} *with rejoicing the hills gird themselves*, cf שְׁאֵרִית חֵמֹת תַּח׳ ψ 76^{11} *with a remnant* (*residue*) *of wraths thou girdest thyself*, so Hi Hup De VB, but very doubtful, 𝔊 Bo Ew rd תָּחֹגֶּךָּ for תַּחְגֹּר; Bae Ka omit line as corrupt, cf further Che and crit n —וְיַחְגְּרוּ 2 S 22^{46} is txt err for וְיַחְרְגוּ, cf ‖ ψ 18^{46}, so Now Hup Kit al

†**חֲגוֹר** **n.**[**m.**] **belt, girdle** (distinct fr אֵזוֹר *waist-cloth*, Che[Je in Pulpit Comm. (1883) 333 Jerem., Life and Times (1888) 161] RS[JQ Jan 1892 299 ff.])—חֲגוֹר for sword 2 S 20^{8} (yet rd prob חָגֻר, Th We Klo Dr), cf 1 S 18^{4}, article of commerce Pr 31^{24} (coll.? or of a richly adorned girdle?)

†[**חָגוּר**] **adj** **girt, girded,** only pl cstr; חֲגוֹרֵי אֵזוֹר Ez 23^{15} *girded with a waist-cloth.*

†**חֲגוֹרָה** **n.f.** **girdle, loin-covering, belt** —חֲגוֹרָה Is 3^{24}; חֲגֹרָה 2 S 18^{11} 2 K 3^{21}, sf חֲגֹרָתוֹ 1 K 2^{5}; Pl חֲגֹרֹת Gn 3^{7},—*girdle, loin-covering* Gn 3^{7} (J); as article of women's dress Is 3^{24}, *belt* of warrior 1 K 2^{5} 2 K 3^{21} (חגר ח׳), cf. 2 S 18^{11}—On חֲגוֹרָה Is 32^{11} v חָגַר **1.**

†**מַחֲגֹרֶת** **n f.** **a girding, cincture,** only cstr.; תַּחַת פְּתִיגִיל מַחֲגֹרֶת שָׂק Is 3^{24} *instead of a mantle a girding of sackcloth*

I. חַד Ez 33^{30} v. אֶחָד

II חַד v. sub חדד

†[**חָדַד**] **vb.** **be sharp, keen** (Aram. חֲדַד; NH חדד *sharpen*; Ar حَدَّ *be sharp* and *sharpen*, As. Pi *uddudu*, *sharpen*, Dl[Pr 174, W 121])—**Qal** *Pf* וְחַדּוּ מִזְּאֵבֵי עֶרֶב consec Hb 1^{8} *are keener than evening wolves* (of impetuous Chaldean horses) **Hiph.** החד (Che Or Brd) or יָחַד (Nag cf Dr[§ 123 a, R]), ins. Is 44^{12} after 𝔊 𝔖: the smith *sharpeneth* an axe. **Hoph.** *Pf* 3 fs הוּחַדָּה Ez $21^{14\,15\,16}$ *be sharpened* (in all, subj חֶרֶב)—Vid also I חדה

†II. [**חַד**] **adj.** **sharp**—only fs. חַדָּה, of חֶרֶב Ez 5^{1}, in fig of tongue ψ 57^{5}, sim. of mouth Is 49^{2}; fig of end of (i e final experience with) strange woman ח׳ כְּחֶרֶב פִּיּוֹת Pr 5^{4} (‖ מָרָה כַלַּעֲנָה)—I. חַד v sub אֶחָד

עֵין חַדָּה v. חַדָּה.

†[**חַדּוּד**] **adj.** **sharpened, sharp, pointed,** only cstr, with superlat. sense = subst. תַּחְתָּיו חַדּוּדֵי חָרֶשׂ Jb 41^{22} *beneath him the sharpest of potsherds*, of scales of crocodile, cf Di VB

†**חֲדַד** **n.pr.m.** (on this and foll. cf Palm n pr חדודן Vog[No. 96], Sab חדד Hal[27]),—a son of Ishmael Gn 25^{15} (cf Baer's n; van d H. חֲדַר) 𝔊 Χοδδαν, 𝔊L Χοδδαδ, = 1 Ch 1^{30} 𝔊 Χονδαν, A Χοδδαδ, 𝔊L Αδαδ.

†**חָדִיד** **n.pr.loc.** in Benj., mentioned with לֹד and אוֹנוֹ Ezr 2^{33} = Ne 7^{37}; with these and other places Ne 11^{34}, prob = Ἀδιδά 1 Macc 12^{38}, Ἀδίδοις 13^{13}, mod. *El-Hadîte* c. 3½ miles N of E from Lydda, Guérin[Judée i 320] (cf Rob[BR iii. 143]).

†I [**חָדָה**] **vb.** **be or grow sharp,**—**Qal** *grow sharp*, *Impf* apoc = juss יִחַד Pr 27^{17a}; **Hiph.** *sharpen* (fig), *Impf apoc.* יַחַד Pr 27^{17b}; בַּרְזֶל בְּבַרְזֶל יָחַד וְאִישׁ יַחַד פְּנֵי־רֵעֵהוּ *let iron by means of iron grow sharp, and let a man sharpen the countenance* (presence, bearing) *of his friend*,—so Ki[Michl 126 a] De Now Ko[Lgb i 373 f.], cf. Str (who however makes both forms Hiph)

†II [**חָדָה**] **vb.** **rejoice** (As *ḫadû* Dl[Pr 153]; Aram حدا, חֲדָא)—**Qal** *Impf* 3 ms וַיִּחַדְּ Ex 18^{9} (E), and Jethro *rejoiced* over (עַל rei), juss. אַל־יִחַדְּ Jb 3^{6} *let it not rejoice* among (בְּ) the days of the year, i.e not take its place joyfully among them (fig of day of Job's birth)—Klo prop. וְלֹא חָדוּ . . . בְּ 1 S 6^{19} for וַיַּךְ . . . בְּ cf. also Dr **Pi.** *Impf* sf. (causat.) תְּחַדֵּהוּ בְשִׂמְחָה ψ 21^{7} *thou makest him joyful* (Che *cheerest him*) *with gladness* (‖ תְּשִׁיתֵהוּ בְרָכוֹת)

†**חֶדְוָה** **n f** (late) **joy** (Aram חדוא).—ח׳ 1 Ch 16^{27} (in the sanctuary); חֶדְוַת י׳ Ne 8^{10} (‖ אַל־תֵּעָצֵבוּ)

†**יַחְדִּיאֵל** **n.pr.m.** (*God giveth joy*) a chief man in Manasseh 1 Ch 5^{24}, 𝔊 Ιελιηλ, A 𝔊L Ιεδιηλ.

†**יֶחְדְּיָהוּ** **n.pr.m.** (*May* י׳ *give joy!*) **1.** a Levite 1 Ch 24^{20}, 𝔊 Ιεδεια, 𝔊L Ιαδαια **2.** officer of David 1 Ch 27^{30} 𝔊 Ιαδ(α)ιας

†**חָדַל** **vb.** **cease** (Sab חדל *be negligent*, Sab. Denkm [76])—**Qal** *Pf.* חָדַל Gn 18^{11} + 4 t; וְחָדַל cousec. Nu 9^{13} ψ 49^{9}, 2 ms. חָדַלְתָּ Ex 23^{5};

pl. הָדְלוּ Ju 5[6] + 4 t; חָדֵלּוּ (cf. Ko[i. 243]) Ju 5[7] 1 S 2[5]; 1 pl. חָדַלְנוּ Je 44[18]; *Impf* יֶחְדַּל Dt 15[11] + (Jb 10[20] Kt יחדל jussive > Qr וַחֲדַל *Imv*); אֶחְדָּל Ju 15[7] + 3 t.; וְאֶחְדְּלָה Jb 16[6]; pl יֶחְדְּלוּ Ez 2[5] + 2 t; יֶחְדָּלוּן Ex 9[29]; וַיֶּחְדְּלוּ Gn 11[8] Ex 9[33], נֶחְדַּל 1 K 22[15], etc., *Inf. cstr* חֲדֹל 1 S 12[23], *Imv.* חֲדַל Ex 14[12] +, etc., חִדְלוּ Is 1[16] 2[22]; חֲדָלוּ Zc 11[12];—**1.** *cease, come to an end* Ex 9[29.33.34] (J), Is 24[8], impers חָדַל להיות לְשָׂרָה Gn 18[11] (J); *cease to be* Dt 15[11] (sq. מִן), and poet. Ju 5[6.7] 1 S 2[5] Jb 14[7]; = *be lacking, fail* Jb 19[14] Pr 10[19]. **2.** *cease, leave off*, sq. inf c. לְ Gn 11[8] (J), 41[49] (E), Nu 9[13] (P), 1 S 12[23] 23[13] Je 44[18] 51[30] Dt 23[23] ψ 36[4] Pr 19[27] Ru 1[18], inf. alone Is 1[16]; so also Ho 8[10], where read וְחָדְלוּ for וַיָּחֵלּוּ 𝔊 Che We, sq. inf. c. מִן Ex 23[5] (JE), 1 K 15[21] = 2 Ch 16[5], sq. subst. c. מִן (*cease regarding*) Is 2[22] (but Che Du al. treat v. as interpol, om. 𝔊), 1 S 9[5] Pr 23[4], sq מֵאלהים 2 Ch 35[21], i.e leave off provoking God; Ex 14[12] (J), sq מִמֶּנּוּ *desist from us*, let us alone; Jb 7[16]; sq acc. Jb 3[17] ח׳ רֹגֶז, Jb 14[6] *have rest* (i e. cease from being troubled, see Di; cf v[1]), no complem expressed, *cease, forbear* Ju 15[7] 20[28] Am 7[5] 1 K 22[6.15] = 2 Ch 18[5.14], Je 40[4] 41[8] Zc 11[12] ψ 49[9] Jb 16[6] 2 Ch 25[16]; specif. of refusal to hear Ez 2[5.7] 3[11.27] (all opp. שָׁמַע). **Hoph.** *Pf* (contracted) c. interrog. part. הֶחֳדַלְתִּי Ju 9[9.11.13] *should I be made to leave*, sq acc. (cf Ko[i. 240 ff.]); but perh rd. הַחֲדַלְתִּי, **Qal** *Pf.* Stu Be, cf, for acc sq, Jb 3[17].

†חָדֵל **adj.** **forbearing, lacking,** הֶחָדֵל as subst. Ez 3[27] *he that forbeareth* (opp שֹׁמֵעַ, cf. חדל **Qal** ad fin.), cstr. חֲדַל אישים Is 53[3] *lacking men* (i e. forsaken by them);—*ceasing, transient* מֶה־חָדֵל אָנִי ψ 39[5], but rd rather חֶלֶד, v. Che[crit. n]

†[חֶדֶל] **n.[m.]** **cessation,** only יוֹשְׁבֵי חָדֶל Is. 38[11] (so Baer) *inhabitants of* (land of) *cessation*, i e of She'ôl; v. Di; but rd. rather חֶלֶד, v. חָלַד.

†חַדְלַי **n.pr.m.** an Ephraimite, 2 Ch 28[12], 𝔊 Χοαδ, A Αδδι, 𝔊L Αδλι.

חדק (√of foll.; NH חָדַק *press* or *thrust in*, Aram חֲדַק *id* (denom.?))

†חֵדֶק **n.[m.]** **brier** (NH *id.*, Aram חִדְקָא Low[p 147, No 104]; cf. Ar. حَدَقٌ a kind of nightshade, v. Lane[532]),—טוֹבָם כְּחֵדֶק Mi 7[4] *the best of them* (si vera l.) *is like the brier* (|| יָשָׁר מִמְּסוּכָה); דֶּרֶךְ עָצֵל כִּמְשֻׂכַת חָדֶק Pr 15[19] *the way of a sluggard is like a brier-hedge.*

†חִדֶּקֶל **n.pr.fl.** **Tigris** (As. *Idiklat, Diklat*, Old Pers. *Tigrâ* Spieg[APK. Gloss.], etc), the famous Assyr river; v esp. Dl[Pa 110 f. 170 ff.]; ח׳ Gn 2[14], חִדָּקֶל Dn 10[4].

†[חָדַר] **vb.** **surround, enclose** (Ph. in deriv.; Ar. خَدَرَ II. *conceal*, خِدْرٌ *curtain* concealing a person, *chamber, house, or tent* as concealing some one; Eth ኀደረ: *dwell*, v also foll.)—only **Qal** *Pt* fs הַחֹדֶרֶת לָהֶם Ez 21[19] *that which surroundeth them* (of the sword),—so 𝔖 Thes Sm Co Da VB.

†חֶדֶר **n.m.** [1 Ch 28.11] **chamber, room** (NH *id*; Ph. חדר, חדרת; Sab חדר Mordt[ZMG 1876, 24], Eth ማኅደር:)—abs חֶדֶר 2 S 13[10] + 11 t.; הַחַדְרָה Gn 43[30] 1 K 1[15], הַחֶדְרָה Ju 15[1] 2 S 13[10]; cstr. חֶדֶר Ct 3[4], חֲדַר Ex 7[28] + 5 t; sf חֶדְרוֹ Jo 2[16]; pl חֲדָרִים Dt 32[25] Pr 24[4], cstr. חַדְרֵי Pr 7[27] + 8 t; sf חֲדָרֶיךָ Is 26[20], חֲדָרָיו Ct 1[4] 1 Ch 28[11],—*room, chamber*, usually private, as bedroom Gn 43[30] (J), Ju 15[1] 16[9.12] 2 S 13[10.10] 1 K 1[15] Ct 1[4] Is 26[20], Ju 14[18] rd. prob הַחַדְרָה *bridal-chamber* for הַחַרְסָה Sta[ZAW 1884, 253], cf. Jo 2[16] (|| חֻפָּתָהּ of bride), ח׳ הוֹרָתִי Ct 3[4] (|| בית אמי), of kings (of Egypt) ψ 105[30], specif.: ח׳ מִשְׁכָּב *bed-chamber* Ex 7[28] (J), 2 S 4[7] 2 K 6[12] Ec 10[20]; other combinations.—ח׳ הַמְּקֵרָה Ju 3[24] = *cool chamber*, ח׳ הַפְּנִימִים 1 Ch 28[11] *inner chamber*; חדרי מַשְׂכִּיתוֹ Ez 8[12] *his chambers of imagery* (del. Hi Co Sgfr), ח׳ בְּח׳ *a chamber within a chamber*, i.e an innermost chamber 1 K 20[30] 22[25] = 2 Ch 18[24], 2 K 9[2], pl = *store-rooms* Pr 24[4], so ח׳ הַמִּטּוֹת 2 K 11[2] = 2 Ch 22[11], i e. room where beds were stored (Ke Th); metaph ח׳ מָוֶת Pr 7[27] (|| דַּרְכֵי שְׁאוֹל); חדרי תֵמָן Jb 9[9] *chambers of south* (where constellations are treasured up, v. Di; Hoffm thinks of n pr. of star or constell.); cf Jb 37[9] a *chamber* whence comes storm-wind (סוּפָה); חַדְרֵי בָטֶן i.e. inner parts of body, only fig Pr 18[8] = 26[22], 20[27.30]; in Dt 32[25] מֵחֲדָרִים = *within*, poet. for מבית, || מחוץ *without*

†חַדְרָךְ **n.pr.terr.** only Zc 9[1] אֶרֶץ ח׳ (|| דַּמֶּשֶׂק), perh. = As. *Ḫatarakka, Ḫatari(k)ka*, a district near Damascus and Hamath; v. Schr[COT ad loc.], Dl[Pa 279].

†[חָדַשׁ] **vb.** only **Pi.** (and **Hithp.**) **renew, repair** (poet. and late) (NH *id*, Ph. חדש; n. חדש *new moon*, also in קרתחדשת *new-city* =

Carthage; Aram חַדֵּת and חֲדַת, Ar حَدَثَ *be new*, Eth ሐደሰ: I 2 *renew;* Sab. החדת, v. Os(Levy)$^{ZMG\ 1865,\ 204}$ Mordt$^{ZMG\ 1876,\ 30}$, As [*addâšu*], *uddiš, renew, eššu, new*, etc Dl$^{W\ 199\ ff}$)—**Pi.** *Pf* וחדשו consec. Is 61^{4}, *Impf* יְחַדֵּשׁ 2 Ch 15^{8}, 2 ms תְּחַדֵּשׁ Jb 10^{17} ψ 104^{30}, וּנְחַדֵּשׁ 1 S 11^{14}; *Imv* חַדֵּשׁ ψ 51^{12} La 5^{21}; *Inf* לְחַדֵּשׁ 2 Ch 24$^{4.12}$,—**1.** *renew, make anew* הַמְּלוּכָה 1 S 11^{14} (editorial), פני אדמה ψ 104^{30}, רוּחַ ψ 51^{12} (|| בְּרָא),=bring back יָמֵינוּ כְּקֶדֶם La 5^{21}, ח׳ עֵדֶיךָ Jb 10^{17} i e *bringest fresh* (*new*) *witnesses* **2.** *repair*, cities Is 61^{4}, temple 2 Ch 24$^{4.12}$, altar 2 Ch 15^{8} **Hithp.** *Impf* 3 fs תתחדש c pl subj כַּנֶּשֶׁר נְעוּרָיְכִי ח׳ ψ 103^{5} *thy youth reneweth itself, like the eagle.*

†**חָדָשׁ** adj new (on format v Lg$^{BN\ 48}$)—abs ח׳ Ex 1^{8}+19 t, f חֲדָשָׁה Lv 23^{16}+19 t, pl חֲדָשִׁים Dt 32^{17}+10 t, f חֲדָשׁוֹת Is 42^{9} 48^{6},—*new*, usu **a.** attrib Ex 1^{8} (E) *a new king;* so of house Dt 20^{5} ^{22}, wife 24^{5}, cords Ju 15^{13} 16$^{11.12}$, cart 1 S 6^{7} 2 S 6$^{3.3}$ (but del. in v^{b}, cf We Dr)=1 Ch 13^{7}, garment 1 K 11$^{29.30}$, vessel 2 K 2^{20}, wine-skins Jos 9^{13} (JE) Jb 32^{19}, threshing instr Is 41^{15}, meal-offering Lv 23^{16} (H) Nu 28^{26} (P); esp (poet) שִׁיר ח׳ *a new song* (of praise) ψ 33^{3} 40^{4} 96^{1} 98^{1} 144^{9} 149^{1} Is 42^{10}, ברית ח׳ Je 31^{31}, שָׁמַיִם חדשים וארץ חדשה Is 65^{17} cf 66^{22}, שם ח׳ Is 62^{2}; לֵב ח׳ 18^{31} +, רוּחַ ח׳ *a new spirit* Ez 11^{19} 18^{31} 36^{26}, פֶּתַח שַׁעַר־י׳ הַח׳ Je 26^{10} *new gate* of (house of) י׳, cf 36^{10} (v. Gf Je 20^{2}), also הֶחָצֵר הַח׳ 2 Ch 20^{5} *the new court* (v Be Ot), אלהים חדשים Ju 5^{8} *new gods? judges?* txt prob corrupt, cf No$^{ZMG\ 1888,\ 477}$, Mull$^{Königsb.\ Stud\ I}$, GACooke$^{Deb\ 34\ ff}$ and conj by Bu$^{RS.\ 103}$, RS in Bla^{Judges}, in gen אֵין כָּל־ח׳ Ec 1^{9} *there is nothing new*, with no subst expr. חָגוּר חֲדָשָׁה 2 S 21^{16} *girt with a new* (sword but txt perh corrupt, cf We Klo Dr), of (food-)products of earth (opp יָשָׁן) Lv 26^{10} (H) Ct 7^{14}, חֲדָשִׁים Dt 32^{17} *new ones* (i e. gods, || מִקָּרֹב בָּאוּ); in gen. f חֲדָשָׁה *a new thing* Is 43^{19} Je 31^{22}, fpl Is 42^{9} (opp הָרִאשֹׁנוֹת), 48^{6}. **b** very rarely predicate of י׳'s compassions חדשים לַבְּקָרִים La 3^{23} they are *new every morning;* כבודי ח׳ עִמָּדִי Jb 29^{20} *my glory* shall be *fresh with me*, ראה זה ח׳ הוא Ec 1^{10} *see, this is new!*

I **חֹדֶשׁ**$_{281}$ **n.m** $^{Gn\ 7,\ 11}$(**f** MT 38^{24} but **m.** Sam Di) (**newness**), **new moon, month** (on format cf Lg$^{BN\ 144}$, on usage, names, etc, Muss-Arnolt $^{JBL\ 1892,\ 72\ ff\ \ 100\ ff}$)—ח׳ abs Gn 7^{11}+, cstr (rare) Gn 29^{14}+; sf חָדְשׁוֹ Nu 28^{14}+2 t, חָדְשָׁהּ Ho 2^{13} Je 2^{24}, pl חֳדָשִׁים Gn 38^{24}+, cstr. חָדְשֵׁי Ex 12^{2} +2 t, sf. חֳדָשָׁיו Jb 14^{5}+2 t; חָדְשֵׁיכֶם Is 1^{14} Nu 28^{11}; חָדְשֵׁכֶם Nu 10^{10},—†**1.** *new moon*=day, time, of new moon, as religious festival 1 S 20$^{5.18.24.27.34}$ (Dr); cf. יאכלם ח׳ Ho 5^{7} *a new moon shall devour them*, Hi St VB, but on txt v We; usu || שַׁבָּת Am 8^{5} 2 K 4^{23} Is 1^{13} (+קְרָא מִקְרָא), מִדֵּי חֹדֶשׁ בְּחָדְשׁוֹ 66^{23}, Ez 46$^{1.6}$ (both יוֹם הַח׳), 1 Ch 23^{31} 2 Ch 2^{3} 8^{13} 31^{3} Ne 10^{34} (all + מוֹעֵד), Ho 2^{13} Ez 45^{17} (both + מועד, חג), || מוֹעֵד alone Is 1^{14} Ez 3^{5}, || יום חַגֵּנוּ ψ 81^{4}, (cf. רֹאשׁ הַח׳ Nu 10^{10} 28^{11}, on religious observance of new moon cf Di$^{Lv\ p\ 578\ f}$ Benz$^{Archäol\ §69}$), as time of augury in Babylon (astrolog. prognost) Is 47^{13} † **2.** *month* (as beginning with new moon, lunar month, cf Benz$^{Archäol\ §30}$, but then, without ref to day of beginning) †**a.** as measure of time during which Gn 38^{24} (J), Nu 11$^{20.21}$ (JE), 9^{22} (P), Ju 11$^{37.38.39}$ 20^{47} 1 S 6^{1} 27^{7} 2 S 2^{11} 5^{5} 6^{11} 24$^{8.13}$ =1 Ch 21^{12}, Am 4^{7} 1 K 4^{7} 5$^{7.28.28.28}$ 11^{16} 2 K 15^{8} 23^{31} 24^{8} Ez 39$^{12.14}$ 1 Ch 3^{4} 13^{14} 2 Ch 36$^{2.9}$ Est 2$^{12.12.12}$ In 1 S 10$^{27\ b}$ rd. prob. כְּמֵחֹדֶשׁ for MT כמחריש, and join to 11^{1}, so 𝔊 We Dr (cf Gn 38^{24}); in combinations, ח׳ יָמִים *a month* (of) *time* (cf. יֶרַח יָמִים Dt 21^{13} 2 K 15^{13}) Gn 29^{14} (J), Nu 11$^{20.21}$ (JE), ימים ארבעה ח׳ Ju 19^{2}, of age מִסְפַּר־ח׳ *number of his months*=length of his life Jb 14^{5} 21^{21}, cf esp בֶּן־ח׳ Lv 27^{6} Nu 3$^{15.22.28.34.39.40.43}$ 18^{16} 26^{62} (all P) † **b.** *calendar months*, †(1) with names ח׳ הָאָבִיב Ex 13^{4} 23^{15} 34$^{18.18}$ (all JE, =1st mo 12^{2} P), Dt 16^{1}, ח׳ זו 1 K 6^{1} (=2nd mo. ib, = יֶרַח זִו v^{37}), cf. 8^{2} (יֶרַח הָאֵתָנִים=הַח׳ הַשְּׁבִיעִי), 6^{38} (יֶרַח בּוּל=הַח׳ הַשְּׁמִינִי), in the postex. books occur Babyl names (v the several words):—ח׳ נִיסָן Ne 2^{1} Est 3^{7} (=1st mo. Est 3^{7}), ח׳ סִיוָן Est 8^{9}=3rd mo, ח׳ כסלו Zc 7^{1} Ne 1^{1} (=9th mo Zc 7^{1}); ח׳ טֵבֵת Est 2^{16}=10th mo, ח׳ שְׁבָט Zc 1^{7}=11th mo; ח׳ אֲדָר Est 3$^{7.13}$ 8^{12} 9^{1} in all=12th mo, 9$^{15.17.19.21}$; (cf also אֱלוּל Ne 6^{15}, without ח׳ or יֶרַח, this was 6th mo, v further Schr $^{COT\ Ne\ 1\ 1}$ Benz$^{l\ c}$).† (2) merely numbered (chiefly P and late) e g. בַּח׳ הַשֵּׁנִי Gn 7^{11}, cf 8$^{4.5.14}$ Lv 16^{29} Nu 1$^{1.18}$ (all P) + oft. P, Dt 1^{3} (P), 1 K 12$^{32.33}$ 25$^{1.3.8.25.27}$ Je 1^{3}+11 t Je, Ez 24^{1} 32^{1} Hg 1$^{1.15}$ Zc 1^{1} 7$^{1.3}$, 1 Ch 12^{15}, cf entire list 27$^{2-15}$ 2 Ch 3^{2} +12 t 2 Ch, Ezr 3^{1}+10 t Ezr; Ne 7^{72} 8$^{2.14}$ Est 3^{12}, note esp הַח׳ הַזֶּה לָכֶם רֹאשׁ חֳדָשִׁים ראשׁוֹן הוא לָכֶם Ex 12^{2} (P), as implying that the 1st mo. was formerly *not* in the spring; observe also usage of omitting ח׳, e.g בַּח׳ הָר׳=בָּרִאשׁוֹן Gn 8^{13}, cf v^{5}, so commonly in Ezek.:—Ez 1^{1} 8^{1} 20^{1} 29$^{1.17}$ 30^{20} 31^{1} 33^{21} 45$^{18.21.25}$ + 26^{1} 32^{17} 45^{20} Co, (ח׳ sts. expr, v. Ez 24^{1} 32^{1} supr, on like usage with יום v יום) (3) special phrases and usages are.—

+עלת חֹדֶשׁ בְּחָדְשׁוֹ לְחָדְשֵׁי שָׁנָה Nu 28[14] (P; cf. יום, and Is 66[23] supr. **1**), מִיּוֹם לְיוֹם וּמֵחֹדֶשׁ לחדש Est 3[7] *from day to day and from month to month*, חָדְשָׁהּ Je 2[24] of wild she-ass's mating time.†

†II. חֹדֶשׁ **n.pr.f.** a wife of Shaharaim of Benj. 1 Ch 8[9], 𝔊 'Αδα, 𝔊L Βαδαα (so v[8]=בַּעֲרָה).

†חֲדָשָׁה **n.pr.loc.** town in Judah Jos 15[37] (site unknown, cf Di)

†חָדְשִׁי in **n.pr.loc.** אֶרֶץ תַּחְתִּים ח׳ 2 S 24[6], rd א׳ הַחִתִּים קָדֵשָׁה v Hi[Gesch Isr 1 29], 𝔊L εἰς γῆν Χεττιειμ Καδης; cf Dr[ad loc] and (in part) Klo, v also קָדֵשׁ

†[חוּב] **vb.** be guilty (NH *id*, *be under obligation, guilty*, Aram. ܚܳܒ, חוב, *be defeated, guilty*, Ar خَابَ *be disappointed, fail*;—Ar حَوْبٌ, حُوبٌ *sin*, is loan-wd acc to Bev Dn 1[10]), —**Qal** not in MT, but rd perh חַבְתִּי (for סַבֹּתִי) 1 S 22[22] *I am guilty*, so 𝔖 Th We Dr **Pi.** *Pf. inculpate* וְחִיַּבְתֶּם אֶת־רֹאשִׁי לַמֶּלֶךְ consec. Dn 1[10] *and inculpate my head with the king*.

†חוֹב **n.[m.]** debt (NH *id.*; Aram. ܚܰܘܒܳܐ, חוֹבָא),—חֲבֹלָתוֹ ח׳ יָשִׁיב Ez 18[7] *his pledge as to indebtedness he restores*, v Hi-Sm Ew[§ 291 b] Ges[§ 128 R 5, b] Ko[Lgb 1. 497 f] and cf Dr[§ 193] (but constr. hard. Co שׁוּב; dittogr. fr. חבל׳ Bev[Dn 1 10], cf v[12 16])

†חוֹבָה **n pr.loc.** Gn 14[15], north of Damascus; mod *Hoba*, 20 hours N of Dam, acc to Wetzst[Del Gn ed 4. 561 ff] so Di.

†[חוּג] **vb.** draw round, make a circle (Aram. ܚܳܓ *circumivit*, n ܚܽܘܓܳܐ, חוּגָא, *circle, vault of heavens*)—**Qal** *Pf.* חֹק חָג עַל־פְּנֵי מַיִם Jb 26[10] (cf Pr 8[27]), *hath drawn as a circle* a bound, etc, of the horizon-line

†חוּג **n.[m.]** vault;—only of vault of the heavens בְּחֻקּוֹ חוּג עַל־ Jb 22[14]; חוּג שָׁמַיִם הִתְהַלָּךְ הַיֹּשֵׁב עַל־חוּג הָאָרֶץ Is 40[22] פְּנֵי תְהוֹם Pr 8[27];

†מְחוּגָה **n.f.** circle-instrument, compass, used by carvers of idols וּבַמְּחוּגָה יְתָאֲרֵהוּ Is 44[13]

I. חוד (✓of foll; Ar حَادَ is *decline, turn aside, avoid*, hence perh *riddle*, as *indirect, obscure*)

†חִידָה **n.f.** riddle, enigmatic, perplexing saying or question,—abs ח׳ Ju 14[12]+6t; sf. חִידָתִי Ju 14[18] ψ 49[5]; חִידָתְךָ Ju 14[13]; pl. abs. חִידוֹת 1 K 10[1]+4t; חידת Nu 12[8], sf. חִידֹתָם Pr 1[6],—**1.** *riddle*=dark, obscure utterance Nu 12[8] (JE; opp פֶּה־אֶל־פֶּה and מַרְאֶה); of something put indirectly and needing interpretation;—an allegory חוּד ח׳ Ez 17[2] (‖מָשָׁל), allegor and fig sayings Pr 1[6] (‖מְלִיצָה מָשָׁל and דִּבְרֵי חֲכָמִים), enigmat. sentences and comparisons, declaring fate cf Chaldeans Hb 2[6] (+ מְלִיצָה, ‖ מָשָׁל), perplexing moral problem ψ 49[5] (c פָּתַח *open, propound*, ‖מָשָׁל), a lesson taught indirectly ψ 78[2] (ח׳ מִנִּי קֶדֶם, c. הִבִּיעַ; ‖מָשָׁל). **2.** *riddle, enigma*, to be guessed, in Ju 14: **a.** with vb חוּד Ju 14[12 13 16] *propound a riddle*. **b.** with vb. הגיד *tell* (give answer to) *a riddle* Ju 14[14 15 17 19]. **c.** with vb מצא *find out a riddle* Ju 14[18] **3.** *perplexing questions* by which queen of Sheba put Sol. to the test (נִסָּה) 1 K 10[1]=2 Ch 9[1] **4.** with הֵבִין skilled in *double-dealing* Dn 8[23] (Bev).

†II [חוּד] **vb. denom.** propound a riddle,—**Qal** *Pf* 2 ms. חַדְתָּה Ju 14[16], *Impf* אָחוּדָה Ju 14[12]; *Imv.* חוּד (חִידָה וּמְשֹׁל מָשָׁל) Ez 17[2], חוּדָה Ju 14[13], always c חידה acc. cogn

I חוה (Ph. חוא *live*=Heb. חָיָה q v.)

†I חַוָּה **n.pr.f.** (*life*, vid. Di Gn 3[20]; >We[Prol 1886, 322, Skizzen III. 217] after No who suggests *serpent* as poss. mng, cf Ar. حَيَّة, but RS[K 177] 'mother of every *hayy*,' v. II חַי sub חיה)—Gn 3[20] *and the man called his wife* חַוָּה, because she was אֵם כָּל־חָי; cf. ח׳ אִשְׁתּוֹ 4[1] (both J)—II. חַוָּה *village*, v. infr sub II חוה

†יְחוּאֵל **n.pr m.** 2 Ch 29[14] Kt; Qr יְחִיאֵל q v sub חיה.

II חוה (✓of foll., Ar. حَوَى, *collect, gather*; حِوَاءٌ *circle of tents* cf. II חַי sub חיה, Ar. حَيٌّ).

†II [חַוָּה] **n.f.** tent-village—Pl. חַוֹּתֵיהֶם Nu 32[41] (JE), cf Di Elsewh. in cpd appellative, almost=n pr חַוֹּת יָאִיר Dt 3[14] Jos 13[30] (D), Ju 10[4] 1 K 4[13] 1 Ch 2[23]—I חַוָּה n pr.f. v. supr.

†חִוִּי **adj. gent.** (=*villagers*?)—**1.** שְׁכֶם בֶּן־חֲמוֹר הַח׳ Gn 34[2] (P), cf. צִבְעוֹן הַח׳ 36[2] (but rd. rather הַחֹרִי Ol Di cf. 𝔊 Jos 9[7]). **2.** c art. as n pr. coll הַחִוִּי *the Hivvites* 'begotten' by Canaan Gn 10[17]=1 Ch 1[15], esp in list of Canaanit. peoples displaced by Hebrews Ex 3[8 17] 13[5] 23[23 28] 33[2] 34[11] Dt 7[1] 20[17] Jos 3[10] 9[1] 12[8] 24[11] (all JED), Ju 3[5] 1 K 9[20]=2 Ch 8[7]; cf עָרֵי הַח׳ וְהַכְּנַעֲנִי 2 S 24[7] (note מִבְצַר־צֹר, צִידוֹן, just preceding), applied specif. to Gibeonites Jos 9[7] (JE), 11[19] (D)—In Jos 11[3] Ju 3[3] rd. prob הַחִתִּי for הַחִוִּי We Mey Bu[Urg 350] v. (partly) 𝔊, Dr on Dt 7[1].

†מַחֲוִים appar. **adj. gent.**, only אֱלִיאֵל הַמַּ׳ 1 Ch 11^{46}, but rd. prob. הַמַּחֲנִי (Be), v. מַחֲנַיִם n.pr.loc. sub חנה; Öt suggests also הַמְּעוֹנִי; 𝔊 ὁ Μιει, A ὁ Μαωειν, 𝔊L ὁ Μαωθε.

†III. [חָוָה] **vb.** only **Pi.** (poet. & late), **tell, declare** (Aram. ܚܘܝ, חַוִּי)—**Pi.** *Impf.* 3 ms. יְחַוֶּה־ ψ 19^{3}; 1 s. אֲחַוֶּה Jb 32$^{10.17}$; sf. אֲחַוְּךָ Jb 15^{17}, אֲחַוֶּנָּה Jb 36^{2}; *Inf. cstr.* חַוּוֹת;—*declare, make known*, c. acc. דָּעַת ψ 19^{3} (subj. לַיְלָה, sq. לְלַיְלָה; || יַבִּיעַ אֹמֶר); c. acc. דֵּעִי Jb 32$^{10.17}$; c. 2 acc. וָאִירָא מֵחַוֹּת דֵּעִי אֶתְכֶם 32^{6}, sq. sf. pers. + obj. cl., וַאֲחַוְּךָ כִּי־עוֹד לֶאֱלוֹהַּ מִלִּים׃ 36^{2} *and I will shew thee that* (there are) *yet words for God;* sq. sf. pers. only Jb 15^{17};—rd. prob. also וַאֲחַוֶּה for וַאֲקַוֶּה ψ 52^{11} Hi Che al.

†[אַחֲוָה] **n.f.** declaration (in form, an Aram. Aphel Inf.)—only sf. וְאַחֲוָתִי בְּאָזְנֵיכֶם׃ Jb 13^{17} (in || line שִׁמְעוּ שָׁמוֹעַ מִלָּתִי).

חוֹזָי 2 Ch 33^{19} v. sub חזה.

חוח (√of foll., meaning dubious).

†חוֹחַ **n.m.**[2 K 14.9] **1.** brier, bramble. **2.** hook, ring, fetter;—ח׳ abs. Ho 9^{6} + 8 t.; pl. חֹחִים 1 S 13^{6} (but v. infr.), חוֹחִים Ct 2^{2}; חֹחִים 2 Ch 33^{11};—**1. a.** *brier, bramble* 2 K 14$^{9.9}$ = 2 Ch 25$^{18.18}$ (allegory of Jehoash); coll., sign of desolation Ho 9^{6} (|| קִמּוֹשׂ), Is 34^{13} (|| קִמּוֹשׂ, סִירִים), Jb 31^{40} (opp. חִטִּים); in sim. of fool's parable ח׳ עָלָה בְיַד־שִׁכּוֹר Pr 26^{9} *a brier cometh into the hand of a drunken man* (De Now Str); כְּשׁוֹשַׁנָּה בֵּין הַחוֹחִים Ct 2^{2}; *briers = thickets* as hiding-places 1 S 13^{6} (but Ew We Dr חֹרִים *holes*, cf. 14^{11}; v. sub III. חרר; || מְעָרוֹת, סְלָעִים, בֹּרוֹת, צְרִחִים; 𝔊 here ἐν τ. μάνδραις; 14^{11} ἐκ τ. τρωγλῶν). **2.** late, **a.** *hook* or *ring*, in jaw of crocodile c. תִּקֹּב Jb 40^{26} (|| הֲתָשִׂים אַגְמֹן בְּאַפּוֹ); of captive וַיִּלְכְּדוּ אֶת־מְנַשֶּׁה בַּחֹחִים 2 Ch 33^{11} (cf. חַח).

†חַח **n.m.** hook, ring, fetter;—חַח abs. Ex 35^{22}; sf. חַחִי Is 37^{29} 2 K 19^{28}; pl. חַחִים Ez 19^{4} + 2 t. + Ez 29^{4} Qr (Kt erron. חחיים, v. infr.);—**1.** *hook, ring*, in nose of captive וְשַׂמְתִּי חַחִי בְּאַפֶּךָ Is 37^{29} = 2 K 19^{28} (cf. בַּחֹחִים 2 Ch 33^{11}, v. חוֹחַ supr.); so of princes of Judah, under fig. of young lions Ez 19$^{4.9}$ (in v^{9} transp., so that בחחים foll. הביא as v^{4}; so Co); in jaws of crocodile (metaph. of Pharaoh), c. נתן Ez 29^{4}, cf. 38^{4} (but 𝔊 om. and sense opposes, cf. Co and—dub.—Da). **2.** *hook, ring* as ornament, perhaps *nose-ring* (others *brooch*, see VB), Ex 35^{22} (P; || כּוּמָז, טַבַּעַת, נֶזֶם).

חוט (of foll.; Ar. خَاطَ, Aram. ܚܛ, חַיֵּט *sew*).

†חוּט **n.m.**[Jos 2.18] **thread, cord, line** (NH *id.*; Ar. خَيْط, Aram. ܚܘܛܐ, חוּטָא)—ח׳ abs. Gn 14^{23} + 2 t.; cstr. Jos 2^{18} + 3 t.;—**1.** *thread*, as easily broken Ju 16^{12} (sim.); as composing a rope or cord; תִּקְוַת ח׳ הַשָּׁנִי הַזֶּה Jos 2^{18} (JE) *this cord of scarlet thread* (lit. the cord of this thread of scarlet); prob. also מִחוּט וְעַד שְׂרוֹךְ נַעַל Gn 14^{23} *from a thread to a sandal-thong;* in sim. כְּח׳ הַשָּׁנִי Ct 4^{3} *like a thread of scarlet* are thy lips. **2. cord,** הַח׳ הַמְשֻׁלָּשׁ Ec 4^{12} *a three-fold cord.* **3.** *line*, as measure of length 1 K 7^{15} *and a line of twelve cubits surrounded* (i.e. would surround) *it* (cf. קָו v^{23}), so Je 52^{21}.

חִוִּי v. sub II. חוה.

†חֲוִילָה **n.pr.terr.** (√dub. Dl[Pa 12] suggests חול *sand-land, downs*, as Heb. popular etym., MV[11] give it as actual etym.; Sta[ThLZ Apr. 28, 1894, 235] compares this, as well as חול *sand*, with Ar. وَحَل *soft mud, [damp sand]*)—אֶרֶץ הַחֲוִילָה Gn 2^{11} (surrounded or bordered—סבב—by river Pishon; noted for excellent gold, bdellium and *shoham*-stone); elsewhere without art. חֲוִילָה 10^{7} = 1 Ch 1^{9} as a 'son' of Cush (between סְבָא and סַבְתָּה); but also as a 'son' of יָקְטָן, a descendant of Shem Gn 10^{29} = 1 Ch 1^{23} (between אופיר and יוֹבָב); מֵח׳ עַד־שׁוּר Gn 25^{18} said of limits of Ishmaelitish territory; cf. same limits of Amalek 1 S 15^{7} (but dub.; We rds. טֶלָם, cf. v^{4} and vid. Dr; Glaser[Skizze ii. 326] rds. חֲכִילָה as 23^{19} 26$^{1.3}$).—Most have supposed several regions named ח׳ to be indicated in these passages:—e.g. Thes 1. Arabian shore of Pers. Gulf Gn 10^{29} etc. 2. Ethiopian coast Gn 10^{7} etc. 3. India Gn 2^{11} (regarded as indef. extension of 1). Di[Gn 10,7] distinguishes 1 and 2 either as quite distinct, or as different settlements of one great people, and (on Gn 2^{14}) thinks that כל ארץ ח׳ Gn 2^{11} implies vague extension eastward. Dl[Pa 12 ff. 57 ff.] identif. ח׳ in all passages with NE. part of Syrian desert, so E. Meyer[Gesch. Alterth. i. 224]; Glaser[Skizze ii. 323 ff.] with central and NE. Arabia. The question is still undecided.

†I. חול [חִיל] **vb. whirl, dance, writhe** (NH, Aram. *id., dance;* Ar. حَالَ *change, turn;* As. *ḫâlu, writhe* in fear Dl[Pr 191] (on *ḫ* = ح v. DHM[ZK i. 357]); on form of Heb. **vb.** v. Nö[ZMG. 1883, 536])—**Qal** *Pf.* 3 fs. חָלָה Mi 1^{12} + 2 t.; וְחָלָה consec. Ho 11^{6}; חַלְתִּי Is 23^{4}; חָלוּ Je 5^{3} (but v. infr.), La 4^{6}; וְחָלוּ

Dt 2^{25}; חַלְנוּ Is 26^{18}; *Impf.* יָחוּל Je 23^{19} 30^{23}; 3 fs. תָּחוּל Ez 30^{16} Qr (Kt Co תחיל); וַתָּחָל Je 51^{29}; אחולה Je 4^{19} Kt (Qr אוֹחִילָה, Hiph. יחל); יָחֻלוּ 2 S 3^{29}; but also יָחִיל ψ 55^{5} (Jb 20^{21} v. II. חול); וַיָּחֶל 1 S 31^{3} = 1 Ch 10^{3} + Gn 8^{10} (where rd. prob. וַיָּחֶל as v^{12}; = וַיְּחַל Ol Di); 3 fs. תָּחִיל Is 26^{17} + 2 t. + Ez 30^{16} Kt (cf. *supr.*); וַתָּחֵל ψ 97^{4}; 2 fs. תְּחִילִין Is 45^{10}; יָחִילוּ ψ 77^{17} + 3t. (ψ 10^{5} v. II. חול); וַיָּחִילוּ Ju 3^{25}; יְחִילוּן Is 13^{8}; תָּחִילוּ Je 5^{22}; *Imv.* fs. חוּלִי Mi 4^{10} ψ 114^{7}; mpl. חִילוּ ψ 96^{9} 1 Ch 16^{30}; *Inf. cstr.* (לָ)חוּל Ju 21^{21} Ez 30^{16} (= Inf. abs.); *Pt.* fs. חוֹלָה Je 4^{31} vid. Gf Gie and Ges $^{§72 R.1}$;—**1.** *dance* Ju 21^{21} (לָחוּל בַּמְּחֹלוֹת). **2.** *twist, writhe:* **a.** in pain, esp. childbirth Is 26^{17} 45^{10} (מה־תוליד ‖ מַה־תח׳); metaph., of sea Is 23^{4} (‖ ילד); Israel 26^{18} (‖ הרה), 54^{1} (‖ ילד); Zion $66^{7.8}$ (‖ *id.*), Mi 4^{10} (‖ גֹּחִי, sim. כיולדה; cf. v. 9), Je 4^{31}. **b.** fig., *be in severe pain*, or *anguish* (mostly poet. and elevated prose), sq. מפני Dt 2^{25} (‖ רגז, cf. also פַּחַד and יִרְאָה v^{a}); Ez 30^{16} ψ 96^{9} Je 5^{22} (‖ ירא); sq. מִלִּפְנֵי 1 Ch 16^{30} ψ 114^{7}; abs. ψ 55^{5} (‖ אימות מָוֶת נפלו עלי), Je 4^{19} Kt, ψ 77^{17} (‖ רגז) 97^{4} Is 13^{8} 23^{5} Je 51^{29} (‖ רָעַשׁ), Jo 2^{6} Zc 9^{5} (‖ ירא), prob. also 1 S 31^{3} (cf. 28^{5}) = 1 Ch 10^{3}, cf. Öt; fig. of mts. Hb 3^{10}. **c.** in contrition Je 5^{3}, חָלוּ der. fr. חול Ew Gf Gie; < 𝔊 Ra Hi Ke al. fr. חלה (wrongly accented; vid. חלה **Qal 2**). **d.** in anxious longing עַד בּוֹשׁ Ju 3^{25}, sq. לְ Mi 1^{12} (on Gn 8^{10}, cf. supr.) **3.** *whirl, whirl about* עַל־ראשׁ יוֹאָב (i.e. blood—דמים—of Abner, from sword) 2 S 3^{29}; of attack of sword itself Ho 11^{6} (‖ כִּלָּה, אכל), cf. La 4^{6} לֹא חָלוּ בה ידים; of tempest על ראש רשעים יחול Je 23^{19} (v^{a} סער מִתְחוֹלֵל) = 30^{23} (v^{a} סַעַר מִתְגּוֹרֵר). **Po'lel.** *Impf.* יְחוֹלֵל ψ 29^{9}; 3 fs. תְּחוֹלֵל Pr 25^{23}; sf. תְּחוֹלֶלְכֶם Is 51^{2}; 2 ms. תְּחוֹלֵל Jb 35^{14}; וַתְּחוֹלֵל ψ 90^{2}; *Inf. cstr.* חֹלֵל Jb 39^{1}; *Pt.* מְחֹלֶלֶךָ Pr 26^{10}; מְחֹלְלֶךָ Dt 32^{18}; מְחוֹלֶלֶת Is 51^{9}; מְחֹלְלוֹת Ju 21^{23};—1 S 18^{6} ψ 87^{7} v. infr.; on חֹלָלָה Jb 26^{13} v. חלל;—**1.** *dance* Ju 21^{23}, so perh. also 1 S 18^{6} (rd. הַמְּחֹלְלוֹת 𝔊 We Dr; and חֹלְלִים pt. (מ om.) ψ 87^{7} RV Pe De Che Bae; cf. **Qal 1**). **2.** *writhe* in travail *with, bear, bring forth* (poet.), of Sarah, mother of Isr., Is 51^{2} (‖ אַבְרָהָם אֲבִיכֶם); of hinds Jb 39^{1} ψ 29^{9} (caus.); fig. of י׳'s producing earth ψ 90^{2} (‖ יֻלָּדוּ); of his bringing forth Isr. (with difficulty, v. Di) Dt 32^{18}; of north wind bringing forth rain Pr 25^{23}; רַב מְחוֹלֵל כֹּל 26^{10} *a master producuth everything* (on trans. see VB; Ew. al. derive fr. חלל *wound*). **3.** *wait anxiously* (cf. **Qal 2 d**), sq. לְ Jb 35^{14} (Elihu). **Po'lal.** *Pf.* חוֹלָלְתִּי ψ 51^{7} + 2 t.; חוֹלָלְתָּ Jb 15^{7}; *Impf.* יְחוֹלָלוּ Jb 26^{5};—**1.** *be made to writhe* Jb 26^{5} (הָרְפָאִים). **2.** *be brought forth* Jb 15^{7} (‖ תִּוָּלֵד), ψ 51^{7} (‖ יחם), metaph. of wisdom Pr $8^{24.25}$. **Hiph.** *Impf.* יָחִיל ψ $29^{8.8}$ *cause to be in anguish*, c. acc. מִדְבָּר, subj. י׳. **Hoph.** *Impf.* יוּחַל Is 66^{8} *be born* (= travailed with, Che), subj. אֶרֶץ (‖ יִוָּלֵד גוי). **Hithpol.** **1.** *Pt.* מִתְחוֹלֵל *whirling* סַעַר מתח׳ Je 23^{19} (= סער מִתְגּוֹרֵר 30^{23}). **2.** *writhing, suffering torture* Jb 15^{20} (of life of wicked). **3.** *Imv.* הִתְחוֹלֵל ψ 37^{7} *wait longingly* sq. לְ *for*, ‖ דּוֹם. **Hithpalp.** *Impf.* 3 fs. וַתִּתְחַלְחַל Est 4^{4} *and she writhed* in anxiety.

†חוֹל **n.m.** $^{Ho\ 2,1}$ sand (perh. as turning or *whirling*; otherwise explained by Sta, vid. sub חֲוִילָה; NH *id.*, Aram. חָלָא, (ﺧﻠ)—ח׳ abs. Gn 22^{17} + 15 t.; cstr. Gn 32^{13} + 6t.;—*sand* Ex 2^{12} (E); set as bound for sea Je 5^{22}; שְׂפֻנֵי טמוני ח׳ Dt 33^{19} *hidden treasures of sand*, poet. for *glass* (regarded as mysteriously produced out of sand, v. Di and reff.); **a.** usu. sand of seashore, sim. of numberlessness, vastness, so of Abraham's seed Gn 22^{17} (J; cf. 15^{5}); Jacob's 32^{13} (E); of a host Jos 11^{4} (JE), Ju 7^{12} 1 S 13^{5} 2 S 17^{11}; a people 1 K 4^{20} Ho 2^{1} Is 10^{22} 48^{19} (‖ וְצֶאֱצָאֵי מֵעֶיךָ כִּמְעֹתָיו), Je 33^{22} Hb 1^{9}; of corn gathered by Joseph Gn 41^{49}; of days of Job Jb 29^{18} (on interpr. = *phœnix*, vid. Di); of birds עוֹף כנף (i.e. quails) ψ 78^{27} (‖ כֶּעָפָר); of vast extent of Sol.'s wisdom 1 K 5^{9}. **b.** in comp., *more than the sand* Je 15^{8} (widows of Judah); thoughts of God ψ 139^{18}. **c.** of weight (in balances), metaph. of Job's vexation (כַּעַשׂ) Jb 6^{3} *heavier than the* sand, cf. כֹּבֶד ‖ וְנֵטֶל הַחוֹל Pr 27^{3} (כַּעַס אֱוִיל, אֶבֶן), said of—Combinations are: כח׳ אשר על שפת הים Gn 22^{17} Jos 11^{4} 1 S 13^{5} 1 K 5^{9}; כח׳ הַיָּם + אשר לא יִמַּד) Gn 32^{13} 41^{49} Is 10^{22} Ho 2^{1} ; כח׳ שֶׁעַל־שפת הים לרב (ולא יִסָּפֵר) ח׳ הַיָּם Je 33^{22}; כח׳ אשר־על־הים לרב Ju 7^{12}; 2 S 17^{11} 1 K 4^{20}; (מ)חול יַמִּים Jb 6^{3} ψ 78^{27} Je 15^{8}.

†חִיל **n.m.** $^{Ex\ 15.14}$ **a writhing, anguish**;—ח׳ abs. Ex 15^{14} + 5 t.—**1.** *writhing* (contortions of fear) Ex 15^{14} (‖ vb. רָגַז). **2.** *anguish*, always in sim. כַּיּוֹלֵדָה ψ 48^{7} (allied kings against Jerus.); Zion, before Assyrians Mi 4^{9}; before Scythians or Chaldeans Je 6^{24} (‖ צָרָה), = 50^{43} (of king of Babylon; ‖ צָרָה); 22^{23} (‖ חבלים q.v.)

†חִילָה **n.f.** anguish, Jb 6^{10}.

†**חֵל, חֵיל** **n.m.** Ob 20 **rampart, fortress** (perh. orig. *surrounding wall*, cf. Sab. Denkm. 91 n. 2)—abs חֵיל Na 3[8], חֵל La 2[8] + 3 t. (+ ψ 10[10] Qr v חלכה), cstr חֵל 1 K 21[23], sf חֵילֵךְ ψ 122[7], חֵילָה Zc 9[4], חֵילָה = חֵלָה ψ 48[14], Ol § 40c 75g 96e Sta § 347c,—**1.** *rampart* (defined by Jews as בֶּן חוֹמָה, i.e. a little wall, cf Ki s v), of an outer fortification 2 S 20[15] (others, by meton., of space between outer and inner fortif., incl moat, v Dr Kit), Is 26[1] La 2[8] (both ‖ חוֹמוֹת), in gen of defences, or sea-power of Tyre וְהִכָּה בַיָּם חֵילָהּ Zc 9[4] (v Sta ZAW i 1881 15), of No-Amon (Thebes) אֲשֶׁר חֵיל יָם מִיָּם חוֹמָתָהּ Na 3[8], of Zion ψ 122[7], also 48[14] (חֵילָה = חֵלָה, cf supr., both ‖ ארמנותיך)—For חֵל 1 K 21[23] rd prob חֵלֶק, q v **2.** *fortress* גָּלֻת הַחֵל הַזֶּה Ob[20] *the exiles of this fortress* (Hi-St; Or AV RV *this army*, חֵל = חַיִל)

†**חֵילָה** ψ 48[14], v חֵל supr.

†**חֵילָם** **n.pr.loc.** E of Jordan 2 S 10[16] (Th *their army*, but 𝔊 𝔖 𝔗 Ew Gesch iii 211 Anm 1—H iii 155 n 2 We Dr)= חֵלָאמָה v[17] (𝔊 Αιλαμ), + חילם Ez 47[16] (𝔊 Ηλιαμ) Co, acc. to this it lay on the border between Damascus and Hamath

†**חִילֵן** **n pr.loc.** in Judah 1 Ch 6[43] = חֹלֹן **2**

†**חֹלֹן, חֹלוֹן** **n.pr.loc** **1.** in Moab חלון Je 48[21] (𝔊 Χελων, Χαιλων) **2.** in Judah חלן Jos 15[51] (𝔊 Χαλου, 𝔊L Χειλου); priestly city 21[15] (𝔊 Γελλα, 𝔊L Ιλων) = חילן 1 Ch 6[43] (𝔊L Χελων)

†**חֵלֹן** **n pr.m.** a man of Zebulon Nu 1[9] 2[7] 7[24.29] 10[16] (𝔊 Χαιλων, 𝔊L Χελων)

†**חַלְחָלָה** **n.f. anguish,** מָלְאוּ מָתְנַי ח׳ Is 21[3], ח׳ בכל מתנים Na 2[11], Ez 30[4.9] (‖ החריד)

†**מָחוֹל** **n.m.** La 5. 15 **dance,**—abs מ׳ ψ 30[12] + 3 t; cstr מחול Je 31[4], מחולנו La 5[15];—*dance,* token of joyousness ψ 30[12] (opp מספד), Je 31[4.13] (cf. v[b]), La 5[15] (opp אבל), act of praise to י׳ ψ 149[3] 150[4], accompanied by timbrel (תֹּף) and sometimes other instruments ψ 149[3.4] Je 31[13]

†[**מְחוֹלָה**] **n.f.** id.,—cstr מחלת Ct 7[1], pl מחלת Ex 32[19], מְחֹלוֹת Ex 15[20] + 5 t., *dancing,* token of joyousness after victory, Ju 11[34] 1 S 18[6] 21[12] 29[5], in worship, at feast Ju 21[21], act of praise to י׳ Ex 15[20] (song), in idolatrous worship Ex 32[19] (E), as graceful and beautiful Ct 7[1]; accomp by timbrel Ex 15[20] Ju 11[34], and by singing Ex 15[20] 1 S 18[6] (where however rd. prob Po'lel Pt. הַמְחֹלְלוֹת, cf vb חול supr.; so 𝔊 We Dr), 21[12] 29[5]

†II [**חִיל, חוּל**] **vb. be firm, strong** (Aram. Pa *strengthen*, חֵילָא, حَيْل *strength;* Palm רב חילא רבא *general-in-chief* Vog No 28 al; Sab. חיל Sab Denkm 91 (on חֵל in Sab. n pr v Hal JAS Juin, 1872, 533); Eth ኀየለ: ኀይለ: *be strong,* ኀይል: *strength, army,* ኀያል: *strong,* As *ḫa(i)ltu, army* Flood Tabl iii 22 (*ḫaiallu* Jager BAS i 461), poss comp Ar خَيْل *horses* (as *strong ones?* cf ψ 33[17]))—only **Qal** *Impf* in לֹא יָחִיל טוּבוֹ Jb 20[21] *his prosperity is not firm* (does not endure), יָחִילוּ דְרָכָו בְּכָל־עֵת ψ 10[5] *his ways are always firm* (stable, prosperous), so Ol De Pe Che al

חַיִל 244 **n.m.** 2 K 10 2 **strength, efficiency, wealth, army,**—abs ח׳ Gn 47[6] +, חָיִל ψ 60[14] +, חָיִל ψ 60[14] +, חיל Is 36[2] 2 K 18[17], cstr. חיל Ex 14[28] + (on ψ 10[10] v חלכה); sf חילי Jb 31[25] + 2 t., חֵילוֹ Ex 14[4] +, etc, pl חֲיָלִים Je 15[13] +; חילך 1 Ch 7[5] + 19 t, sf חיליהם Is 30[6],—**1.** *strength,* usu physical **a.** seld alone (chiefly poet) 1 S 2[4] ψ 18[33.40] = 2 S 22[33.40], also גָּבְרוּ ח׳ Jb 21[7], cf Ec 10[10], מחיל אֶל־חָיִל ψ 84[8], בכֹחַ ח׳ 2 Ch 26[13], cf virility Pr 31[3], of י׳'s power ψ 59[12] 110[3], cf Hb 3[19], strength of horse ψ 33[17]; fig of product of vine and fig-tree Jo 2[22] (‖ פרי) **b.** of result or display of strength עשה ח׳ *achieve might = do valiantly* Nu 24[18] (JE), 1 S 14[48] ψ 60[14] = 108[14], 118[15.16]. **c.** oft. in phrases גִּבּוֹר(הַ)ח׳, גִּבּוֹרֵי(הַ)ח׳ *hero(es) of strength, mighty man (men) of valour* Jos 1[14] (D), 6[2] 8[3] 10[7] (all JE), Ju 6[12] 11[1] 1 S 9[1] 16[18] 1 K 11[28] 2 K 5[1] 15[20] 24[14.16] 1 Ch 5[24] 7[2.9] 8[40] + (very freq. in Ch), note esp הַגִּבּוֹרִים וכל גבורי ח׳ 28[1]; also ג׳ ח׳ 2 Ch 13[3] (‖ מלחמה ;(ג׳ (הַ)חֲיָלִים 1 Ch 7[5.7.11.40] 11[26] (v also גִּבּוֹר, p. 150); בֶּן־(הַ)ח׳, בני(הַ)ח׳ Dt 3[18] Ju 18[2] + (v בן **8**, p 121); אִישׁ ח׳, אַנְשֵׁי ח׳ Ju 3[29] 20[44.46] 1 S 31[12] 11[16] 2 S 23[20] (Qr, Kt חי, on phr בן־איש חיל cf Dr) = 1 Ch 11[22] (Kt חיל), 2 S 24[9] Na 2[4] Je 48[15] 1 Ch 10[12] Ne 11[6] ψ 76[6], ironical אַ׳ ח׳ למסך שֵׁכָר Is 5[22] (‖ גבורים לשתות יין), Ec 12[3] metaph of legs. **2.** *ability, efficiency,* often involving moral worth אַנְשֵׁי ח׳ Gn 47[6] (J), Ex 18[21.25] (both E); of a woman אֵשֶׁת ח׳ Pr 12[4] 31[10] Ru 3[11]; cf 1 K 1[42.52] (opp רעה), and esp אַנְשֵׁי ח׳ יראי אלהים אַנְשֵׁי אמת שׂנאי בֶצַע Ex 18[21] (E), עֲשָׂה חיל Pr 31[29] *do worthily, efficiently,* perh. also Ru 4[11], late (with weakened mng. of גבורי חיל מְלֶאכֶת עֲבוֹדַת בית הָאֱלֹהִים (גבור 1 Ch 9[13], cf איש ח׳ בְּכֹחַ לַעֲבֹדָה 26[8] So also 1 S 10[26] (rd. בני ח׳, v 𝔊 We Dr, *men of worth,* opp. בני בליעל

v[27]) for MT ח׳ *force, band.* **3.** *wealth* Gn 34[29] Nu 31[9] (both P), Dt 8[17 18] 33[11] Is 8[4] 10[14] 30[6] (‖אוֹצְרֹתָם), 60[5] (‖ הֲמוֹן יָם), v[11] 61[6] Mi 4[13] Je 15[13] 17[3] (both ‖ אצרות), Zp 1[13] Ez 26[12] 28[4.5.5] Zc 14[14] Jb 5[5] 15[29] 20[15.18] 31[25] ψ 49[7 11] 62[11] 73[12] Pr 13[22]. **4.** *force, army,* very oft Ex 14[4.9 17 28] (all P), 15[4] (song), 1 S 17[20] 2 S 8[9] 2 K 6[4 15] 25[1.5.10] 2 Ch 13[3] (בחיל גִּבּוֹרי מלחמה), 14[7] 16[7] 23[14]+, so usu. Jer: Je 32[2] 34[1]+; freq. Ezek.: Ez 17[17] 27[10]+; Dn 11[7 13.25.25.26]; = *a band* 1 S 10[26] (MT, but v. **2**, *ad fin*); of train of Queen of Sheba ח׳ גדול 1 K 10[2] = 2 Ch 9[1]; חיל כָּבֵד Is 36[1] = 2 K 18[17] *a powerful army* (on form cf Sta § 194 c), also (late) חיל הַצָּבָא 1 Ch 20[1] 2 Ch 26[13], חֵיל עָם Est 8[11]; הֲמוֹן חֲיָלִים Dn 11[10]; שַׂר־הח׳ 2 S 24[2] *captain of the host,* שָׂרֵי הַחֲיָלִים, [4.4] שָׂרֵי הח׳ *captains of armies* (bands, divisions) 1 K 15[20] = 2 Ch 16[4], 2 K 25[23] Je 40[7 13] 41[11 13.16] 42[1.8] 43[4.5], בקודי החיל Nu 31[14] (P)—חֵילוֹ Ez 32[31] om B Hi Co, for חֵילֵךְ Ez 27[11] rd. prob. a n pr loc, cf Da; Co prop. חתלון (cf 47[15] 48[1]), Hal [Mél. Épigr 1874, 69] חלך = *Cilicia*, v. Lag [M i, 221].

†חוּל **n.pr.m.** a 'son' of Aram Gn 10[23] = 1 Ch 1[17], named between עוּץ and גֶּתֶר 𝔊 Ουλ

חום (√ of foll., meaning dub.; NH חום = *be warm*)

†חוּם **adj. darkened, dark brown or black,** only of colour of sheep (in Gn 30, J).—וכל־שֶׂה־חוּם וכל־חוּם בכשׂבים Gn 30[32], וחום בכ׳ בצאן Gn 30[33.35], Gn 30[40] (cl prob interpol Ol Hup De We Di)

חוֹמָה v. sub חמה

†[חוּס] **vb. pity, look upon with compassion** (Aram. ܚܳܣ, חוּס *pity, spare;* As *ḫâs,* in n pr cf. Dl [Pr 181])—**Qal** *Pf.* 3 fs. חָסָה Ez 16[5], 2 ms. חַסְתָּ Jon 4[10]; *Impf.* 3 ms. יָחוּס Je 21[7]; יָחֹס ψ 72[13], 3 fs תָּחוֹס Is 13[18]; תָּחוֹס Dt 7[16] + 9 t. (Ges § 72 R 4 Bo § 1133 (2)); וַתָּחָס תָּחֹס Gn 45[20] Ez 9[5]; 1 S 24[11] Ez 20[17], 1 s. אָחוּס Je 13[14] + 2 t; *Imv.* חוּסָה Jo 2[17] Ne 13[22]:—**a.** of the eye, עַיִן, עַל (לא) תח(ו)ס the eye *shall* (*not*) *look with compassion, pity, upon* Dt 7[16] 13[9] 19[13] Is 13[18] Ez 7[4] 20[17]; לא חסה עָלַיִךְ עין Ez 16[5]; עֵינְכֶם אַל־תָּחֹס עַל־כְּלֵיכֶם Gn 45[20] (R[JE]) *let not your eye look with regret upon your stuff,* with ellipsis of עין 1 S 24[11] (but rd. וָאָחֹס for וַתָּחָס 𝔊 𝔖 𝔗 We Klo Dr); with ellipsis of עַל Dt 19[21] 25[12] Ez 5[11] 7[9] 8[18] 9[10], (אל) עַל תחס עינכם Ez 9[5]. **b.** of God חוסה על Ne 13[22] Jo 2[17], לא אחוס על נינוה Jon 4[11], ellipsis of עַל Je 13[14] Ez 24[14]. **c.** of man: the Messianic king עַל־דַּל וְאֶבְיוֹן ψ 72[13] *he shall have pity on poor and needy,* Nebuchadrezzar עליהם (i.e. on Zedekiah and the people) Je 21[7]; Jonah, על הקיקיון Jon 4[10]—Vid. also חמל.

חוֹף v. sub II חפף.

†חוּפָם **n.pr.m.** head of a Benjamite family Nu 26[39], not in 𝔊, (= חֻפִּים Gn 46[21], cf also 1 Ch 7[12.15])

†חוּפָמִי **adj. gent.** of foregoing, c art = n coll. הַח׳ Nu 26[39].

I **חוץ** (√ of foll, meaning unknown).

חוּץ **n [m.] the outside, sts, esp. in pl, spec a street, never with sf. in sg, with** ־ָה loc. חוּצָה, חֻצָה, pl. חֻצוֹת, חוצות, with sf חוצֹתָיו etc, Is 15[3] etc,—**1.** *the outside,* of a house, tent, city, camp, etc, oft. used, esp with preps., to express the adv idea of *outside, abroad* (Aram. syn, exc. in sense **2 a**, is בַּר, ܒܰܪ): **a.** as accus after vb. of motion Dt 23[13] יָצָא חוּץ to go forth outside (sc. a camp), v[14] (as adv. accus) בְּשִׁבְתְּךָ חוּץ *outside,* הוֹצִיא הַחוּץ to bring forth *outside* (a house or chamber) Ju 19[25] 2 S 13[18] cf. Ne 13[8], Ju 12[9 §§] בָּנוֹת הביא לְבָנָיו מִן־הַחוּץ from *outside,* from *abroad,* 2 K 4[3] שַׁאֲלִי־לָךְ כלים מִן־הַחוּץ from *outside* (opp. בַּבַּיִת v[2]); as genit. Lv 18[9] מוֹלֶדֶת חוּץ one born *abroad* (i.e by another father or mother, of a half-sister. opp מוֹלֶדֶת בַּיִת) Ez 47[2.2]. With ־ָה *loc.* חוּצָה, after a vb. of motion Ex 12[46] מִן־הַבַּיִת . . . חוּצָה, Pr 5[16] 2 Ch 29[16], 33[15] מִקִּיר הָעִיר חוּצָה לָעִיר *outside of* the city, Nu 35[4] וָחוּצָה from the wall of the city *and outwards;* = *on the outside, without* 1 K 6[6] Is 33[7] צָעֲקוּ חוצה cry *without,* 2 Ch 24[8]: so הַחוּצָה Gn 15[5] ויוצא אתו הח׳ and brought him *outside,* 19[17] 24[29] Jos 2[19]+, 1 K 8[8] לֹא יֵרָאוּ הַחוּצָה were not seen *towards the outside,* Dt 25[5] לֹא תִהְיֶה אֵשֶׁת הַמֵּת הַחוּצָה לְאִישׁ זָר i e. shall not be married into another family, cf. Ju 12[9 §]. **b.** with preps.: *a* †אֶל־הַחוּץ *towards the outside* Ez 41[9], †34[21] pleon. אֶל־החוצה. *b.* בַּחוּץ Gn 9[22] *outside* (opp. בתוך אָהֳלֹה v[21]), 24[31] לָמָּה תַעֲמֹד בַּחוּץ, Dt 24[11] Ex 21[19] אם יקום והתהלך בחוץ (after leaving a sick couch), 2 K 10[24] ψ 31[12] Ez 7[15] (opp. מִבַּיִת), Ho 7[1]+. *c.* †לחוץ ψ 41[7] יצא לחוץ; = *on the outside* Ez 41[17] 42[7], †לְחוּצָה 2 Ch 32[5] *towards the outside.* *d* מחוץ *on* (מִן **3 c**) *the outside* Ez 40[19] 46[2], מִבַּיִת וּמִחוּץ within and *without* (of an ark, building, etc.) Gn 6[14] Ex 25[11] = 37[2] 1 K 7[9], Dt 32[25] מחוץ תְּשַׁכֶּל־חֶרֶב (opp. וּמֵחֲדָרִים

אִיטָּה), La 1[20] (cf Ez 7[15] supr. *b*); so מֵהַחוּץ +Ez 41[25]. מחוץ ל *on the outside of*, Gn 19[16] וַיַּנִּחֻהוּ מחוץ לָעִיר, 24[11] Ex 26[35] 37[27] Lv 8[17] 14[8] Nu 35[5] Jos 6[23] Je 21[4]+, even after a vb of motion 1 K 21[13] וַיֹּצִיאֻהוּ מחוץ לָעִיר, 2 K 23[6], though in this case אל מחוץ ל is more common, Lv 4[12.21] אל מחוץ למחנה, 6[4] 10[4] 14[40.41]+oft P, Dt 23[11]. **e** †מִחוּצָה Ez 40[40] *on the outside*, מחוצה ל v[44] *f.* (late) †חוץ מן *outside of*, Ec 2[25] who can eat, and who enjoy, חוּץ ממני *outside of* me, i e *except* me? (but rd rather, with 𝔊 𝔖 De Now al, חוּץ מִמֶּנּוּ *apart from, without* him, i e God) (So NH חוץ מן *except, without*, v De[Ec 2, 25] Cf the Aram syn בַּר מִן *except* Ex 20[3] 𝔗, *apart from, without* Is 36[10] 𝔗, Syr ܒܠܥܕ ܡܢ *id*)

2. Of a definite locality, viz **a.** that which is outside the houses of a town, i. e *a street* Is 51[23] כַּחוּץ לַעֹבְרִים, Je 37[21] חוּץ הָאֹפִים the Bakers' *street*, Pr 1[20] בַּחוּץ || בָּרְחֹבוֹת · so 7[12] 22[13] Je 9[20]); oft in pl, as חוּצוֹת אַשְׁקְלוֹן the *streets* of Ashkelon 2 S 1[20], ח׳ ירושלם Je 5[1] 7[17.34]+oft Jer, 1 K 20[34] וְחֻצוֹת תָּשִׂים־לְךָ בְדַמֶּשֶׂק and *streets* (i e. bazaars) shalt thou make thee in D, as my father made in Samaria (a concession involving the right of trading), Am 5[16] Is 15[3] 24[11] (as scene of mourning), Is 5[25] Je 51[4] Ez 11[6] 28[23] (as filled with corpses of slain), בראשׁ כָּל־חוצות i e in conspicuous places, Na 3[10] La 2[19] 4[1] Is 51[20], טִיט חוצות mire of *streets* Zc 10[5] (trampled on by warriors), in simile, of foes trodden under foot, ψ 18[43] Mi 7[10] (so כְּחֹמֶר ח׳ Is 10[6]), metaph of cheapness and abundance Zc 9[3] **b.** more gen, that which is outside enclosed cities, the *open country*, Jb 18[17] ולא שֵׁם לו עַל־פְּנֵי־חוּץ (v De), cf Pr 24[27], in the pl Jb 5[10] וְשֹׁלֵחַ מַיִם עַל פני חוצות, Pr 8[26] ψ 144[13] (as place where flocks abound)

†חִיצוֹן **adj. outer, external** (opp פנימי) f חִיצוֹנָה (for חוצון, by dissim, Ba[NB xxix] Phil BAS ii 2 362 Ges[§ 27 3 n 6])—**1.** 2 K 16[18] מְבוֹא הַמֶּלֶךְ הַחִיצוֹנָה the *outer* entry of the king (viz. to the Temple), Ez 44[1] the *outer* gate of the sanctuary, החצר החיצונה the *outer* court (of the Temple) Ez 10[5] 40[17.20.31.34.37] 42[1.3.7.8.9.14] 44[19] 46[9] [20.21], cf. Est 6[4] (of Ahasuerus' palace), 2 Ch 33[14] חומה ח׳ an *outer* wall (built by Manasseh for the עִיר דָּוִיד,) הַחִיצוֹן absol, in לַחִיצוֹן 1 K 6[29.30], בַּחִיצוֹן Ez 41[17] (הַבַּיִת being understood) of the *outer* (part of the Temple), i e. the Holy Place (cf. פְּנִימָה, פנימי, of the Holy of holies) **2.** fig. *outward, external* הַמְּלָאכָה הַחִיצוֹנָה Ne 11[16] 1 Ch 26[29], of business not distinctively sacred, in which Levites were engaged (cf the NH use of ח׳ to denote *extra-canonical*, as *Sanh.* 10[1] [Jost, 11[1] Surenh] ספרים החיצונים)

II. חוץ (√of foll, cf. Ar. خَاصَ *sew together*, Aram שְׁנַץ *bind, compress*, σφίγγειν, ܫܢܰܨ *bandage* خَاطَ iv *encompass*, حَائِط *wall*, which is oft compared, does not correspond phonetically)

†חַיִץ **n.[m.] party-wall** (NH *id*, prob from Ez *l c*)—Ez 13[10], acc to Ki מחיצה גרועה i.e a thin or party-wall

חיק, חוק (√of foll, As. *ḫiku, embrace*, Creation Tabl[iv 16], Ar. حَوْقٌ *ring*, حَوْقٌ *width* of desert, of well, of vulva, أَحْوَقُ *wide;* Di comp also Eth ሐቀፈ: *shore* of sea, fr. *surrounding*, cf As supr)

†[חוק] **n [m.] bosom,** ψ 74[11] Kt חוקך (but rd Qr חֵיקְךָ, v following)

†חֵיק, חֵק **n.[m.] bosom** (NH *id*)—abs חיק Ez 43[17] Pr 16[33]+Ez 43[13] (Co חיקו, cf ZKW 1883, pp. 67 ff, חיקה Dr[8m xxxi]), חק Pr 21[14], cstr חיק 1 K 22[35]+3 t.+Ez 43[14] (Co חיקו) חק Pr 5[20] (om by accident in Baer, cf. Str[ad loc]) 17[23]; sf חיקי 1 K 3[20] ψ 89[51], חקי Jb 19[27] etc., elsewh alw plene c sf, חוקך Kt ψ 74[11] (Qr חֵיקְךָ),—*bosom*, specif **1.** of fold of garment, at breast Ex 4[6.6.7.7.7] (all J), Pr 6[27] 16[33], metaph of י׳ ψ 74[11], שֹׁחַד בַּח׳ Pr 21[14] is a *hidden reward* (concealed in bosom, || מַתָּן בַּסֵּתֶר), שׁחד מחק 17[23] is a *gift secretly given*, fig, *requite into bosom* Is 65[6.7] ψ 35[13] 79[12] Je 32[18]. **2.** *carry* (נָשָׂא) *in bosom*, Moses the people Nu 11[12] (JE), Naomi, Ruth's child Ru 4[16], cf 1 K 3[20.20] 17[19]; ewe lamb 2 S 12[3] Is 40[11] (metaph), La 2[12] of infants dying in their mothers' arms; fig. of carrying insults in one's bosom ψ 89[51] (rd. prob. כְּלִמַּת for כל, v. Bi Che) **3.** *bosom* as part of body. **a.** external, *lie in bosom*, of wife שֹׁכֶבֶת Mi 7[5], cf 2 S 12[8], concubine Gn 16[5] (J) cf 1 K 1[2], אֵשֶׁת חֵיקֶ(ךָ) Dt 13[7] 28[54], cf also Pr 5[20] איש חיקה; תְּחַבֵּק חֵק נָכְרִיָּה Dt 28[56]. **b.** internal, anger resteth בח׳ כסילים Ec 7[9], כָּלוּ כִלְיֹתַי בחקי Jb 19[27] *my reins are consumed within me*, Jb 23[12] (rd. בְּחֵקִי for מֵחֻקִּי, so 𝔊 𝔙 Ol Me Stu Di) *in my breast have I hidden the words of his mouth* (cf בלבי ψ 119[11]), fig. of interior of chariot 1 K 22[35] ח׳ הרכב, of hollow bottom

of altar Ez 43[13.14.17] (Sm *Rinne; Co Grundeinfassung*).

†**חוּקֹק** **n.pr.loc.** city in Asher 1 Ch 6[60] 𝔊 Ικακ, 𝔊L Ακωκ; but rd. prob. חֻלְקָת (as Jos 19[25]) q. v.—חֻקֹּקָה Jos 19[34] v. sub חקק.

†I. [**חָוַר**] **vb. be or grow white, pale** (Ar. حَوِرَ *be white*, حَوَرٌ *whiteness*, Aram. ܚܘܪ, חֲוַר *be white*)—only **Qal** *Impf.* 3 mpl. וְלֹא עַתָּה פָּנָיו יֶחֱוָרוּ Is 29[22] (|| לֹא עַתָּה יֵבוֹשׁ יַעֲקֹב).

†I. **חוּר** **n.[m.]** **white stuff** (dub. whether cotton or linen, cf. כַּרְפַּס), || תְּכֵלֶת:—of Mordecai's garments בִּלְבוּשׁ מַלְכוּת תְּכֵלֶת וָחוּר Est 8[15a] *in a royal garment of violet and white stuff* (cf. וְתַכְרִיךְ בּוּץ וְאַרְגָּמָן v[b]); of furnishings of royal palace of Susa חוּר כַּרְפַּס וּתְכֵלֶת אָחוּז בְּחַבְלֵי־בוּץ וְאַרְגָּמָן 1[6] *white stuff of fine linen(?) held fast by cords of byssus and purple.*

†**חוֹרָי** **n.m.** white stuff, cf. I. חוּר; וְאֹרְגִים חוֹרָי Is 19[9] *and* (those) *weaving white stuff.*

†I. **חֹרִי** **n.[m.]** white bread or cake שְׁלֹשָׁה סַלֵּי חֹרִי Gn 40[16] *three baskets of white bread.*—II. חֹרִי v. III. חרר.

†II. **חוּר** **n.pr.m.** (mng. dub.; cf. Nab. n.pr. חורו Nö in Eut[p.45])—**1.** 𝔊 Ωρ, named with Aaron as compan. of Moses Ex 17[10.12] 24[14] (all E). **2.** 𝔊 Ωρ, a Judahite Ex 31[2] = 35[30], cf. 38[22] (all P) 1 Ch 2[19.20.50] (on div. of verse v. Be VB); also 4[1.4] 2 Ch 1[5]. **3.** 𝔊 Ουρ, a king of Midian Nu 31[8] Jos 13[21] (both P). **4.** 𝔊L Σουρ (B om.) head of fam. of returned exiles Ne 3[9]. **5.** בֶּן־חוּר officer of Sol. 1 K 4[8], v. sub בֵּן p. 122.

III. **חוּר** = **חֹר** v. sub III. חרר.

†**חוּרַי** **n.pr.m.** a hero of David חוּ׳ מִנַּחֲלֵי גָעַשׁ 1 Ch 11[32] 𝔊 Ουρ(ε)ι, 𝔊L Ουρια; = הִדַּי 2 S 23[30] (om. B; A Αθθαι, 𝔊L Αδδαι).

†**חוּרִי** **n.pr.m.** a Gileadite (of Gad) 1 Ch 5[14] (𝔊 Ουρ(ε)ι).

†**חִירָה** **n.pr.m.** (√חור but mng. dub.) an Adullamite, friend of Judah Gn 38[1.12] (both J), 𝔊 Ειρας.

חוּרָם v. חִירָם sub אָח, אחה supr. p. 27 b.

II. **חוּר** (√of foll.; cf. Ar. خَارَ *bend, turn, incline*, of man *be weak*, Lane[820c], خَوْرٌ *hollow, depressed ground between hills*).

†I. **חֹר** **n.[m.]** **hollow**, only in חֹר הַגִּדְגָּד Nu 33[32] *hollow of Gidgad* (v. Di).

II., III. **חוּר**, **חֹר**, (**חוֹרִים**) v. sub II., III. חרר.

†**חַוְרָן** **n.pr.terr.** (meaning unknown; conjectures are:—*black-land* (as basaltic region), supported by حَوَرٌ *black*, dial. of Yemen, Maltzan [ZMG 1874, 230], and tokens of immigration from Yemen into Ḥaurân, Wetzst in De [Job 2, 598; ZKW 1884, 120]; *land of caves*, Thes Hi-Sm, Porter [Dict. Bib.], and *hollow*, GASm [Geogr. 552], who comp. Heb. חוּר *hole*; but this prob. fr. III. חרר, and Ar. خَوْرٌ, *hollow*, diff. fr. حَوْرَان)—district SE. fr. Mt. Hermon, extending between Jaulan and Lejah, toward Syr. desert; only גְּבוּל חַוְרָן Ez 47[16] cf. מִבֵּין חַוְרָן וּמִבֵּין דַּמֶּשֶׂק v[18]; = As. *Ḥaurani* Dl [Pa 294]; 𝔊 Αυρανιτις, and so Jos [Ant. xv. 10. 1 etc.], Ar. حَوْرَان. On this district v. Wetzst [Hauran, (1860)] and in De [Job 2. 597 ff.] Bd [Pal 195 ff.] Schumacher [Across the Jordan, 1889; ZPV xii. 1889, 225 ff. (with map)] GASm [Geogr. 552 f. 609 ff.]

†I. **חוּשׁ** **vb. haste, make haste** (As. *ḫâšu*, Dl [Pr 180], Eth. ሐሰ:; on this vb. v. Nö [ZMG 1883, 538])—**Qal** *Pf.* 3 ms. חָשׁ Dt 32[35] (or *Pt.*, but v. Di), 1 s. חַשְׁתִּי ψ 119[60]; *Impf.* 3 fs. וַתַּחַשׁ (sic!) Jb 31[5] Ges [§ 72 R. 9]; *Imv.* חוּשָׁה 1 S 20[38] + 6 t. ψ, + ψ 71[12] Qr (Kt חִישָׁה); *Inf.* sf. חוּשִׁי Jb 20[2]; *Pt. act.* חָשׁ Hb 1[8] + Is 8[1.3] in n.pr.; *pass.* חֻשִׁים Nu 32[17]; but v. infr.:—*make haste* Dt 32[35] (|| קָרוֹב), ψ 119[60]; in prophetic n.pr. מַהֵר שָׁלָל חָשׁ בַּז Is 8[1.3]; of eagle (in sim. of Chald. army) נשר חש לאכול Hb 1[8]; Jb 31[5] subj. רגל, sq. על־מרמה; חוּשִׁי בִּי Jb 20[2] *my haste in me*, i.e. my inward excitement—esp. *Imv.* 1 S 20[38] (|| מהרה), and in ψψ: sq. לִי 22[20] 38[23] 40[14] 70[2] 71[12] (Qr); sq. לְעֶזְרָתִי 70[6] 141[1]; *pt. pass.* נֵחָלֵץ חֻשִׁים Nu 32[17], but prob. for חֲמֻשִׁים (Kn Di comp. Ex 13[18] etc.); Ba [NB 180] retains חוּשִׁים and regards it as act. (intrans.) = *hastening.* **Hiph.** *Pf.* הֵחִישׁוּ Ju 20[37]; *Impf.* יָחִישׁ Is 28[16]; יָחִישָׁה coh. 5[19] (Ges [§ 48. 3]); אָחִישָׁה coh. ψ 55[9]; *sf.* אֲחִישֶׁנָּה Is 60[22];—**1.** *shew haste, act quickly* Ju 20[37]; *hasten, come quickly* Is 5[19] (subj. מַעֲשֵׂהוּ, || יְמַהֵר; others: *let him hasten on his work*), יָחִישׁ Is 28[16] *hasten away* (flee), or *hasten about* distractedly (si vera l.; Che Guthe rd. ימישׁ *yield, give way*). **2.** transit. c. sf. Is 60[22] *I will hasten it*; c. acc. ψ 55[9] *I would hasten* (= secure quickly) *my escape.*

†**חִישׁ** **adv. quickly**, כי גז חיש ψ 90[10] of passing away of human life.

†II. [**חוּשׁ**] **vb. feel, enjoy** (with the senses) (Now comp. Ar. حَسَّ *feel, perceive* by senses; NH חוש *feel pain*; Aram. ܚܫ, חוּשׁ, *feel pain*;

Eth. ሐወፀ: *perception*)—only **Qal** *Impf.* 3 ms. מִי יֹאכַל וּמִי יָחוּשׁ Ec 2^{25} *who can eat and who can feel* (i.e. *enjoy pleasure*)?

† חוּשָׁה **n.pr.m.** a 'son' of חור = place in Judah 1 Ch 4^{4}.

† חֻשָׁתִי **adj.gent.** of foregoing:—**1.** of individ., c. art. הַח׳ 2 S 21^{18} = 1 Ch 20^{4}, 2 S 23^{27} = 1 Ch 11^{29}, v. also 1 Ch 27^{11}.

† חוּשַׁי **n.pr.m. 1.** ח׳ הָאַרְכִּי 2 S 15^{32} so $17^{5.14}$, called רֵעֶה דוד 15^{37} *friend of David*, so 16^{16a}; cf. $16^{16b.17.18}$ 1 Ch 27^{33}; also 1 S $17^{6.7.8.15}$. **2.** 1 K 4^{16} father of one of Solomon's officers.

† I. חֻשִׁים, חוּשִׁים **n.pr.f.** wife of Shaharaim of Benjamin, חוּשִׁים 1 Ch 8^{8}, חֻשִׁים v^{11}.

† II. חֻשִׁים **n.pr.m.** of Dan, וּבְנֵי דָן ח׳ Gn 46^{23} cf. חֻשִׁם בְּנֵי אַחֵר 1 Ch 7^{12} (v. Be VB); = שׁוּחָם (q.v.) Nu 26^{42} cf. שׁוּחָמִי $v^{42.43}$.

† חֻשָׁם, חוּשָׁם **n.pr.m.** a king of Edom: חֻשָׁם Gn $36^{34.35}$ = חוּשָׁם 1 Ch $1^{45.46}$.

חוֹתָם v. sub חתם.

חֲזָאֵל v. חֲזָהאֵל sub I. חזה.

† I. חָזָה **vb.** (almost wholly poet.) **see, behold** (Aram. ܚܙܐ, חֲזָא, *see, perceive with the eyes;* Palm. Ethp. אתחזי = ἔδοξεν Reckendorf ZMG, 1888, 397; Ar. حَزَى, *perceive with the inner vision,* only; حَازٍ *astronomer, astrologer*)—**Qal** *Pf.* ח׳ ψ 58^{11} + 6 t.; חָזִיתָ Pr 22^{29} 29^{20}; חָזִית Is 57^{8}; חָזִיתִי Jb 15^{17}; חֲזִיתִךָ ψ 63^{3}; חָזוּ Jb 24^{1} + 5 t.; חֲזִיתֶם Jb 27^{12} Ez $13^{7.8}$; *Impf.* יֶחֱזֶה Nu 24^{4} + 2 t.; 3 fs. וְתַחַז Mi 4^{11}; 2 ms. תֶּחֱזֶה Ex 18^{21}; 1 s. אֶחֱזֶה ψ 17^{15} + 4 t.; אָחַז Jb 23^{9}; pl. יֶחֱזוּ Is 26^{11} + 4 t.; יֶחֱזָיוּן Is 26^{11}; תֶּחֱזֶינָה Is 33^{17} + 2 t.; תֶּחֱזוּ Is 30^{10} Ct 7^{1}; 1 pl. וְנֶחֱזֶה Ct 7^{1}; *Imv.* חֲזֵה Is 33^{20} 48^{6}; חֲזוּ ψ 46^{9} Is 30^{10}; *Inf. cstr.* חֲזוֹת ψ 27^{4} Ez 21^{34}; *Pt.* חֹזֶה Ez 12^{27}; pl. חֹזִים Is 47^{13} Ez $13^{9.16}$ 22^{28}. (All other ptc. forms are used as nouns, v. חֹזֶה.) **1.** *see, behold:* **a.** *with the eye,* acc. rei ψ $58^{9.11}$ Pr 22^{29} 29^{20} Is 33^{20} 57^{8}; God in theophany Ex 24^{11} (JE); God, after death, apart from the flesh Jb $19^{26.27}$; the face of God ψ 11^{7} 17^{15} (after death). **b.** subj. *the eyes themselves;* man's eyes: תֶּחֱזֶינָה עֵינֶיךָ *thine eyes will behold* Is 33^{17}; also of God's eyes: ψ 11^{4} 17^{2}. **c.** with בְּ *look on* (intensely, with gratification); a damsel Ct $7^{1.1}$; Zion Mi 4^{11}; נֹעַם י׳ in the temple ψ 27^{4}; the work of God Jb 36^{25}; with investigation בַּכּוֹכָבִים on the stars, as stargazers, in astrology Is 47^{13}. **2.** *see as a seer in the ecstatic state,* with acc. of the vision seen: חזון Is 1^{1} Ez 12^{27} 13^{16}; מחזה Nu $24^{4.16}$ (JE; poet., Balaam); מחזה שׁוא Ez 13^{7}; מַשָּׂא Is 13^{1} Hb 1^{1}; משׂאות שׁוא La 2^{14}; שׁוא Ez $13^{6.9.23}$ 21^{34} 22^{28} La 2^{14}; כזב Ez 13^{8}; שֶׁקֶר Zc 10^{2}; obj. *deceitful things* Is 30^{10}; דבר(ים) Is 2^{1} Am 1^{1} Mi 1^{1}; with לְ, *be a seer, for* any one Is 30^{10}; *see a vision for* one La $2^{14.14}$. **3.** *see, perceive:* **a.** with the intelligence, abs. Jb 34^{32} Pr 24^{32}; acc. rei Is 48^{6}; Yahweh in his temple ψ 63^{3}; in his providential workings Jb 23^{9} ψ 46^{9} Is $26^{11.11}$. **b.** *see,* by experience abs. Jb 27^{12}; acc. rei Jb 15^{17} 24^{1}. **c.** *provide,* תחזה מכל העם אנשי חיל Ex 18^{21} *provide from all the people men of ability* (E).

Note.—בֵּית אֲבָנִים יֶחֱזֶה Jb 8^{17} is difficult: RV renders *he (it) beholdeth the place of stones* (the root of the plant personified) Hengst, cf. Reuss al. after 𝔖 𝔗. Other renderings are: *pierceth* (cf. חָזָז) Bö Ew Hi (יְחַזֶּה), Di De MV; *between* (v. p. 108) *the stones it liveth* (יִחְיֶה) 𝔊 Siegf.

חוֹזָי 2 Ch 33^{19}, v. following.

† חֹזֶה **n.m.** **seer**;—abs. ח׳ Am 7^{12} + 7 t.; cstr. חֹזֵה 1 Ch 21^{9} + 3 t.; חוֹזֵה 2 Ch 35^{15}; pl. חֹזִים Is 29^{10} + 4 t.; חוֹזִים 2 Ch 33^{19} (so rd. with 𝔊; חוֹזָי MT scribal error)—**1.** *seer:* **a.** of unnamed persons, syn. נבא(ים) 2 K 17^{13} Is 29^{10}; רֹאִים Is 30^{10}; קֹסְמִים Mi 3^{7}; historical writers דִּבְרֵי הַחֹזִים 2 Ch 33^{18}, דברי חוזים (𝔊) 2 Ch 33^{19} (MT appar. n.pr.) **b.** named prophets; Gad 2 S 24^{11} = 1 Ch 21^{9}, 1 Ch 29^{29} 2 Ch 29^{25}; Amos Am 7^{12}; Iddo 2 Ch 9^{29} 12^{15}; Jehu 2 Ch 19^{2}. **c.** the singers: Heman 1 Ch 25^{5}; Asaph 2 Ch 29^{30}; Jeduthun 2 Ch 35^{15}. *Note*—It seems best to add **2.** *vision* (cf. רֹאֶה Is 28^{7}) עִם שְׁאוֹל עָשִׂינוּ חֹזֶה Is 28^{15} *with Sheʼôl we made a vision* (had a vision, in connexion with Sheʼôl—i.e. by necromancy, v. Du—which makes us secure; ‖ כרת ברית אֶת־מָוֶת); Ew §156e trans. *oracle* here and 2 K 17^{13}; Hoffm ZAW iii. 95 puts this under **1**: 'we have appointed a prophet with Sheʼôl (SS "Ein bei der Scheol bestellter Seher"), who is answerable to us for it;' 𝔊 𝔙 𝔗 AV RV Che Di al., *are at* (or *have made an*) *agreement* (prophetic advice of seers being taken at time of making treaties; v. חָזוּת **1**). —Vid. also כָּל־חֹזֶה **n.pr.m.** sub כל.

† חָזוֹן **n.m.** Dn 8,1 **vision** (on format. cf. Lg BN 204)—abs. ח׳ Ho 12^{11} + 25 t.; cstr. חֲזוֹן Is 1^{1} + 8 t. **1.** *vision,* as seen in the ecstatic state

|| קסם Mi 3[6]; || מקסם Ez 12[24]; || חלמות Dn 1[17], || נביא Dn 9[24]; 'ראה ח Ez 12[27] 13[16]; 'חזה ח Dn 8[15]; 'ראה בח Dn 8[2.2] 9[21], 'דבר בח ψ 89[20]; חזון מצא ח' נראה אל Dn 8[1] *vision appeared unto;* 'מצא ח מיהוה La 2[9] *find a vision from Yahweh;* also Ez 12[22.23] Dn 8[13 17 26] 10[14] 11[14] **2.** *vision*, in the night חֲזוֹן לַיְלָה Is 29[7] **3.** *divine communication in a vision, oracle, prophecy* 'בקש ח מנביא *seek a vision (prophecy) from prophet* Ez 7[26]; || (דבר(ים 1 S 3[1] 1 Ch 17[15]; חֲזוֹן לִבָּם יְדַבֵּרוּ Je 23[16] *a prophecy of their own hearts (minds) they speak*, חֲזוֹן שֶׁקֶר וְקֶסֶם אֱלִיל וְתַרְמִית לִבָּם הֵמָּה מִתְנַבְּאִים Je 14[14] *false vision and* (v. אליל) *worthless divination & deceit of their own hearts they are prophesying;* 'כתב ח *write the vision* Hb 2[2]; also Ho 12[11] Hb 2[3] Pr 29[18] Ez 7[13] (del. Co). **4.** *vision*, as title of book of prophecy, ספר חזון נחום Na 1[1], 'ח ישעיהו Is 1[1], 'ח עבדיה Ob[1]; of other writings of prophets 2 Ch 32[32].

†[חָזוֹת] **n.[f.]**, only cstr בַּחֲזוֹת יֶעְדּוֹ *in the visions* (prophecies) *of Iddo* 2 Ch 9[29], the title of a collection of prophetic history, v. חָזוֹן **4.**

†חָזוּת **n.f. vision, conspicuousness** (on format cf. Lg [BN 202])—abs. 'ח Is 21[2] Dn 8[5.8], cstr חָזוּת Is 29[11]; sf חָזוּתְכֶם Is 28[18],—**1.** *vision, oracle of a prophet* חָזוּת קָשָׁה הֻגַּד־לִי Is 21[2] *a hard vision is declared to me*, וַתְּהִי לָכֶם חָזוּת הַכֹּל כדברי הַסֵּפֶר הֶחָתוּם Is 29[11] *the vision* (prophecy) *of the whole is become to you as the words of a sealed writing*, חָזוּתְכֶם אֶת־שְׁאוֹל לֹא תָקוּם Is 28[18] *your agreement with Sheol will not stand*, so Thes MV De Che Di al. after Vrss, but Ew [§ 156 e] renders *oracle*, and Siegf. *Hellseherei*, v חזה **2.** **2.** *conspicuousness in appearance*. קֶרֶן חָזוּת *a conspicuous horn* Dn 8[5]=the great horn v[8.21]; so חָזוּת אַרְבַּע Dn 8[8], but < rd. אֲחֵרוֹת *others*, as 𝔊 Gi Bev

חִזָּיוֹן **n.m.** [2 S 7. 17] **vision** (on format cf. Lg [BN 200])—abs 'ח 2 S 7[17] Is 22[1.5]; cstr. חֶזְיוֹן Jb 20[8] 33[15]; sf חֶזְיֹנוֹ Zc 13[4], pl abs חֶזְיֹנוֹת Jb 7[14] Jo 3[1], cstr. id. Jb 4[13],—**1** *vision*, in the ecstatic state 'ראה ח Jo 3[1]; 'ח (גי(א Is 22[1.5] *valley of vision* Is 22[1.5]. **2.** *vision*, in the night חֶזְיֹנ(וֹת) לַיְלָה Jb 4[13] 20[8] 33[15]; || חֲלֹמוֹת Jb 7[14]. **3.** *divine communication in a vision, oracle, prophecy:* || דברים 2 S 7[17] (=חזון 1 Ch 17[15]); יֵבֹשׁוּ אִישׁ מֵחֶזְיֹנוֹ בְּהִנָּבְאוֹתוֹ Zc 13[4] *they will be ashamed, every one of his vision when he prophesieth.*

†חֶזְיוֹן **n.pr.m.** (*vision*) ancestor of Benhadad king of Aram 1 K 15[18] (Klo prop. חֶזְרוֹן and comp. 𝔊 1 K 11[23 f])

†חֲזָהאֵל **n.pr.m.** (*Ēl sees;* As. *Ḫaza'ilu* COT [Gloss]) king of Aram 2 K 8[8.13 15], v[29]=2 Ch 22[6], contr. חֲזָאֵל 1 K 19[15 17] 2 K 8[9 12], v[28]=2 Ch 22[5], 2 K 9[14 15] 10[32] 12[18.18.19] 13[3.3.22.24 25]; בית חזאל Am 1[4].

†חֲזִיאֵל **n.pr.m** (*vision of Ēl*) Levite of the line of Gershon, of the time of Solomon 1 Ch 23[9]

†חֲזָיָה **n.pr.m.** (*Yah hath seen*) one of the chiefs of the בני יְהוּדָה Ne 11[5]

†יַחֲזִיאֵל **n.pr.m.** (*Ēl sees*)—**1.** Benjamite warrior of David 1 Ch 12[4] **2.** priest of David 1 Ch 16[6] **3.** a Levite 1 Ch 23[19] 24[23]. **4.** a Levite of the sons of Asaph 2 Ch 20[14]. **5.** ancestor of one of the families of the restoration Ezr 8[5]

†יַחְזְיָה **n.pr.m.** (*Yah sees*) a prince of the restoration Ez 10[15]

†מַחֲזֶה **n [m.] vision**—abs.'מ Gn 15[1]; cstr מַחֲזֵה Nu 24[4 16] Ez 13[7],—*vision, in the ecstatic state* מַחֲזֵה שָׁוְא (|| מִקְסַם כָּזָב) Ez 13[7] of the false prophets, מַחֲזֵה שַׁדַּי Nu 24[4 16] (JE, poems of Balaam); הָיָה דְבַר י' אֶל־אַבְרָם בַּמַּחֲזֶה Gn 15[1] (R) *the word of* ' *came unto Abram in a vision.*

†מֶחֱזָה **n.f. light, place of seeing, window**, מֶחֱזָה אֶל־מֶחֱזָה *light over against light* 1 K 7[4.5]

†מַחֲזִיאוֹת **n.pr.m.** (*visions*) 1 Ch 25[4] (but on this list cf RS [OTJC 422, ed 2, 143]),=מַחֲזִיאֹת 1 Ch 25[30] a Hemanite chief of a course of singers.

II חזה (√of foll; Ar. حَذَا III., حِذَآءٌ *be opposite*, حِذَآءٌ *front*, Lane [537 b]; v. Lg [BN 50] Di [§ 178], cf. Sab. חדית prep *opposite* DHM in MV)

†חָזֶה **n.m.** [Lv 7. 31] **breast of animals** (Aram حَدْيَا, חַדְיָא)—abs. 'ח Ex 29[26]+4 t., cstr חֲזֵה Ex 29[27]+5 t; pl. חֲזוֹת Lv 9[20.21]—*breast*, only P, and only of sacrificial animals; always as wave-offering; of ram of installation Ex 29[26.27] Lv 8[29], of peace-offering Lv 7[30.30] 9[20.21], of Nazirite sacrif. Nu 6[20], perquisite of Aaron and his sons Lv 7[31 34] 10[14 15], cf Nu 18[18].

†חֲזוֹ **n.pr.m.** son of Nahor Gn 22[22], 𝔊 Αζαυ (cf. As. n pr.loc *Ḫazû*, mentioned with *Bazû*

(v. III. כוז) by Esar. Dl$^{Pa\ 307}$ $^{ZK\ 1885,\ 93\ f.}$ COT on Gn 22^{21}; also Di)

חזז (√of foll, Ar حَزَّ *cut* or *notch*, حَزَّ *pierce* (Frey)).

†[**חֲזִיז**] **n.[m.]** **thunder-bolt, lightning-flash** (NH חָזִיז, Aram חֲזִיזָא *shining cloud*)—only cstr חֲזִיז and pl חֲזִיזִים, וְדֶרֶךְ לַחֲזִיז קֹלוֹת Jb 28^{26} *and a way for thunder-bolts* = 38^{25}, י׳ עֹשֶׂה חֲזִיזִים Zc 10^{1} (|| מְטַר־גֶּשֶׁם)

חָזַק $_{291}$ **vb. be or grow firm, strong, strengthen** (NH *id*, Aram سَأَم, חֲזַק *bind on* or *about*, *gird on*, cf Ar حَزَقَ *bind, squeeze*) —†**Qal** *Pf* ח׳ Gn 41^{57}+4 t, חָזָק 2 Ch 26^{15}; sf חֲזָקוֹ 2 Ch 28^{20}, etc; *Impf* יֶחֱזַק 2 Ch 28^{7} (Baer)+2 t, וַיֶּחֱזַק Gn 41^{56}+, יֶחֶזְקוּ 2 S 10^{11}+2 t, יחזקו Is 28^{22}, *Imv* חֲזַק Dt 12^{23}+, חִזְקוּ Dt 31^{6}+, *Inf cstr* לְחָזְקָה 2 K 12^{13}, sf לְחָזְקָה Ez 30^{21}, *Pt.* חָזֵק Ex 19^{19} 2 S 3^{1}, etc,—**I.** intrans *be* or *grow strong* —**1. a.** of physical strength of hands Ju 7^{11} 2 S 2^{7} 16^{21} Ez 22^{14} Zc 8$^{9.13}$ (on Ez 3^{14} v infr), of arm, sq inf Ez 30^{21}, used of recovery fr illness Is 39^{1}, sq מִן compar *overpower* 1 S 17^{50} (c ב instr), 2 S 13^{14} **b.** of people, army Dt 11^{8} Jos 17^{13} (JE), =Ju 1^{28}, Ezr 9^{12}, sq מִן compar. *be stronger than, too strong for, prevail against* 2 S 10$^{11.11}$=1 Ch 19$^{12.12}$ 1 K 20$^{23.25}$; *id.*, sq acc 1 K 16^{22}, cf. of י׳ as prevailing over man Je 20^{7} (|| יָכֹל), sq עַל 2 Ch 8^{3} 27^{6} **c.** of royal power וְדָוִד הֹלֵךְ וְחָזֵק 2 S 3^{1} (opp הֹלְכִים וְדַלִּים), cf 2 Ch 26^{15} (|| חֶזְקָה v^{16}), Dn 11^{5a}. **d.** *prevail over, upon,* of word of king 2 S 24^{4} (sq. אֶל־)=1 Ch 21^{4} (sq. עַל). **e.** of bonds Is 28^{22}. **f.** of sound of trumpet הוֹלֵךְ וְחָזֵק מְאֹד Ex 19^{19} (E, cf חָזָק v^{16}) *it grew much louder and louder* **2.** *be firm, fast* —**a.** lit *be caught fast*, of Absalom's head 2 S 18^{9} (sq. ב) **b.** *be firm, secure,* of a kingdom 2 K 14^{5} (+בְּיָדוֹ)=2 Ch 25^{3} (+עָלָיו). Oftener **c.** *be firm*=courageous, confident, esp Imv., usually || אֱמַץ (q v), Dt 31$^{6.7.23}$ Jos 1$^{6.7.9.18}$ 10^{25} 23^{6} (all D), 2 S 10^{12} 13^{28} 1 K 2^{2} 1 Ch 19^{13} (|| התחזק), 22^{13} 28$^{10.20}$ 2 Ch 15^{7} 19^{11} 32^{7} Ezr 10^{4} ψ 27^{14} 31^{25} Is 35^{4} 41^{6} Hg 2$^{4.4.4}$ Dn 10$^{19.19}$; sq. לַמִּלְחָמָה 2 Ch 25^{8}. **d.** *hold firmly to, devote oneself to,* sq. ב 2 Ch 31^{4}. **e.** sq Inf. *be firm* not to eat blood, i e *firmly refrain* from it Dt 12^{23}, cf. 1 Ch 28^{7}. **3.** *press, be urgent,* sq עַל+Inf Ex 12^{33} (E), sq עַל of hand of י׳ in prophetic ecstasy Ez 3^{14} (𝔊 Co rd חֲזָקָה, adj, v חָזָק) **4.** in bad sense. **a.** *grow stout, rigid, hard,* with idea of perversity, of Pharaoh's heart Ex 7$^{13.22}$ 8^{15} (all P), 9^{35} (R), cf. חָזְקוּ עָלַי דִּבְרֵיכֶם Mal 3^{13} **b.** *be severe, grievous,* of battle 2 K 3^{26}, of famine Gn 41$^{56.57}$ (E), 47^{20} (J, sq עַל), 2 K 25^{3}=Je 52^{6}. **II.** transit. only לֹא חֲזָקוֹ 2 Ch 28^{20} *strengthened him not,* but txt. very dub (|| וַיָּצַר לוֹ). †**Pi.** *Pf.* חִזַּק ψ 147^{13}+, etc; *Impf* וַיְחַזֵּק Ex 9^{12}+10 t., etc.; *Imv* חַזֵּק Ne 6^{9}+2 t, fs. חַזְּקִי Na 3^{14}; חַזֵּקִי Is 54^{2} etc., *Inf cstr* חַזֵּק 2 K 12^{9}+12 t., *Pt* מְחַזֵּק Ex 14^{17}; מְחַזְּקִים 2 K 12^{9},—**1.** *make strong* (physically) **a.** sq acc. pers Ju 16^{28}; sq עַל 3^{12}, sq. מָתְנַיִם Na 2^{2} (|| אַמֵּץ כֹּחַ, of personif. people) **b.** =*restore to strength* Dn 10$^{18.19}$, *to health* Ez 34$^{4.16}$, c ל *give strength to* 1 Ch 29^{12}; so, sq זְרוֹעֹתָם, Ho 7^{15} Ez 30^{24} (and v^{25} Co, v. **Hiph.**) **c** sq. acc rei Is 41^{7} Je 10^{4} (both c ב instr, of manufacture of idols); of strengthening tent-pegs, in metaph. Is 54^{4}, cf 33^{23}; sq bars of gates ψ 147^{13}, oft of *making strong, fortifying* a town, etc Na 3^{14} 2 Ch 11$^{11.12}$ 26^{9} 32^{5}, =*repair* (wall, obj not expr) Ne 3^{19} v. Hiph; c acc of temple 2 K 12$^{6.7.15}$ 22^{6} 2 Ch 24$^{5.12}$ 29^{3} 34^{8}, cf v^{10} (|| לבדוק), sq לְבֵית י׳ 1 Ch 26^{27}, obj breaches (acc.) 2 K 12$^{8.9.13}$ 22^{5} **d.** of establishing kingdom 2 Ch 11^{17}. **2.** *strengthen* the hands (acc) of any one, i e. *sustain, encourage* (opp רִפָּה) Ju 9^{24} Je 23^{14} Ez 13^{22} Is 35^{3} Jb 4^{3} Ezr 6^{22} Ne 2^{18} 6^{9} 2 Ch 29^{34}, ויח׳ ידו באלהים 1 S 23^{16}; sq. ב Ezr 1^{6} (+ב instr) **3.** *make strong=bold, encourage,* c. acc. Dt 1^{38} 3^{28} 2 S 11^{25} Is 41^{7}, c. acc pers.+ לַעֲבֹדַת בֵּית י׳ 2 Ch 35^{2}. **4.** *make firm*:—**a.** c 2 acc. וְאַבְנֵטְךָ אֲחַזְּקֶנּוּ Is 22^{21} *and with thy sash* (of office) *will I make him firm,* i e. bind it firmly about him (|| הלביש) **b.** *make firm* or *fixed,* = *definitely adopt* יח׳־ לָמוֹ דָּבָר רָע ψ 64^{6}. **5.** *make rigid, hard,* i.e. perverse, obstinate, *harden* (the heart of any one) Ex 4^{21} 10$^{20.27}$ (all E), 9^{12} 11^{10} 14$^{4.8.17}$ (all P), Jos 11^{20} (D), v also ח׳ פניהם מסלע Je 5^{3}† **Hiph.**$_{118}$ *Pf.* הֶחֱזִיק Ju 7^{8}+; 3 fs. הֶחֱזִיקָה Je 49^{24}+, sf הֶחֱזִקַתְנִי Je 8^{21}; הֶחֱזַקְתִּי Ne 5^{16}+3 t, וְהַחֲזַקְתִּי Ez 30^{25}, etc.; *Impf* יַחֲזִיק Jb 8^{15}+2 t; 1 s וְאַחְזִק Is 42^{6}; יַחֲזִיקוּ Je 6^{23}+2 t; יַחֲזִקוּ Dn 11^{32}, etc; *Imv.* הַחֲזֵק 2 S 11^{25}+2 t., etc; *Inf cstr.* הַחֲזִיק 2 K 15^{19} Is 64^{6}, sf הַחֲזִיקִי Je 31^{32} (הַח׳ Cod. Petrop. v. RS$^{JPh\ xvi\ 1888,\ 73}$), *Pt.* מַחֲזִיק Ex 9^{2}+9 t; sf. מַחֲזִקָהּ Dn 11^{6}; fs. מַחֲזֶקֶת Ne 4^{11}; pl. מַחֲזִיקִים Ne 4^{10}+5 t.; cstr. מַחֲזִיקֵי Ez 27$^{9.27}$;—†**1. a.** *make strong, strengthen* Je 51^{12}. **b.** *make firm,* the kingdom 2 K 15^{19} (+בְּיָדוֹ) **c.** *display strength* (late) 2 Ch 26^{8}

(‖ וַיֵּלֶךְ שְׁמוֹ עַד וגו׳), Dn 11^{32} (‖ וְעָשׂוּ). †**2.** *make severe*, of battle 2 S 11^{25}. †**3.** sq. יד = *support* Ez 16^{49}; sq. זְרֹעוֹת 30^{25} (subj. ^; but Co rds. **Pi.** as v^{24})†. **4.** = *repair*, walls of Jerus., Ne 3$^{4.4.4}$ + 31 t. Ne 3; cf. (in gen.) pt. used substant. מחזיקי בדקך Ez 27$^{9.27}$ of Tyre and her ships (‖ מַלָּחִים, etc.) †**5.** *prevail*, abs. Dn 11^{7}; sq. עַל Jb 18^{9}; *prevail upon to* החז׳ בו לֶאֱכָל 2 K 4^{8}. **6.** esp *take* or *keep hold* of, *seize, grasp*. **a.** *take hold* of, *seize, catch*, sq ב Gn 19^{16}(J), 21^{18}(E), Ex 4^{4} (J; ‖ אחז), Ju 7^{20} 1 S 15^{27} 2 S 1^{11} 1 K 1^{50} 2^{28} 2 K 2^{12} 4^{27} Is 4^{1} Zc 8$^{23.23}$ Pr 7^{13} 26^{17}, cf. also Ju 19$^{25.29}$ 2 Ch 28^{15}, with violence Dt 22^{25} 25^{11} 1 S 17^{35} (perh pf. consec. freq, v. Dr), 2 S 2^{16} 13^{11}, sq. לְ 2 S 15^{5}; fig *take hold* in order to lead one (subj ׳י) sq ב Je 31^{32}, c acc. Is 41$^{9.13}$; cf Is 51^{18} (ב; ‖ נַהֵל); sq acc. Na 3^{14} *take hold of the brick-mould*, Je 6^{23} = 50^{42}, Zc 14^{13} (with violence), ψ 35^{2} Ne 4$^{10.11}$, seize the kingdom Dn 11^{21}; in metaph. Mi 4^{9} (הֶחֱזִיקֵךְ חִיל), Je 6^{24} 8^{21} 49^{24} (v. Gie), 50^{43}; of pious laying hold of ׳י, sq. בְּ Is 64^{6}, cf. 27^{5} 56$^{2.4.6}$, of other gods 1 K 9^{9} = 2 Ch 7^{22}; laying hold of wisdom Pr 3^{18}, cf. 4^{13} Jb 2$^{3.9}$ 27^{6} Je 8^{5}. **b.** *have* or *keep hold of*, sq. ב Ju 16^{26} 2 S 3^{29} Je 50^{33} Ne 4^{15} **c.** *hold up*, sq ב, fig. = *sustain, support* Lv 25^{35}; of ׳י holding his servants Is 42^{6} 45^{1}, cf. Jb 8^{20}, v. also pt. used substantively Dn 11^{1} (‖ מָעֹז), v^{6} (‖ מְבִיא, ילד); of Ne holding fast to (ב) his work Ne 5^{16}; cf of wicked, holding to his house Jb 8^{15}; *cleave* or *cling to* (על) one's brethren Ne 10^{30}. hence **c.** *keep, retain*, sq ב Ex 9^{2}(J), Ju 7^{8} 19^{4}; so Ez 7^{13} Sm Co (MT Hithp); sq anger (acc.) Mi 7^{18}. **d.** hence also *hold, contain*, sq. acc. 2 Ch 4^{5}. †**Hithp.** (esp. Ch) *Pf.* הִתְחַזֵּק 2 Ch 13^{7} + 3 t, etc.; *Impf.* וַיִּתְחַזֵּק Gn 48^{2} + 7 t; וַיִּתְחַזֵּק 2 Ch 21^{4} 32^{5}, יִתְחַזָּקוּ Ez 7^{13} (but Sm Co rd. Hiph), etc., *Imv* הִתְחַזֵּק 1 K 20^{22}; הִתְחַזְּקוּ 1 S 4^{9}; *Inf. cstr.* לְהִתְחַזֵּק 2 Ch 13^{8} 16^{9}, *Pt.* מִתְחַזֵּק 2 S 3^{6} Dn 10^{21}; pl. מתחזקים 1 Ch 11^{10};—**1.** *strengthen oneself* 2 S 3^{6} 1 K 20^{22} 2 Ch 1^{1} 12^{13} 13^{21} 21^{4} 23^{1} 25^{11} 27^{6}, sq. עַל *against* 2 Ch 17^{1}, *gain strength* Ezr 7^{28} Dn 10^{19}, cf. התח׳ ביהוה 1 S 30^{6}, fig. = *take courage* 2 Ch 15^{8}. **2.** *put forth strength, use one's strength* Gn 48^{2} (i e he exerted himself, he sat up by a great effort), Nu 13^{20} Ju 20^{22} 1 S 4^{9} 2 S 10^{12} 1 Ch 19^{13} 2 Ch 32^{5}. **3.** sq. לִפְנֵי *withstand* 2 Ch 13$^{7.8}$ **4.** sq. עִם *hold strongly with* 1 Ch 11^{10} Dn 10^{21}, cf. of ׳י, לְהִתְח׳ עִם לְבָבָם שָׁלֵם אֵלָיו 2 Ch 16^{9} —For יִתְחַזָּקוּ Ez 7^{13} rd. Hiph, v. Sm Co Da.

†חָזָק† **adj.** strong, stout, mighty;—ח׳ Ex 10^{19} + 18 t.; f חֲזָקָה Ex 3^{19} + 31 t. + Ez 3^{14} (Co for MT vb. 3 fs.), pl. חֲזָקִים Ju 18^{26} + 2 t.; cstr. חִזְקֵי Ez 2^{4} (del. Co v. infr.) 3^{7};—**1.** *strong*. **a.** of men, rarely pred. Nu 13^{18} (opp. רָפֶה), v^{31} (compar c. מִן), Jos 14^{11} 17^{18} (all JE), Ju 18^{26} (compar c. מן), also of גֹּאֵל Je 50^{34} Pr 23^{11}, of hand of ׳י Jos 4^{24} (D), so Ez 3^{14} 𝔊 Co (v. supr and חָזַק **Qal 3**); cf of Tyre הָיְתָה חֲזָקָה בַיָּם Ez 26^{17} (del. B Co). **b.** usu. attrib; of arm of Pharaoh Ez 30^{22} (opp. נִשְׁבָּרֶת); esp. of hand of ׳י in delivering Isr from Egypt, Ex 3^{19} (gloss? v Di), 6^{1} 13^{9} (all J), Dt 6^{21} 7^{8} 9^{26} Dn 9^{15}; in wonders done by agency of Moses Dt 34^{12}, also בכֹחַ גָּדוֹל וּבְיָד חֲזָקָה Ex 32^{11} (JE), cf Ne 1^{10}, but oftener ביד חזקה ובזרוע נטויה Dt 4^{34} 5^{15} 7^{19} 11^{2} 26^{8} Je 32^{21} ψ 136^{12}; of control of enemies and deliverance from exile Ez 20$^{33.34}$; more gen. Dt 3^{24} (‖ גָּדְלְךָ), 1 K 8^{42} = 2 Ch 6^{32}, of ׳י's opposition to Zedekiah Je 21^{5}, once of Edom, opp Isr בעם כבד וביד חזקה Nu 20^{20} (JE) **c.** of sword of ׳י Is 27^{1} (‖ הַקָּשָׁה וְהַגְּדוֹלָה), of wind Ex 10^{19} (J), 1 K 19^{11}, sound of trumpet (= *loud*) Ex 19^{16} (E) **d.** *severe, sharp, hot*, of war 1 S 14^{52} (pred.), battle 2 S 11^{15}, sickness 1 K 17^{17} (pred.), famine 18^{2}. **e.** *firm, hard*, of face, פנים Ez 3^{8}, forehead, מֵצַח v^{8}, adamant, sim of forehead v^{9} (compar., c מן), of sky Jb 37^{18} (pred.) In pl. cstr. ח׳ לב Ez 2^{4} *hard of heart* (‖ קְשֵׁי פָנִים) but om B Co, ח׳־מצח 3^{7} *hard* (= impudent) *of forehead* (‖ קשי־לב) **2.** as subst, *a strong one*, of ׳י (בְּחָזָק, *as, in the character of, a strong one*) Is 40^{10}, of ׳י's agent Is 28^{2} (‖ אַמִּיץ); v. also וְחָזָק לֹא יְאַמֵּץ כֹּחוֹ Am 2^{14}, c מִן comp = *one too strong for* Je 31^{11} ψ 35^{10}. In Ez 34^{16} MT uses הח׳ in bad sense (‖ הַשְּׁמֵנָה). 𝔊 Co, with diff. text, in good sense (v. VB)

חָזֵק **adj. verb.** v. חָזַק **Qal** *Pt*

†[חֵזֶק] **n.[m.]** strength, only חִזְקִי ׳י ψ 18^{2} (om by error ‖ 2 S 22^{2} where 𝔊L ἰσχύς μου) (De al der fr חָזַק, but [חָזְקָה] favours חֵזֶק)

†[חֶזְקָה] **n.f.** strength, force (strictly Inf form fr חזק v Ges §45.1b)—**1.** of urgency of ׳י's hand in prophetic inspiration בְּחֶזְקַת הַיָּד Is 8^{11} (cf. חָזָק Ez 3^{14}). **2.** of royal power כְּחֶזְקָתוֹ 2 Ch 12^{1} 26^{16} (‖ חָזַק v^{15}), Dn 11^{2}.

†חֹזֶק **n.m.** strength,—ח׳ cstr. Ex 13^{3} + 3 t, חָזְקֵנוּ Am 6^{13},—**1.** of ׳י, ח׳ יָד Ex 13$^{3.14.16}$ (all JE). **2.** national strength Am 6^{13} Hg 2^{22}.

†חָזְקָה **n.f.** strength, force, violence, alw. בְּחָזְקָה, *with strength force*, etc ,—**1.** of oppression Ju 4^{3} *forcibly, violently;* capture *by force* 1 S 2^{16}, Ez 34^{4} of ruling בְּח׳ וּבְפָרֶךְ *with force and with rigour.* **2.** rebuke *severely, sharply* Ju 8^{1}; cry *mightily*, insistently Jon 3^{8}—לְחָזְקָה 2 K 12^{13} v חָזַק **Qal** *Inf.*

†חִזְקִי **n.pr m.** a Benjamite 1 Ch 8^{17}, 𝔊 Αζακ(ε)ι; 𝔊L Εζεκια

יְחִזְקִיָּה, יְחִזְקִיָּהוּ, חִזְקִיָּה, חִזְקִיָּהוּ **n.pr.m** (י׳ *hath strengthened,* י׳ *strengtheneth*, = As *Hazaki(i)au*, Schr ^{COT} on 2 K $18^{1\,ff.}$, Jager $^{BAS\,I\,469}$, cf. n pr. יחזק on seal Gann $^{JAs\,1883\,Feb-Mar,\,134\,No\,7}$, —on format. v Lag $^{BN\,134}$)— **1.** 𝔊 Εζεκιας, *son of Ahaz*, King of Judah, seldom †חִזְקִיָּה 2 K $18^{1\,10\,14\,11\,15\,16\,16}$, also אַנְשֵׁי ח׳ Pr 25^{1}†; elsewh in 2 K (exc 20^{10}) חִזְקִיָּהוּ 16^{20} 18^{9}+34 t, 2 K 18–21 ‖ Is 36^{1}+31 t, Is 36–39; also †Je $26^{18\,19}$ 1 Ch 3^{13} 2 Ch $29^{18.27}$ 30^{24} 32^{15}, in Ch usu יְחִזְקִיָּהוּ 1 Ch 4^{41} 2 Ch 28^{27}+35 t 2 Ch 29–33; also 2 K 20^{10} Je 15^{4}, and in title Is 1^{1}, †יְחִזְקִיָּה Ho 1^{1} Mi 1^{1} †(if י in these three be not txt err for ו) †**2** חִזְקִיָּה great-great-grandfather of proph Zephaniah Zp 1^{1}, 𝔊 τοῦ Εζεκιου, perh = **1.** †**3.** 𝔊 Εζεκια(ς), חִזְקִיָּה man of royal Davidic line 1 Ch 3^{23} prob near time of Chr. †**4.** יְחִזְקִיָּה, 𝔊 Εζεκια(ς), head of a family of returned exiles Ezr 2^{16}=חִזְקִיָּה Ne 7^{21}, cf also ח׳ Ne 10^{18} †**5.** יְחִזְקִיָּהוּ 𝔊 Εζεκιας, an Ephraimite, Ahaz's time 2 Ch 28^{12}

†יְחֶזְקֵאל **n.pr.m.** (*God strengtheneth*, cf foreg; v Lag $^{BN\,134}$)—**1.** the well-known priest and prophet, son of Buzi, 𝔊 Ιεζεκιηλ, Ez 1^{3} 24^{24}. **2.** priest of 19th course (assigned to David's time) 1 Ch 24^{16}, 𝔊 Εζεκηλ, 𝔊L (20th course, cf A) Ιεζεκιηλ.

יְחִזְקִיָּהוּ, יְחִזְקִיָּה v. חִזְקִיָּהוּ supr.

חזר (√of foll, meaning dub, perh cf Ar خَزِرَ *the eye was* or *became narrow, small*, Lane $^{731\,c}$, hence *narrow-eyed* animal)

†חֲזִיר **n.m.** $^{\psi\,80\,14}$ swine, boar (NH *id*; Aram. חֲזִירָא, ܚܙܝܪܐ; Ar. خِنْزِير (Aram loan-wd acc. to Frä ^{110}, yet v. Lag $^{BN\,113}$), Eth ሐንዚር: (only once; = wild boar), v Hom $^{NS\,319\,f\,358,\,366}$)—alw. st abs, 4 t c art הַח׳,—**1.** *swine*, forbidden as food Lv 11^{7} (P), Dt 14^{8}, cf בְּשַׂר הַח׳ Is 65^{4} 66^{17}, and דַּם־ח׳ 66^{3} as heathen offering (RS $^{Sem\,1\,272.325\,338.392}$), with implication of repulsiveness נֶזֶם זָהָב בְּאַף ח׳ Pr 11^{22} sim of fair woman with dub. character. **2.** *wild boar* ח׳ מִיַּעַר ψ 80^{14} fig. of foes of Isr (in fig of vineyard).

†חֵזִיר **n.pr.m.** (cf inscr in RA $^{1887,\,pl\,7}$, Dr $^{Sm\,xxiii}$, No $^{ZMG\,1886,\,162}$ 'pointing ◌ֵ to avoid offence,' but Nbr $^{Acad\,1887,\,Dec\,17}$ comp. Talm. & 𝔗 (חֲזוֹרָא, חיזור, חוזרא etc) *pomegranate* (and *apple*, Syr ܚܙܘܪܐ, ܚܙܘܪ), cf בני רמון 2 S $4^{2.5.9}$)—**1** a priest of 17th course (assigned to David's time) 1 Ch 24^{15}, 𝔊 Χηζειν (16th, v^{14}), but A Ιεζειρ, 𝔊L Χηζειρ. **2.** one of those sealed Ne 10^{21}; 𝔊 Ηζειρ, 𝔊L Αζηρ.

†יְחֵזְרָה **n.pr.m.** 1 Ch 9^{12} cf. אַחְזַי p 28 b.

חַח, חָח v sub חוח.

†חָטָא $_{238}$ **vb.** miss (a goal or way), go wrong, sin (NH *id.*, Aram חֲטָא, ܚܛܐ, As *haṭû*, Zim $^{BP\,46}$, Sab. חטא, החטא, *id*, DHM in MV, Ar خَطِئَ *do wrong, commit a mistake* or *an error*; II *make to miss the mark*; IV. *miss the mark, miss the way*; Eth ኀጥአ: *fail to find* or *have*, sts *sin*, esp. in deriv)—**Qal** *Pf* ח׳ Ex 32^{31}+29 t, 3 fs חָטְאָה Lv 5^{15} La 1^{8}, חָטָאָה Je 50^{14} Ez 16^{51}, חָטָאת Ex 5^{16}, etc, +82 t Pf, *Impf.* יֶחֱטָא Lv 4^{3}+12 t, תֶּחֱטָאוּ Ex 20^{20} ψ 4^{5}, etc + 20 t. Impf, *Inf.* חֲטֹא Ez 3^{21}+8 t, מֵחֲטוֹא ψ 39^{2}, מחטו (txt err for מחטא) Gn 20^{6}, בַּחֲטָאָה Nu 15^{28}, חֲטָאתִי Ez 33^{12} (del. Co); *Pt* חוטא Pr 13^{22}+6 t, חטא Is 1^{4} Ec 9^{2}, חוֹטֶא Is 65^{20}+2 t, חֹטֶא Ec 8^{12}, sf חטאי Pr 8^{36}, pl. חֹטְּאִים 1 S 14^{33}, sf. חטאת Ez $18^{4\,20}$,—**1.** *miss*. לא תחטא *thou shalt not miss anything* Jb 5^{24}, אָץ בְּרַגְלַיִם חוטא Pr 19^{2} *one hastening with his feet misseth* (the way or the goal); חטאי חמס נַפְשׁוֹ Pr 8^{36} *the one missing me* (Wisdom) *is one wronging himself* (opp. מֹצְאִי), *miss*, i e. *endanger*, one's life Pr 20^{2} Hb 2^{10} acc. to De VB (others sub **3** q v) **2.** *sin, miss the goal* or *path of right and duty*. **a.** *against man*, abs Ex 5^{16} (E), 1 S 26^{21} 2 S 19^{21} 1 K 18^{9} 2 K 18^{14}; with ל of the person against whom or towards whom one sins, Gn 40^{1} (E), Ju 11^{27} 1 S 2^{25} 19^{4} 24^{12}, 1 K 8^{31} = 2 Ch 6^{22}; מה חטאתי לך *wherein have I sinned against thee?* Gn 20^{9} (E) Je 37^{18}; with ב, אל תחטאו בילד Gn 42^{22} (E) *do not sin against* the lad, against David 1 S $19^{4.5}$. **b.** elsewhere always *against God*, abs Ex 20^{20} (E), 9^{34} (J) Jos 7^{11} (D) Lv 4^{3} $5^{1\,11\,17\,21\,23}$ Nu 16^{22} (P), Ne 6^{13} Jb $1^{5\,22}$ 7^{20} 10^{14} 24^{19} 35^{6} ψ 4^{5} 78^{32} Is 43^{27} 64^{4} Je 2^{35} La 5^{7} Ez $3^{21\,21}$ 16^{51} 28^{16} 33^{12} Ho 8^{11}

(del We$^{Kl\ Proph}$), v^{11} 10^{9} 13^{2}; לא נתתי לחטא חכי *I have not permitted my palate to sin* Jb 31^{30}; *Pt.* חטא, used as adj, sinful nation Is 1^{4}, sinful person Ez 18$^{4.20}$; but usually as noun, *sinner* Pr 11^{31} 13^{22} 14^{21} Ec 2^{26} 7^{26} 8^{12} 9$^{2.18}$ Is 65^{20} Sin is confessed: חָטָאנוּ *we have sinned* Nu 14^{40} 21^{7} (E) Ju 10^{15} 1 S 12^{10}, 1 K 8^{47} = 2 Ch 6^{37}, Ne 1^{6} ψ 106^{6} La 5^{16} Dn 9$^{5.15}$; חטאתי *I have sinned* Ex 9^{27} Nu 22^{34} (J) 1 S 15$^{24.30}$ 2 S 24$^{10.17}$ 1 Ch 21$^{8.17}$ Jb 33^{27}. Sin is universal: אין אדם אשר לא יחטא *there is no man who sinneth not* 1 K 8^{46} = 2 Ch 6^{36}, כי אדם אין צדיק בארץ אשר יעשה טוב ולא יחטא Ec 7^{20} *for man there is none righteous in the earth who doeth good and sinneth not;* with ל, against God Gn 20^{6}(E), 39^{9}(J), Ex 32^{33} Nu 32^{23}(both JE), Dt 9^{16} 20^{18} 1 S 2^{25} 12^{23} 14$^{33.34}$, 1 K 8$^{33.35.46.50}$ = 2 Ch 6$^{24.26.36.39}$, 2 K 17^{7} Ho 4^{7} Mi 7^{9} Zp 1^{17} Je 40^{3} 44^{23} 50$^{7.14}$ Ez 14^{13} Is 42^{24} Jb 8^{4} ψ 78^{17} 119^{11} Ne 1^{6}; in confession חטאתי ל Ex 10^{16} Jos 7^{20}(J), 2 S 12^{13} ψ 41^{5} 51^{6}, חטאנו ל Dt 1^{41} Ju 10^{10} 1 S 7^{6} Je 3^{25} 8^{14} 14$^{7.20}$ Dn 9$^{8.11}$; with בְּ of instr, lips Jb 2^{10}, tongue ψ 39^{2}; wherein Ez 37^{23} Lv 4^{23} (P), therein Lv 5^{22}(P); ellipsis of ב in phrase עונם אשר ח׳ לי (*their*) *iniquity wherein they sinned against me* Je 33$^{8.8}$, בשגגה *by error, unwittingly* Lv 4$^{2.22.27}$ 5^{15} Nu 15$^{27.28}$ (all P); *against* thy judgments Ne 9^{29}; with על, *with regard to* Lv 5^{5} Nu 6^{11}(P) Ne 13^{26}, with cognate acc. ח׳ חֲטָאָה Ex 32$^{30.31}$(JE); חַטָּאת אשר ח׳ Nu 12^{11} (J) Lv 4$^{3.28.28.35}$ 5$^{6.10.13}$ (all P) 19$^{22.22}$(H), Dt 9^{18} 1 K 14$^{16.22}$ 15^{30} 16$^{13.19}$ 2 K 21^{17} Ez 18^{24} 33^{16}; חטאת אשר ח׳ ל Je 16^{10} Ne 1^{6}, חטאת אשר ח׳ על Lv 4^{14}(P); חטא ח׳ La 1^{8}; חֵטְא אשר ח׳ Dt 19^{15} **3.** *incur guilt, penalty by sin, forfeit* וחטאתי לך כל הימים Gn 43^{9} *I shall incur the blame of sinning against thee all my days*, cf. 44^{32}(J); c. acc. חוטא נפש *forfeiting oneself, one's life* Pr 20^{2} Hb 2^{10} acc. to most, yet v. sub **1.**—והביא אשמו אשר ח׳ Lv 5^{7} *he shall bring his trespass-offering which he has incurred by sin*, קרבנו אשר ח׳ Lv 5^{11}; את אשר ח׳ מן־הקדש ישלם v^{16} *what he hath incurred by taking of the holy thing he shall pay* **Pi.** *Pf.* חטא Lv 14^{52}, sf. חטאו Nu 19^{19}, חטאת Ex 29^{36} + 2 t.; 3 pl. חִטְּאוּ Ez 43$^{22.22}$; *Impf.* ויחטא Lv 8^{15}, sf. וַיְחַטְּאֵהוּ Lv 9^{15}, תחטאני ψ 51^{9}, אֲחַטֶּנָּה Gn 31^{39}, וַיְחַטְּאוּ 2 Ch 29^{24}; *Inf.* חַטֵּא Lv 14^{49} Ez 43^{23}; *Pt.* הַמְחַטֵּא Lv 6^{19};—**1.** *bear loss:* אָנֹכִי אֲחַטֶּנָּה *I bare the loss of it* Gn 31^{39} (E; lit. *I let it be missing*? poss id אֲחֻטֶּנָּה *I was made to miss it*?). **2.** *make a sin-offering*. c sf. referring to שעיר Lv 9^{15}(P); to sin-offering Lv 6^{19}(P); על המזבח *upon the altar* Ex 29^{36} (P, not *cleanse the altar* RV), ח׳ את דמם המזבחה 2 Ch 29^{24} *made a sin-offering with their blood on the altar.* **3.** *purify from sin*: the altar, by putting the blood of the sin-offering on its horns, Lv 8^{15}(P), Ez 43$^{20.22.22.23}$; the sanctuary, by applying to it the blood of the sin-offering Ez 45^{18}. **4.** *purify from uncleanness:* the house of the leper by application of the mixture of living water and blood of the bird Lv 14$^{49.52}$(P), a person, by application of the mixture of living water and ashes of the red heifer Nu 19^{19}(P), by sprinkling with a hyssop sprig ψ 51^{9}. **Hiph.** *Pf.* החטיא 1 K 14^{16} + 17 t., הֶחֱטִי (Kt err for החטיא) 2 K 13^{6}, sf הֶחֱטִיאָם 2 K 17^{21}; pl. הֶחֱטִיאוּ 1 K 16^{13} Ne 13^{26}; *Impf.* יַחֲטִא Ju 20^{16} 2 K 21^{11}, תַּחֲטִיא Dt 24^{4}; וַתַּחֲטִא 1 K 16^{2} 21^{22}; pl יַחֲטִיאוּ Ex 23^{33}, *Inf* הַחֲטִיא Ec 5^{5} 1 K 16^{19} Je 32^{35}(Qr), הַחֲטִי Je 32^{35}(Kt err.); *Pt* pl. cstr. מַחֲטִיאֵי Is 29^{21}, — **1.** *miss the mark*. קֹלֵעַ בָּאֶבֶן אֶל־הַשַּׂעֲרָה וְלֹא יַחֲטִא Ju 20^{16} *slinging with stones at an hair and would not miss* **2.** *induce or cause to sin*: with acc Ex 23^{33}(JE), Ne 13^{26}, elsewh in the phrase החטיא את ישראל (*he*) *caused Israel to sin* 1 K 14^{16} 15$^{26.30.34}$ 16$^{2.13.19.26}$ 21^{22} 22^{53} 2 K 3^{3} 10$^{29.31}$ 13$^{2.6.11}$ 14^{24} 15$^{9.18.24.28}$ 23^{15}; c sf. ref. to Isr. 2 K 17^{21}, החטיא את יהודה 2 K 21$^{11.16}$ Je 32^{35} (sts c. 2nd acc —חטאת, or אשר ref to חטאת.—1 K 15$^{26.34}$ 16^{26} 2 K 17^{21} 21^{16}; prob. also 1 K 14^{16} 15^{30} 16^{13}, no 2nd acc. 1 K 16$^{2.19}$ 21^{22} 22^{53} 2 K 21^{11} 23^{15} Je 32^{35}, the rest are ambiguous). **3.** *bring into guilt, condemnation, punishment*. מחטיאי אדם Is 29^{21} *who bring a man into condemnation;* לא תחטיא את הארץ Dt 24^{4} *thou shalt not bring the land into guilt;* אל תתן את־פיך לחטיא את־בשרך Ec 5^{5} *do not permit thy mouth to bring thy flesh into punishment.* **Hithp.** *Impf* יתחטא Nu 19^{12} + 4 t, יִתְחַטָּאוּ Nu 8^{21}, תִּתְחַטְּאוּ Nu 31^{19}, תתחטאו Nu 31^{20}; יִתְחַטָּאוּ Jb 41^{17}, —**1.** *miss oneself, lose oneself*, fig for *be bewildered, beside oneself*, מִשְּׁבָרִים יִתְחַטָּאוּ Jb 41^{17} *by reason of consternation they are beside themselves* (|| יגורו *are afraid*) **2.** *purify oneself from uncleanness*, only in P. **a.** Levites Nu 8^{21}. **b.** those in contact with the dead Nu 19$^{12.13.20}$ 31$^{19.20}$; with ב, בְּמֵי נִדָּה Nu 31^{23}, by a mixture of ashes of the red heifer with fresh water Nu 19^{12}.

† חֵטְא **n.m.**$^{Dt\ 15,9}$ sin (on format. v. Lag$^{BN\ 142}$)—ח׳ Lv 19^{17} + 15 t.; sf. חֶטְאוֹ Lv 24^{15} + 5 t, חֲטָאָו La 3^{39}, חֶטְאָם Lv 20^{20}; pl. חֲטָאִים Ec 10^{4}; cstr. חֲטָאֵי 2 K 10^{29} Ez 23^{49}; sf חֲטָאַי Gn 41^{9},

חַטָּאַי Is 38^{17} ψ 51^{11}, חַטָּאֵינוּ Dn 9^{16} ψ 103^{10}, חַטָּאֵיכֶם Is 1^{18},—**1.** *sin*. **a.** against man Gn 41^{9} (E) Ec 10^{4} **b.** elsewh ag God, abs. Is 31^{7} Ho 12^{9}, ח׳ חָטָא La 1^{8} cf Dt 19^{15} 2 K 10^{29}, ח׳ משפט מות *sin* worthy of death Dt 21^{22} = ח׳ מות 22^{26}, with בּ, *because of*, Dn 9^{16}; God is entreated. *hide thy face from my sins* ψ 51^{11}, and it is said in faith, *thou wilt cast behind thy back all my sins* Is 38^{17} **2.** *guilt of sin* היה חטא ב *sin* (the guilt of sin) *come on one* Dt 15^{9} 21^{22} 23$^{22.23}$ 24^{15}, בחטאו מת *in his sin* (guilt) *die* Nu 27^{3} (P); איש בחטאו *each for his own sin* Dt 24^{16} = 2 K 14^{6} = 2 Ch 25^{4}, בחטא יחמתני אמי ψ 51^{7} *in sin* (condition of sin and guilt) *my mother conceived me*, אם חטאיכם כשנים Is 1^{18} *though your sins be like scarlet* (in guilt), לא כחטאינו עשה לנו ψ 103^{10} *not according to our sins* (their guilt) *hath he done to us.* **3** *punishment for sin*. נשא ח׳ *bear sin* (its punishment) Lv 20^{20} 24^{15} (H), Nu 9^{13} 18^{22} (P); with עַל, *bear sin because of* Lv 19^{17} 22^{9} (H) Nu 18^{32} (P); bear sins of idols (in worshipping idols) Ez 23^{49}; the ideal servant of Yahweh *bore the sins of many* Is 53^{12}; without נשא, only La 3^{39} גבר על חטאו (wherefore doth) *a man* (complain) *for the punishment of his sin?*

†[חַטָּא] **adj.** and **n.m. 1.** sinful, **2** sinners—as adj f חַטָּאָה Am 9^{8}, elsewhere only pl חַטָּאִים Nu 32^{14} + 15 t, cstr חַטָּאֵי Am 9^{10}, sf חַטָּאֶיהָ Is 13^{9},—**1. adj. a.** *sinful* men Nu 32^{14} (J), kingdom Am 9^{8} **b.** *exposed to condemnation, reckoned as offenders* 1 K 1^{21} (cf Hiph Pt Is 29^{21}). Elsewh. **2. n.m.** *sinners* Nu 17^{3} (P), 1 S 15^{18} Am 9^{10} Is 1^{28} 13^{9} 33^{14} ψ 1$^{1.5}$ 25^{8} 26^{9} 51^{15} 104^{35} Pr 1^{10} 13^{21} 23^{17}, ח׳ ליהוה *sinners against* י׳ Gn 13^{13} (J).

†חַטָּאָה **n.f.** sinful thing, sin, Ex 34^{7} (JE) Is 5^{18}

†חֲטָאָה **n.f** sin, sin-offering (?)—**1.** *sin*, chiefly in the phrase ח׳ גדלה *great sin* Gn 20^{9} (E) Ex 32$^{21.30.31}$ (JE), 2 K 17^{21}, כסוי ח׳ ψ 32^{1} *he whose sin is covered* is blessed, but the *prayer* of the wicked *becomes sin when he is judged* ψ 109^{7}. **2.** *sin-offering* (acc to most) עולה וחטאה ψ 40^{7} *whole burnt-offering and sin-offering* (so Vrss Thes MV SS al., but < *whole burnt-offering with sin* v Br$^{MP\ 329}$)

†חַטָּאת **n.f.**$^{1814\ 38}$ (Gn 4^{7} no exception for רבץ is noun = crouching beast) **sin, sin-offering,** ח׳ Gn 4^{7} + 124 t.; לַחַטָּ֫את Nu 15^{24} (txt err. for לחטאת), לְחַטָּאת Zc 13^{1} (but rd לְחַטָּאת Sta$^{ZAW\ i\ 36}$); cstr. חַטַּאת Ex 30^{10} + 19 t, sf חַטָּאתִי Gn 31^{36} + 16 t, חַטָּאתוֹ 1 K 16^{26}, חַטַּאתְכֶם Ex 32^{30} + 3 t, etc, + 52 t sf, pl חַטָּאוֹת 2 K 12^{17} + 3 t, cstr. חַטֹּאות ψ 25^{7} + 17 t.; חַטֹּאת Nu 5^{6} + 6 t; sf. חַטֹּאותַי ψ 25^{18}, חַטֹּאתָו Ez 18^{21} 33^{16}, etc, + 40 t. sf,—**1.** *sin*. **a.** *against man* Gn 31^{36} 50^{17} (E), Nu 12^{11} (J) 1 S 20^{1}, ח׳ אדם *sins against man* Nu 5^{6} (P). Elsewhere **b.** *against God* Lv 4$^{14.23.28}$ (P), 1 S 2^{17} 14^{38} 1 K 16$^{13.13}$ 2 K 21$^{16.17}$ 2 Ch 33^{19} Is 3^{9} 30^{1} 58^{1} 59$^{2.12}$ Je 5^{25} 16$^{10.18}$ 30$^{14.15}$ 50^{20} La 4$^{6.22}$ Ez 16^{51} 18^{14} 21^{29} 33$^{10.16}$ Am 5^{12} (We$^{Kl\ Proph.}$ ids חטאיכם, as Is 1^{18}—v חֵטְא—on acc. of masc עצומים), Mi 1^{13} 3^{8} ψ 32^{5} 51^{5} 59^{4} Pr 5^{22} 13^{6} 14^{34} 21^{4} 24^{9} Jb 13$^{23.23}$ Dn 9$^{20.20}$, ח׳ נעורי *sins of my youth* ψ 25^{7}, פרי בטני ח׳ נפשי Mi 6^{7} *fruit of my body* (my child as an offering) for the *sin of myself*, sin of divination 1 S 15^{23}, of the mouth ψ 59^{13}, ח׳ עמי יאכלו Ho 4^{8} *the sin of my people they eat* (gain their daily food by means of it, cf We, 𝔗 Hi Or al. *sin-offering*, but this not elsewhere in early proph, and ‖ עָוֹן against it, v. We$^{Prol\ 3.76}$), לפתח חטאת רבץ Gn 4^{7} (J) *at the door* (of Cain) *sin is a crouching beast;* sin of the people is embodied in the golden calf Dt 9^{21}; and the high places of Beth Aven Ho 10^{8}, c בּ *on the ground of sin* Ne 9^{37}, *for sin* Mi 1^{5} 2 K 24^{3} Is 40^{2} Je 15^{13} 17^{3} Ez 16^{52}, *with* or *by sin* 1 K 14^{22} 16^{2} Is 43^{24}; הלך בח׳ *walk in sin* 1 K 15$^{3.26.34}$ 16$^{19.26.31}$ 2 K 17^{22}, דבק בח׳ *cleave unto sin* 2 K 3^{3}, c. עַל, *on account of sin* Dt 9^{18} 1 K 15^{30} 16^{19} Mi 6^{13}; *for sin* Lv 4$^{3.28.35}$ 5$^{6.13}$ (P) 19^{22} 26$^{18.24.28}$ (H), יסף על ח׳ *add unto sin* 1 S 12^{19} 2 Ch 28^{13} Is 30^{1} Jb 34^{37}; c. כְּ *according to sin* Lv 26^{21}, c לְ *to* or *for sin* Lv 16$^{16.21}$ Dt 19^{15} 1 K 12^{30} 13^{34} Pr 10^{16} Zc 13^{1}; c מִן *because of sin* Lv 4^{26} 5$^{6.10}$ 16^{34} (P), 19^{22} (H), La 4^{13}; *more than sin* Jb 35^{3}, טָהַרְתִּי מֵחַטָּאתִי *I am clean from my sin* Pr 20^{9}, מפני ח׳ *because of sin* ψ 38^{4}, בגלל ח׳ *because of sin* 1 K 14^{16}, הלך אחר ח׳ *walk after sin* 2 K 13^{2}. **c.** men should *return from sin* שוב מן 1 K 8^{35} = 2 Ch 6^{26}, Ez 18^{21} 33^{14}, *depart from it* סור מעל 2 K 10^{31} 15^{18}, סור מן 2 K 13$^{6.11}$ 14^{24} 15$^{9.24.28}$, *be concerned about* דאג מן ψ 38^{19}; *confess* הִתְוַדָּה ח׳ Nu 5^{7} (P), התודה על ח׳ Ne 1^{6} 9^{2} **d.** God deals with sin: (1) he *visits punishment* upon it פקד (על) Ex 32^{34} (JE) Ho 8^{13} 9^{9} Je 14^{10}, *inquires after it* דרש ל Jb 10^{6}, *watches over it* שמר על Jb 14^{16}, *hoards it up* Ho 13^{12}, (2) *by forgiveness:* נשא ח׳ Ex 10^{17} 32^{32} (JE), 1 S 15^{25}; נשא עון ח׳ ψ 32^{5}, נשא לח׳

Jos 24^{19}(E), ψ 25^{18}; *pardon* סלח לח׳ Ex 34^{9}(JE) 1 K 8$^{34.36}$ 2 Ch 6$^{25.27}$ 7^{14} Je 36^{3}, *removal* הסר Is 27^{9}; העביר 2 S 12^{13}; *casting into the depths of the sea* Mi 7^{19}; (3) *by covering over, making atonement for* חַטָּאתְךָ תְּכֻפָּר Is 6^{7} *thy sin shall be covered over;* actively, כפר על ח׳ ψ 79^{9}; כסה ח׳ ψ 85^{3} (cf. כסוי חֲטָאָה ψ 32^{1}); לְהָתֵם ח׳ (Qr) *make an end of sins* Dn 9^{24}; (4) *by blotting out* מחה ח׳ Is 44^{22} Je 18^{23} ψ 109^{14} Ne 3^{37}; *cleanse from sin* טַהֲרֵנִי מח׳ ψ 51^{4}; מקור לח׳ *a fountain for sin* Zc 13^{1}; (5) *by not remembering it* לא זכר ח׳ Is 43^{25}; לח׳ לא זכר Je 31^{34}, אַל־תֵּפֶן אֶל־חַטָּאתוֹ Dt 9^{27} *look not unto his sin.* **e.** atonement may be secured for, כפר בעד ח׳ Ex 32^{30} (JE; Moses, by his intercession). **f.** acc. to P (H) the priest is to make atonement for a person (כפר על) by sin-offering or trespass-offering, מח׳ *because of sin* Lv 4^{26} 5$^{6\ 10}$ 16^{34}, על ח׳ 4^{35} 5^{13} (all P), 19^{22} (H, v. We$^{\text{Comp. 89}=\text{JBTh xxii, 427}}$), so that the man is *clean from sin* טהר מח׳ Lv 16^{30}. **2.** *condition of sin, guilt of sin* Gn 18^{20} Nu 16^{26} 32^{23} (J), Ez 3^{20} 18^{24}, ח׳ יְהוּדָה חֲרוּשָׁה עַל־לוּחַ לִבָּם וּלְקַרְנוֹת מִזְבְּחוֹתֵיכֶם *the sin* (guilt) *of Judah is graven upon the table of their heart, and upon the horns of your altars* Je 17^{1} **3.** *punishment for sin:* זאת תִּהְיֶה ח׳ מִצְרָיִם וח׳ כָּל־הַגּוֹיִם Zc 14^{19} *this will be the punishment for sin of Egypt and the punishment for sin of all nations* (the plague with which Yahweh will smite them). **4.** *sin-offering*. one of the kinds of offering of P, Lv 7^{37}, first in the history 2 K 12^{17} (reign of Jehoash), where חטאת of money given to priests; elsewh. only in Chr; 2 Ch 29$^{21.23.24}$ Hezekiah had made a ח׳ of 7 צְפִירֵי עזים at purification of temple; Ezr 8^{35} 12 צְפִירֵי ח׳ were offered; Ne 10^{34} ח׳ ‖ עולות;—in these no evidence of special ritual. Sin-offering elsewh. only in codes of H Ez and P.—On Ho 4^{8} v. **1** supr. In H, Lv 23^{19} a שְׂעִיר עזים, for feast of weeks. In Ez ח׳ in gen ‖ other sacrifices, Ez 40^{39} 45$^{17\ 25}$ 46^{20}; and priests eat them Ez 42^{13} 44^{29} At dedication of altar, the blood of a young bullock was to be applied to horns of altar, the corners of its settle and its border, the bullock itself burnt without the sanctuary; for each of the 7 days following a שעיר עזים was to be offered Ez 43$^{19.21.22.25}$ On first day of first month a young bullock was to be offered to cleanse the sanctuary: its blood put on the door posts of the house and of the gate of the inner court and on the four corners of the settle of the altar; also on the seventh day (𝔊 first day of seventh month) Ez 45$^{17\ 19}$ (cf. v$^{18.20}$) On 14th day of first month the prince was to offer a bullock for himself and the people and on each of the 7 days of the Passover week a שְׂעִיר עִזִּים Ez 45$^{22.23}$. When a priest entered the sanctuary to minister after his cleansing he was to offer his sin-offering Ez 44^{27}. P gives several grades: **a.** a ruler should offer a he-goat Lv 4$^{24\ 25}$ Nu 7$^{16.22.28.34.40\ 46.52.58.64\ 70.76.82.87}$, an ordinary person a she-goat Lv 4^{29} (cf. v^{28}) 5^{6} Nu 15^{27}, ewe lamb Lv 4$^{32.33.33.34}$ 14^{19} Nu 6$^{14\ 16}$, a turtle dove or young pigeon Lv 5$^{7\ 8.9.9}$ 12$^{6.8}$ 14$^{22.31}$ 15$^{15.30}$ Nu 6^{11}, or one-tenth of an ephah of fine flour Lv 5$^{11\ 11\ 12}$; according to ability of the person, and nature of offence. The victim was brought unto the tent of meeting, the hands of the offerer laid on its head, it was slaughtered by the offerer, the priest took some of the blood and put it on horns of altar of burnt-offering and the rest of the blood he poured out at the base of it, to cover over the sin, or cleanse the altar from the sin defiling it All the fat pieces (cf Lv 4$^{22-35}$) and a handful of the flour (cf. Lv 5^{12}) were burned on altar The rest of the flesh and the flour were eaten by priests in court of Holy place Lv 5^{13} 6$^{10\ 18.18.23}$ (cf v$^{11\ 19}$), 7^{7} 10$^{16\ 17\ 19\ 19}$ 14^{13} Nu 18^{9}. **b.** a bullock was offered for priests Ex 29$^{14.36}$ Lv 4$^{3.8.20}$ 8$^{2\ 14\ 14}$ 9$^{2\ 7\ 8.10}$, for Levites at their installation Nu 8$^{8.12}$ and for whole congregation Lv 4$^{14.21}$; but usu offering for congregation was he-goat Nu 15$^{24.25}$, esp at dedication of altar Lv 9$^{3\ 15.22}$, and in ritual of feasts Nu 28$^{15.22.30}$ 29$^{5.11\ 16\ 19.22.25.28.31.34.38}$ Before consecr of tabernacle the blood went to altar of burnt-offering (Lv 9^{9}), but subsequ. some of it was sprinkled seven times before the vail and some of it put on horns of altar of incense to cleanse this higher altar; the fat pieces were burned on altar of burnt-offering, and the rest of the victim burned without the camp (Lv 4$^{3-21}$ 6^{23} 8$^{16\ 17}$ 9$^{10.11}$) **c.** on day of atonement, sin-offering for high priest was a bullock Lv 16$^{3.6}$, and for congregation two he-goats, one לַעֲזָאזֵל (v. עזאזל) Lv 16^{8} (cf. v$^{8.10.20-22}$), the other for sacrifice ליהוה Lv 16^{9} (cf. v^{8}). Some of the blood of Aaron's bullock was first taken into innermost sanctuary and sprinkled on the כפרת and seven times before it; so also blood of the he-goat Lv 16$^{11\ 11\ 15}$ (cf. v$^{12-14\ 16\ 17}$) to cleanse highest altar. then the blood of the two victims was applied to lower altars as in **a** and **b** and so sin was covered over at the three altars Ex 30^{10} (cf Lv 16$^{16-19}$). The fat pieces went to altar of burnt-offering and the rest of the victims was burnt without the camp Lv 16$^{25.27\ 27}$. (Sins which might be covered over were limited to those committed בשגגה Lv 4$^{2.22.27}$ Nu 15^{27}, לשגגה Nu 15^{24}, minor offences Lv 5$^{1-6}$; and ceremonial uncleanness Lv 12$^{6.8}$ 14^{13} 15^{15} Nu 6$^{11\ 14}$.) —Phrases for sacrificing are: עשׂה ח׳ Lv 9$^{7.22}$

14[19] Nu 6[16] Ez 45[17], הקריב ח׳ Lv 10[19] Ez 44[27], שחט ח׳ Lv 14[13] Ez 40[39]. **5.** *purification* from sins of ceremonial uncleanness, all P מֵי ח׳ Nu 8[7] *water of purification from sin*, מי נִדָּה ח׳ הוא *water of* (*cleansing from*) *impurity, it is a purification from sin* Nu 19[9], עֲפַר שְׂרֵפַת הח׳ Nu 19[17] *ashes of the burning of the purification from sin* (RV renders *sin-offering;* but there was no offering made, only water of purification was used)

†I [חָטַב] **vb.** cut or gather wood, usu *firewood* (NH *id.*, Ar. حَطَبٌ *firewood* حَطَبَ *collect firewood* (v Wetzst in De ψ 144, 12), Eth ሐጠበ: *cut* (or gather) *firewood*)—**Qal** *Impf* יַחְטְבוּ Ez 39[10], *Inf* לַחְטֹב Dt 19[5], *Pt* חֹטֵב Dt 29[10], pl חֹטְבִים 2 Ch 2[9], cstr חֹטְבֵי Jos 9[21] +3 t; pass pl f חֲטֻבוֹת Pr 7[16]—*cut or gather* wood, sq acc Dt 19[5] 29[10] (‖ שֹׁאֵב מים), cf Ez 39[10] מִן־היערים (obj in preceding cl), 2 Ch 2[9] (‖ כֹּרְתֵי הָעֵצִים), *Pt* cstr ח׳ עֵצִים Je 46[22], and (‖ שֹׁאֲבֵי מַיִם) Jos 9[21 23.27] **Pu.** *Pt* מְחֻטָּבוֹת ψ 144[12] meaning dub; perhaps *hewn* (so, in substance, Thes MV SS Ew Che Bae, v however II חטב), of corner-pillars (זָוִיּוֹת v זָוִית p 265 supr), sim of beautiful, stately daughters

II חטב (√of foll, cf Ar حَطِبَ be of the colour حُطْبَةٌ, i e. *turbid, dusky, mixed with yellowish red*, etc, Aram *Pt* ܡܚܛܒܐ *variegated* 𝔖 2 S 13[19])

†חֲטֻבוֹת **n.f.pl.** dark-hued stuffs, only in חֲטֻבוֹת אֵטוּן מִצְרָיִם Pr 7[16] *dark-hued stuffs* (of) *yarn of Egypt* (‖ מַרְבַדִּים), v De Now; מְחֻטָּבוֹת ψ 144[12] der fr this √by De (q v, and Wetzt.'s n), but v. I. חטב.

חִטָּה *wheat*, v sub חנט

חָטַט (√of foll, cf Ar خَطَّ *make lines, marks*, خَطٌّ *line, streak, stripe*, Aram. ܚܛ, חֲטַט *dig*, ܚܛܘܛܐ *furrow, trench*)

†חֲטִיטָא **n.pr.m.** head of a Levit family, returned exiles Ezr 2[42] 𝔊 Ατητα, = Ne 7[45] 𝔊 Ατειτα, in both A Ατιτα, 𝔊L Αζιζα

חטל (√of foll, Ar. خَطِلَ = *be flabby* (of ear), *be tall, long, quivering, be light, quick*)

†חַטִּיל **n.pr.m.** head of a family of 'the children of Sol.'s servants' Ezr 2[57] 𝔊 Αττεια, A Αττιλ = Ne 7[59] 𝔊 Εγηλ, A Εττηλ, 𝔊L Αττιλ in both.

†חָטַם **vb.** hold in, restrain (Ar. خَطَمَ *strike the nose, attach the* خِطَامٌ = *camel-halter*, خَطْمٌ n *muzzle, nose of beast*, NH חָטָם *nose-ring of camel*, חוֹטָם, Aram חוּטְמָא *nose*, cf חטם, Inscr Zinj., acc to DHM[Sendsch 34], of taming wild beasts)—**Qal** *Impf* אֶחֱטָם־לָךְ לְבִלְתִּי הַכְרִיתֶךָ: Is 48[9] *I will restrain for thee* (mine anger), *not to cut thee off* (‖ אַאֲרִיךְ אַפִּי)

†חָטַף **vb** catch, seize (Ar خَطِفَ, cf. As *ḫaṭâpu, oppression*, Dl[Pr 181], NH חָטַף, Aram. ܚܛܦ *seize*, חֲטַף *do hurriedly*)—**Qal** *Pf* וַחֲטַפְתֶּם consec Ju 21[21] lit, *seize* wives, *Impf* יַחְטֹף עָנִי ψ 10[9], *Inf* לַחֲטוֹף עָנִי ψ 10[9] both fig of oppressor *catching* the distressed, all sq acc.

†חֲטִיפָא **n pr.m.** head of a family of Nethinim, post-exil, Ezr 2[54] 𝔊 Ατουφα, A Ατιφα = Ne 7[56] 𝔊 Ατειφα, 𝔊L both Ατουφα

חטר (√of foll, cf Ar خَطَرَ *lash with the tail, move spear up and down, shake, quiver* (said of spear), etc, Aram ܚܘܛܪܐ, חוּטְרָא, As *ḫuṭartu*, all = *staff*, Schr[COT Gloss] and on 2 K 9[2], חטר *sceptre*, Inscr. Zinj DHM[Sendsch. 57], on format v Lag[BN 144]).

†חֹטֶר **n.m.** branch or twig, rod—metaph. abs ח׳ *branch, twig*, Is 11[1] (ויצא ח׳ מִגֶּזַע יִשָׁי ‖ נֵצֶר), cstr *rod*, בְּפִי־אֱוִיל חֹטֶר גַּאֲוָה Pr 14[3].

חַטָּאת v. חַטָּאת sub חטא

חטש (√of foll, meaning unknown)

†חַטּוּשׁ **n.pr.m.** **1.** man of Davidic line, post-exil, 1 Ch 3[22] 𝔊 Χαττους 𝔊L Ατους, Ezr 8[2] 𝔊 Τους, A𝔊L Αττους **2.** a builder at the wall of Jerus Ne 3[10], 𝔊 Ατουθ, 𝔊L Αττους **3.** head of a priestly house, post-exil., Ne 10[5] 𝔊 Τους, 𝔊L Αττους, 12[2] 𝔊L Αττους (B om.), relation to **2** dubious

חַי, חִיאֵל v sub חיה infr

חִידָה v sub חוד

חָיָה[283] **vb.** live (NH Ph *id.*; Ar حَيِيَ, حَيَّ; Sab חיו Mordt[ZMG 1876 28], Eth ሐየወ: Aram ܚܝܐ, חֲיָא; Palm חיי *life, life-time*, Vog[32,74])—**Qal**[201] *Pf* חָיָה Ec 6[6] + 4 t, חָיְתָה Je 21[9] 38[2], חַי Gn 5[5] + 23 t. (this and the following form are treated as ע״ע, the original weakness of the stem final admitting of either ל״ה or ע״ע, Ges[§76 (2) b]),

וְחִי Lv 25^{35}(Bö § 1161); 3 fs. חָיְתָה Gn 12^{13} Je 38^{17}; וְחָיָה Ex 1^{16} (for חָיָה Bö § 1123 (3), Sam. חיתה); 2 ms. חָיִיתָ Dt 30^{16}, חָיִתָה Je 38^{17}; 3 m. pl. חָיוּ Nu 14^{38}, וְחָיוּ consec. Nu 4^{19} + Zc 10^{9} (where rd. Pi. וְחִיּוּ Sta ZAW i. 1881, 22 so 𝔊), וִחְיִיתֶם Ez 37^{6} + 2 t.; *Impf.* יִחְיֶה Gn 17^{18} + 27 t.; יְחִי Dt 33^{6} + 10 t., וִיחִי ψ 49^{10} + 2 t., וַיֶּחִי Is 38^{21}, וַיְחִי Gn 5^{3} + 37 t., וַיֶּחִי Dt 4^{33} + 4 t.; 3 fs תחיה Jos 6^{17}, תְּחִי Gn 19^{20} + 5 t.; 2 ms תִּחְיֶה Gn 27^{40} + 7 t, 2 fs תִּחְיִי 2 K 4^{7}; 1 s. אֶחְיֶה 2 K 1^{2} + 8 t, 3 mpl יִחְיוּ Jos 9^{21} + 8 t., 3 fpl תִּחְיֶינָה Ez 13^{19} 37^{3}; 2 mpl תִּחְיוּ Dt 4^{1} + 2 t, תחיון Dt 5^{30} 8^{1}; 1 pl. נִחְיֶה 2 K 7^{4} + 7 t; *Imv.* וִחְיֵה Gn 20^{7} Pr 4^{4}, וֶחְיֵה Pr 7^{2}; fs. חֲיִי Ez 16$^{6.6}$; mpl. וִחְיוּ Gn 42^{18} + 7 t; *Inf abs* חָיֹה 2 K 8^{10} + 6 t.; חָיוֹ Ez 3^{21} + 3 t, *cstr.* לחיות Ez 33^{12}, sf. חֲיוֹתָם Jos 5^{8},—**1.** *live* **a.** *have life*, Gn 31^{32}(E), Ex 33^{20}(J), Nu 4^{19}(P), Dt 30^{16}+; also in phrase וַיְחִי *and he lived* (so many years) with acc of time, Gn 5$^{3-30}$ (16 t.) 9^{28} 11$^{11-26}$ (14 t.) 47^{28} (all P), 50^{22} (E), 2 K 14^{17} = 2 Ch 25^{25} Jb 42^{16}. **b.** *continue in life, remain alive* Gn 20^{7} (E), Lv 25^{35} 2 S 12^{22}+, also †נפש ח׳ *live*, of *the soul* or *the self* Gn 12^{13} 19^{20} (J), 1 K 20^{32} ψ 119^{175} Je 38$^{2.17.20}$ Is 55^{3}; וְחַי הַיָּלֶד *and the boy may live* 2 S 12^{22}, †ח׳ לִפְנֵי *live in the presence of* Gn 17^{18} (P) Ho 6^{2}; †ח׳ ב׳ *live among* La 4^{20}. †**c.** *sustain life, live on* or *upon* (על), of the animal life, by the sword Gn 27^{40} (J), by bread Dt 8^{3}; elsewh. in pregnant sense of fulness of life in divine favour, sustained by (על) everything that issueth out of the mouth of י׳ Dt 8^{3}; his promises (?) Is 38^{16}, of wicked man, by repentance Ez 33^{19}; c ב by the statutes and judgments of י׳ if a man do them, Lv 18^{5} (H) Ez 20$^{11.13.21.25}$ Ne 9^{29}; צַדִּיק בֶּאֱמוּנָתוֹ יִחְיֶה *a righteous man by his faithfulness shall live* Hb 2^{4} †**d.** *live* (prosperously) יְחִי הַמֶּלֶךְ *may the king live* 1 S 10^{24} 2 S 16$^{16.16}$ 1 K 1$^{25.31.34.39}$ 2 K 11^{12} 2 Ch 23^{11}, יחי לְבַבְכֶם ψ 22^{27} 69^{33}; המלך לעולם יחיה Ne 2^{3} †**2.** *be quickened, revive:* **a.** *from sickness* Nu 21$^{8.9}$ Jos 5^{8} (E) 2 K 1^{2} 8$^{8.9.10.14}$, 2 K 20^{17} = Is 38$^{1.9.21}$ **b.** *fr discouragement* of the spirit Gn 45^{27}(E). **c.** *fr. faintness* Ju 15^{19} **d.** *fr. death* 2 K 13^{21} Jb 14^{14} Is 26$^{14.19}$, by return of נפש 1 K 17^{22}, of רוּחַ Ez 37$^{3.5.6.9.10.14}$ (and so Ju 15^{19} c) †**Pi.** *Pf.* 3 ms. חִיָּה ψ 22^{30}, 3 fs. sf. חִיָּתְנִי ψ 119^{50}, 2 ms sf. חִיִּיתַנִי ψ 30^{4}; חִיִּיתָנִי ψ 119^{93}, 3 pl. חִיּוּ Ju 21^{14}, הַחִיִּיתֶם Nu 31^{15}, *Impf* יְחַיֶּה 1 S 27^{9}+, etc.; *Imv.* sf חַיֵּנִי ψ 119^{25} + 8 t, חַיֵּיהוּ Hb 3^{2}, *Inf. cstr.* חַיּוֹת Gn 7^{3} Ez 13^{19}; sf. חַיֹּתֵנוּ Dt 6^{24} +, etc., *Pt.* מְחַיֶּה Ne 9^{6} 1 S 2^{6};—**1.** *preserve alive, let live* Ex 1$^{17.18.22}$ 22^{17} Jos 9^{15} (JE), Gn 12^{12} (J), Nu 31^{15} (P), Dt 6^{24} 20^{16} Ju 21^{14} 1 S 27$^{9.11}$ 1 K 18^{5} 2 K 7^{4} Je 49^{11} Ez 3^{18} Hb 3^{2} Jb 36^{6} ψ 30^{4} 33^{19} 41^{3} 138^{7}, ח׳ נפש *preserve oneself alive* ψ 22^{30} Ez 18^{27}, or *preserve persons alive* Ez 13$^{18.19}$, or *preserve life* 1 K 20^{31}; ח׳ זרע *preserve seed alive* Gn 7^{3} 19$^{32.34}$ (J), *keep in existence* heaven and earth Ne 9^{6}, *nourish*, young cow Is 7^{21}, lamb 2 S 12^{3}. **2.** *give life*, to man when created Jb 33^{4} **3.** *quicken, revive, refresh* **a.** *restore to life*, the dead 1 S 2^{6} Dt 32^{39} Ho 6^{2}, the dying ψ 71^{20}. **b.** *cause to grow*, grain Ho 14^{8} **c.** *restore*, a ruined city 1 Ch 11^{8}, stones destroyed by fire Ne 3^{34} **d.** *revive*, the people of י׳ by י׳ himself with fulness of life in his favour ψ 80^{19} 85^{7} 119$^{25.37.40.50.88.93.107.149.154.156.159}$ 143^{11} Ec 7^{12}. †**Hiph.** *Pf* הֶחֱיָה Jos 6^{25} + 5 t.; 2 ms sf הֶחֱיִתָנוּ Gn 47^{25}, 1 s החייתי Nu 22^{33}, הַחֲיִתֶם Jos 2^{13} Ju 8^{19}; *Imv* sf הַחֲיֵנִי Is 38^{16}; הַחֲיוּ Nu 31^{18}, *Inf abs.* הַחֲיֵה Jos 9^{20}, *cstr* הַחֲיוֹת Gn 6^{20} + 6 t., הַחֲיֹת Gn 6^{19} 50^{20}, sf הַחֲיֹתוֹ Ez 13^{22};—**1.** *preserve alive, let live* Gn 45^{7} 50^{20} (E), 47^{25} Nu 22^{33} Jos 2^{13} 6^{25} (all J), 14^{10} (D); Gn 6$^{19.20}$ Nu 31^{18} Jos 9^{20} (P), Ju 8^{19} 2 S 8^{2} Ez 13^{22}, with נפש Gn 19^{19} (J) **2.** *quicken, revive:* **a.** *restore* to health, a leper 2 K 5^{7}, Hezekiah Is 38^{16}. **b.** *revive* the לב and רוּחַ Is 57$^{15.15}$ **c.** *restore to life*, the dead 2 K 8$^{1.5.5.5}$.

†I. חַי **adj. alive, living**;—ח׳ Gn 25^{6}+, חָי Gn 3^{20}+, חֵי Am 8^{14} + 15 t (Ew § 329 explains as cstr., but Ges § 93, R 7 n al as contracted abs); f חַיָּה Gn 1^{20}+; pl חַיִּים ψ 116^{9}+,—**1. a.** *of God*, as the *living one*, the fountain of life אֵל חַי Jos 3^{10} (J), Ho 2^{1} ψ 42^{3} 84^{3}, אלהים חי 2 K 19$^{4.16}$ = Is 37$^{4.17}$; אלהים חיים Dt 5^{23} 1 S 17$^{26.36}$ Je 10^{10} 23^{36}, חי יהוה *Yahweh is living* ψ 18^{47} = 2 S 22^{47}; גֹּאֲלִי חי *my avenger is living* Jb 19^{25}, the formula of the oath is חַי י׳ Ju 8^{19} Ru 3^{13} 1 S 14$^{39.45}$ 19^{6} 20^{21} 25^{34} 26$^{10.16}$ 28^{10} 29^{6} 2 S 4^{9} 12^{5} 14^{11} 15^{21} 1 K 1^{29} 2^{24} 17$^{1.12}$ 18^{10} 22^{14} = 2 Ch 18^{13}, 2 K 5$^{16.20}$ Ho 4^{15} Je 4^{2} 5^{2} 12^{16} 16$^{14.15}$ 23$^{7.8}$ 38^{16}, חי אֵל Jb 27^{2}; חי י׳ צבאות 2 S 2^{27}; חי אדני י׳ Je 44^{26}; חי האלהים 1 K 18^{15} 2 K 3^{14}; as used by God Himself it is חי אנכי Dt 32^{40}, elsewhere חי אני Nu 14$^{21.28}$ (P) Is 49^{18} Je 22^{24} 46^{18} Ez 5^{11} 14$^{16.18.20}$ 16^{48} 17$^{16.19}$ 18^{3} 20$^{3.31.33}$ 33$^{11.27}$ 34^{8} 35$^{6.11}$ Zp 2^{9}, cf. also חֵי דרך באר שבע, חֵי אלהיך דן Am 8^{14}; with the exception of בְּחֵי הָעוֹלָם *by him who liveth for ever* Dn 12^{7}, חֵי is always (as an artificial distinction of scribes) used of non-sacred oaths, v. b. **b.** *of*

man: אָדָם חַי *a living man* La 3^{39}, in antith. מת: חי חי Is 38^{19}; הַחַי collective Ec 7^{2}; Absalom 2 S 19^{7}; Naboth 1 K 21^{15}; a son or lad 2 S 12^{21} 1 K $3^{22.22.23.23.25.26.26.27}$ 17^{23}, usually pl חיים *alive, living* Nu $16^{30.33}$(J), 17^{13}(P), Dt 4^{4} 5^{3} Is 8^{19} ψ 55^{16} 124^{3} Pr 1^{12} Ec $4^{2.2.15}$ 6^{8} $9^{4.5}$ Ru 2^{20}, taking prisoners *alive* Jos 8^{23}(J) 1 S 15^{8} 1 K $20^{18.18}$ 2 K 7^{12} $10^{14.14}$ 2 Ch 25^{12}, *living* (prosperously) 1 S 25^{6} (We rds. לְחַי=לְאָחִי (v Klo Dr) *to my brother*, after 𝔙 *fratribus meis*), elsewh in phrase כל־הימים אשר הם (אתם) חיים על (פני) האדמה *all the days that they (ye) live upon (the face of) the land* Dt 4^{10} 12^{1} 31^{13} 1 K 8^{40}=2 Ch 6^{31} Note phrases עוד חַי (ים) *yet alive* Gn 25^{6} $43^{7.27.28}$ 45^{28} 46^{30}(J), $45^{3.26}$ Ex 4^{18}(E), Dt 31^{27} 1 S 20^{14} 2 S 12^{22} 18^{14} 1 K 20^{32}, בהיות חי 2 S 12^{18} 1 K 12^{6} 2 Ch 10^{6}, אֶרֶץ (ה)חַיִּים *land of the living* Is 38^{11} 53^{8} Je 11^{19} Ez 26^{20} $32^{23.24.25.26.27.32}$ ψ 27^{13} 52^{7} 142^{6} Jb 28^{13}, ארצות הח׳ ψ 116^{9}, ספר ח׳ ψ 69^{29}, צרור הח׳ *bundle of the living* 1 S 25^{29}, אור הח׳ *light of the living* Jb 33^{30} ψ 56^{14}. In the oath by life of men חי is pointed always חֵי חי אדני המלך *as my lord the king liveth* 2 S 15^{21}, חי פרעה Gn $42^{15.16}$(E), חֵי נַפְשְׁךָ 1 S 1^{26} 17^{55} 2 S 14^{19}; חַי י׳ וחי נַפְשְׁךָ *as Yahweh liveth and as thy soul* (or thyself) *liveth* 1 S 20^{3} 25^{26} 2 K $2^{2.4.6}$ 4^{30} חֵיךָ וחי נ׳ 2 S 11^{11} (but on txt v We Dr) **c.** of animals, *alive, living*. ox Ex 21^{35} 22^{3}(E); goat Lv $16^{10.20.21}$(P), bird Lv $14^{4.5.6.7.51.53}$; dog, לְכֶלֶב חַי הוּא טוב מִן־הָאַרְיֵה הַמֵּת Ec 9^{4} (comp. Ar prov *Kelb hei wa-lâ meijit, a living dog and no dead lion* Wetzst $^{Verhand. Berl Anthrop Ges. 1878, 388}$), reptiles Gn 1^{28}(P), animals in general Gn 9^{3} (P); בשר חי *living, raw flesh* Lv $13^{10.14.15.15.16}$(P) 1 S 2^{15} **d.** *animals* and *man*, phrases for either or both כל חי Gn 3^{20} 8^{21}(J) Jb 12^{10} 28^{21} 30^{23} ψ 143^{2} 145^{16}, כל החי Gn 6^{19}(P), נֶפֶשׁ חַיָּה Gn $1^{20.24.30}$(P) $2^{7.19}$(J), כל נֶפֶשׁ חַיָּה Gn $9^{12.15.16}$(P) Ez 47^{9}, כל נפש החיה Gn 1^{21} 9^{10} Lv $11^{10.46}$(P). **e.** (dub.) of vegetation, as thorns, *green*, ψ 58^{10} (Ges Ew Ol Pe, but De Ri Che Bae *raw flesh*, v. **c** supr ad fin) **f.** of water, *flowing, fresh* מים חיים Gn 26^{19}(J), Lv $14^{5.6.50.51.52}$ 15^{13} Nu 19^{17}(P), Je 2^{13} 17^{13} Zc 14^{8} Ct 4^{15} **2.** (dub.) *lively, active* איש חַי *an active man* 2 S 23^{20} (but Qr איש חַיִל is to be preferred), איבי חיים mine enemies *are lively* ψ 38^{20} (RV, but Houb Ol Ew Hu Che al rd. חִנָּם, ‖ שקר). **3.** *reviving*. כָּעֵת חַיָּה *at the time* (when it is) *reviving*, the spring Gn $18^{10.14}$ (J), 2 K $4^{16.17}$

† II [חַי] **n.[m.] kinsfolk** (Ar حَيٌّ a group of families united by vital ties RS $^{K 36-40}$ Dr $^{Sm 119}$), pl. sf חַיַּי 1 S 18^{18}, incorrectly pointed with the interpretation *my life* RV, but rd. חַיַּי *my kinsfolk*, We Ki Dr RS SS RVm VB It is explained by the gloss משפחת אבי We (Klo rds. אַחַי ו).

† I חַיָּה **n.f. living thing, animal** (Zinj. *wild beast* DHM $^{Sendsch 54}$)—ח׳ Gn 8^{17}+, cstr. חַיַּת Is 57^{10}+, old case ending (poetic) חַיְתוֹ Gn 1^{24} ψ 50^{10} 79^{2} $104^{11.20}$ Is $56^{9.9}$ Zp 2^{14}, sf חַיָּתִי ψ 143^{3}, etc, pl חיות Lv 14^{4}+ 12 t —**1.** *animal*, as a living, active being · **a** *in general*, Gn 8^{17} Lv $11^{2.27.47.47}$ Nu 35^{3} (P) ψ 104^{25} Is 46^{1} Dn 8^{4} **b.** *wild animals*, on account of their vital energy and activity Gn $7^{14.21}$ $8^{1.19}$ 9^{5}(P) Lv 17^{13} 25^{7}(H) Jb 37^{8} ψ 148^{10} Is 40^{16} Ez 14^{15} 33^{27} Zp $2^{14.15}$, ח׳ קנה ψ 68^{31} *wild animal of the reeds*, ח׳ רעה *evil beast* Gn $37^{20.33}$(JE) Lv 26^{6}(H) Ez 5^{17} $14^{15.21}$ 34^{25}, ח׳ טמאה Lv 5^{2}(P) *unclean beast*, ח׳ הארץ Gn $1^{25.30}$ $9^{2.10.10}$(P) 1 S 17^{46} Ez 29^{5} 32^{4} 34^{28} Jb 5^{22}; חיתו ארץ Gn 1^{24}(P) ψ 79^{2}, ח׳ השדה Ex $23^{11.29}$ (covt code) Lv 26^{22}(H) Dt 7^{22} 2 S 21^{10}, 2 K 14^{9} =2 Ch 25^{18}, Ho $2^{14.20}$ 4^{3} 13^{8} Is 43^{20} Je 27^{6} 28^{14} Ez 38^{20} 39^{4} Jb 5^{23} 39^{15}, כל ח׳ השדה Gn $2^{19.20}$ $3^{1.14}$(J) Jb 40^{20} Je 12^{9} Ez $31^{6.13}$ $34^{5.8}$ 39^{17}; חיתו שדי Is 56^{9} ψ 104^{11}; חיתו (ב)יער Is 56^{9} ψ 50^{10} 104^{20}, פריץ חיות Is 35^{9} *destroyer among beasts*. **c.** *living beings*, of the cherubic chariot Ez $1^{5.13.13.14.15.15.19.19.20.20.21.22}$ 3^{13} $10^{15.17.20}$. **2.** *life*, only in late poetry, ψ 143^{3} Jb $33^{18.20.22.28}$ 36^{14} Ez $7^{13.13}$, and (dub.) ψ 74^{19} 78^{50}. **3.** *appetite*, activity of hunger: חית כפרים *appetite of young lions* Jb 38^{39} **4.** *revival, renewal* חַיַּת יָדֵךְ מָצָאת *thou didst find renewal of thy strength* (re-invigoration) Is 57^{10}, v חָיָה **2.**

† II חַיָּה **n.f.** (several) **community** (=fem. of II חַי acc. to No $^{ZMG 1886, 176}$)—וְחַיַּת פְּלִשְׁתִּים חֹנָה *and a community of Philistines* (i.e a group of allied families, making a raid together) *was encamping* 2 S 23^{13} (=מַחֲנֵה 1 Ch 11^{15}), perh also ψ 68^{11} (cf. infr)

Note—Several other passages are dub: וַיֵּאָסְפוּ פלשתים לַחַיָּה 2 S 23^{11} *assembled into a troop*, or *by bands* (RV, but neither rend. justif.: Bo Ew We Klo Dr rightly rd לֶחְיָה to *Lehi*, cf. Ju 15^{9}; wd om by accident in ‖ 1 Ch 11^{13} Dr); חַיָּתְךָ יָשְׁבוּ־בָהּ ψ 68^{11} *thy troop dwelt in it* (Thes SS RVm Hi Ri Che, but 𝔊 𝔖 Jer Pe *thy*

(*living*) *creatures*, of the people; Hup *id.*, ref. to quails; improb.); אַל־תִּתֵּן לְחַיַּת נֶפֶשׁ תּוֹרֶךָ חַיַּת עֲנִיֶּיךָ אַל־תִּשְׁכַּח לָנֶצַח ψ 74^{19} *give not the soul of thy turtle-dove to the wild beasts, the life of thine afflicted do not forget for ever*. RV Hi Pe Bae Sch render thus, giving חית diff. meanings in the two clauses, the former being archaic fem. abs. Ges$^{§80.2.R.2}$, text doubtless corrupt, rd. poss למות Schr Ri, for לחית, or לשחת Kroch; Gr either of these, Che either, or better לחרב

†[חָיֶה] **adj. having the vigour of life, lively** (on format. v. Lag$^{BN 49}$)—fpl חָיוֹת Ex 1^{19}(E), of Hebrew women in childbirth, bearing quickly, easily.

†חַיִּים **n.m.**$^{Dt 28,66}$ **pl. abstr. emph.** life, ח׳ Gn 2^{7}+; חַיִּין Jb 24^{22} (Aramaism Ges$^{§87(1)a}$); חַיֵּי Gn 23^{1}+, sf. חַיַּי Gn 47^{9}+; חַיָּיְכִי ψ 103^{4}, (Ges$^{§91(2)R.2}$), etc;—**1.** *life*. physical Gn 27^{46} Ex 1^{14} (P), Dt 28$^{66.66}$ 2 S 11^{11} 15^{21} Is 38^{12} Je 8^{23} La 3$^{53.58}$ Ez 7^{13} Jb 3^{20} 7^{7} 9^{21} 10^{12} 24^{22} ψ 7^{6} 17^{14} 21^{5} 26^{9} 31^{11} 34^{13} 63^{4} 64^{2} 66^{9} 88^{4} 103^{4} Pr 18^{21} Ec 2^{17} 6^{12} 7^{13} 9$^{9.9}$ 10^{19} Jon 2^{7} 4$^{3.8}$, חַיֵּי שָׂרָה *life of Sarah* Gn 23^{1} (P), שְׁנֵי ח׳ *years of the life of* 2 S 19^{35} Gn 23^{1} 25$^{7.17}$ 47$^{8.9.9.28}$ Ex 6$^{16.18.20}$ (P); שְׁנַת לְח׳ Gn 7^{11} (P); שְׁנוֹת חַיִּים Pr 3^{2} 4^{10} 9^{11}; יְמֵי ח׳ *days of the life of* Ec 2^{3} 5$^{17.19}$ 6^{12} 8^{15} 9^{9}; כל יְמֵי ח׳ Gn 3$^{14.17}$(J) Dt 4^{9} 6^{2} 16^{3} 17^{19} Jos 1^{5} 4^{14}(D) 1 S 1^{11} 7^{15} 1 K 5^{1} 11^{34} 15$^{5.6}$, 2 K 25$^{29.30}$=Je 52$^{33.34}$, Is 38^{20} (poem of Hez.) ψ 23^{6} 27^{4} 128^{5} Pr 31^{12}, בח׳ *in* or *during one's life* Gn 27^{46}(P) Lv 18^{18}(H) Ju 16^{30} 2 S 1^{23} 18^{18} ψ 49^{19} 63^{5} 104^{33} 146^{2} Jb 10^{1} Ec 3^{12} 9^{3}, רוּחַ ח׳ Gn 6^{17} 7^{15} (P); ח׳ רוּחִי Is 38^{16} (poem of Hez), ח׳ בשׂרים Pr 14^{30}; נִשְׁמַת (רוּחַ) ח׳ Gn 2^{7} 7^{22}(J). **2.** *life*: as welfare and happiness in king's presence Pr 16^{15}; as consisting of earthly felicity combined (often) with spiritual blessedness Dt 30$^{6.15.19.19.20}$ 32^{47} ψ 30^{6} 133^{3} Pr 3^{22} 4$^{13.22}$ 8^{35} 10^{16} 11^{19} 12^{28} 19^{23} 21^{21} 22^{4} Mal 2^{5}; used only once distinctly of eternal life (late) ח׳ עולם Dn 12^{2}; אֵל חַיָּי ψ 42^{9} *God of my life*, מעוז ח׳ ψ 27^{1}; מקור ח׳ ψ 36^{10} Pr 10^{11} 13^{14} 14^{27} 16^{22}; עץ (ה)חיים Gn 2^{9} 3$^{22.24}$ (J) Pr 3^{18} 11^{30} 13^{12} 15^{4}, ארח ח׳ ψ 16^{11} Pr 5^{6} 15^{24}; ארח לח׳ Pr 10^{17}; ארחות ח׳ Pr 2^{19}; דֶּרֶךְ (ה)חַיִּים Pr 6^{23} Je 21^{8}; חקות ח׳ Ez 33^{15}; תוצאות ח׳ Pr 4^{23} *sources* (origin and direction) *of life*; תוכחת ח׳ Pr 15^{31}; כָּתוּב לַחַיִּים Is 4^{3} *written unto life* **3.** *sustenance, maintenance*: חַיִּים לְנַעֲרוֹתֶיךָ Pr 27^{27} *maintenance for thy maidens*, v. מִחְיָה infr.

†חַיּוּת **n.f. abstr.** אַלְמְנוּת חַיּוּת 2 S 20^{3}, lit. 'widowhood of livingness,' Dr; We rds. אַלְמְנוֹת חַיּוֹת *living widows* ('grass-widows,' who were separated from their husbands), after 𝔊 χῆραι ζῶσαι, so SS

†מִחְיָה **n.f. preservation of life, sustenance,** מ׳ Gn 45^{5}+4 t, cstr. מִחְיַת Lv 13$^{10.24}$; sf. מִחְיָתְךָ Ju 17^{10},—**1.** *preservation of life* Gn 45^{5} (E), 2 Ch 14^{12}. **2.** *sustenance* Ju 6^{4} 17^{10}. **3.** *reviving*, Ezr 9$^{8.9}$ **4.** *the quick* מִחְיַת (בָּשָׂר) *the quick* (or raw spot) *of the flesh* Lv 13$^{10.24}$(P).

†חִיאֵל **n.pr.m.** (*Ēl lives* (or abbrev. for יחיאל); Sab חיאל, name of coin, after n.pr. of king DHM$^{ZMG 1875, 613, 1883, 15}$; cp. also foll, and Ph כמשיחי, מריחי)—name of the rebuilder of Jericho 1 K 16^{34}, 𝔊 Ἀχ(ε)ιήλ, om. 𝔊L

†יְחִיאֵל **n.pr.m.** (*may Ēl live*; Ph יחואלן, יחומלך v Eut$^{ZMG 1876, 136}$)—𝔊 usu. Ἰειήλ, Ἰαειήλ,—**1.** one of David's chief musicians 1 Ch 15^{18} (𝔊 Ἰειήλ, 𝔊L Ἰαιήλ), v^{20} (𝔊 Εἰθήλ, 𝔊L Ἰειήλ), 16^{5} (𝔊 Ἐιειήλ, 𝔊L Ἰαιήλ) **2.** one of David's chiefs of the Levites 1 Ch 23^{8} (𝔊 Ἰ(ει)ήλ), 29^{8} (𝔊 Βεσιήλ, A 𝔊L Ἰειήλ). **3.** tutor of David's sons 1 Ch 27^{32} (𝔊 Ἰε(ρι)ήλ, 𝔊L Ἰωήλ) **4.** son of Jehoshaphat 2 Ch 21^{2}. **5.** יְחוּאֵל Hemanite of Hezekiah's reign 2 Ch 29^{14} **6.** overseer in Hezekiah's reign 2 Ch 31^{13}. **7.** ruler of the temple in Josiah's reign 2 Ch 35^{8}. **8.** contemporaries of Ezra, Ezr 8^{9} (𝔊 Ἰεμα, A Ἰεειήλ, 𝔊L Ἰειήλ), 10$^{2.21.26}$.

†יְחִיאֵלִי **n.pr.m.** (patronym), 1 Ch 26$^{21.22}$ (𝔊 Ἰειήλ; 𝔊L om. in v^{22}).

†יְחִיָּה **n.pr.m.** (*may Yah live*) keeper of the ark 1 Ch 15^{24} (𝔊 Ἰε(α)ια, 𝔊L Ἰειήλ).

חיל v. I. II חול supr.

חֵיל, חֵיל, חִיל, חִילָה, חִילָם, חֵילָן v sub I. II. חול supr.

חין v. sub חנן.

חַיִץ, חִיצוֹן v. sub I. II חוץ.

חיק v. sub חוק.

חִירָה v. sub I חור.

חִירוֹם, חִירָם v. sub אח, אחה supr p. 27^{b}.

חך v. sub חנך.

†[חָכָה] **vb. wait, await—Qal** *Pt.* pl. cstr. חוֹכֵי Is 30^{18}, with לְ *waiting for him* (י׳). **Pi.** חִכָּה Jb 32^{4}, חִכְּתָה ψ 33^{20}; חִכִּיתִי Is 8^{17}, ψ חִכּוּ 106^{13}; חִכִּינוּ 2 K 7^{9}, *Impf* יְחַכֶּה Is 30^{18}; תְּחַכֶּה 2 K 9^{3}; *Imv.* חַכֵּה־ Hb 2^{3}, חַכּוּ Zp 3^{8}; *Inf. cstr.* כְּחַכֵּי Ho 6^{9} (Ephraimit. for חַכֵּה ?), *Pt.* מְחַכֶּה Dn 12^{12}, cstr מְחַכֵּה Is 64^{3}; pl מְחַכִּים Jb 3^{21},—**1.** *wait, tarry*, abs 2 K 9^{3} *tarry not;* with עַד till morning light 2 K 7^{9}, c. acc את איוב בדברים Jb 32^{4} *tarry for Job with words* **2.** *wait* (in ambush), כְּחַכֵּי אִישׁ גְּדוּדִים Ho 6^{9} *as marauding bands wait for a man* AV RV De, or *as marauders lie in wait* Hi Ew (taking אִישׁ as cstr.) **3** *wait for, long for*, with לְ for י׳ Is 8^{17} 64^{3} Zp 3^{8} ψ 33^{20}, for his counsel ψ 106^{13}; for his vision Hb 2^{3}, for death Jb 3^{21}, יחכה יהוה לחננכם *Yahweh waiteth to be gracious unto you* Is 30^{18} (Di regards this as threatening and refers it to **1**), abs. *waiteth* (and cometh to the days of blessedness) Dn 12^{12}

חַכָּה v sub חנך

חכל (√of foll., cf Ar. حَكِلَ iv. *be confused, vague;* حُكْلَةٌ *barbarousness*, or *impediment in speech*, As *akâlu, be gloomy, êklu, dark, eklitu, darkness*, Dl in Zim[BP 115, W 385 ff.], cf. Jager[BAS ii. 282]).

†חֲכִילָה **n.pr.loc.** (*dark*) a hill in southern Judah, on edge of wilderness of Ziph 1 S 23^{19} $26^{1.3}$ (Glaser[Skizze ii. 326] rds also for חוילה, q v, in 1 S 15^{7}), 𝔊 Εχελα (26^{1} B Χελμαθ, A Αχιλα)

†חַכְלִילִי **adj.** (dark) dull, from wine, ח׳ עֵינַיִם מִיָּיִן Gn 49^{12}

†חַכְלִלוּת **n.f.** dulness, of eyes in drunkenness; לְמִי חַכְ׳ עֵינָיִם Pr 23^{29} (v ^{30} לַמְאַחֲרִים עַל־הַיָּיִן)

†חֲכַלְיָה **n.pr.m.** (mng dub., perhaps חַכֵּה לְיָהּ *wait for Yahweh*, √חכה, so We ?)—father of Nehemiah Ne 1^{1}, 𝔊 Χελκ(ε)ια, 𝔊L Χελκιας(ου), א A Αχαλια, 10^{2} 𝔊 Αχελια, A 𝔊L Αχαλια

†**חָכַם** **vb.** be wise (NH *id*, Aram ܚܟܡ, חֲכַם *id*; Zinj חכמה *wisdom*, DHM[Sendsch 57]; As *hakâmu, know* (with exceptional ה v Dl[Pr 178 f]); Ar. حَكَمَ *restrain from acting in an evil manner, judge, govern*, iv *make firm, sound, free from defect* by the exercise of skill)—**Qal** *Pf* ח׳ Pr 23^{15}; 3 fs חָכְמָה Zc 9^{2}, חָכַמְתָּ Pr $9^{12.12}$, etc + 3 t. Pf, *Impf* יֶחְכַּם Pr 9^{9} 21^{11}, וַיֶּחְכַּם 1 K 5^{11}; יֶחְכָּם Pr 20^{1}+; וֶחְכָם Pr 13^{20}, תֶּחְכַּם Pr 19^{20}; אֶחְכָּמָה Ec 7^{23}, pl יֶחְכָּמוּ Jb 32^{9}, *Imv.* חֲכַם Pr 27^{11}, חֲכָם Pr 6^{6} 23^{19}+ 13^{20} Kt; חַכָּמוּ Pr 8^{33};—*be* or *become wise, act wisely* Dt 32^{29} (poet.) 1 K 5^{11} Jb 32^{9} Pr 6^{6} 8^{33} $9^{9.12.12}$ 13^{20} 19^{20} 20^{1} 21^{11} 23^{19} 27^{11} Ec 2^{15} 7^{23} Zc 9^{2}, אם חכם לבך *if thy mind be wise* Pr 23^{15}, c acc שחכמתי Ec 2^{19} *wherein I have acted wisely* **Pi.** *Impf* יְחַכֵּם ψ 105^{22}, sf יְחַכְּמֵנוּ Jb 35^{11}; תְּחַכְּמֵנִי ψ 119^{98}; all *make wise, teach wisdom*, c acc **Pu.** *Pt.* *made wise*, intensive, as it were the embodiment of wisdom חוֹבֵר חֲבָרִים מְחֻכָּם ψ 58^{6}, pl הֵמָּה חֲכָמִים מְחֻכָּמִים Pr 30^{24} (of intelligent animals). **Hiph.** *Pt* cstr. מַחְכִּימַת פֶּתִי ψ 19^{8} *making wise the simple* **Hithp.** *Impf* נִתְחַכְּמָה לוֹ Ex 1^{10} (E) *let us deal wisely* (*shrewdly*) *toward it* (the people); 2 ms. תִּתְחַכַּם Ec 7^{16} *make or shew thyself wise*

†**חָכָם** **adj.** wise, ח׳ Dt 4^{6}+67 t.; cstr. חֲכַם Is 3^{3}+9 t, pl חֲכָמִים Dt 1^{13}+39 t.; cstr. חַכְמֵי Ex 28^{3}+4 t, sf חֲכָמֶיךָ Is 19^{12} etc.+8 t; f חֲכָמָה 2 S 14^{2} 20^{16}, cstr חַכְמַת Ex 35^{25}, pl. חֲכָמוֹת Je 9^{16}, cstr חַכְמוֹת Ju 5^{29} Pr 14^{1} (but id חָכְמוֹת De),—**1.** *skilful* in technical work, artificers Is 3^{3}, sailors Ez 27^{8}, so (prob.) v ^{9}, mourning women Je 9^{16}, artisans of tabern and temple and their furniture Ex 28^{3} 31^{6} 35^{10} $36^{1.2.4.8}$ (P), 1 Ch 22^{15} 2 Ch $2^{6.12.13.13}$, women in spinning Ex 35^{25} (P); goldsmiths and other artisans Je 10^{9}; makers of idol-images Is 40^{20}. **2.** *wise in the administration of affairs*. Joseph in Egypt Gn $41^{33.39}$ (E), heads of tribes Dt $1^{13.15}$, judges 16^{19}, of David 2 S 14^{20}, of Solomon 1 K 2^{9} 3^{12} 5^{21} = 2 Ch 2^{11}; the prince of Tyre, in satire Ez 28^{3}; of kings in general Pr 20^{26}; class of political advisers of Judah Is 29^{14} Je 18^{18}, appar. also Is 5^{21}; of Egypt Is $19^{11.11.12}$, Edom Ob ^{8}, the nations Je 10^{7}, so of God Is 31^{2}. **3.** *shrewd, crafty, cunning*. Jonadab 2 S 13^{3}; the princesses Ju 5^{29}, אשה חכמה *wise woman* 2 S 14^{2} 20^{16}, gen., Je 9^{22}, intelligent animals Pr 30^{24}, לכד ח׳ בערמם *taking the cunning in their craft* Jb 5^{13}, חכם בעיני *wise in one's own eyes* Pr 3^{7} $26^{5.12.16}$ 28^{11}, חכמי לב *wise of mind* (in their own mind) Jb 37^{24} **4.** pl class of *learned* and *shrewd* men, incl astrologers, magicians and the like, of Egypt Gn 41^{8} (E), Ex 7^{11} (P; cf. Is $19^{11.11.12}$); Babylon Is 44^{25} Je 50^{35} 51^{57}, Persia Est 1^{13} 6^{13}. **5.** *prudent*, towards king Pr 16^{14}; in controversies Pr 11^{29} $29^{8.9.11}$, religious affairs Ho 13^{13} 14^{10} Je 4^{22} $8^{8.9}$ Dt 4^{6} 32^{6} ψ 107^{43}; איש ח׳ Je 9^{11}. **6.** *wise*, ethically and religiously, in Wisd Lt **a.** as adj, חֲכַם לֵב *wise of mind* Pr

10^{8} 16^{21}; לֵב חָכָם Ec 8^{5}; of the son Pr 10^{1}=15^{20}, 13^{1} 23^{24} Ec 2^{19}; ילד ח׳ Ec 4^{13} *wise boy;* גבר ח׳ Jb 34^{34} *wise man;* מוכיח ח׳ *wise reprover* Pr 25^{12}. **b.** = subst.. (1) as a *wise learner* in school of wisdom, he fears God and departs from evil Pr 14^{16}; is silent Pr 17^{28}, hearkens to counsel Pr 12^{15}; hears and increases in learning Pr 1^{5}; his ear seeketh knowledge Pr 18^{15}, he receives it Pr 21^{11}; and stores it up Pr 10^{14}; his ears hearken to the reproof which giveth life Pr 15^{31}, and he becomes wiser through it Pr 9$^{8.9}$. (2) as a *wise teacher, a sage,* he does not answer with windy knowledge Jb 15^{2}, he tells the experience of the past Jb 15^{18}, has knowledge Jb 34^{2}; teaches it Ec 12^{9}; disperses it Pr 15^{7}; his tongue is health Pr 12^{18}; it utters knowledge aright Pr 15^{2}; his mind instructs his mouth and adds learning to his lips Pr 16^{23}, his words are gracious Ec 10^{12}; it is good to hear his rebuke Ec 7^{5}, his instruction is a fountain of life Pr 13^{14}, one walking with him becomes wiser Pr 13^{20}. The חכמים recall the Gk. σοφοί, having their schools, pupils (בן), discipline (מוסר), principles and collections of wisdom, דברי חכמים Pr 1^{6} 22^{17} (cf 24^{23}), Ec 9^{17} 12^{11}; God himself is חכם לבב Jb 9^{4}. (3) *the wise* are prosperous. true, in sceptical view of Ec, they have no advantage over the fool Ec 6^{8}, but die as the fool Ec 2$^{16.16}$ ψ 49^{11}; they will not be able to find the works of God Ec 8^{17}, like others are in the hands of God Ec 9^{1}; they do not secure bread Ec 9^{11}; but elsewhere reverse is true precious treasure is in his dwelling Pr 21^{20}, his lips preserve him Pr 14^{3}; they inherit glory Pr 3^{35}; wealth is their crown Pr 14^{24}; the wise man is strong Pr 24^{5} Ec 7^{19}; his eyes are in his head Ec 2^{14}, his mind is at his right hand Ec 10^{2}; he interprets things Ec 8^{1}. (4) the *wise* man is a blessing to others · he wins men Pr 11^{30}, scales the city of the mighty Pr 21^{22}, though poor he delivers the city Ec 9^{15}, is a reproof to scorners Pr 15^{12}, his mind is in the house of mourning Ec 7^{4}; injustice makes him foolish Ec 7^{7}; Job finds no wise men among his cruel friends Jb 17^{10}

†חָכְמָה **n.f.** wisdom, ח׳ Ex 28^{3}+106 t.; cstr. חָכְמַת Ex 35^{35}+15 t.; sf. חָכְמָתִי Ec 2^{9}, etc. +25 t. sf; pl. abst. emph חָכְמוֹת ψ 49^{4} Pr 1^{20} 9^{1} 24^{7}; חַכְמוֹת Pr 14^{1} (incorrectly pointed as adj. cstr. f.; rd חָכְמוֹת De);—**1.** *skill* in war Is 10^{13}, in technical work Ex 28^{3} 31$^{3.6}$ 35$^{26.31.35}$ 36$^{1.2}$ (P), cf. 1 K 7^{14}, 1 Ch 28^{21}, of sailors ψ 107^{27}. **2.** *wisdom,* in administration Dt 34^{9} Is 29^{14} Je 49$^{7.7}$ 2 S 14^{20}, of prince of Tyre Ez 28$^{4.5.7.12.17}$; Sol.'s wisdom included this with other forms of cleverness and shrewdness 1 K 2^{6} 3^{28} 5$^{9.10.14.14.26}$ 10$^{4.6.7.8.23.24}$=2 Ch 9$^{3.5.6.7.22.23}$, 1 K 11^{41} 2 Ch 1$^{10.11.12}$; the Messiah is to have רוּחַ חָכְמָה וּבִינָה Is 11^{2}. **3.** *shrewdness, wisdom,* 2 S 20^{22} 1 K 5$^{10.10}$ Je 9^{22}; withheld by God from the ostrich Jb 39^{17}; of magicians and prophets Is 47^{10} Dn 1$^{4.17.20}$ **4.** *wisdom, prudence* in religious affairs Dt 4^{6} ψ 37^{30} 51^{8} 90^{12} Pr 10^{31} Is 33^{6} Je 8^{9}. **5.** *wisdom,* ethical and religious: **a.** of God, as a divine attribute or energy, his wisdom is in the skies Jb 38^{36}, by it he numbers the clouds Jb 38^{37}, founded the earth Pr 3^{19}, and made all things Je 10^{12}=51^{15}, ψ 104^{24}; it is with him Jb 12^{13}; not to be found by the most persevering human search Jb 28$^{12.20}$; he alone knows it Jb 28^{23}, gives it Pr 2^{6}; and shews its secrets Jb 11^{6} **b.** the divine wisdom is personified. she was begotten before all things to be the architect and counsellor of God in the creation (Pr 8$^{22-31}$), she builds a palace and spreads a feast for those who will receive her instruction 9^{1} (cf. v$^{2-6}$); she teaches in public places 1^{20} 8$^{1.5.11.12}$ (v context); gives her pupils the divine spirit 1^{23}, by her discipline simple become wise, rulers rule wisely, and those seeking her are richly rewarded 8^{14} (cf. v$^{1-21}$) **c.** of man. to get wisdom is principal thing Pr 4^{7}; its fundamental principle is to fear God ψ 111^{10} Pr 15^{33} Jb 28^{28} (‖סור מרע בינה), and know י׳, the All Holy Pr 9^{10} 30^{3}, it is of inestimable worth Jb 28^{18} Pr 8^{11} 16^{16} 17^{16} 23^{23} 24^{7}, beyond the reach of scorners Pr 14^{6}; God giveth it to the good Ec 2^{26}, men are to incline the ear Pr 2^{2}, attend unto wisdom Pr 5^{1}; seek Ec 7^{25}, know Pr 24^{14} Ec 1^{17} 8^{16}, behold Ec 2^{12} 9^{13}, get her Pr 4$^{5.7}$, treat her as sister Pr 7^{4}, happy the man who finds her Pr 3^{13}, he who has wisdom is איש תבונה Pr 10^{23}; נָבוֹן Pr 10^{13} 14^{33}; מֵבִין Pr 17^{24}, cf. also ψ 49^{4} Jb 4^{21} 12$^{2.12}$ 13^{5} 15^{8} 26^{3} 32$^{7.13}$ 33^{33} Pr 1$^{2.7}$ 2^{10} 4^{11} 11^{2} 13^{10} 14$^{1.8}$ 18^{4} 21^{30} 24^{3} 28^{26} 29$^{3.15}$ 31^{26} Ec 1$^{13.16.16.18}$ 2$^{3.9.13.21}$ 7$^{10.11.12.12.19.23}$ 8^{1} 9$^{10.15.16.16.18}$ 10$^{1.10}$,—on Solomon's wisdom v supr

†חַכְמוֹנִי **n.pr.m.** (*wise*)—**1.** father of one of David's warriors 1 Ch 11^{11}. **2.** father of the tutor of David's sons 1 Ch 27^{32}.

†תַּחְכְּמֹנִי **adj.gent.** 2 S 23^{8}=בן חכמוני 1 Ch 11^{11}, rd. הַחַכְמֹנִי We Klo Dr VB.

חַל v. חַיִל sub I. חול.

חֵל v. sub III. חלל

†I. [חָלָא] **vb. be sick, diseased** (=חלה, v Ges ^{§75,22})—**Qal** *Impf* וַיֶּחֱלָא אָסָא ... בְּרַגְלָיו 2 Ch 16^{12} (=חלה 1 K 15^{23})

†תַּחֲלֻאִים **n.pl.m.**$^{2 Ch 21,19}$ **diseases**, abs ת׳ Je 16^{4} 2 Ch 21^{19}, cstr תַּחֲלוּאֵי Je 14^{18}, תַּחֲלֻאָיְכִי ψ 103^{3}, תַּחֲלֻאֶיהָ Dt 29^{21},—*diseases* Dt 29^{21} 2 Ch 21^{19} ψ 103^{3}, ממותי תחלאים יָמֻתוּ Je 16^{4}, תחלואי רעב Je 14^{18} *diseases of famine* (‖ חַלְלֵי־חֶרֶב)

II. חלא (√of foll, DHM in MV comp. Sab פחטאת ותחלאן *she sinned and defiled herself*)

†I. [חֶלְאָה] **n.f. rust** (perh as *filth* v supr) —חֶלְאָתָהּ Ez 24$^{6.12}$ + v$^{11.12}$ (del Co intern grounds) + v^{6} חֶלְאָתֹה (cf Ges $^{§91.1 R.2}$) *rust* on metal pot, symbol of impurity of Jerusalem.

†II. חֶלְאָה **n.pr.f.** (meaning dub)—wife of Ashhur (of Judah) 'father' of Tekoah 1 Ch 4$^{5.7}$ 𝔊 Αωδα, Αοαδα, Αλαα, Ελαα, Ελεα

חֲלָאִים v חֳלִי sub III חלה

חֶלְאָמָה v חֵילָם sub I חול.

I חלב (√of foll; meaning unknown).

†חָלָב **n.m. milk** (NH *id* (and vb denom), Aram חֲלָבָא, ܚܠܒܐ, Ph חלב, Ar حَلِيبٌ n *fresh milk*, حَلَبَ vb *milk*, As *alibu, milk*, v Dl $^{Pr 174}$; Eth ሐሊብ:)—ח׳ abs. Gn 18^{8} + 35 t + Ez 34^{3} (v. infr), cstr חֲלֵב Ex 23^{19} + 5 t, sf חֲלָבִי Ct 5^{1}, חֲלָבֵךְ Ez 25^{4},—*milk*. **a.** as common food Gn 18^{8} (J; distinct from חֶמְאָה *curd*, q v), חֲלֵב צֹאן Dt 32^{14} (poet, distinct fr. חֶמְאַת בָּקָר), in Ju 5^{25} חָלָב is used parallel with חמאה, elsewhere חֶמְאָה seems to be produced fr. חָלָב— מִיץ חָלָב יוֹצִיא חֶמְאָה Pr 30^{33} *a pressing (squeezing) of milk produces curd;* מרב עֲשׂוֹת חָלָב יֹאכַל חֶמְאָה Is 7^{22} *because of abundant yield of milk he shall eat curd,* cf also חרִצי הֶחָלָב 1 S 17^{18} *cuts of milk,* i e *cheeses*, it was received in buckets or pails (עֲטִינָיו) Jb 21^{24} (v. Ew De Di VB), and kept in skins (נאוד ח׳) Ju 4^{19}; men drank it (שׁתה) Ez 25^{4} (cf. השקה Ju 4^{19}), but also ate it (אכל), if emend הַחֵלֶב Ez 34^{3} (for הֶחָלָב) is right, 𝔊 𝔙 Bo Hi-Sm Co, al; it was poured out, v sim. of formation of the embryo הֲלֹא כֶּחָלָב תַּתִּיכֵנִי Jb 10^{10} *hast thou not poured me out like milk?* specif. (1) חֲלֵב עִזִּים לְלַחְמְךָ Pr 27^{27} *milk of goats for thy food* (RS$^{Sem. I. 204}$) (2) c אֵם *mother's milk:* of kid לא־תבשׁל גדי בַּחֲלֵב אִמּוֹ Ex 23^{19}=34^{26} (JE) = Dt 14^{21}, cf טלה ח׳ 1 S 7^{9} *sucking lamb* (for sacrif), but also of human beings גְּמוּלֵי מֵח׳ Is 28^{9} *weaned from milk* (‖ עַתִּיקֵי מִשָּׁדָיִם); fig. in promise to Zion וְיָנַקְתְּ חֲלֵב גּוֹיִם Is 60^{16} *and thou shalt suck the milk of nations* (‖ וְשֹׁד מְלָכִים תִּינָקִי) (3) ח׳ with wine, as esp. delicacy Ct 5^{1} (v De), fig of י׳'s choicest blessings Is 55^{1} (4) oft. in phr of productiveness of land of Canaan זָבַת חָלָב וּדְבָשׁ (דבשׁ) *flowing with milk and honey* Ex 3$^{8.17}$ 13^{5} 33^{3} Nu 13^{27} 14^{8} 16$^{13.14}$ (all JE), Lv 20^{24} (H), Dt 6^{3} 11^{9} 26$^{9.15}$ 27^{3} 31^{20} Jos 5^{6} Je 11^{5} 32^{22} Ez 20$^{6.15}$, in Messian time the hills תֵּלַכְנָה ח׳ Jo 4^{18} (‖ יִטְּפוּ הֶהָרִים עָסִיס); fig of charms of loved one דְּבַשׁ וח׳ תַּחַת לְשׁוֹנֵךְ Ct 4^{11} *honey and milk are under thy tongue* **b.** *milk* as white לְבֶן־שִׁנַּיִם מֵח׳ Gn 49^{12} *white of teeth, from milk;* צַחוּ מֵח׳ La 4^{7} *they were whiter than milk* (‖ זַכּוּ מִשֶּׁלֶג), so also prob of eyes רֹחֲצוֹת בֶּח׳ (עינים) Ct 5^{12} *bathed in milk*, i e. the white of the eye—On milk as not used by Israel in sacrifice v. RS$^{Sem 204}$.

II. חלב (√of foll, perh. cf As *ḫalâbu, be covered*, VR 8^{53} Lyon$^{Manual, Gloss}$, *ḫallibu, cover, clothe*, IR$^{18.68}$ *ḫallubtu, clothing*, Lyon$^{Sargontexte 14}$, *ḫitlupatu, naḫlapu* (rd. *b* for *p*) Schr$^{COT Gloss}$)

I. חֵלֶב **n.m.**$^{Ex 29, 13}$ **fat** (NH *id.*, *fat*, so Ph. חלב (prob.), Aram. ܚܠܒܐ (also *diaphragm* in Lexx, v. PS^{1274}) orig *diaphragm*, *midriff*; Ar خِلْبٌ, incl *midriff-fat*, RS$^{Sem I 360}$),—ח׳ abs Lv 3^{16} + 40 t; cstr. Gn 45^{18} + 21 t.; sf. חֶלְבּוֹ Lv 3^{9} + 6 t, חֶלְבָּהּ Lv 4$^{31.35}$, חֶלְבָּם Nu 18^{17}, חֶלְבָּמוֹ ψ 17^{10}, חֶלְבְּהֶן Lv 8$^{16.25}$ (rd. n pl חלביהן Sam. Di), pl הַחֲלָבִים Lv 8^{26} + 7 t; cstr חֶלְבֵי Lv 6^{5} + 4 t, sf. חֶלְבֵהֶן Gn 4^{4} (חלביהן Sam Di, cf. Lv 8$^{16.25}$ supr.),—**1.** *fat* of human body Ju 3^{22} (covering intestines), ח׳ גבורים 2 S 1^{22} as smearing warrior's shield, of grossness of wicked כִּסָּה פָנָיו בְחֶלְבּוֹ Jb 15^{27}, *fat* (of midriff) fig. of unreceptive heart ח׳ סָגְרוּ ψ 17^{10}, v also 73^{7} (rd מחלב עוֹנֵמוֹ for מחלב עֵינֵמוֹ 𝔊 𝔖 Hi Ew Ol De Che Bae al.), טָפַשׁ כַּח׳ לִבָּם ψ 119^{70} i. e. their heart is as unresponsive as the midriff-fat near it. **2.** *fat* of beasts: **a.** as rich food (poet.) Dt 32^{14} and in sim. ψ 63^{6} (‖ דֶּשֶׁן); so MT Ez 34^{3} (but rd. הֶחָלָב, v. חָלָב), 39^{19} (𝔖 Co בשׂר). **b.** esp as offered in sacrifice, sg, to י׳ Ex 23^{18} (JE), 1 S 2$^{15.16}$ Ex 29$^{13.13.22.22.22}$

Lv 3$^{3.3.4.9.9.9.10.14.14.15}$ + 23 t. Lv, Nu 18^{17} (all P), Lv 17^{6} (H), 1 S 15^{22} Is 1^{11} 43^{24} Ez 44$^{7.15}$; v. Is 34$^{6.6.7}$ of fat of Edomites slaughtered by 'י's sword (under fig. of lambs, rams, and bulls); as eaten by (strange) gods Dt 32^{38} (poet.), not to be eaten by men Lv 3^{17} 7$^{23.24.24.25}$ (all P); also pl., *fat parts* or *pieces* Gn 4^{4} (J) Lv 6^{5} + 8 t. Lv, 1 K 8$^{64.64}$ 2 Ch 7$^{7.7}$ 29^{35} 35^{14}. **3.** *choicest, best part* of products of land Gn 45^{18} (E), specif. of oil Nu 18^{12} and wine v^{12}; of corn and oil v$^{29.30.32}$; also (poet.) ח' כִּלְיוֹת חִטָּה Dt 32^{14} *kidney-fat of wheat* (i. e. the very choicest, cf. Is 34^{6}), ח' חִטָּה ψ 81^{17}, ח' חִטִּים 147^{14}.

†II. **חֵלֶב** **n.pr.m.** (Sab. n.pr.m. חלבן = *the crafty one* Sab.Denkm. $^{27.28}$)—one of David's heroes 2 S 23^{29} (but rd. (חלד(י, v. Dr), 𝔊 Εσθαει, A Αλαφ, 𝔊L Αλλαν (= חֵלֶד 1 Ch 11^{30} = חֶלְדַּי 27^{15}).

†**חֶלְבָּה** **n.pr.loc.** town assigned to Asher Ju 1^{31}, site unknown, 𝔊 Χεβδα, 𝔊L Ελβα; (comp. As. *Maḫalliba* Schr Dl, but v. אַחְלָב infr.)

†**חֶלְבּוֹן** **n.pr.loc.** place whence wine came (to Tyre) יֵין ח' Ez 27^{18}; so also As. n.pr.terr. *Ḫilbunim* or *Hilbunu*, v. Schr^{COT} and Dl in Co. Mod. *Ḥalbûn*, NW. fr. Damascus, Wetzst $^{ZMG\ xi.\ 1857,\ 490\ f.}$ Bd$^{Pal\ 341}$.

†**חֶלְבְּנָה** **n.f.** (Aram. ܚܶܠܒܳܢܺܝܬܳܐ, חֶלְבְּנִיתָא, 𝔊 χαλβάνη, 𝔙 *galbanum*)—a kind of gum Ex 30^{34}, ingredient of the holy incense, v. Di Löw^{115}.

†**אַחְלָב** **n.pr.loc.** town assigned to Asher Ju 1^{31}, site unknown, 𝔊 Δααλαφ (= Ααλαφ) (WMaxMüller$^{Asien\ u.\ Europa\ 194}$ thinks corrupt. for מחלב, As. *Maḫalliba* (which Schr^{COT} Ju 1^{37} Dl$^{Pa\ 283}$ comp. with אחלב and חֶלְבָּה); he rds. n.pr.loc. מחלב for מֵחֶבֶל Jos 19^{29}, 𝔊 καὶ ἀπὸ Λεβ = וּמֵחֶלְב; this would be on coast, N. of Achzib).

I. **חלד** (√ of foll.; Ar. خَلَدَ *abide, continue*, often in Qor of righteous in Paradise).

†**חֶלֶד** **n.[m.]**$^{Jb\ 11,\ 17}$ **duration, world** (= αἰών) (Ar. خُلْدٌ *perpetual duration, eternity*)—abs. ח' ψ 17^{14}; חָלֶד Jb 11^{17} + 2 t. + Is 38^{11} Che De, sq. Cod. Bab. etc. (Baer (חֶדֶל; sf. חֶלְדִּי ψ 39^{6}; = *duration of life* Jb 11^{17} ψ 39^{6} (|| יָמַי), זְכָר אֲנִי מֶה־חָלֶד 89^{48} *of what duration I am* Dr$^{§\ 189.\ 2}$, or (אני for אדני) *what is life*(?) Hi Ew Now al.; *world* (= αἰών, not κόσμος) ψ 17^{14} 49^{2} (יֹשְׁבֵי ח' || כָּל־עַמִּים), cf. Is 38^{11} (v. supr.; || אֶרֶץ הַחַיִּים).

II. **חלד** (√ of foll.; cf. NH חלד *dig*, or *hollow out*, Aram. ܚܠܰܕ *creep, crawl*).

†**חֵלֶד** **n.pr.m.** (Sab. n.pr. חלד DHM$^{Epigr.\ Denkm.\ 35}$) one of David's heroes, son of בַּעֲנָה 1 Ch 11^{30} A 𝔊L Αλαδ (= חֶלְדַּי 27^{15} = חֵלֶב 2 S 23^{29}).

†**חֹלֶד** **n.[m.]** weasel (NH חוּלְדָּא; Ar. خُلْدٌ *mole* or *blind-rat*, or *a species of rat*; on format. v. Lag$^{BN\ 144}$) — *weasel* Lv 11^{29} (Vrss Ki Thes al. v. esp. Di; > Saad Bo MV SS Lag$^{l.c.}$ *mole*).

†**חֻלְדָּה** **n.pr.f.** prophetess, Josiah's time, 2 K 22^{14} = 2 Ch 34^{22}, 𝔊 Ολδα.

†**חֶלְדַּי** **n.pr.m.** **1.** one of David's heroes 1 Ch 27^{15} (= חֵלֶד 11^{30} = חֵלֶב 2 S 23^{29}) 𝔊 Χολδεια (-δαι), 𝔊L Ολδια. **2.** a returned exile Zc 6^{10} (om. 𝔊) = חֵלֶם v^{14}.

†I. **חָלָה** **vb. be weak, sick** (NH *id.*; Aram. חֲלָא *suffer* (rare); As. *ḫalû, sickness, grief*, Dl$^{Pr\ 181}$)—**Qal** *Pf.* ח' 1 K 14^{1} + 8 t.; 2 fs. חָלִית Is 57^{10}; 1 s. חָלִיתִי 1 S 30^{13} + 2 t.; וְחָלִיתִי consec. Ju 16$^{7.11.17}$, חָלוּ Je 5^{3} (so rd., v. infr.); *Impf.* וַיִּחַל 2 K 1^{2}; *Inf.* sf. חֲלֹתוֹ Is 38^{9}; חַלּוֹתִי ψ 77^{11} cf. sub **Pi.**; חֲלוֹתָם ψ 35^{13}; *Pt.* חֹלֶה Gn 48^{1} + 6 t. + 1 S 22^{8} (v. infr.); חוֹלֶה Ne 2^{2} Mal 1^{13}; f. חוֹלָה Ec 5^{12} + 3 t. (for Je 4^{31} v. I. חול), cstr. חוֹלַת Ct 2^{5} 5^{8};—**1.** *be* or *become weak*, Samson Ju 16$^{7.11.17}$; *feel weak* Is 57^{10} (Che) Ez 34$^{4.16}$. **2.** *become sick, ill* Gn 48^{1} (E) 1 S 19^{14} 30^{13} 1 K 14$^{1.5}$ 15^{23} (of Asa, = חלא 2 Ch 16^{2}) 17^{17} 2 K 1^{2} 8^{7} 13^{14} (c. acc. cogn.) 20^{12} = Is 39^{1}, Is 33^{24} 38^{9} Pr 23^{35} ψ 35^{13} Ne 2^{2}, cf. ψ 77^{11} חַלּוֹתִי for חֲלוֹתִי Che after Bi; *lame and sick*—i. e. imperfect for sacrifice—of animals Mal 1$^{8.13}$; *sick* from effect of wounds 2 K 8^{29} = 2 Ch 22^{6}, cf. Pr 23^{35}, מַכָּה with חָלִי Dt 28$^{59.61}$ Je 6^{7} 10^{19}; hyperbol. *sick* from love חוֹלַת אַהֲבָה אני Ct 2^{5} 5^{8}; *be sick unto dying* חֹלֶה לָמוּת 2 K 20^{1} = Is 38^{1}, ח' עַד־לָמוּת (late) 2 Ch 32^{24}; Je 5^{3} rd. prob. לֹא חָלוּ (for MT חָלוּ, v. I. חול) of the people, unmoved by 'י's chastisements; *thou hast smitten them, but they are not sick* (cf. **Niph.** Am 6^{6}); of sickness of the mind in MT 1 S 22^{8} sq. עַל (but rd. rather חֹמֵל 𝔊 Gr Klo Dr); *pt.* as adj. *severe, sore* רָעָה חוֹלָה Ec 5$^{12.15}$;—on Je 4^{31} v. I. חול. **Niph.** *Pf.* 1 s. נֶחֱלֵיתִי Dn 8^{27}; 3 pl. נֶחְלוּ Am 6^{6} Je 12^{13}; *Pt.* f. נַחְלָה Is 17^{11} + 4 t.; pl. נַחְלוֹת Ez 34^{4} (del. Co) v^{21};—**1.** *make oneself sick*, fig. for *strain oneself* Je 12^{13} (but Gr נִלְאוּ). **2.** *be made sick* Dn 8^{27}; לֹא נֶח' of indifference, apathy Am 6^{6} sq. עַל (cf. **Qal** Je 5^{3});

pt *diseased*, as subst c art. Ez 34[4] (del Co) v[21], = *severe, sore* (pred of מַכָּה) Na 3[19] Je 10[19] 14[17] 30[12]; also (מַכָּה om) Is 17[11]. **Pi.** *Pf* חִלָּה *make sick*, c. acc. cogn + בְּ of land Dt 29[21], *Inf cstr* חַלּוֹתִי הִיא ψ 77[11] rd prob. חֲלוֹתִי, Inf Qal, *my sickness*, so Bi Che (others der. fr חלל *my wounding*, v De) —For other forms of Pi v II חלה **Pu.** *Pf be made weak*, 2 ms חֻלֵּיתָ Is 14[10] **Hithp** *Impf* וַיִּתְחָל 2 S 13[6], *Imv* הִתְחָל 2 S 13[5], *Inf* הִתְחַלּוֹת 2 S 13[2],—*make oneself sick*, of Ammon's morbid passion for his sister 2 S 13[2], sq בַּעֲבוּר; of his pretended sickness of body 2 S 13[5 6] **Hiph.** *Pf* 3 ms הֶחֱלִי Is 53[10], 1 s הֶחֱלֵיתִי Mi 6[13], pl הֶחֱלוּ Ho 7[5] (on txt. v infr.), *Pt* מַחֲלָה Pr 13[12],—**1** *make (sick, i e.) sore thy smiting* הַכּוֹתֶךָ Mi 6[13] (cf Na 3[19], Niph), obj (implic) a person, וי׳ חָפֵץ דַּכְּאוֹ הֶחֱלִי Is 53[10] *it pleased* י׳ *to bruise him, making him sick* = to bruise him *sorely*, v further Di **2** *make sick*, obj לֵב (of hope deferred) Pr 13[12]. **3.** *shew* (signs of) *sickness, become sick*, only הֶח׳ שָׂרִים חֲמַת מִיָּיִן Ho 7[5] *princes are become sick with fever of wine* (Now Che VB; > Vrss Hi-St who rd הֵחֵלּוּ *they begin* the day with wine-fever) **Hoph.** *Pf. be made sick* = *wounded* הָחֳלֵיתִי 1 K 22[34] = 2 Ch 18[33], 2 Ch 35[23]

†חֳלִי **n.m.** [Dt 28, 59] sickness, חֳלִי Dt 28[61] + 8 t; חֹלִי Dt 7[15] + 2 t., sf. חָלְיוֹ Is 38[9] + 7 t + Ec 5[16] (where del. sf, cf Vrss Now), pl חֳלָיִם Dt 28[59], חֳלָיִים 2 Ch 21[15], חֳלָיֵנוּ Is 53[4];—*sickness, disease* Dt 7[15] 28[59 61] 1 K 17[17] 2 K 1[2] 8[8.9] 13[14] Is 38[9] 2 Ch 16[12 12] 21[15 15 19] ψ 41[4] Ec 6[2]; of the suffering servant of י׳ Is 53[3.4] (in both ‖ מַכְאֹב), of rich man Ec 5[16] (rd וָחֹלִי, v supr), *incurable disease* ח׳ לְאֵין מַרְפֵּא 2 Ch 21[18], *recover from sickness* חיה מחלי Is 38[9], metaph of distress of land Ho 5[13] (‖ מָזוֹר), Is 1[5] Je 10[19], = *wound*, of violence in Jerusalem Je 6[7] (‖ מַכָּה)

†[מַחֲלֶה] **n.[m.]** sickness, disease—sf מַחֲלֵהוּ Pr 18[14] *his sickness* (= any sickness of his), of specif disease, cstr. מַחֲלֵה מֵעֶיךָ 2 Ch 21[15] (+ מֵהֳלִי, בָּחֳלָיִים רַבִּים)

†מַחֲלָה **n f** sickness, disease, מַחֲלָה Ex 15[26] + 3 t —*sickness, disease* (in gen) Ex 23[25] (JE); so c כל, 1 K 8[37] = 2 Ch 6[28] (‖ כָּל־נֶגַע), Ex 15[26] (JE; cf. אֲנִי יהוה רֹפְאֶךָ *ad fin*)

†[מַחֲלוּיִים] **n.m.** sickness, suffering (caused by wounds, cf. חלה 2 K 8[29])—only pl intens. מַחֲלֻיִים 2 Ch 24[25].

†II [חָלָה] **vb.** only **Pi.** sq פְּנֵי, פָּנֶיךָ, פָּנָיו = **mollify, appease, entreat the favour of,** lit. *make the face* of any one *sweet* or *pleasant* (cf. Ar حَلَا, حَلِيَ *be sweet, pleasant,* Aram. ܚܠܐ, חֲלִי, *id*, adj חֲלִי *sweet*),—**Pi.** *Pf* חִלָּה 2 Ch 33[12], חִלִּיתִי 1 S 13[12] ψ 119[58], וְחִלּוּ consec Jb 11[19], חִלִּינוּ Dn 9[13], *Impf.* וַיְחַל Ex 32[11] + 3 t, יְחַלּוּ ψ 45[13] Pr 19[6], *Imv* חַל־נָא 1 K 13[6], חַלּוּ־נָא Mal 1[9]; *Inf. cstr* לְחַלּוֹת Zc 7[2] + 2 t, — **1.** ח׳ אֶת־פְּנֵי־י׳: **a.** *mollify, pacify, appease* י׳, i e induce him to shew favour in place of wrath and chastisement Ex 32[11] (JE), 1 K 13[6] (+ הִתְפַּלֵּל), v[6] 2 K 13[4] Je 26[19] (+ וַיִּנָּחֶם), 2 Ch 33[12] (‖ וַיִּכָּנַע מְאֹד מִלִּפְנֵי), Dn 9[13], also ח׳ פְּנֵי־אֵל Mal 1[9] (sq וִיחָנֵנוּ *that he may be gracious to us*) **b.** *entreat the favour of* י׳, i e aim at success, prosperity, etc, through his favour, 1 S 13[12] (in anticipation of war), Zc 8[21.22] (‖ לְבַקֵּשׁ אֶת־י׳, of cities and nations assembling at Jerusalem for worship), Zc 7[2] (‖ לְבַקֵּשׁ אֶת־י׳) of worship at Jerusalem; quite gen, as habit of God-fearing man, ψ 119[58] (+ בְּכָל־לֵב) **2.** *entreat favour* of men (in sense of **1 b**)—רַבִּים יְח׳ פְנֵי־נָדִיב Pr 19[6] *many entreat a prince's favour* (‖ וְכָל־הָרֵעַ לְאִישׁ מַתָּן), ψ 45[13] יְח׳ פָּנַיִךְ of favour of king's bride, וְח׳ פָּנֶיךָ רַבִּים Jb 11[19] favour of Job when absolved and restored

†מַחֲלַת **n.f.** only in ψ titles עַל־מ׳ ψ 53[1] 88[1], appar. a catchword in a song, giving name to tune, mng dub, Aq Symm 𝔙 מחלת *dance;* v. Ol [Psalmen p 27] Bae [Psalmen p xviii].

III חלה (*adorn,* cf Ar. حَلَى *adorn,* حَلْيٌ (neck-)*ornament*)

†I. חֲלִי **n.m.** ornament, נֶזֶם זָהָב וַחֲלִי־כָתֶם Pr 25[12] *a* (nose- or ear-) *ring of gold and* (neck- or breast-) *ornament of fine gold;* pl. חֲלָאִים Ct 7[2], in sim of grace and beauty.

†II. חֲלִי **n.pr.loc.** in Asher Jos 19[25], site unknown (v. conject in Di).

†[חֶלְיָה] **n.f.** jewelry, נִזְמָהּ וְחֶלְיָתָהּ Ho 2[15] (v Now Che).

†חֲלַח **n.pr.loc.** a city or district under Assyr control, whither Isr captives were taken 2 K 17[6] = 18[11], 1 Ch 5[26], cf. *Ḫalaḫḫu* in Meso-

potamia, Schr [COT] on 2 K 17[3]; > Hal [Mél. Epigr. 1874, 70] *Cilicia* (=Ph. חלך, Lag [M. i. 211], As. *Ḫilakku*, Lyon [Sargontexte]) Lag [BN 57].

† חַלְחוּל **n.pr.loc.** town in Judah, Jos 15[58] Lag [Onom. 119, 7, 2nd ed. 152] Elul in tribu Iuda, cf. Alula juxta Chebron; mod. Ḥalḥûl, 1½ hour (3½ miles) N. fr. Hebron, v. Di (and reff.) Bla Rob [BR iii. 281 f.] Guérin [Judée iii. 284 ff.]

חַלְחָלָה **n.f.** v. I. חול.

† [חָלַט] **vb.** only וַיַּחְלְטוּ הֲמִמֶּנּוּ 1 K 20[33], rd. prob. וַיַּחְלְטוּהָ מִמֶּנּוּ (cf. 𝔊 ἀνελέξαν τὸν λόγον ἀπὸ τοῦ στόματος αὐτοῦ and Sta [G i. 445 f.]) *and they snatched it from him*, caught the word fr. his lips; Sta [§ 529a] as **Qal**; Kö [i. 251] Ges [§ 53. 3 R 4] and most as **Hiph.**, with ַ om.

חלך (√ of foll.; poss. (si vera l.) cf. Ar. حَلِكَ *be black* (passing into fig. sense, *unfortunate*, in Heb.), v. Bae [ψ 10, 8]; cf. Aram. חֲשׁוֹךְ).

† חֵלְכָה rd. חֵלְכָּה, חַלְכָּה, חֲלֵכָה, or חֵלְכָּה, **adj. hapless, unfortunate,** only as subst. *hapless, luckless one(s)*—לְחֵלְכָה ψ 10[8], 𝔊 εἰς τὸν πένητα, 𝔖𝔗; חֵלְכָה 10[14] 𝔊 ὁ πτωχός; חלכאים 10[10] Kt, rd. pl. חֵלְכָּאִים (חֵל׳, חָל׳); Qr חֵל כָּאִים, 𝔊 τῶν πενήτων. In all txt. and mng. dub. (MT rds. חֵילְךָ=חֵלְכָה *thine army;* and חֵל כָּאִים v[10] *army of dejected ones*, but this against usage of חֵל, and no such fig. sense of חַיִל, v. Ol Hup De Bae Che, and crit. n.)

† I. חָלַל **vb. bore, pierce** (Ar. خَلَّ *perforate, pierce through, transfix,* Eth. ኅለት: (hollow) *reed;* Aram. חֲלַל *hollow out,* חֲלִילָא *pipe;* ܚܠܝܠܐ adj. *hollow,* ܡܚܠܐ *cave,* ܡܚܠܐ *sheath,* etc.; NH in deriv. חָלָל n. *hollow,* adj. *slain,* חָלִיל *pipe*);—**Qal** *Pf.* לִבִּי חָלַל בְּקִרְבִּי *my heart is pierced* (wounded) *within me* ψ 109[22] (? lit. *one has pierced my heart;* or rd. **Pu.** חֻלַּל); *Inf. cstr.* חַלּוֹתִי הִיא ψ 77[11] *it is my piercing, my wound* (my woe, my cross; so Ew Hi De Bae MV SS Kö [i. 341], but Hu Pe Bi Che rd. חֲלוֹתִי *my sickness*). **Pi.** *Pt.* pl. (Baer) בְּיַד מְחַלְלֶיךָ Ez 28[9] *in the hand of the ones wounding thee* (Sm Co rd. מְחוֹלְלֶךָ). **Pu.** *Pt.* מְחֻלְּלֵי חֶרֶב *pierced by the sword* Ez 32[26]. **Po'el** *Pf.* 3 fs. חֹלֲלָה יָדוֹ נָחָשׁ בָּרִחַ Jb 26[13] *his hand pierced the fleeing serpent;* *Pt.* f. מְחוֹלֶלֶת תַּנִּין Is 51[9] *who pierced the dragon.* **Po'al** *Pt.* מְחֹלָל מִפְּשָׁעֵינוּ Is 53[5] *pierced, wounded because of our transgressions* (of the servant of י׳, ‖ מְדֻכָּא מֵעֲוֺנֹתֵינוּ).

I. חָלָל [90] **n.m. pierced,** ח׳ abs. Dt 21[1] + 25 t.; cstr. חֲלַל Nu 19[16]; pl. חֲלָלִים Nu 23[24] + 28 t.; cstr. חַלְלֵי Is 22[2] + 21 t.; sf. חֲלָלֶיךָ ψ 69[27], etc. + 11 t. sfs.;—**1.** *pierced, fatally wounded* ψ 69[27] Je 51[52] Ez 26[15] 30[24] La 2[12]. Elsewhere **2.** *slain* Nu 19[18] 31[8. 19] (P), etc.; sg. coll. 2 S 23[8. 18] = 1 Ch 11[11. 20] Ez 6[7] 30[11], etc., but usu. pl. 1 S 17[52] (RV *wounded*) Je 51[49], etc.; + חַלְלֵי חֶרֶב Is 22[2] Je 14[18] Ez 31[17. 18] 32[20. 21. 25. 28. 29. 30. 31. 32] Zp 2[12] La 4[9]; חַלְלֵי רעב La 4[9]; חַלְלֵי יהוה Is 66[16] Je 25[33].

† חַלָּה **n.f.** a kind of cake (prob. as *perforated*, v. Di Lv 2[4])—ח׳ abs. Nu 15[20] Lv 24[5]; cstr. חַלַּת Ex 29[23] + 4 t.; pl. חַלּוֹת Lv 2[4] + 2 t.; חַלֹּת Ex 29[2] + 3 t.—used in offerings: **1.** at the sacrif. of David on removal of ark, given to each person as part of peace-offering 2 S 6[19]. **2.** elsewh. only P (H Lv 24[5. 5]): **a.** of the 12 cakes of the table of the holy place, made of סלת Lv 24[5. 5]. **b.** made of ראשית ערסת as an offering of first-fruits Nu 15[20]. **c.** of לחם שמן, to be burnt with the עֹלָה Ex 29[23] = Lv 8[26]. **d.** of מַצָּה burnt on the altar with **c** Lv 8[26], but usu. to be eaten by participants in the several forms of peace-offering Nu 6[19], and as such mingled with oil Ex 29[2] Lv 2[4] 7[12. 12] Nu 6[15]. **e.** ח׳ לחם חמץ to be used by the offerer in connexion with the unleavened cakes of **d** Lv 7[13].

† חַלּוֹן **n.m.** [Jos 2, 18] and **f.** [Ez 40, 16] **window,** abs. הַחַלּוֹן Gn 26[8] + 12 t.; cstr. חַלּוֹן Gn 8[6] Pr 7[6]; sf. חַלּוֹנוֹ Ez 40[22]; mpl. חַלּוֹנִים Ez 40[25] + 3 t.; cstr. חַלּוֹנֵי 1 K 6[4]; sf. חַלּוֹנַי Je 22[14] (defective pl. Ges [§ 87 (1) e], dual Ew [§ 177 a], but rd. ־ָיו סָפוּן Mich Hi Gf Or Gie); חַלּוֹנֵינוּ Je 9[20]; f. חַלּוֹנוֹת Ez 40[16] + 4 t.; חַלֹּנוֹת Ct 2[9] + 3 t.; *window* פָּתַח ח׳ *open the window* Gn 8[6] (P) 2 K 13[17]; עלה בח׳ Je 9[20]; בעד הח׳ *through the window* Gn 26[8] Jos 2[15] (J) Ju 5[28] 1 S 19[12] 2 S 6[16] = 1 Ch 15[29], 2 K 9[30] Jo 2[9]; *latticed windows* 1 K 6[4] Ez 40[16] 41[16. 26]; בח׳ Jos 2[18. 21] (J) Pr 7[6] Zp 2[14]; אֶל־הח׳ 2 K 9[32]; מִן־הח׳ Ct 2[9]; *windows* of palace, קָרַע לוֹ חַלּוֹנָי(ו) Je 22[14] *cutteth him out his windows;* of the gates of Ezek.'s temple Ez 40[16. 22. 25. 25. 29. 33. 36], of the temple itself Ez 41[16. 16].

† חָלִיל **n.m. flute, pipe,** ח׳ 1 S 10[5] Is 5[12] 30[29]; pl. חֲלִלִים 1 K 1[40] Je 48[36. 36].

†II [חָלַל] **vb. denom. play the pipe, pipe**—**Qal** *Pt.* pl וְשָׁרִים כְּחֹלְלִים ψ 87^{7} *as well the singers as the pipe-players*, cf AV, < RV Pe Do Che Bae al **Polel** *Pt* fr 1 חול *dancers* **Pi.** *Pt* וְהָעָם מְחַלְּלִים בַּחֲלִלִים 1 K 1^{40} *and the people piped with pipes* (cf As *ḫâlalu*, acc to Dl in Zim $^{BP\ 117}$)

† [מְחִלָּה] **n.f.** hole, מְחִלּוֹת עָפָר *holes of the dust* Is 2^{19} (‖ מְעָרוֹת צֻרִים *caves of the rocks*)

†III. [חָלַל] **vb. pollute, defile, profane, Hiph.** also begin (lit *untie, loosen, open*, v. Arab) (‎ⅷ حَلَّ *untie, undo, become free, lawful, free from obligation* or *tie*, IV *make lawful;* X. *esteem lawful* or *free, profane, desecrate, violate;* NH חלל *be profane, desecrated* (also Pi Hiph transit), cf Aram. חֲלַל, ܚܰܠܶܠ Pa. is *purify*, ܐܰܚܶܠ Aph is *profane*)—**Niph.** *Pf* נִחַל Ez 25^{3}, נחלת (-תי Co) Ez 22^{16}, נחלו Ez 7^{24}, *Impf* יֵחַל Is 48^{11}, תחל Lv 21^{9}, וָאֵחַל Ez 22^{26}, *Inf.* הֵחֵל Ez 20$^{9.14.22}$, sf לְהֵחַלּוֹ Lv 21^{4}—**1.** reflex *pollute, defile oneself* **a.** ritually, by contact with dead ‖ טמא, Lv 21^{4} (H) **b.** *sexually* ‖ זנה Lv 21^{9} (H) **2.** Pass, *be polluted, defiled*, of holy places Ez 7^{24} 25^{3}, name of God Ez 20$^{9.14.22}$ Is 48^{11} and even God himself Ez 22$^{16.26}$ **Pi.** *Pf* חִלֵּל Lv 19^{8}+3 t., sf חִלְּלוֹ Dt 20^{6}, 2 ms חִלַּלְתָּ Gn 49^{4}+3 t; 2 fs חִלַּלְתְּ Ez 22^{8}, 3 pl. sf. חִלְּלוּהָ Ez 7^{21} etc, + 16 t. Pf, *Impf* יְחַלֵּל Lv 21$^{12.15.23}$, sf יְחַלְּלֶנּוּ Dt 20^{6}, pl יְחַלְּלוּ Lv 21^{6}+4 t, יְחַלֵּלוּ ψ 89^{32} etc, + 13 t Impf, *Inf* חַלֵּל Am 2^{7}+4 t; חַלְּלוֹ Ez 23^{39}+4 t, חַלְּלָם Je 16^{18}, *Pt* מְחַלֵּל Ez 24^{21} pl. מְחַלְּלִים Mal 1^{12} Ne 13^{17}, sf מְחַלְלֶיהָ Ex 31^{14}, f. מְחַלֶּלֶת Lv 21^{9},—**1.** *defile, pollute:* **a.** sexually, Gn 49^{4} (poem) = 1 Ch 5^{1} (the father's bed), a woman = זנה Lv 19^{29} 21^{9} (H); זַרְעוֹ Lv 21^{15} (H). **b.** ceremonially, *profane*, the altar by a tool Ex 20^{25} (JE), sacred places Lv 21$^{12.23}$ (H), Ez 7$^{21.22.22}$ 23^{39} 24^{21} 44^{7} Zp 3^{4} Mal 2^{11} ψ 74^{7} Dn 11^{31}, the holy land Je 16^{18}, sacred things Lv 19^{8} 22$^{9.15}$ (H) Nu 18^{32} (P) Ez 22^{26}, the sabbath Ex 31^{14} (P), Is 56$^{2.6}$ Ez 20$^{13.16.21.24}$ 22^{8} 23^{38} Ne 13$^{17.18}$; and so the sanctity of the prince of Tyre who made himself God, and his holy places, Ez 28$^{7.16.18}$ **c.** the name of God Lv 18^{21} 19^{12} 20^{3} 21^{6} 22$^{2.32}$ (all H), Am 2^{7} Je 34^{16} Ez 20^{39} 36$^{20.21.22.23}$ Mal 1^{12}, God himself Ez 13^{19} **d.** ′י *defiles* or *profanes* his inheritance by giving it over to Babylon Is 47^{6}, the princes of the sanctuary by giving them to Chaldeans Is 43^{28} **2.** *violate the honour of, dishonour*, ′י subj, crown of Davidic kingdom ψ 89^{40} (sq לארץ pregn.), kingdom of Judah La 2^{2}; the גאון כל צבי Is 23^{9} **3.** *violate* a covenant ψ 55^{21} 89^{35} Mal 2^{10}, the חקות of God ψ 89^{32}. **4.** *treat* a vineyard *as common* (v. חֹל) *by beginning to use its fruit* Dt 20$^{6.6}$ 28^{30} Je 31^{5} (v. the law Lv 19$^{23-25}$, H) **Pu.** *Pt* שְׁמִי הַגָּדוֹל הַמְחֻלָּל בַּגּוֹיִם Ez 36^{23} *my great name which is profaned among the nations.* **Hiph. 1. a.** *Impf.* לֹא אַחֵל אֶת־שֵׁם־קָדְשִׁי עוֹד Ez 39^{7} *I will not let my holy name be profaned any more.* **b.** לֹא יַחֵל דְּבָרוֹ *he shall not violate his word* Nu 30^{3} (P) **2.** *begin*, *Pf* החל Gn 6^{1}+15 t, הֵחֵלָּה Ju 20^{40}, הַחִלּוֹתָ Dt 3^{24} Est 6^{13}, הַחִלֹּתִי Dt 2^{31} 1 S 22^{15}, הֵחֵלּוּ Ezr 3^{6}+6 t; *Impf* יָחֵל Ju 10^{18} 13^{5}, וַיָּחֶל Gn 9^{20}+5 t, 3 fs. וַתָּחֶל Ju 13^{25} 16^{19}, 2 ms תָּחֵל Dt 16^{9}, וַתְּחִלֶּינָה, אָחֵל Dt 2^{25} Jos 3^{7}, וַיָּחֵלּוּ Ju 20^{31}+3 t, Gn 41^{54}, תָּחֵלּוּ Ez 9^{6}, *Imv* הָחֵל Dt 2$^{24.31}$, *Inf cstr.* הָחֵל 1 S 3^{12}+2 t; sf הַחִלָּם Gn 11^{6}, *Pt.* מֵחֵל Je 25^{29};—*begin*, Nu 17$^{11.12}$ (P) Dt 16^{9} 2 Ch 29$^{27.27}$, so 2 S 24^{15} 𝔊 We Dr (𝔊 inserts וְהַמַּגֵּפָה הֵחֵלָּה bef וַיָּמָת בָּעָם); c. Inf. (ל) *begin to* Gn 41^{54} (E), Gn 6^{1} 10^{8} = 1 Ch 1^{10}, Gn 11^{6} Nu 25^{1} (all J), Dt 2$^{25.31}$ 3^{24} 16^{9} Jos 3^{7} (D), Ju 10^{18} 13$^{5.25}$ 16$^{19.22}$ 20$^{31.39.40}$ 1 S 3^{2} 14^{35} 22^{15} 2 K 10^{32} 15^{37} 1 Ch 27^{24} 2 Ch 3$^{1.2}$ 29^{17} 31$^{7.10.21}$ 34$^{3.3}$ Ezr 3^{6} Ne 4^{1} Est 6^{13} 9^{23} Je 25^{29} Jon 3^{4}, c ו consec. Gn 9^{20} (J), Ezr 3^{8}; c ב *begin with* Gn 44^{12} (J), Ez 9^{6}, 2 Ch 20^{22}, so 2 S 24^{5}, rd וַיָּחֵלּוּ for וַיַּחֲנוּ 𝔊L We Dr; c. מן *begin from* Ez 9^{6}, הָחֵל רָשׁ *begin! possess!* Dt 2$^{24.31}$; הָחֵל וְכַלֵּה *beginning and ending* 1 S 3^{12} (i e accomplishing my full purpose, v. Dr) **Hoph.** *Pf.* אָז הוּחַל לִקְרֹא בְּשֵׁם ′י *then it was begun* (= men began) *to call on the name of* ′י Gn 4^{26} (J)

Note—וְיָחֵלּוּ מְעַט מִמַּשָּׂא Ho 8^{10} *begin to be minished by reason of the burden* RV Hi al, Wü Now rd וְיָחִילוּ (I. חיל, חול)—for om. of dagh v also ויחלו of Cod Bab—*shall be in anguish a little for the burden*, so Ra AV; Ew וְיָחִלוּ *that they may wait* (?) *a little;* 𝔊 וחדלו מעט ממשח *cease a little from anointing*, so Che We, this probably best

†חֹל **n.[m.] profaneness, commonness,**—דֶּרֶךְ חֹל 1 S 21^{6}, לֶחֶם חֹל v^{6}, in concrete sense, opp קֹדֶשׁ Lv 10^{10} (P), Ez 22^{26} 42^{20} 44^{23} 48^{15}.

II. †חָלָל adj. profaned;—חָלָל רָשָׁע (rd. cstr. חֲלַל SS) *profaned, dishonoured wicked one* Ez 21^{30} (so AV Thes MV SS Co Or; but RV Hä *deadly wounded*, Ew Sm *fallen, slain*); pl. cstr. חַלְלֵי רְשָׁעִים Ez 21^{34}; fs. חֲלָלָה of woman sexually dishonoured Lv 21$^{7.14}$ (H; ‖ זֹנָה).

†חָלִ֫ילָה **subst.** c. ה loc., used as exclam. lit. *ad profanum!* i.e. far be it (for me, thee, etc.)! (v. Ba$^{NB\ 136}$)—ח׳ Gn 44^{7}+17 t., חָלִלָה Gn 18^{25}+2 t.—alone, 1 S 14^{45} 20^{2}; elsewh. c. ל pers.: Gn 18$^{25\,b}$ (J), 1 S 2^{30} 20^{9} 22^{15}; + מִן and inf. of act deprecated Gn 18$^{25\,a}$ 44$^{7.17}$ (all J), Jos 24^{16} (E), 1 S 12^{23} 2 S 23^{17}; + מִמֶּנּוּ ל (peculiarly) Jos 22^{29} (P; = *from it, even to rebel*); + אִם (= *surely not*) 2 S 20^{20} (ח׳ ח׳), Jb 27^{5}; strengthened idiom. by מיהוה ,ח׳ לִי מִי׳ sq. מִן and inf. 1 S 26^{11} 1 K 21^{3}+ 2 S 23^{17} (rd. מיהוה, 𝔊L 𝔖 𝔗) = 1 Ch 11^{19} (מאלהי) sq. אִם 1 S 24^{7}; ח׳ לָאֵל מֵרֶשַׁע Jb 34^{10}.

†תְּחִלָּה **n.f.** beginning, הַתְּחִלָּה Ne 11^{17} (rd. הַתְּהִלָּה 𝔊 𝔙 SS Öt), בַּתְּחִלָּה Gn 13^{3}+10 t.; cstr. תְּחִלַּת Ho 1^{2} Pr 9^{10} Ec 10^{13}, בִּתְחִלַּת 2 K 17^{25} +4 t., תְּחִלַּת 2 S 21^{9}, מִתְּחִלַּת 2 S 21^{10}:—cstr. with nouns תְּ׳ חָכְמָה Pr 9^{10} *the beginning, first principle* of wisdom תְּ׳ דִּבְרֵי Ec 10^{13} *the first word,* sq. rel. clause תְּ׳ דִּבֶּר י׳ *at the beginning of, Yahweh spake* (= when Yahweh first spake) Ho 1^{2}; preceded by prep. מִן 2 S 21^{10}, elsewhere by בְּ *in the beginning,* of the harvest Ru 1^{22} 2 S 21^{9} (Qr), of the kingdom Ezr 4^{6}, of their dwelling there 2 K 17^{25}, of supplications Dn 9^{23}, of the shooting up of vegetation Am 7^{1}, כְּבַתְּ׳ as in the beginning Is 1^{26}; בַּתְּ׳ *at first, first* in order Ju 1^{1} 20$^{18.18}$ 2 S 17^{9}; *at the first, first* (or *former*) *time,* i.e. first in a series of occurrences, Gn 13^{3} (J), 41^{21} (E), 43$^{18.20}$ (J), Dn 8^{1} 9^{21}.

†I. [חָלַם] **vb. be healthy, strong** (NH *id.*; Aram. ܚܠܡ Ethp. *be made healthy, strong,* Aph. causat., also deriv.; חֲלַם *press firmly together*)—**Qal** *Impf.* יַחְלְמוּ בְנֵיהֶם Jb 39^{4} *their young are healthy.* **Hiph.** *Impf.* 2 ms. וְתַחֲלִימֵנִי Is 38^{16} *and restore me to health* (‖ וְהַחֲיֵנִי).

†חֵ֫לֶם **n.pr.m.** (*strength*)—a returned exile Zc 6^{14} = חֶלְדַּי v^{10}.

†II. חָלַם **vb. dream** (NH *id.*; Aram. ܚܠܡ, חֲלַם; Eth. ሐለመ: Ar. حَلَمَ, *dream, experience an emission of the seminal fluid, attain to puberty*)—**Qal** *Pf.* ח׳ Gn 42^{9} Dn 2^{1}, חָלַמְתִּי Gn 37^{9}+3 t., חָלָמְתִּי Gn 37^{6}+2 t., etc., +3 t. Pf.; *Impf.* יַחֲלֹם Is 29^{8}+5 t., יַחְלְמוּ Jb 39^{4}, וַיַּחַלְמוּ Gn 40^{5}, יַחֲלֹמוּן Jo 3^{1}, נַחֲלְמָה Gn 41^{11}; *Pt.* חֹלֵם Dt 13^{4}, חֹלֵם Gn 41^{1} Dt 13$^{2.6}$, חֹלְמִים ψ 126^{1};—*dream:* **a.** of ordinary dreams of sleep Is 29$^{8.8}$ ψ 126^{1}. **b.** of dreams with prophetic meaning: of Jacob Gn 28^{12}, Joseph Gn 37$^{5.6.9.9.10}$ 42^{9}, of Pharaoh and his servants Gn 40$^{5.8}$ 41$^{1.5.11.11.15}$ (all E, not elsewh. in Hex.); of Midianite Ju 7^{13}, Nebuchad. Dn 2$^{1.3}$, old men in latter days Jo 3^{1}. **c.** of dreams of false prophets Dt 13$^{2.4.6}$ Je 23$^{25.25}$. **Hiph.** *Pt.* מַחְלְמִים *dream* (of false prophets, c. acc. cogn.) Je 29^{8} (but rd. חֹלְמִים [מ by dittogr. fr. אַתֶּם], Hi Gf Gie Gr).

†חֲלוֹם **n.m.**$^{Gn\ 37,10}$ dream;—ח׳ abs. Gn 37^{5}+, cstr. Gn 20^{3}, חֲלֹם abs. Gn 20^{6}, cstr. 31^{24}; sf. חֲלוֹמִי Gn 40$^{9.16}$, חֲלֹמִי Gn 41$^{17.22}$, חֲלֹמוֹ Gn 40^{5}+5 t.; pl. חֲלֹמוֹת Je 23^{32}+10 t. etc., +7 t. sf.—*dream* **1.** ordinary dream of sleep Jb 7^{14} 20^{8} ψ 73^{20} Ec 5$^{2.6}$ Is 29^{7}. **2.** dreams with prophetic meaning, the lowest grade of prophecy (v. Br$^{MP\ 6}$): **a.** dream of Abimelek Gn 20$^{3.6}$, of Jacob 31$^{10.11}$, Laban 31^{24}, Joseph 37$^{5.6.8.9.9.10.19.20}$ 42^{9}, Pharaoh and his servants 40$^{5.5.5.8.9.9.16}$ 41$^{7.8.11.11.12.12.15.15.17.22.25.26.32}$; of a lower order of prophets than Moses Nu 12^{6}, (all E, not elsewh. in Hex.), Jb 33^{15}, of Midianite Ju 7$^{13.13.15}$, desired by Saul 1 S 28$^{6.15}$; of Sol. 1 K 3$^{5.15}$; of old men in latter days Jo 3^{1}, of Nebuchad. Dn 2$^{1.2.3.3}$; Daniel הֵבִין בְּכָל־חָזוֹן וַחֲלֹמוֹת Dn 1^{17} *had understanding* in all visions and *dreams.* **b.** of false prophets Dt 13$^{2.4.6}$ Je 23$^{27.28.28.32}$ 27^{9} 29^{8} Zc 10^{2}.

חַלָּמוּת **n.f.** name of a plant, with thick, slimy juice, *purslain,* Jb 6^{6} RVm, so Thes Rob Ges al.; 𝔖 ܚܠܡܘܬܐ, *anchusa* PS$^{i,\ 1284}$; on this, and later interpr. v. Bö Di Löw$^{pp.\ 165,\ 361}$; only אִם־יֶשׁ־טַעַם בְּרִיר חַלָּמוּת Jb 6^{6} *is there any taste in the juice of* ח׳ (fig. of insipid and dull discourse); > AV RV Ew Hi SS after 𝔗 Saad Rabb. *in the white of an egg.*

חלמש (quadrilit. √ of following; meaning unknown).

†חַלָּמִישׁ **n.m.** flint;—חַלָּמִישׁ Dt 8^{15}+3 t.; cstr. חַלְּמִישׁ Dt 32^{13};—*flint* צוּר הַח׳ *rock of flint* = flinty rock, whence water flowed for Isr. in desert Dt 8^{15}, and (no צוּר) ψ 114^{8}; worked by miners Jb 28^{9}; hyperb. *oil out of* ח׳ צוּר Dt 32^{13} *flint of rock* = rocky flint (poet.);—in sim. of firmness עַל־כֵּן שַׂמְתִּי פָנַי כַּחַלָּמִישׁ Is 50^{7}.

חלן, חלון v. sub I. and II. חול.

†**חָלַף vb. pass on or away, pass through** (mostly poet) (NH *id*, *pass by* or *away*, *change*; Ph חלפת *equivalent*, Reinach $^{RÉJ\ 1888,\ 278}$, Hoffm $^{G\ G\ Abh\ xxxvi.\ 1890,\ 20}$, Aram חֲלַף *pass away*, *change*, ܚܠܦ *change*, *substitute*; Nab חלף *change* (?) Eut $^{p.\ 53}$, Ar خَلَفَ *come after*, *succeed*, *replace* [cf 'Caliph' i e *successor* (of Mohammed)] and many deriv. Lane $^{792-799}$, so also ויחלפה MI ^{6} *and his son succeeded him*, Eth ኀለፈ: *pass by*, *across*, *through*)—**Qal** *Pf* חָלַף Ct 2^{11} Hb 1^{11} etc, *Impf* יַחֲלֹף Jb 4^{15} + 4 t.; 3 fs. sf תַּחְלְפֵהוּ Jb 20^{24}; יַחֲלֹפוּ ψ 102^{27}; *Inf cstr.* לַחֲלוֹף Is 21^{1};—**1. a.** *pass on quickly* 1 S 10^{3}; elsewh. only poet., *move* or *sweep on*, of a flood Is 8^{8}, or wind 21^{1} Jb 4^{15} Hb 1^{11}, of God Jb 9^{11} 11^{10}. **b.** *pass away* (*vanish*) Jb 9^{26} (of days), Ct 2^{11} (of rain ‖ עבר), of the heavens ψ 102^{27}, of idols Is 2^{18}, (but perhaps gloss JBL $^{ix\ 1890,\ 86}$) **2.** of grass, *come on anew*, i e *sprout again* (cf **Hiph. 2**) ψ $90^{5\ 6}$, so Thes AV De Hi Che Bae al; less suitably in context, 𝔊 𝔙 Ew *pass away*, supr **1 b** **3.** trans **a.** *pass through*, i e. pierce, sq. acc Ju 5^{26} Jb 20^{24}. **b.** *overstep*, *transgress* Is 24^{5} (‖ עבר), (cf Ar iv to *break* a promise) **Pi.** *Impf* וַיְחַלֵּף (*cause to pass*) *change*, sq. acc. garment Gn 41^{14} (E) 2 S 12^{20}. **Hiph.** *Pf* הֶחֱלִף Gn 31^{7}, *Impf* יַחֲלִיף Jb 14^{7}; sf יַחֲלִיפֶנּוּ Lv 27^{10}; 3 fs. תַּחֲלִיף Jb 29^{20}, 2 ms וַתַּחֲלֵף Gn 31^{41}; sf. תַּחֲלִיפֵם, יַחֲלִיפוּ Is 40^{31} 41^{1}; נַחֲלִיף Is 9^{9},—**1.** *change* (trans.) garments Gn 35^{2} (E) ψ 102^{27}, wages Gn $31^{7\ 41}$ (both E), no obj expr Lv 27^{10} (H), *substitute* i e *cause to succeed* Is 9^{9}, *change* for better, *renew*, obj כֹּחַ Is 40^{31} 41^{1}. **2.** *shew newness*, of tree, putting forth fresh shoots Jb 14^{7}, of bow 29^{20}

†I. **חֵלֶף n.[m.] exchange**, only cstr, as prep. *in return for* (so חֲלַף, ܚܠܦ, common in Aram e g Gn 4^{25} 𝔗𝔖 for Heb תַּחַת—ח׳ עֲבֹדָתָם (עֲבֹדַתְכֶם) Nu $18^{21\ 31}$ (both P)

†II. **חֵלֶף n pr.loc.** in Naphtali, site unknown Jos 19^{33}

†**חֲלוֹף n.m a passing away, vanishing** (properly Inf of חלף)—בְּנֵי ח׳ Pr 31^{8} i e those who are passing away, transitory (cf. **Qal 1 b**).

†[**חֲלִיפָה**] **n.f. a change** (from idea of *replacing*, *changing*, *substituting*, cf Ar., Aram)—sf. חֲלִיפָתִי Jb 14^{14}, pl abs. חֲלִיפוֹת Ju 14^{19} + 3 t; cstr. *id.* Ju 14^{13} 2 K 5^{5}; חֲלִפוֹת Gn 45^{22} + 2 t; חֲלִפֹת Gn 45^{22} Ju 14^{12},—**1.** *change* of raiment ח׳ שְׂמָלֹת Gn $45^{22\ 22}$, elsewhere ח׳ בגדים Ju $14^{12\ 13}$ 2 K $5^{5\ 22.23}$; so without בגדים Ju 14^{19}. **2.** *relays* 1 K 5^{28}; cf ח׳ וצבא Jb 10^{17} (Di). **3.** revival after death, under fig of *relief* from milit service Jb 14^{14}. **4.** *changing*, *varying*, of course of life אֲשֶׁר אֵין חֲלִיפוֹת לָמוֹ ψ 55^{20} of the wicked, *with whom are no changings*, i e they do evil incessantly, steadily (‖ ולא יָרְאוּ אלהים) so Kmp Hu De Sch al; but the expression is peculiar and obscure, Calv *vicissitudes*; Hengst *discharges*, text perhaps corrupt.

†[**מַחֲלָף**] **n.m. knife**, so 𝔙 (cf. Syr. ܚܠܦ *totondit* (in Lex.), ܡܚܠܦܐ, ܡܚܠܦܐ, *knife*, Talm. חליפות *knives*, acc. to Levy, Jastr; Thes as *passing through* (cf. vb **3 a**)), but √ and meaning not certain, only Pl. מַחֲלָפִים Ezr 1^{9}, among temple utensils (v. BeRy Ryle).

†[**מַחְלָפָה**] **n.f. plait** (of hair; so called fr. *intertwining*, *passing through* each other, of the strands)—Pl cstr. מַחְלְפוֹת רֹאשִׁי Ju 16^{13}, cf. v ^{19}.

†I. **חָלַץ vb. draw off or out, withdraw** (NH *id*; Aram. חֲלַץ, ܚܠܨ *despoil*, usu. Pa. etc, Ph. n pr חלצבעל *Baal has rescued*, and חלץ alone; Ar خَلَصَ *withdraw*, *retire*)—**Qal** *Pf* Ho 5^{6}; וְחָלְצָה consec. Dt 25^{9}; חָלְצוּ La 4^{3}; *Impf.* 2 ms תַּחֲלֹץ, *Pt pass* cstr. חֲלוּץ Dt 25^{10},—**1.** *draw*, *draw off*, c. acc. of sandal Dt 25^{9} Is 20^{2} (both sq מִן c רֶגֶל), cf. בֵּית חֲלוּץ הַנָּעַל Dt 25^{10}, *draw out*, *present* the breast, of animal giving suck La 4^{3} **2.** intrans *withdraw* (himself) sq מִן Ho 5^{6} **Niph.** *Pf be delivered* נֶחֱלַץ Pr 11^{8} (sq מִן); *Impf.* יֵחָלֵצוּ Pr 11^{9}; יֵחָלְצוּן ψ 60^{7} = 108^{7} (Ges $^{§\ 51\ 2\ R\ 2}$) **Pi.** *Pf.* חִלֵּץ Lv 14^{43} etc, *Impf.* יְחַלֵּץ Jb 36^{15}; וָאֲחַלְּצָה ψ 7^{5} (but on text vid infr ad fin), sf. אֲחַלֶּצְךָ ψ 50^{15}, אֲחַלְּצֵהוּ ψ 81^{8}, etc, *Imv* חַלְּצָה ψ 6^{5}; חַלְּצֵנִי ψ 119^{153} 140^{2};—**1.** *pull out*, *tear out* Lv $14^{40.43}$ (P; stones fr infested house). **2.** *rescue*, *deliver*, c obj pers, but only poet.,—sq נפשי ψ 6^{5} 116^{8} (מִמָּוֶת); cf. 140^{2} (sq מִן), abs c. acc. ψ 18^{20} = 2 S 22^{20}, ψ 34^{8} 50^{15} 81^{8} 91^{15} 119^{153} Jb 36^{15}; וָאֲחַלְּצָה ψ 7^{5}, sq acc., *but I delivered* AV Hup Ri, cf Ew, *and spoiled*, *despoiled* Ges Hi De Bae (but this only in Aram); < *and oppressed* (rd. וָאֶלְחֲצָה) Krochm Dy Gr Che; (‖ גָּמַלְתִּי רָע).

†[**חֲלִיצָה**] **n.f. what is stripped off a person**, as plunder, in war;—only sf חֲלִצָתוֹ 2 S 2^{21}; חֲלִיצוֹתָם Ju 14^{19}.

†[מַחֲלָצָה] **n.f.** robe of state (*taken off in ordinary life*);—only pl. abs. מַחֲלָצוֹת Is 3^{22} robes of ladies of Jerusalem; Zc 3^{4} of high priest.

†II. [חָלַץ] **vb.** equip for war (primary idea of *strength, vigour*, v. Hiph., n. חֲלָצַיִם, and As. *ḫalṣu, fortification* (Schr $^{COT\ Gloss}$ Asrb $^{Annals\ ii.\ 52}$), cf. *ḫilṣu, belt*, Zehnpfund $^{BAS\ i.\ 499}$; Aram. ܚܠܝܨ *accinctus ad opus, strenuus*, ܚܠܝܨܘܬܐ *fortitudo, strenuitas*, Gk. ἀνδρεία, > Thes Rob Ges SS who regard as = I. חלץ in sense *strip* for battle, *expeditus*)—**Qal** only *Pt. pass.* חָלוּץ Nu 32^{21} + 7 t., cstr. חֲלוּץ Nu 32^{27}; pl. חֲלוּצִים Nu 32^{30} + 2 t., cstr. חֲלוּצֵי 1 Ch 12^{24} + 3 t.; חֲלֻצֵי Is 15^{4};—*equipped*: **1.** as adj. Nu $32^{30.32}$ Dt 3^{18}. **2.** as subst. sg. coll. Nu 32^{21} (JE; v. Niph. v^{20}) 2 Ch 20^{21} 28^{14}, c. art. הֶח׳ Jos $6^{7.9.13}$ (JE); חֲלוּץ צָבָא Nu 32^{27} *men equipped for war* (JE), so ח׳ הַמִּלְחָמָה 32^{29} (P); הֶח׳ לַצָּבָא 1 Ch 12^{24} (v^{23} van d. H); pl. חֲלוּצֵי צָבָא Nu 31^{5} (P) 1 Ch 12^{25} (v^{24} van d. H) 2 Ch 17^{18}; ח׳ הַצ׳ Jos 4^{13} (P); note חֲלֻצֵי מוֹאָב Is 15^{4} *warriors* (*equipped ones*, Che *men-at-arms*) *of Moab*. **Niph.** *Impf.* 2 mpl. תֵּחָלְצוּ Nu 32^{20}, 1 pl. נֵחָלֵץ Nu 32^{17}; *Imv.* הֵחָלְצוּ Nu 31^{3}; *be*, or *go equipped*, sq. לִפְנֵי Nu $32^{17.20}$ (both JE; v. Qal Pt. v^{21}); sq. לַצָּבָא 31^{3} (P; Niph. Imv. here surprising with מֵאִתְּכֶם, v. Di). **Hiph.** *Impf.* עַצְמֹתֶיךָ יַחֲלִיץ Is 58^{11} *he* (י׳) *will brace up, invigorate, thy bones* (MV De Di; Hup Che crit. n. Du al. rd. יַחֲלִיף *renew, rejuvenate*).

†[חָלָץ] **n.[f.]** only dual, loins (as seat of strength, vigour; cf. Aram. חַרְצָא *hip, loin*, Syr. ܚܨܐ, Nö $^{ZMG\ 1886,\ 741}$)—חֲלָצַיִם Is 32^{11}; sf. חֲלָצֶיךָ Gn 35^{11} + 4 t.; חֲלָצָיו Is 5^{27} + 2 t.; + חלצו Kt Jb 31^{20}, Qr חֲלָצָיו;—*loins*: **1.** as seat of virility יצא מן ח׳ Gn 35^{11} (P), 1 K 8^{19} 2 Ch 6^{9}. **2.** as girded אֱזָר־נָא כְגֶבֶר ח׳ Jb 38^{3} 40^{7}; אֵזוֹר חֲלָצָיו Is 5^{27} (v. אֵזוֹר), וַחֲגוֹרָה עַל חֲלָצָיִם 32^{11}, cf. Jb 31^{20} where the clothed loins are conceived as blessing charitable giver; metaph. Is 11^{5} faithfulness waist-cloth of his loins (‖ מתניו). **3.** as seat of pains, like a woman's in travail, Je 30^{6}.

†חֶלֶץ **n.pr.m.** (*vigour*). **1.** one of David's heroes 2 S 23^{26}, 𝔊 Σελλης, A Ελλης, 𝔊L Χαλλης; = 1 Ch 11^{27} 𝔊 Χελλης, 𝔊L Ελλης; also 1 Ch 27^{10} 𝔊 Χεσελης, A 𝔊L Χελλης (in both, Baer חֶלֶץ, van d. H. חָלֶץ). **2.** man of Judah 1 Ch 2^{39} = חָלֶץ v^{39} 𝔊 Χελλης, 𝔊L Αλλαν.

חָלֶץ **n.pr.m.** v. חֶלֶץ supr.

†I. חָלַק **vb.** divide, share (NH *id.*; Aram. חֲלַק *field*, חוּלָקָא *portion*, ܚܠܩ *divide, determine, decree*; Ar. خَلَقَ *measure, measure off*; As. *eḳlu, possession, field*, Jäger $^{BAS\ ii.\ 296}$; Eth. ኈለቈ: I. 2, is *enumerate*, ኍልቍ: ኈልቍ: *enumeration, number*)—**Qal** *Pf.* ח׳ Dt 4^{19} + 5 t.; חָלְקוּ Jos 18^{2}; *Impf.* יַחֲלֹק Jb 27^{17} Pr 17^{2}; 2 ms. sf. וַתַּחְלְקֵם Ne 9^{22}; 3 pl. וַיַּחְלְקוּ Jos 14^{5}; יַחֲלֹקוּ 1 S 30^{24}; וַיֶּחָלְקוּם 1 Ch $24^{4.5}$; תַּחְלְקוּ 2 S 19^{30}; *Imv.* חִלְקוּ Jos 22^{8}; *Inf.* לַחֲלֹק Ne 13^{13}; *Pt.* חוֹלֵק Pr 29^{24};—**1.** *divide, apportion*, sq. acc. (of gods) and לְ pers. Dt 4^{19} 29^{25}; acc. not expressed Ne 13^{13} (ref. to offerings and tithes); c. acc. (of land) Jos 14^{5} (P), 18^{2} (JE), 2 S 19^{30}: obj. people Ne 9^{22}; ח׳ עִם *divide with* others Jos 22^{8} (D ?). **2.** *assign, distribute*: Levites over (עַל) temple 2 Ch 23^{18}, cf. 1 Ch $24^{4.5}$. **3.** *assign, impart*, sq. בִּינָה & לְ Jb 39^{17}. **4.** *share* (in), sq. acc. silver Jb 27^{17}; inheritance Pr 17^{2}; spoil 1 S 30^{24} (obj. om.); sq. עִם *have shares with* ח׳ עִם גַּנָּב Pr 29^{24}. **5.** *divide up* = *plunder* the temple, sq. acc. 2 Ch 28^{21} (v. Be). **Niph.** *Impf.* יֵחָלֵק Nu 26^{55} 1 K 16^{21}; וַיֵּחָלֵק Jb 38^{24}; וַיֵּחָלֵק Gn 14^{15}; 3 fs. תֵּחָלֵק Nu 26^{53} 26^{56}; וַיֵּחָלְקֵם (Baer) 1 Ch 23^{6} 24^{3} cf. Be & infr. sub **Pi.**;—**1.** reflex., *divide oneself* Gn 14^{15} (i.e. one's men). **2.** pass. *be divided*: **a.** *apportioned*, the land Nu $26^{53.55}$ (by lot) v^{56} (*id.*); all P. **b.** of people, *divided into* two factions 1 K 16^{21}. **c.** of light, *parted, spread abroad* Jb 38^{24}. **3.** trans. *assign, distribute* 1 Ch 23^{6} 24^{3}, but trans. Niph. is unlikely, v. infr. **Pi.** *Pf.* 3 pl. חִלְּקוּ Jo 4^{2}; וְחִלַּקְתֶּם consec. Ez 47^{21}; sf. חִלְּקָם La 4^{16}; 3 fs. sf. חִלְּקַתָּה Is 34^{17}; 2 ms. sf. וְחִלַּקְתָּם Ez 5^{1};—*Impf.* יְחַלֵּק Gn 49^{27} + 4 t., etc.; prob. rd. יְחַלְּקֵם 1 Ch 23^{6} 24^{3} (v. supr. **Niph.**), etc.; *Imv.* חַלֵּק Jos 13^{7}; *Inf.* חַלֵּק Jos 19^{51} Pr 16^{19}; sf. חַלְּקָם Is 9^{2};—**1.** *divide, apportion*: food, at festival 2 S 6^{19}, sq. acc. & לְ = 1 Ch 16^{3}, garments ψ 22^{19}, sorrows Jb 21^{17} (no לְ); *give a portion to*, sq. לְ (no acc. expr.) Is 53^{12}; a land Jo 4^{2} (no ind. obj.) Jos 19^{51} (P), also Mi 2^{4}, ψ 60^{8} = 108^{8}, Dn 11^{39}; sq. acc. & לְ Jos 13^{7} 18^{10} 1 K 18^{6} Is 34^{17} Ez 47^{21}; *divide* hair (symbol.) Ez 5^{1}; *divide* spoil (שָׁלָל) Is 9^{2} Pr 16^{19} Gn 49^{27} (poem), Ex 15^{9} (song); Ju 5^{30} ψ 68^{13} Is 53^{12}. **2.** *assign, distribute*: Levites to their service, prob. 1 Ch 23^{6} 24^{3} (v. supr.) **3.** *scatter*, sq. acc. Gn 49^{7} (poem) (‖ הפיץ), La 4^{16}. **Pu.** *Pf.* חֻלַּק Is 33^{23};

וְחָלַק consec Zc 14^{1}, *Impf.* 3fs תְּחֻלָּק Am 7^{17}; *be divided*, of land Am 7^{17}, spoil Is 33^{23} Zc 14^{1} **Hithp.** *Pf* וְהִתְחַלְּקוּ consec Jos 18^{5} *divide* (land) *among themselves* **Hiph.** *Inf* לַחֲלֹק Je 37^{12}; *to receive a portion* (denom. fr. חֵלֶק), but dub

† I. **חֵ֫לֶק n.m.**$^{Jos\ 18,5}$ **portion, tract, territory** —ח׳ abs. Gn 31^{14}+; cstr Gn 14^{24}+; sf חֶלְקִי ψ 16^{5}+6 t; חֶלְקְךָ Nu 18^{20} Ec 9^{9}, חֶלְקֵךְ ψ 50^{18}, חֶלְקֵךְ Is 57^{6}, חֶלְקוֹ Hb 1^{16}+5 t, חֶלְקָם Gn 14^{24} +3 t, pl. חֲלָקִים Jos 18^{5}+5 t, sf חֶלְקֵיהֶם Ho 5^{7},—**1.** *portion, share:* **a.** of booty Gn 14$^{24.24}$ Nu 31^{36} (P) 1 S 30$^{24.24}$. **b.** of food Lv 6^{10} (P); ח׳ כח׳ יאכלו Dt 18^{8}, = food Hb 1^{16} (‖ מַאֲכָל), so (of unrestricted charity) Ec 11^{2} v Now **c.** sq. בְּ, *share* or *interest in* Ec 9^{6}, with idea of *obligation to* Gn 31^{14} (E; in father's house), 2 S 20^{1} = 1 K 12^{16} = 2 Ch 10^{16} (in royal line, all ‖ נַחֲלָה); of *right* (*privilege*) *in* ח׳ ביהוה Jos 22$^{25.27}$ (P), Ne 2^{20} (in Jerus, + צְדָקָה וזִכָּרוֹן). **d.** proper *share* or *part* אַעֲנֶה חֶלְקִי Jb 32^{17} i e I will do my part in replying Esp **2.** *portion, tract*, of land **a.** as distrib at conquest Jos 19^{9}, seven *portions* 18$^{5.6.9}$ (all JE) v^{7} (JE, + נחלה in ‖ cl), 15^{13} 19^{9} (both P); none for tribe of Levi Dt 10^{9} 12^{12} 14$^{27.29}$ 18^{1} Jos 18^{7} (all D; ‖ נחלה), Jos 14^{4} (P), none for priests Nu 18^{20} (P; ‖ vb נחל) **b.** of land possessed by people Ho 5^{7} Mi 2^{4} **c.** portion to be assigned after exile Is 61^{7} Ez 45^{7} 48$^{8.21}$, חֶלְקוֹ עַל־אַדְמַת הַקֹּדֶשׁ Zc 2^{16}. **d.** specif. of *town-land*, district about a town, ח׳ יזרעאל 2 K 9$^{10.36}$ + 1 K 21^{23} (MT חל), הַשָּׂדֶה בח׳ יְ׳ v^{37}. **e.** הַחֵלֶק Am 7^{4} (opp תהום) appar of *land* of Isr. **3.** hence *portion*, i e. (acquired) *possession:* **a.** of people as י׳'s possession Dt 32^{9} (‖ חֶבֶל נחלתו); but esp. **b.** of י׳ as possession of his servants: of priests, as enjoying perquisites of altar Nu 18^{20} (P; ‖ נחלה), in spiritual sense ψ 73^{26} 119^{57} La 3^{24}, ח׳ בְּאֶרֶץ הַחַיִּים ψ 16^{5}; י׳ מְנָת חֶלְקִי 142^{6}, hence ח׳ יעקב of י׳ Je 10^{16} = 51^{19} (שֵׁבֶט נַחֲלָתוֹ in ‖ cl) **4.** chosen *portion*, habitual mode of life עִם־מְנָאֲפִים ח׳ ψ 50^{18} *with adulterers is thy chosen life* (companionship, shewing character), בְּחַלְּקֵי־נַחַל חֶלְקֵךְ Is 57^{6} *among smooth* (things i e. stones) *of a brook-bed is thy chosen life* (of idolatrous habit, v חָלָק), חֶלְקָם בַּחַיִּים ψ 17^{14}. **5.** *portion, award*, from God ח׳ אֱלוֹהַּ Jb 31^{2} (‖ נחלה); specif. of punishment of wicked Is 17^{14} (‖ גּוֹרָל), עִם־אֵל Jb 27^{13}, מֵאֱלֹהִים 20^{29} (‖ נחלה); = *profit, reward* חֶלְקִי מִכָּל־עֲמָלִי Ec 2^{10}, cf v^{21} 3^{22} 5$^{17.18}$ 9^{9}.—לְחֵלֶק Jb 17^{5} is dub.. *a share* of feast, or of booty, Kmp Hi; *a prey, spoil*, Ew Di Da, AV *flattery* does not suit context.

† II. **חֵ֫לֶק n.pr.m.** (portion) a Gileadite Nu 26^{30} Jos 17^{2}. 𝔊 Χελεγ, (κ), Κελεζ, etc; 𝔊L Jos 17^{2} Ελεκ

† **חֶלְקִי adj.gent.** of foreg; only c art as subst. coll after מִשְׁפַּחַת Nu 26^{30}.

† I **חֶלְקָה n.f. portion of ground**,—abs. ח׳ Am 4$^{7.7}$+8 t.; cstr. חֶלְקַת Gn 33^{19}+12 t.; sf. חֶלְקָתִי Je 12^{10}, חֶלְקָתָם Jb 24^{18}, *portion* of ground, **1.** esp **a.** ח׳ הַשָּׂדֶה = the clearly divided *field* Gn 33^{19} Jos 24^{32} (both E), 2 S 23^{11} Ru 2^{3} 4^{3} 2 K 9^{25} 1 Ch 11^{13}. Also **b.** without השדה Am 4$^{7.7}$ 2 S 14$^{30.30.31}$ 23^{12} 2 K 3$^{19.25}$ 9$^{21.25.26}$ 1 Ch 11^{14} Jb 24^{18}; of י׳'s land Je 12$^{10.10}$ (‖ כַּרְמִי); cf also n pr loc חלקת הַצֻּרִים 2 S 2^{16} *field of sword-edges* (Dr), 𝔊 Ew$^{G\ iii.\ 156\ Eng\ tr.\ 114}$ We rd. ח׳ הַצֹּדִים *field of plotters* or *liers-in-wait* (v. Dr) **2.** *portion* of ground assigned to one, ח׳ מחקק Dt 33^{21} *commander's portion.*

† [חֲלֻקָּה] **n.f. part, portion**, חֲלֻקַּת בֵּית־אָב לַלְוִיִּם 2 Ch 35^{5}.

† **חֶלְקַי n.pr.m.** priest, time of Joiakim son of Jeshua, Ne 12^{15} (perh abbrev. for חלקיהו, (q.v.), 𝔊L Χελκιας (B om.)

† **חֶלְקַת n.pr.loc.** (*portion, possession*) city in Asher Jos 21^{31}, 𝔊 Χελκατ, A Θελκαθ, 𝔊L Χαλκαθ, = חֶלְקַת 19^{25} 𝔊 Ελεκεθ, A Χελκαθ, 𝔊L Ελκαθ.

† **חֶלְקַת הַצֻּרִים n.pr.loc.** a place near pool of Gibeon where Ishbosheth's men were killed by Dvd's men under Joab 2 S 2^{16}, 𝔊 Μέρις τῶν ἐπιβούλων, on mng of name v I חֶלְקָה supr.

† **חִלְקִיָּהוּ, חִלְקִיָּה n.pr.m.** (*my portion is* י׳) 𝔊 usu Χελκ(ε)ιας, Χελχιας;—**1.** father of Eliakim, Hezekiah's officer, חלקיהו 2 K 18$^{18.26}$ Is 22^{20} 36$^{3.22}$; חלקיה 2 K 18^{37}. **2.** high priest, Josiah's time, חלקיהו 2 K 22$^{4.8.14}$ 23$^{4.24}$ 2 Ch 34$^{9.14.15.15.18.20.22}$, חלקיה 2 K 22$^{8.10.12}$ 1 Ch 5$^{39.39}$ 9^{11} 2 Ch 35^{8} Ezr 7^{1}, cf also Ne 11^{11}. **3.** חלקיהו father of Jerem Je 1^{1}.—The foll. are all חלקיה. **4.** Levites: **a.** 1 Ch 6^{30} **b.** 1 Ch 26^{11} **5.** a priest, contemp. of Ezra Ne 8^{4} 12$^{7.21}$. **6.** father of Gemariah, an ambassador of Zedekiah to Nebuchadrezzar Je 29^{3}.

מַחֲלֹ֫קֶת n.f. division, course (almost

wholly Chr.)—מ׳ abs. 1 Ch $27^{1.2}$; cstr. 1 Ch 27^{4}; sf. מַחֲלֻקְתּוֹ 1 Ch 27^{2} + 14 t. 1 Ch 27; abs. מַחְלְקוֹת 1 Ch 23^{6} + 6 t. Ch + 1 S 23^{28} (v. infr.); cstr. *id.* 1 Ch 26^{12} + 5 t. Ch + Ne 11^{36}; sf. מַחְלְקוֹתֵיכֶם 2 Ch 35^{4}; מַחְלְקוֹתֵיהֶם 2 Ch $31^{16.17}$; מַחְלְקוֹתָם 1 Ch 24^{1} + 3 t. in Ch; מַחְלְקֹתָם Jos 11^{23} 12^{7} 18^{10} Ez 48^{29};—**1.** *division, part,* of land assigned to the several tribes of Isr. Jos 11^{23} 12^{7} (both D) 18^{10} (JE; others, divisions of Isr., but v.) Ez 48^{29}. **2.** techn. term of organization of priests and Levites (late), 1 Ch 23^{6} 24^{1} $26^{1.12.19}$ 2 Ch $8^{14.14}$ $31^{2.2}$ $35^{4.10}$ Ne 11^{36} + 26 t. in Ch.—סֶלַע הַמַּחְלְקוֹת n.pr. 1 S 23^{28} was popularly connected with this √,=*rock of divisions,* where Saul and David parted from neighbourhood of each other (Dr) so Vrss Th al.; Bö Klo, where their forces lay divided from each other; orig. connex. was perh. with II. חלק, *smooth, slippery;* Ges De W Ke al. expl. here as *rock of escapes,* but this meaning for חלק dubious.

II. חָלַק **vb. be smooth, slippery** (NH adj. חָלָק *smooth, empty,* Ar. خَلَقَ *make smooth, lie, forge, fabricate*)—**Qal** *Pf.* ח׳ Ho 10^{2}; 3 mpl. חָלְקוּ ψ 55^{22};—*smooth, slippery,* only fig.: Ho 10^{2} of heart of faithless Isr. (so Ew Ke Wü Now RVm), We *false;* > Vrss (not 𝔊) Hi St who rd. חָלַק, *divided* is their heart; 𝔊 ἐμέρισαν; of words, *smooth* ψ 55^{22} i.e. deceptive (‖ רַכּוּ דְבָרָיו מִשֶּׁמֶן). **Hiph.** *Pf.* הֶחֱלִיק ψ 36^{3}, הֶחֱלִיקָה Pr 2^{16} 7^{5}; *Impf.* יַחֲלִיקוּן ψ 5^{10}; *Pt.* מַחֲלִיק Pr 28^{23} + 2 t.; *make smooth:* **1.** lit. of idol-maker Is 41^{7} c. acc. instr. פַּטִּישׁ *hammer.* **2.** fig. *the tongue,* i.e. flatter with it ψ 5^{10} Pr 28^{23}, words Pr 2^{16} 7^{5} אֲמָרֶיהָ הֶחֱלִיקָה; abs. *deal smoothly,* sq. אֶל־ ψ 36^{3}, עַל Pr 29^{5}.

†III. חֵלֶק **n.[m.] smoothness, seductiveness** of speech, only sg. cstr. בְּחֵלֶק שְׂפָתֶיהָ תַּדִּיחֶנּוּ Pr 7^{21} *with the seductiveness of her lips she impelleth him* (‖ הִטַּתּוּ בְּרֹב לִקְחָהּ).—I. and II. חֵלֶק v. sub I. חלק.

†חָלָק **adj. smooth**—**1.** lit. אִישׁ חָלָק Gn 27^{11} (J), *smooth man* (opp. אִישׁ שָׂעִר); הָהָר הֶחָלָק Jos 11^{17} 12^{7} *the bald mt.* (both D); southern limit of Jos.'s conquest, identif. dub.; (1) white cliffs 8 m. S. of Dead Sea, and (2) Mt. Mâdara SW. fr. Pass es-Ṣafâ are proposed, v. Di.; as subst. חַלְּקֵי־נַחַל Is 57^{6} (v. I. חֵלֶק, **4**) *smooth* (stones) of a brook-bed (ravine, wady), i.e. thou worshippest common round stones (contempt., v. Che Di). **2.** fig. of mouth uttering smooth words וְחָלָק מִשֶּׁמֶן חִכָּהּ Pr 5^{3} cf. 26^{28}. **3.** as subst. =*flattery* מִקְסַם חָלָק Ez 12^{24} *divination of flattery.*

†II. [חֶלְקָה] **n.f. smooth part, smoothness, flattery;**—cstr. חֶלְקַת Gn 27^{16} Pr 6^{24}; pl. חֲלָקוֹת ψ 12^{3} + 3 t.;—**1.** *smoothness, smooth part* חֶלְקַת צַוָּארָיו Gn 27^{16}. **2.** pl. *slippery places* ψ 73^{18} fig. of situation of wicked. **3.** *smoothness*=*flattery* שְׂפַת ח׳ ψ 12^{3}, cf. v^{4}; חֶלְקַת לָשׁוֹן Pr 6^{24};=subst. pl. *smooth things,* i.e. *agreeable, flattering things* Is 30^{10}.—I. חֶלְקָה v. sub I. חלק.

†[חַלָּק] **adj. smooth,** only pl. cstr. חַלֻּקֵי אֲבָנִים 1 S 17^{40} *smooth ones of (among) stones*=*smooth* (or *smoothest?*) *stones* Ges $^{§§ 132 R 2. 133,2}$ Dr^{Sm}.

†[חֲלַקָּה] **n.f. smoothness, flattery,** only pl. abs.: **fine promises,** וְהֶחֱנִיף בַּחֲלַקּוֹת Dn 11^{32} (perhaps directly from חָלָק, exceptional pl., cf. קְטַנּוֹת, קְטַנִּים, קְטַנָּה, גְּמַלִּים).

†חֲלַקְלַקּוֹת **n.pl.f.abstr. smoothness, slipperiness, flattery, fine promises; 1.** *slipperiness* יהיה דרכם חשך וַחֲלַקְלַקֹּת ψ 35^{6}; יהיה דרכם להם כַּחֲלַקְלַקּוֹת Je 23^{12}. **2.** *fine promises* והחזיק מלכות בַּחֲלַקְלַקּוֹת Dn 11^{21}; cf. 11^{34}.

†II. מַחְלְקוֹת **n.f.pl. smoothness,** סֶלַע הַמּ׳ 1 S 23^{28} *rock of smoothness,* i.e. *slippery rock,* perhaps original meaning of this n.pr., v. further I. מחלקות sub I. חלק.

†[חָלַשׁ] **vb. 1. be weak, prostrate. 2.** (si vera l.) **weaken, disable, prostrate** (Aram. חֲלַשׁ *be weak;* ܚܠܫ, חַלָּשׁ, *weak,* as in Heb.; Ar. مُخْلِس *poor* (Frey))—**Qal** *Impf.* וַיַּחֲלֹשׁ Ex 17^{13}, וַיֶּחֱלָשׁ Jb 14^{10}; *Pt.* חוֹלֵשׁ Is 14^{12}; **1.** וגבר ימות ויח׳ Jb 14^{10} *but man dieth and is prostrate.* **2.** *disable, prostrate,* sq. acc. pers. Ex 17^{13} (E; point as **Hiph.**?); sq. עַל pers. (strangely) Is 14^{12}.

†חַלָּשׁ **adj. weak,** only c. art. as subst., הַחַלָּשׁ יאמר גבור אני Jo 4^{10} *the weak, let him say, I am a mighty man.*

†חֲלוּשָׁה **n.f. weakness, prostration,** אֵין קוֹל עֲנוֹת ח׳ Ex 32^{18} *it is not the sound of the answering of weakness* (JE; opp. גְּבוּרָה).

†I. חָם **n.pr.pers. m.** and **loc.** (cf. Sab. חם Hal^{243})—𝔊 Χαμ:—**1. Ham,** 2nd son of Noah Gn 5^{32} 6^{10} 7^{13} $9^{18.18}$ 1 Ch 1^{4}; called father of

Canaan Gn 9^{22} and of various peoples $10^{1.6.20}$ 1 Ch 1^{8}, cf. מִן־חָם הַיֹּשְׁבִים שָׁם 4^{40}; these peoples were inhabitants of southern lands, or related historically or politically to such inhabitants, v. כוש, פוט, מצרים, כנען, etc **2.** in late ψψ a name (coll) for Egyptians —אָהֳלֵי־ח׳ ψ 78^{51}; אֶרֶץ־ח׳ $105^{23.27}$ 106^{22} (all ‖ מִצְרַיִם, exc 105^{27})—On historical significance, and attempts at etymol. v Di Gen. ed 6, chap 10, esp. pp. 165, 168 f., Hom SV i 427 Bu Urg 323 Wiedemann Aegypt. Gesch i 22.

II. חָם *husband's father*, v חמה.

III חָם **adj.** *warm, hot*, v sub חמם.

חם v. sub חמם

חמא (√of foll, cf Ar. حَمِئَ *be hard*, used of curdled milk, Frey)

†**חֶמְאָה** **n.f.** curd,—ח׳ Gn 18^{8}+6 t; = חֵמָה Jb 29^{6}, cstr חֶמְאַת Dt 32^{14}, *curd, curdled milk*, mod *lebben* מִיץ חָלָב יוֹצִיא ח׳ Pr 30^{33}, elsewhere joined with חָלָב Gn 18^{8} (J) Dt 32^{14} (poem; חֶמְאַת בָּקָר וַחֲלֵב צֹאן), Ju 5^{25} (where served בְּסֵפֶל אַדִּירִים, v. ספל), with דְּבַשׁ 2 S 17^{29} Is $7^{15.22.22}$, cf נַחֲלֵי דְבַשׁ ח׳ fig of abundance Jb 20^{17}; בְּרְחֹץ הֲלִיכַי בְּחֵמָה Jb 29^{6} (‖ צוּר יָצוּק פַּלְגֵי־שָׁמֶן:)

†**חֵמָא** v חֵמָה sub יחם.

†**חָמַד** **vb desire, take pleasure in** (Aram. חֲמַד (not in Syr); Ar. حَمِدَ *praise, eulogize, approve of;* Sab חמדם *in gratitude* [praise] *there-for* DHM ZMG 1875, 595, 1876, 686)—**Qal** *Pf* ח׳ ψ 68^{17} Pr 12^{12}; חָמְדוּ Pr 1^{22}; וְחָמְדוּ consec Mi 2^{2}, חֲמַדְתֶּם Is 1^{29}, *Impf.* יַחְמֹד Ex 34^{24}; 2 ms תַּחְמֹד Ex $20^{16.16}$+3 t (incl. Pr 6^{25} juss); sf וָאֶחְמְדֵם Jos 7^{21}; וְנֶחְמְדֵהוּ Is 53^{2}, *Pt pass.* חֲמוּדוֹ ψ 39^{12} Jb 20^{20}, חֲמוּדֵיהֶם Is 44^{9};—*desire:* **a.** in bad sense of inordinate, ungoverned, selfish desire, sq. acc. Ex $20^{17.17}$ (E)=Dt 5^{18} (v^{18b} has תִתְאַוֶּה), Ex 34^{24} (JE) Dt 7^{25} Jos 7^{21} (JE) Mi 2^{2} Pr 12^{12}, of lustful desire Pr 6^{25}. **b.** = *take pleasure in*, of idolatrous tendency Is 1^{29}, so pt. pl. חֲמוּדֵיהֶם Is 44^{9} *their delightful things* (things in which they delight, v. also v^{11} and Bev JPh xvii 1888, p 126), לֵצִים לָצוֹן חָמְדוּ Pr 1^{22} how long do *scorners delight in scorning* **c.** less often in good sense, said of God הָהָר חָמַד א׳ לְשִׁבְתּוֹ, poet. ψ 68^{17}; obj. the suffering servant of י׳, Is 53^{2} no beauty in him, *that we should desire him* (choose him, be drawn toward him); pt. pass. coll חֲמוּדוֹ ψ 39^{12} *his desired* things, i e. chosen, choice, desirable (v. Niph); so prob. Jb 20^{20}. **Niph.** *Pt.* נֶחְמָד Gn 2^{9}+2 t.; הַנֶּחֱמָדִים ψ 19^{11};—*desirable:* עֵץ נ׳ ψ 19^{11} הַנֶּח׳ מִזָּהָב, 3^{6}, נ׳ לְהַשְׂכִּיל Gn 2^{9}, לְמַרְאֶה which are *more desirable than gold*, אוֹצָר נֶחְמָד Pr 21^{20} *desirable*, i e. costly *treasure*. **Pi.** *Pf* 1 s. *delight greatly* בְּצִלּוֹ ח׳ וְיָשַׁבְתִּי Ct 2^{3} *in his shadow I greatly delighted and sate*, i e sate with great delight

†**חֶמֶד** **n.[m.]** desire, delight—abs ח׳ Am 5^{11}+4 t, only after a cstr; כַּרְמֵי־ח׳ נְטַעְתֶּם Am 5^{11} *vineyards of desire* (i e delightful vineyards) *have ye planted*, so rd also Is 27^{2} (for MT כֶּרֶם חֶמֶר) Codd 𝔖 𝔊 van d H Lo Hi Ew De Di Che Du, so of fields שְׂדֵי ח׳ Is 32^{12}, elsewh. of young men בַּחוּרֵי ח׳ Ez $23^{6.12.23}$ *desirable young men*=*fine, attractive, young men.*

†**חֶמְדָּה** **n.f.** id—ח׳ Ho 13^{15}+8 t.; cstr. חֶמְדַּת 1 S 9^{20}+3 t, sf חֶמְדָּתִי Je 12^{10}, חֶמְדָּתֵךְ Ez 26^{12}; חֶמְדָּתָם Dn 11^{8};—*desire* of Israel 1 S 9^{20} sq לְ before obj of desire; בְּלֹא ח׳ = *without desire* 2 Ch 21^{20} (i e he lived as no one desired), v Ot 𝔊 (not 𝔊L) 𝔙, concrete: כָּל־ח׳ יִשְׂרָאֵל 1 S 9^{20} and for whom is *all that is desirable in Isr?* so 𝔊 𝔙 RV Dr; (>AV and on whom is *all the desire of Isr?*); cf. וּבָאוּ ח׳ כָּל־הַגּוֹיִם Hg 2^{7} (i. e. the desirable, precious things of all nations); elsewh. after cstr. as חֶמֶד; esp. כְּלִי ח׳ Ho 13^{15} Na 2^{10} Je 25^{34} 2 Ch 32^{27} 36^{10} Dn 11^{8}; שְׂכִיּוֹת ח׳ Is 2^{16}, אֶרֶץ ח׳ ψ 106^{24} Je 3^{19} Zc 7^{14}, cf חֶלְקַת ח׳ Je 12^{10}; בָּתֵּי ח׳ Ez 26^{12}; ח׳ נָשִׁים Dn 11^{37}, appar. ref. to some obj. of idolatrous worship, perhaps *Adonis*=*Tammuz* Ew Bev (*Astarte*, Meinh).

†[**חֲמוּדָה**] **n.f. desirableness, preciousness**—*Pl.* abs חֲמוּדוֹת Dn 9^{23}; חמודת Ezr 8^{27}; חֲמֻדוֹת 2 Ch 20^{25}+4 t.; חֲמֻדֹת Gn 27^{15}; cstr. חֲמֻדוֹת Dn 11^{43},—*desirable, choice things* i.e. garments Gn 27^{15} (‖ בְּגָדִים); cf. Dn 11^{38} (‖ אֶבֶן יְקָרָה), 11^{43} (חֲמֻדוֹת מִצְרָיִם), = *precious things* Ezr 8^{27} (as gold); כְּלֵי ח׳ 2 Ch 20^{25}; לֶחֶם ח׳ Dn 10^{3}; of man only אִישׁ־ח׳ Dn $10^{11.19}$, and, without אִישׁ, אַתָּה ח׳ Dn 9^{23} *thou art a precious treasure* (on construction v. Dr § 189, 2; v. Bev and cf. neg. חמד Is 53^{2}).

†**חֶמְדָּן** **n.pr.m.** an Edomite Gn 36^{26} 𝔊 Αμαδα = חַמְרָן 1 Ch 1^{41} (𝔊 Εμερων, 𝔊L Αμαδαμ).

†**מַחְמָד** **n.m. desire, desirable thing**—abs מַחְמָד Ho 9^{6}; cstr. *id.* 1 K 20^{6}+3 t. Ez; pl. מַחֲמַדִּים Ct 5^{16}, cstr. מַחֲמַדֵּי La 2^{4} Ho 9^{16};

sf. מַחֲמַדַּי Jo 4^{5}; מַחֲמַדֵּינוּ Is 64^{10}; מַחֲמַדֶּיהָ 2 Ch 36^{19} La 1^{10}; מַחֲמַדֵּיהֶם La 1^{11} Qr (v. also מַחְמֹד);—*desirable, precious things* כלי־מ׳ 2 Ch 36^{19}; sg. coll. Ho 9^{6}; pl. Jo 4^{5} Is 64^{10} La $1^{10.11\,(Qr)}$, מ׳ בִּטְנָם Ho 9^{16}; v. esp. pl. intens. כֻּלּוֹ מַחֲמַדִּים Ct 5^{16} *all of him is delightfulnesses* (‖מַמְתַקִּים); elsewh. מַחְמַד עינים *desire of the eyes*, i.e. that in which the eyes take delight 1 K 20^{6} Ez 24^{16} (of proph.'s wife), $v^{21.25}$; pl. La 2^{4}.

†[מַחְמֹד] **n.[m.] desirable, precious thing**;—מַחֲמֹדֶיהָ La 1^{7}, מַחֲמוֹדֵיהֶם La 1^{11} Kt (Qr מַחֲמַדֵּיהֶם). Perh. מַחֲמַד׳ to be read in both; cf. Sta$^{§\,273\,a}$.

I. **חמה** (✓of foll.; cf. Ar. حَمَى *protect, guard*, RS$^{K\,136}$ Lag$^{BN\,156}$; Dl$^{Pr\,91;\,BAS\,ii.\,43}$ comp. an As. *êmû, surround, guard*, cf. Mod. Syr. ܚܡܐ *id.*; Eth. ሐመወ: III. 1 means *contract affinity, be joined by affinity*, prob. denom.)

†II. [חָם] **n.m. husband's father** (NH *id.*, of husband's or wife's father, so Aram. חֲמָא; Ar. حَمٌ *husband's male relation* (father, brother, paternal uncle), but also *wife's father*, etc.; Eth. ሐም: As. *êmû*, Zim$^{BP\,48}$);—only sf. חָמִיךְ Gn $38^{13.25}$, of Judah as Tamar's father-in-law; חָמִיהָ 1 S $4^{19.21}$ of Eli, father-in-law of Phinehas' wife.

†[חָמוֹת] **n.f. husband's mother** (NH חָמוֹת, Aram. חֲמָתָא; Ar. حَمَاةٌ *husband's mother*; As. *êmêtu*, Zim$^{BP\,48}$; Eth. ሐማት:)—only sf. חֲמוֹתֵךְ Ru 2^{11} 3^{17}; חֲמוֹתָהּ Ru 1^{14} + 7 t.; חֲמֹתָהּ Mi 7^{6};—of Naomi Ru 1^{14} $2^{11.18.19.19.23}$ $3^{1.6.16.17}$; בַּת קָמָה בְאִמָּהּ כַּלָּה בַּחֲמֹתָהּ Mi 7^{6}.

חוֹמָה $_{133}$ **n.f. wall** (as *protection*; cstr. חמת MI$^{21.21}$)—abs. ח׳ Lv 25^{29} + 59 t. (incl. לְהַחוֹמָה Ne 12^{38}); חֹמָה Ex 14^{29} + 8 t.; cstr. חוֹמַת Jos 6^{5} + 28 t.; sf. חוֹמָתָהּ Na 2^{6} 3^{8}; pl. abs. חוֹמוֹת 2 Ch 8^{5} Is 26^{1}; חֹמוֹת Ct 5^{7}; cstr. חוֹמוֹת ψ 51^{20}; חוֹמֹת 2 K 25^{10} + 9 t.; sf. חוֹמֹתַי Is 56^{5}; חֹמֹתֶיךָ Dt 28^{52} Is 25^{12}; חוֹמוֹתַיִךְ Ez $26^{10.12}$ $27^{11.11}$; חוֹמֹתַיִךְ Is 49^{16} + 2 t.; חֹמֹתַיִךְ Is 60^{10}; חֹמוֹתַיִךְ Ez 26^{9}; חוֹמוֹתֶיהָ Je 50^{15}; חוֹמֹתֶיהָ ψ 55^{11} Je 1^{15}; du. חוֹמֹתַיִם Is 22^{11}; הַחֹמֹתַיִם 2 K 25^{4} = Je 52^{7}; הַחֹמֹתַיִם Je 39^{4} (on form v. Ol$^{§\,113\,a}$);—**1.** usu. term for *wall* of city Dt 28^{52} Jos 2^{15} $6^{5.20}$ (all JE), 1 S $31^{10.12}$ 2 S $11^{20.21.21}$ 2 K $18^{26.27}$ = Is $36^{11.12}$, Am $1^{7.10.14}$ Is 2^{15} $20^{10.11}$ 25^{12} Na 2^{6} 3^{8} Ez 26^{9} +, Je 1^{15} +, Jo $2^{7.9}$; בֵּין הַחֹמֹתַיִם (of Jerus.) i.e. *between the two walls* of the Ophel and the SW. hill respectively, of a reservoir Is 22^{11}, a gate 2 K 25^{4} = Je 34^{4} = 52^{7}; symbol of Isr., Am 7^{7}; 2 Ch 8^{5} 14^{6} 25^{23} $26^{6.6.6}$ ψ 51^{20} Ne 1^{3} + 31 t. in Ne; חוֹמַת אֲנָךְ Am 7^{7} (lit. *wall of a plummet*) is of doubtful mng.: *a wall built plumb*, or *by means of a plumb-line*? We thinks unintelligible; עִיר חוֹמָה = *walled city*, Lv 25^{29}, עִיר אשר לא ח׳ v^{30} (לוֹ = לֹא), opp. הַחֲצֵרִים אשר אין להם ח׳ v^{31} (all H); more elaborately עָרִים בְּצֻרֹת ח׳ גְּבֹהָה דְּלָתַיִם וּבְרִיחַ Dt 3^{5}, cf. 2 Ch 8^{5}; ע׳ גְּדֹלוֹת חוֹמָה וּבְרִיחַ נְחֹשֶׁת 1 K 4^{13}; ח׳ בְּצוּרָה Is 2^{15}; ח׳ sg. of wall of Jerus. 1 K 3^{1} + oft.; contempt. חוֹמַת אַבְנֵיהֶם Ne 3^{35}; less oft. pl. Ne 2^{13} +; of specific portions of wall ח׳ הָעֹפֶל 2 Ch 27^{3} Ne 3^{27}; ח׳ בְּרֵכַת הַשֶּׁלַח Ne 3^{15}; הַח׳ הָרְחָבָה 3^{8} 12^{38}; also (generally) of Babylon Je 51^{58}.—Men *build*, בנה, the ח׳ 1 K 9^{15} +, esp. (of rebuilding), Ne 2^{17} +; fortify it בִּצֵּר Is 22^{10}; it is *joined together* קשר Ne 3^{38}; is *repaired* עָלְתָה אֲרוּכָה לַח׳ Ne 4^{1}; it *falls* נפל Jos $6^{5.20}$ 1 K 20^{30} Ez 38^{20}; the enemy *makes it fall* הִפִּיל 2 S 20^{15} (preceded by מַשְׁחִית si vera l., v. Dr); *destroys* it הִשְׁחִית La 2^{8}; שִׁחֵת Ez 26^{4}; *makes a breach in it* פָּרַץ בְּ׳ 2 K 14^{13} = 2 Ch 25^{23}, cf. פרץ c. acc. 2 Ch 26^{6} Ne 3^{35}, and וַיִּבֶן אֶת־כָּל־הַח׳ הַפְּרוּצָה 2 Ch 32^{5}; also (in sim.) עִיר פְּרוּצָה ואין ח׳ Pr 25^{28}; and Pu. pt. מְפֹרָצֶת Ne 1^{3}; one *breaks it down* נָתַץ 2 K 25^{10} 2 Ch 36^{19} Je 39^{8} 52^{14}; *tears it down* הָרַס Ez 26^{12}, cf. pass. Je 50^{15}; Amos predicts that י׳ will *send fire* into wall (of Gaza, etc.): וְשִׁלַּחְתִּי אֵשׁ בְּח׳ Am $1^{7.10}$; or *kindle fire in* וְהִצַּתִּי אֵשׁ בְּח׳ v^{14}, so Je 49^{27}. **2.** *wall* of a building: **a.** citadel, fortress ח׳ ארמנותיה La 2^{7}. **b.** surrounding new temple Ez 40^{5} 42^{20}. **3.** fig. of waters of Red Sea Ex $14^{22.29}$ (P), cf. Na 3^{8}; of David's men as protectors of Nabal's shepherds 1 S 25^{16}; of prophet as object of assault חוֹמַת נְחֹשֶׁת Je 1^{18}; ח׳ נחשת בְּצוּרָה Je 15^{20}; of strong, virtuous woman Ct $8^{9.10}$; of salvation, יְשׁוּעָה ח׳, as defence Is 26^{1} (‖ חֵל); of י׳ himself ח׳ אֵשׁ Zc 2^{9}; a dangerous polit. scheme is called breach in ח׳ נִשְׂגָּבָה Is 30^{13}; ח׳ נִשְׂגָּבָה in sim. of wealth Pr 18^{11} (‖ קִרְיַת עֻזּוֹ); a reckless man is עִיר פְּרוּצָה אֵין ח׳ Pr 25^{28}.

†**יַחְמַי** **n.pr.m.** (perh. = יַחְמְיָה *may* י׳ *protect!* cf. Sab. יחמאל Hal^{187})—a man of Issachar 1 Ch 7^{2}, 𝔊 Εικαν, A Ιεμου, 𝔊L Ιαμιν.

†**חֲמוּטַל** Qr, **חמיטל** Kt, **n.pr.f.** (meaning dub.; perh., if Kt right, *my husband's father is the dew*, cf. אֲבִיטַל)—𝔊 Αμειται, Μιτατ; A Αμιταλ, Αμιταθ; 𝔊L Αμιταλ;—mother of the kings Jehoahaz and Zedekiah, sons of Josiah 2 K 23^{31} 24^{18} Qr (Kt חמיטל) = Je 52^{1} Qr (Kt *id.*)

חֵמָה *wrath*, v sub יחם, חֵמָה Jb 29^{6}, v חמם v. sub חַמַּת, חַמּוֹן, חַמָּן, חַמָּה, חֶמְאָה

חֲמוּאֵל **n.pr.m.** v sub חמם

חָמוּת v. sub חמה supr.

חמט (√ of foll; cf. As *ḫamâṭu, hasten*, Pra$^{ZMG\ 1874, 88 ff.}$, *ḫamṭu*, swift, Zim$^{BP\ 84n}$; Aram חֲמַט, חֲמִיט is *sink* or *fall to the ground, kneel*)

†**חֹמֶט** **n.[m.]** a kind of lizard, only in list of unclean creeping animals Lv 11^{30} וְהָאֲנָקָה וְהַכֹּחַ וְהַלְּטָאָה וְהַחֹמֶט וְהַתִּנְשָׁמֶת׃ (Aram. ܚܘܡܛܐ is *chameleon*)

†**חֻמְטָה** **n.pr.loc.** city in Judah Jos 15^{54}, 𝔊 Εὔμα, 𝔊L Αμματα, site unknown.

חֲמִיטַל v חמוטל supr

†**חָמַל** **vb. spare** (Ar حَمَلَ is *bear, become responsible*; Aram. ܚܡܠ *comportavit, congessit*),—**Qal** *Pf* ח׳ 1 S 15^{15}+3 t, חָמַל 2 S 12^{6} La 2^{17}, חָמַלְתָּ La 2^{21} 3^{43}, וְחָמַלְתִּי Mal 3^{17}; *Impf* יַחְמֹל Jb 16^{13}+6 t; יַחְמוֹל Jb 6^{10}+3 t, וַיַּחְמֹל 1 S 15^{9}+3 t, 3 fs וַתַּחְמֹל Ex 2^{6}, 2 ms תַּחְמֹל Dt 13^{9} 1 S 15^{3}, אֶחְמוֹל Ez 8^{18} 9^{10}, אֶחְמֹל Je 13^{14}+4 t; וְאֶחְמֹל Ez 36^{21}, יַחְמֹלוּ Is 9^{18}; תַּחְמְלוּ Je 50^{14} 51^{3}, תַּחְמֹלוּ Ez 9^{5}, *Inf cstr* חֶמְלָה Ez 16^{5} (Ges$^{§ 45\ 1\ f}$),—*spare, have compassion*, c על Ex 2^{6} (E), 1 S 15$^{3.9.15}$ 23^{21} 2 S 21^{7} 2 Ch 36$^{15.17}$ Je 15^{5} Ez 16^{5} 36^{21} Jb 20^{13} Zc 11$^{5.6}$ Mal 3$^{17.17}$ Jo 2^{18}, Dt 13^{9} (‖ חוס sq. על), Je 21^{7} (‖ חוס sq על + רחם), Ez 9^{10} (‖ חוס sq על acc to 𝔖 𝔗 Co); sq. אֶל־ Je 51^{3} Is 9^{18}; note poet. אַל־תַּחְ׳ אֶל־חֵץ = *spare no arrow* Je 50^{14}, sq *Inf* 2 S 12^{4}, abs. 2 S 12^{6} Is 30^{14} La 2$^{17.21}$, also v^{2} where appar sq acc., 3^{43} Jb 6^{10} 16^{13} 27^{22} Pr 6^{34} Hb 1^{17}, ‖ חוס Ez 5^{11} 7^{4} (del Co as doubl of v^{9}), 7^{9} 8^{18} 9^{5}, Jer 13^{14} (‖ אחוס and ארחם)

†**חָמוּל** **n.pr.m.** (*spared*),—grandson of Judah Gn 46^{12} = 1 Ch 2^{5}, Nu 26^{1}; 𝔊 Ιεμουηλ, [Ι]αμουηλ.

†**חָמוּלִי** **adj. gent.** of foreg, only c art הַחָ׳, as subst coll Nu 26^{21}.

†[**חֶמְלָה**] **n.f. compassion, mercy,** of י׳ (strictly Inf form from חמל, v. Ges$^{§ 45.1 b}$)—cstr. בְּחֶמְלַת י׳ עָלָיו Gn 19^{16} (J), בְּאַהֲבָתוֹ וּבְחֶמְלָתוֹ הוּא גְאָלָם Is 63^{9}

חֶמְלָה v. חמל *Inf.*

†[**מַחְמָל**] **n.[m.] thing pitied, object of compassion,** only cstr. מַחְמַד עֵינֵיכֶם וּמַחְמַל נַפְשְׁכֶם Ez 24^{21} *object of your eyes' desire, and of your soul's compassion.*

†[**חָמַם**] **vb. be or become warm** (NH id, Pi, *make warm*, Aram ܚܡ, חֲמַם *be warm*; Ar. حَمَّ *become hot*, of water, also *heat, kindle fire in*)—**Qal** *Pf.* חַם ψ 39^{4} Ex 16^{21}, וְחַם consec. 1 K 1^{2} Ec 4^{11}; חַמּוֹתִי Is 44^{16}; *Impf* יָחֹם Is 44^{16}; וַיָּחָם 2 K 4^{34} Is 44^{15}; also יחם 1 K 1^{1}, יֵחַם Dt 19^{6}, יֵחָם Ec 4^{11}; 3 fs תחם Ez 24^{11}; יֶחֱמוּ Ho 7^{7}; וַיֶּחֱמוּ Gn 30^{39}; וַיֵּחַמְנָה v^{38} (last seven forms could be also from יחם q v; but no decisive evidence that this √ is used in Qal; they are placed under חמם by Thes Ew$^{§ 138 a}$ Ol$^{§ 243 b}$; v. also Ko $^{I\ 365, 417\ ff}$, who on account of יחם Pi. Inf Gn 30^{41} 31^{10}, der last two, needlessly, fr. יחם), *Inf* לַחְמָם Is 47^{14}, cf Jb 30^{4} (where, however, ל׳ is fr. לֶחֶם Mich Di unless (Luzz Che) we read לְחַמֵּם Pi. Inf in both); חֹם 1 S 11^{9} Hg 1^{6} Ne 7^{3}, sf. חֻמּוֹ Jb 6^{17}, חָמָם Je 51^{39};—**1.** lit, *be or grow warm* Ex 16^{21} (P, subj. שֶׁמֶשׁ), cf. 1 S 11^{9} Ne 7^{3} and Jb 6^{17} (sf of impers subj), from fire Is 44$^{15.16.16}$ 47^{14} (cf. supr); natural heat 1 K 1$^{1.2}$ (by personal contact), so 2 K 4^{34} Ec 4$^{11.11}$, fr. clothing Hg 1^{6}; of Jerusalem under fig. of pot or caldron Ez 24^{11}. **2.** fig, subj. לִבִּי ψ 39^{4} (‖ בַּהֲגִיגִי תִבְעַר־אֵשׁ), cf Dt 19^{6}, of conspirators Ho 7^{7}, Chaldeans Je 51^{39} **3.** of heat in conception (animals) Gn 30$^{38.39}$ (cf יחם) **Niph.** *Pt* נֵחָמִים בָּאֵלִים Is 57^{5} (Ko$^{I\ 371}$), *inflame oneself with*, of idolatry **Pi.** *Impf* 3 fs תְּחַמֵּם Jb 39^{14} *keep* eggs *warm* (of ostrich) **Hithp.** *Impf* יִתְחַמָּם *warm oneself* Jb 31^{20} מִגֵּז כְּבָשַׂי *by means of fleece of sheep*

†**חֹם** **n.m.** Je 17^{8} **heat**;—חֹם abs. Gn 8^{22}+3 t. + 1 S 21^{7} (v infr.), cstr. Gn 18^{1}+3 t.; of heat of (mid-)day חֹם הַיּוֹם Gn 18^{1} (J), 1 S 11^{11} 2 S 4^{5}; in promise of regular seasons Gn 8^{22} (opp. קֹר); cf Is 18$^{4.4}$ (ח׳ קָצִיר), but as dangerous to plant-life Je 17^{8}; it melts snow Jb 24^{19}; לֶחֶם חֹם 1 S 21^{7} *bread of heat = hot bread*, rd perhaps ל׳ חָם (as Jos 9^{12})

†III. **חָם** **adj. hot,**—לחם ח׳ Jos 9^{12} *hot bread* (JE), i e. freshly baked; בגדים חַמִּים Jb 37^{17} of garments heated by south wind—I. חָם v. supr p 325. II. חָם v sub חמה

†**חַמָּה** **n.f. heat, sun** (poet)—חַמָּה Is 24^{23}+4 t; חַמָּתוֹ ψ 19^{7};—**1.** *heat* of sun ψ 19^{7} **2.**

= *sun* Jb 30^{28}; ‖ לְבָנָה *moon* Is 24^{23} $30^{26.26}$ Ct 6^{10}.

†[חַמָּן] **n.m. sun-pillar**, used in idolatrous worship (v. Thes $^{469 ff.}$ RS $^{Sem. i, 469}$ Lag $^{M i, 228}$ Now $^{Arch. ii, 302}$; = Palm. חמנא Vog $^{No. 123 a}$; Ph. לבעל חמן oft. as epithet of solar Baal);—only pl. abs. חַמָּנִים Is 27^{9} + 4 t.; sf. חַמָּנֵיכֶם Lv 26^{30} + 2 t.; ‖ בָּמוֹת Lv 26^{30} (H), 2 Ch 14^{4}, cf. Ez $6^{4.6}$; ‖ מזבחות הבעלים 2 Ch 34^{4}; ‖ אשרים Is 17^{8} 27^{9}; ‖ אשרים and פְּסִלִים 2 Ch 34^{7}.

†חַמּוֹן **n.pr.loc.** (*hot* spring?)—**1.** town in Asher Jos 19^{28}. **2.** in Naphtali 1 Ch 6^{61} (perh. = I. חַמַּת, חַמַּת דֹּאר, v. Be and Di Jos 19^{35}).

†I. חַמַּת **n.pr.loc.** (*hot* spring)—town in Naphtali Jos 19^{35} (perh. = חַמּוֹן **2** v. Di); 𝔊 Ωμαθαδακεθ (= חַמַּת רַקַּת), A Αμαθ, 𝔊L Αμμαθ; Jos $^{Ant. xviii, 2.3}$ Αμμαθους (ed. Niese), cf. Id. $^{BJ. iv, 1.3}$ Guthe $^{ZPV 1891, xiii, 284}$; prob. = Talm. Ḥamata Nbr $^{Géogr. du Talm. 207}$ (with hot springs), 35 minutes south of Tiberias, v. Rob $^{BR ii, 385}$ Buhl $^{ZPV xiii, 1890, 39 f.}$ Guthe $^{l. c.}$ GASm $^{Geogr. 450}$ (Furrer $^{ZPV ii, 1878, 55; xiii, 1890, 194 ff.}$ al. say north of Tiberias); v. חַמּוֹן, חַמַּת דֹּאר.

†II. חַמַּת **n.pr.m.** father of the house of Rechab 1 Ch 2^{55}.

†חַמֹּת דֹּאר **n.pr.loc.** in Naphtali, Levitical city Jos 21^{32} (perh. = I. חַמַּת, חַמּוֹן **2** v. Di), 𝔊 Νεμμαθ, A Εμαθδωρ, 𝔊L Αμαθδωρ.

†חַמוּאֵל **n.pr.m.** (mng.? comp. Sab. [ל]חמא Hal ^{216})—a Simeonite 1 Ch 4^{26} 𝔊L Αμουηλ.

†[חָמַס] **vb. treat violently, wrong** (NH *id.*, *act violently, treat violently;* Aram. חֲמַס (rare) *violently seize;* Ar. حَمِسَ is *be hard, strict, rigorous*)—**Qal** *Pf.* 3 pl. חָמְסוּ Ez 22^{26} Zp 3^{4}; *Impf.* יַחְמֹס Jb 15^{33}, וַיַּחְמֹס La 2^{6}; תַּחְמֹסוּ Jb 21^{27} Je 22^{3}; *Pt.* חֹמֵס Pr 8^{36};—*treat violently, wrong;*—**1.** of physical wrong: תַּח׳ Je 22^{3} (‖ תֹּנוּ) of wrong to widows and orphans; וַיַּח׳ כַּגַּן שֻׂכּוֹ La 2^{6} *and hath done violence to his pavilion as to a garden* (‖ שִׁחֵת מֹעֲדוֹ); so, fig., of vine, *wrong*, i.e. fail to nourish, kill יַח׳ כַּגֶּפֶן בִּסְרוֹ Jb 15^{33}. **2.** of ethical wrong, obj. תּוֹרָה Zp 3^{4} Ez 22^{26} (both ‖ חִלֵּל קֹדֶשׁ); cf. מְזִמּוֹת עָלַי תַּחְמֹסוּ Jb 21^{27} *the devices* (wherewith) *ye do me violence.* **3.** both physical and ethical חֹטְאִי חֹמֵס נַפְשׁוֹ Pr 8^{36}. **Niph.** *Pf.* 3 pl. נֶחְמְסוּ Je 13^{22} thy heels *suffer violence* (‖ נִגְלוּ שׁוּלַיִךְ).

†חָמָס **n.m.** $^{\psi 7.17}$ **violence, wrong**—abs. ח׳ Gn 6^{11} + 44 t.; cstr. חֲמַס Ju 9^{24} + 7 t.; sf. חֲמָסִי Gn 16^{5} Je 51^{35} (in both = wrong *done to me*); חֲמָסוֹ ψ 7^{17}; pl. חֲמָסִים 2 S 22^{49} + 3 t.;—*violence*, specif. of physical violence Ju 9^{24} 2 S 22^{3} (not ‖ ψ 18^{3}), Ob ^{10}, Hb 1^{9} Je 51^{35} (of Chaldeans), Hb $2^{8.17.17}$ Jo 4^{19} ψ 72^{14}; but also *wrong*, incl. injurious language, harsh treatment, etc. Gn 16^{5} (J, of wrong done to Sarah by Hagar), Jb 19^{7} Mal 2^{16}; in gen. of rude wickedness of men, their noisy, wild, ruthlessness Mi 6^{12} Hb 1^{2} Zp 1^{9} Pr $10^{6.11}$ 13^{2} 26^{6} + Ez 7^{11} (si vera l., v. Co), ‖ שֹׁד Am 3^{10} Hb 1^{3} Je 6^{7} 20^{8} Ez 45^{9} Is 60^{18}, ‖ רִיב ψ 55^{10}, ‖ עָמָל 7^{17}, ‖ גַּאֲוָה 73^{6}, אֹהֵב ח׳ 11^{5} (‖ רָשָׁע), denied, of servant of י׳ Is 53^{9}, ח׳ בארץ Je 51^{46}, cf. Gn $6^{11.13}$ (P), Ez 8^{17} 12^{19}; מָלְאוּ מַחֲשַׁכֵּי־אֶרֶץ נְאוֹת ח׳ ψ 74^{20}, הָעִיר מָלְאָה ח׳ Ez 7^{23} 28^{16}, שֶׁבֶת ח׳ Am 6^{3} is (prob.) *enthronement of violence;* כְּלֵי ח׳ Gn 49^{5} (poem) *instruments, weapons, of violence;*—other phrases are: ח׳ בְּיָדַיִם Jon 3^{8} 1 Ch 12^{17}, cf. Jb 16^{17}, פֹּעַל ח׳ בְּכַפֵּיהֶם Is 59^{6}; ח׳ יְדֵיכֶם ψ 58^{3} and עֵד ח׳ i.e. a witness that promotes violence and wrong Ex 23^{1} (JE), Dt 19^{16}, עֵדֵי ח׳ ψ 35^{11}; עֵדֵי שֶׁקֶר וִיפֵחַ חָמָס ψ 27^{12}; שִׂנְאַת ח׳ ψ 25^{19} = hatred characterized by violence; אִישׁ חָמָס = *violent man* ψ 18^{49} (2 S 22^{49} has the later א׳ חמסים, cf. infr.) 140^{12} Pr 3^{31} 16^{29}; אישׁ חמסים (later) ψ $140^{2.5}$ 2 S 22^{49}; יֵין חֲמָסִים Pr 4^{17} i.e. wine gained by violence (‖ לֶחֶם רֶשַׁע).

†תַּחְמָס **n.[m.]** name of **male ostrich**, acc. to Bo $^{ii. 830}$ Thes (Thes der. fr. *violence* of this bird, cf. Ar. ظَلِيمٌ *violence*, also *ostrich;* other conject. are: *owl* 𝔊 𝔙; *swallow*, Saad: v. also Kn in Di)—mentioned as unclean Lv 11^{16} (P) Dt 14^{15}.

†I. חָמֵץ **vb. be sour, leavened** (NH *id.*, Pi. Hiph. *make sour, leaven;* Ar. حَمُضَ *be sour;* Aram. חֲמַע *be sour, leavened,* ܚܡܥ, *be leavened*)—**Qal** *Pf.* חָמֵץ Ex 12^{39}; *Impf.* יֶחְמָץ Ex 12^{34}; *Inf.* sf. חֻמְצָתוֹ Ho 7^{4};—*be leavened*, of dough (בָּצֵק), Ex $12^{34.39}$ (E), cf. Ho 7^{4}. **Hithp.** *be soured, embittered,* ψ 73^{21} (‖ כִּלְיוֹתַי אֶשְׁתּוֹנָן).

†חָמֵץ **n.m.** $^{Ex 13, 3}$ **that which is leavened**—ח׳ Ex 12^{15} + 10 t.—forbidden at Passover Ex 12^{15} (P), $13^{3.7}$ (JE), Dt 16^{3}, in all sacrifices Ex 23^{18} 34^{25} (both JE); cf. Am 4^{5}; Lv 2^{11} 6^{10} (P; appos.); exceptions are לֶחֶם ח׳ of peace-offering Lv 7^{13} (P), and the wave-loaves (ח׳ appos.) Lv 23^{17} (H).—v. RS $^{Sem 203\ OTJC 2, 345}$.

†חֹמֶץ **n.m. vinegar**—ח׳ abs. Pr 10[26] + 3 t.; cstr. Nu 6[3.3];—a common condiment Ru 2[14], forbidden to Nazirite (ח׳ יין and ח׳ שכר) Nu 6[3.3] (P), offered (in cruelty) to a thirsty man ψ 69[22] (fig. for harshness, lack of sympathy); in sim. of sluggard כַּחֹמֶץ לַשִּׁנַּיִם Pr 10[26], ח׳ עַל־נָתֶר Pr 25[20] *vinegar on nitre* (sim. of merry songs for the heavy-hearted).

†חָמִיץ **adj. seasoned** (viz. with salt, or a salt herb—Ar حُمَّاض, Pun 'Αμουτ [= *חמרן] Blau[ZMG 1873, 522], v Thes—rendering it more tasty), of provender for cattle בליל חָמִיץ יֹאכֵלוּ Is 30[24].

חֲמֻצָה v. I חמץ Inf

†מַחְמֶצֶת **n.f. anything leavened**, only Ex 12[19.20] (P).

†II. [חָמֵץ] **vb. be red** (? cf. Aram ܣܡܩ Ethpa. *blush, be ashamed*, poss orig *be red*),—**Qal** *Pt. pass* cstr חֲמוּץ בְּגָדִים *red of garments* Is 63[1]; poss also *Impf.* 3 fs. תֶּחְמַץ ψ 68[24] *that thy foot may be red with blood* (for MT תמחץ; so Krochm Hi Gr, most, however, rd תרחץ v רחץ).

†III. [חָמֵץ] **vb. be ruthless** (dub √; perh. by-form of חמס, perh err. for it; identif. by most with I. חמץ, *be sour*, hence *sharp, violent*, but connexion improb)—only **Qal** *Pt. act* מִכַּף מעול וחומץ ψ 71[4] *from the hand of the unjust and ruthless* (|| מִיַּד רָשָׁע)

†חָמוֹץ **n.[m.]** coll. **the ruthless**—only אַשְּׁרוּ ח׳ Is 1[17] *set right the ruthless*, so Hi Ew Kn De Che Di, Vrss give passive (perh חָמוּץ) hence AV *relieve the oppressed;* but on form חָמוֹץ = doer of action v Ew[§ 149b].

†חָמַק **vb. turn away** (intr.)—**Qal** *Pf.* 3 ms. ודודי ח׳ עָבָר Ct 5[6] *and my beloved had turned away, passed on* **Hithp.** *Impf* 2 fs עַד־מָתַי תתחַמָּקִין הַבַּת הַשּׁוֹבֵבָה Je 31[22] *turn hither and thither,* v Gf VB.

†[חַמּוּק] **n.m. curving, curve**, חַמּוּקֵי יְרֵכַיִךְ Ct 7[2] *the curvings* (curved lines, curves) *of thy thighs*

†I חָמַר **vb ferment, boil or foam up** (Ar. خَمَرَ *ferment, leaven*, خُمْرَةٌ, خَمِيرَةٌ n. *leaven;* v. Lag[BN 207]),—**Qal** *Pf* 3 ms. וְיַיִן ח׳ ψ 75[9] *and wine which foams*, (others fr. IV. חמר *be red*), 3 pl. חָמְרוּ is suggested by We as poss Hb 3[15] (for MT חֹמֶר q.v) the *great waters foamed; Impf* 3 mpl יֶהֱמוּ יֶחְמְרוּ מֵימָיו ψ 46[4] *let its water roar and foam.* **Pe'al'al** *Pf. pass* 3 pl מֵעַי חֳמַרְמָרוּ La 1[20] *my bowels are in a ferment* (|| נהפך לבי), of distress at calamities of Jerus, so מעי חֳמַרְמָרוּ La 2[11]—Jb 16[16] v. IV. חמר.

†חֶמֶר **n.[m.] wine** (poet) (Aram. ܚܡܪܐ, חַמְרָא, Ar. خَمْرٌ, v. Lag[BN 207])—וְדַם־עֵנָב תִּשְׁתֶּה־חָמֶר Dt 32[14], כֶּרֶם חֶמֶר Is 27[2], but rd here כֶּרֶם חֶמֶד (v. חמד)

†חֵמָר **n.[m.] bitumen, asphalt** (fr I. חמר acc to OBlau[ZMG 1869, 279], bitumen as *seething, swelling up;* Thes MV, fr IV חמר, with ref. to reddish-brown colour)—חֵמָר Gn 11[3] + 2 t; used for cement in building Babel Gn 11[3] (J); abounding in vale of Siddim בֶּאֱרֹת בֶּאֱרֹת ח׳ Gn 14[10]; used in coating Moses' 'ark' of bulrushes Ex 2[3] (E; || זֶפֶת).

†I חֹמֶר **n.m. cement, mortar, clay**,—ח׳ abs Gn 11[3] + 13 t; cstr Is 10[6] + 2 t.;—**1.** *mortar, cement* for holding building-stones (brick) together Gn 11[3] (J), Ex 1[14] (P; both || לבנים), Na 3[14] (|| טיט). **2.** *clay*. **a.** as material of vessels Je 18[4.6], ח׳ היצר Is 29[16], in sim of God's fashioning man Is 45[9] 64[7] Jb 10[9]; as material of human bodies בָּתֵּי ח׳ Jb 4[19] cf. 33[6]; as material of bulwarks (disparagingly) Jb 13[12]; ח׳ חותם = *seal-clay* i.e. clay upon which seal is pressed. **b.** = *mire* ח׳ חוצות Is 10[6], הֹרָנִי לַח׳ Jb 30[19] *he hath cast me into the mire*, i e. deeply humiliated me (עָפָר and אֵפֶר in || cl.); as sim. of commonness, abundance Jb 27[16] (|| עָפָר)

†II. [חָמַר] **vb. denom. cover or smear with asphalt**, only **Qal** *Impf.* 3 fs. sf. וַתַּחְמְרָה Ex 2[3] (E); on form of sf v. Ges[§ 58, 3, R 1].

III. חמר (√ of foll, NH חָמַר *heap up;* Aram חֲמַר *make a ruin-heap;* Ar. خِمَارٌ *great mass of stone, heap of stones*)

II. חֹמֶר **n.[m] heap** (cf I. חֲמוֹר)—ח׳ cstr. ח׳ מַיִם רַבִּים Hb 3[15] *a heap of great waters* (|| יָם) —but txt. dub., v I חמר; pl חֳמָרִים חֳמָרִים Ex 8[10] (J), of dead frogs gathered in *heaps*

†III חֹמֶר **n.m. homer**, a dry measure (perh. fr. above √, but dub; cf. As. *amâru, surround, contain*, II. R 36[19a b] Strm[4760], *imêru, a measure* Zim[BP 6 n])—ח׳ abs Is 5[10] + 5t Ez, cstr Ho 3[2] + 3 t, pl. חֳמָרִים Nu 11[32],—ח׳ of barley Ho 3[2] Ez 45[13], cf. זֶרַע ח׳ שְׂעֹרִים Lv 27[16]

i.e. land on which a ח׳ of barley seed was sown (taxed at 50 shekels), ח׳ of wheat Ez 45^{13}; in gen. זֶרַע ח׳ Is 5^{10}, = 10 ephahs (or baths, v. בַּת sub בתת) Ez $45^{11\,11\,11\,14\,14}$ (in v^{14} del. Co); on actual size of ח׳, = 393 9 litres, v. Hultzsch Metrol. 2nd ed 448, 452 f. See further II. בַּת and reff., Benz Arch. 183 f. Now Arch i, 203 f.

†I. חֲמוֹר **n.[m.]** heap, abs. ח׳ with du חֲמֹרָתָיִם (Baer חמרת׳), as if fr. חֲמֹרָה;— בִּלְחִי הַחֲמוֹר חֲמוֹר חֲמֹרָתָיִם Ju 15^{16} *with the ass's jawbone, a heap, two heaps*, i e so many slain.

חֲמֹרָתָיִם v. I. חֲמוֹר.

†IV. [חָמַר] **vb.** be red (Ar. حَمَّرَ II. *dye red*, حُمْرَةٌ *redness, reddish brown* (appar. *skin-colour*) so Thes MV Ba NB 192 al.)—only **Pe'al'al** *Pf.* pass. פָּנַי חֳמַרְמְרָה Jb 16^{16} *my face is reddened* from weeping —La 1^{20} 2^{11} v I. חמר.

†II. חֲמוֹר **n.m.** Gn 45, 23 (he)-ass (NH *id* (sts. female, but this regularly חֲמוֹרָה); Aram. חֲמָרָא, ܚܡܳܪܳܐ; Ar. حِمَارٌ, Palm חמרא Reckendorf ZMG 1888, 404; As. *imêru*, Schr COT Gloss;—name fr. *reddish* colour)—abs. חֲמוֹר Gn 22^{5} + 43 t.; חֲמֹר Ex 13^{13} Dt 22^{10}, cstr. חֲמוֹר Ex 23^{5} + 4 t; חֲמֹר Gn 49^{14}; sf. חֲמֹרְךָ Dt 5^{14} 28^{31}; חֲמֹרֶךָ Ex 23^{12}; חֲמֹרוֹ Gn 22^{3} + 8 t.; pl. חֲמוֹרִים Ju 19^{10} + 9 t; חֲמֹרִים Gn 12^{16} + 16 t, sf חֲמוֹרֵינוּ Ju 19^{19}; חֲמֹרֵינוּ Gn 43^{18}, חֲמוֹרֵיכֶם I S 8^{16}; חֲמֹרֵיהֶם Gn 34^{28} + 4 t.; חֲמוֹרֵיהֶם Jos 9^{4},—*ass* (*he-ass*; אתון = *she-ass*) found in all periods (coll. only Gn 32^{6} Is 21^{7}),—**1.** as (valuable) property, with oxen, sheep, camels, slaves, etc. Gn 12^{16} 24^{35} 30^{43} 47^{17} Ex 9^{3} (all J) Ex 20^{17} (E), 21^{33} $22^{3.8.9}$ $23^{4.5\,12}$ Nu 16^{15} Jos 6^{21} 7^{24} (all JE); note also Ex 13^{13} = 34^{20} (JE, firstlings belong to י׳); Gn 36^{24} Nu $31^{28.30.34.39.45}$ (all P); Dt $5^{14\,18}$ $22^{3.4}$ Ju 6^{4} I S 8^{16} 12^{3} 15^{3} 22^{19} 27^{9} I Ch 5^{21} Ezr 2^{67} = Ne 7^{68} (Baer), Zc 14^{15}, coll. Gn 32^{6} (J; ‖ שׁוֹר, צֹאן, עֶבֶד, שִׁפְחָה), but pl. (similar ‖) Gn 34^{28} (P), 47^{17} (J); cf. also ח׳ יְתוֹמִים Jb 24^{3} *the orphans' ass* (‖ שׁוֹר אַלְמָנָה); as knowing its master's crib Is 1^{3} (‖ שׁוֹר); found in camp 2 K $7^{7\,10}$ (both ‖ סוּסִים); as harnessed מֶתֶג לַח׳ Pr 26^{3} (‖ סוּס). **2.** used for riding. **a.** by women Ex 4^{20} (J), Jos 15^{18} (JE) = Ju 1^{14} I S $25^{20.23.42}$, cf. 2 Ch 28^{15}. **b.** by men 2 S 16^{2} 17^{23} 19^{27} I K 2^{40} $13^{13\,13.23.24.27.28.29}$ Is 21^{7} Zc 9^{9}. **c** צֶמֶד חֲמוֹרִים *a pair of asses* 2 S 16^{1} (for burdens and for riding); for man and woman Ju $19^{3.10\,19.21}$; carrying dead body v^{28}, cf. ח׳ I K 13^{29}. **3.** beast of burden Gn $22^{3.5}$ (cf v^{6}), $42^{26.27}$ 45^{23} (all E) $43^{18.24}$ $44^{3.13}$ (all J), Jos 9^{4} (JE), I S 25^{18} I Ch 12^{41} Ne 13^{15} (cf. also צֶמֶד ח׳ 2 S 16^{1} supr.); metaph. of Issachar ח׳ גָּרֶם Gn 49^{14} (poem), *an ass of* (strong) *bones*—ח׳ לֶחֶם I S 16^{20} rd. prob. חֲמִשָּׁה *five*, or better עֲשָׂרָה *ten*, v. We Dr. **4.** used in tillage Is 32^{20}; not to be used in ploughing with an ox (שׁוֹר) Dt 22^{10}. **5.** parts of body of ass mentioned are: לְחִי ח׳ Ju $15^{15\,16}$ jawbone, Samson's weapon; רֹאשׁ ח׳ 2 K 6^{25} eaten in famine; בְּשַׂר ח׳ Ez 23^{20} genital organ of ass (contempt. sim) **6.** קְבוּרַת ח׳ Je 22^{19} *burial of an ass*, in fig. of ignominious treatment of a corpse.

†III. חֲמוֹר **n.pr.m.** father of Shechem (*he-ass*; v. RS K 220; Sem I 449)—Gn 33^{19} $34^{2.4.6.8\,13\,18\,18\,20.24.26}$ Jos 24^{32} Ju 9^{28}

†חַמְרָן **n.pr.m.** I Ch 1^{41} (= חֶמְדָּן Gn 36^{26} q v)

†יַחְמוּר **n.[m.]** roebuck (Sam. יחמור, Syr. ܝܰܚܡܽܘܪܳܐ, ℑ יַחְמוּרָא v. Hom NB 392 (and 333), Lag BN 127, name from *reddish* colour?)—as edible Dt 14^{5} I K 5^{3};—on identif with roebuck, v. Tristr Proc Zool. Soc London, May 2, 1876 Conder Tent Work, 1887, p. 91.

I. חמשׁ (√of foll.; meaning unknown).

חָמֵשׁ, חֲמִשָּׁה 342 **n.m.** and **f.** five (NH *id*, *id.*; Aram. חֲמֵשׁ, חַמְשָׁא, ܚܡܶܫ, ܚܰܡܫܳܐ; Ph חמשת, Palm. חמשא, c n. masc., Reckendorf ZMG 1888, 408; As *ḫamšu*, *ḫamiltu* Dl ^{175}, Eth. ኀምስ: ኀምስቱ: Ar. خَمْسٌ, خَمْسَةٌ, Sab. & Lihyân. חמס DHM ZMG xxix. 613, Epigr Denkm 71, 73),—**m.** (c **n.f.**) abs. חָמֵשׁ Gn 5^{6} + 94 t + Ez 40^{30} (del 𝔊B Hi-Sm Co; Co del also in $v^{25.29.33.36}$) + Ez 45^{3} Kt (where rd. **f.** with Qr); cstr. חֲמֵשׁ Gn 5^{10} + 67 t. + Ez 48^{16} Kt, **f.** (c. **n.m.**) abs. חֲמִשָּׁה v. Lag BN 80 Gn 18^{28} + 139 t. (incl. Ez 8^{16} del. B Co al); cstr. חֲמֵשֶׁת Nu $3^{47.47}$ + 26 t.;—on pl. חֲמִשִּׁים *fifty*, see below;—*five*, in Hex. chiefly P;—**1.** without other numeral: **a.** חָמֵשׁ, before fpl. noun Gn 43^{34} + 35 t.; before n coll. ח׳ צֹאן I S 25^{18}; v. also ח׳ בָּאַמָּה *five in cubit(s)* = five cubits I K 7^{23} I Ch 11^{23} 2 Ch 4^{2}; after noun (late) 2 K 8^{16} (בִּשְׁנַת חָמֵשׁ לְיוֹרָם = *in the fifth year*) + 6 t. Ch; no noun expr. I K $7^{39.39.49.49}$ I Ch 3^{20} 2 Ch $4^{7.7}$. **b.** חֲמִשָּׁה before mpl. noun Gn 47^{2} + 18 t.; after noun Ex 36^{38} + 36 t Nu (all P); no noun expr. Gn 14^{9} (only here c. art.) + 20 t. **c.** חֲמֵשׁ before noun (usu. defined; exc. אֲלָפִים, מֵאוֹת, v **3, 4**) Ex $26^{3\,9}$ $36^{10\,16}$ + Ez 42^{16} ח׳ אַמּוֹת Kt, but Qr ח׳ מֵאוֹת, v. infr. **d.** חֲמֵשֶׁת מְלָכִים Jos 10^{5} + 5 t.; ח׳ הָאֲנָשִׁים Ju $18^{7\,14\,17}$; ח׳ שְׁקָלִים Nu 18^{16}; also, distrib, ח׳ ח׳ שְׁקָלִים 3^{47}; ח׳ הַסְּרָנִים Jos 13^{3} Ju 3^{3} I S 6^{18}, ח׳ בְּנֵי מ׳ 2 S 21^{8}. **e.** = ordinal, בִּשְׁנַת חָמֵשׁ לְיוֹרָם 2 K 8^{16} *the fifth* (year) *of Joram*;

בַּחֲמִשָּׁה לַחֹדֶשׁ *on the fifth* (day) *of the month* Ez 1$^{1.2}$ 8^{1} 33^{21}, (so also 15th, 25th, etc.) **2.** ח׳ combined with עשר, עשרה *ten = fifteen:* **a.** חֲמֵשׁ עֶשְׂרֵה (c **n.f.**) Gn 5^{10} 7^{20} Ex 27$^{14.15}$ 38$^{14.15}$ 2 K 14$^{17.23}$ 20^{6} 2 Ch 15^{10} 25^{25} Is 38^{5} **b.** חֲמִשָּׁה עָשָׂר (c. **n.m.**), (1) after noun Est 9^{21}; (2) before noun Ex 16^{1} (= ordinal *fifteenth*, so Lv 23^{6}+) Ho 3^{2}+. **c.** חֲמֵשֶׁת עָשָׂר before n 2 S 19^{18}+. **d.** חֲמֵשֶׁת עָשָׂר, without n = ordinal *fifteenth* 1 Ch 24^{14}+4 t. + Ez 45^{12} (rd חֲמִשִּׁים A Hi Co). **3.** חֲמֵשׁ מֵאוֹת = 500 Gn 5$^{30.32}$+49 t + Ez 42^{16} Qr. **4.** חֲמֵשֶׁת אֲלָפִים = 5000 Nu 31^{32} Jos 8^{12} Ju 20^{45} 1 S 17^{5} Ez 45^{6} 48^{15} 1 Ch 29^{7} 2 Ch 35^{9} Ezr 1^{11} 2^{69},—in 25,000, 35,000 etc. חמשה (usu. without א׳) precedes the 20,000, 30,000, etc. **5.** with other numerals. **a.** חָמֵשׁ before larger numeral (1) noun repeated Gn 5^{6}+4 t.; (2) noun with 2nd num only, Gn 5^{17}+8 t. + Ez 45^{3} Kt; (3) noun c. ב with 2nd num Ez 40^{21}+2 t. **b.** חָמֵשׁ after larger num.: (1) noun repeated Gn 25^{7}; (2) noun foll ח׳ (only) Ju 14^{10}+ (esp in expressions of age and duration); (3) noun before both num, st abs., 2 Ch 3^{15}, st cstr 2 Ch 15^{19}. **c.** no noun expr, ח׳ between other num, e g שש מאות ח׳ ושבעים Nu 31^{37} **d.** חמשה before larger num, noun foll larger num Nu 1^{21}+22 t. **e.** ח׳ follows, and (1) is foll by noun Ju 20^{35}+7 t; (2) noun precedes both 1 K 7^{3} Je 52^{30}. **f.** ח׳ precedes, no noun expr 1 K 5^{12}. **g.** ח׳ follows, no noun expr. Gn 18^{28}+. **h.** no noun expr ח׳ between other num. Ex 38^{28} Ezr 2^{5}.

†I חֹמֶשׁ **n.[m.]** **fifth part**—only לְפַרְעֹה לַחֹמֶשׁ Gn 47^{26}, but connex. with preceding awkward, rd perh. הַחֹמֶשׁ (𝔖), or לַחֹמֶשׁ 𝔊, v. Di

†II [חָמַשׁ] **vb.denom.** only **Pi.** וְחִמֵּשׁ אֶת־אֶרֶץ מִצְרָיִם Gn 41^{34} (E) *and he shall fifth* (take the fifth part of) *the land of Egypt*, i e. the fifth part of the produce (cf Ar. خَمَسَ *take a fifth part*, Eth ኀመሰ: I 2 *quinque facere*).

חֲמִשִּׁים$_{164}$ **n.pl.** (a) **fifty** (Ar. خَمْسُونَ, Aram ܚܡܫܝܢ, Ph חמשם; MI^{28} חמשן; As. *ḫamšâti* Dl in Lotz$^{TP\,80}$)—חֲמִשִּׁים Gn 6^{15}+154 t. (incl Ez 40$^{25.29.33}$, del Co) + Ez 45^{12} (so rd. A Hi Co for חמשה), sf חֲמִשֶּׁיךָ 2 K 1$^{10.12}$, חֲמִשָּׁיו 2 K 1^{9}+4 t., חֲמִשֵּׁיהֶם 2 K 1^{14},—**1.** abs **a.** *a fifty*, a company of fifty Ex 18$^{21.25}$ Dt 1^{15} 1 S 8^{12} 2 K 1$^{9.9}$+13 t 2 K 1 (in v^{14} = *fifties*), Is 3^{3} **b.** elsewhere, without noun expr, (1) without other numeral Nu 31$^{30.47}$ Ez 27$^{15.18}$ Hg 2^{16}; (2) with other num ח׳ preceding Ex 30$^{23.23}$+11 t.; + 1 Ch 12^{34} Baer, van d H v^{33} (sq אלף); (3) ח׳ following Ex 38^{26}+10 t., (4) ח׳ between other num. Nu 1^{23}+23 t. **2.** חֲמִשִּׁים without other num: **a.** before noun Gn 6^{15}+58 t. + ח׳ בָּאַמָּה Ex 38^{12}. **b.** after noun 2 S 24^{24} Ex 26^{11}+4 t Chr. **3.** ח׳ before other num.: **a.** foll. by noun Gn 7^{24}+. **b.** preceded by noun 1 Ch 5^{21}. **4.** ח׳ after other num, and **a.** this after noun 1 Ch 8^{40} Ezr 8$^{3.26}$. **b.** noun repeated e.g Gn 9$^{28.29}$ **5.** ח׳ preceded by cstr. e.g. בשנת ח׳ שָׁנָה 2 K 15$^{23.27}$ Lv 15$^{10.11}$ **6.** ח׳ = ordinal, *fiftieth* Lv 25$^{10.11}$ 2 K 15^{23}, cf. v^{27}.

†חֲמִישִׁי **m.**, חֲמִישִׁית **f.adj.num.ordin.** **fifth**;—**m.** חֲמִישִׁי Gn 1^{23}+22 t.; חֲמִשִׁי Zc 7^{3}+3 t; **f.** חֲמִישִׁית abs. 1 K 14^{25}+4 t; חֲמִשִׁית Lv 19^{25} Je 36^{9}; חֲמִשִּׁית 1 K 6^{31}, cstr. חמישית Lv 27$^{15.19}$; sf. חֲמִישִׁתוֹ Lv 5^{16}+2 t; חֲמִשִׁיתוֹ Lv 22^{14} 27^{31}, חֲמִשְׁתוֹ Lv 27^{27}, cf. חֲמִשְׁתָיו Lv 5^{24}, rd ־תוֹ Sam. Di (q.v.),—*fifth*, usu in enum. days, months, years, sons, etc; definite, exc *masc* Gn 1^{23} 30^{17}, *fem* Gn 47^{24} 1 K 6^{31} Ne 6^{5};—**1. m.** Gn 1^{23} Nu 7^{36} 29^{26} 33^{38} Jos 19^{24} (all P), Gn 30^{17} (E), Ju 19^{8} 2 K 25^{8} Je 1^{3} 28^{1} 52^{12} Zc 7^{3} 1 Ch 27^{8} Ezr 7$^{8.9}$, noun om. 2 S 3^{4} 1 Ch 2^{14} 3^{3} 8^{2} 26$^{3.4}$ (all of בן), 1 Ch 24^{9} 25^{12} (גּוֹרָל), Zc 8^{19} (חֹדֶשׁ), 1 Ch 27^{8} (יוֹם) **2. f.** Lv 19^{25} 1 K 14^{25} Je 36^{9} Ez 1^{2} 2 Ch 12^{2}, פַּעַם ח׳ Ne 6^{5} **3.** חֲמִשִׁית 1 K 6^{31} as subst. *a fifth part*, so חמישית Gn 47^{24} Lv 5$^{6.24}$ 22^{14} 27$^{13.27.31}$ Nu 5^{7}, cstr חמישית כסף Lv 27$^{15.19}$

III. חמשׁ (√of foll, meaning dubious)

†II. חֹמֶשׁ **n.m. belly** (Aram ܚܘܡܫܐ)—הַחֹמֶשׁ 2 S 2^{23}+3 t; וַיַּכֵּהוּ ... אֶל־הַח׳ 2 S 2^{23} *and he smote him in the belly*, 2 S 20^{10}+4^{6}, rd וַתָּנָם ... וַתִּישַׁן *and she slumbered and slept* 𝔊 We Dr.; yet corruption difficult to explain, v. Klo; וַיַּכֵּהוּ שָׁם הַח׳ 2 S 3^{27} (where prob ins. אֶל־ cf. Dr).

IV חמשׁ (√of foll; mng dub; perh. cf. Ar. خَمِيس *army*, Sab חמס men of a tribe who can bear arms; √then poss. = I חמש (e g. army as composed of *five parts*) v. Lane Frey; also Sab Denkm^{24}, which cites *tribus* (fr *tres*), *quartier* (fr. *quartus, quatuor*); > Thes MV al. who comp Ar خَمُسَ *be firm strong*, خَمِيس *be courageous*, etc)

†חֲמֻשִׁים **adj.pl.** **in battle array**, alw this form, Ex 13^{18} (E), Jos 1^{14} 4^{12} (both D), Ju 7^{11}+ Nu 32^{17} (JE), v. חוש.

חמת (√of foll; mng unknown; MV al, very improbably, fr. Ar خَمِتَ *grow rancid, putrid*; see on formation, Lag$^{BN\,184}$)

†חֵמֶת, חֵמֶת **n.[m.]** **waterskin** (NH *id*)

—הַחֵמֶת Gn 21^{15}; הַחֵ֫מֶת Gn 21^{19}; וְחֵ֫מֶת מַ֫יִם Gn 21^{14} (v. Di), [Hb 2^{5} חֲמָתְךָ v. חֵמָה].

†חֲמָת, חֲמַת **n.pr.loc.** (√dub.; Thes MV al. der. fr. חָמָה, חֹמָה = *fortress*, or (v. RS$^{Sem. i, 140}$), *sacred enclosure, temenos, ḥimā*, cf. Hal$^{JAS 7ème Sér. x, 392}$ Lag$^{BN 82, 156}$; but no certainty that name is Shemitic; Ar. حَمَاة, As. *Amattu*, Dl$^{PA 275 ff. Pr 174}$); —mod. Ḥamâ, on *el-ʿÂṣi* (Orontes), 38 h. (c. 115 m.) N. of Damascus, v. Bd$^{Pal 398 f.}$ It had a king, תֹּעִי, in David's time 2 S 8^{9} = 1 Ch 18^{9}, and in 8th cent. B.C. 2 K 19^{13} = Is 37^{13}; gods of its own 2 K 17^{30} 18^{34} = Is 36^{19}; gave its name to land (limits unknown) רִבְלָה בְּאֶרֶץ ח׳ 2 K 23^{33} 25^{21} Je 39^{5} 52$^{9.27}$, cf. 2 Ch 8^{4}; contained Isr. exiles Is 11^{11}; furnished colonists for Samaria 2 K 17^{24} (cf. v^{30} supr.) after being conquered by Sargon, (COT 2 K 17^{24} 18^{34} cf. Is 10^{9}). It is called *great Hamath* by Am 6^{2} (חֲמַת רַבָּה,—חֲמַת only here). ח׳ is mentioned with צִידוֹן, צֹר, דַּמֶּשֶׂק in prophecy against land Hadrach (חַדְרָךְ) Zc 9^{2}, cf. Je 49^{23}. Often in phr. (עַד־) לְבֹא ח׳ = *the entrance to H.*, i.e. *the approach to H.*, as territorial limit Ju 3^{3}; usu. as denoting (ideal) northern limit of Isr. territory Jos 13^{5} Nu 13^{21} 34^{8} Am 6^{14} 1 K 8^{65} = 2 Ch 7^{8}, 2 K 14^{25} 1 Ch 13^{5}; חֲמָ֫תָה 1 Ch 18^{3}; ח׳ צוֹבָה 2 Ch 8^{3}, and הֵשִׁיב אֶת־דַּמֶּשֶׂק וְאֶת־ח׳ לִיהוּדָה 2 K 14^{28}; so also Ez 47, 48: גְּבוּל ח׳ Ez 47^{17}, cf. v^{16b} + v^{16a} (del. Co); לְבוֹא ח׳ 48^{1}, cf. 47^{20}; אֶל־יַד ח׳ 48^{1}.

†חֲמָתִי **adj. gent.** c. art. = subst. הַחֲמָתִי, as descendants of Canaan Gn 10^{18} = 1 Ch 1^{16}.

חַמַּת **n.pr.loc.** v. sub חמם.

חֵן, חֵנָדָד, חַנָּה v. sub חנן.

חָנָה$_{143}$ **vb. decline, bend down, encamp** (Aram. ܚܢܐ *to aim at, incline towards, reach;* Zinj. מחנת cstr. *camp*, Inscr. Panammu$^{13.16.17}$; Ar. حَنَا *bend, curve, bend down;* As. *mânu, mênu* and *tênû, couch, mânîtu, house*, Zim$^{BP 44, 45}$ Dl in Zim^{117})—**Qal** *Pf.* חָנָה 1 S 26^{5} Is 29^{1}; וְחָנִ֫יתִי consec. Is 29^{3} Zc 9^{8}; חָנוּ Nu 2^{34} + 2 t.; וְחָנוּ consec. Nu 1^{52}; *Impf.* וַיִּחַן Gn 26^{17} + 9 t.; 3 fs. תַּחֲנֶה ψ 27^{3}; יַחֲנוּ Nu 1^{50} + 13 t. Nu + Ex 14^{2}: וַיַּחֲנוּ Ex 13^{20} + 79 t. (of which 42 in Nu 33); וַיַּחֲנוּן Ju 11^{18}; 2 mpl. תַּחֲנוּ Ex 14^{2}; 1 pl. וַנַּחֲנֶה Ezr 8^{15}; *Imv.* חֲנֵה 2 S 12^{28}; חֲנוּ Nu 31^{19} Je 50^{29}; *Inf.* חֲנוֹת Ju 19^{9}; חֲנֹת Nu 1^{51}; sf. חֲנֹתוֹ Nu 10^{31}; חֲנֹתְכֶם Dt 1^{33}; *Pt.* חֹנֶה Ex 18^{5} ψ 34^{8}; f. חֹנָה 2 S 23^{13} 1 Ch 11^{15}; חֹנָךְ ψ 53^{6}; pl. חֹנִים Ex 14^{9} + 11 t.; חוֹנִים Nu 2^{2} Na 3^{17};—**1.** *decline*, of day drawing to its close חֲנוֹת הַיּוֹם Ju 19^{9} (|| רָפָה הַיּ׳ v^{11} הַיּוֹם רַד מְאֹד לָעֶרֶב; also נְטוֹת הַיּ׳ v^{8}). **2.** *encamp* (prop. *verge toward, incline to, settle at,* of goal of day's march):—**a.** of single nomad Gn 26^{17} (J; sq. ב), 33^{18} (E; sq. אֶת־פְּנֵי). **b.** of Israel at Exod. and in wilderness Ex 13^{20} (ב) 14^{2} (לִפְנֵי), v^{2} (עַל), + c. 80 t. (Hex. chiefly P); also (abs.) Nu 9$^{18.20.22.23}$ cf. Ezr 8^{15}; Ne 11^{30} *so they encamped* (i.e. *settled*, or *were settled*) from Beersheba to the valley of Hinnom (|| ישבו v^{25}). **c.** of armies: (1) Israel (conquering Canaan, etc.) Jos 4^{19} 5^{10} + oft.; (2) Philistines 1 S 4^{1} 13^{16} 2 S 23^{23} +; usu. sq. ב loc. Nu 10^{31} 1 S 4^{1} 13^{16} Jos 4^{19} 1 S 13^{5} + 63 t. (וַיַּחֲנוּ בְ 2 S 24^{5} rd. וַיָּחֵלּוּ מִן 𝔊L We Dr v. חלל); so of locusts in hedges (in sim.) Na 3^{17}; also sq. עַל = *by, near* Ex 14$^{2.9}$ 15^{27} Nu 1^{52} 2$^{2.5.12.27}$ 3$^{29.35}$ (על ירד), 33^{10} Ju 7^{1} 1 S 4^{1}; על־פני השׂדה (על in diff. sense) 2 S 11^{11}; sq. עַל also = *against, encamp* with hostile purpose Jos 10$^{5.31.34}$ Ju 6^{4} 20^{19} 1 S 11^{1} 2 S 12^{28} 1 K 16^{15} 2 K 25^{1} 2 Ch 32^{1} Je 50^{29} 52^{4} ψ 27^{3}; sq. אֶל־ in same sense Jos 11^{5}; metaph. of God's hostility to apostate Jerusalem (על) Is 29^{3}; sq. also לְ = *at, by* Nu 2^{34} Zc 9^{8}; אשׁר . . . שָׁם Ex 18^{5} 1 S 26^{5}; sq. סביב לְ for protection Nu 1$^{50.53}$, cf. metaph. ψ 34^{8}, but also hostility Jb 19^{12}; also sq. other prep. and prep. phrases, e.g. מֵעֵבֶר Nu 21^{13}; מחוץ Nu 31^{19}; בין 1 S 17^{1}; נגד 1 K 20^{27} etc.; sq. acc. loc. 2 S 17^{26}; sq. sf. acc. with hostile sense חֹנָךְ ψ 53^{6}; without prep. or noun foll., in sense of *encamp, be* or *abide in encampment* Nu 9$^{18.20.22.23}$ Ezr 8^{15} 2 S 11^{11} +; poet. of David in Jerusalem, Is 29^{1} *city in which David fixed his camp.*

†[חָנוּת] **n.f.** cell (as having *curved* or *vaulted roof, arched;* v. Thes Gf, and cf. Aram. ܚܢܘܬܐ *vaulted room*)—הַחֲנֻיוֹת Je 37^{16} (|| בֵּית הַבּוֹר).

†חֲנִית **n.f. spear** (as *flexible?* v. Thes);—*abs.* חֲנִית 2 S 13^{19} + 26 t.; cstr. *id.* 1 S 26^{16} (so v^{22} Qr, where Kt has art.); sf. חֲנִיתֶךָ Hb 3^{11}; חֲנִיתוֹ 1 S 17$^{7.7}$ + 11 t. + 2 S 23^{8}, v. infr.; pl. חֲנִיתִים 2 Ch 23^{9}; חֲנִיתוֹתֵיהֶם Is 2^{4} = חֲנִיתֹתֵיהֶם Mi 4^{3};—**1.** *spear*, as hurled 1 S 18$^{10.11}$ 19$^{9.10.10}$ 20^{33}; held by king 22^{6}; sign of king's presence 26$^{7.8.11.12.16.22}$ (v. RS$^{K 171}$); also 2 S 1^{6} 2^{23} 21^{19} 23$^{18.21.21.21}$ 1 Ch 11^{11} = 2 S 23^{8}, where rd. הוּא עוֹרֵר אֶת־חֲנִיתוֹ (for הוּא עֲדִינוֹ הָעֶצְנוֹ) acc. to Ew Th Ke Klo Dr (not We), 1 Ch 11$^{20.23.23.23}$; pl. 2 Ch 23^{9}; oft. || חֶרֶב 1 S 13$^{19.22}$ 17$^{45.47}$ 21^{9} Is 2^{4} = Mi 4^{3}, Na 3^{3}; || שְׁלָטִים 2 K 11^{10}; || צִנָּה 1 Ch 12^{35} (Baer); סֶפַע

Jb 41^{18}, סִר ψ 35^{3}; ‖ קֶשֶׁת ψ 46^{10}. **2. a.** *shaft of spear* is עֵץ ח׳ 2 S 23^{7} 1 Ch 20^{5} + 1 S 17^{7} Qr (doubtless right; Kt חץ). **b.** *spear-head* ברק ח׳ 1 S 17^{7}, cf. לַהַב ח׳ Jb 39^{23}; לְהַבַת ח׳ Na 3^{3} Hb 3^{11}. **c.** *butt of spear* אַחֲרֵי ח׳ 2 S 2^{23} **3.** metaph of teeth of lions ψ 57^{5} (‖ חִצִּים, fig of Psalmist's enemies)

מַחֲנֶה $_{214}$ **n.m.** $^{Gn 33,8+16t}$ and **f.** $^{ψ 27,3, 1 Ch 11,15}$ (on Gn 32^{9a} v. Di) **encampment, camp**—abs מ׳ Gn 32^{9b} + 126 t. (incl Ez 1^{24}, del Co); cstr. מַחֲנֵה Gn 32^{3} + 56 t, sf מַחֲנֵהוּ Nu 1^{52} + 5 t; מַחֲנֶיךָ Dt 23^{15} 29^{10}, מַחֲנֶךָ Dt 23^{15}, מַחֲנֵיכֶם Am 4^{10}, מַחֲנֵיהֶם Nu 5^{3} Ju 8^{10} (cf infr, and on form of noun c. sf. vid Ges$^{§ 93.3, R 3}$); pl abs מַחֲנוֹת Gn 32^{8} + 9 t; cstr 1 Ch 9^{18} + 2 t, מַחֲנִים Nu 13^{19}; sf. (appar pl n) מַחֲנֵיהֶם Jos 10^{5} + 5 t,—on du v מ׳ **n.pr.** infr **1.** *camp, place of encampment* **a.** of caravan of travellers Gn 32^{22} (J), esp of Isr at Exod and in wildern. Ex 16$^{13.13}$ 19$^{16.17}$ (all P; disting. fr. עָם); שַׁעַר מ׳ Ex 32^{26} (JE); esp מחוץ המ׳ in connexion with uncleanness, etc, Ex 29^{14} Lv 4^{12} (P) + oft, of position of tent of meeting Ex 33$^{7.7}$ (JE), contr Nu 2^{17} (P), where of encampments of several tribes, cf 1^{52} 2^{3} 10$^{2.5.6.25}$ etc, (all P), already passing over to **3** (cf הַחֲנִים 10$^{5.6}$); specif of *camp of Levites*, surrounding tabernacle, so that P can say אהל־מועד מַחֲנֵה הַלְוִים Nu 2^{17}, and so (late) of temple הַשֹּׁעֲרִים לְמַחֲנוֹת בני לוי 1 Ch 9^{18}, as well as שַׁעֲרֵי מַחֲנוֹת י׳ 2 Ch 31^{2}, pl (opp מִבְצָרִים =*fortresses*) Nu 13^{19}. **2.** *camp of armed host* Jos 6$^{11.11.14}$ (JE), 1 S 4$^{3.5.6.6.7}$ 17^{53} 2 K 7^{16} etc **3. a.** *those who encamp* Nu 10$^{5.6}$ 1 Ch 11^{15} ψ 27^{3} (all c vb. חנה), cf (prob) Is 37^{36} = 2 K 19^{35}, etc. **b.** *company, body of people;* people and beasts Gn 32$^{8.9.9.11}$ 33^{8}, funeral company of Jacob Gn 50^{9}, of Isr on march Ex 14$^{19.20}$ cf Nu 10$^{5.6}$. **c.** *army, host* Jos 8^{13} 10^{5} 11^{4} Ju 4$^{15.16.16}$ 7$^{1.8}$ 8$^{10.10.11.11.12}$ 1 S 17$^{1.46}$ 2 K 3^{9} even while in the thick of the fight; 1 K 22^{34} = 2 Ch 18^{33} etc

†מַחֲנֵה־דָן **n.pr.loc.** =*camp of Dan*, name given, Ju 13^{25} 18^{12}, to place where Danites encamped (v. Bla).

†מַחֲנַיִם **n.pr loc** (*two camps*)—E. of Jordan, name from Jacob's meeting angels acc. to Gn 32^{3} (J), place on border of Gad Jos 13^{26}, of Manasseh v^{30} (P), Levit city in Gad 21^{36} (P) = 1 Ch 6^{65}; named also 2 S 2^{8} (מַחֲנָיִם), v$^{12.29}$ (־נָיִם), 19^{33} 1 K 2^{8} (־נָיִם); מַחֲנָיְמָה 2 S 17$^{24.27}$ 1 K 4^{14}, site unknown, v Di^{Gn}, כִּמְחֹלַת הַמַּחֲנָיִם Ct 7^{1} is put here by Ew Hi Ot al *as at a* (the) *dance of Mahanaim; dance of a double choir* Gi Stickel RV.

†תַּחַן **n.pr.m.** (perh abbrev fr תַּחֲנָה)—an Ephraimite Nu 26^{35} 𝔊 Ταναχ, 1 Ch 7^{25} 𝔊 Θαεν, 𝔊L Θααν.

†תַּחֲנִי **adj.gent.** only c art. as subst. coll, הַתּ׳ Nu 26^{35}

†[תַּחֲנָה] **n.f. encamping,** or **encampment,**—pl sf. תַּחֲנֹתִי (si vera l) אֶל־מְקוֹם פְּלֹנִי אַלְמֹנִי 2 K 6^{8}, *unto such and such a place is my encamping;* but form very strange Rd prob. תֵּחָבְאוּ *ye shall hide yourselves,* so 𝔖 Th Klo.

†חָנַט **vb. spice, make spicy, embalm** (NH *id, bud, blossom;* Ar. حَنَطَ *become mature,* II *prepare for burial,* حَنُوطٌ *spices* for a corpse; حَنَّاطٌ *embalmer,* Dozy$^{i, 332}$ after PS^{1320}, Aram. حَنَط, חנט *embalm;* so Eth. ሐነጠ: (loan-word Di^{110})),—**Qal** *Pf* 3 fs. חָנְטָה Ct 2^{13}; *Impf.* 3 mpl. וַיַּחַנְטוּ Gn 50$^{2.26}$; *Inf cstr* לַחֲנֹט Gn 50^{2},— **1.** *spice, make spicy* הַתְּאֵנָה ח׳ פַּגֶּיהָ Ct 2^{13} *the fig-tree spiceth its figs,* so VB De in transl (Ew De in notes Ot al. prefer *reddeneth,* on account of spring season, cf. the less common and perhaps secondary sense in Ar. *become red* (of leather) Lane^{657a}) **2.** *embalm,* sq. acc pers. Gn 50$^{2.2}$ (performed by הָרֹפְאִים), v^{26}.

†חֲנֻטִים **n.[m.]pl.abstr.embalming,** only יְמֵי הַח׳ Gn 50^{3} i e. the days consumed in the embalming process = אַרְבָּעִים יוֹם v. Di.

†חִטָּה **n f. wheat** (NH *id.*, Aram. חִנְטִין, חִיטְּתָא, ܚܶܛܬܳܐ, Ar. حِنْطَةٌ);—abs. ח׳ Ex 9^{32} + 6 t.; pl חִטִּים Gn 30^{14} + 20 t.; חִטִּין Ez 4^{9}, cstr. חִטֵּי Ez 27^{17},—*wheat,* sg chiefly poet, of growing wheat Ex 9^{32} (E), Dt 8^{8} Jb 31^{40} Jo 1^{11}, sown Is 28^{25}, food-product Dt 32^{14} (חֵלֶב כִּלְיוֹת ח׳ *kidney-fat of wheat,* i e the choicest, v. חֵלֶב), חֵלֶב ח׳ ψ 81^{17} (cf 147^{14} infr), elsewh pl.; wheat as sown Je 12^{13}, *wheat-harvest* קְצִיר ח׳ Gn 30^{14} (J), Ex 34^{22} (JE), Ju 15^{1} 1 S 6^{13} 12^{17} Ru 2^{23}, + 2 S 24^{15} where insert acc. to 𝔊 We Dr; wheat threshed Ju 6^{11} 1 Ch 21^{20} cf. v^{23}, measured 1 K 5^{25} = 2 Ch 2^{9} (חִטִּים מַכּוֹת, rd ח׳ מַכֹּלֶת as 1 K 5^{25} = *wheat for food* Th Be Ke after Vrss), v^{14} 27^{5} Ez 45^{13}; stored (with barley, oil and honey) Je 41^{8}, for food 2 S 17^{28}, חֵלֶב חִטִּים ψ 147^{14} (cf 81^{14} supr); לֹקְחֵי חִטִּים 2 S 4^{6} (rd. סֹקְלָה ח׳ 𝔊 We Dr); סֹלֶת ח׳ *fine wheaten flour*

Ex 29[2] (P); Ez 4[9] (חִטִּין, Aram. pl.) mixed with barley, beans, lentils, etc., and made into bread.

חֲנִיאֵל **n.pr.**, and חֲנִינָה v. sub חנן.

חֲנִית v. sub חנה.

I. **חנך** (√of foll. (see Ar. Syr.); meaning unknown).

†**חֵךְ** **n.m. palate, roof of mouth, gums** (NH *id.*; Aram. ܚܶܟܳܐ, חִכָּא; Ar. حَنَكٌ *palate, roof of mouth, jaws, lower part of mouth, lower jaw* of horse, *mouth*, etc. Lane[659] Dozy[i. 332]);—abs. ח׳ Jb 12[11] 34[3]; sf. חִכִּי Pr 8[7] + 6 t., חִכְּךָ Ho 8[1], חִכֵּךְ Ez 3[26] Pr 24[13]; chiefly poet., esp. WisdLt:—חִכֵּךְ Ct 7[10], חִכּוֹ La 4[4] + 2 t., חִכָּהּ Pr 5[3], חִכָּם Jb 29[10];—*palate, roof of mouth:* **a.** אֶל־חִכְּךָ שֹׁפָר Ho 8[1] *a trumpet to thy palate!* (or *gums;* as in Eng., *to thy lips*); oft. c. לָשׁוֹן, *tongue clings* (דבק) *to* חך, expression for speechlessness Ez 3[26] Jb 29[10], as imprecation ψ 137[6]; for the parching of extreme thirst La 4[4] (בַּצָּמָא), cf. ψ 22[16] MT יָבֵשׁ כַּחֶרֶשׂ כֹּחִי, rd. חִכִּי for כחי v. Che[crit. n.] (לְשׁוֹנִי מֻדְבָּק מַלְקוֹחָי ||). **b.** as organ of speech Pr 5[3] 8[7] (both || שְׂפָתַיִם), Jb 31[30] 33[2] (פָּתַחְתִּי פִי || דִּבְּרָה לְשׁוֹנִי בְחִכִּי). **c.** as organ of taste Jb 12[11] 34[3], פִּרְיוֹ מָתוֹק לְחִכִּי Ct 2[3] *his fruit was sweet to my palate*, Pr 24[13] (implied sim. of wisdom as sweet to the soul); fig. of God's words as sweet לְחִ׳ ψ 119[103] (|| פִּי); of taste as distinguishing misfortunes Jb 6[30] (|| לָשׁוֹן; > others of speech); of keeping wickedness בְּתוֹךְ ח׳ Jb 20[13] (|| תַּחַת לְשׁוֹן), i.e. delighting in and prolonging the taste of it. **d.** nearly = *mouth*, as an element in personal sweetness and beauty Ct 5[16] 7[10].

†II. **חָנַךְ** **vb. train up, dedicate** (cf. Ar. حَنَّكَ appar. denom. fr. حَنَكٌ, *rub palate* of child with chewed dates, Lane[659 a], of midwife *rub palate* of new-born child with oil, etc., before it begins to suck, Dozy[ii. 332]; also *make experienced, submissive*, etc. (as one does a horse by a rope in its mouth) Lane; v. also We Skizzen iii, 154; NH חִנֵּךְ *accustom;* Aram. חֲנַךְ *dedicate*, חַנֵּיךְ as NH; Eth. II. ሐነከ: *perceive, understand* (Di[108], ሐንካ: *initiatio* is loan-word Id.[ib.]))—**Qal** *Pf.* 3 ms. sf. חֲנָכוֹ Dt 20[5]; *Impf.* 3 ms. sf. יַחְנְכֶנּוּ Dt 20[5], 3 mpl. וַיַּחְנְכוּ 1 K 8[63] 2 Ch 7[5]; *Imv.* חֲנֹךְ Pr 22[6];—**1.** *train, train up* a (the) youth (לַנַּעַר) Pr 22[6] (cf. NH חִנּוּךְ). **2.** *dedicate*, of formal opening of a new house Dt 20[5.5]; *dedicate, consecrate* temple 1 K 8[63] = 2 Ch 7[5] (all sq. acc.)

†**חֲנוֹךְ** **n.pr.m.** **1.** son of Cain Gn 4[17.17.18] 𝔊 Ενωχ, 𝔊L Ενως. **2.** son of Jered (line of Seth), the pious Enoch, who walked with God and was taken by him Gn 5[18.19.21.22.23.24] 1 Ch 1[3] 𝔊 Ενωχ. **3.** חֲנֹךְ a son of Midian Gn 25[4] 1 Ch 1[33], 𝔊 Ενωχ. **4.** חֲנוֹךְ a son of Reuben Gn 46[9] Ex 6[14] Nu 26[5] 1 Ch 5[3], 𝔊 Ενωχ.

†**חֲנֹכִי** **adj.gent.** of חֲנוֹךְ **4,** only c. art. הַחֲ׳ = subst. coll. Nu 26[5].

†[**חָנִיךְ**] **adj. trained, tried, experienced,** only pl. sf. חֲנִיכָיו יְלִידֵי בֵיתוֹ, Gn 14[14] i.e. his tried and trusty men, born in his house.

†**חֲנֻכָּה** **n.f. dedication, consecration,** as a matter of usage only P and late (NH חֲנֻכָּה Feast of Dedication; so Aram. חֲנֻכְּתָא)—abs. ח׳ Ne 12[27]; cstr. חֲנֻכַּת Nu 7[10] + 6 t.; dedication of wall of Jerus. Ne 12[27.27], by sacrifices and processions, with music; of altar in temple 2 Ch 7[9]; of 'the house' ψ 30[1] (title), i.e. the temple (re-dedication by Judas Maccab., 1 Macc. 4[52 ff.]), v. Ol Bae al. (opp. De), and esp. Che OP 234, 247;—*dedication-offering* for altar in tabernacle Nu 7[10] (acc. c. וַיַּקְרִיבוּ), cf. יַקְרִיבוּ אֶת־קָרְבָּנָם לַחֲנֻכַּת הַמִּזְבֵּחַ v[11], also v[84.88] (all P; v Di Nu 7[20]).

†**חַכָּה** **n.f. hook fastened in jaw, fish-hook** (NH *id.*, Aram. חַכְּתָא)—abs. ח׳ Jb 40[25] + 2 t.; כָּל־מַשְׁלִיכֵי בַיְאוֹר חַכָּה Is 19[8] (|| הַדַּיָּגִים), כֻּלֹּה בְּחַכָּה הֵעֲלָה Hb 1[15] (of אדם, who, v[14], is comp. to דְּגֵי הַיָּם, and רֶמֶשׂ), cf. תִּמְשֹׁךְ לִוְיָתָן בְּחַכָּה Jb 40[25].

חִנָּם v. sub חנן.

†**חֲנַמְאֵל** **n.pr.m.** (perh. = חנן־אל)—Jeremiah's cousin, son of his uncle Je 32[7.8.9], cf. ח׳ דֹּדִי v[12]; 𝔊 Αναμεηλ.

†[**חֲנָמַל**] **n.[m.]** only בַּחֲנָמַל ψ 78[47] (on form v. Dr[Sm p. 98]) as instr. of destroying sycomores (|| בָּרָד); meaning conject.; 𝔊 𝔙 *frost.*

†I. **חָנַן** **vb. shew favour, be gracious** (NH *id.*, Aram. חֲנַן, ܚܢܰܢ; Ar. حَنَّ *yearn towards, long for, be merciful, compassionate, favourable, inclined towards;* Sab. חן in n.pr. חן מסבררהם DHM Epigr. Denkm. 40; Ph. חנן in חן *favour*, and n.pr. as אלחנן, חננבעל; As. in deriv. *annu, grace, favour, unninu, têninu nannu, id.*, Lotz TP Zim BP 23, 86)—**Qal** *Pf.* חָנַן Gn 33[5]; sf. חַנַּנִי Gn 33[11]; יְחָנֵּנִי 2 S 12[22]; חַנֹּתִי Ex 33[19]; חָנָנוּ La 4[16]; *Impf.* יֶחֱנַן Am 5[15]; יָחֹן Dt 28[50]; וַיָּחָן 2 K 13[23]; sf. יָחְנְךָ Gn 43[29] Is 30[19]; וִיחֻנֶּךָּ Nu 6[25];

יְחָנֵּנוּ Is 27^{11} Jb 33^{24}; יְחָנֵּנוּ ψ 67^{2} 123^{2} Mal 1^{9}; תָּחֹן ψ 59^{6}; sf. תְּחָנֵּם Dt 7^{2}; אָחֹן Ex 33^{19}; *Imv.* sf. חָנֵּנִי ψ 4^{2} + 17 t. ψψ; חָנְנֵנִי ψ 9^{14} (Baer pts. חָנְנֵנִי); חָנֵּנוּ Is 33^{2} ψ 123$^{3.3}$; חָנּוּנוּ Ju 21^{22}; חָנֻּנִי Jb 19$^{21.21}$; *Inf. abs.* חָנוֹן Is 30^{19}; *cstr.* חַנּוֹת ψ 77^{10}; חֶנְנָהּ ψ 102^{14}; חֲנַנְכֶם Is 30^{18}; *Pt.* חוֹנֵן Pr 14^{31}; חוֹנֵן ψ 37^{21} + 5 t. ψψ Pr.—*favour, shew favour;* **1.** of man: **a.** Ju 21^{22} *favour us with them* (2 acc.; i.e. by giving them to us). **b.** in *dealing with the poor, needy, and orphans,* abs. ψ 37$^{21.26}$ = 112^{5}; c. acc. Pr 14^{31} 19^{17} 28^{8}; c. לְ ψ 109^{12}. **c.** by *considering and sparing,* c. acc. Dt 7^{2} 28^{50} La 4^{16} Jb 19$^{21.21}$. **2.** of God, **a.** in the bestowal of favours, with acc. Gn 33^{11} (E), 43^{29} (J), Nu 6^{25} (P), 2 S 12^{22}; double acc. Gn 33^{5} (E), תּוֹרָתְךָ חָנֵּנִי *be gracious unto me* (in giving) *thy law* ψ 119^{29}. **b.** usually in the bestowal of redemption from enemies, evils, and sins; abs. ψ 77^{10}, elsewhere c. acc. Ex 33$^{19.19}$ (JE), Am 5^{15} 2 K 13^{23} Is 27^{11} 30$^{18.19.19}$ 33^{2} Mal 1^{9} ψ 4^{2} 6^{3} 9^{14} 25^{16} 26^{11} 27^{7} 30^{11} 31^{10} 41$^{5.11}$ 51^{3} 56^{2} 57$^{2.2}$ 59^{6} 67^{2} 86$^{3.16}$ 102^{14} 119$^{58.132}$ 123$^{2.3.3}$ Jb 33^{24}.—Jb 19^{17} v. II. חנן. **Niph.** *Pf.* 2 fs. נֵחַנְתְּ Je 22^{23} *be pitied* (cf. נֵאַר √ארר) but 𝔊 𝔖 𝔙 express *groan* (i.e. נֶאֱנַחְתְּ), which is favoured by context, and adopted by Hi Ew Gf Gie al. **Pi.** *Impf.* 3 ms. *make gracious, favourable* כִּי־יְחַנֵּן קוֹלוֹ Pr 26^{25}. **Po'el** *Impf.* 3 ms. *direct favour to* (Ges § 55, 1) וְאֶת־עֲפָרָהּ יְחֹנֵנוּ ψ 102^{15}; *Pt.* מְחוֹנֵן עֲנָיִים Pr 14^{21}. **Hoph.** *Impf.* יֻחַן *be shewn favour, consideration* Is 26^{10} Pr 21^{10}. **Hithp.** *Pf.* 2 ms. הִתְחַנַּנְתָּה 1 K 9^{3} + 5 t. Pf.; *Impf.* אֶתְחַנָּן ψ 30^{9} + וַיִּתְחַנֵּן 2 K 1^{13}; וַתִּתְחַנֶּן־ Est 8^{3}; etc. + 6 t. Impf.; *Inf.* לְהִתְחַנֶּן־ Est 4^{8}; בְּהִתְחַנְנוֹ Gn 42^{21}—*seek or implore favour:* **1.** *of man,* with אֶל Gn 42^{21} (E) 2 K 1^{13}; with לְ Jb 19^{16} Est 4^{8} 8^{3}. **2.** of *God,* with אֶל־ Dt 3^{23} 1 K 8$^{33.47}$ = 2 Ch 6^{37}, Jb 8^{5} ψ 30^{9} 142^{2}; with לְ Ho 12^{5} Jb 9^{15}; with לפני 1 K 8^{59} 9^{3} 2 Ch 6^{24}.

†I. **חֵן** **n.m.** ψ 45, 3 **favour, grace;**—ח׳ Gn 6^{8} + 67 t.; sf. חִנּוֹ Gn 39^{21};—**1.** *favour, grace, elegance:* **a.** of *form and appearance,* of a woman יֹפִי‖ Pr 31^{30}; אֵשֶׁת חֵן Pr 11^{16}; זונה טובת חן Na 3^{4}; of a doe Pr 5^{19}; precious stone אבן חן Pr 17^{8}; of ornaments Pr 1^{9} = 4^{9}, 3^{22}. **b.** of *speech,* lips ψ 45^{3} Pr 22^{11}; words Ec 10^{12}. **2.** *favour, acceptance:* **a.** *with men* Pr 13^{15} 22^{1} Ec 9^{11}. **b.** *with God* Zc 4$^{7.7}$ 12^{10}; chiefly in phrases: מצא חן בעיני *find favour in the eyes of:* (1) *men* Gn 30^{27} 32^{6} 33$^{8.10.15}$ 34^{11} 39^{4} 47$^{25.29}$ 50^{4} Nu 32^{5} (all J); Dt 24^{1} Ru 2$^{2.10.13}$ 1 S 1^{18} 16^{22} 20$^{3.29}$ 25^{8} 27^{5} 2 S 14^{22} 16^{4} 1 K 11^{19} Est 5^{8} 7^{3}; (2) *of God* Gn 6^{8} 18^{3} 19^{19} Ex 33$^{12.13.13.16.17}$ 34^{9} Nu 11$^{11.15}$ (all J); Ju 6^{17} 2 S 15^{25} Pr 3^{4}; abs. מצא חן (with man) Pr 28^{23}; (with God) Je 31^{2}; מצא חן לפניו Est 8^{5} (i.e. of the king); נתן חן בעיני *give favour in the eyes of* (1) man Gn 39^{21} Ex 3^{21} 11^{3} 12^{36} (J); abs. נתן חן of man ψ 84^{12}; (2) of God Pr 3^{34}; נשא חֵן בְּעֵינֵי *obtain favour in the eyes of* Est 2^{15}; of the king 5^{2}; so וַתִּשָּׂא־חֵן וָחֶסֶד לְפָנָיו Est 2^{17}.

חִנָּם **subst.,** used chiefly in the accus. as **adv.** (cf. As. *annâma, in vain,* Dl$^{K 7, Pr 44}$; from חֵן, with aff. ־ָם, which is sometimes found in substantives proper, as סֻלָּם, and pr. names, but is more partic. used with substs. applied adverbially, as רֵיקָם, דּוּמָם, אָמְנָם, יוֹמָם: Sta § 293 Ba$^{NB § 216}$)—lit. **out of favour; i.e. a.** *gratis, gratuitously, for nothing,* עֲבַד חִנָּם to serve *for nought* Gn 29^{15} Jb 1^{9}, Is 52^{3} to be sold (fig.) *for nought* v^{5}; Ex 21$^{2.11}$ יָצָא חִנָּם to go out (from slavery) *freely, for nothing,* Nu 11^{5} which we used to eat in Eg. *for nought,* Je 22^{13} 1 Ch 21^{24}; in the genitive 2 S 24^{24} עלות חִנָּם i.e. burnt-offerings *which cost nothing* (in the ‖ 1 Ch 21^{24} the constr. is changed). **b.** *for no purpose, in vain* Pr 1^{17} Mal 1^{10}: once אֶל חִנָּם (cf. אֶל **7**) Ez 6^{10}. **c.** *gratuitously, without cause, undeservedly,* esp. of groundless hostility or attack 1 S 19^{5} לְהָמִית חִנָּם to slay David *without cause,* 25^{31} ψ 35$^{7.7}$ 109^{3} 119^{161} רְדָפוּנִי חִנָּם, Pr 1^{11} 3^{30} 23^{29} Jb 2^{3} לְבַלְּעוֹ ח׳, 9^{17} 22^{6} Ez 14^{23}, ψ 35^{19} and 69^{5} שֹׂנְאַי חִנָּם my haters *without cause,* La 3^{52} אֹיְבַי חִנָּם; in the genitive 1 K 2^{31} דְּמֵי חִנָּם blood shed *without cause* (cf. 1 S 25^{31}), Pr 24^{28} אַל־תְּהִי עֵד ח׳ בְּרֵעֶךָ, 26^{2} קִלְלַת ח׳ the *causeless* curse.

†II. **חֵן** **n.pr.m.** (*favour*) — contemp. of Zerubbabel Zc 6^{14}, so RV SS We, but RVm Ew Hi Ke Or *grace, favour, kindness.*

†**חִין** **n.[m.]** חִין עֶרְכּוֹ Jb 41^{4} the *grace* of his proportions (= חֵן Aram. חִנָּא) so AV RV Thes De Volck Da al.; meaning not very appropr. in context (description of crocodile); but nothing better has been proposed; v. suggestions in Di.

†**חַנָּה** **n.pr.f.** 𝔊 *Ἄννα* (cf. Nab. חנה Eut$^{No. 20}$), mother of Samuel 1 S 1$^{2.2.5.5.8.9.13.15.19.20.22}$ 2$^{1.21}$.

†**חָנָן** **n.pr.m.** (*gracious;* cf. Sab. חנן, Ph. חנא)—**1.** one of the warriors of David 1 Ch 11^{43}. **2.** one of the heads of families of Nethinim Ezr 2^{46} = Ne 7^{49}. **3.** names of Levites Ne 8^{7} 10^{11} 13^{3}. **4.** chiefs of the people: **a.** Ne 10^{23}. **b.** Ne 10^{27}. **5.** Benjamite name 1 Ch 8$^{23.38}$ 9^{44} (cf. n.pr.loc. בֵּית חָנָן,

Mish. (כְּפַר חָנָן). **6.** אִישׁ הָאֱלֹהִים head of a prophetic guild, בְּנֵי חָנָן Je 35⁴.

†חָנוּן **n.pr.m.** (*favoured;* cf. As. *Ḥanunu,* king of Gaza COT on 2 K 15²⁹);—**1.** an Ammonite king 2 S 10¹·²·³·⁴ 1 Ch 19²·²·³·⁴·⁶. **2.** Jewish chiefs, contemporaries of Nehemiah: **a.** Ne 3¹³. **b.** Ne 3³⁰.

†חַנּוּן **adj.** gracious, only used as an attribute of God, as hearing the cry of the vexed debtor Ex 22²⁶ (covt. code), ‖ מְרַחֵם ψ 116⁵; elsewhere in the earlier phrase רַחוּם וְחַנּוּן Ex 34⁶ (JE) = ψ 86¹⁵ 103⁸, or the later חַנּוּן וְרַחוּם 2 Ch 30⁹ Ne 9¹⁷·³¹ ψ 111⁴ 112⁴ 145⁸ Jo 2¹³ Jon 4².

†חֲנִינָה **n.f.** favour לֹא־אֶתֵּן לָכֶם חֲנִינָה *I will shew you no favour* Je 16¹³ (v. on form Ba[NB 136]).

†חֲנִיאֵל **n.pr.m.** (*favour of Ēl;* cf. Ph. חנבעל, חנמלקרת (Hamilcar) *favour of Melqart;* Nab. חנאל Vog[No. 10])—**1.** prince of tribe of Manasseh Nu 34²³. **2.** a chief of the tribe of Asher 1 Ch 7³⁹.

†חֲנַנְאֵל **n.pr.m.** (*Ēl is gracious;* cf. Ph. חננבעל, אלחנן, etc.)—name of a tower at Jerusalem Je 31³⁸ Zc 14¹⁰ Ne 3¹ 12³⁹.

†חֵנָדָד **n.pr.m.** (חֵן+הֲדַד *favour of Hadad*)—Levite chief Ezr 3⁹ Ne 3¹⁸·²⁴ 10¹⁰.

†חֲנָנִי **n.pr.m.** (perh. abbrev. from foll.);—**1.** father of the prophet Jehu 1 K 16¹·⁷ 2 Ch 16⁷ 19² 20³⁴. **2.** brother of Nehemiah Ne 1² 7². **3.** a chief musician of David 1 Ch 25⁴·²⁵. **4.** a chief musician in time of Nehemiah Ne 12³⁶. **5.** a priest of Ezra's time Ezr 10²⁰.

†חֲנַנְיָהוּ, חֲנַנְיָה **n.pr.m.** (י׳ *hath been gracious*)—𝔊 Ἀνανίας; חֲנַנְיָהוּ: (cf. חנניהו on Israel. seal, Ganneau[JAs Fev.-Mars 1883, 128, No. 1])—**1.** father of a prince under Jehoiakim Je 36¹². **2.** captain of Uzziah's army 2 Ch 26¹¹. **3.** chief of one of the divisions of musicians of David 1 Ch 25²³ = חֲנַנְיָה v⁴.—חֲנַנְיָה: **4.** a false prophet of Jeremiah's time Je 28¹·⁵·¹⁰·¹¹·¹²·¹³·¹⁵·¹⁵·¹⁷. **5.** one of the three companions of Daniel Dn 1⁶·⁷·¹¹·¹⁹. **6.** grandfather of an officer of the guard in Jeremiah's time Je 37¹³. **7.** a son of Zerubbabel 1 Ch 3¹⁹·²¹. **8.** a Benjamite 1 Ch 8²⁴. **9.** various postexilic persons. **a.** Ezr 10²⁸. **b.** Ne 3⁸. **c.** Ne 3³⁰. **d.** Ne 7². **e.** Ne 10²⁴. **f.** Ne 12¹²·⁴¹.

†חַנָּתֹן **n.pr.loc.** place in the tribe of Zebulun Jos 19¹⁴; 𝔊 Αμωθ, A Ενναθωθ, 𝔊L Αναθωθ; site unknown; acc. to Conder = Talm. Caphar Hanania (Nbr[Géogr. 176.226]) on the border of Upper and Lower Galilee, mod. Kefr' Anân, Survey[WP i. 205.207].

†I. תְּחִנָּה **n.f.** favour, supplication for favour;—ת׳ Jos 11²⁰ + 4 t.; cstr. תְּחִנַּת 1 K 8³⁰·⁵²·⁵²; תְּחִנָּתִי Je 37²⁰ + 5 t.; תְּחִנָּתָם 2 Ch 6³⁹ etc. + 10 t. sf.;—**1.** *favour,* shewn by Israel Jos 11²⁰ (D); מאת יהוה Ezr 9⁸. **2.** *supplication for favour,* from God 1 K 8⁵²·⁵² 2 Ch 33¹³ ψ 119¹⁷⁰; ‖ תְּפִלָּה 1 K 8²⁸ = 2 Ch 6¹⁹, ψ 6¹⁰ 55²; תפלה (ו)תחנה 1 K 8³⁸·⁴⁵·⁴⁹·⁵⁴ = 2 Ch 6²⁹·³⁵·³⁹ 1 K 9³; ת׳ אשר התפלל 1 K 8³⁰ (= תַּחֲנוּן 2 Ch 6²¹); תִּפֹּל ת׳ לִפְנֵי *let the supplication fall before,* Yahweh Je 36⁷, the king Je 37²⁰, Jeremiah Je 42²; הִפִּיל ת׳ לפני *present supplication before,* Yahweh Je 42⁹ Dn 9²⁰, the king Je 38²⁶.

†II. תְּחִנָּה **n.pr.m.** one in the line of Judah 1 Ch 4¹².

†[תַּחֲנוּן] **n.[m.]** only **pl. abstr.** supplication for favour;—abs. תַּחֲנוּנִים Pr 18²³ + 4 t.; cstr. תַּחֲנוּנֵי Je 3²¹ 2 Ch 6²¹; sf. 1 s. תַּחֲנוּנַי ψ 28² etc., + 9 t. sf.; also תַּחֲנוּנוֹתָי ψ 86⁶;—**1.** made to men: דִּבֶּר ת׳ (a poor man to the rich) Pr 18²³; ת׳ אֶל *supplication unto* (crocodile to man) Jb 40²⁷; elsewhere **2.** to God: ‖ תפלה ψ 143¹ Dn 9³·¹⁷; ת׳ אשר התפלל 2 Ch 6²¹ (= תחנה 1 K 8³⁰); קוֹל ת׳ *voice of supplication* ψ 28²·⁶ 31²³ 86⁶ 130² 140⁷, also 116¹ (for קוֹלִי is old case-ending, and cstr. as 𝔊 𝔙 Che Bae al.); ‖ בְּכִי Je 31⁹; בְּכִי ת׳ Je 3²¹; אֲנַחְנוּ מַפִּילִים ת׳ לְפָנֶיךָ Zc 12¹⁰; רוח חן ות׳ Dn 9¹⁸ *we are presenting our supplications before thee;* בִּתְחִלַּת ת׳ Dn 9²³ *at the beginning of thy supplication.*

†II. [חָנַן] **be loathsome** (cf. Ar. خَنَّ x. *foetorem emisit* (puteus); Syr. ܚܢܝܢܐ *rancid*);—only וְחַנֹּתִי לִבְנֵי בִטְנִי Jb 19¹⁷ *and I am loathsome* to the sons of my womb (‖ זָרָה v. II. זור), so RVm Ew De Di al. (On the tone v. De.)

†חָנֵס **n.pr.loc.** Is 30⁴ in Lower Egypt, on island in Nile, S. of Memphis (‖ צֹעַן) = Egypt. *Ḥnnstn* [*Ḥnênsĕ*], As. *Ḥininši;* Herodot.[ii. 137] Ἄνυσις, afterward *Heracleopolis magna,* now *Ahnâs;* v. Steindorff[BAS i. 602].

†[חָנֵף] **vb.** be polluted, profane (Ar. حَنَفَ *incline, decline,* hence حَنِيفٌ *inclining to a right state,* but in Heb. of *inclining away from right, irreligion, profaneness,* cf. حَنِيفٌ *have a* حَنَفٌ i.e. *distortion of foot;* Syr. in deriv,

be profane, etc, NH Hiph., Aram Aph. *act falsely toward, flatter*, חֲנֻפָּה *hypocrisy*, As *ḫanpu, ruthlessness, ḫanâpu, exercise ruthlessness toward*, Tel Amarna Zim$^{ZA\ vi\ 1891\ 256}$)—**Qal** *Pf* 3 fs חָֽנְפָה Is 24^{5}; 3 pl. חָֽנְפוּ Je 23^{11}, *Impf.* 3 fs תֶּחֱנַף Je 3^{1}; תֶּחֱנַף Mi 4^{11}; וַתֶּחֱנַף Je 3^{9} ψ 106^{38}, *Inf. abs* חָנוֹף Je 3^{1},—**1.** *be polluted:* of land Is 24^{5} Je 3^{1} ^{1} ψ 106^{38}; of Zion Mi 4^{11}. **2.** of prophet and priest = be חָנֵף (cf infr) i.e. *profane, godless* Je 23^{11}—Je 3^{9} appar trans. וַתֶּחֱנַף את הארץ, Gf del את, Gie cites Ges$^{§121.1}$, but rd. rather Hiph וַתַּחֲנִף with Codd 𝔊 Ew al. (v. also Gf Gie) **Hiph.** *Impf* יַחֲנִיף Nu 35^{33} Dn 11^{32}; 2 fs וַתַּחֲנִיפִי Je 3^{2}, 2 mpl תַּחֲנִיפוּ,—**1.** *pollute* the land Nu 35$^{33.33}$ (by blood, P), Je 3^{2} (by idolatry, etc) + Je 3^{9} (v supr) **2.** *make profane, godless* Dn 11^{32} c acc. pers.

† חֹ֫נֶף **n.[m.] profaneness**—לַעֲשׂוֹת ח׳ Is 32^{6} *to practise profaneness* (+ תּוֹעָה, אָוֶן, נְבָלָה).

† חָנֵף **adj profane, irreligious** (Syr ܚܢܦܐ *profane*, hence oft *heathen, apostate;* Ar. حَنِيف *inclining to a right state*, esp. *the true religion, a Muslim*)—abs ח׳ Jb 8^{13} + 10 t; pl חֲנֵפִים Is 33^{14}, חַנְפֵי Jb 36^{13} ψ 35^{16},—*profane, godless* of persons, אָדָם ח׳ Jb 34^{30}, גּוֹי ח׳ Is 10^{6}; as subst. *godless man* Is 9^{16} (‖ מֵרַע) Jb 8^{13} 13^{16} 17^{8} 20^{5} 27^{8} Pr 11^{9}; coll עֲדַת ח׳ Jb 15^{34}, pl Is 33^{14}; חַנְפֵי־לֵב Jb 36^{13}; בְּחַנְפֵי לַעֲגֵי מָעוֹג ψ 35^{16} *as profane men, mockers for cake* (i e table-jesters, on cstr v. Ges$^{§130\ 5}$), but txt. dub. (v Che$^{crit\ n}$ Bae).

† חֲנֻפָּה (so Baer; van d. H חֲנֻפָּה) **n.f. profaneness, pollution,** Je 23^{15}.

† [חָנַק] **vb. strangle** (NH *id*, Aram. חנק, ܚܢܰܩ, Ar خَنَقَ);—**Niph.** *Impf.* וַיֵּחָנַק 2 S 17^{23} *strangled himself* (+ וַיָּמָת) **Pi.** *Pt* מְחַנֵּק Na 2^{13} *strangle*, of lion strangling prey, fig of Ninevitish king (object not expressed)

† מַחֲנָק **n.[m.] strangling, suffocation,** as a mode of death, וַתִּבְחַר מַחֲנָק נַפְשִׁי Jb 7^{15} *and my soul chooseth strangling* (‖ מָוֶת).

חַנָּתֹן v sub חנן

† I [חָסַד] **vb. 1. be good, kind** (NH חָסַד in deriv חָסִיד *pious*, Aram חֲסַד *be kind, mild* (then *beg*), chiefly in deriv חסדא etc.; cf. perh. Ar حَشَدَ usu. pl *they assembled*, sq. لَهُ *they combined for him, and took pains to shew him courtesy* Lane^{574c}, v also RS$^{Proph\ iv\ n\ 9}$ (and Schu AE v in Thes), > Thes al. who find primary meaning in *eager zeal* or *desire* (‖ קנא), whence develop *kindness* (as above), and *envy*, Ar حَسَدَ, حَسَدٌ *envy* (vb & n), Aram. חֲסַד *be put to shame*, ܚܣܕܐ, חִסֵּד *reproach, revile*, v. II. חסד)—only **Hithp.** *Impf.* עִם־חָסִיד תִּתְחַסָּד *thou shewest thyself kind* 2 S 22^{26} = ψ 18^{26}.—On **Pi.** Pr 25^{10} v. II. חסד

† I. חֶ֫סֶד$_{247}$ **n.m.**$^{2\ S\ 16,17}$ **goodness, kindness;**—abs ח׳ Gn 24^{12} + 85 t; חָ֫סֶד Gn 39^{21} + 12 t.; cstr. חֶסֶד 1 S 20^{14} + 8 t., sf. חַסְדִּי ψ 59^{18} + 120 t. sfs, pl. חֲסָדִים Gn 32^{11}, cstr. חַסְדֵי Is 55^{3} + 5 t. (Baer$^{Jes\ p.\ 79}$ Ges$^{§93,R.1F}$); sf חֲסָדַי Ne 13^{14} + 10 t. sfs, (not in H or P). **I.** *of man;* **1.** *kindness* of men towards men, in doing favours and benefits 1 S 20^{15} 2 S 16^{17} ψ 141^{5} Pr 19^{22} 20^{6}, ח׳ יהוה 1 S 20^{14} *the kindness of* י׳ (such as he shews, Thes MV; that sworn to by oath to Yahweh Mich Dathe, shewn out of reverence to Yahweh Th Ke), cf. ח׳ אלהים 2 S 9^{3}; תּוֹרַת־ח׳ Pr 31^{26} *instruction in kindness, kindly instruction* עָשָׂה חֶסֶד עִמָּדִי *do or shew kindness* (in dealing) *with me* Gn 20^{13} 40^{14} (E), 1 S 20^{14} 2 S 10^{2} (עִמִּי in ‖ 1 Ch 19^{2}); c עִם Gn 21^{23} (E), 24$^{12.14}$ Jos 2$^{12.12}$ Ju 1^{24} (J), 8^{35} 1 S 15^{6} 2 S 2^{5} 3^{8} 9$^{1.3.7}$, 10^{2a} = 1 Ch 19^{2a}, 1 Ch 19^{2b} 2 Ch 24^{22}, c. עַל 1 S 20^{8}; c לְ 1 K 2^{7}, נשׂא ח׳ לפני *obtain kindness before* Est 2$^{9.17}$, היטיב ח׳ Ru 3^{10} **2.** *kindness* (especially as extended to the lowly, needy and miserable), *mercy* Pr 20^{28} Jb 6^{14}; אִישׁ חסד *merciful man* Pr 11^{17} (opp אַכְזָרִי), מַלְכֵי ח׳ *merciful kings* 1 K 20^{31}; עשׂה ח׳ ψ 109^{16}; in this sense usu with other attributes (v also infr **II. 2**); ‖ אמת Ho 4^{1} Is 16^{5}; ח׳ ואמת Pr 3^{3} 14^{22} 16^{6} 20^{28}; עָשָׂה ח׳ ואמת Gn 24^{49} 47^{29} Jos 2^{14} (J; RV gives these under **1**), ‖ צדקה Ho 10^{12}; צדקה וח׳ Pr 21^{21}, ‖ משׁפט Mi 6^{8}, ח׳ ומשׁפט Ho 12^{7}; ‖ חוֹנֵן ψ 109^{12}, ח׳ ורחמים Zc 7^{9} Dn 1^{9}.—(On Ho 6$^{4.6}$ v. **3** infr) **3.** (rarely) *affection* of Isr to י׳, *love to God, piety*· ח׳ נְעוּרַיִךְ Je 2^{2} *piety of thy youth* (‖ *love of thine espousals* to Yahweh), poss also חַסְדְּכֶם כַּעֲנַן־בֹּקֶר Ho 6^{4} *your piety is like a morning cloud* (fleeting), and כי חסד חָפַצְתִּי וְלֹא־זָבַח Ho 6^{6} *for piety I delight in and not in peace-offering* (‖ דעת אלהים, cf 1 S 15^{22});—so Wu Now Hi (v^{4}) Che; Ke Hi (v^{6}) al. sub **2** (or **1**),—אַנְשֵׁי חֶסֶד *men of piety* Is 57^{1} (‖ צַדִּיק); pl *pious acts* 2 Ch 32^{32} 35^{26} Ne 13^{14}. **4.** *lovely appearance* כָּל־חַסְדּוֹ כְּצִיץ הַשָּׂדֶה Is 40^{6} *all its loveliness as the flower of the field* (so Thes Hi De Che Di al., but δόξα 𝔊 1 Pet 1^{24} & *gloria* 𝔙 favour an original reading הוֹדוֹ Lo or כְּבוֹדוֹ Ew, see

Br$^{MP\ 375}$; Du חֶדְרוֹ). **II.** *of God: kindness, lovingkindness* in condescending to the needs of his creatures. He is חַסְדָּם *their goodness, favour* Jon 2^{9}; חַסְדִּי ψ 144^{2}; אֱלֹהֵי חַסְדִּי *God of my kindness* ψ 59^{18}; in v^{11} rd. אֱלֹהֵי חַסְדּוֹ *my God with his kindness* 𝔖 𝔙 Ew Hup De Pe Che Bae; his is the kindness ψ 62^{13}; it is with him ψ 130^{7}; he delights in it Mi 7^{18}. **1.** specif. lovingkindness: **a.** *in redemption from enemies and troubles* Gn 19^{19} 39^{21} (J), Ex 15^{13} (song), Je 31^{3} Ezr 7^{28} 9^{9} ψ 21^{8} $31^{17.22}$ 32^{10} 33^{22} $36^{8.11}$ 42^{9} 44^{27} 48^{10} 59^{17} 66^{20} 85^{8} 90^{14} 94^{18} $107^{8.15.21.31}$ $143^{8.12}$ Jb 37^{13} Ru 1^{8} 2^{20}; men should trust in it ψ 13^{6} 52^{10}; rejoice in it ψ 31^{8}; hope in it ψ 33^{18} 147^{11}. **b.** *in preservation of life from death* ψ 6^{5} 86^{13} Jb 10^{12}. **c.** *in quickening of spiritual life* ψ 109^{26} $119^{41.76.88.124.149.159}$. **d.** *in redemption from sin* ψ 25^{7} 51^{3}. **e.** *in keeping the covenants*, with Abraham Mi 7^{20}; with Moses and Israel שֹׁמֵר הַבְּרִית וְ(הַ)חֶסֶד *keepeth the covenant and the lovingkindness* Dt $7^{9.12}$ 1 K 8^{23} = 2 Ch 6^{14}, Ne 1^{5} 9^{32} Dn 9^{4}; with David and his dynasty 2 S 7^{15} = 1 Ch 17^{13}, 2 S 22^{51} = ψ 18^{51}, 1 K $3^{6.6}$ = 2 Ch 1^{8}, ψ $89^{29.34}$; with the wife Zion Is 54^{10}. **2.** חֶסֶד is grouped with other divine attributes: חסד ואמת *kindness (lovingkindness) and fidelity* Gn 24^{27} (J), ψ 25^{10} $40^{11.12}$ 57^{4} 61^{8} 85^{11} 89^{15} 115^{1} 138^{2}; עשׂה ח׳ ואמת עם 2 S 2^{6} 15^{20} (𝔊, v. Dr); רַב ח׳ ואמת Ex 34^{6} (JE), ψ 86^{15}; also ‖ אמת Mi 7^{20} ψ 26^{3} 117^{2}; ‖ אֱמוּנָה ψ 88^{12} 89^{3} 92^{3}; ח׳ ואמונה ψ 89^{25}; אמונה וח׳ ψ 98^{3}; ‖ רחמים ψ 77^{9}; ח׳ ורחמים Je 16^{5} Ho 2^{21} ψ 103^{4}; ח׳ ומשׁפט Je 9^{23} ψ 101^{1}; ‖ צדקה ψ 36^{11}; טוב וח׳ ψ 23^{6}. **3.** the *kindness* of God is **a.** *abundant:* רַב־חֶסֶד *abundant, plenteous in kindness (goodness)* Nu 14^{18} (J), Ne 9^{17} (Qr), Jo 2^{13} Jon 4^{2} ψ 86^{5} 103^{8} (cf. Ex 34^{6} JE; ψ 86^{15}); רֹב חַסְדְּךָ Ne 13^{22} ψ 5^{8} 69^{14} 106^{7} (𝔊 𝔙 Aq 𝔗, to be preferred to MT חֲסָדֶיךָ); רֹב חֲסָדָו La 3^{32} ψ 106^{45} (Kt 𝔊 in both to be preferred). **b.** *great in extent:* גֹּדֶל ח׳ *greatness of thy mercy* Nu 14^{19} (J); גְּדָל־ח׳ ψ 145^{8}; it is kept for thousands Ex 34^{7} (JE), Je 32^{18}, esp. of those connected with lovers of י׳, Ex 20^{6} = Dt 5^{10}; for 1000 generations Dt 7^{9}; it is great as the heavens ψ 57^{11} 103^{11}, cf. 36^{6} 108^{5}; the earth is full of it ψ 33^{5} 119^{64}. **c.** *everlasting:* לעולם חסדו Je 33^{11} 1 Ch $16^{34.41}$ 2 Ch 5^{13} $7^{3.6}$ 20^{21} Ezr 3^{11} ψ 100^{5} 106^{1} 107^{1} $118^{1.2.3.4.29}$ $136^{1-26\ (26\ t.)}$; חסדך לעולם ψ 138^{8}; ח׳ מעולם ועד עולם ψ 103^{17}; ח׳ עולם Is 54^{8}; ח׳ אל כל היום ψ 52^{3}. **d.** *good:* כִּי־טוֹב חַסְדְּךָ ψ 69^{17} 109^{21}; כי טוב חסדך מחיים ψ 63^{4}. **4.** pl. *mercies, deeds of kindness*, the historic displays of lovingkindness to Israel: shewn to Jacob Gn 32^{11} (R); but mostly late Is 63^{7} ψ 25^{6} 89^{2}; כְּרֹב חסדיו Is 63^{7}, see **3 a**; promised in the Davidic covenant ψ 89^{50}; חַסְדֵי דָוִד *mercies to David* Is 55^{3} 2 Ch 6^{42}; *mercies* in general La 3^{22} ψ 17^{7} $107^{43\,f.}$—חֶסֶד in n.pr.m. בן־ח׳ v. sub בֵּן. On Lv 20^{17} Pr 14^{34} v. II. חֶסֶד sub II. חסד.

†**חָסִיד** **adj.m.** kind, pious (so, as denoting active practice of חֶסֶד, kindness, Thes MV De and most, cf. קָצִיר, פָּקִיד etc.; > Hup on ψ 4^{4} RVm who expl. as passive *reception* of י׳'s חֶסֶד, cf. שָׂכִיר, אָסִיר etc.; its use as attribute of God Je 3^{12} ψ 145^{17}, and the context ψ 12^{1} Mi 7^{2} etc., favour active sense)—ח׳ ψ 4^{4} + 9 t.; חֲסִידְךָ Dt 33^{8} ψ 89^{20}; חֲסִידְךָ ψ 16^{10}; pl. חֲסִידִים ψ $149^{1.5}$; sf. חֲסִידָי ψ 50^{5}; חֲסִידָו 1 S 2^{9} + 15 t. sfs.;—**1.** *kind:* **a.** of man עם ח׳ תתחסד *with the kind thou shewest thyself kind* 2 S 22^{26} = ψ 18^{26}. **b.** of wing of ostrich אִם אֶבְרָה חֲסִידָה Jb 39^{13} *is it a kindly pinion?* poss. with play on חֲסִידָה n.f. *stork* (is the ostrich kind like the stork?). **c.** of God, only Je 3^{12} ψ 145^{17}. **2.** *pious, godly*, either as exhibition of 'duteous love' toward God (Che$^{OP\ 378}$), or (in view of rarity of such passages as Ho $6^{4.6}$ Je 2^{2}, and their possible ambiguity) because *kindness*, as prominent in the godly, comes to imply other attributes, and to be a designation of the godly character, *piety:* **a.** as adj.—גּוֹי לא חסיד *a nation, not pious, = ungodly* ψ 43^{1}. **b.** elsewh. as subst.: sing., *a pious man, the godly* ψ 4^{4} 12^{2} 32^{6} 86^{2}, ‖ יָשָׁר Mi 7^{2}; *(thy) pious one(s)* ψ 16^{10} (Kt pl.), 1 S 2^{9} (Qr pl.) Pr 2^{8}, אִישׁ חֲסִידֶךָ *men of thy pious one* Dt 33^{8} (Moses, v. Di; others, *the man, thy godly one*, i.e. Levi); pl. *the pious, godly*, those of the people who were faithful, devoted to God's service, only in Psalter and chiefly, if not entirely, in late Psalms ψ $149^{1.5}$; *his pious ones* ψ 30^{5} 31^{24} 37^{28} 85^{9} 97^{10} 116^{15} 148^{14} 149^{9}; *thy pious ones* ψ 52^{11} 79^{2} 89^{20} 132^{9} = 2 Ch 6^{41}, ψ 145^{10}; *my pious ones* ψ 50^{5}, *her* (Zion's) *pious* ψ 132^{16}.—(In Maccab. age, *συναγωγὴ Ἀσιδαίων* denoted, technically, the party of *the pious*, who opposed the Hellenization of Judaea, v. 1 Macc 2^{42} 7^{13} 2 Macc 14^{6} and Che$^{OP\ 48,\ 56}$; so perhaps ψ 116^{15} $149^{1.5.9}$.)

†I. **חֲסִידָה** **n.f.** stork (so called as kind and affectionate to its young)—Lv 11^{19} = Dt 14^{18}, ψ 104^{17} Je 8^{7} Zc 5^{9}.

†**חֲסַדְיָה** **n.pr.m.** (*Yah is kind*) son of Zerubbabel 1 Ch 3^{20}.

†II [חָסַד] **vb. be reproached, ashamed** (Aramaism, v RS [Proph iv, n 9]; Aram חסד *be put to shame*, ܚܣܕ, חסד *reproach, revile*; חִסּוּדָא, ܚܣܕܐ *shame, reproach*, oft in 𝔗 𝔖 for חֶרְפָּה);—only **Pi.** *Impf* פֶּן־יְחַסֶּדְךָ Pr 25[10] *lest he reproach thee, expose thee to shame.*

†II חֶסֶד **n.m.** shame, reproach, only abs.—ח׳ הוּא Lv 20[17] (H) *it is a shame* (shameful thing), ח׳ לְאֻמִּים חַטָּאת Pr 14[34] *sin is a reproach to peoples*

†חָסָה **vb.** (mostly poet and fig) **seek refuge** (Ar خَشِيَ III is *set aside*; v. *go aside, apart*; خَشَى *shelter, protection*, but ? ش=ס)—**Qal** *Pf* ח׳ ψ 64[11], 3 fs חָסָיָה ψ 57[2], חָסִיתִי ψ 7[2] + 7 t., pl. חָסוּ ψ 37[40] Zp 3[12], חָסָיוּ Dt 32[37], *Impf* יֶחֱסֶה ψ 34[9], תֶּחְסֶה ψ 91[4], אֶחְסֶה ψ 57[2] (see Baer ψ 34[9]), אֶחסה ψ 18[3] + 2 t; pl יֶחֱסוּ Is 14[32], יֶחֱסָיוּן ψ 36[8]; *Imv* חֲסוּ Ju 9[15], *Inf* חֲסוֹת ψ 118[8] + 3 t, *pt* חוסה Is 57[13], חסה Pr 14[32], חוסים ψ 17[7] + 3 t, חוסי Pr 30[5] 2 S 22[31] (see Baer Pr 30[5]), חסים ψ 2[12] 5[12], חסי Na 1[7],—*seek refuge*, c. ב in the shadow of a tree Ju 9[15], בצל מצרים Is 30[2], בָּהּ Is 14[32] in Zion, in gods Dt 32[37] (poem), elsewhere *in God* 2 S 22[3] = ψ 18[3], Na 1[7] ψ 2[12] 5[12] 7[2] 11[1] 16[1] 25[20] 31[2.20] 34[9.23] 37[40] 57[2] 64[11] 71[1] 118[8.9] 141[8] 144[2], Is 57[13], מגן הוא ל(כל ה)חוסים בו *a shield is he to (all) who seek refuge in him* 2 S 22[31] = ψ 18[31], Pr 30[5], ב׳ is probably to be supplied in thought at least: מושיע חוסים ψ 17[7] *saviour of those seeking refuge* (in thee), חסה במותו צדיק Pr 14[32] *a righteous man in his death seeketh refuge* (in Yahweh), בשם י׳ Zp 3[12], בצל כנפיך *in the shadow of thy wings* ψ 36[8] 57[2], בסתר כנפיך ψ 61[5], תחת כנפיו *under his wings* ψ 91[4] = Ru 2[12]

†חֹסָה **1 n.pr.m.** (refuge)—name of one of the Levitical doorkeepers of the temple 1 Ch 16[38] 26[10 11 16]. **2 n.pr.loc.** place in the tribe of Asher Jos 19[29], site unknown; 𝔊 Ιασιφ, A Σουσα, 𝔊L Ωσα.

†חָסוּת **n.f.** refuge;—וְהֶחָסוּת בְּצֵל מִצְרַיִם Is 30[3] (|| מָעוֹז פַּרְעֹה).

†מַחְסֶה **n.m.** [Pr 14 26] **refuge, shelter**;—abs. מַ׳ Jb 24[8] + 5 t; מַחְסֵה ψ 46[2] + 2 t.; cstr. מַחְסֵה Is 28[17]; sf מַחְסִי ψ 62[8] + 5 t, מַחְסִי ψ 71[7] Je 17[17], מַחְסֵהוּ ψ 14[6], מַחְסֵנוּ Is 28[15],—*shelter* **a.** from rain and storm Is 4[6] 25[4] Jb 24[8]. **b.** from danger סְלָעִים מַחְסֶה לַשְׁפַנִּים *rocks a refuge for conies* ψ 104[18], מחסה כזב *refuge of falsehood* Is 28[17], כזב מחסנו *falsehood our refuge* Is 28[15], elsewhere of God as the refuge of his people ψ 14[6] 46[2] 61[4] 62[8.9] 71[7] 73[28] 91[2.9] 94[22] 142[6] Pr 14[26] Je 17[17] Jo 4[16]

†מַחְסֵיָה **n.pr.m.** (*י׳ is a refuge*) ancestor of Baruch and Seraiah Je 32[12] (Baer מַחְסֵ׳) 51[59].

†[חָסַל] **vb. finish off, consume** (Aram חֲסַל *come to an end*, Aph. *bring to an end*)—**Qal** *Impf* יַחְסְלֶנּוּ הָאַרְבֶּה Dt 28[38] of locusts destroying crops

†חָסִיל **n.m.** a kind of **locust** (sg coll), alw abs ח׳, and alw as destructive, 1 K 8[37] = 2 Ch 6[28] ψ 78[46] (all || אַרְבֶּה), Jo 1[4] 2[25] (|| יֶלֶק), (גָּזָם, אַרְבֶּה), cf אֹסֶף הֶחָ׳ Is 33[4] *the gathering of the locust*, in sim of despoiling of Assyria (|| גֵּבִים)

†[חָסַם] **vb. stop up, muzzle** (NH *id.*, חסום *muzzle*, Aram חֲסַם *bind up fast*)—**Qal** *Impf* לא תַחְסֹם שׁוֹר בְּדִישׁוֹ Dt 25[4] *thou shalt not muzzle an ox when it is treading* (i e. threshing), *Pt* וחסמת היא Ez 39[11] *and it shall stop* (the way of) the passers-by, but rd. וְחָסְמוּ אֶת־הַגַּיְא *and they shall stop up the valley*, Co v. 𝔊 𝔖 Hi.

†מַחְסוֹם **n.m. muzzle**, אֶשְׁמְרָה־לְפִי מ׳ ψ 39[2] *let me keep a muzzle for my mouth*, to avoid (hasty and) erring speech

חסן (√of foll; Aram. חֲסַן, ܚܣܢ, ܚܣܢ, *be strong*, also *take possession of*, חַסִּין, ܚܣܝܢܐ *strong*, etc.; Ar خَشُنَ *be rough, hard, coarse*).

†חֹסֶן **n.m.** [Pr 15, 6] **wealth, treasure** (on relation to √mng cf. חַיִל)—ח׳ abs Pr 15[6] + 2 t; cstr Is 33[6] Je 20[5],—*wealth, treasure*, of individuals Pr 15[6] (ח׳ רָב, opp נֶעְכָּרֶת), Pr 27[24] (|| נֵזֶר), Ez 22[25] (|| יְקָר), of city ח׳ הָעִיר הַזֹּאת Je 20[5] (|| אוֹצְרוֹת, יְקָר, יְגִיעַ); in transf sense ח׳ יְשׁוּעֹת, *wealth* (or *abundance* VB) *of salvations*, ח׳ יְשׁ׳ חָכְמַת וָדָעַת יִרְאַת י׳ הִיא אוֹצָרוֹ Is 33[6] and stability of thy times shall be *abundance of salvations* (helps, deliverances), etc

†חָסֹן **adj.** strong, of the Amorite Am 2[9] (ח׳ כָּאַלּוֹנִים, *strong as the oaks*), הֶחָסֹן as subst. *the strong one* Is 1[31].

†חֲסִין **adj. strong, mighty** (Aramaism),—only מִי־כָמוֹךָ חֲסִין יָהּ ψ 89[9].

†[חָסְפַּס] **vb.** only/*Pt. pass.* (**scaled off**) **scale-like** (appar. redupl. fr *חסף for חספסף, v. Ew §158 c Ol §§214, 276 Ges §55.4 Sta §291; Kö i. 250 thinks euphon for מְחֻסְפָּף; to be comp. are Ar خَشِفَ, *have scab, itch* (Frey; but خش = (זס); Aram. חַסְפָּא *potsherd*, חַסְפְּנִיתָא *scale* (of fish), *scurf;* Eth. ሐሠፈ: *scabiosus fuit* Di 587 and Ex 16[14])—hence מְחֻסְפָּס *scaled off, scale-like*, as 𝔊 𝔗 Thes RobGes MV SS VB;—of the manna דַּק מְחֻסְפָּס דַּק כַּכְּפֹר Ex 16[14] *a fine, scale-like thing, fine as the hoar-frost.*

†חָסֵר **vb.** lack, need, be lacking, decrease (v. Lag BN 143, NH חִסֵּר *cause to lack* or *fail, diminish* (act), and deriv; Aram חֲסַר, ܚܣܰܪ, *want, lack*, and deriv, cf. Ph. מחסר, v. מחסור infr; Ar حَسَرَ *remove, strip off; disappear, retire* (of water), *fail* (of sight), etc.; perh also Eth. ኀጸረ: *be inferior, worthless, diminished* Di 590 and deriv)—**Qal** *Pf.* 3 ms. ח׳ 1 K 17[16]; 2 ms חָסַרְתָּ Dt 2[7]; 3 pl. חָסֵרוּ Ne 9[21]; 1 pl חָסַרְנוּ Je 44[18]; *Impf.* יֶחְסַר Dt 15[8] + 2 t; יֶחְסָר Pr 31[11] Ec 9[8]; 3 fs תֶּחְסַר 1 K 17[14] Pr 13[25]; 2 ms תֶּחְסַר Dt 8[9]; 1 s. אֶחְסָר ψ 23[1]; pl. יַחְסְרוּ ψ 34[11] Ez 4[17]; וַיַּחְסְרוּ Gn 8[3]; יַחְסְרוּן Gn 18[28]; *Inf. cstr.* חֲסַר Pr 10[21] Ew §238 a, cf. Ges §45.1 a, *abs* חָסוֹר Gn 8[5]; *Pt.* חָסֵר 1 K 11[22] Ec 10[3] (v חָסֵר infr);—**1.** lack: **a.** c. acc. Gn 18[28](J) *perchance the fifty righteous lack five*, Dt 2[7] *thou hast not lacked anything*, 8[9] Je 44[18] 1 K 11[22] Ez 4[17] ψ 34[11] Pr 31[11], cf also בַּחֲסַר־לֵב Pr 10[21] *by lacking intelligence (sense)*, (Di puts here Dt 15[8], v infr) **b.** abs. *be in want, want* ψ 23[1] Pr 13[25] Ne 9[21]. **2.** *be lacking*, מַחְסֹרוֹ אֲשֶׁר יֶח׳ לוֹ Dt 15[8] *his lack* (i e. thing needed), *which is lacking to him* (possible also is, *which he lacks for himself*, so Di, v. supr.); שֶׁמֶן עַל־רֹאשְׁךָ אַל־יֶח׳ Ec 9[8] *oil on thy head let it not be lacking;* v. also abs Is 51[14] Ct 7[3], and לִבּוֹ חָסֵר Ec 10[3] *his sense is lacking;* of jar of oil 1 K 17[14 16] (abs.) by meton. for the oil itself (cf ‖ כלה *be consumed, exhausted*) **3.** *diminish, decrease*, of waters Gn 8[3] (P), cf הָלוֹךְ וְחָסוֹר v[5] (P), waters *continually diminished* (v. הלך supr. p. 233[b]). **Pi.** *cause to lack*, c acc pers., *Impf.* 2 ms. sf וַתְּחַסְּרֵהוּ מְעַט מֵאֱלֹהִים ψ 8[6] *and thou didst make him lack little of God*, *Pt.* וּמְחַסֵּר אֶת־נַפְשִׁי מִטּוֹבָה Ec 4[8] for whom am I labouring *and depriving myself of good things?* **Hiph.** *Pf.* הֶחְסִיר Ex 16[18], *Impf.* יַחְסִיר Is 32[6],—*cause to be lacking, fail*, c acc. rei מַשְׁקֵה צָמֵא יַחְ׳ Is 32[6]; *the drink of the thirsty he causeth to fail* (‖ לְהָרִיק נפש רָעֵב); abs. Ex 16[18] (P), *he that gathered little caused no lack.*

†חֶסֶר **n.m.** Pr 28. 22 **want, poverty**—alw. abs.; ח׳ יְבֹאֶנּוּ Pr 28[22] *want shall come to him;* ‖ כָּפָן *hunger* Jb 30[3].

†חֹסֶר **n.[m.]** want, lack (Lag BN 144)—only cstr. ח׳ לָחֶם Am 4[6], ח׳ כֹּל Dt 28[48 57].

†חָסֵר **adj.** needy, lacking, in want of—ח׳ abs. Ec 6[2]; cstr. חֲסַר 1 S 21[16] + 13 t;—*needy, in want of* חֲ׳ משגעים אני 1 S 21[16] *am I in want of madmen?* 2 S 3[29] *in need of bread*, so Pr 12[9], usu. חֲסַר־לֵב *lacking understanding, sense* Pr 6[32] 7[7] 9[4 16] 10[13] 11[12] 12[11] 15[21]; אָדָם ח־לב Pr 17[18] 24[30]; נָגִיד ח׳ תְּבוּנוֹת Pr 28[16]; אֵינֶנּוּ חָסֵר לְנַפְשׁוֹ מכל וג׳ Ec 6[2] *neither is he lacking for his soul in aught of* (מִן *part*) *all that he desireth.*

†חַסְרָה **n.pr.m.** grandfather of Shallum who was husband of Huldah the prophetess (𝔊A Εσσερη, 𝔊L Ασερ) = חַרְחַס 2 K 22[14] (𝔊 Αρααs, 𝔊L Αδρα).

†חֶסְרוֹן **n.m.** thing lacking, deficiency (Lag BN 198)—only ח׳ לֹא־יוּכַל לְהִמָּנוֹת Ec 1[15] *what is lacking cannot be counted.*

†מַחְסוֹר, מַחְסֹר **n.[m.]** need, thing needed, poverty;—מ׳ abs Pr 11[24] + 6 t.; cstr. Ju 18[10] 19[19], sf מַחְסוֹרְךָ Ju 19[20]; מַחְסֹרְךָ Pr 6[11]; מַחְסֹרוֹ Dt 15[8]; pl sf. מַחְסֹרֶיךָ Pr 24[34];—**1.** *need* = *thing needed* דֵּי מַחְסֹרוֹ Dt 15[8] *enough for his need* (sq. אשר יֶחְסַר לוֹ, cf חסר vb), כָּל־מ׳ עָלָי Ju 19[20] *all thy need* be *upon me* (for me to provide) **2.** *lack, want* אין מ׳ כָּל־דָּבָר Ju 18[10] *no lack of anything*, 19[19] ψ 34[10]. **3.** in gen., *need, poverty* Pr 6[11] (‖ ראש) = 24[34] (‖ ריש), 11[24] 14[23] 21[5] 22[16] 28[27]; איש מ׳ 21[17] *a man of poverty*

חַף v. II חפף.

†[חָפָא] **vb.** do secretly (prop. cover, = חפה, q v);—only **Pi.** *Impf.* וַיְחַפְּאוּ . . . דברים *and they did things secretly* 2 K 17[9].

†[חָפָה] **vb.** cover (NH *id.*, esp. Pi; Aram. חֲפָא, ܚܦܳܐ (esp. Pa.); Ar. خَفِيَ *be hidden*, خَفَى *hide*)—**Qal** *Pf* חָפוּ 2 S 15[30] + 3 t.; *Pt* חָפוּי 2 S 15[30]; cstr. חֲפוּי Est 6[12];—*cover* the head (ראש), in token of grief 2 S 15[30] Je 14[3.4]; *pt* agrees with ר׳ 2 S 15[30]; חֲפוּי ראש (‖ אָבֵל) Est 6[12]; in token of sentence of death Est 7[8]. **Niph.** *Pt.* f. נֶחְפָּה ψ 68[13] (כנפי יונה נ׳), c. בְּ

of material. **Pi.** *Pf.* (late) חִפָּה 2 Ch $3^{8.9}$; *Impf.* וַיְחַף 2 Ch 3^{7}; sf. וַיְחַפֵּהוּ 2 Ch $3^{5.8}$; *overlay* sq. 2 acc. (one of material) 2 Ch $3^{5.5.7.8.9}$.

I. חֻפָּה, II. חֻפָּה v. sub חפף.

†[חָפַז] **vb. be in trepidation, hurry, or alarm** (Ar. حَفَزَ *hasten, incite, urge*);—**Qal** *Impf.* יַחְפּוֹז Jb 40^{23}; תֵּחָפְזוּ Dt 20^{3}; *Inf. cstr.* sf. בְּחָפְזִי ψ 31^{23} 116^{11}; בְּחָפְזָהּ 2 S 4^{4}; בְּחָפְזָם 2 K 7^{15} Qr (Kt הֵחָפְזָם);—**1.** *be in a hurry* or *alarm*, of hurried flight 2 S 4^{4} 2 K 7^{15}; *Inf.* c. בְּ = noun, *in my alarm* ψ 31^{23} 116^{11}; *be alarmed* Dt 20^{3} (‖תיראו), Jb 40^{23} (of hippopot.) **Niph.** *Pf.* נֶחְפָּזוּ ψ 48^{6} (‖נִבְהֲלוּ) *hurry away in alarm;* so *Impf.* יֵחָפֵזוּן ψ 104^{7} (‖ יְנוּסוּן); *Inf.* הֵחָפְזָם 2 K 7^{15} Kt v. *supr.*; *Pt.* נֶחְפָּז 1 S 23^{26} *hurried* ויהי דוד נ׳ ללכת *and David became hurried to go.*

†חִפָּזוֹן **n.[m.] trepidation, hurried flight** (Lag^BN 200)—always בְּח׳ Ex 12^{11} (P), Dt 16^{3} Is 52^{12} (‖ מְנוּסָה).

חֻפִּים v. sub חפף.

חפן (√of foll.; Ar. حَفَنَ *take with both hands*, حَفْنَةٌ *handful;* NH חָפַן, Aram. חֲפַן *fill the hands* with).

†[חֹפֶן] **n.[m.] hollow of hand** (NH חוֹפֶן, Aram. חָפְנָא, חוּפְנָא, ܚܘܦܢܐ; Eth. ሕፍን:—also Ar. حُفْنَةٌ *hollow in the ground;* and, acc. to Zehnpfund^BAS i. 635, As. *ḫupunnu, bowl*, but ḫ = ح ?)—only du. חָפְנַיִם Ec 4^{6}; cstr. חָפְנֵי Ez 10^{7} (del. Co intern. grounds); sf. חָפְנֶיךָ Ez 10^{2}; חָפְנָיו Lv 16^{2} Pr 30^{4}; חָפְנֵיכֶם Ex 9^{8}; מְלֹא ח׳ Ez 10^{2} + v^{7} (del. Co cf. supr.);—מְלֹא ח׳ = *handful* Ex 9^{8} Lv 16^{12} (both P), Ec 4^{6}, material follows in implic. acc.; מי־אסף רוח בח׳ Pr 30^{4}.

†חָפְנִי **n.pr.m.** (Sab. n.pr. חפן Hal^No 14)—one of Eli's two sons 1 S 1^{3} 2^{34} $4^{4.11.17}$.

†I. [חָפַף] **vb. enclose, surround, cover** (Ar. حَفَّ, *surround*, حِفَافٌ *side*, or *border* of a thing)—only **Qal** *Pt.* חֹפֵף עָלָיו Dt 33^{12} (poem) he (י׳) *is covering him over*, fig. of י׳'s sheltering Benj. (in temple; on omission of subj. v. Ges^§ 116. 5. R. 3).

†חוֹף **n.[m.] shore, coast** (as *surrounding, enclosing*)—ח׳ only cstr. Gn $49^{13.13}$ + 5 t.:—*shore of sea* ח׳ הַיָּם Dt 1^{7} Jos 9^{1} (both D), Ju 5^{17} Je 47^{7} Ez 25^{16}; ח׳ יַמִּים Gn 49^{13} (poem); ח׳ אֳנִיּוֹת v^{13} *the shore of ships*, i.e. to which ships come.

†I. חֻפָּה **n.f. canopy, chamber** (as *covering, enclosing*)—abs. ח׳ Is 4^{5}; sf. חֻפָּתוֹ ψ 19^{6}; חֻפָּתָהּ Jo 2^{16};—**1.** *canopy*, עַל־כָּל־כָּבוֹד ח׳ Is 4^{5} *over all glory a canopy* (for protection). **2.** *chamber*, of bridegroom ψ 19^{6} (metaph. of sun rising); of bride Jo 2^{16} (‖ חֶדֶר of bridegroom).

†II. חֻפָּה **n.pr.m.** 1 Ch 24^{13} priest of 13th course, 𝔊 Οφφα.

†חֻפִּים **n.pr.m.** a son of Benjamin Gn 46^{21} (𝔊 Οφιμ(ε)ιν, Οφμειν), descendant of Benjamin 1 Ch 7^{15} (𝔊 Αμφειν, Αφφειν, 𝔊L Οφερ), and so חֻפִּם v^{15}; v. חוּפָם.

II. חפף (NH חָפַף; Aram. חֲפַף, ܚܦ, ܚܦܦ, all *rub, cleanse*, esp. the head).

†חַף **adj. clean**—only זַךְ אֲנִי בְּלִי פָשַׁע חַף אָנֹכִי Jb 33^{9} *I am pure, without transgression, I am clean* (in speech of Elihu).

†חָפֵץ **vb. delight in** (cf. Ar. حَفِظَ *be mindful of, attentive to, keep, protect*, Aram. ܚܦܛ whence ܚܦܝܛ *eager, zealous*, Ar. حَفِيظَةٌ *anger* (excitement), أَحْفَظَ *enrage* (Aram. and Ar. of *excited* attention, Heb. of *delighted* attention), Dl^Pr 168 Nö^ZMG 1886, 742; NH חֵפֶץ weakened to *thing*, v. De^Ec. Gloss., Ph. in n.pr. חפצבעל);—**Qal** *Pf.* ח׳ Gn 34^{19} + 28 t.; f. חָפְצָה Is 66^{3}; 2 m. חָפַצְתָּ Dt 21^{14} + 4 t.; חָפָצְנוּ Jb 21^{14}, etc., + 14 t. Pf.; *Impf.* יַחְפֹּץ Dt 25^{7} + 7 t.; יֶחְפָּץ ψ 37^{23} 147^{10}; pl. יַחְפְּצוּ Is 13^{17} Je 6^{10}; יֶחְפָּצוּ ψ 68^{31}; יֶחְפָּצוּן Is $58^{2.2}$ etc. + 9 t. Impf.; *Inf. abs.* חָפֹץ Ez 18^{23}; on *Pt.* חָפֵץ = adj. verb., v. infr.;—**1.** of *men:* **a.** *take pleasure in, delight in*, c. בְּ, a woman Gn 34^{19} (J), Dt 21^{14} Est 2^{14}; a man 1 S 18^{22} 19^{1} 2 S 20^{11}; in matters and things 2 S 24^{3} Is 13^{17} 66^{3} Je 6^{10} ψ 109^{17} 112^{1} 119^{35} Pr 18^{2} Est $6^{6.7.9.9.11}$; c. acc. ψ 68^{31} Is 58^{2} Ec 8^{3}; implic. obj. ψ 73^{25}. **b.** *delight, desire, be pleased* to do a thing, *would* do it Dt $25^{7.8}$ 1 K 9^{1} Est 6^{6} Ru 3^{13} ψ 40^{9} Jb 9^{3} 13^{3} 21^{14} 33^{32} Is 58^{2} Je 42^{22}. **c.** abs. עַד שֶׁתֶּחְפָּץ *until it please* (of love) Ct 2^{7} 3^{5} 8^{4}. **2.** *of God:* **a.** *delight in, have pleasure in*, c. בְּ, persons Nu 14^{8} (J), 2 S 15^{26} 22^{20} = ψ 18^{20}, 1 K 10^{9} = 2 Ch 9^{8}, ψ 22^{9} 41^{12} Is 62^{4}; not in the strength of a horse ψ 147^{10}; in doing evil Mal 2^{17}; in the death of the sinner Ez 18^{32} 33^{11}; but in mercy, justice, and righteousness Je 9^{23}; בחר באשר (לא) חפצתי Is 56^{4} 65^{12} 66^{4}; not with (acc.) the blood of bullocks Is 1^{11}; זבח(ים) ψ 40^{7} $51^{18.21}$, or the death of the sinner Ez $18^{23.23}$; but with חסד Ho 6^{6} Mi 7^{18}, אמת

ψ 51^{8}; with the way of a man ψ 37^{23}; כל אשר חפץ ψ 115^{3} 135^{6} Pr 21^{1}; אשר חפץ Is 55^{11} Jon 1^{14} **b.** *pleased* to do a thing c. inf. Ju 13^{23} 1 S 2^{25} Is 53^{10}. **c.** with impf subj. (Ges $^{§120(2)c}$) יהוה חפץ ינדיל תורה *Yahweh was pleased to magnify teaching* Is 42^{21} —On Jb 40^{17} v. חָפֵץ.

†**חָפֵץ adj. verb. delighting in, having pleasure in**;—ח׳ ψ 5^{5} + 4 t; pl. חֲפֵצִים Mal 3^{1} Ne 1^{11}; cstr. חֲפֵצֵי ψ 35^{27} + 2 t., sf. חָפְצֵיהֶם ψ 111^{2}; f. חֲפֵצָה 1 Ch 28^{9},—**1.** *of man*, c. acc. ψ 34^{13} 35^{27} Mal 3^{1}; c. inf. Ne 1^{11}, abs. הֶחָפֵץ *whosoever would* 1 K 13^{33}, אם חפץ אתה *if thou pleasest* 1 K 21^{6}, נֶפֶשׁ חֲפֵצָה *willing soul* 1 Ch 28^{9}; pl. cstr before nouns abs ψ 35^{27} 40^{15} = 70^{3}; דְּרוּשִׁים לְכָל־חֶפְצֵיהֶם *studied of all who take pleasure in them* ψ 111^{2} **2.** *of God*, לֹא אֵל־ חָפֵץ רֶשַׁע אָתָּה *thou art not a God taking pleasure in wickedness* ψ 5^{5}.

†**חֵפֶץ n m.** $^{Pr 3, 15}$ **delight, pleasure**,—ח׳ Is 54^{12} + 20 t; sf. חֶפְצְךָ Is 58^{13} etc. + 13 t. sfs, pl. חֲפָצִים Pr 8^{11}, sf. חֲפָצֶיךָ Pr 3^{15}, חֲפָצֶךָ Is 58^{13}— **1.** *delight* אבני ח׳ Is 54^{12} *delightful stones;* אֶרֶץ ח׳ Mal 3^{12} *delightsome land;* דִּבְרֵי ח׳ Ec 12^{10}, so perhaps also בגדי ח׳ Ez 27^{20} *garments of delight*, i e of beauty and luxury (Gr; MT חֹפֶשׁ q. v.), c. ב of persons ψ 16^{3} Ec 5^{3} Mal 1^{10}; of things 1 S 15^{22} 18^{25} ψ 1^{2} Jb 21^{21} Ec 12^{1}; כְּלִי אין חפץ בו *vessel wherein is no pleasure* Je 22^{28} 48^{38} Ho 8^{8}; הַחֵפֶץ לְשַׁדַּי כִּי Jb 22^{3} *is it a pleasure to Shadday that?* **2.** *desire, longing* מנע מח׳ דלים Jb 31^{16} *withhold the poor from (their) desire;* מחוז חֶפְצָם *the city of their desire* ψ 107^{30}; כל חפץ *all (one's) desire* 2 S 23^{5} 1 K $5^{22.23.24}$ 9^{11}, 10^{13} = 2 Ch 9^{12}; כל חפצים *all things to be desired* Pr 3^{15} 8^{11}. **3.** *the good pleasure, will, purpose*, of Yahweh Is 44^{28} 46^{10} 48^{14}. **4.** *that in* which one takes delight, his *business* (late), or *matter* (very late, cf. in Mish. = *thing*) חֵפֶץ י׳ בְּיָדוֹ יִצְלָח *the good pleasure (cause, business) of Yahweh will prosper in his hands* Is 53^{10}, מצא ח׳ Is $58^{3.13}$; עֲשׂוֹת חֲפָצֶךָ *doing thy affairs* Is 58^{13} (see De in loco), בְּחֵפֶץ כַּפֶּיהָ *in the business of her hands* Pr 31^{13}; עֵת לְכָל־חֵפֶץ *time for every matter, affair* Ec $3^{1.17}$ 8^{6}; אַל־ תִּתְמַה עַל־הַחֵפֶץ *marvel not at the matter* Ec 5^{7}.

Note—חפץ is not used in any of its forms in E D² H P of the Hexateuch.

†**חֶפְצִי־בָהּ n.pr.f.** (*my delight is in her;* cf. Ph. חפצבעל)—**1.** mother of king Manasseh 2 K 21^{1}. **2.** fig. name of Zion Is 62^{4}, here expl. by כי חפץ יהוה בָּךְ *for Yahweh delighteth in thee.*

† [**חָפֵץ**] **vb.** bend down (Ar. حَفَضَ *lower, depress*, as wings Qor 15^{88})—only **Qal** *Impf.* יַחְפֹּץ זְנָבוֹ כְמוֹ־אָרֶז Jb 40^{17}, *he bendeth down (extendeth down stiffly) his tail like a cedar,* v. Wetzst in De $^{Job 526}$ Hi $^{Hiob 299}$.

† I. **חָפַר vb. dig, search for** (Ar. حَفَرَ *id.;* Aram. חֲפַר, ܚܦܰܪ, *id.;* NH חֲפַר *act of digging*) —**Qal** *Pf.* ח׳ Jb 39^{29}, חָפַרְתָּ Jb 11^{18}, חָפַרְתָּה Dt 23^{14}; חָפַרְתִּי Gn 21^{30}; חָפְרוּ Gn 26^{18} + 2 t; חֲפָרוּהָ Gn 26^{32}; חֲפָרוּהָ Nu 21^{18}; *Impf.* וַיַּחְפֹּר Gn $26^{18.22}$; וָאֶחְפֹּר Je 13^{7}; וַיַּחְפְּרוּהוּ ψ 7^{16}; יַחְפְּרוּ Jb Jb 39^{21} (but rd. יַחְפֹּר so 𝔊 𝔅 𝔖 Di) Dt 1^{22}; וַיַּחְפְּרוּ Gn 26^{19} + 2 t., וַיַּחְפְּרֻהוּ Jb 3^{21}, *Inf. cstr* לַחְפֹּר Jos $2^{2.3}$ + Is 2^{20} (cf. infr.); *Pt* חפר Ec 10^{8}; —**1.** *dig:* **a.** a well, c. acc. בְּאֵר Gn 21^{30} (E), $26^{15.18.18.19.21.22.32}$ (J), Nu 21^{18} (E); cf. Ex 7^{24} (E); *dig* (a hole, implied as obj) Dt 23^{14}, a pit, with hostile purpose, as snare or trap, fig. of malicious plan, c acc. בּוֹר ψ 7^{16} (כָּרָה ‖); so c. acc נומץ Ec 10^{8}, cf [שַׁחַת] ח׳ לְנַפְשִׁי ψ 35^{7}; of horse, *dig*, i. e *paw* the ground, יַחְפֹּר בָּעֵמֶק Jb 39^{21} (so rd, v supr) *he paweth in the valley* (cf. Ar. حَافِرٌ *hoof*). **b.** *dig* for something hidden, c. acc. Jb 3^{21} (fig. of longing for death), Je 13^{7} (no obj expr) **2.** *search, search out, explore,* c. acc. הָאָרֶץ Jos $2^{2.3}$ (JE), Dt 1^{22}; of eagle, *search for* food, c. acc ח׳ אכל Jb 39^{29}, with esp. reference to keen vision (מֵרָחוֹק עֵינָיו יַבִּיטוּ ‖); so = *search* or *look carefully about* before going to rest Jb 11^{18} (no obj)—לַחְפֹּר Is 2^{20} v. חֲפַרְפָּרָה infr.

† I. **חֵפֶר n.pr.m. 1.** a Manassite Nu $26^{32.33}$ 27^{1} Jos $17^{2.3}$, 𝔊 Οφερ **2.** a man of Judah 1 Ch 4^{6}; 𝔊 Ηφαλ, 𝔊L Αφερ **3.** one of David's heroes, acc. to 1 Ch 11^{36} (but on txt. v. Be VB and Dr 2 S 23^{36}).

†**חֶפְרִי adj. gent.** of I. חֵפֶר **a**; only c. art. as n pr. coll הַח׳ Nu 26^{32}.

† II **חֵפֶר n.pr.loc. 1.** Canaanitish town, with a king, named just before Aphek Jos 12^{17}, exact site unknown. **2.** 1 K 4^{10} in Judah (ארץ ח׳),—on גִּתָּה ח׳ Jos 19^{13}, גַּת הַח׳ 2 K 14^{25}, v. sub גַּת יגן.

†**חֲפָרַיִם n.pr.loc.** in Issachar Jos 19^{19}, 𝔊 Αγειν, A Αφεραειμ, 𝔊L Αμφαραιμ, = Egypt Ḥa-pu-ru-m-â WMM $^{Asien. 170}$, site dub; 6 m. N. of *Legio* acc. to Lag $^{Onom 223, 2nd ed 241}$.

†[חֲפַרְפָּרָה] **n.f.** mole (as *digger*)—only Is 2^{20}, rd. לַחֲפַרְפָּרוֹת (MT לַחְפֹּר פֵּרוֹת, meaning obscure, **v.** conject in Thes Ges^{Comm} Di)

†II [חָפֵר] **vb. be abashed, ashamed** (𝔗 חֲפַר Pr 13^5, מַחְפַּרְנָא *one causing shame* Pr 19^{26}; Syr سحف, esp Aph *be ashamed, put to shame*, Ar خَفِرَ *be bashful*, خَفِرٌ *shy, bashful*, Eth. ኀፍረ: *be ashamed, blush*)—**Qal** *Pf.* 3 fs חָפְרָה Je 50^{12}, וְחָפְרָה consec Is 24^{23}, חָפְרָה Je 15^9, חָפְרוּ ψ 71^{24}; וְחָפְרוּ consec Mi 3^7; *Impf* יַחְפְּרוּ ψ 35^4+4 t., יֶחְפָּרוּ ψ 34^6, וַיֶּחְפָּרוּ Jb 6^{20}, תַּחְפְּרוּ Is 1^{29},—*be abashed, ashamed*, said of face ψ 34^6 (avoided by looking to י׳), elsewhere always ‖ בּוֹשׁ, of enemies of righteousness ψ 71^{24} $35^{4.26}$ 40^{15}=70^3 83^{18}, of idolaters Is 1^{29}, diviners Mi 3^7, of distressed Jerusalem Je 15^9, so of Babylon 50^{12}, of moon Is 24^{23}, *be put to shame* (disappointment), of caravans looking for water Jb 6^{20}. **Hiph.** *Pf* הֶחְפִּיר Is 33^9, *Impf* יַחְפִּיר Pr 13^5; תַּחְפִּירִי Is 54^4; *Pt* מַחְפִּיר Pr 19^{26},—*display shame*, fig. of Lebanon Is 33^9 (‖ קָמַל 'dried up' Che); of Israel Is 54^4 (‖ בּוֹשׁ Qal), of an unfilial son, *cause shame* Pr 19^{26} (‖ מֵבִישׁ); cf Pr 13^5 of wicked (‖ יַבְאִישׁ. v. באשׁ **Hiph.** supr. p. 93)

†חָפְרַע **n.pr.m. Apries**, reigned in Egypt alone, B C. 589–570 and with Amasis 570–564; named as פַּרְעֹה ח׳ מֶלֶךְ־מִצְרַיִם Je 44^{30} *Pharaoh Hophra' king of Egypt* (v. פַּרְעֹה), 4th king of 26th dynasty, 𝔊 Οὐαφρη, Manetho Οὐαφρις; Egypt Monum *Uah-abra*, Wiedemann$^{Aegypt. Gesch. 602, 636 ff, Gesch Ägypt 163 ff.}$; Gk Ἀπρίης Herodot ii 161 etc (v. Wied$^{Herodot's\ 2tes\ Buch, 569}$), Diodor$^{i\ 68}$, Ἀπρίας Ctesias (Athen. 13^{560})

חֲפַרְפָּרָה v sub I. חפר

†[חָפַשׂ] **vb. search** (𝔗^{Jer} חֲפַס *dig, seek*, Pal Syr. *dig* (Schw), perh As *êppêšu, êtpêšu, sensible*, Lyon$^{Sargontexte\ 65}$)—**Qal** *Impf* 2 ms. sf תַּחְפְּשֶׂנָּה Pr 2^4, יַחְפְּשׂוּ ψ 64^7; נַחְפְּשָׂה La 3^{40}; *Pt* חֹפֵשׂ Pr 20^{27},—*search, search out*, fig.; **1.** *search for*, obj בִּינָה etc. Pr 2^4 (‖ בִּקֵּשׁ). **2.** =*think out, devise*, c acc עוֹלֹת unjust acts ψ 64^7 (cf. also sub **Pu**) **3.** *search*=*test*, La 3^{40} (obj דְּרָכֵינוּ, ‖ חקר), Pr 20^{27} **Niph.** *Pf* נֶחְפְּשׂוּ Ob^6 subj עֵשָׂו coll.; *searched out*=exposed and plundered (‖ נִבְעוּ מַצְפֻּנָיו). **Pi.** *Pf.* וְחִפַּשְׂתִּי 1 S 23^{23}, וְחִפְּשׂוּ 1 K 20^6; *Impf* וַיְחַפֵּשׂ Gn 31^{35}+2 t, אֲחַפֵּשׂ Am 9^3 Zp 1^{12}; *Imv.* חַפְּשׂוּ 2 K 10^{23},—**1.** *search through*, c acc, a house 1 K 20^6, Jerusalem (metaph.) Zp 1^{12}, no obj expr 2 K 10^{23}. **2.** *search for*: **a.** a person c acc 1 S 23^{23}. **b.** a thing, c. acc. Gn 44^{12} (J; Joseph searching for his cup); Gn 31^{35} (E; no obj expr, Laban looking for his teraphim); Am 9^3 (י׳ searching for evildoers), ψ 77^7 (soul searching to understand י׳'s dealings with his servants). **Pu.** *Impf.* יְחֻפַּשׂ Pr 28^{12} *be searched for*=be hidden; *Pt* מְחֻפָּשׂ ψ 64^7 in ח׳ מ׳=*a searched out search*, i e a device well thought out (cf Che; ‖ **Qal** q v.); v also חֵפֶשׂ. **Hithp.** *Pf* הִתְחַפֵּשׂ 2 Ch 35^{22} (but 𝔊 הִתְחַזֵּק, cf also 𝔙 𝔖 3 Esdr 1^{26}, so Be Ot); *Impf.* יִתְחַפֵּשׂ Jb 30^{18}, וַיִּתְחַפֵּשׂ 1 S 28^8+3 t; *Inf. abs* הִתְחַפֵּשׂ 1 K 22^{30}=2 Ch 18^{29};—*disguise oneself* (lit *let oneself be searched for*) 1 S 28^8 1 K $22^{30.30}$=2 Ch $18^{29.29}$, 2 Ch 35^{22} (but v supr), all of disguise by change of garments; 1 K 20^{38} בָּאֲפֵר i e. with headgear over eyes; subj לְבוּשׁ Jb 30^{18}, i e his garment is disguised, no longer looks like the mantle it is.

†חֵפֶשׂ **n** [**m.**] **a (shrewd) device, plot**, only in תָּמְנוּ ח׳ מְחֻפָּשׂ ψ 64^7 (cf. חָפַשׂ supr.)

†[חָפַשׁ] **vb. be free**—only **Pu.** *Pf.* 3 fs. כִּי לֹא חֻפָּשָׁה Lv 19^{20} (H), *because she was not freed* (a freed-woman)

†חֹפֶשׁ **n.**[**m.**] very dub; only בִּגְדֵי־חֹפֶשׁ לְרִכְבָּה Ez 27^{20} *wide-spread* (?) *garments for riding*, i e. saddle-cloths, acc to Thes Sm Co Da al, but mng. *spread* for √ purely conject.; Gr suggests, plausibly, חֵפֶץ (q v)

†חֻפְשָׁה **n.f. freedom**, only ח׳ לֹא נִתַּן־לָהּ Lv 19^{20} (H) *freedom had not been given to her.*

†חָפְשִׁי **adj. free** (NH *id*)—ח׳ Ex 21^5+10 t.+ψ 88^6; pl. חָפְשִׁים Is 58^6+4 t.—**1.** *free* from slavery: of Hebrew bondslave (male or female) set free in 7th year Ex $21^{2.5}$ (JE), Dt $15^{12.13.18}$, cf Je $34^{9.10.11.14.16}$; of slave (male or female) set free on account of injury done Ex $21^{26.27}$ (JE), עֶבֶד ח׳ מֵאֲדֹנָיו Jb 3^{19} *a slave is free from his master* (i.e in She'ôl); but בַּמֵּתִים חָפְשִׁי ψ 88^6 *among the dead* I am *free* (i.e. adrift, cut off from Yahweh's remembrance); more gen, שַׁלַּח רְצוּצִים חָפְשִׁים Is 58^6 *to let oppressed ones go free.* **2.** *free* from taxes, obligations, etc. אֶת בֵּית אָבִיו יַעֲשֶׂה חָפְשִׁי בְּיִשְׂרָאֵל 1 S 17^{25} '*his father's house will he make free in Israel.*

†חָפְשִׁית, חפשׁוּת **n.f.** freedom, separateness, only בֵּית הַחָפְשִׁית 2 K 15^{5} = 2 Ch 26^{21} Qr (Kt החפשות) i.e. (si vera l.) a separate house—a house apart (on account of his disease).

חֵץ v. sub חצץ.

†[חָצַב] חָצֵב **vb.** hew, hew out, cleave (NH *id.*, Aram. חֲצַב, SI$^{4.6}$ pt. pl החצבם; cf. Ph. מחצב = Heb. *id*)—**Qal** *Pf.* חָצַב Is 5^{2}; חָצְבָה Pr 9^{1}; חָצַבְתִּי Ho 6^{5}, etc.; *Impf.* וַיַּחְצֹב 2 Ch 26^{10}; 2 ms. תַּחְצֹב Dt 8^{9}; *Inf. cstr.* לַחְצֹב Je 2^{13}; לַחְצוֹב 1 Ch 22^{2}; *Pt. act* חֹצֵב Is 10^{15} + 4 t., cstr. חֹצְבִי Is 22^{16}, חֹצְבִים 1 Ch 22^{2} + 3 t.; חֹצְבֵי 2 K 12^{13}; pass. חֲצוּבִים Dt 6^{11} Ne 9^{25},—**1.** *hew out, (dig)*, wine-vat יֶקֶב Is 5^{2}; sepulchre (קֶבֶר) Is 22$^{16.16}$; cisterns בֹּרוֹת Dt 6^{11} ^{11} 2 Ch 26^{10} Ne 9^{25}, cf. Je 2^{13}; of mining מהרריה תח׳ נחשת Dt 8^{9} *out of its mountains thou mayst hew out copper.* **2. a.** *hew* stone 1 Ch 22^{2}, metaph. of pillars Pr 9^{1} (subj wisdom); elsewhere pt., *hewer* of stone 2 K 12^{13} 1 Ch 22$^{2.15}$ (v SI$^{4.6}$ supr.); prob. 1 K 5^{29} 2 Ch 2$^{1.17}$ (ח׳ בָּהָר v Be), cf. 24^{12} Ezr 3^{7}. **b.** appar. *hew wood* Is 10^{15} ח׳ בּוֹ (i.e. בַּגַּרְזֶן). **3.** metaph. *hew in pieces* Ho 6^{5} fig. of י׳ attacking people by agency of prophets (‖ הֲרַגְתִּים); *divide, cleave* subj. י׳'s voice ψ 29^{7} obj. להבות אשׁ, i.e. the thunder of his voice sends forked lightnings (but on txt. cf. Che and crit. n.) **Niph.** *Impf.* יֵחָצְבוּן *be cut, hewn, graven* (words on rock) Jb 19^{24}. **Pu.** *Pf.* חֻצַּבְתֶּם Is 51^{1} fig., *hewn* out of rock (of Isr.'s origin; ‖ נֻקַּר). **Hiph.** *Pt.* מַחְצֶבֶת Is 51^{9} *hew in pieces* = **Qal 3**, fig. of destroying רהב = Egypt (cf. ψ 89^{11})

†מַחְצֵב **n.** [**m.**] hewing, alw. אַבְנֵי מ׳ = *hewn stones* 2 K 12^{13} 22^{6} = 2 Ch 34^{11} (in all ‖ עֵצִים).

†חָצָה **vb.** divide (NH *id.*; Ar. حَظِيَ is *be fortunate, happy* with one's husband or wife, etc., i.e. have a *share* in happiness, حُظْوَةٌ *a small arrow;* Di^{134} puts here Eth. ሐጽ: *arrow*, cf. חֵצִי)—**Qal** *Pf.* חָצָה Nu 31^{42}; וְחָצִית consec. Nu 31^{27}; וְחָצוּ consec. Ex 21^{35}; *Impf.* יֶחֱצֶה Is 30^{28}; וַיַּחַץ Gn 32^{8} + 2 t.; וַיֶּחֱצֵם Ju 9^{43}; יֶחֱצוּ ψ 55^{24}, יֶחֱצוּן Ex 21^{35}; יֶחֱצוּהוּ Jb 40^{30},—**1.** *divide*, sq. כֶּסֶף Ex 21^{35}; שׁוֹר v^{35} (both JE), לִוְיָתָן crocodile Jb 40^{30}; prey, מלקוח, Nu 31^{27} (P; c. לְ before parts); a company of people Gn 32^{8} (sq. לְ as foreg.), 33^{1} (both J) Ju 9^{43} (לְ as foreg.) but cf. 7^{16}. **2.** (appar. denom. fr. חֵצִי) ψ 55^{24} לא יח׳ ימיהם *shall not halve their days*, i.e. enjoy even half of the normal number; Is 30^{28} עד צואר יח׳ *shall halve unto the neck* = shall reach to the neck and so divide the man in half. **Niph.** *Impf.* 3 fs. apoc תֵּחָץ Dn 11^{4} *be divided* (of kingdom), sq. לְ, ולא יֵחָצוּ עוד לשׁני גוים Ez 37^{22} (Judah and Isr.); waters of Jordan 2 K 2$^{8.14}$.

†[חָצוֹת] **n.f.** (Inf. form) division, middle—only cstr. חֲצוֹת הַלַּיְלָה Ex 11^{4} (J) = *midnight;* חֲצוֹת לַיְלָה Jb 34^{20} ψ 119^{62}; in all = adverb. phr. of time (בְּ om.)

חֵצִי$_{123}$ **n.m.**$^{Nu\ 12.12}$ half (NH *id.*; Ph. חצי; on format. v. Lag$^{BN\ 113}$)—abs חֵצִי 1 K 3$^{25.25}$ + 3 t., הַחֵצִי 1 K 10^{7}, cf. 16^{21}; וְחֵצִי Ez 40^{42}, וָחֵצִי Dn 12^{7} + 13 t. (usu. c Pashta or Tiphcha), cf. בַּחֲצִי 2 S 10^{4} 1 Ch 19^{4}; cstr. חֲצִי Ex 12^{29} + 84 t.; sf חֶצְיוֹ Ex 38^{4} + 7 t. + Jos 8^{33} וְהֶחֶצְיוֹ (but art suspicious v. Ges$^{§127\ R3,4}$); חֶצְיָהּ Ne 3^{38}; חֶצְיֵנוּ 2 S 18^{3}; חֶצְיָם Zc 14$^{8.8}$ + 2 t.—**1.** *half* of anything:—blood of offering Ex 24$^{6.6}$ (JE), beard 2 S 10^{4}, a hin Nu 15$^{9.10}$ 28^{14} (P); curtain Ex 26^{12} (P); week ח׳ השׁבוע Dn 9^{27} etc.; ח׳ אַמָּה *half a cubit* Ex 26^{16} 36^{21} (P) +; esp. ח׳ שׁבט *half a tribe* Nu 32^{33} 34$^{13.14.15}$ (P) +; half of people 2 S 18^{3} 19^{41} 1 K 16$^{21.21.21}$ +, etc. so ח׳ הַמְּנֻחוֹת 1 Ch 2^{52} and ח׳ הַמָּנַחְתִּי v^{54} (v. Be and מָנַחַת sub נוח).—On כבחצי 1 S 14^{4} v. We Dr. **2.** *middle* ח׳ הלילה Ex 12^{29} (J) *midnight*, so Ju 16$^{3.3}$ Ru 3^{8}; of garments 2 S 10^{4} 1 Ch 19^{4}; altar Ex 27^{5}; of the Mt. of Olives Zc 14^{4}; ח׳ יָמַי ψ 102^{25} *the midst of my days* (when they are but half done), Je 17^{11}.

חֲצִי הַמְּנֻחוֹת 1 Ch 2^{52}, and חֲצִי הַמָּנַחְתִּי v^{54}, v. מָנַחַת sub נוח.

†חֵצִי **n.m.**$^{2\ K\ 9.24}$ arrow (cf. Ar. حُظْوَةٌ, Eth. ሐጽ: *id.*, Di^{134}, and v. Dr on 1 S 20^{36})—abs. הַחֵצִי 1 S 20$^{36.37.37}$ + v^{38} Kt (Qr הַחִצִּים), perh. also v$^{21.22}$ (so 𝔊 We, for MT pl. הַחִצִּים), 2 K 9^{24}; the usual form is חֵץ; v. infr.

†יַחְצְאֵל, יַחְצִיאֵל **n.pr.m.** (*God divideth, apportioneth*)—son of Naphtali; יַחְצְ׳ Gn 46^{24} (𝔊 Ασιηλ, 𝔊L Ιασβηλ), Nu 26^{48} (Σαηλ, Ασιηλ) = יַחְצִי׳ 1 Ch 7^{13} (Ιεισιηλ, 𝔊L Ιασσιηλ).

†יַחְצְאֵלִי **adj.gent.** of foregoing; only c. art. as n pr coll, Nu 26^{48}.

†מֶחֱצָה **n.f.** half, of spoils;—abs מֶחֱצָה Nu 31^{36}; cstr מֶחֱצַת Nu 31^{43} (both P).

†מַחֲצִית **n.f.** half, middle—cstr. מַחֲצִית

Ex $30^{13.13}$+8 t, מַחֲצִית Nu $31^{30.47}$; sf. מַחֲצִיתוֹ Ex 30^{23}, מַחֲצִיתָהּ Lv $6^{13.13}$, מַחֲצִיתָם Nu 31^{29}—**1.** *half* of a shekel Ex $30^{13.15.15}$ cf v^{23} 38^{26}; the flour for offering Lv $6^{13.13}$, of spoils Nu $31^{29.30.42.47}$, of tribe Jos 21^{25} (all P), 1 Ch $6^{46.55}$; of chariots 1 K 16^{9} **2.** *middle* מ׳ היום=*midday, noon* Ne 8^{3} (cf *midnight*, חֲצוֹת, חצי **2**)

חצן (√of foll, meaning dub; denom seem to be Ar حَضَنَ, Eth. ሐፀነ: *carry in the arms* or *bosom, rear, foster;* perhaps also As *êsênu, bring together*, also *drink* or *draw in* sweet odours Flood Tablet $^{iii.49}$ Hpt in KAT$^{2\,Gloss\,i}$)

†[**חֹצֶן**] **n.m** bosom of a garment (Ar حِضْنٌ, Eth. ሕፅን: also Syr ܥܘܒܐ *bosom* (=ܚܨܢܐ*), v Hoffm$^{ZMG\,1878,\,753}$ Lag$^{M\,ii\,361\,ff,\,BN\,46\,f.}$; on this word and foll. v Ba$^{NB\,120,\,ZMG\,1889,\,183}$)—שֶׁלֹּא מִלֵּא כַפּוֹ קוֹצֵר וְחִצְנוֹ מְעַמֵּר ψ 129^{7} (grass) *with which a reaper filleth not his hand, nor a binder his bosom*

†**חֹצֶן** **n.m.** **bosom**,—חָצְנִי נָעַרְתִּי Ne 5^{13} *I shook out my bosom* (the bosom of my garment), והביאו בָנַיִךְ בְּחֹצֶן Is 49^{22} *and they shall bring thy sons in the bosom* (i e. in the arms, clasped to the bosom, like infants, ‖ עַל־כָּתֵף)

†I [**חָצַץ**] **vb. divide** (NH *make a partition;* As. *ḫaṣâṣu, cut in two*, Zim$^{BP\,24\,n}$, Eth ሐጸጸ: *curtail, diminish*)—**Qal** *Pt* חצץ intr Pr 30^{27} of locusts ויצא ח׳ כלו, i e dividing (themselves) into companies or swarms. **Pi.** *Pt* מחצצים v II חצץ. **Pu.** *Pf* מספר חדשיו חֻצָּצוּ Jb 21^{21} *the number of his months, they have been cut in two* (fig for *curtailed*)

†**חָצָץ** **n** [**m.**] **gravel** (as *divided, comminuted;* Aram. חֲצָצָא, ܚܨܨܐ)—only abs ח׳ Pr 20^{17} La 3^{16} [חֲצָצֶיךָ ψ 77^{18} v חֵץ]—ח׳ יִמָּלֵא־פִיהוּ Pr 20^{17} fig of a liar, וַיַּגְרֵס בֶּח׳ שִׁנָּי La 3^{16} *and he hath crushed my teeth with gravel-stones*, fig of י׳'s dealings with sufferer

†**חֵץ** **n.m.** $^{1\,S\,20.20}$ **arrow**, mostly poet. and proph (cf חצי supr sub חצה)—abs ח׳ ψ 91^{5} +9 t + 1 S 17^{7} Kt (Qr עֵץ q v); cstr. *id* 2 K $13^{17.17}$, sf חצי Jb 34^{6}, חִצּוֹ ψ 58^{8} Zc 9^{14}, חִצָּם ψ 11^{2} 64^{4}, *Pl* חִצִּים Gn 49^{23} + 17 t + 1 S 20^{38} Qr (Kt חֵצִי q v) + 2 S 22^{15} (< חִצָּיו ‖ ψ 18^{15}), cstr. חִצֵּי Jb 6^{4} ψ 120^{4} + Ez 5^{16} (Co חִצַּי cf. 𝔊 𝔖 Hi), חִצַּי Dt $32^{23.42}$ (Ez 5^{16} v. supr), חִצֶּיךָ ψ 38^{3} + 4 t; חִצָּיו Is 5^{28} + 5 t,—*arrow*. **1.** lit., shot from bow by hand 1 S $20^{20.21.21.22}$ (𝔊 We sg, i e הַחֵצִי, in $v^{21.22}$, see also Dr) $v^{36.38\,Qr}$ 2 K 19^{32} = Is 37^{33}, Is 5^{28} 7^{24} Je $50^{9.14}$ 51^{11} Ez $39^{3.9}$ 1 Ch 12^{2}; shot from engine of war 2 Ch 26^{15}; used in divination Ez 21^{26} cf. 2 K $13^{15.15.17.17.18}$; בַּעֲלֵי חִצִּים =archers Gn 49^{23}. **2.** fig of Israel's weapons Nu 24^{8}, of the (Messianic) king ψ 45^{6}, of Yahweh's judgments Dt $32^{23.42}$ Jb 6^{4} (cf. חצי=*my wound* 34^{6}), ψ 7^{14} 38^{3} 58^{8} (but on text cf Che$^{crit.\,n}$) 64^{8} 120^{4} (? cf. Che); further Pr 7^{23} La 3^{12} Ez 5^{16}; in theoph ψ 18^{15} = 2 S 22^{15}, cf. Hb 3^{11} Zc 9^{14} ψ 144^{6}, of wicked men's violence ψ 11^{2} cf 91^{5}, under fig of lion's teeth ψ 57^{5}, their words ψ 64^{4} cf. Pr 25^{18} Je 9^{8}, simile, of strength and efficiency derived from one's children, ψ 127^{4}; of a deceiver's words Pr 26^{18}; metaph of servant of י׳ ח׳ בָּרוּר Is 49^{2}.—In 1 S 17^{7} rd עֵץ (for חֵץ) as Qr and ‖ 2 S 21^{19} = *the shaft*, v. עֵץ; so Klo Dr

†**חַצְצוֹן תָּמָר** **n.pr.loc.** (ח׳ *of the palm*);—abode of Amorites Gn 14^{7}, 𝔊 Ασασαν Θαμαρ; חַצְצוֹן תָּמָר הִיא עֵין גֶּדִי 2 Ch 20^{2} base of operations for אֲרָם (rd. אֱדוֹם) ag Judah (vid Jos$^{Ant.\,ix,\,1.2}$); it was on W side of Dead Sea (v. עין גדי); see Rob$^{BR\,i,\,500\text{-}509}$ Bd$^{Pal\,143}$ GASm$^{Geogr\,269\,ff}$; Wady *Ḥuṣâṣâ* (=חצצן?) lies NW. fr Engedi GASm$^{l.c.}$ cf. Rob$^{BR\,i,\,506}$ Bd$^{Pal\,14\,(map)}$; GASm suggests also possibility of finding here תָּמָר 1 K 9^{18} Kt (= תַּדְמֹר Qr and 2 Ch 8^{4}), Ez 47^{19} 48^{28} (v. תָּמָר n.pr.loc.)

† II [**חָצַץ**] **vb denom.** only **Pi.** *Pt* מְחַצְּצִים Ju 5^{11} *archers* (> *those dividing* spoil, since no obj expr. and חלק more suitable for such mng.)

חֲצֹצְרָה, חצצר v. IV. חצר

I. **חצר** (√of foll.; cf Ar حَصَرَ *encompass, surround*, Eth ሐጸረ: *surround, enclose* by wall, etc., ሐጸር: *enclosure*, NH חָצֵר *court*, Ph חצר *id*, Syr ܚܨܪܐ, *id*)

1 **חָצֵר**$_{145}$ **n.m.**$^{Ez\,40.23}$ and (oftener) **f.**$^{1\,K\,8.36}$ **enclosure, court**—abs ח׳ 1 K 7^{8}+, חָצֵרָה Je 36^{20}; cstr. חֲצַר Ex 27^{9}+, sf חֲצֵרוֹ 2 S 17^{18}; חֲצֵרוֹת Ex 8^{9} + 4 t, cstr חַצְרֵי Ne 13^{7}, חַצְרוֹת 2 K 21^{5} + 10 t, sf חֲצֵרַי Is 1^{12} Zc 3^{7}; חֲצֵרֶיךָ ψ 65^{5} 84^{11}; חֲצֵרוֹתַי 1 Ch 28^{6}, חֲצֵרֹתָיו ψ 100^{4}, לְחַצְרוֹתָיו ψ 96^{8}, וּבְחַצְרֹתֵיהֶם Ne 8^{16},—**1.** *enclosures* (in Egypt), perhaps court-yards, or cattle-yards, distinct from houses and from fields Ex 8^{9} (J). **2.** *court* of private house 2 S 17^{18} (containing well), cf Ne 8^{16}; of a palace, חָצֵר הָאַחֶרֶת 1 K 7^{8} *the other court*, immediately surrounding palace, so called in distinct. from (ה)ח׳ הַגְּדוֹלָה $v^{9.12}$ *the great court*, including ח׳ הא׳ and הֶח׳ הַפְּנִימִית of temple (v. **3 b**) in one great enclosure (v.

Sta [Salomos Bauten, ZAW 1883, 152 f]); 2 K 20^{4} (Qr Vrss The Kmp Klo al.; Kt Ke al. הָעִיר), Je 36^{20} Est 1^{5} 2^{11} 4^{11} $5^{1.2}$ $6^{4.4.5}$; ח׳ מַטָּרָה *court of guard*, place of (honourable) confinement Je 32^{2} (in king's house), $v^{8\ 12}$ 33^{1} $37^{21\ 21}$ $38^{6.13.28}$ $39^{14\ 15}$. Esp. **3. a.** *court* of tabernacle חֲצַר הַמִּשְׁכָּן Ex 27^{9}, cf $v^{9.12\ 13}$ + 24 t. Ex (all P; שַׁעַר הח׳ *gate of the court* Ex 35^{17} $38^{15.18.31}$ 39^{40} $40^{8.33}$), Lv $6^{9\ 19}$ Nu $3^{26.26}$ (פֶּתַח הח׳), v^{37} $4^{26.26}$ (פֶּתַח שַׁעַר הַח׳), v^{32}, *courts* of house of י׳ 1 Ch 23^{28}. **b.** *court(s)* of Sol's temple, *inner c* הֶח׳ הַפְּנִימִית 1 K 6^{36} 7^{12} (but on txt. v. Sta [l c]) Ez 8^{16} 10^{3} cf. v^{4}; = *upper c* הֶח׳ הָעֶלְיוֹן Je 36^{10} (v Gf), and ח׳ הַכֹּהֲנִים 2 Ch 4^{9} (where also הָעֲזָרָה הַגְּדוֹלָה, as oft Ezek, also דַּלְתוֹת לָעֲזָרָה); *outer* court הֶח׳ הַחִיצֹנָה Ez 10^{5} = הֶח׳ הַחֲדָשָׁה 2 Ch 20^{5}, v. further 1 K 8^{64} = 2 Ch 7^{7}, 2 Ch 24^{21} 29^{16} Je 19^{14} 26^{2} Ez 8^{7}, *two courts* 2 K 21^{5} = 2 Ch 33^{5}, 2 K 23^{12}; *courts* Ez 9^{7} 1 Ch 28^{12} 2 Ch 23^{5} Ne 8^{16} 13^{7}; oft. poet., *courts* of י׳ Is 1^{12} 62^{9} (ח׳ קדשי), Zc 3^{7} ψ 65^{5} $84^{3\ 11}$ 96^{8} 100^{4} 116^{19} 135^{2}. **c.** *courts* of Ezek.'s temple Ez 40^{14} + 38 t. Ez 40–46 (of these rd. הַשַּׁעַר for החצר $40^{19.32}$ with 𝔊 Hi Co; and החיצון for החצר 41^{15} with 𝔊 Ew Co).

II. חצר (√ of foll; cf Ar حَضَرَ *be present, settle* or *dwell*, v. Lag [BN 47 f.], Sab. חצר *fixed abode* Os (Levy) [ZMG 1863, 189] CIS [iv, 1 2, No 79 8?])

II. [חָצֵר]$_{46}$ **n.m.** [Ne 11 25] **settled abode, settlement, village** (Lag [l c])—always pl, abs. חֲצֵרִים Jos 19^{8} + 5 t; cstr. חַצְרֵי 1 Ch 9^{16} Ne 12^{28}, sf חֲצֵרֶיהָ Jos 21^{12} + 4 t; חצריהם 1 Ch 4^{33} + 6 t; חצריהן Jos 13^{23} + 24 t Jos;—**a.** settlements of Ishmaelites Gn 25^{16} (P, ‖ טירות *circles* of tents); of עַוִּים Dt 2^{23}, of Kedar Is 42^{11} (‖ עָרִים); בָּתֵּי הַחֲצֵרִים אֲשֶׁר אֵין־לָהֶם חֹמָה סָבִיב Lv 25^{31} (H), *houses of the villages which have no wall about them;* מַאְרַב חֲצֵרִים ψ 10^{8} *lurking-place(s) of villages* (i e. where oppressor, as a wild beast, watches his opportunity to attack the defenceless). Usu. **b.** as dependencies of cities Jos 15^{45}, with בְּנֹתֶיהָ (v. supr בַּת **4** p. 123) Jos $15^{45.47\ 47}$ (all JE?); וְכָל־הַח׳ אֲשֶׁר סביבות הֶעָרִים 19^{8} (P), also 21^{12} (P) = 1 Ch 6^{41}, Ne 12^{29}, also Jos $13^{23.28}$ 15^{32} + 23 t. Jos (all P), Ne $11^{25.30}$ (‖ בְּנוֹת $v^{25.27}$ etc), 12^{28} **c.** villages, not contrasted with cities (cf. Is 42^{11} supr.) 1 Ch $9^{16\ 22.25}$ (all of Levites). **d.** ח׳ appar. incl all settlements outside of Jerusalem הַח׳ בִּשְׂדֹתָם Ne 11^{25}.—ח׳ in n pr loc v infr. (and see Bla on Jos 15^{20-32})

† **חֲצַר־אַדָּר** **n.pr.loc.** place on southern border of Canaan (Judah) Nu 34^{4} 𝔊 ἔπαυλις Αραδ; = חֶצְרוֹן (q v.) Jos 15^{3} (+ אַדָּרָה) 𝔊 Σαραδα, A 𝔊L Αδδαρα.

† **חֲצַר גַּדָּה** **n.pr.loc.** in southern Judah Jos 15^{27} 𝔊 Σερει, A 𝔊L Ασεργαδδα.

† **חֲצַר סוּסָה, ח׳ סוּסִים** **n.pr.loc.** (cf *Kefr Susê*, 'Rossdorf,' close to Damascus on the south, No [ZMG, 1875, xxix 476])—in Simeon ח׳ סוסה Jos 19^{5} 𝔊 Σαρσουσειμ, 𝔊L Ασαρσουσιν = ח׳ סוסים 1 Ch 4^{31}, 𝔊 Ἡμισυσεσοραμ, 𝔊L Ασερσουσι.

† **חֲצַר עֵינָן, ח׳ עֵינָן** **n.pr.loc.** on NE. border of Canaan Ez 47^{17}; חֲצַר עֵינָן 48^{1} (Co in both חֲצַרָה עֵינוֹן); ח׳ עֵינָן Nu $34^{9.10}$, where it is said (v^{9}) וְהָיָה לָכֶם גְּבוּל צָפוֹן; 𝔊 Αρσεναιειμ, 𝔊L Ασερναιν,—v. also חֲצַר הַתִּיכוֹן infr.

† **חֲצַר שׁוּעָל** **n.pr.loc.** **1.** place in southern Judah Jos 15^{28} = 1 Ch 4^{28}, Ne 11^{27}. **2.** place in Simeon Jos 19^{3} — 𝔊 Αρσωλα, Χολασεωλα, Ασαρσουλα, Ασαρσουαρ, etc.

† **חֲצַר הַתִּיכוֹן** **n.pr.loc.** Ez 47^{16} 𝔊 Sm Co חֲצַרָה עינון (q v.); it is described as אֲשֶׁר אֶל־גְּבוּל חַוְרָן, Wetzst [ZKW, 1884, v 114] identif. with *Hadar* (حضر) 'at the foot of the eastern corner of Hermon.'

† **חָצוֹר, חֲצֹר** **n.pr.loc.** (Lag [BN 47 f.])—𝔊 Ασωρ, etc; **1.** a royal city of northern Canaan Jos 11^{1} יָבִין מֶלֶךְ־ח׳, cf. 12^{19}, and Ju $4^{2\ 17}$ 1 S 12^{9}; Jos $11^{10\ 10.11\ 13}$ 19^{36} 2 K 15^{29}, חָצֹר 1 K 9^{15}. **2.** places in the Negeb **a.** Jos 15^{23}. **b. c.** Jos 15^{25} וְחָצוֹר חֲדַתָּה וקריות חֶצְרוֹן היא חָצוֹר. **3.** חָצוֹר Ne 11^{33} a Benjamite town, prob = בַּעַל חָצוֹר q.v. **4.** מַמְלְכוֹת חָצוֹר אֲשֶׁר הִכָּה נבוכדראצּוֹר Je 49^{28}, cf. $v^{30.33}$, an Arabian locality, v Winer [BW Hasor] Gf Gie.—עין ח׳ Jos 19^{37}, v. sub עַיִן.

† **חָצוֹר חֲדַתָּה** **n.pr.loc.** (si vera l. perhaps *new Hasôr*, with Aram ת in adj)—Jos 15^{25}, v. חָצוֹר, in *Negeb* of Judah, site unknown.

† I. **חָצִיר** **n.[m.]** **settled abode or haunt** (‖ form of חָצֵר *supr*, or txt. err. for it);—נוה תַנִּים חָצִיר לִבְנוֹת יַעֲנָה Is 34^{13} *a dwelling of jackals (and) a haunt for ostriches;* also בנוה תַנִּים רִבְצָהּ חָצִיר לְקָנֶה וָגֹמֶא 35^{7} *an abode, home, of reeds and rushes* (so Che Di Du al.; others put this under II חָצִיר); Che Du think the v. mutilated, and would emend this line acc. to 34^{13}.

† **חֶצְרוֹ, חֶצְרַי** (**n.pr.m.** cf, Sab. n.pr.m חצר DHM [Epigr Denkm 56])—one of David's heroes, called

the Carmelite, חצרו 2 S 23[35] Kt (חֶצְרַי Qr; 𝔊 Ασαραι) = חֶצְרוֹ 1 Ch 11[37] 𝔊 Ησεραι, Ασαραι, Εσρει.

†חֶצְרֹן, חֶצְרוֹן **n.pr.loc.** et **pers.** (cf. Sab. חצרן n.pr.loc. vel. trib. Hal [No. 661] DHM [ZMG 1883, 15]) —**1. n.pr.loc.** 𝔊 Ασωρων, Ασερων, Εσρωμ: **a.** חֶצְרוֹן Jos 15[3] place in extreme south of Judah, + קְרִיּוֹת = חֲצַר־אַדָּר = אַדָּרָה (q.v.) Nu 34[4]. **b.** חֶצְרוֹן הִיא חָצוֹר Jos 15[25] another town of Judah in south. **2. n.pr.m.** 𝔊 Ασρωμ(ν), Εσρων, etc.: **a.** חֶצְרֹן son of Reuben Gn 46[9] Ex 6[14] Nu 26[6] = חֶצְרוֹן 1 Ch 5[3]. **b.** son of Pereṣ and grandson of Judah Gn 46[12] Nu 26[21] = חֶצְרוֹן Ru 4[18.19] 1 Ch 2[5.9.18.21.24.24.25] 4[1].

†חֶצְרֹנִי, חֶצְרוֹנִי **adj.gent.** only c. art. as n. coll. **1.** הַחֶצְרוֹנִי Nu 26[6], of **2 a** supr. **2.** החצרני v[21], of **2 b** supr.

†חֲצֵרוֹת, חֲצֵרֹת **n.pr.loc.** 𝔊 Ασηρωθ, a station of Isr. in wilderness: חֲצֵרוֹת Nu 11[35.35] 12[16] = חֲצֵרֹת 33[17.18] Dt 1[1].

†חֲצַרְמָוֶת **n.pr.m.** (Ar. حَضْرَمَوْت, Sab. חצרמות, חצֿרמת, Os [ZMG 1865, 239 ff.] DHM [ZMG 1883, 18. 412]) —a 'son' of יָקְטָן, 5th in order from Shem (שֵׁם, 1. אַרְפַּכְשַׁד; 2. שֶׁלַח; 3. עֵבֶר; 4. יָקְטָן; 5. ח׳) Gn 10[26] = 1 Ch 1[20], 𝔊 Ασαρ(α)μωθ; = **n.pr.terr.** a district in southern Arabia, where dwelt the Χατραμωτῖται (Strabo [xvi. 4. 2]); mod. *Ḥaḍramaut* (or *Ḥaḍramût*, see Maltzan [ZMG 1871, 493] Mordt [ZMG 1876, 323], van d. Berg [p. 9], v. infr.) is same land, but not quite co-extensive; v. Di Gn 10[26], Ritter [Erdkunde xii (Arabien i) 609 ff.], de Goeje [Hadhr. 1886], van den Berg [Hadhramout, 1886], Glaser [Skizze ii. 20, 423 ff. etc.]; on its precise limits see esp. Ritter [611 ff.], de Goeje [l. c.] van d. Berg [ch. 1].

III. חצר (√of foll.; Ar. خَضِرَ *be green*).

†II. חָצִיר **n.m.** [Is 15, 6] **green grass, herbage,** abs. חָצִיר Nu 11[5] + 16 t.; cstr. חֲצִיר Is 37[27] = 2 K 19[26], ψ 129[6];—**1.** *grass*, as food for animals 1 K 18[5] Jb 40[15] ψ 104[14] 147[8] Pr 27[25] (‖ דֶּשֶׁא and עֵשֶׂב), Is 15[6] (‖ דֶּשֶׁא and יֶרֶק); spec. of *leeks* (as still sometimes in Aram., v. Löw [pp. 226, 228]) Nu 11[5] (v. Di); in sim. of abundant growth Is 44[4] (v. 𝔊 Ew Che); on Is 35[7] v. I. חָצִיר *supr.* **2.** as type of what is quickly perishing Jb 8[12], hence fig. of perishing enemies חֲצִיר גַּגּוֹת Is 37[27] = 2 K 19[26] (‖ עֵשֶׂב, דֶּשֶׁא), ψ 129[6], i.e. having no depth of root; of wicked, soon to be cut down ψ 37[2]; with special reference to Israel's oppressors Is 40[6] (‖ צִיץ [השׂדה]), v[7] (‖ *id.*), v[7.8] (‖ *id.*), 51[12]; in sim. of frail man ψ 90[5]; man's days ψ 103[15] (‖ צִיץ השׂדה).

IV. חצר (assumed as √ for redupl. חצרצר whence foll.; mng. unknown; perh. onomatop., v. Thes Ol [§ 82 c. 188 a] Sta [§ 124 b]; see also Lag [Or ii. 18]).

†חֲצֹצְרָה **n.f. clarion** (NH חֲצוֹצֶרֶת, Aram. חֲצוֹצְרְתָּא)—mostly P and late;—abs. ח׳ Ho 5[8]; pl. abs. חֲצֹצְרוֹת Nu 10[8] + 22 t.; חֲצֹצְרֹת Nu 10[9.10]; cstr. *id.* Nu 31[6] 2 Ch 13[12]; חֲצוֹצְרֹת Nu 10[2]; *clarion*: **1.** as secular instr. Ho 5[8] (‖ שׁוֹפָר) 2 K 11[14.14] = 2 Ch 23[13.13]. **2.** as sacred instr. 2 K 12[14], esp. for use by priests (only P, ψ 98 and Chr). **a.** תקע בח׳ (of blowing a single long blast) Nu 10[3.4.7.8], to gather congreg. or נשׂיא׳ together, and, on festivals, over sacrif., 'to be remembered before י׳,' v[10]. **b.** תקע תרועה בח׳, or הריע בח׳ (of sounding alarm,—a series of quick blasts) for camps to move Nu 10[5.6], also in battle, v[9], 'to be remembered before י׳;' so Nu 31[6] 2 Ch 13[12] (cf. v[14]), both ח׳ התרועה. **c.** esp. in Chr's descriptions of ceremonies at festivals, to express rejoicing: 1 Ch 13[8] 15[28] (‖ קוֹל שׁוֹפָר), 16[6.42] 2 Ch 15[14] (‖ שׁוֹפָר), 20[28] 29[26.27] Ezr 3[10] Ne 12[35.41], ψ 98[6] (‖ קוֹל שׁוֹפָר); הָרִים קוֹל בח׳ 2 Ch 5[13]; מחצצרים בח׳ 1 Ch 15[24] 2 Ch 5[12.13] 13[14]; in 2 Ch 29[28] this pt. agrees with noun in *sense*, and is masc.; *and the clarions* (= players on the clarions) *sounded*.—The חֲצֹצְרָה, or (sacred) clarion, was a long, straight, slender metal tube, with flaring end, v. Benz [Archäol. 277]; distinguished thus from the שׁוֹפָר which was originally a ram's horn, and prob. always retained the horn-shape; the שׁוֹפָר is mentioned constantly in the earlier lit., and was used by watchmen, warriors, etc., as well as priests (v. Benz [ib. 276] and שׁוֹפָר).

†[חצצר] **vb.** Kt, [חצר] Qr, denominat. from חצצרה = *sound a clarion*—**Pi.** *Pt.* מְחַצְּצְרִים 2 Ch 5[13] (Qr מְחַצְּרִים) = *players on clarions.* **Hiph.** *Pt.* מַחְצְצְרִים (Qr מַחְצְרִים as Hiph. v. Kö [ii. 252]) 1 Ch 15[24] + 3 t. + 2 Ch 5[12] Baer, (van d. H מחצררים); *sound with clarions* מח׳ בחצצרות 1 Ch 15[24] 2 Ch 5[12] 13[14]; abs. *sounded* (*sounding*) 2 Ch 7[6] 29[28], cf. חצצרה *ad fin.* (Kt in all to be pronounced (prob.) מְחַצְּצְרִים).

חֵק v. חֵיק sub חוק; חֹק v. sub חקק.

†חָקָה **vb.** only **Pu. cut in, carve** (NH *represent, imitate*; ‖ חקק)—**Pu.** *Pt.* מְחֻקֶּה 1 K 6[35] Ez 8[10] + 23[14] (Co מְחֻקִּים, after 𝔊 𝔖 𝔗 𝔙), *carved* figure on wall Ez 8[10] 23[14] (where rd. אנשים מחקים, v. supr.) = subst. *carved work* 1 K 6[35] (on doors of temple). **Hithp.** *Impf.* 2 ms. עַל־שָׁרְשֵׁי רַגְלַי תִּתְחַקֶּה Jb 13[27] *thou gravest thee a*

graving (=markest a line) *for* (i e. about) *the soles of my feet*, fixest limits for them (v. Di).

חֻקָּה v. sub חקק

†**חֲקוּפָא** **n.pr.m.** head of a family of returning exiles Ezr 2^{51} = Ne 7^{53}, 𝔊 Αφεικα, Αχειφα, Ακουφα, etc.

†**[חָקַק]** **vb. cut in, inscribe, decree** (NH *id*, Aram. חֲקַק, Zinj חקק, Ph. *id. Pt.* Hiph.; Ar حَقَّ *be just, right, obligatory*, also *make* or *decide to be just*, etc; حَقٌّ *justness, truth, necessity, obligation;* Eth. ሐቅ: adj *moderate, sufficient;* cf also חקה)—**Qal** וְחַקּוֹתָ Ez 4^{1}; sf. חַקֹּתִיךְ Is 49^{16}; *Inf* sf. בְּחֻקוֹ Pr 8^{27}; בְּחוּקוֹ Pr 8^{29} (assim. to בשׂומו); חֻקָּהּ Is 30^{8}; *Pt.* חֹקְקֵי Is 22^{16} (archaic case ending Ges §90.3a); pl. חֹקְקִים Is 10^{1}; cstr. חֹקְקֵי Ju 5^{9} (poss Po'el=מחוקקי with מְ omitted, v. Ges §52(2), note 6), *Pt. pass.* pl חֲקֻקִים Ez 23^{14} (Co חקוקים),—**1.** *cut in*, with בְּ, Is 22^{16}, of a dwelling-place=tomb, in a rock. **2.** *cut in* or *on, upon, engrave, inscribe*, c על on roll of a book Is 30^{8}; representation of city on brick (as in Babylonia) Ez 4^{1}; images on a wall Ez 23^{14}, fig. of Zion's walls on palms of י׳ Is 49^{16}. **3.** *trace, mark out*, a circle, c. על over the face of deep Pr 8^{27}; c. acc., foundations of earth v^{29}. **4.** of a law, *engrave, inscribe* (on a tablet), fig for *enact, decree* חֹקְקִים חִקְקֵי און Is 10^{1} (|| כתב עמל), חוקקי ישׂראל poet =*commanders* (v. **Po'el**) Ju 5^{9} (|| מחקקים v^{14}) **Po'el** *Impf.* יְחֹקְקוּ Pr 8^{15}, *Pt* מְחֹקֵק Gn 49^{10} Nu 21^{18} Dt 33^{21}, sf. מְחֹקְקִי ψ 60^{9} 108^{9}; מְחֹקְקֵנוּ Is 33^{22}; pl מְחֹקְקִים Ju 5^{14},—*inscribe* (as a law), *enact* (poet). c acc. צֶדֶק Pr 8^{15} elsewh. pt. **a.** *prescriber* of laws, hence (as sovereign authority in a warlike clan) *commander* Dt 33^{21} (of warlike tribe of Gad), Ju 5^{14} Is 33^{22} (of י׳; || מַלְכֵּנוּ, שֹׁפְטֵנוּ) **b.** *commander's staff* Gn 49^{10} (|| שֵׁבֶט), Nu 21^{18} (both poet), ψ 60^{9}=108^{9}. **Pu.** *Pt.* מְחֻקָּק *that which is decreed* Pr 31^{5} (late). **Hoph.** *Impf* יֻחַקּוּ Jb 19^{23} *inscribed* in (ב) a book.

חֹק 127 **n.m.** MI 7.11 **something prescribed, a statute or due**,—חֹק Gn 47^{22}+22 t.; חָק Ex 30^{21}+14 t.; sf חֻקִּי Pr 30^{8}+3 t., חָקְךָ Lv $10^{13.14}$ etc.+4 t. sfs; pl. חֻקִּים Dt 4^{5}+31 t., cstr. חֻקֵּי Ex 18^{16}, חוּקֵי Ez 20^{18}; also חִקְקֵי Ju 5^{15} Is 10^{1} (Ges §93.1 R7), חֻקּוֹ Jb 14^{5} etc.+44 t sfs —**1.** *prescribed task*, assigned to Isr in Egypt Ex 5^{14} (E). **2.** *prescribed-portion*, or allowance of food Gn $47^{22.22}$ (J), Pr 30^{8} 31^{15} Ez 16^{27}, מחקי Jb 23^{12} (RV; < 𝔊 𝔙 Ol Me Di SS בְּחֵקִי *in my bosom*). **3.** *action prescribed* for oneself, *resolve*. חִקְקֵי לֵב Ju 5^{15} *resolves of mind* || חִקְרֵי לֵב v^{16}. **4.** *prescribed due* of the priests from offerings Lv 6^{11} $10^{13.13.14.14}$ (P), *due* of י׳ Lv 6^{15} (P); לְחָק׳ עולם Ex 29^{28} Lv 7^{34} 10^{15} Nu $18^{8.11.19}$ (all P), Lv 24^{9} (H); portion of oil for the תרומה Ez 45^{14}. **5.** *prescribed limit, boundary:* of sea Je 5^{22} Pr 8^{29} Jb 26^{10} 38^{10}; of heavens ψ 148^{6}; of land of Israel Mi 7^{11}; of time Jb $14^{5.13}$; so בְּעָרָה פִיהָ לִבְלִי חֹק Is 5^{14} She'ôl *openeth wide her mouth, without limit.* **6.** *enactment, decree, ordinance* of either God or man: **a.** *specific decree:* law of fifth in Egypt Gn 47^{26} (J); of passover Ex 12^{24} (J); lament for Jephthah's daughter Ju 11^{39}; for Josiah 2 Ch 35^{25}, חק ומשפט Ex 15^{25} Jos 24^{25} (both E), 1 S 30^{25}, חק עולם Ex 30^{21}, || מִשְׁפָּט, עדות ψ $81^{5.6}$ (law of a festival). **b.** of י׳ in nature Jb 28^{26}. **c.** respecting Mess king ψ 2^{7}, day of י׳ Zp 2^{2} MT, but on txt. v. We and טֶרֶם, infr.; covenant with Jacob ψ 105^{10}=1 Ch 16^{17}; destiny of man Jb 23^{14}. **d.** *law in general* עלי חק *according to law, right* ψ 94^{20} (others *against law*), לְמד ח׳ ומשפט Ezr 7^{10}; || ברית and תורות Is 24^{5}; || עדות ψ 99^{7}. **7.** pl. חֻקִּים *enactments, statutes* of a law: **a.** of י׳ in nature Je 31^{36} **b.** of the prophets Zc 1^{6}. **c.** *conditions* of deed of purchase Je 32^{11} **d.** *enactments* || מִשְׁפָּטִים: ancestral Ez 20^{18}; given by God as punishment for disobedience 20^{25} **e.** *decrees* of unjust judges חִקְקֵי־אָוֶן Is 10^{1}. **f.** *civil enactments prescribed by God* · חֻקֵּי האלהים Ex 18^{16} (E; || תּוֹרֹתָיו), v^{20} (E; || *id*) **g.** elsewh of prescriptions of the several codes of Hex. Lv 10^{11} Nu 30^{17} (P), Dt 4^{6} 6^{24} 16^{12} ψ 119^{5} +20 t, Mal 3^{7}; || תּוֹרַת י׳ Am 2^{4}; ח׳ ותורות ψ 105^{45}, ח׳ דברי הת׳ והח׳ Dt 17^{19}; || ברית ψ 50^{16}; ח׳ וברית ועדות 2 K 17^{15}; usu. either || משׁפטים Dt $4^{1.5.8.14}$ 5^{1} 11^{32} 12^{1} 26^{16}, 1 K 9^{4}=2 Ch 7^{17}, 1 Ch 22^{13} Ez 11^{12} 36^{27}, or else ח׳ ומשׁפטים combined with other synon (usu. preceding): e g. דבר(ים) ψ 147^{19}; תורה 2 Ch 33^{8} Mal 3^{22}; מצוה Dt 5^{28} 6^{1} 7^{11}, מצות Ne 1^{7} 1 K 8^{58}, מצוה, תורה 2 Ch 19^{10}; עדת Dt 4^{45} 6^{20}, sts. foll: e.g. תורות Lv 26^{46}, מצוה, מ׳ ותורות 2 K 17^{37}, or in different order, e g. תורה ח׳ ומצות Ne 9^{13}; ח׳ ומצות מצות ומ׳ וח׳ Ne 10^{30}; ומ׳ Dt 26^{17}. Apart from משׁפטים it is combined with מצות, e.g. ח׳ ומ׳ מ׳ וח׳ Ex 15^{26} (R), Dt 27^{10}; מ׳ עדות וח׳ Dt 4^{40} 1 K 3^{14} 8^{61}, מ׳ וח׳ ותורה Ne 9^{14}; Dt 6^{17} 1 Ch 29^{19} 2 Ch 34^{31}; דברי מ׳ וח׳ Ezr 7^{11}; it is used c vbs.: נתן Lv 26^{46}+3 t.; צוה Nu 30^{17} +9 t.; לִמֵּד Dt 4^{1}+10 t.; שָׁמַר Dt 26^{17}+16 t.; עָשָׂה Dt 6^{24}+5 t; שׁמר לעשׂות Dt 11^{32}+4 t; הלך ב 1 K 8^{61}+3 t —[On usage of חֹק v. חֻקָּה ad fin.]

†**חֻקָּה** 104 **n.f.** Ex 13.10 **something prescribed, enactment, statute**;—ח׳ Nu 9^{14}+2 t.; cstr. חֻקַּת

Ex 12^{14} + 28 t.; pl. חֻקּוֹת Je 5^{24} + 12 t.; חֻקֹּת Lv 20^{23} Je 31^{35}; sf. חֻקֹּתַי Gn 26^{5} + 14 t.; Lv 18^{4} + 21 t. etc.;—**1.** sg. *statute*, of special ritual laws: of passover Ex 13^{10} (J); elsewhere only in P (and H), חקת הפסח Ex 12^{43} Nu $9^{12.14}$; ח׳ התורה Nu 19^{2} 31^{21}; ח׳ משפט Nu 27^{11} 35^{29}; ח׳ עולם Ex $12^{14.17}$ 27^{21} 28^{43} 29^{9} Lv 3^{17} 7^{36} 10^{9} $16^{29.31.34}$ $23^{21.31}$ 24^{3} Nu 10^{8} 15^{15} 18^{23} $19^{10.21}$ (all P), Lv 17^{7} $23^{14.41}$ (H); חֻקָּה אַחַת לַגֵּר ולאזרח Nu 9^{14} 15^{15}. **2.** pl. *statutes:* **a.** of nature ח׳ שמים Jb 38^{33} Je 33^{25}; of moon and stars Je 31^{35}; of weeks of harvest Je 5^{24}. **b.** fig. of a firmly established custom (ח׳ הגוי(ם Lv 20^{23} (H) 2 K 17^{8}; ח׳ העמים Je 10^{3} ח׳ עמרי Mi 6^{16}; idolatry ח׳ ישׂראל 2 K 17^{19}; sexual offences Lv 18^{30} (H). **c.** ח׳ דוד statutes of David 1 K 3^{3}. **d.** ‖ משפטים 2 S 22^{23} = ψ 18^{23} (of the law known to David); ‖ מצות ψ 89^{32}; ברית וח׳ 1 K 11^{11}; elsewhere of the prescriptions of the codes of D, H, P, Ez: usu. חקות ומשפטים Lv $18^{5.26}$ 19^{37} 20^{22} (H), 25^{18} Nu 9^{3} (P), 1 K 11^{33} Ez 5^{7} 11^{20} 18^{9} $20^{11.13.19.21}$; preceded by מצות Dt 30^{16}; followed by מצות Lv 26^{15} (H), Dt 11^{1} 1 K 6^{12}; תורה ומצוה 2 K 17^{34}; or else משפטים וחקות Lv 18^{4} 26^{43} (H), Ez $5^{6.6}$ 18^{17} $20^{16.24}$ 37^{24}; preceded by מצות Dt 8^{11}; in diff. order, ח׳ מצות ומ׳ ועדות 1 K 2^{3}; frequently also ח׳ ומצות Lv 26^{3} (H), Dt 6^{2} 1 K 11^{38} 2 Ch 7^{19}; or מצות (ו)ח׳ Dt 10^{13} $28^{15.45}$ 30^{10} 1 K 9^{6} 11^{34} Ez 43^{11} (Co), 2 K 17^{13}; foll. by מצות תורות Gn 26^{5} (R); ותורה וח׳ 2 K 23^{3}; ועדות וח׳ תורה וח׳ Je 44^{10}; ועדות תורות יח׳ 44^{23}; ח׳ ותורות Ez 44^{5} 43^{11} (Co); special ordinances are ח׳ המזבח Ez 43^{18}; ח׳ בית י׳ Ez 44^{5}; ח׳ חיים Ez 33^{15} (which are life to those who keep them); ח׳ עולם תמיד (𝔊 𝔖 𝔙 Talm Co del. עולם) Ez 46^{14}. **e.** phrases of obedience are הלך ב׳ Lv 18^{3} 20^{23} 26^{3} (H), 1 K 3^{3} 6^{12} 2 K $17^{8.19}$ Je $44^{10.23}$ Ez $5^{6.7}$ 11^{20} $18^{9.17}$ $20^{13.16.19.21}$ 33^{15}; שמר Lv $18^{4.5.26}$ $19^{19.37}$ $20^{8.22}$ (H), Gn 26^{5} (R), Dt 6^{2} 8^{11} 10^{13} 11^{1} 28^{45} $30^{10.16}$ 1 K 2^{3} 9^{6} $11^{11.34.38}$ 2 K 17^{13} 23^{3} Ez $18^{19.21}$ 37^{24} 43^{11} 44^{24}; עשׂה Lv 25^{18} (P), Dt 28^{15} 1 K 11^{33}; עשׂה כח׳ 2 K 17^{34}; בח׳ אֶשְׁתַּעֲשָׁע ψ 119^{16}; phrases of disobedience are מאס ח׳ Ez 20^{24} מאס בח׳ Lv 26^{15} (H); נעל Lv 26^{43} (H); עזב 2 Ch 7^{19}; חלל ψ 89^{32}.—חֹק and חֻקָּה differ somewhat in shade of meaning and frequency in various writings: e.g. חֹק oftener in Jb ψ Pr (חֻקָּה not at all Pr, once Jb), and in Chr (חֻקָּה only 2 Ch 7^{19}); חֻקָּה oft. in K, rarely in Hex. except in P (H); in proph., חֹק occurs Am 2^{4} Is 5^{14} 24^{5} Mi 7^{11} Je 3 t., Ez 6 t., חֻקָּה only Ez, Je (6 t.) and Mi 6^{16}; חֻקִּים esp. in Dt and ψ 119, חֻקּוֹת esp. in H, Ez and sometimes (8 t.) Dt; חֹק עוֹלָם usu. = *due*, חֻקַּת ע׳ much more often *statute, ordinance*, etc.]

† [חֻקֹּק] **n.pr.loc.** in tribe of Naphtali, only c. ה loc. חֻקֹּקָה Jos 19^{34}; identif. with *Yakûk* c. 4 m. NW. of Lake Tiberias by Rob [BR iii. 81] Survey [WP i. 365].

† חוּקֹק **n.pr.loc.** only 1 Ch 6^{60}, prob. err. for חֶלְקַת (q.v.) Jos 19^{25} 21^{31}.

חֻקְקֵי v. חקק supr.

† [חָקַר] **vb. search** (NH *id.*, Niph. pass., Aram. חֲקַר)—**Qal** *Pf.* 3 ms. sf. וַחֲקָרוֹ consec. Pr 18^{17}; חֲקָרָהּ Jb 28^{27}; וְחָקַרְתָּ Dt 13^{15} etc.; *Impf.* אֶחְקֹר Jb 13^{19}; יַחֲקָר ψ 44^{22}; יַחְקְרֶנּוּ Pr 28^{11}; יַחְקֹר 1 S 20^{12}; נַחְקְרָה תַּחְקְרוּן Jb 32^{11}; La 3^{40} etc.; *Imv.* חָקְרֵנִי ψ 139^{23}; חִקְרוּ Ju 18^{2}; *Inf.* חֲקֹר 2 S 10^{3} + 2 t.; לַחְקוֹר Pr 23^{30}; לַחְקְרָהּ Ju 18^{2};—**1.** *search (for)*, sq. acc. Pr 23^{30} Jb 32^{11}; abs. וְדָרַשְׁתָּ וְחָקַרְתָּ וְשָׁאַלְתָּ הֵיטֵב Dt 13^{15}; lit. Ez 39^{14} (i.e. for bones unburied). **2. a.** *search through, explore*, lit., obj. הארץ Ju 18^{2} (‖ רַגֵּל) v^{2}, 1 Ch 19^{3} (‖ *id.*); city העיר 2 S 10^{3} (‖ *id.*), of mining Jb 28^{3}; *search out* a subject or matter Jb 5^{27} 28^{27} Pr 25^{2} ψ 44^{22}. **b.** *search* a man, find out his sentiments (AV *sound* him) 1 S 20^{12}. **c.** of י׳ *searching* man, c. acc. ψ 139^{1} (‖ ידע), v^{23} (‖ *id.*) Jb 13^{9}, cf. Je 17^{10} (obj. לֵב). **d.** of *examining thoroughly*, so as to expose weakness in a case Jb 29^{16} Pr 18^{17}, cf. 28^{11}; so of self-examination ח׳ דרכים La 3^{40} (‖ חפש). **Niph.** *Pf.* נֶחְקַר 1 K 7^{47} 2 Ch 4^{18}; *Impf.* יֵחָקֵר Je 46^{23}; יֵחָקְרוּ Je 31^{37} *be searched out, found out, ascertained*, 1 K 7^{47} 2 Ch 4^{18} (weight of the bronze used in temple utensils), of forest Je 46^{23}; *searched out*, Je 31^{37} subj. מוסדי ארץ. **Pi.** *Pf.* חִקֵּר Ec 12^{9} *he sought out* many proverbs (‖ אִזֵּן; מְשָׁלִים).

† חֵקֶר **n.m.** [Ju 5, 16] **searching, thing (to be) searched out**;—abs. חֵקֶר Jb 5^{9} + 8 t.; cstr. *id.* Jb 8^{8} + 2 t.; pl. cstr. חִקְרֵי Ju 5^{16};—חִקְרֵי לֵב Ju 5^{16} *searchings, questionings of heart;* Jb 11^{7} canst thou reach ח׳ אֱלוֹהַּ i.e. what is to be explored in him, the whole range of his nature, so ח׳ תהום 38^{16} the range of the deep; esp. אֵין ח׳ i.e. *it is unsearchable* Jb 5^{9} 9^{10} ψ 145^{3} Pr 25^{3} Is 40^{28}, cf. לא ח׳ Jb 34^{24} 36^{26}; ח׳ אבותם 8^{8} i.e. thing searched out by their fathers.

† [מֶחְקָר] **n.m. range** (as place to be explored), מֶחְקְרֵי־אָרֶץ ψ 95^{4} (cf. חֵקֶר Jb 38^{16}).

חֹר *noble*, חר, חַר, חֹר *hole*, v sub II. חרר; חר הַגִּדְגָּד v. sub II. חור

חרא, or חרה (✓of following; meaning unknown).

†[**חֲרָא**], or [**חֲרִי**] **n.[m.]** dung (NH חרא (־ִי), *id.*; Aram. ܚܪܝܐ *id.*; Mand. חרא (on this and cogn. lang. in gen. v. No[M 56]); Ar. خُرْءٌ *id*, whence vb خَرِئَ of act, and n مَخْرَأَة of place; Amh. ሐሬ፡ (Di[Lex. Aeth. 88]))—pl sf. חֲרָאֵיהֶם Is 36[12] Kt (Qr צוֹאָתָם), ‖ 2 K 18[27] has חֲרֵיהֶם (v. sg חרי 6[25]; Qr as above); חֲרֵי יוֹנִים *dove's dung* 2 K 6[25] Kt (Qr דִּבְיוֹנִים), v, further, Gei[Urschrift, 409].

†[**מַחֲרָאָה**] **n.f.** pl. draught house, 2 K 10[27].

†I. [**חָרֵב**] **vb.** be dry, dried up (cf. יָבֵשׁ) (Aram. חֲרוּב *be dry*, חוּרְבָא *drought*);—**Qal** *Pf.* 3 pl. חָרְבוּ Gn 8[13.13], Is 19[6], *Impf.* 3 ms. יֶחֱרַב Ho 13[15] + 2 t, וַיֶּחֱרַב ψ 106[9]; *Imv.* fs. חֳרָבִי Is 44[27];—*be dry, dried up*: **1.** of ground, be freed from waters of flood ח׳ פְּנֵי הָאֲדָמָה Gn 8[13 b] (J). **2.** of waters, *be dried up*, taken away; of waters of flood Gn 8[13 a] (P), of Nile וְנָהָר יֶחֱרַב וְיָבֵשׁ Is 19[5] (‖ וְנִשְּׁתוּ־מַיִם מֵהַיָּם), v. same combination Jb 14[11] (‖ אָזְלוּ מַיִם מִנִּי־יָם); Is 19[6] (‖ דָּלְלוּ) 44[27] (‖ הוֹבִישׁ); of Red Sea ψ 106[9]; fig. of Ephraim's freshness and vigour Ho 13[15]. **Pu.** *Pf.* 3 pl. לֹא חֹרָבוּ Ju 16[7.8], of fresh bow-strings (of gut, v. Bla). **Hiph.** *Pf.* הֶחֱרִיב Na 1[4], of י׳'s *drying up* rivers (‖ וַיַּבְּשֵׁהוּ), perh. also Is 11[15] (for MT החרים) v. 𝔊 𝔖 𝔙 𝔗; וְהַחֲרַבְתִּי the Euphrates Je 51[36] (‖ הוֹבַשְׁתִּי); *Impf* אַחֲרִיב יָם Is 50[2], subj. י׳, *I dry up a sea* (‖ אָשִׂים נְהָרוֹת מִדְבָּר); אַחְרִב Is 37[25] = אַחְרִב 2 K 19[24], of king of Assyria *drying up* rivers of Egypt; *Pt.* fs. הַמַּחֲרֶבֶת Is 51[10] of י׳'s arm *drying up* (Red) Sea.

†I. [**חָרֵב**] **adj.** dry, only fs. חֲרֵבָה Lv 7[10] of meal-offering not moistened (with oil, P), פַּת־ חֲרֵבָה Pr 17[1] *a dry morsel*.

†I. **חֹרֶב** **n.m.**[Gn 31, 40] dryness, drought, heat, abs ח׳ Gn 31[40] + 11 t + Dt 28[22] (for MT חֶרֶב; v. Di, sq 𝔙; 𝔊 and 𝔊L om);—**1.** *dryness* Ju 6[37 39.40] (all of absence of dew); Je 50[38] (‖ יָבֵשׁוּ); so rd. also Zc 11[17] (for MT חֶרֶב, see v[b] and Sta ZAW i 1881, 29), *a drying up upon his arm* (i. e. a *withering*) *and upon his right eye* **2.** *drought* Hg 1[11] + Dt 28[22] v. supr. **3.** *parching heat* (of sun) Gn 31[40] (opp קֶרַח), Je 36[30] (opp. *id.*); Is 4[6] 25[4.5.5]; of fever Jb 30[30]

†**חָרָבָה** **n.f.** dry ground;—abs. ח׳ Gn 7[22] + 7 t.; opp. הַיָּם Ex 14[21] (J), Hg 2[6]; cf. Gn 7[22] (J); opp. water of Jordan Jos 3[17 17] (J), 4[18] (E), 2 K 2[8], of Nile-arms וְנָתַתִּי יְאֹרִים ח׳ Ez 30[12].

†[**חֲרָבוֹן**] **n.m.** drought, only pl. cstr. בְּחַרְבֹנֵי קַיִץ ψ 32[4] metaph of fever heat

†II. [**חָרֵב**] be waste, desolate (NH חָרֵב *id*, Aram חֲרוּב, ܚܪܒ *be laid waste*; Zinj חרב adj.; Ar. خَرِبَ *be in ruins, waste, depopulated*; As. *ḫarâbu*, *be waste*, Dl[Pr 175], *ḫuribtu*, *desert*, Lotz[TP]);—**Qal** *Impf.* 3 fs. תֶּחֱרַב Je 26[9], תֶּחֱרַב Is 34[10]; 3 mpl. יֶחֶרְבוּ Ez 6[6], יֶחֱרָבוּ Am 7[9] Is 60[12], 3 fpl. תֶּחֱרַבְנָה Ez 6[6] 12[20]; *Imv.* חִרְבוּ (so, not חָרְבוּ—Theile—see van d H Hahn Ko[i. 244]) Je 2[12], *Inf. abs* חָרֹב Is 60[12];—*be waste, desolate*; of sanctuaries of Isr. Am 7[9] (‖ נָשַׁמּוּ), of altars Ez 6[6], of cities Je 26[9] Ez 6[6] 12[20] (‖ שׁמם); of nations Is 34[10], חָרֹב יֶחֱרָבוּ 60[12] (‖ יֹאבֵדוּ); fig, in address to the heavens חָרְבוּ מְאֹד Je 2[12]—(‖ שֹׁמּוּ, וְשַׂעֲרוּ), *be very desolate* (at sins of Isr); others, *be amazed, astounded* (on relation of meanings v. שׁמם). **Niph.** *Pt.* f. נֶחֱרֶבֶת Ez 26[19] as adj, *desolate* city, i.e. uninhabited, v. context, נֶחֱרָבוֹת 30[17] of *desolate* countries (‖ נְשַׁמּוֹת) **Hiph.** *Pf.* הֶחֱרִיב Ez 19[17]; 1 s. הֶחֱרַבְתִּי Zp 3[6], 3 pl. הֶחֱרִיבוּ Is 37[18] 2 K 19[17], *Impf* 1 s אַחֲרִיב Is 42[15], *Pt* מַחֲרִיב Ju 16[24]; pl c. sf. מַחֲרִיבַיִךְ Is 49[17],—*lay waste, make desolate*, human subj; nations and lands Is 37[18] = 2 K 19[17], Is 42[15], cf. pt. Is 49[17] (‖ מְהָרְסַיִךְ); add prob. with We Am 4[9] (הֶחֱרַבְתִּי for the untranslateable הַרְבּוֹת) *I have devastated your gardens and vineyards*, pt. Ju 16[24] *desolater of our country* (‖ הִרְבָּה אֶת־חֲלָלֵינוּ); obj cities Ez 19[7]; streets Zp 3[6] (‖ נִצְדּוּ). **Hoph.** *Pf.* 3 fs. הָחֳרָבָה Ez 26[2] *she is laid waste*, of a city; *Pt.* מָחֳרָבוֹת Ez 29[12] *laid waste*, of cities (‖ שׁמם).

†II **חָרֵב** **adj.** waste, desolate;—ms. abs. ח׳ Je 33[10] + 3 t.; fs חֲרֵבָה Ne 2[3] + 2 t.; fpl. הֶחֳרֵבוֹת Ez 36[35.38] (v Ko[i 241]);—of a city, defined מֵאֵין אָדָם וּמֵאֵין בְּהֵמָה Je 33[10], cf v[12]; also Ne 2[3.17], הֶעָרִים הֶחֳרֵבוֹת Ez 36[35] (+ הַנְּשַׁמּוֹת, הַנֶּהֱרָסוֹת; opp. בְּצוּרוֹת יָשָׁבוּ).

†II. **חֹרֶב** **n.[m.]** desolation;—עָרֵי ח׳ Is 61[4] *cities of desolation* (‖ שֹׁמְמוֹת, and, in v[a], חָרְבוֹת); cf. Zp 2[14] Je 49[13], and מִצְרַיִם חָרְבוֹת ח׳ Ez 29[10] Egypt shall be *wastes of desolation* (but 𝔊 𝔙 Co *wastes of the sword*, חֶרֶב for חֹרֶב); + Ez 38[8] Co, who rds. מֵחֶרֶב (or מֵחֳרָבָה).

†חֹרֵב, חורב **n.pr.mont.** **Horeb** (*waste, desert*)—𝔊 Χωρηβ (v Lag$^{BN\,85}$), אֶל־הַר הָאֱלֹהִים חֹרֵבָה Ex 3^{1} (E), cf עַד הַר הָאֱלֹהִים חרב 1 K 19^{8}, הַצּוּר בחרב Ex 17^{6}, הַר חורב 33^{6} (both E), מחרב, בחרב Dt 1$^{2.6.19}$ 4$^{10.15}$ 5^{2} 9^{8} 18^{16} 28^{69}; 1 K 8^{9} 2 Ch 5^{10} ψ 106^{19} Mal 3^{22}, the sacred mountain of the wilderness, no geograph diff from סיני discoverable, but synonym of it in E and (esp) D (except poem Dt 33^{2}, vid סִינַי P)

†חָרְבָּה **n f.** **waste, desolation, ruin**,—abs. ח׳ Lv 26^{31} + 15 t. + Ez 38^{8} (del 𝔊 Co) + Ez 38^{12} חרבה 𝔊 Co for חרבות, pl חֳרָבוֹת ψ 9^{7} + 11 t. (Ez 38^{12}, cf supr), cstr חָרְבוֹת Is 5^{17} + 7 t; sf חָרְבֹתַיִךְ Is 49^{19}; חָרְבֹתָיו Ezr 9^{9}, חָרְבֹתֶיהָ Is 51^{3}; חָרְבוֹתֶיהָ Is 44^{26}, חרבותיהם ψ 109^{10} + 2 Ch 34^{6} (cf. חרב and infr), (chiefly mid. and late Heb Is^{2} 8 t, Je 10 t Ez 14 t—incl 38^{8}, q del. Co),—**1.** *waste, ruin*, of cities of Israel Lv 26$^{31.33}$(H); Judah Is 44^{26} 49^{19} (‖ שממת), 58^{12} (בנה), Je 25^{18} 27^{17} 44$^{2.6}$ Ez 5^{14}; ruins of Jerusalem Is 52^{9} Dn 9^{2}, also Ez 35^{4}; cf Mal 1^{4} (c בנה), Ez 36^{10} (c בנה) v^{33} (*id.*), Egypt Ez 29$^{9.10}$ (in both ‖ שְׁמָמָה, חרבות חֹרֶב in v^{10}), ruin of temple Ezr 9^{9}, =ruined dwellings ψ 109^{10}; cf 2 Ch 34^{6}, where rd perh בְּחָרְבֹתֵיהֶם for בחר בתיהם (v. חָרֵב sub III חרב); Je 22^{5}, in gen *ruins* (si vera l., v Di, obj of בנה) Jb 3^{14}, כוס ח׳ ψ 102^{7} *an owl of a ruin* **2.** of land waste place amid ruins Is 5^{17}, cf 51^{3} (‖ מִדְבָּר, עֲרָבָה), land a desolation Je 7^{34} 44^{22} Ez 25^{13} (Edom) Je 25^{11} Is 64^{10} and Ez 33$^{24.27}$ (of Judah), cf Ez 13^{4}, הח׳ הַשֹּׁמְמוֹת כְּשֻׁעָלִים בח׳ sim of the prophets; Ez 36^{4} (of Israel), of desolation of enemies of Isr. ψ 9^{7} (ח׳ לָנֶצַח), ח׳ עולם = old ruins Is 61^{4} (c בנה), elsewhere perpetual ruin, desolation Je 25^{9} 49^{13} (cities of Bosra); ח׳ מעולם Ez 26^{20} (sim of Tyre)

†III [חָרַב] **vb.** (Aram. and rare) **attack, smite down** (cf Ar حَرَبَ *plunder*, III. *wage war with*, VI *fight together*, حَرْبٌ *war, battle*, Syr ܚܪܒ *smite, slay*)—**Qal** *Imv.* ms. חֲרֹב Je 50^{21} *attack* (+ וְהַחֲרֵם אַחֲרֵיהֶם), mpl חִרְבוּ v^{27} obj. כָּל־פָּרֶיהָ, fig. of men of Babylon. **Niph.** *Pf.* 3 pl נחרבו המלכים (v **Hoph.**) הָחֳרֵב 2 K 3^{23} *the kings have attacked one another, fought together* (‖ וַיַּכּוּ אִישׁ אֶת־רֵעֵהוּ) **Hoph.** *Inf. abs* 2 K 3^{23}, v. **Niph.**, but rd perhaps הַחֲרֵב, cf Dr Lv 19^{20}, note

חֶרֶב$_{411}$ **n.f.**$^{Is\,21.15}$ **sword** (as weapon, Aram. חַרְבָּא, ܚܪܒܐ, Zinj חרב; Ar حَرْبَةٌ *dart, javelin*)—abs חֶרֶב Gn 3^{24}+; חָרֶב Ex 17^{13}+; cstr. חֶרֶב Dt 33^{29}+; sf חַרְבִּי Ex 15^{9} + 13 t.; חַרְבְּךָ Gn 27^{40} + 7 t, חַרְבֶּךָ 1 S 17^{33} ψ 17^{13}; חַרְבּוֹ Nu 22^{23} + 24 t, חַרְבְּכֶם Je 2^{30} Ez 33^{26}, חַרְבָּם ψ 37^{15} 44^{4}, pl. חֲרָבוֹת Is 21^{15} + 5 t; cstr. חרבות Jos 5^{2} + 2 t; sf חַרְבוֹתָיו Ez 26^{9}, חַרְבוֹתָם Is 2^{4} + 5 t.; חרבתיהם Mi 4^{3} + 2 t; —**1. a.** *sword*, as weapon of war Gn 48^{22} (E), Ju 7$^{14.20}$ 1 S 21^{9}, and so in all periods; *two-edged* (short) *sword* ח׳ ולה שני פיות גֹּמֶד אָרְכָּהּ Ju 3^{16}, cf ח׳ ביות Pr 5^{4} (in sim), ח׳ פיפיות ψ 149^{6}; v also צור ח׳ *edge of sword* ψ 89^{44} **b.** *gird on sword* = חָגַר הח׳ 1 S 17^{39} 25$^{13.13.13}$ ψ 45^{4} (הח׳ ח׳ (על יָרֵךְ), שים על ירך Ex 32^{27}, cf esp 2 S 20^{8}. **c.** *draw the sword* הֵרִיק הח׳ Ex 15^{9} Lv 26^{33} Ez 5$^{2.12}$ 12^{14} 28^{7}, הוציא הח׳ Ez 21$^{8.10}$, פתח הח׳ ψ 37^{14} Ez 21^{33}, נטש Is 21^{15} (Gr Che לטש v. infr); usu שלף הח׳ Nu 22$^{23.31}$ Jos 5^{13} Ju 3^{22} 8$^{10.20}$ 9^{54} 1 S 17^{51} 31^{4} = 1 Ch 10^{4} 21^{16}, and as characteristic of warriors שלף ח׳ Ju 20$^{2.15.17.25.35.46}$ 2 S 24^{9} 2 K 3^{26}, 1 Ch 21$^{5.5}$, וַתִּדְבַּק יָדוֹ אֶל־הַח׳ 2 S 23^{10}, ins. also in ‖ 1 Ch 11^{13} (Dr). **d.** *whet, sharpen the sword* לטש הח׳ ψ 7^{13} (cf. Is 21^{15} supr.), but also שנן Dt 32^{41} cf ψ 64^{4}, הוּחַדָּה Ez 21$^{14.16}$. **e.** put up the sword into the sheath השיב הח׳ אֶל־נְדָנָהּ 1 Ch 21^{27} (*sheath* of sword is elsewhere תַּעַר 1 S 17^{51} 2 S 20^{8} Je 47^{6} Ez 21^{8}) **f.** *slay with sword* הרג בח׳ Jos 10^{11} 13^{22}+; in ימותו אנשים 1 S 2^{33}, insert בַּחֶרֶב before אנשים 𝔊 We Dr; rarely הכה בח׳ Jos 11^{10} 2 K 19^{37} = Is 37^{38}, very oft. הִכָּה לפי־ח׳ *smite acc to the mouth of the sword* i e as the sword can devour (2 S 2^{26} 11^{25}) = *without quarter* Nu 21^{24} (E) Dt 13^{16a} 20^{13} Jos 11$^{11.12.14}$ (all D) Ju 18^{27} 21^{10} 1 K 10^{25} Jb 1$^{15.17}$; also c העיר as sole obj Jos 8^{24} 10$^{28.30.32.35.37}$, cf v^{39} 19^{47} Ju 1$^{8.25}$ 20^{37} 1 S 22$^{19.19}$ 2 S 15^{14}, הרג לפי־ח׳ + Gn 34^{26} (J), החרים לפי־ח׳ Dt 13^{16b} (incl. הָעִיר in obj), Jos 6^{21} 1 S 15^{8}, חלש לפי־ח׳ + Ex 17^{13} (E), נפל לפי־ח׳ Jos 8^{24} Ju 4^{16}, וַיָּהָם י׳ . לפי־ח׳ Ju 4^{15},—(לפי־ח׳) is chiefly in Jos and Ju (21 t), in Hexat only JED; but Jb post-ex.). **g.** אכלה הח׳ etc, of the sword as *devouring*—תאכל חַרְבִּי בָּשָׂר Dt 32^{42} (poet.), 2 S 2^{26} 11^{25} 18^{8} Is 1^{20} Je 2^{30} Je 46$^{10.14}$ Na 2^{14}. **h.** *slain by sword* is חֲלַל־ח׳ Nu 19^{16} (P) and frequently Ez, חַלְלֵי־ח׳ 31$^{17.18}$ 32$^{21.25.28.29.30.32}$ 35^{8} מְחֻלְּלֵי ח׳ v^{26} < Co חללי־ח׳ (on text of 32$^{20.22.31}$ v. Co) **i.** שְׁבֻיוֹת ח׳ Gn 31^{26} are *captives of* (taken by) *sword* **j.** sword frequently agent of י׳ Ju 7^{20} Is 34^{6} Je 12^{12} 47^{6} etc, —so Dt 28^{22}, but rd חֹרֶב v sub I. חרב (cf on other hand 1 S 17^{47}), note esp Gn 3^{24} לַהַט הח׳ הַמִּתְהַפֶּכֶת, poet לַהַב ח׳ Na 3^{3}, בְּרַק ח׳ Dt 32^{41}.

†II. **חֲרָדָה** **n.pr.loc.** a station of Isr. in wilderness Nu $33^{24.25}$, site unknown.

†**חָרָה** **vb. burn, be kindled, of anger** (Aram. חרי Pa. *cause* fire *to burn* (rare); Zinj. חרא *anger*, Nö ZMG 1893, 98. 103; Ar. حَرْوَةٌ *burning sensation, in throat*, etc., *fr. rage and pain*)—**Qal** *Pf.* ח׳ Gn 4^{6} + 20 t.; *Impf.* יֶחֱרֶה Ex 32^{11} + 2 t.; יִחַר Gn 18^{30} + 7 t.; וַיִּחַר Gn 4^{5} + 46 t.; *Inf. abs.* חָרֹה 1 S 20^{7}; cstr. חֲרוֹת 2 S 24^{1} ψ 124^{3};— **1.** of man: **a.** חרה אף (one's) *anger was kindled, burned* Gn 39^{19} Nu 22^{27} (J), Ex $32^{19.22}$ (JE), Ju 9^{30} 14^{19} 1 S 11^{6} Jb $32^{2.5}$; c. בְּ *against* Gn 30^{2} (E), 44^{18} (J), 1 S 17^{28} 20^{30} 2 S 12^{5} 2 Ch 25^{10} ψ 124^{3} Jb $32^{2.3}$; c. אֶל Nu 24^{10} (E). **b.** impers., אף omitted; חרה לְ *it was kindled for* (him) *he burned with anger* Gn 31^{36} (E), $4^{5.6}$ 34^{7} Nu 16^{15} (J), 1 S 15^{11} (rd. perh. וַיֵּצַר, Weir in Dr), 18^{8} $20^{7.7}$ 2 S 3^{8} 6^{8} = 1 Ch 13^{11}, 2 S 13^{21} 19^{43} Ne 3^{33} 4^{1} 5^{6} Jon $4^{1.4.9.9}$; ins. ויחר לדוד 2 S 11^{22} 𝔊 We Dr; ח׳ בְּעֵינֵי Gn 31^{35} 45^{5} (E). **2.** of God: **a.** ח׳ אַף Ex 22^{23} Nu 22^{22} (E), Nu $11^{1.10}$ 32^{10} (J); c. בְּ Ex 4^{14} 32^{10} Nu 12^{9} Dt 31^{17} (J), 6^{15} 7^{4} 11^{17} 29^{26} Jos 23^{16} (D), Ju 6^{39} 2 S 6^{7} = 1 Ch 13^{10}, Ho 8^{5} 2 K 23^{26} 2 Ch 25^{15} Jb 42^{7}; בָּעָם Ex 32^{11} Nu 11^{33} (J), Is 5^{25} ψ 106^{40}; בישׂראל Nu 25^{3} 32^{13} (JE); Ju $2^{14.20}$ 3^{8} 10^{7} 2 S 24^{1} 2 K 13^{3}; בבני ישׂראל Jos 7^{1} (R); בנהרים, אף omitted, Hb 3^{8}; c. עַל Zc 10^{3}. **b.** חרה לְ Gn $18^{30.32}$ (J) 2 S 22^{8} = ψ 18^{8}.—*Note:* חרה not in HP (who use קצף); nor in Je Ez Is ² Pr or poetry of Jb. **Niph.** *Pf.* נִחֲרוּ sq. בְּ Ct 1^{6} (acc. to Bö ii. 379 De Kö i. 551) *be angry* with; *Pt.* כֹּל הַנֶּחֱרִים בָּ׳ *all that are incensed against* (*thee*) Is 41^{11}, so 45^{24}. **Hiph.** *Pf.* הֶחֱרָה הֶחֱזִיק Ne 3^{20} *burned with zeal* (?) *in repairing*, but 𝔊 om. החרה; prob. dittogr.; *Impf.* וַיַּחַר עָלַי אַפּוֹ Jb 19^{11} *and kindled his anger against me.* **Hithp.** *Impf.* אַל תִּתְחַר ψ $37^{1.7.8}$ Pr 24^{19} *heat oneself in vexation.*—The foll. forms are somewhat dub.: *Impf.* 2 ms. אֵיךְ תְּתַחֲרֶה אֶת־הַסּוּסִים Je 12^{5} *how canst thou hotly contend* (in a race) *with the horses?* *Pt.* כִּי אַתָּה מְתַחֲרֶה בָאֶרֶז Je 22^{15} *because thou strivest eagerly* (to excel) *in cedar;* expl. as *Tiphʿēl* by Thes Ges § 55, 5 Ew § 122 a Ol § 255 a Sta § 159 b Kö i. p. 537 al., and regarded by most as a rare *causative* stem; but ag. existence of *Tiphʿēl* v. Ba NB § 180 a; ZMG 1894, 20; Ba regards the form as denom. (fr. a noun formed by ת preform., cf. Aram. ܬܚܪܝܐ *contention*); SS would point as Hithp. [cf. Syr. ܐܬܬܚܪܝ *contend with*, ܬܚܪܝܐ *contention*], although meaning of Hithp. is diff., v. supr.

†**חָרוֹן** **n.m.** (burning of) anger (cf. Lag BN 204 Anm. * ×)—ח׳ Ez 7^{12} + 2 t.; cstr. חֲרוֹן Nu 25^{4} + 33 t.; sf. חֲרוֹנִי Ez 7^{14} (Co חרון), חֲרוֹנוֹ ψ 2^{5}; חֲרֹנְךָ Ex 15^{7}; pl. sf. חֲרוֹנֶיךָ ψ 88^{17};—alw. of God's anger (v. note, infr.), חֲרוֹן אַף Ex 32^{12} Nu 25^{4} 32^{14} Jos 7^{26} (J), Dt 13^{18} 1 S 28^{18} 2 K 23^{26} 2 Ch $28^{11.13}$ 29^{10} 30^{8} Ezr 10^{14} Ho 11^{9} Na 1^{6} Zp 2^{2} 3^{8} Is $13^{9.13}$ Je $4^{8.26}$ 12^{13} $25^{37.38}$ 30^{24} 49^{37} 51^{45} Jon 3^{9} ψ 69^{25} 78^{49} 85^{4} Jb 20^{23} La 1^{12} 4^{11}; אף om., Ex 15^{7} (song), Ne 13^{18} ψ 2^{5} Ez 7^{12} (del. Co), v^{14}; pl. *bursts of burning anger* ψ 88^{17}.—*Note:* כְּמוֹ־חָרוֹן ψ 58^{10} *burning anger* 𝔊 𝔙 Jer AV Bae Che; but Thes MV SS DeW Ew Ol Pe, something burning, e.g. thorns, antith. *green* thorns; Hengst De *cooked* flesh, antith. *raw;* Je 25^{38} מפני ח׳ הַיּוֹנָה because of the *fierceness of the oppressor* (? AV) would then be the only use of the word of other than God's anger; here 𝔊 𝔗 Ew Hi Gf Ke Che Gie RV rightly rd. חרב *oppressing sword* (as 46^{16} 50^{16}). חרון is not used in H P D² or E (except song, Ex 15^{7}) of the Hex; nor in Ez except 7^{12} (del. Co), v^{14}.

†**חֳרִי** **n.m.** burning, alw. חֳרִי (הָ)אַף of Moses Ex 11^{8} (J); Jonathan 1 S 20^{34}; army of Ephraim 2 Ch 25^{10}; Rezin Is 7^{4}; of God Dt 29^{23} La 2^{3}.

חַרְהֲיָה v. חרחיה.

†**חֲרוּמַף** **n.pr.m.** father of one of the builders of the wall Ne 3^{10}.

חרז (√of foll.; NH חָרַז *string together*, esp. jewels or pearls; Aram. חֲרַז *id.;* ܚܪܙ *id.;* Ar. خَرَزَ *sew* or *stitch*, خَرَزٌ *beads strung together, neck-ornament*).

†[**חָרוּז**] **n.[m.]** **string of beads,** only pl. צַוָּארֵךְ בַּחֲרוּזִים Ct 1^{10} *thy neck* (is comely) *with strings of beads.*

†**חַרְחֲיָה** (van d. H חרהיה), **n.pr.m.** (√ and mng. unknown)—father of one of the builders of the wall, Neh.'s time Ne 3^{8}.

חַרְחֻר, חַרְחוּר v. sub I. חרר.

†**חַרְחַס** **n.pr.m.** grandfather of Shallum, who was husband of Huldah the prophetess 2 K 22^{14}.

I. **חרט** (√of foll.; Aram. ܚܪܛ *cut, scratch, tear;* cf. Ar. خَرَطَ *peel off bark, strip off leaves* (mod. Ar. *turn* wood), مِخْرَطٌ *iron instrument for doing* this).

†**חֶרֶט** **n.[m.]** **graving-tool, stylus — 1.** *graving-tool*, with which Aaron fashioned (וַיָּצַר)

the molten calf Ex 32^{4} (E). **2.** ***stylus***, for writing on tablet (כְּתֹב עָלָיו בְּחֶרֶט אֱנוֹשׁ · גִּלָּיוֹן) Is 8^{1} *write on it with a man's* (i e. an ordinary) *stylus*=in common characters, intelligible to all (v. Benz$^{Arch\ 290}$).

†[חַרְטֹם] **n.m.** $^{Ex\ 7\ 22}$**engraver, writer,** only in deriv. sense of one possessed of occult knowledge, *diviner, astrologer, magician* (prob = חֶרֶט+ם, v. Di Ol$^{§216.5}$ Sta^{§§295,327a})—only pl. abs. חַרְטֻמִּים Gn 41^{24}+4 t.; חַרְטֻמם Ex 8^{15} 9^{11}, cstr. חַרְטֻמֵּי Gn 41^{8}+2 t ,—**1.** *magicians* of Egypt Gn 41^{8} (E; ‖חֲכָמִים), v^{24} (E), Ex 8$^{3\ 14\ 15}$ 7^{11} (‖מְכַשְּׁפִים, חֲכָמִים), v^{22} 9$^{11\ 11}$ (all P) **2.** *magicians* of Babylon Dn 2^{2} (‖מְכַשְּׁפִים, אַשָּׁפִים, כַּשְׂדִּים).

II. **חרט** (√of foll.; relation to I. חרם obscure).

†[חָרִיט] **n m.**$^{1K\ 5\ 23}$**bag, purse** (cf. Ar. خَرِيطَة *bag* or *purse* made of skin or other material)—only pl abs. שְׁנֵי חֲרִטִים 2 K 5^{23}, containing each a talent of silver; הָחֲרִיטִים Is 3^{22} in list of ladies' finery.

I. **חֹרִי** *white bread* v. sub I חור

II. **חֹרִי, חוֹרִי** **n.pr gent.** v. sub III. חרר.

חֲרֵיהֶם, חֲרֵי יוֹנִים v. [חרי, חרא].

†I. [**חָרַךְ**] **vb. set in motion, start** (cf Ar. حَرَّكَ *move, be agitated,* II *set in motion*)—only **Qal** *Impf* 3 ms לֹא־יַחֲרֹךְ רְמִיָּה צֵידוֹ Pr 12^{27} *slackness* (i e. a slack or slothful man) *doth not start its game* De RVm, cf Now (>Be Ew after Jewish trad , *doth not roast,* Aram. חֲרַךְ, ܚܪܟ *scorch, parch*).

II. **חרך** (√of foll ; meaning unknown)

†**חֲרַכִּים** **n.[m.]pl. lattice or other opening** through which one may look (Aram חֲרַכָּא ℭ Jos 2^{15} al.=Heb. חַלּוֹן; but NH חֲרַךְ is an opening smaller than a window)—only מֵצִיץ מִן־הַח׳ Ct 2^{9} *peeping in at the lattice* (‖מַשְׁגִּיחַ מִן־הַחַלֹּנוֹת).

חרל (√of foll , meaning unknown)

†**חָרוּל** **n.[m.]** a kind of weed, perh chick-pea (*cicercula*), v. Low$^{p\ 153}$ (Syr ܫܥܘܠܐ *fodder for horses;* ℭ Pr 24^{31} gives חוּרְלָא)—abs. ח׳ Jb 30^{6} Zp 2^{9}, pl חֲרֻלִּים Pr 24^{31};—as growing in devastated land, coll Zp 2^{9}; in vineyard of slothful, pl כָּסּוּ פָנָיו ח׳ Pr 24^{31} (‖קִמְּשֹׂנִים); as sole shelter of certain outcast peoples Jb 30^{7} (שִׂיחִים)

†I. [**חָרַם**] **vb. Hiph. ban, devote, exterminate** (MI^{17} החרמתה of *devoting, dedicating* a city to Chemosh, in cl. with כי explaining massacre of all inhabitants; the altar-hearth of י׳ there was dragged before Chemosh; حَرُمَ *be prohibited, forbidden, unlawful, become sacred,* IV. *make, pronounce sacred, inviolable,* Eth ሐረመ: *prohibit from common use, consecrate to God, esteem unlawful;* Palm חרם=*consacré* Vog$^{No\ 35}$; Nab *id* ,Eut$^{p\ 28}$; Sab מחרם *sanctuary, temple,* Os$^{ZMG\ 1865,\ 176.232}$, חרמתן DHM$^{ZMG\ 1875\ 564}$, Aram אַחְרִים, and esp ܚܪܡ *anathematize, excommunicate;* v. also We$^{Skizzen\ iii,\ 165}$, Dr$^{Sm\ 100\ ff.}$, RS$^{Sem\ i\ 140(150)}$)—**Hiph.** *Pf* הֶחֱרִים Jos 8^{26}+5 t., הַחֲרִם Jos 10^{28}; 2 ms. וְהַחֲרַמְתָּה 1 S 15^{18}, 1 s. הֶחֱרַמְתִּי 1 S 15^{20}; וְהַחֲרַמְתִּי Nu 21^{2}; 2 fs. (וְהַחֲרַמְתְּ(י consec Mi 4^{13} (so 𝔊 𝔙 𝔖 ℭ RV most; MT 1 s), v Ges$^{§44.\ R.\ 4}$; pl. הֶחֱרִימוּ 1 S 15^{9} 2 Ch 32^{14} etc.; (1 S 15^{3} rd והחרמתו 𝔊 We Dr), *Impf* יַחֲרִם Lv 27^{28}; וַיַּחֲרֵם Nu 21^{3} Jos 10^{37}; sf וַיַּחֲרִימָהּ Jos 10^{1}, 1 pl וַנַּחֲרֵם Dt 2^{34} 3^{6} etc., *Imv* הַחֲרֵם Dt 13^{16}; pl. הַחֲרִימוּ Je 51^{3}; sf הַחֲרִימוּהָ Je 50^{26}; *Inf. abs* הַחֲרֵם Dt 3^{6}+4 t.; cstr. הַחֲרִים 2 Ch 20^{23} Dn 11^{44}; sf הַחֲרִימָם Jos 11^{20}+4 t.;—*ban, devote* (esp. religiously, sq objects hostile to the theocracy [v esp. Ex 22^{19} Hoph]; this involved gen their destruction, when a city was 'devoted' the inhab were put to death, the spoil being destroyed or not acc. to the gravity of the occasion [contrast Jos 6$^{17\ 21}$ 1 S 15^{3} with Dt 2$^{34\ f.}$ 3$^{6.7}$], cf. MI^{17} לעשתר כמש החרמתה *to Ashtar-Chemosh I devoted it,* i e. the city Nebo),—**1.** most oft. of devoting to destruction cities of Canaanites and other neighbours of Isr , *exterminating* inhabitants, and destroying or appropriating their possessions · **a.** Isr and her leaders subj Nu 21$^{2.3}$ (destruction acc. to vow), Jos 6^{21} (cf חֵרֶם לַיהוה v^{17}, all J); in v^{18} rd. תַּחְמְדוּ (for MT תַּחֲרִימוּ, v Di VB); 8^{26} (𝔊, not 𝔊L, om. v), 10^{1} (JE), Dt 2^{34} 3$^{6.6}$ 7$^{2.2}$ (commanded through Moses, cf. for underlying thought v$^{4.5.6}$), 20$^{17\ 17}$ (commanded by י׳), Jos 2^{10} 10$^{28\ 35.37.39.40}$ (divine command), 11$^{11\ 12.20\ 21}$ (divine command v$^{12.20}$, all D), 1 S 15$^{3.8\ 9\ 9\ 15\ 18.20}$ (divine command v$^{3.18.20}$, cf v$^{11\ 22.23}$); quite secondary is simple *exterminate* 1 K 9^{21}, 1 Ch 4^{41}. **b.** secondary mng *destroy, exterminate,* also with other nations subj —2 K 19^{11}=Is 37^{11}=2 Ch 32^{14}, 2 Ch 20^{23}, Je 50$^{21\ 26}$ (both by divine command), 51^{3} Dn 11^{44}. **c.** *God as subj* , fig. all nations and their armies Is 34^{2}, the nations of Western Asia Je 25^{9}; the tongue of the Egyptian sea (by drying it up)

Is 11[13] (but rd perh. החריב with 𝔊 𝔖 𝔙 𝔗) **d.** so also of *devoting* even Israelites a city of Isr for worshipping other gods Dt 13[16], residents of Jabesh-Gilead for not joining in campaign against Benj Ju 21[11]. **2.** *devote to* י׳ for sacred uses החרים ליהוה the spoil of the nations Mi 4[13], private possessions, whether a man, animal, or field Lv 27[28] (P) **Hoph.** *Impf* יָחֳרַם Lv 27[29] Ezr 10[8]; יָחֳרָם Ex 22[19],—**1.** *be put under the ban, devoted* (to death), for worshipping other gods than י׳ Ex 22[19] (JE; earliest use of word in OT), for some other theocratic offence Lv 27[29] (P, v. Di). **2.** *devoted*, i e *forfeited*, to the temple treasures Ezr 10[8]—On חרם v esp Di (Kn) Lv 27[28], Ew [Antiq 78 78], Dr 1 S 15[33].

†I. **חֵרֶם** **n.m** [Lv 27 28] **1. devoted thing 2. devotion, ban**,—ח׳ abs Jos 6[17]+24 t (most rd חֵרֶם Zc 14[11], Baer חרם), חֵרֶם Jos 7[1], sf חֶרְמִי 1 K 20[42] Is 34[5],—*thing devoted* to י׳ **1.** thing hostile to theocracy, and therefore (in the strictest application) to be either destroyed, or, in the case of certain objects (e g silver and gold, vessels of brass and iron Jos 6[19.24]), set apart to sacred uses, esp **a.** of a Canaan. city, as Jericho, incl all inhab (exc Rahab's family) and spoil Jos 6[17 18.18] 7[1 11 15], Achan by taking מִן־הַחֵרֶם made (camp of) Isr. ח׳ 7[12] cf 6[18], and became himself ח׳, and was stoned and, with his family and possessions, incl the spoil, was burnt 7[1 11 12.13 15] (all JE exc 7[1] P, cf v[1a 24.25]), מָעַל מַעַל בַּח׳ *committed unfaithfulness in the* matter of the *devoted thing* is term for the sin Jos 7[1] 22[20] (both P), cf. מָעַל בַּח׳ 1 Ch 2[7]; Saul and Isr. spared Agag king of Amalek and ראשית הַח׳ i.e of the spoil (sheep and oxen), wh. should have been utterly destroyed 1 S 15[21] (cf v[3.8]; Saul rejected by י׳ for this v[11 26]). so an idolatr. city in Isr. should become ח׳, with all its contents, and be utterly destroyed Dt 13[17] (cf v[13 15 16]). **b.** of individuals, one having relic of Canaanit god in his house should become ח׳, the relic being ח׳ Dt 7[26 26]; every human being who became ח׳ should be killed Lv 27[29 29] (P, v Di). **2.** appar. (so Di) anything *devoted* to sanctuary under specially stringent conditions Lv 27[28] (v Di; and cf. Ezr 10[8]), a field consecrated to י׳ becomes under certain conditions כשדה הַח׳ Lv 27[21], every ח׳ is קֹדֶשׁ קָדָשִׁים ליהוה v[28], and no ח׳ that a man may devote, whether man, beast or field, may be sold or redeemed v[28], every such ח׳ (as in case of metals and metal objects Jos 6[17 19]) went to Aaron and his sons Nu 18[14] (P), to Zadokite priests Ez 44[29] **3.** *devotion, ban*, involving destruction, איש חֶרְמִי 1 K 20[42] *man under my* (י׳'s) *ban* (of Benhadad), עַם חֶרְמִי Is 34[5] (of Edom); נתן לַח׳ Is 43[28] fig. of י׳'s giving over Jud to Chald, ח׳ not to be in future Zc 14[11]; פֶּן־אָבוֹא והכיתי אֶת־הָאָרֶץ ח׳ Mal 3[24] *smite the land with a ban*, i e. utterly destroy it.

† **חֵרֶם** **n.pr loc.** (*sacred*, cf Sab. n pr.loc. אחרם DHM [Epigr Denkm. 43])—a place in tribe of Naphtali Jos 19[38] (P), not identified

† **חָרִם** **n.pr.m.** (*consecrated*; cf Sab n pr m. חרם, יחרמאל Hal [411 504] DHM[1 c])—**1.** priest of the third course, David's time, acc to 1 Ch 24[8] **2.** priest of time of Nehemiah Ne 10[6] **3.** heads of families of returning exiles **a.** Ezr 2[39] = Ne 7[42], Ezr 10[21] Ne 12[15]. **b.** Ezr 2[32] = Ne 7[35], Ezr 10[31] Ne 3[11] **4.** a prince Ne 10[28].

† **חָרְמָה** **n.pr.loc.** (*asylum*, cf. Ar. *id.*, Wetzst [ZKW v 1884 115])—a royal city of Canaanites, in the South, in tribe of Simeon Nu 14[45] (JE; art only here v. Di), 21[3] (J) where name expl. from Israel's *devoting* Canaanites of Arad to destruction; Jos 15[30] 19[4] (P), Dt 1[44] Jos 12[14] (D), 1 S 30[30] 1 Ch 4[30], originally called צְפַת Ju 1[17], where name is said to have been changed to Hormah because Judah and Simeon (after death of Joshua) *devoted* its inhabitants to destruction, v Di Nu 21[3]—On site v צפת.

† **חרמון** **n. pr. mont. Hermon** (*sacred* mountain, cf. Sab מחרם, etc, *temple*, Ar حَرَام *interior of mosque*, حُرْمَة *asylum*, Wetzst [ZKW v 1884, 115] RS [Sem 1. 93, 2nd ed. 94])—the highest peak of Anti-Lebanon range, usually snow-capped, commanding southern Syria & northern Palestine; it is called שיאן by the author of Dt 4[48]; by the Amorites שניר, by the Sidonians שרין Dt 3[9]. It has three peaks, and the names חרמון and שניר, distinguished in 1 Ch 5[23] Ct 4[8], may refer to two of these peaks; חֶרְמוֹנִים ψ 42[7] prob. refers to these different peaks (see Rob [BR iii. 357] Bad [Pal 301]) It is a northern boundary עד הר ח׳ Dt 3[8] Jos 12[1], הר חרמון *mount Hermon* is used also Jos 11[17] 12[5] 13[5 11] 1 Ch 5[23], but חרמון Jos 11[3] ψ 89[13] 133[3] Ct 4[8] Vid. בַּעַל חֶרְמוֹן Ju 3[3] 1 Ch 5[23] (see Wetzst [ib 115]).

חֶרְמוֹנִים v foregoing

†II **[חָרַם]** **vb. slit** (nose, lip, ear, etc), **mutilate**, esp. face (Ar خَرَمَ *perforate, pierce, slit the partition between the nostrils, or the lip, or the lobe of the ear*)—**Qal** *Pt. pass.* איש עִוֵּר או פִסֵּחַ או חָרֻם או שָׂרוּעַ *a man blind or lame or*

mutilated in the face (in nose, lip, ear, etc.), *or too long in a limb* Lv 21^{18} (H), v. Di (Kn).

†II. **חֵרֶם** **n.m. net** (as something perforated; cf Ar. مُخَرَّم *perforated work*, Fl in NHWB $^{\text{ii 208}}$; NH חֵרֶם *net*, Ph. חרם *maker of nets*)—abs. ח׳ Mi 7^{2}; sf. חֶרְמִי Ez 32^{3}, חֶרְמוֹ Hb 1$^{15.16.17}$; pl. חֲרָמִים Ec 7^{26} Ez 26$^{5.14}$ 47^{10};—*hunter's net* Mi 7^{2} Ec 7^{26}; *fisherman's net* Ez 26$^{5.14}$ 32^{3} 47^{10} Hb 1$^{15.16.17}$.

†**חֶרְמֵשׁ** **n.[m.] sickle** (on form v Ges $^{\S 85\text{ xii }55}$)—Dt 16^{9} 23^{26}.

†I. **חָרָן** **n.pr.loc.** city in northern Mesopotamia (As. *ḫarrânu=road, path* COT^{Gloss}; cf Dl$^{\text{Pa 185}}$; Jensen$^{\text{Kosmologie 28}}$ '*junction of trading-routes*'=*cross-roads*)—mentioned as city of Abram's sojourn Gn 11^{31}, where his father Teraḥ died v^{32}, and whence he departed for Canaan 12$^{4.5}$; where Laban, Jacob's uncle, lived, and whither Jacob fled 27^{43} 28^{10} (both חָרָנָה), 29^{4}, as conquered by fathers of Sennacherib 2 K 19^{12}=Is 37^{12}; as place of trade Ez 27^{23}, As *Ḫarrana (-ni)*, Schr^{COT} on Gn 11^{31} 27^{43} 𝔊 Χαρραν. It was an ancient seat of worship of moon-god (Sin), v. Schr$^{\text{KG 555, 556}}$; see further Chwolsohn$^{\text{Ssabier i 303 ff}}$ Wüstenfeld$^{\text{ZMG 1864, 443 f}}$ Schr $^{\text{KG 555, 556}}$ Sachau$^{\text{Reise 217 ff.}}$ Mez$^{\text{Gesch. d. Stadt Harran, 1892}}$.

†II. **חָרָן** **n.pr.m.** son of Caleb of Judah 1 Ch 2$^{46.46}$, 𝔊 Αρραν, 𝔊L Ωρων (Sab. n.pr. חרן DHM$^{\text{Epigr Denkm 56}}$).

חוֹרֹן, **חרן** v. בית חורן p. 111 supr.

חֹרֹנִי **adj.gent.** v. *id*

†**חֹרוֹנַיִם**, **חֹרֹנַיִם** **n.pr.loc.** (poss *two hollows, caves, ravines*, v. בית חורן)—דֶּרֶךְ חרונים Is 15^{5} Je 48^{3}, מוֹרַד חרונים Je 48^{5}, חֹרֹנַיִם 48^{34}, city of Moab;=MI$^{31.32}$ חורנן (i e. prob חורנן); 𝔊 Αρωνιειμ, Ωρωναιμ.—On חֹרֹנַיִם 𝔊 Jos 13$^{10.11}$ 2 S 13^{34} v. We Dr and בית חורן.

†**חַרְנֶפֶר** **n.pr.m.** name in tribe of Asher 1 Ch 7^{36}=**n pr.loc.** v. Be — 𝔊 Αναρφαρ, A Αρναφαρ, 𝔊L Αριαφερ.

חרס (√of foll., meaning dubious)

†I. **חֶרֶס** **n.m.**$^{\text{Ju 14.18}}$ **sun** (NH *id*)—abs ח׳ Jb 9^{7} (‖כוכבים); c ה epenth. בְּטֶרֶם יָבֹא הַחַרְסָה Ju 14^{18} (cf. לַיְלָה, לַיִל) before the *sun* could go down (but rd perh הַחַדְרָה *into the* (bridal) *chamber* Sta$^{\text{ZAW 1884, 253 ff}}$).

†II [**חֶרֶס**] **n.pr.loc. 1.** abode of Amorites, בְּהַר־חֶרֶס בְּאַיָּלוֹן וּבְשַׁעַלְבִים Ju 1^{35}, since חֶרֶס *sun*=שֶׁמֶשׁ, perh.=בית שֶׁמֶשׁ **1.** (q v.), so Stu (who prop עִיר חֶרֶס=עִר), Ke Be Bu$^{\text{RS 17}}$ Ot Bla, 𝔊 ἐν τῷ [ὄρει τοῦ] Μυρσινῶνι(-os)=הַר הֲדַס **2.** place E. of Jordan מִלְמַעֲלֵה הֶחָרֶס Ju 8^{13} *from the ascent of Heres*, 𝔊 Αρες; the point whence Gideon turned back from pursuing Midian, Aq Symm rd הֶהָרִים (v Lag$^{\text{Onom 96, 2nd ed 131}}$) so SS—תִּמְנַת־חֶרֶס Ju 2^{9} v sub תִּמְנַת, √מנה

III. **חֶרֶס**, **חַרְסִית**, **חרכות** v sub חרשׂ.

חרע (√ of foll.; perh. cf. Aram. ܚܪܥ Ethpa *be clever*, ܚܪܝܥܐ *shrewd*, esp in bad sense, Ar. خَرَعَ *split*, VIII *originate, invent*)

†**תַּחְרֵעַ** **n.pr.m.** a great-great-grandson of Saul 1 Ch 9^{41} 𝔊 Θαρα(χ)=תַּאְרֵעַ 8^{35} 𝔊 Θερεε, A Θαρεε, 𝔊L in both Θαραα.

† I. [**חָרַף**] **vb. reproach** (NH Pi. *id.*, Aram. חָרֵף *id*, ܚܪܦ *sharpen*, ܚܪܝܦܐ *sharp, keen, acute*),—**Qal** *Impf.* לֹא־יֶחֱרַף לְבָבִי מִיָּמָי Jb 27^{6}, *Pt. sf* חרפי ψ 119^{42} Pr 27^{11}, חוֹרְפֶיךָ ψ 69^{10} **Piel.** *Pf.* חרף Ju 5^{18}+6 t., חֵרַפְתָּ Is 37^{23}+4 t etc.+10 t. pf., *Impf.* יְחָרֵף 2 S 21^{21} 1 Ch 20^{7}, יְחָרֵף ψ 74^{10}+2 t. sf; *Inf.* לְחָרֵף Is 37^{4}+5 t, בְּחָרְפָם 2 S 23^{9} (but v. infr.), *Pt.* מְחָרֵף ψ 44^{17}, —*reproach*,—prop. *say sharp things against*,—*taunt*, c. acc Ju 8^{15} 1 S 17$^{10.25.26.36.45}$ 2 S 21^{21} +1 Ch 20^{7}; God, by injustice to the poor Pr 14^{31} 17^{5}, Yahweh, by idolatry Is 65^{7}; Yahweh as the God of Israel 2 K 19$^{4.16.22.23}$=Is 37$^{4.17.23.24}$ =2 Ch 32^{17} (c. לְ), c. בְּ, Philistines 2 S 23^{9} MT (but rd. בְּפַס דַּמִּים *at Pas-dammîm*, n pr.loc, as 1 Ch 11^{13} We Dr); *reproach*, Ne 6^{13} ψ 42^{11} 44^{17} 55^{13} 57^{4} 74$^{10.18}$ 79^{12} 89$^{52.52}$ 102^{9} Zp 2$^{8.10}$, poet and fig, *despise, scorn*, ח׳ נפש למות Ju 5^{18}

†**חֶרְפָּה** **n.f. reproach**—ח׳ Gn 34^{14}+35 t, cstr. חֶרְפַּת Jos 5^{9}+15 t; sf. חֶרְפָּתְךָ ψ 74^{22} etc +17 t. sfs; pl חֲרָפוֹת ψ 69^{11} Dn 12^{2}; cstr חֶרְפוֹת ψ 69^{10}—**1.** *taunt* of enemy 1 S 17^{26}, so also 1 S 25^{39}; *reproach* cast upon another, *scorn, contumely* Ne 3^{36} 5^{9} ψ 69$^{20.21}$ 71^{13} 89^{51} 119^{22} Pr 18^{3} Is 51^{7} Ez 21^{33}, שמע ח׳ Je 51^{51} Zp 2^{8} La 3^{61}, נתן ח׳ על Je 23^{40}, נשׂא ח׳ על ψ 15^{3} (slander); נשׂא ח׳ Je 31^{19} Ez 36^{15} Mi 6^{16} (reproach); נשׂא ח׳ על *bear reproach for* ψ 69^{8} Je 15^{15} Zp 3^{18}, השיב ח׳ Ho 12^{15} Ne 3^{36}; חרף ח׳ ψ 69^{10} 79^{12} 89^{51}; הסיר ח׳ מעל 1 S 17^{26} Is 25^{8}, העביר ח׳ ψ 119^{39}; *reproaches against* God ψ 69^{10} (חֶרְפּוֹת חוֹרְפֶיךָ),

74^{22} 79^{12} **2.** *reproach* which rests upon one, condition of *shame, disgrace* **a.** sexual 2 S 13^{13} Is 47^{3} Ez 16^{57} Pr 6^{33}. **b.** barrenness of womb Gn 30^{23} (E) Is 4^{1}; widowhood Is 54^{4} **c.** hunger Ez 36^{30}, disease Jb 19^{5}. **d.** ritual, uncircumcision Gn 34^{14} (P) Jos 5^{9} (JE) **e.** injuries from enemies La 3^{30} 5^{1} Ne 1^{3} 2^{7} Jb 16^{10} Dn $11^{18\,18}$. **3** *a reproach,* the object of reproach, the person or thing reproached חֶרְפַּת אָדָם *a reproach of man* ψ 22^{7}, היה ח׳ ל׳ נבל ח׳ 39^{9}, *become an object of reproach to* 31^{12} 79^{4} 89^{42} 109^{25} Ez 5^{14}, (היה) לח (ל׳) Is 30^{5} Je 6^{10} 20^{8} 42^{18} $44^{8.12}$ 49^{13} ψ 69^{11} Dn 9^{16} 12^{2}, (ל׳) נתן ח׳ Ez 22^{4} Jo 2^{19} ψ 78^{66}, שים ח׳ ל׳ נתן לח׳ Je 24^{9} 29^{18} Ez 5^{14} Jo 2^{17}, ψ 44^{14}, שים ח׳ על 1 S 11^{2}.

†II **חרף** (√of foll, cf Ar حَرَفَ *gather fruit, pluck*)

†**חֹרֶף** **n.m. harvest-time, autumn** (Ar. خَرِيف *freshly gathered fruit, autumn* (also *rain of autumn* or *beginning of winter*) = Sab (ן)חרפ DHM ZMG 1875, xxix 597, Sab חרף, חרפם = *year,* cf Eth. ኀሪፍ: *annus currens* Os(Levy) ZMG 1865 168, 174 DHM ZMG 1883, 369, As *ḫarpu,* Schr JPTh 1875, 341 KAT² 53 n = COT¹ 54 n.)—abs. ח׳ Zc 14^{8} + 5 t, sf חָרְפִּי Jb 29^{4},—קַיִץ וָחֹרֶף Gn 8^{22} (J), ψ 74^{17} Zc 14^{8}, בית הַח׳ *autumn-house* or *palace* Am 3^{15} Je 36^{22} (+ בַּחֹדֶשׁ הַתְּשִׁיעִי *in the 9th month,* i e Nov-Dec); מֵח׳ עָצֵל לֹא יַחֲרֹשׁ Pr 20^{4} *a sluggard ploughs not after harvest,* as implying maturity, בִּימֵי חָרְפִּי Jb 29^{4} *in the days of my autumn* (prime)

III [חָרַף] **vb.denom. remain in harvest-time** (so Ar خَرَفَ, Eng. *to winter*)—only **Qal** *Impf* 3 fs כָּל־בֶּהֱמַת הָאָרֶץ עָלָיו תֶּחֱרָף Is 18^{6} *all the beasts of the earth shall spend the harvest-time upon it*

†**חָרֵף** (dub whether from I or II) **n.pr.m.** a chief of the line of Judah 1 Ch 2^{51}.

†**חָרִף**, **חָרִיף** **n.pr.m** (cf. Ar خَرِيف *autumn,* v. חֹרֶף supr)—**1.** חָרִף head of a family of returned exiles Ne 7^{24} (𝔊 Αρειφ, 𝔊L Ιωρηε) = יוֹרָה (cf יוֹרֶה *early rain*) Ezr 2^{18} (𝔊 Ουρα, A Ιωρα, 𝔊L Ωραι) **2.** חָרִיף one of those sealed Ne 10^{20} 𝔊 Αρειφ(α), 𝔊L Αρηφ.

†**חֲרִיפִי** Qr, הרופי Kt, **adj.gent.** c art, שְׁפַטְיָהוּ הַח׳ 1 Ch 12^{6} (Baer, v⁵ van d H), 𝔊 Χαρα(ι)φ(ε)ι, A Αρουφι, perh, if Qr right, connected with חָרִף Ne 7^{24}

†IV [**חָרַף**] **vb. acquire** (cf Ar حَرَفَ *turn a thing from its proper way or manner,* but also *gain, acquire* [subsistence] for one's family)—only **Niph.** *Pt f* שִׁפְחָה נֶחֱרֶפֶת לְאִישׁ *a maidservant acquired for a man* (viz as his concubine) Lv 19^{20} (H, cf. NH חֲרוּפָה of woman *designated* for a man).

†I **חָרַץ** **vb. cut, sharpen, decide** (NH *id, cut in, decide,* Aram in deriv, As. *ḫarâṣu, dig, decide, ḫarisu, trench,* Zehnpfund BAS I 502, Ph חרץ *decision,* Hoffm AGG xxxvi May 1889, 11)—**Qal** *Pf* 3 ms ח׳ Jos 10^{21}, חָרָצְתָּ 1 K 20^{40}, *Impf.* יחרץ Ex 11^{7}, 2 ms. תֶּחֱרָץ 2 S 5^{24}, *Pt pass.* חָרוּץ Is 10^{22} Lv 22^{22}, pl חֲרוּצִים Jb 14^{5} (v. also חָרוּץ infr)—**1** *cut, mutilate* Lv 22^{22} עַוֶּרֶת אוֹ שָׁבוּר (אוֹ־חָרוּץ אוֹ יַבֶּלֶת **2** *sharpen,* fig. the tongue, לֹא יֶחֱ־כֶּלֶב לְשֹׁנוֹ ל Ex 11^{7} (J), i e utter no sound against Isr, Jos 10^{21} **3.** *decide* 1 K 20^{40} (abs), so pt pass חרוצים ימיו Jb 14^{5} *his days are determined, fixed* (‖ מספר חדשיו), Is 10^{22} כִּלָּיוֹן ח׳, *act with decision* 2 S 5^{24}. **Niph.** *Pt.* נֶחֱרָצָה Is 10^{23} + 3 t, נֶחֱרֶצֶת Dn 9^{26} (both these forms inf cstr acc to Ba NB 90), *decisive* כָּלָה וְנֶח׳ Is 10^{23} 28^{22} Dn 9^{27} a consumption and *strict decision* (i e that which is strictly determined), נֶח׳ שֹׁמֵמוֹת Dn 11^{36}, כי נ׳ נֶעֱשָׂתָה Dn 9^{26} *strict determining of desolation*

†I **חָרוּץ** **adj. sharp, diligent** (on this and foll v Ba NB 173)—חָרוּץ Is 28^{27} + 11 t., pl חֲרוּצִים Pr 10^{4} 12^{24}, חָרֻצִים Pr 13^{4}; חֲרֻצוֹת Am 1^{3},—**1.** *sharp* of threshing instrument מוֹרַג ח׳ חָדָשׁ Is 41^{15}; without מ׳, as subst., 28^{27} (where יוּדַשׁ), ח׳ הַבַּרְזֶל Am 1^{3}, Jb 41^{22} (fig. of crocodile). **2.** fig *diligent* as subst Pr 21^{5}, opp רְמִיָּה Pr 10^{4} $12^{24.27}$; opp. עָצֵל Pr 13^{4}—Dn 9^{25} v IV חרוץ.

†II **חָרוּץ** **n** [**m.**] **strict decision,** only עֵמֶק הֶחָרוּץ Jo $4^{14\,14}$ *valley of strict decision* (v. Ba l.c.).

†III **חָרוּץ** **n.**[**m.**] **trench, moat** (Aram. חֲרִיצָא; As *ḫarisu, ḫirisu, id,* Dl HWB)—only in רחוב וח׳ Dn 9^{25}, si vera l; as above Ges Herzf Ew Zo Meinh (q v), Gr רחוב וחוץ, < 𝔖 Bev רחוב וָחוּץ *with public places and streets.*

†IV. **חָרוּץ** **n.pr.m.** father of king Amon's mother 2 K 21^{19}, 𝔊 Αρους.

†[**חָרִיץ**] **n.m.** 1 S 17. 18 **a cut, thing cut, sharp instrument**;—pl. cstr חֲרִיצֵי 1 S 17^{18} 1 Ch 20^{3}; חריצי 2 S 12^{31},—**1.** ח׳ הֶחָלָב 1 S 17^{18} *cuts of milk* i. e. cheeses. **2.** *sharp instr.* of iron, 2 S 12^{31} =

1 Ch 20³ בַּמְּגֵרָה ובח׳ הַבַּרְזֶל וּבַמְּגֵרוֹת (cf. Am 1³ sub חרץ **1**, and Dr^Sm)

†**חַרְצַנִּים n.m.pl.** some insignificant vine-product, usu. taken as **grape-kernels, grape-stones**, fr. acrid taste, so Thes (after Onk Mishn), v. also זָג p. 260 supr.: מִכֹּל אֲשֶׁר יֵעָשֶׂה מִגֶּפֶן הַיַּיִן מֵחַ׳ וְעַד־זָג Nu 6⁴ *of the wine-vine, including both* חרצנים *and* זג, he shall not eat.

II. **חרץ** *be yellow* (prob. ✓ of foll: Syr. ܚܪܨ *id.* (rare), ܚܪܘܨܐ *yellow;* cf. Aram. חריע *safflower*, Ar إِخْرِيضٌ *id* · v. No ZMG 1886, 728, Low Aram Pflanzenn. 218 Kö II 1, 157)

† v. **חָרוּץ n.m.** Pr 8, 10 gold, poet. (Ph. חרץ, v. Dr Sm xxviii; As. *hurâsu*)—חָרוּץ ψ 68¹⁴ + 5 t.; *gold*, always ‖ כֶּסֶף, Zc 9³, of dove's wings ψ 68¹⁴ בִּירַקְרַק ח׳; elsewh in comparison with value of wisdom, etc Pr 3¹⁴ 8¹⁰ (ח׳ נבחר) v¹⁹ 16¹⁶

חרצב (quadrilit. ✓ of foll, cf Ar. خَضْرَبَ *bind* or *twist powerfully*, Frey)

†[**חַרְצֻבָּה**] **n.[f.]** bond, fetter, pang, only pl. חַרְצֻבּוֹת,—**1.** cstr ח׳ רֶשַׁע Is 58⁶ *bonds of wickedness* i e. imposed by wicked men (‖ אֲגֻדּוֹת מוֹטָה). **2.** *pangs* (cf. חֵבֶל, חֶבֶל), abs. אין ח׳ למותם ψ 73⁴ *they have no pangs* (rd. לָמוֹ תָּם וגו׳).

חַרְצַנִּים v sub I חרץ

†**חָרַק vb. gnash** or **grind the teeth**, only poet. (NH *id;* Ar خَرَقَ *file, rub together, grate* or *grind* (teeth), Aram. ܚܪܩ *id*)—**Qal** *Pf.* 3 ms ח׳ Jb 16⁹; *Impf.* יַחֲרֹק ψ 112¹⁰; וַיַּחַרְקוּ La 2¹⁶; *Inf. abs.* חָרֹק ψ 35¹⁶, *Pt.* חֹרֵק ψ 37¹²;—*grind* the teeth in rage against. ח׳ שניו על ψ 37¹² 35¹⁶, abs without על 112¹⁰ La 2¹⁶ (only here c. שֵׁן sing.); c בְּ instr. (Ges § 119. 3b. R. Da Synt. § 73 R 4) ח׳ בשניו על־ Jb 16⁹.

†I. [**חָרַר**] **vb. be hot, scorched, burn,** poet & late (Ar. حَرَّ *be hot, burn, thirst;* Eth. ሐረረ: Aram חַר, cf. As *arâru, glow*, SASm Assb. i, p. 97 Belser BAS ii. 135)—**Qal** *Pf.* 3 fs. חָרָה Jb 30³⁰, וְחָרָה consec. Ez 24¹¹, חָרוּ Is 24⁶,—**1.** *be hot, scorched*, Jerus, under fig. of caldron Ez 24¹¹. **2.** *burn* = *be burned*, fig. of men, in ׳י's judgment, Is 24⁶. **3.** *burn*, of bones of sick men in fever ח׳ מִנִּי־חֹרֶב Jb 30³⁰. **Niph.** *Pf.* נָחַר Je 6²⁹, נָחָר Ez 15⁴, נחר ψ 69⁴; 3 pl. נִחָרוּ ψ 102⁴ (Kö I 368), *Impf.* יֵחָר Ez 15⁵ יֵחַתּוּ Ez 24¹⁰ (del. Co B al.) **1.** *be scorched*, of bellows מַפֻּחַ in fierce fire Je 6²⁹ (fig), *scorched, charred*, of the vine (as fuel) Ez 15⁴·⁵ middle part charred, the ends devoured (אכל) by fire (sim. of inhab. of Jerus.); bones (sim. *id*) Ez 24¹⁰ (v. supr.) **2.** *burn*, of bones in fever ψ 102⁴ (כְּמוֹקֵד, cf. **Qal** Jb 30³⁰); *be parched*, of throat נח׳ גרוני 69⁴. —Is 41¹¹ 45²⁴ Ct 1⁶ v חרה **Pilp.** *Inf.* לְחַרְחַר־רִיב Pr 26²¹ *to kindle strife*

†[**חָרֵר**] **n.[m.] parched place** (Ar حَرَّاتٌ, Bd Pal 196), only pl. abs. חֲרֵרִים, ח׳ במדבר Je 17⁶ (‖ עֲרָבָה) fig of life of godless

†**חַרְחֻר n.m. violent heat, fever** (v. Ba NB 206)—בַּשַּׁחֶפֶת וּבַקַּדַּחַת וּבַדַּלֶּקֶת וּבַח׳ ובחרב וגו׳ Dt 28²².

†**חַרְחוּר n.pr.m.** head of a family of returning exiles Ezr 2⁵¹ = Ne 7⁵³, 𝔊 Αρου(α)ρ (meaning as above? or fr II חרר?)

II. **חרר** (✓ of foll; Ar حَرَّ *be* or *become free*, حُرٌّ *free, freeborn;* NH חרר Pi. *set free*, חר *freeman*, Aram. חֲרַר, ܚܪ Pa *set free*, חֵרָא, חֵרְתָא *freed-man, -woman;* Sab. חר *freeman, noble* (?) DHM Epigr Denkm. 57, Eth ሐራ: coll *army, troops* (in Amhar. *free, noble*, acc. to Di 85), ሐራዊ: *free, noble*, etc)

† II [**חֹר**] **n.m.** 1 K 21⁸ **noble**, late, esp. Neh, v Dr Intr 519 n (v Lag BN 82)—only pl חֹרִים 1 K 21⁸ + 6 t., חוֹרִים Ec 10¹⁷, Ne 6¹⁷ + 3 t; sf. חֹרֶיהָ Is 34¹²,—*nobles* in Naboth's city 1 K 21⁸·¹¹, nobles of Judah, חרי יהודה 6¹⁷ 13¹⁷ Je 27²⁰ 39⁶ Ne 6¹⁷ 13¹⁷, הח׳ והסגנים (in Jerusalem) Ne 2¹⁶ 4⁸·¹³ 5⁷ 7⁵, Ec 10¹⁷, of Edom Is 34¹²—I. חֹר, v. II. חור.

III **חרר** (✓ of foll., v. As *ḫarâru, bore, pierce, ḫurru, hole, ravine* Dl Pr 150, 182; Ar. خَرَّ *hole* or *mouth* of millstone; NH חִרְחֵר *bore, pierce*)

† III **חֹר**, **חוֹר n.[m.]** hole,—abs חֹר 2 K 12¹⁰ Ez 8⁷ (del Co B etc.), חוֹר Ct 5⁴, חֹרִים 1 S 14¹¹, cstr חֹרֵי Jb 30⁶; sf חֹרָיו Na 2¹³, חוֹרֵיהֶן Zc 14¹²,—*hole* in lid of chest 2 K 12¹⁰ (made by boring, נקב), in door Ct 5⁴; in wall Ez 8⁷ (v. supra), = eye-*socket* עיניו תִּמַּקְנָה בְּח׳ Zc 14¹² (plague of enemies of Jerusalem); *holes* as hiding-places for men 1 S 14¹¹, so also 13⁶ Ew We I r (for MT חוחים), dwelling of outcast people חֹרֵי עָפָר Jb 30⁶; of *dens* of lions Na 2¹³—I חֹר, v. II. חור.

† **חֻר**, **חוּר n.[m.]** id.—coll. חוּר Is 42²² as hiding-places of men, cstr חֻר Is 11⁸ hole of asp (פֶּתֶן).

†II. חֹרִי, חוֹרִי adj., usu. n.pr.gent. et pers. (prob. = *cave-dweller*, so Thes RobGes MV VB; v. also W Max Müll Asien u. Europa 136, 155, 156)—**1.** adj. gent. שֵׂעִיר הַח׳ Gn 36^{20} *Seir the Horite* (P); rd. הַח׳ also v^{2} for MT הַחִוִּי. **2.** n.pr.gent. alw. c. art.; usu. sg. coll. הַחֹרִי, ancient inhabitants of land of Edom Gn 14^{6} (בְּהַרְרָם שֵׂעִיר); in P called בְּנֵי שֵׂעִיר בְּאֶרֶץ אֱדוֹם 36^{21} (vid. v^{20}); cf. $v^{29.30}$; acc. to Dt 2^{12} (where alone הַחֹרִים), v^{22} they were driven out by sons of Esau (yet v. Gn $36^{l.c.}$ and Di); 𝔊 ὁ Χορραῖος, οἱ Χορραῖοι, (Gn $36^{29.30}$ Χορρ(ε)ι). **3.** n.pr.pers.m. **a.** חֹרִי an Edomite Gn 36^{22} = 1 Ch 1^{39}; 𝔊 Χορρ(ε)ι. **b.** חוֹרִי a Simeonite Nu 13^{5}, but 𝔊 Σουρ(ε)ι, 𝔊L Σουδρι.—I. חֹרִי v. sub I. חור.

חרשׂ (√of foll.; cf. Ar. خَرَشَ vb. *scratch, lacerate*, خِرَاش *irritation*, etc.)

†**חֶרֶשׂ** n.[m.] **earthenware, earthen vessel, sherd, potsherd,** P and late (NH חֶרֶס, Aram. חַסְפָּא)—abs. ח׳ Lv 6^{21} + 9 t., חָרֶשׂ Nu 5^{17} + 4 t.; pl. cstr. חַרְשֵׂי Is 45^{9}; sf. חֲרָשֶׂיהָ Ez 23^{34}.—**1.** *earthenware:* כְּלִי־ח׳ *earthen vessel* Je 32^{14}; esp. P Lv 6^{21} 11^{33} $14^{5.50}$ 15^{12} Nu 5^{17}; without כְּלִי Pr 26^{23}; cf. בַּקְבֻּק יוֹצֵר ח׳ Je 19^{1}; לְנִבְלֵי ח׳ La 4^{2} they are reckoned *as earthen vessels*, sim. of sons of Zion; חֶרֶשׂ אֶת־חַרְשֵׂי אֲדָמָה Is 45^{9} *a potsherd* (perh. = *earthen vessel*, v. Pr 26^{23} supr.) *among earthen potsherds* (of men, over against י׳ their potter); sim. of dryness ψ 22^{16}. **2.** *a fragment of earthenware, sherd* Is 30^{14} Ez 23^{34}; ח׳ לְהִתְגָּרֵד Jb 2^{8} *a sherd to scrape himself;* חַדּוּדֵי ח׳ Jb 41^{22} *sharpest potsherds*, fig. of sharp scales on belly of crocodile.

חֲרֶשֶׂת v. קִיר־חֲרֶשֶׂת.

†III. [חֶרֶס] n.[m.] an eruptive disease, itch (Aram. חַרְסָא, ܚܰܪܣܳܐ; also ܚܰܪܽܘܣܳܐ *rough*, etc.)—וּבֶחָרֶס Dt 28^{27} (‖ עפלים Kt, גָּרָב).—I, II. חֶרֶס v. sub חרם.

†**חרסות** Kt, **חַרְסִית** Qr n.f.coll. **potsherd**—פֶּתַח שַׁעַר הַחַרְסוּת Je 19^{2}, designation of a gate in Jerus.; opening of the *gate of potsherds*, i.e. where they were thrown (vid. $v^{10.11}$ and Gf); it led into the valley of Hinnom; 𝔊 χαρσ(ε)ιθ favours Qr.

†I. [**חָרַשׁ**] vb. **cut in, engrave, plough, devise** (NH *id.*, *plough*, so Eth. ሐረሰ: Ph. חרש, Aram. (rare) חֲרַת *engrave*, ܚܪܰܫ *cleave, plough*, Ar. حَرَثَ *plough*)—**Qal** *Pf.* חָרְשׁוּ ψ 129^{3}, חֲרַשְׁתֶּם Ju 14^{18} Ho 10^{13}; *Impf.* יַחֲרֹשׁ Is 28^{24} Pr 20^{4}; יַחֲרוֹשׁ Ho 10^{11} + Am 6^{12} (v. infr.); 2 ms. תַּחֲרֹשׁ Dt 22^{10} Pr 3^{29}; *Inf. cstr.* חֲרֹשׁ 1 S 8^{12}; *Pt.* חֹרֵשׁ Gn 4^{22} + 5 t.; חוֹרֵשׁ Am 9^{13}; pl. חֹרְשִׁים ψ 129^{3}, חֹרְשֵׁי Jb 4^{8} + 3 t., fpl. abs. חֹרְשׁוֹת Jb 1^{14}; *pass.* חֲרוּשָׁה Je 17^{1}:—**1.** *cut in, engrave,* of worker in metals ח׳ נְחֹשֶׁת וּבַרְזֶל Gn 4^{22} (J), ח׳ נחשת 1 K 7^{14}; fig. ח׳ עַל־לוּחַ לִבָּם Je 17^{1} *engraved on the tablet of their heart.* **2.** *plough,* lit., human subj. (animal usu. c. בְּ), no obj. expr. 1 K 19^{19} Dt 22^{10} Is 28^{24}, so יַחֲרוֹשׁ בבקרים Am 6^{12} (but rd. prob. יֵחָרֵשׁ בבקר יָם, v. We al.); c. acc. cogn. ח׳ חֲרִישׁוֹ 1 S 8^{12} *plough his ploughing* (= *do his ploughing*), Pr 20^{4}; fig. of Judah Ho 10^{11}; with ethical ref. ח׳ רֶשַׁע v^{13} (‖ קצר), ח׳ אָוֶן Jb 4^{8} (‖ זרע, קצר); עַל־גַּבִּי חָרְשׁוּ חֹרְשִׁים ψ 129^{3} *upon my back have ploughmen ploughed* (fig. of oppression by wicked); חֹרֵשׁ = *ploughman* Is 28^{24}, Am 9^{13} (‖ קוֹצֵר); ח׳ with oxen subj. only Jb 1^{14}. **3.** *devise* (as one who *works in, practises*), usu. bad sense, obj. רָעָה Pr 3^{29}, 6^{14}; מַחְשְׁבוֹת אָוֶן v^{18}, חֹרְשֵׁי רָע Pr 12^{20} 14^{22}; but also חֹרְשֵׁי טוֹב v^{22}. **Niph.** *Impf.* 3 fs. צִיּוֹן שָׂדֶה תֵּחָרֵשׁ Mi 3^{12} Zion, as a field she *shall be ploughed* = Je 26^{18}. **Hiph.** *Pt.* מַחֲרִישׁ רָעָה עַל־ 1 S 23^{9} *fabricating mischief against* (v. Dr, and cf. We).

†**חָרָשׁ** n.m. Ex 38, 23 **graver, artificer** (Ph. חרש)—abs. ח׳ (= * חַרָּשׁ) Ex 35^{35} + 14 t.; cstr. חָרַשׁ Ex 28^{11} + 2 t.; pl. חָרָשִׁים Ho 13^{2} + 7 t.; חֲרָשִׁים 1 Ch $4^{14.14}$ Ne 11^{35} (v. infr.); cstr. חָרָשֵׁי 2 S 5^{11} + 6 t.;—**1.** *graver, artificer:* **a.** worker in metal 1 S 13^{19} Ho 8^{6} 13^{2} Dt 27^{15} Je 10^{9} (‖ צֹרֵף), Is 40^{19} (‖ *id.*), 54^{16} 1 Ch 29^{5}; ח׳ בַּרְזֶל Is 44^{12} 2 Ch 24^{12}; perh. also Is 41^{7} (+ צֹרֵף); appar. = hammerer Zc 2^{3} (symbol.). **b.** worker in wood ח׳ עֵץ 2 S 5^{11} = 1 Ch 14^{1} (עֵצִים), 2 K 12^{12} 22^{6} = 2 Ch 34^{11}, Je 10^{3} Is 40^{20} 44^{13} (v. also 1 Ch 22^{15} infr.); perh. also Ezr 3^{7} 2 Ch 24^{12} (both ‖ חצב). **c.** worker in stone ח׳ אֶבֶן קִיר 2 S 5^{11} = 1 Ch 14^{1} (om. אבן); also of engraving on gems ח׳ אבן Ex 28^{11} (P; ‖ פִּתּוּחֵי חֹתָם); see also foll. **d.** in gen. ח׳ אֶבֶן וָעֵץ 1 Ch 22^{15}; *idol-maker* ח׳ צִירִים Is 45^{16}, cf. 44^{11} (also $v^{12.13}$ supr.), 2 K $24^{14.16}$ Je 24^{1} 29^{2} (all ‖ מַסְגֵּר), Ex 35^{35} 38^{23} (both P; both ‖ חֹשֵׁב). In גֵּי הַח׳ 1 Ch 4^{14}, גֵּיא חֲרָשִׁים Ne 11^{35} *valley of (the) artificers*, and חֲרָשִׁים *artificers* 1 Ch 4^{14}, ח has ֲ exceptionally, v. Ol § 183 a Kö II, § 60. 5; rd. חָרָשִׁים? **2.** fig. ח׳ מַשְׁחִית Ez 21^{36} *men skilled to destroy.*

† I. **חֲרֹשֶׁת** n.f. **carving, skilful working,** only cstr. חֲרֹשֶׁת עֵץ Ex 31^{5} 35^{33}; ח׳ אֶבֶן 31^{5} 35^{33}.—II. חֲרֹשֶׁת v. p. 361 infr.

†חָרִישׁ **n.m. ploughing, ploughing-time**—abs חָ׳ וְקָצִיר Gn 45[6] (E) *ploughing and harvesting;* also (=*time of ploughing and harvest*) Ex 34[21] (JE); c. sf as acc. cogn. חָרַשׁ חֲרִישׁוֹ 1 S 8[12] (v. supr. חָרַשׁ **2**)

†[מַחֲרֶשֶׁת, מַחֲרֵשָׁה] **n.f. ploughshare**—sg sf. לִלְטוֹשׁ אִישׁ מַחֲרַשְׁתּוֹ v[20] *to sharpen each man his ploughshare* 1 S 13[20] (+ אֶתוֹ, קַרְדֻּמּוֹ)+ מַחֲרֵשָׁתוֹ v[20], rd. prob דָּרְבָנוֹ *his goad* (so 𝔊 𝔖 We Dr, see v[21]), pl abs מַחֲרֵשֹׁת v[21] (+similar list; on txt. of both vv. see Dr)

† II. [חָרַשׁ] **vb. 1.** **be silent, dumb, speechless**, **2.** **be deaf**; chiefly poet. (NH Pi. *make deaf;* Aram. ܚܪܫ, ܚܪܫ *be dumb, deaf;* Ar. خَرِسَ *be dumb, speechless,* cf. As *ḫarâšu, restrain,* acc. to Dl[Pr 100]; v. Lag[BN 120])—**Qal** *Impf.* יֶחֱרַשׁ ψ 50[3], 2 ms. תֶּחֱרַשׁ ψ 28[1] 83[2], תֶּחֱרַשׁ ψ 35[22] 109[1]; תֶּחֱרָשׁ ψ 39[13], 3 fpl. תֶּחֱרַשְׁנָה Mi 7[16], —**1.** *be silent,* alw. of God's keeping silence when men pray ψ 35[22] 50[3] 83[2] 109[1]; sq אֶל־ 39[13]. **2.** *be deaf,* subj י׳, sq. מִמֶּנִּי ψ 28[1]; subj. אָזְנֵיהֶם Mi 7[16]. **Hiph.** *Pf.* הֶחֱרִשׁ Nu 30[15] Gn 34[5]; וְהֶחֱרִישׁ consec. Nu 30[5.8]; וְהחרשׁ consec. Nu 30[12], הֶחֱרַשְׁתִּי Est 7[4] + 2 t etc.; *Impf* יַחֲרִישׁ Nu 30[15] + 2 t. (incl. Zp 3[17] v. infr); 2 ms. תַּחֲרִישׁ Hb 1[13], juss תַּחֲרֵשׁ 1 S 7[8], 2 mpl תַּחֲרִישׁוּן Jb 13[5], תַּחֲרִשׁוּן Ex 14[14], etc.; *Imv* הַחֲרֵשׁ Ju 18[19] + 2 t; הַחֲרִישִׁי 2 S 13[20], הַחֲרִישׁוּ Jb 13[13] Is 41[1], *Inf abs* הַחֲרֵשׁ Nu 30[15] + 2 t, *Pt* מַחֲרִישׁ Gn 24[21] + 2 t (incl 1 S 10[27] v. infr); מַחֲרִישִׁים 2 S 19[11],—**1.** *be silent* (=*exhibit silence*) **a.** almost alw. of men Gn 24[21] 34[5] Ex 14[14] (all J), Ju 18[19] 2 S 13[20] 19[11] 2 K 18[36]=Is 36[21], Je 4[19] Jb 6[24] 13[5.5.19] 33[31.33] Pr 11[12] 17[28] ψ 32[3] Ne 5[8] Est 4[14.14] 7[4]; also וַיְהִי כְּמַחֲרִישׁ 1 S 10[27] (but rd. rather ויהי כמחדשׁ *and it came to pass after about a month,* 𝔊 Dr); יחריש באהבתו Zp 3[17] (𝔊 𝔖 יחדשׁ *he will renew* his love, v esp. Buhl[ZAW v 1885, 183]); ח׳ c ל pers. *keep silence at* one, i e fail to make objection at proper time Nu 30[5.8.12.15.15.15] (all P); הח׳ אלי Is 41[1] pregn =*come silently unto me;* sq. מִן pers *cease to speak with* Je 38[27]; *be silent about, pass by in silence,* sq. acc. אח׳ בַּדָּיו Jb 41[4]. **b.** rarely of God, permitting evil in silence Hb 1[13] Is 42[14] ψ 50[21]. **2.** once causat *make silent,* c. acc Jb 11[3]. **3.** *be deaf, shew deafness.* אַל־תַּחֲרֵשׁ מִמֶּנּוּ מִזְּעֹק 1 S 7[8] *be not deaf* (turning) *from us, so as not to cry.*

†חֵרֵשׁ **adj. deaf**—חרשׁ (=*חֵרֵשׁ) Ex 4[11] + 4 t.; pl. חֵרְשִׁים Is 29[18] + 3 t,—*deaf,* Ex 4[11] (J, ‖ אִלֵּם), ψ 38[14] (‖ *id*), also Lv 19[14] (H), Is 29[18] 35[5] 42[18.19] + v[19 b] (for last עִוֵּר, cf. 43[8], Gr[JQ 1891, Oct p. 2] v. Che[Comm., JQ Jan 1892, 332]), 43[8], פֶּתֶן ח׳ ψ 58[5] *a deaf adder.*

† I חֶרֶשׁ **n.[m.] as adv. silently, secretly**—מְרַגְּלִים ח׳ Jos 2[1] (JE) *exploring secretly.*

III חרשׁ (√of foll; meaning unknown)

†חֹרֶשׁ **n.m.** [Ez 31, 3] **wood, wooded height** (As. *ḫuršu, wooded height* COT[Gloss] Lyon[Sargontexte, Gloss] (v. also Dl[Pr 180] Che[crit n on Is 17, 9]); NH חוֹרֶשׁ *wood, forest;* Aram. חוּרְשָׁא *id*)—abs. ח׳ Is 17[9] Ez 31[3] (but on both v infr); חֹרְשָׁה 1 S 23[16] (v. Dr); בַּחֹרְשָׁה 1 S 23[15.18.19]; pl חֳרָשִׁים 2 Ch 27[4];—*wooded height* 1 S 23[15] (‖ בָּהָר v[14]), v[16.18], so בִּמְצָדוֹת בַּח׳ v[19]; בִּגְבְעַת הַחֲכִילָה וּבֶח׳ בנה בִּירָנִיּוֹת וּמִגְדָּלִים 2 Ch 27[4] *and on the wooded heights he built fortresses and towers* (‖ בְּהַר יְהוּדָה); עֲזוּבַת הַחֹרֶשׁ וְהָאָמִיר Is 17[9] *the forsaken places of the wooded heights and summits* Ges Ew De Di RV, but rd prob ע׳ החוי והאמרי *forsaken places of the Hivites and the Amorites,* so 𝔊 Lag Che Or Brd Du; ח׳ מֵצַל Ez 31[3] *shade-giving wood* or *thicket,* of close branches of cedar (but sense hardly legitimate; del. 𝔊 Co)

IV. חרשׁ (√of foll; meaning unknown, suggestions on etym v. infr)

† II. [חֶרֶשׁ] **n.[m.] magic art, or perh. magic drug** (Aram. ܚܪܫ *practise magic,* חָרָשׁ, ܚܪܫܐ *magician,* ܚܪܫܐ *incantation, magic art, preparation of magic potion,* so Eth. ሐረሰ: *one using incantations,* ሐረሰ: ሐርስ: ሐራስ: *incantation, magic;* comp perh. Ar. خُرْسَةٌ, خُرْسٌ a medicinal broth given to women in childbed; חֶרֶשׁ perh. magical drug, v. RS[JPh xiv 1885, 125])—only חֲכַם חֲרָשִׁים Is 3[3] *skilled in magic arts,* or *drugs* (‖ נְבוֹן לָחַשׁ), (>others gen =*handicraft*).

† III. חֶרֶשׁ **n.pr.m.** a Levite 1 Ch 9[15] 𝔊 Ραραιηλ, A Αρες, 𝔊L Αρης.

†חַרְשָׁא **n.pr m.** head of a family of returning exiles Ezr 2[52] 𝔊 Αρησα, 𝔊L Βασσα, =Ne 7[54] 𝔊 Αδασα

† II. חֲרֹשֶׁת **n.pr.loc.** only in combin ח׳ הַגּוֹיִם, *Harosheth of the nations* (v. גּוֹי), Ju 4[2.13.16]; perh mod *el-Ḥarithiye,* on right bank of lower Kishon, v Thomson[Land and Book, Central Palestine, 1883, 215 ff] Bd[Pal 241] Be Bla Cooke[Hist. Deb 3] GASm[Geog. 393].

הַחֲרָשִׁים v. חָרָשׁ and גַּיְא, also II. חֶרֶשׁ.

† [חָרִישִׁי] **adj.** meaning wholly dub., only רוּחַ קָדִים חֲרִישִׁית Jon 4[8], *a silent east wind* is not suitable in context, *still = sultry* is mere conject.; Hi *autumnal* (√ I. חרשׁ), St prop חֲרִישִׁית = חריסית, fr חֶרֶס *sun* (or √ whence חרס comes) *hot east wind*, We makes no attempt to explain.

† [חָרַת] **vb. grave, engrave,** only **Qal** *Pt pass* חָרוּת עַל הַלֻּחֹת Ex 32[16] (E), *engraved upon the tablets* (by finger of God), but fr absence of ‖ in cogn lang (Ar حَرَتَ is *perforate, bore, slit*) prob error for חָרוּשׁ (Je 17[1]).

† [חֶרֶת] **n.pr.loc.,** only in יַעַר חֶרֶת 1 S 22[5].

† חָשַׂךְ **vb. withhold, refrain** (NH חָסַךְ, Aram חֲסַךְ, ܚܣܟ; Palm חסך *remit, spare*, Vog[Nos 6. 15], Sab. מתחכן *weaned* (child) DHM[ZMG 1875. 608])—**Qal** *Pf.* חָשַׂךְ Gn 39[9] + 4 t. (+ Ez 30[18] Ba, v חשׁך, Is 38[17] v infr.), חָשַׂכְתָּ Is 14[6], חָשְׂכוּ Jb 30[10], חָשָׂכְנוּ Je 14[10], etc.; *Impf* יַחְשֹׂךְ Jb 16[5] + 2 t., 2 ms תַּחְשֹׂךְ Is 58[1], Pr 24[11], 2 fs תַּחְשְׂכִי Is 54[2], etc., *Imv* חֲשֹׂךְ ψ 19[14], *Pt* חוֹשֵׂךְ Pr 10[19] 11[24], חֹשֵׂךְ Pr 13[24] 17[27], sq.—**1. a.** *withhold, keep back, keep for oneself*, acc., Gn 22[12] (E), v[16] 39[9] (sq מִמֶּנִּי, both J), abs Pr 21[26] (opp נָתַן); *withhold the rod* (שׁבט) in discipline, Pr 13[24], no obj. expr. 11[24] 24[11]. **b.** *keep* one from evil, calamity, She'ôl, etc., c. acc. and מִן Gn 20[6] (E), 1 S 25[39] ψ 19[14], ח׳ מִמָּוֶת נַפְשָׁם ψ 78[50] cf Jb 33[18] Is 38[17] (rd חָשַׂכְתָּ or חשׂך for MT חָשַׁקְתָּ, v חשׁק), abs *hinder* (i.e calamities fr coming) Is 14[6]; ח׳ לְמַטָּה מעוננו Ezr 9[13] thou hast *kept back, downward* (= and kept down), *part of our iniquity*, i e hast not punished us according to our full desert. **c.** *hold in check* c. acc. 2 S 18[16] (or *spare* v. infr.), obj רַגְלֵיהֶם Je 14[10], esp. of keeping silence, obj פֶּה Jb 7[11] *restrain my mouth*, שׂפתים Pr 10[19], אמרים 17[27], מִפָּנַי לֹא ח׳ רֹק Jb 30[10] *from my face they have not withheld spittle* (= they have spit in my face). **d.** *refrain* (fr doing what is mentioned in the context), abs Is 54[2] 58[1]. **e.** *spare*, c. acc. pers. 2 K 5[20] *he hath spared* Naaman מִקַּחַת *so as not to take* (= and hath not taken anything) out of his hand, perh also 2 S 18[16] Joab *spared* the people (v. supr.). **f.** *reserve* for, c. acc. + לְ Jb 38[23]. **2.** (abs) *restrain, check* (pain) i e *assuage*, so appar. MT Jb 16[5] (v Di Kau; *I would not restrain condolence of my lips*, 𝔊 𝔖 Me, rdg לא אחשׂך for יחשׂך)—Ez 30[18] v חשׁך.

Niph. *Impf* לְיוֹם אֵיד יֵחָשֶׂךְ רָע Jb 21[30] *at the day of calamity the wicked is spared* (pass. of **Qal 1 e**), יֵחָשֵׂךְ Jb 16[6] *be assuaged*, of pain (pass. of **Qal 2**).

† חָשַׂף **vb. strip off, strip, make bare**—**Qal** *Pf* חָשַׂף Is 52[10], חֲשָׂפָהּ Jo 1[7], חָשַׂפְתִּי Je 13[26] 49[10], *Impf.* וַיֶּחֱשֹׂף ψ 29[9]; *Imv* fs. חֶשְׂפִּי־ Is 47[2], *Inf. abs* חָשֹׂף Jo 1[7], *cstr* לַחְשֹׂף Is 30[14] Hg 2[16]; *Pt pass* חֲשׂוּפָה Ez 4[7], חֲשׂוּפַי Is 20[4] (pl cstr? cf. *infr.*)—**1.** *strip off*, expose oneself by removing (obj שֹׁבֶל, flowing skirt, train) Is 47[2] of Babylon, personified as queen (‖ גַּלִּי שׁוֹק), ח׳ שׁוּלַיִךְ עַל־פָּנַיִךְ Je 13[26]. **2.** *strip, lay bare*, fig of י׳ Is 52[10] obj זרוע קדשׁו, of prophet, Ez 4[7] (but Co del v as interpol); obj pers. Je 49[10] (‖ גִּלֵּיתִי), חָשֹׂף חשׂפה Jo 1[7] of locusts stripping fig-tree; חֲשׂוּפַי שׁת Is 20[4] (pt. either sg coll., with formative ending ־ַי, De Lag[Sem i. 19 (cf. 89). BN 192], or pl cstr, v Ges[§ 87. 1 c.]); ח׳ יְעָרוֹת ψ 29[9] of voice of י׳ (i e a storm) stripping forests. **3.** *draw* (water) Is 30[14], (wine) Hg 2[16]; properly *take from the surface, skim*.

† [חָשִׂיף] **n.m.** only pl cstr כִּשְׁנֵי חֲשִׂפֵי עִזִּים 1 K 20[27] 𝔊 𝔙 𝔗 and most, *two little flocks of goats* (חשׂיף = *segregatum*, strictly *what is stripped off*), but this without other evidence than authority of the Vrss; Klo proposes בַּשְּׁפִי מִשְׁפַּט עִזִּים *on the bare height, after the manner of goats*.

† חֲשׂוּפָא, חֲשֻׂפָא **n.pr.m.** head of a family of Nethinim among the returning exiles חֲשׂוּפָא Ezr 2[43] = חֲשֻׂפָא Ne 7[46].

חֲשׂוּפַי Is 20[4] v חשׂף.

† מַחְשֹׂף **n.m. a laying bare, stripping**—only cstr. מַחְשֹׂף הַלָּבָן Gn 30[37] (J) *a stripping of the white*, i e. so as to shew wood under the bark.

† חָשַׁב **vb. think, account** (NH *id.*; Aram חֲשַׁב, ܚܫܒ; Ar. حَسَبَ; Eth ሐሰበ: *id.*; Ph n חשׁב mng dub v CIS[I 86])—**Qal** *Pf* ח׳ Is 33[8] + 9 t.; חֲשַׁבְתָּה 2 S 14[13] etc.; *Impf* יַחְשֹׁב Is 10[7] + 4 t., יַחֲשָׁב־ 2 S 19[20] ψ 40[18]; sf. יַחְשְׁבֵנִי Jb 19[11] 33[10]; pl יַחְשְׁבוּ ψ 41[8] Dn 11[25]; יַחְשֹׁבוּ Is 13[17]; יַחְשְׁבוּן ψ 35[20], נַחְשְׁבָה Je 18[18], etc. + 9 t. *Impf*, *Inf cstr.* לַחְשֹׁב Ex 31[4] + 3 t.; *Pt.* חשׁב Ex 26[1] + 15 t., חוֹשֵׁב 2 Ch 26[15]; חֹשְׁבִים Ne 6[2] + 3 t., חֹשְׁבֵי Mi 2[1] + 3 t.;—**I.** of man: **1.** *think*,

account לבבו לא כן יחשב Is 10^{7} *not so thinketh his mind;* חשבי שמו Mal 3^{16} those *thinking of his name;* sq. 2 acc. חשבנהו נגוע Is 53^{4} *we thought him stricken;* elsewhere c. acc. + לְ Gn 38^{15} (J), 1 S 1^{13} Jb 19^{15} 35^{2} 41^{24}; so, fig., of crocodile Jb 41^{19} *he reckoneth iron as straw.* **2.** *devise, plan, mean,* c. acc. מַחֲשֶׁבֶת רָעָה Ez 38^{10}, מְזִמּוֹת ψ 35^{4} 140^{3} Zc 7^{10} 8^{17}, תַּהְפֻּכוֹת Pr 16^{30}, רעה ψ 10^{2} 21^{12}, דִּבְרֵי מִרְמוֹת ψ 35^{20}, אָוֶן Mi 2^{1} Ez 11^{2} ψ 36^{5}, הַוּוֹת ψ 52^{4}; ח׳ רע(ה) על *devise evil against* Gn 50^{20} (E), Je 48^{2} Na 1^{11}, ח׳ רעה לְ ψ 41^{8}, ח׳ מַחֲשֶׁבֶת על Je 11^{19} 18^{18} 49^{30} Dn 11^{25} Est 8^{3} 9^{25}, ח׳ כזאת על 2 S 14^{13}; c. inf. 1 S 18^{25} Je 18^{8} 23^{27} Jb 6^{26} Ne 6$^{2.6}$ Est 9^{24} ψ 140^{5}; c. לבלתי + Impf. 2 S 14^{14} (where, however, Ew rds. חוֹשֵׁב for וחשב cf. We Dr; in this case לבלתי carries on לֹא יִשָּׂא). **3.** *charge, impute* ח׳ עון לְ, 2 S 19^{20} *impute iniquity to.* **4.** *esteem, value, regard,* silver Is 13^{17}, a man Is 33^{8}, the servant of ׳י Is 53^{3}. **5.** *invent* ingenious and artistic things, ח׳ להם כלי שיר Am 6^{5} *invent* for themselves instruments of music; ח׳ (כל) מחשבת *invent cunning work* (of artistic devices in constr. of tabern.) Ex 31^{4} 35$^{32.35}$ (all P), so 2 Ch 2^{13}; מַעֲשֵׂה חֹשֵׁב *work of the cunning* (ingenious, inventive) *workman* (of artistic devices in weaving; see esp. VB and Di) Ex 26$^{1.31}$ 28$^{6.15}$ 36$^{8.35}$ 39$^{3.8}$ (all P); מַחְשְׁבֹת חוֹשֵׁב 2 Ch 26^{15} *inventions of inventive men* (of engines of war); חָרָשׁ וְחֹשֵׁב *craftsman and inventive workman* (in constr. of tabern., vid. supr.) Ex 35^{35} 38^{23} (P). **II.** of God: **1.** *think,* c. acc. pers + לְ indirect obj. *account one* לאויב, *for an enemy* Jb 13^{24} 33^{10}; ח׳ לו כצריו Jb 19^{11} *he accounted me unto him as his adversaries.* **2.** *devise, plan, mean,* c. acc. + לְ indirect obj. לטבה *for good* Gn 50^{20} (E); c. לְ pers. לִי *devise for me* ψ 40^{18}; acc. rei + עַל, *devise something against a person* Mi 2^{3} Je 18^{11}; *towards* one Je 29^{11}, c. אל against Je 49^{20} 50^{45}; sq. inf. Je 26^{3} 36^{3} La 2^{8}. **3.** *impute, reckon,* c. acc. rei + לְ pers., the habit of believing in ׳י *he reckoned* to Abram as righteousness Gn 15^{6} (JE; cf. **Niph. 3**); not *impute iniquity to* one ψ 32^{2}. **Niph.** *Pf.* נֶחְשַׁב Nu 18$^{27.30}$, נֶחְשַׁבְתִּי ψ 88^{5} etc. + 10 t. *Pf.; Impf.* יֵחָשֵׁב Lv 7^{18} + 7 t., etc., + 6 t. *Impf.; Pt.* נֶחְשָׁב Is 2^{22} 1 K 10^{21} 2 Ch 9^{20}:—**1.** *be accounted, thought, esteemed,* c. כְּ *as* Ho 8^{12} Is 5^{28} 29^{16} 40^{15} ψ 44^{23} Jb 18^{3} 41^{21}; c. לְ Is 29^{17}=32^{15}, La 4^{2}; עִם *with, among* ψ 88^{5}, בַּמֶּה Is 2^{22} *at what* (value)? (v. prob. interpol.; om. 𝔊); c. acc. Dt 2$^{11.20}$ Pr 17^{28} Ne 13^{13}; נָכְרִיּוֹת נֶחְשַׁבְנוּ לוֹ Gn 31^{15} (E; 𝔊 Sam קָנָה׳) Is 40^{17}. **2.** *be computed, reckoned,* c. לְ Jos 13^{3} (D), עַל Lv 25^{31} (P), 2 S 4^{2}: abs. כסף *was not counted* (so plentiful was it) 1 K 10^{21}=2 Ch 9^{20} 2 K 22^{7}. **3.** *be imputed to any one,* c. לְ Lv 7^{18} Nu 18$^{27.30}$ (all P), Lv 17^{4} (H) Pr 27^{14}; the interposition of Phinehas נח׳ לו לצדקה ψ 106^{31} *was imputed to him for righteousness* (cf. **Qal II 3**). **Pi.** *Pf.* 3 ms. חִשַּׁב Lv 25^{27} + 4 t.; f. חִשְּׁבָה Jon 1^{4}; 1 s. חִשַּׁבְתִּי ψ 77^{6} 119^{59}; *Impf.* יְחַשֵּׁב Pr 16^{9} Dn 11^{24}, תְּחַשְּׁבוּן Na 1^{9}, etc., + 4 t. *Impf.; Pt.* מְחַשֵּׁב Pr 24^{8}:—**1.** *think upon, consider, be mindful of,* c. acc. ψ 77^{6} 119^{59}, (מה) בֶּן־אֱנוֹשׁ וַתְּחַשְּׁבֵהוּ ψ 144^{3} *what* (is) *man's son, and thou thinkest upon him* (‖תֵּדָעֵהוּ). **2.** *think* to do, *devise, plan,* c. acc. Pr 16^{9}, אֶל of persons against whom Ho 7^{15} Na 1^{9}, עַל Dn 11^{24}; c. inf. ψ 73^{16} Pr 24^{8}; so of inanim. object הָאֳנִיָּה חִשְּׁבָה לְהִשָּׁבֵר Jon 1^{4} *the ship was about to* (minded to) *be broken up.* **3.** *count, reckon,* the years since a sale of land Lv 25^{27} (H); c. לְ pers. Lv 25^{52} (H), 27$^{18.23}$ (P); c. עִם Lv 25^{50} (P); c. אֶת 2 K 12^{16}. **Hithp.** *Impf.* בַּגּוֹיִם לֹא יִתְחַשָּׁב Nu 23^{9} (JE) *among the nations it shall not reckon itself.*

†חֵשֶׁב† **n.m. ingenious work,** name of the *girdle* or *band* of the ephod (*cunningly woven band,* RV), only P; alw. in combin., ח׳ האפ(ו)ד Ex 28$^{27.28}$ 29^{5} 39$^{20.21}$ Lv 8^{7}; ח׳ אֲפֻדָּתוֹ Ex 28^{8} 39^{5}.

†חֲשֻׁבָה† **n.pr.m.** (*consideration*)—son of Zerubbabel 1 Ch 3^{20}; 𝔊 Ασουβε, 𝔊 L Ασαβαθ.

†חַשּׁוּב† **n.pr.m.** (*considerate*)—**1.** a Levite chief 1 Ch 9^{14} Ne 11^{15}, 𝔊 Ασουβ. **2.** builders at the wall: **a.** Ne 3^{11} 10^{24}, 𝔊 Ασουβ, Ασουθ. **b.** Ne 3^{23}, 𝔊 Ασουβ.

†I. חֶשְׁבּוֹן **n.m. reckoning, account** (NH Aram. *id.*) Ec 9^{10}, בקש ח׳ Ec 7^{25}, מצא ח׳ Ec 7^{27}.

†II. חֶשְׁבּוֹן **n.pr.loc.** of the city of Sihon king of the Amorites Nu 21$^{26.27.28.30.34}$ 32^{3} (all E); Dt 1^{4} 2$^{24.26.30}$ 3$^{2.6}$ 4^{46} 29^{6} Jos 9^{10} 12$^{2.5}$ 13$^{10.21.27}$ (all D) Ju 11^{19} Je 48^{45} Ne 9^{22}; captured by Israel who dwelt in it Nu 21^{25} (E) Ju 11^{26}; rebuilt by Reuben Nu 32^{37} (E), given to Reuben at the division of the land Jos 13^{17} (P); on the border of Gad, Jos 13^{26} (P), it subsequently fell to Gad and was assigned to Levites out of that tribe Jos 21^{39} (P) 1 Ch 6^{66}; the Moabites gained possession of it Is 15^{4} 16$^{8.9}$ and subsequently

the Ammonites Je 48$^{2.34.45}$ 49^{3}, it was celebrated for its fish ponds Ct 7^{5} —Mod. *Husbân*, Seetzen $^{Reisen\ i\ 407}$ Rob$^{BR\ i\ 551}$ Bd$^{Pal\ 191}$ Survey$^{EP\ 8}$.

†[חֶשְׁבוֹן] **n m. device, invention** (cf Lag $^{BN\ 200}$)—only pl abs עָשָׂה הָאֱלֹהִים ; חִשְּׁבֹנוֹת אֶת־הָאָדָם יָשָׁר וְהֵמָּה בִקְשׁוּ חִשְּׁבֹנוֹת רַבִּים Ec 7^{29} *God made mankind upright but they sought out many devices;* וַיַּעַשׂ חִשְּׁבֹנוֹת מַחֲשֶׁבֶת חוֹשֵׁב 2 Ch 26^{15} *and he made contrivances* (i e. engines of war for hurling stones and arrows, see v^{b}) *the invention of inventive men*

†חֲשַׁבְיָה, חֲשַׁבְיָהוּ **n.pr.m.** (*Yah(u) has taken account*)—**1.** חֲשַׁבְיָהוּ a temple musician 1 Ch 25^{3} = חֲשַׁבְיָה v^{19}, 𝔊 in both Ασαβια **2.** חֲשַׁבְיָה a Levite, David's time 1 Ch 27^{17}, perh. = חֲשַׁבְיָהוּ, officer of David in Hebron 1 Ch 26^{30}, in both 𝔊 Ασαβιας **3.** חֲשַׁבְיָהוּ a Levite, Josiah's time 2 Ch 35^{9}, 𝔊 Ασαβια Elsewhere חשביה **4.** Levite in line of Merari 1 Ch 6^{30} 𝔊 Ασεβ(ε)ι, Ασαβια **5.** Levite 1 Ch 9^{14}, 𝔊 Ασαβια = Ne 11^{15}, A 𝔊L Ασαβιου[ας] **6.** Levite, Ezra's time Ezr 8$^{19.24}$ Ne 10^{12} 11^{22} 12^{24} (𝔊 Ασαβιας etc) = חֲשַׁבְנְיָה **2**, q v. **7.** head of a family of priests Ne 12^{21}, 𝔊 Ασαβιας **8.** a builder at the wall Ne 3^{17}, 𝔊 Ασαβια(ς)

†חֲשַׁבְנָה **n.pr.m.** (this and foll perh txt err for חשביה(ו), yet 𝔊 Εσαβανα, 𝔊L Ασβανα)—a chief of the people, Nehemiah's time Ne 10^{26}. Vid. also following

חֲשַׁבְנְיָה **n pr.m.** (v foregoing),—**1.** father of a builder at the wall Ne 3^{10}, 𝔊 Ασβαναμ, 𝔊L Σαβανιου[-ας]. **2** a Levite Ne 9^{5} (om 𝔊) = חֲשַׁבְיָה **6.**

†מַחֲשָׁבָה **n.f. thought, device** (chiefly poet and late)—abs מ׳ Je 18^{11} 49^{30}, מַחֲשֶׁבֶת Ez 38^{10}, מַחֲשֶׁבֶת Ex 35^{33} 2 Ch 2^{13}, cstr. מַחְשֶׁבֶת Est 8^{5} 2 Ch 26^{15}, sf. מַחֲשַׁבְתּוֹ Est 8^{3} 9^{25}, pl מַחֲשָׁבוֹת Je 11^{19} + 7 t ; מַחֲשָׁבֹת Ex 31^{4} + 3 t , cstr מַחְשְׁבוֹת Is 59^{7} + 13 t ; מַחְשְׁבֹת Gn 6^{5}, sf מַחְשְׁבוֹתַי Is 55^{8} etc + 19 t. sfs ;—**1.** *thought* **a** of man מ׳ אדם ψ 94^{11}, מ׳ לב ψ 33^{11} *thoughts of the mind,* (כל) יצר מ׳ (לב) Gn 6^{5} (J), 1 Ch 28^{9} 29^{18} **b.** of God מ׳ יהוה Mi 4^{12}, c אֶל־ ψ 40^{6}, עַל־ Je 51^{29}, the thoughts of God are exceeding deep ψ 92^{6}, higher than man's thoughts Is 55$^{8.8.9.9}$ **2** *device, plan, purpose* Is 55^{7} 59^{7} 65^{2} 66^{18} Je 6^{19} 18^{12} ψ 56^{6} Pr 19^{21} Jb 21^{27} La 3$^{60.61}$ Est 8^{5}, מ׳ חָרוּץ Pr 21^{5}, מ׳ עֲרוּמִים Jb 5^{12}, מ׳ צדיקים Pr 12^{5}, מ׳ עמים ψ 33^{10}, מ׳ און Is 59^{7} Je 4^{14} Pr 6^{18}, מ׳ רע Pr 15^{26}, מ׳ שָׁלוֹם Je 21^{11}, חשב מ׳ *devise devices* 2 S 14^{14} Je 11^{19} 18$^{11.18}$ 29^{11} 49$^{20.30}$ 50^{45} Ez 38^{10} Dn 11$^{24.25}$ Est 8^{3} 9^{25}, מ׳ as subj of נָכוֹן *be established* Pr 16^{3} 20^{18}, הפר מ׳ *break plans* Pr 15^{22}. **3** *invention* Ex 31^{4} 35$^{32.33.35}$ (all P), 2 Ch 2^{13} 26^{15} (v חָשַׁב **I 5**).

†חֲשַׁבְדָּנָה **n.pr.m.** (etym. dub.)—one of those who stood with Ezra at the reading of the law Ne 8^{4}, B om , A Ασαβααμα, 𝔊L Αβααιας

†[חָשָׁה] **vb. be silent, inactive, still** (chiefly poet and late) (NH *id*, Aram in deriv)—**Qal** *Impf* 2 ms תֶּחֱשֶׁה ψ 28^{1} Is 64^{11}; אחשׁה Is 62^{1} 65^{6}, יֶחֱשׁוּ Is 62^{6}, וַיֶּחֱשׁוּ ψ 107^{29}; —*be silent* Ec 3^{7} (opp לְדַבֵּר); Is 62$^{1.6}$ (= neglect to speak), of י׳ i.e. be unresponsive ψ 28^{1} (‖ חרשׁ), Is 64^{11} (‖ התאפק); but 65^{6} of י׳'s keeping silence at iniquity, i e. overlooking it (cf 57^{11} Hiph), of waves, *be still* ψ 107^{29} (subj גַּלֵּיהֶם) **Hiph** *Pf* החשׁיתי ψ 39^{3} Is 42^{14}, *Imv* החשׁוּ 2 K 2$^{3.5}$, *Pt* מַחְשֶׁה Is 57^{11}, pl. מַחְשִׁים Ju 18^{9} + 3 t.;—**1.** *exhibit silence, be silent* 2 K 2$^{3.5}$ 7^{9} ψ 39^{3} (sq. מִטּוֹב ‖ נֶאֱלַמְתִּי), fig. Is 42^{14} (‖ אחרישׁ); of י׳'s *being silent* at iniquity Is 57^{11} (i e overlooking it, cf Qal 65^{6}), poss also is *be silent*, opp *rescue*, Ges Che Di Du. **2.** *shew inactivity* Ju 18^{9}, הח׳ מִקַּחַת 1 K 22^{3} Gilead is ours, and we *shew inactivity so as not to take it.* **3.** causat *make still, quiet*, sq לְ, of direct obj. Ne 8^{11} (v^{b} הַסּוּ q. v)

חָשִׁים, חֻשִׁם v. supr p. 302 a

†חָשַׁךְ **vb. be, grow dark** (NH *id* ; Aram חֲשַׁךְ, ܚܫܟ ; Ar حَسَكَ *bear rancour*, v. Lag $^{BN\ 30}$) —**Qal** *Pf.* ח׳ Is 5^{30} + 4 t , וְחָשְׁכָה consec. Mi 3^{6} (but v infr), חָשְׁכוּ La 5^{17}, וְחָשְׁכוּ consec. Ec 12^{3}, *Impf* 3 fs תֶּחְשַׁךְ Ec 12^{2}, וַתֶּחְשַׁךְ Ex 10^{15}; 3 mpl יֶחְשְׁכוּ Jb 3^{9}, 3 fpl תֶּחְשַׁכְנָה ψ 69^{24},—**1.** *be, grow dark,* אור Is 5^{30}, cf (fig) Jb 18^{6}, הַשֶּׁמֶשׁ Is 13^{10} (fig), היום Ez 30^{18} (where rd חשך, for MT Baer חשך), Jb 3^{9} (subj כוכבים), cf Ec 12^{2} (subj. השמש, הכוכבים, הירח, האור); impers. Mi 3^{6} (si vera l.; but rd. prob וְחֲשֵׁכָה, corresponding with לילה preceding). **2.** *have a dark colour:* ח׳ משחור תָּאֳרָם La 4^{8} *darker than blackness is their visage;* of the earth הָאָרֶץ Ex 10^{15} **3.** *grow dim* La 5^{17} (subj עינינו), cf. ψ 69^{24} (fig.), Ec 12^{3} subj. הָרֹאוֹת i e the eyes. **Hiph.** *Pf.* הֶחְשִׁיךְ Am 5^{8}, וְהַחֲשַׁכְתִּי Am 8^{9}, *Impf* יַחְשִׁיךְ ψ 139^{12}, יַחְשִׁךְ Je 13^{16}, וַיַּחְשִׁךְ ψ 105^{28}; *Pt.* מַחְשִׁיךְ Jb 38^{2},—**1.**

make dark, יום לילה הח׳ Am 5^{8}; abs. *cause darkness* Je 13^{16} ψ 105^{28}, cf. Am 8^{9} (לארץ). **2.** =*hide, conceal*, sq. מִמֶּךָּ ψ 139^{12}. **3.** fig. *obscure, confuse* Jb 38^{2} (obj. עֵצָה).

†**חֹשֶׁךְ n.m.**$^{Ex 10, 21}$ **darkness, obscurity**;—abs. חֹשֶׁךְ Gn 1^{2} + 75 t. (+ Ez 8^{12} del. Co A B etc.); cstr. *id.* Ex 10^{22}; sf. חָשְׁכִּי ψ 18^{29} = 2 S 22^{29};— **1.** *darkness* (opp. אוֹר) lit. Gn $1^{2.4}$ (P), Is 45^{7} Jb 26^{10} Ec 2^{13}, cf. in imprecation Jb $3^{4.5}$ (ח׳ וצלמות) (ח׳ = לילה) Gn $1^{5.18}$ (P), cf. Jos 2^{5} (JE), Is 45^{19} Jb 17^{12} 24^{16} 38^{19} ψ 104^{20}; *darkness* in mines Jb 28^{3}; of *extraordinary darkness,* in Egypt Ex $10^{21.21}$ (E); ח׳־אֲפֵלָה Ex 10^{22} (E), ψ 105^{28}, from pillar of cloud Ex 14^{20} (J); at Mt. Sinai Dt 4^{11} 5^{20}; of clouds of theophany 2 S 22^{12} = ψ 18^{12}; of darkness in death, or She'ôl, 1 S 2^{9} Jb 10^{21} (אֶרֶץ ח׳ צלמות), 17^{13} 18^{18} ψ 88^{13} Pr 20^{20} (אישׁון ח׳ = *extreme of darkness*). **2.** = *secret place(s)* Is 45^{3} Jb 12^{22} (‖ צלמות); = *hiding-place* Jb 34^{22} (‖ *id.*), cf. ψ $139^{11.12}$;—on Ez 8^{12}, v. supr. **3.** fig., **a.** = distress Is 5^{30} 9^{1} 29^{18} (fig. of blindness), 42^{7} 49^{9} 58^{10} 59^{9} 60^{2} La 3^{2} Mi 7^{8} ψ 18^{29} = 2 S 22^{29}, Jb $15^{22.23.30}$ 20^{26} 22^{11} 23^{17} 29^{3} ψ $107^{10.14}$ (in both ‖ צלמות), 112^{4} Ec 5^{16} 11^{8}. **b.** = dread, terror, symbol. of judgment Am $5^{18.20}$ Zp 1^{15} Na 1^{8} Ez 32^{8} Jo 2^{4} 3^{4}. **c.** = mourning Is 47^{5}. **d.** = perplexity Jb 5^{14} 12^{25} 19^{8}; confusion ψ 35^{6}. **e.** = ignorance Jb 37^{19} Ec 2^{14}. **f.** = evil, sin Is $5^{20.20}$ Pr 2^{13}. **g.** = obscurity Ec $6^{4.4}$.

†**[חָשֹׁךְ] adj.** **obscure, low,** only mpl. as subst.; בַּל־יִתְיַצֵּב לִפְנֵי חֲשֻׁכִּים Pr 22^{29} *he shall not stand before obscure men* (opp. לפני־מלכים).

†**חֲשֵׁכָה n.f. darkness** (chiefly poet.)—ח׳ Gn 15^{12} + 2 t., so rd. also prob. Mi 3^{6} (for MT חָשְׁכָה); חֲשֵׁיכָה ψ 139^{12}; cstr. חֶשְׁכַת ψ 18^{12}; pl. חֲשֵׁכִים Is 50^{10};—*darkness*, opp. light (אוֹרָה) ψ 139^{12}; supernat., ח׳ גדולה Gn 15^{12} (JE); חֶשְׁכַת־מַיִם ψ 18^{12} in theoph. (but ‖ 2 S 22^{12} חַשְׁרַת־מים *a mass of water*); fig. = lack of understanding ψ 82^{5}; = distress Is 8^{22} (‖ צָרָה), 50^{10}.

†**מַחְשָׁךְ n.m. dark place** (poet.)—abs. מ׳ Is 29^{15} 42^{16}; מַחְשָׁךְ ψ 88^{19}; pl. מַחֲשַׁכִּים 88^{7} 143^{3} = La 3^{6}; cstr. מַחֲשַׁכֵּי ψ 74^{20};—*dark place:* **a.** = *hiding-place* מח׳־ארץ 74^{20}. **b.** *dark region,* in which men may lose their way Is 42^{16}. **c.** = *grave,* or שׁאול ψ 88^{19} (v. Che); of dark place of God's wrath (like She'ôl) 88^{7}; cf. 143^{3} = La 3^{6}. **d.** = *secret place, secrecy* (of plots) Is 29^{15}.

†**[חָשַׁל] vb. shatter** (BAram. חֲשַׁל *shatter;* NH Pi., ‖ משׁבר; Syr. ܚܫܠ *forge* a metal, Ar. حَشَلَ *drive* cattle *violently;* As. *ḫašâlu, shatter, destroy* Zim$^{BP 12}$ Dl$^{Pr 42}$)—**Niph.** *Pt.* fig. כָּל־הַנֶּחֱשָׁלִים Dt 25^{18} *all the shattered ones,* i.e. those broken down, worn out, sq. וְאַתָּה עָיֵף וְיָגֵעַ; others think = חלשׁ.

†**חָשֻׁם n.pr.m.** head of a family of returned exiles Ezr 2^{19} = Ne 7^{22}, Ezr 10^{33} cf. Ne 8^{4} 10^{19}.

†**חַשְׁמַל n.[m.]** etym. and exact mng. dub.; evidently some *shining* substance; AV amber; supposed by Thes (q. v.) and most to be a brilliant amalgam of gold and silver, Ⓖ ἤλεκτρον (v. Liddell & Scott s. v. **2**), 𝔙 *electrum;* v. also Dl in Baer$^{Ezech. xii}$; only in the combination כְּעֵין ח׳ *like the appearance of* ח׳ Ez $1^{4.27}$; כְּעֵין הַחַשְׁמַלָה Ez 8^{2} (on ending ָה v. Ges $^{§ 90, 2 R a}$; Co del.)

†**[חַשְׁמַן] n.m.** only pl. חַשְׁמַנִּים ψ 68^{32}; mng. unknown, Ⓖ𝔖𝔙 *ambassadors,* Rabb. *nobles,* conject. from context; doubtless txt. err.; Nes$^{JBL 1891, 152}$ prop. בשׁמנים they shall come *with oils, ointments,* Hilg Che (after Aq Jer) חָשִׁים *hasting.*

†**חֶשְׁמוֹן n.pr.loc.** town in southern Judah, site unknown Jos 15^{27}.

†**חַשְׁמֹנָה n.pr.loc.** a station of Isr. in wilderness Nu $33^{29.30}$, site unknown.

חשׁן (√ of foll.; meaning not certain; Ar. حَسُنَ is *be excellent, beautiful;* حُسْن *beauty, all excellence;* hence poss. חֹשֶׁן either as chief ornament of ephod, or as the most excellent, precious article of high priest's attire).

†**חֹשֶׁן n.m. the breast-piece or sacred pouch,** containing the אורים ותמים, worn on the breast of the high priest when he ministered in the Holy Place to bring the tribes for memorial before י׳. It was made of the same material as the ephod (v. אֵפוֹד), a span square; set in front with twelve jewels in four rows, engraved with the names of the twelve tribes. It was firmly fastened to the shoulders of the ephod by gold chains passing through gold rings, and to the lower part of the ephod just above the girdle by a blue ribbon passing through other gold rings. It was חֹשֶׁן (ה)מִּשְׁפָּט (Ex $28^{15.29.30}$) *pouch of judgment,* because of the decision given by the אוּרִים וְתֻמִּים. The name occurs only in P, Ex 25^{7} $28^{4.15.15.22.23.23.24.26.28.28.29.30}$ 29^{5} $35^{9.27}$ $39^{8.9.15.16.17.19.21.21}$ Lv $8^{8.8}$.—Vid. Now$^{Arch. ii. 119}$.

†**I. חָשַׁק vb. be attached to, love** (NH *press together, desire* (rare); Aram. חֲשַׁק *bind,*

saddle (an ass))—**Qal** *Pf* ח׳ Dt 7[7] + 4 t; חָֽשְׁקָה Gn 34[8]; חָשַׁקְתָּ Is 38[17] (but v infr), וְחָשַׁקְתָּ Dt 21[11],—*be attached to*, only fig. = *love*, a woman sq בְּ Gn 34[8] (P) Dt 21[11], elsewh of י׳'s love for Israel Dt 7[7] 10[15], and of love to י׳ ψ 91[14]; sq acc cogn + לְ and inf כָּל־חֵשֶׁק שְׁלֹמֹה אֲשֶׁר ח׳ לִבְנוֹת 1 K 9[19] = 2 Ch 8[6], חָשַׁקְתָּ נַפְשִׁי מִשַּׁחַת Is 38[17] lit *thou hast loved my soul out of the pit*, i e. lovingly delivered it; but rd חָשַׂכְתָּ *thou hast held back, kept*, from 𝔊 𝔙 Lo Ew Che Di, or חֲשֹׂךְ *hold back* (Imv), so Du

†**חֵ֫שֶׁק** **n.m** **desire** = thing desired—cstr חֵשֶׁק שְׁלֹמֹה 1 K 9[19] = 2 Ch 8[6], 1 K 9[1], sf נֶשֶׁף חִשְׁקִי Is 21[4] *the twilight of my pleasure*.

†[**חָשׁוּק**] **n.**[**m**] **fillet** or **ring** clasping (*binding*) a pillar of the tabernacle, only pl. sf חֲשֻׁקֵיהֶם Ex 27[10] + 5 t, חֲשׁוּקֵיהֶם Ex 38[12, 17], those of the pillars at door of tabernacle (הָאֹהֶל) were overlaid with gold Ex 36[38]; those of the pillars of the court with silver 27[10, 11] 38[10, 11, 12, 17, 19] (all P), v. Di on Ex 27[10], > Thes and most who understand of *connecting-rods*, joining tops of pillars, from which curtains were hung

†II. [**חָשַׁק**] **vb. denom.** only **Pi.** **furnish with fillets or rings**, and **Pu.** pass., **Pi.** *Pf.* 3 ms חִשַּׁק Ex 38[28] (P), subj Bezaleel **Pu.** *Pt* מְחֻשָּׁקִים כֶּסֶף Ex 27[17] 38[17] *furnished with silver fillets*, in agreement with הָעַמּוּדִים (both P)

†[**חִשּׁוּק**] **n.**[**m.**] **spoke** of a wheel (as *binding* felloe to nave)—pl sf חִשֻּׁקֵיהֶם 1 K 7[33].

חשר (√ of foll, cf As *ašâru*, *collect, gather* Zim[BP 39] In Ar., *collect* is حَشَرَ, but ش not usu. = ש)

†[**חַשְׁרָה**] **n.f.** **collection, mass**, only (si vera l) חַשְׁרַת־מַיִם 2 S 22[12] (חַשְׁכַת in ‖ ψ 18[12])

†[**חִשּׁוּר**] **n** [**m.**] **nave, hub of a wheel** (which *gathers in* the spokes)—pl sf חִשֻּׁרֵיהֶם 1 K 7[33].

חשש (√ of foll; cf Ar حَشَّ *hasten, hurry* (trans), حُشَّ *particles of straw, sand, dust*, as flying quickly about, v Lag[BN 40]).

†**חֲשַׁשׁ** **n.m.**[Is 5, 24] **chaff**,—abs. תַּהֲרוּ ח׳ תֵּלְדוּ קַשׁ Is 33[11] *ye conceive chaff, ye bring forth stubble* (fig of vain attempt of Assyr), cstr ח׳ לֶהָבָה יִרְפֶּה Is 5[24] (‖ קַשׁ) *as flaming chaff sinketh down* (sim. of perishing of heedless Judahites).

חִתִּי v. חוּשׁ.

חֵת, חִתָּה v. חתת.

†**חֵת** **n.pr.m.** appar represented as ancestor of the Hittites (etym. and mng unknown; pronounced as fr. √ ע״ע in Heb & As, but not Egypt; v חִתִּי infr)—'begotten' by Canaan Gn 10[15] (J) = 1 Ch 1[13], elsewh only in combin with בְּנֵי, בְּנוֹת, **a.** בְּנֵי־חֵת acc to P lived at Mamre (Hebron), and one of them sold Abraham the cave of Machpelah for a sepulchre Gn 23[3, 5, 10, 10, 16, 18, 20] 25[10] 49[32] **b.** בְּנוֹת(־)חֵת only of wives of Esau Gn 27[46, 46] (P, 𝔊 om. v[b], ‖ בְּנוֹת הָאָ֫רֶץ = בְּנוֹת כְּנָ֑עַן 28[1]).

†**חִתִּי** **adj.** et **n.gent.** **Hittite(s)** (Egypt. *Ḫ-tá*, *Ḫetá*, W Max Müll[Asien u Europa, 319 ff], As. *Ḫatti*, Schr[KG 192 ff] COT on Gn 10[15] Dl[Pa, 269 ff], Tel-el-Amarna *Ḫatti*, *Ḫatta* Bez[Tel el Amarn Brit Mus. 150])—m alw c art הַחִתִּי Gn 23[10] Ex 3[8] +, f חִתִּית Ez 16[3, 45]; mpl. הַחִתִּים Jos 1[4] + 3 t., fpl חִתִּיֹּת 1 K 11[1],—**1. adj.**, of seller of Machpelah to Abr, עֶפְרוֹן הַחִתִּי Gn 23[10] 49[29, 30] 50[13], עֶפְרוֹן בֶּן־צֹחַר הַח׳ 25[9] (all P), of fathers of Esau's wives בְּאֵרִי הַח׳ Gn 26[34], אֵילוֹן הַח׳ v[34] 36[2] (all P), also of warriors of David, אֲחִימֶלֶךְ הַח׳ 1 S 26[6], and esp אוּרִיָּה הַח׳ 2 S 11[3, 6, 17, 21, 24] 12[9, 10] 23[39] 1 K 15[5] 1 Ch 11[41], fs. = subst., only of (religious) ancestry of Jerus Ez 16[3] *thy father was the Amorite, and thy mother was a Hittite woman* חִתִּית, similarly v[45]; fpl = subst. of Sol's foreign wives, חִתִּיֹּת 1 K 11[1] *Hittite women* (+ מוֹאֲבִיּוֹת, עַמֳּנִיּוֹת, אֲדֹמִיֹּת, צֵדְנִיֹּת). **2. n.** usu. **a.** coll. הַחִתִּי *the Hittites*: in lists of Canaanitish peoples Gn 15[20] (JE), Ex 3[8, 17] (both J), 13[5] 23[23, 28] 33[2] 34[11] Nu 13[29] Jos 3[10] (all JE), Dt 7[1] 20[17] Jos 9[1] 12[8] 24[11] (all D), rd also for הַחִוִּי Ju 3[3] (so We Mey Bu[Urg 350]); in Jos 11[3] (D) del הַחִתִּי We Mey Bu[l c], and rd then הַחִתִּי for הַחִוִּי v[b] (so 𝔊, not 𝔊L), further 1 K 9[20] = 2 Ch 8[7], Ezr 9[1] Ne 9[8]. **b. pl** הַחִתִּים· כָּל אֶרֶץ הַחִתִּים Jos 1[4] (D) nearly = land of Canaanites, אֶרֶץ הַח׳ specif of northern home of Hittites Ju 1[26]; so also 2 S 24[6] where rd אֶ֫רֶץ הַחִתִּים קָ֫דְשָׁה (for MT תַּחְתִּים חָדְשִׁי, v. קָדֵשׁ, חָדְשִׁי), מַלְכֵי הַחִתִּים 1 K 10[29] = 2 Ch 1[17] (both + מַלְכֵי אֲרָם), 2 K 7[6] (+ מַלְכֵי מִצְרַיִם, both feared by אֲרָם) Hence it appears that (הַחִתִּי(ם had their proper seat in the north—where also they were encountered by Assyrians from time of TP I (v Schr Dl[l c]), and by Egyptians from time of Tutmes III (v. W Max Müll[l c])—(cf also Ju 3[3] Jos 11[3] supr.), but that individual Hittites were known in Isr.

(cf, besides 1 S 2^{8} 2 S 11^{3} etc, 1 K 9^{20} supr.), that the Hittites were regarded (by JED) as one of the peoples of Canaan, and that the name even came to be used in more gen. sense for Canaanites. Only in P do they appear as having a definite settlement in the south, and are designated by בני־חת (v חת), as well as by the adj הַחִתִּי.

†[חָתָה] **vb.** **snatch up**, usu. fire, coals (NH *id.*; 𝔗 חֲתָא, *id* (rare), As *ḫatû* is *destroy* (i e. *snatch away*?) v SASmith [Asrb L 90]) —**Qal** *Impf.* יַחְתֶּה Pr 6^{27}; sf יַחְתְּךָ ψ 52^{7}, *Inf cstr* לַחְתּוֹת Is 30^{14}, *Pt* חֹתֶה Pr 25^{22};—*snatch up*, c.acc אֵשׁ מִיָּקוּד Is 30^{14} *to snatch up fire from a hearth* (‖ לַחְשֹׂף מַיִם מִגֶּבֶא), אֵשׁ בְּחֵיקוֹ Pr 6^{27} shall a man *snatch up fire in his bosom* and his garments not be burned? (in sim of adulterer); pregn. *seize* (and put) *upon* גֶּחָלִים אַתָּה ח׳ עַל־רֹאשׁוֹ Pr 25^{22}, יַחְתְּךָ וְיִסָּחֲךָ מֵאֹהֶל ψ 52^{7} God . *shall snatch thee away*, and pluck thee up tent-less

†יַחַת **n.pr.m.** (perh for יַחְתֶּה, *he* (God) *will snatch up*)—**1.** grandson of Judah 1 Ch $4^{2.2}$, 𝔊 Ιεθ, 𝔊L Ιαωθ. **2.** Levites **a.** 1 Ch $6^{5.28}$, 𝔊 Ιεεθ, 𝔊L Ιααθ. **b.** 1 Ch $23^{10.11}$, 𝔊 Ιεθ, 𝔊L Ιεειηλ **c.** 1 Ch 24^{22}, 𝔊 Ιναθ, 𝔊L Ιααθ **d.** 2 Ch 34^{12}, 𝔊 Ιε(θ), 𝔊L Ιαεθ

†מַחַת **n.pr.m.** (perh. from מַחְתָּה *thing seized*)—Levites. **a.** 1 Ch 6^{20}, 𝔊 Μεθ, A Μααθ, 𝔊L Αμιωθ. **b.** 2 Ch 29^{12} 31^{13}, 𝔊 Μααθ, Μαεθ, 𝔊L Μααθ, Ααθ.

†מַחְתָּה **n.f.** **fire-holder, censer, snuff-dish**;—abs מ׳ Lv 16^{12} Nu 17^{11}; sf מַחְתָּתוֹ Lv 10^{1} +4 t., pl. abs. מַחְתּוֹת Nu 16^{6}+4 t., מַחְתֹּת Nu 16^{17}+3 t; cstr מַחְתּוֹת Nu $17^{3.4}$; sf מַחְתֹּתָיו Ex 27^{3}; מַחְתֹּתֶיהָ Ex 25^{38}+2 t;—**1.** *snuff-holder*, snuff-dish (Now [Archäol. ii. 43. 65]) of gold Ex 25^{38} 37^{23} Nu 4^{9} (all P) **2.** bronze utensils, *fire-pans*, belonging to altar of burnt-offerings Ex 27^{3} 38^{3}, cf Nu 4^{14} (all P), *fire-pans* of gold 1 K 7^{50} =2 Ch 4^{22}, 2 K 25^{15}=Je 52^{19}. **3.** *censer*, Lv 10^{1} 16^{12} Nu $16^{6.17\,17\,17\,17\,18}$ $17^{2.3.4}$ (of bronze), v^{11} (all P)

חַתְחַת, חִתָּה v sub חתת

†[חָתַךְ] **vb.** **divide, determine** (NH *id.*, *cut, cut off, decide*, so Aram חתך Pa. Ethpa.) —only **Niph.** *Pf* שָׁבֻעִים שִׁבְעִים נֶחְתַּךְ עַל־עַמְּךָ Dn 9^{24} seventy weeks *are determined* upon thy people.

†[חָתַל] **vb.** perh. **entwine, enwrap** (poss. denom., so MV al.; yet cf. NH חוֹתָל *woven date-basket*)—**Pu.** *Pf.* 2 fs. חֻתָּלְתְּ and **Hoph.** *Inf abs* הָחְתֵּל *be swathed, swaddled*;—וְהָמְלֵחַ לֹא הֻמְלַחַתְּ וְהָחְתֵּל לֹא חֻתָּלְתְּ Ez 16^{4} *and not at all wast thou rubbed with salt, and not at all wast thou swaddled*, of Jerusalem under fig. of infant

†[חֲתֻלָּה] **n.f.** **swaddling-band** (v Ba [NB 146])—only בְּשׂוּמִי עָנָן לְבֻשׁוֹ וַעֲרָפֶל חֲתֻלָּתוֹ Jb 38^{9} *when I made cloud its garment, and thick darkness its swaddling-band*, fig. of dark clouds enveloping the sea

†חִתּוּל **n.[m.]** **bandage**—ח׳ Ez 30^{21}, for broken arm (in fig. of Pharaoh's broken arm).

†חֶתְלֹן **n.pr.loc.,** on the extreme northern boundary of Isr territory (in Ezek.'s conception), only דֶּרֶךְ־ח׳ Ez 47^{15} 48^{1}, mod. *Heitela* nearly two hours from sea-coast, acc. to Furrer [ZPV viii 27].

†חָתַם **vb.** **seal, affix seal, seal up** (NH *id.*; Aram חֲתַם, ܚܬܡ; Eth. ኀተመ: Ar. خَتَمَ (whence خَاتَمٌ is loan-word acc. to Fra [252])—**Qal** *Impf.* 3 ms יַחְתֹּם Jb 9^{7} 33^{16}, וַיַּחְתֹּם Jb 37^{7}, Est 8^{10}, etc; *Imv.* חֲתֹם Dn 12^{4}, חֲתוֹם Is 8^{16}, חִתְמוּ Est 8^{8}, *Inf. abs.* חָתוֹם Je 32^{44}, *cstr* לַחְתֹּם Dn 9^{24}, + v^{24} Kt (Qr לְהָתֵם), *Pt act.* חוֹתֵם Ez 28^{12}, *pass* חָתוּם Dt 32^{34}+2 t., etc;—**1.** *seal, affix one's seal*, in attestation, seal with king's seal (בְּחֹתָמוֹ) 1 K 21^{8}, בְּטַבַּעַת הַמֶּלֶךְ Est $8^{8.10}$; of covenant with י׳, *attested by seal* (pass) Ne $10^{1.2}$; fig, of י׳ putting his seal upon (בְּ) discipline, i e ratifying it, Jb 33^{16}; perh. also upon hand of man (that man may know י׳'s ways) 37^{7} v. De; Di sub **2.** *seal up* hand of man, so that he cannot work with it (in winter). **2.** *seal up, fasten up by sealing*, a deed of sale Je $32^{10.11}$ (opp הַגָּלוּי *that which was left open*), $v^{14.44}$, a book of prophecy Dn 12^{4} (‖ סְתֹם הַדְּבָרִים), cf. v^{9} (‖ *id*), $9^{24\,b}$, so in sim. of unintelligible prophecy Is $29^{11.11}$, חֲתוֹם תּוֹרָה בְּלִמֻּדָי Is 8^{16} *seal up the teaching among my disciples*, i e. keep it securely (‖ צוֹר), of י׳'s remembrance of offences חָתֻם בְּאוֹצְרֹתָי Dt 32^{34} (‖ כָּמֻס עִמָּדִי), so חָתֻם בִּצְרוֹר פִּשְׁעִי Jb 14^{17} (‖ וַתִּטְפֹּל עַל־עֲוֺנִי); מַעְיָן חָתוּם Ct 4^{12} *a fountain sealed up*, metaph. of chaste woman (‖ גַּן (גַּל) נָעוּל), וּבְעַד כּוֹכָבִים יַחְתֹּם Jb 9^{7} *and about the stars he putteth a seal* (‖ of forbidding sun

to rise)—אַתָּה חוֹתֵם תָּכְנִית Ez 28[12] is obscure: *thou wast one sealing proportion*, i.e. *perfection*,—wast complete perfection, Ges Sm, wast *a sealer of symmetry* v. Da; wast a *seal* (*ring*)—i.e. חוֹתַם cstr—of proportion Codd. 𝔊 𝔙 Hi cf. Ew, txt perh corrupt, v. suggestions in Co—Dn 9[24 a] rd Qr לְהָתֵם (v. תמם) Jb 33[16] 37[7] v sub **1.** **Niph.** *Pf.* 3 ms [or *Pt* ?] נִכְתָּב וְנֶחְתָּם Est 3[12] (it was) *written and sealed* בְּטַבַּעַת הַמֶּלֶךְ, *Inf abs* ונחתום Est 8[8] (continuing pt נכתב) also + בְּטַבַּעַת הַמ׳; both pass of **Qal 1.** **Pi.** *Pf* 3 pl. יוֹמָם חִתְּמוּ־לָמוֹ Jb 24[16] lit *by day they seal up for themselves*, i.e. acc to most, they shut themselves up, do not shew themselves (‖ לֹא יָדְעוּ אוֹר), 𝔊 C has ἡμέρας ἐσφράγισαν ἑαυτοῖς (B al ἑαυτους), whence Siegf conj plausibly יָמִים ח׳ ל׳ *they seal up the days unto themselves*, i.e. day-time is for them sealed up and unused. **Hiph.** *Pf* 3 ms אוֹ־הֶחְתִּים בְּשָׂרוֹ מִזּוֹבוֹ Lv 15[3] *or hath his flesh* (genital organ) *shewn stoppage by reason of his flux*.

†I **חֹתָם, חוֹתָם** **n.m.**[Jb 41 7] **seal, signet-ring** (Aram ܚܬܡܐ, Eth ማኅተም:—v Lag [BN 116])—abs. חֹתָם Ex 28[11] + 2 t., חוֹתָם Je 22[24] + 8 t; sf חֹתָמְךָ Gn 38[18], חֹתָמוֹ 1 K 21[8],—on supposed cstr. חוֹתַם v foregoing,—*seal, signet-ring*, hung by a cord (פָּתִיל) about the neck Gn 38[18] (J, = חֹתֶמֶת v[25]), or (later ?) worn on (finger of) right hand Je 22[24], (Benz [Archäol 106]), the two customs appar combined Ct 8[6] (עַל־זְרוֹעֶךָ, עַל־לִבֶּךָ), used to attest a royal missive 1 K 21[8] (instr. of vb חתם), a precious article Hg 2[23] (sim of Zerubbabel); פִּתּוּחֵי ח׳ *engravings of a seal*, as model for cutting names and inscr on precious stones and gold plate Ex 28[11 21 36] 39[6 14.30] (all P; v Benz [258 ff.]), חֹמֶר ח׳ Jb 38[14] = *clay of* (under) *a signet*; צַר ח׳ 41[7] *a close signet*, i.e. one that is closely pressed down, sim. of closely joined (סָגוּר) scales of crocodile.

†II. **חוֹתָם** **n.pr.m. 1.** man of Asher 1 Ch 7[32] 𝔊 Χωθαν(μ) (= הֵלֶם v[35], A Ελαμ, 𝔊 L Ιασουλ) **2.** father of two of David's heroes 1 Ch 11[44], 𝔊 Κωθαν, 𝔊 L Χωθαν.

חֹתֶמֶת **n f. signet-ring**—only הַח׳ Gn 38[25] (J; for I חֹתָם v[18]) *the signet-ring* (acc. to Bo [NÄ i 23] fem coll *the sealing-apparatus*).

I. **חתן** (√of foll, prob *circumcise*; cf Ar. خَتَنَ *circumcise*, خِتَانٌ *circumcision*, *circumcision-feast*)

†**חֹתֵן** **n.verb. 1. m. wife's father** (Ar. خَاتِنٌ *a circumciser*, hence father-in-law, with ref to circumcision performed on young men just before marriage; خَتَنٌ *relation on wife's side*; v. We [Prol 1886, 365 Anm 1, Skizzen iii, 154] Sta [ZAW 1886, 143 Anm.] No [ZMG 1886, 167]; otherwise Dl [Pr 91] Lag [BN 116])—cstr. חֹתֵן Ex 18[1] + 9t., חֹתֶנְךָ Ex 18[6], חֹתְנוֹ Ex 3[1] + 9 t,—usu of Moses' *wife's father* Ex 3[1] 4[18] 18[1.2.5.6.7.8.12.12.14.15.17.24.27] (all E), Nu 10[29] (J), Ju 1[16] 4[11], of a Levite Ju 19[4 7 9]. **2. f.** *wife's mother*, only sf. חֹתַנְתּוֹ Dt 27[23].

†**חָתָן** **n.m. daughter's husband, bridegroom** (as one who undergoes circumcision, v. supr, NH *id*, Aram חַתְנָא, and ܚܬܢܐ (also sister's husband, etc), vulg. Ar. خَتَن *daughter's husband*, then more gen wife's and husband's relations; Sab (Lihyân) חתן *daughter's husband* DHM [Epigr Denkm 87], As *ḫatanu*, *daughter's husband* COT [Gloss])—abs ח׳ 1 S 18[18] + 10 t + Gn 19[12] (where rd חֲתָנֶיךָ 𝔊 Ol Di), cstr. חֲתַן Ex 4[25] + 4 t; sf חֲתָנוֹ Ju 19[5]; חֲתָנָיו Gn 19[14 14],—**1.** in relation to a father, *daughter's husband, or bridegroom* Gn 19[12 14] (ח׳ לֹקְחֵי בְנֹתָיו), v[14] (all J), Ju 15[6] 19[5] 1 S 18[18] 22[14] Ne 6[18] 13[28]; v. also חֲתַן בֵּית אַחְאָב 2 K 8[27] *son-in-law of the house of Ahab*, said of Ahaziah, whose mother Athaliah was the daughter of Ahab. **2.** in relation to the bride, *bridegroom* ח׳ דָּמִים אַתָּה לִי Ex 4[25] *a bloody bridegroom art thou to me*, cf v[26] (J; on this v We [Prol 1886, 355]), ‖ כַּלָּה Je 7[34] 16[9] 25[10] 33[11] Jo 2[16], in sim of י׳'s work for and delight in his people Is 61[10] 62[5]; of sun ψ 19[6].

†II [**חתן**] **vb. denom.** only **Hithp. make oneself a daughter's husband** (NH Hithp *id*, Aram Ithpa *id*)—*Pf* 2 mpl וְהִתְחַתַּנְתֶּם consec. Jos 23[12]; *Impf.* וַיִּתְחַתֵּן 1 K 3[1] 2 Ch 18[1]; 2 m תִתְחַתֵּן Dt 7[3] 1 S 18[21], *Imv.* הִתְחַתֵּן 1 S 18[22], הִתְחַתְּנוּ Gn 34[9], *Inf.* הִתְחַתֵּן 1 S 18[23] + 3 t;—**1.** *make oneself daughter's husband* (son-in-law) *to*, c בְּ 1 S 18[21 22 23.26 27], c. אֶת 1 K 3[1], Gn 34[9] (P), c לְ 2 Ch 18[1], of marriage of Jehoshaphat's son and Ahab's daughter (cf 2 K 8[18] = 2 Ch 21[6]). **2.** in gen *form marriage-alliance with*, c בְּ Dt 7[3] Jos 23[12] (D), Ezr 9[14].

†[**חֲתֻנָּה**] **n.f. marriage, wedding** (NH חיתון *id*, Aram חיתונא *id*; Ar. خُتُونَة *marriage-alliance, marriage*)—only בְּיוֹם חֲתֻנָּתוֹ Ct 3[11] *on the day of his marriage*.

†[**חָתַף**] **vb. seize, snatch away** (cf Aram.

ܚܛܦ Pa. *break in pieces; Ar.* حَتْفٌ *death*)—**Qal** *Impf.* no obj. expr. הֵן יַחְתֹּף וּמִי יְשִׁיבֶנּוּ Jb 9^{12} *lo! he seizeth, and who shall turn him back?*

†חֶתֶף **n.[m.]** prey—only אַף־הִיא כְּחֶ׳ תֶּאֱרֹב Pr 23^{28} *she also lieth in wait as* for *prey* (said of strange woman).

†חָתַר **vb.** dig, row (NH *id., bore* (through), so Aram. חֲתַר 𝔗 (rare))—**Qal** *Pf.* ח׳ Jb 24^{16}, חָתַרְתִּי Ez 12^{7}; *Impf.* וָאֶחְתֹּר Ez 8^{8}, יַחְתְּרוּ Ez 12^{12} Am 9^{2}, וַיַּחְתְּרוּ Jon 1^{13}; *Imv.* חֲתָר־ Ez 8^{8} 12^{5};—**1.** *dig into* houses, c. acc. בָּתִּים Jb 24^{16} (of burglary); sq. בְּ into or through a wall Ez 8$^{8.8}$ (Co del. on intern. grounds), 12$^{5.7.12}$; metaph. sq. בשאול Am 9^{2} *dig into Sheʾôl*, i.e. as a refuge. **2.** *row* (as *digging* into the water) Jon 1^{13}.

†מַחְתֶּרֶת **n.m.** breaking in, burglary—אִם־בַּמַּ׳ יִמָּצֵא הַגַּנָּב Ex 22^{1} i.e. caught in the act (JE); so לֹא בַמַּ׳ מְצָאתִים Je 2^{34}, *not in the act of breaking in didst thou find them* (2 fs. sf. Ges$^{§44. 2. R 4}$), i.e. those whom thou hast slain were not detected in crime.

†[חָתַת] **vb.** be shattered, dismayed (As. *ḫattu, terror*, Dl $^{HWB\ 296}$; Talm. חִתִּית *id.*; Eth. ሐተተ: is *scrutari, examinare*, v. Di$^{Lex.\ 105}$)—**Qal** *Pf.* 3 ms. חַת Je 50^{2}; 3 fs. חַתָּה Je 14^{4} + 2 t., וְחַתָּה Je 48^{1}; 3 pl. חַתּוּ Is 37^{27} + 4 t., וְחַתּוּ consec. Is 20^{5} + 2 t., וְחַתּוּ consec. Je 50^{36}; *Impf.* (Kö$^{I.\ 366}$) יֵחַת Is 7^{8} 30^{31}, יֵחָת Jb 39^{22}, אֵחָתָּה Is 31^{4}, יֵחַת Je 17^{18}, יֵחַתּוּ 1 S 2^{10} + 3 t.—On יֵחַתּוּ Jb 21^{13} v. נְחַת;—תֵּחָתּוּ Jos 10^{25} + 2 t., etc.; *Imv.* וָחֹתּוּ Is 8$^{9.9.9}$;—**1.** *be shattered, broken*, fig. of nations under divine judgment Is 7^{8} 30^{31}; so prob. also Is 8$^{9.9.9}$ (but del. in v^{a}), and perh. (of י׳'s foes in gen.) 1 S 2^{10} (song;—others render *dismayed* in all exc. Is 7^{8}); fig. of י׳'s righteousness Is 51^{6} (= be abolished, annihilated); lit. of bows Je 51^{56}, acc. to Gie's rdg. חִתָּה, v. **Pi.** **2.** *be dismayed*, usu. **a.** abs.: ‖ יָרֵא Dt 1^{21} 31^{8} Jos 8^{1} 10^{25} (all D), 1 S 17^{11} Je 23^{4} 30^{10} 46^{27} Ez 2^{6} 3^{9} 1 Ch 22^{13} 28^{20} 2 Ch 20$^{15.17}$ 32^{7}; ‖ בּוֹשׁ Is 20^{5} 37^{27} = 2 K 19^{26} Je 8^{9} 17$^{18.18}$ 48$^{1.20.39}$ 50$^{2.2}$ (others assign 48$^{20.39}$ 50$^{2.2}$ to **1**); fig. of the ground הָאֲדָמָה, *dismayed* for lack of rain Je 14^{4} (‖ בּוֹשׁ of the husbandmen); no ‖ Je 50^{36} Ob^{9} Jb 39^{22}. **b.** *be dismayed at, by reason of*, sq. מִן Is 31$^{4.9}$ 51^{7} (‖ יָרֵא) Je 1^{17} 10$^{2.2}$. **Niph.** *Pf.* only 3 ms. וּמִפְּנֵי שְׁמִי נִחַת Mal 2^{5} and at my name *he is put in awe* (‖ יָרֵא). **Pi.** *Pf. dismay, scare*, 2 ms. sf. וְחִתַּתַּנִי בַחֲלֹמוֹת (Kö$^{I.\ 372}$) consec. Jb 7^{14} *and thou scarest me with dreams* (‖ בְּעֵת); 3 fs. חִתְּתָה Je 51^{56} (of bows) is intrans. [inchoat. Ew$^{§120,\ 2\ d}$], Gf. al., *be shattered*, but txt. prob. erron. Gie חִתָּה (v. **Qal 1**). **Hiph.** *Pf.* 2 ms. הַחִתֹּתָ Is 9^{3}; 1 s. וְהַחְתִּתִּי Je 49^{37} (Kö$^{I.\ 372}$); *Impf.* 3 ms. sf. יְחִתֵּנִי Jb 31^{34}, sf. 3 fpl. יְחִיתַן Hb 2^{17} (Kö$^{I.\ 374}$; but 𝔊 𝔗 𝔖 Ew Ol Sta We יְחִתֶּךָּ); 1 s. sf. אֲחִתְּךָ Je 1^{17} (sq. לפניהם).—**1.** *shatter* c. acc. Is 9^{3}. **2. a.** *cause to be dismayed* Je 49^{37} sq. לִפְנֵי. **b.** *dismay, terrify*, sq. sf. Jb 31^{34} Hb 2^{17}.

†I. [חַת] **n.m.**$^{Gn\ 9.\ 2}$ terror, fear—חַת Jb 41^{25}, חִתְּכֶם Gn 9^{2};—c. sf. as obj. gen., Gn 9^{2} *terror of you* (‖ מוֹרַאֲכֶם); in description of crocodile c. neg., הֶעָשׂוּ לִבְלִי־חָת Jb 41^{25} *one made for fearlessness.*

†II. [חַת] **adj.** shattered, dismayed—mpl. חַתִּים:—**1.** *shattered* קֶשֶׁת גִּבֹּרִים ח׳ 1 S 2^{4} (song; on pl. חַתִּים v. Dr); so fig. Ez 32^{30} acc. to 𝔊 Codd. Co (חַתִּים for MT. חִתִּיתָם) *broken in their might*, of Sidonians in Sheʾôl. **2.** *dismayed* Je 46^{5} of Egyptians defeated by Nebuchadrezzar.

†I. חֲתַת **n.[m.]** terror—only תִּרְאוּ ח׳ וַתִּירָאוּ Jb 6^{21} (> Baer תִּירְאוּ for תִּרְאוּ) *ye see a terror, and fear* (note paronomasia in Heb.; v. Di).

†[חִתָּה] **n.f.** terror—חִתַּת אלהים עַל־הֶעָרִים Gn 35^{5} *a terror of* (= from) *God was upon the cities.*

†II. חֲתַת **n.pr.m.** son of Othniel and grandson of Kenaz (brother of Caleb), חֲתַת 1 Ch 4^{13}.

†[חַתְחַת] **n.[m.]** terror, only pl. חַתְחַתִּים בַּדֶּרֶךְ Ec 12^{5} *terrors are in the way* (‖ ירא).

חִתִּית **n.f.** terror, only Ezek.; abs. ח׳ Ez 32^{23}, but Co rds. חִתִּיתָם (with 𝔊 and v$^{24.26}$); cstr. *id.* 32^{27}; sf. חתיתו 32^{32} Kt (> חִתִּיתִי Qr); חִתִּיתָם 32^{24} + 2 t. + 26^{17} (rd. חִתִּיתָהּ, with 𝔊 Ew Co, see VB), 32^{30} (rd. חַתִּים, v. II. חת);—*terror*, caused by powerful cities, nations, kings, etc.: usu. c. sf. as obj. genit. Ez 26^{17} (of Tyre); elsewh. only Ez 32: v^{27} (ח׳ גִּבּוֹרִים, 𝔊 Co ח׳ נבור תם), v^{30} (חִתִּיתָם, but rd. חַתִּים, v. supr.); esp. in phr. נָתַן ח׳ בארץ חַיִּים *cause one's terror* (terror of oneself) *in the land of the living* v$^{23.24.25}$ (del. 𝔊 Co), v$^{26.32}$.—חִתִּית Ez 16$^{3.45}$ v. חִתִּי sub חת supr. p. 366.

†מְחִתָּה **n.f.** terror, destruction, ruin,

poet (esp. Pr)—abs 'מ Pr 10[14] + 8 t., cstr. מחתת Pr 10[15] 14[28],—**1. a.** *terror*, Is 54[14] (‖ עשק), Je 17[17], = obj of terror, 48[39] (‖ שחק) **b.** *dismay*, Pr 21[15] (opp. שמחה) **2.** *ruin*, of strongholds ψ 89[41], באפס לאם מ׳ רזון Pr 14[28] *without people is ruin to a prince* (opp. הדרת־מלך), מ׳ דלים רישם 10[15] *the ruin of the poor* (is) *their poverty;* as consequence of evil-doing מ׳ לפעלי און Pr 10[29] (opp מָעוֹז), of fools פי כסיל מ׳־לו 18[7], cf. 13[3] (opp שֹׁמֵר נַפְשׁוֹ); פי אויל מ׳ קרבה 10[14] *the mouth of a fool is imminent ruin.*

חת, חִתִּי, חֵת v. supr. p. 366.

ט

ט, *Têth*, ninth letter, = numeral 9 in postB Heb, ט״ו = 15 (9 + 6), ט״ז = 16 (9 + 7), to avoid י״ה and י״ו, v. י, Ges § 5. 4 R 3 Nes ZAW 1884 249.

†[**טאטא**] **vb Pilpēl,** only *Pf* 1 s sf וטאטאתיה במטאטא השמד Is 14[23] *and I will sweep it with the besom of destruction*, of י׳'s laying Babylon waste. (Form of √dub.; ע״ו Ol § 253, ע״ע Sta § 464; undecided Ko i 632 ff. (q v), cf Ew § 118 b)

†**מַטְאֲטֵא** **n.[m.]** **broom, besom,** only Is 14[23], v foregoing

†**טָֽבְאֵל** **n.pr.m.** (Aram, = *God is good*, v טוב, acc to Wkl (v. infr) *God is wise*, cf Aram طب, Eth ጠበበ: *be wise;* Ar طَبَّ *act as physician,* طَبٌّ *expert*)—Persian officer in Samaria Ezr 4[7], 𝔊 Ταβεηλ.

†**טָֽבְאַל** **n.pr.m.** (appar. pointed to mean *good-for-nothing* (אַל as neg) v. De Di Du Sta Gesch i 590, orig. טָבְאֵל; Ol § 91 d Ko ii. 687 al think אַל- simply pausal form)—Aramean, whose son Pekah and Resin proposed to make king of Jerus in place of Ahaz, only בֶּן־טָבְאַל Is 7[6] (Wkl Alttest Untersuch 1892. 74 identif with Resin, comparing טברמן father of Benhadad).

†[**טָבַח**] **vb. slaughter, butcher, slay** (NH *id* (rare) and deriv.; Ph מבח pt.; As *ṭabâḫu* Asrb Annals iii 56; Aram. ܛܒܚ, טבח (rare) and deriv; Ar طَبَخَ *cook* meat, also *bake* bread, Eth. ጦበኀ: *slay*)—**Qal** *Pf* 3 ms sf. וּטְבָחוֹ consec. Ex 21[37], 3 fs טָֽבְחָה Pr 9[2], 2 ms. טָבַחְתָּ La 2[21], 1 s טָבַחְתִּי 1 S 25[11], *Imv* וּטְבֹחַ Gn 43[16], *Inf cstr* טבח Ez 21[15], לִטְבוֹחַ ψ 37[14] + 3 t (so Baer, van d. H לִטְבוֹחַ, exc לִטְבֽוֹחַ Je 51[40]), *Pt. pass* טָבוּחַ Dt 28[31];—**1.** *slaughter, butcher* animals for food Ex 21[37] (E), Pr 9[2] (fig of Wisdom's furnishing her table), so c acc cogn. טְבֹחַ מ׳ Gn 43[16] (J), מ׳ טבחה 1 S 25[11], cf also Dt 28[31], where punishment lies in fact that the owner does not eat of the slain ox; כְּכֶבֶשׂ אַלּוּף יוּבַל לִטְבוֹחַ Je 11[19] *like a mild lamb that is led to slaughter,* sim of the prophet exposed to his enemies, 51[40] sim. of י׳'s vengeance upon Babylon (v also טֶבַח, טבחה), 25[34] of kings and rulers, under fig. of shepherds & choice sheep. **2.** poet & fig, *slay, kill ruthlessly,* c. acc. pers. ψ 37[14], abs La 2[21] (‖ הָרַג; opp. חמל); c acc cogn. מ׳ טֶבַח Ez 21[15] of a sword sharpened for the *slaughter* of Isr. in judgment

†**I. טֶבַח** **n.m.** Is 34. 6 **slaughtering, slaughter**—abs 'ט Gn 43[16] + 6 t.; טָבַח Ez 21[20] + 3 t; sf טבחה Pr 9[2];—**1.** *slaughtering, slaughter,* of animals for food, as acc cogn. after טָבַח (q v.) Gn 43[16] (J), Pr 9[2], כַּשֶּׂה לַטֶּ׳ יוּבָל Is 53[7], sim of suffering servant of י׳, also Pr 7[22] sim. of fatuousness of one following a strange woman, thoughtless of consequences, יָרְדוּ לַטֶּ׳ Je 50[27] metaph. of Babylonian leaders, under fig of bullocks; so prob 48[15], and perh לַטֶּ׳ תִכְרָעוּ Is 65[12] **2.** in poet fig. *slaughter,* to which the nations are given over by י׳ Is 34[2], specif. of Edom v[6] (‖ זֶבַח, v. זבח **6**, p. 258a), of Isr. Ez 21[20], as acc cogn after טָבַח v[15]; of Ammon v[33].

†**II. טֶבַח** **n.pr.m.** son of Nahor by his concubine Gn 22[24], 𝔊 Ταβεκ(χ).

†**טִבְחָה** **n.f. thing slaughtered, slaughtered meat, slaughter—1.** sf. טִבְחָתִי as acc. cogn after טָבַח 1 S 25[11] of meat killed for food **2.** *slaughter for food* (= I. טֶבַח **1**): כְּצֹאן ט׳

ψ 44^{23} *like a flock for slaughter*, sim. of the harassed godly; כְּצֹאן לְטִבְחָה Je 12^{3} sim. of judgment of wicked (|| לְיוֹם הֲרֵגָה).

טַבָּח **n.m.**$^{1\,S\,9.23}$ **1. cook, 2. guardsman**;—†**1.** *cook* (who also killed the animal for food and served it) טַבָּח abs. 1 S 9$^{23.24}$†. **2.** elsewh. only pl. טַבָּחִים *guardsmen, bodyguard* (orig. royal *slaughterers*; v. RS$^{OTJC\,426\,(262);\,Sem.\,I.\,1st\,ed.,\,396}$); alw. in the foll. combinations: שַׂר הַטּ׳ *captain of* Pharaoh's *bodyguard* Gn 37^{36} 39^{1} (both J), 40$^{3.4}$ 41$^{10.12}$ (all E); רַב־טּ׳ *chief of* Nebuchadr.'s *bodyguard* 2 K 25$^{8.10.11.12.15.18.20}$ Je 39^{9} + 16 t. Je (hence Aram. רַב טַבָּחַיָּא Dn 2^{14}).

†[טַבָּחָה] **n.f. female cook**;—only pl. abs. טַבָּחוֹת 1 S 8^{13} (+ רַקָּחוֹת *perfumers* and אֹפוֹת *bakers*, all as menials).

†מַטְבֵּחַ **n.[m.] slaughtering-place** (Ph. מטבח *id.* CIS$^{1.175}$), Is 14^{21}, for Babylonians (under implicit fig. of animals).

†טִבְחַת **n.pr.loc.** a Syrian city; מִטִּבְחַת 1 Ch 18^{8} (𝔊 Μεταβηχα(ς), 𝔊^{L} ταβααθ); so rd. also for II. בֶּטַח 2 S 8^{8} (v. p. 105^{b} supr.)

†I. טָבַל **vb. dip** (NH *id.*; Aram. טְבַל *dip, bathe*; cf. perh. Ar. طَبَلَ *saturavit tinctura vestem*, Frey)—**Qal** *Pf.* וְטָבַל consec. Lv 4^{6} + 5 t.; וְטָבַלְתְּ consec. Ru 2^{14}; וּטְבַלְתֶּם consec. Ex 12^{22}; *Impf.* וַיִּטְבֹּל Lv 9^{9} + 3 t.; 2 ms. sf. תִּטְבְּלֵנִי Jb 9^{31}; וַיִּטְבְּלוּ Gn 37^{31};—*dip*: **1.** trans., *dip* a thing *in*, c. acc. rei + בְּ: in blood Gn 37^{31} (J), so esp. in connexion with sacrifices Lv 4^{6} 9^{9} 14$^{6.51}$ (also in fresh water); in water, for purification Nu 19^{18} (all P); of dipping rod in honey 1 S 14^{27}, bread in vinegar Ru 2^{14}, foot in oil Dt 33^{24} (poem); בַּשַּׁחַת תִּטְבְּלֵנִי Jb 9^{31} *in the ditch dost thou dip me*; acc. omitted Ex 12^{22} (JE; in blood), 2 K 8^{15} (in water); but also + מִן = *moisten with, with some of* Lv 4^{17} (blood), 14^{16} (oil). **2.** intrans., *dip* (*oneself*), sq. בְּ, 2 K 5^{14} in Jordan (|| רָחַץ בְּ v$^{10.12}$).

†טְבַלְיָהוּ **n.pr.m.** (י׳ *hath dipped*, i.e. *purified*)—name of one of the porters, line of Merari 1 Ch 26^{11} (𝔊^{L} Ταβεηλ).

II. טבל (perh. to be assumed as √ of foll.; cf. Eth. ጠብለለ: *wind about, wrap up*; As. *ṭublu, turban*, Dl in Baer's Ezech^{xii}).

†[טְבוּל] **n.m. turban** (v. Sim in Thes Rob Ges Dl$^{l.c.}$)—only סְרוּחֵי טְבוּלִים בְּרָאשֵׁיהֶם Ez 23^{15} extended in respect to *turbans on their heads* = *with pendant turbans* (Dl SS, cf. Da) > Hi-Sm who comp. Ar. طَبَلَ *dye* (v. I. טבל).

†טָבַע **vb. sink, sink down** (NH. *id.*; Aram. ܛܒܰܥ, טְבַע; Ph. טבע *coin*; As. *ṭêbû, sink in, ṭabbi'u, diver*, (water-fowl) etc., v. Muss-Arnolt$^{JBL\,xi,\,1892,\,170}$ Dl^{HWB}; Ar. طَبَعَ *seal, stamp, imprint*; Eth. ጠምዐ: *dip*)—**Qal** *Pf.* טָבַעְתִּי ψ 69^{3}; טָבְעוּ ψ 9^{16} La 2^{9}; *Impf.* וַיִּטְבַּע Je 38^{6}; וַתִּטְבַּע 1 S 17^{49}; אֶטְבָּעָה ψ 69^{15};—*sink, sink down*, intrans., c. בְּ; 1 S 17^{49} (stone into Goliath's forehead); Je 38^{6} (Jerem. in mire of dungeon); La 2^{9} (gates of Jerus. into ground); metaph. of distress; ψ 69^{3} טִ׳ בִּיוֵן מְצוּלָה; 69^{15} (|| הִצִּילֵנִי מִטִּיט); nations into the pit (בַּשַּׁחַת) 9^{16}. **Pu.** *Pf.* טֻבְּעוּ *be sunk* Ex 15^{4} (poem) of Egyptians drowned בְּיַם־סוּף. **Hiph.** *Pf.* הָטְבְּעוּ *be sunk* בַּבֹּץ *in the mire*, of feet, metaph. of entanglements and difficulties Je 38^{22}; הָטְבָּ֑עוּ, of pedestals (אֲדָנִים) of the earth, as *settled, planted* עַל Jb 38^{6} (|| ירה פִּנָּה); abs. of mountains Pr 8^{25}.

טַבַּעַת **n.f. signet, signet-ring, ring** (on format. v. Lag$^{BN\,88}$; As. *ṭimbu'u, seal-ring*, Muss-Arnolt$^{l.c.}$)—abs. טַבַּעַת Ex 26^{24} + 3 t.; cstr. *id.* Est 3^{12} + 3 t.; טַבַּעְתּוֹ Gn 41^{42} + 2 t.; pl. abs. טַבָּעוֹת Is 3^{1} Ex 28^{23}; טַבָּעֹת Ex 25$^{12.12}$ + 14 t.; cstr. טַבְּעוֹת Ex 28^{23} + 2 t.; טַבְּעֹת Ex 25^{12} + 12 t.; sf. טַבְּעֹתָו Ex 28^{28} 39^{21}; טַבְּעֹתֵיהֶם Ex 26^{29}; טַבְּעֹתָם 36^{34};—**1.** *signet-ring*, of king, taken from his hand and given as token of authority Gn 41^{42} (E), Est 3^{10} 8^{2}; used in sealing official missives Est 3^{12} 8$^{8.8.10}$ (vb. חָתַם). **2.** *ring*, as ornament Is 3^{21}; as gift for sacred purposes Ex 35^{22} Nu 31^{50} (both P). **3.** most often (only in Ex.) of rings for staves of ark, for curtains, for ephod, and other sacred furniture Ex 25$^{12.12.12}$ + 35 t. in Ex (all P).

†טַבָּעוֹת **n.pr.m.** a family name among the Nethinim Ezr 2^{43} = Ne 7^{46}.

טבר (√ of foll.; meaning dubious).

†טַבּוּר **n.[m.] highest part, centre** (acc. to 𝔊 𝔙 *navel*, so NH *id.*, and טִיבּוּר, Aram. טִיבּוּרָא, טִיבּוּרָא)—הִנֵּה עָם יֹרְדִים מֵעִם טַבּוּר הארץ Ju 9^{37} *behold people descending from the highest part of the land*; יֹשְׁבֵי עַל־טַבּוּר הארץ Ez 38^{12} those *dwelling upon the navel of the earth*, i.e. upon the mountainous country of Israel, central and prominent in the earth.

†טַבְרִמּוֹן **n.pr.m.** (Aram., =*Ramman is good*, or *is wise*, v Wkl on טבאל supr)—father of Benhadad king of Aram 1 K 15[18].

†טֵבֵת **n.pr.** 10th month=Dec–Jan, Est 2[16] (Nab טבת Eut[No 3] Palm *id.*, Vog[No 66], loan-word from As *Têbêtum*, Schr[COT] on Ne 1[1], Hpt[E-Vowel 10], Jen[ZA iv (1889) 272 f.], √ perh *tebû*=טבע v. esp Hpt[1 c], Muss-Arnolt[JBL xi, 1892, 170], month of *sinking in*=muddy month).

†טַבָּת **n.pr.loc.** Ju 7[22], spot near which Gideon's pursuit of Midianites ended, site unknown.

†טָהֵר **vb. be clean, pure** (Ar طَهُرَ, طَهَرَ *id.*; NH *id*, Pi *make* or *declare ceremonially clean*; Aram טְהַר *emptiness*, טִיהֲרָא *brightness*, Sab טהר Hal[682], Eth ኣጥሀረ: ተጠሀረ: *purify, wash oneself with water*)—**Qal** *Pf* ׳ט Lv 11[32] +12 t, 3 fs טָהֲרָה Lv 12[7] 15[28], טָהֵרָה Lv 12[8] etc, +5 t *Pf*, *Impf* יטהר Lv 15[13] Jb 4[17] etc, +9 t. *Impf*, *Imv* טְהָר 2 K 5[10 13],—**1.** *be clean*, i.e. (miraculously) freed from leprosy by washing in the Jordan 2 K 5[10.12.13.14]. **2.** *be clean ceremonially* (only H P), Lv 15[13.28.28] (P), 22[4] (H), by washing with water, the flesh Lv 22[7] (H), garments Lv 13[6.34 58] Nu 31[24] (all P), both flesh and garments Lv 17[5] (H), 14[8.9] 15[13] Nu 19[19] (all P), other articles Lv 11[32] (P), passing things through the fire Nu 31[23] (P), offering sin-offerings Lv 12[7 8] 14[20] (P), by the ceremony of the two birds Lv 14[53] (P), by ashes of red heifer Nu 19[12 12] (P). **3.** *be clean morally*, of people, made clean by ׳י's scattering clean water upon them Ez 36[25], of Jerus., specif. made clean from idolatry, under fig of adultery Je 13[27], also sq מִן Ez 24[13 13] (purification by ׳י), *made clean* מִכֹּל־חַטֹּאתֵיכֶם Lv 16[30] (P; by the sin-offering of the atonement day); also of the individual, *be clean* מֵחַטָּאוּת Pr 20[9] (‖ זכה), *become clean* by use of hyssop ψ 51[9] (‖ אַלְבִּין), more generally אִם־מֵעֹשֵׂהוּ יִטְהַר־גָּבֶר Jb 4[17] *shall a man be more pure than his maker?* (‖ יִצְדָּק)

Pi. *Pf* טִהַר Lv 13[3] +4 t; sf טִהֲרוֹ Lv 13[6] +5 t, 2 ms טִהַרְתָּ Nu 8[6 15] etc +7 t. *Pf*; *Impf* יְטַהֵר 2 Ch 34[5] etc +4 t *Impf*, *Imv* sf טַהֲרֵנִי ψ 51[4], *Inf.cstr* טַהֵר Ez 39[12] +5 t, sf טַהֲרִי Ez 36[33] etc +4 t *Inf*, *Pt* מְטַהֵר Lv 14[11] Mal 3[3],—chiefly P; **1.** *cleanse, purify* **a.** *physically*, metals from dross Mal 3[3], land from corpses Ez 39[12 14 16]; heavens from clouds Jb 37[21], temple from unclean things 2 Ch 29[15.16 18], land and city from Asherim and images 2 Ch 34[3.5 8], store-chambers of temple from household stuff Ne 13[9], priesthood by exclusion of alien blood Ne 13[30]. **b.** *ceremonially*, the altar of incense by the blood of the annual sin-offering Lv 16[19] (P), the people, gates, and wall (by some undefined ceremony) Ne 12[30], the altar of the court by the blood of sin-offerings Ez 43[26], of consecration of Levites by מֵי חַטָּאת Nu 8[6.7] (P), and חטאת Nu 8[15.21] (P) **c** *morally* Lv 16[30] (P), Ez 37[23] Mal 3[3], מֵחַטָּאת ψ 51[4], מעונ(ות) Je 33[8] Ez 36[33], טמא(ו)ת Ez 24[13] 36[25]. **2.** *pronounce clean*, ceremonially Lv 13[6 13 17 23 28.34.37 59] 14[7.48] (all P) **3.** *perform the ceremony of cleansing* Lv 14[11] (P) **Pu.** *Pf* 3 ms טֹהַר 1 S 20[26] (so rd for MT טהור 𝔊 We Dr, he is not clean, because *he hath not been cleansed*); *Pt* אֶרֶץ לֹא מְטֹהָרָה *a land not cleansed* Ez 22[24] (but 𝔊 Hi Ew Co SS rd. *a land not rained upon*, v. מטר). **Hithp.** *Pf.* 3 pl הִטֶּהָרוּ Ezr 6[20], הִטֶּהָרוּ (Ko[i 271]) 2 Ch 30[18] Nu 8[7], 1 pl הִטַּהַרְנוּ Jos 22[17]; *Impf.* יִטַּהֲרוּ Ne 12[30], *Imv* הִטַּהֲרוּ Gn 35[2], *Pt.* מִטַּהֵר Lv 14[7] +11 t; *pl.* מִטַּהֲרִים Ne 13[22] Is 66[17];—reflexive **1.** *purify oneself* **a.** ceremonially, esp. in preparation for sacred duties Gn 35[2] (R), Nu 8[7] 2 Ch 30[18] Ezr 6[20] Ne 13[22]; also for heathen mysteries Is 66[17]; of purifying priests, people, and wall Ne 12[30] (cf. **Pi. 1 b**) **b.** morally Jos 22[17] (P) **2.** *present oneself for purification*, only pt הַמִּטַּהֵר *the candidate for purification* Lv 14[4.7 8 11 14 17 18 19.25.28.29.31] (P)

†טֹהַר **n.[m.]** purity, purifying—**1.** *purity*, כְּעֶצֶם הַשָּׁמַיִם לָטֹהַר Ex 24[10] (JE), *as the body of the heavens for purity* **2.** sf יְמֵי טָהֳרָהּ Lv 12[4 6] *the days of her purifying* (menstruation).

†[טְהָר] (v. Ges[§ 10 2 B]), or [טֹהַר] (Ol[§ 173 b] Bö[§ 386]) **n.[m.]** clearness, lustre (dub. word; sub טהר Hup Pe SS; so Thes, reading מִטְּהָרוֹ) —only הִשְׁבַּתָּ מִטְּהָרוֹ ψ 89[45], De Hup Pe Sch *thou hast made* (him) *to cease from his lustre*; 𝔖 𝔙 *made his lustre to cease*, so AE Ki al reading מְטֹהָרוֹ or מִטֹּהָרוֹ (D. f. acc. to Ges[§ 20 2 b]), and Schr[SK 1868, 642] who reads הִשְׁבַּתָּה טָהֳרוֹ; Gr prop. עטרתו *his crown*, Bae מַטֵּה מִיָּדוֹ *sceptre from his hand*

†טָהֳרָה **n.f.** purifying, cleansing,—abs. ׳ט Lv 12[4] +2 t.; cstr. טָהֳרַת 1 Ch 23[28] 2 Ch 30[19], sf טָהֳרָתוֹ Lv 13[7] +7 t.;—**1.** *purifying, menstruation* Lv 12[4.5]. **2.** *cleansing, purification*, of leper Lv 13[7 35] 14[2.23.32], of Nazirite Nu 6[9], from an issue Lv 15[13] (all P); from contact with the dead Ez 44[26], of sacred things in gen. 1 Ch 23[28]; of persons for the passover 2 Ch 30[19],

מִשְׁמֶרֶת הַטָּהֳרָה Ne 12^{45} *the charge, requirement of purification.*

†טָהוֹר **adj.** clean, pure,—m. abs ט' Ex 25^{11}+68 t., טָהֹר Lv 11^{47}+4 t.; cstr. טְהוֹר Hab 1^{13}, טְהָוֹר Pr 22^{11}; טְהָר־ Jb 17^{9}, f. טְהוֹרָה Mal 1^{11} +3 t; טְהֹרָה Gn 7^{2}+8 t., mpl טְהוֹרִים Ez 36^{25} Ezr 6^{20}; טהרים Pr 15^{26}; fpl טהרות Lv 14^{4} ψ 12^{7};—**1.** ceremonially *clean*, of animals Gn 7$^{2.2.8.8}$ 8$^{20.20}$ (all J), Lv 14^{4} (P), 20$^{25.25}$ (H), Dt 14$^{11.20}$; places Lv 4^{12} 6^{4} 10^{14} 11^{36} Nu 19^{9} (all P); things Lv 10^{10} 11$^{37.47}$ 14^{57} (P), Ez 22^{26} 44^{23} Is 66^{20} Mal 1^{11}; persons Lv 7^{19} 13$^{13.17.37.39.40.41}$ 15^{8} Nu 5^{28} 9^{13} 18$^{11.13}$ 19$^{9.18.19}$ (all P), Dt 12$^{15.22}$ 15^{22} 23^{11} 1 S 20^{26a} + v.^{26b} MT but rd טֹהַר Pu, see טָהֵר, 2 Ch 30^{17} Ezr 6^{20}. **2.** physically *pure*. of gold זָהָב Ex 25$^{11.17.24.29.31.36.38.39}$ 28$^{14.22.36}$ 30^{3} 37$^{2.6.11.16.17.22.23.24.26}$ 39$^{15.25.30}$ (all P), 1 Ch 28^{17} 2 Ch 3^{4} 9^{17}; כֶּתֶם Jb 28^{19}; of water מַיִם Ez 36^{25}, of incense קְטֹרֶת Ex 30^{35} 37^{29} (P); of lamp stand מְנֹרָה Ex 31^{8} 39^{37} (P), Lv 24^{4} (H); of the table שֻׁלְחָן Lv 24^{6} (H), 2 Ch 13^{11}; *clean*, of turban Zc 3$^{5.5}$. **3.** ethically *pure, clean* Pr 30^{12} Ec 9^{2} Jb 14^{4}; of heart ψ 51^{12} Pr 22^{11}; hands Jb 17^{9}; eyes Hab 1^{13} (of God); words of men Pr 15^{26}; words of God ψ 12^{7}; law of י׳ as object of reverential fear ψ 19^{10}.

†I. טוֹב **vb.** pleasing, good (NH *id*, Hiph.; also deriv., Ar. طاب, med. ى, *be pleasant, delightful, delicious, sweet* or *savoury* in taste or odour, *be pure and clean, cheerful, happy* (Lane); Aram. טִיב, טַב, טאב, ܛܐܒ, ܛܳܒ and esp. deriv. *glad, joyful*; As *ṭâbu, be good, kind, acceptable, joyful, vigorous* Dl$^{HWB\ 299}$)—**Qal** *Pf.* טוֹב Nu 11^{18}+32 t; pl טֹבוּ Nu 24^{5} Ct 4^{10}, (*Impf.* יִיטַב from יָטַב); *Inf. abs* טוֹב Ju 11^{25}; *cstr* טוֹב Je 32^{39}+6 t, כְּטוֹב Ju 16^{25} Qr (Kt כי טוב); *Pt* טוֹב Ju 11^{25} 1 S 2^{26}; (for these forms v. Bö$^{i\ 1133.4}$ SS s v; Ges recognises only *Pfs* and fewer of them than above. It is often difficult to decide between vb. and adj.),—**1.** *be pleasant, delightful*, of tents of Jacob Nu 24^{5} (JE, poet.); of caresses Ct 4^{10} (sq. מִיַּיִן comp.) **2.** *be glad, joyful* טוֹב לֵב Ju 16^{25} (Qr), 1 S 25^{36} 2 S 13^{28} Est 1^{10} (v. טוֹב **2 c**). **3.** of rank, position, claim: הֲטוֹב טוב אתה מבלק Ju 11^{25} *art thou really better than Balak?* **4.** טוֹב לְ *be well with, good for* Nu 11^{18} (J), Dt 5^{30} 15^{16} 19^{13} 1 S 16$^{16.23}$ 2 S 14^{32} ψ 119^{71} 128^{2} Je 22^{15}; so (sc לוֹ) Is 3^{10} it is *well* (with him); אז טוב Je 22^{16} (cf. v^{15}); טוֹב אֶל־ 1 S 20^{12} *there is good toward* David. **5.** *be pleasing* טוֹב בְּעֵינֵי (v. II. טוֹב **2 b c f**) Nu 24^{1} (J) 2 S 3$^{19.36}$ 15^{26} 19^{38}; אם טוב בעיני 1 K 21^{2} Je 40^{4} Zc 11^{12}; later usage is אם טוב על *if it seem good unto* (so As. *ṭâbu eli, be pleasing unto*, Dl$^{HWB\ 300a}$), 1 Ch 13^{2} Ne 2$^{5.7}$ Est 1^{19} 3^{9} 5$^{4.8}$ 7^{3} 8^{5} 9^{13} (cf. טוֹב adj.). **Hiph.** *Pf.* 2 ms הֱטִיבוֹתָ 2 Ch 6^{8}, הֱטִיבֹתָ 1 K 8^{18} 2 K 10^{30};—*do well, act right*, sq. כי *that* 1 K 8^{18} *thou didst well, that it was in thine heart* = 2 Ch 6^{8}; sq inf. c לְ 2 K 10^{30} *thou hast done well in performing what was right in mine eyes.*

†II. טוֹב **adj.** pleasant, agreeable, good (v. Lag$^{BN\ 26}$; Aram טַב, Palm. טב Vog$^{No\ 81}$, טבא Vog$^{No\ 75}$)—m ט' Gn 2^{12}+22 t, טוֹבָם Mi 7^{4}; f. טוֹבָה Est 8^{5}+50 t, טֹבָה Dt 6^{18}+2 t.; cstr. טוֹבַת Gn 26^{7}+6 t, טֹבַת Gn 24^{16}, pl. טוֹבִים Je 44^{17}+28 t.; טֹבִים Gn 27^{9}+4 t; cstr טוֹבֵי Dn 1^{4}+2 t.; pl. טובות Est 2^{2}, טבות Je 24^{2}+6 t., טֹבֹת Gn 6^{2}+4 t.,—**1.** *pleasant, agreeable* to the senses: **a.** to the sight, *fair*, of daughters of men Gn 6^{2} (J); of a son Ex 2^{2} (E), 1 S 9^{2} 1 K 20^{3}, young men (but rd *herds* 𝔊 Th We Klo Dr Bu) 1 S 8^{16}, מראיהם *their appearance* Dn 1^{15}, טֹבַת מראה Gn 24^{16} 26^{7} (both J), 2 S 11^{2} Est 1^{11} 2$^{3.7}$; טוב תאר 1 S 16^{12}; טוב ראי 1 K 1^{6}, טוֹבַת חן Na 3^{4}; טוב לעינים Est 2^{2}, טובות מראה Dn 1^{4}; טובי מראה Ec 11^{7}, טובה בעיניו *fair in his eyes* Est 8^{5}; of mantle Jos 7^{21} (J); goodly houses Is 5^{9} Dt 8^{12}; cities Dt 6^{10}; situation of city 2 K 2^{19}. **b.** to the taste, *good, sweet, agreeable for eating* למאכל Gn 2^{9} 3^{6} (both J), ears of grain Gn 41$^{5.22.24.26}$ (E); figs Je 24$^{2.3.3.5}$; honey Pr 24^{13}; כְּיֵין הטוב Ct 7^{10} *as wine of the best sort* (Hi rds כְּיַיִן); תְּנוּבָתִי הַטּוֹבָה Ju 9^{11} *my sweet fruit* (‖ מָתְקִי). **c.** to the smell, *sweet-scented*, of ointment Ct 1^{3}; קנה הטוב Je 6^{20} *the fragrant cane.* **d.** of *pleasant* shadow of tree Ho 4^{13}. **2.** *pleasant* to the higher nature, giving pleasure, happiness, prosperity, and so *agreeable, pleasing, well*: **a.** of time: יום טוב *good day*, festal day 1 S 25^{8} Est 8^{17} 9$^{19.22}$; of feasts Zc 8^{19}, prosperous years Gn 41^{35} (E). **b.** of place, טוב בית הנשים Est 2^{9} *the best part of the women's house*; בַּטּ' לוֹ Dt 23^{17}, בַּטּ' בעיני Gn 20^{15} (v. **c f** infr.) **c.** of persons, (אתה) טוב בעיני *pleasing in the eyes of* 1 S 29$^{6.6.9}$ טוב בעיני י׳ Mal 2^{17} (cf. **vb. 4**, and **f** infr.); later לפני Ec 2$^{26.26}$ 7^{26}; inserted in 1 S 29^{10} 𝔊 We Dr, cf. ט' עם 1 S 2^{26}. **d.** of word or message, בְּשׂוֹרָה טוֹבָה 2 S 18^{27} *good tidings*; שְׁמוּעָה ט' *good report* 1 S 2^{24} Pr 15^{30} 25^{25}; דבר בעתו Pr 15^{23} *a word in its season*; דבר טוב Pr 12^{25} *an agreeable word* (maketh the heart glad), דבר טוב ψ 45^{2} *a good theme.* **e.** of other things, דֶּרֶךְ טובה 1 S 24^{20} *a pleasant, prosperous journey*;

מנחה כי טוב Gn 49^{15} (poem); of unity of brethren מה טוב ומה נעים ψ 133^{1} *how good and how pleasant it is!* (יהיה) טוב ל *it shall be well for* Ec 2^{3} 6^{12} 8$^{12.13}$ (cf **vb 3**), הֲטוֹב כי Jb 13^{9} *will it be advantageous that* (v **5**) **f.** עשה הטוב בעיני *do what is pleasing in the eyes of* Gn 16^{6} (J), Ju 19^{24} 1 S 1^{23} 3^{18} 14^{40} 2 S 10^{12} = 1 Ch 19^{13}, 2 S 19$^{19.28.39}$ 2 K 10^{5} 20^{3} = Is 38^{3}, 1 Ch 21^{23} = 2 S 24^{22} where obj of העלה, עשה (כ) (כל) (ה)טוב בע׳ Gn 19^{8} (J), Ju 10^{15} 1 S 11^{10} 14^{36} Est 3^{11}, עשה (כ)הטוב ו(כ)הישר בע׳ Dt 12^{28} Jos 9^{25} (D), 2 Ch 14^{1} Je 26^{14}, cf. Est 8^{8}, nouns reversed Dt 6^{18}, עשה הטוב והישר לפני 2 Ch 31^{20}, טוב בע׳ in other combinations Nu 36^{6} (P), Je 40^{4}, ראה הטוב והישר 2 K 10^{3}, דבר ט׳ 1 K 22^{13} = 2 Ch 18^{12}, Nu 10^{29} (J), 1 S 19^{4} Est 7^{9}, דבר מטוב עד־רע *speak either good or bad* Gn 31$^{24.29}$ (E), למרע ועד טוב 2 S 13^{22}, רע או טוב Gn 24^{50} (J), התנבא ט׳ 1 K 22$^{8.18}$ = 2 Ch 18^{17}, cf 1 K 22^{13} = 2 Ch 18^{12} **3.** *good, excellent* of its kind. **a.** of the several creations, וירא אלהים כי טוב *and God saw that it was good, excellent* Gn 1$^{4.10.12.18.21.25}$ (P), כל אשר עשה והנה טוב מאד 1^{31} (P) God saw *all that he had made, and behold it was very excellent* So **b** of land, soil, *fruitful, fertile.* ארץ Ex 3^{8} Nu 13^{19} (both J), 14^{7} (P), Dt 1$^{25.35}$ 3^{25} 4$^{21.22}$ 6^{18} 8$^{7.10}$ 9^{6} 11^{17} Jos 23^{16} (D), Ju 18^{9} 1 Ch 28^{8}; אדמה 1 K 14^{15} Jos 23$^{13.15}$ (D), הר Dt 3^{25}; חלקה 2 K 3$^{19.25}$; שדה Ez 17^{8}, נָוֶה Ez 34^{14}, מרעה 1 Ch 4^{40} Ez 34$^{14.18}$. **c.** of vegetation, *choice, fruitful* זיתים 1 S 8^{14}, עֵץ 2 K 3$^{19.25}$ Ez 31^{16}, שמן טוב 2 K 20^{13} *precious oil* = Is 39^{2}, ψ 133^{2} Ec 7^{1}, of seed, אם שניהם טובים Ec 11^{6} *whether both of them will be fruitful* **d.** of animals, *fat* בקר Gn 18^{7} (J), עזים Gn 27^{9} (J); פרות Gn 41^{26} (E). יָרֵךְ Ez 24^{4} **e.** of minerals, *fine, pure* זהב Gn 2^{12} (J), 2 Ch 3$^{5.8}$, כתם La 4^{1}, brass Ezr 8^{27}, soldering Is 41^{7}. **4.** *good, rich, valuable in estimation* · **a.** in quantity, שֵׂיבה טובה *good old age* Gn 15^{15} (R), 25^{8} (P), Ju 8^{32} 1 Ch 29^{28}, dowry Gn 30^{20} (E, many sons); treasury Dt 28^{12} (from which ׳י sends blessings) **b.** in price, *goodly, valuable:* of the estimation put upon house, beast, and tithe Lv 27$^{10.10.12.14.33}$ (H), profit Pr 31^{18}, hire Ec 4^{9}, מחמדי הטבים Jo 4^{5} *my goodly precious things* **5.** *good, appropriate, becoming,* טוב אשר Ec 7^{18} (cf 5^{4} infr), טובה חכמה עם נחלה Ec 7^{11} *wisdom is good with an inheritance* (other trans. see in VB); ‖ יָפֶה Ec 5^{17}, c עֵצָה 2 S 17$^{7.14}$ *good advice,* טוב פתר Gn 40^{16} (E) that *he interpreted well,* (לא) טוב הדבר Ex 18^{17} (E) *the thing is* (not) *good, wise,* so Dt 1^{14} 1 S 26^{16}, טוב (ה)דבר *the word is good, is well said* 1 S 9^{10} 1 K 2$^{38.42}$ 18^{24} 2 K 20^{19} = Is 39^{8}, for which abbreviated טוב *well! good!* exclamation Ru 3^{13} 1 S 20^{7} 2 S 3^{13} 1 K 2^{18}, followed by כי *it is good that* 2 S 18^{3} Ru 2^{22} La 3^{27} Jb 10^{3} (cf. 13^{9} **2 e**); c inf Gn 2^{18} (J), ψ 73^{28} 92^{2} 147^{1} Pr 25^{27} (cf sub **10**); with ו (strangely) טוֹב וְיָחִיל וגו׳ La 3^{26} *it is good that one wait* (v יָחִיל, דוּמָם), בלא דעת נֶפֶשׁ לא טוב Pr 19^{2} *that a soul be without knowledge is not good.* **6.** c מן compar = *better,* sq. inf Gn 29^{19} (E), Ex 14^{12} (J), ψ 118$^{8.9}$ Pr 16^{19} 25^{7} Ec 6^{9} 7^{2}, inf. om. Pr 21$^{9.19}$ 25^{24}, מן om Nu 14^{3} (J, compar. only implied), c מן pers Ju 15^{2} Ru 4^{15} 1 S 1^{8} 9^{2} 15^{28} 1 K 2^{32} 19^{4} 2 Ch 21^{13} Pr 12^{9} 16^{32} 19$^{1.22}$ 27^{10} 28^{6} La 4^{9} Est 1^{19} Ec 4$^{3.9.13}$ 6^{3} 7$^{5.8}$, c מן rei Ju 8^{2} 1 S 15^{22} 2 S 17^{14} 1 K 21^{2} 2 K 5^{12} Ho 2^{9} Am 6^{2} Is 56^{5} Jon 4$^{3.8}$ ψ 37^{16} 63^{4} 84^{11} 119^{72} Pr 3^{14} 8$^{11.19}$ 15$^{16.17}$ 16$^{8.16}$ 17^{1} 22^{1} 27^{5} Ct 1^{2} Ec 4^{6} 7$^{1.3.8.10}$ 9$^{4.16.18}$, sq מִשֶּׁ־ Ec 5^{4}, מַה־טּוֹב . . . הֲ . . . אם *is it better . . . or?* Ju 9^{2}; הֲטוֹב . . . או 18^{19}; אין טוב מאשר Ec 2^{24} (rd. מִשֶּׁ־ v Comm), טוב שֶׁ־ Ec 3^{22}, אין טוב כי אם Ec 3^{12} 8^{15}, so 1 S 27^{1} 𝔊 We Dr Klo Kit Bu (MT only כי c Impf) **7.** of man's sensuous nature, *glad, happy, prosperous* טוב לב *merry, glad heart* Pr 15^{15} Est 5^{9} Ec 9^{7}, טובי לב 1 K 8^{66} = 2 Ch 7^{10}; וַנִּהְיֶה טובים Je 44^{17} *we were prosperous,* similarly ψ 112^{5}. **8.** of man's intellectual nature, שכל טוב *good understanding* 2 Ch 30^{22} ψ 111^{10} Pr 3^{4} 13^{15}; טוֹבַת שֶׂכֶל 1 S 25^{3}. **9.** *good, kind, benign.* **a.** of men, themselves 1 S 25^{15} 2 S 18^{27} 2 Ch 10^{7}; the eye Pr 22^{9}, דברים טובים *kind words* 1 K 12^{7} = 2 Ch 10^{7}. **b.** of God, himself Na 1^{7} 2 Ch 30^{18} ψ 86^{5}, כי טוב *for he is good, kind* ψ 34^{9} 100^{5} 135^{3} Je 33^{11}; כי טוב כי לעולם חסדו 1 Ch 16^{34} 2 Ch 5^{13} 7^{3} Ezr 3^{11} ψ 106^{1} 107^{1} 118$^{1.29}$ 136^{1}, טוב ל *kind to* 73^{1} 145^{9} La 3^{25}, יד (ה)טובה על Ezr 7^{9} 8^{18} Ne 2$^{8.18}$, רוחך (ה)טובה 9^{20} ψ 143^{10}, שמך כי טוב 52^{11} 54^{8}, כי טוב חסדך 69^{17} 109^{21}, הדבר(ים) הטוב(ים) *the good, kind word(s)* spoken in promise Jos 21^{43} 23$^{14.15}$ (D), 1 K 8^{56} Je 29^{10} 33^{14} Zc 1^{13}. **10.** *good* (ethical), *right:* מה טוב ‖ what Yahweh requires Mi 6^{8}, ‖ משפט Jb 34^{4}· **a.** of man himself ‖ ישר Mi 7^{4}; איש טוב Pr 14^{14}, (ה)טוב(ים) = *(the) good* 2 Ch 19^{11} ψ 125^{4} Pr 2^{20} 12^{2} 13^{22} 14^{19} 15^{3} Ec 9^{2}, man's deeds דברים 2 Ch 2^{12} 19^{3}, מעשה 1 S 19^{4} Ec 12^{14}, מעללים Ez 36^{31}, דֶּרֶךְ הטובה והישרה 1 S 12^{23} *the good and right way;* (הַ)דֶּרֶךְ (ה)טוב(ה) *(the) good way* 1 K 8^{36} = 2 Ch 6^{27}, Is 65^{2} Je 6^{16} ψ 36^{5} Pr 16^{29}, דבריך טובים ונכחים 2 S 15^{3} *good and right is thy case,* דבר טוב *good thing* 1 K 14^{13}, לא טוב

הדבר Ne 5^{9}; אשר לא טוב עשה Ez 18^{18}; so of מאזני מרמה etc., Pr 20^{23}; לא טוב c. inf. (v. **5**) *it is not good or right to:* ענוש לצדיק Pr 17^{26}; שאת פני רשע 18^{5}; הכר פנים 28^{21} 24^{23} (בל טוב). **b.** of God טוב אתה ומטיב ψ 119^{68}; טוב וישר יהוה 25^{8}; משפטיך טובים 119^{39}; his commands מצות Ne 9^{13}; חקים Ez 20^{25} (לא טובים); לקח טוב Pr 4^{2}; מפי עליון לא תצא הרעות והטוב La 3^{38}.

† III. טוֹב **n.m.**$^{Je\ 17,\ 6}$ (cf. טוֹבָה **n.f.**) **a good thing, benefit, welfare;**—ט׳ Gn 26^{29} + 134 t.;— **1.** *welfare, prosperity, happiness:* ‖ שָׁלוֹם Is 52^{7} Je 8^{15} 14^{19}; אם טוב ואם רע 42^{6} *whether prosperity or adversity;* יבוא טוב 17^{6} *prosperity cometh;* שׂמח בט׳ Dt 26^{11} 2 Ch 6^{41}; ראה בט׳ Ec 2^{1} Je 29^{32}; obj. of ראה ψ 4^{7} 34^{13} Ec 2^{24} 3^{13} Jb 7^{7}; of דרשׁ Est 10^{3}; of בקשׁ ψ 122^{9}; מנע 84^{12} Je 5^{25}; נתן ψ 85^{13}; קוה Jb 30^{26}; מצא Pr 16^{20} 17^{20} 18^{22} 19^{8}; נחל Pr 28^{10}; חסר ψ 34^{11}; בשׂר 1 K 1^{42} Is 52^{7}; חול לט׳ Mi 1^{12}; חכמה וט׳ 1 K 10^{7}; טוב וחסד ψ 23^{6}; בטוב *in prosperity* 25^{13} Jb 21^{13} 36^{11} Ec 7^{14}; מטוב *because of prosperity* Zc 1^{17}; *afar from happiness* ψ 39^{3}; כטוב Ho 10^{1}; לטוב Dt 30^{9} Je 15^{11}; לטוב לָנוּ Dt 6^{24} *for good to us,* = *for our good,* 10^{13} (לָךְ), Je 32^{39} (לָהֶם); cf. לרע ל Je 7^{6} 25^{7}). **2.** *good things,* (coll.) ברכ(ו)ת ט׳ *blessing of good things* ψ 21^{4} Pr 24^{25}; מִלְאוּ בָתֵּיהֶם ט׳ Jb 22^{18} *filled their houses with good things;* obj. of שׂבע ψ 104^{28} Pr 12^{14}; מלא ψ 107^{9}; אכל Pr 13^{2} Is 55^{2}; לקח Ho 14^{3}; השׂביע בט׳ ψ 103^{5}; *goods, possessions* 1 S 15^{9}. **3.** *good* = *benefit:* גְּמָלַתְהוּ טוֹב וְלֹא־רָע Pr 31^{12} *she doeth him good and not evil;* תַּאֲוַת צַדִּיקִים אַךְ־טוֹב Pr 11^{23} *the desire of the righteous is only good;* obj. of קבל Jb 2^{10}; מנע Pr 3^{27}; שׁחר 11^{27}; שׁלם 13^{21}; עשׂה Gn 26^{29} (J), ψ 119^{65}; היטיב Nu 10^{32} (J); ערב לט׳ ψ 119^{122}; חֹרְשֵׁי ט׳ Pr 14^{22} *who devise good.* **4.** *moral good,* ידע טוב ורע Gn $2^{9.17}$ $3^{5.22}$ (J), Dt 1^{39}; בין טוב לרע 2 S 19^{36}; in antithesis with רע elsewh. Dt 30^{15} 2 S 14^{17} 1 K 3^{9} Is $5^{20.20}$ $7^{15.16}$ Am $5^{14.15}$ Mi 3^{2} ψ 34^{15} 37^{27} 52^{5}; זנח ט׳ Ho 8^{3} *cast off good;* עשׂה טוב *do good* ψ $14^{1.3}$ = $53^{2.4}$, 37^{3} Ec 7^{20}, in 3^{12} this mng. seems less fitting; rd. perh. לִרְאוֹת ט׳ (Gr, v. also De) and tr. to **1**; רדף ט׳ ψ 38^{21} *pursue good;* מַעְגְּלֵי־ט׳ Pr 2^{9} *path of good.*

† טוֹב אֲדוֹנִיָּה **n.pr.m.** (*good is my Lord,* י׳)—וַאֲדֹנִיָּהוּ וְטוֹבִיָּהוּ וְטוֹב אֲדוֹנִיָּה in list of Levites assigned to reign of Jehoshaphat 2 Ch 17^{8}, but txt. suspicious; 𝔊L *Τωβαδωνια*, but 𝔊 only *Τωβαδωβεια* for all three names.

† טוּב **n.m.**$^{Jb\ 20,\ 21}$ **good things, goods, goodness;**—ט׳ Gn 24^{10} + 17 t.; sf. טוּבִי Ex 33^{19} Je 31^{14}; טוּבְךָ ψ 25^{7} + 4 t.; טוּבוֹ Ho 3^{5} + 2t.; טוּבָהּ Ne 9^{36} Je 2^{7}; טוּבָם Jb 21^{16};—not in H P Chr Ez or post-ex. proph.—**1.** *good things,* coll., produce of the land to be eaten Gn $45^{18.20.23}$ (E), Is 1^{19} Je 2^{7} Ezr 9^{12} Ne $9^{35.36}$, to be enjoyed; good things of י׳ as given by him Ho 3^{5} Je $31^{12.14}$ ψ 27^{13}; of house of י׳ ψ 65^{5}, fig. of spiritual blessings. **2.** *goods, property* Gn 24^{10} (J), Dt 6^{11} 2 K 8^{9} Ne 9^{25}. **3.** abstr.: **a.** *fairness, beauty,* of neck of heifer Ho 10^{11}; of people of י׳ Zc 9^{17}; of י׳ himself Ex 33^{19} (JE). **b.** טוּב לֵב(ב) *joy of* heart Dt 28^{47} Is 65^{14} (v. I. טוֹב **2**, II. ט׳ **7**). **c.** *prosperity* Jb 20^{21} 21^{16}; of Jerusalem ψ 128^{5}; בְּטוּב צַדִּיקִים Pr 11^{10} *in the prosperity of the righteous* the city rejoiceth. **d.** *goodness* of taste, discernment ψ 119^{66}. **4.** abstr., *goodness* of God: **a.** in bestowing good things Ne 9^{25}. **b.** in the salvation of his people Is 63^{7} ψ 25^{7} 145^{7}. **c.** stored up for his saints ψ 31^{20}.

† טוֹבָה **n.f. welfare, benefit, good things, good;**—abs. ט׳ Dt 28^{11} + 54 **t.**; cstr. טוֹבַת ψ 106^{5}; sf. טוֹבָתִי ψ 16^{2} etc. + 4 t. sfs.; pl. טוֹבוֹת Je 12^{6}; טֹבוֹת 2 K 25^{28} Je 52^{32}; sf. טוֹבֹתָיו Ne 6^{19};—**1.** *welfare, prosperity, happiness:* ‖ שׁלום Dt 23^{7} Je 33^{9} Ezr 9^{12} La 3^{17}; יום טובה Ec 7^{14} *day of prosperity;* טוֹבָתִי בַּל־עָלֶיךָ ψ 16^{2} *is not my welfare dependent upon thee?* תְּבוֹאַתְךָ ט׳ Jb 22^{21} *prosperity shall come to thee;* לטובה Gn 50^{20} (E), Dt 28^{11} 30^{9} 2 Ch 18^{7} Je 14^{11}; לרעה ולא לטובה Am 9^{4} Je 21^{10} 39^{16} 44^{27}; obj. of vb. בקשׁ Ne 2^{10}; הביא Je 32^{42}; ראה Jb 9^{25} Ec 5^{17} 6^{6}; אבד Ec 9^{18}; ראה בט׳ ψ 106^{5}; חסר מט׳ Ec 4^{8}; obj. of אכל fig. Jb 21^{25} = *taste happiness;* of שׂבע Ec 6^{3}; after נחם על Je 18^{10}. **2.** *good things* (coll.): **a.** of good words, obj. of דבר 1 S 25^{30} 2 S 7^{28} = 1 Ch 17^{26}, Je 18^{20}; pl. דבר טובות Je 12^{6} 52^{32} = 2 K 25^{28}. **b.** of material possessions ברבות הט׳ Ec 5^{10} *when good things increase.* **3.** *bounty, good* שְׁנַת טוֹבָתֶךָ ψ 65^{12} *year of thy bounty* (harvest bestowed by God), so also טובתך ψ 68^{11}; עשׂה (ה)ט׳ Ex 18^{9} (E), Nu 24^{13} (JE), Ju 8^{35} 9^{16} 1 S 24^{19} 2 S 2^{6} 1 K 8^{66} = 2 Ch 7^{10}, 2 Ch 24^{16} Je 33^{9}; obj. of גמל 1 S 24^{18}; שׁלם 1 S 24^{20}; רעה תחת טובה Gn 44^{4} (J), 1 S 25^{21} ψ 35^{12} 38^{21} 109^{5} Pr 17^{13} Je 18^{20}; ט׳ תחת קללה 2 S 16^{12}; זכר לי לט׳ *remember it for me for good* Ne 5^{19} 13^{31}; לטובה Ezr 8^{22} Ne 2^{18} Je $24^{5.6}$ ψ 86^{17}; pl. טוֹבֹתָיו Ne 6^{19} *his benefits* (i.e. good deeds of Tobiah).

† טוֹבִיָּה, טוֹבִיָּהוּ **n.pr.m.** (*Yah(u) is my*

good)—**1.** טוֹבִיָּהוּ a Levite, assigned to reign of Jehoshaphat 2 Ch 17^{8}, not 𝔊, 𝔊L Τωβιας, elsewhere טוֹבִיָּה 𝔊 Τωβια(ς) **2.** Ammonite adversary of Nehem. Ne 2$^{10.19}$ 3^{35} 4^{1} 6$^{1.12.14.17.17.19}$ 13$^{4.7.8}$. **3.** head of a family of returning exiles of doubtful lineage Ezr 2^{60} = Ne 7^{62}. **4.** a chief of returning exiles Zc 6$^{10.14}$, 𝔊 χρησίμων (-μοις) αὐτῆς, i.e. טוֹבֶיהָ.

†IV. **טוֹב n.pr.loc.** (perh fr above √)—a region beyond Jordan, N or NE of Gilead, prob. Aramean, אֶרֶץ טוֹב Ju 11$^{3.5}$, 𝔊 Τωβ, אִישׁ טוֹב 2 S 10$^{6.8}$ *men of Ṭôb*, 𝔊 (Ε)ιστωβ, = Τουβιον, Τώβιον 1 Macc 5^{13}; identif. by Conder$^{\text{Handb 296}}$ with southern Bashan, where is still *Taiyibeh*, 12 m. SE from Sea of Galilee

†[**טָוָה**] **vb. spin** (NH *id*, Aram טַמְוִיתָא *spider* Jb 8^{14} 𝔗 (but Syr. ܛܘܐ = *roast, broil*, v. Dr$^{\text{JPh xi, 1882, 207}}$), As *ṭamû* (*ṭawû*), *spin*, Hpt$^{\text{ZA. 1887, 274}}$ Dl$^{\text{HWB 302}}$, Ar طَوَى *fold, wind*, Eth ጠወየ: *be twisted*)—**Qal** *Pf.* 3 pl טָווּ work of women of Isr Ex 35^{26} abs, v^{26} sq acc אֶת־הָעִזִּים *goats*, i.e. goats' hair (P)

†מַטְוֶה **n.[m.]** **that which is spun, yarn,** Ex 35^{25} (P)

†[**טוּחַ**] **vb. over-spread, over-lay, coat, besmear** (NH *id*, Aram. *id*, cf. Ar طَاخَ *re foeda contaminatus fuit*, or *contaminavit*, مُطَيَّخ camel *smeared with tar*),—**Qal** *Pf* 3 ms וְטָח consec Lv 14^{42} (on טַח Is 44^{18} v. טחח), 3 pl טָחוּ Ez 22^{28}, טַחְתֶּם Ez 13$^{12.14}$, *Inf cstr* לָטוּחַ 1 Ch 29^{4}, *Pt* pl טָחִים Ez 13^{10} + 2 t, cstr. טָחֵי Ez 13^{11}, only P Ez Ch,—*over-spread, coat* (c acc of house) with earth (clay, עָפָר) Lv 14^{42}, *over-lay* (walls with gold and silver) c acc of wall 1 Ch 29^{4}, metaph. of coating over Jerusalem, under fig. of a wall, with a superficial coating, to hide its real weakness Ez 13^{15} (acc. of wall), v^{12} c acc of coating (טִיחַ); with תָּפֵל (q v) v^{11}, c 2 acc v$^{10.14.15}$; cf וּנְבִיאֶיהָ טָחוּ לָהֶם תָּפֵל Ez 22^{28} where sf ref. to oppressive nobles, i e the prophets 'whitewash' for them (their evil deeds) **Niph.** *Inf cstr* הִטּוֹחַ *be coated* (with עפר) Lv 14^{43}, and, fully, הִטּוֹחַ אֶת־הַבַּיִת 14^{48} (both P).

†טִיחַ **n.[m.]** **a coating,** only אַיֵּה הַטִּיחַ אֲשֶׁר טַחְתֶּם Ez 13^{12}

†טֻחוֹת **n f pl** **inward parts** (as *covered over*, concealed)—טֻחוֹת of seat of faithfulness, אֱמֶת חָפַצְתָּ בַטֻּ׳ ψ 51^{8} *faithfulness thou desirest in the inward parts*, i e. in the heart (|| סָתֻם), of seat of wisdom מִי שָׁת בַּטֻּ׳ חָכְמָה Jb 38^{36} (|| שֶׂכְוִי q.v.), fr. context this can hardly = heart of man (kidneys, 'reins,' 𝔗, Jewish interpr, v. NHWB ii 144 al), but is rather *cloud-layers* (as dark, *hidden* spaces, v Di VB); their 'wisdom' appears in their obedience to natural law.

טוט, טיט (√ of foll, meaning unknown).

†טִיט **n.m.** **mud, mire, clay** (NH *id*; As. *ṭîṭu*, *id*, Flood Tabl iii. 10 25)—abs. טִיט Jb 41^{22} + 6 t, cstr. *id.* Mi 7^{10} + 5 t,—**1.** *mud, mire* of streets (always in sim. of contempt, ignominious treatment) טִ׳ חוּצוֹת Mi 7^{10} ψ 18^{43} = 2 S 22^{43}, Zc 9^{3} 10^{5}, of Jeremiah's dungeon Je 38$^{6.6}$; of mire in which crocodile lies Jb 41^{22}; cast up by sea Is 57^{20} (|| רֶפֶשׁ); of a bog (fig. of distress) ψ 69^{15} and טִ׳ הַיָּוֵן ψ 40^{30}. **2.** poet. of potter's *clay* (|| חֹמֶר) Is 41^{25}, brick-*clay* (|| *id.*) Na 3^{14}.

טֹטָפֹת, טוֹטָפֹת v. טפף.

[**טוּל**] **vb. Pilp.** etc, **hurl, cast** (Ar. طَالَ *be extended, elongated*; v. Hom$^{\text{NS 87}}$ who comp. As *ṭâlu*, Aram. ܛܠܠ, טַיֵּיל all *walk about* (cf *spatiari*, fr. *spatium*); Eth. አጠሎለ: *hang loosely*, አጠሐለ: *expand*)—**Pilp.** *Pt* מְטַלְטֶלְךָ טַלְטֵלָה גָּבֶר Is 22^{17} *hurleth thee* violently. **Hiph.** *Pf* הֵטִיל Jon 1^{4}; וְהֵטַלְתִּי Je 16^{13} 22^{26}; *Impf.* וַיָּטֶל 1 S 18^{11} (but v. infr), 20^{33}; אֲטִילֵךְ Ez 32^{4} (𝔊 Co om.) וַיְטִלוּ Jon 1^{5}; וַיְטִלֻהוּ Jon 1^{15}; *cast, cast out*, of casting a javelin (חֲנִית) 1 S 18^{11} (but id here וַיִּטֹּל, √נטל, *and took up*, so 𝔊 𝔗 Th We Kp Kit, v also Dr); 20^{33} sq עַל pers. aimed at, Jonah אֶל־הַיָּם Jon 1$^{12.15}$; also the cargo כֵּלִים 1^{5}, fig of ׳ casting Pharaoh עַל־פְּנֵי הַשָּׂדֶה Ez 32^{4} (Co del. v. supr.; || וּנְטַשְׁתִּיךָ בָאָרֶץ); *hurl* (send violently), of ׳ sending furious wind Jon 1^{4}; fig of hurling king of Judah, etc. into exile Je 16^{3} sq. acc. + מֵעַל of land from which, and עַל of that to which; Je 22^{26} c acc. + עַל of land to which. **Hoph.** *Pf.* הוּטְלוּ Je 22^{28}; *Impf.* יוּטַל Pr 16^{33}; יוּטָל ψ 37^{24}, יֻטָל Jb 41^{1},—**1.** *be hurled*, e g. into exile Je 22^{28} (|| הֻשְׁלְכוּ); *hurled down, headlong*, כִּי יִפֹּל לֹא יוּטָל ψ 37^{24} *when he falls he shall not be hurled headlong* (fig. of a good man); יֻטָל Jb 41^{1} *be overwhelmed*, at sight of the crocodile. **2.** of inanimate thing, *be cast, thrown*, the lot בַּחֵיק יוּטַל אֶת־הַגּוֹרָל Pr 16^{33}.

†טַלְטֵלָה **n.f.** **a hurling,** Is 22^{17}, v. supr. **Pilp.**, lit. *hurleth thee with a hurling*, O man;

rd. perh (Du), with a diff. word-division, טַלְטֵל הַגֶּבֶר (inf. abs.)

טור (√ of foll, cf. Ar. طَارَ *go* or *hover about, approach*, طَوْرٌ *limit, border*).

†**טוּר n.m.**[Ex 28.17] **row**—abs טו׳ Ex 28[17] + 9 t.; cstr. *id.* 28[17] + 3 t; pl טוּרִים 28[17] + 7 t; טֻרִים 1 K 7[20], cstr. טוּרֵי Ex 39[10] + 2 t.;— **1.** *row, course* of building-stones, in temple and in Solomon's house 1 K 6[36] 7[12], forming enclosures in corner of court Ez 46[23a]; of beams 6[36] 7[12], v. also 7[4] (Th Klo, v שְׁקֻפִים ,שֶׁקֶף); of pillars 7[2.3]. **2.** *row* of jewels, on high priest's breast-piece Ex 28[17 17 17 18.19.20] 39[10.10 10.11 12.13] (all P); of pomegranates on capitals of pillars in temple 1 K 7[20.42] 2 Ch 4[13], so also prob. 1 K 7[18], v. Th Klo, after 𝔊; of knops round the molten sea 7[24], cf. 2 Ch 4[3] (oxen הַבָּקָר, erron for הַפְּקָעִים 1 K 7[24]).

†[**טִירָה**] **n.f. encampment, battlement** (fr. idea of *surrounding*, enclosure; Syr. ܛܝܪܐ *sheepfold*, ἔπαυλις)—cstr. טִירַת Ct 8[9]; טִירָתָם ψ 69[26]; pl. טירות Ez 46[23]; sf. טִירֹתָם Nu 31[10] Gn 25[16]; טירוֹתָם 1 Ch 6[39]; טִירוֹתֵיהֶם Ez 25[4],— **1.** *encampment*, esp. of circular encampment of nomad tribes, mentioned with חצר Gn 25[16]; with ערים Nu 31[10], Ez 25[4] (‖משכניהם); *encampment* (poet.) = habitation ψ 69[26] (‖אהליהם); more gen, 1 Ch 6[39] (‖מושבות) **2.** in metaph. ט׳ כֶּסֶף Ct 8[9] *a battlement of silver.* **3.** *row* of stones, only pl. טירות Ez 46[23], virtually pl. of טור **1**, q.v.

†**יְטוּר n.pr.m.** and **gent.** (perh. connected etymolog. with טִירָה, v. Gn 25[16])—a 'son' of Ishmael Gn 25[15] = 1 Ch 1[31] = tribe with which Reuben, Gad, and half Manasseh made war 1 Ch 5[19]; Ἰτουραῖοί τε καὶ Ἄραβες Strabo[xvi. 2. 18], Ἰτουραίους Joseph[Ant. xiii 11. 3] ed. Niese; they gave name to their region, which was, substantially, Anti-Lebanon, cf. τῆς Ἰτουραίας καὶ Τραχωνίτιδος χώρας Luke 3[1]; on יְטוּר and (later) n pr. terr *Ituraea*, v. esp. GASm[Geogr 544 ff] and reff.

†[**טוּשׁ**] **vb. rush, dart** (Aram ܛܘܫ, טוּס *fly*)—only **Qal** *Impf.* כְּנֶשֶׁר יָטוּשׂ עֲלֵי אֹכֶל Jb 9[26] *like a vulture*, which *rusheth upon its food* (sim. of swiftly passing days of Job's life).

†[**טָחָה**] **vb. hurl, shoot** (NH *id*; Ar. طَحَى *spread, extend, carry far with*, e.g. a ball Lane[1832c])—only **Pil.** *Pt.* (Ges[§ 75 R 16]) pl cstr. הַרְחֵק כִּמְטַחֲוֵי קֶשֶׁת Gn 21[16] (E), lit *making distant like shooters of a bow = about a bowshot off.*

†[**טָחַח**] **vb. be besmeared**—only **Qal** *Pf.* 3 ms טַח מֵרְאוֹת עֵינֵיהֶם Is 44[18] *their eyes have been besmeared so that they do not see*, v. Di Du, and on sg. c subj. pl Ges[§ 145, 7 a]; others regard טַח as metaplastic pointing for טָח, fr. טוח, v. Sta[§ 385 d].

†[**טָחַן**] **vb. grind** (NH *crush*, olives, etc.; Aram. ܛܚܢ, טְחַן *grind*; Ar. طَحَنَ *grind*, Eth. ጠሐነ: *polenta, farina hordacea*)—**Qal** *Pf* וְטָחֲנוּ Nu 11[8]; *Impf.* וַיִּטְחַן Ex 32[20], 3 fs תִּטְחַן Jb 31[10], 2 mpl. תִּטְחָנוּ Is 3[15]; *Inf. abs.* טָחוֹן Dt 9[21]; *Imv.* fs. טַחֲנִי Is 47[2], *Pt.* טוֹחֵן Ju 16[21]; טֹחֲנוֹת Ec 12[3];—*grind*, the work of women, c. acc, with millstones רֵחַיִם Nu 11[8] (JE, obj. the manna), Is 47[2] (obj. קֶמַח), this fig of humiliation of Babylon; abs Ju 16[21], תטחן לאחר אשתי Jb 31[10], i.e serve him as his slave; no obj. expr. Ex 32[20] (E), Dt 9[21] (of golden calf); הַטֹּחֲנוֹת Ec 12[3] = the teeth (cf. Ar. طَوَاحِنُ *molar teeth;* so in Lexx Syr ܛܚܢܬܐ, ܛܚܢܝܬܐ); פני עניים ט׳ Is 3[15] *the face of the poor ye grind*, fig of extreme oppression

†**טְחוֹן n.[m.] grinding-mill, hand-mill;** only בַּחוּרִים ט׳ נָשָׂאוּ La 5[13] *the young men have borne the mill* (i.e been compelled to bear it)

†**טַחֲנָה n.f.** mill = foregoing, בשפל קול הַטּ׳ Ec 12[4] *when the sound of the mill is low* (cf. v[3], sub vb. supr.)

טחר (√ of foll; cf. Ar. طَحَرَ *eject;* Aram. טְחַר, ܛܚܪ *strain at stool*, ܛܚܪܐ *dysentery*)

†[**טְחוֹר**] **n.m.**[1 S 6. 4] only pl. **tumours**, result of dysentery (v. Aram √) (so Aram. טְחוֹרַיָּא, ܛܚܘܪܐ)—chiefly Qr for Kt עֳפָלִים, עפלי, *hemorrhoids* · viz טחרים Dt 28[27] 1 S 5[6.9.12]; טְחֹרֵי זָהָב 6[4]; צַלְמֵי טחריכם 6[5], twice it has found its way into the Kt צלמי טְחֹרֵיהֶם 6[17], טחרי הַזָּהָב 6[11]; We[Sam 27 n.], cf. Gei[Urschrift 408 f.]

טטף (perh. √ of foll.; meaning dub., Dl[Pr 46] comp As. *tatâpu, surround, encircle;* Thes Di prop. √ טוף (cf. Ar. طَافَ *go around*), whence טפטפות = טוטפות, Kn, foll. by Klein[JPTh 1881, 673] al., assumes √ טפף *tap, strike*, comp στίγμα, and thinks of actual sign or mark in the flesh as orig meant).

†**טוֹטָפוֹת n.f.pl. bands** (NH טוֹטֶפֶת, Aram. טוֹטַפְתָּא, and esp. pl. טוטפין *id.*)—alw. *bands, frontlet-bands, between the eyes* (‖ אות על יד; cf. זִכָּרוֹן בֵּין עֵינֶיךָ Ex 13[9] ‖id.), fig. of dedication

of firstborn וְהָיָה . . . לְטוֹטָפֹת בין עיניך Ex 13^{16} (JE); of commandments of י׳, וְהָיוּ לְטֹטָ׳ Dt 11^{18} and וְהָיוּ לְטֹטָפֹת Dt 6^{8}.—This injunction, orig. fig. for *perpetual remembrance* (otherwise Kn, and Klein[l. c. 666 ff.], vid. supr., Benz[Arch. 111] Now[Arch. i. 134]), was taken literally by later Jews, and hence the custom of wearing *phylacteries;* v. Di (on Ex 13^{16}) Winer[RE] Ri[HWB] (art. *Denkzettel*) Smith[Dict. Bib.] (art. *Frontlets*) Sta[ZAW 1894, 312 f., 317].

טִיחַ v. sub טוח.

טִיט v. sub טוט.

טִירָה v. sub טור.

טַל v. sub I. טלל.

†[טָלָא] **vb. patch, spot** (NH *id., patch*)—**Qal** *Pt. pass.* טָלוּא Gn $30^{32.32.33}$; pl. טְלֻאִים $v^{35.39}$; טְלֻאוֹת Ez 16^{16}; טְלֻאָה Gn 30^{35}; chiefly of *spotted, variegated* sheep and goats (Jacob & Laban); || נָקֹד, נְקֻדִּים Gn $30^{32.32.33.35}$; || עקדים Gn 30^{35}; || both, v^{39} (all J); of high places, *variegated* (gaily-coloured shrines) Ez 16^{16}. **Pu.** *Pt.* מְטֻלָּאוֹת *patched,* of sandals Jos 9^{5} (JE).

†I. טְלָאִים **n.pr.loc.** c. art. הַטְּלָ׳, place where Saul mustered his forces 1 S 15^{4}, prob. = טֶלֶם q.v.

II. טְלָאִים v. following.

טלה (√of foll.; mng. dub.; Ar. طلو, طلى is *tie a lamb* to a stake, *confine;* Syr. ܛܠܐ is *make young,* both appar. denom.; Lag[Armen. Stud. § 2229] finds earlier form of טָלֶה in Armenian).

†טָלֶה **n.m.**[1 S 7, 9] **lamb** (NH *id., lamb;* Aram. טַלְיָא *lamb, youth,* טַלְיְתָא *girl,* ܛܠܝܐ *boy, youth,* ܛܠܝܬܐ *girl* (cf. Mk 5^{41} 𝔖); Ar. طَلًا *young* of cloven-footed animals, esp. *young gazelle* Hom[NS 235], Nedj. *tully, male lamb,* Doughty[Arab. Desert. i. 429, ii. 269]; Eth. ጠሊ: *flock of goats, goat, kid*)—טְלֵה חָלָב 1 S 7^{9} *sucking lamb* (for burnt-offering); in prediction זְאֵב וְטָלֶה יִרְעוּ Is 65^{25} *wolf & lamb shall feed;* טְלָאִים pl. of foregoing, only Is 40^{11} in metaph. of י׳ shepherding his people.

טַלְטֵלָה v. sub טול.

I. **טלל** (√of foll.; mng. dub.; perh. denom. are Ar. طَلَّ (the sky) *rained fine rain;* Eth. ጠለ: *be (moist), fat,* II. *fertilize*).

†טַל **n.m.**[Ju 6, 37] **night-mist, dew** (NH טַל *dew;* Aram. ܛܠܐ, טַלָּא *dew;* Ar. طَلّ *light rain, dew;* Eth. ጠል: *dew*)—ט׳ abs. 1 S 1^{21} + 12 t.; טָל Ju 6^{13} + 9 t.; cstr. טַל Gn 27^{28} + 4 t.; sf. טַלֶּךָ Is 26^{19}, טַלָּם Zc 8^{12};—*night-mist,* taking place of our *dew* (v. Che Is 18^{4} & ψ 110^{3}; Lane[1862], Neil[Pal. Explored 129]); as coming from the sky and bringing fertility, טַל הַשָּׁמַיִם Gn 27^{28} (God gives it, נתן), & v^{39} (+ מֵעָל), cf. Dt 33^{28} (heavens distil it, ערף), Hg 1^{10} Zc 8^{12} (heavens give it, נתן); in Dt 33^{13} rd. perh. מֵעָל for מִטָּל (v. || Gn 49^{25} and Di); clouds distil it (רעף) Pr 3^{20}; sq. עַל, it descends (ירד) upon the camp Nu 11^{9} (JE); it is upon the ground Ju $6^{39.40}$, cf. 2 S 1^{21} (+ מָטָר); upon the fleece Ju 6^{37}; is wrung out (מוץ) of the fleece v^{38}; remains through the night (לִן) Jb 29^{19}, cf. שִׁכְבַת הַטּ׳ *the lying of dew* = the dew lying Ex $16^{13.14}$ (P; it goes up (עלה) in morning); it is in drops מִי הוֹלִיד אֶגְלֵי טָל Jb 38^{28}; covers the head of one out at night Ct 5^{2}; it comes (היה) by word of prophet 1 K 17^{1} (+ מָטָר); sim. of stealthy approach כַּאֲשֶׁר יִפֹּל הַטַּל עַל־הָאֲדָמָה 2 S 17^{12}; sim. denoting welcome and gentle refreshment, of speech, which distils (נזל) like it Dt 32^{2} (poem; || רְבִיבִים, שְׂעִירִים); of fraternal unity כְּטַל חֶרְמוֹן ψ 133^{3} (ירד על); of king's favour Pr 19^{12} (עַל); of י׳'s kindness Ho 14^{6}; כְּעָב טַל Is 18^{4} like a *mist-cloud,* of י׳'s quiet watching; of Jacob's influence among nations Mi 5^{6} (ט׳ מֵאֵת י״ || רְבִיבִים); טַל אוֹרֹת טַלֶּךָ Is 26^{19} *a dew of light is thy dew* (v. I. אוֹרָה, p. 21^{b} supr. and Baud[Stud. Sem. Rel. ii. 264 f.]); as transitory, כַּטַּל מַשְׁכִּים הֹלֵךְ Ho 6^{4} *like the dew early departing,* so 13^{3} (both || עֲנַן־בֹּקֶר); fig. of young warriors of king established by י׳, with flashing weapons, like dewdrops טַל יַלְדֻתֶיךָ ψ 110^{3}.

† II. [טָלַל] **vb. cover over, roof,** Aram. loan-word, v. צלל (ܛܠܠ *cover over,* esp. *put on roof,* ܛܠܠܐ *roof,* στέγη: so Palm. v. Eut[SBAk. 1885, 669])—only **Pi.** *Impf.* 3 ms. sf. וִיטַלְלֶנּוּ Ne 3^{15} he built it (kept on building it, i.e. a city-gate) and *covered it over* (laid timbers to cover it, cf. קֵרוּהוּ *they laid its timbers* $v^{3.6}$; v. also בְּצֵל קֹרָתִי Gn 19^{8} *in the shadow of my roof*).

טלם (√of foll.; perh. cf. Ar. ظَلَمَ; Aram. טְלַם, ܛܠܡ; Eth. ጠለመ: all *oppress, injure;* in this case טֶלֶם, טַלְמוֹן will be Aramaic names, since ظ = Heb. צ).

†טֶלֶם **n.pr.loc.** et **pers.** **1. n.pr.loc.** in

the Negeb of Judah, Jos 15[24] = טְלָאִים 1 S 15[4], rd. perh. טְלָאם We Dr. We rds טֶלֶם also for חוילה 1 S 15[7], cf Dr **2. n.pr.m.** one of the porters Ezr 10[24].

†טַלְמֹן, once טַלְמוֹן **n.pr m.** name of porters. **1.** 1 Ch 9[17] Ezr 2[42] = Ne 7[45]. **2.** Ne 11[19] 12[25] (טַלְמוֹן).

†I. **טָמֵא vb. be or become unclean** (NH Pi. *pollute* (ceremonially), Aram טְמָא and esp. deriv., طَمَّا Pa. *pollute*, v. RS [K 307 ff.])—**Qal** *Pf.* 3 ms. ט׳ Lv 11[25] + 22 t, 3 fs טָמְאָה 12[2] + 2 t.; 2 fs טָמֵאת Ez 22[4]; pl. טָמְאוּ Lv 15[18], *Impf.* יִטְמָא Lv 5[3] + 34 t, 3 fs. תטמא 12[2] + 4 t, pl יטמאו ψ 106[39], *Inf.* טָמְאָה Lv 15[32] + 6 t,—*be or become unclean:* **1.** sexually, c ב Lv 18[20.23] (H), Ez 23[17], the land Lv 18[25.27] (H). **2.** religiously, with idols Ez 22[3], c ב v[4]; with necromancers Lv 19[31] (H); by sacrificing children to idols ψ 106[39]. **3.** ceremonially, by contact with carcasses of unclean animals Lv 11[24.27.28.31.32.33.34.34.35.36.40] (P); any carcass 17[15] (H); eating of a carcass 22[8] (H), by issues 15[4.9.20.20.24.27.32] (P), by contact with an unclean man 5[3] 15[4] (P), 22[5] (H), or thing 22[6] (H); by leprosy 13[14.46] 14[36.46] (P), by contact with the dead Nu 6[12] 19[20] (P), Ez 44[25], or with one unclean by such contact Nu 19[22] (P), Hg 2[13.13], by contact with creeping things Lv 22[5] (H); certain animals were alw. unclean 11[26.27] (P) In ordinary cases of uncleanness טמא עד הערב *unclean till even* Lv 11[24.25.27.28.31.32.39.40.40] 14[46] 15[5.6.7.8.10.10.11.16.17.18.19.21.22.23.27] Nu 19[7.8.10.21.22] (all P), Lv 17[15] 22[6] (H); but uncleanness lasted 7 days for woman bearing a son Lv 12[2.2] (P), for man lying with woman having an issue 15[24] (P), or one coming in contact with the dead Nu 19[11.14.16] (P); it lasted 14 days for a woman bearing a daughter Lv 12[5] (P) **Niph.** *Pf.* 3 ms. נִטְמָא Ho 5[3] 6[10], 3 fs. נטמאה Nu 5[27.28]; נִטְמָאָה 5[13] + 5 t., 1 s. נִטְמֵאתִי Je 2[23]; 2 m.pl נִטְמֵתֶם Lv 11[43] (א omitted by scribal error; but Ges al derive from טמה), etc. + 4 t. pf, *Pt* pl נִטְמְאִים Ez 20[30.31];—*defile oneself, be defiled*· **1.** sexually, Lv 18[24] (H), Nu 5[13.14.14.20.27.28.29] (P) **2.** by idolatry conceived as whoredom Ho 5[3] 6[10] Je 2[23] Ez 20[30.31.43] 23[7.13.30]. **3.** ceremonially, by eating creeping things Lv 11[43]. **4.** *be regarded as unclean* (cf. **Pi. 4**), prob. נטמינו Jb 18[3] *we are accounted as unclean*, metapl. form, on another view v. טמה. **Pi.** *Pf.* טִמֵּא Gn 34[5] + 15 t, sf טִמְּאוֹ Lv 13[3] + 3 t.; 2 fs. טִמֵּאת Ez 5[11], etc. + 7 t. Pf., *Impf.* יְטַמֵּא 2 K 23[8], etc + 12 t Impf., *Imv* pl טַמְּאוּ Ez 9[7]; *Inf.* טַמֵּא Lv 13[44] + 2 t, sf. טַמְּאָם 15[31], etc + 4 t. Inf,—*defile*. **1.** sexually Gn 34[5.13.27] (R), Ez 18[6.11.15] 22[11] 33[26]; the land by sexual impurities of the people Lv 18[28] (H); Isr. by spiritual whoredom Ez 23[17]. **2.** religiously: the land, by bloodshed Nu 35[34] (P), by allowing the dead body of the murderer to hang on the tree over night Dt 21[23]; by idolatry Je 2[7] Ez 36[17.18], Isr. defiled the *sacred places* by the sacrifice of children Lv 20[3] (H), Ez 23[38], and God defiled him thereby 20[26], he defileth the sacred places by idolatry 2 Ch 36[14] Je 7[30] = 32[34], Ez 5[11], the holy name of י׳ 43[7.8], Josiah defiled the idolatrous places of worship by destroying them and making them unfit for use 2 K 23[8.10.13.16], of Isr defiling idolatrous images Is 30[22], and the nations the temple of God ψ 79[1] **3.** ceremonially by ceremonial uncleanness, the sacred places Lv 15[31] Nu 19[13.20] (P), the camp Nu 5[3] (P); the temple by dead bodies Ez 9[7], the Nazirite's head of separation by a death occurring in his presence Nu 6[9] (P), the people defile themselves (נפשתיכם) by creeping things Lv 11[44] (P) **4.** *pronounce or declare* ceremonially *unclean:* the leper Lv 13[3.8.11.15.20.22.25.27.30.44.44.59] (P), unclean animals 20[25] (H). **Pu.** *1 t.* נַפְשִׁי לֹא מְטֻמָּאָה Ez 4[14] *myself is not polluted.* **Hithp.** *Impf* יִטַּמָּא Lv 21[1] + 4 t, pl. יִטַּמְּאוּ Ez 14[11] 37[23], יִטַּמָּאוּ Ho 9[4] Ez 44[25], etc + 6 t Impf;—reflexive, *defile oneself*· by eating of an unaccepted peace-offering Ho 9[4], c. ב Lv 18[24.30] (H), 11[43] (P), Ez 14[11] 20[7.18] 37[23], c ל *for* a dead person Lv 21[1.3.11] (H), Nu 6[7] (P), *by* Lv 11[24] (P), without prep 21[4] (H), Ez 44[25] **Hothp.** *Pf.* אַחֲרֵי אֲשֶׁר הֻטַּמָּאָה Dt 24[4] *after that she has been defiled* (sexually); on form v. Ges [§ 54. 3]

†II. **טָמֵא adj. unclean**,—ט׳ Lv 5[2] + 58 t, cstr. טְמֵא 22[4] + 3 t., f טְמֵאָה 5[2] + 11 t., cstr טְמֵאַת Ez 22[5.10], pl. טְמֵאִים Lv 11[8] + 10 t.,—*unclean*, **1.** ethically and religiously ט׳ שפתים Is 6[5.5] *unclean of lips*, ט׳ השם Ez 22[5] *defiled of name, infamous;* טהור מט׳ Jb 14[4]. **2.** ritually. **a.** of persons, ‖ טהור Dt 12[15.22] 15[22] Ec 9[2], ט׳ נפש Lv 22[4] (H), ט׳ לנפש (אדם) *unclean for a (dead) person* Nu 5[2] 9[6.7.10] (P) = ט׳ נפש Hg 2[13]; elsewh for various reasons Dt 26[14]; Lv 5[2] 13[11.36.44.45.45.46] 15[2.25.33] Nu 19[13.17.19.20.22] (all P), 2 Ch 23[19] Is 64[5] Ez 4[13] 22[10] La 4[15]. **b.** of animals Lv 5[2.2.2.2] 7[21.21] 11[4.5.6.7.8.26.27.28.29.31] 27[11.27] Nu 18[15] (all P), Lv 20[25.25] (H), Dt 14[7.8.10.19]. **c.** of things in gen. Lv 11[35.35.38] 15[26] Nu 19[15] (all P), Is 52[11]; food Ju 13[4] Ho 9[3], houses Je 19[13]; leprosy Lv 13[15.51.55] 14[44.57] (P), offering Hg 2[14]. **d.** persons and things in general כל טמא Lv 7[19.21] (P), הבדיל בין הט׳ ובין הטהור Lv 10[10]

11^{47}; הוריע בין (ה)ט׳ לטהור Ez 22^{26} 44^{23}, of aliens Is 52^{1} (‖ עָרֵל), perhaps also 35^{8}. **3.** specif of places: מקום ט׳ *unclean place* (place of refuse away from holy place and human habitation) Lv $14^{40.41.45}$ (P); טמאה ארץ land on the east of the Jordan separated from the land of the tabernacle of י׳ Jos 22^{19} (P), so אדמה ט׳ a foreign land Am 7^{17}.

†טֻמְאָה **n.f. uncleanness**,—abs ט׳ Nu 5^{19} + 4 t., cstr טֻמְאַת Lv 5^{3} + 4 t; sf. טֻמְאָתֵךְ Ez 22^{15} + 2 t. etc, + 18 t sfs, pl טֻמְאֹת Lv $16^{16.19}$; sf טֻמְאוֹתֵיכֶם Ez $36^{25.29}$, טֻמְאֹתָם Lv 16^{16},—**1.** sexual Nu 5^{19} (P), La 1^{9} **2.** of a foul or filthy mass Ez 24^{11} (in a caldron), 2 Ch 29^{16} (in the temple). **3.** ethical and religious Lv 16^{16} (P), Ez 22^{15} 24^{13} 39^{24}, כפר על הקדש מט׳ Lv 16^{16} (P); קדש מט׳ Lv 16^{19} (P), טהר מט׳ Ez 24^{13} 36^{25}, הושיע מכל ט׳ 36^{29}, רוּחַ הט׳ *unclean spirit*, which inspired the prophets to lie Zc 13^{2}. **4.** ritual, of men Lv $5^{3.3}$ $7^{20.21}$ 14^{19} $15^{3.3.31.31}$ Nu 19^{13} (all P), Lv $22^{3.5}$ (H); of women 2 S 11^{4}; וַיִּשְׁכַּב עִמָּהּ והיא מִתְקַדֶּשֶׁת מִטֻּמְאָתָהּ v. Dr; a time favourable to conception RS$^{K\,276}$, Lv $15^{25.26.30}$ (P), 18^{19} (H), Ez 36^{17}, of meats Ju $13^{7.14}$. **5.** local, of the nations Ezr 6^{21} 9^{11}.

†טֻמְאָה **n.f. uncleanness** (טְמֵאָה, Baer, seems to rest upon a misinterpretation of the form) Mi 2^{10} (so Thes MV SS), of ethical uncleanness, from wrong-doing

†[טָמָה] **vb.** only **Niph.** *Pf.* נִטְמִינוּ *we are stopped up, stupid* Jb 18^{3} so Thes MV Di De Zo (Aram. טְמַם, טַמְטֵם *stop up* (e.g. of ear or heart), ܛܡܡ, etc, and deriv, Ar طَمَّ *fill* or *choke up*); 𝔅 Ew Hgst AV RV Da SS take it as metaplastic for נִטְמֵאנוּ *we are regarded as unclean*, see Ew $^{§198\,b}$ Ko $^{i.614}$; 𝔊 rds. נִדְמִינוּ σεσιωπήκαμεν, 𝔗 טְמַעְנָא

• †טָמַן **vb. hide, conceal,** esp. in *earth* (NH *id*, whence perh Aram. טְמַן *keep, preserve*, cf Ar طَمَرَ *bury, hide* (loan-word Frä ^{137}); Aram ܛܡܪ, טְמַר *id*),—**Qal** *Pf* טָמַן ψ 35^{8} + 2 t etc., *Impf* וַיִּטְמֹן Gn 35^{4}, etc; *Imv* sf. טָמְנֵהוּ Je 13^{4}, טָמְנֵם Jb 40^{13}, *Inf. cstr* לִטְמוֹן Jb 31^{33} ψ 64^{6}, *Pt. pass* טָמוּן Jb 3^{16} + 3 t, טמונה Jos 7^{22}; pl. טְמֻנִים Jos 7^{21}, cstr. טמוני Dt 33^{19},—**1.** *hide*, c. acc Gn 35^{4} (E), Ex 2^{12} (E, dead body in sand), Jos 2^{6} (JE; spies under flax-stalks), Jos $7^{21.22}$ (JE, Achan's theft), Je $13^{4.5.6.7}$ (Jer's girdle), $43^{9.10}$ (stones at Tahpanhes), *hide, bury* hand in dish (צַלַּחַת) Pr 19^{24} 26^{15} (of עָצֵל the sluggard); נֵפֶל טָמוּן Jb 3^{16} *hidden abortion*, i.e. a lifeless child at once buried, שְׂפֻנֵי טְמוּנֵי חוֹל Dt 33^{19} (poem); of hiding iniquity עון Jb 31^{33}, hiding the wicked in the dust עפר Jb 40^{13} **2.** often of *hiding, concealing, secretly laying* a snare רֶשֶׁת ψ 9^{16} 35^{8}, sq. לִי 31^{5}, שַׁחַת רִשְׁתָּם 35^{7}, פַּח sq. לִי 140^{6} 142^{4}, sq לְרַגְלִי Je 18^{22}, חֶבֶל Jb 18^{10}; מוקשים ψ 64^{6}. **3.** טָמוּן *that which is darkened* = *darkness*, Jb 40^{13} nearly = שְׁאוֹל. פְּנֵיהֶם חֲבֹשׁ בַּטּ׳ *bind their faces in darkness* (i.e. the wicked); *hide = reserve* Jb 20^{26} *all darkness is held in reserve for his treasures*, i.e. all calamities are stored up for them **Niph.** *Imv* הִטָּמֵן בֶּעָפָר מִפְּנֵי פַּחַד י׳ Is 2^{10} *hide thyself in the dust, from before the terror of* י׳. **Hiph.** (or **Qal**? Ba $^{ZMG\,1888,180}$) *Impf* וַיֵּלְכוּ וַיַּטְמִנוּ 2 K $7^{8.8}$ *and they went and hid* (it), i.e. plunder fr. Aram. camp.

†מַטְמוֹן **n.m. hidden treasure, treasure,**—abs מַטְמוֹן Gn 43^{23}, pl. מַטְמֹנִים Je 41^{8} Pr 2^{4}; מטמונים Jb 3^{21}; cstr. מַטְמֻנֵי Is 45^{3}; (*hidden*) *treasure* Gn 43^{23} (of money in sacks); מַטְמֻנֵי מִסְתָּרִים Is 45^{3} (i.e. treasures now hidden in secret places, shall become spoil of Cyrus; ‖ אוצרות חשך), Je 41^{8}, appos חִטִּים שְׂעֹרִים שֶׁמֶן דְּבַשׁ, in compar. Jb 3^{21} (longing for death more than for treasure), Pr 2^{4} (wisdom sought for like treasure)

טנא (√ of foll; Ph. טנא is *set up, erect*, also *offer, present*, acc. to DHM in MV^{10}, 983).

†טֶנֶא **n.m.** $^{Dt\,28\,5}$ **basket** (NH טני is a large metal vessel)—abs טֶנֶא Dt 26^{4}, טַנְאֲ v^{2}, sf טַנְאֲךָ $28^{5.17}$, in all a receptacle for products of soil (in last two ‖ מִשְׁאֶרֶת)

†[טָנַף] **vb. soil, defile** (NH Pi *id.*, Aram. Pa. טַנֵּף, ܛܢܦ, As. *tanâpu* II, 1, Dl $^{Pr\,83,\,HWB\,302}$; Ar طَنِفَ is *be suspicious, be intrinsically corrupt*)—**Pi.** *Impf* אֲטַנְּפֵם Ct 5^{3} *how should I soil them*, i.e my feet (poet. Aramaism).

†[טָעָה] **vb. wander, stray** (NH *id., err;* Aram טְעָא, ܛܥܐ, Ar طَغَى *exceed just limit, be immoderate, extravagant*, طَاغِيَة *one who deviates from right way;* Eth ጥዕየ: *apostasy, superstition, idolatry*)—**Qal** *Pt.* f. (כ)טֹעִיָּה Ct 1^{7} *like a wandering* (vagrant) *woman*, for MT כְּעֹטְיָה acc to 𝔖 Sym 𝔗 𝔅 Bo Hi Gr al. **Hiph.** *Pf* הִטְעוּ אֶת־עַמִּי Ez 13^{10} fig., *they have led astray my people*.

†טָעַם **vb. taste, perceive** (NH *id*; Aram ܛܥܡ, טְעֵים *taste;* As n *ṭêmû, sense, command,*

Zim[BP 92] Lyon[Sargontexte 67] Asrb[Annals III, 95], Ar. طَعِمَ *eat, taste, examine by tasting;* Eth ጠዐመ: ጠዐመ: *taste, examine by tasting,* etc)—**Qal** *Pf.* 3 ms. ט׳ 1 S 14^{24}; 3 fs. טָעֲמָה Pr 31^{18}; 1 s. טָעַמְתִּי 1 S $14^{29.43}$; *Impf* 3 ms. יטעם 1 S 19^{36} + 2 t., 1 s. אֶטְעַם 2 S 3^{35}; 3 mpl יִטְעֲמוּ Jon 3^{7}; *Imv.* mpl. טַעֲמוּ ψ 34^{9}, *Inf. abs* טָעֹם 1 S 14^{43},—**1.** *taste,* of eating in small quantity, sq. acc. לֶחֶם 1 S 14^{24}, טעם דבשׁ v^{29}, so v^{43} (טָעֹם טָעַמְתִּי), לֶחֶם אוֹ כָל־מְאוּמָה 2 S 3^{35}; מְאוּמָה Jon 3^{7}. **2.** of sense of taste, obj אֶת־אֲשֶׁר אֹכַל וְאֶת־אֲשֶׁר 2 S 19^{36}; so חֵךְ אֹכֶל יִטְעַם־לוֹ Jb 12^{11}, חך אֶשְׁתֶּה יִטְעַם לֶאֱכֹל 34^{3}. **3.** fig Pr 31^{18} *she tasteth that her gain is good* (obj cl. c. כִּי), i.e. she experiences that her trade is profitable; so טַעֲמוּ וּראוּ כי־טוֹב יהוה ψ 34^{9} *taste ye and see that* י׳ *is good*

† טַעַם **n.m.**[Je 48, 11] **taste, judgment**—ט׳ abs. Jb 6^{6} ψ 119^{66}, טָעַם Pr 11^{22} 26^{16}; cstr. טַעַם Nu 11^{8} + 2 t; sf. טַעְמוֹ Ex 16^{31} + 4 t.; טַעְמֵךְ 1 S 25^{33};—**1.** *taste* of manna Ex 16^{31} (P), Nu 11^{8} (JE), cf. v^{8}; in juice of purslain Jb 6^{6}; of Moab under fig. of wine Je 48^{11} (‖ רֵיחַ) **2.** fig *judgment, discretion, discernment,* 1 S 25^{33} Pr 11^{22} Jb 12^{20}, so טוּב טַעַם וָדַעַת לַמְּדֵנִי ψ 119^{66}, מְשִׁיבֵי ט׳ Pr 26^{16} *those answering discretion,* i e discreetly; שַׁנּה טעם *change, disguise one's judgment, sense* 1 S 21^{13} ψ 34^{1}, of David feigning madness. **3.** (late Aramaism, cf. Dn 3^{10} etc.) *decision, decree* טַעַם מֶלֶךְ וּגְדֹלָיו Jon 3^{7}.

† [מַטְעָם] **n.m.** only pl. **tasty or savoury food, dainties**—מַטְעַמִּים Gn $27^{4.7.9.14.17.31}$ (all J); sf. מַטְעַמּוֹתָיו Pr 23^{3}; מַטְעַמֹּתָיו v^{6}.

† I [טָעַן] **vb. load** (NH *id.;* Aram. طعن, טְעַן, טען *carry,* also *load*)—**Qal** *Imv* טַעֲנוּ אֶת־בְּעִירְכֶם Gn 45^{17} (E) *load your beasts*

† II. [טָעַן] **vb. pierce** (Aram. Pa טָעַן *pierce;* Ar. طَعَنَ *pierce, wound, goad*)—only **Pu.** *Pt.* מְטֹעֲנֵי חָרֶב Is 14^{19} *those pierced with a sword.*

טַף v. sub טפף.

† [טָפַח] **vb. extend, spread** (Ar. طَفَحَ *be full to overflowing, abound;* Aram. طفح *extend, spread,* טְפִיחָא *a step, foot-length;* NH טֶפַח *a span* (cf טֶפַח infr))—**Pi.** *Pf.* טִפְּחָה Is 48^{13}, טִפַּחְתִּי La 2^{22},—**1.** *spread out* the heavens Is 48^{13} (‖ יִסְּדָה ארץ). **2.** denom fr טֶפַח *carry on the palms, dandle* La 2^{22} (‖ רִבִּיתִי *I have brought up, reared*).

† טִפֻּחִים **n.[m.] pl. abstr. dandling,** עֹלְלֵי ט׳ La 2^{20}.

† טֶפַח **n.[m.] 1. a span, hand-breadth; 2. coping** (?),—**1.** *a span, hand-breadth,* טֶפַח 1 K 7^{26} = 2 Ch 4^{5} of thickness of the molten sea, pl טְפָחוֹת ψ 39^{6} (a few) *hand-breadths* are my days. **2.** architectural term, perh. *coping,* וּמִמַּסַּד עַד־הַטְּפָחוֹת 1 K 7^{9}.

† טֹפַח **n.m.**[Ez 40, 43] **span, hand-breadth**—alw. abs. טֹפַח Ex 25^{25} 37^{12} (both P), width of border of table in tabernacle; Ez 40^{5} 43^{13} addit to common cubit; Ez 40^{43} width of border (ledge) of four tables in new temple (Sm Co).

† מִטְפַּחַת **n.f. cloak,** abs. הַמִּטְפַּחַת אֲשֶׁר־עָלַיִךְ Ru 3^{15}; pl. הַמִּטְפָּחוֹת Is 3^{22}

† [טָפַל] **vb. smear or plaster (over), stick, glue** (NH *id, besmear, plaster;* Aram. טְפַל *id,* fig. *attack;* טפילא *mortar,* طفل *defile,* As *ṭapâlu, besmear* (?), Dl[Pr 48, HWB])—**Qal** *Pf* 3 pl. טָפְלוּ ψ 119^{69}; *Impf.* 2 ms. וַתִּטְפֹּל Jb 14^{17}, *Pt* pl. cstr. טֹפְלֵי Jb 13^{4},—טָפְלוּ עָלַי שֶׁקֶר זֵדִים ψ 119^{69} *insolent men have plastered falsehood over me,* 'making his real character unrecognisable' (De); טֹפְלֵי שֶׁקֶר Jb 13^{4} ye are *falsehood-plasterers* (‖ רֹפְאֵי אֱלִל); cf. As. *amât taškirti ṭâpilti Ullusum, a speech of falsehood besmearing Ullusum,* Dl[Pr 48], וַתִּטְפֹּל עַל־עֲוֹנִי Jb 14^{17} *and thou hast glued over mine iniquity,* i. e. glued it up, for safe keeping against the day of reckoning (‖ חָתֻם בִּצְרוֹר פִּשְׁעִי).

† טִפְסָר **n.[m.] scribe, marshal** (if meaning correct, then As. loan-word, fr. *dupsarru, tablet-writer, scribe,* v Len[Langue Primit de la Chaldée, 363] Schr[COT] on Je 51^{27}, Lotz[TP 180], *dupšarru,* acc. to Dl[HWB 227])—pl. sf. טַפְסְרַיִךְ Na 3^{17} (as if fr. טִפְסַר) *thy scribes, marshals,* of high officials of Nineveh, abs sg פִּקְדוּ עָלֶיהָ טִפְסָר Je 51^{27} *appoint a marshal against her,* i. e. against Babylon—On military function of those skilled in writing cf. שׁטר.

† [טָפַף] **vb. trip, take quick little steps** (cf. Ar. طَفَّ *pass by quickly,* طَفَّافٌ *light, brisk, quick,* of horse, poss cf. Syr. ܛܦܛܦ *flicker*)—**Qal** *Inf abs.* טָפוֹף Is 3^{16} הָלוֹךְ וְטָפֹף תֵּלַכְנָה, of women of Jerusalem

טַף[42] **n.m.** coll. **children** (as going with *quick, tripping* steps; Eth ጠፍ: Di[1230])—טַף Je 41^{16} + 11 t.; טָף Je 40^{7} + 5 t.; sf. טַפְּנוּ Gn 43^{8}

+5 t.; טַפְּכֶם Gn 45[19] + 10 t.; טַפָּם Gn 34[29] + 6 t.; never cstr. and never pl. (in Gn 47[24] om. 𝔊, cf. Di);—*children, little ones,* Gn 34[29] (E) + 18 t. JE (Gn Ex Nu), also Dt 1[39] + 8 t. D (incl. Jos 1[14] 8[35]); P only Nu 31[9.17.18], where note זָכָר בַּטָּף v[17] = *young boys,* and הַטַּף בַּנָּשִׁים v[18] = *young girls;* also Ju 18[21] 21[10] 2 S 15[22] Je 40[7] 41[16] 43[6] Ez 9[6] 2 Ch 20[13] 31[18] Ezr 8[21] Est 3[13] 8[11]; the words מְתִים וְנָשִׁים וְהַטָּף Dt 2[34] 3[6] incl. all inhabitants; so אֲנָשִׁים וְהַנָּשִׁים וְהַטָּף Dt 31[12] Je 40[7] 43[6]; טַף distinguished from בָּחוּר וּבְתוּלָה Ez 9[6]; also from בְּנֵיהֶם 2 Ch 20[13], and from בְּנֵיהֶם וּבְנוֹתֵיהֶם 2 Ch 31[18].

†**טָפַשׁ vb. be gross** (NH Hithp. *grow stupid,* and deriv.; Aram. טְפֵשׁ, for Heb. שמן Is 6[10], Ithp. *be stupid;* cf. As. *ṭapâšu, be abundant, large,* Guy [JAS 1883, Août-Sept. 189])—metaph. טָפַשׁ כַּחֵלֶב לִבָּם ψ 119[70] *their heart is gross, like fat.*

†**טָפַת n.pr.f.** daughter of Solomon, & wife of בֶּן־אֲבִינָדָב 1 K 4[11].

†[**טָרַד**] **vb. pursue, chase, be continuous** (Ar. طَرَدَ *pursue;* II. *prolong* one's voice; VIII. *continue uninterruptedly;* As. *ṭarâdu, drive away* COT[Gloss], so Aram. טְרַד, טְרַד)—only **Qal** *Pt. act.* וְדֶלֶף טֹרֵד Pr 19[13] *a continuous dripping, dropping,* i.e. one in which one drop *pursues* another; so ד׳ טוֹרֵד 27[15]; in both sim. of a contentious woman.

†**מַטְרֵד n.pr.f.** mother-in-law of Hadar (Hadad) Gn 36[39] 𝔊 Ματρ(α)ι(ι)θ (𝔊 here, not in Ch, makes מ׳ *son* of Mezahab, i.e. n.pr.m.) = 1 Ch 1[50], 𝔊 Ματραδ, Ματρηθ.

טרה (√ of foll.; cf. Ar. طَرُوَ, طَرِىَ *be fresh, juicy, moist;* Eth. ጥሬ: *raw*).

†[**טָרִי**] **adj. fresh,** only fs. טְרִיָּה *fresh,* לְחִי־חֲמוֹר טְרִיָּה Ju 15[15] *the fresh jawbone of an ass,* i.e. not yet dry and brittle; מַכָּה ט׳ Is 1[6] *fresh, raw wound,* not yet healed or even treated (so Ges Ew Brd Di Du; *festering* De Che).

†[**טָרַח**] **vb. toil, be burdened** (NH *id., toil,* Hiph. *weary, importune;* Aram. טְרַח *toil,* etc.; Ar. طَرَحَ is *cast, throw, remove*)—**Hiph.** *Impf.* אַף־בְּרִי יַטְרִיחַ עָב Jb 37[11] *he burdeneth* with moisture the cloud(s).

†**טֹרַח n.m.** burden, fig., הָיוּ עָלַי לָטֹרַח נִלְאֵיתִי נְשֹׂא׃ Is 1[14] *they are become a burden on me, I am weary of bearing;* אֵיכָה אֶשָּׂא טָרְחֲכֶם Dt 1[12] (+ מַשַּׂאֲכֶם וְרִיבְכֶם) *how can I bear the burden of you?*

טֶרֶם [54], once (Ru 3[14] Kt) **טְרוֹם, adv. of time, not yet, ere, before that** (deriv. unknown: not found in cogn. languages)—construed mostly with the impf. (with the pf. only Gn 24[15] (v[45] impf.), 1 S 3[7a] (v[b] impf.), and בְּטֶרֶם ψ 90[2] Pr 8[25]):—**1.** †טֶרֶם in an independent sentence, *not yet,* Gn 2[5] and all the plants of the field טרם יהיה בארץ were *not yet* in the earth, etc., 19[4] טרם ישכבו *not yet* had they lain down, when etc., 24[15.45] Nu 11[33] Jos 2[8] 1 S 3[3.7.7]; of present time, Ex 9[30] 10[7] הֲטֶרֶם תֵּדַע dost thou *not yet* know, etc.?; in a subord. clause, *ere, before that,* Ex 12[34] they took their dough טרם יחמץ *before* it was leavened, Jos 3[1] ψ 119[67]; of future time Is 65[24]. More frequently **2.** בְּטֶרֶם [39], with the same force: of past time, Gn 27[33] I ate of all בטרם תבא *before* thou camest, 37[18] 41[50] Ju 14[18] 1 S 2[15] Je 1[5] 47[1] Ez 16[57]; ψ 90[2] Pr 8[25] (both with pf.); more oft. of pres. or fut., as Gn 27[4] בטרם אמות *before* I die (so 45[28], cf. ψ 39[14] Jb 10[21]), Lv 14[36] Dt 31[21] 1 S 9[13] 2 K 2[9] Is 7[16] 42[9] 48[5] Je 13[16]; the impf. with a freq. force, Ex 1[19] *before* the midwife *cometh,* they are wont to bear, Ru 3[14] Pr 18[13]. Pleon. בְּטֶרֶם לֹא Zp 2[2.2]. Construed with a subst. in the gen., †Is 17[14] בְּטֶרֶם בֹּקֶר = *ere* morning, 28[4] בְּטֶרֶם קַיִץ; with an inf. †Zp 2[2a] (but rd. here with 𝔊 We בְּטֶרֶם לֹא תִהְיוּ כְּמוֹץ עֹבֵר, without יוֹם, 'before ye become as chaff passing away'). **3.** †מִטֶּרֶם Hg 2[15] (sq. inf.) מִטֶּרֶם שׂוּם אֶבֶן *from before* the laying of one stone upon another, etc.

†**טָרַף vb. tear, rend, pluck** (NH *id.,* esp. of wild beasts; Aram. טְרַף *tear, seize,* esp. of creditors; טְרֵיפָא *torn flesh* or *animal;* Ar. طَرَفَ *depasture,* said of camel)—**Qal** *Pf.* טָרַף Jb 16[9]; טָרָף Ho 6[1], etc.; *Impf.* וַיִּטְרֹף ψ 7[3]; יִטְרֹף Am 1[11] (but v. infr.); יִטְרָף Gn 49[27]; אֶטְרֹף Ho 5[14] ψ 50[22]; *Inf.* לִטְרֹף ψ 17[12]; *Pt. act.* טֹרֵף Jb 18[4], etc.;—*tear rend,* of wild beasts, Gn 37[33] (J), 44[28] (J; inf. abs. c. Pu. q. v.), Ex 22[12] (JE; inf. abs. c. **Niph.** q.v.) Elsewh. only in sim. and metaph.; sim. of Gad's fierceness Dt 33[20] (like a lioness, poem); so of Benjamin Gn 49[27] (as a wolf, poem); of the remnant of Jacob, like a young lion among sheep, רָמַס וְטָרַף Mi 5[7]; of the wicked, ψ 17[12] (lion), 7[3] obj. נַפְשִׁי (like a lion); 22[14] psalmist's foes like lion (‖ שֹׁאֵג); Ez 22[25] (טֹרֵף טָרֶף), princes like wolves v[27] (*id.*); metaph. of Israel's princes, like young lion 19[3.6] (c. טָרֶף

acc. cogn.); of Nineveh's king Na 2^{13} (as lion); of God's treatment of the wicked Ho 5^{14} (like a lion), ψ 50^{22}; subj. wrath of God (אַף) conceived as assailing Job, Jb 16^{9} *his wrath teareth* and persecuteth me; cf. טָרָף וְיִרְפָּאֵנוּ Ho 6^{1} subj. ׳י (‖ יַךְ וְיַחְבְּשֵׁנוּ), on tenses v. Dr[§ 84 a, 171, 174 a 1]); subj anger of Edom (abs) Am 1^{11}, but rd. perh. וַיִּטֹּר for ויטרף *and he kept his anger perpetually*, so Ol on ψ 103^{9} We; טֹרֵף נַפְשׁוֹ בְּאַפּוֹ, said of Job by Bildad Jb 18^{4}. **Niph.** *Impf.* of animal *torn* (by wild beasts) טָרֹף יִטָּרֵף Ex 22^{12} (JE); יִטָּרֵף also in prediction of judgment on people of Jerusalem Je 5^{6} **Pu.** *Pf.* טֹרַף טֹרַף יוסף Gn 37^{33} (J) *Joseph has certainly been torn in pieces*, cf. טָרֹף ט׳ 44^{28} (J). **Hiph.** *Imv.* ms sf., note esp. 2nd acc. לֶחֶם, הַטְרִיפֵנִי לֶחֶם חֻקִּי Pr 30^{8} *let me devour my appointed bread* (of men, late; cf טֶרֶף 31^{15}, and ψ 111^{5} Mal 3^{10})

†טָרָף adj fresh-plucked (Aram. ܛܰܪܦܳܐ, טַרְפָּא *fresh leaf*)—עלה זַיִת טָרָף Gn 8^{11} (J) *a fresh plucked olive leaf*

†טֶ֫רֶף n.m.[Na 3, 1] prey, food, leaf;—טֶרֶף Gn 49^{9}+; טָ֑רֶף Jb 4^{11}+, sf טַרְפֵּךְ Na 2^{14}; טַרְפּוֹ Is 31^{4}; pl. cstr. טַרְפֵּי Ez 17^{9};—**1.** *prey* of lion Am 3^{4} Jb 4^{11} 38^{39} ψ 104^{21}; metaph of Judah's conquests Gn 49^{9}, Israel like lion Nu 23^{24} (both poems in JE); of Assyrians Is 5^{29}; of Nineveh and its king Na $2^{13.14}$ 3^{1}; Israel's princes (as young lion) Ez $19^{3.6}$; sim. of false prophet (like lion) 22^{25}; of princes of Judah v ^{27}; sim. of ׳י's descending to battle, like lion Is 31^{4}; cf. ψ 76^{5} coming down from *mountains of prey* (the lion's lair), but rd. perh. עַד, cf. 𝔊 Bi Che[crit. n], fig. of spoil of wicked Jb 29^{17}, cf. ψ 124^{6}. **2.** *food*, of outcasts, under fig. of wild ass פֶּרֶא Jb 24^{5}, of human food (late): for those who fear God ψ 111^{5}; for household Pr 31^{15}, in ׳י's house Mal 3^{10}. **3.** *leaf*, (cf. Gn 8^{11}) טַרְפֵּי צִמְחָהּ Ez 17^{9} metaph. of Judah.

†טְרֵפָה n.f. animal torn (by wild beasts); torn flesh;—abs ט׳ Gn 31^{39} + 8 t. **1.** *animal torn* (by wild beasts), of sheep and goats Gn 31^{39} (E); ox, ass or sheep Ex 22^{12} (JE; del We[Kitr] on Am 3^{12}, as gloss fr. Gn 31^{39}); indef. v ^{31} (JE, forbidden as food); commonly c. נְבֵלָה (i e what dies naturally) as forbidden food, Lv 7^{24} (P), 17^{15} 22^{8} (both H), Ez 4^{14} 44^{31}; *torn flesh*, in metaph. of Nineveh's king as lion Na 2^{13} (‖ טֶ֫רֶף)

י

י, *Yôdh*, tenth letter; used as numeral 10 in postBHeb., יא or י״א = 11; יב, י״ב = 12, etc; 14 and 15, however, are not י״ה, י״ו, which might stand for abbrev of יהוה, but ט״ו, ט״ז, v. ט, and Ges[§ 5. 4 R. 3a].

†[יָאַב] vb. long, desire (Aram ܝܶܐܒ, and esp. Ethpa. and deriv)—**Qal** *Pf.* 1 s יָאַבְתִּי לְמִצְוֹתֶיךָ ψ 119^{131}, late Aramaism

†[יָאָה] vb. befit, be befitting (NH 𝔗 יְאֵי, יָאֶה adj *worthy, fitting, fine*, יָאוֹת adv. *right, well*; Ph יא *fair*; Syr. ܝܳܐܶܐ adj. for נאוה ψ 33^{1}, πρέπει Mt 3^{15})—**Qal** *Pf* לְךָ יָאָתָה Je 10^{7}, *for thee it* (i e fear) *is befitting*, late Aramaism.

יאור v. יאר.

יַאֲזַנְיָה, יַאֲזַנְיָהוּ v. sub אזן p 24^{b} supr.

יָאִירִי, יָאִיר v sub אור p. 22^{b} supr.

†I [יָאַל] vb. be foolish (cf. I. אול)—**Niph.** *Pf.* 3 mpl נוֹאֲלוּ Is 19^{13} Je 5^{4}, וְנֹאָלוּ Je 50^{36}, 1 pl. נוֹאַלְנוּ Nu 12^{11};—*do* or *act foolishly*—**1.** *shew wicked folly* = sin חַטָּאת אֲשֶׁר נוֹאַלְנוּ וַאֲשֶׁר חָטָאנוּ Nu 12^{11} (J), in Je 5^{4} an exhibition of this folly is ascribed to ignorance **2.** *become fools*, lacking insight and judgment. נוֹאֲלוּ שָׂרֵי צֹעַן Is 19^{13} *the princes of Zoan have become fools* (‖ נִשְּׁאוּ שָׂרֵי נֹף), and, in v ^{11} אֱוִילִים שָׂרֵי צֹעַן, etc); חֶרֶב אֶל־הַבַּדִּים וְנֹאָלוּ Je 50^{36} *a sword is against the praters, and they shall become fools*—be shewn up as such (‖ חַתּוּ).

†II. [יָאַל] vb. only **Hiph.** shew willingness, be pleased, determine, undertake to do anything (and do it) (v. Ki Thes; Ar وَأَلَ is *take refuge with, escape, hasten to* a place; cf. II. אול *be in front of*, No[MBAk 1880, 775]; Sab ואל in n.pr. מואלת DHM[Epigr Denkm. 53]; perh. As *âlû*, *accept*, Lyon[Sargontexte 72])—**Hiph.** *Pf* 3 ms. הוֹאִיל Ho 5^{11} + 2 t., 2 ms. הוֹאַלְתָּ 1 Ch 17^{27}; 1 s. הוֹאַלְתִּי Gn $18^{27.31}$, 1 pl. הוֹאַלְנוּ Jos 7^{7}, *Impf.* וַיֹּאֶל Jb 6^{9}

(juss), וַיּוֹאֶל Ex 2[21] + 4 t, וַיֹּאֶל 1 S 17[39] (but v infr), *Imv* הוֹאֶל 2 S 7[29] 2 K 5[23], הוֹאֶל־נָא Ju 19[6], הֹוֹאֶל נָא 2 K 6[3], הוֹאִילוּ Jb 6[28],—**1.** *shew willingness* to do anything, *accept an invitation, acquiesce*, sq inf וַיּוֹאֶל משֶׁה לָשֶׁבֶת אֶת־הָאִישׁ Ex 2[21] (JE) *and Moses was willing to dwell with the man* (and did so), = Ju 17[11] (of Levite), elsewh foll by vb fin, ולוּ הוֹאַלְנוּ וַנֵּשֶׁב Jos 7[7] *and would that we had been willing and had stayed*, esp imv, sq imv הוֹאֶל־נָא וְלִין Ju 19[6] *be willing and spend the night* (kindly accept my invitation) v Ges[§ 110 2a, R 2, 120 2a], 2 K 6[3] and (no ו) 5[23], הוֹאִילוּ פְּנוּ־בִי Jb 6[28] i e be good enough to look upon me **2.** more actively, voluntarily *undertake* to do anything (and do it), sq inf. Gn 18[27] *I have undertaken to speak* = v[31] (both J); so 1 S 17[39] MT, but rd. וַיִּלְא, *and he laboured vainly*, for וַיֹּאֶל, so 𝔊, Gei[Urschrift, 377] We Dr (cf also v[b] לא אוּכַל לָלֶכֶת בָּאֵלֶּה), sq vb. fin הוֹאִיל משֶׁה בֵּאֵר Dt 1[5] i e Moses *took upon himself* to expound the law. **3** more actively still, *be pleased, determine* on one's own responsibility, *resolve*, sq inf: Jos 17[12] (JE) = Ju 1[27] but the Canaanites *were determined* (shewed a determination) to remain in this territory (= *persisted in dwelling there*), Ju 1[35] *the Amorites persisted in dwelling* in Har-Heres, etc; sq vb fin, of irreligious action, הוֹאִיל הָלַךְ Ho 5[11] Ephraim *persisted, he walked* after vanity (rd שָׁוְא for צו, v Che), elsewh only of the divine *good pleasure*: sq inf 1 S 12[22] ׳י *hath been pleased to make you a people for himself*, 1 Ch 17[27], sq vb fin הוֹאַל וּבָרֵךְ 2 S 7[29] *be pleased and bless* the house of thy servant; ויֹאֵל אֱלוֹהַּ וִידַכְּאֵנִי Jb 6[9] *and that Eloah would be pleased and crush me!* (v Ges[§ 120, 2a] Da[Synt § 83b])

†**יְאֹר, יְאוֹר** **n.m.**[Ex 7, 21] **stream** of the Nile, **stream, canal** (Egypt. loan-word = Egypt. *'iotr, 'io'r, watercourse*, Copt ειοορ, ιορ; also *'iotr'o, 'io'r'o*, Copt ειερο, ιαρο, *Nile*, Steindorff[BAS i 612]; in As *ia'uru, stream, 'Iaru'û, river Nile*, Id[ib], Hpt[ib 171] Jäger[ib 466])—abs הַיְאֹר Gn 41[1] + 37 t, הַיְאוֹר Is 19[8], הַיְאֹרָה Ex 1[22], יְאוֹר Is 19[7 7 7] + 2 t; כָּאֹר (err for כַּיְאֹר) Am 8[8]; cstr כִּיאֹר Am 9[5], כִּיאוֹר Am 8[8], sf יְאֹרִי Ez 29[3b] (Co יאר, cf v[9] and 𝔖 𝔗), pl. יְאֹרִים Ex 8[1] + 4 t.; cstr יְאֹרֵי Is 7[18] + 2 t; יְאוֹרֵי 2 K 19[24], sf. יְאֹרֶיךָ Ez 29[4.4.5] + v[4] (del 𝔊 Co) + 29[10] (Co יְאֹרְךָ), יְאֹרָיו Ez 29[3], יְאֹרֵיהֶם Ex 7[19] ψ 78[44],—**1.** *stream* of the Nile, *river Nile*, usu. c art. Gn 41[1 2 3.3 18] Ex 1[22] 2[3.5 5] 4[9.9] 7[15 17 18.18 18. 20.20.21 21 21.24 24.28] 8[5.7] 17[5] (all JE), Am 8[8] 9[5] Is 19[7 7 7 8] 23[3] (‖ שִׁחֹר), v[10] Je 46[7 8] (sim of Egypt invasion), Ez 29[3b] (rd. יאר, v. supr), v[9] Zc 10[11]; more fully יְאֹר מִצְרַיִם Am 8[8] 9[5]. **2.** pl **a.** *Nile-arms, Nile-canals*, יְאֹרֵי מִצְרַיִם Is 7[18]; יְאֹרֵי מָצוֹר 19[6] (‖ נְהָרוֹת), 37[25] = 2 K 19[24], v also Na 3[8] Ex 7[19] 8[1] (both P; ‖ נהרת, אַגְמִים, etc), ψ 78[44] (‖ נֹזְלִים), Ez 29[3.4 4.5 10] + v[4] MT (but del. 𝔊 Co), 30[12] **b.** *watercourses* in gen., יְאֹרִים רַחֲבֵי יָדַיִם Is 33[21] (‖ נְהָרִים); cf NH יְאוֹר, late Aram יְאוֹרָא). **3.** *shafts*, made in mining Jb 28[10] (בַּצּוּרוֹת) **4.** יְאֹר, sg, of *Tigris*, Dn 12[5.5 6.7] (cf. 10[4])

†[**יָאַשׁ**] **vb. despair** (not in **Qal**) (NH Hithp *despair of*, יֵאוּשׁ *desperation*; Aram Pa. יָאֵשׁ, etc., *make despair* (so 𝔗 Ec 2[20]), Ar يَئِسَ *despair*) — **Niph.** *Pf* וְנוֹאַשׁ consec. 1 S 27[1], *Pt.* נוֹאָשׁ Je 2[25] + 3 t.;—*despair*, וְנ׳ מִמֶּנִּי שָׁאוּל לְבַקְשֵׁנִי 1 S 27[1] *and Saul shall despair of me, to seek me*, pt. *desperate, despairing*, of Job, Jb 6[26], elsewh. נוֹאָשׁ (foll אמר) *desperate! = there is no hope!* Je 2[25] 18[12] Is 57[10]. **Pi.** *Inf* לְיָאֵשׁ אֶת־לִבִּי עַל כָּל־הֶעָמָל Ec 2[20] *to make my heart despair, concerning all the toil*

יֹאשִׁיָּה, יֹאשִׁיָּהוּ v. sub אשה p 78[b] supr.

†**יְאָתְרַי** **n.pr.m.** an ancestor of Asaph 1 Ch 6[6] appar = אֶתְנִי v[26]

†[**יָבַב**] **vb.** only **Pi. cry shrilly** (NH Pi *lament*; Aram ܝܰܒܶܒ, יַבֵּב *sound* clarions, *exult*, Eth የበበ: esp. I. 2)—**Pi.** *Impf.* 3 fs. וַתְּיַבֵּב Ju 5[28] through the windows she looked and *shrilly cried*

†**יוֹבָב** **n.pr.m.** (Sab n pr. יהיבב Glaser[Skizze ii 303 ff])—**1.** 'son' of Yoktân Gn 10[29] = 1 Ch 1[23], 𝔊 Ιωβαβ. **2.** a king in Edom Gn 36[33.34] = 1 Ch 1[44 45], 𝔊 Ιω(α)βαβ **3.** king of Madon (Northern Canaan) Jos 11[1], 𝔊 Ιω(β)αβ **4.** Benjamites: **a.** 1 Ch 8[9], 𝔊 Ιωβαβ **b.** 1 Ch 8[18], 𝔊 Ιω(β)αβ.

יְבֻסִי, יְבוּסִי, יְבוּס v. sub בוס p 101[a] supr.

יִבְחַר v. sub בחר p 104[b] supr

יָבִין v sub בין p 108[a] supr.

†[**יָבַל**] **vb. Hiph. conduct, bear along,** esp in *procession* (Aram. יְבַל, אוֹבִיל *id*, ܝܒܠ Pa *lead along*, also Ethpa; Aph. *lead, conduct*, Zinj יבל *id*, DHM[Sendsch Gloss.]; As *abâlu* (ובל), *bring, conduct*, COT[Gloss] Dl[Pr 122 ff], Ar. وَبَلَ is *run vehemently* (of horse), *pursue sharply, pour*

down rain, זֶ֫בֶל *violent rain*)—**Hiph.** *Impf.* 3 ms. sf. יוֹבִלֵנִי ψ 60^{11} 108^{11}; 1 s. sf. אוֹבִילֵם Je 31^{9}; 3 mpl. יוֹבִילוּ ψ 68^{30}; יֹבִילוּ 76^{12} (juss.); יוֹבִלוּן Zp 3^{10}; sf. יֹבִלוּהָ Is 23^{7};—**1.** *bear along* offerings, c. acc. rei, Zp 3^{10}; c. לְ pers. ψ 68^{30} 76^{12}. **2.** *carry away*, only יֹ׳ רַגְלֶיהָ מֵרָחוֹק לָגוּר Is 23^{7} *her feet used to carry her far away to sojourn* (of Tyre as colonizing and trading city). **3.** *lead, conduct*, c. obj. as sf., of returning exiles Je 31^{9}; triumphant army, sq. acc. loc., ψ 60^{11}= 108^{11}. **Hoph.** *Impf.* 3 ms. יוּבַל(־) Is 18^{7} Je 11^{19}; יוּבָל Ho 12^{2} + 3 t.; 3 fs. תּוּבַל ψ 45^{15}; 1 s. אוּבָל Jb 10^{19}; 3 mpl. יוּבָלוּ Jb 21^{30}; 3 fpl. תּוּבַלְנָה ψ 45^{16}; 2 mpl. תּוּבָלוּן Is 55^{12};—**1.** *be borne along*: of things, sq. לְ, a gift Is 18^{7}; idol Ho 10^{6}; oil 12^{2}. **2.** *be borne* to the grave: מִבֶּטֶן לַקֶּבֶר אוּבָל Jb 10^{19}; לִקְבָרוֹת יוּבָל 21^{32}. **3.** *be led, conducted*, sq. לְ, ψ 45^{15} Je 11^{19} Is 53^{7}; abs. ψ 45^{16}; *be led* forth (from captivity in Babylon) Is 55^{12}, abs. (‖ יצא); the wicked (for judgment) abs. Jb 21^{30}.

†I. [יָבָל] **n.[m.]** watercourse, stream (prop. *conduit*), as irrigating;—only pl. cstr. יִבְלֵי(־)מַיִם Is 30^{25} (‖ פְּלָגִים), 44^{4}.

†II. יָבָל **n.pr.m.** son of Lamech by Adah, and founder of pastoral life acc. to Gn 4^{20} (J); 𝔊 Ιωβελ, 𝔊L Ιωβηλ.

†I. יוּבַל **n.[m.]** stream, Je 17^{8} (‖ מַיִם).

†II. יוּבָל **n.pr.m.** son of Lamech by Adah, and inventor of musical instr. Gn 4^{21} (J); 𝔊 Ιωβαλ.

†יְבוּל **n.m.** [Jb 20, 28] produce of soil;—abs. יְ׳ Hb 3^{17}; cstr. *id.* Ju 6^{4} Jb 20^{28}; sf. יְבוּלָהּ Dt 11^{17} + 7 t.; יְבֻלָהּ Dt 32^{22}; יְבוּלָם ψ 78^{46};—*produce*: וְהָאָרֶץ כְּלָאָה Ju 6^{4}; יְ׳ הָאָרֶץ אֶרֶץ וִיבֻלָהּ Dt 32^{22}; וְנָתְנָה הָאָרֶץ יְבוּלָהּ Hg 1^{10}; sf. ψ 78^{46} (‖ יְגִיעַ); esp. יְבוּלָהּ Lv 26^{4} *the land shall yield its produce*, so v^{20} Ez 34^{27} Zc 8^{2} (all ‖ פְּרִי), ψ 67^{7} 85^{13}; also, subj. וְאֵין יְבוּל הָאֲדָמָה Dt 11^{17}; of grapes only בַּגְּפָנִים Hb 3^{17} (‖ תְּאֵנָה לֹא־תִפְרָח and כִּחֵשׁ מַעֲשֵׂה זַיִת); more generally יְבוּל בֵּיתוֹ Jb 20^{28} *the produce* (acquired possessions) *of his house*.

†בּוּל **n.[m.]** produce, outgrowth (abbrev. or scribal err. for foregoing)—only sg. cstr. בּ׳ הָרִים Jb 40^{20}; also בּ׳ עֵץ Is 44^{19} *the produce of a tree*, i.e. a block of wood.

†יוֹבֵל, יֹבֵל **n.m.** [Nu 36, 4] ram, ram's horn, cornet (Ph. יבל *ram*; cf. Di Lv 25^{10} Dl [Pr 124])—abs. יוֹבֵל Jos 6^{5} + 7 t.; יֹבֵל Ex 19^{13} + 13 t.; pl. יוֹבְלִים Jos 6^{4} + 2 t.; יֹבְלִים Jos 6^{13};—**1.** *ram*, only in combin.: בִּמְשֹׁךְ בְּקֶרֶן הַיּ׳ Jos 6^{5} *the ram's horn*, as wind-instrument; so שׁוֹפְרוֹת (ה)י(ו)בלים Jos $6^{4.6.8.13}$ *rams' horns* (v. Benz [Archäol. 276]); יֹבֵל alone, בִּמְשֹׁךְ הַיֹּבֵל Ex 19^{13} *at the sounding of the ram*('s horn). **2.** designation of 50th year, marked by blowing of cornets, AV 'jubile' (so NH יוֹבֵל, 𝔗 יוֹבֵילָא, as loan-word); orig. no doubt שְׁנַת הַיּוֹבֵל *year of the ram*('s horn), as Lv $25^{13.28.40.50.52.54}$ (all H), $27^{17.18.23.24}$ (all P), but then, without שְׁנַת, as יוֹבֵל הִוא תִּהְיֶה לָכֶם 25^{10} *a ram*('s horn blowing) *shall it be to you*; so $v^{11.12.15.28.30.31.33}$ (all H), 27^{18} Nu 36^{4} (both P).

†[יַבָּל] **adj.** running, suppurating—only fs. as subst., יַבֶּלֶת *a running sore* or *ulcer* Lv 22^{22} (+ עַוֶּרֶת, שָׁבוּר, חָרוּץ, גָּרָב, יַלֶּפֶת).

†אוּבָל **n.[m.]** stream, river (= יוּבַל)—only אוּבַל אוּלַי Dn 8^{2} *the river Ulai*.

†תֵּבֵל **n.f.** [Na 1, 5] (appar. **m.** Is 14^{17}) world, poet. synon. of אֶרֶץ (perh. orig. as *productive*, cf. יְבוּל, בּוּל, but this sense not clearly maintained; cf. also As. *tabalu* in *êlî tabali, by land*, ‖ *êlî nâru, by water* (*river*) Meissner [ZA 1889, iv. 3, 261. 263, 265 f.] SASm [As. Letters iv. pl. viii. ix, l. 33]) — usu. abs. תּ׳ (no art.), cstr. Jb 37^{12} Pr 8^{31}; *world*, usu. ‖ אֶרֶץ: 1 S 2^{8} (יְ׳ set תּ׳ on מְצֻקֵי אֶרֶץ), Is 14^{21} 24^{4} 34^{1} Je 10^{12} = 51^{15}, 1 Ch 16^{30} (= ψ 96^{10} infr.) Jb 34^{13} ψ 19^{5} 77^{19} = 97^{4}, 90^{2} 96^{13} (+ עַמִּים), 98^{9} (+ *id.*); תּ׳ וְיֹשְׁבֵי בָהּ Na 1^{5} ψ 24^{1}; יֹשְׁבֵי תּ׳ 33^{8} Is 18^{3} (‖ שֹׁכְנֵי ארץ), $26^{9.18}$ La 4^{12}; תּ׳ וּמְלֹאָהּ 89^{12} (+ שָׁמַיִם), cf. ארץ ומלאה 24^{1}); עַל־פְּנֵי תּ׳ אַרְצָה Jb 37^{12} *upon the face of the world of earth* (earthly world, the whole expanse of earth); בְּתֵ׳ אַרְצוֹ Pr 8^{31}; on the other hand עַפְרוֹת תּ׳ v^{26}; תּ׳ alone Jb 18^{18}; other combin. תּ׳ וּמְלֹאָהּ ψ 50^{12} (cf. 89^{12} supr.); פְּנֵי־תֵ׳ Is 27^{6} (cf. Jb 37^{12} supr.); מוֹסְדוֹת תּ׳ 2 S 22^{16} *foundations of the world* = ψ 18^{16}, cf. תִּכּוֹן תּ׳ ψ 93^{1} 96^{10} (= 1 Ch 16^{30}); world as object of יְ׳'s judgment 9^{9} (‖ לְאֻמִּים; v. also 96^{13} supr.), cf. תּ׳ וישבי בה 98^{7} (‖ יָם), Is 13^{11} (‖ רשעים); as devastated by Babylonian conqueror Is 14^{17} (‖ עָרָיו).

†יִבְלְעָם **n.pr.loc.** a city of Manasseh in West-Jordan land Jos 17^{11} (JE; but יִבְ׳ here dub., v. Bu [RS 13 f.]), Ju 1^{27} 2 K 9^{27}; so rd. also 2 K 15^{10} for MT קָבָל־עָם (𝔊L ἐν Ιεβλααμ; v. Klo);

=בלעם 1 Ch 6^{55}, q v, rd. יִבְלְעָם also in Jos 21^{25} (|| 1 Ch 6^{55}), for MT גַּת רִמּוֹן, 𝔊 Ιεβαθα (𝔊L after MT Γεθρεμμων), v. Di, it lay about 13 m. E of N fr Samaria, three-fifths of the way to Jezreel, mod. ruin *Bel'ame* Bd $^{Pal\ 228}$, cf Schultz $^{ZMG\ III\ 49}$; (Old Egypt *Y-b-ra-'a-mu* WMM^{193}).

יָבַל v **יַבֶּ֫לֶת**

יבם (appar √ of foll; meaning dubious)

†[יָבָם] n.m. husband's brother (NH *id*, 𝔗 יְבָמָא; v Lag $^{BN\ 73}$) — only sf. יְבָמִי Dt 25^{7}, יְבָמָהּ 25^{5}, in law of levirate marriage (cf Gn 38^{8}, v also Di $^{Dt\ 25\ 5-10}$)

†[יְבֵמֶת] n.f. sister-in-law (NH יְבָמָה, 𝔗 יְבִמְתָּא, יבימתא, Syr ܝܒܡܬܐ)—only sf יבמתו Dt 25$^{7.7.9}$ *his brother's wife* (*widow*), (cf Gn 38^{8}) in levirate law; יבמתך Ru 1$^{15.15}$ *thy husband's brother's wife*

†[יָבַם] vb.denom., only **Pi.** *do the duty of* יָבָם *to* a brother's widow, *Pf* וְיִבְּמָהּ consec Dt 25^{5} *and shall do a brother-in-law's office to her*, *Imv* יַבֵּם אֹתָהּ Gn 38^{8} (i.e. אֵשֶׁת אָחִיךָ v^{a}); *Inf. sf* לֹא אָבָה יַבְּמִי Dt 25^{7} (on nominal sf as obj of inf, v. Ges $^{§\ 115\ R.\ 2\ ad\ fin}$)

יִבְנִיָּה, יְבַנְיָה, יַבְנֶה, יַבְנְאֵל v. sub בנה.

יַבֹּק v sub בקק p 132^{b} supr.

יְבֶרֶכְיָ֫הוּ v sub ברך p 140^{a} supr.

יִבְשָׂם v. sub בשׂם p 142^{a} supr.

†I יָבֵשׁ vb. be dry, dried up, withered (NH *id* (rare), 𝔗 יְבֵישׁ, chiefly Pa Ithp, Syr ܝܒܫ; Sab Palm deriv, Ar. يَبِسَ, Eth የብሰ:) —**Qal** *Pf* 3 ms יָבֵשׁ Jos 9^{5}+8 t, וְיָבֵשׁ consec Is 19^{5}+4 t, 3 fs. יָֽבְשָׁה Gn 8^{14}, 3 pl יָֽבְשׁוּ Je 23^{10}+2 t, יָבֵ֑שׁוּ 50^{38}+2 t., *Impf.* 3 ms. יִיבַשׁ Is 19^{7}; יִיבָ֑שׁ Je 12^{4} Jb 8^{12}; וַיִּיבַשׁ 1 K 17^{7}; וַיִּיבָ֑שׁ Jon 4^{7}, 3 fs תִּיבַשׁ Ez 17^{10}, תִּיבָ֑שׁ v^{10}+3 t, etc, *Inf cstr* (ב)יְבֹשׁ Is 27^{11}, יְבֹשֶׁת Gn 8^{7}, *abs* יָבוֹשׁ Zc 11^{17}, יָבֹשׁ Ez 17^{10};—**1.** *be dry, dried up without moisture:* **a.** of bread Jos 9$^{5.12}$ (JE) **b.** of ground lacking rain Am 4^{7}, cf. Am 1^{2} (of Carmel at utterance of י׳'s voice), Je 23^{10}. **c.** of earth after the flood Gn 8^{14} (P), cf חָרֵב. **d.** of grass, herbage, trees and crops (already implied in **b**)=*wither* Is 15^{6} 19^{7} 27^{11} Je 12^{4} Jb 8^{12} Jo 1^{12} Jon 4^{7}; in sim of shortness of life ψ 90^{6} 102^{12} 129^{6}, v. also Is 40$^{7.8}$ (in these two || נָבֵל); of heart under fig of grass ψ 102^{5}; of Judah under fig. of vine Ez 17$^{9.9.10.10.10}$, cf. 19^{12}; of princes under fig. of tree Is 40^{24}; of roots of Ephr. under fig. of tree Ho 9^{16}, so of roots of wicked Jb 18^{16}. **e.** of hand, arm, *dry up, wither*, as judgment from י׳, 1 K 13^{4} Zc 11$^{17.17}$; in distress יָבֵשׁ כַּחֶ֫רֶשׂ כֹּחִי ψ 22^{16} *my strength is dried up like the potsherd;* of skin La 4^{8}, and (fig) of bones Ez 37^{11}. **2.** *be dried up:* of water Gn 8^{7} (J), Is 19^{5} 1 K 17^{7} Je 50^{38} Jo 1^{20} Jb 12^{15} 14^{11}. **Pi.** *make dry, dry up*, only *Impf.* 3 ms sf וַיַּבְּשֵׁהוּ Na 1^{4} *and hath made it dry* (י׳, the sea); 3 fs תְּיַבֵּשׁ Jb 15^{30} the flame *shall dry up* his branches (fig. of wicked); fig תְּיַבֶּשׁ־גָּ֑רֶם Pr 17^{22} a broken spirit *maketh dry* (*the*) *bones* **Hiph.** *Pf* 3 ms הוֹבִישׁ Jos 2^{10}+3 t+Jo 1^{10} (v. infr); הֹבִישׁ Ez 19^{12}+2 t Jo (v infr), 3 fs. הוֹבִ֫ישָׁה Jo 1^{12} (v infr.); 2 ms. הוֹבַשְׁתָּ ψ 74^{15}, 1 s הוֹבַשְׁתִּי Ez 17^{24}; וְהוֹבַשְׁתִּי Je 51^{36}; 3 pl וְהֹבִישׁוּ consec. Zc 10^{11}, *Impf* 1 s אוֹבִישׁ Is 42$^{15.15}$ 44^{27},—*dry up, make dry*: **1.** *dry up water*, י׳ subj, Jos 2^{10} 4$^{23.23}$ 5^{1} (all D), Je 51^{36} (|| הֶחֱרִיב), Is 42^{15} 44^{27} (חָֽרְבִי in ||cl), ψ 74^{15}. **2.** *make dry, wither*. herbage, trees, crops, etc., of י׳, Is 42^{15} (|| החריב); obj Babylon under fig. of tree Ez 17^{24}, of east wind's drying up Judah's fruit Ez 19^{12}. **3.** *exhibit dryness:* of river-deeps laid bare Zc 10^{11}—In like manner might be taken Jo 1$^{10.12.12.17}$, if fr. יבשׁ; but the sense would be difficult, esp in v$^{10.12}$, and הֹבִישׁוּ v^{11} must be fr בושׁ, to which all these cases in Jo may be consistently assigned; v. בושׁ.

†II יָבֵשׁ adj. verb or **pt. dry, dried**, so, ms. abs Na 1^{10}+4 t, fs. יְבֵשָׁה Nu 11^{6}; mpl. (ו)יבשים Nu 6^{3}; fpl יבשות Ez 37$^{2.4}$;—**1.** *dried*, lit. only עֲנָבִים יְבֵשִׁים Nu 6^{3} *dried grapes* (P; opp. עֲ׳ לַחִים); fig. נַפְשֵׁנוּ יְבֵשָׁה 11^{6} (JE) *our soul* (i e. our appetite) *is dried up*, viz for want of fresh, juicy meat. **2.** *dry*, of chaff, קַשׁ Na 1^{10} in sim. of Ninevites under impending judgment; cf in fig of Job, Jb 13^{25}, of tree Ez 17^{24} (fig of Davidic house; opp עֵץ לַח), 21^{3} (in prediction of Judah's devastation by Babylon, opp. *id*), Is 56^{3} fig of eunuch, of the bones in Ezek.'s vision Ez 37$^{2.4}$.

†III יָבֵשׁ, יָבִישׁ n.pr.loc. et pers. 1. n. pr. loc. יָבֵשׁ גִּלְעָד *Jabesh of Gilead*, 𝔊 Ιαβ(ε)ις Γαλααδ, exact site unknown, Ju 21$^{8.9.10.12.14}$ 2 S 21^{12}, 1 Ch 10^{11} (𝔊L Ιαβις της Γαλααδ), יָבִישׁ גִּלְעָד 1 S 11$^{1.9}$ 31^{11} 2 S 2$^{4.5}$ (in these three 𝔊L Ιαβις της Γαλααριδιτος); יָבִישׁ 1 S 11$^{1.3.5.9.10}$; יָבֵשׁ 1 Ch 10^{12}; יָבֵ֫שָׁה v^{12}; || יָבֵ֫ישָׁה 1 S 31$^{12.13}$ **2. n.pr.m.** יָבֵשׁ father of Shallum 2 K 15$^{10.13.14}$

†**יַבָּשָׁה** **n.f. dry land, dry ground** (Sab. יבסם, opp. בחרם *sea*, DHM in MV, Palm. יבשא (*dry*) *land* Vog$^{\text{No.79}}$)—alw abs. sg יַבָּשָׁה: Ex 4^{9} (J); of dry ground as path of Isr. through Red Sea Ex $14^{16.22.29}$ 15^{19} (all P), Ne 9^{11} ψ 66^{6}; through Jordan Jos 4^{22} (D); of dry land, opp. sea, at creation Gn $1^{9.10}$ (P); cf. Jon 1^{9}, specif. of shore of sea Jon 1^{13} 2^{11}; fig of needy Israel, to be refreshed by י׳'s spirit Is 44^{3} (‖ צָמֵא).

†**יַבֶּשֶׁת** **n.f.** id, made by God's hands ψ 95^{5}; water shall become blood בַּיַּבָּשֶׁת Ex 4^{9} (J)

יִגְאָל v. sub I. נאל p. 145^{b} supr.

†**[יָגַב]** **vb. till, be husbandman,** only **Qal** *Pt.* pl לכרמים וּלִיגבים Je 52^{16} 2 K 25^{12} Qr (Kt גבים); v. גוב p 155^{b} supr.

†**[יָגֵב]** **n.m. field,** כְּרָמִים ויגבים Je 39^{10}, but text dub, v. 52^{16} = 2 K 25^{12}, also גּוֹב, II. גב p. 155^{b} supr.

יָגְבְּהָה v. sub גבה p. 147^{a} supr.

יִגְדַּלְיָהוּ v. sub גדל p. 153^{b} supr.

†I. **[יָגָה]** **vb. suffer,** not in **Qal** (cf. Ar. وَجَى *castravit*, وَجِىَ *be abraded* (of the foot), of horse, *have pain in the hoof*)—**Niph.** *Pt.* fpl. נוּגוֹת (on form v. Ko$^{\text{i 582}}$) La 1^{4} (‖ מַר, נֶאֱנָחִים) *grieved*, mpl. cstr. נוּגֵי (v. Ko$^{\text{i o}}$) Zp 3^{18} (sq prep., cf. Ges$^{\text{§130.1}}$); of virgins of Zion La 1^{4}; of exiles Zp 3^{18}. **Pi.** *Impf* וַיַּגֶּה (for וַיְיַגֶּה, v. Ko$^{\text{i. 582. 412}}$) *grieve*, sq. acc. La 3^{33} (‖ עִנָּה) **Hiph.** *Pf* 3 ms הוֹגָה La 1^{12} 3^{32}; sf. הוֹגָהּ La 1^{5}; *Impf.* 2 mpl. תּוֹגְיוּן Jb 19^{2}, *Pt.* pl. sf. מוֹגַיִךְ Is 51^{23};—*cause grief* or *sorrow*, abs. La 3^{32} (opp. רִחַם); sq acc (Zion) La 1^{5}, cf. Is 51^{23}, also La 1^{12} (obj om, but אשר of grief = *wherewith*); sq. נַפְשִׁי Jb 19^{2}.—On 2 S 20^{13} v. II יגה.

†**יָגוֹן** **n.[m.] grief, sorrow;**—abs יָגוֹן Gn 42^{38} + 12 t.; sf. (ט)יגונָם Je 31^{13};—*sorrow*, Gn 42^{38}. 44^{31} (J), ψ 13^{3} Je 8^{18}; ‖ אֲנָחָה ψ 31^{11} Is 35^{10} 51^{11}; cf. ψ 107^{39} (‖ רָעָה, עֹצֶר), 116^{3} (‖ צָרָה), Je 20^{18} (‖ עָמָל), 31^{13} (‖ אֵבֶל, opp. שִׂמַּחְתִּים), 45^{3} (‖ מַכְאֹבִי), Ez 23^{33} (‖ שִׁכָּרוֹן, but Co; שברון with Codd.; cf 21^{11}); Est 9^{22} (opp. שִׂמְחָה).

†**תּוּגָה** **n.f. grief** (poet)—abs ת׳ ψ 119^{28} Pr 14^{13} 17^{21}; cstr. תּוּגַת 10^{1};—*grief* ψ 119^{28}; Pr 10^{1} (opp יְשַׂמַּח), 14^{13} (opp. שִׂמְחָה), 17^{21} (‖ לֹא יִשְׂמַח).

†II. **[יָגָה]** **vb.** only **Hiph.** *Pf* 3 ms. הֹגָה (Ko$^{\text{i 584}}$) **thrust away** (Syr. ܘܓܐ *remove, repel;* Ar. وَجَا iv. *repel*)—כַּאֲשֶׁר הֹגָה מִן־הַמְסִלָּה 2 S 20^{13} *when he had thrust* (him, the murdered Amasa) *out of the highway* (‖ וַיַּסֵּב אֶת־עֲמָשָׂא מִן־הַמְסִלָּה הַשָּׂדֶה v^{12})

יָגוּר v sub I גור p. 158^{b} supr

יָגְלִי v. sub גלה p 163^{b} supr

יגן (√ of foll., cf. Ar. وَجَنَ *beat* cloth (said of a fuller); in Heb. only in deriv. *wine-press*)

†I. **גַּת** **n.f. wine-press** (contracted from *גִּנְתְּ=*יִגְנְתְּ)—abs גַּת Ju 6^{11} + 3 t, גִּתּוֹת Ne 13^{15};—*wine-press*, lit. חֹבֵט חִטִּים בַּגַּת Ju 6^{11} *beating out wheat in the wine-press*, to hide it from Midian; the juice of the grapes was pressed out by treading, דרך בְּגַת Is 63^{2} (in sim), but also as acc דֹּרְכִים גִּתּוֹת Ne 13^{15}; in fig. of judgment, גַּת דָּרַךְ אֲדֹנָי לִבְתוּלַת וגו׳ La 1^{15} *a wine-press hath Adonay trodden for the virgin daughter of Judah;* also רְדוּ כִּי מָלְאָה גַּת Jo 4^{13} (רדה only here with גַּת)—On the form and use of wine-press, and Heb. synonyms, v. Smith^{DB} (art *wine-press*) Benz$^{\text{Arch. 212 f.}}$ Rob$^{\text{BR iii. 137}}$ Schick$^{\text{ZPV x. 1887, 146, 150, and Pl. v vii.}}$ Anderlind$^{\text{ZPV xi. 1888, 168 f.}}$

†II. **גַּת** **n.pr.loc.** (*wine-press*)—Philistine city 𝔊 Γεθ, 𝔙 *Geth*, Jos$^{\text{Ant. vi. 12, 2}}$ etc, Γιττα (ed. Niese), exact site unknown (v. GASm$^{\text{Geog 194 ff.}}$), named with Gaza and Ashdod Jos 11^{22} as home of remaining 'Anakim; named with Ashdod, Gaza, Ashkelon and 'Ekron 1 S 6^{17}; with Ashkelon 1 S 1^{20}; with Ashkelon, Yabne and Ashdod 2 Ch 26^{6}; מֵעֶקְרוֹן וְעַד־גַּת 1 S 7^{14}, cf 17^{52b} and also v^{52a} (rd. גַּת for גַּיְא 𝔊 We Dr); called גַּת פְּלִשְׁתִּים Am 6^{2}, built up by Rehoboam, acc. to 2 Ch 11^{8}; taken by Hazael 2 K 12^{18}; also 1 S 5^{8} $17^{4.23}$ (of Goliath), cf. 2 S $21^{20.22}$ = 1 Ch $20^{6.8}$; 1 S $21^{11.13}$ $27^{2.3.4.11}$ 2 S 15^{18} 1 K $2^{39.39.40.41}$ ψ 56^{1} Mi $1^{10.14}$ 1 Ch 7^{21} 8^{13}, also 18^{1} (but ‖ מֶתֶג אַמָּה 2 S 8^{1}; on change of this into reading in Ch v. We), c ה loc, גַּתָּה 1 K 2^{40}.

†**גַּת הַחֵפֶר** 2 K 14^{25} (*wine-press of digging*) home of Jonah, proph.; גִּתָּה חֵפֶר Jos 19^{13}, perh mod *El-Meshhed*, c. 3 m. E. of N. fr. Nazareth, Rob$^{\text{BR ii 350}}$ Bd$^{\text{Pal 252}}$.

†**גַּת־רִמּוֹן** **n.pr.loc.** in Dan Jos 19^{45}; Levitical city 21^{24} = 1 Ch 6^{54}; site unknown—גַּת רמון in Manasseh Jos 21^{25} is scribal error; rd. יִבְלְעָם, q. v.

† **גִּתִּי adj.gent.** of II גַּת 1, of Obed-edom 2 S 6[10.11] = 1 Ch 13[13], Ittai 2 S 15[19.22] 18[2]; Goliath 21[19] 1 Ch 20[5], pl. c art as subst, הַגִּתִּים 1 S 15[18] *the Gittites* (but read אַחַי הַגִּתִּי We Klo Kit Bu Now[Arch.i.308 n]); sg. c art. as n pr coll הַגִּתִּי Jos 13[3] (with men of Gaza, Ashdod, Ashkelon, Ekron, and the Awwim).

† **גִּתִּית f.** of foregoing (si vera l) only in phr. עַל־הַגִּתִּית in three ψ-titles: ψ 8[1] 81[1] 84[1]; *upon the Gittite (lyre)* so 𝔗, *to the Gittite (melody)* Ew Ol De, or either of these Hup Pe; 𝔊 𝔙 הַגִּתֹּת *wine-presses*, whence Bae al. *at the wine-presses*, i e. (Bae) a song for the feast of booths

† **גִּתַּיִם n.pr.loc.** in Judah;—ג׳ Ne 11[33]; גִּתַּיְמָה 2 S 4[3], site unknown

† [**יָגַע, יָגֵעַ**] **vb.** toil, grow or be weary (NH *id*; As *êgû*, *grow weary* Dl[Pr 140], Ar. وَجِعَ *have pain, suffer*)—**Qal** *Pf* יָגְעָה 2 S 23[10], יָגַעְתָּ Jos 24[13] Is 43[22], יָגַעַתְּ, יָגַעַתְּ 47[12] + 2 t., יָגַעַתְּ Is 47[15]; יָגַעְתִּי ψ 6[7] + 3 t, יָגַעְנוּ La 5[5]; *Impf.* יִיגַע Is 40[28]; 2 ms תִּיגַע Pr 23[4]; אִיגָע Jb 9[29]; יִיגְעוּ Hb 2[13]; יִיגְעוּ Je 51[58] Is 65[23], יִיגָעוּ Is 40[31], יִגְעוּ v[30].—**1.** *toil, labour* for (בְּ), Jos 24[13] (D), Is 62[8], sq acc. (אשר) 47[15], sq. בְּ instr. v[12]; abs. 49[4] (לריק ‖ והבל כחי כליתי), cf 65[23] Je 51[58] (‖ יעף), Hb 2[13] (‖ *id*), La 5[5] (‖ לא־הוּנַח־לָנוּ), Jb 9[29], sq inf Pr 23[4]. **2.** *grow* or *be weary*, from toil, exertion, endurance, 2 S 23[10] (om. by accident in ‖ 1 Ch 11[13] v Dr), *weary of*, sq בְּ, ψ 6[7] 69[4] Is 43[22] 57[10] Je 45[3]; abs. Is 40[28.30.31] (in all ‖ יעף). **Pi.** *Impf* 3 fs. sf. 3 ms תְּיַגְּעֶנּוּ Ec 10[15] *weary, make weary*, subj עֲמַל הכסילים, 2 ms תְּיַגַּע *cause to go toilsomely* Jos 7[3], sq acc **Hiph.** *Pf* 2 ms. sf הוֹגַעְתַּנִי Is 43[24]; הוגעתיך v[23], pl הוֹגַעְתֶּם Mal 2[17], הוֹגַעְנוּ v[17];—*make to toil* (alw. c בְּ instr), c acc pers. *make to toil, weary* Is 43[23] (‖ העביד), obj י׳ v[24] (*weary*, fig), and so Mal 2[17.17]

† **יְגָע n.[m.]** gain (= product of *labour*)—יְגָע Jb 20[18] (‖ תְּמוּרָה)

† **יָגֵעַ adj** weary, wearisome,—יָגֵעַ Dt 25[18] *weary* (‖ עָיֵף), 2 S 17[2] (‖ רפה יָדַיִם), כָּל־הַדְּבָרִים יגעים Ec 1[8] *all things are wearisome* ('full of labour').

† [**יְגִעָה**] **n f.** wearying (late format, Dr Intr[455] Siegf[NH Gram §47 b]) וְלַהַג הַרְבֵּה יגעת בָּשָׂר Ec 12[12] *and studying much is a wearying of flesh*

† [**יָגִיעַ**] **adj.** weary;—pl cstr. וְשָׁם יָנוּחוּ יגיעי כֹחַ Jb 3[17] *and there are resting the weary in strength*, the toil-worn

† [**יְגִיעַ**] **n.m.** toil, product;—cstr יְגִיעַ Gn 31[42] + 5 t, sf יְגִיעֲךָ Dt 28[33], יְגִיעֶךָ Jb 39[11]; יְגִיעֵךְ Ez 23[29], יגיעו ψ 109[11] Ne 5[13]; יגיעה Jb 39[16] Je 20[5], ויגיעכם Is 55[2]; ויגיעם ψ 78[46], pl. sf. יְגִיעָי Ho 12[9] (but יגיעיו 𝔊 Che),—**1.** *toil*, יג׳ כַּפַּיִם Gn 31[42] (E; ‖ עָנְיִי), Jb 39[11] (= husbandry), laying of eggs 39[16] **2.** result of toil, *product, produce, acquired property*: יְגִיעַי Ho 12[9] (‖ און, on text v supr.), Dt 28[33] (‖ פרי אדמתך), ψ 78[46] (‖ יבול), 128[2], Hg 1[11] (‖ דָּגָן, תירושׁ, יִצְהָר), יְגִיעַ כַּפַּיִם (בהמה, אָדָם, אשר תוציא הָאֲדָמָה); Ne 5[13] (‖ בית), ψ 109[11] (‖ כל־אשר־לוֹ), Is 45[14] (יגיע מצרים ‖ סְחַר־כּוּשׁ), 55[2] (‖ כסף), Je 3[24] (‖ צֹאן, בָּקָר, בָּנִים, בָּנוֹת), 20[5] (‖ יְקָר, חֹסֶן, of city), Ez 23[29], of Job as product of God's hands (יג׳ כַּפֶּיךָ) Jb 10[3].

† [**יָגֹר**] **vb.** be afraid, fear (Ph in n pr יגר אשמן = *he feareth Eshmun*, Ar. وَجِرَ *metuens cavit*, Frey; Lag[BN 26 30]; cf III גור)—**Qal** *Pf* 2 ms יָגֹרְתָּ Dt 28[60]; יָגֹרְתִּי 9[19] + 3 t,—*be afraid*, sq מִפְּנֵי *before, of*; of wrath of י׳ Dt 9[19]; of diseases of Egypt 28[60]; *fear*, sq acc Jb 3[25] 9[28] ψ 119[39]

† **יָגוֹר adj. vb.** fearing, men אֲשֶׁר אַתָּה יָגוֹר מִפְּנֵיהֶם Je 22[25] 39[17]

יָד 1604 **n.f.**[Gn 25, 26 + oft.] (**m.** + Ex 17[12] + v Di; on יְרַפּוּ יָדַיִם 2 S 4[1] Zp 3[16] 2 Ch 15[7] Ne 6[9], v. Ges §145. 7 a, R 1) **hand** (NH *id*, Aram. יְדָא, ܐܝܕܐ, Zinj יד DHM[Sendsch Gloss], Ar. يَدٌ, Sab יד DHM ZMG 1883, 343 Mordt[ib 1876, 492], Eth እድ: (v. Lag[BN 22]); Sam ࠉࠃ; As. *idu*, *strength* COT[Gloss],—der by most fr. √ ל״י, on ground of pl and sf. forms in cogn. lang., v esp Philippi[ZMG 1878, 74] Ba[ZMG 1887, 637], but no trace of final י or ו in Heb., and meaning of such √ ל״י not clear; Thes al fr. ידה *extend, throw*, but this in Ar Eth. פ״ו, not פ״י, cf Heb Hiph.; Philippi comp. Ar. يَدَى iv. *strengthen*,—Sta §182. 183 regards יד as bilit)—abs. יָד Gn 38[28] +; cstr. יַד 41[35] +; sf. יָדִי 14[22] +; יָדְךָ 22[12] +; יָדְכֶן, יָדְכָה Ex 13[16]; יֶדְכֶם Gn 9[2] +, יָדִי Ez 13[21 21 23], etc., du. יָדַיִם Gn 34[21] +; cstr. יְדֵי 24[30] +; וידי Ex 15[17] +, etc.; fpl (in fig. senses) abs יָדוֹת Gn 43[34] + 8 t., יָדֹת 47[24] + 2 t.; cstr יְדֹתָיו, ידתיה 1 K 7[32], sf יְדֹתָיו Ex 26[19 19] + 2 t; וידות 1 K 7[35.36]; יְדוֹתָם 1 K 7[33],—**1.** *hand* of man Gn 3[22] 4[11] 8[9] + oft, תַּבְנִית יָד Ez 8[3] *the shape of a hand* (of God in Ezek.'s vision), of cherubim

ת׳ יַד אָדָם 10^{8}, דְּמוּת יְדֵי אָדָם v^{21}: **a.** *right hand* יַד־יְמִינ(וֹ) Gn 48^{17} (JE), Ju 7^{20} 2 S 20^{9} Je 22^{24} Ez 39^{3} ψ 73^{23} 121^{5}; יד[ם] הַיְמָנִית Ex 29^{20} Lv 8$^{23.24}$ 14$^{14.17.25.28}$ (all P); a left-handed man is אִטֵּר יַד־יְמִינוֹ Ju 3^{15} 20^{16} (v. אטר); *left hand* יַד שְׂמֹאל(וֹ) 3^{21} 7^{20} Ez 39^{3}; both hands of one pers. are denoted by du., יָדַיִם Gn 27^{22} 2 K 3^{11} + oft.; occasionally + numeral, שְׁתֵּי יָדַי Dt 9$^{15.17}$, so Lv 16^{21} (P); du. also of hands of several persons Gn 5^{29} Ex 29$^{10.15.19}$ Dt 31^{29} 2 K 11^{16} = 2 Ch 23^{15}, Ez 21^{12} +; yet sts. sg. of hand of several persons Gn 19^{16} Ex 29^{9} Lv 8^{24} Dt 1^{25} 17$^{7.7}$ Ju 7$^{20.20}$ +. **b.** שְׁתֵּי כַּפּוֹת ידיו 1 S 5^{4} *the two palms of his hands;* כַּפּוֹת הידים 2 K 9^{35} Dn 10^{10}; אַצִּילוֹת יָדֶיךָ *armpits* Je 38^{12} Ez 13^{18}; בֹּהֶן יָדָיו Ex 29^{20} (P) = *his thumbs* (opp. בֹּהֶן רַגְלָם); בְּהֹנוֹת יד(יו) ורגל(יו) Ju 1$^{6.7}$; bracelets were worn on *hands,* i.e. wrists Gn 24$^{22.30.47}$ (J), cf. thread bound on *hand* of Zerach 38$^{28.28.29.30}$ (J), and cords on *hands* of Samson Ju 15^{14}; the ring was worn on *hand,* i.e. finger Gn 41^{42} (E), Est 3^{10}. **c.** as to *hands* in use, note זְרֹעֵי ידיו Gn 49^{24} *arms of his hands,* i.e. arms which make his hands serviceable; מִלֵּא יָדוֹ בַּקֶּשֶׁת 2 K 9^{24} *he filled his hand with the bow,* i.e. caused his hand to grasp it, seized it; הַרְכֵּב יָדְךָ עַל־הַקֶּשֶׁת 2 K 13$^{16.16}$; esp. fig. of consecrating or installing (as priest), מִלֵּא יַד *he filled the hand* of any one (perh. orig. gave the selected portions of animal-sacrifices to, v. Lv 8$^{25\,ff.}$, so Di), *installed* as priest Ju 17$^{5.12}$ 1 K 13^{33} (sq. ו subord.); elsewhere only P and late: Ex 28^{41} (‖ קִדֵּשׁ), 29^{9} also v^{29} (‖ מֹשׁח), v^{33} (קדשׁ), v^{35} Lv 8^{33} 2 Ch 13^{9} 16^{33}, sq. inf. Lv 16^{33} מִלֻּאִים (‖ מֹשׁח), 21^{10} (‖ יוּצַק שֶׁמֶן), Nu 3^{3} (‖ מֹשׁח); מִלֵּאתֶם יֶדְכֶם ליהוה 2 Ch 29^{31} = ye have consecrated yourselves to י׳, is addressed appar. to the whole congregation (otherwise Be Öt and Di Ex 32^{29}); so the same expression Ex 32^{29} (poss.) and 1 Ch 29^{5} (certainly) of offering gifts to י׳; מִלְאוּ יָדוֹ Ez 43^{26} of consecrating the altar (‖ טִהַר, כִּפֶּר); שָׁלַח יַד לְ ישלח אֶל־ Ju 5^{26} *stretch out hand to,* so מִשְׁלַח יד(כ)ם 2 S 6^{6} (insert ידו Vrss Dr); hence *that to which one puts the hand,* fig., = undertaking, †Dt 12$^{7.18}$ 15^{10} 23^{21} 28$^{8.20}$†; שלח יד also in hostile sense, c. בְּ, Ex 22^{7} 1 S 24$^{7.11}$ 26^{11} ψ 55^{21} +; cf. מוֹאָב מִשְׁלוֹחַ יָדָם Is 11^{14}; אֶבֶן־יַד Nu 35^{17} (P) *a stone* (*thrown from*) *the hand;* כְּלִי עֵץ־יָד v^{18} *a weapon in the hand;* מַקֵּל יָד Ez 39^{9} *a staff in the hand;* idols are מַעֲשֵׂה יְדֵי וגו׳ Is 2^{8} + oft. v. מַעֲשֶׂה; man is work of God's hand Jb 14^{15}. **d.** special phrases: kissing with the hand וַתִּשַּׁק יָדִי לְפִי Jb 31^{27}; (in silence) יָדִי שַׂמְתִּי לְמוֹ פִי 40^{4} Mi 7^{16} (עַל־פֶּה); the creditor is בַּעַל מַשֵּׁה יָדוֹ Dt 15^{2}; the debt מַשָּׁא כָל־יָד Ne 10^{32}; תְּרוּמַת יֶדְכֶם Dt 12$^{6.11.17}$ *heave-offering of your hand;* the hand is placed תחת יְרֵכוֹ in taking an oath Gn 24^{2} (J); lifted (הרים) to י׳ 14^{22}; so perhaps יָד עַל־כֵּס יָהּ Ex 17^{16} (E) *hand on the throne of Yah!* (but difficult, v. Di VB); oft. c. נשׂא: the hand is lifted (נשׂא) to heaven Dt 32^{40} (of י׳'s oath, poem); elsewh. chiefly Ez and P: simply *lift* (נשׂא) *the hand* (= נשׁבע), sq. inf. Ex 6^{8} Nu 14^{30} (both P), Ez 20$^{28.42}$ 47^{14}; sq. לְ pers. Ez 20$^{5.5}$ (del. Co as gloss); sq. לְ pers. + inf. Ez 20$^{6.15.23}$; abs. 36^{7}; hence (citations) Ne 9^{15} ψ 106^{26}; cf. Ne 8^{6} the people answered אָמֵן אָמֵן בְּמֹעַל יְדֵיהֶם (נשׂא יד(ים)); elsewh. (of men) in prayer ψ 28^{2}; cf. 68^{32}, and יָדִי לַיְלָה נִגְּרָה 77^{3}. Also of God, to give a signal Is 49^{22}; to rescue ψ 10^{12}. יְנֹפֵף יָדוֹ Is 10^{32} *he brandisheth his hand* (Assyrian, in defiance); הֵנִיף יָדוֹ Is 11^{15} (of י׳ in judgment), cf. 19^{16} Zc 2^{13} (sq. עַל); יָנִיעַ יָדוֹ Zp 2^{15} (in derision); הוֹשִׁיעַ יד לְ *one's hand bringing deliverance to, gaining success, by force, for* 1 S 25^{26} + (v. Dr), ins. also v^{31} (𝔊 We Dr); the hand is weary יָגְעָה 2 S 23^{10}, it cleaves (דבק) to the sword (אֶל־הַחֶרֶב) v^{10} (both om. by accident in ‖ 1 Ch 11^{13}, see VB); שֶׁבֶר יָד Lv 21^{19} (H) *fracture of hand* = arm (‖ שֶׁבֶר רגל); after נָתַן: *give a pledge* וַיִּתְּנוּ יָדָם לְהוֹצִיא נְשֵׁיהֶם Ezr 10^{19}; *submit* נָתַן יַד תַּחַת שְׁלֹמֹה 1 Ch 29^{24}, i.e. they acknowledged him as their lord; תְּנוּ־יָד ליהוה 2 Ch 30^{8}; other phr. c. prep. v. infr. **e.** of hand as strong, helpful, etc.:—(1) of man: עֹצֶם יָדִי Dt 8^{17} (‖ כֹּחִי); of fighting power of Edom בְּיָד חֲזָקָה Nu 20^{20} (JE; ‖ בְּעַם כָּבֵד; cf. infr. of God); קִצְרֵי־יָד *small in power* 2 K 19^{26} = Is 37^{27} (cf. infr. of God); Isr. went out of Egypt בְּיָד רָמָה acc. to P, Ex 14^{8} Nu 33^{3} i.e. boldly, defiantly; same phr. of presumptuousness (against י׳) Nu 15^{30} (P, cf. יָדֵנוּ רָמָה Dt 32^{27}). Phrases of *strengthening* are: חִזֵּק יָדָיו Ju 9^{24} Ne 6^{9}; חִזֵּק בְּיָדַיִם Ezr 1^{6}; החזיק בְּיַד Jb 8^{20} (v. חזק); לִהְיוֹת יָדָיו אִתּוֹ 2 K 15^{19} *that his hands might be with him,* to confirm the kingdom in his hand; note also מִי־הוּא לְיָדִי יִתָּקֵעַ Jb 17^{3} *who is he* (that) *will strike his hand into mine,* i.e. give me a pledge (v. sub תקע); strength fails when hands drop: וַיִּרְפּוּ יָדָיו 2 S 4^{1} *then his hands dropped down,* he grew feeble, spiritless (v. רפה); רְפֵה יָדַיִם 17^{2} *weak-handed, weak* (‖ יָגֵעַ). (2) of (mighty) hand of God, pointing to earlier an-

thropomorphism; as strengthening Joseph Gn 49^{24} (poem in J); as stretched out (שׁלח) to smite Ex 9^{15} (J); so of מַלְאַךְ י׳ 2 S 24^{16}, sq. acc. + לְ inf., opp. הֶרֶף יָדֶךָ v^{16}; as smiting (נָגְעָה בְּ) 1 S 6^{9} Jb 19^{21}; as against (בְּ *among, in*) cattle, etc., v^{3} (J); city 1 S 5^{9}; the murrain v^{3} (J); כָּבְדָה יַד־יהוה as heavy against (כבדה אֶל) 1 S 5^{6}; קָשְׁתָה עַל שָׁם v^{11}; v^{7}; of withdrawal of ׳י's chastising hand תָסוּר יָדוֹ מִכֶּם 1 S 6^{3}; and (׳י subj.) יָקֵל אֶת־יָדוֹ מֵעֲלֵיכֶם v^{5}; of ׳י's power to deliver his people:—†יָד חֲזָקָה; †חֹזֶק יָד Ex $13^{3.14.16}$ (all JE)†; $6^{1.1}$ (JE), 13^{9} (JE), Dt 6^{21} 7^{8} Jos 4^{24} (D); esp. in phr. (בְּ)יָד חֲזָקָה וּ(ב)זְרוֹעַ נְטוּיָה Dt 4^{34} + (v. זְרוֹעַ p. 284); כֹּחַ גָּדוֹל + יד חזקה Ex 32^{11} (JE), Ne 1^{10}; הֲיַד י׳ תִּקְצָר Nu 11^{23} (JE) *is the hand of* ׳י *shortened?* Is 50^{2} 59^{1} (both sq. מִן); יָד נְטוּיָה in judgment Is $9^{11.16.20}$ 10^{4}; הָיְתָה יַד־י׳ עָלָי(ו) of grasp of ׳י's hand in prophetic inspiration Ez 1^{3} 3^{22} 37^{1} 40^{1} 2 K 3^{15}; יַד־י׳ עָלַי חזקה Ez 3^{14}; so בְּחֶזְקַת הַיָּד Is 8^{11}; of God's (׳י's) *good hand* = favour, (late) יַד אלה(יו) טוֹבָה עַל(יו) Ezr 7^{9} 8^{18} Ne $2^{8.18}$; without טוֹבָה Ezr $7^{6.28}$ $8^{22.31}$; sq. inf. יַד האלהים לָתֵת לָהֶם 2 Ch 30^{12}; בְּיָדְךָ לְגַדֵּל 1 Ch 29^{12}; in gen. בְּיָדְךָ כֹּחַ וּגְבוּרָה v^{12}; of protection בְּצֵל יָדוֹ Is 49^{2} *in the shadow of his* (׳י's) *hand*.

2. Fig. = *strength, power*:—לֹא הָיָה בָהֶם יָדַיִם לָנוּס Jos 8^{20} (JE) *there was not in them strength to flee*; לֹא מָצְאוּ כָל־אַנְשֵׁי־חַיִל יְדֵיהֶם ψ 76^{6} *none of the men of might have found their hands*, i.e. their powers are paralyzed in death (‖ נָמוּ שְׁנָתָם); with ref. to pecuniary *ability*: תַּגִּיעַ יָדוֹ דֵּי שֶׂה Lv 5^{7} (on this and others c. דֵּי v. דַּי p. 191); תַּגִּיעַ יָדוֹ לִשְׁתֵּי תוֹרִים v^{11} if *his hand* do not *reach to two turtledoves*; אֵין יָדוֹ מַשֶּׂגֶת 14^{21} if *his hand be unable to reach*; so combinations with נשׂג Hiph.: $v^{22.30.31.32}$ Nu 6^{21} (all foregoing P), Lv $25^{26.47.49}$ 27^{8} (all H), Ez 46^{7}; כְּמַתְּנַת יָדוֹ Dt 16^{17} *according to the giving of his hand*, i.e. his ability; similarly מַתַּת יָדוֹ Ez $46^{5.11}$; on יֶשׁ־לְאֵל יָדִי Gn 31^{29}, etc., v. II. אֵל p. 43^{a} supr.; other phr. c. prep. v. infr.; of *dominion* of king לְהָשִׁיב יָדוֹ בְּ 2 S 8^{3} rd. prob. as ‖ 1 Ch 18^{3} לְהַצִּיב יָדוֹ בְּ *to establish his dominion at*; *hand* = *display of strength, action* of ׳י ψ 78^{42} Jb 27^{11} Dt 34^{12}; esp. הַיָּד הַגְּדֹלָה אֲשֶׁר עָשָׂה י׳ Ex 14^{31} (J) = *the great achievement which* ׳י *did*.

3. Fig. = *side*: **a.** of way יַד דֶּרֶךְ 1 S 4^{13} Qr (Kt יַךְ; but rd. prob. לְיַד השׁער v. Dr). **b.** of gate בְּעַד יַד־הַשַּׁעַר 1 S 4^{18} (txt. dub., v. Dr). **c.** of stream or wady כָּל־יַד נַחַל יַבֹּק Dt 2^{37}. Esp. du.: **d.** of land, אֶרֶץ רַחֲבַת יָדַיִם Gn 34^{21} (P) *the land is wide of (on) both hands*, i.e. in both directions, Ju 18^{10} Is 22^{18} 1 Ch 4^{40}; of city Ne 7^{4}; of sea ψ 104^{25}; of streams רַחֲבֵי יָדַיִם Is 33^{21}; מִיַּד כִּתִּים Nu 24^{24} (JE) *from the direction of Kittim*.—Other phr. c. prep. v. infr. **e.** *side* = *place*, properly *place at one side* וְיָד תִּהְיֶה לְךָ מִחוּץ לַמַּחֲנֶה Dt 23^{13}; אִישׁ אֶת־יָדוֹ Je 6^{3} *each (in) his place*; so כָּל־אִישׁ עַל־יָדוֹ Nu 2^{17} (P);—v. other phrases c. prep. infr.

4. יָד is used in various special, technical senses:—**a.** *sign, monument* 1 S 15^{12} 2 S 18^{18}. †**b.** *part, fractional part* or *share*: of seed Gn 47^{24} (J); share in king 2 S 19^{44}; of fighting men 2 K 11^{7}; of people Ne 11^{1}. †**c.** *time, repetition* Gn 43^{34} (J), Dn 1^{20}. Also f. pl. (only in fig. senses):—†**d.** *axle-trees* 1 K $7^{32.33}$ (𝔖 ܐܝ̈ܕܝܐ). †**e.** *stays, supports* for laver 1 K $7^{35.36}$; *stays* at sides of throne 1 K $10^{19.19}$ = 2 Ch $9^{18.18}$. †**f.** *tenons* on sides of boards of tabernacle שְׁתֵּי יָדוֹת Ex 26^{17} (P), also $v^{19.19}$ $36^{22.24.24}$. **g.** יָד חָזִית Is 57^{8} acc. to Hi De Che Or Brd Du and most = *a phallus thou beholdest*; this favoured by context but without support in Heb. usage; Di *a (beckoning) hand*.

5. יָד with prep.:—**a.** אֶל־יַד:—(1) after vb. of motion, *into the charge, custody, of* Est $2^{3.8.8.14}$; (2) אֶל־יַד *by the side of* gate 2 S 18^{4}; אֶל־יָדִי *by my side, next to me* 14^{30}; אֶל־יַד דָּרֶךְ Ez 48^{1a}; אֶל־יַד חֲמָת v^{b} (but on txt. v. Co); cf. also לְיַד, עַל־יַד. **b.** בְּיַד *into the hand*: (1) נָתַן בְּיַד *give into the hand of*, lit., Gn 27^{17}; (2) *into the possession of* נָתַן בְּיַד Ex 10^{25} (JE); esp. (3) נתן ביד = *give into the power of, deliver over to* Jos 6^{2} 7^{7} (both JE), Dt 1^{27} Ju 2^{14a} 13^{1} 15^{12} 1 K 22^{6} 2 K 18^{30} 19^{10}; מָכַר בְּיַד *sell into the hand of* Ju 2^{14b} 3^{8} $4^{2.9}$ 10^{7}; נפל בְּיַד *fall into the hand of* 15^{18} 2 S 24^{14}; וַיְשַׁלְּחֵם בְּיַד פִּשְׁעָם Jb 8^{4} *and he delivered them into the power of their transgression*, gave them over to it; also Is 64^{6}, which read וַתְּמַגְּנֵנוּ for MT וַתְּמוּגֵנוּ; (4) נתן בְּיַד = *entrust to* Gn 30^{35} 32^{17}. **c.** בְּיַד *in the hand of*: (1) lit. מַטְּךָ אֲשֶׁר בְּיָדֶךָ Gn 38^{18} (J) *thy staff which is in thy hand*, Ex 7^{17} (J), 17^{9} (E), 32^{15} Nu $22^{23.31}$ Jos 5^{13} 8^{18} (all JE), 1 S 13^{22} 14^{27} 17^{50} 18^{10} 20^{10} 2 K $11^{8.11}$ = 2 Ch 23^{7}, Am 7^{7} Is 6^{6} Ez $40^{3.5}$ 47^{3} Zc 2^{5} 8^{4}; אֵין בְּיָדִי רָעָה וָפֶשַׁע 1 S 14^{12} *there is not in my hand evil or transgression* (orig. prob. of stains of blood, or other evidences of crime); מַה־בְּיָדִי רָעָה 26^{18}; (2) fig. *in the possession of*, Ex 21^{16} (JE); נִמְצָא בְּיָדִי 1 S 9^{8} *there is found*

in my hand, i.e. I happen to have (¼ shekel), (3) *in the (physical) power of* Gn 16⁶ (J; cf תִּתְעַנִּי תַּחַת יָדֶיהָ v⁹), Jb 1¹²; בְּיַד לָשׁוֹן Pr 18²¹ *in the power of a tongue; in the care* or *charge of, entrusted to*, Gn 39²³ (J), *under the authority of* 2 S 18^{2.2.2} Nu 31⁴⁹ (P),—in Je 41⁹ (AV *because of Gedaliah*), rd ביד גדליהו הוא for בּוֹר גָּדוֹל הוּא 𝔊 Hi Kue Gf Che Gie Di ⁸ᵐ²⁹¹; (4) בְּיַד also with vbs. of *taking*, וַיִּקַּח בְּיָדוֹ אֶת־הָאֵשׁ Gn 22⁶ *and he took the fire in his hand*, Ex 4^{17.20.21} (all E), 1 S 17⁴⁰ 2 K 9¹, thence to denote accompaniment, taking or being *with* one Jos 9¹¹ (JE), 2 S 8¹⁰ 1 K 14³ 2 K 5⁵, אִישׁ שׁוֹרוֹ בְּיָדוֹ 1 S 14³⁴ cf. 16²; קַח בְּיָדְךָ שְׁלֹשִׁים אֲנָשִׁים Je 38¹⁰. **d.** בְּיַד *by the agency* or *instrumentality of* Gn 38²⁰ (J), Ju 6³⁶ 1 S 11⁷ 16²⁰ 2 S 3¹⁸ 10² 11¹⁴ 12²⁵ 2 K 14²⁷ (the orig. lit sense is discernible in some of these), esp. of י׳'s speaking *by the agency* of prophets Ex 9³⁵ (R), Lv 8³⁶ 10¹¹ Nu 4^{37.45} 9²³ 10¹³ 17⁵ Jos 14² 20² 21^{2.8} (all P), 1 S 28^{15.17} 1 K 16^{7.12.34} 2 K 9³⁶ 17^{13.23} 2 Ch 1¹⁷ 7⁶ 10¹⁵ 33⁸ 34¹⁴ 35⁶ Ne 8¹⁴ 9^{14.30}; מוּת בְּיַד י׳ Ex 16³ (P) *die by the hand of* י׳, בְּיַד *by* or *at the side of* (very rare) Zc 4¹² olive-branches *beside* the two golden pipes; =*near to*, in time, נָכוֹן בְּיָדוֹ יוֹם חֹשֶׁךְ Jb 15²³ *ready at his hand is a day of darkness* (i e. near *at hand*). **e.** כְּיַד הַמֶּלֶךְ 1 K 10¹³ *acc. to the hand of the king*, i.e his royal munificence, so Est 2¹⁸ cf. 1⁷. **f.** לְיַד *by the side of* 1 S 19³ 1 Ch 18¹⁷ 23²⁸ Ne 11²⁴ Pr 8³ ψ 140⁶. **g.** מִיַּד *out of the hand*·—(1) *out of the power of*, often nearly = מִן, used idiomat. c many vbs · c. הִצִּיל Gn 32^{12.12} (J), Ex 2¹⁹ 18^{9.10.10} (all JE), 1 S 17³⁷, מִתַּחַת יַד Ex 18¹⁰ (JE; so c פשע 2 Ch 21^{8.10.10}; cf **i.** infr.), of animals מִיַּד 1 S 17^{37.37}, מִיַּד־כֶּלֶב ψ 22²¹, even of inanimate things הציל מִיַּד לֶהָבָה Is 47¹⁴, c. לָקַח Nu 21²⁶ (JE), 1 K 11^{34.35}; c קָרַע v^{12.31}; c. מִלֵּט, מ׳ מִיַּד שְׁאוֹל ψ 89⁴⁹; c. פָּדָה, פ׳ מִיַּד שְׁאוֹל Ho 13¹⁴ (‖ מִמָּוֶת), ψ 49¹⁶, פ׳ מידי חֶרֶב Jb 5²⁰; pregn. יִשְׁפְּטֵנִי מִיָּדֶךָ 1 S 24¹⁶ *may he* (י׳) *judge* (and save) *me out of thy hand*, so 2 S 18¹⁹ and (with רִיב for שפט) 1 S 25³⁹; (2) מִיַּד of separation, מִיָּדְךָ נִגְזָרוּ ψ 88⁶ of wicked, cut off from nearness to God, (3) דָּרַשׁ מִיַּד *exact (at the hand) of* 2 S 4¹¹ Gn 9^{5.5} (P), Ez 33⁶ 34¹⁰ (= דָּרַשׁ מעם Dt 18¹⁹), also of animals Gn 9⁵; בקשׁ מִיַּד Ez 33⁸, קָנָה מִיַּד Ru 4^{5.9} *acquire at the hand of*, with ref to offerings הקריב מִיַּד Lv 22²⁵ (H), רָצָה מִיַּד (י׳ subj.) Mal 1^{10.13}; לָקַח מִיַּד, רָצוֹן מִיַּד 2¹³. **h.** (על־יד(י —(1) *upon the hand(s) of* עַל־יְדֵי תנה אתו Gn 42³⁷ = *entrust him to me* (E; lit. *put him upon my hand*), יַגִּירֻהוּ עַל־יְדֵי־ חֶרֶב ψ 63¹¹ *they shall pour him out upon the hands of the sword = deliver him up to the sword*, so Je 18²¹ Ez 35⁵; (2) עַל־יַד, עַל־יְדֵי *acc. to the hand(s) of* = at the guidance, direction of. עַל־יַד 1 Ch 25^{2.a} 2 Ch 26¹³; עַל־ידֵי Je 5³¹ 33¹³, and esp. Chr · 1 Ch 25^{2b.3.6.6}, עַל־יְדֵי דָּוִיד, על־ידי כְּלֵי דָוִיד 2 Ch 23¹⁸ Ezr 3¹⁰, 2 Ch 29²⁷ *acc. to the guidance of the instruments of David*; (3) *by the side of*, way עַל־יַד דֶּרֶךְ 2 S 15²; river (היאר) עַל־יַד הַשַּׁעַר Ex 2⁵ (E), Nu 13²⁹ (JE; ‖ (עַל־הַיָּם), Je 46⁶ Dn 10⁴; city Jos 15⁴⁶ (JE); person (=*in the company of*) 2 S 15¹⁸, people 2 Ch 21¹⁶; esp. late עַל־יַד *next to* (in a series) 17^{15.16.18} 31¹⁵ Ne 3^{2.2} + 13 t. Ne 3, 13¹³; עַל־יְדֵי *by the side of* Ju 11²⁶; people (אדום) עַל־ידי Nu 34³ (P), 1 Ch 7²⁹, cattle Jb 1¹⁴, הֶעֱמִיד עַל־יְדֵי שִׁיר 1 Ch 6¹⁶ *he stationed them by the side of song*, i e to watch over the singing. **i.** תַּחַת יַד *under the hand* = in the possession, at the disposal of, ואין יֵשׁ־פֹּה תַּחַת־יָדְךָ חֲנִית וגו׳ 1 S 21⁹; = in the power of, subject to Is 3⁶ come, thou shalt be our ruler and this ruin *under thy hand*, pl sq. vb, וְהִתְעַנִּי תַּחַת יָדֶיהָ Gn 16⁹ (J) *and submit thyself under her hands*, her authority, Is 3⁶.— מִתַּחַת יַד v **g.** (1) supr., and sub תַּחַת

† **יִדְאֲלָה** n.pr.loc. in Zebulun Jos 19¹⁵, 𝔊 Ιερειχω, 𝔊L Ιεδαλα, 𝔖 ܐܠܐ; site unknown.

יִדְבָּשׁ v. sub דבשׁ p. 185ᵇ supr

†I. [**יָדַד**] **vb. cast a lot** (cf Eth. ወደየ: *immittere*, etc, Di ⁹³⁵)—only **Qal** *Pf* 3 mpl. יַדּוּ גוֹרָל עַל Na 3¹⁰ Ob¹¹; יַדּוּ גוֹרָל אֶל־ Jo 4³ (Poss. wrongly pointed pfs of ידה **Pi.** q v)

II **ידד** (√of foll; *love*, cf. Ar. وَدّ *love*; Aram. Pa ܝܰܕܶܕ *love*, also deriv., Sab. epith. f. ודת *loving-one, friend, amie*, DHM ᶻᴹᴳ ¹⁸⁸³·³⁹¹; v. also דוד)

†[**יָדִיד**] **adj.** (poet.) **beloved** (NH *id*., Aram. ܝܰܕܺܝܕܳܐ)—cstr. יְדִיד Dt 33¹²; sf. לִידִידִי Is 5¹ Je 11¹⁵, לִידִידוֹ ψ 127²; pl. sf. יְדִידֶיךָ 60⁷ 108⁷; f. ידידת 45¹, ידידות 84²;—**1.** *my beloved*, used by proph of י׳ under fig of husbandman Is 5¹; so *my* (thy, his) *beloved* Je 11¹⁵ ψ 60⁷ = 108⁷, 127², *beloved*, of Benj as beloved by י׳ Dt 33¹². **2.** *lovely*, מַה־יְּדִידוֹת משׁכנותיך ψ 84² *how lovely are thy habitations!* **3.** fpl. as abstr. subst. שִׁיר יְדִידֹת ψ 45¹ = *a song of love*.

† **יְדִדוּת n.f.** love = obj of love,—only cstr. יְדִדוּת נַפְשִׁי Je 12^{7} (׳י speaks) *love* (i.e. beloved) *of my soul*.

† **יְדִידָה n.pr.f.** (*beloved*) mother of Josiah 2 K 22^{1}; 𝔊 Ιεδεια, 𝔊L Ιεδιδα.

† **יְדִידְיָה n.pr.m.** (*beloved of Yah*, cf Sab ודדאל DHM ZMG 1875, 604, 1883 15)—name given to Solomon by Nathan, וַיִּקְרָא אֶת־שְׁמוֹ ידידיָהּ בַּעֲבוּר יהוה 2 S 12^{25}; 𝔊 Ιεδεδι, 𝔊L Ιεδδιδια.

† **יִדּוֹ n.pr.m.** **1.** a Manassite, 1 Ch 27^{21}, 𝔊 Ιαδδαι. **2.** one of those who took foreign wives Ezr 10^{43} Kt (Qr יַדַּי; cf Palm. ידי = *dilectus* Vog$^{No. 5}$), 𝔊 Δια, A Ιαδει, 𝔊L Ιαδιαι.

יַדַּי n.pr m. v יִדּוֹ.

† **מֵידָד n.pr m** one who (with אֶלְדָּד) prophesied in the camp of Isr Nu 11$^{26.27}$ (JE), 𝔊 Μωδαδ.

† [**יָדָה**] **vb. throw, cast** (Ar وَدَى *exeruit, emisit*, II IV. *emisit* (all now in special senses), Eth. ወደየ: *throw, cast* on or in (very oft, cf. ወደደ:), whence **Hiph.** *give thanks, confess* (orig *acknowledge*?) is commonly derived, perhaps from gestures accompanying the act, v Thes Lag$^{Or\ II\ 22}$, yet connexion uncertain; Aram Pa יַדִּי, Aph אוֹדִי *confess*, ܐܘܕܝ, ܬܘܕܝܬܐ *id.*; but Eth. አስተዋደየ: *accuse*, perh. also fr gesture, Palm מודא *render thanks*, oft in votive inscrr., see Vog on No. 79; עבד ומודא Vog$^{No\ 101}$ = εὐχαρίστως ἀνέθηκε, מודן כל יום Vog$^{No\ 93.1}$, ידתא *pious* Vog$^{No\ 29}$)—**Qal** *Imv* יְדוּ אֶל־ *shoot* (arrows) *at* Je 50^{14} (rd prob, with some Codd יְרוּ). **Pi** *Impf* וַיַּדּוּ בִי La 3^{53} *and they cast* (stones) *on me*; *Inf* יַדּוֹת Zc 2^{4} *to cast down* (the horns of the nations).

Hiph. (connex with ידה *throw*, obscure, yet v supr) *Pf.* הוֹדוּ 1 K 8^{33} + 3 t; הוֹדִינוּ ψ 75$^{2\,2}$, *Impf* יוֹדֶה יְהוֹדֶה Ne 11^{17} (on form v. Ges § 53. R. 7); ψ 6^{6}, 1 s sf אֲהוֹדֶנּוּ 28^{7} (Ges$^{l.c}$), אוֹדֶנּוּ 42$^{6\ 12}$ 43^{5}; pl יוֹדוּ 99^{3} + 6 t, sf. יְהוֹדוּךָ 45^{18} (Ges$^{l.c}$); יוֹדֻךָ 49^{19}, etc + 41 t Impf, *Imv* הוֹדוּ Is 12^{4} + 16 t; הֹדוּ ψ 107^{1}; *Inf.* הוֹדוֹת 1 Ch 25^{3} + 11 t.; הוֹדֹת Ezr 3^{11}, הֹדוֹת 1 Ch 16^{7} + 4 t. (see Baer ψ 92^{2}); *Pt* מוֹדֶה Pr 28^{13}, pl. מוֹדִים 1 Ch 29^{13},—**1.** *give thanks, laud, praise*; **a** c acc (1) of men, Judah Gn 49^{8} (poetic play on name), Job (ironical) Jb 40^{14}, the king ψ 45^{18}, the rich 49^{19}, (2) of ׳י, Gn 29^{35} (J expl name יהודה); elsewhere (mostly ψψ and Ch) of *ritual* worship (v. Lag$^{Or\ II\ 22\,f}$), obj שֵׁם ׳י Is 25^{1} ψ 44^{9} 54^{8} 99^{3} 138^{2} 142^{8}; פֶּלֶא ׳י 89^{6}, יהוה 7^{18} 9^{2} 109^{30} 111^{1}; יָהּ 118^{19}; sf ךָ- referring to God 30$^{10.13}$ 35^{18} 43^{4} 52^{11} 67$^{4.4.6.6}$ 71^{22} 76^{11} 88^{11} 118$^{21.28}$ 119^{7} 138^{1} 139^{14} Is 38$^{18\ 19}$ (song of Hez); ־ֶנּוּ ψ 42$^{6\ 12}$ 43^{5}, מִשִּׁירִי אֲהוֹדֶנּוּ 28^{7} *with my song will I praise him*; אוֹדְךָ ׳י *I will praise thee* ׳י 2 S 22^{50} = ψ 18^{50} = 108^{4}, Is 12^{1} (exilic hymn); אדני ψ 57^{10} 86^{12}, cf 138^{4} 145^{10}. **b.** sq לְ, only of the ritual worship: לְשֵׁם ׳י ψ 106^{47} = 1 Ch 16^{35}, ψ 122^{4} 140^{14}; לְזֵכֶר קָדְשׁוֹ 30^{5} 97^{12}, לי׳ 1 Ch 16$^{4.7\ 41}$ 23^{30} 25^{3} 2 Ch 5^{13} 7^{6} 20^{21} ψ 33^{2} 92^{2} 105^{1} = 1 Ch 16^{8} = Is 12^{4}, הודו לי׳ כי טוב *give thanks to* ׳י *for he is good* ψ 106^{1} 107^{1} 118$^{1\ 29}$ 136^{1} 1 Ch 16^{34}; so Je 33^{11} (sq אֶת־י׳); cf הוד(ו)ת לאלהים 2 Ch 7^{3} Ezr 3^{11}; יודו לי׳ חסדו ψ 107$^{8\ 15.21.31}$; Ne 12^{46} ψ 136^{1}; לאדני v^{3}; לאל v^{26}; sfs referring to God. לְךָ 6^{6} 79^{13} 119^{62}; לוֹ 100^{4}; אלהים + לך 75$^{2\,2}$ 1 Ch 29^{13}, abs 2 Ch 31^{2} Ne 11^{17} 12^{24} all of the ritual worship. **2.** *confess*, **a.** the name of God, ‖ התפלל, התחנן, שׁוב, 1 K 8$^{33.35}$ = 2 Ch 6$^{24.26}$. **b.** עֲלֵי פשׁע ψ 32^{5} (‖ לֹא כִסִּיתִי); מודה ועזב (פשׁעיו) Pr 28^{13} *confessing and forsaking* (his transgressions; opp. מְכַסֶּה).

Hithp. *Pf* הִתְוַדָּה Lv 5^{5} 16^{21}; הִתְוַדּוּ 26^{40} Nu 5^{7}, *Impf.* 1 s אֶתְוַדֶּה Dn 9^{4}, pl. יִתְוַדּוּ Ne 9^{2}, *Inf.* sf הִתְוַדֹּתוֹ Ezr 10^{1}; *Pt* מִתְוַדֶּה Ne 1^{6} Dn 9^{20}, pl מִתְוַדִּים 2 Ch 30^{22} Ne 9^{3},—**1.** *confess*, abs. Ezr 10^{1} Ne 9^{3} Dn 9^{4}, c. acc עָוֹן Lv 16^{21} (P), 26^{40} (H); חטאת Nu 5^{7} (P), Dn 9^{20}, אֲשֶׁר חָטָא Lv 5^{5} (P); על חטאות Ne 1^{6} 9^{2}. **2.** *give thanks*, ליהוה, in the ritual worship 2 Ch 30^{22}.

† **הוּיְדוֹת n.f.pl. songs of praise**,—Ne 12^{8}, so Thes MV, but form strange and dub; acc. to Ew § 165 b abstr. הֻיְּדוֹת (many MSS.) *praising*; so Be Ke Ot; Ol § 220 rds inf. הוֹדוֹת, so SS.

† **תּוֹדָה n.f. thanksgiving**, ת׳ Lv 7^{12} + 23 t.; cstr. תּוֹדַת Lv 7$^{13\ 15}$, pl. תּוֹדוֹת ψ 56^{13} + 3 t.; תודֹת Ne 12$^{31\ 40}$;—**1.** *give praise to* ׳י Jos 7^{19} (JE; ‖ שִׂים כָּבוֹד לי׳), Ezr 10^{11}, in both of praise rendered by acknowledging and abandoning sin; v Di on Jos, and on Ezr Ot and esp. Ryle, cf. vb ידה c. לְ, so RVm, > Thes MV SS Be RV al. *confession*. **2.** *thanksgiving in songs of liturgical worship* קול ת׳ ψ 26^{7} 42^{5} Jon 2^{10}; ‖ שיר ψ 69^{31} Ne 12^{27}; ‖ זְמִרוֹת ψ 95^{2}; ‖ קוֹל זִמְרָה Is 51^{3}, ‖ תהלה ψ 100^{4}; ‖ כִּנּוֹר 147^{7}. **3.** *thanksgiving choir, procession, line, company* Ne 12$^{31\ 38.40}$, prob also Je 30^{19} (‖ קוֹל מְשַׂחֲקִים). **4.** *thank-offering* קטר ת׳ Am 4^{5} (‖ נְדָבוֹת), a division of זֶבַח הַשְּׁלָמִים, זבח ת׳ שְׁלָמָיו Lv 7$^{12\,\ast}$ v$^{13\ 15}$,

ת׳ (ה)זבח v ^{12b} (all P), 22^{29} (H), זבחים ותודות 2 Ch 29$^{31\,31}$ זבח זבח(י) ת׳, זבחי שְׁלָמִים ות׳ 33^{16}, ψ 107^{22} 116^{17}, לתודה מבאי(ם) ת׳ Je 17^{26} 33^{11}; ψ 100^{1} (title); in ψψ ‖ נדרים. זֶבַח ת׳ *offer a thank-offering* 50$^{14.23}$ (see Br$^{MP\ 239}$); שלם ת׳ 56^{13}.

†יְדֻתוּן, יְדוּתוּן, יְדִיתוּן **n.pr.m.** usu. יְדוּתוּן; יְדֻתוּן 2 Ch 5^{12} 35^{15}; ידיתון ψ 39^{1} 77^{1} Ne 11^{17} 1 Ch 16^{38}; chief of one of the three choirs of the temple (only Chr & ψ-titles) 1 Ch 9^{16} 16$^{38.41.42}$ 25$^{1.3.6}$ 2 Ch 5^{12}, the king's seer 35^{15}; his descendants formed one of the perpetual temple choirs בני ידותון 1 Ch 16^{42} 25$^{1.3}$ 2 Ch 29^{14}, בֶּן־יְדִיתוּן Ne 11^{17} In ψ-titles על ידותון ψ 62^{1}, 77^{1} (Qr); לִידִיתוּן 39^{1} (לְ error for עַל־), all = *after the manner of* (the choir of) *Yeduthun* (musical term acc. to RS$^{OTJC\ 422,\ 2nd\ ed\ 143}$) —v. also Lag$^{Or\ II\ 16ff}$ and n pr. הֵימָן (sub אמן), אֵיתָן (sub יתן), אָסָף.

†יְדָיָה **n.pr.m.** **1.** a Simeonite chief 1 Ch 4^{37}, 𝔊 Ιδια, 𝔊L Ιεδδαα **2** a builder at the wall Ne 3^{10}, 𝔊 Ιεδαια, 𝔊L Ιεδδεια.

יְדִידְיָה v. sub ידד supr

יְדָיָה v sub ידה supr

יְדִיעֲאֵל v. sub ידע infr.

ידיתון = ידותון v sub ידה

†יִדְלָף **n.pr.m.** son of Nahor Gn 22^{22} (J) (√דלף ? = *he weepeth*?) 𝔊 Ιελδαφ, 𝔊L Ιεδλαφ.

יָדַע $_{T\,943}$ **vb.** know (NH *id.*, Aram. יְדַע, ܝܕܥ, Ph ידע, Eth. አእመረ: II 1. *indicate, announce, narrate;* As *idû, know*, COT^{Gloss}; Sab. ידע, esp. in cpd. n.pr. DHM$^{ZMG\ 1875,\ 612}$)—**Qal** *Pf.* יָדַע Gn 4^{1}+; יָדָע Lv 5^{1}+; sf. יְדָעוֹ Dt 34^{10} Jb 28^{7}; יְדָעָהּ Gn 24^{16} 1 K 1^{4}; יְדָעָנוּ Is 63^{16}; 3 fs. יָדְעָה Ju 11^{39} +4 t; 2 ms. יָדַעְתָּ Gn 30^{26}+; יָדַעְתָּה 2 S 2^{26}; יָדַעַתְּ Ru 2^{11} 1 K 2^{15}; יָדַעַתְּ Je 50^{24}; וְיָדַעַתְּ consec. Ru 3^{4}+6 t. (incl. Ez 22^{16}, Co וידעתם, so 𝔊 𝔗) +Ez 28^{22} Co (for וְיָדְעוּ), so 𝔊; יָדַעְתִּי Gn 4^{9}+; sf. יְדַעְתִּיךָ Ex 33^{12}+2 t; יְדַעְתִּיו Gn 18^{19}, יְדַעְתִּים Pr 30^{18}; ידעתין Is 48^{7}, יָדְעוּ Gn 19^{8}+; יָדָעוּ 2 K 4^{39}+; יְדָעוּן Dt 8$^{3\,16}$ (Dr$^{§6\,n}$); 2 mpl יְדַעְתֶּם Gn 44^{15}+; 2 fpl. יְדַעְתֶּן Gn 31^{6}, וִידַעְתֶּן consec. Ez 13$^{21.23}$, etc; *Impf.* יֵדַע Is 7^{16}+; יֵדָע Jos 22^{22}+ 5 t.; יֵידָע ψ 138^{6} (rd. prob. יֵידַע v. Ges$^{§69,\ 2R.\ 3}$); וַיֵּדַע Gn 4^{17}+; sf. יֵדָעֶנּוּ Je 17^{9}, וְיֵדָעֵם Ho 14^{10}; *Imv* דַּע Gn 20^{7}+10 t; דְּעָה Pr 24^{14}; דָּע Ec 11^{19}, sf דָּעֵהוּ Pr 3^{6}, דעי Je 2^{19}+4 t; דעו Nu 32^{23}+ 15 t.; *Inf. cstr.* דעה Ex 2^{4}, דַּעַת Gn 3^{22}+; דַּעְתִּי Dt 9^{24}, etc, *Inf. abs* יָדוֹעַ Gn 43^{7} Jos 23^{13}; יָדֹעַ Gn 15^{3}+11 t; *Pt. act* יֹדֵעַ Gn 3^{5}+; f. יֹדַעַת Nu 31^{17}+2 t.; יֹדְעִים 2 K 17^{26}+; *pass* וִידוּעַ cstr. Is 53^{3}; pl. וִידֻעִים Dt 1$^{13\,15}$;—**1. a.** *know, learn to know*, good and evil Gn 3^{22} (J), sq. אֶת־אֲשֶׁר 1 S 28^{9}, מִסְפַּר הָעָם 2 S 24^{2}; *anything* מְאוּמָה 1 S 20^{39}; לא יָדַע אתו מאומה Gn 36^{6} (v. II. את **1 b**), so v^{8}; כָּל־דָּבָר 2 S 15^{11}, subj God, knowing fowls ψ 50^{11}; way to wisdom Jb 28^{23}, etc., of bird of prey נָתִיב לֹא יְדָעוֹ עָיִט Jb 28^{7}; the price of wisdom Jb 28^{13}, something future יום מותי Gn 27^{2} (J); esp sq cl. Gn 12^{11} (J) *I know that thou art a woman of fair appearance,* 22^{12} (E), Ec 1^{17}, לא ידעתי Gn 28^{16}, answering qu. Where? without other obj, 4^{9} (both J); sq acc. + בְּ, *in, in the matter of* (v. ב **I 2 b**) לא יָדַע עַבְדְּךָ בְּכָל־ זאת דָּבָר קָטֹן או גדול 1 S 22^{15} *thy servant knoweth not of all this anything, little or much;* sq ב (rare), *gain knowledge of, learn of* or *about*, c inf., הֲתֵדַע בשום־אֱלוֹהַּ עֲלֵיהֶם Jb 37^{15} *dost thou know about God's enjoining upon them?* also c. subst. איש אַל־יֵדַע בַּדְּבָרִים הָאֵלֶּה Je 38^{24} *let not a man know of these words*, similarly sq עַל, only הֲתֵדַע עַל־מִפְלְשֵׂי־עָב Jb 37^{16} *dost thou know concerning the balancings of clouds?* (in Jb 12^{9} בְּ is instr, as Gn 15^{8} ψ 41^{12}), sq. מִן, ראו ודעו מִכֹּל־ הַמַּחֲבֹאִים 1 S 23^{23} *observe and get knowledge of all the hiding-places;* but sq. obj cl + מִן of source, קֶדֶם יָדַעְתִּי מֵעֵדֹתֶיךָ כִּי ψ 119^{152} *long ago I gained knowledge out of thy testimonies that* etc.; sq לְ, *have knowledge of*, + יָדַעְתָּ לְאִוַּלְתִּי ψ 69^{6} *thou knowest my foolishness*, esp. וידע כי אני יהוה *and he shall* (*thou shalt*, etc.) *know that I am Yahweh* Ex 10^{2} (R), 6^{7} 14^{4} 16^{12} 29^{46} (all P), Ez 6$^{7\,10\,13}$ + oft in Ezek, 1 K 20$^{13.28}$, sq. acc, which is really subj of foll. cl., Gn 18^{19} (J) *I know him that he will*, etc. 2 S 3^{25} (Ges$^{§117.\ 1.\ R.\ 6}$). **b.** *perceive* Gn 19$^{33.35}$ (J; obj cl., inf. c. בְּ), with added idea of *observing, taking note of*, a place, acc. Ru 3^{4}, c. ב, יָדַעַתְּ בְּצָרוֹת נַפְשִׁי ψ 31^{8} (‖ רָאָה אֶת־). **c.** ‖ ראה, imv דע וראה *perceive and see* 1 S 12^{17} 24^{12}; *find out and discern* 14^{38} 23^{22}; in reverse order, ראו ודעו only 23^{23} (v. **a** supr.), Je 5^{1} (v. Dr^{Sm}).—Vid. also **g** infr. **d.** *discriminate, distinguish* הַאֵדַע בֵּין־טוֹב לְרָע 2 S 19^{36}, cf. Dt 1^{39} (no בין); לא יָדַע בֵּין־יְמִינוֹ לִשְׂמֹאלוֹ Jon 4^{11} *they cannot distinguish between their right hand and their left.* **e.** *know by experience*, וִידַעְתֶּם בְּכָל־ לְבַבְכֶם וּבְכָל־נַפְשְׁכֶם כִּי Jos 23^{14} (D) *and know in all your hearts, and all your souls, that*, etc.;

learn to know 'י Ho 13^{14}; *learn* (a bitter lesson) Ho 9^{7} Is 9^{8} ψ 14^{4}, *experience* 'י's vengeance Ez 25^{14} ψ 14^{4}(abs.), quietness Jb 20^{20}. **f.** *recognise, admit, acknowledge, confess* Je 3^{13} 14^{20} Is 59^{12} ψ 51^{5} **g.** *consider* דעו מַה־תַּעֲשׂוּ Ju 18^{14}, ‖ ראה, imv דעו וראו, דע וראה, 2 S 24^{13} 1 K 20$^{7.22}$, also וְיָדַעְתָּ עִם־לְבָבֶךָ כִּי Dt 8^{5} *and thou shalt consider with* (*in*) *thy heart, that,* 4^{39} **h.** לא ידע *not know = not expect* Is 47^{11} ψ 35^{8} **2** *know a person, be acquainted with* Gn 29^{5} (J), Ex 1^{8} (E), Jb 42^{11}, *know* 'י 24^{1}; c לא, obj esp other gods, strange land, etc = have no knowledge of, or acquaintance with, have not heard of, esp Dt Je — Dt 11^{28} 13$^{3.7.14}$ 28^{64} 29^{25} 32^{17} (poem), Je 7^{9} 9^{15} 14^{18} 16^{13} 17^{4} 19^{4} 22^{28} 44^{3}; pt act. *acquaintance* Jb 19^{13}, †pt pass *acquainted with* אִישׁ מַכְאֹבוֹת וִידוּעַ חֹלִי Is 53^{3} (lit *known of sickness,* v Thes Ew Che Di Du), *well-known* (with implied trustworthiness) Dt 1$^{13.15}$+, of beasts *knowing* owner and master's crib Is 1^{3} (cf Je 8^{7}); esp of knowing God ('י) לֹא יָדַעְתִּי אֶת־יי Ex 5^{2} (J), involving intelligent worship, obedience, etc Ju 2^{10} 1 S 2^{12} (rd יֹדֵעַ for MT יָדַע, Dr), 3^{7} Ho 2^{22} 8^{2} 5^{4} Jb 18^{21} ψ 79^{6} (v. also דַּעַת **2 b**), of God's *knowing* persons, etc, thoroughly Ho 5^{3} Jb 11^{11}, knowing the heart 1 K 8^{39} 2 Ch 6^{30} ψ 139^{4}; *knowing* his true servants, *recognising* and *acknowledging* them 2 S 7^{20} Na 1^{7} 1 Ch 17^{18}+; יְדַעְתִּיךָ בְשֵׁם Ex 33^{12} (JE), = *take notice of, regard* ψ 1^{6} 31^{7} 37^{18}, so of Isr. as chosen people Am 3^{2} Ho 13^{5} (As *ilu idûšu, God regardeth him,* Hpt$^{BAS I 15}$) cf Gn 18^{19}(J) **3** *know a person* carnally, of sexual intercourse, sq acc: man subj Gn 4$^{1.17.25}$ 24^{16} 38^{26} (all J), 1 S 1^{19} Ju 19^{25} 1 K 1^{4}, woman subj Gn 19^{8} (J), Nu 31$^{17.18.35}$ (all P), Ju 11^{39}; יֹדַעַת מִשְׁכַּב זָכָר Ju 21^{11}, לֹא יָדְעָה אִישׁ לְמִשְׁכַּב זָכָר v^{12}; man subj and obj (of sodomy) Gn 19^{5} (J), Ju 19^{22} **4. a.** *know how* to do a thing, be able to do it, oft c. לא and sq inf לֹא יָדְעוּ עֲשׂוֹת־נְכֹחָה Am 3^{10} *they know not how to do right;* לֹא יָדַעְתִּי דַּבֵּר Je 1^{6} 6^{15} 1 K 3^{7} Is 56$^{11.11}$, c ל 50^{4} Ec 10^{15}, לֹא יָדַע לְהִזָּהֵר Ec 4^{13} *know not how to be admonished* (v^{17} know *that*), inf abs ידע מָאוֹס בָּרָע וּבָחוֹר בַּטּוֹב Is 7$^{15.16}$ **b** *be skilful in,* esp pt., sq acc יֹדֵעַ צַיִד Gn 25^{27} (J) *skilled in hunting,* ידע ספר *skilled in a book, learned* Is 29$^{11.12.12}$, as pl. cstr יוֹדְעֵי נֶהִי Am 5^{16} *knowers of lamentation,* professional mourners, יֹדְעֵי הַיָּם 1 K 9^{27} *skilled in the sea,* 2 Ch 8^{18}; esp sq inf יֹדֵעַ נַגֵּן 1 S 16^{18} *skilled in playing,* 1 K 5^{20} 2 Ch 2$^{6.7.13}$ יֹדֵעַ מְנַגֵּן בַּכִּנּוֹר 1 S 16^{16} *knowing,* (as) *a player on the lyre* (v Dr) **5.** abs *have knowledge, be wise* לַיֹּדְעִים Ec 9^{11} (‖ חֲכָמִים, נבנים); esp have knowledge of God and duty, or in practical affairs Is 1^{3} (‖ בין), 56^{10}, oft. c acc cogn. דַּעַת Pr 17^{27} 30^{3}, בִּינָה Is 29^{24} Pr 4^{1} 2 Ch 2^{12}, cf. יוֹדְעֵי בִינָה לָעִתִּים 1 Ch 12^{33} (Baer), Est 1^{13}, also יֹדְעֵי דַעַת וּמְבִינֵי מַדָּע Dn 1^{4}, יֹדְעֵי דָּת וָדִין v^{13}, obj חָכְמָה וּמוּסָר Pr 1^{2} (‖ בִּין), חָכָם ‖ שֵׂכֶל וּבִינָה 2 Ch 2^{11} (‖ חָכְמָה), הבין אמרי בינה ‖ Pr 24^{14} Ec 8^{16}.

†**Niph.** *Pf* נוֹדַע Gn 41^{21} + 10 t, וְנוֹדַע consec 1 S 6^{3} + 2 t, 3 fs וְנוֹדְעָה Lv 4^{14} Is 66^{14}, etc; *Impf.* יִוָּדַע Gn 41^{31} + 10 t, יִוָּדֵעַ Pr 10^{9}, וַיִּוָּדַע Est 2^{22}, 3 fs תִּוָּדֵעַ Pr 14^{33}; 2 fs תִּוָּדְעִי Ru 3^{3}, וָאִוָּדַע Ez 20^{5}, *Inf.* sf. הִוָּדְעִי Je 31^{19}, *Pt* נוֹדָע ψ 76^{2} + 2 t, —**1.** *be made known, be* or *become known,* of things Gn 41^{31} (sq ב), Ex 2^{14} (both E), Lv 4^{14} (P), Ju 16^{9} 2 S 17^{19} Na 3^{17} Zc 14^{7} (sq ל), ψ 77^{20} 79^{10} (sq. ב), 88^{13} (sq ב); of hand of 'י Is 66^{14} (sq. את), c subj cl. Ex 21^{36} 33^{16} (both JE), Dt 21^{1} 1 S 6^{3} (sq ל), 1 K 18^{36} Ez 36^{32} (sq. ל), Ru 3^{14} Ec 6^{10} Est 2^{22} (sq ל); of pers., Pr 31^{23} (sq ב) Is 61^{9} (sq ב and בתוך); of 'י ψ 76^{2} (sq. ב), = *be revealed, discovered,* of pers 1 S 22^{6} Je 28^{9} Pr 10^{9}, of things Ne 4^{9} Pr 12^{16} 14^{33}. **2.** *make oneself known,* of pers., sq. ל Ru 3^{3}, usu of God ('י) Ex 6^{3} (P; ‖ וָאֵרָא אֶל־), Is 19^{21} Ez 20^{5}, sq. לְעֵינֵי 38^{23}, sq אֶל־ 20^{9}; sq ב 35^{11} ψ 48^{4}; without prep. 9^{17} **3.** *be perceived* (pass of **Qal**), of perception by the eye Gn 41^{21} (E), ψ 74^{5} **4.** *be instructed* (pass of **Hiph.**) Je 31^{19}, in spiritual sense, through chastisement

†**Pi.** *Pf* 2 ms יִדַּעְתָּ, only ידעתה שַׁחַר מקמו Jb 38^{12} Kt, rd with Qr יִדַּעְתָּ הַשַּׁחַר *cause to know,* sq 2 acc; so ψ 104^{19} acc to Bae, who rds. יִדַּע, after Aq Symm

†**Po.** *Pf* 1 s. יוֹדַעְתִּי 1 S 21^{3} *I have caused to know,* i.e directed, sq acc, but rd יוֹעַדְתִּי or יָעַדְתִּי, fr. יעד, so 𝔊 We Dr

†**Pu.** *Pt known* מידעת Is 12^{5} Kt (Qr מוּדַעַת v. **Hoph.**), elsewhere as subst. = *acquaintance* מְיֻדָּעִי ψ 55^{14}; מְיֻדָּעָיו 2 K 10^{11}; מְיֻדָּעַי ψ 88^{9} Jb 19^{14} (‖ קְרוֹבַי), ψ 88^{19} (‖ אהב and רע); מְיֻדָּעַי ψ 31^{12}, Kt מידע Ru 2^{1} (Qr מוֹדַע q.v. infr)

†**Hiph.** *Pf* הוֹדִיעַ ψ 98^{2}; הוֹדִיעַנִי Je 11^{18}, הוֹדַעְתָּ 1 K 1^{27} + 2 t; הוֹדַעְתָּ Jb 26^{3}, etc, *Impf* יוֹדִיעַ ψ 103^{7} Is 38^{19}, *juss.* יֹדַע Nu 16^{5}, וַיֹּדַע Ju 8^{16}; יוֹדִיעֶנּוּ Is 40$^{13.14}$, 2 ms תּוֹדִיעַ Hb 3^{2}; תּוֹדִיעֵנִי ψ 16^{11} 51^{8}; 1 s אוֹדִיעַ ψ 89^{2} Ez 39^{7}; אוֹדִיעָה Pr 1^{23} Is 5^{5}, יוֹדִיעוּ Jb 32^{7}; יוֹדִעֵם Ez 44^{23}; נוֹדִיעָה 1 S 14^{12}, *Imv.* הוֹדַע Pr 9^{9} + 3 t (הוֹדַע ψ 90^{12}), sf. הוֹדִיעֵנִי Jb 10^{2} + 6 t, etc; *Inf cstr* הוֹדִיעַ 2 S 7^{21} + 3 t,

הודיע 1 Ch 17[19]; הוֹדִיעֵנִי 1 S 28[15], etc.; *Pt.* מוֹדִיעֲךָ Dn 8[19]; מוֹדִיעָם Je 16[21], מודיעים Is 47[13] 2 Ch 23[13]; —*make known, declare,* c acc. rei Nu 16[5] (P), Ez 39[7] 1 Ch 17[19] Jb 26[3] ψ 89[2] 98[2] 106[8]; obj. om. Hb 3[2], *teach,* c. acc rei Jb 32[7]; sq inf. ψ 90[12] and (peculiarly) מ׳ להלל 2 Ch 23[13] i.e. *led in praising;* c. לְ pers Pr 9[9]; c. acc pers. Is 40[13] Ju 8[16] (but rd. וַיָּדָשׁ, v. דושׁ); *make known, declare,* c acc. rei, + לְ pers. Ex 18[20] Dt 4[9] Ne 8[12] 9[14], ψ 78[5] 103[7] 145[12] Is 38[19] 64[1], c. cl of thing, + לְ pers. 1 S 10[8]; *make one know,* c. cl. of thing and acc (sf) pers Ex 33[12] Dt 8[3] 1 S 6[2] 16[3] 28[15] Jb 10[2] 37[19], c. acc rei + sf pers הודִעֵנִי נָא אֶת־ דְּרָכֶךָ וְאֵדָעֲךָ Ex 33[13] (JE) *make me, I pray, to know thy ways, that I may know thee;* Je 16[21] Ez 20[4] 22[2] 43[11] Is 40[14] (|| וַיְלַמְּדֵהוּ דַּעַת, also v[a] וַיְבִינֶנּוּ), Pr 22[21] Jb 13[23] ψ 16[11] 25[4] (|| לַמְּדֵנִי), v[14] (on inf. c. לְ v Ges[§ 114. 2. R. 2. Exx]), 39[5] 51[8] 143[8] (|| הַשְׁמִיעֵנִי); עֲוֹנִי לֹא־כִסִּיתִי || חַטָּאתִי אוֹדִיעֲךָ 32[5]; sq. 2 separate acc. Gn 41[39] (E), 1 S 14[12] Is 5[5] Ez 20[11] 16[2] Pr 1[23] Dn 8[19]; acc. pers. om. Ex 18[16] (E); acc. rei om. Jos 4[22] = *teach* one (D), so Is 40[13], 2 S 7[21] 1 K 1[27]; = *answer* Jb 38[3] 40[7] 42[4]; c. sf. pers., acc. rei om Je 11[18] 16[21] Pr 22[19]; sq. acc. rei + בְּ ψ 77[15] *thou hast made known thy might among the peoples,* Is 12[4] 1 Ch 18[8] = ψ 105[1]; sq cl. + בְּ pers. Ho 5[9]; sq. בֵּין, *teach the difference between, to discriminate between* בין הַטָּמֵא לְטָהוֹר Ez 22[26], + sf pers. 44[23] (cf. **Qal 1 d**); sq מִן partit מוֹדִעִים לֶחֳדָשִׁים מֵאֲשֶׁר יָבֹאוּ Is 47[13] *who declare, at the new moons, of (the things) which are to come.*

†**Hoph.** *Pf.* הוֹדַע Lv 4[23.28] (v Ko[i. 427]); *Pt.* מוּדַעַת Qr Is 12[5] (> Kt מְיֻדַּעַת);—*made known* (Pt.) Qr Is 12[5] let this *be made known* in (בְּ) all the earth (> Kt Pu. Pt. which is not elsewhere in this sense); sq אֵלָיו if his sin be *made known unto himself* Lv 4[23.28] (P).

†**Hithp.** *Impf.* אֶתְוַדָּע Nu 12[6] (E), sq. אֶל־ *make oneself known to,* of י׳, *Inf* הִתְוַדַּע אֶל־ Gn 45[1] (E), of Joseph.

†יָדָע **n.pr.m.** (Sab. ידע, epith of king, *the knowing, shrewd one* Mordt[ZMG 1876, 37])—a man of Judah 1 Ch 2[28] (יָדָע), v[32].

†[דֵּעַ] **n** [**m.**] **knowledge, opinion** (late)—only sf דֵּעִי Jb 32[6] + 3 t, and pl. דֵּעִים 37[16]; all in speech of Elihu **1.** *knowledge,* תְּמִים ד׳ Jb 37[16] *one perfect in knowledge* (of God). **2.** *judgment, opinion* Jb 36[3], חַוֹּת דֵּעִי 32[6] *to declare my opinion,* so v[10 17].

†דֵּעָה **n.f. knowledge** (strictly Inf. of ידע)—דֵּעָה ψ 73[11] + 3 t.; pl דֵּעוֹת 1 S 2[3] Jb 36[4];—תְּמִים ד׳ Jb 36[4] (of Elihu), of God's knowledge, אֵל ד׳ י׳ 1 S 2[3] *a God of knowledge is* י׳ (on pl. v. Dr); יֵשׁ דֵּעָה בְעֶלְיוֹן ψ 73[11] (|| אֵיכָה יָדַע־אֵל), *knowledge,* with י׳ as obj. Is 11[9] (where verbal force of noun appears); as taught by proph. Is 28[9], וְרָעוּ אֶתְכֶם דֵּעָה וְהַשְׂכֵּיל Je 3[15] of י׳'s shepherds (i.e. future ideal rulers) Gr prop (plausibly) רָעָה, after 𝔊, v. also Gie.

†דַּעַת **n f.** [ψ 139, 6 Dn 12 4] (**m.** Pr 2[10] 14[6], poss Jb 33[3] Ew[§ 174 g]) **knowledge** (prop Inf, which appears clearly Gn 2[9 17] Je 22[16])—abs דַּעַת Gn 2[9] + 35 t; דָּעַת Jos 20[3] + 35 t, cstr. דַּעַת Nu 24[16] + 10 t.; sf דַּעְתִּי Pr 22[17]; דַּעְתֶּךָ Jb 10[7], דַּעְתֵּךְ Is 47[10]; דַּעְתּוֹ Pr 3[20] Is 53[11]; דַּעְתְּכֶם Jb 13[2]; דַּעְתָּם Is 44[25],—**1. a.** *knowledge, perception* in phrase בִּבְלִי ד׳ Dt 4[42] = *unintentionally,* 19[4] Jos 20[3] (where P's synonym is בִּשְׁגָגָה v[3.9], cf Nu 35[11 15]), v[5]; *without knowing* מִבְּלִי ד׳ Is 5[13] (= before they knew it, suddenly). **b.** = *skill* (in workmanship) Ex 31[3] 35[31] (both P; both || תבונה and חָכְמָה), 1 K 7[14] (sq inf); creative skill Is 40[14] (|| דֶּרֶךְ תְּבוּנוֹת, אֹרַח מִשְׁפָּט). **c.** of proph knowledge יֹדֵעַ ד׳ עליון Nu 24[16] (JE), cf ψ 19[3]. **d.** esp. knowledge with moral quality Gn 2[9 17] (J; in both verbal force, הַד׳ טוֹב וָרָע *the knowing good and evil*) **e.** *knowledge* possessed by God Jb 10[7] ψ 139[6] Pr 3[20] (|| חָכְמָה and תבונה), 21[12]; taught by God to men ψ 94[10] 119[66] (|| טוּב טַעַם), Pr 2[6] (|| חָכְמָה and תבונה) **f.** דַּעַת־רוּחַ = *windy* (unreal) *knowledge* Jb 15[2]. **2.** esp in WisdLt = *discernment, understanding, wisdom:* **a.** Jb 13[2] 33[3] (ד׳ שְׂפָתַי), לֹא בְדַעַת Jb 34[35] (|| חכמה), Pr 8[9 10] (|| מוסר), 10[14] 11[9] 18[15 15] 22[12] 29[7], cf. Is 32[4] 53[11] Je 10[14] = 51[17]; בִּבְלִי דעת Jb 35[16] 36[12], בְּלִי ד׳ 38[2] 42[3], בְּלֹא ד׳ Pr 19[2]; || תבונה Pr 17[27] Is 44[19]; ד׳ מְזִמּוֹת 8[12]; || מְזִמָּה Pr 1[4] 5[2]; חכמה + ת׳ Pr 24[4], || vb. עָרַם 19[25], || מִצְוֹת 22[20]; || מוּסָר 12[1] 19[27] 23[12], || תורה Mal 2[7]; || חכמה Pr 14[6] Ec 1[16 18] 2[21.26] 7[12] 9[10], connected with חָכָם Pr 21[11] Ec 12[9], דברי חכמים Pr 22[17], Is 33[6] (חכמת) Is 44[25] (חכמים), wisdom of magicians 47[10] Dn 1[4] (|| חָכְמָה and מַדָּע). **b.** in highest sense, *knowledge* of God (incl obedience) Ho 4[1.6] (מִבְּלִי הַדָּעַת), v[6] 6[6] Jb 21[14] Pr 2[5] (|| יראת י׳), so Is 11[2] 58[2] Je 22[16] (verbal force, c. acc), Pr 9[10] (|| חָכְמָה, יראת י׳ || ד׳ קדשים), 30[3] (*id,* || חָכְמָה), v. also (|| יִרְאַת י׳) v[22.29], חָכְמָה מוּסָר || 1[7] יראת י׳ ראשית ד׳ 2[10] (|| חָכְמָה) **c.** opp. אִוֶּלֶת Pr 12[23] 13[16] 14[18] 15[2]

cf. v[7], also v[14]. **d.** איש ד׳ שִׂפְתֵי־ד׳ Pr 14[7] 20[15]; 24[5] (|| גֶּבֶר חָכָם).—Dn 12[4] is dub.; 𝔊 Bev rd. ותרבה הָרָעֹת.

†יְדַעְיָה **n.pr.m.** (Sab. n.pr. ידעאל DHM [ZMG 1875, 606]) priestly name;—**1.** 1 Ch 9[10] 𝔊 Ιωαδε, 24[7] 𝔊 (Ανε)ιδεια. **2.** Ezr 2[36] Ne 7[39] 𝔊 Ιεουδα, (Ι)εδδουα, Ιωαδε. **3.** Ne 11[10] 12[6.19] 𝔊 Δαδεια, Ιαδιας, Ιδειας, etc. **4.** Ne 12[7.21] 𝔊L Ωδουιας. **5.** Zc 6[10.14] 𝔊 (παρὰ) τῶν ἐπεγνωκότων αὐτήν.

†יַדּוּעַ **n.pr.m.** **1.** a chief of the people, one of those sealed Ne 10[22] 𝔊L Ιεδδουα. **2.** a priest, prob. the high priest in time of Alexander the Great Ne 12[11.22] 𝔊 Ιαδου, 𝔊L Ιεδδου (whence Lag [BN 113] rds. יִדּוּעַ).

†יְדִיעֲאֵל **n.pr.m.** (Palm. ידיבעל DHM in MV [10, 983] cf. Sab. n.pr. with ידע DHM [ZMG 1875, 612])—**1.** a Benjamite 1 Ch 7[6.10.11], 𝔊 Αδειηλ, Ιεδιηλ, etc. **2.** one of David's heroes acc. to 1 Ch 11[45] appar. = the Manassite captain of 12[21] (Baer; van d. H v[20]), 𝔊 Ελθειηλ, Ιεδιηλ. **3.** a Korahite porter 1 Ch 26[2] 𝔊 Ιδερηλ, Ιεδιηλ.

†דְּעוּאֵל **n.pr.m.** a Gadite, Nu 1[14] 7[42.47] 10[20], but 𝔊 in all Ραγουηλ, so Sam 𝔖; = רְעוּאֵל Nu 2[14], where, however, 𝔙 and Heb. Codd. ד׳ (all P); v. further sub רעה.

†יִדְּעֹנִי **n.m.** **familiar spirit** (prop. either as *knowing, wise* (acquainted with secrets of unseen world), Ew *vielwisserisch*; or as *intimate acquaintance* of soothsayer, v. RS [JPh xiv. 1885. 127])—abs. יִדְּעֹנִי Dt 18[11] + 2 t.; pl. יִדְּעֹנִים 1 S 28[3] + 6 t.; הַיִּדְּעֹנִי מִן 1 S 28[9], rd. הַיִּדְּעֹנִים מִן (v. 𝔊 Th We Klo Dr); *familiar spirit*, always || אוֹב, אֹבוֹת 1 S 28[3.9] Is 8[19] 19[3] 2 K 21[6] (עשׂה אוב || עוֹנֵן, נִחֵשׁ) = 2 Ch 33[6], 2 K 23[24] Lv 19[31] 20[6.27] (all H; on last two cf. Acts 16[16] and Dr [Dt 18. 11]), Dt 18[11] (|| אוב + דֹּרֵשׁ אֶל־הַמֵּתִים).

†מֹדַע, מוֹדַע **n.m.** **kinsman**, מידע לְ Ru 2[1] Kt, but Qr מוֹדַע *a kinsman* of her husband; fig. מֹדָע לַבִּינָה תִקְרָא Pr 7[4] *a kinsman shalt thou call understanding* (|| אֱמֹר לַחָכְמָה אֲחֹתִי אָתְּ).

†[מֹדַעַת] **n.f.** **kindred, kinship**—sg. sf. מֹדַעְתָּנוּ Ru 3[2] is not Boaz (of) *our kindred?*

†מַדָּע **n.m.** [2 Ch 1, 12] **knowledge, thought** (late); מַדָּע 2 Ch 1[10] + 4 t.; מַדָּעֲךָ Ec 10[20];—**1.** *knowledge* (|| חָכְמָה) of Solomon, 2 Ch 1[10.11.12] Dn 1[4] (|| חָכְמָה and דַּעַת), v[7] (|| הַשְׂכֵּל). **2.** *place of knowledge, mind*, (in our idiom also) *thought* Ec 10[20].

מַדּוּעַ [61] and [(Ez 18, 19)] מַדֻּעַ **adv.** **wherefore?** (prob. contr. from מַה־יָּדוּעַ *what being known?* i.e. from what motive? so Ges Ew [§ 325 c] Ol [§ 222 f], cf. in Gk. τί μαθών;)—*wherefore? on what account?* Gn 26[27] מַדּוּעַ בָּאתֶם אֵלָי, 40[7] Ex 1[18] 2[18] 3[3] (in an indirect question), 5[14] 18[14] Lv 10[17] Jos 17[14] (all in Hex), Ju 5[28.28] 2 S 3[7] 11[10] etc., Is 5[4] 50[2] 63[2] (all in Is.); in Jer. 16 t., oft. rhetorically, after a double question introduced by הֲ . . . אִם, expressing affected surprise: + 2[14] (v. Gf) is Israel a slave (unable to defend himself)? *wherefore*, then, is he become a prey? (some other cause must therefore be found for Israel's misfortune), v[31] 8[5.19.22] 14[19] 22[28] 49[1], cf. 30[6]; Jb 3[12] 18[3] (never in ψ).

יָהּ **n.pr.dei**, v. sub הוה p. 219[b] supr.

†[יָהַב] **vb.** **give** (Aram. יְהַב, ܝܗܒ; Ar. وَهَبَ; Eth. ወሀበ: Sab. והב DHM [ZMG xxix. 1875, 614 f.] ול יהב Id [ib. 603])—only **Qal** *Imv.* הַב Pr 30[15.15]; emph. הָבָה Gn 11[3] + 10 t. (6 t. sq. monosyll.); הָבָה Gn 29[21] before gutt. (Di on Gn 28[2] Kö [i. 418]), fs. הָבִי Ru 3[15]; mpl. הָבוּ Gn 47[16] + 16 t.; הָבוּ לִי Jb 6[22] (on these forms v. also Sta [§ 606 a] Bö [i. 225] Ges [§ 69. 2. R. 2]);—**1.** *give*, sq. acc. Gn 29[21] (E) *give* (me) *my wife*, 47[16] (J), Ru 3[15] Zc 11[12] (*price*); of *giving* (i.e. causing to come forth, in deciding by lot) Urim and Thummim 1 S 14[41.41] (𝔊 We Dr, v. אוּרִים); sq. acc. rei + לִי Gn 30[1] (E), Ju 1[15]; acc. rei + לָנוּ Gn 47[15] (J), ψ 60[13] = 108[13]; הָבוּ לִי Jb 6[22] (no acc. expr.); abs. הַב ׀ הַב Pr 30[15]. **2.** = *set*, sq. acc. (Uriah) + אֶל־מוּל פְּנֵי הַמִּלְחָמָה 2 S 11[15] *set Uriah in the fore-front of the battle.* **3.** with reflex. לְ (v. לְ, **5 h**) = *provide*, c. acc. הָבוּ לָכֶם אֲנָשִׁים חֲכָמִים Dt 1[13]; Jos 18[4] (JE), Ju 20[7] 2 S 16[20]. **4.** *ascribe* glory, etc., to י׳ (God): c. כבוד לְ ψ 29[1.1.2] = 96[7.7.8] = 1 Ch 16[28.28.29]; ה׳ גֹּדֶל לאלהינו Dt 32[3] (poem) *ascribe greatness to our God.* **5.** = *come now* (orig. *grant, permit*), before voluntat.: Gn 11[3.4.7] 38[16] (all J), Ex 1[10] (E).

†[יְהָב] **n.[m.]** lot (as that which is *given*)—הַשְׁלֵךְ עַל י׳ יְהָבְךָ ψ 55[23] *cast on* י׳ *thy lot* (the care, anxiety, etc. which are thy portion; cf. גּוֹל עַל־י׳ דרכך ψ 37[5]).

†[הַבְהָב] **n.m.** **gift** (? on form, then comp. צאצא Ges [§ 84 b viii]; but mng. (and √) dub.; poss. fr. NH הִבְהֵב *roast*, Levy [NHWB i. 447 b])—only pl. sf.: זִבְחֵי הַבְהָבַי יִזְבְּחוּ Ho 8[13] *as the sacrifices of my*

gifts (=*my sacrificial gifts*, so Che) *they sacrifice flesh*.

[יהד] **vb.** v. sub יְהוּדָה infr.

יְהֻדִי, יְהֻדַי **n.pr.m.** v sub הדה p. 213^{a} supr.

† יְהֻד **n.pr.loc.** in Dan, Jos 19^{45}; = mod *Yehûdîyeh*, 8 m. E. of Joppa, and 1½ h. [5½ m] W. of N. fr. Lydda, Survey$^{\text{ii 258}}$ Guérin$^{\text{Judée i. 322}}$; 𝔊 A Ιουθ, 𝔊L [Ι]ουδ (on form of name Jastr$^{\text{JBL xii, 1893, 61 ff}}$ comp. *Ia-u-du*, Tel el-Amarna$^{\text{No 39}}$).

יְהוֹ, **n.pr.** cpd. with, v. sub יהוה supr. pp. 219 ff.

יהוא **n.pr.m.** v sub יהוה supr. p. 219.

יְהוּדָה$_{820}$ **n.pr.m.** et **terr. Judah** (treated Gn 29^{35} 49^{8} (q. v. infr) as if der. fr. Hoph. of ידה = *praised, object of praise* (on ה cf. Hiph. אֲהוֹדֶנּוּ ψ 28^{7}, יְהוּדָה Ne 11^{17}), but this dubious; relation to יְהֻד, ii יהודית unexpl; v. further Jastr$^{\text{JBL xii, 1893, 61 ff.}}$; As. *Ia-u-du*, of land; *Ia-u-da-ai, Judaean* COT^{Gloss})—**I. n.pr.m. 1.** *son of Jacob and Leah*, expl by Leah's words *I will praise* י׳ Gn 29^{35} (J); cf Jacob's prediction, *thy brethren shall praise thee* Gn 49^{8} (poem in JE), see also v$^{9\ 10}$; elsewh. Gn 37^{26} 38^{1} + 14 t. Gn 38, 43$^{3.8}$ 44$^{14.16\ 18}$ 46^{28} (all J), 35^{23} (P), 1 Ch 2$^{1.3}$ Ru 4^{12}; בְּנֵי יְהוּדָה *sons of Judah* Gn 46^{12} Nu 26^{19} (P), 1 Ch 2$^{3.4}$ 4^{1}. **2.** *tribe* descended from Judah Dt 33^{7} (poem), Nu 1^{7} (P), Dt 27^{12}+; בְּנֵי יהודה Nu 1^{26} (P), Jos 14^{6} (D), Ju 1^{8}+; שֵׁבֶט יהודה Jos 7^{16} (J), 1 K 12^{20} 2 K 17^{18} ψ 78^{68}, מַטֵּה בְנֵי יהודה Jos 15$^{1\ 20.21}$ 21^{9} (all P), 1 Ch 6^{50}; elsewhere מַטֵּה יהודה Ex 31^{2} 35^{30} 38^{22} Nu 1^{27} 7^{12} 13^{6} 34^{19} Jos 7$^{1\ 18}$ 21^{4} (all P); איש יהודה Ju 15^{10}+; אנשי יהודה 2 S 2^{4}+, (cf *amelûti* [*sabê*] *Ia-u-du* Tel el-Amarna$^{\text{No. 39}}$ Jastr$^{\text{JBL xii, 1893, 64}}$). **3.** *nation*, of southern kingdom under dynasty of David, as distinguished from northern kingdom of Ephraim or Israel Ho 4^{15} Je 2^{28} 2 Ch 12^{12}+; of the returned exiles Ne 4^{4}; עם יהודה 2 K 14^{21} = 2 Ch 26^{1}, Je 25$^{1.2}$ Ezr 4^{4}, בני יהודה Ho 2^{2} Je 7^{30} 2 Ch 13^{18} 25^{12} 28^{10}; בית יהודה Ho 1^{7} Je 3^{18} Ez 4^{6}+; מַלְכוּת יהודה 2 Ch 11^{17}; personified, בַּת י׳ La 1^{15} 2$^{2.5}$. **4.** Levite, Ezra's time, Ezr 10^{23}. **5.** an overseer of Jerus. Ne 11^{9}. **6.** Levite musician Ne 12^{8}. **7.** priest Ne 12^{36}.

II. n.pr.terr. *land of Judah*, **f.** Is 7^{6} Je 23^{6} = 33^{16}, Jo 4^{20} ψ 114^{2}+; ארץ יְהוּדָה 1 S 22^{5} 2 K 23^{24}+, אדמת יהודה Is 19^{17}, עָרֵי יהודה 2 S 2^{1} 1 K 12^{17} 2 K 18^{13} 23$^{5.8}$ Is 40^{9} 44^{26} Zc 1^{12} ψ 69^{36} La 5^{11}, elsewhere 15 t. Chr., 23 t. Jer.; ביהודה Ju 15^{9}+; מיהודה 1 K 13^{1}+, הר יהודה *the hill-country of Judah* Jos 11^{21} (D), 20^{7} 21^{11} (P), 2 Ch 27^{4}; נֶגֶב יהודה *the south* (*country*) *of Judah* 1 S 27^{10} 2 S 24^{7}, מדבר יהודה Ju 1^{16} ψ 63^{1} (title)

† i. יְהוּדִי **adj.gent** **Jewish**, as subst. **a Jew**;—**adj.m.** איש יְהוּדִי Zc 8^{23}; pl אֲנָשִׁים יְהוּדִים *Jewish men* Je 43^{9} Est 2^{5}, as subst Je 34^{9} Est 3^{4}; הַיְּהוּדִי *the Jew* Est 5^{13} 6^{10} 8^{7} 9$^{29.31}$ 10^{3}, *f.* הַיְהֻדִיָּה *the Jewess* 1 Ch 4^{18}, pl *Jews* יְהוּדִים Je 52$^{28.30}$, הַיְּהוּדִים *the Jews* 2 K 16^{6} 25^{25} Je 32^{12} 38^{19} 40$^{11\ 12}$ 41^{3} 44^{1} Ne 1^{2} 2^{16} 3$^{33.34}$ 4^{6} 5$^{1\ 8.17}$ 6^{6} 13^{23} Est 3$^{6\ 10.13}$ 4$^{3\ 13\ 14\ 16}$ 6^{13} 8$^{3.5.8.9\ 11\ 16.17\ 17}$ 9$^{1\ 1\ 2.3.5.6.10\ 12\ 13.16.19\ 20\ 22.23.24.24.25\ 27\ 28.30}$ 10^{3}, הַיְּהוּדִיִּים Est 4^{7} 8$^{1.7\ 13}$ 9$^{15\ 18}$.

† i. יְהוּדִית **adj.gent., f.** of foregoing, but only as **adv. in Jewish** = *in the Jewish language* 2 K 18$^{26.28}$ = Is 36$^{11\ 13}$ = 2 Ch 32^{18}, Ne 13^{24}.

† ii. יְהוּדִי **n.pr.m.** officer of Jehoiakim Je 36$^{14\ 21\ 21.23}$, 𝔊 Ιουδιν (perh. orig. appell. *Jewish*, of one not so by ancestry, v. Gf Gie)

† ii יְהוּדִית **n.pr.f.** (relation to foregoing names obscure)—wife of Esau Gn 26^{34}, daughter of בְּאֵרִי the Hittite (not named Gn 36^{1}), 𝔊 Ιουδιν.

† [יהד] **vb.denom. Hithp. become a Jew**—only pt מִתְיַהֲדִים Est 8^{17} many of the people of the land *were becoming Jews*

יהוה **n.pr.dei,** v. sub הוה p. 217 ff

יְהוּכַל **n.pr.m.** v. sub יהוה p. 220 supr

יְהַלֶּלְאֵל v. sub ii הלל p. 239^{b} supr.

יַהֲלֹם v. sub הלם p 240^{b} supr.

יהץ (√ of foll; Ar. وَهَصَ *break, split; valide calcavit*, وَهْصَةٌ *terra depressa* et *rotunda*)

† יַהְצָה, יַהַץ **n.pr.loc.** in Moab, site unknown (MI$^{19.20}$ יהץ—(יהץ) Is 15^{4} Je 48^{34}; c. ה loc. יַהְצָה, on border of territory of Amorites (under Sihon) Nu 21^{23} Dt 2^{32}; also בְּיָהְצָה Ju 11^{20}, called יַהְצָה Jos 13^{18} (assigned to Reuben); יַהְצָה 1 Ch 6^{63} (Levit city in Reuben), Je 48^{21}.

יהר (√ of foll.; cf. NH יָהַר Hithp. *shew oneself haughty*, adj יָהִיר; Aram יְהַר Pa. *be haughty*, adj. יְהִירָא; cf. Ar. اِسْتَيْهَرَ *be insane*).

† יָהִיר **adj. proud, haughty,** זֵד יָהִיר לֵץ שְׁמוֹ Pr 21^{24} *a presumptuous man*, (who is) *haughty, scoffer is his name* (+ עוֹשֶׂה בְּעֶבְרַת זָדוֹן), גֶּבֶר יָהִיר וְלֹא יִנְוֶה Hb 2^{5}.

יְהוֹ־ = יוֹ־ **n.pr.** cpd. with, v sub יהוה supr p 222 —viz יוֹאָב, יוֹאָח, יוֹאָחָז, יוֹאֵל, יוֹאָשׁ, יוֹיָכִין, יוֹתָם, יוֹרָם, יוֹקִים, יוֹעָשׁ, יוֹעֵד, יוֹיָרִיב, יוֹיָקִים, etc

†**יוֹב** **n pr.m.** son of Issachar Gn 46^{13}, but rd rather יָשׁוּב as Sam. Nu 26^{24} 1 Ch 7^{1} (Qr) 𝔖 Ol al ; 𝔊 Ιασουφ, 𝔊L Ιασουβ

יוֹבָב **n pr.** v יבב ; יוּבַל, יוֹבֵל v יבל

†**יוֹחָא** **n pr m.** (√& mng dub , ?=יוֹאָח)— **1** a Benjamite 1 Ch 8^{16}. **2.** one of David's heroes 1 Ch 11^{45}

יוֹטָה = יֻטָּה q v sub נטה

יוּכַל **n pr m.** v יְהוּכַל sub יהוה supr p 220

יוֹם **n.m.** $^{Gn\,1\,5}$ **day** (NH *id* ; Aram יוֹמָא, ܝܘܡܐ, Ph ים, MI^{5} ימן, sf ימי 1$^{6\,33}$, pl cstr ימי 1^{8}, sf 3 ms ימה 1^{8}, SI^{3} ים, Zinj יום DHM$^{Sendsch\ Gloss}$, Palm יום Vog$^{No\ 123a\ Oxon\ III}$, Ar يَوْمٌ, Eth ዕለት: Sab ים, יום, Mordt$^{ZMG\ 1876,\ 29}$, יומה DHM$^{ZMG\ 1883,\ 328}$ SabDenkm^{61}, As *umⅿu, ûmu* COT^{Gloss}, deriv. unknown , on √and relation of יום to Ph. ימם, Aram יממ, ܐܝܡܡܐ, v. No$^{ZMG\ 1886,\ 721}$ Ba$^{ZMG\ 1887,\ 632\,f}$) —יוֹם abs Gn 1^{5}+, cstr Gn 2^{4}+, sf. יוֹמְךָ Je 50^{31}, יוֹמוֹ Ex 5^{13}+22 t , יוֹמָם Je 50^{27} Ez 21^{34}, du יוֹמַיִם Ex 21^{21}, יוֹמָיִם Ex 16^{29} Nu 11^{19}, 9^{22},+ יָמִין, יָמִים Ho 6^{2}†, pl. יָמִים Gn 4^{3}+, יָמִם Nu 6^{5}, מִימִים יָמִימָה (Aram form; Ges$^{§87\ 1a}$) Dn 12^{13}, Ex 13^{10}+4 t , cstr יְמֵי Gn 3^{14}+, +יְמוֹת Dt 32^{7} ψ 90^{15}†, sf. יָמַי Jb 7^{6}+9 t , יָמֶיךָ Gn 29^{21}+8 t , יָמֵינוּ Je 35^{8}+7 t , etc , — **1.** *day*, opp night, Gn 7$^{4\,12}$ 8^{22} (all J), 31$^{39.40}$ (E), Ex 24^{18} 34^{28} Nu 11$^{32\,32}$ Jos 10^{13} (all JE), Dt 9$^{9\,11\,18\,25}$ 10^{10} (D), Gn 1$^{5.14\,16\,18}$ (P), 1 S 30^{12} Ju 19$^{8\,9\,9\,11}$ Am 5^{8} 1 K 8^{29} 19^{8} Ne 4^{16} Ec 8^{16}, ‖ לִפְנֵי בוֹא־הַשֶּׁמֶשׁ 2 S 3^{35}, חֹם הַיּ׳ Gn 18^{1} (J) *the heat of the day* 1 S 11^{11} 2 S 4^{5}, עוֹד הַיּ׳ גָּדוֹל Gn 29^{7} (J) *the day is still high*, not near its end , רוּחַ הַיּ׳ 3^{8} *cool of the day;* מִן־הָאוֹר עַד־ מַחֲצִית הַיּ׳ Ne 8^{3} *from dawn until mid-day;* so also prob of mid-day הוֹלֵךְ וָאוֹר עַד־נְכוֹן הַיּוֹם Pr 4^{18} *growing lighter and lighter until the full day;* note phr in Ju 19, עַד־נְטוֹת הַיּ׳ Ju 19^{8} *until the declining of the day,* רָפָה הַיּ׳ לַעֲרוֹב v^{9} *the day hath sunk down to become evening*, חֲנוֹת הַיּ׳ v^{9} *the declining of the day*, הַיּ׳ רַד מְאֹד v^{11} *the day has gone down exceedingly* (is far spent).

2. *Day* as division of time · **a.** *working-day* Ex 20$^{9\,10}$ (E)=Dt 5^{13}, Ex 16$^{26.30.30}$(J), 23^{12} (JE), 31^{15}(P), Lv 23^{3} (H), יְמֵי הַמַּעֲשֶׂה Ez 46^{1} **b.** דֶּרֶךְ יוֹם *a day's journey* Nu 11$^{31\,31}$ (JE), 1 K 19^{4}, מַהֲלַךְ יוֹם אֶחָד Jon 3^{4}, דֶּרֶךְ שְׁלֹשֶׁת יָמִים *a three days' journey* Gn 30^{36} Ex 3^{18} 5^{3} 8^{23} (all J), Nu 10$^{33.33}$ (JE), 33^{8}(P); מַהֲלַךְ שְׁלֹשֶׁת יָמִים Jon 3^{3}, so *seven days' journey* Gn 31^{23} (E), 2 K 3^{9}, without דֶּרֶךְ etc , שְׁלֹשֶׁת יָמִים Ex 15^{22} (E) they went *three days*, etc **c.** to denote duration of various other acts or states *seven days* Gn 7$^{4\,10}$ 8$^{10\,12}$, *forty days* 7^{17} 8^{6}(all J), 150 *days* 7^{24} 8^{3}(both P), 1 S 25^{38} 1 K 8$^{65.65}$ Je 42^{7} Ez 4$^{5\,6}$ 1 Ch 9^{25} Ezr 6^{22} Est 1^{4} etc. In Est 4^{16} **1** & **2** are combined · וְאַל־תִּשְׁתּוּ שְׁלֹשֶׁת יָמִים לַיְלָה וָיוֹם *do not eat and do not drink for three days, night or day* (v. Zc 14^{7} sub **3** infr) **d.** day as defined by *evening and morning* Gn 1$^{5.8\,13\,19.23.31}$ (all P; cf further בֹּקֶר, עֶרֶב); v also 2$^{2.2\,3}$ (P), Ex 20$^{11\,11}$(E), 32$^{17\,17}$ (P) **e.** *day* of month (c num ordin), chiefly P and late· Gn 7^{11} 8$^{4\,14}$ Ex 12$^{6.18\,18}$+, 1 K 12$^{32.33}$ Ez 45$^{21.25}$ Zc 1^{7} Hg 1$^{1\,15\,18}$ 2 Ch 29$^{17\,17}$ Ezr 3^{6} Ne 8^{2} 9^{1} Dn 10^{4} Est 3^{12} 9^{1}+, (יוֹם oft om e g Gn 8$^{5\,13}$ Ex 12^{10} 2 K 25$^{1\,3}$ Ez 1$^{1\,2}$ Hg 2$^{1\,20}$ Zc 7^{1} 2 Ch 3^{2} Ezr 6^{19} Est 3^{13}, etc) **f.** יוֹם defined by subst , inf , or other cl (1) cstr יוֹם הַשֶּׁלֶג=*the snowy day* 2 S 23^{20}=1 Ch 11^{22}, יוֹם סַגְרִיר Pr 27^{15}=*rainy d* , יוֹם קָרָה 25^{20}=*cold d* , (so,=*time*) יוֹם צָרָתִי Gn 35^{3} (E) *d of my distress;* Je 18^{17} La 1^{7} Pr 24^{10} 25^{19} 27^{10}), יוֹם מוֹתוֹ etc Ju 13^{7} 2 S 6^{23} 2 K 15^{5} +oft ; cf יוֹם הֻלֶּדֶת אֶת־פַּרְעֹה Gn 40^{20} (E) = *Pharaoh's birthday;* כְּיוֹם הִוָּלְדָהּ Ho 2^{5} cf Ec 7^{1} (v also **7 d** infr , cf יוֹמוֹ Jb 3^{1}), יוֹם חֲתֻנָּתוֹ Ct 3^{11}; of day emphat characterized by proph and others יוֹם מְהוּמָה וּמְבוּסָה וּמְבוּכָה Is 22^{5} (v. מְהוּמָה sub הום), יוֹם צָרָה וְתוֹכֵחָה וּנְאָצָה 37^{3}=2 K 19^{3}, on the other hand יוֹם רָצוֹן לי׳ Is 58^{5} *a day of acceptableness to* י׳; pl sq subst יְמֵי שָׂכִיר Lv 25^{50}(H) *the days of an hireling,* יְמֵי (מִלֻּאֵיכֶם) Lv 8^{33} Nu 6^{13}; sq. rel cl. אָרוּר הַיּוֹם אֲשֶׁר יֻלַּדְתִּי בּוֹ יוֹם אֲשֶׁר־יְלָדַתְנִי אִמִּי וגו׳ Je 20^{14} cf. Jb 3^{3}; also ψ 118^{24} (v. **i**) **g.** particular days defined by n pr.loc.: יוֹם יִזְרְעֶאל Ho 2^{2} i e of judgment, with implied restoration; v also Is 9^{3} Ez 30^{9}, יְמֵי הַגִּבְעָה Ho 9^{9} 10^{9}, i.e of the outrage at Gibeah (Ju 19$^{22\,ff}$); יוֹם יְרוּשָׁלָ‍ִם ψ 137^{7} i e of Jerusalem's calamity, cf. Je 50$^{27.31}$ **h.** c sf , *thy, his,* or *their day*, in sense of (1) day of disaster or death : †בָּא יוֹמְךָ Je 50^{31} *thy day has come;* יוֹמוֹ יָבֹא וָמֵת אוֹ 1 S 26^{10}; בָּא+ in this sense also Ez 21^{30} ψ 37^{13} Jb 18^{20}, יוֹם יוֹמָם Je 50^{27} Ez 21^{34}. **i.** specif a holy day . יוֹם הַשַּׁבָּת *the sabbath day* (v also שַׁבָּת), Ex 20$^{8\,11}$ (E) =Dt 5$^{12\,15}$, Ex 31^{15} 35^{3}+; = יוֹם קָדְשִׁי Is 58^{13}, repetition בְּיוֹם הַשַּׁבָּת בְּיוֹם הַשַּׁבָּת Lv 24^{8} *every sabbath day;* also †יוֹם הַכִּפֻּרִים Lv 23^{27} 25^{9}, יוֹם כִּפֻּרִים 23^{28}, יוֹם הַבִּכּוּרִים Nu 28^{26}, יוֹם חַגֵּנוּ ψ 81^{4}, יוֹם מַלְכֵּנוּ Ho 7^{5}; also of false gods, יְמֵי הַבְּעָלִים 2^{11}.

3. יוֹם י׳ *day of Yahweh,* chiefly as time of his coming in judgment, involving often blessedness for righteous (v. RS[Proph. 396 f.] Dr[Is 28]); Am 5[18.18.20] Is 2[12] 13[6.9] Zp 1[7] (cf. v[8]), v[14.14] (cf. v[15.16]), Je 46[10] Ez 13[5] 30[3] (cf. 36[33] 39[8.11.13]), Ob [15] Zc 14[1] Mal 3[23] (cf. Zc 14[7] Mal 3[2.17.19.19.21]), Jo 1[15] 2[1.11] (cf. v[2.2]), 3[4] 4[14]; יוֹם עֶבְרַת י׳ Zp 1[18]; יוֹם עֶבְרָה Pr 11[4]; יוֹם חֲרוֹן אַפּוֹ Is 13[13] La 1[12]; יוֹם נָקָם Is 34[8] 61[2] 63[4]; יוֹם נְקָמָה Je 46[10]; יוֹם אַף י׳ Zp 2[2.3] La 2[22]; יוֹם אַפּוֹ La 2[1]; cf. also Zc 14[7] (where senses of **1** and **2** are combined, cf. Est 4[16] **2 c** supr.); וְהָיָה יוֹם־אֶחָד הוּא יִוָּדַע לי׳ לֹא יוֹם וְלֹא לָיְלָה *but there shall be one day, known shall it be of* י׳, *not day and not night;* cf. also ביום ההוא **7 g** infr.

4. Pl. *days* of any one: **a.** = his life, his age Gn 6[3] (J), Dt 22[19.29] 23[7] Jos 24[31.31] (D), Ju 2[7.7.18] 1 S 25[28], etc.; Gn 5[4.8.11] 9[29] 11[32] (all P), Jb 7[1.1.6.16] 8[9] ψ 39[5.6] 90[9.10.12.14] 103[15]; כָּל־יְמֵי חַיֶּיךָ Gn 3[14.17] (J), ψ 23[6], so Pr 31[12]; יְמֵי שְׁנֵי חַיִּים 2 S 19[35] Gn 25[7] 47[8.9] (all P); יְמֵי חַיָּיו Ec 5[17.19]; יְמֵי שָׁנָיו 6[3]; יְמֵי שְׁנוֹתֵינוּ ψ 90[10]; מִסְפַּר יְמֵי חַיֵּיהֶם Ec 2[3]; מִסְפַּר יְמֵי חַיֵּי הֶבְלוֹ 6[12] *the number of the days of the years of his vanity,* i.e. his empty, fleeting years; כָּל־הַיָּמִים אֲשֶׁר־הֵם חַיִּים עַל־פְּנֵי הָאֲדָמָה 1 K 8[40]; יָמִים רַבִּים *long life* 1 K 3[11] = 2 Ch 1[11]; בָּא בַּיָּמִים *advanced in days* = of advanced age Gn 18[11] 24[1] (both J), Jos 13[1.1] (JE), 23[1.2] (D), 1 K 1[1]; מִיָּמָיו 1 K 1[6] *from his* (earliest) *days,* so מִיָּמֶיךָ 1 S 25[28] (v. Dr), Jb 38[12]; שְׂבַע יָמִים Jb 42[17] 1 K 8[40]; יַאֲרִכוּן יָמֶיךָ Ex 20[12] (JE) *that thy days may be long* = Dt 5[16], v. further ארך; יָמִים עַל־יְמֵי־מֶלֶךְ תּוֹסִיף ψ 61[7] i.e. prolong the king's life; *outlive* is הֶאֱרִיךְ יָמִים אַחֲרֵי Jos 24[31] (D), Ju 2[7]; אֹרֶךְ יָמִים וּשְׁנוֹת חַיִּים Pr 3[2] *length of days and years of life;* אֹרֶךְ יָמִים v[16]; כְּיָמֶיךָ דבאך Dt 33[25] *according to* (the length of) *thy life shall be* [*thy strength?* rd. רבאך?] v. Di VB; rarely sg. e.g. קְשֵׁה־יוֹם Jb 30[25] *one hard of day,* i.e. whose day (= *life*) was hard; of life as approaching its end, וַיִּקְרְבוּ יְמֵי ישראל לָמוּת Gn 47[29] (J) *and the days of Israel drew near for dying,* so Dt 31[14] 1 K 2[1] (cf. Jb 7[6.16] 8[9] Ec 2[3] supr.) **b.** (*in*) *the days of* (i.e. life-time, reign, or activity of) Gn 10[25] (J), 14[1] Ju 5[6.6] 8[28] 2 S 21[1] 1 K 16[34] 21[29.29] 22[47] 2 K 20[19] 2 Ch 13[20] 35[18] + oft. (so MI[5.8.8.9.33]). **c.** hence in phr. סֵפֶר דִּבְרֵי הַיָּמִים לְ 1 K 14[19.29] + 31 t. K, Ne 12[23] Est 2[23] 10[2]; מִסֵּפֶר דִּבְרֵי הַיָּמִים 1 Ch 27[24]; סֵפֶר הַזִּכְרֹנוֹת דִּבְרֵי הַיָּמִים Est 6[1].

5. *Days:* **a.** indef.: יָמִים אֲחָדִים *some days, a few days* † Gn 27[44] (J), 29[20] (E), Dn 11[20]; יָמִים alone 40[4] (E) they were *days* (a certain time) in the prison 1 K 17[15] Ne 1[4]; עוּל יָמִים Is 65[20] *a suckling of* (a few) *days;* מִיָּמִים Ju 11[4] *after a time,* 15[1]; so מִקֵּץ יָמִים Gn 4[3] (J) *after the end of days,* 1 K 17[7]; יוֹם אוֹ יוֹמַיִם Ex 21[21] (JE) *a day or two.* יָמִים אוֹ עָשׂוֹר Gn 24[55] (J) *some days, or ten* (days or a dekad; on question of txt. v. Di). **b.** of long time, זֶה יָמִים אוֹ זֶה שָׁנִים 1 S 29[3] *these days or these years;* יֹמַיִם אוֹ חֹדֶשׁ אוֹ יָמִים Nu 9[22] (P) *whether two days or a month or days* (an indefinitely long period); יָמִים רַבִּים *many days* Gn 21[34] (JE) 37[34] (J) + ; וַיִּרְבּוּ הַיָּמִים וגו׳ Gn 38[12] (J) *and the days were multiplied* (= time passed) and Judah's wife died, 1 S 7[2]; אָרְכוּ לוֹ שָׁם הַיָּמִים Gn 26[8] (J) *the days were long to him there* = *he had been there a long time;* בְּהַאֲרִיךְ הֶעָנָן ... יָמִים רַבִּים Nu 9[19] (P) *when the cloud prolonged many days* (remained a long time) upon the tabern.—Vid. also **6** infr. **c.** *days of old, former* or *ancient times* (esp. of early period of Isr. hist.): יְמוֹת עוֹלָם Dt 32[7] (poem); יְמֵי עוֹלָם Mi 5[1] 7[14] Is 63[9.11]; יְמֵי קֶדֶם Mi 7[20]; יָמִים מִקֶּדֶם ψ 77[6] 143[5]; cf. הַיָּמִים הָרִאשֹׁנִים Ec 7[10]; *coming days* הַיָּמִים הַבָּאִים Ec 2[16]; *coming time* יוֹם אַחֲרוֹן Pr 31[25]; esp. (ב)אַחֲרִית הַיָּמִים v. p. 31 supr.; לְקֵץ הַיָּמִין Dn 12[13].

6. יוֹם = *time;* **a.** vividly in gen. sense (v. also **5** supr.): *time* of harvest Pr 25[13]; usu. יְמֵי Gn 30[14] (J), Jos 3[15] Nu 13[20.20] (all JE), Ju 15[1] 2 S 21[9]; *proper time* for paying wages Dt 24[15] cf. Jb 14[6]; time of parturition וַיִּמְלְאוּ יָמֶיהָ לָלֶדֶת Gn 25[24]. **b.** appos. to other expr. of time (Dr[§192 (1)] Da[Synt. §29 d]): חֹדֶשׁ יָמִים *a month of time* Gn 29[14] (J; lit. *a month, time*), Nu 11[20.21] (JE); = יֶרַח יָמִים Dt 21[13] 2 K 15[13]; יָמִים ארבעה חדשים Ju 19[2] *time, four months* (si vera l., v. 1 S 27[7]); (מִקֵּץ) שְׁנָתַיִם יָמִים + Gn 41[1] (E) *two years* (*of*) *time,* 2 S 13[23] 14[28] Je 28[3.11]; שְׁלֹשָׁה שָׁבֻעִים יָמִים Dn 10[2.3] *three weeks* (*of*) *time.* **c.** pl. in specific sense, appar. = *year,* lit. יָמִים 1 S 27[7] Lv 25[29] (H); לַיָּמִים Ju 17[10]; זֶבַח הַיָּמִים 1 S 1[21] 2[19] 20[6]; יָמִים וארבעה חדשים 27[7] = *a year and four months* (cf. Ju 19[2] supr. **b**); מִיָּמִים יָמִימָה = *from year to year, yearly* Ex 13[10] (JE), Ju 11[40] (cf. v[b]), 21[19] 1 S 1[3] 2[19]; מִקֵּץ יָמִים לַיָּמִים 2 S 14[26]; יֹמַיִם אוֹ חֹדֶשׁ אוֹ־יָמִים Nu 9[22] (P); distrib. Nu 14[34.34] (P), Ez 4[6.6]; וַיְהִי לְיָמִים מִיָּמִים וּכְעֵת צֵאת הַקֵּץ לְיָמִים שְׁנַיִם 2 Ch 21[19] *and it came to pass at days from days* (= after some days) *even about the time of the outgoing of the end of two* (series of) *days* (i.e. prob. *years,* v. Be).

7. Phrases, without prep. and with, are: **a.** (1) הַיּוֹם = *to-day* Gn 4[14] 31[43.48] Ex 13[4] (JE) + oft.; opp. תְּמוֹל *yesterday* Ex 5[14] 1 S 20[27]; opp. מָחָר

Ex 19^{10}; (2) †(בְּ)יוֹם מָחָר = *to-morrow* Gn 30^{33} Is 56^{12} Pr 27^{1}; (3) יוֹם אֶתְמוֹל ψ 90^{4}; (4) הַיּוֹם שְׁלֹשֶׁת הַיָּמִים 1 S 9^{20} *three days ago* (v. Dr); = הַיּוֹם שְׁלֹשָׁה 1 S 30^{13}; †(5) כַּיּוֹם Ju 13^{10} appar. = *the other day* (v. Be); (6) יוֹם אֶחָד no prep., emphat. = *in one day*, Gn 27^{45} Is 9^{13}; c. בְּ 10^{17} 47^{9}; *for, during, one day* Gn 33^{13} Nu 11^{19}; unemphat., *one day* (= *some day*) 1 S 27^{1}; יוֹם אֶחָד לִפְנֵי 9^{15} *one day, before* Saul came. †**b.** וַיְהִי הַיּוֹם וְ־ *and the day came, that* (or *when*) 1 S 1^{4} (v. Dr), 2 K 4$^{8.11.18}$ Jb 1$^{6.13}$ 2^{1}. **c.** הִנֵּה יָמִים בָּאִים *lo! days are coming*, when, etc.; esp. in Am Je: 1 S 2^{31} Am 4^{2} 8^{11} 9^{13} Is 39^{6} = 2 K 20^{17}, Je 7^{32} + 13 t. Je. **d.** יוֹם in cstr. bef. vbs., both literally, *the day of*, and (oft.) in gen. sense = *the time of* (forcible and pregn., representing the act vividly as that of a single day): (1) bef. inf., †(*a*) sg. without prep. אֶת־יוֹם צֵאתְךָ Dt 16^{3} and thou shalt remember *the day of thy going out* from the land of Egypt, Is 58^{5} Ez 39^{13} Mal 3^{2} cf. Ec 7^{1} (מִן compar.); (β) עַד־יוֹם Jos 6^{10} Ju 18^{30} + 5 t.; (γ) בְּיוֹם Gn 2$^{4.17}$ 3^{5} + 53 t.; †(δ) כְּיוֹם Ho 2$^{5.17}$ Zp 3^{8} Zc 14^{3}; †(ε) מִיּוֹם 1 S 7^{2} 8^{8} 29^{6} 2 S 13^{32} 2 K 8^{6} Dt 9^{24} Lv 23^{15} Ez 28^{15}; †(ζ) לְמִיּוֹם Ju 19^{30} 2 S 7^{6} Is 7^{17}; †(2) pl. cstr. bef. inf.: (*a*) כָּל־יְמֵי Ju 18^{31} 1 S 22^{4} 25$^{7.16}$ Lv 26$^{34.35}$ Nu 6^{6} 2 Ch 36^{21}; (β) בִּימֵי Ru 1^{1} 2 Ch 26^{5}; (γ) כִּימֵי Mi 7^{15}; †(3) sg. cstr. c. prep. bef. finite vb. in pf.: (*a*) cf. בְּ, בְּיוֹם דִּבֶּר י׳ Ex 6^{28} *in the day* (*when*) ׳י *spoke*, so Nu 3^{1} Dt 4^{15}; also Lv 7^{35} 2 S 22^{1} = ψ 18^{1}, ψ 138^{3} Zc 8^{9}; (β) מִיּוֹם Je 36^{2}; †(4) sg. cstr. bef. impf.: בְּיוֹם אֶקְרָא ψ 56^{10} *in the day* (*when*) *I cry*, 103^{3} La 5^{7}; also without בְּ, יוֹם אִירָא ψ 56^{4} (*at the*) *time* (*when*) *I am afraid;* †(5) pl. cstr. bef. pf.: כָּל־יְמֵי הִתְהַלַּכְנוּ אִתָּם 1 S 25^{15}, so Lv 14^{46} (prob., v. Di); כִּימֵי כִּימוֹת ψ 90^{15}; †(6) pl. cstr. bef. impf.: כִּימֵי אֱלוֹהַּ יִשְׁמְרֵנִי Jb 29^{2}; †(7) מִיּוֹם cstr. bef. rel. cl.: מִיּוֹם אֲשֶׁר הָיִיתִי לְפָנֶיךָ 1 S 29^{8} *since the day when* (= *as long as*) *I have been before thee*, Ne 5^{14}; †(8) pl. cstr. bef. rel. cl. כָּל־יְמֵי אֲשֶׁר יִשְׁכֹּן Nu 9^{18} *as long as the cloud remained*, etc. **e.** (1) יוֹם יוֹם *day by day* Gn 39^{10} (J), Ex 16^{5} (P), Pr 8$^{30.34}$ ψ 61^{9} 68^{20} (+ Je 7^{25} ψ 13^{3} Lag, v. יוֹמָם); so (late) †לְיוֹם בְּיוֹם 2 Ch 24^{11}; †יוֹם בְּיוֹם 30^{21} Ne 8^{18}; †לְעֶת־יוֹם בְּיוֹם 1 Ch 12^{22}; עֹלַת יוֹם בְּיוֹם Ezr 3^{4}; בִּדְבַר יוֹם בְּיוֹם 2 Ch 8^{13}; מִיּוֹם אֶל־יוֹם *from day to day* 1 Ch 16^{23} = מִיּוֹם לְיוֹם ψ 96^{2} (Est 3^{7} v. infr.); †יוֹם וָיוֹם Est 3^{4} (very late, v. ן **1 i** (*b*), p. 253 supr. and Dr$^{\text{Intr. 505}}$); בְּכָל־יוֹם וָיוֹם 2^{11}; †כְּיוֹם בְּיוֹם 1 S 18^{10} *as daily = according to daily habit;* (2) מִיּוֹם לְיוֹם Est 3^{7}, is in phr. of casting lots for *one day after another;* (מִיָּמִים יָמִימָה v. **6 c**); (3) of daily duties, observances, etc.: †דְּבַר יוֹם בְּיוֹמוֹ *each day's affair in its day* Ex 5$^{13.19}$ 16^{4} (all J), Lv 23^{37} (H), 1 K 8^{59} 2 K 25^{30} = Je 52^{34}, Ezr 3^{4} Ne 11^{23} 12^{47} Dn 1^{5}; לִדְבַר יוֹם בְּיוֹמוֹ 1 Ch 16^{37} 2 Ch 8^{14} 31^{16}. **f.** †כָּל־הַיָּמִים = *always, continually*, Gn 43^{9} 44^{32} (both J), Dt 4^{40} 5^{26} 6^{24} 11^{1} 14^{23} 18^{5} 19^{9} 28$^{29.33}$ Jos 4^{24} (D), Ju 16^{16} 1 S 2$^{32.35}$ 18^{29} 23^{14} 28^{2} 2 S 13^{37} 19^{14} Je 31^{36} 32^{39} 33^{18} 35^{19} 1 K 5^{15} 9^{3} 11$^{36.39}$ 12^{7} 14^{30} 2 K 8^{19} 13^{3} 17^{37} 2 Ch 7^{16} 10^{7} 12^{15} 21^{7} Jb 1^{5}; also (only in proph. writers and in poetry) †כָּל־הַיּוֹם Gn 6^{5} (J), Ho 12^{2} Dt 28^{32} 33^{12} Je 20$^{7.8}$ Is 28^{24}, 51^{13} 52^{5} (both תָּמִיד כל־היום), 65$^{2.5}$ La 1^{13} 3$^{3.14.62}$ ψ 25^{5} 32^{3} 35^{28} 37^{26} 38$^{7.13}$ 42$^{4.11}$ 44$^{9.16.23}$ 52^{3} 56$^{2.3.6}$ 71$^{8.15.24}$ 72^{15} 73^{14} 74^{22} 86^{3} 88^{18} 89^{17} 102^{9} 119^{97} Pr 21^{26} 23^{17}. **g.** additional phr. c. בְּ = *on* a particular day: בַּיּוֹם הַחֲמִישִׁי Ju 19^{18}, so Gn 2$^{2.2}$ + oft.; בְּכָל־יוֹם *every day* ψ 7^{12} 88^{10} 145^{2}; בַּיּוֹם הַהוּא of definite time in past Gn 15^{18} 33^{16} + (v. also **3** supr.); cf. הַיּוֹם הַזֶּה (no prep.) Ex 13^{3} (JE); בַּיּוֹם הַהוּא of time defined in subsequent context, 1 S 3^{2} *at that time* when Eli was laid down, i.e. at the particular time of the foll. incident (= *at a certain time, on one particular day;* cf. Gn 39^{11} sub **h**; see Da$^{\text{Synt. § 21. e. R. 1, 2}}$ and esp. Dr 1 S 1^{4} 19^{3}); בַּיּוֹם הַזֶּה Gn 7^{11} +; בְּעֶצֶם הַיּוֹם הַזֶּה *on this selfsame day* Gn 7^{13} + (v. עֶצֶם); בַּיּוֹם הַהוּא also of future 1 S 3^{12} Dt 31$^{17.17.18}$; and very oft. in proph., as formula in describing what is to come at time of future blessing, retribution, etc., Am 8$^{3.9}$ Ho 2$^{18.20.23}$ etc., esp. Is 2$^{11.17.20}$ 3$^{7.18}$ 4$^{1.2}$ + oft.; pl. בַּיָּמִים הָהֵם of past Gn 6^{4} (J), Ju 18$^{1.1}$ 19^{1} 21^{25} 1 S 3^{1} + oft.; of future Dt 17^{9} 19^{17} 26^{3}. **h.** c. כְּ: כַּיּוֹם *as* or *like the day* ψ 139^{12}; כַּיּוֹם הַהוּא Jos 10^{14}; כְּיוֹם Ho 2^{5} *as* at *the day of;* כְּיוֹם תָּמִים Jos 10^{13} *about a whole day;* †כַּיּוֹם lit. *at* (*about*) *to-day = now* (v. כְּ) 1 S 9^{27} 1 K 22^{5} = 2 Ch 18^{4} Is 58^{4}; so †כְּהַיּוֹם 1 S 9^{13} + v^{12} We Dr (for MT כי היום), Ne 5^{11}; †כַּיּוֹם = *at once, first of all* Gn 25$^{31.33}$ 1 S 2^{16} 1 K 1^{51}; oft. c. adj. pron. to point out agreement of result with promise or prediction, †כַּיּוֹם הַזֶּה *as* it is *at this day* Gn 50^{20} (E), 1 S 22$^{8.13}$, and esp. Dt Je and subseq. writings: Dt 2^{30} 4$^{20.38}$ 8^{18} 10^{15} 29^{27} Je 11^{5} 25^{18} (gloss, om. 𝔊, cf. esp. Kue$^{\text{Einl. § 56. 1}}$), 32^{20} 44$^{6.23}$ 1 K 3^{6} 8$^{24.61}$ 1 Ch 28^{7} 2 Ch 6^{15} Dn 9$^{7.15}$; so †כְּהַיּוֹם הַזֶּה Dt 6^{24} Je 44^{22} Ezr 9$^{7.15}$ Ne 9^{10}; in Gn 39^{11} (J) this phr. = *on this particular day* (when the incident to be narrated occurred; cf. ביום ההוא **g** supr.) **i.** c. לְ: לְיוֹם *on, at* (lit. *with reference to*) †Ho 9$^{5.5}$ *what will ye do on the day of assembly*, etc., Is 10^{3}; לְיוֹם אֶחָד 1 K 5^{2}

bread *for one day;* הַמְּלָאכָה לֹא לְיוֹם אֶחָד וְלֹא לִשְׁנַיִם Ezr 10^{13}; distrib. phr. נָשִׂיא אֶחָד לַיּוֹם נָשִׂיא אֶחָד לַיּוֹם Nu 7^{11} (P), Jb 21$^{30.30}$; cf. לַיּוֹם Mal 1^{17}; לְיוֹם *against*, i.e. in expectation of Ex 19^{11}, so לְיוֹם קְרָב Jb 38^{23} Pr 21^{31}; לְיוֹם קוּמִי alm.=*until* Zp 3^{8}; לִפְנֵי יוֹם Is 48^{7} *before to-day;* late phr. are †לְיָמִים מִיָּמִים 2 Ch 21^{19}=*in the course of time;* לְיָמִים רַבִּים Dn 8^{26} *at* (the end of) *many days;* לַיּוֹם=*for every day, daily,* †Ex 29$^{36.38}$ Nu 7$^{11.11}$ 28$^{3.24}$ 1 Ch 26$^{17.17}$ Je 37^{21} Ez 4^{10} 43^{25} 45$^{23.23}$ 46^{13}; לַיּוֹם in exclam. הָהּ לַיּ׳ Ez 30^{2} *alas for the day!* אֲהָהּ לַיּ׳ Jo 1^{15}. **j.** c. מִן: מִיּוֹם *since the day (time) of* (or *when*), Ex 10^{6} Lv 23^{15} Dt 9^{24} 1 S 7^{2} etc.; מִיּוֹם הראשׁון Ex 12^{15} *from the first day* (on om. of art. v. Dr$^{§209(1)}$); מִימֵי השׁפטים 2 K 23^{22}, etc.; מִיּוֹם=*from to-day, from this day forth* Is 43^{13} Ez 48^{35}; מֵהַיּוֹם הַהוּא וָמָעְלָה 1 S 16^{13} 30^{25} *from that day forward;* so מֵהַיּ׳ הַה׳ וְהָלְאָה 1 S 18^{9}; מִן־הַיּוֹם הַזֶּה וָמָעְלָה Hg 2$^{15.18}$ *from this day onward* (v. Add. on p. 751^{b}); עַד־הַיּוֹם הַזֶּה Gn 47^{26} *until now;* מִיָּמִים רַבִּים *after many days* Jos 23^{1} Ez 38^{8}; מִיָּמִים *after a time* Ju 11^{4} 14^{8} 15^{1}; but usu. מִקֵּץ י׳, v. קֵץ; מִיֹּמָיִם Ho 6^{2} *after two days;*—מִיָּמִים יָמִימָה v. **e** (4) supr. †**k.** c. לְמִן (v. לְ *ad fin.*): לְמִן הַיּוֹם אֲשֶׁר Dt 4^{32} 9^{7} 2 S 7^{11} Je 7^{25} 32^{31} Hg 2^{18}; twice sq. inf. appos. Ex 9^{18} 2 S 19^{25} (cf. also 2 Ch 8^{16}; v. Dr$^{Sm. \& §190, Obs.}$); לְמִימֵי: לְמִ׳ קֶדֶם 2 K 19^{25} *since days of old=long ago,* cf. Mal 3^{7} *since the days of your fathers.*† **l.** עַד (ה)יּוֹם: עַד יוֹם הָאֶחָד וגו׳ Ex 12^{18} *until the 21st day,* Lv 19^{6}+; עד־יום מותו Ju 13^{7} 1 S 15^{35} 2 S 6^{23}+, etc., v. also (sq. inf.) **c** supr.; עַד־הַיּוֹם *until to-day,* denoting esp. permanence of a name or situation, or of result of an event, †Gn 19$^{37.38}$ (J), 35^{20} (E), 2 K 10^{27} Ez 20^{31}†; more often עַד־הַיּוֹם הַזֶּה *until this day* Gn 26^{33} (J), 32^{33} (P or R), 47^{26} (J), 48^{15} (E), Ex 10^{6} Nu 22^{30} (both J), Dt 2^{22} 3^{14} 10^{8} 11^{4} 29^{3} 34^{6} Jos 4^{9} 5^{9} 6^{25} 7$^{26.26}$ 8$^{28.29}$ 9^{27} 13^{13} 14^{14} 15^{63} 16^{10} (all JE), 22^{3} (D), v^{17} (P), 23$^{8.9}$ (D), Ju 1$^{21.26}$ 6^{24} 10^{4} 15^{19} 18^{12} 19^{30} 1 S 5^{5} 6^{18} 8^{8} 12^{2} 27^{6} 29$^{3.6.8}$ 30^{25} 2 S 4^{3} 6^{8}=1 Ch 13^{11}, 2 S 7^{6}=1 Ch 17^{5}, 2 S 18^{18}+ oft.; עַד־עֶצֶם הַיּוֹם הַזֶּה †Jos 10^{27} (JE), Ez 2^{3} (cf. Lv 23^{14} H); עַד־הַיּוֹם הַהוּא †Ju 18^{1} Ne 8^{17}. **m.** once עַל־יוֹם טוֹב 1 S 25^{8} *upon a good day,* i.e. a day of social cheerfulness, feasting, rejoicing (c. rare עַל temp. cf. Dr; יוֹם טוֹב also Est 8^{17} 9$^{19.22}$, v. טוֹב **adj.**)

יוֹמָם $_{51}$ **subst.** and **adv.** daytime, by day (cf. Aram. יְמָמָא, ܐܺܝܡܳܡܳܐ *day* (as opp. to *night*); 𝔗 יְמָם *by day;* perh. Ph. יממ (in dates, before num.), CIS$^{I. 1. 10. 1 (see\ note)}$; so Nö ZDMG 1886, 721: on ־ָם, v. sub חִנָּם)—**1. subst.** *daytime* (rare) Je 15^{9} בעוד יומם while it is yet *daytime,* 33^{20b} לְבִלְתִּי הֱיוֹת יומם ולילה *daytime* and night, v^{25} בְּרִיתִי י׳ ולילה (? rd. יוֹם as v^{20a}); Ez 30^{16} צָרֵי יוֹמָם foes of *daytime,* i.e. coming by day (cf. Je 15^{8}; but text appar. defective, v. 𝔊 Sm); once (late) בְּיוֹמָם (cf. 𝔗 בְּיֵמָם 1 S 25^{16} Jb 5^{14}), Ne 9^{19} (varied from Ex 13^{21} Dt 1^{33} יומם).—Nu 9^{21} the sense required is (during) *a day* and a night; rd. prob. יוֹם. **2. adv.** *in the day-time, by day,* Nu 10^{34} Jb 24^{16} (but v. חָתַם), Is 4^{6} Ez 12$^{3.4.7}$; mostly c. לַיְלָה, and then oft. poet.=*continually:* so יוֹמָם וָלַיְלָה Ex 13^{21} Jos 1^{8} 1 K 8^{59} ψ 1^{2} 32^{4}+, לַיְלָה וְיוֹמָם †Dt 28^{66} Is 34^{10} Je 14^{17}, in parallel clauses (esp. in poetry) 2 S 21^{10} Is 21^{8} Je 31^{35} ψ 22^{3} 42^{9} 91^{5} 121^{6}+. ψ 13^{3} *by day* yields a lame sense: either add וָלַיְלָה (𝔊 Del Gr Ch), or rd. יוֹם יוֹם (יום יום) Lag$^{Nov. Psalt. Gr. Ed. Spec. 12}$ Now.

I. [ינן] (√of foll.; meaning unknown).

†[יָוֵן] **n.[m.]** mire;—abs. מִטִּיט הַיָּוֵן ψ 40^{3}; cstr. טָבַעְתִּי בִּיוֵן מְצוּלָה 69^{3}.

II. [ינן] (√of foll., mng. unknown; יוֹנָה acc. to Lag$^{Armen. Stud. 7. 53; M. 1. 228}$=Pers. *wanā,* but improb.; Sta^{§259a} conject. יוֹנָה to be fr. אָנָה *mourn,* so Dl$^{Pa 157}$).

†I. יוֹנָה **n.f.** dove (NH *id.;* Aram. *id.,* ܝܘܢܐ)—abs. יוֹנָה Gn 8^{8}+20 t.; cstr. יוֹנַת ψ 56^{1}; sf. יוֹנָתִי Ct 2^{14}+2 t.; pl. יוֹנִים Na 2^{8}+6 t.; cstr. יוֹנֵי Ez 7^{16} (v. infr.);—*dove* Gn 8$^{8.9.10.11.12}$ (all J); oft. of offerings, בֶּן־יוֹנָה Lv 12^{6} (P; an individual of the species; ‖ תֹּר); (ה)יּוֹנִים ‖ בְּנֵי (תֹּרִים) 1^{14} 5$^{7.11}$ 12^{8} 14$^{22.30}$ 15$^{14.29}$ Nu 6^{10} (all P); חֲרֵי יוֹנִים *dove's dung* 2 K 6^{25} (Kt, yet v. Gei$^{Urschrift 409}$); in various similes: Ephr. is כְּיוֹנָה פוֹתָה *like a silly dove* Ho 7^{11} (allowing itself to be snared); sim. of return of exiles, like eager flight of doves 11^{11}, of ships with white outspread sails Is 60^{8}; אֵבֶר כַּיּוֹנָה ψ 55^{7}; v. also כַּנְפֵי יוֹנָה 68^{14}; sim. of fugitive Moab Je 48^{28}; also כְּיוֹנֵי הַגֵּאָיוֹת Ez 7^{16} *like the doves of the valleys* (but on txt. v. Co, who emends כיונים הוגיות, but regards phr. as gloss); sim. of mourning כְּקוֹל יוֹנִים Na 2^{8}; without קול, הנה כיונים Is 38^{14} 59^{11} (from mournful note); fig. of beauty (only Ct): עֵינַיִךְ יוֹנִים *thine eyes are* (those of) *doves* Ct 1^{15} 4^{1}, v. also v^{12}; term of endearment, יוֹנָתִי *my dove* Ct 2^{14} 5^{2} 6^{9}. Elsewh. only ψ 56^{1} (title) (עַל) יוֹנַת אֵלֶם רְחֹקִים prob. name of melody: *To 'the dove of distant*

terebinths' (rd. אֵלִים for אֵלָם; v. אֵלָם supr. p. 48, and Bae[Ψψ. p. xvii]).—On sanctity of dove among Shemites, v. RS[Sem. i. 202, 275].

†II. יוֹנָה **n.pr.m.** prophet, acc. to 2 K 14[25] he was הַנָּבִיא, son of אֲמִתַּי, fr. גַּת הַחֵפֶר, and predicted the recovery of Isr.'s territory which Jerob. II effected; he is also the principal figure of the Book of Jonah: 1[1] (בֶּן־אֲמִתַּי), v[3.5.7.15] 2[1.1.2.11] 3[1.3.4] 4[1.5.6.6.8.9].

III. יוֹנָה v. יָנָה Pt.

†יָוָן **n.pr.gent.** Ionia(ns), Greece (Gk. 'Ιάονες (i.e. orig. 'ΙάϜονες), v. also 𝔊 infr.; OPers. *Yauna* Spieg[APK 237]; As. *Iamanu* (*Iavanu*) Dl[Pa 248 ff.] COT[Gloss]; Egypt. *Yᵉ-vᵃn-(n)a*, v. WMM[369 f. cf. also 24 ff.]; v. esp. on this word Sta[De Populo Javan 1880])—*Ionians*, as traders Ez 27[13], 𝔊 'Ελλάς (named with תֻּבַל, מֶשֶׁךְ; in v[12] תַּרְשִׁישׁ, in v[14] (תּוֹגַרְמָה); cf. יְוָנִי (adj. gent.) infr.; as distant, Is 66[19], 𝔊 'Ελλάς (with תֻּבַל, לוּד, פּוּל, תַּרְשִׁישׁ, and הָאִיִּים הָרְחֹקִים; list to be emended fr. 𝔊 Sta[ib. 5 ff.]); called 'son' of Japhet Gn 10[2](P) = 1 Ch 1[5], and 'father' of אֱלִישָׁא, תַּרְשִׁישׁ, כִּתִּים and רֹדָנִים (so rd. for דֹּדָנִים) Gn 10[4] (P) = 1 Ch 1[7] (in these 𝔊 Ιωυαν, v. Lag[BN 84 Anm.**]); addressed (personif.) בָּנַיִךְ יָוָן Zc 9[13] (opp. בניך ציון) 𝔊 Ἕλληνες, and so in foll.; מֶלֶךְ יָוָן Dn 8[21] (v. מַלְכֵי מָדַי וּפָרָס v[20]) = *king of Greece* i.e. kingdom over which Alexander ruled, whose dominion was afterward divided (see v[22 ff.]); שַׂר־יָוָן 10[20] of the guardian-angel of Greece (v. שַׂר מַלְכוּת פָּרַס v[a]); יָוָן 11[2] (v[b] פָּרָס).—Ez 27[19] וְיָוָן is text. err., v. וְדָן supr. p. 255[a].

†[יְוָנִי] **adj.gent.** only c. art. as n.pr.gent.: וּבְנֵי יְרוּשָׁלַםִ מְכַרְתֶּם לִבְנֵי הַיְּוָנִים Jo 4[6] (𝔊 Ἕλληνες) *and the sons of Jerusalem ye have sold to the sons of the Ionians* (cf. יָוָן Ez 27[13]).—Vid. Sta[ib.]

יוֹסִפְיָה, יוֹסֵף v. sub יסף.

יוֹעֵאלָה v. sub יעל.

יוֹרָה v. sub ירה.

יוֹשַׁב חֶסֶד v. sub שׁוב.

יוֹשָׁה, יֹשַׁוְיָה v. sub ישׁה.

יוז (√ whence first element of foll.; perh. cf. Ar. وَزَى *congregatus, conglomeratus fuit*, Frey).

†[יוזאל, יְזִיאֵל] **n.pr.m.** one of David's heroes וִיזוֹאֵל 1 Ch 12[3].

יַזֶּה v. sub נזה.

[יזן] **vb.** only **Pu.** *Pt.* pl. מְיֻזָּנִים Je 5[8] Qr (< Kt מוּזָנִים v. זון); mng. dub. (comp. by Schu al. with Ar. وَزَنَ *weigh*, whence *furnished with weights*, i.e. testicles, but sense remote and very uncertain).

יָזִיז v. sub I. זוז p. 265[b] supr.

יִזְלִיאָה v. sub זלא p. 272[b] supr.

יְזַנְיָה, יְזַנְיָהוּ v. sub I. אזן p. 24[b] supr.

יזע (√ of foll.; cf. Ar. وَدَغَ *fluxit* aqua (Frey); NH and Aram. in deriv., v. infr.)

†[יֶזַע] **n.[m.]** **sweat** (v. זֵעָה infr.)—לֹא יַחְגְּרוּ בַּיָּזַע Ez 44[18] del. Co, q.v.

†[זֵעָה] **n.f.** **sweat** (NH זֵיעָה (Levy), better זֵיעָה (Jastr); Aram. דֵּיעֲתָא, ܕܘܥܬܐ)—בְּזֵעַת אַפֶּיךָ תֹּאכַל לֶחֶם Gn 3[19] (J).

יִזְרַחְיָה, יִזְרָח v. sub זרח p. 280[b] supr.

יִזְרְעֶאל v. sub זרע p. 283[a] supr.

יחבה v. חֻבָּה sub חבב.

†[יָחַד] **vb.** be united (Ar. وَحَدَ *be alone*, II. *make one*; NH Pi. יִחֵד *make* or *declare one*; Aram. יַחֵד *unite*, ܐܬܝܚܕ *set alone*)—**Qal** *Impf.* 3 fs. Gn 49[6] בִּקְהָלָם אַל־תֵּחַד כְּבֹדִי in their assembly let my glory *not be united* (‖ בְּסֹדָם אַל־תָּבֹא נַפְשִׁי); 2 fs. Is 14[20] לֹא תֵחַד אִתָּם בִּקְבוּרָה. **Pi.** *Imv.* ψ 86[11] יַחֵד לְבָבִי לְיִרְאָה שְׁמֶךָ *unite* my heart (i.e. concentrate its affections, cf. Je 32[39]) to fear thy name (but 𝔊 𝔖 𝔙 Gr Bi Ch יִחַד (from חָדָה) *let* my heart *rejoice*, etc.)

†יָחִיד **adj.** and **subst.** only, only one, solitary (NH *id.*; Aram. יְחִידִי, יְחִיד, ܝܚܝܕܐ, ܝܚܝܕܝܐ *id.*; Arab. وَحِيدٌ *solitary*)—**1.** *only one*, esp. of an only son, Gn 22[2.12.16] את בנך את יְחִידְךָ thy son, thine *only one*, אֵבֶל יָחִיד Am 8[10] Je 6[26] mourning for *an only son*, כמספד על היחיד Zc 12[10], Pr 4[3] רַךְ וְיָחִיד לפני אמי; so fem. יְחִידָה Ju 11[34]. **2.** fem. יְחִידָה as subst. ψ 22[21] 35[17] יְחִידָתִי my *only one*, poet. for *my life*, as the one unique and priceless possession which can never be replaced (in each ‖ נַפְשִׁי). **3.** *solitary*, ψ 25[16] כי יחיד ועני אני; 68[7] מוֹשִׁיב יְחִידִים בַּיְתָה causing *solitary*, *isolated* ones (i.e. friendless wanderers or exiles; ‖ אֲסִירִים) to dwell at home (Lag Ch al. מֵשִׁיב *bringing back* home).

†יַ֫חַד $_{45}$ **n.[m.]** unitedness. **1.** as **subst.** only 1 Ch 12^{17} (peculiar) יִהְיֶה־לִּי עֲלֵיכֶם לֵבָב לְיָחַד I will have a heart toward you *for unitedness*, i.e. my heart shall be ready to become one with yours (cf. v^{38} לב אחד). **2.** elsewhere always in acc. as **adv.** *in union, together* (cf. Ar. وَحْدَ in acc. with sf. *in his solitariness = alone*)—**a.** *together*, of community in action, place, or time (oft. combined, but one usu. more prominent than the others); (1) in action, Jb 38^7 בְּרָן־יַחַד כּוֹכְבֵי אֵל when the stars of God shouted *together*; Ezr 4^3 we *together* will build (opp. to *you*), with נִלָּחֵם 1 S 17^{10}, נִשָּׁפְטָה Is 43^{26}; (2) in place 1 S 11^{11} וְלֹא נִשְׁאֲרוּ בָם שְׁנַיִם יָחַד; 2 S 10^{15} וַיֵּאָסְפוּ יָחַד ψ 2^2 31^{14} 88^{18}, 133^1 שֶׁבֶת יָחַד, Is 50^8, as pred. Mi 2^{12} יַחַד אֲשִׂימֶנּוּ; (3) in place and time at once, 2 S 21^9 וַיִּפְּלוּ יָחַד and they perished *together*, 14^{16} to destroy אתי ואת בני יחד; (4) of time alone (poet.) Is 42^{14} אֶשֹּׁם וְאֶשְׁאַף יחד I will gasp and pant *together*, 45^8 Jb 6^2 17^{16} ψ 141^{10} יחד אנכי עד אעבור while *I* at the same time pass on. **b.** *all together, altogether* (poet. syn. of כֻּלָּם, but more forcible, suggesting oft., esp. with כל, *all at once*, as well as *altogether*), Is 44^{11} יפחדו יבשו יחד (cf. ψ 40^{15}), ψ 62^{10} הֵמָּה מֵהֶבֶל יָחַד they are *all together* (made) of vanity, Is 22^3 כל קציניך נדדו יחד (with כל also ψ 41^8 Jb 34^{15}): oft. in poet. beginning a clause with emph., Dt 33^5 Jb 3^{18} יחד אסירים שאננו, 16^{10} 19^{12} יחד יבאו גדודיו, 24^4 31^{38} ψ 41^8 98^8 Ho 11^7 (with a neg.), v^8; in connexion with a sf., or obj. of a vb., Is 27^4 אציתנה יָחַד I will burn it *altogether*, ψ 33^{15} הַיֹּצֵר יַחַד לִבָּם who formeth the hearts of them *all together*, 74$^{6.8}$ Jb 10^8 יַחַד סָבִיב *altogether* round about (but rd. perh. with 𝔊 𝔖 Del Di אַחַר תְּסוֹב), 40^{13}. **c.** *together*, in the sense of *alike*, the one as well as the other, ψ 49$^{3.11}$ יחד כסיל ובער יאבדו, Jb 21^{26} 34^{29}. More frequent is

יַחְדָּו $_{92}$ (Je 46$^{12.21}$ 49^3 יַחְדָּיו), **adv. together** (prop. (in) *his* or *its unitednesses* (cf. Ar. وَحْدَهُ *alone*; and for the form אַשְׁרָיו), but, the orig. of the term. being forgotten, applied gen. as an adv., without regard to number, gender, or person: so Ges Ol §135 c Sta §370 a)—*together*: **a.** of community in action, ψ 34^4 ונרוממה שמו יחדו let us exalt his name *together*, Is 52^9, with נוֹעַץ *take counsel*, 45^{21} ψ 71^{10} 83^6 Ne 6^7; נִצָּה to *struggle* Dt 25^{11}; in place, as with ישב Gn 13^6 Dt 25^5, הלך Gn 22$^{6.8}$ Am 3^3, בוא Je 3^{18} Jb 9^{32}, קרב Is 41^1, נפל 2 S 2^{16}, אכל Ju 19^6 Je 41^1, התקבץ Jos 9^2, נאסף Ju 6^{33}, etc.; Dt 22^{10} בשור ובחמור יחדו; coupling pairs, and so strengthening וְ (mostly poet.), v^{11} Am 1^{15} הוא ושריו יחדו (cf. Je 48^7 Qr [Kt יחד], 49^3) Je 6$^{11.12}$ שדות ונשים ׳, v^{21} (accents), 13^{14} 31$^{8.13}$ 50$^{4.33}$ Is 41^{19}, cf. 65^7; in time (rare: but v. infr.), ψ 4^9 in peace יחדו אשכבה ואישן will I *at once* lie down and sleep (i.e. lie down and fall asleep immediately). **b.** emph. (esp. poet.) = *all together* 1 S 31^6, Is 10^8 הלא שרי יחדו מלכים are not my princes *all together*, all alike, kings? 18^6 40^5 41$^{20.23}$ 45^{16} (|| כֻּלָּם), 46^2 קרסו כרעו יחדו, 48^{13} 66^{17} ψ 14^3 (|| הַכֹּל), 19^{10} צדקו יחדו (of J.'s ordinances), 35^{26} 37^{38}; sts. (like יַחַד **b**) suggesting *all at once*, as well as *all together*, Ex 19^8 ויענו כל העם יחדו (so, with כל, Is 22^3 31^3 Zc 10^4), Is 1$^{28.31}$ ובערו שניהם יחדו. Prefixed to a clause (like יחד), Dt 33^{17} (cf. יחד v^5), Is 9^{20} 11$^{7.14}$ 31^3 43^{17} 45^{16} 52^8 Je 46^{12} 51^{38} La 2^8 Jb 24^{17} (strengthening לָמוֹ). **c.** *alike*, the one as well as the other, Dt 12^{22} (= 15^{22}) the unclean and the clean *alike* may eat it, 1 S 30^{24} יַחְדָּו יַחֲלֹקוּ they shall share *together*, i.e. *alike*.

† יַחְדַּי Baer, יַחְדּוֹ van d. H, **n.pr.m.** a Gileadite, 1 Ch 5^{14}, 𝔊 Ιουραι, A Ιεδδαι, 𝔊L Ιεδδω.

יֶחְדִּיָּהוּ, יַחְדִּיאֵל v. sub חדה.

יְחוּאֵל v. sub חיה.

יַחֲזִיָּה, יַחֲזִיאֵל v. sub חזה.

יְחֶזְקֵאל, יְחִזְקִיָּה(וּ) v. sub חזק.

†יַחְזֵרָה **n.pr.m.** a priest 1 Ch 9^{12} (for which אַחְזַי (q.v.) Ne 11^{13}), v. now also Ryle on Ne 11^{13}.

יְחִיאֵל, יְחִיאֵלִי, יְחִיָּה v. sub חיה.

†[יָחַל] **vb. Niph.** wait; **Pi.** await (cf. NH יִחוּל *expectation*);—**Niph.** *Pf.* 3 fs. נוֹחֲלָה Ez 19^5 (yet v. infr.); *Impf.* וַיִּיָּחֶל Gn 8^{12} + 1 S 13^8 Kt (v. Dr; Qr Hiph. וַיּוֹחֶל);—*wait*: Gn 8^{12} *and he waited* yet seven days; so 1 S 13^8 Kt; of Isr. under fig. of lioness, וַתֵּרֶא כִּי נוֹחֲלָה אָבְדָה תִּקְוָתָהּ Ez 19^5 *when she saw that her hope tarried, was lost* (but dub.; Sm comp. Aram. ܐܬܚܠ *be weak*, whence perh. *sink down*; Hi (perh. after 𝔊) כִּי נִדַּח לָהּ *that he was thrust away from her*; Co plausibly נוֹאֲלָה that *she had acted foolishly*). **Pi.** *Pf.* 2 ms. sf. יִחַלְתָּנִי ψ 119^{49}; 1 s. יִחַלְתִּי v^{43} + 4 t. ψ 119; 3 mpl. יִחֲלוּ Jb 29^{23} Ez 13^6; יִחֵלוּ Jb 29^{21}; 1 pl. יִחַלְנוּ ψ 33^{22}; *Impf.* יְיַחֵל Mi 5^6;

אֵחַל Jb 6[11] + 3 t.; אֵיחֲלָה 30[26]; יְיַחֵלוּ Is 42[4], יְיַחֵלוּן 51[5]; *Imv* יַחֵל ψ 130[7] 131[3], *Pt* מְיַחֵל 69[4], מְיַחֲלִים 31[25] + 2 t.,—**1.** *wait, tarry* for, sq לְ Mi 5[6] (of rain, ‖ יְקַוֶּה), so 1[12] acc to We, who reads יחלה (Pf) for חָלָה; abs *wait* Jb 14[14] **2.** *wait for=hope for*, sq. לְ Is 42[4] Jb 29[21.23] 30[26] (‖קויתי), ψ 31[25] 33[18.22] 69[4] 119[43.49.74.81.114.147], sq לְ inf ויח׳ לְקַיֵּם דָּבָר Ez 13[6], sq אֶל Is 51[5] ψ 130[7] 131[3]; abs *hope*, Jb 6[11] 13[15] ψ 71[14]. **Hiph.** *Pf.* הוֹחַלְתִּי Jb 32[11], etc., וְהוֹחַלְתִּי (consec, v. Hi De[2] Dr[§§106.119γ]) Jb 32[16], *Impf* וַיּוֹחֶל 1 S 13[8] Qr, 2 ms תּוֹחֵל 10[8], אוֹחִיל 2 K 6[33] La 3[21.24], אוֹחִילָה Je 4[19] Qr (Kt אֹחוּלָה), Mi 7[7], אחילה 2 S 18[14],—*wait, tarry*, abs (prop *shew a waiting* attitude): 1 S 10[8] (sq עַד בּוֹאִי), 13[8] (Qr, cf Niph); 2 S 18[14] Jb 32[16] Je 4[19] (but v. חול), *wait for, hope for* (as **Pi.**), sq לְ 2 K 6[33] Mi 7[7] La 3[24] Jb 32[11] ψ 38[16] 42[6.12] 43[5] 130[5] (‖קויתי), abs *hope*, La 3[21].

†יָחִיל **adj.verb.** waiting, so Thes SS Buhl, but very dub,—only טוב וְיָחִיל ודוּמָם לְ La 3[26] *good* is it that one be *waiting and that silently* (but v דּוּמָם) *for* the salvation of י׳; construct with ו and adj hardly poss, Ew Ke Löhr Kö[ii 407] al regard as ׳ib (fr חול); rd perh וְיָחִיל Hiph Impf fr יחל (cf v[24]).

†תּוֹחֶלֶת **n.f.** hope, abs ת׳ Pr 13[12], cstr. *id* Pr 10[28] 11[7], sf תּוֹחַלְתִּי ψ 39[8] La 3[18]; תֹּחַלְתּוֹ Jb 41[1],—*hope*, sq subj. gen Jb 41[1] Pr 10[28] 11[7] La 3[18], sq subj gen. + לְ ψ 39[8] (תוחלתי לך); alone Pr 13[12].

†יַחְלְאֵל **n.pr.m.** (*wait for God!*);—a Zebulunite Gn 46[14] Nu 26[26] (𝔊 Αλοηλ, Αιηλ, Αλληλ)

†יַחְלְאֵלִי **adj.gent.** of foregoing: only c art. as n pr coll. Nu 26[26].

†[יָחַם] **vb.** be hot, **Pi.** conceive (Ar وَحِمَ v *incaluerunt* pecora, Frey; Aram יְחַם *be hot*, usu of sexual impulse of animals)—**Qal** v. חמם. **Pi.** *Pf* 3 fs. sf. יֶחֱמַתְנִי ψ 51[7] in sin my mother *conceived me* (‖חוֹלָלְתִּי), *Inf. cstr* of *heat* of cattle in breeding, conception; בְּכָל־יַחֵם Gn 30[41] *at every breeding-heat* of the flock (J), בְּעֵת יַחֵם 31[10] *at the time of* the flock's *being hot in breeding* (E); sf 3 fpl לְיַחְמֵנָּה 30[41] *in order that they might have breeding-heat* (J).

חֵמָה (once חֵמָא) [121] **n f** heat, rage (for יֶחֱמָה; NH *id*; Aram. חֵמָא, יְחֵמָא *poison*, ܚܡܬܐ *heat, wrath, poison*, Brock[Lex 116], also Nö[§105]; Ar حُمَةٌ *poison*, Lane[651], As *imtu, spittle, breath, poison*, Dl[HWB 78] Muss-Arnolt[CD 62])—abs. חֵמָה Na 1[2] + 39 t.; חֵמָא + Dn 11[44]; cstr. חֲמַת Gn 27[44] + 25 t, sf חֲמָתִי Je 4[4] + 36 t, חֲמָתְךָ Je 10[25] + 8 t.; חֲמָתֶךָ ψ 88[8] 89[47]; חֲמָתוֹ Is 51[17] + 8 t; חֲמָתָם Jb 6[4], pl חֵמוֹת Pr 22[24], חֵמֹת ψ 76[11],—**1.** *heat:* **a.** *fever*, חֲמַת מִיָּיִן Ho 7[5] *fever from wine, wine-fever* (on st cstr v. Ges[§130.1]) **b.** *venom, poison* (fig.): ח׳ זֹחֲלֵי עָפָר Dt 32[24], ח׳ תַּנִּינִם v[33]; ח׳ נָחָשׁ ψ 58[5] cf v[5], ח׳ עַכְשׁוּב ψ 140[4]; *poison* of arrows (of י׳) Jb 6[4]. **2.** *burning anger, rage*: **a.** of man: Gn 27[44] (J), 2 S 11[20] 2 K 5[12] Est 1[12] 2[1] 3[5] 5[9] (against, עַל), 7[7.10] ψ 37[8] (‖אַף), 76[11] (yet on txt v Che), Pr 6[34] 15[1.18] (אִישׁ חֵמָה *man of rage*= raging or wrathful man), 16[4] 19[19] (גְּדָל־ח׳ Qr =*one great in rage*, v De Now), 27[4] (‖אַף), Is 51[13.13] Ez 23[25]; אִישׁ חֵמוֹת Pr 22[24] (‖בַּעַל אַף); בַּעַל חֵמָה 29[22] (‖אִישׁ אַף), חֵמָה עַזָּה *strong rage* Pr 21[14] (‖אַף), חֲמַת רוּחִי Ez 3[14] *the rage of my spirit.* **b.** of the he-goat in Daniel's vision, בַּחֲמַת כֹּחוֹ Dn 8[6] *in the fury of his power.* **c.** of God (י׳), oft. Je Is[2] Ez ψ Je 4[4] + 16 t Je; 2 K 22[13.17] Is 27[4] (Hi Ew Di Du; on other interpr, and on txt v. Di), 63[5] La 2[4] Ez 5[13] + 29 t. Ez; Nu 25[11] (P), 2 Ch 12[7] 34[21.25] 36[16] ψ 59[14] 79[6] 88[8] 89[47] 106[23] Jb 21[20]; appar. also 19[29] 36[18] v. Di; oft ‖אַף, Mi 5[14] Dt 9[19] 29[22] Is 42[25] (אַפּוֹ as appos, + עֱזוּז מִלְחָמָה), 63[3.6] Dn 9[16] ψ 6[2] 78[38] 90[7], לְהָשִׁיב בְּחֵמָה אַפּוֹ Is 66[15] (‖וְגַעֲרָתוֹ בְּלַהֲבֵי־אֵשׁ), + Je 23[19] 30[23] of the whirlwind of י׳, ‖ אַף + קֶצֶף גָּדוֹל Dt 29[27] Je 21[5] 32[37], ‖ אַף + תוכחות חמה Ez 5[15], cf תּוֹכְחוֹת חֵמָה alone 25[17], ‖ אַפּוֹ חֲרוֹן Na 1[6] La 4[11], ‖ קֶצֶף Is 34[2] (of fury *against*, עַל), ψ 38[2], ‖ גְּעָרָה Is 51[20]; חֵמָה גְדוֹלָה קִנְאָתִי Ez 36[6], cf ‖ גְּמוּל 59[18], ‖ קִנְאָה Zc 8[2] (‖ קִנְאָה גְדוֹלָה), דַּם חֵמָה וְקִנְאָה Ez 16[38] (on txt v. Co); חֲמַת קֶרִי Lv 26[28] *rage of meeting*, i e. *encountering* them *in rage;* כּוֹס חֲמָתוֹ (־תִי) Is 51[17.22] *the cup of his (my) fury;* כּוֹס הַיַּיִן הַחֵמָה הַזֹּאת Je 25[15]; בַּעַל חֵמָה *a possessor of fury= furious* Na 1[2] (‖אֵל קַנּוֹא, נֹקֵם); חֵמָה עַל=*rage against* one. Is 34[2] 2 Ch 28[9] —Vbs used with חֵמָה are: **2 a.**. שׁוּב Gn 27[44], הֵשִׁיב Pr 15[1], עָלָה 2 S 11[20], בָּעַר Est 1[12], שָׁכַךְ 2[1] 7[10]; **2. c.**. הֵשִׁיב *turn away* wrath of י׳ Nu 25[11] ψ 106[23] Je 18[20] (but הָשִׁיב בְּחֵמָה אַפּוֹ Is 66[15] *to recompense his anger in fury*, give it as requital); ח׳ י׳ *is kindled against* one יצת ב Niph 2 K 22[13.17], it *burns* בָּעֲרָה Je 4[4] 21[12] 44[6] ψ 89[47], *arises* עלה 2 Ch 36[16], cf. as obj. of עלה Hiph. Ez 24[8], *is*

poured out נִתְּכָה בְּ 2 Ch 12^{7} 34$^{21.25}$ Je 7^{20}, נִתְּכָה עַל 42$^{18.18}$ 44^{6}, נִתְּכָה כָאֵשׁ Na 1^{6}; י׳ *pours it out* ψ 79^{6} שָׁפַךְ אֶל Is 42^{25} Je 10^{25} Ez 7^{8} 9^{8} 14^{19} 16^{38} (acc. to Co's conject), 20$^{8.13.21}$ 22^{22} 30^{15} 36^{18}; שָׁפַךְ כָּאֵשׁ La 2^{4}; חֵמָה שפוכה Ez 20$^{33.34}$; הניח ח׳ ב *bring to rest* (i e satisfy) *one's fury upon* Ez 5^{13} 16^{42} 24^{13}; כִּלָּה ח׳ La 4^{11}; + בְּ Ez 5^{13} *I have accomplished my fury upon them* (in their case), 6^{12} 13^{15}]

יַחְמוּר v. sub iv. חמר

יַחְמַי v. sub חמה.

יחף (√of foll.; orig mng unknown; NH Aram. יָחֵף adj as Heb, Syr Aph. ܐܚܦܝ *discalceatus fuit*, cf. perh. Ar. حفى (transp.) *walk barefoot*, also *become chafed*, of foot or hoof).

† **יָחֵף adj. barefoot**, alw abs יָחֵף Is 20^{2} + 4 t.;—הלך עָרוֹם וְיָחֵף Is 20^{2} (נַעַלְךָ תַּחֲלֹץ מֵעַל רַגְלֶךָ in preceding cl), v^{3}; הֹלֵךְ יָחֵף 2 S 15^{30}; נָהֵג יָחֵף Is 20^{3}, appar = subst., מנעי רַגְלֵךְ מִיָּחֵף Je 2^{25} *withhold thy foot from bareness* (Syr. ܚܦܝܘܬܐ *discalceatio*)

יַחְצְאֵל, יַחְצִיאֵל, יַחְצְאֵלִי v. sub חצה.

(ו)יחר Kt 2 S 20^{5} (Qr וַיּוֹחֶר), v. אחר supr. p. 29^{b} and Dr^{Sm}.

יחשׂ (√of foll.; meaning unknown; deriv. common in NH and Aram)

† **יַחַשׂ n.[m.] genealogy** (NH יָחַס, יחוּס, Aram. יִחוּס)—סֵפֶר הַיַּחַשׂ Ne 7^{5} *book of genealogy*.

† **[הִתְיַחֵשׂ] vb. Hithp. denom. enrol oneself or be enrolled by genealogy** (NH oft. in Pi. (also Hithp), Aram. Pa. (Ithpa.))—*Pf.* 3 mpl. הִתְיַחְשׂוּ 1 Ch 5^{17} 9^{1}; *Inf. cstr.* הִתְיַחֵשׂ 5^{1} + 5 t; sf. הִתְיַחְשָׂם 1 Ch 4^{33} + 7 t; *Pt.* pl. הַמִּתְיַחְשִׂים Ezr 2^{62} Ne 7^{64};—*be enrolled by genealogy* 1 Ch 5^{17} 9^{1} Ne 7^{5}; perh. also לְהִתְי׳ 2 Ch 12^{15} (tr. to 11^{16} acc. to Hi Be, v. VB); וְלֹא לְהִתְי׳ לַבְּכֹרָה 1 Ch 5^{1} *but he is not to be enrolled in the place of first-born*; sq בְּ (*among, of, consisting in*) 7^{40}, without לְ 7^{7} Ezr 8^{1}; הִתְי׳ הַכֹּהֲנִים 2 Ch 31^{17}; *Inf* = *genealogical enrolment* 1 Ch 4^{33} these were their dwellings and they had (לָהֶם) *genealogical enrolment*, cf. 7$^{5.9}$, בהתי׳ 5^{7} *at the enrolment* of (לְ) their generations, הֵמָּה בְּחַצְרֵיהֶם הִתְיַחְשָׂם 1 Ch 9^{22} *as for them, in their villages was their enrolment*; nearly = *genealogical list* 2 Ch 31^{16} (לִזְכָרִים); i.e. the males whose names were in the list), so Ezr 8^{3}, cf. 2 Ch 31$^{18.19}$ (all sq. בְּ *among, of*); *Pt.* pl c. art בִּקְשׁוּ כְתָבָם הַמִּתְיַחְשִׂים Ezr 2^{62} = Ne 7^{64} *they sought their writing* (their book), namely *the enrolled*, i e their genealogical record.

יַחַת v. sub חתת

† **[יָטַב] vb. be good, well, glad, pleasing** (Aram יְטַב; Zinj. יטב DHM$^{Sendsch 57}$)—**Qal** (*Pf* not in use, v. טוֹב **vb.**) *Impf* יִיטַב Gn 12^{13} + 34 t, יִטַב 1 S 24^{5} + 3 t, תִּיטַב Est 2^{4} + 2 t; תִיטבי (incorrect for תֵּיטְבִי Ges$^{§70 R}$) Na 3^{8}; pl. ייטבו Gn 34^{18}; for *Inf* and *Pt.* v טוב—**1.** *be glad, joyful*, לב Ju 18^{20} 19$^{6.9}$ 1 K 21^{7} Ru 3^{7} Ec 7^{3}. **2.** *be well placed*, הֲתִיטְבִי מנא אָמוֹן Na 3^{8} *art thou better placed than No of Amon?* **3.** impers. c. לְ, *be well for* or *with, go well with* Gn 12^{13}(J), 40^{14}(E), Dt 4^{40} 5$^{16.26}$ 6$^{3.18}$ 12$^{25.28}$ 22^{7} 2 K 25^{24} Ru 3^{1} Je 7^{23} 38^{20} 40^{9} 42^{6}. **4.** *be pleasing* בְּעֵינֵי Gn 34^{18}(J), 41^{37} 45^{16} (E), Dt 1^{23} Lv 10$^{19.20}$ Jos 22$^{30.33}$ (P), 1 S 18^{5} 24^{5} 2 S 3^{36} 18^{4} 1 K 3^{10} Est 1^{21} 2$^{4.4.9}$, c לְ, *be pleasing to*, ψ 69^{32}, c. לִפְנֵי (late) Ne 2$^{5.6}$ Est 5^{14}. **Hiph.** *Pf* היטיב Gn 12^{16} Jos 24^{20}; הֵיטַב 1 S 25^{31}; sf הֵיטִבְךָ Dt 30^{5}, הֵיטַבְתְּ Je 1^{12}; הֵיטַבְתְּ Ru 3^{10}, etc; וְהֵטִבֹתִי Ez 36^{11} (for הֵיטַבְתִּי as if from טוב Ges$^{§70 R}$); *Impf* יֵיטִיב Nu 10^{32} + 3 t.; יֵיטִב Pr 15^{13} + 2 t., ייטיב Jb 24^{21} (Ges$^{§70 R}$), וַיֵּיטִב 1 K 1^{47} (Ges$^{§70 R}$), וַיֵּיטֶב Ex 1^{20}, sf. וְיטִיבְךָ Ec 11^{9}, etc.; *Imv.* הֵיטִיבָה ψ 51^{20}; הֵיטִיבִי Is 23^{16}, etc.; *Inf. abs* היטיב Je 7^{5} 10^{5}; הֵיטֵב Gn 32^{13} + 10 t., *Inf cstr.* היטיב Lv 5^{4} + 7 t, הֵטִיב Je 32^{41}; sf היטיבי Je 32^{40}, etc; *Pt.* מֵיטִיב 1 S 16^{17}; מֵטִיב ψ 119^{68}, מטב Ez 33^{32}, etc.;—**1.** *make glad, rejoice* לב Ju 19^{22}, פנים Pr 15^{13}; the person Ec 11^{9}. **2.** *do good* to, *deal well* with, a person, usu. c prep c לְ, Ex 1^{20} Jos 24^{20} (both E), Gn 12^{16} Nu 10$^{29.32}$ (all J), Ju 17^{13} 1 S 25^{31} ψ 49^{19} 125^{4}; c. עם, Gn 32$^{10.13.13}$ Nu 10^{32} (all J), Mi 2^{7}; c. acc. Dt 8^{16} 28^{63} 30^{5} 1 S 2^{32} Je 18^{10} 32$^{40.41}$ Zc 8^{15} Jb 24^{21} ψ 51^{20}; abs. Ez 36^{11}, opp. הֵרַע (in prov. phr, cannot *do good or ill*, = cannot do anything at all; test of deity) Zp 1^{12} Is 41^{23} Je 10^{5}. **3.** *do well* or *thoroughly*: הטיבו (כל)אשר דברו *they have done well* (all) *that they have spoken* Dt 5^{25} 18^{17}, על הרע כפים להיטיב Mi 7^{3} *their hands are upon the evil to do it well*, i e. *diligently, thoroughly*, lit *make* (*it*) *good*, with play on הרע; esp as auxil. sq inf., היט׳ דעת Pr 15^{2} = *know well*; לראות Je 1^{12} *see well*; (לְ)נַגֵּן *play well, skilfully* 1 S 16^{17} Is 23^{16} Ez 33^{32}, cf. pt. cstr. sq. subst. מטבי צַעַד Pr 30^{29} *marching well*,

in a stately manner, so מיטבי לֶכֶת v^{29}, inf. abs. היטיב as adv = *thoroughly*, c. vbs כתת Dt 9^{21}, שאל 13^{15}, דרש 17^{4} 19^{18}, באר 27^{8}, שבר 2 K 11^{18} **4.** *make a thing good, right, beautiful*. c acc rei the head 2 K 9^{30}, *dress, trim*: a lamp Ex 30^{7} (P), מַצֵּבוֹת Ho 10^{1}, גהה Pr 17^{22} a glad heart *maketh a good cure*, sq. מִן compar., obj שׁם 1 K 1^{47} (= *make it more glorious than*), חֶסֶד Ru 3^{10}, sq דֶּרֶךְ = *course of life* or *action* Je 2^{33} (in order to win love); *amend* one's ways and doings Je 7^{3} 18^{11} 26^{13} 35^{15}, היטיב תיטיבו את־ד׳ 7^{5} **5.** *do well, right*, ethically, abs. **a.** of men, Gn 4$^{7\,7}$ (J), Lv 5^{4} (P), ψ 36^{4} Is 1^{17} Je 4^{22} 13^{23} **b.** of God, טוב ממיב *good and doing good* ψ 119^{68}, so inf abs as adv הַהֵיטֵב חָרָה לָךְ Jon 4$^{4\,9}$ *art thou rightly angry?* sq לי v^{9} In כִּי־יִיטַב אֶל־אָבִי 1 S 20^{13} vb. is appar intrans, = **Qal**, *if it be pleasing unto my father*, but **Hiph.** not elsewh in this sense, point rather יִיטַב, on this and on foll. אֶת־ v We Dr.

†יָטְבָה **n.pr.loc.** (*pleasantness*) city prob. in Judah 2 K 21^{19}, site unknown.

†יָטְבָתָה **n.pr.loc.** (*pleasantness*) station of Isr in wilderness Nu 33$^{33.34}$ (P), Dt 10^{7}, site unknown

†מְהֵיטַבְאֵל **n pr.pers.** (= מיטיב אל *God benefits*)—**1. f.** an Edomite princess Gn 36^{39} (P), 1 Ch 1^{50} **2. m** ancestor of the false prophet Shemaiah Ne 6^{10}.

†(מֵיטָב) **n.[m.]** the best, only cstr. מֵיטַב and as superl, *the best* of a thing. מ׳ שָׂדֵהוּ ומ׳ כַּרְמוֹ Ex 22^{4} (JE) *the best* of his field and *the best* of his vineyard (choicest fruit); מ׳ הַצֹּאן *the best of the sheep* 1 S 15$^{9\,15}$, בְּמ׳ הָאָרֶץ *in the best of the land* Gn 47$^{6\,11}$ (P).

יוֹטָה, יֻטָּה v sub נטה

יטור v sub טור.

יין (√ of foll, meaning unknown, regarded as loan-word by Lag$^{\text{Armen Stud §484}}$ al., Hom$^{\text{ZMG 1889 653 ff Aufsätze 1892, 102}}$ comp Georgian *g'wino, wine*, whence also (acc to him) Armen *gini*, Gk ϝοῖνος, Lat *vinum*, cf on the other hand Jen$^{\text{l c infr}}$)

יַיִן $_{-141}$ **n m** $^{ψ\,75\,9}$ wine (NH *id*, Eth ወይን: *vitis, vinea, vinum*, Ar وَيْن (*black*) *grapes*, v Hom$^{\text{ZMG 1889 654}}$, Sab ויין *vineyard*, Mordt$^{\text{ZMG 1887 364}}$ Hom$^{\text{l c 649}}$ (both after Glaser), As *inu* in vocabularies, but this loan-word from western Shemites, acc to Hom$^{\text{Aufsätze 102}}$; Jen$^{\text{ZA 1 1886 f., ZMG 1890. 705}}$ argues to the contrary)—abs. יָ֑יִן Gn 9^{21} + 84 t; יַ֫יִן Gn 14^{18} + 33 t, cstr יֵין ψ 60^{5} Ct 8^{2}; יֵין Dt 32^{18} + 9 t, sf. ייני Ct 5^{1}, etc;—*wine*: **a.** common drink, for refreshment Gn 14^{18} (E?) 27^{25} (J), Ju 19^{19} 2 S 16^{2} Am 5^{11} 9^{14} Ho 14^{8} Jb 1$^{13.18}$ Dn 1^{5} +, tonic Pr 31^{6}, art of commerce Ez 27^{18} Ne 13^{15}, among supplies in strongholds 2 Ch 11^{11}; as making merry 2 S 13^{28} Zc 9^{15} 10^{7} Est 1^{10} Ec 9^{7} 10^{19} ψ 104^{15}. †**b.** used for rejoicing before י׳ Dt 14^{26}, cf Ho 9^{4}, as drink-offering in prescribed ritual Ex 29^{40} Lv 23^{13} Nu 15$^{5\,7\,10}$ 28^{14}; among temple stores 1 Ch 9^{29}, used also in heathen ceremonial, v Dt 32^{33} **c.** intoxicating 1 S 1^{14} 25^{37} Gn 9$^{21\,24}$ 19$^{32.33.34.35}$ (all J), Is 5$^{11\,22}$ Pr 21^{17} 23$^{30.31}$ +; ‖ תירוש Ho 4^{11}, ‖ שֵׁכָר 1 S 1^{15} Mi 2^{11} Is 24^{9} 28$^{7\,7}$ 56^{12} + 12 t; forbidden to Nazirites †Nu 6$^{3.3}$ (חֹמֶץ יַיִן וְחֹמֶץ שֵׁכָר), v$^{4.20}$, cf. Am 2^{12}; to Rechabites †Je 35$^{2.6\,f}$, to mother of Samson †Ju 13$^{4.7\,14}$; to priests entering sanctuary †Lv 10^{9} (P), Ez 44^{21}; unfitting for kings Pr 31^{4}. †**d.** combinations are יֵין הַטּוֹב Ct 7^{10} = *the best wine* (rd. כַּיַּיִן? Ges$^{\text{§ 133. 3, R 1}}$, יֵין מַלְכוּת Est 1^{7} *royal wine*; אצרות הַיַּיִן 1 Ch 27^{27} *stores of wine, wine-supply*; יַיִן הָרֶקַח Ct 8^{2} *spiced wine*; משתה הַיַּיִן *wine-feast* Est 5^{6} 7$^{2\,7\,8}$, סבאי יין Pr 23^{20} *wine-bibbers*; נאד יין *wine-skin* Jos 9$^{4\,13}$ 1 S 16^{20}, נבל יין *id.* 1 S 1^{24} 10^{3} 25^{18} 2 S 16^{1} Je 13$^{12\,12}$, בית הַיַּיִן Ct 2^{4} either *wine-house*, where wine is drunk, feasting-house (De al), or *place of wine* = vineyard (Ew al.; cf גֶּפֶן יַיִן Nu 6^{4}). †**e.** metaph of wisdom's drink Pr 9$^{2\,5}$, cf. Is 55^{1}, of י׳'s wrath Je 25^{15} (כוס היין); of confusion sent by י׳, יַיִן תַּרְעֵלָה *wine of reeling* ψ 60^{5}, cf 75^{9}; of י׳'s awaking for vengeance, like a wine-shouter ψ 78^{65}; of Babylon's fierce power Je 51^{7}, of love Ct 5^{1}, יֵין חֲמָסִים Pr 4^{17}, in sim of one bursting with words Jb 32^{19}, of disheartened proph. Je 23^{9} (כְּגֶבֶר עֲבָרוֹ יָיִן); of lover's mouth Ct 7^{10} (v. supr.), love is better than wine Ct 1^{2} 4^{10}

יך 1 S 4^{13} Kt; err for יד Qr

†[יָכַח] **vb. Hiph.** decide, adjudge, prove, (NH Pi וִכֵּחַ *argue with* (עם), cf. Hithp, Hiph *prove, correct*, Aram Pa וַכַּח, Aph אוֹכַח, *id*)—**Hiph.** *Pf* הוכיח Is 2^{4} + 5 t; הֹכִיחַ Gn 24^{44}, הוֹכַח Gn 21^{25}; 2 ms הֹכַחְתָּ Gn 24^{14}, 1 s. sf הוֹכַחְתִּיו 2 S 7^{14}, *Impf.* יוֹכִיחַ Is 11^{3} + 5 t, יוכח Ho 4^{4} + 4 t, יוֹכַח 1 Ch 12^{17}; sf. יוכיחני ψ 141^{5} + 12 t. Impf, *Imv* הוֹכַח Pr 9^{8}; *Inf. abs* הוכח Lv 19^{17} + 5 t, cstr. הוֹכִיחַ Hb 1^{12}, הַלְהוֹכַח Jb 6^{26}, *Pt.* מוֹכִיחַ Ez 3^{26} + 8 t; pl מוֹכִיחִים Pr 24^{25};—**1.** *decide, judge*, abs Gn 31^{42} (E), 1 Ch 12^{17} Is 11^{3} ψ 94^{10}, c לְ, *decide for*

Is 2^{4}=Mi 4^{3}, Is 11^{4}; c. בֵּין, Gn 31^{37} (E), Jb 9^{33}; לְגֶבֶר עִם אֱלוֹהַּ Jb 16^{21}. **2.** *adjudge, appoint,* c. לְ, Gn 24$^{14.44}$(J). **3.** *shew to be right, prove,* c. acc. rei and עַל pers. *against* Jb 19^{5}; c. אֶל pers. *unto* Jb 13^{15}; so *argue* before v^{3}, and (abs.) 15^{3}. **4.** *convince, convict,* c. acc. pers. ψ 50^{21} בְּ pers. Pr 30^{6}; c. לְ pers. Jb 32^{12}. **5.** *reprove, chide:* **a.** of God, c. acc. pers. Jb 22^{4} ψ 50^{8} 105^{14} =1 Ch 16^{21}; c. בְּ obj. 2 K 19^{4}=Is 37^{4}. **b.** of man, abs. Ho 4^{4} Ez 3^{26} Jb 6$^{25.26}$ Pr 24^{25} 25^{12}; מוֹכִיחַ בַּשַּׁעַר Am 5^{10} Is 29^{21}; c. acc. pers. Gn 21^{25}(E), Lv 19$^{17.17}$ (H), Pr 9^{8} 28^{23} Je 2^{19}; מוֹכִיחַ אֱלוֹהַּ Jb 40^{2}; acc. rei Jb 6^{26}; c. לְ, Pr 9$^{7.8}$ 15^{12} 19^{25}. **6.** *correct, rebuke,* of God, abs. Hb 1^{12}; c. acc. pers. ψ 141^{5} Jb 13$^{10.10}$; בְּשֵׁבֶט 2 S 7^{14}; happy the man whom God corrects Jb 5^{17}; for God loves him Pr 3^{12}; God is entreated not to correct in anger ψ 6^{2} 38^{2}. **Hoph.** *Pf.* וְהוּכַח בְּמַכְאוֹב *he is chastened also with pain* Jb 33^{19}. **Niph.** *Impf.* לְכוּ־נָא וְנִוָּכְחָה Is 1^{18} *come now and let us reason together; Pt.* שָׁם יָשָׁר נוֹכָח עִמּוֹ Jb 23^{7} *there an upright man might reason with him;* f. (pass.) וְנֹכַחַת Gn 20^{16} (E), but Di SS rd. וְנֹכַחַתְּ 2 fs. *Pf. and thou art set right, righted, justified.* **Hithp.** *Impf.* עִם־יִשְׂרָאֵל יִתְוַכָּח Mi 6^{2} *with Israel he will argue* (‖ רִיב לי׳ עִם).

†**תּוֹכֵחָה** n.f. rebuke, correction;—יוֹם ת׳ Ho 5^{9}; יוֹם צרה ות׳ 2 K 19^{3}=Is 37^{3}; pl. תּוֹכֵחוֹת ψ 149^{7} (‖ נקמה).

†**תּוֹכַחַת** n.f. argument, reproof;—ת׳ Pr 10^{17}+9 t.; sf. תּוֹכַחְתִּי Hb 2^{1}+5 t.; תּוֹכַחְתּוֹ Pr 3^{11}; pl. תּוֹכָחוֹת ψ 38^{15}+3 t.; cstr. תּוֹכְחוֹת Pr 6^{23} Ez 25^{17}; תֹּכְחוֹת 5^{15} (but latter del. Co; given by SS under תּוֹכֵחָה);—**1.** *argument, impeachment,* spoken by lips and mouth ψ 38^{15} Jb 13^{6} 23^{4} Hb 2^{1}. **2.** *reproof, chiding* Pr 1^{23} 27^{5}; ‖ עצה 1$^{25.30}$; ‖ מוסר 3^{11} 5^{12} 10^{17} 12^{1} 13^{18} 15$^{5.10.32}$; ת׳ מוסר 6^{23} *reproofs for discipline;* ת׳ חיים 15^{31} *reproof that giveth life;* איש תוכחות 29^{1} *man of reproofs* (who deserves them). **3.** *correction, rebuke* ψ 39^{12} 73^{14}; שֵׁבֶט ות׳ Pr 29^{15}; ת׳ חֵמָה Ez 5^{15} 25^{17}.

יָכֹל, יָכוֹל 193 **vb. be able, have power, prevail, endure** (NH *id.*; Aram. יְכִיל; As. *akâlu*, Hpt in KAT^{2} Gloss I.)—**Qal** *Pf.* יָכֹל Gn 32^{26} +8 t.; יָכוֹל 1 S 4^{15}+2 t.; 3 fs. יָכְלָה Gn 36^{7} Ex 2^{3}; 2 ms. וְיָכָלְתָּ Ex 18^{23}; 1 s. יָכֹלְתִּי Gn 30^{8}+2 t.; sf. יְכָלְתִּיו ψ 13^{5}; 3 pl. יָכְלוּ Gn 13^{6}+27 t.+Jos 15^{63} Qr; יָכֹלוּ Ex 8^{14}+2 t.; *Impf.* 3 ms. יוּכַל Gn 13^{16}+34 t.; יוּכָל Jb 4^{2}+4 t.; וַיּוּכַל Ho 12^{5}; 3 fs. תּוּכַל Am 7^{10}+2 t.; 2 ms. תּוּכַל Gn 15^{5}+16 t.; 1 s. אוּכַל Gn 19^{19}+30 t., etc. (on these Impf. forms as irreg. Qal, v. Ges §69, 2, R. 3 Kö I. 407 W SG 237; others **Hoph.**); *Inf. cstr.* יְכֹלֶת Nu 14^{16} Dt 9^{28}; *Inf. abs.* יָכוֹל Nu 13^{30} 2 Ch 32^{13}; יָכֹל Nu 22^{38} 1 S 26^{25}; P 8 t. (not Lv), Ez 3 t.; oft. JED Je Is^{2}, not seld. SK Ch;—**1.** *be able,* to do a thing, whether ability be physical, moral, constitutional, or dependent on external authority; usu. of man Gn 13^{16}(J)+, but also of gods 2 Ch 32$^{13.15}$, and of י׳ Nu 14^{16} (JE), Dt 9^{28} Je 44^{22}; occasionally of inanimate things Am 7^{10} Gn 36^{7} (P), Ct 8^{7} Ec 1$^{15.15}$, etc.: **a.** usu. sq. inf. c. לְ (122 t.), Gn 31^{35} *I am not able to rise up;* 45^{1} *Joseph was not able to restrain himself,* v^{3} 48^{10}; Ex 7$^{21.24}$ *were not able to drink,* 12^{39} Jos 24^{19} (all E); Gn 13^{16} *if a man can number the dust,* 19$^{19.22}$ 43^{32} 44$^{22.26.26}$ Ex 10^{5} 19^{23} (all J), Gn 15^{5} Ex 15^{23} Nu 11^{14} (all JE)+10 t. JE; Dt 7^{17}+10 t. D; Gn 13^{6} *they could not dwell together,* 34^{14} 36^{7} Ex 9^{11} 40^{35} Nu 9^{6} Jos 9^{19} (all P); 1 S 3^{2} 6^{20} 1 K 9^{21} (on ‖ 2 Ch 8^{8} and text of Ju 1^{19} v. Bu RS 8), Am 7^{10} Ho 5^{13} Zp 1^{18} Je 6^{10} 11^{11} 13^{23} 18^{6} 19^{11}+. †**b.** sq. inf. without לְ (27 t.; not P): Gn 37^{4} Ex 2^{3} 18$^{18.23}$ (all E), Gn 24^{50} 44^{1} (J), Nu 22$^{37.38}$ (JE), Dt 1^{9} 7^{22} 14^{24} 22^{29} Ju 8^{3} Je 49$^{10.23}$ Hb 1^{13} Is 46^{2} 47$^{11.12}$ 57^{20} La 1^{14} ψ 18^{39} 36^{13} 78^{20} Pr 30^{21} Jb 4^{2} 33^{5}. †**c.** c. inf. implic., alw. neg., Gn 29^{8} go and feed them; and they said, *We are not able, cannot* (J), Ex 8^{14} (P), Is 29^{11} Je 20^{9} ψ 21^{12} Jon 1^{13}. **d.** c. neg.=*may not* (of moral inability): Gn 43^{32} (J) the Egyptians *might not eat* bread with the Hebrews; Ju 21^{18} *we may not give* them wives; esp. D, Dt 7^{22} 12^{17} 14^{24} 16^{5} 17^{15} 22^{3} 28$^{27.35}$. †**e.** *be able,* sq. impf.: אוּלַי אוּכַל נַכֶּה Nu 22^{6} (JE) *perchance I am able* (so that) *we smite* (v. Di; rd. perh. נוּכַל for אוּכַל Ges §120. 1 b); לֹא יוּכְלוּ יִגְּעוּ La 4^{14} *they are unable, they touch=are unable to touch* (Dr §163, Obs.) †**f.** *be able,* sq. pf. consec., only very late, אוּכַל וְרָאִיתִי Est 8$^{6.6}$, lit. how *shall I be able and see?*—Also in various combinations where English idiom would make it an auxiliary to another verb: †**g.** *able to gain, accomplish:* sq. acc. לֹא יוּכְלוּ נִקָּיֹן Ho 8^{5} how long *will they be unable* (to gain) *innocence?* יָדַעְתָּ כִּי־כֹל תּוּכָל Jb 42^{2} *I know that thou art able* (to do) *all things;* אֵין הַמֶּלֶךְ יוּכַל אֶתְכֶם דָּבָר Je 38^{5} *the king is not* (one who is) *able* (to do) *anything with* (אִתְּכֶם for אֶתְכֶם v. Gf, i.e. *against*) *you.* †**h.** *able to endure:* לֹא אוּכַל אָוֶן וַעֲצָרָה Is 1^{13} *I cannot endure iniquity and* (with) *a solemn assembly,* ψ 101^{5}. †**i.** *able to reach,* sq. לְ, ψ 139^{6} it is high, לֹא אוּכַל לָהּ *I cannot* (*reach*) *to it.*

†**2.** *prevail:* **a.** abs. *prevail, overcome, be victor* Gn 30^{8} (E), 32^{29} (J), Ho 12^{5} 1 S 26^{25} 1 K 22^{22} = 2 Ch 18^{21} Je 20$^{7.11}$; of waves 5^{22}; *succeed* Is 16^{12}, Je 3^{5} (VB *hast had thy way*). **b.** sq. לְ pers., *prevail against, over* Gn 32^{26} (J), Nu 13^{30} (JE), Ju 16^{5} 1 S 17^{9} Je 1^{19} 15^{20} 20^{10} 38^{22} Ob^{7} ψ 129^{2} Est 6^{13}. **c.** once c. sf., יְכָלְתִּיו ψ 13^{5} *I have prevailed over him*, + Zc 9^{15} (where rd. וְיָכְלוּם for וְאָכְלוּ with 𝔊 𝔗 Klo$^{Th\ LZ\ 1879.\ 564}$ Sta$^{ZAW\ 1881,\ 18}$). †**3.** abs. *have ability, strength*, only neg. מִשְּׂאֵתוֹ לֹא אוּכָל Jb 31^{23} *because of his loftiness I have no ability*, am inadequate (to anything).

יוּכַל **n.pr.m.** v. יְהוּכַל supr. p. 220^{b}.

†**יְכָלְיָה, יְכָלְיָהוּ** **n.pr.f.** (י׳ *hath been able;* cf. Sab. יכלאל Hal^{165}) mother of king Azariah: יכליהו 2 K 15^{2}, 𝔊 Χαλεια, 𝔊^{L} Ιεχελια; יכליה 2 Ch 26^{3} (Qr; Kt יכיליה), 𝔊 Χααια, A 𝔊^{L} Ιεχελια.

יְכָנְיָה(וּ), **יְכוֹנְיָה** v. יְהוֹיָכִין p. 220^{b}.

יָלַד$_{\ T\ 497}$ **vb. bear, bring forth, beget** (NH *id.*; Aram. יְלֵיד, יְלִיד, ܝܠܕ; Ar. وَلَدَ *bear, bring forth*, so Eth. ወለደ: As. *alâdu*, COT^{Gloss})—**Qal** *Pf.* יָלַד Gn 4$^{18.18.18}$ + 16 t.; יָלְדָה Je 17^{11}; וְיָלַד consec. ψ 7^{15}; sf. יְלָדְךָ Dt 32^{18}; 2 ms. sf. ילדתני Je 2^{27} Kt; Qr יְלִדְתָּנוּ (Kö$^{I.\ 410}$ Ges$^{§\ 70.\ 2.\ R.\ 4}$); 1 s. sf. יְלִדְתִּיךָ ψ 2^{7}; יְלִדְתִּיהוּ Nu 11^{12}, etc.; *Impf.* (יום) יֵלֶד Pr 27^{1}; 3 fs. תֵּלֵד Gn 17^{17} + 6 t.; וַתֵּלֶד 4^{1} + 61 t.; 2 fs. תֵּלְדִי 3^{16}; אֵלֵד 18^{13}; וָאֵלֵד 1 K 3^{17}; יֵלֵדוּ Is 65^{23}; 3 fpl. תֵּלַדְנָה Je 29^{6}; וַתֵּלַדְנָה Ez 23^{4}; וַתֵּלַדְןָ Gn 30^{39}, etc.; *Inf. abs.* יָלֹד Jb 15^{35}; cstr. לֵדָה Ho 9^{11} + 3 t.; לֶדֶת Gn 4^{2} + 10 t.; לָלֶת 1 S 4^{19} (Kö$^{I.\ 402}$, but prob. txt. err. Dr); sf. לִדְתִּי 1 K 3^{18}, etc.; *Pt. act.* יֹלֵד Pr 17^{21} Je 30^{6}, etc.; f. יוֹלֵדָה Ho 13^{13} + 12 t.; יֹלֶדֶת Gn 17^{19} + 4 t.; יֹלַדְתְּ 16^{11} + 2 t. (Kö$^{I.\ 404\ f.}$; perh. יָלֶדֶת intended by Kt, cf. Sta$^{§\ 213\ b}$); sf. Pr 23^{25}; יוֹלַדְתּוֹ Pr 17^{25}, etc.; pl. יֹלְדוֹת Je 16^{3}; *Pt. pass.* יָלוּד 1 K 3$^{26.27}$; cstr. יְלוּד Jb 14^{1} + 2 t.; pl. יְלוּדִים 1 Ch 14^{4};—**1.** *bear, bring forth:* **a.** (a mother a child,) so commonly, c. 208 t.; sq. acc. Gn 3^{16} 4^{1} & constantly; acc. om. 6^{2} etc. = *be delivered of a child*, 1 K 3$^{17.18}$ 2 K 19^{3} = Is 37^{3} (in proverb c. neg., i.e. human power exhausted); of animals Gn 30^{39} 31$^{8.8}$ Je 14^{5} 17^{11} (bird laying eggs, or hatching out young), Ez 31^{6} Jb 39$^{1.2}$; but also of whole process of labour (cf. חול) וַתְּקַשׁ בְּלִדְתָּהּ Gn 35^{16} cf. v^{17}, 38$^{27.28}$, cf. 1 S 14^{19} Je 31^{18} Mi 5^{2} (of a man, as preposterous, Je 30^{6}, cf. Moses as mother of Israel Nu 11^{12}). **b.** hence in simile of distress Mi 4$^{9.10}$ Is 13^{8} 21^{3} 42^{14} Je 6^{24} 13^{21} 22^{23} 30^{6} 49^{24} 50^{43} ψ 48^{7}, cf. Ho 13^{13}; ילד על־ברכים (Sta$^{ZAW\ 1886,\ 143\ ff.}$) Gn 30^{3} 50^{23} (cf. Jb 3^{12}). **c.** fig. of wicked וְהָרָה עָמָל וְיָלַד שָׁקֶר ψ 7^{15} cf. Jb 15^{35} also Is 33^{11}; of Israelites, bringing forth wind (of vain efforts for deliverance) 26^{18}; כְּפֹר שָׁמַיִם מִי יְלָדוֹ Jb 38^{29}; of Tyre as mother of her inhabitants Is 23^{4}; of Jerus. Is 51^{18} 54^{1} 66$^{7.8}$ Ez 16^{20}, Isr. *bearing* disloyal children Ho 5^{7}; Jerus. and Sam., as Oholibah and Oholah Ez 23^{37}; of Babylon Je 50^{12}; of a day, as producing events לֹא־תֵדַע מַה יֵּלֶד יוֹם Pr 27^{1}; perh. of God (fig. of rock צוּר), as mother of Isr. bringing forth with labour Dt 32^{18} yet v. **2.** **2.** less often *beget:* **a.** lit., c. 22 t., alw. c. acc.; in Hex a mark of J; Gn 4$^{18.18.18}$ 10$^{8.13.15.24.24.26}$ = 1 Ch 1$^{10.11.13.18.18.20}$, Gn 22^{23} 25^{3} (Dt 32^{18} & Nu 11^{12} E are dub.; P uses **Hiph.**), elsewh. Pr 17^{21} 23$^{22.24}$ Dn 11^{6}. **b.** *beget*, fig. ψ 2^{7} of י׳'s formally installing king into theocratic rights. **3.** Zc 13$^{3.3}$, of both parents (lit.); Pt. pass. 3 t. = *child* 1 K 3$^{26.27}$ where mother is named, 1 Ch 14^{4} where father named. †**Niph.** *Pf.* נוֹלַד 1 Ch 2^{3} + 6 t. + הִנּוֹלַד Gn 21^{3} acc. to points, but rd. Pt. (v. Di); נוֹלְדוּ 3^{5} 20^{8} (cf. Ol$^{§\ 263\ b}$ Ges$^{§\ 70.\ 2,\ R.\ 5}$); *Impf.* יִוָּלֵד Gn 17^{17} + 4 t.; יִוָּלֶד Is 66^{8}; וַיִּוָּלֵד Gn 4^{18} + 2 t., etc.; *Inf.* הִוָּלֵד Gn 21^{5}; הִוָּלְדוֹ Ec 7^{1}; הִוָּלְדָהּ Ho 2^{5}; *Pt.* נוֹלָד 1 K 13^{2} + 3 t. (Gn 21^{3} v. supr.); נוֹלָדִים 48^{5} 1 Ch 7^{21};—*be born:* of human beings, sq. לְ (born to such and such a man), Gn 4^{18} 10^{1} 17^{17} 21$^{3.5}$ 46^{20} 48^{5} Nu 26^{60} Dt 23^{9} 2 S 3^{2} (Qr), 5^{13} 14^{27} 1 Ch 2$^{3.9}$ 3$^{1.4.5}$ 20$^{6.8}$ 22^{9} 26^{6} Jb 1^{2} cf. 1 K 13^{2}; without לְ, Jb 3^{3} 38^{21} ψ 78^{6} 1 Ch 7^{21} Ec 7^{1} (טוֹב שֵׁם מִשֶּׁמֶן טוֹב וְיוֹם הַמָּוֶת מִיּוֹם הִוָּלְדוֹ:); metaph. of Israel (under fig. of unfaithful wife) Ho 2^{5}; of nation, גּוֹי, Is 66^{8}, people, עָם, ψ 22^{32}; of animals Lv 22^{27} Dt 15^{19}; *Pt.* כָּל־נָשִׁים וְהַנּוֹלָד מֵהֶם Ezr 10^{3}; c. pred. or appos. on which emph. rests, נ׳ רָשׁ Ec 4^{14} *he was born poor;* אֹהֵב הָרֵעַ וְאָח לְצָרָה יִוָּלֵד Pr 17^{17}; עַיִר פֶּרֶא אדם יִוָּלֵד Jb 11^{12} 15^{7}. †**Pi.** *Inf.* יַלֶּדְכֶן Ex 1^{16}; *Pt. abs.* מְיַלֶּדֶת Gn 35^{17} + 2 t.; *pl. abs.* מְיַלְּדוֹת Ex 1^{15} + 5 t. in Ex 1;—*cause* (or *help*) *to bring forth*, viz., *assist* or *tend as midwife* Ex 1^{16} sq. acc.; elsewh. only *Pt. f.* as subst. = *midwife;* Gn 35^{17} (E), 38^{28} (J), Ex 1$^{15.17.18.19.19.20.21}$ (E). †**Pu.** *Pf.* יֻלַּד Gn 4^{26} + 13 t.; יוּלַּד Ju 18^{29}; יֻלַּד Gn 41^{50}; יוּלָּד Jb 5^{7}; יֻלְּדוּ Gn 6^{1} + 4 t. + 2 S 3^{2} Kt (Qr וַיִּוָּלְדוּ); יֻלָּדוּ ψ 90^{2}, etc.; *Pt.* (? cf. Kö$^{I.\ 433}$; Ges$^{§\ 52.\ 2,\ R.\ 6}$) הַיּוּלָּד Ju 13^{8} (Bö$^{II.\ p.\ 244}$ pass. Qal); i. q. Niph. *be born*, sq. לְ of father Gn 4^{26} 6^{1} 10$^{21.25}$ 24^{15} (all J), 41^{50} (E), 35^{26} 36^{5} 46$^{22.27}$ (all P),

Ju 18[29] 2 S 3[2.5] 21[20.22] 1 Ch 1[19] Je 20[15]; sq. לְ before grandmother's name Ru 4[17] cf. לָנוּ Is 9[5]; sq. לְ of purpose, destiny, אדם לעמל יוּלָּד Jb 5[7]; יֻלְּדוּ עַל־בִּרְכֵּי יוֹסֵף Gn 50[23] (E; Sam. בִּימֵי יו׳, cit. Di) denoting recognition of children as his; no prep. Je 20[14] 22[26], cf. Ju 13[8] (v. supr.); fig. of foreigners incorporated in spiritual Zion ψ 87[4.5.6]; of production of mountains ψ 90[2]. **Hiph.** *Pf.* הוֹלִיד Gn 11[27] +; הוֹלִד Nu 26[58]; הֹלִיד 1 Ch 2[36] +; sf. וְהוֹלִידָהּ consec. Is 55[10]; הוֹלַדְתָּ Gn 48[6], etc.; *Impf.* יוֹלִיד Gn 17[20] Ec 6[3]; וַיּוֹלֶד Gn 5[3] +; 2 ms. תּוֹלִיד Dt 4[25] + 4 t.; אוֹלִיד Is 66[9]; *Imv.* הוֹלִידוּ Je 29[6]; *Inf. abs.* הוֹלִיד Is 59[4]; *cstr.* sf. הוֹלִידוֹ Gn 5[4] + 16 t.; *Pt.* מוֹלִיד Is 66[9]; מוֹלִדִים Je 16[3];—**1.** *beget* (a father a child) Gn 5[3.4.4] + 56 t. in Gn., Lv 25[45] Nu 26[29.58] (all these P, v. sub **Qal**) + Dt 4[25] 28[41] (v. Di), 1 Ch 2[10.10.11.11] + 84 t. Chr.; Ru 4[18] + 8 t., Ju 11[1] 2 K 20[18] = Is 39[7], Je 29[6] Ez 18[10.14] 47[22] Ec 5[13] 6[3], cf. Is 45[10]; also Je 16[3] אֲבוֹתָם הַמּוֹלִדִים אוֹתָם, cf. freq. Assyr. *abu banûa*, e.g. VR 1[8]; fig. of producing dewdrops Jb 38[28]; of causing the earth to bear grain Is 55[10]; causing Zion to bring forth 66[9]. **2.** *bear*, only fig. 59[4] (‖ הָרוֹ), of wicked, bringing forth iniquity (this favoured by context; others, *beget*). †**Hoph.** *Inf.* הֻלֶּדֶת Gn 40[20] Ez 16[5]; הוּלֶּדֶת Ez 16[4] (Co as foregoing); only יוֹם ה׳ אֶת־ Gn 40[20] Ez 16[4.5] *day of one's being born* = birthday. †**Hithp.** *Impf.* וַיִּתְיַלְדוּ Nu 1[18] denom. fr. תולדת *declared their pedigree* (v. Di).

†**וָלָד** **n.m.** **offspring, child,** only אֵין לָהּ וָלָד Gn 11[30] (J); si vera l. = Ar. وَلَد; Eth. ወልድ፡ (with orig. ו);—in 2 S 6[23], where some edd. have ולד Kt, יֶלֶד Qr, Baer and van d. H give יֶלֶד Kt.

†**יֶלֶד** [89] **n.m.** [Gn 21, 8] **child, son, boy, youth**;—יָלֶד יֶלֶד abs. Gn 4[23] +; cstr. Je 31[20]; יָלֶד Gn 21[16] +; pl. יְלָדִים 33[1] +; cstr. יַלְדֵי Ex 2[6] + 2 t.; יַלְדֵי־ Is 57[4]; sf. יְלָדַי Gn 30[26] 2 K 4[1]; יַלְדֵיהֶם Jb 21[11]; יַלְדֵיהֶן Gn 33[2] + 4 t., etc.;—**a.** *child* = *son, boy*, Gn 21[8.14.15.16] 37[30] 42[22] (all E), 32[23] (Dinah not included), cf. 30[26] 33[1.2.2.5.5.6.7.13.14] 44[20] (all J); Ex 1[17.18] (‖ בֵּן v[16]), 2[3.6.6.7.8.9.9.10] (all E), 21[4] (E; app. = sons + daughters, but ‖ בָּנַי v[5]); pl. = offspring 21[24] (E; Hex, only Gn & Ex, JE); also Ru 1[5] 4[16] 2 S 12[15.18.18.18.18.18.19.19.21.21.22.22] 1 K 3[25] (cf. v[20]), 14[12] 17[21.21.22.23] 2 K 4[1] (cf. v[5]) v[18.26.34.34] Is 8[18] 9[5] (‖ בֵּן), Jo 4[3] (opp. יַלְדָּה), Zc 8[5] (*id.*); of *young* of raven Jb 38[41]; of wild goats and hinds 39[3]; of cow and bear Is 11[7]. **b.** (little) *child, children* 1 S 1[2.2] 2 S 6[23] Ezr 10[1] Ne 12[43] Jb 21[11] (‖ עֲוִילִים), Ho 1[2] La 4[10] Is 57[5]. **c.** *descendants* Is 29[23], יַלְדֵי נכרים (cf. בֵּן) 2[6]. **d.** *youth* Gn 4[23] (J), 1 K 12[8.10.14] = 2 Ch 10[8.10.14], Dn 1[4.10.13.15.17] cf. 2 K 2[24] (‖ נְעָרִים קְטַנִּים v[23]), Ec 4[13.15]. **e.** fig. of apostate Israelites יַלְדֵי־פֶשַׁע Is 57[4] (‖ זֶרַע שָׁקֶר); cf., in good sense, ילד שַׁעֲשֻׁעִים Je 31[20] of Ephraim (‖ בֵּן יַקִּיר).

†**יַלְדָּה** **n.f.** **girl, damsel**;—abs. יַלְדָּה Gn 34[4] Jo 4[3]; וִילָדוֹת Zc 8[5];—*marriageable girl:* of Dinah, daughter of Jacob Gn 34[4]; opp. יֶלֶד Zc 8[5] Jo 4[3].

†**יַלְדוּת** **n.f.** **childhood, youth**;—abs. יַלְדוּת Ec 11[10] (‖ שַׁחֲרוּת); יַלְדוּתֶךָ 11[9]; = young men טַל יַלְדֻתֶךָ ψ 110[3].

†**יִלּוֹד** **adj.** born (irreg. punctuation for יָלוּד, Dr 2 S 5[14])—יִלּוֹד Ex 1[22] 2 S 12[14]; יִלֹּדִים Jos 5[5] 2 S 5[14]; יִלּוֹדִים Je 16[3]; הַבֵּן הַיִּל׳ Ex 1[22] (E), 2 S 12[14] (לְךָ +); הָעָם הַיִּל׳ בַּמִּדְבָּר Jos 5[5] (D); עַל־הַבָּנִים וְעַל־הַבָּנוֹת הַיִּלוֹדִים בַּמָּקוֹם הַזֶּה Je 16[3]; הַיִּלּוֹדִים לוֹ 2 S 5[14].

†[**יָלִיד**] **adj.** **born**, only *cstr.* יְלִיד Gn 17[12] + 4 t.; pl. יְלִידֵי 14[14] + 6 t.; בִּילִדֵי 2 S 21[18];—*born*, esp. of slave יְלִיד בַּיִת born in (one's) house (opp. purchased by money) Gn 17[12.13.27] Lv 22[11] (all P), cf. Je 2[14] where denied of Israel; יְלִידֵי בַיִת *id.* Gn 14[14]; pl. elsewh. subst. = *children, sons* יל׳ הרפה 2 S 21[16.18] cf. יל׳ הָרְפָאִים 1 Ch 20[4]; יל׳ הענק Nu 13[22.28] Jos 15[14] (all JE).

†**מוֹלֶדֶת** **n.f.** **kindred, birth, offspring**;—מ׳ cstr. Lv 18[9.11]; sf. מוֹלַדְתִּי Gn 24[4] + 3 t., etc.; pl. sf. מוֹלְדוֹתַיִךְ Ez 16[4]; מְלֹרֹתַיִךְ v[3];—**1.** *kindred* Gn 12[1] (‖ בית אביך, ארצך), 24[4] (‖ ארץ), Nu 10[30] (‖ *id.*), Gn 31[3] (‖ ארץ אבותיך), 43[7] (all J); ‖ עַם Est 2[10.20] 8[6]; esp. אֶרֶץ מ׳ *land of one's kindred* Gn 11[28] 24[7] (both J), 31[13] (E), Je 22[10] 46[16] Ez 23[15] Ru 2[11]. **2.** pl. *circumstances of birth, birth* (fig. of origin of Jerus.) מְכֹרֹתַיִךְ וּמ׳ מֵאֶרֶץ הַכְּנַעֲנִי Ez 16[3], cf. v[4]. **3.** (female) *offspring, one born* Lv 18[9.9], *begotten* v[11] (all H); coll. = *issue, offspring* מוֹלַדְתְּךָ אֲשֶׁר הוֹלַדְתָּ Gn 48[6] (P).

†**מוֹלָדָה**, **מֹלָדָה** **n.pr.loc.** town in Simeon מול׳ Jos 19[2] = 1 Ch 4[28]; inhabited after exile Ne 11[26]; name occurs also Jos 15[26] (where prob. interpol. from Ne 11[26] v. Di); 𝔊 Μωλαδα, etc.; identified by Rob [BR ii. 201] Guérin [Judée iii. 184 ff.] with Tel *Milḥ*, 4 hours E. from Beersheba = Μαλαθα Jos [Ant. xviii. 6. 2]; Μαλα(α)θων, *Malatha* Lag [Onom. 214. 266. 87. 119], v. also Di.

†מוֹלִיד **n.pr.m.** a Judahite 1 Ch 2[29]

[תולדות] **n.f.pl.** generations, esp in genealogies=**account of a man and his descendants**,—cstr תולדות Gn 2[4] Ru 4[18]; תולדת Gn 5[1]+6 t; תלדות 36[1]+2 t, תלדת 25[12]; sf תלדתיו 1 Ch 26[31], תולדתם Ex 28[10]+16 t, תולדתם 1 Ch 5[7]+5 t, תלדתם Ex 6[16.19];—**a.** *account of men and their descendants* Gn 5[1] 6[9] 10[1] 11[10.27] 25[12.19] 36[1.9] 37[2] Nu 3[1] Ru 4[18] 1 Ch 1[29]; *successive generations* (in) of families (משפחת) Gn 10[32] cf. 25[13], Ex 6[16.19] 28[10], *genealogical divisions*, by parentage Nu 1[20] (ת׳ למשפחתם)+11 t Nu 1; ואחיו למשפחתיו בהתיחש לתולדותם 1 Ch 5[7] cf 7[9] and prob also 7[2] v Be, 7[4] 8[28] 9[9.34] 26[31] **b.** metaph תולדות השמים והארץ Gn 2[4] lit *begettings of heaven and earth*, i e. **account of heaven and earth and that which proceeded from them** (cf. Dr[Intr 5 n]) In Hex always P.

†תּוֹלָד **n.pr.loc.** in Simeon 1 Ch 4[29], 𝔊 Θουλαεμ, A Θωλαδ, 𝔊L Θολαθ, appar=אֶלְתּוֹלַד q v supr p. 39

†[יָלַל] **vb. Hiph.** howl, make a howling (onomatop)—**Hiph.** *Pf.* והילל consec Je 47[2], והילילו consec Am 8[3], *Impf.* יְיֵלִיל Is 15[2]+3 t. (Ges § 70 2, R. 2 Kö I 457 421), אֲיֵלִיל Je 48[31], ואילילה Mi 1[8], יְיֵלִילוּ Ho 7[14] (Kö I 421), יְהֵילִילוּ Is 52[5], תילילו Is 65[14], *Imv* הילל Ez 21[17] Zc 11[2], הילילי Is 14[31] 49[3]+Je 48[20] Kt, הילילו Is 13[6]+13 t.+ Je 48[20] Qr, +Ez 30[2] (del. 𝔊 Co),—*utter* or *make a howling, give a howl*, in distress, ‖ זעק Ho 7[14] Je 47[2] Is 14[31] Je 25[34] 48[20.31] (sq על), Ez 21[17]; ‖ צעק Is 65[14] (sq מן of occasion, source); ‖ ספד Mi 1[8] Je 4[8] Jo 1[13], ‖ הביש Jo 1[11]; ‖ בכה 1[5] (cf. Is 15[2.3]+בְּכִי); sq על Je 51[8] Is 15[2.3]; We prop ילילו for יגילו Ho 10[5] (others יחילו, v ניל supr. p 162), sq ל Is 16[7], abs והילילו שירות היכל Am 8[3] *and palace-songs shall become howlings*, Is 13[6] 16[7] 23[1.6.14] Je 48[39] 49[3] (Ez 30[2] v. supr), Zp 1[11] Zc 11[2.2], in cruel exultation Is 52[5] cf De Che Di —On הילל בן־שחר Is 14[12] cf. sub I. הלל supr p 237

†יְלֵל **n.**[**m.**] howling (of beasts);—ובתהו יְלֵל ישמן Dt 32[10] *in a waste of howling of a desert* (=*in the howling waste of a desert*; v. Dr).

†יְלָלָה **n.f. howling**,—וִילָלָה Zp 1[10], cstr. יִלְלַת Je 25[36] Zc 11[3], ילְלָתָהּ Is 15[8.8],—*howling* in distress Is 15[8.8] (‖ זְעָקָה), Je 25[36] (of leaders of flock, metaph for princes; ‖ קול צעקה), Zp 1[10] (‖ id), קול יִלְלַת הרעים Zc 11[3] (רעים metaph for princes)

יָלִיץ Pr 20[25] v. לעע

ילף (√of foll; mng. dub, Ar وَلَفَ III is *conjunctus fuit* cum aliquo, etc, Frey; whence ילפת as an *accretion*? so Thes 'ab adhaerendo')

†יַלֶּפֶת **n.f.** scab, scurf, an eruptive disease, Lv 21[20] 22[22] (in both ‖ גָּרָב).

ילק (√of following; meaning dubious; Thes al comp לקק *lick*; Ar. وَلَقَ is *hasten*, etc)

†יֶלֶק **n.m.** [Na 3, 16] a kind of **locust**, abs יֶלֶק Na 3[16]+5 t, יָלֶק Jo 1[4]+2 t.,—alw. coll. **a.** as devouring ‖ חסיל, ארבה, גָּזָם, Jo 1[4.4] 2[25]; ‖ אַרְבֶּה ψ 105[34] (of Egyptian plague), cf. Na 3[16a] (but del We) **b** in sim. of multitude of men Na 3[15b] Je 51[14], of horses v[27] (יֶלֶק סָמָר) **c.** in sim. of scattering and disappearing Na 3[16]

יַלְקוּט v לקט

†יְמוּאֵל **n.pr.m.** son of Simeon Gn 46[10] Ex 6[15] (𝔊 Ιεμουηλ)=נְמוּאֵל (q v) Nu 26[12] 1 Ch 4[24]

†יְמִימָה **n.pr.f.** (cf. perh Ar يَمَامَةٌ *dove*, nom unit of يَمَام Frey)—daughter of Job Jb 42[14]

יִמְלָה **n.pr.** v. יִמְלָא sub מלא.

ימם (√assumed for foll, actual existence and meaning dubious, v infr)

יָם [390] **n.m.** [Ex 14, 27] **sea** (Ph ים, Ar يَمّ; Palm. בימא *on the sea*, Vog[No 79], on As. *idmu*, (*āmu*), *sea*, v Dl[HWB 307] M-A[CD 52] Hpt[BAS I 171 n])—abs. יָם 1 S 13[5]+; יָמָּה Gn 28[14]+, cstr יָם Gn 14[3]+23 t., also יָמָּה סוּף Ex 10[19], but alw. יַם־סוּף Ex 13[18]+22 t; sf יַמָּהּ Je 51[36]; pl. יַמִּים Ju 5[17]+29 t;—*sea*: esp. **1.** *Mediterranean* Nu 13[29] (E), 34[5] (P), Dt 1[7] Jos 5[1] 1 K 5[23.23] Jon 1[4]+oft; the Mediterr is called also הַיָּם הַגָּדוֹל Nu 34[6.7] Jos 15[12.47] Ez 48[28]+, cf. הַיָּם הַג׳ מבוא ψ 104[25] הַיָּ׳ גּ׳ ורחב ידים; הַשֶּׁמֶשׁ Jos 1[4] 23[4] (v As name of Mediterr, *tiamtu rabitu ša sulmu šamši*, etc, Schr[Namen der Meere 171 ff]), הַיָּ׳ הָאַחֲרוֹן, Jos 9[1] הַיָּ׳ הַג׳ אל־מול הַלְּבָנוֹן *the hinder sea* Dt 11[24] 34[2] Zc 14[8] Jo 2[20] (in the last two opp הַיָּ׳ הַקַּדְמֹנִי, v infr), of Mediterr. in particular part יָם פלשתים Ex 23[31] (JE); יָם יָפוֹ 2 Ch 2[15]= יָם יָפוֹא Ezr 3[7] **2.** יַם־סוּף 'Red Sea' (v סוף) Ex 13[18] (cf 10[19]), 15[4] Nu 14[25] Dt 1[40] Jos 2[10] Ju

11[16]+oft.; also הַיָּם Ex 14[2.2.9] Is 51[10.10] 63[11]+; prob. also יַם־מִצְרַיִם 11[15]; 'Red Sea' named or referred to c. 66 t.; יַם־סוּף clearly of Ælanitic Gulf 1 K 9[26] (cf 2 Ch 8[17]). **3.** *Dead Sea*, יָם מֶלַח *sea of salt* Gn 14[3] Nu 34[3.12] Dt 3[17] Jos 3[16] 12[3] 15[2.5] 18[19]; יָם הָעֲרָבָה Dt 3[17] 4[49] Jos 3[16] 12[3] 2 K 14[25]; הַיָּ׳ הַקַּדְמֹנִי Ez 47[18] Zc 14[8] Jo 2[20] (v. supr.); simply יָם Is 16[8] Je 48[32];—in יָם יַעְזֵר Je 48[32] יָם is text. error, del. c. Gf Gr Che Gie. **4.** *Sea of Galilee* יָם כִּנֶּרֶת Nu 34[11] Jos 13[27], יָם כִּנְרוֹת 12[3]; simply יָם Dt 33[23]. **5.** more gen *sea*, opp. earth and (or) sky Gn 1[26.28] 9[2] (P), Ex 20[11] (E), Hg 2[6]+oft Jb ψ Is[2] etc; Am 6[12] rd. בַּבָּקָר יָם for בבקרים (v. בָּקָר); *sea* as under earth ψ 24[2] (cf. Gn 1[10] 6[11] Ex 20[4]=Dt 5[8]); fig. of *flood* of invaders, עָלָה עַל־בָּבֶל הַיָּם Je 51[42]. **6.** of a *mighty river*, the Nile Na 3[8.8] Is 19[5] (‖נָהָר); cf. הַתַּנִּין אֲשֶׁר בַּיָּם 27[1] and כַּתַּנִּים בַּיַּמִּים Ez 32[2] (sim. of Pharaoh); of Euphrates Is 21[1] Je 51[36] (acc. to Che Gf al.; Is 21[1] perhaps better of Persian Gulf, v. Di). **7.** the great basin in temple-court, called *the sea*. וַיַּעַשׂ אֶת־הַיָּם מוּצָק 1 K 7[23] =2 Ch 4[2], יָם הַנְּחֹשֶׁת 2 K 25[13] 1 Ch 18[8] Je 52[17]; הַיָּם alone 1 K 7[24.25]+10 t. K Ch+Je 52[20]. **8.** combinations are. **a.** *shore of sea, sea-shore* שְׂפַת הַיָּם Jos 11[4] 1 K 5[9], and in sim Gn 22[17] Ju 7[12] 1 S 13[5]; חוֹף הַיָּ׳ Jos 9[1] Ez 25[16]; חוֹף יַמִּים Gn 49[13] Ju 5[17]; cf. חֶבֶל הַיָּם Zp 2[5] *region by the sea*; so v[6] but dub, v. I. חֶבֶל **3.** **b.** *sand of the sea* (*shore*) חוֹל הַיָּם (in sim) Gn 32[13] 41[49] Ho 2[1] Is 10[22]+oft. (v. חוֹל); חוֹל גְּבוּל לַיָּם Je 5[22]. **c.** לְשׁוֹן הַיָּם *tongue* (*arm* or *gulf*) *of sea* Jos 15[5] 18[19] Is 11[15]. **d.** מִיָּם עַד־יָם Am 8[12] Zc 9[10] ψ 72[8], cf. Mi 7[12] Zc 14[8.8] Jo 2[20.20] Dn 11[45]. **9.** =*west, westward* (orig. *sea-ward*, fr. position of Mediterr. with ref. to Palestine, and this sense still often perceptible): with other three points of compass Gn 13[14] 28[14] (J), Nu 2[18] 35[5] (P), Dt 3[27] 1 K 7[25] 1 Ch 9[24] 2 Ch 4[4] Ez 42[19]+6 t. Ez, Zc 14[4] Dn 8[4] ψ 107[3] (מִמִּזְרָח וּמִמַּעֲרָב מִצָּפוֹן וּמִיָּם; but rd. perh. וּמִיָּמִין *from the south*, Hu Pe Bi Che); opp. east Jos 11[2] 16[6]+16 t. Ez 48; *west* alone Gn 12[8] (J); רוּחַ יָם Ez 10[19] (J) *west wind*, מִיָּם לְ *westward* Jos 8[9.12.13]+; יָמָּה *westward*, oft of tabernacle Ex 26[22.27] Nu 3[23]+(all P), and of land Jos 5[1] 15[8.10] etc., +oft. Ez; דֶּרֶךְ הַיָּם=*westward* Ez 41[12], פְּאַת־יָם גְּבוּל יָם *western border* Nu 34[6.6] Jos 15[2]; פְּאַת דרך *west side* Ex 27[12] 38[12] Nu 35[5] Jos 18[14]; הים Ez 41[12] (v. further פאה)

†**יֵמִם** **n.[m.]** appar. pl., meaning dub, only in הוּא עֲנָה אֲשֶׁר מָצָא אֶת־הַיֵּמִם בַּמִּדְבָּר Gn 36[24] *that is the 'Ana that found the* יֵמִם *in the wilderness* when he was pasturing the asses of Ṣib'ōn his father; perh. *hot springs*, 𝔙 *aquae calidae*; so Thes MV Dechent[ZPV vii. 1884, 172] al; yet no suitable √ ימה (or ימם) known; v. further Di Buhl [Edomiter 46].

ימן (√of foll.; found in deriv. in all cogn, but orig mng dubious; Thes al. comp. אמן *confirm*, whence *right hand* as the *stronger*; others fr. use of right hand in *confirming* by an oath)

I **יָמִין** [T 137] **n.f.** [Ex 15 6] (Pr 27[16] no exc., v. Now Str) **right hand** (NH *id*, SI[3] מימין *on the right*; Aram. יַמִּינָא, ܝܡܝܢܐ; Ar. يَمِين *right, right side, right hand, south*; Eth የማን: *right hand*, ይማን: *right side*; Sab ימן *right hand*, ימנת *south*, are also quoted; As. *imnu, right, right side, on the right*, Dl[HWB 307])—abs. יָמִין Gn 13[9] +40 t.; cstr. יְמִין 1 S 23[24]+19 t; sf. יְמִינִי Je 22[24]+6 t., etc, always sg·—**1.** *right hand*· **a.** lit. of man, oft. opp. שְׂמֹאל Gn 48[13.14] (cf v[18]), Dn 12[7]; יָדַע בֵּין־יְמִינוֹ לִשְׂמֹאלוֹ Jon 4[11] *distinguish between one's right hand and one's left*, שׁלח ימין Ju 5[26] (‖יד); as holding the lot Ez 21[27]; also of right hand as skilful ψ 137[5]; as receiving bribes 26[10] (‖יָדַיִם), used in false swearing יְמִינָם ימין שָׁקֶר 144[8.11] *their right hand is a right hand of falsehood*; oft. also c. יַד, יַד־יְמִינוֹ Gn 48[17] (E) *hand of his right*=*his right hand* Ju 7[20] 2 S 20[9], אִטֵּר יַד־יְמִינוֹ Ju 3[15] 20[16] *bound as to one's right hand*, i e. left-handed. **b.** fig, of right hand as held by ׳י Is 41[13] 45[1]; so יַד־יְמִינִי ψ 73[23]. **c.** *right hand of* ׳י, as instr of delivering Israel Ex 15[6.6.12]+, cf. בִּגְבֻרוֹת יֵשַׁע יְמִינוֹ ψ 20[7]; שְׁנוֹת יְמִין עֶלְיוֹן 77[11], ‖ זרוע 98[1]; as acquiring the temple-site 78[54]; as holding his servant 18[36] (line om in ‖ 2 S 22[36]), cf 63[9] & בִּימִין צדקי Is 41[10]; as finding, lighting upon (מצא) his enemies ψ 21[9] (‖יד); as full of צֶדֶק 48[11]; as dispensing blessings 16[11] נעימות בימינך (cf. Pr 3[16] of wisdom, personified), used in divine oath Is 62[8] (‖זְרוֹעַ) **2.** of situation on, or direction toward, *the right*: **a.** of situation, c מִן, מִימִינָם וּמִשְּׂמֹאלָם Ex 14[22.29] a wall *on their right hand and on their left hand*; similarly 2 S 16[6] 1 K 7[39.49]=2 Ch 3[17] 4[6], 1 K 22[19] (=2 Ch 18[18] c עַל), 2 Ch 4[7.8] ψ 91[7] (‖מצדך); for protection 16[8]; מִימִין לְ 2 K 23[13] Ez 10[3], c. לְ, וַתֵּשֶׁב לִימִינוֹ 1 K 2[19], so ψ 110[1] 45[10] 109[31], c. עַל־ Zc 3[1] 1 Ch 6[24] 2 Ch 18[18] (=1 K 22[19] c מִן), Ne 8[4] Jb 30[12] ψ 109[6] cf. 110[5]; without prep יְמִין הָעִיר 2 S 24[5] Jb 23[9]. **b.** of direction toward, lit נָטָה יָמִין Nu 20[17] 22[26] (both

JE), סור ימין Dt 2^{27} 1 S 6^{12}, פָּרַץ ימין וש׳ Is 54^{3}, also (vb. הפרד in prev cl) Gn 13^{9}, הַבִּיט ימין ψ 142^{5}, and *looking* is implied also in Ez 1^{10} (c. נטה (לָלֶכֶת) על הַיָּמִין ,על ,אל־, opp (מֵהַשְּׂמֹאל); c. 2 S 2$^{19.21}$, פנה על־ימין Gn 24^{49}; sq אֶל, of course לְיָמִין מֵעַל לַחוֹמָה ,ל c (הלך) of boundary Jos 17^{7}; Ne 12^{31} (vb. om, *went*) *to the right above the wall*, fig of moral deviation, סוּר מִן־הַדָּבָר . . . יָמִין וּשׂמאול Dt 17^{11}, so 5^{29} 17^{20} 28^{14} Jos 1^{7} 23^{6} 2 K 22^{2} = 2 Ch 34^{2}, נטה ימין וש׳ Pr 4^{27}; also (very late) of *the right* as morally good, לב חָכָם לימינו (opp. שמאל) Ec 10^{2} De Reuss Now †**3.** of other parts of the body, besides hand (v יַד־ימינו etc supr) *right* thigh יֶרֶךְ ימינו Ju 3$^{16.21}$, eye עֵין יָמִין 1 S 11^{2}, עין ימינו Zc 11$^{17.17}$, esp שׁוֹק הַיָּמִין i e *the right* (upper) *leg* of sacrificial animal Ex 29^{22} Lv 7$^{32.33}$ 8$^{25.26}$ 9^{21} Nu 18^{18}. †**4.** = *south*, because when facing east the right hand is toward the south: ישב מימין הַיְשִׁימוֹן 1 S 23^{19}, אֶל־ימין v^{24}; מימינך Ez 16^{46} (|| על־שׂמאולך), צָפוֹן וְיָמִין ψ 89^{13}, perh also 107^{3}, v יָם **9.**

†I **יְמִינִי** **adj.** Kt *right hand, on the right:* שם הימיני יָכִין 2 Ch 3^{17} the name of *the one on the right* was Yakin, צדך הימיני Ez 4^{6} *thy right side* (Qr in both הַיְמָנִי, v infr.)

†II **יְמִינִי** **adj. gent.** fr. בִּנְיָמִן, abbrev for בֶּן־יְמִינִי (q v),—אֶרֶץ יְמִינִי 1 S 9^{4}, אִישׁ יְמִינִי 2 S 20^{1} Est 2^{5}, בֶּן־אִישׁ ימיני 1 S 9^{1}.

†II **[יָמַן]** **vb. denom. Hiph.** **go to or choose the right, use the right hand,**—*Impf* 1 s. coh וְאֵימְנָה Gn 13^{10} (J) *then I will go to the right* (opp וְאַשְׂמְאִילָה), 2 mpl תַּאֲמִינוּ Is 30^{21}, fig of turning aside from right course of life (|| תַשְׂמְאִילוּ); *Inf. cstr.* in phr אִם־אִשׁ לְהֵמִין וּלְהַשְׂמִיל מִכֹּל אֲשֶׁר דִּבֶּר אֲדֹנִי הַמֶּלֶךְ 2 S 14^{19} it is surely impossible *to turn to the right or to the left*, etc, *Imv* fs הֵימִינִי Ez 21^{21} *go to the right!* (opp הַשְׂמִילִי), *Pt* pl *use the right hand* מַיְמִינִים וּמַשְׂמִאלִים בָּאֲבָנִים וּבַחִצִּים בַּקָּשֶׁת 1 Ch 12^{2} *using the right hand and the left hand with stones and with arrows in the bow* (i.e in throwing and shooting)

†**יְמָנִי** **adj.** **right hand, right**—m of pillar הָעַמּוּד הַיְמָנִי 1 K 7^{21} = הַיְמָנִי in || 2 Ch 3^{17} Qr (Kt הימיני); f of side of house (temple). כֶּתֶף הַבַּיִת הַיְמָנִית 1 K 6^{8} 7^{39} (|| כֶּתֶף הבית מִיָּמִין), 2 K 11^{11} (opp הַשְּׂמָאלִית), Ez 47^{1}, cf v^{2} 2 Ch 4^{10} 23^{10} (opp הַשְּׂמָאלִית), elsewhere of parts of body (P). *right ear, hand and foot* [ה]אֹזֶן הַיְמָנִית + יד(ם) הי׳ + רגל(ם) הי׳ Ex 29^{20} Lv 8$^{23.24}$ 14$^{14.17.25.28}$, *right finger* אֶצְבָּעוֹ הַי׳ 14$^{16.27}$, cf. also *right side*, m. צדך הַיְמָנִי Ez 4^{6} Qr (Kt הימיני)

†II **יָמִין** **n.pr.m.** **1.** son of Simeon Gn 46^{10} Ex 6^{15} Nu 26^{12} 1 Ch 4^{24}. **2.** man of Judah 1 Ch 2^{27}. **3.** Levite (?) name, time of Ezra Ne 8^{7}.

† **יָמִינִי** **adj. gent.** of II. ימין **1**, only c art. as subst. coll Nu 26^{12}.

†**יִמְנָה** **n pr.m.** (cf perh. Ar. يُمْن *good fortune*, يُمْنَة *right side*)—**1.** a son of Asher Gn 46^{17} Nu 26^{44}, also (for adj gent.) הַיִּמְנָה v^{44} = the family of *the Yimnites* 1 Ch 7^{30}. **2.** a Levite 2 Ch 31^{14}.

†I. **תֵּימָן** **n.f.**$^{1.43.6}$ **south, south wind,** chiefly poet, P & Ez (lit. *what is on the right* (hand), i e. as one faces east, v Wetzst$^{Verhandl\ d.\ Berl.\ Anthrop\ Ges\ 1878,\ 390}$)—abs. ת׳ Zc 9^{14} + 6 t (הַתּ׳ only Zc 6^{6}), תֵּמָן Jb 9^{9}, c ה loc תֵּימָנָה Ex 26^{18} + 12 t.;—**1. a.** *south, southern quarter* of sky, לַתֵּימָן Jb 39^{26} (of flight of bird); of constellations חַדְרֵי ת׳ 9^{9}; סַעֲרוֹת ת׳ Zc 9^{14} *whirlwinds of the south;* of territory, *the south* Is 43^{6} (opp צָפוֹן), also אֶרֶץ הַתּ׳ Zc 6^{6} (opp. אֶרֶץ צָפוֹן); נֶגְבָּה מִקְצֵה ת׳ Jos 15^{1} *southward at the end of* the *south,* i e. in the remotest south (of the land);—see also II ת׳. **b.** c. ה loc. *toward the south,* esp in topograph description (oft. with other points of compass), פְּאַת נֶגְבָּה תֵימָנָה Ex 26^{18} (P), פ׳ ת׳ נ׳, Ez 47^{19}, פ׳ נגב ת׳ Ex 27^{9} 36^{23} 38^{9} (all P), Ez 47^{19} 48^{28}; + צלע *side* Ex 26^{35}, ירך Nu 3^{29} (both P); also Nu 2^{10} 10^{6} (P); יָמָּה וְצָפֹנָה וְת׳ וּמִזְרָחָה Dt 3^{27}; ה loc. is redundant in דֶּרֶךְ תֵּימָנָה Ez 21^{2} turn thy face *southward* (|| דָּרוֹם and נֶגֶב) **2.** *south wind* ψ 78^{26} (in || קָדִים cl), Ct 4^{16} (in || צָפוֹן cl.)

†II. **תֵּימָן** **n.pr. (m. et) loc.** **a** N district of Edom, poet often = Edom Am 1^{12} (|| אֱדוֹם v^{11}, and בָּצְרָה), Ob^{9} (|| הַר־עֵשָׂו), Je 49$^{7.20}$ Ez 25^{13} (all || אדום); Hb 3^{3} (|| הַר־פָּארָן); prob. also Jos 12^{3} 13^{4} (both D); in Gn 36 (P) as name of an Edomite chief, son of אֱלִיפַז and grandson of Esau v^{11} = 1 Ch 1^{36}, v^{42} = 1 Ch 1^{53}; so תּוֹמָן Gn 36^{15}.—Vid. further Buhl$^{Edomiter\ 30}$.

†**תֵּימָנִי** **adj.gent.** alw. c. art. אֱלִיפַז הַתֵּימָנִי (v supr.) Jb 2^{11} 4^{1} 15^{1} 42$^{7.9}$ = אֱלִ׳ הַתֵּמָנִי 22^{1}; = n pr.coll. אֶרֶץ הַתּ׳ Gn 36^{34} *the land of the Temanites* = 1 Ch 1^{45}.

†**תֵּימְנִי** appar. **n.pr.m.** in Judah 1 Ch 4^{6}

יְמַנַּע v. sub מנע.

ימר **vb.** assumed in Thes to expl. **Hiph.** הֵמִיר=הֵימִיר Je 2^{11}, and **Hithp.** תִּתְיַמָּרוּ Is 61^{6}; but on הימיר v. מור (Kö$^{\text{I. 457}}$), and תִּתְיַמָּרוּ is prob. from אמר q. v. supr. p. 56^{b}.

יְמִרָה v. sub מרה.

† **יָמַשׁ** **vb.** (si vera l.) touch, **Hiph.** *Imv.* sf. והימשני Kt (i.e. וַהֲיִמִשֵׁנִי) Ju 16^{26} (וַהֲמִשֵׁנִי Qr) *and let me touch* (no doubt txt. error for הֲמִשֵּׁנִי from מָשַׁשׁ, q. v.)

† [**יָנָה**] **vb. suppress** (?), **oppress, maltreat** (NH Hiph. *vex* with words; so Aram. Aph. אוֹנִי, but also 𝔗 for Heb. הוֹנָה *maltreat;* Ar. وَنَى is *laxus, debilis fuit,* IV. *debilitavit, defatigavit,* but connex. dub.)—**Qal** *Impf.* 1 pl. sf. נִינָם ψ 74^{8}; *Pt.* יוֹנָה Je 25^{38} + 3 t. + ψ 123^{4} (v. infr.);—*suppress* (?), sq. acc. ψ 74^{8} (text dub.); elsewhere *oppress; Pt.* abs. as adj. הָעִיר הַיּוֹנָה Zp 3^{1}; subst. f. coll. הַיּוֹנָה *oppressors* Je 25^{38} (but rd. חֶרֶב for חֲרוֹן, with 𝔊 Ew Hi Gf Ke etc., as 46^{16} 50^{16}); ψ 123^{4} Qr לִגְאֵי יוֹנִים *proudest oppressors* (st. cstr. in superlat., cf. Ges$^{\S 133, 3, R. 1}$; yet most follow Kt לגאיונים, and der. from גַּאֲיוֹן q. v. p. 145 supr.) **Hiph.** *Pf.* הוֹנָה Ez 18$^{12.16}$; הוֹנוּ 22$^{7.29}$; *Impf.* יוֹנֶה 18^{7}; 2 ms. תוֹנֶה Ex 22^{20}; תּוֹנֶנּוּ Dt 23^{17}; יוֹנוּ Ez 45^{8}; תוֹנוּ Lv 19^{33} + 2 t.; תֹּנוּ Je 22^{3}; *Inf.* sf. הוֹנֹתָם Ez 46^{18}; *Pt.* מוֹנַיִךְ Is 49^{26};—*oppress, maltreat,* sq. acc., esp. of ill-treatment of poor and weak, partic. of the גֵּר, the 'stranger,' sojourner, by the rich and powerful, Ex 22^{20} (JE), Lv 19^{33} 25$^{14.17}$ (H), Dt 23^{17} Je 22^{3} Ez 18$^{7.12.16}$ 22$^{7.29}$ 45^{8} 46^{18}; of a foreign oppressor only Is 49^{26}.

יָנוֹחַ v. נוח; **יָנוּם** v. נום.

† [**יָנַק**] **vb. suck** (NH *id.;* Aram. יְנַק, ܝܢܩ, and deriv.; As. *êniḳu, suck,* SASm$^{\text{Asrb. 1, Gloss}}$ *mušeniḳtu, nurse,* Jen$^{\text{ZA. 1886, 402}}$)—**Qal** *Pf.* וְיָנַקְתְּ consec. Is 60^{16}; וִינַקְתֶּם 66^{12}; *Impf.* יִינָק Jb 20^{16}; אִינַק 3^{12}; תִּינְקִי Is 60^{16}; יִינָקוּ Dt 33^{19}; תִּינְקוּ Is 66^{11}; *Pt.* יוֹנֵק Dt 32^{25} + 7 t.; יֹנֵק Nu 11^{12}; יוֹנְקִים ψ 8^{3}; יוֹנְקֵי Jo 2^{16};—*suck,* of infant at mother's breast, abs. Jb 3^{12}; metaph. of abundance and honour of Jerusalem in future, Is 66^{11} abs.; sq. acc. of breast 60^{16}, acc. of milk v^{16} 66^{12}; sq. acc. ראשׁ פְּתָנִים Jb 20^{16} of punishment of wicked; pt. sq. acc. יוֹנֵק שְׁדֵי אִמִּי Ct 8^{1}; cstr. יֹנְקֵי־שָׁדָיִם Jo 2^{16}; elsewh. as subst., *suckling, babe* Nu 11^{12} Dt 32^{25} (opp. אִישׁ שֵׂיבָה); ‖ עוֹלֵל 1 S 15^{3} 22^{19} ψ 8^{3} Je 44^{7} La 2^{11}; ‖ עוֹלָל 4^{4}, cf. Jo 2^{16}; ‖ גָּמוּל Is 11^{8};—on Is 53^{2} v. יוֹנֵק infr. **Hiph.** *Pf.* הֵינִיקָה Gn 21^{7}; הֵינִיקוּ La 4^{3}; *Impf.* sf. וַיֵּנִקֵהוּ Dt 32^{13}; 3 fs. תֵּינִק Ex 2^{7}; וַתֵּינֶק 1 S 1^{23}; וַתְּנִיקֵהוּ Ex 2^{9}; *Imv.* fs. sf. הֵינִקִהוּ v^{9}; *Inf.* לְהֵינִיק 1 K 3^{21}; *Pt.* מֵינֶקֶת Ex 2^{7}; cstr. *id.* Gn 35^{8}; מֵינִקְתּוֹ 2 K 11^{2}; מֵינִקְתּוֹ 2 Ch 22^{11}; מֵנִקְתָּהּ Gn 24^{59}; מֵינִיקוֹת 32^{16}; מֵינִיקֹתַיִךְ Is 49^{23};—*give suck to, nurse,* sq. acc. Gn 21^{7} 1 K 3^{21} Ex 2$^{7.9}$ 1 S 1^{23}; cause to suck honey, fig. Dt 32^{13} (2 acc.); of animals La 4^{3} sq. acc.; pt. fem.=*nursing,* אִשָּׁה מֵינֶקֶת Ex 2^{7} lit. *a nursing woman, a nurse;* מ׳ alone as subst.=*nurse* Gn 24^{59} (J), 35^{8} (E; דְּבֹרָה), 2 K 11^{2} 2 Ch 22^{11}; metaph. Is 49^{23}; of camels גְּמַלִּים מֵינִיקוֹת Gn 32^{16}.

† **יוֹנֵק** **n.m. young plant, sapling** (*sucker*)—Is 53^{2} (‖ שֹׁרֶשׁ) in sim. of the suffering servant of י׳.

† [**יוֹנֶקֶת**] **n.f. young shoot, twig** (=foregoing)—יוֹנַקְתּוֹ Jb 8^{16} + 2 t.; יוֹנְקוֹתָיו Ho 14^{7}; יְנִקוֹתָיו Ez 17^{22}; יוֹנְקוֹתֶיהָ ψ 80^{12};—*shoot, twig,* of tree Jb 14^{7}; of wicked under fig. of tree Jb 8^{16} 15^{30}; Israel under fig. of olive-tree Ho 14^{7}, of cedar Ez 17^{22}, of vine ψ 80^{12}.

† [**יְנִיקָה**] **n.f.** id., only pl. sf. יְנִיקוֹתָיו Ez 17^{4} of Israel under figure of cedar.

יַנְשׁוּף, יַנְשׁוֹף v. sub נשף.

† **יָסַד** **vb. establish, found, fix** (NH *id.,* esp. Pi.; Aram. יְסַד; perh. orig. *fix firm* or *close;* Ar. وِسَادٌ *pillow;* vb. denom. II. *fix as a pillow against one;* V. *lean against, recline,* Lane^{2940} Saad Gn 28^{11}; in Heb. usu. *fix firm* so as to *found*)—**Qal** *Pf.* יָסַד ψ 104^{5} Pr 3^{19}; sf. יְסָדָהּ ψ 24^{2} + 3 t.; 3 fs. יָסְדָה Is 48^{13}; יָסַדְתָּ ψ 104^{8}; יָסַדְתָּ 102^{26}; sf. יְסַדְתּוֹ Hab 1^{12}; יְסַדְתָּם ψ 89^{12} 119^{152}; וִיסַדְתִּיךְ consec. Is 54^{11}; *Inf.* וִיסוֹד 2 Ch 24^{27}; 31^{7} (v. Ges$^{\S 69, 2, R. 1}$; Baer לְיִסּוֹד); לִיסֹד Is 51^{16}; יָסְדִי Jb 38^{4}; יָסְדוֹ Ezr 3^{12}; *Pt.* יֹסֵד Is 51^{13} Zc 12^{1} + Is 28^{16} (Che$^{\text{crit. n.}}$, MT יִסַּד);—*found, establish,* c. acc., the earth ψ 24^{2} (‖ כונן), cf. 78^{69} (obj. om.), 89^{12} 102^{26} 104^{5} cf. v^{8} (sq. לְ), Pr 3^{19} Is 48^{13} Jb 38^{4} Is 51$^{13.16}$ Zc 12^{1}, vault of heaven Am 9^{6}; of *founding* the second temple Ezr 3^{12}, of restoration under Joash, Inf. יְסוֹד 2 Ch 24^{27}; metaph. of future Israel Is 54^{11}; of י׳, *establish* the Chaldaean (as his instrument) להוכיח for correction Hb 1^{12} (‖ שִׂים), his commandments ψ 119^{152}; in weakened sense (si vera l.) יְסַד לְצִיִּים Is 23^{13} *appoint* a city for desert-creatures (on meaning in context, v. Di); *appoint, fix* Ezr 7^{9}

emend. (v. יָסַד); *found, begin*, heaps of offerings in י׳'s house 2 Ch 31⁷. **Niph.** *Pf.* 3 pl. נוֹסְדוּ ψ 2²; *Impf.* 2 ms. תִּוָּסֵד Is 44²⁸; *Inf.* הִוָּסְדָהּ Ex 9¹⁸; הִוָּסְדָם ψ 31¹⁴;—**1.** *fix* or *seat themselves close together, sit in conclave* ψ 2² 31¹⁴ (> Bae from ܣܘܕܐ, ὁμιλία), but Lag's emend. נוֹעֲדוּ is prob. (cf. Ne 6²). **2.** *be founded*, Is 44²⁸ (temple), Ex 9¹⁸ (Egypt). **Pi.** *Pf.* יִסַּד Is 14³² + 3 t.; יִסְּדָהּ 1 K 16³⁴; יִסַּדְתָּ ψ 8³; יִסְּדוּ Zc 4⁹ Ezr 3¹⁰; *Impf.* יְיַסְּדֶנָּה Jos 6²⁶; *Inf.* לְיַסֵּד 1 K 5³¹;—**1.** *found* (= **Qal**), sq. acc., city Jos 6²⁶ (JE), 1 K 16³⁴, temple 1 K 5³¹ Zc 4⁹ Ezr 3¹⁰; Zion Is 14³² 28¹⁶ הִנְנִי יִסַּד (rd. יֹסֵד; v. supr.) **2.** *establish* ψ 8³ sq. עֹז; *appoint, ordain* (late) 1 Ch 9²² (sq. acc.), Est 1⁸ (abs.) **Pu.** *Pf.* יֻסַּד 1 K 6³⁷ + 2 t.; יֻסָּד Ezr 3⁶; *Pt.* מְיֻסָּד 1 K 7¹⁰; מְיֻסָּדִים Ct 5¹⁵; *be founded, be laid*, of a foundation 1 K 6³⁷ Ezr 3⁶ Hg 2¹⁸ Zc 8⁹; *Pt.* = subst. foundation 1 K 7¹⁰, cf. מוסד infr.; pillars set on bases, sim. of legs Ct 5¹⁵. **Hoph.** *be founded: Inf.* הוּסַד 2 Ch 3³ Ezr 3¹¹; *Pt.* מוּסָּד Is 28¹⁶;—*the being founded, founding*, עַל הוּסַד בֵּית י׳ Ezr 3¹¹ *because of the founding* (*laying the foundation*) *of the house of* י׳; וְאֵלֶּה הוּסַד שְׁלֹמֹה לִבְנוֹת וגו׳ 2 Ch 3³ and *this is* (lit. these are) *the founding of Solomon to build* the house of God, i.e. *this is the foundation which Solomon laid for building*, etc.; *Pt.* מוּסָד מוּסָּד Is 28¹⁶ *a foundation founded*, i.e. *well laid* (cf. חָכָם מְחֻכָּם, חֵפֶשׂ מְחֻפָּשׂ).

† **יְסֻד** n.[m.] **foundation, beginning,** Ezr 7⁹ יְסֻד הַמַּעֲלָה, but rd. rather, c. 𝔊, יָסַד (הוּא = Ezra subj.), v. Ry.

† **יְסוֹד** n.f.^Ezr 13, 17^ (m.^Jb 22, 16^) **foundation, base,** abs. יְסוֹד Hb 3¹³ + 2 t.; cstr. *id.* Ex 29¹² + 9 t.; sf. יְסֹדוֹ Ez 13¹⁴; יְסוֹדָם Jb 4¹⁹ 22¹⁶; וִיסֹדֶיהָ Mi 1⁶; יְסֹדֹתֶיהָ La 4¹¹; יְסוֹדוֹתֶיהָ Ez 30⁴;—**1.** *foundation* of city (wall) Mi 1⁶ ψ 137⁷, cf. La 4¹¹; fig. of Egypt Ez 30⁴; שַׁעַר הַיְסוֹד 2 Ch 23⁵ one of gates of temple (but rd. שׁ׳ סוּר 2 K 11⁶ or שׁ׳ סוּס [rather שׁ׳ הַסּוּסִים] Th Klo); fig. of men שֹׁכְנֵי || יְס׳ בֶּעָפָר בָּתֵּי חֹמֶר Jb 4¹⁹, cf. 22¹⁶; of righteous Pr 10²⁵; of hostile prince under fig. of house Hb 3¹³ (details obscure, v^b^ prob. corrupt, v. We); of false prophecies under fig. of wall of defence Ez 13¹⁴. **2.** *base, bottom*, of altar Ex 29¹² Lv 4^7.18.25.30.34^ 5⁹ 8¹⁵ 9⁹ (all P).

† [**יְסוּדָה**] n.f. **foundation = city founded;** אֹהֵב י׳ שַׁעֲרֵי צִיּוֹן || יְסוּדָתוֹ בְּהַרְרֵי־קֹדֶשׁ) ψ 87¹).

† **מוּסָד** n.m.^Is 28, 16^ **foundation, foundation-laying;**—מוּסָד Is 28¹⁶ (v. יסד Hoph.); עַד־הַיּוֹם מוּסַד בֵּית י׳ 2 Ch 8¹⁶ *until the day* (of) *the foundation-laying of the house of* י׳.

† **מוּסָדָה** n.f. **foundation, appointment,** מַטֵּה מוּסָדָה Is 30³² *rod of appointment* (cf. Hb 1¹² יָסַד), *appointed rod* (of punishment); pl. cstr. מוּסְדוֹת Ez 41⁸ Qr, must mean *foundations* (si vera l.); Kt perhaps intends **Pu.** *Pt.* מְיֻסָּדוֹת *founded, furnished with foundations* (conject. emendation by Co).

† [**מוֹסָד**] n.m. ^ψ 18, 8^ **foundation;**—pl. abs. מוֹסָדוֹת Je 51²⁶; cstr. מוֹסְדוֹת ψ 18¹⁶ + 2 t.; מֹסְדוֹת 2 S 22¹⁶; מוֹסְדֵי Dt 32²² + 6 t.; מֹסְדֵי Mi 6²;—*foundations* אֶבֶן לְמ׳ Je 51²⁶; מוֹסְדֵי אָרֶץ *foundations* of the earth Mi 6² Is 24¹⁸ Je 31³⁷ ψ 82⁵ Pr 8²⁹; מ׳ הא׳ Is 40²¹; מ׳ תֵּבֵל ψ 18¹⁶ = 2 S 22¹⁶; מ׳ הרים Dt 32²² ψ 18⁸; 2 S 22⁸ has (less well) מ׳ שמים; מ׳ דור־ודור Is 58¹² (|| חָרְבוֹת עולם) i.e. ancient foundations, now ruined.

† **מַסָּד** n.[m.] **foundation;**—מִמַּסָּד 1 K 7⁹ || עַד־הַטְּפָחוֹת; Co rds. מַסָּד also Ez 41⁸ (for MT מוּסְדוֹת).

† **יסך**, only in יִיסָךְ Ex 30³², rd. יוּסָךְ, v. סוך (Kö ^I. 436^).

† **יִסְכָּה** n.pr.f. (etym. dubious)—a daughter of הָרָן, and sister of מִלְכָּה Gn 11²⁹, 𝔊 Ιεσχα.

יִסְמַכְיָהוּ v. sub סמך.

יָסַף ^214^ vb. **add** (NH *id.*, Hiph.; Aram. Aph. אוֹסִף, ܐܘܣܦ; Ph. יסף; MI²⁹ יספתי, l²¹ לספת; Sab. וסף Hom^ZMG 1892, 580^; As. *esêpu* dub. (*eṣêpu* Dl)—† **Qal** *Pf.* יָסַף Gn 38²⁶ +; יָסְפָה Gn 8¹²; וְיָסְפָה consec. 2 K 19³⁰ = Is 37³¹; יָסַפְתָּ Is 26¹⁵ 2 Ch 9⁶; וְיָסַפְתָּ Dt 19⁹, etc.; *Imv.* סְפוּ Is 29¹ Je 7²¹; + *Inf. cstr.* לִסְפֹּת for MT לִסְפּוֹת Nu 32¹⁴ Is 30¹ (Ges ^§ 69. 2. R^); *Pt.* יוֹסֵף (rd. יוֹסִף) Is 29¹⁴ 38⁵ (Kö ^I. 403^ adds Ec 1¹⁸ יוֹסִיף, fr. form and connexion less likely); pl. יֹסְפִים Dt 5²²;—*add*, sq. acc. + עַל 1 S 12¹⁹ Je 7²¹ 45³ Is 29¹ 30¹ 38⁵ Dt 19⁹ (+ עוד), Lv 22¹⁴ 26²¹ 27^13.15.19.27^; sq. acc. 2 K 19³⁰ = Is 37³¹, Nu 32¹⁴ 2 Ch 9⁶ sq. עַל (no acc.; יָסַפְתָּ עַל־הַשְּׁמוּעָה אֲשֶׁר שָׁמָעְתִּי); sq. לְ (no acc.) = *increase* Is 26^15.15^ (יָסַפְתָּ לַגּוֹי); sq. acc. *increase, have more* 29¹⁹ (וְיָסְפוּ עֲנָוִים בַּיהוה שִׂמְחָה); 14 t. sq. inf. Gn 8¹² (לֹא יָסְפָה שׁוּב אֵלָיו עוֹד, i.e. it *did not again return unto him*), 38²⁶ (+ עוד), Lv 26¹⁸ Nu 32¹⁵ (+ עוד), Dt 5²² (+ עוד), 20⁸ Ju 8²⁸ 13²¹ (+ עוד), 1 S 7¹³ (+ עוד), 15³⁵ 27⁴ (וְלֹא יָסַף עוֹד), 2 S 2²⁸ (+ עוד), 2 K 6²³ (+ עוד), Is 29¹⁴; cf. Nu 11²⁵ Dt 5¹⁹, where

inf. not expressed, but implied from context; both c. לֹא *and did not do it again.* †**Niph.** *Pf.* נוֹסַף Je 36[32]; וְנ׳ consec. Ex 1[10] Nu 36[3]; 3 fs. וְנוֹסְפָה consec. Nu 36[4]; *Pt.* וְנוֹסָף Pr 11[24]; נוֹסָפוֹת Is 15[9];—**1.** *join* (intr.), *join oneself to* (עַל) Ex 1[10]. **2.** *be joined, added to* (עַל) Nu 36[3.4] Je 36[32]; pt. abs. *is increased* Pr 11[24]; pt. fem. pl.=*things added, additions* (i.e. additional calamities) Is 15[9]. **Hiph.** $_{172}$ *Pf.* הֹסִיף 2 K 24[7]; הוֹסַפְתָּ 1 K 10[7], etc.; *Impf.* $_{164}$ יוֹסִיף Jos 23[13]+; *juss.* יוֹסֵף Gn 30[24]+; יוֹסֶף (bef. tone) Pr 1[5] 9[9]; וַיּוֹסֶף Is 7[10]+; וַיֹּאסֶף 1 S 18[29]; 2 ms. תּוֹסִיף Am 7[13]+; *juss.* תֹּסֵף Dt 13[1]; תּוֹסַף Jb 40[32]; תּוֹסְףְּ Pr 30[6]; אוֹסִיף Ho 1[6]+; volunt. אוֹסִףָ 9[15]; אֹסֵף Dt 18[16]+Ez 5[16] (del. Co); אֹסְפָה 2 S 12[8]+prob. Dt 32[23] (for MT אַסְפֶּה); 3 mpl. יוֹסִפוּן 1 K 19[2]; 2 mpl. תּוֹסִיפוּ Is 1[5]+; תֹּסִפוּן Gn 44[23]+2 t.; תֹּאסִפוּן Ex 5[7] (per contr. 2 S 6[1] ψ 104[29], cf. sub אסף), etc.; *Pt.* pl. מוֹסִיפִים Ne 13[18]; *Inf. cstr.* הוֹסִיף Lv 19[25]+3 t.;—**1.** *add* (=**Qal**), sq. acc.+עַל 2 K 20[6] Lv 5[16.24] 27[31] Nu 5[7] Jb 34[37] (Elihu), ψ 61[7] Pr 16[23] Ez 5[16] (v. supr.), Ne 13[18]+Dt 32[23]; sq. acc.+לְ Gn 30[24] Pr 3[2] 9[11]; sq. acc.+אֶל 1 K 10[7] (i.e. thou hast more wisdom and prosperity than is reported); sq. acc.+אִם Pr 10[22]; cf. וְהוֹסַפְתִּי עַל־כָּל־תְּהִלָּתֶךָ ψ 71[14] (i.e. increase); וְהוֹסַפְתִּי חכמה על כל־אשר־היה לְפָנַי Ec 1[16] (‖ הִגְדַּלְתִּי) (i.e. gain more); cf. 2[9] (‖ וְגָדַלְתִּי); וַיּוֹסֶף ה׳ לכם תבואתו Lv 19[25] (i.e. yield more); וַיּוֹסֶף אַחְאָב לַעֲשׂוֹת לְהַכְעִים אֶת־יהוה . . . מִכֹּל וגו׳ 1 K 16[33] (*did more to provoke*); *add to, increase* (sq. עַל), no obj. expr. ה׳ עַל־חַטֹּאתֵנוּ 2 Ch 28[13]; ה׳ עַל־אַשְׁמַת יִשְׂרָאֵל Ezr 10[10]; עליו אֵין להוֹסִיף Ec 3[14] (opp. לִגְרֹעַ), cf. Dt 4[2] 13[1] 1 K 12[11.14] 1 Ch 22[14] 2 Ch 10[11.14] Pr 30[6] ψ 115[14]; sq. אֶל (no other obj. expr.) Ez 23[14]; =*give in addition* וְאֹסִפָה לךָ 2 S 12[8]; מַה־יֹּסִיף לָךְ ψ 120[4] (‖ מַה־יִּתֵּן לְךָ); esp. in phr. כה יעשה אלהים (י׳) לך (לי) וכה יוסיף 1 S 3[17] *so may God do to thee and more also,* 14[44] 20[13] 25[22] 2 S 3[9] (וכה יוסיף לו), v[35] 19[14] 1 K 2[23] 2 K 6[31] Ru 1[17]; subj. heathen gods 1 K 19[2] 20[10]; c. acc. ה׳ אֹמֶץ *add strength*=grow stronger Jb 17[9], cf. Pr 1[5] 9[9] Ec 1[18.18], also Is 1[5] Pr 16[21]; also, where subj. different from indirect obj. Pr 10[27] (יראת י׳ יוסיף ימים), 19[4] 23[28]; =*multiply* ה׳ עליכם כָּכֶם אלף פעמים Dt 1[11] cf. 1 Ch 21[3]; וְיוֹסֵף י׳ אלהיךָ אל־העם כָּהֵם וְכָהֵם וַיֹּסֶף י׳ את־כל־אשר לְאִיּוֹב מֵאָה פְעָמִים 2 S 24[3]; cf. לְמִשְׁנֶה Jb 42[10]. **2. a.** sq. inf. (with or without לְ) *add to do*=*do again* or *more* (in Hex only JE & D); +עוֹד Gn 8[21.21] 18[29] 37[5.8] Ex 10[29] 14[13] Nu 25[15] Dt 3[26] 17[16] 19[20] 28[68] Ju 9[37] 20[28] 1 S 3[6] 18[29] (increase), 23[4] 27[4] (Kt), 2 S 2[22] 5[22] 7[20] (inf. om. in ‖ 1 Ch 17[18]), 14[10] 18[22] 2 K 24[7] Am 7[8.13] 8[2] Is 8[5] 10[20] 23[12] 51[22] Na 2[1] Zp 3[11] Je 31[12] Ez 36[12] ψ 10[18] 78[17]; inf. om. Pr 19[19] 1 Ch 17[18]; עוֹד om. Gn 4[2.12] 8[10] 44[23] Ex 5[7] 8[25] 9[28.34] 10[28] Nu 25[19.25] Dt 13[12] 18[16] 25[3] Jos 7[12] 23[13] Ju 2[21] 3[12] 4[1] 10[6.13] 13[1] 20[22.23] 1 S 3[8.21] 9[8] 19[8] 20[17] 2 S 3[34] 7[10] 24[1] 2 K 21[8] Is 1[13] 7[10] 24[20] Ho 9[15] 13[2] Am 5[2] 1 Ch 17[9] 2 Ch 28[22] 33[8] Jb 27[1] 29[1] ψ 41[9] 77[8] La 4[15.16.22] Jon 2[5]; inf. om. Ex 11[6] Dt 25[3] Jb 20[9] 34[32] (Elihu), 38[11] 40[5.32] Jo 2[2]; cf. also ה׳ עֲבוֹר Nu 22[26] i.e. *went on further.* **b.** sq. Impf. c. וְ (of past time) Gn 25[1] 1 S 19[21] Est 8[3] Jb 36[1] (Elihu), Dn 10[18]; +עוֹד Gn 38[5] Ju 11[14] 1 Ch 14[13]. **c.** sq. Impf. asynd. (Ges[§ 120, 1 b, 2 b]) לא תוסיפי יקראו־לָךְ Is 47[1.5]; אוסיף אֲבַקְשֶׁנּוּ עוד Pr 23[35]; לא אוסיף עוד אֲרַחֵם אֶת־בֵּית ישראל Ho 1[6]; לא יוסיף יָבֹא־בך עוד Is 52[1].

יוֹסֵף $_{212}$ and יְהוֹסֵף († ψ 81[6] v. Ges[§ 53. 3. R. 7]). **n.pr.m.** (*he adds, increases,* v. יוספיה infr.;—on n.pr. loc. in Pal. *Yšap'ara* (Egypt. form,=יוסף אל) v. Mey[ZAW vi. 8] WMM[Asien u. Europa 162])—**1.** elder son of Jacob and Rachel; **a.** as an individual Gn 30[24] (name expl. v[23] (E) from אָסַף=*take away,* but v[24] (J) from יָסַף *add*) +155 t. Gn, chiefly in narrative of JE, also poem 49[22.26] and, dependent on this, 1 Ch 5[1.2]; P only 35[24] 37[2a] 41[46.46] 46[19.20.27] 47[5.7.11] 48[3]; also Ex 1[5.6] (P), v[8] 13[19] Jos 24[32] (all E), 1 Ch 2[2] ψ 105[17]. †**b.** as founder of a tribal division מַטֵּה יו׳ (=Manasseh) Nu 13[11]; usu. בְּנֵי־יו׳ 1[32] (=Ephraim), commonly =Ephraim and Manasseh 1[10] 26[28.37] 34[23] Jos 14[4] 16[1.4] 17[14.16] 18[11], cf. 24[32] 1 Ch 7[29], but also of E. Jordan Israel (where half Manasseh settled) Nu 36[1]=מַטֵּה בני יו׳ v[5]; cf. חֲצִי שֵׁבֶט מנשׁה בֶן־יוֹסֵף 32[33] cf. 36[12], and Jos 17[1.2]; בֵּית יו׳ (Manasseh and Ephraim) 17[17] (so orig. v[14] acc. to Di), 18[5] Ju 1[22.23.35], occupying the great central region of Palestine; 2 S 19[21] 1 K 11[28]; ultimately=**c.** the northern kingdom Am 5[6] Zc 10[6] (‖ בֵּית יְהוּדָה); so יוֹסֵף alone Am 5[15] 6[6] Dt 27[12] 33[13.16] Ob[18] (‖ בית יעקב), Ez 37[16.19] 47[13] 48[32]; בְּנֵי יַעֲקֹב ויוסף ψ 77[16]; אֹהֶל יוֹסֵף 78[67] (‖ שֵׁבֶט אֶפְרָיִם). **d.**=entire nation ψ 80[2] (‖ ישראל); so יְהוֹסֵף 81[6] (‖ *id.*) †**2.** a man of Issachar Nu 13[7]. †**3.** a son of Asaph 1 Ch 25[2.9]. †**4.** one of those who took strange wives Ezr 10[42]. †**5.** a priest Ne 12[14].

†יוֹסִפְיָה **n.pr.m.** (י׳ *adds*)—father of one of Ezra's companions Ezr 8[10].

†[יָסַר] **vb. discipline, chasten, admonish** (Talm. 𝔗 (י)סוּר chastisement; but Aram. יְסַר is *bind*)—**Qal** *Impf.* 3 m. sf. וְיִסְּרֵנִי Is 8[11] (Di De SS

see Bo^{§1103} Ew^{§249d}, but Thes MV Che al. **Pi.** Pf.); 1 s. sf. וְאֶסֳּרֵם Ho 10^{10} (Ges^{§71}); *Inf. abs.* יַסֹּר 1 Ch 15^{22} (noun Ke, point as pt. Öt); *Pt.* יֹסֵר Pr 9^{7} ψ 94^{10}; יסורי Je 17^{13} Kt v. סוּר;—**1.** *admonish* Is 8^{11} (sq. sf. + מִלֶּכֶת *away from walking*, i.e. not to walk), Pr 9^{7} (‖ מוֹכִיחַ). **2.** *instruct*, 1 Ch 15^{22}. **3.** *discipline*, of God Ho 10^{10} ψ 94^{10}. **Niph.** *Impf.* יִוָּסֵר עָבֶד Pr 29^{19}; אִוָּסֵר Je 31^{18}; תִּוָּסְרוּ Lv 26^{23}; *Imv.* f. הִוָּסְרִי Je 6^{8}; mpl. הִוָּסְרוּ ψ 2^{10};—(Niph. *tolerat.*, Ges$^{§51.2}$), *let oneself be corrected, admonished* by words of man ψ 2^{10} Pr 29^{19}; *let oneself be chastened* by discipline of God Je 6^{8} 31^{18} Lv 26^{23}. **Pi.** *Pf.* יִסַּר 1 K 12^{11} + 3 t.; sf. יִסְּרַנִּי ψ 118^{18}; יִסְּרוֹ Is 28^{26}; 3 f. sf. יִסְּרַתּוּ Pr 31^{1}; 2 m. יִסַּרְתָּ ψ 39^{12} Jb 4^{3}, etc. + 8 t. Pf.; *Impf.* יְיַסֵּר Dt 8^{5}; 2 m. sf. תְּיַסְּרֶנּוּ ψ 94^{12}, etc. + 5 t. Impf.; *Imv.* יַסֵּר Pr 19^{18} 29^{17}; sf. יַסְּרֵנִי Je 10^{24}; *Inf. abs.* יַסֹּר ψ 118^{18}; *cstr.* יַסְּרָה Lv 26^{18}; sf. יַסְּרֶךָּ Dt 4^{36}; *Pt.* מְיַסְּרֶךָּ Dt 8^{5};—**1.** *discipline, correct* (the moral nature, with more or less severity acc. to circumstances): **a.** of God, c. acc. Ho 7^{15} (of *training* arms), Dt 4^{36} (v. Dr), 8^{5} (Israel as son), Is 28^{26}, happy the man אשׁר תיסרנו יה ψ 94^{12}, $118^{18.18}$. **b.** of man, c. acc. Dt 8^{5} Pr 19^{18} 29^{17} (all of a father his son), Jb 4^{3} Pr 31^{1}, ψ 16^{7} my reins (the emotions of my own heart) *correct, admonish* me. **2.** more severely, *chasten, chastise*: **a.** of God, sq. acc. pers., Je 31^{18}; אַל־בַּחֲמָתְךָ תְיַסְּרֵנִי ψ 6^{2} 38^{2}; בְּמִשְׁפָּט אל באף Je 10^{24}; למשׁפט 30^{11} = 46^{28}; על חטאת Lv $26^{18.28}$; בתוכחות על עון ψ 39^{12}. **b.** of man, a father his son Dt 21^{18}; elders a man Dt 22^{18} (including, as perh. 21^{18}, bodily chastisement); a king his subjects בַּשּׁוֹטִים and בָּעַקְרַבִּים 1 K $12^{11.14}$ = 2 Ch $10^{11.14}$. **c.** תְּיַסְּרֵךְ רָעָתֵךְ Je 2^{19} *thy badness will chastise thee.* **Nithp.** *Pf.* נִוַּסְּרוּ Ez 23^{48} (for נִתְיַסְּרוּ Ges$^{§55 R.7}$); *pass. be disciplined, corrected.* **Hiph.** *Impf.* 1 s. sf. אַיְסִרֵם (Ew^{§131c}, but error for אֲיַסְּרֵם Bö^{§437f} SS), c. acc. *chasten* Ho 7^{12}.

†יִסּוֹר **n.m.** one who reproves, fault-finder, הֲרֹב עִם־שַׁדַּי יִסּוֹר Jb 40^{2} *shall a reprover contend with Shadday?*

†מוּסָר **n.m.** $^{Pr 15, 10}$ discipline (of the moral nature), chastening, correction;—מ׳ Je 2^{30} + 31 t. (Ez 5^{15} del. Co); cstr. מוּסַר Dt 11^{2} + 14 t. (for Jb 12^{18} see אסר); sf. מוּסָרִי Pr 8^{10}; מוּסָרְךָ Is 26^{16}; מֹסָרָם Jb 33^{16} (for מֻסָרָם Di SS);—*discipline, correction*, of God, Dt 11^{2} מוּסַר י׳ the *discipline* of י׳ (of Y.'s wonders, as exercising a disciplinary, educating influence upon Israel, cf. Dr); לקח מ׳ Je 7^{28} 32^{33} 35^{13} Zp $3^{2.7}$; ψ 50^{17} Jb 33^{16} 36^{10}; מ׳ כְּלִמָּתִי the *correction* of (i.e. which leadeth to) my shame Jb 20^{3}. **b.** מ׳ הבלים עֵץ הוּא the *discipline* of unreal gods is wood (is like themselves, destitute of true moral force) Je 10^{8}; Ez 5^{15} = *warning example* (?) Ew Sm (‖ שַׁמָּה; del. 𝔊 Co). **c.** in Proverbs, *discipline* in the school of wisdom: חכמה ומ׳ $1^{2.7}$ 23^{23}; מ׳ חכמה *discipline of wisdom* 15^{33}; מ׳ הַשְׂכֵּל 1^{3}; תוכחות מ׳ 6^{23}; הָבִיאָה לַמּ׳ לִבֶּךָ 23^{12} *apply thy mind to discipline;* לקח מ׳ 1^{3} 8^{10} 24^{32} (cf. Je supr.); קבל מ׳ 19^{20}; קנה מ׳ 23^{23}; שמע מ׳ 8^{33} 19^{27}; שמר מ׳ 10^{17}; אהב מ׳ 12^{1}; החזק במ׳ 4^{13}; the reverse שׂנא מ׳ 5^{12}; פרע מ׳ 13^{18} 15^{32}; בוזה מ׳ 1^{7}; באין מ׳ *for lack of discipline* 5^{23} מ׳ אֱוִלִים אִוֶּלֶת (‖ בְּרֹב אִוַּלְתּוֹ) 16^{22} *the discipline of fools is folly;* of paternal discipline, correction, Pr. 1^{8} 4^{1} 13^{1}. **2.** more severely, *chastening, chastisement:* **a.** of God, מ׳ יהוה Pr 3^{11} *chastening of Yahweh;* מ׳ שַׁדַּי Jb 5^{17}; מוּסָרְךָ Is 26^{16}; מ׳ שְׁלוֹמֵנוּ עָלָיו Is 53^{5} *chastisement of* (i.e. leading to) *our peace was upon him;* לקח מ׳ Je 2^{30} 5^{3} 7^{28}; מ׳ אַכְזָרִי Je 30^{14} *chastisement of a cruel one*, MT, but rd. מוּסָר א׳ *cruel chastisement*, Gf and esp. Gie; אני מ׳ לְכֻלָּם Ho 5^{2} *I am a chastisement for them all.* **b.** of man, Pr 15^{5} 23^{13}; שֵׁבֶט מ׳ 22^{15}; שְׁחָרוֹ מ׳ 13^{24}; מ׳ אויל 7^{22} *chastisement of a fool;* מוּסָר רָע 15^{10} *grievous chastisement.*

[מֹסֵר] v. מוּסָר.

יָעַ v. sub יעה; יַעְבֵּץ v. sub עבץ.

†יָעַד **vb.** appoint (NH *id.*, *appoint, assign*, esp. of acquiring or designating as wife; Aram. *id.*; Ar. وَعَدَ *promise, threaten, predict*, III. *appoint a time* or *place*; perh. As. *âdu, decide*, M-A^{17} Dl$^{HWB 230}$; Ph. n. pr. אשמניעד)—**Qal** *Pf.* sf. יְעָדוֹ 2 S 20^{5}; יְעָדָהּ Ex 21^{8} + 2 t.; *Impf.* 3 m. sf. יִיעָדֶנָּה Ex 21^{9};—*appoint*, a time 2 S 20^{5}; place Je 47^{7}; a rod Mi 6^{9}; *assign* or *designate* as concubine Ex $21^{8.9}$ (JE). **Niph.** *Pf.* נוֹעַדְתִּי Ex 25^{22}; נֹעַדְתִּי Ex 29^{43}; pl. נוֹעֲדוּ ψ 48^{5} Nu $10^{3.4}$; נוֹעָדוּ Am 3^{3}; *Impf.* אִוָּעֵד Ex 29^{42} + 3 t.; 3 pl. וַיִּוָּעֲדוּ Jos 11^{5} Jb 2^{11}; 1 pl. נִוָּעֵד Ne 6^{10}; וְנִוָּעֲדָה v^{2}; *Pt.* pl. נוֹעָדִים Nu 14^{35} + 3 t.; נֹעָדִים 16^{11};—**1.** reflexive, *meet at an appointed place*, with לְ, of Yahweh *meeting* Moses at the Tent of 'Meeting' Ex $29^{42.43}$ 30^{36} (P); at the throne of the Kapporeth 25^{22} 30^{6} Nu 17^{19} (P). **2.** *meet by appointment* Am 3^{3} Jb 2^{11}; with בְּ of place Ne 6^{2}; אֶל of place v^{10}. **3.** *gather, assemble by appointment*, kings for a campaign (abs.) Jos 11^{5} (D), ψ 48^{5};

with אֶל, unto Moses Nu 10^{4} (P); to the door of the tent of meeting v^{3} (P); with עַל, unto Solomon 1 K 8^{5} = 2 Ch 5^{6}; against Yahweh Nu 14^{35} 16^{11} 27^{3} (P). **Po'ēl** *Pf.* 1 s. יוֹעַדְתִּי (for MT יוֹדַעְתִּי) 1 S 21^{3} sq. acc. pers. + אֶל of place, acc. to 𝔊 We Dr Kit Bu. **Hiph.** *Impf.* מִי יוֹעִדֵנִי Je 50^{44} = מִי יְעִידֵנִי 49^{19} מִי יוֹעִדֵנִי Jb 9^{19} *who will make me meet him at the appointed place* (of judgment)? i.e. *who will summon* or *arraign me?* **Hoph.** *Pt.* מוּעָדִים לְפָנֵי Je 24^{1} *be set, placed before;* אָנָה פָּנַיִךְ מֻעָדוֹת Ez 21^{21} *whither thy face is set.*

עֵדָה$_{149}$ **n.f.** congregation (prop. *company assembled together by appointment*, or *acting concertedly*)—ע׳ Nu 16^{2} + 85 t.; cstr. עֲדַת Ex 12^{3} + 52 t.; sf. עֲדָתִי Jb 16^{7} + 9 t. sfs.;—**1.** עֲדַת־אֵל ψ 82^{1} *congregation of Ēl*, of company of angels (|| בקרב אלהים); ע׳ לְאֻמִּים 7^{8} *congregation of peoples;* ע׳ צַדִּיקִים 1^{5} *congregation of the righteous;* || סוֹד יְשָׁרִים 111^{1}; || קהל Pr 5^{14}; כָּל־עֲדָתִי Jb 16^{7} (of Job's circle of dependents); in a bad sense, ע׳ מְרֵעִים *company of evil doers* ψ 22^{17}; ע׳ עריצים 86^{14}; ע׳ חנף Jb 15^{34}; ע׳ קֹרַח *company of Korah* Nu 26^{9} 27^{3} (P), so עֲדָתוֹ, עֲדָתְךָ 16$^{5.6.11.16}$ 17^{5} (P), and הָעֵדָה 26^{10} 27^{3} (P); ע׳ אֲבִירָם ψ 106^{17}, cf. v^{18}. **2.** of *animals* ע׳ אַבִּירִים ψ 68^{31} (fig. of nobles); ע׳ דְּבֹרִים Ju 14^{8} *a swarm of bees.* **3.** elsewhere of Israel Ho 7^{12} עֲדָתָם i.e. the whole assemblage of them; 1 K 8^{5} (= 2 Ch 5^{6}) כל עדת יש׳ of those gathered to Sol.; 12^{20} העדה of assembly at Shechem; Je 6^{18} (text very dub.); עֲדָתוֹ 30^{20} of restored people; עֲדָתְךָ ψ 74^{2} (|| שבט נחלתך); elsewhere in P, except possibly Nu 20^{11} (R), in technical sense, of the *company* of Israel of the Exodus, the *congregation* (115 t.), esp. in the phrases †ע׳ יהוה† Nu 27^{17} 31^{16} Jos 22$^{16.17}$; †ע׳ ישראל† Ex 12$^{3.6.19.47}$ Lv 4^{13} Nu 16^{9} 32^{4} Jos 22$^{18.20}$; †ע׳ בני ישראל† Ex 16$^{1.2.9.10}$ 17^{1} 35$^{1.4.20}$ Lv 16^{5} 19^{2} (H), Nu 1$^{2.53}$ 8$^{9.20}$ 13^{26} 14$^{5.7}$ 15$^{25.26}$ 17^{6} 19^{9} 25^{6} 26^{2} 27^{20} 31^{12} Jos 18^{1} 22^{12}; הָעֵדָה Lv 8^{4} + 29 t. (cf. Ju 20^{1} 21^{10}); כל־הע׳ Lv 8^{3} + 33 t. (cf. Ju 21^{13}); †נְשִׂיאֵי (ה)ע׳ *princes of the congregation* Ex 16^{22} Nu 4^{34} 16^{2} 31^{13} 32^{2} Jos 9$^{15.18}$ 22^{30}; כָּל־הַנְּשִׂאִים בָּע׳ Ex 34^{31}; זִקְנֵי הע׳ *elders of the congregation* Lv 4^{15} (cf. Ju 21^{16}); ראשי אבות הע׳ Nu 31^{26}.

מוֹעֵד$_{223}$ **n.m.**$^{ψ 102, 14}$ appointed time, place, meeting; מ׳ Ex 9^{5} + 183 t.; מֹעֵד Dt 31^{10}; מוֹעֲדוֹ Nu 9^{2} + 2 t.; מֹעֲדוֹ La 2^{6} + 3 t. + 5 t. sfs.; pl. מוֹעֲדִים Dn 12^{7} + 6 t.; מֹעֲדִים Zc 8^{19} 1 Ch 23^{31}; מוֹעֲדוֹת 2 Ch 8^{13}; cstr. מוֹעֲדֵי Lv 23^{2} + 6 t.; מֹעֲדֵי Lv 23^{44}; sfs. מוֹעֲדַי Ez 44^{24}; מֹעֲדֵיכֶם Nu 15^{3} + 6 t. sfs.;—†**1.** *appointed time:* **a.** in general with prefix לְ, *at an* or *the appointed time* Gn 18^{14} Ex 13^{10} (J), Ex 23^{15} 34^{18} Jos 8^{14} (all JE), Gn 17^{21} 21^{2} (P), 1 S 9^{24} 13^{8} (after אשר insert either אָמַר 𝔊 𝔗 or שָׂם Dr), v^{11} 2 K 4$^{16.17}$ Hb 2^{3} Dn 8^{19} 11$^{27.29.35}$; למ׳ דוד *at the time appointed* with David 1 S 20^{35} (Thes SS *place appointed*); c. prefix בְּ Ho 2^{11} Lv 23^{4} Nu 9$^{2.3.7.13}$ 28^{2} (P); c. מִן 2 S 20^{5}; עַד עֵת מ׳ 24^{15} *unto the time appointed* (but dub., v. Dr); c. vbs. בא מ׳ ψ 102^{14}; לקח מ׳ 75^{3}; שׂים מ׳ Ex 9^{5} (J); העביר המ׳ Je 46^{17}; the stork ידעה מ׳ Je 8^{7} *knows her appointed time;* מ׳ צאתך Dt 16^{6} *time of thy going forth* (from Egypt). **b.** in particular (cf. Ex 13^{10} 23^{15} 34^{18}), *sacred season*, RV usu. *set feast* or *appointed season* (wider than חַג, which was only a feast celebrated by a *pilgrimage*), יוֹם (ימי) מ׳ *day(s) of appointed season* (i.e. *festivals*) Ho 9^{5} 12^{10} La 2$^{7.22}$; sg. indef. 1^{4}; of the feast of booths Dt 31^{10}; || חג חדש שבת Ho 2^{13}; || שבת La 2^{6}; usu. pl. מ׳ יהוה Lv 23$^{2.4.37.44}$ (P), 2 Ch 2^{3} Ezr 3^{5}; with sfs. referring to י׳ Lv 23^{2} (P); במ׳ Nu 15^{3} 29^{39} (P), Ez 36^{38} 46^{9}; קרית מ׳ *city of our solemnities* (sacred seasons) Is 33^{20}; למ׳ טובים Zc 8^{19}; || שבתות Ez 44^{24}; || חדשים Is 1^{14} 1 Ch 23^{31} 2 Ch 8^{13} 31^{3} Ne 10^{34}; || חגים Ez 46^{11}; חגים חדשים Ez 45^{17}; || ראשי חָדְשֵׁכֶם Nu 10^{10} (P).—*Notes.* It is most probable that in Gn 1^{14} (P), where מ׳ || אֹתֹת, the reference is to the sacred seasons as fixed by the moon's appearance; and so also עשה ירח למ׳ *he made the moon for sacred seasons* ψ 104^{19}, although many Lexx. & Comm. refer these to the *seasons* of the year.—למועד מועדים וחצי Dn 12^{7} *for a set time, times, and a half* = 3½ appointed times = half the prophetic week of years, cf. Br$^{MP 453 f.}$—ויאכלו את המ׳ they ate throughout the *sacred season* (of Maṣṣoth) 2 Ch 30^{22} AV RV, but Thes SS Be Ke Öt they ate *the offerings of the sacred season;* 𝔊 וַיְכַלּוּ. **2.** *appointed meeting:* בֵּית מ׳ לְכָל־חָי Jb 30^{23} *house of meeting for every living* (of She'ol); קְרִאֵי מ׳ Nu 16^{2} (P) *called to the assembly* = קְרִאֵי הָעֵדָה; קרא עלי מ׳ La 1^{15} *called a festal meeting against me;* בקרב מ׳ ψ 74^{4} *in the midst of thine assembly;* הַר מוֹעֵד Is 14^{13} *mount of meeting* or *assembly* (of the gods; the mountain of the gods in the extreme north, the oriental Olympus, Persian *Alborg*, Hindu *Meru*, Babylon. *Aralli*, cf. Len$^{Origines II, ch. ix}$). **3.** *appointed place:* **a.** the temple, || שֻׂכּוֹ La 2^{6}, נוּגֵי מִמּ׳ *afflicted* (and driven) *from the place of assembly* Zp 3^{18} (cf. Br$^{MP 225}$). **b.** synagogues, כָּל־מוֹעֲדֵי־אֵל בָּאָרֶץ *all*

the appointed places of Ēl in the land ψ 74⁸ = בית וַעַד *Sota* 9¹⁵ **4.** *appointed sign, signal,* Ju 20³⁸. **5.** אהל מועד *tent of meeting* (of God with his people: see יָעַד Niph **1**), the sacred tent of the Exodus (see אהל **3**) Ex 33⁷ ⁷ Nu 12⁴ Dt 31¹⁴ ¹⁴ (E), Nu 11¹⁶ (J), oft in P, as Ex 27²¹ 29⁴ Lv 1¹ ³ Jos 18¹ 19⁵¹, etc (131 t), elsewhere only 1 S 2²²ᵇ (om 𝔊), 1 K 8⁴ = 2 Ch 5⁵, 1 Ch 6¹⁷ 9²¹ 23³² 2 Ch 1³·⁶ ¹³.

†[מוֹעָד] **n.[m.] appointed place** (of soldier in army), pl sf מוֹעָדָיו i e *his ranks* Is 14³¹, so Thes SS RVm Ew De Che Dr Du, *his places of assemblage* Di, *at his appointed times* RV.

†מוּעָדָה **n.f.** עָרֵי הַמּ׳ *cities appointed* (for refuge) Jos 20⁹ (P)

†נוֹעַדְיָה **n.pr.** (*meeting with Yah*) — **1. m.** Levite, cotemp Ezra Ezr 8³³ **2. f.** a prophetess hostile to Nehemiah Ne 6¹⁴

יֶעְדּוֹ Qr, ידעי Kt **n.pr.m.** 2 Ch 9²⁹ v. עדו sub עדד.

†יָעָה **vb. sweep together** (with collat idea of *carrying away*) (Ar. وَعَى is *collect, gather*)—**Qal** *Pf.* וְיָעָה consec. Is 28¹⁷ subj בָּרָד c acc (ויעה ב׳ מַחסה כָזָב)

†[יָע] **n [m.] shovel** (𝔗ᴶᵉʳ יָעֵי Ex 27³)—pl הַיָּעִים Ex 38³ + 7 t, יָעָיו 27³;—utensils for cleaning altar, *shovels* Ex 27³ 38³ Nu 4¹⁴ (all P), 1 K 7⁴⁰·⁴⁵ 2 K 25¹⁴ 2 Ch 4¹¹ ¹⁶ Je 52¹⁸ (only in lists of utensils)

†יעואל, יעיאל, יְעוֹאֵל **n.pr.m. 1.** יעואל son of Zerah 1 Ch 9⁶, 𝔊 Επειηλ, A 𝔊L Ιειηλ **2** יְעִיאֵל. **a.** a companion of Ezra Ezr 8¹³, 𝔊L Ιειηλ. **b.** a chief of the Reubenites 1 Ch 5⁷, 𝔊 Ιωηλ **c.** Levites, 𝔊 Ιωηλ, Ιειηλ, etc. (1) 1 Ch 15¹⁸ ²¹ 16⁵·⁵ 2 Ch 20¹⁴; (2) 2 Ch 35⁹. **d.** one of those who took strange wives Ezr 10⁴³, 𝔊 Ιαηλ, Ιειηλ, etc. **3.** יעואל Kt, יעיאל Qr: **a** man of Gibeon, ancestor of Saul 1 Ch 9³⁵, 𝔊 Ιηλ, Ιε(ι)ηλ **b.** one of David's heroes 11⁴⁴, 𝔊 (Ι)εια, A 𝔊L Ιειηλ **c.** the סופר (q v.) of King Uzziah 2 Ch 26¹¹, 𝔊 Ιειηλ. **d.** a Levite 29¹³ A 𝔊L Ιειηλ

יעוץ v sub עוץ, יעור v. sub עור.

יעורים v יַעַר.

יעוש v sub עוש.

†[יָעַז] **vb.** only **Niph.** *Pt.* as adj. (precise mng dub., Ar وَعَزَ is *give a nod* or *sign*, then *command*, whence Heb might have meaning *nodding, making signs* (not intelligibly speaking), so Hi—Che *barbarous*, De '*ungeberdig*'—which context favours, or *arrogant*, Thes prop *durus, saevus*, and comp עזז)—in phr עַם נוֹעָז Is 33¹⁹ *a barbarous* (?) *people*, of foreign invader.

יעזיאל, יעזיהו v sub עזז

יַעֲזֵר v sub עזר

†[יָעַט] **vb. cover**,—only **Qal** *Pf.* 3 ms. sf מעיל צְדָקָה יְעָטָנִי Is 61¹⁰ (|| הלבישני בגדי־ישע), but cf עָטָה

יָעִיר v sub עור.

יָעִיש v sub עוש

יַעְכָּן v sub עכן.

†I. [יָעַל] **vb.** only **Hiph. profit, avail, benefit**,—**Hiph.** *Pf.* הועיל Hb 2¹⁸; *Impf* יועיל Je 2¹¹ + 2 t, אעיל Jb 35³, יוֹעִילוּ 1 S 12²¹ + 6 t, יוֹעִלוּ Je 2⁸ 12¹³; יועילוך Is 57¹²; נועיל Jb 21¹⁵; *Inf. abs* הועיל Je 23³²; cstr הועיל 7⁸ + 4 t, *Pt.* מועיל 16¹⁹.—*profit, avail, benefit*, always (exc. Jb 30¹³ where in bad sense, Is 47¹²) c neg, or in question implying neg; esp of idols or false gods (as *unprofitable*), so Hb 2¹⁸ Is 44⁹ ¹⁰ 57¹² Je 2⁸ המיר כבודו בלוא יועיל v¹¹, אחרי לא יועילו הלכו 16¹⁹, ואין בם מועיל 1 S 12²¹, of vain confidences Je 7⁸, or promises 23³² ³² (sq ל), of Egypt as ally Is 30⁵ (sq ל), v⁵·⁶, of *wickedness* Pr 10², *wealth* 11⁴; *worthless* men Jb 30¹³ (לְהַיָּתִי יועילו i e promote it), of words Jb 15³ (|| דָּבָר לא יסכון); in gen. *gain profit* Is 47¹² 48¹⁷ Je 12¹³ Jb 21¹⁵ 35³.

†יוֹעֵאלָה **n.pr.m.** (perh from *יוֹעִלָה *may he avail!*)—one of David's heroes 1 Ch 12⁸ (Baer, v⁷ van d H)

II יעל (✓of foll, Ar وَعَلَ *eminuit, prominuit*, v *ascend*, Kam Frey).

†I [יָעֵל] **n.[m.] mountain-goat** (NH *id*, 𝔗 יַעֲלָא, Syr ܝܥܠܐ, Ar. وَعْلٌ, وَعِلٌ, As. *ya'ilu* Dl⁸⁵³ (but Hpt ᴮᴬ ¹ ¹⁷⁰, Jager ᴵᵇ· ⁴⁶⁵); Eth. ወዕል: v Hom ᴺˢ ²⁹⁰)—*Pl* יְעֵלִים ψ 104¹⁸ (|| שְׁפַנִּים), צורי הַי׳ 1 S 24³; יַעֲלֵי־סָלַע Jb 39¹ (|| אַיָּלוֹת, cf I. יַעֲלָה)

†II יָעֵל **n.pr f.** wife of Heber the Kenite, slayer of Sisera Ju 4¹⁷ ¹⁸·²¹·²² 5²⁴, prob also v⁶ (others find here name of a man, a 'judge')

†I [יַעֲלָה] **n.f.** = I. יָעֵל (female);—אַיֶּלֶת אֲהָבִים וְיַעֲלַת חֵן Pr 5¹⁹ fig of wife.

†II. יַעְלָא, יַעֲלָה **n.pr.m.** *head of a family of returning exiles*, יַעְלָא Ne 7^{58}=יַעֲלָה Ezr 2^{56}.

יַעְלָם v. sub עלם.

I יַ֫עַן **prep. and conj.** v. sub I. ענה.

II. יַעַן in דָּנָה יַעַן 2 S 24^6 v. supr. p. 193.

יען (√of foll., acc. to Ges Ew $^{GGA\ 1864,\ No.\ 27}$ Aram. ‎تعْنَ, تعْنَا *avidus, cupidus*; hence בַּת יַעֲנָה=*daughter of greed*, of ostrich as voracious bird; but Wetzst $^{Del\ Jb\ 31,\ 39}$ = *daughter of the desert* or *steppe*, from وَعْنَةٌ *hard, unproductive soil*; cf. the Arab name أبو ٱلْمَعَارَى *father of the plains*.)

†[יָעֵן] **n.[m.]** ostrich (i.e. *voracious one*?);—only pl. abs כִּי עֲנִים בַּמִּדְבָּר La 4^3 Kt; Qr כַּיְעֵנִים.

†יַעֲנָה **n.f. greed**(?);—only in בַּת־הַיַּעֲנָה Lv 11^{16} Dt 14^{15}; בְּנוֹת־יַעֲנָה Mi 1^8+5 t.;—*ostrich*, (vid. √יען supra), as wailing (sim. of mourning) Mi 1^8 (‖תַּנִּים); symbol of loneliness Jb 30^{29} (אָח הָיִיתִי לְתַנִּים וְרֵעַ לִבְ׳ יַעֲ׳); of desolation, as dwelling among ruins Is 13^{21} 34^{13} (‖תַּנִּים), Je 50^{39}; dwelling in desert Is 43^{20} (‖תַּנִּים), unclean fowl Lv 11^{16} Dt 14^{15}.

יַעְנַי **n.pr.** v. sub ענה.

†I. [יָעֵף] **vb. be weary, faint** (Ar. وَغَفَ *run* and *shew weariness*)—**Qal** *Pf.* וְיָעֵפוּ consec. Je $51^{58.64}$; *Impf* יִיעַף Is 40^{28}; וַיִּעָף 44^{12}; יִעֲפוּ 40^{30}, יִיעָפוּ v^{31} Je 2^{24}; יִעָפוּ Hb 2^{13};—*be* or *grow weary* Je 2^{24} (in seeking);=exhaust oneself fruitlessly Hb 2^{13} (‖ינע), hence Je $51^{58.64}$ (repeated by error from v^{58}); of י׳ (neg.) Is 40^{28} (‖ינע); youth 40^{30} (‖*id.*), the god-fearing v^{31} (‖ *id*); *be faint* from lack of water 44^{12} (‖ אֵין כֹּחַ from hunger) **Hoph.** *Pt wearied* Dn 9^{21} מֻעָף בִּיעָף (v. יְעָף).

†יָעֵף **adj.** weary, faint;—always as subst., exc. Ju 8^{15} אֲנָשֶׁיךָ הַיְּעֵפִים (of physical fatigue from lack of bread); הַיָּעֵף 2 S 16^2 (from lack of drink); of mind and spirit Is 40^{29} (‖ אֵין אוֹנִים), 50^4.

†יְעָף **n.[m.]** weariness, faintness (Aramaism, acc. to Lag $^{BN\ 175}$);—מֻעָף בִּיעָף *weary with weariness*, utterly weary Dn 9^{21} (from winged flight, said of Gabriel).

II. **יעף** (√of following; cf. Ar. يَفَعَ *ascend a mountain*, يَفَعٌ *hill*).

†[תּוֹעָפָה] **n.f.** eminence, of *towering* horns (? v Di) כְּתוֹעֲפֹת רְאֵם לוֹ Nu 23^{22} 24^8, sim. of strength of Israel, of peaks תּוֹעֲפוֹת הָרִים לוֹ ψ 95^4 (‖ מֶחְקְרֵי־אָרֶץ); of silver Jb 22^{25} כֶּסֶף תּוֹעָפֹת לָךְ, very dubious, perhaps *heaps* or *bars* (ingots)

†**יָעַץ** **vb.** advise, counsel (only twice in Hex) (Aram. יְעַט; Ar. وَعَظَ *exhort, admonish*)—**Qal** *Pf.* 3 ms יָעַץ Is 7^5+11 t.; יָעָ֑ץ 14^{27}+2 t.; sf יְעָצַנִי ψ 16^7, יְעָצָהּ Is 23^9+ יְעָצֻהוּ Baer 2 Ch 10^8; 3 pl. יָעֲצוּ ψ 62^5, sf יְעָצֻהוּ 1 K 12^8+2 t (incl. 2 Ch 10^8, Baer יְעָצֻהוּ), etc., *Impf* אִיעָצָה ψ 32^8 (Ol Che אִיעָצְךָ); אִיעָ֫צְךָ Ex 18^{19} Nu 24^{14} (not elsewhere Hex), Je 38^{15}, cf also foregoing; ‏ו׳אִיעצך 1 K 1^{12}, *Pt act* יוֹעֵץ Is 3^3+9 t, cstr. יֹעֵץ Na 1^{11}, יוֹעֵץ 2 S 15^{12}, יוֹעֲצָךְ Mi 4^9, pl. יוֹעֲצִים Jb 12^{17}+3 t, יֹעֲצִים Ez 11^2; cstr. יֹעֲצֵי Is 19^{11}+2 t, etc., fs sf יוֹעַצְתּוֹ 2 Ch 22^3, *Pt. pass* f יְעוּצָה Is 14^{26},—*advise, counsel*, c acc Is $32^{7.8}$ 23^9 (subj. י׳) Mi 6^5; sq בְּלִיַּעַל Na 1^{11} 7^5 (sq עַל=*against*), 19^{12} (sq. *id.*), 23^8 (sq *id*), Hb 2^{10} (sq לְ); oft. c. acc cogn. 2 S 16^{23} 17^7 Ez 11^2; sq. אֶל *against* Je 49^{20} 50^{45} (in both of י׳), sq עַל *against* 49^{30} Is 19^{17} (of י׳), cf pass pt. Is 14^{26}, c acc cogn + sf. pers. 1 K $12^{8\ 12\ 13}$ 2 Ch 10^8; c. acc pers. 2 S 17^{15} ψ 16^7 Ex 18^{19} Nu 24^{14} (+rel. cl) Je 38^{15}; abs (of י׳) Is 14^{24} (c. adv כַּאֲשֶׁר), v^{27}; of man 2 S 17^{15} (כְּזֹאת וּכְזֹאת), v^{21} (עַל+כֹּכָה), sq. inf. ψ 62^5 2 Ch 25^{16} (of אלהים); sq cl without connective 2 S 17^{11}; sq לְלֹא חָכְמָה Jb 26^3,—אִיעָצָה עָלֶיךָ עֵינִי ψ 32^8 (v supr) —*Pt act.* as subst.=*counsellor*, king's adviser 2 S 15^{12} 1 Ch 27^{33} 2 Ch 22^4 25^{16} Ezr 7^{28} 8^{25} Is 19^{11}, so fem. 2 Ch 22^3; prob also 1 Ch 27^{32} (‖אִישׁ מֵבִין וְסוֹפֵר); cf. Mi 4^9, also Is 1^{26} (‖שֹׁפְטִים), Jb 12^{17} (‖ *id*),—in these three, of importance for people, so also Is 3^3 Pr 11^{14}=24^6; cf. Jb 3^{14}, and particularly פֶּלֶא יוֹעֵץ Is 9^5 *wonder of a counsellor*, of the ideal ruler predicted. More generally, *counsellor, adviser* Pr 15^{22}, יוֹ׳ בְּשֶׂכֶל 1 Ch 26^{14} (specific reason for title unknown); יֹעֲ׳ שָׁלוֹם Pr 12^{20};=*prophet* Is 41^{28}, nearly=*agents* (hired by adversaries of Judah) Ezr 4^5. **Niph.** (reflex. or recipr.) *Pf* נוֹעַץ Is 40^{14}; נוֹעֲצוּ ψ 71^{10} 83^6; *Impf.* וַיִּוָּעַץ 1 K 12^6+10 t.; יִוָּעֲצוּ Is 45^{21}; וַיִּוָּעֲצוּ 2 Ch 30^{23}; נִוָּעֲצָה Ne 6^7; *Pt.* pl. נוֹעָצִים 1 K 12^6+4 t,—*consult together, exchange counsel*, of king with advisers, sq. אֶת־ 1 K $12^{6.8}$= 2 Ch $10^{6.8}$; and so of י׳ Is 40^{14}; sq אֶל־ 2 K 6^8 2 Ch 20^{21}; sq עִם 1 Ch 13^1 2 Ch 32^3; abs. *consider* 1 K 12^{28} 2 Ch 25^{17} 30^2; cf. 1 K 12^6 (sq inf.)= 2 Ch 10^6, 1 K 12^9 (sq. Impf + ו subord.)=2 Ch

10⁶, in gen *consult, take counsel*, abs. Pr 13¹⁰, יַחְדָּו ψ 71¹⁰ Ne 6⁷ Is 45²¹, sq לֵב יַחְדָּו (with heart together) ψ 83⁶ nearly = *determine*, sq inf. 2 Ch 30²³ †**Hithp.** *Impf* יִתְיָעֲצוּ ψ 83⁴ *conspire against*, sq עַל (‖ יַעֲרִימוּ סוֹד עַל)

†עֵצָה **n.f.** counsel, advice (= (י)עצה) — ע׳ Ju 20⁷ + 28 t; cstr. עֲצַת Is 5¹⁹ + 33 t; sf עֲצָתִי Pr 1²⁵ + 5 t. (+ Is 46¹¹ Qr; Kt עצתו better), עֲצָתְךָ ψ 20⁵ 73²⁴, עצתו Ho 10⁶ + 7 t (incl Is 46¹⁰ Kt v. supr); עֲצָתָם Je 18²³ + 4 t., pl עֵצוֹת Dt 32²⁸ + 2 t, עֲצָתַיִךְ Is 47¹³, — *counsel, advice* 2 S 15³¹ ³⁴ 16²³ ²³ 17¹⁴ ¹⁴ ¹⁴ ²³ 1 K 12⁸ ¹³ ¹⁴ = 2 Ch 10⁸ ¹³ ¹⁴, 2 Ch 22⁵ 25¹⁶ Ezr 10³ (where rd ע׳ אֲדֹנָי Reuss Ry), v⁸ Jb 29²¹, political *consultation* Is 47¹³; as acc. cogn. 2 S 17⁷ 1 K 1¹² Is 8¹⁰ Ez 11² (עֲצַת־רָע, ‖ אָוֶן); c הָבִיא ע׳ *give counsel* Ju 20⁷ 2 S 16²⁰; עֲשׂה ע׳ Is 16³, 30¹, עֲשׂוֹת עֵצוֹת בְּנַפְשִׁי ψ 13³, = *design, purpose* Ezr 4⁵ Ne 4⁹ 1 Ch 12²⁰ (Baer), ψ 14⁶ 20⁵ Je 18²³ (sq עַל = *against*), 49³⁰ (‖ מַחֲשָׁבָה), עֲצַת־גּוֹיִם ψ 33¹⁰, suitable *counsel* for war (= generalship) 2 K 18²⁰ = Is 36⁵ (cf. Pr 20¹⁸ infr); also עֲצַת שָׁלוֹם Zc 6¹³ *counsel of peace*, practical wisdom, *sagacity* Is 19³, cf v¹¹, Je 19⁷ Dt 32²⁸ (‖ תְּבוּנָה), Ho 10⁶. Esp in WisdLt and proph, *counsel = good counsel, wisdom* Jb 38² 42³ Pr 12¹⁵ 20⁵ (its seat בְּלֶב־אִישׁ); ‖ תּוּשִׁיָּה Pr 8¹⁴ Is 28²⁹ (of י׳); ‖ חָכְמָה Je 49⁷, ‖ חָכְמָה and תְּבוּנָה Jb 12¹³ Pr 21³⁰, ‖ מוּסָר 19²⁰; ‖ תַּחְבֻּלוֹת 20¹⁸ (cf Is 36⁵ supr.); ע׳ נִפְתָּלִים Jb 5¹³, רוּחַ ע׳ וּגְבוּרָה Is 11² (‖ ר׳ חָכְמָה וּבִינָה), *hearty counsel* ע׳ נֶפֶשׁ Pr 27⁹; *counsel of wisdom*, when wisdom is personif Pr 1²⁵ ³⁰ (‖ תּוֹכַחַת); in bad sense ע׳ רְשָׁעִים Jb 10³ 21¹⁶ 22¹⁸ ψ 1¹, cf. Jb 18⁷ ψ 106⁴³ Is 29¹⁵, of plan of י׳: ע׳ י׳ ψ 33¹¹ Pr 19²¹ Is 19¹⁷ 14²⁶ (הָע׳ הַיְּעוּצָה), 25¹ 46¹⁰ ¹¹; ע׳ קְדוֹשׁ יִשְׂרָאֵל 5¹⁹; also Mi 4¹² Je 32¹⁹ (גְּדֹל הָעֵצָה), 49²⁰ 50⁴⁵ ψ 106¹³, ע׳ עֶלְיוֹן ψ 107¹¹, instruction, guiding wisdom of י׳ ψ 73²⁴, אִישׁ־עֲצָתוֹ i e. counsellor of י׳ Is 40¹³, in fig אַנְשֵׁי עֲצָתִי ψ 119²⁴ = *my counsellors*, said of testimonies of God, = *prophecy*, ע׳ מַלְאָכָיו Is 44²⁶ (‖ דְּבַר עַבְדּוֹ); תֹּאבַד ע׳ מִזְּקֵנִים Ez 7²⁶ (cf 1 K 12⁸, ‖ תּוֹרָה, חָזוֹן), מֵחֲכָם Je 18¹⁸ (‖ תּוֹרָה, דָּבָר)

†[מוֹעֵצָה] **n.f.** counsel, plan, principle, device, — pl abs מֹעֵצוֹת Pr 22²⁰ (‖ דַּעַת), in good sense, in bad sense מוֹעֵצוֹת Je 7²⁴ (‖ שְׁרִרוּת לִבָּם); הָרָע מוֹעֲצוֹתֵיהֶם Ho 11⁶ ψ 5¹¹, מוֹעֲצוֹתֵיהֶם ψ 81¹³; מֹעֲצֹתֵיהֶם Pr 1³¹, מֹעֲצוֹתָם Mi 6¹⁶.

יַעֲקֹב, יַעֲקֹבָה v. sub עקב

יַעְקָן v. עֲקָן.

I. יער (√ of foll, Ar وَعُرَ is *be rugged*, of mountain, etc, *be difficult*; وَعْرٌ *rough* or *difficult place, mountain*).

†I. יַעַר **n.m.** ²⁸ ¹⁵ ⁸ wood, forest, thicket (MI²¹ pl היערן (= n pr. loc ?), Ph. יער and יר, cf DHM in MV⁽¹⁰⁾ ⁹⁸³, Aram. יַעְרָא, ܝܥܪܐ *wood, thicket*; As. *âru* Dl^HWB 230, cf. Jager^BAS I. 476) — abs יַעַר Is 7² +, יָעַר Mi 3¹² +, c. ה loc. יַעְרָה Jos 17¹⁵; cstr. יַעַר 2 S 18⁶, יַעְרָה Je 46²³, etc., pl יְעָרִים Ezr 2²⁵ + 4 t (incl. Ez 34²⁵ Qr, so Co), יְעָרוֹת ψ 29⁹, — **a.** *wood, forest, wooded height*, with trees to be felled Jos 17¹⁵ (c עלה *go up* to), v¹⁸ (J), Dt 19⁵ (not elsewhere Hex), עֵץ מִיַּעַר כְּרָתוֹ Je 10³ *as wood out of a forest he hath cut it*; יחטבו מן־היערים Ez 39¹⁰ (‖ עצים מן־השדה cl), as producing trees יַעַר צוֹמֵחַ עֵצִים Ec 2⁶, in designation of Solomon's palace בֵּית יַעַר הַלְּבָנוֹן 1 K 7² (on structure of this house v. Sta^Salomos Bauten ZAW 1883, 150), 10¹⁷ ²¹ = 2 Ch 9¹⁶ ²⁰; cf בֵּית הַיַּעַר Is 22⁸; fig. of foes to be cut down and destroyed נִקַּף סִבְכֵי היער Is 10³⁴; כָּרְתוּ יַעְרָהּ Je 46²³; so Is 32¹⁹ and יער הַבָּצוֹר Zc 11² (rd Kt הַבָּצִיר *inaccessible forest*). **b.** as hiding-place for fugitive 1 S 22⁵, lurking-place of wild beasts Am 3⁴ Mi 5⁷ 2 K 2²⁴ Je 5⁶ 12⁸ Is 56⁹ ψ 50¹⁰ 80¹⁴ 104²⁰, cf Ez 34²⁵ (rd Qr, v. supr) **c.** stripped by voice of י׳ ψ 29⁹, devoured by fire Is 9¹⁷ (סִבְכֵי הַיַּ׳; fig. of the people); so in metaph or sim of י׳'s judgments Is 10¹⁸ (כְּבוֹד יַעְרוֹ, fig of Assyr), Je 21¹⁴ Ez 21² ³ (v. infr) ψ 83¹⁵. **d.** opp כַּרְמֶל (*garden-land*) Is 29¹⁷ 32¹⁵; but also יַעַר כַּרְמִלּוֹ *his garden woodland* 2 K 19²³ = Is 37²⁴, and יַעַר בְּתוֹךְ כַּרְמֶל Mi 7¹⁴ (secluded and fertile abode for flock, fig. of people, v. Che, Hi-St thinks of *sacred grove*) **e.** = *thicket*, esp. as symbol of desolation Ho 2¹⁴; בָּמוֹת יער *thicket-covered heights* (overgrown with bushes and trees) Mi 3¹² = Je 26¹⁸, also בַּיַּעַר בַּעְרַב Is 21¹³ *in the thicket* (or *bushes*, so VB) *in Arabia* must ye lodge, caravans of Dedanites. **f.** עֲצֵי (ה)יער *trees of the forest* Is 7² (in sim), 10¹⁹ (שְׁאָר עֵץ יַעְרוֹ, fig.), 44¹⁴ Ez 15², also v⁶ (עֵץ היער), Ct 2³ (in sim), fig, as singing before י׳ ψ 96¹² = 1 Ch 16³³, Is 44²³ (יער וְכָל־עֵץ בּוֹ). **g.** particular forests are. יער אפרים 2 S 18⁶, see אֶפְרַיִם p. 68 supr., cf v¹⁶ ¹⁷ (v. also Jos 17¹⁵ ¹⁸); יַעַר חֶרֶת 1 S 22⁵ (v supr), יַעַר לְבָנוֹן (v supr.); יַעַר הַשָּׂדֶה נֶגֶב and יַעַר הַנֶּגֶב Ez 21² ³ (v. supr) fig. of Judah

(land and people); v also יְעָרִים infr.—שְׂדֵי־יָעַר ψ 132^{6} is a n pr loc (but Bae thinks appellat. 'auf waldigem Gefilde'), v. קִרְיַת יְעָרִים. On 1 S $14^{25.26}$, v. II. יער.—יעורים Ez 34^{25} Kt, rd. יְעָרִים Qr, v. supr.

II. יער (√of following; meaning dubious, MV identif. with I, from roughness and porousness (?) of honeycomb, cf. Buhl.

†II יַעַר n.[m.] honeycomb,—abs. יַעַר 1 S $14^{25.26}$; sf יַעְרִי Ct 5^{1},—*honeycomb*, containing honey 1 S 14^{25} (where rd וַיַּעַר הָיָה עַל־פְּנֵי הַשָּׂדֶה with 𝔊 We Dr Kit in Kau^{AT}, instead of v as in MT); וַיָּבוֹא העם אֶל־הַיַּעַר 1 S 14^{26} (|| דבש v^{25}) *and when the people came to the honeycomb* behold its bees had departed (v. 𝔊 We Dr Kit VB); אָכַלְתִּי יַעְרִי עִם־דִּבְשִׁי Ct 5^{1}; v. also I. יַעְרָה.

†I [יַעְרָה] n f. honeycomb, only cstr. יַעְרַת הַדְּבַשׁ 1 S 14^{27} (v. II יער)—יְעָרוֹת v. I. יַעַר.

†II. יַעְרָה n.pr.m. a descendant of Saul 1 Ch $9^{42.42}$, prob. corrupt, v. יְהוֹעַדָּה p. 221 supr.

†יַעְרֵי אֹרְגִים n.pr.m. father of Elhanan 2 S 21^{19} (= יָעוּר 1 Ch 20^{5}), א׳ prob scribal err. anticipating א׳ in foll. line (We Dr), and יַעְרֵי error for יָעִיר (We) q v. sub עור

†יְעָרִים n.pr.mont. only הַר־יְעָרִים Jos 15^{10} (𝔊 πόλιν Ιαρειν), where explained as = כְּסָלוֹן (𝔊 Χασ(α)λων), mod *Kesla*, NE. of Beth Shemesh, cf. Rob$^{BR\ II\ 30\ n\ ;\ III.\ 154}$.—קִרְיַת יְעָרִים v sub קִרְיַת.

יַעֲרֶשְׁיָה v. sub ערש

יַעֲשַׂי, יעשׂו, יַעֲשִׂיאֵל v. עשׂה.

יִפְדְיָה v. sub פדה.

†[יָפָה] vb. be fair, beautiful (NH *id.* Pi. and deriv; Aram. Aph. ܐܘܦܝ is *suffice, finish, fail*, cf. Aram. ܦܐܐ (PS ^{3018}) *beautiful, fit*, No$^{§172\ c\ Anm}$ G H[offmann]$^{LCB\ 1882,\ 321}$; Ar. وَفَى *fulfil, perform*; Eth ወፈየ: II 2, *give* (entirely) *over to, into power of*, Di^{949})—**Qal** *Pf.* יָפִית Ct 7^{7}; יָפוּ 4^{10} 7^{2}; *Impf.* 2 fs. וַתִּיפִי (Ko$^{Leh\ i\ 581}$) Ez 16^{13}; 3 ms apoc וַיִּיף 31^{7},—*be beautiful*, subj pers. Ct 4^{10} 7^{7}; of feet v^{2}; of Jerus under fig of woman Ez 16^{13}, Egypt under fig of tree 31^{7}. **Pi.** *Impf.* 3 ms sf יְיַפֵּהוּ Je 10^{4} *beautify* an idol. The (**Pe'al'al**?) *Pf.* form יָפְיָפִיתָ מִבְּנֵי אָדָם ψ 45^{3} is contrary to all anal.: rd. either יָפִיתָ or יְפֵיפִיתָ Ges$^{§55.3}$ Sta$^{§156\ B}$ Now (Kö$^{i.\ 483\ f.}$ defence is artificial) *thou art more beautiful than*, etc. **Hithp.** *Impf.* 2 fs. תִּתְיַפִּי *beautify thyself* Je 4^{30}

†יָפֶה adj. fair, beautiful,—m. abs. יָפֶה 2 S 14^{25} + 4 t; cstr. יפה Gn $39^{6.6}$ + 6 t; f. יָפָה 12^{14} + 14 t, cstr יְפַת 2^{11} + 6 t; sf יָפָתִי Ct $2^{10.13}$; pl. יָפוֹת Jb 42^{15} Am 8^{13}, cstr יְפוֹת Gn 41^{2}, יְפֹת $v^{4.18}$;—*fair, beautiful*, as attribute of woman 2 S 13^{1} 1 K 1^{3} Am 8^{13} Pr 11^{22}; cf. Jb 42^{15} Ct 6^{10} (כַּלְּבָנָה ׳י); pred. Gn 12^{14} 1 K 1^{4} Ct $1^{15.15}$ $4^{1.1.7}$ 6^{4}, = subst. *fair one* 1^{8} $2^{10.13}$ 5^{9} 6^{1}; oft cstr יְפַת־מַרְאֶה Gn 12^{11} 29^{17} 2 S 14^{27}; יְפַת־תֹּאַר Gn 29^{17} 1 S 25^{3} Dt 21^{11} Est 2^{7}: of kine יְפוֹת־מַרְאֶה Gn 41^{2}, cf. v^{4}; יפות־תאר v^{18}, less oft. of boy, young man אִישׁ יָפֶה 2 S 14^{25}; pred. Ct 1^{16}, יפה תאר Gn 39^{6}, ויפה מַרְאֶה v^{6} (of Joseph), of Jerusalem יפה נוֹף ψ 48^{3}, of a singer יְפֵה קוֹל Ez 33^{32}; of trees: olive יְפֵה פרי־תאר Je 11^{16}, cedar (fig. of Egypt) יְפֵה עָנָף Ez 31^{3}, cf. v^{9}; יָפֶה of everything in its time Ec 3^{11}; of various acts 5^{17}.—In עִם יְפֵה עֵינַיִם 1 S 16^{12}, עִם יְפֵה מַרְאֶה 17^{42}, either יפה = subst. abstr. *with beauty of eyes*, or עִם is textual error (Gr Krenkel$^{ZAW.\ 1882,\ 309}$ Bu עֶלֶם *youth*), v. Dr.

†יְפֵה־פִיָּה, rd. יְפֵהפִיָּה, or better יְפֵיפִיָּה (Ol$^{§186\ a}$ Gr Gie, reduplicated, with the force of a diminutive, Sta^{§156}; cf יְרַקְרַק, אֲדַמְדָּם), adj. f. pretty, עֶגְלָה יְפֵה־פִיָּה מִצְרַיִם Je 46^{20} Egypt is a *pretty* heifer (𝔊 κεκαλλωπισμένη).

יפי v. יֳפִי.

†[יֳפִי] n.m. beauty;—abs. יֹפִי Is 3^{24} + 5 t.; cstr. יְפִי Ez 28^{7}; sf יָפְיֵךְ v^{17}; יָפְיֵךְ ψ 45^{12} + 5 t., יָפְיוֹ Is 33^{17} + 2 t, יָפְיָהּ Pr 6^{25} Est 1^{11}; *beauty* of a woman Is 3^{24} ψ 45^{12} Est 1^{11} Pr 6^{25}, cf Pr 31^{30}, of Jerus under fig of woman Ez $16^{14.15.25}$; Tyre 27^{3} (כְּלִילַת יֹפִי), cf $v^{4.11}$; prince of Tyre, *beauty* of (his) wisdom 28^{7}; king of Tyre v^{12} (כְּלִיל יֹפִי), v^{17}, ideal beauty of king of Judah Is 33^{17}, Zion (מִכְלַל־יֹפִי) ψ 50^{2}, cf La 2^{15} (כְּלִילַת יֹפִי); of Egypt under fig of tree Ez 31^{8}, of ransomed people of ׳י Zc 9^{17}.

†יָפוֹ, יָפוֹא n.pr.loc. Joppa (Ph יפי; As. *Ja(p)pu* COT^{Gloss} Bez$^{Tel-el-Amarna\ Tabl\ in\ Brit.\ Mus.\ 146}$; Egypt. *Ye-pu* WMM^{159})—seaport town of Palestine (Jerusalem), יָפוֹ Jos 19^{46} Jon 1^{3} 2 Ch 2^{15} = יָפוֹא Ezr 3^{7}, 𝔊 Ιοππα, mod *Jaffa*.

[יָפַח] **vb. breathe, puff** (by-form of פּוּחַ, q v; see Ba[NB 189], cf Talm יפח *breath*)—only **Hithp.** *Impf* 3 fs. תִּתְיַפֵּחַ Je 4[31] she *gaspeth for breath*

†[יָפֵחַ] **adj.** breathing or puffing out, cstr. וִיפֵחַ חָמָס ψ 27[12] *puffing out violence* (cf Che)

יַפְלֵט v. sub פלט

יְפֻנֶּה v. sub פנה

†[יָפַע] **vb.** only **Hiph. shine out or forth, send out beams, cause to shine** (NH *id*, in fig senses, 𝔗 יְפַע, As Shaph *šûpû, shine, cause to shine, glorify*, Lotz[TP Col vii 93] Zim[BP 97 105] SAS[Asb ii 18]; cf Ar وَفَعَ *aedificium elatum*, kindred seem to be يَفَعَ *ascendit montem, adultus fuit*, Sab יפע *raise, heighten* Os[ZMG 1865, 210f], יפע name of a temple DHM[ZMG 1883, 330])—**Hiph.** *Pf* הוֹפִיעַ Dt 33[2] ψ 50[2], וְהוֹפִיעַ consec. Jb 37[15], 2 ms הוֹפָעְתָּ 10[3], *Impf.* 3 fs תּוֹפַע 3[4], וַתֹּפַע 10[22], *Imv* הוֹפִיעַ ψ 94[1], הוֹפִיעָה 80[2],—**1.** *shine out, forth, display beams* of י׳ Dt 33[2] ψ 50[2] 80[2] 94[1] Jb 10[3] (sq עַל), subj נְהָרָה *light* Jb 3[4], 10[22] וַתֹּפַע כְּמוֹ אֹפֶל (of She'ôl) **2.** *cause to shine* וְהוֹפִיעַ אוֹר עֲנָנוֹ Jb 37[15], subj י׳

†[יִפְעָה] **n.f. brightness, splendour,** יִפְעָתֶךָ Ez 28[7 17] of prince and king of Tyre

†יָפִיעַ **n.pr.pers. et loc. 1. n.pr.m.** (cf. Sab יפעאל Hal[1.0])—**a.** a king of Lachish Jos 10[3], 𝔊 Ιεφθα, A 𝔊L Ιαφ(α)ιε. **b.** a son of David 2 S 5[15] (𝔊 Ιεφιες, 𝔊L Ναφεθ) = 1 Ch 3[7] (𝔊 Ιανουε, A Ιαφιε, 𝔊L Αχικαμ) = 14[6] (𝔊 Ιανουου, A Ιαφιε, 𝔊L Ιαβεγ) **2. n.pr loc.** on border of Zebulun Jos 19[12], perh = mod *Yâfa*, ½ hour fr. Nazareth, Rob[BR ii 343f], but 𝔊 Φαγγαι, A Ιαφαγαι, 𝔊L Ιαφφιε

†מֵיפַעַת **n.pr.loc.** (Sab n pr loc מיפעת, מיפע DHM[ZMG 1876, 679, 1883, 362]) —1 Ch 6[64] Levitical city in Reuben, in Reuben מֵפָעַת Jos 13[18], מוֹפָעַת Je 48[21] in Moab

יֶפֶת v. sub פתה

יִפְתָּח, יִפְתַּח־אֵל v sub פתח

יָצָא[1068] **vb. go or come out** (NH *id*, Aram יְצָא, Eth ወፅአ:, ወፅአ: As *âsû* Dl[HWB 237], all = *go out, forth;* Syr ܢܦܩ *go forth* (in sense of *germinate*), *grow*, Ph יצא *march out;* cf SI[5] המוצא *the source* (of water), Sab וצא *go out*, DHM in MV, Ar وَضُؤَ is *be* or *become fair, beautiful, neat, clean*, cf No[ZMG 1886, 725])—**Qal** *Pf.* יָצָא Gn 10[11] + 92 t, 3 fs יָצְאָה Nu 16[35] + 13 t, יָצָאָה Is 28[29], 2 ms. יָצָאתָ Gn 24[5] + 7 t., 2 fs וְיָצָאת Je 31[4], 2 mpl יְצָאתֶם Ex 13[3] Dt 11[10], וִיצָאתֶם Ju 21[21] Mal 3[20], 3 pl sf יְצָאֻנִי Je 10[20], etc, *Impf* יֵצֵא Gn 15[4] + 64 t, וַיֵּצֵא 4[16] + 132 t; 3 fs תֵּצֵא Ex 21[7] + 22 t, וַתֵּצֵא Gn 30[16] + 14 t; 2 ms תֵּצֵא Dt 20[1] + 16 t, 3 pl יֵצְאוּ Gn 15[14] +, יֵצֵאוּ 17[6] +, 3 fpl וַתֵּצֶאנָה 1 S 18[6] 2 K 2[24], וַתֵּצֶאןָ Ex 15[20], 2 fpl תֵּצֶאנָה Am 4[3], etc., *Imv* צֵא Gn 8[16] + 15 t, וָצְאָה Ju 9[29], fs צְאִי Ct 1[8], mpl צְאוּ Gn 19[14] + 11 t, צֶאוּ Is 49[9] Ez 9[7] + Je 58[8] Qr (Kt צְאֶינָה (יצאו Ct 3[11], *Inf abs* יָצוֹא Gn 8[7] + 2 t, יָצֹא 27[30] + 3 t, *Inf cstr* צֵאת 24[11] + 31 t, sf. צֵאתִי Ex 9[29] + 3 t, צֵאתְנוּ Jo 9[12], צֵאתְךָ Dt 16[3] + 10 t, etc, *Pt* יוֹצֵא (יוצא) Gn 2[10] + 62 t, fs יֹצֵאת Ec 10[5], יֹצֵאת (יו׳) Gn 24[15] + 11 t, יֹצֵת Dt 28[57], etc,—**1** *go* or *come out* or *forth*. **a** from (מִן) a place, e.g a tent Gn 31[33] (E, opp בּוֹא ב), מִפֶּתַח אֹהֶל מוֹעֵד Lv 8[33] 10[7] (P), cf. מִן־הַמִּקְדָּשׁ 21[12] (H), from a house 2 S 11[8], the doors (דלתי) of a house Jos 2[19] (JE), Ju 11[31], מִפֶּתַח ביתו Ex 12[22] (JE), from a camp 1 S 13[17] 2 K 7[12], a city Gn 19[14] (J), 12[4] (P), 1 K 11[29] 20[17] Mi 4[10], a cave 1 S 24[9], the ark Gn 9[18] (J), 8[16 19] (both P), out of vineyards Ju 21[21]; sq acc אֶת־הָעִיר Gn 44[4] (E), Ex 9[29] (J), c בּ also, of gate Je 17[19] Ne 2[13], sq acc. local לֹא אֵצֵא פָּתַח Jb 31[34], pt cstr. יֹצְאֵי הַתֵּבָה Gn 9[10] (P), יֹצְאֵי שַׁעַר עִירוֹ 34[24] (P), abs Jos 2[5] (JE), Ju 3[24] Ex 34[34] (P), Nu 33[3] (P, Israel going out [from Egypt]), 2 Ch 26[20] +, specif., of going out (מִן) from a land (of emigration) Gn 10[11 14] 24[5] (all J), partic of *coming forth* from (the land of) Egypt (the Exodus) Ex 12[41] (J), 13[3.8] 23[15] 34[18] Nu 11[20] 22[5] (all JE), and esp D, Dt 4[45 46] 9[7] 11[10] 16[3.3.6] 23[5] 24[9] 25[17] Jos 2[10] 5[4 5 6] (all D), Nu 33[1] (P), 1 K 6[1] 8[9] = 2 Ch 5[10], 2 K 21[15] Je 7[25] Hg 2[5] ψ 114[1] **b.** *go forth* from (the presence of) a person · Ex 8[26] 9[33] 10[6] (all sq. מעם), Gn 44[28] Ex 5[20] Je 2[37] (מאת), Ju 3[19] (מֵעָלָיו); sq מִלִּפְנֵי Gn 4[16] (J), 41[46] 47[10] Est 8[15] Ec 10[5]; sq מֵעִם פְּנֵי Jb 1[12], מֵאֵת פְּנֵי 2[7], sq sf יְצָאֻנִי Je 10[20] (v. De Ec 7[18]) **c.** in technical senses. abs *go forth*, of emancipation Ex 21[2.3.3.4.5.7.7.7.11] (all JE), cf. יֹצֵא מִתַּחַת יַד־אֲרָם 2 K 13[5], of release in the year of jubilee, land, etc. Lv 25[28.30.31.33] (all H), 27[21] (P); also of a debtor-slave 25[54] (H), of divorce וְיָצְאָה מִבֵּיתוֹ Dt 24[2], of condemnation בְּהִשָּׁפְטוֹ יֵצֵא רָשָׁע ψ 109[7] *when he is judged let him go out as a criminal*, i e be condemned,

of bowels (מֵעִים) falling out by reason of disease 2 Ch 21$^{15.19}$. **d.** of flight, involving escape: sq. נוס ‖ הַחוּצָה, *flee* Gn 39$^{12.15}$ (J), כִּי נָצֹא תֵּצֵא Je 48^{9}; opp. taken (by lot) 1 S 14^{41}; רָעָה אֲשֶׁר לֹא־יוּכְלוּ לָצֵאת מִמֶּנָּה Je 11^{11} *calamity from which they shall not be able to escape;* perh. also יְרֵא אֱלֹהִים יֵצֵא אֶת־כֻּלָּם Ec 7^{18} *he that feareth God shall escape* (or *be freed from*, v. De Hi-Now Mishn) *all of them* (see VB),—on acc. with יצא v. De. **e.** *depart* בְּצֵאת נַפְשָׁהּ Gn 35^{18} i.e. *when she was expiring;* so תֵּצֵא רוּחוֹ ψ 146^{4}; בְּצֵאת הַיַּיִן מִנָּבָל 1 S 25^{37} i.e. *when Nabal became sober;* also fig. וַיֵּצֵא לִבָּם Gn 42^{28} (E) i.e. *their heart failed* (‖ וַיֶּחֶרְדוּ); rust from (מִן) caldron Ez 24^{16} (v. Co Ez 12^{5}); of glory of ׳י 10^{18}; וַיֵּצֵא מִן בַּת־צִיּוֹן כָּל־הֲדָרָהּ La 1^{6}; hence inf.=*exit, end* בְּצֵאת הַשָּׁנָה Ex 23^{16} (JE), and, redundantly, כְּעֵת צֵאת הַקֵּץ לְיָמִים שְׁנַיִם 2 Ch 21^{19} i.e. *at the end of two years.* **f.** of inanimate things: river out of Eden Gn 2^{10} (J), water out of rock Ex 17^{6} (E), Nu 20^{11} (JE), from Leḥi Ju 15^{19}; of molten calf out of fire Ex 32^{24} (E); of gold (after refining) Jb 23^{10} (abs., in sim.); in prophecy of fountain from house of ׳י Ez 47$^{1.8.12}$ Zc 14^{8} Jo 4^{18}; of seed (semen virile) from man Lv 15$^{16.32}$ (P), 22^{4} (H); of weapon which has pierced body 2 S 2^{23} (מֵאַחֲרָיו), 2 K 9^{24} (מִלִּבּוֹ), Jb 20^{25} (מִגֵּוָה); וַתֵּצֵא אַחֲרָיו מַשְׂאַת הַמֶּלֶךְ 2 S 11^{8} *and there went out* (=was sent out) *after him the king's portion* (i.e. the food given by the king); idiomatically of expenditure of money 2 K 12^{13} (abs., cf. Hiph. v^{12}); of swift movement of arrow from bow Zc 9^{14} (like lightning), of lightning out of fire Ez 1^{13}; abs. of *sunrise* (subj. שֶׁמֶשׁ) Ju 5^{31} (in sim.), Gn 19^{23}, cf. Is 13^{10} (so As., e.g. *ultu ṣît šanši adi êrib šanši* COT Gn 19^{23}); of rising of stars (כּוֹכָבִים) Ne 4^{15}; of sentence of judge Hb 1$^{4.4}$ ψ 17^{2}; of judgment, or right appearing (with sim. of light) Hos 6^{5} (rd. וּמִשְׁפָּטִי כָאוֹר יֵצֵא), Is 62^{1}; of a lot וַיֵּצֵא הַגּוֹרָל לִבְנֵי יוֹסֵף Jos 16^{1} (JE), and esp. P, Nu 33^{54} Jos 19$^{1.17.24.32.40}$ 21^{4}, cf. also ויצא גְּבוּל גּוֹרָלָם 18^{11} (P). **g.** with especial emphasis on idea of origin, source: hyssop out of the wall 1 K 5^{13}; מיהוה יצא הדבר Gn 24^{50} (J) *from* ׳י *has the thing proceeded*, of a providential arrangement, so מֵעִם ׳י Is 28^{29}; מֵרְשָׁעִים יֵצֵא רֶשַׁע 1 S 24^{14} (an ancient proverb); of pollution proceeding from (מֵאֵת) prophets Je 23^{15}; of fire from Heshbon Nu 21^{28} (JE), Je 48^{45}, cf. Ju 9$^{15.20.20}$; of fire מִלִּפְנֵי ׳י Lv 9^{24} 10^{2}, מֵאֵת ׳י Nu 16^{35} (all P); in theophany יצא רֶשֶׁף לְרַגְלָיו Hb 3^{5}; iniquity from unreceptive heart ψ 73^{7} (v.ı. חֵלֶב 𝔊); wrath מִלִּפְנֵי ׳י Nu 17^{11} (P); abs. Je 4^{4}=21^{12}, 23^{19}=30^{23}; so salvation Is 51^{5}; וְנִשְׁמַת־מִי יָצְאָה מִמֶּךָּ Jb 26^{4}; of words *going forth* from mouth of speaker (of solemn or formal speech) לֹא יֵצֵא דָּבָר מִפִּיכֶם Jos 6^{10} (JE), Ju 11^{36} 1 S 2^{3} Je 44^{17} Jb 37^{2} Est 7^{8}, also Nu 30^{3} 32^{24} (both P); of ׳י's words going forth from his mouth, or from him Is 45^{23} 48^{3} 51^{4} 55^{11} Ez 33^{30}; of ׳י's words, instruction, command, etc., going forth Is 2^{3}=Mi 4^{2} (from Jerusalem), Dn 9^{23}; of human commandment Est 1^{19}, cf. v^{17}. **h.** of children as *going forth* from loins (of father) מִמֵּעִים 2 S 7^{12} 16^{11}; מֵחֲלָצִים Gn 35^{11} (P), 1 K 8^{19}=2 Ch 6^{9}; sq. מִן alone 2 K 20^{18}=Is 39^{7}; also יֹצְאֵי יְרֵכוֹ Ju 8^{30} Gn 46^{26} Ex 1^{5} (both P); also of birth מֵרֶחֶם (אִמּוֹ) Nu 12^{12} (JE), Je 1^{5} 20^{18} Jb 3^{11}; fig. of sea 38^{8}, of ice v^{29}; מִבֶּטֶן אִמּוֹ Jb 1^{21} Ec 5^{14}; lit., source not expr., Gn 25$^{25.26}$ 38$^{28.29.30}$ (all J); of untimely birth Ex 21^{22} (JE); cf. הַיּוֹצֵת מִבֵּין רַגְלֶיהָ Dt 28^{57} (‖ תֵּלֵד); of family or race connexion (sq. מִן) Na 1^{11} Is 48^{1} 1 Ch 1^{12} 2^{53}; יצא also of produce of vine (מִגֶּפֶן) Ju 13^{14}, cf. הַיֹּצֵא הַשָּׂדֶה Dt 14^{22} (rd. יצא Sam., v. Di); אֶרֶץ מִמֶּנָּה יצא לָחֶם Jb 28^{5}; of viper proceeding from serpent's root Is 14^{29}; further, with idea of unfolding, growth Jb 8^{16} 14^{2} 31^{40}; וְיָצָא חֹטֶר מִגֵּזַע יִשָׁי Is 11^{1}; of the little horn Dn 8^{9}; so of branches of candlestick in tabernacle Ex 25$^{32.33.35}$ 37$^{18.19.21}$ (all P); then simply *project* (tower from wall) Ne 3$^{25.26.27}$; of measuring-line *going forth* (abs.) in a particular direction Je 31^{39}; of a boundary(-line) *going out* (abs.) so as then to turn and make an angle Nu 34$^{4.9}$ Jos 15$^{3.4.9.11.11}$ 16$^{2.6.7}$ 18$^{15.15.17.17}$ 19$^{12.13.27.34.47}$. **2. a.** *go forth* to a place Gn 27^{3} (J), Je 14^{18} Ez 3^{22} Zc 6$^{6.6.7}$+; so וַיֵּצֵא הַפַּרְשְׁדֹנָה Ju 3^{22} (see VB); go forth in surrender 1 S 11^{3} (sq. אֶל pers.), 2 K 18^{31}=Is 36^{16}, Je 38$^{17.21}$; אֵין פֶּרֶץ וְאֵין יוֹצֵאת ψ 144^{14}; into captivity לֹא יָצְאוּ אִתָּכֶם יָצָא מִן־הַמָּקוֹם בַּגּוֹלָה Je 29^{16}, cf. 48^{7} Zc 14^{2}; also הַזֶּה Je 22^{11}, cf. בָּנַי יְצָאֻנִי 10^{20}. **b.** *go forward, proceed* to or toward something, fig., מֵרָעָה אֶל־רָעָה יָצָאוּ Je 9^{2} *from evil to evil they go on;* in like manner 2 S 20^{8} si vera l., but read rather וְהִיא יָצְאָה *and it* (i.e. the sword) *came out* (of the sheath) *and fell* 𝔊 We Dr Kit Bu. **c.** *come* or *go forth*, with esp. ref. to purpose or result: וְיָצָאתִי אַחֲרָיו וְהִכִּתִיו 1 S 17^{35}, cf. 24^{15}; יָצָא שָׁאוּל לְבַקֵּשׁ נַפְשׁוֹ 23^{15}, cf. 26^{20}, further 2 S 2^{13} 18^{4} 1 K 20$^{16.18.19.39}$ 2 K 5^{2} Mi 1^{11} Je 37^{5} Zc 14^{3} Dn 11$^{11.44}$+; of an adulteress Pr 7^{15}; of an angel Nu 22^{32} (JE),

Dn 9[22]; for אִתְּכֶם . . . יֵצֵא 1 S 22[3] (*let* my father etc. *go forth* [to be] *with you*, cf. Klo) rd. perh. יֵשְׁבוּ as 𝔊 𝔙 Kit, v. also Dr; of army marching out to form battle line יֹצֵא אֶל־הַמַּעֲרָכָה 1 S 17[20] (c.art., MT, < om. We Dr Kit Bu); בְּכֹל אֲשֶׁר יָצְאוּ Ju 2[15] *in all to which they went forth*, יָצָא לְפָנֵי 1 S 8[20] of king going out at the head of his soldiers; so of יי before his people Ju 4[14] 2 S 5[24] ψ 68[8], cf. 108[12] 1 Ch 14[15]; of יי going out from Seir Ju 5[4], cf. Hb 3[13]; of the hand of יי, in hostility יָצְאָה בִי יַד־יי Ru 1[13]; abs. of fire *breaking out* Ex 22[5] (JE). **3.** of combinations, note esp.: יָצוֹא וָשׁוֹב (inf. abs.) Gn 8[7] *going out and returning*, nearly = *to and fro;* אִישׁ יוֹצֵא . . . יָצֹא יָצוֹא וּמְקַלֵּל 2 S 16[5] = *coming forth, cursing as he came;* יצא ובא, lit. אֵין יוֹצֵא וְאֵין בָּא Jos 6[1] *none went out and none came in*, i.e. there was no free egress or ingress (of besieged city), cf. 1 K 15[17] = 2 Ch 16[1], 2 Ch 15[5]; to *go out* and *come in* before, of leader in war Nu 27[17] 1 S 18[16], cf. 29[6]; fig. Dt 28[6] blessed shalt thou be בבואך ובצאתך, i.e. when thou completest and beginnest any undertaking, so v[19] 31[2] לא אוכל לצאת ולבוא, i.e. I can no more engage in active undertakings; similarly Jos 14[11] 1 K 3[7] Is 37[28] (+ שִׁבְתְּךָ) = 2 K 19[27], ψ 121[8].

† **Hiph.** [278] *Pf.* הוֹצִיא Gn 14[18]+; וְהוֹצִיא consec. Dt 22[14]; הוֹצֵאתָ Ex 32[11] + 7 t.; וְהוֹצֵאתָ Nu 20[8] + 3 t.; 2 fs. וְהוֹצֵאת 1 K 17[13]; sf. הוֹצִיאַנִי Ez 42[15]; הוֹצִיאָנוּ Ex 13[14] + 2 t.; הוֹצִיאֲךָ Dt 6[12] 16[1], הוֹצִאֲךָ Ex 13[9] Dt 7[19]; הוֹצִיאָם Ex 32[12] + 2 t., etc.; *Impf.* יוֹצִיא (יֹצִא) Lv 16[27] + 9 t.; וַיּוֹצֵא (וַיֹּצֵא) Gn 15[5] + 23 t.; וַיּוֹצֵא (וַיֹּצֵא) Dt 4[20] + 4 t.; sf. יוֹצִיאֵנִי Mi 7[9]; וַיּוֹצִאֲךָ Dt 4[37] 5[15]; וַיּוֹצִאָהּ Ex 4[6.7]; 3 fs. תּוֹצִיא Is 61[11] Hg 1[11]; juss. תּוֹצֵא Gn 1[24]; וַתּוֹצֵא v[12] Ru 2[18]; 2 ms. תּוֹצִיא Ex 12[46] + 5 t.; הֲתֹצִיא Jb 38[32]; וַתֹּצֵא Je 32[21]; וַיֹּצִיאוּ (וַיּוֹצִיאוּ) Lv 24[23]+; sf. וַיּוֹצִאֻהוּ 2 K 12[12]; וַיֹּצִאֻהוּ Gn 19[16]; וַיֹּצִיאֻהוּ 1 K 21[13]; יוֹצִיאוּם 1 Ch 9[28], etc.; *Imv.* הוֹצֵא Gn 19[12] + 5 t. + 8[17] Kt (Qr הַיְצֵא); הוֹצִיא Is 43[8]; הוֹצִיאָה ψ 142[8]; sf. הוֹצִיאֵנִי 25[17] 1 K 22[34], etc.; *Inf. cstr.* הוֹצִיא Ex 6[13] +; sf. הוֹצִיאִי (הוֹצָאִי) Ex 16[32] +; לְהוֹצִאֵהוּ Je 39[14], anom. (Kö[I. 642]), etc.; *Pt.* מוֹצִיא Ex 6[7] + 11 t.; מוֹצֵא ψ 135[7]; sf. מוֹצִיאִי 2 S 22[49], מוֹצִיאֲךָ Dt 8[14] 13[11], etc.;—**1.** *cause to go* or *come out, bring out, lead out:* **a.** a person from a place, + מִן loc., out of prison, etc. Gn 40[14] (E), Je 20[3], 52[31] (not ‖ 2 K 25[27]); so with the servant of יי subj. Is 42[7]; out of house Jos 6[22] (JE), a city Gn 19[12] (J), Ez 14[22] (so 𝔊 𝔖 𝔙 Co VB; MT Hoph.); of יי bringing people of Jerusalem out of city to deliver them to enemy Ez 11[7] (MT (*one*) *shall bring*, but rd. 1 s., see VB), v[9]; fr. a land Je 26[23]; esp. of Moses bringing Israelites out of Egypt Ex 3[10.11.12] (E), 14[11] (J); of Moses and Aaron 6[13.26.27] (P); of יי bringing Israelites out of (מִן) Egypt Ex 18[1] 20[2] Jos 24[5] (all E), Ex 13[3.9.14.16] 32[11] Nu 20[16] 23[22] 24[8] (all JE), Dt 1[27] 4[20.37] 5[6.15] 6[12.21.23] 8[14] 9[12.26.28] 13[6.11] 16[1] 26[8] (all D), Lv 19[36] 22[33] 23[43] 25[38.44.55] 26[13.45] (all H), Ex 6[6.7] (מִתַּחַת סִבְלֹת מצרים), 7[4.5] 12[17.42.51] 16[6.32] 29[46] Nu 15[41] (all P), Ju 2[12] 6[8] 1 S 12[8] 1 K 8[16] = 2 Ch 6[5], 1 K 8[21.51.53] 9[9] Je 7[22] 11[4] 31[32] 32[21] 34[13] Ez 20[6.10], cf. v[9] (del. Co), 2 Ch 7[22] ψ 136[11] Dn 9[15]; abs., same sense, Jos 24[5] (E), Dt 7[8.19] Ez 20[14.22] ψ 105[37.43]; of יי bringing Israelites out of exile (sq. מִן) Ez 20[34.41] 34[13]; obj. rebels (out of, מִן, land) Ez 20[38]; of charioteer bringing Ahab out of battle 1 K 22[34] = 2 Ch 18[33]; of Joseph's bringing out his sons from between Jacob's knees Gn 48[12] (E). **b.** of bringing *from* a place *for a particular purpose* (human subj.) Ex 19[17] (מִן); also (point of departure not expr., and purpose sometimes only implied) Gn 38[24] (J), Jos 2[3] 6[23.23] Ju 6[30] 2 S 12[31] = 1 Ch 20[3], 2 K 11[12] = 2 Ch 23[11], 2 Ch 23[14] Is 43[8]; יי subj., of bringing Israelites out of Egypt to slay them Ex 32[12] (JE), Dt 9[28.29]; obj. Gog Ez 38[4]; subj. יַד יי Ez 37[1]. **c.** *lead out* as an army 2 S 10[16] = 1 Ch 19[16], so of יי Is 43[17]; hence with הֵבִיא, of a ruler's function to *lead people out and in* 2 S 5[2] = 1 Ch 11[2], Nu 27[17] (P). **d.** הוֹצִיא מֵרֶחֶם of God's agency in birth Jb 10[18]. **e.** = *remove* (from a person's presence) הוֹצִיאוּ כָל־אִישׁ מֵעָלָי Gn 45[1] 2 S 13[9]; without ‖ מעל v[18]. **f.** of *putting away* wives and children Ezr 10[3.19] (opp. הוֹשִׁיב v[2], cf. יצאה מביתו Dt 24[2]). **g.** *bring out* person unto (אֶל) a place (human subj.) Jos 10[22.23] (JE), Dt 17[5] 22[21.24] (all D), Lv 24[14.23] (H), Nu 15[36] (P; all אֶל־מִחוּץ), 1 K 21[10.13] (מִחוּץ of motion to), 2 K 11[15] = 2 Ch 23[14]; לְהוֹצִאֵהוּ אֶל־הַבָּיִת Je 39[14]; subj. angels in form of men Gn 19[16.17] (J), Ez 42[1.15] 46[21] 47[2]; also Gn 15[5] (JE; יי subj.); for a specific purpose Ex 16[3] (P). **h.** unto a person Gn 43[23] (J), with purpose expressed or implied Ho 9[13] Gn 19[5.8] (J), Ju 19[22.24]; Jos 10[24] (JE), Je 38[23] Ezr 8[7] (c. על) Kt (but read Qr אַצִּיָה). **i.** unto a place and a person Jos 10[22.23] (JE), Dt 21[19] Ju 19[25]. **2.** fig., obj. persons, *bring out of* (מִן) distress, etc. ψ 25[17] 68[7] 107[14.28] 142[8] 143[11]; deliver from enemies 2 S 22[49] (but ‖ ψ 18[49] מְפַלְּטִי); one's feet out of net ψ 25[15] 31[5]; bring out into a large place 2 S 22[20] = ψ 18[20], cf. ψ 66[12]. **3.** *bring out* animals: horses out of Egypt 1 K 10[29] = 2 Ch 1[17] (but read **Qal** יֵצְאוּ 𝔊 Klo Kmp in Kau[AT]), 2 Ch 1[17] 9[28]; animals

(from ark, no מִן) Gn 8^{17} (P); for sacrifice, to a place Nu 19^{3}. **4.** inanimate obj.: **a.** *carry* or *bring out* (with and without מִן) Ex 12^{39} (E) Am 6^{10} 2 S 12^{30} = 1 Ch 20^{2}, 2 K 10^{26} 23$^{4.6}$ 24^{13} 1 Ch 9^{28} 2 Ch 29$^{5.16.16}$ 34^{14} Je 8^{1} 17^{22} 50^{25} (subj. ׳י), Ez 12$^{4.7}$ (in v$^{5.6.7b.12}$ read **Qal**, cf. v^{4b}, so Co), also 24^{6} (Co 24^{10}); obj. הָאֶבֶן הָרֹאשָׁה Zc 4^{7}; Lv 26^{10} (H), Ezr 1$^{7.7.8}$. **b.** *take* or *draw out* (from one's person or luggage) Gn 24^{53} (J); draw out hand from one's bosom Ex 4$^{6.7}$ (J), cf. Ru 2^{18} (food from one's cupboard). **c.** = *draw* חַרְבִּי מִתַּעְרָהּ Ez 21$^{8.10}$ (subj. ׳י). **d.** *bring out to* a place Dt 28^{38} Lv 4$^{12.21}$ 6^{4} 14^{45} 16^{27} Ez 46^{20}, cf. Dt 14^{28}. **e.** *bring out* to (or for) a person Gn 14^{18} Ju 6^{19} cf. v^{18}, 1 K 17^{13} 2 K 10$^{22.22}$. **f.** *bring out* from (מִן) a place to people Nu 17^{24} (P). **g.** *bring out* in payment, *pay* (money, tribute, etc.) 2 K 12^{12} 15^{20} (עַל = in behalf of: or *put it forth, imposed it, on* Israel). **h.** *bring forth* (= cause to rise or appear) the heavenly bodies Is 40^{26} Jb 38^{32}; see also וְתַעֲלֻמָהּ יֹצִא אוֹר 28^{11} *and hidden things he* (the miner) *bringeth forth to light.* **i.** *bring forth* by miracle: Moses, water out of rock Nu 20$^{8.10}$ (JE); ׳י, id. Dt 8^{15} Ne 9^{15} ψ 78^{16}. **j.** = *produce, generate, bring into being:* of magicians trying to produce lice Ex 8^{14} (P); a smith producing weapon Is 54^{16}; see the threefold הוציא Pr 30$^{33.33.33}$; of ׳י causing לֶחֶם to proceed out of (מִן) earth ψ 104^{14}; elsewhere of earth as producing Gn 1$^{12.24}$ (both P), Is 61^{11} Hg 1^{11}; of Aaron's rod bringing forth blossoms Nu 17^{23} (P). **k.** *bring forth* words (out of mouth, etc.), i.e. *speak* Jb 8^{10} 15^{3} Pr 10^{18} 29^{11} Ne 6^{19} Is 48^{20} (‖ השמיע, הגיד); abs. Ec 5^{1}; of *publishing* a report הו׳ עָלֶיהָ שֵׁם רָע Dt 22^{14} (‖ שָׂם לָהּ עֲלִילֹת דְּבָרִים), cf. v^{19}; הו׳ דִּבַּת הָאָרֶץ (רָעָה) Nu 13^{32} 14^{37}; so 14^{36} (דִּבָּה עַל־הָאָרֶץ). **5.** fig., subj. ׳י, *bring forth* from (מִן) Bel's mouth what he has swallowed Je 51^{44}; wind, out of treasuries 10^{13} 51^{16} ψ 135^{7}; fire, out of Tyre Ez 28^{18}; curse, over the land Zc 5^{4}; of Jeremiah, אִם תּוֹצִיא יָקָר מִזּוֹלֵל Je 15^{19} *if thou bring forth the precious from* (Gie *without*) *the base*, i.e. if thou free that which is pure in thee from base admixture (Gf; Gie *if thou produce the noble without the base*); bring forth, i.e. *exhibit*, righteousness (innocence Che) ψ 37^{6} Je 51^{10} (cf. **Qal 1 f** end); וַיֹּצֵא לָאוֹר צַלְמָוֶת Jb 12^{22}, cf. Mi 7^{9}; subj. servant of ׳י, of publishing מִשְׁפָּט (i.e. religion) to the world Is 42$^{1.3}$.

† **Hoph.** *Pf.* 3 fs. הוּצָאָה Ez 38^{8} (del. Co); *Pt.* fs. מוּצֵאת Gn 38^{25}; m.pl. מוּצָאִים Ez 14^{22} 47^{8} (but v. infr.); f.pl. מוּצָאוֹת Je 38^{22};—*be brought forth* Gn 38^{25} (J; of Tamar); of women as captives Je 38^{22}; remnant out of Jerusalem Ez 14^{22} MT (but rd. Hiph., v. supr.); exiles, from among the peoples 38^{8} (om. 𝔖 Co); of waters, אֶל־הַיָּמָּה הַמּוּצָאִים Ez 47^{8} *which are caused to flow into the sea* (but 𝔖 Co אֶל־הַמַּיִם הַחֲמוּצִים *into the sour* (*bitter, salt*) *waters*, see Field VB).

† [יָצִיא] **adj. coming forth**; only c. מִן and sf., ומיציאו מֵעָיו 2 Ch 32^{21} Kt (וּמִיצִיאֵי Qr), *and some of those who came forth from his loins* (בניו in ‖ Is 37^{38}).

† [צֶאֱצָא] **n.m.** $^{Jb\ 27,\ 14}$ only pl., **issue, offspring, produce** (Nö$^{ZMG\ 1886,\ 725}$ comps. ضِنْضِئ *origin, root, stock*)—**1.** *offspring* of men, abs. הַצֶּאֱצָאִים וְהַצְּפִעוֹת Is 22^{24}; elsewhere only Is$^{2.3}$ and Job: cstr. צֶאֱצָאֵי מֵעֶיךָ Is 48^{19} (‖ זַרְעֶךָ); sf. צֶאֱצָאַי Jb 31^{8}, צֶאֱצָאֶיךָ 5^{25} (‖ זַרְעֲךָ), Is 44^{3} (‖ *id.*); צֶאֱצָאָיו Jb 27^{14} (‖ בָּנָיו); צֶאֱצָאֵיהֶם 21^{8} (‖ זַרְעָם), Is 61^{9} (‖ *id.*), 65^{23}. **2.** *produce* of earth, sf. תֵּבֵל וְכָל־צֶאֱצָאֶיהָ Is 34^{1}; הָאָרֶץ וְצ׳ 42^{5}.

† I. מוֹצָא **n.m.** $^{Ho\ 6,\ 3}$ **place or act of going forth, issue, export, source, spring**;—abs. מ׳ Jb 28^{1} ψ 75^{7}; cstr. מ׳ Nu 30^{13} + 9 t.; מֹצָא Jb 38^{27} Dn 9^{25}; sf. מוֹצָאֲךָ 2 S 3^{25}; מֹצָאוֹ Ho 6^{3}; מוֹצָאוֹ ψ 19^{7}; pl. cstr. מוֹצָאֵי Is 41^{18} + 5 t.; sf. מוֹצָאָיו Ez 43^{11}; מוֹצָאֵיהֶם Nu 33$^{2.2}$; מוֹצָאֵיהֶן Ez 42^{11};—**1.** *a going forth:* **a.** the act, of ׳י Ho 6^{3}; of the sun = *rising* ψ 19^{7} (v. יצא **1 f**); of a man 2 S 3^{25} (opp. מָבוֹא Kt); מ׳ דָּבָר Dn 9^{25} *going forth of a command.* **b.** concrete, מוֹצָאֵי גוֹלָה Ez 12^{4} *goings forth of* exile, i.e. *those going forth into* exile (in sim.). **c.** *way out, exit:* concrete, of chambers in temple Ez 42^{11} 43^{11} (opp. מוֹבָאָיו); מוֹצָאֵי הַמִּקְדָּשׁ Ez 44^{5} (opp. מְבוֹא הַבַּיִת). **2.** *that which goes forth:* **a.** *utterance* of mouth or lips (esp. of solemn or formal speech), מוֹצָא פִּי־י׳ Dt 8^{3}; מ׳ שְׂפָתַי Je 17^{16} ψ 89^{35}; so Dt 23^{24} Nu 30^{13} (P). **b.** *export* of horses 1 K 10^{28} = 2 Ch 1^{16}. **3.** *place of going forth:* **a.** *source* or *spring* of water 2 K 2^{21} Is 58^{11} (in sim.), ψ 107^{33} (‖ נְהָרוֹת), v^{35} (‖ אֲגַם־מַיִם) = Is 41^{18} (‖ *id.*); מוֹצָא מֵימֵי גִּיחוֹן הָעֶלְיוֹן 2 Ch 32^{30}. **b.** *place of departure* of Israel on march Nu 33$^{2.2}$ (P). **c.** מוֹצָא = *east* (place of sun's going forth) ψ 75^{7} (opp. מַעֲרָב); zeugmatically, 65^{9} מוֹצָאֵי בֹקֶר וָעֶרֶב i.e. *the east and the west* (cf. *the two Orients*, Qor 43^{37}). **d.** place whence silver comes = *mine* Jb 28^{1}; וּלְהַצְמִיחַ מֹצָא דֶשֶׁא 38^{27} and to cause the *growing-place* (others, *the growth*) of young grass to sprout.

† II מוֹצָא n.pr.m. **1.** son of Caleb by Ephah his concubine 1 Ch 2[46], 𝔊 Ιωσα(ν), 𝔊L Μουσα **2.** a descendant of Saul 1 Ch 8[36.37] (𝔊 Μαισα) = 9[42.43] (𝔊 Μασσα 𝔊L in both Μωσα)

† [מוֹצָאָה] **n.f.** only pl **a.** Mi 5[1] מוֹצָאֹתָיו (cf future ruler out of Bethlehem), *his origin* **b.** 2 K 10[27] Qr מוֹצָאוֹת *places of going out to*, i e *a privy* (cf. Ar مَخْرَجٌ; Germ *Abtritt*), euphemistically for Kt מַחֲרָאוֹת

† [תּוֹצָאָה] **n. f. outgoing, extremity, source** (?), **escape**, only pl, chiefly P and late,—abs תּוֹצָאוֹת ψ 68[21], cstr תוצאות Pr 4[23] + Jos 18[19] Qr (Kt תוצאותיו), תוצאת Nu 34[5] Ez 48[30]; תצאות Jos 15[4] + 2 t, sf תוצאתיו Nu 34[4] + 3 t, תֹּצְאֹתָיו Jos 15[7] + 8 t + 16[3] Qr (Kt תצאתו), תוצאותם 1 Ch 5[16],—**1.** *outgoing, extremity* of border of territory Jos 16[3] 17[18] (both JE), elsewhere P: Nu 34[4 5.8.9 12] Jos 15[4 7 11] 16[8] 17[9] 18[12 14 19] 19[14.22.29 33], *outskirts* of city Ez 48[30], cf 1 Ch 5[16]. **2.** ת׳ חַיִּים Pr 4[23] (? read מוצאות) *sources of life*. **3.** לַמָּוֶת ת׳ ψ 68[21] *escapes from* (lit *for*, i e. *in view of*) *death*

† [יָצַב] **vb.** only **Hithp. set** or **station oneself, take one's stand** (𝔗 יצב Pa & deriv; Ar وَصَبَ *be constant, firm*)—**Hithp.** *Pf* 3 pl הִתְיַצְּבוּ 2 Ch 11[13], והת׳ consec. Nu 11[16], *Impf* יִתְיַצֵּב Dt 7[24] + 6 t, יִתְיַצָּב Jb 41[2], יִתְיַצָּב Pr 22[29], וַיִּתְיַצֵּב 1 S 3[10] + 5 t, 3 fs וַתֵּתַצַּב Ex 2[4] (but read וַתִּתְיַצֵּב, cf Sam Ges[§71] Ko[i 430]); 2 ms תִּתְיַצֵּב 2 S 18[13]; וְאֶתְיַצְּבָה Hb 2[1], יִתְיַצְּבוּ ψ 2[2] + 2 t, וַיִּתְיַצְּבוּ Ex 19[17] + 4 t, *Imv* הִתְיַצֵּב 8[16] + 5 t, הִתְיַצְּבוּ 1 S 10[19] + 6 t; *Inf cstr* (מ)הִתְיַצֵּב 2 S 21[5] + 4 t,—*station oneself, take one's stand, stand* **a** c phr of place, Ex 2[4] (E, c מֵרָחֹק), 2 S 18[13] (c. מִנֶּגֶד), fig = *stand aloof* (VB Dr), v[30] (c כֹּה || עֲמֹד), c בְּ loc Ex 19[17] Nu 22[22] (both E), Ju 20[2] Dt 31[14 14], also (in sense of *having a place* or *position*) נִשְׁמַדְנוּ מֵהִתְיַצֵּב בְּכָל־גְּבֻל יִשְׂרָאֵל 2 S 21[5], c בְּתוֹךְ pers 1 S 10[23], loc 2 S 23[12] = 2 Ch 11[14], c עַל loc, *at, by* Nu 23[3 15] (JE), *upon* Hb 2[1] (|| עמד), ψ 36[5] (fig), c עַל pers v infr, c שָׁם and עִם pers Ex 34[5] (subj י׳), Nu 11[16] (both JE) **b.** abs 1 S 3[10] (י׳ subj), esp of standing quiet and passive, to see the mighty deliverance of י׳ Ex 14[13] (J), 1 S 12[7 16] 2 Ch 20[17] (|| עמד); of taking a stand to fight 1 S 17[16] ψ 2[2], in military array Je 46[4] (c בְּ accomp), v[14] (|| הָכֵן לָךְ), to answer a charge Jb 33[5], וְיִתְיַצְּבוּ כְּמוֹ לְבוּשׁ 38[14] *and they* (terrestrial things) *stand forth* (in the light) *like a garment* **c.** c. לִפְנֵי pers = *present oneself before* Ex 8[16] 9[13] (both J), Pr 22[29.29], לִפְנֵי י׳ Jos 24[1] (E), 1 S 10[19] (v. also **d**); so as servants or courtiers (v עַל **6 c**), with implication of readiness for service, עַל־אֲדֹנֵי Zc 6[5]; עַל י׳ Jb 1[6] 2[1]. **d.** c. עַל pers *take one's stand on the side of* 2 Ch 11[13]; c עִם, לְ מִי־יִתְיַצֵּב לִי עִם ψ 94[16] *who will take a stand for me against* the workers of iniquity (|| מִי יָקוּם לִי עִם), of *holding one's ground*, maintaining one's position before י׳, (לְנֶגֶד עֵינֶיךָ) ψ 5[6], so c לִפְנֵי Jos 1[5] (D), Dt 9[2] Jb 41[2], c בְּפָנֶיךָ Dt 7[24] 11[25], abs. וְאֵין עֹמֵד לְהִתְיַצֵּב 2 Ch 20[6]

† [יָצַג] **vb. Hiph. set, place,** a vivid and forcible syn. of שִׂים (Ko[i 430] Ges[§71])—**Hiph.** *Pf.* sf הִצִּיגַנִי Je 51[34] Qr (Kt הציגנו), Jb 17[6], 1 s. sf הִצַּגְתִּיו Gn 43[9], וְהִצַּגְתִּיהָ consec. Ho 2[5], *Impf.* וַיַּצֵּג Gn 30[38] Ju 8[27], sf וַיַּצִּגֵם Gn 47[2], 2 ms תַּצִּיג Ju 7[5], etc., *Imv* הַצִּיגוּ Am 5[15], *Inf cstr* הַצֵּג Dt 28[56] (Ges[§53, 3, R. 2] Ko[i e.]); *Pt* מַצִּיג Ju 6[37];—*set, place*, c. acc + בְּ loc. Gn 30[38] (J, + לְנֹכַח צֹאן), Ju 6[37] 8[27] 2 S 6[17] (+ בְּתוֹךְ), c בְּתוֹךְ in || 1 Ch 16[1], + אֵצֶל 1 S 5[2]; of setting foot on (עַל) ground Dt 28[56], Gn 33[15] (J, sq עִם) = *station with* thee some of my retinue; + לִפְנֵי Gn 43[9] (J), so with idea of *presenting, introducing to* Gn 47[2] (J), *set* (so that all may see) + לְ Jb 17[6], sq 2 acc. (= *set as*) Je 51[34], וְהִצַּגְתִּיהָ כְּיוֹם הִוָּלְדָהּ Ho 2[5] *and* (lest) *I set* (= *exhibit*) *her as in the day when she was born* (|| אֲשִׂימֶהָ כַמִּדְבָּר וְשַׁתִּהָ כְּאֶרֶץ צִיָּה) — fig. *set up, establish*, הַצִּיגוּ בַשַּׁעַר מִשְׁפָּט Am 5[15] (opp. v[7] לָאָרֶץ הִנִּיחוּ). **Hoph.** *Impf* יֻצַּג Ex 10[24] (E) *be stayed, stopped, detained* (of herds, etc)

יִצְהָר, יִצְחָק, יִצְהָר v. sub צהר, צחק, צהר.

† [יָצַע] **vb. Hiph. lay, spread,** late (Ges §71, Aram. יצע Pa Aph *id*, also *expound*, '*auslegen*,' Ar وَضَعَ is *put* or *lay* (down, on a place, etc), but وص = Aram. ע)—**Hiph.** *Impf* יַצִּיעַ Is 58[5], אַצִּיעָה ψ 139[8], *lay, spread out*, sq. acc שַׂק וָאֵפֶר Is 58[5], שְׁאוֹל ψ 139[8] *if I spread out She'ôl* (as my couch) **Hoph.** *Impf.* יֻצַּע (**Pu.** *Pf* De Di al) *be laid, spread*, subj שַׂק וָאֵפֶר Est 4[3], subj רִמָּה worm, as couch for king of Babylon Is 14[11]

† [יָצוּעַ] **n.[m.] couch, bed** (poet.),—sf יְצוּעִי Gn 49[4]; pl cstr. יְצוּעֵי 1 Ch 5[1]; sf יְצֻעָי Jb 17[13] + 2 t. (+ 1 K 6[5 6.10] Kt, v. יָצִיעַ), *couch, bed,*

of wedlock or concubinage, Gn 49^{4} (J), hence 1 Ch 5^{1}; in gen. ψ 63^{7}, עֶרֶשׂ יְצוּעָי 132^{3}; בַּחֹשֶׁךְ רִפַּדְתִּי יְצוּעָי Jb 17^{13} (‖אִם־אֲקַוֶּה שְׁאוֹל בֵּיתִי); cf. ψ 139^{8}).

†[יָצִיעַ] **n.m.**$^{1 K 6.10}$ only Qr, properly *flat surface*, only of lower projecting story of temple, יָצוֹעַ 1 K 6$^{5.10}$; v^{6} rd. הַצֵּלָע *the side-chamber*, as 𝔊 Bö$^{§ 656}$ Sta$^{ZAW 1883, 136}$, v. also v$^{5.8}$ Ez 41$^{5.6}$.

†מַצָּע **n.m.** couch, bed; קָצַר הַמּ׳ מֵהִשְׂתָּרֵעַ Is 28^{20} *the bed is too short for one to stretch oneself* (מַסֵּכָה *coverlet* in ‖ cl.).

†יָצַק **vb.** pour, cast, flow (Talm. *id.*)—**Qal** *Pf.* יָצַק Lv 8^{15} + 2 t.; וְיָצַק consec. 2^{1} 14^{15}; sf. יְצָקָם 1 K 7^{46} 2 Ch 4^{17}, etc.; *Impf.* יִצֹק Lv 14^{26} Nu 5^{15}; וַיִּצֹק Gn 28^{18} + 8 t.; וַיִּצֶק 1 K 22^{35} (intrans. sense); 3 fs. וַתִּצֹק 2 S 13^{9}; אֶצָּק Is 44^{3}; אֶצָּק־ v^{3}; וַיִּצְקוּ 2 K 4^{40}; *Imv.* יְצֹק Ez 24^{3}; צַק 2 K 4^{41}; יִצְקוּ 1 K 18^{34}; *Inf.* צֶקֶת Ex 38^{27} Jb 38^{38}; *Pt. pass.* יָצוּק Jb 28^{2} + 5 t.; pl. יְצוּקִים 2 Ch 4^{3}; יְצֻקִים 1 K 7^{24}; יְצֻקוֹת v^{30};—**1.** *pour, pour out*, oil, in anointing, sq. acc. (שמן) + על Gn 28^{18} (E), 35^{14} (J); sq. מִשֶּׁמֶן + על Lv 8^{12} (P); sq. על (שמן implied from context) Ex 29^{7} (P), 1 S 10^{1} 2 K 9^{3}; sq. אֶל־ + שֶׁמֶן v^{6}; fig., c. רוּחִי + על Is 44^{3}; oil in sacrifice, + על Lv 2$^{1.6}$ Nu 5^{15}; in cleansing, + על Lv 14$^{15.26}$ (upon his palm; all P); oil into (על) vessels 2 K 4^{4}; water, for washing, + על 3^{11}; for drenching, + על 1 K 18^{34}; for boiling (into (בְּ) the caldron), symbol., Ez 24^{3}; for satisfying thirst (fig.) + על Is 44^{3}; blood (of sacrifice) + אֶל־יְסוֹד Lv 8^{15} 9^{9} (P); pottage, for eating, 2 K 4$^{40.41}$; cakes (לְבִבוֹת) 2 S 13^{9}; fig. of disease יָצוּק בּוֹ ψ 41^{9} *infused into him* (al. less prob. as **3** *molten*, i.e. *fixed upon*). **2.** *cast* (objects of metal) Ex 25^{12} 26^{37} 36^{36} 37$^{3.13}$ 38$^{5.27}$ (all P), 1 K 7^{46} = 2 Ch 4^{17}, 1 K 7$^{24.30}$ 2 Ch 4^{3}. **3.** *Pt. pass.* as adj. fig. *cast, hard*, of crocodile's scales Jb 41^{15}; of crocodile's heart v$^{16.16}$ (as stone). **4.** intrans. *flow, pour*, only וַיִּצֶק 1 K 22^{35} (of blood), Jb 38^{38} בְּצֶקֶת עָפָר לַמּוּצָק. **Hiph.** *Impf.* וַיַּצִּקוּ 2 S 15^{24}; וַיַּצִּקֻם Jos 7^{23}; *Pt. f.* מוֹצֶקֶת 2 K 4^{5};—*pour* (oil) 2 K 4^{5}, fig. of shekels of silver, etc., *pour out* Jos 7^{23}; of the ark, 2 S 15^{24} *set down* (?); but read וַיַּצִּגוּ (Dr Gr). **Hoph.** *Pf.* הוּצַק ψ 45^{3}; *Impf.* יוּצַק Lv 21^{10} Jb 22^{16}; *Pt.* מוּצָק 1 K 7$^{23.33}$ 2 Ch 4^{2} Jb 37^{18}; מֻצָּק 11^{15}; cstr. מֻצַק 1 K 7^{16};—**1.** *be poured*, subj. שֶׁמֶן, sq. על (in anointing), Lv 21^{10} (H); fig. of foundation of wicked Jb 22^{16}, v. Di; of grace חֵן, on lips, ψ 45^{3} (sq. בְּ), v. Che. **2.** *Pt.* = *cast, molten* הַיָּם הַמּ׳ 1 K 7^{23} = 2 Ch 4^{2}; as predicate 1 K 7^{33}; cstr. as subst. מֻצַק נְחֹשֶׁת 1 K 7^{16}. **3.** *Pt.*, fig. *firmly established*, pred. of pers., וְהָיִיתָ מ׳ Jb 11^{15} *and thou shalt be established* (‖ לֹא תִירָא).

†[יְצֻקָה] **n.f.** a casting (of metal);—יְצֻקִים 1 K 7^{24} *cast at its casting* (בִּיצֻקָתוֹ in ‖ 2 Ch 4^{3}).

†I. מוּצָק **n.m.** a casting; מ׳ אֶחָד 1 K 7^{37} (of metal); of dust compacted into clod בְּצֶקֶת עָפָר לַמּוּצָק Jb 38^{38}.—II. מוצק v. sub צוק.

†[מוּצָקֶת] **n.f.** **1.** pipe (through which oil is *poured*) מוּצָקוֹת Zc 4^{2}. **2.** a casting (cf. יְצֻקָה), יְצוּקִים בְּמֻצַקְתּוֹ 2 Ch 4^{3}.

†יָצַר **vb.** form, fashion (NH in pt. יוֹצֵר *potter, creator*, and deriv.; Ph. יצר *potter*; 𝔗 יצר; Syr. ܝܨܪ = יָצַר, etc.; Ar. وَصْرٌ *covenant, contract*; As. *êṣêru*, as Heb., Dl$^{HWB 309}$)—**Qal** *Pf.* י׳ Is 44^{10}; יָצַר Gn 2^{8}; sf. יְצָרָהּ Is 45^{18}; 2 m. יָצַרְתָּ ψ 104^{26} + 8 t. Pf.; *Impf.* 3 m. וַיִּיצֶר Gn 2^{7}; וַיִּצֶר v^{19}; sf. יִצְּרֵהוּ Is 44^{12}; 1 s. sf. אֶצָּרְךָ Je 1^{5}; *Pt.* יוֹצֵר Is 41^{25} + 20 t.; יֹצֵר 45^{18} + 6 t.; sf. יֹצְרִי 49^{5} + 11 t. sf.; pl. יוֹצְרִים 30^{14} 1 Ch 4^{23}; cstr. יֹצְרֵי Is 44^{9};—**1.** of *human activity*: **a.** of a potter who forms out of clay a vessel Is 29^{16} 41^{25} Je 18$^{4.4.6.6}$ 1 Ch 4^{23} La 4^{2} Zc 11$^{13.13}$ (these last two acc. to Thes SS et al. error for אוֹצָר); כְּלִי (ה)י׳ *potter's vessel* 2 S 17^{28} ψ 2^{9} Je 19^{11}; חֹמֶר הַי׳ *potter's clay* Is 29^{16}; נֵבֶל י׳ 30^{14}; בַּקְבֻּק י׳ Je 19^{1}; בֵּית הַי׳ 18$^{2.3}$. **b.** of a carver of wood, graven images Is 44$^{9.10.12}$ Hb 2$^{18.18}$. **c.** *frame, devise* in the mind י׳ עָמָל ψ 94^{20}. **2.** of *divine activity*: **a.** (as a potter) forming Adam out of עפר from ארמה Gn 2$^{7.8}$ (J), beasts and birds, also from ארמה v^{19} (J); Israel as a people Is 27^{11} 43$^{1.21}$ 44^{21} 45$^{9.9.11}$ 64^{7}, even from the womb 44$^{2.24}$; the servant of Yahweh from the womb 49^{5}; of the formation of the individual man 43^{7}; Jeremiah in the womb Je 1^{5}; the eye of man ψ 94^{9}; the locust Am 7^{1}; Leviathan ψ 104^{26}; the dry land 95^{5}; the earth Is 45$^{18.18}$; the mountains Am 4^{13}; הַכֹּל Je 10^{16} = 51^{19}. Fig. perh. lost sight of in some of the above, and quite certainly in the forming of light Is 45^{7}, of summer and winter ψ 74^{17}, the רוּחַ of man Zc 12^{1}, and the לב of men ψ 33^{15}. **b.** fig. for *frame, pre-ordain, plan* (in divine purpose), of a situation מֵרָחוֹק Is 22^{11}; of an

occurrence מִימֵי קֶדֶם 37^{26} = 2 K 19^{25}; יְצַרְתִּי אַף אֶעֱשֶׂנָּה *I have planned, I will also do it* 46^{11}, רעה על 'י Je 18^{11}, לַהֲבִינָהּ *devised it to establish it* 33^{2} **Niph.** *Pf* לְפָנַי לֹא־נוֹצַר אֵל Is 43^{10} *before me a god was not formed* (created). **Pu.** *Pf* יָמִים יֻצָּרוּ *days* (that) *were pre-ordained* (in the divine purpose) ψ 139^{16} (cf **Qal, 2 b**) **Hoph.** *Impf* כָּל־כְּלִי יוּצַר עָלַיִךְ לֹא יִצְלָח Is 54^{17} *any weapon that is formed against thee will not prosper*

† I יֵצֶר **n.m.**$^{1\cdot 26}$ **form, framing, purpose;**—'י Gn 6^{5} + 5 t, יצרו Dt 31^{21} Hb 2^{18}; יצרנו ψ 103^{14};—**1.** *pottery*, formed by the potter Is 29^{16} **2.** form of a graven image Hb 2^{18} **3.** form of man as made of the dust ψ 103^{14}. **4.** of what is framed in the mind (cf יָצַר **1 c, 2 b**), *imagination, device, purpose* יצר מחשב(ו)ת לב(ב) Gn 6^{5} (J), 1 Ch 29^{18}, 'י מחשבות 28^{9}, 'י לב Gn 8^{21} (J), יֵצֶר alone Dt 31^{21} (J), יצר סָמוּךְ Is 26^{3} *a stedfast purpose* (or *frame* of mind) (In NH יצר is common in sense of *impulse* יצר הטוב and יצר הרע of good and bad tendency in man.)

† II יֵצֶר **n.pr.m.** son of Naphtali Gn 46^{24} = 1 Ch 7^{13}, Nu 26^{49} (P)

† יִצְרִי **n.pr.m.** **a.** chief of one of the Levitical choirs of singers 1 Ch 25^{11} **b. adj. gent.** of II. יצר, c art = subst coll Nu 26^{49} (P)

† [יְצֻרִים] **n.m.pl.** sf וִיצֻרַי *my forms, members* of my body Jb 17^{7}

† [יָצַת] **vb. kindle,** burn (intr) (NH *id.* (rare))—**Qal** *Impf* 3 fs וַתִּצַּת Is 9^{17}; יִצָּתוּ 33^{12} Je 51^{58} (Kö$^{I\ 431}$), 3 fpl תִּצַּתְנָה Je 49^{2},—*kindle*, intr, fig of wickedness, Is 9^{17}, sq בָּאֵשׁ *be kindled with fire* (= set on fire), of thorns (in sim) 33^{12}, Je 49^{2} (of dependent towns and villages of Rabbah, under fig of daughters), 51^{58} (of gates of Babylon) **Niph.** *Pf.* נִצְּתָה 2 K 22^{13} Je 9^{11} + 2^{15} Kt (Qr נִצְּתוּ), וְנִצְּתָה consec 2 K 22^{17} Je 46^{19}, נִצְּתוּ Ne 1^{3} + 2 t + Je 2^{15} Qr (cf. supr),—*be kindled*, fig of wrath of 'י, 2 K $22^{13.17}$; *be burned*, of gates of Jerusalem, sq בָּאֵשׁ, Ne 1^{3} 2^{17}, = *desolated* Je 2^{15} (of cities of Israel), cf 46^{19}, 9^{9} (of mountains and pastures); of land 9^{11} (‖ אָבְדָה) **Hiph** *Pf* הצית Je 11^{16}, 1 s וְהִצַּתִּי consec Je 17^{27} + 5 t, והציתיה 2 S 14^{30} Kt, (< Qr וְהַצִּיתוּהָ *Imv*, Ges^{§71} Kö$^{I\ 431}$), הציתו v^{31} Je 51^{30}, והציתו consec 32^{29}, *Impf* וַיַּצֵּת־ La 4^{11}, אַצִּיתֶנָּה Is 27^{4} (rd אֲצִיתֶנָּה Kö$^{l\ c}$ Ges$^{l\ c}$), וַיַּצִּיתוּ Jos 8^{19} + 2 t., תַּצִּיתוּ v^{8}, *Imv* 2 S 14^{30} Qr, cf supr; *Pt* מַצִּית Ez 21^{3},—*kindle, set on fire,* sq acc, בָּאֵשׁ + עיר Jos $8^{8.19}$ (JE), Je 32^{29} (+ שׂרף); field of corn, + בָּאֵשׁ 2 S $14^{30.30.31}$; dwellings (no באש) Je 51^{30}, cf. also Ju 9^{49}, also sq acc. אשׁ + prep. עַל, Je 11^{16} (of Jerusalem under fig. of olive-tree), elsewh + בְּ, Am 1^{14}, והצתי אשׁ בְּ (hence Je 17^{27} 21^{14} 43^{12} 49^{27} 50^{32}) La 4^{11} Ez 21^{3}.

יקב (√ of foll; comp Ar وَقَبَ *be sunk, depressed,* وَقْبٌ *hollow, cavity*)

† יֶקֶב **n.m.**$^{Pr\ 3\ 10}$ **wine-vat** (a trough or hollow excavated (חצב Is 5^{2}) in the rock for receiving the juice trodden out in the גַּת · Benz ^{212f}), sometimes also **wine-press** (the trough in which the grapes were trodden out),—abs. יֶקֶב Is 5^{2} + 4 t; יָקֶב Nu 18^{30}, cstr. יֶקֶב Ju 7^{25}; sf יִקְבְךָ Dt 15^{14} 16^{14}, pl. יְקָבִים Jb 24^{11} + 4 t.; יקבי Zc 14^{10}; יְקָבֶיךָ Pr 3^{10},—*wine-vat*, Is 5^{2} Hg 2^{16} Jo 4^{13} (‖ גַּת), Pr 3^{10}, oft ‖ גֹּרֶן, Nu $18^{27.30}$ Dt 15^{14} 16^{13} 2 K 6^{27} Ho 9^{2} Jo 2^{24}; appar. of the *wine-press* Jb 24^{11} יְקָבִים דָּרְכוּ, Is 16^{10} (hence Je 48^{33}) Designating particular localities, Ju 7^{25} יֶקֶב זְאֵב, Zc 14^{10} יִקְבֵי הַמֶּלֶךְ (near Jerusalem).

יְקַבְצְאֵל v. sub קבץ.

† [יָקַד] **vb. be kindled, burn** (Aram. יְקַד, ܝܩܕ, *burn*, intrans.; Ar. وَقَدَ, *id*)—**Qal** *Impf* 3 ms יֵקַד Is 10^{16}; 3 fs. וַתִּיקַד Dt 32^{22}; *Pt. act.* f. יֹקֶדֶת Is 65^{5}; *pass* יָקוּד 30^{14},—*be kindled,* fig. of judgment, יֵקַד יקד כיקוד אשׁ Is 10^{16}, so *burn,* Dt 32^{22} *a fire hath been kindled* (קָדְחָה) *in my wrath,* וַתִּיקַד עַד־שְׁאוֹל *and it burneth unto She'ôl;* fig of people displeasing to 'י, אֵלֶּה עָשָׁן בְּאַפִּי אֵשׁ יֹקֶדֶת כָּל־הַיּוֹם Is 65^{5}, pt. יָקוּד *kindled,* as subst. לַחְתּוֹת אשׁ מִיָּקוּד 30^{14} *to take fire from that which is kindled,* i e. from the hearth (Lg$^{BN\ 60}$) **Hoph.** *Impf* 3 fs תוקד Lv $6^{2.5.6}$; תּוּקָד Je 15^{14} 17^{4},—*be burning, burn,* of (perpetual) altar-fire Lv $6^{2.5.6}$ (P), fig of 'י's judgment, אשׁ קָדְחָה בְּאַפִּי עֲלֵיכֶם תּוּקָד Je 15^{14}, similarly 17^{4} (cf. Dt 32^{22} supr., as prob. source of both).

† יְקוֹד **n.[m.]** **a burning** (properly *Inf. cstr.* of יָקַד)—only Is 10^{16}, abs and cstr., fig of 'י's judgment, v [יָקַד] supr.

† מוֹקֵד **n.[m.]** **a burning mass;**—abs. עַצְמוֹתַי כְּמוֹקֵד נִחָרוּ ψ 102^{4} *my bones are scorched through like a burning mass;* pl. cstr, fig of 'י's judgment, מוֹקְדֵי עוֹלָם Is 33^{14} (‖ אֵשׁ אוֹכֵלָה).

† מוֹקְדָה **n.f. hearth** (=*place of burning*), only of *altar-hearth*, the plate or top of altar, on which burnt-offering was laid and consumed, הוּא הָעֹלָה עַל מ׳ עַל הַמִּזְבֵּחַ Lv 6^{2} (sq. ואשׁ הַמִּזְבֵּחַ תּוּקַד בּוֹ).

† יָקְדְעָם **n.pr.loc.** a city of Judah Jos 15^{56}; site unknown. 𝔊 Ιαρεικαμ, A Ιεκδααμ, 𝔊L Ιεκνααμ.

יקה (√of following, cf. Ar. وَقَى *preserve* (from evil, or fear); VIII *be pious, careful of one's religious duties* (Lane^{3059}))

† יָקֶה **n.pr.m.** father of Agur, אָגוּר בִּן־יָקֶה הַמַּשָּׂא Pr 30^{1} (read probably מִמַּשָּׂא or הַמַּשָּׂאִי: v. Be-Now$^{xvi\,ff}$)

† יְקוּתִיאֵל **n.pr m.** (Impf. from √ע״ו + אל acc. to Ol$^{§277\,h\,2}$, meaning dubious, perhaps better regard יקות as n abstr. from יקה, and render *Preservation of God*) a man of Judah 1 Ch 4^{18}; 𝔊 Χετιηλ, A* Ιεκθιηλ, 𝔊L Ιεφθιηλ — Vid יָקְתְאֵל

יקה (√of following; cf Ar. وَقِهَ *be obedient;* so As. *âkû* (וקה ? יקה) Dl$^{HWB\,123}$; Sab וקה *hear* (favourably), *hear* (and answer), also in n.pr. יקהמלך, יקהאל, וקהאל DHM in MV).

† [יְקָהָה] **n.f. obedience,**—cstr יִקְּהַת עַמִּים Gn 49^{10} c. subject. genit. (Daghesh forte dirim. Ges$^{§20.\,2b}$ Lag$^{BN\,82}$), לִיקְּהַת אֵם Pr 30^{17} c. object genit.

יָקוּט Jb 8^{14} v. קוט.

יְקָמְעָם, יְקַמְיָה, יְקַמְיָם, יָקִים, יָקוּם v. sub קום.

יְקוּתִיאֵל v. sub יקה.

† יָקְטָן **n.pr.m.** son of Eber, descendant of Shem (DHM in MV comp. his name in Arab tradition, viz *Ḳaḥṭân;* the √√ قحط and وقط being both expl. in *Muḥîṭ* by ضرب *strike, beat,* v. Lane$^{1777\,ff.}$)—Gn 10$^{25.26.29}$ = 1 Ch 1$^{19.20.23}$, 'father' of various tribes of Yemen; 𝔊 Ιεκταν

† יָקְנְעָם **n.pr.loc.** Canaanitish city, with a king, defined by לַכַּרְמֶל Jos 12^{22}; in Zebulun 19^{11}; Levitical city 21^{34}.

† יָקַע **vb. be dislocated, alienated** (Ar وَقَعَ is *fall, fall down, fall upon, befal, happen*) —**Qal** *Impf* 3 fs. תֵּקַע Je 6^{8}; וַתֵּקַע Gn 32^{26} + 2 t; *dislocated* Gn 32^{26} (Jacob's thigh); elsewhere fig. of נפשׁ; *torn away, alienated* from any one, sq. מִן Je 6^{8} Ez 23^{17}; sq מֵעַל v^{18}. **Hiph.** *Pf.* וְהוֹקַעֲנוּם consec. 2 S 21^{6}; *Impf* וַיֹּקִיעֻם v^{9}; *Imv.* הוֹקַע Nu 25^{4}; of some solemn form of execution, but mng. uncertain: Aq Ges *impale;* 𝔊𝔖 *expose* (ἐξηλιάζειν, παραδειγματίζειν); 𝔗𝔙 *crucify;* RS$^{Rel\,Sem\,398\,(419)}$ *throw down* (Ar. أَوْقَعَ) a rock (cf. 2 Ch 25^{12}). + ליהוה 2 S 21^{6} (לִפְנֵי י׳ v^{9}), Nu 25^{4}. **Hoph.** *Pt.* הַמּוּקָעִים 2 S 21^{13}, pass. of Hiph

† [יָקַץ] **vb. awake** (Ar يَقِظَ *wake, be awake*)—**Qal** *Impf.* יִקַץ 1 K 18^{27}; וַיִּיקַץ Gn 28^{16} + 3 t; וַיִּקַץ Ju 16^{20} ψ 78^{65} 1 K 3^{15} (v. Baer), וָאִיקָץ Gn 41^{21}; יִקְצוּ Hb 2^{7},—*awake,* Gn 41$^{4.7.21}$ (E), 1 K 3^{15}, of Baal 18^{27}, sq מִשְּׁנָתוֹ Gn 28^{16} (J), Ju 16$^{14.20}$; of Noah, מִיֵּינוֹ Gn 9^{24} (J), i.e. from drunken sleep, fig. of י׳ ψ 78^{65}, i.e. *become suddenly active,* of enemies Hb 2^{7}—Vid. also קיץ **Hiph.**

† [יָקַר] **vb. be precious, prized, appraised** (NH *id.*, Pi, Hiph; Aram יְקַר, ܝܩܰܪ, *be heavy, precious;* Pa. *honour;* יַקִּיר, ܝܰܩܺܝܪ *weighty, precious, honoured;* cf. As. *akâru, be precious, costly,* and deriv, Dl$^{HWB\,240}$; Ar. وَقُرَ *be heavy,* II. *honour;* وَقَارٌ *dignity,* Sab. n וקר *honour* DHM$^{ZMG\,1883,\,402}$)—**Qal** *Pf.* 3 fs. יָקְרָה 1 S 26^{21}; 2 ms יָקַרְתָּ Is 43^{4}, 1 s. יָקַרְתִּי Zc 11^{13}; 3 pl. יָקְרוּ ψ 139^{17}; *Impf* וַיֵּיקַר 1 S 18^{30}; וְיֵקַר ψ 49^{9}, וְיֵיקַר 72^{14}; juss. תֵּיקַר(־נָא) 2 K 1$^{13.14}$;—**1.** *be precious:* **a.** = *highly valued, esteemed,* David's name, וַיֵּיקַר שְׁמוֹ מְאֹד 1 S 18^{30}; of Israel, יָקַרְתָּ בְעֵינַי Is 43^{4} (+ אֲהַבְתִּיךָ, נִכְבַּדְתָּ), of God's thoughts וְלִי מַה־יָּקְרוּ רֵעֶיךָ ψ 139^{17} (Ew Hi Hup render *hard, difficult.* cf יַקִּירָה Dn 2^{11}) **b.** esp of life (נֶפֶשׁ), in phr. יָקְרָה נַפְשִׁי בְּעֵינֶיךָ 1 S 26^{21}, i.e. thou hast spared it, so (juss) 2 K 1$^{13.14}$; similarly וְיֵיקַר דָּמָם בְּעֵינָיו ψ 72^{14} (‖ מִתּוֹךְ וּמֵחָמָס יִגְאַל נַפְשָׁם). **c.** *be costly,* וְיֵקַר פִּדְיוֹן נַפְשָׁם ψ 49^{9}. **2.** *be appraised, valued,* אֶדֶר הַיְקָר אֲשֶׁר יָקַרְתִּי מֵעֲלֵיהֶם Zc 11^{13} *the magnificence of the price at which I was appraised* (and dismissed) *from them!* **Hiph.** *Impf* 1 s. אוֹקִיר אֱנוֹשׁ מִפָּז Is 13^{12} *I will make men more rare* (lit. *precious*) *than fine gold.* *Imv.* הֹקַר Pr 25^{17} *make rare* (i e. *withhold*) thy foot from the house of thy friend.

† יָקָר **adj. precious, rare, splendid, weighty,**—abs יָקָר 1 S 3^{1} + 9 t.; cstr. יְקַר־ Pr 17^{27} Qr (Kt וקר; v. infr.); כִּיקַר ψ 37^{20}; f. יְקָרָה 2 S 12^{30} + 14 t; cstr. יִקְרַת Is 28^{16}; mpl יְקָרִים La 4^{2}; fpl. יְקָרוֹת 1 K 5^{31} + 2 t. + Zc 14^{6} (v infr.); sf בְּיִקְּרוֹתֶיךָ ψ 45^{10} (so Baer; van d. H בִּיק׳);—**1.** *precious* **a.** *costly,* אֲבָנִים יְקָרוֹת

of costly building-stones 1 K 5^{31} 7$^{9\,10\,11}$ cf פִּנַּת יִקְרַת מוּסָד מוּסָּד Is 28^{16} *a costly corner*(-stone) of a foundation,—on cstr v Da $^{Synt\,§\,24,\,R\,3,\,6}$, הוֹן יָקָר *costly wealth* Pr 1^{13} 12^{27}, הוֹן יָקָר וְנָעִים 24^{1} **b.** *precious, highly valued:* נֶפֶשׁ יְקָרָה Pr 6^{26} *precious life;* opp זוֹלֵל Je 15^{19} (of choice elements of character), יָקָר בְּעֵינֵי י׳ הַמָּוְתָה לַחֲסִידָיו ψ 116^{15}, יְקָרָה הִיא מִפְּנִינִים Pr 3^{15} *she* (wisdom) *is more precious than rubies* (v. also **c**), *prized*, of חסד י׳ ψ 36^{8}, = subst בְּנוֹת מְלָכִים בִּיקְּרוֹתֶיךָ ψ 45^{10} *king's daughters are among thy precious* (= *dear*) *ones* **c** אֶבֶן יְקָרָה coll *precious stones, jewels* 2 S 12^{30} = 1 Ch 20^{2}, 1 K 10$^{2\,10\,11}$ = 2 Ch 9$^{1\,9\,10}$, 1 Ch 29^{2} 2 Ch 3^{6} 32^{27} Ez 27^{22} 28^{13} (list of precious stones follows), Dn 11^{38}, so also La 4^{2}, read אַבְנֵי צִיּוֹן הַיְקָרִים (for MT בְּנֵי וגו׳), see VB, שֹׁהַם יָקָר Jb 28^{16} (v also Pr 3^{15} sub **b**) **2.** *rare*, 1 S 3^{1} (cf √ Hiph I, 13^{12}) **3.** *glorious, splendid* (cf Aram), cf the moon Jb 31^{26}, as subst = *glory*, the wicked perish, כִּיקַר כָּרִים ψ 37^{20} *like the glory of the pastures* (i e like gay, but short-lived, flowers) **4.** (late and Aram) *weighty, influential*, יָקָר מֵחָכְמָה Ec 10^{1} *weightier than wisdom* and honour is a little folly —In Pr 17^{27} read Kt וְקַר־רוּחַ *and one cool of spirit* (see VB), in Zc 14^{6} read לֹא יִהְיֶה אוֹר וְקָרוֹת וְקִפָּאוֹן *there shall not be light but cold and congelation* (see *id.* and Vrss), **v.**, however, also Addenda.

† יְקָר **n.m.** **preciousness, price, honour** (late cf BA 𝔗 יְקָר, ܐܝܩܪܐ *glory*),—abs יְקָר Zc 11^{13} + 5 t, בִּיקָר etc ψ 49^{13} + 3 t; cstr יְקָר Est 1^{4}, sf בִּיקָרוֹ 6^{6} + 4 t, יְקָרָהּ Je 20^{5};—**1.** *preciousness* **a.** = *precious (costly) things* (coll) Je 20^{5} (om 𝔊), חֹסֶן וִיקָר Ez 22^{25}, כָּל־יְקָר Jb 28^{10}. **b.** כְּלִי יְקָר Pr 20^{15} *a jewel of preciousness* = *precious jewel* (|| פְּנִינִים, זָהָב) **2.** *price* Zc 11^{13}, v יָקָר **2.** **3.** *honour*, ψ 49$^{13.21}$, elsewhere only Est יְקָר תִּפְאֶרֶת גְּדוּלָּתוֹ Est 1^{4} (|| כְּבוֹד מַלְכוּתוֹ), יִתְּנוּ יְקָר לְ v^{20} all wives *give honour to* their lords, עשה לְ 6^{3}, c מַה־נַּעֲשָׂה יְקָר וּגְדוּלָּה לְמָרְדֳּכַי also v^{6}, (הָ)אִישׁ ; 8^{16} לַיְּהוּדִים הָיְתָה אוֹרָה וְשִׂמְחָה וְשָׂשֹׂן וִיקָר אֲשֶׁר הַמֶּלֶךְ חָפֵץ בִּיקָרוֹ *the man in whose honour the king delighteth* 6$^{6.7\,9\,9\,11}$.

† יַקִּיר **adj.** intrans **very precious, dear**, only הֲבֵן יַקִּיר לִי אֶפְרַיִם Je 31^{20} *is Ephraim a very precious son unto me?* (|| יֶלֶד שַׁעֲשֻׁעִים)

† [יָקֹשׁ] **vb.** **lay a bait or lure** (v. מוֹקֵשׁ), then gen. **lay snares** (v also נקשׁ, קושׁ)—**Qal** *Pf* יָקֹשְׁתִּי Je 50^{24}, יָקְשׁוּ ψ 141^{9}, *Pt* pl יוֹקְשִׁים 124^{7},—*lay snares*, fig of devices of wicked 141^{9} (c. acc cogn); of י׳'s plan to destroy Babylon Je 50^{24} יָקֹשְׁתִּי לָךְ וְגַם נִלְכַּדְתְּ, *Pt* as subst *bait-layers, foulers* ψ 124^{7} (cf. 141^{9}) sim. **Niph.** *Pf* נוֹקַשְׁתָּ Pr 6^{2}, וְנוֹקְשׁוּ consec Is 8^{15} 28^{13}, *Impf.* 2 ms תִּוָּקֵשׁ Dt 7^{25}; *be caught by a bait, ensnared*, in business entanglements Pr 6^{2}, in disastrous consequences of idolatry Dt 7^{25} (|| נלכד), of those ensnared by י׳'s plans (sq וְנִלְכְּדוּ) Is 8^{15} 28^{13}. **Pu.** *Pt* יוּקָשִׁים (for מְיוּקָשִׁים, unless this should be read Ges $^{§\,52\,R\,6}$, Sta $^{§\,220}$) *entrapped*, in circumstances of life Ec 9^{12}

† יָקוּשׁ **n.[m.]** **bait-layer, fowler**, פַּח יָקוּשׁ Ho 9^{8} *the snare of a fowler*

† יָקוֹשׁ **n.[m.]** id, פַּח יָקוּשׁ ψ 91^{3}; כְּצִפּוֹר מִיַּד יָקוּשׁ Pr 6^{5}, pl יְקוּשִׁים Je 5^{26} (in sim)

† מוֹקֵשׁ **n.m.** $^{Pr\,12,\,13}$ prop. **a bait or lure** in a fowler's net, then fig **snare**—abs מוֹקֵשׁ Ex 10^{7} + 15 t., cstr Pr 18^{7} 20^{25}, pl מוֹקְשִׁים ψ 64^{6} Jb 40^{24}, מֹקְשִׁים ψ 140^{6}, cstr. מוֹקְשֵׁי 18^{6} + 3 t.; מֹקְשֵׁי 2 S 22^{6}, *f.* מֹקְשׁוֹת ψ 141^{9}, *bait* or *lure*, in a net for birds Am 3^{5}, will not pierce nostril of hippopotamus Jb 40^{24}; elsewhere fig. of what allures and entraps any one to disaster or ruin, Moses a *snare* to Egyptians Ex 10^{7} (J), מוֹקְשֵׁי עָם Jb 34^{30}, of men who are the ruin of their people, idols and idol-worship a pernicious *lure* to Israel Ex 23^{33} (JE), Dt 7^{16} Ju 2^{3} 8^{27} ψ 106^{36}; so alliances with Canaanites Ex 34^{12} (JE), Jos 23^{13} (D), Michal, to David 1 S 18^{21}; of י׳ as cause of ruin to evildoers Is 8^{14}, of plots of wicked ψ 64^{6} 140^{6} (vb שִׁית; || רֶשֶׁת, חֲבָלִים, פַּח), 141^{9} (|| פַּח), a *lure* or *snare* for wicked in their transgressions Pr 29^{6} ψ 69^{23} (|| פַּח), consisting in transgressions of lips Pr 12^{13}, cf 18^{7} 20^{25}, in wrathfulness 22^{25}, in fear of man 29^{25}, מ׳ מָוֶת ψ 18^{6} = 2 S 22^{6} (|| חֶבְלֵי שְׁאוֹל), Pr 13^{14} 14^{27}.

† יָקְשָׁן **n.pr.m.** son of Abraham and Keturah Gn 25$^{2.3}$ = 1 Ch 1$^{32.32}$, 𝔊 Ιεξαν; 𝔊L Gn 25$^{2.3}$ Ιεκταν

† יָקְתְאֵל **n.pr.loc.** (acc to Ol $^{§\,277\,k.\,3}$ יקת is Impf from √ קות, meaning dubious; poss = יְקוּתִיאֵל q v, see Wetzst in De $^{Is\,3,\,703\,f}$)—**1.** in the *Shephelah* of Judah Jos 15^{38}, site unknown; 𝔊 Ιακαρεηλ A Ιεκθαηλ, 𝔊L Ιεχθαηλ. **2.** name given to סֶלַע (= Petra) by King Amaziah, its captor 2 K 14^{7}, 𝔊 Καθοηλ, A Ιεκθοηλ

† **יָרֵא** **vb. fear** (NH *id.*; As. *irû*, *id.*; Hpt KAT[2, Gloss i], COT[Gloss])—**Qal**[328] *Pf.* יר׳ Gn 19[30] + 14 t.; 3 f. יָרְאָה Je 3[8] ψ 76[9]; יָרֵאָה Gn 18[15]; pl. 2 m. יְרֵאתֶם Nu 12[8] + 2 t.; + 23 t. Pf.; *Impf.* יִירָא Am 3[8] + 3 t.; וַיִּירָא Gn 28[17] + 5 t.; יִרָא Je 26[21] + 5 t.; pl. יִירְאוּ (יִרְאוּ) 23[4] +; יִרָאוּן Dt 13[12], +, etc.; 136 t. Impf.; *Imv.* יְרָא Pr 3[7] + 3 t.; יראו Jos 24[14] + 2 t.; *Inf. cstr.* יְרֹא Jos 22[25]; לֵרֹא 1 S 18[29] (Ges[§ 69, R. 1]); לְיִרְאָה Dt 4[10] + 13 t.; sf. יִרְאָתוֹ 2 S 3[11]; יִרְאָתָם Is 29[13]; יְרֹאתָם Jos 4[24] (rd. יִרְאָתָם Bö[§ 1081 a] Ew[337 b] Di etc.); *Pt.* יָרֵא Gn 32[12] + 15 t.; cstr. יְרֵא 22[12] + 10 t.; pl. יְרֵאִים Je 42[11] + 6 t.; cstr. יִרְאֵי Ex 18[21] + 12 t.; f. cstr. יִרְאַת Pr 31[30];—**1.** *fear, be afraid* (not in P): **a.** abs. Gn 3[10] 18[15] 32[8] 43[18] Ex 14[10] (J), Gn 20[8] 28[17] 42[35] Ex 2[14] Jos 10[2] (E), Dt 20[8] 31[8] Ju 7[3] 8[20] 1 S 4[7] 17[11.24] 23[3] 28[5] 31[4] = 1 Ch 10[4], 2 K 10[4] 2 Ch 20[3] Ne 2[2] 6[13] Is 54[14] Je 3[8] 23[4] 26[21] Am 3[8] Jon 1[5.10] ψ 27[3] 46[3] 49[6] (but Bae reads ראה) 56[4.5.12] 64[5.10] 76[9] 112[8] 118[6] Pr 14[16] Jb 6[21] 11[15]; אַל־תִּירָא(י, ו) *fear not* Gn 15[1] 21[17] 35[17] 50[19.21] Ex 20[20] Jos 10[25] (E), Gn 26[24] 43[23] Ex 14[13] Jos 8[1] (J), Dt 1[21] 20[3] 31[6] Ju 4[18] 6[23] 1 S 4[20] 12[20] 22[23] 23[17] 28[13] 2 S 9[7] 13[28] 1 K 17[13] 2 K 6[16] 1 Ch 22[13] 28[20] 2 Ch 20[17] Is 7[4] 35[4] 40[9] 41[10.13.14] 43[1.5] 44[2] 54[4] Je 30[10] 46[27.28] Jo 2[21.22] Zp 3[16] Hg 2[5] Zc 8[13.15] ψ 49[17] La 3[57] Dn 10[12.19] Ru 3[11]; יִשְׁמְעוּ וי׳ *hear and fear* Dt 13[12] 17[13] 19[20] 21[21]; (י)ראו וי׳ *see and fear* ψ 40[4] 52[8] Is 41[5] Zc 9[5]. †**b.** c. acc. rei or pers. Nu 14[9.9] (J), 21[34] (E), Dt 3[2.22] Ju 6[27] 1 S 15[24] 2 S 3[11] 1 K 1[51] Is 8[12] 51[7] 57[11] Ez 3[9] 11[8] Hb 3[2] (acc. פעלך in corrected rhythm), ψ 23[4] Dn 1[10]; acc. of God (י׳) 1 S 12[18] 2 S 6[9] = 1 Ch 13[12] Is 57[11] Je 5[22] Jon 1[16] Jb 9[35] 37[24]. **c.** with מִן *be afraid of*, Dt 1[29] 2[4] 7[18] 20[1] 28[10] Jos 10[8] (D) 1 S 28[20] 2 K 25[24] Is 10[24] 51[12] Je 10[5] 42[11.16] Ez 2[6.6.6] Mi 7[17] ψ 3[7] 27[1] 65[9] 91[5] 112[7] 119[120] Pr 3[25] 31[21] Jb 5[21.22] Ec 12[5]; with מִפְּנֵי Dt 5[5] 7[19] Jos 9[24] 11[6] (D), 1 S 7[7] 18[29] 21[13] 1 K 1[50] 2 K 1[15] 19[6] (= Is 37[6]) 25[26] 2 Ch 20[15] 32[7] Ne 4[8] Je 1[8] 41[18] 42[11.11]; מִלִּפְנֵי 1 S 18[12], with בְּ *because of, for* Je 51[46]. **d.** with inf. and לְ *fear to do* a thing Gn 19[30] 26[7] (J), Nu 12[8] (E), Ju 7[10] 2 S 1[14] 10[19] 12[18]; with infin. and מִן, *afraid of doing* Gn 46[3] Ex 3[6] (E), 1 S 3[15] Je 40[9] Jb 32[6]. **e.** with פֶּן *fear lest* Gn 31[31] (E) 32[12] (J). **2.** *stand in awe of*, with מן and inf. וַיִּירְאוּ מִגֶּשֶׁת אֵלָיו Ex 34[30] (P) *and they stood in awe of drawing nigh unto him;* יִירְאוּ מֵיהוה וגו׳ ψ 33[8] let all the earth *stand in awe of Yahweh;* וְיָרֵאתָ מֵאֱלֹהֶיךָ *and thou shalt stand in awe of thy God* Lv 19[14.32] 25[17.36.43] (all H); with מִפְּנֵי, of the king Solomon 1 K 3[28]; מִפְּנֵי י׳ Ex 9[30] (J?); מפני י׳ Hg 1[12]; מלפני (אלהים) אלהים *stand in awe before* (God) Ec 3[14] 8[12.13]. **3.** *fear, reverence, honour*, e.g. parents Lv 19[3] (H), Moses and Joshua Jos 4[14.14], the oath 1 S 14[26] Ec 9[2], commandment Pr 13[13], the sanctuary Lv 19[30] 26[2] (H), other gods Ju 6[10] 2 K 17[7.35.37.38]; elsewhere of God: **a.** abs. Je 44[10]. **b.** with acc. (ה)אלהים Gn 22[12] 42[18] Ex 1[17.21] 18[21] (E), Dt 25[18] ψ 55[20] 66[16] Jb 1[1.8.9] 2[3] Ec 5[6] 7[18] 8[12] 12[13] Ne 7[2]; יהוה יר׳ Ex 14[31] (J), Jos 22[25] (P), 24[14] (E), 1 S 12[14.24] 1 K 18[3.12] 2 K 4[1] 17[25.28.32.33.34.41] Is 50[10] Je 5[24] 26[19] Ho 10[3] Jon 1[9] Mal 3[16.16] ψ 15[4] 22[24] 25[12] 34[10] 112[1] 115[11.13] 118[4] 128[1.4] 135[20] Pr 3[7] 14[2] 24[21] 31[30]; יר׳ י׳ אֱלֹהֶיךָ (and other sfs.) Dt 6[2.13.24] 10[12.20] 14[23] 17[19] 31[12.13] Jos 4[24] (D), 2 K 17[39]; with sfs. referring to Yahweh or Elohim Dt 4[10] 5[26] 8[6] 13[5] 1 K 8[40.43] = 2 Ch 6[31.33], 2 K 17[36] Is 25[3] 29[13] Je 10[7] 32[39] Mal 2[5] 3[5] Zp 3[7] ψ 22[26] 25[14] 31[20] 33[18] 34[8.10] 60[6] 67[8] 72[5] 85[10] 103[11.13.17] 111[5] 119[63.74.79] 145[19] 147[11]; הַיָּרֵא אֶת־דְּבַר י׳ Ex 9[20] *he that feared the word of Yahweh* (J); *the name* (*of Yahweh*) Dt 28[58] Is 59[19] Mal 3[20] ψ 61[6] 86[11] 102[16] Ne 1[11].

Niph.[45] *Impf.* 2 m. תִּוָּרֵא ψ 130[4]; *Pt.* נוֹרָא Gn 28[17] + 33 t.; f. נוֹרָאָה Is 21[1]; pl. נוֹרָאוֹת 64[2] + 5 t.; נוֹרָאֹת Dt 10[21]; נֹרָאוֹת 2 S 7[23]; sf. נוֹרְאוֹתֶיךָ ψ 145[6];—**1.** *be fearful, dreadful*, e.g. wilderness Dt 1[19] 8[15], land Is 21[1], people 18[2.7] Hb 1[7], ice (in sim.) כְּעֵין הַקֶּרַח הנ׳ Ez 1[22] (del. 𝔊 Co). **2.** *cause astonishment and awe:* of Yahweh himself ψ 47[3] 68[36] 76[8]; נוֹרָא תְהִלֹּת *awe-inspiring in praises* Ex 15[11] (song); עַל־אלוה נוֹרָא הוֹד *awe-inspiring majesty* (*is*) *upon Eloah* Jb 37[22]; c. לְ, to kings of the earth ψ 76[13]; c. על of hostile nations Zp 2[11]; of י׳'s doings Ex 34[10] (J) ψ 66[3.5]; (ה)נוראות *wonderful, glorious things*, of Messianic king 45[5]; of Yahweh himself Dt 10[21] 2 S 7[23] = 1 Ch 17[21] Is 64[2] ψ 106[22] 145[6]; נו׳ adverbially in ψ 65[6] 139[14] Ges[§ 118.5.b] Da[Synt. § 70(b)]; יום י׳ הגדול והנורא *the great and awful day of Yahweh* Jo 3[4] Mal 3[23] cf. Jo 2[11]. **3.** *inspire reverence, godly fear, and awe:* **a.** as attribute of God, לְמַעַן תִּוָּרֵא *that thou mightest be revered* ψ 130[4]; (ה)גָּדוֹל ו(ה)נוֹרָא (the) *great and awful* (God) Dt 7[21] 10[17] Ne 1[5] 4[8] 9[32] Dn 9[4]; with עַל, *above* all gods ψ 96[4] = 1 Ch 16[25]; above the angels round about him ψ 89[8]. **b.** of the name of Yahweh Dt 28[58] ψ 99[3] 111[9] Mal 1[14]. **c.** of sacred things: מלאך האלהים Ju 13[6]; place of theophany Gn 28[17] (E).

Piel.[5] *Pf.* 3 m. sf. יֵרְאֻנִי 2 S 14[15]; *Inf. sf.* לְיָרְאֵנִי Ne 6[19]; לְיָרְאָם 2 Ch 32[18]; *Pt.* pl. מְיָרְאִים Ne 6[9.14] *make afraid, terrify*, with acc.

יָרֵא **adj. verb.** v. supr. *Pt.*

†יִרְאָה **n.f.** fear, —יר׳ Ez 30^{13} + 6 t., cstr יִרְאַת Gn 20^{11} + 27 t, sf יִרְאָתִי Je 32^{40}, יִרְאָתוֹ Ex 20^{20}, יִרְאָתְךָ Jb 4^{6} + 3 t; ψ 5^{8} + 2 t,—**1.** *fear, terror* Is 7^{25} Ez 30^{13}, י׳ גדולה *great fear* Jon 1$^{10.16}$, ‖ פַּחַד Dt 2^{25}, ‖ רעד(ה) ψ 2^{11} 55^{6} **2.** *a terror = obj. of terror,* ‖ גֹּבַהּ Ez 1^{18} (del Co). **3.** *fear of God, reverence, piety* יִרְאַת אלהים Gn 20^{11} (E), 2 S 23^{3} Ne 5^{15}, יר׳ שַׁדַּי Jb 6^{14}; יר׳ אלהינו Ne 5^{9}; יר׳ יהוה 2 Ch 19^{9} Is 11^{3} 33^{6} ψ 34^{12} Pr 10^{27} 14$^{26.27}$ 15^{16} 19^{23} 22^{4} 23^{17}; ‖ the knowledge (of God) Pr 1^{29} 2^{5} Is 11^{2}, is the beginning of wisdom ψ 111^{10} Pr 9^{10}, and knowledge 1^{7}; the instruction of wisdom 15^{33}, is to hate evil 8^{13}, and it involves departing from evil 16^{6}, י׳ אֲדֹנָי is wisdom Jb 28^{28}; יִרְאָה is defined by context 15^{4}, with sfs these are usually obj, *fear of him* Ex 20^{20} (E), *of thee* ψ 5^{8} 90^{11} 119^{38} Is 63^{17}, *of me* Je 32^{40}, but subj, *thy fear* (i e thy religion) Jb 4^{6} 22^{4} **4.** יִרְאַת יהוה ψ 19^{10} the *fear of* י׳ = the law as *revered*

†יִרְאוֹן **n.pr. loc.** city in Naphtali Jos 19^{38}, prob *Jarûn* Bd$^{Pal\ 261}$ Survey$^{i\ 204}$.

†מוֹרָא **n.m.** $^{Dt\ 4\ 34}$ fear, מ׳ Mal 2^{5} + 3 t, מֹרָא Dt 26^{8}, sfs מוֹרָאִי Mal 1^{6}, מוֹרָאוֹ Is 8^{12}; מוֹרַאֲכֶם v^{13} + 2 t; pl. מוֹרָאִים Dt 4^{34};—**1.** *fear, terror,* ‖ חַת Gn 9^{2} (P), ‖ פַּחַד Dt 11^{25}. **2.** *reverence* אַיֵּה מוֹרָאִי *where is the reverence due to me* Mal 1^{6} **3.** *object of reverence,* esp God Is 8$^{12.13}$ ψ 76^{12}, ‖ ברית Mal 2^{5} **4.** *awe-inspiring spectacle* or *deed* (ה)מ׳ (ה)גדול(ים) Dt 4^{34} 26^{8} 34^{12} Je 32^{21}

†מוֹרָה **n.**[**m.**] שִׁיתָה מוֹרָה לָהֶם ψ 9^{21}, prob *appoint* (Hos 6^{11}) *terror* (i.e some awe-inspiring exhibition of power) *for them* Thes SS RV Ew De Hu Pe Che after Mas 𝔗 Aq Jer (מוֹרָה a variation of or prob error for מוֹרָא), poss *set them a teacher, master* Bae after 𝔊 𝔙 𝔖 מוֹרֶה, νομοθέτην, neither altogether satisfactory.

תִּירְיָא **n.pr.m.** (in Judah) 1 Ch 4^{16} van d H, appar. der fr √ירא, cf MV Buhl; but Baer תִּרְיָא (𝔊B om, A Θηρια, 𝔊L Εθρια)

†[יָרָא] **vb. shoot, pour** (Aram. orthogr of יָרָה q v)—**Qal** *Inf cstr* לִירוֹא בַּחִצִּים 2 Ch 26^{15} *shoot with arrows* **Hiph.** *Impf.* וַיֹּראוּ 2 S 11^{24} *and they shot at* (אֶל־), *Pt* pl הַמּוֹרְאִים v^{24} *the shooters, archers;* Kt to be read וַיֹּרְאוּ, הַמּוֹרְאִים, but Mas. noting א as superfluous, would read וַיֹּרוּ, הַמּוֹרִים from יָרָה (Bo$^{i\ 1063\ (8),(9)}$) **Hoph.** *Impf* only in וּמַרְוֶה גַּם הוּא יוֹרֶא Pr 11^{25} he that watereth *shall* himself also *be watered* (Fl De MV al derive—'non bene,' Thes—from √רוה, q. v, יוֹרֶא for *יֻרְוֶה; but v Thes Ew$^{§\ 131\ f.}$ Bo$^{§\ 161\ (4)}$ SS Buhl Ko$^{i\ 583}$, cf ירה **4**)

יְרִאִיָּה **n.pr.m.** v. sub ראה

יָרִב, יְרֻבַּעַל, יָרָבְעָם, יְרֻבֶּשֶׁת v. sub ריב.

יָרַד ^{380} **vb.** come or go down, descend (NH *id;* MI^{32} וארד and רד, As. *arâdu,* Dl$^{HWB\ 240}$, Ar وَرَدَ *come to, arrive at,* also *descend,* Eth. ወረደ: *descend;* Sab ורד and הורד *id,* DHM in MV)—**Qal**$_{306}$ *Pf* יָרַד Ex 19^{18}+; ירד Ju 5$^{13.13}$ (but read יָרַד or ירד), רַד 19^{11} (read יָרַד), etc; *Impf* ירד Gn 42^{38}+; וַיֵּרֶד Gn 11^{5}+, תֵּרֵד 2 S 22^{10} + 2 t., 3 fs (אשׁ) תֵּרֵד 2 K 1$^{10.12}$, וַיֵּרַד Je 13^{17} La 3^{48}; תֵּרֵד Is 34^{5} 63^{14}; תֵּרֵד Ez 26^{11} (יוֹרִיד Vrss Co), וַתֵּרֶד Gn 24^{16} + 7 t, 2 ms. תרד Gn 26^{2} + 5 t + 1 S 20^{19}, where rd. תִּפָּקֵד We Dr, cf 𝔊 𝔖 𝔗, 1 s. ארד Gn 37^{35} + 3 t, וָאֵרֵד Ex 3^{8} + 3 t, cohort אֵרְדָה־נָּא Gn 18^{21}; יֵרְדוּ 1 S 13^{12} + 4 t, וַיֵּרְדוּ Gn 42^{3} + 19 t.; 3 f. pl. תֵּרַדְנָה Je 14^{17} + 2 t, 1 pl. נרד Gn 43^{5}, cohort. נֵרְדָה Gn 11^{7} + 2 t., וַנֵּרֵד 2 K 10^{13}; *Imv* רד Ex 19^{21}+; רדה Gn 45^{9} Ez 32^{19}; רְדָה 2 K 1$^{9.11}$, fs. רְדִי Je 48^{18} Is 47^{1}, mpl. רדו Gn 42^{2} + 5 t; *Inf abs* יָרֹד Gn 43^{20}; *cstr.* רֶדֶת Gn 44^{26}+, (מ)רדה Gn 46^{3} (v Ko$^{i\ 402}$); sf רדתי ψ 30^{10}, etc (in ψ 30^{4} rd. Kt מִיּוֹרְדִי, so 𝔊 𝔖 Che Bae, v Ol$^{§§\ 180\ b,\ 245\ d}$); *Pt.* יורד Ju 9^{36}+; fs ירדה La 1^{16}; (הַ)יֹּרֶדֶת Ec 3^{21} 1 S 25^{20}, etc,—**1. a.** *come* or *go down* · from (מן) a mountain Ex 19^{14} 32$^{1.15}$ (all E), 34$^{29.29}$ (JE), Dt 9^{15} 10^{5} Nu 20^{28} (P)+; abs Ex 19$^{21.24}$ (J), v^{25} (J, c. אל pers.); from the air, of birds, sq עַל Gn 15^{11} (JE) **b.** *go down* (usu. from mountain or hill-country into plain), to battle, abs. Ju 5^{14}; sq לָעֵמֶק Ju 1^{34}, sq לַשְּׁעָרִים Ju 5^{11}; sq. אֶל v$^{10.11}$, cf 1 S 17^{8} (sq אֶל pers.); sq. לִקְרַאת Ju 7^{24}; sq אַחֲרֵי pers 1 S 14^{36}; sq ב loc Ju 7^{9}; בַּמִּלְחָמָה ירד ונספה 1 S 26^{10}, cf. 29^{4} 30^{24}; of single combat, וַיֵּרֶד אֵלָיו בַּשָּׁבֶט 2 S 23^{21} = 1 Ch 11^{23} **c.** *go down* to (acc) threshing-floor, Ru 3$^{3.6}$, (from David's palace) to Uriah's house (אל) 2 S 11$^{9.10.10.13}$; from temple to (acc.) king's house Je 36^{12} (+ עַל־לִשְׁכַּת הַסֹּפֵר); רד בית־מֶלֶךְ יְהוּדָה 22^{1}, etc. **d.** *go down* (abs.) from Palestine to Egypt Gn 42^{3} (E), v^{38} (J) + 6 t JE, †sq אֵלַי Gn 45^{9} (E); sq. מִצְרַיְמָה Gn 46$^{3.4}$ (E), 12^{10} 26^{2}

(both J), Nu 20^{15} (JE); sq. מִצְרַ֫יִם Jos 24^{4} (E), Gn 43^{15} (J), Is 30^{2} 31^{1} 52^{4}; sq. שָׁ֫מָּה Gn 42^{2} (E)†; so to Philistine cities Ju 14^{19} 16^{31} 1 S 13^{20} Am 6^{2}. **e.** from Jerusalem, abs. Ju 1^{9} 1 K 1^{25} Ne 6^{3} 2 Ch 20^{16} (to battle); to Jezreel 2 K 8^{29} = 9^{16} = 2 Ch 22^{6}; to Samaria 1 K 22^{2} = 2 Ch 18^{2}; (to Gihon) 1 S 1^{38}, etc. †**f.** from altar ירד מֵעֲשׂוֹת הַחַטָּאת Lv 9^{22} (P); from chariot, c. מֵעַל Ju 4^{15}; from ass, c. מֵעַל 1 S 25^{23}; from throne, c. מֵעַל Ez 26^{16}, abs. Is 47^{1}, cf. רְדִי מִכָּבוֹד Je 48^{18}; from ships, c. מִן Ez 27^{29}; from bed, c. מִן 2 K $1^{4.6.16}$ (all opp. עלה). †**g.** *go down* הָעַ֫יְנָה Gn $24^{16.45}$ (J); sq. לִרְחֹץ עַל הַיְאֹר Ex 2^{5} (E), cf. (abs.) 2 K 5^{14}; sq. acc. הַסֶּ֫לַע 1 S 23^{25}; יוֹרְדֵי הַיָּם Is 42^{10}; יוֹרְדֵי הַיָּם בָּאֳנִיּוֹת ψ 107^{23}; abs. (into pit or well) 2 S 23^{20} = 1 Ch 11^{22}, sq. שָׁם (i.e. בְּאֵר) 2 S 17^{18}.—וְיָרַדְתִּי Ju 11^{37}, rd. וְרַדְתִּי (√ רוד, *wander about*), RS in Bla. †**h.** = *sink*, in water יָרְדוּ בִמְצוֹלֹת כְּמוֹ־אָ֑בֶן Ex 15^{5} (song in E); לְקִצְבֵי הָרִים יָרַדְתִּי Jon 2^{7}; more gen., opp. rising, יַעֲלוּ הָרִים יֵרְדוּ בְקָעוֹת ψ 104^{8} *mountains rise, valleys sink;* יַעֲלוּ שָׁמַיִם יֵרְדוּ תְהוֹמוֹת 107^{26}. **i.** *go down* to She'ôl: †sq. שְׁאֹ֫לָה Gn 37^{35} (J; + אֶל־בְּנִי), Nu $16^{30.33}$ (JE), Ez $31^{15.17}$; sq. שְׁאוֹל Ez 32^{27} ψ 55^{16} Jb 7^{9} (opp. עלה); בַּדֵּי שְׁאֹל תֵּרַדְנָה Jb 17^{16}; abs. Is 5^{14} Ez 32^{19} (|| הָשְׁכְּבָה), $v^{21.30}$, ψ 49^{18} (sq. אַחֲרָיו); אֶל־שַׁחַת Ez 32^{24}; sq. שַׁחַת Jb 33^{24}, יָרְדוּ עֲרֵלִים ψ 30^{10}; sq. בּוֹר ψ 30^{4} Qr (Kt יורדי) יוֹרְדֵי; אֶל־אַבְנֵי־בוֹר Is 14^{19}+; יוֹרְדֵי בוֹר ψ 28^{1} Ez $26^{20.20}$ + 11 t. (v. בּוֹר); + יוֹרְדֵי עָפָר ψ 22^{30}; (|| אֶ֫רֶץ תַּחְתִּיּוֹת) רַגְלֶיהָ יֹרְדוֹת מָ֫וֶת (|| הַמֵּתִים) Pr 5^{5}, יוֹרְדֵי דוּמָה ψ 115^{17}; cf. 7^{27} (|| דַּרְכֵי שְׁאוֹל); note also מִי יוֹדֵעַ . . . רוּחַ הַבְּהֵמָה הַיֹּרֶדֶת הִיא לְמַטָּה לָאָרֶץ Ec 3^{21} (opp. הָעֹלָה הִיא לְמָ֑עְלָה; rd. הַעֹלָה, הֲיֹרֶדֶת, with Vrss, see VB). **j.** fig. יָרַד בַּבֶּ֫כִי Is 15^{3} *going down* (dissolving) *in tears* (|| יְיֵלִיל; cf. **3 c**). †**k.** = *be prostrated*, abs., of horses and riders Hg 2^{22}, cf. Is 34^{7}, perh. also Je 48^{15} 50^{27} (+ לַטָּ֑בַח); forest Is 32^{19} Zc 11^{2}; city Dt 20^{20} La 1^{9}; wall Dt 28^{52}; nation תֵּרֵד מָ֑טָּה Dt 28^{43} (opp. עלה); לָאָרֶץ מַצְּבוֹת Ez 26^{11} + מָ֑טָּה (where Co ויחרדו). †**2.** of divine manifestations: *descend*, of י׳ in theoph. [= יָרַד עֶלְיוֹן [על ההר] בָּאֵשׁ י׳ Ex $19^{11.18}$ (E), v^{20} (J; אֶל־רֹאשׁ הָהָר), cf. Ne 9^{13}; יֵרֵד י׳ צְבָאוֹת לִצְבֹּא עַל־הַר־צִיּוֹן Is 31^{4}; abs. Gn $11^{5.7}$ 18^{21} Ex 3^{8} (all J), Nu 11^{17} (JE), 2 S 22^{10} = ψ 18^{10} (cf. 144^{5}), Mi 1^{3} Is 63^{19} 64^{2}; וַיֵּרֶד י׳ בֶּעָנָן Ex 34^{5} Nu 11^{25}, cf. 12^{5} (all JE); of pillar of cloud Ex 33^{9} (JE); מִי עָלָה־שָׁמַיִם וַיֵּרַד Pr 30^{4}; of angels on סֻלָּם; עֹלִים וְיֹרְדִים בּוֹ Gn 28^{12} (E). **3.** of inanimate things: **a.** hail c. עַל pers. Ex 9^{19} (J); dew c. עַל loc. Nu 11^{9} (JE), ψ 133^{3}; rain (as אָבָק and עָפָר), sq. עַל + מִן הַשָּׁמַיִם pers. Dt 28^{24}, so in sim. of future king יֵרֵד כְּמָטָר עַל־גֵּז ψ 72^{6}; of גֶּשֶׁם and שֶׁלֶג, c. מִן הַשָּׁמַיִם Is 55^{10}; manna (c. עַל loc.) Nu 11^{9} (JE); fire from (מִן) heaven 2 K $1^{10.10.12.12.14}$ 2 Ch 7^{1}, abs. 2 Ch 7^{3}. **b.** waters, flowing down הַנַּחַל הַיֹּרֵד מִן־הָהָר Dt 9^{21}, cf. Jos 3^{13} (sq. מִלְמָ֑עְלָה), v^{16}; sq. עַל־יָם הָעֲרָבָה v^{16}; עַל־הָעֲרָבָה Ez 47^{8}; sq. מִן 47^{1}. **c.** tears, פַּלְגֵי־מַיִם יָרְדוּ עֵינָי ψ 119^{136}, and so La 3^{48}; also עֵינִי יֹרְדָה מַּיִם La 1^{16}, and so Je 9^{17} 13^{17} 14^{17} (cf. also Is 15^{3}, **1 j**). **d.** of oil descending upon (עַל) beard, etc. ψ $133^{2.2}$. **e.** of shadow on dial 2 K 20^{11} = Is $38^{8.8}$. **f.** of boundary *going down* (from or to a place) Jos 16^{3} (JE), elsewhere P, Nu $34^{11.11.12}$ Jos 15^{10} 16^{7} 17^{9} $18^{13.16}$. **g.** *come down*, abs. of headdresses, in sign of humiliation Je 13^{18}. **h.** pride of power Ez 30^{6}. **i.** of calamity מֵאֵת י׳ Mi 1^{12}; עַל־קָדְקֳדוֹ חֲמָסוֹ יֵרֵד ψ 7^{17}; of sword descending on (עַל) Edom Is 34^{5}. **j.** *fig.* of words of talebearer; יָרְדוּ חַדְרֵי־בָ֑טֶן Pr 18^{8} = 26^{22}.—Vid. also supr. **1 k.**

†**Hiph.** *Pf.* 3 ms. הוֹרִיד 2 K 16^{17}; וְהוֹרִיד consec. Am 3^{11} (We וְהוּרַד); 2 ms. וְהוֹרַדְתָּ 1 K 2^{9}; 2 fs. sf. הוֹרַדְתִּ֫נִי Jos 2^{18} (v. $Baer^{n.}$ and $Kö^{1.412}$); הוֹרִידוּ 1 S 6^{15} La 2^{10} etc.; *Impf.* 3 ms. וַיּ֫וֹרֶד Ju 7^{5} + 5 t. (+ 1 K 6^{32} Klo, who rds. וַיֹּ֫רֶד for וַיָּ֫רֶד, v. רדד); sf. יוֹרִידֵ֫נִי Ob^{3}; וַיֹּרִדֵהוּ 1 S 30^{16} 1 K 17^{23}; וַיֹּרִדֵם 1 K 18^{40}; 2 ms. וְלֹא תוֹרֵד 1 K 2^{6}; sf. (הֲ)תוֹרִדֵ֫נִי 1 S 30^{15}, תּוֹרִדֵם ψ 55^{24} etc.; *Imv.* ms. הוֹרֵד Ex 33^{5} + 2 t.; sf. הוֹרִדֵהוּ Ez 32^{18}; הוֹרִידֵמוֹ ψ 59^{12}; fs. הוֹרִידִי La 2^{18}; mpl. הוֹרִידוּ Gn $43^{7.11}$; sf. הוֹרִדֻהוּ Gn 44^{21}; *Inf. cstr.* לְהוֹרִיד Gn 37^{25}; sf. הוֹרִדִי Ez 31^{16}; *Pt.* מוֹרִיד 1 S 2^{6}; מֹרִיד 2 S 22^{48};—*cause to come or go down:* **1. a.** *bring down* (to Egypt), c. acc. pers. + שָׁ֫מָּה Gn 39^{1} (J); + הֵ֫נָּה 45^{13} (E); + אֵלַי 44^{21}; abs. 43^{7}; c. acc. rei 43^{11}; + מִצְרַ֫יְמָה 37^{25}; abs. 43^{22} (all J); from Canaan to desert Dt 1^{25} (sq. אֵלֵינוּ); to (אֶל) Amalekites 1 S $30^{15.15}$; abs. v^{16}; *bring down* (obj. pers. vel rei) אֶל־הַמַּיִם Ju $7^{4.5}$; אֶל־נַחַל Dt 21^{4} 1 K 18^{40}; יָ֫פוֹ 1 K 5^{23}; to Gaza (עַזָּ֫תָה) Ju 16^{21}; from Jerusalem to Gihon, c. עַל (Qr אֶל) 1 K 1^{33}; to valley of Jehosh. (אֶל) Jo 4^{2}; from (מִן) temple (to king's house) 2 K 11^{19} = 2 Ch 23^{20}; from (מֵעַל) altar 1 K 1^{53}; from (מִן) upper chamber, sq. הַבַּ֫יְתָה 1 K 17^{23}; from

(מן) the heavens Am 9[2], Edom, from (מן) nest in rocks Je 49[16] Ob[4]; cf of Isr. כְּעוֹף הַשָּׁמַיִם Ho 7[12]; c. acc of limit (אֶרֶץ) Ob[3]; *bring down* (from Babylon) into (ב) ships Is 43[14] (v VB) **b.** *send down* rain (הַגֶּשֶׁם) Ez 34[26], cf Jo 2[23], =*cause to flow down*, obj spittle, וַיּוֹרֶד רִירוֹ אֶל־זְקָנוֹ 1 S 21[14], tears הורידי כַנַּחַל דִּמְעָה La 2[18], water-streams וַיּוֹרֶד כַּנְּהָרוֹת מָיִם ψ 78[16] **c.** =*lay prostrate*, *prostrate* הוריד ממך עֻזֵּךְ Am 3[11] (where however We rds. והוּרַד), cf Pr 21[22], ואוריד כְּאַבִּיר יושבים Is 10[13], of God's casting down peoples ψ 56[8] Is 63[6] (sq לָאָרֶץ), מוריד עַמִּים תַּחְתֵּנוּ 2 S 22[48] (in וַיַּדְבֵּר ‖ ψ 18[48]), so perhaps Babylonians, like lambs, לִמְבוֹחַ Je 51[40], so ψ 59[12] (si veral; 𝔊 וְהַנִידֵמוֹ *make them vagabonds*, v Lag[Proph Chald (1872) xlviii] VB Hup Now Che Bae Dr[2 S 15, 20]) **d** *bring down* to She'ôl: ׳י ממית וּמְחַיֶּה מוריד שאול וַיָּעַל 1 S 2[6], sq. שאו(ו)ל also 1 K 2[6,9], sq שְׁאוֹלָה (obj grey hair) Gn 42[38] 44[29 31] (all J), cf Ez 26[20] 31[16] 32[18], sq לבאר שַׁחַת ψ 55[24], לַשַּׁחַת Ez 28[8] **2.** *take down* (from cart) 1 S 6[15], the sea from upon (מעל) the brazen oxen 2 K 16[17]; corpse from (מן) tree Jos 8[29], and (מעל) 10[27] (both JE), the מִשְׁכָּן Nu 1[51] (P), the פָּרֹכֶת Nu 4[5] (P), *take off* ornaments עֶדְיְךָ מֵעָלֶיךָ Ex 33[5] (JE) **3.** *let down* וַתֹּרֶד כַּדָּהּ עַל־יָדָהּ Gn 24[18], so, with מֵעָלֶיהָ v[46], to give one a drink, וַיּוֹרִדוּ איש את־אַמְתַּחְתּוֹ אָרְצָה Gn 44[11] (all J), obj pers. Jos 2[15], בַּחֶבֶל בעד החלון v[15] (both JE), הורידו בְּעַד הַחַלּוֹן 1 S 19[12], cf also לָאָרֶץ רֹאשָׁן בתולת ירושָׁלִָם La 2[10] *the virgins of Jerusalem have bowed down their heads to the ground*

†**Hoph.** *Pf* הוּרַד Gn 39[1] + 2 t + 1 S 30[24] Kt (Qr **Qal** *Pt*), והוּרַד consec Zc 10[11]; 2 ms והוּרַדְתָּ Ez 31[18], *Impf* 2 ms תּוּרַד Is 14[15],—**1.** *be brought down* מִצְרַיְמָה Gn 39[1] (J), בַּמִּלְחָמָה 1 S 30[24] Kt (v supr), to She'ôl הוּרַד שאול גְּאוֹנֶךָ Is 14[11] (of king of Babylon), אֶל־שְׁאוֹל תּוּרָד v[15], אֶל־יַרְכְּתֵי־בוֹר והוּרַדְתָּ אֶל־אֶרֶץ תַּחְתִּית Ez 31[18], והוּרַד גְּאוֹן אַשּׁוּר Zc 10[11].—In Am 3[11] We rds. והוּרַד ממך (v **Hiph.** supr) **2.** *be taken down*, of the מִשְׁכָּן Nu 10[17] (P)

†**יֶרֶד** **n.pr.m.** **1.** son of Mehall'ēl, fourth generation from Seth Gn 5[15 18 19 20], יָרֶד v[15] 1 Ch 1[2], 𝔊 Ἰαρέδ (v Lag[BN] ה״) **2.** יֶרֶד man of Judah 1 Ch 4[18], 𝔊 *id.*

†**מוֹרָד** **n.[m.]** descent, slope; abs ׳מו Mi 1[4] + 2 t, cstr מוֹרַד Jos 10[11] Je 48[5],—**1.** *descent*, *slope*, as designation of locality Jos 7[5] 10[11] (בְּמ׳ חֹרֹנִים, בית־חורן, both JE), בְּמ׳ חֹרוֹנַיִם Je 48[5], + כַּמַּיִם בְּמוֹרָד ins in 2 S 13[34] 𝔊 We Dr; in gen כְּמַיִם מֻגָּרִים במורד Mi 1[4]. **2.** מַעֲשֵׂה מוֹרָד 1 K 7[29] *work of descent*, i e *hanging-work* (VB)

יַרְדֵּן[182] **n.pr.fl.** **Jordan** (acc to Rel Ol[§ 215 e], fr. ירד with ן— for orig ן—, cf 𝔊 ὁ Ἰορδάνης, =river as flowing *downward, descending*, then of particular stream as river κατ' ἐξοχήν See also Sta[§ 294 e] (ן— for ן—, but name acc to Sta non-Hebr))—abs alw. ׳הַיַּר in prose Gn 13[10] + 162 t; c ה loc הַיַּרְדֵּנָה Ju 8[4] + 3 t, יַרְדֵּן only ψ 42[7] Jb 40[23], cstr. יַרְדֵּן Nu 26[3] + 11 t Nu Jos + 1 Ch 6[63];—the river of Palestine in all periods, chiefly Hex (122 t Gn 5 t J, Nu 20 t. P, 1 t JE, Dt 26 t, Jos 34 t JE, 20 t. D, 16 t P), Ju (12 t.), and S (18 t.), in K 13 t; Ch 7 t, elsewh 10 t;—הַיַּרְדֵּן הַזֶּה Gn 32[11] (J), Dt 3[27] 31[2] Jos 1[2 11] 4[22] (all D); בעבר הַיַּרְדֵּן Gn 50[10.11] (J), Jos 7[7] 24[8] (both JE), + 20 t D + Ju 5[17] 10[8] 1 S 31[7], P has also מעבר הַיַּרְדֵּן Nu 32[19], and מע׳ לְיַרְדֵּן v[19 32] 35[14] Jos 14[3], also Jos 17[5] (JE), 18[7] (D), Ju 7[25] 1 Ch 12[37] 26[30], in P peculiarly יַרְדֵּן יְרֵחוֹ *the Jordan of* (at) *Jericho*, with על Nu 26[3 63] 31[12] 33[48.50] 35[1] 36[13], with מֵעֵבֶר ל Nu 22[1] 34[15] Jos 13[32] 20[8] (=1 Ch 6[63]), with מִן Jos 16[1] (E ?), עֵבֶר הַיַּרְדֵּן Is 8[23] Dt 4[49] Jos 13[27] (P); see sub עבר, מֵי הַיַּרְדֵּן Jos 3[13.13] 4[18.23] (all JE), 3[8] 5[1] (both D), מִימֵי הַיַּרְדֵּן 4[7] (JE), גְּאוֹן הַיַּר׳ Je 12[5] 49[19] 50[44] Zc 11[3] (v גאון p. 145 a, supr.), שְׂפַת הַיַּר׳ 2 K 2[13], יושב עַל־הַיָּם וְעַל יַד הַיַּרְדֵּן Nu 13[29] (JE; elsewh in Nu, P); כִּכַּר הַיַּרְדֵּן *the circle of Jordan*, i.e. the plain about Jericho Gn 13[10.11] (J), 1 K 7[46] 2 Ch 4[17]; מַעְבְּרוֹת הַיַּר׳ Ju 3[28] 12[5.6] *fords of the Jordan*, אֶל־גְּלִילוֹת הַיַּרְדֵּן אל־עבר בני יִשְׂרָאֵל Jos 22[11], cf. v[10] (both P, v גלילות supr p. 165), אֶרֶץ יַרְדֵּן ψ 42[7] (without art only here and in foll); יָגִיחַ יַרְדֵּן אֶל־פִּיהוּ Jb 40[23] *a Jordan bursteth forth into his mouth.*

† **יָרָה** **vb. throw, shoot** (NH *shoot*, Hiph. *teach*; Aram Aph. אורי *teach*, Eth. ወረወ: *jecit*, Amh *warê* is *information, news*, v. No[ZMG 1886 724], As *ârû*, *lead, guide*, Dl[HWB 241]; *têrtu*, *law*, Dl[HA 49], Zinj ירי *set, found*, DHM[Sendsch 57], cf. **2** infr — Buhl distinguishes **3** √ √ ירה. I. = *throw*, cf mod Ar. *warra*; II. Hiph =*moisten*, cf רוה; III Hiph =*teach*, cf ראה, Ar. رَأَى, رَوَى, but evidence for this division hardly sufficient)—**Qal** *Pf* ׳יר Ex 15[4] + 3 t.; 1 s יָרִיתִי Gn 31[51] Jos 18[6]; *Impf* 1 pl. sf. וַנִּירָם Nu 21[30] (SS after

(𝔊 וניִנָם, see Ges[§ 76 (2) a]); *Imv.* יְרֵה 2 K 13[17]; *Inf. abs.* יָרֹה Ex 19[13]; cstr. לִיר(וֹ)ת ψ 11[2] 64[5]; *Pt.* יֹרֶה Pr 26[18]; pl יורים 1 Ch 10[3]; יֹרִים 2 Ch 35[23]; —**1.** *throw, cast,* with acc.: cast lots Jos 18[6] (E); army into (בְּ) the sea Ex 15[4] (song) **2.** *cast* (=*lay, set*), corner-stone Jb 38[6]; pillar Gn 31[51] (E, v. Zinj. supr.) **3.** *shoot arrows,* abs. Ex 19[13] (E) 2 K 13[17]; acc. of arrows 1 S 20[36.37] Pr 26[18], acc. pers Nu 21[30] (song, E) ψ 64[5]; with לְ pers. 11[2]; יֹ(וֹ)רִים *archers* 1 Ch 10[3] 2 Ch 35[23]. **4.** *throw water, rain:* Ho 6[3], but v. יוֹרֶה *early rain* (cf **Hiph. 3**). **Niph.** *Impf.* יִיָּרֶה *shot through* (with arrows) Ex 19[13] (E). **Hiph.** *Pf* 3 ms sf הֹרָנִי Jb 30[19] (הֹרַנִי Baer); הוֹרָהוּ 2 K 12[3], הוֹרֵתָנִי ψ 119[102]; 1 s וְהוֹרֵיתִי Ex 4[15] 1 S 12[23]; sf הֹרֵיתִיךָ Pr 4[11]; הוריתיך Ex 4[12]; *Impf* יוֹרֶה ψ 25[8] + 5 t; וַיֹּור 2 K 13[17] (for this and other forms see Ges[§ 76 (2) a]); וַיֹּרֵנִי Pr 4[4]; יורנו Ju 13[8] + 2 t.; יוֹרֵנוּ ψ 25[12] Is 28[26]; וַיּוֹרֵהוּ Ex 15[25], יֹרֵם 2 K 17[27] ψ 64[8]; 2 f. sf. תּוֹרְךָ ψ 45[5]; תֹּרֶךָּ Jb 12[7, 8], 2 m. sf. תּוֹרֵם 1 K 8[36]=2 Ch 6[27], 1 s אֹרֶה 1 S 20[20] Jb 27[11]; sf אורך ψ 32[8]; 3 mpl יורוּ Dt 24[8] + 3 t., יֹרוּ 2 S 11[20] 2 Ch 35[23]; יֹרֻהוּ ψ 64[5]; יוֹרוּךָ Dt 17[10] + 2 t.; *Imv.* sf. הֹרֵנִי Jb 34[32], הוֹרֵנִי ψ 27[11] + 2 t., pl. sf. הוֹרוּנִי Jb 6[24]; *Inf cstr.* הורת Gn 46[28] + 3 t.; הורֹתָם Ex 24[12], *Pt* מוֹרֶה 1 S 20[36] + 5 t.; מֹרֶה Pr 6[13]; pl. מורים 1 S 31[3] + 2 t., sf. מוֹרָי Pr 5[13]; מוֹרֶיךָ Is 30[20.20];—**1.** *throw, cast,* with לְ, into the mire Jb 30[19]. **2.** *shoot* (arrows) 1 S 20[20.36] 2 S 11[20] 2 K 13[17] 19[32]=Is 37[33]; with לְ, of pers. 2 Ch 35[23], acc. pers. ψ 64[5.8]; מורים *archers* 1 S 31[3.3] 1 Ch 10[3]. **3.** *throw water, rain:* וְיֹרֶה צֶדֶק לָכֶם Ho 10[12] *and rain righteousness for you* (Thes al under **5**), hence מורה *early rain* (cf **Qal 4**) **4.** *point out, shew:* לְהוֹרֹת לְפָנָיו גֹּשְׁנָה Gn 46[28] (J) *to point out before him* (the way) *to Goshen,* מֹרֶה בְּאֶצְבְּעֹתָיו Pr 6[13] *pointing out with his fingers;* acc. pers. et rei Ex 15[25] (JE) ψ 45[5] Jb 6[24]. **5.** *direct, teach, instruct:* **a.** of men, abs Bezalel in handicraft Ex 35[34] (P); c acc pers, a father his son Pr 4[4]; the ancients Job Jb 8[10]; the animals and the earth, the friends of Job 12[7 8], c. 2 acc. Is 28[9]; בְּדֶרֶךְ in the way 1 S 12[23] ψ 25[8] 32[8] Pr 4[11]; בְּיַד־אֵל *concerning the hand of El* Jb 27[11].—מוֹרֶה שֶּׁקֶר *teaching lies* is used of prophet Is 9[14]. **b.** specially of the authoritative *direction* (v תּוֹרָה) given by priests on matters of ceremonial observance, with acc. rei and לְ pers. Dt 33[10] (song), they *teach* thy judgments to Jacob, and thy direction (law) to Israel, double acc. 17[10 11] according to the direction, wherewith they *direct* thee; 24[8] (on leprosy), Lv 10[11] (P), abs. 14[57] (P), 2 Ch 15[3] כֹּהֵן מוֹרֶה, Ez 44[23] the Zadokite priests אֶת־עַמִּי יוֹ׳ בֵּין קֹדֶשׁ לְחֹל, Mi 3[11] the priests give such 'direction' for hire; less technically, of Moses Ex 24[12] (E), of Jehoiada 2 K 12[3], of the Samaritan priests 2 K 17[27 28]. **c.** of God · c. acc. pers. Is 28[26] ψ 119[102], double acc Ex 4[12 15] (J), Ju 13[8] Jb 34[32] 1 K 8[36] (=אֶל הַדֶּרֶךְ 2 Ch 6[27]), ψ 27[11] 86[11] 119[33]; acc pers בְּדֶרֶךְ ψ 25[12]; מִדְּרָכָיו *of his ways* Is 2[3]=Mi 4[2] **d.** of idol-image Hb 2[18] (מוֹרֶה שָׁקֶר), v[19].

†**יֹרָה n.pr.m.** בְּנֵי ^ one of the families of the restoration Ezr 2[18] (𝔊 Ουρα, Ιωρα)=חָרִיף Ne 7[24] (𝔊 Αρειφ).

†**יוֹרֶה n.[m.]** **early rain**, which falls in Palestine from the last of October until the first of December, opp מַלְקוֹשׁ: Dt 11[14] Je 5[24] Ho 6[3] (where MT makes 'יו Pt, or Hiph. Impf., but v. We); cf also I. מוֹרֶה. Vid further Rob BR i. 429 f. Chaplin PEF 1883. 8 ff Klein ZPV iv. 72 f.

†I. **מוֹרֶה n.m.** ψ 84.7 (early) **rain** (cf. יוֹרֶה);—Jo 2[23] (|| מַלְקוֹשׁ, גֶּשֶׁם) v[23] (del. We), ψ 84[7].

†II. **מוֹרֶה n m.** Is 30. 20 **teacher**;—abs. in אֵלוֹן מוֹרֶה Gn 12[6] (J)=אֵלוֹנֵי מֹרֶה Dt 11[30] (Sam 𝔊 אֵלוֹן), *the teacher's terebinth* (see אֵלוֹן) near Shechem, cf. גִּבְעַת הַמּוֹרֶה Ju 7[1] *teacher's hill* near the plain of Jezreel, prob Little Hermon, *Nebî Dahî* Bd Pal 244, the terebinth being a holy tree from which divine teaching was given, and the hill of the teacher the seat of a holy place whence divine teaching was given; see also (of God) Jb 36[22]; here belong prob likewise מוֹרָי Pr 5[13], and מוֹרֶיךָ Is 30[20.20]

†**תּוֹרָה n.f.** Dt 1.5 **direction, instruction, law** (poss. in first instance from *casting* lots, We G i, 410; ii 394 (less confidently We Skizzen iii, 167), SS Sm AT Rel Gesch. 36 Benz Arch. 408 Now Arch. ii, 97, opp. by Ko Offenb. ii, 347 Baud Priesterthum 207);—ת׳, Ex 12[49] + 88 t.; cstr תּוֹרַת Ex 13[9] + 65 t; sfs. תּוֹרָתִי ψ 78[1] + 16 t.; תֹּרָתְךָ Je 32[23]; תֹּרָתוֹ 44[23] + 34 t. sfs; pl תּוֹרוֹת Ne 9[13], תֹּרֹת Is 24[5] + 2 t.; sf. תּוֹרֹתַי Ez 44[24]; תּוֹרֹתָיו 43[11] 44[5] + 5 t. sfs.,—**1.** *instruction:* **a.** human: of a mother Pr 1[8] 6[20.23]; of a father 3[1] 4[2] 7[2]; of sages 13[14] 28[4.4.7.9] 29[18]; of a poet ψ 78[1]; תּוֹרַת חֶסֶד *kind instruction* (of a wise wife) Pr 31[26] **b.** divine || אֲמָרִים Jb 22[22]; through his servants Is 30[9] Je 8[8]; || אִמְרָה Is 5[24]; || דָּבָר Is 1[10], || תְּעוּדָה 8[16 20], || חָזוֹן La 2[9], pl. תורות Dn 9[10]. **c.** *a body of prophetic* (or sometimes perh. priestly) *teaching* Is 42[21 24] Je 9[12] 16[11], in the heart Is 51[7]

ψ 37^{31} 40^{9}; ‖ מִשְׁפָּט Hb 1^{4}; ‖ מִשְׁפָּטִים ψ 89^{31}; ‖ דְּבָרִים Je 6^{19} 26^{4} Zc 7^{12}; ‖ חקים Am 2^{4}; ‖ חקות Je 44$^{10.23}$; myriads of precepts Ho 8^{12}. **d.** *instruction in Messianic age* Is 2^{3}=Mi 4^{4}, Is 42^{4} 51^{4} Je 31^{33}. **e.** *a body of priestly direction* or *instruction* relating to sacred things Ho 4^{6} Je 2^{8} 18^{18} Ez 7^{26} Hag 2^{11} Mal 2$^{6.7.8.9}$ Zp 3^{4} Ez 22^{26}; לֹא תוֹרָה ‖ לֹא כֹהֵן מוֹרֶה 2 Ch 15^{3}. **2.** *law* (prop. *direction*): viz. **a.** of *special laws*, sg. of Feast of Maṣṣoth Ex 13^{9} (J), sabbath 16^{4} (J); of direction given by priests in partic. case Dt 17^{11}; of statutes of priest's code Ex 12^{49} (P), Lv 6$^{2.7.18}$ 7$^{1.7.11.37}$ 11^{46} 12^{7} 13^{59} 14$^{2.32.54.57}$ 15^{32} Nu 5$^{29.30}$ 6$^{13.21.21}$ 15$^{16.29}$ 19$^{2.14}$ 31^{21} (P); תּוֹרַת הַבַּיִת Ez 43$^{12.12}$; בֵּין ת׳ לְמִצְוָה 2 Ch 19^{10}; pl. תּוֹרֹת *laws*, ‖ חקים Ex 18$^{16.20}$ (E; of decisions in civil cases given by Moses), ψ 105^{45}; ‖ מצות Ex 16^{28} (J); ‖ חקות, מצות Gn 26^{5} (J); ‖ חקים משפטים Lv 26^{46} (H); ‖ חק, ברית Is 24^{5}; ‖ משפטים חקים, מצות Ne 9^{13}; the laws of the new temple Ez 43^{11} 44$^{5.24}$; those laws in which men should walk Je 32^{23} (Kt). **b.** of *codes of law*, (1) הַתּוֹרָה as *written in the code of the covenant*, ‖ הַמִּצְוָה Ex 24^{12} (E); ספר תּוֹרַת אלהים Jos 24^{26} (E); prob. also Dt 33^{4}, ‖ משפטים v^{10}, ‖ בְּרִית Ho 8^{1} ψ 78^{10}, ‖ עֵדוּת v^{5}; (2) *the law of the Deuteronomic code*, in D and Deuteronomic sections of Kings and sources of Chr., הַתּוֹרָה הַזֹּאת Dt 1^{5} 4$^{8.44}$ 17^{18} 31$^{9.11}$; דִּבְרֵי הַתּ׳ הזאת 27^{26} 31^{24}, + כל 17^{19} 27$^{3.8}$ 28^{58} 29^{28} 31^{12} 32^{46}; סֵפֶר הַתּ׳ הזאת 28^{61}; ספר התורה הזה 29^{20} 30^{10} 31^{26} Jos 1^{8}; ספר התורה 8^{34} 2 K 22^{8} = 2 Ch 34^{15}; דברי התורה Jos 8^{34} 2 K 23^{24}; so התורה אשר צוך משה Jos 1^{7}, similarly 22^{5} 2 K 17$^{13.34.37}$ 21^{8}; (ספר) תּוֹרַת משה Jos 8$^{31.32}$ 23^{6} 1 K 2^{3} 2 K 14^{6} = הַתּ׳ בספר מ׳ 2 Ch 25^{4}, 2 K 23^{25}; דִּבְרֵי סֵפֶר הַתּ׳ 2 K 22^{11} = דברי הַתּ׳ 2 Ch 34^{19}; תּוֹרַת יהוה 2 K 10^{31}. It is probable that ת׳ in ψ 1$^{2.2}$ 94^{12} and some other parts of Chr., e.g. 1 Ch 22^{12} 2 Ch 6^{16} (= 1 K 8^{25} without ת׳), refers to Deuteronomic code. (3) other passages of Chr. may refer to code of D, but most of them certainly refer to *the law of the Priests' code*. The same is true of Mal Dn and late ψψ. The phrases are: (ספר) תורת משה 2 Ch 23^{18} 30^{16} Ezr 3^{2} 7^{6} Ne 8^{1} Mal 3^{22} Dn 9$^{11.13}$; (ספר) תורת יהוה Ezr 7^{10} Ne 9^{3} 1 Ch 16^{40} 2 Ch 12^{1} 17^{9} 31$^{3.4}$ 34^{14} 35^{26} ψ 19^{8} 119^{1}; (ספר) תורת האלהים Ne 8^{18} 10$^{29.30}$; סֵפֶר הַתּ׳ 8^{3}; דִּבְרֵי הַתּ׳ v$^{9.13}$; הַתּוֹרָה 2 Ch 14^{3} 31^{21} 33^{8} Ezr 10^{3} Ne 8$^{2.7.14}$ 10$^{35.37}$ 12^{44} 13^{3}; תּ׳ פִּיךָ ψ 119^{72}; תורתך Ne 9$^{26.29.34}$ Dn 9^{11} ψ 119$^{18.29.34.44.51.53.55.61.70.77.85.92.97.109.113.126.136.142.150.153.163.165.174}$; תּוֹרָה (indef.) ‖ מצוות, חקים Ne 9^{14}. **3.** *custom, manner*: תּוֹרַת הָאָדָם 2 S 7^{19} *the manner of man*, not of God, i.e. deal with me as man with man, Thes, *law for man* RV, but Ew [Gesch. iii. 180] reads (וַתַּרְאֵנִי) דּוֹרֹת hast shewed me *generations of men*; so We Dr.—On ת׳ v. further Dr on Dt 1^{10} 24^{8} 33^{10} and reff.

† יוּרַי (= יוֹרְיָה whom *Yah teacheth*) **n.pr.m.** chief of the tribe of Gad 1 Ch 5^{13}, 𝔊 Ιωρεε.

† יְרוּאֵל (*founded of Êl*) **n.pr.loc.** מִדְבַּר י׳ 2 Ch 20^{16}, 𝔊 Ιεριηλ, not identified, prob. part of wilderness of Judah, near Ziz (*Wady Ḥăṣâṣah*).

† יְרִיאֵל (= יְרוּאֵל) **n.pr.m.** chief of tribe of Issachar, 1 Ch 7^{2}, 𝔊 Ρειηλ, Ιερεηλ; 𝔊L Ιαρουηλ.

יְרִיָּהוּ 1 Ch 23^{19} 24^{23}, יְרִיָּה 26^{31} **n.pr.m.** (cf. יְרִיאֵל) chief of one of the Levitical courses, 𝔊 Ιδουδ, Ιερια, Ιεδδι, Ιεδειμος, etc.

† [יָרָה] **vb.** only **Qal** *Impf.* 3 mpl. תִּרְהוּ Is 44^{8} (van d. H Baer, but prob. תִּרְהוּ si vera l., so Thes); ? *be stupefied* (cf. Ar. وَرِهَ, Thes al.), but Frey *fatuus et stolidus fuit*; < Ew al. who rd. תִּירְאוּ fr. ירא (‖ פחד).

יְרוּשָׁלַםִ, יְרוּשָׁלַיִם $_{644}$ **n.pr.loc. Jerusalem** (in As. *Urusalim*, Tel Amarna, Zim [ZA. 1891, 252, 254]; *Ursalimmu*, COT [Gloss.]; 𝔊 Ιερουσαλημ; √ and mng. dub.; Rel Ew al. der. fr. יְרוּשׁ שלם *possession of peace* (or *Salem's possession*); Thes al. fr. יָרָה, i.e. יְרוּ + שָׁלֵם *a foundation of peace*; Grill [ZAW, 1884, 134 ff.] *foundation of Shalem* (Sh. = God of peace, = י׳); but name not certainly Hebr.; acc. to Sayce [Acad. Feb. 7, 1891, 138; Higher Crit. 176] (opposed by Zim [ZA. 1891, 263]), Jastr [JBL xi, 1892, 105] = *Uru* (*city*) + *Salim*, n.pr.div.);—usu. יְרוּשָׁלַםִ (*Qr perpetuum*), Jos 10^{10}+; יְרוּשָׁלָםִ 1 S 17^{54}+; -לַיִם 5 t. acc. to Mas. (vid. Frensdorff [Mass. Magna, 293]), viz. Je 26^{18} 1 Ch 3^{5} 2 Ch 25^{1} 32^{9} (c. ה loc.), Est 2^{6}, (but -לָםִ 1 Ch 3^{5} van d. H Baer), so Maccab. coins, Levy [Gesch. d. jüd. Münz. 42 f.]; c. ה loc. יְרוּשָׁלַ֫יְמָה 1 K 10^{2} Is 36^{2} Ez 8^{3}; (-לַ֫יְמָה 2 Ch 32^{9} supr.); -לָ֫מָה 2 K 9^{28}; with prefixes: בִּירו׳ 2 S 9^{13}+; לִירו׳ 2 K 18^{22}+; מִירו׳ 2 S 15^{11}+; וִירו׳ 1 K 23^{1}+;—*Jerusalem*, renowned as capital of all Israel, afterwards of southern kingdom, seat of central worship in temple, first named as city of Canaanite Adoni-Ṣedeḳ †Jos 10$^{1.3.5.23}$ (all JE), cf. 12^{10} (D); inhabited by Jebusites Jos 15$^{63.63}$ (P), Ju 1$^{21.21}$, cf. v^{7} (Adoni-Bezeḳ); identif. with יְבוּס Ju 19^{10}, and הַיְבוּסִי (q.v.) Jos 15^{8} 18^{28} (both P); captured by Judah Ju 1^{8}; first named in connexion with David 1 S 17^{54}†; taken pos-

session of by David as king 2 S 5[6]; David's royal seat v[6.13.14] 8[7] 11[1]+; it remained the capital until taken by Nebuchadrezzar, B C 588, 2 K 25[1]+; it became the chief home of the returned exiles Ezr 1[11] 2[11] Ne 2[11 17]+; mentioned S 31 t., K 92 t, Ch 151 t, Ezr 25 t., Ne 38 t., Is[1] 27 t., Is[2.3] 22 t, Je 107 t., Ez 26 t., Zc 41 t., etc.—Vid also n pr loc. שָׁלֵם, יְבוּס.

ירח (√of foll; meaning dub.; acc. to MV Bubl=ארח, of moon as *wanderer*, so Lag[BN 46]).

† יָרֵחַ **n.m.**[Jos 10 13] moon, esp. poet. (NH *id*, Ph. ירח; As. *irihu*, acc. to Pinches [BOR Aug 1888, 207]; Eth ወርኅ: *moon, month*, cf sub יֶרַח)—abs. יָרֵחַ Gn 37[9] + 25 t.; sf. וִירֵחֵךְ Is 60[20]:—*moon*, usually named with sun Jos 10[12.13] (poem in JE), ψ 72[5] (עִם־שָׁמֶשׁ וְלִפְנֵי יָרֵחַ), 89[38] (in these two, a symbol of permanence), 121[6] Is 60[19] Hb 3[11] Jo 3[4], obj. of idolatrous worship Jb 31[26] (+sun); in same sense also+sun and stars Dt 4[19] 17[3] 2 K 23[5] Je 8[2]; as determiner of feast-times ψ 104[19] (‖ sun); +stars, as shining by night ψ 136[9] (‖ sun, by day), so חֻקֹּת יָרֵחַ Je 31[35] (‖ *id.*); elsewh +sun and stars Gn 37[9] (E), Is 13[10] Ez 32[7] Jo 2[10] 4[15] ψ 148[3] Ec 12[2]; +stars ψ 8[4] Jb 25[5]; with neither sun nor stars only עַד־בְּלִי יָרֵחַ ψ 72[7].

† I. יֶרַח **n.m.**[Zc 11, 8] month (Aram. יַרְחָא, ܝܰܪܚܳܐ *new moon, month*; Palm. ירח Vog[No 1], As *arhu* COT[Gloss.] Muss-Arnolt [JBL xi 1892, 73, 163], cf. Ph. Eth. sub יָרֵחַ; Sab ורח *month*, DHM[ZMG 1876, 603; 1883, 369] Hal[JAS vii, 1, 516])—abs. יֶרַח 1 K 6[37]+3 t; cstr. *id* Dt 21[13] 2 K 15[13], pl יְרָחִים Ex 2[2]+3 t.; cstr. יַרְחֵי Jb 7[3] 29[2],—**1.** *month*, as measure of time, during, or in which Ex 2[2] (E), Zc 11[8] Jb 39[2], יַרְחֵי שָׁוְא Jb 7[3]; יַרְחֵי קֶדֶם 29[2]; pleon. יֶרַח יָמִים *a month (of) days=a month of time* Dt 21[13] 2 K 15[13]. **2.** *calendar month*, with name יֶרַח זִו 1 K 6[37] (2nd mo., cf. v[1]); יֶרַח בּוּל v[38] (8th mo.), יֶרַח הָאֵתָנִים 1 K 8[2] (7th mo.); cf. בְּמִסְפַּר יְרָחִים Jb 3[6]; גֶּרֶשׁ יְרָחִים Dt 33[14] *produce of months*, i e of various seasons of year.—Cf. synon. חדשׁ

† II. [יֶרַח] **n.pr.m.** 'son' of Joktan, only יָרַח Gn 10[26] (𝔊 Ιαραδ, 𝔊L Ιεραχ)=1 Ch 1[20] (𝔊L Ιαρε)

† יָרוֹחַ **n.pr.m.** a Gadite, 1 Ch 5[14]; 𝔊 Ιδαι, 𝔊L Αρουε

יְרֵחוֹ v. יְרִיחוֹ

יְרַחְמְאֵל, יְרֹחָם v. sub רחם.

† יַרְחָע **n.pr.m.** an Egyptian slave 1 Ch 2[34.35]; 𝔊 Ιωχηλ, 𝔊L Ιερεε.

† **ירט** vb. be precipitate, precipitate (trans) (cf. Ar. وَرَّطَ *conjecit, praecipitem dedit in puteum, exitium*, Frey)—**Qal** *Pf.* יָרַט Nu 22[32], app c subj. הַדֶּרֶךְ, the way *is precipitate*, (RV[m] *headlong*) *before me*. but transit עַל־יְדֵי רשׁעים ירטני Jb 16[11] *into the hands of wicked men he precipitates me* (v Di, יִרְטֵנִי=ירטני; Baer's text יִרְטֵנִי points to √רטה q v); hence perh. rd. יָרַטְתָּ Nu 22[32]; *thou hast precipitated the journey* in front of me, i e. rushed recklessly in front of me; v. Di; Kau[AT] leaves untransl.

ירחו, יְרִיחוֹ, יְרִיחֹה, יריחו [57] **n.pr.loc.** Jericho (on form see Baer on Jos 2[1] Je 39[5] Ko[Einl 49]; √ and mng. dub.; acc to Thes al. from רֵיחַ, =*regio fragrans*, the district abounding in palms, rose-gardens, balsam, etc);—יְרִיחוֹ Jos 2[1] +27 t. Jos. (19 t. JE, 3 t D, 6 t P). +5 t 2 K 2; ירחו Jos 18[21] 2 S 10[5] Je 39[5] 52[8]; יְרִיחֹה 1 K 16[34]; יְרֵחוֹ Dt 34[1] (P), v[3] (D), Nu 22[1] (P)+9 t. P, 2 K 25[5] Ezr 2[34] Ne 3[2] 7[36]+3 t. Ch;—Canaanit city taken by Josh. Jos 6[1] (JE)+; having a king 2[2.3] 8[2] 10[1] (all JE), 10[28.30] 12[9] (all D); near Jordan, whence (יְרִיחוֹ) ירדן ירחו, v יַרְדֵּן supr.; Mt. Nebo is described as עַל־פְּנֵי יְרֵחוֹ Dt 32[49] 34[1] (P); (called עִיר הַתְּמָרִים Jud 1[16] 3[13]; so in appos. Dt 34[3] 2 Ch 28[15]); the adjacent plain is called בִּקְעַת יְרֵחוֹ Dt 34[3] (JE); עַרְבוֹת ירחו 2 K 25[5]=Je 39[5]=52[8]; ע׳ יְרִיחוֹ Jos 4[13] 5[10] (both P), among returning exiles appear בני ירחו Ezr 2[34]=Ne 7[36], and among builders of wall אַנְשֵׁי ירחו Ne 3[2] (BeRy Ryle *ad loc.* and Ezr 2[34]);—mod. (*E*)*rîḥâ*; see also GASm[Geogr 266 ff]

ירך (√of foll.; meaning dubious).

† יָרֵךְ **n.f.**[Nu 5, 27] thigh, loin, side, base (NH *id.*; Aram יַרְכָא, Zinj. ירך *loin*; As *arku, arkâtu, back, rear, hereafter* Dl[HWB 242]; Ar. وَرِكٌ *hip*)—abs. יָרֵךְ Ju 15[8]+6 t., cstr. יֶרֶךְ Gn 24[9]+11 t. +2 S 3[27] (v. infr); sf. יְרֵכִי Gn 24[2] 47[29], יְרֵכְךָ Nu 5[21]; יְרֵכוֹ Gn 32[26]+6 t.; יְרֵכָהּ Ex 25[31]+3 t.; du. יְרֵכַיִם Ex 28[42]; sf יְרֵכַיִךְ Ct 7[2];—**1.** *thigh*, **a.** outside of thigh, where sword was worn, וַיַּחְגֹּר אֹתָהּ עַל־יֶרֶךְ Ex 32[27] (E); שִׂים חַרְבּוֹ עַל־יְרֵכוֹ יְמִינוֹ Ju 3[16] *and he girded it upon his right thigh*, v[21] ψ 45[4] Ct 3[8]; כַּף הַיָּרֵךְ Gn 32[33] *hollow of the thigh*, v[26.26.33] (all J); חַמּוּקֵי יְרֵכַיִךְ Ct 7[2] *the roundings of thy thighs*; מִמָּתְנַיִם וְעַד־יְרֵכַיִם Ex 28[42] (P); ‖ בֶּטֶן Nu 5[21.22.27] (P); צַלְעָ עַל־יְרֵכוֹ

Gn 32[32](J), *limping upon his thigh*, צֹלֵעַ עַל־יְרֵכוֹ Je 31[19] and (c. אֶל־) Ez 21[17], *smite upon thigh*, in token of consternation; וַיַּךְ אוֹתָם שׁוֹק עַל־יָרֵךְ Ju 15[8] *and he smote them, hip upon thigh*, a great slaughter. **b.** *thigh=loins*, as seat of procreative power (RS[K. 34, Sem 1, 360 (380)]) יֹצְאֵי יֶרֶךְ *those proceeding from the loins of* any one Gn 46[26] Ex 1[5] (both P), Ju 8[30], hence שִׂים יַד תַּחַת יָרֵךְ *place the hand under thigh*, in taking oath Gn 24[2.9] (J), 47[29]. **2.** *side* (flank) of altar 2 K 16[14] Lv 1[11] (P), of tabernacle Ex 40[22.24] Nu 3[29.35] (all P), also יֶרֶךְ הַשַּׁעַר (for MT תּוֹךְ הַשּׁ׳) 𝔊 Th We Dr Bu Kit. **3.** *base* (loins) of candlestick Ex 25[31] 37[17] Nu 8[4] (all P)

†[יַרְכָה, or יַרְכָה Ol[§107 c]] **flank, side, du extreme parts, recesses**,—sf יַרְכָתוֹ Gn 49[13], du יַרְכָתַיִם Ex 26[27] 36[32] + Ez 46[19] Qr (Kt ירכתם), יַרְכָתָיִם Ex 26[23] 36[28], cstr. יַרְכְּתֵי Ju 19[1] + 20 t + 1 K 6[16] Qr (Kt ירכותי),—**1.** *side*, i e *further side* of Zebulun, poet for more distant border of his territory Gn 49[13] **2.** elsewhere always du *the two thighs*, i e fig *angle, recess, extreme parts* as *recesses* of Mt Ephr Ju 19[1.18], of Lebanon 2 K 19[23] = Is 37[24], of *recesses* or *innermost part* of a cave 1 S 24[4], a house Am 6[10] ψ 128[3]; the pit (בּוֹר) Is 14[15] (‖ שְׁאוֹל), Ez 32[23], a ship Jon 1[5], יַרְכְּתֵי צָפוֹן *remote parts of the north* Is 14[13] Ez 38[6.15] 39[2] ψ 48[3] (but here Lag prop יר׳ רצון), יַרְכְּתֵי אָרֶץ *remote parts of earth* Je 6[22] 25[32] 31[8] 50[41], of a long building, *extreme* or *hinder part*, so of tabernacle Ex 26[22.23.27] 36[27.28.32] (all P), of temple 1 K 6[16]; of Ezek's temple Ez 46[19]

†יַרְמוּת **n.pr.loc.** **1.** 𝔊 Ιερ(ε)ιμουθ, Canaanitish city, with a king, named between Hebron and Lachish Jos 10[3.5.23] (JE), 12[11] (D), named with Adullam 15[35] (P), cf Ne 11[29] **2.** 𝔊 Ρεμμαθ, A 𝔊L Ιερμωθ, Levitical city in Issachar Jos 21[29] (P).

†יְרֵמַי **n pr.m.** one of those who had strange wives Ezr 10[33], 𝔊 Ιεραμει(μ)

†יְרֵימוֹת, יְרֵמוֹת, יְרִימוֹת **n.pr.m.** 𝔊 Αρειμωθ, Ιεριμουθ, etc,—**1.** Benjamites **a.** יְרִימוֹת 1 Ch 7[7] **b.** יְרִימוֹת 1 Ch 7[8] **c.** יְרֵמוֹת 1 Ch 8[14] **2.** Levites **a** יְרֵמוֹת 1 Ch 23[23]. **b.** *id.* 1 Ch 25[22] = **c.** יְרִימוֹת 24[30]. **d.** יְרִימוֹת 1 Ch 25[4]. **e.** *id* 2 Ch 31[13] **3.** *id* Naphtalite 1 Ch 27[19]. **4.** *id* son of David and father of Rehoboam's wife 2 Ch 11[18]. **5** יְרֵמוֹת, men who had strange wives **a** Ezr 10[26], 𝔊 Ιερειμωθ (-μωθ) **b.** Ezr 10[27], 𝔊 Αμων, א Αρμων, A Ιαρμωθ, 𝔊L Ιεριμωθ **c.** Ezr 10[29] Kt (Qr וְרָמוֹת), 𝔊 Μημων, A Ρημωθ, 𝔊L Αριμωθ.

יִרְמְיָה, יִרְמְיָהוּ v sub רמה.

†[יָרַע] **vb** quiver (cf Ar وَرِعَ *be timid, weak*, وَرَعٌ *pious fear*, 𝔗 ירע *be disheartened*) —**Qal** *Pf* 3 fs נַפְשׁוֹ יָרְעָה לּוֹ Is 15[4] *his soul quivereth* to him, i e is in terror and distress

יְרִיעָה **n f. curtain** (𝔗 יְרִיעֲתָא, Syr ܝܪܝܥܬܐ) —abs יְרִיעָה Ex 26[2] + 24 t, pl. abs יְרִיעֹת Ex 26[1] + 17 t, יְרִיעוֹת 1 Ch 17[1], cstr יְרִיעֹת Ex 26[7] + 4 t, יְרִיעוֹת Hb 3[7] + 2 t., sf יְרִיעֹתַי Je 4[20] 10[20]; יְרִיעוֹתֵיהֶם Je 49[29];—*curtain*, of tabern Ex 26[1.2] [2.2.8.8] + 38 t. Ex 26 and 36; Nu 4[25] (all P); 2 S 7[2] = 1 Ch 17[1],—in gen. (*tent-*) *curtains* Je 4[20] 10[20] 49[29] Hb 3[7] Ct 1[5] (in all ‖ אֹהֶל), יְרִיעֹת . . . יַטּוּ Is 54[2] (‖ הַרְחִיבִי מְקוֹם אָהֳלֵךְ), fig of Jerusalem's prosperity, in sim נוֹטֶה שָׁמַיִם כַּיְרִיעָה ψ 104[2]

†יְרִיעוֹת **n.pr.m.**(?) only 1 Ch 2[18], where id perh בַּת־יר׳ for MT וְאֶת־יר׳, see We VB, 𝔊 Ελιωθ, A 𝔊L Ιερ(ε)ιωθ

יִרְפְּאֵל v sub רפא

I ירק (✓of foll, NH Hiph, Aram. Aph אוריק *grow green*; ܝܪܩ *be pale*, and deriv, As *arâku*, *grow pale* (of face), *arku*, yellow, green, etc, Dl[HWB 243], Ar وَرَقٌ *leaf*, وَرَّقَ *put forth leaves*, cf وُرْقَةٌ *ash-colour*, أَوْرَقُ *dusky-white*, of camel, وَرِقٌ *silver coin* Lag[BN 30], Sab. ורק *gold* (כתם וורק), Hal[Ét. JAs. Déc 1874 Nos 47 et] DHM[ZMG 1883, 26 f], and Eth. ወርቅ: *gold*, both from colour acc to DHM Dl)

†יֶרֶק **n.m.**[Is 15, 6] **green, greenness** (on ܝܘܪܩܐ in gardens, v No[ZMG 1876, 777] Low[P 236 f])—abs. Ex 10[15] Is 15[6], cstr Gn 1[30] + 3 t.,—יֶרֶק עֵשֶׂב Gn 1[30] 9[3] (both P), יֶרֶק הַשָּׂדֶה, ψ 37[2] יֶרֶק דֶּשֶׁא Nu 22[4] (E) = *green thing, grass*; alone Ex 10[15] (J) *green thing*, incl עֵץ and עֵשֶׂב, Is 15[6]

†יָרָק **n.[m.]** **herbs** (coll), **herbage** (green, greens)—abs יָרָק Dt 11[10] + 2 t.; cstr יְרַק Is 37[27] = 2 K 19[26],—גַּן־יָרָק Dt 11[10] 1 K 21[2], אֲרֻחַת יָרָק Pr 15[17], as subst, יְרַק דֶּשֶׁא Is 37[27] = 2 K 19[26] *green shoots of grass* (‖ עֵשֶׂב שָׂדֶה, etc)

יַרְקוֹן only in מֵי הַי׳ Jos 19[46] v sub מַי

†יָרוֹק **n.[m.]** **green thing** (=יֶרֶק), only as food of wild ass Jb 39[8]

†יֵרָקוֹן **n.m. mildew, paleness, lividness;** **1.** *mildew* Am 4^{9} Dt 28^{22} 1 K 8^{37} Hg 2^{17} 2 Ch 6^{28} (all ‖ שִׁדָּפוֹן). **2.** *paleness* (of face) Je 30^{6}.

†יְרַקְרַק (Sta$^{§156, 234}$) **adj. greenish, pale-green** (cf As. *rakrakku*, Zim$^{BP 37}$)—Lv 13^{49} ψ 68^{14}; fpl. יְרַקְרַקֹּת Lv 14^{37},—of plague spots Lv 13^{49} 14^{37}; as subst., ψ 68^{14} the *green-shimmering* (Che) of gold.

†יָרְקְעָם **n.pr m.** a name in Judah 1 Ch 2^{44}; 𝔊 Ιακλαν, A Ιερκααν, 𝔊L Ιερακαμ (and so for רֶקֶם v^{b}; otherwise רקם v^{43})

†II. יָרַק **vb. spit** (Eth. ወረቀ: *id.*; acc. to Lag$^{BN 200}$ II ירק is not separate √; cf. יֵרָקוֹן, and Ar يَرَقَانٌ *robigo*)—**Qal** *Pf* and *Inf abs* יָרֹק יָרַק בְּפָנֶיהָ Nu 12^{14}, 3 fs consec וְיָרְקָה בְּפָנָיו Dt 25^{9}; both, as token of contempt. Cf רֹק, רָקַק.

יָרַשׁ$_{229}$ **vb. take possession of, inherit, dispossess** (MI^{7} וירש *take possession of*, Aram יְרֵית, ܝܪܬ, *take possession of*, and *be heir to*, *inherit*, so Eth ወረሰ: Ar وَرِثَ *inherit*, v also Sab ורת *inherit*, CIS$^{iv 37, 5}$), esp D (62 t. Qal, 1 t Pi, 7 t Hiph in Dt+13 t. D in Jos);—**Qal** *Pf.* 3 ms יָרַשׁ Je 49^{1}, וְיָרַשׁ consec. Je 49^{2} Nu 27^{11}, 2 ms יָרַשְׁתָּ 1 K 21^{19}; וְיָרַשְׁתָּ Dt 6^{18}+2 t.; sf וירשׁתה consec Dt 17^{14}+2 t. (on this and kindred forms v Kö$^{I. 408, 411}$); וירשׁתם consec Dt 19^{1} 31^{3}, 3 pl. יָרְשׁוּ Dt 3^{20}+, sf וִירֵשׁוּךָ consec Ez 36^{12} (Kö$^{l c}$); וירשׁוה consec. Is 34^{11}+3 t., 2 mpl. וירשׁתם consec. Dt 4^{1}+7 t.; 1 pl יָרַשְׁנוּ Dt 3^{12}, etc., *Impf* 3 ms. יִירַשׁ Gn 21^{10} ψ 25^{13}, 2 mpl תירשׁ Lv 20^{24} 1 Ch 28^{8}, תִּירָשׁוּ Ez 33$^{25.26}$, תִּירָשׁוּן Dt 5^{30}, etc., *Imv.* ms. יְרָשָׁה Dt 33^{23}, רשׁ Dt 1^{21} 1 K 21^{15}; רָשׁ Dt 2$^{24.31}$; mpl רשׁו Dt 1^{8} 9^{23}, *Inf. cstr.* לָרֶשֶׁת Dt 2^{31}+17 t.; לָרֶשֶׁת Ne 9^{23}; sf לרשׁתךָ Gn 28^{4}; לרשׁתו 1 K 21$^{16.18}$, לרשׁתה Gn 15^{7}+28 t.; *Pt* יורשׁ Gn 15^{3}+6 t., pl י(ו)רשׁים Dt 12^{2} Je 8^{10}; sf יֹרְשָׁיו Je 49^{2},—**1.** *take possession of*, esp. by force, *have as a possession*, often with collat. idea of *taking in place of* others, *succeeding to inheriting* (cf **2**): **a.** land, sq acc. Gn 15$^{7.8}$ Nu 13^{30} 21$^{24.35}$ Jos 18^{3} (all JE), 24$^{4.8}$ (E), Ju 2^{6} 11$^{21.22.23.24.24}$ 18^{9} Dt 1$^{8.21.39}$+25 t. Dt,+†Dt 11^{31} 17^{14} 26^{1} (all *possess* land *and dwell therein*), similarly Is 65$^{9.9}$ ψ 69^{36}; בְּאַרְצָם מִשְׁנֶה יִירָשׁוּ Is 61^{7} *in their land they shall possess the double*, הָחֵל רָשׁ Dt 2^{24}; הָחֵל רָשׁ לָרֶשֶׁת אֶת־אַרְצוֹ v^{31}, esp. phr. (הארץ) אֲשֶׁר אַתֶּם בָּאִים (עֹבְרִים etc.) שָׁמָּה לְרִשְׁתָּהּ Dt 4$^{5.14.26}$ +12 t. Dt, also Ezr 9^{10}, v. Dt 30^{18} Jos 1$^{11.11.15.1.}$ 12^{1} 13^{1} 21^{41} 23^{5} (all D), Am 2^{10} Ob$^{19.19}$ Hb 1^{6} Ez 33$^{24.25.26}$ Lv 20$^{24.24}$ (H), Gn 28^{4} Nu 33^{53} (both P), 1 Ch 28^{8} Ne 9$^{15.22.23.24}$; ψ 25^{13} 37$^{9.11.22.29.34}$; +בְּ instr. 44^{4}, also וַעֲמַל לְאֻמִּים יִירָשׁוּ 105^{44} (‖ וַיִּתֵּן לָהֶם אַרְצוֹת גּוֹיִם), †*take possession of* fields Je 8^{10} (obj. not expr.), 1 K 21$^{15.16.18.19}$ ψ 83^{13}, inheritance (in land) Nu 27^{11} 36$^{8.8}$ (all P): city (cities), Jos 19^{47} (JE), Ju 3^{13} Ob^{20}; so הַר־קָדְשִׁי Is 57^{13} (‖ נחל ארץ), 63^{18} where rd. prob הַר־קָדְשֶׁךָ (for MT עַם־ק׳, see 𝔊 VB and ‖ cl); *possess* city and dwell therein 2 K 17^{24} Is 34^{17}, Is 34^{11} yea the pelican and bittern shall *possess* it, so of nettles Ho 9^{6}, וְיִרַשׁ זַרְעֲךָ את שַׁעַר אֹיְבָיו Gn 22^{17}, cf 24^{60} (both J), *possess* houses Ez 7^{24} (del Co), Ne 9^{25}, יוֹרֵשׁ עֶצֶר Ju 18^{7} *possessing wealth* (? see VB)† †**b.** a *people* (with collat. idea of *being their heir* (**2**), and so *dispossessing them*), so esp. in Dt 2$^{12.21.22}$ 9^{1} (+cities), 11^{23} 12$^{2.29.29}$ 18^{14} 19^{1} 31^{3}, Nu 21^{32} (Kt וַיִּירַשׁ, JE), Am 9^{12}, מַדּוּעַ יָרַשׁ מַלְכָּם אֶת־גָּד Je 49^{1} (on text see VB), v^{2} (in these 3 perh play on meaning *inherit*, cf v^{1a}), Ez 36^{12} Ob^{17} Is 54^{3}, nations+countries Ez 35^{10}. †**2.** *inherit*, sq acc pers = *be one's heir* Gn 15$^{3.4.4}$ (JE); שִׁפְחָה כִּי־תִירַשׁ גְּבִרְתָּהּ Pr 30^{23} (or, *dispossess*?), abs. *be heir*, sq. עִם pers = jointly with 21^{10} (E), הַיּוֹרֵשׁ (*the*) *heir* 2 S 14^{7} Je 49^{1} (‖ בָּנִים); Mi 1^{15} (= possessor, captor), where paronom with n pr.loc מָרֵשָׁה, *inherit* persons, as slaves לָרֶשֶׁת אֲחֻזָּה Lv 25^{46} (H). †**3.** = *impoverish*, הַלְיָרְשֵׁנוּ קְרָאתֶם Ju 14^{15} *to impoverish us did ye call* (us)?

†**Niph.** *Impf* יִוָּרֵשׁ Pr 23^{21}; 2 ms תִּוָּרֵשׁ Gn 45^{11} Pr 20^{13}, אִוָּרֵשׁ Pr 30^{9};—*be* (*dispossessed* =) *impoverished, come to poverty* Gn 45^{11} (E), Pr 20^{13} 23^{21} 30^{9} (opp אֶשְׂבַּע).

†**Pi.** *Impf.* פְּרִי אַדְמָתְךָ יְיָרֵשׁ הַצְּלָצַל Dt 28^{42} *the fruit of thy ground shall the cricket get full possession of* (cf. Qal Ho 9^{6} Is 34^{11}), i e. *devour*

†**Hiph.** *Pf.* 3 ms. הוֹרִישׁ Ju 1^{27}+; 2 ms הוֹרַשְׁתָּ 2 Ch 20^{7} ψ 44^{3}, etc.; *Impf* 3 ms יוֹרִישׁ Jos 3^{10}, וַיּ(ו)רֶשׁ Ju 1^{19}+; 3 fs. sf. 3 mpl. תּוֹרִישֵׁמוֹ Ex 15^{9}, etc., *Inf abs.* הוֹרֵשׁ Jos 3^{10} 17^{13}; הוֹרִישׁ Ju 1^{28}, *cstr.* לְהוֹרִישׁ Dt 4^{38}+, etc.; *Pt* מוֹרִישׁ 1 S 2^{7} Dt 18^{12}, sf מוֹרִישָׁם Dt 9$^{4.5}$;—**1.** *cause to possess*, or *inherit* Ju 11^{24}; מִירֻשָּׁתְךָ אֲשֶׁר הוֹרַשְׁתָּנוּ 2 Ch 20^{11}, sq לְ pers, וְהוֹרַשְׁתֶּם לִבְנֵיכֶם Ezr 9^{12} *and cause your sons to inherit* (it), fig. תּוֹרִישֵׁנִי עֲוֹנוֹת נְעוּרָי Jb 13^{26} *thou makest me to inherit* (the consequences of) *the iniquities of my youth.*

2. *cause* (others) *to possess* or *inherit*, then gen. *dispossess* **a.** sq acc gent vel pers, Jos 13^{13} 16^{10} (both JE), Ju 1$^{29.30.31\ 32.33}$ (all opp ישב בְּקֶרֶב), Jos 14^{12}(JE), 17^{13} (JE; הוֹרֵשׁ לֹא הוֹרִישׁוֹ), Ju 1^{28} (*id*), opp ישב את Jos 15^{63}; opp ישב ב Ju 1$^{21\ 27}$, also Nu 21^{32} Qr, 32^{39} Jos 17^{13} (all JE), 13^{12} (D), Ju 1^{19b} 2^{23}, also 1^{19a} וַיֹּרֶשׁ אֶת־הָהָר (= והוֹרַשְׁתָּם את־יושבי ההר see v^{b}), Dt 7^{17} ψ 44^{3}, וְהַאֲבַדְתָּם Dt 9^{3}, sq acc. + מפני Ex 34^{24} Nu 32^{21} Jos 3^{10} (הוֹרֵשׁ יוֹרִישׁ, all these JE), Dt 4^{38} 9$^{4\ 5}$ 18^{12} Jos 13^{6} 23^{9} (both D), Nu 33$^{52.55}$ (both P), Ju 2^{21} 11$^{23.24}$ 1 K 14^{24} 21^{26} 2 K 16^{3} 17^{8} 21^{2} (all D), 2 Ch 28^{3} 33^{2}, acc + מלפני Dt 11^{23} Jos 23$^{5\ 13}$ (D, ∥ הָדַף), 2 Ch 20^{7}, acc + מִשָּׁם Jos 15^{14} (JE) = Ju 1^{20}; of *cities* (i e. their inhabitants) Jos 8^{7} 17^{12}, so of a *land* = Nu 33^{53} (P). see v$^{52\ 55}$ [𝔊 + יושבי]. **b.** sq acc rei, מבטנו ירשנו אל Jb 20^{15} *God shall cast them out of his belly*, i e. riches (∥ חַיִל בָּלַע וַיְקִאֶנּוּ) **3.** = *impoverish*, יהוה מוריש וּמַעֲשִׁיר 1 S 2^{7} (song) *'י impoverisheth and maketh rich*, sq acc (of Tyre) אֲדֹנָי יוֹרִשֶׁנָּה Zc 9^{4} (see v^{3}) **4.** nearly = *bring to ruin, destroy*, sq. acc gent. אָרִיק חַרְבִּי תורישמו יָדִי Ex 15^{9} (poem in E), so perh also Nu 14^{12} (JE, AV *disinherit*, ∥ אַכֶּנּוּ בַדֶּבֶר) **5.** = **Qal** *take possession of* a land Nu 14^{24} (JE), but rd prob. יִרָשֶׁנָּה.

†יְרֵשָׁה **n.f. a possession**, used of nation וְהָיָה אֱדוֹם יְרֵשָׁה וְהָיָה יְרֵשָׁה שֵׂעִיר אֹיְבָיו Nu 24^{18} (JE)

†יְרוּשָׁא, יְרוּשָׁה **n pr.f.** (*taken possession of*, i e *married*?) mother of king Jotham יְרוּשָׁא 2 K 15^{33} = יְרוּשָׁה 2 Ch 27^{1}

†יְרֻשָּׁה **n f.** (a) **possession, inheritance**,—abs יר׳ Dt 2^{5} + 7 t, cstr. יְרֻשַּׁת Ju 21^{17} ψ 61^{6} (but on text v infr); sf יְרֻשַּׁתְךָ 2 Ch 20^{11}; ירשתו Dt 2^{12} 3^{20}, יְרֻשַּׁתְכֶם Jos 1^{15},—used of land Dt 2$^{5.9.9\ 19\ 19}$ 3^{20}, אֶרֶץ יְרֻשָּׁתוֹ 2^{12} *the land of his possession*, so Jos 1^{15}; further, 12$^{6\ 7}$ Ju 21^{17} (but Bu$^{RS\ 152}$ נִשְׁאָרָה), Je 32^{8} ψ 61^{6} (but < אֲרֶשֶׁת *request*, cf Che$^{crit\ n}$), 2 Ch 20^{11}

†רֶשֶׁת **n f**$^{Ex\ 27\ 5}$ **net**,—abs רֶשֶׁת Ho 5^{1} + 11 t, רָשֶׁת Pr 1^{17}, cstr רֶשֶׁת Ex 27^{4} 38^{4}, sf רִשְׁתִּי Ho 7^{12} + 2 t, רשתו ψ 10^{9} 35^{8}, רִשְׁתָּם Ez 19^{8} ψ 35^{7},—**1.** *net*: **a.** for catching (birds, etc.) חִנָּם מְזֹרָה הָרָשֶׁת Pr 1^{17} *to no purpose is the net spread* in the eyes of any bird, elsewhere fig (1) of judgment of ׳י, all c. פרשׂ Ho 7^{12} (∥ כְּעוֹף הַשָּׁמַיִם אוֹרִידֵם), Ez 12^{13} 17^{20} (both ∥ מְצוּדָתִי), 32^{3} (of ׳י catching Pharaoh, under fig of sea-monster; ∥ 11. חֶרֶם); (2) of nations capturing king of Israel under fig of lion 19^{8} (c. פרשׂ, ∥ שַׁחְתָּם); (3) of priests and rulers (as entangling people in sin) Ho 5^{1} (∥ פַּח) **b.** spread for feet of man (fig): (1) by ׳י La 1^{13} (c פָּרַשׂ); (2) by wicked (= *plot*) Pr 29^{5} (c פרשׂ), ψ 140^{6} (c *id*, ∥ טָמַן פַּח), 10^{9} 25^{15}, שֻׁלַּח בְּרֶשֶׁת בְּרַגְלָיו Jb 18^{8} (∥ שְׂבָכָה), elsewh. c טמן ψ 9^{16} (∥ שַׁחַת), 31^{5} 35^{7} (שַׁחַת רִשְׁתָּם), v^{8}, c. הכין 57^{7} (∥ שִׁיחָה) **2.** brazen *network* for altar of tabern מִכְבַּר מַעֲשֵׂה ר׳ נחשת הָרֶשֶׁת Ex 27$^{4.5}$, 27^{4} = 38^{4} (all P) —On Inf רֶשֶׁת, v. ירש supr

†[מוֹרָשׁ] **n.[m.] a possession**,—cstr מוֹרַשׁ וַיַּ֫שִׁי בית קפד Is 14^{23} *a possession for bitterns*, יַעֲקֹב את מוֹרָשֵׁיהֶם Ob^{17} *and the house of Jacob shall possess their possessions* (but rd perhaps מורישיהם *their dispossessors*, 𝔊 𝔙 𝔗 al); fig מוֹרָשֵׁי לְבָבִי Jb 17^{11}, i e *my cherished thoughts* (∥ זִמֹּתַי), but fig is questionable, v Di, who derives from ארשׁ *desire*, so Buhl

†מוֹרָשָׁה **n.f. a possession**,—מ׳ Ex 6^{8} + 8 t;—of land Dt 33^{4} (poem), Ex 6^{8} (P), Ez 11^{15} 25^{10} 33^{24} 36$^{2.5}$, of people Ez 25^{4} 36^{3}.

†מוֹרֶשֶׁת **n.pr.loc.** apparently in neighbourhood of Gath Mi 1^{14} (גַּת vocative, acc to We, > most, who render *M. of Gath*), prob home of prophet Micah, v foll.

†מ(ו)רַשְׁתִּי **adj. gent.** only מִיכָה הַמֹּרַשְׁתִּי Mi 1^{1}, מִיכָיָה הַמּוֹ׳ Je 26^{18}, v. foregoing.

†תִּירוֹשׁ **n m.**$^{Ju\ 9.13}$ **must, fresh** or **new wine**,—abs תירוש Nu 18^{12} + 24 t.; תירש Gn 27^{28} + 3 t., sf. תירושי Ju 9^{13} Ho 2^{11}, תִּירֹשְׁךָ Dt 7^{13} + 4 t Dt, תירושך Is 62^{8}, תִּירוֹשָׁם ψ 4^{8},—*must, new wine*, as enlivening ת׳ הַמְשַׂמֵּחַ אֱלֹהִים וַאֲנָשִׁים Ju 9^{13}, as injurious זְנוּת וְיַיִן ות׳ יִקַּח־לֵב Ho 4^{11}; poet regarded as contained in the grapes יִמָּצֵא הַתּ׳ בָּאֶשְׁכּוֹל Is 65^{8}, cf 24^{7} (∥ גֶּפֶן); as yielding wine (∥ יַיִן) תִּדְרֹךְ זַיִת וְלֹא תָסוּךְ שֶׁמֶן ות׳ ולא תשתה יָיִן Mi 6^{15}, usu as a sign of fertility, or as valuable product. ות׳ יְקָבֶיךָ יִפְרֹצוּ Pr 3^{10} *with must thy vats shall burst open*; + דָּגָן (q v.) Gn 27$^{28.37}$ (both J) Ho 2^{11} 7^{14} Zc 9^{17} ψ 4^{8} Is 62^{8}; ת׳ Ho 9^{2} (∥ גֹּרֶן ,יֶקֶב, cf דָּגָן v^{1}), אֶרֶץ ד׳ ות׳ Dt 33^{28}; + יִצְהָר Jo 2^{24} Ne 10^{38} (+ פְּרִי כָל־עֵץ), + דָּגָן and יִצְהָר Ho 2^{10} 3^{24} Dt 7^{13} 11^{14} 12^{17} 14^{23} 18^{4} 28^{51} Je 31^{12} Hg 1^{11} Jo 1^{10} 2^{19} 2 Ch 32^{28} Ne 5^{11} 10^{40} 13$^{5\ 12}$, חֵלֶב ת׳ Nu 18^{12} (v. ח׳; + *id*.); ת׳ 2 Ch 31^{5} + דגן, יצהר, and דְּבַשׁ; אֶרֶץ דָּגָן ות׳ אֶרֶץ לֶחֶם וּכְרָמִים Is 36^{17} = 2 K 18^{32} (+ ארץ זית יצהר ודבש)

[וַיִּשֶׂם] **vb.** *Impf.* וַיִּישֶׂם Gn 50^{26}, and so 24^{33} Kt, v. שׂוּם, שִׂים.

יִשְׂרָאֵל **n.pr.**, and deriv., v. sub 1 שׂרה.

יְשַׂרְאֵלָה **n.pr.m.** a son of Asaph 1 Ch. 25^{14} = אֲשַׂרְאֵלָה (q.v.) v^{2} (etym dubious)

†יִשָּׂשכָר$_{43}$ (so always MT, Qr perpet., Ben Napht. יִשָּׂכָר Baer$^{Gn\ p.\ 84f.}$) **n.pr.m. Issachar** (etym. and mng. dub., MT as if Niph. Impf. √שׂכר; Kt = יֵשׁ שָׂכָר *there is recompense* (cf. Gn 30^{18}), so Thes al; this the true etym. acc. to Ol $^{§§ 69 e; 277 f.}$ Ko$^{I\ 120}$ v יֵשׁ שָׂכָר Je 31^{16} 2 Ch 15^{7}; = אִישׁ שָׂכָר (a more prob. combination in n pr.) We $^{Sam\ 95}$; > יִשָּׂכָר (MT), or יִשָּׂא שׂכר; 𝔊 Ισσαχαρ, see esp. Gn 30^{18} Ισσαχαρ, ὅ ἐστιν μισθός) — **1.** fifth son of Jacob and Leah (appar. ninth son of Jacob) Gn 30^{18} 35^{23} 46^{13} 49^{14} Ex 1^{3} Nu 1^{8}; בני יש׳ Nu 1^{28} 2^{5} 26^{23} Jos 19^{17} 1 Ch 7^{1} 12^{33} (v^{32} van d. H); מִשְׁפְּחוֹת יש׳ Nu 26^{25} 1 Ch 7^{5}; מַטֵּה יש׳ Nu 1^{29} 2^{5} 13^{7} Jos 21$^{6.28}$ 1 Ch 6$^{47.57}$; מטה בני יש׳ Nu 10^{15} 34^{26} Jos 19^{23}; בית יש׳ 1 K 15^{27}, hence יש׳ alone = *tribe* of Issachar, Nu 7^{18} Dt 27^{12} 33^{18} Jos 19^{17} Ju 5$^{15.15}$ 10^{1} Ez 48^{33} (שער יש׳), 1 Ch 27^{18} 2 Ch 30^{18}, = *territory* of the tribe Jos 17$^{10.11}$ 1 K 4^{17} 1 Ch 12^{41} (v^{40} van d H.), transit. fr *tribe* to *territory* Ez 48$^{25.26}$. **2.** 7th son of Obed-Edom 1 Ch 26^{5}.

יֵשׁ$_{137}$ **subst.** being, substance, existence (on etym. v **2**)—יֵשׁ Gn 18^{24} etc., יֶשׁ־ 31^{29} + oft.; הֲיֵשׁ 24^{23} + 18 t. (so אִשׁ 2 S 14^{19}†, הַאִשׁ Mic 6^{10}†, v. p. 78), with sf יֶשְׁךָ v^{42} + 2 t.; יֶשְׁכֶם v^{49}†; הֲיִשְׁכֶם Dt 13^{4}†; יֶשְׁנוֹ (Ol$^{§ 97 b}$ Sta$^{§ 370 b}$) 29^{14} 1 S 14^{39} (+ v^{41} 𝔊 We Dr), 23^{23} Est 3^{8}†,—**1.** *substance*, only Pr 8^{21} לְהַנְחִיל אֹהֲבַי יֵשׁ to cause them that love me to inherit *substance* (so Sir 42^{3}). **2.** elsewhere (prop. as a subst. in the *st c*), it asserts *existence*, and so corresponds to the *verb substantive*, is (**are, was, were, will be**), lit. *the being, presence of* . . . (so BA אִתַי, Aram. איתא, אית, ܐܝܬ [whence ܐܝܬܝܐ (self-)*existent*, ܐܝܬܘܬܐ *essence, substance*], with לָא contr. לֵית, לית, ܠܝܬ; Mand. עת, עית, לאית, Ar. [with irreg. س] لَيْسَ (inflected as a verb, لَيْسَتْ, لَسْتُ, etc.; W$^{AG\ I\ § 182,\ II,\ § 42}$) *is not* (أَيْسَ is known only in two proverbial sayings, as a secondary form, Fl$^{Kl.\ Schr\ I\ 146f}$), As. *išû, be, have* Dl$^{HWB\ 310}$; with affix 1 s. *la-a i-ša-a-ku, I have not*, TP $^{I,\ 57f.}$. On this word, see esp. No$^{M\ § 213}$, who exemplifies its different constructions in Semitic, and shews how it tends to pass into a verb;—(1) in BAram. Syr. Bab 𝔗, with possessive sf, (2) in later Pal. diall, Jer. 𝔗, Jer. Talm, sts. also in Bab 𝔗 and Syr, with independent pers. pron. (as לית הוא, לית אנא); (3) in Mand. Bab. Talm., sometimes in Syr. and Ar., and in Heb. יֶשְׁנוֹ, with object. (verbal) sf.; (4) in Ar., as a true verb. In Eth. ቦ: lit. *therein*, Germ. *es gibt*, is similar in use (Di$^{Gr\ § 167\ 1}$), though not of course in origin. In Heb. the corresponding neg is אַיִן, q.v, the construction of which is quite similar)—**is, are, was, were,** etc., not, however, as a mere copula, but implying existence with emph (hence in Engl. to be often represented by the subst verb in italics): **a.** with a pred. following, Gn 28^{16} אכן יש י׳ במקום הזה surely Y. *is* (emph.) in this place! 44^{26} אם יֵשׁ אָחִינוּ אִתָּנוּ, Ex 17^{7} הֲיֵשׁ יהוה בקרבנו אם אָיִן, Nu 22^{29} לו יש חרב בידי Oh that there *were* a sword in my hand! Dt 13^{4} הֲיִשְׁכֶם אֹהֲבִים whether you *do* love, 29^{17} פן יש בכם איש, v^{18} 1 S 9$^{11f.}$ and they said, *Is* the seer here? and they said יֵשׁ *He is*, 20^{8} 23^{23} Je 27^{18}. Alone, in answer to a question (asked with הֲיֵשׁ), *He* (*it*) *is*: †1 S 9^{12} 2 K 10^{15} Je 37^{17}. But Je 23^{26} (where יש has no subst. or sf) text must be corrupt: cf. Gie. **b.** absolutely, *there is* (*es gibt, il y a*), Gn 18^{24} אולי יש חמשים צדיקים בעיר perhaps there *are* fifty righteous in the city, 24^{23} הישׁ בית אביך מקום לנו ללין, 42^{1} כי יש שבר במצ׳ that there *was* corn in Egypt, Ju 4^{20} היש פה איש, 2 S 9^{1} 2 K 5^{8} he shall know that there *is* (emph) a prophet in Israel, Ru 3^{12} there *is* a kinsman nearer than I, ψ 58^{12} surely there *are* gods judging on the earth: so in aphorisms, asserting the existence of a partic. character, quality, etc, Pr 11^{24} יש מפזר ונוסף עוד, 12^{18} 13$^{7.23}$ 14^{12} 16^{25} 18^{24} 20^{15} Ec 2^{21} 4^{8} 5^{12} 6$^{1.11}$ 7$^{15.15}$ 8$^{14.14.14}$ 10^{5}. In questions, or protestations, יֵשׁ often implies a doubt whether what is asked about is to be found or exists: 1 K 18^{10} Je 5^{1} and see אם יש איש if there *is* (emph.) a man doing justice, etc. (cf. ψ 14^{2}), 14^{22} Is 44^{8} היש אלהים *is* there a god beside me? ψ 7^{4} אם יש עול בכפי if there *is* iniquity in my hands! 73^{11} *is* there knowledge in the Most High? Jb 5^{1} 6^{30} La 1^{12}. **c.** special phrases:—(*a*) after אם and a ptcp, where an abiding *intention* is to be emphasized, †Gn 24^{42} אם־ישך־נא מצליח דרכי if thou *art* (really) prospering my way, v^{49} 43^{4} Ju 6^{36} (cf. II. אַיִן **2 b**). (*b*) יֵשׁ לְ = *has* (*had*), esp. with prons. יֵשׁ לִי, יֵשׁ לְךָ, etc., Gn 33^{9} יֶשׁ־לִי רָב *I have* plenty, v^{11} 43^{7} היש לכם אח, 44^{20} יש לנו אב זקן, 1 S 17^{46} that they may know כי יש אֱלֹהִים לְיִשׂראל that Israel *has* (emph) a god, 2 K 4^{2} מַה־יֶּשׁ־לָכִי what *hast* thou? Jb 14^{7} for a tree *has* (emph.) hope (cf. Ru 1^{12}), 25^{2} 28^{1} 38^{28} היש למטר אב: Gn 39$^{4.5.8}$

כל אשר יֶשׁ־לוֹ all that he had (v[4] without אשר, prob. error) (*c*) with inf and ל, *is it possible to . . ?* 2 K 4[13] היש לדבר־לך *can* (I) *speak* for thee to the king? 2 Ch 25[9], so אש ל 2 S 14[19] (cf אין ל, sub II אַיִן **5**) (*d*). יֵשׁ אֲשֶׁר (if) *it was* that . . . †Nu 9[20.21], there *were* some who. (with ptcp) †Ne 5[2.3.4] (cf Syr ܐܝܬ ܕ for ὁ μὲν . . . ὁ δὲ. Mt 13[8], ܐܝܬ ܕܐܦ PS[172]) (*e*) יֶשׁ־לְאֵל יָדִי Gn 31[29] al, v II אֵל **7**, p. 43 (*f*) 2 K 10[15] וָיֵשׁ *and* (if) *it be*. (cf Pr 5[17] 2 S 13[26]), so Ju 6[13] ויש י׳ אִתָּנוּ (*g*) pleon אין יֵשׁ †ψ 135[17]. (*h*) לא יש †Jb 9[33] (cf لَيْسَ ܠܝܬ: but 𝔊 𝔖 Me al לֵא)—As a rule, יש precedes its subst (from which, however, like אין, it may be separated: Gn 24[23] 43[7] הֲיֵשׁ לָכֶם אָח, 44[19.20] 1 S 20[8] etc), but occasionally, for greater emphasis, this is prefixed: 1 S 21[5] כי אם לחם קדש יש but holy bread *there is!* Is 43[8] the blind people, ועינים יש though it *has* eyes, Ju 19[19] לחם ויין יש לי (cf אַיִן **2 c**)

יָשַׁב [1090] **vb. sit, remain, dwell** (NH *id.*, Aram יתיב, ܝܬܒ, MI[10.31] ישב, I[8.19] וישב, I[13] ואשב, *dwell*, Ph ישב *dwell*, Zinj ישב *sit* DHM[Sendsch 58], As *ašābu, sit, dwell*, Dl[HWB 244], Ar وَثَبَ *leap, jump*, Himyer dial *sit*, Lane[2919], Eth ወሰበ: II 1 *secum cohabitare facere, marry, consummate marriage*, cf **Hiph. 4)**—**Qal** *Pf* 3 ms יָשַׁב Gn 13[12]+, 2 ms יָשַׁבְתָּ Ju 5[16], וְיָשַׁבְתָּה בָּהּ consec Dt 17[14], 2 mpl יְשַׁבְתֶּם Dt 1[46] Lv 18[3], וישבתם consec Lv 25[18]+7 t, etc, *Impf* יֵשֵׁב 1 S 5[7]+, יֵשֶׁב־ Gn 44[33] Ez 44[3], יֵשֶׁב before monosyll. 1 K 7[8] Jb 22[8], וַיֵּשֶׁב Gn 4[16]+, וַתֵּשֶׁב Ru 4[1], 1 s אשב Ju 6[18]+, וָאֵשֵׁב Dt 9[9]+3 t+Ez 3[15b] (but Co אשר Kt); אֵשְׁבָה 1 S 27[5], אֵשֵׁבָה Is 49[20]; וָאֵשְׁבָה Ez 9[3], 3 mpl יֵשְׁבוּ Gn 47[4]+; 3 fpl תישבנה Ez 35[9] Kt (i e תֵּישַׁבְנָה Ol[§242d] Ko [1 401]), Qr תָּשׁוּבְנָה (√שוב), Co prop תִּוָּשַׁבְנָה, 1 pl נשב Je 42[13.14], וְנֵשֶׁב Nu 20[15]+5 t, *Imv.* ms שֵׁב Gn 20[15]+, שֶׁב־ Gn 35[1], שְׁבָה Gn 27[19]+, fs שְׁבִי Gn 38[11]+, mpl שְׁבוּ Gn 22[5]+, etc., *Inf. abs* יָשׁוֹב 1 S 20[5], *cstr* שֶׁבֶת 1 S 7[2]+; שֶׁבֶת Is 40[22]+, sf שִׁבְתִּי 2 S 7[5]+, etc, *Pt* m י(ו)שב Gn 4[20] 24[3]+, etc.; f יֹשֶׁבֶת Na 3[8], י(ו)שבת Ju 4[5]+, יֹשַׁבְתְּ Jos 2[5] 2 K 4[13], יֹשַׁבְתִּי Je 22[23], י(ו)שבתי Je 10[17] La 4[21] Ez 27[3] (Kt preferable in all these, v. Ol[§123d] Ges[§90.3a]), fpl ישבות 1 S 27[8],—**1. a.** *sit* on (עַל) a seat 1 S 20[25], stone Ex 17[12], teraphim Gn 31[34], couch 48[2] (all E), Ez 23[41], knees 2 K 4[20], throne Ex 11[5] 12[29] (J), Dt 17[18] 1 S 1[9] 4[13] 1 K 1[13.17.20]+, v abs. infr.; of י׳, הַיּשֵׁב עַל־חוּג הָאָרֶץ Is 40[22], dust Is 47[1], ground (אֶרֶץ) Ez 26[16], ashes Jon 3[6] (these in token of humiliation), *sit down* by (עַל) a well Ex 2[15] or pool 2 S 2[13]; c אֶל 1 S 28[23], *sit* in (ב) house, street, doorway, assembly, etc 2 S 7[1] Ju 19[15] Gn 38[14] (J), Je 15[17] 26[10] ψ 1[1] Ct 2[3] so Ez 31[6.17] (fig); of No of Amon (personif city) הַיּשְׁבָה בַּיְאֹרִים Na 3[8] *she who sate amid the rivers*, c ל *sit on to* (pregn.) לָאָרֶץ Is 3[26] 47[1] La 2[10], לכסא ψ 9[5], *at*, לפתח בית Pr 9[14], (י)לימינו 1 K 2[19], ψ 110[1]; לַמַּבּוּל ψ 29[10]; c לפני Gn 43[33] (J), + שָׁם Ju 20[26] 21[2] 2 S 7[18] = 1 Ch 17[16], c עם 1 S 20[5] Pr 31[23]; c אֶת־ Je 16[8] Jb 2[13], c תַּחַת Ju 6[11] Mi 4[4], וַיֵּשֶׁב תַּחְתֶּיהָ בַּצֵּל Jon 4[5], c מנגד Gn 21[16.16] (E), נֶגֶד Is 47[14], מִקֶּדֶם לָעִיר Jon 4[5]; c מִצַּד 1 S 20[25] Ru 2[14]; c. acc cogn. Ez 28[2], לשפט Ex 18[13] Jo 4[12] (cf ψ 9[5] Is 28[6]), hence abs of *sitting* as *king* or *judge* Ex 18[14] ψ 61[8] Mal 3[3], יושבים Is 10[13], perh. Am 1[5.8], esp of י׳ *sitting* (enthroned), ψ 2[4] 9[8] 29[10] 55[20] 102[13] La 5[19], so in ישב (הַ)כרובים 1 S 4[4] 2 S 6[2] = 1 Ch 13[6], 2 K 19[15] ψ 99[1]; ישב תהלות יִשְׂרָאֵל ψ 22[4] (v c עַל, supr.), by meton of thrones, for the judges sitting on them שָׁמָּה יָשְׁבוּ כִסְאוֹת לְמִשְׁפָּט ψ 122[5], הַיּשְׁבִים Ru 4[4], i e in the gate (cf v[11]), those in whose presence purchase of land took place **b.** *sit, sit down*, abs, Ju 19[6] Ru 4[1.2] Ne 1[4] Je 36[15] (sq cl of purpose, *to eat*, etc.) Gn 37[25] Est 3[15]+; opp קום Ex 32[6] (JE) ψ 139[2], מאחרי שבת ψ 127[2] (opp מַשְׁכִּימֵי קוּם), so Is 37[28] = 2 K 19[27] (rd. לְפָנֶי קָמְךָ at end of v[27] = 2 K 19[26] We in Bl[Einl. 4. 257] RS[Proph 361, and n 9]), but also קוּמִי שְּׁבִי Is 52[2], expl. by (הִתְנַעֲרִי מֵעָפָר וַיָּשַׁב) מֵהָאָרֶץ אל־רַמֶּטָּה 1 S 28[23] and) 2 S 19[9] †**c.** *sit down* outside (חוּץ), i e. perform a necessity of nature Dt 23[14] †**d.** *sit* = *be set* (as a jewel), יֹשְׁבוֹת עַל־מִלֵּאת Ct 5[12] *set on a filling* (i e in a setting, De al), in description of eyes, (> others *sitting by full streams*). **2. a.** *remain, stay, tarry* (for a limited or indef time), c אֵת pers Gn 24[55] (J), Ju 19[4] 2 S 16[8]; c. עם pers Gn 27[44] (J), עִמָּדִי 29[19] (E), Ju 17[10], c ב loc 1 S 7[2] (of ark), 13[16] 14[2] 24[4] (23[29] rd אֲשֶׁר for וַיֵּשֶׁב 𝔊 We Dr Klo Kit Bu), 2 S 10[5] 19[25] (where rd. שבתו for שִׁיבָתוֹ Dr Klo Bu, v We), Nu 35[25] (P), Jb 24[13], c. שָׁם עַד־עוֹלָם 1 K 11[16], 1 S 1[22]; c. על (*by*) 1 S 25[13] 30[24]; שְׁבוּ לָכֶם פֹּה עִם־ 2 K 7[4], בה Gn 22[5] (E); c בין Ju 5[16], מחוץ ל Lv 14[8] (P), אֵצֶל 1 S 20[19], c. acc. בית 2 S 6[11] 13[20] Ru 2[7], abs 1 S 1[23.23]; *abide, endure* Mi 5[3], ויהודה לעולם תשב Jo 4[20], so of Mt. Zion ψ 121[1]. **b.** with

special emphasis on qualifying phr, וַתֵּשֶׁב בְּאֵיתָן קַשְׁתּוֹ Gn 49^{24} *and his bow abode as a firm one* (poem in J); 1 K 22^{1} *and they continued* three years without war; of woman *remaining* ברמי טָהֳרָה Lv 12^{4}, על־דמי וגו׳ v^{5} **3.** *dwell, have one's abode* in (ב) a land, city, house, etc., Gn 4^{16} 13$^{7.12.12}$ 19^{29} 24$^{37.62}$ Dt 1^{4} 3^{2} Jos 20^{6} 2 S 7^{6} + oft. (on 2 S 21^{16} v. ישבו בְנֹב, p 444); in tents Je 35$^{7.10}$ 1 Ch 5^{10}; fig. of justice (צְדָקָה) Is 32^{16} (‖וְשָׁכַן מִשְׁפָּט); in the midst of (בְּקֶרֶב) Gn 24^{3} Jos 13^{13} 16^{10} Ju 1$^{30.32.33}$ 3^{5}; so c. בְּתוֹךְ Gn 23^{10} (P); c. על + הארץ, of God 1 K 8^{27} = 2 Ch 6^{18}; of people Lv 25$^{18.19}$ 26^{35} (H); c. לְ Jb 15^{28}; c. בין Gn 20^{1} (E); *dwell with* (אֶת) Gn 34$^{16.22}$ (P), Ex 2^{21} (E), Jos 15^{63} (JE), Ju 1$^{16.21}$ 17^{11}; יֵשְׁבוּ יְשָׁרִים אֶת־פָּנֶיךָ ψ 140^{14}; so c. עִם Jos 20^{4} Dt 23^{17} (+בקרב), ψ 26^{4} (i e *assoc with*, c. יַחְדָּו Gn 13$^{6.6}$ (J), 36^{7} (P), Dt 25^{5}, שֶׁבֶת גַּם יָחַד ψ 133^{1}; *dwell* in their stead (תַּחְתָּם) Dt 2$^{12.21.22.23}$ 1 Ch 4^{41} 5^{22}; abs לָשֶׁבֶת יְצָרָהּ Is 45^{18} *for dwelling he formed it* (the earth); (*thy*) *dwelling-place* is מְקוֹם שִׁבְתְּךָ 1 K 8^{30} = 2 Ch 6^{21}, also מכון ש׳ 1 K 8$^{39.43.49}$ = 2 Ch 6$^{30.33.39}$, so ψ 33^{14}; מָכוֹן לְשׁ׳ Ex 15^{17} 1 K 8^{13} = 2 Ch 6^{2}. *Pt.* ישב = subst., *dweller, inhabitant*, very oft (c. 215 t) e g. ישב אהלים Gn 25^{27} (J); oft. coll ישב אהל Gn 4^{20} (J), ישב הָאָרֶץ 34^{30} 50^{11} (both J), Ex 34$^{12.15}$ (JE); also poet f., (as coll., v Dr on 1 S 17^{21}) יוֹשֶׁבֶת שָׁפִיר etc, Mi 1$^{11.11.12.13.15}$, יוֹשֶׁבֶת צִיּוֹן + Is 12^{6} Je 51^{35}, similarly + 10^{17} 21^{13} 22^{23} 48^{19} (cf La 4^{21}) Zc 2^{11}, with בת in app (Da$^{§28 R 6}$), יוֹשֶׁבֶת בַּת־מִצְרַיִם + Je 46^{19}, so 48^{18}; more usu pl. ישבי הערים Gn 19^{25} (J), cf Dt 13^{14}; ישבי הָאָרֶץ Ex 23^{31} (JE), cf. Ex 15$^{14.15}$ (poem in E); יֹשְׁבֵי תבל Is 18^{3}, יוֹשְׁבֵי חָדֶל 38^{11}, etc.; ישביה Lv 18^{25} 25^{10} (H), Nu 13^{32} (P); abs. יושב (coll) Am 1$^{5.8}$ Is 49^{19}; הַיּוֹשְׁבִים 1 Ch 9^{2}; also (strangely) יֹשְׁבוֹת הארץ 1 S 27^{8} = *the populations of the land* We Dr (elsewhere in this sense only fs. and poet., v. supr.), freq in phr *without inhabitant* (i e. so that there shall be no inhab.), מֵאֵין יושב Is 5^{9} 6^{4} Je 4^{7} 26^{9} 33^{10} 34^{22} 44^{22} 46^{19} 51$^{29.37}$ Zp 2^{5} 3^{6}; מֵאֵין יושב בָּהֵן Je 48^{9}, לְבִלְתִּי; 50^{3}; לא יִהְיֶה יושב בָּהּ, 9^{10}, 2^{15} מבלי ישב הֱיוֹת־בּוֹ יושב 51^{62} **4.** of a land or city, *sit, abide seated in its place*, fig. for *be inhabited* Je 17$^{6.25}$ 50$^{13.39}$ Ez 26^{20} 29^{11} 36^{35} Is 13^{20} (‖לא תשכון), Zc 2^{8} 9^{5} 14^{11}; וְיָשְׁבָה תַחְתֶּיהָ 12^{6} 14^{10}; Ez 35^{9} Kt is תשבנה, Qr תָּשׁוּבֶנָה; Co תושבנה, i.e Niph. תֵּוָשַׁבְנָה (cf 36^{10}), or Hoph תּוּשַׁבְנָה (cf Is 44^{26}), of palace, וְאַרְמוֹן עַל־מִשְׁפָּטוֹ יֵשֵׁב Je 30^{18}.

†Niph. *Pf* 3 fs נוֹשָׁבָה Je 6^{8}; 3 pl וְנֹשְׁבוּ consec Ez 36^{10}, נוֹשָׁבוּ Ez 26^{19}, נוֹשָׁ֑בָה Je 22^{6}; *Pt* f. נוֹשֶׁבֶת Ez 26^{17} (> נִשְׁבַּת 𝔊 Co, √שבת), נוֹשֶׁבֶת Ex 16^{35}; pl. נוֹשָׁבוֹת Ez 12^{20} 38^{12};—*be inhabited*, of land Ex 16^{35} (perh. = *be habitable*), Je 6^{8}; of cities Je 22^{6} Ez 12^{20} 26^{19} 36^{10}; חֳרָבוֹת נוֹשָׁבוֹת Ez 38^{12};—Ez 26^{17} v. supr; 35^{9} v **Qal 4.**

†Pi. *Pf* 3 mpl וְיִשְּׁבוּ טִירוֹתֵיהֶם בָּךְ Ez 25^{4} *and they shall set their encampments in thee* (𝔊 𝔖 Co וְיָשְׁבוּ *inhabit*)

†Hiph. *Pf* 3 ms הֹשִׁיב Ezr 10^{14}, sf הוֹשִׁיבַנִי La 3^{6} ψ 143^{3}; 1 s. הוֹשַׁבְתִּי Lv 23^{43}, וְה(וֹ)שַׁבְתִּים consec. Ho 11^{11} Je 32^{37}; והושבותים consec Zc 10^{6} (Ko$^{i, 413}$, but prob. txt err., vid Thes and Ges$^{Lgb 464}$; rd prob. וַהֲשִׁבוֹתִים as v^{10}, so Sta$^{ZAW 1881, 21}$ We), etc; *Impf* 3 ms. וַיּוֹשֶׁב Gn 47^{11}, וַיּוֹשֶׁב 2 Ch 8^{2} ψ 107^{36}; sf. וַיּוֹשִׁיבֵנִי 1 K 2^{24} (Ko$^{i, 414, 224}$); וַיֹּשִׁיבֵם Jb 36^{7}; 1 pl. וַנֹּשֶׁב Ezr 10^{2}, etc; *Imv.* ms. הושב Gn 47^{6}, mpl. ה(וֹ)שִׁיבוּ 1 K 21$^{9.10}$; *Inf cstr.* ה(וֹ)שִׁיב 1 S 2^{8} Ne 13^{27}; הוֹשִׁיבִי ψ 113^{8} (Ol^{§123d}; rd -בוֹ, v Che), *Pt.* abs. מוֹשִׁיב ψ 68^{7}, cstr. מוֹשִׁיבִי ψ 113^{9} (Ol$^{l.c.}$ Ges$^{l.c.}$);—**1.** *cause to sit* c. acc. pers + על כסא 1 K 2^{24} 2 Ch 23^{20} so (without על כסא) + לָנֶצַח Jb 36^{7}; *set, place* c acc. pers. + נגדו 1 K 21^{10}, also v$^{9.12}$ (בְּרֹאשׁ הָעָם) **2.** *cause to abide* (acc pers.) *at* (ב) 1 S 30^{21}. **3. a.** *cause to dwell*, c. acc. pers. + ב loc. 1 S 12^{8} 2 K 17^{6} Ho 12^{10}, Gn 47$^{6.11}$ (P), Lv 23^{43} (H), La 3^{6} ψ 143^{3}, בְּאֶרֶץ תַּחְתִּיּוֹת Ez 26^{20}; acc. pers. om. 2 K 17$^{24.26}$; acc pers. + שָׁם 2 Ch 8^{2} ψ 107^{36}, acc. pers. + עַל־הַבָּתִּים Ho 11^{11} (but rd וַהֲשִׁבֹתִים We), acc pers. om, c. עִם pers. 1 S 2^{8} ψ 113^{8}; מוֹשִׁיב יְחִידִים בַּיְתָה ψ 68^{7} *causing solitary ones to dwell in a house* (or is מושיב for משיב Bae?), c. acc. pers only מוֹשִׁ׳ עֲקֶרֶת הַבַּיִת ψ 113^{9} *giving a dwelling to her that is barren of house;* abs. c. לָבֶטַח Je 32^{37} ψ 4^{9}; abs. c כְּקַדְמוֹתֵיכֶם Ez 36^{11}. On Zc 10^{6}, v. supr. **b.** *cause* cities (עָרִים) *to be inhabited* Ez 36^{33} Is 54^{3} **4.** *marry* (prop. *give a dwelling* to, cf. ψ 113^{9}), only Ezr Ne, and only c. acc נָשִׁים נָכְרִיּוֹת *strange* or *foreign women* Ezr 10$^{2.10.14.17.18}$ Ne 13^{27}; so הֹשִׁיבוּ נָשִׁים אַשְׁדֳּדִיּוֹת Ne 13^{23}.

†Hoph. *Pf* וְהוּשַׁבְתֶּם לְבַדְּכֶם בְּקֶרֶב הָאָרֶץ Is 5^{8} *and ye be made to dwell alone in the midst of the land* *Impf.* הָאֹמֵר לִירוּשָׁלַםִ תּוּשָׁב Is 44^{26} *he who saith of Jerusalem, she shall be inhabited.* Ez 35^{9} v. **Qal 4.**

† **I. שֶׁבֶת n.f. seat, dwelling, place** (properly Inf Qal from ישב)—מְקוֹם הַשָּׁבֶת 1 K 10^{19} = 2 Ch 9^{18} *the place of the seat;* שֶׁבֶת חָמָס Am 6^{3} *a seat* (*throne*, or *enthronement*) *of violence;* לְשֶׁבֶת עָר Nu 21^{15} *toward the dwelling* (i.e. *place*,

location) *of* ʿ*Âr*; יִשָּׂרְפוּ בַּשָּׁבֶת 2 S 23[7] *they are burned in the* (same) *place*, i e. *on the spot*, but del. ׳ש We Dr Bu, שִׁבְתּ׳ Ob[3] *his* (thy) *dwelling-place*.—II שֶׁבֶת v sub שבת

† I [שִׁיבָה] **n.f.** sojourn (=*ישִׁיבָה acc to Thes)—only בשיבתו 2 S 19[33] *during his sojourn*, but rd בְּשִׁבְתּוֹ, v יָשַׁב **Qal 2.**—II שִׁיבָה v sub שוב.

† יֶשֶׁבְאָב **n.pr.m.** Levite of the 14th course 1 Ch 24[13], but 𝔊 Γελβα, A 𝔊L Ισβααλ

† יֹשֵׁב בַּשֶּׁבֶת **n.pr.m.** one of David's heroes 2 S 23[8] 𝔊 Ιεβοσθε, 𝔊L Ιεσβααλ (‖ 1 Ch 11[11] has יָשָׁבְעָם, q v. sub שוב), id אישבשת q v.

† ישבו בנב Kt, יִשְׁבִּי בְנֹב Qr, **n pr.m.** a gigantic Philistine 2 S 21[16]; but read וַיֵּשְׁבוּ בְנֹב *and they dwelt in Gob*, and tr to v[15] We Dr Bu.

† יָשְׁבְּקָשָׁה **n pr.m** a son of Heman 1 Ch 25[4.24], 𝔊 Ιειβασακα(ταν), Βακατα, 𝔊L Ιεσβοκ

† יוֹשִׁבְיָה **n.pr.m.** (׳י *setteth, causeth to dwell*, cf Ph n pr ישבעל (?=ישבבעל))—a Simeonite 1 Ch 4[35] 𝔊 Ισαβια, 𝔊L Ιωσαβια

† מוֹשָׁב **n.m.** [2 K 2, 19] **seat, assembly, dwelling-place, dwelling, dwellers**,—abs מ׳ ψ 107[4] +4 t, cstr מושב Ex 12[40]+9 t, sf מוֹשָׁבִי Jb 29[7] etc, pl cstr מושבי Ez 34[13]; sf. 2 mpl מושבתיכם etc. Ex 12[20]+11 t; sf. 3 mpl מוֹשְׁבֹתָם etc 10[23]+5 t, מושבתיהם Ez 37[23], but read מְשׁוּב׳ *their apostasies* 𝔊 Comm, see VB, מושבותיהם Ez 6[14],—**1. a.** *seat* 1 S 20[18.25.25] Jb 29[7], fig מ׳ אלהים יָשַׁבְתִּי Ez 28[2] **b.** *sitting*=*those sitting, sitting company* or *assembly*, מושב עֲבָדָיו 1 K 10[5] (‖ מַעֲמַד מְשָׁרְתָיו)=2 Ch 9[4], so ψ 1[1] 107[32] (‖ קהל) **2. a.** *dwelling-place* of people, tribe, etc, oft.=territory, district, or, later, city, Gn 10[30] 27[39] (both J), Ex 10[23] (E), Nu 24[21] (JE), Gn 36[43] (P), Ez 6[14] 48[15] 1 Ch 4[33] 6[39] 7[28]; מ׳ הָאָרֶץ Ex 34[13]=*habitable places of the land*, distinct from city עָרֵיהֶם במושבתם Nu 31[10], cf Ez 6[6], but also עיר מושב ψ 107[4.7.36], of Zion as מ׳ ׳י ψ 132[13] **b** alm.=abstr *dwelling* בית מושב Lv 25[29] (P); אֶרֶץ מ׳ Nu 15[2] *land of your dwelling-places* or *dwelling* (P) **c.** =house Ex 12[20] (‖ בית v[19]), 35[3] Lv 3[17] 7[26] 13[46] 23[3.14.21.31] Nu 35[29] (all P), Lv 23[17] (H) **3.** *situation* of city 2 K 2[19], *location* of image Ez 8[3] **4.** *time of dwelling* Ex 12[40] (P) **5.** coll = *those dwelling*, כל מושב ונו׳ 2 S 9[12] *all those dwelling* in the house of Siba—Ez 37[23] v. supr. and מְשׁוּבָה sub שוב

† תּוֹשָׁב **n.m.** [Lv 25 45] sojourner, only P (H) and late; abs ת׳ Gn 23[4]+6 t, cstr. תושב Lv 22[10], sf תּוֹשָׁבְךָ 25[6], pl תושבים v[6]+2 t.; cstr. תשבי 1 K 17[1], but read תִּשְׁבֶּה (q v.) 𝔊 Ew Th Hi,—*sojourner*, appar of a more temporary and dependent (Lv 22[10] 25[6]) kind than the גר (with which it is often joined)· ‖ שָׂכִיר Ex 12[45] (P), Lv 22[10] (ת׳ כֹּהֵן a priest's *sojourner*), 25[6.40] (all H); הַתּוֹשָׁבִים הַגָּרִים עִמָּכֶם v[45] (c. pt גָּר also v[6]), c עם, also Lv 25[47 47] (H); c בתוך Nu 35[15] (P) Fig of one enjoying only a temporary tenure, c. עם Gn 23[4], with ׳י Lv 25[23] ψ 39[13], c לִפְנֵי 1 Ch 29[15].—1 K 17[1] v supr

יִשְׁבָּח **n.pr.m.** v שבח.

יָשָׁבְעָם, יָשֻׁבִי v שוב.

יִשְׁבָּק v שבק

ישה (√of following, meaning uncertain; acc to Fl De [Pr 2.7]=Ar أَسَا, III. آسَى, var وَاسَى, *assist, support*: but this dubious, v. Lane [60] (cf Wetzst [ZDMG 1868, 119]) acc to whom this is a second sense from *to make equal* (viz by giving to another of one's own property, etc.))

† תּוּשִׁיָּה **n f.** sound, efficient wisdom, abiding success (on der, v. supr; acc to Fl De prop *advancement*, or mental aptitude that *advances*: for the form, cf תּוּגָה and תַּאֲנִיָּה, Sta [§ 262]), a technical term of the WisdLt;—**a.** *sound, efficient wisdom* Is 28[29] (of ׳י) הפליא עצה הגדיל תושיה; Pr 3[21] נצר ת׳ וּמְזִמָּה, 8[14] לִי עֵצָה ות׳ (Wisdom speaks); 18[1] לכל ת׳ יִתְגַּלָּע; Jb 11[6] (of ׳י v. Di), 12[16] עמו עז ות׳; 26[3] ות׳ לָרֹב הוֹדַעְתָּ ‖ עֵצָה לְלֹא חָכְמָה. **b.** of the *effect* of sound wisdom, *abiding success* (for the combination of meanings, cf. השׂכיל *to shew wisdom*, and also *to achieve success*), Jb 5[12] ולא תעשינה ידיהם ת׳ do not achieve *abiding success*; 6[13] and *abiding success* (‖ עֶזְרָתִי) is driven from me, Pr 2[7] יִצְפֹּן לַיְשָׁרִים ת׳; Mi 6[9] ותושיה יראה שמך, i e (si vera l) he that seeth (heedeth) thy name is *well-advised* (Ges [§ 155, 2 b 3]; Dav [§ 29 e])—הֻשִּׁיָּה Jb 30[22], v sub שוא.

† יוֹשָׁה **n.pr.m.** a Simeonite 1 Ch 4[34]; 𝔊 Ιωσ(ε)ια, A Ιωσιας, 𝔊L Ιωας.

† יוֹשַׁוְיָה **n.pr.m.** one of David's heroes 1 Ch 11[46], 𝔊 Ιωσ(ε)ια, 𝔊L Σωσια.

יָשׁוּב v. שׁוּב ; יִשְׁוָה v. שׁוה ; יְשׁוֹהָיָה v. שׁוח.

יִשְׁוִי v. שׁוה ; יֵשׁוּעַ v. יְהוֹשֻׁעַ supr. p. 221.

ישח (√ of following, si vera l.)

† [יֶשַׁח] **n.[m.]** ? **emptiness** (of hunger), meaning conjectured from context; Mi 6[14] וְיֶשְׁחֲךָ בְּקִרְבֶּךָ (|| תאכל ולא תִשְׂבָּע).

† [יָשַׁט] **vb.** only **Hiph.** *Impf.* **extend, hold out** (late) (NH Hiph. *id.;* Aram. Aph. אוֹשִׁיט, ܐܘܫܛ *id.;* ? As. *ašṭu, extended, mighty* Lyon[Sargontexte 60] Dl[HWB 144]; Ar. وَسَطَ is *penetrate into the middle of*)—יוֹשִׁיט שַׁרְבִיט הַזָּהָב לְ Est 4[11] *hold out the golden sceptre to*, so (וַיּוֹשֶׁט) 5[2] 8[4].

יִשַׁי[41] **n.pr.m.** father of David (etym. dub.; Ol[§ 277 f.] conj. יֵשׁ יָהּ; We[1 S 14,49] אבישי = אישי = ישי (but see this))—יִשַׁי 1 S 16[3] + 29 t.; יִשָׁי v[19] + 10 t.; 𝔊 Ιεσσαι; (וְ)אִישַׁי 1 Ch 2[13];—יִשַׁי בֵּית־הַלַּחְמִי *Jesse the Bethlehemite* 1 S 16[1.18] (בֶּן־ישי וגו׳ of David), 17[58] †; ישי also 16[3] + 14 t. 1 S 16, 17; † son of עוֹבֵד acc. to Ru 4[17.22.22] = 1 Ch 2[12]; דָּוִ(י)ד בֶּן־ישי 2 S 23[1] 1 Ch 10[14] 29[26] ψ 72[20]; אֱלִיאָב בֶּן־יִשַׁי 2 Ch 11[18]; elsewhere בֶּן־ישי alone = David, 1 S 20[27.30.31] 22[7.8.9.13] 25[10] 2 S 20[1] 1 K 12[16] = 2 Ch 10[16], 1 Ch 12[18]; גֶּזַע יִשָׁי Is 11[1]; שֹׁרֶשׁ יִשַׁי v[10] of Jesse as ancestor of future (Messianic) king†.

יָשִׁיב **n.pr.** v. יָשׁוּב sub שׁוב.

יְשִׁיָּה(וּ) v. נשה.

† [יָשַׁם] **vb. be desolate** (cf. שָׁמֵם)—**Qal** *Impf.* 3 fs. תֵּשַׁם Ez 12[19]; תֵּשָׁם Gn 47[19]; וְתֵּשַׁם Ez 19[7]; 3 fpl. תִּישַׁמְנָה 6[6] (Co תֵשַׁמְנָה);—*be desolate*, subj. ארץ Ez 12[19] 19[7]; subj. אֲדָמָה Gn 47[19] (J); subj. במות Ez 6[6].

† [יְשִׁימָה] **n.f. desolation**, only intens. pl. יְשִׁימוֹת ψ 55[16] Kt (Qr יַשִּׁיא מָוֶת), so Ges Hup al., cf. n.pr.loc. בית הישימות supr. p. 111 b; 𝔊 Ew Ol Pe De Bae al. follow Qr, *let death come deceitfully upon them*, v. נשא.

† יְשִׁימוֹן **n.m. waste, wilderness**;—abs. יְשִׁימוֹן 1 S 23[19] + 5 t.; יְשִׁמוֹן Nu 21[20] + 3 t.; יְשִׁמֹן Is 43[19]; יְשִׁמֹן Dt 32[10]; cstr. יְשִׁימוֹן ψ 107[4];—*waste, wilderness:* **a.** c. art., alm. n.pr. Nu 21[20] (commanded by Pisgah), 23[28] (by Peʿor; both JE), frequented by David as an outlaw 1 S 23[19.24] 26[1.3]. Probably some part of the wilderness of Judah, bordering on Dead Sea (Conder[Tent Work, ch. 15]; Buhl[Geogr. § 61]); acc. to others, at least in Nu. (v. Di), part of the ʿArábah, NE. of the Dead Sea (in which was בֵּית הַיְשִׁימֹת Nu 33[49] al.) **b.** without art., a *waste* or *wilderness* (only poet.), of scene of Israel's wanderings (after the Exodus), בְּאֶרֶץ מִדְבָּר || בְּתֹהוּ יְלֵל יְשִׁ׳ Dt 32[10], ψ 68[8] 78[40] 106[14]; with ref. to returning exiles Is 43[19.20]; יְ׳ דֶּרֶךְ ψ 107[4] *waste of a way* (= desert way).

† יִשְׁבָּא **n.pr.m.** a name in Judah 1 Ch 4[3]; 𝔊 Ραγμα, A Ιεσμα, 𝔊L Σαμαα.

יִשְׁמָעֵאל, יִשְׁמַעְיָה(וּ) v. שׁמע.

יִשְׁמְרַי v. שׁמר.

† [יָשֵׁן] **vb. sleep** (NH *id.;* Aram. n. ܫܢܬܐ *sleep;* Ar. وَسِنَ *be sleepy*, وَسَنٌ, سِنَةٌ *sleep;* As. *šittu, sleep*, Dl[HWB 246], *šunatu, šuttu, dream*, Id[ib], Flood[iv. 22] Asrb[Annals, v R. 2, 97])—**Qal** *Pf.* יָשַׁנְתִּי Jb 3[13]; וְיָשְׁנוּ consec. Je 51[39] + 2 t.; *Impf.* יִישַׁן Is 5[27] ψ 121[4]; וַיִּישַׁן 1 K 19[5], etc.; *Inf. cstr.* לִישׁוֹן Ec 5[11];—*sleep, go to sleep*, and *be asleep*, Gn 2[21] (J), 41[5] (E), Ez 34[25] Jb 3[13] ψ 3[6] 4[9] Pr 4[16] Ec 5[11], also 2 S 4[6] 𝔊 We Dr Kit Bu, vid. חָמֵשׁ; c. לֹא, of Ass. army Is 5[27] (|| נום); of Baal 1 K 19[5]; of ׳י, עוּרָה לָמָּה תִישַׁן אֲדֹנָי ψ 44[24]; לֹא יִישָׁן 121[4] (|| נום); c. acc. cogn. יָשְׁ׳ שְׁנַת עוֹלָם Je 51[39.57] (v. שֵׁנָה), of death, cf. אִישַׁן הַמָּוֶת ψ 13[4]. **Niph.** only in deriv. sense of *become inactive* or *stationary; Pf.* וְנוֹשַׁנְתֶּם consec. Dt 4[25] *and ye be grown old* בָּאָרֶץ, i.e. (v. Di Dr) have lost freshness of first impressions; of inanimate things, *be old, stale*, only *Pt.* יָשָׁן נוֹשָׁן Lv 26[10] (H), f. צרעת נוֹשֶׁנֶת Lv 13[11] = *old leprosy* (P); these poss. denom. from יָשָׁן. **Pi.** causat. *Impf.* וַתְּיַשְּׁנֵהוּ Ju 16[19] *and she made him sleep.*

† I. יָשֵׁן **adj. sleeping**;—ms. יָשֵׁן 1 S 26[7] + 3 t., fs. יְשֵׁנָה 1 K 3[20] Ct 5[2]; pl. יְשֵׁנִים 1 S 26[12] Ct 7[10]; cstr. יְשֵׁנֵי Dn 12[2];—*asleep, sleeping* 1 S 26[7.12] 1 K 3[20] Ct 5[2] 7[10]; so, fig., Ho 7[6], expl. as = עָשֵׁן *smoketh*, cf. Dt 29[19], by RS[J Phil. xvi. 1888, 72; Proph. iv. n. 19] Che with אַפֵּהֶם (Ges[§ 91. 1. R. 1a]) for אֹפֵהֶם; but < We, *their anger sleepeth;* of Baal 1 K 18[27]; in sim. of ׳י ψ 78[65]; of dead, as sleeping in dust, Dn 12[2].

† II. יָשֵׁן **n.pr.m.** one of David's heroes, 2 S 23[32] = הָשֵׁם 1 Ch 11[34] (in both del. בְּנֵי as dittogr., We Dr Bu); v. הָשֵׁם, and גּוּנִי.

† יָשָׁן **adj. old** (orig., as it seems, *withered, flabby*, like a lifeless plant with top hanging down, as if in sleep; cf. **Niph.** supr., and NH יִשֵּׁן Pi. *let a thing grow old*)—יָשָׁן Lv 25[22] + 3 t.; f. יְשָׁנָה Is 22[11] + 2 t.; pl. יְשָׁנִים Ct 7[14];—*old:* הַבְּרֵכָה

הַיְשָׁנָה Is 22[11], שַׁעַר הַיְשָׁנָה Ne 3[6]; so 12[39], of choice fruits. Ct 7[14] (opp חדש), subst. *old harvest, store*, Lv 25[22.22] 26[10.10] (H; opp. חדש).

† יְשָׁנָה **n.pr.loc.** town on southern border of N. Israel, near Bethel, 2 Ch 13[19]; so rd also 1 S 7[12] for MT הַשֵּׁן We Dr Klo Kit Bu; mod. *ʿAin Sinîya*, 5 m. N. of Beitin, Cl Ganneau JAs Avr.-Juin, 1870, 490-601 Socin ZPV i 1878, 41 Buhl Geogr § 85 p 173.

† שֵׁנָה, שֵׁנָא, שְׁנַת, שֵׁנָה **n.f.** sleep,—שֵׁנָה ψ 90[5] + 3 t; שֵׁנָא ψ 127[2], שְׁנַת ψ 132[4] (Ges § 80 g. h.), cstr. שְׁנַת Je 51[39] + 3 t, שְׁנָתִי Gn 31[40] Je 31[26], etc; pl abs שְׁנוֹת Pr 6[10] 24[33],—*sleep* Gn 28[16] (J), Ju 16[14.20] Pr 3[24] 6[9] 20[13] Ec 5[11] Je 31[26] Zc 4[1], Pr 6[4] (‖ תנומה); מְעַט שֵׁנוֹת מְעַט תְּנוּמוֹת Pr 6[10] = 24[33] (these two of sluggard אִישׁ עָצֵל, v. also 6[9] 20[13]), note also וַתִּדַּד שְׁנָתִי מֵעֵינָי Gn 31[40] (E) *and my sleep fled from mine eyes*, נָדְדָה שְׁנַת הַמֶּלֶךְ Est 6[1]; וְנִגְזְלָה שְׁנָתָם Pr 4[16], וּשְׁנָתוֹ נִהְיְתָה עָלָיו Dn 2[1], שֵׁנָה בְעֵינָיו אֵינֶנּוּ רֹאֶה Ec 8[16], אִם אֶתֵּן שְׁנַת לְעֵינָי ψ 132[4] (all of lack of sleep), יִתֵּן לִידִידוֹ שֵׁנָא ψ 127[2] = *he giveth to his beloved in sleep*, cf Ges § 118. 5, of sleep of death (so Ar. وَسَنٌ Dozy ii 806) Jb 14[12] ψ 90[5] (cf De Che), so, as acc cogn., ψ 76[6] Je 51[39.57] (in these two שְׁנַת־עוֹלָם)

† [יָשַׁע] **vb. Hiph.** deliver, **Niph.** intrans and pass. (Ar وَسِعَ *be capacious*, ii. *make wide, spacious*, iv. *make sufficient*, v viii *be or live in abundance* (v. Dr 1 S 14. 45) Ph n pr ישע, Sab יתע (royal epith.), n pr. עמיתע, יתעאל, אליתע, e g Mordt ZMG 1876, 37, 1893, 409 416 417, etc (yet note strange equiv., ת = س), not in Aram., MI[4] השעני *he delivered me*, l[3] (ב)משע *deliverance*, Sm and So, (but במת ClGann Dr), n pr m משע l[1], also l[3 [4]] Sm and So, but ישע *deliverance*, ClGann Dr)—**Niph.** *Pf* 3 m נוֹשַׁע Dt 33[29] Is 45[17], 2 pl נוֹשַׁעְתֶּם Nu 10[9], 1 pl נוֹשָׁעְנוּ Je 8[20], *Impf* 3 ms יִוָּשֵׁעַ Je 30[7] Pr 28[18] + 1 S 14[47] (for MT יַרְשִׁיעַ) 𝔊 We Klo Dr Kit Bu; 3 fs. תִּוָּשַׁע Je 23[6] 33[16], אִוָּשֵׁעָה ψ 119[117] Je 17[14] + 8 t. Impf; *Imv.* pl. הִוָּשְׁעוּ Is 45[22], *Pt* נוֹשָׁע ψ 33[16] Zc 9[9];—**1.** *be liberated, saved* (prop *placed in freedom;* cf for the fig. מֶרְחָב, הרחיב), from external evils Pr 28[18], by God Is 30[15] 45[22] 64[4] Je 4[14] 8[20] 17[14] 23[6] 33[16] ψ 80[4.8.20] 119[117], with מִן, Je 30[7], מֵאֹיְבִים Nu 10[9] (P), 2 S 22[4] = ψ 18[4] **2.** *be saved* in battle, *victorious* Zc 9[9] ψ 33[16] + 1 S 14[47] v supr; עַם נוֹשַׁע בַּיהוה Dt 33[29] *a people victorious in* ׳י (poem), cf Is 45[17]. **Hiph** *Pf* 3 ms הוֹשִׁיעַ 1 S 9[16] ψ 20[7], הוֹשַׁע Zc 12[7]; sf הוֹשִׁיעוֹ ψ 34[7], 1 S הוֹשַׁעְתִּי Is 43[12] + 4 t., + 14 t. Pf.; *Impf.* יְהוֹשִׁיעַ 1 S 17[47] (v Dr) ψ 116[6], יוֹשִׁיעַ Is 45[20] + 6 t; יוֹשַׁע (juss.) Pr 20[22]; וַיּוֹשַׁע Ex 14[30] + 7 t; וַיֹּשַׁע 1 S 23[5] + 2 t., sf. יוֹשִׁיעֲךָ Ho 13[10], יוֹשִׁיעֵנוּ Is 46[7]; יֹשִׁעֵנוּ 1 S 10[27], יֹשִׁעֲכֶם Is 35[4] (juss., Dr § 47 n 4), etc; *Imv* הוֹשַׁע Je 31[7] ψ 86[2], הוֹשִׁיעָה 2 K 6[26] + 8 t; הוֹשִׁעָה 2 S 14[4] + 19 t Imv; *Inf abs.* הוֹשֵׁעַ 1 S 25[26] + 2 t.; cstr הוֹשִׁיעַ 1 S 14[6] + 14 t + 2 S 3[18] (where rd אוֹשִׁיעַ Vrss Ke We Klo Dr Bu al), + 7 t. Inf; *Pt* מוֹשִׁיעַ Dt 22[27] + 21 t; sf. מוֹשִׁיעָם ψ 106[21] + 8 t. sf; pl מוֹשִׁעִים Ob[21] Ne 9[27],—**1.** *deliver, save* (prop *give width and breadth to, liberate*), in peril, c acc pers vel loc Ex 2[17] (E) Ju 6[31] 1 S 23[2.5] 2 S 10[19] = 1 Ch 19[19], 2 K 6[27.27] ψ 36[7] 72[13] Jb 26[2]; with לְ pers. Jos 10[6] (E) Dt 22[27] Ju 10[14] 2 S 10[11] = 1 Ch 19[12] (with acc.), Je 11[12.12] ψ 72[4] 116[6]; abs. הוֹשִׁיעָה הַמֶּלֶךְ *Help, O king* 2 S 14[4] 2 K 6[26] Specif *save*, from evils and troubles: **a.** of heroic men, saving the nation in war Ju 3[31] 6[15] 10[1] 1 S 10[27] Ho 13[10] Je 14[9], these are named מוֹשִׁיעַ *saviour* Ju 3[9.15] 2 K 13[5] Is 19[20] Ob[21] Ne 9[27]; phr when they are lacking אֵין מוֹשִׁיעַ Ju 12[3] 1 S 11[3] 2 S 22[42] = ψ 18[42], Dt 28[29.31] Is 47[15]; they save מִיַּד *from the hand of* Ju 2[16] 8[22] 12[2] 13[5] 1 S 9[16] Ne 9[27]; מִכַּף Ju 6[14] 1 S 4[3] 2 K 16[7]. **b.** of God, who saves his people from external evils Dt 20[4] Jos 22[22] Ju 3[9] 6[36.37] 7[7] 10[13] 1 S 14[23.39] 2 K 14[27] 19[34] = Is 37[35], Is 25[9] 33[22] 35[4] 43[12] 49[25] 63[9] Je 31[7] Ez 34[22] Ho 1[7.7] Hb 1[2] Zp 3[17.19] Zc 8[7.13] 9[16] 10[6] 12[7] ψ 28[9] 69[36] 106[8] 118[25] 2 Ch 20[9], or the pious among them Is 38[20] Je 2[27] 17[14] ψ 3[8] 6[5] 7[2] 31[17] 54[3] 55[17] 57[4] 69[2] 71[2.3] 106[47] = 1 Ch 16[35], ψ 109[26] 119[94.146] 138[7] Pr 20[22]; and especially the king ψ 20[7.10]; David 2 S 8[6.14], thy servant ψ 86[2.16], חָסִיד 12[2], דַּכְּאֵי־רוּחַ 34[19]; צַדִּיקִים 37[40], יִרְאֵי ׳י 145[19]; חוֹסִים 17[7], עַם עָנִי 18[28] = 2 S 22[28], שַׁח עֵינַיִם Jb 22[29]; יִשְׁרֵי לֵב 7[11]; עַנְוֵי־אֶרֶץ ψ 76[10]; accordingly God is מוֹשִׁיעַ *saviour* Is 43[11] 45[15.21] 63[8] Ho 13[4], מֹשִׁעִי 2 S 22[3], מוֹשִׁיעָם ψ 106[21]; מוֹשִׁיעוֹ Je 14[8], מוֹשִׁיעֵךְ Is 43[3] 49[26] 60[16] Je 30[10] = 46[27], is with his people לְהוֹשִׁיעַ Je 15[20] 30[11] 42[11], רַב לְהוֹשִׁיעַ Is 63[1], בֵּית מְצוּדוֹת לְהוֹשִׁיעֵנִי ψ 31[3]; Isr prays הוֹשִׁיעָה יְמִינְךָ *O save with thy right hand* ψ 60[7] = 108[7], cf. Is 59[1], that fr. wh. one is saved constr c. מִן מִיַּד Ex 14[30] (J) Ju 2[18] 10[12] 1 S 7[8] 2 S 3[18] 2 K 19[19] = Is 37[20], ψ 106[10] 2 Ch 32[22], מֵחָמָס 2 S 22[3]; מֵחֶרֶב Jb 5[15] מִכָּל־צָרוֹת ψ 34[7]; מִכָּל־רָעוֹת 1 S 10[19], מִצָּרֵינוּ ψ 44[8], מִפִּי אַרְיֵה 22[22]; מִשֹּׁפְטֵי נַפְשׁוֹ 109[31], מֵאַנְשֵׁי דָמִים 59[3]; מִמְּצוּקוֹת 107[13.19]. **c.** there is no other salvation, the sword saves not ψ 44[7], or a nation La 4[17], or astrologers Is 47[13], or Asshur Ho 14[4], or other gods Is 45[20] 46[7] Je 2[28] **2.** *save from moral troubles*, only in Ez.

מִכֹּל מוֹשְׁבֹתֵיהֶם (rd, with Co Da al., מְשׁוּבוֹתֵיהֶם) 37^{23}, מִכֹּל טֻמְאוֹתֵיכֶם 36^{29}. **3.** *give victory to*. **a.** of *man*, c. לְ pers., *give victory to*, c. agent subj יָד Ju 7^{2} 1 S 25$^{26.33}$, יָד om. v^{31}; יָמִין Jb 40^{14}; זְרוֹעַ ψ 44^{4}. **b.** of *God*, with לְ pers., subj. יָמִין ψ 98^{1}; זְרוֹעַ Is 59^{16} 63^{5}. Yahweh 1 Ch 18^{6}, with acc. v^{13}, abs *gain victory* 1 S 14^{6} 17^{47}, וַיּוֹשַׁע תְּשׁוּעָה גְדוֹלָה 1 Ch 11^{14}.

†יֶשַׁע **n.m.** Is 51,5 **deliverance, rescue, salvation, also safety, welfare,**—יֶשַׁע ψ 20^{7} + 4 t.; יֵשַׁע Jb 5^{11} + 4 t., sf יִשְׁעִי 2 S 22^{3} + 11 t., + 14 t sfs;—**1.** *safety, welfare, prosperity* 2 S 23^{5} ψ 12^{6} Jb 5$^{4.11}$. **2.** *salvation*, i.e. primarily physical rescue, by God, oft. with added spiritual idea. Is 62^{11} ψ 69^{14} 85$^{8.10}$; יֵשַׁע אֱלֹהִים *salvation from God* ψ 50^{23}; used as infin. with acc. לְיֵשַׁע Hb 3$^{13.13}$ (see Ew §238a); accordingly Yahweh is אורי וְיִשְׁעִי *my light and my salvation* ψ 27^{1}; צור ישעי 95^{1}, קֶרֶן ישעי 18^{3} = 2 S 22^{3}, אֱלֹהֵי ישעי Is 17^{10} Mi 7^{7} Hb 3^{18} ψ 18^{47} = אֱלֹהֵי צור ישעי 2 S 22^{47}, ψ 24^{5} 25^{5} 27^{9} 65^{6} 79^{9} 85^{5} 1 Ch 16^{35}, מָגֵן יֶשׁ׳ ψ 18^{36} = 2 S 22^{36}, על אלהים ישעי ψ 62^{8}, || צְדָקָה Is 45^{8} 51^{5} 61^{10}; שְׂשׂוֹן יִשְׁעֶךָ ψ 51^{14} *joy of thy salvation;* כֹּהֲנֶיהָ אַלְבִּישׁ יֶשׁ׳ 132^{16} *her priests will I clothe with salvation.* **3.** *victory*: גבורות יֵשַׁע יְמִינוֹ ψ 20^{7} *the mighty deeds of the victory of his right hand*

†יְשׁוּעָה **n.f.** **salvation;**—יְשׁ׳ ψ 119^{155} + 18 t., יְשׁוּעָתָה 3^{3} Jon 2^{10}, יְשֻׁעָתָה ψ 80^{3}; cstr. יְשׁוּעַת Ex 14^{13} + 4 t.; sf יְשֻׁעָתִי Jb 30^{15}; יְשׁוּעָתִי ψ 62^{2} + 12 t, + 25 t. sfs.; pl. יְשׁוּעוֹת 2 S 22^{51} + 6 t; יְשׁוּעֹת 42^{12} + 3 t, יְשֻׁעוֹת 53^{7};—**1.** *welfare, prosperity*: כעב עברה ישעתי Jb 30^{15} *as a cloud my prosperity passed away* **2.** *deliverance*: והיתה לי לישועה *and thou wilt be to me for deliverance* 2 S 10^{11} = 1 Ch 19^{12}. **3.** *salvation* by God, primarily from external evils, but often with added spiritual idea: Gn 49^{18} (poem), Is 33^{2} 52$^{7.10}$ 59^{11} 60^{18} Jon 2^{10} ψ 3$^{3.9}$ 14^{7} = 53^{7}, 22^{2} 35^{3} 62^{2} 69^{30} 70^{5} (= תשועה 40^{17}), 78^{22} 80^{3} 91^{16} 96^{2} = 1 Ch 16^{23}, 106^{4} 140^{8} Jb 13^{16}; with verbs of rejoicing בישועה 1 S 2^{1} Is 25^{9} ψ 9^{15} 13^{6} 35^{9}; יְשׁוּעָה יָשִׁית חומות Is 26^{1} *salvation will he set as walls*, cf. phr. אֱלֹהֵי יְשׁ׳ ψ 88^{2}, אל יְשׁ׳ Is 12^{2}, צור יְשׁ׳ Dt 32^{15} (song), ψ 89^{27}, cf. צורי וישועתי 62$^{3.7}$, יום יְשׁ׳ Is 49^{8}; מַעַיְנֵי הַיְשׁ׳ 12^{3} *wells of salvation*; pl. יְשׁוּעוֹת (intensive), of ״י: יְשׁוּעוֹת פָּנָי ψ 42^{6} *the salvation of my face* (person, פניו MT error, פני 𝔊 𝔖), v^{12} 43^{5}, כוס ישועות 116^{13} *cup commemorating saving acts* (of drink-offering); further ψ 119$^{123.155.166.174}$; || צְדָקָה Is 51$^{6.8}$ 56^{1} 62^{1} ψ 98$^{2.3}$, יְשׁוּעָתִי עַד־קְצֵה הָאָרֶץ Is 49^{6} *my salvation unto the ends of the earth;* בְּכָל־גּוֹיִם יְשׁוּעָתֶךָ ψ 67^{3} *among all nations thy salvation.* **4.** *victory*. c. עָשָׂה *work victory* 1 S 14^{45} Is 26^{18}, elsewhere of victories wrought by Yahweh for his people Ex 15^{2} (song) Is 12^{2} Hb 3^{8} ψ 20^{6} 21$^{2.6}$ 44^{5} 68^{20} 118$^{14.15.21}$; phrases: פעל יְשׁוּעוֹת *do victories* 74^{12}; חֹסֶן יְשׁוּעֹת Is 33^{6} *store of victories;* מִגְדּוֹל ישועות 2 S 22^{51} Qr *tower of victories* (Kt מַגְדִּיל and so || ψ 18^{51}); מָעוֹז ישועות ψ 28^{8} *stronghold of victories*, ראו אֶת־יְשׁוּעַת ״י Ex 14^{13} (J) *see the victory of Yahweh*, 2 Ch 20^{17}; כובע יְשׁוּעָה Is 59^{17} *helmet of victory;* יְפָאֵר עֲנָוִים בִּישׁוּעָה ψ 149^{4} *he will beautify the meek with victory.*—Cf. the syn. תְּשׁוּעָה, infr.

†I. שׁוֹעַ **adj.** **(free), independent, noble** (in station) (acc. to most from second √שׁוע = ישע, in sense of Ar. وَسِعَ (cf תְּשׁוּעָה infr.), but actual existence of such a √ not proven; Thes allows שׁוֹעַ = ישׁוֹעַ)—*noble*, of rank (and, by implic., of character) Is 32^{5} (|| נָדִיב, opp כִּילַי), Jb 34^{19} (Di al *rich*, but || שָׂרִים, opp דַּל)—שׁוֹעַ II. Is 22^{5}, v. sub [שׁוּעַ] III שׁוֹעַ **n.pr.gent** Ez 23^{23}, v. שׁ׳.

†I. שׁוּעַ **n.pr.m.** father of Judah's wife, 𝔊 Σαυα, Gn 38^{2} and (after cstr בַּת) v^{12} 1 Ch 2^{3}; v בַּת־שׁוּעַ p. 124 supr, and cf. on mng. (אֲבִי)שׁוּעַ p. 4, (אֱלִי)שׁוּעַ p 46.

II. שׁוּעַ **n.[m.]** **opulence?** (cf. Ar. سَعَةٌ)—so AE al Jb 30^{24} 36^{19}; but < v. sub [שָׁוַע].

†שׁוּעָא **n.pr.f.** a woman of Asher 1 Ch 7^{32}; 𝔊 Σωλα, 𝔊L Σουα

†יִשְׁעִי **n.pr.m.** (*salutary*)—**1.** one of the line of Jerahmeel 1 Ch 2$^{31.31}$, 𝔊 Ισεμιηλ, A Ιεσει, 𝔊L Ιεσσουει. **2.** a chief of Manasseh 1 Ch 5^{24}, 𝔊 Σεει, Ιεσ(σ)ει. **3.** a chief of Judah 1 Ch 4^{20}. **4.** a chief of Simeon 1 Ch 4^{42}.

יְשַׁעְיָהוּ **n.pr.m.** (*salvation of Yah*, cf אֱלִישָׁע p 46 supr; ישעאל on scarab ClGann JAs 1883, Fev-Mars, 135 No. 8)—**1.** Isaiah, son of 'Âmôs, the prophet Is 1^{1} + 15 t. Is., 2 K 19^{2} + 12 t K., 2 Ch 26^{22} 32$^{20.32}$, 𝔊 Ησαιας, 𝔙 *Isaias*. †**2.** one of the children of Jeduthun 1 Ch 25$^{3.15}$, 𝔊 Ισαια, etc. †**3.** a Levite ancestor of one of David's treasurers 1 Ch 26^{25}, 𝔊 Ωσαιας, 𝔊L Ιωσηε.

†יְשַׁעְיָה **n.pr.m.** (*salvation of Yah*)—**1.** grandson of Zerubbabel 1 Ch 3^{21}, 𝔊 Ιασαβα, Ιεσεια **2.** chief of the sons of Elam, who went up with Ezra Ezr 8^{7}, 𝔊 Ιοσεια, Ησαια, etc. **3.** chief of sons of Merari in time of Ezra

Ezr 8[19], 𝔊 Ωσαια, etc **4.** a Benjamite Ne 11[7], 𝔊 Ιεσια, etc

†**הוֹשֵׁעַ n.pr.m.** (*salvation*, on form, cf הַמְשֵׁל, הַשֹּׁטֵר, on pronunciation v. Hpt ZA ii 261 Anm 2 Jager BAS i. 468) — **1.** orig name of Joshua acc to Nu 13[8.16] (P), 𝔊 Αυση, cf Dt 32[44] (J, prob. err, v. Dr), 𝔊 Ιησους, v. יהושׁע p. 221 supr. **2.** last king of Israel 2 K 15[30] 17[1.3.4.6] 18[1.9.10], 𝔊 Ωσηε. **3.** the prophet Hosea Ho 1[1.2], 𝔊 Ωσηε. **4.** an Ephraimite chief under David 1 Ch 27[20], 𝔊 Ωση(ε) **5.** a chief under Nehemiah Ne 10[24], 𝔊 Ωσηθα, Ωσηε

†**הוֹשַׁעְיָה n.pr.m.** (*Yah has saved*)—**1.** a prince of Judah Ne 12[32], 𝔊 Ωσαια **2** father of Azariah or Jezaniah, a chief in time of Jeremiah Je 42[1] 43[2], 𝔊 Μαασ(σ)αιος, etc

יֵשׁוּעַ, יְהוֹשֻׁעַ n pr., see p 221

†**[מוֹשָׁעָה] n.f.** only pl מוֹשָׁעוֹת *saving acts* ψ 68[21]

†**מֵישַׁע n.pr.m.** (*deliverance*) — Mesha, king of Moab 2 K 3[4] = משע MI[1], 𝔊 Μωσα — v Sm and So MI 1846 Di Sm lxxxv ff

†**מֵישָׁע n.pr m.** (*deliverance*) — son of Caleb 1 Ch 2[42], 𝔊 Μαρεισα, 𝔖L Μουσα.

†**תְּשׁוּעָה** (+תְּשֻׁעָה 2 S 19[3]) **n.f. deliverance, salvation** = יְשׁוּעָה (formed by false anal, as if from √ שׁוע, in sense of ישׁע; most assign it to שׁוע, but no sufficient evidence for existence of such a √, cf. Ko ii 200)—abs ת׳ 1 S 11[9] + 19 t., cstr Je 3[23] + 5 t; sf תְּשׁוּעָתִי Is 46[13] + 2 t, תשׁוּעָתְךָ ψ 40[11] + 2 t; תְּשׁוּעָתֶךָ v[17] 71[15];—**1.** *deliverance*, usually by God, through human agency, esp. from oppression 1 S 11[9], and in battle 1 Ch 19[12] (הושׁיע in ‖ cl), = *victory* Ju 15[18] (נָתַתָּ ת׳ בְּיַד וגו׳), 2 K 5[1], י׳ עשׂה ת׳ 1 S 11[13] *wrought a great victory*, so 19[5] 2 S 19[3] 23[10.12] 1 Ch 11[14] (as acc cogn after הושׁיע), Pr 21[31] ψ 33[17] (נושׁע in ‖ v[16]), הַנּוֹתֵן ת׳ לַמְּלָכִים 144[10], so in phr. חֵץ־ת׳ ליהוה 2 K 13[17], חֵץ־ת׳ בַּאֲרָם v[17], of national *deliverance*, from exile, נוֹשַׁע יִשְׂרָאֵל ת׳ עולמים Is 45[17] (Da Synt §67 b), 46[13] (‖ צְדָקָה), v[13] (c. נתן, ‖ תִּפְאֶרֶת); in gen of national *success* and *prosperity* Je 3[23] Pr 11[14] = 24[6], of deliverance fr personal trouble ψ 37[39] La 3[26] (תשׁועת י׳), or of national deliverance under fig of personal ψ 40[11] (‖ אֱמוּנָתְךָ), v[17] 71[15] (‖ צְדָקָה), so י׳ תשׁוּעָתִי 38[23], contrasted with י׳'s deliverance is תְּשׁוּעַת אָדָם *deliverance of (through) man* ψ 60[13] = 108[13], cf 146[3] **2.** more exclusively spiritual in sense, = *salvation*, appear to be אֱלֹהֵי תְּשׁוּעָתִי ψ 51[16], 119[41] (‖ חַסְדְּךָ), v[81], and כֹּהֲנֶיךָ יִלְבְּשׁוּ ת׳ 2 Ch 6[41] (from כהניה אלביש יֶשַׁע ψ 132[16]).

†**יָשְׁפֵה n.[m.]** jasper (loan-word fr. Pers. يَشْم, so Ar يَشْبٌ Lane 2978, also (and on forms يَشْم, يَشْف) Frey, perh As *ašpû* Dl HA 38 HWB 147)—וְיָשְׁפֵה תַּרְשִׁישׁ וְשֹׁהַם Ex 28[20] 39[13] (both P), *beryl and onyx and jasper* (v. Di), וְיָשְׁפֵה (+ *id*) Ez 28[13] (v Sm)

יִשְׁפָּה v sub שׁפה, **יִשְׁפָּן** v. sub שׁפן

†**יָשַׁר vb. be smooth, straight, right** (NH *id.*, and deriv, Ar يَسَرَ *be gentle, tractable, easy*, II *make easy*, يَسْرٌ *manageable, easy*; but Sab. ותר, הותר, אהל יתרן Os ZMG 1865, 270 CIS iv. 29 2, As *išâru*, *be* or *go straight, right*, *mêšêru*, *justice*, *mêšêriš*, *righteously*, Dl HWB 310) — **Qal** *Pf.* יָשַׁר Je 18[4] + 2 t; 3 f יָשְׁרָה Ju 14[3] Hb 2[4], 3 mpl יָשְׁרוּ 1 K 9[12]; *Impf.* ייֹשַׁר Nu 23[27] + 2 t; יִשַׁר 1 S 18[20.26], 3 fs תישׁר Ju 14[7]; 3 fpl. ישׁרנָה 1 S 6[12] (Ges §47 n 3, 71)—**1.** *go straight*, בַּדֶּרֶךְ *in the way* 1 S 6[12] **2.** fig, *be pleasing, agreeable, right* (בעיני *in the eyes of*), said of a woman Ju 14[3.7]; a man Je 27[5], of matters and things (הַדָּבָר) 1 S 18[20.26] 2 S 17[4] 1 Ch 13[4] 2 Ch 30[4]; of cities 1 K 9[12]; a place בעיני הָאֱלֹהִים Nu 23[27] (E), with כַּאֲשֶׁר Je 18[4]. **3.** in ethical sense, *straightforward, upright*; לֹא־יָשְׁרָה נַפְשׁוֹ בּוֹ Hb 2[4] *his soul is not upright in him* (opp. עֻפְּלָה *swollen*). **Pi.** *Pf.* 1 יִשַּׁרְתִּי ψ 119[128] (יִשְּׁרֵהוּ Jb 37[3], 3 m. sf Thes; but < Ew Di Hi De Da, *Impf.* fr שָׁרָה), *Impf.* יְיַשֵּׁר Pr 3[6]; יְיַשֶּׁר־ 15[21], sf. וַיְיַשְּׁרֵם (Mas abbrev. וַיִּשְׁרֵם) 2 Ch 32[30], 3 fs תְּיַשֵּׁר Pr 11[5]; 1 s. אֲיַשֵּׁר Is 45[13]; אֲיַשֵּׁר v[2] Qr (Kt Hiph אושׁר Ges §70, 2 doubtless copyist's error), *Imv* pl יַשְּׁרוּ 40[3], *Pt.* pl. מְיַשְּׁרִים Pr 9[15];—**1.** *make smooth, straight*, acc מְסִלָּה Is 40[3]; הֲדוּרִים 45[2]; fig, with דֶּרֶךְ, *make smooth* or *straight*, i e. free from obstacles, successful v[13] Pr 11[5], ארח 3[6], in ethical sense, הַמְיַשְּׁרִים אֹרְחוֹתָם 9[15] *those making straight their paths*, going straightforward on their paths; יְיַשֶּׁר־לָכֶת 15[21] *maketh straight his going, goeth straightforwards* **2.** *lead straight along, direct*, waters of an aqueduct 2 Ch 32[30]; (of the thunder Jb 37[3] acc. to some; but v. rather שָׁרָה). **3.** *esteem right, approve* ψ 119[128] (rd. כל פקודיך לי יִשַּׁרְתִּי). **Pu** *Pt* זָהָב מְיֻשָּׁר עַל־הַמְּחֻקֶּה 1 K 6[35] *gold made level, laid smoothly out, upon the graven work.* **Hiph.** *Impf.* 3 pl עַפְעַפֶּיךָ יַיְשִׁרוּ נֶגְדֶּךָ Pr 4[25] *let thine eyelids look straight before thee; Imv.* הַיְשַׁר דַּרְכֶּךָ *make thy way even* ψ 5[9] Qr (Kt הוֹשַׁר, v. Ges 70 (2))

†יָשָׁר **adj.** **straight, right**;—׳י 1 S 29[6] + 70 t., cstr. יְשַׁר Pr 29[27]; f. יְשָׁרָה Ez 1[7] + 4 t.; pl. יְשָׁרִים Nu 23[10] + 31 t.; cstr יִשְׁרֵי ψ 7[11] + 8 t.; f. יְשָׁרוֹת Ez 1[23] (del. Co);—**1.** *straight, level*, of a way Is 26[7] Je 31[9] ψ 107[7] Ezr 8[21], foot Ez 1[7], wings v[23] (? v supr.) **2.** *right, pleasing*: **a.** *to God*, הַיָּשָׁר בעיני *that which is right, pleasing in the eyes of, agreeable to* (either cstr. before ׳י, or with sfs. referring to him), esp. in Deut. writers, Ex 15[26] (R), Dt 12[25] 13[19] 21[9] 1 K 11[33.38] 14[8] 15[5.11] 22[43] = 2 Ch 20[32], 2 K 10[30], 12[3] 14[3] 15[3.34] 16[2] 18[3] 22[2] = 2 Ch 24[2] 25[2] 26[4] 27[2] 28[1] 29[2] 34[2], Je 34[15], הטוב והישר בעיני ׳י Dt 6[18]; הישר והטוב בעיני ׳י 12[28] 2 Ch 14[1], הטוב והישר והאמת לפני ׳י 31[20]. **b.** *to man*, (ה)ישר בעיני Dt 12[8] Ju 17[6] 21[25] 2 S 19[7] Je 40[5] Pr 12[15] 21[2]; (ה)טוב ו(ה)ישר בעיני Jos 9[25] (D), Je 26[14] 40[4], יֵשׁ דֶּרֶךְ יָשָׁר לִפְנֵי־אִישׁ Pr 14[12] *there is a way which is pleasing before a man* = 16[25]. **3.** *straightforward, just, upright*: **a.** *of God*, צַדִּיק וְיָשָׁר הוּא Dt 32[4] (song); טוב וישר ׳י ψ 25[8]; ישר ׳י 92[16]; his ways Ho 14[10]; his משפטים Ne 9[13] ψ 119[137], פקודים 19[9]; דָּבָר 33[4]; the words of divine wisdom Pr 8[9] **b.** *of man*, God made him *upright* Ec 7[29], but יָשָׁר בָּאָדָם אָיִן Mi 7[2] *an upright man among men there is none*, and yet Job is תָּם וְיָשָׁר Jb 1[1] (v. Da), v[8] 2[3], cf ψ 37[37]; זך וישר Jb 8[6]; so earlier of David as an upright man 1 S 29[6]; of man's doings ‖ זך Pr 20[11], cf. 21[8]; of his way of life ‖ טובה 1 S 12[23]; יְשַׁר־דַּרְכּוֹ Pr 29[27], יִשְׁרֵי־דָרֶךְ ψ 37[14]; of his heart, mind, and will, יִשְׁרֵי לֵבָב *upright of heart* 2 Ch 29[34], ישרי־לב ψ 7[11] 11[2] 32[11] 36[11] 64[11] 94[15] 97[11]; יְשָׁרִים בְּלִבּוֹתָם 125[4]. **c.** as a noun, (1) with ref. to things, יָשָׁר הֶעֱוֵיתִי *the right I have perverted* Jb 33[27], הַיְשָׁרָה יְעַקֵּשׁוּ Mi 3[9] *pervert the right* (lit. *twist* that which is *straight*); דֹּבֵר יְשָׁרִים *speaketh right things* Pr 16[13], cf. 2 K 10[15]. (2) more commonly of men, in sg (ה)יָשָׁר Mi 2[7] 7[4] 2 K 10[3] Pr 21[29] Jb 23[7]; collective, ψ 11[7]; also in סֵפֶר הַיָּשָׁר *book of the upright* Jos 10[13] 2 S 1[18] (cf. 1 K 8[53] 𝔊; Dr[Intr 182]), a collection of ancient national poetry; in pl. יְשָׁרִים *the upright*, of pious Israel Nu 23[10] (song E); elsewhere of the upright among the people of God as distinguished from the wicked, in WisdLt, Jb 4[7] 17[8] Pr 2[7.21] 3[32] 11[3.6.11] 12[6] 14[9.11] 15[8.19] 16[17] 21[18] 28[10] 29[10], in late ψψ 33[1] 49[15] 107[42] 111[1] 112[2.4] 140[14] and Dn 11[17]. **4.** abstr, *uprightness*, ישר בֶּאֱמֶת וְיָשָׁר ψ 111[8] (Thes), but read rather יֹשֶׁר with Hi Ri Bae, after 𝔊 𝔖 𝔗 Jer

†יֹשֶׁר **n.m.** ψ 25. 21 **straightness, uprightness**;—יֹשֶׁר Pr 2[13] + 11 t.; sf יָשְׁרוֹ Jb 33[23] Pr 14[2],—**1.** *straightness, evenness*, of paths (with moral implication) Pr 2[13] 4[11]. **2.** *rightness, uprightness* Pr 17[26]; תם וָיֹשֶׁר ψ 25[21]; of words, spoken Jb 6[25], written Ec 12[10]; of the moral walk (ו)בישר 1 K 9[4] Pr 14[2], ישר־לבי Jb 33[3]; ישר לבב Dt 9[5] ψ 119[7] 1 Ch 29[17].—on ψ 111[8] v. יָשָׁר **4.** **3.** *what is due, right* Jb 33[23] Pr 11[24].

†יֵשֶׁר **n.pr.m.** (*uprightness*) son of Caleb 1 Ch 2[18] (on pointing v. Baer), 𝔊 Ιωασαρ, 𝔊L Σαρ.

†[יְשָׁרָה] **n.f.** uprightness;—בְּיִשְׁרַת לֵבָב 1 K 3[6] (for form see Bo[§ 644 a] Ko[§ 90 (ii, 170)]).

†יְשֻׁרוּן **n.pr.m.** (*upright one*) Dt 32[15] 33[5.26] Is 44[2]; poetic name of Israel, designating it under its *ideal* character, 𝔊 ὁ ἠγαπημένος, Aq Sym Theod εὐθύς, 𝔙 *rectissimus, dilectus*; Thes Ew[§ 167 a] Lag[BN 33] regard it as dimin. fr. יָשׁוּר = *good little people*, but no evidence that ־וּן has a dimin. force, and most recent scholars De Di Dr MV Ges[§ 86 (2) 4] take as denom. = *Rechtvolk*; Bacher[ZAW v 1885, 161 ff.] and Che rightly compare סֵפֶר הַיָּשָׁר (see יָשָׁר **3 c**).

†[מֵישָׁר] **n.m.** evenness, uprightness, equity,—only pl: מֵשָׁרִים Pr 1[3]; elsewhere מֵישָׁרִים Is 26[7] + 17 t.,—**1.** *evenness, level* Is 26[7], of path of righteous (in the future), fig. for free from difficulties, *smoothness*, of the flow of wine, במ׳ Pr 23[31]; למ׳ Ct 7[10]. **2.** in ethical sense, *uprightness, equity*, as taught in the school of wisdom Pr 8[6], ‖ צֶדֶק 1[3] 2[9], of government (ב)מ׳ ψ 9[9] 58[2] 75[3] 96[10] 98[9] 99[4]; of speech Is 33[15] Pr 23[16]; of Yahweh's promises Is 45[19]; רצה מ׳ 1 Ch 29[17] *have pleasure in equity*; עשׂה מ׳ Dn 11[6] *make an equitable arrangement*. **3.** adv. *rightly*, with חזה ψ 17[2], אהב Ct 1[4].

†מִישׁוֹר **n.m.** Je 48, 8 **level place, uprightness**;—מ׳ ψ 27[11] + 9 t; מִישֹׁר Zc 4[7] (v. Baer) + 12 t;—**1.** *level country, table-land, plain*: antith הר(ים) 1 K 20[23.25] Zc 4[7]; עָקֹב Is 40[4]; מַעֲקַשִּׁים 42[16]; + שְׁפֵלָה 2 Ch 26[10]; ‖ עֵמֶק Je 21[13], הַמִּישׁוֹר specifically of the elevated plateau or *table-land* between the Arnon and Heshbon Dt 3[10] 4[43] Jos 13[9.16.17.21] 20[8] Je 48[8.21]. **2.** *level place* (free from obstacles), fig. for place of safety, comfort, and prosperity ψ 26[12]; ארח מ׳ 27[11]; אֶרֶץ מ׳ 143[10]. **3.** *uprightness* (cf. מֵישָׁר **2**), in government ψ 67[5]; שֵׁבֶט מ׳ 45[7]; ‖ צֶדֶק Is 11[4]; שָׁלוֹם Mal 2[6].

† שָׁרוֹן **n.pr.loc.** **Sharon** (plausibly connected with √ישר by Thes Ges[12] al., cf. GASm Geogr 52, = *יִשְׁרוֹן, Ph שרן)—strictly **n.m.** Is 65. 10 **plain, level**;—**1.** הַשּׁ׳ (with art.), name of maritime plain on Mediterr., fr. Joppa northward, noted for fertility, Is 33^9 (‖ כַּרְמֶל, בָּשָׁן, 𝔊 ὁ Σαρων), cf הֲדַר כַּרְמֶל וְהַשָּׁרוֹן 35^2, 65^{10} (‖ עֵמֶק עָכוֹר, 𝔊 τῷ δρυμῷ); חֲבַצֶּלֶת הַשּׁ׳ Ct 2^1 (𝔊 ἄνθος τοῦ πεδίου), הַבָּקָר הָרֹעִים בַּשּׁ׳ 1 Ch 27^{29}, so also Jos 12^{18}, where rd. מֶלֶךְ אֲפֵק לַשּׁ׳, so Di We Sam 55 Ges[12] after 𝔊, cf. RS OTJC 2, 273, 435.—On this plain v. GASm Geogr 147 ff Buhl Geogr § 65. **2.** מִגְרְשֵׁי שָׁרוֹן, region E of Jordan 1 Ch 5^{16} (‖ בָּשָׁן, גִּלְעָד, 𝔊 τὰ περίχωρα Γεριαμ, 𝔊A Σαρων), identified by many with הַמִּישׁוֹר (Dt 3^{10} etc., v. supr.)

ישש (√of foll., cf Ar وَتْوَاتٌ *weak* or *impotent* man, وَتْوَتَةٌ *weakness, impotence*, Lane 2919)

† יָשֵׁשׁ **adj. aged, decrepit**, only זָקֵן וְיָשֵׁשׁ 2 Ch 36^{17}

† יָשִׁישׁ **adj. aged**, only Jb (NH once יְשִׁישִׁים *old, venerable* men, Levy Jastr),—abs יָשִׁישׁ Jb 15^{10}, pl יְשִׁישִׁים 32^6 + 2 t.,—*aged*, as pred adj Jb 32^6 (opp צָעִיר לְיָמִים); as subst. 15^{10} (‖ שָׂב); 29^8 (opp נְעָרִים), בִּישִׁישִׁים חָכְמָה 12^{12} *among aged men is wisdom* (‖ אֹרֶךְ יָמִים תְּבוּנָה)

† יְשִׁישַׁי **n.pr.m.** a Gileadite name 1 Ch 5^{14}

יתד (√of foll.; mng. dub.; Ar. وَتَدَ *drive in peg, be firm* (of peg), is appar. denom.)

† יָתֵד **n.f.** Dt 23. 14 **peg, pin** (NH id., Ar. وَتِدٌ)—יָתֵד Dt 23^{14} + 9 t., cstr יְתַד Ju 4^{21} 16^{14} (where c art but v Ges § 127 R 4 a), pl. יְתֵדֹת Ex 38^{20}, cstr יִתְדֹת 27^{19} + 4 t., sf יְתֵדֹתַיִךְ Is 54^2, יִתְדֹתָיו Ex 27^{19} Is 33^{20}; וִיתֵדֹתֶיהָ Ex 39^{40}, וִיתֵדֹתָם Nu 3^{37} 4^{32},—*pin, peg*, esp **a.** *tent-pin* Ju 5^{26} 4^{21}, יְתַד הָאֹהֶל v 22, rd perh also Jb 4^{21} (fig; cf. II. יֶתֶר); oft. of tabernacle Ex $27^{19\,19}$ $35^{18\,18}$ $38^{20.31\,31}$, ‖ מֵיתָרָיו 39^{40}, cf Nu 3^{37} 4^{32} (all P); of Zion under fig of tent Is 33^{20} 54^2, fig. of ruler as support of state Zc 10^4. **b.** a peg for hanging Ez 15^3, so fig of Eliakim Is $22^{23.24}$, of secure position Ezr 9^8 (cf Ar, v. Thes Hi Hariri 361 Der, ثابت الأَوْتَادِ of a king) **c.** for digging Dt 23^{14} (= spade) **d.** the *pin* or stick used in beating up the woof in the loom Ju 16^{14*}, vid GFM PAOS, Oct 1889 clxxvi ff., in הַיְתַד הָאֶרֶג v b, del. הַיְתַד (Id 1b and in Comm ad loc.)

יְתוּר Jb 39^8, v. תּוּר.

יִתְלָה v. תלה.

יתח (assumed by Thes as √of foll., cf Ar وَتَخَ *beat with a club, chastise*; مِيتَخَةٌ *club*, Ba NB 294 der. תותח as loan-word fr As *tartaḫu* = *club* (or *javelin*, cf Dl HWB 630))

† תּוֹתָח **n.m.** name of a weapon, perh. **club, mace** (or *dart, javelin*, ‖ כִּידוֹן),—Jb 41^{21}.

יתם (√of foll., cf. Ar يَتِمَ, يَتَمَ *be alone, bereaved*, Aram. adj. and subst. ܝܰܬܡܳܐ, 𝔗 יָתֵם = יָתוֹם; vid. Lag BN 30 Ba NB 194)

† יָתוֹם **n** [**m.**] **orphan** (NH id.; Aram. יַתְמָא, ܝܰܬܡܳܐ, Ph יתם; Ar يَتِيمٌ *pupil, orphan*)—יָתוֹם Ex 22^{21} + 29 t.; pl יְתוֹמִים v 23 + 8 t.; sf יְתוֹמֶיךָ Je 49^{11}; יְתֹמָיו Is 9^{16}, לִיתוֹמָיו ψ 109^{12},—*orphan*, i.e. fatherless (‖ אַלְמָנָה) Ex 22^{23} ψ 109^9 La 5^3 (‖ אֵין אָב), Jb 24^9 ψ 109^{12}, prob. also Ex 22^{21} Dt 10^{18} 14^{29} $16^{11\,14}$ $24^{17\,19\,20.21}$ $26^{12.13}$ 27^{19} ψ 94^6 146^9 Je 7^6 22^3 Zc 7^{10} Mal 3^5 (in all these, mentioned as helpless, exposed to injury, ‖ אַלְמָנָה and גֵּר); similarly, ‖ אַלְמָנָה Jb 22^9 24^3 29^{12} 31^{17} ψ 68^6 Is $1^{17\,23}$ 9^{16} 10^2 Je 49^{11} Ez 22^7; without אלמנה Ho 14^4 Jb 6^{27} 31^{21} ψ $10^{14\,18}$ Pr 23^{10} Je 5^{28} (in no case clear that both parents are dead).

† יִתְמָה **n.pr.m.** one of David's valiant men, called הַמּוֹאָבִי 1 Ch 11^{46}, 𝔊 (Ι)εθαμα, 𝔊L Ιεθαμ

יתן (√of foll., cf. Ar. وَتَنَ *be perpetual, never-failing*, esp. of water, وَاتِنٌ *a permanent thing*: Ph. ירח אתנם CIS I 1 86 A; W PSBA 1886 (Iz) 47).

† I. אֵיתָן, אֵתָן **adj. perennial, ever-flowing, fig permanent, as subst. steady flow, permanence**,—abs. אֵיתָן Gn 49^{24} + 8 t.; אֵתָן Jb 33^{19}; sf אֵיתָנוֹ Ex 14^{27}; pl. אֵיתָנִים Jb 12^{19}, אֵתָנִים 1 K 8^2 Mi 6^2; (in form, an 'elative,' Ew § 162 b = Arab. compar. and superl.),—**1.** *ever-flowing* (opp. אַכְזָב), נַחַל אֵיתָן Am 5^{24} an *ever-flowing* wādy, Dt 21^4 (v. Dr), as subst in נַהֲרוֹת אֵיתָן ψ 74^{15} *rivers of steady flow*; as subst. also Ex 14^{27} (J), the sea returned לְאֵיתָנוֹ to its *steady flow*, יֶרַח הָאֵתָנִים 1 K 8^2 month of *steady flowings* = 7th mo., Oct.–Nov. (post-Bibl. Tisri) **2.** fig *permanent, enduring* גּוֹי אֵיתָן הוּא Je 5^{15}, i.e. a nation whose numbers never dwindle or fail, *imperishable*, וְרִיב עֲצָמָיו א׳ Jb 33^{19} Kt the strife of his bones is *constant*, Gn 49^{24} his bow abode בְּא׳ as an *enduring, firm*, one, א׳ מוֹשָׁבֶךָ Nu 24^{21} (‖ שִׂים בַּסֶּלַע), נְוֵה אֵיתָן Je 49^{19} = 50^{44} an

abode of *permanency* (of Edom, and Babylon, suddenly depopulated by foe, figured as lion); האיתנים מוסדי ארץ Mi 6^{2} ye *ever-enduring* ones, the foundations of the earth (but rd. prob. with We הַאֲזִינוּ), Jb 12^{19} אֵיתָנִים יְסַלֵּף he subverteth them that are *firmly seated* (i.e men established in hereditary offices or dignities) Very uncertain is Pr 13^{15} דֶּרֶךְ בֹּגְדִים אֵיתָן, perh. *firm, hard, rugged* (Ew De Hi Now. acc. to Str. the text is corrupt).

†II. אֵיתָן **n.pr.m.** a wise man 1 K 5^{11} (where called הָאֶזְרָחִי) named with הֵימָן, כַּלְכֹּל, דַּרְדַּע; cf. 1 Ch 2^{6} (where these 4 with זִמְרִי are בְּנֵי זֶרַח); also 2^{8} 6^{27}; called בֶּן־קוּשָׁיָהוּ 6^{29} = בֶּן־קִישִׁי 15^{17}, where, and v^{19}, named as Levit. singer with הֵימָן and אָסָף (q.v; יְדוּתוּן for אֵיתָן in this group 1 Ch 25$^{1.6}$ 2 Ch 5^{12} 35^{15}, v. ידותון); לְאֵיתָן הָאֶזְרָחִי ψ 89^{1} (title).

יַתְנִיאֵל v. תנה.

†יִתְנָן **n.pr.loc.** (etym. dub.) city in the Negeb of Judah Jos 15^{23} (foll. by זִיף v^{24}), 𝔊A Ιθναζιφ, 𝔊L Ιθναν, Ζειφ; site unknown.

[יָתַר]$_{107}$ **vb. remain over** (NH *id.*, Aram יְתַר, [Syriac] *id*; Zinj. יתר n. *rest, remainder*; Eth. [Ethiopic]: As [*atâru*], *remain over*, in der conj, Dl^{HWB}, in Sab. ותר CIS$^{iv. 15. 46. p. 77}$; esp n. ותר as epithet of king = *noble one*, and as n pr. ותרם Mordt$^{ZMG, 1876, 37, 292}$ DHM$^{ZMG, 1883, 15}$ CIS$^{iv. 10}$; Ar. وَتَرَ is *make single, make to be one*, or *an odd number*)—†**Qal** *Pt.* הַיּוֹתֵר 1 S 15^{15} *the remainder*†. **Niph.** *be left over, remain over; Pf.* נוֹתַר Ex 10^{15} + 8 t, etc; *Impf* יִוָּתֵר 2 K 20^{17} + 2 t.; יִוָּתֶר בָּהּ Zc 13^{8}; וַיִּוָּתֵר Gn 32^{25} + 2 t., וָאִוָּתֵר 1 K 19$^{10.14}$, etc.; *Pt.* נוֹתָר 1 S 2^{36} + 17 t., נֹתָר Ex 12^{10}, fs. נוֹתֶרֶת Lv 2^{3} + 3 t.; mpl. נוֹתָרִים Ju 8^{10} + 24 t., etc.;—*be left over, remain (over)*, abs. Ex 10^{15} (J), Jos 11$^{11.22}$ (D), Ju 9^{5} Is 1^{8} 30^{17} 1 K 18^{22} 2 K 20^{17} = Is 39^{6}; sq. לְבַדּוֹ *be left alone* Gn 32^{25} (J), so 1 K 19$^{10.14}$; sq. מִן *be left from* (= *of*) 2 S 13^{30} Ex 29^{34} Nu 26^{65} (both P), ψ 106^{11}; pt sq מִן Ju 8^{10} + 10 t P, 1 K 9^{20} = 2 Ch 8^{7}, Zc 14^{16} 1 Ch 6^{46}; sq. לְ, *be left (surviving) to*, 1 S 25^{34} 2 S 9^{1}, *of those belonging to* Gn 44^{20} (J, לְבַדּוֹ לְאִמּוֹ), sq בְּ *be left in* (= *of*) 2 S 17^{12} Jos 18^{2} (JE), also pt. Lv 8^{32} 14^{18} (P), Ez 48$^{15.18}$; oft. sq. בְּ loc. Am 6^{9} + 11 t.; sq. בית *in the house of* Je 27^{21}; sq. על־פני הארץ Ez 39^{14} (pt.); sq. אַחֲרֵי = *be left behind* (of sons) 1 K 9^{21} = 2 Ch 8^{8}; sq. אֵצֶל + שָׁם Dn 10^{13} *I was left over there beside the kings* (i. e. I had nothing more to do; cf VB); elsewh. pt. abs, as adj. Gn 30^{36} (J), Jos 17$^{2.6}$ (JE), Lv 10$^{12.16}$ 27^{18} Jos 21$^{5.26.34}$ (all P), Je 34^{7} 1 Ch 6$^{55.62}$ 22^{20}; as subst. Ju 21$^{7.16}$ 1 S 30^{9} Ex 28^{10} 29^{34} Lv 19^{6} (all P), 1 K 20$^{30.30}$ 2 K 4^{7} Ez 34^{18} 48^{21} 2 Ch 31^{10}.

†**Hiph.** *Pf.* הוֹתִיר Ex 10^{15} Is 1^{9}, etc; *Impf* יוֹתִיר Dt 28^{54}; juss יוֹתֵר Ex 16^{19}; וַיּוֹתֵר 2 S 8^{4} 2 Ch 18^{4}; 3 fs וַתֹּתַר Ru 2^{14}; 2 ms. juss. תּוֹתַר Gn 49^{4}, 1 s אוֹתִיר Ez 39^{28}; 3 mpl. וַיּוֹתִרוּ Ex 16^{20} 2 K 4^{44}; 2 mpl תותירו Ex 12^{10} + 2 t; *Imv.* הוֹתֵר ψ 79^{11}; *Inf. abs.* הותר 2 K 4^{43} + 2 t.; *cstr.* הותיר Je 44^{7};—**1. a.** *leave over, leave* Ex 10^{15} (J), Ru 2^{14} (obj.om.), v^{18} 2 K 4^{43} (אָכוֹל וְהוֹתֵר, v. infr.), v^{44} (obj.om. in both), 2 Ch 31^{10}; יֶתֶר בָּנָיו אֲשֶׁר יוֹתִיר Dt 28^{54}; sq. obj. שָׂרִיד + לְ pers. Is 1^{9}; obj. שְׁאֵרִית + לְ pers. Je 44^{7}; sq. מִן *from* (= *of*), 2 S 8^{4} = 1 Ch 18^{4}, Nu 33^{55} (P), Ez 12^{16}; + עַד temp Ex 12^{10} 16$^{19.20}$ (all P), Lv 22^{30} (H); + שָׁם loc. Ez 39^{28}. **b.** abs *leave a remnant* Ez 6^{8} (denom. fr. יֶתֶר?). **c.** *save over, i e preserve alive* ψ 79^{11}. **2.** *excel, shew pre-eminence* Gn 49^{4} (poem in J). **3.** *shew excess = have more than enough* Ex 36^{7} (P; vid. also 2 K 4^{43} 2 Ch 31^{10} supr.); *make abundant* Dt 28^{11} 30^{9} (sq sf. pers. + בְּ rei)

יָתֵר Pr 12^{26}, v. תור.

I. יֶתֶר$_{94}$ **n.m.**$^{Ne 2.16}$ **remainder, excellence, excess,**—abs יֶתֶר Ne 2^{16} + 2 t.; יָתֶר Pr 17^{7}; cstr. יֶתֶר Gn 49^{3} + 84 t; יָתֶר Is 56^{12} (vid. Baer's note); sf יִתְרוֹ Is 44^{19}, יתרם Ex 23^{11} + 2 t. (not Jb 4^{21}, q.v. sub II. יֶתֶר);—**1.** †**a.** *remainder, remnant* (with implied inferiority in number or quality), of crops, etc. יִתְרָם Ex 23^{11} (JE), *their remnant*, i.e. what they (the enemy) leave, so יֶתֶר הַגָּזָם Jo 1^{4}; יֶתֶר הָאַרְבֶּה v^{4}, יֶתֶר הַיֶּלֶק v^{4}, יֶתֶר הַפְּלֵטָה Ex 10^{5} (J); of vessels, יֶתֶר הַכֵּלִים הַנּוֹתָרִים Je 27^{19}; of a tree Is 44^{19} (= שְׁאֵרִית v^{17}); elsewh. of pers. Dt 3^{11} = Jos 12^{4} 3^{13} (both D), Dt 28^{54} Jos 23^{12} (D), 2 S 21^{2} 2 K 25^{11} = Je 52^{15}, Ez 34^{18}, of a rescued remnant of Israel (Judah) Mi 5^{2} Zp 2^{9} (∥ שְׁאֵרִית), Zc 14^{2}; יֶתֶר הַקָּדֵשׁ אֲשֶׁר נִשְׁאַר 1 K 22^{47}; יֶתֶר הָעָם הַנִּשְׁאָרִים Je 39$^{9.9}$ 2 K 25^{11} = Je 52^{15}†. **b.** *remainder, rest, other part* of people, elders, etc, 2 S 10^{10} = 1 Ch 19^{11}, 2 S 12^{28} 1 K 12^{23} Je 29^{1} Hb 2^{8} Ez 48^{23}; sts. incl. a majority Ju 7^{6} 1 S 13^{2}; of common people (opp. rulers) Ne 2^{16} 4$^{8.13}$, cf. 6^{1}; of land Dt 3^{13} Jos 13^{27} (P); of other inanimate things Lv 14^{17} (P), Nu 31^{32} (*id.*), of years Is 38^{10}; elsewhere in phr.

יֶתֶר דברי *the rest of the affairs of*, in summaries of reigns of kings of Israel and Judah 1 K 11^{41} + 41 t K Ch, יֶתֶר דְּבָרָיו 1 K 15^{23}; יֶתֶר כָּל־דִּבְרֵי 2 Ch 28^{26}. †**2. a.** *excess*, שְׂפַת יֶתֶר Pr 17^{7} *a lip of excess*=arrogant speech (see VB) **b.** in adv. phrases, עַל יֶתֶר ψ 31^{24} *on the basis of abundance=abundantly*, as adv. accus גָּדוֹל יֶתֶר מְאֹד Is 56^{12} great, *in abundance*, exceedingly, Dn 8^{9} וַתִּגְדַּל־יֶתֶר and grew great *in excess, exceedingly* (cf ܝܬܝܪ *much*, ܝܬܝܪ ܡܢ *more than*) **c.** specif. *what is over and above* immediate necessities, *abundance, affluence* Jb 22^{20} ψ 17^{14} †**3.** *superiority, excellency* יֶתֶר שְׂאֵת וְיֶתֶר עָז Gn 49^{3}.—On Jb 4^{1} v ii יֶתֶר

†ii **יֶתֶר n.m.**$^{Ju\ 16,7}$ **cord** (prop. as *hanging over* or *down*, Aram יִתְרָא part of the intestines, 𝔗 יַתְרַיָּא *ropes*, ܝܬܪܐ *cord, rope, chord* of arc; Ar. وَتَرٌ bow-*string*, lute-*string*; Eth. ወተር: *sinew, cord*; ወተረ: *stretch bowstring, strain* (eyes), *be intent, eager*, etc)—יֶתֶר ψ 11^{2}+3 t, sf. יתרו Kt Jb 30^{11} (יתרי Qr), יִתְרָם Jb 4^{21},—*cord*, for binding a man Ju 16$^{7.8.9}$; *bowstring* ψ 11^{2} Jb 30^{11} (acc to Qr, opp 29^{20b}; Kt=*his cord*, with which he reins in my assailants; cf Di Da). Jb 4^{21} *tent-cord* Ew De Di RV, yet rd perh. יְתֵדָם *their tent-peg*, so Ol Hi Sgfr (>AV *their excellency*, fr i. יֶתֶר)

†iii **יֶתֶר n.pr.m.** (*abundance*; on form and mng of this and the foll n pr v Lag$^{BN\ 52,\ 196}$)—**1.** father of Moses' wife Ex 4^{18a} (E; prob. txt. err, elsewhere יִתְרוֹ, q.v.) **2.** eldest son of Gideon Ju 8^{20}, 𝔊 Ιεθερ. **3.** father of Amasa 1 K 2$^{5.32}$ 1 Ch 2^{17}, 𝔊 Ιεθερ; =יִתְרָא 2 S 17^{25}, 𝔊 Ιοθερ, Ιοθορ, 𝔊L Ιεθερ. **4.** men of Judah, 𝔊 Ιεθερ. **a.** 1 Ch 2$^{32.32}$ **b.** 1 Ch 4^{17}. **5.** a man of Asher 1 Ch 7^{38} (=יִתְרָן v^{37}), 𝔊 Ιεθερ, A Ιεθηρ, 𝔊L [v^{39}] Εθραν

†**יִתְרָא n pr.m.** father of Amasa 2 S 17^{25} (v iii יֶתֶר **3**).

†**יִתְרָה n.f. abundance, riches**,—יִתְרָה עָשָׂה Is 15^{7}=יִתְרַת עָשָׂה Je 48^{36} (on cstr. cf. Da$^{Synt.\ \S 25}$) *the abundance* (which) *he hath gotten*

†**יִתְרוֹ n pr.m.** father of Moses' wife Ex 3^{1} 4^{18b} 18$^{1.2.5.6.9\ 10\ 12}$ (all E), =יֶתֶר 4^{18}, in all 𝔊 Ιοθορ.

†**יִתְרִי adj. gent.**, alw c art הַיִּתְרִי 2 S 23^{38}, 𝔊 Αιθειραιος, etc, v^{34}, 𝔊 Εθθεναιος, 𝔊L Ιεθεμ, rd. perh הַיַּתִּרִי Th Klo Kit Bu, =1 Ch 11$^{40.40}$, 𝔊 Ηθηρει, Ιεθ(ε)ρι, etc., coll 1 Ch 2^{53}, 𝔊 Αιθαλειμ, 𝔊L Εθρι.

†**יֹתֵר, יוֹתֵר n.m. superiority, advantage, excess** (late) (prop **Qal** pt of יתר)—abs. יותר Ec 7^{16}+2 t; יֹתֵר Ec 2^{15}+4 t.,—*superiority, advantage* מַה־יּוֹתֵר לֶחָכָם מִן־הַכְּסִיל Ec 6^{8} *what advantage hath the wise over the fool?* prob. also יֹתֵר מֵהֵמָּה 12^{12} (as to) *what is more than these* (see VB), abs. מַה־יֹּתֵר לָאָדָם 6^{11}; יֹתֵר לְרֹאֵי הַשָּׁמֶשׁ Ec 7^{11}, elsewh. adv *to excess, overmuch* Ec 2^{15} 7^{16}, sq מִן (as oft. in NH), יוֹתֵר מִמֶּנִּי Est 6^{6} *more than me*; יֹתֵר שׁ׳=*besides that* Ec 12^{9}.

†**יֹתֶרֶת n.f. appendage** (term. techn. of P),—most prob. (fat) *appendage*, a (fatty) mass at opening of liver of sacrificial animal, extending to kidneys (v. Di Dr$^{Polychr\ Bible,\ Lv\ 3,\ 4}$),—הַיֹּתֶרֶת עַל־הַכָּבֵד Ex 29^{13} Lv 3$^{4.10.15}$ 4^{9} 7^{4}; הַיּ׳ מִן־הַכָּבֵד Lv 9^{10}, cstr יֹתֶרֶת הַכָּבֵד Ex 29^{22} Lv 8$^{16.25}$ 9^{19} (all P).

†**יִתְרוֹן n.[m.] advantage, profit, only Ec**;—abs Ec 1^{3}+4 t., cstr Ec 2^{13}+4 t,—*advantage* to (ל) any one, מַה־יִּתְרוֹן לָאָדָם Ec 1^{3}, i e *what advantage hath a man?* 5^{15} 10^{11}; sq מִן compar=*advantage beyond, more than* 2$^{13.13}$; cstr. יִתְרוֹן הָעוֹשֶׂה 3^{9} *advantage of* (for) *him that worketh*, יִתְרוֹן אֶרֶץ 5^{8}; יִתְרוֹן דַּעַת 7^{12} *advantage of knowledge*; וְיִתְרוֹן הַכְשֵׁיר חָכְמָה Ec 10^{10} *an advantage for giving success is wisdom*; abs. אֵין יִתְרוֹן תַּחַת הַשָּׁמֶשׁ Ec 2^{11}.

†**יִתְרָן n.pr.m. 1.** an Edomite Gn 36^{26}=1 Ch 1^{41}, 𝔊 Ι(ε)θραν, etc. **2.** a man of Asher 1 Ch 7^{37} (v iii יֶתֶר **5**), 𝔊 Θερα, A Ιεθερ, 𝔊L [v^{38}] Ιεθραν.

†**הוֹתִיר n.pr.m.** (*abundance, superabundance*)—a son of Heman, acc. to 1 Ch 25$^{4.28}$ (but on the ostensible list of names v. Ew$^{\S 274\ b}$ We$^{Prol.\ 229,\ Hist\ Isr\ 219}$ RS$^{OTJC\ 224,\ 2nd\ ed.\ 143}$)

†**מוֹתָר n.m.**$^{Pr\ 14,23}$ **abundance, pre-eminence**,—**1.** *abundance, plenty* מוֹתָר Pr 14^{23} 21^{5} (in both opp מַחְסוֹר). **2.** *pre-eminence, superiority*, מוֹתַר הָאָדָם מִן־הַבְּהֵמָה אָיִן Ec 3^{19} *the superiority of man over beast is nothing*

†**[מֵיתָר] n.m. cord, string** (cf. ii יֶתֶר); of tent-*cords* מֵיתָרַי Je 10^{20}; מֵיתָרַיִךְ Is 54^{2}; specif of *cords* of tabernacle, מֵיתָרָיו Ex 39^{40} Nu 3^{26}; מיתריהם Ex 35^{18} Nu 3^{37} 4$^{26.32}$ (all P), of bow-*strings* מֵיתָרֶיךָ ψ 21^{13}.

†**יַתִּיר, יַתִּר n.pr.loc.** town in Judah (√ dub),—יַתִּיר Jos 15^{48}, 𝔊 Ι(ε)θερ, elsewh יַתִּר,

Levitical city Jos 21^{14} (both P), 𝔊 Αιλωμ, A 𝔊L Ιεθερ, 1 Ch 6^{42}, 𝔊 [v^{43}] Ιεθθαρ, A Ιεθερ; prob. = יַתִּר 1 S 30^{27}, 𝔊 Γεθθορ, A Εειθερ;—acc. to Onom. = Ιεθειρα, village 20 miles from Eleutheropolis, Lag Onom. 266, 133; ed. 2, p. 268; identified by Rob BR i. 494 (who, however, questions ' (ע)=י) Bd Pal. 3, 153 with 'Attîr, halfway between Hebron and Milḥ; so, 'perh.,' Buhl Geogr. § 91, p. 164; this not certain, cf. Di.

† יִתְרְעָם **n.m.** 6th son of David 2 S 3^{5} = 1 Ch 3^{3}, 𝔊 Ιθ(α)ραμ, Ιεθρααμ, etc.

† יְתֵת **n.pr.m.** an Edomite chief Gn 36^{40}, 𝔊 Ιεβερ = 1 Ch 1^{51}, 𝔊 Ιεθετ; 𝔊 L in both Ιεθερ.

כ

כ, ך, eleventh letter; used as numeral 20 in postB Heb.; כא = 21, כב = 22, etc.

כְּ prop. **subst. the like of, like, as** (Aram. כ, Ph. כ, Ar. كَ, Sab. in כעד דא *as* till now DHM ZMG xxix. 615, As. *ki, kima*, Dl HWB 325 f.)—before tone-syll. כָּ, as כָּזֶה, כָּאֵלֶּה, כָּהֵמָּה; c. sf. כָּכֶם Nu 15^{15} + 7 t. (Jb 16^{4} כְּכֶם: Kö ii. 1. 285), כָּהֶם † 2 K 17^{15}, כָּהֵן † Ez 18^{14} [also with nom. forms, כְּהֵמָּה, כָּהֶם, כָּהֵנָּה; v. הֵמָּה **8**; cf. Arab. كَأَنَا, كَأَنْتَ, etc.], before light sf., in the form כְּמוֹ (q.v.), viz. כָּמוֹנִי, כָּמֹנִי Gn 44^{15} + 16 t., כָּמוֹךָ Gn 41^{39} + 28 t., כָּמֹכָה † Ex $15^{11.11}$, כָּמֹהוּ 9^{18} + 23 t., כָּמוֹהָ 11^{6} + 2 t., כָּמֹנוּ Gn 34^{15} + 3 t.; also כְּמוֹכֶם † Jb 12^{3}, כְּמוֹהֶם † Ju 8^{18} ψ 115^{8} 135^{18}. Prop. an undeveloped *subst.*, capable of standing in any case and followed (like كَ) always by a gen., as 1 S 20^{3} כי כפשׂע for there is (nomin.) *the like of* a footstep (Ar. كَخَطْوَةٍ) between me and death, Gn 41^{38} הנמצא כזה shall we find (accus.) *the like of* this one? (v. esp. Fleischer Kl. Schrr. i. 376 ff. Mühlau, *ap.* Bö ii. 64 f., with many Arabic exx.; also W AG i. § 356 R. c.; ii. § 63 Ges § 118. 6; compare, for both usage and constr., the Lat. *instar:* this view criticized by Kö ii. 1. 279 ff., who treats כְּ as demonstr. adv.); but Heb. having no case-endings, its proper sense was doubtless forgotten, and כְּ became practically equivalent to a prep. *like, as*:—**1. a.** *quantitatively* (like the Ar. قَدْرُ *measure, number, size, of* . . .: قَدْرُ مِائَةٍ *as many as* 100), to express exact or approx. equality, in the latter case *the like of* is = *about*: Dt 1^{11} Yahweh add to you ככם אלף פעמים *the like of you* (Saad. مِثْلَكُمْ) 1000 times (cf. 2 S 24^{3}), Ex 12^{37} כשׁשׁ מאות אלף רגלי *the like of* (i.e. *about*) 600,000 footmen, 32^{28} כִּשְׁלֹשֶׁת אלפי אישׁ, Jos 4^{13} 7^{3} 1 S 9^{22} 25^{38} ויהי כעשׂרת הימים (nomin.) and there was *the like of* (= *about*) 10 days, and, etc. Ru 2^{17} כאיפה שׂערים, etc., cf. כַּמָּה *the like of* what? = *how many?* (v. מָה); as accus. of space or time, Nu 11^{31} כדרך יום *the like of* a day's journey, Jos 3^{4}; Jos 10^{13} כיום תמים *about* a whole day (Ar. نَحْوَ يَوْمٍ كَامِلٍ), Ru 1^{4} כעשׂר שׁנים. So (as adv. accus.) with words denoting a *point* of time: often with עֵת, as כָּעֵת הַזֹּאת lit. at *the like of* this time = *about* this time, Jos 11^{6} al., כָּעֵת מָחָר at *the like of* the time, (being) to-morrow = *about to-morrow*, Ex 9^{18}+, כָּעֵת חַיָּה (v. חי), Is 8^{23} כעת הראשׁון *at* the former time, כָּעֵת alone = *at the* (present) *time, now* Nu 23^{23} Ju 13^{23}, Is 23^{5} (unusual) כְּשֵׁמַע צֹר; so כַּיּוֹם, כְּהַיּוֹם (v. יוֹם **7 h**), כְּרֶגַע, כִּמְעַט; and esp. with inf., v. **3 b**. **b.** *qualitatively* (like Ar. مِثْلُ *likeness of* . . .), to express resemblance in respect of some attribute, action, character, appearance, etc.: so very often; as subj. of a sentence, Nu 9^{15} כמראה אשׁ *the like of* (= *as it were*) an appearance of fire was, etc. (cf. Ez $1^{4.26 a.27}$ Dn 8^{15} 10^{18}), 23^{22} כתועפות ראם לו, Ex 24^{10}, Dt 4^{32} הנהיה כדבר הגדול הזה hath there been *the like of* this great thing? 9^{10} Jos 10^{14}; Ho 9^{1} Is 23^{15} ψ 58^{5} Pr 16^{27} La 1^{20} כְּבֵית מָוֶת, Ec 8^{14}; Lv 14^{35} כְּנֶגַע נראה בביתי *the like of* (i.e. *a kind of*) mark; מִי כָמוֹכָה who is *the like of* thee? Ex 15^{11} (Saad. مَنْ مِثْلُكَ) +; as gen. אֵין כָּמוֹךָ 1 S 10^{24} 2 S 7^{22}+; as pred., Ju 8^{21} כָּאִישׁ גְּבוּרָתוֹ, Hb 2^{5} וְהוּא כַמָּוֶת, ψ 17^{14} 89^{30} וכסאו כימי שׁמים (of time: so v^{37}), 125^{1}, etc.; after a verb, היה כְּ to become *the like of* (*like*), Gn 3^{5} + oft. (v. היה **II. 2 c**), cf. after שִׂים Gn 13^{16}+, נתן 42^{30}+, שִׁית ψ 83^{12}+, שָׁוָה, 18^{34}, נֶחְשַׁב 44^{23}+, נִמְשַׁל 49^{13}, הִרְבָּה Gn 22^{17}+; add כָּזֹאת, כָּאֵלֶּה *the like of* this (these), i.e. *tale, talia* (whether nom. or accus.) Ju 13^{23} 15^{7} 20^{30} Lv 10^{19}+ (v. אֵלֶּה, זאת). Cases such as to give or

reward a man כרעתו ,כמעשׂהו, etc., *the like of* his doings, etc., 2 S 3^{39} 1 K 8^{32} ψ 18^{25} 28^{4}, to speak כדבר הזה or כדברים האלה Gn 18^{25} 24^{28} + oft., form the transition to **c.** as an accus. of mode or limitation, *in* or *with the like of* (=*like, as, according to, κατά*);—(1) expressing conformity to a standard or rule: Gn 1^{26} let us make man כדמותנו *according to* our likeness, 9^{3} Jos 19^{47} Ju 20^{10} 1 S 13^{14} hath looked out אישׁ כלבבו a man *according to* his own heart (Je 3^{15}); to do a thing כמשׁפט הזה Jos 6^{15}, cf. Gn 40^{13} 2 K 11^{14}, etc., כדבר פ׳ Gn 44^{2} + oft., כְּצִדְקִי ψ 7^{9}, כְּחַסְדֶּךָ 51^{3}, כַּכָּתוּב *according to* what is written Jos $8^{31.34}$ +, בלא ככתוב (late) † 2 Ch 30^{18}, etc. (2) in comparisons: qualifying an adj., Ex 16^{14} דַּק כַּכְּפֹר, Ct 6^{10} יָפָה כַּלְּבָנָה, cf. Gn 13^{10}; a verb ψ 7^{3} פֶּן־יִטְרֹף כְּאַרְיֵה, 19^{6} יָשִׂישׂ כְּגִבּוֹר, Is 42^{13}, etc.; with the *tertium compar.* attached in a relative clause, Dt 32^{11} כְּנֶשֶׁר יָעִיר קִנּוֹ *like* the great vulture, (that) stirreth up its nest, Jb 9^{26} 11^{16} Is 61^{10} *like* the bride, who putteth on, etc., 62^{1} כְּלַפִּיד יִבְעָר *like* a touch (that) burns (on the presence or absence of the art. in such cases, v. הַ **1 f**), ψ 42^{2} 83^{15} (infr. **2 d**) + oft. (cf. Dr $^{§ 34}$: כְּ is not in these cases to be construed as a conj. [=כַּאֲשֶׁר] with the verb: v. De $^{ψ 38, 14}$ Ges $^{§ 155, 2 b, 1 R.}$). **d.** sometimes כְּ is used in partic. to compare an object with the *class* to which it belongs, and express its correspondence with the idea which it ought to realize: Is 13^{6} (=Jo 1^{15}) of the יום י׳, כְּשֹׁד מִשַּׁדַּי יָבוֹא i.e. it comes as a *veritable*, or *ideal*, destruction from Shaddai, 29^{2} of Ariel (v^{1}) והיתה לי כאריאל i.e. shall be to me as a *true* Ariel (cf. Ges $^{§ 118 x}$): so also, acc. to Hi De, 10^{13} Ez 26^{10} Zc 14^{3} 2 S 9^{8} ψ 122^{3} Ct 8^{10} (v. De), Ec 10^{5} Ne 7^{2}. The older grammarians called this the *Kaph veritatis* (a translation of Ki's כ״ף לאמת הדבר ,כ״ף הָאֲמִתּוּת, Michl $^{45 a (Lyck)}$, Comm $^{Jos 3, 4, 1 S 9, 13, Is 1, 7, Ho 5, 10}$, or כ״ף הָאֲמִתִּי, Lex s. v. יוֹם): they extended it unduly (e.g. to Nu 11^{1} La 1^{20} Ho 11^{4}). **2.** repeated, כְּ . . . כְּ, to signify the completeness of the correspondency between two objects (peculiar to Heb.): **a.** in a principal clause, Gn 18^{25} וְהָיָה כַצַּדִּיק כָּרָשָׁע lit. that *the like of* the righteous be *the like of* the wicked, i.e. that the righteous be *as* the wicked, 44^{18} כמוך כפרעה *the like of* thee is *the like of* Pharaoh, i.e. *thou* art as Pharaoh, Lv 24^{22} כַּגֵּר כָּאֶזְרָח יִהְיֶה, 1 K 22^{4} כָּמוֹנִי כָמוֹךָ כְּעַמִּי כְעַמֶּךָ (Van Dyck مَثَلِي مَثَلُكَ شَعْبِي كَشَعْبِكَ), Hg 2^{3} הֲלוֹא כָמֹהוּ כְּאַיִן בְּעֵינֵיכֶם is not *the like of* it *the like of* nothing in your eyes? i.e. is it not like nothing in your eyes? ψ 139^{12} כַּחֲשֵׁיכָה כָּאוֹרָה i.e. the darkness (to thee) is *as* the light. Usu. the first term is the subj. and the second is the standard with which it is compared: but occas. the terms are inverted, as Lv 7^{7} Nu 15^{15} Ju 8^{18} כמוך כמוהם (Van Dyck مَثَلُهُمْ مَثَلُكَ), Ho 4^{9} Is 24^{2}, cf. 59^{18} (*Note*, infr.) **b.** in a subordinate clause (to be regarded as subordinated in the accus. to the principal verb); (*α*) attached to the *subj.* of the principal vb., Lv 24^{16} כגר כאזרח . . . יומת he shall be put to death, *the like of* the stranger (being) *the like of* the homeborn, Jos 8^{33}. (*β*) attached to its *object*, Dt 1^{17} כקטן כגדל תשׁמעון lit. ye shall hear (them), *the like of* the small (being) *the like of* the great. **c.** occas., for כְּ . . . כְּ, there occurs כְּ . . . וכ: Jos 14^{11} כְּכֹחִי אָז וּכְכֹחִי עָתָּה *the like of* my strength then, and *the like of* my strength now, i.e. they are similar (cf. וְ **1 j**) 1 S 30^{24} Ez 18^{4} Dn 11^{29}. **d.** yet more distinct than כְּ . . . כְּ, is כְּ . . . כֵּן; in a nominal sentence (Ges $^{§ 140-1}$), 'כְּ with its genit. forming the predic., and כֵּן resuming it with emph. and connecting it with the subject;' 1 S 25^{25} כִּי כִשְׁמוֹ כֶּן־הוּא for *the like of* his name, *such* (or *so*) is he, Gn 44^{10} Jos 2^{21} Je 18^{6} ψ 48^{11} 127^{4} Pr 10^{26} +; in a verbal sentence, 'כְּ preceding, as an accusative of state, and giving the *secundum comparationis*, and כֵּן resuming it,' Jo 2^{4} כפרשׁים כן ירוצון '*instar* (accus.) equitum, *sic* currunt' (Fl $^{l. c.}$), Ho 4^{7} lit. *with* (or *in*) *the likeness of* their multiplying, *so* they sinned against me, Gn 6^{22} 1 S 8^{8} Is 38^{14} Ez 22^{22} ψ 42^{2} 83^{15} + oft. **3.** before an inf.: **a.** *like* (lit. *with* or *in the likeness of* . . .), Ju 14^{6} כְּשַׁסַּע הַגְּדִי *like* the rending of a kid, i.e. *as when* a kid is rent (by a lion), 2 S 3^{34} Is 5^{24} ψ 66^{10} 68^{3} Jb 2^{10}, etc.; =*as if*, Is 10^{15} or shall the saw magnify itself against him that wieldeth it כהניף שׁבט את־מרימיו *with the like of* a staff's shaking (=*as if* a staff were to shake) him that lifted it! **b.** of time, *about*, *at*, whether of the past or of the future: Gn 19^{17} כהוציאם אותם *at* their bringing them forth, i.e. *as* or *when* they brought them forth 24^{30} 29^{13} $39^{10.13}$ + very often; of the future, $44^{30.31}$ Dt $20^{2.9}$ 2 S 13^{28} +; Is $28^{20 b}$ (different from $v^{20 a}$) and the covering is (too) narrow *when one gathers oneself* in. Occasionally with the verbal noun, Ho 13^{6} כמרעיתם *at the time of* their feeding, Is 30^{19} כְּשָׁמְעָתוֹ; וּכְחֶזְקָתוֹ † 2 Ch 12^{1} 26^{16} Dn 11^{2} (Ew $^{§ 238 a, 239 a}$): cf. Is $23^{5 b}$ כְּשֵׁמַע צֹר. With the ptcp. † Gn 38^{29} (si vera l.), perh. 40^{10}; cf. Dr $^{§ 135, 6, Obs. 2}$.

Note—כּ is rarely prefixed to preps., the only exx. which occur being the idiomatic כְּבָרִאשֹׁנָה, †Ju 20^{32} 1 K 13^{6} Is 1^{26} Jer 33$^{7.11}$; כְּבַתְּחִלָּה in the ‖ clause †Is$^{1 c}$; כְּבַחֲצִי † 1 S 14^{14} (apparently corrupt), כְּמִשְׁלֹשׁ חֳדָשִׁים † Gn 38^{24} (and prob כְּמֵחֹדֶשׁ 1 S 10^{27} 𝔊), כְּמִפְּנֵי † Lv 26^{37}; † כְּעַל (late): **a.** pleon for כְּ (עַל=*according to*), Is 63^{7} כְּעַל כֹּל־אֲשֶׁר עָשָׂה, 59^{18} כְּעַל גְּמֻלוֹת כְּעַל יְשַׁלֵּם *the like of* their deeds is *the like of* (that which) he will repay (ellipse of rel, as Jb 34^{32}, etc); **b.**=*as over* ψ 119^{14},=*as concerning* 2 Ch 32^{19}. Where logically a prep. would seem to be required after כ, it is in Heb. regularly omitted (Ges$^{§ 118. 3 R}$), the nature of כְּ, as explained above, not in fact admitting it; thus Is 1^{25} I will purge away thy dross כַּבֹּר [not, as in Engl, *like as with* lye, but] (with) *the like of* lye (כ being an accus defining the mode in which אצרף takes place); 5^{17} כְּדָבְרָם in Engl. as *in* their pasture, Ju 20^{39}, כיום as *in* the day of, Is 9^{3} ψ 95^{8}+, כִּימֵי Jb 29^{2} who will set me as *in* the days of old! Is 51^{9}+, כְּנֹקֶף זַיִת as *at*, etc, 17^{6}: so with לְ ψ 83^{10} Jb 29^{23}, על 30^{5}. כְּ is used also pregnantly with substs, ψ 18^{34} who maketh my feet *like hinds* (for *like the feet of hinds*), Is 29^{4} 63^{2} בנדיך כדורך בגת, Je 50^{9} Jb 40^{9} al. Cf. Ges$^{§§ 118. 6; 141 2 R. *}$.

כַּאֲשֶׁר **conj.** according as, as, when (cf. for the combin Aram. כְּדִי, כַּד)—**1.** *according to that which, according as, as*: **a.** Gn 34^{12} I will give כאשר תאמרו אלי *according as* ye shall (*or* may) say unto me, 44^{1} Ex 8^{23} Nu 22^{8} 1 S 2^{16}; Gn 34^{22} if we are circumcised כאשר הם נמולים; 41^{21} כאשר בתחלה *as* at the beginning, so כ׳ בראשונה Jos 8$^{5.6}$ 2 S 7^{10}; Ex 5^{13} כאשר בהיות התבן: Gn 7^{9} they came in two by two כאשר צוה אלהים, *as* God commanded Noah; so, or similarly, very oft., esp. in P, v^{16} 8^{21} 12^{4} 17^{23} 21$^{1.1}$ Ex 16^{24} 39$^{1.5.7}$ Nu 3$^{16.42}$ etc.; כאשר דבר י׳ Dt 1^{21} 2^{1} 6$^{3.19}$+ oft. Dt. **b.** answered, for increased emph., by כן (cf. כְּ **2 d**), Gn 50^{12} ויעשו כן כאשר צִוָּם, Ex 7$^{10.20}$; Gn 18^{5} (J) כן תעשה כאשר דברת, Ex 10^{10} (iron), Am 5^{14} (do.); in opp order, Ju 1^{7} כאשר עשיתי כן שלם לי, Ex 7^{6} כאשר צוה י׳ כן עשו, cf. 12$^{28.50}$ 39^{43} Nu 5^{4} 17^{26} 36^{10} (all P); with impf. (freq) Nu 2^{17} (P) כאשר יחנו כן יסעו; of degree=*the more* .. *the more*, Ex 1^{12} וכאשר יענו אתו כן ירבה וכן יפרץ, cf 17^{11} (JE) והיה כאשר ירים ... וגבר ישר׳ *according as* he held up, etc., Israel prevailed; in an oath or solemn promise, Nu 14^{28} אם לא כאשר דברתם כן אעשה, Dt 28^{63} (Je 31^{28}), 1 K 1^{30} Is 10^{11} 14^{24} 52^{14f} + (v. כן **2 b**) **c.** answered by ·וְ (Dr$^{§ 127 γ}$) † Ex 16^{34} Nu 1^{19}. **d.** oft. in *similes* (sq. impf. of habit) Ex 33^{11} כאשר ידבר איש אל רעהו, Nu 11^{12} Dt 1^{44} Is 9^{2} 66^{20}+, answered by כֵּן Is 31^{4} 55^{10} 66^{22} Am 3^{12}+; a second verb is, in such cases, in the pf. with וְ consec. (Dr$^{§ 115}$) Dt 22^{26} Is 29^{8} כאשר יחלם ... והקיץ, 65^{8} Am 5^{19}. **e.** הָיָה כַּאֲשֶׁר (cf. הָיָה כ) to be *as if*, Jb 10^{19} כאשר לא הייתי אהיה, Zc 10^{6} והיו כאשר לא זנחתים. **2.** with a *causal* force, *in so far as, since* (Germ. *demgemass dass*), Gn 26^{29} if thou doest us no harm כאשר לא נגענוך *according as, in so far as*, we have not touched thee; Nu 27^{14} כאשר מריתם פי *inasmuch as* ye have defied my mouth, Ju 6^{27} 1 S 28^{18} (answered by על כן), 2 K 17^{26} Mi 3^{4}. **3.** with a *temporal* force, *when*, Gn 18^{33} and Y. went away כאשר כלה *when* he had finished, etc., 32$^{3.32}$ 1 S 8^{6} 2 S 12^{21}+; answered by ·וְ (Dr$^{§ 127 β}$), 1 S 6^{6} 12^{8}, ויהי כאשר ... and it came to pass, when ... Gn 12^{11} 20^{13} 24$^{22.52}$ 27^{30} Ex 32^{19}+ oft.; Gn 43^{14} כאשר שכלתי שכלתי when I am bereaved, I am bereaved! an expression of resignation, so Est 4^{16} כאשר אבדתי אבדתי. Jos 2^{7} אחרי כאשר is a 'conflate' reading, omit either אחרי or כ. Of future time, Gn 27^{40} 40^{14} כאשר ייטב לך, Ho 7^{12} Ec 4^{17} 5^{3}, and without a verb Is 23^{5} כאשר שמע למצרים.—Mi 3^{3} כאשר is simply *as that which*, Jb 29^{25} *as one who*.

כְּמוֹ **adv.** and **conj.** like, as, when (lit. *the like of what* (viz.) . ., a pleon. form of כְּ (v. מוֹ), and, like it, prop a **subst.**: cf. Aram כְּמָא *like* ψ 78^{69} Levy, usually כְּמָא דְ *like as*; ܐܝܟܡܐ (i e. ܐܝܟ ܡܐ) *like what, like*, usu. sq ܕ *like as*; Sam ࠊࠌࠅ, Ar كَمَا, Eth. ከመ: *kama, like as*, Di$^{Gr § 63 a}$ Sab. כמו $^{ZMG 1883, 394}$)—used **1.** (56 t.) as an indep. word (exc. Gn 19^{15} Ne 9^{11}, only in poetry); **2.** as an equivalent for כְּ before sfs, always before light ones, and occasionally before heavy ones (v כְּ *ad init.*):—**1. a.** adv., as poet. syn. of כ, *like, as*, Ex 15^{5} they went down כמו־אבן *like* a stone (hence in prose Ne 9^{11}), v^{8} (ψ 78^{13}), Is 30^{22} 51^{6} (v. כֵּן), 26^{17} כְּמוֹ הָרָה תַּקְרִיב לָלֶדֶת (see כְּ **1 c** (2), on the constr: so 41^{25} ψ 58$^{5.8a.9}$), v^{18} we have brought forth *the like of*, *as it were*, wind, Je 13^{21} 15^{18} 50^{26} Ez 16^{57} (כמו עת as *at* the time of: v. כְּ *Note*), Ho 7^{4} 8^{12} 13^{7} Hb 3^{14} (*as it were*), Zc 9^{15} 10$^{2.7}$ (as *with* wine: v. ib) Elsewhere chiefly in ψψ (19 t) and Jb (11 t), as ψ 29^{6} 61^{7} 63^{6} 78^{69} 79^{5} 88^{6} 90^{9}, Jb 6^{15} 10$^{22.22}$ 12^{3} כמו אלה *the like of these things*, 14^{9} Ct 6^{10} 7^{2} La 4^{6} כמו רגע (in prose כרגע). Repeated,

(appar. sign of dawn); numbered by God ψ 147^{4}; sim. of abundant posterity, Gn 15^{5} 22^{17} 26^{4} Ex 32^{13} (all JE); of Isr. Dt 1^{10} 10^{22} 28^{62} 1 Ch 27^{23} Ne 9^{23}; of number of merchants of Nineveh Na 3^{16}; as lofty, Jb 22^{12}; so in fig. of haughty nations Ob^{4} Is 14^{13}; cf. symbolic vision of Dn (צְבָא הַשָּׁמַיִם, צָבָא‖) Dn 8^{10}; sim. of brightness of righteous Dn 12^{3}; not pure (זַכּוּ) before God Jb 25^{5} (‖ moon); darkened in Yahweh's judgment Jo 2^{10} 4^{15} Ez 32^{7} (‖ sun and moon; so) Is 13^{10} (‖also כְּסִילֵיהֶם); personified: as fighting Ju 5^{20}; shouting Jb 38^{7} (בְּרָן־יַחַד כּוֹכְבֵי בֹקֶר, ‖ בְּנֵי אֱלֹהִים); praising ψ 148^{3} (כּוֹכְבֵי אוֹר, ‖ sun and moon).—On stars in Arab. mythol. v. We Skizzen III. 173 f.

†**כָּבֵד** **vb. be heavy, weighty, burdensome, honoured** (NH Pi. *honour*, and deriv., כֹּבֶד *weight*; Ph. n.pr.f. כבדת = *honoured one*, and in cpd. n.pr.; Eth. ከበደ: *be heavy*, etc.; As. *kabâdu* or *kabâtu*, *grow* or *be heavy*, Dl HWB; cf. Ar. كَبَدٌ *difficulty, distress*; كَابَدَ III. *struggle with difficulties*, etc.; Zinj. כבדו *honour*, DHM Sendsch. 58; Sab. כבודת *gifts of honour*, = Heb. נדבה *freewill offering* DHM ZMG 1883, 341 f.)—**Qal** *Pf.* כ׳ Is 24^{20}; 3 fs. כָּבְדָה Gn 18^{20} + 4 t.; כָּבֵדָה Ju 20^{34}; 3 mpl. כָּבְדוּ Gn 48^{10}; *Impf.* יִכְבַּד Ex 9^{7} Is 66^{5}; יִכְבָּד Jb 6^{3} 33^{7} + 10 t. Impf. (כָּבֵד Gn 12^{10} + is given as 3 m. Pf. by some; but it is prob. taken better as adj. SS make כָּבֵד ψ 38^{5} inf. abs.; < Thes adj.).—**1.** *be heavy*, in weight, of misfortune, heavier than sand Jb 6^{3}; of God's hand in punishment 1 S 5^{11}, with אֶל 1 S 5^{6}; עַל ψ 32^{4}; of man's hand in war Ju 1^{35}; יָדִי כָּבְדָה עַל־אַנְחָתִי *my hand is heavy upon my groaning* Jb 23^{2} is explained by 𝔗 Hrz Schlottm as *hand smiting me*; but read rather with 𝔊 𝔖 Ew De Reu Di יָדוֹ of God's hand; of pressure אַכְפִּי Jb 33^{7} (𝔊 כַּפִּי); = *vehement, sore*, of battle Ju 20^{34}; c. אֶל 1 S 31^{3} = עַל 1 Ch 10^{3}; *burdensome, grievous*; וְלֹא נִכְבַּד עָלֶיךָ *lest we be burdensome unto thee* 2 S 13^{25}; of work laid upon one, bondage, with עַל Ex 5^{9} (JE) Ne 5^{18}; of sin conceived as a burden Gn 18^{20} (J), iniquities ψ 38^{5}; transgressions, with עַל Is 24^{20}. **2.** *heavy, insensible, dull*, of the eyes, so as to be unable to see Gn 48^{10} (JE); of the ears Is 59^{1}; of the לֵב, *hard, insensible* Ex 9^{7} (J; P and E's syn. is חָזַק, q.v.) **3.** *be honoured* (cf. βαρύς) of a man Jb 14^{21} (opp. יצערו: cf. Hiph. **3**), of Tyre Ez 27^{25}, of Yahweh Is 66^{5}.

Niph. *Pf.* נִכְבַּד 2 S 6^{20}, נִכְבָּד 2 S 23$^{19.23}$ 1 Ch 11^{21}; נִכְבַּדְתָּ Is 43^{4}; + 2 t. Pf.; *Impf.* אֶכָּבֵד Lv 10^{3} Is 49^{5}; אִכָּבְדָה Ex 14$^{4.17}$; אִכָּבֵדָה 2 S 6^{22}; אִכָּבְדָה Hg 1^{8}; *Imv.* הִכָּבֵד 2 K 14^{10}; *Inf.* הִכָּבְדִי Ex 14^{18} Ez 39^{13}; *Pt.* נִכְבָּד Gn 34^{19} + 6 t.; pl. נִכְבָּדִים Nu 22^{15}; cstr. נִכְבַּדֵּי Is 23$^{8.9}$ Ps 8^{24}; נִכְבַּדֶּיהָ Na 3^{10}; נִכְבְּדֵיהֶם ψ 149^{8}; *Pl. f.* נִכְבָּדוֹת ψ 87^{3}—**1.** pass. **a.** *be made heavy* fr. abundance, מַעְיְנוֹת נִכְבַּדֵּי־מָיִם *fountains abounding in water* Pr 8^{24}. **b.** *be honoured, enjoy honour*, of man 1 S 9^{6} 22^{14} 2 S 6$^{20.22}$ 23^{19} = 1 Ch 11^{21}, 2 S 23^{23} 2 K 14^{10} Is 43^{4} 49^{5} 1 Ch 4^{9} וַיְהִי נִכְבָּד, 11^{25} נִכְבָּד הוּא (altered from 2 S 23^{23}); but more frequent in *pt.* as subst. *honourable, honoured, distinguished man* Gn 34^{19} Nu 22^{15} (JE) Is 3^{5} 23$^{8.9}$ Na 3^{10} ψ 149^{8}; נִכְבָּדוֹת ψ 87^{3} *glorious things*; הַשֵּׁם הַנִּכְבָּד וְהַנּוֹרָא Dt 28^{58} *the glorious and awe-inspiring name* (of Yahweh). **2.** medial, *get oneself glory* (*or honour*), of God Is 26^{15} Ez 28^{22} 39^{13} Hg 1^{8}; with בְּ *in* or *by* any one Ex 14$^{4.17.18}$ (P); עַל־פְּנֵי Lv 10^{3} (P).

Piel *Pf.* 2 m. sf. כִּבַּדְתָּנִי Is 43^{23}; 3 mpl. כִּבְּדוּ 1 S 6^{6}; + 3 t. Pf.; *Impf.* יְכַבֵּד Mal 1^{6} + 3 t.; sf. יְכַבְּדָנְנִי ψ 50^{23}; 3 fs. sf. תְּכַבְּדֵנִי Is 43^{20}; אֲכַבְּדָה ψ 86^{12}; + 12 t. Impf.; *Imv.* כַּבֵּד Ex 20^{12} + 2 t.; + 3 t. Imv.; *Inf. abs.* כַּבֵּד Nu 22^{17}; + 2 t. Inf.; *Pt.* מְכַבֵּד 2 S 10^{3}; + 4 t. Pt.;—**1.** *make heavy, insensible* (cf. **Qal 2**) the לב(ב) 1 S 6$^{6.6}$. **2.** *make honourable, honour, glorify*, usu. c. human subj.: **a.** human obj., parents Ex 20^{12} = Dt 5^{16} (Dec.), Mal 1^{6}; Balaam Nu 22$^{17.17.37}$ 24$^{11.11}$ (JE); sons of Eli 1 S 2^{29}; Saul 1 S 15^{30}; Nahash 2 S 10^{3} = 1 Ch 19^{3}; Jerusalem La 1^{8}; more gen. ψ 15^{4}; subj. God 1 S 2^{30b} ψ 91^{15}, cf. Pr 4^{8}. **b.** obj. things, sacred place Is 60^{13} (God subj.); the Sabbath Is 58^{13}. **c.** God obj. 1 S 2^{30a} Is 24^{15} 25^{3} 43^{20} ψ 22^{24} 50$^{15.23}$ Pr 14^{31}; + acc. rei זבחיך Is 43^{23}; + בְּ instr. (lips) Is 29^{13}; + מִן (מֵהוֹנֶךָ) Pr 3^{9}; obj. the name of י׳, c. acc. ψ 86^{12}; c. לְ ψ 86^{9}; obj. the מַלְאַךְ י׳ Ju 13^{17}. **d.** subj. indef. (si vera l.), obj. God and man Ju 9^{9} (of olive; on text, esp. בּוֹ for בִּי, v. GFM). **e.** obj. a heathen god לֶאֱלֹהַּ Dn 11$^{38.38}$.

Pu. *be made honourable, honoured. Impf.* יְכֻבָּד Pr 13^{18} 27^{18}; *Pt.* מְכֻבָּד Is 58^{13}.

Hiph. *Pf.* הִכְבִּיד La 3^{7} + 5 t.; 2 f. הִכְבַּדְתְּ Is 47^{6}; + 4 t. Pf.; *Impf.* וַיַּכְבֵּד Ex 8^{28} 9^{34}; *Imv.* הַכְבֵּד Is 6^{10}; *Infin. abs.* הַכְבֵּד Ex 8^{11}; *cstr.* הַכְבִּיד 2 Ch 25^{19}; *Pt.* מַכְבִּיד Hb 2^{6}.—**1.** *make heavy*, a yoke 1 K 12$^{10.14}$ = 2 Ch 10$^{10.14}$, Is 47^{6}; ellipt. with עַל Ne 5^{15}; a chain La 3^{7}; pledges, with

על Hb 2^{6}. **2.** *make heavy, dull, unresponsive,* the ears Is 6^{10} Zc 7^{11}, the לב Ex $8^{11.28}$ 9^{34} 10^{1}(J). **3.** *cause to be honoured,* of depopulated districts of N.E. Israel, Is 8^{23}, of restored nation Je 30^{19} (‖לא יצערו); *shew* or *display honour,* 2 Ch 25^{19} לְהַכְבִּיד (in ‖ 2 K 14^{10} הִכָּבֵד).

Hithp. *Imv* הִתְכַּבֵּד Na 3^{15}, *f* הִתְכַּבְּדִי Na 3^{15}, *Pt.* מִתְכַּבֵּד Pr 12^{9},—**1.** *make oneself heavy, dense, numerous* (cf כָּבֵד **1 b**) as locusts Na $3^{15.15}$ **2.** *honour oneself* Pr 12^{9}.

†כָּבֵד **adj.** heavy,—כ׳ Gn 41^{31} + 34 t.; cstr. כְּבַד Ex $4^{10.10}$, כבד Is 1^{4}, pl כבדים Ex 17^{12}, cstr. כִּבְדֵי Ez $3^{5.6}$,—**1 a.** *heavy,* a burden ψ 38^{5}; hands (weary of holding up) Ex 17^{12} (E), hair of head 2 S 14^{26}, a corpulent old man 1 S 4^{18}, עם כֶּבֶד עָוֹן Is 1^{4} *a people heavy with* (*the burden of*) iniquity; a cloud charged with rain Ex 19^{16} (E); a rock of large size Is 32^{2}, *oppressive, grievous, burdensome,* a yoke 1 K $12^{4.11}$ = 2 Ch $10^{4.11}$, a famine Gn 12^{10} 41^{31} 43^{1} $47^{4.13}$ (J), the *vexation* (כַּעַס) of a fool Pr 27^{3}, *vehement, sore,* of a mourning Gn 50^{11} (J) **b.** *massive, abundant, numerous,* of a people עַם Nu 20^{20} (J) 1 K 3^{9}; army חיל 2 K 6^{14} 18^{17} = Is 36^{2}; insect swarm Ex 8^{20} (J) **c.** *heavy, dull* of speech and tongue Ex $4^{10.10}$ (JE), of the לב, *hard* Ex 7^{14} (J). **d.** *hard, difficult,* of a thing to be done Ex 18^{18} (E) Nu 11^{14} (J); of a language to be understood Ez $3^{5.6}$. **2.** in the usage of J כָּבֵד מאד is frequent: **a.** *very oppressive, grievous,* of hail Ex $9^{18.24}$, murrain Ex 9^{3}, lamentation Gn 50^{10}. **b.** *very numerous,* cattle Ex 12^{38}, army, מַחֲנֶה Gn 50^{9}, locusts Ex 10^{14}, so חַיִל 1 K 10^{2} = 2 Ch 9^{1}. **c.** *very rich,* במקנה *in cattle* Gn 13^{2}.

†כָּבֵד **n.m.**$^{La\ 2,11}$ liver (explained by Thes (quoting Galen) as the *heavy* organ, *par excellence,* of the body; NH כָּבֵד; Aram כַּבְדָּא, ܟܒܕܐ, Ar. كَبِدٌ, cf. أَكْبَدُ (anything) *large, thick* in the middle; Eth ከብድ: As. *kabittu* Dl^{HWB} *temper, heart* (fig), Aram. כְּבַד, ܐܬܟܒܕ *be angry,* because the liver was regarded as seat of emotions)—כ׳ Ex 29^{13} + 11 t., כבדו Pr 7^{23}, כְּבֵדִי La 2^{11};—*liver* of man, as pierced by arrow Pr 7^{23}; poured out in sorrow La 2^{11}; of animals as consulted by divination רָאָה בַכּ׳ Ez 21^{26}; elsewhere in P, in phrases (ה)יֹּתֶרֶת (עַל־)הַכָּבֵד Ex $29^{13.22}$ Lv $3^{4.10.15}$ 4^{9} 7^{4} $8^{16.25}$ 9^{19}, הַיֹּתֶרֶת מִן־הַכּ׳ Lv 9^{10}, of the animals suited for sacrifice.

†כֹּבֶד **n.**[**m.**] **1.** heaviness, *weight* of a stone Pr 27^{3}. **2.** *mass, abundance,* of corpses Na 3^{3}. **3.** *vehemence,* of war Is 21^{15}, of storm Is 30^{27}.

†I [כָּבוֹד] **adj.** glorious, only fs כְּבוּדָּה, of a bed Ez 23^{41}, a queen in bridal array ψ 45^{14}. See also כְּבוּדָּה **n.f.** infr

†II כָּבוֹד **n.m.**$^{Is\ 60,1}$ and †**f.**$^{Gn\ 49,6}$ **abundance, honour, glory,**—כ׳ Jos 7^{19} + 70t; כָּבֹד Gn 31^{1} Na 2^{10}; cstr כְּבוֹד Ex 16^{7} + 62 t., כבד Pr $25^{2.2}$; sf כבודי Gn 45^{13} + 17 t; כבֹדִי Gn 49^{6} + 3 t, + 40 t. sfs —**1.** *abundance, riches* Gn 31^{1} (J), Is 10^{3} 61^{6} $66^{11.12}$ Na 2^{10} ψ $49^{17.18}$. **2.** *honour, splendour, glory,* of external condition and circumstances **a.** of men: of Joseph in Egypt Gn 45^{13} (E); of Job Jb 19^{9} 29^{20}; of Ephraim Ho 9^{11}, Samaria Ho 10^{5}; עֹשֶׁר וְכָבוֹד *wealth and splendour* 1 Ch $29^{12.28}$ 2 Ch 17^{5} 18^{1} 32^{27} Pr 3^{16} 8^{18} 22^{4}, עשר (ו)נְכָסִים וכ׳ 2 Ch $1^{11.12}$ = גם ע׳ גם כ׳ 1 K 3^{13}, Ec 6^{2}; ‖ עֹשֶׁר Pr 11^{16}, man was crowned with כ׳ וְהָדָר at his creation, ψ 8^{6}, the king is given כ׳ ‖ הוד וְהָדָר ψ 21^{6}. **b.** of things, כ׳ עָשְׁרוֹ Est 5^{11} *splendour of his wealth,* of a throne 1 S 2^{8} (poem), Is 22^{23} Je 14^{21} 17^{12}; a kingdom Est 1^{4}, chariots Is 22^{18}; priestly robes Ex $28^{2.40}$ (P); Lebanon Is 35^{2} 60^{13}; forest Is 10^{18} (fig of royal might), trees Ez 31^{18}; temple Hg $2^{3.9}$; restored holy land ψ 84^{12} Is $4^{2.5}$, Jerus. Is 62^{2}. **c.** of God, *glory,* (1) in historic theophanies: to Moses Ex $33^{18.22}$ (J), ‖ אֹתֹת Nu 14^{22} (JE); ‖ גָּדְלוֹ Dt 5^{21}. P uses כ׳ יהוה for theophanies of the Exodus Ex $16^{7.10}$ $24^{16.17}$ $40^{34.35}$ Lv $9^{6.23}$ Nu 14^{10} 16^{19} 17^{7} 20^{6}, cf 2 Ch 5^{14} = 1 K 8^{11}, 2 Ch $7^{1.2.3}$, so Ezek, Ez 1^{28} $3^{12.23}$ $10^{4.4.18}$ 11^{23} $43^{4.5}$ 44^{4}; with the variation כ׳ אֱלֹהֵי יִשְׂרָאֵל Ez 8^{4} 9^{3} 10^{19} 11^{22} 43^{2}, and הַכָּבוֹד Ez 3^{23}; the sacred tent was sanctified by the Glory Ex 29^{43} (P), and the temple was מקום משכן כ׳ ψ 26^{8}; when the ark was captured, the Glory went into exile from Israel 1 S $4^{21.22}$. (2) *in historic and ideal* manifestations to the pious mind Yahweh's name is a name of glory ψ 72^{19} Ne 9^{5}; his eyes eyes of glory Is 3^{8}; in the temple his glory is seen ψ 63^{3}; it is על השמים ψ 113^{4}, על כל הארץ ψ $57^{6.12}$, in a thunderstorm he is אֵל הַכָּבוֹד ψ 29^{3}; his glory is לְעוֹלָם ψ 104^{31}; it is great ψ 138^{5}; above all the earth ψ 108^{6}; the whole earth is full of it Is 6^{3}; the heavens are declaring כְּבוֹד אֵל ψ 19^{2}; with reference to the divine reign כ׳ הֲדַר מַלְכוּתוֹ, ψ 145^{12}, הֲדַר כ׳ הוֹדֶךָ ψ 145^{5}. (3) he is מֶלֶךְ הַכָּבוֹד ψ $24^{7.8.9.10.10}$;

he will appear in his glory ψ 102[17], his glory will be revealed in a march through the wilderness to the holy land Is 40[5], the land will see it Is 35[2], shine with it Ez 43[2], and it will dwell in the land ψ 85[10], it will be to the rearward of Israel Is 58[8]; it will arise and be seen upon Jerusalem Is 60[1.2]; Yahweh will be the glory in the midst of her Zc 2[9]; the temple will be filled with it Hg 2[7]; the earth will be filled with a knowledge of it Hb 2[14], and with it Nu 14[21] (JE) ψ 72[19]; it will be declared among the nations and all will see it Is 66[18.19 19] ψ 97[6] and peoples and kings revere it ψ 102[16] Is 59[19]; י׳ will reign before his elders in glory Is 24[23], the resting-place of the Messiah will be כָבוֹד Is 11[10]. **3.** *honour, dignity* of position מנע מִכּ׳ *withhold from honour* Nu 24[11] (E); ירד מכ׳ *descend from* Je 48[18]; שלח אחר כ׳ *send after* Zc 2[12]; תמך כ׳ Is 14[18], שכב בכ׳ ψ 112[9]; רום בכ׳ Pr 29[23]; יַרְבֶּה כ׳ Dn 11[39], לקח כ׳ *take me to honour* ψ 73[24]; not becoming to fools Pr 26[1]; לפני כ׳ ענוה *before honour* (goeth) *humility* Pr 15[33] 18[12]; antithesis קלון Ho 4[7] Hb 2[16] Pr 3[35], קִיקָלוֹן Hb 2[16]; כָבוֹד is used as collective, of honoured men, *dignitaries, nobility* כבוד ישראל Mi 1[15], elsewhere as cstr. before various nations or with sfs. only Is 5[13] 8[7] 10[16] 16[14] 17[3.4] 21[16] 22[24]. **4.** *honour, reputation*, of character, of man וְלֹא־לְךָ לְכ׳ 2 Ch 26[18] *neither will it be for thine honour;* ‖ חכמה Ec 10[1]; צדקה Pr 21[21]; antith. כְּלִמָּה ψ 4[3]; וְחֵקֶר כְּבֹדָם כָּבוֹד Pr 25[27] *and searching out of their glory is* (not) *glory* כ׳ לאיש Pr 20[3]; כ׳ אֱלֹהִים הַסְתֵּר דָּבָר וכ׳ מְלָכִים חֲקֹר דָּבָר Pr 25[2] *the honour of God is to conceal a thing, but the honour of kings is to search out a thing.* **5.** *my honour*, poet. of the seat of honour in the inner man, the noblest part of man ‖ נפשי Gn 49[6] (poem) ψ 7[6]; לבי ψ 16[9] 108[2]; it is called upon to זמר ψ 30[13] (rd. כְּבוֹדִי for כָבוֹד); עוּרָה ψ 57[9]. **6.** *honour, reverence, glory*, as due to one or ascribed to one: **a.** of men, due to a father Mal 1[6]; honour done to David by Nathan's prophecy 1 Ch 17[18]; עשה כ׳ לְ 2 Ch 32[33] *do honour to;* נתן כ׳ לְ Pr 26[8]; ‖ ישע ψ 62[8]. **b.** of God, כְּבוֹדִי *the honour due to me* (Yahweh) Is 42[8] 43[7] 48[11] נתן כ׳ לְ 1 S 6[5] Je 13[16] Mal 2[2] ψ 79[9]; כ׳ שְׁמֶךָ ψ 115[1]; שים כ׳ לְ Jos 7[19] (J), Is 42[12]; שים כ׳ תהלתו ψ 66[2]; יהב כ׳ ועז לְ ψ 29[1] 96[7] = 1 Ch 16[28]; זמר כ׳ שְׁמוֹ יהב כ׳ שְׁמוֹ לְ ψ 29[2] 96[8] = 1 Ch 16[29]; ψ 66[2]; ספר כבודו בגוים ψ 96[3] = 1 Ch 16[24]; אמר נתן כבודי בגוים Ez 39[21]; כ׳ מלכותך ψ 145[11]; אמר כָּבוֹד ψ 29[9] *say Glory;* יַעְלְזוּ בְכ׳ *exult with* (ascriptions of) *glory* ψ 149[5]. **7.** *glory* as *the object* of honour, reverence and glorifying, כבודי ψ 3[4] *my glory* (the one whom I glorify); כְּבוֹדָם ψ 106[20] *their glory;* כְּבוֹדוֹ Je 2[11]

†כְּבוּדָּה **n.f.** *abundance, riches* Ju 18[21]. See also 1. [כָּבוֹד].

כְּבֵדֻת **n.f. heaviness,** וַיְנַהֲגֵהוּ בִּכ׳ Ex 14[25] (J) *and they drave them with heaviness (difficulty).*

†[כָּבָה] **vb. be quenched, extinguished,** go out, of fire or lamp (NH *id;* Aram. כְּבָא *id.* of light of eyes (rare))—**Qal** *Pf.* 3 pl כָּבוּ Is 43[17], *Impf.* יכבה 1 S 3[3] Pr 21[18]; 3 fs. תִּכְבֶּה Lv 6[5] + 10 t; *Inf. cstr* כַּבּוֹתְךָ Ez 32[7] 𝔊𝔖𝔙 Co (MT כב׳ Pi.)—*be quenched, extinguished* (c. neg. exc. 1 S 3[3] Pr 26[20] Is 43[17]), of lamp (נֵר אֱלֹהִים) in sanctuary 1 S 3[3]; of altar-fire Lv 6[5.6]; of נֵרָהּ Pr 31[18], of bodies of renegade Israelites Is 66[24] (cf. גֵּיא בֶן־הִנֹּם); subj. אֵשׁ fig. of contention Pr 26[20], fig., subj. fire kindled by י׳ Ez 21[3.4]; subj. wrath (חֵמָה) of י׳ 2 K 22[17] = 2 Ch 34[25], Je 7[20]; wrath under fig. of fire (אש) Je 17[27]; so of burning land of Edom Is 34[10]; of annihilation of Yahweh's enemies Is 43[17] (כַּפִּשְׁתָּה; ‖ דָּעֲכוּ), cf. Pharaoh Ez 32[7] (v supr.) **Pi.** *Pf.* וְכִבּוּ consec. 2 S 14[7]; *Impf.* 3 ms. sf. יְכַבֶּנָּה Is 42[3]; 2 ms. תְּכַבֶּה 2 S 21[17]; וַיְכַבּוּ 2 Ch 29[7]; *Inf* כַּבּוֹת Ct 8[7]; also MT כַבּוֹתְךָ Ez 32[7] (but cf. supr); *Pt.* מְכַבֶּה Is 1[31] + 3 t;—*quench, extinguish,* fig. except 2 Ch 29[7] (of extinguishing lamps, נֵרוֹת, in temple); sq נֵר יִשְׂרָאֵל (fig. for life of David) 2 S 21[17]; sq. גַּחַלְתִּי (*coal* = family-hope) 2 S 14[7] (of killing widow's only son); sq. פשתה כֵהָה Is 42[3] *dimly-burning* wick (fig. of spiritually weak); implied obj. ref. to wrath of י׳ Am 5[6] Je 4[4] 21[12], to people and idols Is 1[31]; sq. love אַהֲבָה Ct 8[7] (subj. מַיִם רַבִּים); Ez 32[7] cf. supr.

†כָּבוּל **n.pr.loc. 1.** city on border of Asher Jos 19[27], mod. *Kâbûl*, 4 h. (9 miles) SE. from Akko, Rob[BR iii. 88] Guérin[Gal. i. 422 f.] **2.** אֶרֶץ כָּבוּל district in Galilee 1 K 9[13] containing 20 cities given by Sol. to Hiram (popular etymol. poss. כְּ *as* + בַּל = בֵּל *not*, i.e. *as good as nothing*, cf. v[13], so Ew Th, Klo conject. (ארץ גָּלִיל), Buhl[Geogr § 116].

כבל (√of foll. = *bind;* NH כָּבַל *bind*, כֶּבֶל *fetter;* Aram כְּבַל *id*, כַּבְלָא *id.*, ܟܒܠ, ܟܒܠܐ; Ar. كَبَلَ *bind*, كَبْلٌ *fetter*).

†כֶּבֶל **n.[m.]** fetter(s), late;—sg coll. עִנּוּ בַכּ׳ רגליו ψ 105[18] *they humbled his feet with*

fetters (‖בַּרְזֶל), pl cstr אסר בכבלי בַרְזֶל 149[8] (‖זִקִּים)

כבן (√of foll, mng dub.; NH כָּבַן, Aram כבן, كَبَنَ = *wrap round, wrap up*)

†**כַּבּוֹן** **n.pr.loc.** in Judah Jos 15[40] poss. = foll, 𝔊 Χαβρα, 𝔊L Χαββω.

†**מַכְבֵּנָה** (van d H מַכְבֵּנָא) **n.pr.loc.** 1 Ch 2[49] (represented as having שְׁוָא for father, poss = foregoing), 𝔊 Μαχαβηνα, 𝔊L Μαχβανα

†**מַכְבַּנַּי** **n.pr.m.** a hero of David 1 Ch 12[14].

[כָּבַס][51] **vb.** (tread), **wash** (NH *id*; Ph. כבס as pt, As *kabâsu, tread (down), subjugate, kibšu, step, path*, Dl[HWB]) — **Qal** *Pt* only מְסִלַּת שׂדה כובס *highway of fuller's* (= *treader's, washer's*) *field* Is 7[3] 36[2] = 2 K 18[17]. **Pi.** *Pf* וְכִבֶּס consec Lv 13[6] + 11 t., כִּבֵּס Gn 49[11] 2 S 19[25], etc, *Impf* יכבס Lv 11[25] + 16 t; 2 ms sf תְּכַבְּסֵנִי ψ 51[9], etc; *Imv* sf כַּבְּסֵנִי 51[4]; fs כַּבְּסִי Je 4[14]; *Pt.* pl מְכַבְּסִים Mal 3[2], —**1.** *wash* garments (i e by *treading*) Ex 19[10.14] (E), 2 S 19[25], fig of Judah Gn 49[11], elsewhere chiefly P: Lv 6[20] 11[25.28] 13[6.34] 15[11] Nu 8[9] +; ‖ רָחַץ (which = *wash person*) Lv 14[8.9] 15[5.6.7 8 10.11] + (כ׳ in Lv 27 t, ‖ ר׳ 15 t, in Nu 8 t, ‖ ר׳ 3 t); Pt = *fuller* (cf Qal), only ברית מכ׳ Mal 3[2]. †**2.** *wash* person, only poet. and fig. כַּבְּסִי מֵרָעָה לִבֵּךְ Je 2[22], אם תכבסי בַּנֶּתֶר 4[14]; c sf ψ 51[4] (‖ טהר; + מֵעָוֹן); v[9] (‖ חִטֵּא). †**Pu.** *Pf* וְכֻבַּס consec Lv 13[58] 15[17] *be washed*, of garment. †**Hothp.** (Ges§54.3) *Inf* אַחֲרֵי הֻכַּבֵּס אֶת־הַנֶּגַע Lv 13[55] *after the plague is washed out*, so v[56].

† I. **[כָּבַר]** **vb. be much, many** (As *kabâru, be great, mighty; kabru, great, huge*; Ar. كَبُرَ *be great*, in body, rank, or age, كَبِيرٌ *great, noble, aged*, Eth ከበረ: *be honoured, magnified*, ክቡር: *honoured, glorious*; Sab. epith. כבר Hal[Et Sab JAs Dec 1874, No 90], Syr. ܟܒܪ, ܟܒܪ, ܟܒܪ̈ for Heb רַבָּה, הרבה, ܟܒܪ̈ (rare) *much*, Zinj *be abundant, numerous*) — **Hiph.** (only Elihu) *make many*, Jb 35[16] בבלי דַעַת מלין יַכְבִּר (cf וְיַרְב אֲמָרָיו 34[37]) > *make great*, Bu[Beitr 138], comparing 8[2], מַכְבִּיר with the force of a subst (Ew§160e) 36[31] לְמַכְבִּיר יתן אכל *giveth food in abundance* (= prose לָרֹב, e g 2 Ch 11[23])

†**כַּבִּיר** **adj.** great, mighty, much, only poet., and only Jb Is[1] — Is 10[13] Qr (but rd as Kt כְּאַבִּיר), 17[12] and 28[2] מים כבירים (usu. מַיִם רַבִּים), Jb 8[2] ורוח כביר אמרי פיך a *mighty* wind, 15[10] כביר מאביך ימים (Ges§131. R 5a) = *aged*: of God, 34[17] כ׳ כֹּחַ לֵב v[b], כַּבִּיר צַדִּיק the just *mighty* one, 36[5a], *mighty* in strength of understanding; 34[24] כבירים *mighty men*; of quantity = *much*, Is 16[14] שְׁאָר מְעַט מִזְעָר לוֹא כַבִּיר, Jb 31[25] וכי כביר מצאה ידי had gotten *much*

†**[כִּבְרָה]** **n.f.** appar. **distance,** only in the phr. כִּבְרַת (ה)ארץ a *distance of land* or *length of way*, Gn 35[16] וַיְהִי עוֹד כ׳ ה׳ לָבוֹא אֶפְרָתָה, 48[7] בְּעוֹד כ׳ א׳ לָבֹא אֶפְרָתָה, 2 K 5[19] וַיֵּלֶךְ מֵאִתּוֹ כ׳ אָרֶץ. The distance meant is uncertain, but fr 2 K 5[19] it would seem to have been a short one, v. further Di[Gn 35, 16] and Thes (As *kibrâti* is a (widely extended) *territory, quarter of the world*, etc, Dl[HWB 315]; according to Hoffm[GGAbh xxxvi (1890), 23-25] perhaps the distance that one can see).

†I. **כְּבָר** **adv.** (late) **already** (freq. in Mish. and NH, 𝔗 כבר (rare), Syr. ܟܒܪ usu *perhaps*, occas. *already* (Mt 11[21] Hb 10[2]); Mand. כבאר *already*, Nö[M p. 202]. Der uncertain, connexion with √כבר being dub) — *already*, Ec 1[10] כְּבָר הָיָה it hath *already* been, 2[12 16] 3[15 15] 4[2] 6[10] 9[6.7].

†II **כְּבָר** **n.pr.fl. Kĕbār,** a river (or perhaps a canal) of Babylonia, not at present identified, by wh. the exiles, among whom Ez ministered, were settled; always in the phr. נְהַר כְּבָר Ez 1[1.3] 3[15 23] 10[15 20.22] 43[3] (cf Sm[Ez 1.1] Del[Par 47 f., 184]).

II. **כבר** (√of foll., ? *to intertwine, net*; NH כָּבַר *sift* is denom fr כְּבָרָה)

†**[כָּבִיר]** **n.[m.]** prob something *netted*, i e. either a quilt or (Ew[H. 3 77] Ke) a **fly-net** (κωνωπεῖον) spread over the face while a person was asleep; 1 S 19[13 16] כְּבִיר הָעִזִּים a *quilt* (or *fly-net*) of goats(' hair). Vid. further Dr[ad loc.]

†**כְּבָרָה** **n.f. a sieve** (a *net*-like implement), Am 9[9] כַּאֲשֶׁר יִנּוֹעַ בַּכְּבָרָה as it (corn) is shaken (i.e. sifted) in a *sieve*. Cf Wetzst[ZPV xiv 1 ff.]

†**מַכְבֵּר** **n.[m.] a netted cloth or coverlet;** 2 K 8[15] of the cloth which Hazael dipped in water, and spread over Ben-hadad's face to smother him.

מִכְבָּר **n.m. grating or lattice-work,** cstr. מִכְבַּר, — Ex 27[4] and thou shalt make for it (the altar of burnt-offering in the tab) מִכְבָּר מַעֲשֵׂה רֶשֶׁת נחשׁת a *grating*, (even) a network of bronze, which surrounded the lower half of the altar (v[5b]): so 38[4]; מִכְבַּר הַנְּחֹשֶׁת 35[16] 38[5.30] 39[39].

כֶּבֶשׂ$_{107}$ **n.m.** $^{Ex\,29.\,38}$ **lamb** (√dub.: NH *id., battering-ram;* As *kabšu, lamb* acc. to COT ^{Gloss}, Ar. كَبْش is *ram, leader;* Syr ܟܒܫܐ *lamb,* with anom. ܫ, is very rare, and prob. loan-word, No in Fra^{109})—כ׳ abs Ex 29^{39}+43 t.; pl. כְּבָשִׂים v^{38}+61 t., sf כְּבָשָׂי Jb 31^{20};—**1.** *lamb,* for sacrif.: Is 1^{11}; of daily offering Ex 29$^{38.39.39.40.41}$ Nu 28$^{3.4.4}$+12 t. Nu 28; sin-offering Lv 4^{32}; purification 12^{6} 14^{10}+5 t. Lv 14; dedication of altar Nu 7^{15}+25 t. Nu 7; offerings in 7th month 29^{2}+22 t. Nu 29, etc. (87 t. Ex Lv Nu all P); in Ezekiel's temple Ez 46^{4}+6 t. Ez 46, 1 Ch 29^{21} 2 Ch 29$^{21.22.32}$ 35^{7} Ezr 8^{35}, cf. sim. Je 11^{19}. **2.** *lambs,* as grazing; symb of devastation Is 5^{17} (cf Gie$^{Beitr\,1890}$), sim of Isr. Ho 4^{16}; in predict. וְגָר זְאֵב עִם־כ׳ Is 11^{6} **3.** *lambs,* as furnishing wool for clothing: Jb 31^{20} גֵּז כ׳, Pr 27^{26} כ׳ לִלְבוּשֶׁךָ.

†כַּבְשָׂה, כִּבְשָׂה, כִּבְשָׂה **n.f.** ewe-lamb, כ׳ 2 S 12$^{3.6}$; כַּבְשָׂה Lv 14^{10} Nu 6^{14}; cstr כִּבְשַׂת 2 S 12^{4}; pl כְּבָשֹׂת Gn 21$^{29.30}$; cstr כִּבְשׂת v^{28},—*ewe-lambs* (7) set in witness Gn 21$^{28.29.30}$ (E); used in sacrif. Lv 14^{10} (purif.), Nu 6^{14} (Nazirite; both P, and both ‖ כֶּבֶשׂ); for food, in Nathan's parable 2 S 12$^{3.4.6}$.

†כֶּשֶׂב **n.[m.]** lamb (transp fr preceding)—כ׳ abs. Lv 3^{7}+5 t.; pl. כְּשָׂבִים Gn 30^{32}+6 t.;—*lamb,* as property Gn 30$^{32.33.35.40}$ (J), for sacrif. Lv 1^{10} 3^{7} 4^{35} 22^{19} Nu 18^{17}, cf Lv 22^{27}; for food Lv 7^{23}, cf 17^{3} (all P); Dt 14^{4}.

†כִּשְׂבָּה **n.f.** ewe-lamb Lv 5^{6} (P).

†[כָּבַשׁ] **vb.** subdue, bring into bondage (NH *id, press, oppress;* Aram. כְּבַשׁ, ܟܒܫ *tread down, beat* or *make a path, subdue;* Ar. كَبَسَ *press, squeeze, knead* (body or limb, as in the bath, *massage*), also *attack, assault*)—**Qal** *Pf.* 3 pl וְכָבְשׁוּ consec. Zc 9^{15}; *Impf.* יִכְבֹּשׁ Mi 7^{19}; וַיִּכְבְּשׁוּם Je 34^{11} Qr (Kt Hiph), etc; *Imv* pl. sf כִּבְשֻׁהָ Gn 1^{28}; *Inf.* כְּבוֹשׁ 2 Ch 28^{10} Est 7^{8}; *Pt* כֹּבְשִׁים Ne 5^{5};—**1.** *bring into bondage,* sq. acc. + לַעֲבָדִים Je 34$^{11.16}$ 2 Ch 28^{10} Ne 5^{5} **2.** (late) *subdue, force,* a woman Est 7^{8} (= earlier עִנָּה) **3.** *subdue, dominate,* the earth Gn 1^{28} (P), Zc 9^{15} (of conquest); *tread down,* sq אַבְנֵי־קֶלַע; fig *subdue,* sq. עֲוֺנֹתֵינוּ Mi 7^{19}. **Niph.** *Pf.* 3 fs. נִכְבְּשָׁה Jos 18^{1}+3 t; *Pt.* fpl. נִכְבָּשׁוֹת Ne 5^{5},—pass of **Qal 1,** subj בְּנֹתֵינוּ Ne 5^{5}; of **Qal 3,** subj. הָאָרֶץ (of conquest) Nu 32$^{22.29}$ Jos 18^{1} (all P), 1 Ch 22^{18}. **Pi.** *Pf.* כִּבֵּשׁ 2 S 8^{11}, obj. גּוֹיִם (of conquest) **Hiph.** *Impf bring into bondage,* sq. acc. + לַעֲבָדִים Je 34^{11} Kt (Qr **Qal**).

†כֶּבֶשׁ **n.[m.]** footstool (late) (NH *id., step, stair;* Aram. כִּבְשָׁא, etc, a rude *seat* (rare))—כ׳ הַזָּהָב 2 Ch 9^{18} (of Solomon's throne).

†כִּבְשָׁן **n.m.** kiln, for lime or pottery (so Ki, AW; Mishn$^{Kel\,viii\,9}$, √and original mng. dub., acc. to Thes as *subduing, reducing* its contents, cf. *igne ferrum domatur* Plin$^{Nat.\,Hist.\,36.\,27}$)—alw. abs, only in קִיטֹר הַכ׳ Gn 19^{28} (J; sim. of smoke of כִּכָּר, Sodom and Gom.); עֶשֶׁן הַכ׳ Ex 19^{18} (E; sim of smoke of Sinai); פִּיחַ כ׳ ashes of kiln Ex 9^{8}, cf. v^{10} (both P).

כדד (√of foll.; Ar كَدَّ is *toil severely;* كَدَّ *fatigue, weary, harass, tread;* كُدّ *mortar* in which things are *pounded, bruised;* كُدَادَة *what remains in bottom of cooking-pot*).

†כַּד **n.f.** jar (NH *id.;* Aram. כַּדָּא)—כַּד abs 1 K 17^{12} Ec 12^{6}, cstr 1 K 17$^{14.16}$, כַּדָּהּ Gn 24$^{14.17.43}$ etc, pl. כַּדִּים Ju 7$^{16.16}$+3 t;—water-*jar,* carried on woman's shoulder Gn 24$^{14.15.16.17.18.20.43.45.46}$ (all J), 1 K 18^{34} Ec 12^{6}; empty (of water), containing lamps Ju 7$^{16.19.20}$; containing meal 1 K 17$^{12.14.16}$. (On extra-Palest hist of this word cf. Lag $^{BN\,104}$.)

†[כִּידוֹר] **n.m.** spark (fr. above √, = *strike out* a spark, acc to Thes RobGes, cf. Sta^{§216} (doubtfully), Lag$^{BN\,182}$ Ko$^{ii.\,147,\,§71.\,1}$, NH כָּדוּר = *rod* (of iron, etc), כדוריות שֶׁל אֵשׁ i.e. *red-hot rods;* but Ba$^{NB\,§142,\,139}$ der. this and כַּדְכֹּד fr. √כיד = Ar كَادَ, كَيْد *emit fire* (said of a fire-stick, زَنْد, Lane$^{2639\,b,\,cf.\,1257\,b}$), and so Buhl)—only pl. cstr כִּידוֹדֵי אֵשׁ Jb 41^{11} of breath of crocodile (‖ לַפִּידִים)

†כַּדְכֹּד **n.[m.]** a precious stone, perh. ruby (fr. *sparkle?;* Aram ‖ is כַּדְכְּדָנָא); כ׳ Ez 27^{16} as article of commerce; כַּדְכֹּד Is 54^{12} fig in promise to Zion.

כְּדֵי v. דַּי.

כדר (√of foll; cf. Ar. كَدَرَ vii. *shoot* or *rush down* (of hawk, star, etc.; also of an attacking force) so Thes Fl in De$^{Job\,15.\,24}$ Buhl Di al, v. also mod. Ar. كدر *annoy, vex, reprimand,* Spiro^{Vocab}, كدر oftener *be dark, gloomy, turbid,* whence > כִּידוֹר = *seething* tumult, of battle, cf. Ko$^{ii.\,147,\,§71\,1}$).

†כִּידוֹר **n.[m.]** onset, מֶלֶךְ עָתִיד לַכִּ׳ Jb 15^{24} *a king ready for the onset.*

†כַּדּוּר **n.[m.]** ball, acc to Bo[NA ii. 134] De Or al Is 22[18], as in Talm., circle, cordon (As *kudûru*), acc to Jastr[PAOS. Oct. 1888, xcvi]; v. also דּוּר p 189 b

†כְּדָרְלָעֹמֶר **n.pr.m.** king of Elam (= Babylon *Kudar-Laga[mar]* (*Lagamaru*=n pr. div.), v Pinches[Vict Inst Jan. 20 1896] Say[PSBA, June 1896, 178] Scheil[Rev Bibl. 1896, 600 f], cf Schr[COT])—Gn 14[1.4.5.9.17]

כֹּה **demonstr. adv. thus, here** (BA כָּה; 𝔗𝔖 [Jerus] Mand כָּא *here*. in Syr with prefixes ܠܟܐ *hither*, ܡܟܐ (𝔖 [Jerus] مكا) *hence*, ܐܟܐ *where?* cf אֵיכָה, p. 32, and Kö[ii 1. 252])—**1.** of manner, *thus* (so most freq., and usually pointing to what is to follow, while כֵּן points commonly to what has preceded), Gn 15[5] כֹּה יִהְיֶה זַרְעֶךָ *thus* shall thy seed be, Nu 6[23] 1 K 2[30] כֹּה דִבֶּר יוֹאָב וכה עָנָנִי, 5[25] Is 24[13] (answered by כְּ, as Je 23[29]), with a subst. Is 20[6] הִנֵּה כֹה מַבָּטֵנוּ, Je 9[21] (si vera l), 23[29] 1 S 27[11]. Mostly confined to particular phrases thus **a.** with diff forms of אמר, כה תאמר *thus* shalt thou say Ex 3[14.15] 19[3] 20[22] etc.; esp כה אמר י״י thus saith (or said) ׳י Ex 4[22] 5[1] 7[17.26] 8[16] etc., and continually in the prophets, as Is 7[7] 8[11] 18[4] etc., Je 2[2.5] 4[27] 6[16] etc; also in the idiom formula אִם כֹּה יֹאמַר *if he say* (or *used to say*) (the words spoken following) †Gn 31[8] 1 S 14[9.10] 20[7] 2 S 15[26] **b.** with עשה to do *thus*, Ex 5[15] Dt 7[5], pointing back, Nu 22[30] Jos 6[14] 1 S 27[11] al.; esp in the phrase כה יעשה אלהים וכה יוסיף (with variations), 1 S 3[17]+(v יסף), in which כה points to an imprecation understood but not expressed With ב prefixed †1 K 22[20] ויאמר זה בכה וזה אמר בכה and one spake *in this wise*, and another spake *in that wise* (‖ 2 Ch 18[19] כָּכָה...כָּכָה; prob rightly) †**2.** of place, *here* (rare, chiefly in E), Gn 31[37] שִׂים כֹּה place it *here* before my brethren, Nu 23[15.15] 2 S 18[30] Ru 2[8]. Repeated, Ex 2[12] וַיִּפֶן כֹּה וָכֹה and he turned *this way* and *that way*, כֹּה...כֹּה *on this side ... on that side* Nu 11[31]. With עַד Gn 22[5] and we will go עַד־כֹּה *as far as here* (δεικτικῶς) i e *yonder* †**3.** of time, עַד כֹּה *hitherto*, Ex 7[16] (cf עַד־הֵנָּה), Jos 17[14], עַד־כֹּה וְעַד־כֹּה till *now* and till *then*, i. e. meanwhile, 1 K 18[45]

כָּכָה [37] **adv** thus (NH abbrev to כָּךְ, with preps בֵּין כָּךְ *meanwhile*, לְפִיכָךְ *therefore*; prob either from כָּה and כְּ, lit. *as thus*, Ol[§ 223 h], or from כָּה כָּה Kö[ii 1 253]), somewhat more emph. than כֹּה, usu prefixed to word which it qualifies —Ex 12[11] וככה תאכלו אתו and *thus* shall ye eat it, 29[35] Nu 8[26] 11[15] ואם ככה את עשה לי, 15[11.12.13] Dt 25[9] 29[23] (cf 1 K 9[8] Je 22[8]); so often with עשה. 1 S 19[17] למה ככה רמיתני why hast thou *thus* deceived me? 2 S 17[21] 1 K 1[6.48], Je 13[9] 19[11] 28[11] 51[64]; once with an adj 2 S 13[4] מדוע אתה כָּכָה דל why art thou *thus* lean? Ec 11[6] answering to כַּאֲשֶׁר, ψ 144[15] הָעָם שֶׁכָּכָה לּוֹ the people to which it is *thus*. Once 2 Ch 18[19] repeated, *in this way ... in that way* (‖ 1 K 22[20] בכה . . . בכה) Comp. the syn כָּזֹאת. With a prep. once, in late Hebrew, Est 9[26] עַל־כָּכָה concerning such a matter. With the interrog. אי, אֵיכָכָה *how?* (p. 32).

†I [כָּהָה] **vb. be** or **grow dim, faint** (NH *id*, Aram כְּהָא, cf Ar. كَهِىَ *be* اَكْهَى, i e. *weak, cowardly*)—**Qal** *Pf* 3 fs. כָּהֲתָה Dt 34[7], *Impf* יכהה Is 42[4], 3 fs תכהה Zc 11[17], וַתֵּכַהּ Jb 17[7]; וַתִּכְהֶיןָ, Gn 27[1], *Inf abs* כָּהֹה Zc 11[17];—*grow dim*, of eye Gn 27[1] (J), Dt 34[7] Jb 17[7]; of violent putting out of eye Zc 11[17.17], *he shall not grow dim* Is 42[4], of servant of ׳י under fig of lamp or fire (v. Kay Che De), or *grow faint* (cf. Di) **Pi.** *Pf.* 3 fs וְכִהֲתָה consec Ez 21[12] (subj וְנָמֵס כָּל־לֵב ‖ כָּל־רוּחַ) *grow faint* (Pi intrans, Ges[§ 52 k], Kö[i 187], but rd. perh. כָּהֲתָה).

†[כֵּהֶה] **adj. dim, dull, faint**; only f כהה Lv 13[6]+6 t, pl כֵּהוֹת Lv 13[39] 1 S 3[2],—*dim*, of eyes 1 S 3[2], of burning wick (פִּשְׁתָּה כ׳) Is 42[3]; *dull* (in colour, of plague-spots) Lv 13[6.21 26.39.56]; fig =*faint* רוּחַ כ׳ Is 61[3] (opp. מַעֲטֵה תְהִלָּה).

†כֵּהָה **n.f. (dimming), lessening, alleviation**,—אין כ׳ לשברך of Nineveh Na 3[19] (read גֵּהָה, *healing*?)

†II [כָּהָה] **vb. Pi. rebuke** (Syr. ܟܐܐ, Mand. כהא (Nö[M 72]) *id.*), only 1 S 3[13] sq ב, וְלֹא כִהָה בָּם

כהן (✓of foll., mng dub., v. Dr[2S 8, 18]; Ar. vb كَهَنَ is *divine*, and كَاهِنٌ (Qor 52[29]) is *a seer*, the organ (mostly) of a jinn, rarely of a god: the كَاهِنٌ and the כֹּהֵן must have been orig. identical (both alike being guardians of an oracle, at a sanctuary); but their functions diverged the كَاهِنٌ gradually lost his connexion with the sanctuary, and sank to be a mere diviner, the כהן acquired fuller sacrif. functions: v. RS[Enc. Brit ed. 9, xix 727], We[Skizzen iii 130 ff.],

^{167}; Now $^{\text{Arch. ii. 80 f.}}$; Ph. כהן is *priest*, כהנת *priestess*).

כֹּהֵן $_{750}$ **n.m.** priest (NH כֹּהֵן; Aram. כָּהֵין, כָּהֲנָא, ܟܳܗܢܳܐ, ܟܗܶܢ; Eth. ካህን: all *id.*; on Ph. and Ar. v. supr.);—כ׳ Gn 14^{18} + 439 t.; pl. כֹּהֲנִים Ex 19^{6} + 272 t.; cstr. כֹּהֲנֵי 1 S 5^{5} + 13 t.; sf. כֹּהֲנַי La 1^{19} + 22 t. sfs.—†**1.** *priest-king:* e.g. Melchizedek Gn 14^{18} (E?), cf. ψ 110^{4} (the Messianic priest-king like Melchizedek); Zc 6^{13} (Messianic priest and king); Israel מַמְלֶכֶת כֹּהֲנִים Ex 19^{6} (E) *a kingdom of priests* (priests and kings at once in their relation to the nations); cf. Is 61^{6} (of Israel ministering as a priest); or *a chieftain* (exercising priestly functions) כֹּהֵן מִדְיָן Ex 2^{16} 3^{1} 18^{1} (all JE); so also probably the sons of David 2 S 8^{18}, his grandson 1 K 4^{5}, and Ira the Jairite 2 S 20^{26}, who as princes performed priestly functions. With these we may class the כהנים Ex 19$^{22.24}$ (J). †**2.** *priests of other religions than* י׳*'s:* Potiphera כ׳ אֹן Gn 41$^{45.50}$ (E), 46^{20} (P); Egyptian כהנים Gn 47$^{22.22.26}$ (J); כ׳ דָגוֹן 1 S 5^{5}; Philistine כהנים וקסמים 1 S 6^{2}; כֹּהֲנָיו *his priests:* e.g. of Baal 2 K 10^{19} = of Ahab 2 K 10^{11}; of Chemosh Je 48^{7}; of Malcam Je 49^{3}; Mattan was כ׳ הבעל 2 K 11^{18} = 2 Ch 23^{17}; הכמרים עם הכהנים Zp 1^{4}; Josiah burned the bones of the priests of the Baalim and Asherim 2 Ch 34^{5}. †**3.** *priests of special orders in Israel:* **a.** Micah in the hill-country of Ephraim consecrated his own son וַיְהִי־לוֹ לְכֹהֵן Ju 17^{5}; but so soon as he could secure Jonathan ben Gershom, a descendant of Moses (see VB Ju 18^{30}), he consecrated him, הַכֹּהֵן היה לי׳ לכהן Ju 17$^{10.12.13}$ 18$^{4.19}$; v$^{6.17.18.20.24.27}$. He was captured by the Danites, and he and his line became priests at Dan until the Exile, v$^{19.19.30}$. **b.** Jeroboam עשה כהנים 1 K 12^{31} of those not מבני לוי, as כ׳ (הַ)בָּמוֹת *priests of (the) high places* 1 K 12^{32} 13$^{2.33.33}$ = כ׳ לבמות 2 Ch 11^{15}; Amaziah (of this class) was כ׳ בית־אל Am 7^{10}; v. also 2 Ch 13^{9}; called by Chr כ׳ לְלֹא אלהים v^{9}; yet Hosea rebukes them as priests of י׳ Ho 4$^{4.9}$ 5^{1} 6^{9}; at the Exile they were deported by the Assyrians 2 K 17$^{27.28}$. **c.** the people imported into Samaria made some of themselves כ׳ במות to worship י׳ the God of the land 2 K 17^{32}. †**4.** *priests in Israel* הכהנים who bore the ark and the trumpets Jos 3$^{13.14.15.17}$ 4$^{3.9.10.17.18.18}$ 6$^{4.4.6.6.8.9.12.13.16}$ (all JE), 1 K 8$^{3.6.10.11}$; Eli was הכהן 1 S 1^{9} 2^{11}; כ׳ יהוה 14^{3}; and his sons כ׳ ליהוה 1 S 1^{3}; a מִשְׁפַּט הַכֹּהֲנִים 1 S 2^{13} mentions the ministering priest הכהן and the נַעַר הַכֹּ׳ 1 S 2$^{13.14.15.15}$, Ahijah was הַכֹּ׳ in time of Saul 1 S 14$^{19.19.36}$; Abimelech הַכֹּ׳ at Nob, a priestly centre, 1 S 21$^{2.3.5.6.7.10}$ 22^{11}; where were many כֹּהֲנֵי י׳ 1 S 22$^{17.17.21}$, all slain by Saul except Abiathar son of Ahimelech 1 S 22$^{11.18.18.19}$, who became הַכֹּ׳ 1 S 23^{9} 30^{7} 1 K 1$^{7.19.25.42}$ 2$^{22.26}$; Zadok later was הַכֹּ׳ 2 S 15^{27} 1 K 1$^{8.26.32.34.38.39.44.45}$ 2^{35} 3^{2} 1 Ch 16^{39} 24^{6}: so that the two were (ה)כהנים 2 S 8^{17} = 1 Ch 18^{16} (rd. וְאֶבְיָתָר בֶּן־אח׳ 2 S 8^{17} 𝔖 We Dr, and correct 1 Ch 18^{16} accordingly) 2 S 15$^{35.35}$ 17^{15} 19^{12} 20^{25} 1 K 4^{4}; Sol. removed Abiathar 1 K 2^{27} and Zadok was anointed לְכֹהֵן acc. to 1 Ch 29^{22}; cf. prediction of rejection of house of Eli and selection of כ׳ נֶאֱמָן 1 S 2$^{28.35}$; Jehoiada הַכֹּ׳ led the revolution against Athaliah 2 K 11$^{9.9.10.15.15.18}$ 12$^{3.8.10}$ = 2 Ch 22^{11} 23$^{8.8.9.14.14}$ 24$^{2.20.25}$, perh. also Je 29^{26}; הכהנים sustaining him in his reforms 2 K 12$^{5.6.7.8.9.10.17}$; Uriah was הַכֹּ׳ in the reign of Ahaz 2 K 16$^{10.11.11.15.16}$ Is 8^{2}; Hilkiah of Josiah 2 K 22$^{10.12.14}$ 23^{24} 2 Ch 34$^{14.18}$. Other individual priests are named, e.g.: Pashhur of Jehoiachin Je 20^{1}; Zephaniah of Zedekiah Je 21^{1} 29$^{25.26.29}$ 37^{3}; הַכֹּ׳ is Ezekiel's title Ez 1^{3}. Priests are classed with officials of state: prophets and priests 2 K 23^{2} Is 28^{7} Je 5^{31} 6^{13} 8^{10} 14^{18} 23$^{11.33.34}$ 26$^{7.8.11.16}$ 29^{1} La 2^{20} 4^{13}; priests and elders La 1^{19} 4^{16}; king and priest La 2^{6}; kings, priests, and prophets Je 13^{13}; kings, princes, and priests Je 1^{18}; princes, eunuchs, and priests Je 34^{19}; priest, sage, and prophet Je 18^{18}; chiefs, priests, and prophets Mi 3^{11}; prophets, priests, and elders Ez 7^{26}; kings, princes, priests, and prophets Je 2^{26} 4^{9} 8^{1} 32^{32}; princes, judges, prophets, and priests Zp 3^{4}; seeming to exclude any other officials. Apparently in the same generic sense הכהנים Je 1^{1} 2^{8} 27^{16} 28$^{1.5}$ 29^{25} 31^{14}; כַּכֹּהֵן Is 24^{2}; כהנים Jb 12^{19}; כהניה La 1^{4} Ez 22^{26}; כהניו ψ 78^{64}. *Moses and Aaron among his priests* ψ 99^{6} includes Moses (against P). Zion's priests clothed with righteousness and salvation ψ 132$^{9.16}$ = 2 Ch 6^{41}, prob. here also. †**5.** *Levitical priests* הַכֹּהֲנִים הַלְוִיִּם Dt 17$^{9.18}$ 18^{1} 24^{8} 27^{9} Jos 3^{3} 8^{33} (all D), Je 33^{18} (inverted), v^{21} (neither in 𝔊), 2 Ch 5^{5} (= הַכֹּ׳ וְהַל׳ 1 K 8^{4}: Chronicler retains original Deuteronomic reading), Ez 43^{19} 44^{15} (**cf. 6**); הַכֹּ׳ בְּנֵי לֵוִי Dt 21^{5} 31^{9}; לקח לכ׳ לל׳ Is 66^{21} *take for priests, for Levites* (of the nations in Messianic age). Doubtless of same class are: הַכֹּהֲנִים Dt 18^{3} 19^{17} Jos 3$^{6.8}$ 4^{11} (D); and הַכֹּהֵן, the priest officiating on a partic. occasion Dt 18^{3} 20^{2}; or holding a partic. dignity 17^{12} 26$^{3.4}$. The כהנים of the other cities of Judah, כ׳ הבמות, who were not allowed to minister in Jerusalem 2 K 23$^{8.8.9.20}$,

may be an attempt to enforce an exclusion from the priesthood of all but Levitical priests †**6.** *Zadokite priests*. Ezekiel distinguishes among הכהנים הלוים those of the seed of Zadok, בְּנֵי צָדוֹק, all but the latter excluded by him from priesthood 40^{46} 43^{19} 44^{15} 48^{11}, the priests of his code being all Zadokites 40$^{45.46}$ 42$^{13\ 14}$ 43$^{24\ 27}$ 44$^{21\ 22.30.30.31}$ 45$^{4\ 19}$ 46$^{2\ 19.20}$ 48$^{10\ 13}$ **7.** *Aaronic priests* In H. it is taken for granted that a priest is of the seed of Aaron, the pl is never used, כֹּהֵן is used for any priest Lv 21^{9} 22$^{10\ 11\ 12\ 13}$, הַכֹּהֵן for Aaron Lv 21^{21}, and for the official priest (acting for the priesthood, almost collective) Lv 17$^{5.6}$ 22^{14} 23$^{10.11\ 20.20}$ 27$^{8.8.8\ 11\ 12.12\ 14\ 14\ 18.21\ 23}$. The priests of P are בְּנֵי אַהֲרֹן Lv 1$^{5.8.11}$ 2^{2} 3^{2} 21^{1} Nu 3^{3} 10^{8} Jos 21^{19}, so in Chronicles 2 Ch 13$^{9\ 10}$ 26^{18} 29^{21} 31^{19} 35$^{14\ 14}$, הַכֹּהֵן is used of Aaron 22 t, Eleazar 29 t, Phinehas Jos 22^{30} and elsewhere, 180 t. of ministering priests, or generic of the priests, הכהנים Lv 6^{22} 7^{6} 13^{2} 16^{33} Jos 4^{16}, כהן Lv 6^{16} Chronicles distinguishes הַכֹּהֲנִים וְהַלְוִיִּם 1 Ch 13^{2} 15$^{11\ 14}$ 23^{2} 24$^{6.31}$ 28$^{13.21}$ 2 Ch 8^{15} 11^{13} 13$^{9\ 10}$ 23^{4} 24^{5} 29^{4} 30$^{15.25}$ 31$^{2.2.4\ 9}$ 34^{30} 35$^{8.18}$ (the variants without ו 2 Ch 23^{18} 30^{27} are due to copyists' errors), Ezr 1^{5} 2^{70} 3$^{8.12}$ 6^{20} 7^{7} 8$^{29.30}$ 9^{1} Ne 7^{72} 8^{13} 11^{3} 12$^{1.30.44.44}$ 13^{30}; הלוים והכהנים 2 Ch 19^{8} 30^{21}; priests, Levites, and others 1 Ch 9^{2} Ezr 10^{5} Ne 10$^{1.29.35}$ 11^{20}; בְּנֵי לֵוִי antith to הַכּ׳ Ezr 8^{15}, הכהן בן אהרן עם הלוים Ne 10^{39}, (ה)כהנים in Chr 67 t has the same reference, as also כֹּהֲנֵינוּ Ezr 9^{7} Ne 9$^{32.34}$, כהן Ezr 2^{63}=Ne 7^{65}; כ׳ ליהוה 2 Ch 26^{17}; כהניו *His* (God's) *priests* 2 Ch 13^{12}, כ׳ מוֹרֶה *teaching priest* 2 Ch 15^{3}; הַכֹּהֵן is used of Jehoiada in time of David 1 Ch 27^{5}, and Azariah in the reign of Uzziah 2 Ch 26^{17}. In the literature of the restoration הַכֹּהֵן is used of Ezra, Ezr 7^{11} 10$^{10\ 16}$ Ne 8$^{2\ 9}$ 12^{26}, Uriah Ezr 8^{33}; Eliashib Ne 13^{4}, Shelemiah Ne 13^{13}, הכהנים Jo 1$^{9\ 13}$ 2^{17} Hg 2$^{11\ 12.13}$ Zc 7^{5} Mal 1^{6} 2^{1}; priests and prophets Zc 7^{3}, כהן Mal 2^{7} **8.** *the high priest*: הַכֹּהֵן is frequently used (see **4**) to designate the priest who was at the head of priestly affairs. The adj הַגָּדוֹל first appears of Jehoiada 2 K 12^{11}, then of Hilkiah 2 K 22$^{4\ 8}$ 23^{4} 2 Ch 34^{9}, after the exile, of Joshua Hg 1$^{1\ 12\ 14}$ 2$^{2\ 4}$ Zc 3$^{1.8}$ 6^{11}, and Eliashib Ne 3$^{1\ 20}$ 13^{28} But P uses it of Aaron and his eldest descendants who are anointed with holy oil Lv 21^{10} (H, הכ׳ הַגָּדוֹל מֵאֶחָיו), Nu 35$^{25.28\ 28}$ Jos 20^{6}, and so הַכֹּ׳ הַמָּשִׁיחַ Lv 4$^{3.5\ 16}$ 6^{15}, cf 16^{32} כ׳ הָרֹאשׁ is used of Seraiah 2 K 25^{18}=Je 52^{24}; and, in Chronicler, of Amariah 2 Ch 19^{11}, Jehoiada 2 Ch 24^{11}, Azariah 2 Ch 26^{20} 31^{10}, of Aaron, Ezr 7^{5}. (We also supposes הרואה in 2 S 15^{27} to be a corruption of **הראש**, which he regards as postexilic insertion The text is corrupt [see Dr$^{Sm\ l\ c}$], but this correction is improbable. Lists of high priests occur 1 Ch 5$^{30-41}$ 6$^{35-38}$.) A priest of second rank (כֹּהֵן (ה)משנה) appears in 2 K 23^{4} (cstr. pl. incorrect), 25^{18}=Je 52^{24}, זִקְנֵי הַכֹּ׳ 2 K 19^{2}=Is 37^{2}, Je 19^{1}; שָׂרֵי הַכֹּ׳ 2 Ch 36^{14} Ezr 8$^{24.29}$ 10^{5}, רָאשֵׁי הַכֹּ׳ Ne 12^{7}.

† II. [כָּהַן] **vb.** only **Pi. denom.** act as priest;—*Pf.* כהן Ex 40^{13} 1 Ch 5^{36}, 3 mpl. כִּהֲנוּ Ex 28^{41} 40^{15}, *Impf* 3 ms יְכַהֵן Nu 3^{4}+2 t, pl יְכַהֲנוּ 1 Ch 24^{2}, *Inf. cstr* כַּהֵן Ex 29^{1}+11 t.; sf. כַּהֲנוֹ Ex 28$^{1.3.4}$.—**1.** *minister as a priest*, abs. Ex 31^{10} 35^{19} 39^{41} Lv 16^{32} Nu 3$^{3.4}$ (all P), כ׳ לי *minister to me* (׳י) Ex 28$^{1.3.4.41}$ 29$^{1\ 44}$ 30^{30} 40$^{13.15}$ (all P), Ez 44^{13} Ho 4^{6}, כ׳ ליהוה Lv 7^{35} (P), 1 Ch 5^{36} 24^{2} 2 Ch 11^{14} (alw. of Aaron and his sons, exc. Ez 44^{13} 2 Ch 11^{14}, where Levites are forbidden to minister; and Ho 4^{6} of Israel, whose national priesthood is taken away). **2.** *be* or *become priest* Dt 10^{6} (E?). **3.** *play the priest*: כֶּחָתָן יְכַהֵן פאר Is 61^{10} *as a bridegroom (that) priests it with his turban*, decks himself with a splendid turban such as the priests wore.

†כְּהֻנָּה **n.f.** priesthood;—abs כ׳ Ex 29^{9} +5 t., cstr. כְּהֻנַּת Nu 25^{13}+2 t.; sf. כְּהֻנַּתְכֶם Nu 18$^{1\ 7\ 7}$, כְּהֻנָּתָם Nu 3^{10}, pl. כְּהֻנּוֹת 1 S 2^{36}—כהנת יהוה *priesthood of* ׳י, the portion of the Levites Jos 18^{7} (D); pl *priest's offices* 1 S 2^{36}, elsewhere Ex 29^{9} 40^{15} Nu 3^{10} 16^{10} 18$^{1\ 7\ 7}$ 25^{13} (all P), Ezr 2^{62} =Ne 7^{64}, Ne 13$^{29.29}$.

† כּוּב **n.pr gent.** Ez 30^{5}, rd לוּב 𝔊 Sta$^{Pop.\ Jav\ 6}$ Co, cf Sm.

†כּוֹבַע **n.m.** helmet (√ dub., NH כּוֹבַע, Aram כּוֹבְעָא *turban;* cf קוֹבַע Ez 23^{24})—abs. כ׳ Ez 27^{10}, כּוֹבַע 38^{5}, cstr כּוֹבַע (Ew$^{§\ 213,\ f}$) 1 S 17^{5} Is 59^{17}; pl כּוֹבָעִים Je 46^{4} 2 Ch 26^{14};—*helmet*, of bronze כ׳ נחשת עַל־ראשו 1 S 17^{5}; Je 46^{4} Ez 27^{10} 38^{5} 2 Ch 26^{14}, fig. of ׳י, וַיִּלְבַּשׁ צְדָקָה כַּשִּׁרְיָן וכ׳ יְשׁוּעָה בראשו Is 59^{17}

†[כָּוָה] **vb.** burn, scorch, brand (NH *id.;* Aram. ܟܘܳܐ esp. Pa, Ar كَوَى *cauterize*)—**Niph.** *Impf* 2 ms תִּכָּוֶה Is 43^{2} thou shalt not *be scorched* (fig. of Isr, ‖ בָּעַר), 3 fpl. וְרַגְלָיו לֹא תִכָּוֶינָה Pr 6^{28} shall a man walk on the coals *and his feet not be burned?* (‖ שָׂרַף of garments v^{27})

†כִּי n.[m.] burning, branding (for form, cf. רִי from רָוָה, אִי, צִי, עִי: Kö[ii. 1. 64])—only כִּי תַּחַת יֹפִי Is 3^{24} *branding instead of beauty*, in judgment on women of Jerusalem.

†כְּוִיָּה n.f. id.; כ׳ תַּחַת כ׳ Ex 21^{25}.

†מִכְוָה n.f. burnt-spot, scar of a burn; מִכְוַת־אֵשׁ Lv 13^{24}; מִכְוָה $v^{24.25.28.28}$ (all P).

כּוֹכָב v. sub ככב.

†[כּוּל] vb. comprehend, contain (NH, Aram. *id., measure, measure out*, of dry or liquid measure; Syr. Aph. ܐܟܝܠ *id.*; Ar. كَالَ *measure* grain)—**Qal** *Pf.* only Is 40^{12} מִי . . . כָּל בַּשָּׁלִשׁ עֲפַר הָאָרֶץ *who hath comprehended the dust of the earth in a shalish-measure?* **Pilp.** *Pf.* כִּלְכֵּל 2 S 19^{33}; sf. כִּלְכְּלָם 1 K 18^4; 2 ms. sf. כִּלְכַּלְתָּם Ne 9^{21}, etc.; *Impf.* יְכַלְכֵּל Zc 11^{16}+, etc.; *Inf. cstr.* כַּלְכֵּל Je 20^9+, etc.; *Pt.* מְכַלְכֵּל Mal 3^2;—*sustain, maintain, contain*: **1.** *sustain, support, nourish*, sq. acc. pers. Gn 45^{11} 50^{21} (both E), 2 S $19^{33.34}$ 20^3 1 K 4^{7a} (v^b abs.), 5^7 $17^{4.9}$ Ne 9^{21} Ru 4^{15} ψ 55^{23} Zc 11^{16} (of sheep); sq. acc. pers. + rei (food) Gn 47^{12} (J), 1 K $18^{4.13}$. **2.** *contain*, sq. acc. pers. 1 K 8^{27} 2 Ch 2^5 6^{18} (heavens cannot contain י׳); *hold in, restrain* Yahweh's word within one, Je 20^9. **3.** *support, endure*, sickness רוּחַ אִישׁ יְכַלְכֵּל מַחֲלֵהוּ Pr 18^{14} Mal 3^2 (obj. אֶת־יוֹם בּוֹאוֹ); of *sustaining* a cause, in court, יְכַלְכֵּל דְּבָרָיו בְּמִשְׁפָּט ψ 112^5. **Polp.** *Pf.* 3 pl. כָּלְכְּלוּ *were supplied with food* 1 K 20^{27} (Klo prop. בְּגִלְבֹּעַ). **Hiph.** *Impf.* יָכִיל 1 K 7^{26} + 2 t. etc.; *Inf. cstr.* הָכִיל Je 6^{11} + 5 t.;—*contain, hold, hold in, endure*; **1.** *contain*, sq. acc. (of liquid) 1 K $7^{26.38}$ 2 Ch 4^5; in fig. Je 2^{13}, abs. Ez 23^{32}; (of burnt-offering) 1 K 8^{64} 2 Ch 7^7; *hold in* (wrath of י׳, obj. not expr., subj. Jeremiah) Je 6^{11} (opp. שְׁפֹךְ). **2.** *sustain, endure*, sq. acc. Am 7^{10} Je 10^{10} Jo 2^{11}.

†כַּלְכֹּל n.pr.m. one of the wise men whom Solomon surpassed 1 K 5^{11} 1 Ch 2^6 (on format. v. Ba[NB 206]).

כום (√ of foll.; Ar. كَامَ II. is *heap up, accumulate*; كُومَةٌ *heap*; كَوْمٌ *herd* of camels, hence perh. כִּימָה as a *group, herd*, or *flock* of stars, but uncertain (v. כִּימָה)).

†כִּימָה n.f. perh. **Pleiades** (v. supr.; NH *id.*; 𝔗 כִּימָא, 𝔖 ܟܝܡܐ)—as made by י׳, Am 5^8 (‖ כְּסִיל), Jb 9^9 (‖ עָשׁ, כְּסִיל, חַדְרֵי תֵמָן); and under his control, מַעֲדַנּוֹת כ׳ Jb 38^{31} (‖ מֹשְׁכוֹת כְּסִיל).—(Stern [Jüd. Zeitschr. f. Wissen. u. Leben, iii. (1864-65) 258 ff.] Nö in Schenkel[BL] Hoffm[ZAW iii. 107 ff.] interpret עשׁ as Pleiades, and כימה as Sirius).

†I. [כּוּן] [218] vb. prob. be firm, only in der. conj. (NH Aram. כּוּן, in der. conj., כַּיֵּן *arrange, direct*; ܩܘܢ *put right, correct*; As. *kânu, be firm, right* Dl[HWB 321]; Ar. كَانَ (med. و) *exist, occur, be*; so Eth. ኮነ: Sab. כון DHM[ZMG 1875, 599], Ph. כון *be* (oft.));—**Niph.** *Pf.* (on 3 ms. v. *Pt.* infr.), 3 fs. נָכֹ֫ונָה 1 K 2^{46}; 3 pl. נָכֹ֫ונוּ Pr 19^{29}; נָכֹ֫נוּ Ez 16^7; *Impf.* יִכּוֹן Pr 12^3+; 3 fs. תִּכּוֹן Je 30^{20}+; וַתִּכֹּן 1 K 2^{12} 2 Ch 8^{16}, etc.; *Imv.* הִכּוֹן Am 4^{12}; הִכֹּן Ez 38^7; pl. הכונו 2 Ch 35^4 Kt (Qr הָכִינוּ Hiph.); *Pt.* נָכוֹן Gn 41^{32}+ (in ψ 93^2 and perh. elsewh. the *Pf.* would be poss.); cstr. נְכוֹן Pr 4^{18}; f. נְכוֹנָה ψ 5^{10} + 2 t.; pl. נְכֹנִים Ex 19^{11} + 2 t.; pass. or neut., and (less oft.) reflex.:—**1.** *be set up, established, fixed*: **a.** lit., of house upon (עַל) pillars Ju $16^{26.29}$, so, in metaph., of temple-mt., sq. בְּרֹאשׁ Is 2^2 = Mi 4^1; *be firm*, of breasts at puberty Ez 16^7; *firmly established*, of תֵּבֵל ψ 93^1 = 96^{10} = 1 Ch 16^{30}; *firm*, i.e. a strong support, of י׳'s hand יָדִי תִּכּוֹן עִמּוֹ ψ 89^{22} (‖ זְרוֹעִי תְאַמְּצֶנּוּ). **b.** fig., of throne 2 S 7^{16} = 1 Ch 17^{14}, 1 K 2^{45} ψ 89^{38} 93^2 Pr 16^{12} 25^5 29^{14}; of king, royal family, kingdom 1 S 20^{31} 1 K $2^{12.46}$ 2 S 7^{26} = 1 Ch 17^{24}. **c.** of any persons, *be established, stable, secure, enduring* Jb 21^8 (c. לִפְנֵי), Pr 12^3, also v^{19} (subj. שְׂפַת אֱמֶת), ψ 101^7 (c. לְנֶגֶד עֵינָי), 102^{29} (c. לְפָנֶיךָ), 140^{12} (c. בָּאָרֶץ); of plans Pr 16^3 20^{18}; נְכוֹן הַיּוֹם 4^{18} *the established, stable*, (part) *of the day*, i.e. mid-day, when the sun seems motionless in mid-heaven.—2 S 6^6 v. נָכוֹן n.pr. infr. **d.** *fixed, securely determined* כ׳ הַדָּבָר מֵעִם הָאֱלֹהִים Gn 41^{32} (E); so כְּשַׁחַר נָכוֹן מֹצָאוֹ (‖ אֱמֶת) Ho 6^3 MT, but rd. כְּשַׁחֲרֵנוּ כֵּן נִמְצָאֵהוּ Gie[Beiträge 206] We[ad loc.]; *substantiated, certain*, of an allegation Dt 13^{15} = 17^4; עַל־נָכוֹן *acc. to* (what is) *certain*, = certainly, assuredly 1 S 23^{23} 26^4 (v. Dr). **2.** in moral sense, *be directed aright*, of ways Pr 4^{26} ψ 119^5 (cf. Hiph. **3**); *be fixed aright, stedfast* נָכוֹן ψ $57^{8.8}$ 108^2, so 112^7; לִבָּם לֹא נָכוֹן עִמּוֹ 78^{37}; לֹא נָכוֹן לַעֲשׂוֹת כֵּן Ex 8^{22} (J) it is not *right, proper*, etc.; pt. f. נְכוֹנָה as subst. = *what is right, the right* Jb $42^{7.8}$; = *uprightness* ψ 5^{10}. **3.** *prepare, be ready*, pers. Am 4^{12} (c. ל inf.); words Pr 22^{18}; הִכֹּן וְהָכֵן לְךָ Ez 38^7; 2 Ch 35^4 Kt (Qr Hiph.); pt. as adj. = *prepared*,

ready, oft. c הָיָה, of persons Ex 19$^{11.15}$ 34^{2} Jos 8^{4} (all JE); of things, sq לְ pers Jb 12^{5} Ne 8^{10}, לְ loc. Jb 18^{12}, לְ nom act ψ 38^{18}, בְּ loc Jb 15^{23}, **4** pass. *be prepared*, of judgments Pr 19^{29} (לְ pers), of work *be arranged, settled* 2 Ch 8^{16}, fig of prayer ψ 141^{2} *be arranged, set in order*, as incense before thee (> *present itself* as incense); *be arranged, ordered*, of temple service 2 Ch 29^{35} 35$^{10.16}$.

Hiph. *Pf.* הכין Jos 4^{4}+; sf הכינני 1 K 2^{24}, הֱכִינוּ 2 S 5^{12} 1 Ch 14^{2}; הכינה Jb 28^{27}, 2 ms. הֲכִינוֹתָ Jb 11^{13}+; 3 pl הכינו 1 Ch 12^{39}+, והכינו consec Ex 16^{5}, 1 pl הֲכִינוֹנוּ 1 Ch 29^{16}, הכִנּוּ (Ges$^{§72.R.6}$) 2 Ch 29^{19}, etc; *Impf* יָכִין Ju 12^{6}+; וַיָּכֶן 1 Ch 15^{1}+3 t., etc; *Imv* הָכֵן Gn 43^{16}+; pl הָכִינוּ Jos 1^{11}+; *Inf abs* הָכֵן Jos 3^{17}, so הָכִין 4^{3} (rd הָכֵן, v. Di), Je 10^{23} (v Gie), Ez 7^{14} (v. Sm Co and infr, see on all Kön$^{i.468}$); *cstr.* הָכִין Is 9^{6}+, sf הֲכִינוֹ Na 2^{4} Pr 8^{27}; הֲכִינָהּ Je 33^{2}; *Pt* מֵכִין Je 10^{12}+4 t;—(favourite word in Ch, in various applications) **1.** *establish, set up*. **a.** king (or, one as king) 2 S 5^{12} 1 K 2^{24} 1 Ch 14^{2}, royal seed ψ 89^{5}, kingdom 1 S 13^{13} 2 S 7^{12}=1 Ch 17^{11}, 1 Ch 28^{7} 2 Ch 12^{1} 17^{5}, throne 1 Ch 22^{10}; the world תבל Je 10^{12}=51^{15}, mts ψ 65^{7}; heavens Pr 8^{27}, an altar upon (עַל) its base Ezr 3^{3}. **b.** God's faithfulness ψ 89^{3}; heart of humble 10^{17} **c.** =*accomplish, do* Je 33^{2} (‖ עשׂה), =*make* Is 40^{20} Jb 28^{27}. **d.** *make firm*, only inf. abs, as adv =*firmly* הָכֵן Jos 3^{17}; הָכִין 4^{3} (v supr) **2.** **a** *fix*, so as to be ready, *make ready, prepare*, a gift Gn 43^{25} (J), place Ex 23^{20} (JE), 2 Ch 3^{1}, c לְ rei 1 Ch 15$^{1.3}$, also (obj om) v^{12} (vid Be, and Da$^{Synt.§144}$), 2 Ch 1^{4} (בַּהֵכִין, v. Ges$^{§138.3.b}$); oft *prepare* food, acc + לְ pers Jos 1^{11} (D), ψ 78^{20}; לְ om Pr 6^{8} 30^{25}, obj om 1 Ch 12^{39} 2 Ch 35$^{14.14.15}$, both om Gn 43^{16} (J), 1 Ch 9^{32}; *prepare* a road Dt 19^{3} a sacrifice Zp 1^{7}, ambuscades Je 51^{12}, one's work Pr 24^{27}, materials for (לְ) temple 1 Ch 22$^{3.14}$, also v^{14b} (no לְ), 29$^{2.3}$, weapons (c לְ pers) 2 Ch 26^{14} and (hostile purpose) ψ 7^{14}, cf. 57^{7}, Is 14^{21} *prepare slaughter-place for* (לְ) *his children*, store-rooms 2 Ch 31^{11a}, also v^{11b} (obj. om), gallows (c לְ pers) Est 6^{4} 7^{10}, corn (produce of land) ψ 65^{10}, land v^{10}, so (=*restore*) 68^{11}, c acc pers 2 Ch 35^{6}, fig. of belly preparing deceit Jb 15^{35}, *make preparation* (for, לְ rei) 1 Ch 22^{5}, and v^{5} (לְ om), sq. לבנות 1 Ch 28^{2}, c acc material+לבנות 1 K 5^{32} 1 Ch 29^{16}, without לְ, *make ready* 1 S 23^{22} Na 2^{4}, Ez 7^{14} (rd. הָכִינוּ הָכֵן Co, for ה׳ הַכֹּל MT)=*make full preparation! make thee ready!* Je 46^{14} (לְ dat. eth), Ez 28^{7} (id), 2 Ch 35^{4}. **b.** *provide for, provide, furnish* Nu 23$^{1.29}$ 29^{7} Jos 4^{4} (all JE), Jb 27$^{16.17}$, food for (לְ) raven Jb 39^{41}, rain for (לָ) earth ψ 147^{8}, 1 Ch 29^{19} 2 Ch 2^{6} ψ 74^{16} **3.** *direct* one's face towards (אֶל־) Ez 4$^{3.7}$, in moral and spiritual sense, *direct* one's step (צַעֲדוֹ)=*order aright*, Je 10^{23} (v supr), Pr 16^{9}, so (פְּעָמַי) ψ 119^{133}, הֵכִין דרכיו לפני י׳ אלהיו 2 Ch 27^{6}, also (sq דרכיו only) Pr 21^{29} Kt (Qr יָבִין), עַל הַהֵכִין הָאֱלֹהִים לָעָם 2 Ch 29^{36} *that which God had ordered aright for the people* (on art.=pron rel v Ges$^{§138.3.b}$), sq לֵב Jb 11^{13} ψ 78^{8}; +לְ, לא הכין לבו לדרוש את־י׳ 2 Ch 12^{14}, so 19^{3} 30^{19}, + הכין לבב לדרוש אֶת־תּוֹרַת י׳ Ezr 7^{10}; אֶל־י׳ 1 S 7^{3} *direct the heart towards* י׳, 1 Ch 29^{18} (י׳ subj.), so (c. לאלהים) 2 Ch 20^{33}, hence (no obj expr)=*give attention*, sq inf. Ju 12^{6} **4.** *arrange, order* 2 Ch 29^{19} (of sacred vessels, +הקדשנו), 35^{20} (of temple).

Hoph. *Pf* הוּכַן Is 30^{33}, והוּכַן consec Is 16^{5} Zc 5^{11}, וְהֻכַן Na 2^{6}, *Pt* מוּכָן Pr 21^{31}, pl מוּכָנִים Ez 40^{43},—**1.** *be established*, of throne Is 16^{5}, *be fastened*, of hooks Ez 40^{43}. **2.** *be prepared* for (לְ pers.) Is 30^{33} and (לְ temp) Pr 21^{31}, abs Na 2^{6}, *be ready* Zc 5^{11}

Po'lēl. *Pf.* 3 ms כּוֹנֵן ψ 9^{8}+3 t, וְכוֹנֵן consec Hb 2^{12}; sf כּוֹנְנָהּ Is 45^{18}; 2 ms כּוֹנַנְתָּ ψ 99^{4} 119^{90}, כּוֹנָ֑נְתָּה ψ 8^{4}, etc.; *Impf* 3 ms יְכוֹנֵן Is 62^{7}, sf. וַיְכֹנְנֶךָ Dt 32^{6}, יְכוֹנְנֶהָ ψ 24^{2}+, sf. 1 pl וַיְכֻנֶנּוּ Jb 31^{15} (וַיְכוֹנְנֵנוּ van d H), 2 ms תְּכוֹנֵן ψ 7^{10} 21^{13}, etc, *Imv* כונן Jb 8^{8} (but on text v. infra), כּוֹנְנָה ψ 90^{17}, sf. כּוֹנְנֵהוּ ψ 90^{17};—orig *make firm*;—**1.** *set up, establish*. **a.** of men, *found*, a city Hb 2^{12} (‖ בנה), ψ 107^{36}. **b.** of God, *establish*, king's throne 2 S 7^{13}=1 Ch 17^{12}, his own throne ψ 9^{8} (למשפט), sanctuary Ex 15^{7} (song), a nation Dt 32^{6} (poem, ‖ עשה, קנה), a city ψ 48^{9} 87^{5}, תבל ψ 24^{2} (c עַל ‖ יָסַד), אֶרֶץ 119^{90}, cf Is 45^{18}, also ψ 68^{10} (obj. om, rd perh. אֶרֶץ צִיָּה Bi Che), heavens Pr 3^{19} (‖ יָסַד־אָרֶץ), moon and stars ψ 8^{4}; fig, steps of men 40^{3}, work of men's hands 90$^{17.17}$, justice 99^{4}, *establish*, i e. vindicate and make secure to righteous (צדיק) 7^{10}. **2.** *constitute, make*, a man (in womb) Jb 31^{15} (‖ עשה), cf ψ 119^{73} (‖ id); c acc +לְ rei+לְ pers. reflex 2 S 7^{24} *thou hast made*

for thyself (לְךָ), thy people (אֶת־עַמְּךָ) Israel for thyself (לְךָ) into a people (לְעָם) for ever. **3.** *fix*, so as to be ready, arrow upon (עַל) string ψ 11^{2}, so (חֵץ om.) ψ 21^{13} (c. עַל־פְּנֵיהֶם), and poss. (חֵץ om.) Is 51^{13} (Di Che al.; but dub., cf. Du; verse corrupt acc. to Che$^{Intr. Is. 427}$), a bow ψ 7^{13}. **4.** *direct* (sc. לֵב), sq. לַחְקֹר Jb 8^{8}, i.e. give attention to (but no ‖ in Po'l.; rd. perh. בּוֹנֵן, cf. Dt 32^{10}, v. Ol Di). **Po'lal.** *Pf. be established:* מי׳ מִצְעֲדֵי־גֶבֶר כּוֹנָנוּ ψ 37^{23} *from* י׳ *are a man's steps established;* =*be prepared* כּוֹנָנוּ Ez 28^{13} but del. Co Da after A B 𝔊 al. **Hithpo'l.** *Impf.: be established,* of house, 3 ms. יִתְכּוֹנָן Pr 24^{3} (‖ יִבָּנֶה), of nation, 2 fs. תִּכּוֹנָנִי (Ges$^{§54.2.b}$) Is 54^{14}; 3 fs. תִּכּוֹנֵן = *be restored,* of city Nu 21^{27} (JE; ‖ תִּבָּנֶה); *set oneself, take one's stand* 3 mpl. יִכּוֹנָנוּ ψ 59^{5}.

†I. כֵּן **adj.** right, veritable, honest (prop. *firm, upright;* Syr. ܟܐܢ *recte* PS^{1662})—abs. כֵּן Ex 10^{29} + (on poss. cstr. v. **2** ad fin.); pl. כֵּנִים Gn 42$^{11.19.31.33.34}$;—**1.** *right,* usu. indecl., oft. as subst. *a right thing,* esp. c. vbb. *dicendi* Ex 10^{29} (J) כֵּן דֹּבְרֹת Nu 27^{7}, כֵּן דִּבֶּרֶת 36^{5} (both P); כֵּן יַאֲרִיךְ Pr 28^{2} (the) *right* (i.e. order and justice) *shall last long* (v. De Now VB); =adv. *aright,* of pronunciation Ju 12^{6}; also c. vb. *agendi* Ec 8^{10} (on Is 33^{23} v. III. כֵּן sub כנן); *right well* ψ 65^{10}; (Che; al.=*so*); c. לֹא, as adj., *not right* דְּבָרִים אֲשֶׁר לֹא־כֵן 2 K 17^{9} *things which were not right* (vb. *agendi*); of heart of a fool Pr 15^{7}; Je 23^{10}; as subst.=*what is not right, upright* Je 8^{6}; c. vb. *agendi* לֹא־כֵן 2 K 7^{9} *that which is not right we are doing,* Je 48^{30b}. **2.** *veritable, true,* כֶּן־צְדָקָה Pr 11^{19} *the veritable of righteousness*= *true righteousness;* Is 16^{6}=Je 48^{30a} may be either *their boastings are not true* or (Thes Che Di Du Gr Gie al.) *the untruth of their boastings* (לֹא־כֵן as cpd. cstr.); abs., in assent to something already said, *Right! Correct! True!* Jos 2^{4}. **3.** pl. concr. *honest* (men) Gn 42$^{11.19.31.33.34}$ (all E).—I. כֵּן *thus, so,* v. p. 485 infr.; III. כֵּן *place, base,* v. sub כנן; IV. [כֵּן], כַּנּוֹ, כַּנָּם, v. sub כנן.

†II. כּוּן **n.pr.loc.** city of Hadarezer (מִטִּבְחַת וּמִכּוּן עָרֵי ה׳ 1 Ch 18^{8}, 𝔊 ἐκ τῶν ἐκλεκτῶν πολέ(μ)ων (=בֵּרֹתַי 2 S 8^{8}); =mod. *Kuna,* near *Bereitan* (betw. Laodicea and Heliopolis), acc. to Furrer$^{ZPV viii. 34}$, v. בֵּרוֹתָה p. 92 supr., and Thes.

†כּוֹנַנְיָהוּ Kt, כָּנַנְיָהוּ Qr, **n.pr.m.** Levites. **1.** 2 Ch 31$^{12.13}$ (v. Baer's note). **2.** 2 Ch 35^{9}.— 𝔊 Χωμενιας, Χωνενιας, A Χωχενιας.

†יָכִין **n.pr.m.** (*he will establish*);—**1.** a Simeonite Gn 46^{10}=Ex 6^{15}, Nu 26^{12}, 𝔊 Ιαχειμ(ν). **2.** name of right-hand pillar before temple 1 K 7^{21}=2 Ch 3^{17}, 𝔊 Ιαχουμ (opp. בֹּעַז, q.v. p. 126 f. supr.; v. also RS$^{Sem. i. 191 (208)}$).

†יָכִינִי **adj. gent.** of יָכִין **1,** with art. as n. coll. הַי׳ Nu 26^{12}.

†יְכוֹנְיָה **n.pr.m.** (י׳ *is firm, enduring*);— Je 27^{20} = יְכָנְיָהוּ 24^{1} = יְכָנְיָה 28^{4} 29^{2} 1 Ch 3$^{16.17}$ Est 2^{6} = כָּנְיָהוּ Je 22$^{24.28}$ 37^{1} (𝔊 Ιεχονιας throughout), all of last king but one of Judah, v. יְהוֹיָכִין p. 220 supr.

†מָכוֹן **n.m.**$^{Dn 8, 11}$ **fixed or established place, foundation** (chiefly poet.);—abs. מ׳ Ex 15^{17} + 2 t.; cstr. מְכוֹן 1 K 8^{39} + 10 t.; sf. מְכוֹנִי Is 18^{4}, מְכוֹנוֹ Ezr 2^{68}; pl. sf. מְכוֹנֶיהָ ψ 104^{5};—**1.** *fixed place* of י׳'s abode on earth Ex 15^{17} (song), 1 K 8^{13}=2 Ch 6^{2} (poet. fragm.: v. 𝔊 and Dr$^{Intr. 182}$); =*place,* or *site* of God's house Ezr 2^{68}; כָּל־מְכוֹן הַר־צִיּוֹן Is 4^{5}, appar.=*all the extent* of Mt. Zion; redund. (si vera l.) וְהֻשְׁלַךְ מְכוֹן מִקְדָּשׁוֹ Dn 8^{11} *and the place of his sanctuary shall be thrown down* (on difficulties of v., see Bev); of heavens מְכוֹן שִׁבְתְּךָ 1 K 8$^{39.43.49}$=2 Ch 6$^{30.33.39}$, cf. ψ 33^{14}; מְכוֹנִי alone Is 18^{4}; fig. צֶדֶק וּמִשְׁפָּט מְכוֹן כִּסְאֶךָ ψ 89^{15}, so 97^{2}. **2.** *foundation,* only pl., poet. יָסַד אֶרֶץ עַל־מְכוֹנֶיהָ ψ 104^{5}.

מְכֹנָה, מְכוֹנָה$_{25}$ **n.f. fixed resting-place, base;**—abs. מ׳ 1 K 7^{27} + 5 t.; מְכֹנָה 1 K 7$^{34.34.35}$; sf. מְכֻנָתָהּ Zc 5^{11} (Ges$^{§27,3.R.1}$); pl. מְכוֹנוֹת Je 27^{19}, מְכֹנֹת 1 K 7^{27} + 12 t.; sf. מְכוֹנֹתָו Ezr 3^{3};—*base* or *stand* of laver כִּיּוֹר 1 K 7$^{27.27}$ + 13 t. 1 K 7, 2 K 16^{17} 25$^{13.16}$ = Je 52$^{17.20}$, Je 27^{19} 2 Ch 4$^{14.14}$; of altar Ezr 3^{3}; of the symbol. ephah Zc 5^{11}.

†נָכוֹן **n.pr.m.** only in גֹּרֶן נ׳ 2 S 6^{6}; 𝔊 Νωδαβ, A Ναχων, 𝔊L Ορνα τοῦ Ἰεβουσαίου;=כִּידֹן 1 Ch 13^{9}.

†תְּכוּנָה **n.f. arrangement, preparation, fixed place;**—**1.** *arrangement, disposition* תְּכוּנָתוֹ Ez 43^{11}, i.e. the arrangement of the house (del. Co with 𝔊 codd.) **2.** *preparation,* וְאֵין קֵצֶה לַתְּכוּנָה Na 2^{10} *and no end to the preparation* (i.e. things prepared, supply, store). **3.** *fixed place,* i.e. dwelling-place, of God (=מָכוֹן) תְּכוּנָתוֹ Jb 23^{3}.

†[כַּוָּן] **n.[m.] cake, sacrificial cake** (? √כון; cf. Hiph. **2. a.** *prepare* food, etc.)—only pl.

abs. עָשִׂינוּ לַעֲשׂוֹת כַּוָּנִים לִמְלֶכֶת הַשָּׁמַיִם Je 7^{18}; לָהּ כ׳ לְהַעֲצִבָה 44^{19}.

†I. כּוֹס **n.f.**$^{La\ 4.21}$ cup (√unknown; perh. kindred with כִּיס, q.v.; NH *id.*; Ph. כסת; Aram. כָּס, ܟܣܐ; Ar. كَأْسٌ is Aram. loan-wd. acc. to Frä^{171}, but see DHM$^{VOJ\ i.\ 27}$)—כ׳ abs. Gn 40^{11}+; כֹּס Pr 23^{31}; cstr. Gn 40^{11}+; sf. כּוֹסִי ψ 16^{5} 23^{5} etc.; pl. abs. כֹּסוֹת Je 35^{5};—*cup* 2 S 12^{3}; for wine Gn $40^{11.11.11.13.21}$ (all E), Pr 23^{31} Je 35^{5}; שְׂפַת־כּוֹס 1 K 7^{26} 2 Ch 4^{5}; כ׳ תַּנְחוּמִים Je 16^{7} the *cup* offered to mourners; fig. (wine-) *cup* of judgment of י׳, from which the nations, or Isr., must drink כ׳ הַיַּיִן Je 49^{12} La 4^{21} ψ 75^{9}; כ׳ חֲמָתוֹ Is $51^{17.22}$; כ׳ הַתַּרְעֵלָה Is $51^{17.22}$; כ׳ הַחֵמָה Je 25^{15}, cf. v$^{17.28}$; כ׳ שַׁמָּה וּשְׁמָמָה Ez 23^{33}, cf. v$^{31.32.33}$; כ׳ יְמִין י׳ Hb 2^{16}; by bold metaph. Babylon is such a cup כ׳ זָהָב בְּיַד י׳ Je 51^{7}; so of wicked persons, fire, brimstone, and burning wind are מְנָת־כּוֹסָם ψ 11^{6} *the portion of their cup;* כ׳ in good sense, *cup* of blessing ψ 23^{5} (overflowing); י׳ מְנָת חֶלְקִי וְכוֹסִי ψ 16^{5}; כ׳ יְשׁוּעוֹת ψ 116^{13}.

†II. כּוֹס **n.**[**m.**] a kind of owl (acc. to Vrss.; v. Kn-Di Lv 11^{17}; wd. perh. onomatop.)—unclean bird Lv 11^{17} Dt 14^{16}, dwelling in ruins כ׳ חֳרָבוֹת ψ 102^{7}.

I. כור (√of foll.; perh. *be* or *make round,* hence *furnace, pot, basin,* fr. shape; Ar. كَارَ *wind about* (e.g. a turban), كَوَّرَ *turn* or *twist* (of turban), كُورٌ *blacksmith's fire-place, hornets'* or *bees' nest,* كَارَةٌ *bundle;* > Thes comp. Syr. ܐܬܟܘܪ *incaluit* (Lexx. *aestuavit, calefactus est*)).

†I. [כַּר] **n.**[**m.**] **basket-saddle,** בְּכַר־הַגָּמָל Gn 31^{34} *in the camel-basket,* i.e. the basket-saddle of the camel, a sort of palankeen bound upon the saddle proper (cf. Kn in Di and reff.). II. כַּר v. in alphabetical order.

†כּוּר **n.**[**m.**] **smelting-pot or furnace** (Ar. كُور; NH *id.;* Aram. *id.,* ܟܘܪܐ; Eth. ኮር:)—*pot* or *furnace* for smelting metals, but alw. in metaph. or sim. of human sufferings in punishment or discipline: iron (fig. of Egypt as place of bondage) מִכּוּר הַבַּרְזֶל Dt 4^{20} Je 11^{4}, מִתּוֹךְ כ׳ הַבּ׳ 1 K 8^{51}; gold כ׳ לַזָּהָב Pr 17^{3} = 27^{21} (|| מַצְרֵף); various metals Ez $22^{18.20.22}$; once בְּכוּר עֹנִי Is 48^{10} *in a smelting-pot of affliction.*

כּוּר־עָשָׁן **n.pr.loc.** v. בּוֹר עָשָׁן supr. p. 92^{b}.

†[כִּיר] **n.**[**m.**] **cooking-furnace** (Mishn. כִּירָה)—frangible, only du. כִּירַיִם Lv 11^{35} (c. תַּנּוּר), perh. as supporting two pots (Ki); 𝔊 *χυτρόποδες.*

†כִּיֹּר, כִּיּוֹר, כִּיֹּר **n.m.**$^{1\ K\ 7.38}$ **pot, basin** (NH כִּיּוֹר *wash-basin,* so Aram. כִּיּוֹרָא)—abs. כִּיֹּר 1 K 7^{30} + 8 t.; כִּיּוֹר 1 S 2^{14} + 5 t.; cstr. כִּיּוֹר Ex 30^{18} + 2 t.; pl. abs. כִּיֹּרוֹת 1 K 7^{40} (but v. infr.), 2 Ch 4^{14}; כִּיֹּרֹת 1 K 7^{43}; כִּיּוֹרִים 2 Ch 4^{6}; cstr. כִּיֹּרוֹת 1 K 7^{38};—**1.** *pot* for cooking 1 S 2^{14} (|| דּוּד, קַלַּחַת, פָּרוּר). **2.** *fire-pot* כִּיּוֹר אֵשׁ Zc 12^{6} (|| לַפִּיד אֵשׁ; fig. of chiefs of Judah). **3.** *basin* of bronze for washing, *laver;* set on a bronze support **a.** before tabernacle Ex $30^{18.28}$ 31^{9} 35^{16} 38^{8} 39^{39} $40^{7.11.30}$ Lv 8^{11} (all P). **b.** 10 in number, 5 at each front corner of temple 1 K $7^{30.38.38.38.43}$ = 2 Ch 4^{14}, 2 Ch 4^{6} (1 K 7^{40} rd. הַסִּירוֹת as v^{45} and || 2 Ch $4^{11.16}$, so Heb. Codd. 𝔊 𝔙 Th Ke Sta Klo al.) **4.** *platform* or *stage* of bronze (prob. round, bowl-like in shape) on which, acc. to Chr, Solomon stood and kneeled 2 Ch 6^{13}.

†II. [כּוּר] **vb.** mng. dub., perh. *bore,* or *dig,* or *hew* (Dl$^{Prol.\ 121}$ comp. As. *kâru, fell* trees (Dl$^{HWB\ 324}$))—only **Qal** *Pf.* 3 pl. כָּארוּ = כארו for כָּרוּ ψ 22^{17} (MT כָּאֲרִי, v. אֲרִי) *they have bored* (*digged, hewn*) my hands and my feet (si vera l.; cf. Vrss De Pe Che Bae al.; some, however, deriving from כרה in this sense); hence perhaps following.

†[מְכוּרָה, מְכֹרָה] **n.f.** origin (i.e. *place of digging out?*)—sg. sf. אֶרֶץ מְכוּרָתָם Ez 29^{14}; of a people, persons: pl. sf. בְּאֶרֶץ מְכֻרוֹתַיִךְ 21^{35} (|| בִּמְקוֹם אֲשֶׁר נִבְרֵאת); of Jerus., מְכֹרֹתַיִךְ וּמֹלְדֹתַיִךְ מֵאֶרֶץ הַכְּנַעֲנִי 16^{3}.

†[מְכֵרָה] **n.**[**f.**] prob. the name of a weapon, only pl. sf. כְּלֵי חָמָס מְכֵרֹתֵיהֶם Gn 49^{5} *weapons of violence are their* מ׳ (other conjectures v. in Di).

†כּוֹרֶשׁ and (Ezr $1^{1.2}$) כֹּרֶשׁ **n.pr.m. Cyrus** (Pers. *K'ur'u(š),* Spieg$^{APK\ 215}$; Bab. *Kuraš* COT on Ezr 1^{1}, Dl in Baer$^{Dn.\ p.\ x}$)—king of (Anzan = Susiana, Tiele$^{Bab.-Assyr.\ Gesch.\ 469}$, and) Persia, conqueror of Babylon (Tiele$^{ib.\ 468\ ff.}$), restorer of Jews to Palestine Is 44^{28} 45^{1} Ezr 1^{7}; called מֶלֶךְ פָּרַס 2 Ch $36^{22.22.23}$ Ezr $1^{1.1.2}$, also Ezr 1^{8} $4^{3.5}$ Dn 10^{1}; simply הַמֶּלֶךְ Dn 1^{21}.

†I. כּוּשׁ **n.pr.pers.m., gent. et terr.** (Egypt. *Kôš,* Steindorff$^{BAS\ i.\ 593}$, As. *Kûsu,* Id$^{ib.}$ Dl$^{Pa\ 251}$; *Kaši* in Tel Amarna tablets, vid. Wkl

Tel Am 39a);—**1.** 1st 'son' of חָם Gn 10[6.7](P)=1 Ch 1[8.9], 𝔊 Χους, 𝔙 *Chus*, from whom descended acc to these vv. the southernmost peoples known to Hebrews. **2.** land and people of southern Nile-valley, or Upper Egypt, extending from Syene (Ez 29[10]) indefinitely to the south, 𝔊 Αἰθιοπία, Αἰθίοπες· **a.** the land Is 11[11] 18[1] Zp 3[10] Ez 29[10] Jb 28[19] Est 1[1] 8[9]. **b.** the people Is 20[4] Je 46[9] Ez 38[5]; personif. ψ 68[32]. **c.** indeterminate, either land or people, or including both: Is 20[3.5] 43[3] 45[14] 2 K 19[9]=Is 37[9] Na 3[9] Ez 30[4.5.9] ψ 87[4] (𝔊 λαὸς Αἰθιόπων). **3.** in Gn 10[8](J)=1 Ch 1[10] כּוּשׁ is err. for כַּשׁ=Bab *Kaššu*, acc. to Schr[COT] on Gn 10[6], Dl[Pa 51 ff. 72 f.] and most Assyriol.; so perh. also Gn 2[13] (J), yet v. Hpt[Über Ld u Meer, 1894-5, No. 15].

†II. כּוּשׁ **n.pr.m.** a Benjamite, ψ 7[1] (title), 𝔊 Χουσει υἱοῦ Ιεμενει.

†I. כּוּשִׁי **adj.gent.** of I. כּוּשׁ;—m. כּוּשִׁי Je 13[23]+13 t., f כֻּשִׁית Nu 12[1], pl. כּוּשִׁים Zp 2[12] +6 t.; כֻּשִׁים Dn 11[43]; כֻּשִׁיִּים Am 9[7];—**a.** sg. agreeing with noun Nu 12[1] (E; only here fem.). **b.**=subst, *a Cushite* Je 13[23] **c.** id. c. art., *the Cushite*, of Joab's adjutant 2 S 18[21.21] (where rd. חֻ׳, for MT כּ׳, We Dr Kit Bu), v[22.23.31.31.32.32]; in appos. with n.pr. Je 38[7.10.12] 39[16] 2 Ch 14[8]. **d.** pl. (הַ)כּוּשִׁים = subst. Zp 2[12] 2 Ch 12[3] 14[11 11 12] 16[8] 21[16]; so כֻּשִׁים Dn 11[43], כֻּשִׁיִּים (si vera l.) Am 9[7].

†II. כּוּשִׁי **n.pr.m.** 𝔊 Χουσει—**1.** Je 36[14] great-grandfather of יְהוּדִי, q.v. (perh. orig appellat. *Cushite*). **2.** father of prophet Zephaniah Zp 1[1].

† כּוּשָׁן **n.pr., gent.** vel **terr.**, only אָהֳלֵי כ׳ Hb 3[7] (‖ מִדְיָן), 𝔊 Αἰθιόπων

†כּוּשַׁן רִשְׁעָתַיִם **n.pr.m.** king of Aram Naharaim Ju 3[8.8.10 10]; otherwise unknown, 𝔊 Χουσαρσαθαιμ, 𝔊L Χουσανρεσαμωθ.

כּוֹשָׁרוֹת v [כּוֹשָׁרָה] sub כָּשֵׁר.

†כּוּתָה, כּוּת **n.pr.loc.** whence king of Assyria (Sargon) transported colonists into N. Israel, מִכּוּתָה 2 K 17[24], אַנְשֵׁי־כוּת v[30]; Bab. *Kûtû, Kûtê*, mod Tel-Ibrahim, c 20 m NE. fr. Babylon, v. COT[2 K 17. 24] Dl[Par 217] M-A[JBL 1892, xi 169].

†[כָּזַב] **vb.** lie, be a liar (Ar كَذَبَ, Aram. כְּדַב, ܟܰܕܶܒ *id* chiefly Pa; NH כָּזַב)—**Qal** *Pt.* כֹּזֵב ψ 116[11] (cf. כָּזָב 62[10]). **Niph.** *Pf.* כָּל־הָאָדָם כֹּזֵב 3 fs. תּוֹחַלְתּוֹ נִכְזָבָה Jb 41[1] *his hope has been made deceptive*, i.e been shewn to be so, 2 ms consec. וְנִכְזָבְתָּ Pr 30[6] lest he convict thee *and thou be proven a liar* **Pi.** *Pf.* 3 ms. כִּזֵּב Mi 2[11]; *Impf.* 3 ms יְכַזֵּב Hb 2[3] Pr 14[5]; וִיכַזֵּב Nu 23[19], etc, *Inf. cstr.* sf. (בּ)כַזֶּבְכֶם Ez 13[19];—**1.** *lie, tell a lie*, abs., Nu 23[19] (JE), Mi 2[11] Jb 6[28] 34[6] Pr 14[5] Is 57[11]; sq. לְ pers. *lie to* Ez 13[19] ψ 78[36] 89[36], sq בְּ pers. *tell a lie with*, i.e. in intercourse, conversation with 2 K 4[16]. **2.** *disappoint, fail*, of a divine revelation Hb 2[3]; waters of a spring Is 58[11]. **Hiph.** *Impf* 3 ms. sf. יַכְזִיבֵנִי Jb 24[25] who *will make me a liar?* i.e prove me to be so (cf **Niph.**)

†כָּזָב **n.m.**[Am 2.4] lie, falsehood, deceptive thing,—abs. כ׳ Ho 12[2]+19 t.; pl abs. כְּזָבִים Ju 16[10]+9 t; sf כִּזְבֵיהֶם Am 2[4];—*lie, falsehood*, c דִּבֶּר Ju 16[10.13] Ho 7[13] Zp 3[13] Dn 11[27] ψ 5[7] 58[4], so Ez 13[8] Co (by transp. כ׳ with שָׁוְא, cf v[6.7.9]); c יָפִיחַ (in Pr) Pr 6[19] 14[5.25] 19[5.9], of false prophecies (divinations) c אָמַר, כ׳ מִקְסַם Ez 13[7], c קָסַם v[9] 21[34] 22[28]+13[6] 𝔊 Co (קְסוּם כ׳, for MT קֶסֶם כ׳); c. שָׁמַע 13[19], בִּקֵּשׁ ψ 4[3]; c. רָצָה *delight in* 62[5]; so in the phr. דְּבַר־כ׳ Pr 30[8], אִישׁ כ׳ 19[22] =*liar*, עֵד כְּזָבִים 21[28]=*false witness*, of idols as a *lie* (*res ementita*) Am 2[4], so prob. שָׂטֵי כ׳ *those turning aside to a lie* ψ 40[5] (cf. אֱלִיל, אָוֶן, שֶׁקֶר, הֶבֶל); then of empty human pretensions כ׳ וָשֹׁד יַרְבֶּה Ho 12[2], Is 28[15] (‖ שֶׁקֶר), v[17] (מַחְסֵה כ׳), ψ 62[10] (‖ הֶבֶל, cf כֹּזֵב 116[11]), לֶחֶם כְּזָבִים Pr 23[3] =*deceptive* (disappointing) *bread*.

†כְּזִיב **n.pr.loc.** in plain of Judah Gn 38[5], 𝔊 Χασβι, = אַכְזִיב **1.** v. infr.

†כֹּזֵבָא **n.pr.loc.** 1 Ch 4[22] 𝔊 Σωχηθα, A𝔊L Χωζηβα, = אַכְזִיב **1.** v. infr.

†כָּזְבִּי **n.pr.f.** a woman of Midian Nu 25[15.18], 𝔊 Χασβ(ε)ι.

†אַכְזָב **adj.** deceptive, disappointing (elative; opp אֵיתָן q.v. sub יתן)—only abs. sg.:—Mi 1[14] (with play on n pr. אַכְזִיב); of a deceptive, disappointing stream (cf. Is 58[11]) Je 15[18] (‖ מַיִם לֹא נֶאֱמָנוּ; on meaning cf. Jb 6[15 ff])

†אַכְזִיב **n.pr.loc.** **1.** in lowland of Judah Jos 15[44] (𝔊 Ακιεζει καὶ Κεζειβ, 𝔊L Αχζειβ), Mi 1[14] (𝔊 οἴκους ματαίους; v. also כְּזִיב, כֹּזֵבָא) **2.** in Asher Ju 1[31] (𝔊 Ασχαζει), and (אַכְזִיבָה) Jos

19^{29} (𝔊 Εχοζοβ, A Αχζειφ, 𝔊L Αχαζειβ), it lay on the coast S of Tyre, in As *Akzibi*, COT Jos 19 29 Dl Par 284, Gk Εκδιππα; mod *ez-Zîb*, Bd Pal 272 Buhl G § 120 and (on pronunciation) Kasteren ZPV xiii 101

כזר (√ of foll , Aram Ethpe *be cruel* (𝔗 Jb 10^{1}), cf. Syr ܟܙܝܪܐ, *miles, vir strenuus* PS 1718, who comp Pers گزیر *athleta, heros* (Vullers))

†**אַכְזָר** **adj.** **cruel, fierce,** of poison (ראשׁ) Dt 32^{33}, elsewh of men, *fierce* Jb 41^{2}, as subst. = *a cruel one* Jb 30^{21} (of God), La 4^{3}.

†**אַכְזָרִי** **adj.** **cruel,** always in this form,—Pr 12^{10} 17^{11} Je 6^{23} 50^{42}, also 30^{14} (rd מוּסַר א׳, for MT מוּסַר, Gf Gie); as subst Pr 5^{9} 11^{17}, perhaps also, in appos with יוֹם י׳, Is 13^{9}

†**אַכְזְרִיּוּת** **n.f.** **cruelty, fierceness,** only א׳ חֵמָה וְשֶׁטֶף אָף Pr 27^{4} *fierceness of rage and outpouring of anger.*

†I. **כֹּחַ** **n.[m.]** a small reptile, prob a kind of lizard, in list of unclean creeping things Lv 11^{30}, 𝔊𝔙 AV *chameleon,* on various opinions v Di.

II **כֹּחַ** v sub כחח

†[**כָּחַד**] **vb** not in **Qal**, **Pi. Hiph.** **hide, efface,** **Niph.** (usu) pass (Aram אתכחדו *be effaced* 𝔗 Jb 4^{7}, ܟܚܕ is *revere*, Pt *venerable*, Pa *put to shame*, Ethpa *be ashamed;* Eth. ክሕደ: *deny, apostatize*)—**Niph.** *Pf.* 3 ms נִכְחַד Ho 5^{3} + 2 t., 3 pl. נִכְחֲדוּ Jb 4^{7} ψ 69^{6}, *Impf* 3 ms יִכָּחֵד 2 S 18^{13}, etc , *Pt* נִכְחֶדֶת Zc 11^{9}; pl נִכְחָדוֹת Zc 11^{16} Jb 15^{28},—**1.** *be hidden*, sq. מִן pers , 2 S 18^{13} Ho 5^{3} ψ 69^{6} 139^{15}. **2.** *be effaced, destroyed* Zc 11^{9} Jb 4^{7} 15^{28} (עָרִים נִכְחָדוֹת), 22^{20}, sq. מִן־הָאָרֶץ Ex 9^{15} (J), *Pt* intrans of incomplete process = *going to ruin* Zc 11$^{9.16}$ **Pi.** *Pf* כִּחֵד 1 S 3^{18}, 1 s כִּחַדְתִּי Jb 6^{10} ψ 40^{11}, 3 pl. כִּחֲדוּ Jb 15^{18}, כִּחֵדוּ Is 3^{9}, *Impf* 2 ms. תְּכַחֵד Jos 7^{19} + 4 t , 2 fs תְּכַחֲדִי 2 S 14^{18}, 1 s אֲכַחֵד Jb 27^{11}, 2 mpl תְּכַחֲדוּ Je 50^{2}, 1 pl נְכַחֵד Gn 47^{18} ψ 78^{4},—*hide*, sq מִן pers Gn 47^{18} (J), Jos 7^{19} (JE), 1 S 3$^{17\ 17\ 18}$ 2 S 14^{18} Je 38$^{14\ 25}$ ψ 78^{4}, sq לְ pers. ψ 40^{11} *conceal toward, with ref to,* i e *from,* without prep. Is 3^{9} Je 50^{2} Jb 15^{18} 27^{11}, = *disown* Jb 6^{10} **Hiph.** *Pf* 1 s consec sf וְהִכְחַדְתִּיו Ex 23^{23}, *Impf* 3 ms וַיַּכְחֵד 2 Ch 32^{21}, sf יַכְחִידֶנָּה Jb 20^{12}; 1 s וָאַכְחִד Zc 11^{8}; 1 pl sf וְנַכְחִידֵם ψ 83^{5}; *Inf cstr* לְהַכְחִיד 1 K 13^{34},—**1.** *hide,* in fig יַכְחִידֶנָּה תַּחַת לְשׁוֹנוֹ Jb 20^{12} (obj wickedness) **2.** *efface, annihilate* Ex 23^{23} (E), 1 K 13^{34} (‖ הַשְׁמִיד), Zc 11^{8} 2 Ch 32^{21}, sq מִגּוֹי ψ 83^{5}, i e *from being* (so that they be not) *a nation*

כחח (√assumed by Thes Buhl al for foll. Ba NB 79 prop √כוח).

†II **כֹּחַ** and (†Dn 11^{6}) **כּוֹחַ** **n.m.** Dt 4.37 **strength, power** (NH *id*),—כ׳ abs Dt 8^{18} +, cstr. Nu 14^{17} +, sf. כֹּחִי Gn 31^{6} +, כֹּחֲךָ Ju 16^{6} +, כֹּחֶךָ Pr 5^{10}, כֹּחֶכָה Pr 24^{10}, etc ; alw sg ,—**1.** *human strength* · **a.** physical, of Samson Ju 16$^{5.6.9.15.17.19.30}$, strength in toil Is 44^{12} (זְרוֹעַ כֹּחוֹ), v^{13} Lv 26^{20} Ne 4^{4}; of manly vigour (in procreation) אַתָּה כֹּחִי וְרֵאשִׁית אוֹנִי Gn 49^{3} (poem in J; said to Reuben); vigour in gen Jos 14$^{11\ 11}$ (JE), Ju 6^{14} 1 S 28^{22} Jb 6$^{11\ 12}$ ψ 31^{11} 38^{11} 71^{9} 102^{24} Pr 20^{29}, as sustained by food 1 K 19^{8}, lack of such vigour is לֹא־כֹחַ Jb 26^{2}, cf מִכֹּחַ Je 48^{45} *without strength,* בְּלֹא־כ׳ La 1^{6}; יְגִיעֵי־כ׳ Jb 3^{17}; כֹּחַ לֹא־הָיָה בוֹ 1 S 28^{20}, cf Dn 10$^{8\ 17}$, in ψ 22^{16} rd חִכִּי, so Ew Ol Che al ; specif of *power* of voice Is 40^{9} **b.** more inclusively, *ability, efficiency:* sq inf , *ability* to weep 1 S 30^{4}, to get wealth Dt 8^{18}; to bring forth (a child; in fig) 2 K 19^{3} = Is 37^{3}; sq לַעֲמֹד Dn 1^{4} Ezr 10^{13}, cf. Dn 11^{15}; without inf 1 Ch 29^{2} Ezr 2^{69}, of *efficiency* in battle 2 Ch 14^{10} 20^{12} 26^{13}, for porter's service in temple אִישׁ־חַיִל בַּכֹּחַ לַעֲבֹדָה 1 Ch 26^{8}; *ability* or *efficiency* in gen. Gn 31^{6} Pr 24$^{5.10}$ Ec 4^{1} 9^{10}, so prob. כֹּחַ יְדֵיהֶם Jb 30^{2}; עָצַר כֹּחַ (late, cf. עצר) *retain ability* or *strength,* sq inf , נַעְצֹר כ׳ לְהִתְנַדֵּב 1 Ch 29^{14} that *we should retain* (have) *ability to make freewill-offerings,* to build 2 Ch 2^{5}, c neg , without inf, Dn 10$^{8.16}$ (cf. 11^{6}, **c**). **c.** *power* of a people, or king, Jos 17^{17} Na 2^{2} Hb 1^{11} Is 49^{4} (of servant of י׳), La 1^{14} Dn 8$^{22.24\,a}$, also v$^{24\,b}$ (si vera l, v. Bev), 11^{25} (‖ לְבָב), c עָצַר 2 Ch 13^{20} 22^{9} Dn 11^{6} (לֹא תַעְצֹר כ׳ הַזְּרוֹעַ, cf **b**), in Ho 7^{9} fig of body seems combined with that of land yielding produce (v. **5** infr) **d.** *power* opp. to that of God Am 2^{14} Is 10^{13} (כ׳ יָדִי), Dt 8^{17} 1 S 2^{9} Zc 4^{6} Jb 36^{19} ψ 33^{16}. **e** *power* conferred by God Is 40^{29}, cf. v^{31} 41^{1}, of prophetic power Mi 3^{8} **2** *strength* of angels ψ 103^{20} **3.** *power* of God: in creation Je 10^{12} 51^{15} (see also 32^{17} infr.), ψ 65^{7}; in governing the world 1 Ch 29^{12} 2 Ch 20^{6} ψ 29^{4}; in acts of deliverance and judgment Ex 9^{16} 15^{6} 32^{11} Nu 14$^{13\ 17}$ (JE), Is 50^{2} 2 Ch 25^{8} Jb 9^{19} 24^{22} 26^{12} 30^{18} 36^{22}, in combin כֹּחַ גָּדוֹל Dt 4^{37}, ‖ יָד חֲזָקָה Ex 32^{11} (JE), Ne 1^{10}, ‖ זְרוֹעַ נְטוּיָה Dt 9^{29} 2 K 17^{36}

Je 27^{5} 32^{17}; he is רַב־כֹּחַ ψ 147^{5}, cf. רֹב כֹּחוֹ Is 63^{1} Jb 23^{6}; also גדול־כּח Na 1^{3}; אַמִּיץ כֹּחַ Is 40^{26} Jb 9^{4}, שַׂגִּיא־כֹחַ 37^{23}; כֹּחַ מַעֲשָׂיו ψ 111^{6} *the power of his works;* קוֹל י׳ בַּכֹּחַ ψ 29^{4} (of thunder); specif. of his wisdom (rather peculiarly, Elihu) כַּבִּיר כֹּחַ לֵב Jb 36^{5} *mighty in strength of mind.* **4.** of animals: wild ox Jb 39^{11}, horse v^{21}, hippopot. 40^{16}, bullock Pr 14^{4}; he-goat Dn 8^{6}, ram v^{7}. **5.** *strength,* of soil i.e. *produce,* Gn 4^{12} (J), Jb 31^{39}; (Ho 7^{9} v. **1. c** supr.); = *wealth* (cf. חַיִל) Pr 5^{10} Jb 6^{22}.

†[כָּחַל] **vb. paint** (eyes) (NH *id.;* Aram. כְּחַל, ܟܚܰܠ; Eth. ኰሐለ: Ar. كَحَلَ)—only in רָחַצְתְּ כָּחַלְתְּ עֵינַיִךְ וגו׳ Ez 23^{40} (Co rds. 3 pl.);—v. also פּוּךְ.

†כָּחַשׁ **vb. be disappointing, deceive, fail, grow lean** (NH כָּחַשׁ *grow lean;* Hiph. *convict of falsehood, refute;* Aram. כְּחַשׁ *grow lean;* כַּחְשָׁא *leanness,* כְּחִישׁוּתָא *leanness, weakness;* Aph. as NH Hiph.)—**Qal** *Pf.* 3 ms. וּבְשָׂרִי כָּחַשׁ מִשָּׁמֶן ψ 109^{24} *my flesh hath grown lean* (away) *fr. fatness* (|| בִּרְכַּי כָּשְׁלוּ מִצּוֹם). **Niph.** *Impf.* וְיִכָּחֲשׁוּ אֹיְבֶיךָ לָךְ Dt 33^{29} *thine enemies shall cringe* (come cringing, i.e. orig. *act deceptively, feigning obedience*) *to thee* (cf. also **Pi. 3, Hithp.**) **Pi.** *Pf.* 3 ms. כִּחֵשׁ 1 K 13^{18} Hb 3^{17}; וְכִחֶשׁ consec. (bef. monosyll.) Lv 5^{22} Jb 8^{18}, etc.; *Impf.* (בָּהּ) יְכַחֶשׁ Ho 9^{2}; 3 fs. וַתְּכַחֵשׁ Gn 18^{15}, etc.; *Inf. abs.* כַּחֵשׁ Ho 4^{2} Is 59^{13}; *cstr.* Zc 13^{4};—**1.** *deceive,* abs. Gn 18^{15} (J), Jos 7^{11} (JE), Ho 4^{2} (אלה וכחש together = *false swearing* acc. to We$^{Kl. Pr.}$; + וְרָצֹחַ וְגָנֹב וְנָאֹף), cf. לֹא תִּגְנֹבוּ וְלֹא־תְכַחֲשׁוּ וְלֹא תְשַׁקְּרוּ אִישׁ בַּעֲמִיתוֹ Lv 19^{11} (H); לְמַעַן כ׳ Zc 13^{4} *in order to deceive;* sq. לְ pers. 1 K 13^{18} Jb 31^{28}; sq. בְּ pers. et rei Lv 5^{21}, בְּ rei v^{22}. **2.** *act deceptively* against (i.e. seem to acknowledge, but not really do so), sq. בְּ pers. Jos 24^{27} (E), Je 5^{12} Is 59^{13} Jb 8^{18}, appar. also וְתִירוֹשׁ יכ׳ בָּהּ Ho 9^{2} *and new wine shall deny her* (Isr.; i.e. refuse to acknowledge her as its mistress, not yield itself to her); abs. Pr 30^{9}. **3.** *cringe* = *come cringing* (make shew of obedience, v. Niph.), sq. לְ pers. ψ 18^{45} (Hithp. in || 2 S 22^{45}); sq. לְ pers. ψ 66^{3} 81^{16}. **4.** *disappoint, fail,* abs. כִּחֵשׁ מַעֲשֵׂה זַיִת Hb 3^{17} *the product of the olive hath failed* (in sense comp. Ho 9^{2} supr.)

Hithp. *Impf.* יִתְכַּחֲשׁוּ לִי 2 S 22^{45} *shall come cringing to me* (|| ψ 18^{45}, v. supr.)

†כַּחַשׁ **n.m.**$^{Jb\ 16,8}$ **1. lying. 2. leanness;**—abs. כ׳ Ho 12^{1} + 2 t.; כָּחַשׁ Ho 10^{13}; sf. כַּחֲשִׁי Jb 16^{8}; pl. sf. כַּחֲשֵׁיהֶם Ho 7^{3};—**1.** *lying,* אֲכַלְתֶּם פְּרִי כ׳ Ho 10^{13} *ye have eaten the fruit of lying;* 7^{3} (|| רָעָה), 12^{1}; of Nineveh, כ׳ פֶּרֶק מְלֵאָה Na 3^{1} *of lying* (and) *robbery it is full;* ψ 59^{13} (|| אָלָה). **2.** of Job's affliction Jb 16^{8} *my leanness hath risen up against me* (cf. ψ 109^{24}; 𝔗 J Gn 41^{27}, Ec 12^{5}; Talm. כחשא; > *my lying,* i.e. my affliction regarded as a lying witness, Di Buhl al.)

†[כֶּחָשׁ] **adj. deceptive, false** (on format. v. Ba$^{NB\ 50}$ Ges$^{§\ 84\ b}$)—בָּנִים כֶּחָשִׁים Is 30^{9} (|| עַם מְרִי).

כִּי **conj. that, for, when** (Moab. *id.:* Ph. כ. Prob. from the same demonstr. basis found in كُمَّ *here,* and in certain pronouns, as Aram. דֵּךְ *this* (W$^{SG\ 110\ f.}$); perh. also ultim. akin with كَيْ *that, in order that,* and كَمَ *then,* enclit., like Lat. *nam* in *quisnam?*)—**1.** *that* (ὅτι, Germ. *dass*): **a.** prefixed to sentences depending on an active verb, and occupying to it the place of an accus.: so constantly, after vbs. of seeing, as Gn 1^{10} וַיַּרְא אֱלֹהִים כִּי טוֹב and God saw *that* it was good, 3^{6} $6^{2.5}$ 12^{14} + oft., hearing 14^{14} 29^{33}, knowing 22^{12} 24^{14}, telling 3^{11} 12^{18}, repenting $6^{6.7}$, swearing Gn 22^{16} Je 22^{5}, believing Ex 4^{5} La 4^{12}, remembering ψ 78^{35}, forgetting Jb 39^{15}; אָמַר = *command* (late; in early Heb. the words said are quoted) Jb $36^{10.24}$ (זְכֹר in a command) $37^{20\,b}$ 1 Ch 21^{18} (contrast 2 S 24^{18}) etc.; טוֹב כִּי it is good *that* ... 2 S 18^{3} + (v. p. 374^{b}: usu. the inf. c., as Gn 2^{18}; v. ibid.); Gn 37^{26} מַה־בֶּצַע כִּי נַהֲרֹג what profit *that* we should slay (impf.) ...? Mal 3^{14} what profit כִּי שָׁמַרְנוּ *that* we have kept (pf.)...? Jb 22^{3} הַחֵפֶץ לְשַׁדַּי כִּי is it pleasure to Shaddai that ...? after a pron., as ψ 41^{12} by *this* I know that thou hast pleasure in me, *that* my enemy cannot triumph over me, 42^{5} *these* things will I remember ... *that* (or *how*) I used to go, etc., 56^{10} *this* I know *that* God is for me, Jb 13^{16} (הוּא). And with כִּי repeated pleon. after an intervening clause 2 S 19^{7} Je 26^{15} +; וְכִי ... כִּי Gn 3^{6} 29^{12} Ex 4^{31} Jos 2^{9} 8^{21} 10^{1} 1 S 31^{7} 2 S 5^{12} 1 K 11^{21} Je $40^{7.11}$; וְכִי ... לֵאמֹר Gn 45^{26} Ju 10^{10}. **b.** כִּי often introduces the *direct* narration (like ?, إِنَّ, and the Gk. ὅτι *recitativum,* e.g. Luke 4^{21}), in which case it cannot be represented in English (except by inverted commas), Gn 21^{30} 29^{33} and she said, כִּי שָׁמַע י׳ Yahweh hath heard, etc.; Ex 3^{12} = Ju 6^{16} and he said, כִּי אֶהְיֶה עִמָּךְ I will

be with thee, Jos 2^{24} 1 S 2^{16} (v Dr) 10^{19} and ye have said to him, כִּי מֶלֶךְ תָּשִׂים עָלֵינוּ Thou shalt set a king over us, 2 S 11^{23} 1 K 1^{13} 20^{6} Ru 1^{10}, cf 2^{21} (but in reply to a qu כי may = *because*, v sub **3**; and so also in sentences giving the expl of a proper name, Gn 26^{22} 29^{32} (but De *surely*. v. infr.), Ex 2^{10} (cf Gn 4^{25} $41^{51.52}$), in כִּי מָה, introducing an expostulation, 1 S 29^{8} 1 K 11^{22} 2 K 8^{13}, it gives the reason for a suppressed 'Why do you say this?'). **c.** esp after an oath חַי אָנִי, חַי י׳, etc, introducing the fact sworn to, Gn 42^{16} by the life of Pharaoh, כִּי מְרַגְּלִים אַתֶּם (I say) *that* ye are spies, but though Heb. usage prob gave it an asseverative force, Engl idiom does not require it to be expressed: Nu 14^{22} 1 S 20^{3} as י׳ liveth, כִּי כְפֶשַׂע בֵּינִי וּבֵין הַמָּוֶת there is but a step between me and death! 26^{16} 29^{6} Is 49^{18}+, 1 S 14^{44} כה־יַעֲשֶׂה אלהים וכה יוסיף כי מות תָּמוּת thus may God do and more also: thou shalt surely die! 2 S 3^{35} 1 K 2^{23} Ru 1^{17} al—Note that כי when thus used is oft repeated after an intervening clause, in order that its force may be fully preserved Gn 22^{16f} 1 S 14^{39} 25^{34} חַי י׳ כי (אם־יֶשְׁנוֹ ביוֹנָתָן בני) כי מות יָמוּת 2 S 2^{27} כִּי (לוּלֵא דִבַּרְתָּ) כי אָז וגו׳, 3^{9} 15^{21} Qr 1 K 1^{30} Je 22^{24} **d.** כִּי is used sts with advs and interjs to add force or distinctness to the affirmation which follows: (*a*) so esp in אַף כִּי (v. אַף), הֲכִי+ *is it that . . . ?* (as a neutral interrog) 2 S 9^{1}, (expecting a neg. answer) Gn 29^{15} *is it that* thou art my brother, and shalt (therefore) serve me for nothing? Jb 6^{22} *is it that* I have said, Give unto me? expressing surprise Gn 27^{36} *is it that* he is called Jacob, and has (hence) supplanted me twice? 2 S 23^{19} an affirm answer is required (wh. would imply הֲלֹא כִי) rd. prob with the ‖ 1 Ch 11^{25} הִנּוֹ *behold, he*, etc, אִם־לֹא כִי+ Dt 32^{30} were it not *that* , אָמְנָם כִּי+ Jb 12^{2} of a truth (is it) *that* ye are the people, etc, אַךְ כִּי+ 1 S 8^{9}, אפס כי Nu 13^{28}+; גַּם כִּי +Ru 2^{21}, הֲלֹא כִי+, 1 S 10^{1} (but v 𝔊 Dr), 2 S 13^{28}, הנה כי+ ψ 128^{4}; cf ψ 118^{10-12} בְּשֵׁם י׳ כִּי אֲמִילַם in the name of י׳ (is it) *that*—or (I say) *that*—I will mow them down, Jb 39^{27} doth the vulture mount up at thy command, וכי יָרִים קִנּוֹ *and* (is it) *that* it (so) makes high its nest? Is 36^{19} have the gods of the nations delivered each his land etc? . . . וכי הצילו i e (Hi) *and* (is it) *that* they have delivered Samaria out of my hand? > (Ew ^{354e} De Di) *and that* they have delivered Samaria out of my hand! = how much less (אַף כִּי) have they, etc! (‖ 2 K 18^{34} כִּי alone, perhaps conformed by error to v^{35}, 2 Ch 32^{15} אַף כִּי, which however does not decide the sense of the orig. וְכִי) 1 Ch 29^{14} וכי מִי rd. ומי or כי מי (*b*) in introducing the apodosis, esp. in כִּי עַתָּה (chiefly after לוּלֵא) *indeed* then , Gn 31^{42} 43^{10} for unless we had tarried כִּי עַתָּה שַׁבְנוּ *surely* then we had returned twice, Nu 22^{33} (rd. לוּלֵי for אוּלַי); so 1 S 14^{30} 𝔊 (after לוּא), and 13^{13} Hi We (לֹא for לוּ); after אם Jb 8^{6} *surely* then he will awake over thee, etc. (But elsewhere כִּי עַתָּה is simply *for now*, Gn 29^{32} Jb 7^{21}+, or *for then* = *for in that case*, Ex 9^{15} Nu 22^{29} Jb 3^{13} 6^{3}+). It is dub whether כִּי אָז has the same sense: for 2 S 2^{27} 19^{7} the כִּי in כִּי אָז may be merely resumptive of the כִּי *recitat.* preceding (vid. **a, c**). Rare otherwise. Ex 22^{22} if thou afflict him כִּי אִם־צָעֹק יִצְעַק 'tis *that* (= *indeed*), if he cries unto me, I will hear him, Is 7^{9} if ye believe not: כִּי לֹא תֵאָמֵנוּ *indeed* ye will not be established. **e.** there seem also to be other cases in which כִּי, standing alone, has an intensive force, introducing a statement with emph., *yea, surely, certainly* (Germ. *ja*—a lighter particle than these Engl. words) see in AV RV Ex 18^{11} Nu 23^{23} 1 S 17^{25} 20^{26} 2 K 23^{22} Is 32^{13} 60^{9} Je 22^{22} 31^{19} Ho 6^{9} 8^{6} 9^{12} 10^{3} Am 3^{7} ψ 76^{11} 77^{12} (Ew Che), Pr 30^{2} (but not if construed as RVm), Ec 4^{16} $7^{7.20}$ Jb 28^{1}+; La 3^{22} (𝔖 𝔗 Ew Th Ot) the mercies of י׳, *surely* they are not consumed (rd prob. תַּמּוּ or תָּמְמוּ for תמנו), Ru 3^{12} כִּי אָמְנָם *yea*, indeed. But it is doubtful whether כִּי has this force in all the passages for which scholars have had recourse to it, and whether in some it is not simply = *for*. De$^{Pr\ 30,1}$ would restrict the usage to cases in which a suppressed clause may be understood **f.** *that*, expressing consecution, esp. after a question implying surprise or deprecation: sq perf, Gn 20^{9} what have I sinned against thee כִּי הֵבֵאתָ עָלַי *that* thou hast brought upon me? 1 S 22^{8} Is 22^{1} what aileth thee, *that* thou art gone up, etc.? v^{16} 36^{5} 52^{5} Mic 4^{9} Hb 2^{18}, sq. ptcp. Ju 14^{3} 1 S 20^{1} 1 K 18^{9} how have I sinned *that* thou art giving, etc? 2 K 5^{7} Ez 24^{19}, usu sq. impf. Ex 3^{11} who am I כִּי אֵלֵךְ *that* I should go, etc? 16^{7} Ju 8^{6} 9^{28} 2 K 8^{13} Is 7^{13} 29^{16} (also pf.), ψ 8^{5} what is man כִּי תִזְכְּרֶנּוּ? Jb 3^{12} or why the breasts: כִּי אִינָק *that* I should suck? 6^{11} מַה־כֹּחִי כִּי אֲיַחֵל, $7^{12.17}$ 10^{6f} 13^{25f} $15^{12f.14}$ 16^{3} 21^{15}+, after a neg., Gn 40^{15} here also I have done nothing

כִּי שָׂמוּ *that* they should have placed me in the dungeon, ψ 44$^{19f.}$ our heart has not turned backward, etc. כִּי דִכִּיתָנוּ *that* thou shouldst have crushed us, etc., Is 43^{22} not *me* hast thou called on, כִּי יָגַעְתָּ בִּי *that* thou shouldst have wearied thyself with me, Ho 1^{6} (v. RV), Jb 41^{2} Ru 1^{12} I am too old to have an husband כִּי אָמַרְתִּי *that* I should have said, etc. (cf. Ew ^{§337a}; Dr ^{§39d}). **g.** added to preps. כִּי converts them, like אֲשֶׁר, into conjs...., as יַעַן כִּי because *that*...: v. sub יַעַן, עַד, עַל, עֵקֶב, תַּחַת.

2. a. Of time, *when*, of the past וַיְהִי כִּי Gn 6^{1} (cf. Bu$^{Urg. 6}$), 26^{8} 27^{1} 2 S 6^{13} 7^{1} 19^{26}+ (כַּאֲשֶׁר, and esp. בְּ c. inf., are more freq.); וְהָיָה כִּי (simple וְ) 1 S 1^{12} 17^{48}; Jos 22^{7} Ju 2^{18}; 12^{5} והיה כי יאמרו and it would be, whenever (freq.) they said, Je 44^{19} (ptcp.), Ho 11^{1} ψ 32^{3} כי החרשתי *when* I was silent, Jb 31$^{21.26.29}$; of present (usu. with impf.) as Ex 18^{16} כִּי יִהְיֶה לָהֶם דָּבָר *when* they have a matter, 1 S 24^{20} Is 1^{12} 30^{21} Je 14^{12} Zc 7$^{5.6}$ Mal 1^{8} ψ 49^{19} and men praise thee כִּי תֵיטִיב לָךְ *when* thou doest well to thyself, 102^{1} 127^{5}+, with pf. Ez 3$^{19-21}$ 33^{9} Pr 11^{15} 23^{22}; esp. of future, as Gn 4^{12} כִּי תַעֲבֹד אֶת־הָאֲדָמָה *when* thou shalt till the ground it shall not, etc., 24^{41} 30^{33} 31^{49} 32^{18} Ex 7^{9} *when* Pharaoh shall speak unto you, Dt 4^{25} 6^{20}+; in phrase וְכִי תֹאמְרוּ (תאמר וג׳) Lv 25^{20} Dt 18^{21} Is 8^{19} 36^{7} Je 13^{22}; and esp. in ... וְהָיָה כִּי Gn 12^{12} 46^{33} Dt 6^{10} 15^{16} 1 S 10^{7} 25^{30} Is 8^{21} 10^{12}+oft.; with pf. Is 16^{12} 1 Ch 17^{11} (altered fr. impf. 2 S 7^{12}); with ptcp. (unusual) Nu 33^{51} 34^{2} Dt 11^{31} 18^{9}. **b.** elsewhere כִּי has a force approximating to *if*, though it usu. represents a case as more likely to occur than אִם:—(mostly with impf.) Gn 38^{16} Nu 5^{20} 10^{32} Dt 6^{25} 7^{17} 28$^{2.13}$ 1 S 20^{13} 2 S 19^{8} 2 K 4^{29} 18^{22} Je 38^{15} Pr 4^{8} Jb 7^{13} (כי אמרתי *when* I say), 19^{28}; oft. in laws, as Ex 21$^{14.33.35.37}$ 22$^{4.5}$ etc., Dt 13^{13} 14^{24} 15$^{7.12}$ 17^{2} 18$^{6.21}$ etc.; sometimes, in particular, to state a principle broadly, after which special cases are introduced by אִם, as Ex 21^{2} *when* (כִּי) thou buyest a Hebrew servant, he shall serve thee six years, after which v$^{3-5}$ follow four special cases with אִם *if*: so 21^{7} (כי), v$^{8-11}$ (אם); v^{18} (כי), v^{19} (אם); v^{20} (כי), v^{21} (אם); v$^{22f.28-32}$; Lv 1^{2} (כי), v$^{3.10}$ (אם) 4$^{2.3.13.27.32}$ 13$^{2ff.}$ Nu 30$^{3ff.}$+; though this distinction is not uniformly observed, contrast e.g. Ex 21^{5} with Dt 15^{16}; Nu 5^{19} and v^{20}.—N.B. with כִּי = *when* or *if*, the subject is oft. prefixed for distinctness and emph.: 1 K 8^{37} רָעָב כִּי־יִהְיֶה בָאָרֶץ דֶּבֶר כִּי יִהְיֶה וג׳, Is 28^{18} Mi 5^{4} אשור כִּי־יָבֹא בְּאַרְצֵנוּ, ψ 62^{11} Ez 3^{19} (וְאַתָּה), 14$^{9.13}$ 18$^{5.18.21}$ 33^{6} (cf. v^{2}); and esp. in laws of P, as אָדָם ... כִּי Lv 1^{2} 13^{2}, ... נֶפֶשׁ כִּי ... 2^{1} 4^{2} 5$^{1.4.15}$, similarly 15$^{2.16.19.25}$ 22$^{12.13.14}$ etc., rather differently Nu 5^{20}. **c.** *when* or *if*, with a concessive force, i.e. *though:*—(*a*) with impf. Je 4$^{30.30.30}$ 14^{12} 49^{16} כִּי־תַגְבִּיהַּ כַּנֶּשֶׁר קִנֶּךָ *though* thou make high like the vulture thy nest, I will bring thee down thence, 51^{53} Ho 13^{15} Zc 8^{6} ψ 37^{24} 49$^{19f.}$ *though* in his lifetime he bless himself... he shall come, etc., perh. also Je 46^{23} Ew (but Hi Gf Ke *for*), 50^{11} Ew Ke (Hi *yea*); and strengthened by גַּם, גַּם כִּי Is 1^{5} ψ 23^{4} (cf. Dr ^{§143}); (*b*) with perf. (rare) Mi 7^{8} כִּי נָפַלְתִּי קָמְתִּי *though* I have fallen, I rise, Na 1^{10} (si vera l.), ψ 21^{12} (Hi Ew Now), 119^{83} (Ew De).

3. *Because, since* (ὅτι)—**a.** Gn 3^{14} *because* thou hast done this, cursed art thou, etc., v^{17} 18^{20} the cry of S. and G.—*because* it is great ... (subj. prefixed for emph.: cf. **2** N.B.) Is 28^{15}; in answer to a qu., Gn 27^{20} Ex 1^{19} 18^{15} 2 S 19^{43}+. Enunciating the conditions under which a fut. action is conceived as possible (Germ. *indem*) Lv 22^{9} Dt 4^{29} כי תדרשנו, 12^{20} (v.^{Dr}), v$^{25.28}$ 13^{19} 14^{24} 16^{15} 19$^{6.9}$+, 1 K 8^{35} (cf. v^{33} אֲשֶׁר), v^{36} כִּי תוֹרֵם, Pr 4^{8b}. **b.** more commonly the causal sentence follows, as Gn 2^{3} and God blessed the seventh day כִּי בוֹ שָׁבַת וג׳ *because* on it he rested, etc., 4^{25} etc., in which case it may oft. be rendered *for*, Gn 2$^{5.23}$ 3^{20} 5^{24} 6$^{7.12.13}$ ψ 6^{3} heal me כִּי נִבְהֲלוּ עֲצָמָי *for* my bones are vexed, 10^{14} 25^{16} 27^{10}+very oft. Spec. after vbs. expressive of mental emotions, as rejoicing Is 14^{29} ψ 58^{11}, being angry Gn 31^{35} 45^{5}, fearing 43^{18} ψ 49^{17} etc. Iron. 1 K 18^{27} *for* he is a god etc. (4 t.); Pr 30^{4} Jb 38^{5} כִּי תֵדָע *for* or *since* thou knowest. With subj. prefixed ψ 128^{2}. Repeated (with anacol.) Is 49^{19}. **c.** the causal relation expressed by כִּי is sometimes subtle, esp. in poetry, and not apparent without careful study of a passage. Thus sts. it justifies a statement or description by pointing to a pregnant fact which involves it, as Is 3^{8a} Jb 6^{21} (ground of the comparison v$^{15-20}$), 14^{16} (*For* ...: ground of the wishes expressed v$^{13-15}$), 16^{22} (ground of v$^{20f.}$) 30^{26} (*For* ...), or by pointing to a general truth which it exemplifies Jb 5^{6} (reason why complaining v$^{2-5}$ is foolish), 15^{34} 23^{14}; sts. it is *explicative*, justifying a statement by unfolding the particulars wh. establish or exemplify it 2 S 23^{5a} Is 1^{30} 5^{7} 7^{8} 9^{4} 10$^{8-11}$ 13^{10} (development of v^{9a}), 32$^{6f.}$ (developing the characters of the נָבָל and כִּילַי, and so explaining why they will no longer be esteemed v^{5}); Jb 11$^{16ff.}$ (explic. of v^{15b}), 18$^{8ff.}$ (justifying v^{7}), 22$^{25ff.}$ (justifying v^{25}); elsewhere the cause is expressed indirectly or figuratively Is 2^{6} (reason

why invitation v^5 is needed), 5^{10} (sterility of the soil the cause of the desolation v^9), 18^5 28^8 (proof of the intoxication v^7), 31^7 (reason for the exhortation v^6: the certainty that the folly of idolatry will soon be recognized), Jb 7^{21} (for soon it will be too late to pardon), 27^{8-10} (Job wishes his enemy the lot of the wicked, *because* this is so hopeless); or כִּי relates not to the v. which immed. precedes or follows, but to several, as Is $7^{16f.}$ (v^{17} specially the ground of the people being reduced to simple fare v^{15}), $21^{6ff.}$ (ground of the statements v$^{1-5}$), Jb 4^5 (ground of v^2), 14^{7-12} (v$^{10-12}$ specially the ground for the appeal in v^6), 23^{10-13} (ground why God cannot be found v$^{8f.}$), ψ 73^{21} (ground not of v^{20}, but of the general train of thought v$^{2-14}$); similarly Gn 4^{24} Dt 18^{14} Je 30^{11} the reason lies not in the words immed. after כִּי, but in the second part of the sentence; or, on the other hand, it may state the reason for a partic. word, Is 28^{20} (justifying 'nought but terror' v^{19}), Jb 23^{17} (*God's* hostility v^{16} the cause of his misery, not the calamity as such). Sometimes also כִּי, in a poet. or rhet. style, gives the reason for a thought not expressed but implied, esp. the answer to a qu.; Is 28^{11} (the mockeries of v^{10} have a meaning) '*for* with men of strange lips, etc. he will speak unto this people,' who will retort the mockeries, charged with a new and terrible meaning, upon those who uttered them (v^{13}); = (no,) *for* Is 28^{28} (see RVm), Jb 22^{2b} *no*, he that is wise is profitable to himself, 31^{18} 39^{14} (see v^{13b}), ψ 44^{24} (he cannot do this, v^{23}) *for* for thy sake are we killed, etc., 130^4 *no*, with thee is forgiveness; = (yes,) *for* Is 49^{25} (see the qu. v^{24}), 66^8. **d.** כִּי . . . כִּי ἀσυνδέτως sts. introduce the proximate and ultimate cause respectively, Gn 3^{19} 26^7 43^{32} 47^{20} Ex 23^{33} *for* [else] thou wilt serve their gods, *for* it will be a snare to thee, Is $2^{6.6}$ $3^{8.8}$ $6^{5\,a.b}$ $10^{22f.}$ Jb $6^{3f.}$ $8^{8.9.9}$ $24^{17.17}$ $29^{11f.}$; sts. they introduce two co-ordinate causes (where we should insert *and*), Ex $23^{21.22}$ Is $6^{5\,b.c}$ I am undone, *because* I am of unclean lips . . ., *because* mine eyes have seen ׳י of hosts, $15^{5.5.6.6.8.9}$ Zp $3^{8f.}$ Jb $15^{25.27}$ $20^{19f.}$ $31^{11f.}$. But כִּי . . . וְכִי also occurs, Gn 33^{11} Nu 5^{20} (if), Jo 7^{15} Ju 6^{30} 1 S 19^4 22^{17} 1 K 2^{26} Is 65^{16}+. **e.** after a neg. כִּי *for* becomes = *but* (Germ. *sondern*): Gn 17^{15} thou shalt not call her name Sarai, כִּי שָׂרָה שְׁמָהּ *for* (= *but*) Sarah shall be her name, $24^{3f.}$ 45^8 Ex 1^{19} 16^8 not against us are your murmurings, כי על־׳י *for* (they are) agst. ׳י = *but* agst. ׳י, Dt 21^{17} 1 S 6^3 (אַל), 27^1 (v. Dr), 1 K 21^{17} Is 10^7 28^{27} 29^{23} 30^5 ψ 44^8 118^{17}+oft.; so in לא כי *nay, for* = *nay, but*, as Gn 18^{15} לֹא כִּי צָחָקְתְּ *nay*, *but* thou didst laugh, 19^2 42^{12} Jos 5^{14} 1 S 2^{16} MSS 𝔊 (v. Dr), 12^{12} 2 S 16^{18} 24^{24} 1 K 2^{30} 3^{22} 11^{22} Is 30^{16} *nay, but* we will flee upon horses.

Note.—כִּי is sts. of difficult and uncertain interpretation, and in some of the passages quoted a different expl. is tenable. Authorities esp. read the Heb. differently, when the choice is between *for* and *yea*. E.g. Is 8^{23} Ges Ew $^{§ 330 b}$ *doch (no, but)*; Hi Di *for* (taking v^{22} as RVm); Ch *surely:* 15^1 Ges Ew Hi Di *surely;* De *for:* 39^8 Ges Hi De *surely;* Di *for* (expl. of טוֹב): Ez 11^{16} Hi Ke Co *surely;* Ew Sm *because*.—In Ex 20^{25} the tense of וַתְּחַלְלֶהָ makes it prob. that כִּי is *for* (Dr $^{§ 153}$). Jb 22^{29} is taken with least violence to usage (גֵּוָה) as Hi: *When* they humble thee, and thou sayest (= complainest) Pride! he will save, etc.

כִּי אִם־ (the אִם always foll. by makkeph, except Gn 15^4 Nu 35^{33} Ne 2^2, where כִּי־אִם is read by the Mass.: Fr $^{MM\,241}$)—**1.** each part. retaining its independent force, and relating to a *different* clause: **a.** *that if* Je 26^{15}; after an oath (כִּי not translated: v. כִּי **1 c**) *if* 1 S 14^{39} Je 22^{24}, *surely not* (אִם **1 b** 2) 2 S 3^{35} 1 S 25^{34} (כִּי being resumptive of the כִּי before לוּלֵי: v. כִּי **1 c**); Ex 22^{22} (in apod.) *indeed if* . . . (v. כִּי **1 d**). **b.** *for if* Ex 8^{17}-9^2 10^4 Dt 11^{22} +, *for though* Is 10^{22} Je 37^{20} Am 5^{22}, *but if* Je 7^5.

2. (About 140 t.) the two particles being closely conjoined, and relating to the *same* clause—**a.** *limiting* the prec. clause, **except** (after a negative, or an oath, or question, the equivalent of a negative)—the most usual term for expressing this idea: sq. vb. Gn 32^{27} I will not let thee go; כִּי אִם־בֵּרַכְתָּנִי lit. *but* (כִּי **3 e**) *if* thou bless me (sc. I will let thee go), i. e., subordinating the second clause to the first, 'I will not let thee go, *except* thou bless me;' Lv 22^6 he shall not eat of the holy things כִּי אִם־רָחַץ *except* he have washed his flesh, Is 65^6 Am 3^7 Ru 3^{18} La $5^{21f.}$ (Ew Näg Ke Che Öt), turn thou us unto thee, etc., *unless* thou have utterly rejected us, (and) art very wroth with us (= *Or* hast thou utterly rejected us? etc. Ew Öt); sq. a noun, *except, but*, Gn 28^{17} this is nothing כִּי אִם־בֵּית הָאֱ׳ *but* the house of God, 39^9 he withholds from me nothing כִּי אִם־אוֹתָךְ *except* thee, Lv 21^2 Nu 14^{30} (after אִם), 26^{65} (cf. 32^{12} בִּלְתִּי), Jos 14^4 1 S $30^{17.22}$ 2 S 12^3 אֵין כֹּל כִּי אִם־ (so 2 K 4^2), 19^{29} 1 K 17^1 (after אִם), 22^{31} 2 K 5^{15} 9^{35} 13^7 Je 22^{17} 44^{14}+; after אַל, 2 Ch 23^6; sq. an adv. clause, Gn 42^{15} Nu 35^{33} 2 S 3^{13} (but כִּי אִם and לִפְנֵי are mutually ex-

clusive: rd. prob. with 𝔊 (כי אם־הֲבִיאתָ); after an interrog. Is 42[19] who is blind כִּי אִם־עַבְדִּי *but* my servant? (who is blind in comparison with him?), Dt 10[12] Mi 6[8] Ec 5[10] 2 Ch 2[5]. **b.** the *if* being neglected, and treated as pleonastic (cf. **אם 1 c**), so that the clause is no longer a limitation of the preceding clause but a contradiction of it: **but rather, but** (=a slightly strengthened כִּי), Gn 15[4] this man shall not be thy heir; כִּי אִם־אֲשֶׁר וגו׳ *but* one that shall come forth from thy own bowels, he shall be thy heir (cf. 1 K 8[19]), 32[29] thy name shall no more be called Jacob כִּי אִם־יִשְׂרָאֵל *but* Israel (cf. כִּי alone 17[15]), 47[18] we will not hide it from my lord, *but* the money . . . is all made over to, etc., Ex 12[9] not boiled in water, *but* roast with fire, Dt 7[5] 12[5] 16[6] Jo 23[8] 1 S 2[15] he will not take of thee boiled flesh כִּי אִם־חָי: *but* raw, 8[19] לֹא כִּי אִם־מֶלֶךְ יִהְיֶה עָלֵינוּ nay, *but* a king shall be over us (cf. כִּי alone, 10[19] 12[12]), 21[6] 2 S 5[6] 1 K 18[18] 2 K 10[23] (פֶּן), Is 33[21] 55[10, 11] 59[2] Je 3[10] 7[32] 9[23] 16[15] 20[3] Ez 36[22] 44[10] Am 8[11] ψ 1[2, 4] Pr 23[17] (אַל)+; with the principal verb repeated (as Gn 15[4] 1 K 8[19]), Lv 21[14] Ez 44[22] Nu 10[30] 2 K 23[23] Je 39[12] Kt (Qr om. אם), cf. 7[23]. Occas. in colloq. language, the neg., it seems, is left to be understood: 1 S 26[10] as י׳ liveth, (by no means,) כִּי אִם *but* י׳ shall smite him, 2 S 13[33] Kt (by no means,) *but* Amnon alone is dead (Qr om. אם). Sq. imv. Is 65[18] Ez 12[23] Je 39[12] 2 Ch 25[8]. Sts also, though rarely (and not certainly), כִּי אִם appears to have the force of *only* even without a previous neg.: Gn 40[14] כִּי אִם־זְכַרְתַּנִי אִתְּךָ *only* have (?) me in remembrance with thyself (but rd. perh. אַךְ for כִּי; v Dr[§ 119 δ n], the use of a bare pf., without לוּ, or even waw consec., to express a wish or command is unexampled), Nu 24[22] כִּי אִם־יִהְיֶה לְבָעֵר קָיִן: *only, nevertheless,* the Kenite shall be for extermination (cf. Di), Jb 42[8] (De Di) כִּי אִם־פָּנָיו אֶשָּׂא. **c.** after an oath כִּי אִם appears to=a strengthened כִּי (cf. בִּלְתִּי אם, עַד אִם: **אם 1 c**), introducing the fact sworn to (v. **כִּי 1 c**). 2 K 5[20] as י׳ liveth, כִּי אִם־רַצְתִּי *surely* I will run (pf of certitude) after him, etc, Je 51[14] (Ges Hi Gf RV) *surely* I will fill thee with men (viz. assailants), etc. (but Ew Ke Ch treat the particles as separate (כִּי as **כִּי 1 c**): though I have filled thee with men—i. e. increased thy population—, yet shall they—the assailants—lift up the shout against thee), 2 S 15[21] Kt (Qr omits אם); after an assever part. Ru 3[12] Kt וְעַתָּה כִּי אָמְנָם כִּי אִם גּוֹאֵל אָנֹכִי and now, yea indeed, *surely* I am thy kinsman (Qr omits אם), the oath being understood, Ju 15[7] if ye do thus, כִּי אִם־נִקַּמְתִּי *surely* (Ges *hercle*) I will avenge myself, 1 S 21[6] כִּי אִם־אִשָּׁה עֲצֻרָה לָנוּ *of a truth* women have been kept from us, etc, 1 K 20[6] *surely* tomorrow I will send, etc, Pr 23[18] (v. De) *surely* there *is* a reward; perh. also Jb 42[8].

†כִּי עַל כֵּן *forasmuch as*, a peculiar phrase found Gn 18[5] 19[8] 33[10] 38[26] Nu 10[31] 14[43] Ju 6[22] 2 S 18[20] Qr (rightly), Je 29[28] 38[4]—lit *for therefore,* emphasizing the ground pleonastically (Ew[§ 353 a]). The orig. force of the phrase is traceable in some of the passages in which it occurs, as Gn 18[5] let me fetch a morsel of bread, and comfort your heart; כִּי־עַל־כֵּן עֲבַרְתֶּם עַל עַבְדְּכֶם *for therefore* (sc. to partake of such hospitality) are ye come to your servant, Nu 14[43] the Amalekite and the Canaanite are there, and ye will fall by the sword, כִּי־עַל־כֵּן שַׁבְתֶּם *for therefore* (to encounter such a fate) have ye turned back from י׳, etc: but in process of time the distinct sense of its component parts was no doubt gradually obscured, and it thus came to be used conventionally, as a *mere* particle of causation, even where there was no preceding statement to which עַל כֵּן *therefore* could be explicitly referred. אֲשֶׁר עַל כֵּן appears to be used similarly (cf **אֲשֶׁר 8 c**) †Jb 34[27].

II. כִּי, *branding*, v. sub כוה.

†[כִּיד] **n.[m.]** only sf. כִּידוֹ Jb 21[20], meaning unknown; rd prob פִּידוֹ *his misfortune* (as 12[5] etc.)

כיד (√ of foll; cf perh Ar. كَادَ in sense *labour, take pains, strive,* or *struggle* with, كَيْدٌ *war*).

†I. כִּידוֹן **n.[m.]** **dart, javelin** (NH *id*)—abs כ׳ Jos 8[18] + 6 t, כִּידֹן Je 50[42]; cstr. כִּידוֹן 1 S 17[6];—*dart, javelin* (distinct fr. חֲנִית *spear, lance,* q v), נטה בכ׳ אשר ביד(ך) Jos 8[18, 18], cf. v[26], בְּהֶרֶב רַעַשׁ כ׳ Jb 41[21] *the rushing sound of a dart*, בַּחֲנִית וּבְכ׳ 1 S 17[45] (weapons of Goliath), כ׳ נחשת בין כתפיו v[6] (חֲנִית in v[7]); + חֲנִית Jb 39[23] also; קֶשֶׁת וכ׳ Je 6[23] 50[42].

†II כִּידֹן **n.pr.m.** 1 Ch 13[9], 𝔊L Χειδων, A Χειλω, = נָכוֹן 2 S 6[6] (𝔊 Νωδαβ, A Ναχων, 𝔊L Ορνα).

כִּידוֹר v. sub כדר, כִּידוּד v. sub כדד.

†כִּיּוּן **n.pr dei** Am 5[26], prob = As *kaiwânu*, planet *Saturn* (Ar. and Pers. كَيْوَانُ, Syr. ܟܐܘܢ),

regarded as god; orig. pronunc. כֵּיְוָן Schr COT ad loc., cf. Kö ii. 151 (pointing כִּיּוּן intended to suggest √כון as something *established, firm*); *kaimânu=kaiânu*, acc. to Jen Cosm. iii. 502 who der. fr. כון (cf. Thes; so Zim BP 17); >Hpt ZA ii. 266, 281 f. rds. כֵּיָוָן (for כָּאָמָן*), reading the Babyl. name *Ka'âmânu;* v. also M-A JBL 1892, xi. 86 n. 39.

כִּיּוֹר, v. sub I. כור.

כִּילַי, כֵּלַי Is 32[5.7] v. נכל (Kö ii. 118).

†**כֵּילַפּוֹת** n.[f.] axe (loan-word (cf. Frä[74]) fr. As. *kalappatu* v. Dl HWB 333)—בְּכַשִּׁיל וְכֵ׳ יַהֲלֹמוּן ψ 74[6] (|| קַרְדֻּמּוֹת v[5]).

כִּימָה v. sub כום.

†**כִּיס** n.m. Pr 1, 14 bag, purse (perh. kindred with כּוֹס, q.v.; Ar. كِيسٌ (prob. fr. Pers. كيسه Lane 2640); Eth. ኪስ: NH כִּיס; Aram. כִּיסָא, ܟܝܣܐ; Palm. מן כיסה *from his purse*=at his own expense, Vog p. 13 al.)—*bag*, in which were carried: **a.** weights (v. אֶבֶן **5**) Dt 25[13] Mi 6[11] Pr 16[11]; **b.** money, i.e. *a purse* Is 46[6] Pr 1[14].

כִּיר, [כִּיר], כִּירַיִם v. sub I. כור.

כִּישׁוֹר v. sub כשר.

כָּכָה v. sub כה p. 462 supr.

כִּכָּר v. sub כרר; **כֹּל** v. sub I. כלל.

†**[כָּלָא]** vb. **shut up, restrain, withhold** (NH *id.;* Aram. כְּלָא, ܟܠܐ; Eth. ከልአ: *restrain, hinder;* As. *kalû, id.;* Ar. كَلَأَ *protect* Qor 21[43] cf. Ba ZMG 1887, 605 Anm. 4)—**Qal** *Pf.* 3 ms. sf. כְּלָאוֹ Je 32[3]; 3 fs. כָּלְאָה Hg 1[10]; 2 fs. sf. כְּלִתַנִי 1 S 25[33]; 1 s. כָּלָאתִי ψ 119[101]; 3 pl. כָּלְאוּ Hg 1[10], כָּלוּ 1 S 6[10]; *Impf.* 3 ms. יִכְלֶה Gn 23[6]; 2 ms. תִּכְלָא ψ 40[12]; 2 fs. תִּכְלָאִי Is 43[6]; 1 s. אֶכְלָא ψ 40[10]; *Imv.* sf. כְּלָאֵם Nu 11[28]; *Inf. cstr.* לִכְלוֹא Ec 8[8]; *Pt. pass.* כָּלוּא Je 32[2], כָּלֻא ψ 88[9]; (on the metapl. forms, as if fr. כלה, v. Ges § 75, 21 c Kö i. 611);—**1.** *shut up*, c. acc. 1 S 6[10] (+ בְּ loc.), Je 32[3]; pt. pass. Je 32[2] (בְּ loc.), fig. ψ 88[9] (opp. יצא). **2.** *restrain*, c. acc. 1 S 25[33] (+ מִבּוֹא בְדָמִים), ψ 119[101] (+ מִכָּל־); כְּלָאֵם (sc. מִתְנַבְּאִים) Nu 11[28]; כ׳ אֶת־הָרוּחַ ψ 40[10]; כ׳ שְׂפָתַי Ec 8[8]. On כ׳ אֶת־קִבְרוֹ ψ 74[11] v. כלה **Pi. 2.** **3.** *withhold*, מִמְּךָ מִקְּבֹר מֵתֶךָ Gn 23[6] (P), כ׳ רַחֲמֶיךָ מִמֶּנִּי ψ 40[12], Hg 1[10 b], prob. also v[a] (rd. טַל for MT 𝔊 מִטָּל, We); abs. אַל־תִּכְלָאִי (sc. exiles) Is 43[6] (|| תְּנִי). **Niph.** *Impf.* וַיִּכָּלֵא הַגֶּשֶׁם מִן־הַשָּׁמַיִם Gn 8[2] (J), *and the rain from heaven was restrained*, cf. וַיִּכָּלְאוּ מַיִם רַבִּים Ez 31[15] (in fig.; || מנע); וַיִּכָּלֵא הָעָם מֵהָבִיא Ex 36[6] (P). **Pi.** [Pf. כִּלָּא and] *Inf. cstr.* לְכַלֵּא v. כלה **Pi.**

†**כֶּלֶא** n.[m.] **confinement, restraint, imprisonment**;—abs. כ׳ 1 K 22[27] + 6 t.; sf. כִּלְאוֹ 2 K 25[29] Je 52[33]; pl. כְּלָאִים Is 42[22];—*confinement*, in combin. בֵּית (ה)כ׳ (cf. As. *bit kili, prison*, Dl HWB 328) 1 K 22[27] = 2 Ch 18[26], 2 K 17[4] Je 37[15.18] Is 42[7]; בָּתֵּי כְלָאִים v[22] (cf. בַּיִת **1** (ε) (2) p. 109 supr.; v. also כלוא infr.); בִּגְדֵי כִלְאוֹ 2 K 25[29] = Je 52[33] *garments of imprisonment* = prison-garb.

†**כלוא** Kt, **כְּלִיא** Qr n.[m.] id.;—בֵּית הַכ׳ Je 37[4] 52[31] (v. כֶּלֶא supr.)

†I. **מִכְלָה** (incorrect for מכלא) n. [m.] **enclosure, fold**;—גָּזַר מִמִּ׳ צֹאן Hb 3[17]; pl. cstr. לקח מִמִּכְלְאֹת צֹאן ψ 78[70] (obj. David); pl. sf. לקח מִמִּכְלְאֹתֶיךָ 50[9] (obj. he-goats).—II. מִכְלָה v. sub כלה.

†**כִּלְאַיִם** n.[m.] du. **two kinds** (Ar. كِلَا، كِلَا *both;* Eth. ክልኤ: *two;* perh. also כלאי MI[23] *both, two*, Nö LCB 1886, 61, cf. Dr Sm xcii; Sm u. So MI, 1886 suggest *reservoirs;* v. also כְּלִי)—בְּהֶמְתְּךָ לֹא תַרְבִּיעַ כ׳ Lv 19[19] *not cause thy cattle to breed* (in) *two kinds;* שָׂדְךָ לֹא תִזְרַע כ׳ v[19] (H); לֹא תִזְרַע כַּרְמְךָ כ׳ Dt 22[9] (both כִּלְאָיִם); בֶּגֶד כ׳ Lv 19[19] (H);—only in law of H and D against mixtures.

†**כִּלְאָב** n.pr.m. second son of David, 2 S 3[3] = דָּנִיֵּאל 1 Ch 3[1], v. דָּנִיֵּאל **1.** p. 193 supr.

כלב (√of foll.; meaning unknown; Thes regards כֶּלֶב as onomatop.)

†**כֶּלֶב** n.m. 1 S 24, 15 **dog** (NH *id.;* Ph. כלב; Aram. כַּלְבָּא, ܟܠܒܐ; Ar. كَلْبٌ; Eth. ከልብ: As. *kalbu* Dl HWB 328) — abs. כ׳ Ju 7[5] + 16 t., כָּלֶב ψ 59[7.15]; pl. כְּלָבִים 1 K 14[11] + 12 t.; cstr. כַּלְבֵי Jb 30[1]; sf. כְּלָבֶיךָ ψ 68[24];—*dog:* **a.** lit. 1 K 14[11] 16[4] 21[19.19.23.24] 22[38] 2 K 9[10.36] (all of fierce, hungry dogs, devouring dead bodies and licking blood); cf. Je 15[3] and לְשׁוֹן כְּלָבֶיךָ ψ 68[24]; eating torn flesh, Ex 22[30] (E), כַּלְבֵי צֹאנִי = *my sheep-dogs*, only Jb 30[1] (in both these with implied inferiority); dog-sacrifice was a heathen rite Is 66[3] (Di al.); v. esp. RS Sem. i, 273 (291), 325 (343); in various sim. Ju 7[5] Pr 26[11.17] ψ 59[7.15]; in proverbial sayings: לֹא יֶחֱרַץ־כ׳ לְשֹׁנוֹ Ex 11[7] (v. I. חרץ); לְכ׳ חַי הוּא טוֹב מִן

הָאַרְיֵה הַמֵּת Ec 9[4]. **b.** applied, fig., to men, in contempt 1 S 17[43], so of psalmist's enemies ψ 22[17.21], or in excessive humility 2 K 8[13]; still more emphatically הַכ׳ הַמֵּת כ׳ מֵת *a dead dog*, 2 S 9[8] 16[9]; also רֹאשׁ כ׳ 3[8], כְּלָבִים אִלְּמִים Is 56[10] (of misleading prophets), הַכ׳ עַזֵּי נֶפֶשׁ v[11] (*id.*); כ׳ was name given to male temple-prostitutes Dt 23[19] (v. Dr; cf קָדֵשׁ)

†כָּלֵב **n.pr.m.** (Nab n.pr כלבא Eut(No)[p 55]. כלבו Vog[Nab. 6]; cf. also We[Skizzen u Vorarbeiten iii. 217]; on כָּלֵב = *dog-clan*, v RS[K 17 190 f., 219 254]);—son of יְפֻנֶּה (𝔊 Χαλεβ; cf. Lag[BN 78]), called הַקְּנִזִּי (v. קְנַז) in JE, Nu 32[12] Jos 14[6.14], cf 15[17] = Ju 1[13], Ju 3[9] (where קְנַז is brother of כ׳), also 1 Ch 4[15]; treated as full Judahite only in P Nu 13[6] (v. GFM[Jud p 30 f.]) the one of the spies who (with Joshua) reported well of Canaan 14[6.24.30.38]; also 26[65] 34[19] Dt 1[36] Jos 14[13] 15[13 14 16 18] 21[12] (P = 1 Ch 6[41]) Ju 1[12 14.15.20] (‖ with Jos 15); = clan of Caleb 1 S 30[14] (disting. from Judah) Caleb is called בְּכָלֵב v[9], כְּלוּבָי = v[19.42 46.48.49.50] בֶּן־חֶצְרוֹן 1 Ch 2[18], cf. אֶפְרָתָה 1 Ch 2[24], rd. perh. בָּא כ׳, so 𝔊 𝔙, cf. Kau[AT] (v. אֶפְרָתָה p 68 supr.)

†כָּלִבִּי **adj.gent.** of כָּלֵב 1 S 25[3] Qr (Kt כָּלִבּוֹ).

†כְּלוּב **n.pr.m.** **1.** a name in Judah 1 Ch 4[11], 𝔊 Χαλεβ (acc to We[Gentib 20 Hist 218] = כָּלֵב בֶּן־חֶצְרוֹן; rd also for כַּרְמִי v[1]). **2.** father of one of David's officers, acc. to 1 Ch 27[26] (𝔊 Χοβουδ, A Χελουβ, 𝔊L Χαλουβ)

†כְּלוּבַי **n.pr.m.** a son of Hezron of Judah, acc. to 1 Ch 2[9] (𝔊 Χαβελ, A Χαλεβ, 𝔊L Χαλωβι). = כָּלֵב v[18] etc. (see כָּלֵב **2**).

†כְּלוּב **n.m.**[Je 5, 27] basket, cage (√dub; NH *id.*, כְּלִיבָה; Aram. ܟܠܘܒܐ in Lexx.; Tel Am. *kilubi, bird-net*, cf. Zim[ZA vi. 145, 147])—abs. כִּכְלוּב מָלֵא עוֹף Je 5[27] *like a cage full of birds*; cstr. כְּלוּב קָיִץ Am 8[1.2] *a basket of summer fruit*

I כָּלָה[208] **vb. be complete, at an end, finished, accomplished, spent** (NH *id.*, Pi; Ph. כלה; As *kalû, put an end to*, and *cease, vanish* Dl[HWB 329]; late Aram. כְּלָא *cease, perish* (not 𝔗), on root-meaning *enclose* cf. כלא and Ba[ZMG 1887 606])—†**Qal** *Pf.* כ׳ 1 K 6[38] +; 3 fs כָּלְתָה 1 S 20[7] +; 1 s. כָּלִיתִי ψ 39[11]; 3 pl. כָּלוּ Jb 19[27] +; 2 mpl. כִּלִּיתֶם Mal 3[6], וְכִלִּיתֶם consec. Ez 13[14]; 1 pl. כָּלִינוּ ψ 90[7], etc; *Impf* יִכְלֶה Pr 22[8], juss יִכֶל Jb 33[21] (v. Dr[§ 171-173] Ges[§ 109 2 b Anm.] Da[Synt. § 51 R. 5, 64 R. 6]), 3 fs תִּכְלֶה 1 K 17[14], וַתֵּכֶל Ex 39[32] + 2 S 13[39] (v. infr); 3 mpl יִכְלוּ Is 1[28] +, יִכְלָיוּן Is 31[3], etc.; *Inf. cstr* כְּלוֹת Ru 2[23] +, etc.,— **1. a.** *be complete, at an end*, of a period of time Gn 41[53] (E; opp. III. חלל Hiph *begin* v[54]), Je 8[20] (‖ עבר); so of action or event, with emphasis on time Is 10[25] 24[13] Ru 2[23] 2 Ch 29[28] (opp החל v[27]), v[34] Dn 12[7] (‖ קֵץ v[6.9]);—vid also **2 b** infr. **b.** *be completed, finished*, of a work. temple 1 K 6[38] 1 Ch 28[20] 2 Ch 8[16] (‖ שָׁלֵם), tabernacle Ex 39[32] (P). **c.** *be accomplished, fulfilled*, only of purposed wrath, or prediction of י׳, Ez 5[13] (‖ כִּלֵּיתִי v[b], see **Pi.**), Dn 11[36] 2 Ch 36[22] = Ezr 1[1]. **d.** be ideally complete, *be determined*, always in bad sense, *plotted*, subj הָרָעָה sq מֵעִם of agent 1 S 20[7], also v[9] (+ לָבוֹא עַל), + v[33] (rd. כָּלְתָה, for MT כָּלָה הִיא, 𝔊 We Dr Kit Bu); כ׳ הָרָעָה אֶל־אֲדֹנֵינוּ וְעַל־כָּל־בֵּיתוֹ 25[17]; sq. מֵאֵת of agent Est 7[7] (+ אֵלָיו). **2. a.** *be spent, used up* (prop. *come to an end*), of water Gn 21[15] (E), meal 1 K 17[14 16] **b.** *waste away, be exhausted, fail*, lit. of fading grass Is 15[6] (‖ לא היה ,יָבֵשׁ), of vintage 32[10] (opp בּוֹא), of vanishing cloud Jb 7[9] (in sim, ‖ הלך), fig. of fleeting days of life v[6] (‖ קלל), cf. ψ 102[4] and כָּלוּ בְיָגוֹן חַיַּי ψ 31[11], Je 20[18]; v. also **1 a** supr.; of flesh Jb 33[21], cf. כ׳ בְּשָׂרִי וּשְׁאֵרִי ψ 71[9], Pr 5[11], of vital strength ψ 73[26], שְׁאֵרִי וּלְבָבִי subj רוּחִי 143[7], once of י׳'s compassion לֹא־כָלוּ רַחֲמָיו La 3[22] (‖ חמם, on txt. see VB); esp of eyes exhausted by weeping La 2[11], strained by looking (fig) for relief or refreshment, *pine, languish* 4[17] ψ 69[4] Jb 11[20] 17[5] Je 14[6] (of wild asses); sq. לְ La 4[17] and, in spiritual sense, ψ 119[82.123]; similarly (sq. לְ) of נפש exhausted by *longing* ψ 84[3] (‖ נכסף), 119[81], כָּלוּ כִלְיֹתַי בְּחֵקִי Jb 19[27]; so also 2 S 13[39] where rd. וַתְּכַל רוּחַ הַמֶּלֶךְ (for MT וַתְּכַל דָּוִד הַמּ׳) *and the spirit of the king pined* to go forth unto Absalom, cf 𝔊L We Klo Dr Kit Bu. **c.** *come to an end, vanish = perish, be destroyed*, by י׳'s judgment Is 1[28] (‖ שֶׁבֶר), 16[4] (‖ אָפֵס ,תָּמַם), 29[20] (‖ אָפֵס ,נִכְרַת), 31[3] (‖ נפל ,כשל), וּבַחֶרֶב וּבָרָעָב יִכְלוּ Je 16[4], cf 44[27] (‖ תָּמַם), Ez 5[12] (‖ נָפַל ,מוּת), 13[14] Mal 3[6] ψ 37[20 20] (‖ אבד), Jb 4[9] (‖ *id.*), ψ 71[13] (‖ בוש); hyperbol., of severe discipline 39[11] 90[7] (‖ נבהל), of prosperity of a people Is 21[16]; שֵׁבֶט עֶבְרָתוֹ יִכְלֶה Pr 22[8] *the rod of his wrath perishes*

(>Ew al. *is accomplished*, of God's wrath).—Dn 12^{7} rd. perh. וְכִכְלוֹת יַד נֹפֵץ עַם קֹדֶשׁ *and when the power of the shatterer of the holy people should come to an end*, so Bev after 𝔊 (for difficult MT וּכְכַלּוֹת נַפֵּץ יַד־עַם־קֹדֶשׁ)+.

Pi.$_{140}$ *Pf.* כִּלָּה Gn 18^{33}+, כִּלָּא Pr 16^{30} Baer (van d. H כִּלָּה), sf. כִּלָּנוּ 2 S 21^{5}, כִּלָּם La 2^{22}; 3 fs. וְכִלָּתָה consec. Ho 11^{6}, sf. וְכִלַּתּוּ consec. Zc 5^{4}; 1 s. כִּלִּיתִי Nu 25^{11}, כִּלִּיתִי Is 49^{4}, וְכִלֵּיתִי Ez 6^{12}+ 2 t.; sf. כִּלִּיתִים Ez 22^{31}, וְכִלִּיתִךָ consec. Ex 33^{5}; 3 pl. כִּלּוּ Gn 24^{19}+, etc.; *Impf.* יְכַלֶּה Is 10^{18}; וַיְכַל Gn 2^{2}; 3 fs. וַתְּכַל Gn 24^{19}+2 S 13^{39} (but rd. וַתֵּכֶל We Dr al., and v. **Qal 2 b**); 1 s. אֲכַלֶּה Gn 24^{25}+4 t.; וָאֲכַל Ez 43^{8}; sf. אֲכֶלְךָ Ex 33^{3} (Kö$^{i.545}$); 3 mpl. יְכַלּוּ Jb 36^{11}+21^{13} Qr (Kt יבלו; v. בלה p. 115 supr.), +, etc.; *Imv.* כַּלֵּה ψ 59$^{14.14}$+74^{11} (but text dub., v. infr., **2**); mpl. כַּלּוּ Ex 5^{13}; *Inf. abs.* כַּלֵּה 1 S 3^{12}+5 t.; *cstr.* לְכַלֵּא Dn 9^{24} (metapl. form), כַּלּוֹת 1 S 2^{33}+, etc.; *Pt.* מְכַלֶּה Je 14^{12} Jb 9^{22}; fpl. מְכַלּוֹת Lv 26^{16};—**1.** †**a.** *complete, bring to an end, finish* a thing, task, work, etc., c. acc. rei Ex 5$^{13.14}$ (+inf.; both J), 1 K 6$^{9.14}$ 7^{1} Ez 42^{15}, Gn 2^{2} 16^{16} Ex 40^{33} (P), Ru 2^{21} 1 Ch 31^{1} 2 Ch 7^{11} Ezr 9^{1}, so לְכַלֵּא הַפֶּשַׁע Dn 9^{24} *to make an end of the transgression* (cf. VB Bev); Lv 23^{22} (modified from 19^{9} q.v. infr.); acc. om. 2 Ch 31^{7} (opp. הֵחֵל לְ), 24$^{10.14}$ Ne 3^{34}. †**b.** *complete* a period of time יָמִים Ez 4$^{6.8}$; *complete* one's days, enjoy the full measure of human life Jb 21^{13} 36^{11}, or *bring* one's years *to an end* ψ 90^{9}, with added idea of transitoriness. **c.** *finish* doing a thing, usu. sq. לְ inf. Gn 18^{33} 24$^{15.19.19.22}$ (all J), 17^{22} Ex 31^{18} Nu 4^{15} (all P), Am 7^{2} 1 K 1^{41} 2 Ch 29^{29} Ru 3^{3}+31 t. incl. 2 S 11^{19}, where obj. of infin. precedes it, v. Dr, so Lv 19^{9} (cf. 23^{22} supr.); +1 Ch 27^{24} (לְ inf. om.; opp. הֵחֵל לְ), 2 Ch 29^{17}; +Dn 12^{7} (inf. without לְ; but see **Qal 2 c** ad fin.); sq. מִן inf., 1 S 10^{13} 2 S 6^{18}=1 Ch 16^{2}, Ex 34^{33} Lv 16^{20} Jos 19^{51} (all P), Ez 43^{23}. †**d.** *make an end, end*, sq. בְּ *make an end with*, finish dealing with 2 Ch 20^{23} Ezr 10^{17}; abs., opp. הֵחֵל, בַּגָּדוֹל הֵחֵל וּבַקָּטֹן כִּלָּה Gn 44^{12} (J) *he began with the eldest and with the youngest he ended;* so inf. abs. adverb. הָחֵל וְכַלֵּה 1 S 3^{12} *a beginning and an ending*, i.e. doing it thoroughly (v. Dr); also עַד־כַּלֵּה=*utterly* 2 K 13$^{17.19}$, *to extremity* Ezr 9^{14} (of י׳'s anger), עַד־לְכַלֵּה (late) =*completely* 2 Ch 24^{10} (until all had given), 31^{1} (until all were destroyed). †**e.** *accomplish, fulfil, bring to pass*, a thing Ru 3^{18}; c. acc. of י׳'s wrath (חֲמָתוֹ) La 4^{11}; so (אַפִּי, חֲמָתִי) +בְּ pers. Ez 5^{13} 6^{12} 7^{8} 13^{15} 20$^{8.21}$. †**f.** *accomplish* in thought, *determine* (cf. **Qal 1 d**) sq. רָעָה Pr 16^{30} (‖ חשב).
†**2. a.** *put an end to, cause to cease* Nu 17^{25} (+מֵעָלַי); וַיְכַל־בַּהֶבֶל יְמֵיהֶם ψ 78^{33} *and he consumed (caused to vanish) as vanity their days.* **b.** *cause to fail, exhaust, use up, spend,* חִצַּי אֲכַלֶּה־בָּם Dt 32^{23} *my arrows will I exhaust against them;* exhaust one's strength כֹּחַ Is 49^{4} (‖ יָגַע); the eyes (by weeping; cf. **Qal 2 b**) 1 S 2^{33} Jb 31^{16}; of a disease, *consume* the eyes Lv 26^{16} (H). **c.** *destroy*, sts. *exterminate:* (1) men subj., c. acc. pers. 2 S 21^{5} 22^{39} (‖ מחץ), Dt 7^{22} 2 Ch 8^{8} Je 10^{25} (‖ אכל), La 2^{22} ψ 119^{87}; esp. in phr. עַד כַּלּוֹתָם 1 S 15^{18} (on txt. v. Dr), 2 S 22^{38} (‖ השמיד)=ψ 18^{38}, 1 K 22^{11}=2 Ch 18^{10}; (2) God subj., c. acc. pers. Jos 24^{20} (E), Is 10^{18} (Assyrian host, under fig. of forest); Je 5^{3} Ex 32^{10} 33$^{3.5}$ (JE), Nu 16^{21} 17^{10} 25^{11} (all P), Lv 26^{44} (H), Ez 20^{13} 22^{31} 43^{8} Jb 9^{22}; עַד כַּלֹּתוֹ אֹתְךָ Dt 28^{21}, עַד כַּלּוֹתִי אוֹתָם Je 9^{15} 49^{37}; abs. ψ 59$^{14.14}$; so also (si vera l.) 74^{11} (see VB; Bi Che בְּקֶרֶב חֵיקְךָ תְּכַלֵּא and thy right hand (why) *keepest thou in thy bosom*); acc.+בְּ instr. Je 14^{12} (by sword, famine, and pestilence); sts. the instrument of י׳'s judgment becomes grammat. subj.; subj. הַחֶרֶב Ho 11^{6} (obj. בַּדָּיו, of city; ‖ אכל), subj. עֵגֶל Is 27^{10} (obj. סְעִפֶיהָ; ‖ רָעָה), subj. flying roll Zc 5^{4} (obj. house). †**Pu.** *Pf.* 3 pl. כָּלּוּ ψ 72^{20} *be finished, ended;* *Impf.* 3 mpl. וַיְכֻלּוּ Gn 2^{1} *be completed* (P).

†כָּלָה **n.f. completion, complete destruction, consumption, annihilation**; alw. this form;—**1.** *completion*, but only as adv., and dubious: *completely, altogether* Gn 18^{21} (J; rd. כֻּלָּם Ol Kau Buhl), Ex 11^{1} (si vera l.) **2.** *complete destruction, consumption, annihilation:* **a.** almost alw. by God, esp. עָשָׂה כ׳ Is 10^{23} (+וְנֶחֱרָצָה), Na 1^{8} (2 acc., si vera l.; Buhl$^{ZAW\ 1885,\ 181}$ prop. בְּקָמָיו for מְקוֹמָהּ v. Id$^{HWB\ 12}$ Kau$^{AT,\ Text\ Krit.\ Erläut.\ p.\ 65}$; v. also מָקוֹם sub קום), v^{9} Je 4^{27} Ne 9^{31} (2 acc.); +אֶת pers.=*with*, pregn. sense,=*in dealing with* (cf. II. אֵת **1 d**), Zp 1^{18} (כ׳ אַךְ נִבְהָלָה), Je 5^{18} 30^{11}=46^{28} (אִתְּךָ=אֹתְךָ), Ez 11^{13} 20^{17} (אִתָּם=אוֹתָם); +בְּכָל־גּוֹיִם Je 30^{11} 46^{28}; without עשׂה: כ׳ וְנֶחֱרָצָה שָׁמַעְתִּי Is 28^{22}, עַד־כ׳ וְנ׳ Dn 9^{27} (on both cf. Is 10^{23} Zp 1^{18}); לְכָלָה *for annihilation* Ez 13^{13} (si vera l., v. Co), וְלֹא לְהַשְׁחִית לְכ׳ 2 Ch 12^{12}. **b.** by men, וְכ׳ אַל־תַּעֲשׂוּ Je 5^{10}; וְכ׳ בְּיָדוֹ Dn 11^{16} *and* (i.e. *with*) *annihilation in his hand.*

†[כָּלֶה] **adj.** failing with desire, longing, only fpl. וְעֵינֶיךָ רֹאוֹת וְכָלוֹת אֲלֵיהֶם Dt 28^{32} *while thine eyes look and fail longingly for them* (cf. vb. כלה **Qal 2 b**, and כִּלָּיוֹן infr.)

†כלוהי Kt, כְּלוּהוּ Qr **n.pr.m.** (? √ I. כלה)—one of those who had strange wives Ezr 10^{35}, 𝔊 Χελκεια, A Χελια, 𝔊L Χελιασουβ.

†כִּלָּיוֹן **n.m. 1.** failing, pining; **2.** annihilation (on format cf. Lag$^{BN\,200}$),—**1.** cstr. כִּלְיוֹן עֵינַיִם Dt 28^{65} *failing of eyes* (in longing, cf. foregoing, and v. Dr) **2.** כִּלָּיוֹן חָרוּץ Is 10^{22} *annihilation, strictly decided.*

†כִּלְיוֹן **n.pr.m.** one of Naomi's sons Ru $1^{2.5}$ 4^{9}, 𝔊 Κελαιων, Χελαιων, Χελεων, 𝔊L Κελλαιων (on etym. cf. Jer , vid Lag$^{Onom.ed\,2,62,8}$).

†II [מִכְלָה] **n.[f.]** completeness, perfection;—only pl. cstr. intens. מִכְלוֹת זָהָב 2 Ch 4^{21} *perfections of gold* = purest gold.—I. מִכְלָה v. sub כלא.

†תִּכְלָה **n.f.** completeness, perfection;—לְכָל־תִּ׳ רָאִיתִי קֵץ ψ 119^{96} *to all perfection have I seen an end.*

†תַּכְלִית **n.f.** end, completeness;—ת׳ abs. Jb 11^{7} 28^{3}, cstr. Ne 3^{21} + 2 t.;—**1.** *end*, וְעַד־תּ׳ בית וגו׳ Ne 3^{21} *even unto the end of the house of* Eliashib; עַד־תּ׳ אוֹר עִם־חֹשֶׁךְ Jb 26^{10} *unto the end of* (= boundary betw) *light and darkness*, וּלְכָל־תּ׳ הוּא חוֹקֵר 28^{3} *and to every end* (= to the farthest limit) *he exploreth;* עַד־תּ׳ שַׁדַּי תִּמְצָא Jb 11^{7} *unto the end of Shadday wilt thou reach* (so as to know him fully)? **2.** *completeness*, as acc of manner (Da$^{Synt.\,§\,70\,b}$) ת׳ שִׂנְאָה שְׂנֵאתִים ψ 139^{22} *with completeness of hatred I hate them.*

כְּלִי$_{324}$ **n.m.**$^{Ho\,8,8}$ **article, utensil, vessel** (NH *id*; acc. to Thes fr. כלה = *conficere*, like Ger. *Zeug* fr. *zeugen*, prop. therefore anything *finished, made, produced;* acc. to Ba$^{ZMG\,1887,\,603}$ fr. meaning *enclose, contain;* he finds pl of כלי in כלאי M-I^{23} (cf. כלאים))—כ׳ abs Je 18^{4}+, כֶּלְיָךְ 1 S 17^{49} 21^{6}; cstr כְּלִי Ho 13^{15}+, sf. הַכֵּלִי Dt 23^{25}; pl. כלים Ex 22^{6}+; cstr. כְּלֵי Gn 24^{53}+; sf. כֵּלַי Gn 31^{37} + 2 t; כֵּלֶיךָ Gn 27^{3} Ez 12^{4}; כֵּלָיו 1 S 9^{7}; כְּלֵיכֶם Gn 43^{11}+, כֵּלֵיהֶם Jos 7^{11}+;—**1.** in gen, *article, object*, made of any material, *thing*, esp. thing of value כ׳ זָהָב 1 S $6^{8.15}$ (images of mice, etc.), personal or household property כְּלֵי בית־ Gn $31^{37.37}$ (E; v^{b} כֹּל כְּלֵי־בֵיתֶךָ), 45^{20} (E), טוֹבִיָּהוּ Ne 13^{8}, Jos 7^{11} (JE), כֶּסֶף אוֹ כֵלִים Ex 22^{6} (E) *money* or *articles* (property), כְּלִי־פָז Jb 28^{17} (appar. coll.); *things carried*, pl. = *stuff, load, baggage* (*impedimenta*) 1 S $17^{22\,22}$, appar = *baggage-train* 10^{22} 25^{13} 30^{24} Is 10^{28}, (cf Gn 31^{37} supr.); כְּלִי גוֹלָה *things of exile*, i e the most necessary articles, such as exiles may take, Je 46^{19} Ez $12^{3.4\,b\,7\,b}$, cf v$^{4\,a\,7\,a}$, = *ornaments* or *jewels* Gn 24^{53} (J; כ׳ כֶּסֶף וכ׳ זָהָב, prob = ornaments), כ׳ כסף וכ׳ זהב also Ex 3^{22} 11^{2} 12^{35} (all E); Is 61^{10}, Ex 35^{22} Nu 31^{50}, כְּלִי מַעֲשֶׂה v^{51} (all P), כְּלִי יְקָר Pr 20^{15} (in fig.), כ׳ תִפְאַרְתֵּךְ Ez $16^{17.39}$ 23^{26} (all in fig); כְּלִי נְחֹשֶׁת as merchandise Ez 27^{13}; כסף וזהב וּכְלֵי נחשת כלים as cargo of ship Jon 1^{5}; וּבַרְזֶל Jos $6^{19\,24}$ (JE; spoil of war); of any household article (on which one sits) Lv $15^{4.6.22.23.26}$ (all P), of skin Nu 31^{20}, or wood v^{20} (P); כְּלִי חֶמְדָּה Na 2^{10} *precious thing*, so Ho 13^{15} (fig.), Je 25^{34} (sim.), 2 Ch 32^{27} Dn 11^{8}, כְּלֵי חֲמֻדוֹת 2 Ch 20^{25} (appar. = ornaments), also כְּלִי אֵין־חֵפֶץ בּוֹ Je 22^{28} (fig. of Coniah, ‖ עֶצֶב נִבְזֶה נָפוּץ), Ho 8^{8} (sim; cf. Je 48^{38} infr); † specif of *garments* (one's 'things'): כְּלִי־גֶבֶר Dt 22^{5} (‖ שִׂמְלַת אִשָּׁה), so כְּלִי־עוֹר Lv 13^{49} (cf מְלָאכֶת עוֹר v^{48}), v$^{52.53.57.58.59}$ (all P) **2.** *utensil, implement, apparatus:* † **a.** *implement* of hunting and (esp) war, = *weapon* Gn 27^{3} (J), 1 S 20^{40} 21^{9} (גַּם חַרְבִּי וְגַם כֵּלַי), 1 K 11^{8} = 2 Ch 23^{7}, 1 K 11^{11} Is $54^{16\,17}$ Je 22^{7}; prob. also כְּלִי Nu 35^{22}, כְּלִי עֵץ־יָד v^{16}, כְּלִי בַרְזֶל v^{18} (all P), כ׳ מַפָּצוֹ Gn 49^{5} (poem); כְּלִי מַשְׁחֵתוֹ Ez 9^{1}, חָמָס v^{2}, fig. of God's weapons כְּלֵי־מָוֶת ψ 7^{14} (‖ חִצָּיו); כ׳ וְעָמוֹ Is 13^{5} Je 50^{25}, of entire equipment of warrior, *armour* or *armament* offensive and defensive 1 S 17^{54} (cf. v$^{5\,ff}$), $21^{6\,6}$ (v. Dr$^{Sm\,139.293}$), $31^{9\,10}$ = 1 Ch $10^{9\,10}$; hence נשא כֵּלִים (כֵּלָיו) *armour-* or *weapon-bearer* Ju 9^{54} 1 S $14^{1\,6.7\,12\,12\,13.13.14\,17}$ 16^{21} $31^{4.4.5\,6}$ = 1 Ch $10^{4.4.5}$, 2 S 18^{15} 23^{37} = 1 Ch 11^{39}; fig. וכלי כֵּלָיו רָעִים Is 32^{7} *and a knave, his weapons* (i e devices, Che 'machinations') *are evil;* more precisely כְּלִי מִלְחָמָה Ju $18^{11\,16\,17}$ 1 S 8^{12} 2 S 1^{27} Dt 1^{41} Je 21^{4} 50^{20} (fig.), Ez 32^{27} 1 Ch 12^{34} (van d. H v^{33}); כְּלֵי צְבָא מִלְחָמָה 1 Ch 12^{38} (van d. H v^{37}); בֵּית כֵּלָיו 2 K 20^{13} = Is 39^{2} is perh. *armoury;* כְּלִי קְרָב Ec 9^{18}; כ׳ Ez 40^{42} is sacrificial knife † **b.** *instrument* of music כְּלֵי (הַ)שִּׁיר Am 6^{5} 1 Ch 15^{16} 16^{42} 2 Ch 5^{13} 7^{6} 23^{13} 34^{12}; כְּלֵי דָוִיד $29^{26.27}$, כ׳־שִׁיר דָּוִיד Ne 12^{36}; כְּלִי נֶבֶל ψ 71^{22}, כ׳ נְבָלִים 1 Ch 16^{5}; כלים alone 1 Ch 23^{5},

cf. Nu 31[6] (P; כְּלֵי הַקֹּדֶשׁ);—for (לַיהוה) בִּכְלִי עֹז 2 Ch 30[21] rd בְּכָל־עֹז (Kau[AT], cf Be) †**c.** *implement* of labour, *tool* כ׳ בַּרְזֶל 1 K 6[7], or of one's calling, pursuit קַח־לְךָ כְּלִי רֹעֶה אֱוִלִי Zc 11[15] (otherwise 1 S 17[40], v **3**) †**d** *equipment* of oxen (yoke, etc) 2 S 24[22] 1 K 19[21]. †**e.** כְּלִי רִכְבּוֹ 1 S 8[12] *his chariot-equipments* **f.** as gen term for *utensils* and *furniture* of Sol's palace 1 K 10[21] = 2 Ch 9[20], esp (very oft.) of tabern Ex 25[9.39] 27[3]+ (in Hex alw. P), and temple 1 K 7[45.47.48] 2 K 12[14]+, of both palace and temple Je 27[18.19.21], combinations are כְּלֵי הַמִּשְׁכָּן Ex 27[19], כ׳ בֵּית י׳ 38[3], כ׳ יהוה Is 52[11], כ׳ הַמִּזְבֵּחַ Je 27[16] 28[3.6] Ezr 1[7], כְּלֵי חֶמְדַּת בֵּית י׳ 2 Ch 36[10], כ׳ בֵּית הָאֱלֹהִים 2 Ch 28[24.24] 36[18] Ne 13[9] Dn 1[2], כ׳ הַמִּקְדָּשׁ Ne 10[40], כ׳ הַשָּׁרֵת Nu 4[12] *utensil of ministry*, כ׳ עֲבֹדַת בֵּית י׳ Nu 4[26] 1 Ch 9[28] 28[14.14], כ׳ עֲבֹדָתָם 1 Ch 28[13], כ׳ מִשְׁמֶרֶת מַשָּׂאָם Nu 4[32]; also כְּלֵי הַקֹּדֶשׁ 1 K 8[4] 1 Ch 9[29], of *appliances* of idol-worship 2 K 23[4] **3.** *vessel, receptacle*, of various materials and for various purposes Gn 43[11] (J); 1 S 9[7] Dt 23[25], = *sack* Gn 42[25] (E, in ‖ שַׂק cl, cf אַמְתַּחַת v[27]), כְּלִי הָרֹעִים *shepherd's bag* or *wallet* 1 S 17[40], cf. v[49], כ׳ חֶרֶשׂ Je 32[14] is *earthenware receptacle* for deed of sale, for liquids 1 K 17[10] 2 K 4[3.3.4.6.6.6], כ׳ מַשְׁקֶה 1 K 10[21] = 2 Ch 9[20], כְּלֵי שְׁמָנָה Nu 4[9], cf v[10], וְלֹא הוּרַק מִכְּלִי אֶל־כֶּלִי Je 48[11] (fig), cf. v[12] (‖ נְבָלִים), for cooking Lv 6[21] (כ׳ חֶרֶשׂ), v[21] (כ׳ נְחֹשֶׁת); v. also (הַ)יּוֹצֵר 2 S 17[28] Je 19[11] (sim), ψ 2[9] (sim), לַצֹּרֵף כֶּלִי Pr 25[4]; כ׳ פָּתוּחַ Nu 19[15] *an open* (*uncovered*) *vessel*. כ׳ טָהוֹר Is 66[20] *a clean vessel*; fig of Eliakim's relatives כֹּל כְּלֵי הַקָּטָן מִכְּלֵי הָאַגָּנוֹת וְעַד כָּל־כְּלֵי הַנְּבָלִים Is 22[24] *the vessels of smallness* (Da[Synt § 32, R 5]), *from the basin-vessels to all the pitcher-vessels* †**4.** specif. כְּלֵי־גֹמֶא Is 18[2] *vessels* (boats) *of paper-reed*

II. **כלה** (√ of foll; meaning unknown).

†[**כִּלְיָה**] **n f.** only pl. **kidneys** (NH כִּלְיָה (pl); Aram כּוּלְיָא or כּוּלְיָא (only pl.), ܟܘܠܝܬܐ; Eth ኵሊት: 𝔊 οἱ νεφροί),—abs. pl כְּלָיוֹת Je 11[20] + 5 t, כְּלָית Ex 29[13] + 13 t.; cstr כִּלְיוֹת Dt 32[14] Is 34[6], sf כִּלְיוֹתַי Jb 16[13] + 2 t; כִּלְיֹתַי Jb 19[27]; כִּלְיוֹתָי ψ 16[7] Pr 23[16], כִּלְיֹתָי ψ 139[13] La 3[13]; כִּלְיוֹתֵיהֶם Je 12[2],—*kidneys* **1.** lit., as physical organ, **a.** of man, only poet, as created by י׳ ψ 139[13], as the most sensitive and vital part, in metaph of one wounded by י׳'s arrows Jb 16[13] La 3[13] **b.** of sacrificial animals, offered as choice part to י׳ Lv 3[4.10.15] 4[9] 7[4] 9[10.19]; שְׁתֵּי הַכ׳ Ex 29[13.22] Lv 3[4.10.15] 4[9] 7[4] 8[16.25] (all P); in fig of sacrif. Edomites חֵלֶב כִּלְיוֹת אֵילִים Is 34[6], transferred to wheat, חֵלֶב כִּלְיוֹת חִטָּה Dt 32[14] *kidney-fat* (i e the choicest, richest) *of wheat* **2.** fig, as seat of emotion and affection Jb 19[27] Pr 23[16] ψ 16[7] 73[21]; קָרוֹב אַתָּה בְּפִיהֶם וְרָחוֹק מִכּ׳ Je 12[2] *near art thou in their mouth, and far from their affections;* hence, as involving character, the obj of God's examination, alw. ‖ לֵב: בֹּחֵן כ׳ וָלֵב Je 11[20] cf ψ 7[10], בֹּחֵן צַדִּיק רֹאֶה כ׳ וָלֵב Je 17[10], חֹקֵר לֵב בֹּחֵן כ׳ 20[12], צָרְפָה כ׳ וְלִבִּי ψ 26[2].

כְּלוּלָה,כַּלָּה v sub II. כלל

כלח (√ of 1 כֶּלַח, mng dub.; Ar كَلَحَ is *contract the face, look hard, stern;* كَلَحٌ ,كَلَاحِ *a hard year* (through dearth, etc)).

†I **כֶּלַח** **n.m.** poss **firm or rugged strength** (v. √supr), תָּבוֹא בְכֶלַח אֱלֵי־קָבֶר Jb 5[26] *thou shalt come in firm strength* (with thy body vigorous, powers unimpaired) *unto the grave;* עָלֵימוֹ אָבַד כָּלַח 30[2] *upon whom vigour has perished.*

†II. [**כֶּלַח**], **כָּלַח** **n.pr.loc.** city in Assyria Gn 10[11.12] = As *Kalḫu*, Schr[COT ad loc] Dl[Par 261], mod. *Nimrûd*, at NE. angle of Upper Zab and Tigris (v. Billerbeck u Jeremias BAS[III 1895, 130 ff])

†**כָּל־חֹזֶה** **n.pr.m. 1.** father of one of the builders, Shallun Ne 3[15] **2.** a name in Judah Ne 11[5] (relation to **1** unknown).

כְּלִי, כִּלָּיוֹן, etc, v. sub I. כלה.

כִּלְיָה v. sub II כלה

כלכל **vb.**, **כַּלְכֹּל** **n.pr.m.** v. sub כול.

†I **כָּלַל** **vb. complete, perfect** (NH *comprehend, include*, Pi *complete*, כְּלָל *a general rule*, בִּכְלָל *in general;* BAram and Syr Shaph שַׁכְלֵל, ܫܰܟܠܶܠ *complete, finish;* As *kalâlu* III 1. 2 *complete;* Ar كَلَّ is *be wearied, fatigued;* Aram. כְּלִילָא, ܟܠܝܠܐ is *a crown*, hence den אַכְלִיל, ܟܰܠܶܠ *to crown*, Eth. I. 2 ከለለ: *to crown*, አክሊል: *a crown*, ተከለለ: *crowning* (of bride), *nuptials*, Ar. إكليل *a crown*, loan-word (Fra[62])).—Ez 27[4] בֹּנַיִךְ כָּלְלוּ יָפְיֵךְ thy builders have *perfected* thy beauty (of Tyre, under fig. of ship), v[11]

כֹּל once כּוֹל (Je 33^{8} Kt.), **n.m. the whole, all** (Moab., Ph., *id.;* Aram. כּוֹל, ܟܠ; Ar. كُلٌّ; Sab. כל, cf. DHM$^{Epigr. Denk. 36-38}$; Eth. ኵሉ: As. *kullatu*)—abs. כֹּל, cstr. כֹּל Gn 2$^{5.16.20}$ + oft., once כָּל־ ψ 138^{2} (v. Ba), but more usu. כָּל־ (with makk.: without it, † ψ 35^{10} Pr 19^{7}; Kö$^{i. 84, 95}$); sf. 2 ms. in p. כֻּלָּךְ † Mi 2^{12}; 2 fs. כֻּלֵּךְ † Is 14$^{29.31}$, כֻּלָּךְ † Is 22^{1} Ct 4^{7} (perh. for assonance with accompanying בָּךְ, לָךְ); 3 ms. כֻּלֹּה 2 S 2^{9} (v. Dr) + 17 t. (never in Pent.), כֻּלּוֹ Gn 25^{25} + 16 t.; 3 fs. כֻּלָּהּ Gn 13^{10} + 15 t., כֻּלָּא † Ez 36^{5}; כֻּלָּנוּ (16 t.); כֻּלְּכֶם (18 t.); כֻּלָּם (oft.), כּוּלָּם † Je 31^{34}, כֻּלָּהֶם † 2 S 23^{6} (and prob. Je 15^{10} (כֻּלְּהֶם); 3 fpl. כֻּלָּנָה † Gn 42^{36} Pr 31^{29}; כֻּלְהֶנָה: † 1 K 7^{37}:—*the whole,* **1.** with foll. gen. (as usually) *the whole of,* to be rendered, however, often in our idiom, to avoid stiffness, *all* or *every:* **a.** Gn 2^{1} כָּל־צְבָאָם *the whole of* their host, v^{13} כָּל־אֶרֶץ כּוּשׁ *the whole of* the land of Kush; כָּל־הַלַּיְלָה *the whole of* the night; כָּל־יִשְׂרָאֵל *the whole of* Israel = *all* Israel; Dt 4^{29} בְּכָל־לְבָבְךָ with *the whole of* thy heart = with *all* thy heart; + very oft. With a *plural* noun, usu. determined by the art. or a genitive: Gn 5^{5} כל־ימי אדם *the whole of* (= *all*) the days of Adam, 37^{35} כל־בניו *the whole of* (= *all*) his sons, Is 2^{2} כל־הגוים *all* the nations; Gn 43^{9} + oft. כל הימים = *continually.* In poetry, however, the noun may remain undetermined, כָּל־יָדַיִם *the whole of* hands = *every* hand, Is 13^{7} Jer 48^{37} Ez 21^{12}; כל־פנים i.e. *every* face Is 25^{8} Joel 2^{6}; כל שלחנות Is 28^{8}; כל חוצות 51^{20} La 2^{19} al. Before an inf. † Gn 30^{41} Dt 4^{7} 1 K 8^{52} 1 Ch 23^{31}. Freq. with sfs., as כֻּלּוֹ (כֻּלֹּה) *the whole of him* Gn 25^{25} Jb 21^{23} Ct 5^{16}, *the whole of it* Lv 13^{13} Je 2^{21} Na 2^{1} Pr 24^{31}; כֻּלָּהּ *the whole of it* Gn 13^{10} Ex 19^{18} 25^{36} Am 8^{8}; כֻּלָּךְ *all of thee* Ct 4^{7} + (v. ad init.); כֻּלָּנוּ *the whole of us* Gn 42^{11} Dt 5^{3} Is 53$^{6.6}$; כֻּלְּכֶם Dt 1^{22} 4^{4} 1 S 22$^{7.7}$; כֻּלָּם Gn 11^{6} 43^{34} Jos 8^{24} ויפלו כֻלָּם, Ju 11^{6} בְּיַד כֻּלָּם, Is 7^{19} 31^{3} + oft.—Twice, strangely, with hyperb. intensive force, ψ 39^{6} כָּל־הֶבֶל *the whole of* vanity, are all men (? om. כל, as v^{12}), 45^{14} כָּל־כְּבוּדָּה *the whole of* gloriousness is the king's daughter. **b.** followed often by a singular, to be understood *collectively,* whether with or without the art.: Gn 1^{21} את כל נפש החיה *the whole of* living souls = every living soul, 2^{9} כל עץ נחמד למראה *the whole of* trees (every kind of tree) pleasant to view, 6^{12} + כָּל־בָּשָׂר, 7^{14} כל צפור כל כנף *all* birds of *every kind of* wing (so Ez 17^{23}), v^{21} כל האדם the whole of mankind (so Nu 12^{3} 16^{29} Ju 16^{17} al.); poet. כל־אדם ψ 39^{6} 64^{10} +; 1 S 14^{52} כל איש גבור וכל־בן־חיל, 17$^{19.24}$ כל איש ישראל, 22^{2}; Is 9^{16} כל פה *the whole of* mouths = every mouth, 15^{2} 24^{10} כָּל־בַּיִת + oft. (in 2$^{12-16}$ the sg. and pl. interchange); ψ 7^{12} + בכל־יום, 10^{5} + בכל־עת = at *all* seasons. So כל־העץ Gn 1^{29}, כל־הבן Ex 1^{22} = *all* the sons, כל־המקום 20^{24} Dt 11^{24} = *all* the places, כל־המרכב Lv 15^{9}, v^{26} Dt 4^{3} כל־האיש אשר = all the *men* who..., 15^{19} כל־הבכור, Je 4^{29} כל־העיר עזובה *all* the cities (notice the foll. בָּהֵן); כל־היום = *all* the days (v. יום **7 f**), etc. In late Heb. extended to such phrases as בְּכָל־דּוֹר וָדוֹר ψ 45^{18} + 145^{13} Est 9^{28}; בכל־עיר ועיר † 2 Ch 11^{12} 28^{25} 31^{19} Est 8$^{11.17}$ 9^{28}; † 2 Ch 32^{28} Est 2^{11} 3^{14} 4^{3} 8$^{13.17}$ 9$^{21.27.28.28.28}$ (cf. וְ **1 i** *b*). **c.** the gen. after כל is oft. a rel. sentence, introduced by אשר: Gn 1^{31} את כל אשר עשה *the whole* of what he had made, 7^{22} 13^{1} + very oft. Sts., with a prep., כל אשר has the force of *wheresoever, whithersoever,* as Jos 1^{7} בְּכֹל אֲשֶׁר תֵּלֵךְ *wheresoever* thou goest, v^{16} אֶל־כָּל־אֲשֶׁר *whithersoever* (see אֲשֶׁר **4 b** γ). Very rarely in such cases is there ellipse of the rel., as Gn 39^{4} וְכָל־יֶשׁ־לוֹ נָתַן בְּיָדִי (contrast v$^{5.8}$), Ex 9^{4} מכל־לבני ישראל, Is 38^{16} וּלְכָל־בָּהֶן חַיֵּי רוּחִי ψ 71^{18} לְכָל־יָבוֹא (74^{3}, v. **2 a**), 2 Ch 32^{31}; peculiarly also in Chr (Dr$^{Intr\ 505}$), 1 Ch 29^{3} מִכָּל־הֲכִינוֹתִי, 2 Ch 30$^{18 f.}$ Ezr 1^{6}; cf. with כֹּל (**2 a**) 1 Ch 29^{11a} 2 Ch 30^{17} Ezr 1^{5}. **d.** with a *suffix* two idiomatic uses of כל have to be noticed: (*a*) כל is often made more independent and emphatic by being placed with a suffix *after* the word which it qualifies, to which it then stands in apposition (cf. in Syr., Ar., Eth.), as 2 S 2^{9} יִשְׂרָאֵל כֻּלֹּה, Jer 13^{19} 48^{31} Is 9^{8} 14$^{29.31}$ פלשת כלך Philistia, *all of* thee! Mi 2^{12} Hb 2^{6} Jb 34^{13} ψ 67$^{4.6}$; esp. in Ezek., as 14^{5} 29^{2} מצרים כֻּלָּהּ 32$^{12.30}$; with change of person (cf. the idiom in Is 22^{16} 48^{1} 54^{1} etc.), 1 K 22^{28} = Mi 1^{2} שמעו עמים כלם Hear, nations, *all of* them! Mal 3^{9} הַגּוֹי כֻּלּוֹ. So even with כל preceding: Nu 16^{3} כָּל־הָעֵדָה כֻּלָּם, Is 14^{18} Jer 30^{16} Ez 11^{15} כל בית ישראל כֻּלֹּה *the whole of* the house of Israel, *the whole of* it (so 20^{40} 36^{10}), 35^{15} 36^{5} ψ 8^{8} (cf. Sab. DHM$^{l.c.}$); (*b*) with the sf. of 3 ms., understood as referring

to the *mass* of things or persons meant, כֻּלָּה or כֻּלּוֹ, lit *the whole of it*, is equivalent to *all of them, every one*, †Ex 14[7] and captains עַל־כֻּלּוֹ upon *the whole of it* (the רֶכֶב collectively)=*all of them*, Is 1[23] *the whole of* it (the people) loveth bribes, 9[16] 15[3] Jer 6[13 13] 8[6 10 10] 20[7] Hab 1[9 15] ψ 29[9] and in his temple כֻּלּוֹ אֹמֵר כָּבוֹד *the whole of* it (= every one there) says, Glory! 53[4] (‖ 14[3] הַכֹּל); perh Is 16[7] Je 48[38], + Pr 19[6] Ew Hi (וְכֻלֹּה רֵעַ) Je 15[10] rd. כֻּלְּהֶם קִלְלוּנִי **e.** Heb idiom in certain cases affirms, or denies, of an *entire* class, where Engl idiom affirms, or denies, of an *individual* of the class, thus in a compar or hypoth sentence כל is=*any*, and with a neg. =*none* (*a*) Gn 3[1] the serpent was more subtil מכל חית השדה than *all* beasts of the field (in our idiom than *any* beast of the field), Dt 7[7] 1 S 9[2], (*b*) Lv 4[2] a soul when it sins through ignorance מכל מצות י״י in *all* the commandments of Jehovah (= in *any* of the commandments, etc), 19[23] when ye plant כל־עץ מאכל=*any* tree for food, Nu 35[22] or if he have cast upon him כָּל־כְּלִי=*any* weapon, 1 K 8[37 b], joined with a ptcp in a hypoth sense (Dr § 121 n Ges § 116. 5 R 5), Gn 4[14] כל מצאי *all my finders* (= if any one find me), he will slay me, v[15 a] Nu 21[8] כָּל־הַנָּשׁוּךְ =*whosoever* (= if *any one*) is bitten, 1 S 2[13]; (*c*) with a neg, Gn 2[5] *all* plants of the field טֶרֶם יִהְיֶה were not as yet=no plant of the field as yet was, 4[15 b] לבלתי הכות־אתו כל־מצאו for the not-smiting him of all finding him = that none finding him should smite him, Ex 10[15] ולא־נותר כל ירק = and no green things were left, 12[16] כל־מלאכה לא יעשה *all* work shall not be done=no work shall be done, Dt 28[14] Ju 13[4] אַל־תֹּאכְלִי כָּל־טָמֵא eat not of *all that is* unclean, 19[19] אין מַחְסוֹר כָּל־דָּבָר there is no lack of *all things* i e of *any thing*, ψ 143[2] כי לא־יצדק לפניך כָל־חָי, + very oft. (so οὐ πᾶς, as a Hebraism, in the N T, e g Mk 13[20] οὐκ ἂν ἐσώθη πᾶσα σάρξ, Lk 1[37] οὐκ ἀδυνατήσει . . . πᾶν ῥῆμα, as Jer 32[17] לֹא־יִפָּלֵא מִמְּךָ כָּל־דָּבָר, Gal 2[16] οὐ δικαιωθήσεται πᾶσα σάρξ, etc) Usu, in such cases, כל (or its gen.) is without the art., being left purposely indef in ψ 49[18] (**2 b** *a*) הַכֹּל is emph (In Nu 23[13] וְכֻלּוֹ לא תראה the context shews that כל is opp to a part) **f.** very anomalously, severed from its gen, † 2 S 1[9] כִּי־כָל־עוֹד נַפְשִׁי בִּי, Jb 27[3] כִּי־כָל־עוֹד נשמתי בי, Ho 14[3] (si vera l) כָּל־תִּשָּׂא עָוֺן On Ec 5[15] כָּל־עֻמַּת־שֶׁ v. עֻמָּה

Note.—When the gen. after כל is a noun fem. or pl, the pred usu agrees with this (as being the really important idea), e.g. Gn 5[5] ויהיו כל ימי אדם, Nu 14[1] וַתִּשָּׂא כָּל־הָעֵדָה, Nah 3[1] ψ 150[6] כל הַנְּשָׁמָה תְּהַלֵּל, exceptions being very rare, Is 64[10 b] Pr 16[2] (Ges § 146. 1 R. 2)

2 Absolutely: †**a.** without the art., *all things, all* (mostly neuter, but sts m), the sense in which 'all' is to be taken being gathered fr. the context, Gn 9[3] נתתי לכם את כל, 16[12] וְיַד כֹּל בּוֹ, 20[16] ואת כל ונוכחת, 33[11] וכי יש לי כל, Nu 8[16] בכור כל מבני ישראל, 11[6] אין כל *nought of all things!* = *there is nothing* (so † 2 S 12[3] Pr 13[7], cf. 2 K 4[2]), 13[2] כל נשיא בהם (cf 2 S 23[28] 1 Ch 3[9]. usu so הַכֹּל), Dt 28[47] מרב כל, v[48. 57] בְּחֹסֶר כֹּל (cf Je 44[18]), Is 30[5] כל הבאיש *all* exhibit shame, 44[24] י״ עֹשֶׂה־כֹּל, Je 44[12] ותמו כל (unusual), Zp 1[2] ψ 8[7] 74[3] (rd כל הֵרַע), 145[15] עיני כל, Pr 16[4] 26[10] 28[5] Jb 13[1] הן כל ראתה עיני, 42[2] 1 Ch 29[11 b] 2 Ch 32[22] (m), Dn 11[37] (v. also **1 c** *end*); מכל Gn 6[19 20 b] שְׁנַיִם מִכֹּל, 14[20] 27[33] Je 17[9] עָקֹב הלב מכל, Dn 11[2] (m) After a neg = *anything*, Dt 4[25] תְּמוּנַת כֹּל the likeness of *anything*, 8[9] 28[55] Pr 30[30]. In the gen. also, very rarely, to express the idea of *all* as comprehensively as possible Ez 44[30] כָּל־בִּכּוּרֵי כֹל וְכָל־תְּרוּמַת כֹּל; ψ 119[128] (si vera l) כָּל־פִּקּוּדֵי כֹל all the statutes *about everything* †**b.** with art. הַכֹּל: (*a*) where the sense is limited by the context to things (or persons) just mentioned, Ex 29[24] ושמת הַכֹּל ביד אהרן, Lv 1[9] הקטיר את הַכֹּל, v[13] 8[27] Dt 2[36] את הַכֹּל נתן י״ לפנינו, Jos 11[19] (cf 2 S 19[31] 1 K 14[26] = 2 Ch 12[9]), 21[43] הַכֹּל בָּא (cf 23[14]), 1 S 30[19] הַכֹּל השיב דוד, 2 S 17[3] (corrupt v 𝔊 Dr), 24[23] (1 Ch 21[23]), 1 K 6[18] הַכֹּל ארז (cf 7[33] 2 K 25[17]=Je 52[22]), 2 K 24[16] הַכֹּל גבורים, Is 65[8] לבלתי השחית הַכֹּל, ψ 14[3]; or implied, Gn 16[12] יָדוֹ בַכֹּל, 24[1] ברך את אברהם בַּכֹּל, 2 S 23[5] (poet.) עֲרוּכָה בַכֹּל, Is 29[11] (peculiarly) חָזוּת הַכֹּל the vision *of the whole*, Je 13[7 10] לא יצלח לַכֹּל, Ez 7[14] וְהָכִין הַכֹּל (but Co וְהָכִינוּ הָכֵן), ψ 49[18] לא במותו יקח הַכֹּל. more freq later, viz. 1 Ch 7[5] (as regards *all*), 28[19] 29[19] 2 Ch 28[6] 29[28] 31[5] 35[7] 36[17 18] Ezr 1[11] 2[42] 8[34. 35] 10[17] וַיְכַלּוּ בַכֹּל (v Be Ry), Ec 5[8] (בַּכֹּל, appar = *in all respects*), 10[19] 12[13] (*b*) in a wider sense, *all*, whether of all mankind or of all living things, the universe (τὸ πᾶν), or of all the circumstances of life (chiefly late), Je 10[16]=51[19] כי יוצר הַכֹּל הוא,

ψ 103[19] (cf. 1 Ch 29[12]), 119[21] הַכֹּל עֲבָדֶיךָ, 145[9] טוֹב י׳ לַכֹּל, 1 Ch 29[12.14.16] Dn 11[2], and esp. in Ec., as 1[2.14] 2[11.17] 3[19] 12[8] הַכֹּל הָבֶל, 2[16] הכל נשכח, 3[1] לַכֹּל זְמָן, v[11.19.20] 6[6] 7[15] 9[1.2.2.3] 10[3.19] 11[5]. כַּכֹּל, †Jb 24[24] (si vera l.) כַּכֹּל יִקָּפְצוּן like *all* men (i.e. like men in general).

†כָּלִיל **adj.** and **subst.** **entire, whole, holocaust**, cstr. כְּלִיל, fem. constr. כְּלִילַת;—**1. adj.** Ez 16[14] (of Jerus.) the report בְּיָפְיֵךְ כִּי כָּלִיל הוּא, 28[12] כְּלִיל יֹפִי (of the king of Tyre) *entire, perfect* in beauty; 27[3] אֲנִי כְּלִילַת יֹפִי (of Tyre), La 2[15] (of Jerus.) הֲזֹאת הָעִיר שֶׁיֹּאמְרוּ כְּלִילַת יֹפִי. **2. subst. a.** *entirety, whole,* Ex 28[31] thou shalt make the robe of the ephod כְּלִיל תְּכֵלֶת a *whole* of purple (i.e. wholly purple); so 39[22]; Nu 4[6] בֶּגֶד כְּלִיל תְּכֵלֶת; Ju 20[40] והנה עלה כְּלִיל־הָעִיר השמימה the *whole* of the city (perh. with allusion to mng. **b**); as adv. acc., Is 2[18] וְהָאֱלִילִים כָּלִיל יַחֲלֹף will pass away *in entirety, wholly.* **b.** as a sacrif. term, *entire-* or *whole-*offering, *holocaust,* of a sacrifice consumed *wholly* on the altar (cf. Ph. כלל CIS[I. 1. 165, 167]; RS[Rel. Sem. 237]), usu. a descriptive syn. of עוֹלָה: Dt 33[10] יָשִׂימוּ קְטוֹרָה בְּאַפֶּךָ וְכָלִיל עַל מִזְבְּחֶךָ; ψ 51[21] אז תחפץ זבחי צדק עולה וְכָלִיל, in app. 1 S 7[9] ויעלה עולה כָּלִיל ליהוה; of the priests' מִנְחָה, Lv 6[15] ליהוה כָּלִיל תָּקְטָר, v[16] וְכָל־מִנְחַת כֹּהֵן כָּלִיל תִּהְיֶה לֹא תֵאָכֵל; fig. Dt 13[17] (of idol. city) ושרפת באש את־העיר ואת־כל שללה כָּלִיל לי׳ אלהיך and thou shalt burn the city and all its spoil as *a whole-offering* to י׳.

†מִכְלוֹל **n.m.** **perfection, i.e. (prob.) gorgeous attire,** Ez 23[12] 38[4] (of warriors) לְבֻשֵׁי מִכְלוֹל.

†[מַכְלֻל] **n.m.** **a thing made perfect, i.e. (prob.) gorgeous garment (or stuff),** Ez 27[24] הֵמָּה רֹכְלַיִךְ בְּמַכְלֻלִים בִּגְלוֹמֵי תְּכֵלֶת וְרִקְמָה וגו׳.

†מִכְלָל **n.m.** **completeness, perfection,** ψ 50[2] מִצִּיּוֹן מִכְלַל יֹפִי out of Zion, the *perfection* of beauty (cf. כָּלִיל **1**), hath God shined.

II. כלל (assumed as √ of foll., but dubious; cf. NH כַּלָּה; Aram. כַּלְּתָא, ܟܰܠܬܳܐ; Ar. كَنَّة; As. *kallâtu,* expl. by Dl[Prol. 130 f.] (cf. Id[HWB 330]) as prop. *closed bridal chamber* (ideogr.=*closed chamber*), fr. √ כלא or כלה, thence *bride* (cf. *harem*); acc. to RS[K 136 f. 292] כַּלָּה=*one closed in,* or *reserved* (sc. for her husband); Ges al. *one crowned* (cf. Aram. etc. כלילא *crown*), but form much against this; Nö[ZMG 1886, 737] 'ventures no explanation').

†כַּלָּה **n.f.** **daughter-in-law, bride**;—abs. כ׳ Je 2[32]+14 t.; sf. כַּלָּתוֹ Gn 11[31]+5 t.; כַּלָּתָהּ Ru 1[22]+2 t., etc.; pl. sf. כַּלֹּתֶיהָ Ru 1[6.8], כַּלּוֹתֶיהָ 1[7], כַּלּוֹתֵיהֶם Ho 4[13.14];—**1.** *daughter-in-law,* in ref. to husband's father Gn 38[11.16.24] (J), cf. 1 Ch 2[4], 1 S 4[19] Ez 22[11] Mi 7[6] Gn 11[31] (P), Lv 18[15] 20[12] (both H); husband's mother Ru 1[6.7.8.22] 2[20.22] 4[15]. **2.** *bride,* usu. **a.** just before marriage Is 49[18] 61[10] 62[5] Je 2[32] (all in sim., etc.), ‖ חָתָן 7[34] 16[9] 25[10] 33[11] Jo 2[16]; Ct 4[8.9.10.11.12] 5[1]. **b.** also just after marriage=*young wife* Ho 4[13.14]; rd. הַכַּלָּה likewise 2 S 17[3] (for MT הַכֹּל), 𝔊 We Dr Klo Kit Bu.

†[כְּלוּלָה] **n.f.** **betrothal**;—only pl. כְּלוּלֹתָיִךְ (cf. '*espousals*') Je 2[2] *thy betrothal-time* (‖ נְעוּרַיִךְ).

†כְּלָל **n.pr.m.** one of those who took strange wives Ezr 10[30], 𝔊 Χαηλ, A Χαληλ, 𝔊L Χαλαμαναι.

†[כָּלַם] **vb.** only **Niph. Hoph.** be humiliated, **Hiph.** humiliate (NH Hiph., *id.*; Aram. כְּלַם Aph. Ithpe.; Ar. كَلَمَ is *wound*; كَلَّمَ also *speak to, converse with*);—**Niph.** *Pf.* 2 fs. וְנִכְלַמְתְּ consec. Je 22[22]+2 t.; 1 s. נִכְלַמְתִּי Je 31[19] Ezr 9[6], נִכְלָמְתִּי Is 50[7]; 3 pl. נִכְלְמוּ Is 45[16]+2 t.; *Impf.* 3 fs. תִּכָּלֵם Nu 12[14]; 2 fs. תִּכָּלְמִי Is 54[4]; 3 mpl. יִכָּלְמוּ Is 41[11]+5 t.; 2 mpl. תִּכָּלְמוּ Is 45[17]; *Imv.* mpl. הִכָּלְמוּ Ez 36[32]; *Inf. cstr.* הִכָּלֵם Je 3[3] 8[12]; *Pt.* נִכְלָם ψ 74[21]; mpl. נִכְלָמִים 2 S 10[5]+2 t.; fpl. נִכְלָמוֹת Ez 16[27];—*be humiliated, ashamed, put to shame, dishonoured, confounded*: **1.** *be humiliated, ashamed,* before men Nu 12[14] (E), 2 S 10[5]=1 Ch 19[5], 2 S 19[4], cf. ψ 74[21]; before enemies (by defeat, etc.) Is 45[17] (‖ בוש), 50[7] 54[4] (‖ חפר, בוש); before God, sq. לְ inf., וְנִכְלַמְתִּי אֱלֹהַי לְהָרִים פָּנַי אֵלֶיךָ Ezr 9[6] (‖ בוש); Je 3[3] Ez 16[27.54] (‖ נָשָׂא כְלִמָּה), 43[10.11] (all+מִן caus.) 16[61], so prob. Levites, at Hezekiah's reforms 2 Ch 30[5]. **2.** *be put to shame, dishonoured, confounded,* by judgments of י׳, all ‖ בוש: Je 22[22] (מִן of cause), Ez 36[32] (*id.*), Je 31[19] (כִּי of cause), 8[12] Is 41[11] 45[16] (+הָלְכוּ בַכְּלִמָּה), ψ 35[4] 69[7]; +חפר ψ 40[15] 70[3]. **Hiph.** *Pf.* 3 ms. sf. הִכְלִמוֹ 1 S 20[34]; 3 mpl. sf. הֶכְלַמְנוּם (Ges[§ 53. 3 R. 6]) 1 S 25[7]; *Impf.* 2 ms. sf. וַתַּכְלִימֵנוּ ψ 44[10]; 2 mpl. יַכְלִים Pr 28[7]; 2 ms. sf. וַתַּכְלִימֵנוּ ψ 44[10]; 2 mpl.

sf. תַּכְלִימוּנִי Jb 19^{3}, ־מוּהָ Ru 2^{15}; *Inf. cstr.* הַכְלִים Je 6^{15} Pr 25^{8}; *Pt.* מַכְלִים Ju 18^{7} (but v. infr.), מַכְלִם Jb 11^{3};—**1.** *put to shame = insult, humiliate*, c. acc. 1 S 20^{34} 25^{7} (cf. Hoph. v^{15}) Ru 2^{15} Jb 19^{3}; *humiliate* by rebuke Jb 11^{3}; *humiliate* by defeat Pr 25^{8} ψ 44^{10}; *cause shame to* Pr 28^{7};—Ju 18^{7} is crpt. (see Be VB GFM; Be prop. מַחְסוֹר כל־דבר there was no *lack of anything*, for MT מַכְלִים ד׳; GFM conjectures מַכְלִא מְדַבֵּר *there is no one to restrain* (us) *from anything* in the land). **2.** *exhibit shame* Je 6^{15} (‖ בּוֹשׁ). **Hoph.** *Pf.* **1.** 1 pl. לֹא הָכְלַמְנוּ 1 S 25^{15} *we were not insulted, humiliated* (cf. **Hiph. 1**). **2.** 3 pl. הָכְלְמוּ Je 14^{3} *they were put to shame, dishonoured, confounded* (‖ בּוֹשׁ).

† כְּלִמָּה **n.f.** insult, reproach, ignominy;—abs. כ׳ Is 45^{16} + 9 t.; cstr. כְּלִמַּת Je 20^{11} + 3 t.; sf. כְּלִמָּתִי Jb 20^{3} + 3 t., etc.; pl. כְּלִמּוֹת Mi 2^{6} Is 50^{6};—**1.** specif., *insult, reproach*, לֹא יִסַּג כ׳ Mi 2^{6} *reproaches do not cease*; מוּסַר כְּלִמָּתִי Jb 20^{3} = *my beshaming* (*insulting*) *correction*, i.e. the correction which insults me. **2.** in gen., *reproach, ignominy*, opp. כָּבוֹד ψ 4^{3}; הלך בַּכּ׳ Is 45^{16} *go into ignominy* (+ בּוֹשׁ, נִכְלַם); oft. ‖ בֹּשֶׁת Is 30^{3} 61^{7} ψ 44^{16}, subj. of כִּסָּה Je 3^{25} *our ignominy covereth us*, so under fig. of garment, after לָבַשׁ ψ 35^{26} (+ בּוֹשׁ, חפר in v^{a}), 109^{29}; ‖ חֶרְפָּה ψ 69^{8} (subj. of כִּסְּתָה פָּנָי), Je 51^{51} (*id.*; בוש in ‖ cl.), ψ 71^{13} (+ בוש in ‖ cl.); ‖ חֶרְפָּה + בֹּשֶׁת 69^{20}; אִוֶּלֶת ‖ Pr 18^{13}; ‖ רֹק Is 50^{6}; כ׳ עוֹלָם Je 20^{11} (בוש in ‖ cl.); כְּלִמָּתֵךְ Ez 16^{63} (*id.* ‖); oft. in Ezek. נשׂא כ׳ *bear ignominy*, Ez 16$^{52.52}$ (‖ בּוֹשׁ), v^{54} (נִכְלַם in ‖ cl.); 32$^{24.25.30}$ (all + אֶת־יוֹרְדֵי בוֹר *with those who go down to the pit*; ref. to ignominious death), 36^{7} 39^{26} (si vera l. = *bear the humiliating sense* of undeserved kindness from י׳; but txt. dub., Hi Co, q.v., [כ׳] נשׁו; Sm Da defend); נשׂא כְּלִמַּת הַגּוֹיִם, i.e. caused by the nations, 34^{29} 36^{6}, also v^{15} (‖ חֶרְפַּת עַמִּים), prob. also ψ 89^{51} (rd. כְּלִמַּת, cf. VB Che Bae); וְנ׳ כְּלִמָּתָם וְתוֹעֲבוֹתָם אֲשֶׁר עָשׂוּ Ez 44^{13}.

† כְּלִמּוּת **n.f.** ignominy;—only cstr. וּכְלִמּוּת עוֹלָם Je 23^{40} (‖ חֶרְפַּת עוֹלָם).

† כִּלְמַד **n.pr.loc.** (si vera l.) Ez 27^{23}, named after אַשּׁוּר, 𝔊 Χαρμαν; = mod. *Kalwâdha* near Bagdad, acc. to G. Smith$^{TSBA\ i.\ 61}$ Dl$^{Pa\ 206}$, cf. Schr^{COT}; but txt. dub. v. Co; 𝔗 ומדי, whence Mez $^{Stadt\ Harrân\ 34}$ כָּל־מָדַי *all Media*; JKi Hi Co כְּלָמּוּד (רְכֻלָּתֵךְ) Asshur was *as thine apprentice* (v. sub למד) *in trading*; but sense not very prob.

† כַּלְנֵה (van d. H, so Norzi; Baer כַּלְנֶה) **n.pr.loc.** in Babylonia, Gn 10^{10} (J), 𝔊 Χαλαννη; Dl$^{Pa\ 225}$ prop. identif. with Bab. *Kul-unu*=*Zirlab* (conquered by Sargon in 710: COT$^{Gn\ 10,\ 10;\ Am\ 6,\ 2}$), but dubious, and site of Zirlab unknown.

† כַּלְנֵה Am 6^{2}, prob. = כַּלְנוֹ Is 10^{9} **n.pr.loc.** city (conquered by Assyria under Sargon?) poss. = כַּנֶּה (q.v.) Ez 27^{23}, 𝔊 om. in Am 6^{2}, Χαλαννη Is 10^{9}; perh. = Kullani (Wkl$^{Gesch.\ Bab.\ 225}$) i.e. (Tomkins$^{PSBA\ Jan.\ 1883,\ 61}$) Kullanhou, near Aleppo, conquered by Tiglath-Pileser III in 738 (COT$^{ii,\ 195}$); or (Di) Kunulua (KG^{217} KB$^{i,\ 107}$), SE. of Antioch (cf. Dr$^{Am\ 6,\ 2}$).

† כָּמַהּ **vb.** faint (Ar. كَمِهَ is *be pale* of face, *gray* (of daylight), *weak-eyed*, أَكْمَهُ *blind from birth*; Syr. ܟܡܗ *be blind*), only fig.—**Qal** *Pf.* 3 ms. כ׳ לְךָ בְשָׂרִי ψ 63^{2} *faint* (with longing) *for thee* (‖ צָמְאָה לְךָ נַפְשִׁי).

† כִּמְהָם **n.pr.m. 1.** attendant of David 2 S 19$^{38.39}$ = כִּמְהָן v^{41}; 𝔊 in all Χιμααμ, 𝔊L Αχιμααμ. **2.** in **n.loc.** גֵּרוּת כִּמְהָם Je 41^{17} Qr (Kt כמוהם), cf. גֵּרוּת p. 158 supr.

כִּמְהָן 2 S 19^{41}, v. foregoing.

כַּמָּה v. מָה. כְּמוֹ v. sub כְּ p. 455 supr.

כמוהם Je 41^{17} Kt, v. כִּמְהָם.

† כְּמוֹשׁ **n.pr.div.** Chemosh (כמש MI$^{3.5.9.12.13.14.18.19.32.33}$ also עשתר כמש l^{17} and n.pr.m. כמשמלך l^{1}; As. *Kammusunadbi*, a king of Moab Schr. $^{COT\ i,\ 281;\ =KAT\ 2,\ 288}$; cf. further Bae$^{Rel\ 13\ f.\ 238,\ 256}$ Nö$^{ZMG\ 1888,\ 471}$; 𝔊 Χαμώς);—god of the Moabites to whom Solomon erected a high place 1 K 11$^{7.33}$ 2 K 23^{13} Je 48^{7} (Kt כמיש), v^{13}. Moab is עַם־כ׳ Nu 21^{29} (ode) *people of Chemosh*, and Moabites his sons and daughters, cf. Je 48^{46}. He is said to be also the God of the Ammonites Ju 11^{24} (probably an error Bae$^{Rel\ 15}$ GFM).

כמז (√ of foll.; mng. dub.; Ar. كُمْزَةٌ is *bunch, heap*).

† כּוּמָז **n.[m.]** name of a golden ornament;—אֶצְעָדָה וְצָמִיד טַבַּעַת וְכ׳ Ex 35^{22}; חָח וָנֶזֶם וְטַבַּעַת וְכ׳ עָגִיל וְכ׳ Nu 31^{50} (both P).

כמיש Je 48^{7} Kt, v. כְּמוֹשׁ.

כמן (√ of foll. (si vera l.); perh. *be hidden*; cf. Aram. כְּמַן, ܟܡܢ, *lie in ambush*; Ar. كَمَنَ *id.* is denom. fr. loan-word كمّين acc. to Frä^{243}).

†[מִכְמָן] **n.[m.]** only pl. **hidden stores,** מִכְמַנֵּי הַזָּהָב וְהַכֶּסֶף Dn 11^{43} (? rd מַטְמֹנֵי)

†כַּמֹּן **n.m. cummin,** plant grown as condiment (𝔊 κύμινον, *cuminum cyminum;* Plin. $^{NH\ xix.\ 8}$; Germ. '*römischer Kümmel,*' $Low^{No\ 152}$, √dub, NH *id.;* Aram כַּמּוֹנָא, ܟܡܘܢܐ; Ar كَمُّونٌ, Eth. ከሙን: on format. cf. $Lag^{BN\ 89}$, loan-word acc. to Di^{832});—Is $28^{25.27.27}$.

†[כָּמַס] **vb. store up** (si vera l.), in **Qal** *Pt. pass.* כָּמֻס Dt 32^{34} is not this *stored up* (*laid up in store*) with me (‖ חָתוּם בְּאוֹצְרֹתָי); but rd prob. כָּנֻס in same mng (v. כנס, and $Dr^{Dt\ 32,34}$)

†מִכְמָס **n.pr.loc.** Ezr 2^{27} = Ne 7^{31}, = מִכְמָשׁ (v. Baer's notes) 1 S 13^{2} + 6 t. 1 S, + 2 t.,—city in Benjamin, N. fr. Geba and Jerusalem 1 S $13^{2.5}$ (E. fr. Bethaven), $v^{11\ 16.23}$ $14^{5.31}$ Is 10^{28} Ne 11^{31}; אַנְשֵׁי מ׳ Ezr 2^{27} = Ne 7^{31}. 𝔊 Μαχ(ε)μας, etc. (On *Mikmās* v. $Rob^{BR\ i\ 440\ ff}$ $Buhl^{Geogr\ §\ 96}$.)

†I. [כָּמַר] **vb. Niph. grow warm and tender, be or grow hot** (NH *id.* Pi. *heat* fruit in the ground, making it ripe, over-ripe, tender, Aram. כְּמַר *id.*, and more gen. *make warm* (one's flesh, or food); cf. *kemr, fermentation,* etc., in mod. Syria $Wetzst^{ZPV\ xiv\ (1891),\ 6}$)—**Niph.** *Pf.* 3 pl. נִכְמְרוּ Gn 43^{30} + 2 t., נִכְמָרוּ La 5^{10};— **1.** *grow warm* and *tender,* fig., subj. רַחֲמִים, נ׳ רַחֲמָיו אֶל־אָחִיו Gn 43^{30} (J), so נ׳ רַחֲמֶיהָ עַל־בְּנָהּ 1 K 3^{26}, (רַחֲמַי We) יַחַד נ׳ נִחוּמָי Ho 11^{8} (‖ נֶהְפַּךְ עָלַי לִבִּי). **2.** *be* or *grow hot,* עוֹרֵנוּ כְּתַנּוּר נ׳ מִפְּנֵי וגו׳ La 5^{10} *our skin has become hot like a furnace,* because of the famine.

II כמר (? √ of foll.; cf. Syr. ܟܡܝܪ *black, dark,* usu. *gloomy, sad;* ܟܡܪ, ܐܬܟܡܪ *be sad*).

†[כִּמְרִיר] **n.m. darkness, gloominess** (?), pl. intens. cstr. כִּמְרִירֵי יוֹם Jb 3^{5} *the deep gloom of day* (‖ עֲנָנָה, צַלְמָוֶת, חשֶׁך),—rd. כַּמ׳, v. $Di\ Sta^{§\ 231}$.

III כמר (√ of foll.; cf. As. *kamâru, overthrow, lay prostrate,* whence n. *kamâru, net, snare* $Dl^{HWB\ 336}$ and כֹּמֶר *priest* acc. to $Dl^{HA\ 42}$, i.e. one who prostrates himself; also Mand. כמר *turn round, bring back* $No^{M\ 443\ f.}$ and N. Syr. ܟܡܪ *pursue* No^{ib} PS^{1759}).

†מִכְמָר **n.[m.] net, snare,** bringing an animal to its fall, כְּתוֹא מ׳ Is 51^{20} *like an antelope of* (*in*) *a net* or *snare* (cf. II. חֵרֶם p. 357, II. רֶשֶׁת p. 440).

†[מַכְמֹר] **n.[m.] net, snare** (v. foregoing)— pl. sf. יִפְּלוּ בְמַכְמֹרָיו רְשָׁעִים ψ 141^{10}, so Gr Che 140^{11} (במכמרות for MT בְּמַהֲמֹרוֹת, v. p. 243)

†[מִכְמֶרֶת] **n.f. net, fishing-net;** sg. sf. מִכְמַרְתּוֹ Hb 1^{15} (‖ חַכָּה, and חֵרֶם), v^{16}, both in fig. of conquering Chaldeans.

†מִכְמֹרֶת **n.f.** *id.*, וּפֹרְשֵׂי מ׳ עַל־פְּנֵי־מַיִם Is 19^{8} (‖ מַשְׁלִיכֵי בַיְאוֹר חַכָּה).

†[כֹּמֶר] **n.m. (idol-)priest** (so NH כּוֹמֶר; Aram. כּוּמְרָא, ܟܘܡܪܐ, is also priest of God; Nerab כמר $Hal^{Rev\ Sém\ 1896,\ 280,\ 282}$, Nab. כמר *priest* $CIS^{ii,\ No.\ 170}$, Teima כמרא *id.* $CIS^{ii,\ No\ 113\ a,\ b,\ b\ bis}$, so כמר Neo-Pun. $Eut^{ZMG\ 1875,\ 238,\ 239}$ Berger $^{JAs\ Apr\ June,\ 1887,\ 465}$, perh. Tel Am. *kamiru* $Bez^{BM\ Tabl\ xxvi,\ Or\ Dipl.\ 92}$; $Wkl^{TA\ 1\ 16,33}$ leaves untransl.),— pl. abs., in O.T. only of idol-priests, הַכְּמָרִים 2 K 23^{5}, כְּמָרָיו Ho 10^{5}, הַכּ׳ עִם־הַכֹּהֲנִים Zp 1^{4}. In Ho 4^{4} Beck (in Wu^{142}) We prop וְעַמִּי כִּכְמָרָיו (for MT וְעַמְּךָ כִּמְרִיבֵי)

כמת (√ of foll., meaning unknown)

†מִכְמְתָת **n.pr.loc.** alw. הַמ׳, Jos 16^{6} (𝔊 Ικασμων, 𝔊L εις Αχθωθ, A Μαχθωθ), 17^{7} (מֵאָשֵׁר הַמ׳; 𝔊 Δηλαναθ, A ἀπὸ Ασηρ Μαχθωθ, and similarly 𝔊L), place in NE. Ephraim, near border of Manasseh, between Shechem and Taanath Shilo, $Buhl^{Geogr\ 109}$ conj. *Khirbet kefr beita.*

I כֵּן **adv. so** (Ph. NH 𝔗 *id.*, Syr. ܟܝܢ is *then,* Ar. لٰكِنْ, لَكِنْ, *but*: prob. from the demonstr. √*ka*, found in כִּי etc., $Kö^{ii\ 1\ 254}$); כֶּן־הוּא (הִיא) Gn 44^{10} + 4 t.:—*so* (i.e. usu., as has been described or commanded, with ref. to what has preceded), mostly of manner, but sts. also of quantity, quality, or degree. **1. a.** Ju 5^{31} כֵּן יֹאבְדוּ *so* perish thy enemies, Jb 5^{27} כֶּן־הִיא, 8^{13} כֵּן אָרְחוֹת כָּל שֹׁכְחֵי אֵל, Pr 6^{29} 8^{13} 2 S 16^{23} Is 36^{6} 47^{15} כֵּן הָיוּ לָךְ, Nu 13^{33} וְכֵן הָיִינוּ בְעֵינֵיהֶם; Nu 9^{16} כֵּן יִהְיֶה תָמִיד, Ex $10^{14.14}$ לֹא הָיָה כֵן אַרְבֶּה כָּמֹהוּ וגו׳ (i.e. in such numbers), 1 K 10^{12} לֹא בָא כֵן עֲצֵי אַלְמֻגִּים, v^{20} 2 Ch $1^{12.12}$, Ju 21^{14} וְלֹא מָצְאוּ לָהֶם כֵּן and they did not suffice for them *so* (viz. in such numbers of them as there were); 1 K 6^{26} וְכֵן הַכְּרוּב הַשֵּׁנִי, Ez 41^{7}; וְכֵן לְ׳ Ex 27^{11} 1 K 10^{29} Ez 40^{16} 2 Ch 35^{12}, cf. 1 Ch 23^{30}, כֵּן לְ׳ Ex 25^{33} (cf. 26^{24}), Jos 21^{40}. **b.** the force of כֵּן has sts. to be elicited from the context: 1 K 2^{7} כִּי כֵן קָרְבוּ אֵלַי (sc. with kindness such as that enjoined in v^{a}), 20^{40} כֵּן מִשְׁפָּטֶךָ, Je 14^{10} כֵּן אָהֲבוּ לָנוּעַ (i.e. not less than י׳ has withdrawn from

them v^{9}, Gf Ke; Gie prop. אָכֵן, ψ 61^{9} כֵּן אֲזַמְּרָה שִׁמְךָ (Hi כְּצִדְקָתְךָ, implied in v$^{6-8}$), 63^{3} כֵּן בַּקֹּדֶשׁ חֲזִיתִךָ (sc. with the longings of v^{2}), v^{5} כֵּן כִּי כֵן תְּכִינֶהָ (sc. כְּרֹב חַסְדְּךָ v^{4}), 65^{10} אֲבָרֶכְךָ בְחַיָּי (i.e. so generously, v^{10}), 90^{12} לִמְנוֹת יָמֵינוּ כֵּן הוֹדַע (Hi כְּיִרְאָתְךָ v^{11}), 127^{2} כֵּן יִתֵּן לִידִידוֹ שֵׁנָא (sc. as abundantly; but Che אָכֵן), Pr 24^{14} (see v^{13}), Is 52^{14} כֵּן מִשְׁחַת מֵאִישׁ מַרְאֵהוּ (sufficiently to justify שממו עליך רבים). **c.** כן *occurs* freq. in partic. phrases, as (*a*) with הָיָה, esp. ויהי כן and it was *so* Gn $1^{7.9.11}$ +, 2 K 2^{10} if thou seest me taken from thee יהי־לך כן let it be to thee *so* (sc. as thou desirest), 7^{20}, with עשה (esp. וַיַּעַשׂ, וַיַּעֲשׂוּ) Gn 29^{28} 42^{20} 45^{21} + oft., Ju 7^{16} מִמֶּנִּי תִרְאוּ וְכֵן תַּעֲשׂוּ, + ל׳ Gn 42^{25} ויעש להם כן, Ex 22^{29} 23^{11} כן תעשה ל׳, Dt 22^{3} 2 S 12^{31} 1 K 11^{8} (cf. 6^{33} 7^{18}); Gn 29^{26} לֹא יֵעָשֶׂה כן במקומנו, 34^{7} 2 S 13^{12}; rarer usages, דִּבֶּר כֵּן Ex 6^{9}, 1 K 22^{8} אמר כן, כן אמרתם Ez 11^{5} 33^{10}, אָמֵן כֵּן יֹאמַר י׳ 1 K 1^{36} (cf. Je 28^{6}), 1 S 23^{17} וגם שאול אבי יֹדֵעַ כֵּן; אָהַב כֵּן (idiom.) to love (it) *so*, †Je 5^{31} Am 4^{5}; (*b*) Gn 50^{3} כי כן ימלאו ימי החנטים (cf. Ju 14^{10} 2 S 13^{18} Est 2^{12}); (*c*) alone, אִם כֵּן if it be *so* †Gn 25^{22} 43^{11}; † וַיִּרְאוּ כִּי־כֵן 1 S 5^{7}, יָדַעְתִּי כִּי־כֵן Jb 9^{2}; (*d*) לא כן not *so* (viz. as has been described or implied), with a subst. Nu 12^{7} לא כן עבדי משה, 2 S 20^{21} 23^{5} ψ 1^{4} Jb $9^{35\,b}$ כי־לא־כן אנכי עמדי not *so* am I with myself (i.e. I am not conscious of being one who would fear him, v^{a}), with a vb. Dt 18^{14} ואתה לא כן נתן לך י׳ (not *so*,—viz. as implied in v^{a}), 2 S 18^{14} Is 10^{7} לא כן יחשב, לא כן יְדַמֶּה, absol. Gn 48^{18} לא כן אבי, Ex 10^{11}.

2. Often, to emphasize the agreement, in answer to כְּ, and כַּאֲשֶׁר: viz. **a.** כְּ . . . כֵּן, (*a*) Gn 44^{10} = Jos 2^{21} כדבריכם כֶּן־הוּא acc. to your words, *so* be it, 1 S 25^{25} כִּי כשמו כֶּן־הוּא, ψ 48^{11} Pr 23^{7} כֶּן־הוּא (after conj. כְּמוֹ), Ez 42^{11} כְּאָרְכָּן כֵּן רָחְבָּן; (*b*) Lv 27^{12} כְּעֶרְכְּךָ כֵּן יִהְיֶה, 2 S 13^{35} Nu 8^{4} 9^{14} 15^{20} Dt 8^{20} Ju 11^{10}, so after כְּפִי Nu 6^{21}; (*c*) כְּכֹל . . . כֵּן . . . 1 S 8^{8} 2 S 7^{17} Je 42^{5}; (*d*) in similes, (*α*) 2 S 14^{17} כמלאך הא׳ כן אדני המלך, Je 18^{6} ψ 123^{2} 127^{4} Pr 10^{26} $26^{8.19}$ $27^{8.19}$ Ct $2^{2.3}$; (*β*) Jo 2^{4} כְּפָרָשִׁים כֵּן יְרוּצוּן, Is 31^{5} 38^{14} ψ 103^{15} Pr $26^{1.2}$; (*γ*) ψ 42^{2} כאיל תערג . . . כן נפשי ונ׳ like the hind which etc., 83^{16} Is 61^{11} 63^{14} Jb 7^{3}, so after כמו Is 26^{17}; (*δ*) Je 2^{26} כְּבֹשֶׁת גַּנָּב . . . כֵּן הוֹבִישׁוּ, 6^{7} 34^{5} (rd. כְּמִשְׂרְפוֹת), Ez 22^{22} (cf. v^{20}), 23^{44} 34^{12}; cf. (of degree) 35^{15} (om. 𝔊 Co), Ho 4^{7} כְּרֻבָּם כֵּן חָטְאוּ לִי. Of *time* (uncommon) 1 S 9^{13} כְּבֹאֲכֶם הָעִיר כֵּן תִּמְצְאוּן אֹתוֹ. **b.** †Ezr 10^{12} כן כדבריך עלינו לעשות. **c.** כַּאֲשֶׁר . . . כֵּן, (*a*) Ex 7^{6} כאשר צוה י׳ כן עשו, $12^{28.50}$ 39^{43} (cf. 27^{8}), Nu 8^{22} (cf. 5^{4}), 17^{26} 36^{10} Jos 14^{5} (all P); Gn 41^{13} כאשר פתר כן היה, Jos $10^{1.39}$ 11^{15} Ju 1^{7} $15^{11\,b}$ ψ 48^{9}; (*b*) (freq.) Nu 2^{17} כאשר יַחֲנוּ כֵּן יִסָּעוּ, Ex 1^{12} (of degree = *the more . . . the more*) כַּאֲשֶׁר יְעַנּוּ אֹתוֹ כֵּן יִרְבֶּה וְכֵן יִפְרֹץ; (*c*) Gn 6^{22} ככל אשר צוה אתו אלהים כן עשה, Ex $39^{32.42}$ 40^{16} Nu 1^{54} 2^{34} 8^{20} 9^{5} (all P), cf. Ex 25^{9} (וְכֵן), simil. 2 S 9^{11} 2 K 16^{11}, cf. Jos 1^{17} Je 42^{20}; (*d*) Ex 27^{8} כאשר הֶרְאָה אתך כן יעשו, 2 S 16^{19} 1 K 2^{38} Is 20^{4} $52^{14\,f.}$; with the same vb. repeated Lv $24^{19.20}$ Dt 28^{63} כאשר שׂשׂ . . . . כן יָשִׂישׂ, Jos 23^{15} 1 S 15^{33} 26^{24} 1 K 1^{37} Is 10^{11} Je 5^{19} 31^{28} 32^{42} 42^{18} Ez 12^{11} 20^{36} Zc 7^{13} Pr 24^{29}; Nu 14^{28} אם לא כאשר דברתם כן אעשה, Is 14^{24}, so after הלא 10^{11}, after asseverative כי 2 S 3^{9} 1 K 1^{30}; so כֵּן . . . . כְּכָל־עֻמַּת שֶׁ׳ † Ec 5^{15}; (*e*) Ju $7^{17\,b}$ כאשר אעשה כן תעשון, Lv 27^{14} Nu 15^{14}, cf. Je 39^{12}; (*f*) in similes, Dt 12^{22} 22^{26} Am 3^{12} Is 65^{8} Je 13^{11}. †**d.** כן כאשר . . . ., (*a*) Ex 7^{10} ויעשו כן כאשר צוה י׳, v^{20} Jos 4^{8} 2 S 5^{25} Ez 12^{7}, cf. Gn 50^{12} Nu 8^{3}; iron. Am 5^{14} יהי כן י׳ אתכם כאשר אמרתם, Ex 10^{10}; (*b*) Gn 18^{5} כן תעשה כאשר דברת, Ne 5^{12}.—Occasionally in poetry כאשר is not expressed: Is 54^{9} (De), 55^{9} Je 3^{20} Jb 7^{9} Ho 11^{2} קראו להם כן הלכו מפניהם (of degree: *so* = in the same proportion), ψ 48^{6} המה ראו כן תמהו (i.e. in the same measure that they saw); Je 33^{22} (acc. to many, but dub.; rd. prob. כאשר Gie) it is represented by אשר (so Is 54^{9} Hi Ew Di): Ju 5^{15} כ is not expressed.—Na 1^{12} is prob. corrupt; Zc 11^{11} for כן עניי rd. כְּנַעֲנֵי.—כָּכָה, כֹּה, כָּזֹאת are syn., but differ considerably in usage.

3. With prepositions:—**a.** אַחֲרֵי־כֵן, אַחַר־כֵּן, מֵאַחֲרֵי־כֵן, lit. *after so*, i.e. *afterwards*: v. אַחַר. **b.** †בְּכֵן (late), lit. *in such circumstances*, i.e. *thereupon, then*, Ec 8^{10} Est 4^{16} (𝔗 בְּכֵין oft. for אָז; e.g. Ex 15^{1}; Syr$^{Jerus.}$ ܒܟܝܢ = τότε). **c.** †כְּמוֹ־כֵן Is 51^{6}, acc. to some, *like so*, i.e. (Vrss Rabb) *in like manner*, or (De) *like this* (accompanied by a contemptuous gesture) = like a mere nothing: but v. IV. כֵּן. **d.** לָכֵן $_{200}$ *according to such conditions, that being so, therefore* Nu 16^{11} 1 S 27^{6} ψ 16^{9} $73^{6.10}$; esp. in proph., where it often introduces, after statement of the grounds, a divine declaration or command: Ju 10^{13} 2 K 1^{6} Am 4^{12} Is $5^{13.14.24}$ 7^{14} 10^{16} 16^{7} 27^{9} Je 6^{15} 8^{10} etc.; לכן כה אמר י׳ 2 K 21^{12} Is 10^{24} 28^{16} 29^{22} 30^{12} 37^{33} Je 5^{14} 6^{21} + oft.; sq. נאם האדון Is 1^{24}; נאם י׳ 1 S 2^{30} Je 2^{9}; לכן הנה ימים באים נאם י׳ Je 7^{32} 16^{14} 19^{6} +; לכן חי אני נאם י׳ Ez 5^{11} $35^{6.11}$ Zp 2^{9}; לכן הנני . . . . 1 K 14^{10} Ho $2^{8.16}$ Is 29^{14} Je 16^{21} Ez 16^{37} $22^{19\,b}$ $25^{4.7.9}$ +; לכן אֱמֹר † Ex 6^{6} Nu 25^{12} (both P),

Ez 11$^{16.17}$ 14^{6} 20^{30} 33^{25} 36^{22}, לָכֵן דַּבֵּר † Ez 14^{4} 20^{27}; לָכֵן שִׁמְעוּ..., † Ez 11^{4} 36$^{3.6}$ 37^{12} 38^{14}, לָכֵן הִנָּבֵא Is 28^{14} 51^{21} Je 6^{18} 44^{26}+. In answer to יַעַן. Nu 20^{12} (P), 1 K 14^{10} 2 K 1^{16} 21^{12} 22^{20} Is 29^{14} 30^{13} Je 19^{6}+, Ez 5^{8} 13^{23}+; so, once, וְלָכֵן Is 8^{7}; to כי Is 28^{16} Je 35^{17}, על Je 9^{14}; אם 23^{38} 42^{15}. Special usages:—(*a*) idiom, in conversation, in reply to an objection, to state the ground upon which the answer is made; Gn 4^{15} *therefore*—this being so—whoso killeth Cain, etc, 30^{15} Ju 8^{7} 11^{8} 1 S 28^{2} 1 K 22^{19} Jb 20^{2} (𝔊 in Gn K Jb, not perceiving the idiom, renders οὐχ οὕτως (as though לא־כן) · so also strangely, elsewhere, as 1 S 3^{14} 2 K 1$^{4.6}$ 21^{12}) (*b*) inferring the cause from the effect, or developing what is logically involved in a statement, Is 26^{14b} (cf. De) *therefore* thou hast visited and destroyed them (not a consequence of v^{a} 'the dead rise not,' but the development of what is implicit in it), 61^{7} Je 2^{33} 5^{2} (because viz. אין אמונה v^{1}), Jb 34^{25} 42^{3}.—Zc 11^{7} rd. לִכְנַעֲנֵי הַצֹּאן. **e.** † עַד־כֵּן *hitherto* (of time), *as yet* Ne 2^{16}. **f.** עַל־כֵּן$_{143}$ *upon ground of such conditions, therefore* (introducing, more generally than לָכֵן, the statement of a *fact*, rather than a *declaration:* never used in the phrases noted under לָכֵן), Gn 20^{6} 42^{21} Ex 5$^{8.17}$ 16^{29} 20^{11} 1 S 20^{29} 28^{18} 2 S 7$^{22.27}$ 1 K 20^{23} Is 5^{25} 9^{16} 13$^{7.13}$ 15$^{4.7}$ 16$^{9.11}$ 17^{10} 21^{3} Je 5$^{6.27}$ 10^{21} 12^{8} 20^{11} 31$^{3.20}$ Ez 7^{20} 22^{4} 31^{5} etc, ψ 1^{5} 42^{7} 45^{3c} (the poet's inference from v$^{a.b}$), v^{8} 110^{7} Jb 6^{3} 9^{22} 17^{4} 20^{21} etc, Ct 1^{3}; and regularly where the origin of a name, or custom, or proverb is assigned, Gn 2^{24} על־כן יעזב איש וג׳, 10^{9} על־כן יֵאָמַר, 11^{9} על־כן קרא שמה בבל, 16^{14} 19^{22} 21^{31} 25^{30} 26^{33} 29$^{34.35}$ 30^{6} 32^{33} 47^{22} Ex 13^{15} 15^{23} Nu 18^{24} 21$^{14.27}$ Dt 10^{9} (cf. 15$^{11.15}$ 19^{7} 24$^{18.22}$), Jos 7^{26} 14^{14} Ju 15^{19} 18^{12} 1 S 5^{5} 10^{12} 23^{28} (? rd. so 27^{6}) 2 S 5$^{8.20}$ etc.; הַעַל־כֵּן † Hb 1^{17}.—Est 9^{26} the 2nd על כן (unless dittogr.) points unusually onwards to על כל דברי האגרת *on this account, on account, viz.*, etc.

II כֵּן v. כון; III. כֵּן v I. כנן; IV. כֵּן v. II. כנן.

† [כָּנָה] **vb. Pi.** **betitle, title, give an epithet or cognomen** (NH *id.*, Aram. כַּנָּא, ܟܢܐ, Ar. كَنَى)—**Pi.** *Impf.* 1 s. sf. וָאֶקְרָא לְךָ בִשְׁמֶךָ אֲכַנְּךָ Is 45^{4} *I have called thee by thy name, giving thee a title* (of honour; cf. for construction Dr^{§163}); 3 ms וּבְשֵׁם יִשְׂרָאֵל יְכַנֶּה 44^{5}, *and with the name Israel he titles* (himself), is hardly poss.; abs. *he betitles*, or *makes use of a title*, is unlikely; rd. prob. **Pu.**, v. infr, in bad sense *=give a flattering title:* וְאֶל־אָדָם לֹא אֲכַנֶּה Jb 32^{21} *and unto man I do not give flattering titles* (‖ אַל־נָא אֶשָּׂא פְּנֵי אִישׁ); abs v^{22}. **Pu.** *Impf.* יְכֻנֶּה Is 44^{5} *he is betitled* (v. supr.; so 𝔗 Bi Che Du; ‖ יקרא בשם יעקב, etc)

כַּנָּה ψ 80^{16} v sub כנן p 488.

† כַּנֵּה **n.pr.loc.** appar. in Mesopot., חָרָן וכ׳ וָעֶדֶן Ez 27^{23}, 𝔊 Χαναα; identif dub.; =כַּלְנֵה Thes and most, Co *rds.* כַּלְנֵה; Mez$^{\text{Stadt Ḫarrân 34}}$ prop. בני עֶדֶן.

כְּנָוֹת v. כנת p 490.

כְּנָיָהוּ v. יְהוֹיָכִין p 220, and יכוניה sub כון.

כִּנָּם, כִּנִּם v. IV כן sub II. כנן

I. כנן (√of foll., parallel form of כון; *be firm, substantial*)

† III. כֵּן **n.m.** **base, pedestal, office** (NH כַּנָּה; Aram. כַּנְתָּא, ܟܢܐ)—abs. כ׳ Is 33^{23} 1 K 7^{31} (but v. infr); sf. כַּנּוֹ Ex 30^{18}+11 t; כַּנֶּךָ Gn 40^{13}, כַּנִּי 41^{13},—**1.** lit. *base, pedestal*, 1 K 7^{31} (like) the work of *a pedestal* (Th VB), acc. to Sta$^{\text{ZAW iii, 1883, 161, 162}}$ מַעֲשֵׂה־כֵן is in wrong place, being orig. part of a gloss to v^{33},—כ׳ in v^{29}=*thus*, or is txt err.;—כֵּן־תָּרְנָם Is 33^{23} *the base* (*support* or *socket*) *of their mast* (so Thes and most), esp. of base of laver of tabernacle Ex 30$^{18.28}$ 31^{9} 35^{16} 38^{8} 39^{39} 40^{11} Lv 8^{11} (all P). **2.** *office, place* Gn 40^{13} 41^{13} (both E); hence (late) עַל־כַּנּוֹ *in his place* Dn 11$^{20.21.38}$ (i.e. in his stead, as his successor, cf Germ. *an seiner Stelle*); על om. v^{7}.

† כְּנַנְיָהוּ **n.pr.m.** (י׳ *is firm*),—**1.** a Levite 1 Ch 15^{22} 𝔊 Κωνενια, A Χωνενια, 𝔊L Ιεχονιας; =כְּנַנְיָה v^{27}, 𝔊 Ιεχονιας, A Χενενιας, 𝔊L Χονενιας. **2.** an Izharite 1 Ch 26^{29}, 𝔊 Χωνεν(ε)ια(ς).

† כְּנָנִי **n pr.m.** a Levite Ne 9^{4}, א$^{c.a}$ A Χανανι, 𝔊L Χωνενιας (B om)

כָּנַנְיָהוּ Qr **n.pr.m.** v. כּוֹנַנְיָהוּ sub כון.

II כנן (√of foll.; meaning dubious; v. conj. in Ko$^{\text{ii 1 100 Anm}}$)

† IV. כֵּן (?) כִּנָּם, כִּנִּם **n.**[**m.**], mng. dub.; either **gnat, gnats, gnat-swarm** (so 𝔊 𝔙 Philo$^{\text{Vita Mos. i, p. 97}}$, Origen$^{\text{Hom. 4, 6 in Ex.}}$, and most moderns), or [**louse,**] **lice** (so 𝔖 𝔗 Jos$^{\text{Ant. ii 14. 13}}$ Boch$^{\text{Hieroz II, ii, 572 f}}$, as NH כִּנָּה, pl. כִּנִּים=*maggots*, and esp *lice*)—abs. perh. כֵּן Is 51^{6} (v. infr.); pl. כִּנִּים Ex 8$^{13.14}$ ψ 105^{31}, כנם Ex 8^{12}; Ex 8$^{13.14}$ has, also, כִּנָּם prob a mere Mas. device for כִּנִּם (cf. Di), on account of preceding וַתְּהִי (on which see Ges$^{§145.4}$ Da$^{\text{Synt §116}}$); Sam. has כנים throughout:—of Egyptian plague Ex 8$^{12.13.13.14.14}$ (all P),

hence ψ 105^{31}, כמרכן ימותון Is 51^{6} *like a gnat-swarm* (?) *shall they die* (cf Di Du, Weir Che rd. כנים, cf Buhl$^{p\ 355}$, >Brd De *like this*)

Note — No$^{M\ 74}$ Ba$^{NB\ §\ 15,\ ES\ 63}$ Buhl$^{Ges\ HWB\ ed\ 12}$ connect this word etymol with Aram כלמתא *vermin*, Ba and Buhl also with As *kalmatu*, *id* [Dl$^{HWB\ 333}$], and even with Aram קלמתא, ܩܠܡܬܐ, Ar قَمْلٌ, etc, Eth ቍማል: *louse*, but these connexions, as well as that with NH כִּנִּימָה, all involving radical מ, are most improb

†כַּנָּה ψ 80^{16} **n.f.** (si vera l.) **support** (of tree), i.e. *root, stock* (fem of III כֵּן, cf Syr ܟܢܐ m *id*, Che^{Psalms}, so Ges), al take as vb, but 𝔊 κατάρτισαι is ag gramm (should be כּוֹנְנָה), and √כנן = كَنَّ *protect* (Hu Ri De; rd then כֹּנָּה) is improb Txt. dubious

†[כָּנַס] **vb. gather, collect** (NH *id*, Aram כְּנַס (v also כנש), Eth ከነሰ: in der conj *assemble for worship*, etc, Ar كَنَسَ is *sweep, sweep away, destroy*) — **Qal** (late) *Pf* 1 s כָּנַסְתִּי Ec 2^{8}, *Imv* כְּנוֹס Est 4^{16}, *Inf. cstr* 1 Ch 22^{2} + 3 t, *Pt* כֹּנֵס ψ 33^{7}; — *gather* people 1 Ch 22^{2} Est 4^{16}, כ׳ כַּנֵּד מֵי הַיָּם נֹתֵן באוצרות תהומות ψ 33^{7} (rd. perh, for כַּנֵּד, כַּנֹּאד *as in a wine skin*, v נאד, נד), *gather, collect* portions of harvest for priests and Levites Ne 12^{44}; stones Ec 3^{5} (opp הִשְׁלִיךְ), silver and gold = *amass* wealth Ec 2^{8}, abs v^{26} (‖ אסף) **Pi** *Pf* 1 s וְכִנַּסְתִּי אֶתְכֶם Ez 22^{21} *and I will gather you together* (for punishment, Co tr to v^{20} and rds for וְהִנַּחְתִּי ‖ קִבֵּץ v$^{19.20}$), of restoration וְכִנַּסְתִּים אֶל־אַדְמָתָם 39^{28}, and יְכַנֵּס ψ 147^{2} **Hithp.** *Inf cstr.* וְהַמַּסֵּכָה צָרָה כְּהִתְכַּנֵּס Is 28^{20} *and the covering is (too) narrow when one gathers oneself together* (‖ קָצַר הַמַּצָּע מֵהִשְׂתָּרֵעַ), i.e. the bed is too short to stretch oneself at full length, and when one (perforce) draws up the feet, the covering becomes too narrow.

†[מִכְנָס] **n m** $^{Ez\ 44\ 18}$ only du (or pl) **drawers** (connex with above √כנס obscure, Di der fr כנס = גנז *cover up, hide* (cf Du Is 28^{20}), which Thes also comp) — only cstr מִכְנְסֵי, — a priestly garment of linen מִכְנְסֵי פִשְׁתִּים Ez 44^{18}, מִכְנְסֵי (הַ)בָּד Ex 28^{42} 39^{28} Lv 6^{3} 16^{4} (all P)

†[כָּנַע] **vb. be humble**, only in der conj (Aram כְּנַע *id*, Ar كَنِعَ is *be contracted, wrinkled*, also *fold wings* (of eagle)) — **Niph.** *Pf* 3 ms. נִכְנַע 1 K 21^{29} + 3 t, 3 pl. נִכְנְעוּ 2 Ch 12^{7} 30^{11}, נִכְנָ֑עוּ 2 Ch 12^{7}, *Impf* יִכָּנַע Lv 26^{41} + 3 t; 3 fs וַתִּכָּנַע Ju 3^{30}; 2 ms וַתִּכָּנַע 2 K 22^{19} + 2 t, 3 mpl וְיִכָּנְעוּ 2 Ch 7^{14} + 5 t, יִכָּנֵ֑עוּ 1 Ch 20^{4}, *Inf* הִכָּנַע 2 Ch 33^{23}, sf הִכָּנְעוֹ 2 Ch 12^{12} 33^{19}, — **1.** reflex *humble oneself* Lv 26^{41} (H, subj לְבָבָם), 2 Ch 7^{14} 12$^{6.7.7.12}$ 30^{11} 32^{26} 33$^{19.23}$; *before* some one, לִפְנֵי 2 Ch 34^{27}; מִלְּפָנַי 1 K 21^{29} 2 Ch 33$^{12.23}$ 34^{27} 36^{12}, מִפָּנַי 1 K 21^{29} 2 K 22^{19} **2.** pass *be humbled, subdued* 1 S 7^{13} 1 Ch 20^{4} 2 Ch 13^{18}, sq לִפְנֵי pers Ju 8^{28}, מִפְּנֵי Ju 11^{33}, *under* some one תַּחַת Ju 3^{30} ψ 106^{42}. **Hiph.** *Pf* 3 ms. הִכְנִיעַ 2 Ch 28^{19}, 1 s הִכְנַעְתִּי 1 Ch 17^{10}; *Impf* 3 ms. וַיַּכְנַע Ju 4^{23} ψ 107^{12}, sf יַכְנִיעֵם Dt 9^{3} + 2 t, 2 ms. תַּכְנִיעַ Is 25^{5}; וַתַּכְנַע Ne 9^{24}, 1 s אַכְנִיעַ ψ 81^{15}; *Imv.* הַכְנִיעֵהוּ Jb 40^{12}, — **1.** *humble* 2 Ch 28^{19} Jb 40^{12} ψ 107^{12} (obj לֵב), Is 25^{5} (obj שְׁאוֹן זָרִים) **2** *subdue* enemies 2 S 8^{1} = 1 Ch 18^{1}, 1 Ch 17^{10} ψ 81^{15}, sq לִפְנֵי Dt 9^{3} Ju 4^{23} Ne 9^{24}.

†[כִּנְעָה] **n f. bundle, pack** (cf Ar sense of √, supr), — sf אִסְפִּי מֵאֶרֶץ כִּנְעָתֵךְ Je 10^{17} *pack thy bundle* (and take it) *out of the land*

I כְּנַעַן$_{90}$ **n.pr.m. et terr. Canaan** (𝔊 Χαναάν, Ph. כנען = *Phoenicia*, Χνα = כנע, Hecataeus, v Muller$^{Fr\ Hist.\ Gr\ i\ 17}$ al., Egypt *Ka-n-'-na* WMM$^{Asien\ u\ Europa,\ 205\ ff}$, Tel Amarna *Kinahna*, *Kinahhi*, etc, Bezold$^{BM\ Tablets,\ 150}$ Wkl$^{TA\ 39*}$; etym dub GFM$^{PAOS\ Oct.\ 1890\ lxvii\ ff}$, v. also GASm$^{Geogr\ 4\ f}$ Buhl$^{Geogr\ §\ 42}$), — †**1.** as **n.pr.m.**, son of Ham Gn 9$^{18.22.25.27}$ 10^{15} (as ancestor of Canaanites and Phoenicians; all J); 10^{6} (P); 1 Ch 1$^{8.13}$ (fr Gn 10$^{6.15}$) **2. a.** land, W. of Jordan, into wh Hebrews came, and where they settled, subduing the inhabitants, מַלְכֵי כְנַעַן Ju 5^{19}, מֶלֶךְ כ׳ Ju 4$^{2.23.24.24}$, hence מַמְלְכוֹת כ׳ ψ 135^{11}, יֹשְׁבֵי כ׳ Ex 15^{15} (song in E); cf. מִלְחֲמוֹת כ׳ Ju 3^{1}; עֲצַבֵּי כ׳ ψ 106^{38} *idols of Canaan*, i.e. of the former inhabitants, esp אַרְצָה כ׳, אֶרֶץ(־) כ׳ Gn 44^{8} 46^{31} 47$^{1.4.13.14.15}$ 50$^{5.13}$ (all J), 35^{6} 42$^{5.7.13.29.32}$ 45$^{17.25}$ Jos 24^{3} (all E), Gn 11^{31} 12$^{5.5}$ 13^{12} (opp. עָרֵי הַכִּכָּר vb), 16^{3} 17^{8} (all P) + 40 t. P, Ju 21^{12} 1 Ch 16^{18} = ψ 105^{11}, also הָאָרֶץ כ׳ Nu 34^{2} (P); בְּנוֹת כ׳ Gn 28^{1} *daughters of Canaan* = women of the land, so v$^{6.8}$ 36^{2} (all P), כנען is personif Ho 12^{8} = apostate Israel, שְׂפַת כ׳ Is 19^{18} = the Hebrew lang (without evil implication). **b.** the coast, esp Phoenicia Is 23^{11}, cf. כ׳ אֶרֶץ פְּלִשְׁתִּים Zp 2^{5}.

†II כְּנַעַן **n** [**m.**] **merchant(s)** (because Canaanites, esp. Phoenicians, were traders), — כָּל־עַם כְּנַעַן Zp 1^{11}, אֶרֶץ כ׳ Ez 16^{29} (om 𝔊B al Co), 17^{4} *a land of merchants*, cf כְּנַעֲנִי *ad fin*

†I. כְּנַעֲנִי **adj. et nom. gent.** of I. כְּנַעַן, —usu. ms. (הַ)כְּנַעֲנִי Gn 38[2] Nu 21[1] +, fs. הַכְּנַעֲנִית Gn 46[10] = Ex 6[15] 1 Ch 2[3]; mpl (הַ)כְּנַעֲנִים Ob [20] Ne 9[24]; —**1. adj.** אִישׁ כ׳ Gn 38[2] (J). **2.** c. art. as **subst., a.** of individual, הַכ׳ מֶלֶךְ־עֲרָד Nu 21[1] (J) and hence 33[40] (P or R), f. בַּת־שׁוּעַ הַכְּנַעֲנִית Gn 46[10] = Ex 6[15] (P) הַכְּנַעֲנִית 1 Ch 2[3] **b.** usu. coll. (c. art.) of pre-Isr. inhabitants of כְּנַעַן (q. v.) Gn 12[6] 24[3.37] 50[11] (all J), Nu 21[3] (J), Jos 13[3] (D), Ju 1[1.3.9.10.17], many of whom continued to live in the midst of Isr., v[27.28.29.29.30.32.33] Jos 16[10.10] 17[12.13.16.18] (all JE), 1 K 9[16]; pl. only Ob[20], and יֹשְׁבֵי הָאָרֶץ הַכְּנַעֲנִים Ne 9[24]; מִשְׁפְּחוֹת הַכ׳ Gn 10[18], גְּבוּל הַכ׳ v[19] (both J), אֶרֶץ הַכ׳ Ex 13[11] (JE), Ez 16[3], oft. of *part* of the inhabit., הַכ׳ וְכֹל יֹשְׁבֵי הָאָרֶץ Jos 7[9] (JE), Dt 11[30]; with other n pr gent, + הַפְּרִזִּי Gn 13[7] 34[30] (both J), Ju 1[4.5], + הָאֱמֹרִי Dt 1[7] Jos 5[1] 13[4] (all D); + הַחִוִּי 2 S 24[7]; + (ה)עֲמָלֵק Nu 14[25.43.45]; esp. in the list of peoples dispossessed by Isr., Gn 15[21] Ex 3[8.17] 13[5] 23[23.28] 33[2] 34[11] Nu 13[29] (הַכ׳ dwelling by the sea and along Jordan [cf. Dt 1[7] 11[30] Jos 5[1] 11[3] 13[4]]; all these JE), Dt 7[1] 20[17] Jos 3[10] 9[1] 11[3] 12[8] 24[11] (all JED), Ju 3[3.5], hence Ezr 9[1] Ne 9[8]. Cf. Dr [Dt. p. 11, 13f, 97, 133].

†II. כְּנַעֲנִי **n.m. trader, merchant** (cf. II כְּנַעַן); only sg. (but v. infr.)—וְלֹא יִהְיֶה כ׳ עוֹד בְּבֵית י׳ Zc 14[21] (prob.); חֲגוֹר נָתְנָה לַכ׳ Pr 31[24] (‖ סָדִין עָשְׂתָה וַתִּמְכֹּר) In Zc 11[7.11] rd perh. (לְ)כְנַעֲנִיֵּי for (לָ)כֵן עֲנִיֵּי, 𝔊 Χαναναῖοι, Χαναανῖτιν, Sta [ZAW. 1881, 26] (who comp. as to sense Ho 12[8]), cf. Klo We Marti.

†כְּנַעֲנָה **n.pr.m.** **1.** father of proph Zedekiah 1 K 22[11.24] = 2 Ch 18[10.23] (𝔊 Χαναav, Χaava, Χavava) **2.** a Benjamite 1 Ch 7[10] (𝔊 Χavaav, Χavavav)

כנף √ of foll. (mng. dub.; Ar كَنَفَ *fence in, enclose*, and Aram. כְּנַף *collect, assemble*, are denom.)

כָּנָף [109] **n.f.** [1 K 6, 27] (**m.** Ez 7[2] Kt, but cf. Qr and Co; also appar. 2 Ch 3[11.13], but v. Be), **wing, extremity** (NH *id.*; Aram. כַּנְפָּא, ܟܢܦܐ; Zinj. אחז בכנף מראה, fig. for *attached himself to the party of his lord*, Panammu [Inscr 1 11], cf. Zc 8[23] (**2 a** infr); DHM [Sendsch 58]; Ar. كَنَفٌ, As. *kappu*, Eth. ክንፍ);—abs. כ׳ Gn 1[21] +, cstr כְּנַף 1 K 6[24] +; sf. כְּנָפִי Ez 16[8], כְּנָפֶךָ Ru 3[9], כְּנָפוֹ Hg 2[12]; du. כְּנָפַיִם 1 K 8[7] + (even of more than two, Is 6[2.2] Ez 1[6.21]); cstr. כַּנְפֵי Ex 19[4]; sf. כְּנָפֶיךָ Ez 5[3], כְּנָפַיִךְ Je 2[34], כְּנָפָיו Is 8[8] +; כְּנָפֶיהָ Ho 4[19] Mal 3[20]; כַּנְפֵיהֶם 1 K 6[27] +; כַּנְפֵיהֶן Ez 1[24.25]; pl cstr. כַּנְפוֹת Dt 22[12] + 4 t; —**1.** *wing*, †**a.** of birds Is 10[14] (in fig.), Ex 19[4] (E? R? fig) Dt 32[11] (in sim.), Zc 5[9] Lv 1[17] (P), Jb 39[13.26] ψ 68[14], in fig. of invading king Je 48[40] 49[22] Ez 17[3.7]; so appar. Is 8[8] of invader as overflowing river (but Du Che separate וְהָיָה מֻטּוֹת כְּנָפָיו from preceding), of riches, as flying away Pr 23[5], in phr צִפּוֹר כָּנָף = *winged birds* Dt 4[17] ψ 148[10], (עַיִט)צִפּוֹר כָּל־כ׳ Ez 39[4.17], כֹּל צִפּוֹר כָּל־כ׳ Gn 7[14] (P), Ez 17[23], עוֹף כ׳ Gn 1[21] (P), ψ 78[27]; also בַּעַל כ׳ Pr 1[17] = *winged thing*, cf. בַּעַל־הַכְּנָפַיִם Ec 10[20]. †**b.** of insects (prob.), אֶרֶץ צִלְצַל כְּנָפָיִם Is 18[1] *buzzing*, or *humming of wings*, i. e. Ethiopia, so called from its swarms of flies, with especial ref. poss. to the tsetse-fly (so Du, cf. Che; id., in gen., Hi De, > Kn Di of the tropical *shadow falling both ways*, Thes [1167 b] of *noise of the wings* of an army; ref. to sails as wings—cf. v[2]—would be suitable, but צלצל does not favour this). **c.** of cherubim 1 K 6[24.24.24.24] + 8 t. K, cf. 2 Ch 3[11.11.11.11] + 6 t. Ch, Ez 1[6] + 17 t. Ez, Ex 25[20.20] 39[9.9] (all P) †**d.** of seraphim Is 6[2.2]. †**e.** of women in Zec.'s vision Zc 5[9.9] †**f.** fig. of the wind, Ho 4[19] ψ 18[11] = 2 S 22[11], ψ 104[3]. †**g.** fig. of the dawn (winged sun-disc?) ψ 139[9], cf. of sun of righteousness Mal 3[20] †**h.** fig. of י׳, as protector of his people ψ 17[8] 36[8] 57[2] 61[5] 63[8] 91[4] Ru 2[12]. †**2.** *extremity.*—**a.** of garment = *skirt, corner*, or loose flowing end, 1 S 15[27] 24[5.6.12.12] Dt 22[12] 23[1] 27[20] Je 2[34] (fig.), Ez 5[3] 16[8] (in fig.), Hg 2[12.12] Zc 8[23] Nu 15[38.38] (P; cf. RS [Sem. 1 416, 2nd ed 437]) **b.** of the earth, מִכְּנַף הָאָרֶץ Is 24[16] *from the end of the earth;* elsewhere pl. כַּנְפוֹת הָא׳ Jb 37[3] 38[13], and, def. אַרְבַּע כ׳ הָא׳ Is 11[12] *the four corners of the earth;* so of the holy land Ez 7[2].—עַל־כְּנַף שִׁקּוּצִים מְשֹׁמֵם Dn 9[27] is obscure; Meinh. reads, after Vrss, כָּנָף, *on the corner* (of the altar) *is a devastating abomination*, < Kue [Onderzoek 2, II. 472] Bev, who rd עַל־כַּנּוֹ *in its place, instead of it.*

† [כָּנַף] **vb. denom.** fr. כָּנָף **2.** only **Niph. be cornered, thrust into a corner, or aside;**— *Impf.* 3 ms וְלֹא יִכָּנֵף עוֹד מוֹרֶיךָ Is 30[20] *and no more shall thy teachers be thrust into a corner* (cf. Di), > others, who render *hide themselves*, (cf. Ar. كَنَفَ *enclose, guard*, but this rather for protection).

כנר (poss. √ of foll.; meaning unknown)

†כִּנּוֹר **n.m.** $^{81.3}$ **lyre** (on formation cf. Lag$^{BN\ 89,\ Anm}$; NH *id*, Aram כִּנָּרָא, ܟܢܪܐ, Mand (א)כינאר No$^{M\ §\ 104}$ (who questions Shemitic origin), Ar كَنَّارَةٌ, كِنَّارٌ; as loan-word in Hellen. Gk. κινύρα (𝔊 and Joseph); in Egypt. *kn-an-aul* acc to Bondi^{79})—abs כ׳ Gn 4^{21}+; sf כִּנֹּרִי Jb 30^{31}, pl. כִּנֹּרוֹת 1 K 10^{12}+, sf כִּנּוֹרֶיךָ Ez 26^{13}, כִּנֹּרוֹתֵינוּ ψ 137^{2},—*lyre*, stringed instrument used for popular as well as sacred music (cf Benz$^{Arch\ 273\ ff}$ Now$^{Arch.\ i.\ 273\ ff}$),—כ׳ איש ידע מְנַגֵּן בַּכ׳ Gn 4^{21}, בתף ובכ׳ 31^{27}; ועוּגָב 1 S 16^{16} *a man skilled in playing on the lyre*, cf v^{23} (ונגן בידו); at banquets Is 5^{12} (+ נֵבֶל, תֹּף, חָלִיל), token of merriment 24^{8} (+ תֻּפִּים), Ez 26^{13}, cf. וַיְהִי לְאֵבֶל כִּנֹּרִי וְעֻגָבִי לְקוֹל בֹּכִים Jb 30^{31}, יִשְׂאוּ כְּתֹף וכ׳ וְיִשְׂמְחוּ לְקוֹל עוּגָב Jb 21^{12}, carried by a loose woman Is 23^{16} (fig. of Tyre), in sim. Is 16^{11} (of murmuring sound of bowels = heart, in pity), used also in praising י׳, usu. as accompaniment of song (cf 1 Ch 15^{16}) נֵבֶל ותף וְחָלִיל וכ׳ 1 S 10^{5}, Is 30^{32} (‖ תֻּפִּים), esp before the ark 2 S 6^{5} (+ תֻּפִּים, נְבָלִים, etc) ‖ 1 Ch 13^{8}, and in sanctuary (usu + נֵבֶל, etc) 1 K 10^{12}, but esp Chr ψψ—1 Ch 13^{8} (pl, and so chiefly in Chr), $15^{16.21.28}$ 16^{5} $25^{1.3.6}$ 2 Ch 5^{12} 9^{11} 20^{28} 29^{25} Ne 12^{27}, ψ 33^{2} (sg, and so chiefly in ψψ), 43^{4} 49^{5} 57^{9} 71^{22} 81^{3} 92^{4} $98^{5.5}$ 108^{3} 147^{7} 149^{3} 150^{3}; cf כִּנּוֹרוֹתֵינוּ ψ 137^{2}—Vbs used with כ׳ are—תָּפַשׂ Gn 4^{21}, נִגֵּן בְּ 1 S 16^{16}, מְשַׂחֵק בְּ 2 S 6^{5} = 1 Ch 13^{8}, מְשַׁמְּעִים בְּ 1 Ch 15^{16}, מְשֹׁרְרִים בְּ v^{28}, נִבָּא בְּ $25^{1.3}$, הוֹדָה בְּ ψ 33^{2} 43^{4}, זִמֵּר בְּ ψ 71^{22} 98^{5} 147^{7} 149^{3}, הַלְלוּהוּ בְּ 150^{3}—On ancient lyres v reff ap Dr$^{Amos,\ p\ 236\ f}$

†כִּנֶּרֶת, כִּנְּרוֹת **n.pr.loc.** in Galilee (Naphtali), כִּנֶּרֶת Dt 3^{17} Jos 13^{27} Nu 34^{11}; כִּנֶּרֶת Jos 19^{35}, כִּנְּרוֹת (so Baer, כִּנְרוֹת Norzi) Jos 11^{2} 12^{3} 1 K 15^{20},—**1.** a city Jos 19^{35} (P; 𝔊B Κενερεθ, A Χενεροθ, 𝔊L Χενερεθ, as always exc. Jos 13^{27}), so prob 11^{2} (D ?; B Κενερωθ, A Χενερεθθι), Dt 3^{17} (B Μαχαναρεθ,—Μαχ- = מִכּ׳) **2.** יָם־כִּנֶּרֶת, lake near the city, Nu 34^{11} (P; 𝔊B Χεναρα, A Χενερεθ), Jos 13^{27} (P; 𝔊B Χενερεθ; A𝔊L Χενερωθ), יָם כִּנְּרוֹת Jos 12^{3} (D, 𝔊B Χενερεθ; A Χεννερεθ), כָּל־כִּנְּרוֹת 1 K 15^{20} = all the territory about the city and lake, cf. πᾶσαν τὴν γῆν Χενερεθ 𝔊L,—𝔗 has גְּנֵּסַר, גְּנֵיסַר, גִּינֵסַר, cf. τὸ ὕδωρ τοῦ Γεννησαρ 1 Makk 11^{67}, Γεννησαρετ Mk 6^{53} Mt 14^{34} Lu 5^{1}, etymol connexion with כִּנֶּרֶת disputed by GASm$^{Geogr\ 443\ n}$ Buhl$^{Geogr\ 113\ n}$—On the lake and surrounding region v. GASm$^{Geogr\ ch.\ xxi}$, Ld$^{Pal\ 254}$ Buhl$^{Geogr\ 113\ f.\ 225}$ Furrer $^{ZPV\ 1879\ (ii.),\ 52-74}$ Frei $^{ib\ 1886\ (ix.),\ 81-145}$ van Kasteren $^{ib\ 1888\ (xi.),\ 212-248}$.

†[כְּנָת] **n.** [of men, but **f** in form, Ges$^{§\ 122.4\ b}$] **associate, colleague** (loan-wd fr. BAram כְּנָת; Syr ܟܢܬܐ, cf also Schwally$^{Idiot\ 46}$; on format v. Lag$^{BN\ 82}$);—only Aram. pl שְׁאָר כְּנָוָתוֹ Ezr 4^{7} *the rest of his associates*

כֵּס Ex 17^{16}, v. כסא.

†כֶּסֶא Pr 7^{20}, כֶּסֶה ψ 81^{4} **n.[m.] full moon** (cf. Aram ܟܣܐ, orig dubious, cf Lag$^{Symm\ i.\ 93}$, perh As loan-word, cf. As. *kusêu, headdress* or *cap*, = *agû*, *id*, and also *full moon* (as tiara of moon-god ?), Dl^{HWB}, sub *kusêu, kubšu, agû;* yet v. Brock)—לְיוֹם הַכ׳ Pr 7^{20}; as a feast-day, בַּכ׳ ψ 81^{4} (opp. בַּחֹדֶשׁ, *at the new moon*).

כִּסֵּא, כִּסֵּה $_{133}$ **n.m.** $^{287.16}$ **seat** of honour, throne (NH *id.;* Ph. (pl.) כרסים, Aram. כּוּרְסְיָא, ܟܘܪܣܝܐ, BAram כָּרְסֵא, Zinj כרסא DHM$^{Sendsch\ 58.\ 44}$, Ar كُرْسِيٌّ; but As. *kussu;* perh Akkad loan-word, ideogr. *is* GU. ZA, cf Dl$^{HWB\ 343}$),—abs כִּסֵּא Gn 41^{40}+, כִּסֵּה 1 K $10^{19.19}$ Jb 26^{9}, הַכִּסֵּא Ez 1^{26}, cstr. כִּסֵּא 2 S 3^{10}+, כֵּס Ex 17^{16} (si vera l, v infr); sf כִּסְאִי 1 K 1^{13}+, כִּסְאֲךָ 2 S 7^{16}+, כִּסְאוֹ 1 K 5^{19}+, כִּסְאוֹ Ex 11^{5}+; pl כִּסְאוֹת ψ $122^{5.5}$; sf. כִּסְאוֹתָם Ez 26^{16} Is 14^{9};—*seat of honour*, usually **1. a.** of king = *throne* Gn 41^{40} (E), Ex 11^{5} 12^{29} (both J) 1 K 2^{19} Is 47^{1} Ez 26^{16}; of queen-mother 1 K $2^{19\,b}$; כ׳ מַלְכוּתוֹ Est 5^{1} *his royal throne;* of future (Messianic) prince Zc $6^{13\,a}$ (in v^{b} read עַל־יְמִינוֹ 𝔊 Sta$^{ZAW\ 1881,\ 10}$), of dead kings in She'ôl Is 14^{9}; נָתַן כ׳, in, or against a place, said of king himself, (only Je) is a sign of conquest (Je 1^{15}); so שִׂים כ׳ 43^{10}, and (of י׳) 49^{38}; in Ju 3^{20}, though of king, not seat of office, 12 t. elsewhere, lit. †**b.** *throne* of י׳ (אלהים) as heavenly king, Is 6^{1} Ez $1^{26.26}$ 10^{1} 1 K 22^{19} = 2 Ch 18^{18}; Jb 26^{9} ψ 11^{4} Is 66^{1} *heaven is my throne;* as seat of judgment ψ $9^{5.8}$; in oath יָד עַל־כֵּס יָהּ Ex 17^{16} (cf. Di; > Cler JDMich Ges Buhl SS נֵס *banner*, 𝔊 κρυφαίᾳ √ כסה, favours כֵּס); Jerusalem called throne of י׳ Je 3^{17}, so the sanctuary 17^{12} (כ׳ כָּבוֹד מָרוֹם), Ez 43^{7}. †**2.** of high priest 1 S 1^{9} $4^{13.18}$; of honoured guest 2 K 4^{10}; of governor Ne 3^{7}, of (unjust) judge כ׳ הַוּוֹת ψ 94^{20}; = conspicuous seat (lit.) Pr 9^{14}, = seat of distinction, explicitly כ׳ כָּבוֹד Is 22^{23}, כ׳ alone 2 K $25^{28.28}$ = Je $52^{32.32}$ Est 3^{1}.

3. a. fig. = *royal dignity, authority, power,* לְדָוִד וּלְזַרְעוֹ וּלְבֵיתוֹ וּלְכִ׳ 2 S 14^{9}; הַמֶּלֶךְ וְכִסְאוֹ נָקִי 1 K 2^{33}; esp. *kingdom,* c. vbs. of *setting up, establishing,* י׳ subj., הָקִים כ׳ דָּוִד 2 S 3^{10}, וּבָנִיתִי לְדֹר־וָדוֹר כִּסְאֲךָ ψ 89^{5}, so c. שִׂים v^{30}; king subj., סָעַד בַּחֶסֶד כִּסְאוֹ Pr 20^{28}; pass. כ׳ דָּוִד יִהְיֶה נכון 1 K 2^{45} *the throne of David shall be established,* cf. 2 S 7^{16} = 1 Ch 17^{14}; וְהוּכַן בַּחֶסֶד כ׳ Is 16^{5} (of Mess. reign); so (in gen.) בִּצְדָקָה יִכּוֹן כ׳ Pr 16^{12}, cf. 25^{5} 29^{14}; intrans. (c. הָיָה) ψ 89^{37}; more fully, י׳ subj., וְכֹנַנְתִּי אֶת־כ׳ מַמְלַכְתּוֹ 2 S 7^{13} (כֹּנַן כסאו in ‖ 1 Ch 17^{12}), וַהֲקִמֹתִי אֶת־כ׳ מַמְלַכְתְּךָ עַל־יִשְׂרָאֵל 1 K 9^{5}, cf. ‖ 2 Ch 7^{18} and וַהֲכִינוֹתִי כ׳ מַלְכוּתוֹ עַל־יִשְׂרָאֵל 1 Ch 22^{10}; also מגר כ׳ ψ 89^{45} *cast down throne,* of Gentile nations וְהָפַכְתִּי כ׳ מַמְלָכוֹת Hg 2^{22}; יָשַׁב עַל־כ׳ *sit on the throne of* any one (esp. David) = be his successor 1 K 1$^{13.17.20.24.27.30.35.48}$ 2^{12} 3^{6} 2 K 13^{13}, esp. Je 13^{13} 17^{25} 22^{2} + 5 t. Je; יֵשְׁבוּ לְכִ׳ לָךְ ψ 132^{12}; more fully 1 Ch 29^{23}; †caus. הוֹשִׁיב עַל־כ׳ 1 K 2^{24} 5^{19} 2 K 10^{3}; הוֹשִׁיב לַכּ׳ fig. Jb 36^{7}, of placing in honour; מִפְּרִי בִטְנְךָ אָשִׁית לְכִ׳ לָךְ ψ 132^{11}; + ישב עַל־כ׳ also = *take one's seat as king, become actual king, possess royalty* 1 K 16^{11}, oft. sit on the *throne of Isr.* 1 K 8$^{20.25}$ = 2 Ch 6$^{10.16}$, 1 K 10^{9} 2 K 10^{30} 15^{12}, Je 33^{17}; without ישב 1 K 2^{4} 9^{5}, cf. also Is 9^{6} (Mess.); ישב על־כסא מַמְלַכְתּוֹ לְשִׁבְתּוֹ Dt 17^{18}, על־כסא הַמְּלוּכָה 1 K 1^{46}, and even ישב עַל־כִּסֵּא מַלְכוּת י׳ עַל־יִשְׂרָאֵל 1 Ch 28^{5}; also עַל־כ׳ הַמְּלָכִים 2 K 11^{19}, ‖ כ׳ הַמַּמְלָכָה 2 Ch 23^{20}; of (royal) throne as judgment seat Pr 20^{8}, cf. also ψ 122^{5}; set one upon the throne of Isr. נתן פ׳ על־כ׳ יש׳ 1 K 10^{9} cf. ‖ 2 Ch 9^{8}; in compar. sentence יְגַדֵּל אֶת־כִּסְאוֹ מִכּ׳, i.e. make him a more powerful king than, 1 K 1^{37}, cf. v^{47}; of king of Babylon, מִמַּעַל לְכוֹכְבֵי־אֵל אָרִים כִּסְאִי Is 14^{13}. In ψ 45^{7} כִּסְאֲךָ אלהים וגו׳ the text is prob. corrupt: AE Hi Ew Bae read *thy throne is (a throne) of God;* Bi Che insert נכונה יסודתו הקימו *thy throne [its foundation is firmly fixed],* God [has established it]; v. further Dr$^{§ 194, Obs.}$. †**b.** throne of י׳ (אלהים) = his royal dignity, sovereignty, La 5^{19} ψ 93^{2} 103^{19} (הֵכִין כ׳ ‖ מַלְכוּת); כ׳ כְּבוֹדֶךָ Je 14^{21}; יָשַׁב עַל־כ׳ קָדְשׁוֹ ψ 47^{9}; צֶדֶק וּמִשְׁפָּט מְכוֹן כִּסְאֶךָ ψ 89^{15} cf. 97^{2}.

†I. [כָּסָה] **vb.** cover (NH כִּסָּה Pi; Aram. כַּסָּא chiefly Pa; ܟܰܣܺܝ Pa. *hide, cover;* ܟܣܳܝܳܐ *covering,* ܐܶܣܛܠܳܐ *garment;* Ar. كَسَا (كسو) *clothe,* كِسَاءٌ *garment;* As. *kusû,* cover; *kusîtu,* garment Dl$^{HWB 342}$)—**Qal,** only *Pt. act.* כֹּסֶה;—**1.** *conceal* shame Pr 12^{16}; knowledge Pr 12^{23}. **2.** *pass.* (cstr.) כְּסוּי חֲטָאָה ψ 32^{1} *covered* in respect of sin (by God, which he thus puts out of sight) (‖ נְשׂוּי־פֶּשַׁע). **Niph.** *Pf.* 3 fs. נִכְסָתָה, *covered,* with waves Je 51^{42}; *Inf. cstr.* הִכָּסוֹת Ez 24^{8}, (blood) not to be covered. **Pi.** *Pf.* 3 ms. כִּסָּה Nu 9^{15} + 12 t.; sf. כִּסָּהוּ Lv 17^{13} Nu 17^{7}; כִּסָּמוֹ Ex 15^{10}; 3 fs. כִּסָּתָה Gn 38^{15} + 5 t.; 1 s. כִּסִּיתִי ψ 32^{5} + 3 t.; כִּסֵּתִי Ez 31^{15} (del. Co); כִּסֵּיתִי Ez 32^{7} + 13 t. Pf.; *Impf.* 3 ms. יְכַסֶּה Is 6^{2} + 8 t.; וַיְכַס Ex 10^{15} + 4 t.; sf. יְכַסֶּךָּ Hab 2^{17}; יְכַסֶּנָּה Ez 30^{18}; 3 mpl. sf. יְכַסְיֻמוּ Ex 15^{5} + 41 t. Impf.; *Imv.* sf. כַּסּוּנוּ Ho 10^{8}; *Inf. cstr.* כַּסּוֹת Mal 2^{13} + 11 t.; כַּסֹּת Nu 4^{15}; sf. כַּסֹּתוֹ Ex 26^{13}; *Pt.* מְכַסֶּה Pr 10^{18} + 12 t.; pl. מְכַסִּים Is 11^{9}; fpl. מְכַסּוֹת Ez 1$^{11.23.23}$;—**1.** *cover, clothe* Ju 4^{19} Ez 16^{10} (2 acc.), v^{18}; Jon 3^{6} is appar. reflex., c. acc. of garment (strange; rd. perh. וַיִּכַּס); nakedness Gn 9^{23} (J), Ex 28^{42} (P), Ez 16^{8} Ho 2^{11}; the naked Is 58^{7} Ez 18$^{7.16}$ (+ acc. rei); the face and legs of seraphim Is 6$^{2.2}$; bodies of cherubim Ez 1$^{11.23.23}$; the face Gn 38^{15} (J), Ez 12$^{6.12}$, fig. Jb 23^{17}; earth with the great deep ψ 104^{6}; heavens with glory Hab 3^{3}; with בְּ of the clothing Gn 38^{14} (J), Dt 22^{12}, these two appar. reflex., cf. Jon 3^{6} supr.; Ju 4^{18} 1 K 1^{1}; heaven with clouds ψ 147^{8}, with glory Ez 32^{7}. **2.** *cover, conceal* blood Gn 37^{26} (J), Jb 16^{18}; human ordure Dt 23^{14}; mts. conceal men from God Ho 10^{8}; *cover* transgressions Jb 31^{33} Pr 17^{9} 28^{13}; iniquity ψ 32^{5}; righteousness ψ 40^{11}; hatred Pr 10^{18}; a thing Pr 11^{13}; face of judge so that he cannot see justice Jb 9^{24}; rulers and seers Is 29^{10}; with בְּ of covering Lv 17^{13} (H), 1 S 19^{13}; face by fat Jb 15^{27}; sun by a cloud Ez 32^{7}; with מִן from whom Gn 18^{17} (J), Jb 33^{17}. **3.** *cover* (with covering of protection), a pit Ex 21^{33} (Covt. code); with cloud of incense, the Kapporeth Lv 16^{13} (P); coverings of the sacred tent, tabernacle, and their furniture Ex 26^{13} Nu 4$^{9.15}$ (P); with בְּ of the covering Nu 4$^{5.8.11.12}$ (P); Zion בְּצֵל יָדִי Is 51^{16}. **4.** *cover, spread over,* fat, the inwards Ex 29$^{13.22}$ Lv 3$^{3.9.14}$ 4^{8} (with עַל), 7^{3} (P); leprosy, the skin and flesh Lv 13$^{12.13}$ (P); the cloud of the theophany, the mount Ex 24$^{15.16}$ (P), the tent of meeting Ex 40^{34} Nu 17^{7} (P), and the tabernacle Nu 9$^{15.16}$ (P); altar with tears Mal 2^{13} (2 acc.); Jerusalem with multitude of camels Is 60^{6}; of handiwork 1 K 7$^{18.41.42}$ = 2 Ch 4$^{12.13}$. **5.** *cover, overwhelm,* sq. accus., the sea the Egyptians Ex 14^{28} (P), 15$^{5.10}$ (song), Jos 24^{7} (E), ψ 78^{53} 106^{11}; waters Jb 22^{11} 38^{34} ψ 104^{9} Je 46^{8} Ez 26^{19}; locusts the eye of the land Ex

$10^{5.15}$ (J), also Israel Nu $22^{5.11}$ (J); frogs the land Ex 8^{2} (P), quails the camp Ex 16^{13} (P), cloud the land Ez 30^{18} $38^{9.16}$, darkness the earth Is 60^{2}, dust a city Ez 26^{10}, the depths of the sea by God Jb 36^{30}, with a reference to a person's shame ψ 44^{16} 69^{8} Je 51^{51} Ob ^{10} Mi 7^{10}, horror ψ 55^{6} Ez 7^{18}, violence Pr $10^{6.11}$ Hb 2^{17}, confusion Je 3^{25}, mischief ψ 140^{10}, God *covers sin* ψ 85^{3} (‖ נשא עון), cf. 32^{1} (Qal) **6.** sq על of person or thing covered, *cover over*. cherubim over the ark 2 Ch 5^{8}; over the dead, the earth Nu 16^{33} (JE), ψ 106^{17} Is 26^{21}, worms Jb 21^{26}; dust over blood Ez 24^{7}, waters over the sea Hb 2^{14}, cf. לַיָּם Is 11^{9}, (v. Dr $^{§135.7\,Obs}$), love covereth over all sins Pr 10^{12}, God covereth over iniquity Ne 3^{37}, people not to cover over a guilty person Dt 13^{9}, + acc. of obj covering (Da $^{Synt.\,§75}$), fig covering over the garment with violence Mal 2^{16}, God's hands with light Jb 36^{32}, + ב of covering ψ 44^{20}.

Note—כסתי (אֵלֶיךָ) ψ 143^{9} is error for חָסִיתִי acc to 𝔊 *κατέφυγον* SS, but חסה not cstr with אֶל־, חכיתי Bae; האבלתי כסתי עָלָיו אֶת־תהום Ez 31^{15} acc to Co *I caused the deep to mourn for them* (del כסתי) **Pual.** *Pf* 3 mpl כֻּסּוּ ψ 80^{11} Pr 24^{31}, *Impf* יְכֻסֶּה Ec 6^{4}, *pl.* וַיְכֻסּוּ Gn $7^{19.20}$, *Pt* pl מְכֻסִּים 1 Ch 21^{16}, fpl מְכֻסּוֹת Ez 41^{16}. **1.** sq accus *be covered*, hills with shadow ψ 80^{11}, mountains with water Gn $7^{19.20}$ (P), field with nettles Pr 24^{31}, abs, windows of temple Ez 41^{16} **2.** sq ב, *be clothed*, with sackcloth 1 Ch 21^{16}, name with darkness Ec 6^{4}.

Hithp. *Impf* וַיִּתְכַּס Is 37^{1} = 2 K 19^{1}, 3 fs. תִּתְכַּסֶּה Pr 26^{26}; וַתִּתְכָּס Gn 24^{65}, pl יִתְכַּסּוּ Is 59^{6} Jon 3^{8}, *Pt* מִתְכַּסֶּה 1 K 11^{29}, pl מִתְכַּסִּים Is 37^{2} = 2 K 19^{2},—*cover, clothe oneself*, abs (of veil) Gn 24^{65} (J), with ב, of new garment 1 K 11^{29}, sackcloth 2 K $19^{1.2}$ = Is $37^{1.2}$, fig of works Is 59^{6}, of hatred with guile Pr 26^{26}, with acc Jon 3^{8} (שַׂקִּים)

†[כָּסוּי] **n.**[m] covering, only cstr כְּסוּי עוֹר *covering of skins* Nu $4^{6.14}$ (P)

• †כְּסוּת **n.f.** covering—כ׳ Gn 20^{16} + 3 t, sf כְּסוּתְךָ Dt 22^{12} + 3 t sfs,—**1.** *covering, clothing* Ex 21^{10} 22^{26} (Cov t code), Dt 22^{12} Jb 24^{7} 31^{19}, of שַׂק as clothing of heavens Is 50^{3} in fig **2.** *covering* for concealment, of Abaddon, the subterranean abode of the dead Jb 26^{6}; כ׳ עֵינַיִם, *covering of the eyes* Gn 20^{16} (so that they cannot see the wrong, fig of a present offered in compensation for it, E)

†מִכְסֶה **n.**[m.] covering,—מ׳ Ex 26^{14} 36^{19}; cstr. מִכְסֵה Gn 8^{13} + 10 t, sf. מִכְסֵהוּ Ex 35^{11} + 2 t,—**1.** *covering* of the ark, deck-roof (𝔊 *στέγη*) Gn 8^{13} (J) **2.** of the skins of the tent of meeting Ex $26^{14.14}$ 35^{11} $36^{19.19}$ $39^{34.34}$ 40^{19} Nu 3^{25} $4^{8.10.11.12.25.25}$ (all P)

†מְכַסֶּה **n m.** $^{Is\,23,18}$ covering,—מ׳ Lv 9^{19} Is 23^{18}, sf. מְכַסֵּךְ Ez 27^{7}; pl sf מְכַסֶּיךָ Is 14^{11}, of fat covering (the inwards) Lv 9^{19}; worms, covering the dead Is 14^{11}, deck of a ship Ez 27^{7} (Co *Kajutenwand*); garment Is 23^{18}.

II כסה (√of foll; prob *bind*, cf As *kasû, take captive*, **Pi.** *fetter, kasîtu, kisittu, a fetter*, Zehnpfund $^{BAS\,i\,536}$ Dl $^{Baer's\,Ezech\,xii,\,HWB\,342}$)

†[כֶּסֶת] **n.f.** band, fillet (= charm or amulet acc. to Ephr Syr, *φυλακτήρια* acc to ὁ Ἑβραῖος of Hexapl, cf RS $^{JPh\,xiii,\,286}$, in NH כסת usu = *cushion, bolster, pillow*), only pl. מְתַפְּרוֹת כְּסָתוֹת עַל־ Ez 13^{18} women *sewing bands upon* elbows; c sf 2 fpl כִּסְּתוֹתֵיכֶנָה v^{20}.

כֶּסֶה v כֶּסֶא

כסה v. כסא

כְּסוּחָה Is 5^{25} v סוּחָה.

כְּסוּי, כְּסוּת v sub I. כסה

†[כָּסַח] **vb.** cut off or away, a plant (NH *id*, Aram כְּסַח, ܟܣܚ (for Heb זָמַר); Ar. كَسَحَ *sweep off, away, destroy, do away with*, cf. Sab כסח *overpower, conquer*, Hom $^{ZMG\,1892,\,532}$)—only **Qal** *Pt pass*, fs כְּסוּחָה ψ 80^{17}, *cut away*, of Isr under fig of vine, mpl. קוֹצִים כְּסוּחִים Is 33^{12} *thorns cut away*, fig. of peoples destroyed by divine judgment

†[כָּסַל] **vb** be or become stupid (NH Aram in deriv, Ar كَسِلَ *be sluggish*, so N Syr. in deriv; orig mng possibly *thick, plump, fat*; hence in good sense כִּסְלָה, כֶּסֶל, כְּסָלִים *loins, confidence*; in bad sense: כְּסִילוּת, כִּסְלָה, כֶּסֶל, כְּסִיל *stupidity, folly*, כסיל *stupid fellow*)—**Qal** *Impf* יִכְסָלוּ *they become stupid* Je 10^{8} (‖ יִבְעֲרוּ *they become brutish*)

†כֶּסֶל **n.m.** **1.** loins, **2.** stupidity, **3.** confidence (NH *id* loin, Aram. כִּסְלָא *id*);—**1.** *loins* כֶּסֶל Jb 15^{27}, pl. כְּסָלִים Lv $3^{4.10.15}$ 4^{9} 7^{4}, sf. כְּסָלַי ψ 38^{8}. **2.** *stupidity, folly* כ׳ Ec 7^{25} (‖ סכלות), כסל ψ 49^{14}. **3.** *confidence*, sf כִּסְלִי Jb 31^{24}; כִּסְלֶךָ Pr 3^{26}; כִּסְלוֹ Jb 8^{14}, כִּסְלָם ψ 78^{7}

† כִּסְלָה **n.f.** (Gie [ZAW i. 1881. 304]). **1. stupidity** ψ 85⁹ (but rd. לְכִסְלָה ⁶ Bae Che). **2. confidence**, sf. כִּסְלָתֶךָ Jb 4⁶.

I. כְּסִיל 70 **n.m. stupid fellow, dullard, fool**;—כ׳ ψ 49¹¹ + 44 t.; pl. כְּסִילִים ψ 94⁸ + 25 t.;—‖ בער ψ 49¹¹ 92⁷ 94⁸, elsewh. only in Wisd Lt.; he hates knowledge Pr 1²²; delights not in understanding 18²; it is his sport to do mischief 10²³; his heart proclaimeth אִוֶּלֶת 12²³; his mouth poureth it forth 15², and feedeth on it 15¹⁴.

† כְּסִילוּת **n.f. stupidity**;—Pr 9¹³ אֵשֶׁת כ׳, *the woman Stupidity*, in antithesis with חָכְמוֹת the Supreme Wisdom personified as a woman.

† II. כְּסִיל **n.m. Orion** (relation to above √ obscure);—Am 5⁸ Jb 9⁹; also מֹשְׁכוֹת כ׳ תְּפַתֵּחַ 38³¹ *the cords of Orion wilt (canst) thou let out?* (appar. some mythological allusion, v. Di Che, to giant bound in skies; cf. Hom. 'Ωρίωνα δοκεύει, and σθένος 'Ωρίωνος); both times associated with the Pleiades; sf. כְּסִילֵיהֶם *their Orions* Is 13¹⁰, Orion and other constellations of the same brilliancy.

† III. כְּסִיל **n.pr.loc.** in S of tribe of Judah Jos 15³⁰, prob. corrupt for בְּתוּל Jos 19⁴; see בְּתוּאֵל.

† כְּסָלוֹן **n.pr.loc.** on border of tribe of Judah = הַר־יְעָרִים Jos 15¹⁰; = *Kesla* 10 miles W. Jerus., Guérin [Jud. ii. 11 ff.] Mem [iii. 25. 26] Buhl [G. § 92, p. 166].

† כִּסְלוֹן **n.pr.m.** a prince of Benjamin Nu 34²¹.

† כְּסֻלּוֹת **n.pr.loc.** in the tribe of Issachar Jos 19¹⁸, = כִּסְלֹת תָּבֹר (loins or flanks of Tabor), on the W. foot of Mt. Tabor, Jos 19¹²; = תָּבוֹר Jos 19²² 1 Ch 6⁶²; = mod. *Iksâl* Rob [BR iii. 182], Mem [i. 365] Buhl [G. § 113, p. 216].

† כִּסְלֵו **n.pr.[m.] Kislew,** ninth month (postex.) = Nov.–Dec., Zc 7¹; בְּחֹדֶשׁ כ׳ Ne 1¹ (𝔗 *id.*; loan-word from Bab. *kislimu, kislivu*, Muss-Arn [JBL 1892, 167]; conj. on etym. by Jen [ZA ii. 210, Anm. 3] Hpt [ib. 265, Anm. 2]; Palm. כסלול Vog [No. 24]; Gk. χασελευ 1 Makk 1⁵⁴).

† כַּסְלֻחִים **n.pr.gent.** Gn 10¹⁴ (𝔊D Χασμωνιειμ, 𝔊L Χασλωνιειμ, E Χαλοειμ) = 1 Ch 1¹² (A Χασλωνιειμ, 𝔊L Χασλωειμ), among the sons of מִצְרַיִם; not identif.; conject. in Thes Di.

כִּסְלֹת תָּבוֹר v. כְּסֻלּוֹת supr.

† [כָּסַם] **vb. shear, clip** (As. *kasâmu, cut in pieces*, acc. to Dl [HWB 344]);—only **Qal** *Impf.* and *Inf. abs.* כָּסוֹם יִכְסְמוּ אֶת־רָאשֵׁיהֶם Ez 44²⁰ *they shall by all means clip their heads* (opp. יְגַלֵּחוּ *shave* and יְשַׁלֵּחוּ, i.e. *let grow freely*).

† כֻּסֶּמֶת **n.f. spelt,** *triticum spelta* (NH pl. כּוּסְמִין, cf. 𝔗 𝔖 כונתא, ܟܘܢܬܐ; cf. Löw [p. 104 ff.] Di [Ex 9. 32] Now [Arch. i. 111]);—abs. כ׳ Ex 9³² Is 28²⁵ pl. כֻּסְּמִים Ez 4⁹ (in all disting. from wheat, barley, etc.)

† [כִּרְסֵם] **vb. quadril.** = **Pi.**, tear off (cf. קִרְסֵם NH *cut* or *eat away*, Dt 28³⁸ 𝔗 ᴶ for חָסַל; on form v. Ges [§ 56]);—only *Impf.* 3 ms. sf.:—יְכַרְסְמֶנָּה חֲזִיר מִיָּעַר ψ 80¹⁴ *teareth it off* (sc. the vine, fig. of Israel).

† [כָּסַס] **vb. compute** (perh. orig. *divide up, make small, fine*; NH *chew*; Aram. ܟܣܣ *break small* (rare), usu. (Aph. etc.) *correct, convict*; Ar. كَسَّ *pulverize*; As. *kasâsu*, perh. *cut in two*, or *up*, whence *kissatu, fodder*)—only **Qal** *Impf.* 2 mpl. אִישׁ לְפִי אָכְלוֹ תָּכֹסּוּ עַל־הַשֶּׂה Ex 12⁴ (P) *each one according to his eating shall ye compute for the lamb.*

† מֶכֶס **n.m. computation, proportion to be paid, tax** (Palm. מכסא Reckendorf [ZMG 1888, 379 ff.]; NH מֶכֶס, Aram. מַכְסָא, ܡܟܣܐ *tax* (hence Ar. مَكْس as loan-word Frä [283]); As. *miksu*, Dl [HWB 407] (√ מכס); NH מוֹכֵס *tax-collector*; so As. *makkasu*, cf. Ar. (مَكَّاس)—Nu 31²⁸ וַהֲרֵמֹתָ מ׳ לי׳ and thou shalt separate a *tax* (duty levied on the spoil) for י׳, v [37. 38. 39. 40. 41] (all P).

† מִכְסָה **n.f. computation** (f. of מֶכֶס); hence —**a.** *number*, Ex 12⁴ (P). **b.** *valuation, worth*, Lv 27²³ (P).

† [כָּסַף] **vb. long** (for) (Ar. كَسَفَ *be colourless, obscure, be eclipsed* (of sun or moon); also *be depressed* in appearance Ba [ZS 61]; mod. Ar. *disappoint*; refl. conj. *be disappointed, ashamed*, v. Spiro [Vocab.]; NH כסף Hiph. *shew pallor, be pale, white*; Qal *be ashamed, long for*, cf. Aram. כְּסַף)—**Qal** *Impf.* 2 ms. לְמַעֲשֵׂה יָדֶיךָ תִכְסֹף Jb 14¹⁵ *for the work of thy hands thou wouldest long*; 3 ms. כְּאַרְיֵה יִכְסוֹף לִטְרֹף ψ 17¹² *like a lion that longeth to rend.* **Niph.** *Pf.* 2 ms. + *Inf. abs.* נִכְסֹף נִכְסַפְתָּה לְבֵית אָבִיךָ Gn 31³⁰ *thou didst long sorely for thy father's*

house, *Pf.* 3 fs ψ 84[4] נִכְסְפָה . . . נַפְשִׁי לְחַצְרוֹת י׳ *my soul longeth* . . *for the courts of* י׳ ; *Pf* 3 ms הַגּוֹי לֹא נִכְסָף Zp 2[1] very dub, but perhaps (Ges Ew Hi Ke al.), O nation *not turning pale*, = *not ashamed*, cf. etym supr; We thinks whole v. corrupt

כֶּסֶף 402 **n.m.** Gn 23, 9 **silver, money** (NH *id*, Ph Zinj כסף; Aram כַּסְפָּא, ܟܣܦܐ, Palm כספא Vog No. 23, As *kaspu*, prob the *pale* metal Thes al, cf. RS JPh xiv. 125)—כ׳ abs Gn 20[16] +, כָּסֶף Ex 21[11] +, cstr 43[21] +; sf כַּסְפִּי Gn 42[28] + 3 t, כַּסְפְּךָ 1 K 20[3] + 2 t, כַּסְפֵּךְ Gn 17[13] Is 30[22], כַּסְפֵּךְ Is 1[22], כַּסְפֵּנוּ Gn 31[15] + 2 t, כַּסְפָּם Ho 8[4] + 6 t; pl. sf כַּסְפֵּיהֶם Gn 42[25.35],—*silver*, †**1.** = silver ore, raw silver (rare and mostly late) Jb 28[1], also (in fig) Ez 22[20.22] Zc 13[9] Pr 2[4] 17[3] 27[21] Mal 3[3.3] ψ 12[7] 66[10] Is 48[10], הָגוֹ סִינִים מִכ׳ Pr 25[4] *remove dross from silver*, cf. כ׳ סִינִים 26[23] and כ׳ סִנִים Ez 22[18] (MT, 𝔊 כ׳ ס׳; Co del. in view of v[20]); כַּסְפֵּךְ הָיָה לְסִינִים Je 6[30] (cf. v[29]), כ׳ נִמְאָס Is 1[22] †**2.** silver as bright, shining, fig. of dove's wings כַּנְפֵי יוֹנָה נֶחְפָּה בַכֶּסֶף ψ 68[14]. **3.** silver, as wealth, Gn 13[2] (J) + oft (c 54 t in all, frequently with gold, etc, v. זהב), מְלֹא בֵיתוֹ כ׳ וזהב Nu 22[18] 24[13], fig. of a slave as valuable, כַּסְפּוֹ הוּא Ex 21[21] (all JE); silver as less valuable than gold 1 K 10[21] = 2 Ch 9[20], cf also 1 K 10[27] = 2 Ch 1[15] 9[27], כ׳ נִבְחָר *choice silver*, Pr 18[19] 10[20] **4.** silver as spoil of war (c. זהב, q v) Ju 5[19] 2 S 8[11] = 1 Ch 18[11] + 11 t †**5.** silver as merchandise Ez 27[12] Pr 3[14] (סְחַר־כ׳), Zp 1[12], cf also 1 K 10[22] = 2 Ch 9[21]. **6.** silver as costly gift (c. זהב, q v) 1 K 15[18.19] = 2 Ch 16[2.3], 2 K 16[8] 18[15] 2 Ch 9[14] 17[11] 21[3] Is 60[9] Dn 11[38] (other instances under **8**) **7.** silver as material (c. 117 t in all; oft c זהב, q v), of cup Gn 44[2] cf v[8] (J), trumpets Nu 10[2] (P), כְּלֵי־כ׳ Gn 24[53] (J)+, of idols Ex 20[23] Is 2[20] Dt 29[16] Ez 16[17] ψ 115[4] 135[15] + 4 t, cf Dt 7[25] Je 10[4] Hb 2[19]; esp of fittings of tabern Ex 26 27. 36 38 (19 t), and those offered by chiefs of people Nu 7 (28 t), etc **8.** silver as measure of weight and value (c 184 t.):—†**a.** shekels—כ׳ שְׁלֹשִׁים שְׁקָלִים Ex 21[32] (JE), cf. 2 S 24[24] Lv 5[15] Nu 18[16] (both P), Ne 5[15], also (diff. order) חֲמִשָּׁה שְׁקָלִים כ׳ Lv 27[6.6] (P), cf Jos 7[21] (JE), 2 K 15[20], and אַרְבַּע מֵאֹת שֶׁקֶל י׳ Gn 23[15.16], cf. Lv 27[3.16] (all P), 1 S 9[8], once שִׁבְעָה שְׁקָלִים וַעֲשָׂרָה הַכ׳ Je 32[9] **b.** more oft om שֶׁקֶל Gn 20[16] 45[22] (E), 37[28] (J), Ho 3[2] Ct 8[11] + 17 t †**c.** talents—כִּכַּר (הַ)כ׳ Ex 38[27] (P), cf. 1 K 20[39] 2 K 5[22] 15[19] 18[14] 23[33] = 2 Ch 36[3], 1 Ch 19[6] 2 Ch 25[6] 27[5] Est 3[9], 1 K 16[24] 2 K 5[23], כִּכְּרַיִם כ׳ 2 K 5[5]; עֶשֶׂר כִּכְּרֵי־כ׳ 1 Ch 22[14] cf. 29[7] Ezr 8[26], כ׳ אֶלֶף אֲלָפִים כִּכָּרִים †**d.** minas—כ׳ מָנִים חֲמֵשֶׁת אֲלָפִים Ezr 2[69] cf. Ne 7[70.71]. **e.** more oft = *money*, measure of value and exchange (c 112 t; not necess *coined*) Gn 31[15] 42[25.27] (E), 43[12.12.15.18] (J), Gn 23[13] Lv 27[18] Nu 3[48] (P), Ju 16[18] 1 K 21[2] 2 K 12[5] etc; so ψ 68[31] Che, but see De Grill Bae, and Che crit. n, מִקְנַת כ׳ *one bought for money* Gn 17[12.13.23.27] Ex 12[44] (all P); מִקְנָתוֹ כ׳ Lv 25[51] (H) *money for which he was bought*, כ׳ מָלֵא *full price* Gn 23[9] (P) 1 Ch 21[22.24]; כַּסְפֵּנוּ בְּמִשְׁקָלוֹ Gn 43[21] i.e. our money in full; כ׳ מִמְכָּרוֹ Lv 25[50] *the price of his sale*; כ׳ אָשָׁם 2 K 12[7] *trespass-money*, כ׳ חַטָּאוֹת v[7] *sin-money*, כ׳ הַכִּפֻּרִים Ex 30[16] *atonement-money*, כ׳ הַפִּדְיוֹן Nu 3[49] *redemption-money* (both P); כ׳ עֶרְכְּךָ Lv 27[15.19] i e estimated value, etc. **9.** among vbs. and phr. with כ׳ are—צרף *try, refine*, Zc 13[9] Is 48[10] Mal 3[3a] ψ 12[7] 66[10]; זקק Mal 3[3b], (cf. הִתּוּךְ Ez 22[22], נתך √, see v[20.21]); יפה בכ׳ *beautify* Je 10[4], תָּפוּשׂ כ׳ Hb 2[19] *encased with* gold and *silver*, שָׁקַל אֶת־הַכ׳ לְ *weigh out the silver to* or for a person Je 32[9] Gn 23[16] (P) Ezr 8[25], without לְ Je 32[10], cf Ex 22[16] (E), 1 K 20[39], שקל כ׳ ב׳ Is 55[2] = *spend money for*; לֹא יִשָּׁקֵל כ׳ מְחִירָהּ Jb 28[15], כ׳ בְּקָנֵה יִשְׁקְלוּ Zc 11[12], וַיִּשְׁקְלוּ אֶת־שְׂכָרִי שְׁלֹשִׁים כ׳ Is 46[6], of weighing material for idol; מָכַר בכ׳ *sell for money* Am 2[6] Gn 37[28] (J), Dt 21[14], נָתַן בכ׳ Dt 2[28b] 1 K 21[6.15] Gn 23[9] (P), 1 Ch 21[22], also, of food, השׁביר בכ׳ Dt 2[28a], נתן כ׳ השׂדה Gn 23[13] (P) *pay the price of the field*; קָנָה בכ׳ *buy* something *for money* Am 8[6] Je 32[25.44] Is 43[24] 1 Ch 21[24], cf קָנָה נֶפֶשׁ קִנְיַן כ׳ Lv 22[11] (H); שבר בכ׳ Dt 2[6a] Is 55[1], כרה בכ׳ Dt 2[6b], peculiar is its use with פָּדָה, *redeem* (q.v) in Nu 18[16], לקח כ׳ *receive money* 2 K 5[26] 12[8.9], לָוָה כ׳ Ne 5[4] *borrow money*; הִלְוָה Ex 22[24] (JE) *lend* money *to* (c 2 acc), נתן כ׳ בְּנֶשֶׁךְ *give money on usury* Lv 25[37] (H), ψ 15[5], cf. לֹא תַשִּׁיךְ לְאָחִיךָ נֶשֶׁךְ כ׳ Dt 23[20]

†**כָּסִפְיָא** **n pr.loc.** in Babylonia, site unknown·—בכ׳ הַמָּקוֹם Ezr 8[17.17] 𝔊 B ἐν ἀργυρίῳ, 𝔊L ἐν Μασφεν Esdr α, τῶν γαζοφυλακίων, γαζοφύλαξιν Esdr β.

כֶּסֶת v sub II. כסה.

†**כָּעַס** **vb. be vexed, angry** (NH כָּעַס, Aram כְּעַס (not Syr)),—**Qal** *Pf* כ׳ ψ 112[10] Ec 5[16], *Impf* וַיִּכְעַס Ne 3[33] 2 Ch 16[10], 1 s אֶכְעַס Ez 16[42],

Inf. לִכְעוֹס Ec 7[9].—**1.** *be vexed, indignant* ψ 112[10] Ne 3[33] Ec 5[16]. **2.** *be angry* Ez 16[42] Ec 7[9], c. אֶל pers. 2 Ch 16[10]. **Piel.** *Pf.* 3 fs. sf כִּעֲסַתָּה 1 S 1[6]; 3 mpl. sf. כִּעֲסוּנִי Dt 32[21] *provoke to anger*

Hiph. *Pf.* הכעיס Ho 12[15] 1 K 15[30]; sf. הִכְעִיסוּ 2 K 23[26] + 4 t. Pf.; הִכְעִסוּנִי Je 25[7]; (scribal error for הִכְעִיסוּנִי acc to SS); *Impf* וַיַּכְעֵס 1 K 22[54] 2 Ch 28[25]; 3 fs. sf. תַּכְעִיסֶנָּה 1 S 1[7] + 6 t. Impf.; *Inf. cstr.* הַכְעִיס 1 K 16[13] + 5 t; sf. הַכְעִ(י)סֵנִי Je 7[18] + 11 t, + 6 t. sfs.; *Pt.* pl. מַכְעִיסִים Je 7[19] + 4 t.—**1.** *vex*, c acc. pers. 1 S 1[7] Ez 32[9]. **2.** *vex, provoke to anger*, esp. of provoking Yahweh by worship of other gods Ju 2[12] 1 K 14[9.15] 16[33] 22[54] 2 K 17[11] 23[19] 2 Ch 28[25] Ne 3[37] Je 7[18.19] 11[17] 32[29.32] 44[3] Ez 8[17] 16[26] Is 65[3] Ho 12[15], c. בְּ instr. בתועבת Dt 32[16]; בְּהַבְלֵיהֶם Dt 32[21] 1 K 16[13.26]; בחטאתם 1 K 16[2]; במעש(י) יד(יו) Dt 31[29] 1 K 16[7] Je 25[6.7] 32[30] 44[8]; בכל מעש(ה) ידיהם 2 K 22[17] = 2 Ch 34[25]; בבמות ψ 78[58]; בפסיליהם Je 8[19]; במעלליהם ψ 106[29]; cf. the phrases עשה הרע(ה) בעיני י׳ להכעיס(ו) *do the evil in the eyes of Yahweh to provoke* (him) *to anger* Dt 4[25] 9[18] 31[29] 1 K 16[7] 2 K 17[17] 21[6] = 2 Ch 33[6]; so מכעסים 2 K 21[15] Je 32[30]; כעס(ים) אשר הכעיס 1 K 15[30] 21[22] 2 K 23[26]—The phrase is characteristic of D Je and the compiler of Kings; see Dr[Intr 191, Dt 4 25] Holz[Einl Hex 287].

†כַּעַס **n.m.** vexation, anger,—כ׳ Dt 32[27] + 13 t.; כָּעַס Pr 21[19] Ec 1[18]; sf. כַּעְסִי 1 S 1[16], כַּעַסְךָ ψ 85[5], כַּעְסוֹ Pr 12[16] 1 K 15[30]; *pl.* כְּעָסִים 2 K 23[26].—*vexation*. **1.** of men, esp caused by unmerited treatment, 1 S 1[6.16] Pr 12[16] 17[25] 21[19] 27[3] Ec 7[9]. **2.** *vexation, anger of* Yahweh (caused esp. by worship of other gods) 1 K 15[30] 21[22] 2 K 23[26]; כ׳ עִמָּנוּ ψ 85[5] *anger (of Yahweh) with us;* כ׳ בָּנָיו Dt 32[19] *anger against his sons,* כ׳ אוֹיֵב v[27] *anger against the enemy* (both obj gen. see Di; RV *provocation of*, cf. Dr); כ׳ קָרְבָּנָם Ez 20[28] *provocation of their offering* (so RV but Co del, rightly). **3.** *vexation, grief* ψ 6[8] 10[14] 31[10] Ec 1[18] 2[23] 7[3] 11[10], also כעס 5[16] acc. Ew al.

†כַּעַשׂ **n.m.** (dialectic variation of כַּעַס, only in Jb);—כ׳ Jb 17[7], כָּעַשׂ Jb 5[2]; sf. כַּעְשִׂי Jb 6[2]; כַּעַשְׂךָ Jb 10[17],—**1.** *vexation, grief* of men Jb 5[2] (cf. Pr 12[16] 27[3]), 6[2] 17[7]. **2.** *vexation, anger*, of God; c כַּעַשְׂךָ עִמָּדִי Jb 10[17] *thine anger with me.*

כַּף v. sub כפף

†[כֵּף] **n.[m.]** rock (As *kâpu* Dl[HWB 346]; Aram. כֵּיפָא, ܟܐܦܐ; perh. Aram. loan-word in Heb.; √ dub),—only pl כֵּפִים Je 4[29] as place of refuge; Jb 30[6] as dwelling-place.

†[כָּפָה] **vb.** prob. subdue (NH *overturn, hold under, compel;* Aram כְּפָא, *id.;* ܟܦܐ *incline* (as face to ground), *overturn;* As *kapû* perh. *id*, Dl[HWB 346]; cf Ar. كفأ *overturn, turn back*);—only **Qal** *Impf.* מַתָּן בַּסֵּתֶר יִכְפֶּה־אָף Pr 21[14] *a gift in secret subdueth anger* (so Thes RobGes; Ew *beugt:* Fl De *averteth*, from the Ar., is more remote; 𝔊 ἀνατρέπει, cf NH).

כִּפָּה v. sub כפף.

†כָּפַל **vb.** double, double over (late) (NH *id*, Aram. כְּפַל; 𝔗 כּוּפְלָה, כִּיפְלָא, Nab. כפל Eut[Nab No 20,7] *the double;* Christ. Pal. Aram. ܟܦܠ, Schwally[Idiot. 46]; NSyr. *id*, Ar. كِفْلٌ *the double,* كَفَلٌ *posteriors, buttocks;* Eth. ከፈለ: is *divide*, ክፍል: *a part*)—**Qal** *Pf.* 2 ms. וְכָפַלְתָּ Ex 26[9] *and thou shalt double over* the sixth curtain, i.e. prob. use it double (Di); *Pt pass.* כָּפוּל *folded double*, of the breastpiece (חֹשֶׁן) Ex 28[16] 39[9.9]. **Niph.** *Impf.* 3 fs וְתִכָּפֵל Ez 21[19] *and let* the sword *be doubled*, but very dub; Co rds plausibly תְּשַׁכֵּל *let* the sword *bereave* (cf VB)

†כֶּפֶל **n.[m.]** the double:—כ׳ cstr: בְּכֶ׳ רִסְנוֹ Jb 41[5] *within the double of his jaw* (i e. his double jaws) who can come? elsewhere du. כִּפְלַיִם (cf. Ar. كِفْلَانِ), לְתוּשִׁיָּה 11[6] *double* in sound wisdom (beyond what Job imagines), of retribution Is 40[2].

†מַכְפֵּלָה **n.pr.loc.** near Hebron, where the patriarchs and their wives were buried, only in P, alw c art; שדה אשר בַּמ׳ Gn 23[17], מְעָרַת הַמ׳ *the cave of Machpelah* v[9], 25[9], מְעָרַת שדה הַמ׳ 23[19] 50[13], מְעָרָה אֲשֶׁר בשדה המ׳ 49[30].—cf. Buhl[Geogr 160, 161].—(Evidently orig. appell., but meaning dub; 𝔊 τὸ διπλοῦν; acc to Thes = *part, lot, portion*, as Eth. መክፈልት:)

†[כָּפַן] **vb.** be hungry, hunger, perh. also hungrily desire (Aram. loan-word; cf. Aram. כְּפַן, כְּפֵין, ܟܦܢ *be hungry;* Ar. كفن is *spin* wool, *wrap* a corpse *in the shroud*),—only **Qal** *Pf.* 3 fs. כָּפְנָה עַל Ez 17[7] (si vera l) this vine *stretched* its roots *hungrily* toward (|| שִׁלְּחָה לוֹ).

†כָּפָן **n.[m.]** hunger, famine (Aramaism; on form cf. Lag[BN 144]), Jb 5[22] 30[3].

כפס (perh. √ of foll; cf 𝔗 כְּפַס Est 1[6] *bind, fasten* (so Levy, Jastrow)).

†כָּפִים **n m** appar. (si vera l) term techn for some beam in a house, perhaps **rafter**, or **girder** (NH *id*, Levy, Jastrow, but acc to Hoffm$^{ZAW\ ii\ 1881, 71}$ it is changed fr oblong block of wood (O T) to a *building-stone*, or *brick* in Mish.), —only Hb 2^{11} *for a stone out of the wall crieth out*, וכ׳ מעץ יַעֲנֶנָּה *and a rafter out of the timber-work answereth it*

†**כָּפַף** **vb. bend, bend down, be bent, bowed** (NH *bend, overturn*, As *kapâpu, bend, bow*, Dl$^{HWB\ 347}$, Ar كَفَّ *fell* a seam, also *turn back, avert*, كُفَّةٌ *selvage*, كِفَافٌ *circuit, rim*, Aram כְּפַף, ܟܦ *bend, curve*, Palm כבתא *niche*, from כפף *curve* acc to Vog$^{No. 70, p 60}$), —**Qal** *Pf* כ׳ נַפְשִׁי ψ 57^{7} *my soul is bowed down*; *Inf cstr* (trans) לָכֹף כְּאַגְמֹן ראשׁו Is 58^{5} *to bend down, like a rush, his head* *Pt pass* (הַ)כְּפוּפִים *those bowed down*, in distress, humiliation, etc, ψ 145^{14} 146^{8} **Niph.** *Impf* 1 s אִכַּף לאלהי מָרוֹם Mi 6^{6} with what *shall I bow myself* (in worship) *toward the high God?*

כַּף$_{192}$ **n.f.**$^{1\ K\ 8\ 54}$ **hollow, or flat of the hand, palm, sole of foot, pan** (NH *id*, Aram *id*, ܟܦܐ, As *kappu, hand, pan, kippatu, hollow*; Ar كَفّ *palm, hand*)—abs. כ׳ Jb 29^{9}+, so rd prob also Ez 29^{7b} for MT כָתֵף (𝔊 𝔖 Sm Co, cf v^{a}), כָּף 2 K 11^{12}+, more oft cstr כַּף Gn 40^{11}+, sf כַּפִּי Ju 12^{3}, כַּפְּךָ Jb 13^{21}, etc, in Ez 29^{7} rd כַּף Qr for כפך Kt (so Ew Hi Sm Co Du), du כַּפַּיִם Is 49^{16}+, cstr. כַּפֵּי Ex 29$^{24.24}$+ 3 t., sf כַּפַּי Gn 20^{5}+, כַּפָּיו Nu 24^{10}+, כַּפֵּיהֶם Is 59^{6}+2 t, כַּפֵּימוֹ Jb 27^{23}, etc; pl כַּפּוֹת (esp. of *soles*, and in metaph. senses) abs Nu 4^{7}+; cstr 2 K 9^{35}+, sf כַּפֹּתָיו Ex 25^{29} 37^{16},—**1. a.** of human beings, *hollow* or *flat of hand, palm*, (c 116 t) 2 K 4$^{34.34}$, נָתַן את הַכּוֹס עַל־כַּף פ׳ Gn 40$^{11\ 21}$ (E), *set the cup upon the palm of Pharaoh* (cf v^{11a} וכוס פרעה בְּיָדִי), similarly Lv 8$^{27\ 27}$ (P)+, הַשֶּׁמֶן אֲשֶׁר עַל־כַּפּוֹ Lv 14$^{15.17\ 18.27\ 28}$, as disting from wrist and arm, Dt 25^{12}, rarely c ידים (always כַּפּוֹת), שְׁתֵּי כַּפּוֹת ידיו 1 S 5^{4} (of Dagon), כַּף הַשְּׂמָאלִית 2 K 9^{35}, cf Dn 10^{10}; כ׳ הַיָּדַיִם Lv 14$^{15\ 26}$, note esp מְלֹא כ׳ קֶמַח 1 K 17^{12} *a handful of meal* (lit *palmful*), cf Ec 4^{6} (where disting fr. מלא חָפְנַיִם *a double fistful*, in both these passages of a very small quantity), cf וַיְמַלֵּא כַפּוֹ מִן Lv 9^{17} (ref to מלא קֻמְצוֹ 2^{2} 5^{12} cf 6^{8}) In Ex 4^{4} (JE), Pr 31^{19} Ez 21^{16} ψ 129^{7}, etc, the thought is that of grasping. **b.** anthropomorph. of י׳, covering Moses over with his palm, וְשַׂכֹּתִי כַפִּי עָלֶיךָ Ex 33^{22} (J), and so fig (c. שׁית) ψ 139^{5}, withdrawing (הסיר) his hand Ex 33^{23}(J); removing (הרחיק) his afflicting hand Jb 13^{21}, עַל־כַּפַּיִם כִּסָּה אוֹר Jb 36^{32}, i e he (God) hath filled his palms with light. **c.** once of animals, הוֹלֵךְ עַל־כַּפָּיו Lv 11^{27} *going upon their palms*, i e paws (cats, dogs, etc). **d.** phrases are —†(1) הִכָּה כַף = *clap the hands*, in applause 2 K 11^{12} so תִּקְעוּ כ׳ ψ 47^{2}, מָחָא כ׳ Is 55^{12} (fig of trees), ψ 98^{8} (fig. of rivers); but esp in scorn, contempt, etc, סָפַק את־כַּפָּיו Nu 24^{10} (J), יִשְׂפֹּק עָלֵימוֹ כַפֵּימוֹ Jb 27^{23}, so תָּקְעוּ כַף על־ Na 3^{19}, הִכָּה כַפֵּי אֶל־ Ez 22^{13} (of י׳); abs, הַכֵּה בְכַפְּךָ Ez 6^{11} (as מחא יד 25^{6}), הַכֵּה כַף אֶל־כַף 21^{19}, אַכֶּה כַפִּי אֶל־כַּפִּי v^{22} (of י׳) †(2) תָּפַשׂ בַּכַּף *grasp, seize with the hand* Ez 29^{7} cf v^{7} (on text v. supr) †(3) of *hand-grasp* as pledge, תָּקַעְתָּ לַזָּר כַּפֶּיךָ Pr 6^{1} (*if*) *thou hast smitten thy palms* (given a double hand-grasp), *for another* (so De; ‖ עָרַבְתָּ לְרֵעֶךָ); so abs תקע כף 17^{18} 22^{26} (cf תקע ליד Jb 17^{3}). (4) oft of hand *spread out* in prayer, as sign of longing to receive, c. פָּרַשׂ אֶל־ Ex 9$^{29.33}$ (J), 1 K 8^{38} = 2 Ch 6^{29}, etc. (v. ψ יד 143^{6} La 1^{17} and יָד **1 d,** supr p 389, also שׁטח, נשׂא, פרשׂ). †(5) שִׂים כַּף לפה, in respectful silence, Jb 29^{9}. †(6) fig וָאָשִׂימָה נַפְשִׁי בְכַפִּי Ju 12^{3} = *I have taken my life in my hand* (i e hazarded it), so 1 S 19^{5} 28^{21} Jb 13^{14} and (without vb) ψ 119^{109} †(7) נִקְיֹן כ׳ Gn 20^{5} *cleanness of palms* is fig for purity of act, cf. ψ 26^{6}, also Jb 9^{30} 22^{30} ψ 24^{4} 73^{13}; conversely, (לא)חָמָס בְּכַפַּי Jb 16^{17} 1 Ch 12^{18} Is 59^{6} Jon 3^{8}, cf Is 59^{3} (so ידים 1^{15}), Jb 31^{7} ψ 7^{4}.—In many cases כַּף is not to be distinguished from יָד; so in phr †יגיע כ׳ *toil of the hands* Gn 31^{42} Hg 1^{11} Jb 10^{3} ψ 128^{2}, פֹּעַל כ׳ ψ 9^{17}, חֵפֶץ כ׳ Pr 31^{13}; ψ תְּבוּנוֹת כ׳ 78^{72}, פְּרִי כ׳ Pr 31^{16}+, cf. Mi 7^{3}. †**2.** = *power* (i.e grasp) of any one, נתן בכף Ju 6^{13} = *deliver into the power of*, so Je 12^{7}, cf בוא בכף Pr 6^{3}; usu. הוֹשִׁיעַ, פָּדָה, הִצִּיל etc, c מִכַּף = *out of the power of* Ju 6^{14} 1 S 4^{3} 2 S 14^{16} 19$^{10\ 10}$ 22^{1} = ψ 18^{1} (title), 2 K 16^{7} 20^{6} = Is 38^{6}, Mi 4^{10} Je 15^{21} 2 Ch 30^{6} 32^{11} Ezr 8^{31} ψ 71^{4} (cf יָד **5 g**, p 391 supr) †**3.** כַּף רַגְלָהּ, etc, = *sole of foot*, Gn 8^{9} (J), Jos 3^{13} 4^{18} (both JE), 1 K 5^{17} 2 K 19^{24} = Is 37^{25}, Dt 11^{24} 28$^{56\ 65}$ Jos 1^{3} (D), Ez 43^{7} Mal 3^{21}; מִכַּף רַגְלוֹ וְעַד קָדְקֳדוֹ 2 S 14^{25} Jb 2^{7}, cf. Is 1^{6} (fig), מִדְרַךְ כ׳ ר׳ Dt 2^{5} *treading place for the sole of a foot*; of the cherubim Ez 1^{7}, of a calf, (in sim.) v^{7}, (acc.

to MT; cf however Co) **4.** of various *hollow, bending* or *bent* objects.—†**a.** *hollow* (i e socket), *of the thigh*-joint, כ׳ יָרֵךְ Gn $32^{26.26.33.33}$ (J) **b.** *pan, vessel* (as hollow), used in ritual, Ex 25^{29} 37^{16} Nu 5^{7} 7^{14} + 15 t Nu 7; 1 K 7^{50} = 2 Ch 4^{22}, 2 K 25^{14} = Je 52^{18}, Je 52^{19}, 2 Ch 24^{14}. †**c.** *hollow* of sling, 1 S 25^{29} †**d.** כַּפּוֹת תְּמָרִים Lv 23^{40} = of huge *hand-shaped branches* (or *fronds*) *of palm-trees* **e.** כַּפּוֹת הַמַּנְעוּל Ct 5^{5} *the* (bent) *handles of the bolt*

† כִּפָּה **n.f.** branch, frond (prob. of palm-tree, cf. כַּף **3 d**),—כ׳ Is 9^{13} 19^{15} fig. of nobles, rulers (both opp אַגְמוֹן *rush*, i e. high and low, ‖ רֹאשׁ וְזָנָב); c. sf כִּפָּתוֹ Jb 15^{32} (of wicked under fig of palm-tree)

I. **כפר** (of foll, orig mng. dub., but most prob *cover*, cf. Ar. كَفَرَ *cover, hide;* > RS who thinks of Aram כַּפַּר, ܟܦܪ Pa. *wash away, rub off*, whence כֹּפֶר, לְכַפֵּר of *washing away, obliteration* of sin: NH כִּפֵּר, Aram כַּפַּר and deriv.; Ar كَفَّارَة *an expiation* (see RS$^{OTJC\ 438;\ 2.381}$ Kn on Lv4^{20} Ri$^{Begr\ der\ Sühne}$ We$^{Comp\ 335\ f}$ Sm$^{AT\ Rel\ Gesch.\ 321}$ Now$^{Arch.\ II.\ 192}$ Dr$^{Dt\ 425}$ Schmoller$^{St.\ Kr\ 1891,\ 205\ ff}$ Lag$^{BN\ 230\ ff}$))

† I. כֹּפֶר **n.m.** the price of a life, ransom (ποινή, *wergeld*);—כ׳ Ex 21^{30} + 10 t.; sf. כָּפְרְךָ Is 43^{3}; כָּפְרוֹ ψ 49^{8},—**1.** *a price for ransom of a life* Jb 33^{24} 36^{18}; כ׳ עַל Ex 21^{30} (Covt. code; ‖ פִּדְיֹן נַפְשׁוֹ), כ׳ נפשׁ Pr 13^{8}, כ׳ לְ *ransom for* Pr 6^{35} 21^{18} Nu $35^{31.32}$ (P), כָּפְרוֹ *his ransom* ψ 49^{8} (‖ פדה); כָּפְרְךָ *thy ransom* Is 43^{3} (‖ תַּחְתֶּיךָ); כֹּפֶר alone 1 S 12^{3} Am 5^{12}. **2.** in the ritual of P כ׳ נַפְשׁוֹ Ex 30^{12} is a half shekel of the sanctuary paid by each male above twenty years at the census in order that there might be no plague upon them It was offered to Yahweh, לְכַפֵּר עַל *to atone for them.*

† כָּפַר **vb. Pi.** etc **denom.** cover over (fig.), pacify, make propitiation;—**Pi.** *Pf.* כִּפֶּר Ex 30^{10} + 31 t; 2 ms sf כִּפַּרְתָּהוּ Ez 43^{20}; 3 mpl, יְכַפְּרוּ Ez 43^{26}; 2 mpl. כִּפַּרְתֶּם Ez 45^{20}, *Impf.* יְכַפֵּר Ex 30^{10} + 10 t., יְכַפֵּר Lv 7^{7} Nu 5^{8}; sf. יְכַפְּרֶנָּה Pr 16^{14}, 1 s אֲכַפֵּר 2 S 21^{3}; אֲכַפְּרָה Gn 32^{21} Ex 32^{30}, etc.; *Imv.* כַּפֵּר Dt 21^{8} + 4 t, *Inf* כַּפֵּר Ex 30^{15} + 28 t.; sfs כַּפְּרִי Ez 16^{63}, כַּפֶּרְךָ Ex 29^{36}; כַּפְּרָהּ Is 47^{11},—**1.** *cover over, pacify, propitiate;* אֲכַפְּרָה פָנָיו בַּמִּנְחָה Gn 32^{21} *let me cover over his face by the present* (so that he does not see the offence, i.e. *pacify* him; E; RS$^{OTJC,\ 2d\ ed\ 381}$ 'wipe clean the face,' blackened by displeasure, as the Arabs say 'whiten the face'), וְתִפֹּל עָלַיִךְ הֹוָה לֹא תוּכְלִי כַּפְּרָהּ Is 47^{11} *and disaster will fall upon thee, thou wilt not be able to propitiate it* (by payment of a כֹּפֶר, see Is 43^{3}), pacify the wrath of a king Pr 16^{14} (e g by a gift) **2.** *cover over, atone for sin,* without sacrifice. **a** man as subj, בַּמָּה אֲכַפֵּר 2 S 21^{3}, *with what shall I cover over* (viz the bloodguiltiness of the house of Saul, says David. The answer is by a death penalty of seven sons of the guilty house), בְּעַד חַטַּאתְכֶם Ex 32^{30} *on behalf of your sins* (JE, Moses, by intercession); c עַל of persons Nu $17^{11.12}$ (P; by incense), 25^{13} (P when Phinehas slays the ringleaders). **b.** with God as subj, c. acc. pers, *cover,* i. e. treat as covered, view propitiously, Yahweh's land Dt 32^{43} (song); לְ pers. Dt 21^{8} (bloodguiltiness flows away in the stream), Ez 16^{63}, בְּעַד of person 2 Ch 30^{18}; c acc of *the sin* ψ 65^{4} 78^{38}, prob also Dn 9^{24} (‖ חתם חטאת); עַל of sin, ψ 79^{9} Je 18^{23} (‖ מחה). It is conceived that God in his sovereignty may himself provide an atonement or covering for men and their sins which could not be provided by men **3.** *cover over, atone for sin and persons by legal rites,* in the codes of H, P, and Ez: abs וכ׳ הַכֹּהֵן *and the priest shall make atonement* Lv 16^{32}, **a.** c. acc. of sacred places (by the great sin-offering of the day of atonement), Lv $16^{20.33.33}$, also Ez $43^{20.26}$ 45^{20} (by the blood of the sin-offering ‖ טִהַר, חִטֵּא) **b.** usually c. עַל (1) of things, e g. of the altar to which the blood of the sin-offering was applied Ex $29^{36.37}$ 30^{10} Lv 8^{15} (‖ קִדֵּשׁ), 16^{18}; and specifically the horns of the altar Ex 30^{10}; the holy place of the tabernacle Lv 16^{16} (by the great sin-offering, because of (מִן) the uncleannesses of the children of Israel and because of their transgressions), for the leprous house by ceremony of purification Lv 14^{53} (‖ טִהַר), for the goat לַעֲזָאזֵל Lv 16^{10} (which was presented before Yahweh to consecrate him for the bearing away of the sins of the people) (2) of persons, עַל־נַפְשֹׁתֵיכֶם, *for your persons, yourselves,* e.g. by the payment of atonement-money כֶּסֶף הַכִּפֻּרִים at the census Ex $30^{15.16}$; by the קרבן of the spoils Nu 31^{50}; by the blood upon the altar Lv 17^{11}; in the ritual עָלָיו, עֲלֵיהֶם by ministry of priest through the blood of the sin-offering Lv $4^{20.31}$ 8^{34} 10^{17} $12^{7.8}$ $14^{19.31}$ $16^{30.33}$ 23^{28} Nu $8^{12.21}$ $15^{25.28.28}$ $28^{22.30}$ 29^{5} 2 Ch 29^{24} Ne 10^{34}; of the trespass-offering Lv $5^{16.18.26}$ 7^{7} 14^{21} 19^{22} Nu 5^{8}; the whole burnt-offering Lv 1^{4} 14^{20} 16^{24}, by the oil

used in purifying a leper Lv $14^{18.29}$; by the תרומה Ez 45^{15}; by the priestly ministry in general 1 Ch 6^{34}; by the substitution of the Levites for the firstborn Nu 8^{19}. Underlying all these offerings there is the conception that the persons offering are covered by that which is regarded as sufficient and satisfactory by Yahweh. (The purpose of the covering is stated Lv 16^{30} יְכַפֵּר עֲלֵיכֶם לְטַהֵר אֶתְכֶם מִכֹּל חַטֹּאתֵיכֶם לִפְנֵי י׳ תִּטְהָרוּ = *shall atonement be made for you to cleanse you, from all your sins shall ye be clean before Yahweh*, and Nu 8^{21} וַיְכַפֵּר עֲלֵיהֶם לְטַהֲרָם *and* (*Aaron*) *made atonement for them to cleanse them.*) **c.** the need of the atonement is expressed by מִן: מֵחַטָּאתוֹ *because of his sin* Lv 4^{26} $5^{6.10}$ 16^{34}; מטמאתו Lv 14^{19} 16^{16}; מזוב Lv $15^{15.30}$; מֵאֲשֶׁר חָטָא Nu 6^{11}; also עַל, עַל־חַטָּאתוֹ *on account of his sin* Lv 4^{35} 5^{13} 19^{22}; על־שגגתו Lv 5^{18}. **d.** c. בְּ instr. בְּאֵיל Lv 5^{16} 19^{22} Nu 5^{8}; *with* a trespass-offering Lv 7^{7}; כִּי־הַדָּם הוּא בַּנֶּפֶשׁ יְכַפֵּר Lv 17^{11} *for it is the blood with the living being that covers over* (H, see נפשׁ **3** (*a*); RV *by reason of the life* after De Di Kn Bähr Kau and most moderns; AV follows 𝔊 𝔙 𝔗, so Ges Ew$^{§ 282 a. Anm. 1}$: *'for the soul'*); c. בְּ loc. בַּקֹּדֶשׁ Lv 6^{23} $16^{17.27}$. **e.** c. בְּעַד pers., *on behalf of* Lv $9^{7.7}$ $16^{6.11.17.24}$ (by Aaron), Ez 45^{17} (by the prince). **Pu.** *Pf.* כֻּפַּר Ex 29^{33} Is 28^{18} (but rd. תֻּפַר,—√ I. פרר,—so 𝔗 Hu We Che SS al. v. Br$^{MP 209}$); *Impf.* יְכֻפַּר Nu 35^{33} + 3 t.; 3 fs. תְּכֻפָּר Is 6^{7} *be covered over, atoned for.* **1.** apart from the ritual, חטאתך תכפר Is 6^{7} thy sin *shall be covered over* (‖ וְסָר עֲוֺנֶךָ; by the touch of the live coal from the altar); אִם־יְכֻפַּר הֶעָוֺן הַזֶּה לָכֶם Is 22^{14} *surely this iniquity shall not be covered over for you;* c. בְּ instr. בזאת יכפר עון Is 27^{9} by *this* shall the iniquity *of Jacob be covered over* (‖ הסר חטאתו; namely by the destruction of idolatrous objects); בחסד ואמת יכפר עון Pr 16^{6} *by mercy and fidelity iniquity is covered over.* **2.** c. לְ *for* whom, לארץ לא יכפר לדם Nu 35^{33} *for the land atonement cannot be made, in view of the blood* shed in it, except by the blood of the shedder of blood; in the ritual of P, c. בְּ instr. אֲשֶׁר כֻּפַּר בָּהֶם Ex 29^{33} *wherewith atonement was made* (ram of consecration).

Hithp. *Impf.* יִתְכַּפֵּר 1 S 3^{14}; c. בְּ instr. אִם־יִתְכַּפֵּר עֲוֺן בֵּית־עֵלִי בְּזֶבַח וּבְמִנְחָה *the iniquity of the house of Eli shall not be covered by peace-offering or minchah* (in other words there was no atonement for it; cf. **Pu.** Is. 22^{14}).

Niph. *Pf.* וְנִכַּפֵּר לָהֶם הַדָּם Dt 21^{8} *and the blood shall be covered for them.*

† כִּפֻּרִים **n.pl.abstr.** atonement, only in P: חַטַּאת הַכִּ׳ *sin-offering of the atonement* Ex 30^{10} Nu 29^{11}; יוֹם (ה)כ׳ *day of* (*the*) *atonement* Lv $23^{27.28}$ 25^{9}; אֵיל הַכִּ׳ Nu 5^{8}; עַל־הַכִּ׳ Ex 29^{36}; כֶּסֶף הכ׳ Ex 30^{16} *money of atonement.*

† כַּפֹּרֶת **n. propitiatory,** late techn. word from כפר *cover over sin:* the older explan. *cover, lid* has no justification in usage; 𝔊 ἱλαστήριον; only P: Ex $25^{17.18.19.20.20.21.22}$ 26^{34} 30^{6} 31^{7} 35^{12} $37^{6.7.8.9.9}$ 39^{35} 40^{20} Lv $16^{2.2.13.14.14.15.15}$ Nu 7^{89}, and 1 Ch 28^{11}; it was a slab of gold 2½ cubits × 1½ c. placed on top of the ark of the testimony. On it, and a part of it, were two golden cherubim facing each other, whose outstretched wings came together above and constituted the throne of Yahweh. When the high priest entered the Holy of Holies on the day of atonement it was necessary that this highest place of atonement should be enveloped in a cloud of incense. The blood of the sin-offering of the atonement was then sprinkled on the face of and seven times before it. The temple proper, as distinguished from porch etc., was called בֵּית הַכִּ׳ 1 Ch 28^{11}.

II. כפר (√ of following).

† II. כֹּפֶר **n.m. pitch** (Ar. كُفْر (loan-wd., cf. Frä^{150}), Syr. ܟܘܦܪܐ, 𝔗 כּוּפְרָא; As. *kupru, kupur* Dl$^{HWB 348}$; cf. גֹּפֶר ?)—Gn 6^{14} (P).

† II. [כָּפַר] **vb. denom.** (from II. כֹּפֶר)—*Pf.* 2 ms. וְכָפַרְתָּ בַּכֹּפֶר Gn 6^{14} *and thou shalt pitch it with pitch* (P).

III. כפר (√ of following).

† כְּפִיר **n.m.** young lion;—כ׳ Ju 14^{5} + 16 t.; pl. כְּפִרִים Je 2^{15} + 3 t.; כְּפִירִים Zc 11^{3} + 7 t.; sf. כְּפִירַיִךְ Na 2^{14}; כְּפִירֶיהָ Ez 38^{13} (Co rds. כנעניה);—lit. כ׳ אֲרָיוֹת Ju 14^{5} *young lion of lions;* Am 3^{4} ψ 17^{12}. It differs from whelp גּוּר Ez $19^{2.3}$ as old enough to hunt its prey, Je 25^{38} Is 11^{6} Zc 11^{3} ψ 104^{21}; in sim. of roar of hostile army Is 5^{29} (‖ לָבִיא) cf. Je 51^{38} (‖ גּוֹרֵי אריות); sim. of י׳'s invincible might Is 31^{4} (‖ אַרְיֵה); of Isr. among the nations, Mi 5^{7}; of Assyr. princes Na 2^{12}; of prince of Isr. Ez $19^{5.6}$; other cases are: ‖ לָבִיא Jb 38^{39}; ‖ שַׁחַל Ho 5^{14} ψ 91^{13} Jb 4^{10}; of bloodthirsty enemies ψ 34^{11} 35^{17} 58^{7} Je 2^{15}; כ׳ גוים Ez 32^{2}, of young warriors Na 2^{14} Ez 38^{13} (?; v. Co supr.); righteous compared with, Pr 28^{1}; king's wrath like roaring of, Pr 19^{12} 20^{2}; of one of faces of cherubim Ez 41^{19}.

† III. כֹּפֶר **n.m.** name of a plant, *El Henna* (√dub; NH כּוֹפֶר; Aram. כּוּפְרָא, ܟܘܦܪܐ; Ar. *El Henna*, see Löw[No. 169])—a shrub or low tree, with fragrant whitish flowers growing in clusters like grapes, אֶשְׁכֹּל הַכֹּפֶר *cluster of Henna* Ct 1^{14} (fragrant, fig. of a beloved one), pl. כְּפָרִים Ct 4^{13}.

† [כָּפָר] **n.m. village** (√dub; NH כָּפָר; Aram. כַּפְרָנָא; Syr ܟܦܪܐ, ܟܦܪܢܐ; As. *kapru* Dl[HWB 348]);—sg. cstr. כְּפַר הָעַמֹּנִי Jos 18^{24} Kt *village of the Ammonites*, or כ׳ הָעַמֹּנָה Qr, a village of Benjamin, possibly *Kefr 'Âna'*, 3 miles N. of Bethel Surv[ii. 299]; *pl* כפרים Ct 7^{12} 1 Ch 27^{25}

† IV. כֹּפֶר **n.[m.] village**,—only sg. cstr. כֹּפֶר הַפְּרָזִי 1 S 6^{18} *villages of the peasantry*.

כְּפַר הָעַמֹּנִי v. כָּפָר supr.

† כְּפִירָה **n.pr.loc.** city of the Hivites subsequently assigned to Benjamin, Jos 9^{17} 18^{26} Ezr 2^{25} = Ne 7^{29}; 𝔊 Κεφειρα, etc; = mod. *Kefireh* Rob[BR iii. 146] Guérin[Jud i 283 ff] Mem[iii. 36] Buhl[G § 94, p 169]

† כְּפִירִים Ne 6^{2}, prob. = foregoing (𝔊 al. n appell. = *villages*).

IV. **כפר** (√of foll, = *dig*? cf. Sab. כפר, vb. *dig*, n. *cave*, DHM[Anzeiger d. Wiener Ak., phil. hist. Cl., Dec. 17, 1884], quoted by Eut[Nab 27]; No[ib.] comp. also Eth. ከፈር: *basket, measure;* Nab כפר *cave, sepulchre*, synon. of קברא No in Eut[Nab ib])

† I. כְּפוֹר **n.m. bowl** (NH *id.*; 𝔗 כְּפוֹרָא)—*bowl* of gold or silver, used in the temple (late), כ׳ 1 Ch $28^{17\ 17\ 17\ 17}$; pl. cstr. כְּפוֹרֵי 1 Ch $28^{17\ 17}$ Ezr $1^{10\ 10}$ 8^{27}.

† II כְּפוֹר **n.m. hoar frost** (NH *id.*)—כ׳ ψ 147^{16}, כְּפֹר Ex 16^{14} (P), Jb 38^{29}.

† [כָּפַשׁ] **vb.** only **Hiph. make bent, press or bend together** (NH Hiph. *id*; כָּפַשׁ *furnish* a vessel *with a bent rim*, כּוֹפֶשׁ *a broad-rimmed vessel;* Ar. كَبِسَ *have bent* or *crooked feet;* Tel Am. *kapâšu*, *sole* of foot Dl[HWB 348] (doubtfully), but inf. fr. כבש acc. to Wkl[Tel Am. Letters, Vocab.]),—**Hiph.** *Pf* 3 ms. sf. הִכְפִּישַׁנִי בָּאֵפֶר La 3^{16} *he made me cower in the ashes*.

† I. כַּפְתֹּר, כַּפְתּוֹר **n.m. 1. capital, 2. knob, bulb** (**2.** perhaps earlier mng, Hoffm ZAW[iii. (1883), 124], comp. Syr. ܦܬܘܪܐ *pear* (Low[No. 153]), from shape);—**1.** כַּפְתּוֹר Am 9^{1} *capital* of pillar; so pl. sf. כַּפְתֹּרֶיהָ Zp 2^{14}. **2.** כַּפְתֹּר, *knob* or bulb, ornament on the golden lampstand in tabernacle; 𝔊 σφαιρωτήρ, Jos[Arch. iii. 6, 7] ῥοΐσκος, *small pomegranate;* 𝔙 *sphaerula*.—Ex $25^{33.33.33.35.35}$ = $37^{19\ 19.21\ 21\ 21}$; sf. כַּפְתֹּרֶיהָ $25^{31.34}$ = $37^{17\ 20}$, כַּפְתֹּרֵיהֶם 25^{36} = 37^{22} (all P).

† II. כַּפְתֹּר, כַּפְתּוֹר **n.pr.terr.** prob **Crete**, so Ew Kiep Di[Gn 10. 14] Gie[Je 47. 4] al, cf. A. J. Evans[Cretan Pictographs (1895), 100 ff.], (> 𝔊 𝔖 𝔙 𝔗 *Cappadocia*, certainly wrong; Mich *Cyprus;* Eb[ÄgM 127 ff] al. the coast of the *Nile-Delta;* WMM[As. Eu. 387 f.] Philistines, originally pirates from SW. coast of Asia Minor, and the Ægean islands);—כַּפְתּוֹר Am 9^{7} (orig. home of Philistines), כַּפְתֹּר Dt 2^{23} (home of Caphtorim, v. infr.); שְׁאֵרִית אִי כַּפְתֹּר Je 47^{4} *the rest of the coast-land of Caphtor*.—Vid. also כְּרֵתִי infr

† [כַּפְתֹּרִי] **adj.gent.**, only pl. as subst כַּפְתֹּרִים **Cretans**, Gn 10^{14} (J) = 1 Ch 1^{12}; as expellers of the 'Awwim' from their homes about Gaza, Dt 2^{23}.

I. כַּר *basket-saddle*, v. sub כור.

† II. כַּר **n.m.** ψ 65, 14 **pasture** (√dub.; Thes der fr. כַּר *lamb* (= lamb-pasturage); Schwally ZAW[x (1890) 186] fr. כרה, and comp As. *kirû* [which however = *nursery of trees, grove* Dl[HWB 353]], Ar. كُرّ *cistern;* Hom[NS 100] from כרר q. v, orig = *round enclosure*);—sg. only כַּר נִרְחָב Is 30^{23} *a roomy pasture;* pl כָּרִים ψ 37^{20}, לָבְשׁוּ כ׳ הַצֹּאן 65^{14} *the pastures are clothed with the sheep* (> Schwally[l. c] who tr. *lambs* ψ 37^{20} after Aq 𝔖 𝔗, and 65^{14}, and underst. Is 30^{23} of a def. pl).—III. כַּר *lamb* v. sub כרר.

† כֹּר **n.[m.]** kōr, a measure (usu. dry), = חמר (Ez 45^{14} cf. v^{11}) (NH כּוֹר, Aram כּוֹרָא, ܟܘܪܐ; hence, as loan-words, Gk. κόρος, Ar. كُرّ Fra[207]; √dub; כרה, Lag[Or ii. 30], cf. Id[BN 80, 156]; כרר, No[ZMG 1886, xl. 734]; Dl[Prol. 113] comp. As. *kâru*, and der fr כור (but see now *kâru* Dl[HWB 349]));—כ׳ סֹלֶת 1 K 5^{2}; כ׳ קֶמַח v^{2}; of חִטִּים v^{25a}; pl. כֹּרִים of ח׳ and שְׂעֹרִים 2 Ch 2^{9} 27^{5}; הַכֹּר as liquid measure (of oil) Ez 45^{14}. See further Benz[Arch 183 ff.] Now[Arch i. 203], and, on capacity, v. III חֹמֶר p. 330 f. supr.; in 1 K 5^{25b} rd. בַּת שֶׁמֶן for MT כֹּר שׁ׳ (cf. 𝔊 and 2 Ch 2^{9})

† [כרבל] **vb.** either **denom. be-mantle** (from BAram. כַּרְבְּלָא Dn 3^{21}, *if* this = *mantle*, and not (Marti[Gl]) = Ass. *karballatu, cap* (but 'Kriegs[?]-mantel,' Zehnpfund[BAS ii. 535])), or

poss. **quadril.** bind round (from כבל, with ins ר),—only **Pu.** *pt pass* מְכֻרְבָּל בִּמְעִיל בּוּץ 1 Ch 15^{27} *bemantled* with a robe of byssus.

†I. **כָּרָה** **vb** dig (NH *id*, Aram כְּרָא, Eth ከረየ: Ar كَرَا (c و and esp ى, Dozy$^{\text{ii 461}}$), Syr ܟܪܳܐ is *be short, cut off* (i e *rounded off* ?), Ar كُرَةٌ *ball;* ℑ כרי *heap* Dalm$^{\text{Gr 109}}$, Syr ܟܪܳܐ, Mish. כרי *id*, As *karê*, large vessels for holding corn, etc, Dl$^{\text{HWB 353}}$, cf *kirû* (dub) Wkl$^{\text{Tel Am Vocab}}$, Ba$^{\text{ZMG 1887 615}}$ conjectures *be round* as orig √ mng, and comp Ar. كَرِبَ السَّاقُ *the leg is round*),—**Qal** *Pf* 3 ms כָּרָה 2 Ch 16^{14} ψ 7^{16}, 2 ms. כָּרִיתָ ψ 40^{7}, 1 s כָּרִיתִי Gn 50^{5}, 3 pl כָּרוּ Je 18^{20}+3 t, sf כָּרוּהָ Nu 21^{18}, *Impf* 3 ms יִכְרֶה Ex 21^{33}, 3 mpl וַיִּכְרוּ Gn 26^{25}, *Pt* כֹּרֶה Pr 16^{27} 26^{27},—*dig* a grave, קֶבֶר Gn 50^{5} (J), cf 2 Ch 16^{14}; a well, בְּאֵר Gn 26^{25} (J), Nu 21^{18} (song in JE); a pit, בּוֹר Ex 21^{33}, fig of plotting against others ψ 7^{16}, so sq שׁוּחָה Je 18$^{20.22}$, sq שִׁיחָה 57^{7} 119^{85}, sq שַׁחַת Pr 26^{27}, hence כֹּרֶה רָעָה Pr 16^{27} *one digging a calamity*, אָזְנַיִם כ׳ לִי ψ 40^{7} ears *hast thou dug* (with allusion to the cavity of the ear) *for me*, thou hast given me the means of hearing and obeying thy will —On ψ 22^{17} v. II כּוּר. **Niph.** *Impf* 3 ms עַד יִכָּרֶה שַׁחַת ψ 94^{13} *until the pit be digged* for the wicked, fig of judgment.

†[**כֵּרָה**] **n.f. cistern** (or **well**), only pl cstr in נוֹת כְּרֹת רֹעִים Zp 2^{6} pastures of (=with) *wells of shepherds*, but text dub; כ׳ a gloss acc to Ko$^{\text{ii 176, (§ 94 a) Anm}}$, 𝔊 κρήτη; We (והיתה כרת נות רעים, as 𝔊) *kereth*=Philistia, v further כְּרֵתִי, Bohme$^{\text{ZAW vii 1887, 212}}$ views כרת, plausibly, as erron variant of preceding נוֹת, so Schwally$^{\text{ib. x 1890, 185, 186}}$, Rothstein in Kau^{AT}.

†[**מִכְרֶה**] **n.m. pit** (?), only cstr מִכְרֵה־מֶלַח Zp 2^{9} *salt-pit* (but not certain).

†II [**כָּרָה**] **vb. get by trade, trade** (NH כִּירָה *act of buying, purchase* (so 'in den Kustenlandern,' Levy$^{\text{NWB ii 323 f}}$), Ar. كَرَى *let for hire*),—only **Qal** *Impf.* 1 s sf. וָאֶכְּרֶהָ Ho 3^{2} (d f dirim, si vera punctat, Ges$^{\text{§ 20. 2. b}}$, but cf We), 3 mpl יִכְרוּ Jb 40^{30}, 2 mpl תִּכְרוּ Dt 2^{6} Jb 6^{27},—*get by trade, buy*, c. acc. Ho 3^{2} Dt 2^{6}, sq עַל־ *trade in, make trade of* Jb 6^{27} 40^{30}.

†III [**כָּרָה**] **vb give a feast** (lit perhaps *bring* (guests), *invite*, cf As *karû, bring, kirêtu, feast, kireti iškun, he gave a feast*, Dl$^{\text{HWB 352}}$),—only **Qal** *Impf* c acc. cogn., וַיִּכְרֶה לָהֶם כֵּרָה גְדוֹלָה 2 K 6^{23} *and he gave a great feast for them* (the context requires this sense, but text dubious, No$^{\text{ZMG 1886, 724}}$, cf. Klo)

†**כֵּרָה** **n f a feast**, 2 K 6^{23} (si vera l.; v foregoing)

כְּרוּב **n.m. cherub**,—כ׳ Ex 25^{19}+26 t, pl כְּרוּבִים ψ 99^{1}+33 t, כְּרֻבִים Ex 25^{18}+29 t., (NH *id*; Aram כְּרוּבָא, ܟܪܘܒܐ, √ dub, As *karâbu = be gracious to, bless* Dl$^{\text{HWB 350}}$, but adj *karûbu* is *great, mighty*, Id$^{\text{ib 352}}$, on poss connex. with כְּרוּב cf. Dl in Baer$^{\text{Ezech xiii}}$, As *kirubu=šêdu* (name of winged bull in Assyr, v. Len$^{\text{Origines i 118, Eng Tr 126}}$ Dl$^{\text{Par 154}}$) has not been verified, cf v F$^{\text{ZA i. 68 f}}$ Budge$^{\text{Expos Apr May, 1884}}$ Telon$^{\text{ZA vi 124 ff}}$; the older view, connecting כ׳ with γρύψ, and deriving from Pers *griften, griffen*, lacks evidence and probability.—Possibly the *thunder-cloud* underlies the conception),—**1.** the living chariot of the theophanic God; possibly identified with the storm-wind ψ 18^{11}=2 S 22^{11} וַיִּרְכַּב עַל־כְּרוּב *and he rode upon a cherub* (‖ flew swiftly on the wings of the wind) **2.** as the guards of the garden of Eden Gn 3^{24} (J) **3.** as the throne of Yahweh Sabaoth, in phrase י׳ (צְבָאוֹת) ישֵׁב הַכְּרוּבִים *Yahweh Sabaoth throned on the cherubim* 1 S 4^{4} 2 S 6^{2}=1 Ch 13^{6}; the context shews that the cherubim of the ark of the covenant are referred to, and it is probable that the same reference is in 2 K 19^{15} = Is 37^{16}, ψ 80^{2} 99^{1}. **4.** P gives an account of. **a.** two cherubim of solid gold upon the slab of gold of the כַּפֹּרֶת facing each other with wings outstretched above, so as to constitute a basis or throne on which the glory of Yahweh appeared, and from whence He spake Ex 25$^{18-22}$ 37$^{7-9}$ Nu 7^{89}, **b.** numerous cherubim woven into the texture of the inner curtains of the tabernacle and the veils Ex 26$^{1.31}$ 36$^{8.35}$. **5.** K and Ch describe the cherubim of the temple. **a.** two gigantic images of olive wood plated with gold, ten cubits high, standing in the דְּבִיר facing the door, whose wings, five cubits each, extended, two of them meeting in the middle of the room to constitute the throne, two of them extending to the walls 1 K 6$^{23-28}$ 8$^{6-7}$ 2 Ch 3$^{10-13}$ 5$^{7-8}$; Ch (doubtless influenced by Ez) represents them as the chariot of Yahweh 1 Ch 28^{18}; **b.** images of cherubim were carved on the gold plated cedar planks which constituted the inner walls of the temple, and upon the olive wood doors 1 K 6$^{29-35}$ 2 Ch 3^{7}; and on the bases of the portable lavers, interchanging

with lions and oxen 1 K 7^{29-36}; Ch also represents that they were woven in the veil of the דְּבִיר 2 Ch 3^{14}. **6.** Ezekiel describes the cherubim: **a.** as four living creatures, each with four faces, lion, ox, eagle, and man, having the figure and hands of men, and the feet of calves. Each has four wings, two of which are stretched upward, meeting above and sustaining the throne of Yahweh; two of them stretched downwards so as to cover the creatures themselves. The cherubim never turn but go straight forward, as do the wheels of the cherubic chariot, and they are full of eyes and are like burning coals of fire, Ez 1^{5-28} 9^{3} 10^{1-20} 11^{22}; the king of Tyre is scornfully compared with one of these, and is assigned a residence in Eden and the mountain of God Ez $28^{14.16}$; **b.** Ez knows of no cherubic statues in the new temple, but represents the inner walls of the temple as carved with alternating palm trees and cherubim, each with two faces, the lion looking on one side, the man on the other. It is evident that the number and the form of the cherubim vary in the representations (cf. Ez 41^{18-25}). It is probable that the שְׂרָפִים of Is 6^{2-6} are another form of the cherubim. The Apoc of the seals Rev 4–6 combines them in four ζῷα.

†כָּרִי **adj. gent.** prob = **Carian**, only c art. as subst. coll *Carians*, name given to foreign body-guard of king (cf. RS OTJC 349, 2d ed. 262) לַכָּרִי וְלָרָצִים 2 K 11^{4} cf. v^{19}; הכרי 2 S 20^{23} Kt (< Qr הַכְּרֵתִי, which We Dr Bu prefer).

כְּרִית **n.pr.loc** and כְּרִיתוּת v sub כרת.

כרך (√ of following; cf. Aram. כְּרַךְ, ܟܪܰܟ *enwrap, surround*, כְּרִיכָא, ܟܪܺܝܟܳܐ *bundle*, כְּרַכָּא, ܟܪܰܟܳܐ *city* (+many other deriv.); כְּרִיכָא, ܟܪܺܝܟܳܐ, NH כֶּרֶךְ, *scroll*, etc)

†תַּכְרִיךְ **n.m.** robe וְתַכְרִיךְ בּוּץ וְאַרְגָּמָן Est 9^{15}.

כרכב **quadril.** (√ of following, cf NH כרכב, *furnish with a rim, enclose, set*).

†כַּרְכֹּב **n.[m.]** border, rim, of altar (NH *id*),—cstr. כ׳ הַמִּזְבֵּחַ Ex 27^{5}, c sf. כַּרְכֻּבּוֹ 38^{4} (both P)

†כַּרְכֹּם **n.[m.]** saffron (*crocus sativus*) (NH *id*; and vb denom. כרכם; Hithp *grow yellow, pale*; Aram כּוּרְכְּמָא, ܟܘܪܟܡܐ; Ar كُرْكُم = κρόκος, *crocus*; Lag Ges. Abh 58, No. 147, so also JHMordt Sab Denkm 83 f.; otherwise DHM ib, who comp. Sab כמכם, Ar كُمْكَام = Gk. κάγκαμον);—Ct 4^{14}, on meaning v esp. Löw No. 162.

†כַּרְכְּמִישׁ, כַּרְכְּמִשׁ **n.pr.loc.**, city on Euphrates (As. *Kargamis, Gargamis*, cf Dl Par 265 ff.; Egypt. *Ḳa-ri-ka-mạı(?)-šạ* WMM Asien u Europa 263, etym dub.; acc. to Hoffm Auszüge Act Pers Märt 163 RS Proph. I, n 5 = '*Castle of Mish*,' cf Dl l c);—כַּרְכְּמִישׁ Is 10^{9} 2 Ch 35^{20} (𝔊L Χαρχαμεις), כַּרְכְּמִשׁ Je 46^{2} (𝔊 Χαρμεις, Καρχαμεις). Hittite capital, E. bank of Euphr., mod. *Jerabîs*, or *Jerbâs*; Schr KGF 221 ff., COT on Is 10 9 Dl l c.; Jen ZA vii (1892), 365 thinks he reads *G(K)ar-g(k)a-mi-si(e)-ras* = 'king of Karkemish' on ('Hittite') inscr from Karkemish.

†כַּרְכַּס **n.pr.m. Pers.**, a eunuch of Ahasuerus, Est 1^{10}.

כִּרְכָּרוֹת v [כִּרְכָּרָה] sub כרר.

כֶּרֶם 92 **n.m** Dt 28, 30 (**f.** Is 27, 2) **vineyard** (NH *id*, Aram. כַּרְמָא, ܟܰܪܡܳܐ; Zinj. כרם DHM Sendsch 58; Ar كَرْم, كَرْمَة *vine*, Eth ከርም: ከርም: *vine*, Jen ZA vii (1892) 217 comp As *karânu, vine*,—etym. dub; Thes al. comp. Ar كَرُمَ *noble, generous, fertile*, but precarious);—abs כ׳ Ex 22^{4}+, כָּרֶם Gn 9^{20}+; cstr. כֶּרֶם 1 K 21^{7}+, sf. כַּרְמִי Is 5^{3}+, כַּרְמְךָ Ex 23^{11}+, etc., pl. כְּרָמִים Jos 24^{13}+; cstr. כַּרְמֵי Am 5^{1}+2 t.; sf. כְּרָמֵנוּ Ne 5^{3}+3 t.; כַּרְמֵיכֶם Am 4^{9}+2 t., etc.,—*vineyard* Gn 9^{20} (J), 1 K 21^{1}+9 t. 1 K 21, Ct $2^{15.15}$+; so even Ju 15^{5} (where rd. כ׳ וזית, cf. GFM, who however doubts genuineness); + זַיִת Ex 23^{11} (E) and oft. (v. זית); + שָׂדֶה Ex $22^{4.5}$ (E), and oft, fig of Isr under י׳'s care Is $5^{1 ff}$, cf. 3^{14} Je 12^{10}; fig of Shulamite's complexion Ct 1^{6}, of her heart 8^{12}—Vbs governing כ׳ are.—נָטַע Gn 9^{20} Am 5^{11}+16 t., cf. מַטָּעֵי כ׳ Mi 1^{6}; זָרַע Dt 22^{9} (c. 2 acc.); חִלֵּל = *begin to use fruit of*, Dt $20^{6.6}$ 28^{30} Je 31^{5}; זָמַר *prune*, Lv $25^{3.4}$; בָּצַר *gather, harvest* (lit. *cut off*, i.e. grapes, Lv $25^{5.11}$), Dt 24^{21} Ju 9^{27}, cf. לָקַשׁ Jb 24^{6}, עולל *glean*, Lv 19^{10} Dt 24^{21}; אָכַל Jos 24^{13} (usu. 'eat *fruit* of' Is 65^{21}, etc); locusts *devour* Am 4^{9} (si vera l.) On **n.pr.loc.** אָבֵל כְּרָמִים v. II. אָבֵל **4**; בֵּית הַכֶּרֶם v. p. 111 b.

†[כָּרַם] **vb. denom.** tend vineyards, dress vines, only **Qal** *Pt.* pl *vinedressers* כֹּרְמִים 2 K 25^{12} = Je 52^{16} (‖ יֹגְבִים), Jo 1^{11} 2 Ch 26^{10} (both ‖ אִכָּרִים), כֹּרְמֵיכֶם Is 61^{5} (‖ *id.*)

†I. כַּרְמִי **n.pr.m. 1.** a son of Reuben Gn 46^{9} Ex 6^{14} Nu 26^{6} 1 Ch 5^{3}. **2.** a Judaite Jos $7^{1.18}$ 1 Ch 2^{7}; so 4^{1}, but rd. perh כְּלוּבַי We (cf. 2^{9})—𝔊 throughout Χαρμ(ε)ι.

†II. כַּרְמִי **adj. gent.** of I. כַּרְמִי **1**; only c. art. הַכּ׳, as subst. Nu 26⁶.

†I. כַּרְמֶל **n.m.** Is 29.17 **1. plantation, garden-land. 2. fruit, garden-growth** (כֶּרֶם + ל, cf. Ges § 85.52 Sta § 299);—abs. כ׳ Is 16¹⁰ + 12 t.; sf. כַּרְמִלּוֹ Is 10¹⁸ + 2 t.;—**1.** *garden-land*, Is 16¹⁰ (|| כְּרָמִים), 10¹⁸ (|| יַעַר), 29¹⁷·¹⁷ (opp. לְבָנוֹן, יַעַר), 32¹⁵·¹⁵ (opp. יַעַר, מִדְבָּר), v¹⁶ Je 4²⁶ (opp. מִדְבָּר), 48³³ 2 Ch 26¹⁰ (opp. הֶהָרִים); אֶרֶץ הַכּ׳ Je 2⁷ *the country of garden-land*, i.e. fertile; יַעַר כַּרְמִלּוֹ 2 K 19²³ = Is 37²⁴, *the garden-like forest of it* (viz. of Lebanon). On Mi 7¹⁴ v. II. כַּרְמֶל. **2.** by meton. (*fresh*) *fruit, garden-growth*, 2 K 4⁴² (+ לֶחֶם שְׂעוֹרִים); Lv 2¹⁴ (+ אָבִיב, and גֶּרֶשׂ, q. v.), לֶחֶם וְקָלִי וכ׳ Lv 23¹⁴.

†II. כַּרְמֶל **n.pr.mont. et urb. Carmel**:—**1.** mt.-promontory on Mediterranean, with fertile slopes, Tel el-Amarna (*Ginti-*)*Kirmil*, Jastrow JBL xi. 1892, 115; Jos 19²⁶, הַר־הַכּ׳ 1 K 18¹⁹·²⁰ 2 K 2²⁵ 4²⁵; רֹאשׁ הַכּ׳ Am 1² 9³ 1 K 18⁴²; c. art. also Jos 12²²; and, + בָּשָׁן, Je 50¹⁹, as pasturage (in fig. of Isr. as flock of י׳), cf. (כ׳ without art.) Mi 7¹⁴ (less prob. rend. *garden-land*, I. כַּרְמֶל, so We GASm); הַכּ׳ Is 35² (+ הַשָּׁרוֹן, הַלְּבָנוֹן); כ׳ Is 33⁹ (+ לְבָנוֹן, הַשָּׁרוֹן and בָּשָׁן, marking extent of land), Na 1⁴ (+ לְבָנוֹן, בָּשָׁן); כְּכַרְמֶל בַּיָּם Je 46¹⁸ (sim. of Nebuchad.); Ct 7⁶ רֹאשֵׁךְ עָלַיִךְ כַּכּ׳ (but v. כַּרְמִיל);—on Carmel v. GASm G. 337 ff. Buhl G. 23. **2.** city, 3 h. S. of Hebron, כַּרְמֶל Jos 15⁵⁵; בַּכּ׳ 1 S 25²·²·⁷; כַּרְמֶ֫לָה v⁵ (= *to Carmel*); הַכַּרְמֶ֫לָה 15¹² 25⁴⁰.—Mod. *Kurmul*, Rob BR i. 492–498, ii. 97 Buhl G. 163.

†כַּרְמְלִי **adj. gent.**, c. art., **the Carmelite**, of Nabal הַכּ׳ 1 S 30⁵ 2 S 2² 3³, so also 1 S 27³ (𝔊 We Klo Dr Bu Kit; MT הַכַּרְמְלִית, of Abigail); of חצרו 2 S 23³⁵ = 1 Ch 11³⁷. **f.** הַכַּרְמְלִית *the Carmelitess*, 1 Ch 3¹, of Abigail.

†כַּרְמִיל **n.[m.]** crimson, carmine, i.e. crimson stuff, cloth; late (prob. Pers. loan-word, and a deriv. fr. Pers. كِرْم *worm*, v. De ZLuth. Th. 1878, 593);—only 2 Ch 2⁶·¹³ 3¹⁴ (in all + אַרְגְּוָן(-ן), תְּכֵלֶת, 2¹³ 3¹⁴ + בּוּץ also); rd. perh. also for כַּרְמֶל Ct 7⁶ (|| אַרְגָּמָן): so Gi, of hair formed spirally, like shell-fish; Gr, of glossy hair).

†כְּרָן **n.pr.m.**, an Edomite Gn 36²⁶ = 1 Ch 1⁴¹.

כִּרְסֵם v. sub כסם.

†כָּרַע **bow down** (NH *id.*; Aram. כְּרַע; Ar. كَرَعَ *put one's mouth* into water, or water-vessel; i.e. kneel to drink? denom. fr. foll.?);—**Qal** *Pf.* 3 m. כ׳ Gn 49⁹ + 6 t.; 3 mpl. כָּֽרְעוּ Ju 7⁶ + 4 t.; *Impf.* יִכְרַע Ju 7⁵ + 3 t.; 1 s. וָאֶכְרְעָה Ezr 9⁵; 3 mpl. יִכְרְעוּן Jb 31¹⁰; 2 mpl. תִּכְרָ֑עוּ Is 65¹²; 1 pl. וְנִכְרָ֫עָה ψ 95⁶ + 6 t. Impf.; *Inf. cstr.* כְּרֹעַ 1 K 8⁵⁴; *Pt.* כֹּרֵעַ Est 3⁵; pl. כֹּרְעִים Est 3²; f. כֹּרְעוֹת Jb 4⁴.—**1.** *bow* על ברכים to drink Ju 7⁵·⁶, in supplication to Elijah 2 K 1¹³; in the worship of God 1 K 8⁵⁴ Ezr 9⁵; c. ברכים subj. and לְ of God 1 K 19¹⁸ Is 45²³; without ברכים c. לִפְנֵי ψ 22³⁰ 72⁹; || השתחוה 2 Ch 7³ 29²⁹ ψ 95⁶, worship of God, but Est 3²·²·⁵ in obeisance to Haman. **2.** *bow down*, of the couching lion Gn 49⁹ Nu 24⁹ (both poetry). **3.** preg. c. עַל, *bow down over* (in order to lie with) a woman Jb 31¹⁰. **4.** *bow down*, of a woman in childbirth 1 S 4¹⁹, so of animals Jb 39³; idols, removed by enemies Is 46¹·²; בִּרְכַּיִם כֹּרְעוֹת Jb 4⁴ *tottering* (feeble) knees; of enemies in death, כרע [ו]נפל *bow and fall down* Ju 5²⁷·²⁷·²⁷ ψ 20⁹, preg. without נפל 2 K 9²⁴ Is 65¹², c. תַּחַת Is 10⁴.—**Hiph.** *Pf.* 3 ms. הִכְרִיעַ ψ 78³¹; 2 fs. sf. הִכְרַעְתִּנִי Ju 11³⁵; *Impf.* 2 ms. תַּכְרִיעַ 2 S 22⁴⁰ = ψ 18⁴⁰; *Imv.* sf. הַכְרִיעֵהוּ ψ 17¹³; *Inf. abs.* הַכְרֵעַ Ju 11³⁵.—**1.** cause to *bow in grief* Ju 11³⁵·³⁵. **2.** cause to *bow down in death* ψ 17¹³ 78³¹, c. תַּחַת 2 S 22⁴⁰ = ψ 18⁴⁰.

†[כֶּרַע] **n.[f.]** leg, (NH כֶּרַע, Aram. כַּרְעָא, ܟܪܥܐ);—only dual fem. כְּרָעַיִם Lv 11²¹ + 3 t.; כְּרָעַיִם Lv 9¹⁴; sf. כְּרָעָיו Ex 12⁹ + 3 t.;—*two* (bending) *legs*, of animals in ritual phrase of P, רֹאשׁוֹ עַל־כְּרָעָיו Ex 12⁹ *his head with his legs*, Lv 4¹¹; (ה)קרב(ו) ו(ה)כרע(יו) (*his*) *inwards* and (*his*) *legs* Ex 29¹⁷ Lv 1⁹·¹³ 8²¹ 9¹⁴; Am 3¹² (of legs of lamb in mouth of lion); of the long bending hinder legs of the Saltatorial Orthoptera (v. Tristr Nat. Hist. Bib. 309; Dr Joel 84) Lv 11²¹ אשר לוֹ כְּרָעַיִם מִמַּעַל לְרַגְלָיו לְנַתֵּר בָּהֵן עַל הָאָרֶץ which have *bending legs* above their feet, etc.

†כַּרְפַּס **n.m.** cotton (or fine linen) (loan-word fr. Sk. *karpâsa, cotton*, Pers. كَرْپَاس *fine linen*; hence also κάρπασος, *carbasus*, Ar. كِرْبَاس, Talm. כַּרְפְּסָא; cf. Lag Arm. Stud. § 1148);—חוּר כ׳ וּתְכֵלֶת Est 1⁶ (𝔊 καρπασίνοις): cf. Cels. Hierob. ii. 157 ff.

†[כָּרַר] **vb.** √ of foll. (NH כִּרְכֵּר *use circumlocution*; 𝔗 pl. כִּרְכְּרָן *dances*; Ar. كَرَّ *return, repeat, attack anew, advance and retreat*; كَرْكَرَ *id.*; II. *whirl about*; orig. perh. *move around*,

then *surround, enclose, recur*, etc.; Eth. ከርከረ: *turn* a mill, only pt.; ኵርኵረ: v. *rotate, revolve, roll*, and deriv. Di[838 f.]);—only **Pilpēl**, *Pt.* מְכַרְכֵּר *dancing* (lit. *whirling*) 2 S 6[14.16] (‖ מְפַזֵּז).

†II. **כַּר n.[m.] he-lamb, battering-ram** (As. *kirru*, Zim in Schwally[ZAW x. (1890). 186]; perh. *lamb* fr. *dancing, skipping, galloping* in field; (*battering-*)*ram* as in Eng., fr. butting; cf. Ar. كَبْش *ram* and *buttress*, Lane; also *battering-ram* cf. Dozy[ii. 440]);—sg. only Is 16[1] *the lamb of the ruler* (as tribute); elsewh. pl. כָּרִים Am 6[4] 1 S 15[9] 2 K 3[4] Je 51[40] (in sim.), Ez 27[21] 39[18]; חֵלֶב כ׳ Dt 32[14] *the fat of lambs*; דַּם כ׳ וְעַתּוּדִים Is 34[6] *the blood of lambs and goats*; כָּרִים = *battering-rams* Ez 4[2] 21[27.27] (in v[a] Co rds. שָׂרִים, cf. AV; MT RV as above).—Vid. also בֵּית כַּר p. 111 supr.

†[**כִּרְכָּרָה**] **n.f.** '*dromedary* (acc. to Ki Thes; perhaps from constantly *repeated undulating* movement);—only pl. abs. וּבַכִּרְכָּרוֹת Is 66[20] (+ בַּסּוּסִים וּבָרֶכֶב וּבַצַּבִּים וּבַפְּרָדִים; the whole list is a gloss acc. to Du Che[Intr. Is.]).

כִּכָּר n.f.[Gn 13, 10 Ex 29, 32]; **a round**: hence **1. a round district. 2. a round loaf. 3. a round weight, talent** (NH *id.*; *loaf, weight, talent*; Aram. כַּכְּרָא, ܟܰܟܪܳܐ, *talent*; Tel Am. *gaggaru* kaspu Wkl[No. 35, Rev. 14] Christ.-Pal.-Aram. ܟܟܪܐ, of honey-*comb* Schwally[Idiot. 46]; on format. v. Ba[NB 204]);—abs. כ׳ Gn 13[12]+; cstr. כִּכַּר 1 S 2[36]+; du. כִּכְּרַיִם כֶּסֶף 1 K 16[24] 2 K 5[23], כִּכָּרַיִם v[23]; pl. כִּכָּרִים 1 Ch 22[14.14]+7 t. Chr; cstr. כִּכְּרֵי 2 K 5[5] + 2 t. Chr; כִּכְּרוֹת (*loaves*) Ju 8[5] 1 S 10[3];—†**1.** *the round* (or *oval*) esp. of the Jordan valley, כִּכַּר הַיַּרְדֵּן Gn 13[10.11] 1 K 7[46]=2 Ch 4[17]; abs. הַכִּכָּר Gn 19[17.25] Dt 34[3] 2 S 18[23]; אֶרֶץ הַכּ׳ Gn 19[28]; עָרֵי הַכּ׳ 13[12] 19[29], v. GASm[G. 505] Buhl[G. 112]; district of Jerus., הַכּ׳ Ne 3[22] 12[28]. †**2.** *loaf* of bread (from round shape), כִּכַּר לֶחֶם 1 S 2[36] Pr 6[26], cf. Ex 29[23] Je 37[21] 1 Ch 16[3]; כִּכְּרוֹת לֶחֶם 1 S 10[3] Ju 8[5]. **3.** †**a.** *a weight* (also fr. shape), כִּכַּר עֹפֶרֶת Zc 5[7] *a weight of lead*, serving as cover of an ephah. **b.** a particular unit of weight, *talent*, usu. of gold or silver:—כ׳ זָהָב 2 S 12[30] 2 K 9[14]+18 t.; כ׳ כֶּסֶף 1 K 20[39] 2 K 5[5]+21 t.; but also of iron, בַּרְזֶל 1 Ch 29[7], and bronze נְחֹשֶׁת Ex 38[29] 1 Ch 29[7].—The weight of the talent was 58·944 kilogr. (=129·97 lbs.) acc. to older (Bab.) standard, later 49·11 kg. (=108·29 lbs.) and less; v. Benz[Arch. 187 ff. 194] Now[Arch. i. 208 f.].—See also שֶׁקֶל.

כרשׁ √ of foll. (Ar. كَرِشَ *be wrinkled*).

†[**כָּרֵשׂ**] **n.[m.]** belly (NH כֶּרֶס *id.*; Aram. כַּרְסָא, ܟܪܣܐ *id.*; Mand. כרא‍ס, כארסא, *uterus*, Nö[M 151, 157]; Ar. كَرِش, Eth. ከርሥ: *wrinkled* or *folded stomach* of cud-chewing animals; cf. Lag[BN 20, 44]; As. *karšu, body, belly*);—only sf. כְּרֵשׂוֹ Je 51[34] of Nebuchadrezzar under fig. of sea-monster.

כֹּרֶשׁ n.pr.m. v. כּוֹרֶשׁ.

†**כַּרְשְׁנָא n.pr.m.** a Pers. prince Est 1[14].

†**כָּרַת**[291] **vb. cut off, cut down** (NH *id.*; As. *karâtu*, II. *hew off* Dl[HWB 357]);—**Qal** *Pf.* כ׳ Gn 15[18] + 19 t.; 2 ms. כָּרַתָּ Dt 20[20]; 1 s. כָּרַתִּי Ex 34[27] + 15 t.; + 8 t. Pf.; *Impf.* יִכְרֹת Jb 40[28] + 21 t.; 2 ms. תִּכְרָת־ Is 57[8]; 1 s. אֶכְרוֹת Is 61[8] 1 S 11[2]; אֶכְרְתָה Is 55[3]; 3 mpl. יִכְרֹתוּ Ho 12[2] ψ 83[6]; 1 pl. נִכְרְתָה Gn 26[28] 31[44]; sf. נִכְרְתֶנּוּ Je 11[19]; + 31 t. Impf.; *Imv.* כְּרָת־ 1 S 11[1]; כִּרְתָה 2 S 3[12]; + 4 t. Imv.; *Inf. abs.* כָּרֹת Ho 10[4]; כָּרוֹת Ne 9[8]; *cstr.* כְּרֹת Je 34[8] + 2 t.; כְּרָת־ Is 44[14] + 2 t.; כְּרוֹת 2 Ch 2[7] 29[10]; sf. כָּרְתִי 1 S 24[12]; *Pt. act.* כֹּרֵת Ex 34[10] + 3 t.; + 3 t. Pt. act.; *pass.* כָּרוּת Lv 22[24]; cstr. כְּרוּת Dt 23[2]; pl. כְּרֻתֹ[וֹ]ת 1 K 7[12] + 3 t.;—**1.** *cut off*: **a.** *things*: c. acc. foreskin Ex 4[25] (J); privy member Lv 22[24] (H) Dt 23[2]; cluster of grapes Nu 13[23.24] (E); bough of tree Ju 9[48.49]; skirt 1 S 24[5.6.12]; head of man 1 S 17[51] 31[9] 2 S 20[22]; garments 2 S 10[4] = 1 Ch 19[4]; palms of hands 1 S 5[4]; sprigs Is 18[5]. **b.** *persons*, c. acc. pers. מִן *loc.* Je 11[19] 50[16]. **2.** *cut down*, c. acc. trees Dt 19[5] 20[19.20] 2 K 19[23]=Is 37[24], Is 44[14] Je 6[6] 10[3] 22[7] 46[23] Ez 31[12]; *asherim* Ex 34[13] (J) Ju 6[25.26.30] 1 K 15[13] = 2 Ch 15[16]; 2 K 18[4] 23[14]. **3.** *hew*, timber 1 K 5[20.20] = 2 Ch 2[7.15], Is 14[8]; כֹּרְתֵי הָעֵצִים *hewers of timber* 2 Ch 2[9]; כְּרֻת(וֹ)ת *hewn beams* 1 K 6[36] 7[2.12]. **4.** כ׳ בְּרִית *cut, or make a covenant* (because of the cutting up and distribution of the flesh of the victim for eating in the sacrifice of the covenants, see בְּרִית); הָעֵגֶל אֲשֶׁר כ׳ *the calf which they cut* Je 34[18] (referring to Gn 15[10]); עֲלֵי־זָבַח ψ 50[5]; abs. Gn 21[27.32] 31[44] (E) 1 S 18[3] 1 K 5[26] Ho 10[4]; c. אֶת *with* Gn 15[18] Ex 34[27] Dt 31[16] (J) Dt 5[3] 28[69.69] 29[13] 2 S 3[12.13.21] 2 K 17[15.35.38] Is 28[15] Je 11[10] 31[31.32.33] 34[8.13] Ez 17[13] Zc 11[10] ψ 105[9] = 1 Ch 16[16]; c. עִם Gn 26[28] (J) Ex 24[8] (E) Dt 4[23] 5[2] 9[9] 29[11.24] 1 K 8[21] = 2 Ch 6[11] 2 Ch 23[3] Ne 9[8] Ho 2[20] 12[2] Jb 40[28]; בְּ׳ omitted 1 S 20[16] 22[8] 1 K 8[9] = 2 Ch 5[10]; c. לְ Ex 23[32] 34[12.15] Jos 9[6.7.11.15.16] 24[25] (JE) Dt 7[2] Ju 2[2] 1 S 11[1] 2 S 5[3] 1 K 20[34]

2 K 11^{4} 1 Ch 11^{3} 2 Ch 21^{7} 29^{10} Ezr 10^{3} Is 55^{3} 61^{8} Je 32^{40} Ez 3^{25} 37^{26} Jb 31^{1} ψ 89^{4}; ב׳ omitted 1 S 11^{2} 2 Ch 7^{18}, נגד Ex 34^{10} (J), לפני 1 S 23^{18} 2 K 23^{3} = 2 Ch 34^{31} Je 34$^{15.18}$; בין ובין 2 K 11^{17}, 2 Ch 23^{16}, c על *against*, ψ 83^{6}, אֲמָנָה is used for ברית Ne 10^{1}, and דָּבָר Hg 2^{5}

Note—וַתִּכְרָת־לָךְ מֵהֶם Is 57^{8} is usually rendered as RV *made for thee a covenant with them*, with ellipsis of ב׳ as above. But מן is not used in such a construction. The clause is commonly regarded as corrupt by recent critics. Gr emends עִמָּהֶם for מהם, this is easiest and gives the usual construction; Du, followed by Buhl, reads וַתִּכְרִי after Ho 3^{2}

Niph. *Pf* 3 ms נִכְרַת Jo 1^{5} + 5 t, נִכְרָת Jo 1^{16} + 2 t, 3 fs נִכְרְתָה Gn 17^{14} + 16 t, ψ 37^{38}; 2 ms נִכְרַתָּ Ob^{10}, + 8 t Pf, *Impf* יִכָּרֵת Gn 9^{11} + 21 t, יִכָּרֵת־ Ob^{9}, 3 mpl יִכָּרֵתוּ Zc 13^{8}, יִכָּרֵתוּן Jos 3^{13} ψ 37^{9}, + 9 t Impf, *Inf.* הִכָּרֵת Nu 15^{31} ψ 37^{34};—**1.** *be cut off*: **a.** of *things*, froward tongue Pr 10^{31}, burden from a nail Is 22^{25}, chariots Zc 9^{10}, dwelling Zp 3^{7}. **b.** *of persons*, the people of the land by a famine (ב) Gn 41^{36} (E), all flesh by waters of deluge (מִמֵּי) Gn 9^{11} (P), the anointed Dn 9^{26}, enemies Is 11^{13} Mi 5^{8}, the wicked Is 29^{20} Ho 8^{4} Na 2^{1} ψ 37$^{9.22.28.34.38}$ Pr 2^{22}, others Ob$^{9.10}$ Zp 1^{11} Zc 13^{8} 14^{2}. **c.** in the technical phrases of H and P וְנִכְרְתָה הַנֶּפֶשׁ הַהִוא *that person shall be cut off* (by death penalty) מֵעַמֶּיהָ Gn 17^{14} Lv 7$^{20.21.25.27}$ Nu 9^{13} Lv 19^{8}, מִיִּשְׂרָאֵל Ex 12^{15} Nu 19^{13}, מֵעֲדַת ישראל Ex 12^{19}, מִקֶּרֶב עַמֶּיהָ Ex 31^{14} Nu 15^{30} (עַמָּהּ), מִתּוֹךְ הַקָּהָל Nu 19^{20}, מִלְּפָנַי Lv 22^{3}, similarly with variation of subject Ex 30$^{33.38}$ Lv 17$^{4.9}$ 18^{29} 20^{18} 23^{29}, and with omission of word with מן Lv 17^{14} 20^{17} Nu 15$^{31.31}$. **2.** *be cut down*, a tree Jb 14^{7}. **3.** *be chewed* between the teeth Nu 11^{33} (J). **4.** *be cut off*, in a more general sense, *fail*: of waters Jos 3$^{13.16}$ (JE) 4$^{7.7}$ (D); new wine Jo 1^{5}, meat v^{16}, hope Pr 23^{18} 24^{14}, a name Is 48^{19} 56^{5} Ru 4^{10}, a sign Is 55^{13}; faithfulness Je 7^{28}, לֹא יִכָּרֵת לְךָ אִישׁ *there shall not fail thee a man* 1 K 2^{4} 8^{25} = 2 Ch 6^{16}, 1 K 9^{5} = 2 Ch 7^{18}, Je 33$^{17.18}$ 35^{19}, לא יכרת מן *there shall not fail of* Jos 9^{23} (J) 2 S 3^{29}

Pual *Pf* כָּרַת Ez 16^{4}, 3 fs כֹּרָתָה Ju 6^{28},—**1.** *be cut off*, navel string Ez 16^{4}. **2.** *be cut down*, Asherah Ju 6^{28}

Hiph. *Pf* הִכְרִית 1 S 28^{9} 1 K 11^{16}; 3 fs הִכְרִיתָה Lv 26^{22}, 1 s הִכְרַתִּי Jos 23^{4} + 32 t, + 4 t. Pf, *Impf* יַכְרִית Dt 12^{29} + 2 t, juss יַכְרֵת ψ 12^{4} + 4 t, 1 s וָאַכְרִתָה 2 S 7^{9}, 1 pl. sf וְנַכְרִיתֶנָּה Je 48^{2}, + 9 t Impf, *Inf* הַכְרִית Je 44^{8} + 15 t.; הַכְרִת 1 S 20^{15}; + sf. 2 t.—**1.** *cut off*, flattering lips ψ 12^{4}. **2.** *cut off*, destroy the life of: **a.** animals c acc., cattle Lv 26^{22} (H), c. acc. and מן frogs Ex 8^{5} (J), horses Mi 5^{9} Zc 9^{10}. **b.** of men abs ψ 109^{13}, by men, c acc. enemies Ju 4^{24} 1 S 24^{22} 1 K 11^{16} 14^{14} 18^{4} 2 Ch 22^{7} Is 10^{7} Ez 17^{17} Ob^{14}, c acc and מן enemies Jos 11^{21} Je 48^{2}; the wicked ψ 101^{8}, a clan Nu 4^{18} (P), young men by death Je 9^{20}, people by the sword Na 3^{15}; necromancers 1 S 28^{9}; the name Jos 7^{9}. **c.** of men, by God c acc. (הַ)גּוֹיִם Dt 19^{1} Jos 23^{4} (D) Zp 3^{6}, various persons and things Is 48^{9} Je 44^{11} 51^{62} Ez 25^{16} 30^{15} Zc 9^{6}, c acc. and מן Ez 25^{7} Am 1$^{5.8}$ 2^{3}; מֵאֶרֶץ Na 2^{14} ψ 34^{17} = 109^{15}, מִיִּשְׂרָאֵל Is 9^{13}; מִיַּד Mi 5^{11}; מִפָּנֶיךָ Dt 12^{29} 2 S 7^{9} = 1 Ch 17^{8}, מֵעַל פְּנֵי הָאֲדָמָה 1 S 20^{15} 1 K 9^{7} Zp 1^{3}, מִקֶּרֶב עַמּוֹ Lv 17^{10} 20$^{3.5.6}$ (H), מִתּוֹךְ עַמִּי Ez 14^{8}, Ez says also הכ׳ מן אָדָם וּבְהֵמָה . . . 14$^{13.17.19.21}$ 25^{13} 29^{8}, צדיק ורשׁע 21$^{8.9}$, עבר ושׁב 35^{7}, c acc. and לְ, *cut off, to*, or *from* Is 14^{22} Je 44$^{7.8}$ 47^{4}, כ׳ לְ׳ מַשְׁתִּין בקיר 1 K 14^{10} 21^{21} 2 K 9^{8}, כ׳ לְ׳ מעם מזבח 1 S 2^{33}; יַכְרֵת י׳ לָאִישׁ מֵאָהֳלֵי יַעֲקֹב Mal 2^{12} *may Yahweh cut off to the man—from the tents of Jacob*. **3.** *cut down, destroy*, cities Mi 5^{10}, sun-pillars Lv 26^{30} (H), and other things used in idolatry Na 1^{14} Zp 1^{4}, מן הארץ Zc 13^{2}, מִקֶּרֶב Mi 5^{12}. **4** *take away*, חסד מעם *kindness from* 1 S 20^{15}. **5.** *permit to perish*, מֵהַבְּהֵמָה (some) *of the cattle* 1 K 18^{5}

Hoph. *Pf* הָכְרַת מִנְחָה וָנֶסֶךְ מִבֵּית י׳ Jo 1^{9}

†כְּרִיתוּת **n.f.** divorcement,—כ׳ Is 50^{1}; כריתת Dt 24$^{1.3}$, pl sf כְּרִיתֻתֶיהָ Je 3^{8}; סֵפֶר כ׳ *writing* (i.e deed) *of divorcement*, Dt 24$^{1.3}$ Is 50^{1} Je 3^{8}

†כְּרִית **n.pr.** the brook where Elijah was hidden 1 K 17$^{3.5}$, identif. dub; acc Rob $^{BR\ II.\ p.\ 288}$ Wady *el-Kelt*, near Jericho; acc Buhl $^{Handw\ 12}$ Wady *'Ajlun*, E of Jordan, yet v. Buhl $^{G\ 121}$.

כרת Zp 2^{6} v [כָּרָה] sub I. כרה

†כְּרֵתִי **adj gent.**, always c. art., or pl, as subst, **Kerethites**, a name for Philistines or a part of them (perhaps = *Cretans*, cf. 𝔊 Zp 2^{5} Ez 25^{15}, on *Crete* as orig home of Philistines, v (פְּלִשְׁתִּי, כַּפְתֹּר),—הַכְּרֵתִי = subst. coll; נֶגֶב הַכ׳ 1 S 30^{14} (cf Dr, 𝔊B Χολθει, 𝔊L Χορρι, A Χερηθει), of soldiers of David's guard, הַכ׳ וְהַפְּלֵתִי 2 S 8^{18} (rd עַל־הַכ׳ Th We Dr al) = 1 Ch 18^{17}, 2 S 15^{18} 20^{7} + v^{23} Qr (> Kt הכרי), 1 K 1$^{38.44}$ (𝔊 Χελεθθει, Χερεθθει, etc.); pl כרתים Ez 25^{16} (‖ פְּלִשְׁתִּים,

(𝔊 Κρῆτας); גּוֹי כְּרֵתִים Zp 2^{5} (𝔊 Κρητῶν; ‖ ארץ פלשׁתים): in v^{6} We rds. כְּרֵת = Philistia (v. [כָּרָה], sub I. כרה).

כִּשְׂבָּה כֶּשֶׂב v. כֶּבֶשׂ, etc.

† **כֶּשֶׂד** n.pr.m. son of Nahor acc. to Gn 22^{22} (J; perh. orig. personif., or assumed ancestor, of following, v. Di Dl $^{Par\,201}$).

† **כַּשְׂדִּים** n.pr. gent. et terr. **Kasdim = Chaldeans, Chaldea,** 𝔊 Χαλδαῖοι and (Je 50^{10}) ἡ Χαλδαία (As. (mat) *Kaldu, Kaldû*; fr. earlier (Bab.) form [**Kašdu*]—*š* before dental becoming *l*, Dl $^{Par\,128\,f.\,200\,f.;\,As.\,Gr.\,\S51,3}$; Schr $^{KGF\,94\,ff.;\,COT\,on\,Gn\,11,28}$);—**1.** *Chaldeans:* **a.** people dwelling on lower Euphrates and Tigris; in n.pr.loc. אוּר כ׳ Gn 11^{28} (J), v^{31} (P), 15^{7} (J), Ne 9^{7}. **b.** esp. the people ruled by Nebuchadrezzar;—כ׳ Je 37^{10} 39^{5} Ez 23^{23} 2 K 24^{2} 25$^{4.5.10.13}$ = Je 52$^{7.8.14.17}$ (2 K 24$^{5.10}$ = also Je 39$^{5.8}$), 2 K 25^{26} Is 13^{19} 43^{14} 48$^{14.20}$ Jb 1^{17}; Kt. כַּשְׂדִּיִּים Ez 23^{14} 2 Ch 36^{17}; הַכּ׳ Je 21$^{4.9}$ 22^{25} 32$^{4.5.24.25.28.29.43}$ 33^{5} 35^{11} 37$^{5.8.9.11.13.14}$ 38$^{2.18.19.23}$ 39^{8} 40$^{9.10}$ 41$^{3.18}$ 43^{3} 50^{35} Hb 1^{6} 2 K 25$^{24.25}$; בַּת־כ׳ Is 47$^{1.5}$ = Babylon (in dirge); אֶרֶץ כ׳ ἡ γῆ Χαλδαίων (on locality v. Schr Dl $^{l.c.}$) Je 24^{5} 25^{12} 50$^{1.8.25.45}$ 51$^{4.54}$ Ez 1^{3} 12^{3}, also Is 23^{13} (inauthentic, Di Che; rd. כְּנַעֲנִים Ew Schr, or כִּתִּים Du); סֵפֶר וּלְשׁוֹן כ׳ Dn 1^{4}; מַלְכוּת כ׳ 9^{1}. **c.** *Chaldeans* as learned class, skilled in interpretations Dn 2^{2} (+ מְכַשְּׁפִים, אַשָּׁפִים, חַרְטֻמִּים), v^{4}. **2.** *Chaldea,* וְהָיְתָה כַשְׂדִּים לְשָׁלָל Je 50^{10} *and Chaldea shall be despoiled;* יוֹשְׁבֵי כ׳ 51$^{24.35}$; כַּשְׂדִּים אֶרֶץ מוֹלַדְתָּם Ez 23^{15}; c. ה loc.: כַּשְׂדִּימָה Ez 11^{24} 16^{29} 23^{16}.

† **[כָּשָׂה]** vb. **be sated, gorged with food** (cf. Ar. كَشِيَ *be filled with food; As. kissatum, sustenance, provender, food,* Zehnpf $^{BAS\,I.\,503}$);—only **Qal** *Pf.* 2 ms. שָׁמַנְתָּ עָבִיתָ כָּשִׂיתָ Dt 32^{15} *thou grewest fat, becamest thick, wast gorged!* fig. of Isr. as fat beast (cf. Dr).

כַּשִּׁית, כֻּשִׁיִּים v. כּוּשִׁי.

† **כָּשַׁל** vb. **stumble, stagger, totter** (NH *id.*; Syr. [ܟܫܠ] *give offence* (occasion for stumbling), σκανδαλίζω, (chiefly Ethpe. Aph.), v. PS Brock Schwally; Ar. كَسِلَ is *be heavy, sluggish*);—**Qal** *Pf.* כ׳ Ne 4^{4}+, (Ho 5^{5b} rd. יִכָּשֵׁל, cf. We), כָּשְׁלָה Is 3^{8} 59^{14}; כָּשְׁלוּ Je 46^{6}+, כָּשַׁלְנוּ Is 59^{10}, etc.; *Impf.* 3 mpl. יכשׁלו Pr 4^{16} Kt (but rd. Hiph., q.v., so Qr); יכשלו Na 3^{3} Kt (but rd. Pf. וְכָשְׁלוּ, so Qr); *Inf. abs.* כָּשׁוֹל Is 40^{30} (c. Niph. Impf.); *Pt. act.* כּוֹשֵׁל Is 5^{27} + 2 t., כֹּשֵׁל 2 Ch 28^{15} ψ 105^{37}; fpl. כֹּשְׁלוֹת Is 35^{3};—**1.** *stumble* at, over, something, c. ב (lit. *by means of*); Na 3^{3}, גִּבּוֹר בְּגִבּוֹר כ׳ Je 46^{12} (+ נָפַל), cf. Lv 26^{37}; וּנְעָרִים בָּעֵץ כ׳ La 5^{13} i.e. *stagger* (of toil in captivity); abs. Is 5^{27} (‖ עָיֵף), כָּשְׁלוּ וְנָפָלוּ Je 46^{6}, cf. הִרְבָּה כּוֹשֵׁל גַּם־נָפַל אִישׁ וגו׳ v^{16} (strange; Gie, foll. in part 𝔊 𝔖, עֶרְבֵּךְ כָּשַׁל וְנָפַל *thy mixed people*—cf. 25^{20}, etc.—*hath stumbled and hath fallen*); oft. fig. of overthrow, through divine judgment, c. בְּ *at,* (v. supr.) Je 6^{21}, so Is 8^{15} (+ נָפַל etc.) acc. to Ges Hi Buhl Che Di; < בָּם = *among them,*—Isr. and Judah,—as ב in v^{16}, so Ew De Du EV; Ho 4$^{5.5}$ 5^{5} 14^{2} (בַּעֲוֺנֶךָ, בְּ prob. instr.); abs. of Babylon, under fig. of זָדוֹן, כ׳ ונפל Je 50^{32}; כ׳ ונפל ψ 27^{2} Is 3^{8} 31^{3} (both ‖ נפל); of אֱמֶת Is 59^{14}; in metaph. of anxiety, distress Is 59^{10}, ψ 107^{12}. **2.** *totter,* of knees, lit. בִּרְכַּי כ׳ מִצּוֹם ψ 109^{24} *my knees totter from fasting;* fig. Is 35^{3} (‖ יָדַיִם רָפוֹת); כּוֹשֵׁל *tottering one,* lit. Jb 4^{4} 2 Ch 28^{15} ψ 105^{37}; hence fig., *fail,* of strength (כֹּחַ), Ne 4^{4} ψ 31^{11};—Inf. abs. כָּשׁוֹל, v. sub Niph. **Niph.** *Pf.* consec. וְנִכְשַׁל Dn 11^{9}, וְנִכְשְׁלוּ v^{33}, וְנִכְשָׁלוּ v^{14}; *Impf.* יִכָּשֵׁל Ez 33^{12} + Ho 5^{5b} (𝔊 as v^{a}, so We; MT כָּשַׁל), 2 ms. תִּכָּשֵׁל Pr 4^{12}, יִכָּשְׁלוּ Ho 5^{5a} + 9 t.; יִכָּשֵׁלוּ Is 40^{30} + 3 t.; *Inf. cstr.* sf. בִּכָּשְׁלוֹ Pr 24^{17} (yet v. Ges $^{\S51,R.1}$), בְּהִכָּשְׁלָם Dn 11^{34}; *Pt.* נִכְשָׁל Zc 12^{8}; pl. נִכְשָׁלִים 1 S 2^{4};—**1.** *stumble* (= **Qal**) Na 2^{6} Is 63^{13} Je 31^{9}; usu. fig.: **a.** of misfortune Pr 24^{17} (‖ נפל), neg. 4^{12}. **b.** of divine judgment (c. בְּ *at*) Pr 4^{19} 24^{16}, neg. Ez 33^{12}; see also Ho 14^{10} (בְּ loc.), Je 20^{11} Dn 11$^{14.35}$, יִכָּשְׁלוּ וְיֹאבְדוּ מִפָּנֶיךָ ψ 9^{4}; esp. = *be overthrown,* of nations, armies, etc., Ho 5^{5} (c. בַּעֲוֺנָם, cf. 14^{2} **Qal**), Je 6^{15} (‖ נפל), cf. 8^{12} (‖ *id.*), Dn 11^{19} (+ נפל), v^{33} (בְּ instr.), v$^{34.41}$. **2.** *be tottering, feeble,* כָּשׁוֹל יִכָּשֵׁלוּ Is 40^{30} (opp. יַחֲלִיפוּ כֹחַ v^{31}); so pt. 1 S 2^{4} Zc 12^{8}. **Pi.** only apparent, תְּכַשְּׁלִי Ez 36^{14}, rd. תְּשַׁכְּלִי with Qr Vrss EV Sm Co Da (v. also **Hiph.** *ad fin.*). **Hiph.** *Pf.* הִכְשִׁיל La 1^{14}, הִכְשַׁלְתֶּם Mal 2^{8}; *Impf.* 3 ms. sf. יַכְשִׁילְךָ 2 Ch 25^{8}; 2 fs. תַּכְשִׁלִי Ez 36^{15} (but del. 𝔊 Co; rd. תשכלי, as v^{14} other Vrss Sm Da); 3 mpl. יַכְשִׁילוּ Pr 4^{16} Qr (Kt v. sub **Qal**), וַיַּכְשִׁילֻהוּ ψ 64^{9}, וַיַּכְשִׁלוּם Je 18^{15} (so 𝔗; Gie, after 𝔊 𝔖, וַיִּכָּשְׁלוּ, [< וַיִּכָּשְׁלוּ]); *Inf. cstr.* הַכְשִׁיל 2 Ch 25^{8}, sf. הַכְשִׁילוֹ 2 Ch 28^{23};—**1.** *cause to stumble,* fig.: **a.** = *bring injury* or *ruin to,* abs. Pr 4^{16}; of pun-

ishment ψ 64[9] (indef subj; si vera l, text prob corrupt, v Che Bae). **b.** = *overthrow*, of nation, army, etc, 2 Ch 25[8] (sq לִפְנֵי אוֹיֵב), cf. v[8] (opp עזר), *cause overthrow* 2 Ch 28[23] —On Ez 36[15] v supr. **c.** morally, Je 18[15] (ב loc), Mal 2[8] (ב instr.) **2.** *make feeble, weak*, הכשיל כחי La 1[14] (of God's dealing with Jerus) **Hoph.** only *Pt* והיו מֻכְשָׁלִים לְפָנֶיךָ Je 18[23] either *and let them be ones who have stumbled before thee*, i e. regard them as such (Hi Gf VB), or *and let them be ones overthrown before thee* (Gie; so Qr acc to Gf). So also in Ez 21[20] acc to Co, cf Sm Da (MT מכשלים, v. מכשול)

†כַּשִּׁיל **n.[m.]** axe (acc to Vrss and context, NH *id*; 𝔗 Je 46[22], prob fr. *felling*, Aram. loan-word acc to Fra[74], but word not common in Aram)—בְּכ׳ וכילפות יַהֲלֹמוּן ψ 74[6].

†כִּשָּׁלוֹן **n.[m.]** a stumbling; fig = calamity Pr 16[18]

†מִכְשׁוֹל **n m** [Je 6 21] a stumbling, means or occasion of stumbling, stumbling-block,—מ׳ abs Is 8[14] + 3 t, מכשל Lv 19[14]; cstr. מכשול 1 S 25[31] + 6 t Ez, pl. מִכְשֹׁלִים Je 6[21] + Ez 21[20] MT (Co al מֻכְשָׁלִים, v *infr*),—**1.** *stumbling*, צור מ׳ Is 8[14] (fig.) *a rock of stumbling* (i.e. over which one stumbles); lit. הַרְבֵּה הַמִּכְשֹׁלִים Ez 21[20] *an abundance of stumblings, falls* (si vera l.; 𝔊 οἱ ἀσθενοῦντες, appar. reading pt., cf Sm, so Co Da (as a possibility), i e. מֻכְשָׁלִים **Hoph.** *Pt* of כשל = *those who have stumbled* or *been overthrown*) **2.** *means*, or *occasion of stumbling, stumbling-block*, **a.** lit. Lv 19[14]. **b.** fig of misfortune, calamity ψ 119[165]; in divine judgment Je 6[21] Ez 3[20], as a hindrance to restoration of people Is 57[14] **c.** in ethical sense מ׳ עֲוֹנָם Ez 7[19] *a stumbling-block of* (i e. occasioning) *their iniquity*, so 14[3.4.7] 18[30] 44[12] (mostly with ref to idols) **d.** מ׳ לב 1 S 25[31] *a stumbling-block of heart* i e. ground for remorse.

†מַכְשֵׁלָה **n.f. 1. overthrown mass. 2. stumbling-block**,—**1.** fig of kingdom Is 3[6] **2.** pl הַמַּכְשֵׁלוֹת Zp 1[3] *stumbling-blocks* = idols (cf מִכְשׁוֹל **2 c**), but rather dub; We thinks a gloss. Schwally [ZAW x (1890), 169] rds והכשלתי *and I will cause* the wicked to *stumble*

I כשף (√ of foll, cf Ar كَشَفَ *cut off, cut up*, Syr ܐܬܟܫܦ *to pray* (lit prob *to cut oneself*, v. 1 K 18[28]). so RS [J Phil xiv 125, 126] No [ZMG 1886, 723], acc to RS כֶּשֶׁף is prop herbs etc *shredded* into a magic brew)

†[כֶּשֶׁף] **n m.** [2 K 9 22] sorcery, only **pl.** (As *kišpu, id*),—כְּשָׁפִים Mi 5[11] Na 3[4], sf. כְּשָׁפַיִךְ Is 47[9.12], כְּשָׁפֶיהָ Na 3[4] 2 K 9[22],—*sorceries*: **1.** lit. והכרתי כ׳ מִיָּדֶךָ Mi 5[11], said of Isr; רב כ׳ Is 47[9.12] (‖ חֲבָרַיִךְ), said of Babylon **2.** fig of seductive and corrupting influences: of Jezebel 2 K 9[22] (‖ זְנוּנִים); of Nineveh personif. as harlot Na 3[4] (‖ *id*), called בַּעֲלַת כ׳ v[4] (following מרב זְנוּנֵי זוֹנָה)

†כשף **vb. Pi. denom. practice sorcery** (As *kašâpu, id*),—*Pf* 3 ms: וְעוֹנֵן וְנִחֵשׁ וְכִשֵּׁף וְעָשָׂה אוֹב וידעוני 2 Ch 33[6] (of Manasseh), elsewh only *Pt* as subst. ms *sorcerer*, in Israel, מְכַשֵּׁף Dt 18[10] (following קֹסֵם קְסָמִים מעונן וּמְנַחֵשׁ); fs. מכשפה = *sorceress* Ex 22[17] (E); mpl מְכַשְּׁפִים Mal 3[5] (named with adulterers and false-swearers), of diviners, or astrologers in Egypt (חַרְטֻמִּים q v) Ex 7[11] (P; ‖ חֲכָמִים), in Babylon Dn 2[2] (+ חַרְטֻמִּים, אַשָּׁפִים, כַּשְׂדִּים).

†[כַּשָּׁף] **n.m.** sorcerer, only pl. sf. (As. *kaššapu, id.; kaššaptu, sorceress*),—אַל־תִּשְׁמְעוּ אֶל־נְבִיאֵיכֶם וְאֶל־קֹסְמֵיכֶם וְאֶל חֲלֹמֹתֵיכֶם ואל־עֹנְנֵיכֶם ואל־כַּשָּׁפֵיכֶם Je 27[9].

II כשף (√ of following)

†אַכְשָׁף **n.pr.loc.** in (Northern) Canaan, with a king, Jos 11[1] 12[20], situated on the border of Asher 19[25], Egypt *'A-k-sap* WMM [As. u. Eur 181]; 𝔊B Ἀζείφ, A Ἀχσαφ, 𝔊L ('A)χασαφ, etc; site dub; mod *Iksâf* or *Kesâf*, Rob [BR iii 55], c 17 m. E. of Tyre, and nearly 3 m. SW. of the great bend of the Litâny, is phonetically suitable, but much too far NE for Jos 19[25], poss. there were two *Akšaphs*; cf. Di [Jos 11 1] Buhl [Geogr 237]. Vid. further Krall [Tyrus u Sidon 10], Lag [Onom 218 91 3, 2d ed 239].

†כָּשֵׁר **vb.** be advantageous, proper, suitable, succeed, late Aram (NH *id.*; Aram. כְּשַׁר, ܟܫܰܪ),—**Qal** *Pf* 3 ms וְכָשֵׁר הַדָּבָר לִפְנֵי הַמֶּלֶךְ Est 8[5] *and the thing be proper in the view of the king*; *Impf.* יִכְשָׁר Ec 11[6] thou knowest not whether this *shall succeed*, or this. **Hiph.** *Inf. cstr* וְיִתְרוֹן הַכְשֵׁיר חָכְמָה Ec 10[10] *an advantage for giving success is wisdom*.

†כִּשְׁרוֹן **n.[m.]** skill, success;—**1.** *skill,* כָּל־כִּשְׁרוֹן בְּחָכְמָה וּבְדַעַת וּבְכִשְׁרוֹן Ec 2^{21}; cstr. כִּשְׁרוֹן הַמַּעֲשֶׂה 4^{4} *all skill of work* = skilful work. **2.** *success, profit,* וּמַה־כִּשְׁרוֹן לִבְעָלֶיהָ Ec 5^{10} *and what profit have the owners of it?*

†[כּוֹשָׁרָה] **n.f.** prosperity (cf. ܟܘܫܪܐ, *id.*). Only pl. intens. בַּכּוֹשָׁרוֹת ψ 68^{7} he bringeth out captives *into prosperity.*

†כִּישׁוֹר **n.[m.]** distaff (etym. dub.; perh., if meaning correct, fr. כשר (cf. Sta ^{§216} Lag$^{BN 182}$) = *be straight,* because it stands erect, De Str; 𝔖 ܟܘܫܪܐ *industry;* whence 𝔗 כּוּשְׁרָא, and likewise 𝔗 כּוּנְשְׁרָא, also Pr 3^{8}, (for Heb. שֹׁר), where Levy *Wirbelsäule,* Str $^{ad loc.}$ Jastr *navel;* but Str doubts etymological connexion with כישור);—only in יָדֶיהָ שִׁלְּחָה בַכִּישׁוֹר Pr 31^{19} (‖ פֶּלֶךְ: *whirl* of spindle).—As above De Now Str RV SS al.; > Ki AW Thes RobGes *whirl* of spindle (AV *spindle*); vid. פֶּלֶךְ.

כָּתַב$_{223}$ **vb.** write (NH *id.;* Ph. כתב; Aram. כְּתַב, ܟܬܒ; Nab. כתב, v. esp. Nö in Eut $^{Nab. p. 43}$; thence Ar. كَتَبَ, Eth. ጸሐፈ: *book,* Di $^{Lex. 852}$ (as loan-wds., Frä ^{249} DHM $^{VOJ i (1887), 29}$); MV Buhl comp. Ar. كَتَبَ *draw* or *sew together, conjoin* (letters), etc., cf. Fl $^{ZMG 1873, 427}$)—**Qal** *Pf.* כ׳ Jos 8^{32}+, כָּתַבְתָּ Je 36^{6}+, sf. וּכְתַבְתָּם consec. Dt 6^{9} 11^{20}, etc. (Pf. 27 t.); *Impf.* יִכְתֹּב Is 44^{5}, וַיִּכְתֹּב Ex 24^{4}+, etc. (Impf. 39 t.); *Imv.* כְּתֹב Is 8^{1} + 5 t., כְּתָב־ Ex 34^{27} + 2 t.; sf. כָּתְבָהּ Is 30^{8}, כָּתְבֵם Pr 3^{3} 7^{3}; pl. כִּתְבוּ Dt 31^{9} + 3 t.; *Inf. abs.* כָּתוֹב Je 32^{44}; *cstr.* כְּתוֹב ψ 87^{6}, לִכְתֹּב Dt 31^{24} Jos 18^{8}; sf. כָּתְבוֹ Je 45^{1}; *Pt. act.* כֹּתֵב Je 36^{18}, pl. כֹּתְבִים Je 32^{12} Ne 10^{1}; *pass.* (113 t.), כָּתוּב Jos 1^{8}+, f. כְּתוּבָה 2 S 1^{18}+, pl. כְּתוּבִים 1 K 15^{7}+, כְּתֻבִים 1 K 11^{41}+; fpl. כְּתוּבוֹת 2 Ch 34^{24};—**1.** *write:* **a.** c. acc., words Ex 34^{27}, commandments 24^{12}, etc.; acc. cogn. מכתב Ex 39^{30}, cf. כַּמִּכְתָּב Dt 10^{4}; with בְּ, giving purport of writing, also Est 8^{8}; but obj. also a book, סֵפֶר Ex 32^{32} Dt 24^{1}; מְגִלָּה Je 36^{6}, cf. pt. pass., וְהִיא כְתוּבָה פָּנִים וְאָחוֹר Ez 2^{10} (of מגלה; i.e. written on both sides); a letter, סֵפֶר 2 S 11^{14} 2 K 10^{1} + 4 t., אִגֶּרֶת 2 Ch 30^{1}; a divorce-certificate סֵפֶר כְּרִיתֻת Dt 24^{1}, etc.; even לֻחֹת כְּתֻבִים *tablets inscribed* by the finger of God Ex 31^{18} cf. Dt 9^{10}; לֻ׳ כ׳ מִשְּׁנֵי עֶבְרֵיהֶם Ex 32^{15} *tables inscribed on both sides* (cf. Ez 2^{10} supr.) Here belongs (prob.) וְזֶה יִכְתֹּב יָדוֹ לי״ Is 44^{5} *and this one shall inscribe his hand, 'Yahweh's,'* so 𝔊 Hi Kn Che Br Du Di, > Ges Ew De, *shall sign* (with) *his hand unto* י׳. **b.** more often *write* something *on,* or *in* (עַל־ 85 t., בְּ 44 t., אֶל־ 3 t.) a tablet, roll, book, etc. (obj. various, as above):—(1) כ׳ עַל־ sq. סֵפֶר = *book* Dt 17^{18} + 55 t., esp. in phr. כתובים על־ספר דברי וגו׳ 1 K 11^{41} + oft. K Ch; כ׳ עַל־מְגִלָּה Je $36^{2.28.32}$ 38^{29}; עַל־לוּחַ(ות) Ex 34^{1} + 7 t., עַל־אֶבֶן Dt 27^{3} + 2 t., עַל־גִּלָּיוֹן Is 8^{1}; עַל־מְזוּזוֹת בֵּית Dt 6^{9} 11^{20}; עַל־מַטֶּה *on a rod* Nu $17^{17.18}$; עַל־עֵץ Ez $37^{16.16}$, עַל־צִיץ (high priest's plate) Ex 39^{30}; even (only Ch) עַל־ sq. name of book or its contents:—כ׳ עַל־דִּבְרֵי נָתָן 2 Ch 9^{29} cf. 33^{19}; עַל־מִדְרַשׁ וגו׳ 24^{27}; עַל־הַקִּינוֹת 35^{25}; fig., כ׳ עַל־לִבָּם Je 31^{33} *I will write them upon their heart;* cf. כ׳ עַל־לוּחַ לִבֶּךָ Pr 3^{3}. (2) כ׳ אֶל־ appears for כ׳ עַל־ only Je 36^{2} cf. Ez 2^{10}, Je 51^{60}. (3) כ׳ בְּ sq. ספר = *book* Jos 24^{26} (E) + 35 t.; = *letter, bill, deed,* 1 K 21^{9} + 5 t.; בִּמְגִלַּת סֵפֶר כָּתוּב עָלָי ψ 40^{8} *it is prescribed to me,* על as 2 K 22^{13} (N.B. כ׳ עַל־ not used with סֵפֶר = *letter,* and כ׳ בְּ not used with לוּחַ, אבן or עֵץ). **c.** other uses of prep. with כ׳ are:—בְּ instr., כ׳ בְּחֶרֶט אֱנוֹשׁ Is 8^{1}, כ׳ בְּעֵט בַּרְזֶל Je 17^{1}; כְּתֻבִים בְּאֶצְבַּע אֱלֹהִים Dt 9^{10} Ex 31^{18}; כ׳ אֶל־ *unto,* of person to whom letter, etc., is addressed 2 S 11^{14} 2 K 10^{6} Est 9^{13}; עַל־ subst. for אֶל־ (late) 2 Ch 30^{1} Ezr 4^{7} Est 8^{8}; the fuller construction is כ׳ ספר וישלח (אֶל־) 2 K 10^{1} Est 8^{10} 9^{20} +; כ׳ אֶל־ *write down for* the benefit or use of some one, Ju 8^{14}; לְ *to* or *for,* Dt 17^{18} 24^{1} +; note esp. אֶכְתָּוב־לוֹ רֻבּוֹ תּוֹרָתִי Ho 8^{12}, i.e. either, *I write (keep writing) for them ever so many* (We, רֹב, cf. רֻבֵּ; Ew and most רִבּוֹ(א) a myriad) *of my directions,* or *'Though I write,' 'Were I to write,'* etc.; כ׳ sq. לְ c. inf. of purpose 2 Ch 32^{17} Est 8^{5}; c. מִן in phr. כ׳ מִפִּי פ׳ *write from the mouth of* any one, i.e. from dictation, †Je $36^{2.32}$ $38^{6.17.27}$ 45^{1}. **2.** = *write down, describe in writing,* כ׳ אֶת־הָאָרֶץ Ju $18^{4.6.8.8.9}$. **3.** = *register, enroll* Is 10^{19} (= record the number), 1 Ch 24^{6}; esp. pass. הַכְּתֻבִים Nu 11^{26} *those enrolled* cf. Ne 12^{22}; הַכ׳ בְּשֵׁמוֹת 1 Ch 4^{41} *those recorded by name;* in prediction, כ׳ אֶת־הָאִישׁ הַזֶּה עֲרִירִי Je 22^{30} *register this man as childless;* with eschatol. reference, כָּל־הַכָּתוּב לַחַיִּים Is 4^{3} *all those enrolled* (i.e. appointed) *unto life;* and, more explicitly, כָּל־הַנִּמְצָא כָּתוּב בַּסֵּפֶר Dn 12^{1}; י׳ יִסְפֹּר בִּכְתוֹב עַמִּים ψ 87^{6} י׳ *shall reckon, when he registers* (note absence of suffix) *the*

peoples, etc **4** = *decree*, תִּכְתֹּב עָלַי מְרֹרוֹת Jb 13[26] *thou* ('י) *decreest against me bitter things* †**Niph.** (chiefly late, esp Est), *Impf* יִכָּתֵב Est 1[19]+, 3 fs. תִּכָּתֶב זֹאת ψ 102[19], 3 mpl. יִכָּתֵבוּ Je 17[13]+3 t, יִכָּתְבוּן Jb 19[23], *Pt.* נִכְתָּב Est 3[12] +2 t,—**1.** *be written*, subj words, Jb 19[23], book Mal 3[16], *be written* בַּסֵּפֶר Est 2[23] 9[23], *in*, or *among* (ב) the laws Est 1[19], once, c עַל־, וְעַל־סִפְרְךָ כֻּלָּם יִכָּתֵבוּ ψ 139[16] *in thy* ('י's) *book all of them* (my members) *are written*, i e *written down, recorded* (v infr), abs. כְּתָב אֲשֶׁר נִכְתָּב בְּשֵׁם הַמֶּלֶךְ Est 8[8] *a writing which is written in the king's name*, cf (impers) 3[12], impers also וַיִּכָּתֵב כְּכָל־אֲשֶׁר צִוָּה Est 3[12] 8[9], יִכ׳ sq לְ = *for* ψ 102[19], sq לְ + inf (really = a subject-cl,—the contents of the letter) Est 3[9] 8[5]. **2.** *be written down, recorded*, Ezr 8[34], *enrolled*, בִּכְתָב בֵּית יִשְׂרָאֵל לֹא יִכָּתֵבוּ Ez 13[9] *in the enrolment of the house of Israel they are not enrolled* (eschatolog), יִמָּחוּ מִסֵּפֶר ‖) ψ 69[29] וְעִם־צַדִּיקִים אַל־יִכָּתֵבוּ), בָּאָרֶץ יִכָּתֵבוּ—(חַיִּים Je 17[13] is difficult, Giesebrechts, plausibly, מֵאֶרֶץ יִכָּרֵתוּ (cf ψ 34[17] 101[8], etc) †**Pi.** frequent, *Pf.* and *Pt*, only וּמְכַתְּבִים עָמָל כִּתֵּבוּ Is 10[1] and *busy writers that make a business of writing* oppression (i e. register unjust sentences, cf **Qal 4**; ‖ הַחֹקְקִים חִקְקֵי־אָוֶן)

†כְּתָב **n.m.** Ezr 4,7 writing (late Aram, BA כְּתָב, Syr ܟܬܒܐ),—כ׳ abs 1 Ch 28[19]+4 t, cstr Ez 13[9]+4 t, sf כְּתָבָהּ Est 1[22]+2 t, כְּתָבָם Ezr 2[62]+3 t,—*writing* **1.** *register, enrolment*, Ez 13[9] Ezr 2[62]=Ne 7[64] **2.**=*mode of writing, character, letter*, וּכ׳ הַנִּשְׁתְּוָן כָּתוּב אֲרָמִית Ezr 4[7] *and the writing of the letter was written in Aramaic* (characters, so prob, v. Be-Ry Ryle, cf NH Hoffm ZAW i (1881), 334 ff), cf. Est 1[22] 3[12] 8[9 9] **3.**=*letter*, 2 Ch 2[10] Est 9[27] **4.** of a royal enactment, edict 2 Ch 35[4] (‖ מִכְתָּב), Est 3[14] 8[8 13]; more fully כְּתָב־הַדָּת 4[8]. **5.** of a writing with divine authority 1 Ch 28[19]; כ׳ אֱמֶת Dn 10[21], i e a book of truth

†כְּתֹבֶת **n.f.** only cstr וּכְתֹבֶת קַעֲקַע לֹא תִתְּנוּ בָּכֶם Lv 19[28] i e *a writing* (mark or sign) *of imprintment*, scriptio stigmatis, perh of tattooing, cf Di (v also Ba NB 61)

†מִכְתָּב **n.m.** 2 Ch 21 12 writing,—abs מ׳ Dt 10[4]+5 t, cstr מִכְתַּב Ex 32[16]+2 t,—**1.**=*handwriting* וְהַמִּכְתָּב מִכְתַּב אֱלֹהִים הוּא Ex 32[16]. **2.** = thing written, Ex 39[30] (acc cogn c כָּתַב), Dt 10[4], specif a royal enactment or edict (= כְּתָב 4), 2 Ch 35[4] (‖ כְּתָב), 36[22]=Ezr 1[1], a prophetic writing 2 Ch 21[12]. **3.** in a title, מ׳ לְחִזְקִיָּהוּ Is 38[9] *Writing of Hezekiah.*

†[כִּתִּי] **adj.gent** alw pl כִּתִּיִּים, כִּתִּים; usu. as **n.gent.** = **Cypriotes** (cf Ph n pr.loc. כת, כתי, *Citium*, on a connexion with *Kheta*, *H-tā*, *Hattê*, חתי, v WMM Asien u Europa, 345,—on *Citium* v Cesnola Cyprus 46 ff),—אֶרֶץ כִּתִּים Is 23[1], כִּתִּיִּים v[12]; כִּתִּים (as son of Yawan) Gn 10[4]=1 Ch 1[7], וְצִים מִיַּד כ׳ Nu 24[24] *ships from the side* (direction) *of Kittim*, more generally, of coast-lands of Mediterranean, אִיֵּי כִתִּיִּים Je 2[10], אִיֵּי כִּתִּים Ez 27[6], even of Macedonian Greece, צִיִּים כִּתִּים Dn 11[30] (only here as adj, cf. Bev) i e. Grecian ships.

כָּתִית v sub כתת

כתל (√of foll, cf. Ar. كَتَلَ *make into firm lumps* or *blocks, make compact*, Frey also *bind, imprison*, كَتِلَ *be joined together*).

†[כֹּתֶל] **n.[m.]** wall of house (NH כּוֹתֶל, Aram. כּוּתְלָא),—only sf כָּתְלֵנוּ Ct 2[9]

†כִּתְלִישׁ **n.pr.loc.** a city of Judah Jos 15[40], site unknown, 𝔊B Μααχως, A Χαθλως, 𝔊L Καθαλεις

†I [כָּתַם] **vb.** only **Niph.** be stained (NH Niph *id* (Jastr); כֶּתֶם *blood-stain*; 𝔗 כְּתִים (blood-)*stained* Is 1[18], כִּיתְמָא *blood-stain* Je 2[22]; Syr ܟܬܡ *stain, defile*, Pt, also Pa. Ethpa, and deriv., Ar كَتَمَ is *cover, conceal*, so As *katâmu*; Zinj כתם (?), DHM Sendsch p. 37),—**Niph.** *Pt*, fig, נִכְתָּם עֲוֹנֵךְ לְפָנַי Je 2[22] *stained is thine iniquity before me* (cf Eng. phr *iniquity of deepest dye*).

II **כתם** (√of foll, meaning unknown).

†מִכְתָּם **n.[m.]** **Mikhtām**, a term. techn. in ψ-titles, meaning unknown (𝔊 στηλογραφία. cf Bae Ps p xiii f), alw c לְדָוִד—מ׳ לְדָוִד ψ 16[1] 60[1]; לְדָוִד מ׳ 56[1] 57[1] 58[1] 59[1]

†כֶּתֶם **n.m.** La 4, 1 gold, poet and late (perh. loan-word in Heb; Ph has n pr.m. כתם, Sab. כתם Hal Et. Sab. 190, *kaθamā* as loan-wd. in Egypt., Bondi 80 f),—כ׳ abs Jb 28[19]+3 t, כָּתֶם Pr 25[12]; cstr. כתם Is 13[12]+3 t,—כ׳ אוֹפִיר Is 13[12] *gold of Ophir* (‖ פָּז), so Jb 28[16] ψ 45[10]; כ׳ אוּפָז Dn 10[5] (rd perh אוֹפִיר for אוּפָז q v.), כ׳ alone Jb 31[24] (‖ זָהָב), חֲלִי־כ׳ Pr 25[12] *ornament of gold* (‖ נֶזֶם זָהָב), כ׳ פָּז Ct 5[11], כ׳ טָהוֹר Jb 28[19]; הַכ׳ הַטּוֹב La 4[1] (‖ זָהָב)

כתן (√of foll., =*clothe?* so Zehnpf.[BAS i. 531], who der. therefrom As. *kitinnê, linen, cloth*, = Ar. كَتَّان, v. also Aram. כִּיתָּנָא, ܟܬܢܐ and infr.)

†**כְּתֹנֶת, כֻּתֹּנֶת, כֻּתֹנֶת** **n.f.** tunic (NH *id.*; Aram כתונא, etc ܟܘܬܝܢܐ, etc , Eth ከታን: *tunic, linen*; cf. also √ supr),—abs. כְּתֹנֶת Gn 37^{31} + 2 t ; כתנת Ex 28^{39}, cstr. כְּתֹנֶת Gn 37^{3}+9 t ; sf. כֻּתָּנְתּוֹ Gn 37^{23} 2 S 15^{32}, כֻּתָּנְתֶּךָ Is 22^{21}, כֻּתָּנְתִּי Jb 30^{18} Ct 5^{3}; pl. abs. כֻּתֳּנֹת Ex 28^{40} + 3 t , הַכֻּתֳּנֹת 39^{27}, cstr. כָּתְנוֹת Gn 3^{21} + 2 t , כָּתְנֹת Ezr 2^{69}, sf. כֻּתֳּנֹתָם Lv 10^{5},—*tunic*, principal ordinary garment (v. Benz[Arch. 98 f.] Now[Arch. i. 121, 133]) of man and woman, worn next the person, כָּתְנוֹת עוֹר Gn 3^{21} *tunics of skin*, of man 2 S 15^{32}; פִּי כ׳ Jb 30^{18} *mouth of any tunic* (i.e. its collar); כ׳ פַּסִּים Gn 37^{3} $^{23.32}$ i.e tunic with long skirts and sleeves (v פַּס), cf v[23.31 31 32.33], of woman Ct 5^{3} (put off at night), כ׳ פַּסִּים 2 S $13^{18.19}$ (of king's daughter, rent, as sign of grief, cf. also 15^{32}, and v. קרע) Specif of priest's tunic Ex $28^{4.39}$ (embroidered, v. שבץ, תַּשְׁבֵּץ), v[40] $29^{5.8}$ 39^{27} (made of שֵׁשׁ, q.v.), 40^{14} Lv $8^{7\ 13}$ 10^{5}, כ׳־בַּד קֹדֶשׁ 16^{4} *a holy linen tunic*, of high priest; כ׳־כֹהֲנִים Ezr 2^{69} Ne $7^{69.71}$ (van d H v[70 72]); of Shebna's official tunic Is 22^{21}

כתף (√of following, meaning unknown)

†**כָּתֵף** **n.f.**[Ex 27. 15] shoulder, shoulder-blade, side (NH *id* , Aram. כַּתְפָּא, ܟܬܦܐ, Ar كَتِفٌ), —abs כ׳ Zc 7^{11}+; cstr כֶּתֶף 1 K 6^{8}+, app כָּתֵף Is 11^{14} (but regard as appos., or rd כֶּתֶף), sf כתפי Jb 31^{22}; כְּתֵפָם 1 Ch 15^{15}, pl. abs. כְּתֵפֹת Ex 28^{7}+, כְּתֵפוֹת 1 K $7^{30.34}$, cstr כתפת Ex 28^{12}+, כתפות Ez 41^{2}+, du sf כְּתֵפָיו Dt 33^{12} + 3 t., כתפיה 1 K 7^{34};—**1. a.** of man, *shoulder, shoulder-blade* (while שְׁכֶם, q v =*neck and shoulders*), כידון נחשת בין כתפיו 1 S 17^{6}; cf fig of י׳'s dwelling *between the shoulders* of Benj Dt33^{12} (v. Dr); כתפי משִׁכְמָה תפול Jb 31^{22} *my shoulder-blade, from the shoulder let it fall*, as support for burdens Ju 16^{3} Ez $12^{6\ 7\ 12}$ Is 46^{7} 49^{22} (in fig.), Ex 28^{12} Nu 7^{9} (both P), 1 Ch 15^{15} 2 Ch 35^{3}, cf כָּל־כ׳ מרוטה Ez 29^{18} *every shoulder was rubbed bare* (of Nebuch.'s soldiers chafed by armour and toil), as aim of bird of prey Is 11^{14} (fig), cf. *shoulder of Moab* Ez 25^{9} (fig , i e. the side of M. exposed to invasion) Ez 29^{7b} rd. prob. כַּף (𝔊 𝔖 SmCo, cf v[a]) **b.** of beasts, Is 30^{6} (carrying), Ez 34^{21} (thrusting, in fig), כ׳ סֹרָרֶת Zc 7^{11} *a refractory shoulder* (refusing the yoke, fig.), so Ne 9^{29}; of choice meat Ez 24^{4} (‖ יָרֵךְ) **c.** = *shoulder-pieces* (alw pl.) of ephod Ex $28^{7\ 12.25.27}$ = $39^{4\ 7\ 18.20}$ (P) **2. a.** *slope, side*, of mountain, כֶּתֶף יָם־כִּנֶּרֶת Nu 34^{11}, i e. the mt -slopes NE. of the lake, cf Jos $15^{8\ 10\ 11}$ $18^{12\ 13.16\ 18\ 19}$ (all P). **b.** *opposite side(s)*, sc of door or entrance, of tabernacle-court Ex $27^{14\ 15}$ = $38^{14\ 15}$ (all P), of temple 1 K 6^{8} $7^{39.39.39}$ = 2 Ch 4^{10}, 2 K $11^{11\ 11}$ = 2 Ch $23^{10.10}$, cf. Ez $40^{18.40.40.41\ 44.44}$ $41^{2.26}$ 46^{19} $47^{1\ 2}$. **3.** *supports* of the bases for the lavers beside the temple 1 K $7^{30.30.34.34}$.

†**[כָּתַר]** **vb.** surround (in **Pi.**), (Aram. כַּתַּר Pa , *wait, hope* for, ܟܬܪ Pa. *wait, await, remain*, i.e perh. *surround expectantly*, v. Jb 36^{2} infr)—**Pi.** *Pf* 3 pl כִּתְּרוּ Ju 20^{43} of *surrounding* an enemy, sf כתרוני ψ 22^{13} (in fig , ‖ סְבָבוּנִי); *Imv* כַּתַּר־לִי Jb 36^{2} *wait, I pray* (as in Aram) **Hiph.** *Impf.* 3 mpl. בִּי יַכְתִּרוּ צדיקים ψ 142^{8} dub , *throw out crowns* (Ges[§ 53 s]), i e appear with crowns (denom fr. כֶּתֶר, but this very late—only in Est), fig. for *triumph*, because of me, but Gr Che יִתְפָּאֲרוּ (v I. פאר), יַכְתִּרוּ דָעַת Pr 14^{18} dub , Thes De al *throw out knowledge as a crown*, make knowledge their crown (denom fr. כֶּתֶר; but v. supr), Now, *encompass knowledge*, i e possess it (‖ נָחֲלוּ), sense good, but meaning of כ׳ without ‖. *Pt* מַכְתִּיר *surrounding* (as **Pi.**) Hb 1^{4} (c. acc. of enemy)

†**כֶּתֶר** **n.m.** crown ((perh Pers loan-word Lag[Ges. Abh 207]), NH *id* , Aram כִּתְרָא; Ar. كَثَرٌ *the higher hump* of a camel),—always cstr , in combin כ׳ מַלְכוּת *royal crown* Est 1^{11} 2^{17} (both of queen), 6^{8} (of king)

כֹּתֶרֶת, כּוֹתֶרֶת **n.f.** capital of pillar (as *surrounding, crowning* its top?);—abs. כֹּתֶרֶת 1 K $7^{16\ 16}$ + 10 t ; הַכּוֹתֶרֶת Je 52^{22c} ; pl. abs. כֹּתָרֹת 1 K 7^{16} + 7 t., כֹּתָרוֹת 2 Ch $4^{12\ 12\ 13}$;—*capitals* of pillars יָכִין and בֹּעַז 1 K $7^{16\ 16\ 16}$ + 12 t. 1 K 7 = 2 Ch $4^{12\ 12.13}$; 2 K $25^{17\ 17\ 17}$ = Je $52^{22\ 22.22}$.

†**[כָּתַשׁ]** **vb.** pound, pound fine, bray (NH *id.*, Aram כְּתַשׁ; Syr. ܟܬܫ is *strive, contend*; Zinj כתש *break in pieces, shatter*, DHM[Sendsch. 58]), —**Qal** *Impf* אִם־תִּכְתּוֹשׁ אֶת־הָאֱוִיל בַּמַּכְתֵּשׁ Pr 27^{22} *if thou shouldest bray the fool in the mortar*.

†**מַכְתֵּשׁ** **n.m.** mortar (place of pounding, braying, cf. Palm n.pr.m. מכתש = *contundens* Vog[No 97])—abs. מ׳ Pr 27^{22} (v. foregoing), hollow resembling a mortar Ju 15^{19} (whence came forth a water-spring; cf GFM), Zp 1^{11} = a part of Jerusalem, cf. Schwally[ZAW x. (1890) 173 f.]

†[כָּתַת] **vb. beat, crush by beating** (NH *id*, Aram. כְּתַת),—**Qal** *Pf.* 1 s וְכַתּוֹתִי ψ 89[24], *Impf.* 1 s. וָאֶכֹּת Dt 9[21], *Imv.* mpl כֹּתּוּ Jo 4[10], *Pt. pass* כָּתוּת Is 30[14] Lv 22[24],—**1.** *beat* or *crush fine*, of a potter's vessel Is 30[14], the golden calf Dt 9[21] (+ טָחוֹן היטב), a sacrificial victim Lv 22[24] (i e. its testicles, + מָעוּךְ, נָתוּק, כָּרוּת), fig of enemies ψ 89[24]. **2.** *beat, hammer* (ploughshares into swords, cf. **Pi. 2**) Jo 4[10]. **Pi.** *Pf* 3 ms כִּתַּת 2 K 18[4] 2 Ch 34[7], 3 mpl. וכתתו consec Is 2[4] + 2 t.,—as **Qal 1** *beat* or *crush fine* 2 K 18[4] 2 Ch 34[7] (of images), fig of devastating the land Zc 11[6]. **2.** *beat, hammer* (swords into ploughshares, cf **Qal 2**) Is 2[4] = Mi 4[3] **Pu.** *Pf.* 3 mpl וְכֻתְּתוּ 2 Ch 15[6] *and they were beaten in pieces*, one nation against another **Hiph.** *Impf* 3 mpl. וַיַּכְּתוּ Dt 1[44] *beat in pieces* an enemy, sf וַיַּכּוּם וַיַּכְּתוּם Nu 14[45]. **Hoph.** *Impf.* 3 ms. וּשְׁאִיָּה יֻכַּת־שָׁעַר Is 24[12] *and to ruins is the gate crushed;* 3 mpl. יֻכַּתּוּ Mi 1[7] (of idol-images); fig of warriors Je 46[5], of frail man Jb 4[20].

†כָּתִית **adj. beaten**;—only in combin. שֶׁמֶן כָּתִית *beaten oil*, i.e oil made by beating or pounding the olives in a mortar; esp fine and costly (cf Levy[NHWB ii 443] sub כָּתִית),—1 K 5[25] Ex 29[40] Nu 28[5]; שֶׁמֶן זַיִת זָךְ כ׳ לַמָּאוֹר Ex 27[20] *pure beaten olive oil for the lamp* = Lv 24[2] (Hex only HP)

†[מְכִתָּה] **n.f. the crushed or pulverized** = coll **crushed fragments**;—sg. sf. מְכִתָּתוֹ Is 30[14] (result of כָּתוּת, v[a])

ל

ל, twelfth letter, used as numeral 30 in postB Heb

ל prep. to, for, in regard to (Moab. Ph. ל, Aram ל, ܠ, Arab. لِ, Eth. ለ: As *la* in *lapân* = לפני, Dl[HWB 630]), before tone-syllables usu לָ (Ko[ii 276 t]), with suff לִי; לְךָ, לָכָה †Gn 27[37] 2 S 18[22] Is 3[6], לָךְ; f. לָךְ, לָכִי †2 K 4[2] Ct 2[13] Kt (prob N Pal dialect: cf. Syr. ܠܟܝ); לוֹ (15 t., acc to Mas, written incorrectly לֹא. v. לא *note*); לָהּ, לָה †Nu 32[42] Zc 5[11] Ru 2[14], לָנוּ; לָכֶם, לָכֵנָה †Ez 13[18] (לָכֶן does not occur); לָהֶם, poet לָמוֹ (55 t, incl a few cases where, acc. to many, it stands for לוֹ· cf. Ges[§103 2a, n], Di[Is 44 15 53, 8]), [also לָהֵמָּה †Je 14[16]]; [לָהֶן] לָהֵן (q v) †Ru 1[13 13], לָהֵנָּה 5 t, v. [הֵמָּה] **Prep.** denoting direction (not properly *motion*, as אֶל) **towards**, or **reference to**; and hence used in many varied applications, in some of which the idea of *direction* predominates, in others that of *reference* (cf. Giesebrecht[Die Präp. Lamed, 1876]).—**1.** very often, with various classes of verbs, *to, towards, for.* viz **a.** verbs of *looking, listening, attending, waiting*, etc, as האמין, הטה אזן, כלה (ψ 84[3]+), נכסף, הוחיל, יחל, התחלל, שמע, הקשיב, קִוָּה, נתן (נטה, הבין, שׂת) לב (sts), צמא to thirst *for* (Ex 17[3] ψ 42[3]), השתחוה (*to* Gn 37[10], *towards* ψ 99[5]), sts also with האזין, הבים, נִבַּט, ראה, נפש, נשא (see these verbs, many are also construed with other preps.); Is 51[6] ψ 44[21]; pregn. Is 38[14]; השתאה ל †Gn 24[21], החריש ל Nu 30[5.8]: sts. without a vb, as Ju 5[9] לבי ל, Je 5[3] עיניך ל, ψ 33[18] (|| אל), 39[8] נפשי, 130[6], תוחלתי לך היא, 120[7] המה למלחמה, לאדני (cf Is 26[8]), 143[6] Dn 11[27] 2 Ch 3[13] 32[2]. **b.** with verbs of *saying, calling, singing, vowing, sacrificing*, etc, as אמר, דבר (chiefly with God as subj = *promise*, Gn 24[7] 1 K 5[26]+, esp. in D כאשר דבר ל Dt 1[11] (v. Dr), v[21] etc.; with human subj Gn 49[28] Ju 14[7] 1 K 2[19] al (Gie[42 f]: דבר אל is more common), הגיד, הודה, זמר, זבח, נדר, נשׂא יד (in oath) Ez 20[5.6 23] ψ 106[26], קִטֵּר, שָׁר, נשבע, הריע etc. **c.** with vbs. of *giving, leaving, bringing, offering* etc, as הביא, הביל, *allot* (Jos 13[6]), נתן, הסגיר, עזב ψ 16[9] abandon *to* Sheol, Is 18[6], הקריב Lv 17[4], שׁוּב = *to be returned* Dt 28[31], השיב = *bring back* 22[1], = *requite* 2 S 16[12], שִׁלַּח, etc **d.** with vbs of dealing, acting *towards* (whether with friendly or hostile intent), as עשה ל Gn 19[8]+oft, גמל ל Is 3[9], so with הֵיטִיב, הֵרַע, הֵמַר, חָטָא to sin *against* (Gn 20[9]+), אָשַׁם to be guilty *towards* (Lv 5[19]), כחש, שִׁקֵּר to lie *to*, כִּזֵּב, with vbs of mocking or laughing, *against, at*, as לעג ל ψ 2[4], שחק ל 37[13], שׂמח ל to rejoice *over* 35[19] Ez 35[15], caus שִׂמַּח ל ψ 30[2], עלץ ל +25[2]. with other verbs denoting hostility (less common than ב or על), Gn 27[42] מתנחם לך להרגך, 2 K 5[7], Ex 11[7]

(so Jos 10[21]: cf. Jb 16[9]), Je 25[31] 50[9] ψ 7[14] 37[12] 56[3] 106[16] קנא לְ (usu. in good sense, **5 g** *c*) Jb 20[27] 34[37]. And with adjj., as ψ 73[1] טוב לְ good *to*, Gn 13[13] רָעִים וְחַטָּאִים לי׳ *towards* ׳י, 2 S 22[24] (עִמּוֹ ψ 18[24] ||) תָּמִים לוֹ, ψ 89[29] נֶאֱמֶנֶת לוֹ; with subst. (rare) Ex 32[12] La 3[60] (syn. v[61] עַל). **e.** with words denoting what is pleasurable or the reverse, as נעם לְ 2 S 1[26], ערב לְ Ho 9[4], יֵמַר לְ Is 24[7], טוֹב לְ (adj.) 1 S 1[8], נָקֵל לְ 2 K 20[10], also סכן לְ, הועיל לְ, to be profitable *to;* and with neuter vbs., to denote the subj. of a sensation or emotion, as טוֹב לְ to be well *to* (with), Dt 5[30] 19[13] +, מַר לְ Ru 1[13], צַר לְ 1 S 13[6] + oft., חַם לְ to be warm *to*, 1 K 1[1], רָוַח לְ 1 S 16[23], קֹרֹב לְ Ho 10[1], רַע לְ ψ 106[32], חָרָה לְ it was hot (=anger arose) *to* Gn 4[6] + oft., חָשְׁכָה לְ Mi 3[6]. And with pass. vbs., נִסְלַח לוֹ it is forgiven *to him* = he is forgiven Lv 4[26] + oft.; otherwise rare, נִרְפָּא לָנוּ 1[4] נִרְצָה לְ it is healed *to us* = we are healed Is 53[5], הונח לְ La 5[5], יְבֻלַּע לְ 2 S 17[16] (v. Dr). **f.** with verbs of *reaching to, touching, attaching* etc., as אסר לְ to bind *to*, חבשׁ, דבק ψ 44[26], מצא to reach *to* Is 10[10.14] ψ 21[9], הגיע Ex 4[25], נצמד Nu 25[5], קרוב (adj.) Ru 2[20]; out of connexion with a vb. (almost = עַד), Jos 16[1] ψ 59[14] Jb 28[3] Ne 3[15] 2 Ch 33[14], and correl. to מִן (v. מִן **5**). **g.** with vbs. of *motion*, as הלך, בא, שָׁב etc. (not so common as אל, or the simple acc. with or without ה *loc.*)—(*a*) with *places*, rare in early prose, Jos 1[15] 8[14] Ju 1[34] 20[10] (but v. GFM), 1 S 9[12] 20[25] 2 K 3[27], exc. in partic. phrases, viz. למקומו Gn 18[33], לדרכו 32[2], לאהליו 1 S 4[10] (also with other sfs.: all these + oft., esp. with שוב and הלך, or preceded by distrib. איש; לאהליו(ך), also, without vb., as exclam., 2 S 20[1] 1 K 12[16]), לארצו Gn 30[25] +, איש לנחלתו Jo 24[28] +, אִישׁ לִירֻשָּׁתוֹ Dt 3[20], לעירו 1 S 8[22] Ne 13[10]: oft. in late Heb., as Jb 4[5], 1 Ch 4[39.42] 5[26] 12[1.9] 22[18] 24[19] 2 Ch 1[3] 8[17] + oft. Chr, Ezr 2[68] +, Ne 10[35 ff.] Est 6[4] ψ 96[8] 132[7] 146[4]: לירושלם Je 3[17 b] (om. 𝔊), Zc 1[16], and oft. Ch Ezr Ne (as 2 Ch 11[14] 19[1] 30[3.11]), לשמרון 2 Ch 18[2] 28[8.9], לבבל Je 51[2] Ezr 2[1] 1 Ch 9[1] 2 Ch 36[7] (but earlier always שמרון, ירושלם, בבל or בבלה); and poet. Ju 5[11] Is 22[1] 23[17] 49[18] 51[14] (pregn.) ימות לשחת, 59[20] 60[4.5.7] 65[12] Je 31[17] 48[15] 50[27] Mi 1[12] Zc 9[12] ψ 7[8] 68[19] 74[3] Ct 4[16] 5[1] 6[2] 7[13] (pregn.) נשכימה לכרמים, Jb 10[19] 20[6]; הוציא לְ ψ 18[20] 66[12], לאור Mi 7[9] Jb 12[22]; יובל לְ Ho 10[6] +: without a vb., Is 23[5] Ho 7[12]. Also לָאָרֶץ, with many vbs., both in sense *down to* the earth, Is 14[12] 21[9] 28[2] Am 3[14] 5[7] Ez 26[11] ψ 7[6] +, c. חִלֵּל (pregn.) 74[7] 89[40], and idiom. c. ישב to sit *on* the earth, Is 3[26] 47[1] Jb 2[13] +, without vb. Is 26[9]: so לֶעָפָר Jb 7[21] ψ 7[6], הוריד לשחת Ez 28[8]. (*b*) with *persons*, not very common, Dt 32[35] Is 31[6] 57[9] Je 3[22] אָתָנוּ לָךְ, ψ 45[15] 119[79] Jb 18[14] 1 Ch 12[16] Ne 6[19], לְעַמִּי Nu 24[14] Ru 1[10]: בא לְ, esp. with pron. לָךְ, לָהּ etc. (friendly) 2 S 12[4] Zc 9[9] Am 6[1], (hostile) 2 S 5[23] Je 46[22] 49[9] 50[26] 51[48.53]; with a *thing* as subj. Dt 33[16] (לראשׁ), 2 S 24[13] Is 47[9] Jb 3[25] (cf. Is 66[4]), Je 4[12] 22[23] בְּבֹא לָךְ חֲבָלִים (so Ho 13[13] Is 66[7]). And with vbs. of placing (where על would be more usu.) ψ 21[4] תָּשִׁית לְרֹאשׁוֹ עֲטֶרֶת פָּז, 22[16] 66[12], with לְכִסֵּא ψ 9[5] 132[11.12] Jb 36[7]: cf. הִשְׁתַּחֲוָה, נָפַל לְאַפָּיו, Gn 48[12] + (also על א׳). **h.** expressing *direction towards* (without contact), לאחור back*wards* Je 7[24], לחוץ out*wards* ψ 41[7], למעלה up*wards*, למטה down*wards;* to scatter לכל רוח Je 49[32] cf. v[36] Ez 5[10] +, לארבע רוחות (שמים) Ez 42[20] Dn 8[8] 11[4] 1 Ch 9[24]: of the points of the compass (without vb.) ...לִפְאַת *towards* the quarter of (the N., S., etc.) Ex 26[18] + oft. P (so Ez 47[15]), לדרום, למזרח etc. (late: earlier ממזרח, or מזרחה etc.) Ez 40[23] 41[11.14] 42[4] Ne 3[26] 1 Ch 5[9] 6[63] 7[28] 12[15] 26[16–18] 2 Ch 31[14], למדבר 2 Ch 20[24]; also (peculiarly) 1 S 14[40] 1 K 20[38] 2 K 11[11]. **i.** expressing *addition* (rare); Is 28[10.13] צַו לָצָו, קַו לָקָו, 56[8] (resuming על), Ec 7[27] אחת לאחת (adding) one *to* another, Ezr 8[24] Ne 11[17] (על is more usual in this sense).

2. Expressing *locality, at, near*, idiom. in the phrases לִפְנֵי = *before* (sts. after vbs. of motion, as 1 K 1[23], but very oft. otherwise), לְעֵינֵי *in the sight of*, לְיַד, לִימִין, לִשְׂמֹאל (only Ec 10[2]), לפתח *at the entrance* (*of*), Gn 4[7] Nu 11[10] +; in other, rarer connexions, Nu 20[24] ... לְמֵי (usu. על), Ju 5[16] (|| v[15] ב), לְחוֹף + Gn 49[13.13] Ju 5[17], לְפִי + ψ 141[7] Pr 8[3], Ho 5[1] לְמִצְפָּה, 2 Ch 35[15]. לִפְנִימָה = *within*, 1 K 6[30] Ez 40[16].

3. To denote the *object* of a vb.—**a.** with the Hif., mostly of intrans. vbs., properly (as it seems) a *dat. commodi*, as הֵנִיחַ לְ to *give rest to*, הִרְחִיב to *give width to*, הֵצַר לְ, הֵצִיק לְ, exceptionally also with other words, as הִרְגִּיז, הוֹכִיחַ, הִצְדִּיק to *give righteousness to*, Is 53[11], הֶחֱיָה Gn 45[7], הֵבִין *give understanding to* (late), הִצְלִיחַ (do.), הִרְבָּה Ho 10[1], הִשְׂגִּיא Jb 12[23], הִפְתָּה Gn 9[27] *give breadth to*. **b.** with other vbs., sporadi-

cally early (if the text be sound), but mostly late, in conseq. of Aram. influence (in Aram. the accus. being constantly denoted by ל), as אהב Lv 19$^{18.34}$ 2 Ch 19^{2}, הרג 2 S 3^{30} Jb 5^{2}, בוז (mostly), בזה 2 S 6^{16}, sts. also זכר *to remember*, עבד *to serve* (work or do service *for*), עזר (2 S 8^{5}, and esp. late), דרשׁ (esp. Chr), הִלֵּל (only Chr Ezr), רפא (prob. the dat. comm.), שִׁחֵת 1 S 23^{10} Nu 32^{15}, נִדָּה Am 6^{3}, גִּדֵּל ψ 34^{4}, פִּתַּח 116^{16}, כִּבֵּד 86^{9} Dn 11^{38}, חִזֵּק 1 Ch 26^{27} 29^{12}, בֵּרַךְ 29^{20} Ne 11^{2}, חֵרֵף 2 Ch 32^{17}; see also 1 S 22^{7} 2 K 8^{6} Je 16^{6} 40^{2} Jon 4^{6} ψ 69^{6} 73^{18} 135^{11} 136$^{19.20}$ Pr 17^{26} Jb 12^{23b} La 4^{5} 1 Ch 16^{37} 18^{6} (הושׁיע, altered fr. 2 S 8^{6}: so ψ 116^{6}), 25^{1} 29$^{22.22}$ 2 Ch 5^{11} 6^{42} 17^{7} 24^{5} 34^{13} (usu. על), Ezr 8^{16}; at the end of an enumeration, 1 Ch 28^{1b} 2 Ch 24^{12b} 26^{14b} 28^{23}; marking the defin. obj. in appos., 1 Ch 29^{18} 2 Ch 2^{12} 23^{1} ψ 135^{11} 136$^{19.20}$ (= earlier את, Gn 26^{34} Ju 3^{15} Is 7^{6} 8^{2}); after a sf. (in Syr. fashion), 1 Ch 5^{26} וַיַּגְלֵם לְ׳, 23^{6} 2 Ch 25$^{5.10}$ 28^{15}, cf. Ne 9^{32}; defining anom. the sf. of a *noun*, Nu 29$^{18.21.24\,etc.}$ 1 Ch 7^{5} הִתְיַחְשָׂם לַכֹּל, 2 Ch 31$^{16.18}$ Ezr 9^{1} 10^{14}. (But in sentences of the type אֵין דּוֹרֵשׁ לְנַפְשִׁי ψ 142^{5b} 72^{12} Is 51^{18} Je 14^{16} 49^{5} La 1$^{7.9.17.21}$, the ל belongs prob. to אין: cf. the ‖ types אֵין לִי מַכִּיר ψ 142^{5a} Dt 28^{31} Je 50^{32} La 1^{2}, דֹּרֵשׁ אֵין לָהּ Je 30^{17} La 4^{4}.) Cf. Ges$^{\S 117n}$.

4. *Into* (εἰς), of a transition into a new state or condition, or into a new character or office:— **a.** Gn 2^{22} וַיִּבֶן אֶת־הַצֵּלָע לְאִשָּׁה *into* a woman, 12^{2} וְאֶעֶשְׂךָ לְגוֹי גָּדוֹל *into* a great nation, and very oft. with this and similar verbs, as Ex 26^{7} Is 44$^{17.19}$, שָׂם Gn 46^{3} Is 5^{20} make bitter *into* sweet etc., 28^{17}, נָתַן 42^{6}, also in such phrases as שָׂם לְשַׁמָּה to make *into* a desolation Is 13^{9} Je 4^{7} etc. 19^{8}; הפך ל to change *into* Ex 7^{15} Dt 23^{6}+, to cut or divide *into* Gn 32^{8} Ju 19^{29} Is 11^{15}+, שָׂרַף לְ to burn *into* Am 2^{1}, Dt 9^{21} דַּק לְעָפָר, פעל ψ 7^{14} maketh *into* (or *to be*) flaming ones; היה ל *to become*, in many diff. connexions, as Gn 2^{7} ויהי האדם לנפשׁ חיה *became* a living soul (see היה **II. 2 e**, p. 226^{a}); משׁח למלך (לנגיד) to anoint *so as to be* king, *as* king (Germ. 'zum König': cf. Old Engl. *to*, as Ju 17^{13} and 'We have Abraham *to* our father'), 1 S 9^{16} 15^{1} etc., צִוָּה לְ to appoint *as* 13^{14} 25^{30}; שׁת ל ψ 45^{17}; even more freely, as דִּבֶּר עָלַי לְמֶלֶךְ 1 K 14^{2}, cf. 2 S 3^{17} 1 Ch 29^{23}; חשׁב ל to count *for* (or *as*) Gn 38^{15} + oft.; Ex 21^{7} when a man sells his daughter לְאָמָה *for, as,* a female slave, Dt 6^{8} to bind לְאוֹת *for, as* a sign, הִתְיַצֵּב (יָצָא) לְשָׂטָן *so as to be* an adversary Nu 22$^{22.32}$, קוּם (הקים) לְאֹרֵב 1 S 22$^{8.13}$, עמד לְ Is 11^{10} Dn 11^{1}, יצא לַחָפְשִׁי to go forth *into the state of* one free Ex 21^{2} (cf. v$^{26.27}$ after שׁלח), 2 K 25^{12} Is 14^{2} Je 34^{11}, ψ 48^{4} נודע לְ hath made himself known *as*, 87^{4} הזכיר לְ to mention *as*, Ez 13^{20}; poet. Jb 39^{16} הִקְשִׁיחַ בָּנֶיהָ לְּלֹא־לָהּ treats her young ones hardly (turning them) *into* none of hers: without a vb. (poet., or late prose) Mi 1^{14} Na 1^{7} Hb 1^{11} זוּ כֹחוֹ לֵאלֹהוֹ, Zc 4^{7} La 4^{3} Jb 13^{12} Hg 1^{9} 1 Ch 21^{12} 26^{29} 28^{18b} 2 Ch 23^{4}. **b.** this usage is also combined idiomatically, with great freq., with a 2nd לְ, of reference (**5 a d**), giving rise to such phrases as Gn 1^{29} לָכֶם יִהְיֶה לְאָכְלָה to you it shall be *for food* (see היה **II. 2 f**, p. 226^{b}), 45^{8} וַיְשִׂימֵנִי לְאָב לְפַרְעֹה, 47^{26} Dt 28$^{9.25}$ Ju 1^{33} 1 S 2^{28} Is 21^{4} 28^{18b} וְהָיִיתֶם לוֹ לְמִרְמָס, 49^{5} יֹצְרִי מִבֶּטֶן לְעֶבֶד לוֹ, 63$^{8.10}$ וַיֵּהָפֵךְ לָהֶם לְאוֹיֵב (Jb 30^{21}), Je 15$^{4.20}$ 20^{4} 21^{9} Hb 2^{7} ψ 33^{12} 94^{22} 132^{13} 139^{22} Jb 13^{24} ותחשׁבני לאויב לך, 16^{12} etc.

5. *With reference to*, viz. **a.** defining those in reference to whom a predicate is affirmed, hence oft. = *belonging to, of*: (*a*) Dt 23^{3} דור עשׂירי לא יבא לו, v$^{4.9}$ La 1^{10}; הכרית לְ 1 S 2^{33} 1 K 14^{10}+; השׁבית לְ Je 48^{35}; לֹא יִכָּרֵת אִישׁ לְ 1 K 2^{4} 8^{25}+; 1 S 25^{34} אִם נוֹתַר לְ, Gn 17^{10} המול לכם כל בשׂר, 34$^{15.22}$ Ex 12^{48} 1 S 11^{2}; 1 K 14^{13}; ישׁב על כסא לְ 2 K 10^{30} 15^{12} Je 13^{13} 22^{4} ψ 132^{12} cf. v^{11}; ראה בנים לְ Gn 50^{23} ψ 128^{6}; אבד לְ to perish *belonging to* 1 S 9$^{3.20}$ Is 26^{14}; מצא לְ to find *belonging to* Dt 22^{14} 1 S 13^{22}; Gn 23^{16} money עֹבֵר לַסֹּחֵר current *to* (= with) the merchant, Nu 9^{10} Am 9^{1} Is 33^{14} Jb 12^{6}: note further the pron. in Ex 10^{5} הַצֹּמֵחַ לכם מן השׂדה, 12$^{2.5}$ 26^{33} Lv 11^{29} וְזֶה לָכֶם הַטָּמֵא (cf. v$^{4-8}$), 19^{23} 25^{30} 26$^{5.26}$ בְּשִׁבְרִי לָכֶם מַטֵּה לֶחֶם (Ez 14^{13}), Nu 28^{19} 32^{21} 34^{4} Dt 28^{66} Jos 2^{6} הָעֲרֻכוֹת לָהּ עַל הַגָּג, Ju 16^{9} 19^{14} (cf. זָרַח לְ Gn 32^{32}+), 1 S 5^{9} 2 S 15^{30} 2 K 4^{27b} נַפְשָׁהּ מָרָה־לָהּ (cf. Is 15^{4} Je 4^{19}), Is 23^{7} Je 2^{21} Mi 2^{4} אֵיךְ ימישׁ לי, Ez 16^{14} 29^{7} ψ 110^{3}; also 40^{7} ears hast thou digged *to* (or *for*) me, 51^{12} (cf. 1 S 10^{9}), Is 50$^{4.5}$ יעיר לי אזן. (*b*) in such phrases as Nu 1^{4} אִישׁ אִישׁ לַמַּטֶּה a man *for* (or *of*) a tribe, 7^{11} 31^{4}, Dt 1^{23} Jos 3^{12} 18^{4} Ju 20^{10} ten men לַמֵּאָה *of* 100, 100 *of* 1000 etc.; רִאשׁוֹן לְ = first *of* Ex 12^{2} 2 S 19^{21}. (*c*) spec. of relationship, to define a man's family or tribe, esp. in genealogies, Nu 1^{6} לראובן אליצור, v$^{7.8}$ etc., v$^{22.24}$ etc., 3$^{21.27}$ 1 Ch 24$^{20.21}$ etc., 26$^{23.25}$ etc. + oft.; in the opp. order Ex 31^{2} Lv 24^{11} Nu 17^{23} אהרן לבית לוי 1 K 15^{27} etc., cf. 2 S 3$^{2.3.5}$, also 9^{3a} Gn 20^{18} 46$^{26.27}$; similarly הנשׁארים לְ 2 K 10$^{11.17}$, הַמֵּת לְ 1 K 14^{11}

16^{4}+. (*d*) denoting *relation* (to be *to* or *towards* one in a particular regard or capacity) Ex 19^{5} והייתם לי סְגֻלָּה ye shall be *to me* a special possession, 22^{30} ,אנשי קדש תהיון לי, 1 S 18^{18} 2 S 19^{29} 1 K 5^{15} 2 K 19^{15} Je 12^{9} 15^{8} 22^{6} גלעד אתה לי, 51^{20} Is 54^{9} Ez 24^{19} ψ 12^{5} מִי אָדוֹן לָנוּ, 35^{14} כְּרֵעַ כְּאָח לִי, 99^{8} Jb 24^{17} 30^{29} Ne 6^{18}; with a ptcp. Nu 10^{25} 25^{18} 35^{23} Dt 4^{22} $19^{4.6}$ Is 11^{9} 14^{2} (Dr $^{§135, 7 Obs.}$); מלך לְ Nu 22^{4}; רַב לָכֶם it is (too) much *to* you, מְעַט לְ (too) little *to* . . .; in the phr. (מָה) מִי אֵלֶּה לְּךָ who (what) are these *to* thee? = *what meanest thou* by these things? Gn $33^{5.8}$ 2 S 16^{2} Ez 37^{18}, cf. Ex 12^{26} Jos 4^{6} Ez 12^{22}; חלילה לי away be it *to* (or *for*) me! למה לי to what purpose *to* me is . . .? Gn 27^{46} Is 1^{11} Je 6^{20} Jb 30^{2}: oft. also in such phrases as מָגֵן לְ a shield *to* Gn 15^{1} ψ 18^{31}, a strength *to* ψ 28^{8}, an abomination *to* Gn 43^{32} Is 1^{13}+, a grief *to* Pr 10^{1} 17^{21}; cf. Je 15^{10} Mal 2^{9} ψ 89^{28} etc.: note also Jon 3^{3} עיר גדולה לאלהים a city great *to* God (i.e. in his estimation: cf. Acts 7^{20} ἀστεῖος τῷ θεῷ, and לפני Gn 10^{9}), Est 10^{3}. And with כְּ Ju 17^{11} 2 S 12^{3} וַתְּהִי לוֹ כְּבַת, Ex 22^{24} (cf. **4 b**), Am 9^{7} כבני כֻשִׁיִּים אַתֶּם לִי Ho 11^{4} Is 29^{2} Jb 33^{6} הֵן־אֲנִי לָאֵל כְּפִיךָ lo, I am *to* God as thou art, etc. **b.** denoting possession, *belonging to*;—(*a*) as predicate, in הָיָה לְ (cf. Lat. *est mihi*), יֵשׁ לְ, אֵין לְ constantly (see these words); also alone, as Gn $31^{16.43}$ לי הוא it is *mine*, 48^{5} לי הם, Ex 19^{5b} כי לי כל הארץ, 1 K $20^{3.4}$ Is 43^{1} לי אתה, 44^{5} לי׳ אני, Ez 29^{3} ψ 47^{10} $50^{10.12}$ Jb $12^{13.16}$ Ct 2^{16} 6^{3}; 1 S 1^{2} ולו שתי נשים and *he had* two wives, $25^{7.36}$ Ju 3^{16} 17^{5} Jb 22^{8} 2 S 17^{18} Ho 6^{10}, +oft.; with לא, 1 K 22^{17} Is 53^{2} לא הדר לו, Je 5^{10}+; with a neut. adj. (rare) Is 63^{2} Je 30^{10} אָנוּשׁ לְשִׁבְרֵךְ; note also such phrases as 2 K 10^{19} זבח גדול לי לבעל, Is 2^{12} כִּי יוֹם לי׳ על וג׳ for י׳ *hath* a day against, etc., 22^{5} 28^{2} הִנֵּה חָזָק וְאַמִּיץ לי׳ י׳ *hath* a strong and mighty one (sc. at his disposal), 34^{2} קֶצֶף לי׳ על וג׳, $v^{6b.8}$; Ho 4^{1} . . . כִּי רִיב לי׳ עם, 12^{3} Mi 6^{2}: מַה־לִּי וָלָךְ what is there *to* me and *to* thee? (i.e. what have we to do with each other?), v. מָה; שלום לך peace be *to thee!* Of that which *pertains to* one as a right, Lv $25^{31.48}$ Dt 1^{17} כי המשפט לאלהים הוא, 21^{17} 1 S 17^{47} Je 10^{23} $32^{7.8}$ Ez 21^{32} ψ 3^{9} לי׳ הישועה, Jon 2^{10}; with an inf. 1 S 23^{20} וְלָנוּ הַסְגִּירוֹ and it shall be *for us* (or *our place*) to deliver him, Mi 3^{1} הלא לכם לדעת, Ezr 4^{3} 2 Ch 13^{5} 20^{17} 26^{18}, cf. ψ 50^{16} מַה־לְּךָ לְ. (*b*) here also belongs the so-called *Lamed auctoris*, Is 38^{9} מִכְתָּב לְחִזְקִיָּהוּ a writing *belonging to, of,* or *by* H., Hb 3^{1}, ψ 3^{1} and oft. מזמור לדוד a Psalm *of* or *by* D. (but possibly denoting orig., at least in some cases, a Psalm *belonging to* a collection known as David's: so certainly in לבני קרח ψ 42^{1} al., and prob. also in לאסף ψ 50^{1} al.); so לדוד מזמור 24^{1}+, לדוד alone 10^{1} 14^{1}+. Comp. on Ph. coins לצדנם *of* the Sidonians, i.e. belonging to them, לצור (= Gk. Σιδονίων, Τύρου). Heb. idiom also uses the לְ of possession where we should write the simple name, as Ez 37^{16} (written on a stick) ליהודה, v^{17} ליוסף, in English 'Judah,' 'Joseph,' Is 8^{1} למהר־שלל־חש־בז 'Maher-shalal-hash-baz.' **c.** as periph. for the *st. c.*:—(*a*) אשר לְ, as Ex 29^{29} $39^{1.39}$ Lv $7^{20.21}$ $16^{6.15}$ (see further exx. sub אשר **7**, p. 82 f.); so שֶׁלִּי +Ct 1^{6} 8^{12}, שֶׁלָּנוּ +2 K 6^{11}. (*b*) without אשר—(*α*) where it is desired to keep the first noun indeterm., 1 S 16^{18} ראיתי בן לישי a son *to* or *of* Jesse, 22^{20} Gn 41^{12} Nu 1^{4} 7^{24} 1 K 2^{39} שני עבדים לשמעי, 18^{22} 2 K 3^{11} Ru 2^{1} etc.; (*β*) where the genit. is a *compound* term, to avoid a series of nouns in the *st. c.*, Nu 1^{4} ראש לבית אבותיו, $7^{24.30.36}$ etc., 1^{21} פקדיהם למטה ראובן, $v^{23.25}$ etc., $2^{9.16}$ etc., Jos 21^{38}; 1 Ch 9^{23} הראש לְ 27^{3}, הַשְּׁעָרִים לְבֵית י׳, 2 Ch 19^{11} Ne 10^{39} etc., occas. also besides, as 1 S 14^{16} הצופים לשאול, Ex 31^{7} (usu. ארון העדות); (*γ*) where the regens is a pr. name, or a compound term, which does not readily admit of being placed in the *st. c.*, as דברי הימים למלכי ישראל (יהודה) 1 K $14^{19.29}$ +oft., 1 K 5^{30} שרי הנצבים לְ, 2 K 11^{4} שרי המאות לְ; ראשי האבות לְ Nu 36^{1} Jos 19^{51} 1 Ch 8^{13} + oft. Ch Ne Ezr; in dates, as באחד לחדש Gn $8^{5.14}$ Ex $12^{3.6}$, Gn 7^{11} לחיי נח . . . בשנת, 16^{3} Ex 19^{1} 1 K . . . בשנת שתים לאסא, בחדש השלישי לצאת $15^{25.28}$ 16^{8} (all + oft.); other cases, Ex $20^{5.6}$ Lv 13^{46} Nu 16^{22} (= 27^{16}) 18^{15} Ju 20^{10} 2 K 5^{9} Ez 45^{19} Ru 2^{3} 1 Ch 4^{43} $9^{19.21}$ 26^{19} 2 Ch 22^{10} 23^{4}; (*δ*) with a neg., Gn 15^{13} בארץ לא לכם, Je 5^{19} Pr 26^{17} Hb 1^{6}, poet. even alone, 2^{6} who increaseth לא לו (that which is) not *his*, Jb 18^{15} בְּלִי לוֹ, 39^{16} ללא לָהּ as (**4**) those which are not *hers;* (*ε*) poet., Is 16^{2} 26^{7} ארח לצדיק Je 47^{3} Ho 9^{6} ψ 37^{16} 49^{14} 55^{19} (Hi De Ch), 58^{5} 73^{6} 105^{36} 116^{15} המותה לחסידיו, 123^{4} Jon 2^{3} Ec 5^{11}; cf. also מלך לְ Jos 12^{18} (but v. 𝔊 Di), 2 K 19^{13} (cf. Aram. Ezr 5^{11}): v. further Ew ^{§292}, Ges ^{§129}, Giesebr ^{§19}. **c.** attached to advbs., esp. those compounded with מִן, it forms preps., as מִקֶּדֶם לְ Gn 3^{24} lit. off the front *with reference to* (or *of*) = *in front of:* so מִבַּיִת לְ = *within,* מִחוּץ לְ = *without,*

סָבִיב לְ, מִצָּפוֹן לְ, מֵהָלְאָה לְ, מֵעֵבֶר לְ, מֵעַל לְ, מִמַּעַל לְ (all oft.); more rarely, מֵאַחֲרֵי לְ, מִבַּעַד לְ, מִבֵּינוֹת לְ, אֶל בֵּינוֹת לְ, מִזֶּה וּמִזֶּה לְ Ex 38^{15}, הֵנָּה לְ Dn $12^{5.5}$, תַּחַת לְ, מִסָּבִיב לְ, מִנֶּגֶד לְ, מִימִין לְ, מִזְרָח לְ, poet. נֶגְדָה־נָּא לְ †ψ $116^{14.18}$. See בית, חוץ, etc.; and cf. Ju $7^{1.8}$. **d.** construed with *passive* verbs, the ל of reference notifies the *agent*, as בָּרוּךְ לְ blessed *by*, Gn 14^{17} + oft.; otherwise not very common, Gn 31^{15} נֶחְשַׁב לְ to be reckoned *by* (so Is 40^{17}), Ex 12^{16} אַךְ אֲשֶׁר יֵאָכֵל לְכָל־נֶפֶשׁ הוּא לְבַדּוֹ יֵעָשֶׂה לָכֶם, 1 S 2^{3} 25^{7} 2 S 19^{43} Je 8^{3} נִבְחַר לְ (Pr 21^{3}), 29^{22} ψ 73^{10} 111^{2} Pr 13^{13} יֵחָבֶל־לוֹ is pledged *by it*, 14^{20} Ne $6^{1.7}$ נִשְׁמַע לְ, 13^{26} אָהוּב לְ, Est 4^{3} 5^{12} Ec 5^{12} שָׁמוּר לְ. So with נִרְאָה Ex 13^{7} (=Dt 16^{4}), נוֹדַע 1 S 6^{3} Ez 36^{32} Ne 4^{9} (but usu. with these words לְ is rather the dat. comm. *be known, appear, to*), נעתר Gn 25^{21} +, נדרשׁ and נמצא Is 65^{1} + to let oneself be *entreated, sought, found, by*, נוֹסַר †Lv 26^{23}, נענה †Ez $14^{4.7}$ (?). (Comp. in Syr. Nö § 247, esp. with pass. ptcp. § 279 (so Talm., Luz § 90), which in Mand. and New Syr. even unites with the ל to form a new tense, v. Nö M § 263; NS § 104.) Analogously Gn 38^{15} וַתַּהַר לוֹ and was pregnant *by*, v^{18} הָרָה לְ (adj.) pregnant *by* (lit. *to*). **e.** *regarding, in respect of*, viz. (*a*) with verbs of *speaking, commanding, hearing*, etc.; *concerning, about* (syn. עַל, which is more usu.); so with אָמַר Gn 20^{13} Dt $33^{12.13}$+ Ju 9^{54} Is 41^{7} ψ 3^{3} 41^{6}+, דִּבֶּר Ez 44^{5}, סִפֵּר ψ 22^{31}, דרשׁ Dt 12^{30} 2 S 11^{3}, חָלַם Gn 42^{9}, הִטִּיף Mi 2^{6}, צִוָּה Nu 8^{20} ψ 91^{11}+, שָׁמַע Gn 17^{20}, and oft. in the adjunct לאשׁר..., לכל אשׁר... Gn 27^{8} Jos 1^{18} 22^{2}+; שׁאל Gn 26^{7}+, esp. in phr. שׁאל לפ׳ לְשָׁלוֹם to ask *about* any one *with ref. to* (his) welfare; in the phr. לַדָּבָר הַזֶּה *in regard to* this thing (idiom.), Gn 19^{21} 1 S 30^{24}+, Ju $21^{5.7}$ לנשׁים, 1 K 20^{7}; without a vb., Lv 7^{37} 14^{54} Dt 33^{7}, and in titles Je 23^{9} 46^{2} 48^{1} $49^{1.7.23.28}$. (*b*) limiting the application of a term, esp. with כְּ to denote the *tertium comparationis*, as Gn 41^{19} לֹא רָאִיתִי כָהֵנָּה... לָרֹעַ *as regards, in respect of* (in our idiom, simply *in* or *for*) badness, Ex 24^{10} כְּעֶצֶם הַשָּׁמַיִם לָטֹהַר *in brightness*, Dt $34^{11.12}$ Ez 3^{3} (rd. לְמֹתֶק) Pr 25^{3} 1 Ch 24^{4}; with an inf., Gn 3^{22} היה כאחד ממנו לדעת *in respect of* knowing, etc., 34^{15} Is 21^{1} כַּסּוּפוֹת לַחֲלוֹף as whirlwinds *in respect of* sweeping through, Jos 10^{14} 2 S $14^{17.25}$ Ez $38^{9.16}$ Pr 26^{2} כצפור לָנוּד כדרור לָעוּף, 1 Ch 12^{9} כצבאים לְמַהֵר; with לָרֹב *in* multitude, Dt 1^{10} ככוכבי השׁמים לרב Ju $7^{12.12}$+ oft.; less freq. in comparisons with מִן, 1 K 10^{23} וַיִּגְדַּל... מִכֹּל... לְעֹשֶׁר וּלְחָכְמָה, Ct 1^{2} Jb 30^{1} צעירים ממני לימים (cf. the accus. 15^{10}), $32^{4.6}$, cf. 11^{6} כִּפְלַיִם לְתוּשִׁיָּה; rarely after substs., 2 Ch 16^{8} 21^{3}, 3^{8} לְכִכָּרִים, $v^{9.11}$ Ezr 8^{26} (where the earlier language would use appos., or the accus. of specification, Dr § 194). (*c*) somewhat differently, Lv 5^{4b} and be guilty לְאַחַת מֵאֵלֶּה *as regards* one of these things, v^{5} 22^{5b} Nu 18^{7} (cf. 1 Ch 26^{32} 27^{1} 2 Ch $19^{11.11}$) Je 2^{37} (peculiar) thou shalt not prosper להם *as regards* them, Ez 44^{14}, cf. Jb 9^{19}; after substs. Gn 47^{26} לַחֹמֶשׁ (but cf. 𝔖 Di) *with ref. to* the fifth, Lv 7^{26} 11^{46b} Nu 19^{11} 29^{39} 30^{13} Dt 19^{15} 23^{19} Ezr 8^{34} 1 Ch 27^{1} (לכל ח׳), 2 Ch 8^{15} Ne 11^{24}. (*d*) לְכֹל... (לְכָל־), at the close of a description or enumeration, with a generalizing force, *as regards all*... =*namely, in brief* (Ew § 310a), chiefly in P and Chr (prob. a juristic usage): Gn 9^{10b} all that go out of the ark לְכֹל חַיַּת הָאָרֶץ *as regards* (=*namely, even*) all beasts of the earth, 23^{10b} Ex 14^{28} (cf. v^{9} וְ), $27^{3.19}$ 28^{38} 30^{1b} Lv $5^{3.4}$ (cf. 13^{51}) 11^{42} $16^{16.21}$ 22^{18} Nu 3^{26b} ($v^{31.36}$ וְ), $4^{27.31.32}$ 5^{9} $18^{4.8.9.11}$ (all P), 2 K 12^{6} Je 19^{13} Ez 44^{9} 1 Ch 13^{1} 2 Ch 5^{12} (לְכֻלָּם), 25^{5} 31^{16} 33^{8b} (‖ 2 K 21^{8} ולכל) Ezr 1^{5}. (*e*) introducing a new subj. (rare, and text sts. dub.; chiefly Chr), *as regards*..., Is 32^{1} ולשׂרים (rd. prob. וְשָׂרִים; ל by error from foll. למשׁפט), Lv 11^{26} 1 Ch 3^{2} (rd. prob. אבשׁלום), 5^{2} (? v. Ke), 7^{1} (Ke ובני), v^{5a} (?), 24^{1} $26^{1.23.25.26.31a\beta}$ 2 Ch 5^{12} 7^{21} לְכָל־עֹבֵר עליו ישׁרק (‖ 1 K 9^{8} כָּל־עֹבֵר), cf. Dt 24^{5} (peculiar); Ec 9^{4} כִּי לְכֶלֶב חַי הוּא טוב וג׳; cf. ψ 17^{4} (on 16^{3} v. Comm.). In Chr sts. used peculiarly as a periphr., 1 Ch $28^{1b.21}$ לכל נדיב *as regards* every liberal man = every liberal man (cf. Ke), $29^{5a.6b}$; cf. Ezr 6^{7} (Aram.), 7^{28}. **f.** in connexion with terms designating a cause or occasion, *with reference to* or *in view of* (Germ. *auf...hin*) becomes nearly equivalent to *on account of, through* (not common): so to cut oneself לָנֶפֶשׁ Lv 19^{28} *on account of* a (dead) person, Dt 14^{1} Je 16^{6b}, Lv 11^{24} לְאֵלֶּה תִּטַּמָּאוּ *on account of* these ye shall become unclean, $21^{1.2.3}$+, Ez 20^{31} נִטְמָא לְ, Nu 5^{2} כָּל־טָמֵא לָנֶפֶשׁ Nu $9^{6.7.10}$, cf. 2 Ch 23^{19}; לְשֵׁם י׳ *in view of* (i.e. determined by), *because of* י׳'s name, Jo 9^{9} Je 3^{17} Is 55^{5} (‖ לְמַעַן), Ez 36^{22} (do.); Gn 4^{23a} I have slain a man לְפִצְעִי *because of* my wound, v^{23b} Ex 4^{26} לַמּוּלֹת, Nu 35^{33} לַדָּם; לָכֵן = *therefore* (syn. עַל כֵּן), constantly (v. כֵּן); Job 30^{24} (si vera l.) לָהֶן: of the cause of an emotion, Is 15^{5} לִבִּי לְמוֹאָב

יִזְעַק because of Moab, $16^{7.11}$ Je 31^{20} (עַל) הָמוּ מֵעַי לוֹ Ct 5^{4}), Ho 10^{5}, לְזֹאת Jb 37^{1}. Cf. Nu 16^{34} נסו לקולם fled *at* the sound of them, Ez 27^{28} Hb 3^{16} ψ 42^{8}.

g. marking the aim, object, or consequence of an action or thing, *in view of, for, unto:* (*a*) Gn 1^{16} לממשלת היום *for* the rule of the day, 22^{7} where is the sheep לְעֹלָה? 42^{25} provision לַדָּרֶךְ *for* the way; Ex 20^{7} לַשָּׁוְא i.e. *for* a vain or frivolous purpose, similarly לָרִיק and לַשֶּׁקֶר; Lv 1^{3}+ לִרְצֹנוֹ *for* his acceptance; Nu 21^{23} and oft. יצא למלחמה *for* battle; יָשַׁב לְ to sit (wait) *for*, Ex 24^{14} Hos 3^{3} Je 3^{2}; 1 S 8^{16} to use לִמְלַאכְתּוֹ *for* his business; 2 S 15^{2}+ בָּא לַמִּשְׁפָּט *for* judgment; ψ 69^{22} לִצְמָאִי *for* (i.e. to quench) my thirst, Ne 9^{15}; Ex 29^{36}+ לַיּוֹם *for* each day; Is 4^{3} כָּל־כָּתוּב לַחַיִּים *for* life; Ho 9^{4} לַחְמָם לְנַפְשָׁם; לרעה and לטובה Je 21^{10}+; Is 58^{4} ψ 63^{10} לְשׁוֹאָה יבקשו נפשי: in the sense of *to secure, compass,* Gn 41^{55} cried to Ph. לַלֶּחֶם *for* bread, 1 S 2^{36} Am 8^{11} Jb 15^{23} Is 10^{3}: so in לְמַעַן *for* the purpose of; and with an inf. oft. (v. **7 a**). (*b*) corresponding to the Lat. *dat. commodi,* (*α*) with vbs., Gn 2^{18} אעשה לו I will make *for* him, etc., v^{20} 3^{21}, etc., absol. עָשָׂה לְ 1 S 14^{6} Is 64^{3}, פָּעַל לְ ψ 68^{29}; מָצָא לְ Gn 8^{9}; בָּנָה לְ, Je $16^{5.6}$, נוּד, סָפַד לְ $24^{3.4}$+ oft.; לָקַח לְ 22^{10}, etc.; Ju 16^{25} וִישַׂחֶק־לָנוּ to sport *for* us (for our pleasure); Ho 2^{25} Mi 5^{1}, etc.; with a pron. of the same pers. as the vb., as 1 K 20^{34} תשים לך, 2 K 6^{7} 10^{24}, Zc 9^{13}, leading on to **h** *a*, below; oft. with prons. and imv., Nu 11^{16} אֶסְפָה־לִּי gather *me* 70 men, 22^{6} אָרָה־לִּי curse *me* this people, 23^{1} בְּנֵה לִי, 1 K 1^{28} קראו לי לבת־שבע call *me* B., 3^{24} 13^{13} 17^{10} Ct 2^{15} אֶחֱזוּ לָנוּ catch *us* the foxes, Is 49^{20} גְּשָׁה־לִּי retire *for* me, that I may dwell, 2 S 18^{5} לְאַט לִי לַנַּעַר (act) gently (**5 i** *b*) *for my sake* towards the young man, 2 K 4^{24} אַל־תַּעֲצָר־לִי לִרְכֹּב AV slacken *me* not the riding; (*β*) with substs., e.g. in such phrases as פסח הוא לי׳ Ex 12^{11} a passover is it *unto* י׳, חַג לי׳ 13^{6}, שַׁבָּת לי׳ 16^{25}, קֹדֶשׁ לי׳ Is 23^{18}+, Lv 1^{9} and oft. אִשֵּׁה רֵיחַ ניחוח לי׳, 1 S 1^{3} כהנים לי׳, etc.; (*γ*) also as a *dat. incommodi,* as to lie in wait, lay snares, dig a pit, etc., *for* any one, Ju 9^{25} 16^{2} ψ 35^{7} 57^{7} etc.; with vbs. of withholding or removing (rare), Ju 17^{2} לָקַח לָךְ 1 S 21^{6} (cf. 𝔊 (כִּי)) ψ 40^{11} 84^{12} Jb 12^{20}; note also the phr. לְכַד הַמַּיִם (הַמַּעְבָּרוֹת) לְ Ju 3^{28} (RV), 7^{24} 12^{5}: זכר לְ, in both senses, to remember *for* (in one's favour) Je 2^{2}+, *against* ψ 137^{7}+, cf. גער לְ Mal 3^{11} and 2^{3}. (*c*) more distinctly *on behalf of,* as with קִנֵּא to be jealous *for*, Nu 11^{29}+, רִב לְ, 7^{12}+, שָׁמַר Dt 3^{22}+, נִלְחַם to contend *for* Ju 6^{31}, יָרֵא Jos 9^{24}, הִתְפַּלֵּל 1 S 2^{25}+, דִּבֶּר to speak *for* one 2 K 4^{13}, Jb 13^{7} הַלְאֵל תְּדַבְּרוּ עַוְלָה will ye speak wickedness *on God's behalf?* שָׁאַל to ask 1 S 22^{13}+, עָבַר to pass over *for* (=to pardon) Am 7^{8}; Dt 30^{12} מי יעלה לנו, v^{13} Ju 1^{1} 20^{18} Is 6^{8} מִי יֵלֶךְ־לָנוּ; see also Ex 2^{19} 4^{16a} Nu 35^{31} Dt 23^{6} Jos 18^{6} Ju 5^{13} $7^{4.20}$ 2 S 15^{34b} Is 33^{21} Pr 16^{26} 31^{8}, etc.; ψ 94^{16} מִי יָקוּם לִי עִם מְרֵעִים; היה לי׳ to be *on one's side,* Hos 1^{9} ואנכי לא אהיה לכם, ψ $124^{1.2}$, and without היה Gn 31^{42} Ex 32^{26}, מִי לי׳ אֵלָי who is on י׳'s side? (let him come) to me! Jos 5^{13b} 2 S 20^{11} 2 K 10^{6} אִם לִי אַתֶּם (syn. אִתִּי 9^{32}), ψ 56^{10} זה ידעתי כי י׳ לי, $118^{6.7}$ י׳ לִי.

h. used reflexively (the 'ethical' dative, or dative of feeling), throwing the action back upon the subj., and expressing with some pathos the interest, or satisfaction, or completeness, with which it is (or is to be) accomplished, esp. (but not exclusively) with imv. and 1 pers. impf. (oft. not expressible in Engl., sts. to be expressed by a paraphr.);—(*a*) with *trans.* verbs (a choice idiom, a development of **g** *b a*, common, esp. with imv., in best prose), עֲשֵׂה לְךָ Gn 6^{14} Nu 21^{8} + oft., וַיַּעֲשׂוּ לָהֶם, עֲשִׂיתֶם לָכֶם Dt $4^{16.23}$ 9^{16} Am 5^{26}, Gn 3^{7} Ex 32^{31} Ho 13^{2}, Je 11^{17} the evil which עשו להם they have *loved to do* (cf. Hi), Gn 11^{4} Ju 3^{16} 2 S 15^{1}, etc.; קְחוּ לָכֶם, קַח־לְךָ Gn 6^{21} + oft., ויקח לו Gn 15^{10}, etc.; בָּזֶז לוֹ Dt 2^{35} 20^{14}+; תְּנוּ לָכֶם, שִׂימוּ Ex 7^{9} Jos 20^{2}; הָבוּ לָכֶם Dt 1^{13} (cf. Dr) +, בַּחֲרוּ לָכֶם Ju 19^{30}, cf. 2 K 10^{24} Ho 2^{2}; בְּחַר לוֹ, לָכֶם etc. Gn 13^{11} 2 S 17^{1} 𝔊 (v. Dr) + oft.; קְנֵה לְךָ Je 32^{7}+, דַּע לָךְ, Jb 5^{27}, cf. Ct 1^{8}; Dt $10^{1.1}$ $16^{9.13.18}$ $19^{2.3.9}$, Jos 22^{23} לִבְנוֹת לָנוּ, 1 S 20^{20} לְשַׁלַּח לִי לְמַטָּרָה, 2 K 4^{3} שַׁאֲלִי לָךְ (cf. Is 7^{11}), 18^{23} Is 44^{7} יַגִּידוּ לָמוֹ, 59^{8} עִקְּשׁוּ לָהֶם, Je 2^{13} 22^{14} אֶבְנֶה־לִּי, 31^{21} 46^{14} Ho 10^{1} פְּרִי יְשַׁוֶּה־לּוֹ maketh fruit *freely,* $v^{11.12.12}$ Am $6^{5.13}$ ψ 44^{11} שָׁסוּ לָמוֹ=plunder *at their will,* 64^{6} 83^{13} Pr 1^{22} Ec 8^{12} מַאֲרִיךְ לוֹ (denoting satisfaction), Jb 7^{3} הָנְחַלְתִּי לִי, 12^{11} יִטְעַם לוֹ, 13^{1} וַתָּבֶן־לָהּ, 24^{16}, etc.: rarely separated from the vb., Ho 12^{9} Pr 23^{20} Jb 3^{14}. (*b*) with verbs of *motion,* Gn 12^{1} 22^{2} לֶךְ־לְךָ *get thee* away, 27^{43} בְּרַח לְךָ Am 7^{12}, Nu 22^{34} אשובה לי lit. I will return *for myself,* Dt 1^{7} (cf. Dr) סְעוּ לָכֶם, v^{40} 2^{13} עברו לכם, 5^{27} שובו לכם, 1 S 22^{5} 26^{11} נְטֵה לְךָ 2 S 2^{21}, וַיֵּלְכוּ לָהֶם v^{12}, וְנֵלְכָה לָּנוּ v^{22} 1 K 17^{3} Is 31^{8} נָס לוֹ, 40^{9} עֲלִי לָךְ, Je 5^{5} אֵלְכָה לִּי, Hos 8^{9} a wild ass בּוֹדֵד לוֹ going alone *at its*

pleasure, Mi 1^{11} ψ 58^{8} כמים יתהלכו למו that *run apace*, Pr 20^{14} אזל לו=*goeth his way*, Jb 39^{4} Ct 1^{8b} 2$^{10\,11\,13}$ 4^{6}. (*c*) with *neuter* verbs, esp those signifying a state of mind or feeling (chiefly poet.), ψ 66^{7} אל ירומו למו, 80^{7} ילעגו למו mock *as they please*, 120^{6} רַבַּת שָׁכְנָה לָהּ נַפְשִׁי has *had her* dwelling with, etc, 122^{3} שֶׁחֻבְּרָה לָּהּ is *well* compacted, 123^{4} שָׂבְעָה לָהּ is *but too* full, Is 2^{22} חִדְלוּ לָכֶם, 2 Ch 25^{16} 35^{21} Je 7^{4} אַל־תִּבְטְחוּ לָכֶם, v^{8} 2 K 18^{21}, Ez 37^{11} נִגְזַרְנוּ לָנוּ we are *quite* cut off, Jb 6^{19} קִוּוּ לָמוֹ (implying that they *fed themselves* on hope), 15^{28} יָשְׁבוּ לָמוֹ which should not sit (be inhabited), 19^{29} גּוּרוּ לָכֶם, Ct 2^{17} 8^{14} דמה לך, and the freq. הִשָּׁמֶר־לְךָ take heed *to* thyself Gn 24^{6}+; with an adj., Am 2^{13} הַמְלֵאָה לָהּ עָמִיר (Cf Ew$^{§\,315a}$ Very common in Syriac, esp *b* No$^{§\,224}$) **i.** of reference to a norm or standard, *according to, after, by* —(*a*) Gn 1^{11} + oft P למינו *acc to* its kinds, 8^{19} + לְמִשְׁפְּחֹתֵיהֶם *acc. to* their families, 10^{5} איש לִלְשֹׁנוֹ, v$^{31.32}$, Ex 30^{12}+ לִפְקֻדֵיהֶם *acc to* them that are numbered of them, Nu 1^{2} לְבֵית אֲבֹתָם *by* their fathers' houses, v^{2} לְגֻלְגְּלֹתָם, v^{3} לְצִבְאֹתָם, v^{20}+ oft, esp. in enumerations and classifications, Gn 13^{3} Abram went לְמַסָּעָיו *by* his journeyings (stages), so לְמַסְעֵיהֶם Ex 17^{1}+; Gn 13^{17} go through the land לְאָרְכָּהּ וּלְרָחְבָּהּ *acc to* (i e. to the full extent of) its length and breadth (cf Hb 1^{6}), 41^{47} לִקְמָצִים *by* handfuls, Nu 24^{2}+ לִשְׁבָטָיו *by* its tribes, 1 S 29^{2} עברים למאות ולאלפים *by* hundreds and thousands, 2 S 18^{4}, Nu 32^{33} לְעָרֶיהָ Jos 18^{9}; Ju 19^{19} לַעֲצָמֶיהָ *acc to* her bones (i.e. limb by limb), Ez 24^{6} לִנְתָחֶיהָ piece by piece; ψ 140^{12} to hunt לְמַדְחֵפֹת thrust-*wise*, with thrust upon thrust, Is 27^{12} לְאַחַד אֶחָד (Ges Ew) *by* one, one (i e one by one), hence, esp. with plurals, it acquires sts a *distributive* force, as לַבְּקָרִים Is 33^{2} *by* mornings = *every* morning (cf. **6**), so לַבְּקָרִים ψ 73^{14} 101^{8}+, לִרְגָעִים Is 27^{3}+ *every* moment, לֶחֳדָשָׁיו Is 47^{13} *every* month, Ez 47^{12} 1 K 10^{22} אַחַת לְשָׁלֹשׁ שָׁנִים once *every* three years, Am 4^{4} לשלשת ימים *every* three days (but v. We), 1 Ch 9^{25}; in Chr לשער ושער, לְעִיר וָעִיר, 2 Ch 8^{14} 19^{5}, 26^{11}. (*b*) denoting the *principle*, with regard to which an act is done, לְמִסְפַּר *acc. to* the number of. Dt 32^{8} Ju 21^{23}+, Is 11^{3} to judge לְמַרְאֵה עֵינָיו, לְמִשְׁמַע אָזְנָיו *acc to* that which his eyes see, his ears hear (cf Lv 13^{12} Jb 42^{5}), 28^{26}, 32^{1} a king will reign לְצֶדֶק *acc to* justice (‖ למשפט), 42^{3} לֶאֱמֶת = *faithfully*, Je 9^{2} לֶאֱמוּנָה = *honestly*, 15^{15} 30^{11} (= 46^{28}) וְיִסַּרְתִּיךָ לַמִּשְׁפָּט (synon. 10^{24} במשפט), Ho 2^{12} (‖ לְפִי), Jo 2^{23} לִצְדָקָה; Gn 38^{24} pregnant לִזְנוּנִים = *unchastely*, Nu 15^{24} לשגגה *by* error (elsewhere בשגגה), 2 Ch 30^{3} 35^{6}, Ct 7^{10} flowing down למישרים *straightly* (Pr 23^{31} ב׳), לָרֹב Jb 26^{3} 2 Ch 14^{14}, poet לְמַכְבִּיר Jb 36^{31} *in* abundance, לְאַט = *gently* 2 S 18^{5}+; Ex 16^{3} ψ 78^{25} לָשֹׂבַע *acc to* satiety, לְרֶגֶל *acc. to* the foot (pace) of Gn 33^{14}+ (v רֶגֶל), 1 S 23^{20} לְכָל־אַוַּת נַפְשְׁךָ (Dt 12^{15} al. ב׳), 2 S 15^{11} לְתֻמָּם *acc. to* their simplicity, i.e. unsuspectingly (so 1 K 22^{34}), 1 K 9^{11} לְכָל־חֶפְצוֹ, Is 54^{15} Ez 22^{6} לִזְרֹעוֹ, Jb 12^{5} ψ 119$^{91\,134}$ לְאִמְרָתֶךָ (‖ כְּ׳ v$^{58\,116\,170}$), Ec 1^{10} long ago לְעֹלָמִים *acc. to* (measured by) the ages etc. (v. Hi): so also in the phr לפי חֶרֶב *acc to* a sword's mouth, i e. as the sword would devour, without quarter, Jos 6^{21} + oft; . . . . לפי itself also, in various fig. applications, has the force of *acc to*, Gn 47^{12}, etc. (v פֶּה), and in יֵשׁ (אין) לְאֵל יָדְךָ it is (not) *acc. to* the power of thy hand (v. p. 43). Similarly Dt 11^{11} לִמְטַר הַשָּׁמַיִם *after the manner of* the rain of heaven, i. e. as the rain permits (opp. to the artificial irrigation of v^{10}), Ju 21^{12}+ לְמִשְׁכַּב זָכָר, Ez 12^{12} לְעַיִן i.e. *as* the eye sees it **j.** designating a condition or state: לָבֶטַח *in a state of* confidence = confidently, Lv 25^{18} + oft.; לְבָדָד, לְבַד, *in a state of* separation (= apart), so לְבַדּוֹ (v pp 94, 95); לְשָׁלוֹם Gn 44^{17}+, לְפֶתַע suddenly †Is 29^{5} 30^{13}; לבלי *in a condition of* no . . = without, Is 5^{14}+ (v בלי), so . . . לְאֵין (late, v p 35), לְלֹא †2 Ch 15^{3}, further Is 1^{6} לָחֳלִי *in a state of* sickness, 50^{11} לְמַעֲצֵבָה, ψ 45^{15} לִרְקָמוֹת, Ezr 2^{63} = Ne 7^{65} a priest לאורים ולתמים *having relation to* (i.e. *with*) U. and Th., 2 Ch 20^{21} לְהַדְרַת קֹדֶשׁ = *in* holy adornment (cf. ב׳ ψ 29^{2} 96^{9}) And of a concomitant circumstance (Germ. *bei*), *in presence of, at*, Jb 29^{3} לְאוֹרוֹ, Hb 3^{11}, . . . לקול Jb 21^{12} Ezr 3^{13}.

6. Of time **a.** *towards, against*, sts with collat idea of *in view of*, much rarer than ב, but expressing concurrence (*at*) rather than duration (*in*): Gn 3^{8} לְרוּחַ הַיּוֹם *at* the breeze of the day, לְעֵת in various connexions, as לעת עֶרֶב Gn 8^{11}+ (v עת), לְעִתִּים מְזֻמָּנִים † Ezr 10^{14} Ne 10^{35}, לְעִתּוֹת בַּצָּרָה † ψ 9^{10} 10^{1}; . . . לְיוֹם *at, on* the day of, ψ 81^{4} Pr 7^{20}+, . . . מה תעשו לְיוֹם Is 10^{3} Ho 9^{5}

לְיוֹם אֲשֶׁר... (cf. Je 5[31]), ... לְיָמִים אֲשֶׁר + Ez 22[14], ... לִתְקוּפַת לִתְשׁוּבַת הַשָּׁנָה + Mal 3[17]; 2 S 11[1] +; הַיָּמִים † 1 S 1[20], לִתְקוּפַת הַשָּׁנָה + 2 Ch 24[23] (Ex 34[22] without לְ), לְקֵץ שָׁנִים (יָמִים) (late) 2 Ch 18[2] Ne 13[6] Dn 11[6.13] (in early Heb מִקֵּץ יָמִים); ... לִשְׁנַת + 2 Ch 15[10]; לַבֹּקֶר ψ 30[6] 49[15] + (Ex 34[2] after הָיָה נָכוֹן = *against, for*; cf. 19[11] Pr 21[31]); לַבְּקָרִים Is 33[2], v. **5 i**); לָעֶרֶב Gn 49[27] (‖ בַּבֹּקֶר) +; לְמָחָר + Ex 8[6] (in answer to v[5] לְמָתַי), v[19] Est 5[12] (Nu 11[18] Jos 7[13] after הִתְקַדְּשׁוּ = *against*), לְמָחֳרָת Jon 4[7] (cf. 1 Ch 29[21]); לְמוֹעֵד ... לַמּוֹעֵד, Jb 24[14], לָאוֹר Gn 17[21] Ex 23[15] +; לְפָנִים and לִפְנֵי *before* (oft.); לְאָחוֹר *hereafter*, † Is 41[23] 42[23], ψ 32[6b]; with inf. (rare), in the phr. לִפְנוֹת (הַ)בֹּקֶר (עֶרֶב) Gn 24[63] +, 2 S 18[29] Is 7[15] לְדַעְתּוֹ *when* he knoweth. **b.** to denote the *close* of a period (rare), Gn 7[4] לְיָמִים עוֹד שִׁבְעָה, v[10] Ex 19[15] 2 S 13[23] Am 4[4] לִשְׁלֹשֶׁת יָמִים (We); Ezr 10[8.9] Ne 6[15] Dn 12[7] (cf. עַד 7[25]) 2 Ch 21[19] (so Syr. v PS ⟍ 5). **c.** *towards, to*, Ex 34[25] לֹא יָלִין לַבֹּקֶר (usu. עַד, as 23[18]), Dt 16[4] 1 S 13[3] (after נוֹחַל), Am 4[7] בְּעוֹד שְׁלֹשָׁה חֳדָשִׁים לַקָּצִיר *to* the harvest; oft. in the expressions לְעוֹלָם, לְדֹר דֹּר, לְדוֹר וָדוֹר, לָנֶצַח; rather differently in מִיּוֹם לְיוֹם ψ 96[2] (‖ 1 Ch 16[23] אֶל), Est 3[7] (i. e. passing from day to day), cf. 2 S 14[26] (Gie [30c]). **d.** *for, during*, Is 63[18] לַמִּצְעָר (si vera l.), 2 Ch 11[17] לְשָׁנִים שָׁלוֹשׁ, 29[17].

7. With an *inf.* (Ges [§ 114. 2]), לְ denotes **a.** most commonly the end or purpose of an action (= the Lat. gerund with *ad*, e.g. *ad faciendum*, to do): Gn 1[17] and he placed them in the firmament לְהָאִיר ... וְלִמְשֹׁל ... וּלְהַבְדִּיל *to* give light..., and *to* rule.., and *to* divide, etc., 2[15] set him in the garden לְעָבְדָהּ וּלְשָׁמְרָהּ *to* till it, and *to* keep it, v[9] brought them to Adam לִרְאוֹת *to* see, etc., + very oft.; Gn 19[20] קְרֹבָה לָנוּס שָׁמָּה near *for* fleeing thither, Ec 3[2] עֵת לָלֶדֶת a time *for* bringing forth. The neg. is expressed by לְבִלְתִּי, q. v. **b.** *with reference to*, limiting or qualifying the idea expressed by the principal vb., and so resolvable sts. into *so as to, to*, sts. into *in respect of, in*:—(*a*) *so as to, to*, Dt 8[6] and keep the commands of י׳ לָלֶכֶת בִּדְרָכָיו וּלְיִרְאָה אֹתוֹ *to* walk in his ways, and *to* fear him, 10[12] 11[22] 19[9] 1 K 2[3.4] 11[2] 1 S 20[20.36] Jo 2[26] אֲשֶׁר עָשָׂה עִמָּכֶם לְהַפְלִיא *so as to* do wondrously, Ez 5[6]; Ju 5[18] עַם חֵרֵף נַפְשׁוֹ לָמוּת *so as to* die, *for* dying [not '*unto* death'], 16[16] 2 K 20[1] חָלָה לָמוּת, Gn 2[3] לַעֲשׂוֹת *so as to* make (or *in* making) which, he created; and in the very freq לֵאמֹר, introducing the words spoken, *so as to say* = *saying* (Germ. *indem* er sagte), Gn 1[22], etc. (*b*) *in respect of, in* (cf. **5 e** (*b*)) Gn 34[7] 1 S 12[17] your evil is great that ye have done לִשְׁאוֹל לָכֶם מֶלֶךְ *in* asking for yourselves a king, v[29] 14[33] the people sin against J. לֶאֱכֹל עַל־הַדָּם *in* eating with the blood, 19[5] 2 S 19[7] 2 K 4[24] Je 44[18] ψ 36[3] 63[3] 78[18] 101[8] 103[20] Ne 13[18]. And with the *tert. compar.*, above, **5 e** (*b*). Esp. with verbs expressing what with us would be denoted by an adv. adjunct, but in Heb. idiom forms the principal idea, as 1 S 1[12] הִרְבְּתָה לְהִתְפַּלֵּל lit. did much *in respect of* praying (= prayed long *or* much), Is 55[7] כִּי יַרְבֶּה לִסְלוֹחַ +; 2 K 2[10] הִקְשִׁיתָ לִשְׁאוֹל thou hast done hardly *in respect of* asking (= asked a hard thing), 1 K 14[9] הֵרַע לַעֲשׂוֹת; so with הִקְרִיב Gn 12[11], מִהַר 27[20], הִרְחִיק Ex 8[24] הֶעְפִּיל Nu 14[44], הֵחֵל Dt 1[5], בֹּשֵׁשׁ Ju 5[28], הִפְלִיא 13[19] 2 Ch 26[15] (with *pass.* vb.), שׁוּב 1 K 13[17] Ezr 9[14], הֵיטִיב Je 1[12] + (without לְ 1 S 16[17]), הֶעְמִיק Is 29[15] +, קָרֵב Ez 36[8], הִגְדִּיל Jo 2[20] +, קִדַּמְתִּי לִבְרֹחַ Jon 4[2], הִגְבִּיהַּ ψ 113[5], הַשְׁפִּיל v[6], Gn 31[27] נַחְבֵּאתָ לִבְרֹחַ hast hidden thyself *in regard to* fleeing = hast fled secretly, 2 S 19[4] וַיִּתְגַּנֵּב לָבוֹא = come in stealthily. (*c*) by an extension of (*b*), the inf. with לְ so forms the complement of a verb that, if the verb be trans., it becomes virtually its *object*: so very oft. with such verbs as הוֹסִיף *to add* Gn 4[2.12], הֵחֵל *to begin* 6[1], חָדַל 11[8], יָכֹל 13[6], נָתַן 18[7], *to permit* 20[6], אָבָה 24[5], בִּקֵּשׁ Ex 2[15], מִהֵר 7[14], לָמַד Dt 14[23], חָפֵץ 25[8], יָדַע 1 K 5[20] (these all occur also without לְ); הוֹאִיל *to undertake, consent*, Gn 18[27.31], כִּלָּה *to finish*, תָּמַם Dt 2[16] (to come to an end *in respect of*), קִוָּה Is 5[2]; also צִוָּה Gn 50[2], אָמַר Ex 2[14], דִּמָּה Nu 33[56], חָשַׁב 1 S 18[25], יָעַץ ψ 62[5], לִמֵּד Je 12[16], אָהֵב Ho 12[8]: Dt 10[12] what doth י׳ ask of thee כִּי אִם לְיִרְאָה except *to* fear etc.? (cf. Mi 6[8] after דָּרַשׁ without לְ). (*d*) as the *subj.* of a sentence (rare): Is 10[7] לְהַשְׁמִיד בִּלְבָבוֹ, 1 Ch 29[12]; with טוֹב 1 S 15[22] ψ 118[8.9] Ec 7[2.5] Pr 21[9] (usu. without לְ, as v[19] 25[24] Ex 14[12]); cf. Ex 8[22] לֹא נָכוֹן לַעֲשׂוֹת כֵּן; 2 S 18[11] וְעָלַי לָתֶת, Ne 13[13] Ezr 10[12], Mi 3[1] הֲלֹא לָכֶם לָדַעַת, Ezr 4[3] 2 Ch 13[5] 20[17] 26[18]. (*e*) with יֵשׁ, אֵין (late), and (more rarely) לֹא, in sense of *it is* (*not*) *possible to*..., or (sts.) *there is no need to*...: see יֵשׁ **2 c c** (p. 442), אַיִן **5** (p. 34[b]), adding Hag 1[6] Est 8[8] 2 Ch 22[9]; לֹא **1 a b** (p. 518): and cf. Dr [§ 202] Ges [§ 114 l] Dav [§ 94 b, 95 b]. (*f*) with הָיָה, to express the idea of *destination*, as Nu 24[22] וְקִין יהיה

לְבָעֵר shall be *for consuming*, Dt 31[17] Is 5[5] 6[13] 37[26] Ez 30[16] ψ 109[13]+. Cf. מָה לַעֲשׂוֹת *what is* (*was*) *to be done?* Is 5[4] 2 K 4[13] 2 Ch 25[9]+ (Dr [§ 203]). (*g*) expressing (acc. to the context) *tendency, intention,* or *obligation* (the 'periphrastic' future):—Ho 9[13] וְאֶפְרַיִם לְהוֹצִיא אֶל הֹרֵג בָּנָיו *is for* bringing forth (=*must* bring forth), Is 10[32] עוד היום בנב לעמד *is he for* tarrying (*must he* tarry), 38[20] י׳ להושיעני *is* (*ready*) *to* save me, 44[14] (si vera l.), Jer 51[49] Hb 1[17] ψ 32[9] 49[15] צוּרָם לְבַלּוֹת שְׁאוֹל = *must* Sheol waste away, 62[10] בְּמֹאזְנַיִם לַעֲלוֹת, Pr 18[24] 19[8] שומר תבונה למצא טוב *will be finding* prosperity, 20[25] Jb 30[6] 1 Ch 22[5] (לִבְנוֹת), Ec 3[15]: of past time, Gn 15[12] ויהי השמש לבוא *was about to* go down, Jos 2[5] 1 S 14[21b] (txt. dub.: Dr [§ 206 Obs.]), 2 Ch 26[5] (strangely) ויהי לדרש אלהים RV *set himself to* seek; usu. without היה, 2 S 4[10] אֲשֶׁר לְתִתִּי לוֹ to whom *it was for my* giving (*I ought to have* given), 2 K 13[19] לְהַכּוֹת *percutiendum erat*, 1 Ch 9[25], and more freely 2 Ch 11[22] כי להמליכו for (he was) *for making* him king, 12[12] ולא להשחית and *was no longer for* destroying him, 36[19](?): in a question, Gn 30[15] וְלָקַחַת and *art thou for* taking? Est 7[8] 2 Ch 19[2] הֲלָרָשָׁע לַעְזֹר *wilt thou help* the wicked? Cf. Dr [§ 204], Ges [§ 114 h-k], Dav [§ 94]. (*h*) with וְ, in contin. (mostly) of a finite vb. or ptcp., Ex 32[29] מַלְאוּ יֶדְכֶם . . . וְלָתֵת and *be for placing* etc. Lv 10[10 f.] (?), 1 S 8[12] יִקַּח . . . וְלָשׂוּם, Je 19[12] עשׂה . . . וְלָתֵת, 44[14] Ho 12[3] ψ 25[14] 109[16] Jb 34[8] Ec 7[25] 9[1] (si vera l.), Dn 12[11] Neh 8[13] 1 Ch 10[13] 2 Ch 2[8] 7[17] 8[13] 30[9], Ez 13[22]; Am 8[4] הַשֹּׁאֲפִים אֶבְיוֹן וְלַשְׁבִּית וג׳ *and* (that are) *for making* the poor to cease, Is 44[28] הָאֹמֵר . . . וְלֵאמֹר, 56[6] ψ 104[21] Je 17[10] 44[19] 1 Ch 6[34] (cf. Dr [§ 206] Dav [§ 96 R. 4]).—On לְמַן, v. מַן.

Note.—1 K 6[19] לְתִתֵּן שָׁם, the supposition that לְ is a conj. (=למען) is too alien to Heb. usage to be justified by the Ar. لِ for لِكَيْ, and the view that תִּתֵּן here and 17[14] is an anom. form for תֵּת (Ew [§ 238 c] Kö [I. 305]) is against analogy: rd. with Ol [§ 224 d], Ges [§ 67 A. 3], Klo, לָתֵת (as 17[14] Qr).

†**לְמוֹ** poet. for לְ (v. מוֹ) Jb 27[14] 29[21] 38[40] 40[4].

לֹא or **לוֹא** **adv.** not (Ar. لا, Aram. לָא, لا, Sab. לא, Ass. *lâ;* not in Eth.: cf. Kö [ii. 1. 236] Walker [AJSL 1896, 237 ff.])—לוֹא, acc. to Mass. (Fr [MM 248]), 35 t., besides בְּלוֹא 6 t., and הֲלוֹא, the orthogr. of which varies much (*ib.* [p. 251]), e. g. in S always הֲלוֹא, in Chr always הֲלֹא, on the whole הֲלוֹא 141 t., הֲלֹא 128 t.; twice, acc. to Mass., written לו (Qr לֹא), 1 S 2[16] 20[2], once לה Dt 3[11] Kt:—*not*—denying objectively, like οὐ (not μή = אַל):—**1.** in predication: **a.** with a *verb;* so most freq., and nearly always (*a*) with the finite tenses, whether pf. (Gn 2[5b] 4[5] etc.) or impf. (3[4] 8[21.22] etc.); in short circumst. clauses, as Gn 44[4] לא הרחיקו, Is 40[20] לֹא יִמּוֹט, and with a final force 41[7] Ex 28[32] (v. Ges [§ 156. 3 R. b, c] Dr [§ 162]). Governing two closely connected verbs (Dr [§ 115, לא]) Ex 28[43] וְלֹא יִשְׂאוּ עָוֹן וָמֵתוּ, Lv 19[12.29b] Dt 7[25.26] 19[10] 22[1] al.; and two parallel clauses (Ges [§ 152. 3]) Is 23[4b] ψ 9[19] 44[19] Jb 3[11] al. With the impf., esp. with 2 ps., לא often expresses (not, like אַל, a deprecation, *do not . . ., let not . . .,* but) a *prohibition,* as Gn 2[17] לֹא תֹאכַל מִמֶּנּוּ thou *shalt not* eat of it, 3[1.3] Ex 20[3] לֹא־יִהְיֶה לְךָ there *shall not* be to thee, etc., v[13] לא תגנב, etc. With the coh. and juss. moods (which are negatived regularly by אַל), it occurs only exceptionally (Ges [§ 109. 1 b R. 1]), Gn 24[8] 1 S 14[36] 2 S 17[12] 18[14] 1 K 2[6] Ez 48[14]. (*b*) with the inf. (which is negatived by בִּלְתִּי, q.v.), only once, in בְּלֹא (**4 a**), and with לְ, in the sense of *cannot,* or *must not;* †Ju 1[19] כי לא להוריש for it *was not* (possible) *to* dispossess, etc. Am 6[10] לא להזכיר בשם י׳, 1 Ch 5[1] 15[2] (Dr [§ 202. 2]); cf. Aram. לָא Dan 6[9] Ezr 6[8]. On its use with the ptcp., see **b** *c*. (*c*) לא always negatives properly the word immed. following: hence, in a verbal sentence, where this is not the verb, some special stress rests upon it, Gn 32[29] לֹא יַעֲקֹב יֵאָמֵר עוד וג׳ *not Jacob* shall thy name be called any more, but Israel, 45[8] לֹא אַתֶּם שְׁלַחְתֶּם אֹתִי *Not ye* (in our idiom: It is not ye who) have sent me hither, but God, Ex 16[8] 1 S 8[7] כִּי לֹא אֹתְךָ מָאָסוּ כִּי אֹתִי וג׳, ψ 115[17]; without a foll. correcting clause, Gn 38[9] Nu 16[29] לֹא י׳ שְׁלָחָנִי: *Not* י׳ (but another) hath sent me, Dt 32[27] לא י׳ פָּעַל זֹאת, 1 Ch 17[4] Dt 8[9] Is 28[28] . . . לא לנצח *not for ever* (but only for a while) . . . (so 57[16] ψ 9[19] 49[18] 103[9]; but Is 13[20] לא תשב לנצח is, will *not be inhabited* for ever), Is 43[22] Jb 13[16] 32[9]; hence rhetorically, insinuating something very different, not named, 2 K 6[10] *not* once, and *not* twice (but repeatedly), Ezr 10[13] Je 4[11] a wind לֹא לִזְרוֹת וְלוֹא לְהָבַר: *not* to winnow, and *not* to cleanse (but to exterminate), Is 45[13] 48[1b] Jos 24[12] Dn 11[20.29] Jb 34[20] לֹא בְיָד (but by a Divine agency: cf. Dn 2[34]; also Jb 20[26] אֵשׁ לֹא נֻפָּח fire *not* blown upon [but kindled from heaven],

Lam 4[6]; and אין Is 47[14]). (*d*) standing alone: (*α*) אִם־לֹא *if not*, Gn 18[21] וְאִם־לֹא אֵדָעָה, 29[49] 42[16] Jb 9[24] 24[25]; (*β*) הֲ . . . אִם־לֹא, *or not*, Gn 24[21] waiting to know הַהִצְלִיחַ י׳ דַּרְכּוֹ אִם־לֹא, 27[21] 37[32] Ex 16[4] Nu 11[23] Dt 8[2] Ju 2[22] (cf. אִם אַיִן, אַיִן **2 d** *β, δ*). In answer to a question or request, to deny, or decline, *Nay, No:* Ju 12[5] ויאמר לא, Hg 2[12]; לא אדני Gn 23[11] 42[10] 1 S 1[15]+; oft. sq. כי, *No: for* ... = *No: but* ..., Gn 18[15] ויאמר לֹא כִּי צָחָקְתְּ, 19[2] Jos 5[14] 24[21] 1 S 2[16] Qr (v. Dr), 10[19] (𝔊 MSS), 2 S 16[18] 24[24] 1 K 3[22.22]+; Jb 23[6] (strangely). (Cf., in deprecation, אַל.) (*e*) with an interrog. force, which however does not lie in לא as such, but (as in other cases) in the contrast with a preceding clause, or in the tone of voice (cf. וְ **1** *f;* Ew § 324 a Ges § 150. 1 Dr § 8 11, 12): Jon 4[11] אַתָּה חַסְתָּ . . . וַאֲנִי לֹא אָחוּס וגו׳, Jb 2[10]; 22[11]; Ex 8[22]; 2 K 5[26] Je 49[9] (‖ Ob [5] הֲלוֹא), Mal 2[15] La 3[38]; and in passages, exeg. or text. doubtful (v. Comm.), 1 S 20[14] 2 S 23[5] (but v. Bu), Ho 10[9] (Ew We), 11[5] (Ew), Jb 14[16b] (but 𝔊 Ew Di תַּעֲבֹר), La 1[12] (Ew Ke), 3[36] (Ke Bä). **b.** with *adjs.* and *substs.:* (*a*) Gn 2[18] לֹא טוֹב הֱיוֹת הָאָדָם לְבַדּוֹ *not good* is man's being alone, Ex 18[17]+oft. (*b*) Ex 4[10] לֹא אִישׁ דְּבָרִים, Am 7[14] לא נביא אנכי, Nu 23[19] לֹא אִישׁ אֵל וִיכַזֵּב, Dt 17[15] (v. אשר **2** *b*) 20[20] 32[47] 1 S 15[29] 2 S 18[20] לֹא אִישׁ בְּשֹׂרָה אַתָּה הַיּוֹם, 21[2] 1 K 22[33] 2 K 6[19] לא זה הדרך, Mi 2[10] Is 27[11] Ho 8[6]; והמה לא אלהים Je 2[11] 16[20] 2 K 19[18]; 1 K 19[11.11] לֹא בָרַעַשׁ י׳, Dt 30[12.13] Jb 15[9] 28[14] לֹא בִי הִיא (‖ אֵין עִמָּדִי), ψ 74[9] Je 5[10] לוא לי׳ המה, 10[16]; Dt 32[21] בָּנִים לֹא אֵמֻן בָּם, Je 10[14] Hb 1[14] Jb 16[17] 38[26] מִדְבָּר לֹא אָדָם בּוֹ; 1 K 22[17] לֹא אֲדֹנִים לָאֵלֶּה, Je 49[31] ψ 22[3] וְלֹא דוּמִיָּה לִי, Jb 18[17.19] 29[12] ולא עֹזֵר לוֹ, 30[13] 33[9]; Je 2[19] וְלֹא פַחְדָּתִי אֵלַיִךְ and (that) my terror reached not unto thee, Jb 21[9]; abs. Gn 29[7] לֹא־עֵת הֵאָסֵף הַמִּקְנֶה (Hg 1[2]), Nu 20[5] 2 K 4[23] לא חדש ולא שבת, Is 44[9] Je 5[12] ויאמרו לוא הוא, Jb 9[32] 22[16] 36[26] 41[2]; Pr 19[7] (si vera l.) מְרַדֵּף אֲמָרִים לֹא־הֵמָּה words which *are not*, which *are nought.* (*c*) with the ptcp. לא is rare, a finite vb. being usu. preferred (Ex 34[7] וְנַקֵּה לֹא יְנַקֶּה: Ew § 320 c Dr § 162): 2 S 3[34] יָדֶךָ לֹא אֲסֻרוֹת, Ez 4[14] 22[24] Dt 28[61] ψ 38[15] כְּאִישׁ אֲשֶׁר לֹא שֹׁמֵעַ who is *not hearing*, Jb 12[3] 13[2] לֹא נֹפֵל אָנֹכִי מִכֶּם, Zp 3[5] (very anom.); 1 K 10[21] לא is prob. text. err. In לֹא שֹׂנֵא הוּא לוֹ or וְהוּא לֹא שֹׂנֵא לוֹ, Dt 4[42] 19[4.6] Jos 20[5] (cf. אֹיֵב Nu 35[23]), שֹׂנֵא is best construed as a subst., he being a *not-hater* to him aforetime.—In most of the cases under *b, c,* אין could have been employed; but the negation by לא is more pointed and forcible.

2. Not in predication: **a.** coupled to an adj. to negative it, like the Gk. ἀ-, but usu. by way of litotes: Ho 13[13] בן לא־חכם an *unwise* son, ψ 36[5] דֶּרֶךְ לֹא טוֹב a way *not good*, 43[1] גוי לא חסיד, Pr 16[29] 30[25.26] Ez 20[25] 2 Ch 30[17]: Is 16[14] לוֹא כַבִּיר, cf. 10[7] לֹא מְעַט. **b.** with a ptcp. Je 2[2] ארץ לא זרועה, 18[15] (the finite verb is more common: see Is 62[12] עִיר לֹא נֶעֱזָבָה (cf. 54[11]), Je 6[8] אֶרֶץ לוֹא נוֹשָׁבָה, 15[18] 22[6] 31[18] Zp 2[1]). **c.** †Gn 15[13] בארץ לא להם, Je 5[19] Hab 1[6] מִשְׁכָּנוֹת לֹא־לוֹ, Pr 26[17] רִיב לֹא־לוֹ. **d.** with a subst., in poetry, forming a kind of compound, expressing pointedly its antithesis or negation (Germ. *un-* is sts. used similarly): Dt 32[5(?).17.21a] they made me jealous בְּלֹא אֵל with a *not-God* (with what in no respect deserved the name of God), v[b] בְּלֹא עָם i.e. with an unorganized horde, Am 6[13] הַשְּׂמֵחִים לְלֹא דָבָר i.e. at a thing wh. *is not*, an unreality (of their boasted strength), Is 10[15] כְּהָרִים מַטֶּה לֹא עֵץ like a rod's lifting up *what is no wood* (but the agent wielding it), 31[8] חרב לא איש, חרב לא אדם, 55[2] בלוא לחם for *what is not bread*, בלוא לשבעה for *what is not* for satiety, Je 5[7] וַיִּשָּׁבְעוּ בְּלֹא אֱלֹהִים by *not-gods*, in late prose 2 Ch 13[9] כֹּהֵן לְלֹא אֱלֹהִים; ψ 44[13] תִּמְכֹּר עַמְּךָ בְלֹא־הוֹן for *no-value* (i.e. cheaply), Pr 13[23] Jb 10[22] צלמות וְלֹא סְדָרִים darkness and *disorder;* so לֹא־עַמִּי Ho 1[9] 2[25]: still more pregnantly Jb 26[2a] מֶה־עָזַרְתָּ לְלֹא־כֹחַ (poet. for לאשר אין לו כח) the *powerless*, v[2b.3a] (Ew § 286 g Ges § 152. 1 n.), 39[16] הִקְשִׁיחַ בָּנֶיהָ לְלֹא לָהּ useth hardly her young ones (making them) into *none of hers;* and even Hb 2[6] הַמַּרְבֶּה לֹא־לוֹ *what is not his own* (cf. Jb 18[15] מִבְּלִי לוֹ). Cf. with a verb, and ellipse of אשר, Is 65[1] לְלוֹא שָׁאָלוּ to those who have not asked, v[b] Je 2[8] אַחֲרֵי לֹא יוֹעִלוּ, v[11b]; also לֹא רֻחָמָה Ho 1[6.8] 2[25], and prob. Jb 31[31] לֹא נִשְׂבָּע (pf. in p.) one *not satisfied.* **e.** in circ. clauses (Dr § 164), poet. and rare: qualifying a subst., 2 S 23[4] בֹּקֶר לֹא עָבוֹת a morning *without clouds*, Job 12[24] בְּתֹהוּ לֹא דָרֶךְ in a *pathless* waste, 38[26a]; and a verb Jb 34[24] יָרֹעַ כַּבִּירִים לֹא חֵקֶר *without inquiry*, ψ 59[4] לא פשעי ולא חטאתי (cf. v[4] בלי עון), in late prose, twice, 1 Ch 2[30.32] וימת לא בנים (אַיִן and בְּלִי, q.v., are more usual in such cases).

3. Once (acc. to many MSS), as a subst., Jb 6^{21} כִּי־עַתָּה הֱיִיתֶם לֹא for now are ye become *nothing*, Hi De Kö (cf. Dn 4^{32} (Aram.) כְּלָה חֲשִׁיבִין, 𝔗 here הֲוֵיתוּן כְּלָא, and אַל Jb 24^{25}); but reading fluctuates (Orientals לֹא, Qr לוֹ, Westerns, Baer (v. pp. 37, 56) לוֹ ['now are ye become *that*,' viz. the נַחַל אַכְזָב of v^{15}]; but even לוֹ yields a forced sense; and text is prob. wrong: Mich Ew Ol Sgf Bu כֵּן . . . לִי (𝔊 𝔖 also rd. לִי); Bö Di כִּי . . . לְאַיִן. Cf. Kö $^{ii.1.286f.}$

4. With prefixes:—**a.** †בְּלֹא$_{81}$ (chiefly poet. or late), acc. to the varying signif. of בְּ: (*a*) usu. *with not=without*, Je 22^{13} בונה ביתו בלא־צדק *without* justice (‖ בלא משפט; so Ez 22^{29} Pr 16^{8}), Is $55^{1.1}$ Pr 19^{2}, Jb 8^{11} הֲיִגְאֶה־גֹּמֶא בְּלֹא בִצָּה *without* mire (‖ בלי מים), 30^{28} בְּלֹא חַמָּה (= not *through* the sun), La 1^{6} וילכו בלא־כח, Nu 35^{22} בְּלֹא צְדִיָּה . . . בְּלֹא אֵיבָה, v^{23} (sq. inf.) בְּלֹא רְאוֹת, 2 Ch 21^{20} Ec 10^{11}; ψ 17^{1} תְּפִלָּתִי בְּלֹא שִׂפְתֵי מִרְמָה; used more freely in Chr, 1 Ch 12^{18} בְּלֹא חָמָס בְּכַפַּי, v^{34} בְּלֹא לֵב וָלֵב, 2 Ch 30^{18} בְּלֹא כַכָּתוּב. With ellipse of rel., La 4^{14} בְּלֹא יוּכְלוּ יִגְּעוּ *without* (that) men are able to touch, etc. (*b*) of time, *in not*, i.e. *outside of*, Lv 15^{25} בלא עֶת־נִדָּתָהּ, *before* Jb 15^{32} בלא־יומו, Ec 7^{17} בְּלֹא עִתֶּךָ. (*c*) where לֹא belongs to the foll. word, and is only accidentally preceded by ב (v. supr. **2 d**), Dt $32^{21.21}$ Je 5^{7} Pr 13^{23} בלא משפט through *injustice;* with בְּ *pretii*, ψ 44^{13} Is $55^{2.2}$ Je 2^{11} בְּלוֹא יוֹעִיל *for* (that which) *profiteth not*.

b. הֲלֹא *nonne?* Gn 4^{7} + oft. Inviting, as it does, an affirmative answer, it is often used, (*a*) esp. in conversation, for pointing to a fact in such a way as to arouse the interest of the person addressed, or to win his assent: Gn 13^{19} *Is not* the whole land before thee? 19^{20} 20^{5} 27^{36} 29^{25} Ex 4^{11} Who maketh dumb or deaf, etc.? *Do not* I? 33^{16} Ju $4^{6.14}$ 8^{2} $9^{28.38}$ 1 S $9^{20.21}$ 15^{17} etc.; with a vb. in 1 ps., Jos 1^{9} הלא צויתיך, Ju 6^{14} הלא שלחתיך, 1 S 20^{30} 2 S 19^{23} Ru 2^{9}: similarly in a poet. or rhet. style, Ju 5^{30} הלא ימצאו יחלקו שלל, Is 8^{19} $10^{8.9.11}$ 28^{25} 29^{17} $40^{21.23}$ 42^{24} 43^{19} etc., Jb $4^{6.21}$ 7^{1} $10^{10.20}$, etc. (*β*) it has a tendency to become little more than an affirm. particle, declaring with some rhetor. emph. what is, or might be, well known: Dt 3^{11} הֲלֹה הִיא בְּרַבַּת בְּנֵי עַמּוֹן, 11^{30} 1 S 21^{12} הלוא זה דוד וג׳ (cf. $29^{3.5}$ 2 S 1^{18}), 23^{19} 26^{1} 2 S 15^{35}; it is thus nearly = הִנֵּה (𝔊 sts. represents it by ἰδού, as Jos 1^{9} Ju 6^{14} Ru 2^{9} 2 S 15^{35}); so esp. in the phrase of the compiler of K, And the rest of the acts of . . ., הֲלֹא הֵם (הֵמָּה) כְּתוּבִים *are* they *not* written in, etc.? 1 K 11^{41} 14^{29} + oft. (with which there interchanges הִנָּם כְּתוּבִים 1 K 14^{19} 2 K 15^{11} $15^{26.31}$, which is gen. used by the Chr, 2 Ch 16^{11} 20^{34}, etc.), Jos 10^{13} (cf. 2 S 1^{18} הִנֵּה), 1 K 8^{53} 𝔊, Est 10^{2}; ψ 56^{14} (strangely: contr. 116^{8}).—הֲלֹא הִנֵּה + Hb 2^{13} 2 Ch 25^{26} (הִנָּם).—On Ju 14^{15}, see הֲ **1** *end*.

c. †וְלֹא *and not=and if not*, 2 S 13^{26} 2 K 5^{17}. Comp. וְיֵשׁ. **d.** †כְּלוֹא Ob^{16} והיו כלוא היו, poet. for כאשׁר, *as though* they had not been.

e. †לְלֹא *without*, lit. *in the condition of no* . . . 2 Ch 15^{3} (comp. לְאַיִן, also in Chr). Elsewhere לא belongs to the foll. word, Am 6^{13} 2 Ch 13^{9} Is $65^{1.1}$ Jb $26^{2.3}$ 39^{16} (v. supr. **2 d**).

Note.—Fifteen times, acc. to Mas. (v. De ψ $^{100.3}$ Fr $^{MM\,247}$ Str $^{Prol.\,Cr.\,84}$), לא is written by error for לוֹ, viz. Ex 21^{8} Lv 11^{21} 25^{30} 1 S 2^{3} 2 S 16^{18} 2 K 8^{10} Is 9^{2} 63^{9} ψ 100^{3} 139^{16} Jb 13^{15} 41^{4} Pr 19^{7} 26^{2} Ezr 4^{2} (always with Qr לוֹ). The passages must be considered each upon its own merits: in some לוֹ yields a preferable sense; but this is not the case in all. There is the same קרי (rightly) on Is 49^{5} 1 Ch 11^{20}; but these were not considered to rest upon equal authority, and are hence not reckoned with the fifteen.—In Ju 21^{22} (v. GFM), 1 S 13^{13}. $20^{14.14}$, and in Jb 9^{33} (לֹא יֵשׁ), rd. prob. לֻא for לֹא.

†**לוֹ דְבָר, לֹא דְבָר** **n.pr.loc.** in Gilead, near, perh. east of, Mahanaim (q.v.);—לֹא ד׳ 2 S 17^{27} (𝔊 Λωδαβαρ, Λαδαβαρ); Gr We rd. also לֹא דְבָר Am 6^{13} = same city (but v. Dr); = לוֹ ד׳ 2 S $9^{4.5}$ (𝔊 Λαδαβαρ); perh. also intended in מִמַּחֲנַיִם עַד־גְּבוּל לִדְבִר Jos 13^{26} (cf. Di Bla; 𝔊 Δαιβων, A Δαβειρ, 𝔊L Δεβηρ); v. II. דְּבִיר, p. 184 supr.

לֹא עַמִּי **n.pr.m.** (*not my people*: see לא **2 d**) symb. name of Hosea's son, Ho 1^{9}, cf. 2^{25} (v. also $2^{1.3}$).

לֹא רֻחָמָה **n.pr.f.** (*uncompassionated:* Ges $^{§\,152\,a,\,N}$) symb. name of Hosea's daughter, Ho $1^{6.8}$, cf. 2^{25} (v. also 2^{3}).

לא 2 S 18^{12} Kt (Qr לוּ) **if**: v. לוּ.

לאב (√of foll., cf. Ar. لَابَ (med. و) *be thirsty*, لُوبَةٌ, لَابَةٌ *a stony tract* of land (v. Wetzst $^{Reiseberischt\,99}$)).

†**[תַּלְאֻבָה]** **n.f. drought;**—only pl. intens., בַּמִּדְבָּר בְּאֶרֶץ תַּלְאֻבוֹת Ho 13^{5}.

†[לָאָה] **vb.** be weary, impatient (cf. Ar. لَأَى *be slow, hesitating* (Frey); بَعْدَ لَأْيٍ *after difficulty,* لَأْيًا *with difficulty* (Lane[3007]); Aram. לְאֵי, לְאָא, (لَأَى);—**Qal** *Impf.* 2 ms. תִּלְאֶה Jb 4²; וַתֵּלֶא Jb 4⁵; 3 pl. וַיִּלְאוּ Gn 19¹¹;—*be weary* (in vain endeavour) sq. Inf. Gn 19¹¹; *be weary, impatient* at attempted consolation abs. Jb 4²; at calamity abs. Jb 4⁵ (‖ בָּהַל). **Niph.** *Pf.* נִלְאָה Pr 26¹⁵ + 2 t.; 2 fs. נִלְאֵית Is 47¹³; נִלְאֵיתִי Is 1¹⁴ + 3 t., etc.;—sq. inf. *be weary* of doing a thing, Ex 7¹⁸ (JE), *make oneself weary* in doing something Pr 26¹⁵ (of sluggard's laziness), *weary* (i.e. strenuously exert) *oneself* to Je 9⁴ 20⁹; abs. of eager and hopeless prayer נִלְ׳ עַל־הַבָּמָה Moab, Is 16¹² (‖ בָּא אֶל־מִקְדָּשׁוֹ לְהִתְפַּלֵּל, נִרְאָה); of vain consultations, (sq. בְּ) Babylon Is 47¹³; subj. י׳, sq. inf. Is 1¹⁴; Je 6¹¹ 15⁶, always of exhausted patience; fig. of parched soil (abs.) ψ 68¹⁰. **Hiph.** *Pf.* 3 ms. sf. הֶלְאָנִי Jb 16⁷; 3 fs. הֶלְאָת Ez 24¹² (del. 𝔊 Co), 1 s. sf. הֶלְאֵתִיךָ Mi 6³; *Impf.* וַיַּלְאוּךָ Je 12⁵; תַּלְאוּ Is 7¹³; *Inf. cstr.* הַלְאוֹת Is 7¹³;—*weary, make weary, exhaust,* sq. acc. Jb 16⁷ (subj. God); *exhaust patience of,* obj. God Is 7¹³; obj. men Is 7¹³ Je 12⁵ Mi 6³.

תְּלָאָה† **n.f. weariness, hardship**;—ת׳ Ex 18⁸ + 4 t.; of distress of Isr. in Egypt Nu 20¹⁴; in wilderness Ex 18⁸ (both JE); from Assyr., Bab., etc. Ne 9³²; cf. La 3⁵ (‖ רֹאשׁ, gall); Mal 1¹³.

לֵאָה 34 **n.pr.f. Leah**, elder daughter of Laban, and wife of Jacob (perh. = *wild-cow,* Ar. لَأًى, (לְאוֹ) [cf. רָחֵל *ewe*], Dl[Prol. 80] RS[K 219] and (doubtfully) Nö[ZMG xl. 1886, 167]; also Gray[Heb. Names, 96]; others, as Hpt[GGN 1883, 100] comp. As. *li'at,* in sense *mistress;* on poss. relation of לֵאָה to לֵוִי v. לֵוִי);—mother of Reuben, Simeon, Levi, Judah, Issachar, Zebulun and Dinah; Gn 29^{16.17.23.24.25.30.31.32} (cf. vv^{33.34.35}) 30⁹ + 15 t. Gn 31, 32; 33^{1.2.7} 34¹ 35^{23.26} 46^{15.18} 49³¹ Ru 4¹¹; 𝔊 Λ(ε)ια.

†לָאַט **vb. cover,** only **Qal** *Pf.* 3 ms. וְהַמֶּלֶךְ לָ׳ אֶת־פָּנָיו 2 S 19⁵, rd. perh. לָאַט, fr. לוט We Dr Bu.

לָאט Ju 4²¹, etc., v. לוט.

לְאַט, לָאַט *gently,* v. אַט sub אטט p. 31 supr.

לאך (√ of מְלָאכָה, מַלְאָךְ, cf. Ar. أَلَكَ, لَأَكَ *send,* مَأْلَكٌ *messenger,* Eth. ለአከ: *send a messenger,* v. ተለአከ: *be sent, wait on, minister;* መልአክ: = Heb. מַלְאָךְ; cf. Ph. מלאך *messenger;* NH מַלְאָךְ, Aram. מַלְאֲכָא, as in Heb.)

מַלְאָךְ 214 **n.m. messenger**;—מ׳ Ex 23²⁰ + 48 t.; cstr. מַלְאַךְ Gn 16⁷ + 69 t.; sfs. מַלְאָכִי Ex 23²³ + 3 t.; מַלְאָכוֹ Gn 24^{7.40}; pl. מַלְאָכִים Gn 32⁴ + 63 t. + מלאכים 2 S 11¹ Kt (< Qr מְלָכִים); cstr. מַלְאֲכֵי Gn 28¹² + 11 t.; מַלְאָכֶיךָ Nu 24¹², 2 K 19²³; מַלְאָכֵכֵה Na 2¹⁴ error for מַלְאָכַיִכִי = מַלְאָכַיִךְ Ges § 91, (2) Anm. 2 or < for מַלְאָכֵךְ by dittogr. fr. foll. ה Kö[II. 1. 571]); מַלְאָכָיו 2 Ch 36¹⁵ + 8 t.;—**1.** *messenger,* **a.** one sent with a message Gn 32⁴ + 8 t. JE; Dt 2²⁶, (not in P); Ju 6³⁵ + 8 t.; 1 S 6²¹ + 51 t. S K, 1 Ch 14¹ 19^{2.16} 2 Ch 18¹² 35²¹ Ne 6³ Jb 1¹⁴ Pr 13¹⁷ 17¹¹ Is 14³² 18² 30⁴ 37^{9.14} Je 27³ Ez 17¹⁵ 23^{16.40} 30⁹ Na 2¹⁴; מלאכי שלום, messengers of peace Is 33⁷. **b.** a prophet Is 42¹⁹ 44²⁶ 2 Ch 36^{15.16} Hg 1¹³; the herald of the advent מלאכי Mal 3¹. **c.** priest Mal 2⁷, prob. Ec 5⁵ (RV *angel*). **d.** ‖ מֵלִיץ Jb 33²³, a messenger from God acting as an interpreter and declaring what is right (*angel* of RV too specific). **e.** fig. מ׳ רָעִים *messengers of evil* ψ 78⁴⁹; מ׳ מות *messengers of death* Pr 16¹⁴; ‖ רוחות *winds his messengers* ψ 104⁴. **2.** *angel,* as messenger of God, מלאכים with God in theophanies Gn 19^{1.15} 28¹² 32² (JE), praising him; ψ 103²⁰ 148²; in his sight not without error Jb 4¹⁸ charged with the care of the pious ψ 91¹¹; elsewhere *sg.* sent to a prophet 1 K 13¹⁸ 19^{5.7} 2 K 1^{3.15} Zc 1⁹ + 18 t. in Zc 1–6; excellent, wise, powerful 1 S 29⁹ 2 S 14^{17.20} 19²⁸ Zc 12⁸; encamping about the faithful ψ 34⁸; chasing his enemies ψ 35^{5.6}; destroying by judgment of Yahweh 2 S 24^{16.17} = 1 Ch 21^{12-30}; 2 K 19³⁵ = Is 37³⁶ = 2 Ch 32²¹. †**3.** *the theophanic angel* מ׳ (ה)אלהים in the story of E: Gn 21¹⁷ 31¹¹ Ex 14¹⁹, also in Ju 6²⁰ 13^{6.9}; מ׳ יהוה in the story of J: Gn 16^{7.9.10.11} 22^{11.15} Ex 3² Nu 22^{22.23.24.25.26.27.31.32.34.35} and in Ju 2^{1.4} 5²³ 6^{11.12.21.21.22.22} 13^{3.13.15.16.16.17.18.20.20.21}; הַמַּלְאָךְ Gn 48¹⁶ (E); מַלְאָךְ Ex 23²⁰ (E), 33² Nu 20¹⁶ (JE), Ho 12⁵; מַלְאָכִי Ex 23²³ (E), 32³⁴ (J); מַלְאָכוֹ Gn 24^{7.40} (J), מ׳ פניו Is 63⁹ (referring to the ancient מלאך); מ׳ הברית Mal 3¹ (referring to the advent of י׳ for judgment, see Br[MP 473]). The theophanic angel is not mentioned in D and P.

מְלָאכָה 167 **n.f. occupation, work** (for *מַלְאָכָה; cf. Ph. מלאכת *labour*)—מ׳ Ex 12¹⁶ + 102 t.; מְלָאכֶת 2 Ch 13¹⁰; cstr. מְלֶאכֶת Ex 35²⁴ + 42 t.; sf. מְלַאכְתְּךָ Jon 1⁸; מְלַאכְתֶּךָ Ex 20⁹ + 2 t.;

מְלַאכְתּוֹ Gn 2^{2} + 13 t.; pl. cstr. מַלְאֲכוֹת 1 Ch 28^{19}; sf. מַלְאֲכוֹתֶיךָ ψ 73^{28};—**1.** *occupation, business*, מַה מְּלַאכְתְּךָ *what is thy occupation* Jon 1^{8}; business of a steward Gn 39^{11} (J); diligent in business Pr 22^{29}; slack in business 18^{9}. **2.** *property* in which one is occupied, מ׳ רעהו *his neighbour's property* Ex 22$^{7.10}$ (E); possessions of herds and flocks Gn 33^{14} (J), 1 S 15^{9} (cf. מִקְנֶה); מ׳ רבה *great property* 2 Ch 17^{13}. **3.** *work* as something done or made: **a.** of God in creation Gn 2$^{2.2.3}$ (P), in judgment Je 50^{25}, in general ψ 73^{28}. **b.** of men, מ׳ עור *leather-work* Lv 13$^{48.51}$ (P), מ׳ השדה *work in the field* 1 Ch 27^{26}; in building Pr 24^{27} +, the walls of Jerusalem Ne 4^{5} +, making the tabernacle and its furniture Ex 36^{2} +, the temple 1 K 5^{30} +; work of the potter Je 18^{3}, of the seaman ψ 107^{23}, of the Levites 1 Ch 26^{29}, of priests in the sacrifices 2 Ch 29^{34}; †מְלֶאכֶת (הָ)עֲבֹדָה phrase of P, Ex 35^{24} 36$^{1.3}$ Lv 23$^{7.8.21.25.35.36}$ Nu 28$^{18.25.26}$ 29$^{1.12.35}$ also 1 Ch 9$^{13.19}$ 28$^{13.20}$ 2 Ch 24^{12}; המ׳ לעבדה 1 Ch 23^{24}; עֹשֵׂה המ׳ עבדה למ׳ Ex 36^{5} (P); cf. the phrase עֹשֵׂה המ׳ *workmen* Ezr 3^{9} Ne 2^{16}; עֹשִׂים במ׳ 1 K 5^{30} 9^{23} +; כל מ׳ *any work* forbidden on the Sabbath Ex 20$^{9.10}$ Lv 23^{3} (P) Dt 5$^{13.14}$ Je 17$^{22.24}$; on holy convocations Ex 12^{16} Lv 16^{29} 23$^{28.30.31}$ Nu 29^{7} (P). †**4.** *workmanship*, כל מלאכה *in every kind of workmanship*, phrase of P: Ex 31$^{3.5}$ 35$^{29.31.33.35}$; and Chr: 1 Ch 22^{15} 28^{21} 29^{5}; 1 K 7^{14}. †**5.** *service, use* Lv 7^{24} 11^{32} Ju 16^{11} Ez 28^{13}. †**6.** *public business*: **a.** *political* 1 K 11^{28} 1 Ch 29^{6} Dn 8^{27} Est 3^{9} 9^{3}. **b.** *religious*, putting away foreign wives Ezr 10^{13}; מ׳ יהוה 1 Ch 26^{30}; מ׳ הַקֹּדֶשׁ Ex 36^{4} 38^{24} (P), מ׳ קדש הקדשים 1 Ch 6^{34}; מ׳ אהל מועד Ex 35^{21} (P), מ׳ בית י׳ 1 Ch 23^{4} Ezr 3^{8} 6^{22} Ne 10^{34} 11^{22}.

†[מַלְאָכוּת] **n.f.** message, cstr. מַלְאֲכוּת Hg 1^{13}.

†מַלְאָכִי appar. **n.pr.m.** Malachi, Mal 1^{1}, but in fact not historical name of author, nor pseudonym for Ezra; prob. a conjecture based on 3^{1}; so many moderns; see Dr$^{Intr.}$

†לָאֵל **n.pr.m.** (*belonging to God*; cf. Palm. לשמש: v. Nö$^{WZKM.\ 1892,\ 314}$ Gray$^{Heb.\ Names,\ 207}$) a Gershonite-Levite; Nu 3^{24}, 𝔊 Δαηλ, Δαουηλ.

לאם (√ of foll.; cf. Ar. لَأَمَ *bind up*, or *together*, III. *reconcile, bring together* (Thes Ba$^{NB\ §\ 65\ n.\ 2}$); > Lag$^{BN\ 180}$ who comp. لَوُمَ *be low, ignoble*, إِيَّامٌ [pl.] *common ones*, hence לְאֹם prop. *common, vulgar people*).

†לְאֹם, לְאוֹם **n.m.** $^{Gn\ 25,\ 23}$ people, poet. and chiefly late;—ל׳ abs. Gn 25$^{23.23}$ Pr 14^{28}, לְאוֹם Pr 11^{26}; sf. לְאוּמִּי Is 51^{4}; pl. לְאֻמִּים Gn 25^{23} + 28 t.; לְאוּמִּים Is 55^{4};—*people*, both of Isr. and of Edom, Gn 25$^{23.23.23}$ (J; Jacob and Esau; ‖ גּוֹי); elsewhere of Isr. only Is 51^{4} (sg. ‖ עַם); usu. pl. of other peoples:—שְׁאוֹן ל׳ Is 17^{12} (‖ הֲמוֹן עמים), cf. v^{13}; ‖ גּוֹיִם Is 34^{1} 43^{9} ψ 2^{1} 44$^{3.15}$ 105^{44} 149^{7}, cf. Is 55$^{4.4}$ (גּוֹי in v^{5}); ‖ עַמִּים Gn 27^{29} (J), Hb 2^{13} Je 51^{58} ψ 47^{4} 57^{10} 67$^{5.5}$ 108^{4} Pr 24^{24}; further Is 41^{1} 49^{1} (both ‖ אִיִּים), 43^{4} (‖ אָדָם), 60^{2} (‖ אֶרֶץ), ψ 9^{9} (‖ תֵּבֵל), 148^{11} (‖ מַלְכֵי אֶרֶץ, etc.); הֲמוֹן ל׳, ψ 7^{8}, עֲדַת לְאֻמִּים 65^{8}; of any and all *peoples* Pr 14^{34}; sg. indef. = *people* in gen., as making public opinion, 11^{26} (coll., c. pl. vb.); = *population*, as subjects of prince 14^{28} (‖ עַם).

†לְאֻמִּים **n.pr.gent.**, as 'son' of Dedan Gn 25^{3}. A𝔊L Λοωμ(ι)ειμ. (Sab. n.pr. trib. לאימם, לאמם SabDenkm^{11}).

לֵב v. sub לבב infr.

לבא (√ of foll.; v. Ar. لَبْوَةٌ, لَبْأَةٌ, لَبَاءٌ *lioness*, cf. לְבִיא; v. perh. also Ph. n.pr. לבא CIS$^{I.\ 147}$; Jastrow$^{JBL\ xi.\ (1892)\ 120\ f.}$ comp. Tel el-Am. n.pr. *Labâ'* (Bez$^{BM.}$ *Labay[a]*); poss. is also *Lapaya*, which Wkl$^{TA,\ 1896}$ rds.; deriv. only poet.)

†[לָבִי] **n.[m., f.]** lion;—only pl. and fig. of foes נַפְשִׁי בְּתוֹךְ לְבָאִם ψ 57^{5}; of Assyrians לְבְאֹתָיו Na 2^{13} (‖ גֹּרֹתָיו; sf. ref. to אַרְיֵה).

†לְבִיָּא **n.f.** lioness (on format. v. Lag$^{BN\ 93}$);—Ez 19^{2} (‖ אֲרָיוֹת) fig. of mother of Isr.

†לָבִיא **n.[m.]** lion, poss. also **[f.]** lioness (cf. Ar. usage, and Gn 49^{9} Nu 24^{9} Jb 4^{11}, etc.; but this by no means certain);—ל׳ abs. Gn 49^{9} + 10 t.;—Is 30^{6} (‖ לַיִשׁ), Jb 38^{39} (‖ כְּפִיר); Gn 49^{9} in sim. of victor's repose (‖ אַרְיֵה; רָבַץ), cf. Nu 24^{9} (c. שָׁכַב; ‖ אֲרִי), Dt 33^{20} (שָׁכֵן וְטָרַף); v. also Nu 23^{24} (‖ אֲרִי; קוּם); fig. of Nineveh Na 2^{12} (‖ אַרְיֵה), cf. Is 5^{29} (שְׁאָגָה in sim.; ‖ כְּפִירִים); fig. of wicked Jb 4^{11} (+ לַיִשׁ, כְּפִיר, שַׁחַל, אַרְיֵה, v$^{10.11}$); sim. of י׳, devouring (אָכַל) in judgment Ho 13^{8}; fig. of locusts שִׁנֵּי ל׳ מְתַלְּעוֹת Jo 1^{6} (‖ אַרְיֵה).

†לְבָאוֹת **n.pr.loc.** a city in S. Judah, Jos 15^{32}, 𝔊 Λαβως, A𝔊L Λαβωθ = בֵּית ל׳ (q.v. p. 111 supr.) Jos 19^{6}, 𝔊 Βαθαρωθ, 𝔊L Βηθλεβαωθ. Site unknown.

†לבב (mng dub; Dl$^{Pr\ 88\ ff}$ finds orig. mng. in As. *labâbu, in unruhiger Bewegung sein*;—√ of לֵב, לֵבָב; cf NH *id*, As *libbu*, Aram לִבָּא, ܠܶܒܳܐ, Eth ልብ: Ar لُبّ, Sab לב, Sab Denkm $^{p. 13, No. 1, l 7}$),—the literary usage of לֵב and לֵבָב is: **1.** earliest poetry, J and E chiefly, Eph doc. of Ju S K chiefly, Am Ho Zc 9–11 Is 15 use לֵב **2.** לֵבָב first appears in Is and certain strata of E and Eph doc. of Ju S K, and is continued in Zp Na (prob) D H Dt editors and some ψψ **3.** Je Ez Jb prefer לֵב but use occasionally לֵבָב. **4.** Is$^{2.3}$ La and exilic ψψ use לֵב. **5.** Is 13–14^{23} Je 50–51 Hg Zc 1-8 Jo Jon ψ 25, 90, 104, use לֵבָב. **6.** Mal Ob Zc 12–14 Memorials of Ezr and Ne Pr Ru Ct and many ψψ of Persian period use לֵב. **7.** Chr and Dn use לֵבָב. **8.** Ec Est and latest ψψ use לֵב. Exceptions will be noted and suspected passages indicated by ? under לבב and לב which are treated apart. See Br. 'Study of the use of לב and לבב in the O T.' in *Semitic Studies in Memory of Dr. Kohut*, Berlin, 1897

†לֵבָב 251 **n.m.** ψ $^{104,\ 15}$ **inner man, mind, will, heart,**—abs ל׳ Dt 28^{28} + 31 t., cstr. לְבַב Dt 20^{8} + 22 t, sf. לְבָבִי Is 21^{4} + 24 t.; לְבָבְךָ Dt 4^{29} + 35 t., לְבָבֶךָ Dt 4^{39} + 21 t, לְבָבֵךְ 1 S 1^{8} + 3 t., לְבָבוֹ Dt 2^{30} + 37 t., לְבָבָהּ Zp 2^{15} + 3 t; לְבָבֵנוּ Dt 1^{28} + 3 t., לְבַבְכֶם Dt 10^{16} + 37 t; לְבָבָם Lv 26^{41} + 22 t., pl לִבְבֵהֶן Na 2^{8} (Sta$^{§\ 353\ a}$ rds לְבָבֶהֶן, but see Kö$^{ii\ 78}$), pl. לְבָבוֹת 1 Ch 28^{9}.—*The inner, middle, or central part.* **I.** seldom of *things* בלבב יַמִּים *in the midst of the seas*, Jon 2^{3} (poetry), עד לבב השמים *unto the midst of heaven* Dt 4^{11} (so Sam but MT לב). **II.** usu *of men*: **1.** *the inner man* in contrast with the outer, כלה שארי ולבבי *my flesh and my heart* (*soul*) *doth fail* ψ 73^{26}; antithesis with garments Jo 2^{13}; hands ψ 73^{13} La 3^{41}(?), eyes Nu 15^{39} (H) 1 S 16^{7}, ears Ez 3^{10}; mouth Dt 30^{14}, speech ψ 28^{3} 78^{18}, מְתֹפְפֹת עַל־לִבְבֵהֶן *tabering upon their breasts* Na 2^{7} (inner for outer). **2.** the *inner man*, indef. the *soul*, comprehending mind, affections and will, or, in connexion with certain verbs, having more specific reference to some one of them בכל־לבב ובכל־נפש *with all the heart and with all the soul* Dt 4^{29} 6^{5} 10^{12} 11^{13} 13^{4} 26^{16} 30$^{2.6.10}$ Jos 22^{5} 23^{14} 1 K 2^{4} 8^{48} (= 2 Ch 6^{38} לב ?) 2 K 23^{25} 2 Ch 15^{12} 34^{31} (= 2 K 23^{3} לב ?) Je 32^{41}, abbr בכל־לבב 1 S 7^{3} 12$^{20.24}$ 1 K 14^{8} 2 K 10^{31} 2 Ch 15^{5} 22^{9} 31^{21} ψ 86^{12} 111^{1} Je 29^{13} Jo 2^{12}, אשר בלבב *what is in the heart* (mind) Dt 8^{2} 1 S 9^{19} 14^{7} 2 S 7^{3} (= 1 Ch 17^{2}) 2 K 10^{30}; 2 Ch 32^{31}, cf. Jb 10^{13}, ψ 84^{6} (?); עם לבב *with the heart* (mind), c ידע Dt 8^{5}, שִׂיחַ ψ 77^{7}, usu c. (היה), of a thought or purpose, Dt 15^{9} Jos 14^{7} 1 K 8$^{17.18.18}$ (= 2 Ch 6$^{7.8.8}$) 10^{2} (= 2 Ch 9^{1}) 1 Ch 22^{7} 28^{2} 2 Ch 1^{11} 29^{10} (cf 24^{4} לב); כלבב *according to the heart* 1 S 13^{14} 14^{7} ψ 20^{5}. We may add Dt 5^{26} 11$^{16.18}$ 17^{17} 1 S 2^{35} 2 S 19^{15} 1 K 8$^{39.39}$ (= 2 Ch 6$^{30.30}$) 11$^{2.3}$ (לב an error) v$^{4.9}$ 1 Ch 12^{17} 22^{19} 28^{9} ψ 62^{9} 86^{11} 139^{23} Is 7^{2} Dn 11$^{27.28}$. **3.** specific ref to *mind* (characteristic of לבב). **a.** אַנְשֵׁי לֵבָב *men of mind* Jb 34$^{10.34}$; גם לי לבב *I also have a mind* Jb 12^{3}, הוללות בל׳ *madness is in* (*their*) *mind* Ec 9^{3}(?), וַתִּגְנֹב לְבָבִי *and thou didst steal my mind* Gn 31^{26} (E, the לֵב of v^{20} should be corrected to לבב cf 'steal me' v^{27}). **b.** *knowledge*, c. ידע Dt 8^{5} 23^{14} 1 K 2^{44}; הבין Is 6^{10} 32^{4}; חֲכַם לֵבָב *wise of mind* Jb 9^{4}; לְבַב חָכְמָה *mind of wisdom* ψ 90^{12}. **c.** *thinking, reflection*, c. חשב Is 10^{7} Zc 7^{10} 8^{17}; (שיח ψ 77^{7} supr); יצר מחשבות ל׳ *conception of thoughts of mind* 1 Ch 29^{18}; מַשְׂכִּיּוֹת ל׳ *imaginations of* (*their*) *mind* ψ 73^{7}; מוֹרָשֵׁי ל׳ *possessions* (*thoughts*) *of* (*my*) *mind* Jb 17^{11}; שׂם לבב *set the mind, consider* Hg 2$^{15.18.18}$, c. לְ Dt 32^{46}, על Hg 1$^{5.7}$. **d.** of *memory* שׂם בלבב *lay up in the mind* 1 S 21^{13} Jb 22^{22}, השיב אל ל׳ *lay to heart, call to mind* Dt 4^{39} 30^{1} 2 Ch 6^{37} (= 1 K 8^{47} לב ?); עלה על ל׳ *come upon the mind* Je 51^{50} Ez 38^{10} (cf. לב **3 d**); סור מל׳ *depart from the mind* Dt 4^{9}, שמר בתוך ל׳ *keep in the midst of* (*thy*) *mind* Pr 4^{21}, על ל׳ *upon the mind* Dt 6^{6} **4.** spec. ref to *inclinations, resolutions, determinations of the will* (characteristic of ל׳). הכין ל׳ *set the mind*, c. אֶל 1 S 7^{3} 1 Ch 29^{18}, לְ 2 Ch 20^{33} לדרש 2 Ch 19^{3} 30^{19} Ezr 7^{10}, הטה ל׳ אֶל Jos 24^{23} (E) 1 K 8^{58}; נתן ל׳ לדרש 1 Ch 22^{19}, cf 2 Ch 11^{16}, ל׳ פנה מעם *mind turn away from* Dt 29^{17} 30^{17}, יֵהָפֵךְ ל׳ פ׳ *Pharaoh's mind was changed* Ex 14^{5} (E). **5.** spec ref. to *conscience* לא יחרף לבבי *my heart* (*conscience*) *shall not reproach me* Jb 27^{6}. **6.** spec ref. to *moral character* (characteristic of ל׳): God tries the ל׳ 1 Ch 29^{17}. **a.** יֹשֶׁר ל׳ *uprightness of heart* Dt 9^{5} 1 Ch 29^{17}, ψ 119^{7} (?); יִשְׁרֵי ל׳ 2 Ch 29^{34}, יִשְׁרַת ל׳ 1 K 3^{6}, יָשָׁר ל׳ 2 K 10$^{15.15.15}$; תָּם־ל׳ *integrity of heart* Gn 20$^{5.6}$ (E) 1 K 9^{4} ψ 78^{72} 101^{2}, ל׳ שָׁלֵם (עם) *heart perfect* (with) 1 K 8^{61} 11^{4} 15$^{3.14}$ (= 2 Ch 15^{17}) 2 K 20^{3} (= Is 38^{3} לב ?)

1 Ch 12^{39} 29^{19} 2 Ch 16^{9} 19^{9} 25^{2}, בַּר־לֵ׳ *pure in heart* ψ 24^{4}, בָּרֵי לֵ׳ ψ 73^{1}. We may add 2 K 22^{19} = 2 Ch 34^{27}, Ne 9^{8} Je 32^{40} **b.** it is the seat of naughtiness 1 S 17^{28} (?), erring ψ 95^{10}; is froward ψ 101^{4}. **c.** seat of pride, ψ 101^{5} Is 9^{8} 10^{12}, 60^{5} (?) Ez 28$^{2.5.6(?)}$ Dn 8^{25}; רָם לֵ׳ *heart is lifted up* Dt 8^{14} 17^{20} Ez 31^{10} Dn 11^{12}. **d.** is circumcised Dt 10^{16} 30^{6} Je 4^{4}, or uncircumcised Lv 26^{41} (H); is hardened אמץ לֵ׳ Dt 2^{30} 15^{7} 2 Ch 36^{13}; כבד לֵ׳ 1 S 6^{6} (?); הקשה לֵ׳ ψ 95^{8} **7.** = *the man himself* (meaning characteristic of נפש) אמר בלֵ׳ *say in the heart* (*to oneself*) Dt 7^{17} 8^{17} 9^{4} 18^{21} ψ 4^{5} Is 14^{5} 47^{8} 49^{21} Je 5^{24} 13^{22} Zp 1^{12} 2^{15}; ללבב Ho 7^{2} (?), דבר בלֵ׳ ψ 15^{2}, ברכו בלֵ׳ Jb 1^{5}; התברך בלֵ׳ Dt 29^{18}, יחי לְבַבְכֶם *let your heart* (you yourselves) *live* ψ 22^{27} 69^{33} (cf. 119^{175}). **8.** spec as the *seat of the appetites* (for which usually נפש) סעד לֵ׳ *stay the heart* (with food) ψ 104^{15} Ju 19^{8} (?), יִיטַב לְבָבֶךָ *that thine heart may be merry* (with wine) Ju 19^{9} (?), יַיִן יְשַׂמַּח לֵ׳ *wine gladdens the heart* ψ 104^{15} **9.** spec of *seat of the emotions and passions* (for which usually נפש): **a.** of joy Is 30^{29} Je 15^{16} Ez 36^{5}, gladness Dt 28^{47}, desire Pr 6^{25} (?); דבר על לֵ׳ *speak into the heart* (comfortably) 2 Ch 32^{6} (elsewhere לב) **b.** of trouble 1 K 8^{38} ψ 25^{17} 73^{21}, weakness, faintness Lv 26^{36} (H) Dt 20$^{3.8}$ 2 Ch 13^{7} Is 1^{5} 7^{4} Je 51^{46}, grief Dt 15^{10} 1 S 1^{8}, sorrow ψ 13^{3}, fear Dt 28^{67}, dismay Is 21^{4}, astonishment Dt 28^{28}, anger 19^{6}, hate Lv 19^{17} (H), ימס לֵ׳ *the heart melteth* Dt 20^{8} Jos 2^{11} 5^{1} 7^{5} (all D) Is 13^{7} 19^{1}; המס לֵ׳ Dt 1^{28} (so rd prob also Jos 14^{8}, where לב error). **10.** *seat of courage* (for which usually רוּחַ), יָעֵר כֹּחוֹ וּלְבָבוֹ *stir up his power and his courage* Dn 11^{25}, יַאֲמֵץ לְבַבְכֶם *let your heart take courage* ψ 31^{25}.

לֵב 699 **n. m.** $^{Pr\ 23\ 15}$ (†**f.** Pr 12^{25}, fr. influence of נֶפֶשׁ v De Now) **inner man, mind, will, heart,** abs and cstr לב Gn 8^{21} + 239 t, לֶב־ Ex 15^{8} + 15 t, sf לבי Gn 24^{45} + 102 t, לבך Ex 9^{14} + 28 t, לִבֵּךְ Ju 19^{6} + 25 t, לבך Is 47^{7} + 7 t; לבו Gn 6^{5} + 93 t, לִבָּהּ Ju 19^{3} + 7 t, לבנו Is 41^{22} + 5 t.; לבכם Gn 8^{5} + 2 t, לִבָּם Gn 42^{28} + 56 t, לִבְּהֶן Ez 13^{17}, לִבָּן Ex 35^{26}, pl לבות ψ 7^{10} Pr 15^{11} + 3 t Pr.; sf לבותם Is 44^{18}, לִבּוֹתָם ψ 125^{4} — *inner part, midst* **I.** seldom of things, בְּלֶב־יָם *in the midst of the sea* Ex 15^{8} Pr 23^{34} 30^{19}, בלב יַמִּים ψ 46^{3} Ez 27$^{4.25.26.27}$ 28$^{2.8}$ בלב האלה 2 S 18^{14}, בלב אֹיְבֵי *in the midst of the enemies of* ψ 45^{6} (v. Br $^{MP\ in\ loco}$; AV RV al *in the heart of*). **II.** elsewhere of men: †**1.** *the inner man* in contrast with outer לבי ובשרי ירננו *my heart and my flesh cry out* ψ 84^{3}; ‖ מעים ψ 22^{15} Je 4^{19}, the inner for outer מעים Je 49^{22}, as within the breast על לב Ex 28$^{3.29.30.30}$ (P); מלב 2 K 9^{24}, בלב ψ 37^{15} 2 S 18^{14}, סְגוֹר לִבָּם Ho 13^{8}; antithesis with בָּשָׂר Pr 14^{30} Ec 2^{3}; head Is 1^{5}, face Ez 14$^{3.4.7}$; arm Ct 8^{6}, hands Ez 22^{14}; bones ψ 102^{5}, eyes 1 K 9^{3} (= 2 Ch 7^{16}) Je 22^{17}; ear Pr 22^{17} 23^{12}, mouth ψ 55^{22}, lips Is 29^{13}, אֲנִי יְשֵׁנָה וְלִבִּי עֵר *I slept but my heart waked* Ct 5^{2}. **2.** *the inner man*, indef., *soul*, comprehending mind, affections and will, with occasional emphasis of one or the other by means of certain verbs. †בכל לב 1 K 8^{23} (= 2 Ch 6^{14}) ψ 9^{2} 119$^{2.10.34.58.69.145}$ 138^{1} Pr 3^{5} Je 3^{10} 24^{7}, †עם לב 2 Ch 24^{4} (see לבב **2**); †בלב 2 S 7^{21} (= 1 Ch 17^{19}) Je 3^{15}, תַּעֲלֻמוֹת לֵב *secrets of the heart* ψ 44^{22}; לב מְלָכִים אין חֵקֶר *the heart of kings is unsearchable* Pr 25^{3}; הֵיֹּצֵר יַחַד לִבָּם ψ 33^{15} etc **3.** specific reference to *mind*. **a.** †מלב *of one's own mind* Nu 16^{28} 24^{13} (JE) 1 K 12^{33} Ne 6^{8} Ez 13$^{2.17}$; †חֲסַר לב *destitute of mind* Pr 6^{32} 7^{7} 9$^{4.16}$ 10$^{13.21}$ 11^{12} 12^{11} 15^{21} 17^{18} 24^{30}; לב אין Ec 10^{3}, אין לב Je 5^{21} Ho 7^{11}; לבו חָסֵר כֹּחַ לב Pr 17^{16}, קנה לב *get a mind* Pr 15^{32} 19^{8}, *power of mind* Jb 36^{5}, רחב לב *breadth of mind* 1 K 5^{9}, לב גנב 2 S 15^{6} Gn 31^{20} (E? see לבב **3 a**). **b** *knowledge*, c †ידע Dt 29^{3} Pr 14^{10} 22^{17} Ec 1^{17} 7$^{22.25}$ 8$^{5.16}$ Je 24^{7}; ראה ψ 66^{18} Ec 1^{16}; חֲכַם לב *mind is wise* Pr 23^{15}; †לב חָכָם *wise mind* 1 K 3^{12} Pr 16^{23} Ec 8^{5}, †חֲכַם לב Ex 31^{6} 35^{10} 36$^{1.2.8}$ (P) Pr 10^{8} 11^{29} 16^{21}; †חַכְמֵי לֵב Ex 28^{3} (P) Jb 37^{24}; †חכמת לב Ex 35$^{25.35}$ (P); לב חכמים Ec 7^{4} 10^{2}; לב כסילים Pr 12^{23} 15^{7} Ec 7^{4} 10^{2}; c חכמה Ex 36^{2} (P) 1 K 10^{24} (= 2 Ch 9^{23}) Pr 2^{10} 17^{16} Ec 2^{3}; †לב נָבוֹן *intelligent mind* Pr 14^{33} 15^{14} 18^{15}; with הבין Pr 8^{5}; תְּבוּנָה Pr 2^{2}; שֶׂכֶל Jb 17^{4} etc **c.** *thinking, reflection*, c. חשב ψ 140^{3} Pr 16^{9}; מחשבות Gn 6^{5} (J) ψ 33^{11} Pr 6^{18} 19^{21} cf. Gn 8^{21} (J), הגיון הגה *muse, study* Pr 15^{28} 24^{2} Is 33^{18} 59^{13}; ψ 19^{15}; הָגוּת ψ 49^{4}; †שם לב *set the mind, consider* Is 41^{22} Ez 44^{5}, c לְ 1 S 9^{20} 2 S 13^{20} Ez 40^{4} 44^{5}, אֶל Ex 9^{21} (J) 1 S 24^{28} 2 S 18$^{3.3}$ Jb 2^{3} 34^{14}; לְ †שת לב ψ 62^{10} Pr 22^{17} 24^{32}, c על Jb 1^{8}, אל Ex 7^{23} (JE) 1 S 4^{20} ψ 48^{14} Pr 27^{23} Je 31^{21}, Jb 7^{17} **d.** *memory* †השיב אל לב *call to mind* Is 44^{19} La 3^{21}, על לב Is 46^{8}, †עלה על לב *come into mind* (occur to one) Is 65^{17} Je 3^{16} 7^{31}

19[5] 32[35] (cf. Acts 7[23]), so בא על לב 2 Ch 7[11]; †שׂם על לב *lay to heart* Is 42[25] 47[7] 57[1.11] Je 12[11] Mal 2[2.2] Dn 1[8]; כתב על לב 2 S 13[33] 19[20] אל לב Je 31[33]; קשר על לב Pr 6[21]; †לוּחַ לֵב *tablet of the memory* Pr 3[3] 7[3] Je 17[1]; נִשְׁכַּחְתִּי כְּמֵת מִלֵּב *I am forgotten as a dead man out of mind* ψ 31[13]. **4.** spec. ref. to *inclinations, resolutions and determinations of the will;* †הכין לב *set the mind* 2 Ch 12[14] ψ 10[17] 78[8] Jb 11[13]; †נכון לב ψ 57[8.8] (=108[2]) 78[37] 112[7]; †נתן לב ל Ec 1[13.17] 7[21] 8[9.16]; †נתן אל לב Ec 7[2] 9[1]; Ne 2[12] 7[5], בלב Ex 35[34] (P) Ezr 7[27] Ec 3[11]; †אֲשֶׁר־נְשָׂאוֹ לִבּוֹ *whose heart stirred him up* Ex 35[21] 36[2] cf. 35[26] (all P); †נְדִיב לֵב *willing of mind* Ex 35[5.22] (P) 2 Ch 29[31] cf. Ex 25[2] 35[29] (P); †נטה לב אחרי *inclined to follow* Ju 9[3] ψ 119[112]; †הטה לב 1 K 11[3] ψ 119[36] 141[4] cf. 2 S 15[13]:—גְּדֹלִים חִקְקֵי־לֵב *great resolves of heart* Ju 5[15] etc. **5.** spec. ref. to *conscience,* וַיַּךְ לֵב דָּוִד אֹתוֹ *and David's heart (conscience) smote him* 1 S 24[6]; מִכְשׁוֹל לֵב *offence of conscience* 1 S 25[31]. **6.** spec. ref. to *moral character,* God tries the heart ψ 17[3] Je 12[3]; sees the heart and reins Je 20[12], tries them ψ 7[10] Je 11[20], refines them ψ 26[2]; searches the heart and tries the reins Je 17[10]. **a.** †יִשְׁרֵי לֵב ψ 7[11] 11[2] 32[11] 36[11] 64[11] (all c. דָּוִד in title), 94[15] 97[11]; יֹשֶׁר־לִבִּי Jb 33[3]; †לֵב שָׁלֵם 1 Ch 28[9] 29[9] Is 38[3] (all originally לבב, see לבב **6 a**); נִשְׁבְּרֵי־לֵב *broken of heart* ψ 34[19] Is 61[1]; לֵב־נִשְׁבָּר ψ 51[19]; שְׁבוּרֵי לֵב ψ 147[3]; נִדְכָּאִים Is 57[15]; לֵב טָהוֹר *clean heart* ψ 51[12]; †לֵב חָדָשׁ *new heart* Ez 18[31] 36[26] (prob. also 11[19] for אֶחָד see Co) etc. **b.** לֵב רָע *evil heart* Pr 26[23]; עִקְּשׁ(י) לב; חַנְפֵי־לֵב *godless in heart* Jb 36[13]; *perverse in heart* Pr 11[20] 17[20]; †תַּרְמִת לִבָּם *deceit of their heart* Je 14[14] 23[26]; בלב ולב *with a double heart* ψ 12[3] etc. **c.** seat of pride Pr 21[4] Je 48[29] 49[16] Ho 13[6] Ob [3] גְּבַהּ לֵב 2 Ch 32[26]; גְּבַהּ־לֵב Pr 16[5]; †גָּבַהּ לֵב 2 Ch 26[16] 32[25] ψ 131[1] Pr 18[12] Ez 28[2.17]. **d.** the heart is uncircumcised Je 9[25] Ez 44[7.7.9] and hardened: †חזק לב Ex 4[21] 10[20.27] (E), 9[12] 11[10] 14[4.8.17] (P), Jos 11[20] (D[2] ?); †יֶחֱזַק לֵב Ex 7[13.22] 8[15] 9[35] (P); חִזְקֵי־לֵב Ez 2[4]; †הקשה לב Ex 7[3] (P) Pr 28[14]; קְשֵׁי־לֵב Ez 3[7]; הכביד לב Ex 8[11.28] 9[34] 10[1] (J); כָּבֵד לֵב Ex 7[14] 9[7] (J); כבד לב 1 S 6[6]; הַשְׁמֵן לֵב־הָעָם הַזֶּה *make the heart of this people fat* Is 6[10] (?); †שְׁרִ(י)רוּת לֵב Dt 29[18] ψ 81[13] after Je 3[17] 7[24] 9[13] 11[8] 13[10] 16[12] 18[12] 23[17]; †לב האבן *the heart of stone* Ez 11[19] 36[26] etc. **7.** for *the man himself,* †אמר בלב Gn 17[17] (P), 27[41] (JE), 1 K 12[26] Est 6[6] ψ 10[6.11.13] 14[1] (=53[2]) 35[25] 74[8] Ec 2[1.15] 3[17.18] Is 47[10] Ob [3] Zc 12[5]; †דבר בלב Gn 8[21] (J) 1 S 27[1]; אֶל־לֵב Ec 2[15]; אֶל־לֵב Gn 24[45] (J); עַל לֵב 1 S 1[13] (?); עם לב Ec 1[16]; נְאֻם־פֶּשַׁע לָרָשָׁע בְּקֶרֶב לִבִּי ψ 36[2]. **8.** as *seat of appetites,* סְעַד לֵב *stay the heart* (with bread) Gn 18[5] (J) Ju 19[5]. **9.** as *seat of the emotions and passions:* **a.** of joy and gladness, in various combinations of †טוב, Ju 16[25] 18[20] 19[6.22] Ru 3[7] 1 S 25[36] 2 S 13[28] 1 K 8[66] (=2 Ch 7[10]) 21[7] Est 1[10] 5[9] Pr 15[15] Ec 7[3] 9[7] 11[9] Is 65[14]; various combinations of †שׂמח, Ex 4[14] (J) 1 Ch 16[10] (=ψ 105[3]) ψ 4[8] 16[9] 19[9] 33[21] Pr 15[13.30] 17[22] 27[9.11] Ec 2[10.10] 5[19] Ct 3[11] Is 24[7] Zc 10[7]; שׂושׂ ψ 119[111] Is 66[14] La 5[15]; עליץ 1 S 2[1]; עלז ψ 28[7] Zp 3[14]; רנן Jb 29[13]; גיל ψ 13[6] 24[17] Zc 10[7]; of desire, ψ 21[3] 37[4]; †דבר על לב *speak unto the heart* (kindly) Gn 34[3] 50[21] (JE) Ju 19[3] 2 S 19[8] 2 Ch 30[22] Is 40[2] Ho 2[16] Ru 2[13]. **b.** of trouble 2 K 6[11] Is 65[14], sorrow Ne 2[2] Pr 14[3], pain ψ 55[5], vexation Ec 11[10], trembling Dt 28[65] (?) 1 S 28[5], faintness La 5[17]; it is wounded ψ 109[22], dies within one out of fear 1 S 25[37] etc.; †לב נמס *the heart melteth* (in fear) 2 S 17[10] ψ 22[15], Ez 21[12] Na 2[11]. †**10.** *seat of courage:* יַאֲמֵץ לִבֶּךָ *let thine heart take courage* ψ 27[14]; אַמִּיץ לִבּוֹ Am 2[16]; אַבִּירֵי לֵב *stout-hearted* ψ 76[6] Is 46[12]; לִבּוֹ יָצוּק כְּמוֹ־אָבֶן *his heart as firm as a stone* Jb 41[16]; לִבּוֹ כְּלֵב הָאַרְיֵה *his heart as the heart of the lion* 2 S 17[10].

†[לִבָּה]† *sf.* לִבָּתֵךְ Ez 16[30] should be corrected to לִבְרִיתֵךְ (see Co). >older view, as fem. of לֵב.

לֵב קָמָי prob. late Atbash (cf. שֵׁשַׁךְ) for כשׂדים the original reading (𝔊) Je 51[1].

†I. [לבב] **vb. denom. Niph.** *Impf.* יִלָּבֵב get a mind; וְאִישׁ נָבוּב יִלָּבֵב וְעַיִר פֶּרֶא אָדָם יִוָּלֵד *shall an empty man get a mind or a wild ass's colt be born a man?* Jb 11[12]. **Pi.** encourage; *Pf.* לִבַּבְתִּנִי . . . . לִבַּבְתִּנִי בְּאַחַד מֵעֵינַיִךְ Ct 4[9.9] *thou hast encouraged me, thou hast encouraged me with one of thine eyes* Ew Gi Gr RVm (AV RV Ges Hi De Öt (cf. 5[6]) *ravished my heart,*— Pi. *priv.* Ges[§ 52 h]).

†[לְבִבָה]† **n.pl.** cakes (prob. *pancakes,* from shape ?) לְבִבוֹת 2 S 13[6.8.10].

†II. [לבב] **vb. denom. Pi.** make cakes. *Impf.* תְּלַבֵּב 2 S 13[6.8].

לְבַד *alone* v בַּד sub בדד p. 94 supr.

[לָבָה], לַבַּת Ex 3^{2} v לֶהָבָה sub להב

[לָבַט] **vb. thrust down, out, or away** (NH *id*, Ar لَبَطَ *strike the ground* with a person, i.e. throw one down; Syr Pa ܠܰܒܶܛ *incitavit, stimulavit*),—only **Niph** *Impf be thrust down, away*, i.e. ruined, עָם לֹא יָבִין יִלָּבֵט Ho 4^{14}, אֱוִיל שְׂפָתַיִם יִלָּבֵט Pr $10^{8.10}$

לְבִיא, לָבִיא, לְבִי v sub לבא

לוּבִים v **לְבִים**.

†**[לָבַן]** **vb be white** (on — v Ba$^{NB\ 166}$, Lag$^{BN\ 33,\ cf.\ 83,\ 84}$ infers *לָבָן from לְבָנָה; NH *id*, Pi Hiph, and deriv, Ph לבן *white*, Ar. لَبَنٌ *milk*, لبن also *be white*, dial of Yemen, Maltzan ZMG xxvii, 1873, 247; appar. √ of foll. fourteen words, but this dub. esp. in case of II III לָבָן, לִבְנָא, לְבֹנָה II, לִבְנָה I. II. לִבְנִי);—**Hiph.** *Pf* 3 pl. הִלְבִּינוּ Jo 1^{7}; *Impf* 1 s. אַלְבִּין ψ 51^{9}; 3 pl יַלְבִּינוּ Is 1^{18}, *Inf. cstr.* וְלַלְבֵּן (=וּלְהַלְבֵּן) Dn 11^{35},—**1.** *make white*=purify (ethical) Dn 11^{35} (no object expr, ‖ צָרַף, בָּרַר). **2.** *shew whiteness, grow white*, of fig-tree, stripped by locusts, Jo 1^{7}, fig of moral purity, כַּשֶּׁלֶג יַלְבִּ׳ Is 1^{18}, מִשֶּׁלֶג אַלְבִּ׳ ψ 51^{9}. **Hithp.** *Impf* יִתְלַבְּנוּ Dn 12^{10} *be purified* (ethical, ‖ יִתְבָּרְרוּ)—לָבֵן, *make brick*, v. infr.

† I. **לָבָן adj. white**,—ל׳ abs Gn 30^{35} + 13 t, cstr לְבֶן־ Gn 49^{12} (cf Ges $^{§93.2.R\ 1}$ Ko$^{Lgb\ II.74}$ Ba$^{NB\ 166}$), f לְבָנָה Lv 13^{4} + 6 t., pl לְבָנִים Zc 1^{8} + 3 t, לְבָנוֹת Gn 30^{37} + 2 t;—*white*, of wood under bark Gn $30^{37.37}$ (cf Jo 1^{7}), of spots on goats v^{35} (all J), of manna Ex 16^{31} (P); garments Ec 9^{8} (sign of cheerfulness and joy); of teeth וּלְבֶן־שִׁנַּיִם מֵחָלָב Gn 49^{12} (poem in J, ‖ חַכְלִילִי עֵינַיִם מִיָּיִן) of Judah (on interpr. v. Di and, differently, Marc. Jastr JBL xi (1892), 178); of horses Zc 1^{8} $6^{3.6}$ (in vision), chfly. of diseased skin or flesh on body (בַּהֶרֶת Lv $13^{4.19.24.25.26.38}$) Lv $13^{4.10.13.16.17.19.24.38}$; and of hair on such spots $13^{3.4.10.20.21.25.26}$, + אֲדַמְדֶּמֶת $13^{19.24.43}$, cf. v^{42}; + כֵּהָה v^{39} (all P)

† I **לְבָנָה n.f.** moon, poet. (NH *id*),—ל׳ Is 24^{23} + 2 t, shall pale before י׳ Is 24^{23} (‖ חַמָּה), shall become like sun (חַמָּה) in day of י׳'s redemption 30^{26} (אוֹר הַלּ׳), sim of woman's beauty, יָפָה כַלּ׳ Ct 6^{10} (‖ חַמָּה)

II. **לָבָן** $_{54}$ **n.pr.m.** son of Bethuel, brother of Rebekah, and father-in-law of Jacob (𝔊 Λαβαν), Gn $24^{29.29.50}$ 27^{43} $28^{2.5}$ + 17 t J (Gn 29, 30, 31, 32), $29^{15.16.19.21.22.26}$ + 18 t E (Gn 31, 32, ל׳ הָאֲרַמִּי 31^{24}); 25^{20} (ל׳ הָאֲרַמִּי) 28^{5} (*id*), also 28^{2} $29^{24.29}$ $46^{18.25}$ (all P)

† III. **לָבָן n.pr.loc.**, connected with desert-journey of Israelites Dt 1^{1}, 𝔊 Λοβον; poss.= לִבְנָה **2**, q. v.

† **לְבָנָא** Ne 7^{48} = II. לְבָנָה Ezr 2^{45},—head of a family of returning exiles, 𝔊 *Λαβανα, Λαβανω*, 𝔊L *Λοβνα*.

† **לִבְנָה n.pr.loc.** **1.** city in SW Judah, exact site unknown, captured by Joshua, acc. to D, Jos $10^{29.29.31.32.39}$ 12^{15} (all D), 15^{42} (P), Levit. city 21^{13} (P) = 1 Ch 6^{42}, further 2 K 8^{22} = 2 Ch 21^{10}, 2 K 19^{8} = Is 37^{8}, 2 K 23^{31} 24^{18} = Je 52^{1}; 𝔊 *Λεβνα* Vid Lag$^{Onom\ 274,\ 135,\ 28,\ 2nd\ ed.\ 273}$ *Λεβνα*; Buhl$^{Geogr\ 193}$. **2.** station of Isr. in wilderness, between רִמֹּן פֶּרֶץ and רִסָּה Nu $33^{20.21}$ (perh.= לָבָן Dt 1^{1}), 𝔊 *Λεμωνα*, A𝔊L *Λεβωνα*.

† I **לְבֹנָה, לְבוֹנָה n.f. frankincense** (from *white* colour, cf. Lag$^{BN\ 33}$, NH *id*; Aram. *id*, ܠܒܘܢܐ, לְבוֹנְתָא; Ph. לבנת, Ar لُبَانٌ (Lane^{3007}), Eth ሉብን: is fr. λίβανος),—ל׳ Ex 30^{34} + 18 t.; לְבֹנָתָהּ Lv $2^{2.16}$,—used in prep. of holy incense Ex 30^{34} (‖ סַמִּים), used as incense Je 6^{20}, on meal-offering Lv $2^{1.2.15.16}$ 6^{8}, cf. 5^{11} Nu 5^{15}, also Je 17^{26} 41^{5} Is 43^{23} 66^{3}, with shew-bread Lv 24^{7}, Ne $13^{5.9}$ 1 Ch 9^{29} (‖ בְּשָׂמִים), burned as perfume (art. of luxury) Ct 3^{6} (‖ מֹר), גִּבְעַת הַלְּבוֹנָה 4^{6} (‖ הַר הַמּוֹר), עֲצֵי לְבוֹנָה v^{14} (‖ נֵרְדְּ, כַּרְכֹּם, קָנֶה, קִנָּמוֹן, מֹר, אֲהָלוֹת); as tribute to Zion Is 60^{6} (‖ זָהָב).—In Hex only P.

† II. **לְבוֹנָה n.pr.loc.**, by which, among other places, loc of Shiloh is fixed Ju 21^{19}, 𝔊 *Λεβωνα*; mod *Lubban*, c 3 m WNW. fr. Shiloh (Seilûn), Rob$^{BR\ ii\ 271\ f}$ Guérin$^{Sam.\ ii,\ 164\ f}$ Bd$^{Pal\ 217}$ Buhl$^{Geogr\ 173}$.

† I. **לִבְנִי n.pr.m.** a Levite, son of Gershom, Ex 6^{17} Nu 3^{18} 1 Ch $6^{2.5.14}$ (𝔊 *Λοβεν[ε]ι*).

† II. **לִבְנִי adj. gent.** of foregoing, always c art. הַלּ׳ as subst. coll., Nu 3^{21} 26^{58}.

† **לְבָנוֹן** (Dt 3^{25} הַלְּבָנוֹן van d H.) $_{71}$ **n.pr.mont.** **Lebanon** (Ph לבנן; As *Labnanu*, etc, Schr^{COT} on 1 K 5^{13}, Dl$^{Par\ 103\ ff.}$, Egypt. *Ra-m^{e} n-n* WMM

Asien u Europa, 197 ff; Ar. لُبْنَانُ, cf. further Rob BR II 435 ff.493 GASm Geogr 45 ff Buhl Geogr 110 and reff.; name prob. fr. *whiteness* of its cliffs Rob BR II, 493); —wooded mountain-range on northern border of Isr. [usu. c. art הַלּ׳ (51 t), without art. לְבָנוֹן, poet. and late Ho 14[8] Na 1[4] 2 K 19[23]=Is 37[24], Ez 31[15 16] Is 14[8] 29[17] 33[9] 40[16] Je 18[14] Hb 2[17] Zc 10[10] 11[1] ψ 29[6] Ct 4[8.8.11 15], c ה loc לְבָנוֹנָה 1 K 5[28a]]; perh first mentioned in defining a locality, as הַר הַלְּבָנוֹן, Ju 3[3] (E acc to GFM; this combination only here), but also in early proph., then in D, and later;—in defining a locality Jos 9[1]; בִּקְעַת הַלּ׳ Jos 11[17] 12[7] (side of Baal Gad); as a marked feature, in describing extent of land Dt 1[7] 3[25] 11[24] Jos 1[4] 13[5] (כָּל־הַלּ׳) v[6] (all D), 1 K 9[19]=2 Ch 8[6], Je 22[20] Zc 10[10], רֹאשׁ הַלּ׳ Je 22[6] (fig of royal house of Judah), as a height Ct 4[8.8]; מִגְדַּל הַלּ׳ Ct 7[5] i e. a tower built on Lebanon, שֶׁלֶג ל׳ Je 18[14] *snow of L;* L. as source of streams Ct 4[15]; יֵין ל׳ Ho 14[8]; most often, however, as bearing forests, esp of cedars, אַרְזֵי הַלּ׳ Ju 9[15] (in allegory; perh. J, acc. to GFM), Is 2[13] 14[8] ψ 29[5] 104[16], cf 1 K 5[13.20.23.28.28] 2 Ch 2[7 7 15], 2 K 14[9.9]=2 Ch 25[18.18] (in allegory), Je 22[23] Ez 17[3] 27[5] 31[3.15 16] Zc 11[1] Ezr 3[7] ψ 92[13] Ct 3[9] 5[15] (sim. of majestic figure); פֶּרַח ל׳ Na 1[4]; כְּבוֹד הַלּ׳ Is 35[2] 60[13], וְשָׁב ל׳ לְכַרְמֶל 29[17] (יַעַר‖); יַרְכְּתֵי ל׳ with the same ref Is 37[24]=2 K 19[23]; הַלּ׳=trees of Lebanon Ho 14[6] Is 10[34] 40[16] ψ 29[6] 72[16]; ל׳ Is 33[9] fig, as mourning; חֲמַס ל׳ Hb 2[17] i.e *violence done to Lebanon*, prob. by cutting down its trees; בֵּית יַעַר הַלּ׳ a royal mansion of Sol., 1 K 7[2] and 10[17 21]=2 Ch 9[16.20]; ל׳ as home of wild beast 2 K 14[9]=2 Ch 25[18] (in allegory); רֵיחַ לְבָנוֹן, of the odour of cedar forests Ct 4[11], cf. Ho 14[7] (in sim., We thinks ל׳ here to be a specific plant)

†לִבְנֶה **n.[m.] poplar** (appar.=Ar. لُبْنَى, Eth. ልብን: *styrax officinalis;* but 𝔊 λεύκη, cf. 𝔖 and Low No 107),—Gn 30[37] מַקַּל לִ׳ לַח וְלוּז וְעַרְמוֹן, as marking places of idolatrous incense-burning תַּחַת אַלּוֹן וְלִבְנֶה וְאֵלָה Ho 4[13].

†לְבֵנָה† **n.f. brick, tile** (NH *id.;* Aram. לְבֵינְתָא, ܠܒܶܢܬܳܐ; Zinj. לבן (?) DHM Sendsch. 37 59; As. *libittu;* Ar. لَبِنَةٌ, لِبْنَةٌ, لِبِنٌ, لَبِنٌ, لِبْنٌ (loan-words acc. to Fra[47]); acc. to Thes and most from *whiteness* of clay, or light colour of sun-baked bricks; so No ZMG xl 1886, 735 Lag BN 139; >others regard as As. loan-word VOJ L 22 ff.; in As. a deriv fr. *labânu, throw down, prostrate,* is sought Dl Pr 93 f.(cf. HWB 369)),—ל׳ Gn 11[3] Ez 4[1]; cstr. לִבְנַת Ex 24[10]; pl. לְבֵנִים Gn 11[3]+7 t.; sf. מַלְבְּנֵיכֶם Ex 5[19],—**1. brick**, as building-material, Gn 11[3] (sg. coll, elsewh. pl.) v[3]; Ex 1[14]; straw used in making Ex 5[7], cf. v[8.16 18.19]; Is 9[9] (fig.; as inferior to גָּזִית *hewn stone*); incense burnt on Is 65[3] (=roof-tiles? cf. Che Di). **2.**=*tile*, on which plan of city could be engraved (חקק) Ez 4[1]. **3.**=*pavement*, Ex 24[10] (cf Di)

†[לָבַן] **vb.denom.** make brick (as As. *labânu* fr. *libittu* Dl HWB 370),—**Qal** *Impf* 1 pl. נִלְבְּנָה Gn 11[3] (c. acc. cogn.); *Inf. cstr* לִלְבֹּן Ex 5[7] (c. acc. cogn.), v[14] (abs.)

†מַלְבֵּן **n.[m.] 1. brick-mould; 2. quadrangle** (on meaning *brick-mould*, and fig. something *rectangular*, v. Hoffm ZAW 1882, 53-72 Dr 2 S 12 31, cf. NH מַלְבֵּן; Ar. مِلْبَن; Syr. ܡܰܠܒܢܳܐ);—**1.** *brick-mould*, 2 S 12[31] Qr (Kt, by error, מלכן), Na 3[14]. **2.** *quadrangle*, Je 43[9] (at Tahpanhes).

לַבֵּן in עַל־מוּת ל׳ ψ 9[1] of dubious meaning, v. Thes Bae Psalmen, p xvii.

לִבְנַת, v. שִׁיחוֹר לִבְנָת Ar.

†לָבֵשׁ, לָבַשׁ **vb. put on** (a garment), **wear, clothe, be clothed** (NH *id;* Aram. לְבֵישׁ, ܠܒܶܫ, As *labâšu;* Ar لَبِسَ, Eth. ለበሰ:);—**Qal** *Pf.* 3 ms לָבֵשׁ ψ 93[1], לָבַשׁ Jb 7[5]+2 t, וְלָבַשׁ (consec) Lv 6[3]+3 t; sf. וּלְבֵשָׁם (consec.) Lv 16[4]; 3 fs לָבְשָׁה Ju 6[34]+2 t., etc. (Ez 42[14] rd. prob וְלָבְשׁוּ Qr, for ילבשו Kt, but cl. perhaps interpol, v. Co), *Impf.* 3 ms. יִלְבַּשׁ Dt 22[5]+; sf. וַיַּלְבִּשֵׁנִי Jb 29[14], יִלְבָּשֵׁם Ex 29[30]; 1 s. sf. אֶלְבָּשֶׁנָּה Ct 5[3]; 3 fpl. תִּלְבַּשְׁןָ 2 S 13[18], etc.; *Imv.* ms. לְבַשׁ 1 K 22[30], etc., *Inf. abs* לָבוֹשׁ Hg 1[6]; *cstr.* לִלְבֹּשׁ Gn 28[20] Lv 21[10], *Pt. act.* pl. הַלֹּבְשִׁים Zp 1[8]; *pass.* abs לָבוּשׁ 1 S 17[5] Dn 10[5], לָבֻשׁ Ez 9[2]+3 t.; cstr. לְבוּשׁ Dn 12[6.7], לְבֻשׁ Ez 9[11]+3 t.; pl cstr. לְבֻשֵׁי Ez 23[6]+2 t;—**1. a.** lit. *put on* (one's own) garment (acc.) Gn 38[19] 1 S 28[8] 2 S 14[2] 1 K 22[30]=2 Ch 18[29], Ex 29[30] Lv 6[3.4] 16[4 4 23.24.32] 21[10] Dt 22[5] Ez 44[17 19], and so 42[14] Qr (v. supr.), Jon 3[5] Ct 5[3] Est 4[1] 5[1], c. acc. garment + עַל־בְּשָׂרוֹ Lv 16[3]; of putting on armour Je 46[4], =*wear* (more or less habitually), c acc. of garment,

Is 4^{1} Dt 22^{11} Zp 1^{8} Zc 13^{4}; of Jerus. under fig. of woman Je 4^{30}, of rulers under fig. of shepherds Ez 34^{3}, cf. בֵּן תִּלְבָּשְׁךָ 2 S 13^{18} (no acc.) **b.** very oft. fig., *put on, be clothed with*, c. acc. of garment;—לָבַשׁ בְּשָׂרִי רִמָּה Jb 7^{5} *my flesh is clothed* (i.e. covered) *with worms;* of Jerus., *be clothed with* inhabitants Is 49^{18}; of pasture, with flocks ψ 65^{14}; more oft. the garment is some abstract quality, e.g. righteousness, majesty, beauty, strength, etc.;—וַיִּלְבַּשׁ צְדָקָה כַּשִּׁרְיָן Is 59^{17} he (י׳) *hath put on righteousness as a breastplate*, cf. v^{17} (vengeance), ψ 93^{1} (majesty), v^{1} (strength), 104^{1} (honour and majesty), Is 51^{9} (strength); also Jb 40^{10}; said of men, 2 Ch 6^{41} (salvation), ψ 132^{9} (righteousness), Jb 29^{14} (*id.*); of Zion Is 52$^{1.1}$; also in bad sense, clothed with terror, trembling, shame, etc., Ez 7^{27} 26^{16} Jb 8^{22} ψ 35^{26} 109^{29}, cf. v^{18} (cursing). **c.** lit. *put on*, obj. om., נָתַן ... בֶּגֶד לִלְבֹּשׁ Gn 28^{20} Jb 27^{17}; *Inf. abs.* לָבוֹשׁ Hg 1^{6} (there is) *a clothing*, but he has nothing for warmth. **d.** once c. בְּ, אֲשֶׁר לָבַשׁ בּוֹ ... לְבוּשׁ Est 6^{8}. **e.** *Pt. pass., clothed with*, chiefly Ezek.;—c. acc. of garment, Ez 9$^{2.3}$ Zc 3^{3} Pr 31^{21} Dn 10^{5}; of wearing armour 1 S 17^{5}; cstr. before garment, לְבֻשׁ הַבַּדִּים Ez 9^{11} 10$^{2.6.7}$, cf. 23$^{6.12}$ 38^{4} Dn 12$^{6.7}$. **f.** fig.:—וְרוּחַ י׳ לָבְשָׁה אֶת־גִּדְעוֹן Ju 6^{34} *and the spirit of* י׳ *clothed itself with Gideon*, i.e. (GFM) took possession of him (cf. ܠܒܝܫܐ *possessed*); so 1 Ch 12^{18} 2 Ch 24^{20}; צֶדֶק לָבַשְׁתִּי וַיִּלְבָּשֵׁנִי Jb 29^{14} and it *clothed itself* in me, as it were, became incarnate in me. **Pu.** only *Pt.* pl. מְלֻבָּשִׁים *arrayed*, c. acc. of garment 1 K 22^{10} = 2 Ch 18^{9}, 2 Ch 5^{12}; abs. *in full apparel* Ezr 3^{10}. **Hiph.** *Pf.* 3 ms. sf. הִלְבִּישַׁנִי Is 61^{10}; 3 fs. הִלְבִּישָׁה Gn 27^{16}; 2 ms. וְהִלְבַּשְׁתָּ Ex 28^{41} + 3 t.; sf. וְהִלְבַּשְׁתָּם (consec.) Ex 29^{8} Nu 20^{26}; 1 s. sf. וְהִלְבַּשְׁתִּיו Is 22^{21}; 3 pl. הִלְבִּישׁוּ 2 Ch 28^{15}, וְהִלְבִּשׁוּ (consec.) Est 6^{9}; *Impf.* 3 ms. וַיַּלְבֵּשׁ Gn 41^{42} + 5 t.; sf. וַיַּלְבִּשֵׁם Gn 3^{21} Lv 8^{13}; 3 fs. תַּלְבִּישׁ Pr 23^{21}, etc.; *Inf. abs.* הַלְבֵּשׁ Zc 3^{4}; cstr. הַלְבִּישׁ Est 4^{4}; *Pt.* sf. הַמַּלְבִּשְׁכֶם 1 S 1^{24};—*clothe, array with.* **1.** usu. c. 2 acc., **a.** lit. וַיַּלְבֵּשׁ אֹתוֹ בִּגְדֵי־שֵׁשׁ Gn 41^{42} 2 S 1^{24} Is 22^{21} Ex 28^{41} 29$^{5.8}$ 40$^{13.14}$ Lv 8$^{7.13}$ Nu 20$^{26.28}$ Zc 3$^{4.5}$; of clothing Jerus. under fig. of infant Ez 16^{10}; of putting armour on some one 1 S 17$^{38.38}$. **b.** fig., Jb 10^{11} *thou hast clothed me with skin and flesh;* cf. 39^{19} (quivering of horse's neck); Is 50^{3} 61^{10} ψ 132$^{16.18}$. **2.** c. acc. garment only, Gn 27^{16} (+ עַל־יָדָיו); fig., Pr 23^{21}. **3.** c. acc. pers. only, Gn 3^{21} 27^{15} 2 Ch 28$^{15.15}$ Est 4^{4} 6$^{9.11}$.

† לְבוּשׁ, לְבֻשׁ **n.m.** $^{Jb 30,18}$ **garment, clothing, raiment** (on format. cf. Ges $^{§ 84a, 12}$ Lag $^{BN 64, 179}$);—לְבוּשׁ abs. 2 K 10^{22} + 9 t.; cstr. לְבוּשׁ Est 4^{2} + 2 t., לְבֻשׁ Is 14^{19}; sf. לְבוּשִׁי Jb 30^{18} + 3 t.; לְבוּשֶׁךָ Is 63^{2} Pr 27^{26}; לְבוּשׁוֹ Is 63^{1} Jb 41^{5}, לְבֻשׁוֹ 2 S 20^{8} + 2 t.; לְבוּשָׁהּ ψ 45^{14} + 2 t.; לְבוּשְׁכֶן 2 S 1^{24}; לְבוּשָׁם Je 10^{9}; pl. sf. לְבֻשֵׁיהֶם La 4^{14};—*garment, clothing*, Gn 49^{11} (poem in J; ‖ סוּתֹה), Jb 24^{7} (‖ כְּסוּת), v^{10} 30^{18} 31^{19} Pr 27^{26} ψ 22^{19} La 4^{14}; of women's raiment 2 S 1^{24} Pr 31^{22}, also fig. עֹז וְהָדָר לְבוּשָׁהּ v^{25}; specif. of princess ψ 45^{14}; of warrior's tunic 2 S 20^{8}, cf. Is 63$^{1.2}$ (י׳ as warrior); raiment for worshippers 2 K 10^{22}; for mourners, לְבוּשִׁי שָׂק ψ 35^{13}, cf. 69^{12}; בִּלְבוּשׁ שָׂק Est 4^{2}; of royal apparel ל׳ מַלְכוּת Est 6^{8} 8^{15}, cf. (without מ׳) 6$^{9.10.11}$; scaly coat of crocod. פְּנֵי לְבוּשׁוֹ Jb 41^{5}; cover garment with violence Mal 2^{16}, fig. of putting away a wife, cf. RS $^{K. 269}$ We; in other fig. uses:—as changed ψ 102^{27} (sim. of heavens and earth), as covering 104^{6} (sim. of deep upon earth); of cloud as garment of sea Jb 38^{9}, sim. of terrestrial objects in the light v^{14}.

† מַלְבּוּשׁ, [מַלְבֻּשׁ] **n.m.** $^{Zp 1, 8}$ **raiment, attire**;—abs. 2 K 10^{22} + 2 t.; sf. מַלְבּוּשֵׁךְ Ez 16^{13}; pl. sf. מַלְבּוּשַׁי Is 63^{3}; מַלְבּוּשֵׁיהֶם 2 Ch 9$^{4.4}$, מַלְבֻּשֵׁיהֶם 1 K 10^{5};—*raiment*, 2 K 10^{22} (for worshippers, ‖ לְבוּשׁ), Jb 27^{16} (as wealth); of Jerus. under fig. of infant Ez 16^{13}; מַל׳ נָכְרִי Zp 1^{8} *foreign attire* (acc. with לָבַשׁ); pl. of *garments* of Sol.'s servants 1 K 10^{5} = 2 Ch 9^{4a}, + 2 Ch 9^{4b}; of י׳ under fig. of warrior Is 63^{3}.

† תִּלְבֹּשֶׁת **n.f.** raiment;—וַיִּלְבַּשׁ בִּגְדֵי נָקָם ת׳ Is 59^{17} *and he put on garments of vengeance as raiment* (of י׳ as champion of Israel).

† לֹג **n.m.** $^{Lv 14, 10}$ a liquid measure (NH *id.;* Aram. לוּגָּא; also ܠܓܬܐ, ܠܓܐ *a (dessert-)dish*, etc.; mng. of √dub.; Thes comp. Ar. لَجَّ *be deep*, لُجّ *depth, abyss*);—ל׳ abs. Lv 14^{10}; cstr. v^{12} + 3 t. Lv 14; always of oil (שֶׁמֶן) Lv 14$^{10.12.15.21.24}$ (P; all in law of purif. of leper); acc. to Talm. = $\frac{1}{12}$ hin (v. הִין supr. p. 228; Zuckermann $^{Jüd. Massystem, 49}$) i.e. c. $\frac{1}{2}$ litre; Benz $^{Arch. 182, 184}$ Now $^{Arch. i. 204 f.}$

† לֹד **n.pr.loc.** = Λυδδα, 1 Makk 11^{34} Acts 9$^{32.35.38}$, **Lydda**, mod. *Ludd*, c. 11 miles SE. fr. Jaffa, toward Jerusalem; Rob $^{BR ii. 244-248}$ GASm $^{Geogr. 160 ff.}$ Buhl $^{Geogr. 197}$ 1 Ch 8^{12} (ל׳ וּבְנֹתֶיהָ), Ezr 2^{33} (בְּנֵי לֹד) = Ne 7^{37}, cf. 11^{35}; 𝔊 Λωδ, Λοδ, Λυδδων, Λυδδα.

†לְדְבִר n.pr.loc. only in גְּבוּל לְ׳ Jos 13[26]; E. of Jordan, in tribe of Gad; 𝔊B Δαιβων, A Δαβειρ, 𝔊L Δεβηρ; perh = לֹא דְבָר q.v., and cf. II. דְּבִיר 2 b.

לְדָה v. ילד, *Inf. cstr.*

לֹה v. לֹא.

להב √ of foll. (cf Ar. لَهِبَ *be thirsty* [prob. *burn with thirst* Lane[2674]], II. *make* a fire *blaze fiercely*, cf. IV; V. *blaze fiercely* (of fire), cf VIII; Aram. [להב, ܠܗܒ] *burn*, in Shaph. Ishtaph. and deriv; also לַהֲבָא, לְהָבוּתָא *flame*; Eth. ለሀበ:, As *la'abu, flame*, Dl[HWB 384]).

†לַ֫הַב n.m. flame, blade;—לְ׳ abs. Ju 3[22.22] + 2 t.; cstr. Ju 13[20] + 5 t; pl. לְהָבִים Is 13[8], cstr. לַהֲבֵי Is 66[15];—**1.** *flame*, of altar, Ju 13[20.20] (לְ׳ הַמִּזְבֵּחַ), לְ׳ אֵשׁ אוֹכְלָה, of י׳'s judgment Is 29[6] 30[30] 66[15] (in all ‖ forces of nature, whirlwind, thunder, earthquake, rain, hail, etc.); fig. פְּנֵי לְ׳ פְּנֵיהֶם Is 13[8] (i.e hot with excitement, cf. Di); sim. Jo 2[5] כְּקוֹל לְ׳ אֵשׁ (of rush of locusts), fig of breath of crocodile Jb 41[13]. **2.** of *flashing point* of spear Jb 39[23]; *blade* of sword Na 3[3], in prose, Ju 3[22.22].

†לֶהָבָה n.f. id.,—לְ׳ Nu 21[28] + 13 t, לֶהָבַת abs. Jb 15[30], cstr. Ez 21[3], לַבַּת Ex 3[2] (= לַהֶבֶת; Sam. להבת, v. Di), pl. לֶהָבוֹת ψ 105[32], cstr. לַהֲבוֹת ψ 29[7];—**1.** *flame*, poet. (‖ or + אֵשׁ, exc. ψ 29[7] Dn 11[33]), of fire consuming (לָהַט) Dathan, etc. ψ 106[18] (cf Nu 16[35]); wasting (לָהַט) mts. 83[15]; consuming (בָּעַר, אָכַל) chaff (in sim.) Is 5[24]; cf lightning (with hail) אֵשׁ לְ׳ ψ 105[32] (cf. Ex 9[24]), ψ 29[7] לְ׳ אֵשׁ (on text of v. cf. Che); sim. of judgment, אֵשׁ לְ׳ La 2[3] (vb. אָכַל) Ho 7[6] (vb. בָּעַר) Is 47[14] (מִיַּד לְ׳), cf. 10[17] Ob[18], לְ׳ שַׁלְהֶ׳ Ez 21[3]; fig. of drought Jo 1[19], of locusts' ravages 2[3] (vb לָהַט in both); of war Nu 21[28] Je 48[4] (both vb. אָכַל), cf. Dn 11[33] (‖ חֶרֶב); of calamity Is 43[2]; symb נֹגַהּ אֵשׁ לְ׳ of י׳'s presence Is 4[5] (cf. Ex 13[21]); לַבַּת אֵשׁ Ex 3[2]. **2.** *point, head* of spear 1 S 17[7].

לַבַּת אֵשׁ Ex 3[2] v. לֶהָבָה.

†שַׁלְהֶ֫בֶת n.f. flame (Aram. שַׁלְהוֹבִיתָא, ܫܠܗܒܝܬܐ)—in לַהֶבֶת שׁ׳ Ez 21[3], of judgment; so שַׁלְהֶבֶת Jb 15[30]; רְשָׁפֶיהָ רִשְׁפֵּי אֵשׁ שַׁלְהֶבֶתְיָה Ct 8[6] i e. *Yahweh-flame* = powerful flame (> Jager[BAS I.471] Jastrow[JBL xiii (1894), 111] expl יָה־ here as encl part.)

†לְהָבִים n.pr.gent. Gn 10[13] = 1 Ch 1[11], prob. = לוּבִים q.v.; 𝔊 Λαβιειμ.

להג √ of foll. (Ar. لَهِجَ *be devoted, attached* to a thing, *apply oneself assiduously* to it).

†לַ֫הַג n.m. (late) study, i.e devotion to books; לְ׳ הַרְבֵּה יְגִעַת בָּשָׂר Ec 12[12] (cf. Now).

†לַ֫הַד n.pr.m. son of יַחַת of Judah 1 Ch 4[2], 𝔊 Λααθ, 𝔊L Λααδ (etym. and mng. unknown).

†[לָהָה] vb. languish, faint (= לָאָה) (𝔗 לְהֵי, *id.*);—**Qal** *Impf.* 3 fs. apoc. וַתֵּלַהּ אֶרֶץ Gn 47[13] (of famine)

[לָהְלַהּ] vb.quadril. amaze, startle (cf Syr. Palp. ܠܗܠܗ *confudit, obstupefecit*, Ethpalp. *stupore percussus est*; ܡܠܗܠܗܢܘܬܐ *consternatio*, all in Lexx, PS[1891])—**Hithpalp.** *Pt.* מִתְלַהְלֵהַּ as subst. = *madman*, sq. הַיֹּרֶה זִקִּים Pr 26[18] (v. Now).

†[לָהַט] vb. blaze up, flame (NH *id.*, Syr ܠܗܛ, As. *la'âtu*, in der. forms),—**Qal** *Pt. act* אֵשׁ לֹהֵט ψ 104[4] *a flaming fire* (so Bae; אֵשׁ וָלַהַט Bi Che, cf. Ol), made into י׳'s servants; pl. לֹהֲטִים 57[5] (fig. of enemies, cf. לְבָאִם v[a]). **Pi.** *Pf.* 3 ms וְלִהַט Mal 3[19]; 3 fs. לִהֲטָה Jo 1[19]; *Impf.* 3 fs. תְּלַהֵט Jo 2[3] + 4 t.; וַתְּלַהֵט Dt 32[22]; sf. וַתְּלַהֲטֵהוּ Is 42[25];—*set ablaze*, usu. c. acc;—foundation of mts., Dt 32[22] (subj אֵשׁ, fig. of י׳'s judgment, ‖ אָכַל, יָקַד, קָדַח), cf. תְּלַ׳ הָרִים ψ 83[15] (in sim, subj. לֶהָבָה; ‖ כְּאֵשׁ תִּבְעַר־יַעַר); of flame (לֶהָבָה) consuming trees Jo 1[19] (of effects of drought; ‖ אֵשׁ אָכְלָה); persons Mal 3[19] (subj. הַיּוֹם הַבָּא ‖ כְּבַעַר); cf. ψ 97[3] (subj. אֵשׁ), 106[18] (subj. לֶהָבָה, ‖ וַתִּבְעַר־אֵשׁ); hyperb. of י׳'s wrath (חֵמָה אַפּוֹ וֶעֱזוּז מִלְחָמָה) consuming Jacob Is 42[25]; of crocodile (hyperb.), נַפְשׁוֹ גֶּחָלִים תְּלַהֵט Jb 41[13] *his breath setteth coals ablaze*; abs. Jo 2[3], fig. of devastation by locusts (subj. לֶהָבָה; ‖ אָכְלָה אֵשׁ)

†לַ֫הַט n.[m.] flame;—only cstr. לַהַט הַחֶרֶב הַמִּתְהַפֶּכֶת Gn 3[24] *the flame of the whirling sword.*

לְהָטִים v. לוּט.

†[לָהַם] vb. swallow greedily (= Ar. لَهِمَ; Di[Lex Eth 25] comp. Eth. ለህም: *ox, cow*);—only **Hithp.** *Pt.* מִתְלַהֲמִים Pr 18[8] i e *bits greedily*

swallowed, dainties, = 26[22], sim. of tale-bearer's words.

†לָהֵן **conj. on this account, therefore,** Ru 1[13 13] (either from ל and הֵן (v sub הֵמָּה), or the Aram לָהֵן Dn 2[6.9] 4[24]. see the Aram Lex.)

†[לַהֲקָה] **n.f.** dub; acc to 𝔊𝔖𝔗 Aq Symm **band, company** (perh by transp from קְהִלָּה, cf. Thes (קְהִלָּה) The Klo Bu, v also HPS).— לַהֲקַת הַנְּבִיאִים 1 S 19[20].

לוֹ (Kt 1 S 2[16] 20[2]), לוּא, v לֹא.

†לוּ[17] and לוּא (†1 S 14[30] Is 48[18] 63[19]), also לֵא (Qr לוּ), †2 S 18[12] 19[7] (Ar لَوْ, Aram. ܠܘ, לְוַי, Mishn. לוּי, As. *lû*, with opt. force, Dl[§ 78 end. 83,145], cf. Ko[ii 533]), **conj. if, O that.**— **1.** *if* (stating a case which has not been, or is not likely to be, realized): **a.** sq pf (so mostly), Dt 32[29] לוּ חכמו ישכילו זאת *if* they had been wise (which they are not), they would understand this; Mi 2[11] (apod. וְהָיָה); Ju 8[19] 13[23] לוּ חפץ י׳ להמיתנו לא לקח *if* J. had desired to slay us, he would not have taken, &c., 1 S 14[30] 2 S 19[7]. **b.** sq impf Ez 14[15] *if* I were to send, &c. (but rd. prob. אוֹ, cf v[17 19]). **c.** sq ptcp, 2 S 18[12] וְלֹא אָנֹכִי שֹׁקֵל and *though* I should be weighing 1000 pieces of silver upon my hand, I would not, &c.; ψ 81[14-17] לוּ עמי שמע לי *if* my people were hearkening to me, . . . quickly would I bow down, &c. **d.** sq. יֵשׁ Job 16[4].— With the apod omitted, Gn 50[15] לוּ יִשְׂטְמֵנוּ *if* Joseph were to hate us (how should we fare then?)

2. *If only* . . ! i e. *O that! would that!* (cf εἰ γάρ, εἴθε) usu sq perf, as Nu 14[2.2] לוּ מַתְנוּ *if only* we had died in the land of Egypt! 20[3] Jos 7[7] וְלוּ הוֹאַלְנוּ וַנֵּשֶׁב Is 48[18] 63[19], sq יש Nu 22[29]; sq impf. Gn 17[18] לוּ יחיה *O that* Ishmael might live before thee! Jb 6[2], sq. juss Gn 30[34] לוּ יהי כדברך; sq imv. 23[13] אם אתה לוּ שמעני if thou—*O that* thou wouldst hear me! (+ prob. v[5] לאמר לוֹ: שׁ׳ for לאמר: לוּ שמעני, and similarly v[15])—Rd also prob. לֵא for Mas לֹא Ju 21[22] (with כי עַתָּה for כָּעֵת), 1 S 13[13] 20[14 14] Jb 9[33] (sq. יֵשׁ); and perh 14[4] (Ew Ko).

†לוּלֵא Gn 43[10] Ju 14[18] 2 S 2[27] ψ 27[13], elsewhere לוּלֵי[10] **if not, unless** (fr. לוּ *if*, and לֹא, by dissim (Ko[ii 236 459]) for לֹא *not*, cf Ar. لَوْلَا), the neg of לוּ, and used similarly —**a.** sq pf, Ju 14[18] לולא חרשתם . . . לא מצאתם *unless* ye had ploughed with my heifer, ye would not have found out my riddle, 1 S 25[34] (second כי resumptive: כי **1 d**), ψ 106[23]; with apod. introd by כי עַתָּה Gn 31[42] 43[10]; by אָז 2 S 2[27] (כי resumptive); by כמעט Is 1[9]; with an aposiop ψ 27[13] *if I had not believed . . !* **b.** sq impf. Dt 32[27] לולי . . . אמרתי אגור I should have said, &c. . . . *except* I dreaded, &c **c.** sq ptcp, 2 K 3[14]. **d.** without a verb, ψ 94[17] (apod. כמעט), 119[92] (apod. אָז). In the later language, ψ 124[1 2] לוּלֵי י׳ שֶׁ- (apod. אֲזַי) *except that* . . . (cf. Aram. ψ 106[23], ܐܠܘܠܐ . . . דִּי ψ 27[13] 𝔗).— Rd. also לוּלֵי for אוּלַי in Nu 22[33] (apod. כי עַתָּה) See further on לוּ and לולא Dr[§§ 139-145] Ko[iii. 467 f. 565].

†לְמוֹ poet. for לְ, Job 27[14] 29[21] 38[40] 40[4], like כְּמוֹ for כְּ, בְּמוֹ for בְּ: see מוֹ.

†[לוּב] לוּבִים, לֻבִים **n.gent.pl. Lybians,** in N. Africa, W. of Egypt;— Na 3[9] (+ פוּט), 2 Ch 12[3] (𝔊 Λίβυες, + כּוּשִׁים, סֻכִּיִּים, מִצְרַיִם), 16[8] 𝔊 Λίβυες; (+ כּוּשִׁים); לֻבִים Dn 11[43] (v. Baer, c. כֻּשִׁים, מִצְרַיִם), Theod. Λιβύων; prob. = לְהָבִים (q.v.) Gn 10[13] = 1 Ch 1[11] A𝔊L Λαβιειμ; read לוּבִים perh. also Je 46[9] (for 𝔐 לוּדִים, cf Sta[Javan 5 f]), 𝔊 Λυδοί (פוּט *ib* = Λίβυες); 𝔊 Sm Co Sta[Javan 6] Berthol rd. לוּב Ez 30[5] (for 𝔐 כּוּב, q v.) See WMM[As Eur 115].

†לוּד, לוּדִים **n.pr.m.** et **gent. 1. Lud, Lydia,** As *Luddu* —אַרְפַּכְשַׁד וְלוּד וַאֲרָם Gn 10[22] = 1 Ch 1[17] 𝔊 Λουδ. **2.** appar. a people in NE. Africa תַּרְשִׁישׁ פּוּל וְלוּד Is 66[19], 𝔊 Λουδ; פָּרַס וְל׳ Ez 27[10]; כּוּשׁ וּפוּט וְלוּד 30[5] (+ לוּב q.v.), in both 𝔊 Λ(ο)υδοί; also pl לוּדִים a 'son' of Misraim, Gn 10[13] 𝔊 Λυδιειμ (|| לְהָבִים) = 1 Ch 1[11] (לוּדִיִּים); Je 46[9] (|| כּוּשׁ, פּוּט) v לוּב supr.—On this African לוּד v. Di[Gn 10. 13], opp. Sta[Javan 5 ff.] cf WMM[As. Eur 115].

לוֹ דְבָר **n.pr.loc.** v. לֹא דְבָר.

†I. [לָוָה] **join** (intr), **be joined** (NH Pi. לִוָּה (ליוה) trans, Hithp intr.; Aram. לְוֵי *accompany;* so ܠܘܐ, Ba[ES 12] comp. Ar. وَلِيَ *be near*),—**Qal** (late) *Impf* 3 ms. sf יִלְוֶנּוּ Ec 8[15], *be joined to, attend* (of mirth). **Niph.** נִלְוָה ψ 83[9] Is 14[1], 3 mpl. consec. וְנִלְווּ Nu 18[4] + 2 t, + Je 50[5] (Ges[Lbg] Bo Ko[i. 588] Gf Gie; > *Imv* Ki Ew[§ 226 c] Ol[§ 204]), *Impf.* יִלָּוֶה Gn 29[34]; יִלָּווּ Nu 18[2]; *Pt* נִלְוָה Is 56[3] (pointed as Pf, rd. prob. נִלְוֶה); pl. נִלְוִים Est 9[27] Is 56[6];—*join oneself* or *be joined* unto, sq עַל Nu 18[2.4] מַטֵּה לֵוִי to Aaron, by

word-play), Is 14[1] (strangers to Isr), Dn 11[34] (flatterers to the people), cf. Est 9[27]; Is 56[6] (to י׳); sq. אֶל־ Is 56[3] (to י׳), Zc 2[15] (to י׳), Je 50[5] (to י׳), Gn 29[34] (J; husband to wife); sq. עִם ψ 83[9] (Asshur with enemies of Isr.)

†II. [לָוָה] **vb.** borrow (NH *id*; cf. Ar. لَوَى *delay payment of debt* (cf. Ba[ES 12]));—**Qal** *Pf.* 1 pl. לָוִינוּ Ne 5[4]; *Impf.* 2 ms. תִּלְוֶה Dt 28[12]; *Pt.* לֹוֶה Pr 22[7]+2 t.,—*borrow*, עֶבֶד לֹוֶה לְאִישׁ מַלְוֶה Pr 22[7] *a borrower is slave to a man who lends*; abs. Dt 28[12] Is 24[2] ψ 37[21]; sq כֶּסֶף Ne 5[4]. **Hiph.** *Pf.* 2 ms. consec. וְהִלְוִיתָ Dt 28[12]; *Impf.* 3 ms. sf. יַלְוְךָ Dt 28[44]; 2 ms. תַּלְוֶה Ex 22[24]; sf. תַּלְוֶנּוּ Dt 28[44]; *Pt* מַלְוֶה ψ 37[26]+3 t., cstr. מַלְוֵה Pr 19[17],—*cause to borrow*, i.e. *lend to*, c. acc. pers.+rei Ex 22[24] (E); c. acc pers. Dt 28[12.44.44]; abs. ψ 37[26] 112[5]; אִישׁ מַלְוֶה Pr 22[7] (v. **Qal** supr.); as subst. Is 24[2]; מַלְוֵה י׳ Pr 19[17] *a lender to* י׳ is one shewing favour to the poor.

III. לוה (✓of foll., cf. Ar. لَوَى *turn, twist, wind*, As. *lamû*, *surround, encircle*, Dl[HWB 368] Jen[ZMG xliii (1889), 201])

†[לִוְיָה] **n.f.** wreath;—cstr. לִוְיַת חֵן only fig. Pr 1[9] (‖ עֲנָקִים) of instruction of parents, 4[9] (‖ עֲטֶרֶת תִּפְאֶרֶת) of work of Wisdom.

†[לֹיָה] **n.f.** wreath? (mng. dubious, cf Sta ZAW iii. 1883, 161; poss =לִוְיָה);—pl. לֹיוֹת 1 K 7[29.30.36] of carved work on bases of lavers in Solomon's temple.

†לִוְיָתָן **n.m.** [Jb 40, 25] serpent, dragon, leviathan, poet and rare (on format. fr. לוה c. fem. ת+ן ָ—v Thes and cf. Ges[§ 85, 54] Kö[ii, p. 99] Ba[NB § 207 c]; Lag[BN 205] thinks foreign loan-word);—*sea-monster*=crocodile Jb 40[25]; whale ψ 104[26] (v. Che), *dragon* producing eclipses (mythol.) Jb 3[8]; fig of Egypt as all-engulfing ψ 74[14] (‖ תַּנִּינִים v[13]); cf. Is 27[1.1] (‖ נָחָשׁ עֲקַלָּתוֹן, נָחָשׁ בָּרִחַ), v. Che Di and esp. (on ל׳ in gen.) Barton[Tiamat, JAOS xv (1891), 22 ff.] Gunkel[Schöpf. u. Chaos 46].

†[לוּז] **vb.** (poet., mostly WsdLt) turn aside, depart (NH Niph., Hiph.; Ar. لَاذَ *have recourse* to, *take refuge in*);—**Qal** *Impf* אַל־יָלֻזוּ מֵעֵינֶיךָ Pr 3[21] *let them not* (i.e. sound wisdom, etc, si vera l, cf. VB) *depart from thine eyes* (v. Hiph.). **Niph.** *Pt* נָלוֹז Pr 3[32] Is 30[12]; cstr. נְלוֹז Pr 14[2]; pl נְלוֹזִים 2[15],—fig, *devious, crooked*, נ׳ בְּמַעְגְּלוֹתָם Pr 2[15] (‖ עִקְּשִׁים); נ׳ דְּרָכָיו 14[2]; as subst. of pers. 3[32]; of course of action Is 30[12] (‖ עֹשֶׁק), i e. *crookedness*=*craftiness, cunning*, cf. De Che Di. **Hiph.** *Impf.* אַל־יַלִּזוּ מֵעֵינֶיךָ Pr 4[21] (subj. דְּבָרַי) *let them* [my words] *not depart* (on form v. Ges[§ 72 R. 9]) *from thine eyes* (strictly, *let them not practise, exhibit, deviation*, direct causat., Kö[i 205]).

†[לָזוּת] **n.f.** deviation, crookedness (fig);—only cstr. לְזוּת שְׂפָתַיִם Pr 4[24] (on form cf. Ol § 219 a Kö[ii. 166, 474]).

†I. לוּז **n.[m.]** almond-tree, almond-wood (NH *id*; Aram. לוּזָא, ܠܘܙܐ *almond* (Löw[No 319]), whence Ar. لَوْز as loan-wd. (Fra[145] Lag[BN 157 t]), Eth. ሎዝ:),—Gn 30[37] (J; + עַרְמוֹן ,לִבְנֶה) of rods stripped by Jacob.

†II. לוּז **n.pr.loc.** **1.** former name of Bethel Gn 28[19] (J), 35[6] (E), 48[3] (P), Jos 18[13.13] (P), Ju 1[23]; appar. distinct fr. B. מִבֵּית־אֵל לוּזָה Jos 16[2] (JE; but ל here perh. explan. gloss, v. Di); 𝔊 Λουζα, Gn 28[19] [Ουλαμ]λους. **2.** city in hands of Hittites Ju 1[26] (on conject. as to site v. GFM); 𝔊 Λουζα.

לוח (✓of foll., mng. unknown; cf. perh. Ar. لَاحَ *shine, gleam, flash* (of star, lightning, etc.), or Syr. ܠܚܐ *wipe out, efface*, with ref. to smooth surface; but this=לחה).

†לוּחַ **n.m.** tablet, board or plank, plate (NH *id*., Aram. לוּחָא, ܠܘܚܐ; Ar. لَوْح (mod. pron. *lûh, lôḥ*, cf. e g. Spiro[Arab.-Eng Vocab.] Buhl), Eth. ሉሕ:, but As. *lî'u* (as if from לחה) in Dl[HWB 366], see, however, *lêjum* (*lêyum*) Jäger[BAS i, 466]);—ל׳ abs. Is 30[8]; cstr. Pr 3[3]+4 t; du. לֻחֹתַיִם Ez 27[5]; pl. לוּחֹת (לֻחֹת ,לֻחוֹת) abs. Ex 32[16] +17 t.; cstr. Dt 4[13]+16 t.;—**1.** chiefly of stone tablets on which ten words were written Ex 24[12] 31[18b] 32[16.16.19] (all E), 34[1.1.1.4.4.28] (all J), Dt 4[13] 5[19] 9[9.10.11.17] 10[1.2.2.3.3.4.5] 1 K 8[9] 2 Ch 5[10]; ל׳ הָעֵדֻת Ex 31[18a] 32[15] cf. v[15], 34[29] (all P); ל׳ הַבְּרִית Dt 9[9.11.15]; tablet for writing prophecy Is 30[8] (‖ סֵפֶר), Hb 2[2], and fig., לוּחַ לִבֶּךָ Pr 3[3] 7[3] (for writing wise counsel), cf Je 17[1] (inscribing sin of Judah); (vb mostly כָּתַב Ex 31[18b] 32[15] Dt 9[10]; כ׳ עַל Ex 34[1.28] Dt 4[13] 5[19] 10[2.4] Pr 3[3] 7[3] Is 30[8]; חָרַשׁ עַל Je 17[1]; כָּרַת sq acc Dt 9[9] cf. 1 K 8[9]=2 Ch 5[10]; חָרַת עַל Ex 32[16], בֵּאר עַל Hb 2[2]). **2.** wooden *boards*, composing altar of tabern. Ex 27[8] 38[7]; *planks* composing ship (fig. of Tyre) Ez 27[5]; cf. נָצוּר עָלֶיהָ לוּחַ אָרֶז Ct 8[9], of door. **3.** (metal)

plates on bases of lavers in Solomon's temple 1 K 7^{36}.

†לוּחִית **n.pr.loc.** in Moab; c. art מַעֲלֵה הַלּוּחִית Is 15^{5} Je 48^{5} Qr (הַלֻּחִית; Kt. הלחות), it lay S of the Arnon; cf Buhl$^{Geogr\ 24.272}$ and reff; 𝔊 Λουειθ.

[לוּט] **vb. wrap closely, tightly, enwrap, envelope** (Ar لَطَّ *cleave, stick* to a thing; also trans *make to stick*, or *adhere*),—**Qal** *Pf* 3 ms לָאט 2 S 19^{5} (so rd, for MT לָאַט, We Klo Dr Bu), *Pt act* לוֹט Is 25^{7} (cf Kö$^{I\ 445}$), *Pt pass* f לוּטָה 1 S 21^{10},—לוּטָה בַשִּׂמְלָה 1 S 21^{10} it is *wrapped up in a garment* (of sword of Goliath); fig of covering as sign of mourning, פְּנֵי־הַלּוֹט הַלּוֹט עַל־כָּל־הָעַמִּים Is 25^{7} *the surface of covering which covereth over all the peoples* (‖ הַמַּסֵּכָה הַנְּסוּכָה). **Hiph.** *Impf envelope, wrap* וַיָּלֶט פָּנָיו בְּאַדַּרְתּוֹ 1 K 19^{13}.

†לָט, לָאט **n.[m.]** **secrecy, mystery**;—abs לָט 1 S 18^{22}+2 t, לָאט Ju 4^{21}, pl sf לָטֵיהֶם Ex 7^{22}+2 t., לַהֲטֵיהֶם Ex 7^{11},—alw c בּ· **1.** בַּלָּט =*secretly* 1 S 18^{22} 24^{5} Ru 3^{7}, so בַּלָּאט Ju 4^{21} **2.** בְּלָטֵיהֶם *with their mysteries*=enchantments (i e of חַרְטֻמֵּי מִצְרַיִם) Ex 7^{22} $8^{3.14}$=בְּלַהֲטֵיהֶם 7^{11} (all P)

†I לוֹט **n.m.** **envelope, covering**,—Is 25^{7} v sub vb supr.

II לוֹט$_{33}$ **n pr.m.** **Lot** son of Haran, and nephew of Abram; 𝔊 Λωτ,—Gn $11^{27.31}$ $12^{4.5}$ $13^{1.5.7.8.10.11.11.12.14}$ $14^{12.16}$+15 t. Gn 19, †בְּנֵי לוֹט= Moabites Dt 2^{9}, = Ammonites Dt 2^{19}, = both, ψ 83^{9}.

†לוֹטָן **n.pr.m.** 𝔊 Λωταν; a son of שֵׂעִיר Gn $36^{20.22}$=1 Ch $1^{38.39}$, and father of חֹרִי etc. Gn 36^{22} =1 Ch 1^{39}, called a chief (אַלּוּף) of הַחֹרִי Gn 36^{29}.

†I. לֵוִי **n.pr.m.** **Levi** (√and mng dubious; Gn 29^{34} (J) interpr as *joined*, i e husband to wife, Nu $18^{2.4}$ (P, appar. in word-play) of Levites as *joined to, attendant upon*, Aaron, orig as *attached to, accompanying* Isr fr Egypt, Lag$^{Or\ ii\ 20\ f}$; as *attached to, attending upon* the ark, Bau$^{Priest\ 74}$, in this case I לֵוִי would be derived fr II לֵוִי in priestly sense, Hom$^{A\ u\ A\ 1890.30\ f}$ prop Minaean לוא, *lau'ăn, priest*, cf. Id$^{Süd\ Arab\ Chrest\ 127}$, ag all such views v Kau$^{SK\ 1890\ 771\ f}$, We$^{Prol\ ed\ 5\ 141,\ Hist\ Isr\ 145}$ Sta$^{ZAW\ i\ (1881),\ 112\ ff}$ Gray$^{Prop\ Names,\ p\ 96}$, cf No$^{ZMG\ xl\ (1886),\ 167}$, make לֵוִי n gent. fr לֵאָה (q. v.); cf a further sugg We$^{Skizzen\ iii\ 114}$)—𝔊 Λευ(ε)ι(ν),—**1. a.** *Levi*, son of Jacob and Leah, as individual, Gn 29^{34} $34^{25.30}$ 35^{23} 49^{5} (all J); 35^{23} 46^{11} Ex 1^{2} $6^{16.16}$ Nu 3^{17} 16^{1} (all P), 1 Ch 2^{1} 5^{27} $6^{1.4.23.28.32}$ 23^{6} Ezr 8^{18}; so [אֶת־] בַּת־לֵ׳ Ex 2^{1} (E), Nu 26^{59} (P) **b.** as head of a family of descendants, in phr בֵּית לֵוִי Ex 2^{1} (E), and (with ref. to tribe, late) Nu 17^{23}, מִשְׁפַּחַת בֵּית לֵ׳ Zc 12^{13}. **c.** oft בְּנֵי(־)לֵ׳ Ex $32^{26.28}$ (E), Jos 21^{10} (P), בני(־)לֵ׳ with tribal ref. Nu 3^{15} 4^{2} 18^{21} (charged with service of tabern, and hence to receive tithes, all P), as priests הַכֹּהֲנִים בְּנֵי לֵוִי Dt 21^{5} 31^{9}, cf. Mal 3^{3}, and לֹא הָיוּ מִבְּנֵי לֵ׳ 1 K 12^{31}, from the בְּנֵי לֵ׳ the Zadokites are selected as priests Ez 40^{46}, acc to 1 Ch 9^{18} $23^{24.27}$ בְּנֵי לֵ׳ are subordinate officials in temple (cf. $v^{28\ f}$), cf 24^{20}; sharply disting from priests Ezr 8^{15}, Ne 12^{23} (cf. v^{22}); so also in later stratum of story of Korah's revolt Nu $16^{7.8.10}$ (P²). **2.** as name of tribe, שֵׁבֶט לֵ׳ Dt 18^{1} (priestly tribe), מַטֵּה לֵ׳ Nu 1^{49} (in charge of tabern.), 3^{6} 18^{2} (ministers unto Aaron), לֵוִי alone=(tribe of) Levi Dt 27^{12} 33^{8} (earlier poem), Nu 26^{58} (P), Ez 48^{31} Mal 2^{4} (priestly tribe, cf v^{1}), 1 Ch 21^{6} 27^{17}, מַטֵּה לֵ׳=*rod* of (the tribe of) *Levi* Nu 17^{18} (P); also (no inheritance, because charged with service of tabernacle) Dt 10^{9}.

II לֵוִי$_{291}$ **adj.gent** **Levite**,—לֵוִי, 40 t, pl. לְוִיִּם 250 t.; sf 1 pl לְוִיֵּנוּ Ne 10^{1},—†**1.** sg of individual, אִישׁ לֵ׳ Ju 19^{1} *a certain Levite*, pred. וְהוּא לֵ׳ Ju 17^{7} *and he was a Levite*, so v^{9}; c art. הַלֵּ׳ as subst *the Levite* Ex 4^{14} (J), Ju $17^{10.11.12.13}$ (as priest), Dt 18^{6} 2 Ch 20^{14} $31^{12.14}$, Ezr 10^{15}; הָאִישׁ הַלֵּ׳ Ju $18^{3.15}$, הַנַּעַר הַלֵּ׳ 20^{4}. Sg usu †**2.** c art הַלֵּוִי as subst coll *the Levites*. Ex 6^{19} Nu $3^{20.32}$ 26^{57} (all P), 18^{23} (P, charged with service of tabern), esp D, Dt $12^{12.18.19}$ $14^{27.29}$ $16^{11.14}$ $26^{10.12.13}$; also 1 Ch 24^{6}, Mal 2^{8} (as priestly tribe); שֵׁבֶט הַלֵּ׳ Dt 10^{8} *tribe of the Levites* (set apart for service), cf Jos $13^{14.33}$ 1 Ch 23^{14}, בְּנֵי־הַלֵּוִי 1 Ch 12^{27} (van d H v^{26}) *sons of the Levites* (i e. of the tribe); so Ne 10^{40} (as tithe-collectors); בֵּית הַלֵּוִי ψ 135^{20} *house* (family, tribe) *of the Levites*. **3.** pl. הַלְוִיִּם לְוִיִּם chiefly Chr and P;—alw. c. art. except sf לְוִיֵּנוּ Ne 10^{1}, the art. is om by 𝔊𝔙 and most in Is 66^{21}, always=subst. *Levites*,—**1.** †**a.** earlier usage:—as bearing the ark 1 S 6^{15} 2 S 15^{24} Dt 31^{25}, so (with priests) 1 K 8^{4} =2 Ch 5^{5} (𝔊 הכהנים הַלֵּ׳; rd prob וְהַלֵּ׳ as in K, 𝔊𝔖𝔙 cf. Ot VB), also 1 Ch $15^{2.26.27}$ 23^{26} 2 Ch 5^{4} (for הכהנים ‖ 1 K 8^{3}). †**b.** not disting. from priests by D: הַכֹּהֲנִים הַלֵּ׳ Dt $17^{9.18}$ 18^{1} 24^{8} 27^{9},

Jos 3[3] 8[33] (both D; as bearing ark), also Je 33[18.21] (הַל׳ הַכּ׳), Ez 43[19] 44[15]; cf. Dt 18[7] 27[14] Je 33[22]; הַכּ׳ הַל׳ likewise 2 Ch 23[18] 30[27] (but rd. prob. וְהַל׳ after 𝔊𝔖𝔙, cf. Öt and infr.) †c. as tribal designation, Ex 6[25] Nu 3[39] 4[18.46] Jos 21[1] (all P), 1 Ch 9[33.34] 15[12] 2 Ch 35[5] Ne 11[15.16] 12[24]; with ref. to share in land Lv 25[32.32.33.33] (H), Nu 1[47] 2[33] Jos 14[3.4] 21[3.4.8.20.27.34.38.39] (all P), 18[7] (D), 1 Ch 6[49]; cf. also 2 Ch 11[14]†. **d.** set apart for service in tabern., Ex 38[21] Nu 1[50.51.51.53.53] 2[17] 7[5.6] 8[6] + 18 t. Nu 8 (all P), cf. 1 Ch 6[33] 16[4]; ministers to Aaron and his sons Nu 3[9] 8[19] 18[6] (P); set apart for ׳י (as redemption for first-born) Nu 3[12.12] + 7 t. Nu 3 (P); with certain perquisites Nu 18[24.26.30] + 9 t. Nu (P). **2.** in Chr. the tribal idea is in the background, and thought of Levites as official class is prominent: **a.** disting. from priests הַכּ׳ וְהַל׳ 1 Ch 9[14] (cf. v[10]), 13[2] 15[4.11.14] 23[2] 24[6.31] + 67 t. Chr.; also Is 66[21] (acc. to Vrss., but dub.), Ez 44[10] 45[5] (cf. v[4]), 48[11.12.13.22]. **b.** as porters, 1 Ch 9[26] 26[17], cf. 34[9]; as in charge of music, 1 Ch 15[16.17.22] 2 Ch 5[12] 29[25.30] 34[12] Ne 12[27]; yet disting. fr. porters and singers, Ne 7[1] 13[5.10]; disting. also fr. נְתִינִים 1 Ch 9[2] Ezr 8[20] Ne 10[29]; further (with various official functions) 1 Ch 9[31] + 29 t. Chr.; of groups of individuals, 2 Ch 17[8.8] 29[12] 34[12] Ezr 2[40] = Ne 7[43], Ezr 8[33] Ne 3[17] 9[5] 10[10] 12[8], also 8[7] (om. ו; 𝔙 BeRy Ryle). **c.** בְּנֵי־הַלְוִיִּם 1 Ch 15[15] (bearing ark), 24[30] (tribal designation).—See, on Levites, esp. Gf [Gesch. d. Stammes Levi] in Me [Archiv i. 68 ff. 208 ff.] We [Prol. Cap. iv] RS [OTJC. 435 f., 2nd ed., 360 f.] Bau [Priesterthum 50 f., 68 f., and oft.]

†[לוּל] **n.[m.]** shaft or enclosed space (poss. in wall), with steps or ladder, only pl. לוּלִים 1 K 6[8] (וּבְלוּלִים יַעֲלוּ), on mng. v. Sta [ZAW iii. 1883, 136 ff.] > 𝔊𝔙 *winding-stair*, cf. Buhl, v. Sta [l.c.] (NH לוּל *winding passage* or *stair*, or enclosed space in which is *a winding stair*, acc. to Levy [NHWB ii. 486], but v. Sta [l.c.]; √ dubious; hardly לולו infr.)

לוּלֵא, לוּלֵי v. sub לוּ.

לולו (appar. secondary √ from III. לוה *turn, twist, wind*, whence following).

†[לוּלַי] **n.f.** loop (probably from לולו; cf. [דּוּדַי] p. 188 supra; Zehnpf [BAS i. 635], comp. As. *lu-lu*, '*Schleife*');—only pl. abs. לֻלָאֹת Ex 26[5.5.5] + 8 t., cstr. לֻלְאֹת Ex 26[4] 36[11];—*loops* on edges of curtains of tabernacle, matching the hooks (קְרָסִים), for joining the curtains: Ex 26[4.5.5.5.10.10.11] 36[11.12.12.12.17.17] (all P).

לוּלֵי v. לוּלֵא sub לוּ.

I. לִין, לוּן **vb.** lodge, pass the night, fig. abide (NH לִינָה n. *lodging, spending the night*; cf. Nö [ZMG xxxvii (1883), 533 ff.]; acc. to Thes kindred with לַיְלָה (q.v. infra), with change of ל and ן)—**Qal** *Pf.* לָן Gn 32[22] 2 S 12[16]; 3 fs. וְלָנָה consec. (before monosyl.) Zc 5[4]; 1 pl. וְלַנּוּ consec. Ju 19[13] (v. Ges [§ 73. R. 1] Kö [i. 508]); *Impf.* יָלִין Ex 23[18] + 13 t. + 2 S 17[8], but cf. **Hiph.**; וַיָּלֶן Gn 28[11] + 4 t.; 3 fs. תָּלִין Lv 19[13] + 4 t.; תָּלֶן Jb 17[2] (v. Kö [i. 509]); 2 ms. juss. אַל־תָּלֶן 2 S 17[16]; תָּלֶן Ju 19[20] (v. Kö [l.c.]), etc.; *Imv.* לִין Ju 9[6.19], etc.; *Inf. cstr.* לָלוּן Gn 24[25] + 5 t.; לָלִין 24[23]; *Pt.* pl. לֵנִים Ne 13[21];—**1.** *lodge, pass the night*: **a.** lit., human subj., oft. c. prep. or adv. of place, Gn 19[2] 28[11] Ju 19[13.15] 2 S 17[16] Jb 24[7] + oft. (on 2 S 17[8] v. **Hiph.**); c. ה loc., וְלָן וְשָׁכַב אַרְצָה 2 S 12[16]; c. ב loc. + ב temp. בַּלַּיְלָה הַהוּא Gn 32[14.22] Jos 8[9]; c. הַלַּיְלָה (accus. temp.), Nu 22[8] Jos 4[3] 2 S 17[16] 19[8] Ru 3[13]; of the wicked ψ 59[16], acc. to Hup De Pe al.; < fr. II. לון 𝔊𝔙 Aq Che Bae al., cf. AV; sim. of temporary sojourn Je 14[8] (of ׳י in Isr.) **b.** of animals: wild ox (רְאֵם) Jb 39[9] (sq. עַל־אֲבוּסֶךָ), porcupine (קִפֹּד) Zp 2[14]. **c.** inanim. subj. = *remain all night*: of fat of sacrifice Ex 23[18] (E; sq. עַד־בֹּקֶר), passover meal 34[25] (P; sq. לַבֹּקֶר), Dt 16[4] (sq. לַבֹּקֶר; all these without local designation), wages of hireling Lv 19[13] (H; אֵת = *with* + עַד־בֹּקֶר); of dead body Dt 21[23] (עַל loc.); dew Jb 29[19] (ב loc.); bunch of myrrh Ct 1[13] (בֵּין loc.) **d.** fig. בָּעֶרֶב יָלִין בֶּכִי ψ 30[6] *at evening weeping may come to lodge* (opp. וְלַבֹּקֶר רִנָּה). †**2.** fig. *abide, remain*, subj. עַיִן (= *look upon*), c. ב Jb 17[2]; of error; 19[4] (c. prep. אֵת pers.), strength 41[14] (of crocod.; c. ב); of righteousness, Is 1[21] (c. ב); נַפְשׁוֹ בְּטוֹב תָּלִין ψ 25[13]; of hearkening ear Pr 15[31], c. בְּקֶרֶב; of thoughts Je 4[14], c. id.; abs., of man, *continue, endure*, ψ 49[13], שָׂבֵעַ יָלִין Pr 19[23] *he shall continue satisfied*. **Hiph.** *Impf.* יָלִין *cause to rest, lodge*, sq. acc., 2 S 17[8] v. Kö [i. 509]. **Hithpalp.** *Impf.* יִתְלוֹנָן Jb 39[28] *dwell, abide*, of eagle; fig. בְּצֵל שַׁדַּי יִתְלוֹנָן ψ 91[1] of one trusting in ׳י.

†מָלוֹן **n.m.** lodging-place, inn, khan;—abs. מ׳ Gn 42[27] + 5 t.; cstr. מְלוֹן 2 K 19[23] Je 9[1];—*lodging-place, inn, khan* (?) Gn 42[27] 43[21] Ex 4[24]; מְ׳ אֹרְחִים Je 9[1]; = camp (of Isr.) for a night, Jos 4[3] (+ לין), v[8]; of Assyrians Is 10[29]; fig. מְלוֹן קִצֹּה 2 K 19[23], i.e. its (Lebanon's) remotest camping-ground, hyperb. of Assyrian conquest; so rd.

prob. in ‖ Is 37[24] for MT מְרוֹם ק׳, cf. Di Du Kit Che[Hpt.]

† מְלוּנָה **n.f.** lodge, hut;—מ׳ בְּמִקְשָׁה Is 1[8] (i.e. a watchman's hut); sim. of frail, insecure structure וְהִתְנוֹדְדָה כַּמְּלוּנָה Is 24[20] *and it* [the earth] *shall shake* (or *totter*) *like a hut.*

† II. [לוּן] **vb.** murmur, only Ex 15, 16, 17, Nu 14, 16, 17, and Jos 9[18] (Sam. always defect., hence Nö[ZMG xxxvii. 1883, 535 n.] thinks poss. לנן [cf. רנן ?]; from limited occurrence, he supposes it disappeared early; but found chiefly in P);—**Niph.** *Impf.* 3 mpl. וַיִּלֹּנוּ Ex 15[24] + 3 t. + Ex 16[2] Qr (Kt (וילינו)) + Nu 14[36] Kt (Qr וַיַּלִּינוּ, **Hiph.**); 2 mpl. תִּלּוֹנוּ Ex 16[7] Nu 16[11], both Kt (Qr תַּלִּינוּ); on forms v. Ges[§ 72 Anm. 8] Kö[i. 509];—*murmur* against, sq. עַל Ex 15[24] (JE), 16[2.7] Nu 14[2] 16[11] 17[6] Jos 9[18] (all P; all of people Isr.); abs. ψ 59[16] (v. I. לון **1 a**). **Hiph.** *Pf.* 2 mpl. הֲלִינֹתֶם Nu 14[29]; *Impf.* וַיָּלֶן Ex 17[3]; וַיַּלִּינוּ Ex 16[2] Kt, Nu 14[36] Qr; 2 mpl. תַּלִּינוּ Ex 16[7] Qr, Nu 16[11] Qr (on all vid. supr.); *Pt.* pl. מַלִּינִים Ex 16[8] + 3 t.;—*murmur* = Niph., sq. עַל Ex 17[3] (E), elsewhere P: 16[8] Nu 14[27.27.29] 17[20]; *cause to murmur*, sq. acc. + עַל Nu 14[36] Qr; (cf. also supra **Niph.**)

† [תְּלֻנָּה] **n.f.** murmuring;—pl. cstr. תְּלֻנּוֹת (תְּלוּנֹּת) Ex 16[12] + 2 t.; sf. תְּלֻנֹּתֵיכֶם 16[7] + 3 t.; תְּלוּנֹּתָם Nu 17[25];—*murmurings* of Isr. against ׳י (only P); Ex 16[9.12] Nu 17[25]; sq. עַל Ex 16[7.8], cf. v[8], Nu 14[27] 17[20] (+ מַלִּינִם עַל).

† I. [לוּעַ, or לָעַע] **vb.** swallow, swallow down (Syr. ܠܥܐ, ܠܥܐ *lap* or *lick up* Ju 7[5-7]);—**Qal** *Pf.* 3 pl. וְלָעוּ consec. Ob[16] (Ges[§ 67 R. 12]);—abs., fig. of nations drinking (cup of judgment).—Hi De *talk wildly*, vid. II. לוע; We Now נָעוּ *reel, totter* (cf. Is 24[20] 29[9]).

† [לֹעַ] **n.[m.]** prob. throat (external) (cf. NH לוֹעַ *jaw, cheek*, Aram. לוֹעָא, ܠܘܥܐ *id.*);—וְשַׂמְתָּ שַׂכִּין בְּלֹעֶךָ Pr 23[2] *and thou shalt put a knife to thy throat* (fig. for restraining oneself from indulgence in food).

† II. [לוּעַ, or לָעַע] **vb.** talk wildly (MT יָלַע, לָעוּ; perh. better wd. be יִלְעֶה, לָעוּ (√לעה), cf. Thes and Ar. لَغَا, لَغِيَ *make mistakes in talking*, Ba[ZMG xli. 1887, 605, 614]);—**Qal** *Pf.* 3 mpl. לָעוּ Jb 6[3], subj. דברים (v. Di); *Impf.* מוֹקֵשׁ אָדָם יָלַע קֹדֶשׁ Pr 20[25] it is *a snare to a man that he should rashly cry, Holy!* (construction unusual, and perh. text. err., cf. Frankenberg; on form v. Ol[§ 243 a Anm.]; Bö[i. 296] Kö[i. 375 f.] der. fr. לעע; Str., Hiph. fr. לעע).

לוץ v. ליץ.

† לוּשׁ **vb.** knead (NH *id.*; Aram. לוּשׁ, ܠܫ, Eth. ለውሰ: or ለሰ:);—**Qal** *Impf.* 3 fs. וַתָּלָשׁ 1 S 28[24] 2 S 13[8] Qr (Kt וַתָּלוֹשׁ-); *Imv.* fs. לוּשִׁי Gn 18[6]; *Inf. cstr.* מִלּוּשׁ Ho 7[4]; *Pt.* fpl. לָשׁוֹת Je 7[18];—*knead* (obj. not expr. = קֶמַח סֹלֶת) Gn 18[6] (J), cf. 1 S 28[24]; obj. בָּצֵק *dough* Ho 7[4] Je 7[18] cf. 2 S 13[8].

לוּשׁ (Kt) **n.pr.m.**, לַיִשׁ v. ליש.

לָז, לָזֶה, לֵזוּ v. הַלָּז etc., p. 229 supra.

לְזוּת v. לוז supra.

לַח v. sub לחח.

לחה (√ of foll., poss. fr. *smoothness*, cf. Ar. لَحَى *peel off;* Syr. ܠܚܐ *strip off, erase*).

† I. לְחִי **n.m.** [Ct 1, 10] jaw, cheek (NH *id.;* Aram. לוֹחָא; Ar. لَحْيٌ; on As. *laḫû* cf. Dl[HWB 375], but ح = *ḫ ?*);—ל׳ abs. Ju 15[17] Mi 4[14]; cstr. Ju 15[15] + 2 t.; לְחִי 1 K 22[24] + 3 t. + Ju 15[19.19]; *sf.* לְחָיוֹ Jb 40[26]; לְחֱיָהּ La 1[2]; du. לְחָיַיִם Dt 18[3]; cstr. לְחָיֵי Is 30[28]; sf. לְחָיַי Is 50[6], cf. Jb 16[10], etc.; לְחֵיהֶם Ho 11[4];—**1.** *jaw, jawbone*, of animal, Ju 15[15.16.16.17] (under jaw of ass), cf. n.pr.loc. רָמַת לְחִי v[17]; in sim. כִּמְרִימֵי עֹל עַל־לְחֵיהֶם Ho 11[4] *like those lifting up a yoke from upon* (rd. מֵעַל ?) *their jaws* (Isr. under fig. of oxen); of sacrificial ox or sheep Dt 18[3]; of crocodile Jb 40[26]; of Pharaoh under fig. of תַּנִּים Ez 29[4] (cf. v[3]); cf. 38[4] Is 30[28]. **2.** *cheek*, of man 1 K 22[24] = 2 Ch 18[23], Jb 16[10] ψ 3[8] Ct 5[13] Is 50[6] La 3[30] Mi 4[14]; of woman Ct 1[10] La 1[2] (fig. of Jerusalem).

† II. לְחִי **n.pr.loc.** scene of an exploit of Samson;—ל׳ Ju 15[19.19] (𝔊 Σιαγων), לֶחִי v[14]; c. art. בַּלֶּחִי v[9] (𝔊 Λευει, 𝔊L Λεχει), cf. רָמַת לְחִי v[17] = *height of Leḥi* (expl. as fr. לְחִי *jawbone*, cf. GFM, 𝔊 Ἀναίρεσις σιαγόνος); also 2 S 23[11], where read לְחָיָה *to Leḥi*, for לַחַיָּה, vid. II. חַיָּה, p. 312 supr.; (𝔊 θηρία; 𝔊L σιαγόνα). It must have lain in the Shephelah, near the border of the hill-country of Judah (Buhl[Geogr. 91]); site unknown; conjectures are cited and criticized by GFM[Ju 15, 19] q.v.

לחח (√of foll.; cf. Eth. ለለሐ: II. I. *moisten, cool;* ተለሐለሐ: *be moistened* Di$^{Lex.30}$; NH לִחְלֵחַ Pilp. *moisten thoroughly,* Aram. לַחְלַח *id.,* NH לַח *moist, fresh;* לֵיחָה *moisture, freshness,* etc.)

† **לַח** adj. moist, fresh, new;—לַ׳ Gn 30^{37} Ez 21^{3}; לָח 17^{24}; pl. לַחִים Nu 6^{3}+2 t.;—**1.** *moist, fresh,* of trees, fruit, etc.; לִבְנֶה לַח Gn 30^{37} (J); עֵץ לַ׳ Ez 17^{24} 21^{3}; grapes עֲנָבִים לַ׳ Nu 6^{3}. **2.** *new,* of cords, יְתָרִים לַ׳ Ju $16^{7.8}$, prob. made of *fresh* sinews of animal (cf. Syr. ܠܐܟܐ PS^{1652}; GFM$^{ad loc.}$)

†[**לֵחַ**] n.m. moisture, freshness (i. e. *force, vigour*);—sf. וְלֹא נָס לֵחֹה Dt 34^{7} *and his freshness had not fled;* rd. prob. also בְּלֵחוֹ for MT בְּלַחְמוֹ Je 11^{19} (v. לֶחֶם ad fin.; on Zp 1^{17} v. לְחוּם).

לְחִי, לֶחִי v. sub לחה.

†[**לָחַךְ**] vb. lick (NH *id.;* so Aram. לְחַךְ, ܠܚܟ; Ar. لَحِكَ);—**Qal** *Inf. cstr.* כִּלְחֹךְ Nu 22^{4} (E), sq. acc.; of ox licking up grass. **Pi.** *Pf.* 3 fs. לִחֵכָה 1 K 18^{38}; *Impf.* 3 mpl. יְלַחֲכוּ Nu 22^{4} Mi 7^{17}; יְלַחֵכוּ ψ 72^{9} Is 49^{23}; *lick up* (sq. acc.), fire fr. heaven the water in trench 1 K 18^{38}; of Isr. consuming produce of land Nu 22^{3} (E); esp. לִ׳ עָפָר *lick the dust,* sign of humiliation Mi 7^{17} ψ 72^{9} Is 49^{23}.

I. [**לָחַם**]$_{171}$ vb. fight, do battle (NH Hithp.; ואלתחם MI$^{11.15.19}$; perh.=*order the battle,* cf. Nö$^{ZMG\ xl.\ 1886,\ 721}$; Ar. لَحَمَ *fit close together,* so NH לחם Pi., Syr. ܠܚܡ Pa. *unite,* ܠܚܝܡ *fit;* also *threaten;* Gerber$^{Verb.\ Denom.\ 59}$ thinks vb. in Heb. denom. fr. מִלְחָמָה *battle-line,* but dub.);—†**Qal** (poet.) only *Imv.* ms. and *Pt. act.*—*fight, do battle* with, rare, only ψψ, appar. later usage:—לְחַם אֶת־לֹחֲמָי ψ 35^{1} *do battle with those battling with me* (dub. whether את is acc. sign or prep. *with,* cf. Ol; ‖ רִיבָה אֶת־יְרִיבַי); לֹחֲמִים לִי 56^{3} *doing battle against me;* לֹחֵם v^{2} as subst. *fighter.*† **Niph.**$_{167}$ *Pf.* נִלְחַם Ju 9^{17}+, וְנִלְחַמְתָּ 11^{8} 1 S 15^{18}, וְנִלְחַמְנוּ Dt 1^{41} consec., etc.; *Impf.* יִלָּחֵם Ex 14^{14} Dt 1^{30}; יִלָּחֶם לָנוּ Ne 4^{14}, וַיִּלָּחֶם Ex 17^{8}+19 t.; 3 fs. תִּלָּחֵם Zc 14^{14}; 3 mpl. וַיִּלָּחֲמוּ Ju 1^{5}+13 t.; sf. וַיִּלָּחֲמוּנִי ψ 109^{3}; 2 mpl. תִּלָּחֲמוּ 1 K 22^{31}+4 t.; תִּלָּחֲמוּן 1 K 12^{24}, etc.; *Imv.* הִלָּחֲמוּ Ex 17^{9} 1 S 18^{17}; הִלָּחֶם בּוֹ Ju 9^{38}; pl. הִלָּחֲמוּ 2 K 10^{3} Ne 4^{8}; *Inf. abs.* נִלְחֹם Ju 11^{25}; *cstr.* הִלָּחֵם 1^{9}+35 t.; הִלָּחֶם בּוֹ etc., Nu 22^{11}+6 t.; sf. הִלָּחֲמוֹ 2 K 8^{29}+3 t.; *Pt.* נִלְחָם Ex 14^{25}+10 t.; pl. נִלְחָמִים Jos 10^{25}+10 t. (but 1 S 31^{1} rd. rather נִלְחֲמוּ, so ‖ 1 Ch 10^{1} We Klo Bu, cf. Dr);—*engage in battle* (recipr.), sometimes *wage war* (Jos 10^{5} Ju 11^{5} 1 K 14^{19} 22^{46} 2 K 6^{8} 14^{28} etc.), oft. c. בְּ of enemy (60 t.) Ex 1^{10} $17^{9.10}$ Nu $21^{23.26}$ 22^{11} (all E), Ju $11^{8.25}$ 1 S 15^{18} 2 S 8^{10}+(49 t.); less oft. c. בְּ of city attacked or besieged †Ju 9^{45} 1 S 23^{1} 2 S $12^{26.27.29}$ Is 20^{1} Jos 10^{31} (D), 1 K 20^{1} Ne 4^{2}; of tower Ju 1^{52}; sq. בְּאַרְצִי 11^{12}†; also c. עִם of enemy (26 t.): Ju 5^{20} $11^{4.5.20}$ Jos 11^{5} (JE), 1 S 13^{5} 17^{19}, also 1 S $17^{32.33}$ (of single combat), Dt 20^{4} Jos 9^{2} (both D), 2 K 13^{12} 14^{15} 2 Ch 11^{1} 17^{10} 27^{5} Dn 10^{20} 11^{11}+; c. עִם of city †Jos 10^{29} (D), 19^{47} (JE)†; c. אֶת־=*with,* of enemy, †Jos 24^{8} (E), 1 S 17^{9} (single combat), Je 21^{5} 1 K 20^{23} 2 K 19^{9} =Is 37^{9}, Je 37^{10}; also Ju 12^{4} 2 S 11^{17} 21^{15} 1 K 22^{31} 2 K 8^{29} 9^{15} Je 21^{4} 32^{5} 33^{5} 2 Ch 18^{30} 22^{6}, and c. אוֹתָם (=אִתָּם) Jos 10^{25} (D), 1 K 20^{25} (Kö$^{Lgb.\ ii.\ 296}$)†; c. עַל, *against,* of enemy only Je 21^{2}; elsewhere (16 t.) of city: †Jos 10^{5} (JE), Is 7^{1} 2 K 12^{18} 19^{8} =Is 37^{8}; esp. D and Je: Dt $20^{10.19}$ Jos $10^{34.36.38}$ (all D), Je $32^{24.29}$ $34^{1.7.8.22}$†; c. אֶל־ of enemy †Je 1^{19} 15^{20}†; c. sf. וַיִּלָּחֲמוּנִי †ψ 109^{3} *and they have fought against me*†; c. יַחַד i.e. fight *together* =with (against) one another †1 S 17^{10}; abs. c. acc. cogn. מִלְחָמוֹת *fight battles* †1 S 8^{20} 18^{17} 25^{28} 2 Ch 32^{8}†; abs. elsewhere Ju $5^{19.19.20}$ Dt 1^{41} Zc 10^{5} +26 t.+וַיָּסֻרוּ עָלָיו לְהִלָּחֵם 1 K 22^{32}; †c. עַל *for, in behalf of,* Ju 9^{17} 2 K 10^{3} Ne 4^{8}; c. לְ=*id.,* Ex 14^{14} (J), v^{25} (J; + בְּ of enemy), Dt 1^{30} 3^{22} 20^{4} (+ עִם of enemy, vid. supra), Jos $10^{14.42}$ $23^{3.10}$ (all D), Ne 4^{14}†; יָכֹל לְהִלָּ׳ *be able to fight,* c. את of enemy 1 S 17^{9}, c. בְּ of enemy Nu 22^{11}, =*be successful in fighting,* prevail against; so c. עַל of city Is 7^{1}, and abs. 2 K 16^{5} (after וַיָּצֻרוּ עַל *besiege*).

† **לָחֶם** n.[m.] only in אָז לָחֶם שְׁעָרִים Ju 5^{8} (so Mass.; Codd. לְחֶם, לָחֶם), usu. tr. *then* was there *war* of (=at) the *gates,* but improb.; text and meaning dub.; A𝔊L rd. ὡς ἄρτον κρίθινον, whence Bu$^{RS\ 103}$ אָז לֶחֶם שְׂעֹרִים *then* they used to eat *barley bread;* but Bu$^{Comm.}$ אָזַל לֶ׳ שְׂ׳ *the barley bread was exhausted;* Mayer Lambert$^{RÉJ\ xxx,\ 115}$ אז לחמש ערים *then for* (*in*) 5 *cities* no shield was seen, etc.; other conj. in Kau^{AT}; cf. GFM$^{ad loc.}$

†[**לְחוּם**] n.[m.] perh. intestines, bowels (mng. and √ not wholly certain, cf. Nö$^{ZMG\ xl.\ 1886,\ 721}$; from לחם=*press together,* acc. to Dl$^{Prol.\ 193}$);—

only sf.: וּלְחֻמָם כַּגְּלָלִים Zp 1[17] their blood shall be poured out like water, *and their bowels like dung*, Hi-St (cf 2 S 20[10]), Dl[l.c.] We ('ihr Mark'), Rothstein[KauAT] Di[Jb 20, 23]; Gr חֵלְבָּם cf. v[12] (to wh. Now incl), Now suggests also וְלֵחָם *and their moisture* (*freshness, vigour*, cf. Dt 34[7]), >al who render *flesh*, 𝔊 τὰς σάρκας (cf. Ar لَحْمٌ *flesh, meat*, v. sub לֶחֶם); וְיַמְטֵר עָלֵימוֹ בִּלְחוּמוֹ Jb 20[23] to fill his belly, God sendeth into him his burning anger, *and raineth it upon him, into his* (very) *bowels* Hi Dl[l.c.] Bae[KauAT] (cf Di, and *into his flesh* De, v. supr.); >disting. from Zp 1[17] Di (in transl.) Da Hoffm Bu *his food* (as obj of יַמְטֵר; rd then לַחְמוֹ), 𝔊 ὀδύνας, whence Me Sgfr חֲבָלִים, Schwally[ZAW x. 1890, 179] בַּלָּהָה; No[l.c.] *wrath*, cf Syr. ܚܣܡ *threaten*.

מִלְחָמָה [319] **n.f. battle, war**;—abs מ׳ Gn 14[2.8] Ex 1[10]+, cstr. מִלְחֶמֶת 1 S 13[22] (מ׳ מִכְמָשׂ) 𝔊 Th We Bu HPS Ew § 188 c Ko ii. 182 > abs. Thes al), sf מִלְחַמְתִּי 2 Ch 35[21]; מִלְחַמְתְּךָ 2 S 11[25], מִלְחַמְתֶּךָ Is 41[12], etc; pl מִלְחָמוֹת Is 42[13]+7 t Ch ψψ, cstr מִלְחֲמוֹת Ju 3[1]+, etc,—*battle*, Gn 14[8] 1 S 17[1.2.8] 31[3] 1 K 20[14.18.29.39]+oft; *war*, Gn 14[2] Ex 1[10] Dt 20[12] Jos 11[23] 14[15] 2 S 3[1] (וַתְּהִי הַמִּלְחָמָה) סֵפֶר מִלְחֲמֹת י׳ Nu 21[14] (JE), acc cogn. c נלחם +1 S 8[20] 2 Ch 32[8] and (מִלְחֲמוֹת י׳) 1 S 18[17] 25[28]+; = *art of war*, לְמֹד מ׳ Is 2[4] *learn war* = Mi 4[3]; לַמֵּד מ׳ Ju 3[2] *teach war, fighting*; מְלַמֵּד יָדַי לַמ׳ 2 S 22[35] = ψ 18[35], cf. ψ 144[1], לְמוּדֵי מ׳ 1 Ch 5[18], מְלֻמְּדֵי מ׳ Ct 3[8] *instructed in war*; once = *battlefield* וַיָּבֹאוּ עַד הַמ׳ 1 S 14[20] (so Kit[KauAT]). The most freq. phrases are †אִישׁ מ׳ Is 3[2] 1 S 16[18] 17[33] 2 S 17[8] Ez 39[20] Jos 17[1] (P), also (coll) Ju 20[17], of י׳ Ex 15[3] (poem), אַנְשֵׁי הַמ׳ Jos 6[3] 10[24] (both JE), Dt 2[14.16] Jos 5[4.6] (all D), Je 38[4] 39[4] 41[3.16] 49[26] 51[32] 52[7.25], also 1 K 9[22] 2 K 25[4] Nu 31[28.49] (P), Jo 4[9], late אַנְשֵׁי מ׳ Jo 2[7] 1 Ch 12[39] (v[38] van d. H) 2 Ch 8[9] 17[13], אַנְשֵׁי מִלְחַמְתָּהּ Is 42[13] 1 Ch 28[3], אִישׁ מִלְחָמוֹת Je 50[30] *her men of war*, cf. Is 41[12] Ez 27[10.27]; אִישׁ מִלְחֲמוֹת תֹּעִי 2 S 8[10] *a man of battles of Toi*, i e. his frequent opponent (v Dr), = 1 Ch 18[10], seldom גִּבּוֹר מ׳ ψ 24[8] (of י׳), גִּבּוֹרֵי מ׳ 2 Ch 13[3]; שָׂרֵי מִלְחָמוֹת 2 Ch 32[6], עַם הַמ׳ Jos 8[1.3] 10[7] 11[7], cf. 8[11] (all JE), cf also 1 S 13[16] add 𝔊 We Dr, cf. Klo; אַנְשֵׁי חַיִל לַמ׳ Je 48[14], צְבָא מ׳ *battle-host* Is 13[4], so צ׳ הַמ׳ Nu 31[14] (P); also גְּדוּדֵי צְבָא מ׳ 1 Ch 7[4], אַנְשֵׁי צָבָא לַמ׳ 1 Ch 12[9] v[11] יֹצְאֵי צ׳ לַמ׳ (v[8] van d H)†, *weapons of war*, כְּלֵי (ה)מ׳ Ju 18[11.17] Je 21[4] 51[20] 1 Ch 12[34] (v[33] van d. H), also fig 2 S 1[27] (‖ גִּבּוֹרִים), כְּלֵי צְבָא מ׳ 1 Ch 12[38] (v[37] van d H), קֶשֶׁת מ׳ Zc 9[10] 10[4]; כְּלֵי מִלְחַמְתּוֹ *his weapons of war* 1 S 8[12] Dt 1[41], cf Ju 18[16] Ez 32[27]; דִּבְרֵי הַמ׳ = *the news of the battle* 2 S 11[18.19] + v[22] add. 𝔊 The We Klo Dr Bu Freq combin. with vbs. are, עָרַךְ מ׳ *draw up battle-*line Ju 20[22]+, sq. אֵת *with* = *against* Gn 14[8] Ju 20[20], sq עִם 2 Ch 13[3]; אָסַר הַמ׳ i e begin the battle 1 K 20[14], cf 2 Ch 13[3], וַתִּקְרַב הַמ׳ 1 K 20[29] *and the battle was joined*; עָשָׂה מ׳ *make war* Pr 20[18] 24[6] 1 Ch 22[8], sq אֵת *with* Gn 14[2] Jos 11[18] (D), sq עִם Dt 20[12.20] 1 Ch 5[10.19]; יָצָא לַמ׳ עִם† Ju 20[14.20.28], c עַל 1 K 8[44] 2 Ch 6[34]; נִגַּשׁ לַמ׳ עִם 2 K 8[28], הָלַךְ לַמ׳ עִם Ju 20[23], c בְּ 1 S 7[10] 2 S 10[3], abs Je 46[3]+, וַתְּהִי הַמ׳ עִם 2 S 21[18.19], c. בֵּין 2 S 3[1], cf v[6]+, †קִדֵּשׁ מ׳ *consecrate war*, i e. open a campaign (with sacred rites, Che) Mi 3[5] Je 6[4] (both c. עַל), Jo 4[9], cf †הִדְבִּיקַתְהוּ הַמ׳ Ju 20[42] *and the battle clung to them*; וַתַּעַל הַמ׳ 22[35] *and the battle rose* (high) = 2 Ch 18[34], וַתִּטֹּשׁ הַמ׳ 1 S 4[2], rd. וַתֵּט הַמ׳ (𝔊 We Klo Bu, cf Dr) *and the battle inclined* (in favour of one side); נָפֹצֶת הַמ׳ 2 S 18[8] Qr *the battle was spread* (extended), so read 1 S 14[23] add. 𝔊 The We Klo Dr, תָּקוּם עָלַי מ׳ ψ 27[3] *if war rise against me*†, הַמ׳ כָּבְדָה Ju 20[34] *the battle was severe*, cf וַתִּכְבַּד הַמ׳ אֶל־שָׁאוּל 1 S 31[3] = 1 Ch 10[3] (אל for על), so וַתְּהִי הַמ׳ חֲזָקָה 1 S 14[52], חָזַק מִמֶּנּוּ הַמ׳ 2 K 3[26], וַתְּהִי הַמ׳ קָשָׁה 2 S 2[17]: cf. כֹּבֶד מ׳ Is 21[15], עֱזוּז מ׳ 42[25].

†II. **[לָחַם]** **vb. use as food, eat, poet** (so Thes Buhl, cf. Fra[30] Guidi[Della Sede 33]; this would explain diff. between לֶחֶם and لَحْمٌ; yet verb rare and chiefly late),—**Qal** *Pf.* 3 pl לָחֲמוּ Pr 4[17]; *Impf* 2 ms תִּלְחַם Pr 23[6], 1 s אֶלְחָם ψ 141[4]; *Imv.* mpl. לַחֲמוּ Pr 9[5], *Inf. cstr.* לְחוּם Pr 23[1], *Pt pass* pl. cstr. לְחֻמֵי Dt 32[24], *eat* (mostly Pr), abs. Pr 23[1], sq acc. cogn. לֶחֶם 4[17] 23[6], sq בְּלַחְמִי 9[5], sq בְּמַנְעַמֵּיהֶם ψ 141[4] eat *of their dainties*, לְחֻמֵי רֶשֶׁף Dt 32[24] (poem) *eaten up with the Fire-bolt*, fig. of pestilence (Dr)

לֶחֶם [296] **n.m.**[1 S 9 7] and (rarely) **f.**[Gn 49, 20] (vid. infr, and Dr[1 S 10, 4]) bread, food (Ph. לחם *bread*; NH לֶחֶם, Aram לַחְמָא, ܠܰܚܡܳܐ, as Heb.; Ar. لَحْمٌ *flesh, meat* (cf. Fra[30])),—abs ל׳ Gn 3[19]+; לָחֶם Gn 31[54]+; לָחֶם ψ 14[4]+2 t.; cstr. לֶחֶם Ho 9[4]+; sf לַחְמִי Jb 3[24]+, לַחְמְךָ Ob[7]+, לַחְמָם Ho 9[4b], +v[4a] (for MT לָהֶם), We GASm Now, + etc.,—**1. a.**

bread, the ordinary food of early Hebrews (Benz $^{Arch. 84 ff.}$ Now$^{Arch. i. 109 ff.}$) Ex 21^{14} (E), Nu 21^{5} Jos 9$^{5.12}$ (JE), Dt 8^{3} 23^{5} Ex 16^{3} (P) +; כִּכַּר־ל׳ *loaf of bread* 1 S 2^{36} + (vid. כִּכָּר sub כרר), and without ככר (always c. num.) †1 S 10^{4} 16^{20} (v. Dr), 17^{17} 21^{4} 25^{18} 2 S 16^{1} 1 K 14^{3} 2 K 4^{42}†; חַלַּת ל׳ *cake of bread* 2 S 6^{19} Ex 29^{23} + (v. חַלָּה sub I. חלל); made from barley (שְׂעֹרִים) Ju 7^{13} 2 K 4^{42} (v. also לֶחֶם supr.); from wheat-flour (סֹלֶת חִטִּים) Ex 29^{2} (P); cf. the mixture Ez 4^{9}; made by baking (אפה) Is 44$^{15.19}$ Lv 26^{26} (H; cf. Je 37^{21}); פַּת־ל׳† *a bit of bread* 1 S 2^{36} 1 K 17^{11} Pr 28^{21}, cf. Ez 13^{19}, as modest term for a hospitable meal Gn 18^{5} (J), Ju 19^{5} 1 S 28^{22}†; disting. from meat (flesh), Gn 27^{17} (J), 1 S 25^{11} 1 K 17$^{6.6}$ Ex 16$^{8.12}$ (also v^{3} supr.), 29$^{32.34}$ Lv 8^{31} (all P), 23^{18} (H), 1 Ch 12^{40} ψ 78^{20} Dn 10^{3}; = a meal 1 S 20^{27}, אָכַל ל׳ = *take a meal* Gn 31$^{54.54}$ 37^{25} 43$^{25.32}$ +; אכל לַחְמִי ψ 41^{10} *eat my bread*, establishing an obligation, cf. Ob^{7} (rd. אֹכְלֵי ל׳ acc. to Marti ^{KauAT}; del. ל׳ 𝔊 Hi We, cf. VB) עֹשֶׂה ל׳ מַטֵּה = *make a feast* Ec 10^{19}; *staff of bread* (as *support* of life), only late †Ez 4^{16} 5^{16} 14^{13} Lv 26^{26} (H), ψ 105^{16}; cf. מִשְׁעַן ל׳ Is 3^{1} (gloss)†; *leavened bread* is ל׳ חָמֵץ Lv 7^{13}; *unleavened bread* is ל׳ מַצּוֹת Ex 29^{2} (both P); †(הַ)פָּנִים ל׳ *bread of the face* (of י׳; i.e. in his presence, Di$^{Lv 24.9}$ Dr$^{1 S 21.7}$): in the sanctuary 1 S 21^{7} 1 K 7^{48} = 2 Ch 4^{19}, Ex 25^{30} 35^{13} 39^{36}, without פ׳ 40^{23} (all P); = ל׳ הַתָּמִיד Nu 4^{7} (P), ל׳ קֹדֶשׁ 1 S 21^{5}; in Chr ל׳ הַמַּעֲרֶכֶת 1 Ch 9^{32} cf. 23^{29} Ne 10^{34}, מ׳ ל׳ 2 Ch 13^{11}; opp. ל׳ חֹל 1 S 21^{5}†; ל׳ תְּנוּפָה Lv 23^{17} *wave-loaf*; ל׳ (הַ)בִּכּוּרִים v^{20} 2 K 4^{42} *bread of first-fruits*. †**b.** = *bread-corn*, the material from which bread is made, i.e. wheat, barley, etc.: Gn 41$^{54.55}$ (E), 47$^{13.15.17.17.19}$ (J), 49^{20} (poem in J), Is 28^{28} 30^{23} 55^{10} Je 5^{17} Ez 48^{18} Jb 28^{5} Pr 28^{3} ψ 104^{14}; ל׳ הָאָרֶץ Nu 15^{19} (P), ארץ ל׳ 2 K 18^{32} = Is 36^{17}†. **2.** *food* in general: **a.** of man, Ju 13^{16} (kid, v^{15}), 1 S 14$^{24.24.28}$ (honey), 28^{20} 30^{12} Pr 22^{9} 27$^{27.27}$ (goat's milk) +; נֹתֵן ל׳ לְכָל־בָּשָׂר ψ 136^{25}. †**b.** of animals, Pr 6^{8} 30^{25} 65^{25} Jb 24^{5} ψ 147^{9}†. **c.** of God (in sacrifices): †ל׳ אֱלֹהֵיהֶם (cf. RS$^{Sem. i. 207, 2nd ed., 224}$) Lv 21^{6} cf. v$^{8.17.21.22}$, 22^{25} (all H), cf. Nu 28^{2} (P), Ez 16^{19} 44^{7}, and ל׳ מְגֹאָל Mal 1^{7}; also (ל׳) ל׳ אִשֶּׁה Lv 3$^{11.16}$ Nu 28^{24} (all P)†. **3.** other phrases and fig. uses are: **a.** ל׳ רֶשַׁע Pr 4^{17} (acc. cogn. c. לָחַם), prob. = *food gained by wickedness* (‖ יֵין חֲמָסִים), cf. ל׳ שֶׁקֶר 20^{17}, ל׳ כְּזָבִים 23^{3}; ל׳ עַצְלוּת 31^{27} = *bread of idleness*, i.e. unearned; ל׳ חֻקִּי Pr 30^{8} (opp. to riches and poverty, v. חֹק); ל׳ לַחַץ 1 K 22^{27} = 2 Ch 18^{26}, vid. לַחַץ infr.; ל׳ הָעֲצָבִים ψ 127^{2}, vid. II. עָצָב; ל׳ אוֹנִים Ho 9^{4}, vid. אָוֶן, p. 20 a; ל׳ אֲנָשִׁים Ez 24$^{17.22}$ of food offered to mourners, cf. Je 16^{7} (where ins. ל׳ 𝔊 Gf Gie); שַׁלַּח לחמך על־פני המים Ec 11^{1} usually interpr. of benevolent giving (cf. Now); De al. of sea-commerce in bread-stuffs, cf. Pr 31^{14}. **b.** fig. לַחְמֵנוּ הֵם Nu 14^{9} (JE) *our food are they*, i.e. we will devour, destroy, them (cf. Dt 7^{16}); ל׳ דִּמְעָתִי ψ 42^{4} cf. 80^{6} (vid. אכל, p. 37^{b} supr.); ל׳ of evil deeds of wicked Jb 20^{14}; עֵץ בְּלַחְמוֹ Je 11^{19} appar. fig. of destroying the *prophet and his house*, but read prob. בְּלֵחוֹ *in its freshness* (i.e. untimely), so Hi Gf Che Gie (vid. לֵחַ sub לחח supra).

†לַחְמִי **n.pr.m.** brother of Goliath of Gath (q.v.) slain by Elhanan, acc. to 1 Ch 20^{5} (את לחמי; 𝔊 Ελεμεε, Λεεμει, Λοομι); orig. reading prob. (as in ‖ 2 S 21^{19}) בֵּית הַלַּחְמִי q.v. p. 112^{a} supra.

†לַחְמָס **n.pr.loc.** in Judah (32 Codd. לחמם);—Jos 15^{40}, 𝔊 Μαχες, A𝔊L Λαμ(μ)ας; perh. = *El-laḥm*, c. 13 miles WNW. from Hebron, Kn$^{ad loc.}$ PEF$^{Mem. iii. 261}$ Buhl$^{Geogr. 192}$.

†לָחַץ **vb. squeeze, press, fig. oppress** (Ar. لَخَصَ; Chr.-Pal. لحص Schwally $^{Idioticon 48}$ (with which Nö$^{M 74}$ comp. Mand. הלאצא, *torture*, NS. لخص *press together, urge, exert oneself*); see also rare deriv. in Syr. PS^{1932});—**Qal** *Pf.* ל׳ Ju 4^{3} + 2 t. etc.; *Impf.* sf. יִלְחָצֵנִי ψ 56^{2}; 3 fs. וַתִּלְחַץ Nu 22^{25}, etc.; *Pt.* pl. לֹחֲצִים Ex 3^{9} + 2 t., etc.—**1.** *squeeze, press:* sq. acc. + אֶל Ju 1^{34} Nu 22^{25b} (J); sq. acc. + בְּ instr. 2 K 6^{32} shut the door *and press him* (back, out) *with the door.* **2.** *oppress:* sq. acc. pers. Ex 22^{20} (‖ הוֹנָה), 23^{29} (both E), ψ 56^{2}; of people Ex 3^{9} (E; + acc. cogn.), Ju 2^{18} 4^{3} 6^{9} 10^{12} 1 S 10^{18} Am 6^{14} 2 K 13$^{4.22}$ Je 30^{20} ψ 106^{42}; abs. Is 19^{20}. **Niph.** *Impf.* 3 fs. וַתִּלָּחֵץ Nu 22^{25a} (J) *squeeze oneself*, of Balaam's ass, sq. אֶל־הַקִּיר.

†לַחַץ **n.m. oppression, distress**;—ל׳ abs. 1 K 22$^{27.27}$ + 5 t.; cstr. 2 K 13^{4} + 2 t.; sf. לַחֲצֵנוּ Dt 26^{4} ψ 44^{25};—*oppression* of Isr. Ex 3^{9} (E; + vb. cogn.), 2 K 13^{4} cf. Dt 26^{7} (‖ עָנְיֵנוּ, עֲמָלֵנוּ) ψ 44^{25} (‖ עָנְיֵנוּ); *oppr. of* (i.e. by) an enemy, ψ 42^{10} 43^{2}; in gen. Jb 36^{15} (‖ עֳנִי); לֶחֶם ל׳ וּמַיִם ל׳ 1 K 22^{27}

= 2 Ch 18[26] *bread of oppression and water of oppression*, i.e. prison-fare (> Klo *scanty* fare); cf. לֶחֶם צַר וּמַיִם לַ׳ Is 30[20], appar. of privations of a siege (cf. Che Di Du; on the apposition in these passages v. Ges § 131. 2 (b) Kö iii. § 333 p. q. Da Synt. § 29. e).

†[לָחַשׁ] **vb. whisper, charm** (NH *id.*; Aram. לְחַשׁ, ܠܚܫ; Eth. ለሐሰ: *whisper*, v. RS JPh xiv. 1885, 122, possibly originally serpent-charming);—**Pi.** *Pt.* pl. קוֹל מְלַחֲשִׁים ψ 58[6] *voice of whisperers* (i.e. *serpent-charmers*; ‖ חוֹבֵר חֲבָרִים). **Hithp.** *whisper together*, *Impf.* יִתְלַחֲשׁוּ c. עַל ψ 41[8]; *Pt.* pl. מִתְלַחֲשִׁים 2 S 12[19].

†לַחַשׁ **n.[m.]** a whispering, charming;—לַ׳ Is 26[16]; לָחַשׁ Ec 10[11] Is 3[3] Je 8[17]; pl. לְחָשִׁים Is 3[20].—**1.** *serpent-charming* Ec 10[11]; נְבוֹן לָחַשׁ Is 3[3] (prob. more general). **2.** *charms, amulets*, worn by women, Is 3[20]. **3.** *whisper of prayer*, צָקוּן לַחַשׁ Is 26[16] *they pour forth a whisper of prayer* (but Koppe Bö Gr Di Du rd. צֹקֶן לַחַשׁ '*Zauberzwang*,' *compulsion of* (*by*) *magic*).

†לוֹחֵשׁ **n.pr.m.** (=*whisperer*) only c. art. הַלּ׳, a chief of the people Ne 3[12] 10[25].

לָט v. sub לוט.

†לֹט **n.[m.]** myrrh, or '*ladanum*' (Gk.), an aromatic gum exuded by leaves of *cistus-rose*, *cistus villosus*, Tristr FFP. 235, and esp. Nat. Hist. Bib., 458 ff.; Ri HWB 897, cf. Löw No. 79 Di Gn 37, 25 Now Arch. i. 64 (Sab. לדן, Sab. Denkm.[84]; As. *ladunu* (fr. Damascus) cf. Schr COT Gn 37, 25, MBAk. 1881, pp. 413 ff.; Ar. لَاذَن, whence Gk. λήδανον, λάδανον Hdt iii. 112);—נְכֹאת וּצְרִי וָלֹט Gn 37[25], merchandise of Ishmaelite caravan, cf. 43[11], present to Joseph (both J; 𝔊 στακτή).

לטא (√of following; meaning unknown).

†לְטָאָה **n.f.** a kind of lizard (NH *id.*);—named as unclean Lv 11[30] (with כֹּחַ, אֲנָקָה, צָב, חֹמֶט, תִּנְשָׁמֶת), 𝔊 χαλαβώτης, 𝔙 *stellio*.—Vid. Di ad loc. Tristr Nat. Hist. Bib. 266 ff.

†[לָטַשׁ] **vb. hammer, sharpen, whet** (NH *id., hammer, tap*; Aram. לְטַשׁ, ܠܛܫ *sharpen*; Ar. لَطَسَ *strike, tap*);—**Qal** *Impf.* יִלְטוֹשׁ Jb 16[9] ψ 7[13]; *Inf. cstr.* לִלְטוֹשׁ 1 S 13[20]; *Pt.* לֹטֵשׁ;—**1.** *hammer*, only *Pt.* = *hammerer*, sq. כָּל־חֹרֵשׁ Gn 4[22] (J). **2.** *sharpen* sword, חֶרֶב (acc.) ψ 7[13]; cf. 1 S 13[20], obj. קַרְדֹּם, אֵת, מַחֲרֶשֶׁת, מַחֲרֵשָׁה; fig. יִ׳ עֵינָיו לִי Jb 16[9] my foe *whets his eyes for me*. **Pu.** *Pt.* תַּעַר מְלֻטָּשׁ ψ 52[4] *a sharpened razor* (in sim. of evil tongue).

†לְטוּשִׁם **n.pr.gent.** Gn 25[3], descendants of Abraham and Keturah; 𝔊 Λατουσιειμ.

[לִיָה], לִיוֹת v. sub III. לוה.

לַיִל, לַ֫יְלָה 242 **n.m.** Gn 40, 5 **night** (NH *id.*; MI[15] (ב)ללה; Aram. לֵילְיָא, ܠܠܝܐ, ܠܶܠܝܳܐ; Ar. لَيْلٌ, لَيْلَةٌ; Eth. ሌሊት: all=*night*; As. *lîlâtu, evening* Dl HWB; meaning of √dubious; form probably לַיְלַי, and ending ־ָה radical, and not ה loc., Nö M 127 Dl Prol. 128 Ges § 90. 2. c. R. Kö ii. p. 57, R. 1);—abs. לַ֫יְלָה Gn 19[33] + 214 t. + 2 t. Qr (v. infr.); לָ֑יְלָה Gn 1[5] + 3 t.; לַיִל Is 16[3] + Pr 31[18] La 2[19] Kt (Qr לַיְלָה); לֵיל Is 15[1.1] 21[1]; cstr. לֵיל Ex 12[42] Is 30[29]; pl. abs. לֵילוֹת 1 S 30[12] + 4 t.; cstr. *id.*, Is 21[8] + 5 t.;—**1.** lit. *night*, opp. day, Gn 8[22] (J), Dt 1[33] + very oft. (v. יוֹם); alternation of day and night divinely ordained Gn 1[5] (P), Je 33[20.20.25] +; מִיּוֹם עַד־לַ׳ Is 38[12.13] i.e. within one whole day; as close of day, עַד־לַ׳ 2 Ch 35[14]; as time of sacred חַג (לֵיל) Is 30[29]; of suffering and weeping לֵילוֹת עָמָל Jb 7[3], cf. ψ 6[7] 77[3] etc.; of pious desires, prayer, praise, meditation, etc. (sts. ‖ *by day*) Is 26[9] Jb 35[10] ψ 1[2] 22[3] 42[9] 77[7] 88[2] 92[3] 119[55], cf. 16[7] 17[3]; of night-service in Temple 134[1]; of sudden assault, or destruction, Is 15[1] Je 6[5] Ob[5] Jb 27[20] 34[20.25] 36[20]; divided into watches ψ 90[4]; לֵיל שִׁמֻּרִים Ex 12[42] v. sub שמר; c. num., denoting duration of time, †*forty days and forty nights* Gn 7[4.12] Ex 24[18] 34[28] Dt 9[9.11.18.25] 10[10] 1 K 19[8]; *three days and three nights* (שְׁלֹשָׁה לֵילוֹת) 1 S 30[12] Jon 2[1]; *seven days and seven nights* (שִׁבְעַת לֵילוֹת) Jb 2[13] †; מַרְאֹת הַלּ׳ † חֲלוֹם הַלּ׳ Gn 20[3] 31[24] (both E), 1 K 3[5]; Gn 46[2] (E); חֶזְיוֹן לַ׳ Jb 20[8] 33[15], חֶזְיֹנוֹת לַ׳ 4[13], חֲלוֹם חֲזוֹן לַ׳ Is 29[7] (cf. Mi 3[6] infr.) †; בִּן־לַ׳ Jon 4[10.10] v. בֵּן **8.** p. 121 b. Chiefly in adverb. phr.:—בַּחֲצִי הַלּ׳ *at midnight* Ex 12[29] + (v. חֲצִי, חָצוֹת p. 345 b), cf. בְּתוֹךְ הַלּ׳ † 1 K 3[20], בְּאִישׁוֹן לַ׳ Pr 7[9] †; בַּלּ׳ הַזֶּה Ex 12[8.12] *on this night* (P; the night of which one is speaking); בַּלּ׳ הַהוּא *on that night* Gn 19[35] (J) + oft., (P only Nu 14[1]); בַּלּ׳ הוּא Gn 19[33] 30[16]; so הַלּ׳ alone † 1 S 14[34], but del. 𝔊 We Kit, cf. Dr; Klo Bu rd. לַיהוה; הַלּ׳ *to-night* † Gn 19[5.34] 30[15] (all J), Nu 22[8.19] (E), Jos 2[2] 4[3]

(both JE), 2 S 17^{16} 19^{8} Ru 1^{12} 3$^{2.13}$, opp. מָחָר *to-morrow* 1 S 19^{11}; הַלּ׳ = *this night* just past, *last night* 1 S 15^{16} (cf Dr), כָּל־הַלּ׳ *all night* Ho 7^{6} (opp. בֹּקֶר), Ex 14$^{20.21}$ (J), Nu 11^{32} Jos 10^{9} (both JE), Ju 16$^{2.2}$ 19^{25} 1 S 15^{11} 31^{12} 2 S 2$^{29.32}$ 4^{7}; opp. כל־היום ההוא (of continuous action) 1 S 19^{24} 28^{20} Is 62^{6}, opp. יוֹמָם ψ 78^{14}; בְּכָל־לַ׳ ψ 6^{7} *every night* (prob.); cf כָּל־הַלֵּילוֹת Is 21^{8} *all the nights* (opp יוֹמָם)†; esp. לַיְלָה *by night* Nu 22^{20} (E) Jos 8^{3} (JE), Dt 16^{1} Nu 9^{16} (P) + 51 t.; of these Gn 14^{15} and Ex 13$^{21.22}$ (J) + 25 t. opp. יוֹמָם, covering all the time; otherwise Ju 6^{27} (opp. יוֹמָם), לַיְלָה וָיוֹם *night and day* 1 K 8^{29} Is 27^{3} Est 4^{16}, less oft. לילות ψ 16^{7}; הַלּ׳ *by night* †2 K 25^{4} (לֹ׳ in ‖ Je 52^{7}), Zc 1^{8} Ne 4^{16} (opp. הַיּוֹם)†; בַּלּ׳ *id.*, Je 6^{5} + 18 t. (chfly late; oft. opp יוֹמָם, בַּיּוֹם, etc.); בַּלַּיְלָה ψ 92^{3} (opp. בַּבֹּקֶר), 134^{1} Ct 3$^{1.8}$; בַּלֵּילוֹת† Ne 9^{19} (opp. בְּיוֹמָם); בְּלִיל Is 15^{1}, כַּלּ׳ *as at night* Jb 5^{14} (opp. צָהֳרַיִם)†. **2.** fig. שִׁיתִי כַלַּיִל צִלֵּךְ Is 16^{3} sim. of shadow of Zion as protection; more oft in gloomy sense, of avenging calamity without divine guidance or comfort לַיְלָה מֵחָזוֹן Mi 3^{6}, personal distress Jb 35^{10}, judgment perh. also Jb 36^{20} (Ew De Di Da; night of death Bu; 'unintelligible' Siegf); מַה־מִּלַּיְלָה מַה־מִּלֵּיל Is 21^{11} i.e. what hour of the night of calamity is it? cf. v^{12} (opp. בֹּקֶר).

†**לִילִית** **n.f. Lilith** (Milton Che *night-hag*), name of a female night-demon haunting desolate Edom; prob. borrowed fr. Bab., Is 34^{14} (NH *id.*, As. *lilîtu*, Dl$^{HWB\ 377}$; Syr. ܠܠܝܬܐ PS^{1951}; on the development of legends of Lilith in later Judaism, v. Bux$^{Lex\ Talmud.,\ s.v.}$ Che$^{ad\ loc.}$ Grünbaum$^{ZMG\ xxxi.\ 1877,\ 250\ f.}$—Connexion with לילה perhaps only apparent, a popular etymology).

לִין v. לוּן.

†[**לִיץ**] **vb. scorn** (NH *id.*; vb. not in cognates, cf. Ph. מליץ *interpreter* CIS$^{22.44.88}$; Ar. لَاصَ is *turn aside* (intrans.); hence perh. prop *speak indirectly* or *obliquely*, Fl$^{De\ Pr.\ 1,\ 6}$);—**Qal** *Pf.* 3 m. לָצְתָּ Pr 9^{12}; *Impf.* יָלִיץ 3^{34} + 2 t., *Pt.* לֵץ 9^{7} + 11 t.; pl. לֵצִים ψ 1^{1} + 3 t.;—*scorn*, וְלַצְתָּ לְבַדְּךָ תִשָּׂא Pr 9^{12} *if thou scornest thou alone shalt bear it* (opp. חָכַמְתָּ), c. acc 14^{9} 19^{28}; c. לְ, לַלֵּצִים הוּא־יָלִיץ *scorners he (God) scorneth* 3^{34}, הַלֵּץ the scorner is proud and haughty 21^{24}, delights in scorning 1^{22}, is incapable of discipline 9^{7}, reproof 9^{8} 15^{12}, or rebuke 13^{1}, cannot find wisdom 14^{6}; is an abomination 24^{9}, should be avoided ψ 1^{1}; smitten and punished for the benefit of the simple Pr 19^{25} 21^{11} and banished for the removal of contention 22^{10}; judgment is prepared for him 19^{29}; ‖ עָרִיץ Is 29^{20}; wine is a scorner Pr 20^{1}.—**Hiph.** *Pf.* 3 mpl. sf הֱלִיצֻנִי ψ 119^{51}; *Pt* מליץ Gn 42^{23} Jb 33^{23}; pl. cstr מְלִיצֵי 2 Ch 32^{31}, sf. מְלִיצַי Jb 16^{20}; מְלִיצֶיךָ Is 43^{27};—**1.** *deride* Jb 16^{20} ψ 119^{51}. **2.** Pt *interpreter* Gn 42^{23} (E), fig. of intermediaries between God and man, Jb 33^{23} Is 43^{27}; *ambassador* 2 Ch 32^{31}. **Po'lel** *Pt* pl. לֹצְצִים (מְ dropped Ko$^{ii\ 479}$) *scorners* Ho 7^{5}. **Hithp.** *Impf.* תִּתְלוֹצָצוּ *act as a scorner, shew oneself a mocker*, Is 28^{22}.

†**לָצוֹן** **n.[m.] scorning**, Pr 1^{22}; אַנְשֵׁי לָצוֹן *men of scorning, scorners* = לֵצִים 29^{8} Is 28^{14}.

†**מְלִיצָה** **n.[f.] satire, mocking-poem** Hb 2^{6}, also Pr 1^{6} (al. here *figure, enigma*)

ליש (√ of foll., Thes לוּשׁ; perhaps = *be strong* (Thes) cf. Ar. لَثَّ, لَوْثٌ, **strength**; لَاثَ (med. ى) III v. *be strong*, etc., appar. denom. = *be lion-like*).

†I **לַיִשׁ** **n.m.**$^{Jb\ 4.\ 11}$ **lion** (Ar. لَيْثٌ, 𝔗 לֵיתָא; As. *nešu*, *lion* is comp by Hal (cf. Hpt$^{KAT\ 2.\ 510}$) Ba$^{ZA\ iii\ 1888,\ 60}$);—*lion* Jb 4^{11} Is 30^{6} (‖ לָבִיא), לַ׳ גִּבּוֹר בַּבְּהֵמָה Pr 30^{30}.

†II. **לַיִשׁ** **n.pr.loc.** (on meaning *lion*, cf. RS$^{Sem.\ i.\ 156\ (om\ 2nd\ ed.)}$);—former name of Dan, in extreme north of Canaan, Ju 18$^{7.14.27.29}$ (v. דָּן p. 192 b); 𝔊 Λαισα, = לֶשֶׁם q.v., cf Buhl$^{Geogr.\ §\ 124}$.

†III **לַיִשׁ** **n.pr.m.** father of Michal's second husband, 1 S 25^{44} + 2 S 3^{15} Qr (Kt לוּשׁ), 𝔊 Αμεις, Σελλης, A Λα(ε)ις, 𝔊 L Ιωας, Σελλειμ.

†**לַיְשָׁה** **n pr.loc.** N. of Jerus. Is 10^{30} (perh. akin to III. לַיִשׁ, v. Di); site unknown; v. Kasteren$^{ZPV\ xiii.\ 101}$ conj *'Isawiye*, village two miles NE. fr. Jerus. (PEF$^{Map;\ Mem.\ iii\ 37}$ Rob$^{BR\ i.\ 437}$ cf Buhl$^{Geogr.\ 175}$), 𝔊 ἐν Σα, Λαισα.

לְכָה = **לֵךְ** *Imv.* of הָלַךְ q.v.

לָכַד $_{121}$ **vb. capture, seize, take** (by lot) (Ph. לכד *take out, choose* (?); 𝔗 לְכַד as BH; Ar لَكَدَ is *strike, push*, with the hand, etc., مِلْكَد *pestle*, cf mod. لَكَّد *attack* Wetzst$^{ZMG\ xxii.\ 1868,\ 140}$,

לָכַד stick or cleave to), —**Qal** *Pf.* לׅ' Jos 8^{1}+, לָכַדְתִּי 2 S 12^{27} etc; *Impf.* 3 ms יִלְכּוֹד Am 3^{5}, וַיִּלְכֹּד Ju 8^{12}+, etc, *Imv.* ms sf. לָכְדָהּ 2 S 12^{28}, mpl לִכְדוּ, *Inf abs.* לָכוֹד Am 3^{5}; *cstr* sf לְלָכְדֵנִי Je 18^{22}, לְלָכְדָהּ 32^{24}; *Pt* לֹכֵד Jb 5^{13} Pr 16^{32},—**1.** *capture, seize* (not in P) c acc., usu a city or town, in war Ju 1$^{8.12}$ Jos 8^{21} 10^{1} (JE), Dt 2^{34}+48 t (but Ju 1^{18} del. as gloss Bu Kit GFM al); land Jos 10^{42} (D), Dn 11^{18}; water-courses (fords), Ju 3^{28} 7$^{24\,24}$ 12^{5}; obj men (usu. princes, kings) in battle Ju 7^{25} 8$^{12\,14}$ Jos 11$^{12.17}$ (D), 2 Ch 22^{9} 33^{11}; captives and spoils 2 S 8^{4} = 1 Ch 18^{4}; of Saul's seizing the kingdom (הַמְּלוּכָה), i e acquiring it actually by force of arms 1 S 14^{47}, also of Samson's *catching* the foxes Ju 15^{4}; of a lion *catching* his prey Am 3^{4}; of a trap, snare, לָכוֹד יִלְכּוֹד 3^{5}. †**2.** fig of entrapping men Je 5^{26} ψ 35^{8}, cf Pr 5^{22} Jb 5^{13} and (of a pit) Je 18^{22}. †**3.** of *taking* by lot Jos 7$^{14\,14\,14\,17}$ (JE; v. **Niph. 3**).

†**Niph.** *Pf* נִלְכַּד La 4^{20}; 3 fs. נִלְכְּדָה 1 K 16^{18}+, etc, *Impf* יִלָּכֵד Is 24^{18} Je 48^{44}; יִלָּכֶד בָּהּ Ec 7^{26}, וַיִּלָּכֵד Jos 7^{16}+, etc, *Pt* נִלְכָּד Jos 7^{15};— **1.** *be captured* in war, of city 1 K 16^{18} 2 K 18^{10} Je 38$^{28\,28}$ 48$^{1\,41}$ 50$^{2\,9.24}$ 51$^{31\,41}$ Zc 14^{2}, of men Je 51^{56} La 4^{20} (cf. **Qal 1**). **2.** of men, *be caught*, viz. in a snare or trap, only fig, usu by divine judgment Is 8^{15} 24^{18} 28^{13} ψ 9^{16} 59^{13} Pr 6^{2} 11^{6} Je 6^{11} 8^{9}; so of Moab Je 48$^{7\,44}$, of being *ensnared* by a woman Ec 7^{26}; of being *caught* by cords of distress, בְּחַבְלֵי עֹנִי, Jb 36^{8}. **3.** *be taken* by lot Jos 7$^{15\,16.17\,18}$ (all JE), 1 S 10$^{20.21\,21}$ 14$^{41.42}$ (cf. **Qal 3**).

†**Hithp.** *Impf.* 3 mpl, יִתְלַכְּדוּ וְלֹא יִתְפָּרָדוּ Jb 41^{9} *they grasp each other, and cannot be separated*, of crocodile's scales (‖ אִישׁ בְּאָחִיהוּ יְדֻבָּקוּ), פְּנֵי תְהוֹם יִתְלַכָּדוּ Jb 38^{30} *the face of the deep compacts* (of freezing; ‖ כָּאֶבֶן מַיִם יִתְחַבָּאוּ, vbs transp, plausibly, by Me Bi Siegf Bu)

†[לֶכֶד] **n** [**m.**] **a taking, capture** (cf. ψ 9^{16}) וְשָׁמַר רַגְלְךָ מִלָּכֶד Pr 3^{26} (subj י׳).

†[מַלְכֹּדֶת] **n.f. a catching instrument,** i e **a snare, trap,** only fig, sf מַלְכֻּדְתּוֹ עֲלֵי נָתִיב Jb 18^{10} of the wicked (‖ טָמוּן בָּאָרֶץ חַבְלוֹ)

לְכָה, לְכָה *Imv* fr הָלַךְ q v.; לְכָה also for לְךָ *to thee* †Gn 27^{37}.

†לֵכָה **n.pr.loc.** in Judah 1 Ch 4^{21}; unknown. 𝔊 Ληχα, Λαιχα

†לָכִישׁ **n.pr.loc.**—so Jos 10^{3}+; c ה loc. לָכִישָׁה Jos 10^{31}+5 t.,—Canaanitish (Amorit) city, with king, Jos 10$^{3.5.23}$ (all JE), v^{31} 12^{11} (both D); (=Tel el-Amarna *Lakiša, Lakisi* Wkl$^{TA\ Tablets,\ Nos.\ 217,\ 218,\ 180,\ 181}$); captured by Jos 10$^{32.33.34\,35}$ (all D); reckoned to Judah Mi 1^{13} Je 34^{7} Jos 15^{39} (P), cf. 2 K 14$^{19\,19}$ = 2 Ch 25$^{27\,27}$, 2 Ch 11^{9} Ne 11^{30}, base of Assyrian operations 2 K 18^{14}, cf. 2 Ch 32^{9}, also 2 K 18^{17} 19^{8} = Is 36^{2} 37^{8} (=As *Lakisu* Schr$^{COT\ 2\ K\ 18,\ 13}$), prob = mod. *Tell el-Hesy*, c 33 miles SW. from Jerusalem FJB$^{Mound\ of\ Many\ Cities,\ 1893}$ Buhl$^{Geogr\ §\ 103}$ GASm$^{Geogr\ 234}$, > *Umm el-Lâkis* vdVelde$^{Mem\ 320}$ Guérin$^{Judée\ II\ 299\ ff}$, *Um Lâkis* opp by Rob$^{BR\ II\ 47}$.—𝔊 Λαχεις

לוּלֵי sub [לוּלֵי] v. לְלָאוֹת כֵּן v לָכֵן

†לָמַד **vb. exercise in, learn** (NH *id.*, *be accustomed to, learn*, Aram לְמַד (rare) *learn;* Syr. ܠܡܰܕ Pa *accustom, combine;* Ettaph *be taught*, etc; As *lamâdu, learn*, Dl$^{Prol.\ 29}$);— **Qal** *Pf* 3 ms. לׅ' Is 26^{10}, 1 s לָמַדְתִּי Pr 30^{3}+3 t. Pf, *Impf* 3 ms יִלְמַד Dt 17^{19}, 1 s אֶלְמְדָה ψ 119^{73}; 3 pl יִלְמְדוּן Dt 4^{10}+12 t Impf; *Imv* לִמְדוּ Is 1^{17}, *Inf abs.* לָמֹד Je 12^{16}, *cstr.* sf. לָמְדִי ψ 119^{7}, *Pt. pass* cstr. לְמוּדֵי 1 Ch 5^{8},—*learn* something, c. acc Dt 5^{1} ψ 119$^{7\,71.73}$ 106^{35} Pr 30^{3} Is 2^{4} 26$^{9.10}$ 29^{24} Je 12$^{16\,16}$ Mi 4^{3}, c. אֶל Je 10^{2}, c *inf.* Dt 18^{9} Is 1^{17} Ez 19$^{3.6}$, לְיִרְאָה Dt 4^{10} 14^{23} 17^{19} 31^{13}, וְיָרְאוּ Dt 31^{12}, לְמוּדֵי מִלְחָמָה *trained* to war 1 Ch 5^{18} **Piel** *Pf* 3 ms. לִמַּד Ec 12^{9}, 2 m sf. לִמַּדְתַּנִי ψ 71^{17} +7 t. Pf, Impf. יְלַמֵּד ψ 25^{9}, יְלַמֵּד Jb 21^{22}; 2 ms sf. תְלַמְּדֶנּוּ ψ 94^{12}; 1 s. אֲלַמְּדָה ψ 51^{15}, 3 mpl יְלַמְּדוּן Dt 4^{10}+12 t Impf; *Imv.* sf. לַמְּדֵנִי ψ 25^{4}+12 t Imv., *Inf* לַמֵּד Je 32^{33}+9 t, *Pt.* מְלַמֵּד Dt 4^{1}+7 t. Pt,—*teach*, abs 2 Ch 17$^{7\,9.9}$ ψ 60^{1}, *teach* some one something, c double acc. Dt 4$^{5\,14}$ 5^{28} 11^{19} 31$^{19.22}$ Ju 3^{2} 2 S 1^{18} (?), ψ 25$^{4\,9}$ 34^{12} 51^{15} 94^{10} 119$^{12.26.64\,66.68.108.124\,135.171}$ 132^{12} Ec 12^{9} Is 40^{14} Je 2^{33} 9$^{13\,19}$ 13^{21} Dn 1^{4}; c acc. pers Dt 4^{10} ψ 25^{5} 71^{17} Ct 8^{2} Is 48^{17} Je 31^{34} 32$^{33.33}$ Ezr 7^{10}, acc. rei Jb 21^{22}, acc pers לְ rei 2 S 22^{35} = ψ 18^{35}, ψ 144^{1}; acc. rei לְ pers. Jb 21^{22}, acc. pers מִן rei ψ 94^{12}, acc pers בְּ rei Is 40^{14}; acc. pers. inf. rei Dt 4^{1} 6^{1} 20^{18} ψ 143^{10} Je 9^{4} 12^{16}; מְלַמְּדַי *my teachers* ψ 119^{99} Pr 5^{13}. **Pual** *Pf.* 3 ms. לֻמַּד Je 31^{18}, *Pt* pl cstr מְלֻמְּדֵי 1 Ch 25^{7} Ct 3^{8}; f מְלֻמָּדָה Is 29^{13} Ho 10^{11},—*trained*, as soldiers Ct 3^{8}, singers 1 Ch 25^{7}, a bullock to the yoke Ho 10^{11}; *taught*, of a human command Is 29^{13}.

לָמֻד **adj.** taught;—לִ׳ Je 2^{24}; pl. למודים Is $50^{4.4}$; cstr. לִמּוּדֵי Is 54^{13}, לִמֻּדֵי Je 13^{23}; sf. לִמֻּדָי Is 8^{16};—**1.** *taught*, as disciples Is 8^{16} $50^{4.4}$ 54^{13}. **2.** *accustomed to* something, לִמֻּד מדבר Je 2^{24} (wild ass) *accustomed to the wilderness*; לִמֻּדֵי הָרֵעַ 13^{23} *accustomed to do evil.*

† [מַלְמָד] **n.[m.]** ox-goad,—cstr. מַלְמַד Ju 3^{31}.

† תַּלְמִיד **n.[m.]** scholar (late; NH) 1 Ch 25^{8}.

לָמָּה, לָמָה, לָמָּה, לָמָה v מָה **4 d.**

לְמוֹ poet. for לְ, v. p. 518 a.

† לְמוּאֵל, לְמוֹאֵל **n.pr.m.** king of Massa (prob., v. מַשָּׂא); לְמוּ׳ Pr 31^{1}, לְמוֹ׳ v^{4}.

לְמוֹאֵל Ne 12^{38} rd לִשְׂמֹאל, v. שׂמאל.

† לֶמֶךְ **n.pr.m.** (on orig form cf. Lag$^{BN 77}$, conj. as to meaning Bu$^{Urgesch\ 102, 129}$);—לֶ׳ Gn 4^{19} + 7 t; לָמֶךְ 4^{18} + 2 t;—**1.** son of מְתוּשָׁאֵל (Cainite) Gn $4^{18.19.23.23.24}$ (all J). **2.** son of מְתוּשֶׁלַח (Sethite) Gn $5^{25.26.28.30.31}$ (all P), 1 Ch 1^{3}.—𝔊 Λαμεχ.

לְמִן, לְמִנִּי v. מִן **9 b.**

לְמַעַן v. מַעַן sub ענה.

לַע v. sub I. לוע.

† [לָעַב] **vb.** jest (NH Hiph. *id.*; 𝔗 לְעַב Ethpa. *id.*; Syr. ܠܥܒ Ethpa. *mock, delight oneself, be greedy*; Ar. لَعِبَ *play, sport, jest*);—only **Hiph.** *Pt.* וַיִּהְיוּ מַלְעִבִים בְּ׳ 2 Ch 36^{16} *and they were* (continually) *making jest at* the messengers of God.

† [לָעַג] **vb.** mock, deride; also (Niph.) stammer, poet. (NH Hiph. *id.*; 𝔗 לעג Aph *id*, ܠܓܠܓ *stutter* (cf. NH לגלג *mock*, 𝔗 לַגְלֵג *id*, Syr. ܠܓܠܓ *stutter*, Ar. لَجْلَجَ *id*)),—**Qal** *Pf.* 3 fs. לָעֲגָה 2 K 19^{21} Is 37^{22}; *Impf.* יִלְעֲגוּ Jb 22^{19} ψ 2^{4}, יִלְעַג Jb 9^{23}, 3 fs. תִּלְעַג Pr 30^{17}; 2 ms. תִּלְעָג ψ 59^{9}, וַתִּל׳ Jb 11^{3}, 1 s. אֶלְעַג Pr 1^{26}; 3 mpl. יִלְעֲגוּ־ ψ 80^{7}, *Pt.* לֹעֵג Pr 17^{5} Je 20^{7},—*mock, deride, have in derision*, of Jerus. triumphing over enemy (c לְ pers vel rei) 2 K 19^{21} = Is 37^{22} (‖ בזה), of the innocent Jb 22^{19} (‖ שׂמח); of God (c. לְ) 9^{23} ψ 2^{4} 59^{9}, abs. of wisdom Pr 1^{26} (‖ שׂחק), of wicked (c. לְ) Pr 17^{5} (‖ שׂמח), 30^{17} (‖ בוז), Je 20^{7} (‖ שׂחק); so also perh ψ 80^{7} (read לָנוּ for לָמוֹ with 𝔊 𝔖 𝔙), cf (abs.) Jb 11^{3}. **Niph.** *Pt.* עַם . . . נִלְעַג לָשׁוֹן Is 33^{19} *a people stammering of tongue* (i.e. barbarians, cf v^{8}; but rd. נעלג [√עלג] Gr$^{Monatsschr\ 1884\ 45}$, ‖ עִמְקֵי שָׂפָה). **Hiph.** (late; cf NH) *Impf.* 3 ms. וַיַּלְעֵג Ne 3^{33}; 2 ms. תַּלְעִיג Jb 21^{3}, 3 mpl. יַלְעִגוּ ψ 22^{8}, וַיַּלְעִגוּ Ne 2^{19}; *Pt* מַלְעִגִים 2 Ch 30^{10},—*mock, deride*, always in bad sense: c לְ pers Ne 2^{19} (‖ בזה), ψ 22^{8}; c. עַל־ pers. Ne 3^{33}; c. בְּ pers. 2 Ch 30^{10} (‖ השׂחיק); abs Jb 21^{3}—So also יַלְעִיג (or יִלְעַג) Pr 18^{1} for MT יִתְגַּלָּע Gr$^{1\ c.}$ (v גלע, p. 166 supra).

† לַעַג **n.[m.]** mocking, derision, (barbarous) stammering,—abs. לַ׳ Jb 34^{7} + 2 t + ψ 123^{4} (הַלּ׳ MT cstr. c. art.—so Kö$^{Synt\ §\ 303\ e}$—but prob insert לְ foll Hup Now Bae, cf. also Ges$^{§\ 127\ g}$), + Ez 23^{32} (but del. 𝔊B Hi Co Berthol), + 36^{4} (where Co reads בלע, but less prob., cf. Berthol); sf. לַעְגָּם Ho 7^{16} (v. infr); pl cstr לַעֲגֵי Is 28^{12} (v. infr.);—**1. a.** *mocking, derision*, ψ 123^{4} (‖ בוז), so appar. c. sf as gen obj Ho 7^{16} (but very dub, probably corrupt, cf. We Now); nearly = *blasphemy* Jb 34^{7}. **b.** = obj. of derision ψ 44^{14} = 79^{4} (‖ קֶלֶס, חֶרְפָּה); so also Ez 23^{32} (‖ צחק; si vera l., v. supr), 36^{4}. **2.** *stammerings* (of barbarous language), לַ׳ שָׂפָה Is 28^{11} (‖ לָשׁוֹן אַחֶרֶת; so Ew Brd Di Hup-Now$^{\ast\ 33,\ 19}$, De al. sub לָעֵג); but Gr$^{Monatsschr\ 1884,\ 45}$ reads עִלְּגֵי, √עלג.

† [לָעֵג] **adj.** mocking, only pl. cstr. as noun (si vera l), לַעֲגֵי מָעוֹג ψ 35^{16} *mockers of* מָעוֹג (q v), but text dub.; Che reads לַעֲגֵי, Schwally ZAW xi 1890, 258 לָעֲגוּ—To [לָעֵג] is also referred לַעֲגֵי Is 28^{11} by Ges De Che Du, < sub לַעַג q v.

† לַעְדָּה **n.pr.m.** a man of Judah 1 Ch 4^{21}, 𝔊 Μαδαθ, A Λαδα, 𝔊L Λαδηι.

† לַעְדָּן **n.pr.m. 1.** an Ephraimite 1 Ch 7^{26} 𝔊 Λαδ(δ)αν. **2.** a Gershonite 1 Ch $23^{7.8.9}$ $26^{21.21.21}$ 𝔊 Εδαν, A Λ(ε)αδαν, Χαδαν, 𝔊L Λααδαν.

לעה v. לוע.

† [לָעַז] **vb.** talk indistinctly, unintelligibly (NH *id*, in deriv (לַעַז *foreign language*, לֹעֵז *foreigner*), also *murmur, remonstrate*; Syr. ܠܥܙ *talk indistinctly*; Ar. لَغَزَ *distort*; IV. *talk obscurely, ambiguously*),—only **Qal** *Pt* עַם לֹעֵז ψ 114^{1} *a people talking unintelligibly* (‖ מִצְרַיִם).

†[לָעַט] **vb. swallow (greedily)** (NH *id.*, Hiph. *stuff* cattle with food; Syr. [illegible] *jaw;* cf. Ar. لَغَطَ *speak confusedly, utter indistinct sounds*);—only **Hiph.** *Imv.* ms. sf. causat. הַלְעִיטֵנִי Gn 25^{30} (J) *let me swallow*, sq. מִן rei.

†לַעֲנָה **n.f. wormwood** (NH *id.;* Ar. لَعْن is *curse* (vb. لَعَنَ *id.*), so Nab. לענת (vb. לען) cf. Cook$^{Gloss.}$);—only fig. of bitter things:—of perverted justice, Am 5^{7} 6^{12} (‖ ראשׁ); of result of idolatry, Dt 29^{17} (‖ *id.*); of י׳'s chastisement Je 9^{14} (‖ מֵי־ראשׁ), 23^{15} (‖ *id.*), La 3^{15} (‖ מְרוֹרִים), v^{19} (‖ ראשׁ); sim. of bitter (מָרָה) result of intercourse with strange woman Pr 5^{4}.—On *wormwood* (*Artemisia absinthium*, etc., Gk. ἀψίνθιον) cf. Löw$^{80 f. 401, 421}$ Tristr$^{Nat. Hist. Bib. 493}$.

לָעַע v. לוע.

לפד (√ of following; meaning unknown).

†לַפִּיד **n.m.**$^{Ju 15, 4}$ **torch** (NH *id.*);—ל׳ abs. Ju 15^{4} Is 62^{1}; cstr. Gn 15^{17} Zc 12^{6}; pl. לַפִּידִים Ju 15^{5} + 2 t., לַפִּדִים Ex 20^{18}, לַפִּדִים Ju 7^{16} + 3 t.; cstr. לַפִּידֵי Dn 10^{6}:—*torch*, Ju 7$^{16.20}$ 15$^{4.4.5}$ (kindled, הִבְעִיר אֵשׁ בְּ׳); לַפִּיד אֵשׁ Gn 15^{17} (+ תַּנּוּר עָשָׁן; JE), Zc 12^{6} (sim. of conquering power of [chiefs of] Judah; ‖ כִּיּוֹר אֵשׁ), לַפִּידֵי אֵשׁ Dn 10^{6} (sim. of eyes of angel in vision; ‖ וּפָנָיו כְּמַרְאֵה בָרָק); sim. of flashes (reflected from) darting chariots Na 2^{15} (‖ בְּרָקִים); ל׳ of lightning-flashes Ex 20^{18} (E; + קולת *thunder-peals*); of flashing water-drops expelled by snortings of crocodile Jb 41^{11} (‖ כִּידוֹדֵי אֵשׁ); of flame between cherubim Ez 1^{13} (‖ גַּחֲלֵי־אֵשׁ, אֵשׁ); sim. of Zion's glorious deliverance Is 62^{1} (‖ נֹגַהּ).—לַפִּיד Jb 12^{5} v. sub פִּיד.

†לַפִּידוֹת **n.pr.m.** husband of Deborah Ju 4^{4}; 𝔊 Λαφ(ε)ιδωθ.—On fem. form cf. GFM.

לִפְנֵי 1 K 6^{17} v. sub [פָּנֶה], פָּנִים.

לִפְנִים 1 K 6^{29} v. sub פְּנִימָה.

†[לָפַת] **vb. twist, turn, grasp with a twisting motion** (Ar. لَفَتَ *twist, wring;* As. *lapâtu, overthrow*, Dl$^{HWB 382}$);—**Qal** *Impf.* וַיִּלְפֹּת Ju 16^{29} sq. acc., Samson *grasped* the two middle columns. **Niph.** *Impf.* 3 ms. וַיִּלָּפֵת Ru 3^{8} the man started up *and twisted himself;* 3 mpl. יִלָּפְתוּ Jb 6^{18} the paths of their way [i.e. of the streams] *turn aside* (*twist, wind*, with lessening force), so AV Hi De Da Bu > Ew Ol Di Siegf Du, who read Qal יִלְפְּתוּ or Pi. יְלַפְּתוּ, making ארחות, =*caravans*, subj.

לָצוֹן, לֵץ v. sub ליץ.

†לַקּוּם **n.pr.loc.** northern border-town of Naphtali, Jos 19^{33} (P), 𝔊 Δωδαμ, 𝔊L Λακουμ. so also Lag$^{Onom. 275, 24}$; site unknown.

לָקַח 965 **vb. take** (NH *id.*, esp. *buy*, and (Niph.) *be taken in marriage;* MI$^{17.20}$ Impf. ואקח; Ph. לקח; As. *liḳû, laḳû* Dl$^{HWB 384}$; Ar. لَقِحَ *conceive* (of female), IV. *impregnate;* Eth. ለቀሐ: *receive;* Zinj. לקח DHM$^{Sendsch. 59}$; Aram. also Inscr. of Carpentr.^{3} (Imv. קחי); cf. Cook$^{Gloss. Aram. Inscr.}$);—**Qal** *Pf.* ל׳ Gn 2^{22}+, לָקָח 27^{36}+ (קָח Ez 17^{5} is textual error; om. 𝔊 𝔖 Co, cf. Ges$^{§ 19, 3, a}$); sf. לְקָחַנִי Gn 24^{7}, לְקָחָם Je 27^{20} (for קָחָם Ho 11^{3} rd. prob. אֶקָּחֵם 𝔊 𝔗 Ew St Sta$^{§ 384, 4}$ Now Che Or We); 2 ms. לָקַחְתָּ Gn 20^{3}+, etc.; *Impf.* יִקַּח Ex 21^{10}+, וַיִּקַּח Gn 2^{15}+ (Nu 16^{1} read וַיָּקָם Bö We Di Dr$^{2 S 18, 18}$; 1 S 30^{20} read וַיִּקְחוּ We Dr Kit Bu); sf. יִקָּחֵנִי 2 S 22^{17}+; יִקָּחֲךָ Jb 15^{12}; 3 fs. תִּקַּח Gn 38^{28}+; 1 s. אֶקַּח 14^{23}+, וָאֶקְחָה, Zc 11^{13}; 1 pl. נִקַּח Gn 34^{6}+, נִקְחָה 1 S 4^{3}+; וַנִּקַּח Dt 3^{8} 29^{7}; *Imv.* לְקַח Ex 29^{1} Pr 20^{16} + Ez 37^{16} (Co וְלָקַחְתָּ, after 𝔊); fs. לִקְחִי 1 K 17^{11}; usually קַח Gn 6^{21}+, קְחָה 15^{9}, sf. 3 ms. קָחֶנּוּ 1 S 16^{11} + 2 t.; sf. 3 fs. קָחֶנָּה Je 36^{14}; sf. 3 mpl. קָחֶם־נָא Gn 48^{9} (cf. Kö$^{I. 330}$ Ges$^{§ 61, 2}$); fs. קְחִי Is 23^{16} + 3 t.; mpl. קְחוּ Gn 42^{33}+, sf. 3 ms. קָחֻהוּ 1 K 20^{33}; *Inf. abs.* לָקוֹחַ Je 32^{14} + 2 t., לָקֹחַ Dt 31^{26}; *cstr.* קַחַת Je 5^{3}+; קַחַת־ 2 K 12^{9} (Kö$^{I. 318}$); usually c. prep. לָקַחַת Gn 4^{11}+, מִקַּחַת 1 K 22^{3}+, etc.; sf. קַחְתִּי Ez 24^{25}, קַחְתֵּךְ Gn 30^{15}+, etc.; *Pt. act.* לֹקֵחַ 27^{46}+, etc.; *pass.* pl. לְקֻחִים Pr 24^{11};—**1.** *take, take in the hand*, sq. acc. rei, Ex 7^{15} (J), 17^{5} (E), Nu 25^{7} (P), 2 K 4^{29} (all c. בְּיָד) 2 S 18^{14} (c. בְּכַף), cf. Gn 8^{9} (J), Ex 4^{17} 12^{22} (JE), Dt 15^{17} + oft.; Gn 40^{11} (E; of plucking grapes. 2 S 4^{6} read סֹקְלָה for לֹקְחֵי, v. חִטָּה, p. 334 supra, and סקל). This easily passes into **2.** *take and carry along* with oneself, כֶּסֶף קְחוּ בְיֶדְכֶם Gn 43^{12} (J), Jos 9^{11} (JE), 1 K 14^{3} 2 K 5^{5} 8$^{8.9}$ 9^{1} Pr 7^{20} (all c. בְּיָד); cf. Gn 43^{15} Jos 9^{4} (both JE), +. **3. a.** *take* from, or out of, sq. acc. rei vel pers., + מִן loc.: Gn 2^{22} (rib from man), 3^{22} (man from ground; both J); Dt 19^{12} 1 S 17^{49} 1 K 17^{19}+; וַיִּקַּח אֶת־הַחֶרֶב מֵעַל יְרֵךְ יְמִינוֹ Ju 3^{21} (i.e. *drew* it); c. ב instr. בְּמֶלְקָחַיִם ל׳ מֵעַל הַמִּזְבֵּחַ Is 6^{6}; sq. מִן partit. 2 S 12^{4}. **b.** *take, carry away:* Ez 3^{14} *spirit lifted me up and carried me away;* fig. of passion carrying one away Jb 15^{12}. **c.** *take away* from, so as to

deprive of, sq. acc. Gn 42^{36} (E); sq. acc. + מִן, Gn 44^{29} (מֵעִם; J), 1 K 11^{34} ψ 51^{13}; י׳ לֹקֵחַ אֶת־אֲדֹנֶיךָ מֵעַל רֹאשֶׁךָ 2 K 2^{3} *is about to take away thy lord from over thy head,* so v^{5}; cf. abs. אֵינֶנּוּ כִּי־לָ׳ אֹתוֹ אלהים Gn 5^{24} (P); more oft. without מִן, Gn 27$^{35.36}$ 30$^{15.15}$ 31^{1} (all J), Ju 11$^{13.15}$ 15^{6} 18^{24} 1 S 12$^{3.3}$ 2 S 12^{4} 1 K 11^{34} Jb 12^{20}; abs. Jb 1^{21}; אֶתֶּן־לְךָ מֶלֶךְ בְּאַפִּי וְאֶקַּח בְּעֶבְרָתִי Ho 13^{11}; of the sword, taking away its victims Ez 33$^{4.6}$; fig. of taking away understanding Ho 4^{11}. **d.** esp. *take away* life 1 K 19$^{10.14}$ ψ 31^{14} Pr 1^{19} Jon 4^{3}. **4.** *take* to or for a person: **a.** for oneself, sq. acc. + לְ, = *appropriate* to oneself Dt 7^{25} Nu 8^{16} (P), Dt 22^{7} 2 K 12^{6}; c. לְ as dat. comm., Zc 11^{7}; לָ׳ אֶת־שְׁנֵי יְלָדַי לוֹ לַעֲבָדִים 2 K 4^{1} *to take my two sons for himself for slaves;* so (without לְ reflex.), תִּקָּחֶנּוּ לְעֶבֶד עוֹלָם Jb 40^{28} *wilt thou take him as slave for ever?* **b.** = *procure, get,* sq. acc. + לְ, קְחוּ לָכֶם תֶּבֶן Ex 5^{11} (J) *get you straw;* לֹקֵחַ לוֹ קָלוֹן Pr 9^{7} *getteth to himself shame;* so oft., esp. קַח לְךָ, etc., Gn 6^{21} 12^{19} 16^{21} 45^{19} +; without לְ, Ne 5^{2} *let us procure corn,* and eat and live; of acquiring a field Pr 31^{16}. **c.** *take possession of,* sq. acc., of land Dt 29^{7} Jos 11$^{16.23}$ (all D), 2 Ch 16^{6}; cf. פְּקֻדָּתוֹ יִקַּח אַחֵר ψ 109^{8} *his office let another take;* fig. הַלַּיְלָה הַהוּא יִקָּחֵהוּ אֹפֶל Jb 3^{6} *that night—let darkness take possession of it!* **d.** = *select, choose,* וְאֶתְכֶם לָקַח י׳ Dt 4^{20}, cf. v^{34} (+ לוֹ), 1 K 11^{37}; of men Dt 1^{15} Jos 3^{12} (JE; + לָכֶם); + מִן Dt 1^{23} Jos 4^{2} (JE). **e.** esp. *take* in marriage: (1) for another, esp. a son, c. לְ, וְלָקַחְתָּ אִשָּׁה לִבְנִי Gn 24^{4} *and thou shalt take a wife for my son,* so v$^{7.38.40.48}$ (all J), 21^{21} (E), Je 29^{6b}; (2) more oft. for oneself, usu. c. לְ reflex. (sts. + לְאִשָּׁה), Gn 4^{19} 6^{2} 11^{29} 12^{19} (all J), + oft.; without לְ Gn 20$^{2.3}$ (E), etc. **f.** = *receive, accept,* esp. a bribe, gift, ransom, etc., 1 S 8^{3} 12$^{3c.4}$ (both sq. מִן), Am 5^{12} 2 K 5$^{15.16.20.23.26.26}$ ψ 15^{5}; interest-money Ez 18$^{13.17}$ 22^{12}; inheritance Jos 13^{8} 18^{7} (both D), Nu 34$^{14.14.15}$ (P); of earth, receiving Abel's blood Gn 4^{11} (J); chastisement Is 40^{2}; of *perceiving* a sound, Jb 4^{11} *mine ear received a whisper of it;* *receive* mentally: וְלָקַח בְּעָלָיו Ex 22^{10} (E) i.e. shall accept the oath as satisfactory; בָּרֵךְ לָקָחְתִּי Nu 23^{20} (JE), i.e. *I have received* (commandment by revelation) *to bless;* *receive* instruction Pr 24^{32} Je 2^{30} +; entanglements of temptation Pr 22^{25}. **g.** *take,* as preliminary to further action: Gn 31^{34} (E), *she took them* and put them; Ju 3^{25} *take* key and open; Jos 2^{4} *she took* the two men and hid them; 1 K 18^{4} Obadiah *took* 100 prophets and hid them; 19^{21} Elisha *took* the yoke of oxen and slew them, cf. 2 S 17^{19} 18^{18}; sts. wholly redundant, קְחוּ וַעֲשׂוּ עֲגָלָה חֲדָשָׁה 1 S 6^{7} *take and prepare a new cart,* etc.; somewhat different is הַלֹּקְחִים לְשׁוֹנָם וַיִּנְאֲמוּ נְאֻם Je 23^{31}, i.e. *they take* (= make use of) their own tongues, and talk oracles. **5.** *take* up, upon = *put* upon, sq. עַל: וַתִּקַּח תָּמָר אֵפֶר עַל־רֹאשָׁהּ 2 S 13^{19} *and Tamar put ashes upon her head;* וַיִּקָּחֶהָ עַל־הַחֲמוֹר Ju 19^{28}; cf. יִפְרֹשׂ כְּנָפָיו יִקָּחֵהוּ Dt 32^{11} *he spreadeth his wings, he taketh him up.* **6.** = *fetch:* קְחִי־נָא לִי מְעַט־מַיִם 1 K 17^{10} *fetch me, pray, a little water,* cf. v$^{11.11}$, 2 K 2^{20} 4^{41}; וְקַח־לִי מִשָּׁם שְׁנֵי גְּדָיֵי עִזִּים Gn 27^{9} *and fetch me thence two kids,* cf. v^{13} (J); + בְּיָדִי 1 S 21^{9}; an offering Lv 12^{8} (P; ‖ הֵבִיא v^{6}); c. human obj. oft. nearly = *summon,* לָקֹב אֹיְבַי לְקַחְתִּיךָ Nu 23^{11} (JE) *to curse mine enemies did I summon thee,* Ju 11^{5} 1 S 16^{11}; שְׁלַח וְקַח אֹתוֹ אֵלַי 1 S 20^{31} *send and bring him unto me;* 2 K 3^{15} 6^{13} +; of י׳, summoning his people from exile, מִשָּׁם יִקָּחֶךָ Dt 30^{4}. **7.** *take* = *lead, conduct* (with or without contact): וַיִּקַּח אֶת־שְׁנֵי בָנָיו עִמּוֹ Gn 48^{1}; גַּם בְּקַרְכֶם קְחוּ Ex 12^{32} (both E); וְאֶת־עַמּוֹ לָקַח עִמּוֹ Ex 14^{6} (J) *and his people he took with him;* cf. v^{7} (J), Jos 8^{1} (JE), Ju 4^{6}; אֶקָּחֲךָ אֶל־מָקוֹם אַחֵר Nu 23^{27} *I will take thee unto another place,* cf. v$^{14.28}$ (all JE); י׳ subj., וָאֶקַּח אֶת־אֲבִיכֶם Jos 24^{3} (E) *and I took your father* Abraham from beyond the river; הַצֵּל לְקֻחִים לַמָּוֶת Pr 24^{11} *rescue those led to death.* **8.** *take* = *capture, seize:* לָקַחְתִּי בְחָזְקָה 1 S 2^{16} *I will take by force,* sc. flesh; of spoils, בֶּצַע כֶּסֶף לֹא לָ׳ Ju 5^{19} *gain of silver they took not;* of capture of ark 1 S 5^{1}; bronze 2 S 8^{8}, etc.; territory Gn 48^{22} (E), Dt 3^{14}; cities Nu 21^{25} (JE), Dt 3^{14} Jos 11^{19} (D), 1 S 7^{14} 2 S 8^{1}; of capture of hippopotamus Jb 40^{24}; of seductions of woman, וְאַל־תִּקָּחֲךָ בְּעַפְעַפֶּיהָ Pr 6^{25} *and let her not capture thee with her eyelids.* **9.** *take* = *carry off:* **a.** as booty Gn 14^{11} 1 S 27^{9} 30$^{16.18.19.20}$ 1 K 14$^{26.26}$. **b.** as prisoners Gn 14^{12} 2 K 18^{32} = Is 36^{17}, 2 K 23^{34} = 2 Ch 36^{4}. **10.** in phr. *take* vengeance: וְנִקְחָה נִקְמָתֵנוּ מִמֶּנּוּ Je 20^{10} *and we will take our vengeance upon him;* abs. נָקָם אֶקָּח Is 47^{3} *vengeance will I take.*

†**Niph.** *Pf.* נִלְקַח 1 S 4^{22}; נִלְקָח 4^{11} Ez 33^{6}; 3 fs. נִלְקְחָה 1 S 4^{17}; *Impf.* 3 fs. וַתִּלָּקַח Est 2$^{8.16}$; 1 s. אֶלָּקַח

2 K 2^9, *Inf cstr.* הִלָּקַח 1 S $4^{19.21}$, sf. הִלָּקְחוֹ 1 S 21^7,—**1.** *be captured*, of ark 1 S $4^{11\ 17\ 19\ 21\ 22}$. **2.** *be taken away, removed*, of shewbread 1 S 21^7; of removal by death Ez 33^6, of translation of Elijah 2 K 2^9 (c. מֵעִם pers.) **3.** *be taken, brought* unto (אֶל־), only Est $2^{8\ 16}$

†**Pu.** *Pf* לֻקַּח Gn 3^{23}+, 3 fs לֻקְּחָה־ 2^{23}, 2 ms לֻקָּחְתָּ 3^{19}, etc.,—**1.** *be taken* from, out of (מִן of source) Gn 2^{23} $3^{19.23}$ (all J), cf וְלֻקַּח מֵהֶם קְלָלָה Je 29^{22} *and there shall be taken from them* (derived from their case) *a curse-formula*. **2.** =*be stolen* from, Ju 17^2 (לְ pers.) **3.** *be taken captive*, Je 48^{46}, cf Is 52^5 **4.** *be taken away, removed* (=**Niph. 2**), of Elijah's translation 2 K 2^{10} (c מֵאֵת pers.), of death Is 53^8 (c מִן, prob. instr.)

†**Hoph.** *Impf* יֻקַּח Gn 18^4+, etc.,—**1.** *be taken, brought* unto Gn 12^{15} (J, sq בֵּית *to the house of*), 18^4 (abs.) **2.** *be taken* out of Jb 28^2 (מִן of source), from, of Ez 15^3 (מִן partit.) **3.** *be taken away* from Is 49^{24} (מִן pers.), abs v^{25}.

†**Hithp** *Pt.* fs. אֵשׁ מִתְלַקַּחַת lit fire *taking hold of itself*, of lightning Ex 9^{24} (JE), Ez 1^4, exact signif dub., *in close succession, incessant* Di Sm, *infolding itself*, i e a mass of fire, Thes RobGes AV VB SS, > of *quivering* flashes Buhl, of *forked* or *zigzag* lightning Da.

†לֶקַח **n.m.** [Pr 4, 2] **learning, teaching** (concrete, prob *what is received*),—לֶ׳ abs Is 29^{24}+ 5 t; sf לִקְחִי Dt 32^2 Jb 11^4, לִקְחָהּ Pr 7^{21},—**1.** *instruction*, subjective, as personal acquirement, יִלְמְדוּ לֶקַח Is 29^{24}, they *shall learn instruction* (‖ בִּינָה), וְיוֹסֶף לֶקַח Pr 1^5 a wise man will hear *and will increase* (his) *learning*, so 9^9 **2.** *teaching*, obj., as thing taught, יַעֲרֹף כַּמָּטָר לִקְחִי Dt 32^2 (‖ אִמְרָתִי), Jb 11^4; לֶ׳ טוֹב נָתַתִּי לָכֶם Pr 4^2, also =*teaching-power, persuasiveness*, מֶתֶק שְׂפָתַיִם יֹסִיף לֶ׳ Pr 16^{21} *sweetness of lips increaseth persuasiveness* (v מתק), וְעַל שְׂפָתָיו יֹסִיף לֶקַח v^{23}, in bad sense, of seductive words of adulteress, בְּרֹב לִ׳ Pr 7^{21} (‖ בְּחֵלֶק שְׂפָתֶיהָ).

†לִקְחִי **n pr.m.** a Manassite, 1 Ch 7^{19}, 𝔊 Λακεειμ, A Λακεια, 𝔊L Λοκεειμ.

†I. מַלְקוֹחַ **n m.** [Is 49, 25] **booty, prey** (cf. לָקַח 9),—הֲיֻקַּח מִגִּבּוֹר מַ׳ Is 49^{24} (‖ שְׁבִי), cf. v^{25} (‖ *id.*), Nu 31^{26} (‖ *id.*), 31^{11} (‖ שָׁלָל), v^{12} (‖ *id* + שְׁבִי, i e here, only, disting. fr captives), v^{32} (‖ יֶתֶר הַבָּז), v^{27}

†II. [מַלְקוֹחַ] **n.[m.] jaw** (as *taking, seizing* food),—du sf. וּלְשׁוֹנִי מֻדְבָּק מַלְקוֹחָי ψ 22^{16} *and my tongue is made to cleave to my jaws*, i.e my gums

†מַלְקָחַיִם, [מֶלְקָחַיִם] **n.[m.]du. tongs, snuffers**;—**1.** tongs used at altar of temple, for lifting coal, in Is.'s vision, Is 6^6. **2.** lamp-*snuffers*, in temple 1 K 7^{49} = 2 Ch 4^{21}, in tabern. sf (ref to lamp-stand, מְנוֹרָה) מַלְקָחֶיהָ Ex 25^{38} 37^{23} Nu 4^9 (all P)

†[מִקָּח] **n.[m.]** **a taking, receiving**,—cstr. מִקַּח־שֹׁחַד 2 Ch 19^7 *a taking of a bribe*

†[מַקָּחָה] **n.f. ware** (prop thing *received*, sc. in trade; cf. לָקַח in NH); only pl הַמַּקָּחוֹת Ne 10^{32} (*their*) *wares*

†[לָקַט] **vb. pick or gather up,** specif. **glean** (NH *id.* and נָקַט, Ar لَقَطَ *pick up* (as a bird, grains, etc.); Aram. לְקַט, and נְקַט; ܠܩܛ, Mand לגט (No [M 54], also on Talm נקט); cf As *lakâtu* Dl [HWB 385] (but ט = *t*?)),—**Qal** *Pf* 3 pl לָקְטוּ Ex 16^{22} Nu 11^8, וְלָ׳ consec. Ex 16^4, לָקְטוּ Ex 16^{18}, *Impf.* 3 mpl יִלְקְטוּ Ex 16^5, וַיִּלְקְטוּ Ex $16^{17\ 21}$, יִלְקֹטוּן ψ 104^{28}, 2 mpl.sf. תִּלְקְטֻהוּ Ex 16^{26}, *Imv* mpl. לִקְטוּ Gn 31^{46} Ex 16^{16}, *Inf. cstr* לִלְקֹט Ex 16^{27} + 2 t.;—**1.** *pick up, gather*, c acc., stones Gn 31^{46} (J), lilies Ct 6^2, usu. the manna· Ex $16^{4\ 5.26}$ (J), $v^{21\ 22}$ (P); sq מִן partit v^{16} (P), so abs. v^{27} Nu 11^8 (both JE), Ex $16^{17\ 18}$ (P), of animals gathering food תִּתֵּן לָהֶם יִלְקֹטוּן ψ 104^{28}. **2.** specif *glean*, abs., Ru 2^8 (c בְּ loc.; usu. Pi in this sense) **Pi.** *Pf* 3 fs וְלִקְּטָה consec. Ru 2^{18}, לִקֵּטָה Ru $2^{17\ 18}$, 2 fs לִקַּטְתְּ Ru 2^{19}, *Impf* וַיְלַקֵּט Gn 47^{14} + 2 t., 3 fs תְּלַקֵּט Ru 2^{15}, וַתְּ׳ Ru $2^{3\ 17}$; 2 ms. תְּלַקֵּט Lev 19^9 + 2 t; 1 s. אֲלַקֲּטָה Ru $2^{2.7}$ (cf. Ba [NB 102. 489]), *Inf. cstr* לְלַקֵּט Ru 2^{15} + 2 t, *Pt* מְלַקֵּט Is 17^5, pl מְלַקְּטִים Ju 1^7 Je 7^{18},—**1.** *gather, gather up*, fallen grapes, Lv 19^{10} (H), arrows 1 S 20^{38}, (fire-)wood Je 7^{18}; abs. (food from ground) Ju 1^7 (cf. GFM); = *pick, pick off*, 2 K $4^{39.39}$ (+ מִן of source) **2.** fig. *collect* (money) Gn 47^{14} (J) **3.** specif *glean*, after the reapers, usu. abs. Ru $2^{3.7}$ (‖ אָסַף), v^{17} (all c בְּ loc.), v^{15} (בֵּין loc.), v^{19} (adv. loc.), also v^2 (where בְּ may be loc. or partit., cf. Be), also $v^{15\ 16.23}$, c acc. Is 17^5 (שִׁבֳּלִים, sim. of devastation of land, ‖ אָסַף קָצִיר), Ru $2^{17\ 18}$, c acc. cogn לֶקֶט Lv 19^9 = 23^{22} (H). **Pu.** *Impf.* 2 mpl תְּלֻקְּטוּ

Is 27^{12} *ye shall be picked up* (of Isr. under fig. of grains or berries, after the threshing process of י׳'s judgment). **Hithp.** *Impf.* וַיִּתְלַקְּטוּ Ju 11^{3} and *there collected themselves* worthless men unto (אֶל) Jephthah (*were raked together* GFM).

†לֶקֶט **n.[m.] gleaning**, i.e. what is or may be gleaned, only cstr. ל׳ קְצִירְךָ, as acc. cogn. with לקט Pi., (q. v.) Lv $19^{9} = 23^{22}$ (H).

†יַלְקוּט **n.[m.] receptacle, wallet**(?) (prop. *collector*) (on form cf. Lag$^{BN\ p.\ 127}$ Ba$^{NB\ §\ 156\ b}$ Kö$^{ii.\ 1,\ §\ 76,\ 4}$)—only in 1 S 17^{40} and he put them [the stones] בִּכְלִי הָרֹעִים אֲשֶׁר־לוֹ וּבַיַּלְקוּט *in the shepherd's receptacle which he had, even* (?) *in the wallet* (? such as every shepherd carried, hence art.); but prob. del. ו before בַּיַּל׳ (𝔊 The We Klo Bu HPS), and regard בִּכְלִי . . . לוֹ as gloss (We Bu HPS).

†[לָקַק] **vb. lap, lick** (NH *id.*, Pi.; Ar. لَقَّ *lick, lap* of dog (Wahrm));—**Qal** *Pf.* 3 ms. לָקְקוּ 1 K 21^{19}; *Impf.* 3 ms. יָלֹק Ju $7^{5.5}$; 3 mpl. יָלֹקּוּ 1 K 21^{19}, וַיָּלֹקּוּ 1 K 22^{38};—*lap*, יָלֹק בִּלְשׁוֹנוֹ מִן־הַמַּיִם Ju 7^{5}, like a dog v^{5} (abs.); of dogs *lapping up* blood (acc.), 1 K $21^{19.19}$ 22^{38}. **Pi.** *Pt.* pl. c. art. הַמְלַקְקִים Ju 7^{6} (בְּיָדָם אֶל־פִּיהֶם is erron. gloss, v. GFM), v^{7}; in both = *lap, lap up* (= **Qal** v^{5}).

לקשׁ (√ of foll.; NH לקשׁ *be late* (Hiph. and deriv.); Aram. ܠܩܫ *make* or *do late*, לַקְּשָׁא, ܠܩܫܐ *late;* vulg. Ar. لقّس *be late* (Hauran), Wetzst in De$^{Job\ 24,\ 6}$, so 11. Wahrm; لَقِيس *late*, Dozy$^{Suppl.\ ii.\ 543}$).

†לֶקֶשׁ **n.[m.]** prob. **after-growth, aftermath, i.e. spring-crop** (cf. GASm$^{12\ Proph.\ i.\ 109}$);—only (2 t.) Am 7^{1}, בִּתְחִלַּת עֲלוֹת הַלָּ֑קֶשׁ וְהִנֵּה לֶקֶשׁ אַחַר גִּזֵּי הַמֶּלֶךְ׃.—> Other interpr. are: *late-rain growth* (fr. מַלְקוֹשׁ q. v.), Hoffm$^{ZAW\ iii.\ (1883)\ 116}$; *leaf-and-herb-gathering* in spring, We after Klein$^{ZPV\ iv.\ 1881,\ 83}$; Anderlind$^{viii.\ 1886,\ 62}$.

†מַלְקוֹשׁ **n.m.**$^{Je\ 3,\ 3}$ **latter-rain, spring-rain** (i.e. showers of March–April; important, as strengthening and maturing crops); מ׳ Ho 6^{3} + 7 t.;—related to גֶּשֶׁם as particular to general, opp. יוֹרֶה (*former rain*, q.v.): Ho 6^{3} Je 5^{24}; so opp. מוֹרֶה Jo 2^{23}; particular under מָטָר Dt 11^{14} (opp. יוֹרֶה), Zc 10^{1} (+ מְטַר־גֶּשֶׁם), Jb 29^{23}; ‖ רְבִבִים Je 3^{3}; עָב מ׳ Pr 16^{15} *spring-rain-cloud* (sim. of king's favour).

†[לִקֵּשׁ] **vb.** only **Pi.** 3 mpl., prob. denom. fr. לֶקֶשׁ = **take the aftermath**, i. e. *take everything* (Wetzst in De$^{Hiob\ 24,\ 6}$) (> Buhl 11. לקשׁ, cf. Ar. لَقَشَ *schnell zusammenraffen* [cf. Lane^{2668}]);—*despoil;* וְכֶרֶם רָשָׁע יְלַקֵּשׁוּ׃ Jb 24^{6} *and the vineyard of the wicked* (but rd. prob. עָשִׁיר *the rich* Bu Du) *they despoil* (‖ קָצַר).

לשׁד (√ of foll., cf. Ar. لَسَدَ *suck, lick* (Eth. ለሰድ: *butter*); so Thes and on ψ 32^{4} De Bae, also Di$^{Nu\ 11,\ 8}$).

[לָשָׁד] **n.m. juice, juicy or dainty bit, dainty**;—cstr. כְּטַעַם לְשַׁד הַשָּׁמֶן Nu 11^{8} (J) sim. of taste of manna (𝔊 ἐγκρίς, 𝔙 *panis oleatus*), i.e. a dainty prepared with oil (cf. Di); נֶהְפַּךְ לְשַׁדִּי בְּחַרְבֹנֵי קַיִץ ψ 32^{4} *my juice* (sap, life-moisture) is transformed, etc.

לשׁך (√ of foll.; meaning unknown).

†לִשְׁכָּה **n.f. room, chamber, hall, cell, lishka** (NH *id.* 𝔗 לִשְׁכְּתָא; cf. also נִשְׁכָּה; on the *lishka* v. Now$^{Arch.\ ii.\ 37,\ 52,\ 79}$; Bo$^{Geogr.\ I.\ xvii.\ 438\ (ed.\ Leusd.)}$ comp. Gk. λέσχη, cf. RS$^{Sem.\ i.\ 236\ (2nd\ ed.\ 254)}$ al.);—ל׳ Ez 40^{38}+; cstr. לִשְׁכַּת 2 K 23^{11}+; c. ה loc. לִשְׁכָּ֫תָה 1 S 9^{22}; pl. לְשָׁכוֹת Ez 40^{17}+; cstr. לִשְׁכוֹת Ne 10^{38}+;—**1. a.** of room connected with a sanctuary (בָּמָה), where sacrif. meal was eaten 1 S 9^{22}, insert also prob. 1^{18} (𝔊 We Dr Klo Bu). **b.** connected with Sol.'s temple, where wine offered to Rechabites Je $35^{2.4}$, cf. $v^{4.4}$; one where prophecy read 36^{10} (both these appar. open, cf. Gie$^{Je\ 35,\ 2}$); cf. לִשְׁכַּת נְתַן־מֶלֶךְ הַסָּרִיס . . בַּפַּרְוָרִים 2 K 23^{11}; used of Levites' cells 1 Ch 9^{33}; = store-rooms v^{26} (‖ אֹצָרוֹת), 23^{28} 28^{12} 2 Ch 31^{11}. **c.** in Ezek.'s temple, cells for priests, singers, etc. Ez $40^{17.17.38.44.45.46}$ + 41^{10}(del. Co Bthl), $42^{1.4.7.7.8.11}$ + v^{12} (del. Co Bthl); in three tiers, cf. הַלְּ׳ הָעֶלְיוֹנֹת 42^{5} (vid. v^{3}), (45^{5} rd. עָרִים לָשֶׁבֶת 𝔊 Sm Co Sgfr$^{Kau AT}$ Bthl); לְ׳ הַקֹּדֶשׁ for sacred uses $42^{13.13.13}$ 44^{19} 46^{19}. **d.** in second temple, as store-rooms Ezr 8^{29} Ne $10^{38.39}$ (‖ בֵּית הָאוֹצָר), v^{40}; used by individuals Ezr 10^{6} Ne 13^{5} (לְ׳ גְדוֹלָה), v^{8}, in gen. $v^{4.9}$. **2.** of scribe's room in royal palace Je $36^{12.20.21}$.

†I. לֶשֶׁם **n.[m.]** a precious stone in h. p.'s breast-plate Ex 28^{19} 39^{12} (√ and mng. dub.; 𝔊 λιγύριον, Joseph$^{Ant.\ iii.\ 7,\ 5}$ λίγυρος, 𝔙 *ligurius*, and this (= λυγκούριον, *lyncurion*?) compared with *carbuncle* Plin$^{NH\ viii.\ 57\ (38)}$; identif. with *amber*

Demostratus in Plin[NH xxxvii 11(2)], or with *jacinth* (Rev 21[20]) Braun[De Vest Sacerd ii 14] Winer[BWB 332]; cf. further, Di[Ex 28 19])

†ii לֶשֶׁם **n.pr.loc.** variant of לַיִשׁ (whence We[De gent 37] Di rd לֶשֶׁם, Lag[BN 20 Anm] thinks ם remnant of *Mimmation*, לֶשֶׁם fr. לַיִשׁ = *Laišum*), old name of city דָּן (v לַיִשׁ), Jos 19[47 47] (cf Di), 𝔊B Λαχεις, לֶשֶׁם דָּן = Λασεννδακ, A𝔊L Λεσεν(μ)

לשן (√of foll, Thes conj orig mng *lick* (cf لَسَّ, لسب, لسم), so Hup-Now[ψ 32 4])

†לָשׁוֹן **n.m.**[Jos 7 29] and (more oft) **f.**[Is 28. 11] **tongue** (NH *id*; also As *lišânu*; Ar لِسَانٌ, Eth ልሳን:, Aram לִשָּׁן, לִשְׁנָא, ܠܶܫܳܢܳܐ (all *li*-), Zinj. לשן DHM[Sendsch 59]), — abs ל׳ Ex 4[10] +, הַלָּשׁוֹן Jos 15[2]; cstr לשון Jos 7[21] +, sf לשוני 2 S 23[2], לשנו Ex 11[7] + 2 t, לְשׁוֹנוֹ Ju 7[5] Est 1[22], לְשׁוֹנְךָ ψ 34[14], לשונכם Is 59[3], etc; pl לשנות abs ψ 31[21] Is 66[18], cstr Zc 8[23], sf לשׁנֹתָם Gn 10[20.31], — **1.** *tongue* of men, **a.** used in lapping Ju 7[5], cleaving to the palate (חך), in thirst La 4[4], so as to produce dumbness Jb 29[10] (‖ קול נחבא), ψ 137[6] Ez 3[26] (‖ נֶאֱלַם), cleaving to jaws (מַלְקוֹחַ) ψ 22[16], ל׳ בַּצָּמָא נָשָׁתָּה Is 41[17] *their tongue for thirst is parched*, ל׳ תִּמַּק בְּפִיהֶם Zc 14[12] (of י׳'s judgment); a choice morsel is held תַּחַת ל׳ Jb 20[12] (fig of mischief), cf. ψ 10[7] (ready to be uttered), 66[17] (‖ פֶּה), Ct 4[11]. **b.** usu as organ of speech, both good and bad (esp. ψ Pr, oft ‖ פֶּה, שָׂפָה), — כבד ל׳ Ex 4[10] (J) *heavy of tongue*; מַעֲנֵה ל׳ Pr 16[1], מִלָּתוֹ עַל־לְשׁוֹנִי 2 S 23[2], cf Pr 31[26], ψ 139[4] (כל׳), הֲיֵשׁ בִּלְשׁוֹנִי עַוְלָה Jb 6[30], מָוֶת וְחַיִּים בְּיַד ל׳ Pr 18[21], cf 21[23] 25[15], of (false) proph, הַלֹּקְחִים ל׳ Je 23[31], subj of vb. of speaking, דִּבְּרָה לְשׁוֹנִי — Jb 33[2] ψ 12[4] 37[30], cf (Je 9[7] infr. and) ל׳ . . תְּמַהֵר בחכי Is 32[4], לְדַבֵּר לשוני עט ספר מָהִיר ψ 45[2], i e as swift as a rapid scribe's stylus, subj. of הָגָה Is 59[3] Jb 27[4] ψ 35[28] 71[24], subj of נִשְׁבַּע Is 45[23], ל׳ תִּהֲלַךְ בָּאָרֶץ ψ 73[9], of hostile speech, insolence, etc., Jos 10[21] (JE, obj of 1 חָרַץ q v, cf. **3** infr), Je 18[18] Is 3[8], זַעַם ל׳ Ho 7[16] (but text dub, cf We Now), שָׁנְנוּ ל׳ כמו חֶרֶב חַדָּה ψ 57[5], cf 64[4], ל׳ האריך 57[4], כָּל־ל׳ תָּקוּם אִתָּךְ Is 54[17]; נָחָשׁ 140[4]; further, Je 9[2.4], as instr of seductive flattery (הֶחֱלִיק), without ב, ψ 5[10] Pr 28[23], cf חלקת ל׳ נָכְרִיָּה Pr 6[24], of falsehood ψ 78[36] (cf infr), of slander (cf רָגַל עַל־ל׳ (לושן) ψ 15[3], אִישׁ לָשׁוֹן 140[12], cf לְ׳ סֵתֶר Pr 25[23]; חֲטֹא בל׳ ψ 39[2], cf. 64[9] (text dub., v Hup Che Bae), moral qualities ascribed to — as arrogant ψ 12[5] (cf v[4] supr.), as devising injuries, הַוּוֹת תַּחְשֹׁב ל׳ ψ 52[4], cf ל׳ הַוֹּת Pr 17[4], נצר ל׳ ψ 50[19] *nectere fraudem*; ל׳ תַּצְמִיד מרמה מֵרָע ψ 34[14] (‖ וּשְׂפָתֶיךָ מִדַּבֵּר מִרְמָה); oft of lying tongue. לשון שֶׁקֶר Pr 6[17] 12[19] 21[6] 26[28] ψ 109[2]; לְ׳ תַּרְמִית Mi 6[12] ψ 120[2.3], לְ׳ רמיה 52[6]; ל׳ מִרְמָה Zp 3[13]; ל׳ תַּהְפֻּכוֹת Pr 10[31], and נֶהְפָּךְ בל׳ Pr 17[20], ל׳ עֲרוּמִים Jb 15[5]; also מרמה דִבֵּר Je 9[7]; on the other hand ל׳ צַדִּיק Pr 10[20]; ל׳ חֲכָמִים 12[18] 15[2], ל׳ לִמּוּדִים, v[4] מַרְפֵּה לְ׳, Is 50[4]. — Note phrases שׁוֹט ל׳ Jb 5[21] *scourge of* (the) *tongue*, ריב לְשֹׁנוֹת ψ 31[21], פַּלַּג לְשׁוֹנָם ψ 55[10]. also בַּעַל הַל׳ Ec 10[11] (of serpent-charmer), and וַתֵּעָלוּ עַל־שְׂפַת ל׳ Ez 36[3]. — On tongue of י׳ (once), v **4** infr †**c.** organ of singing, subj of רָנַן ψ 51[16] 126[2] Is 35[6], עָנָה ψ 119[172]. **2.** = *language* Dt 28[49] Je 5[15] and later, viz: Ez 3[5.6] (‖ עִמְקֵי שָׂפָה, כבדי ל׳), but del. 𝔊 Codd Co Sgfr[KauAT]), Is 28[11] (‖ ל׳ אַחֶרֶת, לַעֲגֵי שָׂפָה, fig. of י׳'s unintelligible dealings); (עמקי שָׂפָה ‖) עַם . . . נִלְעַג ל׳ 33[19], 66[18] (‖ גּוֹיִם), Zc 8[23] Gn 10[5.20.31] (all P), Ne 13[24] Est 1[22.22] 3[12] 8[9.9] Dn 1[4] **3.** *tongue* of animals dog Ex 11[7] (J, obj of 1 חָרַץ q v., cf **1 b**), ψ 68[24], adder Jb 20[16] (subj of תַּהַרְג); crocodile 40[25]. **4.** *tongue* of fire, devouring, כֶּאֱכֹל קַשׁ לשון אשׁ Is 5[24]; cf. of י׳, (שְׂפָתָיו מָלְאוּ זַעַם ‖) ולשונו כאשׁ אֹכָלֶת 30[27] **5.** = (*tongue*-shaped) *wedge* of gold Jos 7[21 24] (JE) **6.** = (*tongue*-shaped) *bay* of sea Is 11[15] Jos 15[2 5] 18[19] (all P)

†[לָשַׁן] **vb denom. use the tongue**, only specif, **slander**, — **Po'el** *Pt* מְלָשְׁנִי בַסֵּתֶר רֵעֵהוּ ψ 101[5] (on form, cf Ges[§ 90, 3] Kö[Lgb i § 26]) **Hiph.** *Impf.* 2 ms juss אַל־תַּלְשֵׁן עֶבֶד וגו׳ Pr 30[10].

†[לֶשַׁע] **n pr.loc.** near Sodom and Gomorrah, only לָשַׁע Gn 10[19], 𝔊D Λασα; E𝔊L Λασα; site unknown, = *Kallirrhoe*, with hot-springs, Jerome[Quaest in Gen (10, 19)], cf. Buhl[Geogr 123 and reff]

לַשָּׁרוֹן Jos 12[18] v. שָׁרוֹן.

לתח (√of foll, meaning unknown, Thes conj *spread out*, cf Sam נתח *spread out garment*, v also Di[Lex. Eth 45 f], but this word very dubious)

†מֶלְתָּחָה† **n.f.** appar. **wardrobe, wearing apparel** (Eth. ልብስ: *tunic*);—only in וַיֹּאמֶר לַאֲשֶׁר עַל־הַמֶּ׳ הוֹצֵא לְבוּשׁ 2 K 10[22]; 𝔊 ἐπὶ τοῦ [οἴκου] μεσθααλ (μισθ'); 𝔙 *super vestes.*

לתך (√ of foll., mng. unkn., cf Lag[Or. ii. 32 f.]).

†לֶתֶךְ† **n.[m.] a barley-measure** (NH *id*, a corn-measure); only in חֹמֶר שְׂעֹרִים וְלֶ׳ שְׂעֹרִים Ho 3[2]; acc. to 𝔙 = ½ כֹּר = ½ חֹמֶר (q v.), cf. Mish. (Levy[NHWB ii. 531]), but this tradition is uncertain (cf. Now[Arch i. 203]), 𝔊 νέβελ οἴνου, for לֶ׳ שׂ׳.

מ

מ, **ם**, *Mêm*, thirteenth letter; used as numeral 40 in postB. Heb.

מַ־ v. מָה. מִ־ v. מִן.

מוֹאָב v. מֹאָב. [מַאֲבוּס] v. אבס.

מאד (√ of following As. *ma'âdu, be many, increase, ma'adu, many; ma'adiš, in abundance,* Dl[HWB. 388 f]; cf Sab. מאד *to add,* DHM [ZMG 1883, 342 f.] Hom[Süd-Ar Chr 127]; Ar. مَأَدَ *begin to grow,* of plant)

מְאֹד n.m. muchness, force, abundance, exceedingly (cf As *mu'du, abundance,* Hom [ZMG 1878, 711] ('treasures *ana mu'di, in abundance*') Dl[HWB 399]).—**1.** *force, might,* †Dt 6[5] וּבְכָל־מְאֹדֶךָ and with all thy *might;* hence 2 K 23[25]. **2.** in diff. idioms (298 t.) to express the idea of *exceedingly, greatly, very* (whether of magnitude or degree): **a.** (so mostly) as adv. acc, qualifying both adjj and vbs., Gn 1[31] טוֹב מְאֹד good *exceedingly,* 4[5] וַיִּחַר לְקַיִן מְאֹד and Cain was wroth *exceedingly,* 7[18] וַיִּגְבְּרוּ הַמַּיִם וַיִּרְבּוּ מְאֹד, 12[14] 13[2] v[13] חַטָּאִים לַי׳ מְאֹד, וְאַבְרָם כָּבֵד מְאֹד בַּמִּקְנֶה, 18[20] 19[3 9] 21[11] 24[16.35], + oft, ψ 46[2] עֶזְרָה בְצָרוֹת נִמְצָא מְאֹד as a help in troubles, to be found (= present) *exceedingly;* with an inf. Is 47[9] בְּעָצְמַת חֲבָרַיִךְ מְאֹד despite of thy spells being *very* numerous, Jos 9[13] מֵרֹב הַדֶּרֶךְ מְאֹד, 1 K 7[47], הַרְבֵּה מְאֹד Gn 15[1] 41[49] Dt 3[5] +, for which in the later language is found לָרֹב מְאֹד †Zc 14[14] 2 Ch 4[18] 9[9] (in 1 K 10[10] הַרְבֵּה מְאֹד), 24[24] 30[13], and even לְהַרְבֵּה מְאֹד †2 Ch 11[12] 16[8]. מאד is not usually separated from the word it qualifies by more than one or two words (as Gn 20[8] וייראו האנשים מאד, Nu 11[10] ויחר אף י׳ מאד); see, however, Dt 30[14] Ju 12[2] 2 S 12[5] 1 K 11[19] ψ 31[12]. It precedes its verb, †ψ 47[10] מְאֹד נַעֲלָה (hence 97[9]), 92[6]. **b.** עַד־מְאֹד *up to abundance, to a great degree, exceedingly,* †Gn 27[33] חֲרָדָה גְּדֹלָה עַד־מְ׳, v[34] 1 S 11[15] וישמח . . . עד מ׳, 25[36] והוא שִׁכֹּר עַד־מְ׳, 2 S 2[17] 1 K 1[4] Is 64[8] (cf. La 5[22]), v[11] ψ 38[7 9] 119[8.43.51 107] Dn 8[8] 11[25]. **c.** עַד־לִמְאֹד (v עַד לְ)† 2 Ch 16[14]. **d.** duplicated (Ges[§ 133 k]), †Gn 7[19] וְהַמַּיִם גָּבְרוּ מְ׳ מְ׳, 30[43] Nu 14[7] 1 K 7[47] 2 K 10[4] Ez 37[10] **e.** בִּמְאֹד מְאֹד lit. *with muchness, muchness,* †Gn 17[2 6.20] Ex 1[7] (all P), Ez 9[9] 16[13].

I **מֵאָה**[583] **n.f. hundred** (NH *id.;* MI[20] מאתן (du); SI[5] מאתים, מאת (du); Ph. מאת, מאתם (du.), As. *mê* (prob, Dl[§ 75]), TelAm. *mê-at* Wkl[TelAm 20*]; Ar. مِائَةٌ; Sab. מאת, מאתם Os [ZMG x 1856, 49, CIS iv l. 6, 4, 46, 6]; מאה Eut[Sin 457]; Eth. ምእት:; Aram מְאָה, مْأا; Palm. תלת מאה 300 Vog[Palm 6, 4]; Nab. מאה Eut[Nab 8, 9]);—מ׳ Gn 6[3] + 144 t.; cstr. מְאַת 5[3] + 30 t. (on מְאַת Ec 8[12] v. **2 d** infr); pl. abs. מֵאוֹת Gn 5[9] + 324 t. (מֵאת only 5[4.30]); המאיות Kt 2 K 11[4] + 3 t. 2 K 11; du. מָאתַיִם (־תַּ֫יִם) Gn 11[19] + 76 t. (but 1 S 18[27] rd. מֵאָה (מְאַת) 𝔊 We Dr Kit Bu HPS);—*hundred*.—**1.** as simple number: **a.** abs. sg., (1) foll. by sg. of noun enumerated: מֵאָה קְשִׂיטָה Gn 33[19] Jos 24[32] (both E); מ׳ אִישׁ Ju 7[19] 1 K 18[13] 2 K 4[43]; מ׳ אַמָּה 1 K 7[2] Ez 40[19] +; מ׳ כִּכָּר 2 K 23[33] 2 Ch 25[6] 27[5] 36[3] Ezr 8[26]; מ׳ אֶלֶף = 100,000 1 K 20[29] + 6 t K Ch; cf also Gn 17[17] (P), 2 S 8[4] Is 65[20.20], and sq n. coll. רֶכֶב 2 S 8[4] = 1 Ch 18[4], צֹאן 1 K 5[3]; (2) less oft. sq pl מֵאָה שְׁעָרִים Gn 26[12] (J), מ׳ נְבִיאִים 1 K 18[4], מ׳ פְּעָמִים 2 S 24[3] = 1 Ch 21[3], etc.; (3) seldom, and late, preceded by n pl.: אַמּוֹת הַמֵּאָה Ez 42[2], cf. Ezr הָרִמֹּנִים מֵאָה Je 52[23], 2[69] 2 Ch 3[16] 4[8] 29[32]; (4) exceptional is כְּלֵי כֶסֶף מֵאָה לְכִכָּרִים Ezr 8[26]; also, with ellipsis, מֵאָה כֶסֶף Dt 22[19] (i e. shekels); מֵאָה קַיִץ 2 S 16[1] (i e cakes),

(5) מֵאָה without noun enumerated, esp = *a hundred* (men, persons) Ju 20[10.10] Am 5[3.3] Lv 26[8.8] (H), 1 Ch 12[14], מ׳ Pr 17[10] = 100 (blows), Ec 6[3] = 100 (children), 8[12] = 100 (times) —On Ne 3[1] 12[39] v. infr. **b.** abs du, (1) foll. by sg, מָאתַיִם איש 1 S 18[27] 30[10] 2 S 15[11], מ׳ לֶחֶם 1 S 25[18] 2 S 16[1], מ׳ צִנָּה 1 K 10[16] = 2 Ch 9[15], מ׳ אֶלֶף 1 S 15[4] +, מ׳ שָׁנָה Gn 11[23] (P); (2) less oft sq pl מ׳ שְׁקָלִים Jos 7[21] (JE), 2 S 14[26], מ׳ דבלים 1 S 25[18], מ׳ אֲנָשִׁים 1 S 30[21], cf. Ezr 8[4]; (3) also preceded by n pl עִזִּים מ׳ Gn 32[15], רחלים מ׳ v[15] (E), הָרִמּוֹנִים מ׳ 1 K 7[20], cf 1 Ch 15[8] 2 Ch 29[32] Ezr 2[69], (4) c ellipsis מ׳ כֶּסֶף Ju 17[4], (5) as pred, רָאשֵׁיהֶם מ׳ 1 Ch 12[32] (v[33] van d H). **c.** abs pl. מא(ו)ת — (1) alone, = *hundreds*, למאות 1 S 29[2] *by hundreds*, so 2 S 18[4] (both + thousands), esp שָׂרֵי (הַ)מ׳ *captains of (the) hundreds* Ex 18[21.25] (E), 2 K 11[4.9.10.15] +, (2) multiplied, sq noun enumerated, in sg. שְׁלֹשׁ מ׳ אִישׁ Ju 7[6] 300 *men*, cf. v[7.8.16] 8[4] Ex 12[37] (E), etc, אַרְבַּע מ׳ שָׁנָה Gn 15[13] (JE) 400 *years*, חֲמֵשׁ מ׳ אֶלֶף 2 S 24[9] 500,000, cf 2 Ch 13[17], שֵׁשׁ מ׳ רֶכֶב Ex 14[7] (J) 600 *chariots*; שְׁבַע מ׳ אִישׁ Ju 20[15.16] 700 *men*; שְׁמֹנֶה מ׳ חָלָל 2 S 23[8] 800 *slain*, תְּשַׁע מ׳ רֶכֶב Ju 4[3.13] 900 *chariots*, (3) less oft sq n pl שְׁלֹשׁ מ׳ שׁוּעָלִים Ju 15[4] 300 *foxes*, חֲמֵשׁ מ׳ אֲתוֹנוֹת Jb 1[3] 500 *she-asses*, etc, (4) rare, and chiefly late, after n pl. פִּלַגְשִׁים שְׁלֹשׁ מ׳ 1 K 11[3] 300 *concubines*, cf 7[42] = 2 Ch 4[13], 1 Ch 4[42] 2 Ch 14[8] etc, after n coll בָּקָר חָמֵשׁ מ׳ 2 Ch 35[9], (5) rare is חֲמֵשׁ מ׳ בַּשֶּׁקֶל Ex 30[24] (P), (6) ellipsis of n, שְׁלֹשׁ מ׳ כֶּסֶף Gn 45[22] (E), etc **d.** cstr. sg, only sq sg, and late. מְאַת־שָׁנָה Gn 11[10] 21[5] 25[7] (all P) + 25 t P, 1 Ch 25[9] Est 1[4] (Dr[Intr 124]) (also c. other numerals, v **2** infr); מְאַת Ec 8[12] = *100 times* (מאה פעמים), sc פַּעַם, or perhaps only appar. cstr (Ko[II 228] cf. Ew[§ 269 b 279 e]) — Ne 5[11] v. **3** infr. **2.** as part of larger number. **a.** usually preceding tens and units, (1) with noun expressed once, or not at all, earlier usage, usu c ו before ten if no unit follows, otherwise without וְ before ten (see Ko[II 218 ff]). מֵאָה וְעֶשְׂרִים Ju 2[8]; שֵׁשׁ מֵאוֹת שִׁשִּׁים וָשֵׁשׁ כִּכַּר 1 K 10[14] 666 *talents*, etc (exceptions are Ne 7[24] and v[31]), (2) chiefly late, with noun and וְ repeated: מֵאָה שָׁנָה וְעֶשְׂרִים שָׁנָה וְשֶׁבַע שָׁנִים Gn 23[1] (P) (cf ואלף אמה ומאת אמה Sl[5.6] Da[Expos Times, May, 1898]). **b.** less oft, foll tens and units, chiefly late, c ו repeated.— עשרים ומאה Nu 7[86] (P), שֶׁבַע וּשְׁלֹשִׁים וּמְאַת שָׁנָה Ex 6[16] (P), etc, c noun after ten and after hundred, חָמֵשׁ וְשִׁשִּׁים שָׁנָה וּשְׁלֹשׁ מֵאוֹת שָׁנָה Gn 5[23] (P), etc —On these usages v, further, Ko[II 217 ff] Da[Synt §§ 36 R. 3. 37 (d)] Ges[§§ 97 134] and esp. Herner[Synt d Zahlwörter im AT (1893)]. †**3.** מְאַת הַכֶּסֶף Ne 5[11] = *a hundredth* part *of the money;* but read quite poss. מַשַּׁאת *the debt* (Gei[Jüd Zeitschr viii 1870, 227] Gr)

†II. מֵאָה **n.f.** used as n pr of tower on northern wall of Jerus, מִגְדַּל הַמֵּאָה Ne 3[1] 12[39].

[מַאֲוַי], מַאֲוַיֵּי v. sub I אוה, p. 16 supr.

מאם (✓of following, mng. unkn., Ol[§ 205] prop ✓אום = חום *black*, cf already Ew[§ 160 d])

†**מְאוּם** **n.m.** [Jb 31, 7] blemish, defect (for מְאוּם, which, although found only late, is (si vera l.) appar. original form, Ko[II 146]),—מ׳ abs.: **1.** of physical defect Dn 1[4]. **2.** fig בְּכַפַּי דָּבַק מ׳ Jb 31[7] of moral stain, usually

†**מוּם** **n.m.** [Lv 21, 17] (= foregoing; quiesc א om) (NH *id*, Aram מוּמָא, ܡܘܡܐ),—abs. מ׳ Lv 21[17] + 16 t., sf. מוּמוֹ Pr 9[7]; מוּמָם Dt 32[5],—*blemish, defect* (chiefly H). **1.** physical, **a.** in man, as excluding from priestly service, Lv 21[17.18.21.21.23], disfiguring man 2 S 14[25], woman Ct 4[7], (in all היה מ׳ ב), as caused by man upon man Lv 24[19.20]. **b.** in beast (ref. to sacrifice) Lv 22[20.21.25] Nu 19[2] Dt 15[21.21] 17[1] (in all היה מ׳ ב) **2.** fig of moral blemish Dt 32[5] (but text very dubious, cf. Dr), תִּשָּׂא פָנֶיךָ מִמּוּם Jb 11[15]; of shame of repulse Pr 9[7] (‖ קָלוֹן)

מְאוּמָה [32] **pron. indef.** anything (acc. to Thes from מָה וּמָה, like *quidquid*, against which is the *Mil'el* tone; acc to Ol[254 256 384] Ko[II. 146] an old accus from מאום in sense of *speck*, *particle*, cf. Fr *point*. in As. *manman* (prop. *who? who?*), assim *mamman*, or *manma* (*man*, *who?* + generalizing *ma*), *mamma*, is *any one*, *minma* (*min*, *what?* + *ma*), *mimma*, is *anything*, Dl[§ 60, HWB 418 f] WSG[125 f]),—*anything*, usually in negative sentences, as Gn 22[12] ואל־תעש לו מאומה; לא־תתן־לי מאומה (euphem. for *something bad*), 30[31], 39[6.9] 40[15] (euphem), 1 S 12[4.5] 20[26.39] 25[7.15.21] 29[3] etc, Ju 14[6] ומאומה אין בידו, Ec 5[14] ומ׳ לא ישא בעמלו, 1 K 18[43] אין מ׳ lit. nought of *anything!* Je 39[12] ואל תעש לו מאומה רָע; strengthened by כל + Gn 39[23] 2 S 3[35], after אם = *surely not*, 2 S 3[35]; in interrog sentence Nu 22[38]; in affirm. sentence Dt 24[10] כִּי־תַשֶּׁה בְרֵעֲךָ מַשַּׁאת מ׳ a pledge of (= consisting in)

anything, 2 S 13[2] (euphem.), 2 K 5[20]. Used adverbially, 1 S 21[3] איש אל ידע מ׳ את הדבר let no one know of the matter *in anything at all.*

מָאוֹר, [מְאוּרָה] v אור

[מאזן], מֹאזְנַיִם v. II אזן

מְאִיוֹת Kt v. מֵאָה.

מַאֲכָל, מַאֲכֹלֶת, מַאֲכֶלֶת v אכל

[מַאֲמַצִּים, מַאֲמָץ] v. אמץ

[מַאֲמָר] v. אָמַר.

†[מָאֵן] **vb. Pi. refuse** (**Qal** perhaps *be distasteful*, cf. Syr. ܡܐܢ *taeduit, pinguit*, Aph. *be slothful;* NH Pi., as term techn. of girl, *refuse* to acknowledge marriage contract; poss. akin to Eth. **መነነ:** *reject;* Ar. مَانَ is *sustain, maintain*),—**Pi.** *Pf* מאן Ex 7[14] + 4 t.; fs. מֵאֲנָה Je 15[18] + 3 t.; מֵאַנְתָּ Ex 10[3], etc.; *Impf.* יְמָאֵן Ex 22[16]; וַיְמָאֵן Gn 37[35] + 8 t etc; *Inf. abs.* מָאֵן Ex 22[16];—*refuse,* (sq. Inf. except 6 t. v. infr) human subj Gn 37[35] (J), Je 31[15] Ex 22[17 17] Nu 20[21] 22[14] (all E), Dt 25[7] 1 S 8[19] 2 S 2[23] 13[9] 1 K 20[35] 21[15] Est 1[12] Je 50[33] cf Jb 6[7] ψ 77[3] Pr 21[25] Je 15[18], without Inf. וַיְמָאֵן וַיֹּאמֶר Gn 39[8] 48[19] (both J), 1 S 28[23]; also 2 K 5[16]; esp. of refusing to obey ׳י's commands Ex 4[23] 7[14] 10[3] 16[28] (all J), Ne 9[17]; also ψ 78[10] Pr 21[7] Ho 11[5], v. esp. Je 3[3] 5[3.3] 8[5] 9[5] 11[10] cf. 25[28], Zc 7[11]; without Inf. = *be recusant* Pr 1[24] Is 1[20], once subj ׳י Nu 22[13] (E).

†מָאֵן **adj. verb. refusing,** sq Inf, and alw. of disobeying ׳י, Ex 7[27] 9[2] 10[4] (all J), Je 38[21].

†[מֵאֵן] **adj.** id pl. מֵאֲנִים sq. Inf., of disobeying ׳י Je 13[10].

†I. [מָאַס] **vb. reject** (NH *id;* Aram. מְאַס *reject, despise,* BA[Ezr 6 12] comp (dub.) Ar. مَعَسَ *lightly esteem* (Kam.); As. *ma'âsu* is perhaps *destroy* Meissn[Suppl. 56]);—**Qal** *Pf.* 3 ms. מָאַס Is 8[6] + 4 t.; sf מְאָסָם ψ 53[6]; 2 ms. מָאַסְתָּ Je 14[19] + 3 t, מְאַסְתָּה Ju 9[38] 1 S 15[26] + 22 t. Pf; *Impf.* יִמְאַס Jb 8[20] + 3 t; יִמְאָס ψ 36[5] Jb 36[5]; sf. וַיִּמְאָסְךָ 1 S 15[23.26]; for וְאֶמְאָסְךָ Ho 4[6] (so Baer, cf. De Complut Var 18 f.; not וְא׳ van d H) rd וָאֶמְאָסְךָ; 3 mpl יִמְאָסוּ Je 6[19] + 2 t; יִמְאָסוּן Is 31[7]; + 12 t. Impf.; *Inf. abs.* מָאוֹס Is 7[15 16] מָאֹס Je 14[19] La 5[22], *cstr.* מָאָסְכֶם Is 30[12], מָאֳסָם Am 2[4]; *Pt.* מוֹאֵס Pr 15[32]; מֹאֵס Is 33[15], f. מֹאֶסֶת Ez 21[15] (text dub., Co מוֹאֵס; Berthol וּמֹאֵסְ), v[18] (also dub, Co מִמְאָסָם; Berthol מאסף),—**1.** *reject, refuse,* **a.** c acc.: God rejects men Ho 4[6] 9[17] 1 S 15[23.26] 16[1 7] 2 K 23[27] Je 7[29] 14[19 19] 33[24 26] Lv 26[44] (H), ψ 53[6] Jb 8[20] 10[3] La 5[22.22]; זָנַחְתָּ וַתִּמְאָס ψ 89[39], men reject God Nu 11[20] (J), 1 S 8[7] 10[19], men 1 S 8[7] Jb 30[1], idols Is 31[7], evil ψ 36[5], knowledge Ho 4[6], divine תורה Am 2[4] Is 5[24]; דבר 1 S 15[23.26], חקות Ez 20[24], חקים 2 K 17[15]; מוסר Jb 5[17] Pr 3[11], var things Is 8[6] Ez 21[15] ψ 118[22] Jb 31[13]. **b.** c בְּ God rejects men 2 K 17[20] Je 6[30] 31[37] ψ 78[59.67], that in which man confides Je 2[37]; men reject evil Is 7[15 16], divine תורה Je 6[19], דבר Is 30[12] Je 8[9], חקות Lv 26[15] (H), משפטים v[43] (H), Ez 5[6] 20[13.16]; var. things, Nu 14[31] (J) Is 33[15] Je 4[30] ψ 106[24]. **2.** *despise,* c. acc, God subj. שנאתי מאסתי חגיכם Am 5[21] *I hate, I despise your feasts;* elsewhere men subj. גם עוילים מ׳ בי Jb 19[18] *even young children despise me;* אמ׳ חיי 9[21] *I despise my life,* cf. מואס נפשו Pr 15[32], הלא זה העם אשר מ׳ בו Ju 9[38] *is not this the people that thou despisedst?* מ׳ עָרִים Is 33[8], obj. om Jb 7[16] (< join to preceding Me Siegf Du); 34[33] 36[5] 42[6] (𝔖 Siegf אֶשְׁתַּק; 𝔊 𝔙 Symm Bo אֶמְאַס) Ez 21[18] (but v. supr.)—**Niph.** *be rejected:* *Impf.* תִּמָּאֵס Is 54[6] (wife); *Pt.* נִמְאָס Je 6[30] (silver), ψ 15[4] (= *reprobate;* opp. יִרְאֵי י׳); + f נִמְאֶסֶת, נִמְאָסָה 1 S 15[9] *rejected,* i.e *worthless* (for 𝔊 נָמֵס) acc to We Klo Dr Kit Bu HPS (|| נִבְזָה, rd. נמבזה; cf בזה, מסס **Niph.**)

†מָאוֹס **n.** [m.] **refuse** סְחִי וּמָאוֹס תְּשִׂימֵנוּ La 3[45] *offscouring and refuse thou makest us*

†II. [מָאַס] **vb. Niph. flow, run** (Aram *id*, but rare and dub;—secondary form of מסס q.v);—*Impf.* 3 ms וַיִּמָּאֵס Jb 7[5] my skin hath hardened *and run* (i e again, afresh; > GHoffm Du rd. וַיִּמַּס, Bu וַיִּמָּאֵס, √מסס); 3 mpl. יִמָּאֲסוּ כְמוֹ מַיִם ψ 58[8] (fig. of annihilation of wicked).

[מַאֲפֶה] v. אפה

מַאֲפֵלְיָה, מַאֲפֵל v. אפל.

מאץ (cf. Ar. مَأْصٌ a kind of *white* camel, whence Lag[BN 29] prop. מָאֹץ for the difficult אָמֹץ (אֲמֻצִּים) Zc 6[3.7]).

†[מָאַר] **vb.** (cf. Ar. مَأَرَ *excite hostility, irritate,* مُئِرّ *break open,* of a wound),—**Hiph. prick, pain** *Pt.* מַמְאִיר Ez 28[24]; f. מַמְאֶרֶת Lv 13[51] + 2 t.;—of thorn סלון מ׳ Ez 28[24] (fig of oppressors of Isr., || קוֹץ מַכְאִב); elsewh. of leprosy (צָרַעַת) = *malignant?* Lv 13[51.52] 14[44] (all P; but Sam. in all these has מראת, √מרא = מרה *be obstinate,* cf. Thes[816 b] Di).

מַאֲרָב v ארב מְאֵרָה v ארר.

[מִבְדָּלָה], מִבְדְּלוֹת v בדל.

מָבוֹא v בוא. מְבוּכָה v. בוך.

†**מַבּוּל** **n.m.**[Gn 7 6] flood in time of Noah (NH *id*; Jew-Aram. מַבּוּלָא; Syr ܡܰܒܘܽܠܳܐ; der. dub.; Thes al √יבל, but improb, v Dl [Prol 122 f], poss. old As (Bab) loan-word (yet form unkn in As), or fr. √נבל = As *nabâlu, destroy* Dl [HWB 443 f], cf Dl[Par 156, Prol. 122] Che[ψ 29, 10 crit. n., Hbr III. 3. 175 f], O. Whitehouse[COT II. 293]),—מ׳ only Gn and ψ 29[10], alw. abs. and alw c art. exc Gn 9[11 15]; וַיְהִי הַמּ׳—Gn 7[17], לֹא יִהְיֶה עוֹד מ׳ 9[11]; foll. by מַיִם as appos Gn 6[17] 7[6]; מֵי הַמּ׳ Gn 7[7 10] 9[11]; לֹא־יִהְיֶה עוֹד הַמַּיִם לְמ׳ Gn 9[15], as epoch, in phr. אַחַר הַמּ׳ Gn 9[28] 10[1.32] 11[10] (del as gloss Bu Di), י׳ לַמּ׳ יָשָׁב ψ 29[10] *at the flood sat enthroned* (so most; Che[v crit n] '*at the storm*' (*destruction = destructive storm* Id[Hbr I c.]), but הַמּ׳ seems in all the other passages to be almost = n. pr. of the flood; cf also מֵי נֹחַ Is 54[9 9]).

מְבוּנִים Kt v. בין. מְבוּסָה v בוס

מַבּוּעַ v. נבע מְבוּקָה v. בוק.

[מְבוּשִׁים, מְבוּשׁ] v. בוש

מִבְחוֹר, I, II מִבְחָר v. בחר

מַבָּט v. נבט. מִבְטָא v. בטא.

מִבְטָח v בטח. [מַבְלִיגִית] v בלג

מְבַלְּקָה v. בלק [מִבְנֶה] v. בנה.

מְבֻנַּי v. סבכי I מִבְצָר v. בצר.

II. **מִבְצָר** **n.pr.m.** Edomite chief Gn 36[42] = 1 Ch 1[53]; A𝔊L Μαζαρ, A (in Ch) Μαβσαρ;—on n pr loc *Mabsar* (Onom [277, 63, 137, 11]) cf. Buhl [Edom 34])

[מִבְרָח] v ברח מְבַשָּׂם v. בשׂם

[מְבֻשִׁים] v. בוש. מְבַשְּׁלוֹת v בשל.

†**מָג** **n.m.** soothsayer, magian (loan-word fr. As. *mahhu, soothsayer*, Dl[HWB 397]; perh. orig Sumerian, Dl[HA 14]),—רַב־מָג Je 39[3.13] *chief-soothsayer*, in train of Nebuchadrezzar.

מַגְבִּישׁ v גבשׁ מִגְבָּלֹת v. גבל.

מִגְבָּעוֹת v נבע.

מגד (√of foll., cf Ar مَجَدَ, مَجُدَ, *be glorious, excel in glory*)

†**מֶגֶד** **n.m.** excellence (NH *id.*, *choice fruit*; Syr. ܡܓܕܐ *fruit*; Ar. مَجْدٌ *glory, honour, nobility*);—מ׳ cstr. Dt 33[13] + 4 t. Dt 33; pl מְגָדִים Ct 4[13] 7[14]; sf. מְגָדָיו Ct 4[16]—*excellence*: excellent or choice things, always of gifts of nature: מ׳ שָׁמַיִם Dt 33[13] i.e (natural) gifts of heaven; מ׳ תְּבוּאֹת שָׁמֶשׁ v[14], מ׳ גֶּרֶשׁ יְרָחִים v[14], מ׳ גִּבְעוֹת עוֹלָם v[15] (|| רֹאשׁ הַרְרֵי קֶדֶם); מ׳ אֶרֶץ וּמְלֹאָהּ, pl abstr. פְּרִי מ׳ (= excellent fruit) Ct 4[13 16]; מ׳ alone = foreg, 7[14]

†[**מִגְדָּנָה**] **n.f.** choice or excellent thing,—pl abs מִגְדָּנוֹת, as gifts, Gn 24[53] 2 Ch 21[3] 32[23] (|| מִנְחָה), Ezr 1[6]

†**מַגְדִּיאֵל** **n.pr.m.** a chief of Edom, Gn 36[43] = 1 Ch 1[54], 𝔊[B] Μεδιηλ (Ch), 𝔊[A] Μετοδιηλ (Gn), Μαγεδιηλ (Ch, cf 𝔊L)—(cf. Sab. מגדעל Derenb [Études I 65], Palm. מגדת (מגרת?) Cook [Aram Gloss 70]).

מִגְדּוֹ, מְגִדּוֹן v. גדד.

מִגְדָּל, מִגְדּוֹל, מִגְדָּל v גדל.

מָגוֹג n pr. v גוג.

I, II. מָגוֹר, מְגוּרָה v. I, III. גור.

[מְגוּרָה] v. גור. מַגָּל v. נגל.

מְגִלָּה v. גלל. [מְגַמָּה] v. גמם.

מָגֵן, מִגֵּן, מְגִנָּה v. גנן

מִגְעֶרֶת v. גער. מַגֵּפָה v. נגף.

†**מַגְפִּיעָשׁ** **n pr.m.** a chief of the people, Ne 10[21], 𝔊 Βαγαφης, A Μαιαφης, 𝔊L Μεγαιας.

†[**מָגַר**] **vb.** cast, throw, toss (Aram. ܡܓܰܪ *lapsus est et cecidit* Lexx., 𝔗 Pa מַגַּר *hurl down* 2 K 9[33], *overthrow*);—**Qal** *Pt* pass. pl. cstr. מְגוּרֵי אֶל־חֶרֶב הָיוּ Ez 21[17] *they are thrown to the sword* (on cstr. before prep v. Ges[§ 130 1] Da[Synt. § 28 R 1]) **Pi.** *Pf* 2 ms. וְכִסְאוֹ לָאָרֶץ מִגַּרְתָּה: ψ 89[45] and his throne to earth *thou hast hurled.*

†**מִגְרוֹן** **n.pr.loc.** **1.** 1 S 14[2] district (?) near Gibeah (home of Saul), cf. Buhl[Geogr 178]; 𝔊 Μαγων, 𝔊L Μαγεδδω (We thinks n.pr. not required, and prop. מִגֹּרֶן (= 𝔖 גֹּרֶן *threshing-floor*, so Bu, but word not in Hebrew; Klo, improb, מִגְרָשׁ). **2.** Is 10[28], place north of Michmash (and Gibeah), 𝔊 Μαγεδω, perhaps modern ruin *Makrun* Di[ad loc] Bd[Pal 3 121] Buhl[l c].

מְגֵרָה v. נרר.

[מְגֵרָעָה], מִגְרָעוֹת v. גרע.

[מְגֵרָפָה] v. גרף. מִגְרָשׁ v. גרשׁ.

מַד v. מדד. I, II. מִדְבָּר v. דבר.

מָדַד ^{53} **vb.** measure (NH *id.*; Ph. מדד; Ar. مَدَّ *extend, stretch,* مُدّ *a corn-measure,* etc.; As. *madâdu, measure*; Jew.-Aram. n. מְיּדָּה *measure, proportion, rule*);—**Qal** *Pf.* מ׳ (מָדַד) Is 40^{12} + 9 t. Ez; sf. מְדָדוֹ Ez $42^{15.20}$; 1 s. וּמַדֹּתִי Is 65^{7}; וּמָדְדוֹ consec. Dt 21^{2} Ez 43^{10}; וּמַדֹּתֶם consec. Nu 35^{5}; *Impf.* וַיָּמָד Ru 3^{15} + 22 t. Ez; 2 ms. תָּמוֹד Ez 45^{3}; וַיָּמֹדּוּ Ex 16^{18}; תָּמֹדּוּ Ez 47^{18}; *Inf.* לָמֹד Zc 2^{6};—*measure,* chiefly lit. (usu. sq. acc. *rei*; obj. om. Ex 16^{18} Dt 21^{2} Ez 40^{35}, cf. 47^{18} (but v. Co); sq. acc. of measure Ru 3^{15} Ez 42^{19} $47^{3.4.4.5}$);—**1.** measure of length, distance Nu 35^{5} (P), Dt 21^{2} (D), Ez $40^{5.6.8.20}$ + 32 t. Ez 40–47 Zc 2^{6}. **2.** of dry measure Ex 16^{18} (P), Ru 3^{15}. **3.** fig. of measuring waters Is 40^{12} (of י׳); of requital Is 65^{7}. †**Niph.** *Impf.* יִמַּד Ho 2^{1} Je 33^{22}; יִמַּדּוּ Je 31^{37};—*be measured,* of sand of sea Ho 2^{1} Je 33^{22}; of heavens Je 31^{37}. †**Pi.** *Pf.* וּמִדַּד־ consec. Jb 7^{4} (cf. Ges$^{\S 52.2R.1}$); *Impf.* וַיְמַדֵּד 2 S 8^{2}; וַיְמַדְּדֵם v ^{2}; אֲמַדֵּד ψ 60^{8} 108^{8};—**1.** *extend, continue* (=make extent *or* continuation), subj. עָרֶב Jb 7^{4}. **2.** *measure, measure off,* בַּחֶבֶל, of apportioning Moabites to death and life, sq. sf. 2 S 8^{2}; also obj. חֲבָלִים v ^{2}; metaph. of conquest, sq. acc., ψ 60^{8} = 108^{8} (‖ חִלֵּק). **Po.** *Impf.* וַיְמֹדֶד Hb 3^{6} (subj. God, obj. אֶרֶץ), *measured* (viz. with eye) 𝔙 Hi AV RV, but dub.; 𝔊 ἐσαλεύθη, 𝔗 אֲזִיעַ, hence *shook* Ew Ke Or al. (fr. √[מוּד =] מוֹט, but rd. then rather וַיְמֹטֵט, although מוט not elsewhere in this conj.; We, plausibly, וַיְמֹגֵג √מוג, cf. Na 1^{5}). †**Hithpo.** וַיִּתְמֹדֵד sq. עַל־הַיֶּלֶד; 1 K 17^{21} *measured* (=extended, stretched) *himself* upon the boy.

[מַד] **n.m.** $^{1\S 4.12}$ **measure, also cloth garment** (as *extended, wide*);—sf. מִדּוֹ ψ 109^{18}; מִדּוֹ Lv 6^{3} 2 S 20^{8} (מִדָּה Jb 11^{9}, v. sub מִדָּה); pl. מִדִּין Ju 5^{10} (v. infr.), 2 S 21^{20} Kt (Qr מָדוֹן; rd. perh. מִדָּה, v. 1 Ch 20^{6}, cf. Dr); sf. מִדֶּיךָ Je 13^{25}; מַדָּיו 1 S 4^{12} + 4 t.;—**1.** *measure* (only pl.) = apportionment Je 13^{25}, מְנָת־מִדַּיִךְ (of lot of Judah, ‖ גּוֹרָל); cf. lit. 2 S 21^{20} Kt (but v. מִדָּה). **2.** perh. *cloth, carpet* (for sitting on), Ju 5^{10} (so most, conj. fr. context; on pl. in ִין, v. Ges$^{\S 87.1.a}$). **3.** *garment,* outer garment Ju 3^{16} 1 S 4^{12}, cf. (sim.) ψ 109^{18}; of fighting-attire 1 S 17^{38} (c. vb. הִלְבִּישׁ), v ^{39} 18^{4} 2 S 20^{8} (‖ לְבוּשׁ); of priest's garment וְלָבַשׁ הַכֹּהֵן מִדּוֹ בַד Lv 6^{3}; cf. [מַדְוֶה, מָדוּ] sub מדה.

†I. **מִדָּה** **n.f.** **measure, measurement, stature, size, garment** (mostly late)—מ׳ Ex 26^{2} + 35 t.; cstr. מִדַּת Ez 40^{21} + 2 t.; pl. מִדּוֹת Ez 41^{17} + 12 t.; מִדּוֹתָיו ψ 133^{2}; מִדּוֹתֶיהָ Ez 48^{16};—**1.** *measure, act of measurement,* i.e. long measure Ez 41^{17} (del. Co), 42^{15} $48^{30.33}$; cf. Jos 3^{4} (P), 1 Ch 23^{29}, v. also Lv 19^{35} (H); once of liquid measure, fig., Jb 28^{25}; קַוֵּה הַמּ׳ Je 31^{39} *measuring-line*; חֶבֶל מ׳ Zc 2^{5} (*id.*); קְנֵה הַמּ׳ *measuring-reed* Ez $40^{3.5}$ 42^{16} (del. Co), v$^{16.17.18.19}$. **2.** *measurement, size* of curtains in tabern. Ex $26^{2.8}$ $36^{9.15}$ (all P); cf. 1 K 6^{25} 7^{37} (both ‖ קֶצֶב), v$^{9.11}$ 2 Ch 3^{3} Ez $40^{10.10.21.22.24.28.29.32.33.35}$ 43^{13} 46^{22} 48^{16}; once of time, מִדַּת יָמַי ψ 39^{5}; prob. also Jb 11^{9} (fig. of God's wisdom) where מִדָּתָהּ = מִדָּהּ, cf. Sta$^{\S 347.c.2}$; בֵּית מִדּוֹת = *house of size* Je 22^{14}; אִישׁ מִדָּה = *man of size, stature,* 1 Ch 11^{23} 20^{6}; so also prob. ‖ 2 S 21^{20} (for 𝔊 מדין, Qr מָדוֹן, v. [מַד]), We Dr Kit Bu; pl. Nu 13^{32} Is 45^{14}. **3.** *measured portion, extent,* stretch (of wall) Ne $3^{11.19.20.21.24.27.30}$, cf. Ez 45^{3}. **4.** *garment* (pl. poet.) ψ 133^{2}.

†[מֵמַד] **n.**[**m.**] **measurement**;—מִי שָׂם מְמַדֶּיהָ Jb 38^{5}, i.e. of the earth (‖ מִי־נָטָה עָלֶיהָ קָו).

†**מִדִּין** **n.pr.loc.** city of Judah Jos 15^{61}, site unknown, A Μαθων; 𝔊L Μαδδειν.

†II. [מִדָּה] **n.f.** **tribute** (loan-word fr. As. *mandattu, id.,* √ *nadânu* = נָתַן Dl$^{HWB 451}$, cf. Schr$^{COT Ezr 4, 13}$; also in BAram. מִדָּה, מִנְדָּה *id.*);—מִדַּת הַמֶּלֶךְ Ne 5^{4}.

מדה (secondary form of מדד; √of foll.)

†[מָדוּ], I. [מַדְוֶה] **n.m.** **garment**;—pl. sf. מַדְוֵיהֶם 2 S 10^{4} = 1 Ch 19^{4}.

†מַדְהֵבָה† Is 14^{4}, rd. מַרְהֵבָה v. רהב.

†II. [מַדְוֶה] v. דוה. מַדּוּחִים v. נדח.

I, II. מָדוֹן v. דין.

† III. מָדוֹן **n.**[**m.**] 2 S 21^{20} Qr, v. I. מִדָּה.

מַדּוּעַ v. ידע, p. 396.

מְדוּרָה v. דור. מִדְחֶה v. דחה.

[מַדְחֵפָה], מַדְחֵפֹת v. דחף.

†מָדַי **n.pr.gent.** et **terr. Medes, Media** (OPers. *Mâda* Sp[APK], As. *Madai* COT[Gloss. and on Gn 10. 2] Dl[Par. 247]);—**1.** people, as 'son' of Japhet Gn 10[2] (P) = 1 Ch 1[5]; as hostile power Is 13[17] 21[2]; זֶרַע מָדַי Dn 9[1]; land and people, מַלְכֵי מָדַי Je 25[25] (+מַלְכֵי עֵילָם), 51[11.28]; מַלְכֵי מ׳ וּפָרַס Dn 8[20]; cf. פָּרַס וּמָדַי Est 1[3.14.18.19] 10[2]; 𝔊 Μαδαι. **2.** of land alone = *Media* 2 K 17[6] 18[11] (both עָרֵי מָדָי).

†מָדִי **adj.gent. Mede, Median,** דָּרְיָוֶשׁ הַמָּדִי Dn 11[1].

מַדַּי (i.e. מַה־דַּי) 2 Ch 30[3], v. מה **1 e.**

מִדֵּי v. דַּי.

מִדְיָן, מְדִינָה v. דין.

מַדְוֶה v. דוה. — מִדְיָנִים v. I. מדון.

מַדְמֵן, מַדְמֵנָה, מַדְמֵנָּה I, II. v. דמן.

מְדָנִים v. מדון, מִדְיָנֵי. — מְדָן v. דין.

מַדָּע, מֹדַע, מֹדַעַת v. ידע.

[מַדְקָרָה], pl. cstr. מַדְקְרוֹת v. דקר.

מְדֻרָה v. דור. — מַדְרֵגָה v. דרג.

[מִדְרָשׁ] v. דרש. — [מִדְרָךְ] v. דרך.

[מְדֻשָּׁה] v. דוש.

מָה, rarely **מָה־** (e.g. Gn 31[43] Jos 22[16] Ju 8[1]), **מַה־, מָה, מֶה, מַה·, מָ·** (†Ex 4[2] Is 3[15] Mal 1[13] 1 Ch 15[13] 2 Ch 30[3]), **מָ** (only in מָהֵם †Ez 8[6] Kt., Qr. מָה הֵם)—on the distinction in the use of these forms, see Ges[§ 37]—**pron. interrog.** and **indef. what? how? aught;** used of things, as מִי of persons (Aram. ܡܳܐ, מָא, Ar. مَا; prob. apoc. from a longer form with *n* or *nt*, As. *minû* (Dl[HWB 417 f.]), Eth. ምንት: *ment;* cf. W[CG 123 ff.] Kö[II. 368]):—**1.** interrog. *what?* **a.** in a direct question, before either verbs or nouns Gn 4[10] מֶה עָשִׂיתָ *what* hast thou done? 15[2] מַה־תִּתֶּן־לִי *what* wilt thou give me? Ex 3[13] מַה־שְּׁמוֹ, 12[26] 13[14] and so very often: מַה־הִיא Zc 5[6]; מה אלה Zc 1[9]; מָה אַתָּה רֹאֶה Je 1[11] Am 7[8]+; Jl 4[14] מה אתם לי; Ju 18[8] מה אתם vid. Comm., v[24] מה לי עוד *what* have I still? Is 21[11] מַה־מִּלַּיְלָה *what* (= how much) of the night (is past)? = *as what? (qualem?)* Hg 2[3] (cf. מִי Am 7[2]); to express surprise, Jb 9[12] who shall say to him, מה תעשה *what* doest thou? 22[13] Ec 8[4] Is 45[9.10]; sq. כִּי, Gn 20[10] מה ראית כי עשית *what* hadst thou in view, that thou hast done, etc.? 31[36] Ex 16[7] וְנַחְנוּ מָה כִּי and *what* are we, that . . .? 32[21] Nu 22[28] Hb 2[18], etc. Note in partic.—(*a*) מָה is followed sometimes by a subst. in appos. (against Arabic usage, which does not permit this: W[AG. ii. § 170]), so that it becomes virtually an adj.: מַה־בֶּצַע *what* profit . . .? Gn 37[26] ψ 30[10] Mal 3[14]; Is 40[8] מַה־דְּמוּת, Mal 1[13] ψ 89[48] זְכָר־אֲנִי מֶה חָלֶד (inverted for מֶה חֶלֶד אָנִי) remember (of) *what* (short) duration I am, Ec 1[3] 5[10.15] 6[8.11] (Da[§ 8, R. 2] Kö[III. 23 f.]); as exclam., ψ 89[48 b] Jb 26[14]. And with the subst. idiom. at the end (in Arabic preceded then by مِنْ: W[AG. ii. § 49. 7]), 1 S 26[18] וּמַה־בְּיָדִי רעה and what is there in my hand, evil? 20[10] (vid. **3**), 2 S 19[29] 24[13] 1 K 12[16] Je 2[5] מַה־מצאו אבותיכם בי עָוֶל, Ec 11[2] Est 6[3]. (*b*) מַה־זֶּה *what, now?* 1 S 10[11], contr. מַזֶּה †Ex 4[2] (זֶה **4 c**); Gn 3[13] מַה־זֹּאת עָשִׂית; 12[18] 29[25] מַה־זֹּאת עָשִׂיתָ לִּי; similarly 26[10] 42[28]+, either *what, now,* hast thou done? or *what is this* that thou hast done? (vid. זֶה **4 d**). (*c*) מַה־לְּךָ *what* to thee? i.e. *what aileth* thee? or *what dost thou want?* Gn 21[17] מַה־לָּךְ הָגָר; Jos 15[18] 2 S 14[5] 1 K 1[16] 2 K 6[28] Ez 18[2] (accents); sq. כִּי, Ju 18[23] מה־לך כי נזעקת, Gn 20[9] (cf. 1 S 11[5] מה לעם כי יבכו), Is 22[1] מַה־לָּךְ כִּי עָלִית (cf. τί παθὼν τοῦτο ποιεῖς;), ψ 114[5]; without כִּי Is 3[15] (cf. Qor 57[8.10]); with a ptcp., Jon 1[6] *what is it to thee* as a sleeper? (accus.: Da[§ 70 a] cites Qor 74[50]), Ez 18[2] (if אתם be treated as strengthening לכם). (*d*) מַה־לְּךָ (לִּי) פֹּה = *what* hast thou (have I) here? Ju 18[3] 1 K 19[9] Is 22[16] 52[5]. (*e*) in the genit., Jer 8[9] וְחָכְמַת־מֶה לָהֶם, and wisdom of *what* (= what kind of wisdom) is theirs? Nu 23[3] (v. infr. **3**). **b.** often in an *indirect* question, as after ראה, Gn 2[19] to see מה־יקרא־לו *what* he would call it, 37[20] וְנִרְאֶה מה־יהיו חלמתיו *to what* his dreams will come, Nu 13[19 f.] Hb 2[1]; הַכִּיר Gn 31[32]; ידע 39[8] Ex 2[4] לדעת מה־יֵּעָשֶׂה לו, 16[15] 32[1] Jb 34[4]; שמע Nu 9[8] וְאשמעה מה־יצוה י׳ (cf. ψ 85[9]), 2 S 17[5]; פֵּרֵשׁ Nu 15[34]; שאל 1 K 3[5] 2 K 2[9]; הֵבִין Jb 6[24] 23[5]: Nu 13[18] וראיתם את הארץ מה היא, ψ 39[5] Is 41[22] הָרִאשֹׁנוֹת מָה הֵנָּה הַגִּידוּ.—In some such cases it approximates in meaning to the simple rel., as Jer 7[17] 33[24] Mi 6[5.8] Jb 34[33]. **c.** = *of what kind?* (Germ. *was für ein . . .?*), with an insinuation of blame, or reproach, or contempt: Gn 37[10] מה החלום הזה *what* is this

dream which thou hast dreamt? 44[15] Jos 22[16] Ju 8[1] 15[11] 20[12] 1 S 29[3] מָה הָעִבְרִים האלה, 1 K 9[13] מה הערים האלה אשר נתתה לי, 2 K 9[22] 18[19]. **d.** מה is often used in questions to which the answer *little*, or *nothing*, is expected, and it thus becomes equivalent to a *rhetorical negative* (cf. הֲ **b**, מִי **f** *c*): (*a*) Gn 23[15] land worth 400 shekels..., מה היא *what is it?* (i.e. it is something quite insignificant), 27[37] Ju 8[2] ומה־יכלתי עשות ככם, 14[18] Ho 9[5] 10[3] ψ 30[10] 56[5] Jb 15[9] 16[6] 21[21] 22[13.17] La 2[13] Ct 5[9] מַה־דּוֹדֵךְ מִדּוֹד *what* is thy beloved (more) than a(nother) beloved? ‖ לא, 1 K 12[16] מַה־לָּנוּ חֵלֶק בְּדָוִד וְלֹא־נַחֲלָה בְּבֶן יִשַׁי (2 S 20[1] אֵין־לָנוּ חֵלֶק וגו׳), Jb 16[6]. (*b*) sq. כִּי (כִּי **1 f**), Gn 20[9] 37[26] מַה־בֶּצַע כִּי נַהֲרֹג *what* profit (is it) that we should slay him? Ex 16[7] Nu 16[11] Hb 2[18] 2 K 8[13] *what* is thy servant, the dog, *that he should do*, etc.? and often in poetry, as ψ 8[5] מָה אנוש כי תזכרנו *what* is man *that* thou rememberest him? Jb 6[11] מַה־כֹּחִי כִּי אֲיַחֵל, v[11 b] 7[17] 15[12f.14] 16[3] 21[15] + (cf. מִי **f** *b*). Hence, (*c*) in the formula of repudiation, or emphatic denial, מַה־לִּי וָלָךְ (וְלָכֶם) *what* is there (common) to me and to thee? i.e. what have I to do with thee? †Ju 11[12] 2 S 16[10] מה לי ולכם, 19[23] 1 K 17[18] 2 K 3[13] 2 Ch 35[21]; cf. Jos 22[24] 2 K 9[18.19]; rather differently, without וְ, †Je 2[18] מה לך לדרך מ׳ *what* is there to thee *with reference to* the way to Egypt? Ho 14[9] מַה־לִּי לָעֲצַבִּים, cf. ψ 50[16] (לְסַפֵּר); with את, †Je 23[28] מַה־לַתֶּבֶן אֶת־הַבָּר *beside* (or *in comparison with*) the wheat? cf. τί ἐμοὶ (ἡμῖν) καὶ σοί; Mt 8[29] Mk 5[7] Jn 2[4]; and Ar. مَا لِي وَلَكَ. **e.** =*whatsoever* (cf. מִי **g**): (*a*) Ju 9[48] מה אתם ראיתם עשיתי מהרו עשו כמוני, lit. *what* do you see (that) I have done? hasten, and do like me (=*whatever* ye see, etc.), 2 S 21[4] מה אתם אמרים אעשה לכם, Jb 6[24]; with the apod. introd. by וְ, 1 S 20[4] מה תאמר נפשך ואעשה לך; Est 5[3] מַה־בַּקָּשָׁתֵךְ ... וְיִנָּתֵן לָךְ, v[6] 7[2] 9[12]; hence in the late and strange idiom of Ch., it sinks twice almost to the rel. *what*, 1 Ch 15[13] כי לְמַבָּרִאשׁוֹנָה לא אתם because ye were not (employed) for *what* was at first (on the former occasion), J. etc., 2 Ch 30[3] לְמַדַּי acc. to *what* was sufficient (=in sufficient numbers), cf. Est 9[26]. (*b*) מַה־שֶּׁ־ (late: frequently in Mishn., etc.), *whatever*, *what* (cf. מִי, מִי אֲשֶׁר **g** *end*): †Ec 1[9] מַה־שֶּׁהָיָה הוא שֶׁיִּהְיֶה, lit. *what* is that which hath been? it is that which shall be (=*whatever* hath been, it is that which shall be), v[9] 3[15.22] 6[10] 7[24] 8[7] 10[14].

2. Used adverbially: **a.** as an *interrogative*: (*a*) *how?* especially in expressing what is regarded as an impossibility, Gn 44[16] מַה־נִּצְטַדָּק *how* shall we justify ourselves? Nu 23[8.8] 1 S 10[27] מַה־יֹּשִׁעֵנוּ זֶה, 2 K 4[43] Jb 9[2] 25[4.4] 31[1] I made a covenant with my eyes, וּמָה אֶתְבּוֹנֵן עַל ב׳ and *how* should I look upon a maid? (𝔊 οὐ, 𝔙 *non*), Pr 20[24] וְאָדָם מַה־יָּבִין דַּרְכּוֹ; in an indirect question, Ex 10[26] ψ 39[5] אֵדְעָה מֶה־חָדֵל אָנִי; מַה־זֶּה *how, now?* (in surprise), Gn 27[20] מַה־זֶּה מִהַרְתָּ לִמְצֹא בְּנִי, Ju 18[24] 1 K 21[5] 2 K 1[5]. (*b*) *why?* Ex 14[15] מַה תִּצְעַק אֵלָי, 17[2.2] 2 K 6[33] 7[3] ψ 42[6] מַה־תִּשְׁתּוֹחֲחִי עלי, Jb 15[12] +; Ct 8[4] I adjure you מַה־תָּעִירוּ וּמַה־תְּעֹרְרוּ, *why* will ye stir up, etc.? (i.e. *do not*: ‖ אִם 2[7] 3[5]).—The transition from the interrog. to the neg., to which in Heb. there is an approx. (v. supr.: esp. 1 K 12[16] Jb 31[1] Ct 8[4]), is in Ar. complete, مَا being there used constantly in the sense of *not* (cf. Walker[Hbr. xii. 244 ff.]; Kö[iii. 478]). **b.** as an *exclam.*, *how...!* with adjectives and verbs, Gn 28[17] מַה־נּוֹרָא הַמָּקוֹם הַזֶּה *how* dreadful is this place! 38[29] Nu 24[5] מַה־טֹּבוּ אֹהָלֶיךָ, Is 52[7] ψ 3[2] מה רבו, 8[2] מה אדיר, 21[2] 36[8], etc., Ct 4[10.10] 7[2]; ironically, 2 S 6[20] Je 2[33.36] Jb 26[2.3].

3. Indef. pron. *anything*, *aught*, Nu 23[3] וּדְבַר־מַה־יַּרְאֵנִי וְהִגַּדְתִּי לָךְ and he will shew me the matter of *aught*, and I will tell thee (=if he shew me... I will, etc., Dr[§ 149]), 1 S 19[3] וְרָאִיתִי מָה וְהִגַּדְתִּי לָךְ=and if I see aught, I will, etc., 20[10] אוֹ מַה־יַּעַנְךָ אָבִיךָ קָשָׁה if perchance thy father shall answer thee *aught* that is harsh (order, **1 a** *a*), 2 S 18[22] וִיהִי־מָה אָרוּצָה־נָּא but let there happen *what may* (lit. *aught*), I will run, v[23] (cf. Jb 13[13] וְיַעֲבֹר עָלַי מָה), v[29] וְלֹא יָדַעְתִּי מָה (cf. Pr 9[13]), Pr 25[8]. Cf. Kö[iii. § 65].

4. With preps.: **a.** בַּמֶּה[9], בַּמָּה[19] *wherein?* Ex 22[26] Ju 16[5] 1 S 14[38] (indirect question; We בַּמִּי); and so acc. to the various senses of בְּ: *whereby?* Gn 15[8] Ex 33[16] Mal 1[2.6.7] 2[17] 3[7-8]; *wherewith?* 1 S 6[2] 2 S 21[3] Mi 6[6]; *by what means?* Ju 16[5] וּבַמֶּה נוּכַל לוֹ; *at what* (worth)? Is 2[22]; *for what?* 2 Ch 7[21] (‖ 1 K 9[8] עַל־מָה). **b.** יַעַן מֶה †Hg 1[9] *because of what?* †**c.** כַּמֶּה, כַּמָּה, prop. *the like of what?* (Ar. كَمْ, Syr. ܟܡܐ); hence (*a*) *how much? how many?* כַּמָּה יְמֵי וגו׳ Gn 47[8] 2 S 19[35] ψ 119[84] Jb 13[23]; עַד כַּמָּה פְעָמִים 1 K 22[16] (=2 Ch 18[15]); כַּמָּה *how often?* Jb 21[17] (i.e. how seldom!); in an indirect question, *how much?* Zc 2[6.6]. As an exclamation, Zc 7[3] as

I have done זֶה כַּמֶּה שָׁנִים now (זֶה **4 i**), *how many* years! ψ 78^{40} כַּמָּה *how often!* (*b*) *for how long?* ψ 35^{17} כמה תראה, Jb 7^{19}. **d.** לָ֫מָּה, לָמָ֫ה (לָ֫מָּה) mostly before the gutturals א, ה, ע, and י׳ [i.e. אֲדֹנָי], but twice besides, ψ 42^{10} 43^{2}; לָ֫מָּה also occurs before gutt., in five places noted by Mas. on ψ 43^{2}, viz. 1 S 28^{15} 2 S 2^{22} 14^{31} ψ 49^{6} Je 15^{18}, and before ה †Gn 4^{6} 2 S 14^{13} 24^{3} Ec 2^{15}), לָ֫מָּה †Jb 7^{20}, לָ֫מָּה † 1 S $1^{8.8.8}$, *for what reason? why?* Gn 4^{6} למה חרה לך *why* art thou angry? 24^{31}, etc.; often strengthened by זֶה (זֶה **4 e**), Gn 18^{13} 32^{30} (=Ju 13^{18}) למה זה תשאל לשמי, 33^{15} Ex 2^{20} 5^{22} 17^{3}, etc., Je 6^{20} 20^{18}+; Gn 25^{22} אם כן למה־זה אנכי if so, *why, then,* am I? (why do I continue to live?); =*to what purpose* (sq. לְ pers.), Gn 27^{46} למה לי חיים, Is 1^{11} Je 6^{20} Am 5^{18} למה זה לכם יום י׳, Jb 30^{2}; in an indirect question, 1 S 6^{3} Dn 10^{20}. Note especially (*a*) in expostulations, Gn 12^{18} למה לא הגדת לי *why* didst thou not tell me, etc.? v^{19} 29^{25} 31^{27} 42^{1} 43^{6} 1 S 21^{15} 22^{13} 24^{10} ψ 22^{2} $44^{24.25}$ $74^{1.11}$+ oft.; (*b*) with an impf., oft. deprecating, or introducing rhetorically, the reason why something should, or should not, be done, *why should ...?* 1 S $19^{5.17}$ 20^{8} but to thy father (emph.) למה זה תביאני, *why shouldst* thou bring me? 20^{32} למה יומת מה עשׂה *why should* he be put to death? 2 S 13^{26} 16^{9} 20^{19} 2 K 14^{10}, etc.: in such cases, it approximates in meaning to *lest* (cf. Ph. CIS$^{1.2.21}$ לָם יסגרינם אלנם *ne* tradant eos dii), and is in 𝔊 often rendered by μήποτε, as Gn 27^{45} למה אשכל *why should* I be bereaved, etc.? Ex 32^{12} למה יאמרו מצרים Ne 6^{3} ψ 79^{10} 115^{2} Ec 7^{16}, μή, Jer 40^{15}, ἵνα μή, Gn 47^{19} 2 S 2^{22} 2 Ch 25^{16} Ec 5^{5} 7^{17}, or ὅπως μή, Jo 2^{17} (in 1 S 19^{17} 2 S 13^{26}, paraph. by εἰ μή); and, connected with the foreg. sentence by אשׁר, or שֶׁ, in late, or dial., Heb. it actually has that mng., Dn 1^{10} אֲשֶׁר לָמָּה יִרְאֶה *lest* he see, Ct 1^{7} שַׁלָּמָה אֶהְיֶה *lest* I become (so in Aram. דִּי לְמָה Ezr 7^{23}, דִּילְמָא 𝔗, Syr. ܕܠܡܐ, both regularly=*lest*). **e.** עַד־מָה (ψ 4^{3} עַד־מֶה) *until when? how long?* †Nu 24^{22} (aposiop.), ψ 4^{3} 79^{5} 89^{47}; in indirect qu., ψ 74^{9} (cf. עד מתי, עד אנה). **f.** עַל־מָה, and עַל־מֶה, *upon what?* Jb 38^{6} 2 Ch 32^{10}; *upon what ground? wherefore?* Nu 22^{32} עַל־מָה הִכִּיתָ אֶת־אֲתֹנְךָ, Dt 29^{23} (cf. 1 K 9^{8} Je 22^{8}), Is 1^{5} Je 8^{14} 9^{11} 16^{10} Ez 21^{12} ψ 10^{13} Jb 13^{14} (probably dittogr. from v^{13}); עַל־מַה־זֶּה Ne 2^{4}. In an indirect question, Jb 10^{2} הוֹדִיעֵנִי עַל מַה־תְּרִיבֵנִי, Est 4^{5} לָדַעַת מַה־זֶּה וְעַל־מַה־זֶּה.

†[מָהַהּ] **vb.** only **Hithpalp.** linger, tarry (cf. Ar. مَهْمَهَ *slow walk, delay* (Kam.));—**Hithpalp.** *Pf.* 1 s. הִתְמַהְמָ֫הְתִּי ψ 119^{60}; 3 pl. הִתְמַהְמָ֫הוּ Ju 19^{8}; 1 pl. הִתְמַהְמָ֫הְנוּ Gn 43^{10}; *Impf.* יִתְמַהְמַהּ Hb 2^{3}; וַיִּתְמַ׳ Gn 19^{16}; *Imv.* mpl. הִתְמַהְמְהוּ Is 29^{9}; *Inf.* לְהִתְמַהְמֵהַּ Ex 12^{39}; *Pt.* מִתְמַהְמֵהַּ 2 S 15^{28};—*linger, tarry, wait,* of pers., Gn 19^{16} 43^{10} (J), Ex 12^{39} (E), Ju 3^{26} 19^{8} 2 S 15^{28} Is 29^{9} ψ 119^{60} (c. לֹא, opp. חַשְׁתִּי); subj. חָזוֹן *vision* Hb 2^{3}.

מְהוּמָה v. הום. מְהוּמָן v. אמן.

מְהֵיטַבְאֵל v. יטב.

†[מָהַל] **vb. circumcise, weaken** (si vera l.; cf. NH מָהַל *circumcise,* Aram. מְהַל *id.*);—only fig. **Qal** *Pt. pass.* סָבְאֵךְ מָהוּל בַּמָּיִם Is 1^{22} *thy choice wine weakened with water,* so Thes De Che^{Comm} Di Du; cf. *vinum castrare,* Plin$^{xix.53}$: Ba$^{Erkl.\,d.\,Jes.}$ Che^{Hpt} (cf. Nö$^{ZMG\,xl.\,1886,\,741}$) comp. NH מוהל, *juice* (of fruit, esp. olives); Ar. مُهْلٌ *oil, liquid pitch, suppurating matter;* v. against this Di.

[מַהֲלָךְ] v. הלך.

[מַהֲלָל], מַהֲלַלְאֵל v. II. הלל.

מַהֲלֻמוֹת v. הלם.

[מַהֲמֹרָה], מַהֲמֹרוֹת v. המר.

[מַהְפֵּכָה], מַהְפֶּ֫כֶת v. הפך.

†I. [מָהַר] **vb.** hasten (NH Pi., and deriv.; Ar. مَهَرَ *be practised, skilled* (with As. *mâru, send, order, govern,* cf. II. מהר); Eth. ᠐ᠰᡃ: *train, teach;* Syr. ܡܗܪ Pa. *id.;* cf. also Egypt. *māhar, trained warrior* Bondi^{57});—**Niph.** *Pf.* 3 fs. נִמְהָרָה Jb 5^{13}; *Pt.* נִמְהָר Hb 1^{6}; pl. נִמְהָרִים Is 32^{4}; cstr. נִמְהֲרֵי Is 35^{4};—*be hurried*=anxious, disturbed נִמְהֲרֵי־לֵב Is 35^{4}; *hasty, precipitate,* subj. עֵצָה Jb 5^{13}; so pt. as subst. Is 32^{4}; *impetuous,* of Chaldeans, Hb 1^{6} (‖ מַר). **Pi.** *Pf.* מִהַר 1 S 4^{14} Is 51^{14}; 3 fs. מִהֲרָה Je 48^{16} etc.; *Impf.* יְמַהֵר Is 5^{19}+2 t.; וַיְמַהֵר Gn 18^{6}+8 t. (1 S 28^{30} v. infr.); 3 fpl. תְּמַהֵרְנָה Je 9^{17} etc.; *Imv.* ms. מַהֵר Gn 19^{22}+; מַהֲרָה 1 S 23^{27} 1 K 22^{9}, etc.; *Inf. cstr.* מַהֵר Pr 7^{23}+; *Pt.* מְמַהֵר Gn 41^{32} Mal 3^{5} (on מַהֵר Zp 1^{14} [1 S 23^{22}] cf. Kö$^{i.\,268}$, Schwally$^{ZAW\,x.\,1890,\,176}$ vid. 1. מַהֵר infra), fpl. מְמַהֲרוֹת Pr 6^{18};—**1.** *hasten, make haste,* =go or come quickly Gn 18^{6} 1 S 9^{12} (but del. 𝔊 We

Dr Kit Bu HPS), Na 2[6] Is 49[17] 1 Ch 12[9]; =go eagerly, (sq. Inf. of purpose) Pr 1[16] Is 59[7]; *Pt.* =swift, prompt Mal 3[5]; of bird Pr 7[23]; fig. of calamity Is 5[19] (‖חוּשׁ), Je 48[16], cf. מַהֵר שָׁלָל חָשׁ בַּז Is 8[1.3], infr. **2.** *hasten* + vb, (מ׳ having really adverbial force): sq Inf Gn 18[7] (מהר לַעֲשׂת); cf. 27[20] 41[32] (subj God), Ex 2[18] 10[16] 12[33] 2 S 15[14] Is 32[4] 51[14] Pr 6[18] Ec 5[1]; more often sq. vb. c ו Gn 24[18.20.46] 44[11] (all J), 45[9.13] (E), prob. 43[30] (J), also Ex 34[8] (J), Jos 4[10] 8[14.19] (all JE), Ju 13[10] 1 S 4[14] 17[48] 23[27] 25[18.23.34.34] 28[24] 2 S 15[14] 19[17] 1 K 20[33.41] 2 K 9[13] Je 9[17], so even when act. is not wholly voluntary 1 S 28[20] (but rd. prob. וַיִּבָּהֵל 𝔊 We Dr Kit Bu); also, ו om, ψ 106[13], esp. c. Imv. Gn 19[22] (J), Ju 9[48] Est 6[10]; so also מַהֵר עֲנֵנִי ψ 69[18] 102[3] 143[7]; cf. 79[8] (v. Ol[ad loc.]). **3.** trans *hasten*, = prepare quickly Gn 18[6]; =bring quickly 1 K 22[9]=2 Ch 18[8], Est 5[5]; = do quickly 2 Ch 24[5.5].

† I. מַהֵר **adj. hastening, speedy, swift** (strictly **Pi.** *Pt* for מְמַהֵר v. sub מהר);—of יוֹם י׳ קָרוֹב וּמ׳ מְאֹד, (בַּגִּלּוֹ) הַמַּהֲרָה Zp 1[14], rd also f. 1 S 23[22] *his swift foot* (for MT (ר׳ מִי רָאָהוּ) Th We Dr Bu, deeper corruption assumed by HPS.

† II. מַהֵר **adv. quickly, speedily** (strictly **Pi.** inf. abs) always immediately after vb.; Ex 32[8] (J), Dt 4[26] 7[4.22] 9[3.12.12.16] 28[20] Jos 2[5] (J), Ju 2[17.23] Pr 25[8] (on ψ 69[18] 79[8] 102[3] 143[7], where מ׳ precedes, v. supr. sub מָהַר).

† מָהִיר **adj. quick, prompt, ready, skilled**,—אִישׁ מ׳ בִּמְלַאכְתּוֹ; ψ סוֹפֵר מ׳ 45[2] Ezr 7[6]; Pr 22[29], cstr. מְהִר צֶדֶק Is 16[5] *prompt in justice*.

† מְהֵרָה **n.f. haste, speed**;—usually as adverb. acc. *hastily, quickly:* Jos 8[19] 10[6] 23[16] (all JE), Nu 17[11] (P), Dt 11[17] Ju 9[54] 2 S 17[16.18.21] Je 27[16] Ec 8[11] (in all these cases after vb.); before vb. (poet) Is 5[26] (‖קַל), ψ 31[3] 37[2] Is 58[8] Jo 4[4] (‖קַל); so also 1 S 20[38] מ׳ הוּשָׁה (cf. Dr); 2 K 1[11] מ׳ רֵדָה,—but perhaps rd. מַהֲרָה, i e. *Pi. Imv* of מהר (cf. 1 S 23[27]); c. prep (late): בִּמ׳ *in haste*=quickly Ec 4[12]; עַד־מ׳, *id.* ψ 147[15].

† מַהֲרַי **n.pr.m.** one of David's heroes, 2 S 23[28] 1 Ch 11[30] 27[13]; 𝔊 Νοερε, Μαελαι, Μααραυ, Μααρι, etc.

† מַהֵר שָׁלָל חָשׁ בַּז as **n.pr.m.** Is 8[1.3] (lit. *Swift is booty, speedy is prey*).

II. מהר (√ of foll; cf prob As *mâru*; *send*, whence *tamirtu, tumartu*, (*missive*,) *gift*, Dl[HWB 389 f.]; v. No[ZMG xl. 1886, 154]).

† מֹהַר **n.m. purchase-price of wife** (NH *id.*; Ar. مَهْر RS[K 78 f. Proph iv n. 13] No[l c.] Sta[Gesch i 381] Dr[Dt 22, 23] and reff., Aram. מוֹהֲרָא, ܡܗܪܐ),—abs מ׳ Gn 34[12] (J, ‖ מַתָּן) 1 S 18[25], cstr. מֹהַר הַבְּתוּלֹת Ex 22[16] (E).

† III. [מָהַר] **vb. denom. acquire by paying purchase-price** (Ar. مَهَرَ *give a dowry, marry for a* مَهْر; cf. Gerber[Verb denom 12] Buhl SS);—**Qal** *Pf.* 3 pl. מָהָרוּ ψ 16[4] usu. *obtain* another *in exchange* (or, by paying a price, cf. Che), but txt. dub; *Impf* 3 ms. sf. + *Inf. abs.* מָהֹר יִמְהָרֶנָּה לּוֹ לְאִשָּׁה Ex 22[15] (E).

מַהֲתַלּוֹת v. תלל.

I. מוֹ a paragogic syllable, attached to בְּ, כְּ, לְ (q. v.), so as to form with them independent words, לְמוֹ, כְּמוֹ, בְּמוֹ (q. v.) These forms, except sometimes כמו, are exclusively poetical. In origin מו is identical with מָה *what*, Ar. مَا, which is used similarly, pleonastically, with certain prefixes, e.g بِمَا, كَمَا, عَمَّا See Qor 3[153] 71[25]; Fl[Kl. Schr i. 473 f., 479, 558]; W[AG ii § 70, Rem / SG 128 f.], Ko[ii 250 f.]; and cf. Eth. ከመ:, Syr. ܐܝܟܡܐ, Sab. במו=بمه, DHM[ZDMG 1883, 396 f.], Hom[Chrest. § 18].

II. [מוֹ]=מַי *water.*

מוֹאָב, מֹאָב[180] **n.pr. gent. et terr. Moab** (MI[1.2.5.6.12.20] מאב; As *Ma'aba, Ma'bu, Mu'âba*, etc., Schr[COT Gloss. and on Gn 19, 37] Dl[Par 294 f., 298];—on etym. cf. Lag[BN 90 Anm.], Ne[SK 1892, 573], Gray[Prop N 25]);—מוֹ׳ Gn 19[37] + 178 t.; מֹאָב 2 S 8[12]; 𝔊 Μωαβ,—**1.** *Moab* as son of Lot by his elder daughter acc. to Gn 19[37]. **2.** *Moab:* **a.** = nation of which Lot's son is represented as ancestor Gn 19[37] Nu 21[29] 22[3.3] Am 2[1.2] Je 48[1.2] + 30 t. Je 48 + oft.; having a king, Nu 21[26] 22[4.10] Ju 3[12] 1 S 12[9] +. **b.** = territory of Moab Nu 21[11.13.13.15] +; שְׂדֵה מ׳ † Gn 36[35] Nu 15[20] Ru 1[1.2.6.6.22] 2[6] 4[3] 1 Ch 1[46] 8[8]; אֶרֶץ מ׳ † Dt 1[5] 28[69] 32[49] 34[5.6] Ju 11[15.18.18] Je 48[24.33]; מִדְבַּר מ׳ † Dt 2[8]; עַרְבוֹת מ׳ † Nu 26[3.63] 31[12] 33[48.49.50] 35[1] 36[13] Dt 34[1.8] Jos 13[32].

† מוֹאָבִי, מוֹאָבִיָּה **adj. gent. Moabitish**;—מ׳ Dt 23[4] + 2 t, מֹאָבִי Ezr 9[1]; pl. מֹאָבִים Dt 2[11], מֹאָב׳ Dt 2[29]; fs. מוֹאֲבִיָּה Ru 1[22] + 4 t.; מֹאָב׳ Ru 4[10], מוֹאָבִית 2 Ch 24[26]; fpl. מוֹאֲבִיּוֹת 1 K 11[1] Ne

13²³; מֹאָבִי Ru 1⁴ —m. =*a Moabite* Dt 23⁴ Ne 13¹, הַמּ׳ =*the Moabite* 1 Ch 11⁴⁶; coll =*the Moabites* Ezr 9¹, so pl. Dt 2¹¹·²⁹, fpl as adj נָשִׁים מ׳ Ru 1⁴, as subst., 1 K 11¹ Ne 13²³, fs as adj 2 Ch 24²⁶; esp רוּת הַמּ׳ Ru 1²² 2²·²¹ 4⁵·¹⁰, מ׳ as n fs Ru 2⁶.

מואל v מול.

[מִיבָא] v מָבוֹא sub בוא.

†מוּג vb. melt (𝔗 מוּג Ithp., ψ 46⁷ 107²⁶, cf Ar مَاجَ *surge* (of the sea), Qor 18⁹⁹, مَوْجٌ *a wave*),—**Qal** *Impf* 3 fs תָּמוּג ψ 46⁷, וַתָּמוֹג Am 9⁵, 2 ms sf וַתְּמוּגֵנוּ Is 64⁶ (but rd. prob וַתְּמַגְּנֵנוּ, v. [מָגַן] p 171 supr, and cf. Di > Du תמוגננו), *Inf* לָמוּג Ez 21²⁰,—**1.** *melt*, subj אֶרֶץ, at touch of י׳ Am 9⁵, at voice of ה׳ ψ 46⁷, =*faint* (of heart), Ez 21²⁰. **2.** trans. *cause to melt* Is 64⁶ (but v supr.) **Niph.** *Pf* נָמוֹג Na 2⁷+2 t, 3 pl נָמֹגוּ Ex 15¹⁵+3 t, *Pt* pl נמגים ψ 75⁴,—*melt away*, fig for be helpless, disorganized (through terror, etc) Ex 15¹⁵ (cf context), Jos 2⁹·²⁴ 1 S 14¹⁶ (cf We Dr), Je 49²³, cf Na 2⁷ Is 14³¹ ψ 75⁴. **Po'l.** *soften, dissolve*, act. only Impf. 2 ms sf. (subj. God). ברביבים תמגגנה ψ 65¹¹ *thou softenest it* [the earth] *with showers;* fig, =*dissipate* וּתְמֹגְגֵנִי Jb 30²²—We rds וימגג Hb 3⁶ for וַיְמֹדֶד, v מדד **Po'**. **Hithpo'l.** *Pf* 3 pl התמגגו Na 1⁵, *Impf* 3 fs. תתמוגג ψ 107²⁶, 3 fpl תתמוגגנה Am 9¹³,—*melt*, subj hills (before י׳) Na 1⁵, subj נפש ψ 107²⁶ (in terror), hyperb for *flow* Am 9¹³ (of fertile hills, || הטיפו הרים)

I מוד (√of foll, appar. secondary form of מדד, cf Ba^NB § 190c, and Ar مَادَ *stretch, extend*, also *prolong, make to continue*)

†תָּמִיד n.m.^Dn 12 11 continuity (perh. orig. *extent*, NH as BH, Ecclus תמיד 45¹⁴),—ת׳ alw. abs,—**1.** earliest and oftenest as adv., *continually* **a.** of going on without interruption =*continuously*, Ho 12⁷ Je 6⁷ Na 3¹⁹ Is 21⁸ 49¹⁶ 51¹³ (+ כָּל־הַיּוֹם), 52⁵ (+*id.*), 60¹¹ (|| יוֹמָם וָלַיְלָה), 62⁶ (+ כָּל־הַיּוֹם וְכָל־הַלַּיְלָה), 65³ Ob¹⁶ Hb 1¹⁷ Dt 11¹² 1 K 10⁸=2 Ch 9⁷, 1 Ch 16¹¹·³⁷, esp (sometimes hyperbol) in ψψ ψ 16⁸ 25¹⁵ 34² (|| בְּכָל־עֵת), 35²⁷ cf 40¹⁷ 70⁵, 38¹⁸ 40¹² 50⁸ 51⁵ 69²⁴ 71⁶·¹⁴ 72¹⁵ 73²³ 74²³ 105⁴ 109¹⁵·¹⁹ 119⁴⁴ (+ לְעוֹלָם וָעֶד:), v¹⁰⁹·¹¹⁷ (so also ψ 16⁵, for MT תּוֹמִיךְ, Bi Che, תוסיף Ol Bae); Pr 5¹⁹ (|| בְּכָל־עֵת), 6²¹ 15¹⁵ 28¹⁴, also Ez 38⁸ (del. 𝔊 Co Toy^Hpt Berthol), Lv 6⁶ (P, of fire, || לֹא תִכְבֶּה), and 46¹⁴ (but חֻקַּת ת׳ 𝔊 Co Berthol); also in ritual, Lv 24³ (H), cf. Ex 25³⁰ (P, shew-bread), Lv 24²·³·⁴ (H), cf. Ex 27²⁰ (P, of lamp), Ex 28²⁹·³⁰·³⁸ **b.** of regular repetition: meals 2 S 9⁷·¹⁰·¹³ 2 K 25²⁹=Je 52³³; journeys 2 K 4⁹, cf Nu 9¹⁶ ψ 71³, of ritual sacrifice, לַיּוֹם תָּמִיד Ex 29³⁸; cf. 1 Ch 16⁴⁰ 23³¹ 2 Ch 24¹⁴. **2.** as subst **a.** of uninterrupted continuity, אַנְשֵׁי ת׳ Ez 39¹⁴ *men of continuity*, i e men continually employed for the purpose; לֶחֶם הַת׳ Nu 4⁷ *the bread of continuity*, i.e. the bread that is always there, so מַעֲרֶכֶת ת׳ 2 Ch 2³, and perh חֲצֹצְרוֹת ת׳ 1 Ch 16⁶ **b.** of regular repetition אֲרֻחַת מ׳ 2 K 25³⁰, i e. a regular allowance, =Je 52³⁴, esp of ritual: קְטֹרֶת ת׳ Ex 30⁸ (P), most often עֹלַת ת׳ Ez 46¹⁵ (every morning), Ex 29⁴² (morning and evening, so) Nu 28⁶ Ezr 3⁵, so rd. also Nu 28³ (Di) for MT עולה ת׳ (ליום); עֹלַת הַת׳ Nu 28¹⁰·¹⁵·²³·²⁴·³¹ 29⁶·¹¹·¹⁶·¹⁹·²²·²⁵·²⁸·³¹·³⁴·³⁸ Ne 10³⁴; rarely מנחת ת׳ Nu 4¹⁶ (P), Ne 10³⁴, as appos, מִנְחָה ת׳ Lv 6¹³ *meal-offering as a regular observance* (cf Ges § 131, 2 (b) Da^Synt. § 29 (b), on text v. Di, Now^Arch II. 124 f.), (and Nu 28³ MT, but v. supr) **c.** (late) הַתּ׳ alone= *daily* (morning and evening) *burnt-offering* (Now^Arch II 221 f) Dn 8¹¹·¹²·¹³ 11³¹ 12¹¹ (so Talm, even in pl תמידין).

†II מוד vb. assumed by Ke Or al. (=מוט) as √of וַיְמֹדֶד Hb 3⁶, but v. מדד **Po**.

מוֹדַע v ידע.

†[מוֹט] vb. totter, shake, slip (usu. poet) (NH *id*, der species, Aram. מוט, ܡܛ, Ar مَاطَ (med. י) *remove, retire; deviate from right course; repel, push, thrust*, Eth. ሞጠ: *turn*, As *matû* is *dwindle, diminish, grow weak* Dl^HWB 405, > denom. fr. מוט *pole, bar* Dl^Prol 184 Gerber^Verb denom 195 f., cf Buhl);—**Qal** *Pf.* 3 fs. מָטָה ψ 60⁴+2 t.; 3 pl מָטוּ ψ 46⁷, *Impf* 3 fs. תָּמוּט Dt 32³⁵ Is 54¹⁰; 3 fpl. תְּמוּטֶינָה Is 54¹⁰, *Inf. cstr.* מוט ψ 38¹⁷ 46³, *abs* id. Is 24¹⁹; *Pt* מָט Pr 25²⁶; pl מָטִים Pr 24¹¹,—*totter, slip*, subj רֶגֶל (fig of insecurity) Dt 32³⁵ ψ 38¹⁷ 94¹⁸: cf (without רֶגֶל) Pr 24¹¹ מ׳ לַהֶרֶג, מ׳ לִפְנֵי־רָשָׁע 25²⁶, *shake*, intr, subj יָד Lv 25³⁵ (H, of feebleness), subj גְּבָעוֹת Is 54¹⁰ (|| מוּשׁ), מ׳ הָרִים בְּלֵב יַמִּים ψ 46³ (|| הָמִיר, cf מור) (both symb of extreme insecurity), cf subj ברית Is 54¹⁰, subj מַמְלָכוֹת ψ 46⁷, subj אֶרֶץ (=land) ψ 60⁴; cf Is 24¹⁹ (v. sub Hithp.) **Niph.** *Pf* 3 pl. נָמוֹטוּ ψ 17⁵,

Impf. יִמּוֹט ψ 15[5]+8 t., etc.;—all poet., mostly c. neg. (בַּל 13 t.; לֹא 6 t.), *be shaken, moved, overthrown,* of idols Is 40[20] 41[7]; of scales of crocodile Jb 41[15]; of תֵּבֵל 1 Ch 16[30]=ψ 93[1] 96[10]; of אֶרֶץ ψ 104[5]; of הַר־צִיּוֹן ψ 125[1], cf. 46[6]; fig. of general disorder (no neg.), subj. מוֹסְדֵי אֶרֶץ ψ 82[5]; oft. of righteous, as secure, ψ 10[6] 15[5] 16[8] 21[8] 30[7] 62[3.7] 112[6] Pr 10[30] 12[3] (subj. שֹׁרֶשׁ צַדִּיקִים); cf. (without neg.) ψ 13[5] 140[11] Qr (so appar. 𝔊 AV RV; but mng. of Niph. not suitable; Kt Hiph. q.v.); fig. of steadfast obedience (subj. פְּעָמַי) ψ 17[5]. **Hiph.** *Impf.* 3 mpl. יָמִּיטוּ ψ 55[4] 140[11] Kt (Qr **Niph.**);—*dislodge, let fall, drop* יָמִיטוּ עָלַי אָוֶן ψ 55[4]; cf. וימיטו עֲלֵיהֶם גֶּחָלִים 140[11] Kt, *and may they drop coals upon them,* De al.; < rd. יַמְטֵר (Hup Gr Bae Dr), wh. Bi Che *insert.* **Hithpo'l.** *Pf.* 3 fs. מוֹט הִתְמוֹטְטָה Is 24[19] *be greatly shaken* (subj. אֶרֶץ, in judgment of י׳; ‖ רעע, פרר, Hithp.)

†מוֹט **n.[m.]** **shaking, pole, bar of yoke;**—abs. מ׳ Nu 4[10]+5 t.; sf. מֹטֵהוּ Na 1[13];—**1.** *a shaking, tottering* (c. neg., of security) לֹא־יִתֵּן מ׳ לַצַּדִּיק ψ 55[23]; לֹא נָתַן לַמּוֹט רַגְלֵנוּ ψ 66[9], cf. 121[3]. **2.** *pole,* or *bar* for carrying (named from springing motion) Nu 4[10.12] cf. esp. 13[23]. **3.** *bar* of yoke Na 1[13] (אֶשְׁבֹּר מֹטֵהוּ מֵעָלַיִךְ), fig. of oppression. Cf. following.

†מוֹטָה **n.f.** **pole, bar** of yoke, mostly late (cf. מוט);—מ׳ Je 28[10]+4 t.; pl. מֹטוֹת etc., abs. Je 27[2] 1 Ch 15[15]; cstr. Ez 30[18]+4 t.;—**1.** *pole,* pl., staves, for bearing ark 1 Ch 15[15]. **2.** *bar* of yoke, symb., of oppression Je 27[2] (‖ מוֹסֵרוֹת, cf. עֹל v[8.11.12]), 28[10.12] (cf. עֹל v[11]); מ׳ עֵץ 28[13]; מ׳ בַּרְזֶל v[13] (cf. עֹל v[14]); fig. of oppression, Is 58[6.9] Ez 30[18]; cf. (thongs of yoke) אֲגֻדּוֹת מ׳ Is 58[6]; מֹטֹת עֻלְּכֶם Lv 26[13] cf. Ez 34[27].—On form of yoke v. Schumacher[ZPV xii. 1889, 160], Benz[Arch. 207].

†[מוּךְ] **vb.** **be low, depressed, grow poor** (NH *id.*, Niph.; Aram. מוּךְ, *sink* or *bend down;* cf. מְכַךְ, Syr. ܡܟ, ܡܟܟ, *be brought low, humble*);—**Qal** *Pf.* consec. וּמָךְ Lv 27[8] (P); *Impf.* יָמוּךְ Lv 25[25.35.39] (all H); *Pt.* מָךְ Lv 25[47] (P): all of impoverished Israelites.

†I. מוּל, מוֹל (+Dt 1[1]), מוֹאל (+Ne 12[38]) **subst.** and **prep.** **front, in front of** (deriv. dub.; acc. to Ol[§ 223 c] Sta[§ 378 a], for מְאוֹל from אול *to be in front:* v. further Kö[ii. 300 f.] Hpt[BAS i. 172]):—**1. subst.** only 1 K 7[5] (si vera l.: v. Sta[ZAW 1883, 151]) וּמוּל מֶחֱזָה אֶל־מֶחֱזָה and the *front* of (one) window was towards (the other) window, and Ne 12[38] לְמוֹאל = *in the opposite direction* (but rd. prob. לִשְׂמֹאול, cf. לְיָמִין v[31]). **2.** as **prep.**, Dt 1[1] 2[19] מוּל בני עמון *in front of* the Ammonites, 3[29] (=4[46] 34[6]) מוּל בית פעור, 11[30] Jos 18[18] 19[46] מוּל יָפוֹ, 1 S 14[5.5]; fig. Ex 18[19] הֱיֵה אַתָּה לעם מוּל האלהים *in front of* God, i.e. representing God to them. With prefixes:—**a.** אֶל־מוּל *towards the front of,* 1 S 17[30] וַיִּסֹּב מֵאֶצְלוֹ אֶל־מוּל אַחֵר *to the front of* another; *on the front of,* Ex 34[3] (pregn.) וְאַל־יִרְעוּ אל־מוּל ההר, Jo 8[33.33] 9[1] 22[11] (v. WAW[JPh. xiii. 117 ff.]); spec. אֶל־מוּל פְּנֵי *towards* or *on the forefront of,* Ex 26[9] 28[25] (‖ 39[18]), v[37] Lv 8[9] Nu 8[2.3] 2 S 11[15] set ye Uriah אל־מוּל פני המלחמה. **b.** מִמּוּל:—(*a*) *from the front of,* Mi 2[8] (text dub.: rd. prob. מֵעַל). (*b*) of position, *off* (v. מִן **1 c**) *the front of,* Lv 5[8] מִמּוּל עָרְפּוֹ *off the front of* its neck, i.e. close in front of it, Nu 22[5] והוא יושב מִמֻּלִי *close in front of* me, 2 S 5[23] (1 Ch 14[14]) ובאת להם ממול בכאים come to them *off the front of* the mulberry-trees, 1 K 7[39] (2 Ch 4[10]) מִמּוּל נֶגֶב; מִמּוּל פָּנָיו *on the forefront of,* Ex 28[27] (‖ 39[20]).

†II. [מוּל] **vb.** **circumcise** (NH *id.;* 𝔗 מוּל *cut off* (grass, etc.: only for III. מָלַל, q.v.); cf. NH מָהַל, Aram. מְהַל, acc. to Thes Nö[ZMG xl. 1886, 741] Ba[ib. xli. 1887, 626] v. also מהל supr.);—**Qal** *Pf.* 3 ms. מָל Jos 5[4]+2 t.; 2 ms. מַלְתָּה Ex 12[44]; 3 mpl. מָלוּ Jos 5[5.7]; 2 mpl. מַלְתֶּם Dt 10[16]; *Impf.* וַיָּמָל Gn 17[23]+2 t.; *Imv.* מֹל Jos 5[2]; *Pt. pass.* מוּל Je 9[24]; pl. מֻלִים Jos 5[5];—*circumcise,* c. acc. בשׂר ערלה (flesh of foreskin) Gn 17[23] (P), acc. pers. Gn 21[4] Ex 12[44] (P), Jos 5[2.3] (J), v[4.5.7.7] (D); fig. ערלת לבב (foreskin of the heart) Dt 10[16]; לבב Dt 30[6]; pass. מוּל בערלה Je 9[24]; מֻלִים Jos 5[5] (D). **Niph.** *Pf.* 3 ms. נִמּוֹל (Ges[§ 72. R. 9]) Gn 17[26]; 3 mpl. נִמֹּלוּ Gn 17[27]; 2 mpl. וּנְמַלְתֶּם (consec.) Gn 17[11] (for וּנְמַלְתֶּם √ מלל Ew[§ 234. e.] Ges[§ 67. R. 11]; but Bö[1146 B] for וּנְמוֹלֹתֶם); *Impf.* יִמּוֹל Gn 17[12]+3 t.; 3 mpl. וַיִּמֹּלוּ Gn 34[24]; *Imv.* הִמֹּלוּ Je 4[4]; *Inf.* הִמּוֹל Gn 17[10]+5 t.; הִמֹּל Gn 34[15]; sf. הִמֹּלוֹ Gn 17[24.25]; *Pt.* pl. נִמֹּלִים Gn 34[22];—*be circumcised,* of בשׂר ערלה Gn 17[14.24.25] Lv 12[3]; elsewhere of pers. Gn 17[10.10.12.13.13.26.27] 34[15.17.22.24] Ex 12[48] (P), Jos 5[8] (J): reflex. הִמֹּלוּ לי׳ Je 4[4] *circumcise yourselves to Yahweh* (and take away the foreskin of

your heart). **Hiph.** *Impf* 1 s בשם י׳ כי אֲמִילַם ψ $118^{10\ 11\ 12}$ *in the name of* י׳, *yea I will make them to be circumcised* (enemies, by force of arms, but De *cut to pieces* (from מָלַל=מול), Che *mow*, Bae *annihilate* (?), 𝔊 Aq ἠμυνάμην, Symm διέθρυψα, Jer *ultus sum eas*). **Hithp.** *Impf* 3 mpl יִתְמֹלָלוּ ψ 58^{8} *be cut off*, of arrows, i.e made blunt

†[מוּלָה] **n.f.**, only pl **circumcision** חתן דמים למולת Ex 4^{26} (J) *a bridegroom of blood because of* (or *in regard of*) *the circumcision*, cf. We$^{Prol\ ed\ 4\ (1895)\ 345\ f\quad Hist.\ 340}$

מוֹלֶדֶת, מוֹלִיד, מוֹלָדָה v ילד.

מומכן Kt, v. מְמוּכָן · מוּם v מאום

מוּסַב v סבב · מוּן v מִן.

[מוּסָד] v. יסד · מוּסָד, מוּסָדָה, מוּסָד

[מוּסָךְ] v סכך. · מוּסָר v יסר

[מוסר], מוֹסֵרָה v אסר.

מוּסָר v יסר

מוֹעֵד, [מוֹעָד], מוֹעָדָה v יעד.

מוֹעַדְיָה v מַעַדְיָה.

[מוֹעֵצָה] v יעץ · מוּעָף v. II עוף.

מוּפָז v. פזז · מוּעָקָה v. עוק.

מופעת Kt, v מיפעת sub יפע

מוֹפֵת v. אפת.

מוץ (√of following, meaning unknown)

†[מוֹץ], מֹץ **n.m.**$^{Is\ 29\ 5}$ **chaff** (Talm. 𝔗 מוֹצָא, Ar مَوْصٌ *straw*),—מ׳ abs. Ho $13^{3}+6$ t, cstr Is 17^{13},—*chaff*, always as driven by wind, and alw c כ, in sim, of wicked Jb 21^{18} (תֶּבֶן לִפְנֵי‖ רוּחַ), cf ψ 1^{4} 35^{5} Ho 13^{3}; of hostile nations Is 17^{13} (מ׳ הָרִים), 29^{5} (‖ אָבָק דַּק), hyperb of Judah's power, תָּדוּשׁ ‖ גְּבָעוֹת כַּמֹּץ תָּשִׂים Is 41^{15} (הָרִים וְתָדֹק); of passing time, יוֹם Zp 2^{2}.

I, II. מוֹצָא, [מוֹצָאָה] v. יצא.

I. מוּצָק, [מוּצֶקֶת] v יצק.

II מוּצָק v צוק.

†[מוּק, מִיק] **vb. mock, deride** (Aram. Pa. מַיֵּיק, ܡܝܩ, and Aph אָמֵיק),—*Impf* 3 mpl. (prob Hiph) יָמִיקוּ ψ 73^{8} (‖ וִידַבְּרוּ בְרָע)

מוֹקְדָה, מוֹקֵד v יקד.

מוֹקֵשׁ v. יקשׁ.

†[מוּר] **vb. change** (NH *id*, Hiph.; Ar مَارَ (med و) is *move to and fro* (intransitive); مَارَ (med ي) *procure* food, Aram. ܡܐܪ *buy* or *import* food, No$^{ZMG\ xl\ 1886,\ 154}$),—**Niph.** *Pf.* נָמַר (as if fr מרר) *be changed*, Je 48^{11} subj ריחו (of wine, fig of Moab), **Hiph.** *Pf* המיר Je 2^{11}; on הֵהֵימִיר *ib.*, v Ko$^{i,\ 457}$; *Impf* יָמִיר ψ $15^{4}+3$ t., juss יָמֵר Ez 48^{14}, sf יְמִירֶנּוּ Lv $27^{33.33}$; אָמִיר Ho 4^{7}, וַיָּמִירוּ ψ 106^{20}; *Inf cstr.* הָמִיר ψ 46^{3}, abs. הָמֵר Lv $27^{10.33}$;—**1.** *change, alter*, Mi 2^{4} (obj. חֵלֶק עַמִּי; but 𝔊 יִמַּד בַּחֶבֶל, so Sta$^{ZAW\ 1886,\ 122\ f.}$), ψ 15^{4} (no obj expr), Hiph declar. 46^{3} (ארץ subj, Hup Che Bae al., Ges$^{§\ 115\ 2,\ R.\ 2}$) *when the earth shews change*, Krochm Gr prop הָמוֹג (cf מוג $v^{7\ b}$ ‖ מוט), but needless **2.** *exchange* (sq. acc of obj. relinquished, + ב before obj. acquired) Lv $27^{10\ 10\ 10.10}$ (2 t. as Inf abs); Ho 4^{7} ψ 106^{20}; cf c one obj Lv $27^{33.33.33}$ (once as Inf. abs.), Je $2^{11\ 11}$ (cf. supr.); without obj Ez 48^{14} (but Ew Co יוּמַר, Hoph). **Hoph.** *Impf* יוּמַר Ez 48^{14} Ew Co, cf Berthol.

†תְּמוּרָה **n.f. exchange, recompense**;—ת׳ Ru 4^{7}, sf. תמורתו Lv $27^{10}+3$ t; תמוּרָתָהּ Jb 28^{17},—*exchange*=thing acquired by exchange Lv $27^{10\ 33}$ Jb 28^{17}; חיל תמורתו Jb 20^{18} *wealth acquired by exchange* (fig; rd poss. חֵילוֹ as *his wealth* (so) *his exchange*, Bu); *recompense* (for worldliness) Jb 15^{31}; abstr. *exchanging* Ru 4^{7} (‖ גְּאוּלָּה).

מוֹר, מֹר v. מרר

מוֹרָא, I מוֹרֶה v. יָרֵא.

†מוֹרַג **n.m.**$^{Is\ 41\ 15}$ **threshing-sledge** (NH *id*, 𝔗 *id*, S Ar نَوْرَجٌ, نَيْرَجٌ, Fra ^{133}, cf. Ba $^{ZA\ ii.\ 117}$ (loan-word in Ar = *ploughshare*); mod مَوْرَج Dozy$^{ii\ 623}$, and نَوْرَج Wetzst$^{Z\ für\ Ethnol\ 1873,\ 270\ ff}$, Anderlind$^{ZPV\ ix\ 41\ f}$ (*ploughshare* and *harrow*));—abs. מ׳ Is 41^{15}; pl. מֹרִגִּים 2 S 24^{22} (+ כְּלֵי הַבָּקָר); מורגים 1 Ch 21^{23};—*threshing-sledges* of Araunah, given by him to David for wood of sacrifice 2 S 24^{22} = 1 Ch 21^{23}; fig of Israel as instr. of י׳'s judgment Is 41^{15}. On form of threshing-sledge (mod; slightly turned up in front, and set with sharp stones or pieces of iron), and threshing-rollers, v. Benz$^{Arch\ 209\ f.}$ Now$^{Arch\ i\ 232\ f.}$ Dr$^{Amos,\ 227\ f}$

מוֹרָד v. ירד.   I. מוֹרָה v. יָרֵא.

†II. מוֹרָה **n.m.** razor (√dub.; We$^{Sm\ p\ 146}$ thinks = (מְעָרָה);—*razor*, always in phr. מ׳ לא יַעֲלֶה (עָלָה) עַל־רֹאשׁ Ju 13^{5} 16^{17} 1 S 1^{11}.

I, II. מוֹרֶה v. ירה.   מוֹרִיָּה v. מֹרִיָּה.

[מוֹרָשׁ], מוֹרָשָׁה, מוֹרֶשֶׁת, מוֹרַשְׁתִּי v. ירשׁ.

†I. [מוּשׁ, מישׁ Bö$^{ii\ 512\ f}$, but Thes Kö$^{i\ 511}$ think purely ע״ו] **vb. depart, remove** (Ar. مَاسَ (ى) is *walk with elegant, proud, self-conceited gait*);—**Qal** *Pf.* מָשׁ consec. Zc 14^{4}; וּמַשְׁתִּי Zc 3^{9}; מָשׁוּ Nu 14^{44}, *Impf.* יָמוּשׁ Jos 1^{8} Is 54^{10}, etc.,—*depart*, mostly of inanimate things (= *be removed*) sq. מִן Jos 1^{8} Is 59^{21} Je 31^{36}; without prep Pr 17^{13} Qr, Is 22^{25} 54$^{10\ 10}$ (|| מוט); sq ה loc. Zc 14^{4}; sq מִן pers Ju 6^{18}, of both Nu 14^{44}, trans. *remove*, sq. acc. Zc 3^{9}. **Hiph.** *Impf* יָמִישׁ Ex 13^{22} + 6 t, etc.; *remove, take away*, sq. מִן Mi 2^{3}, sq. לְ v^{4} (but 𝔊 Sta$^{ZAW\ vi.\ 1886,\ 122\ f}$ אין מֵשִׁיב for אֵיךְ יָמִישׁ); *depart*, sq מִן pers Ex 33^{11}; fig. *recede* Jb 23^{12}; of idol, *leave its place*, Is 46^{7}; of other inanimate things, sq מִן Ex 13^{22}; fig. ψ 55^{12} Pr 17^{13} Kt (Qr יָמוּשׁ), without prep, abs., Na 3^{1}, subj. טָרֶף; of righteous under fig. of tree, לֹא יָמִישׁ מֵעֲשׂוֹת פֶּרִי Je 17^{8}, i e. shall not cease.

†II. [מוּשׁ] **vb. feel** (NH *id*; Aram. ܡܫ, מוּשׁ *id*; secondary form of משׁשׁ q.v.);—**Qal** *Impf.* 1 s sf. וַאֲמֻשְׁךָ Gn 27^{21} draw near *that I may feel thee.* **Hiph.** *Impf.* 3 mpl. יְדֵיהֶם וְלֹא יְמִישׁוּן ψ 115^{7} *as for their hands, they do not feel* (of idols; || רַגְלֵיהֶם וְלֹא יְהַלֵּכוּ); *Imv.* sf וַהֲמִישֵׁנִי Ju 16^{26} Qr (Kt והימשׁני, v ימשׁ), but rd וַהֲמִשֵּׁנִי, v. משׁשׁ.

מוֹשָׁב v. ישׁב.

†I. מוּשִׁי, מֻשִׁי **n.pr.m.** a Levite, son of Merari, מוּשִׁי Ex 6^{19} Nu 3^{20} 1 Ch 6^{32} 23$^{21.23}$ 24$^{26.30}$; מֻשִׁי 1 Ch 6^{4}; 𝔊 Ομουσ(ε)ι, rarely Μουσ(ε)ι, Μοουσι.

†II. מוּשִׁי **adj. gent.** c. art. as n. coll. מִשְׁפַּחַת הַמּ׳ Nu 3^{33} 26^{58}.

[מוֹשָׁעָה], מוֹשָׁעוֹת v. ישׁע.

מוּת **vb. die** (NH *id.* (rare); As. *mâtu* Dl$^{HWB\ 396}$, Ar. مَاتَ, Eth ሞተ:, Aram. מוּת, מִית, ܡܝܬ; Nab מות Eut$^{Nab\ 14,\ 6}$; Zinj. מת DHM Sendsch Gloss.),—**Qal** *Pf.* 3 ms. מֵת Gn 42^{38} +, 3 fs. מֵתָה Gn 35^{18} +; 2 ms. מַתָּה Ez 28^{8}, 1 s. וָמַתִּי Gn 19^{19}; 3 mpl. מֵתוּ Gn 7^{22} +; 1 pl. מַתְנוּ Nu 14^{2} 2 K 7^{4}; מָתְנוּ Nu 14^{9} +, *Impf.* יָמוּת Gn 38^{11} +; יָמֹת Dt 33^{6} +, וַיָּמָת Gn 11^{28} +; 1 s אָמוּת Gn 26^{9} +; אָמֻת 2 S 19^{38}; אָמוּתָה Gn 46^{30}, 3 mpl. יָמוּתוּ 1 S 2^{33} +; יְמֻתוּן Nu 16^{29}, 3 fpl. תְּמוּתֶנָה Ez 13^{19} (Ges $^{§72.5}$) +; *Imv.* מֻת Dt 32^{50} Jb 2^{9}; *Inf. abs.* מוֹת Gn 2^{17} +; *cstr.* מוּת Gn 25^{32} +; sf. מוּתִי 2 S 19^{1}, מֻתָן 2 S 20^{3}, etc., *Pt* מֵת Gn 20^{3} +; sf. מֵתִי Gn 23^{4} +, fs מֵתָה Gn 30^{1} Zc 11^{9}; pl מֵתִים Ex 12^{33} +, cstr. מֵתֵי Is 22^{2} +, sf. מֵתֶיךָ Is 26^{19};—**1.** *die*, of natural or other causes: **a.** (1) of man, †וַיִּגְוַע וַיָּמָת *and he expired and died* Gn 25^{8} (+ בְּשֵׂיבָה טוֹבָה, v. infr), v^{17} 35^{29} (P); †וַיָּמָת וַיִּקָּבֵר Ju 10$^{2.5}$ 8^{32} 12$^{7\ 10\ 12\ 15}$ 2 S 17^{23}, †וימת וימלך תַּחְתָּיו *and he died and — reigned in his stead* Gn 36$^{33.34.35.36.37\ 38.39}$ (P), 2 S 10^{1} = 1 Ch 19^{1}, 2 K 1^{17} 8^{15} 13^{24} 1 Ch 1$^{44.45.46.47\ 48.49\ 50}$; וימת בשׂיבה טובה *and he died in a good old age* 1 Ch 29^{28} (+ Gn 25^{8}, v. supr.); as the result of smiting הכה Ex 21$^{18.20\ 22}$ (E), +במלחמה Dt 20$^{5.6.7}$ 2 S 19^{11}; בַּחֶרֶב Je 11^{22}; ברעב v^{22}, מפני הרעב 38^{9}; בַּדֶּבֶר 21^{6}; באבן Nu 35$^{17\ 23}$ (P); †בַּמַּגֵּפָה Nu 14^{37} 17^{14} 25^{9} (P) (2) fig. of wisdom, עִמָּכֶם תָּמוּת חָכְמָה Jb 12^{2}; of courage, וַיָּמָת לִבּוֹ בְּקִרְבּוֹ *and his heart died within him* 1 S 25^{37}.—2 S 2^{31} del. מֵתוּ We Dr Kit Bu, cf. 𝔊. **b.** of animals Lv 11^{39}; cattle Gn 33^{13} (J), fish Ex 7^{18} (E), frogs Ex 8^{9} (J), lion Ec 9^{4}, worm Is 66^{24}; כֶּלֶב מֵת, *dead dog* (in proverb) 1 S 24^{15} 2 S 9^{8} 16^{9}. **c.** a tree Jb 14^{8}. **d.** זִבְחֵי מֵתִים ψ 106^{28} *sacrifices to the dead* (idols). **2.** *die* as a penalty = *be put to death:* **a.** by human authority Gn 42^{20} Ex 10^{28} 21^{14} (E), Gn 44^{9} Jos 2^{14} (J), Lv 20^{20} (H), Nu 35$^{12.30.30}$ (P), esp. D, Dt 17$^{2.6}$ 18^{20} 19^{12} 22$^{22\ 25}$ 24^{7} Ju 6^{30} 1 S 14$^{43.45.45}$ 19^{24} Je 38^{24}; מוֹת יָמוּת, *die = be put to a violent death* (> AV RV *surely die*), 1 S 14$^{39.44}$ 22^{16} 1 K 2$^{37.42}$ (all Judaic), Je 26^{8}, all of capital punishment; 2 K 8^{10} (Ephr.) of assassination; מוֹת יוּמָת *be put to a violent death*, in the codes of Ex 21$^{12.15\ 16.17}$ 22^{18} (E), Lv 20$^{2.9.10\ 11\ 12.13\ 15\ 16.27}$ 24$^{16\ 17}$ (H), Ex 31$^{14.15}$ Nu 15^{35} 35$^{16\ 17\ 18.21.31}$ Lv 27^{29} (P, never in D; D uses verb, either Qal or Hiph., without inf abs.); it is used in narratives Gn 26^{11} (J), Ex 19^{12} (E), Ju 21^{5}. מ׳ is preceded by רגם Nu 15^{36} (P), Dt 21^{21} 1 K 12^{18} = 2 Ch 10^{18}, 1 K 21^{13}; סקל Dt 13^{11} 17^{5} 22$^{21.24}$ 1 K 21$^{10.13.14\ 15}$; פגע 1 K 2$^{25.46}$; רמס 2 K 7$^{17\ 20}$; בְּיַד גֹּאֵל Jos 20^{9} (P) **b.** inflicted by God, Gn 20$^{3\ 19}$ Jos 10^{11} (E), Gn 3^{3} 38^{11} Ex

11^{5} 12^{36} (J), 28^{35} $30^{20\,20}$ Lv 8^{35} $10^{2.6\,7\,9}$ $16^{1\,2\,13}$ Nu 3^{4} $4^{19.20}$ 14^{35} $17^{14\,28.35}$ $18^{3.32}$ $26^{11\,61}$ (P), Dt $5^{22.22}$ 18^{16} Ju 6^{23} 1 S 5^{12} 12^{19} $25^{17\,38.39}$ 2 S 6^{7} 12^{13} 1 K 19^{4} 2 K 14^{6} = 2 Ch 25^{4}, 1 Ch 24^{2} 2 Ch 13^{20} 2 K 19^{35} = Is 37^{36}, Ez 3^{20} $18^{4.20.21\,28}$ 33^{13}; מוּת יָמוּת Gn 2^{17} 3^{4} (J), 20^{7} (E), Ju $13^{21\,22}$ 2 S 12^{14} 14^{14} 2 K $1^{4\,6\,16}$ (all Judaic), Nu 26^{65} (P), Ez 3^{18} $33^{8\,14}$, מוֹת יוּמַת 18^{13}, ביד יהוה Ex 16^{3} (P); בחטא Lv 22^{9} (H), Nu 27^{3} (P), 2 K 14^{6} = 2 Ch 25^{4}; לשאת חטא למות Nu 18^{22} (P), בחטאת Ez 3^{20} 18^{24}, בטמאה Lv 15^{31} (P), לֹא ישאו עון ומתו Je 31^{30} Ez $3^{18\,19}$ $18^{17\,18}$ $33^{8\,9}$, בעון Ex 28^{43} Nu 4^{15} (P), בעול Ez 18^{26} $33^{13\,18}$, על עול 18^{26}, במעל 1 Ch 10^{13} **c.** *die, perish*, of a nation by divine judgment, Moab Am 2^{2}, Ephraim Ho 13^{1}; בית ישראל Ez 18^{31} 33^{11}. **d.** *die prematurely*, by neglect of wise moral conduct Pr 5^{23} 10^{21} 15^{10} 19^{16} 23^{13} Ec 7^{17} —*Note* On עַל־מוּת (לַבֵּן) ψ 9^{1} 48^{15} v עַלְמָה sub II. עלם

Po'lel. *Pf* 3 ms sf מוֹתְתַנִי Je 20^{17}, 1 s מֹתַתִּי 2 S 1^{16}, *Impf.* 3 ms sf יְמוֹתְתֵהוּ 1 S 17^{51}, 3 fs. תְּמוֹתֵת ψ 34^{22}, 1 s sf. אֲמֹתְתֵהוּ 2 S 1^{10}, *Imv* sf. מוֹתְתֵנִי Ju 9^{54}; מֹתְתֵנִי 2 S 1^{9}, inf. מוֹתֵת ψ 109^{16}; *Pt* מְמוֹתֵת 1 S 14^{13},—*kill, put to death, despatch* (intens.), abs 1 S 14^{13}, elsewhere c. acc. Ju 9^{54} 1 S 17^{51} 2 S $1^{9\,10\,16}$ Je 20^{17} ψ 34^{22} 109^{16}.

Hiph. *Pf.* 3 ms הֵמִית Ju 16^{30}+, sf. הֱמִיתָתְהוּ 2 S 14^{32}, הֱמִיתָם Je 41^{8}, 3 fs. sf וְהֵמִתַנִי 2 Ch 22^{11}, 2 ms הֵמַתָּה Nu 14^{15}, 1 s sf הֲמִיתִיו (rd הֲמִתִּיו) 1 S 17^{35}, 3 mpl. הֵמִיתוּ 1 S 30^{2}+, etc., *Impf.* יָמִית Nu 35^{19}+, וַיָּמֶת Gn 38^{10}+; sf. יְמִיתֵהוּ 1 K 13^{24}+, יְמִתֶנּוּ Nu 35^{19}+; *Imv* sf. הֲמִיתֵנִי 1 S 20^{8}; pl. הָמִיתוּ 1 S 22^{17}; *Inf abs* הָמֵת 2 K 11^{15}+, *cstr.* הָמִית Lv 20^{4}+; *Pt* מֵמִית 1 S 2^{6}, pl מְמִיתִים 2 K 17^{26} Jb 33^{22}, מְמִתִים Je 26^{15},—*kill, put to death*. **1.** abs. Jb 9^{23}, elsewhere c acc, subj man, **a.** of killing men in personal combat, or in war, often preceded by הכה smite Jos 10^{26} 11^{17} 17^{30}+, cf destroying a city 2 S 20^{19} (‖ השחית v ^{20}) **b.** by authority, espec. in capital punishment Ex 1^{16} (E), Lv 20^{4} (H), Nu $35^{19\,19\,21}$ (P), Dt 9^{10} 17^{7} Ju 20^{13} 1 S 11^{12} 28^{9} 2 S $14^{7\,32}$ 21^{4} 1 K $2^{26.34}$ 11^{40} $19^{17\,17}$ 2 K 14^{6} = 2 Ch 25^{4}, Is 11^{4} Je $26^{15\,21\,24}$ $38^{15\,16.25}$ Est 4^{11}; בַּחֶרֶב 1 K 1^{51} 2^{8} 2 K 11^{20} = 2 Ch 23^{21}, הָמֵת יָמִית Ju 15^{13} 1 K $3^{26\,27}$ Je 26^{19} 38^{15} **2.** subj. God, by inflicting penalty, abs. Dt 32^{39} 1 S 2^{6} 2 K 5^{7}, elsewh c. acc Gn 18^{25} $38^{7\,10}$ Ex 4^{24} Nu 14^{15} (J), Dt 9^{28} Ju 13^{23} 1 S 2^{25} $5^{10\,11}$ 1 Ch 2^{3} 10^{14} Is 65^{15} Ho 9^{16}, ברעב Is 14^{30}, בצמא Ho 2^{5}, of killing fish ψ 105^{29}, מְמִיתִים Jb 33^{22} *executioners*, angels of death **3.** of animals killing men, e g ox Ex 21^{29} (E), lion 1 K $13^{24\,26}$ 2 K 17^{26} **4.** bring to a premature death Pr 19^{18} 21^{25}

Hoph. *Pf.* הוּמַת 2 K 11^{2}+; 3 mpl הֻמְתוּ 2 S 21^{9}; *Impf* יוּמַת Lv 20^{10}+, יוּמָת Gn 26^{11}+, *Pt* מוּמָת 1 S 19^{11}, pl מוּמָתִים 2 K 11^{2} (Qr), 2 Ch 22^{11},—*be killed, put to death*. **1.** by conspiracy 2 K $11^{2.2}$ = 2 Ch 22^{11}, 2 K $11^{8.15\,16}$ 2 Ch $23^{7\,14}$. **2.** by capital punishment Ex 21^{29} (E), 35^{2} Nu 1^{51} $3^{10.38}$ 18^{7} (P), Lv 19^{20} $24^{16.21}$ (H), Dt 13^{6} $17^{6.6}$ 21^{22} $24^{16\,16\,16}$ = 2 K $14^{6.6}$, Jos 1^{18} (all D) Ju 6^{31} 1 S 11^{13} $19^{6\,11}$ 20^{32} 2 S $19^{22.23}$ 21^{9} 1 K 2^{24} 2 Ch 15^{13} Je 38^{4}, and the phrase מוֹת יוּמַת (see **Qal 2 a**) **3.** by divine infliction, in the phrase מוֹת יוּמַת (see **Qal 2 b**) **4.** *die prematurely* Pr 19^{16}

מָוֶת $_{161}$ **n.m.** $^{Ez\ 10,\ 17}$ **death**,—abs. מ׳ Dt 19^{6}+; מָוְתָה ψ 116^{15}, cstr מוֹת Gn 25^{11}+; sf. מוֹתִי Gn 27^{2}+, pl. cstr. מוֹתֵי Ez 28^{10}; sf בְּמֹתָיו Is 53^{9},—**1.** *death*, opp. life, Dt $30^{15.19}$ 2 S 15^{21}; †מ׳ כל האדם *the death of all men* (that all go to) Nu 16^{29} (J), as distinguished from violent death; יוֹם מ׳ *day of death* Gn 27^{2} (J) Ju 13^{7} 1 S 15^{35}+; שְׁנַת מ׳ Is 6^{1} 14^{28}; עד מ׳ Nu $35^{25.28.32}$ Jos 20^{6} (P), 1 K 11^{40}; לפני מ׳ Gn $27^{7\,10}$ 50^{16} (JE); אחרי מ׳ Gn 26^{18} (J), 25^{11} Lv 16^{1} Nu 35^{28} (P), Dt $31^{27\,29}$ (D)+, בכור מ׳ Jb 18^{13} *firstborn of death* (deadly disease); of flies Ec 10^{1}, unclean animals Lv $11^{31\,32}$ (P) **2.** *death by violence* as a penalty: †מִשְׁפַּט מ׳ + לְ or בּ pers: *a case of death to*, or *in* a man, guilty of capital crime Dt 19^{6} 21^{22} Je $26^{11\,16}$; †חֵטְא מ׳ Dt 22^{26}, †בנ(י) מ׳ 1 S 20^{31} 26^{16} 2 S 12^{5}, אִישׁ מ׳ 2 S 19^{29}; אנשי מ׳ 1 K 2^{26}, מַלְאֲכֵי מ׳ Pr 16^{14} *messengers of death*; בְּמוֹתָיו Is 53^{9} *in his (martyr-)death* (v Br $^{MP\ 369}$). †**3.** *state of death* or *place of death* (‖ שְׁאוֹל) Is $28^{15\,18}$ 38^{18} Ho 13^{14} Hb 2^{5} ψ 6^{6} 49^{15} Ct 8^{6} Pr 5^{5} 7^{27}, (‖ אבדון) Jb 28^{22}, שַׁעֲרֵי מ׳ *gates of death* ψ 9^{14} 107^{18} Jb 38^{17}.

†[**מָמוֹת**] **n.[m.]** only pl **death** (cf Ar. مَمَاتٌ);—cstr מְמוֹתֵי תַחֲלֻאִים Je 16^{4} of painful *death by diseases*, מ׳ חָלָל Ez 28^{8}.—For הַמְּמוֹתִים (Kt) 2 K 11^{2}, *the slain*, Qr הַמּוּמָתִים is certainly correct (v מות **Hoph.** supr.)

†**תְּמוּתָה** **n.f.** death,—בְּנֵי ת׳ *children of death*, those worthy of death and appointed to death, ψ 79^{11} 102^{21} (see מָוֶת **2**)

מוֹתָר v יתר **מִזְבֵּחַ** v. זבח.

מַזְבֵּל v 1 זְבֻל sub זבל

מזג (√of foll. = *mix*, cf. Syr. ܡܙܓ, and deriv.; 𝔗 מְזַג *mix, prepare by mixing*.—Ar. مَزَجَ *id.* is denom. fr. مِزَاج v. foll., Frä[172]).

[מֶ֫זֶג] **n.m. mixture,** i.e. mixed wine (NH *id.*, Aram., and thence מִזְגָּא, מְזִיגָא, ܡܘܙܓܐ; Ar. مِزَاج *water mixed with wine, mixture* (Frä l.c.), cf. مَزْج, مِزْج);—אַל־יֶחְסַר הַמָּזֶג Ct 7[3] (Tosafoth here *spiced wine*: cf. Levy[NHWB iii. 61]).

מזה (√of foll.; prob. cf. Ar. مَزَّ *suck out*, cf. Dr[Dt 32, 24]).

†[מָזֶה] **adj.** (si vera l.) **sucked out, empty,** מְזֵי רָעָב Dt 32[24] *sucked out, empty, from hunger* (‖ לְחֻמֵי רֶשֶׁף) so Is 5[13] Ew De Che Di Du (for MT מְתֵי; 𝔊𝔙 מֵתֵי).

†מִזָּה **n.pr.m.** grandson of Esau Gn 36[13.17] (𝔊 Μοζε); 1 Ch 1[37] (𝔊 Ομοζε, 𝔊L Μαζε).

[מָזוּ], מְזָוֵינוּ v. זוה. מְזוּזָה v. זוז.

מָזוֹן v. זון. I. מָזוֹר v. III. זור.

II. מָזוֹר v. II. מזר infra.

†מֵזַח **n.m. girdle** (acc. to Bondi[11] WMM[As. u. Eur. 104] loan-word fr. Egypt *mdḥ*, cf. Lag[GGN 1889, 310]);—abs. מ׳:—in sim. of curse enfolding the wicked ψ 109[19] (‖ בֶּגֶד); fig. = restraint Is 23[10] (but text dubious).

†[מְזִיחַ] **n.m.** *id.* (of like orig.):—only cstr. מ׳ אֲפִיקִים רִפָּה Jb 12[21] *loosen the girdle of mighty*; i.e. weaken them, make them defenceless, by ungirding.

מַזְכִּיר v. זכר.

†מַזָּלוֹת **n.[f.]pl. constellations,** perhaps **signs of the zodiac** (prob. loan-word fr. As. *manzaltu, mazaltu, station, abode* (of gods) Dl[HWB 457; Prol. 142] Jen[Kosmologie 348]; cf. NH מַזָּלוֹת, *id.*; מַזָּל Aram. מַזָּלָא, *star of fortune* or *fate*, Ph. [מ]זל נעם CIS[95, 8] (Vogüé; bilingual inscr.; Gk. ἀγαθῇ τύχῃ); Syr. ܡܘܙܠܬܐ *zodiac* PS[109] ܡܙܠܬܐ *mansiones lunae*, Lexx, PS[2332]; Ar. مَنَازِل (loan-word acc. to Hoffm[ZAW iii. 1883, 110]. Suidas μαζουρωθ = ζῴδια);—only לַמַּזָּלוֹת 2 K 23[5] as obj. of worship (+ לַבַּעַל, לַשֶּׁמֶשׁ, לַיָּרֵחַ, and לְכֹל צְבָא הַשָּׁמָיִם) 𝔊 τοῖς μαζουρωθ; prob. = מַזָּרוֹת Jb 38[32].

מַזְלֵג, [מִזְלָגָה] v. זלג. מְזִמָּה v. זמם.

מִזְמוֹר v. I. זמר.

מַזְמֵרָה, מְזַמֶּרֶת v. II. זמר.

מִזְעָר v. זער.

I. **מזר** (? √of foll. so Thes[781] cf. Ba[NB § 164 c]; otherwise Gei[Urschrift 52]: NH מָזַר and Aram. ܡܙܪ *be bad* (of eggs), Ar. مَذِرَ *be foul, corrupt*).

†מַמְזֵר **n.m. bastard,** specif. **child of incest** (NH *id.* (v. Levy), מַמְזֵרוּת *incest*; Aram. (loan-word) מַמְזֵרָא *bastard*):—**1.** lit. *bastard*, Dt 23[3] (v. Dr). **2.** perh. fig. coll., of mixed population Zc 9[6] 𝔊 ἀλλογενεῖς (cf. also Gei[Urschrift, 52 f.]).

II. **מזר** (√of foll., si vera l.; poss. = *spread out*; Aram. ܐܬܡܙܪ *stretch oneself*, cf. Ar. مَزَرَ *aequaliter distendit* utrem).

†II. מָזוֹר **n.m.** Ob[7] יָשִׂימוּ מָזוֹר תַּחְתֶּיךָ, very dub., perh. net (as something *extended*): 𝔊 (ἔνεδρα), 𝔖𝔙 *ambush* (? מָצוֹד or מְצוֹדָה *net*, Vollers[ZAW 1884, 16]; מָצוֹר *siege* Prince[JBL xvi. 1897, 177]), Aq Theod *fetter, bond*, 𝔗(תקלא) *stumbling-block*; Gr מַכְמֹר, מִכְמָר; We Now leave untranslated; Dl[Prol. 67, HWB 396] comp. As. *mazûru*, appar. *a pole with an iron hook*, but improb.—I. מָזוֹר v. sub II. זור, p. 267.

מִזְרֶה v. זרה.

†מַזָּרוֹת **n.[f.]pl.** prob. = מַזָּלוֹת q.v. supr. (on ר = ל v. W[SG 67], yet also Nö[ZMG xl. 1886, 185]) only הֲתֹצִיא מ׳ בְּעִתּוֹ Jb 38[32], where treated as ms., and perh. understood of some particular star or constellation. 𝔊 μαζουρωθ.

מִזְרָח v. זרח. מְזָרִים v. זרה **Pi. 1.**

[מִזְרָע] v. I. זרע. מִזְרָק v. זרק.

[מֵחַ], מֹחַ v. מחח.

†[מָחָא] **vb. strike,** only = **clap** (the hand) (Aram. form of II. מָחָה q.v.);—**Qal** *Impf.* 3 mpl. only fig., of joy of inanimate things before י׳: נְהָרוֹת יִמְחֲאוּ־כָף ψ 98[8]; וְכָל־עֲצֵי הַשָּׂדֶה יִמְחֲאוּ־כָף Is 55[12].—**Pi.** *Inf. cstr.* sf. *id.*, of exultation over foe יַעַן מַחְאֲךָ יָד Ez 25[6] (‖ וַתִּרְקַע בְּרֶגֶל).

מַחֲבֵא, [מַחֲבֹא] v. חבא.

מְחַבְּרֶת, [מְחַבְּרָה] v. חבר.

מַחֲבַת v. חבת. מַחֲגֹרֶת v. חגר.

†I. מָחָה **vb. wipe, wipe out** (NH *id.;* Ar. مَحَا, *efface, erase, cancel, obliterate;* Aram. מְחָא (I), cf. Ph. למחת *acc. to stroke = exactly* Hoffm [Ph. Inschr., Abh. GGW. xxxvi. May 1889, 9]).—**Qal** *Pf.* 3 ms. מָחָה Nu 5^{23} + 3 t.; 3 fs. מָחֲתָה Pr 30^{20} + 4 t. *Pf.; Impf.* יִמְחֶה 2 K 21^{13}; וַיִּמַח (Baer; var. וַיִּמֶּח) Gn 7^{23}; 1 s. sf. אֶמְחֶנּוּ Ex 32^{33}; + 4 t. Impf.; *Imv.* מְחֵה ψ $51^{3.11}$; sf. מְחֵנִי Ex 32^{32}; *Inf. abs.* מָחֹה Ex 17^{14}; *cstr.* לִמְחוֹת 2 K 14^{27}; *Pt.* מֹחֶה Is 43^{25}; fpl. (לְ)מֹחוֹת Pr 31^{3} (Ges Fl Nö De Str for MT לַמְחוֹת);—**1.** *wipe,* the mouth Pr 30^{20}; tears from (מעל) the face Is 25^{8}; written curse, into the water (אל־מים) for drinking Nu 5^{23} (P); Moses' name from the book (מספר) of God Ex $32^{32.33}$ (J); וּמָחִיתִי אֶת־יְרוּשָׁלִַם כַּאֲשֶׁר יִמְחֶה אֶת־הַצַּלַּחַת מָחָה וְהָפַךְ עַל־פָּנֶיהָ 2 K 21^{13} *and I will wipe Jerusalem as one wipeth a dish,—he doth wipe and turn it* (but rd. prob. מָחֹה וְהָפֹךְ) *upside down.* **2.** *blot out = obliterate* from the memory, מִתַּחַת הַשָּׁמַיִם *from under heaven* e.g. the name Dt 9^{14} 29^{19} 2 K 14^{27}; the remembrance Ex $17^{14.14}$ (J), Dt 25^{19}; the name for ever ψ 9^{6}; transgressions (פשע; no more remembered by God against sinner) ψ 51^{3} Is 43^{25} 44^{22}; עָוֹן ψ 51^{11}. **3.** *blot out = exterminate,* כל־היקום all existing things Gn 7^{23} (J) and mankind, מֵעַל פְּנֵי הָאֲדָמָה Gn 6^{7} 7^{4} (J); מֹחוֹת מְלָכִין Pr 31^{3} (with the text-change, v. supr.) = *destroyers of kings* (i.e. impure women), but expression strange and dubious.

Niph. *Pf.* 3 mpl. נִמְחוּ Ez 6^{6}; *Impf.* יִמָּחֶה Dt 25^{6} Ju 21^{17}; יִמַּח ψ 109^{13}; 3 fs. תִּמָּח ψ 109^{14}; + 4 t. Impf.;—**1.** *be wiped out* מִסֵּפֶר חַיִּים ψ 69^{29}. **2.** *be blotted out,* מִיִּשְׂרָאֵל of a name Dt 25^{6}, a tribe Ju 21^{17}; name (‖ posterity) ψ 109^{13}; from memory, of sins Ne 3^{37} ψ 109^{14}; reproach, Pr 6^{33}. **3.** *be exterminated,* מִן־הָאָרֶץ Gn 7^{23} (J); of idolatrous works of Israel Ez 6^{6}.

Hiph. *Impf.* 2 ms. תֶּמַח Ne 13^{14}; תֶּמְחִי Je 18^{23} (but tone suggests תֶּמַח cf. Ges [§ 75, R. 17]; Gie reads Qal and doubts Hiph. altogether); *Inf.* לִמְחוֹת Pr 31^{3} (= לְהַמְחוֹת but see **Qal 3**);—*blot out,* from the memory; pious acts Ne 13^{14}; sins Je 18^{23}.

†II. מָחָה **vb. strike** (Aram. מְחָא (II), ܡܚܐ; acc. to L Gei [Urspr. d. Spr. 416] Lag [Sem. i. 26, BN 142] Nö [ZMG xxxii. 1878, 409] weakened fr. ܡܚܨ = مخض, Heb. מָחַץ q.v., cf. Dr [§ 178 n.]; As. *maḫû = crush, oppress,* acc. to Dl [HWB 396]);—*Pf.* 3 ms. consec., וּמָחָה עַל־כֶּתֶף וגו׳ Nu 34^{11} (P) *and* the border *shall strike upon (reach unto) the shoulder of the sea of Chinnereth* (> Di al. der. fr. I. מָחָה *rub along by, brush past, skirt*).

†מְחִי **n.[m.]** only in מְחִי קָבָלּוֹ Ez 26^{9} *the stroke of his battering ram* (cf. (מ)מחיו Ecclus 42^{5} *smiting* a deceitful servant, marg. מוסר).

III. מחה v. מֹחַ sub מחח. מְחוּגָה v. חוג.

†[מָחוֹז] **n.[m.]** city (As. loan-word; fr. *maḫâzu, city,* Asrb [Annals iii. 116] and oft.; v. Dl [HWB 271]; cf. 𝔗 מְחוֹזָא *market-place, province,* ܡܚܘܙܐ *small town*)—only cstr. וַיַּנְחֵם אֶל־מְחוֹז חֶפְצָם ψ 107^{30} *and he guided them unto the city of their desire.*

†מְחוּיָאֵל **n.pr.m.** great-grandson of Cain Gn 4^{18a} = מְחִיָּיאֵל v ^{18b} (J; A 𝔊L in both Μαιηλ, E Μαουιηλ; cf. further Lag [Or. ii. 35 BN 96] (Μαουιαηλ) Bu [Urgesch. 125]).—(Etym. dub.; Thes [Add. 97] perhaps *smitten of Ēl* √ מחה; Bu [Urgesch. 128] Kerber [Eigennam. d. AT. 91] מְחִיָּאֵל, or מַחְיִיאֵל *Ēl maketh alive;* DHM [MV 10] thinks of n. pr. div. יאל,—cf. Ph. n. pr. יאלפעל, and CIS [i. 132, 4; esp. p. 163 b], = *god* יאל *giveth life* (against this Gray [Prop. N. 164])).

מַחֲוִים v. sub II. חוה. I. מָחוֹל v. I. חול.

†II. מָחוֹל **n.pr.m.** father of Heman, etc., 1 K 5^{11}, 𝔊 Μαλ, A Μαουλ, 𝔊L Μααλα.

מְחֹלָה v. II. אָבֵל p. 6 supr.; v. also מְחֹלָה.

מַחֲזִיאוֹת, מֶחֱזָה, מַחֲזֶה v. חזה.

מחח (√ of foll.; cf. Ar. مخ IV. *be fat,* also *contain marrow*).

†[מֵחַ] **n.[m.]** fatling (Ph. מח *fat* (adj.); NH מֵיחָא fig. of *choice flour*);—only pl. abs.: עֹלוֹת מֵיחִים ψ 66^{15} *burnt offerings of fatlings;* so מֵחִים Is 5^{17} (‖ כְּבָשִׂים) acc. to Hi Du Che [Hpt] (rd. חֳרָבוֹת and del. גָּרִים); most, *fat ones,* fig. for *rich men.*

†מֹחַ **n.m.** marrow (NH מוֹחַ, Ar. مُخّ, Aram. מוֹחָא, ܡܘܚܐ all *marrow, brain*);—only cstr. מֹחַ עַצְמוֹתָיו יְשֻׁקֶּה Jb 21^{24} fig. of prosperity.

†III. מָחָה **vb. denom.** only **Pu.** *Pt.* מְמֻחָיִם (Ges [§ 75. R. 13]) in phr. שְׁמָנִים מ׳ Is 25^{6} fat pieces *full of marrow.*

מְחִי v. II. מחה.

†מְחִידָא **n.pr.m.** head of a family of returning exiles Ezr 2[52] (𝔊 Μαουδα, 𝔊L Μεειδα) = Ne 7[54] (𝔊 Μεειδα).

מחיה v. חיה. מחייאל v. מְחוּיָאֵל.

†מַחְלָה **n.pr.f. 1.** a daughter of Zelophehad Nu 26[33] 27[1] 36[11] Jos 17[3], 𝔊 Μα(α)λ(α)α. **2.** a Gileadite name (poss. **m.**) 1 Ch 7[18] 𝔊 Μαελα, 𝔊L Μααλαθ.

[מַחֲלֶה], מַחֲלָה v I. חלה.

מחלה v. I. חול. [מחלה] v. I. חלל.

†מַחְלוֹן **n.pr.m.** son of Elimelech and Naomi, first husband of Ruth, Ru 1[2.5] 4[9.10], 𝔊 Μααλων.

†I. מַחְלִי **n.pr.m. 1.** Levite, son of Merari Ex 6[19] Nu 3[20] 1 Ch 6[4.14] 23[21.21] 24[26.28] Ezr 8[18] (prob.), 𝔊 Μοολλει **2.** son of Mushi, and grandson of Merari 1 Ch 6[32] 23[23] 24[30], 𝔊 Μοολει, Μοολ(λ)ι.

†II. מַחְלִי **adj.gent.** of above; only c. art. as coll הַמּ׳ Nu 3[33] 26[58].

מַחֲלֻיִים v. [מַחֲלוּי] sub I. חלה.

[מַחֲלָף], [מַחֲלָפָה] v. חלף.

מַחֲלָצוֹת v. [מַחֲלָצָה] sub I. חלץ.

II. מַחְלְקוֹת v. II. חלק. מַחֲלֹקֶת v. I. חלק.

I. מַחֲלַת v. sub II. חלה.

†II. מַחֲלַת **n.pr.f. 1.** daughter of Ishmael Gn 28[9], 𝔊 Μαελεθ. **2.** granddaughter of David 2 Ch 11[18], 𝔊 Μολλαθ; 𝔊L Μαελλεθ.

מחלת v. מְחוֹלָה sub I. חול.

†מְחֹלָתִי **adj.gent.** only c. art. הַמְּ׳ *the Mĕḥolathite*, of 'Adriel 1 S 18[19], A τῷ Μοουλαθειτῃ; 𝔊L τοῦ Μαολλαιου; of Barzillai 2 S 21[8]; 𝔊 τῷ Μωουλαθει, 𝔊L τοῦ Μαυθει.

†מַחְמָאֹת **n.f.pl.** only (appar. cstr.) חָלְקוּ מ׳ פִּיו ψ 55[22], acc. to Ew De Hup = *curd-like* (i.e. smooth, hypocritical) *words, smooth are the butter-words of his mouth*, but read prob. חלק(ו) מֵחֶמְאֹת (מֶחֶמְאָה or) פיו (פניו) *his face is smoother than curds* (Vrss Ki Thes Ol Che Bae We).

מַחְמָד [מַחְמֹד, מַחֲמַדִּים] v. חמד.

[מַחְמָל] v. חמל. מַחְמֶצֶת v I. חמץ

מַחֲנֶה, מַחֲנֵה־דָן, מַחֲנַיִם v. חנה.

מַחֲנָק v. חנק. מַחְסֶה, מַחֲסֶה v. חסה.

מַחְסוֹם v. חסם. מַחְסוֹר v. חסר.

מַחְסֵיָה v. חסה.

†מָחַץ **vb. smite through, wound severely, shatter** (poet.) (As *maḥâṣu, smite, wound*, Dl[HWB 398]; Ar. مَحَضَ *churn; beat* or *agitate* the milk, etc., Sab. מחץ DHM[ZMG xxx. 1876, 684; xxxvii 1883, 338], Burgen u. Schlösser (SB xcvii. 1881), 965 (of stone-cutter's work), Hom[Chrestom. 127]; Eth. ምሕጸ:),—**Qal** *Pf.* 3 ms. מ׳ Jb 26[12] + 3 t.; וּמָחֲצָה Ju 5[26] etc.; *Impf.* יִמְחַץ Jb 5[18] ψ 68[22]; 1 s. sf. אֶמְחָצֵם ψ 18[39]; וָאֶ׳ 2 S 22[39],—*smite through*, sq. ראשׁוֹ, of Jael, Ju 5[26] (‖ מָחַק, הָלַם, חָלַף), of Isr., *shattering* enemies, חִצָּיו יִמ׳ Nu 24[8] (obj om., ‖ עַצְמֹתֵיהֶם יְגָרֵם) cf. v[17] (obj. פַּאֲתֵי מוֹאָב); cf ψ 18[39] = 2 S 22[39]; of י׳, *smiting through* or *shattering* his foes, ψ 110[6], their heads v[6] 68[22] Hb 3[13], loins Dt 33[11]; cf. Jb 26[12] obj. רַהַב q v; abs, Dt 32[39] (opp רָפָא, ‖cl. אָמִית וַאֲחַיֶּה) cf. Jb 5[18] (opp רָפָא, ‖cl. יַכְאִיב וְיֶחְבָּשׁ). For תִּמְחַץ (רגלך בדם) ψ 68[24], rd. תִּרְחַץ (58[11]), Ol Br Che Bae We.

†מַחַץ **n.[m.]** severe wound,—only cstr מַחַץ מַכָּתוֹ יִרְפָּא Is 30[26] of י׳'s restoration of his people (‖ חֲבֹשׁ שֶׁבֶר עַמּוֹ).

מַחְצֵב v. חצב. מֶחֱצָה, מַחֲצִית v. חצה.

†[מָחַק] **vb. utterly destroy, annihilate** (cf. GFM) (NH *id*, *wipe* or *rub off, erase*; Aram. מְחַק מחק *id.*; Ar مَحَقَ *utterly destroy, annihilate*);—only 3 fs מָחֲקָה ראשׁוֹ Ju 5[26] (‖ הָלַם, חָלַף, מָחַץ).

[מֶחְקָר] v. חקר.

מחר (✓of foll., *be in front of, meet*, cf. As *maḥâru*, Dl[HWB 400] *come to meet, receive* [cf. קבל], and Id[Prol. 93]; Sab. מחר *receive*, etc., n. *id.*, *token of favour*, ‖ *gift*, נחלת; DHM[ZMG xxxvii. 1883, 408]).

מָחָר[52] **n.m.,** used oft. as **adv., to-morrow, in time to come** (Aram. מְחָר, ܡܚܪ; prob. properly *time in front*, Ko[ii. 253], cf. ✓, and As *maḫru, front*, oft. of time, though alw of *former time, of old*, Dl[HWB 402]):—**1.** *to-morrow* (the day following the *present* day), **a.** as *subst.* Ex 16[23]

שַׁבָּתוֹן שַׁבַּת קֹדֶשׁ לַי׳ מָחָר *to-morrow* is a sabbath, etc., 1 S 20^{5} חֹדֶשׁ מָחָר׳ *to-morrow* is the new moon, v^{18}; in יוֹם מָחָר †Gn 30^{33} Pr 27^{1} Is 56^{12}; in the idiom. phr. כָּעֵת מָחָר at the like of the time, (being) *to-morrow*, = *about to-morrow* (v. כְּ **1a**) †Ex 9^{18} 1 S 9^{16} 20^{12} 1 K 19^{2} 20^{6} 2 K 7$^{1.18}$ 10^{6}; and in לְמָחָר †Ex 8^{19} לְמָחָר יִהְיֶה הָאֹת הַזֶּה, = *for, against, to-morrow*, Ex 8^{6} Nu 11^{18} Jos 7^{13} Est 5^{12}. **b.** as *adv. acc.* Ex 8^{25} 9^{5} מָחָר יַעֲשֶׂה 17^{9} 32^{5}, הִנְנִי מֵבִיא מָחָר אַרְבֶּה 10^{4}, י׳ הַדָּבָר הַזֶּה Nu 14^{25} 1 S 11^{9} etc., Jos 11^{6} מָחָר כָּעֵת הַזֹּאת; opp. to הַיּוֹם Ex 19^{10} הַיּוֹם וּמָחָר, Jos 22^{18} 2 S 11^{12a}; rhetorically, Is 22^{13} כִּי מָחָר נָמוּת. **2.** = *in future time*, Ex 13^{14} כִּי יִשְׁאָלְךָ בִנְךָ מָחָר לֵאמֹר = Dt 6^{20}, Jos 4$^{6.21}$ 22$^{24.27.28}$; so בְּיוֹם מָחָר Gn 30^{33}.

†מָחֳרָת **n.f.** the morrow (the day following a *past* day)—abs. מ׳ Gn 19^{34}+, cstr. מָחֳרַת Lv 23^{11}+;—*the morrow*, Nu 11^{32} וְכֹל יוֹם הַמָּחֳרָת; מִמָּחֳרָת = *on the morrow*, so וַיְהִי מִמָּחֳרָת, Gn 19^{34} Ex 18^{13} 32^{30} Nu 17^{23} Ju 9^{42} 21^{4} 1 S 11^{11} 18^{10} 31^{8} (= 1 Ch 10^{8}) 2 K 8^{15} Je 20^{3}; וַיַּשְׁכֵּם (וַיַּשְׁכִּימוּ) מִמָּחֳרָת, Ex 32^{6} Ju 6^{38} 1 S 5$^{3.4}$; Ex 9^{6} ויעש י׳ את הדבר הזה ממ׳, Nu 17^{6} Jos 5^{12}; 2 S 11^{12b}: מִמָּחֳרַת הַשַּׁבָּת *on the morrow of* (= *after*) the sabbath, Lv 23$^{11.15.16}$, מִמ׳ הַפֶּסַח Nu 33^{3} Jos 5^{11}, מִמָּחֳרַת הַחֹדֶשׁ [𝔊 בַּיּוֹם] הַשֵּׁנִי (MT falsely מִמָּחֳרַת) 1 S 20^{27}; of the morrow after a day specified in a law, Lv 19^{6} בְּיוֹם זִבְחֲכֶם יֵאָכֵל וּמִמָּחֳרָת, 7^{16}. Twice (late) with לְ, Jon 4^{7} לַמָּחֳרָת *on the morrow*, 1 Ch 29^{21} לְמָחֳרַת הַיּוֹם הַהוּא.—1 S 30^{17} strangely וַיַּכֵּם דָּוִד מֵהַנֶּשֶׁף וְעַד־הָעֶרֶב לְמָחֳרָתָם from the dawn to the evening *of their following day* (We Bu לְהַחֲרִימָם).

† I. **מְחִיר** **n.m.** price, hire (as that which is *placed in front* of one, *presented, offered*; As. *maḫîru, price; maḫirânu, buyer*, Dl$^{HWB\ 404,\ Prol.\ 94}$);—מ׳ abs. Mi 3^{11} + 9 t.; cstr. Dt 23^{19} + 2 t.; sf. מְחִירָהּ Jb 28^{15}; pl. sf. מְחִירֵיהֶם ψ 44^{13};—**1.** *price*, oft. בִּמְחִיר *for a price*; in trade 2 S 24^{24} 1 K 10^{28} 2 Ch 1^{16}; cf. La 5^{4} (‖ בְּכֶסֶף), also (no בְּ) 1 K 21^{2} and מ׳ שָׂדֶה עַתּוּדִים Pr 27^{26}; of wisdom Jb 28^{15} (‖ סְגוֹר כֶּסֶף) cf. Pr 17^{16} (no בְּ); fig. בְּלוֹא־כֶסֶף וּבְלוֹא מ׳ Is 55^{1} in purchase of blessings fr. י׳; of price of people, fig. ψ 44^{13}, cf. Je 15^{13}. **2.** hire, מ׳ כֶּלֶב (i.e. of male prostitute) Dt 23^{19} (‖ אֶתְנַן זוֹנָה) v. Di Dr; of venal priests Mi 3^{11} (‖ שֹׁחַד); = *reward, gain*, denied of Cyrus Is 45^{13} (‖ *id.*); affirmed of Ant. Epiph. Dn 11^{39}.

† II. **מְחִיר** **n.pr.m.** 1 Ch 4^{11}, 𝔊 Μα(χ)ειρ.

[מַחֲרָאָה], מַחֲרָאוֹת v. חרא.

[מַחֲרֶשֶׁת, מַחֲרֵשָׁה] v. I. חרשׁ.

מַחְשֹׂף v. חשׂף.

מַחֲשָׁבָה, מַחֲשֶׁבֶת v. חשׁב.

מַחְשָׁךְ v. חשׁך. מַחְתָּה, מְחִתָּה v. חתה.

מְחִתָּה v. חתת. מַחְתֶּרֶת v. חתר.

מַט v. מַטֶּה sub נטה.

מַטְאֲטֵא v. טאטא. מַטְבֵּחַ v. טבח.

מַטֶּה, מִטָּה, מֻטָּה, מַטָּה v. נטה.

מַטְוֶה v. טוה.

מטל (√ of foll.; cf. Ar. مَطَلَ *strike, beat, extend by beating, shape iron into a helmet*, Frey, مِمْطَل iron, or a sword, *beaten into a long shape*, Lane^{3021}).

†מְטִיל **n.m.** wrought-metal rod (Aram. (𝔗) מְטַל);—cstr. מְטִיל בַּרְזֶל Jb 40^{18} fig. of bones (עֲצָמָיו אֲפִיקֵי נְחֻשָׁה ‖ גְּרָמָיו) of hippopot.

מַטְמוֹן v. טמן. מַטָּע v. נטע.

[מַטְעָם], מַטְעַמִּים v. טעם.

מִטְפַּחַת v. טפח.

†מָטָר **n.m.**$^{Ex\ 9,33}$ rain (As. *meṭru*, Dl$^{HWB\ 406}$; Ar. مَطَر; Sab. (Min.) מטר Hom$^{Chrestom.\ 127}$; Aram. מִטְרָא, ܡܛܪܐ;—מ׳ Ex 9^{33} + 30 t.; cstr. מְטַר Dt 11^{11} + 5 t.; pl. cstr. מִטְרוֹת Jb 37^{6};—*rain*, as watering earth, esp. Canaan, Dt 11^{11} מ׳ הַשָּׁמַיִם; as blessing sent (vb. usu. נָתַן) and withheld by י׳, Dt 11^{14} (‖ יוֹרֶה, מַלְקוֹשׁ); v^{17} (here מ׳ אַרְצְכֶם); 28^{12} 1 K 8$^{35.36}$ 17^{1} (‖ טַל), 18^{1} 2 Ch 6$^{26.27}$ 7^{13} Jb 5^{10} (‖ מַיִם), cf. 28^{26} 36^{27} ψ 147^{8} (vb. הֵכִין); so מ׳ זַרְעֲךָ Is 30^{23} Zc 10^{1} (‖ מַלְקוֹשׁ), v^{1} מְטַר־גֶּשֶׁם; גֶּשֶׁם מָטָר Jb 37^{6}, (‖ שֶׁלֶג) v^{6} גֶּשֶׁם מִטְרוֹת עֻזּוֹ; 38^{28} (‖ אֶגְלֵי־טָל); ψ 135^{7} Je 10^{13} = 51^{16} (‖ הֲמוֹן מַיִם) בְּרָקִים לַמָּ׳; also in יִתֵּן אֶת מְ׳ אַרְצְךָ אָבָק וְעָפָר Dt 28^{24}; cf. Is 5^{6} (where acc. cogn. with הִמְטִיר); wish of David 2 S 1^{21} (‖ טַל); מ׳ בַּקָּצִיר sim. of the unseasonable, Pr 26^{1} (‖ שֶׁלֶג בַּקַּיִץ); sent by extraord. supernat. power as sign Ex 9$^{33.34}$ (J; both ‖ קֹלוֹת, בָּרָד) cf. 1 S 12$^{17.18}$ (‖ קֹלוֹת); sim. of refreshment Dt 32^{2} (‖ טַל), Jb 29^{23} (‖ מַלְקוֹשׁ), ψ 72^{6} (‖ רְבִיבִים), cf. 2 S 23^{4}; as destructive Pr 28^{3} (מָטָר סֹחֵף); also fig., Is 4^{6} (‖ זֶרֶם).

†[מָטַר] **vb. denom.** (cf. Gerber$^{Verb.\ denom.\ 106}$) [rain] (Ar. مَطَرَ; Syr. ܡܛܪ; 𝔗 Aph. אַמְטַר);—**Niph.** *Impf. be rained upon* חֶלְקָה אַחַת תִּמָּטֵר Am 4^{7}. **Hiph.** *Pf.* הִמְטִיר Gn 2^{5} 19^{24}; וְהִמְטַרְתִּי Am 4^{7}; *Impf.* יַמְטֵר ψ 11^{6} Jb 20^{23}; וַיַּמְטֵר Ex 9^{23} + 2 t.; 3 fs. תַּמְטִיר Am 4^{7} (but rd. תַּמְטִיר 𝔊 𝔙); 1 s. אַמְטִיר Am 4^{7} + v^{7} (for תַּמְטִיר), Ez 38^{22}; *Inf. cstr.* הַמְטִיר Is 5^{6} Jb 38^{26}; *Pt.* מַמְטִיר Gn 7^{4} + 2 t.;—*send rain, rain* (sq. עַל exc. Ex 9^{18} 16^{4}); subj. ׳י (no dir. obj.) Gn 2^{5} 7^{4} (both J), Am $4^{7.7.7}$, cf. Jb 38^{26}; subj. clouds עָבִים by divine command Is 5^{6} (acc. cogn. מָטָר); לֶחֶם Ex 16^{4} (J; מִן־הַשָּׁמַיִם; no עַל); הַמ׳ מָן ψ 78^{24}; שְׁאֵר v^{27}; as act of judgment הִמ׳ בָּרָד *rain hail, send hail,* subj. ׳י Ex 9^{23} (J); cf. v^{18} (J; no עַל); obj. גָּפְרִית וָאֵשׁ Gn 19^{24} (J), cf. Ez 38^{22} וְגֶשֶׁם שׁוֹטֵף וְאַבְנֵי אֶלְגָּבִישׁ אֵשׁ וְגָפְרִית אַמ׳; fig. ψ 11^{6} (obj. פַּחִים; but rd. פַּחֲמֵי אֵשׁ v. Ew Che Bae al.); Jb 20^{23} (‖ cl. יְשַׁלַּח בּוֹ חֲרוֹן אַפּוֹ).

†מַטְרִי **adj. gent.** only c. art. as subst. coll. הַמ׳ 1 S 10^{21a} + v^{21b} 𝔊 The We Klo Dr Kit Bu HPS. 𝔊 Ματταρι.

מַטְרֵד v. טרד. מַטָּרָה, מַטָּרָא v. נטר.

[מַי] **n.m.** $^{2814.14}$ only pl. מַ֫יִם **waters, water** (NH *id.*; MI^{23} [מ]ין; SI^{5} המים; Aram. מַיִן, מַיָּא, ܡܰܝܳܐ; As. *mû*, pl. *mê*, also *mâmu* Dl$^{HWB\ 394}$; Ar. مَآءٌ; Eth. ማይ፡, pl. ማያት፡; Sab. [מו], מום, pl. מון, Min. [מה], pl. מהן DHM$^{6th\ Or.\ Congr.\ (Leiden)\ ii,\ 1,\ 451\ f.}$ (v. on these forms Ba$^{ZMG\ xlii.\ 1888,\ 341\ ff.}$));—מַיִם (מָ֫יִם) Gn 1^{2} +; הַמָּ֫יְמָה Ex 7^{15} 8^{16}; cstr. מֵי Gn 7^{7} + 71 t.; מֵימֵי Ex 4^{9} + 10 t. + Qr 2 K 18^{27} = Is 36^{12}; sf. מֵימַי Ho 2^{7} + 1 S 25^{11} (but rd. here יֵינִי 𝔊 Ew Th We Klo Dr Kit Bu); מֵימֶיךָ Ex 23^{25} + 3 t.; מֵימָיו Nu 20^{8} + 6 t.; מֵימֶיהָ Je 6^{7} 50^{38}; מֵימֵינוּ La 5^{4}; מֵימֵיהֶם Ex 7^{19} + 4 t.;—*waters, water* (c. adj. pl. Gn 26^{19} Ex 15^{10} Lv $14^{5.6.50}$ + oft., so alw. c. adj.; also c. pt. pl. Nu $5^{18.19.24}$ 2 K 3^{20} +; c. pron. pl. Nu 20^{13} 27^{14} 2 K 2^{21} +; cf. sf. Jos 4^{18}; before pl. vb. Gn $1^{9.20.21}$ 7^{17} + oft.; after pl. vb. Jos 3^{13} Is 28^{17} Pr 9^{17} Ez 31^{4} +; rarely c. sg. vb.; before, Gn 9^{15} Lv 11^{34} Nu 20^{2} 24^{7} 33^{14} 2 K 3^{9}; after, Nu $19^{13.20}$);—**1. a.** *water,* of a spring or well (בְּאֵר, עַיִן) Gn 16^{7} $24^{11.13.13.43}$ Ex $15^{27.27}$ (J), Gn $21^{19.25}$ Nu 20^{17} 21^{16} (E), etc.; for drinking, also Am 4^{8} 8^{11} Jon 3^{7} + oft.; out of rock Ex 17^{6} (E), Nu $20^{8.8.10.11}$ (P), Dt 8^{15} etc.; מֵי מְרִיבָה (RS$^{Sem.\ i.\ 165;\ 2nd\ ed.\ 181}$) Nu $20^{13.24}$ 27^{14} (P), Dt 33^{8} ψ 81^{8} 106^{32}; cf. Dt 32^{51} Ez 47^{19} 48^{28}; for washing (hands, feet, person) Gn 18^{4} 24^{32} 43^{24} (J), 2 K 3^{11}, Ex 29^{4} 30^{20} Lv $15^{5.6}$ + (P); (victims) Lv $1^{9.13}$ 8^{21} (P); (vessels) Lv 6^{21} $12^{32.34}$ (P); (garments) Lv 15^{17} Nu 19^{8} (P); for cooking Ex 12^{9} (P), cf. Is 64^{1} Ez 24^{3} (symbol.); for purification Nu 8^{7} (מֵי חַטָּאת), 19^{9} (מֵי נִדָּה), cf. $v^{13.18.20.21.31}$ $31^{23.23}$ (all P), Ez 36^{25} (fig.). **b.** of a river, Nile Ex 2^{10} $4^{9.9}$ (J), Je 2^{18} etc.; Jordan Jos 3^{8} (D), $v^{15.16}$ (JE), etc.; Euphrates Is 8^{7} (fig.), Je 2^{18}; Ezek.'s river Ez $47^{1.1.2}$ +, etc.; of streams, canals, etc., esp. as condition of fertility Dt 8^{7} 10^{7} Is 1^{30} Pr 30^{16} 2 K 3^{17} +, etc. **c.** of sea Am 5^{8} 9^{6}; Red Sea Ex $15^{8.10.19}$ (song), $14^{21.22.26}$ + (P), Jos 2^{10} (D), etc. **d.** of flood Gn $7^{7.10}$ $8^{3.7.8.9.11}$ (J), 6^{17} $7^{6.17.18.18.19}$ 8^{5} $9^{11.15}$ (P); so מֵי־נֹחַ Is $54^{9.9}$ *waters of Noah.* **e.** subterranean Ex 20^{4} (E), Dt 4^{18} 5^{8}, cf. Jb 26^{5} ψ 136^{6}. **f.** in clouds Je 10^{13} Jb 26^{8} ψ $29^{3.3}$ 104^{3} 148^{4}, etc. **g.** of rain Ju 5^{4} 2 S 21^{10} Dt 11^{11} ψ 65^{10} Jb 5^{10} (‖ מָטָר), etc. **h.** of dew Ju 6^{38}. **i.** primæval deep Gn $1^{2.6}$ (P). **2.** c. nomm. pr. loc. (q. v.), to denote springs, streams, or seas belonging to, near, such places: מֵימֵי מִצְרַיִם Ex 7^{19} 8^{2}; מֵי מְרִיבָה (v. supr. **1 a**); מֵי מֵרוֹם Jos $11^{5.7}$; מֵי עֵין־שֶׁמֶשׁ Jos 15^{7}; מֵי נֶפְתּוֹחַ 15^{9} 18^{15}; מֵי יְרִיחוֹ 16^{1}; מֵי מְגִדּוֹ Ju 5^{19}; מֵי נִמְרִ(י)ם Is 15^{6} Je 48^{34}; מֵי דִימוֹן Is 15^{9}; cf. מֵי הַשִּׁלֹחַ Is 8^{6}; מֵימֵי גִיחוֹן הָעֶלְיוֹן 2 Ch 32^{30}; cf. also n. pr. loc. מִשְׂרְפוֹת מַיִם Jos 11^{8} 13^{6}. **3.** special uses are: מֵי רַגְלַיִם *water of the feet* = urine 2 K 18^{27} = Is 36^{12}; cf. בְּמֵי מַדְמֵנָה Is 25^{10} Kt *in water of a dunghill* (> Qr בְּמוֹ); מַיִם לַחַץ *water* (which is) *distress,* because drunk in imprisonment 1 K 22^{27} (‖ לֶחֶם לַחַץ) = 2 Ch 18^{26}; בְּמֵי־שָׁלֶג *in snow-water* Jb 9^{30} Qr (Kt במו; Me Hoffm Siegfr כְּמוֹ), מֵימֵי שֶׁלֶג 24^{19}; מַיִם קְדֹשִׁים †Nu 5^{17} *holy water* (cf. RS$^{Sem.\ 165,\ 2nd\ ed.\ 181}$, but text dubious, v. Di); מֵי הַמָּרִים *bitter water* †Nu $5^{18.19.23.24}$; cf. Ex 15^{23} (כִּי מָרִים הֵם), opp. וַיִּמְתְּקוּ הַמָּיִם v^{25} *and the waters were sweetened;* מֵי חַטָּאת, מֵי נִדָּה v. supr. **1 a**; מַיִם חַיִּים *living* (i.e. running) *water* Lv $14^{5.6.50.51.52}$ Nu 19^{17}, also (fig.) Zc 14^{8} (cf. Ez 47), and (fig.) Je 2^{13} 17^{13}. See also infr. (cf. Nu $21^{17.18}$; v. RS$^{Sem.\ i.\ 127,157;\ 2nd\ ed.\ 135,\ 176}$). **4.** among fig. uses are: **a.** of distress Is 43^{2} ψ 66^{12} (‖ אֵשׁ), 69^{2} La 3^{54}; usu. *many waters* 2 S 22^{17} = ψ 18^{17}, cf. Jb 22^{11} ψ 32^{6} 144^{7}, or *deep waters* ψ $69^{3.15}$, cf. v^{16}; also מֵי־רֹאשׁ *water of gall* Je 8^{14} 9^{14} 23^{15}. **b.** פֶּרֶץ מַיִם 2 S 5^{20} = 1 Ch 14^{11} of outbursting force. **c.** שְׁאוֹן מַיִם Is $17^{12.13}$ of rushing nations. **d.** of what is impetuous, violent, overwhelming Is $28^{2.17}$ Ho 10^{7} Jb 27^{20} ψ $124^{4.5}$ 88^{18}; sim. of impetuousness פַּחַז כַּמַּיִם Gn 49^{4}. **e.** (as running away) of heart in timidity Jos 7^{5}, cf. ψ 22^{15}, of knees Ez 7^{17} 21^{12}. **f.** of transitoriness Jb 11^{16} 24^{18} ψ 58^{8}. **g.** of refreshment Is 32^{2} 49^{10}; spiritual 12^{3}. **h.** מֵי מְנֻחוֹת ψ 23^{2} in fig. of rest and peace, cf. Je 31^{9}. **i.** of reckless bloodshed (poured out

like water) ψ 79^{3}; cf. pouring away (and not eating) blood Dt 12$^{16.24}$ 15^{23}. **j.** בְּאֵר מַיִם חַיִּים Ct 4^{15} fig. of bride; מַיִם מִבּוֹרֶךָ Pr 5^{15} of enjoyment of one's own wife; of harlotry מַיִם גְּנוּבִים Pr 9^{17} *stolen waters.* **k.** of outpoured wrath of י׳ Ho 5^{10}. **l.** of abundant justice Am 5^{24}. **m.** of outpoured feelings Jb 3^{24}; שִׁפְכִי כַמַּיִם לִבֵּךְ La 2^{19}.—Is 48^{1} rd. prob. מִמְּעֵי for MT מִמֵּי, so Secker Du Che ^{Hpt} Skinner, cf. Di.

†מֵי זָהָב **n.pr.m.** an Edomite Gn 36^{39} (𝔊 Μεζοοβ, 𝔊L Μαιζοοβ) = 1 Ch 1^{50} (𝔊L Μαιζααβ).

†מֵי הַיַּרְקוֹן **n.pr.loc.** in Dan, near Joppa Jos 19^{46} (reading dubious; 𝔊 ἀπὸ θαλάσσης [i.e. מִיָּם = מים] Ιερακων).

מִי $_{423}$ **pron. interrog.** who? of persons, as מָה (q.v.) of things (Eth. ሚ: but only = *What?* and *How?* As. *mî, me* (rare) Jäger $^{BAS. ii. 277}$, the usu. Sem. form for *Who?* has *n*, viz. As. *mannu, manu* (Dl $^{HWB 419}$), Eth. መኑ: *manū*, Aram. ܡܰܢ, Arab. مَنْ, vulg.-Arab. *min, mīn*, from a form resembling which, by rejection of *n*, prob. Heb. מִי: W $^{SG 123 f.}$):—*who?* (τίς; *quis?*) Gn 3^{11} מִי הִגִּיד לְךָ *who* told thee? 24^{65} מִי הָאִישׁ הַלָּזֶה *who* is this man? 27^{18} מי אתה בני *who* art thou, my son? Nu 22^{9} Ju 1^{1} 6^{29} 15^{6} 18^{3} 20^{18} 2 S 1^{8} + oft.; Ru 3^{9} מִי אָתְּ *who* art thou (fem.)? Is 51^{12}; of more than one, מִי אֵלֶּה *who* are these? Gn 33^{5} 48^{8} Is 60^{8}; מי אתם 2 K 10^{13}; once, more explicitly, מִי וָמִי הַהֹלְכִים Ex 10^{8}; =*as who?* (i.e. in what condition, or capacity), Am 7^{2} מי יקום יעקב, v^{5} Is 51^{19} מִי אֲנַחֲמֵךְ (but Vrss Che Lag Brd Du מִי יְ׳, as ‖ מִי יָנוּד), Ru 3^{16} (Be Ke Kö $^{iii. 388}$). Note in partic.: **a.** מִי is rarely used of *things*, and usually where persons are understood or implied: Gn 33^{8} מי לך כל־המחנה הזה *who* (or *what*) to thee is all this camp? Dt 4^{7} Ju 9^{28} מִי שְׁכֶם *who* is Shechem (i.e. the Shechemites)? Mi 1^{5} מִי־פֶשַׁע יַעֲקֹב הֲלֹא שֹׁמְרוֹן, v^{b} Ct 3^{6} Ju 13^{17} מִי שְׁמֶךָ (but מה Gn 32^{28} Ex 3^{13}: with מי cf. מַן in Aram. Ezr 5^{4} Gn Ex. *ll. cc.* 𝔗; and see Nö $^{M. p. 341}$). On 1 S 18^{18}, v. II. חַי. **b.** in the gen., בַּת־מִי אַתְּ *whose* daughter art thou? Gn 24$^{23.47}$ 1 S 12$^{3.3.3}$ 17^{55} Je 44^{28} Jb 26^{4} 33^{28}; after various preps., as אַחֲרֵי מִי 1 S 24$^{15.15}$; אֶל־מִי 1 S 6^{20} 2 K 9^{5} +; בְּמִי by *whom?* † 1 K 20^{14}, לְמִי$_{20}$ *to whom? whose?* Gn 32^{18} לְמִי אַתָּה, 38^{25} Pr 20^{29} (6 t.) +; מִמִּי + Ez 32^{19} ψ 27$^{1.1}$; עַל־מִי 2 K 18^{20} 19^{22} Is 57^{4} +; אֶת־מִי (so alw. in acc.), 1 S 12$^{3.3}$ 28^{11} Is 6^{8}; =*with whom?* Jb 12^{3}. **c.** in an indirect qu., as Gn 21^{26} 43^{22} לֹא ידענו מי שׂם we do not know *who put*, etc., Dt 21^{1} ψ 39^{7} Jos 24^{15} בַּחֲרוּ . . . אֶת־מִי תַּעֲבֹדוּן choose *whom* ye will serve, after ראה 1 S 14^{17}, שׁאל 17^{56}, הגיד 1 K 1^{20}, הוריע v^{27}. **d.** מי ב׳ *who among . . . ?* 1 S 22^{14} Is 36^{20}; 43^{9} 48^{14} (בהם); 42^{23} 50^{10} Hg 2^{3} (all בכם); מי מן *who of . . . ?* Ju 21^{8} 2 K 6^{11} Is 50^{1}. **e.** strengthened and emph. forms of interrog.: (*a*) מי זה (v. זה **4 b**), מי הוא (v. הוא **4 b** β), מי הוא זה † ψ 24^{10} Je 30^{21} Est 7^{5} (v. *ibid.*); (*b*) מִי אֶחָד *what single one . . . ?* Ju 21^{8}, cf. 2 S 7^{23} (= 1 Ch 17^{21}). **f.** various *rhetorical* uses (oft. *repeated* in ‖ cl., as ψ 15^{1} 18^{32} Is 28^{9} 29^{15}):—(*a*) sq. impf. it expresses a *wish* (the question implying a desire that the person asked for were present), 2 S 15^{4} מִי יְשִׂמֵנִי שֹׁפֵט *who* will set me judge? i.e. *would that* some one would make me judge! 23^{15} מִי יַשְׁקֵנִי מַיִם = *O that* one would give me to drink, etc.! cf. Nu 11$^{4.18}$ Mal 1^{10} ψ 4^{7} 60^{11} 94^{16} Is 42^{23}, and very oft. in the phr. מִי יִתֵּן *who will give?* i.e. *would that there were . . . !* as Nu 11^{29} ומי יתן כל עם י׳ נביאים = and *would that* all י׳'s people were prophets! Dt 28^{67} מי יתן ערב = *would it were* even! Ju 9^{29} + (v. נָתַן). (*b*) it expresses *contempt* (*who?* implying the answer *no one at all*), Ex 5^{2} מי י׳ אשר אשמע בקולו *who* is י׳ that I should listen to his voice? Ju 9^{28} מִי אֲבִימֶלֶךְ וּמִי שְׁכֶם כִּי נַעַבְדֶנּוּ, v^{38} 1 S 17^{26} *who* is this Phil. that he should have reproached, etc.? 25^{10} מי דוד ומי בן ישי, Is 28^{9} Jb 26^{4} Pr 30^{9} מי י׳; or *modesty* (real or assumed), Ex 3^{11} מִי אָנֹכִי כִּי אֵלֵךְ אֶל־פַּרְעֹה, 1 S 18^{18} מי אנכי ומי חיי who am I, and who is my clan (חַיַּי), that I should be the king's son-in-law? 2 S 7^{18} 1 Ch 29^{14} 2 Ch 2^{5}; or *surprise*, Is 44^{10} 49^{21}. (*c*) in impassioned prose, and esp. in poetry, implying the answer *few* or *none*, it is equiv. to a rhetorical negative, Dt 9^{2} מִי יִתְיַצֵּב לִפְנֵי בְּנֵי עֲנָק *who* can stand, etc.? 30^{12} מִי יַעֲלֶה־לָּנוּ הַשָּׁמַיְמָה, v^{13} 1 S 4^{8} מִי יַצִּילֵנוּ וגו׳, 6^{20} 22^{14} 26$^{9.15}$ 2 S 16^{10}; מי יאמר *who* shall (or can) say? Jb 9^{12} Pr 20^{9} Ec 8^{4}; with the perfect (of experience), *who has ever . . . ?* Nu 23^{10} Dt 5^{23} Is 36^{20} 66$^{8.8}$ Je 18^{13} מִי שָׁמַע כָּאֵלֶּה, 23^{18} (MT), 30^{21} Jb 4^{7} 9^{4} מִי הִקְשָׁה אֵלָיו וַיִּשְׁלָם, 41^{3} Pr 30^{4} La 3^{37}; poet., very oft., as Gn 49^{9} וּכְלָבִיא מִי יְקִימֶנּוּ *who* can rouse him up? (i.e. no one), Ex 15$^{11.11}$ מִי כָמוֹךָ (so ψ 35^{10} al.), Nu 24$^{9.23}$ 1 S 2^{25} מי יתפלל לו *who* shall intercede for him? (i.e. no one), Is 1^{12} 10^{3} 40$^{13.14.18}$ 41^{26} 42^{19} 43^{9} 48^{14} 50^{1} 53^{1} מִי הֶאֱמִין לִשְׁמֻעָתֵנוּ (i.e. few or none), etc.; ψ 18^{32} מִי אֱלוֹהַּ מִבַּלְעֲדֵי י׳, 76^{8} 89^{7} 130^{3} Jb 21^{31}

34^{29} Je 17^{9} Jo 2^{11} Mal 3^{2}; . . . מִי לֹא Am 3^{8} Je 10^{7} Jb 12^{9} (cf. 25^{3} Na 3^{19}); מִי יְשִׁיבֶנּוּ (יְשִׁיבֶנָּה) *who* shall (can) turn it back? †Jb 9^{12} 11^{10} 23^{13} Is 14^{27} 43^{13} Je 2^{24}; implying the answer, *no one but God*, Is 40^{12} 41^{2} Jb $38^{5.6.25}$, etc.; defiantly, Is 50^{9} מִי הוּא יַרְשִׁיעֵנִי, Je 21^{13} 49^{4} מִי יָבוֹא אֵלָי, v^{19} Ob^{3} ψ 12^{5} מִי אָדוֹן לָנוּ, 59^{8} 64^{6} Jb 9^{19} וְאִם לְמִשְׁפָּט מִי יוֹעִידֵנִי, 13^{19} מִי הוּא יָרִיב עִמָּדִי *who* is he that will contend with me? 17^{3} 41^{2}. Notice in examples of this kind the freq. *order* of words: Pr 20^{6} ואיש אמונים מי ימצא, 24^{22} ופיד שניהם מי יודע, 31^{10} Na 1^{6} לפני זעמו מי יעמד, ψ 147^{17} לפני קָרָתוֹ מִי יעמד, Jb 4^{2} וַעְצֹר בְּמִלִּין מִי יוּכָל, 26^{14} 38^{37} 39^{5} $41^{5.6}$ ψ 6^{6} בִּשְׁאוֹל מִי יוֹדֶה־לָּךְ, 19^{13}; and with the *nom. pendens*, Je 2^{24} תַּאֲנָתָהּ מִי יְשִׁיבֶנָּה, Pr 18^{14} Jb 17^{15} וְתִקְוָתִי מִי יְשׁוּרֶנָּה, 38^{29} וּכְפֹר שָׁמַיִם מִי יְלָדוֹ. (*d*) מִי יוֹדֵעַ *who knoweth?* (ψ 90^{11} Pr 24^{22}), sq. a verbal clause, becomes (cf. *nescio an*) = *it may be, perchance*, †2 S 12^{22} מִי יוֹדֵעַ יְחָנַּנִי י׳ (Qr וְחַנַּנִי), Jo 2^{14} (= Jon 3^{9}) מי יודע ישוב ונחם, Est 4^{14} מי יודע אם. (*e*) especially in poetry, a question with מִי, to which the answer follows, is an effective mode of affirming a fact, or introducing a description: ψ $15^{1.1}$ (see v^{2-5}), $24^{3.8.10}$ Is 23^{8} מי יעץ זאת וג׳ (v^{9} the answ., י׳ צ׳ יְעָצָהּ), 33^{14} (see $v^{15f.}$), 37^{23} $41^{2.4}$ 60^{8} 63^{1} Je 46^{7} Ct 3^{6}, cf. 6^{10} 8^{5}; answered by הֲלֹא Ex 4^{11} Is 42^{24} 45^{21} Mi $1^{5.5}$. **g.** מִי may sometimes be rendered *whosoever*, though, as the examples will shew, it does not really mean it: Ex 24^{14} מִי בעל דברים יִגַּשׁ אליהם, lit. *Who* hath a cause? let him draw nigh unto them, i.e. *whoso* hath a cause, let him, etc., Is 50^{8b} מִי בַעַל מִשְׁפָּטִי יִגַּשׁ אֵלָי, 54^{15} Ju 7^{3} מִי יָרֵא וְחָרֵד יָשֹׁב וג׳ *who* is fearful and trembling? let him return, Pr $9^{4.16}$ מִי־פֶתִי יָסֻר הֵנָּה, Ezr 1^{3} (cf. with וְ in apod. Je 9^{11} Ho 14^{10} ψ 107^{43}; Zc 4^{10} is dubious, on account of anom. tense and construct.); so with מי האיש אשר . . . Dt $20^{5.6.7}$ Ju 10^{18}, cf. ψ 25^{12}. With 1 ps. in apod., Ex 32^{33} מִי אֲשֶׁר חָטָא לִי אֶמְחֶנּוּ מִסִּפְרִי, Je 49^{19} (= 50^{44}) וּמִי בָחוּר אֵלֶיהָ אֶפְקֹד and *who* is chosen? I will appoint him over her! Is 50^{8a}; with an imv. in the apod. Ex 32^{24} (against accents; v. Ra) למי זהב התפרקו *who* hath gold? break it off you! Gn 19^{12} 1 S 11^{12}, cf. ψ $34^{13f.}$; without a verb, Ex 32^{26} מי לי׳ אלי *who* is on J.'s side? (let him come) to me! so 2 S 20^{11} (מי אשר); Ec 5^{9} 9^{4} (מי אשר). **h.** once, following a verb (cf. מָה **3**), *any one*, 2 S 18^{12} שִׁמְרוּ־מִי בַּנַּעַר באבשלום Have a care, *whosoever ye be*, of, etc. (but 𝔊𝔖𝔙 Bu לִי; cf. v^{5}).

†מִיכָאֵל **n.pr.m.** Michael, 𝔊 Μειχαηλ, Μιχαηλ (*Who is like God?* cf. מִיכָיְהוּ, and As. proper names, as *Mannu-kî-Rammân*, 'Who is like Rammân?' *Mannu-kî-ilu-rabu*, 'Who is like the great God?' Dl $^{\text{Prol. 210; HWB 419}}$; Schr $^{\text{COT 478}}$; cf. Cook $^{\text{Aram. Gloss. 74}}$):—**1.** Nu 13^{13} (P). **2.** 1 Ch 5^{13}. **3.** 5^{14}. **4.** 6^{25}. **5.** 7^{3}. **6.** 8^{16}. **7.** 12^{21}. **8.** 27^{18}. **9.** 2 Ch 21^{2}. **10.** Ezr 8^{8}. **11.** the 'prince,' or patron-angel, of Israel, Dn $10^{13.21}$ 12^{1} (cf. Jude^{9} Rev 12^{7}; Levy $^{\text{NHWB iii. 100}}$).

†מִיכָיְהוּ **n.pr.** (*Who is like Yah?* cf. מִיכָאֵל):—**1. m.** a prince under Jehosh. 2 Ch 17^{7}. **2. f.** 2 Ch 13^{2} f. l. for מַעֲכָה **2 b**, q. v. Of this name, the following are abbreviated, or softened, forms—

†מִיכָיְהוּ **n.pr.m.** (so on an Isr. scarab, Ganneau $^{\text{JAS 1883, 156, No. 42}}$)—**1.** an Ephraimite, Ju $17^{1.4}$ (in $17^{5ff.}$ $18^{2ff.}$ called מִיכָה). **2.** a prophet, the son of Imlah (𝔊 Μειχαίας), 1 K 22^{8-28} (9 t.), ‖ 2 Ch 18^{7-25} (7 t.) + v^{8} Qr (Kt מיכהו). **3.** a contemp. of Jer., Je 36^{11} (מִכָיְהוּ), v^{13}.

†מִיכָיָה **n.pr.m.** **1.** the canon. prophet, Micah, Je 26^{18} Kt (Qr מִיכָה, as Mi 1^{1}). **2.** Ne 12^{35} (called מִיכָא, $11^{17.22}$). **3.** Ne 12^{41}. **4.** 2 K 22^{12} (‖ 2 Ch 34^{20} מִיכָה).

†מִיכָה **n.pr.m.** **1.** Micha, the Ephraimite (𝔊 Μειχαίας), Ju $17^{5.8.9.10.12.12.13}$ $18^{2ff.}$ (12 t.), called מִיכָיְהוּ $17^{1.4}$. **2.** the prophet Micah (𝔊 Μειχαίας), Mi 1^{1} (Je 26^{18} Kt מִיכָיָה). **3.** 1 Ch 5^{5}. **4.** son of Meribbaal (Mephibosheth) $8^{34f.}$ (𝔊 Μιχια), $9^{40f.}$ (𝔊 Μειχα), called מִיכָא 2 S 9^{12}. **5.** 23^{20} (𝔊 Μειχας), $24^{24.25}$ (𝔊 Μειχα). **6.** 2 Ch 18^{14} (= מִיכָיְהוּ **2**). **7.** 34^{20} (‖ 2 K 22^{12} מִיכָיָה).

†מִיכָא **n.pr.m.** (so in Palm., Vog $^{\text{No. 36a}}$). **1.** son of Mephibosheth (𝔊 Μειχα), 2 S 9^{12} (= מִיכָה **4**). **2.** Ne 10^{12}. **3.** Ne 11^{17} (= 1 Ch 9^{15}), v^{22} (called מִיכָיָה 12^{35}).

†מִישָׁאֵל **n.pr.m.** (*Who is what God is?* Ass. form., cf. מְתוּשָׁאֵל: note also in Thothmes' list of towns *Ba'-t'-ša-'-rạ*, i.e. prob. בֵּיתְשָׁאֵל, Heb. בֵּיתְאֵל WMM $^{\text{As. Eur. 193}}$):—**1.** a cousin of Moses Ex 6^{22} Lv 10^{4} (P). **2.** one of Daniel's companions Dn $1^{6.7.11.19}$ + 2^{17} (Aram.), elsewhere in c. 2–3 called מֵישַׁךְ (1^{7}). **3.** Ne 8^{4}.

†מֵידְבָא **n.pr.loc.** city in Moab (MI^{8} מהדבא)—Nu 21^{30} Is 15^{2}; Jos $13^{9.16}$ assigned to

Reuben (𝔊 Δαιδαβαν, Μαιδαβα, 𝔊L Μεδαβα); 1 Ch 19[7] meeting-place of Ammonites (𝔊 Μαιθαβα, A 𝔊L Μηδαβα).

מֵידָד v. II. ידד.

מידע Kt Ru 2[1] v. מודע sub ידע.

מֵיחִים v. מֵחַ sub מחח.

[מֵיטָב] v. יטב.

מִיכָא, מִיכָה, מִיכָיָה, מִיכָיְהוּ v. מִי.

מִיכָאֵל v. מִי.

† [מִיכָל] **n.[m.] brook, stream(?)** (dubious word, cf. Dr[ad loc.] HPS), cstr. מִיכַל הַמָּ֑יִם 2 S 17[20].

† מִיכַל **n.pr.f.** (acc. to Ol[§ 277 f.], contr. from מִיכָאֵל):—younger daughter of Saul, wife of David (𝔊 Μελχολ), 1 S 14[49] 18[20.27.28] 19[11.12.13.17.17] 25[44] 2 S 3[13.14] 6[16] = 1 Ch 15[29], 2 S 6[20.21.23]; also 21[8] (𝔊 Μιχολ), but err. for מֵרַב (𝔊L Μεροβ).

מַיִם v. מַי.

† מִיָּמִן, מִיָּמִין, מִנְיָמִן, מִנְיָמִין **n.pr.m.** **1.** priestly name: **a.** מִיָּמִן assigned to David's time, 1 Ch 24[9]. **b.** Neh.'s time Ne 10[8] = מִנְיָמִין 12[17.41]. **c.** מִנְיָמִן assigned to Hezekiah's time 2 Ch 31[15]. **d.** מִיָּמִין went up with Zerub. Ne 12[5]. **2.** one of those who took strange wives Ezr 10[25].—𝔊 Βενιαμειν and (esp. A𝔊L) Μιαμειν.

מון, מין (√ of foll.; dubious; Fl in Levy NHWB iii. 310, comp. Ar. مَانَ (med. *i*) *split* the earth (in ploughing), cf. Dr[Dt 14, 13]).

† [מִין] **n.[m.] kind, species** (NH *id.* (Ecclus 43[25] *id.*), also *schismatic, heretic*; Jewish-Aram. מִינָא, *species*, so Syr. (Edessa) ܡܙܢܐ; Palest. Syr. = *nation* PS[2094] Schwally[Idioticon 50]; yet not Aram. loan-wd. in Heb.; v. Lag[BN 183 f.]);—alw. sf. + prep. לְמִינֵהוּ Gn 1[12.12] + 2 t.; לְמִינוֹ Gn 1[11] (om. 𝔊) + 3 t.; לְמִינָהּ Gn 1[24.24] + 9 t.; לְמִינָה Ez 47[10] (del. Co); לְמִינֵהֶם Gn 1[21];—*kind, species*, of plant Gn 1[11.12.12]; usu. of animal (beast, bird, fish, insect) Gn 1[21.22.24.24.25.25.25] 6[20.20.20] 7[14.14.14.14]; Lv 11[14.15.16.19.22.22.22.22.29] (all P); also Dt 14[13.14.15.18] (cf. Lv) Ez 47[10] (on text, cf. Co).

† תְּמוּנָה **n.f. likeness, form**;—ת׳ Ex 20[4] + 4 t.; cstr. תְּמוּנַת (תְּמֻנַת) Dt 4[16] + 3 t.; sf. תְּמוּנָתֶ֑ךָ ψ 17[15];—*likeness, representation* (‖ פֶּסֶל) Ex 20[4] = Dt 5[8], cf. 4[16.23.25]; *form, semblance* of י׳ Nu 12[8] ψ 17[15], cf. Dt 4[12] (vid. Dr), v[15]; of nocturnal apparition Jb 4[16].

מֵינֶ֫קֶת v. ינק **Hiph.**

מיסך v. [מוּסָךְ] sub סכך.

מֵיפַ֫עַת, מֵפָ֫עַת, מופעת v. יפע.

† [מִיץ] (√ of foll. = *press, squeeze*, cf. NH *id.*, *press, suck*; Ar. مَاصَ (med. و) is *wash gently, rub* with the hand).

† מֵץ **n.m. squeezer**, i. e. **extortioner, oppressor**, only הַמֵּץ Is 16[4].

† מִיץ **n.m. squeezing, pressing, wringing** (3 t.) מִיץ חָלָב יוֹצִיא חֶמְאָה וּמ׳־אַף יוֹצִיא דָ֑ם וּמ׳ אַפַּיִם יוֹצִיא רִיב׃ Pr 30[33] *the squeezing of milk produceth curd* (v. Thomson[Land and Book, Centr. Pal. 456] Rob[BR i. 485; ii. 418]), *and the squeezing of the nose produceth blood*, and (so) *the squeezing of anger* (i. e. pressure, insistence) *produceth strife.*

מִישׁ v. מושׁ.

† מֵישָׁא **n.pr.m.** of Benjamite in Moab 1 Ch 8[9]. 𝔊 Μισα; A Μωσα.

מִישָׁאֵל v. מִי.

מִישׁוֹר, [מֵישָׁר], מֵישָׁרִים v. ישׁר.

† מֵישַׁךְ **n.pr.m.** (acc. to Dl[Baer, Dan. xi] for *Mi-sha-aku* 'who is what Aku (the moon-god) is?' cf. מִישָׁאֵל, p. 567);—the new (Bab.) name given to Mishael, Dn 1[7] (+ Aram. 2[49] and c. 3).

מֵישַׁע, מֵישָׁע v. ישׁע. [מֵיתָר] v. יתר.

מַכְאוֹב v. כאב. מַכְבִּיר v. I. כבר **Hiph.**

מַכְבַּנַּי, מַכְבֵּנָא v. כבן.

מִכְבָּר, מַכְבֵּר v. II. כבר.

מַכָּה v. נכה. מִכְוָה v. כוה.

מְכוֹנָה, מָכוֹן v. כון.

[מְכֹרָה, מְכוּרָה] v. II. כור.

† מָכִי **n.pr.m.** a Gadite Nu 13[15]. 𝔊 Μα(κ)χι.

† [מָכַךְ] **vb. be low, humiliated** (Aram. מְכַךְ, ܡܟ; Ar. مَكَّ is *suck entirely out, diminish, consume*)—**Qal** *Impf.* וַיָּמֹכּוּ ψ 106[43] of perverse Isr. **Niph.** *Impf.* יִמַּךְ Ec 10[18] *sink* (in decay) of house-timbers. **Hoph.** *Pf.* וְהֻמְּכוּ Jb 24[24] *be brought low*, of wicked.

I. מִכְלָה v. כלא. II. [מִכְלָה] v. כלה.

מִכְלוֹל, מִכְלָל, [מַכְלֻל] v. כלל.

מַאֲכֹלֶת v. אכל. [מִכְמָן], מִכְמַנֵּי v. כמן.

מִכְמָס, מִכְמָשׂ v. כמס.

מִכְמֹרֶת, [מִכְמֶרֶת], [מִכְמֹר], מַכְמָר v. III. כמר.

מִכְמְתָת v. כמת.

†מַכְנַדְבַי **n.pr.m.** one of those who had taken strange wives Ezr 10^{40} (Gray Expos. Times, Feb 1899, p. 233 prop. מכרנבו = *possession of Nebo*), 𝔊 Μαχαδναβου, A Μαχναδααβου; 𝔊L Ναδαβου.

†מְכֹנָה **n.pr.loc.** in Judah Ne 11^{28}. 𝔊L Μαμη.—מְכֹנָה = מְכוֹנָה v. כון

[מִכְנָס], מִכְנְסֵי v. כנס.

מֶכֶס, [מִכְסָה] v. כסס.

מִכְסֶה, מְכַסֶּה v. I. כסה.

מַכְפֵּלָה v. כפל.

†מָכַר **vb. sell** (NH *id.*; Ph. מכר; Zinj. מכרו *price*, DHM Sendsch. 60; Aram. מְכַר, ܡܟܰܪ *marry* (i.e. *buy* as a wife); cf. As. *makkûru*, *namkur(r)u*, *nakkuru*, *possession*, *property*, Dl HWB 408);—**Qal** *Pf.* מ׳ Lv 27^{20} + 2 t.; sf. מְכָרוֹ Ex 21^{37} + 2 t.; 1 s. מָכַרְתִּי Is 50^{1} + 2 t., etc.; *Impf.* יִמְכֹּר Ex 21^{7} +, etc.; *Imv.* מִכְרָה Gn 25^{31}; fs. מִכְרִי 2 K 4^{7}, *Inf abs* מָכֹר Dt 14^{21} 21^{14}; *cstr.* מְכֹר Ne 10^{32}; sf. מָכְרָהּ Ex 21^{8}; מִכְרָם Am 2^{6} Ne 13^{15} (cf Ba NB 104); *Pt.* מֹכֵר (מוֹכֵר) Lv 25^{16} + 3 t.; f. מֹכֶרֶת Na 3^{4}, etc.;—*sell* (c. ב *pret.* Am 2^{6} Jo 4^{3} ψ 44^{13}) sq. acc. e g. land Gn $47^{20.22}$ (J), Lv 25^{14} (acc. cogn.), v^{25} (H; sq. מֵאֲחֻזָּתוֹ) cf Ez 48^{14} (sq. מִן partit.), Lv 25^{15} (no obj. expr), so v^{27}; 27^{20} (H), Ru 4^{3}; house Lv 25^{29} (H), beast Ex $21^{35.37}$ (E); flesh Dt 14^{21} (no obj); crop Lv 25^{16} (H); food Ne 10^{32} $13^{15.16}$, cf v^{20} (sq. מִמְכָּר); oil 2 K 4^{7}; linen Pr 31^{24}; birthright Gn $25^{31.33}$ (J); most oft. human beings, e.g. as slaves Gn $37^{27\ 28.36}$ $45^{4.5}$ (all JE), Ex 21^{16} (E), Dt $21^{14\ 14}$ 24^{7}, cf Am 2^{6} Ne 5^{8} Zc 11^{5} Jo $4^{3.6.7\ 8.8}$; esp. daughters Ex $21^{7.8}$ (E), in marriage Gn 31^{15} (E); *Pt.* = *seller* Is 24^{2} Ez $7^{12\ 13}$; fig., obj. truth Pr 23^{23}; of Nineveh, selling nations גּוֹיִם Na 3^{4}; esp. י׳ selling his people (to enemies), i.e. giving it entirely into their power: Dt 32^{30} ψ 44^{13} Is 50^{1}, also (מ׳ בְּיַד) Ju 2^{14} 3^{8} 4^{2} 10^{7} 1 S 12^{9}; cf. Ju 4^{9} (Sisera to woman); also Ez 30^{12} (del. Co after B al) **Niph.** *Pf.* נִמְכַּר Lv 25^{48} + 5 t, etc.; *Impf.* יִמָּכֵר Lv 25^{34} + 3 t., etc; *Inf.* הִמָּכְרוֹ Lv 25^{50}, *Pt* pl. נִמְכָּרִים Ne 5^{8};—*be sold*, of land Lv $25^{23.34}$; beast Lv 27^{27}; cf. v^{28} (all P); of human beings as slaves Ex 22^{2} for (בְּ) theft (E), Lv 25^{42} (P), ψ 105^{17} Est 7^{4}; *sell oneself* Lv $25^{39.47\ 48.50}$ (PH), Dt 15^{12} Je 34^{14} Ne $5^{8.8}$; fig. of Isr., *sold* by י׳, Is 50^{1} for (בְּ) their sins, 52^{3}; cf. Est 7^{4} = *given over* to death. **Hithp.** *Pf* הִתְמַכֵּר 1 K 21^{25}; וְהִתְמַכַּרְתֶּם consec. Dt 28^{68}; וַיִּתְמַכְּרוּ 2 K 17^{17}; *Inf.* הִתְמַכֶּרְךָ 1 K 21^{20}; *sell oneself* as slave Dt 28^{68}; fig. 1 K $21^{20.25}$ 2 K 17^{17}, all sq. לַעֲשׂוֹת הָרַע.

†מֶכֶר **n.m.** Pr 31, 10 **merchandise, value;**—מ׳ abs. Ne 13^{16}; מִכְרָהּ Pr 31^{10}; מִכְרָם Nu 20^{19}; prob. also מְכָרָיו (rd. מִמְכָּרָיו) Dt 18^{8}, v DiDr,—**1.** *merchandise* Ne 13^{16}; *value, price*, of water Nu 20^{19} (JE), cf. Dt 18^{8} (v. supr.); of capable woman Pr 31^{10}.

†מָכִיר **n.pr.m.** 𝔊 Μαχειρ (Sab מכר Hal⁴). **1.** eldest son of Manasseh;—Gn 50^{23} Nu $26^{29\ 29}$ 27^{1} $32^{39.40}$ 36^{1} Dt 3^{15} Jos $13^{31.31}$ $17^{1\ 1}$, cf. 1 Ch $1^{21\ 23}$ $7^{14\ 15\ 16\ 17}$; v also Ju 5^{14} (poet.) where = Manasseh. **2.** son of ʽAmmiel 2 S $9^{4.5}$ 17^{27}.

†מָכִירִי **adj.gent.** only c. art. הַמּ׳ as subst. coll. *the Machirites* Nu 26^{29}.

†מִכְרִי **n.pr.m.** a Benjamite 1 Ch 9^{8}. 𝔊 Μαχειρ; A Μοχορι; 𝔊L Μαχειρι

†מִמְכָּר **n.m.** Lv 25, 28 **sale, ware,**—abs. מ׳ Lv 25^{14} + 2 t; cstr. מִמְכַּר Lv $25^{25.33}$; מִמְכָּרוֹ Lv 25^{27} + 3 t.; pl. sf. מִמְכָּרָיו Dt 18^{8} (but v. sub מֶכֶר);—*sale* Lv $25^{27.29.50}$; *thing sold* Lv 25^{14} (acc. cogn.), $v^{25\ 28}$ Ez 7^{13} Ne 13^{20}; מִמְכַּר בַּיִת Lv 25^{33} (Hex. only PH). On Dt 18^{8} v. מֶכֶר.

†מִמְכֶּרֶת **n.f.** sale,—cstr. יִמָּכְרוּ מִמְכֶּרֶת עָבֶד Lv 25^{42} (H)

[מַכָּר] v. נכר. [מְכֵרָה] v. I. כרה

[מְכֹרָה], [מְכוּרָה] v. II. כור.

†מְכֵרָתִי **adj.gent.** 1 Ch 11^{36}. 𝔊 Μοχορ, 𝔊L ὁ Μεχωραθι.

מִכְשׁוֹל, מִכְשֹׁל, מַכְשֵׁלָה v. כשל.

מִכְתָּב v. כתב [מְכִתָּה] v. כתת.

מִכְתָּם v. II. כתם. מַכְתֵּשׁ v. כתשׁ.

מָלֵא 249 **vb. be full, fill** (NH *id.* (Pi. trans.); Zinj. מלא (Pi trans) DHM Sendsch 60; As. *malû*

(trans. and intrans.) Dl $^{HWB\ 409}$; Ar. مَلَأَ (trans.) مَلُؤَ, مَلِئَ (intrans.); Eth. መልአ: (trans. and intrans.); Aram. ܡܠܐ (trans.), מְלָא (intrans. and trans.), Palm. n.pr. מלא = *plenitude*, Vog $^{Palm\ 7,2\ al.}$; Sab. מלא Os ^{14} Levy-Os $^{ZMG\ xix.\ 1865,\ 211\ f.}$ DHM $^{ZMG\ xxix.\ 1875,\ 595}$); — **Qal**$_{99}$ *Pf.* מ׳ Ex 40^{34} +; sf. מְלָאוֹ Est 7^{5}; מְלֵאתָ Jb 36^{17}; מָלֵאתִי Mi 3^{8} Je 6^{11}; מָלֵתִי Jb 32^{18}; מָלְאוּ Gn 29^{21} +; מָלוּ Ez 28^{16} (מָלְאתָ 𝔊 𝔖 Co); מָלֵאוּ Is 1^{15}, etc.; *Impf.* 3 fs. sf. תִּמְלָאֵמוֹ Ex 15^{9}; יִמְלְאוּ Gn 50^{3} + 2 t.; וַיִּמְלְאוּ Gn 25^{24} 50^{3}; *Imv.* מִלְאוּ Gn 1^{22} + 5 t.; *Inf. cstr.* מְלֹאת (מְלֹאות) Lv 8^{33} + 12 t.; *Pt.* מָלֵא Je 23^{24}; מְלֵאִים Is 6^{1}; (cf. also sub מָלֵא *adj.*);—**1.** *be full*, usu. c. acc. material: **a.** lit., subj. houses Ex 8^{17} 10^{6} (both J) Ju 16^{27} Is 13^{21} 2 Ch 5^{13}, cf. Ez 10^{4} (del. Co); winepress Jo 4^{13}; threshing-floor Jo 2^{24}; vessel 2 K 4^{6} Jb 21^{24}, etc.; Jb 20^{22} מְלֹאות (cf. מְלֹא), i.e. *fulness, abundance.* **b.** fig., earth full of violence Gn 6^{13}, cf. Lv 19^{29} (both P), Mi 6^{12} Is 1^{15} Je 23^{10} 51^{5} ψ 26^{10} Ez 7$^{23.23}$ Ec 9^{3}, etc.; earth full of glory, mercy, goodness, knowledge, of י׳ ψ 33^{5} 119^{64} Is 11^{9} Hb 3^{3}; cf. also ψ 48^{11} 104^{24}, etc.; subj. נֶפֶשׁ = desire be satisfied (full) c. sf. Ex 15^{9}; וְדִין רָשָׁע מ׳ Jb 36^{17} *and of judgment on the wicked art thou full* (hast thou thy fill), cf. Di Du; מָלֵא לֵב לַעֲשׂוֹת רָע Ec 8^{11}; esp. of days, years, *be full, accomplished, ended,* Gn 25^{24} 29^{21} 50$^{3.3}$ (JE); Lv 8^{33} 12$^{4.6}$ 25^{30} Nu 6$^{5.13}$ (P); 1 S 18^{26} 2 S 7^{12}; Je 25^{12} 29^{10} La 4^{18} Ez 5^{2} 1 Ch 17^{11} Est 1^{5} 2^{12} Dn 10^{3}; cf. also with other subj. (lit.) Je 25^{34} Is 40^{2}. **2.** trans. *fill*, of populating sea and earth Gn 1$^{22.28}$ 9^{1} (all P); *consecrate* מִלְאוּ יֶדְכֶם ליהוה; (lit. fill the hand) Ex 32^{29} (cf. infr.); esp. of glory of י׳ filling tabern. and temple; Ex 40$^{34.35}$ (P) 1 K 8$^{10.11}$, cf. Is 6^{1}; v. also Je 23^{24}, esp. lit. Ez 10^{3} 43^{5} 44^{4} 2 Ch 5^{14} 7$^{1.2}$; sq. 2 acc. *fill* jars (with) water 1 K 18^{34}; abs. *overflow* מ׳ עַל־כָּל־גְּדוֹתָיו Jos 3^{15} (cf. 1 Ch 12^{16} **Pi.**); fig. *fill* land with sin Je 16^{18}, cf. 19^{4} Ez 8^{17} 28^{16}, cf. 30^{11}; מְלָאוֹ לִבּוֹ לַעֲשׂוֹת־כֵּן Est 7^{5} (cf. Ec 8^{11} supr.); מִלְאוּ הַשְּׁלָטִים Je 51^{11} meaning obscure, v. [שֶׁלֶט]; Gie prop. מִרְטוּ הַשּׁ׳ *polish.*

†**Niph.** *Pf.* נִמְלָא־ Ct 5^{2}; *Impf.* יִמָּלֵא 2 S 23^{7} + 9 t.; וַיִּמָּלֵא Ex 7^{25} + 5 t.; יִמָּלְאוּ Pr 3^{10} + 2 t.; יִמָּלְאוּ Pr 24^{4}; יִמָּלְאוּן Ez 32^{6};—**1.** *be filled*, usu. c. acc. mat. (c. מִן of source Ec 1^{8}, cf. Ez 32^{6}; c. לְ Hb 2^{14}); land, with people Ex 1^{7}; cf. 2 K 3$^{17.20}$ Is 2$^{7.7.8}$; house with smoke Is 6^{4}, cf. Ez 10^{4}; v. also Pr 3^{10} 24^{4} Je 13$^{12.12}$ Zc 8^{5} Ct 5^{2} Ec 11^{3} 2 K 10^{21} Ez 32^{6}; = *be armed* 2 S 23^{7} (lit. *be filled* or *fill himself*, i.e. his hand, with weapon, cf. **Pi. 2**); *be satisfied*, subj. נֶפֶשׁ = appetite Ec 6^{7}; subj. אֹזֶן Ec 1^{8}; fig. earth filled with violence (cf. **Qal**) Gn 6^{11}, cf. Ez 9^{9} 23^{33}; with glory and knowledge of י׳ Nu 14^{21} Hb 2^{14} ψ 72^{19}; v. also 1 K 7^{14} ψ 71^{8} 126^{2} Est 3^{5} 5^{9} Pr 20^{17}; abs. Ez 26^{2} (but Co sub מָלֵא *adj.*, so 𝔊 𝔗) 27^{25}. **2.** *be accomplished, ended*, subj. days Ex 7^{25}; of an exchange, requital, Jb 15^{32}.

Pi.$_{112}$ *Pf.* מִלֵּא Ex 35^{35} +; מִלָּא Je 51^{34}; מִלֵּאתָ Dt 6^{11} +; מִלְּאוּ Nu 32^{11} +, etc.; *Impf.* יְמַלֵּא Lv 8^{33} +; יְמַלֶּה Jb 8^{21}; וַיְמַלְאוּ Gn 42^{25} Ex 39^{10}; יְמַלְאוּ Ez 7^{19}, etc.; *Imv.* מַלֵּא Gn 29^{27} + 5 t.; מַלְאוּ Je 4^{5} Ez 9^{7}; *Inf. cstr.* מַלֵּא Ex 29^{29} + 5 t.; מַלֹּאות (-את) Ex 31^{5} + 5 t.; sf. מַלְּאָם Je 33^{5}; *Pt.* מְמַלֵּא Je 13^{13} 1 Ch 12^{15}; pl. מְמַלְאִים Is 65^{11} + 2 t.;—**1.** *fill* (oft. c. 2 acc.; lit., c. בְּ 2 K 9^{24} Ezr 9^{11} Jb 40^{31}; c. מִן Je 51^{34} ψ 127^{5}): Gn 21^{19} 24^{16} 26^{15} 42^{25} 44^{1} Ex 2^{16} Dt 6^{11} Jos 9^{13} 1 K 18^{35} 20^{27} 2 K 3^{25} 23^{14} Is 23^{2} Jb 3^{15} 22^{18} Je 41^{9} Ez 3^{3} 7^{19} 9^{7} 10^{2} 24^{4} Na 2^{13} Hg 2^{7} ψ 129^{7} 2 Ch 16^{14}, etc. (indef. subj.); *fill* (cup) *with drink* for libation Is 65^{11}; fig. *fill with spirit* Ex 28^{3} 31^{3} 35^{31} cf. v^{35}, ψ 107^{9} Is 33^{5} Je 15^{17}; fill (with blood) 2 K 21^{16}; with abominations Ezr 9^{11} (c. בְּ). **2.** special uses are: *satisfy* appetite Jb 38^{39} ψ 17^{14} Pr 6^{30} Jb 20^{23} Je 51^{14} (fig.); *take a handful of* מ׳ כַּפּוֹ מִן Lv 9^{17}; *grasp* מ׳ יָדוֹ בְּ 2 K 9^{24}, cf. (of laying arrow on bow) fig. מ׳ הַקֶּשֶׁת בְּאֶפְרַיִם Zc 9^{13}; *overflow* מְמַלֵּא עַל־כָּל־גִּדְיוֹתָיו 1 Ch 12^{16} (cf. Jos 3^{15} **Qal**); *give in full* וַיְמַלְאוּם לַמֶּלֶךְ 1 S 18^{27} (rd. וַיְמַלְאֵם A𝔊L 𝔙 We Dr Kit Bu); מִלֵּא יַד פ׳ fig. for *institute to a priestly office, consecrate* Ex 28^{41} 29$^{9.29.33.35}$ Lv 8^{33} 16^{32} 21^{10} Nu 3^{3} Ju 17$^{5.12}$ 1 K 13^{33} Ez 43^{26} (altar), 1 Ch 29^{5} 2 Ch 13^{9} 29^{31} (cf. As. *umallu katu, confer upon,* Dl $^{HWB\ 409}$); מ׳ אַחֲרֵי *wholly follow* י׳ Nu 14^{24} 32$^{11.12}$ Dt 1^{36} Jos 14$^{8.9.14}$ 1 K 11^{6}; *fill in*, i.e. *set* precious stones Ex 28^{17} (מ׳ בּוֹ מִלֻּאַת אֶבֶן) cf. 31^{5} 35^{33} 39^{10} (all P); etc. **3.** *fulfil, accomplish, complete*, obj. week, year, day, Gn 29$^{27.28}$ Ex 23^{26} Is 65^{20} Jb 39^{2} 2 Ch 36^{21} Dn 9^{2}; obj. word, promise, etc.; subj. י׳ 1 K 8$^{15.24}$ 2 Ch 6$^{4.15}$ ψ 20$^{5.6}$; subj. men 1 K 2^{27} Je 44^{25} 2 Ch 36^{21}. **4.** *confirm* words 1 K 1^{14}.

†**Pu.** *Pt. filled*, i.e. *set* with jewels מְמֻלָּאִים בַּתַּרְשִׁישׁ Ct 5^{14}.

†**Hithp.** *Impf.* עָלַי יִתְמַלָּאוּן Jb 16^{10}, *mass themselves* against me; perh. denom. fr. מְלֹא **2**.

†מָלֵא **adj.** full;—מ׳ Gn 23^{9} + 15 t.; cstr. מְלֵא Je 6^{11}; f. מְלֵאָה Nu 7^{14} + 20 t.; cstr. מְלֵאַתִי Is 1^{21} cf. Ges $^{§90.3a}$; pl. מְלֵאִים Nu 7^{13} + 18 t.;

f. מְלֵאוֹת (-אֹת) Gn 41^{7}+4 t.;—*full*, abs. of ears of corn Gn 41$^{7.22}$; of value, price, Gn 23^{9} 1 Ch 21$^{22.24}$; of wind (=strong) Je 4^{12} sq. acc. mat., bowls of fine flour (סֹלֶת) Nu 7$^{13.19.25.31.37.43.49.55.61.67.73.79}$; spoons of incense Nu 7$^{14.20.26.32.38.44.50.56.62.68.74.80.86}$; bowls of wine Je 35^{5}, cf. fig. ψ 75^{9}; houses, of contents Dt 6^{11} Ne 9^{25} cf. Pr 17^{1}; cage, of birds Je 5^{27} (in sim., v. infr.); cart, of sheaves Am 2^{13} (in sim.) 1 Ch 11^{13} 2 K 7^{15}; Ez 1^{18} 10^{12} 17^{3} 36^{38} 37^{1}; as pred., of storehouses ψ 144^{13}; cf. fig. of Naomi Ru 1^{21}; of sea Ec 1^{7}; with art., of *full vessel* 2 K 4^{4}; מְלֵאָה pregnant woman Ec 11^{5}; fig. *full* of blessing Dt 33^{23}; wisdom 34^{9}; justice Is 1^{21}; commotion 22^{2}; fury 51^{20}; lies, etc. Na 3^{1}; wisdom Ez 28^{12} (del. A B Co); only twice in cstr. before that with which a thing is filled Is 1^{21} מ׳ מִשְׁפָּט; Je 6^{11} מְלֵא יָמִים (as subst.); as subst. in genit. (Ges $^{§ 128 n}$) ψ 73^{10} מֵי מָלֵא; as adv. = *fully* Na 1^{10} Je 12^{6} (loudly, cf. 4^{5}).

†מְלֹא, [מְלוֹא] n.m. $^{Is 31.4}$ **fulness, that which fills** (Ar. مِلْءٌ Lane ^{2729});—מ׳ cstr. Gn 48^{19} + 19 t.; מְלוֹ Ez 41^{8}; sf. מְלוֹאוֹ Is 42^{10} + 3 t.; מְלֹאָהּ Dt 33^{16} + 12 t.;—**1.** *fulness* of hand (= handful) Ec 4$^{6.6}$ sq. acc. mat. מ׳ חָפְנֵיכֶם פִּיחַ Ex 9^{8} cf. Lv 16^{12} 1 K 17^{12}; so homer-full of manna; Ex 16^{33} cf. Lv 16^{12} Nu 22^{18} 24^{13} Ju 6^{38}; simil. מְלֹא בִגְדוֹ 2 K 4^{39}; rarely sq. מִן Lv 2^{2} 5^{12}, cf. Ex 16^{32} (but rd. perh. מְלֹאוֹ so 𝔊 Sam. v. Di). **2.** *mass* of shepherds Is 31^{4} (in sim.); *multitude* of nations Gn 48^{19} (cf. Ar. مَلَأٌ Qor 2^{247} al.) **3.** *fulness = that which fills, entire contents*, of אֶרֶץ Dt 33^{16} ψ 24^{1} Is 6^{3} 8^{8} 34^{1} Mi 1^{2} Je 8^{16} 47^{2} Ez 12^{19} 19^{7} 30^{12} 32^{15}; תֵּבֵל ψ 50^{12} 89^{12}; יָם Is 42^{10} 1 Ch 16^{32} ψ 96^{11} 98^{7}; עִיר Am 6^{8}. **4.** phrases:—מ׳ קוֹמָתוֹ = *at full length* 1 S 28^{20}; *full line*, or portion מ׳ הַחֶבֶל 2 S 8^{2}; מ׳ הַקָּנֶה Ez 41^{8} *full rod* (reed).

†מְלֵאָה n.f. fulness, full produce;—מ׳ Nu 18^{27} Dt 22^{9}; מְלֵאָתְךָ Ex 22^{28}; = *full produce* of field Ex 22^{28}, מ׳ הַזֶּרַע *the full produce of the seed* Dt 22^{9}; of winepress Nu 18^{27}.

†[מִלֻּאָה] n.f. setting of jewel (cf. **vb. Pi. 2, Pu.**);—cstr. מִלֻּאַת Ex 28^{17} מ׳ אֶבֶן (as acc. cogn. with מִלֵּא); cf. sf. מִלּוּאֹתָם (מִלֻּא׳) Ex 28^{20} 39^{13}.

†[מִלֻּא, מִלּוּא] n.m. setting, installation; (cf. **vb. Pi. Pu.**);—pl. מִלֻּאִים (מִלּוּ׳) Ex 25^{7} + 13 t.; מִלֻּאֵיכֶם Lv 8^{33};—**1.** *setting*, אַבְנֵי מ׳ *stones for setting* Ex 25^{7} 35$^{9.27}$ cf. 1 Ch 29^{2} (אַבְנֵי שֹׁהַם וּמ׳). **2.** installation (of priests): Lv 7^{37} 8^{33}; = installation-offering 8^{28} (אִשֶּׁה ‖) cf. סַל־הַמּ׳ v^{31}; אֵיל הַמּ׳ Ex 29$^{22.26.27.31}$ Lv 8$^{22.29}$; בְּשַׂר הַמּ׳ Ex 29^{34}.

†מִלּוֹא n. pr. loc. (Thes *'fill'* of earth, earthwork, but v. GFM $^{Ju 9.6}$);—**1.** בֵּית מִלּוֹא Ju 9^{6} (בַּעֲלֵי שְׁכֶם ‖) so v$^{20.20}$; near Shechem, site unknown; 𝔊 οἶκος Βηθμααλων. **2.** citadel in Jerus. הַמִּלּוֹא 2 S 5^{9} 1 K 9$^{15.24}$ 11^{27} 1 Ch 11^{8} 2 Ch 32^{5}. 𝔊 usu. ἡ ἄκρα (A 1 K 9$^{15.24}$ also Μελω). **3.** בֵּית מִלֹּא 2 K 12^{21} (+ הַיֹּרֵד סִלָּא) dub.; = **2**? 𝔊 οἴκῳ Μααλω.

†מִלֵּאת n.f. dub.: only יֹשְׁבוֹת עַל־מ׳ Ct 5^{12} of lover's eyes; A E De Bae ^{Kau} **setting**, perh. better **border, rim**, Öt Wild *fulness, abundance*, of surrounding of eye.

†יִמְלָא, יִמְלָה n.pr.m. father of prophet Micaiah of Isr.:—יִמְלָה 1 K 22$^{8.9}$ 𝔊 Ιεμια, 𝔊L Ναμαλι; = יִמְלָא 2 Ch 18$^{7.8}$. 𝔊 Ιεμαα, A Ιεμλα, 𝔊L Ναμαλι.

מַלְאָךְ, מְלָאכָה, [מַלְאָכוּת], מַלְאָכִי v. לאך.

מִלְבַד v. II. בַּד. **מַלְבּוּשׁ** v. לבשׁ.

מַלְבֵּן v. לבן. **מִלָּה** v. I. מלל.

מִלּוֹ v. מלא. **מְלוּנָה, מָלוֹן** v. לון.

מַלּוֹתִי n. pr. v. I. מלל.

†I. [מָלַח] vb. tear away, fig. dissipate (cf. Ar. مَلَخَ *pull out* eye, tooth, &c.; esp. Dozy *tear off branch* to plant it, &c. so Eth. መለኀ: *evellere*);—**Niph.** fig. *be dispersed in fragments, dissipated, Pf.* שָׁמַיִם כֶּעָשָׁן נִמְלָחוּ Is 51^{6}.

†I. [מֶלַח] or [מְלָח] n.[m.] rag; only pl. מְלָחִים Je 38$^{11.12}$ (סְחָבוֹת ‖).

II. מלח (√ of foll.; meaning dubious).

†II. מֶלַח n.m. salt (NH *id.*; Ar. مِلْحٌ; Aram. ܡܶܠܚܳܐ, מִלְחָא);—מ׳ abs. Gn 19^{26} +; cstr. Lv 2^{13};—*salt* for seasoning food Jb 6^{6}; offering Lv 2$^{13.13.13}$ cf. Ez 43^{24}; בְּרִית מֶלַח Nu 18^{19} 2 Ch 13^{5} (cf. Lv 2^{13} v. Di); used in purifying waters 2 K 2$^{20.21}$; strewn on site of devoted city Ju 9^{45} cf. Zp 2^{9} (מִכְרֵה־מ׳) Dt 29^{22} (גָּפְרִית ‖); produced in marshes reserved for purpose Ez 47^{11}; pillar of salt נְצִיב מ׳ Gn 19^{26}; usu. in combin. יָם(־) הַמֶּלַח Gn 14^{3} (עֵמֶק הַשִּׂדִּים), Nu 34$^{3.12}$ Dt 3^{17}

(יָם הָעֲרָבָה ||), Jos 3[16] 12[3] 15[2.5] 18[19], also גיא־מ׳ 2 S 8[13] 2 K 14[7] Qr, ψ 60[2] (title), גיא הַמּ׳ 1 Ch 18[12] 2 Ch 25[11] 2 K 14[7] Kt.

†III [מָלַח] **vb denom.** salt, season, **Qal** *Impf* 2 ms. תִּמְלָח sq. acc. Lv 2[13] (obj. offering) **Pu** *Pt* מְמֻלָּח Ex 30[35] *salted*, i e the incense (v. Di) **Hoph.** *Pf.* 2 fs. + *Inf abs* הָמְלֵחַ לֹא הֻמְלַחַתְּ Ez 16[4], i e *rubbed* or *washed with salt* (of infant, in personification)

†מְלֵחָה **n.f.** saltness, barrenness,—Jb 39[6] (עֲרָבָה ||) as dwelling-place of wild ass, *salt-plain;* אֶרֶץ מְלֵחָה Je 17[6] (לֹא תֵשֵׁב ||), ψ 107[34] (opp אֶרֶץ פְּרִי)

†מַלּוּחַ **n.[m.]** mallow, plant growing in salt-marsh, Jb 30[4] (cf Now[Arch i 67, 112])

†[מַלָּח] **n.m.** mariner (loan-word from As *malahu* Dl[HWB 412] cf Id[Prol 178], Hal[ZA iv 1889, 53], so also Aram ܡܠܚܐ (v Brock), whence Ar مَلَّاح Fra[221]),—pl. מַלָּחִים Jon 1[5] Ez 27[29], מַלָּחַיִךְ Ez 27[27], מַלָּחֵיהֶם v[9] (Ba[NB 49 Anm 3]),—*mariners, sailors* of ship going to Tarshish Jon 1[5] (cf רַב הַחֹבֵל v[6]), to Tyre Ez 27[9], cf. v[27, 29] (חֹבְלִים ||)

מִלְחָמָה v I לחם

†[מָלַט] **vb. slip away** (not in **Qal**) (NH מִילוּט *rescue;* 𝔗 מלט (rare) = BH, Ar. مَلِطَ is *have scanty hair; IV. cast the foetus without hair;* [*slip away, escape* fr hand is اِمَّلَصَ]),—**Niph.** *Pf.* 3 ms נִמְלַט Ju 3[26] + 6 t., 3 fs נִמְלְטָה ψ 124[7], with וְ cons וְנִמְלָ֫טָה Je 48[19]; 3 mpl. נִמְלָ֫טוּ 2 S 4[6] + 8 t Pf; *Impf.* יִמָּלֵט Am 9[1] + 13 t; וַיִּמּ׳ Ju 3[26] + 7 t; 1 s. אִמָּלְטָה Gn 19[20] +; 3 mpl וַיִּמָּלֵ֫טוּ Mal 3[15] + 12 t. Impf; *Imv* הִמָּלֵט Gn 19[17, 17, 22], f הִמָּלְטִי Zc 2[11]; *Inf abs* הִמָּלֵט 1 S 27[1] (but rd אִם אִמָּלֵט 𝔊 We Dr Lohr HPS, > Th Kit Bu ins אִם bef הִמּ׳), cstr *id*, Gn 19[19] Est 4[3], *Pt* נִמְלָט 1 K 19[17, 17];—**1.** *slip away* אִמָּלְטָה נָּא וְאֶרְאֶה אֶת־אֶחָי 1 S 20[29] *let me slip away to see my brethren; slip through,* or *past* (into the house) 2 S 4[6] (cf. Dr HPS and **Pi. 1, Hiph. 2**; > Klo נִלְאָ֫טוּ*, √לאט, after 𝔊 ἔλαθον). **2.** *escape,* Ju 3[29] 1 S 19[10] (נוּס ||), v[12, 18] (both בָּרַח ||), v[17] 22[20] (בָּרַח ||), 30[17] 1 K 18[40] 20[20] (נוּס ||), 2 K 10[24] Is 20[6] (נוּס, נִצַּל ||), 49[24, 25] Je 46[6] 48[8, 19] (נוּס ||), Ez 17[15, 18, 18] Am 9[1] Jo 3[5] Zc 2[11] Mal 3[15] ψ 124[7] Pr 19[5] Jb 1[15, 16, 17, 19], c. מִן of place whence 1 S 23[13] 2 S 1[3] ψ 124[7], c אֶל־ = whither 1 S 22[1] 27[11]; c. עַד Ju 3[26]; c. ־ָה loc, Gn 19[17, 19, 20, 22] (J), Ju 3[26]; c acc. 2 K 19[37] = Is 37[38], Est 4[13]; c מִן of person fr. whom Ec 7[26]; c. מִיַּד 1 S 27[1] 2 Ch 16[7] Je 32[4] 34[3] 38[18, 23] Dn 11[41], מִפְּנֵי Je 41[15]; מֵחֶרֶב 1 K 19[17, 17], c. עַל־נֶפֶשׁ *for one's life* Gn 19[17] **3.** pass. *be delivered* ψ 22[6] Pi 11[21] 28[26] Jb 22[30] Dn 12[1] (later usage) **Pi.** *Pf* 3 ms. מִלֵּט Ez 33[5]; וּמִלַּט־ Ec 9[15]; sf מִלְּטָ֫נוּ 2 S 19[10]; *Impf* יְמַלֵּט Am 2[14] + 8 t, sf יְמַלְּטֵהוּ ψ 41[2], + 5 t. Impf, *Imv.* מַלְּטָה ψ 116[4]; f. מַלְּטִי 1 K 1[12], + 4 t Imv, *Inf. abs* מַלֵּט Is 46[2] Je 39[18], *Pt.* מְמַלֵּט 1 S 19[11], pl מְמַלְּטִים 2 S 19[6],—**1.** *lay* (eggs; i.e. let them slip out; of arrow-snake) Is 34[15]. **2.** *let escape* · וימלטו עצמתיו 2 K 23[18] *and so they let his bones* (the prophet's) *escape* (from the burning) **3.** *deliver,* abs. Is 46[4], c. acc Is 46[2] Je 39[18, 18] ψ 41[2] Jb 22[30] 29[12] Ec 8[8] 9[15], c מִיַּד Jb 6[23]; מִכַּף 2 S 19[10] משחיתותם ψ 107[20], elsewh מלט נפש *deliver, save, life* 1 S 19[11] 2 S 19[6] 1 K 1[12] Je 48[6] 51[6, 45] Ez 33[5] Am 2[14, 15] ψ 89[49] 116[4], נפש om. Am 2[15] ψ 33[17] Jb 20[20].—(This form not in Hex., Ju, Ch., Is [1]) **Hiph.** *Pf.* 3 ms המליט Is 31[5], 3 fs הִמְלִיטָה Is 66[7]. **1.** *give birth to* a male child Is 66[7] (יָלְדָה ||, cf. **Pi 1)** **2.** *deliver* abs Is 31[5] (הציל, גָּנַן ||, פָּסֹחַ) **Hithp.** *Impf* 1 s וָאֶתְמַלְּטָה Jb 19[20]; 3 mpl יִתְמַלָּטוּ Jb 41[11] **1.** *slip forth, escape* (sparks of fire from jaws of crocodile; RV *leap forth*) Jb 41[11]. **2.** *escape* (with the skin of the teeth, the gums; only these left unattacked by leprosy) Jb 19[20]

†מֶ֫לֶט **n.[m.]** mortar, cement (etym dub.; Aram. ܡܠܛܐ *id.*, whence Ar مِلَاط Fra[10]),—Je 43[9]

†מְלַטְיָה **n.pr.m.** (*Yahweh delivered,* cf. Gray[Prop N 267, 294]) a Gibeonite, a builder at the wall Ne 3[7], 𝔊L Μαλτιας

מְלִיצָה v לִיץ

I מלך (√of foll, mng. dub., Thes comp. Ar مَلَكَ *possess, own exclusively,* cf. Eth መልከ: so Bae[Rel 144] (cf בַּעַל), and No[ZMG xl 1886, 727]; Lyon[Bib Sacr Apr 1884] Dl[Prol 30] al comp. As *malāku, counsel, advise* Dl[HWB 412], BH and NH מָלַךְ, Aram. מְלַךְ, ܡܠܟ, whence king as orig. *counsellor,* he whose opinion is decisive)

I מֶ֫לֶךְ[2513] **n.m.** king (NH *id;* MI[1.5.10.18.23] מלך, 1[4] המלכן, Ph מלך; Zinj. מלך DHM[Sendsch 60],

As. *maliku, malku, prince* (As. *šarru* = *king*); Ar. مَلِكٌ *king* (orig. Heb.* מֶלֶךְ inferred, Lag$^{\text{BN 73}}$ Ba$^{\text{NB §112}}$ WMM$^{\text{As. u. Europ. 76}}$); Sab. מלכן Sab Denkm$^{\text{No. 1}}$; cstr. מלך, pl. אמלך CIS$^{\text{iv. 37}}$; cf. Eth. አምላክ: *God* (and Nö$^{\text{l.c.}}$); Aram. מְלֵךְ, ܡܠܟܐ; Palm. מלך מלכא Vog$^{\text{No. 28}}$; Nab. מלכא Eut$^{\text{Nab. 1}}$);—מ׳ abs. Gn 14^{7}+ (ins. also 2 S 13^{17} 𝔊 Th We Dr Kit Bu, and v^{34} 𝔊 We Dr Kit Bu); in p. alw. מָ֫לֶךְ Gn 49^{20} + 238 t. (so also n. pr. in מָלֶךְ-); cstr. Gn 14^{1}+; sf. מַלְכִּי 2 S 19^{44} + 6 t., etc.; pl. מְלָכִים Gn 14^{9}+; מְלָכִין Pr 31^{3}; cstr. מַלְכֵי Gn 17^{16}+; sf. מְלָכֶיהָ Is 7^{16} + 3 t.; מַלְכֵיהֶם Dt 7^{24} + 16 t., etc.;—**1.** *king:* of Egypt Gn 39$^{20f.}$ Ex 1$^{8f.}$ Dt 11^{3} 1 K 3^{1}; of Mesopotamia, Shinar, Assyr., Babyl., Pers., etc. Ju 3$^{8.10}$ Gn 14$^{1f.}$ 2 K 15$^{19.20.29}$ 17$^{3f.}$ 18$^{13f.}$ 24$^{1.11f.}$ Ezr 1$^{1f.}$ 4$^{3f.}$ Est 1^{2}+, 1 K 11$^{18.40}$ 14^{25} 2 K 17$^{4f.}$ 23^{29}+; of Canaan, Philist., Edom, Moab, etc. (often of single city): Gn 14$^{2f.}$ v^{18} 20^{2} 26$^{1.8}$ 36^{31} Nu 20^{14} 21$^{1f.}$ 22$^{4.10}$ Dt 1^{4} 3$^{1f.}$ Jos 2^{2} (oft. in Jos), Ju 1^{7} 5^{19} 8$^{5.12}$ 11$^{12f.}$ 2 K 3$^{4f.}$+; of Aram, Hamath, etc. 2 S 8$^{3f.}$ v^{9} 1 K 15^{18} 20$^{1f.}$ 22^{3} 2 K 5$^{1f.}$ 8$^{7f.}$ v^{29} 9$^{14.15}$ 15^{37} 16$^{5f.}$+; of Tyre, etc. 2 S 5^{11} 1 K 5^{15} 9^{11} 16+, etc.; esp. of Israel (undivided, and of both divisions) Gn 36^{31} Nu 23^{21} 24^{7} Dt 17$^{14f.}$ Ju 17^{6} 18^{1} 19^{1} 21^{25} 1 S 2^{10} 8$^{5f.}$ 2 S 2$^{4f.}$ 1 K 1$^{33.34f.}$ + very often; cf. also Ju 9^{6}.—2 S 18^{29b} del. הַמּ׳ We Klo Dr Kit Bu. Note that in early books המלך דוד is nearly always said; in late books usually דויד המלך (שׁלמה וגו׳); cf. Aram. כּוֹרֶשׁ מַלְכָּא, etc. **2.** of Davidic king, as under divine protection, 1 S 2^{10} (‖ מְשִׁיחוֹ), ψ 2^{6} 18^{51} 89^{19} 61^{7}, cf. 99^{4}; so in (Messianic) prediction Ho 3^{5} Is 32^{1} Je 23^{5} Ez 37$^{22.24}$ Zc 9^{9}. **3.** used of י׳ as king of Israel 1 S 12^{12}; poet. Dt 33^{5} cf. ψ 5^{3} 10^{16} 29^{10} 44^{5} 48^{3} 68^{25} 74^{12} 84^{4} 145^{1} 149^{2} Is 41^{21} 43^{15} 44^{6} Zp 3^{15}; מֶלֶךְ הַכָּבוֹד ψ 24$^{7.8.9.10.10}$; universal king ψ 47$^{3.8}$ 95^{3} 98^{6} Je 10$^{7.10}$, cf. 46^{18} 48^{15} 51^{57} Zc 14$^{9.16.17}$ Mal 1^{14}; of false god Am 5^{26}. **4.** in fable, king of trees Ju 9$^{8.15}$; fig. of crocodile Jb 41^{26}; מ׳ אֵין לָאַרְבֶּה Pr 30^{27}; of death, מֶלֶךְ בַּלָּהוֹת Jb 18^{14}. **5.** combinations are:—**a.** הַמּ׳ הַגָּדוֹל 2 K 18$^{19.28}$ = Is 36$^{4.13}$ (of Assyrian king: cf. As. *šarru rabu*); מ׳ גָּדוֹל Ec 9^{14} (indef.); of י׳ Mal 1^{14}, מ׳ ג׳ עַל־כָּל־אלהים ψ 95^{3}; מ׳ עוֹלָם Je 10^{10} (of י׳); מ׳ מְלָכִים Ez 26^{7} (king of Babyl.) **b.** יְחִי הַמֶּלֶךְ 1 S 10^{24} 2 S 16$^{16.16}$ 1 K 1$^{34.39}$ 2 K 11^{12} 2 Ch 23^{11}; מֶלֶךְ בירושׁלם Ec 1^{1}, cf. 15^{26} 2 S 5^{2} 1 K 14^{2} 1 Ch 29^{25} 2 S 2^{11} (היה מ׳ בחברון על־) 1 K 11^{37} 2 Ch 28^{4} Ec 1^{12}. **c.** following a verb (one or two acc.) שׂים מ׳ על Dt 17$^{14.15.15}$ 1 S 10^{19}; שִׂים לָנוּ מ׳ 1 S 8^{5}; שִׂים לְמ׳ 1 K 10^{9}; נָתַן מ׳ לְ 1 S 8^{6} Ho 13$^{10.11}$; נָתַן עַל 1 S 12^{13} 2 Ch 2^{10} Ne 9^{37} 13^{26}; הִמְלִיךְ לְמֶלֶךְ Ju 9^{6} 1 S 15^{11}; מָשַׁח מ׳ 1 S 8^{22}; הִמְלִיךְ מ׳ לְ 1 S 12^{1}; הִמְלִיךְ מ׳ על Ju 9^{8}; מָשַׁח לְמ׳ על 1 K 1^{45}; מָשַׁח לְמ׳ על Ju 9^{15} 1 S 15$^{1.17}$ 2 S 2^{4} 5$^{3.17}$ 12^{7} 1 K 1^{34} 1 Ch 11^{3} 14^{8}; הֵכִין לְמ׳ 2 S 3^{17}; בִּקֵּשׁ למ׳ על 1 S 8^{19}; מ׳ יִהְיֶה על 2 S 5^{12} 1 Ch 14^{2}; הֵקִים מ׳ על 1 K 14^{14} Dt 28^{36}; יָשַׁב עַל־כִּסֵּא י׳ לְמ׳ תַּחַת וגו׳ 1 Ch 29^{23}, cf. Pr 20^{8}; נָתַן עַל־כִּסֵּא לְמ׳ לי׳ אלהיך 2 Ch 9^{8}. **d.** מַעֲדַנֵּי־מֶלֶךְ Gn 49^{20} *royal dainties*, fig.; מִשְׁתֵּה הַמּ׳ 1 S 25^{36} *royal feast* (in sim.); אֶבֶן הַמּ׳ 2 S 14^{26} *king's weight*; יַד־הַמּ׳ 1 K 10^{13} *royal bounty* (in sim.); גִּזֵּי הַמּ׳ Am 7^{1} *king's mowings*; מִקְדַּשׁ מ׳ Am 7^{13} *royal sanctuary*; עֲטֶרֶת מַלְכָּם 2 S 12^{30} *crown of their king* = 1 Ch 20^{2} (but rd. מִלְכֹּם 𝔊 We Klo Dr Kit Kau—not Bu Kit$^{\text{Chr. Hpt}}$); cf. also בַּיִת, עֵמֶק, גַּן, שָׁוֵה, etc.—N.pr. אבימלך, אחימלך, אלימלך, נתן מלך, עבד מלך, v. sub אב, אח, etc.

מַלְכָּה$_{35}$ **n.f.** queen:—abs. מ׳ Est 1^{9} + 24 t. Est.; cstr. מַלְכַּת 1 K 10^{1} + 7 t.; pl. מְלָכוֹת Ct 6$^{8.9}$;—*queen* of Sheba 1 K 10$^{1.4.10.13}$ = 2 Ch 9$^{1.3.9.12}$; of Persia, Vashti Est 1^{9} + 7 t. Est 1; Esther Est 2^{22} + 16 t. Est 4–9 (in Esther mostly appos. of n.pr.; it precedes n.pr. Est 1$^{12.15}$; follows n.pr. Est 1^{9} + 17 t.); of Isr. queens only pl. and only Ct 6$^{8.9}$ (both ‖ פִּילַגְשִׁים). Cf. גְּבִירָה.

† **מְלֶ֫כֶת** **n.f.** queen (form difficult; cf. Ol §147 d Kö$^{\text{ii, 169 n.}}$ Gie$^{\text{Je 7, 18}}$ Ba$^{\text{NB 165, Anm. 2; ZMG xli. 1887, 606}}$);—only cstr. מ׳ הַשָּׁמַיִם Je 7^{18} + 4 t. Je = *queen of the heavens*, a goddess; identif. dub.; perhaps = Ištar, Venus, cf. Schr$^{\text{infr.}}$ al.; (> = מְלֶאכֶת (Codd.), cstr. of מְלָאכָה (v. לאך), *worship of the heavens* (Cast$^{\text{Lex. Syr.}}$), or creative *work of the heavens*, coll. = צְבָא הַשּׁ׳ *host of heaven*, Sta$^{\text{infr.}}$ (cf. 𝔊); v. Schr$^{\text{COT Je 7, 18; SBAk 1886, 477 ff.; ZA iii. 1888, 353 ff., iv. 1889, 74 ff.}}$ Sta$^{\text{ZAW 1886, 123 ff. 289 ff.}}$ Kue$^{\text{Ges. Abh. 186 ff.}}$ We$^{\text{Skizzen iii. 38}}$ Nö$^{\text{ZMG xli. 1889, 710 f.}}$ RS$^{\text{Sem. i. 57, 172 (ed. 2, 57, 189)}}$ Grünb$^{\text{ZMG xlii. 1888, 45}}$);—only as worshipped by people of Jerusalem לַעֲשׂוֹת כַּוָּנִים לְמ׳ הַשּׁ׳ Je 7^{18} (‖ הַסֵּךְ נְסָכִים לֵאלֹהִים אֲחֵרִים); לְקַטֵּר לְמ׳ הַשּׁ׳ Je 44$^{17.18.19.25}$ (all ‖ הַסֵּךְ לָהּ נְסָכִים).

II. **מָלַךְ**$_{346}$ **vb. denom.** be, or become king, or queen, reign;—**Qal**$_{296}$ *Pf.* מ׳ Jos 13^{10}+, etc.; *Impf.* יִמְלֹךְ (-לוֹךְ) Ex 15^{18}+; וַיִּמְלֹךְ Gn 36^{32}+; 2 ms. תִּמְלֹךְ Gn 37^{8}+, (הֲתִתְמַלֵּךְ Je 22^{15} Baer); *Imv.* מְלָךְ־ Ju 9^{14}; מָלְכָה Ju 9^{8}; מָלְכִי Ju 9$^{10.12}$; *Inf. abs.* מָלֹךְ Gn 37^{8} 1 S 24^{21}; *cstr.*

מָלַךְ 1 K 2^{15}+, sf. מָלְכוֹ 1 S 13^{1}+, *Pt* מֹלֵךְ Je 22^{11}+2t, מֹלֶכֶת 2 K 11^{3} = 2 Ch 22^{12},—*be* (become) *king, reign,* mostly of Hebrew kings, 2 S 2^{10} 1 K 16^{22} 2 K 3^{1} 9^{13}, but also gen Pr 8^{16} 30^{22}, of Can., Edom., Aram., Assyr., Pers kings, etc. Ju 4^{2} Gn 36^{31} 1 K 11^{25} 2 K 8^{15} 19^{37} Est 1^{1}+; sq בְּ loc. (usu city) Jos $13^{10.12}$ Ju 4^{2} 2 S 5^{5} 1 K 11^{24} 14^{21}+oft; but also Gn $36^{31.32}$ 1 Ch 1^{43} בארץ, and even בכל אֲשֶׁר־תְּאַוֶּה נַפְשֶׁךָ 2 S 3^{21}, sq עַל c. people or land 1 S $8^{9.11}$ 12^{14} 13^{1} 1 K $15^{1.9}$ 16^{23}+ oft., sq בְּ loc + עַל territ (or pop) 2 S 5^{5} 1 K 11^{42}, sq. תַּחַת (תַּחְתָּיו) 2 S 16^{8} Gn 36^{33f} = 1 Ch 1^{44f}, 1 K $14^{20.31}$ 2 K 8^{15} 13^{24} Je 22^{11}+oft.; †subj God, sq. עַל ψ 47^{9} Mi 4^{7} Ez 20^{33} 1 S 8^{7}, sq בְּ Is 24^{23}, abs. Ex 15^{18} Is 52^{7} ψ 93^{1} 96^{10} = 1 Ch 16^{31}, 97^{1} 99^{1} 146^{10}†, subj future (Mess) king Is 32^{1} Je 23^{5}, †subj a woman (= *be queen*) 2 K 11^{3} = 2 Ch 22^{12} (both sq. עַל), Est 2^{4} sq תַּחַת†, Imv only in fable, king of trees, Ju $9^{8.10.12.14}$ all sq. עַל, בְּמָלְכוֹ esp. = *when he began to reign, became king* 1 S 13^{1} 2 S 2^{10} 1 K 14^{21}+oft, Inf also = *reign:* בשׁנת שׁמנה לְמָלְכוֹ 2 K 24^{12} 25^{1}, cf v^{27}, 1 K 6^{1} 2 Ch 16^{13} 17^{7} 29^{3} $34^{3.8}$, cf. עַד מֶלֶךְ דָּוִד 1 Ch 4^{31}, עַד מְלֹךְ מַלְכוּת פָּרַס 2 Ch 36^{20}, *began to reign and reigned* מָלַךְ וַיִּמְלֹךְ 1 K 15^{25} 16^{29} 2 K 3^{1}+; oft. מָלַךְ alone with *same meaning* 1 K 16^{23} 2 K $13^{1.10}$ 14^{23}+.

†**Hiph.** *Pf.* הִמְלִיךְ 1 S 15^{35}+2t; הִמְלַכְתָּ 1 K 3^{7}, etc; Impf. וַיַּמְלֵךְ 2 K 23^{34}+4t, וַיַּמְלִיכוּ Ju 9^{6}+ etc; *Inf cstr* הַמְלִיךְ 1 K 12^{1}+etc; *Pt.* מַמְלִיךְ Ez 17^{16},—*make king,* or *queen, cause to reign,* sq acc pers. Ju 9^{16} 1 S 11^{15} 1 K 1^{43} 12^{1} 16^{21} 2 K 10^{5} 11^{12} (anointing and coronation) = 2 Ch 23^{11}, 2 K 17^{21} 1 Ch 11^{10} $12^{32.39}$ 2 Ch 10^{1} 11^{22} Ez 17^{16}, sq. לְ (of dir. obj, as Aram) 1 Ch 29^{22}; sq acc cogn 1 S 8^{22} (+לָהֶם), 12^{1} (+עַל), Is 7^{6} (+בתוך), sq לְמֶלֶךְ Ju 9^{6} 1 S 15^{11}, sq acc. pers. +בְּ loc Je 37^{1}, +עַל Ju 9^{18} 1 S 15^{35} 1 K 12^{20} 16^{16} 2 K 8^{20} 1 Ch 12^{38} 28^{4} (acc om.), 23^{1} 2 Ch $1^{9.11}$ 21^{8} $36^{4.10}$, cf 2 S 2^{9} (3 t אֶל־, 3 t. עַל־); +תַּחַת 1 K 3^{7} 2 K 14^{21} 21^{24} 23^{30} (anointing), v^{34} 24^{17} 2 Ch 1^{8} 22^{1} 26^{1} 33^{25} 36^{1}, Est 2^{17} (= *make queen* at coronation), abs Ho 8^{4} †**Hoph.** *Pf* הָמְלַךְ עַל מַלְכוּת כַּשְׂדִּים Dn 9^{1}

†II. מֹלֶךְ **n pr.m.** son of Micah, a Benjamite (on מ׳ as individ name v. Gray[Prop. N 116, 122 n 4], cf Ph n pr מלך (v Bloch), Sab n. pr מלכם CIS[iv 1], Palm n pr. מלכו Vog[Palm 92 al] Nab *id*, Eut[Nab 21.4 al] Vog[Nab 1.2]),—1 Ch 8^{35} (𝔊 Μελχηλ), 9^{41} (𝔊 Μαλαχ, 𝔊L Μελχιηλ in both).

†מֹלֶךְ **n.pr.div.** Molech (𝔊 Μολοχ, 𝔙 *Moloch*) (= מֶלֶךְ i e (*divine*) *King,* with vowels of בֹּשֶׁת to denote abhorrence, Hoffm[ZAW iii 1883, 124] RS[Sem I 353, 2nd ed 372]; cf Hoffm[GG Abh. xxxvi 1890 (May 1889), 23], Ph n. pr. div. מלך *Milk,* in n. pr cf Bloch, Dr[Dt 222 f.]),—c art. הַמּ׳ —the god to whom Isr. sacrif children with fire (in valley of Hinnom); העביר לַמּ׳ 2 K 23^{10}, העביר בָּאֵשׁ לַמּ׳ Je 32^{35} (|| הַבַּעַל), Lv 18^{21} (H); נתן לַמּ׳ Lv $20^{2.3.4}$ (H); more gen לזנות אַחֲרֵי הַמּ׳ v^{5} (H) In 1 K 11^{7} rd. prob. מלכם, q.v

†מֹלֶכֶת **n.pr.f.** c. art הַמֹּלֶכֶת 1 Ch 7^{18} (of Manasseh) 𝔊 ἡ Μαλέχεθ, 𝔊L Μελχαθ.

†מִלְכָּה **n.pr.f.** 𝔊 Μελχα (= מַלְכָּה? No ZMG xlii 1888, 484 comp. Ph n pr. deæ מלכת; cf. Gray[Prop. N 116]);—**1.** wife of Nahor Gn $11^{29.29}$ $22^{20.23}$ $24^{15.24.47}$ (all J) **2.** daughter of Zelophehad (of Manasseh), Nu 26^{33} 27^{1} 36^{11} Jos 17^{3} (all P)—Perhaps orig town-name, Gray[l.c]

†מְלוּכָה **n.f. kingship, royalty;**—מ׳ abs 1 S 10^{16}+23 t.,—*kingship, kingly office, royalty:* 1 S $10^{16.25}$ 11^{14} 18^{8} 1 K $2^{15.15.22}$ 11^{35} 1 Ch 10^{14} Is 34^{12}, belonging to י׳ Ob[21] ψ 22^{29} (|| וּמשׁל בַּגּוֹיִם); לָכַד מ׳ עַל 1 S 14^{47} *assume sovereignty over;* נָתַן מ׳ בְּיַד 2 S 16^{8} *give kingship to* (subj. י׳); הֵשִׁיב מ׳ לְ 1 K 12^{21} *restore kingship to,* עָשָׂה מ׳ עַל 1 K 21^{7} *exercise kingship over,* metaph of Jerus. וַתִּצְלְחִי לִמְלוּכָה Ez 16^{13} (del 𝔊 Co), עִיר הַמּ׳ 2 S 12^{26} = *royal city,* cf. כסא הַמּ׳ 1 K 1^{46}, זֶרַע הַמּ׳ 2 K 25^{25} so Je 41^{1} Ez 17^{13} Dn 1^{3}, צְנוֹף מ׳ Is 62^{3} (|| עֲטֶרֶת תִּפְאֶרֶת)

†מַלְכוּת **n.f royalty, royal power, reign, kingdom** (chiefly late),—מ׳ abs Est 1^{9}+; cstr. 1 Ch 12^{23}+, sf מַלְכוּתִי 1 Ch 17^{14}, etc., pl. מַלְכֻיּוֹת Dn 8^{22},—**1.** *royal power, dominion* Nu 24^{7} (c. תִּנַּשֵּׂא), 1 S 20^{31} (c. תִּכּוֹן), 1 K 2^{12} (c. *id*), cf. Je 10^{7} Ec 4^{14}, 1 Ch 11^{10} 12^{23} 29^{30} (|| גְּבוּרָה), 2 Ch 33^{13} Est 1^{19}, *royal* (queenly) *dignity* 4^{14}, 1 Ch 14^{2} (c. נשׂאת); c לָכַד Dn 11^{21}, c. הֵכִין (subj. י׳) 1 Ch 17^{11} 28^{7}; 2 Ch 12^{1} (subj Rehob.), Isr. royalty as belonging to י׳ 1 Ch 17^{14}; dominion of י׳ ψ 103^{19} (c. מָשְׁלָה), ψ $145^{13.13}$, כְּבוֹד מ׳ v^{11}; כבוד הדר מ׳ v^{12}, שֵׁבֶט מ׳ ψ 45^{7}, כִּסֵּא מ׳ 1 Ch 22^{10} 28^{5} 2 Ch 7^{18}, of Pers. Est 1^{2} 5^{1}, בית לַמּ׳ 2 Ch 1^{18} 2^{11}, בית מ׳ Est 1^{9} 2^{16} 5^{1} (cf As. *bit šarruti* Dl[HWB 171]), יֵין מ׳ *royal wine* Est 1^{7}, דְּבַר מ׳ *royal command* Est 1^{19}; הוד מ׳ *royal honour, majesty* 1 Ch 29^{25} Dn 11^{21}; so perh also

הֲדַר מ׳ Dn 11^{20} v. Bev; עֹשֶׁר כְּבוֹד מ׳ Est 1^{4}; כֶּתֶר מ׳ *royal crown* Est 1^{11} 2^{17} 6^{8}; לְבוּשׁ מ׳ *royal apparel* Est 6^{8} 8^{15}; מ׳ (לְבוּשׁ om.) Est 5^{1} (*queenly attire*). **2.** *reign:* 40th year of reign of David 1 Ch 26^{31} cf. 2 Ch 3^{2} 15$^{10.19}$ 16$^{1.12}$ 35^{19} Je 49^{34} Dn 1^{1}; also 2 Ch 29^{19}; of Babyl. and Pers. kings Je 52^{31} (בִּשְׁנַת מ׳ ‖ 2 K 25^{27} מָלְכוֹ) Dn 2^{1} 8^{1} Ezr 4$^{5.6.6}$ 7^{1} 8^{1} Ne 12^{22} Est 2^{16}; cf. עַד־מְלֹךְ מַלְכוּת פָּרָס 2 Ch 36^{20}. **3.** *kingdom, realm* 2 Ch 1^{1} 11^{17} 20^{30} Ne 9^{35}; esp. realm of Babyl. and Pers. 2 Ch 36^{22} = Ezr 1^{1}, Est 1$^{14.20}$ 2^{3} 3$^{6.8}$ 5$^{3.6}$ 7^{2} 9^{30} Dn 8^{22} 9^{1} 10^{13}; cf. 11$^{2.4.4.9.17}$; v^{20} הֶדֶר מ׳ = Jerus. acc. to Hi., but v. **1** supr.

†מַמְלָכָה **n.f.** **kingdom, sovereignty, dominion, reign**;—abs. מ׳ Jos 10^{2}+; cstr. מַמְלֶכֶת Ex 19^{6} + 11 t. (incl. Mi 4^{8} before לְ); sf. מַמְלַכְתִּי Gn 20^{9}+, etc.; pl. מַמְלָכוֹת Dt 3^{21}+; cstr. מַמְלְכוֹת Dt 28^{25}+;—**1.** *kingdom, realm,* chiefly non-Isr.: Gn 10^{10} (J), 20^{9} (E), Nu 32$^{33.33}$ (P), Dt 3$^{4.10.13.21}$ 28^{25} Jos 11^{10} (D), 1 S 10^{18} 1 K 5^{1} 10^{20} 18$^{10.10}$ (both ‖ גּוֹי), Is 10^{10} 1 Ch 16^{20} = ψ 105^{13} (‖ עַם and גּוֹי), ψ 135^{11} Is 14^{16} 19$^{2.2}$ 23^{11} 2 Ch 9^{19} 14^{4} 29^{21} 32^{15} (‖ גּוֹי), Ne 9^{22} (‖ עַם), ψ 46^{7} (‖ גּוֹי), 79^{6} (‖ *id.*), 102^{23} (‖ עַם), Is 60^{12} (‖ גּוֹי), so Je 1^{10} 18$^{7.9}$ 27^{8} 28^{8}; Je 49^{28} 51$^{20.27}$ Am 6^{2} Na 3^{5} Zp 3^{8} Hg 2^{22} Ez 17^{14} 29$^{14.15}$ 37^{22}; מַמְלְכוֹת הַגּוֹיִם 2 Ch 20^{6}, cf. Is 13^{4}; מַמְלְכוֹת הָאָרֶץ 2 K 19$^{15.19}$ = Is 37$^{16.20}$, 2 Ch 36^{23} = Ezr 1^{2}, ψ 68^{33} Is 23^{17} Je 15^{4} 24^{9} 25^{26} 29^{18} 34$^{1.17}$; מַמְלְכוֹת הָאֲרָצוֹת 1 Ch 29^{30} 2 Ch 12^{8} 17^{10} 20^{29}; of Isr. Am 9^{8} Dt 17^{20} 2 S 3^{28} La 2^{2} 2 Ch 21^{4}; cf. מַמְלֶכֶת כֹּהֲנִים Ex 19^{6} (‖ גּוֹי קָדוֹשׁ); of Mess. king Is 9^{6}; צְבִי מַמְלָכוֹת (of Babylon) Is 13^{19}, גְּבֶרֶת מ׳ (*id.*) 47^{5}; מִשְׁפְּחוֹת מַמְלְכוֹת צָפוֹנָה Je 1^{15}. **2.** *sovereignty, dominion* 1 S 13^{14} (Isr.; c. תָּקוּם), cf. 24^{21}; 2 Ch 13^{8} מ׳ י׳ בְּיַד בְּנֵי דָוִיד; לְךָ י׳ הַמַּמ׳ 1 Ch 29^{11}; חָזְקָה בְּיָד 2 K 14^{5}; ח׳ עַל 2 Ch 25^{3} הֶחֱזִיק בְּיָד 2 K 15^{19} cf. 2 Ch 22^{9}; הֵכִין מ׳ אֶל (subj. י׳) 1 S 13^{13} (Isr.), cf. 2 S 7$^{12.16}$ (‖ בַּיִת); 2 Ch 17^{5} (בְּיָד) cf. 1 K 2^{46} (נָכוֹנָה בְּיָד); נִשָּׂא מ׳ (subj. י׳) 2 S 5^{12}; נָתַן מ׳ לְדָוִד עַל (subj. י׳) 2 Ch 13^{5}, cf. 21^{3}; קָרַע הַמַּ׳ מִן (subj. י׳) 1 S 28^{17} (Isr.), 1 K 11^{11} (sq. מֵעַל), v^{31} 14^{8}; מִן om. 11^{13}; לָקַח מִיָּדוֹ 11^{34} (or = *kingdom*?), הֶעֱבִיר מ׳ מִן (subj. י׳), 2 S 3^{10} (Isr.); נִשְׁבַּת מ׳ מִן Is 17^{3}; cf. תָּשׁוּב הַמַּ׳ לְ 1 K 12^{26}; עָדֶיךָ תאתה ובאה...מ׳ Mi 4^{8}; הֵשִׁיב מ׳ לְ 2 Ch 11^{1}; כִּסֵּא מ׳ Dt 17^{18} (Isr.; יָשַׁב עַל), 2 S 7^{13} (כּוֹנֵן י׳), 1 K 9^{5} (הֵקִים י׳) 2 Ch 23^{20}, כִּסֵּא מַמְלָכוֹת Hg 2^{22}; בֵּית מ׳ *royal house* Am 7^{13}; עָרֵי הַמַּ׳ *royal cities* Jos 10^{2} cf. 1 S 27^{5}; זֶרַע הַמַּ׳ *royal seed, children,* 2 K 11^{1} = 2 Ch 22^{10}. **3.** *reign,* בְּרֵאשִׁית מ׳ Je 27^{1} 28^{1} *in the beginning of the reign of* (cf. מַלְכוּת **2**, מַמְלָכוּת **3**).

†[מַמְלָכוּת] **n.f.** **kingdom, dominion, reign** (on form cf. We[1 S 15, 28] Dr[ad loc. id.]);—cstr. מַמְלְכוּת Jos 13^{12} + 8 t.; **1.** *kingdom* of Og Jos 13$^{12.30.31}$; of Sihon v$^{21.27}$. **2.** *dominion, royal power* c. קָרַע מֵעַל (subj. י׳) 1 S 15^{28}; c. הֵשִׁיב לְ (hum. subj.) 2 S 16^{3}; c. הִשְׁבִּית Ho 1^{4}. **3.** *reign* בְּרֵאשִׁית מַמ׳ Je 26^{1} (cf. מַמְלָכָה **3**, מַלְכוּת **2**).

†מַלְכִּיאֵל **n.pr.m.** son of Beriah (of Asher) (*my king is Ēl;* cf. Tel Am. *Milkili* Wkl[Tel Am. 39*], v. Jastr[JBL 1892, 120; 1893, 61 f.]; cf. further, Gray[Prop. N. 118 f., 206], v. also Ph. n.pr. מלכבעל, Palm. n.pr. מלכבל Vog[Palm. 3, 4; 140] and BH אֱלִימֶלֶךְ);—Gn 46^{17} Nu 26^{45} 1 Ch 7^{31}. 𝔊 Μελχιηλ.

†מַלְכִּיאֵלִי **adj.gent.** c. art. as subst. coll. מִשְׁפַּחַת הַמַּ׳ Nu 26^{45}.

†מַלְכִּיָּהוּ (only Je 38^{6}), מַלְכִּיָּה **n.pr.m.** (*my king is Yah;* cf. Gray[Prop. N. 119 f., 146 al.]);—𝔊 Μελχ(ε)ια(ς).—**1.** father of Pashhur Je 21^{1} 38^{1}, cf. 1 Ch 9^{12} (priest), Ne 11^{12}. **2.** a prince Je 38^{6}. **3.** priests: **a.** 1 Ch 24^{9}. **b.** Ne 12^{42}. **4.** one of the sealed Ne 10^{4}; perh. also 8^{4}. **5.** a Levite 1 Ch 6^{25}. **6.** various men: **a.** Ezr 10^{25a}. **b.** Ezr 10^{25b}. **c.** Ezr 10^{31} = Ne 3^{11}. **d.** Ne 3^{14}. **e.** Ne 3^{31}.

†מַלְכִּי־צֶדֶק **n.pr.m.** king of שָׁלֵם (q.v.), (*my king is Ṣedeḳ*)—Gn 14^{18} ψ 110^{4}. 𝔊 Μελχισεδεκ.

†מַלְכִּירָם **n.pr.m.** son of Jeconiah (= Jehoiakin) (*my king* (= Yahweh) *is high,* cf. Gray[Prop. N. 146 f.]; Ph. n. pr. מלכרם);—1 Ch 3^{18}. 𝔊 Μελχ(ε)ιραμ.

†מַלְכִּישׁוּעַ **n.pr.m.** son of Saul (*my king* (= י׳) *is opulence,* cf. Gray[Prop. N. 147]);—1 S 14^{49} 31^{2} 1 Ch 8^{33} 9^{39} 10^{2} (in Ch. מַלְכִּי־שׁוּעַ). 𝔊 Μελχεισα, Μελχεσουε, etc.

†מַלְכָּם **n.pr.m.** a Benjamite 1 Ch 8^{9}. 𝔊B Μελχας, A Μελχαμ, 𝔊L Μελχομ. On Je 49$^{1.3}$ Zp 1^{5} v. מִלְכֹּם.

†מִלְכֹּם **n.pr.div.** **Milcom,** god of Ammonites (cf. RS[Sem. i. 67])—מ׳ שִׁקֻּץ עַמֹּנִים 1 K 11^{5} (‖ עַשְׁתֹּרֶת); cf. מ׳ אֱלֹהֵי בְנֵי עַמּוֹן v^{33} (‖ כְּמוֹשׁ + ע׳), so rd. also (for MT מֹלֶךְ) v^{7} (‖ כְּמוֹשׁ); מ׳ תּוֹעֲבַת בְּנֵי־עַמּוֹן 2 K 23^{13} (‖ as 1 K 11^{33}); rd. מִלְכֹּם also

for מַלְכָּם Je 49[1.3] (𝔊 Μελχολ, Μελχομ), cf Gie, and Zp 1[5] (𝔖 ܡܠܟ, cf. Now), prob 2 S 12[30]= 1 Ch 20[2] (v מֶלֶךְ **5 d**), and perh Am 1[15] (whence Je 49[3], cf Dr Now,—not We GASm).

†יַמְלֵךְ **n.pr.m.** a Simeonite (cf Palm n pr ימלכו Vog[Palm 36a]),—1 Ch 4[34] 𝔊 Ιεμολοχ

†מַלּוּךְ **n.pr.m.** 𝔊 Μαλωχ, Μαλουχ, etc **1.** Levites: **a.** 1 Ch 6[29] **b.** Ne 12[2] (priest?) **2.** various men **a.** Ezr 10[29] **b.** Ezr 10[32]. **c.** Ne 10[5]. **d** Ne 10[28]

†מלוכי Kt, מליכו Qr **n.pr.m.** a priest Ne 12[14]. 𝔊 Μαλουχ, 𝔊L Μαλουκ.

†II [מָלַךְ] **vb counsel, advise** (loan-wd from Aram ܡܠܟ, מלך, cf As. *malâku*, Dl [HWB 412]),—only **Niph.** (so NH) *Impf* וַיִּמָּלֵךְ לִבִּי עָלַי i.e. I considered carefully, Ne 5[7].

[מַלְכֹּדֶת] v לכד.

מַלְכֵּן v מַלְבֵּן sub לבן.

†I. [מָלַל] **vb. Pi. speak, utter, say** (NH Pi *id*; Aram ܡܰܠܶܠ (and many deriv), מַלֵּל, perh. cf Ar مَلَّ iv *dictate* (a letter, etc), (ملو) مَلَا iv. *id* No[ZMG xl 1886, 723]),—**Pi.** *Pf* מלל Gn 21[7], cf 1 s. מִלּוֹתִי (Ew[§274 b N]) as **n pr** infr, מִלֵּלוּ Jb 33[3], *Impf* יְמַלֵּל ψ 106[2], תְּמַלֶּל־ Jb 8[2],—**say**, sq dir quot. + לְ of ind obj Gn 21[7], utter, obj דַּעַת Jb 33[3]; cf. 8[2], obj ^ גְּבוּרוֹת ψ 106[2].

†מִלָּה **n.f. word, speech, utterance** (poet, esp Jb; common in Aram.);—מ׳ ψ 139[4] Jb 30[9], sf מִלָּתִי Jb 13[17]+3 t.; מִלָּתוֹ 2 S 23[2], pl. מִלִּים Jb 6[26]+9 t. (all Jb); מִלִּין Jb 4[2]+12 t (all Jb), pl sf. מִלָּי Jb 19[23]+4 t; מִלֶּיךָ Jb 4[4] Pr 23[9], מִלֵּיהֶם ψ 19[5],—*word* בלשוני *in* (*on*) *my tongue* ψ 139[4]; *word* (of י׳) עַל־לְשׁוֹנִי *on my tongue* 2 S 23[2], שכל מ׳ Pr 23[9], fig ψ 19[5] (|| קַוָּם, but rd קוֹלָם v. Che crit n); elsewhere only Jb (34 t); sg *speech, utterance* Jb 13[17] 21[2] 24[25] 29[22]; also *word = by-word*, וָאֱהִי לָהֶם לְמִלָּה Jb 30[9]; pl. *words*, Jb 4[4] 6[26] 8[10] 12[11] 15[3] (|| דְּבָר), 16[4] 19[2.23] 32[11 14] 33[1 8] (קוֹל מ׳), 34[2.3 16] (קוֹל מ׳), 36[2 4]; words of God Jb 23[5]; *words = speech, speaking*, וְעצר במלין מי יוכל Jb 4[2], cf. 29[9]; *utter words*, הִגַּדְתָּ מ׳ 26[4]; והצאת מפיך מלין 15[13]; *lay snares for words* השימון קִנְצֵי לְמִלִּין Jb 18[2], cf. Jb 32[15] הֶעְתִּיקוּ מהם מלים, מָלֵתִי מִלִּים Jb 32[18] *I am full of words*, cf אֲשִׁיבְךָ מִלִּין 33[32], אִם־יֵשׁ־מִלִּין הֲשִׁיבֵנִי Jb 35[4], בִּבְלִי־דַעַת מִלִּין יַכְבִּר 35[16], cf. 38[2].

†מַלּוֹתִי as **n pr.m.** a son of Heman (*I have uttered* = מִלֵּלְתִּי Ew[§274 b. N] v מלל);—1 Ch 25[4] (on this appar. list of names v Ew[1 c] RS[OTJC 422, 2nd ed 143]) v[26].

†מִלֲלַי **n.pr.m.** a priest's son, Ne 12[36].

†II. [מָלַל] **vb. rub, scrape** (NH *id*, *rub* ears of wheat, *scrape*),—only **Qal** *Pt* מולל in קֹרֵץ בעינו מולל ברגלו מֹרֶה באצבעתיו Pr 6[13] *he that winketh with his eyes, that scrapeth with his feet* (making signs), etc., so De Now Str < Ew Wild fr. I. מלל *that speaketh with his feet.*

†[מְלִילָה] **n.f. ear** of wheat, etc (perh. as *rubbed* or *scraped*, cf. NH הַמּוֹלֵל מְלִילוֹת);—only pl. abs מְלִילוֹת Dt 23[26] (cf. Di).

†III. [מָלַל] **vb. languish, wither, fade** (apparently secondary ✓of אמל q v);—**Qal** *Impf* 3 ms יִמַּל Jb 18[16], וַיִּמָּל Jb 14[2]; 3 mpl. יִמָּלוּ Jb 24[24] ψ 37[2] (so Hup De and most; > Niph. fr IV. מלל Thes);—*hang down, wither*, fig. of man Jb 14[2] (כציץ); of wicked מִתַּחַת שָׁרָשָׁיו יִבָשׁוּ וּמִמַּעַל יִמַּל קְצִירוֹ 18[16], כְּרֹאשׁ שִׁבֹּלֶת יִמָּלוּ 24[24] (יבולון ||) כֶּחָצִיר מְהֵרָה יִמָּלוּ ψ 37[2] (הֻמְּכוּ, יִקָּפְצוּן ||); **Po'l.** *Impf.* ימולל ψ 90[6] *it withereth* (of grass; + וְיָבֵשׁ).

†IV [מָלַל] **vb. circumcise** (= מוּל),—to this are sts. assigned. **Qal** *Imv* מֹל Jos 5[2]. **Niph.** *Pf* נְמַלְתֶּם Gn 17[11]. **Hithpo.** *be cut off*: *Impf.* יִתְמֹלָלוּ ψ 58[8]. Vid. מוּל

[מַלְמַד, מַלְמָד] v. למד

†[מָלַץ] **vb.** prob **be smooth, slippery** (Ar مَلِصَ *slip*),—**Niph.** *Pf* מַה־נִּמְלְצוּ לְחִכִּי אִמְרָתֶךָ ψ 119[103] *how smooth* (agreeable, pleasant) *are thy words to my palate* (|| מִדְּבַשׁ לְפִי).

†מֶלְצַר **n.m.** a Bab title; dubious; perhaps **guardian**? (Schr[COT Dn 1 11] Dl[Baer Dn xi] conj loan-word fr As. *maṣ(s)aru*, *keeper, guardian*, cf Dl [HWB 423]; hardly connected with (mod) Pers. *mulsaru* 'kellermeister' (cf Meinh), v against this Bevan),—only c art. הַמּ׳ Dn 1[11 16].

†**מָלַק** **vb.** nip, nip off (head of bird; without *necessarily* severing it fr. body, cf. Lv 5[8]) (NH *id.*, Aram. מְלַק, ܡܠܰܩ);—**Qal** *Pf.* consec. וּמָלַק אֶת־רֹאשׁוֹ Lv 1[15], i. e. head of dove; cf. וּמָלַק אֶת־רֹאשׁוֹ מִמּוּל עָרְפּוֹ וְלֹא יַבְדִּיל Lv 5[8]. Cf. Di-Ry. 𝔊 ἀποκνίζω.

I, II. **מַלְקוֹחַ, מַלְקָחַיִם, מֶלְקָחַיִם** v. לקח.

מַלְקוֹשׁ v. לקשׁ. **מֶלְתָּחָה** v. לתח.

[**מַלְתָּעוֹת**] v. מְתַלְּעוֹת sub תלע.

מַמְּגֻרוֹת v. I. גור. [**מֵמַד**] v. מדד.

†**מְמוּכָן** **n.pr.m.** a prince of Persia and Media—Est 1[14.21] also v[16] Qr; Kt מומכן. 𝔊 Μουχαιος, Μαμουχαιος.

[**מָמוֹת**], **מְמוֹתִים** v. מות.

מַמְזֵר v. I. מזר.

מִמְכָּר, מִמְכֶּרֶת v. מכר.

מַמְלָכָה, [מַמְלְכוּת] v. מלך.

מִמֶּנִּי, etc. v. מִן. **מִמְסָךְ** v. מסך.

מֶמֶר, [**מַמְרוֹר**], **מַמְרוֹרִים** v. מרר.

†**מַמְרֵא** **n.pr.m. et loc.** Mamre, only in Gn: **1.** in J only אֵלֹנֵי מַמְרֵא *terebinths of M.* (n.pr.m.?), Gn 13[18] (defined by אֲשֶׁר בְּחֶבְרוֹן), 18[1] (in both the dwelling-place of Abraham). **2.** **n.pr.m.** in Gn 14[13] (אֵלֹנֵי מ׳ הָאֱמֹרִי), cf. v[24] (where ally of Abr.) **3.** **n.pr.loc.** in P: near Abr.'s place of burial Gn 23[17] 25[9] 49[30] 50[13]; appar. identified with Hebron 23[19] 35[27], cf. Di.—𝔊 Μαμβρη.

מִמְשַׁח v. משׁח.

מִמְשָׁל, מֶמְשָׁלָה, מֶמְשֶׁלֶת v. משׁל.

[**מִמְשָׁק**] v. משׁק. **מַמְתַקִּים** v. מתק.

†I. **מָן** **n.m.**[Nu 11, 9] manna (=Ar. مَنّ, known to Beduin in Sin. Penin.; a juice exuding in heavy drops from twigs (some say also the leaves) of *Ṭarfa* (Ṭŭrfa) tree (*tamarix gallica mannifera*) in W. Sin. Penin., end of May and in June, sweet, sticky, honey-like; cf. Di[Ex 16, 36] Rob[BR i. 75, 115, 590] Eb[GS 233 ff., 574 ff.] Soc[ZMG xxxv. 1881, 254]);—מ׳ abs. Ex 16[15] + 12 t., sf. מַנְךָ Ne 9[20]:—*manna*: וַיֹּאמְרוּ מָן הוּא כִּי לֹא יָדְעוּ מַה־הוּא Ex 16[15]; v[31.33.35.35] Nu 11[6.7.9] (described Ex 16[14.31] Nu 11[7]; accomp. dew Ex 16[14] Nu 11[9]); ceased after Israel reached Canaan Jos 5[12.12]; as 2nd acc. הַמַּאֲכִלְךָ מָן Dt 8[3], cf. v[16]; וַיַּמְטֵר עֲלֵיהֶם מָן לֶאֱכֹל ψ 78[24]; וּמַנְךָ לֹא־מָנַעְתָּ מִפִּיהֶם Ne 9[20].

†II. **מָן** in Ex 16[15] (with reference to the manna) וַיֹּאמְרוּ אִישׁ אֶל־אָחִיו מָן הוּא כִּי לֹא יָדְעוּ מַה־הוּא, most prob. 'What is it?' the question being intended as a popular etym. of מָן 'manna,' based upon the *late* Aram. ܡܰܢ *What?* (*man* is 'Who?' in Arab., Aram. (ܡܰܢ, מַן), Mand. (מאן), Eth. (*manu*), 'What?' in these dialects being מָה, ما, ܡܳܐ, מָא (Eth. *ment*); מָן in the sense of 'What?' must correspond to the later Syr. ܡܰܢ, contr. from ܡܳܐ ܗܽܘ, 𝔗 מָדֵין: Nö[§ 68] W[SG 125]).

†I. [**מֵן**] **n.**[**m.**] string (of harp) (prob. loan-word fr. Aram. ܡܶܢܬܳܐ, *hair, string* PS[2163]); pl. מִנִּים ψ 150[4], so also prob. 45[9] (rd. מִנִּים for MT מִנִּי, cf. Che Bae We > Ges[§ 87. 1. b] Hup al., who think מִנִּי an apoc. pl.)

II. [**מֵן**], **מִנְּהוּ** v. מנן.

מִן־, and **·מִ**, before ; (exc. Dn 12[2] 2 Ch 20[11]) contr. to מִי (as מִידֵי from מִיְּדֵי), before gutt. and ר, mostly מֵ, occasionally מִ (Ges[§ 102. 1 R.]; more fully Kö[ii. 291 ff.]), מִן before art. in all books much commoner than -מֵ; מִן before other words most freq. in Ch [51 t.: elsewhere 47 t. (Kö[292])]; poet. also מִנִּי, with the old י of the gen. (Ges[§ 90. 3 a]) Ju 5[14.14] Is 46[3.3] ψ 44[11.19] 68[32] 74[22] 78[2.42] 88[10] + 19 t. Jb, and in לְמִנִּי + Mi 7[12.12], and מִנֵּי־ (on anal. of עֲלֵי, עֲדֵי) + Is 30[11.11], **prep.** expressing the idea of *separation*, hence out of, from, on account of, off, on the side of, since, above, than, so that not (Ph. מ; Aram. ܡܶܢ; Ar. مِنْ; Eth. እምነ: ; Sab. בן (DHM[ZMG xxix. 606 ff.; xxxvii. 375])); with suff. מִמֶּנִּי (the מִן reduplicated, Ol[§ 223 c], al., Kö[ii. 289 f.]), poet. מִנִּי + Is 22[4] 30[1] 38[12] Jb 16[6], מֶנִּי + ψ 18[23] 65[4] 139[19] Jb 21[16] 22[18] 30[10]; מִמְּךָ, מִמֶּךָּ, מִמֵּךְ; מִמֶּנּוּ (+ Jb 4[12] מֶנְהוּ); מִמֶּנָּה; 1 pl. מִמֶּנּוּ (acc. to Orientals מִמֵּנוּ: v. Baer[Job, p. 57] Kö[290]); מִכֶּם; מֵהֶם (מִנְּהֶם + Jb 11[20]), מֵהֵמָּה + Je 10[2] Ec 12[12]; מֵהֵנָּה 7 t. (v. הֵמָּה **8 c**), מֵהֶן (edd. מֵהֵן) + Ez 16[47.52] (v. Zerweck[Heb. Präp. Min, 1894]):—**1.** with verbs expressing (or implying) *separation* or *removal*, whether from a person or place, or in any direction, also from guilt, calamity, etc.:—thus **a.** to descend *from* a mountain Ex 19[14], to fall *from* a roof Dt 22[8], *from* heaven Is 14[12], to go up *from* a valley

Jos 10^{7}, to raise up *from* the dunghill 1 S 2^{8}, or the ground 2 S 12^{17}. So constantly with vbs. of *going*, as ברח ,שׁב ,הלך ,בא (sq. a person, usu. מפני), of *calling*, as Is 24^{14} צָהֲלוּ מִיָּם, 42$^{10.11}$ ψ 148^{1}, of *asking* or *exacting*, as בקשׁ ,שׁאל, דרשׁ ,נָקַם ,הִנָּקֵם, of *delivering*, as הוֹשׁיע ,הציל, etc., of *hiding*, as נעלם ,העלים, etc., of *taking* or *withholding*, as לקח ,חשׂך ,מנע, of *keeping* (*from*), as נצר ,שׁמר, of *being far*, or *desisting*, as רחק Ex 23^{7}, חֲדַל מִמֶּנּוּ desist *from* us, 14^{12}, so הֶרֶף Dt 9^{14}, הֵנִיחַ 12^{10}, השׁקיט ψ 94^{13}, שׁבת Gn 2^{2}, cf. 5^{29}; note esp. the pregn. constructions, שׁפט to judge (and save) *from* ψ 43^{1}, sq. מִיַּד 1 S 24^{16}+, ענה to answer (and save) *from* ψ 22^{22}, חרשׁ and חשׁה to be silent (turning) *from* ψ 28$^{1.1}$, החרישׁו ממני Jb 13^{13} Je 38^{27}, ψ 18^{22} ולא רשׁעתי מאלהי nor did wickedly (turning) *from* my God, 30^{4} Kt., 73^{27} כל־זוֹנֶה ממך, Je 3^{20} בָּגַד מִן (𝔊 εἰς=ב), 31^{13} c. שִׂמַּח (2 Ch 20^{27}), Ez 27^{34} Pr 25^{17} הֹקַר רַגְלְךָ מִבֵּית רֵעֶךָ, Is 29^{4} 63^{17} Jo 1^{12}; Je 51^{5} אַלְמָן מֵאֱלֹהָיו widowed (and severed) *from* etc., Ez 44^{22}; also Ju 7^{17} מִמֶּנִּי תִרְאוּ וְכֵן תַּעֲשׂוּ ye shall *see from* me, i. e. learn what to do by observing me. Some of the verbs mentioned above are construed more precisely with מֵאֵת, מֵעִם ,מֵעַל, q.v.: and others, esp. לקח ,דרשׁ, הושׁיע ,הציל ,פדה ,פִּלֵּט, idiom. with מִיַּד. With inff., v. infr. **7 b**. Often also with adverbs, as מִשָּׁם *thence*, מֵאַיִן *whence?* מִזֶּה ,מִפֹּה *hence*. Cf. also חָפְשִׁי מִן free (safe) *from* Jb 3^{19}, עֵזֶר מִצָּרָיו a help *from* his foes Dt 33^{7}, Na 3^{11} מָעוֹז מֵאוֹיֵב, ψ 32^{7} סֵתֶר מִצַּר, 60^{13} עֶזְרָת מִצָּר, Is 4^{6} צֵל מֵחֹרֶב a shadow *from* the heat, 25^{4}. Here also belong Is 40^{15} מַר מִדְּלִי a drop *from* (hanging from) a bucket; Ct 4^{1} goats שֶׁגָּלְשׁוּ מהר גלעד that sit up (seeming to hang) *from* the hills of Gilead (cf. Od. 21. 420 ἐκ δίφροιο καθήμενος: also the Arabic idiom قَرِبَ مِنْ, lit. to be near *from* a thing): prob. also the difficult passage Dn 8^{9}, and from one of them there came forth קֶרֶן אַחַת מִצְּעִירָה a horn *from* (being) a little one, i. e. gradually increasing from small beginnings (but ? rd. אַחֶרֶת צְעִירָה Bev cf. 7^{8}). **b.** מן also, without a verb of similar significance, sometimes expresses the idea of separation, *away from*, *far from* (cf. Il. 2. 162 φίλης ἀπὸ πατρίδος αἴης): Pr 20^{3} שֶׁבֶת מֵרִיב to sit *away from* strife (cf. قَعَدَ عَنْ *ap.* De), Nu 15^{24} if the thing be done מֵעֵינֵי הָעֵדָה *away from* the eyes of etc., Ju 5^{11} De RV (but Be RVm *because of*), Is 14^{19} cast out מִקִּבְרְךָ *away from* thy sepulchre, Jb 28^{4} דַּלּוּ מֵאֱנוֹשׁ, Gn 4^{11} cursed art thou מִן־הארמה, De Di *away from* the (tilled) soil, cf. v^{14} (but Kn Ke *from*, cf. v^{12a}), 27^{39} (prob.) מִשְׁמַנֵּי הָאָרֶץ *away from* the fatness of the earth shall be thy dwelling; almost=*without*, Jb 11^{15} then shalt thou lift up thy face מִמּוּם *away from*, *without* spot, 19^{26} (prob.) מִבְּשָׂרִי *without* my flesh shall I see God, 21^{9} בָּתֵּיהֶם שָׁלוֹם מִפָּחַד are at peace *without* fear, Pr 1^{33} Je 48^{45} fleeing עָמְדוּ מִכֹּחַ they stand *without* strength, Is 22^{3} מִקֶּשֶׁת אֻסָּרוּ (Hi De Di Che) they were bound *without* the bow (being used) (but Ges as **2 e**: *by* the bowmen), Zp 3^{18}. (On 2 S 13^{16} v. We or Dr). See also **7 b**. **c.** of position, *off*, *on the side of*, *on*, esp. with ref. to quarters of the heavens (cf. πρὸς Νότου, ἐκ δεξιῶν, *a* fronte, *a* tergo, etc.): Gn 2^{8} י׳ planted a garden in Eden מִקֶּדֶם *off*, *on* the east, 12^{8} בֵּיתְאֵל מִיָּם וְהָעַי מִקֶּדֶם Bethel *off* (*on*) the West and ʿAi *off* (*on*) the East; so מִמִּזְרָח ,מִצָּפוֹן ,מִנֶּגֶב Jos 11^{3} 15^{8} 18^{5} 1 S 14^{5}, etc.: similarly מִיָּמִין *on* the right, מִשְּׂמֹאול *on* the left, מִמּוּל and (more rarely) מִפָּנִים *on* the front, מֵאָחוֹר = behind (2 S 10^{9}), מִסָּבִיב Dt 12^{10}+ *round about*, מִמַּעַל ,מִלְמַעְלָה, and מֵעַל (rare) = *above*, מִתַּחַת Ex 20^{4}+ *beneath*, מִבַּיִת *on* the inside, מִחוּץ *on* the outside Gn 6^{14}+, מִנֶּגֶד *in front*, *at* a distance, Gn 21^{16}+, מֵרָחוֹק Ex 2^{4}+ *afar off*, מִפְּנִימָה *within*, מִזֶּה . . . מִזֶּה and מִפֹּה . . . מִפֹּה *on* this side . . . *on* that side. And so even with verbs of motion, as Gn 11^{2} ויהי בנסעם מִקֶּדֶם as they journeyed—not *from*, but—*on the side of* the east, virtually=*eastwards*, 13^{11} and Lot journeyed מקדם *east*, Is 17^{13} 22^{3} מֵרָחוֹק ברחו they fled—not *from* afar but—*afar*, 23^{7} whose feet used to carry her מֵרָחוֹק *afar off* to sojourn, 57^{9} thou didst send thy messengers עד־מרחוק *even to afar*. With a foll. לְ (or sf.), most of these words are freq. in the sense of *on the east* (*west*, etc.) *of* . . ., as Jos 8^{13} מִיָּם לָעִיר *on* the west of the city, מִקֶּדֶם לְ Gn 3^{24}, מִצָּפוֹן לְ (cstr. Ges $^{§130a,n.}$) Jos 8$^{11.13}$ 24^{30}, מִימִינֶךָ ψ 91^{7}, מִתַּחַת לְ Gn 1^{7}, מִמַּעַל לְ 22^{9}, מִבֵּית לְ Lv 16^{2}: מֵאַחֲרֵי *behind* Ex 14^{19}, מִצַּד בֵּיתְאֵל *beside* Bethel Jos 12^{9}, מִצִּדּוֹ *beside* it 1 S 6^{8}, מֵעֵבֶר לַיַּרְדֵּן *on* the other side of Jordan Nu 21^{1}+; מֵהָלְאָה לְ *beyond* Am 5^{27}; tablets written מִשְּׁנֵי עֶבְרֵיהֶם *on* both their sides, מִכָּל־עֲבָרָיו Je 49^{32}+ (v. further the words cited). So מֵהַבַּיִת *on the side of the* house Ez 40$^{7.8.9}$, מֵאֵצֶל *beside* Ez 40^{7}; 1 S 20^{21} the arrows

are מִמְּךָ וָהֵנָּה *from thee* and hither=on this side of thee, v[22] מִמְּךָ וָהָלְאָה, cf Nu 32[19.19].

2. Out of, Gk. ἐκ, Lat. *ex:* thus **a.** מִמִּצְרַיִם *out of* Egypt: so (*a*) with verbs of *proceeding, removing, expelling*, etc, as יָצָא, הוֹצִיא (v. יָצָא), שִׁלַּח Gn 3[23], לָקַח 34[26], גָּנַב 40[15], הִכְרִית Ex 8[5] ψ 101[8], גרשׁ Ju 11[7], etc., to draw *out of* water, a pit, etc. Ex 2[10] ψ 40[3]; to cast *out of* the hand Ju 15[17]; to rescue *out of* the mouth Am 3[12]; to drink מכוס 2 S 12[3]; Dt 30[3] וְקִבֶּצְךָ מִן־הָעַמִּים, Ez 11[17] 36[24]+: pregn. with חָרַד Ho 10[10.11], רגז Mi 7[17] to tremble (and come) *out of*, חרג ψ 18[46] (|| 2 S 22[46] חגר), 74[11] Is 38[17] חָשַׂךְ (ni חָשַׁק leg.), Ez 28[16] חִלֵּל, Ezr 2[62]; cf. נִשְׁכַּח מִפֶּה Dt 31[21], מִלֵּב ψ 31[13]. In this applic., often made more definite by the use of . . . מִקֶּרֶב, . . . מתוך *out of* the midst of (*b*) of the place *out of* which one looks, speaks, exerts power, etc., Gn 4[10] Nu 24[19] (ψ 110[1]), Dt 4[36] מן־השמים השמיעך את־קלו, Am 1[2] י׳ מציון ישאג, ψ 14[2] 20[3] send thee help מִקֹּדֶשׁ, v[7] יַעֲנֵהוּ מִשְּׁמֵי קָדְשׁוֹ, 42[7] 68[36] 85[12] 109[10] ודרשו מחרבותיהם seek (their bread) *out of* their desolate homes (but Ew De as **1 b** *far from;* 𝔊 Gr Che יְגֹרְשׁוּ let them *be driven from*), 128[5] 130[1] Jb 27[23] Is 29[18] to see *out of* darkness, Ct 2[9] to look out מִן־הַחַלֹּנוֹת *from* the windows (usu. בעד), 5[4] he put forth his hand מִן־הַחוֹר *from* (i.e. *in through*) the hole (in the door or wall) (*c*) with בָּחַר to choose *out of*, Ex 18[25]+oft., cf. with הבדיל Dt 29[20] 1 K 8[53], with יָדַע Am 3[2], Ex 19[5] ye shall be to me סְגֻלָּה מכל־העמים a treasure (chosen) *out of* all peoples (cf. with בָּחַר Dt 7[6] 14[2]) **b.** of the material *out of* which anything is formed, or from which it is derived: (*a*) Gn 2[19] to form מן־האדמה *out of the* soil, v[23] עֶצֶם מֵעֲצָמַי וּבָשָׂר מִבְּשָׂרִי, Ex 39[1] Nu 6[4] Ho 13[2] to make images מִכַּסְפָּם, ψ 16[4] נִסְכֵּיהֶם מִדָּם, 45[14] Ct 3[9]; Is 40[17] מאפס ותהו נחשבו־לו as *made of* nought and unreality are they reckoned by him (|| כְּאַיִן נֶגְדּוֹ), 41[24] הֵן אַתֶּם מֵאַיִן (|| מֵאָפַע, rd. מֵאָפֶס), ψ 62[10] מֵהֶבֶל (*al.* **6 c**), Pr 13[11]; Ex 25[19.31] its cups, its knops, etc., ממנה יהיו shall be *from it* (i.e. of one piece with it), so v[34.36] 27[2] 30[2] *al.*; (*b*) with verbs of eating, filling, etc., as שתה Gn 9[21], Jb 21[20] מֵחֲמַת שַׁדַּי יִשְׁתֶּה, Ct 8[2] הִשְׁקָה, רָוָה ψ 36[9]+, מִלֵּא, שבע Is 34[7], שבע Pr 18[20]+, הִשְׂבִּיעַ ψ 81[17]+, רִוָּה (rare) 127[5]. cf. Dt 32[42] אַשְׁכִּיר חִצַּי מִדָּם, Is 51[21]; ψ 28[7] (peculiar) וּמִשִּׁירִי אֲהוֹדֶנּוּ *out of* my song I will thank him (69[31] ב׳), also (unusual) Is 2[3] וְיֹרֵנוּ מִדְּרָכָיו i e. *out of* (the treasure of) his ways (*al.* part.=*some of*), ψ 94[12b] מִתּוֹרָתְךָ תְלַמְּדֶנּוּ; Ec 7[10] to speak מֵחָכְמָה (cf Rabb. מתוך). **c.** of the *source* or *origin:* viz. (*a*) of parents, Gn 16[2] אִבָּנֶה ממנה I shall be built up *out of* her (so 30[3]), 17[16] מלכי עמים ממנה יהיו, 35[11a]: often of coming forth מִבֶּטֶן Jb 1[21], מֵחֲלָצֶיךָ Gn 35[11b], ממעיך 15[4], 1 S 2[20] י׳ give thee seed *from* this woman; cf. Jb 14[4] מִי יִתֵּן טָהוֹר מִטָּמֵא. (*b*) of the tribe or people, *from* which a person comes (cf. **1 a**), Nu 3[12] כל בכור . . . מבני ישׂ׳, Jos 12[4] 2 S 4[2] 21[2] Je 1[1]+; and so of a person's native place, as Ju 12[8] אבצן מבית לחם Ibzan *from* B., 13[2] איש מִצָּרְעָה, 17[1.7] 1 S 1[1] 9[1] 2 S 23[20.30] Am 1[1]+, cf. Je 46[25] אָמוֹן מִנֹּא; Is 48[1] וּמִמֵּי יְהוּדָה יָצָאוּ, v[2] מֵעִיר הַקֹּדֶשׁ נִקְרָאוּ, 58[12] וּבָנוּ ממך (those) *from* thee shall build, ψ 68[27] מִמְּקוֹר ישׂראל ye (sprung) *from* the fountain of Israel, Mi 5[1] Na 1[11] (v[14] fig. מִשִּׁמְךָ), Zp 3[18]; Je 30[21] Zc 10[4]. (*c*) of beasts and things, Gn 2[7] עָפָר מִן־הָאֲדָמָה, Je 5[6] אַרְיֵה מִיַּעַר a lion *from* the forest, ψ 80[14] חֲזִיר מִיַּעַר; cf. 10[18] אֱנוֹשׁ מִן־הָאָרֶץ man *from* the earth (*terrenus*), 72[16] יָצִיצוּ מֵעִיר; Jb 28[12] וְהַחָכְמָה מֵאַיִן תִּמָּצֵא (*d*) מִלֵּב Is 59[13] Jb 8[10], esp with reference to what is self-devised, Nu 16[28] כי לא מלבי, 24[13] 1 K 12[33] Ne 6[8]; נביאי מִלִּבָּם Ez 13[2]. **d.** of the *source* or *author* of an action, counsel, or event. 1 S 24[14] מֵרְשָׁעִים יֵצֵא רֶשַׁע, 2 S 3[37] לא היתה מהמלך it was not *from* the king to, etc.; spec. of י׳, Gn 24[50] כי מי׳ יצא הדבר, Ju 14[4] knew כי מי׳ הוא that it was *from* J., 1 K 2[15] כי מי׳ היתה לו, Pr 16[1] 20[24] מי׳ מִצְעֲדֵי גָבֶר, ψ 37[39] 62[2] מִמֶּנּוּ יְשׁוּעָתִי, Ho 8[4] they have made kings, וְלֹא מִמֶּנִּי not *from me*, i.e. not at my prompting, Is 30[1] 50[11] (מִיָּדִי), Ez 3[17 end]=33[7] and warn them *from me*, 1 Ch 5[22] 13[2] 2 Ch 22[7] 25[20] (syn. מֵאֵת, מֵעִם, which are more frequent in this sense); poet. Ho 7[5] חֲמַת מִיַּיִן heat *from wine*, ψ 9[14] עָנְיִי מִשֹּׂנְאַי *at the hands of* my haters, 74[22] Jb 4[13] שְׂעִפִּים מֵחֶזְיֹנוֹת לָיְלָה thoughts (arising) *out of*, etc, 6[25] הוֹכֵחַ מִכֶּם reproof *proceeding from* you, 20[29.29], ψ 78[2] חִידוֹת מִקֶּדֶם indirect lessons (springing) *out of* antiquity; Dn 11[31] וּזְרֹעִים מִמֶּנּוּ (Ko[iii 241]) As marking the author of a judgment or estimate (rare), Nu 32[22] נְקִיִּם מי׳ וּמִיִּשְׂרָאֵל guiltless *at the hands of* (=in the judgment of) J. and Israel (cf מֵעִם 2 S 3[28] Jb 34[33]), Jb 4[17] shall man be just מֵאֱלוֹהַּ *at God's hands?* (|| מֵעֹשֵׂהוּ), Je 51[5b] (Ges Gf); so in חָלִילָה לִּי מי׳. **e.** of the immediate, or *efficient*, cause (chiefly poet.), *in consequence of, at, by* (cf. Gk. ἀπό, as Hd. 2[54]

(ζήτησιν ἀπὸ σφέων γενέσθαι): (*a*) the cause, a *person* Gn 19^{36}+ הָרָתָה מִן to be pregnant *by*, 49^{25} 1 S 31^{3} וַיָּחֶל מֵהַמּוֹרִים was in anguish *from* the archers, Ho 7^{4} בֹּעֵרָה מֵאֹפֶה (ni בֹּעֵר הֵם leg.: v. We), ψ 18^{9} Na 1^{5} הרים רעשו ממנו, Dn 11^{31} (accents); with pass.vb., Na 1^{6} הצורים נִתְּצוּ ממנו, ψ 37^{23} (cf. Pr 20^{24} **d**), Jb 24^{1} Ec 12^{11} Dn 8^{11}. (*b*) the cause, a *thing*, Gn 49^{24} his arms were agile מידי אביר יעקב *from* the hands, etc., Is 6^{4} the thresholds shook מִקּוֹל הַקּוֹרֵא (so מקול elsewhere, as 30^{31} 33^{3} Je 8^{16}), 28^{7} תָּעוּ מִן־הַשֵּׁכָר (|| ב), 31$^{4.9}$ Je 10^{10} Ez 19^{10} became fruitful מִמַּיִם רַבִּים, 31^{5} Jb 4^{9} מִנִּשְׁמַת אֱלוֹהַּ יֹאבֵדוּ *at* the breath of God, 14^{9} מֵרֵיחַ מַיִם יַפְרִחַ, 31^{23} 39^{26} הֲמִבִּינָתְךָ יַאֲבֶר־נֵץ, ψ 39^{11} 73^{19} סָפוּ תַמּוּ מִן־בַּלָּהוֹת, 78^{65} מִתְרוֹנֵן מִיָּיִן, 104^{15} להצהיל פנים משמן *from* oil, 107^{39}, cf. Jb 7^{14} (|| ב); so with מִגַּעֲרַת י׳ *at* J.'s rebuke, 18^{16} 76^{7}+; with a pass. vb., Gn 9^{11} to be cut off מִמֵּי הַמַּבּוּל, 2 S 7^{29} וּמִבִּרְכָתְךָ יְבֹרַךְ, Is 28^{7} נבלעו מן־היין are undone *through* wine (22^{3} is dub.: see **1 b**), Ob^{9} Jb 28^{4} הַנִּשְׁכָּחִים מִנִּי רָגֶל; cf. Is 34^{3} Ho 6^{8}. (*c*) with verbs of *fearing*, to express the source of the emotion, as ירא ψ 3^{7}+ oft. (also c. מִפְּנֵי), פָּחַד 27^{1}, נִבְהַל Ez 26^{18}, גור Dt 18^{22} Jb 41^{17}, Est 5^{9} ולא־קם ולא זָע ממנו; with בּוֹשׁ *to be disconcerted* or *disappointed*, to express the source of the disappointment, Is 1^{29} +oft.; with שָׂמֵחַ +Pr 5^{18} Ec 2^{10}. **f.** of the remoter cause, the ultimate ground *on account of* which something happens or is done. (N.B. The line between **e** and **f** is not always clearly defined): Ex 2^{23} they sighed מן־העבדה *on account of* the bondage, 6^{9} 15^{23} Dt 7^{7} not מֵרֻבְּכֶם *through, by reason of,* your numbers did J. set his love upon you, Jos 22^{24} to do a thing מִדְּאָגָה *out of* carefulness, 2 S 23^{4} מִנֹּגַהּ, 1 K 14^{4} Is 53^{5} wounded מִפְּשָׁעֵנוּ *on account of* our transgressions, bruised מֵעֲוֺנֹתֵינוּ, v^{8} Jb 4^{19} Ob^{10} Hb 2^{17} ψ 6^{8} עששה עיני מִכַּעַס *from* vexation (cf. Jb 17^{7}: ψ 31^{10} ב׳), 31^{12} 38^{19} I am concerned *on account of* my sin, Pr 20^{4} מֵחֹרֶף עצל לא יחרש *by reason of* the winter, Jb 22^{4} הֲמִיִּרְאָתְךָ יֹכִיחֶךָ *on account of* thy fear of him? Ct 3^{8} Ru 1^{13} כִּי־מַר־לִי מְאֹד מִכֶּם *because of you:* see also Dt 28$^{34.67}$ 32^{19} Ju 2^{18} Is 65^{14} Je 12^{4} 24^{2} מֵרֹעַ, 50^{13} 51$^{5 b}$ (Ew Ke), Ez 7^{27} (but read prob. with 𝔊 𝔖 𝔙 Co כְּדַרְכָּם), 16^{61} 35^{11} (AV *out of*), 45^{20} Mi 2^{12} 7^{13} ψ 5^{11} 12^{6} 107^{17} 119^{53}; Gn 49^{12} red of eyes מִיָּיִן, and white of teeth מֵחָלָב. Often also in מֵרֹב *from* the abundance of, abs. *for* abundance, with many different verbs, as Gn 16^{10} לֹא יִסָּפֵר מֵרֹב Jos 9^{13} 1 S 1^{16}, etc. Similarly in מִבִּלְתִּי, מִבְּלִי, מֵאֵין (pp. 35, 115, 117); and before an inf. (**7 a**), and in מֵאֲשֶׁר (p. 84). **g.** the cause being conceived as regulative, מן occasionally approaches in sense to *according to* (cf. Lat. *ex* more, *ex* lege), Jon 3^{7} proclaimed in Nineveh מטעם המלך וגדליו *at, by, in accordance* with, the decree of the king (cf. Aram. Ezr 6^{14} Dn 2^{8}): so Jb 39^{26} (**2 e** (*b*)) acc. to Ges Hi.

3. *Partitively* (a sense connecting with **2 a** (*c*), above):—**a.** Gn 6^{19} שְׁנַיִם מִכֹּל two *out of, from,* all, 7^{8}; 39^{11} ... איש מן a man (or one) *of* ... (so Nu 25^{6} 1 S 24^{28}+, ... אנשים מן Nu 16^{2} Jos 2^{2}+, 2 K 2^{7}, etc.); Gn 42^{16} send מִכֶּם אֶחָד Lv 1^{2} 17^{12} כָּל־נֶפֶשׁ מִכֶּם, 19^{34} 26^{8}, Ju 8^{14} נַעַר מֵאַנְשֵׁי סֻכּוֹת, 1 S 22^{8}, etc.; Ju 14^{19} 2 K 2^{24} Is 66^{19}; אַחַד מִן ..., 1 S 16^{18}+, ... אֶחָד מִן (Ges § 130, 1) Dt 25^{5}+; ψ 34^{21} Is 34^{16} אַחַת מֵהֵנָּה; ... מִי מִן Jb 5^{1} Is 50^{1}, ... אֵין מִן 1 S 14^{39} Is 51^{18}; Is 21^{11} מַה־מלילה how much *of* the night? 2 Ch 31^{3} וּמְנָת הַמֶּלֶךְ מִן־רְכוּשׁוֹ. **b.** the number being omitted, מִן is used indefinitely:—(*a*) = *some of*,—as subj. Ex 16^{27} יצאו מן־העם there went out (some) *of* the people, Lv 25^{49} 2 S 11$^{17.24}$, esp. in late Hebrew Ezr 2$^{68.70}$ 7^{7} Ne 11$^{4.25}$ 1 Ch 4^{42} 9$^{30.32}$ 2 Ch 17^{11} 32^{21} Dn 11^{35}; more freq. as obj., esp. with לקח, Gn 4^{3} וַיָּבֵא מִפְּרִי האדמה brought *of* the fruit of the ground, 30^{14} give me מִדּוּדָאֵי בְּנֵךְ (some) *of* thy son's love-apples, 33^{15} Ex 12^{7} 17^{5} Lv 18^{30} 20^{2} Nu 11^{17} 13^{23} 1 K 12^{4} Is 39^{7} 47^{13} Am 2^{11} Dn 8^{10}+, Ct 1^{2} ישקני מִנְּשִׁיקוֹת פִּיהוּ let him kiss me (with) *some of* the kisses etc., ψ 72^{16} 137^{3} מִשִּׁיר צִיּוֹן (some) of the songs of Zion, Jb 11^{6} (Ges RVm) +oft.; in late Hebr. note also ... יֵשׁ מִן ... there are *some of* ... Ne 5^{5}; ... מֵהֶם ... מֵהֶם ... *some* ... *others* ... 1 Ch 9$^{28 f.}$ (as in Aram. Dn 2^{33}, and PS^{2155}); ... מִקְצָת *some of* ... (as in NH) +Dn 1^{2} Ne 7^{69}. (*b*) to designate an individual (rare), Gn 28^{11} and he took מֵאַבְנֵי הַמָּקוֹם (one) of the stones of the place (see v^{18}), Ex 6^{25} מבנות פוטיאל (one) *of* the daughters of P., Ez 17$^{5.13}$ Ne 13^{28} ψ 132^{11}; as subj. Lv 25^{33} Dn 11^{5} the king of the south וּמִן־שָׂרָיו and (one) of his captains, v^{7}, cf. Je 41^{1} Est 4^{5} 2 Ch 26^{11}; Ru 2^{20} מִגֹּאֲלֵנוּ הוּא he is (one) of our kinsmen, Ex 2^{6}. (*c*) in a neg. or hypoth. sentence (whether subject or object) = *any, aught,* Dt 16^{4} ולא ילין מן־הבשׂר and there shall *not* remain *any* of the flesh, 1 K 18^{5} ולא נכרית

מן־הבהמה and we shall not destroy *any* of the beasts, 2 K 10^{10} (cf. Jos 21^{45} 23^{14} 1 S 3^{19} 1 K 8^{56} Est 6^{10}), v^{23} מִשְׁפַּט עַבְדֵי י׳ לֹא יֶחֱרַף לְבָבִי מִיָּמָי, Jb 27^{6} my heart reproacheth not *one* of my days: with אִם, etc. Ex 29^{34} Lv 4^{2a} (cf. v$^{22.27}$), 11^{32} (מהם), v$^{33.35.37-39}$ 18^{29} 25^{25} Nu 5^{6}; מִכֹּל *anything whatever*, Lv 5^{24} 11^{34}; cf. 1 S 23^{23} (?). (*d*) peculiarly, with a noun of unity, esp. אֶחָד, to express forcibly the idea of a *single one*: Dt 15^{7} if there be a poor man in thy midst, מֵאַחַד אַחֶיךָ *any one* of thy brethren, Lv 4^{2b} if he doeth מֵאַחַת מֵהֵנָּה *any one* of these things, 5^{13} Ez 18^{10} וְעָשָׂה אָח מֵאַחַד מֵאֵלֶּה (where אח is a *vox nihili*) and doeth *aught* of these things; 1 S 14^{45} if there shall fall מִשַּׂעֲרַת ראשׁוֹ אַרְצָה *a single* hair of his head to the ground! (for שַׂעֲרָה as a nom. unit. v. Ges^{§122d} Dr), cf. 2 S 14^{11} 1 K 1^{52}. (Probably a rhetorical application of the partitive sense, though the explanation '*starting from* one' = '*even* one' would also be possible. مِنْ is used similarly after neg. and interrog. particles, not merely with collective nouns, as مَا لَهُمْ مِنْ عِلْمٍ nought have they of knowledge (Qor 18^{4}), but also with nouns of unity, as Qor 3^{55} Ye have not مِنْ إِلَهٍ *aught of* (= *any*) god, except Him; 19^{19} dost thou perceive مِنْهُمْ مِنْ أَحَدٍ *even one* of them? 6^{59} there falleth not مِنْ وَرَقَةٍ *even a single* leaf (nom. unit.) without His knowing it. See further Thes, and W$^{AG. ii. § 48 f. b}$). (*e*) (rare) specifying the objects, or elements, of which a genus consists (the Ar. مِنْ لِلْبَيَانِ, *min of explication*, W$^{AG. ii. § 48 e}$): Gn 6^{2} מכל אשׁר בחרו *consisting of* all whom they chose, 7^{22} 9^{10} Lv 11^{32} (מכל), 1 Ch 5^{18} Je 40^{7} (מאשׁר); 44^{28} and they shall know דְּבַר־מִי יָקוּם מִמֶּנִּי וּמֵהֶם whose word shall stand, *consisting of me and of them* (defining the genus embraced by מי: cf. كُلٌّ مِنْ هَابِيلَ وَقَابِيلَ both (of them), Abel as well as Cain, and Qor 3^{193}: W$^{l.c.}$).—On מֵאֵין Je 10$^{6.7}$, v. אַיִן *ad fin.*, p. 35.

4. Of *time*—viz. **a.** as marking the *terminus a quo*, the anterior limit of a continuous period, *from, since* Dt 9^{24} מִיּוֹם דַּעְתִּי אֶתְכֶם *from* the day of my (first) knowing you (so 1 S 7^{2} 8^{8}+); 1 S 18^{9} מהיום ההוא וָהָלְאָה *from* that day and onwards, simil. †Lv 22^{27} Nu 15^{23} Ez 39^{22}; Is 18$^{2.7}$ (where מֵאֲשֶׁר הוּא = מִן־הוּא; cf. Na 2^{9} מהיום ההוא וָמָעְלָה (מִימֵי אֲשֶׁר הִיא = מִימֵי הִיא); †1 S 16^{13} 30^{25} (Hg 2$^{15.18}$ appar. of time *backwards*); מֵאָז *from* the time of .... (v. p. 23); מִבֶּטֶן אִמִּי מִן־הַבֶּטֶן *from* the womb Ju 13$^{5.7}$, 16^{17}+; .... מִימֵי Ho 10^{9} Is 23^{7} Je 36^{2}+; מִיָּמֶיךָ idiom. = *since* thou wast born †1 S 25^{28} 1 K 1^{6} (מִיָּמָיו), Jb 38^{12}; מִקֶּדֶם *from* antiquity Hb 1^{12} ψ 74^{12}, Is 42^{14} הֶחֱשֵׁיתִי מֵעוֹלָם I have been silent *since* old time; מֵעַתָּה *from* now, hence-*forth* Je 3^{4}+, מִיּוֹם *from* to-day †Is 43^{13} Ez 48^{35}, מן־היום הזה Hg 2^{19}. See also **5 c, 7 c.** Cf. Ex 33^{6} מֵהַר חוֹרֵב *from* Horeb, Ho 13^{4} I am י׳ thy God מֵאֶרֶץ מִצְרָיִם. **b.** as marking the period immediately succeeding the limit, *after*: Gn 38^{24} כְּמִשְׁלֹשׁ חֳדָשִׁים *after* about three months it was told Judah, מִיָּמִים רַבִּים †Jos 23^{1} Ez 38^{8}, מִיָּמִים *after* (some) days, †Ju 11^{4} 14^{8} 15^{1}, מִיֹּמַיִם *after* two days †Ho 6^{2}; מֵרֹב יָמִים Is 24^{22}: more freq. with קֵץ or קָצֶה, Gn 4^{3} מִקֵּץ יָמִים, 8^{3} Jos 3^{2} +oft.; Dt 14^{28} מִקְצֵה שָׁלֹשׁ שָׁנִים, 15^{1} מִקֵּץ שֶׁבַע שָׁנִים (by which is meant not the actual *end* of the three or seven years, but the period when the third or seventh year has arrived); מִמָּחֳרַת *after* the morrow (had arrived) = *on* the morrow, Gn 19^{34}+oft.; מֵהַבֹּקֶר 2 S 2^{27}.—2 S 23^{4} מִמָּטָר; Is 53^{11} מֵעֲמַל נַפְשׁוֹ; perhaps 29^{18} (Kö^{581}). Cf. 2 S 20^{5} and he delayed מן־המועד *beyond* the appointed time. **c.** in such phrases, however, מִן sometimes (cf. **1 c**) loses its signif.: thus מֵאָז 2 S 15^{34} Is 16^{13} not *from* former time, but *in* former time, formerly, Gn 6^{4} הַגִּבֹּרִים אֲשֶׁר מֵעוֹלָם which were *of old*, Jos 24^{2} dwelt *of old*, ψ 77^{6} days מִקֶּדֶם *aforetime*, מֵאַחֲרֵי Dt 29^{21} (p. 30).—†מִקָּרוֹב lit. *from near*, i.e. recently Dt 32^{17}, of short duration Jb 20^{5}, shortly Ez 7^{8}; at hand (in a *local* sense, **1 c**) Je 23^{23}.

5. (וְעַד) מִן ... עַד *from ... even to*: very oft.:—**a.** in geogr. or local sense, Gn 10^{19} 15^{18} מנהר מצרים עד הנהר הגדול, 25^{18} Ex 23^{31} Dt 2^{36} 1 S 3^{20} 2 S 5^{25} Je 31^{38} ψ 72^{8}+oft.; so with מִלְּבוֹא †1 K 8^{65} (2 Ch 7^{8}), 2 K 14^{25} Am 6^{14}; Dt 13^{8} מִקְצֵה הָאָרֶץ וְעַד קְצֵה הָאָרֶץ, 28^{64} Je 12^{12}; Gn 47^{21} מִקְצֵה גְבוּל־מִצְרַיִם וְעַד־קָצֵהוּ, 1 K 6^{24} 7^{23} מִשְּׂפָתוֹ וְעַד שְׂפָתוֹ; Lv 13^{12} מראשׁו ועד רגליו, Dt 28^{35} מכף רגלך ועד קדקדך (similarly 2 S 14^{25} Jb 2^{7} Is 1^{6}). Cf. 1 S 9^{2} מִשִּׁכְמוֹ וָמַעְלָה, 2 S 5^{9} Jos 15^{46}. **b.** metaph. not of actual space, but of *classes of objects*, to express idiomatically the idea of *comprehension*, so that the two preps. may be often represented by *both ... and*: Gn 19^{4} מִנַּעַר וְעַד־זָקֵן *from* young *to* old (i.e. both included) = *both* young *and* old, v^{11} 1 S 5^{9}+ מִקָּטֹן וְעַד־גָּדוֹל = *both* great *and* small, Je 6^{13} מִקְּטַנָּם וְעַד־גְּדוֹלָם *from* the least

of them *even to* the greatest of them, ib. מִנָּבִיא וְעַד־כֹּהֵן *from* the proph *even to* the priest every one dealeth falsely, Ex 9^{25}+ מאדם ועד בהמה *both* man *and* beast, 11^{5} מבכור פרעה . . . עד מחטב עציך ,בכור השפחה וגו׳ 13^{15} Nu 6^{4} Dt 29^{10} ,עד שאב מימיך, Jos 8^{25}+ מאיש ועד אשה, 1 S 15^{3} (4 pairs), 22^{19} 1 K 5^{13} 2 K 17^{9} = 18^{8}, Is 10^{18} מנפש ועד בשׂר = *both* soul *and* body, Je 9^{9}; after a word implying a negative = *either . . . or* Gn 14^{23} 31$^{24.29}$ מטוב עד רע *either* good *or* evil. The עד may be repeated, if required: Gn 6^{7} מאדם עד־בהמה עד רמש ועד־עוף השמים (so 7^{23}), Ex 22^{3} Jos 6^{21} Ju 15^{5} ,מִגָּדִישׁ וְעַד־קָמָה וְעַד־כֶּרֶם זָיִת, 20^{48} 1 S 30^{19}. without מן, Lv 11^{42} Nu 8^{4}. Similar is the use of מן in the idiom מִבֶּן . . . שָׁנָה וָמַעְלָה (וָמָטָּה) (also וְעַד־בֶּן . . . שָׁנָה): v p 122^{a}, and cf. 2 K 3^{21}. **c.** of *time*, Gn 46^{34} מִנְּעוּרֵינוּ וְעַד עַתָּה *from* our youth even until now, 1 S 12^{2} Je 3^{25}, Nu 14^{19}; Ex 10^{6}, 18^{13} ,מִן־הַבֹּקֶר עַד־הָעָרֶב, 1 S 30^{17} 1 K 18^{26}, Is 9^{6} ψ 90^{2}; +oft, with two inff Hos 7^{4}. and implying *intervals* (not duration) Ez 4$^{10.11}$ (cf with ל Est 3^{7}) **d.** there occur further (1) מִן . . . אֶל־, Jos 15^{21}, Ex 26^{28} = 36^{33} מִן־הַקָּצֶה אֶל־הַקָּצֶה *from* end *to* end, Ez 40$^{23.27}$ Ezr 9^{11} ; מִפֶּה־אֶל־פֶּה ψ 144^{13} מִזַּן אֶל זַן *from* kind *to* kind = kinds of every sort; with a verb of motion, Je 48^{11} ψ 105^{13} 1 Ch 17^{5}, and expressing a climax, ψ 84^{8} יֵלְכוּ מֵחַיִל אֶל־חָיִל, Je 9^{2} (cf Rom 1^{17}): of time, מיום־אל־יום + Nu 30^{15}, cf 1 Ch 16^{23} (‖ ψ 96^{2} לְ); implying *intervals,* מֵעֵת אֶל־עֵת + 1 Ch 9^{25} (2) מִן . . . לְ Ex 32^{27} Ez 40^{13} Zc 14^{10} of time ψ 96^{2}, Jb 4^{20}: with *intervals*, 2 S 14^{26}. (3) מִן . . . ־ָה Nu 34^{10} Ez 6^{14} ממדבר רִבְלָתָה (so Ges Ew Hi etc.) *from* the wilderness *to* Riblah, 21^{3} 25^{13} מתימן ודְּדָנָה (Co Ko Berthol), without ־ָה, 1 K 5^{1}. And of time in the phrase (implying *intervals*) מִיָּמִים יָמִימָה Ex 13^{10}+4 t

6. In *comparisons, beyond, above,* hence in Engl *than:* so constantly; viz. **a.** when an object is compared with another distinct from itself, Ju 14^{18} מַה־מָּתוֹק מִדְּבַשׁ what is sweet *away from, beyond, in excess of,* honey? i e. in our idiom, what is *sweeter than* honey? Lv 21^{10} הַכֹּהֵן הַגָּדוֹל מֵאֶחָיו the priest that is great *above* his brethren, Nu 14^{12} Ez 28^{3} חָכָם מִדָּנִאֵל wiser *than* Daniel, ψ 119^{72}+very oft., Ho 2^{9} ,כִּי טוֹב לִי אָז מֵעָתָּה, with an inf (sts c לְ) as subj, Gn 29^{19} טוב תתי אֹתָהּ לָךְ מתתי אתה וגו׳ better is my giving her to thee *than* my giving her to another, Ex 14^{12} 1 S 15^{22} Pr 21$^{9.19}$ 25^{7} ψ 118$^{8.9}$+; with verbs, Gn 19^{9} עתה נָרַע לְךָ מהם now we will harm thee *beyond* them, *more than* them, 25^{23} ,לאם מלאם יֶאֱמָץ, 26^{16} 29^{30} ויאהב גם־את־רחל מלאה, יִגְדַּל מִמֶּנּוּ 48^{19}, צָדְקָה מִמֶּנִּי 38^{26}, Ju 2^{19} השחיתו מאבותם they have done corruptly *more than* their fathers, 1 S 2^{29} 2 S 20^{6} 1 K 1^{37} 14^{9} Je 5^{3} Ez 5^{6}+oft, = *in preference to, above,* ψ 45^{8} 52$^{5.5}$ Ho 6^{6} Hb 2^{16}, after בחר Je 8^{3} Jb 7^{15} 36^{21} ψ 84^{11} (מדור)+: note also נפל מן Jb 12^{3} 13^{2} = inferior *to* (Ew Ges: al Hi; al. De); שׁנה מן different *from* Est 1^{7} 3^{8}. **b.** when an obj. is compared with a group or multitude of which it forms one, esp. with מכל, Gn 3^{1} עָרוּם מכל חַיַּת הַשָּׂדֶה subtil *out of* all beasts of the field, or *beyond, above* all (other) beasts, v^{14} cursed *above* all cattle (but without implying any judgment whether other cattle are cursed likewise), 37^{3} Israel loved Joseph מִכָּל־בָּנָיו *out of* all his sons, or *above* all his (other) sons, Dt 7^{7} 33^{24} בָּרוּךְ מִבָּנִים אָשֵׁר blessed above sons be Asher, Ju 5^{24} תְּבֹרַךְ מִנָּשִׁים blessed *above* women be Jael, 1 S 9^{2b} 15^{33} ,כֵּן תִּשְׁכַּל מִנָּשִׁים אִמֶּךָ, 18^{30} Je 17^{9} עָקֹב מכל deceitful *above* all things, ψ 45^{3} Ct 5^{10} דָּגוּל מרבבה (cf בָּחַר מִן supr. **2 a** *c.* *ex* in eximius, egregius; Il. 18^{431} ὅσσ', ἐμοὶ ἐκ πάσεων Κρονίδης Ζεὺς ἄλγε' ἔδωκεν, 3^{227} ἔξοχος Ἀργείων . . . κεφαλήν) **c.** sometimes in poetry the idea on which מן is logically dependent, is unexpressed, and must be understood by the reader, Is 10^{10} ופסיליהם מירושלם and their idols are (more) *than* (those of) Jerusalem, Mi 7^{4} יָשָׁר מִמְּסוּכָה the uprightest is (sharper) *than* a thorn-hedge (but We *from*), Jb 11^{7} 28^{18}; ψ 4^{8} מֵעֵת *beyond* (that of) the time when etc Ec 4^{17} 9^{17}, cf. Ez 15^{2}. **d.** מן not unfrequently expresses the idea of a thing being *too much for* a person, or surpassing his powers. Gn 18^{14} הֲיִפָּלֵא מי׳ דָּבָר can a thing be *too hard for* J? (so Dt 17^{8}+, cf. ψ 131^{1} 139^{6}+), 32^{11} קָטֹנְתִּי מִן, Dt 14^{24} כִּי יִרְבֶּה מִמְּךָ הַדֶּרֶךְ = is *too great for* thee (1 K 19^{7}), 32^{47} רק מכם : so c עָצַם Gn 26^{16}, כָּבֵד be *too heavy for* Ex 18^{18} ψ 38^{5}, מָךְ Lv 27^{8} (too poor to pay), קָשָׁה Dt 1^{17}, צַר be *too narrow for,* 2 K 6^{1} Is 49^{19}, קצר Is 50^{2}, אָמֵץ ψ 18^{18}, ירום ממני is *too high for* me 61^{3}, 65^{4} גָּבַר, הַמְעַט מִמְּךָ +Jb 15^{11} *too little for* thee? הַמְעַט מִכֶּם +Nu 16^{9} Is 7^{13} Ez 34^{18} (v מְעַט; also on 16^{20}); oft. with an inf, as Gn 4^{13} גָּדוֹל עֲוֹנִי מִנְּשׂוֹא is *greater than* I can bear, 36^{7} their substance was רַב מִשֶּׁבֶת יַחְדָּו lit. *great beyond* dwelling together = *too great for* (their) dwelling together, Ex 12^{4} Ju 7^{2} רַב מתתי = *too great for* me to give, 1 S 25^{17b} 1 K 8^{64} ,רַב מֵהָכִיל, Is 28^{20} 33^{19} 59^{1} Hb 1^{13} ψ 40^{6} Ru

1^{12}: note esp. רַב מִן it is *more than that* . . . (= there is enough of), Ex 9^{28} 1 K 12^{28}, sq. subst. Ez 44^{6} (v. רַב); and Is 49^{6} נָקֵל מִהְיוֹתְךָ לִי עֶבֶד לְהָקִים וגו׳ *too light for thy being* my servant was it to raise up, etc., Ez 8^{17} הֲנָקֵל לְבֵית יִשׂר׳ מֵעֲשׂוֹת וגו׳ was it *too trifling* to the house of Isr. *for* the doing etc. (less than the doing etc. deserved)? (but ?rd. עֲשׂוֹת on anal. of 1 K 16^{31}).

7. מִן is prefixed to an *infin.*: **a.** with a *causal* force (rare), *from, on account of, through* (cf. **2 f**): Dt $7^{7.8}$ מֵאַהֲבַת י׳ אֶתְכֶם *through* J.'s loving you = *because* J. *loved* you, 9^{28} (cf. 1^{27} בְּ) 2 S 3^{11} מִיִּרְאָתוֹ אֹתוֹ = *because* he feared him, Is 48^{4} . . . מִדַּעְתִּי = *because* I knew . . . So in מִבִּלְתִּי, מִבְּלִי . . . . **b.** after verbs implying *restraint, prevention, cessation*, etc., as עֲצָרַנִי מִלֶּדֶת Gn 16^{2} hath restrained me *from* bearing, 29^{35} וַתַּעֲמֹד מִלֶּדֶת 30^{9}: so with חשׂך 20^{6} +, חדל Ex 23^{5} +, כָּלָה 34^{33} +, נִכְלָא 36^{6}, מָנַע 1 S 25^{26} +, שָׁמְרוּ מִן־הַחֵרֶם Je 31^{36} +, יָרֵא מֵהַבִּיט Ex 3^{6} +, שׁבת †Jos 6^{18}, 2 Ch 25^{13} הֵשִׁיב מִלֶּכֶת. Esp. (*a*) after similar verbs, expressing concisely a *negative consequence*, lit. *away from* . . ., i.e. *so as not to, so that not*: Gn 23^{6b} 27^{1} Jacob's eyes were dim, מֵרְאֹת *away from* seeing = *so that* he could not see, 31^{29} נִשָּׁמֶר מִן (‖ v^{24} פֶּן), Ex 14^{5} Lv 26^{13} Nu 32^{7} Dt 28^{55} (his eye shall be envious etc.) מִתֵּת *from* giving = *so that he will not* give, Ju 6^{27} 1 S 2^{31} 7^{8} do not be silent from us מִזְּעֹק *so as not to* call (cf. 1 K 22^{3}), 8^{7} me have they rejected מִמְּלֹךְ עליהם, 16^{1} (Ho 4^{6}), 2 S 14^{11} (rd. מֵהַרְבּוֹת), Is 5^{6} 8^{11} 21^{3} 23^{1} is destroyed מִבּוֹא *so that none* can enter in, 24^{10} 33^{15} 44^{18} 49^{15} 54^{9} 56^{6} 58^{13} Je 10^{14} נִבְעַר . . . מִדַּעַת is stupefied *so that he has no knowledge*, 13^{14} $33^{21.24.26}$ Ez 20^{17} Mi 3^{6} Zc $7^{11.12}$ ψ 30^{4} Qr, 39^{2} 69^{24} 102^{5} (after שָׁכַח, peculiarly), 106^{23} La 3^{44} 4^{18} Jb 34^{30a} 2 Ch 36^{13}. So in חָלִילָה־לִּי מֵעֲשׂוֹת *that I should not* do Gn 44^{17} +. (*b*) still more concisely, esp. in poetry, with a noun alone: 1 S 15^{23} has rejected thee מִמֶּלֶךְ *from* (being) king (v^{26} מִהְיוֹת מֶלֶךְ), Lv 26^{43} מֵהֶם, Is 7^{8} יֵחַת מֵעָם shall be shattered *from* (being) a people, *that it be no more* a people, 17^{1} מוּסָר מֵעִיר, 25^{2b} 52^{14} כֵּן מִשְׁחַת מֵאִישׁ מַרְאֵהוּ marred *away from* (being) a man('s), Je 2^{25} מִיָּחֵף, 17^{16} מֵרֹעֶה, 48^{2} וְנַכְרִיתֶנָּה מִגּוֹי, v^{42} מֵעָם, ψ 8^{6} hast made him lack but little מֵאלהים *ut non esset* Deus, 83^{5} מִגּוֹי, Pr 30^{2} בַּעַר אָנֹכִי מֵאִישׁ *too* boorish *to be* a man; cf. Dn 4^{13}; 1 K 15^{13} וַיְסִרֶהָ מִגְּבִירָה removed her *from* (being) queen-mother, Ez 16^{41} וְהִשְׁבַּתִּיךְ מִזּוֹנָה; and even to express absol. the non-existence of a thing not named in the principal clause, as Is 23^{1} כִּי שֻׁדַּד מִבַּיִת *so that there is no* house, Ez 12^{19} (32^{15}), 25^{9} מֵהֶעָרִים, Ho $9^{11.11.11.12}$ Mi 3^{6} Hg 1^{10} Zc 7^{14} 9^{8} ψ 39^{3} 49^{15} מִזְּבֻל־לוֹ, מִטַּל *so that it has no* dwelling, 52^{7} יִסָּחֲךָ מֵאֹהֶל pluck thee up *tentless*, 109^{24} is lean מִשָּׁמֶן *so that there is no* fatness, Jb 28^{11} 33^{21} 34^{30b}. Oft. strengthened by pleon. אֵין or בְּלִי, as מֵאֵין יוֹשֵׁב Is 5^{9}, מִבְּלִי יוֹשֵׁב v. pp. 35^{a}, 115^{b}. Cf. Kö$^{iii. 592 ff.}$ **c.** with a *temporal* force, *since, after* (cf. **4**), chiefly late: Nu 24^{23} מִשֻּׂמוֹ אֵל *after* God's establishing him, Is 44^{7} מִשּׂוּמִי עַם־עוֹלָם *since* I appointed the ancient people, Ho 7^{4} Hg 2^{16} (?) Ru 2^{18} Ne 5^{14} 1 Ch 8^{8} מִן־שִׁלְחוֹ אוֹתָם (cf. 6^{16}) 2 Ch 31^{10} Dn 11^{23} 12^{1} (cf. 9^{25}), ψ 73^{20} כַּחֲלוֹם מֵהָקִיץ *after* (one's) awaking, Jb 20^{4}.

8. Once Dt 33^{11} as a **conj.** before a finite verb. Smite . . . his haters מִן־יְקוּמוּן *that* they rise not again, poet. for מִקּוּם (**7 b**): cf. Dr$^{\S 41}$.—On מֵאֲשֶׁר **adv.** and **conj.**, v. p. 84.

9. In compounds:—**a.** מֵאַחֲרֵי, מֵאֵת, מִבֵּין, מִבַּלְעֲדֵי, מִבַּעַד, מִכָּל (common in NH, esp. before inf.; in O.T. only in מִלְּבַד, מִלְּבוֹא (supr. **5 a**), מִלְמַעְלָה, מִלְמַטָּה, מִלְּעֻמַּת, מִלְּפָנִים, מִלִּפְנֵי, and, si vera l., מִלְמַעְלֵה הֶחָרֶס Jd 8^{13}, v. מַעֲלֶה), מִנֶּגֶד, מֵעַל, מֵעִם, מִתַּחַת; see אַחֲרֵי, אֵת, etc. **b.** לְמִן (לְמִנִּי +Mi $7^{12.12}$), with לְ pleon., *from* = מִן, but used almost exclusively of the *terminus a quo*, whether of space or time (cf. מִן **5**);—(1) of *space*, Dt 4^{32} Ju 20^{1} לְמִדָּן וְעַד־בְּאֵר שֶׁבַע, Mi $7^{12.12}$ (both לְמִנִּי), Zc 14^{10} 1 Ch 5^{9}; לְמֵרָחוֹק *from* afar Jb 36^{3} 39^{29} (on Ezr 3^{13} 2 Ch 26^{15}, v. sub עַד לְ); לְמִתַּחַת לְ = *underneath* 1 K 7^{32}. Idiom., esp. sq. וְעַד, to denote comprehensively an entire class, לְמֵאִישׁ וְעַד בְּהֵמָה +Ex 11^{7} Je 51^{62} (לְמֵאָדָם), לְמִקָּטֹן וְעַד גָּדוֹל, לְמֵאִישׁ וְעַד אִשָּׁה +2 S 6^{19} 2 Ch 15^{13}, †2 K 23^{2} Je 42^{8}, simil. 2 Ch 15^{13} Je 31^{34} Est $1^{5.20}$, לְמִבֶּן עֶשְׂרִים שָׁנָה +2 S 13^{22} לְמֵרַע וְעַד־טוֹב, וּלְמַטָּה +1 Ch 27^{23}, cf. 2 Ch 25^{5}.—On לְמִבֵּית Nu 18^{7}, see p. 110^{b}. (2) of *time* (oft. foll. by עַד), לְמִן הַיּוֹם אֲשֶׁר . . . *from* the day when . . ., †Dt 4^{32} 9^{7} 2 S 7^{11} (‖ 1 Ch 17^{10} וּלְמִיָּמִים אֲשֶׁר) Je 7^{25} 32^{31} Hg 2^{18}; לְמִקְצָת הַיָּמִים אֲשֶׁר . . . †Dn 1^{18}; לְמִן הַיּוֹם sq. inf. (in appos.) †Ex 9^{18} 2 S 19^{25}; לְמִיּוֹם sq. inf. (genit.) †Ju 19^{30} 2 S 7^{6} Is 7^{17}; לְמִימֵי . . . †2 K 19^{25} (‖ Is 37^{26} מימי) Mal 3^{7}; לְמִן־עולם ועד עולם +Je 7^{7} 25^{5}; לְמֵרָחוֹק *from* afar = long before, 2 S 7^{19} = 1 Ch 17^{17}, 2 K 19^{25} = Is 37^{26}.

מְנָאוֹת v. מְנָת sub מנה.

[מְנִגִינָה] v. נגן.

†**מָנָה** **vb.** count, number, reckon, **assign** (NH *id.*; As *manû* Dl$^{HWB\ 416}$; Ar مَنَى *assign, apportion;* Aram. ܡܢܳܐ, מְנָא);—**Qal** *Pf.* מָנָה Nu 23^{10}, וּמָנִיתִי Is 65^{12}; *Impf.* 2 ms תִּמְנֶה־ 1 K 20^{25}; וַיִּמְנוּ 2 K 12^{11}; *Imv.* מנה 2 S 24^{1}; *Inf cstr.* לִמְנוֹת Gn 13^{16} + 4 t; *Pt* מוֹנֶה Je 33^{13} ψ 147^{4},—**1.** *count, number* (cf סָפַר) dust (grains) Gn 13^{16} (J), cf. עֲפַר יַעֲקֹב Nu 23^{10} (JE); money 2 K 12^{11}; stars (מ׳ מִסְפָּר לַכּוֹכָבִים) ψ 147^{4}, flock Je 33^{13} (symb of peace); days ψ 90^{12}, people, army 2 S 24^{1} 1 Ch $21^{1\ 17}$, cf. 27^{24} (object om), 1 K 20^{25}. **2.** *reckon, assign, appoint* לַחֶרֶב Is 65^{12} (with play on מְנִי v^{11}). **Niph.** *Pf.* נִמְנָה Is 53^{12}; *Impf* יִמָּנֶה Gn 13^{16} 1 K 3^{8}, יִמָּנוּ 1 K 8^{5} = 2 Ch 5^{6}; *Inf. cstr* הִמָּנוֹת Ec 1^{15};—**1.** *be counted, numbered,* of descendants Gn 13^{16} (J), of people 1 K 3^{8} (‖ יִסָּפֵר); of sacrificial animals 1 K 8^{5} = 2 Ch 5^{6} (both ‖ *id*), indef. Ec 1^{15}. **2.** *be reckoned, assigned* (a place), of servant of י׳ Is 53^{12} (c. אֶת פֹּשְׁעִים). **Pi.** (late and poet) (B Aram and 𝔗 מַנִּי);—*Pf.* מִנָּה Dn $1^{10\ 11}$; מִנּוּ Jb 7^{3}, *Impf.* וַיְמַן Jon 2^{1} + 4 t; *Imv.* מַן ψ 61^{8}, *appoint, ordain,* food Dn 1^{10}, v^{5} (sq. לְ), officer v^{11} (sq. עַל); nights of weariness (לֵילוֹת עָמָל) Jb 7^{3} (subj indef.; sq לְ); in story of Jonah, obj. fish Jon 2^{1}, ricinus 4^{6}, worm v^{7}, wind v^{8} (all subj. י׳); obj חֶסֶד וֶאֱמֶת ψ 61^{8} (subj י׳) **Pu.** *Pt* pl מְמֻנִּים 1 Ch 9^{29} *appointed,* of porters (sq. עַל).

†**מָנָה** **n f.** part, portion;—מ׳ Ex 29^{26} + 4 t; (on מְנָת־ Je 13^{25}, cf ψ 16^{5}, v. מְנָת), pl. מָנוֹת 1 S 1^{4} + 5 t., sf. מָנוֹתֶהָ Est 2^{9};—*part, portion,* esp. choice portion, Ex 29^{26} Lv 7^{33} 8^{29} (all of sacrificial animal; all P); cf 2 Ch 31^{19}; also 1 S $1^{4.5}$, of distrib of choice bits Ne $8^{10\ 12}$ Est $9^{19\ 22}$, cf also Est 2^{9} (v Dn $1^{5\ 10}$)

†**מָנֶה** **n.m.** maneh, mina, a weight (perh. orig *a specific part;* NH *id;* As. *manû* Dl $^{HWB\ 417}$; Aram ܡܢܝܐ, מַנְיָא);—מ׳ Ez 45^{12}; מָנִים 1 K 10^{17} + 3 t, = 50 shekels Ez 45^{12} (on חֲמִשִּׁים for חֲמִשָּׁה v. Hi Co); of gold 1 K 10^{17}; of silver Ezr 2^{69} Ne $7^{71\ 72}$.—The weight of the mina was $\frac{1}{60}$ of talent, i e acc. to older (Bab.) standard, 982·2 grammes (= 60 shekels at c. 16·37 g) = c 2 lbs.; in Ezekiel's time the mina = 50 shekels = 818 6 g. = c. $1\frac{2}{3}$ lb (cf. כִּכָּר, שֶׁקֶל). Vid Benz$^{Arch.\ 187\ ff\ 194}$ Now$^{Arch\ i.\ 208\ f.}$

†**[מֹנֶה]** **n.[m.]** counted number, time;—only הֶחֱלִיף . . . עֲשֶׂרֶת מֹנִים Gn $31^{7\ 41}$ *changed ten times*

†**מְנִי** **n.pr.div.** Meni, god of fate (*award, apportionment;* cf Ar. n. pr div. *Maniyyât,* and perh. *Manât,* We$^{Skizzen\ iii.\ 22\ f.\ 189}$, مَنَوَاتُ No ZMG xl 1886,709; in Nab מנותו Eut$^{Nab\ No.\ 2,\ l.\ 5}$, etc.),—הַמְמַלְאִים לַמְנִי מִמְסָךְ Is 65^{11} (‖ לַגַּד)—v. Che Di Bae Sem. Rel 79.

†**[מְנָת]** **n.f.** portion (= מָנָה, chiefly late; on form cf. Ges$^{§ 95\ n}$ Lag$^{BN\ 81,\ 150}$),—cstr. מְנָת 2 Ch 31^{3} + 5 t; *Pl.* cstr. מְנָאוֹת Ne 12^{44}; מְנָיוֹת Ne 12^{47} 13^{10},—*portion* of king, for sacrifice, 2 Ch 31^{3}; of priest v^{4}; also Ne 12^{44} מְנָאוֹת הַתּוֹרָה לַכֹּ׳, of Levites 13^{10}; of singers 12^{47}; fig. מְנָת כּוֹסָם ψ 11^{6} (of judgment of wicked), cf. מ׳ שֻׁעָלִים ψ 63^{11}; so מְנָת־מִדַּיִךְ Je 13^{25} *portion of thy measure* = thine allotted portion; rd. also מְנָתוֹ(-ה) for מִנֵּהוּ ψ 68^{24} (so Ol Dy Bi Che We); in good sense, י׳ מְנָת חֶלְקִי וְכוֹסִי ψ 16^{5} *is the portion of my lot and my cup*

†**תִּמְנָה, תִּמְנָתָה** **n.pr.loc.** (prob. = *portion, territory*),—(תִּמְנָה) Jos $15^{10\ 57}$ 2 Ch 28^{18}; תִּמְנָתָה [as nomin. v. GFM$^{Ju\ 14,\ 1}$] Jos 19^{43} Ju $14^{1\ 2.5}$; c ה loc. תִּמְנָתָה Gn $38^{12\ 13\ 14}$ Ju $14^{1.5}$, 𝔊 Θαμνα, Θαμναθα):—**1.** place in hill-country of Judah Gn $38^{12\ 13\ 14}$ prob = Jos 15^{57} Site unknown (cf. Di$^{Gn\ 38,\ 12}$ Rob$^{BR\ ii\ 17\ n}$) **2.** place on border of Judah Jos 15^{10} 19^{43} (assigned to Dan), Ju $14^{1.2.5.5}$ 2 Ch 28^{18}. Mod. *Tibneh,* c. 15 m. S. of W. fr. Jerusalem cf. Rob$^{BR\ ii\ 17}$ Buhl$^{Geogr\ 196}$.

†**תִּמְנִי** **adj.gent.** הַתּ׳ Ju 15^{6} *the Timnite.*

†**תִּמְנַת חֶרֶס** **n.pr.loc.** (prob = (sacred) *territory of the Sun;* WMM$^{As.\ u.\ Eur\ 165}$ thinks perh. Eg. *Ḥi-ra-tà*); in hill-country of Ephr., westward, Ju 2^{9} = foll (cf. GFM) = Θαμναθα 1 Makk 9^{50} = mod. *Tibneh,* c. 17 m. W. of N. fr. Jerusalem, v also Buhl$^{Geogr\ 170}$.

†**תִּמְנַת סֶרַח** **n pr.loc.** by metath. from foregoing, to avoid idolatr. suggestion (GFM $^{Ju\ 2,\ 9}$), Jos 19^{50} 24^{30}.

מִנְהָג v. נהג. **[מִנְהָרָה]** v. II. נהר.

מָנוֹד v. נוד

I, II. **מְנוּחָה, מָנוֹחַ** v. נוח.

†**מָנוֹן** **n.m.** dub.; only in וְאַחֲרִיתוֹ יִהְיֶה מ׳ Pr 29^{21} Ew Now *thankless one* (Eth. ምንን: Di^{189}),

De "*Brutstatte*" i.e. father of numerous progeny (√נק); < Be Str (who cites A. Müller), cf. Wild., rd. מָדוֹן *strife*.

מְנוּסָה, מָנוֹס v. נוס. מָנוֹר v. ניר.

מְנוֹרָה v. נור. [מִנְּזָרִים] v. נזר.

מנח (√of foll.; cf. Ar. مَنَحَ *lend, give a gift*, مِنْحَة *loan, gift* esp. of she camel, sheep, or goat for milking, Ph. מנחת, *gift, offering*).

מִנְחָה [211] **n.f. gift, tribute, offering** (NH *id.*; Ph. מנחת; 𝔗 מִנְחָתָא; on Ar. v. supr.);—abs מ׳ Gn 4^{3}+81 t.; cstr. מִנְחַת Lv 2^{7}+22 t.; sf. מִנְחָתִי Gn 33^{10}+3 t.;+41 t. sfs. sg.; pl. sf. מִנְחֹתֶיךָ ψ 20^{4}; מנחתיכם Nu 29^{39} Am 5^{22};—**†1.** *gift, present* Gn $32^{14\ 19\ 21.22}$(E), 33^{10} $43^{11\ 15.25.26}$ (J), Ju 6^{18} 1 S 10^{27} 1 K 10^{25}=2 Ch 9^{24} 2 K $8^{8.9}$ 20^{12}=Is 39^{1}, ψ 45^{13} 2 Ch 32^{23}. **†2.** *tribute* Ju $3^{15\ 17\ 18.18}$ 2 S $8^{2.6}$=1 Ch $18^{2.6}$, 1 K 5^{1} 2 K $17^{3.4}$ 2 Ch $17^{5\ 11}$ 26^{8} Ho 10^{6} ψ 72^{10}. **†3.** *offering* made to God, of any kind, whether grain or animals Gn $4^{3.4.5}$ Nu 16^{15} (J), 1 S $2^{17\ 29}$ 26^{19} Is 1^{13} ψ 96^{8} Zp 3^{10}; + (prob.) (לְ)עֲלוֹת הַמִּנְחָה 1 K $18^{29\ 36}$ 2 K 3^{20} (Ephr.; usually regarded as = מִנְחַת עֶרֶב, but that much later usage). This gen. meaning poss. also in foll.: זבח ומנחה 1 S 2^{29} (see v^{29b}), 3^{14} Is 19^{21}; עלה ומנחה Je 14^{12}; ‖ עולה ψ 20^{4}; ‖שְׁלָמִים Am 5^{22} (עלות gloss, to explain אֲרִיחַ); or these may shew early stage of discrimination. **†4.** *grain offering* (whether raw, roasted, ground to flour, or prepared as bread or cakes, see below. AV *meat offering*, misleading < RV *meal-offering*. GFM [Judges 322] renders *cereal oblation*);—יָבִיאוּ אֶת־הַמִּנְחָה בִּכְלִי טָהוֹר Is 66^{20} *they bring the grain offering in clean vessels* (restored Jews are brought as such an offering), cf. מנחה טהורה Mal 1^{11}; brought in hands Je 41^{5} (late addit. Co); received from hands Mal 1^{10}; חִטִּים למנחה 1 Ch 21^{23} *wheat for grain offering*; סֹלֶת 1 Ch 23^{29}, mixed with oil Ez 46^{14}, baked v^{20}; disting. from other offerings 1 K $8^{64.64}$=2 Ch 7^{7}, 2 K $16^{13.15\ 15\ 15}$ Is 43^{23} 57^{6} 66^{3} Je 17^{26} 33^{18} 41^{5} (late editors Co), Ez 42^{13} 44^{29} $45^{15\ 17\ 17.25}$ Dn 9^{27} ψ 40^{7}; used alone Ne $13^{5\ 9}$ Ez 45^{24} $46^{5.5.7\ 11\ 14.14\ 15}$ Mal 1^{13} $2^{12\ 13}$ $3^{3.4}$ Ju $13^{19\ 23}$ (R, GFM [Judges 322]); מִנְחַת (הָ)עֶרֶב *evening grain offering* 2 K 16^{15} Ezr $9^{4.5}$ Dn 9^{21} ψ 141^{2}; מנחת הַתָּמִיד *continual grain off.* Ne 10^{34}, cf. Lv 6^{13} Nu 4^{16} (all cases under **4** exilic or post-exilic). **5.** *grain-offering*, always with this meaning in P, in classifications Ex 30^{9} 40^{29} Lv 7^{37} 23^{17} Nu 18^{9} 29^{39} Jos $22^{23.29}$:—**a.** אָבִיב grain in the ear parched with fire, with oil and frankincense Lv $2^{14\ 15}$. **b.** סֹלֶת fine flour with oil and frankincense Lv 2^{1} 6^{7}; elsewhere בְּלוּלָה בַשֶּׁמֶן mingled with oil Lv $14^{10.21}$ 23^{13} Nu 7^{13+10t} 8^{8} $15^{4.6.9}$ Nu 28^{5+6t} $29^{3.9\ 14}$, except sin offering of very poor where offered without oil and frankincense Lv 5^{11-13}. **c.** סֹלֶת baked in an oven as חַלּוֹת perforated cakes, or רְקִיקִים flat cakes Lv 2^{4} 7^{9} Nu 6^{15}, עַל הַמַּחֲבַת *on a flat pan* Lv 2^{5} 6^{14} 7^{9}, or מַרְחֶשֶׁת *frying pan* Lv 2^{7} 7^{9}. All these always unleavened (מַצּוֹת) and mixed with oil and salt Lv 2^{11-13}. **d.** at Pentecost to consecrate new bread, מִנְחָה חֲדָשָׁה *new grain offering* of two loaves of leavened bread Lv $23^{16\ 17}$ Nu 28^{26}. **e.** barley meal without oil or incense; מִנְחַת קְנָאֹת *grain offering of jealousy*, מ׳ זִכָּרוֹן Nu $5^{15\ 18.25}$. Cf. phrases מִנְחַת הַבֹּקֶר *morning oblation* Ex 29^{41} Nu 28^{8}; מ׳ בִּכּוּרִים Lv 2^{14}; קָרְבַּן מ׳ Lv $2^{1.4.13}$, מ׳ בִּכּוּרִים Lv 6^{14}. **6.** vbs. of *offering* are הֵבִיא Gn 4^{3} (J), Lv $2^{2.8}$ (P), Is 1^{13} $66^{20.20}$ Je 17^{26} Mal 1^{13}; הִקְרִיב Lv $2^{1.8.11}$ 6^{7} Nu 5^{25}, עשה Nu 6^{17} 28^{31} 1 K 8^{64}=2 Ch 7^{7}, Ez 45^{24} $46^{7\ 14\ 15}$; הקטיר 2 K $16^{13\ 15}$ Je 33^{18}; העלה Is 57^{6} 66^{3} Je 14^{12}; הגיש Am 5^{25} Mal 2^{12} 3^{3}, הוביל Zp 3^{10}; נשׂא ψ 96^{8}, also (מ׳ = *tribute*) 2 S $8^{2.6}$ and ‖.

מְנֻחָה v מְנוּחָה sub נוח. מְנַחֵם v. נחם.

מָנַחְתִּי, מְנֻחוֹת, מְנֻחַת v. נוח.

מִנִּי v. מנה.

†I. מִנִּי **n.pr.terr.** region of Armenia;—Je 51^{27} (‖ אֲרָרָט, אשכנז); = As. *Mannai* Schr. COT ad loc; KGF 174 212.520.

II מִנִּי, מִנֵּי v. מן. מִנִּי ψ 45^{9} v. I [מֵן].

מְנָיוֹת v. מָנָת sub מנה.

מִנְיָמִין, מִנְיָמִן v. מִיָּמִן.

מִנְלָם v. [מִנְלֶה] sub נלה.

מנן (of foll; Ar. مَنَّ is *praecidit* funem, *diminuit* numerum, *debilitavit*; also *be bounteous*, Qor 3^{158} al., مَنّ *a gift*; whence Zerweck [Präp. Min 4] *assumes* a primary mng. *to separate*—either *from* or *for* ("zutheilen"), as the case might be)

†II [מֵן] **n.[m.] portion** (Sim Hup al.);—מִנֵּהוּ ψ 68^{24}, but rd מְנָתוֹ (ָ—ה) Ol Dy Bi Che We (v. מְנָת supr.)—ψ 45^{9} 154^{4} v. I. מֵן supr.

†מִנִּית **n.pr.loc.** in Ammonite territory, site unknown (4 Rom. m. fr. Heshbon Euseb.

Onom. 253, 33; cf. Buhl $^{Geogr. 266}$);—Ju 11^{33} (𝔊 ἄχρις Ἀρνών, A εἰς Σεμωειθ, 𝔊L Σεμενειθ); חִטֵּי מ׳ Ez 27^{17} *wheat of Minnîth* (cf. wheat fr. Ammon 2 Ch 27^{5}) so Berthol, but dub.; Co conj. חִטִּים וּנְכֹאת *wheat and storax.*

[מְנָסָה] v. מְנוּסָה sub נוס.

†מָנַע **vb. withhold, hold back** (NH *id.*; Zinj. מנע DHM $^{Sendsch. 60}$; Ar. مَنَعَ; Sab. מנע Levy-Os $^{ZMG\ xix.\ 1865,\ 268}$; Aram. מְנַע);—**Qal** *Pf.* מ׳ Gn 30^{2}; sf. מְנָעֲנִי 1 S 25^{34}; מָנַעְתָּ ψ 21^{3} Ne 9^{20}, etc.; *Impf.* יִמְנַע־ ψ 84^{12}; sf. יִמְנָעֵנִי 2 S 13^{13} etc.; *Imv.* מְנַע Pr 1^{15}; מִנְעִי Je 2^{25} 31^{16}; *Pt.* מֹנֵעַ Pr 11^{26} Je 48^{10};—*withhold,* sq. מִן Gn 30^{2} (obj. פְּרִי־בָטֶן), Am 4^{7} (rain), Ne 9^{20} (manna; all subj. י׳); Jb 22^{7} (bread), 1 K 20^{7} (obj. om.; both hum. subj.), so Je 48^{10} (sword), Ec 2^{10} (heart), Je 5^{25} (good), Pr 3^{27} (*id.*), 1^{15} (foot); Je 2^{25} (*id.*) 31^{16} (voice); further, 2 S 13^{13} (woman), Je 42^{4} (knowledge), Jb 31^{16} (poor), Pr 23^{13} (correction), obj. om. י׳ subj. Pr 30^{7}; מִן om. Pr 11^{26} (obj. corn); cf. ψ 21^{3} subj. י׳ (obj. אֲרֶשֶׁת שְׂפָתָיו ‖ נָתַן תַּאֲוַת לִבּוֹ), Jb 20^{13} fig. (wickedness), Ez 31^{15} י׳ subj. (obj. rivers); obj. pers. י׳ subj. sq. מן Nu 24^{11}; sq. מִן + inf. 1 S 25$^{26.34}$; sq. לְ, subj. י׳ ψ 84^{12} (good). **Niph.** *Pf.* נִמְנַע Jo 1^{13}; *Impf.* יִמָּנַע Jb 38^{15}, etc.; *be withholden* sq. מִן, subj. מִנְחָה etc. Jo 1^{13}; light from wicked Jb 38^{15}; Nu 22^{16} (sq. מִן + inf.); subj. showers (רְבִבִים) Je 3^{3}.

†יִמְנָע **n.pr.m.** son of Helem (of Asher) 1 Ch 7^{35}. 𝔊 Ιμανα, 𝔊L Ιαμνα.

†תִּמְנָע **n.pr.m.** and **f.** Edomite name. 𝔊 Θαμνα:—**1.** תִּמְנָע **n.pr.m. a.** a chief of Edom Gn 36^{40} = 1 Ch 1^{51}. **b.** son of Eliphaz 1 Ch 1^{36} (for Korah Gn 36$^{15.16}$). **2.** תִּמְנָע **f.** Gn 36^{22} = 1 Ch 1^{39} sister of Lotan (of Seîr); Gn 3^{12} concubine of Eliphaz son of Esau.

מְנֻעוֹל, [מִנְעָל] v. נעל.

[מַנְעַמִּים] v. נעם.   מְנַעַנְעִים v. נוע.

[מְנַקִּית], מְנַקִּיָּה v. נקה.

מֵינֶקֶת v. ינק **Hiph.**

מְנֹרָה v. מְנוֹרָה sub נור.

מְנַשֶּׁה 136 **n.pr.m. et trib. Manasseh** (interpr. Gn 41^{51} as Pi. causat. √II. נשה q. v.);—מ׳ Gn 46^{20} +; מְנַשֶּׁה 41^{51} + (on Ju 18^{30} v. מֹשֶׁה); c. art. (strangely), הַמְ׳ Jos 1^{12} + 10 t. (v. infr.); 𝔊 Μαν(ν)ασση;—**1.** †**a.** *Manasseh,* eldest son of Joseph Gn 41^{51} 48$^{1.13.14.14.17.20.20}$, also 50^{23} (father of Machir; all E), 46^{20} 48^{5} (both P). **b.** of tribe, oft. + Ephraim (v. אֶפְרַיִם): (1) the part W. of Jordan: †*a.* בְּנֵי מ׳ Jos 16^{9} 17^{2a} (בני־מ׳), v$^{2b.6.12}$ (all JE), 1 Ch 7^{29} 9^{3} (בְּנֵי אֶפְרַיִם וּמ׳); הַנּוֹתָרִים Jos 13^{29} v. infr.); *β.* מ׳ alone, Jos 17$^{5.8.8.9b.11.17}$ Dt 34^{2} (אֶרֶץ אֶפְרַיִם וּמ׳; all JE), 2 Ch 30^{10} (*id.*), Jos 16^{4} 17$^{7.9a.10}$ (all P), also appar. Dt 33^{17} (poem), Ju 1^{27} 6$^{15.35}$ 7^{23} Is 9$^{20.20}$ ψ 80^{3} + 10 t. Chr; †*γ.* מַטֵּה מ׳ 1 Ch 6^{55}; חֲצִי מַטֵּה מ׳ Jos 21$^{6.25}$ 1 Ch 12^{32} (van d. H v^{31}); מַחֲצִית מַטֵּה חֲצִי מ׳ 6^{46} (but on text v. Kit); שְׁנֵי מַטּוֹת מ׳ וְאֶפְרַיִם Jos 14^{4} (P); †*δ.* חֲצִי שֵׁבֶט מ׳ 1 Ch 27^{20}; c. art. הַשֵּׁבֶט הַמְ׳ Jos 13^{7} (D). †(2) of Manasseh E. of Jordan; *a.* בְּנֵי מ׳ Jos 22$^{30.31}$ (P); *β.* מ׳ alone, Ju 11^{29} (distinctly of territory), 12^{4} (but on text v. GFM), ψ 60^{9} = 108^{9}; חֲצִי הַמְ׳ 1 Ch 27^{21}; *γ.* מַטֵּה מ׳ Jos 17^{1a} 20^{8} (both P), 1 Ch 6^{47}; חֲצִי מַטֵּה מ׳ Jos 22^{1} (D), Nu 34^{14} Jos 21$^{5.27}$ (all P), 1 Ch 6^{56}; חֲצִי מַטֵּה בְּנֵי מ׳ Jos 13^{29} (P); *δ.* חֲצִי שֵׁבֶט מ׳ Dt 3^{13} (D), Jos 13^{29} 22$^{13.15}$ (all P), 1 Ch 15$^{18.23.26}$ 12^{38} (van d. H v^{37}); חֲצִי שֵׁבֶט מ׳ בֶּן־יוֹסֵף Nu 32^{33} (P); c. art. חֲצִי שֵׁבֶט הַמְ׳ Jos 1^{12} 4^{12} 12^{6} 18^{7} 22$^{1.7}$ (all D), 22$^{9.10.11.21}$ (all P). Here belong also (chiefly) reff. to מ׳ as father of Machir (cf. Gn 50^{23} supr.): + Nu 27^{1} 32$^{39.40}$ 36^{1} Jos 13^{31} 17$^{1.3}$ (all P), 1 Ch 7$^{14.17}$; and of Jair Dt 3^{14} (D), Nu 32^{41} (P), 1 K 4^{13} (cf. יָאִיר, מָכִיר). †(3) of undivided tribe (never שֵׁבֶט מ׳): *a.* בְּנֵי מ׳ Nu 1^{34} 2^{20} 7^{54} 26^{29} 36^{12} (all P); *β.* מ׳ alone, Nu 1^{10} 26$^{28.34}$ 27^{1b} (all P), Ez 48$^{4.5}$; *γ.* מַטֵּה מ׳ Nu 1^{35} 2^{20} 13^{11}, מַטֵּה בְּנֵי מ׳ Nu 10^{23} 34^{13} (all P). **2.** son of Hezekiah, and king of Judah (As. *Menasê, Minsê* Schr $^{COT\ 2\ K\ 21,\ 1}$);—2 K 20^{21} 21^{1} + 9 t. Kings, 12 t. Chr, Je 15^{4}. †**3.** two who had taken strange wives: **a.** Ezr 10^{30}. **b.** 10^{33}.

†מְנַשִּׁי **adj. gent.** of מ׳ **1**; only c. art. הַמְ׳, as n. coll., of tribe E. of Jordan: Dt 4^{43} 2 K 10^{33}; שֵׁבֶט הַמְ׳ Dt 29^{7} 1 Ch 26^{32}.

מְנָת v. מנה.

†I. מַס **n.m.** $^{1\ K\ 5,\ 27}$ usu. **coll. body of forced labourers, task-workers, labour-band** or **gang,** also (late) **forced service, task-work, serfdom** (𝔗 מִסָּא, esp. in phr. מַסְּקֵי מִסִּין (implying late and [for BH] false sense 'tribute,' so NH מַעֲלֵי מִסִּים; ✓ unknown, prob. loan-wd.; follows anal. of ע״ע);—abs. מ׳ 1 K 5^{27} +; לָמַס Jos 17^{13} +, הַמַּס 2 S 20^{24} +; pl. מִסִּים Ex 1^{11};—**1.** *labour-band, labour-gang,* body of task-workers for public service, formed

by levy upon the people by Sol. וַיַּעַל הַמֶּלֶךְ שְׁלֹמֹה מַס מִכָּל־יִשְׂרָאֵל 1 K 5^{27}, amounting to 30,000 men v^{27}; וַיַּעֲלֵם שׁ׳ 9^{15} הַמ׳ אֲשֶׁר הֶעֱלָה; לְמַס עֹבֵד v^{21} *and Sol. levied them for a toiling labour-band* (cf. Gn 49^{15} Jos 16^{10}) = וַיַּעֲלֵם שׁ׳ לְמַס 2 Ch 8^{8}; appar. instituted, earlier, by David, cf. וַאֲדֹרָם עַל־הַמַּס 2 S 20^{24}, i.e. had charge of the body of labourers, so 1 K 4^{6} 5^{28} 12^{18} = 2 Ch 10^{18}. **2. a.** of *labour-bands, slave-gangs* of Isr. in Egypt, only שָׂרֵי מִסִּים Ex 1^{11} (J) *gang-overseers.* **b.** of conquered populations, subject to forced labour: יִהְיוּ לְךָ לָמַס וַעֲבָדוּךָ Dt 20^{11} cf. Ju $1^{30.33.35}$ (v. GFM), Is 31^{8} La 1^{1}; so ויהי לָמַס עֹבֵד Jos 16^{10} (cf. Gn 49^{15} 1 K 9^{21}); וַיִּתְּנוּ אֶת־הַכְּנַעֲנִי לָמַס Jos 17^{13}, cf. (וַיָּשֶׂם וגו׳) Ju 1^{28}. **3.** in gen: וַיְהִי לְמַס־עֹבֵד Gn 49^{15} *and he* (Issachar) became *a slaving labour-band* (poem in J; cf. Jos 16^{10} 1 K 9^{21}); cf. רְמִיָּה תהיה לָמַס Pr 12^{24} (here appar. of individ.) **4. forced service,** *serfdom* (or poss. (in late passage) *tribute = enforced payment,* cf NH, 𝔗, v. supr.), only of Ahasuerus: וַיָּשֶׂם הַמֶּלֶךְ מַס עַל־הָאָרֶץ וגו׳ Est 10^{1}.

II מַס v. מסס. מֵסַב, מסב v. סבב.

מַסְגֵּרֶת, מסגר v. סגר.

מַסַּד v. יסד [מִסְדְּרוֹן] v. סדר.

†[מָסָה] **vb. melt, dissolve, be liquefied** (Eth መሰወ: *liquefy;* Aram מְסָא *melt away,* ܡܣܐ *dissolve, decay, coagulate,* As *masû* is *wash,* v. also מסס),—only **Hiph.** *Pf.* 3 pl. הִמְסִיו Jos 14^{8} (on form v. Ges $^{§75\,R.\,17}$). *Impf.* sf. יַמְסֵם ψ 147^{18}; 2 ms. וַתֶּמֶס ψ 39^{12}; אַמְסֶה ψ 6^{7},—*cause to dissolve, melt,* ice ψ 147^{18}, hyperb בְּדִמְעָתִי עַרְשִׂי אַמְסֶה ψ 6^{7} *with my tears I cause my bed to dissolve;* וַתֶּמֶס כָּעָשׁ חֲמוּדוֹ ψ 39^{12} = *consume, cause to vanish;* fig. sq. לב = *intimidate* Jos. 14^{8}.

I [מַסָּה] v. מסס. II, III. מַסָּה v. נסה.

[מִסָּה] v. מִסַּת. מַסְוֶה v. סוה.

מסוכה = מְשׂוּכָה v. I. סוך (שׂוך).

†מַסָּח dub. word, only in וּשְׁמַרְתֶּם אֶת־מִשְׁמֶרֶת הַבַּיִת מַסָּח 2 K 11^{6}; Thes al. sub √נסח = *for plucking away,* i. e. repulse, defence, but very uncertain; prob. text. err.; om. 𝔊 ^{B} We Sta $^{p\,304}$; 𝔊L Μεσσαε.

[מִסְחָר] v. סחר.

†מָסַךְ **vb. mix, produce by mixing** (cf. perh. מָזַג, מזג Ba $^{ZS\,33,51}$);—**Qal** *Pf.* 3 ms. מ׳ Is 19^{14}; מָסְכָה Pr 9^{2}; מָסָכְתִּי Pr 9^{5} ψ 102^{10}; *Inf. cstr.* מְסֹךְ Is 5^{22},—**1.** *pour,* only fig., מ׳ בְּקִרְבָּהּ רוּחַ עִוְעִים Is 19^{14} (subj י׳), *mix,* c. acc. שֵׁכָר Is 5^{22}; i. e. make a choice drink by mixing with spices, etc. (mixing with water came later, cf. 2 Macc 15^{39}) Low $^{p\,419}$ Fra $^{162\,f\,171\,f.}$ Now $^{Arch\,1,\,120}$ Benz $^{Arch\,90}$; obj. יַיִן fig., subj. wisdom Pr $9^{2.5}$; שִׁקּוּי בִּבְכִי מָסָכְתִּי ψ 102^{10} *my drink with weeping have I mixed* (v. As. [*akâl*] *ul âkul, bikîtum kurmati, mê ul ašti, dîmtu maštîtî* Zim $^{BP\,34}$).

†מֶסֶךְ **n.[m.] mixture,** i. e. wine mixed with spices; ψ כוס בְּיַד י׳ וְיַיִן חָמַר מָלֵא מ׳ 75^{9} (fig of י׳'s judgment).

†מִמְסָךְ **n.m. mixed drink** (v. מָסַךְ),—מִמְסָךְ Pr 23^{30} *mixed* (wine), as beverage; Is 65^{11} as libation to Menî.

מָסָךְ, [מְסֻכָּה] v. סכך.

I. מַסֵּכָה v. I. נסך.

II. מַסֵּכָה, [מַסֶּכֶת] v. II. נסך.

†מִסְכֵּן **adj.** poor, only Ec (NH *id;* Aram. *id.*, ܡܣܟܝܢܐ PS ^{2632}, Ar. مِسْكِين; Eth ምስኪን: Di ^{382}; √dub; usu. der. fr. III. סכן q.v.; perh. loan-wd; acc to Jen $^{ZA\,iv\,(1889),\,271\,f}$ Zim $^{ib\,vii\,(1892),\,353}$ = As. *muškênu, beggar, needy one*);—alw abs. מ׳ Ec 4^{13} (opp. מֶלֶךְ זָקֵן וּכְסִיל); יֶלֶד מ׳ וְחָכָם—מ׳ 9^{15}, הָאִישׁ הַמ׳ v^{15}; as subst. אִישׁ מ׳ חָכָם v^{16} *the poor man.*

†מִסְכֵּנֻת **n.f. poverty, scarcity,** Dt 8^{9}.

מסכנות v. I. סכן.

מְסִלָּה, מַסְלוּל v. סלל.

[מַסְמֵר], מַסְמְרִים etc. v. סמר (שׂמר).

†[מָסַס] **vb. dissolve, melt, intr.** (𝔗 מְסַס; cf מסה, and II מאס),—**Qal** *Inf. cstr.* כִּמְסֹס נֹסֵס Is 10^{18}; *like the melting* (wasting away) of a נֹסֵס (q.v.) **Niph.** *Pf.* וְנָמַס consec. Ez 21^{12}; וְנָמֵס Ex 16^{21} ψ 112^{10}; נָמַסּוּ ψ 97^{5} + 2 t.; *Impf.* יִמַּס Dt 20^{8} +; וַיִּמַּסּוּ Ju 15^{14}; *Inf. abs.* הִמֵּס 2 S 17^{10}; *cstr id.* ψ 68^{3}; *Pt.* נָמֵס ψ 22^{15} + 2 t.;—**1.** *melt* (intr.) of manna Ex 16^{21}; wax ψ 68^{3} (sim. of wicked); manacles Ju 15^{14} (= *vanished, dropped off*); wicked ψ 112^{10} (*melt away*); esp. of hills and mts Mi 1^{4} ψ 97^{5} Is 34^{3}. **2.** most oft. fig. of heart = *faint, grow fearful,* Na 2^{11} 2 S $17^{10\,10}$ (cf. Dr), Dt 20^{8} Jos 2^{11} 5^{1} 7^{5} Is 13^{7}

19^1 Ez 21^{12} ψ 22^{15}. **3** *Pt.* = *wasted, consumptive* (?), 1 S 15^9 (‖ נִבְזָה) נמבזה, rd נִבְזָה v. בזה **Niph.**) < rd. נְמָאֶסֶת *worthless*, lit. *rejected* (v. מאס **Niph.**) **Hiph.** *Pf* 3 pl הֵמַסּוּ אֶת־לְבָבֵנוּ Dt 1^{28} *cause to melt* (= intimidate).

†II [מָס] **adj. despairing** (lit. *melting*, i e *failing, collapsing*),—לַמָּס Jb 6^{14} *to him who despaireth* belongeth kindness, etc.

†I. [מַסָּה] **n.f. despair** (lit. *melting, failing*);—only לְמַסַּת נקיים ילעַג Jb 9^{23} *at the despair of innocent ones he mocketh*, so 𝔗 Ew Di Bu Du > Ges Hi al *trial* (by calamity), √ נסה.

†תֶּמֶס **n.m. melting** (away);—כְּמוֹ שַׁבְּלוּל ת׳ יַהֲלֹךְ ψ 58^9 like a snail that goeth *into melting* (leaving slimy track)

מַסָּע, I. מַסָּע v. I נסע. II. מַסָּע v. II. נסע.

מִסְעָד v. סעד. מספד v ספד.

מספוא v. ספא.

מִסְפָּחוֹת, מִסְפַּחַת v ספח

I, II מִסְפָּר, מִסְפֶּרֶת v ספר.

†[מָסַר] **vb.** si vera l. **deliver up, offer** (NH מָסַר; Aram ܡܣܰܪ *deliver up, denounce, betray*, מְסַר; Hom$^{ZMG\ xlvi\ 1892,\ 530}$ comp Sab מסר *take away*);—**Qal** *Inf cstr.* לִמְסָר־מַעַל בי׳ Nu 31^{16} *offer* (commit) *a trespass against* י׳, but rd. לִמְעָל, cf Thes Di (v. Nu 5^6 2 Ch 36^{14}). **Niph.** *Impf* וַיִּמָּסְרוּ Nu 31^5 *delivered over to, assigned to* (of warriors), rd. perh וַיִּסָּפְרוּ (𝔊 ἐξηρίθμησαν) cf Thes

מָסֹרֶת, מסרות v. אסר.

[מוּסָר] v. מוּסָר sub יסר.

†מִסַּת **n. sufficiency** (der. obscure · Aram מִיסַת, ܡܣܰܬ, common in 𝔗 𝔖, both absol. and cstr, in sense of *sufficiency, enough*; e.g for Heb רַב 2 S 24^{16} 𝔗, דַּי Ex 36^7 𝔗 𝔖, Ob^5 𝔗 𝔖, for לְפִי Ex 12^4 𝔖; ܡܣܰܬ ܚܰܘܒܳܐ the *amount* of the debt, PS^{2153}),—Dt 16^{10} and thou shalt keep the pilgrimage of weeks מִסַּת נדבת יָדְךָ *acc. to* (adv. acc) *the sufficiency of* the free-will offering of thy hand, which thou shalt give, i e. with the full amount that thou canst afford (cf. די שה Lv 5^7 12^8; 𝔗 כְּמִיסַת אִימְרָא).

מסתור, מִסְתָּר, מַסְתֵּר v. סתר

[מַעְבָּד] v. עבד. [מַעֲבֶה] v. עבה.

[מַעֲבָר], מַעְבָּרָה v. עבר.

מַעְגָּל, מַעְגָּלָה v. עגל.

†[מָעַד] **vb. slip, slide, totter, shake** (only Heb),—**Qal** *Pf* 3 pl. מָעֲדוּ 2 S 22^{37} = ψ 18^{37}; *Impf.* 3 fs. תִּמְעַד ψ 37^{31}; אָמְעָד ψ 26^1; *Pt.* pl. cstr. מוֹעֲדֵי Jb 12^5,—*slip*, subj. feet, (fig.) 2 S 22^{37} = ψ 18^{37}, Jb 12^5; subj. אֲשֻׁרָיו ψ 37^{31}; cf. ψ 26^1. **Pu.** *Pt* מוּעֶדֶת (= מְמֹעֶדֶת Ges$^{§ 52 s}$, or old **Qal** *Pt. pass*,—cf Ba$^{NB\ 273}$;—but pass. not needed here, read perh מֹ׳ **Qal** *Pt act.* v. Schwally$^{ZAW\ x,\ 1890,\ 176}$),—רֶגֶל מ׳ Pr 25^{19} (sim. of untrustworthiness). **Hiph.** *Pf.* וְהַמְעַדְתָּ (so rd. for 𝔐 והעמדת, cf. Sm Co Da Berthol) Ez 29^7; *cause to shake* obj. כָּל־מָתְנַיִם, i. e. *make them totter*; cf *Imv.* הַמְעַד (obj *id.*) ψ 69^{24}.

†מַעֲדַי (van d. H מַעְדִי) **n.pr.m.** one of those who had taken strange wives Ezr 10^{34}. 𝔊 Μοδεδ(ε)ια, A 𝔊 L Μοο(υ)δεια (perh. = foll., q.v.)

†מַעַדְיָה **n.pr.m.** a priest of Zerubbabel's time acc. to Ne 12^5, 𝔊א Μααδιας, 𝔊 L Μαασιας; appar. = מוֹעַדְיָה v^{17}, 𝔊 L Μαςαι (etym. dub.; Thes puts sub עדה = *ornamentum Jovae*, but prop מַע׳ = מוֹע׳, √ יעד = *conventus Jovae*).

מֹעֵד v. מוֹעֵד sub יעד.

[מַעֲדָן], מַעֲדַנִּים v. עדן.

†מַעֲדַנּוֹת **n.[f.]pl.** Jb 38^{31} v. sub ענד; מַעֲדַנֹּת 1 S 15^{32} is dub; = above, as adv. acc. *in bonds, fetters*, Ki Gr Klo; 𝔗 Sym We Dr assign to √ עדן = *delicately, voluptuously*; but 𝔊 τρέμων, whence Lag$^{Proph\ Chald\ ii}$ prop. מַעֲדַנִּית (cf אֲחֹרַנִּית) √ מעד = *totteringly*, so HPS.

מַעְדֵּר v. עדר.

מעה (√of foll; meaning dubious)

†[מֵעָה] **n.m.** $^{Is\ 16,11}$ only **pl. internal organs, inward parts (intestines, bowels), belly** (NH *id*; Aram מְעָא, מְעָיָא, ܡܥܰܝܳܐ, ܡܰܥܝܳܐ, Ar. مِعًى; Eth አምዕት:;—on form cf. Lag$^{BN\ 186}$ Ba$^{ZMG\ xlii\ 1888,\ 345}$),—pl [מֵעִים] cstr. מְעֵי ψ 71^6 + 3 t., sf. מֵעַי 2 S 16^{11} + 9 t, מֵעָי ψ 22^{15} 40^9; מֵעֶיךָ Gn 15^4 + 6 t, מֵעַיִךְ Gn 25^{23} Nu 5^{22}; מֵעָיו 2 S 20^{10} + 5 t, מֵעֵיהֶם Ez 7^{19};—**1.** lit: **a.** וַיִּשְׁפֹּךְ מֵעָיו אַרְצָה 2 S 20^{10} *and he poured out his inward parts on the ground* (through a wound); cf. מַחֲלַה מ׳ 2 Ch $21^{15.18}$, יֵצְאוּ מ׳ v$^{15.19}$. **b.** as digestive organs, but without precision, nearly = *stomach*,

belly, Jb 20[14]; Ez 3[3] (|| בֶּטֶן), 7[19] (|| נֶפֶשׁ; both c. מִלֵּא), Nu 5[22]; so of fish that swallowed Jonah Jon 2[1.2]. **2.** source of procreation: אשר יצא מִמֵּ׳ (said of offspring) Gn 15[4] (JE), 2 S 7[12] 16[11]; צֶאֱצָאֵי מ׳ Is 48[19] (|| *id.*); מִיצִיאֵי מ׳ (|| וְזַרְעֲךָ), 2 Ch 32[21]. **3.** = *womb*, שְׁנֵי לְאֻמִּים מִמֵּעַיִךְ יִפָּרֵדוּ Gn 25[23] (J; || בֶּטֶן), cf. Is 49[1] (|| *id.*), ψ 71[6] (|| *id.*), Ru 1[11]. **4.** in gen. = *inwards, inward part*, ψ 22[15], cf. תּוֹרָתְךָ בְּתוֹךְ מ׳ 40[9]. לִבִּי . . . נָמֵס בְּתוֹךְ מ׳ **5.** fig. = seat of emotions: pity, Is 16[11] (|| קֶרֶב); of God's compassion, Je 31[20] (|| רחם; in both subj. of vb. הָמוּ); הֲמוֹן מֵעֶיךָ Is 63[15] (|| רַחֲמֶיךָ); distress, Je 4[19.19] (|| לֵב), מֵעַי חֳמַרְמָרוּ La 1[20] (|| לֵב), 2[11] (|| כָּבֵד *liver*); מֵעַי רֻתְּחוּ Jb 30[27] (dub., v. Bu); love, מֵעַי הָמוּ עָלָיו Ct 5[4]. **6.** the external belly, מֵעָיו עֶשֶׁת שֵׁן Ct 5[14].

†[מָעָה] **n.f. grain** (of sand), si vera l. (NH מָעָה, *seed* (of melon, etc.), *coin*, Aram. ܡܥܐ, מָעָא *coin*);—only fpl. sf.: וַיְהִי כַחוֹל זַרְעֶךָ וְצֶאֱצָאֵי מֵעֶיךָ כִּמְעֹתָיו Is 48[19] *and thy seed had been like the sand, and the offspring of thy bowels like the grains thereof*, cf. 𝔙 𝔗 De Di Du al. > pl. of [מֵעָה] *the entrails of it* (i.e. the sea) AE Ges Hi Che[Comm.].—𝔊 ὡς ὁ χοῦς τῆς γῆς, whence Gr כְּעפרותיו.

מָעוֹג v. עוג. מָעוֹז, מָעֹז v. עוז (cf. עזז).

I, II. מָעוֹן, מְעֹ(וֹ)נָה, מְעוֹנֹתַי v. עון.

†מְעוּנִים **n.pr.gent.** Me'unim, Me'unites (usu. connected with מָעוֹן (v. עון), but dub., cf. Buhl [Edom. 41 f.]); — a people S. (SE?) of Canaan (cf. Buhl [l.c.]);—הַמְּ׳ 2 Ch 26[7] and 1 Ch 4[41] Qr (Kt המעינים, 𝔊[B] τοὺς Μιναίους, 𝔊L τ. Κιναίους); rd. also מֵהַמְּעוּנִים 2 Ch 20[1] (for MT מֵהָעַמּוֹנִים), so 𝔊[BA] (𝔊L Ἀμμανιειμ), Ew Be Ke Öt Kau Kit; בְּנֵי־מְעוּנִים (among Nethinim who went back with Zerub.) Ezr 2[50] = Neh 7[52] are perhaps descendants of those named above (2 Ch 26[7]). 𝔊 οἱ Μιναῖοι, but against מ׳ = Minæans (Glaser [Skizze ii. 450 f.] al.) v. Sprenger [ZMG xliv (1890), 505].

[מָעוּף] v. I. עיף. מָעוֹר v. II. עור.

מעז (√ of following).

†מַעַזְיָה, מַעַזְיָהוּ **n.pr.m.** of priests. **1.** 1 Ch 24[18] ascribed to David's time, A Μοοζαλ, 𝔊L Μοοζια. **2.** Neh 10[9], Nehemiah's time, A Μααζεια, 𝔊L Μααζίας.

†[מָעַט] **vb.** be or become small, diminished, few (NH, Talm., *id.*; Ar. مَعِطَ is *to be without hair on the body*) — **Qal** *Impf.* יִמְעַט Ex 12[4], 2 mpl. תִּמְעָטוּ Je 29[6], 3 mpl. יִמְעָטוּ Is 21[17] +, וַיִּמְעֲטוּ ψ 107[39]; *Inf.* מְעֹט Lv 25[16];— Ex 12[4] אִם־יִמְעַט הַבַּיִת מִהְיוֹת מִשֶּׂה if the house be *too small* for a lamb; Ne 9[32] אַל־יִמְעַט לְפָנֶיךָ אֵת כָּל־הַתְּלָאָה (cf. Ges [§ 117 l]); of a people, Je 29[6] וּרְבוּ שָׁם וְאַל־תִּמְעָטוּ and *become* not *few*, 30[19] וְהִרְבִּתִים וְלֹא יִמְעָטוּ, Is 21[17] ψ 107[39]; Pr 13[11] הוֹן מֵהֶבֶל יִמְעָט *diminishes* (opp. יַרְבֶּה); Lv 25[16] וּלְפִי מְעֹט הַשָּׁנִים acc. to the *fewness* of the years. **Pi.** *become few* (Ges [§ 52 k]), *Pf.* 3 pl. Ec 12[3] וּבָטְלוּ הַטֹּחֲנוֹת כִּי מִעֵטוּ. **Hiph.** *Pf.* 3 fs. consec. וְהִמְעִיטָה (Ges [§ 49 k]), Lv 26[22], 1 s. with sf. וְהִמְעַטְתִּים Ez 29[15]; *Impf.* 2 ms. תַּמְעִיט Lv 25[16], תַּמְעִטֵנִי Je 10[24], 2 fs. תַּמְעִיטִי 2 K 4[3], etc.;—*make small* or *few, diminish*: **a.** Lv 26[22] (of the sword) וְהִמְעִיטָה אֶתְכֶם, Ez 29[15] וְהִמְעַטְתִּים, Je 10[24] אַל־בְּאַפְּךָ פֶּן־תַּמְעִטֵנִי lest thou *make me* (the people) *small*, ψ 107[38] וּבְהֶמְתָּם לֹא יַמְעִיט; Lv 25[16] וּלְפִי מְעֹט הַשָּׁנִים תַּמְעִיט מִקְנָתוֹ acc. to the smallness (fewness) of the years, thou shalt *make small* its price, Nu 26[54] לָרַב תַּרְבֶּה נַחֲלָתוֹ וְלַמְעַט תַּמְעִיט נַחֲלָתוֹ and to the small (few) thou shalt *make small* his inheritance (so 33[54]). **b.** qualifying an *action* (sts. to be understood from the context), Ex 16[17] וַיִּלְקְטוּ הַמַּרְבֶּה וְהַמַּמְעִיט and they gathered, he that made much, and he that *made little* (sc. לִלְקֹט), v[18] Nu 11[32] הממעיט אסף עשׂרה חמרים, 2 K 4[3] כֵּלִים רֵקִים אַל־תַּמְעִיטִי empty vessels *make not few* (sc. in borrowing); Ex 30[15] הֶעָשִׁיר לֹא יַרְבֶּה וְהַדַּל לֹא יַמְעִיט מִמַּחֲצִית הַשָּׁקֶל לָתֵת וגו׳ *shall not diminish* from the half shekel to give, i.e. shall not give less, Nu 35[8] מֵאֵת הָרַב תַּרְבּוּ וּמֵאֵת הַמְעַט תַּמְעִיטוּ and from the few ye shall *make few* (sc. לָתֵת), i.e. ye shall give few (cities).

מְעַט[101] **subst.** a little, fewness, a few;— מ׳ abs. and cstr., מְעַט Is 10[7] +, pl. מְעַטִּים ψ 109[8] Ec 5[1];—**1. a.** Gn 30[30] מעט אשר היה לך לְפָנַי *the little* that thou hadst, 47[9] מעט ורעים היו ימי שני חיי *few* and evil, Lv 25[52] Nu 26[54] (cf. 33[54]) וְלַמְעַט תמעיט נחלתו and *to the small* (few) thou shalt make small his inheritance, v[56] 35[8] וּמֵאֵת הַמְעַט תמעיטו, Dt 7[7] כי אתם הַמְעַט מכל־ העמים ye are *the fewest* out of all peoples, 1 S 14[6] כִּי נִשְׁאַרְנוּ מְעַט מֵהַרְבֵּה, Je 42[2] לְהוֹשִׁיעַ בְּרַב אוֹ בִמְעָט we are left *as few* out of many, Ez 5[3] וְלָקַחְתָּ מִשָּׁם מְעַט בְּמִסְפָּר, Hg 1[6] זְרַעְתֶּם הַרְבֵּה וְהָבֵא מְעָט (cf. v[9]), ψ 8[6] ותחסרהו מעט מאלהים, 37[16] טוֹב מְעַט לַצַּדִּיק

(cf Pr 15[16] 16[8]), 2 Ch 29[34] רַק הַכֹּהֲנִים הָיוּ לִמְעָט; as pred Nu 13[18] הַמְעַט הוּא אִם־רָב, Jos 7[3] כִּי מְעַט הֵמָּה, Jb 10[20] Ru 2[7] Ne 7[4]; Is 16[14] וּשְׁאָר מְעַט מִזְעָר. — Ho 8[10] וַיָּחֵלּוּ מְּעַט and they begin *as littleness* (= *to be minished*) because of, &c, but rd prob (𝔊) וְיֶחְדְּלוּ מְעַט מִמְּשֹׁחַ and they shall cease *for a little* (**d**) from anointing, etc. **b.** as subst with foll gen, Gn 18[4] מְעַט מַיִם *a little of* water, 24[17.43], 43[2] 44[25] מְעַט אֹכֶל 1 S 14[43] 17[28] מְעַט הַצֹּאן הָהֵנָּה lit. *the fewness of* those sheep, Pr 6[10]+; as gen to a previous subst, מְתֵי מְעָט men *of fewness* †Dt 26[5] 28[62], in appos., †Is 10[7] לְהַכְרִית גּוֹיִם לֹא מְעָט, Ezr 9[8] מִחְיָה מְעַט, Ne 2[12] וַאֲנָשִׁים מְעַט עִמִּי, Ec 9[14], either gen or appos, 10[1] Dn 11[34] יֵעָזְרוּ עֵזֶר מְעָט with a help *of smallness*. **c.** twice declined as an adj, ψ 109[8] יִהְיוּ יָמָיו מְעַטִּים, Ec 5[1] עַל־כֵּן יִהְיוּ דְבָרֶיךָ מְעַטִּים. **d.** as adverb acc, of place, 2 S 16[1] וְדָוִד עָבַר מְעַט, of time, Jb 10[20 b], of degree, 2 K 10[18] אַחְאָב עָבַד אֶת־הַבַּעַל מְעָט, Ez 11[16] and have been to them for a sanctuary *but little*, Zc 1[15]; repeated מְעַט מְעַט *by little, by little* = gradually, Ex 23[30] Dt 7[22]. **e.** phrases — *a* with the interr הֲ, †Gn 30[15] הַמְעַט קַחְתֵּךְ אֶת־אִישִׁי וְלָקַחַת was thy taking my husband (too) little? and (wilt thou be) for taking also my son's love-apples? Nu 16[9-10] הַמְעַט מִכֶּם כִּי הִבְדִּיל . . . וּבִקַּשְׁתֶּם גַּם כְּהֻנָּה is it *too little for you* that J hath separated, etc, . . . and do ye seek, etc? v[13] הַמְעַט כִּי הֶעֱלִיתָנוּ . . . כִּי תִשְׂתָּרֵר גַּם הִשְׂתָּרֵר, Jos 22[17 f.] הַמְעַט לָנוּ . . . וְאַתֶּם תָּשֻׁבוּ וגו׳, Is 7[13] הַמְעַט מִכֶּם הַלְאוֹת אֲנָשִׁים כִּי תַלְאוּ וגו׳ is wearying men *too little* for you, that you will weary also my God? Ez 34[18] (as Ew Co AV RV), Jb 15[11] הַמְעַט מִמְּךָ תַּנְחֻמוֹת אֵל. But Ez 16[20] (si vera l.) was it (too) little *because of* thy whoredom? (was that insufficient for thee? Ko[iii 406m]) *b* עוֹד מְעַט וְ׳, †Ex 17[4] עוֹד מְעַט וּסְקָלֻנִי *yet a little, and* they will stone me, Je 51[33] Ho 1[4] ψ 37[10]; עוֹד מְעַט מִזְעָר וְ׳ †Is 10[25] 29[17]; cf Hg 2[6] Jb 24[24].

2. †כִּמְעַט *like a little* hence **a.** *within a little, almost* (cf ὀλίγου), Gn 26[10] . . . כִּמְעַט שָׁכַב *almost* had lain, ψ 73[2] Qr, 94[17] 119[87] Pr 5[14] (all sq pf), Ez 16[47] כִּמְעַט קָט וַתַּשְׁחִתִי מֵהֶן *like a little*, and thou hadst done more corruptly than they; Ct 3[4] כִּמְעַט שֶׁעָבַרְתִּי מֵהֶם = *hardly* had I passed. **b.** with impf, *just*, 2 S 19[37] כִּמְעַט יַעֲבֹר עַבְדְּךָ *just* would thy servant pass over, *lightly, easily, quickly* (cf δι' ὀλίγου), ψ 2[12] כִּי יִבְעַר כִּמְעַט אַפּוֹ, 81[15] Jb 32[22]. **c.** = *shortly*, 2 Ch 12[7] **d.** = *little worth*, Pr 10[20] וְלֵב רְשָׁעִים כִּמְעָט. **e.** pleon for מְעַט, Is 1[9] (accents) שָׂרִיד כִּמְעָט a *little* remnant, ψ 105[12] (= 1 Ch 16[19]) כִּמְעַט וְגָרִים בָּהּ; כִּמְעַט רֶגַע *like the littleness of* a moment = *for a little* moment, Is 26[20] Ezr 9[8].

מְעֻטָּה Ez 21[20] textual error, v. sub מרט.

מַעֲטֶה v עטה   [מַעֲטָפָה] v. I עטף.

† מְעִי only in וְהָיְתָה מְ׳ מַפָּלָה Is 17[1], acc. to AV RV Thes al **n.[m.]** = עִי *ruin-heap*, but form very strange, 𝔊 om (ἔσται εἰς πτῶσιν); Gr prop כְּעִי, Di לְעִי, < dittogr. from מעיר Lag[Sem. i 29] Che No[ZMG xxxii 1878, 401] Brd SS Buhl Gu[in Kau] Du

† מָעַי **n.pr.m.** a musician Ne 12[36]; 𝔊א[c.a] Μααι, 𝔊L Μαια.

מֵעִים v מעה   מַעְיָן v. sub עין.

מעינים 1 Ch 4[41] Kt v. מְעוּנִים.

†[מָעַךְ] **vb. press, squeeze** (NH *id.*; 𝔗 מְעַךְ, Ar. مَعَكَ *rub*), — **Qal** *Pt. pass* וּמָעוּךְ וְכָתוּת וְנָתוּק וְכָרוּת Lv 22[24] (H), not to be offered to י׳, reference to emasculation (cf. Di), וַחֲנִיתוֹ מְעוּכָה־בָאָרֶץ 1 S 26[7] *and his spear pressed* (thrust) *into the ground.* **Pu.** *Pf.* 3 mpl שָׁמָּה מֹעֲכוּ שְׁדֵיהֶן Ez 23[3] *there were their breasts squeezed* (|| עִשּׂוּ, unchastely; fig. of intercourse of Samaria and Jerus with Egypt, involving idolatry).

† מָעוֹךְ **n.pr.m.** father of Achish of Gath (on form cf Lag[BN 32]), — 1 S 27[2] (𝔊 Αμμαχ, A Μωαβ, 𝔊L Αχιμααν) = מַעֲכָה 1 K 2[39] (𝔊 Αμησα, A 𝔊L Μααχα).

† מַעֲכָה **n.pr.m., f. et gent.** **1. n.pr.m.** 𝔊 Μ(ο)ωχα, Μα(α)χα: **a** son of Nahor by his concubine רְאוּמָה Gn 22[24] (J), ancestor of people v. **3.** **b.** father of חָנָן, a hero of David 1 Ch 11[43] **c.** Simeonite name 1 Ch 27[16]. **d.** father of Achish 1 K 2[39] (v מָעוֹךְ supra). **2. n pr.f.** 𝔊 Μ(ο)ωχα, Μααχα, etc **a.** Geshurite princess, wife of David, mother of Absalom, 2 S 3[3] = 1 Ch 3[2] **b.** daughter of Absalom, wife of Rehoboam, mother of Abijam, 1 K 15[2] 2 Ch 11[20.21.22]; rd. also מ׳ 2 Ch 13[2] (so 𝔊 𝔖) for MT מִיכָיָה, where called daughter of Uriel of Gibeah (on this difficulty v. Be Ot, and cf. **c**). **c.** mother of Asa, and called also daughter of Absalom (as **b**) 1 K 15[10], cf. v[13] = 2 Ch 15[16], (on this difficulty v. Th Kmp[in Kau]) **d.** concubine of Caleb acc. to 1 Ch 2[48]. **e.** wife of

Machir 1 Ch 7^{16}, cf. v^{15} (corrupt, v. Be) **f.** wife of (יעיאל), father of Gibeon, 1 Ch 8^{29} 9^{35}. **3. n.pr.gent.**, 𝔊 *Μοοχα, Μωχα, Μα(α)χα*; dwelling W. of Bashan, near *Soba*, and *Geshur* (cf esp. adj. gent. infr.), 2 S 10$^{6.8}$ = 1 Ch 19^{7}, אֲרַם מ׳ v^{6} (cf. Gn 22^{24} supr); = מַעֲכָת Jos 13^{13} (+ גְּשׁוּר), 𝔊 *ὁ Μαχατει, Μαχαθι*.—אָבֵל בֵּית מַעֲכָה v. sub בַּיִת, p. 112 supr, and אָבֵל, p. 5.

מַעֲכָת v. supr מַעֲכָה **3.**

† מַעֲכָתִי **adj.gent.** הַמּ׳ 1 Ch 4^{19}; so בֶּן־הַמַּעֲכָתִי 2 S 23^{34} of one of David's heroes, We del. בן; rd. prob. בית הַמּ׳ Klo HPS; v. also Dr; of associate of Ishmael the Judaean 2 K 25^{23} = Je 40^{8}, coll. = *the Maachathites* Dt 3^{14} Jos 12^{5} 13$^{11.13}$ (all + הַגְּשׁוּרִי, cf. מַעֲכָה **3**).—𝔊 *Μαχ(ε)ι, Μαχατ(ε)ι, Μααχαθι*, etc

† מָעַל **vb. act unfaithfully, treacherously,** a priestly word (P Ez. Ch.), chiefly late (NH *id., act unfaithfully;* Ar. مَغَلَ *whisper, backbite,* مَغَالَةٌ *perfidy, fraud*);—**Qal** *Pf.* 3 ms מָעַל Jos 22^{20} + 4 t; 3 fs. מָֽעֲלָה Lv 5^{21} Nu 5^{12} + 13 t. Pf; *Impf* יִמְעַל Pr 16^{10} 2 Ch 26^{16}; 3 fs תִּמְעֹל Lv 5^{15} Nu 5^{27}; 3 mpl יִמְעֲלוּ Jos 7^{1}, וַיִּמְעֲלוּ 1 Ch 5^{25}; 2 mpl. תִּמְעָ֑לוּ Ne 1^{8}; *Inf. cstr.* לִמְעֹל, so rd for 𝔐 למסר Nu 31^{16} Thes Di;—*act unfaithfully, treacherously,* usu. **1.** מָעַל מַ֫עַל: **a.** abs. בַּחֵרֶם *in the matter of the devoted thing* (the sin of Achan) Jos 7^{1} (JE), 22^{20} (P), cf. Lv 5^{15} (P), 2 Ch 36^{14} Ez 14^{13} 15^{8} 18^{24}. **b.** wife against (ב) husband Nu 5$^{12.27}$ (P; marital infidelity) **c.** elsewhere ag. (בְּ) God, Lv 26^{40} (H), 5^{21} Nu 5^{6} 31^{16} (?) Jos 22$^{16.31}$ (all P), 1 Ch 10^{13} 28^{19} Ez 17^{20} 20^{27} 39^{26} Dn 9^{7}. **2.** usage without מַ֫עַל (only late): **a.** במשפט לא ימעל פיו Pr 16^{10} *let not his* (the king's) *mouth act treacherously against justice* (RV *in judgment*). **b.** elsewhere against God, c ב, Dt 32^{51} (P), 1 Ch 5^{25} 1 2^{2} 26^{22} 30^{7} Ezr 10^{2} Ne 13^{27} Ez 39^{23}, without בְּ, 2 Ch 26^{18} 29^{6} Ezr 10^{10} Ne 1^{8}; בַּחֵרֶם 1 Ch 2^{7}

† I. מַ֫עַל **n.m.** $^{Ezr\ 9.2}$ **unfaithful, treacherous act** (NH מְעִילָה);—מ׳ Lv 5^{15} + 16 t.; מָ֑עַל Nu 5^{12} + 2 t; sf מַעֲלוֹ Ez 17^{20} + 4 t.; מַעֲלָם Ez 39^{26} + 3 t.,—**1.** ag man: נשאר מעל Jb 21^{34} *faithlessness remains* (cf. Nu 5$^{12.27}$ Pr 16^{10} under מָעַל) **2.** elsewhere ag. God, c. ב, Jos 22^{22} (P), without בְּ, 1 Ch 9^{1} 2 Ch 29^{19} 33^{19} Ezr 9$^{2.4}$ 10^{6}.—מַעַל elsewhere only c. מָעַל q v. (**1**; all cited).

† מְעִיל **n.m.** $^{1\ S\ 2.19}$ **robe** (Thes conj. orig. meaning *cover* for √מעל, cf. בגד; Ba$^{ES\ 15}$ comp. Ar. مِعْوَلٌ *an outer garment*, but against this Sta$^{ThLz,\ Apr\ 28,\ 1894,\ 230}$);—מ׳ Ex 28^{31} + 18 t.; sf. מְעִילוֹ 1 S 15^{27}; מעלו Jb 1^{20} 2^{12} + 4 t sg; pl. מְעִילִים 2 S 13^{18}, (but del. We Klo Kit Bu SS; orig gloss מֵעוֹלָם We Kit Bu); מְעִילֵיהֶם Ez 26^{16};—exterior garment, *robe*, worn over the inner tunic כְּתֹנֶת: **1.** worn by men of rank: Saul and Jonathan 1 S 18^{4} 24$^{5.12.12}$, princes of the sea Ez 26^{16}; Job Jb 1^{20} 2^{12}; Samuel 1 S 15^{27} 28^{14}; Ezra Ezr 9$^{3.5}$; David clothed with מ׳ בוּץ 1 Ch 15^{27} (in the procession of the ark); the child Samuel had מ׳ קָטֹן 1 S 2^{19};—(it had a skirt כנף 1 S 15^{27} 24$^{5.12.12}$) **2.** worn by the daughters of David 2 S 13^{18} (but prob del., v supr.) **3.** robe of high priest (only P) מְעִיל הָאֵפוֹד, made of purple stuff, Ex 28^{31} 29^{5} 39^{22}; אפוד ומעיל 28^{4}; הַמְּעִיל Lv 8^{7}, having שׁוּלֵי הַמְּעִיל skirts Ex 28^{34} 39$^{24.25.26}$, around which were alternate coloured pomegranates and golden bells, and פִּי הַמְּעִיל, an opening or hole by which it might be drawn over the head 39^{23}. **4.** fig of attributes (of י׳, and of men), קנאה Is 59^{17}, צדקה 61^{10}; משפט Jb 29^{14}; בשת ψ 109^{29}.

II. מַ֫עַל v sub עלה. מעל v. עַל.

[מֹ֫עַל], מַעֲלָה, מַעֲלֶה v. sub עלה.

[מַעֲלָל, מַעֲלִיל] v. עלל.

[מַעֲמָד], מַעֲמָד v. עמד מַעֲמָסָה v עמס.

מַעֲמַקִּים v. עמק. מַ֫עַן v. מַעֲנֶה sub I. עָנָה.

מַעֲנֶה, מַעֲנָה, מַעֲנִית v. I. ענה

מְעֹנָה v. עון.

מעץ (√ of foll; perhaps = *be wrathful*, cf. Ar. مَعِصَ *be enraged*, cf. also **n.pr.m.** אֲחִימַ֫עַץ, supr. p 27).

† מַ֫עַץ **n.pr.m.** in Judah 1 Ch 2^{27}; 𝔊 *Maas.*

מַעֲצֵבָה v. עצב. מַעֲצָד v. עצד.

[מַעֲצָה] v. [מוֹעֵצָה] sub יעץ.

מַעְצוֹר, מַעְצָר v עצר. מַעֲקֶה v. עקה.

מַעֲקַשִּׁים v. עקש מַ֫עַר, מַעֲרֶה v. ערה.

I. מַעֲרָב v. I. ערב.

II. מַעֲרָב, מַעֲרָבָה v. III. ערב.

מַעֲרָה v. I. ערר.

מערות 1 S 17^{23} Kt v מערכה sub ערך.

[מַעֲרִיץ] v. ערץ.

מַעֲרֶכֶת, מַעֲרָכָה, מַעֲרָךְ v. ערך.

[מַעֲרֻמִּים] v II. עור. מַעֲרָצָה v. ערץ

מַעֲרַת v. ערה.

מַעֲשֶׂה, מַעֲשַׂי, מַעֲשֵׂיָה, מַעֲשֵׂיָהוּ v. עשה

מַעֲשֵׂר v. עשׂר. מַעֲשַׁקּוֹת v עשק.

† מֹף **n.pr.loc. Memphis** (Eg *Mr-nfr*, i.e. *Mĕnnūfĕr*, **Mĕnnúfĕ*, Steindorff$^{BAS\ i.\ 594\ f}$; As. *Mêmpi*, *Mimpi*, Schr$^{COT\ Is\ 19,\ 13}$ Dl$^{Par\ 314}$; cf. Erman$^{Aegypten\ 48,\ 243}$ Eb$^{Cicerone\ i\ 114\ f}$, 𝔊 (and Gk) Μεμφις, on coins Μενφι(ς) Steind.$^{l.\ c.}$),—מ׳ Ho 9^{6} = נֹף Is 19^{13} Je 2^{16} 44^{1} 46$^{14.19}$ Ez 30^{13}, and וְנֹף צָרִי יוֹמָם v^{16} (without clear meaning, prob. txt. err. Siegfr$^{in\ Kau}$; 𝔊 (appar.) וְנָפֹצוּ מֵימֵיהֶם *and their waters shall be dispersed* (cf Na 3^{8}); Co ונפרצו חומותיה *and its walls shall be torn down*); נֹף also v^{15} (for MT נא) 𝔊 Co.

מִפְגָּע v. פגע. מַפָּח, מַפַּח v. נפח.

מְפִ(י)בֹשֶׁת v. מְרִיב׳ sub ריב.

† מֻפִּים **n.pr.m.** family name in Benjamin, Gn 46^{21}, 𝔊 Μαμφειν; but 1 Ch 7^{12} שֻׁפִּם q v

מֵפִיץ v. פוץ, פצץ, נפץ.

מַפָּל, מַפָּלָה, מַפֶּלֶת v. נפל.

[מִפְלָאָה] v פלא. [מִפְלַגָּה] v. פלג

מִפְלָט v. פלט. מִפְלֶצֶת v. פלץ.

[מִפְלָשׂ] v. פלש = פלס.

[מִפְעָל, מִפְעָלָה] v. פעל.

מֵיפַעַת v מִיפַּעַת sub יפע.

[מַפָּץ], מַפֵּץ v. נפץ. מִפְקָד v. פקד.

[מִפְרָץ] v פרץ [מַפְרֶקֶת] v פרק.

[מִפְרָשׂ] v פרשׂ. מִפְשָׂעָה v פשׂע.

מַפְתֵּחַ, [מִפְתָּח] v. פתח.

מִפְתָּן v פתן. מֵיץ Is 16^{4} v. מיץ

מֵץ v. מוץ.

מָצָא^{452} **vb. attain to, find** (NH *id.*, As. *maṣû*, Dl$^{HWB\ 421}$, Eth መጽአ: *come, arrive;* Aram. [ܡܛܳܐ *find*], Pt. pass ܡܨܶܐ *able, powerful,* and deriv; cf. No$^{ZMG\ xl\ 1886,\ 736}$ Dr$^{1\ S\ 23,\ 17}$);—**Qal** *Pf.* מ׳ Gn 2^{20}+, sf. מְצָאוֹ Jb 31^{29}, 3 fs. מָֽצְאָה Gn 8^{9}+, sf מְצָאַתְנוּ Ju 6^{13} Ne 9^{32}, מצָאָתַם Ex 18^{18}, 2 ms. מָצָאתָ Gn 31^{37}+; 1 s. מָצָאתִי Gn 18^{3}+, מָצָתִי Nu 11^{11}, sf מצָאתִיו Ct 3$^{1.2}$, מְצָאתִיהוּ Ct 5^{6}; 3 pl. מָֽצְאוּ Ju 21^{14}+, sf. מְצָאֻהוּ Jb 37^{23}, etc.; *Impf.* יִמְצָא 1 S 24^{20}+, 3 fs. תִּמְצָא 1 S 1^{18}+; 3 mpl. יִמְצְאוּ Ju 5^{30}+, sf יִמְצָאֻהוּ Jb 20^{8}, יִמְצָאֻנְנִי Pr 1^{28} 8^{17}, יִמְצָאוּנְהָ Je 2^{24}; 3 fpl. תִּמְצֶאןָ Dt 31^{21} etc.; *Imv* מְצָא 1 S 20$^{21.36}$, וּמְצָא־ Pr 3^{4}; mpl. מִצְאוּ Je 6^{16}; fpl וּמְצֶאןָ Ru 1^{9}, *Inf.* מצא, מְצוֹא ψ 32^{6} Gn 19^{11}+, sf בְּמֹצַאֲכֶם Gn 32^{20} [= מָצְאֲכֶם Ges §74, 3, R 2], *Pt* מוֹצֵא ψ 119^{162}, מוֹצֶה Ec 7^{26}, sf מֹצְאִי Gn 4^{14} Pr 8^{35}, fs abs. מֹצֵאת 2 S 18^{22}, מוֹצֵאת Ct 8^{10}, mpl. מֹצְאִים Nu 15^{33}, cstr מֹצְאֵי Pr 8^{9}; fpl abs. מֹצְאוֹת Jos 2^{23}, etc.;—**1.** *find:* **a.** thing sought, c. acc. rei, straw Ex 5^{11} (J), water Gn 26^{32} (J), cf. v^{19}, Ex 15^{22} (J), grass 1 K 18^{5}, help, consort, Gn 2^{20} (J), cf. Pr 18^{22}+; with idea of attaining to, arriving at, a resting-place Gn 8^{9} (J) Is 34^{14} cf. צִפּוֹר מָֽצְאָה בַיִת ψ 84^{4}, Je 45^{3} La 1^{3}; of marriage Ru 1^{9}; of finding place for temple ψ 132^{5}; fig. וּמִצְאוּ מַרְגּוֹעַ לְנַפְשְׁכֶם Je 6^{16} *and find quiet for yourselves;* find grave Jb 3^{22}; reach cities 2 S 20^{6} (where rd יִמְצָא Vrss Th Dr Kit Bu), cf. ψ 107^{4}; *find* = secure prey, booty, plunder Gn 27^{20} (J), Ju 5^{30} 21^{12} 1 S 14^{30} cf 2 Ch 20^{25} Pr 1^{13} ψ 119^{162}; of securing gain Ho 12^{9} (+ לִי, ‖ עֹשֶׁר), Jb 31^{25}, so perhaps also abs. אֵין בְּשׂוֹרָה מֹצֵאת 2 S 18^{22} *there is no news securing* gain i.e such as to bring you a reward (cf. Th Dr; but text dub); secure as crop Gn 26^{12} (J), cf Ec 11^{1}; = *acquire, get* wounds and dishonour Pr 6^{33}; מ׳ חן בעיני פ׳ *find* (= gain, secure) *favour in the eyes of* any one: of י׳, †Gn 6^{8} Ex 33$^{12.13}$ $^{13.16.17}$ 34^{9} (all J), Nu 11$^{11.15}$ (JE), Ju 6^{17} 2 S 15^{25}†; oftener of men Gn 18^{3} 19^{19} 30^{27} 32^{6} + 8 t. Gn (all J), Nu 32^{5} (JE), Dt 24^{1} 1 S 1^{18} + 7 t. S, 1 K 11^{19} Ru 2$^{2.10.13}$ Est 5^{8} 7^{3}; מ׳ חֵן לִפְנֵי פ׳ †Est 8^{5}, אָז הָיִיתִי בְעֵינָיו כְּמוֹצְאֵת שָׁלוֹם †Ct 8^{10}; abs. מָצָא חֵן †Je 31^{2} Pr 3^{4} 28^{23}†: = *seek and find* 1 S 20^{21} (arrows), so v^{36}; fig. of grounds of accusation Jb 33^{10} *he succeeds in finding;* so also Is 58$^{3.13}$; *find* knowledge of God Pr 2^{5} cf. 8^{9}, word of י׳ Am 8^{12}, words of wisdom Pr 4^{22}, wisdom Jb 32^{13} Pr 24^{14} (v. also infr), ransom Jb 33^{24}; life Pr 8^{35} (Qr מָצָא; > Kt מֹצְאֵי, i.e. מֹצְאַי De Str Wild), 21^{21}; c. acc. pers. Gn

18$^{26.28.30}$ (J), 41^{38} (E), 1 S 9$^{13.13}$ 1 K 1^{3} 13^{14} cf. v^{28}, +; of pursuit Jos 2^{22} (J); *find* י׳ +Ho 5^{6} Dt 4^{29} Je 29^{13} Jb 23^{3} ψ 32^{6} + Ho 6^{3} (rd. כְּשַׁחֲרֵנוּ כֵּן נִמְצָאֵהוּ, for MT כְּשַׁחַר נָכוֹן מֹצָאוֹ Gie$^{Beitr. z. Jes. Krit. 208}$ We Now); so poss. also (obj. om.) Je 10^{18} (so Gf.; 𝔅 Or rd. Niph.; Gie יִמָּצְאוּ), (Jb 37^{23} 11$^{7.7}$ v. infr.); *find* wisdom (personif.) Pr 1^{28} 8$^{17.35}$ cf. 3^{13}. **b.** what is lost, missed, c. acc. rei, Gn 31$^{32.33.34.35.37}$ (E), 1 S 9$^{4.4}$ Dt 22^{3} Lv 5$^{22.23}$ (P), Gn 36^{24} (P)+; וַיִּלְאוּ לִמְצֹא הַפָּתַח Gn 19^{11} *and they grew weary in finding the door; find* a word (to say) Ne 5^{8} Ec 12^{10}, answer Jb 32^{3}, vision from י׳ La 2^{9}; c. acc. pers. Gn 38$^{20.22.23}$(J), 2 S 17^{20} 1 K 18$^{10.12}$ 21$^{20.20}$ 2 K 2^{17} Ez 22^{30} Pr 7^{15} Ct 3$^{1.2.4}$ 5^{6}+. **c.** *meet, encounter*, c. acc. pers. (one expected), Gn 32^{20} (E), 2 K 9^{21} Je 41^{12} 2 Ch 20^{16}; cf. also Nu 35^{27} (P). **d.** *find* a condition, *find* one in a situation; וְלֹא מ׳ לָהּ בְּתוּלִים Dt 22^{14} cf. v^{17} 24^{1}; וַיִּמ׳ אֶת־מֶלֶךְ . . . נִלְחָם 2 K 19^{8} *and he found the king* of Assyria *warring* against Lachish = Is 37^{8}; וּמ׳ אֶת־לְבָבוֹ נֶאֱמָן Ne 9^{8}; מ׳ כָּתוּב בספר Ne 7^{5} 8^{14}; esp. late, 1 Ch 20^{2} 2 Ch 25^{5} Dn 1^{20} Ec 7^{26}. **e.** = *learn, devise* Ec 7$^{27.27.29}$. **f.** = *experience* sorrow ψ 116^{3}, cf. Ec 7^{14}. **2.** *find out:* **a.** find out thoroughly, explore: obj. God Jb 11$^{7.7}$ 37^{23}; God's works Ec 3^{11} 8$^{17.17.17}$, cf. 7^{24}. †**b.** = *detect* sin, crime, usu. *in* (ב) one, 2 K 17^{4} 1 S 29$^{3.6.8}$ Ho 12^{9}; לֹא מ׳ בְּיָדִי מְאוּמָה 1 S 12^{5}; detect evil in God Je 2^{5}; subj. God Je 2^{34} 23^{11}; מ׳ עֲוֹן עֲבָדֶיךָ Gn 44^{16}(J), cf. ψ 36^{3}; abs. ψ 10^{15} 17^{3}†. **c.** = *guess*, solve riddle Ju 14$^{12.18}$ cf. Pr 8^{12}. **3.** = *come upon, light upon:* **a.** often unexpectedly = *happen upon*, c. acc. rei, money Gn 44^{8} (J), book 2 K 22^{8} 23^{24} = 2 Ch 34$^{14.15}$, cf. Ne 7^{5}; honey Pr 25^{16}, ship Jon 1^{3}; a plain Gn 11^{2}(J), jawbone Ju 15^{15}; ark of י׳ ψ 132^{6} (acc. to some, but dub.; Bae prop. הוֹצֵאתוּהָ); indef. Ez 3^{1} (del. 𝔊 Co); c. acc. pers. = *meet, fall in with* Gn 4$^{14.15}$ cf. Je 50^{7} Gn 37$^{15.17}$ (all J), 1 S 9^{11} 30^{11} Dt 22$^{23.25.27.28}$ 1 K 13^{24} 20^{36} 2 K 4^{29} 10$^{13.15}$ Ct 3^{3} 5$^{7.8}$ 8^{1}; come upon = *discover*, Nu 15$^{32.33}$; of י׳ meeting (finding) Isr. in desert Ho 9^{10} cf. 12^{5} Dt 32^{10}; angel finding Hagar Gn 16^{7} (J); י׳ finding David ψ 89^{21}. **b.** *hit*, c. acc. pers., subj. bowmen 1 S 31^{3} = 1 Ch 10^{3}; subj. axe Dt 19^{5}. **c.** subj. hand Is 10^{14} (fig., in metaph., of reaching nests), cf. v^{10}, 1 S 23^{17} (cf Saul's taking David), ψ 21^{9} (sq. לְ), v^{9} (c. acc.); כֹּל אֲשֶׁר תִּמְצָא יָדְךָ לַעֲשׂוֹת Ec 9^{10}; sin (i.e. its punishment) *will light upon* you Nu 32^{23}. **d.** †subj. fire, כִּי תֵצֵא אֵשׁ וּמָצְאָה קֹצִים Ex 22^{5} (E). †**e.** *befal*, c. acc. pers. Jos 2^{23} (JE); of evil Gn 44^{34} (J), Dt 4^{30} 31$^{17.17.21}$ Ju 6^{13} 2 K 7^{9} Jb 31^{29} ψ 116^{3} 119^{143} Est 8^{6}; subj. תְּלָאָה Ex 18^{8} (E), Nu 20^{14} (JE), Ne 9^{32}†. **4.** noteworthy phrases are: כַּאֲשֶׁר תִּמ׳ יָדֶךָ Ju 9^{33} *acc. to what thy hand findeth*, i.e. as the occasion may demand, so 1 S 10^{7} (c. acc.; cf. Ec 9^{10} **3 c**); but 25^{8} = *what thou chancest to have*, cf. אֲשֶׁר מ׳ כְּלִי זָהָב Nu 31^{50} (P); וְלֹא יִמְצָאֻהוּ Jb 20^{8} = *and he shall not be*, shall no longer exist, cf. Is 41^{12}; Ec 9^{15} *they found in it* = there happened to be in it; מ׳ אֶת־לִבּוֹ לְהִתְפַּלֵּל 2 S 7^{27} *he found the heart* (took courage) *to pray* = 1 Ch 17^{25} (om. את־לבו, perh. ancient text. err.); לֹא מָצְאוּ יְדֵיהֶם ψ 76^{6} *they did not find their hands*, were not able to use them, were paralyzed; חַיַּת יָדֵךְ מָצָאת Is 57^{10} = (perh.) *experience renewal of thy strength* (cf. 1. חַיָּה p. 312 supr. Che$^{Comm.}$; for other interpr. of ח׳, ידך, v. Ew Di Du Che^{Hpt}); וּמָצָא כְּדֵי גְאֻלָּתוֹ Lv 25^{26} = *and he find* (that he has) *enough for its redemption* (cf. דַּי), so מָצְאָה יָדוֹ דֵּי הָשִׁיב v^{28}, תִּמ׳ יָדָהּ דֵּי שֶׂה 12^{8} (cf. תַּגִּיעַ 5^{7}); without דַּי, וְלֹא מָצְאוּ לָהֶם כֵּן Ju 21^{14} = (prob.) *and they* (the Israelites) *did not find* enough *for them*, even *so* (cf. GFM); also וּמָצָא לָהֶם Nu 11$^{22.22}$ (JE) *and so one find* (= there be found) enough *for them* (cf. Niph. Jos 17^{16} Zc 10^{10}).

†**Niph.** *Pf.* נִמְצָא 1 S 13^{22}+; 3 fs. נמצאה Je 48^{27} Kt Gf; < נִמְצָא Qr Gie; 2 fs. נִמְצֵאת Je 50^{24}; 1 s. נִמְצֵאתִי Is 65^{1}, וְנִמְצֵאתִי consec. Je 29^{14}; 3 pl. נִמְצְאוּ Dt 22^{20}+, הַנִּמְצְאוּ 1 Ch 29^{17} (הַ = rel., cf. Da$^{Synt. § 22 R. 4}$ Kö$^{Synt. § 52}$); *Impf.* יִמָּצֵא Gn 44^{9}+; 3 fs. תִּמָּצֵא Ex 22^{3}+; 2 fs. תִּמָּצְאִי Ez 26^{21}; 3 mpl. יִמָּצְאוּן Gn 18$^{29.30.31.32}$, וַיִּמָּצְאוּ 1 Ch 24^{4} 2 Ch 4^{16}; 3 fpl. תִּמָּצֶאינָה Je 50^{20}; *Inf.* הִמָּצֵא Ex 22^{3} (= Inf. abs. cf. Ba$^{NB 74}$), sf. הִמָּצְאוֹ Is 55^{6}; *Pt.* נִמְצָא Ju 20^{48}+, fs. נִמְצָאָה 2 K 19^{4} = Is 37^{4}; pl. נִמְצָאִים 1 S 13^{15} + 11 t.; נִמְצְאִים only Ezr 8^{25}; sf. 2 fs. נִמְצָאַיִךְ Is 22^{3}; נִמְצָאוֹת Gn 19^{15} Ju 20^{48};—pass. of Qal, *be found:* **1. a.** of a thing lost (asses) 1 S 9^{20} 10$^{2.16}$; stolen Gn 44$^{9.10.12.16.17}$ (J), Ex 21^{16} (all c. בְּיַד); sought, wisdom Jb 28$^{12.13}$ Pr 10^{13}. **b.** of thing found unexpectedly, book 2 K 22^{13} 23^{2} = 2 Ch 34$^{21.30}$; of corpse Dt 21^{1}. **c.** = *be lighted upon, encountered;* of breaches in temple 2 K 12^{6}; of cities Ju 20^{48b}; of persons in captured city 2 K 25$^{19.19}$ = Je 52$^{25.25}$, Dt 20^{11}, cf. Ex 9^{19} (J), Ju 20^{48a} Is 13^{15} 22^{3} Je 41^{8}; *be discovered*, of a condition, situation Dt 22^{20} (בתולים); נִמְצָא־בוֹ דָּבָר טוֹב 1 K 14^{13}, cf. 2 Ch 19^{3}. **d.** *be found* written (כתוב), Ne 13^{1} Est 6^{2}; of persons Dn 12^{1}.

e. = *appeared, were recognised*, of words of 'י Je 15^{16}. **f.** of persons sought Gn 18$^{29.30.31.32}$ (J), Jos 10^{17} (JE), 1 S 10^{21} 2 S 7^{12} 1 Ch 26^{31}; in geneal. register Ezr 2^{62} = Ne 7^{64}; of 'י, specif., *let himself be found of* (*by*) any one: sq. לְ pers. Is 65^{1} Je 29^{14} 1 Ch 28^{9} 2 Ch 15$^{2.4.15}$, abs. Is 55^{6}. **g.** = *be discovered, detected*: (1) of iniquity, crime: Ex 22$^{3.3}$ (E), 1 S 25^{28} 1 K 1^{52} Je 2^{34} Ez 28^{15} Jb 19^{28} Mal 2^{6}, cf. Mi 1^{13}, 2 Ch 36^{8} Est 2^{23}. (2) of wrong-doers Ex 22$^{1.6.7}$ (E), Dt 22$^{22.28}$ 24^{7} Je 2^{26} 48^{27} 50^{24} (נִלְכַּדְתְּ ‖ נִתְפַּשְׂתְּ), Pr 6^{31} Ezr 10^{18}. **h.** = *be gained, secured*, as a crop, of fruit, fig. מִמֶּנִּי פֶּרְיְךָ נִמְצָא Ho 14^{9} (cf. Qal Gn 26^{12} Ec 11^{1}). **i.** = *be discoverable, to be found* Jb 42^{15} Dn 1^{19} (cf. Is 55^{6} supr. **1 f**). **2.** *be found* = *be*: **a.** c. בְּיַד *be found in* one's *hand* = one happens to have 1 S 9^{8} 13$^{22.22}$, cf. (without ביד) 23^{4}. **b.** c. לְ pers., = be in the possession of: Dt 21^{17}, c. אֶת־ (prep.) pers. Ex 35$^{23.24}$ 1 Ch 29^{8}. **c.** *be found in* (בְּ) a place, esp. of wealth, treasure, Gn 47^{14} (J), 2 K 12$^{11.19}$ 14^{14} 16^{8} 18^{15} 20^{13} = Is 39^{2}, 2 K 22^{9} 2 Ch 21^{17} 25^{24} 34^{17}; cf. Ex 12^{19} Je 41^{3} 1 Ch 4^{41}; = *happen to be, be*, Dt 17^{2} 18^{10} Je 5^{26} Is 35^{9} 51^{3} 65^{8}; c. neg. = *be no more* Zp 3^{13} Ez 26^{21} ψ 37^{36} (‖ אֵינֶנּוּ), Dn 11^{19}. **d.** = *be left* after war, violence, etc., 1 S 13^{19} 2 S 17^{13} Is 30^{14} 2 K 19^{4} = Is 37^{4}. **e.** = *be present* Gn 19^{15} (J), 1 S 13$^{15.16}$ 21^{4}; esp. late, 1 Ch 29^{17} 2 Ch 5^{11} 29^{29} 30^{21} 31^{1} 34$^{32.33}$ 35$^{7.17.18}$ Ezr 8^{25} Est 1^{5} 4^{16}. **f.** = *prove to be*, after numbering, 1 Ch 24^{4} 2 Ch 2^{16}; of 'י, עֶזְרָה בְצָרוֹת נִמְצָא ψ 46^{2}. **3.** *be* (*found*) *sufficient*: לֹא יִמָּצֵא לָנוּ הָהָר Jos 17^{16} (JE), cf. Zc 10^{10} (also Qal Nu 11^{22} Ju 21^{14}).

†**Hiph.** *Pf.* 1 s. sf. הִמְצֵיתִךָ 2 S 3^{8}; 3 mpl. הִמְצִיאוּ Lv 9^{13}; *Impf.* 3 ms. sf. 3 ms. יַמְצִאֶנּוּ Jb 34^{11}, יַמְצִאֵהוּ Jb 37^{13}; 3 mpl. וַיַּמְצִאוּ Lv 9$^{12.18}$; *Pt.* מַמְצִיא Zc 11^{6};—**1.** *cause to find, attain*, c. acc. pers. Jb 34^{11} (subj. God). **2.** *cause to light upon, come upon, come* c. acc. of cloud Jb 37^{13} (dub.) **3.** *cause to encounter*, deliver up to, c. acc. pers., + בְּיַד 2 S 3^{8} (subj. man), Zc 11^{6} (subj. God). **4.** *present* unto (אֶל־), of Aaron's sons ministering unto him, c. acc. of offering, and of blood, Lv 9$^{12.13.18}$.

מֹצָא v. מוֹצָא sub יצא.

מַצָּב, מֻצָּב, מַצָּבָה, מַצֵּבָה, מַצֶּבֶת v. נצב.

†**מְצֹבָיָה** c. art. 'הַמּ 1 Ch 11^{47}, dub.; the preceding n.pr. seems to call for adj. gent., but form not suitable, and poss. deriv. unknown; Be conj. מִצֹּבָה, *from Ṣôba*; 𝔊 ὁ Μειναβεια, Μεσωβια, Μασαβια; 𝔙 *de Masobia*.

מְצַד, [מְצָדָה], מְצָדָה v. צוד.

†**[מָצָה]** **vb.** drain, drain out (NH *id.*, *press* or *drain out*; Aram. מְצָא, ܡܨܳܐ *id.*; Ar. مصو II. *drain to the last drop* (Dozy); cf. מָצַץ);—**Qal** *Pf.* 2 fs. מָצִית Is 51^{17}, וּמָצִית consec. Ez 23^{34}; *Impf.* 3 ms. apoc. וַיִּמֶץ Ju 6^{38}, 3 mpl. יִמְצוּ ψ 75^{9};—*drain, drain out*, וַיִּמֶץ טַל מִן־הַגִּזָּה Ju 6^{38} *and drained dew out of the fleece*; so fig., obj. קֻבַּעַת *bowl, goblet*, of bewilderment fr. 'י, Is 51^{17} (+ שׁתה; of personif. Jerusalem), cf., obj. כּוֹס, Ez 23^{34} (+ שׁתה); obj. שְׁמָרֶיהָ *the dregs of it* (viz. כּוֹס) ψ 75^{9} (subj. the wicked). **Niph.** *Pf.* וְנִמְצָה consec. Lv 1^{15} *and* the blood (of the bird) *shall be drained out*; so *Impf.* יִמָּצֵה 5^{9} (both P); וּמֵי מָלֵא יִמָּצוּ לָמוֹ ψ 73^{10} *water of abundance is drained* (i. e. drunk) *by them* (Gr Che Buhl rd. יָמֹצּוּ or יָמֹצוּ (מצץ) *they drain*).

I. **מַצָּה** v. מצץ. II. **מַצָּה** v. נצה.

†**מֹצָה** **n.pr.loc.** in Benj., Jos 18^{26}; 𝔊 Αμωκη, A Αμωσα, 𝔊L Μασσα. Site unknown.

[מִצְהָלָה] v. צהל.

[מָצוֹד], מְצוֹדָה, מְצוּדָה v. צוד.

מִצְוָה v. צוה.

[מְצוֹלָה], מְצוּלָה, מְצֻלָה v. צול.

מָצוֹק, מְצוּקָה v. I. צוק.

מָצוֹק v. II. צוק.

I. **מָצוֹר, מְצוּרָה** v. I. צור.

II. **מָצוֹר** *Egypt*, v. מִצְרַיִם, מצר.

[מַצּוֹת] v. נצה.

מצח (√ of foll.)

†**מֵצַח** **n.m.**$^{Ez\,3.8}$ brow, forehead;—'מ abs. Ez 3^{7}, cstr. Ex 28^{28} Je 3^{3}; sf. מִצְחֲךָ Ez 3^{8} Is 48^{4}, מִצְחֵךְ Ez 3^{9}; מִצְחוֹ Ex 28^{38} + 4 t.; מִצְחָם Ez 3^{8}; pl. cstr. מִצְחוֹת Ez 9^{4};—*brow, forehead*, struck by stone fr. David's sling 1 S 17$^{49.49}$; Aaron's forehead Ex 28$^{38.38}$; place where leprosy appears 2 Ch 26$^{19.20}$; place for a distinguishing mark or cross Ez 9^{4}; חִזְקֵי־מ' 3^{7} the house of Isr. are *stout of forehead* (i. e. obstinate; ‖ קְשֵׁי־לֵב), cf. v^{8}; so מִצְחֲךָ נְחוּשָׁה Is 48^{4} *thy brow* (is) *brass*

(גִּיד בַּרְזֶל עָרְפֶּךָ ||); also of boldness, firmness of prophet v^{8}, and v^{9} (but del. 𝔊 Co); מ׳ אִשָּׁה זוֹנָה הָיָה לָךְ Je 3^{3}, i. e. thou wast shameless (מֵאַנְתְּ הִכָּלֵם ||).

†[מִצְחָה] **n.f.** greave(s);—only sg. cstr. וּמִצְחַת נְחֹשֶׁת עַל־רַגְלָיו 1 S 17^{6} *and greaves of bronze upon his legs;* < מִצְחוֹת Vrss Th We Klo Dr Bu.

[מְצִלָּה], מְצִלְתַּיִם v. I. צלל.

מְצֻלָּה v. צול. מִצְנֶפֶת v. צנף.

[מַצָּע] v. יצע. [מִצְעָד] v. צעד.

מִצְעָר v. צער.

I, II. מִצְפֶּה, מִצְפָּה v. צפה.

[מַצְפּוּנִים] v. צפן.

†[מָצַץ] **vb. drain out** (cf. מָצָה; NH *id.*; Ar. مَصَّ *suck, suck up;* Aram. מְצַץ, ܡܨ *suck* or *press out*);—only **Qal** *Impf.* 2 mpl. תָּמֹצּוּ וְהִתְעַנַּגְתֶּם מִזִּיז כְּבוֹדָהּ Is 66^{11} that *ye may drain out and delight yourselves,* etc. (|| תִּינְקוּ וּשְׂבַעְתֶּם).

†I. מַצָּה **n.f. unleavened bread, or cake(s);**—abs. מ׳ Lv 2^{5} 8^{26} (חַלַּת מ׳ אַחַת), Nu 6^{19} (*id.*), v^{19}; usu. pl. מַצּוֹת Ex 12^{15}+44 t.; מַצֹּת Ex 12^{18} +3 t.;—*unleavened bread,* prepared in form of לֶחֶם Ex 29^{2}; חַלָּה Ex 29^{2}+4 t. P; רקיקים Ex 29^{2} 1 Ch 23^{29}+4 t. P; עֻגֹת Ex 12^{39}; used at ordinary meals (prepared hastily): אפה מ׳ Gn 19^{3} (J), Ex 12^{39} (J), 1 S 28^{24}; prob. also Ju 6$^{19.20.21.21}$; elsewhere at sacrificial meals, e. g. ritual peace-offerings Lv 2$^{4.4.5}$ 6^{9} 7$^{12.12}$ 10^{12}; consecration of priesthood Ex 29$^{2.2.2.23}$ Lv 8$^{2.26.26}$; at peace-offering of Nazirite Nu 6$^{15.15.17.19.19}$; at Passover Ex 12^{8} Nu 9^{11} (all P); esp. at feast of *unleavened bread* [*cakes*] for 7 days after Passover שמר חג המ׳ Ex 23^{15} (E), 34^{18} (J); שמר מ׳ Ex 12^{17} (P), עשׂה חג (ה)מ׳ 2 Ch 30$^{13.21}$ 35^{17} Ezr 6^{22}; בחג המ׳ Dt 16^{16} 2 Ch 8^{13}; חג המ׳ לי׳ Lv 23^{6}. During these seven days all Israel ate מצות Ex 12$^{15.18.20}$ (P), 23^{15} (E), 13$^{6.7}$ 34^{18} (J), Lv 23^{6} Nu 28^{17} (P), Dt 16$^{3.8}$ Jos 5^{11} Ez 45^{21}.—2 K 23^{9} rd. prob. מִצְוֹת or מְנָיוֹת for MT (אכל) מ׳; so Gei Kue Kmp Bu.

[מָצֹק] v. מָצוֹק sub II. צוק.

[מְצֻקָה] v. מצוקה sub I. צוק.

[מֻצֶּקֶת] v. מוצ׳ sub יצק. מֵצַר v. I. צרר.

מצר (√ of foll.)

מִצְרַיִם$_{681}$ **n.pr.terr. et gent. f.**$^{Ex 10,7}$, **m.**$^{Ex 12,33}$, **mpl.**$^{Gn 41,55}$ etc. (v. infr. **2**), **Egypt, Egyptians** (Ph. מצרם; As. *Mûṣûr(u), Muṣru, Miṣir,* Dl$^{Par 308}$ Schr$^{COT Gloss. KGF 246 ff.}$, Tel Am *Miṣri,* Wkl$^{TA 39*}$ Bez$^{BM 152}$, and *Mašrî* Wkl$^{l.c.}$; Ar. مِصْر Cairo, Egypt (Spiro); Min. *Miṣru* Hom$^{A. and A. (1892), 125}$; v. also Eb$^{ÄgM 71 ff.}$; 𝔊 Αἴγυπτος;—deriv. and form dub.; ־ַיִם usu. regarded as dual term. (Upper and Lower Egypt? cf. Di$^{Gn 10,6}$), but as loc. ending EMey$^{Gesch. i. § 42}$ Ba$^{NB p. 319 R. 5}$; Jen$^{ZA iv (1889), 268 ff.}$ thinks מִצְרַיִם abs. formed by anal. of מַיִם, שָׁמַיִם from *Miṣrî* (cf. Tel Am); v. further Wkl$^{infra, ad fin.}$);—מ׳ Gn 13^{1}+; מִצְרָיִם 37^{36}+; מִצְרַיְמָה 12^{10}+12 t., מִצְרָיְמָה 12^{11}+14 t.;—**1. a.** of land, *Egypt,* Gn 13^{1}+500 t., +, in all periods, incl. אֶרֶץ מ׳ 13^{10} +c. 220 t. (of course f., 47$^{6.13}$); אַדְמַת מ׳ *the soil of Egypt* †47$^{20.26}$; מֵימֵי מ׳ †Ex 7^{19} 8^{2}; נְהַר מ׳ †Gn 15^{18}; יְאֹר מ׳ †Am 8^{8} 9^{5}; יְאֹרֵי מ׳ †Is 7^{18} (cf. מָצוֹר); שִׁיחוֹר מ׳ †1 Ch 13^{5}; לְשׁוֹן יָם־מ׳ †Is 11^{15}; נַחַל מ׳ Jos 15^{4}+6 t. (v. these various wds.); land as productive Gn 45^{20} 49^{23}, cf. שֵׁשׁ בְּרִקְמָה מִמּ׳ Ez 27^{7}, אֵטוּן מ׳ Pr 7^{16}; oft. || כּוּשׁ, esp. in proph. and poet. Is 20$^{3.4.5}$ 45^{14} Ez 30$^{4.9}$+; || אַשּׁוּר Ho 11^{11} 12^{1} Is 7^{18} Je 2^{18}+; incl. Upper Egypt (פַּתְרוֹס), as well as Lower, Je 44^{1}, cf. Ez 29^{10} 30^{6}; appar. disting. fr. Upper Egypt Is 11^{11}, and poss. also Je 44^{15} (cf. Gf Gie Buhl SS Che$^{Hpt Isaiah}$); but פתרוס etc. in these vv. somewhat dub. (cf. Du Gie). **b.** combinations are: (1) מ׳ as limit of motion: יָרַד מצרים(ה) Gn 43^{15} Jos 24^{4}+c. 12 t.; בּוֹא מ׳ 1 S 12^{8} +c. 26 t., בוא בְּמ׳ †Is 19^{23}, בוא לְמ׳ †Je 44^{28}; שׁוּב מ׳ Ho 8^{3}+9 t., שׁוּב אֶל־מ׳ †Ho 11^{5}, שׁוּב לְאַרְצוֹ מ׳ †Je 37^{7}; בָּרַח מ׳ †1 K 11^{40}; שָׁלַח מ׳ †Je 26^{22}, so (+ אֶל־) v^{22}. In Je 42$^{16 b}$ rd. בְּמ׳ with Gie. (2) מ׳ as point of departure (הֶעֱלָה) עָלָה מִן־(ארץ) מ׳ Gn 13^{1}+c. 43 t.; (הוֹצִיא) יָצָא מִן־(ארץ) מ׳ Ex 12^{39}+c. 96 t.; פָּדָה מִמּ׳ †2 S 7^{23} (but del. Gei$^{Urschr. 288}$ We Dr Kit Bu) = 1 Ch 17^{21}; בוא מִמּ׳ †2 Ch 12^{3} 20^{10}; שׁוּב מִמּ׳ †Je 44^{28} 2 Ch 10^{2}; אָתָה מִמּ׳ †ψ 68^{32}; קָרָא מִמּ׳ †Ho 11^{1}. **2.** of people: **a.** in table of nations, personif. as second son of Ham †Gn 10^{6} = 1 Ch 1^{8}, cf. Gn 10^{13} = 1 Ch 1^{11}. **b.** = *Egypt* (as a people), *Egyptians* Gn 41^{56}+c. 134 t., incl. use = Egyptian kingdom, empire, i. e. land and people as political power; so c. vb. fs. אָבְדָה מ׳ Ex 10^{7}, cf. Ho 9^{6} Jo 4^{19} and (pron. fs.) Ez 30^{18}; c. vb. ms. Ex 12^{33} 14^{25} Is 19$^{16.23.25}$ Je 46^{8}; oft. c. vb. mpl. Gn 41^{55} Is 19$^{21.23}$+22 t.; בְּנֵי מ׳ Ez 16^{26};

בְּתוּלַת בַּת מ׳ † Je 46[11], cf. v[19.24].—In 1 K 10[28] = 2 Ch 1[16.17], 2 K 7[6] Wkl[Alttest. Unters. 171 f.] thinks of As. *Muṣri* in N. Syria. (On מִצְרַיִם as oft. = *Muṣri* in N. Arabia v. Wkl [Altor. Unters. i. 24 ff., ii. 195, iii. 289, iv. 337 f.; MVG 1898, 1. 4]).

† מָצוֹר n.pr.terr. = מִצְרַיִם; only poet.: יְאֹרֵי מ׳ Is 19[6] 2 K 19[24] = Is 37[25]; וְעָדֶיךָ יָבוֹא לְמִנִּי אַשּׁוּר וְעָרֵי מ׳ וּלְמִנִּי מ׳ וְעַד נָהָר Mi 7[12] (𝔊 misunderstands everywhere).

† מִצְרִי adj.gent. Egyptian;—ms. מ׳ Gn 39[1] + 16 t.; fs. מִצְרִית 16[1] + 3 t.; mpl. מִצְרִים 12[12] + 5 t.; fpl. מִצְרִיֹּת Ex 1[19];—**1.** adj. אִישׁ מ׳ = *an Egyptian* Gn 39[1] Ex 2[11.19] Lv 24[10] 1 S 30[11] 2 S 23[30]; הָאִישׁ הַמּ׳ 1 Ch 11[23]; עֶבֶד מ׳ נַעַר מ׳ 1 S 30[13], 1 Ch 2[34]; שִׁפְחָה מִצְרִית Gn 16[1], הַנָּשִׁים הַמִּצְרִיֹּת Ex 1[19]. **2.** c. art. = subst. *the Egyptian* Gn 39[2.5] Ex 2[12.14] 2 S 23[30.30] 1 Ch 11[23.23]; so once without art. מִצְרִי Dt 23[8]; הַמִּצְרִי once (late) coll. = *the Egyptians* Ezr 9[1] (where with Canaanitish peoples); pl. = *the Egyptians*, הַמִּצְרִים Gn 12[12.14] 43[32] Dt 26[6] Jos 24[7]; fs. הָגָר הַמִּצְרִית *Ḥagar the Egyptian woman* Gn 16[3] 21[9] 25[12].

[מְצֻרָה] v. מְצוּרָה sub I. צור.

מַצְרֵף v. צרף. [מַצַּת] v. מַצּוֹת sub נצה.

מַק, מָק v. מקק. מַקֶּבֶת I, II. v. נקב.

† מַקֵּדָה n.pr.loc. in Judah Jos 15[41], near Beth Horon Jos 10[10], and Libnah v[29], where was a cave v[16.17], cf. v[21], captured by Joshua v[28], with a king v[28] 12[16]. 𝔊 Μακηδα. Site dubious, Warren [Survey Mem. ii. 411 ff., 427] comp. *El-mughâr*, c. 2¾ miles SW. from Ekron.

מִקְדָּשׁ v. קדשׁ.

מַקְהֵלִים, מַקְהֵלֹת I, II. v. קהל.

מִקְוֶא, מִקְוָה, מִקְוֶה I, II. v. קוה.

מָקוֹם v. קום. מָקוֹר v. קור.

[מִקָּח, מַקָּחָה] v. לקח.

[מִקְטָר], מִקְטֶרֶת v. קטר.

† מַקֵּל n.m. [Zc 11, 7] (appar. **f.** Gn 30[37], where בָּהֶן, but Sam. בָּהֶם) rod, **staff** (√ dub.; Thes assumes √ מקל *sprout*; Schwally [ZAW xi. 1891, 170 f.] from קלל = *shake*, with ref. to oracle of the lot (cf. קִלְקַל בַּחִצִּים Ez 21[26]); Ba [ZMG xli. 1887, 616] gives √ קל, and comp. قَلَّةٌ *stick driven* by another, in sport; Frä [ZA iii. 52], comp. Eth. በቈልት፡ *growth, stem, palm-tree* (interchange of ב and מ));—מ׳ abs. Nu 22[27]; cstr. Je 1[11] + 2 t., מַקַּל Gn 30[37]; sf. מַקְלִי 32[11] + 2 t.; מַקְלוֹ 1 S 17[40] Ho 4[12]; מַקֶּלְכֶם Ex 12[11]; pl. abs. מַקְלוֹת Gn 30[37] + 6 t.;—**1.** branch of tree as *rod, stick*, used by Jacob in breeding his flocks, Gn 30[37] (מ׳ לִבְנֶה לַח), v[37.38.39.41.41]; of symbolic rod (מ׳ שָׁקֵד *almond-rod*) in Jerem.'s vision Je 1[11]; symbolic rods or staves, with names, used by proph. Zc 11[7.10.14]; fig. of Moab מ׳ תִּפְאָרָה Je 48[17] (‖ מַטֵּה־עֹז). **2.** *staff*, used in journeying Gn 32[11] Ex 12[11], 1 S 17[40] cf. v[43]; carried even when riding Nu 22[27]; so also מַקֵּל יָד Ez 39[9] (= *riding-stick*) acc. to Hi Da Berthol; < a weapon (+ חִצִּים, קֶשֶׁת, מָגֵן, צִנָּה, רֹמַח). **3.** *wand* of diviner Ho 4[12].

† מִקְלוֹת n.pr.m. **1.** a Benjamite 1 Ch 8[32] (read perh. also v[31 ad fin.], so 𝔊, cf. 9[37]), 9[37.38].—𝔊 Μακαλωθ, Μακελλωθ, etc. **2.** an officer of David acc. to 1 Ch 27[4] (om. 𝔊B; 𝔊L Μακελλωθ).

מִקְלָט v. II. קלט.

מִקְלַעַת v. קלע. מָקֹם v. מָקוֹם sub קום.

מִקְנֶה, מִקְנָה, מִקְנֵיָהוּ v. קנה.

[מִקְסָם] v. קסם. מַקָּפִים v. נקף.

† מָקַץ n.pr.loc. in Israel, site unknown, 1 K 4[9]; 𝔊 Μαχεμας, A Μαχμας (i. e. מִכְמָס), 𝔊L Μαγχας.

מִקְצוֹעַ, מִקְצָע, [מַקְצוּעָה, מִקְצֹעַת] v. קצע.

מִקְצָת v. קָצָת.

† [מָקַק] vb. decay, rot, fester, fig. **pine away** (NH *id.*; Aram. (𝔗) מְקַק);—**Niph.** *Pf.* 3 pl. נָמַקּוּ ψ 38[6], וְנ׳ consec. Is 34[4] Ez 4[17]; 2 mpl. וּנְמַקֹּתֶם consec. Ez 24[23]; *Impf.* 3 fs. תִּמַּק Zc 14[12]; 3 mpl. יִמַּקּוּ Lv 26[39], יִמָּקּוּ v[39]; 3 fpl. תִּמַּקְנָה Zc 14[12]; *Pt.* pl. נְמַקִּים Ez 33[10];—**1.** *fester*, of wounds ψ 38[6] (+ הִבְאִישׁוּ, v. באשׁ). **2.** *rot, rot away*, עֵינָיו תִּמַּקְנָה בְחֹרֵיהֶן וּלְשׁוֹנוֹ תִּמַּק בְּפִיהֶם׃ Zc 14[12] (plague upon foes of Jerusalem). **3.** *moulder away*, of צְבָא הַשָּׁמַיִם Is 34[4] (‖ וְנָגֹלּוּ כַסֵּפֶר הַשָּׁמָיִם). **4.** of *pining away* by reason of (בְּ), as punishment for, iniquity Ez 4[17] 24[23] 33[10] Lv 26[39.39]. **Hiph.** *Inf. abs.* הָמֵק, trans. ה׳ בְּשָׂרוֹ Zc 14[12] *a causing his flesh to rot.*

†מַק (c. art. מָק) **n.m.** **decay, rottenness**;—תַּחַת בֹּשֶׂם מַק יִהְיֶה Is 3^{24} *instead of perfume rottenness shall there be*; fig. שָׁרְשָׁם כַּמָּק יִהְיֶה 5^{24} (|| וּפִרְחָם כָּאָבָק יַעֲלֶה).

מִקְרָא v. I. קרא. מְקָרֶה, מִקְרֶה v. קרה.

מְקֵרָה v. קרר. I. מִקְשֶׁה, מִקְשָׁה v. קשה.

II. מִקְשָׁה v. [קִשֻּׁאָה]

I. מַר, מֹר, מָרָא Ru 1^{20}, v. I. מרר.

II. מַר v II. מרר.

†I. [מָרָא] **vb.** only **Hiph.** *Impf.* 3 fs: mng dub, perh. *beat* the air, or *flap* the wings, cf. Di De (and Wetzst in De), Bu Du (cf Ar. مَرَى *whip, urge on* a horse?),—תַּמְרִיא תִּשְׂחַק לַסּוּס וּלְרֹכְבוֹ׃ Jb 39^{18} *she* (the ostrich) *flaps away*, she laughs at the horse and his rider.

II. מרא (√ of foll, *be fat*; cf. As. *marû* III. causat., adj. *marû*, *well-fed, fat*; Ar. مَرِئَ *be digestible, agree with* (of food)).

†מְרִיא **n.[m.]** **fatling, fatlings**;—abs. מ׳ 2 S 6^{13} + 3 t; pl abs. מְרִיאִים Is 1^{11}, cstr. מְרִיאֵי Ez 39^{18}, sf מְרִיאֵיכֶם Am 5^{22},—*fatling*: עֵגֶל וּכְפִיר וּמְרִיא Is 11^{6}; elsewh. only of sacrificial animals, שֶׁלֶם מְרִיאֵיכֶם Am 5^{22} (|| מִנְחֹתֵיכֶם, עֹלוֹת); חֵלֶב מְרִיאִים Is 1^{11} (|| דַּם פָּרִים, עלות אילים, etc); מְרִיאֵי בָשָׁן Ez 39^{18} (+ אֵילִים, פָּרִים, etc.); also sg coll., וַיִּזְבַּח שׁוֹר וּמְרִיא 2 S 6^{13}, so (+ צֹאן וּבָקָר) 1 K 1^{9}, and (+ צאן, שׁוֹר) v$^{19.25}$.

†[מֻרְאָה] **n.f.** **crop** or **alimentary canal**, of bird, cf Di-Ry (on form cf. Lag$^{BN\ 81}$);—וְהֵסִיר אֶת־מֻרְאָתוֹ בְּנֹצָתָהּ Lv 1^{16}.

מֹרָא v. מוֹרָא sub ירא.

מְרֹאדַךְ v. מְרֹדַךְ.

מַרְאֶה, מַרְאָה v. ראה.

מֹרְאָה v. מרה pt. f. מֵרוֹן v. שִׁמְרוֹן.

מְרַאֲשָׁה v. מָרֵשָׁה [מְרַאֲשׁוֹת] v. ראש.

†מֵרַב **n.pr.f.** elder daughter of Saul 1 S 14^{49}, promised to David 18^{17}, but given to Adriel v^{19} (rd. also 2 S 21^{8} for מִיכַל 𝔊L 𝔖 Th Dr Klo Kit Bu Lohr HPS). 𝔊 Μεροβ.

מַרְבַדִּים v. II. רבד.

מַרְבִּית, מַרְבֶּה, מִרְבָּה v. רבה.

מַרְבֵּץ v. רבץ. מַרְבֵּק v. רבק.

מַרְגּוֹעַ v. II. רגע. [מַרְגְּלוֹת] v. רגל.

מַרְגֵּמָה v. רגם. מַרְגֵּעָה v. II רגע.

†[מָרַד] **vb.** **rebel** (NH *id.*; Ar. مَرُدَ *be bold and audacious in acts of rebellion or disobedience*; Eth. መረደ: *run strenuously, attack*; መረድ: *rebellion*, Pra$^{Beiträge\ iii.\ 44}$; Sab. מרד *rebellion* Hal^{535,16} Sab Denkm.^{38} Hom$^{Chrestom\ 127}$, Aram. ܡܪܕ, מְרַד; *rebel*),—**Qal** *Pf* 3 ms. מָרַד 2 Ch 36^{13}, 2 ms. מָרַדְתָּ 2 K 18^{20} = Is 36^{5}, etc; *Impf.* וַיִּמְרֹד 2 K 18^{7} + 3 t., וַיִּמְרָד 2 K 24^{1} Ez 17^{15}, etc.; *Inf. cstr.* לִמְרֹד Jos 22^{29}, לִמְרוֹד Ne 6^{6}; *Pt.* pl מֹרְדִים Ne 2^{19} Ez 20^{38}, מֹר׳ Ez 2^{3}; cstr מֹרְדֵי Jb 24^{13},—*rebel, revolt*: **1.** against human king, c. בְּ pers 2 K 18$^{7.20}$ = Is 36^{5}, 2 K 24$^{1.20}$ = Je 52^{3}, cf. Ez 17^{15} 2 Ch 36^{13}, Ne 9^{26}; less oft. (late) c. עַל pers. 2 Ch 13^{6} Ne 2^{19}; abs. Gn 14^{4} Ne 6^{6}. **2.** against God, c. בְּ Nu 14^{9} (JE), Jos 22$^{16.18.19.29}$ (all P), Ez 2^{3} (Co מָרוּ), Dn 9^{9}; abs. Ez 2^{3} (pt., Co מוֹרִים), 20^{38} Dn 9^{5}. **3.** poet., against light, only מֹרְדֵי אוֹר Jb 24^{13}.

†I. מֶרֶד **n.[m.]** **rebellion, revolt,** against י׳, אִם בְּמֶרֶד וְאִם־בְּמַעַל בַּיהוה Jos 22^{22} (P, cf. מָרַד **2**).

†II. מֶרֶד **n.pr.m.** name in Judah acc to 1 Ch 4^{17}, מֶרֶד v^{18}. 𝔊 Πωραδ, Νωρωηλ, A Μωραδ, Μωρηδ, 𝔊L Βαραδ, Μαρω.

†מַרְדּוּת **n.f.** **rebellion, rebelliousness,** only in בֶּן־נַעֲוַת הַמּ׳ 1 S 20^{30}, where read prob. בֶּן־נַעֲרַת הַמַּרְדּוּת *son of a girl of rebelliousness* = *rebellious girl*, cf. 𝔊 𝔙 Th We Dr HPS; > Lag$^{M\ i\ 236\ f.}$ Bu (cf. also Dr Kit) der. מ׳ fr. רדה, and, retaining MT, rd. *a woman gone astray* (v. II. עָוָה) *from discipline* (Aram. sense: √ רְדָא).

†מְרֹדָךְ **n.pr.div.** chief god of Babylon in Nebuchadrezzar's time (As. *Mar(u)duk(u)* Schr$^{COT\ Gloss}$ Tiele$^{Bab.-Ass.\ Gesch.\ 530\ ff}$ Say$^{Rel.\ Bab.\ 96\ ff}$; cf. Muss-Arnolt$^{JBL\ xi\ 1892,\ 164\ f.}$);—נִלְכְּדָה בָבֶל הֹבִישׁ בֵּל חַת מְרֹדָךְ Je 50^{2} (𝔊 Μαιωδακ).

†מְרֹדַךְ בַּלְאֲדָן **n.pr.m.** king of Babylon (As. *Marduk abal-idinna, Marduk has given a son* Schr$^{COT\ 2\ K\ 20\ 12}$),—Is 39^{1} (> van d. H מְרֹאדַךְ ב׳, v. Baer's n.) = 2 K 20^{12} (where read מרדך for בראדך); 𝔊 (in both) Μαρωδαχ(χ) Βαλ(α)δαν; cf. also בַּלְאֲדָן.

†מָרְדֳּכַי (van d H מָרְדְּכַי) **n.pr.m.** **Mordecai** (perh fr. n div. *Marduk* (מְרֹדָךְ), Zim$^{ZAW\ xi\ 161ff}$; cf further Wild (citing Jensen)$^{Comm.\ Est\ 173f}$),—מ׳ Ezr 2^{2} Est 2^{5}+; מָרְדֳּכָ֑י Est 2^{22}+;—**1.** companion of Zerub., acc to Ezr 2^{2} = Ne 7^{7}. 𝔊 Μαραθχαιος, Μαρδοχαιος, etc. **2.** cousin and adoptive father of Esther Est $2^{5.7.10}$ + 55 t Est. 𝔊 Μαρδοχαιος.

מִרְדָּף v רדף, רדה.

†מָרָה **vb. be contentious, refractory, rebellious** (NH *id*, Hiph; Ar مَرَى III. *dispute with*; Syr ܡܪܐ Pa *contend with*);—**Qal** *Pf* 3 ms. מָרָה 1 K 13^{26}; f מָרְתָה Ho 14^{1}; מָרָ֑תָה Je 4^{17}; 2 ms מָרִיתָ 1 K 13^{21} + 11 t. pf, *Inf. abs.* מָרוֹ La 1^{20}, *Pt* מֹרָה 2 K 14^{26} (but rd מַר, √מרר, Kmp^{Kau} כִּי מַר הוּא), מוֹרֶה Dt 21^{18} + 3 t., f. מֹרְאָה Zp 3^{1} (rd. מֹרָה; metapl. form acc. to Ges $^{§ 75\ R\ 22}$), pl מֹרִים Nu 20^{10},—*be disobedient, rebellious*: **1** בֵּן סוֹרֵר וּמוֹרֶה Dt $21^{18.20}$ *stubborn and rebellious son* (towards father) **2.** elsewhere towards God. לֵב סוֹרֵר וּמ׳ ψ 78^{8}, דּוֹר סוֹרֵר וּמֹרֶה Je 5^{23}; מֹרְאָה וְנִגְאָלָה הָעִיר Zp 3^{1}; הַמֹּרִים Nu 20^{10} *ye rebels* (P); abs Is 50^{5} 63^{10} La $1^{20.20}$; ‖ מאן Is 1^{20}, פשׁע La 3^{42}; c. ב pers Ho 14^{1} ψ 5^{11}, elsewh acc. pers. Je 4^{17}; י׳'s words ψ 105^{28}, מרה (את) פי Nu 20^{24} 27^{14} (P), 1 S 12^{15} 1 K $13^{21.26}$ (D^{2}) La 1^{18} —In Ho 4^{4} rd. perh. מָרוּ בִי *have rebelled against me* (for MT כִּמְרִיבֵי), so RS$^{Proph\ iv\ n\ 8}$ Che (for other views v. ריב) **Hiph.** *Pf* 3 mpl הִמְרוּ ψ 106^{33} 107^{11}, *Impf* יַמְרֶה Jos 1^{18}, f וַתֶּמֶר Ez 5^{6}; 2 ms תֶּמֶר (as if √מרר) Ex 23^{21}, rd. תַּמֵּר Di al; 3 mpl. יַמְרוּ ψ 106^{43} + 6 t.; sf יַמְרוּהוּ ψ 78^{40}; 2 mpl תַּמְרוּ 1 S 12^{14} + 3 t; *Inf. cstr* לַמְרוֹת Is 3^{8} ψ 78^{17}, sf. הַמְרוֹתָם (Ges$^{§ 20.2b}$) Jb 17^{2}, *Pt.* pl מַמְרִים Dt 9^{7} + 2 t,—*shew disobedience, rebelliousness*, always toward God: abs. Ne 9^{26} (‖ מרד), ψ $106^{7.43}$ Jb 17^{2}; c. ב pers. Ex 23^{21} Ez $20^{8.13.21}$, עם Dt $9^{7.24}$ 31^{27}; elsewhere acc. of God or his commands: Is 3^{8} Ez 5^{6} ψ $78^{17.40.56}$ 107^{11}; המרה את פי Dt $1^{26.43}$ 9^{23} Jos 1^{18} 1 S 12^{14} (D^{2}), את־רוחו ψ 106^{33} (cf Eph 4^{30}), perh 139^{20} (v. אָמַר **1**).

†מְרִי **n.m.**$^{Pr\ 17.11}$ **rebellion**;—מְרִי Is 30^{9} + 10 t.; מֶ֫רִי Nu 17^{25} + 9 t, sf מֶרְיְךָ Dt 31^{27}, מֶרְיָם Ne 9^{17},—*rebellion* Dt 31^{27} 1 S 15^{23} Ne 9^{17} Jb 23^{2} עם מרי *rebellious people* Is 30^{9}, בית (ה)מרי *rebellious house* (referring to Israel) Ez $2^{5.6.8}$ $3^{9.26.27}$ $12^{2.2.3.9.25}$ 17^{12} 24^{3}, בית omitted (restored by Co) 2^{7} 44^{6}, בני מרי *rebellious sons* Nu 17^{25} (P), with omission of בן (or abstr. for concrete), אל תהי מֶרִי *be not a rebellious person* Ez 2^{8}; אך מרי יבקשׁ רע *a rebellious man seeketh only evil* Pr 17^{11}.

†יִמְרָה **n.pr.m.** 1 Ch 7^{36} a chief of Asher. 𝔊 Ιμαρη, A Ιεμρα, 𝔊L Ιεμβρα.

מָרָה, מָרָה, מָרָה, מָרָה v I מרר.

מֹרֶה v. ירה **Hiph.** Pt, and II. מוֹרָה p 435

[מָרוּד] v. רוד. מרוז v אח.

†[מְרוֹחַ] **n.**[**m.**] dub., only cstr. מְרוֹחַ אָשֶׁךְ Lv 21^{20}, √ either מָרַח *rub* = *a rubbing away of the testicle*; or רָוַח *be roomy, enlarged* = *enlargement* (read then מְרֻוָח); v. further Di

מָרוֹם v רום

†מֵרוֹם **n.pr.loc.** only in מֵי מֵרוֹם Jos $11^{5.7}$ *waters of Merom*, in N Canaan; = Lake *Ḥule*, acc to Rel and many, but dub, cf. Di Bad$^{Pal\ 3\ 259}$ GASm$^{Geogr\ 481}$ Buhl$^{Geogr\ 113}$.

מֵרוֹן v. שִׁמְרוֹן. מֵרוֹץ, I [מְרוּצָה] v. רוץ.

II. מְרוּצָה v. רצץ. [מְרוּקִים] v. I. מרק.

†מָרוֹת **n.pr loc.** in (Shephelah of) Judah Mi 1^{12}, form attested by 𝔊 ὀδύνας (√ מרר)

מַרְזֵחַ v רזח.

†[מָרַח] **vb. rub** (NH *id.*; Aram. (Talm) מְרַח, cf. Ar مَرَخَ *anoint, smear*);—**Qal** *Impf.* יִשְׂאוּ דְּבֶלֶת תְּאֵנִים וְיִמְרְחוּ עַל־הַשְּׁחִין Is 38^{21} let them take a cake of figs *and rub* it upon the eruption (שִׂים in ‖ 2 K 20^{7})—On מרוח v. supr.

מֶרְחָב, מֶרְחַבְיָה v רחב.

מֶרְחָק v. רחק. מַרְחֶשֶׁת v רחשׁ.

†[מָרַט] **vb. make smooth, bare, bald; scour, polish** (NH *id.*; *pull out, off* (feathers, hair), Aram ܡܪܛ, מְרַט *id*; Ar مَرِطَ *have little hair*, مَرَطَ *pluck out hair*);—**Qal** *Impf* 1 s. וָאֶמְרְטָה Ezr 9^{3}, sf 3 mpl. וָאֶמְרְטֵם Ne 13^{25}; *Inf cstr* מָרְטָה Ez 21^{16}, *Pt* pl מֹרְטִים Is 50^{6}; *pass* f מְרוּטָה Ez 21^{14} + 2 t.,—**1.** *make bare* כָּל־כָּתֵף מְרוּטָה Ez 29^{18} *every shoulder is laid bare* (fr. chafing of burden; ‖ כָּל־רֹאשׁ מֻקְרָח); the cheek (by plucking out beard) גֵּוִי נָתַתִּי לְמַכִּים וּלְחָיַי לְמֹרְטִים Is 50^{6}; c. acc. pers וָאֶמְרְטֵם Ne 13^{25} (both acts of violence); of hair and beard וָאֶמְרְטָה מִשְּׂעַר רֹאשִׁי וּזְקָנִי Ezr 9^{3} (sign of grief) **2.** *scour, polish*, a sword, only Ez 21:

v^{14} (+ התחדה; Co rds. ׳מ as Pu), v^{16} (del. Co), v^{33}, + v^{20} מְרֻטָּה for MT מְעֻטָּה (Ew Sm Co Bertho1). **Niph.** *Impf.* יִמָּרֵט רֹאשׁוֹ Lv 13$^{40.41}$ *his head is made bald* (by leprosy). **Pu.** *Pf.* 3 fs. מֹרָטָה Ez 21$^{15.16}$; *Pt.* מְמֹרָט 1 K 7^{45}, מוֹרָט Is 18$^{2.7}$ (Ges$^{§ 52 R. 6}$)·—*scoured, polished,* of bronze utensils of temple 1 K 7^{45}; of human skin Is 18$^{2.7}$; of sword Ez 21$^{15.16}$ (both + הוחדה, v. **Qal** supr.)

מְרִי v. מרה.

מְרִיב־בַּעַל, מְרִי־בַּעַל v. ריב.

I, II. מְרִיבָה v. ריב.

†מְרָיָה **n.pr.m.** a priest in days of h p. Joiakim Ne 12^{12}, 𝔊 Μαρεα, Μαρ(α)ια, 𝔊L Αμαριας.

†מֹרִיָּה, מוֹרִיָּה **n.pr.loc.** ׳אֶרֶץ הַמ Gn 22^{2} (E), place for sacrificing Isaac, 𝔊 τ. γῆν τ. ὑψηλήν (text dub., v. Di); ׳הַר הַמ 2 Ch 3^{1} site of temple, 𝔊 Αμορ(ε)ια (cf Jos$^{Ant. I. 13, 1 f.}$)

†מְרָיוֹת **n.pr.m.** (on form cf Lag$^{BN 81}$);—**1.** descendant of Aaron: **a.** grandfather of Ahitub and great-grandfather of Zadok 1 Ch 5$^{32.33}$ 6^{37} Ezr 7^{3}; 𝔊 Μαρειηλ, Μαρερωθ, Μαραιωθ, etc **b.** as son of Ahitub and father of Zadok 1 Ch 9^{11} Ne 11^{11}; 𝔊 Μαρμωθ Μαρ(α)ιωθ. **2.** name of a priestly house Ne 12^{15} (prob. err. for מרמות, q v., 12^{3}), 𝔊L Μαριμωθ

†מִרְיָם **n.pr.f.** et **m.** **1. f.** sister of Aaron Ex 15^{20} (E), and of Moses and Aaron Nu 26^{59} (P), 1 Ch 5^{29}; named also Ex 15^{21} (E), Nu 12$^{1\,4.5\,10\,10\,15\,15}$ 20^{1} (all JE), Dt 24^{9} Mi 6^{4}. 𝔊 Μαριαμ. **2. m.** (prob) a Judahite 1 Ch 4^{17}. 𝔊 τὸν Μαιων, 𝔊L Μωεωρ.

מְרִירוּת, מְרִירִי v. מרר.

מֹרֶךְ v. רכך. מֶרְכָּבָה, מֶרְכָּב v. רכב.

[מַרְכֹּלֶת] v. רכל I. מִרְמָה v. רמה.

†II מִרְמָה **n.pr.m.** a Benjamite 1 Ch 8^{10}; 𝔊 Ιμαμα, A 𝔊L Μαρμ(ι)α.

†מְרֵמוֹת **n.pr m.** **1.** priest, time of Zerub. Ne 12^{3} (= מְרָיוֹת, q.v., v^{15}) 𝔊L Μαρειμωθ. **2.** priest, time of Ezra and Neh, Ezr 8^{33} Ne 3$^{4.21}$ 10^{6} (prob same). 𝔊 Μερειμωθ, Μεραμωθ, etc. **3.** one of those who had taken strange wives Ezr 10^{36}. 𝔊 Ιεραμωθ, A Μαρεμωθ.

מִרְמָס v. רמס.

†מֵרֹנֹתִי **adj. gent.** (deriv. unknown) c.art. as subst. = *the Merothonite* **1.** 1 Ch 27^{30}; 𝔊 ὁ ἐκ Μεραθων. **2.** Ne 3^{7}; 𝔊L ὁ Μηρωναθαιος.

†מֶרֶס **n.pr.m.** a Persian noble Est 1^{14}.

†מַרְסְנָא **n.pr.m.** a Persian noble Est 1^{14}.

[מֵרַע] v. רעה.

מִרְעֶה, [מַרְעִית] v. רעה.

†מַרְעֲלָה **n.pr.loc.** on border of Zebulun Jos 19^{11}. 𝔊 Μαραγελδα, A Μαριλα, 𝔊L Μαραλα.

מַרְפֵּא, מַרְפֵּה v. רפא.

[מִרְפָּשׂ] v. רפשׂ.

†[מָרַץ] **vb.** be sick, only in der species (As. II. *marâṣu* Dl$^{HWB 426}$, Ar. مَرِضَ; Sab מרץ *sick person, sickness,* Mordt$^{ZMG 1876, 32}$; Aram. vb. מְרַע, ܡܪܰܥ);—**Niph.** *Pf.* 3 pl נמרצו Jb 6^{25} (but v. infr); *Pt.* נִמְרָץ Mi 2^{10}; f. נִמְרֶצֶת 1 K 2^{8};—חֶבֶל נִמְרָץ Mi 2^{10} *a sore, grievous* destruction (lit. *made sick,* cf. מַכָּה נַחְלָה Je 14^{17}); קְלָלָה נִמְרֶצֶת 1 K 2^{8} *a grievous curse*—In Jb 6^{25} this mng. unsuit., Bu *are strong, effective* [cf. As. I. *marâṣu, be difficult, inaccessible* Dl$^{HWB 425 f.}$, always of something repelling]. More prob נמרצו = נמלצו *be sweet* (cf. ψ 119^{103}) or rd. נמלצו (q.v.), Che$^{JQ July, 1897}$ Du. **Hiph.** *Impf* sf. מַה־יַּמְרִיצְךָ Jb 16^{3} *what sickens thee* (what disturbs, vexes thee) that thou answerest?

[מְרֻצָה] v. מְרוּצָה sub רוץ.

מַרְצֵעַ v. רצע. מַרְצֶפֶת v. רצף.

†I. [מָרַק] **vb.** scour, polish (NH *id.;* Aram. מְרַק, ܡܪܰܩ, cf. Ar مَرَقَ *scrape off wool* from a skin);—**Qal** *Imv.* מִרְקוּ הָרְמָחִים Je 46^{4} *polish the lances! Pt. pass.* מָרוּק 2 Ch 4^{16} *polished,* of bronze utensils of temple (= מְמֹרָט 1 K 7^{45}). **Hiph.** *Impf.* 3 fs. תַּמְרִיק only Pr 20^{30} Kt, fig., in cl. חַבֻּרוֹת פֶּצַע ת׳ בְּרָע *blows that cut in, cleanse away evil* (cf. De Now Wild VB); Qr תַּמְרוּק i e. (are) *a cleansing.* (𝔊 συναντᾷ κακοῖς, whence Gr תקרים, Frankenb. תַּקְרִינָה, but improb.). **Pu.** *Pf.* וּמֹרַק consec. Lv 6^{21} *be well scoured,* of bronze vessel (‖ וְשֻׁטַּף בַּמָּיִם).

†[מָרוּק] (Ko$^{ii. 138}$) **n.[m.]** a scraping, rubbing;—only pl. sf. יְמֵי מְרוּקֵיהֶן Est 2^{12} lit. *the days of their* (bodily) *rubbings,* i.e. the year's preparation of girls for the harem.

†תַּמְרוּק **n.[m.]** id ,—abs. sg. only Pr 20[30] Qr, v. מרק **Hiph.**, elsewhere pl cstr. תַּמְרוּקֵי הַנָּשִׁים Est 2[12]; sf. תַּמְרוּקֶיהָ v[9], תַּמְרוּקֵיהֶן v[3].

II **מרק** (✓ of foll.; cf Ar مَرَقَ *fill a pot with rich broth* (Frey Wahrm)).

†מָרָק (van d. H מְרַק) **n.m.** juice stewed out of meat, or broth (on form cf Lag[BN 50]),—וְאֶת־הַמָּרָק שָׂם בַּפָּרוּר Ju 6[19] (v. GFM), וְהַמָּרָק שְׁפוֹךְ v[20]; cstr מְרַק Is 65[4] Qr, so Vrss (Kt פרק) *broth* of unclean things.

[מִרְקַחַת ,מֶרְקָחָה ,[מֶרְקָח] v. רקח.

†I **מָרַר** **vb.** be bitter (NH *id*; As *marâru* and deriv. Dl[HWB 427], Ar. مُرَّ *become roused* (of bile), II *make bitter*, IV. *become bitter*; مُرّ *bitter*; Eth መረረ: ; Aram מְרַר, ܡܪ);—**Qal** *Pf* 3 ms מַר Is 38[17] + 2 t; 3 fs. מָרָה 1 S 30[6] 2 K 4[27]; *Impf* 3 ms יֵמַר Is 24[9],—*be bitter*: **1.** lit. יֵמַר שֵׁכָר לְשֹׁתָיו Is 24[9]. **2.** fig נֶפֶשׁ מָרָה 1 S 30[6] *the soul* of all the people *was bitter* against (עַל־), נַפְשָׁהּ מָרָה־לָהּ 2 K 4[27] *her soul, it is bitter to her* (i.e she is in bitter distress), impers מַר־לִי מְאֹד מִכֶּם Ru 1[13] *it is very bitter to me on your account* (I am much distressed), cf La 1[4].—לְשָׁלוֹם מַר־לִי מָר Is 38[17] is dub.; Che[Comm] *for (my) welfare was it (so) bitter to me, (so) bitter*, cf. Brd; so De Kau (treating מר appar. as adj), < Drechsl. Di *for my welfare did the bitter become bitter to me* (מָר adj), Lo Gr, cf Buhl (sub מַר adj.), rd מָר for מַר (✓מור), the bitter *is changed* for me into welfare, Che[Hpt] del מָר; Du (after 𝔊) del. cl as gloss.

Pi. *Impf* 1 s אֲמָרֵר Is 22[4]; 3 mpl. וַיְמָרְרוּ Ex 1[14], sf. וַיְמָרֲרֻהוּ Gn 49[23],—*make bitter, shew bitterness* —**1.** וַיְמ׳ Gn 49[23] (poem) and the archers *shewed bitterness* (i.e. bitter hostility) *toward him* (sf. of indir obj), אֲמָרֵר בַּבֶּכִי Is 22[4] *I will shew bitterness in weeping* (=weep bitterly). **2.** וַיְמ׳ אֶת־חַיֵּיהֶם Ex 1[14] (P) *and they made their lives bitter* by slavery.

Hiph. *Pf* 3 ms הֵמַר Ru 1[20] Jb 27[2]; *Impf.* 2 ms תַּמֵּר Ex 23[21] (but rd. תַּמְרֵ ✓מרה **Hiph.** q.v.); *Inf abs.* הָמֵר Zc 12[10 10],—*make bitter, shew bitterness* **1.** שַׁדַּי הֵמַר נַפְשִׁי Jb 27[2] *Shadday, who hath embittered my soul;* הֵמַר שַׁדַּי לִי מְאֹד Ru 1[20] **2.** וְהָמֵר עָלָיו כְּהָמֵר עַל־הַבְּכוֹר Zc 12[10] *and a bitter outcry* (=lit shewing bitterness, ‖ סָפַד, מִסְפֵּד) over him, like a *bitter outcry* over the first-born

Hithpalp. *Impf* וְיִתְמַרְמַר Dn 11[11] *and the* king of the south *shall embitter himself* (be enraged); וַיִּתְמ׳ אֶל־ 8[7] *and he was enraged against.*

†I. **מַר** **adj.** and **subst.** bitter, bitterness;—abs. מ׳ Pr 27[7] +, הַמַּר, Hb 1[6], מָר ψ 64[4] +; cstr מַר 1 S 22[2] +, f מָרָה Gn 27[34] +, מָרָא Ru 1[20]; cstr. מָרַת 1 S 1[10]; mpl. מָרִים Ex 15[23] +; cstr. מָרֵי Ju 18[25] Pr 31[6],—*bitter*: **1.** lit, of water Ex 15[23] (J), food Pr 27[7] (opp מָתוֹק), wormwood (לַעֲנָה) Pr 5[4] (in sim. of end of harlot, cf Ec 7[26] infr); as subst. pl, of physical pain, result of curse לַמָּרִים Nu 5[24.27], whence מֵי הַמָּרִים v[18] (cf. Di) v[19.23.24]; of harmful result of ruthless fighting 2 S 2[26], of wickedness Je 2[19] 4[18]; = *injurious, hurtful* Is 5[20.20] (opp מָתוֹק). **2.** fig, **a.** of cry (זְעָקָה, צְעָקָה) Gn 27[34] (J), Est 4[1], מִסְפַּד מָר Ez 27[31] (del Co); דָּבָר מָר ψ 64[4], as adv. (cry, weep) *bitterly* Ez 27[30] (מָרָה), Zp 1[14] Is 33[7] (both מַר) **b.** of feeling, temper, esp c נֶפֶשׁ: אֲנָשִׁים מָרֵי נֶפֶשׁ Ju 18[25] *men fierce* (GFM *acrid*) *of temper*, so 2 S 17[8] (like a bear robbed of whelps); הַגּוֹי הַמַּר Hb 1[6] *the fierce nation*, מַר־נֶפֶשׁ = *discontented* 1 S 22[2], מָרֵי נֶפֶשׁ = *the bitterly wretched* Jb 3[20] Pr 31[6], so מָרַת נ׳ 1 S 1[10], cf. יוֹם מָר Am 8[10], as subst. abstr. מַר־נֶפֶשׁ *bitterness of soul* Is 38[15] Ez 27[31] (del. Co), Jb 7[11] 10[1] = נֶפֶשׁ מָרָה 21[25]; cf מָרָא Ru 1[20] (name given to Naomi by herself); מַר־הַמָּוֶת 1 S 15[32] *the bitterness of death;* מַר־מִמָּוֶת Ec 7[26] (metaph. of harlot), in Ez 3[14] *I went bitterly*, del מַר Co.—Is 38[17] v. מרר.

†מֹר, **מוֹר** **n.m.**[Ct 5, 5] myrrh (fr *bitter* taste; As *murru* Meissn[Suppl 60]; Ar مُرّ; cf. Lag[BN 40]),—abs. מֹר ψ 45[9] + 5 t., מוֹר Ct 4[6] + 3 t. Ct; cstr. מָר־ Ex 30[23]; sf. מוֹרִי Ct 5[1],—*myrrh* (late), an Arabian gum, exuding from the bark of a tree, *Balsamodendron Myrrha* (v. Sigismund[Aromata 12 f] Ri[HWB s.v.]) —as flowing, i.e. fine, choice (carefully prepared by pressing and mixing, cf. Di[Ex 30, 23] Ri[HWB]): מָר־דְּרוֹר Ex 30[23] (v I דְּרוֹר), ingredient of sacred oil; מוֹר עֹבֵר Ct 5[5 13] (as perfume); cf (as perfume) Ct 1[13] 4[14] 5[1.5]; הַר־הַמּוֹר 4[6], i.e. where it is gathered; as perfume also ψ 45[9] Pr 7[17], as incense מְקֻטֶּרֶת מֹר וּלְבוֹנָה Ct 3[6], שֶׁמֶן הַמֹּר as unguent Est 2[12].

מָרָא Ru 1[20], v. I. מַר supr.

†**מָרָה** **n.pr.f.** of bitter spring in Sinaitic penins. Ex 15[23.23] (J), Nu 33[8.9] (P), + ־ָה loc. מָרָתָה Ex 15[23] (J); prob mod *'Ain Hawwâra*[ten]. (Cf Rob[BR I 67] Palmer[Desert I 40] Eb[GS 125 f])

†[מָרָה] **n.f.** bitterness (on form v. Ges $^{§ 82, 5 R}$);—cstr. לֵב יוֹדֵעַ מָרַּת נַפְשׁוֹ Pr 14^{10} the heart knoweth *the bitterness of its soul* (its own misery).

†[מֹרָה] **n.f.** id., cstr. מֹרַת רוּחַ Gn 26^{35} (P) *bitterness of spirit* (= grief of mind)

†[מָרֹר] **n.m.** bitter thing, bitter herb (cf NH *id*, *bitter herb*; on form v. Ba$^{NB\ 194}$);—only pl. מרֹרים Ex 12^{8} Nu 9^{11}, מְרוֹרִים La 3^{15};—*bitter herbs*, in Passover meal Ex 12^{8} Nu 9^{11} (both P), cf. הִשְׂבִּיעַנִי בַמּ׳ La 3^{15}, fig. of distress inflicted (‖ לַעֲנָה).

†[מְרֵרָה] **n.f.** bitter thing, gall, poison; cstr. מְרוֹרַת Jb 20^{14}; sf. מְרֵרָתוֹ v^{25}; pl. מְרֹרֹת Dt 32^{32}, מְרֹרוֹת Jb 13^{26},—**1.** *gall*, i.e. seat of gall, gall-bladder Jb 20^{25} (‖ גֵּוָה *back*, cf. מְרֵרָה 16^{30}) **2.** =*poison*, מ׳ פְּתָנִים Jb 20^{14}. **3.** מְרֹרוֹת *bitter things* Jb 13^{26} (of God's edict of judgment). **4.** pl. abstr. = *bitterness*; אַשְׁכְּלֹת מ׳ Dt 32^{32} *clusters of bitterness* (‖ עִנְּבֵי רוֹשׁ).

†[מְרֵרָה] **n.f.** gall; only sf. יִשְׁפֹּךְ לָאָרֶץ מְרֵרָתִי Jb 16^{13} *he poureth on the ground my gall* (‖ יְפַלַּח כִּלְיוֹתַי), fig. of God's cruel treatment (cf. מְרֵרָה 20^{25}).

†מְרִירִי **adj.** bitter,—קֶטֶב מ׳ Dt 32^{24} *bitter destruction*. (On Jb 3^{5} v. כִּמְרִיר sub II. כמר.)

†מְרִירוּת **n.f.** bitterness;—וּבִמ׳ תֵּאָנַח Ez 21^{11} *and in bitterness* (bitterly) *shalt thou groan*.

†מֶמֶר **n.[m.]** bitterness;—מ׳ לְיוֹלַדְתּוֹ Pr 17^{25} of a fool-son (‖ כַּעַס לְאָבִיו).

†[מַמְרוֹר] **[n.m.]** bitter thing;—only pl. יַשְׂבִּעַנִי מַמְּרֹרִים Jb 9^{18} (on dagh. f. dirim. cf. Ges $^{§ 20. 2. b}$), he sateth me with *bitter things* (bitter experiences; cf. מָרֹר La 3^{15}).

†I. [תַּמְרוּר] **n.m.** bitterness;—only pl. intens. תַּמְרוּרִים Ho 12^{15} + 2 t.;—מִסְפַּד ת׳ Je 6^{26} *mourning of bitterness* (bitter mourning), so בְּכִי ת׳ 31^{15} (cf the vb. Is 22^{4} Zc 12^{10}); as adv. *bitterly* Ho 12^{15} (si vera l.).—II [תַּמְרוּר] v. sub ת.

†I. מְרָרִי **n.pr.m.** a son of Levi, and head of a chief Levit. family: 𝔊 Μεραρ(ε)ι, Μαραρει;—Gn 46^{11} Ex 6$^{16.19}$ Nu 3$^{17.20.33.33.35.36}$ 4$^{29.33.42.45}$ 7^{8} 10^{17} 26^{57} Jos 21$^{7.34.38}$ (all P), 1 Ch 5^{27} 6$^{1.4.14.29.32.48.62}$ 9^{14} 15$^{6.17}$ 23$^{6.21}$ 24$^{26.27}$ 26$^{10.19}$ 2 Ch 29^{12} 34^{12} Ezr 8^{19}.

†II מְרָרִי **adj. gent.** of above, only c. art. as subst. coll. הַמּ׳ Nu 26^{57}.

II. מרר (√ of foll; perhaps (so Thes) cf Ar. مَرَّ *pass by, go*, sts *flow*, مَرْمَرَ *cause to flow*, مَمَرّ *water-course*).

†II. מַר **n.[m.]** drop, only גּוֹיִם כְּמַר מִדְּלִי Is 40^{15} *nations* are *like a drop* hanging *from a bucket*

†מָרֵשָׁה and (Jos 15^{44}) מָרֵאשָׁה **n.pr.loc.** (etym. dub.) in (the Shephelah of) Judah, Mi 1^{15} (where named with אַכְזִיב etc), Jos 15^{44} (*id.*), cf. 2 Ch 11^{8} 14$^{8.9}$ 20^{37}; so appar. (as n pr m. in geneal. scheme) 1 Ch 2^{42} 4^{21}.—Cf. 2 Macc. 12^{35} (Μαρισα), 1 Macc 5^{66} (rd. Μαρισα for Σαμαρια, cf. Var Apocr.).—Joseph$^{Ant.\ xii.\ 8,\ 6}$ (Μαρισσα). 𝔊A Jos 15^{44} Μαρησα; 𝔊L Βαρσηα, 𝔊 1 Ch 2^{42} Μαρ(ε)ισα 𝔊L Μαρησα, etc. Prob = mod. *Merāsh* 1 m. S. of Beit Jibrin (Eleutheropolis), cf. Rob$^{BR\ ii.\ 51}$ Be$^{1\ Ch\ 2,\ 42}$ GASm$^{Geogr\ 233}$ (who identif. with (גַּת) מוֹרֶשֶׁת Mi 1^{14} q.v. sub ירשׁ p 440 supr, but v. Lag$^{Onom.\ 139,\ 141,\ 279,\ 282}$) Buhl$^{Geogr\ 192}$.

מַרְשַׁעַת v. רשׁע. מֹרַשְׁתִּי v. ירשׁ.

†מְרָתַיִם used as **n.pr.f.** = Babylon, עַל־הָאָרֶץ מ׳ עֲלֵה עָלֶיהָ Je 50^{21}; perh. = *Double rebellion* (du.) √ מרה q.v.; De$^{Par\ 182}$ thinks = Bab. *Marrâtim*, i e., land by the *nar Marrâtu*, *the bitter river* (Pers. Gulf) = Southern Babylonia.

†I. מַשָּׂא **n.pr.gent. et terr.** **1.** 'son' of Ishmael Gn 25^{14} = 1 Ch 1^{30}. 𝔊 Μασση, Μασσα, etc. **2.** realm of king Lemuel Pr 31^{1} De Now Str Wild.—Perh. = N. Arab. *Mas'u* Schr$^{COT\ Gn\ 25,\ 14,\ KGF\ 102.\ 262\ ff.,\ 364}$ Dl$^{Par\ 302\ f.}$

II, III. מַשָּׂא, מַשֹּׂא, מַשָּׂאָה, מַשְׂאֵת v. נשׂא

מַשָּׂאוֹת v מַשּׁוּאוֹת sub נשׁא.

מִשְׂגָּב v. שׂגב. [מְשׂוּכָה] v. II. שׂכך.

מַשּׂוֹר v. נשׂר.

†מְשׂוּרָה **n.f.** measure, of water, Ez 4$^{11.16}$ (‖ מִשְׁקָל), capacity in gen, Lv 19^{35} (+ מִדָּה, מִשְׁקָל), 1 Ch 23^{29} (deriv dub)

מָשׂוֹשׂ v. שׂושׂ. מִשְׂחָק v. שׂחק.

מַשְׂטֵמָה v. שׂטם. [מְשֻׂכָּה] v. שׂוך.

מַשְׂכִּיל v. שׂכל. מַשְׂכִּית v. שׂכה

[מַשְׂכֹּרֶת] v. שׂכר. [מַשְׂמֵר] v. שׂמר.

מִשְׂפָּח v. שׂפח. מִשְׂרָה v. שׂרה.

[מִשְׂרְפוֹת], מִשְׂרְפוֹת מַיִם v. שׂרף.

מַשְׁרֵקָה v. שׁרק.

†מַשְׂרֵת n.m. appar = pan, dish, Pal-Aram. מסרית, only וַתִּקַּח הַמּ׳ 2 S 13[9] *and she took the pan*; perh. = *מִשְׁאֶרֶת, orig *dough*-pan (שׂאר), kneading-trough, Gei[Urschr 392 f.] We (not Dr); > Klo Bu Ry in Di[Ex 12, 34 (Ste Aufl)] (וַתִּקְרָא (אֶת־ הַמְשָׁרֶת *and she called the servant* (HPS del. v)

†מַשׁ n.pr.loc. vel **gent.** מַשׁ Gn 10[23], as son of Aram, Sam. משא, 𝔊 Μοσοχ; so rd in ‖ 1 Ch 1[17] for MT מֶשֶׁךְ A 𝔊L Μοσοχ, v. Kau Kit Loc. dub. Bo Mich *Mons Mas-ius*, N. of Nisibis (between Armen. and Mesop), but name not certainly old Aram (unknown in As) cf Di[ad loc.]. As *Maš* (Syro-Ar desert Dl[Par 242 f.]) is hardly poss, cf. מֵשָׁא.

מַשָּׁא, מַשָּׂאָה v. I נשא.

†מֵשָׁא n.pr.loc. limiting territory of Joktanites, Gn 10[30]; Dl[Par 243] identif with As. *Maš* (Syro-Ar. desert), > district *Mesene*, on Pers Gulf, Thes[823] (cf. Di), 𝔊 Μασση(ε), whence Di I. מַשָּׁא q v. (after Hal[Mél. 91 f.])

[מַשְׁאָב] v. שׁאב. מְשׁוֹאָה v. מַשָּׁאָה.

מַשָּׁאוֹן, מַשָּׁאוֹת v. II נשא.

†מִשְׁאָל n.pr.loc. in Asher (Eg. *Mi-ša'a-ra* WMM[As. u Eur 181]),—Jos 19[26] (𝔊 Μαασα, A Μασαψ, 𝔊L Μασαλ) 21[30] (𝔊 Βασελλαν, A Μασααλ, 𝔊L Μισαλα); = (1) מָשָׁל 1 Ch 6[59] (𝔊 Μαασα, A Μασαλ, 𝔊L Μασιλ)

[מִשְׁאָלָה] v. שׁאל.

†[מִשְׁאֶרֶת] n.f. a household vessel, AV (Ex), RV *kneading-trough*; vessel in which was dough before it was leavened (Ex 12[34]) (hence usu der fr שׂאר *leaven* (with שׁ—by error?—for שׂ), but this not certain; cf. מַשְׂרֵת supr.),—only sf מִשְׁאַרְתֶּךָ Dt 28[5.17] (both + טַנְאֲךָ); pl. sf. מִשְׁאֲרוֹתֶיךָ Ex 7[28] (J, + תַנּוּרֶיךָ), מִשְׁאֲרֹתָם 12[34] (E)

מִשְׁבְּצוֹת v. שׁבץ. מַשְׁבֵּה v. מְשׁוּבָה

מַשְׁבֵּר, [מִשְׁבָּר] v. שׁבר.

[מִשְׁבָּת] v. שׁבת. מִשְׁגֶּה v. שׁנה

†[מָשָׁה] vb. draw (Ar مَسَى *cleanse uterus* of camel, Aram ܡܫܐ *clean, stroke, the face*, etc; מְשָׁא (Talm) *wash* the hands, Zinj [י]משי perhaps *wash* oneself, DHM[Sendsch 60]);—**Qal** *Pf.* sf מִן־הַמַּיִם מְשִׁיתִהוּ Ex 2[10] *out of the water I drew him* (used to explain מֹשֶׁה, but v. this infr) **Hiph.** *Impf.* sf. = **Qal**, fig. יַמְשֵׁנִי מִמַּיִם רַבִּים 2 S 22[17] = ψ 18[17] (subj י׳).

מֹשֶׁה[767] n.pr.m. Moses, the great Hebrew leader, prophet and lawgiver (prob. = Eg. *mes, mesu, child, son*, Eb[GS 539], cf. Di[Ex 2, 10], where see also older (abandoned) etymol),—מ׳ Ex 2[10] + מֹשֶׁה v[15] +; name occurs 706 t in Hex. (Ex. 290 t, Lv. 86 t, Nu 233 t, Dt. 38 t, Jos. 59 t), Ju 4 t. + 18[30] where read מֹשֶׁה for מְנַשֶּׁה (cf. GFM); 1 S 12[6.8], Kings 10 t., Mi 6[4] Je 15[1] Is 63[11.12] Mal 3[22] ψ 77[21] + 7 t.; Chr. 3 t, Dn 9[11.13],—*Moses* was son of Amram and Jochebed Ex 6[20] Nu 26[59] (both P), 1 Ch 5[29] 23[13]; of tribe of Levi Ex 2[1] (E; cf also foregoing), (younger) brother of Aaron 4[14] (J), 7[1.2.7] (P), etc, and brother of Miriam Nu 26[59] (P), 1 Ch 5[29] (cf. Ex 15[20] E); called prophet Dt 18[15.18] 34[10]; agent by whom י׳ gave law Ex 20[19.20.21.22] (E)+; esp. P (כַּאֲשֶׁר צִוָּה י׳ אֶת־מ׳, etc.), Ex 39[1.5.7.21.26.29.31] 40[19.21.23.27.29.32] Lv 7[38] 8[9.13.17.21.29] + oft; lawgiver Dt 33[4] Jos 1[7.13] (D) +; priest, מ׳ וְאַהֲרֹן בְּכֹהֲנָיו ψ 99[6]. Phrases are—(עַבְדִּי, עַבְדּוֹ, etc.) מ׳ עֶבֶד י׳ Ex 14[31] (J), Nu 12[7] (E), Dt 34[5] (JE), Jos 1[1] (D) + 15 t. Jos (D); 1 K 8[53.56] 2 K 18[12] 21[8] Mal 3[22] 2 Ch 1[3] 24[6] Ne 1[8] 9[14] ψ 105[26], מ׳ עֶבֶד אלהים 1 Ch 6[34] 24[9] Ne 10[30] Dn 9[11]; מ׳ אִישׁ הָאֱלֹהִים Ezr 3[2] ψ 90[1]; תּוֹרַת מ׳ Jos 8[32] (D), 1 K 2[3] 2 K 23[25] Mal 3[22] 2 Ch 23[18] 30[16] Ezr 3[2] 7[6] Dn 9[11.13], סֵפֶר מ׳ 2 Ch 25[4] 35[12] Ne 13[1], סֵפֶר תּוֹרַת מ׳ Jos 8[31] (D), 23[6] (D), 2 K 14[6] Ne 8[1].

[מַשֶּׁה] v נשה.

מַשָּׁאָה, מְשׁוֹאָה v. II. שׁוא.

מַשּׁוּאוֹת v. II. נשא. מְשׁוֹבֵב v. שׁוב.

מְשׁוּבָה v שׁוב. [מְשׁוּגָה] v שׁוג.

מָשׁוֹט, [מִשּׁוֹט] v. שׁוט.

מְשׁוּסָּה Kt. = מְשִׁסָּה v. שׁסס.

†מָשַׁח vb. smear, anoint (NH *id*; orig. prob as Ar مَسَحَ *wipe* or *stroke with the hand* (cf RS[Sem 1 215, 2nd ed, 233]), *anoint*, Aram. ܡܫܚ, מְשַׁח *anoint*, on משח, *id* (?) in Aram. inscr v. CIS[II. 1 No. 145, C, 1], Palm משחא *oil* Vog[No 16]; Eth መሰሐ: *anoint, feast, dine* Di[Lex 176]; (As *mašâhu* is *measure*, Aram מְשַׁח *id*; Ar. مساحة *measure*-

ment, cf. Dl[Prol. 178] Frä[292]));—**Qal** *Pf.* 3 ms. מ׳ Nu 3[25] + 2 t.; sf. מְשָׁחֲךָ ψ 45[8] 1 S 10[1]; מְשָׁחוֹ 2 Ch 22[7]; 2 ms. מָשַׁחְתָּ Gn 31[13] + 12 t., + 9 t. Pf.; *Impf.* 3 ms. יִמְשַׁח Lv 16[32] + 6 t.; 3 mpl. יִמְשָׁחוּ Am 6[6], + 13 t. Impf.; *Imv.* sf. מָשְׁחֵהוּ 1 S 16[12]; pl. מִשְׁחוּ Is 21[5]; *Inf. abs.* מָשׁוֹחַ Je 22[14]; *cstr.* מְשֹׁחַ Ju 9[8] Dn 9[24] + Ho 8[3] 𝔊 We GASm Now; מָשְׁחָה Ex 29[29]; sf. מָשְׁחֲךָ 1 S 15[1] (Baer); מָשְׁחוֹ Lv 7[36]; מָשְׁחָתָם Ex 40[15]; *Pt.* pl. משחים Ju 9[15]; *pass.* מָשׁוּחַ 2 S 3[39] (We suggests deriv. from שׁח, defect. משח (מָשֻׁחַ), wrongly read as מָשֻׁחַ; or by transposition משוח may have been mistaken for an unexampled מוּשׁח Hoph. Pt. of שׁוח); מָשִׁיחַ 2 S 1[21] (but rd. מָשֻׁחַ (or נמשח) Codd. We Dr Kit Bu HPS); pl. מְשֻׁחִים Ex 29[2] + 4 t.;—**1.** *smear*, house with colour (paint) Je 22[14]; shield with oil (anoint) Is 21[5] 2 S 1[21] (cf. Dr; Gr כְּלִי מָשׁוּחַ *weapon anointed;* Peters[JBL 1893, 56] כְּלֵי מָשׁוּחַ *weapons of one* (the king) *anointed*); the person, with ointments Am 6[6]; unleavened cakes, with oil Ex 29[2] Lv 2[4] 7[12] Nu 6[15] (P). **2.** *anoint*, as consecration, solemn setting apart to an office, always by the use of oil poured on the head: לנביא as a prophet 1 K 19[16] (Elisha by Elijah) Is 61[1]; elsewh. of king, c. acc., מֶלֶךְ Ju 9[8] (E), so Ho 8[3] reading מִמְּשֹׁחַ מֶלֶךְ (for MT מִמַּשָּׂא מ׳) We GASm Now; also Ho 7[3] reading יִמְשָׁחוּ (for MT יְשַׂמְּחוּ) We Now; elsewhere acc. pers. 1 S 16[3.12.13] 1 K 1[39] 2 K 11[12] 23[30] 2 Ch 22[7] 23[11]; בְּשֶׁמֶן קָדְשִׁי ψ 89[21] *with my holy oil;* שמן שָׂשׂוֹן ψ 45[8] (fig.); c. עַל, 2 S 19[11] whom *we have anointed over* us; לְמֶלֶךְ 1 K 1[45] 5[15]; c. עַל, לְמֶלֶךְ Ju 9[15] 2 S 2[4.7] 1 K 19[15]; על ישראל *over Israel* 1 S 15[1.17] 2 S 5[3] = 1 Ch 11[3], 2 S 5[17] 12[7] 1 K 1[34] 19[16]; אֶל־ישׂראל 2 K 9[3.6.12] (Ephr.); לנגיד 1 Ch 29[22]; על 1 S 9[16] 10[1]; מָשׁוּחַ מֶלֶךְ 2 S 3[39] (? v. supr.) **3.** *anoint, consecrate* to religious service: **a.** Aaronic priests, only P, c. acc. pers. Ex 28[41] 29[7] 30[30] 40[13.15.15.15] Lv 7[36] 8[12] 16[32]; abs. Ex 29[29]; הכהנים הַמְּשֻׁחִים Nu 3[3]. **b.** sacred things: מַצֵּבָה Gn 31[13] (E); tabernacle and its sacred vessels Ex 29[36] 30[26] 40[9.10.11] Lv 8[10.11] (all P); קדשׁ קדשׁים Dn 9[24]. **Niph.** *Pf.* 3 ms. נִמְשַׁח 1 Ch 14[8]; *Inf.* הִמָּשַׁח Lv 6[13] + 3 t.;—*be anointed*, למלך על כל ישראל 1 Ch 14[8]; Aaron and his sons Lv 6[13] (P); altar Nu 7[10.84.88].

† מִשְׁחָה **n.f.** **1.** ointment; **2.** consecrated portion;—abs. מ׳ Ex 25[6] +; cstr. מִשְׁחַת Ex 30[25] +;—**1.** *ointment*, the holy oil used in the consecration of the Aaronic priests, only in P; שֶׁמֶן הַמִּשְׁחָה Ex 25[6] 29[7.21] 31[11] 35[8.15.28] 37[29] 39[38] 40[9] Lv 8[2.10.12.30] 21[10] Nu 4[16]; שׁ׳ מִשְׁחַת קֹדֶשׁ Ex 30[25.25.31]; שׁ׳ מ׳ יהוה Lv 10[7]; שׁ׳ מ׳ אֱלֹהָיו 21[12]. **2.** *consecrated portion*, of Aaron and his sons Lv 7[35.35] (P).

† מָשְׁחָה **n.f.** consecrated portion (Ew[§ 238 a] poss. error of pointing);—Nu 18[8] (P).

† מָשִׁיחַ **n.m.** anointed;—abs. מ׳ Lv 4[3] + 5 t.; cstr. מְשִׁיחַ La 4[20] + 11 t.; sf. מְשִׁיחִי ψ 132[17] 1 S 2[35]; מְשִׁיחֶךָ Hb 3[13] + 5 t.; מְשִׁיחוֹ ψ 2[2] + 9 t.; pl. sf. מְשִׁיחָי 105[15] 1 Ch 16[22];—**1.** king of Israel *anointed* by divine command, מ׳ יהוה 1 S 24[7.7.11] 26[9.11.16.23] 2 S 1[14.16] 19[22] La 4[20]; מ׳ אלהי יעקב 2 S 23[1]; so c. sfs. ref. to י׳, 1 S 12[3.5] 16[6] ψ 20[7] 28[8] Hb 3[13]; Davidic dynasty with Messianic ideals attached ψ 2[2] 18[51], = 2 S 22[51], ψ 89[39.52] 132[10] = 2 Ch 6[42], ψ 132[17] 1 S 2[10.35]. **2.** high priest of Israel, הַכֹּהֵן הַמָּשִׁיחַ, Lv 4[3.5.16] 6[15] (P); מְשִׁיחֶךָ ψ 84[10]. **3.** Cyrus as commissioned by י׳, מְשִׁיחוֹ Is 45[1]. **4.** *Messianic prince*, עַד־מָשִׁיחַ נָגִיד Dn 9[25] = מָשִׁיחַ v[26] (see Br[MP 422 f.]; others disting. מ׳ v[25] fr. v[26] and refer v[25] to Cyrus [as **3**; so Ew v. Leng Schü Co Behrm], or h.p. Joshua [as **2**; so Gr Bev], v[26] to Seleucus IV [Ew v. Leng], or h.p. Onias III. [Hi Gr Co Bev Behrm]). **5.** patriarchs, regarded as anointed kings ψ 105[15] = 1 Ch 16[22].

† מִמְשַׁח **n.[m.]** dub.; only in כְּרוּב מִמְשַׁח הַסּוֹכֵךְ Ez 28[14] *cherub of expansion* (then cf. As. *mašâḫu, measure*, Aram. מְשַׁח *id.*, etc.) *that covereth*, after 𝔙 *cherub extentus* (far-reaching wings), "*far-covering cherub*," Ew (Or "*umspannender*"); *the anointed cherub that covereth*, AV RV, so Hä. Co thinks gloss, and reads אֶת־כְּרוּב נְתַתִּיךָ; text dub. acc. to Siegf[Kau] SS Buhl Berthol.

מַשְׁחִית, [מַשְׁחֶת], מִשְׁחַת, [מָשְׁחָת] v. שׁחת.

מִשְׁחָר v. שׁחר.

מִשְׁטוֹחַ, [מִשְׁטָח] v. שׁטח.

[מִשְׁטָר] v. שׁטר.

† מֶשִׁי **n.[m.]** a costly material for garments, acc. to Rabb. **silk**, (so Now[Arch. i. 124]); whether this is based on actual tradition is dub. (etym. unknown);—abs. מ׳ Ez 16[13] (‖ שֵׁשׁ), מֶשִׁי v[10] (‖ *id.*) Vid., further Thes Sm Da Berthol. 𝔊 τρίχαπτα.

מֹשִׁי v. מוּשִׁי.

†**מְשֵׁיזַבְאֵל** **n.pr.m.** Jewish name in Persian period (*God delivers*, from Aram. שֵׁיזִב, ܫܰܘܙܶܒ *deliver*, As. *šûzubu*, Shaph. from *ezêbu*, *deliver*, Dl$^{HWB\ 35}$; cf. the Bab. names *Mušêzib-Marduk*, 'Marduk delivers,' *Mušêzib-ilu*, KB $^{ii.\ 261\ iv\ 129}$).—grandfather of one of the wall-builders Ne 3^{4}; one of those sealed 10^{22}, father of royal officer (a Judaean) 11^{24}; the relation of these to each other is unknown, 𝔊 Μασεζεβηα, Μεσωζεβηλ, 𝔊L Μασσιζαβελ, etc.

†**מָשַׁךְ** **vb. draw, drag** (NH *id.*; Aram. מְשַׁךְ (rare) *be extended*, also *conduct, take*, Syr ܡܫܰܟ is *be dry, shrivelled* (of fruit, etc); Eth. መሰከ: *bend* (the bow); Ar. مَسَكَ *grasp and hold* I. Frey; IV. Frey Lane; cf also As. *mašku, skin* (perh. also *march* Dl$^{HWB\ 431}$), Ar مَسْكٌ *id*, Aram. ܡܫܟܐ, מַשְׁכָּא *id*);—**Qal** *Pf.* 3 ms. מ׳ 1 K 22^{34} + 2 t, וּמָשַׁךְ consec Jb 24^{22}, 3 fs. מָשְׁכָה Dt 21^{3}, etc, *Impf.* יִמְשׁוֹךְ Jb 21^{33}, וַיִּמְשֹׁךְ Ju 20^{37}; 2 ms sf. תִּמְשְׁכֵנִי ψ 28^{3}; 1 s. sf. אֶמְשְׁכֵם Ho 11^{4}, etc; *Imv* מְשֹׁךְ ψ 36^{11}, sf. מָשְׁכֵנִי Ct 1^{4}; mpl. מִשְׁכוּ Ex 12^{21}, מָשְׁכוּ Ez 32^{20}; *Inf. cstr.* מְשֹׁךְ Ex 19^{13} Jos 6^{5}, לִמְשׁוֹךְ Ec 2^{3}; *Pt* מֹשֵׁךְ Am 9^{13} ψ 109^{12}; pl. מֹשְׁכִים Ju 5^{14}; cstr. מֹשְׁכֵי Is 5^{18} 66^{19},—**1.** *draw* and lift out of (מִן), c acc. pers, וַיִּמְשְׁכוּ וַיַּעֲלוּ אֶת־יוֹסֵף מִן הַבּוֹר Gn 37^{28} (E), so Jeremiah (+ בַּחֲבָלִים ,ב instr.) Je 38^{13}, cf תִּמְשֹׁךְ לִוְיָתָן בְּחַכָּה Jb 40^{25}; *draw, drag along* מֹשְׁכֵי עָוֺן בְּחַבְלֵי הַשָּׁוְא Is 5^{18} (fig); בְּמָשְׁכוֹ בְרִשְׁתּוֹ ψ 10^{9} (fig. of wicked catching and *dragging* the poor); *draw, lead along* (with hostile purpose) c. acc. pers. Ju 4^{7} (subj י׳, + אֶל־ pers. et rei); *lead* or *drag off* (to doom, subj י׳) ψ 28^{3} (cf. 26^{9}); similarly, or = *draw down* to death, מָשְׁכוּ אוֹתָהּ וגו׳ Ez 32^{20} (si vera l; ref. to fall of Egypt), but rd. perh. a form of שׁכב for מִשְׁכוּ, 𝔊 Co Berthol, cf. Sm.; abs., subj. heifer, מָשְׁכָה בְּעֹל Dt 21^{3} (ב instr); *draw, lead* (in love), (fig, subj י׳) בְּחַבְלֵי אָדָם אֶמְשְׁכֵם Ho 11^{4}, cf Je 31^{3} (al as **5** infr.) **2.** *draw* the bow, מ׳ בַּקֶּשֶׁת 1 K 22^{34} = 2 Ch 18^{33}, but מֹשְׁכֵי ק׳ Is 66^{19} (where text dub, 𝔊 Μοσοχ καὶ εἰς (Θοβελ), so Lo Sta$^{Javan\ 8}$ Du Che^{Hpt},—not Gr Che^{Comm} Di). **3.** *proceed, march* (cf Germ. *ziehen*) וּמָשַׁכְתָּ בְּהַר תָּבוֹר Ju 4^{6} cf 20^{37} (abs), Jb 21^{33} (אַחֲרָיו); so also (perh) Ex 12^{21} *proceed* (i e. forthwith), and take you a sheep, and prob. מֹשְׁכִים בְּשֵׁבֶט Ju 5^{14} *those marching with the staff*, etc. (most under **2.** *drawing with*, i.e. wielding). **4.** *draw out* a sound, *give a sound*, בִּמְשֹׁךְ הַיֹּבֵל Ex 19^{13} (E) *when the ram('s horn) sounds*, בִּמ׳ בְּקֶרֶן הַיֹּבֵל Jos 6^{5} (JE) **5.** *draw out, prolong, continue*, מְשֹׁךְ חַסְדְּךָ לְיֹדְעֶיךָ ψ 36^{10} *prolong, continue thy kindness to them that know thee*; אַל־יְהִי לוֹ מֹשֵׁךְ חָסֶד 109^{12}, (so poss מְשַׁכְתִּיךְ חָסֶד Je 31^{3} *I have prolonged kindness to thee*, cf. Ryle Ne 9^{30}; al as **1** supr); cf וַתִּמ׳ עֲלֵיהֶם שָׁנִים תִּמ׳ אַפְּךָ לְדֹר וָדֹר Ne 9^{30} (חֶסֶד omitted); רַבּוֹת 85^{6} (הַלְעוֹלָם תֶּאֱנַף בָּנוּ ‖); וּמ׳ אַבִּירִים בְּכֹחוֹ Jb 24^{22} i e. *he* (God) *prolongeth* the life of *the mighty* (Du *draggeth* them *off*, as ψ 28^{3} **1** supr.,—reading also אֹבְדִים for אַב׳, with 𝔊 Bi); cf. **Niph.** **6.** *trail* seed (draw along in sowing) Am 9^{13} (opp דֹּרֵךְ עֲנָבִים, cf. מֶשֶׁךְ infr.) **7.** (late) *cheer* (draw, attract, gratify) מ׳ בַּיַּיִן אֶת־בְּשָׂרִי Ec 2^{3},—so De (who cites NH, Chag$^{14\ a}$) Now Wild—מָשַׁךְ יָדוֹ אֶת־לֹצְצִים Ho 7^{5} is difficult, 𝔊 AV RV *he stretcheth out his hand with*, maketh common cause with, is hardly poss, text prob. corrupt We Now. **Niph.** *Impf* 3 mpl. לֹא יִמָּשֵׁכוּ Is 13^{22} *they shall not be prolonged* (days of Babylon); 3 fs. לֹא תִמָּשֵׁךְ Ez 12$^{25.28}$ *it shall not be postponed.* **Pu.** *Pt. long drawn out*· מְמֻשָּׁךְ Is 18$^{2.7}$ of persons, = *tall*; תּוֹחֶלֶת מְמֻשָּׁכָה Pr 13^{12} *hope postponed, deferred.*

†I. [מֶשֶׁךְ] **n.[m.]** **a drawing, drawing up, a trail**,—**1.** cstr. מֶשֶׁךְ חָכְמָה מִפְּנִינִים Jb 28^{18} *the drawing up* (fishing up, i e. securing after effort) of wisdom is beyond corals. **2.** cstr. *a trail* (of seed), מֶ׳ הַזָּרַע ψ 126^{6} bearing the *trail* of seed, cf. מָשַׁךְ **6.**

†II. מֶשֶׁךְ **n.pr.gent. the Moschi** (Gk. Μόσχοι, v. infr.; As *Mušku, Muški*, Dl$^{Par\ 250}$ Schr$^{COT\ Gn\ 10,\ 2;\ KGF\ 155\ ff}$; cf. Sab משך Hal^{243});—'son' of Japheth Gn 10^{2} (P), between תֻּבַל and תִּירָס, = 1 Ch 1^{5}; also, מֶשֶׁךְ, prob. err., v^{17} (v. מַשׁ), מֶשֶׁךְ ψ 120^{5} (קֵדָר ‖; here without תֻּבַל); תּוּבַל וּמ׳ Ez 27^{13} cf. 32^{26} 38^{2} (both + תֻּבַל); so also 𝔊 Is 66^{19} (Lo Sta$^{Javan\ 8}$ Du Che^{Hpt}; v. supr. **2**); מֶשֶׁךְ גּוֹג נְשִׂיא רֹאשׁ מ׳ וְתֻבָל Ez 38^{3} 39^{1}. 𝔊 Μοσοχ (Μεσοχ), Sam. מוש(י)ך.—On identif cf. Boch.; in Assyr. times they dwelt in W. (or NW) Armenia (cf. Schr$^{l\ c}$); in Pers. times appar. farther NE. (SE. of Euxine Sea), cf. Μόσχοι καὶ Τιβαρηνοί Herod$^{iii\ 94,\ vii\ 78}$; also Di $^{Gn\ 10,\ 2}$ and Che$^{Encycl.\ Bib.\ Art.\ Geogr\ (Biblical)}$.

†[מֹשֶׁכֶת] **n.f. cord**;—only pl cstr. מֹשְׁכוֹת כְּסִיל Jb 38^{31} *the cords of Orion*, i e. prob. those by which (acc to some legend) he is dragged along in the sky (cf. Di).

מִשְׁכָּב v. שׁכב. מִשְׁכָּן v. שׁכן.

I. מָשָׁל n.pr.loc. v. מִשְׁאָל.

†I. [מָשַׁל] **vb. represent, be like** (Ar. مَثَلَ *stand erect* (cf. Fl$^{De Pr 1,1}$), II. *effigiavit, repraesentavit* (rem alicui), V. *imitate, use a verse as a proverb;* مَثَل *description by way of comparison;* As. *mašâlu*, Dl$^{HWB 431 f.}$; Eth. መሰለ: *become like;* Aram. מְתַל *be like,* ܡܬܠ *compare*). **Niph.** *Pf.* 3 ms. נִמְשַׁל ψ 49$^{13.21}$; 2 ms. נִמְשַׁלְתָּ Is 14^{10}; 1 s. נִמְשַׁלְתִּי ψ 28^{1} 143^{7}:—*be like, similar,* c. אֶל Is 14^{10}; עִם ψ 28^{1} = 143^{7}; כְּ ψ 49$^{13.21}$. **Hiph.** *Impf.* 2 mpl. sf. וְתַמְשִׁלוּנִי *compare* Is 46^{5}. **Hithp.** *Impf.* 1 s. וָאֶתְמַשֵּׁל Jb 30^{19} (c. כְּ) *and I have become like dust.*

†II. מָשָׁל **n.m.**$^{Is 14,4}$ **proverb, parable** (of sentences constructed in *parallelism*, usu. of Hebrew Wisdom, but occas. of other types);—abs. מ׳ Ez 17^{2} + 20 t.; cstr. מְשַׁל 1 S 24^{14}; sf. מְשָׁלוֹ Nu 23^{7} + 8 t.; pl. מְשָׁלִים Ec 12^{9} + 2 t.; cstr. מִשְׁלֵי Pr 1^{1} + 3 t.;—**1.** *proverbial saying,* brief terse sentence of popular sagacity 1 S 10^{12} Ez 12$^{22.23}$ 18$^{2.3}$; מ׳ הַקַּדְמֹנִי 1 S 24^{14} *proverb of the ancients.* **2.** *by-word* ψ 44^{15} 69^{12}; לְמָשָׁל וְלִשְׁנִינָה Dt 28^{37} 1 K 9^{7} 2 Ch 7^{20} Je 24^{9}; לְאוֹת וּלְמְשָׁלִים Ez 14^{8}. **3.** prophetic figurative discourse: נָשָׂא מָשָׁל *lift up, utter a* מ׳ Nu 23$^{7.18}$ 24$^{3.15.20.21.23}$ (all of Balaam); Is 14^{4} Mi 2^{4} (‖ נהי) Hb 2^{6} (‖ חידה), (cf. Jb 27^{1} 29^{1} for same phrase under **6**). **4.** *similitude, parable,* Ez 17^{2} 21^{5} 24^{3}. **5.** *poem,* of various kinds: the ode (Nu 21$^{27-30}$), the 3,000 pieces traditionally ascribed to Solomon 1 K 5^{12}, didactic psalms ψ 49^{5} 78^{2}. **6.** *sentences of ethical wisdom* דִּבְרֵי חֲכָמִים collected in the מִשְׁלֵי שְׁלֹמֹה Pr 10^{1} 25^{1} (10^{1}–22^{16} consisting of 376 couplets chiefly antithetical; 25–29 chiefly couplets of an emblematic type, but also occasional tristichs, tetrastichs, pentastichs, and decastichs. To these are appended דְּבָרִים of a more mixed character as to size and content in 22^{7}–24^{22}; 24$^{23-34}$; 30$^{1-14}$; v$^{15-33}$; 31$^{1-9}$; v$^{10-31}$; the Praise of Wisdom 1$^{8-9}$ is prefixed, and an introduction to the whole 1$^{1-7}$, in which the whole contents are represented as) משלים Pr 1^{1}, cf. v^{6}. The references in Jb 13^{12} 27^{1} 29^{1} Pr 26$^{7.9}$ Ec 12^{9} are to the same type of wisdom.

†II. מָשַׁל **vb. denom. use a proverb, speak in parables or sentences of poetry,** esp. Ezek.;—**Qal** *Impf.* יִמְשֹׁל Ez 16^{44}; 3 mpl. יִמְשְׁלוּ 12^{23}; *Imv.* מְשֹׁל 17^{2} 24^{3}; *Inf. cstr.* מְשֹׁל 18^{3}; *Pt.* מֹשֵׁל 16^{44}, pl. מֹשְׁלִים 18^{2} Nu 21^{27};—*use a proverb:* מָשַׁל מ׳ Ez 12^{23} 18^{3}; a parable c. אֶל־ 17^{2} (‖ חוּד חִידָה), 24^{3}; c. עַל־ 18^{2}, and (מָשָׁל appar. om.) הִנֵּה כָּל־ הַמֹּשֵׁל עָלַיִךְ יִמְשֹׁל 16^{44} (but this is awkward; point הִנֵּה כֹּל הַמָּשָׁל); מֹשְׁלִים Nu 21^{27} (JE). **Pi.** *Pt.* הֲלֹא מְמַשֵּׁל מְשָׁלִים הוּא Ez 21^{5} *is he not a maker of parables?*

†I. [מֹשֶׁל] **n.[m.] likeness, one like;** only sf. מָשְׁלוֹ Jb 41^{25} *his likeness,* i.e. *one like him.*

†מְשֹׁל **n.[m.] by-word,** only cstr. (strictly Inf.) לִמְשֹׁל עַמִּים Jb 17^{6} (they) *have made me a by-word of the peoples.*

†III. מָשַׁל **vb. rule, have dominion, reign** (NH *Pt. id.;* Ph. משל);—**Qal** *Pf.* 3 ms. וּמָשַׁל consec. Zc 6^{13} + 2 t., מָשָׁל Dn 11^{4}, וּמָשַׁל consec. v^{5}; 3 fs. מָשָׁלָה ψ 103^{19}; 2 ms. מָשַׁלְתָּ Is 63^{19}, וּמָשַׁלְתָּ Dt 15^{6}; 3 pl. מָשְׁלוּ Is 3^{5} La 5^{8}; *Impf.* 3 ms. יִמְשֹׁל Ex 21^{8} + 3 t., יִמְשׁוֹל Pr 22^{7}; יִמְשָׁל־ Gn 3^{16}, etc.; *Imv.* מְשָׁל־ Ju 8^{22}; *Inf. abs.* מָשׁוֹל Gn 37^{8}; *cstr.* מְשֹׁל Ju 9^{2} +, לִמְשָׁל־ Jo 2^{17}, etc.; *Pt.* מֹשֵׁל Gn 45^{26} +, etc.;—**1.** human subj., *rule, have dominion* over (בְּ) Gn 3^{16} 4^{7} 24^{2} (all J), 45$^{8.26}$ (E), מָשׁוֹל תִּמְשֹׁל בּ׳ 37^{8} (E); Dt 15$^{6.6}$ Jos 12^{5} (D); Ju 8$^{22.23.23}$ 9$^{2.2}$ 14^{4} 15^{11} 2 S 23^{3} (Pt. abs. = *when one ruleth,* cf. Dr), 1 K 5^{1} 2 Ch 7^{18} 9^{26} 23^{20} Is 3$^{4.12}$ 19^{4} Mi 5^{1} Hb 1^{14} Je 22^{30} La 5^{8} Jo 2^{17} Pr 16^{32} (מֹשֵׁל בְּרוּחוֹ), 17^{2} 19^{10} 22^{7} ψ 19^{14} 105^{21} 106^{41} Dn 11^{43} Ec 9^{17}; rarely other preps.: לְ (c. inf.) Ex 21^{8} (E); עַל־ Pr 28^{15} Ne 9^{37}, אֶל־ Je 33^{26}; c. sf. Is 52^{5} Je 30^{21}; c. acc. cogn. מ׳ מִמְשָׁל רָב Dn 11$^{3.4}$; מֹשֵׁל מִן . . . וְעַד Jos 12^{2} (D); abs. 2 S 23^{3} (cf. Dr), Ez 19^{14} Zc 6^{13} (עַל loc.), Pr 12^{24} 29^{2} Dn 11^{5}; esp. Pt. as subst. = *ruler,* מֹשֵׁל־אֶרֶץ Is 16^{1}, מֹשֵׁל עַמִּים ψ 105^{20}; abs. Is 14^{5} 49^{7} Je 51$^{46.46}$ Ez 19^{11} Pr 6^{7} 23^{1} 29$^{12.26}$ Ec 10^{4}; מֹשְׁלֵי הָעָם הַזֶּה Is 28^{14}. **2.** of heavenly bodies, c. בְּ Gn 1^{18}. **3.** of God, c. בְּ Ju 8^{23} Is 63^{19} ψ 22^{29} 59^{14} 89^{10} 103^{19} 1 Ch 29^{12} 2 Ch 20^{6}; abs. ψ 66^{7}; וּזְרֹעוֹ מ׳ לוֹ Is 40^{10} *his arm ruling for him.* **Hiph.** *Pf.* 3 ms. sf. consec. וְהִמְשִׁילָם Dn 11^{39}; *Impf.* 2 ms. sf. תַּמְשִׁילֵהוּ ψ 8^{7}; *Inf. abs.* הַמְשֵׁל Jb 25^{2};—*cause to rule,* sq. acc. pers. + בְּ ψ 8^{7} (subj. י׳), Dn 11^{39}; *exercise dominion,* only inf. abs. as n. abstr. *the exercise of dominion* Jb 25^{2} (attrib. of God).

†II. [מֹשֶׁל] **n.[m.]** dominion,—sf. מָשְׁלוֹ מִיָּם כִּמְשָׁלוֹ אֲשֶׁר מָשַׁל עַד־יָם Zc 9[10] (of Mess king), Dn 11[4] (of Alexander).

†מִמְשָׁל **n** [m.] dominion, ruler (late);—abs. מ׳ Dn 11[3.5], pl הַמִּמְשָׁלִים 1 Ch 26[6],—**1.** מָשַׁל מ׳ רב *great dominion* Dn 11[3] (acc. cogn c מָשַׁל), v[5] (pred. of מֶמְשַׁלְתּוֹ) **2.** abstr for concr. (pl) = *rulers* 1 Ch 26[6] (? rd הַמֹּשְׁלִים).

†מֶמְשָׁלָה **n.f.** rule, dominion, realm (cf Dr[JPhil. xi 1882, 215]), —abs. מ׳ Mi 4[8], cstr. מֶמְשֶׁלֶת ψ 136[8] (before בּ Ges[§ 130. 1] Ko[ii. 182]), Je 34[1] + 2 t.; sf. מֶמְשַׁלְתְּךָ Is 22[21] ψ 145[13], מֶמְשַׁלְתּוֹ 1 K 9[19] + 6 t., pl. cstr מֶמְשְׁלוֹת ψ 136[9], sf מַמְשְׁלוֹתָיו ψ 114[2],—**1.** *rule, dominion* (human) Is 22[21] Mi 4[8]; וְכָל־מֶמְשַׁלְתּוֹ עִמּוֹ 2 Ch 32[9] *and all his imperial might with him* (i e. display of might—soldiers, court, luxury, etc, of Sennach); כֹּל אֶרֶץ מֶמְשַׁלְתּוֹ 1 K 9[19] = 2 Ch 8[6], Je 51[28], מַמְלְכוֹת אֶרֶץ מֶמְשֶׁלֶת יָדוֹ Je 34[1]; hence מ׳ alone = *realm, domain* 2 K 20[13] = Is 39[2], Dn 11[5]. **2.** *rule* of heavenly bodies לְמֶמְ׳ הַיּוֹם Gn 1[16] the sun *for the rule of the day*, cf. v[16]; also sq בּ ψ 136[8.9] **3.** God's *rule, dominion:* ψ 145[13] (‖ מַלְכוּת), כָּל־מְקֹמוֹת מֶמְשַׁלְתּוֹ 103[22], pl. = *realm* הָיְתָה יְהוּדָה לְקָדְשׁוֹ יִשְׂרָאֵל מַמְשְׁלוֹתָיו: 114[2].

[מִשְׁלָח], מִשְׁלַח, מִשְׁלַחַת v שׁלח.

מְשֻׁלָּם, מְשִׁל(י)מוֹת, מְשֶׁלֶמְיָה(ו) v. שׁלם.

מְשֻׁלֶּמֶת, מְשִׁלֵּמִית v. שׁלם.

מִשֶּׁלָּנוּ v שֶׁ. מְשֻׁלָּשׁ Gn 38[24] v שׁלשׁ.

מְשַׁמָּה v. שׁמם.

מַשְׁמַנִּים, מְשַׁ׳, מִשְׁמַנָּה, מִשְׁמָן v. שׁמן.

I, II. מִשְׁמָע, [מִשְׁמַעַת] v שׁמע.

מִשְׁמָר, [מִשְׁמֶרֶת] v שׁמר.

מִשְׁנֶה v שׁנה. מְשִׁסָּה v. שׁסס.

משׁע (cf As *mısû, cleanse, wash*, cf Dl[HWB], whence *might* come foll—though שׁ = s is surprising—cf Dl[Baer Ezech xiv])

†מִשְׁעִי **n.f.** (? = מִשְׁעִית cf Thes Sm) cleansing, only לֹא רֻחַצְתְּ לְמִ׳ Ez 16[4] *thou wast not washed for cleansing* (cf 𝔗 Thes and Add[98] Sm RV al., 𝔙 *ad salutem*, as if from ישׁע, 𝔊 om, and so Co Be SS, cf Buhl, form strange, and word at best dub.)

מִשְׁעוֹל v. I. שׁעל.

†מִשְׁעָם **n.pr.m** name in Benjamin 1 Ch 8[12]. 𝔊 Μεσσααμ, 𝔊L Μεσοαμ.

מִשְׁעֶנֶת, מַשְׁעֵנָה, מַשְׁעֵן, מִשְׁעָן v שׁען

מִשְׁפָּט v. שׁפט. מִשְׁפָּחָה v. שׁפח.

מִשְׁפְּתַיִם v. שׁפת.

משׁק (assumed as √ of two following, but wholly dubious).

†מֶשֶׁק **n.[m.]** acquisition, possession (?; meaning conject. fr. context, fr. analogy of מִמְשָׁק q.v, and of משׁך), only וּבֶן־מֶשֶׁק בֵּיתִי הוּא דַּמֶּשֶׂק אֱלִיעֶזֶר Gn 15[2] (cf. בֵּן 8 (λ), supr. p. 121[b]; Ges[§ 128. 2, R. 2. c]) *and the son of acquisition* (= *he who is to acquire, the heir of*) *my house is*, etc; מ׳ poss. changed from משׁך (cf Jb 28[18]) for word-play with דמשׂק, Kau and So[Gn Anm 62], or by copyist's error, but very dubious. 𝔊 Μασεκ (n.pr, cf. Lag[BN 78]).

†[מִמְשָׁק] **n.[m.]** possession (? so RV), perh. better *place of possession, place possessed by;* only cstr. מִמְשַׁק חָרוּל Zp 2[9] *a place possessed by* chickpeas (> AV *breeding* of nettles), 𝔊 Δαμασκος. Word very dubious (We GASm), text prob. corrupt, Schwally[ZAW x 1890, 188] conj meaning *place of growth;* Gr (so Now) prop. קִמּוֹשׂ, or קמשׂנים.

מַשָּׁק v. שׁקק. מַשְׁקֶה v. שׁקה.

מִשְׁקָל, מִשְׁקֹלֶת, מִשְׁקֶלֶת, מִשְׁקוֹל v. שׁקל.

מַשְׁקוֹף v. שׁקף. [מִשְׁקָע] v שׁקע.

מִשְׁרָה v. שׁרה.

מֵשָׁרִים v. מֵישָׁרִים sub ישׁר.

†מִשְׁרָעִי **adj gent.** (deriv unknown), only c art. as n.coll הַמִּ׳ 1 Ch 2[53] *the Mishra'ites*, a family of Kirjath Jearim, 𝔊 Ἡμασαρειμ, 𝔊L Μασερεθι.

†[מָשַׁשׁ] **vb.** feel, grope (NH *id.* Pi.; Ar مَسَّ *feel;* Eth. መረሰሰ: Di[166]; Aram ܡܫ, מְשַׁשׁ Pa, Palp—v also ימשׁ, II. (מושׁ);—**Qal** *Impf* 3 ms sf יְמֻשֵּׁנִי Gn 27[12] perhaps my father *will feel me;* וַיְמֻשֵּׁהוּ v[22] *and he felt of him* (both J). **Pi.** *Pf* 2 ms מִשַּׁשְׁתָּ; *Impf* 3 ms. יְמַשֵּׁשׁ Dt 28[29], וַיְמַשֵּׁשׁ Gn 31[34]; 3 mpl. יְמַשְׁשׁוּ Jb 5[14] 12[25], *Pt.* מְמַשֵּׁשׁ Dt 28[29],—*feel over* or *through, grope:*—

1. וַיְמַ׳ לָבָן אֶת־כָּל־הָאֹהֶל Gn 31[34] *and Laban felt through the whole tent* (i.e. searched it); so (obj. כֵּלַי) v[37] *thou hast felt through* all my possessions (or baggage; both E). **2.** *grope*, of blind Dt 28[29b] (in sim.), periphr. conj., וְהָיִיתָ מְמַשֵּׁשׁ v[29a] *and thou shalt become one that gropes* at noonday (fig. of judicial blindness); cf. Jb 5[14] 12[25]. **Hiph.** *Impf.* וְיָמֵשׁ חֹשֶׁךְ Ex 10[21] *that one may feel* (the) *darkness;* rd. also *Imv.* sf. הֲמִשֵּׁנִי (for והימשני, v. ימשׁ, p. 413 supr.) Ju 16[26] *and let me touch* the pillars (2 acc.)

מִשְׁתֶּה v. שׁתה. מֵת v. מות.

†[מַת] **n.m. male, man** (מְתוּ־ in n.pr.; Zinj. מת coll. *males, male offspring;* As. *mutu, husband;* Eth. ምት: *id.;* cf. Eg. *m-t, phallus, male,* Steindorff in Ba[NB § 2b. d]);—only pl. מְתִים Jb 11[3] + 3 t., מְתִם Dt 2[34] 3[6] + Ju 20[48] (probably), for MT מְתֹם, so GFM; cstr. מְתֵי Gn 34[30] + 13 t.; sf. 2 fs. מְתַיִךְ Is 3[25]; 3 ms. מְתָיו Dt 33[6];— **1.** *males, men,* Is 3[25] (‖ גְּבוּרָתֵךְ); more distinctly, עִיר מְתִם (וְ)הַנָּשִׁים וְהַטַּף Dt 2[34] 3[6] every *city of males* (male population, cf. Dr), *and the women,* etc.; Ju 20[48] (v. supr.; opp. בְּהֵמָה). **2.** usu. less emphasis on sex, in prose only phr.: **a.** מְתֵי מִסְפָּר *men of number* (numerable, i.e. few) Gn 34[30] (J; appos. of אֲנִי = Jacob, representing his family), Dt 4[27] Je 44[28], also ψ 105[12] = 1 Ch 16[19]; cf. וִיהִי מְתָיו מִסְפָּר Dt 33[6] *and (but) let his men be few.* **b.** בִּמְתֵי מְעָט = *consisting of a few men* Dt 26[5] 28[62]. **3.** elsewhere only poet., sex usually not emph.: **a.** Jb 11[3] 24[12] ψ 17[14.14] (but text prob. corrupt, cf. Bae We; at least om. ממתים ידך Ol Bi Che, cf. Hup-Now); מְתֵי יִשְׂרָאֵל Is 41[14]. **b.** poet. phr.: מְתֵי שָׁוְא *men of falsehood* Jb 11[11] ψ 26[4]; מ׳ אָוֶן 22[15] *men of wickedness;* מ׳ סוֹדִי 19[19] *men of my circle;* מ׳ אָהֳלִי Jb 31[31] *men of my tent* (household); מ׳ רָעָב Is 5[13] *men of hunger,* but read probably מְזֵי ר׳ *sucked out, empty* from hunger (as Dt 32[24]) Ew De Che Di Du (cf. מָזֶה).

†מְתוּשָׁאֵל **n.pr.m.** descendant of Cain (Bab. form., *mutu-ša-ili* 'man of God,' Len Orig. ed. 2, i. 262 f. Eng. Tr. 268);—Gn 4[18.18] (J), 𝔊 Μαθουσαλα (i.e. מְתוּשֶׁלַח? so Di; otherwise Bu[Urgesch. 125 f.])

†מְתוּשֶׁלַח **n.pr.m.** descendant of Seth (? *man of the dart:* more prob. Bab.; see conj. in Hom[PSBA 1893, 243 ff.]);—מ׳ Gn 5[22.25.26.27] (P), 1 Ch 1[3], מְתוּשָׁלַח Gn 5[21] (P). 𝔊 Μαθουσαλα.

מַתְבֵּן v. תבן.

מתג (√ of foll.; meaning unknown).

†מֶתֶג **n.m. bridle** (Aram. (𝔗) מִתְגָּא; NH מֶתֶג of secondary accent ֽ; מִתֵּג Pi. denom. *put on a bridle*);—**1.** lit. *bridle,* for animals; מֶתֶג לַחֲמוֹר Pr 26[3] a whip for the horse, *a bridle for the ass,* etc.; בְּמ׳ וָרֶסֶן ψ 32[9] *with bridle and halter* (on text of verse cf. Che); of י׳'s *bridle* for Sennach. (under fig. of beast), וּמִתְגִּי בִּשְׂפָתֶיךָ 2 K 19[28] and I will put (וְשַׂמְתִּי) my hook in thy nose *and my bridle in thy lips* = Is 37[29] (v. Dr Is. ed. 2, 220). **2.** fig. = *control, authority,* only in מ׳ הָאַמָּה 2 S 8[1] *authority of the mother city,* acc. to MV Buhl, cf. esp. We Dr; Bu om. as corrupt (v. I. אַמָּה, p. 52 supr.); vid., further, HPS.

מְתוּשָׁאֵל, מְתוּשֶׁלַח v. sub מַת supr.

†[מָתַח] **vb. spread out** (NH *id.;* Aram. מְתַח, ܡܬܚ; Ar. مَتَحَ *be long,* مَتَّاح *long* (prob. loan-word); cf. perhaps As. *matâḫu, direct* the eyes toward);—only **Qal** *Impf.* 3 ms. sf. וַיִּמְתָּחֵם Is 40[22] *and he* (י׳) *hath spread them* (the heavens) *out* as a tent to dwell in.

†אַמְתַּחַת **n.f. sack,** only Gn 42–44;—א׳ constr. Gn 44[2.12]; sf. אַמְתַּחְתִּי 42[28], אַמְתַּחְתּוֹ 42[27] + 2 t.; pl. cstr. אַמְתְּחֹת 44[1]; sf. אַמְתְּחֹתֵינוּ 43[18] + 3 t.; אַמְתְּחֹתֵיכֶם 43[12.23];—*sack*(s) in wh. brethren of Joseph carried corn from Egypt; in phr. בְּפִי אַמ׳ Gn 42[27] *in the mouth of the sack,* so 43[12.21] 44[1.2.8]; elsewhere 42[28] 43[18.21.22.23] 44[1.11.11.12] (all J).

מָתַי 43 **interrog. adv. when?** (Ar. مَتَى; As. *mati:* in NH and Aram. with the interrog. ܐܡܬܝ, אֵימַת, אֵימָתַי, אֵי), in OT only of future time: **a.** alone, †Gn 30[30] מָתַי אעשה גם אנכי לביתי *when* shall I also do, etc.? Am 8[5] ψ 41[6] 42[3] 94[8] 101[2] 119[82.84] Pr 6[9b] 23[35] Jb 7[4] מָתַי אָקוּם, Ne 2[6]. **b.** לְמָתַי *against when?* †Ex 8[5] לְמָתַי אַעְתִּיר לְךָ. **c.** עַד־מָתַי *until when? how long?* sq. impf. Ex 10[7] עד מתי יהיה זה לנו למוקש, 1 S 1[14] Je 4[14.21] ψ 74[10] 82[2] 94[3] Pr 1[22] +, sq. ptcp. 1 S 16[1] 1 K 18[21] עַד־מָתַי אַתֶּם פֹּסְחִים עַל־שְׁתֵּי הַסְּעִפִּים, sq. pf. †Ex 10[3] ψ 80[5]; עַד מָתַי לֹא †2 S 2[26] Ho 8[5] Zc 1[12]; alone, Is 6[11] וָאֹמַר עַד־מָתַי אֲדֹנָי, Hb 2[6] הוֹי הַמַּרְבֶּה לֹּא־לוֹ עַד־מָתַי; with an aposiop., ψ 6[4] וְאַתָּה י׳ עַד־מָתָי, 90[13]. **d.** אַחֲרֵי מָתַי עוֹד *after how long yet?* †Je 13[27].

מְתִים v. מַת. מַתְכֹּנֶת v. תכן.

מַתְלָאָה v. תְּלָאָה. מְתַלְּעוֹת v. תלע.

מתם v תמם; Ju 20⁴⁸ v. מַת.

מתן (√of foll., Ar مَتُنَ be stout, firm, enduring (Frey Wahrm), II. make stout, firm (Lane))

†מָתְנַיִם n.m.du. loins (Ar مَتْنٌ back, مَتْنَانِ the two sides of the back, etc.; Syr. ܡܰܬܢܳܐ),—abs מ׳ Dt 33¹¹ + 7 t, מָתְנָיִם Ez 29⁷ 47⁴; cstr מָתְנֵי Je 13¹¹ + 3 t; sf מָתְנַי Is 21³, מָתְנֶיךָ Je 13², מָתְנֵיהֶם 1 K 20³² + 4 t, etc.,—loins: **1. a.** place of wearing girdle 1 K 2⁵ 2 K 1⁸ Je 13¹·²·⁴·¹¹ Ez 23¹⁵; fig Is 11⁵ *righteousness shall be the girdle of his loins.* **b.** hence place of things attached to girdle:—sword girded on (חגר על, אסר) 2 S 20⁸ Ne 4¹², opp, וּמָתְנֵי מְלָכִים אֲפַתֵּחַ Is 45¹ *and the loins of kings I will loosen*, i e. will disarm them (׳י before Cyrus; cf. Che), ink-horn Ez 9²·³·¹¹. **c.** girding up *loins* = make ready for action, וַיְשַׁנֵּס מָתְנָיו 1 K 18⁴⁶; more oft חֲגֹר מ׳ 2 K 4²⁹ 9¹ Ex 12¹¹ (P), Dn 10⁵, אֱזֹר מ׳ Je 1¹⁷. **d.** זַרְזִיר מ׳ Pr 30³¹ that which is *girt in the loins*, i. e. prob either a *greyhound* Ew Bo De (contracted, as if by a belt), or a war-horse, charger, Bo Ges Hi Str Wild (with a saddle); cf. also זרזיר, p 267 supr; text perh. corrupt (Wild). **e.** girded with sackcloth (in mourning) Gn 37³⁴ (J), Am 8¹⁰ Is 20² 1 K 20³¹·³² Je 48³⁷ **f.** linen breeches of priests were to extend מִמָּתְנַיִם וְעַד יְרֵכַיִם Ex 28⁴² (P), to be עַל־מָת׳ Ez 44¹⁸, loins of slaves are girt with waistcloth, cf Jb 12¹⁸ (v. also אזור). **g.** in gen. of the middle of the body, מֵי מָת׳ Ez 47⁴ (i. e. water reaching to the loins), so of the appearance of ׳י in Ezek.'s visions Ez 1²⁷·²⁷ 8²·². **2. a.** *loins* as seat of strength, Dt 33¹¹ 1 K 12¹⁰ = 2 Ch 10¹⁰; חַזֵּק מָתְנַיִם Na 2² (|| אַמֵּץ כֹּחַ), כֹּחוֹ בְמָתְנָיו Jb 40¹⁶ (of hippopotamus), in combin. with **1 a** (fig.) חָגְרָה בְעוֹז מ׳ Pr 31¹⁷ *she girdeth her loins with strength*, she puts on energy with her girdle, cf. also בשברון מ׳ Ez 21¹¹ sigh *with breaking of loins*, i e in entire collapse of strength; so וּמ׳ תָּמִיד הַמְעַד ψ 69²⁴ *and make their loins continually to shake*, make them totter; cf. Ez 29⁷ (where rd. וְהַמְעַדְתָּ for וְהַעֲמַדְתָּ, v מָעַד). **b.** as seat of keenest pain, due to grief or dread Na 2¹¹ Is 21³ (as in travail), so prob also ψ 66¹¹ (cf. Bae, and v מוּעָקָה sub עוק)

†מִתְנִי adj.gent. (deriv. unknown);—only יוֹשָׁפָט הַמִּ׳ 1 Ch 11⁴³. 𝔊 ὁ Βαιθανει, A Μαθθανει, 𝔊L Μαιθανι

מַתָּן, מַתָּנָה, מַתְּנַי, מַתַּנְיָה(וּ) I, II. I, II v נתן.

†[מָתֹק] vb. become or be sweet, pleasant (NH מתק, esp. Pi.; As. [*matâku*] *be sweet*, in deriv.; Eth. ጥዑም: *sweet*; Aram. ܡܬܩ *suck* (with pleasure), מְתַק *id*, *be sweet*; Ar. مطق (ط before ق) v. *smack* the lips (with pleasure), مُطْقَةٌ *sweetness*);—**Qal** *Pf* 3 ms sf. מְתָקוֹ Jb 24²⁰, 3 pl מָתְקוּ 21³³; *Impf.* 3 mpl. יִמְתָּקוּ Pr 9¹⁷, וַיִּמְתְּקוּ Ex 15²⁵,—**1.** lit *become sweet*, of water (opp מָרִים) 15²⁵ (J), *are* (i. e. taste) *sweet*, מַיִם גְּנוּבִים יִמ׳ Pr 9¹⁷ (fig. of delights of illicit pleasure). **2.** = *be pleasant*, מָתְקוּ לוֹ Jb 21³³ *sweet* (pleasant) *to him* are the clods of the valley (said of one resting in the grave) **3.** *suck* (Aram. sense, cf Syr supr.) מְתָקוֹ רִמָּה Jb 24²⁰ the worm *doth suck him*, feast on him (on vb. masc cf. Ges§ 145.7 Ko^Synt. § 345a Da^Synt § 113(b)), Di De Buhl (cf. Kau Da; also SS who render 'angenehm finden'), but this sense in Heb dub.; txt. perh crpt (cf conject. by Bu Du) **Hiph.** *Impf.* 3 fs. אִם תַּמְתִּיק בְּפִיו רָעָה Jb 20¹² *if evil gives a sweet taste in his mouth* (declarative Hiph), 1 pl אֲשֶׁר יַחְדָּו נַמְתִּיק סוֹד ψ 55¹⁵ *we who used to make sweet* (our) *intimacy.*

†מֶתֶק n.m.^Pr 16. 21 sweetness; cstr. מֶ׳ שְׂפָתַיִם Pr 16²¹ i.e agreeable, attractive speech, so prob. מ׳ רֵעֵהוּ 27⁹ *the sweetness of one's friend*, i.e of his speech.

†[מֹתֶק] n.[m.] sweetness,—only sf מָתְקִי Ju 9¹¹ *my sweetness* (fig-tree loquitur), i.e. sweetness of the fruit.

†מָתוֹק adj. sweet, and n.[m.] sweetness (on form v. Lag^BN 30, 60, cf. Ba^NB 13, 36);—abs. מ׳ Ju 14¹⁴ + 9 t; f. מְתוּקָה Ec 5¹¹; pl מְתוּקִים ψ 19¹¹,—**1.** *sweet*, of honey Ju 14¹⁴ (where מ׳ = subst. *a sweet thing*), v¹⁸ (both Samson's riddle), Pr 24¹³; so = *sweetness*, Ez 3³, more gen., כָּל־מַר מ׳ Pr 27⁷ *every bitter thing is sweet* to one hungry; fig. ψ 19¹¹ (God's commandments, sweeter than honey), cf. Pr 16²⁴ (sim. of pleasant words) וּפִרְיוֹ מ׳ לְחִכִּי Ct 2³ (i.e his caresses); שָׂמִים מַר לְמ׳ וּמ׳ לְמָר Is 5²⁰ *making bitter into sweet and sweet into bitter* (obscuring moral distinctions, || הָאֹמְרִים לָרַע טוֹב וְלַטּוֹב רָע).

2. =*pleasant*, sleep of the toiler Ec 5^{11}; light 11^{7} (טוב לָעֵינַיִם לִרְאוֹת אֶת־הַשָּׁמֶשׁ ||).

†מִתְקָה **n.pr.loc.** a station of Isr. in desert Nu $33^{28.29}$. 𝔊 Ματεκκα, A Μαθεκκα, 𝔊L Ματτεκα.

†מַמְתַקִּים **n.[m.]pl. sweetness=sweet things**;—of drinks וּשְׁתוּ מ׳ Ne 8^{10} (|| אִכְלוּ מַשְׁמַנִּים); of lover's kisses חִכּוֹ מ׳ Ct 5^{16} (|| כֻּלּוֹ מַחֲמַדִּים).

†מִתְרְדָת **n.pr.m.** name of two Persians; **1.** Cyrus' time Ezr 1^{8}. **2.** Artaxerxes' time Ezr 4^{7}.—𝔊 Μιθρα[ι]δατης in both.

מַתָּת, מַתָּנָה, מַתִּתְיָה(וּ) v. נתן.

נ

נ, ן, *Nûn*, fourteenth letter; used as numeral 50 in postB. Heb.

I. נָא **part. of entreaty** or **exhortation, I (we) pray, now** (enclitic) (Syr ܢܳܐ, ܢܳܝ; cf Eth. ንዒ: *veni, age!* Di§160 ¹ Lex^{675} Kö$^{II. 244}$);—attached: **1.** to the imv, esp. in colloquial style, when it expresses an entreaty or admonition, as Gn 12^{13} אִמְרִי־נָא say, *I pray*, 13^{9} הִפָּרֶד־נָא מֵעָלַי, v^{14} שָׂא־נָא עֵינֶיךָ, 15^{5} הַבֶּט־נָא השמימה, 24^{2}+oft., Nu 20^{10} שמעו־נא המורים, Ju 13^{4} $16^{6.10.28}$ 18^{5}, etc., Is 1^{18} 5^{3} Am $7^{2.5}$; rarely in a command, Gn 22^{2} Is 7^{3}. Ironically, in a challenge, Is 47^{12} Jb 40^{10}. Once anomalously attached to a subst., or (accents) prefixed to a verb, Nu 12^{13} אֵל נָא רְפָא נָא (Ew§246a Di אַל־נָא; v **3 b**) **2.** to the pf with *waw* consec, in a precative sense (Dr§119δ) Gn 40^{14}. **3.** to the impf., when leave is asked, or a prayer or desire expressed; **a.** in 1 pers, esp with ה cohort., Gn 19^{8} אוציאה־נא let me, *I pray*, bring out, v^{20} אִמָּלְטָה־נָּא שָׁמָּה, 24^{12} הַקְרֵה־נָא לְפָנַי, v^{14} הַטִּי־נָא, v$^{17.23.43.45}$ 25^{30} $32^{12.30}$+oft, Ex 3^{18} נלכה־נא let us go, *I pray*, Nu 20^{17} Is 5^{1}; and in self-deliberation, Gn 18^{21} ארדה־נא I will go down, *now!* Ex 3^{3} אסורה־נא ואראה I will turn aside, *now*, and see, 2 S 14^{15} Ct 3^{2} Is 5^{1}; with אַל Jb 32^{21}. **b.** in 2 pers, with אַל, in deprecation, Gn 18^{3} אל־נא תעבר מעל עבדך, 19^{7} 47^{29} Nu 10^{31}, etc.; hence ellipt אל־נא do not, *I pray*, (do this,) Gn 19^{18} 33^{10} Nu 12^{13} Ew Di. **c.** in 3 pers., Gn 18^{4} יֻקַּח־נָא let there be brought, *I pray*, 26^{28} 33^{14} $44^{18.33}$, etc., 2 S $14^{11.12.17}$ 1 K 17^{21} 2 K 2^{9} ψ 7^{10} $118^{2.3}$; ironically Is 19^{12} 47^{13}, or defiantly Jer 17^{15} where is the word of J? יָבוֹא נָא; with אַל, Gn 13^{8} אַל־נָא תְהִי מְרִיבָה, 18^{30} אַל־נָא יִחַר לַאדֹנָי, 37^{27} Nu 12^{12}. **4.** joined to conjunctions and interjections **a.** [אָה־נָא, contr] אָנָּא; v. p. 58. **b.** אַל־נָא, see above **3 b, c.** **c.** אִם־נָא, esp. in the phrase אם נא מצאתי חן בעיניך, used by one craving a favourable hearing †Gn 30^{27} 33^{10} Ju 6^{17} 1 S 27^{5}, and with נא repeated in the request itself †Gn 18^{3} 47^{29} 50^{4} Ex 33^{13} 34^{9}; otherwise Gn 24^{42}. **d.** הִנֵּה־נָא behold, *I pray*, craving a favourable consideration of the fact pointed to by הנה, and of the request founded upon it (with which נא is often repeated), Gn 12^{11} 16^{2} $18^{27.31}$ $19^{2.8.19.20}$ 27^{2} Ju 13^{3} 19^{9} 1 S 9^{6} 16^{15} 2 S 13^{24} 2 K $2^{16.19}$ 4^{9}+, Jb 13^{18} 33^{2} $40^{15.16}$. **e.** אוֹי־נָא לִי (לנו) Woe, *now*, to me (us)! †Je 4^{31} 45^{7} La 5^{16}. **f.** אַיֵּה־נָא where, *pray?* †ψ 115^{2}. **g.** נֶגְדָה־נָּא, peculiarly, †ψ $116^{14.18}$ my vows to J. I will perform, נגדה־נא לכל־עמו *O that* (it may be) before all his people!

II. נָא **adj.** v. ניא.

†נֹא **n.pr.loc.** No=Thebes (Eg *nt, city*, i.e. prob. *nē(t)*, v. Steind$^{BAS\ I.\ 596\ f.}$; As. *Ni-'u*, *Ni-i'* Dl$^{Par\ 318}$ Steind$^{l.c.}$ Schr$^{COT\ gloss}$; Tel Am. Ni (Ni-i) Wkl$^{Tel\ Am\ 39*}$ Bez$^{Tel\ Am.\ in\ BM\ 153}$),—הִנְנִי פוקד אֶל־אָמוֹן מִנֹּא Je 46^{25} *Amon from* (*of*, 𝔊 ἐν =ב) *No*; נֹא אָמוֹן Na 3^{8} *No of Amon* (=*city of god Ammon*, =𝔊 Διόσπολις Ez $30^{14.16}$ Steind$^{l.c.}$; v. also Jerem. and Billerbeck$^{BAS\ III.\ 104\ f.}$); Ez 30^{14} (|| צֹעַן, פַּתְרוֹס), וְהִכְרַתִּי אֶת־הֲמוֹן נֹא v^{15} (|| סִין; but 𝔊 Co Berthol נֹף q v for נא) v^{16} (|| סִין, Co סון). It lay on the right bank of the Nile, c. 400 miles (by the river) S. of Memphis.

†נֹאד (Ju 4^{19} Kt נאוד, i.e. prob. נְאוֹד), **n.m.**$^{Jos\ 9,4}$ **skin-bottle, skin** (√unknown; NH נוד; As. *nâdu*, Dl$^{HWB\ 433}$; Aram. נוֹדָא);—נ׳ abs. ψ 119^{83}, cstr. Ju 4^{19} 1 S 16^{20}; sf. נֹאדְךָ ψ 56^{9}; pl. נֹאדוֹת Jos $9^{4.13}$,—*skin*, נ׳ יַיִן Jos $9^{4.13}$ 1 S 16^{20}; נ׳ הֶחָלָב Ju 4^{19}; for tears ψ 56^{9} (fig.; v. Che); נ׳ בקיטור i e shrivelled and useless ψ 119^{83} (in sim., cf [De] Che Schu DeWitt We >as thrust

aside, out of the way Now (in Hup), cf De, or as black and wrinkled outwardly, while retaining the choice wine within Bae, after Rosenm. Hup).—Vid Winer$^{BWB\ Art. Schlauch}$ Kmp$^{Bi HWB\ id}$

†[נָאָה] **vb.** only **Pi'lel** be comely, befitting (Thes Ol$^{§251\,a.\,187\,a}$ Sta^{§416b} Ges$^{§73.2\ R\ 4}$ SS Bae$^{\psi 33\ 1}$ > AE Ki Hartm$^{Pluralb. bildungen (1875) 13 ff}$ No$^{ZMG\ xxx\ 1876,\ 185}$ Now Hup$^{\psi 31,1\ 93,5}$ Buhl **Niph.** √ I. אוה *desire*, i e. *desirable, beautiful;* NH נאה Pi Hithp ; 𝔗 נוֹאי *beauty*),—**Pi'lel** *Pf* נַאֲוָה ψ 93^{5} (so van d. H Ginsb; Mass Baer De$^{ad\ loc}$ נַאֲוָה = נָאֲוָה v. נָאוֶה **adj.**, but v. Sta $^{§155\,b.n}$); נָאווּ Is 52^{7} Ct 1^{10} (on form cf. Ges$^{l.c.}$),—**1.** *be comely;* of feet of messenger, (fig) Is 52^{7}, of cheeks Ct 1^{10}. **2.** *be befitting* לְבֵיתְךָ נ׳־קֹדֶשׁ ψ 93^{5}.

†נָאוֶה **adj.** comely, seemly;—נ׳ m Ct 2^{14} + 3 t, f. נָאוָה ψ 33^{1} + 4 t, נָוָה Je 6^{2},—**1.** *comely, beautiful,* of woman Ct 1^{5} 6^{4} (‖ יָפָה); of face 2^{14} (מַרְאֶה); so נָוָה Je 6^{2} (fig of Jerus, ‖ מְעֻנָּגָה); of mouth Ct 4^{3} (‖ שִׂפְתוֹת). **2.** *seemly,* of praise תהלה ψ 33^{1} 147^{1}, subj שְׂפַת־יֶתֶר Pr 17^{7} (cf Ct 4^{3}), תַּעֲנוּג 19^{10}, כָּבוֹד 26^{1}. So also ψ 93^{5} Mass (anom. fem) v. [נאה] supr.

נאות v II. [נָוָה] sub II. נוה.

נאם (√ of foll, cf نَأَمَ *groan, sigh;* perhaps also NH נום *speak*)

נְאֻם $_{376}$ **n.m.** utterance (Ba$^{NB\ 82\,a}$ Ko$^{Lgb\ ii\ 501}$ > older expl as *Pt pass*);—נ׳ always thus, as cstr —**1.** *utterance, declaration, revelation,* of prophet in ecstatic state נ׳ בִּלְעָם Nu 24$^{3\ 15}$, נ׳ הַגֶּבֶר v$^{3\ 15}$ 2 S 23^{1} Pr 30^{1}, נ׳ שֹׁמֵעַ אִמְרֵי אֵל v$^{4\ 6}$, נ׳ דָּוִד 2 S 23^{1}; נ׳ פֶּשַׁע ψ 36^{2} (transgression personified, speaking with proph. voice בקרב לִבּוֹ), elsewh alw **2.** before divine names (exc Je 23^{31} see **vb.**) נ׳ יהוה *utterance, declaration* of י׳ (prophet citing divine word given through him), Gn 22^{16} (J), Nu 14^{28} (P), 2 K 9$^{26\ 26}$ 19^{33} = Is 37^{34}, 2 K 22^{19} = 2 Ch 34^{27}, Is 14^{22} 30^{1} 31^{9} Ez 13$^{6\ 7}$ 16^{58} 37^{14} Ho 2$^{15\ 18.23}$ 11^{11} Jo 2^{12} Ob$^{4.8}$ Mi 4^{6} 5^{9} Zp 1$^{2.3\ 10}$ 3^{8} Zc 8^{17} 10^{12} 11^{6} 12^{14} 13^{8} Mal 1^{2} + Is^{2} 12 t, Je 162 t, Am 14 t., Hg 5 t, Zc^{1} (1–8) 6 t; sq אלהי ישראל י׳ 1 S 2^{30} Is 17^{6}, י׳ אלהי (הַ)צבאות Am 6$^{8\ 14}$, נ׳ י׳ צבאות Is 14$^{22.23}$ 17^{3} 22^{25} Je 8^{3} 25^{29} 30^{8} 49^{26} Na 2^{14} 3^{5} Zc 13$^{2.7}$ + Hg 5 t, Zc^{1} (1–8) 7 t; sq אלהי ישראל י׳ צ׳ Zp 2^{9}, האדון י׳ צ׳ Is 1^{24} 19^{4}, אֲדֹנָי י׳ אלהי הַצ׳ Am 3^{13}, אדני י׳ צ׳ Is 3^{15} Je 49^{5}; הַמֶּלֶךְ י׳ צ׳ 46^{18} 48^{15} 57^{67}, נ׳ אדני יהוה Is 56^{8} Je 2^{22} Am 4^{5} 8$^{3\ 9\ 11}$ + Ez 82 t. נְאֻם begins sentence only Is 56^{8} ψ 110^{1}; often in middle Is 49^{18} Am 3^{10} +; most frequently at end Is 54^{17} Am 2^{11} 4^{3} +; found in all proph. except Hab, Jon; not in HD of Hex., Chr. (except ‖ Kings), Dan., Job or the five Megilloth.

†[נָאַם] **vb. denom.** utter a prophecy, speak as prophet,—**Qal** *Impf.* 3 mpl. וַיִּנְאֲמוּ נְאֻם Je 23^{31} *and they uttered* (in the prophetic manner), it *as an utterance* (of י׳); they used the prophetic formula (cf. אֹמְרִים נְאֻם י׳ Ez 13$^{6.7}$).

†[נָאַף] **vb.** commit adultery (NH *id.;* Aram נְאַף (rare)),—**Qal** *Impf* 3 ms. יִנְאַף Lv 20$^{10\ 10}$, 3 mpl וַיִּנְאָפוּ Je 5^{7} + 3 t. Impf; *Inf. abs* נָאוֹף 23^{14}; נָאֹף Ho 4^{2} Je 7^{9}, *Pt* נֹאֵף Pr 6^{32} Jb 24^{15}; fs. נֹאֶפֶת Lv 20^{10}; fpl. נֹאֲפוֹת Ez 16^{38} + 2 t,—**1.** lit *commit adultery:* **a.** usu. of *man,* always with wife of another; c. acc. woman, Lv 20$^{10\ 10}$ (H), Pr 6^{32}, elsewh. abs Ex 20^{14} = Dt 5^{17} (Ten Words), Je 5^{7} 7^{9} 23^{14} Ho 4^{2}, pt. m. Lv 20^{10} (H), Jb 24^{15}. **b.** of *women,* only pt. Lv 20^{10} (H), Ez 16^{38} 23$^{45\ 45}$. **2.** fig of *idolatrous worship,* את האבן ואת העץ Je 3^{9}.

Piel *Pf.* 3 fs. נִאֲפָה Je 3^{8}, 3 mpl נִאֵפוּ Ez 23$^{37\ 37}$, *Impf.* 3 mpl. יְנָאֲפוּ Je 29^{23}, 3 fpl. תְּנָאַפְנָה Ho 4$^{13.14}$; *Pt* מְנָאֵף Is 57^{3}, pl מְנָאֲפִים Je 9^{1} + 4 t, f. מְנָאֶפֶת Pr 30^{20} + 2 t.,—**1.** lit. *commit adultery.* **a.** of *man,* c acc woman, Je 29^{23}; abs. Ez 23^{37}; pt pl. Je 9^{2} 23^{10} Ho 7^{4} Mal 3^{5} ψ 50^{18}. **b.** of *woman,* abs Ho 4$^{13\ 14}$; pt. 3^{1} Pr 30^{20}; pl Ez 16^{32}. **2.** fig of *idolatrous worship,* אֶת־גִּלּוּלֵיהֶם Ez 23^{37}; abs. Je 3^{8}, זֶרַע מְנָאֵף Is 57^{3}

†[נִאֻף] **n.[m.]** adultery,—only pl נִאֻפִים Ez 23^{43} (but 𝔊 𝔖 Co נִאֲפוּ, cf Berthol); sf. נִאֻפַיִךְ Je 13^{27} (Ko$^{i\ 151}$), fig of idolatrous worship

†[נַאֲפוּף] **n.[m.]** adultery,—only pl sf. נַאֲפוּפֶיהָ Ho 2^{4} (Ba$^{NB\ 216}$), of idolatrous worship of Baal

†**נָאַץ** **vb.** contemn, spurn (NH *id*, Pi.; 𝔗 נִיאוּצָא *reviling*),—**Qal** *Pf* נ׳ Pr 5^{12}; 3 pl נָאֲצוּ Pr 1^{30}; נָאָצוּ ψ 107^{11}; *Impf* יִנְאַץ Pr 15^{5}; יִנְאָצוּן Je 33^{24}, etc ,—*contemn,* subj wicked and foolish, obj תוכחת Pr 1^{30} 5^{12}, obj. מוּסַר Pr 15^{5}; עֵצָה ψ 107^{11}, Je 33^{24} (obj. עַם י׳; cf Gie); subj. י׳ Dt 32^{19} Je 14^{21} La 2^{6}. **Pi.** *Pf* נִאֵץ ψ 10$^{3\ 13}$, יְנָאֵץ ψ 74^{10}; sf. יְנַאֲצֻנִי, etc, *Impf* נִאֵצְתָּ 2 S 12^{14}, Nu 14^{11}, *Inf abs* נִאֵץ (Sta^{§221}) 2 S 12^{14}, *Pt.* sf. מְנַאֲצַי Nu 14^{23}; מְנַאֲצַי Je 23^{17}, מְנַאֲצַיִךְ Is 60^{14};—

contemn, spurn, subj. men, obj 'י, etc.: Nu $14^{11.23}$ 16^{30} (all J), Dt 31^{20} Is 1^{4} ψ $10^{3.13}$ Je 23^{17}; obj. שם י' ψ $74^{10.18}$; אמרת י' Is 5^{24}, מִנְחַת י' 1 S 2^{17}; once obj. Jerus. Is 60^{14}, *cause to contemn* (blaspheme AV RV) 2 S $12^{14.14}$ (but אֹיְבֵי prob interp; v. Comm).

Hiph. *Impf.* יְנֹאץ v. נצץ.

Hithpo'el *Pt.* כל־היום שמי מִנֹּאָץ Is 52^{5} *every day is my name contemned.*

†**נְאָצָה** **n.f.** contempt, contumely;—יוֹם־צָרָה וְתוכחה ונ' 2 K 19^{3} = Is 37^{3}.

†[**נֶאָצָה**] **n.f.** contempt (toward 'י), blasphemy;—pl. נֶאָצוֹת Ne $9^{18.26}$ c עָשָׂה, of Isr; נֶאָצוֹתֶיךָ Ez 35^{12} of Mt. Seir, spoken against הרי ישראל.

†**נָאַק** **vb.** groan (Aram. נְאַק (rare));—**Qal** *Pf* וְנָאַק consec Ez 30^{24} c. acc. cogn. fig. of Pharaoh before king of Babylon (emend. Co v. נְאָקָה) *Impf* Jb 24^{12} יִנְאָקוּ.

†[**נְאָקָה**] **n.f.** groan, groaning;—cstr. נַאֲקַת Ex 6^{5}; sf. נַאֲקָתָם Ex 2^{24} Ju 2^{18}; pl cstr נַאֲקוֹת Ez 30^{24};—*groaning* of oppressed people Ex 2^{24} 6^{5} Ju 2^{18}; of a wounded man Ez 30^{24}, (𝔊 Co וּבְזוֹ בִזָּה for MT וְנָאַק נַאֲקוֹת, but cf Berthol).

[**נָאַר**] **vb.** only **Pi.** exact mng uncertain; prob. (from context) abhor, spurn (De comp. Ar. نار *abhor*, but this is med. و),—**Pi.** *Pf.* subj 'י, נאר La 2^{7} (obj מִקְדָּשׁוֹ, ‖ זָנַח); 2 ms נֵאַרְתָּה ψ 89^{40} (obj. ברית עבדך ‖ חִלַּלְתָּ, and זָנַחְתָּ, מָאַס v^{39}; doubts cast on text by Hup (reading נאץ), Now, $Bu^{La\ 2,7}$).

†**נֹב** **n.pr.loc.** **1.** ancient priestly city 1 S 22^{19} cf. v^{11} c ה loc. נֹבֶה ($Ges^{§90,2\,ad\,fin}$), 21^{2} 22^{9}; 𝔊 Νομβα, Νομμα, Νοβα, etc.; perh = נְבוֹ (q v.) Ezr 2^{29} = Ne 7^{33}, Ezr 10^{43}, 𝔊 Ναβου, Ναβια, etc. Site dub, on Jerome's identif. with *Nobe* near Lydda cf. $Buhl^{Geogr\ 189}$, a Bêt Nûbâ lies c. 13 m. WNW. fr. Jerus, c. 10 SE. fr. Lydda. **2.** Is 10^{32} just N of Jerus, station in (ideal) Assyr. march; cf. Ne 11^{32} (inhab. by Benjamites); perhaps = **1.**—2 S 21^{6} read נֹב (q v. p. 146 supr.)

נבא (√of foll, Ew Fl De $Ko^{Lehrb\ ii.\ 1,133}$ al comp. Ar نَبَأَ [نَبَّأَ *utter a low voice*, or *sound*, (esp. of dog); *announce;* but also *be exalted, elevated* (نَبْوَة *eminence*), III, IV. *acquaint, inform*, نَبَأٌ *information, announcement, intelligence*]; As. *nabû, call, proclaim, name*, Dl $^{HWB\ 441}$; Eth. ነበበ: *speak;* Sab. תנבא? cf. Levy-$Os^{ZMG\ xix\ 1865,\ 208}$ $CIS^{iv\ 1,\ No\ 31}$, Ges Kue al. think weakened form of נבע *bubble up, pour forth* (of flow of words under excitement of inspiration); Hup Ri Sch cf. נאם; v careful discussions by $RS^{Proph.\ ii,\ n.\ 18}$ $Ko^{OB\ i,\ 71\,ff}$)

נָבִיא $^{†\,306}$ **n.m.** spokesman, speaker, prophet —נ' Gn 20^{7} + 155 t.; sf. נְבִיאֲךָ Ex 7^{1}; pl. נְבִיאִים Nu 11^{29} + 82 t.; נבאים Je 27^{18} + 16 t; sf. נְבִיאַי ψ 105^{15}; נְבִיאָיו 1 K 22^{22}; נבאיו 2 K 17^{13}, etc.;— **1.** genuine *prophet* of 'י, נביא, anciently called רֹאֶה, 1 S 9^{9} (antiquarian note); change prob. occurred in times of Elijah and is first reflected in Ephr. lit. as applied to Abraham Gn 20^{7}; Moses Dt 34^{10}, M. and other early proph. Ho 6^{5} $12^{11.11.14.14}$ Am $2^{11.12}$; of proph. in ecstatic state Nu 12^{6} (E), 11^{29} (JE). So in Judaic lit., of prophet like Moses Dt $18^{15.18}$ (D), of Aaron (as mouthpiece of M) Ex 7^{1} (P), of Sam. 1 S 3^{20}, an unknown Ju 6^{8}; in time of Sam. proph. were organized in bands: †חֶבֶל נביאים 1 S $10^{5.10}$; †לַהֲקַת הנ' 1 S 19^{20}; and in time of Elijah were †בְּנֵי הַנְּבִיאִים = members of prophets' guilds 1 K 20^{35} 2 K $2^{3.5.7.15}$ $4^{1.38.38}$, נָבִיא, of genuine proph. (besides phrases), in Judaic prophets, only of Jer, Je 1^{5}; Ezekiel, Ez 2^{5} = 33^{33}; of ancient prophets Je $28^{8.9.9.9}$ Zc 1^{6} 8^{9}; esp. †הנביאים הראשנים Zc 1^{4} $7^{7.12}$, cf †עבדי(ו) הנביאים *my* (*his*) *servants the prophets* 2 K 9^{7} $17^{13.23}$ 21^{10} 24^{2} (all R^{D}) Ezr 9^{11} Dn 9^{10} Je 7^{25} 25^{4} 26^{5} 29^{19} 35^{15} 44^{4} Am 3^{7} Zc 1^{6}, cf. Ez 38^{17} Dn 9^{6}; †עבדו הנ' *his servant the prophet* 1 K 14^{18} 2 K 14^{25}; הַנָּבִיא with n. pr Jer, 2 Ch 36^{12} Dn 9^{2} + 31 t. Je (but 𝔊 only 4 t, the rest prob. redactional, see $Gie^{Jer\ xxvii}$); Elijah 1 K 18^{36} (om 𝔊), 2 Ch 21^{12} Mal 3^{23}; Nathan 2 S 7^{2} + 10 t S. and K.; 4 t Chr. ψ 51^{2} (title); Isaiah, 2 K 19^{2} $20^{1.14}$ = Is 37^{2} 38^{1} 39^{1}; 2 K 20^{11} 2 Ch 26^{22} $32^{20.32}$; Habakkuk Hb 1^{1} 3^{1} (titles); Haggai, Hg $1^{1.3.12}$ $2^{1.10}$; Zech., Zc $1^{1.7}$ (titles); elsewh. several others in S, K. and Chr. 15 t.; נביא is used elsewh. of genuine proph only 1 S 9^{9} + 34 t. S and K., 1 Ch 16^{22} = ψ 105^{15}, + 13 t Chr; ψ 74^{9} complains of absence of נ'; לַחְתֹּם חָזוֹן וְנָבִיא Dn 9^{24} v. חתם. **2.** *false prophets:* †prophets as official class, beside priests, charact. as false prophets: Is 28^{7} Je 2^{26} 4^{9} 6^{13} $8^{1.10}$ 13^{13} 14^{18} 18^{18} $23^{11.33.34}$ $26^{7.8.11.16}$ 32^{32} Zc 7^{3}, app also 2 K 23^{2} Ne 9^{32} La 2^{20} Je 29^{1} Ez 7^{26} (in these not characterized); alw. false (exc. of ancient and special prophets given above) in Am 7^{14} Ho 4^{5} $9^{7.8}$ Mi $3^{5.6.11}$ Is 3^{2} 9^{14} 29^{10} Je $2^{8.30}$

5$^{13.31}$ 14$^{13.14.15.15}$ 23$^{9+16t.}$ 27$^{9.14.15.16.18}$ 29$^{9.15}$ 37^{19} Ez 13$^{2.2.3.4.9.16}$ 14$^{4.7.9.9.10}$ 22$^{25.28}$ Zp 3^{4} La 2$^{9.14}$ 4^{13}, especially discredited Dt 13$^{2.4.6}$ 18$^{20.20.22.22}$ Zc 13$^{2.4.5}$; such a prophet Hananiah called הַנָּבִיא Je 28$^{1.5.10.12.15.17}$ (𝔊 omits in all but v^{1}, where ψευδοπροφήτης). Usage of prophets themselves gives such a bad flavour to נביא, that we are not surprised that it is absent from exilic Isaiah, the Wisd. Lit., and ψψ (except for special reasons in 3 ψψ given under **1**). **+3.** *heathen prophets* 1 K 18^{20} 19^{1} 2 K 3$^{13.13}$, נביאי האשרה 1 K 18^{19}; נביאי הבעל 1 K 18$^{19.22.25.40}$ 2 K 10^{19}; 1 K 22$^{6.10.12.13.22.23}$ = 2 Ch 18$^{5.9.11.12.21.22}$.

†[נָבָא] **vb. denom.** **prophesy** (in oldest forms, of religious ecstasy with or without song and music; later, essentially religious instruction, with occasional predictions),—**Niph.** *Pf* 3 ms. נִבָּא Je 20^{1} + 7 t., 2 ms. נִבֵּאתָ Je 20^{6} + 2 t., נִבֵּית Je 26^{9}, 1 s נִבֵּאתִי Ez 37^{7}; 3 pl נִבְּאוּ Je 2^{8} + 3 t., נִבָּאוּ Je 23^{21}, *Impf.* 3 ms יִנָּבֵא Am 3^{8} + 9 t Impf.; *Imv.* הִנָּבֵא Am 7^{15} + 27 t., *Inf.* הִנָּבֵא Am 7^{13}, sf הִנָּבְאוֹ Zc 13^{3}, הִנָּבְאוֹתוֹ Zc 13^{4}, + 4 t. Inf., *Pt* נִבָּא Je 26^{18} + 20 t. Pt;—**1.** *prophesy* under influence of divine spirit. **a.** in the ecstatic state, with song 1 S 10^{11} 19^{20} and music 1 Ch 25$^{1.2.3}$. **b.** the word of י׳ abs Am 2^{12} 3^{8} (emend יחרד We Now needless), 7$^{12.13}$ Jo 3^{1} Je 19^{14} 26^{18} 28^{9} 32^{3} Ez 11^{13} 12^{27} 21^{19} 37^{7} 38^{17} but esp in phr הִנָּבֵא וְאָמַרְתָּ Ez 12^{27} 21$^{14.33}$ 30^{2} 34^{2} 36^{3} 37$^{7.12}$ 38$^{14.17}$, c. acc. Je 20^{1} 25^{30} 28^{6}, sq עַל *against* Am 7^{16} Je 25^{13} 26^{20} Ez 4^{7} 11^{4} 13^{17} 25^{2} 28^{21} 29^{2} 34^{2} 35^{2} 36^{6} 38^{2} 39^{1}, *unto* Ez 37^{4}, אֶל *unto* Am 7^{15} Je 26$^{11.12}$ 28^{8} Ez 36^{1} 37^{9}, *against* 6^{2} 13^{2} 21$^{2.7}$; בשם י׳ Je 11^{21} 14^{15} 23^{25} 26^{9}. **2.** of false prophets. abs. Je 23^{21} Ez 13^{2} Zc 13$^{3.3.4}$, c acc. 1 K 22^{12} = 2 Ch 18^{11}, שׁקר Je 14^{14} 23^{25} 27$^{10.14.16}$ 29^{21}, לַשֶּׁקֶר 27^{15}, לְ 5^{31} 20^{6} 29^{9}, נבאי הש׳ 23^{26}, cf v^{32}; c בַּשֶּׁקֶר 14^{16} 23^{16} 27$^{15.16}$ 29^{31} 37^{19}, sq. אֶל *concerning* Ez 13^{16}. **3.** of *heathen prophets*, בַּבַּעַל Je 2^{8} 23^{13}. **3.** of false prophets 1 K 22^{10} = 2 Ch 18^{9}, Je 14^{14} Ez 13^{17}.

Hithp. *Pf* 2 ms הִתְנַבִּיתָ 1 S 10^{6}, 1 s. הִנַּבֵּאתִי Ez 37^{10}, *Impf* יִתְנַבֵּא 1 S 10^{10} + 7 t; 3 mpl יִתְנַבְּאוּ Nu 11^{25} + 5 t; *Imv.* הִנַּבְאוּ Je 23^{13}, *Inf* הִתְנַבּוֹת 1 S 10^{13}, *Pt.* מִתְנַבֵּא Je 26^{20} + 9 t Pt,—**1.** *prophesy* under influence of divine spirit: **a.** in the ecstatic state Nu 11$^{25.26.27}$ (J), with music 1 S 10$^{5.6.10.13}$, in frenzy 1 S 19$^{20.21.21.23.24}$, excited to violence 1 S 18^{10} (= מְשֻׁגָּע *mad* 2 K 9^{11}); Je 29^{26}. **b.** apart from ecstatic state, abs. Ez 37^{10}, c. לְ 1 K 22^{8} Je 29^{27}, עַל 1 K 22^{18} = 2 Ch 18^{17}, 2 Ch 18^{7} 20^{37}, בשם י׳ Je 26^{20}. **2.** of heathen prophets of Baal in ecstatic state 1 K 18^{29}; בַּבַּעַל Je 23^{13} **3.** of false prophets 1 K 22^{10} = 2 Ch 18^{9}, Je 14^{14} Ez 13^{17}.

†נְבוּאָה **n.f.** **prophecy** (late: earlier syn. חָזוֹן),—**1. a.** specific and genuine 2 Ch 15^{8}. **b.** false Ne 6^{12}. **2.** prophetic writing עַל־נְבוּאַת אֲחִיָּה 2 Ch 9^{29}.

†נְבִיאָה **n.f.** **prophetess**;—**1. a.** of the ancient type endowed with gift of song, Miriam Ex 15^{20}; Deborah Ju 4^{4}. **b.** of the later type consulted for a word of י׳, Huldah 2 K 22^{14} = 2 Ch 34^{22}. **2.** false prophetess, Noadiah Ne 6^{14} **3.** wife of Isaiah Is 8^{3}.

†[נָבַב] **vb.** **hollow out** (cf. As. *imbubu, flute*, Dl$^{HWB 443}$, NH אַבּוּב *id*, Aram אַבּוּבָא, ܐܒܘܒܐ *id.*; hence also Ar. أُنْبُوب *knots* in reed, *part of* reed *between knots, reed*; vid. Hoffm$^{LCB 1882, 321}$ Fra^{23} Fl in Levy$^{TW I 417}$),—**Qal** *Pt pass* נָבוּב Jb 11^{12} Je 52^{21}, נְבוּב Ex 27^{8} 38^{7};—*hollowed, hollow* of altar of tabern. נְבוּב לֻחֹת Ex 27^{8} 38^{7} (P), of pillar in temple Je 52^{21}; fig אִישׁ נָבוּב Jb 11^{12}, i e. *empty, hollow-minded* man

נֹבַה v. נֹב.

†I. נְבוֹ **n.pr loc.** (prob. connex, at least for **2**, with (Bab) god *Nebo, Nabû*, cf. II נבו and Bae$^{Rel 15.89.259}$; yet not certain, No$^{ZMG xlii 1888, 470}$ comp. Ar. النَّبَاوَة *the height*, etc.) 𝔊 Ναβαυ,—**1. a.** city in Moab Nu 32$^{3.38}$ (where assigned to Reuben; both JE = נבה MI^{14}) Is 15^{2} Je 48$^{1.22}$ 1 Ch 5^{8}; prob. on or near Mt. Nebo (v infr.), cf Buhl$^{Geogr 266 f}$ Tristr$^{Moab 338}$. **b.** city in Judah, בני נ׳ Ezr 2^{29} = אַנְשֵׁי נ׳ אַחֵר Ne 7^{33} (*the men of the other N*, so disting.—si vera l., cf Ryle—fr. **a** ? or fr. another נב ?), Ezr 10^{43};—this נבו in Judah perhaps = נֹב **1** q v. **2.** mt in Moab, where Moses died Nu 33^{47} Dt 32^{49} (הַר־נְבוֹ), 34^{1} (*id.*; all P), six miles W. of Heshbon acc. to Onom. (ed. Lag^{283}). Prob = mod *Nebâ* at NE corner of Dead Sea, Survey$^{E Pal. I 198 ff}$ GASm$^{Geogr 562 ff}$ Buhl$^{Geogr 266 f}$ Tristr$^{Moab 318, 338}$ Merrill$^{E of Jordan 242 ff}$—Cf. פִּסְגָּה.

†II. נְבוֹ **n.pr.div.** **Nebo** (loan-wd in Heb., cf Ph. n pr.m נבו, = As *Nabû*, Schr$^{COT Gloss and Is 46 1}$ Jastrow$^{Rel. Bab 124 ff}$ Jen$^{Kosmol pass.}$ Tiele$^{Ass. u Bab Gesch 532 f.}$ Say$^{Rel Bab. 112 ff}$ (cf Palm. n pr. נבוזבד, ברנבו Vog$^{Palm. No 73}$), and this perh. √*nabû, call, name*, v. נבא),—Babylonian god כָּרַע בֵּל קֹרֵס נְבוֹ Is 46^{1}.

†נְבוּזַרְאֲדָן **n.pr.m.** (= *Nabû-zêr-iddin, Nebo hath given seed*, Schr[COT 2 K 25, 8]);—general of Nebuchadrezzar, always entitled רַב־טַבָּחִים 2 K 25[8.11.20] = Je 52[12.15.26]; Je 39[9.10.11.13] 40[1] 41[10] 43[6] 52[16.30].

†נְבוּכַדְרֶאצַּר and (incorrectly) נְבוּכַדְנֶאצַּר (v. also infr.) **n.pr.m.** **Nebuchadrezzar, Nebuchadnezzar** (Bab. *Nabû-kudurri-uṣur* = (prob.) *Nebo, protect the boundary!* Dl[Calwer BL] Budge[Nebuchadn.] (on *kudurru, boundary*, v. Dl[HWB 319]); poss. is also *crown*, and so Schr[COT 2 K 24, 1]; Jäger[BAS i. 471] prop. (*thy*) *servant*);—𝔊 Ναβουχοδονοσ(σ)ορ; Can. Ptol. Ναβοκολασσαρου Schr[COT 490], Abydenos etc. Ναβουκοδρόσορος, v. Schr[ib. 2 K 24, 1];—the great king of Babylon (reigned B.C. 605–562), who captured Jerus. and carried Judah captive: most oft. נְבוּכַדְרֶאצַּר מֶלֶךְ בָּבֶל (נ׳ oft. om. in 𝔊) Je 21[2.7] (but om. 𝔊 Gie), 22[25] 25[1.9] 29[21] 32[28] 34[1] (v. Baer's note; van d. H נבוכדנ׳), 35[11] 37[1] 39[1.5] (v. on 34[1]), v[11] 43[10] 44[30] 46[2.13.26] 49[30] 50[17] 51[34] 52[4.12] Ez 26[7] 29[18.19.30]; so Qr Je 49[28] (Kt נבוכדראצור מ׳ ב׳); נְבוּכַדְרֶאצַּר (מֶלֶךְ בָּבֶל om.) Je 32[1] 52[28.29.30]. Spelt corruptly with *n*, נְבוּכַדְנֶאצַּר מ׳ ב׳ (cf. Schr[COT 2 K 24, 1 n.]) 2 Ch 36[6] Dn 1[1] Je 27[6.8.20] 28[3] 29[3] Ezr 2[1] Qr (Kt נבוכדנצור מ׳ ב׳, cf. Je 49[8] supr.); נְבוּכַדְנֶאצַּר alone 2 Ch 36[7.10.13] (הַמֶּלֶךְ נ׳), Je 29[1]; נְבֻכַדְנֶאצַּר מ׳ ב׳ 2 K 24[1.10.11] 25[1.8.22] Je 28[11.14]; נְבוּכַדְנֶאצַּר 1 Ch 5[41]; נְבוּכַדְנֶצַּר מ׳ ב׳ Ne 7[6] Est 2[6]; נְבוּכַדְנֶצַּר Ezr 1[7] (מ׳ ב׳ om.), נְבֻכַדְנֶצַּר Dn 2[1.1], נְבֻכַדְנֶצַּר 1[18] (v. also Tobit 14[5], Jud 1[1] + oft., as 𝔊 supr.)—On N. v. further Tiele[Bab.-Ass. Gesch. 421 ff., 454 ff.]

†נְבוּשַׁזְבָּן **n.pr.m.** (= *Nabû-šêzib-anni, Nebo delivers me*, Schr[COT Je 39, 13]);—officer of Nebuchadrezzar, called רַב־סָרִיס (q.v.) Je 39[13].

נָבוֹת 22 **n.pr.m.** a Jezreelite;—1 K 21[1.2.3] + 16 t. 1 K 21; 2 K 9[21.25.26]. 𝔊 Ναβουθαι.

†[נָבַח] **vb.** **bark** (of dogs) (NH *id.*; Ar. نَبَحَ; Eth. ነብሐ:; Aram. ܢܒܚ, נְבַח);—**Qal** *Inf. cstr.* only כֻּלָּם כְּלָבִים אִלְּמִים לֹא יוּכְלוּ לִנְבֹּחַ Is 56[10] fig. of helpless prophets.

†נֹבַח **n.pr.m. et loc.** **1. m.** a Manassite Nu 32[42] (JE), 𝔊 Ναβαυ. **2. loc.** in Gilead Ju 8[11], 𝔊 Ναβαι, Ναβε(θ); Nu 32[42] (formerly קְנָת, q.v.), 𝔊 Ναβωθ.

†נִבְחַז **n.pr.div.** god of men of Avva, 2 K 17[31]; name otherwise unknown, cf. Sch[COT ad loc.]; 𝔊B τὴν Ἐβλαζερ, 𝔊L Ἐβλαιεζερ, A Ἀβααζερ καὶ τὴν Ναιβας; Thes comp. Mand. denom. נבאז = ܢܒܙ (Cod. Nasar. Norberg.) Codd. give variant נבחן cf. Baer[ad loc.] Frensdorff[Mas. Magna i. 306].

†[נָבַט] **vb.** **Pi., Hiph.** look (NH Pi. *id.*; Ar. نَبَطَ is *well* or *issue forth* (of water). As. *nabâṭu* is *shine* Dl[HWB 443]; Sab. epith. נבט *protector* (? lit. looking with consideration upon Mordt[ZMG xxx. 1876, 37]); n.pr. נבטאל *God has seen*, i.e. *considered* Levy-Os[ZMG xix. 1865, 231]);—**Pi.** *Pf.* consec. וְנִבַּט Is 5[30] *look* (lit.), sq. לְ. **Hiph.** *Pf.* הִבִּיט Nu 21[9] + 3 t.; וְהִבַּטְתָּ 1 S 2[32], etc.; *Impf.* יַבִּיט Nu 12[8] + 4 t.; וַיַּבֵּט 1 S 17[42] + 4 t., etc.; *Imv.* הַבֵּט 1 K 18[43] +; הַבִּיט ψ 142[5] (or *Inf. abs.*), cf. La 5[1] Kt; הַבִּיטָה ψ 13[4] +, etc.; *Inf. cstr.* הַבִּיט Ex 3[6] +, etc.; *Pt.* מַבִּיט ψ 104[32];—*look*: **1.** lit., **a.** human subj., sq. אֶל־ Ex 3[6] (E), Nu 21[9] (JE), Is 8[22] (|| פָּנָה לְמָעְלָה v[21]), cf. 51[6], Jon 2[5]; sq. עַל־ Hb 2[15]; sq. אַחֲרֵי Gn 19[17.26] (J), Ex 33[8] (E), 1 S 24[9]; sq. ־ָה loc., Gn 15[5] (שָׁמַיְמָה), cf. Jb 35[5] (שָׁמַיִם); sq. דֶּרֶךְ־יָם 1 K 18[43]; sq. acc. = *look upon, behold* Nu 12[8] (E), Is 38[11]; abs. Jb 6[19] 1 S 17[42] (|| רָאָה), 1 K 18[43] 19[6] (sq. הִנֵּה), 1 Ch 21[21] (|| רָאָה), so ψ 22[18]. **b.** subj. eagle, abs. Jb 39[29] (sq. adv. לְמֵרָחוֹק). **2.** fig.: sq. אֶל *regard, shew regard to* 1 S 16[7] (אֶל־מַרְאֵהוּ), cf. 2 K 3[14] (|| רָאָה); *pay attention to*, sq. אֶל־ Is 22[8]; = *consider* Is 51[1.2]; *look unto* י׳, sq. אֶל־ ψ 34[6] (read Imv. pl. 𝔊 𝔖 Che), Is 22[11] Zc 12[10]; cf. ψ 119[6] sq. אֶל־כָּל־מִצְוֹת; cf. also Jb 36[25] (abs., sq. מֵרָחוֹק); sq. acc. אֹרְחֹתֶיךָ ψ 119[15], cf. v[18], Is 5[12]; sq. acc. וַתַּבֵּט בְּשׁוּרָי בְּ׳ עֵינִי, אָוֶן Nu 23[21] (|| רָאָה); subj. ψ 92[12] *see its desire upon, gloat over* (cf. רָאָה בְּ), diff. 1 S 2[32]; sq. acc. adv. ψ 142[5] (יָמִין) *to the right*; || רָאָה); abs. Is 42[18] (sq. לִרְאוֹת of purpose); 63[5] Hb 1[5] (|| רָאָה), so ψ 91[8] (בְּעֵינֶיךָ), cf. Pr 4[25], sq. לְנֹכַח (subj. עֵינֶיךָ || יַיְשִׁרוּ נֶגְדֶּךָ). **3.** subj. י׳: sq. מִשָּׁמַיִם + אֶל ψ 102[20]; sq. אֶל־ = *look upon*, i.e. endure to see Hb 1[13] (|| רָאָה); so sq. acc. v[13], cf. 1[3] (or *causat.* Ew; || תַּרְאֵנִי); sq. לְ, ψ 104[32] Jb 28[24]; ψ 74[20] (לַבְּרִית); sq. acc. Is 64[8] (|| הֵן), La 3[63] ψ 10[14] (|| רָאָה); = *regard, shew regard to*, Am 5[22] ψ 84[10] La 4[16], cf. ψ 13[4]; sq. אֶל־ *id.* Is 66[2]; abs. ψ 94[9] i.e. *have power of sight*, Is 18[4]; sq. מִשָּׁמַיִם ψ 33[13] 80[15] Is 63[15] (|| רְאֵה), La 1[11] (|| רְאֵה), so v[12] 2[20] 5[1].

† [מַבָּט] **n.m.**[Zc 9, 5] **expectation** = object of hope or confidence (lit. *thing looked to*);—sf. מַבָּטֵנוּ Is 20[6], מַבָּטָם v[5], מֶבָּטָהּ Zc 9[5];—of Cush

as ally of Judah Is 20[5.6]; of Tyre as ally of Philistia Zc 9[5].

†נְבָט n.pr.m. father of Jerob I (cf. Sab. נבט, נבטאל, v. נָבַט supr.),—only in phrase יָרָבְעָם בֶּן־נְבָט 1 K 11[26] 12[2.15] 15[1] 16[3.26.31] 21[22] 22[53] 2 K 3[3] 9[9] 10[29] 13[2.11] 14[24] 15[9.18.24.28] 17[21] 23[15] 2 Ch 9[29] 10[2.15] 13[6]. 𝔊 Ναβαθ, Ναβατ

†נְבָיוֹת n.pr.gent. (Nab נבטו=*Nabataean* and *Nabataeans*, Eut[Nab I 4] and oft, cf. נבט of Jewish trad. No[ZMG xxv 1871, 124], נבט 𝔗[Is 60,7] (on form of name, and on ט=ת cf Lag[BN 81 f]), in As. *Nabaitai*, etc, Schr[COT Gn 25, 13 KGF 99 ff] Dl[Par 296 f]),—as (eldest) son of Ishmael (brother of Kedar) Gn 25[13] 28[9] 36[3] (all P), 1 Ch 1[29], people (‖ Kedar) Is 60[7], cf *Nabataei + Cedrei* Plin[NH v 11, 65], 𝔊 Ναβαιωθ; Gk Ναβαταῖοι—See further No[ZMG xxv 1871, 122 f] Eut[Nab p 78] GASm[Geogr 547–629 pass]

†[נֵבֶךְ] n.[m.] spring (si vera l) (√unknown),—only pl cstr. נִבְכֵי־יָם Jb 38[16] *the springs, sources of the ocean* (‖ חֵקֶר תהום),—Ol Siegf נבלי, Bu suggests מַבְּעֵי = נבעי as poss; but Gi Perles rd נבכי Jb 28[11], also, for Mass מבכי, cf נָהָר **2**

†I. נבל (√of foll, meaning dubious)

I. נֵבֶל n m.[Je 13.12] **1. skin-bottle, skin, 2 jar, pitcher,**—נֵבֶל abs. 1 S 10[3]+, cstr v[3]+(on נֶבֶל v Baer[181 24]),—**1.** *skin of wine*, נֵבֶל יַיִן 1 S 1[24] 10[3] 2 S 16[1], cf also Je 13[12.12], pl נִבְלֵי יַיִן 1 S 25[18] fig נִבְלֵי שָׁמַיִם Jb 38[37] i.e *clouds* (‖ שחקים) **2** earthen *jar, pitcher*. fig of connexions of Eliakim כלי נבלים Is 22[24], נִבְלֵיהֶם יְנַפֵּצוּ Je 48[12] נִבְלֵי־חֶרֶשׂ (‖ כלים יריקו) in fig of Moab (cf. ψ 2[9]), La 4[2] sim of men of Judah (‖ מַעֲשֵׂה ידי יוצר); sim of destruction of Judah, שֵׁבֶר נֵבֶל יוצרים Is 30[14]

†II נֵבֶל, נֶבֶל n.m.[ψ 57, 9] a musical instrument, either a portable **harp, or a lute, guitar** (with bulging resonance-body at lower end); (perh = I נבל, and then shape seems to favour *lute*, perh independent word, e g Egyptian loan-word, cf *nfr, lute*, We[Hpt 222]),—abs נֵבֶל 1 S 10[5]+3 t, נֶבֶל ψ 71[22]+3 t, נֵבֶל Am 6[5]+2 t, pl נְבָלִים 2 S 6[5]+4 t, sf נְבָלֶיךָ Am 5[23] Is 14[11],—*harp* (or *lute*), played at feasts and religious ceremonies, probably less simple, cheap and common than כִּנּוֹר (q v, oft named with נ׳)—as mark of luxury, revelry Am 5[23] 6[5] Is 14[11], so 5[12] (כִּנּוֹר נ׳ תֹּף חָלִיל), also (not in bad sense) 1 K 10[12], played by wandering band of prophets 1 S 10[5] (list as Is 5[12]); in worship 2 S 6[5], elsewh only ψψ Chr always in worship · ψ 57[9] 81[3] 92[4] 108[3] 150[3], כְּלִי נֶבֶל 71[22]; נ׳ עָשׂוֹר *a harp with ten strings* 33[2] 144[9]; 1 Ch 13[8] 15[16.20.28] 16[5] (כְּלֵי נְבָלִים), 25[1.6] 2 Ch 5[12] 9[11] 20[28] 29[25] Ne 12[27]—Cf. further Benz[Arch 273 ff] Now[Arch I 273 ff] Dr[Amos 234 ff.] We[Hpt 222 ff]

†II נָבֵל vb. be senseless, foolish (NH נַבְלוּת, נְבָלָה of immodesty, Ar نَبُلَ = (per contra) *be noble, distinguished*, نَبُلَ also *be gracious* (Frey); Aram נבל Pa *reject, despise*, v. 𝔗 Ne 3[6] Je 14[21]; in deriv as NH);—**Qal** *Pf.* 2 ms. נָבַלְתָּ Pr 30[32] *if thou hast been foolish* in lifting up thyself (opp זַמּוֹתָ) **Pi.** *Pf* 1 s sf. consec וְנִבַּלְתִּיךְ Na 3[6], *Impf* 3 ms. וַיְנַבֵּל Dt 32[15], 2 ms. תְּנַבֵּל Je 14[21]; *Pt.* מְנַבֵּל Mi 7[6],—*regard* or *treat as a* נָבָל (q.v.), i e. *with contumely*, c acc בֵּן מְנַבֵּל אָב Mi 7[6] *son treateth father as a fool* (with contumely), וַיְנ׳ צוּר Dt 32[15] *and he treated with contumely the Rock* of his salvation (i e י׳; ‖ נטש); י׳ subj, Na 3[6] *I will treat thee* (Nineveh) *with contumely* (‖ וְהִשְׁלַכְתִּי עָלַיִךְ שִׁקֻּצִים); Je 14[21] do not *treat with contumely* the throne of thy glory (‖ נאץ).

†I נָבָל adj. foolish, senseless, esp. of the man who has no perception of ethical and religious claims, and with collat idea of *ignoble, disgraceful*,—abs נ׳ 2 S 3[33]+14 t., mpl נְבָלִים 13[13] Ez 13[3] (𝔊 Co מִלִּבָּם), fpl נְבָלוֹת Jb 2[10],—*senseless*, esp of religious and moral insensibility עַם נ׳ Dt 32[6] (of Isr, unappreciative of J.'s benefits, opp. חָכָם), so of heathen nation ψ 74[18] (blaspheming name of י׳), גּוֹי נ׳ Dt 32[21] (‖ לֹא עָם); הַנְּבִאִים הַנּ׳ Ez 13[3] (si vera l, v. supr); elsewh as **subst** (impious and presumptuous) fool, Is 32[5] (opp. נָדִיב *noble-minded*), characterized as at once irreligious and churlish, v[6]; denying God ψ 14[1]=53[2], insulting God 74[22], and God's servant 39[9], Pr 17[7] arrogant speech becometh not *the* (impious and presumptuous) *fool* (whose faults it only makes the more conspicuous), much less do lying lips him that is noble (נדיב), v[21] (‖ כסיל), 30[22] ונבל כי ישבע לחם (one of the things under which the earth trembles), בְּנֵי נָבָל Jb 30[8] i.e ignoble men (‖ בני בלי־שם), as one who might be expected

to have a contumelious end, הַכְּמוֹת נ׳ יָמוּת אבנר 2 S 3^{33} was Abner (destined) to die, as a נ׳ dieth? of the man who amasses riches unjustly ובאחריתו יהיה נבל Je 17^{11} i.e. will prove himself to be a נ׳; as acting immorally (with collat. idea of disgracefully) 2 S 13^{13} ואתה תהיה כְּאַחַד הַנְּבָלִים בישראל (cf. נְבָלָה); f only in כדבר אַחַת הַנְּבָלוֹת Jb 2^{10} (of Job's wife). Cf. Dr$^{Dt\ 22,21\ 32,6\ 15.21,\ Psalt\ 457}$.

II. נָבָל **n.pr.m.** (on popular etymol. see 1 S 25^{25} infr);—a churlish man of Carmel, whose widow David married 1 S $25^{3.4.5.9\ 10.14\ 19.25\ 26}$ (כשמו כֶּן־הוּא נָבָל שְׁמוֹ וּנְבָלָה עִמּוֹ), v^{26} + 10 t. 1 S + 2 S 2^{2} 3^{3}. 𝔊 Ναβαλ.

† נְבָלָה **n.f. senselessness** (as shewn in disregard of moral and religious claims), esp. of disgraceful sins, also **disgrace**,—alw abs. נ׳,—**1.** *disgraceful folly*, esp of sins of unchastity Ju 19^{23} (*wanton deed* GFM), so דָּבָר הַנּ׳ הַזֹּאת v^{24}, 2 S 13^{12}, oft. עָשָׂה נ׳ בְּיִשְׂרָאֵל i.e do a thing disgraceful acc to Isr.'s standard Gn 34^{7} (J), Dt 22^{21} (cf Dr on mng of wd.; only here of woman), Ju 20^{6} (+ זִמָּה), v^{10} Je 29^{23} (cf. לא יֵעָשֶׂה כן בישראל 2 S 13^{12}), also of inhospitable churlishness 1 S 25^{25} (v I, II נָבָל, and esp. Is 32^{6}); of profane action Jos 7^{15} (Achan; עָשָׂה נ׳ בְּיִשְׂרָאֵל), of senseless and irreligious language Is 9^{16} דֹּבֵר, 32^{6} (יְדַבֵּר) **2.** *contumely, disgrace* עֲשׂוֹת עִמָּכֶם נ׳ Jb 42^{8} (of י׳), i.e. *deal out to you disgrace*, expose you and punish you as נְבָלִים (cf 2 S 3^{33}, sub נָבָל), because of your utterances about me.

† נַבְלוּת **n.f. immodesty, shamelessness,** *lewdness* of Isr under fig. of adulteress Ho 2^{12}.

† נָבֵל **vb. sink or drop down, languish, wither and fall, fade** (NH *id.*; As. *nabâlu*, *destroy*, Dl$^{HWB\ 443\ f.}$ Ar نَبَلَ v, viii *die*, Aram נבילא *corpse*),—**Qal** *Pf.* 3 ms. נ׳ Is $40^{7\ 8}$ Je 8^{13}; 3 fs נָבְלָה Is $24^{4\ 4}$, *Impf* 3 ms. יִבּוֹל ψ 1^{3} + 4 t (on form cf. Ges$^{§\ 43,\ 8,\ R\ 1\ b}$ Ol$^{§\ 246\ e}$), 2 ms. תבל Ex 18^{18}; 3 mpl יִבֹּלוּ 2 S 22^{46} = ψ 18^{46}, יִבּוֹלוּן ψ 37^{2}, 1 pl. וַנָּבֶל Is 64^{5} (on form cf. Di and Ol$^{§\ 236\ e}$); *Inf abs.* נָבֹל Ex 18^{18}; cstr נְבֹל Is 34^{4}, *Pt.* נבל Is $28^{1\ 4}$, f. נֹבֶלֶת abs Is 34^{4}; cstr. Is 1^{30},—**1.** *sink* or *drop down*, fr exhaustion נָבֹל תִּבֹּל Ex 18^{18} (Moses and Isr); fr. discouragement 2 S 22^{46} = ψ 18^{46} (of foreigners, foes of Isr.); of mt הַר־נֹפֵל יִבּוֹל Jb 14^{18} (but נָפוֹל יִפּוֹל Lag$^{Proph.\ Chald}$ Siegf Baer, after 𝔊, so Bu [or יִבְלֶה]; Du נָבוֹל יִבּוֹל) **2.** usu. *fall* like a leaf, or flower *wither and fall, fade:* כְּאֵלָה נֹבֶלֶת עָלֶהָ Is 1^{30} *like an oak falling as to its leaves* (sim. of people of Jerus.); the host of heaven יִבּוֹל כִּנְבֹל עָלֶה מִגֶּפֶן וּכְנֹבֶלֶת מִתְּאֵנָה Is 34^{4}, לא יִבּ׳ עָלֵהוּ Ez 47^{12} (trees in Ezek.'s vision), so fig of good man ψ 1^{3}, of Isr. Je 8^{13}, וַנָּבֶל כֶּעָלֶה Is 64^{5}; also ציץ נבל $40^{7.8}$ (both ‖ יָבֵשׁ חָצִיר), צִיץ נֹבֵל 28^{1}, cf. v^{4}, of wicked כְּיֶרֶק דֶּשֶׁא יִבּ׳ ψ 37^{2} (‖ כְּחָצִיר יִמָּלוּ); of devastated earth אָבְלָה נָבְלָה הָאָרֶץ אֻמְלְלָה נָבְלָה תֵבֵל Is 24^{4}.

† נְבֵלָה **n.f. carcass, corpse** (as *inert, flabby*);—נ׳ abs. 1 K 13^{24} +; cstr. נִבְלַת v^{29} +; sf. נִבְלָתִי Is 26^{19}, נִבְלָתְךָ Dt 28^{26} 1 K 13^{22}, נִבְלָתוֹ Jos 8^{29} + 6 t.; נִבְלָתָהּ Lv $11^{39.40.40}$; נִבְלָתָם Is 5^{25} + 14 t.;—*carcass, corpse:* **1. a.** human (not in Ez P, (H), which use פֶּגֶר); Jos 8^{29} (JE), 1 K $13^{22.24.24.25.25.28.28.28.29.30}$ 2 K 9^{37} Je 26^{23} 36^{30} Dt 21^{23} 28^{26}; coll. *corpses* Is 5^{25} 26^{19} (wish for restoration to life), Je 7^{33} 9^{21} 16^{4} 19^{7} 34^{20} ψ 79^{2}. **b.** of lifeless idols, coll. נִבְלַת שִׁקּוּצֵיהֶם וגו׳ Je 16^{18}. **2.** of animals (clean and unclean, wild animals, cattle, birds and reptiles, chiefly Lv Ez), Dt 14^{8}; Lv $5^{2.2.2}$ $11^{8\ 11\ 24\ 25.27\ 28.35.36.37.38}$ 17^{15} (all P); נ׳ specif. = body of animal dying of itself Dt 14^{21}; Lv 7^{24} $11^{39.40.40}$ (P), 22^{8} (H), Ez 4^{14} 44^{31}.

† נְבַלָּט **n.pr.loc.** place where Benjamites dwelt Ne 11^{34} 𝔊L Ναβαλλατ. Mod. Beit Nebâlâ, 6 m. NE from Lydda, acc. to Guérin$^{Sam\ II\ 67\ f.}$; Mishn בית נבלטא Buhl$^{Geo\ 12;\ Geogr\ 197}$.

† [נָבַע] **vb. flow, spring, bubble up,** poet. and late (NH *id.* (rare); As. *nabû*, *id*, Dl$^{HWB\ 442}$, Ar. نَبَعَ *well* or *issue forth* (of water); Aram. ܢܒܰܥ, נְבַע; Eth. ነቦዐ: II. *weep*, አንብዕ: *tear(s)*),—**Qal** *Pt.* נַחַל נֹבֵעַ Pr 18^{4} *a flowing wady*, metaph of מְקוֹר חָכְמָה. **Hiph.** *Impf.* יַבִּיעַ ψ 19^{3} + 3t., אַבִּיעָה ψ 78^{2} Pr 1^{23}; יַבִּיעוּ ψ 94^{4} 145^{7}, יַבִּיעוּן ψ 59^{8}; 3 fpl. תַּבַּעְנָה ψ 119^{171};—*pour out, emit, cause to bubble, belch forth:* **1.** *pour out*, fig אַבִּיעָה לָכֶם רוּחִי Pr 1^{23} (‖ אוֹדִיעָה דְבָרַי אֶתְכֶם) **2.** *cause to bubble, ferment* זְבוּבֵי מָוֶת יַבְאִישׁ יַבִּיעַ שֶׁמֶן רוֹקֵחַ Ec 10^{1}. **3.** fig, usually of speech, *pour forth, emit, belch forth*, emphat. expression: פִּי רְשָׁעִים יַבִּיעַ רָעוֹת Pr 15^{28} (opp לֵב צַדִּיק יֶהְגֶּה לַעֲנוֹת) i.e. the righteous

considers before he speaks, the wicked bursts out with reckless utterance; כי כסילים יַבִּיעַ אִוֶּלֶת Pr 15^{2} (opp לְשׁוֹן חֲכָמִים תֵּיטִיב דָּעַת); יַבִּיעוּ יְדַבְּרוּ עָתָק ψ 94^{4} (|| יִתְאַמְּרוּ כָּל־פֹּעֲלֵי אָוֶן); יַבּ׳ בפיהם 59^{8} (|| חֲרָבוֹת בשפתותֵיהֶם); in good sense, אַבִּיעָה חידות 78^{2} (|| אֶפְתְּחָה בְמָשָׁל פִּי); תַּבַּעְנָה שְׂפָתַי תְּהִלָּה 119^{171}, זכר רַב־טוּבְךָ יַבִּיעוּ 145^{7} (|| וצדקתך יְרַנֵּנוּ, cf. also v^{6}), metaph. יום ליום יַבּ׳ אֹמֶר 19^{3}, i.e though silent, it really *pours forth* speech.

†מַבּוּעַ n.[m.] spring of water (As. *nambaʾu* Dl$^{HWB 442}$, Ar. مَنْبَعٌ, Syr ܡܰܒܽܘܥܳܐ),—abs מ׳ Ec 12^{6}; pl cstr. מַבּוּעֵי מַיִם Is 35^{7} 49^{10} (for returning exiles)

נבשן v. בשן.

נגב (√of foll. = *be dry, parched*, NH נָגַב, Aram נְגֵיב, נגוב, ܢܓܰܒ)

†נֶגֶב n.[m.] south-country, Negeb, south (cf. Lag$^{BN 78}$),—נ׳ abs Gn 20^{1}+, cstr Jos 11^{2}+; נֶגְבָּה Gn 13^{14}+,—**1.** *south-country*, i e **a.** specif. the region S. of Judah, boundaries not exactly defined (see cities in it Jos 15$^{21-32}$), but c. fr. hills S. of Hebron to Kadesh, אֶרֶץ הַנּ׳ Gn 20^{1} (E), 24^{62} (J), Nu 13^{29} (JE), Ju 1^{15} Jos 15^{19}, alm = n pr הַנּ׳, הַנֶּגְבָּה, Gn 12^{9} 13^{1} Nu 13$^{17.22}$ 21^{1} (all J), Dt 34^{3} (JE), Dt 1^{7} Jos 10^{40} 11^{16} 12^{8} (all D), Nu 33^{40} Jos 15^{21} (both P), Ju 1^{9} 1 S 20^{41} (but rd. הָאַרְגָּב, i.e. *the mound* 𝔊 (ἀργαβ) Th We Klo Dr Kit Bu HPS), Je 13^{19} 17^{26} 32^{44} 33^{13} Zc 7^{7} Ob^{20} ψ 126^{4} (sim), Ez 21^{3} (= Judah), נ׳ (no art) Gn 13^{3} (J), 1 S 30^{1}, Is 30^{6} (cf. Di); of particular districts in the Negeb: נ׳ עֲרָד Ju 1^{16} (cf GFM), נ׳ יהודה etc. 1 S 27$^{10.10.10}$ (cf. Dr), 30$^{14.14}$ 2 S 24^{7} 2 Ch 28^{18}; v also Zc 14^{10}; רָמַת נ׳ Jos 19^{8}, רָמוֹת נ׳ 1 S 30^{27}; coll. c pl vb = *people of south-land* Ob^{19}. **b.** land S. of Babylon Is 21^{1} (cf. Di) **c.** = Egypt Dn 11$^{5.6.9.11.14.15.25.25.29.40}$ (v Meinh Bev Behrm, cf v^{43}) **2.** hence *south* (opp. N., E, W.) Gn 13^{14} 28^{14} (both J), Jos 17^{10} (P), 1 K 7^{25} = 2 Ch 4^{4}, 1 Ch 9^{24} 26$^{15.17}$ (cf. v$^{14.16.18}$), Ez 21$^{3.b.9}$ Dn 8$^{4.9}$, further 1 K 7^{39} Zc 14^{4}, פְּאַת נֶגְבָּה תֵימָנָה Ex 26^{18}, cf 27^{9} 36^{23} 38^{9} 40^{24} (of S side of tabernacle), פְּאַת נ׳ שַׁעַר נ׳ Ez 46$^{9.9}$; *south side* or *border* Nu 34^{3} 35^{5} Jos 18^{15} (all P), Ez 47^{19}, cf v^{19} 48$^{16.28.33}$, גְּבוּל נ׳ *south boundary* Nu 34^{3} Jos 15$^{2.4}$ 18^{19} (all P), cf (הַגְּבוּל) מִנֶּגֶב לְ *on the south of* Nu 34$^{4.4}$ Jos 15^{3} (אֶל־מִנּ׳ לְ), v$^{3.7}$ 18^{3} (all P), Ju 21^{19}, מִנּ׳ abs *on the south* Jos 18^{5} (JE), 19^{34} (P), 1 S 14^{5} Ez 40^{2}; כֶּתֶף הַיְבוּסִי מִנּ׳ Jos 15^{8}, cf. 18$^{13.16}$ (all P); נֶגְבָּה 15$^{1.2}$ 18$^{14.14.19}$ (all P), 2 Ch 4^{10} Ez 21^{2} (Co; 𝔊 נגב), 48$^{10.17}$, נֶגְבָּה לְ Jos 17^{9} (P) —For נ׳ כנרות Jos 11^{2} rd. נֶגֶר (𝔊 Di).

[נָגַד]$_{363}$ **vb. be conspicuous** (NH in deriv; Ph. n pr.m. נגד; Ar. نَجَدَ *conquer, overcome,* also *be apparent, conspicuous;* نَجْدٌ *high land* or *country;* نَجُدَ *be courageous, vigorous, effective,* نَجِدٌ *courageous, efficient;* Aram נְגַד, ܢܓܰܕ *drag, draw, lead,* נָגוֹדָא, ܢܳܓܽܘܕܳܐ *leader;* Eth. ነገደ: is *travel*);—**Hiph.**$_{328}$ *Pf* הִגִּיד Gn 3^{11}+, 3 fs. הִגִּידָה 1 S 25^{19}+, הִגַּדְתָּ Gn 12^{8}+, etc, *Impf* יַגִּיד 1 S 9^{6}+, וַיַּגֵּד Gn 9^{22}+; sf. יַגִּידֶהָ Is 44^{7}, יַגִּדָהּ Je 9^{11}, יַגֶּדְךָ Dt 32^{7} (juss), etc, *Imv.* הַגֵּד 2 S 18^{21}+; הַגִּידָה Gn 29^{15}+, etc, *Inf abs* הַגֵּד Ju 14^{12}+ 2 t.; הַגִּיד Je 36^{16}, *cstr* לְהַגִּיד Gn 32^{6}+; לגיד 2 K 9^{15} Kt (Qr לְהַגּ׳), *Pt.* מַגִּיד Gn 41^{24}+; f. מַגֶּדֶת Est 2^{20}; pl. cstr. מַגִּידֵי Ju 14^{19},—*declare, tell* [usu. sq לְ of indir. obj. Gn 3^{11}+oft., ins also 1 S 12^{7} 2 S 13^{34} 𝔊 Th We Klo Dr Kit Bu, so HPS 2 S 13^{34} (1 S 12^{7} he foll 𝔊 as more diff.); sq. אֶל Ex 19^{9} 1 S 3^{15}, sq. לִפְנֵי 1 S 17^{31} ψ 142^{3}; עַל־פָּנָיו Jb 21^{31}; בְּאָזְנֵי Je 36^{20}; sq. בְּ loc. (instead of indir obj) chiefly proph Je 4^{5} 5^{20} 31^{10}+; also 1 S 4^{13} 2 S 1^{20} 2 K 9^{15} Mi 1^{10}; rarely sq. acc. pers 2 S 15^{31} (but rd. וּלְדָוִד הִגִּיד HPS (indef. subj), or וּלד׳ הֻגַּד We Dr Kit, 𝔊𝔙 Th Klo Bu favour הֻגַּד), 2 K 7$^{9.11}$ Ez 43^{10} Jb 17^{5} 26^{4} 31^{37}; sq. dir obj. in acc Gn 45^{13}+oft; sq cl wi. כִּי Gn 3^{11}+oft; sq. cl wi. כִּי=אֲשֶׁר (late) Est 3^{4} 6^{2}; sq. cl wi מָה Gn 29^{15} Ju 16^{15} Est 8^{1}+; sq cl wi. מִי 2 K 6^{11}, sq cl wi. אֵיכָה Ct 1^{7}, once sq. cl wi הֲ Gn 43^{6}, etc; oft no dir. obj, sq. לֵאמֹר Ex 13^{8} 1 S 25^{14}+; sq. וַיֹּאמֶר Gn 47^{1}+; אמר then foll. by *orat. rect.;* הִגּ׳ alone sq *orat. rect.* Zc 9^{12}, sq עַל *concerning,* 1 S 27^{11} Est 6^{2}, oft indir obj om. 1 S 24^{19}+; dir. obj. om. Ju 13^{10}+; both om. Lv 5^{1}+] In Hex. rarely P, †Lv 5^{1} 14^{35} Ex 16^{22}†; J, Gn 3^{11} 12^{18} Ex 13^{8}+18 t, E, Gn 21^{26} 31^{20} 41^{25}+15 t.; D, Dt 17^{9} 26^{3} 30^{18}+5 t.;—**1.** *tell, announce, report,* usu. human subj Gn 9^{22} 24^{23} 32^{6} Lv 14^{35} Ju 13^{6} 1 S 3^{18} 1 K 1^{23} Ne 2^{12} Est 2$^{10.10}$ Jb 12^{7} ψ 142^{3} Is 19^{12} Je 5^{20} Ez 24^{19}+. **2.** *declare, make known, expound,* esp. of something before not understood, concealed or mysterious, Gn 3^{11} 12^{18}, etc; 1 K 10^{3} = 2 Ch 9^{2}; a riddle Ju 14$^{12.13.15.16.16.16.19}$; dream Dn 2^{2}, secret Jb 11^{6}, etc.; of י׳ as revealing, Gn 41^{25} 2 S 7^{11} 2 K 4^{27} Mi 6^{8} Je 42^{3} ψ 147^{19}, of declaring by י׳'s agents Dt 5^{5} Mi 3^{8} 1 S 15^{16} 2 S 24^{13} Je 50^{28} Is 58^{1}; by divin. Ho 4^{12}.

3. *inform of* (play the informer concerning) Jos 2[14.20] Je 20[10] Jb 17[5] Lv 5[1] Pr 29[24]. **4.** *publish, declare, proclaim*, esp. of proclaiming wisdom, power, loving-kindness, etc., of י׳ (esp. ψψ): ψ 9[12] 22[32] 51[17] 92[3.16] 145[4]+, subj. heavens ψ 19[2] 50[6] 97[6]; Is 42[12] 57[12]. **5.** *avow, acknowledge, confess:* Is 3[9] ψ 38[19], cf. Is 48[6].—Pt.=*messenger* 2 S 15[13] Je 51[31.31] cf. הַנַּעַר הַמַּגִּיד 2 S 1[5.6.13]; הָאִישׁ הַמּ׳ 2 S 18[11]. †**Hoph.** *Pf.* הֻגַּד Jos 9[24]+; *Impf.* וַיֻּגַּד Gn 22[20]+; *Inf. abs.* הֻגֵּד Jos 9[24] Ru 2[11];—*be told, announced, reported*, alw. sq. לְ (sts. impers., logical subj. in acc., cf. Gn 27[42] 2 S 21[11], c. fem. Is 21[2]; not in P): Gn 27[42] (J), 31[22] (E), Dt 17[4] Jos 9[24.24] (D), Ru 2[11.11] Ju 9[25] 2 S 10[17] 19[2] 21[11] 1 K 10[7] 18[13] 1 Ch 19[17] 2 Ch 9[6] Is 21[2] 40[21]; sq. לֵאמֹר Gn 22[20] 38[13.24] (all J), Jos 10[17] (JE), 1 S 15[12] 19[19] 2 S 6[12] 1 K 1[51] 2 K 6[13] 8[7] Is 7[2]; sq. cl. with כִּי Ex 14[5] (J), Ju 9[47] 1 S 23[7.13] 27[4] 1 K 2[29.41].

נֶ֫גֶד 151 **subst. what is conspicuous or in front, always as adv. or prep. in front of, in sight of, opposite to,** נֶ֫גֶד, cstr. נֶגֶד, sf. נֶגְדִּי ψ 38[11]+, נֶגְדְּךָ 38[10]+, etc.; with ה *loc.* נֶ֫גְדָּה †ψ 116[14.18];—**1.** as adv. accus. *in front of*, **a.** locally (rather stronger and distincter than לִפְנֵי), (*a*) Gn 31[32] נֶגֶד אַחֵינוּ הַכֶּר־לְךָ *in front of* our brethren own it, now, v[37] 47[15] ולמה נמות נגדך why should we die *in thy sight?* Ex 19[2] Isr. encamped נגד ההר *in front of* the mountain, 34[10] נגד כל־עמך אעשׂה נִפְלָאֹת *before, in sight of, all thy people* (cf. ψ 78[12]), Jos 3[16] the people passed over נגד ירחו *in front of* J., 1 K 20[27], etc.; Ne 3[23] *in front of* their house, v[29]; נגד (כל) ישׂראל Dt 31[11] Jos 8[35] 1 S 15[30] 2 S 12[12]+; 1 K 21[13] set Naboth נֶגֶד הָעָם; נגד י׳ 1 S 12[3] 16[6] נֶגְדּוֹ 18[13]; so נֶגְדִּי ψ 89[37], אַךְ נֶגֶד י׳ מְשִׁיחוֹ; נגד השׁמשׁ Nu 25[4] 2 S 12[12]; ψ 22[26] נ׳ יראיו, 52[11] (so poet. נֶגְדָּה לְ ψ 116[14.18]); hostilely, Jb 10[17]; with collat. idea of *to the mortification of*, ψ 23[5] 31[20], cf. Jo 1[16]; with collat. idea of being *open* or *known to*, Pr 15[11] שׁאול ואבדון נגד י׳, Jb 26[6]; ψ 38[10] נגדך כל־תאותי (‖ ממך לא נסתרה), 69[20] (‖ יָדַעְתָּ), 119[168] Is 59[12]; so נֶגֶד פָּנַי הָיוּ Ho 7[2]. (*b*) with reflex. sf., and vb. of motion, to go *in front of oneself*, i.e. *straightforward*, Jos 6[5] ועלו העם אישׁ נגדו each *straightforward*, v[20] Am 4[3] Je 31[39] Ne 12[37], cf. Pr 4[25]. **b.** mentally,= vividly present to, ψ 38[18] ומכאובי נגדי תמיד, 44[16] 51[5] וחטאתי נגדי תמיד, 109[15] נ׳ י׳ (remembered by): nearly = בְּעֵינָיו, כְּאַיִן נֶגְדּוֹ Is 40[17] ψ 39[6]; so וְנ׳ פְּנֵיהֶם נְבֹנִים Is 5[21]. But Ex 10[10] כי רעה נגד פניכם *before your face* is = in your view, or purpose (cf. לא אשׁית לְנֶגֶד עֵינַי דבר־בליעל ψ 101[3]).

2. With preps.: **a.** †כְּנֶגֶד *acc. to what is in front of*=*corresponding to*, Gn 2[18] I will make him עֵזֶר כְּנֶגְדּוֹ a help *corresponding to* him i.e. equal and adequate to himself, v[20] among the animals there was no עֵזֶר כְּנֶגְדּוֹ. **b.** לְנֶגֶד *in front of, before*, Gn 33[12] וְאֵלְכָה לְנֶגְדֶּךָ, Nu 22[32] 2 K 1[13] fell on his knees לנגד אליהו, Is 1[7] your ground לנגדכם זרים אכלים אותה; with עָמַד Jos 5[13] Dn 8[15] 10[16], in a hostile sense v[13], cf. Pr 21[30]; *in the sight* or *presence of*, Hb 1[3] וְשֹׁד וְחָמָס לְנֶגְדִּי, ψ 39[2] בעוד רשׁע לנגדי, 50[8] ועולתיך לנגדי תמיד, Ne 3[37]; *opposite to* (prob. of opposite choirs), Ne 12[9.24]; =*parallel to*, 1 Ch 5[11]; =*over, for*, a business (peculiar) Ne 11[22]; fig. of what is visible morally, ψ 18[23] כי כל משׁפטיו לנגדי (‖ לֹא אָסִיר מֶנִּי), with *to set* or *place* ψ 16[8] 54[5] לא שׂמו אלהים לנגדם (cf. 86[14]), 90[8]; oft. in the phrase ... לְנֶגֶד עֵינַי, both lit., as Jb 4[16] תְּמוּנָה לנ׳ עֵינָי, ψ 5[6] לא יתיצבו הוללים לנ׳ עיניך (cf. 101[7]); and in a moral sense, ψ 18[25] כְּבֹר ידי לנ׳ עיניו, 26[3] כי חסדך לנ׳ עיני i.e. is ever present to my mind, 36[2] אין פחד אלהים לנ׳ עיניו i.e. he has no eye to discern God's awe-inspiring judgments (cf. 10[5]); with לא אשׁית i.e. have in view, purpose (‖ שׂנאתי) 101[3]. **c.** †מִנֶּגֶד (*a*) **adv.** *off* (מִן **1 c**) *the front, in front, opposite, ex adverso*, Gn 21[16] ותשׁב לה מנגד sat her down *opposite*, v[16], 2 K 2[7]; Dt 28[66] והיו חייך תלואים לך מנגד shall be hung up for thee *in front* (i.e. suspended, as by a thread, in front of thee); Ju 9[17] וישׁלך נפשׁו מנגד and flung away his life *in front* or *straight away* (i.e. hazarded it);=*some way off, from* or *at a distance*, Nu 2[2] Dt 32[52] כי מִנֶּגֶד תראה את הארץ, 2 K 2[15] וַיִּרְאֻהוּ מנ׳ *at a distance*, 3[22] 4[25]; *aloof*, 2 S 18[13] ואתה תתיצב מנגד, Ob 1[11]. (*b*) as a **prep.** (*α*) *from the front of, away from*, Ct 6[5] הָסֵבִּי עֵינַיִךְ מִנֶּגְדִּי, 1 S 26[20] אל־יפל דמי ארצה מנ׳ פני י׳; מנגד עיני *from before the eyes of*, with verbs of removing Is 1[16], cutting off ψ 31[23] Jon 2[5], hiding Am 9[3] Je 16[17]. (*β*) *opposite to*, Ne 3[19.25.27]; *at a distance from*, ψ 10[5] מרום משׁפטיך מנגדו, 38[12] מנגד נגעי יעמדו. (*γ*) מִנֶּגֶד לְ *from before*, Pr 14[7], *in front of* Ju 20[34]. **d.** †עַד נֶגֶד *as far as the front of*, Ne 3[16.26].

†נָגִיד **n.m. leader** (lit. prob. *one in front*), **ruler, prince**;—abs. נ׳ 1 S 9[16]+31 t.; cstr. נְגִיד (נְגִד) 2 K 20[5]+6 t.; pl. נְגִידִים Jb 29[10]+3 t.; נְגִידֵי 2 Ch 35[8];—*ruler, prince* ψ 76[13] Pr 28[16] Jb

29^{10} 31^{37} (in sim) Esp **1.** of king of Isr.: of Saul מָשַׁח לנ׳ על (+acc. pers), 1 S 9^{16} (subj. proph), cf. of Sol., subj people, 1 Ch 29^{22}, 10^{1} (subj ׳י); of David צִוָּהוּ לנ׳ על 1 S 13^{14} 25^{30}, צִוָּה נ׳ על 2 S 6^{21} (in these ׳י subj), היה לנ׳ על 5^{2}, היה נ׳ על 7^{8} 1 Ch 11^{2} 17^{7}; cf. also 5^{2} 2 Ch 6^{5}; of David also נָתַן נ׳ ל׳ Is 55^{4}; of Sol צִוָּה אתו להיות נ׳ על 1 K 1^{35} (׳י subj), of Jerob נתן נ׳ על (+acc. pers) 1 K 14^{7} (׳י subj), so 16^{2} of Baasha, of Hezekiah הֶעֱמִיד נ׳ עַמִּי 2 K 20^{5}; לנ׳ בְּאֶחָיו (+acc. pers) 2 Ch 11^{22} (of Abijah, subj Rehob), of Judah 1 Ch 28^{4} **2.** of a foreign *ruler* or *prince* Ez 28^{2} Dn $9^{25.26}$ **3** the title of some high official connected with the temple Je 20^{1} (of Pashhur) וְהוּא פָקִיד נָגִיד בבית ׳י and he was *prince-overseer* in, etc. (for פ׳ see 29^{26}), hence נ׳ בית האלהים 1 Ch 9^{11} 2 Ch 31^{13} 35^{8} (three נגידי ב׳ ה׳, including the high-priest), Ne 11^{11}, of high-priest Dn 11^{22} נ׳ ברית **4.** *ruler* in other capacities (late): of tribe 1 Ch 27^{16} 2 Ch 19^{11}; of Korahites 9^{20}, of Aaronite warriors 12^{27}, of division of army 1 Ch 13^{1} 27^{4} 2 Ch 11^{11} (commandant of fortress), 32^{21} (in Ass. army: ‖ שַׂר); of temple-treasuries 1 Ch 26^{24}, cf. 2 Ch 31^{12}; נ׳ הבית 2 Ch 28^{7} (i.e. of palace?). **5.** *princely things*, pl abstr Pr 8^{6}

†**נָגַהּ** **vb. shine** (As *nagû*, *shine, beam, be joyful*, Dl$^{HWB\ 446}$, Eth **ነጎሀ:** Aram. ܢܓܗ; NH ‎ ‎𝔗 נוֹגַהּ planet *Venus*)—**Qal** *Pf* ועל־דרכיך נ׳ אור Jb 22^{28}, אור נ׳ עליהם Is 9^{1}; *Impf* ולא־יִגַּהּ שביב אשׁו Jb 18^{5}. **Hiph.** *Impf* **1** *enlighten* יהוה אלהי יַגִּיהַּ חשׁכי = 2 S 22^{29} ויהוה יַגִּיהַּ חָשְׁכִּי ψ 18^{29} **2.** *cause to shine* (of moon) וְיָרֵחַ לֹא־יַגִּיהַּ אורו: Is 13^{10} (‖ חָשַׁךְ).

†I **נֹגַהּ** **n.f.**$^{Hb\ 3,4}$ **brightness**,—נ׳ abs Am 5^{20}+, cstr Is 4^{5}+, sf נָגְהָם Jo 2^{10} 4^{15},—*brightness* of a (clear, sunshiny) day Am 5^{20} (‖ אור, opp חֹשֶׁךְ, אֹפֶל), 2 S 23^{4} (מִמָּטָר *after rain*); so fig of Zion's dawning, נ׳ זַרְחֵךְ Is 60^{3} (‖ אור), of her righteousness כַּנֹּגַהּ 62^{1} (c art only here and Ez 1^{28}) ‖ כְּלַפִּיד יִבְעָר, of moon Is 60^{19}, of stars Jo 2^{10} 4^{15}, of theophany 2 S 22^{13} = ψ 18^{13} (in storm), cf Ez $1^{4.27.28}$, נ׳ כבוד ׳י 10^{4}, כָּאוֹר נ׳ Hb 3^{4}, נ׳ בָרָק Ez 1^{13}, נ׳ אשׁ לֶהָבָה Is 4^{5}, נ׳ לְאֵשׁ Hb 3^{11} (of glitter of ׳י's spear, ‖ אור חִצֶּיךָ חֲנִיתֶךָ), of individ, ואין נ׳ לו Is 50^{10} (fig of distress ‖ חֲשֵׁכִים), so וְאֹרַח צדיקים כאור נ׳ Pr 4^{18} *the path of righteous men is like a light of brightness*

†II **נֹגַהּ** **n.pr m.** a son of David acc to 1 Ch 3^{7} 14^{6}. 𝔊 Ναγαι, Ναγεθ, etc

†[**נְגֹהָה**] **n.f. brightness**; fig. of prosperity,—pl. לַנְּגֹהוֹת Is 59^{9} (opp אֲפֵלוֹת ‖ אור).

†**נָגַח** **vb. push, thrust, gore** (NH *id*; Ar. نَجَحَ *succeed, attain, make progress*; 𝔗 as BH),—**Qal** *Impf.* יִגַּח Ex $21^{28.31.32}$ (E), יִגָּח v^{31},—*gore*, subj שׁור, sq. acc. pers. **Pi.** *Impf* יְנַגַּח Dt 33^{17}; 2 ms תְּנַגַּח 1 K 22^{11} 2 Ch 18^{10}, תְּנַגְּחוּ Ez 34^{21}; ננגח ψ 44^{6}; *Pt* מְנַגֵּחַ Dn 8^{4},—*push* or *thrust at*, sq. acc. of Joseph under fig of wild ox Dt 33^{17}, cf. 1 K 22^{11} = 2 Ch 18^{10} ψ 44^{6} (‖ בוס), v also Ez 34^{21} (of Isr. under fig of sheep), cf. Dn 8^{4} (of ram in vision; obj. not expr). **Hithp.** *Impf.* יִתְנַגַּח עמו מֶלֶךְ הַנֶּגֶב Dn 11^{40} *engage in thrusting with*, wage war with.

†**נַגָּח** **adj.** addicted to goring, pred. of שׁור Ex $21^{29.36}$ (E), cf. Ba$^{NB\ 49}$.

נגל (√ of foll, mng unknown; Ar نَجَلَ is *strike, split, pierce*, but v infr)

†**מַגָּל** **n.[m.]** sickle (Ar. مِنْجَل (yet poss. Aram loan-word Fra^{133}), Aram ܡܓܠܐ,—c. תָּפַשׂ *handle, wield* Je 50^{16} (‖ זָרַע), c שָׁלַח Jo 4^{13} fig of judgment.

†[**נָגַן**] **vb.** touch (strings), play a stringed instrument (NH Pi.; Aram. נַגֵּן Pa),—**Qal** *Pt* נֹגְנִים ψ 68^{26} *players* (‖ שָׁרִים, עֲלָמוֹת תּוֹפֵפוֹת). **Pi.** *Pf* וְנִגֵּן 1 S 16^{16} (consec.), v^{23}; *Impf* 1 pl. נְנַגֵּן Is 38^{20}; *Inf cstr* נַגֵּן 1 S 16^{17} + 5 t, *Pt* מְנַגֵּן 1 S 16^{16} + 4 t.,—*play* בְּיָדוֹ 1 S 16^{16}, $v^{16.23}$ (בכנור in context), 18^{10} 19^{9}; c acc cogn Is 38^{20}; in sim מֵטִב נַגֵּן Ez 33^{32} (‖ שִׁיר עֲגָבִים יְפֵה־קוֹל, אִישׁ), מֵיטִיב לנ׳ 1 S 16^{17}, cf. ψ 33^{3} Is 23^{16} (both ‖ שִׁיר), יֹדֵעַ נ׳ 1 S 16^{18}, also 2 K 3^{15}; Pt = *player, minstrel* (cf Qal) 2 K $3^{15.15}$, cf. also אִישׁ יֹדֵעַ מְנַגֵּן בַּכִּנּוֹר 1 S 16^{16} (Ges^{§120b})

†[**נְגִינָה**] **n f.** music,—abs נגינת ψ 61^{1} (v. infr), sf. נגינָתִי ψ 77^{7}, נגינָתָם Jb 30^{9} + 2 t.; pl נגינות ψ 4^{1} + 6 t, נגינותַי Is 38^{20}, ־תָי Hb 3^{19};— **1.** *music* (of stringed instr) acc cogn. Is 38^{20}; as occupation La 5^{14}; esp בנגינות in ψ-titles; ψ 4^{1} 6^{1} 54^{1} 55^{1} 67^{1} 76^{1}, so Hb 3^{19}; cf. עַל־נגינַת ψ 61^{1} (rd perh pl Ges^{§80f}) **2.** *song* (with string accomp?) ψ 77^{7}, *subject of* mocking *song* Jb 30^{9} (‖ מִלָּה), ψ 69^{13} (נ׳ שׁוֹתֵי שֵׁכָר), La 3^{14} (‖ שְׂחֹק).

†[**מַנְגִּינָה**] **n f.** (mocking, derisive) song (cf foreg.);—מַנְגִּינָתָם La 3^{63}, i.e. *subject of their mocking song*

נָגַע $_{150}$ **vb. touch, reach, strike** (NH *id.*; Ar. نَجَعَ is *agree* with one (of food), *produce effect*; Aram. נְגַע Ithpa. *be struck* (sc. w. leprosy), cf. Pi. infr.);—**Qal** *Pf.* נ׳ Gn 32^{33}+; נָגְעָה Ju 20^{41}+; 1 pl. sf. נְגַעֲנוּךָ Gn 26^{29}; *Impf* יִגַּע Lv 5^{3}+; וַיִּגַּע Gn 32^{26}+, etc.; *Imv.* גַּע ψ 144^{5} + 2 t.; *Inf. cstr.* נְגֹעַ, לִנְגּוֹעַ Gn 20^{6} + 3 t; גַּעַת 2 S 14^{10} Ez 17^{10}; sf. נָגְעֵךְ Ru 2^{9}, etc.; *Pt. act* נֹגֵעַ 1 K 19^{5}+; נֹגְעִים Je 12^{14}; f. נֹגַעַת Nu 19^{22} + 2 t.; pl. נֹגְעֹת 1 K 6^{27}; *pass.* נָגוּעַ ψ 73^{14} Is 53^{4},—**1. a.** *touch*, usu sq בְּ Gn 3^{3} (J), $32^{26.33}$ Ex $19^{12\ 12.13}$ (all E), 29^{37} 30^{29} (P), Lv $5^{2.3}$ + 25 t. Lv; Nu 16^{26} + 7 t. Nu (P) + 19^{22} (no בְּ or obj.), Dt 14^{8} Ju 6^{21} 2 S 23^{7} 1 K $6^{27\ 27}$ $19^{5.7}$ 2 K 13^{21} Est 5^{2} Dn $8^{5\ 18}$ $10^{10\ 18}$ La 4^{14}, sq. אֶל־ Hg 2^{12} Nu 4^{15} 1 K 6^{27} Dn 9^{21}, cf. Ho 4^{2}; sq. עַל־פֶּה Is 6^{7}, עַל־שְׂפָתַי Dn 10^{16}; sq. acc. Is 52^{11}; abs. (no obj. expr) Jb 6^{7} La 4^{15}. **b.** of י׳ *touching* earth, mountains, etc., sq בְּ Am 9^{5} ψ 104^{32} 144^{5}; fig of י׳ *touching* the heart, sq בְּ 1 S 10^{26}. **2.** nearly = *strike*, pass. *stricken*, ψ 73^{14} Is 53^{4} (‖ מֻכֵּה), of wind Jb 1^{19} Ez 17^{10}; of divine chastisement 1 S 6^{9} Jb 1^{11} 19^{21}, sq. אֶל 2^{5}. **3.** *touch* = harm, sq בְּ, Gn 26^{11} (J), Jos 9^{19} 2 S 14^{10} 1 Ch 16^{22} (‖ הָרַע) = ψ 105^{15}, Je 12^{14} Zc $2^{12\ 12}$; sq אֶל־ Gn 20^{6} (*touch* a woman), so Pr 6^{29} (sq בְּ), sq. acc. Gn 26^{29} (J, sf), so Ru 2^{9}; v. also Jb 5^{19} (subj. רָע, sq בְּ), Ju $20^{34.41}$ (both subj. רָעָה, sq. עַל־). **4.** *reach, extend to*, 2 S 5^{8}, sq. בְּ (but crpt v. Dr HPS), in metaph., sq עַד, of vine Is 16^{8} Je 48^{32}, of sword Je 4^{10}, cf. v^{18}; of chastisement Mi 1^{9}, cf Jb 4^{5} (‖ בּוֹא אֶל־); also (sq. אֶל) Je 51^{9}; = *come*, sq. אֶל־ Jon 3^{6}; *arrive* (of time), abs. Ezr 3^{1} Ne 7^{73}.

†**Niph.** *Impf* וַיִּנָּגְעוּ Jos 8^{15} *be stricken, defeated* (in battle), i.e. feign to be so, but rd. prob. וַיִּנָּגְפוּ, v. נגף **Niph.**

†**Pi.** *Pf.* sf. נִגְּעוֹ 2 Ch 26^{20} *strike* (with leprosy, 2 acc.), subj. י׳; so *Impf.* וַיְנַגַּע 2 K 15^{5}; Gn 12^{17} (subj. י׳, acc. pers + acc. cogn.).

†**Pu.** *Impf* יְנֻגָּעוּ *be stricken* by diseases (?; cf **Pi.** and נֶגַע **2. 3.** esp 2 S 7^{14}) ψ 73^{5}.

†**Hiph.** *Pf.* הִגִּיעַ Is 25^{12} + 6 t.; 2 fs. הִגַּעַתְּ Est 4^{14}; 1 s sf וְהִגַּעְתִּיהוּ Ez 13^{14}, etc, *Impf.* יַגִּיעַ Is 8^{8} + 3 t; וַיַּגַּע Is 6^{7} Je 1^{9}, etc; *Inf cstr* הַגִּיעַ Est $2^{12\ 15}$, *Pt* מַגִּיעַ Gn 28^{12}+; f מַגַּעַת 2 Ch 3^{11};—*cause to touch; reach, approach, arrive*: **1.** *cause to touch, apply*, Ex 12^{22} (JE; אֶל־, מִדָּם); *cause to touch* (sq לָאָרֶץ, עַד עָפָר), i.e. bring to ground, Is $25^{5\ 12}$, cf La 2^{2}, Ez 13^{14} (sq. אֶל־), Ex 4^{25} (J, sq לְרַגְלָיו), sq עַל־פֶּה Is 6^{7} Je 1^{9}, sq בְּ Is 5^{8}. **2.** intr. *reach, extend*, Gn 28^{12} (sq. ה‍ָ loc.); sq אֶל־ Zc 14^{5}, sq. עַד Is 8^{8}; cf. תַּגִּ׳ יָדוֹ דֵּי שֶׂה Lv 5^{7} *if his hand do not reach enough for a lamb* (i.e. he be not able to furnish a lamb); sq. לְ Jb 20^{6} (hyperb) 2 Ch $3^{11\ 11\ 12}$; sq. עַד לְ 28^{9}; *attain*, sq לְ Est 4^{14}, *arrive, come*, sq. acc. loc. Is 30^{4} Est 4^{3} 8^{17}, sq לְ (of time) Dn 12^{12}, sq. אֶל־ 1 S 14^{9}, sq. עַד־ ψ 107^{18}, abs. Est 6^{14}; sq. אֶל Dn 8^{7}. **3.** *approach*, of time, abs. Ec 12^{1} Ct 2^{12} Ez 7^{12} (‖ בּוֹא); v. also Est 9^{1} (sq Inf), cf. $2^{12.15}$ ψ 88^{4} (sq. לְ). **4.** of fate or lot, = *befal*, sq. אֶל־ Est 9^{26} Ec $8^{14.14}$ ψ 32^{6}.

נֶ֫גַע $_{78}$ **n.m.** $^{Gn\ 12,17}$ **stroke, plague, mark, plague-spot**;—נ׳ abs. Ex 11^{1}+, נָ֑גַע Lv 13^{13}+; cstr. Dt 24^{8}+; sf. נִגְעִי ψ 38^{12}, נִגְעֶךָ 39^{11}; נִגְעוֹ Lv 13^{44} 2 Ch 6^{29}; pl. נְגָעִים Gn 12^{17} ψ 89^{33}; cstr. נִגְעֵי 2 S 7^{14};—**1.** *stroke, wound*, inflicted by man on man Dt 17^{8} 21^{5} (‖ רִיב), Pr 6^{33}. **2.** *stroke*, metaph., esp of a disease, regarded as sent by a divine chastisement, Gn 12^{17} (J), Ex 11^{1} (E), 2 S 7^{14} (‖ שֵׁבֶט אֲנָשִׁים, נ׳ בְּנֵי אָדָם, i.e. customary, ordinary), 1 K 8^{37} = 2 Ch 6^{28} (both ‖ מַחֲלָה); 1 K 8^{38} (נ׳ לְבָבוֹ) = 2 Ch 6^{29} (נִגְעוֹ); ψ 91^{10} (‖ רָעָה); of Israel 38^{12} 39^{11} (‖ תִּגְרַת יָדְךָ), 89^{33} (‖ שֵׁבֶט); v also Is 53^{8} (of suffering servant of י׳, נֶגַע לָמוֹ) **3.** *mark* (60 t Lv 13, 14), indeterm. Lv $13^{5\ 6}$ (מִסְפַּחַת), $v^{17\ 29.30.32.43.44}$; of leprosy, regarded as the *heavy touch* or *stroke* of a disease, נ׳ צָרַ֫עַת Lv 13^{2}+; v^{51} (צָרַעַת מַמְאֶרֶת הַנ׳), v^{59} $14^{3.32.54}$, Dt 24^{8}; also נ׳ הַנֶּתֶק Lv 13^{31}; נ׳ לְבָן אֲדַמְדָּם v^{42}; identif. with person having it $13^{4\ 12.13\ 17\ 31}$, in garment, etc. v^{47} + 15 t Lv 13; in house $14^{34.35.36.43.44.48.48}$; i.e. house-wall $v^{37\ 37\ 39}$; in stones of wall v^{40}, = garment, etc., with plague-spot 13^{50}.

†**נָגַף** **vb.** strike, smite (Aram. נְגַף);—**Qal** *Pf* נ׳ 2 Ch 13^{15} Is 19^{22} (ו consec.); sf. נְגָפוֹ 2 Ch 21^{18}, etc; *Impf.* יִגֹּף Ex 21^{35} + 2 t; וַיִּגֹּף Ex 32^{35} + 4 t., אֶגּוֹף ψ 89^{24}+, etc.; *Inf. abs.* נָגֹף Is 19^{22}; *cstr.* לִנְגֹּף Ex $12^{23.23}$; נָגְפוֹ v^{27},—*strike, smite*, of serious (even fatal) injury, sq. acc pers. Ex $21^{22.35}$ (E); one's foot against (בְּ) stone ψ 91^{12}, abs. (stumble) Pr 3^{23}, esp. of judgment, subj י׳, obj individ. (fatal stroke) 1 S 25^{38} 26^{10} 2 S 12^{15} 2 Ch 13^{20} 21^{18} (לָחֳלִי), obj people (abs.) Ex $12^{23.23.27}$ (JE), 32^{35} Jos 24^{5} (E), Is 19^{22}, cf. v^{22}; v. also ψ 89^{24}, cf c acc cogn. מַגֵּפָה Zc $14^{12.18}$ 2 Ch 21^{14} (sq also בְּעַמֶּךָ), c. בְּ instr. Ex 7^{27}; of causing defeat in battle, sq. acc. + לִפְנֵי Ju 20^{35} 1 S 4^{3} 2 Ch 13^{15} 14^{11}.

Niph. *Pf* נִגַּף 2 S 10^{15}; נִגְּפוּ v^{19} + 2 t., etc; *Impf* יִנָּגֵף 2 Ch 6^{24}, וַיִּנָּגֵף 1 S 4^{2} + 4 t, *Inf abs* נִגּוֹף Ju 20^{39}; cstr הִנָּגֵף 1 K 8^{33}; *Pt* נִגָּף Dt 28^{25} Ju 20^{39}, etc.;—*be smitten*, bef. enemy, in battle, sq לִפְנֵי Ju 20$^{32.39.39}$ 1 S 4^{2} 7^{10} 2 S 10$^{15.19}$ 18^{7} 1 K 8^{33} 2 K 14^{12} 1 Ch 19$^{16.19}$ 2 Ch 6^{24} 25^{22} Lv 26^{17} Nu 14^{42} Dt 1^{42}; abs. Ju 20^{36} 1 S 4^{10} 2 S 2^{17} 2 Ch 20^{22}, Pt after נָתַן, sq לִפְנֵי Dt 28$^{7.25}$ Vid נָגַע **Niph.**

Hithp. *Impf* יִתְנַגְּפוּ Je 13^{16} = *stumble*, subj רַגְלֵיכֶם, sq עַל (loc), cf. **Qal** (ψ 91^{12}) and נגף **2.**

†נֶ֫גֶף **n.m.**$^{Ex\ 12.13}$ **blow, striking** (as judgment, only P),—נ׳ abs Ex 12^{13} + 6 t.;—**1.** *fatal blow, plague*, Ex 12^{13} (death of first-born), 30^{12} Nu 8^{19} (indef); = pestilence Nu 17$^{11.12}$ Jos 22^{17}. **2.** *striking*, אֶבֶן נ׳ Is 8^{14} i.e. against which the foot strikes and so stumbles (‖ צוּר מִכְשׁוֹל)

†מַגֵּפָה **n.f. blow, slaughter, plague, pestilence**,—מ׳ abs Nu 14^{37} + 23 t; cstr. מַגֵּפַת Zc 14^{15}; pl sf מַגֵּפֹתַי Ex 9^{14};—**1.** *blow*, = fatal stroke Ez 24^{16}, in divine judgment (plague) Ex 9^{14} (J). **2.** *slaughter* in battle, 1 S 4^{17} 2 S 17^{9} 18^{7}. **3.** *plague, pestilence* (divine judgment), of tumours on Philistines 1 S 6^{4}; against Isr Nu 14^{37} 17$^{13.14.15}$ 25$^{8.9.18.19}$ 31^{16} 2 S 24$^{21.25}$ (ins. also v^{15} 𝔊 Th We Klo Dr Kit Bu), 1 Ch 21^{22} ψ 106$^{29.30}$; specif. disease of bowels 2 Ch 21^{14}, מ׳ = infected people 1 Ch 21^{17}, wasting of flesh, eyes and tongue, of hostile peoples Zc 14$^{12.18}$; attacking beasts v$^{15.15}$

†[נָגַר] **vb. pour, flow, run** (Aram. نجر *be long* (of time), Aph. *prolong, protract*, נגר *endure, flow, stream*),—**Niph.** *Pf.* 3 fs נִגְּרָה ψ 77^{3} La 3^{49}, *Pt* pl נִגָּרִים 2 S 14^{14}; נִגָּרוֹת Jb 20^{28},—**1.** *be poured, spilt*, 2 S 14^{14} (כַּמַּיִם הַנִּגָּרִים אַרְצָה in sim. of mortality). **2.** *pour oneself, flow, trickle*, of eye (in tears) La 3^{49} **3.** fig *vanish*, Jb 20^{28} (‖ גָּלָה) **4.** *be stretched out* (?) יָדִי לַיְלָה נִגְּרָה ψ 77^{3} (or rd עֵינִי?) **Hiph.** *Pf* וְהִגַּרְתִּי Mi 1^{6}; *Impf* וַיַּגֵּר ψ 75^{9}, וְתַגֵּר Ez 35^{5}, יַגִּירֻהוּ ψ 63^{11}, *Imv* sf הַגִּרֵם Je 18^{21},—*pour down, hurl down* the stones of Samaria, subj י׳ Mi 1^{6}, *pour out*, fig of י׳'s wine-cup, ψ 75^{9}; sq עַל־יְדֵי חֶרֶב = *deliver over to* Je 18^{21} ψ 63^{11} Ez 35^{5} **Hoph.** *Pt* כְּמַיִם מֻגָּרִים בְּמוֹרָד Mi 1^{4} in sim, of mountains melting at theophany

†[נָגַשׂ] **vb. press, drive, oppress, exact** (As. *naḳâšu, throw down, overthrow*, Dl$^{HWB\ 418}$, Ar نجش *rouse* and *drive* game, *drive vehemently*, Eth ነገሠ: *reign, wield power*, ንጉሥ: *king*);—**Qal** *Pf.* נ׳ 2 K 23^{35}; *Impf.* יִגֹּשׂ Dt 15^{2}, 2 ms תִגֹּשׂ Dt 15^{3}; 2 mpl. תִּנְגֹּשׂוּ Is 58^{3};—*Pt.* נֹגֵשׂ Is 9^{3} +, etc.,—**1.** *press, drive* to work (obj עַצְּבֵיכֶם your workmen), Is 58^{3} (Ges^{Comm}, De Di Du; *exact* [changing ע׳, q. v.] Che, etc.); v. **3.** **2.** *exact* c. acc כֶּסֶף, 2 K 23^{35}, sq acc pers. only Dt 15$^{2.13}$. **3.** Pt. (= subst) *driver, taskmaster* Ex 3^{7} 5$^{6.10.13.14}$ Jb 3^{18}; (ass-)driver Jb 39^{7}; of (arbitrary) *ruler* Is 3^{12}, *ruler* (good sense) Zc 10^{4}; = foreign *oppressor, tyrant* Is 9^{3} (c ב) 14$^{2.4}$ Zc 9^{8}; *exactor* of tribute, Dn 11^{20}; pl. abstr *lordship* = *lord, ruler*, fig of צְדָקָה (personif) Is 60^{17} (‖ פְּקֻדָּתֵךְ שָׁלוֹם) **Niph.** *Pf.* נִגַּשׂ 1 S 13^{6} + 2 t + Is 3^{5} (וְ consec.),—*hard pressed* by enemy 1 S 13^{6}, and so 14^{24} (but om. by emend, after 𝔊, Th We Dr Kit Bu HPS); *treated harshly*, of suffering servant of י׳ Is 53^{7}, recipr *tyrannize over* (ב׳) *each other* Is 3^{5}.

[נָגַשׁ]$_{125}$ **vb. draw near, approach**, less freq syn. of קרב q v. (NH *id.* Hiph. (rare) and deriv),—**Qal**$_{68}$ *Impf* יִגַּשׁ Ex 24^{14} +, יִגָּשׁ ψ 91^{7}, וַיִּגַּשׁ Gn 18^{23} +; 3 fs. וַתִּגַּשׁ Gn 33^{7}, 2 ms תִּגַּשׁ־ Is 65^{5}, 3 mpl. יִגְּשׁוּ Is 41^{1} +, יִגָּ֑שׁוּ Ex 24^{2}, יִגְּשׁוּ Jb 41^{8} (Baer; van d H. יִגָּשׁוּ), 3 fpl. וַתִּגַּשְׁןָ, Gn 33^{6}, etc, *Imv* גַּשׁ 2 S 1^{15}, גֶּשׁ־ Gn 19^{9}, גְּשָׁה Gn 27^{21} + 2 t; fs. גֹּשִׁי Ru 2^{14}, etc; *Inf. cstr.* לָגֶשֶׁת Ju 20^{23} +; sf. גִּשְׁתּוֹ Gn 33^{3}; גִּשְׁתָּם Ex 28^{43} + 2 t,—*draw* or *come near*, **1.** human subj.: sq אֶל־ pers. Gn 27^{22} 43^{19} 44^{18} 45^{4} (all J), Ex 19^{15} (of sexual intercourse), 24^{2} Nu 32^{16} Jos 14^{6} (all E), Ex 34^{30} Jos 21^{1} (P), + 10 t. elsewh. (not D), + ψ 91^{7} (subj pestilence personif.); of priestly approach to י׳ Ez 44^{13}, cf Je 30^{21b}, also sq. אֶל־ of altar Ex 28^{43} 30^{20} Lv 21^{23} and abs, v^{21} (all P or H), sq אֶל־ rei also Nu 8^{16}, sq עַד־ pers. Gn 33^{3} (J), rei Ju 9^{52}; sq עַל־ pers. Ez 9^{6}, rei 44^{13}, sq. ב pers. Is 65^{5} (‖ קְרַב אֶל־), in Am 9^{10} rd תַּגִּישׁ בַּעֲדֵנוּ (for MT תַּגִּישׁ **Hiph.** cf. We GASm Dr Now, ‖ קִדֵּם); sq לַמִּלְחָמָה *draw near for battle* Ju 20^{23} Je 46^{3} 2 S 10^{13} = 1 Ch 19^{14} (+ לִפְנֵי pers); sq. acc. pers. 1 S 9^{18} 30^{21}, rei Nu 4^{19} (P), but acc difficult; Dr rds אֶל־ for אֶת־ 1 S 9^{18} Nu 4^{19}, cf. Klo, HPS; in 1 S 30^{21} Dr takes אֶת־ = *with*, sq. הֲלֹם *hither*, 1 S 14^{38} Ru 2^{14}; abs. Gn 18^{23} 27^{21} 29^{10} 33$^{6.7}$ 45^{4} (all J), Ex 24^{2} (E), Jos 8^{11} (E; + וַיָּבֹאוּ), + 9 t. (not P, D), + Gn 27$^{26.27}$ (E), Jos 3^{9} (J), 2 S 1^{15} 2 Ch 29^{31} (all Imv. sq. 2nd Imv), + Gn 19^{9} (J), Lv 21$^{21.21}$ (H), 2 K 4^{27} (all sq Inf. purpose). Note esp גֶּשׁ־הָלְאָה Gn 19^{9} lit *approach thither!*

i.e. move away! cf. גְּשָׁה־לִּי וְאֵשֵׁבָה Is 49^{20} *move away for me* (make room for me) *that I may dwell* (צַר־לִי הַמָּקוֹם‖). **2.** inanim. subj. אֶחָד בְּאֶחָד יִגַּשׁוּ Jb 41^{8} *one to another they approach* (fit closely together, of scales of crocodile)—**Qal** not in D

Niph. *Pf.* נִגַּשׁ Gn 33^{7}+; 3 fs. וְנִגְּשָׁה Dt 25^{9}; 3 mpl. נִגְּשׁוּ Ex 34^{32}+, נִגַּשְׁתֶּם 2 S $11^{20.21}$; *Pt* pl. נִגָּשִׁים Ex 19^{22};—*draw near* = **Qal** (and substit. for it in D):—sq. אֶל־ pers. Dt 25^{9} 1 K 20^{13} Ezr 9^{1}, of priestly approach to Yahweh Ex 19^{22} (J), Je 30^{21}; sq. אֶל־ rei Ex 20^{21} 24^{2} (both E), 2 S $11^{20.21}$, אֶל־הַמִּשְׁפָּט Dt 25^{1}; sq בְּ pers. Am 9^{13}; sq. לַמִּלְחָמָה 1 S 7^{10}, abs. Gn 33^{7} (J), Dt 20^{2} (קרב‖), 21^{5} Ex 34^{32} (P), so fig. of worship Is 29^{13}.

†**Hiph.** *Pf.* 3 ms. sf. consec. וְהִגִּישׁוֹ Ex $21^{6.6}$, הִגִּשְׁתֶּם והגישה Lv 2^{8}; 3 pl. הִגִּישׁוּ 2 S 17^{29}; 2 mpl. הִגַּשְׁתֶּם Am 5^{25}; *Impf.* juss יַגֵּשׁ Jb 40^{19}; וַיַּגֶּשׁ Gn 27^{25}; וַיַּגֵּשׁ Ju 6^{19}, 3 fs. תַּגִּישׁ Am 9^{10}, וַתַּגֵּשׁ 1 S 28^{25} 2 S 13^{11}; 3 mpl. יַגִּישׁוּ Is 41^{22}; 2 mpl. תַּגִּישׁוּ Mal 1^{8}, תַּגִּישׁוּן v^{8}, וַתַּגִּישׁוּן Am 6^{3}, etc.; *Imv.* ms. הַגִּישָׁה Gn 27^{25}+; mpl הַגִּישׁוּ 1 S 13^{9}+; *Pt.* מַגִּישׁ Mal 2^{12}; pl. cstr. מַגִּישֵׁי Mal 3^{3}, etc.,—*cause to approach, bring near, bring,* sq. אֶל־ pers. (usu. obj acc rei, rarely pers Ex $21^{6.6}$ 1 S 15^{32} Gn 48^{10} cf. v^{13}):—Gn $48^{10.13}$ (E), Ex $21^{6.6}$ (E), 1 S 13^{9} 14^{34} 15^{32} 2 S 13^{11} (+Inf. purpose), 2 K $4^{5.6}$; sq אֶל־הַמִּזְבֵּחַ Lv 2^{8} (P, of sacrifice); עַל־מִזְבְּחִי Mal 1^{7} (sacrif.); לְ pers. Gn $27^{25.25}$ (E), 1 S 30^{7} 2 S 17^{29} (rd וַיַּגִּישׁוּ 𝔊 Th We Klo Kit, cf Dr), of sacrifice Am 5^{25} Mal 2^{12} 3^{3}, לִפְנֵי pers. 1 S 28^{25} 2 Ch 29^{23}; no prep Ex 32^{6} (J), 1 S $14^{18.34}$ 23^{9} 30^{7} Ju 6^{19} (foll. הוציא אֶל־), Am 6^{3} 1 K 5^{1} Lv 8^{14} (P), of sacrif. also Mal 1^{8} (לִזְבֹּחַ), v^{8} (הקריב‖); fig. (obj. *proofs, evidences*) Is 41^{21} (קרב‖), v^{22} (+וְיַגִּידוּ), cf. 45^{21} (הַגִּידוּ‖); הָעֹשׂוֹ יַגֵּשׁ חַרְבּוֹ Jb 40^{19} let him that made him (the hippot.) *draw near* his sword, is dub, Du הָעָשׂוּ[י] נֹגֵשׂ חֲבֵרָיו *wh. is made ruler of its fellows* (other conject. v. Di Bu); Am 9^{10} rd. תִּגַּשׁ **Qal** q.v.). †**Hoph.** *Pf.* 3 mpl. לֹא־לִנְחֻשְׁתַּיִם הֻגָּשׁוּ 2 S 3^{34} (Ginsb הֻגָּשׁוּ) thy feet *have not been brought near* (put into) *fetters; Pt* מֻגָּשׁ לִשְׁמִי Mal 1^{11} *it* (impers) *is offered to my name.* †**Hithp.** *Imv.* mpl. הִתְנַגְּשׁוּ Is 45^{20} *draw near!* (הִקָּבְצוּ וָבֹאוּ‖).

נֵד v. II. נדד. נֵד v. נוּד.

†[נָדָא] **vb. drive away, thrust aside** (‖form of נדה, q.v., or text. err.; Eth. ነድአ: *drive* cattle, etc),—only **Hiph.** *Impf.* 3 ms. וידא . . . אֶת־יִשְׂרָאֵל מֵאַחֲרֵי י׳ 2 K 17^{21} Kt (Qr וַיַּדַּח √נדח **Hiph.**).

†נָדַב **vb. incite, impel** (NH *id.*; Ar. نَدَبَ *call, impel, incite* (نَدُبَ *be noble, willing, generous,* is denom. fr. [نَدْبٌ cf.] נָדִיב acc. to Ba $^{NB\,§\,125\,e}$); VIII. نتدب *ready, willing;* As. *nidbu, freewill-offering* Dl$^{HWB\,448}$; Aram נדב *be willing* Pa. Ithpa.; Zinj. נדב *inciting, instigation* DHM$^{Sendsch\,60}$);—**Qal** *Pf* 3 ms. נָדַב Ex 35^{29}; 3 fs. נָדְבָה v^{21}; *Impf.* 3 ms. sf. יִדְּבֶנּוּ 25^{2},—אֲשֶׁר יִדְּבֶנּוּ לִבּוֹ 25^{2} *whose heart incited,* cf 35^{29}; subj. רוּחַ 35^{21} (all P). **Hithp.** *Pf.* 1 s. הִתְנַדַּבְתִּי 1 Ch 29^{17}, 3 mpl. הִתְנַדְּבוּ Ezr 2^{68} 1 Ch 29^{9}, *Impf.* 3 mpl יִתְנַדְּבוּ v^{6}; *Inf.* הִתְנַדֵּב Ju 5^{2} + 2 t.; הִתְנַדֶּב־ 1 Ch 29^{17}; sf. הִתְנַדְּבָם v^{9}, *Pt* מִתְנַדֵּב Ezr 3^{5}+2 t; pl. מִתְנַדְּבִים Ju 5^{9} Ne 11^{2};—**1.** *volunteer* for war Ju $5^{2.9}$; for service of other kinds 2 Ch 17^{16} Ne 11^{2}. **2.** *offer freewill-offerings* for the first temple 1 Ch $29^{5.6.9.9.14.17.17}$; for the second Ezr 1^{6} 2^{68} 3^{5} (cf. BAram)

†נָדָב **n.pr.m.** (*generous, noble*)—**1.** eldest son of Aaron Ex 6^{23} $24^{1.9}$ 28^{1} Lv 10^{1} Nu $3^{2.4}$ $26^{60.61}$ 1 Ch 5^{29} 24^{1}. 𝔊 Ναδαβ (so **3, 4**). **2.** son of Jeroboam I 1 K 14^{20} $15^{25.27.31}$. 𝔊 Ναβατ, Ναβαθ, 𝔊L Ναδαβ. **3.** a Jerahmeelite 1 Ch $2^{28.30}$. **4.** a Gibeonite 1 Ch 8^{30} 9^{36}.

†נְדָבָה **n.f. voluntariness, freewill-offering**;—abs. נ׳ Ex 35^{29}+14 t; cstr. נִדְבַת Dt 16^{10}; pl. נְדָבוֹת Am 4^{5} ψ 68^{10}, נְדָבֹת 110^{3}; cstr. נִדְבוֹת 119^{108} 2 Ch 31^{14}; sf. נִדְבֹתֶיךָ Dt 12^{17} +4 t. sfs.;—**1.** *voluntariness* אֹהֲבֵם נְדָבָה Ho 14^{5} *I* (י׳) *will love them freely;* עַמְּךָ נְדָבֹת בְּיוֹם חֵילֶךָ ψ 110^{3} *thy people will be* (all) *voluntariness in the day of thy host* (be ready to volunteer, v. Br$^{MP\,153}$); גֶּשֶׁם נדבות 68^{10} *generous* (copious) *rain;* בנדבה 54^{8} *voluntarily,* and adverb. acc. נדבה Dt 23^{24} (v. Dr). **2.** *freewill, voluntary, offering:* **a.** incl. gifts used in erection and furnishing of tabernacle Ex 35^{29} 36^{3} (P), for first temple 2 Ch 31^{14}, second Ezr 1^{4} 8^{28}. **b.** incl. עולה and שלמים Ez 46^{12}; prob. also Am 4^{5}, נדבות פי ψ 119^{108}. **c.** usu. a זֶבַח for festival meals, at Passover 2 Ch 35^{8}, Pentecost Dt 16^{10}, Tabernacles Ezr 3^{5} (besides the ritual offerings); disting from נֶדֶר votive offering Lv 7^{16} Nu 15^{3} 29^{39} (P), Lv $22^{18.21.23}$ 23^{38} (H), Dt $12^{6.17}$.—(Verbs used are הביא נ׳ Ex 35^{29} 36^{3}, הקריב נ׳ Lv 22^{18}; עשה נ׳ Nu 15^{3} Ez 46^{12}; נתן נ׳ Lv 23^{38} Dt 16^{10}.)

†נָדִיב **adj.** and **n.m.**$^{\text{Is 32.8}}$ **inclined, generous, noble**,—abs. נ׳ Is 32^{5}+6 t; cstr. נדיב Ex 35^{5}+2 t, f. נדיבה ψ 51^{14}, pl נדיבים Is 13^{2} +9 t, cstr נדיבי Nu 21^{18}+2 t, sf נדיבמו ψ 83^{12},—**1.** *incited, inclined, willing*, נדיב לב Ex $35^{5.22}$ (P), 1 Ch 29^{31} (v נָדַב **Qal**), נְדִיב בְּחָכְמָה 28^{21}; רוּחַ נדיבה ψ 51^{14} *a willing spirit.* **2.** *noble, princely*, in rank 1 S 2^{8} (poem), Jb 12^{21} = ψ 107^{40}, Jb 34^{18} Pr 8^{16} ψ 47^{10} 83^{12} $113^{8.8}$ 118^{9} 146^{3}, פני נדיב Pr 19^{6} 25^{7}, בית נ׳ Jb 21^{28}; פתחי נ׳ Is 13^{2}, בת נ׳ Ct 7^{2}, נדיבי הָעָם Nu 21^{18} (poem). **3** *noble* in mind and character ‖ צדיק Pr 17^{26}, opp נָבָל Is $32^{5.8}$

†[נְדִיבָה] **n f. nobility, nobleness**,—sf. נְדִבָתִי Jb 30^{15}, pl נדיבות Is $32^{8.8}$,—**1.** *nobility* of rank, *honour* Jb 30^{15} **2.** pl = *noble things* as counselled by the נדיב in character Is $32^{8.8}$.

†נוֹדָב **n.pr.gent.** Arab tribe acc. to 1 Ch 5^{19} (+ יטור, נָפִישׁ q v Gn 25^{15} 1 Ch 1^{31}), 𝔊 Ναδαβαιων. (Connex. with above √ quite uncertain.)

†נְדַבְיָה **n pr.m.** (*whom Yah impels;* in As. *Na-ad-bi-ia-a-u* Jager$^{\text{BAS I 468}}$); — son of Jeconiah 1 Ch 3^{18}. 𝔊 Δενεθει, 𝔊L Ναδαβια

†I [נָדַד] **vb. retreat, flee, depart, stray, wander, flutter** (NH *id;* Ar. ندّ *flee, run away,* Aram نَدّ *hate, abominate, shrink from,* Aph *put to flight,* etc., נדד *flee*),—**Qal** *Pf.* 3 fs נָדְדָה Is 10^{31} Est 6^{1}, 3 pl נָדְדוּ Ho 7^{13}+4 t, נָדָדוּ Is 21^{15} Je 4^{25}, *Impf* יִדּוֹד Na 3^{7}; 3 fs וַתִּדַּד Gn 31^{40}, 3 mpl. ידדון ψ $68^{13.13}$, *Inf cstr.* נדד ψ 55^{8}, *Pt* נדד Je 49^{5}+; f. נוֹדֶדֶת Pr 27^{8}, pl נֹדְדִים Ho 9^{17},—**1.** *retreat, flee* Is 21^{15} *fr before* (מפני) *swords;* 33^{3} *at the sound* (מקול) *of tumult,* abs 10^{31} 22^{3} ψ $68^{13.13}$, of birds and beasts Je 4^{25} 9^{9} (+ הָלָכוּ); pt = *fugitive* Is 16^{3} 21^{14}, of fleeing in horror, disgust, c. מן pers. Na 3^{7} ψ 31^{12} **2.** *flee, depart*, Isr. fr (מן) י׳ Ho 7^{13}, of sleep (מעיני) Gn 31^{40} (E), abs Est 6^{1} **3.** *wander, stray* (homeless, cf נוד), עוף נודד Is 16^{2} (in sim), so Pr 27^{8} (מן loc, in sim), cf v^{8} (מן loc), of scattered Isr. Ho 9^{17} Je 49^{5}, (searching) for food Jb 15^{23} (wicked man), ארחיק נדד ψ 55^{8} *I will wander afar* **4.** trans. *flutter* wings (of bird, in fig) Is 10^{14}. **Po'ēl** *Pf* consec שֶׁמֶשׁ זָרְחָה וְנֹדַד Na 3^{17} the sun hath arisen and it (the locust swarm) *fleeth away.* **Hiph.** *chase away, Impf.* 3 mpl sf וּמתבל יְנִדֻהוּ Jb 18^{18} (of wicked, ‖ יֶהְדְּפֻהוּ מֵאוֹר). **Hoph.** *be chased away, Impf* 3 ms. וְיֻדַּד כְּחֶזְיוֹן Jb 20^{8} (of wicked), קוֹץ מֻנָּד 2 S 23^{6} *thorns thrust away* (si vera l., cf Dr, Klo Bu HPS (ק׳ מדבר) **Hithpo'l** *Impf.* יתנודדו ψ 64^{9} *flee away* (in horror, disgust, cf **Qal** Na 3^{7} ψ 31^{12}).

†[נְדוּד] **n.[m.]** tossing of sleeplessness, only pl נְדֻדִים Jb 7^{4} I am sated with *tossings.*

†נִדָּה **n.f.** impurity (as *abhorrent, shunned*);—abs נ׳ Ez 18^{6}+, cstr נִדַּת Lv 12^{2}+; sf נִדָּתָהּ v^{5}+,—*impurity* (esp P and Ezek): **1.** of ceremonial impurity, as union with brother's wife, Lv 20^{21}; esp. of menstruation Ez 18^{6} (rd אשה בנדתה for MT א׳ נדה 𝔊 Co), טֻמְאַת הַנּ׳ 22^{10}, cf 36^{17}, נדת דותה Lv 12^{2}, cf v^{5} $15^{19.20.24.25}$ (עֶת־נד׳), v$^{25.25}$, v^{26} (מִשְׁכַּב נִד׳), v^{26} (טֻמְאַת נד׳), v^{33} 18^{19}; of defilement contracted by contact with a corpse, מֵי (הַ)נִּדָּה *water of impurity* (i e to remove it, cf. Di) Nu $19^{9.13.20.21.21}$ 31^{23}. **2.** fig. (with allusion to cerem. usage), *impure thing,* Ez $7^{19.20}$ (of gold), La 1^{17} (of Jerus); of idolatry, immorality, etc, 2 Ch 29^{5} Ezr 9^{11} (אֶרֶץ נדה), v^{11}, Zc 13^{1} (לְחַטָּאת וּלְנִדָּה).

†נִידָה **n.f. id.** (on form cf. Ges$^{\S 20.3.R1}$ Ko$^{\text{II 1.497}}$),—of Jerusalem La 1^{8} (= נִדָּה v^{17})

II נדד (√of foll, v Ko$^{\text{II 1.42}}$, cf Ar. نَدّ *high hill, hill rising high into the sky,* Lane^{2778}; also *earth-heap, sand-heap*).

†נֵד **n.m.**$^{\text{Jos 3.13}}$ heap of waters, of Red Sea Ex 15^{8} (song), ψ 78^{13}, of Jordan Jos $3^{13.16}$ ψ 33^{7} (sim). נד קציר Is 17^{11} *harvest-heap* is perhaps corrupt: Ges Ew Di Du der from נוד, reading (probably) נָד (Di) *fled is the harvest;* Che^{Hpt} proposes לָכֵן *therefore;* Buhl$^{\text{Lex 13}}$ עַד, after 𝔊 𝔗.

†I [נָדָה] **vb. Pi. put away, exclude** (NH Pi (*excommunicate*) Hithp Niph; As. *nadû, throw, overthrow, destroy,* etc., Dl$^{\text{HWB 448}}$),—**Pi.** *Pt.* הַמְנַדִּים לְיוֹם רָע Am 6^{3} *they that thrust off the evil day* (i e refuse to think of it), lit מְנַדֵּיכֶם Is 66^{5} *thrust away, exclude* from association in worship (on usage v Che).

II. נדה (√of foll., cf Ar. نَدِيَ *be moist, moistened,* and also *betide, befal;* نَدًى *rain, dew,* and also *bounty, liberality, a gift,* Lane^{3030})

†נֵדֶה (so Baer Ginsb; van d H. נֵדָה), **n.m.** gift (on format. cf. Ges$^{\S 84a\,c}$ Ol$^{\S 146a}$ Ko$^{\text{II 1.65}}$ Ba$^{\text{NB §12a}}$), —לְכָל־זֹנוֹת יִתְּנוּ־נֵדֶה Ez 16^{33} (‖ נְדָנַיִךְ).

†[נָדַח] **vb. impel, thrust, banish** (esp. Dt. Je. and later) (NH *id., beguile*, Hiph. Niph.; Aram. נְדַח (rare)=BH; Eth. ነደሐ: *thrust;* Ar. نَدَخَ is *drive* a ship to *shore*);—**Qal** *Impf.* יִדַּח 2 S 14^{14}; *Inf.* לִנְדֹּחַ Dt 20^{19};—trans. **1.** *impel* (i.e. *wield*) an axe, sq. עַל־ Dt 20^{19}; **2.** *thrust away, banish*, sq. מִן־ 2 S 14^{14}. **Niph.** *Pf.* 3 fs. נִדְּחָה Jb 6^{13}, etc.; (*Impf.* יִדַּחוּ Je 23^{12} v. דחח); *Pt.* נִדָּח 2 S 14^{14}; נִדָּחָה Mi 4^{6} + 2 t.; נִדַּחַת Ez $34^{4.16}$, etc. On נִדְּחֵי Is 11^{12} 56^{8} ψ 147^{2} v. Ki Kö $^{I.317}$;—**1.** *be impelled:* וְנִדְּחָה יָדוֹ בַגַּרְזֶן *be impelled* with the axe Dt 19^{5}. **2.** *be thrust out, banished:* of dispersion in exile, sq. שָׁם Je 40^{12} 43^{5} (‖ שׁוב); sq. לְפָנֵי 49^{5} (‖ קִבֵּץ); cf. also fig. תֻּשִׁיָּה נִדְּחָה מִמֶּנִּי Jb 6^{13} *is banished from me*, i.e. is non-existent; esp. Pt. *banished one(s), outcast(s)*, as acc. cogn. c. נִדָּח 2 S 14^{14}; c. קִבֵּץ Mi 4^{6} Dt 30^{4} Zp 3^{19} Ne 1^{9}; נִ׳ יִשְׂרָאֵל, c. אָסַף Is 11^{12} (‖ נְפֻצוֹת יְקַבֵּץ); c. קִבֵּץ 56^{8}; c. כִּנֵּס ψ 147^{2}; c. הֵשִׁיב 2 S 14^{13} Ez $34^{4.16}$ (both ‖ אֹבֵד); c. בּוֹא Is 27^{13} (‖ *id.*); v. also Is $16^{3.4}$ Je 49^{36}; *outcast = neglected one*, fig. of Zion 30^{17} (‖ דֹּרֵשׁ אֵין לָהּ). **3.** *driven away* (fr. herd, i.e.) *straying* Dt 22^{1}. **4.** *thrust away, aside*, from י׳ to idolatry Dt 4^{19} 30^{17} (sq. וְהִשְׁתַּחֲוָה).

Pu. *Pt.* אֲפֵלָה מְנֻדָּח Is 8^{22} *thrust into darkness*.

Hiph. *Pf.* הִדַּחְתִּי; וְהִדִּיחַ consec. 2 S 15^{14}; Je 23^{3} 29^{14}, etc.; *Impf.* sf. וַיַּדַּח 2 Ch 21^{11} + 2 K 17^{21} Qr; וַיַּדִּיחוּ Dt 13^{14}, etc.; *Imv.* sf. הַדִּיחֵמוֹ ψ 5^{11}; *Inf.* הַדִּיחַ 62^{5}, etc.;—**1.** *thrust, move, impel*, fig., obj. רָעָה 2 S 15^{14} (sq. עַל־). **2.** *thrust out, banish*, esp. of exile, subj. י׳, c. acc. sq. שָׁמָּה Dt 30^{1} Je 46^{28}; 16^{15} (‖ הֶעֱלָה); sq. שָׁם Je 8^{3} 24^{9} 29^{18} Dn 9^{7} + Ez 4^{13} (om. 𝔊 Co); Je 23^{3} (‖ קִבֵּץ), v^{8} (‖ הֵבִיא, הֶעֱלָה), 29^{14} (‖ הֵשִׁיב, קִבֵּץ), so 32^{37}; also 27^{10} (‖ הִרְחִיק), v^{15} (‖ אִבֵּד), cf. 23^{2} (Judah under fig. of flock, subj. evil shepherd, ‖ הֵפִיץ), 50^{17} (Isr. as sheep, subj. enemies as lions); of driving out priests 2 Ch 13^{9}; invader Jo 2^{20} (sq. אֶל־); wicked ψ 5^{11} (‖ הַאֲשִׁימֵם); good man from his eminence ψ 62^{5} (sq. מִן). **3.** *thrust away, aside*, from י׳ to idolatry, c. acc., Dt 13^{14}; sq. מִן־הַדֶּרֶךְ v^{6}; מֵעַל י׳ v^{11}; מֵאַחֲרֵי י׳ 2 K 17^{21} Qr (Kt v. נדא); cf. 2 Ch 21^{11} (‖ הִזְנָה). **4.** *compel, force*, subj. adulteress (by flattery), sq. acc. Pr 7^{21} (‖ הִטָּה).

Hoph. *Pt.* מֻדָּח *chased, hunted*, צְבִי מ׳ Is 13^{14}, sim. of fugitive Babylonians.

†[מַדּוּחַ] **n.[m.] a thing to draw aside, enticement** (cf. √ **Hiph. 3, 4**);—pl. מַדּוּחִים La 2^{14}, וַיֶּחֱזוּ לָךְ מַשְׂאוֹת שָׁוְא וּמ׳ (cf. ‖ שָׁוְא וְתָפֵל v^{a}).

† I. [נֵדֶן, נֶדֶן, נָדָן] **n.[m.] gift** (prob. As. loan-word, cf. As. *nudnu, dowry* Dl $^{HWB\ 451}$, √*nadânu*=נתן, Dl $^{Baer\ Ezech.\ xiv}$);—נְדָנַיִךְ Ez 16^{33}, of bribe from harlot (‖ נֵדֶה), metaph. of Jerusalem.

† II. [נָדָן] **n.[m.] sheath** (NH *id.;* Aram. נִדְנָא (𝔗 Talm.); Pers. loan-word Nö $^{GGA,\ 1884,\ 1022}$);—וַיָּשֶׁב חַרְבּוֹ אֶל־נְדָנָהּ׃ 1 Ch 21^{27}.

†[נָדַף] **vb. drive, drive asunder** (NH *id., spread, be diffused, disseminated* (of odour); Ar. نَدَفَ *strike, beat*, esp. bow-string with mallet, to clean cotton; also *play* the lyre; Aram. נְדַף = NH; Eth. ነደፈ: *throw, hurl*);—**Qal** *Impf.* sf. יִדְּפֶנּוּ Jb 32^{13} (juss.); 3 fs. sf. תִּדְּפֶנּוּ ψ 1^{4}; 2 ms. תִּנְדֹּף ψ 68^{3};—*drive about*, chaff, subj. wind ψ 1^{4}; wicked, subj. God 68^{3} (כְּהִנְדֹּף עָשָׁן, v. infr.); cf. Jb 32^{13} (= defeat, anguish).

Niph. *Pf.* נִדָּף Is 19^{7}; *Inf.* כְּהִנְדֹּף ψ 68^{3} (v. Kö $^{I.\ 306\ f.}$); *Pt.* נִדָּף Lv 26^{36} + 3 t.;—*be driven, driven about* (esp. by wind) ψ 68^{3}, v. supr. (like a driving [Che *drift*] of smoke); of breath (הֶבֶל) fig. of deceitful gain Pr 21^{6} (𝔊 Hi Ew רֹדֵף; v. De Now); of withered plant Is 19^{7} (where subj. עָרוֹת, מִזְרָע i.e. place; whence Che trans. נ׳ *vanish;* but ref. prob. to plant-life in these places, v. Di); of leaf Lv 26^{36} (as making slight sound), Jb 13^{25} (fig. of sufferer, ‖ קַשׁ יָבֵשׁ), of chaff (קַשׁ) Is 41^{2} (sim. of bow of hostile kings ‖ עָפָר).

†נָדַר **vb. vow** (NH *id.;* Ph. נדר; ‖ form of נָזַר, q.v.);—**Qal** *Pf.* 3 ms. נ׳ ψ 132^{2} 2 S 15^{8}; נָדַרְתָּ נֶדֶר Ju 11^{39}; 3 fs. נָדְרָה Nu 30^{11}; 2 ms. נָדַרְתָּ Gn 31^{13} + 5 t. Pf.; *Impf.* 3 ms. יִדֹּר Nu 6^{21} + 5 t.; 2 ms. תִּדֹּר Dt 12^{17} + 4 t., תִּדּוֹר Ec 5^{4} + 4 t. Impf.; *Imv.* pl. נִדְרוּ ψ 76^{12}; *Inf.* לִנְדֹּר Nu 6^{2} Dt 23^{23}; Pt. נֹדֵר Lv 27^{8} Mal 1^{14};—*vow a vow* נָדַר נֶדֶר Gn 28^{20} 31^{13} (both E), Nu 21^{2} (J), Nu 6^{2} $30^{3.4}$ (P), Ju 11^{30} 1 S 1^{11} 2 S $15^{8.7}$ Is 19^{21}; נֶדֶר om. Lv 27^{8} Nu 30^{11} (P); Dt 23^{23} ψ 76^{12} Ec $5^{4.4}$; c. לְ *to whom* Nu 6^{21} Dt 23^{24} Mal 1^{14} ψ 132^{2} Ec 5^{3}; נֶדֶר אֲשֶׁר נָדַר *vow which he vowed* Dt $12^{11.17}$ $23^{22.22}$ Ju 11^{39} Je 44^{25} Jon 1^{16}; cf. אֲשֶׁר נ׳ אֲשַׁלֵּמָה Jon 2^{10}, אֵת אֲשֶׁר תִּדֹּר שַׁלֵּם Ec 5^{3}.

†נֶדֶר, נֵדֶר **n.m.** $^{Nu\ 30,\ 5}$ **vow;**—נֶדֶר Gn 28^{20} + 17 t.; נֵדֶר Nu 30^{10} + 4 t.; sf. נִדְרִי 2 S 15^{7} + 5 t. sfs.; pl. נְדָרִים Jon 1^{16} Pr 20^{25}; sf. נְדָרַי ψ 22^{26}

+3 t., נדריהֶם Lv 22[18] + 24 t. sfs.;—*vow:* **1.** of personal service to י׳ Gn 28[20] 31[13] (of Jacob at Bethel), 2 S 15[7.8] (at Hebron), Lv 27[2] (P, any one), of Nazirite Nu 6[2.5.21]; Hannah's consecration of her son 1 S 1[11], cf. בר נדרי Pr 31[2] **2.** in gen. of any kind of votive offerings or promised gifts to י׳ Nu 30[3.4 5.5.6.7 8.9 10 12.13 14 15] (P) Dt 12[11 17 26] 23[19.22] Is 19[21] Na 2[1] ψ 22[26] 61[6 9] 65[2] 116[14 18] Pr 20[25] Jb 22[27] Ec 5[3]. **3.** Jephthah's daughter as עולה Ju 11[30.39]. **4.** the ban Nu 21[2] (E). **5.** ‖ עולה ψ 66[13], תוֹדָה ψ 50[14] 56[13], שְׁלָמִים Nu 15[8], opp. נדבה Lv 7[16] Nu 15[3] 29[39] (P), Lv 22[18.21 23] 23[38] (H), Dt 12[6 17] 1 S 1[21] Jon 1[16]. **6.** once of idolatry Je 44[25] (נ׳ לְקַטֵּר לִמְלֶכֶת הַשָּׁמַיִם).—Vbs. used are: נָדַר q.v.; שִׁלֵּם *pay* 2 S 15[7] + 12 t; עשׂה Ju 11[39] Je 44[25]; נשׂא Dt 12[26]; קום Nu 30[5.8 12 15], הקים Je 44[25]; אסר Nu 30[14]; פלא Lv 22[21] 27[2] Nu 15[3.8] פלא לנ׳ נ׳ Nu 6[2]; הפר Nu 30[9]. (See these vbs)

נֹהַּ v. נוה.

†I. **נָהַג** **vb. drive, conduct** (NH *conduct oneself, behave, be accustomed;* Ar. نَهَجَ *go along the road, keep to the road,* Aram נְהַג *lead*),—**Qal** *Pf* נ׳ La 3[2]; נָהֲגוּ 1 S 30[20]; *Impf* יִנְהַג Is 20[4], etc., *Imv* נְהַג 2 K 4[24]; *Pt. act* נֹהֵג Is 11[6] + 2 t., etc., *pass.* נהוגים Is 60[11];—**1.** *drive*, flocks Ex 3[1], cf (in predict) Is 11[6] (sq. בְּ); fig, obj. Joseph, ψ 80[2] (sim. of flock); hence, obj human being, *lead on*, Ct 8[2] (‖ הביא אֶל־); also fig., subj. י׳, La 3[2] (‖ הוליך); pass pt of kings *led* in procession Is 60[11] cf. Di (rather than as captives, Che, as earlier usage; ‖ הביא); *drive away, off*, (obj מקנה) Gn 31[18] (of Jacob, going by stealth), usually as booty (obj. flocks and herds) 1 S 23[5], חמור יתומים ינהגו Jb 24[3] (unjustly); cf. 1 S 30[2.20] (rd וַיִּנְהֲגוּ We Dr Kit Bu, cf. Th, not HPS q.v.), v[22] (no obj expr. but really captives ‖ הָלַךְ), Is 20[4], *drive* an ass for riding 2 K 4[24] (‖ הָלַךְ); a cart (עֲגָלָה) 2 S 6[3] = 1 Ch 13[7] (where בְּעֶ׳); abs of driving chariot 2 K 9[20], *lead out* an army to battle (late) 1 Ch 20[1] 2 Ch 25[11]. **2.** fig. וְלִבִּי נֹהֵג בַּחָכְמָה Ec 2[3] my heart *behaving itself* in wisdom (cf NH supr.) **Pi.** *Pf.* נִהַג Ex 10[3], נִהַגְתָּ Is 63[14], *Impf* יְנַהֵג Dt 4[27], etc.;—**1.** *drive away, lead off*, sq acc, daughters of Laban Gn 31[26] (‖ גָּנַב), of י׳, *leading off* people into exile, sq שָׁמָּה Dt 4[27] (‖ הפיץ), 28[37] (‖ הוליך) **2.** *lead on, guide*, sq acc, subj י׳, ψ 78[52] (כַּעֵדֶר ‖ הסיע כַּצֹּאן); Is 49[10] (‖ נהל, cf. ψ 23[2]); 63[14], ψ 48[15]; *guide on*, a wind, Ex 10[13] (sq בָּאָרֶץ), ψ 78[26] (‖ הסיע) **3.** *cause to drive* (cf. **Qal**, 2 K 9[20]) Ex 14[25] (JE, subj. י׳, v. Di).

†**מִנְהָג** **n.m. driving, charioteering**;—abs. מ׳ 2 K 9[20]; cstr מִנְהַג v[20].

†II. **[נָהַג]** **vb. Pi. moan, lament** (Ar. نَهَجَ *be out of breath, pant, breathe heavily;* Aram ܢܗܓ *sigh, groan*);—**Pi.** *Pt* fpl. מְנַהֲגוֹת Na 2[8] (כְּקוֹל יונים)

†**נָהָה** **vb. wail, lament** (prob. onomatop, cf. Sta[Gesch. I 388]; Aram. ܢܗܐ, (in Lexx); Eth. ንህየ: is *recreari, respirare*, etc Di[632]),—**Qal** *Pf.* וְנָהָה Mi 2[4] *lament* sq acc. cogn; *Imv* נהה Ez 32[18], sq. עַל, *concerning, for.* **Niph.** *Impf* וַיִּנָּהוּ 1 S 7[2] sq אַחֲרֵי *went mourning after* (so most, cf. Th Dr, who argue against Thes *were gathered*), < rd וַיִּפְנוּ (ויפנ(ה)), *turned after* = *submitted* to (as Ez 29[16]) 𝔊 (perh), We Kit Bu HPS.

†**נְהִי** **n.[m.] wailing, lamentation, mourning song**,—נ׳ abs Am 5[16] + 5 t; וּנְהִי Je 9[9],—*wailing*, at י׳'s judgment Mi 2[4] as acc. cogn.; Je 9[9] (c. בכי + נָשָׂא עַל־, ‖ קִינָה), v[17] (c. *id.*, ‖ דִּמְעָה), v[18] (קול נ׳), 31[15] (‖ בְּכִי, תַּמְרוּרִים); *mourning song* יודעי נ׳ Am 5[16] of professional mourners, skilled in mourning song; cf Je 9[19], where taught (‖ קִינָה), also הי Ez 2[10] (‖ אֵבֶל, מִסְפֵּד) q.v. (Ol Co rd. נהי, cf. Berthol)

†**נִהְיָה** **n.f.** *id.* (si vera l),—only Mi 2[4] נָהָה נהי נִהְיָה, where, however, Thes al. der. נהיה fr. היה (Niph, v. p. 228a supr.); but prob. corrupt, del. 𝔊 Sta[ZAW 1886, 122 f] We Now as dittogr.

†**[נִי]** **n.[m.]** si vera l., **wailing** (AV RV) (=נהי);—ונשׂאו אליך בניהם קינה Ez 27[32], but improb; 𝔊 𝔖 בְּנֵיהֶם, v MV, so Co, who, however, del. as gloss, cf. Buhl Berthol.

†**הִי** **n.[m.]** si vera l, **wailing** (=(נ)הי q v) Ez 2[10] וָהִי, where probably read ונהי Ol Co, cf Berthol (‖ קינים והגה)

†**[נָהַל]** **vb. Pi. lead, guide to a watering-place or station, and cause to rest there; bring to a station or place of rest; lead, guide; refresh** (cf. Ar. مَنْهَلٌ *watering-place,* نَهَلَ *take a first drink;* likewise (Dozy) مَنْهَلَةٌ *station, stage* of the road, perh also As. *nâlu, lie down* Dl[HWB 458]; Dl[HA 51, Prol. 178] tries to ex-

plain all the passages from this As. *nâlu;* against him v. Pra $^{LOPh\ i.\ 196}$ Che $^{Acad.,\ April\ 12,\ 1884}$ DHM $^{ZKF\ i\ 357\ f.}$ No $^{ZMG\ xl\ 1886,\ 723}$; *two* √√ prop. by RDWilson $^{Presb.\ Rev\ (N\ Y),\ April,\ 1885}$ (careful art.), cf. Che $^{\psi\ 23.\ 2,\ crit\ n}$);—**Pi.** *Pf* 2 ms. נֵהַלְתָּ Ex 15^{13}; *Impf* 3 ms. יְנַהֵל Is 40^{11}, sf. יְנַהֲלֵנִי ψ 23^{2}, יְנַהֲלֵם Is 49^{10}; וַיְנַהֲלֵם Gn 47^{17} 2 Ch 32^{22}; 2 ms. sf. תְּנַהֲלֵנִי ψ 31^{4}; 3 mpl. sf וַיְנַהֲלוּם 2 Ch 28^{15}; *Pt.* מְנַהֵל Is 51^{18},—**1.** *lead to a watering-place (or station), and cause to rest there,* subj. ′י as shepherd, Is 49^{10} (עַל־ loc., ‖ נהג), ψ 23^{2} (c. עַל־ loc.; ‖ הרביץ), Is 40^{11} (‖ רעה, קבץ) **2.** *lead* or *bring to a station, a goal,* ′י subj. Ex 15^{13} (song; no obj expressed, אֶל־ loc., ‖ נחה), human subj. 2 Ch 28^{15} *and they conducted* all the feeble of them *by means of* (ב) *asses* (‖ הביא). **3.** *lead, guide:* fig, אין מְנַהֵל לָהּ Is 51^{18} *there is no one to be a guide for her,* i e for Jerus, drunk with cup of ′י's fury (‖ מַחֲזִיק בְּיָדָהּ); ′י subj. ψ 31^{4} *lead me* (‖ תַּנְחֵנִי). **4.** *give rest to* (?) וַיְנ׳ מִסָּבִיב 2 Ch 32^{22} *and he gave them rest on every hand,* cf. 𝔊 𝔙 (=וַיָּנַח לָהֶם מִס׳ 1 Ch 22^{18}+, prob. so read here, v. Be DHM Ot) **5.** *refresh* with food, וַיְנ׳ בַּלֶּחֶם Gn 47^{17} (J).

Hithp. *Impf* prob *journey by stations, stages,* only 1 s. אֶתְנַהֲלָה Gn 33^{14} (J), *I will proceed, journey on, by stages* (i.e. deliberately, with family and cattle)

נַהֲלָל v. n. נַהֲלָל.

†I. **נַהֲלֹל** **n.m.** pasture, or perh. (EncBi ^{614}) *watering-place* (see √), only pl. נַהֲלֹלִים Is 7^{19}.

II. **נַהֲלֹל** **n.pr.loc.** Ju 1^{30} in Zebulun, 𝔊 Δωμανα, A Εναμμαν, 𝔊L Αμμαν; = נַהֲלָל Jos 19^{15} 21^{35}, 𝔊 Ναβααλ, Νααλωλ, 𝔊L Αναλωθ, Αλωμ;—site unknown, cf GFM $^{Ju\ 1.\ 30}$.

†[**נָהַם**] **vb.** growl, groan (NH *id.;* Ar. نَهَمَ; Aram. ܢܗܡ, נהם),—**Qal** *Pf.* וְנָהַמְתָּ Pr 5^{11}; וּנְהַמְתֶּם Ez 24^{23}, *Impf* יִנְהֹם Is $5^{29.30}$; *Pt* נֹהֵם Pr 28^{15};—**1.** *growl,* of a lion (viz. while it is devouring its prey. opp. שׁאג, of *roar* with which it springs upon it RS $^{Proph\ 243}$) Pr 28^{15}, of Assyr. (under fig. of lion) Is 5^{29}; sq עַל (*over*), v^{30}. **2.** *groan,* of sufferer Pr 5^{11} Ez 24^{23}.

†**נַהַם** **n.[m.]** growling of lion;—fig. of king's wrath Pr 19^{12}, cf. 20^{2}.

†[**נְהָמָה**] **n.f.** growling, groaning,—only cstr. נַהֲמַת: **1.** Is 5^{30} of sea, in sim. of growling of Assyr. lion. **2.** fig. *groaning* ψ 38^{9} of heart (שָׁאַגְתִּי מִנ׳).

†[**נָהַק**] **vb.** bray, cry (NH *id;* Ar. نَهَقَ *bray* (of ass); Aram נהק *cry out* (of men), נְהִיקָא *braying*),—**Qal** *Impf.* יִנְהַק Jb 6^{5} of wild ass; יִנְהָקוּ 30^{7} of cries of destitute outcasts.

†I. [**נָהַר**] **vb.** flow, stream (Ar. نَهَرَ *run, flow;* perh. denom. fr. نَهْر *river,* and this loan-wd. (cf. Fra ^{286}), As. *nâru, stream, river,* Dl $^{HWB\ 449}$; Aram. ܢܗܪܐ, נַהֲרָא *river*),—**Qal** *Pf.* 3 pl. consec. וְנָהֲרוּ Is 2^{2}+2 t.; *Impf.* 3 mpl יִנְהֲרוּ Je 51^{44};—*flow, stream,* only fig: of restored Isr. streaming אֶל־טוּב ′י עַל־דָּגָן וגו׳ Je 31^{12}; nations to (אֶל־) Bel 51^{44}; to temple-hill at Jerus. Is 2^{2} (אֵלָיו) = Mi 4^{1} (עָלָיו).

נָהָר $_{120}$ **n.m.** $^{Gn\ 2.\ 10}$ stream, river;—abs. נ׳ Gn 2^{10}+; cstr נְהַר Dt 1^{7}+; pl. נְהָרִים Is 18^{2} +4 t., cstr. נַהֲרֵי Is 18^{1}+2 t; but oftener נְהָר(וֹ)ת Is 19^{6}+23 t.; cstr. נַהֲרוֹת 2 K 5^{12}+2 t.; sf. נַהֲרֹתֶיךָ Ez 32^{2}, נַהֲרֹתַיִךְ Is 44^{27}, נַהֲרֹתֶיהָ Ez $31^{4.15}$, נַהֲרֹתָם Ex 7^{19}, נַהֲרוֹתָם Ez $32^{2\ 14}$; appar. du. נַהֲרַיִם Gn 24^{10}+2 t., נַהֲרָיִם Ju 3^{8} (v. infr.) (all in אֲרַם נ׳),—**1.** *stream, river,* Nu 24^{6} (JE), Jb 14^{11} 40^{23} ψ 105^{41} (in sim.), Is 48^{18} (*id.*), 59^{19} (*id*)+oft.; freq of partic. rivers; r. of Eden Gn 2^{10} and its branches $v^{13.14}$ (all J); נְהַר מִצְרַיִם 15^{18} (J; i e, si vera l., the Nile) but rd. prob. נַחַל מ׳, whence נהר through infl. of foll. נהר—cf. 2 K 24^{7}—No $^{ZMG\ xl\ 1886,\ 699}$ (alternat.), Lag $^{BN\ 140}$ Ball ^{Hpt}; נָהָר of Nile Is 19^{5}; esp. of Euphrates נְהַר פְּרָת Gn 15^{18} Dt 1^{7} (both + הַנָּ׳ הַגָּדוֹל) Jos 1^{4} +8 t. + 2 S 8^{3} (Qr 𝔊 and ‖ 1 Ch 18^{3}; Kt om. פרת;—cf also Gn $2^{14\ b}$ supr.); oftener (of Euphr) without פ׳ · הַנָּהָר κατ' ἐξοχήν, Gn 31^{21} Ex 23^{31} Nu 22^{5} Jos $24^{2.3.14\ 15}$ (all E), poss. also Gn 36^{37} (P; cf. Di) = 1 Ch 1^{48}, +13 t. + 2 S 8^{3} Kt (v. supr), and even without art. (poet.) + Is 7^{20} Je 2^{18} Mi 7^{12} Zc 9^{10} ψ 72^{8}; הַנּ׳ הַגּ׳ once of Tigris + Dn 10^{4}; + נְהַר גּוֹזָן (חבור) 2 K 17^{6} 18^{11} cf 2 Ch 5^{26}; pl. נַהֲרֵי כוּשׁ Zp 3^{10}; perh. of a *canal:* נְהַר־כְּבָר Ez $1^{1.3}$+6 t. Ez; הַנָּהָר אַהֲוָא Ezr 8^{21}, נהר א׳, v^{31}; cf נַהֲרוֹת בָּבֶל ψ 137^{1}; *canals* poss. also in שַׁעֲרֵי הַנּ׳ Na 2^{7} (of Nineveh); of *canals* of Egypt Ex 7^{19} (‖ יְאֹרִים etc.), 8^{1} (‖ *id.*). **2.** (מִבְּכִי) נְהָרוֹת Jb 28^{11} usu. understood of (*underground*) *streams;* Szold $^{Comm.\ Jb}$ Gr $^{Monatsschr\ 1887,\ 410}$ and Perles $^{Analekten\ 69}$ prop. נִבְכֵי נ׳ *sources of rivers* (cf. 36^{16}), Wetzst Hoffm Bu מִבְּכִי נ׳

(not elsewh.) with similar meaning. **3.** fig. of 'י's favour ψ 46^{5}.—On נַהֲרַיִם ending appar. du., v. אֲרָם; Tel Am. *Na-ri-ma, Naḥrima* (Wkl [Tel Am. 40*]), and Eg. *Nhrina* (WMM [As. u. Eur. 249 ff.]) point however to orig. ending ־ַיִם; this inconsistent with view of EMey [Gesch. § 180] that ־ַיִם here a *locative* ending (cf. Ba [§ 194 c. Anm. 1] Buhl [Ges 12]), v. also Di [Gn 24, 10].

†II. **נָהַר** **vb. shine, beam** (Aram.) (NH *id.*, esp. in deriv.; As. *nûru, light*, Dl [HWB 440]; Ar. نَهَرٌ *daytime*, نَهَارٌ *day, daytime;* Aram. ܢܗܰܪ *shine*, נְהַר *id.;* Palm. נהירא *illustrious*, e. g. Vog [Palm. No. 22]);—**Qal** *Pf.* 2 fs. consec. וְנָהַרְתְּ Is 60^{5}; 3 pl. נָהָרוּ ψ 34^{6};—*beam, be radiant*, fig. of joy: תִּרְאִי וְנ׳ Is 60^{5}, הִבִּיטוּ אֵלָיו וְנ׳ ψ 34^{6} (rd. הַבִּ׳, וּנְהָרוּ, v. 𝔊 𝔖 𝔙 Che Bae Du).

†**נְהָרָה** **n.f. light, daylight** (as Aram. נְהוֹרָא, ܢܘܗܪܳܐ m.);—וְאַל־תּוֹפַע עָלָיו נ׳ Jb 3^{4} (opp. חֹשֶׁךְ).

†[**מִנְהָרָה**] **n.f.** dub., only pl. הַמִּנְהָרוֹת אֲשֶׁר בֶּהָרִים Ju 6^{2} (+ הַמְּעָרוֹת *caves*, הַמְּצָדוֹת *strongholds*)—(clearly, si vera l., fr. a √ נהר, but with what meaning? Schultens [Jb 49] comp. Ar. مِنْهَرٌ, مِنْهَرَةٌ [which means *a place hollowed out by water*], and rend. *crevices, ravines*, so Thes al.; Rashi Ki Wetzst [Hauran, 46] think of caves with a *light*-opening; R. Levi ben Gerson *beacons*, i.e. towers for fire-signals, GFM; but II. נהר late in Heb.; 𝔊 τρυμαλίας, 𝔙 *antra;* Bu thinks הַמְּעָרוֹת a gloss explaining הַמִּנ׳).

†[**נוּא**] **vb. hinder, restrain, frustrate** (Ar. (نوأ) نَآءَ (or نَآءَ) *rise with difficulty, rise against one* (Frey), III. *contend with*, Lane [2861]);—**Qal** *Impf.* 2 mpl. תנואון Nu 32^{7} Kt, but read Hiph. (so Qr), cf. Di. **Hiph.** *Pf.* הֵנִיא Nu 30^{6}, etc.; *Impf.* יָנִיא v^{9}, יָנִי ψ 141^{5}, תְּנִיאוּן Nu 32^{7} Qr;—**1.** *restrain, forbid* (performance of vow), sq. acc. pers. Nu $30^{6.6.9.12}$; *frustrate* (device of people), subj. 'י, sq. acc. rei, ψ 33^{10} (‖ הֵפִיר); *refuse* 141^{5} (text dub. v. Che). **2.** *restrain, make averse* the heart (acc.) Nu 32^{7} (sq. מֵעֲבֹר), v^{9} (sq. לְבִלְתִּי־בֹא).

†[**תְּנוּאָה**] **n.f. opposition;**—sf. תְּנוּאָתִי Nu 14^{34} *my opposition*, of 'י; pl. תְּנוּאוֹת עָלַי יִמְצָא Jb 33^{10} = occasions for hostility (‖ count as enemy).

†[**נוּב**] **vb. bear fruit** (poet.) (Aram. נוֹבָא *fruit* (rare));—**Qal** *Impf.* יָנוּב ψ 62^{11} Pr 10^{31}; יְנוּבוּן ψ 92^{15};—only fig., abs. of righteous under fig. of tree ψ 92^{15}; חַיִל כִּי יָנוּב 62^{11} if wealth *beareth fruit;* Pr 10^{31} פִּי צַדִּיק יָנוּב חָכְמָה *beareth the fruit of* wisdom. **Po'l.** *Impf.* יְנוֹבֵב Zc 9^{17}, דָּגָן בַּחוּרִים וְתִירוֹשׁ יְנ׳ בְּתֻלוֹת fig. for *makes to flourish*.

†**נוֹב** Kt (Qr נִיב, q.v.) **n.[m.] fruit;**—cstr. Is 57^{19} *fruit of lips* (fig. for thanksgiving).

†[**נִיב**] **n.[m.] fruit;**—נִיב cstr. Is 57^{19} Qr, v. supr.; נִיבוֹ Mal 1^{12} of offerings to 'י as fruit of his table (‖ אכלו).

†**נוֹבַי** **n.pr.m.** a chief of people Ne 10^{20} Qr נֵיבָי (Baer; נֵיבַי van d. H., Ginsb; 𝔊 Νωβαι (cf. Palm. נבי n.pr.f. Cook [124] Lzb [321]).

תְּנוּבָה **n.f. fruit, produce;**—abs. Is 27^{6}; cstr. תְּנוּבַת Ez 36^{30}; תְּנוּבָתִי Ju 9^{11}; pl. תְּנוּבֹת Dt 32^{13}, ־וֹת La 4^{9}; esp. ת׳ שָׂדָי *fruit, produce, of field* Dt 32^{13} La 4^{9}; cf. ת׳ הַשָּׂדֶה Ez 36^{30} (‖ פרי העץ); of fig-tree Ju 9^{11}; metaph. of Isr. וּמָלְאוּ פְנֵי־תֵבֵל ת׳ Is 27^{6} (‖ יַשְׁרֵשׁ יעקב יציץ ופרח ישׂ׳).

†**נוּד** **vb. move to and fro, wander, flutter, shew grief** (NH *id.* (rare); Aram. נוּד, ܢܘܕ, *shake, move to and fro, be disturbed, agitated;* BAram. *flee* (v. infr.); Ar. (نود) نَادَ *waver, totter*);—**Qal** *Pf.* 3 ms. נָד, so rd. for MT נֵד Is 17^{11} Ges Hi Ew Di Kit Che [Hpt] RV; 3 pl. נָדוּ Je 50^{3}; *Impf.* 3 ms. יָנוּד 1 K 14^{15} + 3 t.; 2 ms. תָּנוּד Je 4^{1}, juss. תָּנֹד 16^{5}; 3 mpl. וַיָּנֻדוּ Jb 42^{11}; 2 mpl. תָּנֻדוּ Je 22^{10}; *Imv.* fs. נוּדִי ψ 11^{1} Qr (Kt נודו); mpl. נֻדוּ Je 48^{17} + 2 t. Je; *Inf.* לָנוּד Jb 2^{11} + 2 t.; *Pt.* נָד Gn $4^{12.14}$;—**1. a.** *move to and fro, wander* aimlessly, as fugitive, נָע וָנָד Gn $4^{12.14}$ (J), Je 4^{1} (Gie, as apod., so RV; but Ew Hi Gf Che Ke, as prot., *if thou wanderest not* [morally], and swearest, etc.,—Ew Hi reading with 𝔊 שקוציך מִפִּיךָ וּמִפָּנַי לא תנוד; Co del. $v^{1.2}$); *take flight* (perh. metaplast. form of נדד q.v.), נָסוּ נָדוּ מְאֹד Je 49^{30} (on dagh. v. Ges [§ 20 g]), of harvest Is 17^{11} i.e. be destroyed, in fig. (v. supr.); Je 50^{3} (‖ הלך), v^{8} (sq. מִתּוֹךְ; ‖ יצא). **b.** *flutter*, of bird Pr 26^{2} (‖ עוּף); fig. of soul ψ 11^{1}. **c.** *waver, wave, shake*, of reed 1 K 14^{15} (sim. of smitten Isr.). **2.** *shew grief* (i.e. by shaking or nodding head), usu. sq. לְ pers.: **a.** *lament* for the dead (Josiah) Je 22^{10} (‖ בכה), for Jerus. Je 15^{5} (‖ חמל), 16^{5} (‖ ספד), Is 51^{19}; for Nineveh Na 3^{7}; Moab Je 48^{17}. **b.** *condole, shew sympathy* with Jb 2^{11} 42^{11}; abs. ψ 69^{21}. **Hiph.** *Impf.* 3 ms. יָנִיד Je 18^{16}; 3 fs. sf. תְּנִידֵנִי ψ 36^{12}; *Imv.* ms. sf. הֲנִידֵמוֹ ψ 59^{12} (so rd. for MT הורידמו 𝔖 Lag [Proph. Chald. xlviii.] Dr [2 S 15, 20] cf. Che [crit. n.] Hup-Now Bae Du); *Inf.* לְהָנִיד 2 K 21^{8};—

1. *cause to wander* aimlessly, as fugitives, c. acc. pers. ψ 36^{12} 59^{12} (v. supr.), sq. רֶגֶל 2 K 21^{8}. **2.** *make a wagging, wag* with the head, בְּרֹאשׁ Je 18^{16}. **Hoph.** *Pt.* כְּקוֹץ מֻנָד 2 S 23^{6} and the worthless, *like briers made to flutter* (tossed away) are they (text dub.; Klo Bu HPS rd. מִדְבָּר). **Hithpo'lel** *Pf.* 3 fs. וְהִתְנוֹדְדָה consec. Is 24^{20}; *Impf.* 2 ms. תִּתְנוֹדָד Je 48^{27}; *Pt.* מִתְנוֹדֵד Je 31^{18};—**1.** *move oneself to and fro, sway, totter,* Is 24^{20} (of earth). **2.** *shake oneself,* in excitement Je 48^{27} (perh. of scorn = *wag* the head, as Hiph. Je 18^{16} cf. Gf RV). **3.** *bemoan oneself* (cf. **Qal 2**), Je 31^{18} (the lament follows in orat. recta).

†I. [נוֹד, נֹד] **n.[m.]** **wandering** of aimless fugitive;—only sf. נֹדִי ψ 59^{9} *my wandering* (word-play with נֹאדֶךָ v^{b}).

†II. נוֹד appar. **n.pr.terr.** אֶרֶץ־נ׳ Gn 4^{16} of region into which Cain wandered (cf. $v^{12.14}$); 𝔊 (strangely) Ναιδ; 𝔙 appellat., *profugus* in terra, cf. Symm Theod, v. Ne[Marg. 9].

† נִיד **n.m.**[(v. infr.)] **quivering motion of lips**;—only cstr. נִיד שְׂפָתַי Jb 16^{5} *the motion of my lips* (in expressing sympathy).—MT makes subj. of יַחְשֹׂךְ, but rd. prob. אֶחְשֹׂךְ, v. חשׂך.

נִידָה v. נִדָּה sub נדד.

†[מָנוֹד] **n.[m.]** **a shaking, wagging**;—only cstr. מְנוֹד רֹאשׁ ψ 44^{15} *object of head-shaking,* in derision (of Isr.; ‖ מָשָׁל; v^{14} חֶרְפָּה, לַעַג, קֶלֶס).

נוה (prob. √of foll., si vera l., cf. Ar. نَاهَ (نوه) *be high, eminent*).

† נֹהַּ **n.[m.]** **eminency, distinction**;—לֹא נֹהַּ בָּהֶם Ez 7^{11} *no eminency is left in them* (so A𝔊 Theod Symm Ges Ke), < del. 𝔊B Co Berthol Toy, cf. also Da.

†I. [נָוָה] **vb.** only **Hiph.** (si vera l.) lit. **beautify** (then connected with נאה *be comely,* so Buhl SS; cf. NH נוה Niph. *shew oneself beautiful,* Nithp. *adorn oneself,* נָוֶה adj. *beautiful,* Levy[NHWB]);—*Impf.* 1 s. sf. אַנְוֵהוּ Ex 15^{2} *I will beautify, adorn him* (with praises; obj. י׳; ‖ רוממ; 𝔊 δοξάσω, 𝔙 *glorificabo*).—Adj. נָוֶה Je 6^{2}, v. נָאוֶה sub [נָאָה].

II. **נוה** (√of foll., mng. dub.; Ar. نَوَى is *aim at, propose to oneself as aim* (e.g. of journey), VIII. *betake oneself to a place of alighting,* or *abode;* نِيَّةٌ, نَوًى *place to which one purposes journeying* Lane[3040]; hence poss. I. נָוֶה as goal of shepherd; cf. Sab. נוי *meadow, pasture,* DHM [Südar. Alt. 32]; see however Dr[1 S 19.18] HPS[ib.]; NH נָוֶה *dwelling, habitation*).

†I. נָוֶה **n.m.**[Is 27.10] **abode of shepherd, or flocks, poet. habitation**;—abs. Is 27^{10}+; cstr. נְוֵה Ex 15^{13}+; נְוַת Jb 8^{6} (as if fr. נָוָה; or rd. נְוֵה ?); sf. נָוְךָ Jb 5^{24}, נָוֵהוּ 2 S 15^{25}+, נְוֵהֶם Je 49^{20} Ez 34^{14} (cf. Sta[§ 351 c.]), נְוֵהֶן Je 23^{3} (so Baer Ginsb; נְוִיהֶן van d. H., pl. acc. to Kö[II. 1, p. 77]);—**1.a.** *abode,* of sheep 2 S 7^{8} (‖ מֵאַחַר הַצֹּאן) = 1 Ch 17^{7}; Is 65^{10} (‖ רֵבֶץ); of people under fig. of sheep Je 23^{3} 49^{20} = 50^{45}, 50^{19} Ez $34^{14.14}$ (‖ רֵבֶץ, מִרְעֶה); of camels Ez 25^{5} (‖ מִרְבַּץ צֹאן). **b.** *abode of shepherds* Je 33^{12} (+ מַרְבִּיצִים צֹאן). **c.** = *meadow,* in fig. of Ephr. planted (שְׁתוּל) as tree Ho 9^{13}. **2.** *habitation,* usu. of country, or of domains in the country (chiefly poet.), Jb 5^{3} 8^{6} (נְוַת צִדְקֶךָ, v. supr.), Pr 21^{20}; ‖ אֹהֶל Jb 5^{24} 18^{15}; ‖ בַּיִת Pr 3^{33}; ‖ רֵבֶץ 24^{15}; of י׳ in Canaan 2 S 15^{25}; of Can. as place of י׳'s sanctuary, נ׳ קָדְשֶׁךָ Ex 15^{13}; fig. of י׳ himself, נ׳ צֶדֶק Je 50^{7}; habit. of nation Je 10^{25} 25^{30} Is 32^{18} (נ׳ שָׁלוֹם), ψ 79^{7}; = city Is 27^{10}, esp. Jerus. Is 33^{20} (נ׳ שַׁאֲנָן ‖ אֹהֶל); נ׳ אֵיתָן Je 49^{19} (fig. of Edom) = 50^{44} (of Bab.); of land of Isr., נ׳ צֶדֶק Je 31^{23} (‖ הַר הַקֹּדֶשׁ). Twice of habitation of jackals Is 34^{13} 35^{7} (both ‖ חָצִיר).

†I. [נָוָה] **vb. denom.** **dwell, abide** (si vera l.);—only **Qal** *Impf.* 3 ms. לֹא יִנְוֶה Hb 2^{5} *he shall not abide,* so Ke; Hi *rest* (cf. Da); We prop. יִרְוֶה *be satiated,* cf. 𝔖; Krochm יָנוּחַ.

†II. [נָוָה] **adj.** **dwelling, abiding**;—only (si vera l.) נְוַת בַּיִת ψ 68^{13} *she that is abiding at home.*—נָוָה Je 6^{2} v. נָאוָה sub [נָאָה].

†II. [נָוָה] **n.f.** **pasture, meadow**;—pl. cstr. נְוֹת Zp 2^{6}, usu. נְאוֹת ψ 23^{2}+11 t.;—**1.** *pasture, meadow:* נ׳ הָרֹעִים Am 1^{2}, cf. Zp 2^{6} (‖ גִּדְרוֹת צֹאן; v. also [כָּרָה] p. 500 supr.); esp. נְאוֹת (הַ)מִּדְבָּר Je 9^{9} 23^{10} ψ 65^{13} Jo $1^{19.20}$ 2^{22}; נ׳ דֶּשֶׁא ψ 23^{2} *grassy pastures;* נ׳ אֱלֹהִים ψ 83^{13} *pastures of God,* i.e. the land of Canaan, נ׳ יַעֲקֹב La 2^{2}; נ׳ הַשָּׁלוֹם Je 25^{37} *meadows of peace;* נ׳ חָמָס ψ 74^{20} appar. *habitations* (?) *of violence,* but rd. prob. נְאֻוָה וְח׳, so Bi Che (v. 73^{6}).—Je 6^{2} v. foll.; Jb 8^{6} v. I. נָוֶה.

† נוית Kt (i.e. נָוִית, or נְוָיֹת, Ginsb), נָיוֹת Qr; prob. **n.pr.loc.** in Ramah (poss. = *habitations,* but dub., v. Dr[1 S 19.18] HPS);—abode of prophets 1 S $19^{18.19.22.23.23}$ and 20^{1} (where Baer

נוות Kt); sq. בָּרָמָה (exc 19^{18}), 𝔊 Ἀυαθ (ν dropped out after ιν), so 𝔊 L; Α Ναυιωθ

† **נוּחַ** **vb. rest** (NH *id*; Aram. נוּחַ, نَاحَ, Ph נחת n *rest*; poss also vb. ינח (Iph. Pf), cf Levy cited CIS$^{i. 118}$ Lzb^{322}; As *nâhu*, *rest* (*inûh*), and deriv; Eth ኖኀ: *be extended, long*, rarely *rest*, Ar ناخ iv. is *make camel lie down* on his breast; مُنَاخ *resting-place of camel*, cf Doughty$^{Arab. Des i, 397 ii, 63, 486 642}$),—**Qal** *Pf.* 3 fs. נָחָה Is 7^{2} + 2 t, consec וְנָחָה Is 11^{2}, 1 s נַחְתִּי Jb 3^{26}; 3 pl נָחוּ Est 9^{22}, consec וְנָחוּ Is 7^{19}, *Impf* 3 ms יָנוּחַ Ex 23^{12} + 6 t, וַיָּנַח Ex 10^{14} 20^{11}, 3 fs תָּנוּחַ Is 25^{10} Pr 14^{33}, וַתָּנַח Gn 8^{4} Nu 11^{26}, 2 ms תָּנוּחַ Dn 12^{13} etc; *Inf abs.* נוֹחַ Est 9$^{16\ 17\ 18}$; *cstr.* לָנוּחַ 2 S 21^{10}, כנוח Nu 11^{25} Jos 3^{13} Ne 9^{28}, sf 3 ms בנחה Nu 10^{36},—לְנוּחֶךָ 2 Ch 6^{41} v. מְנוּחָה.—**1.** *rest, settle down and remain*, sq עַל, of birds 2 S 21^{10}, ark Gn 8^{4} (P), נָחָה אֲרָם עַל־אֶפְרָיִם Is 7^{2} *Aram hath settled down upon Ephraim*, of spirit of י׳ Nu 11$^{25\ 26}$ (E), Is 11^{2}; spirit of Elijah 2 K 2^{15}, sceptre of wicked ψ 125^{3} (in fig), sq בְּ loc: of insects Ex 10^{14} (J), Is 7^{19} (fig. of invaders), of soles of feet *resting* in water Jos 3^{13} (JE); hand of י׳ Is 25^{10}, wisdom Pr 14^{33}, anger Ec 7^{9}; בִּקְהַל רְפָאִים יָנוּחַ Pr 21^{16} *in the assembly of Shades shall he settle down*; abs., = *stop*, of ark at stages of journey Nu 10^{36} (JE); *cease* speaking 1 S 25^{9}. **2.** *repose, be quiet, have rest:* after labour Ex 20^{11} (E, of God), 23^{12} (E; of cattle), Dt 5^{14} (of slave); *have rest from* (מִן) enemies Est 9^{16} (inf. abs. נוֹחַ + עָמוֹד, הָרוֹג), v^{22}, cf (abs.) v$^{17\ 18}$ (in both + עָשֹׂה), Ne 9^{28}, *be at rest* (from trouble), abs, Jb 3^{26} (+ שָׁקַטְתִּי, שָׁלַוְתִּי), of the earth Is 14^{7}, in couch of the grave 57^{2}, in Sheʾôl Jb 3^{17}, so prob Dn 12^{13}, also לֹא תָנוּחַ לָךְ Is 23^{12} = *thou shalt not be at rest*, cf. impers יָנוּחַ לִי Jb 3^{13} = *I should be at rest* (in Sheʾôl).—אָנוּחַ לְיוֹם צָרָה Hb 3^{16} is dub.: *I wait quietly for the day of distress* De Ke Hi-St SS, so Now, doubtfully; We conj. אֶנָּחֵם as Is 1^{24} *I will appease me*, GASm leaves untransl **Hiph. A.** *Pf* 3 ms הֵנִיחַ Jos 22^{4} +; 1 s וַהֲנִיחֹתִי 2 S 7^{11} +, הֵנִיחוּ Zc 6^{8}, *Impf* 3 ms יָנִיחַ Ex 17^{11} +; וַיָּנַח Jos 21^{42} +; sf. וַיְנִיחֵנִי Ez 37^{1} 40^{2}, 3 fs sf. תְּנִיחֶנּוּ Is 63^{14} (but v infr), etc, *Imv* mpl. הָנִיחוּ Is 28^{12}; *Inf. cstr.* הָנִיחַ Is 14^{3} +, sf הֲנִיחִי Ez 24^{13}, *Pt.* מֵנִיחַ Jos 1^{13},—**1.** *cause to rest* = *give rest* to. **a.** sq. acc. יָדוֹ Ex 17^{11} (E), רוּחִי Zc 6^{8}, so appar. sq בְּ + חֲמָתִי pers., *quiet* (i e sate) *my fury by* (wreak it upon) Ez 5^{13} (del Co), 16^{42} 24^{13}, also 21^{22} (Co adds בְּ pers.) **b.** usu. sq. לְ pers.: (1) *give rest to* i e. bring to resting-place Ex 33^{14} (J), Dt 3^{20} Jos 1$^{13\ 15}$ 22^{4} (all D), 1 Ch 23^{25}; so, c sf, Is 63^{14} (si vera l, Vrss Lo Ew Brd Che^{Hpt} rd תַּנְחֶנּוּ, *leadeth him*, √נחה), (2) of freedom from enemies, Is 28^{12} 2 Ch 14^{5}, + מִכָּל־אֹיְבִים [מִסָּבִיב] Dt 12^{10} 25^{19} Jos 23^{1} (D), 2 S 7$^{1\ 11}$ 1 Ch 22^{9}; so + מִסָּבִיב alone 1 K 5^{18} Jos 21^{42} (P), 1 Ch 22^{18} 2 Ch 14^{6} 15^{15} 20^{30}, so also prob. 32^{22} (for MT וַיְנַהֲלֵם מסביב), (3) of freedom from suffering, + מֵעָצְבְּךָ וגו׳ Is 14^{3}. **c.** *make quiet* in mind, *set at rest* וִינִיחֶךָ Pr 29^{17} discipline thy son, *that he may give thee quiet* (of mind, ‖ יִתֵּן מַעֲדַנִּים לְנַפְשֶׁךָ) **2.** *cause to rest* (i e *light*) upon, c. acc *staff* + עַל pers. Is 30^{32}; c acc. *blessing* + אֶל־ Ez 44^{30}, *cause to alight, set down*, c sf pers. + בְּתוֹךְ loc Ez 37^{1}; + אֶל־ loc. 40^{2}.—For this mng. v. esp **B.** infr **B.** *Pf.* 3 ms הִנִּיחַ Ju 3^{1} +, הִנַּח 1 K 8^{9}, sf וְהִנִּיחוֹ Dt 26^{4}, והניחם Lv 16^{23} both consec., 2 ms. וְהִנַּחְתָּ Dt 14^{28}, sf וְהִנַּחְתּוֹ 26^{10} consec., etc.; *Impf.* 3 ms. יַנִּיחַ Lv 7^{15}, וַיַּנַּח Ju 2^{23} +, sf. וַיַּנִּיחֵהוּ Ex 16^{34}, 3 fs. וַתַּנַּח Gn 39^{16}; 2 ms juss אַל־תַּנַּח Ec 7^{18} + 2 t, etc, *Imv.* ms הַנַּח Ho 4^{7} + 2 t, הַנִּיחָה Ex 32^{10} Ju 16^{26}, etc; *Inf cstr.* sf לְהַנִּיחוֹ Nu 32^{15}, לְהַנִּיחָם Est 3^{8}; *Pt* מַנִּיחַ Ec 5^{11};—**1.** *lay* or *set down, deposit, let lie*, c acc. rei, usu. + word of place: stones at ford of Jordan Jos 4$^{3.8}$ (JE), ark 1 S 6^{18}, garments Gn 39^{16} (J), Lv 16^{23} (P), Ez 42^{14} 44^{19}; cf Ex 16$^{23.24.33.34}$ Nu 17$^{19\ 22}$ (all P), Dt 26$^{4.10}$ 1 K 8^{9} 13^{31} Ez 40^{42} 42^{13}; so, acc. om, Ju 6$^{18.20}$ Dt 14^{28} Nu 19^{9} (P), 1 S 10^{25}, *place, put*, sq acc. pers + local modif, Gn 2^{15} (J), 19^{16} (J), Jos 6^{23} (JE), Lv 24^{12} Nu 15^{34} (both P), Is 14^{1} 46^{7} Ez 37^{14}; prob. also Zc 5^{11} (rd. וְהִנִּיחֻהָ, v. Ges$^{§ 72\ ee}$), rd. וַיַּנִּיחֵם also 2 K 18^{11} (𝔊 ἔθετο; for MT וַיַּנְחֵם; cf. וַיֵּשֶׁב אוֹתָם ‖ 2 K 17^{6}); *place* corpse on (אֶל־) ass 1 K 13^{29}, in grave v^{30}, horsemen and chariots in cities 2 Ch 1^{14} 9^{25}, so rd also ‖ 1 K 10^{26} (𝔊 ἔθετο, for MT וַיַּנְחֵם), tables in temple 2 Ch 4^{8}, idols in shrines 2 K 17^{29} (acc. om). Here belongs perh also וְגַם מִזֶּה אַל־תַּנַּח אֶת־יָדֶךָ Ec 7^{18} *and also from this do not let thy hand lie* (idle), i.e. engage in it, cf. 11^{6}, *lay down forcibly, thrust down* הִנִּיחַ לָאָרֶץ בְּיָד Is 28^{2}, cf. Am 5^{7}; perh also Ez 22^{20} (abs; but del Co Berthol, after 𝔊). **2.** *let remain, leave* (in present condition), obj nations Ju 2^{23} 3^{1} Je 27^{11}, people in wilderness Nu 32^{15} (JE); וְהִנִּיחוּךְ עֵירֹם וְעֶרְיָה

Ez 16^{39}; sq. acc. rei Lv 7^{15} 1 K 7^{47} (leave unweighed); *leave behind* sq.acc. pers. Gn 42^{33}(E), 2 S 16^{21} 20^{3} 1 K 19^{3} Je 43^{6}; + אֶת־פְּנֵי 1 S 22^{4} (rd. וַיַּנְחֵם, for MT וַיַּנְחֵם, *and he left them with* 𝔖𝔗𝔙 We Dr Klo Bu Löhr HPS; *leave* name, for a curse Is 65^{15}; *leave* or *bequeath* to (לְ), c. acc. rei, ψ 17^{14} Ec 2^{18}. **3.** *leave* = depart from, מְקוֹמְךָ אַל־תַּנַּח Ec 10^{4} *do not leave thy place.* **4.** *abandon*, sq. acc. pers. Je 14^{9}; בַּל־תַּנִּיחֵנִי לְעֹשְׁקָי ψ 119^{121} *abandon me not to my oppressors.* **5.** *let alone* (refrain from interfering with), sq. לְ pers. Ex 32^{10}(JE; obj. י׳), Ho 4^{17} 2 S 16^{11} 2 K 23^{18}; sq. acc. pers. Est 3^{8}; = *avoid* יַנִּיחַ חֲטָאִים גְּדוֹלִים Ec 10^{4} (but rd. perh. יָנִיחַ, *causeth to rest* = *allayeth* cf. Wild). **6.** *permit*, c. acc. pers. Ju 16^{26}; + inf. לֹא הִנִּיחַ אָדָם לְעָשְׁקָם ψ 105^{14} = 1 Ch 16^{21}, but here הִנִּיחַ לְאִישׁ, cf. לְיִשׁוֹן מַנִּיחַ לוֹ Ec 5^{11}. **Hoph. A.** *Pf.* 3 ms. הוּנַּח־לָנוּ La 5^{5} i.e. *no rest is granted to us;* for 3 fs. וְהֻנִּיחָה Zc 5^{11} [so Baer Ginsb; van d. H. וְהֻנּ׳] rd. prob. וְהִנִּיחָהּ v. supr. **Hiph. B 1.** **B.** *Pt.* מֻנָּח as subst. = *space left, open space* Ez $41^{9.11.11}$.

נֹחַ v. נוח *Inf. abs.* נוֹחַ 2 Ch 6^{41} v. מְנוּחָה.

†**נוֹחָה** **n.pr.m.** 4th son of Benjamin acc. to 1 Ch 8^{2}. 𝔊 Ιωα, A Νωα, 𝔊L Νουαα.

†**I. נַחַת** **n.[f.]** (appar. **m.** Jb 36^{16}, but v. infr.) **quietness, rest** (under this √ Thes Ol §164 e Sta §201 d Kö ii. 172 f.; > sub נחת Dl Prol. 118 ff.);—נ׳ Is 30^{15} + 2 t., נָחַת Jb 17^{16} + 2 t.; cstr. נַחַת Jb 36^{16};—**1.** *quietness, quiet attitude* Is 30^{15} (‖ הַשְׁקֵט); דִּבְרֵי חֲכָמִים בְּנ׳ נִשְׁמָעִים Ec 9^{17}; opp. עָמָל וּרְעוּת רוּחַ 4^{6}; opp. שָׂחֹק רָנַּן, Pr 29^{9}; of comfort of one's table, i.e. its satisfying plenty, וְנ׳ שֻׁלְחָנְךָ מָלֵא דָשֶׁן Jb 36^{16} *the comfort of thy table, which* (i.e. the table) *was full of fat* (Di, cf. Bu; > *that which is set on thy table shall be*, etc. De al., making נ׳ subj. of מָלֵא, and so masc.). **2.** *rest* of death Jb 17^{16}; of a stillborn child Ec 6^{5}.—II, III. נַחַת v. נחת.

נֹחַ $_{46}$ **n.pr.m. Noah** (Nab. n.pr. נוח Lzb 322, Syr. n.pr. ܢܘܚ Meissn VOJ viii. (1894), 303 ad fin. (No. 116));—Gn 5^{29} (where trad. etym.), + 40 t. Gn 5–10 (not in ED); 1 Ch 1^{4}; נֹחַ דָּנִאֵל וְאִיּוֹב Ez $14^{14.20}$; מֵי נֹחַ = flood Is $54^{9.9}$; 𝔊 Νωε.—On hist. of interpret. of name v. Goldziher ZMG xxiv. (1870), 207 ff.

נִיחֹחַ and (Lv 1^{9}) **נִיחוֹחַ** $_{43}$ **n.[m.] a quieting, soothing, tranquillizing** (cf. I. נַחַת Jb 36^{16}) (ריח ניחח also Ecclus 45^{16c}; on format. v. Ol §187 b Sta §233 Ba NB §142 Kö ii. 1, 151. 489, where, after Philippi BAS ii. 362, ִ—י expl. as dissim. from וֹ);—abs. נ׳ Gn 8^{21} +; sf. נִיחֹחִי Nu 28^{2}, נִיחֹחֲכֶם Lv 26^{31}, נִיחוֹחֵיהֶם Ez 20^{28};—*a soothing, tranquillizing,* only in phr. רֵיחַ נ׳ = *soothing, tranquillizing odour* of sacrifices acceptable to י׳ Gn 8^{21} (J), Ex $29^{18.25.41}$ Lv $1^{9.13.17}$ + 32 t. P. Ez 20^{41}; of sacrif. to idols †Ez 6^{13} 16^{19} 20^{28}.

†**הֲנָחָה** **n.f. a giving of rest, i.e. perh. holiday-making** (cf. נוח **Hiph. A;** prop. Inf., Sta §621 e Ba NB 90, cf. Kö ii. 1, 402);—וַה׳ לַמְּדִינוֹת עָשָׂה Est 2^{18} *and a holiday-making for the provinces be enacted,* 𝔙 *requies;* but 𝔊 ἄφεσις, whence al. *release* from taxes, or *amnesty.*

†**יָנוֹחַ** **n.pr.loc.** in extreme N. of Isr. 2 K 15^{29}; site dub., *Yânûḥ* (Conder Lists 38) near Tyre is prob. too far W.; Guérin Gal. ii. 371 f. prop. *Hunîn*, W. of upper Jordan, cf. Buhl Geogr. 237; 𝔊 Αναωχ, A 𝔊L Ιανωχ.

†**יָנוֹחָה** **n.pr.loc.** on border of Ephraim Jos $16^{6.7}$, identif. with *Yânun* SE. fr. Shechem Rob BR iii. 297 cf. Buhl Geogr. 178; 𝔊 Ιανωχα, Ιανωκα.

†**I. מָנוֹחַ** **n.m. resting-place, state, or condition of rest;**—abs. מ׳ Gn 8^{9} + 4 t.; cstr. מְנוֹחַ 1 Ch 6^{16}; pl. sf. 2 fs. מְנוּחָיְכִי ψ 116^{7} (Ges §91 l);—**1.** *resting-place* לְכַף רַגְלָהּ Gn 8^{9} (J), cf. Dt 28^{65} La 1^{3}; Is 34^{14} (cf. also מְנֻחָה Gn 49^{15}). **2.** *rest, repose* of soul ψ 116^{7} (pl. abstr. vel intens.); *condition of rest* and security attained by marriage Ru 3^{1}. **3.** with force of inf. (cf. Aram. inf. c. מ pref.) מִמְּנוֹחַ הָאָרוֹן 1 Ch 6^{16} *from the coming to rest of the ark.*

II. **מָנוֹחַ** $_{18}$ **n.pr.m.** father of Samson Ju $13^{2.8}$ + 15 t. Ju 13, 16^{31}, 𝔊 Μανωε.

†**מְנֻחָה, מְנוּחָה** **n.f. resting-place, rest;**—abs. מ׳ Mi 2^{10} +, מְנֻחָה Gn 49^{15} (but v. infr.), 2 S 14^{17}; sf. מְנוּחָתִי ψ 95^{11} + 2 t., מְנוּחָתֶךָ ψ 132^{8} = 2 Ch 6^{41} (where rd. as in ψ, for anom. לְנוּחֶךָ MT), מְנֻחָתוֹ Is 11^{10} Zc 9^{1}; pl. מְנוּחֹת Is 32^{18}, מְנֻחוֹת ψ 23^{2};—**1.** *resting-place* Mi 2^{10} Nu 10^{33} (JE), Dt 12^{9} (+ הַנַּחֲלָה) so ψ 95^{11} (י׳'s resting-pl.), cf. 132^{8} = 2 Ch 6^{41} (v. supr.), ψ 132^{14} Is 66^{1} בֵּית מ׳ 1 Ch 28^{2} (‖ בַּיִת אֲשֶׁר תִּבְנוּ לִי), cf. לַאֲרוֹן וגו׳ (בַּיִת מ׳), also Is 11^{10}; prob. also Gn 49^{15} (‖ הָאָרֶץ); טוֹב here is appar. subst., Sam. rds. adj. טוֹבָה; but rd. perh. מְנֻחוֹ, *his resting-place*, fr. מָנוֹחַ, Ball Hpt Holz after 𝔖); מְנוּחֹת שַׁאֲנַנּוֹת Is 32^{18} (+ נְוֵה שָׁלוֹם, מִשְׁכְּנוֹת מִבְטַחִים); of י׳'s word Zc 9^{1}; resting-

place on journey, in שַׂר מ׳ Je 51[59] (Ew Gf Gie al.), fig for security, assurance 2 S 14[17] (taken from *resting*, equilibrium, of scale acc to Klo) **2.** *rest, quietness*, pl. מֵי מְנֻחוֹת ψ 23[2], = refreshment Is 28[12] (‖ מַרְגֵּעָה), *rest* (fr. enemies) = peace 1 K 8[56] (cf. 5[18]), אִישׁ מ׳ 1 Ch 22[9] *a man of peace* (cf הֵנִיחַ vb); = relief fr sorrow Je 45[3], *condition of rest* and security attained by marriage Ru 1[9] (= מָנוֹחַ 3[1]) —מ׳ Ju 20[43] is perh. n. pr., cf. GFM.

מְנֻחוֹת **n.pr.** v מָנַחְתִּי infr

†1. [מָנַחַת] **n. pr. loc.** (= *resting-place, settlement*), מָנָ֑חַת 1 Ch 8[6], site unknown, 𝔊 Μαχαναθει, 𝔊L Μανουαθ.

†מָנַחְתִּי **adj.gent.** perh fr foregoing, only c art as n coll חֲצִי הַמ׳ 1 Ch 2[54] of a Judaean tribe (𝔊 Μαλαθει, A 𝔊L Μαναθ(ι)); so rd. also prob for חֲצִי הַמְּנֻחוֹת v[52] (𝔊 Μωναιω, A Αμμανιθ).

†II מָנַחַת **n.pr.m.** in Edom Gn 36[23] = 1 Ch 1[40]; 𝔊 Μαν(ν)αχαθ, Μαναα θ

†[נוּט] **vb. dangle, shake** (𝔗 [נוט] Aph. *scare*, sld, Levy[ChWB II 97] Jastr[Dict. 886], Ar نَوْطٌ *a bag hanging down*, نَاطَ *suspend, hang*),—**Qal** *Impf* 3 fs תָּנוּט ψ 99[1] *let* (the earth) *shake* (‖ יִרְגְּזוּ) —Ol We prop. תָּמוּט.

נְוִית v. sub I נוה

†נוּם **vb. be drowsy, slumber** (NH נוּם, נמנם *id*, Aram נוּם, نَمْ, Ar نَامَ (نوم) *id*, Eth ኖመ:),—**Qal** *Pf* 3 pl. נָמוּ Na 3[18] ψ 76[6] (Ges[§ 72 l]), *Impf.* יָנוּם ψ 121[3] + 2 t.; 3 fs וַתָּנֹם 2 S 4[6] (so rd. for 𝔐 וַיַּכֻּהוּ, with other radical changes, 𝔊 Th We Dr Kit Bu HPS); *Inf. cstr.* לָנוּם Is 56[10] —*be drowsy, slumber*, lit. וַתָּנֹם וַתִּישָׁן 2 S 4[6] (emend, v supr) *and she grew drowsy and slept*; fig. of inactivity, indolence, Is 5[27] (‖ ישׁן), ψ 121[3.4] (of י׳; ‖ *id*); Na 3[18] (‖ שָׁכְנוּ); אֹהֲבֵי לָנ׳ Is 56[10] (‖ שֹׁכְבִים), sq. acc. cogn. שְׁנָה ψ 76[6] (of death, ‖ נִרְדָּם)

†נוּמָה **n f.** somnolence, fig. for indolence, Pr 23[21]

†תְּנוּמָה **n f.** slumber,—abs ψ 132[4] Pr 6[4], pl. תנומות Pr 6[10] + 2 t,—*slumber* as time of visions Jb 33[15] (‖ תַּרְדֵּמָה), of indolent slumber ψ 132[4] (‖ שְׁנָת) Pr 6[4] (‖ שנה) in both c נָתַן, sq acc + לְ; 6[10] 24[33] (both ‖ שְׁנוֹת, שכב)

†יָנוּם **n.pr loc.** city in Judah, Jos 15[53] Qr, Kt ינים (so van d H Ginsb; Baer only יָנוּם), 𝔊 Ιεμαειν, A 𝔊L Ιανουμ.

†[נִין, נוּן] **vb.** propagate, increase (si vera l) (> denom. fr נִין Hup-Now SS,—NH נוּן = *fish*, so Aram נוּנָא, نُونٌ, As *nunu*),—**Qal** (or **Hiph.** ?) *Impf.* ינין Kt; > **Niph.** יִנּוֹן Qr ψ 72[17] let his name *have increase* (or, if Niph, *be propagated, spread*), but dub, Vrss perh. יִכּוֹן *be established, endure.*

†נוּן and (1 Ch 7[27]) נוֹן **n.pr.m.** father of Joshua 1 Ch 7[27]; elsewh. alw. (יְהוֹשֻׁעַ) בִּן־נוּן Ex 33[11] Nu 11[28] 13[8.16] + 22 t. Nu Dt Jos (JEDP); also Ju 2[8] 1 K 16[34] Ne 8[17], 𝔊 Ναυη (for Ναυν by err., cf Thes).

†נִין **n.[m.]** offspring, posterity;—abs. Jb 18[19] Is 14[22], sf. נִינִי Gn 21[23] (all ‖ נֶכֶד).

מָנוֹן v p. 584 supr.

נוּס [160] **vb.** flee, escape (Syr. ܢܳܣ *tremble* (rare), cf Brock, Ar نَاسَ, نوس *move to and fro, be in commotion, dangle*, Lane[2866]),—**Qal** *Pf* נָס Nu 35[25] +; נַסְתָּה 2 K 9[3], נַסְתִּי 1 S 4[16], etc, *Impf* יָנוּס Ex 21[13] +; וַיָּנָס Gn 39[12] +, יְנוּסוּן ψ 104[7], etc.; *Imv mpl* נֻסוּ Je 48[6] + 4 t. Je Zc, *Inf abs* נוס 2 S 18[3], *cstr.* (לָנֻס) לָנוּס Gn 19[20] +, *Pt.* נָס Am 9[1] +, נָסִים Ex 14[27] +;—**1.** *flee*, abs Gn 39[12.15] Nu 16[34] (all J), Jos 10[16] (JE), Lv 26[17.36] (H), fig of sea ψ 114[3.5] cf 104[7]; sq acc cogn. מָנוֹס Je 46[5], sq דֶּרֶךְ Jos 8[15] (J), 2 K 9[27], sq. בדרך Dt 28[7.25]; נ׳ אֶל־נַפְשָׁם 2 K 7[7] *flee for their life*, נ׳ בְּרַגְלָיו Ju 4[15] *flee on foot*, + 44 t abs. (not elsewh. Hex); sq. אֶל־ loc Dt 4[42] 19[5.11] (D), Nu 35[32] Jos 20[4] (both P), Ju 4[17] 1 K 2[28.29] Is 13[14], sq לְ 1 S 4[10] + 6 t. + לִקְרָאתוֹ Ex 14[27] (E; not elsewh. Hex), sq עַד Ju 7[22] + Pr 28[17] (עַד־בּוֹר, v. בור), sq עַל־ Is 10[3], sq ָ—ה loc Gn 14[10] + 4 t. JE, Nu 35[6] + 6 t P, Dt 4[42] 19[3.4] (D), + 6 t, sq. שָׁם Is 20[6], sq. acc. loc Jos 8[20] (J), + 4 t., sq מִמֶּרְחָק Is 17[13] = *far away*, sq. מִן *from*, Jos 20[6] (P), 1 S 4[16] + 3 t; מִתּוֹךְ Je 51[6], esp מִפְּנֵי *from before* Ex 4[3] 14[25] Nu 10[35] Jos 10[11] (all JE), 1 S 17[24] Je 48[44] (Qr הַנָּס, > Kt הנים), + 19 t, sq. מִלִּפְנֵי Jos 7[4] 8[5.6] (all J), 1 S 4[17] 2 S 24[13], לִפְנֵי 1 Ch 19[18]. **2.** *escape* Am 9[1] (‖ נמלט) so Je 46[5]; hence **3.** *take flight, depart, disappear*, only fig, Dt 34[7] (JE) *his freshness* (לחה *vigour*) *was not gone* (‖ לֹא כָהֲתָה עֵינוֹ), of shadows (at evening), Ct 2[17] 4[6]; of sorrow etc. Is 35[10] 51[11] **4.** נ׳ עַל־סוּס Is 30[16] *fly* (to the attack) *on horseback* †**Po'lel** *Pf* Is 59[19] רוּחַ י׳ נֹסְסָה בוֹ *the breath of* י׳ *driveth at it, driveth it on* (cf.

Hiph. 2). †**Hithpo'l.** *Inf. cstr.* לְהִתְנוֹסֵס מִפְּנֵי ψ 60[6] *in order to take flight before* the bow (so Vrss Hup-Now Che Bae al.). †**Hiph.** *Pf.* הֵנִיס Ex 9[20]; *Impf.* יָנִיסוּ Dt 32[30] + Ju 7[21] Kt (Qr וַיָּנוּסוּ **Qal**); *Inf. cstr.* לְהָנִיס Ju 6[11];—**1.** *put to flight*, sq. acc. Dt 32[30] (‖רדף). **2.** *drive hastily* to a safe place Ex 9[20], sq. acc. + אֶל־. **3.** *cause to disappear, hide* Ju 6[11] (no obj. expr.) sq. מִפְּנֵי.

†מָנוֹס **n.m.**[Am 2, 14] **1.** flight. **2.** place of escape, refuge;—abs. מ׳ Am 2[14] + 5 t.; sf. מְנוּסִי 2 S 22[3] Je 16[19];—**1.** *flight*, acc. cogn. c. נוס Je 46[5]. **2.** (*place of*) *escape*; אָבַד מ׳ מִן *escape perished from*, = *there was no escape for*, Am 2[14] Je 25[35] Jb 11[20] ψ 142[5]; of י׳ as a *refuge* 2 S 22[3] (‖משגב; מנוס וגו׳ not ‖ ψ 18[3]; txt. disputed, Kit Bu retain in Sm, Klo Bae Löhr Du ins. in ψ; < del. in Sm De Hup-Now HPS cf. Che), ψ 59[17] (‖*id.*); Je 16[19] (‖מעז, מעוז).

†מְנוּסָה **n.f.** flight;—מ׳ Is 52[12] (‖חִפָּזוֹן); מְנֻסַת־חֶרֶב Lv 26[36] = *flight from sword*, acc. cogn. c. נוס.

†נוּעַ **vb.** quiver, wave, waver, tremble, totter (NH Pilp. נִעְנַע *shake*, Aram. נוּע *waver, stagger* (rare); Ar. نَاعَ, نوع *bend* (of boughs), v. commotus fuit (of *id.*), so Kam Frey; also *change*, نَوْعٌ *kind, species, variety*; Di cp. Eth. ነዐወ: *hunt*);—**Qal** *Pf.* נָעוּ Jb 28[4] +; וְנָעוּ Am 4[8] + 2 t.; *Impf.* וַיָּנַע Is 7[2]; 3 fs. תָּנוּעַ Is 24[20]; אֲנוּעֶךָ 2 S 15[20] Kt (but rd Qr Hiph q.v.); יְנוּעוּ ψ 109[10]; יְנוּעוּן ψ 59[16] Kt (so rd.; not Qr Hiph.), etc.; *Inf. abs.* נוֹעַ Is 24[20] ψ 109[10]; *cstr.* נוּעַ Ju 9[9] + 3 t.; נוֹעַ Is 7[2]; *Pt.* נָע Gn 4[12.14]; נָעִים Pr 22[19]; נָעוֹת 1 S 1[13]:—**1.** *wave*, of trees, sq. עַל Ju 9[9.11.13]; sq. מִפְּנֵי of cause Is 7[2]; *quiver, vibrate*, of lips 1 S 1[13]; *swing* (to and fro) of miners Jb 28[4] (‖דללו); *stagger* like drunkard, of mariners in storm ψ 107[27] (‖חגג), cf. Is 29[9] (‖שכר); hence *be unstable*, fig. of ways of harlot Pr 5[6]; *tremble*, of doorposts, Is 6[4] (sq. מִן caus.), idols 19[1] (sq. מִפְּנֵי), earth Is 24[20] (‖התנודד), people Ex 20[18] (E); fig. of heart Is 7[2]. **2.** *totter, go tottering* (faint and uncertain) La 4[14] v[15] (‖נוד), Am 8[12] (‖שוטט); as beggars ψ 109[10] (‖שָׁאֵל), cf. 59[16]; Am 4[8] sq. אֶל־; *pt. vagabond* Gn 4[12.14] (both ‖נָד); fig. = *err, sin*, Je 14[10]. **Niph.** *Impf.* יִנּוֹעַ Am 9[9] *be tossed about* (of corn) in a sieve; יִנּוֹעוּ *id.*, of bulwarks as fig-trees Na 3[12] (‖נפל). **Hiph.** *Pf.* 3 fs. הֵנִיעָה 2 K 19[21] = Is 37[22]; וַהֲנִעוֹתִי Am 9[9]; *Impf.* יָנִיעַ Zp 2[15]; juss. יָנַע 2 K 23[18]; אֲנִיעֲךָ 2 S 15[20] Qr (cf. **Qal**); יְנִיעוּן ψ 109[25] + 59[16] Qr (rd. Kt **Qal** q.v.), etc.; *Imv.* sf. הֲנִיעֵמוֹ ψ 59[12];—**1.** *toss about* Am 9[9] subj. י׳, obj. Isr. sq. בַגּוֹיִם (cf. **Niph.**). **2.** *shake, cause to totter*: = *set me tottering* Dn 10[10] *on my knees and hands*; esp. *shake* or *wag* the head, in mockery 2 K 19[21] = Is 37[22] (‖בוז, לעג) cf. ψ 22[8] 109[25]; sq. עַל־ Jb 16[4] (בְּמוֹ ר׳ [Ges § 119 q]), also La 2[15] (‖שרק), Zp 2[15] יָדוֹ (‖*id.*), [v. also Ecclus 12[18] 13[7] (ר׳ב)]. **3.** (*shake*), *disturb*, bones of dead 2 K 23[18]. **4.** *cause to wander* Nu 32[13] (J); 2 S 15[20] (sq. ללכת); ψ 59[12] (‖הוריד, for which Lag[Proph. Chald. xlviii.] prop. הניד).

†נֵעָה **n.pr.loc.** in Zebulun; הַנֵּעָה Jos 19[13], 𝔊 Aοζα, A Aννουα, 𝔊L Nουα; site unknown.

†נֹעָה **n.pr.f.** a daughter of Zelophahad (of Manasseh), Nu 26[33] 27[1] 36[11] Jos 17[3], 𝔊 Nουα.

†[מְנַעְנֵעַ] **n.[m.]** appar. a kind of rattle, only וּבִמְנַעַנְעִים 2 S 6[5], in list of musical instruments; 𝔊 κύμβαλα, but this usu. (12 t.) = מְצִלְתַּיִם; 𝔙 *sistra*; the sistrum (Gr. σεῖστρον, fr. σείω) was much used in Egypt; it was a small metal frame with loose metal bars carrying loose rings, borne and *swung* or *shaken* in the hand, v. Wilkinson Anc. Egyptians (1878), i. 497 ff. Now Arch. i. 273 Benz Arch. 278 We ψψ Eng. Trans. p. 233.

נוֹעַדְיָה v. יעד.

I. [נוּף] **vb.** move to and fro, wave, besprinkle (NH Hiph., Pilp. *wave, blow, fan*, cf. נָפָה *sift*, נָפָה n. *sieve* (as BH); 𝔗 Aph. as BH; Syr. ܢܳܦ *bend, wave, shake*; Di cp. Eth. quadril. ነጠብጠበ: *distil, drop like dew*; ነፈየ: *sift*);—**Qal** *Pf.* 1 s. נַפְתִּי מִשְׁכָּבִי מֹר וגו׳ Pr 7[17] *I have besprinkled my couch with myrrh*, etc. **Po'lel** *Impf.* 3 ms. יְנֹפֵף יָדוֹ הַר וגו׳ Is 10[32] *he brandisheth his hand toward the mt.* (on acc. הַר cf. Ges § 118 f. Da[Synt. § 69, R 2]). **Hiph.** *Pf.* 3 ms. הֵנִיף Jos 8[31] +, 2 ms. הֲנֵפֹתָ Ex 20[25] (Ges § 72 k), וְהֵנַפְתָּ Ex 29[24] + 3 t.; 1 s. הֲנִיפֹתִי Jb 31[21]; *Impf.* וַיָּנֶף Lv 8[27] Nu 8[21], sf. וַיְנִיפֵהוּ Lv 8[29]; 2 ms. תָּנִיף Dt 23[26] + 2 t., etc.; *Imv.* mpl. הָנִיפוּ Is 13[2]; *Inf. cstr.* הָנִיף Is 10[15] + 2 t.; לַהֲנָפָה Is 30[28] (Ges § 72 z BA[NB 90], v. also הֲנָחָה), etc.; *Pt.* מֵנִיף Is 19[16] Zc 2[13], etc.;—*swing, wield, wave*:—**1.** *wield*, move tool to and fro in using it, c. עַל־ of material: כִּי חַרְבְּךָ הֵנַפְתָּ עָלֶיהָ Ex 20[25] (E), i.e. over stone, so Dt 27[5] Jos 8[31] (D), and Dt 23[26]

a sickle *thou shalt not wield over* the standing grain of thy neighbour; abs מְנִיפוֹ Is 10[15] against *him that wieldeth it* (i e a saw), and כְּהָנִיף שֵׁבֶט וְאֶת־מְרִימוֹ v[15] (rd. אֶת־) *like a rod's wielding him that lifteth it*

2 *Shake* or *wave* the hand, **a.** *wave* hand אֶל־הַמָּקוֹם 2 K 5[11], in healing ceremony (i e prob toward sanctuary Kmp[Kau]; > *toward the spot* [where leprosy appears], so most). **b.** c עַל־, *shake* or *brandish against*, Is 11[15] 19[16] Zc 2[13] (all of י׳), Jb 31[21] [cf. Ecclus 12[18] (without עַל) in mockery]. **c.** *wave* hand, as a signal, Is 13[2]. **3.** *swing* to and fro בְּנָפָת, *in a sieve*, Is 30[28] (fig, of nations).

4. Oft term. techn. in P (H), of rite in which originally the priest lifted his share of offering and *waved* it, i e. moved it toward altar and back, in token of its presentation to God and its return by him to priest: in H, והניף אֶת־הָעֹמֶר לִפְנֵי י׳ Lv 23[11 a] cf. v[11 b 12], also v[20] (on text v Di Dr-Wh[Hpt]), in P, והנַפְתָּ אתוֹ תנופה לפני י׳ Ex 29[26], so Lv 7[30] 8[29] 9[21] 10[15] (obj. om), Nu 6[20], thus also Levites are set apart for service of the priests Nu 8[11] (Di del. v), v[13.21], cf v[14] (לפני י׳ om); but same phr of entire lamb, with oil, Lv 14[12.24], and of offerings wh. were burnt, entirely Ex 29[24] (cf. v[25]), Lv 8[27] (cf v[28]), or in part Nu 5[25] (הניף הַמִּנְחָה לִפְנֵי י׳), —in these the orig signif. seems lost; so, clearly, of contributions for tabernacle, = *offer*, הניף תְּנוּפַת זָהָב לַי׳ Ex 35[22].—Cf תְּנוּפָה infr.

5. *Shed abroad* (si vera l) גֶּשֶׁם נְדָבוֹת תָּנִיף ψ 68[10] *bounteous rain thou didst shed abroad* [cf Ecclus 43[17 e]], but vb. not wholly suitable; Lag Gr prop תַּטִּיף, yet this also questionable. **Hoph.** *Pf.* 3 ms הוּנַף, *be waved*, Ex 29[27] (P), pass of **Hiph. 4.**

†I [נָפָה] **n.f. sieve** or other winnowing implement, Di Du *Schwinge*, Che[Hpt] *fan* (as *swung*),—only cstr לַהֲנָפָה גוֹיִם בְּנָפַת שָׁוְא Is 30[28] *to swing* nations in a sieve of worthlessness.

תְּנוּפָה[30] **n.f. a swinging, waving, wave-offering, offering**,—abs. ת׳ Is 30[32]+; cstr תְּנוּפַת Is 19[16] Ex 35[22], pl. cstr תנופת Nu 18[11],— **1.** *a swinging, brandishing*, ת׳ יַד י׳ Is 19[16] *the brandishing of* י׳*'s hand* (in hostility); מִלְחֲמוֹת ת׳ 30[32] *battles of brandishing* (brandished weapons) **2. a.** *waving, wave-offering*, term techn. in P (H), orig. of priest's share of sacrifice (cf נוף **Hiph. 4**), לְכָל־תְּנוּפֹת בְּנֵי יִשׂ׳ לְךָ נְתַתִּים Nu 18[11], oft. as 2nd acc. after הֵנִיף Ex 29[26]+5 t.; even of Levites Nu 8[11 13.15.20] (on all v. נוף **Hiph. 4**), חֲזֵה הַתּ׳ Ex 29[27] *the wave-breast*, so Lv 7[34] 10[14.15] Nu 6[20] (all + שׁוֹק הַתְּרוּמָה), 18[18] (+ שׁוֹק הַיָּמִין); עֹמֶר הַתּ׳ Lv 23[15], לֶחֶם הַתּ׳ v[17]; ת׳ alone v[20] (all H), less accurately Ex 29[24] Lv 8[27] 14[12 21 24] (v נוף[l.c.]). **b.** *offering*, of gold and brass for tabern., Ex 35[22] 38[24 29]—On ת׳ v. Di[Lv 7.30] Benz[Arch 459 f.] and esp Now[Arch ii 239 f.]; also תְּרוּמָה

II. נוף (√of foll., cf Ar نَافَ, نوف I, IV. *overtop* (Frey), نَوْفٌ *camel-hump* (ib); مُنِيفٌ *high, lofty* (of mt and building, Lane[3039]).

†נוֹף **n.[m.] elevation, height** (NH נוֹף is *tree-top, bough*, so 𝔗 נוֹפָא),—יְפֵה נ׳ ψ 48[3] *beautiful in elevation* (of Mount Zion)

II [נָפָה] **n.f. height**,—only cstr in combin נָפַת דּוֹר Jos 12[23] = נ׳ דּאר 1 K 4[11], pl. cstr. נָפוֹת ד׳ Jos 11[2], cf II דּוֹר, and Di[Jos 11 2], v. also [נֶפֶת].

†[נֶפֶת] **n.f.** id;—only הַנָּפֶת Jos 17[11] (but rd. perh הַנָּפַת, fr. foregoing, v. Di; 𝔊 Μαφετα, A Ναφεθα, 𝔊L Νοφεθ, cf. 12[23] [supr. sub II. נָפָה], 𝔊L Ναφαθδωρ).—נֹפֶת *honey*, v. נפת

נוֹצָה v I. נצה

[נוק] **vb.** whence (si vera l.) might come, **Hiph. suckle, nurse**;—*Impf.* 3 fs. sf וַתְּנִיקֵהוּ Ex 2[9], but v. ינק and Ges[§ 70 e]; rd. prob. וַתֵּינ׳ (Sam. ותיניקהו).

נור (√of foll; cf NH נוּר, *flame, fire*, 𝔗 *id*, Ar نَارَ, نور *give light, shine*, I. (Kam Frey), IV. Lane[2864], نَارٌ *fire*, نُورٌ *light*; Syr. ܢܘܪܐ *fire*; also in n.pr Palm. Pun. v. Lzb[322] Cook[81]; Min. מנורת *torches* (?) Hom[Südar Chrest 128]; As. *tinûru*, *furnace, oven* (Dl[HWB 711]) belongs here acc. to Jager[BAS ii 294])

I. נֵר[43] **n.m.**[Ex 25, 37] **lamp**,—נ׳ abs. Ex 27[20]+, cstr. 1 S 3[3]+, sf נֵרִי ψ 18[29], +נִירִי‎ ‖ 2 S 22[29], etc; pl. נֵרוֹת abs. Lv 24[4]+, cstr Ex 39[37], sf. נֵרֹתֶיהָ Ex 25[37 37]+, נרתיהֶם 1 Ch 28[15] 2 Ch 4[20];—*lamp* in shrine at Shiloh 1 S 3[3]; esp. of *lamps* in temple 1 K 7[49]+7 t. Ch, and in tabern. Ex 25[37 37]+15 t P; cf. in Zech.'s vision Zc 4[2.2]; as token of merrymaking Je 25[10]; used in search Zp 1[12], cf (fig) נֵר י׳ נִשְׁמַת אָדָם Pr 20[27]; used in household work Pr 31[18]; fig of prosperity נ׳ יִשְׂרָאֵל 2 S 21[17] (embodied in David); also Jb 18[6] 21[17] 29[3] ψ 18[29] = 2 S 22[29], ψ 132[17] Pr 13[9] 20[20] 24[20], of God's word as a guide ψ 119[105], cf. Pr 6[23].

†II. **נֵר** **n.pr.m.** 𝔊 Νηρ. **1.** father of Abner 1 S $14^{50.51}$ $26^{5.14}$ 2 S $2^{8.12}$ $3^{23.25.28.37}$ 1 K $2^{5.32}$ 1 Ch 26^{28}. **2.** father of Kish 1 Ch 8^{33} $9^{36.39}$.

†I. **נִיר** **n.[m.]** lamp;—alw. fig. לְמַעַן הֱיוֹת־נ׳ לְדָוִיד 1 K 11^{36}, i.e. that his family may remain on the throne; cf. 15^{4} 2 K 8^{19} = 2 Ch 21^{7}, = happiness, delight (cstr.) נִר רְשָׁעִים Pr 21^{4} (so Vrss Thes Buhl Now Wild, > Ew Del SS Frankenb = II. נִיר sub II. ניר infr.).

†**נֵרִיָּה, נֵרִיָּהוּ** **n.pr.m.** father of Baruch: נריהו Je $36^{14.32}$ 43^{6} 45^{1}, = father of Seraiah 51^{59}; נֵרִיָּה $32^{12.16}$ $36^{4.8}$ 43^{3}, 𝔊 Νηριου, cf Gray$^{Prop\ N.\ 294}$.

מְנֹרָה, מְנוֹרָה $_{42}$ **n.f.** lampstand (Ecclus מנורה *fire*, 43^{4d}),—abs מְנֹרָה 2 K 4^{10} + 9 t., מנורה Ex $25^{32.32}$ + 19 t.; cstr. מְנוֹרַת Zc 4^{2} 2 Ch 13^{11}, מְנֹרַת Ex 25^{31} + 2 t; pl. מְנֹרוֹת abs. 1 K 7^{49} + 2 t.; cstr. 1 Ch $28^{15.15}$ 2 Ch 4^{7},—*lampstand*: **1.** in private house 2 K 4^{10} **2.** ten *lampstands* in temple, pl 1 K 7^{49} = 2 Ch 4^{7}, Je 52^{19} (so also 𝔊; om. ‖ 2 K $25^{14.15}$, del here Now $^{Arch\ ii\ 40}$ < retain Gf Gie), cf. 2 Ch 4^{20}, also 1 Ch $28^{15.15.15.15.15.15.15}$, but 2 Ch 13^{11} has מ׳ in sg. (as **3**); cf. sg in Zech.'s vision Zc 4^{2}. **3.** seven-branched *lampstand* in tabern. Ex 25 $^{31.31.32.33}$ + 15 t. Ex, Lv 24^{4} (with lamps upon it), Nu 3^{31} 4^{9} $8^{2.3.4.4}$ (all P)—מָנוֹר v. II. ניר.

†**[נָרַשׁ]** **vb.** be sick, si vera l (= I. אנש acc. to Thes who comp. Syr. ܢܪܫ);—**Qal** *Impf.* 1 s. וָאָנוּשָׁה ψ 69^{21}, but rd. perh [מַכַּת נַפְשִׁי] וָאָנוּשָׁה (‖ חֶרְפָּה שָׁבְרָה לִבִּי), Bi Che$^{crit.\ n}$, cf. 𝔊, v. I. אנש; or (< קִוָּה) ואנוש הוא קוה (with different word-division), Weir$^{Acad\ 1870\ 257}$ (who cp. Je 17^{9} 8^{18})

†I. **[נָזָה]** **vb.** spurt, spatter; **Hiph.** sprinkle (NH **Hiph.** *sprinkle;* Aram. נְדָא, אַדִּי Lv 4^{6} and oft, for הִזָּה; Syr. ܢܕܐ is *erupit, stillavit* Is 63^{3}, also *prominuit*, etc. PS^{2291});— **Qal** *Impf.* 3 ms יִזֶּה Lv $6^{20.20}$, יֵז Is 63^{3} (but rd. וַיֵּז Che Di Du Ges$^{§\ 53,\ p\ n,\ 107\ b\ n}$ al.), וַיִּז 2 K 9^{33},— *spurt, spatter*, alw. of blood:—וַיִּז מִדָּמָהּ אֶל־ 2 K 9^{33} *and some of her blood spurted against* the wall; so ויז נִצְחָם Is 63^{3} (c. עַל־ rei, in metaph), יִזֶּה מִדָּמָהּ Lv 6^{20}, cf. v^{20} (both c. עַל־ rei) **Hiph.** *Pf* 3 ms. וְהִזָּה consec. Lv 4^{6} + 12 t.; 2 ms. וְהִזֵּיתָ Ex 29^{21}; *Impf.* יַזֶּה Lv 16^{14} (Is 52^{15}, v. infr.); וַיַּז Lv $8^{11.30}$; *Imv.* הַזֵּה Nu 8^{7}; *Pt.* cstr. מַזֵּה Nu 19^{21},—*cause to spurt, sprinkle* upon, in ceremonials of P: c. acc. + עַל־ pers. Nu 8^{7} (water), + עַל־ rei, לִפְנֵי rei Lv 16^{15}; obj. oft. מִן partit, or implied in context; sq. עַל־ Lv 5^{9} 14^{7} $16^{14.19}$ (all of blood); 8^{11} (oil); Nu $19^{18.19}$ (water), Ex 29^{21} Lv 8^{30} (both blood and oil); sq. אֶל־ Lv 14^{51} (blood and water), אֶל־נֹכַח פְּנֵי Nu 19^{4} (blood); sq. לִפְנֵי Lv $4^{6.17}$ 16^{14} (blood), $14^{16.27}$ (oil); once without prep מַזֵּה Nu 19^{21} *the sprinkler of* the water.—Is 52^{15} v. II. נזה.

†**יְזִיָּה** **n.pr.m.** (*may* י׳ *sprinkle*, rd. prob. יִזִּ׳, 𝔊 Αζεια, ℵ Αδεια, 𝔊L Ιαζιας);—one of those who took strange wives Ezr 10^{25}.

II. **[נָזָה]** **vb.** (dub.) spring, leap (cf. Ar. نَزَا *leap, leap up, upon,* Thes Frey$^{Prov.\ Ar\ i,\ 171.\ 297,\ 22,\ 138,\ 26,\ 11}$);—hence, acc. to many, **Hiph.** *Impf.* 3 ms. כֵּן יַזֶּה גּוֹיִם רַבִּים Is 52^{15} *so shall he cause to leap* (i.e. in joyful surprise, or = *startle*) *many nations;* but perh. crpt; Che$^{Comm.}$ יַתִּר in like sense; < יִרְגְּזוּ (for יהגוים) *many shall tremble* (v. רגז), GFM$^{JBL\ 1890,\ 216\ ff.}$ cf. Che^{Hpt}.

זיד v. נָזִיד.

†**[נָזַל]** **vb.** flow, trickle, drop, distil (poet.) (𝔗 נְזַל of *flowing* water; Syr. ܢܙܠ *descendit, defluet* PS^{2331}; Ar. نَزَلَ *descend* (milk into udder, but also in gen)),—**Qal** *Pf* נָזְלוּ Ju 5^{5}; *Impf.* יִזַּל Nu 24^{7}, etc; *Pt.* נֹזְלִים Ex 15^{8} +, etc.;— **1.** *flow*, subj. water, Nu 24^{7} (JE); ψ 147^{18}, cf. Je 18^{14}; subj clouds, Jb 36^{28} sq. rain as acc. mat. Ges$^{§\ 117\ z}$ (‖ רעף and, v^{27}, זקק), cf Je 9^{17} (of eyelids); so fig. Is 45^{8} sq צֶדֶק (‖ רעף); of mts. (i e. their torrents) Ju 5^{5} acc. to 𝔙 Ew GFM al., but v. I. זלל; esp pt as subst., = *streams, floods*, Ex 15^{8} (‖ תהום, מים of Red Sea); ψ 78^{44} (‖ יְאֹר); for drinking ψ 78^{16} (‖ תהום, מים כַּנהרות v^{15}), Pr 5^{15} out of well (‖ מים), for irrigation Is 44^{3} (‖ מים); fig. of Shulamite נ׳ מִן־לְבָנוֹן Ct 4^{15} (‖ באר מים, מעין גנים). **2.** *distil*, of spices בְשָׂמָיו Ct 4^{16}; fig. of words, like dew Dt 32^{2} (‖ ערף). **Hiph.** *Pf.* הִזִּיל Is 48^{21} *cause to flow*, water from rock (‖ זוב).—Vid. also I. זלל.

נזם (√ of foll., meaning unknown).

†**נֶזֶם** **n.m.**$^{Jb\ 42,\ 11}$ ring, always of gold when material mentioned;—נ׳ abs. Gn 24^{30} +; cstr. v^{22} +; sf. נִזְמָהּ Ho 2^{15}; pl. נְזָמִים Gn 35^{4}; cstr. נִזְמֵי Ex 32^{2} +;—**1.** *nose-ring* (Syr. ܩܕܫܐ) woman's ornament, נ׳ עַל־אַפָּהּ Gn 24^{47} cf. $v^{22.30}$ (J); נִזְמֵי הָאָף Is 3^{21} (‖ טַבַּעַת seal-ring); perh. also Ho 2^{15}; Ez 16^{12} fig. of י׳'s adorning Jerus (‖ עֲגִילִים עַל־אָזְנַיִךְ); cf. נ׳ בְּאַף חֲזִיר Pr 11^{22}.

2. *earring*, ornament of men and women, Gn 35^{4}, נ׳ אֲשֶׁר בְּאָזְנֵיהֶם so Ex $32^{2.3}$ (all E), cf Pr 25^{12} (in sim of wise reprover), and perh. Ex 35^{22} (P; ‖ טַבַּעַת), prob also Ju $8^{24.24.25.26}$ (of men, cf. GFM), Jb 42^{11} —Cf further Gei^Jüd Zeitschr x (1872), 45 ff^ RS^Sem i. 434, 2d ed 453^, also ref. sub נזר.

†[נֵ֫זֶק] **n.[m.] injury, damage** (Aram. loan-word v BAram),—only cstr. בְּנֵזֶק הַמֶּלֶךְ Est 7^{4} *at the price of injury to the king*

[נָזַר] **vb. dedicate, consecrate,** (cf We^Skizzen iii 118^), **separate**, in relig and ceremonial sense (NH only as denom, cf II נזר, Ar نَذَرَ *make a vow*, cf. We^Skizzen iii 117 f^, RS^i 463 f., 2d ed. 482 f.^; Sab נדר *vow* Levy^ZMG xxii (1868), 196^ Min. *id*, Hom^Südar Chrest 128^; Aram נְדַר, ܢܕܪ, *vow*, As. *nazâru*, *curse* Dl^HWB 457^),—**Niph.** *Impf* יִנָּזֵר Ez 14^{7}, וְיִנָּזְרוּ Lv 22^{2}, וַיִּנָּזְרוּ Ho 9^{10}; *Inf. abs* הִנָּזֵר Zc 7^{3},—*devote, dedicate oneself* unto (לְ), הַבֹּשֶׁת, i.e Ba'al Ho 9^{10}; from (מִן) י׳ Ez 14^{7} (of apostasy), *hold sacredly aloof* from, (מִן) Lv 22^{2} (H), abs. Zc 7^{3} *consecrating my(self)*, i e by fasting. **Hiph.** *Pf.* וְהִזַּרְתֶּם אֶת־בְּנֵי־יִשׂ׳ מִטֻּמְאָתָם Lv 15^{31} (P) *and ye shall keep the sons of Isr. sacredly separate from their uncleanness* (but rd. perh וְהִזְהַרְתֶּם *warn* away from—as Ez 3^{18} $33^{8.9}$,—so Sam 𝔊—as to sense—Di Kau) —Vid. also II. [נָזַר].

†נֵ֫זֶר **n m.**^ψ 132, 18^ **consecration, crown, Naziriteship**;—נ׳ abs 2 S 1^{10}+; cstr. Ex 29^{6}+, sf. נִזְרוֹ ψ 89^{40}+, נִזְרֵךְ Je 7^{29},—**1.** *crown* (sign of consecration, We^Skizzen iii. 118^ cp. Syr ܩܕܫܐ [ܩܕܫܐ], *earring*; v also Gei^Jüd Zeitschr x 45 ff^ on נֶזֶם) **a.** of kg 2 S 1^{10} 2 K 11^{12} = 2 Ch 23^{11}, symbol of royal power ψ 89^{40} 132^{18}; cf. Pr 27^{21}; אַבְנֵי נ׳ Zc 9^{16} *stones of a crown, diadem* (prob.; > We Now—who del, cf GASm—*stones of charming*, fr. use of precious stones as charms **b.** of high priest, נ׳ הַקֹּדֶשׁ Ex 29^{6}, made of gold 39^{30} Lv 8^{9} (all P) **2.** woman's *hair* (orig. prob of long hair as sign of consecration, as in Nazirite vow, cf Nu 6^{19} infr., and נָזִיר, also We^Skizzen iii 117, 167, Arab Heidenthum2 p.143^ RS^Sem i. 464, 2d ed 483^), Je 7^{29} (of personif. Jerus) **3.** *consecration* **a.** of h p נ׳ שֶׁמֶן מִשְׁחַת אֱ׳ עָלָיו Lv 21^{12} (P) *the consecration of the oil of anointing of his God is upon him* **b.** in Nu 6 (P), specif of Nazirite consecration (cf נָזִיר) · נ׳ אֱלֹהָיו עָלָיו Nu 6^{7}, נֶדֶר נִזְרוֹ v^{5}, טִמֵּא נ׳ v^{12}, רֹאשׁ נ׳ (because of unshorn hair) $v^{9.18.18}$, (כָּל־) יְמֵי נ׳ $v^{4.8.12.13}$, תּוֹרַת נ׳ v^{21b} cf עַל־נ׳ v^{21a}, in v^{19} נ׳ = *the hair of his consecration* (cf Je 7^{29} supr)

†נָזִיר **n.m.**^Gn 49, 26^ **one consecrated, devoted** (נזיר י׳ Ecclus 46^{13e} (of Samuel); cf Syr. ܢܙܝܪܐ RS^Sem i 465, 2d ed 485^);—נ׳ abs Nu 6^{2}+5 t, cstr נְזִיר Gn 49^{26}+4 t.; sf נְזִירֶךָ Lv 25^{5}; pl נְזִרִים Am $2^{11.12}$, sf. נְזִירֶיהָ Lv 25^{11}, נְזִירֶיהָ La 4^{7},—**1.** of prince, ruler, as *consecrated*. נְזִיר אֶחָיו Gn 49^{26} (poem in J), *one consecrated among his brethren*, = Dt 33^{16}; cf נְזִירֶיהָ La 4^{7} *her princes*. **2.** specif. of one dedicated to י׳ by vow involving abstinence fr. intoxicants, fr touching corpse, and fr. cutting hair (cf נזר **2**), *devotee* (GFM), *Nazirite*: נ׳ אלהים *God's devotee*, of Samson Ju $13^{5.7}$ 16^{17} (exceptionally, from birth); usu. voluntary Am $2^{11.12}$, and for limited time, cf. נֶדֶר נ׳ Nu 6^{2} (of man or woman; cf. Peritz^JBL xvii (1898), 128^), תּוֹרַת נ׳ $v^{13.21}$, also $v^{18.19.20}$ (all P; cf also נזר) —On Naz. v. GFM^Ju 13, 5^ Dr^Am 2, 11^, esp. Grill^JPTh. 1880. 645–680^ Now^Arch. ii. § 97^ Benz^Arch. 429 f^ Gray^JThS Jan. 1900, 201 ff.^ **3.** = *untrimmed vine* (like Nazirite with unshorn hair) Lv $25^{5.11}$ (HP).

† [נָזַר] **vb. denom. Hiph.** *be a Nazirite, live as Nazirite*, sq. מִן (abstaining) *from* (so NH),—only Nu 6 in law of Naz: *Pf.* וְהִזִּיר לַי׳ consec v^{12}; *Impf.* יַזִּיר לַי׳ v^{5}, also מִיַּיִן . . . יַזִּיר v^{3} *from wine . he shall abstain as a Nazirite*; *Inf.* לְהַזִּיר לַי׳ v^{2}, כָּל־יְמֵי הַזִּירוֹ לַי׳ v^{6}.

†[מִנְזָר] **n.[m.]pl.** perh. **consecrated** (i e. anointed) **ones, princes**,—only sf. מִנְּזָרַיִךְ Na 3^{17} with d. f dirim. Ges^§ 20 h^ (of Nineveh),—form dub.; Ko^ii 1, 90^ prop. מִנְזָרַיִךְ = *thy crowned ones*; Gr רוֹזְנַיִךְ; Now GASm leave untranslated.

נַחַ **n.pr.** v. נוח   נַחְבִּי **n.pr.** v חבה.

†[נָחָה] **vb. lead, guide** (Ar. نَحَا *go in direction of, turn* (eyes) *toward*);—**Qal** *Pf.* sf. נָחַנִי Gn 24^{27}+2 t., וְנָחֲךָ Is 58^{11}, נָחָם Ex 13^{17}; 2 ms נָחִיתָ Ex 15^{13} ψ 77^{21}; *Imv.* נחה Ex 32^{34}; sf. נְחֵנִי ψ 5^{9}+2 t,—*lead, bring*, sq acc. pers, subj. man Ex 32^{34} (sq. אֶל־), cf. ψ 60^{11} 108^{11} (both sq. עַד־; ‖ הוביל); usu subj י׳ Gn 24^{27} (J; also sq. בַּדֶּרֶךְ + acc. loc), Ex 13^{17} (E; sq. דֶּרֶךְ), 15^{13} (song, ‖ נהל), ψ 77^{21}; fig. of guidance in prosperity and righteousness ψ 5^{9} (‖ הושר דרך), 27^{11} (sq. בְּאֹרַח ‖ הורה דרך), 139^{24} (sq בדרך עולם); cf Is 58^{11} **Hiph.** *Pf* sf. הִנְחַנִי Gn 24^{48}, 2 ms. sf הִנְחִתָם Ne 9^{12}, *Impf.* sf. יַנְחֵנִי Nu 23^{7} ψ 23^{3}, יַנְחֵנוּ Dt 32^{12} Pr 18^{16}; 3 fs. תַּנְחֶה Pr 6^{22}, etc; *Inf. cstr.* sf לְהַנְחֹתָם Ne 9^{19}, לַנְחֹתָם Ex

13[21];—*lead, guide* (=Qal) sq. acc pers Nu 23[7] (JE; +מִן) —1 S 22[4] (+אֶת־פְּנֵי), 1 K 10[26] 2 K 18[11] v. sub נוח **Hiph.** B —; of guiding=treating kindly (the helpless) Jb 31[18], of guiding constellations 38[32] (‖הוציא); usu. subj. י׳ Gn 24[48] (J; sq בְּדֶרֶךְ) Dt 32[12] ψ 78[14.53.72] (Isr. as flock; ‖רעה); Is 57[18] ψ 107[30] (sq אֶל־); cf. of pillar of cloud Ex 13[21] (J), Ne 9[12.19]; also Jb 12[23] (‖שטח), ψ 67[5], esp. in path of blessing ψ 23[3] 31[4] (‖נהל), 61[3] (sq בְּ), 73[24]; cf. 43[3] 139[10] (‖אחז), 143[10] (sq. בְּ); also of instruction, etc., Pr 6[22] 11[3] 18[16] (sq לִפְנֵי)

I. **נחל** (√of foll; cf. Ar نَحَلَ *give for one's own, bestow,* so Sab נחל Sab. Denkm No 9, 1 10, No 15, 1 4, cf. pp. 41, 65; hence נַחֲלָה orig. *gift,* as Sab נחלת Levy-Os ZMG xix (1865), 284 Sab. Denkm. l.c.; Min. *id*, Hom Südar Chrest. 128)

נַחֲלָה 224 **n.f. possession, property, inheritance** (orig *gift;* NH=BH);—נ׳ Nu 18[23]+; נַחֲלַת ψ 16[6] (Ges § 80 g), rd. נַחֲלָתִי Ew SS We Ko ii 1, 42a; cstr. נַחֲלַת Jos 13[23], sf נַחֲלָתִי Ru 4[6]; נַחֲלַתְכֶם ψ 105[11]; pl. נחלות Is 49[8], נְחָלֹת Jos 19[51];—**1.** *property:* **a.** in Canaan given by י׳ to Israel, †נחלת ישראל Ju 20[6]; †נ׳ יעקב Is 58[14], esp. †אֲשֶׁר נֹתֵן לְךָ נַחֲלָה Dt 4[21] 15[4] 19[10] 20[16] 21[23] 24[4] 25[19] 26[1] (all D); הנחלה אשר הנחלתי את עמי Je 12[14]. **b.** distrib among tribes. נתן נ׳ לְ Nu 16[14] 36[2] Jos 14[3] (restore לְ), 17[4.14] 19[49] (all P); נתן לנ׳ לְ Dt 29[7] Jos 11[23] 14[13] (all D[2]); נָפְלוּ נחלה Jos 17[6] (J), תחלק בנ׳ Nu 26[53.54] (P), נפל בנחלה Nu 34[2] (P), Ju 18[1] Ez 47[22], הפיל בנ׳ Jos 13[6] 23[4] (D[2]), Ez 45[1] 47[22], also v[29] (Co rds. ב for מ). **c.** nations as possession of the people, ψ 111[6], of the king 2[8]. **d.** Levites have no property in the land Nu 18[23.24] Dt 10[9] 12[12], their possession is י׳ Nu 18[20] (P), י׳ הוא נחלתו Dt 10[9] 18[2] Jos 13[14.33] (all D), the tithes Nu 18[21.24.26] (P) **e.** †י׳ takes Isr. as his property, 1 S 10[1] 1 K 8[53] 2 K 21[14] Is 19[25] Mi 7[18] ψ 33[12] 68[10] 106[5], עם נחלה Dt 4[20] (D[2]), עַמְּךָ וְנַחֲלָתְךָ Dt 9[26.29] (D), 1 K 8[51], ‖ עם Is 47[6] Jo 2[17] 4[2] Mi 7[14] ψ 28[9] 78[62.71] 94[5.14] 106[40]; נחלת י׳ 1 S 26[19] 2 S 20[19] 21[3]; נ׳ אלהים 2 S 14[16], יעקב חבל נ׳ Dt 32[9]; שבט נ׳ Je 10[16]=51[19], ψ 74[2], שבטי נ׳ Is 63[17]; also, the holy mt. Ex 15[17] (song), temple Je 12[7] ψ 79[1], land Je 2[7] 12[8.9] 16[18] 50[11]. †**2.** *portion, share:* **a.** assigned by God, Is 54[17] ψ 37[18] 127[3], elsewh ‖ חלק Jb 20[29] 27[13] 31[2]. **b.** by choice, ‖חֵלֶק, לא נ׳ לנו בבן ישי 2 S 20[1] *we have no share in the son of Jesse*=1 K 12[16]=2 Ch 10[16]. **3.** *inheritance* (45 t.) חֵלֶק וְנַחֲלָה בְּבֵית אָבִינוּ Gn 31[14] (E) *portion or inheritance in the house of our father;* העביר נ׳ לְ Nu 27[7.8] (P) *cause the inheritance to pass unto;* נתן נ׳ ל Nu 27[9.10.11] (P), Jb 42[15], †נחלת אבות Nu 36[3.8] 1 K 21[3.4] Pr 19[14], נ׳ לבניו תהיה Ez 46[16].

†**נָחַל** **vb. denom. get or take as a possession** (cf Gerber 236 ff; Ecclus נחל 45[22b]+; NH *id.* (rare));—**Qal** *Pf.* נ׳ Zc 2[16], 2 ms נָחַלְתָּ Ex 23[30]+8 t. Pf.; *Impf.* 3 ms. יִנְחַל Is 57[13]; 3 mpl. יִנְחָלוּ Nu 18[23]+5 t.; יִנְחֲלוּ 26[55]+2 t; +8 t. Impf.; *Inf.* נְחֹל Nu 34[18] Jos 19[49],—**1.** *take possession, inherit* · **a.** land of Canaan, Ex 23[30] (E), 32[13] (J), Is 57[13] Ez 47[14]; Zion and Judah ψ 69[37]. **b.** special sections in the land, of tribes and individuals, נחל נחלה Jos 17[6] (J); נחלה אשר נ׳ Dt 19[14] (D), Nu 35[8] (P), cf. Jos 14[1] (P); without acc, *have or get a* (landed) *property,* Nu 18[20.23.24] 26[55] 32[19] Jos 16[4] 19[9] (all P), Ju 11[2]. **c.** land of Moab and Ammon by conquest Zp 2[9]; landed property בכל הגוים ψ 82[8]. **d.** God takes possession of Israel as his private property Ex 34[9] (J); Judah Zc 2[16]. **2.** fig. *have or get as a possession, property* testimonies ψ 119[111], glory Pr 3[35], good things 28[10], lies Je 16[19], wind Pr 11[29], simplicity 14[18]. **3.** *divide the land for a possession,* Nu 34[17.18] Jos 19[49] (all P; incorrect pointing for Piel, so SS)

Pi. *divide for a possession* · *Pf.* 3 ms. נִחַל Jos 13[32]; 3 pl. נִחֲלוּ Jos 14[1] 19[51]; *Inf.* נַחֵל Nu 34[29] (all P), also Nu 34[17.18] Jos 19[49] (v. **Qal 3**)

Hithp. *Pf.* 3 pl sf הִתְנַחֲלוּם Is 14[2]; 2 mpl. הִתְנַחַלְתֶּם Lv 25[46] Nu 33[54]; *Impf.* תִתְנַחֲלוּ Nu 34[13] Ez 47[13]; תתנחלו Nu 33[54]; *Inf* הִתְנַחֵל Nu 32[18]; *possess oneself of* land (acc), Nu 33[54] 34[13] (P) Ez 47[13]; נחלה Nu 32[18] (P); slaves Lv 25[46] (P) Is 14[2], abs., ref. to land Nu 33[54] (P), all c. לְ pers. (for whose benefit), exc. Nu 32[18] 34[13] Is 14[2].

Hiph. *Pf.* 1 s הִנְחַלְתִּי Je 3[18]+3 t. Pf.; *Impf* 3 ms יַנְחִיל Dt 3[28], יַנחל Ez 46[18]; 2 ms sf תַּנְחִילֶנָּה Dt 31[7]+5 t. Impf, *Inf. cstr.* הַנְחִיל Is 49[8] Pr 8[21], בְּהַנְחֵל Dt 32[8] (on form cf Ew § 238 d Ko i. 335 Ges § 53 k; rd. בהנחל?); sf. הַנְחִילוֹ Dt 21[16], *Pt.* מַנְחִיל Dt 12[10];—**1.** *give as a possession:* **a.** land of Canaan (given by י׳ or his servants), acc pers et rei, Dt 1[38] 3[28] 12[10] 19[3] 31[7] Jos 1[6] (all D), Je 3[18] 12[14]. **b.** various things, acc. pers et rei, espec blessings, Zc 8[12] 1 S 2[8] Pr 8[21]; acc. rei Is 49[8]; acc. pers Dt 32[8]. **2.** *cause to inherit, give as an inheritance,* c. acc. pers et rei, Dt 21[16]; acc. pers.+מן rei, Ez 46[18], acc. pers. Pr 13[22]; לְ

pers. 1 Ch 28[8]. **Hoph.** *Pf.* 1 s. הָנְחַלְתִּי Jb 7[3] *made to possess*, c. acc. rei, e.g. *months of vanity*.

[נְחִילָה] **n.f.** meaning unknown; only pl. in phr. אֶל־הַנְּחִילוֹת ψ 5[1] (title); most conj. = נְחִלוֹת √חלל = חָלִיל *flute*; v. against this Bae[Einl. xi], who thinks (cf. 𝔊 ὑπὲρ τῆς κληρονομούσης = אֶל־הַנַּחֲלָת [cf. 𝔙], Jerome [Aq. Symm] *pro hereditatibus* = אֶל־הַנַּחֲלֹת) possibly designation of a melody.

II. נחל (√ of foll.; meaning unknown).

†I. נַחַל **n.m.**[2 K 3.16] **torrent, torrent-valley, wady** (Ecclus 40[13.16]; NH *id.*, *stream* (rare); 𝔗 נַחְלָא, Syr. ܢܰܚܠܳܐ, = BH; As. *naḫlu* = BH; Lag[BN 140 Anm.] thinks Νεῖλος may be from Νεέλ = נחל pronounced *נְחֵל; on נ׳ in Sab. n.pr.loc., v. Hal[Rev. Sémit. iv (1896), 80, l. 14]);—abs. נ׳ Gn 32[24]+, נַחְלָה ψ 124[4]; cstr. נַחַל Gn 26[17]+; c. ה loc. Nu 34[5]; so read also Ez 47[19] 48[28] (where MT נַחֲלָה; v. Thes); du. נַחְלַיִם Ez 47[9], but rd. הַנַּחַל 𝔊 𝔗 𝔖 𝔙 Co Berthol; pl. נְחָלִים Nu 21[4]+; נַחֲלֵי Dt 8[7]+; sf. נְחָלֶיהָ Is 34[9];—**1.** *torrent*, of rushing water in narrow channel Ju 5[21.21.21] 4[7.13] ψ 83[10] (all of קִישׁוֹן, q.v.); mountain torrent Dt 9[21] (cf. Ex 32[20]); so Am 5[24] (sim. of righteousness); הַנּ׳ הַשּׁוֹטֵף 2 Ch 32[4] (|| מַעְיָנוֹת); נֶהְפְּכוּ נ׳ לְזֶפֶת Is 34[9]; sim. of tears La 2[18]; hyperb. נ׳־שָׁמֶן Mi 6[7] *torrents of oil*, cf. of honey and curd Jb 20[17] (|| פְּלַגּוֹת, נְהָרִים); fig. נ׳ בְלִיַּעַל 2 S 22[5] *torrents of worthlessness* (|| מִשְׁבְּרֵי מָוֶת), = ψ 18[5]; נ׳ שׁוֹטֵף sim. of glory of nations Is 66[12], fig. of invaders Je 47[2] (|| מַיִם), or foes ψ 124[4] (נַחְלָה, v. supr.); 1 K 17[4.6] (for drinking), drying up in summer v[7] (יָבֵשׁ; all of Elijah's stream כְּרִית, q.v.); for drinking also ψ 110[7], and (fig.) נ׳ עֲדָנֶיךָ 36[9]; Jb 6[15.15] (אֲפִיק; נְחָלִים in sim.); of water bursting from rock ψ 78[20] (מַיִם || שָׁטַף), cf. 74[15] (+ מַעְיָן); fig. of מְקוֹר חָכְמָה Pr 18[4] (מַיִם עֲמֻקִּים || נ׳ נֹבֵעַ); more gen. = stream, brook, river (chiefly late) Is 11[15] (divisions of river, נָהָר), in desert 35[6] (|| מַיִם), Je 31[9] (נַחֲלֵי מַיִם), Ez 47[5.5.9b] (all del. Co), v[6.7.9a] (rd. הַנַּחַל, v. supr.), v[12]; containing fish, etc. Lv 11[9.10] (|| יַמִּים, מַיִם), Ec 1[7.7]; fig. of רוּחַ י׳ Is 30[28] (נ׳ שׁוֹטֵף), 30[33] (נ׳ גָּפְרִית).

2. *Torrent-valley, wady*, as stream-bed 1 S 17[40] Ne 2[15] Is 57[6]; with torrent flowing through it, נ׳ אֵיתָן Dt 21[4.4.6], אֶרֶץ נַחֲלֵי מַיִם Dt 8[7] (|| עֲיָנֹת וּתְהֹמֹת יֹצְאִים בַּבִּקְעָה מַעְיָנֵי וּבָהָר); cf. 10[7], 1 K 18[5] (|| הַמַּיִם), ψ 104[10]; abode of Elijah 1 K 17[3.5] (cf. v[4.6.7] supr.); עֹרְבֵי נ׳ Pr 30[17] (cf. 1 K 17[4.6]); נ׳ הַבַּתּוֹת Is 7[19] as home of bees; fertile, נ׳ אֶשְׁכֹּל Nu 13[23.24] (E); אִבֵּי הַנּ׳ Ct 6[11]; עַרְבֵי־נ׳ *poplars of the wady* Lv 23[40] (H), Jb 40[22]; נ׳ עֲרָבִים Is 15[7]; needing water Gn 26[17] (נ׳ גְּרָר), v[19] (J), cf. 2 K 3[16.17]; place for refuse, ruins, etc. 2 S 17[13]; poet., also as wild, remote *ravine* Jb 30[6], cf. בְּצוּר הַנְּחָלִים 22[24]; place of child-sacrifice Is 57[5]; burial-place Jb 21[33] (רִגְבֵי נ׳).—Nu 24[6] v. II. נַחַל.

Particular wadys designate localities: אַרְנוֹן Nu 21[14] (E), Dt 2[24.36.36] 3[8.12.16.16] 4[48] Jos 12[1.2.2] 13[9.9] (all D), v[16.16] (P), 2 K 10[33]; אֶשְׁכֹּל Nu 32[9] (J), Dt 1[24]; בְּשׂוֹר 1 S 30[9.10.21]; גָּד 2 S 24[5]; זֶרֶד Nu 21[12] (E), Dt 2[13.13.14]; יַבֹּק Gn 32[24] (J), Dt 2[37] 3[16] Jos 12[2] (all D); קִדְרוֹן 2 S 15[23] 1 K 2[37] 15[13] 18[40] 23[6.6.12] 2 Ch 15[16] 29[16] 30[14] Je 31[40]; קָנָה Jos 16[8] 17[9.9.9] (all P); שׂוֹרֵק Ju 16[4]; נ׳ הַשִּׁטִּים Jo 4[18]; נ׳ מִצְרַיִם is SW. limit of Pal. (As. *naḫal* [*mat*] *Muṣri*, Dl[Par. 310] Schr[COT Nu 34, 5]) Nu 34[5] (P), Jos 15[4] (D), v[47] (P), 1 K 8[65] 2 K 24[7] 2 Ch 7[8] Is 27[12], + (om. מצרים) Ez 47[19] 48[28] (v. supr.); so rd. also poss. Am 6[14] (v. עֲרָבָה: usually identified with *Wâdy el-Arîsh*; on Wkl's different view, v. reff. sub מִצְרַיִם *ad fin.*); on identif. of נ׳ Jos 15[7] 19[11] (both P), 2 S 23[30] = 1 Ch 11[32], 2 Ch 20[16] 33[14], v. Comm.; אֶשֶׁד הַנְּחָלִים Nu 21[15], v. אֶשֶׁד.

3. *Miner's shaft*, פָּרַץ נ׳ Jb 28[4].

†II. [נַחַל] **n.[m.]** perh. **palm-tree** (Ar. نَخْلٌ, n. unit. نَخْلَةٌ; v. Perles[JQ. July, 1899, 688]);—only pl. abs., כִּנְחָלִים נִטָּיוּ Nu 24[6] *like palm-trees, which are stretched out, spread out* (as to foliage). So Perles[l.c.], who compares כערבי נחל Ecclus 50[12e], 𝔊 ὡς στελέχη φοινίκων.

†נַחֲלִיאֵל **n.pr.loc.** (= *valley*—or *palm*—*of Ēl*);—station of Isr. E. of Dead Sea Nu 21[19.19] (JE), poss. (if = *valley*) one of main tributaries of Arnon, e.g. *W. Wâle* (v. Bliss[PEF 1895, 204, 215]).

†נֶחֱלָמִי **adj.gent.** (noun not found);—Je 29[24]; also v[31.32] (where van d. H. נֶחְלָמִי).

נַחֲלָת v. נַחֲלָה.

†[נחם] **vb. Niph. be sorry, console oneself**, etc. (only in der. species) (NH Pi. *comfort*; Ph. in n.pr. Lzb[322]; 𝔗 Pa. = NH, and deriv.; Chr Pal Aram. Pa. *id.*, Schwally[Idiot. 54]; Ar. نَحَمَ *breathe pantingly* (of horse));—**Niph.** *Pf.* נִחַם Am 7[3] + 4 t.; נִחָם Je 20[16] + 2 t.; 1 s. נִחַמְתִּי Gn 6[7] + 8 t.; נִחָמְתִּי Zc 8[14]; 2 mpl. נִחַמְתֶּם Ez 14[22]; *Impf.* יִנָּחֵם Ex 13[17] + 6 t.; וַיִּנָּחֶם Gn 6[6] + 6 t.; + 5 t. Impf.; *Imv.* הִנָּחֵם Ex 32[12] ψ 90[13]; *Inf.* הִנָּחֵם Je 31[15] 1 S 15[29]; *Pt.* נִחָם Ju 21[15] + 3 t.;

—**1.** *be sorry, moved to pity, have compassion,* for others, abs. Je 15^{6}; c. על ψ 90^{13}; אֶל Ju 21^{6}; לְ v^{15}; מִן 2^{18}. **2.** *be sorry, rue, suffer grief, repent,* of one's own doings, abs. Ex 13^{17} (E), ψ 106^{45} Je 20^{16} Jo 2^{14} Zc 8^{14}; ‖ שׁקר 1 S 15$^{29.29}$; מאס Jb 42^{6}; שׁוב Je 4^{28} 31^{19} Jon 3^{9}; חוס Ez 24^{14}; לא נ׳ ‖, נשׁבע ψ 110^{4}; c. על Am 7$^{3.6}$ Je 8^{6} 18^{10}; על־הרעה for ill done to others Ex 32$^{12.14}$(J), Je 18^{8} Jo 2^{13} Jon 3^{10} 4^{2}; אל־הרעה 2 S 24^{16} = 1 Ch 21^{15} (על), Je 26$^{3.13.19}$ 42^{10}; כִּי Gn 6$^{6.7}$ (J), 1 S 15$^{11.35}$. **3.** *comfort oneself, be comforted:* abs. Gn 38^{12} (J) ψ 77^{3} Ez 31^{16}; c. על 2 S 13^{39} Je 31^{15}; על הרעה, *concerning the evil* Ez 14^{22} 32^{31}; אחרי Gn 24^{67} (J). **4.** *comfort oneself, ease oneself,* by taking vengeance c. מן Is 1^{24}; על 57^{6}.

Piel *Pf.* נִחַם Is 49^{13}; + 8 t. Pf.; *Impf.* יְנַחֵם Jb 29^{25}; 3 mpl. יְנַחֲמוּ Jb 42^{11}; יְנַחֵמוּן Zc 10^{2} + 13 t. Impf.; *Imv.* נַחֲמוּ Is 40$^{1.1}$; *Inf.* נַחֵם Is 61^{2}; sf. נַחֲמוֹ Gn 37^{35} + 9 t. Inf.; *Pt.* מְנַחֵם La 1^{2}, pl. מְנַחֲמִים ψ 69^{21}, + 11 t. Pt.—*comfort, console,* abs. Gn 37^{35} (J), 1 Ch 19^{3} = 2 S 10^{3}; ψ 69^{21} Ec 4$^{1.1}$ Zc 10^{2} Na 3^{7} La 1^{16}; c. acc. pers. Gn 50^{21} (E) 2 S 12^{24} 1 Ch 7^{21} 19^{2} Jb 2^{11} 7^{13} 21^{34} 29^{25} Ru 2^{13} ψ 23^{4} 71^{21} 119$^{76.82}$ Is 12^{1} 22^{4} 40$^{1.1}$ 51$^{3.3.12.19}$ 61^{2} 66$^{13.13}$ Ez 14^{23} 16^{54} Zc 1^{17} La 2^{13}; ‖ עזר ψ 86^{17}; רִחֵם Is 49^{13}; גאל Is 52^{9}; שׂמּח Je 31^{13}; מן rei Gn 5^{29} (J); על Je 16^{7} 42^{11}; אל 2 S 10^{2} = על 1 Ch 19^{2}; מְנַחֲמֵי עמל Jb 16^{2}; אֵין מְנַחֵם לְ La 1$^{2.9.17.21}$.

Pual *Pf.* נֻחָמָה Is 54^{11}; *Impf.* תְּנֻחָמוּ Is 66^{13}; *be comforted, consoled.*

Hithpa. Pf. 1 s. וְהִנֶּחָמְתִּי (for הִתְנ׳; but del. Co) Ez 5^{13}; *Impf.* יִתְנֶחָם Dt 32^{36} + 2 t.; 1 s. אֶתְנֶחָם ψ 119^{52}; *Inf.* הִתְנַחֵם Gn 37^{35}; *Pt.* מִתְנַחֵם Gn 27^{42}—**1.** *be sorry, have compassion* עַל־עֲבָדָיו *upon his servants* Dt 32^{36} = ψ 135^{14}. **2.** *rue, repent of,* ‖ כזב, Nu 23^{19} (poem). **3.** *comfort oneself, be comforted,* abs. Gn 37^{35} (J), ψ 119^{52}. **4.** *ease oneself,* by taking vengeance Ez 5^{13} (?); c. לְ pers. Gn 27^{42} (JE): cf. **Qal 4.**

† נַחַם **n.pr.m.** (*comfort*), a chieftain of Judah 1 Ch 4^{19}; 𝔊 Ναχεθ, A Ναχεμ, 𝔊L Ναουμ.

† נֹחַם **n.m.** *sorrow, repentance,* Ho 13^{14}.

† נַחוּם **n. pr. m.** (*comfort*) the prophet Nahum, Na 1^{1}, 𝔊 Ναουμ.

† נְחוּם **n.pr.m.** (*comfort*) a returned exile Ne 7^{7} 𝔊 Ναουμ = רְחוּם Ezr 2^{2}.

† [נִחוּם] **n.m. 1.** *comfort,* pl. נִחֻמִים Is 57^{18} Zc 1^{13}. **2.** *compassion,* sf. נִחוּמָי Ho 11^{8} (We rds. רַחֲמַי).

† נְחֶמְיָה **n.pr.m.** (*Yah comforts,* 𝔊 Νεεμιας (-ου), etc.;—n.pr. נחמיה(ו) on Isr. scarab in BM, Cl-Gann$^{JAs 1883, Fév.-Mars. 156 No. 42}$);—**1.** the son of Hachaliah, governor of Judah under Artaxerxes Longimanus Ne 1^{1} 8^{9} 10^{2} 12$^{26.47}$. **2.** ruler of half the district of Bethzur Ne 3^{16}. **3.** one of twelve heads of people who returned with Zerubbabel Ezr 2^{2} = Ne 7^{7}.

† נַחֲמָנִי **n.pr.m.** (*compassionate*) a returned exile Ne 7^{7}; 𝔊 Νεεμιου (gen.).

† [נֶחָמָה] **n.f. comfort,** sf. נֶחָמָתִי ψ 119^{50} Jb 6^{10}.

† מְנַחֵם **n. pr. m.** (*comforter*), king of Northern Israel, 2 K 15$^{14.16.17.19.20.21.22.23}$; 𝔊 Μαναημ.

† [תַּנְחוּם] **n.m.**$^{ψ 94.19}$ *consolation,* only in pl. (usually abstr. and intensive) תַּנְחוּמִים Je 16^{7}; sf. תַּנְחוּמֶיךָ ψ 94^{19}; תַּנְחֻמֶיהָ Is 66^{11}; תַּנְחוּמוֹת Jb 15^{11}; תַּנְחוּמֹתֵיכֶם 21^{2}.

† תַּנְחֻמֶת **n.pr.m.** (? Lag$^{BN 126 f.}$ thinks **f.**) parent of Seraiah, a Hebr. captain, after fall of Jerus. Je 40^{8} = 2 K 25^{23} (Lag$^{l.c.}$ conj. תסחמת, Egyptian name).

נַחְנוּ v. אֲנַחְנוּ p. 59 b supr.

† [נָחַץ] **vb. urge** (?), whence (si vera l.);—**Qal** *Pt. pass.* (*active* Pt. in *u*, acc. to Ba$^{NB 175}$), דְּבַר הַמֶּלֶךְ נָחוּץ 1 S 21^{9} *the king's business was urgent* (𝔊 κατὰ σπουδήν, A κατασπεῦδον). (Thes cp. Ar. نَحَصَ *ursit institique rogando* [Kam Frey]); text dub.; HPS נָאוֹץ (from אוץ), > נחושׁ.

נחר (prob. onomatop. √ of foll.; cf. As. *naḫîru, nostril;* Ar. نَخَرَ *snort,* نُخْرٌ *nostril;* Eth. ንኅር: *snort;* Syr. ܢܚܪ *id.,* ܢܚܝܪܐ *nostril;* 𝔗 נְחִירָא *id.;* also NH Pi. *snort*).—נְחַר Je 6^{29} etc., v. I. חרר.

† [נַחַר] **n.[m.] a snorting;** sf. נַחְרוֹ Jb 39^{20} (of horse).

† [נַחֲרָה] **n.f.** id.;—cstr. נַחֲרַת סוּסָיו Je 8^{16}.

† נָחוֹר **n.pr.m.** (connexion with √ obscure);—**1.** father of Teraḥ Gn 11$^{22.23.24.25}$ (all P), 1 Ch 1^{26}. **2.** son of Teraḥ and brother of Abr. Gn 11$^{26.27}$ (P), v$^{29.29}$ 22$^{20.23}$ 24$^{15.24.47}$ cf. 29^{5} (all J), Jos 24^{2} (E); עִיר נ׳ Gn 24^{10} (J); אֱלֹהֵי נ׳ 31^{53} (E).—𝔊 always Ναχωρ.

†[נָחִיר] **n.[m.]** **nostril** (appar. fr. above √, and not connected with Ar. نَحَرَ *stab* camel in wind-pipe, etc, Aram. נחר *kill by stabbing* in nose or throat, cf NH נָחַר *perforate, kill by stabbing*, so that נָחִיר would = *perforation*, and נחר *snort* wd be denom),—only du sf מִנְּחִירָיו יֵצֵא עָשָׁן Jb 41[12] (of crocodile)

†נַחְרַי **n.pr m.** one of David's heroes, 2 S 23[37], 𝔊 Γελωρε, 𝔊L Αραια; = †נַחְרַי 1 Ch 11[39], 𝔊 Ναχωρ, A Naapai, 𝔊L Noapai.

I. **נחש** (appar onomatop. √ of foll. = *hiss*, so Thes Bau[Sem Rel i 287] al)

†I **נָחָשׁ** **n.m.**[Gn 3,1] **serpent** (NH *id*, Ar حَنَش *serpent, viper* (Lane[406] anything *hunted*) is cp by Lag[M i 230, BN 50, 188] Ba[ES 48], but improb.; Ar نَحِسَ v. sub [נָחַשׁ] infr, on formation cf Lag[BN 50]),—abs נ׳ Am 5[19]+; cstr נחשׁ Nu 21[9]+ 2 t; pl נְחָשִׁים Nu 21[6] Je 8[17],—**1.** *serpent*: **a.** as biting, Am 5[19] Ec 10[8], in spite of charm (לָחַשׁ) v[11] [cf Ecclus 12[13]], Je 8[17] (+צפענים; fig of enemies), so הַנְּחָשִׁים הַשְּׂרָפִים Nu 21[6] (deadly; JE, cf. Jacob[Arab. Dicht iv 10 ff]), and sg. v[9], also (coll) v[7], cf נ׳ שָׂרָף Dt 8[15] (+עַקְרָב), נ׳ fig of oppressor, מִשֹּׁרֶשׁ נָחָשׁ יֵצֵא צֶפַע וּפִרְיוֹ שָׂרָף מְעוֹפֵף Is 14[29], fig of Dan Gn 49[17] (poem in J, ‖ שְׁפִיפֹן), חֲמַת נ׳ ψ 58[5] (sim of perniciousness of ungodly), cf נ׳ 140[4], sim of effect of wine Pr 23[32] (‖ צִפְעֹנִי) **b.** rod becomes נ׳ Ex 4[3] (J), cf 7[15] (E), דֶּרֶךְ נ׳ עֲלֵי צוּר Pr 30[19] **c.** נ׳ (appar) as hissing Je 46[22] (in sim, cf Gie); as eating dust Is 65[25] cf Mi 7[17] (in sim., v also Gn 3[14]) **d** as crafty tempter Gn 3[1 2.4 13 14] **2.** נ׳ (הַ)נְּחֹשֶׁת, bronze image of serpent Nu 21[9 9] 2 K 18[4] (cf נְחֻשְׁתָּן) **3** mythol נ׳ בָּרִחַ Jb 26[13] *fleeing serpent*, of eclipse-dragon (cf לִוְיָתָן 3[8]), also ... לִוְיָתָן נ׳ בָּרִחַ לִוְיָתָן נ׳ עֲקַלָּתוֹן Is 27[1] (symbol of world-powers); נ׳ of sea-monster Am 9[3] —נ׳ c vb. נָשַׁךְ *bite* Nu 21[6]+8 t On supernat. character of serpents in Arab belief v Nö[Zeitschr für Völkerpsychol i (1860), 412-416] RS[Kinship 197, Sem i. 421 f, 2d ed 442] We[Skizzen iii 147, Arab Heid 2. 152 f.] Jacob[Arab Dicht iv 5].

†II **נָחָשׁ** **n pr m.** **1.** king of Ammon 1 S 11[1 1.2] 12[12] 2 S 10[2] 1 Ch 19[1 2], perh also 2 S 17[27], 𝔊 Naas. **2.** father of Abigail and Zeruiah 2 S 17[25], si vera l 𝔊 Naas, but 𝔊L Ιεσσαι (cf. 1 Ch 2[16]), We[Gesch 2 57 Anm 1] Lohr defend נחשׁ; dub We[Sm] HPS **3.** giving name to a city, עִיר נ׳ 1 Ch 4[12], 𝔊 πολεως Naas, 𝔊L Ηρναας

†נַחְשׁוֹן **n.pr.m.** son of Amminadab, of Judah, brother-in-law of Aaron Ex 6[23] Nu 1[7] 2[3] 7[12.17] 10[14] (all P), Ru 4[20.20] 1 Ch 2[10 11]. 𝔊 Ναασσων (DHM[ZMG xxxvii (1883), 15] cp Sab. tribal name נחסן).

†II **[נָחַשׁ]** **vb.** only **Pi.** *practise divination, divine, observe signs* (denom from נָחָשׁ acc. to Nö[Zeitschr f. Völkerpsychol. i (1860), 413] Bau[Sem Rel i 287] Lag[BN 188] Gerber[Verb Denom 29], otherwise We[Skizzen iii 147] Me[Chrest Targ s.v] Ba[ES 48] (agst him v. Sta[Th Lz. April 28, 1894, 235]), chief difficulty is that Aram., which has נְחַשׁ, has no נָחָשׁ, cf. RS[JPh xiv 116],—NH Qal Pt. נוֹחֵשׁ, and Pi; Aram Pa. נַחֵשׁ, ܢܰܚܶܫ, all = *divine, learn by omens*; perh cp also Ar نَحِسَ *be unlucky* Lane[2775] cf Me[l c]),—*Pf.* 3 ms. וְנִחֵשׁ 2 K 21[6] 2 Ch 33[6], 1 s נִחַשְׁתִּי Gn 30[27], *Impf.* יְנַחֵשׁ Gn 44[5 15], 3 mpl. יְנַחֲשׁוּ 1 K 20[33], וַיְנַחֲשׁוּ 2 K 17[17]; 2 mpl תְנַחֲשׁוּ Lv 19[26], *Inf abs* נַחֵשׁ 1 K 20[33], *Pt.* מְנַחֵשׁ Dt 18[10] (cf. esp. RS[JPh. xiv 113 ff]),—**1.** *practise divination* Gn 44[5] (J; by means of cup, i e by hydromancy), with implied power to learn secret things v[15]; condemned by proph. writer 2 K 21[6] = 2 Ch 33[6] (+ עוֹנֵן וְעָשָׂה אוֹב וידענים), 2 K 17[17] (‖ וַיִּקְסְמוּ קְסָמִים); forbidden in D and H Dt 18[10] (+ קסם קסמים מעונן ומכשׁף), Lv 19[26] (H, ‖ תְעוֹנֵנוּ) **2.** *observe the signs* or *omens* Gn 30[27] (J), so prob יְנַחֲשׁוּ 1 K 20[33] now the men *were observing the signs*

†**נַחַשׁ** **n.[m.]** **divination, enchantment,** only abs. נ׳ Nu 23[23] (JE, ‖ קֶסֶם), and pl abs נְחָשִׁים Nu 24[1] (JE), both in story of Balaam

III **נחש** (√ of foll, meaning unknown).

I **נְחֹשֶׁת** **n.m.**[1 K 7,45] (cf Albrecht[ZAW xvi (1896), 106], **f.** 1 Ch 18[8]) **copper, bronze** (NH = BH; Ph. נחשת; Palm נחשא Lzb[322], Syr. ܢܚܳܫܳܐ, 𝔗 נְחָשָׁא, Ar. نُحَاسٌ, Eth. ንሐስ: (so also OEth DHM[Epigr Denkm aus Abess (1894), 52]), WMM[As. u Eur 127] cites Egypt *teh(h)ost, copper* (= *tenhost*), as loan-wd. fr נחשת + fem art.),—נ׳ abs Gn 4[22]+, cstr. Ex 38[29], sf נְחֻשְׁתִּי La 3[7], נְחֻשְׁתֵּךְ Ez 16[36], נְחֻשְׁתָּהּ 24[11], נְחֻשְׁתָּם 2 K 25[13]+2 t., du נְחֻשְׁתַּיִם Ju 16[21] +6 t,—**1.** *copper*, as ore Dt 8[9], cf Zc 6[1], worked by artificer Gn 4[22] (J) 1 K 7[14 14] 2 Ch 24[12], material—doubtless hardened with alloy, prob tin, making *bronze*, cf Now[Arch. i 243] Benz[Arch 214]—of armour 1 S 17[5.6] 1 K 14[27], utensils 2 K 25[14] = Je 52[18], Lv 6[21] Nu 17[4] + very oft, altar 2 K 16[14 15] Ex 38[30] 39[39], etc, and other objects Nu 21[9.9] (JE), 2 K 18[4] 1 K 4[13] 7[15 ff] +, esp. in description of tabernacle and temple; cast 1 K 7[14], polished מְמֹרָט v[45], מָרוּק 2 Ch 4[16] (cf Lv 6[21]), and shining מֻצְהָב Ezr 8[27]. On

נ׳ קָלָל Ez 1[7] Dn 10[6] v. קלל; נ׳ as spoil of war 2 S 8[8] 2 K 25[13] = Je 52[17 20] etc. †**2.** *fetters of copper* or *bronze*, usu. du Ju 16[21] 2 S 3[34] 2 K 25[7] = Je 39[7] 52[11] 2 Ch 36[6], also 33[11]; sg. only La 3[7] (fig. of oppression). **3.** as less in value than gold but more than wood Is 60[17 17]; fig of worthless people Je 6[28] (+ בַּרְזֶל), *id.* (as dross of silver) Ez 22[18] (+ בדיל, בַּרְזֶל, עוֹפֶרֶת). —On Ez 16[36] v. IV. נחשׁ. **4.** fig. of pitiless sky Dt 28[23].

†נָחוּשׁ **adj.** of bronze;—אִם־בְּשָׂרִי נ׳ Jb 6[12] *or is my flesh of bronze?* fig. for strong, enduring (‖ אֲבָנִים; cf. 40[18]).

†נְחוּשָׁה and (Lv 26[19] Jb 40[18]) נְחֻשָׁה **n.f.** copper, bronze (only poet.; cf. I. נְחֹשֶׁת);—נ׳ alw. abs;—**1.** *copper* produced from ore by melting Jb 28[2]. **2.** *copper*, doubtless hardened with alloy, = *bronze*, as material of bow 2 S 22[35] = ψ 18[35], Jb 20[24]; gates Is 45[2], fig of strength Jb 40[18] (bones of hippopotamus), cf. 41[19], Mi 4[13] (hoofs of Zion), of obstinate brow Is 48[4] (‖ גִּיד בַּרְזֶל עָרְפֶּךָ); unproductive earth Lv 26[19].

†נְחֻשְׁתָּא **n.pr.f.** mother of king Jehoiakin 2 K 24[8]; 𝔊 Νεσθα, A Ναισθα, 𝔊L Νεεσθαν.

†נְחֻשְׁתָּן **n.pr.** given to bronze serpent 2 K 18[4] prob. = *bronze*-god (so Thes, v. also Bau[Sem. Rel 1.288]; cf. נחשׁ נחשת v[4] Nu 21[9 9]);—chief arg ag this are vocalization of 𝔊 Νεσθαλει, A𝔊L Νε(ε)σθαν, and comparat. unimportance of material of wh image was made; others think of נָחָשׁ *serpent* (No[ZMG xlii (1888), 482] נחש + תן, Klo[ad loc] נחש + יתן); Lag[BN 188, 205] thinks loan-wd.

IV. נחשׁ (poss √of foll, si vera l.; but precise meaning uncertain; Gei[Urschrift 392] cp. Ar نَحَسَ [= *goad, prick;* نِحَاسٌ a certain piece of *perforated wood* (Frey)], NH נחשת [*bottom* of vessel, Levy[NHWB iii 374]]).

†II. [נְחֹשֶׁת] **n.[f.]** sf. נְחֻשְׁתֵּךְ Ez 16[36] where context (‖ עֶרְוָה) favours mng. *lust, harlotry*, or specif sens obscoen. (Co [citing Ki Ra] Berthol, v. also Da); text perh. crpt (cf. No[ZMG xl (1886), 730]), Sm prop תַּזְנוּתַיִךְ, so appar. Toy[Hpt], Or בָּשְׁתֵּךְ.

†[נָחַת] **vb.** (Aram. and poet) go down, descend (Aram נחת, ܢܚܬ; Palm. נחת Lzb[323]);—**Qal** *Impf.* 3 ms. יֵחַת Je 21[13]; 3 fs תֵּחַת Pr 17[10], וַתִּנְחַת ψ 38[3], 3 mpl. יֵחָתּוּ Jb 21[13] (forms יֵחַת, יֵחָתּוּ v also חתת),—**1.** *go down, descend*, to attack Je 21[13]; into She'ôl Jb 21[13]. **2.** fig. *descend* in chastisement ψ 38[3] (hand of י׳; ‖ **Niph.** v. infr.); sq בְּ *descend into* i.e make impression on, Pr 17[10] (of reproof). **Niph.** *Pf.* 3 mpl. נִחֲתוּ sq. בְּ = *penetrate* ψ 38[3], (of arrows of י׳). **Pi.** *Pf.* 3 ms. consec. וְנִחַת 2 S 22[35] (v. Ges[§ 145. 7]), = 3 fs וְנִחֲתָה ψ 18[35]; *Inf. abs* נַחֵת ψ 65[11];—*cause to descend = press down*, acc. to most, in וְנ׳ קֶשֶׁת נְחוּשָׁה זְרֹעֹתָי 2 S 22[35] = ψ 18[35] *so that my arms press down, stretch*, a bow of bronze, but dub; Bu conj Hiph. יַנְחִת; HPS וַיָּשֶׁת *and makes my arms a bow of bronze;* of *pressing down*, smoothing out, furrows of land ψ 65[11]. **Hiph.** *Imv* הַנְחַת Jo 4[11] thither *bring down* thy heroes, י׳! (on form cf Ges[§ 64 R 3] Ko[i 314 f]).

†II נַחַת **n.[m.]** descent;—only cstr, of י׳'s arm in judgment Is 30[30]—I. נַחַת v. sub נוח.

†[נָחֵת] **adj.** descending,—mpl נְחִתִּים (on form cf Ko[ii 81]), 2 K 6[9] (to battle); but rd. prob. with Th Klo Benz after 𝔊 נֶחְבִּים *hidden*.

†III. נַחַת **n.pr.m.** **1.** son of Reuel, grandson of Esau Gn 36[13.17] (P; 𝔊 Ναχομ, Ναχοθ, 𝔊L Ναχεθ), 1 Ch 1[37] (𝔊 Ναχες, A 𝔊L Ναχεθ) **2.** grandson of Elkanah 1 Ch 6[11], 𝔊 Καιναθ, 𝔊L Νααθ;—prob. crpt. for תּוֹחַ v[19], or תֹּחוּ 1 S 1[1] (v. these words and We[de gent. 37 f.] [who prop תַּחַת for נַחַת], Dr[1 S 1]). **3.** an overseer, Hezekiah's time 2 Ch 31[13], 𝔊 Μαεθ, A Ναεθ, 𝔊L Νααθ.

נָטָה [215] **vb.** stretch out, spread out, extend, incline, bend (NH *id*, *incline, spread tent*, etc; Ar نطو, نَطَا *stretch out*),—**Qal**[137] *Pf.* 3 ms נ׳ Gn 33[19]+, 3 fs. נָטְתָה Nu 22[33]; 2 ms. נָטִיתָ Ex 15[12]; 3 pl. נָטוּ ψ 21[12] Is 45[12], נָטָיוּ ψ 73[2] Qr, etc.; *Impf.* יִטֶּה Jb 15[29], juss. יֵט Zp 2[13]; וַיֵּט Gn 12[8]+, וַיֶּט־ Gn 26[25] 1 Ch 15[1]; 3 fs. תִּטֶּה Jb 31[7], וַתֵּט Nu 22[23] + 2 t.; 2 ms. juss. תֵּט Pr 4[5.27], 3 mpl וַיִּטּוּ 1 S 8[3]; 1 pl. נִטֶּה Nu 20[17] 21[22]; *Imv.* נְטֵה Ex 8[1]+; *Inf cstr* נְטוֹת Ju 19[8] + 4 t., נְטֹת Ex 23[2], sf. נְטֹתִי Ex 7[5], נְטוֹתוֹ ψ 109[23]; *Pt. act.* נֹטֶה Je 10[20] + 6 t., נוֹטֶה Ez 25[16] + 3 t.; sf נוֹטֵיהֶם Is 42[5], *pass.* נְטוּי ψ 62[4] + 2 t, + ψ 73[2] (v. infr.); fs. נְטוּיָה Is 5[25] + 24 t.; pl. נְטֻיוֹת Is 3[16] Qr (Kt נְטוּוֹת):—**1. a.** *stretch out, extend*, hand, rod, usu c. acc. + עַל of direction Ex 9[22.23] 10[12.13.21.22] (all E), 7[19] 14[16.21 26.27] (all P), abs. Jos 8[19] (JE), Ex 8[12] (P), c בְּ of dart or rod נ׳ בַּכִּידוֹן אֶל־ Jos 8[18 18] (JE), נ׳ יָדְךָ בְּמַטֶּךָ עַל־ Ex 8[1] (P), cf. v[2] and (עַל om) v[13] (all P), Jos 8[26] (JE), fig of hostility to God נ׳ יָדוֹ אֶל־ Jb 15[25];

esp. of God *stretching out* his hand *over* (עַל), oft with idea of *against*, i.e. in judgment, Is 5^{25} 23^{11} Zp 1^{4} 2^{13} Ez 6^{14} + 7 t. Ez, Ex 7^{5} (P); c. אֶל־ *against* Je 51^{25}, cf sword Ez 30^{25}, abs. Ex 15^{12} (song); pt pass נ׳ גָּרוֹן Is 3^{16} *outstretched of neck;* oft. זְרוֹעַ נְטוּיָה *arm stretched out* (of י׳) to deliver, Dt 4^{34} + 14 t (v זרוע), אזרוע נ׳ Je 32^{21}, יָד נ׳, to oppose, Je 21^{5}, עוֹד יָדוֹ נְטוּיָה in judgment, Is 5^{25} (|| לֹא שָׁב אַפּוֹ), so $9^{11.16.20}$ 10^{4} (all || *id.*), cf 14^{27}, הַיָּד הַנְּטוּיָה עַל־ v^{26}, נָטִיתִי יָדִי Pr 1^{24} (of wisdom's appeal, || קָרָאתִי) **b.** *stretch* line and plummet, c עַל, 2 K 21^{13} (subj י׳, fig of destruction), cf. Is 34^{11} La 2^{8}; line, of artisan's measurements (abs.) Is 44^{13}, and (c עַל) Jb 38^{5}. **c.** = *offer*, only שָׁלוֹשׁ אֲנִי נֹטֶה עָלֶיךָ 1 Ch 21^{10} *three* things *do I offer unto thee* (so rd. prob. also || 2 S 24^{12}, v. נטל)

2. *Spread out*, i.e. *pitch*, tent Gn 12^{8} 26^{25} 35^{21} (all J), 33^{19} (E), Ju 4^{11}, cf Je 43^{10}; fig of establishing people Je 10^{20}, of sacred tent Ex 33^{7} (JE), 2 S 6^{17} = 1 Ch 16^{1}, 1 Ch 15^{1} 2 Ch 1^{4}, obj heavens (spread out by י׳ as tent) Je 10^{12} + 9 t, cf. Jb 26^{7}, obj. likeness of firmament in Ezek.'s vision Ez 1^{22}.

3. *Bend, turn, incline:* **a.** intrans., of wady Nu 21^{15} (JE; c. לְ); *turn aside*, of Balaam's ass 22^{23} (מִן־הַדֶּרֶךְ), v^{33} (מִפָּנַי), cf v^{33} (לְפָנַי), c adv acc. 22^{26}, so of Isr. 20^{17}, and (c מֵעָלָיו) v^{21}, c בְּ *into*, 21^{22}, of individ. 2 S 2^{19} (לָלֶכֶת עַל), v^{21} (עַל), Je 14^{8} (c inf); cf. Gn 38^{1} (עַד), v^{16} (אֶל־); fig of deviating from path of loyalty 1 K 2^{28} (c אַחֲרֵי), cf Ju 9^{3} (of heart), or of righteousness Ex 23^{2} [yet on text cf Bu ZAW xi (1891) 113 Ry ad loc], 1 S 8^{3} (all c. אַחֲרֵי), c מִן Jb 31^{7} ψ 44^{19}, cf Pr 4^{5} and (c. adv. acc.) v^{27}, מעם י׳ 1 K 11^{9} (of heart), cf ψ $119^{51.157}$, *incline*, of heart, c לְ 1 S 14^{7} (rd לְבָבְךָ נָטָה or לְ׳ נטה Th We Dr Klo Bu HPS Lohr), *decline*, of shadow on dial 2 K 20^{10} (|| הָלַךְ, opp שׁוּב אֲחֹרַנִּית), fig of failing life ψ 102^{12} 109^{23}, of day Ju 19^{8} + v^{9} (txt emend., v. GFM), *bend down*, יִטֶּה לָאָרֶץ Jb 15^{29}, לִנְטוֹת בָּאָרֶץ ψ 17^{11} (both dub., v. Comm.); appar וַיֵּט בְּכֹחַ Ju 16^{30} *and he bowed with* all his *might* (after וַיִּסְמֹךְ, וַיִּלְפֹּת; al *stretched himself*, i.e. *gave a thrust*, Be GFM, but vb less oft. intrans in this sense); of י׳, וַיֵּט אֵלַי ψ 40^{2} *and he inclined unto me*,—וַתִּטֹּשׁ הַמִּלְחָמָה is rd 1 S 4^{2} by 𝔊 Dr Klo Bu, cf נָטַשׁ **b.** less oft trans., *bend, bow*, וַיֵּט שִׁכְמוֹ לִסְבֹּל Gn 49^{15} (Issachar under fig. of ass), קִיר נָטוּי ψ 62^{4} (sim. of fate of wicked; || גָּדֵר הַדְּחוּיָה); here belongs also prob וַאֲנִי כִּמְעַט נָטוּי רַגְלָי ψ 73^{2} (Kt) *and I was almost prostrated as to my feet* (i.e. by stumbling, Qr נָטָיוּ Pf. 3 mpl. but needless, cf. Ol Bae; || כְּאַיִן שֻׁפְּכָה אֲשֻׁרָי:), נ׳ לִבִּי ψ 119^{112} *I have inclined my heart* (c. inf.), of י׳, וַיֵּט שָׁמַיִם וַיֵּרַד 2 S 22^{10} = ψ 18^{10}, also fig., *hold out, extend* unto, of י׳, obj. חֶסֶד Gn 39^{21} (J), שָׁלוֹם, etc., Is 66^{12} (both c. אֶל־), of men רָעָה ψ 21^{12} (עַל)

†**Niph.** *be stretched out;*—*Pf* 3 mpl. נִטָּיוּ Nu 24^{6} (JE; cf II. נַחַל); *Impf* 3 ms יִנָּטֶה עַל־ Zc 1^{16} (of measuring line, for building), *stretch themselves out*, i.e. grow long, 3 mpl. יִנָּטוּ Je 6^{4} (of shadows, || פָּנָה הַיּוֹם).

Hiph. 73 *Pf.* הִטָּה Ezr 7^{28} ψ 116^{2}, sf הִטָּהוּ; 3 fs sf הִטַּתּוּ Pr 7^{21}; 1 s. הִטִּיתִי Pr 5^{13}, 3 pl הִטּוּ Am 5^{12} + 8 t; 2 mpl. הִטִּיתֶם Je 25^{4} 35^{15}; *Impf.* יַטֶּה Is 31^{3}, וַיֵּט 2 S 9^{15} Ezr 9^{9}, 2 ms. תַּטֶּה Ex 23^{6} + 3 t, juss. תַּט ψ 27^{9} 141^{4}; 1 s. אַטֶּה Je 6^{12} ψ 49^{5}, אַט Jb 23^{11}, וָאַט Ho 11^{4}, but rd perh. וְאַט (cf. Now) as Je 15^{6}; etc.; *Imv* הַטֵּה 2 K 19^{16} + 7 t., הַט ψ 17^{6} + 5 t. ψψ Pr; fs הַטִּי Gn 24^{14} ψ 45^{11}; mpl הַטּוּ Jos 24^{23} + 3 t., *Inf cstr.* לְהַטּוֹת Is 10^{2} + 4 t, לְהַטֹּת Ex 23^{2}, sf לְהַטּוֹתָהּ Nu 22^{23}, *Pt.* מַטֶּה Dt 27^{19}, mpl. מַטִּים ψ 125^{5}, cstr. מַטֵּי Mal 3^{5},—**1.** rarely *stretch out* (as **Qal 1**), hand Is 31^{3} (of י׳ in hostility), c עַל Je 6^{12} 15^{6}. **2.** rarely *spread out* cloth on (אֶל) rock 2 S 21^{10}; as **Qal 2**: tent 16^{22} (+ לְ pers), tent-curtains (fig of growth) Is 54^{2} **3.** usu *turn, incline*, c. acc., in many senses: **a.** lit *turn* ass into (acc.) road Nu 22^{23} (JE); *take aside* 2 S 3^{27} (acc. pers + אֶל־), 6^{10} (acc. rei + acc = *to*) = 1 Ch 13^{13} (אֶל־), *incline, turn* jar of water Gn 24^{14} (J; to give drink); intrans. only יַטּוּ עַל־ Am 2^{8} *on* garments taken in pledge *they recline*, and הַטּוּ מִנִּי־אֹרַח Is 30^{11} *turn aside, out of the path* (i.e. do not interfere with us; || סוּרוּ מִנֵּי־דֶרֶךְ). **b.** fig, הַמַּטִּים עֲקַלְקַלּוֹתָם ψ 125^{5} *those turning aside their crooked* (ways), i.e. making their ways crooked; cf (neg) Jb 23^{11}. **c.** *turn*, = influence, heart 2 S 19^{15}; *turn* (away) heart (cause to apostatize) 1 K $11^{2.4}$ (c. אַחֲרֵי), v^{3} (abs); לֵב subj., c. acc. pers. Is 44^{20} cf. Jb 36^{18} (acc. pers); of persuasion, c acc. pers Pr 7^{21} (|| תַּדִּיחֶנּוּ) **d.** *incline* one's own heart unto (אֶל) God and his commands, Jos 24^{23} (E), cf. Pr 2^{2} (לְ); subj י׳, 1 K 8^{58} ψ 119^{36}, c עַל־ Pr 21^{1}, neg (c. לְ) ψ 141^{4}. **e.** esp. *incline* the ear, of men (in obedience to God), usu. || שָׁמַע: abs.

Je 7^{24} + 6 t. Je (all neg.), so 25^4 44^5 (+inf.), Is 55^3; to inspired teacher Pr 4^{20} (‖ הַקְשִׁיב), 5^1 (‖ *id.*) v^{13} (all c. לְ), 22^{17} ψ 45^{11} 78^1 (‖ הַאֲזִינָה); to receive revelation ψ 49^5; of God, listening to men, sts. ‖ שְׁמַע: 2 K 19^{16} = Is 37^{17}, Dn 9^{18}, c. לְ ψ 17^6; also (c. אֶל־) 31^3 71^2 102^3, c. לְ 88^3 116^2, abs. 86^1; once וְאַט אֵלָיו Ho 11^4 *and I used to incline* etc. (either rare intrans., or obj. om., e.g. אָזְנִי; rd. perh. וְאַט (וְאֵט?) *and I inclined*, after וָאֶהְיֶה). **f.** *bend down* heavens, of י׳ (cf. **Qal 3 b**), ψ 144^5; = *hold out, extend* unto (from above, עַל) Ezr 7^{28} 9^9 (obj. חֶסֶד). **g.** *thrust aside*, esp. c. acc. מִשְׁפָּט, of *perverting* or *wresting* justice: Ex 23^6 (E), 1 S 8^3 Dt 16^{19} 24^{17} 27^{19} La 3^{35}, cf. Am 2^7; לְהַטּוֹת אָרְחוֹת מִשְׁפָּט Pr 17^{23}; also c. acc. pers. לְהַטּוֹת מִדִּין דַּלִּים Is 10^2 Am 5^{12} Is 29^{21} Mal 3^5, יַטּוּ אֶבְיוֹנִים מִדָּרֶךְ Jb 24^4, לְהַטּוֹת צַדִּיק בַּמִּשְׁפָּט Pr 18^5; here belongs prob. לְהַטּוֹת Ex 23^2 (E; abs.), perh. ins. מִשְׁפָּט (cf. Bu$^{ZAW\ xi.\ (1891),\ 113}$ Ry$^{ad\ loc.}$). **h.** *thrust away*, of י׳, אַל־תַּט בְּאַף עַבְדֶּךָ ψ 27^9; cf. עֲוֹנוֹתֵיכֶם הִטּוּ־אֵלֶּה Je 5^{25} *your iniquities have thrust away* (deprived you of) these (harvests).

†יֻטָּה Jos 21^{16}, יוּטָּה (so Baer) 15^{55} **n.pr. loc.** town in Judah (15^{55} 𝔊 Ἰταν, A 𝔊L Ἰεττα, 21^{16} 𝔊 Τανυ, 𝔊L Ἰεττα).

†מַטָּה, מָ֫טָּה **adv.** **downwards** (from [מַט] for [מַטֶּה] *a place of declension* (cf. נָטָה, **3 a**), with ה — *loc.*, Ol$^{222\ b}$ Kö$^{ii.\ 280}$: cf. the opp. מַ֫עְלָה, sub עָלָה):—**1.** alone, Dt 28^{43} and thou shalt descend מַטָּה מָּטָּה *downwards, downwards*, i.e. lower and lower, Pr 15^{24} לְמַעַן סוּר מִשְּׁאוֹל מ׳. **2.** לְמַ֫טָּה: **a.** *downwards* Dt 28^{13} וְלֹא תִהְיֶה לְמ׳, Is 37^{31} = 2 K 19^{30} שֹׁרֶשׁ לְמ׳ (cf. Ph CIS$^{i.\ 1.\ 3,\ 11\ f.}$ אל יכן לם שרש למט ופר למעל let them not have root *downwards*, or fruit upwards), Je 31^{37} Ec 3^{21} 2 Ch 32^{30}; Ezr 9^{13} כי אתה חָשַׂכְתָּ לְמַטָּה מֵעֲוֹנֵנוּ either (Be) hast kept back, *downward*, part of our iniquity (prevented it from appearing, and being counted against us), or, held us (Ges), or thy anger (Ke), back, *below* (cf. לְמַעְלָה מֵעַל *above*, 2 Ch 34^4) our iniq. (punished us less than our iniq. deserved). **b.** וּלְמַ֫טָּה, (*a*) of space, *and downwards*, Ez 1^{27} וּמִמַּרְאֵה מָתְנָיו ול׳, 8^2; (*b*) of age, *and under*, 1 Ch 17^{23} לְמִבֶּן עֶשְׂרִים שָׁנָה ול׳. **3.** מִלְּמַ֫טָּה *beneath* (v. מִן **9 a**: opp. מִלְמַ֫עְלָה *above*), Ex 26^{24} = 36^{29}, 27^5 = 38^4, 28^{27} = 39^{20}.

מַטֶּה$_{251}$ **n.m.**$^{Ex\ 4,\ 17}$ (**f.** Mi 6^9 acc. to MT, but dub., v. infr.) **1. staff, rod, shaft.** **2. branch.** **3. tribe** (Ecclus 48^2 *staff*, $45^{6.25}$ *tribe*);—abs. מ׳ Gn 38^{25}+; cstr. מַטֵּה Ex 4^{20}+; sf. מַטְּךָ Gn 38^{18} + 5 t., מַטֶּ֑ךָ Ex 8^1, מַטֵּהוּ Is 10^{24} + 10 t.; pl. מַטּוֹת 1 K 8^1+, etc.; sf. מַטּוֹתָם Ex 7^{12} Nu 17^{21}; also מַטָּיו Hb 3^{14} (but rd. מַטֶּיךָ, or—Gr—מַטּוֹתֶיךָ);—**1.** (cf. מַקֵּל, שֵׁבֶט) *staff* of traveller Gn $38^{18.25}$ (J); in gen. Is 10^{15} (sim.; ‖ שֵׁבֶט); from staff as support comes fig. מַטֵּה־לֶחֶם *staff of bread* (food supply) Ez 4^{16} 5^{16} 14^{13} Lv 26^{26} ψ 105^{16}; of staff or rod, Moses as shepherd Ex $4^{2.4}$ 7^{15} (J), 4^{17} $7^{17.20}$ 9^{23} 10^{13} 17^5 (all E); cf. also Is 10^{26}; Ex 14^{16} Nu $20^{8.9.11}$ (all P); called מ׳ הָאֱלֹהִים Ex 4^{20} 17^9 (both E), because of miraculous power connected with it; cf. mirac. rod of Aaron $7^{9.10.12.19}$ $8^{1.12.13}$ (all P), and of Egyptian magicians $7^{12.12}$ (P); cf. Aaron's rod that budded Nu $17^{18.21.23.25}$ (cf. RS$^{Sem.\ i.\ 180;\ 2d\ ed.\ 197}$); carried even by warrior 1 S $14^{27.43}$; מַטֵּה שִׁכְמוֹ Is 9^3 i.e. rod that strikes his shoulder, task-master's rod (‖ שֵׁבֶט הַנֹּגֵשׂ בּוֹ), cf. 10^5 and v^{24} 14^5 (‖ שֵׁבֶט), all fig. of oppression; מַטֵּה מוּסָדָה 30^{32} *appointed rod* (of punishment); cf. מ׳ Ez $7^{10.11}$ (but text obscure, Co—q.v.—*sceptre*), also Mi 6^9 acc. to MT, but v. sub **3**; used in beating out (חבט) fennel Is 28^{27}; *staff* as badge of leader or ruler מַטֵּה־עֹז Je 48^{17} (‖ מַקֵּל), cf. ψ 110^2; so Nu $17^{17.17.17.17}$ + 10 t. Nu 17; appar. *shafts*, i.e. arrows or spears, Hb $3^{9.14}$ (cf. Now Da GASm). †**2.** *branch* of vine Ez $19^{11.12.14.14}$. **3.** *tribe* (183 t.), orig. company led by chief with *staff*: specif. of tribes of Isr. in both sg. and pl., 1 K 7^{14} 8^1 = 2 Ch 5^2, Ex 31^2 + 5 t. Ex; Lv 24^{11}; Nu 1^4 + 89 t. Nu; Jos 7^1 + 56 t. Jos (all P); 1 Ch 6^{45} + 21 t. 1 Ch 6, 12^{31}; prob. also Mi 6^9 (vocative; so 𝔊 We Now GASm).—Cf. שֵׁבֶט, and on relation of these two words for *tribe* in Hebr. usage Dr$^{JPh.\ xi.\ (1882),\ 213\ f.}$

†מִטָּה **n.f.** **couch, bed** (*place of reclining*; מטותם Ecclus 48^6);—abs. מִטָּה Am 3^{12} + 14 t.; cstr. מִטַּת 2 K 4^{21}; sf. מִטָּתִי ψ 6^7, מִטָּתֶךָ Ex 7^{28}, מִטָּתוֹ 2 S 4^7 + 6 t.; pl. מִטּוֹת abs. 2 K 11^2 2 Ch 22^{11}, cstr. Am 6^4 Est 1^6;—*couch, bed*, common article of furniture 2 K 4^{10}, cf. v$^{21.32}$ 1 K 17^{19}, for repose, esp. at night, or in illness Gn 47^{31} (J; רֹאשׁ הַמִּ׳), cf. 48^2 (J), 49^{33} (P), ψ 6^7 Pr 26^{14} 2 Ch 24^{25} (prob.), and for sitting, or reclining by day 1 S 28^{23} 1 K 21^4; פְּאַת מ׳ Am 3^{12}; seat of King Solomon Ct 3^7; in bed-chamber (חֲדַר מִשְׁכָּב) Ex 7^{28} (J), 2 S 4^7; sts. portable 1 S 19^{15} cf. v$^{13.16}$, hence = *bier*

2 S 3[31]; sts high 2 K 1[4.6.16] (עָלָה שָׁם, opp. יָרַד מִן), sts. costly, (with frames) of ivory Am 6[4], for reclining at feasts, made of gold and silver Est 1[6], cf מ׳ כבוּדָה Ez 23[41] *glorious couch*, חֲדַר הַמִּטּוֹת 2 K 11[2] = 2 Ch 22[11] (v. חֶדֶר)—Cf. also עֶרֶשׂ (שׁכב), מִשְׁכָּב

†[מֻטָּה] **n f. spreading, outspreading;**—only pl cstr. מֻטּוֹת כְּנָפָיו Is 8[8] *the outspreading of his wings* (cf. Ges§ 147 7 a Ko ii. 1, 192, 390), fig of invading Assyrian army

†מֻטֶּה **n [m.] that which is perverted, perverted justice** (see √**Hiph 3 g**),—only וְהָעִיר מָלְאָה מ׳ Ez 9[9] (as above Ke Sm Da Berthol Toy RV > *perverseness* AV) > Co חָמָס (as 7[23])

†נטל **vb.** lift, bear (rare synon of נָשָׂא; BAram 𝔗 נטל *lift;* hence specif, Syr. ܢܛܠ *sustulit* (aquam), further, *be heavy;* also borrowed and denom forms in Ar. and NH, cf Frä[65 f]),—**Qal** *Pf.* 3 ms נ׳ La 3[28], *Impf.* 3 ms יִטּוֹל Is 40[15], *Pt act.* נוֹטֵל 2 S 24[12],—*lift*, c acc Is 40[15] (fig subj ׳י), *lift over thee* (עַל) i e. offer 2 S 24[12], but rd נוֹטֶה (as ‖ 1 Ch 21[10]) We Bu HPS, *lift (and lay) upon* (עַל) La 3[28]. **Pi.** *Impf* sf. וַיְנַטְּלֵם Is 63[9] *and he bare them*, fig of ׳י bearing his people (‖ וַיְנַשְּׂאֵם)

†נֵטֶל **n.[m.] burden, weight;**—נ׳ cstr, of sand, Pr 27[3] (‖ כֹּבֶד)

†[נָטִיל] **adj.** laden, only pl. cstr. נְטִילֵי כָסֶף Zp 1[11] *those laden with silver*

†נָטַע **vb. plant** (NH *id*, and deriv., cf. Sab נטעת *pavilion* [? as planted, established] DHM ZMG xxxvii (1883), 337, 349),—**Qal** *Pf* 3 ms Nu 24[6]+, 2 ms נָטַעְתָּ Dt 6[11], sf 3 mpl נְטַעְתָּם Je 12[2], 1 s נָטַעְתִּי Je 45[4]+2 t, וְנָטַעְתִּי, Je 42[10] Ec 2[5], sf. נְטַעְתִּיךְ Je 2[21], וּנְטַעְתִּיו consec 2 S 7[10] = 1 Ch 17[9], וּנְטַעְתִּים consec Am 9[15]+2 t, etc; *Impf* 3 ms יִטַּע Dn 11[45], וַיִּטַּע Gn 2[8]+2 t, sf וַיִּטָּעֵהוּ Is 5[2], 2 ms תִּטַּע Dt 16[21]+2 t., sf 3 fs וַתִּטָּעֶהָ ψ 80[9], sf 3 mpl וַתִּטָּעֵמוֹ Ex 15[17], וַתִּטָּעֵם ψ 44[3], etc; *Imv* נִטְעוּ Je 29[5]+3 t; *Inf.* לִנְטֹעַ Is 51[16] Je 18[9], לִנְטוֹעַ Je 1[10] 31[28], לָטַעַת Ec 3[2], *Pt. act.* נוֹטֵעַ Je 11[17], נֹטֵעַ ψ 94[9] (shewing orig *a* acc. to Lag BN 84), pl נֹטְעִים Je 31[5]; *pass* נָטוּעַ Ec 3[2], pl נְטוּעִים Ec 12[11],—**1.** *plant*, c acc. of tree or vine Nu 24[6] (JE, subj. ׳י), Gn 21[33] (J), Lv 19[23] (H), Is 44[14] ψ 106[16] (subj. ׳י), Ec 2[5] also (fig of people) Je 2[21] 11[17] ψ 80[9.16]; c acc of vineyard Gn 9[20] (J), Am 5[11] 9[14] 2 K 19[29] = Is 37[30] Zp 1[13] Dt 20[6] 28[30.39] Je 31[5.5.5] 35[7] Ez 28[26] Is 65[21] Pr 31[16] ψ 107[37] Ec 2[4], olive trees and vineyards Dt 6[11] Jos 24[13] (D), garden Gn 2[8] (׳י), Je 29[5.28], so c acc. אֲשֵׁרָה כָּל־עֵץ Dt 16[21], נ׳ נִטְעֵי נַעֲמָנִים Is 17[10] (fig of idolatry); abs. (lit.) Is 65[22] Ec 3[2] (opp עָקַר); c. 2 acc. Is 5[2] (*plant vineyard with vine*) **2.** *plant*, fig = establish, usu. of establishing people, c acc 2 S 7[10] = 1 Ch 17[9] Am 9[15] (opp נָתַשׁ), Ez 36[36] Ex 15[17] (song), esp. Je 24[6] 32[41] (ב loc), 42[10] (opp נָתַשׁ), 45[10] (opp *id*), ψ 44[3] (all of establishing Isr.); of establishing wicked Je 12[2]; abs. of establishing people Je 1[10] 18[9] 31[28]; more lit, *establish* heavens Is 51[16] (‖ לִיסֹד אֶרֶץ), *plant* i e fix (late use) tents Dn 11[45]; מַשְׂמְרוֹת נְטוּעִים Ec 12[11] *nails planted*, i.e. fixed in; even נ׳ אֹזֶן ψ 94[9] *he that planted the ear.* **Niph.** *Pf* 3 pl נִטָּעוּ Is 40[24] *be planted*, fig., = be established.

†[נֶטַע] **n. [m.] plantation, planting, plant,**—abs. נֶטַע Jb 14[9], cstr נְטַע Is 5[7]; sf. נִטְעֵךְ Is 17[11]; pl cstr. נִטְעֵי Is 17[10];—**1.** *plantation* Is 5[7] (fig. of Judah, planted by ׳י); 17[10] (fig of idolatry), so **2.** act of *planting* Is 17[11]. **3.** *plant* Jb 14[9] (in sim).

†נְטָעִים **n. pr. loc.** 1 Ch 4[23], 𝔊 Αζαειμ, A Αταειμ, 𝔊L Εταειμ

†[נָטִיעַ] **n.[m.] plant,**—only pl נְטִעִים ψ 144[12] (fig. of vigorous sons).

†מַטָּע **n.m. place, or act of planting; plantation,**—abs. מ׳ Ez 34[29], cstr. מַטַּע Is 61[3], sf מַטָּעוֹ Is 60[21] (Kt; Qr מַטָּעַי); מַטָּעָהּ Ez 17[7], also 31[4], but rd. מַטָּעָה 𝔊 Hi Co Berthol Toy; pl cstr מַטָּעֵי Mi 1[6],—**1.** *planting-place*, מַטָּעֵי כָרֶם Mi 1[6] *planting-place for a vineyard*, so Ez 31[4] (id. מַטָּעָה, v. supr.), prob also מ׳ לְשֵׁם < rd מ׳ שָׁלֹם 𝔊 Co Berthol Toy i.e. *peaceful (fruitful) planting-place;* cf עֲרֻגוֹת מ׳ 17[7] = *beds where it was planted* **2.** act of *planting* נֵצֶר מ׳ Is 60[21] *shoot of his (my) planting* (fig of people) **3.** מ׳ ׳י Is 61[3] *plantation of* ׳י (*id*).

†[נָטַף] **vb. drop, drip,** fig. (esp. of prophet) **discourse** (NH *id*, 𝔗 נטף *drop, drip;* Syr ܢܛܦ *drip*, ܢܛܘܦܐ *drop* (No Syr Gr § 105) etc.; Ar. نَطَفَ *id;* Eth. ነጠፈ: *id*, ንጥፈ: *colare (stillando), expercolare*);—**Qal** *Pf* 3 mpl נָטְפוּ Ju 5[4]+2 t, נָטָפוּ Ju 5[4]; *Impf* 3 fs. תִּטֹּף Jb 29[22], 3 mpl יִטְּפוּ Jo 4[18], 3 fpl. תִּטֹּפְנָה Pr 5[3] Ct 4[11];

Pt. נֹטְפוֹת Ct 5^{13};—*drop, drip,* usu. trans., c. acc., of clouds *dropping* water (מַיִם), in storm Ju 5^{4}, ‖ heavens v^{4} (obj. om.), ψ 68^{9} (*id.;* all theoph.); of hands *dripping* myrrh (מוֹר) Ct 5^{5}; in predict. יִטְּפוּ עָסִיס Jo 4^{18} the mts. *shall drip must;* fig. of (seductive) speech נֹפֶת תִּטֹּ׳ Pr 5^{3} the lips of the strange woman *drop honey,* so perh. Ct 4^{11} (Bu of kisses); שִׂפְתוֹתָיו נ׳ מוֹר 5^{13} *his lips drip myrrh* (perh. of sweet breath). Intrans. only עָלֵימוֹ תִּטֹּף מִלָּתִי Jb 29^{22} *upon them my speech used to drop.* **Hiph.** *Pf.* 3 mpl. וְהִטִּיפוּ consec. Am 9^{13}; *Impf.* 2 ms. תַטִּיף Am 7^{16}; 1 s. אַטִּף Mi 2^{11}; 3 mpl. יַטִּיפוּן v^{6}; 2 mpl. תַּטִּיפוּ v^{6}, תַּטִּפוּ v^{6}; *Pt.* מַטִּיף Mi 2^{11};—**1.** *drip,* וְהִטּ׳ עָסִיס Am 9^{13} and the mts. *shall drip must* (=**Qal** Jo 4^{18}). **2.** of speech, esp. prophecy (without acc.): c. עַל *against,* Am 7^{16} (‖ הִנָּבֵא), c. אֶל־ *toward,* Ez 21^{2} (‖ *id.*), v^{7} (‖ *id.*); c. לְ *concerning* Mi 2^{11} cf. v^{11};—אַל־תַּטִּפוּ יַטִּיפוּן לֹא־יַטִּפוּ לָאֵלֶּה Mi 2^{6} *'talk not'—so they talk—'they* (rd. *ye?*) *shall not talk of these things'* (where תַּטּ׳, יַטִּפוּ ref. to prophets).

†I. [נָטָף] **n.m.** drop;—נִטְפֵי־מָיִם Jb 36^{27} (‖ מָטָר, *rain*).

†II. נָטָף **n.[m.]** an odorif. gum (gathered in *drops*), used in sacred incense Ex 30^{34} (P). Identif. dub.; 𝔊 στακτή, 𝔙 *stacte,* i.e. (Hesych.) a kind of myrrh, so Kn, cf. Ri^{HWB}; Rosenm Thes Ke al. *storax;* Rabb. *opobalsamum* (cf. Di$^{ad\ loc.}$ Now$^{Arch.\ ii.\ 64,\ 248}$).

†[נְטִיפָה?] **n.[f.]** drop, i.e. pendant, an ornament (or *pearl* = Ar. نُطْفَةٌ, fr. likeness to drop of water; cf. GFM);—only pl. abs. נְטִיפוֹת Ju 8^{26}, נְטִפוֹת Is 3^{19}.

†נְטֹפָה **n.pr.loc.** in Judah (*dropping, dripping,* cf. Lewy$^{Sem.\ Fremdwörter\ 40}$);—Ezr 2^{22} = Ne 7^{26}; 𝔊 Νετωφα, 𝔊^L Νετωφατι (as adj. gent. Ne 12^{28}).

†נְטֹפָתִי, נְטוֹפָתִי **adj. gent.**;—נְטֹפָ׳ 2 S 23^{28} + 5 t., נְטוֹפָ׳ 1 Ch 2^{54} + 4 t. Ch;—הַנְּ׳ *the Netophathite* 2 S $23^{28.29}$ 2 K 25^{23} = Je 40^{8} 1 Ch $11^{30.30}$; sg. coll. (the) *Netophathites* (no art.) 1 Ch 2^{54} 9^{16} Ne 12^{28}.

†[נָטַר] **vb. keep** (less common ‖ of נָצַר) (NH *id.;* 𝔗 נְטַר, Syr. ܢܛܪ *id.;* Nab. in n.pr. Lzb^{323} (cf. also infr.), Ar. نَطَرَ *id.* (obj. garden, etc.));—**Qal** *Pf.* 1 s. נָטַרְתִּי Ct 1^{6}; *Impf.* 3 ms. יִטּוֹר ψ 103^{9}, יִנְטוֹר Je 3^{5}; rd. וַיִּטֹּר also Am 1^{11} (for MT וַיִּטְרֹף) Ol$^{ψ\ 103.9}$ We Now GASm Dr; 2 ms. תִּטֹּר Lv 19^{18}; 1 s. אֶטּוֹר Je 3^{12}; *Pt. act.* נוֹטֵר Na 1^{2}; f. נֹטֵרָה Ct 1^{6}; mpl. נֹטְרִים Ct $8^{11.12}$;—**1.** *keep, maintain* (sc. wrath), of י׳, Je $3^{5.12}$ Na 1^{2} (c. לְ *for*), ψ 103^{9}; of Edom Am 1^{11} (rdg. וַיִּטֹּר לָעַד אַפּוֹ *and he kept his anger perpetually,* v. supr.). **2.** *keep, guard* a vineyard Ct $1^{6.6}$ (in fig.), abs. 8^{11}, obj. פִּרְיוֹ v^{12}.

†מַטָּרָה and (La 3^{12}) מַטָּרָא **n.f. 1. guard, ward, prison. 2. target, mark** (as *kept* in the eye, *watched,* cf. נָצַר Pr 23^{26}, and σκόπος (*watcher, mark*) from σκέπτομαι; perh. Nab. [מט]רתא Lzb^{323});—always abs.:—**1.** *guard, ward, prison,* usu. חֲצַר הַמּ׳ *court of guard* (v. 1. חָצֵר) Je $32^{2.8.12}$ 33^{1} $37^{21.21}$ $38^{6.13.28}$ $39^{14.15}$; שַׁעַר הַמּ׳ Ne 12^{39}. **2.** *target, mark* Jb 16^{12} (fig. of י׳'s chastisement), כַּמַּטָּרָא לַחֵץ La 3^{12} (sim. *id.*); lit. only 1 S 20^{20}.

†נָטַשׁ **vb. leave, forsake, permit** (𝔗 *forsake; draw off* skin of dead animal; Ar. نَطَسَ = *abstinens ab impuro* acc. to Ḳam (Frey));—**Qal** *Pf.* 3 ms. נ׳ 1 S 10^{2}, sf. 1 pl. נְטָשָׁנוּ Ju 6^{13}; 2 ms. נָטַשְׁתָּ 1 S 17^{28}, נָטַשְׁתָּה Is 2^{6}, sf. נְטַשְׁתַּנִי Gn 31^{28}, וּנְטַשְׁתָּהּ consec. Ex 23^{11}, etc.; *Impf.* יִטֹּשׁ 1 S 12^{22} ψ 94^{14}, יִטּוֹשׁ Ho 12^{15}, sf. 1 pl. יִטְּשֵׁנוּ 1 K 8^{57}; 1 pl. נִטֹּשׁ Ne 10^{32}, etc.; *Imv.* נְטוֹשׁ Pr 17^{14}; *Pt. pass.* f. נְטוּשָׁה Is 21^{15}; mpl. נְטֻשִׁים 1 S 30^{16};—**1.** *leave, let alone* Ex 23^{11} (E; =let field lie fallow, ‖ שָׁמַט), cf. וְנִטֹּשׁ אֶת־הַשָּׁנָה הַשְּׁבִיעִית וּמַשָּׁא כָל־יָד Ne 10^{32} (i.e. leave field fallow and debts unclaimed); obj. quails, *let them lie,* (עַל loc.) Nu 11^{31} (JE), of Amalekites נְטֻשִׁים עַל־פְּנֵי כָל־הָאָרֶץ 1 S 30^{16} *left to themselves over all the land;* וְדָמָיו עָלָיו יִטּוֹשׁ Ho 12^{15} and his mortal guilt *shall he leave upon him; leave* in charge of, *entrust* to (עַל pers.): sheep 1 S $17^{20.28}$; baggage v^{22}. **2.** usu. *forsake, abandon,* נ׳ דִּבְרֵי הָאֲתֹנוֹת 1 S 10^{2} thy father *hath abandoned the matter of the asses* (ceased to be concerned about them); הָרִיב נְטוֹשׁ Pr 17^{14} *abandon contention;* oft. subj. י׳, c. acc. pers. Ju 6^{13} Is 2^{6} 1 S 12^{22} 1 K 8^{57} (‖ עָזַב) 2 K 21^{14} Je 7^{29} 12^{7} (‖ עָזַב), $23^{33.39}$ ψ 27^{9} (‖ עָזַב), 94^{14} (‖ *id.*); of י׳ leaving Phar. forsaken (on ground, cf. **Niph. 1**) Ez 29^{5} (+ ה loc.), 32^{4} (+ ב loc.); abandoning the sanctuary at Shiloh ψ 78^{60}; of men *forsaking* God Dt 32^{15} (poem), Je 15^{6}; cf. אַל־תִּטֹּשׁ תּוֹרַת אִמֶּךָ Pr 1^{8} 6^{20}; of men *abandoning* kg. (under fig. of cedar)

Ez 31[12.13] **3.** *permit*, only ולא נטשתני לְנַשֵּׁק לְבָנַי וגו׳ Gn 31[28] (E) *and hast not permitted me to kiss my sons*, etc —For וַתִּטֹּשׁ הַמִּלְחָמָה 1 S 4[2] rd prob וַתֵּט (𝔊 ἔκλινεν) Dr Klo Bu, or < וַתִּקְשֶׁה (קשה) *grew fierce* HPS (Lohr prop. תִּנָּטֵשׁ cf Ju 15[9] etc) For חֶרֶב נְטוּשָׁה Is 21[15] (‖קֶשֶׁת דְּרוּכָה) rd perh. ח׳ לְטוּשָׁה. **Niph.** *Pf* 3 fs נטשה Am 5[2], 3 pl. נטשו Is 16[8] 33[23]; *Impf* 3 mpl וַיִּנָּטְשׁוּ Ju 15[9] + 2 t;—**1.** *be forsaken*, Am 5[2] *she* (Isr) *lieth forsaken* (עַל loc) **2.** *be loosened* or *loose* (prop. *be let alone*, left to hang down) of ship's tackle Is 33[23]. **3.** *be let go, spread abroad*, of warriors, Ju 15[9] 2 S 5[18 22] (all c ב loc, for purpose of plunder), of tendrils of vine Is 16[8] (fig of Moab) **Pu.** *Pf* only אַרְמוֹן נֻטָּשׁ Is 32[14] *palaces are abandoned, deserted* (‖הֲמוֹן עִיר עֻזָּב)

†[נְטִישָׁה] **n f. twig, tendril of vine** (as *spreading*, cf. √**Niph. 3**),—only pl הַנְּטִישׁוֹת הסיר התז Is 18[5] *the tendrils he hath removed*, cf הָסִירוּ נטישׁוֹתֶיהָ Je 5[10] (appar cited from Is; expl by Finn[Journ Trans. Vict Inst. xxii 306 f] from use by shepherds of *poterium spinosum*, called *nettsh*, as defence of sheepfolds),—in both of destroying city (under fig of vineyard), נטישׁתיך עָבְרוּ יָם Je 48[32] *thy tendrils went over the sea* (fig of prosperity of Moab)

[נִי] v. נהה

ניא (√of foll, cf Ar. نِيءَ (med י), *be raw*)

†II **נָא** **adj. raw**, of flesh Ex 12[9] (P, opp בשׁל)

[נִיב], נִיבַי, נִיבָי v. נוב.

נִיד v נוד   נִידָה v II. נדד

נָיוֹת v נוית sub I נוה

נִיחֹחַ, נִיחוֹחַ v נוח.   נִין v. נון

†**נִינְוֵה** **n.pr.loc Nineveh**, capital of Assyria (As *Ninâ, Ninua, Ninû*, cf. Schr COT Gloss. Dl[Par 260]),—Gn 10[11 12] (J), 2 K 19[36] = Is 37[37], Na 1[1] 2[9] 3[7] Zp 2[13] Jon 1[2] 3[2.4.5.6.7], called הָעִיר הַגְּדוֹלָה v[3b] 4[11] (cf 3[4f]), 𝔊 Νινευη, 𝔊L Νινευι. Site on E bank of Tigris marked by mounds *Neby Yunus* and *Kuyundjik*, opposite Mosul Cf. Layard[Nineveh and its Remains, 1848, Monuments of N 1849 f] Billerbeck u Jeremias[BAS III 1 (1895), 107 ff]

נִיס v נוס **Qal 1.** ad fin

†**נִיסָן** **n.pr.** of 1st month (loan-wd. fr Bab. *Nisannu*, cf. Schr[COT Ne 1. 1] Muss-Arnolt[JBL xi. 1 (1892), 76], NH = BH, so Nab Palm. v. Lzb[323]);—only post-exil.: חֹדֶשׁ נ׳ Ne 2[1] Est 3[7] (+ הַחֹדֶשׁ הָרִאשׁוֹן), = pre-exil. (חֹדֶשׁ) הָאָבִיב —On sacredness of Nisan cf also RS[Sem. i 387, 2d ed 406 f.]

נִיצוֹץ v. נצץ.   נִיר v נר.

†I [נִיר] **vb. break up, freshly till**;—**Qal** *Imv.* mpl נִירוּ, c. acc cogn ניר Ho 10[12] Je 4[3].

†II. **נִיר** **n.[m.] the tillable, untilled** or **fallow ground**;—נ׳ abs. as acc cogn נירו לָכֶם נִיר Ho 10[12] Je 4[3] *till you the untilled ground* (fig. of unaccustomed moral action), cstr only רָב־אֹכֶל ניר ראשים Pr 13[23] *abundant food* (yields) *the fallow ground of poor men* (i e. with י׳'s blessing) —I. ניר v. נור

II **ניר** (√of foll, cf. NH נִיר, Ar نِيرٌ, Syr. ܢܝܪܐ (in Lexx), all = the system of *heddles* or 'apparatus [of small cords with loops, or eyes] by wh the threads of the warp are raised and lowered to make an opening for the passing of the woof' GFM[PAOS Oct 1889 clxxix. f], cf. As *nîru*, Syr ܢܝܪܐ, *yoke*)

†[מָנוֹר] **n.m. beam** (prob round) carrying the heddles (in loom), = Lat *jugum*, so GFM[l. c.];—only cstr. in phr כמנור ארגים *beam of weavers* 1 S 17[7] 2 S 21[19] = 1 Ch 20[5], 1 Ch 11[23], all sim of thick and heavy shaft of spear

†[נָכָא] **vb. smite, scourge** (rare Aramaizing form of נָכָה),—only **Niph.** *Pf* 3 pl. נִכְּאוּ מִן־הָאָרֶץ Jb 30[8] *they are scourged out of the land.*

†[נָכָא] **adj stricken**,—mpl נְכָאִים Is 16[7] (Ko[ii. 1, 73]), of Moab prostrated by conquest.

†[נָכֵא] **adj. id**, alw. f רוּחַ נכאה *a stricken spirit*, Pr 15[13] 17[22] (both opp לֵב שָׂמֵחַ), 18[14]

†**נְכֹאת** **n f.** a spice, (usu. understood of *tragacanth gum*, exuding fr *astralagus* bush, Di[Gn 37, 25] and reff; Now[Arch i 64 (and 249)], cf. also Löw[§ 24], but = Ar. نَكَعَة = نُكَاعَة *summitas rubicunda sive flores plantae* (i e a certain plant, Frey), acc to Hom[Aufsätze 4]),—abs. נ׳ Gn 37[25] (+ צֳרִי, לֹט, as merchandise), 43[11] (+ *id.*, also דְּבַשׁ, בָּטְנִים, שְׁקֵדִים, as gift).

נכר (√of foll, mng. uncertain, Eth ንኵር = *gens, stirps*, [cf. Sam נגר Gn 21[23]]).

†נֶ֫כֶד† n.[m.] progeny, posterity, alw. c. נִין in standing phr. (Ecclus 41⁵ 47²²ᵉ, both c. שֵׁם);—abs. לֹא נִין לוֹ וְלֹא נ׳ בְּעַמּוֹ Jb 18¹⁹, cf. (נין) וּשְׁאָר וְנִין וְנ׳ Is 14²², sf. לִי וּלְנִינִי וּלְנֶכְדִּי Gn 21²³ *to me and to my offspring and to my posterity.*

[נָכָה]₅₀₁ **vb.** smite (not in **Qal**) (NH Hiph. *id*; Pf. 3 pl. הכו SI⁴, Inf. [ת]להכ ib.²; Syr. ܢܟܐ, *laesit, nocuit, repugnavit*; Aph. *laesit, vulneravit*; Eth ነከየ: *laesit, nocuit*; cf. Ar. نَكَى *be defeated*, نِكَايَةٌ *the inflicting of injury* on an enemy Lane³⁰³⁸);—†**Niph.** *Pf.* וְנִכָּה וָמֵת consec 2 S 11¹⁵ *and he shall be smitten* [struck by weapon in battle] *and die.*

†**Pu.** *Pf.* 3 fs נֻכְּתָה Ex 9³¹; 3 pl. נֻכּוּ v³² (J), both *be smitten down* by the hail.

Hiph.₄₈₁ *Pf.* 3 ms. הִכָּה Ex 9²⁵+; sf. וְהִכַּנִי consec. Gn 32¹², הִכָּם Je 5³, 2 ms. הִכִּיתָ Ex 17⁵+; 1 s. הִכֵּיתִי Ju 15¹⁶+, וְהִכֵּיתִי Ex 3²⁰+; 3 pl. הִכּוּ Gn 19¹¹+; 2 mpl. הִכִּיתֶם Je 37¹⁰+3 t. consec.; etc., *Impf.* 3 ms. יַכֶּה Ex 21²⁰+, יַךְ Ho 6¹ (but rd וְיַךְ We Now GASm); יַךְ Ho 14⁶ (v. infr.), יַכֶּ֫הָ Jos 10⁴⁰+, usu. וַיַּךְ Ex 2¹²+; sf. 2 ms. וַיַּכְּכָה Je 40¹⁵+2 t., 3 ms. וַיַּכֵּהוּ 2 S 14⁶ (but rd. וַיַּךְ 𝔊𝔖𝔙 Th We Dr Klo Kit Bu HPS), יַכֵּנוּ 1 S 17²⁵ +2 t; usu. וַיַּכֵּהוּ Nu 21²⁴+; 3 fs. וַתַּךְ Jon 4⁷ ⁸; 2 ms. תַּכֶּה Ex 2¹³+, sf 3 ms. תַּכֶּנּוּ Pr 23¹³ ¹⁴; 1 s אַכֶּה 1 S 18¹¹+; וָאַכֶּה Ne 13²⁵, וָאַךְ Ex 9¹⁵; 3 mpl יַכּוּ Mi 4¹⁴; usu וַיַּכּוּ Gn 14⁵+ (1 S 4² rd. prob. **Hoph.** q.v.); 1 pl נַכֶּה־ Nu 22⁶; וַנַּךְ Dt 2³³, etc; *Imv.* הַכֵּה Ez 6¹¹, הַךְ Am 9¹+; mpl. הַכּוּ 2 S 13²⁸, etc, *Inf. abs* הַכֵּה Dt 3¹⁶+, הַכּוֹת 2 K 3²⁴ (Ges^§75ff); *cstr* הַכּוֹת Gn 4¹⁵+, etc.; *Pt.* מַכֶּה Ex 2¹¹+, cstr. מַכֵּה Ex 21¹²+; pl. מַכִּים 1 S 4⁸+, etc.,—**1. a.** lit., *smite* (with a single, non-fatal, blow), *strike*, sq. acc, ass Nu 22²³ ²⁵.²⁷ (בַּמַּקֵּל), v²⁸.³² (all J); man Ex 21¹⁵ ¹⁹ (E); cheeks Jb 16¹⁰; man (on) cheek (2 acc.) La 3³⁰ ψ 3⁸, man עַל־לְחִי Mi 4¹⁴ (ב instr.), 1 K 22²⁴ = 2 Ch 18²³; eye Ex 21²⁶ (E); שֵׁבֶט מַכֵּךְ Is 14²⁹ (fig of conqueror); with (ב) stone or fist Ex 21¹⁸ (E), cf. (fig) Is 58⁴ (abs.); *smite* lion or bear 1 S 17³⁵, *strike* river (with rod מַטֶּה) 7¹⁷ (c. עַל obj, +ב instr.), v²⁰ Ex 17⁵ (E; ב instr.), also (with mantle) 2 K 2⁸.¹⁴ ¹⁴, cf ׳י *smiting* Euphrates into (ל) seven streams Is 11¹⁵, dust Ex 8¹² ¹³ (P); rock 17⁶ (E), Nu 20¹¹ (P; ב instr.), ψ 78²⁰; fig *smite* earth בְּשֵׁבֶט פִּיו Is 11⁴ (of future Davidic kg.), *strike* on ground (אַ֫רְצָה; with arrows) 2 K 13¹⁸, also (abs) v¹⁸ ¹⁹; *strike* weapons out of (מִן) hands, Ez 39³ (׳י; fig. of making powerless); lintel of door Am 9¹; barley-loaf *strikes* tent Ju 7¹³ (in dream); in fig. of regret, remorse וַיַּךְ לֵב דָּוִד אֹתוֹ 2 S 24¹⁰ *and David's heart smote him*, so 1 S 24⁶ (+עַל־אֲשֶׁר *because*); of goat smiting (butting with horn) the ram, so as to break its horns Dn 8⁷ (in vision), *smite* = *hit* with missile, sling-stone 1 S 17⁴⁹ (c acc. pers. +אֶל־מִצְחוֹ), cf. 2 K 3²⁵ (but text perh corrupt, v. Benz); arrow, 1 K 22³⁴ = 2 Ch 18³³ (c acc pers +בֵּין), 2 K 9²⁴ (c. *id*); of piercing, הַכּוֹת בַּחֲנִית בְּדָוִד וּבַקִּיר 1 S 19¹⁰ *smite with the dart into D. and into the wall*, pin D. to the wall, וַיַּךְ אֶת־הַח׳ בַּקִּיר v¹⁰, cf. 18¹¹, אַכֶּה בַחֲנִית וּבָאָרֶץ 26⁸. **b.** *smite* repeatedly, *beat*, a man Ex 2¹¹ ¹³ (E), 5¹⁶ (J), Ne 13²⁵ (מִן partit), cf. Dt 25¹¹; here prob also 1 K 20³⁵.³⁵.³⁷ ³⁷ (הַכֵּה וּפָצֹעַ *beating and bruising him*); of Assyr. under fig. of taskmaster Is 10²⁴; *beat* a woman so as to bruise her (פָּצַע) Ct 5⁷; *beat* by authority, *scourge* Je 20² 37¹⁵ Dt 25².³ (c. acc. pers.+acc. cogn. מַכָּה רַבָּה), v³ cf. בִּן הַכּוֹת v² i e *worthy of scourging*, bastinado, (cf. Dr); 2 Ch 25¹⁶; Pr 17¹⁰ 19²⁵ 23¹³ ¹⁴ (ב instr.); cf גֵּוִי נָתַתִּי לְמַכִּים Is 50⁶; of hail, *beat down* herbage etc Ex 9²⁵.²⁵ (cf. **Pu.**). **c.** וַיַּכּוּ כָף 2 K 11¹² *and they clapped hands* (in applause); elsewhere only Ezek, in mockery; (רקע ברגלך ‖) 6¹¹ בְּכַפּוֹ; כַּף אֶל־כַּף Ez 21¹⁹.²²; acc. כַּפִּי 22¹³ **d.** *give a thrust* (with fork) into (ב) pot 1 S 2¹⁴; *strike* roots Ho 14⁶ (in fig., but וְיֵלְכוּ We Now). **e.** rarely *smite* (in battle) so as (merely) to wound 1 K 8²⁸, so (+acc. cogn. מַכָּה) v²⁹ 9¹⁵ = 2 Ch 22⁶; fig of ׳י's wounding Isr Ho 6¹ (opp. חָבַשׁ, *bind up*), Je 30¹⁴ (c. acc. cogn.) Cf. *smite with* (ב) *the tongue* Je 18¹⁸. **f.** *smite*, of sun, etc, c. acc. pers Is 49¹⁰ ψ 121⁶; c. עַל Jon 4⁸.

2. *Smite* fatally: **a.** (subj. man) *smite*, c. acc., +word of killing (dying):—obj. lion and bear 1 S 17³⁶, man Ex 21¹².²⁰ (E), Jos 10²⁶ (JE), 11¹⁷ (D), 1 S 17⁵⁰ 2 S 1¹⁵ 2³¹ (מִן partit. +ב *among*), 4⁷ 14⁶ 18¹⁵ 21¹⁷ 1 K 16¹⁰ 2 K 12²² 15³⁰ 25²¹ = Je 52²⁷, 2 K 25²⁵ Je 41² Nu 35¹⁶ ¹⁷ ¹⁸.²¹ (P; all c. ב instr.), c. acc.+אֶל־הַחֹמֶשׁ+ב instr. 2 S 2²³ *smote him* (fatally) *in the belly with* (on text v HPS), 20¹⁰, cf. 3²⁷ 4⁶ (but del. 𝔊 Ew Th We Dr Bu HPS); וְהִכָּהוּ נֶפֶשׁ Dt 19¹¹ *and he smite him in his life* (mortally), and he die, cf. (without word of dying) v⁶ Gn 37²¹ (J), Je 40¹⁴ ¹⁵ [otherwise Lv 24¹⁷ ¹⁸ Nu 35¹¹ ¹⁵.³⁰ Dt 27²⁵ Jos 20³.⁹]; with prolepsis לְהַכּוֹת חֲלָלִים *smite the slain*

Ju 20$^{31.39}$; + אַ֫רְצָה *smite to the ground* i.e. kill 2 S 2^{22} 18^{11}. **b.** *smite*, of worm gnawing or boring so as to kill plant Jon 4^{7}. **c.** very oft. = *kill, slay, man or beast* (c 150 t) · Gn 4^{15} 8^{21} (exterminate; both J), Ex 2^{12} Nu 21^{35} (E), Jos 7^{5} (מִן partit), v^{6} (JE), Dt 19^{6} 21^{1} 27$^{24.25}$ Jos 11^{10} (ב instr; all D), Lv 24$^{17.18.21.21}$ (H), Nu 35$^{11.15.21.24.30}$ Jos 9^{18} 20$^{3.9}$ (all P), Ju 15^{16} 1 S 17$^{9.9.36}$ 2 S 12^{9} (ב instr), 2 K 9^{7} (exterminate), etc, c ב *among* 1 S 23^{5}, מִן partit Ju 14^{19} 20^{45}; c ב partit *slay at, work slaughter among* 2 S 23^{10} (ins also in ‖ 1 Ch 11^{13} v Be$^{ad loc}$ Dr$^{2 S 23.10}$), but also ב of dir obj 1 S 18^{7} 21^{12} 29^{5}, subj lion 1 K 20$^{36.36}$ cf Je 5^{6} (fig of judgment), ׳י subj 1 S 6$^{19 b}$ (ב *among*, + acc cogn; 1 S 6$^{19 a}$ וַיַּךְ crpt v 𝔊 Th We Dr Kl Kit Bu HPS), *slay* firstborn Ex 12^{2} (J), v^{29} Nu 3^{13} 8^{17} 33^{4} (all P), ψ 78^{51} 105^{36} 135^{8}, God *slays* for (עַל) sin 2 S 6^{7} = 1 Ch 13^{10} (עַל־אֲשֶׁר), *slay* לְפִי־חָ֫רֶב Dt 13^{16} 20^{13} Jos 11$^{11.12.14}$ (all D), Ju 18^{27} 21^{10} 1 S 22^{9} 2 K 10^{25} Je 21^{7} Jb 1$^{15.17}$, *kill, slay*, c. acc. cogn. (מַכָּה) 1 S 14^{14} 1 K 20^{21} (ב *among*), 2 Ch 13^{17} (בָּהֶם), 25^{13} (מֵהֶם); c. acc. pers + acc cogn Jos 10^{20} (JE), Est 9^{5}, etc., *kill unwittingly, unintentionally* הִכָּה בִבְלִי דַ֫עַת Dt 19^{4} Jos 20^{5} (both D).

3. *Smite* = *attack, attack and destroy* a company Gn 32$^{9.12}$ 34^{30} Jos 8^{21} Ju 8^{11} 9^{43} 2 K 8^{21} 2 Ch 21^{9}, *attack and capture* a city Ju 1^{8} v^{12} = Jos 15^{16} (JE), Jos 7^{3} 10^{4} (JE), 1 S 30^{1} 1 K 15^{20} = 2 Ch 16^{4}, 2 K 15$^{16.16}$ 1 Ch 20^{1} 2 Ch 14^{13} Je 47^{1}; tents 1 Ch 4^{41} 2 Ch 14^{14}, = *sack* a city לְפִי־חָ֫רֶב (slaying inhab.), Jos 8^{24} 19^{47} (both JE), 10$^{28.30.32.35.37}$ cf v^{39} (all D), Ju 1^{25} 20^{37} 2 S 15^{14}, esp *defeat* kg or army (involving oft. overthrow, pursuit and slaughter),—c 95 t,—Gn 14$^{5.15.17}$ Nu 14^{45} 21^{24} (JE), Jos 8^{12} 10^{10} (+ acc cogn), v^{10} (עַד loc), 11$^{8.8}$ (all JE), Dt 1^{4} 2^{33} 3^{3} 4^{46} 7^{2} 29^{6} Jos 10$^{33.40}$ (מִן—ועד loc), 12$^{1.6.12}$ 13^{12} (all D), Ju 1$^{5.17}$ 1 S 11^{11} (עַד temp.), 1 K 13^{17} (עַד־כַּלֵּה), 2 K 3$^{24 a}$ + v$^{24 b}$ (where rd. וַיָּבֹאוּ בוֹא וְהַכּוֹת *and they went on defeating*), Is 10^{20} Je 37^{10}, etc.; ins. וַיַּךְ or הִכָּה in 2 S 8^{13} Th Ke Kit Bu cf Dr, after 𝔊, c ב obj 1 S 14^{31} 23$^{2.2}$ (ה loc — מִן), + לְפִי חָ֫רֶב Ju 20^{48}, etc; of gods *causing defeat* 2 Ch 28^{23}; *smite* land = conquer, subjugate, sts ravage, Gn 14^{7} Jos 10^{40} (D), 1 S 27^{9} Je 43^{11} 46^{13}, cf Is 14^{6} (acc cogn); subj ׳י Nu 32^{4} (P), of ׳י *smiting* sea וְהִכָּה בַיָּם גַּלִּים Zc 10^{11} (Bev$^{JPh\ xviii\ 35\ (1889)\ 88}$ prop נבלים)

4. Of God, **a.** *smite* with (ב) a plague, disease, etc —blindness Gn 19^{11} (J), 2 K 6$^{18.18}$ cf. Zc 12$^{4.4}$ (symbol.); of Egyptian plagues Ex 3^{20} 9^{15} (both J), 1 S 4^{8}, without ב Ex 7^{25} (J), 12^{13} (P), ψ 136^{10} (acc + בִּבְכוֹרֵיהֶם); other plagues Nu 14^{12} (JE), Dt 28$^{22.27.28.35}$ 1 S 5^{6} 2 S 24^{17} Jb 2^{7} Am 4^{9} Hg 2^{17} Mal 3^{24}, without ב, 1 S 5^{9} 2 K 19^{35} = Is 37^{36}; Nu 11^{33} (JE, בָּעָם + acc. cogn.), *smite* vines with (ב) blight ψ 105^{33}. **b.** *smite* = *chastise*, or *send judgment upon*, usu. c acc, 1 K 14^{15} 1 Ch 21^{7} Is 5^{25} 9^{12} 27^{7} (הַכְּמַכַּת מַכֵּהוּ הִכָּהוּ), 30^{31} (ב instr) 57^{17} 60^{10} (opp. רִחַם) Je 2^{30} 5^{3} 14^{9} Ez 32^{15} (𝔊 Co זרה scatter), c עַל *punish for*, (sin) Lv 26^{24} (H) **c.** of God's *destroying* palaces Am 3^{15} 6^{11} (2 acc), cf Zc 9^{4}.

†**Hoph.** *Pf* הֻכָּה Ho 9^{16} Nu 25^{14}, הוּכָּה ψ 102^{5}, וְהֻכָּה consec. Ex 22^{1}, 3 fs. הֻכְּתָה Ez 33^{21} 40^{1}, 1 s הֻכֵּ֫יתִי Zc 13^{6}; 3 pl. הֻכּוּ 1 S 5^{12}; *Impf.* 3 mpl וַיֻּכּוּ Ex 5^{14}; 2 mpl תֻכּוּ Is 1^{5}, *Pt* מֻכֶּה Nu 25^{14}, cstr מֻכֵּה Is 53^{4}, f. מֻכָּה Nu 25$^{15.18}$; pl מֻכִּים Ex 5^{16}, cstr. מֻכֵּי־ Je 18^{21},—*be smitten*· **1.** = *receive a blow* Is 1^{5} (Judah under fig. of man) **2.** *be wounded* Zc 13^{6}. **3.** *be beaten* Ex 5$^{14.16}$ (J) **4.** *be* (fatally) *smitten* + vb of dying Ex 22^{1} (E); *be killed, slain* Nu 25$^{14.14.15.18}$ (c עַל, *for*), מֻכֵּי־חֶ֫רֶב Je 18^{21} (‖ הֲרֻגֵי מָוֶת), so also (abs) prob 1 S 4^{2} (rd. וַיֻּכּוּ 𝔊 𝔖 𝔙 Th Dr Klo Kit, for MT וַיַּכּוּ) **5.** *be attacked and captured*, of city Ez 33^{21} 40^{1}. **6.** *be smitten* with disease (by God) 1 S 5^{12}, abs, of ׳י's servant Is 53^{4}. **7.** *be blighted*, of plant (in fig) Ho 9^{16} (Ephr), ψ 102^{5} (heart, כָּעֵשֶׂב; both + יָבֵשׁ).

†[נָכֶה] **adj.** smitten, stricken (cf [נָכָא]),—only cstr. נְכֵה רַגְלַיִם 2 S 4^{4} 9^{3} *crippled of feet*; נְכֵה־רוּחַ Is 66^{2} *contrite of spirit* (+ עָנִי).

†[נָכֶה] **adj.** id;—pl נֵכִים ψ 35^{15} *smitten ones*, but rd prob נָכְרִים *aliens* Ol Che Bae al.

†I נָכוֹן **n.[m.]** = blow Jb 12^{5} acc to Schult Di Bu, but precarious; < Niph. fr. כון q v.

מַכָּה† **n.f.** blow, wound, slaughter,—abs מ׳ 1 S 4^{8}+, cstr. מַכַּת Is 10^{26}+, sf מַכָּתִי Je 10^{19} 15^{18}, etc., pl. מַכּוֹת abs 2 K 8^{29}+, cstr. Dt 29^{21}+, sf. מַכֹּתֶךָ Dt 28^{59}, מַכּוֹתַיִךְ Je 30^{17}, etc;—**1. a.** *blow, stripe*, lit. of scourging, chastising Dt 25^{3} Pr 20^{30} (‖ חַבֻּרוֹת פֶּצַע), מַכַּת חֶ֫רֶב Est 9^{5} (as acc cogn). **b.** *beating, scourging*, fig of defeat of Midian Is 10^{26} (‖ עוֹרֵר שׁוֹט). **c.** oft. *wound* 1 K 22^{35} 2 K 8^{29} 9^{15} = 2 Ch 22^{6} (rd. מִן־הַמּ׳), Zc 13^{6} (בֵּין יָדֶיךָ), symbol of violence Je 6^{7} (+ חֳלִי), פֶּצַע וְחַבּוּרָה וּמַכָּה טְרִיָּה Is 1^{6} (of Judah, under fig of maltreated man), cf. Mi 1^{9} (מ׳ אֲנוּשָׁה),

Na 3^{19} (|| שֶׁבֶר; of Nineveh), esp. in Je (of Judah): Je 10^{19} 14^{17} 30^{12} (all + נַחְלָה *severe*; || שֶׁבֶר), 15^{18} (מ׳ אֲנוּשָׁה), 19^{8} 47^{17} 50^{13}, as acc. cogn. 30^{14}, c. vb. רָפָא *heal* v^{17}; also מַחַץ מ׳ Is 30^{26} (|| שֶׁבֶר); of wounds made by י׳'s arrows ψ 64^{8}. **2.** = *slaughter* 1 S 4^{10} 14^{30}, usu. as acc. cogn. c. הִכָּה Jos 10^{20} 1 S 6^{19} 14^{14} 19^{8} 23^{5} 1 K 20^{21} 2 Ch 13^{17}. **3.** = *defeat*, as acc. cogn. c. הִכָּה Jos 10^{10} 11^{33} 15^{8} 2 Ch 28^{5}; = *conquest* (of י׳) Is 14^{6}. **4.** *plague*, esp. disease, as punishment (of י׳), 1 S 4^{8} Dt $28^{59.59.59}$ (|| חֳלִי), v^{61} (|| *id.*), 29^{21} (|| תַּחֲלֻאִים), Lv 26^{21} (H), as acc. cogn. Nu 11^{33}.—מַכּוֹת 2 Ch 2^{9} rd. מַכֹּלֶת (v. אכל) as || 1 K 5^{25}, so 𝔊𝔙 Be Öt and Th[1 K 5, 25].

†נְכוֹ, נְכֹה **n.pr.m.** Necho (II), king of Egypt (Egypt. *Nkw*, i.e. (Steindorff[BAS i. 346 f.]) *Nekawō*; As. *Nikû* Id.[ib.] Schr[COT 2 K 23, 29] is grandfather of Bibl. Necho);—contemp. of Josiah and Nebuchad. [B.C. 611–605]: נְכוֹ 2 Ch 35^{20} (𝔊 Φαραω Νεχαω), נְכֹה 2 Ch 35^{22} 36^{4} (𝔊 Φαραω Νεχαω); פַּרְעֹה נְכוֹ Je 46^{2}, פַּרְעֹה נְכֹה 2 K $23^{29.33.34.35}$ (all 𝔊 *id.*).

II. נָכוֹן **n.pr.m.** v. sub כון, and v. כִּידֹן.

נכח (√of foll.: prob. *be in front of;* Lag[BN 30] cp. Ar. نَكَحَ *marry* (perh. orig. in phys. sense); Syr. ܢܟܺܝܚ is *gentle*, ܢܰܟܺܝܚܽܘܬܳܐ *gentleness*).

†נֹכַח **subst.** front, always in **prep.** or **adv.** phrases, with sf. נִכְחוֹ Ex 14^{2} Ez 46^{9}:—**1.** as adv. acc. *in front of, opposite to*, Ex 14^{2} נִכְחוֹ תַחֲנוּ, 26^{35} the candlestick נֹכַח הַשֻּׁלְחָן, 40^{24}, Jos 18^{17} (in the || 15^{7}, נֹכַח לְ : v. לְ **5 c**), 1 K 20^{29} וַיַּחֲנוּ אֵלֶּה נֹכַח אֵלֶּה, 22^{35} (= 2 Ch 18^{34}), Est $5^{1.1}$; Ez 46^{9} Qr כִּי נִכְחוֹ יֵצֵא shall go out *in front of himself*, i.e. straightforward; cf. נֶגֶד, נֶגְדּוֹ **1 a**(*b*). Fig. Pr 5^{21} כִּי נֹכַח עֵינֵי י׳ דַּרְכֵי אִישׁ *in the sight* of י׳'s eyes are, etc., Ju 18^{6} נֹכַח י׳ דַּרְכְּכֶם *before* י׳ is your way, i.e. under his eye and favourable regard. In the phr. נֹכַח פְּנֵי, Je 17^{16} מוֹצָא שְׂפָתַי נֹכַח פָּנֶיךָ הָיָה was *before* thy face, La 2^{19}, Ez 14^{3} מִכְשׁוֹל עֲוֹנָם נָתְנוּ נֹכַח פְּנֵיהֶם (i.e. they contemplate it with pleasure), $v^{4.7}$. **2.** combined with preps.:—**a.** אֶל־נֹכַח, Nu 19^{4} וְהִזָּה אל־נ׳ פני אהל מועד and sprinkle it *towards the front* of, etc. **b.** לְנֹכַח: (*a*) as **adv.** Pr 4^{25} עיניך לנ׳ יביטו let thine eyes look *to the front* or *right on* (|| ועפעפיך יַיְשִׁרוּ נֶגְדֶּךָ); (*b*) as **prep.** Gn 30^{38} לְנֹכַח הַצֹּאן *in front of* the flocks, 25^{21} וַיֶּעְתַּר . . . לְנֹכַח אִשְׁתּוֹ *in front of*, i.e. *on behalf of* (cf. *pro*), his wife; (*c*) עַד־נֹכַח, Ju 19^{10} וַיָּבֹא עַד־נ׳ יְבוּס *as far as in front of* Jebus, 20^{43} Ez 47^{20} (עַד־נֹכַח לְ). Syn. נֶגֶד, q.v.

†[נָכֹחַ] **adj.** and **subst.** straight, right, straightness, f. נְכֹחָה, pl. נְכֹחִים, ־וֹת:—Is 57^{2} הֹלֵךְ נְכֹחוֹ he that walks *in* (cf. 33^{15} 50^{10}) *his straightness* (Ges 'der seinen *geraden* Weg geht'), fig. for straightforwardly (cf. Pr 4^{25}); נְכֹחָה *what is straight in front*, fig. *straightforwardness, honesty*, Am 3^{10} לֹא יָדְעוּ עֲשׂוֹת נ׳, Is 59^{14} (|| אֱמֶת) ונ׳ לא תוכל לָבוֹא; 2 S 15^{3} דבריך טובים ונכחים thy pleadings are good and *right* (i.e. *true*), Pr 8^{9} (of words of Wisdom) כֻּלָּם נְכֹחִים לַמֵּבִין i.e. they lead *straight* to the right goal (|| ישרים; comp. v^{8b} אֵין בָּהֶם נִפְתָּל וְעִקֵּשׁ), 24^{26} מֵשִׁיב דְּבָרִים נְכֹחִים i.e. either *correct* (leading to the right point), or *honest* answers; Is 30^{10} לֹא־תֶחֱזוּ לָנוּ נְכֹחוֹת *true* things (opp. חֲלָקוֹת, מַהֲתַלּוֹת *illusions*), 26^{10} בְּאֶרֶץ נְכֹחוֹת יְעַוֵּל in a land of *rectitude* (Che) he will do wickedly.

†[נָכַל] **vb. be crafty, deceitful, knavish** (As. *nakâlu, be crafty, cunning;* 𝔗 נְכֵל *be crafty*, Pa. *deceive;* Syr. ܢܟܰܠ *deceive, plot;* cf. perh. ወነኰለ *act faithlessly*, ወነጌለ *faithless*, Prä[Amhar. Spr. 90]);—**Qal** *Pt.* נוֹכֵל Mal 1^{14} *knave.* **Pi.** *Pf.* 3 mpl. c. acc. cogn. נִכְלֵיהֶם אֲשֶׁר נִכְּלוּ לָכֶם Nu 25^{18} *their wiles with which they beguiled you.* **Hithp.** *Impf.* וַיִּתְנַכְּלוּ אֹתוֹ לַהֲמִיתוֹ Gn 37^{18} *they knavishly planned* against him (Kö[iii. 9]), etc.; *Inf. cstr.* לְהִתְנַכֵּל בְּ ψ 105^{25} *to deal knavishly with.*

†[נֵכֶל] **n.**[**m.**] **wiliness, craft, knavery;**—only pl. sf. נִכְלֵיהֶם Nu 25^{18} *their craft, their wile* (as acc. cogn. c. נִכֵּל).

†כֵּלַי, כִּילַי **n.m.** knave (for נְכִילַי v. Kö[ii. 1, 118]);—abs. כִּילַי Is 32^{5} (opp. שׁוֹעַ, || נָבָל); כֵּלַי v^{7} (assonance with כֵּלָיו, fr. כְּלִי q.v.).

†[נֶכֶס] **n.m.**[Jos 22, 8] only pl. נְכָסִים **riches, treasures** (prob. As. or Aram. loan-word, cf. As. *nikâsu, property, wealth, gain*, Dl[HWB 463], Syr. ܢܶܟܣܶܐ *wealth;* on deriv. fr. As. *nikâsu, cut off, hew down, behead*, etc., Syr. ܢܟܰܣ *slay*, 𝔗 נְכַס, NH נֶכֶס *id.*, through meaning *cattle for slaughter*, cf. Frä[98] Hpt[Hbr. iii (Jan. 1887), 107 ff.] Schwally[Idiot. 120 f.] Brock[ad voc.]);—Jos 22^{8} (P), 2 Ch $1^{11.12}$ Ec 6^{2} (all || כָּבוֹד, עֹשֶׁר), 5^{18} (|| עֹשֶׁר).

†I. [נָכַר] **vb.** (not **Qal**) **regard, recognize** (NH Hiph. *know, be acquainted with;* 𝔗 Aph.

id; Syr Aph. ܐܟܪ *id.*, cf. also Ar نَكِرَ in sense *be shrewd, cunning*),—**Niph.** *Pf* 3 mpl. לא נכרו La 4^{8} *they are not recognized* **Pi.** *Pf.* לא נִכַּר שׁוֹעַ לִפְנֵי־דָל Jb 34^{19} *he regardeth not the opulent above the poor* (|| לֹא־נָשָׂא פְּנֵי שָׂרִים), *Impf* לא תְנַכֵּרוּ Jb 21^{29} *do ye not recognize their tokens* **Hiph.** *Pf* הכיר Dt 33^{9} Dn 11^{39} Kt, sf. הִכִּירוֹ Gn 27^{23}, 3 pl. הכירו Ju 18^{3} + 2 t, sf הכירהו Jb 2^{12}, הִכִּרֻהוּ Gn 42^{8}, *Impf* יַכִּיר Dt 21^{17} + 3 t + Dn 11^{39} Qr, וַיַּכֵּר Gn 38^{26} +; sf. וַיַּכִּרֵהוּ 1 K 18^{7}, יַכִּירֶנּוּ Jb 7^{10}, וַיַּכִּירָהּ Gn 37^{33}, etc.; *Imv.* הַכֶּר־ Gn 31^{32} + 2 t, *Inf abs* הַכֵּר־ (Ginsb van d H הַכֵּר־) Pr 24^{23} 28^{21}, *cstr.* sf. הַכִּירֵנִי Ru 2^{10}, *Pt* מַכִּיר ψ 142^{5}, sf מַכִּירֵךְ Ru 2^{19}, etc,—**1.** *regard, observe*, esp with a view to recognition, c obj. cl, Gn 31^{32} 37^{32} 38^{25}, *pay attention to*, c. acc. pers Ru $2^{10.19}$, acc. rei (of God) Jb 34^{25}; acc rei om 2 S 3^{36}, ׳י subj כן אַכִּיר ... לְטוֹבָה Je 24^{5} *so will I regard* the exiles . *for good*, Antiochus subj Dn 11^{39}, הכיר פָּנִים *pay regard to* (shew partiality, = (נָשָׂא פני פ׳ || הִטָּה משפט) Dt 1^{17} 16^{19}), Pr 24^{23} 28^{21}.

2. *Recognize* (as formerly known) c acc pers vel rei, Gn 27^{23} 37^{33} 38^{26} (all J), $42^{7.8.8}$ (E), 1 K 18^{7} 20^{41} Jb 2^{12}, proverb. בטרם יַכִּיר איש את־רעהו Ru 3^{14} *before a man could recognize his fellow* (i e. before dawn); *recognize* voice (קול), Ju 18^{3} 1 S 26^{17}, = *perceive* the true situation, וָאַכִּירָה והנה Ne 6^{12} *and I perceived, and lo!* God had not sent him

3. *Be willing to recognize, acknowledge* Dt 21^{17} 33^{9} Is 63^{16} (|| יָדַע), ψ 142^{5}, *acknowledge with honour* Is 61^{9}.

4. *Be acquainted with*, לא יַכִּירֶנּוּ עוֹד מְקוֹמוֹ Jb 7^{10} *his place shall be acquainted with him no more* (he shall be gone and forgotten), cf ψ 103^{16}; c acc rei Jb 24^{17}

5. *Distinguish, understand*, הכיר קול ... לקול Ezr 3^{13} could not *distinguish*, etc.; cf Jb 4^{16} *could not distinguish its appearance*, הכיר לְדַבֵּר Ne 13^{24} *understand* how *to speak*, etc

Hithp. *Impf* יִתְנַכֶּר־נַעַר Pr 20^{11} by his deeds *a youth maketh himself known*, whether his doing be pure, etc.

†[הַכָּרָה] **n f.** look (or **expression**?);—cstr הַכָּרַת פְּנֵיהֶם Is 3^{9} *a look at their face* witnesses against them (𝔅 Che^Comm al), or *the expression of their face* (Ges^Comm De Gu SS, cf Kit-Di), > *their regarding of persons* 𝔖 𝔗 Thes Hi Du Che^Hpt (v against this Kit-Di); Ew Di *the impudence of their face* (√הכר), but this very dub.

†[מַכָּר] **n m. acquaintance, friend** (dub, cf Benz^ad loc),—sf מַכָּרוֹ 2 K 12^{6}; pl sf. מַכָּרֵיכֶם v^{8}

II. **נכר** (√of foll, poss = I נכר, whence the *foreign, strange*, as that which is intently regarded, so Thes, but precarious, cf. As. *nakâru, rebel*, Pa *change, nakiru*, and *nakaru, enemy, nukurtu, enmity*, etc., Ar. نَكِرَ in sense *be bad, evil;* II. *change, alter* a thing; Sab. נכר II. *reject, injure*, etc., נכרם *injury* Sab Denkm [76] CIS^IV 81 9, 29 5, Min נכר *alter* Hom^Südarab Chrest 128; Syr ܢܟܪ *reject*, ܢܘܟܪܝܐ *alienus*, etc; 𝔗 נוּכְרִי *strange, foreign*).

†[נֹכֶר], נֵכֶר **n.[m.]** misfortune, calamity,—abs נֵכֶר Jb 31^{3} *calamity* (|| איד), sf נָכְרוֹ Ob ^{12} *his calamity*

†נֵכָר **n.[m.]** that which is foreign, foreignness (on format. cf. Lag^BN 61, 154),—abs נ׳ Ju 10^{16} +, cstr נֵכַר־ Dt 31^{16},—*foreignness* (of another family, tribe, or nation), esp. **1.** אֱלֹהֵי (הַ)נֵּכָר = *foreign gods* Gn $35^{2.4}$ Jos $24^{20.23}$ (all E, = א׳ אחרים of D, cf אַחֵר), Ju 10^{16} 1 S 7^{3} Je 5^{19} 2 Ch 33^{15}, א׳ נֵכַר־הָאָרֶץ Dt 31^{16} = *foreign gods of the land*, sg. אל נכר Dt 32^{12} Mal 2^{11} ψ 81^{10}, אֱלוֹהַּ נ׳ Dn 11^{39} **2.** בֶּן־(הַ)נֵּכָר = *foreigner* Gn 17^{12} (|| לֹא מִזַּרְעֲךָ), v^{27} Ex 12^{43} (all P), Lv 22^{25} (H), Ez $44^{9.9}$ Ne 9^{2} Is 56^{3}, בני (ה)נ׳ 2 S $22^{45.46}$ = ψ $18^{45.46}$, Ez 44^{7} Is 56^{6} 60^{10} 61^{5} 62^{8} ψ $144^{7.11}$ **3.** other combin . הַבְלֵי נ׳ Je 8^{19} *foreign vanities* (idolatries), מזבחות הַנּ׳ 2 Ch 14^{2} *foreign altars*, אַדְמַת נ׳ ψ 137^{4} *foreign soil;* מִכָּל־נ׳ Ne 13^{30} *from everything foreign*

†נָכְרִי **adj.** foreign, alien (NH נָכְרִי = *Gentile*),—נ׳ abs. m Zp 1^{8} +; f. נָכְרִיָּה Ex 2^{22} +; mpl נָכְרִים Is 2^{6} + 2 t + Pr 20^{16} Kt (> Qr נָכְרִיָּה), + 27^{13} (so read for MT נָכְרִיָּה); fpl. נָכְרִיּוֹת Gn 31^{15} +,—**1. a.** *foreign:* עַם נָכְרִי Ex 21^{8} (E) *a foreign* (non-Isr) people, איש נ׳ Dt 17^{15} (|| לֹא אָחִיךָ); מַלְבּוּשׁ נ׳ Zp 1^{8}, אֶרֶץ נָכְרִיָּה Ex 2^{22} (J) *foreign land*, so 18^{3} (E), esp. נָשִׁים נָכְרִיּוֹת *foreign* (non-Isr) *women* 1 K $11^{1.8}$ Ezr $10^{2.10.11.14.17.18.44}$ Ne $13^{26.27}$. **b.** as subst נָכְרִי *foreigner* (non-Isr.) Ju 19^{12} (+ אֲשֶׁר לֹא מִבְּנֵי יִשְׂרָאֵל), 1 K 8^{41} (+ אֲשֶׁר לֹא מֵעַמְּךָ), = 2 Ch 6^{32} (+ *id*), 1 K 8^{43} = 2 Ch 6^{33}, Dt 14^{21} (|| גֵּר), 15^{3} 23^{21} (opp. אָחִיךָ), 29^{21} (+ אֲשֶׁר יָבֹא מֵאֶרֶץ רְחוֹקָה), as predicate, 2 S 15^{19} (|| גֹלֶה), נָכְרִיָּה Ru 2^{10}, pl. נָכְרִים *foreigners* La 5^{2} (|| זָרִים), Ob ^{11} (|| *id*); cf יַלְדֵי נָכְרִים Is 2^{6}, fpl *alien women* Gn 31^{15} (E; i.e. not of one's

father's family). **2.** נָכְרִיָּה *foreign woman*, as term. techn., in Pr, for *harlot* (perh. because harlots were orig. chiefly foreigners): Pr 2[16] (|| אִשָּׁה זָרָה), 7[5] (|| *id.*), 5[20] (|| זָרָה), 6[24] (|| אֵשֶׁת רָע), 23[27] (|| זוֹנָה).—On 20[16] 27[13] v. infr. **3.** fig. *unknown, unfamiliar:* נָכְרִי הָיִיתִי בְעֵינֵיהֶם Jb 19[15] *an alien am I become in their eyes;* נ׳ לִבְנֵי אִמִּי ψ 69[9] (|| מוּזָר הָיִיתִי לְאֶחָי); אִישׁ נ׳ Ec 6[2]; of ׳י's judgment, נָכְרִיָּה עֲבֹדָתוֹ Is 28[21] *strange is his task!* (|| זָר מַעֲשֵׂהוּ); גֶּפֶן נָכְרִיָּה Je 2[21] *an alien vine* (opp. זֶרַע אֱמֶת), fig. of degenerate Israel; as subst., נָכְרִים Pr 20[16] Kt (> Qr נָכְרִיָּה), *aliens*, persons unknown to him (|| זָר), so read also (for MT נָכְרִיָּה) || 27[13].

†[נכר] **vb.denom.** act or treat as foreign, or strange; disguise, misconstrue;—**Niph.** *Impf.* יִנָּכֵר Pr 26[24] with his lips a hater *disguiseth himself* (dissembles, speaks what is *foreign* to his thought). **Pi.** *Pf.* נִכַּר 1 S 23[7], but v. infr.; *Impf.* וַיְנַכְּרוּ Je 19[4] *and they have treated* this place *as foreign* (profane); יְנַכְּרוּ צָרֵימוֹ Dt 32[27] lest *their adversaries should misconstrue* (it).—נִכַּר אֹתוֹ א׳ בְּיָדִי 1 S 23[7] *God hath alienated him into my hand*, but improbable; 𝔊 מָכַר (cf. Ju 4[9]) *hath sold him*, so Th Klo HPS (cf. We); < סִכַּר (as Is 19[4]) Krochm Dr; Kit either of these; > סִגַּר Bu; Löhr either סִגַּר or סִכַּר. **Hithp.** *Impf.* וַיִּתְנַכֵּר אֲלֵיהֶם Gn 42[7] *he acted as a stranger toward them; Pt.* f. מִתְנַכֵּרָה 1 K 14[5,6] *feign to be a stranger-woman.*

†[נְכֹת] **n.**[**f.**] **treasure** (so context demands) (𝔊L 2 K 20[13] τῆς ὑπάρξεως, cf. 𝔖 𝔗; der. uncertain; Dl[Prol. 141] cp. As. *bit nakamti* (*nakanti*), *house of treasure*, √ *nakâmu, heap up* [Dl[HWB 462]], whence ב׳ נ׳ perh. borrowed; this favoured by Nö[ZMG xl (1886), 731] Hpt[ZA ii. 266] (reading *nakavâti* = *nakamâti*, and Heb. ב׳ נְכֹתָיו or ב׳ נְכוֹתוֹ).—Only sf. בֵּית נְכֹתֹה = *his treasure-house* 2 K 20[13] = Is 39[2].

נלה doubtful √ (Ar. نيل, نَالَ is *obtain, attain,* نَيْلٌ *what one obtains* by another's bounty, Lane[3040]);—for supposed **Hiph.** *Inf.* sf. כַּנְּלֹתְךָ Is 33[1] = כְּהַנְלֹתְךָ (Ki Ges[Lgb. 87] Kö[i. 574]), read כְּכַלֹּתְךָ (**Pi.** Inf. of כלה; so Ra Capp Ges[Thes] Ew Kn Che Brd Di Du), cf. || כַּהֲתִמְּךָ.

†[מִנְלָה] **n.**[**m.**]? **gain, acquisition**?—Only sf. מִנְלָם לֹא יִטֶּה לָאָרֶץ מִנְלָם Jb 15[29] (si vera l.) *their acquisition*, but very dub.; Di (formerly) שִׁבֳּלִים, Hi מְלִלִים *ears*, cf. Bu; other conj. v. in Di; Du thinks hopelessly corrupt.—𝔊 σκιάν [i.e. צִלָּם], 𝔖 *their word* [מִלָּתָם].

נְמִבְזָה 1 S 15[9] v. בזה **Niph.**

†**נְמוּאֵל** **n.pr.m.** (cf. Gray[Prop. N. 307]);—**1.** son of Simeon Nu 26[12] 1 Ch 4[24] (= יְמוּאֵל, q.v., Gn 46[10] Ex 6[15]), 𝔊 Ναμουηλ. **2.** a Reubenite (brother of Dathan and Abiram) Nu 26[9], 𝔊 *id.*

†**נְמוּאֵלִי** **adj.gent.** of **1** supr., only c. art. הַנּ׳ as n.coll. Nu 26[12], 𝔊 Ναμουηλει.

נמל (√ of following, meaning unknown).

†**נְמָלָה** **n.f.unit.** (Lag[BN 81]) ant (NH *id.*; Ar. نَمْلَةٌ (nom. unit. of نَمْلٌ); Syr. ܢܡܠܐ);—abs. נ׳ Pr 6[6]; pl. הַנְּמָלִים 30[25].

נמר (√ of foll., meaning dub.; poss. cp. As. *namâru, shine, gleam* (fr. glossy coat of panther and leopard), [v. Ar. نَمِرٌ *pardus*, and *limpidus, purus* (of water; cf. infr. נמרים)] so Hom[NS 294 f.]; ag. this Nö[ZMG xl (1886), 736] Schwally[Idiot. 121]; נָמֵר is comm. Sem.: As. *nimru* Dl[HWB 468]; Ar. نَمِرٌ, نِمْرٌ Lane[2853]; Eth. ነምር: Syr. ܢܡܪܐ, 𝔗 נִמְרָא; NH נָמֵר).

†**נָמֵר** **n.m.**[Is 11, 6] **leopard**;—abs. נ׳ Ho 13[7] + 3 t.; pl. נְמֵרִים Hb 1[8] Ct 4[8];—*leopard*, as spotted Je 13[23], swift Hb 1[8], keen-eyed Je 5[6] (symb. of calamities of Isr.), so Ho 13[7] (sim. of ׳י); נ׳ עִם־גְּדִי יִרְבָּץ Is 11[6] (predict.); הַרְרֵי נְמֵרִים Ct 4[8] (|| מְעֹנוֹת אֲרָיוֹת).

†**נִמְרָה** **n.pr.loc.** place E. of Jordan Nu 32[3] (+ חֶשְׁבּוֹן, דִּיבֹן, עֲטָרוֹת, etc.), 𝔊 Ναμβρα, A Αμβραμ, 𝔊L Μαμβραν. Perh. = *Tel Nimrîn*, c. 6 m. E. of Jordan, nearly opp. Jericho, cf. Buhl[Geogr. 264]. —Cf. בֵּית נ׳ (q.v.), also in NH (cf. נמרה n.pr.m. Sinait. Inscr. SACook[81] Lzb[323]; meaning dub.; Nö[ZMG xxix (1875), 437] thinks from *spotted* or *striped* appearance of ground; *place of leopard* also Gray[Prop. Names 92] (on tribal names from leopard v. RS[K 201] also Sab n. pr. אנמרם Levy-Os[l.c.], etc.); We[Held. 2, 82] thinks of *clear water* [cf. foll.]).

†**נִמְרִים** **n.pr.loc.** in Moab (cf. Sab. נמרן attrib. of Bark[m], DHM[ZMG xxix (1875), 592], v. also CIS[iv. No. 103, p. 169]; مَآءٌ نَمِيرٌ *wholesome water* Lane[2853], also We[l.c.]);—only מֵי נִמְרִים Is 15[6] Je 48[34]; prob. = Βηνναμαρειμ Lag[Onom. 284, 33], in *Wady Numêre* at SE. end of Dead Sea, Buhl[Geogr. 272].

†נִמְרֹד, נִמְרוֹד **n.pr.m.** Nimrod (etym. and meaning wholly unknown; Thes (dub.) sub מָרַד *rebel* (of which Hebr. may have thought [cf. Lag[BN 105]]); in fact prob. Bab. name; **1.** = a god e.g. Marduk, We[Comp. Hex. (2), 308 f.; Nimrod, Encycl. Brit. (9), xvii. 511], RS[Sem. i. 91 n.; 2d ed. 92]; Hom[PSBA xv (1893), 291–300] prop. *Narûdu* = **Namra-uddu*, a star-god. **2.** < name of Bab. king or prince: *Nu-marad* = 'Man of Marad' cf. Dl[Pa 220] De[Gn 10, 8 [1887]]; more plausibly = *Nazi-maraddash* (*marattash, murudas*), Hpt[Andover Rev. July, 1884, 93 f.] Dl[K (1884)] Say[Athen. Feb. 16, 1895, Acad. Mar. 2, 1895] (cf. Che[ib. Mar. 9]),—i.e. a Kashite kg., B.C. 1378, but dub., cf. Hpt[BAS i (1889), 183], Jeremias[Izdubar-Nimrod, 1891, 1 ff.]);—son of כּוּשׁ (q.v.), hero and hunter Gn 10[8.9] (J; kg. in Babylonia, builder of Nineveh, etc. v[10 f.]), נִמְרוֹד 1 Ch 1[10]; אֶרֶץ נִמְרֹד Mi 5[5] (‖ אֶרֶץ אַשּׁוּר); 𝔊 Νεβρωδ.

†נִמְשִׁי **n.pr.m.** grandfather of Jehu 2 K 9[2.14]; יֵהוּא בֶּן־נ׳ 1 K 19[16] 2 K 9[20] 2 Ch 22[7]; 𝔊 Ναμεσθει, Ναμεσ(σ)ει.

נֵס v. נסס. נְסִבָּה v. סבב.

נָסָה v. נשׂא.

†[נָסָה] **vb. Pi.** test, try (NH *id.*, Pi.; 𝔗 Pa. נַסִּי; Syr. Pa. ܢܰܣܺܝ; cf. Eth. መንሱት: *temptation*);—**Pi.** *Pf.* 3 ms. נִסָּה Dt 4[34] + 3 t.; sf. נִסָּהוּ Ex 15[25]; 3 fs. נִסְּתָה Dt 28[56]; 1 s. נִסִּיתִי Ec 7[23], + 4 t. Pf.; *Impf.* 3 ms. sf. יְנַסֵּם Dn 1[14]; 1 s. אֲנַסֶּה Ju 6[39]; sf. אֲנַסְּכָה Ec 2[2]; 3 mpl. יְנַסּוּ Nu 14[22]; 2 mpl. תְּנַסּוּן Ex 17[2], + 7 t. Impf.; *Imv.* נַס Dn 1[12]; sf. נַסֵּנִי ψ 26[2]; *Inf. cstr.* נַסּוֹת Ex 20[20], + 8 t. Inf.; *Pt.* מְנַסֶּה Dt 13[4];—**1.** *test, try* (syn. בחן), abs. 1 S 17[39] (a sword); c. בְּ Ju 7[39] Ec 2[1]; c. acc. Dn 1[12.14]; acc. + בְּ 1 K 10[1] = 2 Ch 9[1], Ec 7[23]. **2.** *attempt, assay, try* to do a thing, c. Inf. Dt 4[34] 28[56]; c. acc. Jb 4[2] (*venture* a word). **3.** *test, try, prove, tempt* [but not in modern sense of the word: v. Dr[Dt 6, 16; ψψ 453, 483]] **a.** God *tests* or *proves* Abr. Gn 22[1] (E), Isr. Ex 15[25] 20[20] (E), 16[4] (J), Dt 8[2.16] 13[4]; c. בְּ Ju 2[22] 3[1.4]; tribe of Levi Dt 33[8] (poem); Hezekiah 2 Ch 32[31]; psalmist ψ 26[2]. **b.** Isr. *tests*, or *tries* God: Ex 17[2.7] Nu 14[22] (J), Dt 6[16] ψ 78[18.41.56] 95[9] 106[14]; so Ahaz, Is 7[12].

†II. מַסָּה **n.f.** test, trial, proving;—מ׳ ψ 95[8]; cstr. מַסַּת Jb 9[23]; pl. מַסֹּת Dt 4[34] 7[19], מַסּוֹת Dt 29[2];—*testings* or *provings* of Pharaoh and Egyptians at Exodus, Dt 4[34] (v. Dr), 7[19] 29[2] (‖ אֹתֹת);—*test, trial*, of innocent person Jb 9[23] acc. to Hi al., but v. I. מַסָּה sub מסס.

†III. מַסָּה **n.pr.loc.** where Israel tried י׳ in the wilderness, Ex 17[7] (JE), Dt 6[16] 9[22] ψ 95[8] (all 𝔊 (ὁ) πειρασμός), where Levi was tested Dt 33[8] (𝔊 πείρᾳ).

†[נָסַח] **vb.** pull or tear away (NH נָסַח, 𝔗 נְסַח both *remove*; As. *nasâḫu* = BH, so OAram. נסח Cook[82] Lzb[323]; Ar. نَسَخَ *annul, supersede, change by substitution, copy*; cf. As. *nisḫu, nusḫu, extract, excerpt* Dl[HWB 472] Meissn[ZA iv (1889), 267]; NH נֻסְחָה, Nab. נסחת *id.*, also Aram. נוסחא (whence Ar. نُسْخَة) Hoffm[ZMG xxxii. 760] cf. Frä[251]; Syr. ܢܣܚ *copy*);—**Qal** *Impf.* 3 ms. בֵּית גֵּאִים יִסַּח י׳ Pr 15[25] *the house of proud men will* י׳ *tear down*; יִסָּחֲךָ מֵאֹהֶל ψ 52[7] *yea, he* [י׳] *shall tear thee away, without a tent*; 3 mpl. יִסְּחוּ מִן Pr 2[22] transgressors *shall* (men) *tear away from* the land (rd. perh. יִנָּסְחוּ *shall be torn away*; ‖ יִכָּרֵתוּ; cf. Ges[§ 144, 3 b. R] Da[Synt. § 108. b]). **Niph.** *Pf.* 2 mpl. consec. וְנִסַּחְתֶּם מֵעַל הָאֲדָמָה Dt 28[63] *and ye shall be torn away from off the land*.

מַסָּח 2 K 11[6], v. p. 587 a supr.

†I. נָסַךְ **vb.** pour out (NH *id.*, *pour, cast* (metals, Pi. *make libation*; Ph. נסך *cast* gold or iron Lzb[323 f.]; 𝔗 נְסַךְ *make libation*; Syr. ܢܣܟ *pour out*; Ar. نَسَكَ, orig. *be-pour, water* Nö[ZMG xli (1887), 719] (rare), usu. *worship* Lane[3032] (cf. RS[Sem. i. 213; 2d ed. 229]), i.e. *pour out* blood of victim, *pour out* wine We[Heid. 2, 114, 118, 142]);—**Qal** *Pf.* 3 ms. נָסַךְ Is 29[10] 40[19]; נָסָךְ 44[10]; *Impf.* 3 mpl. יִסְּכוּ Ho 9[4]; 2 ms. תִסְּכוּ Ex 30[9]; *Inf.* לִנְסֹךְ Is 30[1]; *Pt. pass.* f. נְסוּכָה 25[7];—**1.** *pour out*, c. עַל (the spirit of deep sleep) Is 29[10]. **2.** *pour out libations*, c. acc. נֶסֶךְ Ex 30[9] (P); מַסֵּכָה Is 30[1]; יַיִן Ho 9[4]. **3.** *cast metal images*, c. acc. פֶּסֶל Is 40[19] 44[10].

Piel *Impf.* יְנַסֵּךְ 1 Ch 11[18] *pour out as libation*, c. acc. מַיִם + לַיהוה (= 2 S 23[16] Hiph.).

Hiph. *Pf.* 3 mpl. הִסִּכוּ Je 32[29]; *Impf.* 3 ms. וַיַּסֵּךְ Gn 35[14] + 2 t.; 1 s. אַסִּיךְ ψ 16[4]; 3 mpl. וַיַּסִּיכוּ Ez 20[28]; *Imv.* הַסֵּךְ Nu 28[7]; *Inf. abs.* הַסֵּיךְ Je 44[17]; הַסֵּךְ Je 7[18] + 3 t.; *cstr.* לְהַסֵּךְ Je 44[19.25] (Kö[i. 309]);—*pour out libations*, c. acc. נֶסֶךְ Gn 35[14] (E), 2 K 16[13] Nu 28[7] (P), מַיִם 2 S 23[16] לַיהוה; elsewhere, נְסָכִים to other gods Je 7[18] 19[13] 32[29] 44[17.18.19.19.25] Ez 20[28] ψ 16[4].

Hoph. *Impf.* 3 ms. יֻסַּךְ *be poured out*, Ex 25[29] 37[16], of holy wine, c. בְּ of vessels.

† נֶ֫סֶךְ **n.m. drink-offering**,—abs נ׳ Gn 35^{14} + 6 t; נָ֑סֶךְ Ex 29^{40} 30^{9} Ez 45^{17}; נָ֫סֶךְ Nu 4^{7} Jo 1^{13}; cstr. נֶ֫סֶךְ Nu 28^{7}; sf נִסְכִּי Is 48^{5}, etc.; pl. נְסָכִים Je 7^{18} + 9 t.; sf נִסְכָּהּ Nu 29^{31}, נִסְכֵּיכֶם v^{39}, etc.,—**1.** *drink-offering*, c. עַל (on Jacob's מַצֵּבָה at Bethel) Gn 35^{14} (E); elsewhere in worship of י׳ only P and related doc.; once of vessels of holy table קְשׂוֹת הַנָּ֑סֶךְ Nu 4^{7}; elsewh. in classifications Lv 23^{37} Nu 29^{39}, usu offered with the עלה Ex 29^{40} Lv 23$^{13.18}$ Nu 15$^{5.7.10.24}$ 28$^{7.14.31}$ 29$^{18.21.24.27.30.33.37}$, esp. עֹלַת הַתָּמִיד 28$^{9.10.15.24}$ 29$^{6.11.16.19.22.25.28.31.34.38}$; מִנְחַת הַבֹּקֶר Ex 29^{41} Nu 28^{8}; but sts. also with זבח (שׁלמים) 6$^{15.17}$ 15$^{5.10}$; usu. + מנחה; elsewhere only 1 Ch 29^{21} 2 Ch 29^{35} Ez 45^{17}, מנחה ונ׳ Jo 1$^{9.13}$ 2^{14}. Offered to other gods 2 K 16$^{13.15}$ Is 57^{6} Je 7^{18} 19^{13} 32^{29} 44$^{17.18.19.19.25}$ Ez 20^{28} ψ 16^{4}. **2.** *molten images*, Is 41^{29} 48^{5} Je 10^{14} 51^{17}.—Combinations are: נָסַךְ נ׳, הסיך נ׳ (see vb.); שָׁפַךְ נ׳ Is 57^{6}.

† I. [נָסִיךְ] **n.m. 1. libation; 2. molten image**,—**1.** sf יֵין נְסִיכָם *wine of their drink-offering* Dt 32^{38}. **2.** *molten image*, sf. נְסִכֵיהֶם Dn 11^{8}.

† I. מַסֵּכָה **n.f. 1. molten metal, or image; 2. libation**;—מ׳ Ex 32^{4}+; cstr מַסֵּכַת Is 30^{22}; pl. מַסֵּכוֹת 1 K 14^{9}+; sf מַסֵּכֹתָם Nu 33^{52},—**1.** *libation*, with covenant sacrif in making covenant Is 30^{1} (= **1.** נֶסֶךְ, see, however, sub II. [נָסַךְ]). **2.** *molten metal, or image*: עֵגֶל מַסֵּכָה *molten calf* Ex 32$^{4.8}$ Dt 9^{16} Ne 9^{18}, cf. ψ 106^{19}; אֱלֹהֵי מַסֵּכָה *molten gods* Ex 34^{17} Lv 19^{4}; צַלְמֵי מ׳ Nu 33^{52}, פֶּסֶל וּמַסֵּכָה Dt 27^{15} Ju 17$^{3.4}$ 18^{14} Na 1^{14} 2 Ch 34$^{3.4}$, elsewh. (variously) Dt 9^{12} Ju 18$^{17.18}$ 1 K 14^{9} 2 K 17^{16} 2 Ch 28^{2} Is 30^{22} 42^{17} Ho 13^{2} Hb 2^{18}.

† II. [נָסַךְ] **vb. weave** (Ar. نَسَجَ has same meaning);—**Qal** *Pt. pass.* f נְסוּכָה Is 25^{7}; perh. also *Inf. cstr.* לִנְסֹךְ 30^{1}; on both v. foll.

† II. מַסֵּכָה **n.f. woven stuff, web, esp. as covering**,—abs. הַמּ׳ הַנְּסוּכָה עַל־ Is 25^{7} *the web that is woven over* all the nations (i.e *mourning-veil*, symb. of distress; ‖ הַלּוֹט הַלּוֹט), = *bed-covering* 28^{20} (in fig). Perhaps also לִנְסֹךְ מ׳ 30^{1} *weave a web* (‖ לַעֲשׂוֹת עֵצָה), ref. to negotiations with Egypt (so 𝔙 Aq Ew De Che Di; > 𝔊 Ges Hi Kn Brd Du *pour a libation*; מ׳ not elsewhere = נֶסֶךְ).

† [מַסֶּ֫כֶת] **n.f. web** of unfinished stuff, on loom (v. GFM$^{PAOS, Oct 1889, clxxvii}$),—only abs. מַסָּ֑כֶת Ju 16$^{13.14}$.—סכך v מְסֻכָה, מָסָךְ.

† III. [נָסַךְ] **vb. set, install** (As *nasâku*, *id*, whence *nasiku*, *prince*, Dl$^{HWB\,472}$, v. also Muss-Arnolt$^{Hbr\,vi\,89,\,B.17}$ and reff);—**Qal** *Pf* 1 s. נָסַכְתִּי מַלְכִּי עַל־צִיּוֹן ψ 2^{6} *I have installed my king upon Zion.* **Niph.** *Pf* 1 s נִסַּכְתִּי Pr 8^{23} *I was installed* (of Wisdom).

† II [נָסִיךְ] **n.m. prince**,—pl. cstr. נְסִיכֵי Jos 13^{21} Ez 32^{30} Mi 5^{4}, sf. נְסִיכֵמוֹ ψ 83^{12}.

נִסְמָן v. סמן

† I. [נָסַס] **vb. be sick** (?; cf. Syr. ܢܣ *id.*, and esp. ܢܣܝܣܐ *debilis, infirmus, aegrotans*, etc, PS^{2367}, 𝔗 נְסַס *be sad;* As *nasâsu*, *wail, lament* Dl$^{HWB\,472}$, Ar. نَسَّ is *go at a gentle pace*);—only **Qal** *Pt act.* (si vera l) כִּמְסֹס נֹסֵס Is 10^{18} like the wasting away *of a sick man* (so Thes Ew De Che Di Du)

II. נסס (√ of foll. = *be high* or *conspicuous?* **Hithpo'l.** *Inf.* לְהִתְנוֹסֵס ψ 60^{6}, acc to some denom from נֵס *that it may be displayed*, AV, cf. De; < v. נוס; *Pt* מִתְנוֹסְסוֹת Zc 9^{16} *raised? prominent?* (עַל־אַדְמָתוֹ; of precious stones, in fig.) very dub.; We Now del.; Gr מִתְנוֹצְצוֹת)

† נֵס **n. [m.] standard, ensign, signal, sign** (NH *id*, *flag*, usu *sign*, i e. *miracle;* 𝔗 נֵס, נִסָּא *sign, miracle*);—נ׳ abs Nu 21^{8}+, cstr. Is 11^{10}; sf. נִסִּי Ex 17^{15} Is 49^{22};—**1. a.** *standard*, as rallying-point, י׳ נִסִּי Ex 17^{15} (E), *י׳ my standard* (name of altar), conspicuously set on hill Is 30^{17} (sim. of solitariness; ‖ תֹּרֶן עַל־רֹאשׁ הָהָר); signal of war [v. Schumacher$^{ZPV\,ix\,232,\,Across\,the\,Jordan,\,104\,f}$] (esp. to the nations, for destruction or deliverance of Judah, Is Je), נָשָׂא נ׳ לַגּוֹיִם Is 5^{26} 11^{12} cf. 18^{3} (on mts, ‖ תְּקֹעַ שׁוֹפָר); אָרִים נ׳ 49^{22} (‖ אֶשָּׂא אֶל־גּוֹיִם יָדִי), אֶל־עַמִּים—in all these subj י׳; cf. עֹמֵד לְנֵס עַמִּים Is 10^{11} (of Mess kg.); שְׂאוּ נ׳ 13^{2} (on mt.), Je 50^{2} 51^{12} (c. אֶל־ *against*), v^{27} (‖ תִּקְעוּ שׁוֹפָר בַּגּוֹיִם), הָרִימוּ נ׳ עַל־הָעַמִּים Is 62^{10}, cf Je 4^{21} (‖ קוֹל שׁוֹפָר); נָתַתָּה ... נ׳ לְהִתְנוֹסֵס ψ 60^{6} *thou hast set a standard* (only) *for fleeing.* **b.** *signal*, שְׂאוּ נ׳ צִיּוֹנָה Je 4^{6} (i.e. to direct refugees to Zion). **2.** *standard*, as pole, supporting serpent of bronze Nu 21$^{8.9}$ (JE). **3. a.** *ensign, signal*, שֵׁשׁ ... מִמִּצְרַיִם הָיָה מִפְרָשֵׂךְ לִהְיוֹת לָךְ לְנֵס Ez 27^{7} *byssus from Egypt was thy sail, to serve*

thee for an ensign (so DaToy; on lack of pennon on ancient ships v Co; > del. Co Berthol); so **b.** (since sails were the only ensign) = *sail* Is 33^{23} (Che Di al, > *pennon* Ges Hi Ew De Du) **4.** *sign* (cf. NH) = *warning* Nu 26^{10} (P).

I **נָסַע** $_{147}$ **vb.** **pull out or up, set out, journey** (NH *id*, *move, march;* As *nisû, set out, withdraw*, etc Dl$^{HWB 470}$, No$^{ZMG xl (1886), 723}$ cp also Ar. نَزَعَ, Eth ነሰአ: [rare] *pull up, away*, so Ba$^{ES 51}$), — **Qal**$_{137}$ *Pf.* 3 ms נ׳ Gn 33^{17}+, 3 mpl. נָסְעוּ Dt 10^{6}, נָסָעוּ Nu 2^{34}+, etc.; *Impf* יִסַּע Is 33^{20}, וַיִּסַּע Gn 12^{9}+, sf וַיִּסָּעֵם Ju 16^{3}, 3 mpl יִסָּעוּ Ex 40^{36}+, יִסָּעוּ Nu 2^{9}+; 2 mpl תִּסָּעוּ Jos 3^{3}, 1 pl. נִסְעָה cohort Gn 33^{12}, וַנִּסַּע Dt 1^{19} 2^{1}, וְנִסְעָה Ezr 8^{31}, etc.; *Imv.* סְעוּ Dt 2^{24}+; *Inf abs* נָסוֹעַ Gn 12^{9}, *cstr.* נְסֹעַ Jos 3^{14}+; sf נָסְעָם Gn 11^{2} Nu 10^{34}, *Pt* נֹסֵעַ Ex 14^{10} Nu 10^{33}, pl נֹסְעִים Nu 10^{29},—**1.** *pull out* or *up*, city-gate and gate-posts Ju 16^{3}, loom v^{14} (on text cf. GFM), tent-pegs Is 33^{20} (*fig. of Jerusalem;* cf. also **Niph.**) **2.** hence (from pulling up tent-pegs), **a.** *set out* Gn 35^{5} Nu 12^{15} (both E), Je 4^{7} (‖ יָצָא מִמְּקֹמוֹ); even of lifeless things, e g. the ark, הָאָרוֹן Nu 10^{35} (JE); oft. in P: Ex 14^{15} 40^{37} Nu 1^{51} $4^{5.15}$ 9^{17} + 8 t. Nu 9, $10^{5.6.17.18.21.22.25}$, so prob also 2^{8} + 6 t Nu 2 (v. infr.; even of lifeless things, אֹהֶל מוֹעֵד 1^{51}, מִשְׁכָּן $10^{18.22}$, דֶּגֶל 2^{17}), 33^{3}, וַיִּסַּע . . . וַיָּבֹא Gn 46^{1} (E) *and* Isr. *set out, and came*, etc, Ex 16^{1} 19^{2} Nu 20^{22} Jos 9^{17} (all P), Dt 1^{7}, נִסְעָה וְנֵלְכָה 33^{12} (J); (וַיַּעֲלוּ . . .) וַיִּסְעוּ Ju 18^{11}, סְעוּ ועברו Dt 2^{24}; נ׳ oft c. מִן Gn 35^{16} (E), Nu 10^{34} (JE), נ׳ מֵאָהֳלֵיהֶם לַעֲבֹר Jos 3^{14} (JE), *set out from their tents, to cross*, etc., cf. נ׳ מִן . . . לָלֶכֶת Ezr 8^{31}; c. בוא + מִן, Jos 3^{1} (JE), Nu 33^{9} (P), + וַיֵּלֶךְ v^{3} (D), Dt 1^{19}, + וַיַּעַבְרוּ Nu 33^{8} (P); + וַיֵּשֶׁב + וַיַּחֲנוּ Nu 33^{7} (P). **b.** *depart*, c מִן Gn 37^{17} (J), 2 K 3^{27} $19^{8.36}$ = Is $37^{8.37}$; even of עַמּוּד הֶעָנָן Ex 14^{19} (J); of angel v^{19} (E; + וַיֵּלֶךְ) **3.** *journey, march* (by stages) Gn 12^{9} 35^{21} (both J), Nu $10^{13.14.28}$ (P), (poss also Nu 2^{9} etc, cf. **2** supr), + לְמַסְעֵיהֶם *acc to their stations*, i.e by stages Ex 17^{1} Nu 10^{12} (+ מִן), cf Ex 40^{36} (all P); sq ה loc Gn 12^{9} 33^{17} (both J), Dt 1^{40} 2^{1}, סְעוּ לָכֶם הַמִּדְבָּר Nu 14^{25} (JE), sq מִקֶּדֶם *eastward* (v. מִן **1.** **c**) Gn 11^{2} 13^{11} (both J), אַחֲרֵי Ex 14^{10} (J), אֶל־ Nu 10^{29}, לִפְנֵי v^{33} (of ark; all J), sq. מִן + ה loc Gn 20^{1} (E), Dt $10^{6.7}$ Ex 12^{37} (P), + acc. loc. Nu 11^{35} (JE), sq מִן + acc of distance, דֶּרֶךְ 10^{33} (JE), 21^{4} (P), esp וַיִּסְעוּ מִן . . . וַיַּחֲנוּ Nu $21^{12.13}$ (JE), Ex 13^{20} Nu 21^{11} 33^{5} + 37 t. Nu 33 (all P); of shepherds Je 31^{24} —נָסְעוּ כְּמוֹ צֹאן Zc 10^{2} is dub, We נָעוּ or יָנֻעוּ, so Now. **4.** of wind, נ׳ רוּחַ מֵאֵת י׳ Nu 11^{31} *there set forth* (sprang up) a wind from י׳.

†**Niph.** *Pf. be pulled up, removed:* 3 ms. דּוֹרִי נִסַּע וְנִגְלָה מִנִּי כְּאֹהֶל רֹעִי Is 38^{12}; of tent-peg הֲלֹא נִסַּע יִתְרָם Jb 4^{21} (reading יְתֵדָם for יִתְרָם, v. II. יֶתֶר).

†**Hiph.** *Impf* 3 ms וַיַּסַּע יַסַּע ψ 78^{26}, Ex 15^{22} + 2 t; 2 ms תַּסִּיעַ ψ 80^{9}, 3 fs. תַּסִּיעִי 2 K 4^{4}; 3 mpl וַיַּסִּעוּ 1 K 5^{31}, *Pt.* מַסִּיעַ Ec 10^{9}; — **1.** *cause to set out, lead out*, c. acc. pers. Ex 15^{22} (J; + וַיֵּצְאוּ ,מִן), ψ 78^{52} (כַּצֹּאן ‖ וַיְנַהֲגֵם), 80^{9} (מִן; fig of vine), fig. of a wind, *cause to spring up*, יַסַּע קָדִים ψ 78^{26} (‖ וַיְנַהֵג); cf **Qal 4**). **2.** *remove*, c acc rei 2 K 4^{4}; וַיַּסַּע כָּעֵץ תִּקְוָתִי Jb 19^{10}; specif, *remove* from quarry, *quarry* 1 K 5^{31} *and they quarried* great stones, cf. Ec 10^{9}.

† **מַסַּע** **n.** [**m.**] **pulling up, breaking camp, setting out, journey**;—abs. מ׳ Nu 10^{2} Dt 10^{11}; pl. cstr מַסְעֵי Nu 10^{28} 33^{1}, sf. מַסָּעָיו Gn 13^{3}, מַסְעֵיהֶם Ex 17^{1} + 6 t;—**1. a.** *pulling up, breaking* camp (c. acc. מַחֲנֶה, Ges$^{§ 45 e 115 d}$) Nu 10^{2}. **b.** *setting out* Nu 10^{6}, cf. v^{28} **2.** *station, stage, journey* (by stages), וַיֵּלֶךְ לְמ׳ Gn 13^{3} *and he went by* (acc. to) *his journeyings* (cf. הלך, p 231a supr.); לְמַסְעֵיהֶם Ex 17^{1} cf $40^{36.38}$ Nu 10^{12} (all P; all c. נָסַע), $33^{1.2}$ (‖ מוֹצָאֵיהֶם), v^{2} (‖ *id*), קוּם לֵךְ לְמַסַּע Dt 10^{11} *for journeying* (v. Dr).

†I. **מַסָּע** **n.** [**m.**] **quarry or quarrying**;—only abs. as adv. acc., אֶבֶן שְׁלֵמָה מַסָּע 1 K 6^{7} *stone perfect* (at the) *quarry* (or *at quarrying*, i e when it was quarried; cf. Benz, text dub.).

II **נסע** (√ of foll.; poss Ar. نَسَغَ *throw* (*puncture, wound*, etc), Kam Frey, so Buhl^{13})

†II **מַסָּע** **missile, dart**;—only abs. Jb 41^{18} (+ חֲנִית, שִׁרְיָה).

נסק whence אֶסַּק ψ 139^{8} acc. to Thes al; but v סלק

† **נִסְרֹךְ** **n.pr.div.** Assyr. god, worshipped by Sennach., 2 K 19^{37} = Is 37^{38}; 𝔊 Εσδραχ, A Εσθραχ, 𝔊L Ασραχ (K); 𝔊 Νασαραχ, א Ασοραχ, A Ασαραχ (Is); Jos$^{Ant. x 1 5}$ Αρασκη; no such god in cuneif. inscr; see views in Meinh$^{Jesaiaerzählungen (1898) ad loc}$; crpt form of *Nusku* (= נסוך) acc to Hal$^{JAs xiii (1879) 387 = Mél de Crit. 177}$ Muss-Arnolt$^{JBL xi 1 (1892), 86, Hbr vii 89 B 17}$, *Nusku* is a solar deity, cf. Jastr$^{Rel Bab. 220 f.}$

נעה, נָעָה v. נוע.

†נְעִיאֵל n.pr.loc. on border of Asher Jos 19^{27}; 𝔊 Ιναηλ, A Ανιηλ, 𝔊L Naειηλ.

†נָעַל vb. bar, bolt, lock (NH *id.*);—**Qal** *Pf.* 3 ms. נָעַל 2 S 13^{18}, נָעָ֑ל Ju 3^{23}; *Imv.* נְעֹל 2 S 13^{17}; *Pt. pass.* נָעוּל Ct $4^{12\,12}$; fpl נְעֻלוֹת Ju 3^{24};—*bar, bolt, lock,* usu c. acc. דֶּלֶת, דַּלְתוֹת: Ju 3^{23}, + אַחֲרֵי *after, behind,* v^{24} 2 S $13^{17\,18}$, elsewh. only גַּן נָעוּל Ct 4^{12} *a garden barred* (fig of Shulamite), so also $v^{12\,b}$ (reading גַּן for גַּל, Vrss Gr Bu).

†נַ֫עַל n.f.$^{Jos\,9.5}$ **sandal, shoe** (NH *id.*; Ar. نَعْل *id.* (also *horse-shoe*, etc.); Syr. ܢܥܠܐ appar. only *horse-shoe* (rare, also NS) PS^{2405}, cf. poss Eth. ነዐለት: (obsol.) *wife of Levirate marriage* Di^{676}),—abs. נ׳ Gn 14^{23}, נָ֑עַל Dt 25^{10}; sf. נַעֲלִי ψ 60^{10} 108^{10}, נַעַלְךָ Jos 5^{15}, etc, du. נַעֲלַיִם Am 2^{6} 8^{6}, pl. נעילם Is 11^{15} Ct 7^{2}, נְעָלוֹת Jos 9^{5}; sf. נְעָלֶיךָ Ex 3^{5} Ez 24^{17}, נְעָלָיו Is 5^{27}, נעלינו Jos 9^{13}, נַעֲלֵיכֶם Ex 12^{11} Ez 24^{23};—*sandal* Ju 9^{13}, Am 2^{6} 8^{6} (du. = pair of sandals, mentioned as of little worth), Dt 29^{4}, on (בְּ) feet Jos 9^{5} (JE), 1 K 2^{5} Ez 24^{23} Ex 12^{11} (P); cf פְּעָמַיִךְ בַּנְּעָלִים Ct 7^{2}, וְהִדְרִיךְ בַּנּ׳ Is 11^{15}; *put on sandal* is שׂים נ׳ ברגל Ez 24^{17}, *loose the sandal* is חָלַץ Is 20^{2} Dt 25^{9} cf. v^{10}, שַׁל (Imv.) Ex 3^{5} (E), Jos 5^{15} (JE); שָׁלַף Ru $4^{7\,8}$ (cf. Burton$^{Midian\,ii\,197}$), *sandal-thong* is שְׂרוֹךְ Gn 14^{23} Is 5^{27}, עַל־אֱדוֹם אַשְׁלִיךְ נַעֲלִי ψ 60^{10} *upon Edom do I cast my sandal* = 108^{10}, denotes either contempt (Hup; עַל = *unto*, fig. of slave), or taking possession of (Fl in De, Che Bae), ||מוֹאָב סִיר רַחְצִי favours former —On symbolic use of sandal v. further Goldziher$^{Abh.\,z.\,Arab.\,Philol\,i\,47\,f}$ Jacob$^{Arab\,Dicht.\,iv\,23}$.

†[נָעַל] vb.denom. furnish with sandals, shoe (𝔗 נעל (rare), *bind on sandal;* Ar. نَعَّلَ *furnish with sandals, shoe* horse or camel, Syr. ܢܥܠ *shoe* horse),—**Qal** *Impf* 1 s sf וָאֶנְעָלֵךְ תַּחַשׁ Ez 16^{10} *and I shod thee with* תחש (q v.). **Hiph.** *Impf* 3 mpl sf. וַיַּנְעִלוּם 2 Ch 28^{15} *and gave them sandals.*

†מַנְעוּל n.[m.] bolt;—abs. כַּפּוֹת הַמּ׳ Ct 5^{5} (of house-door); pl. sf מַנְעֻלָיו מַנְעוּלָיו Ne 3^{3}, $v^{6.13.14\,15}$, all of city-gates, in phr. דַּלְתֹתָיו (וּ)מַנְ׳ וּבְרִיחָיו.

†[מִנְעָל] n.m. id, only sf בַּרְזֶל וּנְחֹשֶׁת מִנְעָלֶךָ Dt 33^{25} (song)

†I. [נָעֵם] vb. be pleasant, delightful, lovely (Ph. נעם *good* Lzb^{324} (and many n pr.); Ar. نَعِمَ be *plentiful, easy, pleasant;* أَنْعَمَ على *shew gracious favour toward,* oft. in Qor; Sab נעם *be lovely, agreeable, well* Levy-Os$^{ZMG\,xix\,(1865),\,176}$ CIS$^{iv\,19,\,11}$, so Min. Hom$^{Südar\,Chrest.\,128}$, OAram. in n pr. Lzb$^{222,\,324}$ Cook^{82} (נעמתי *my darling* [or *my songs,* cf. II. נ׳]); 𝔗 נְעִים *pleasant, lovely,* נְעִימְתָא *loveliness;* Pra$^{BASi\,46\,f.}$ cp. Eth. አጤመ: *be pleasant,* = *ኣነዐመ:);—**Qal** *Pf.* 3 fs נָעֵ֫מָה Gn 49^{15} (poem in J, of land); 2 ms. (of delightful friend) נָעַמְתָּ לִּי מְאֹד 2 S 1^{26}, also (of physical beauty) מִמִּי נָעָ֑מְתָּ Ez 32^{19}; 2 fs. (*id*) מַה־נָּעַמְתְּ Ct 7^{7} *how lovely art thou!* (||מַה־יָּפִית); 3 pl, of pleasant words, נָעֵ֑מוּ ψ 141^{6}; *Impf.* 3 ms. ינעם: לֶחֶם סְתָרִים יִנְ׳ לְנַפְשְׁךָ יִנְ׳ Pr 2^{10} (of knowledge), 9^{17} (||יִמְתָּ֑קוּ), יִנְ׳ 24^{25} is impers. c. לְ, *to them ... shall be delight.*

†נֹ֫עַם n.m.$^{\psi\,90,\,17}$ **delightfulness, pleasantness** (Ecclus נועם תירוש 32^{6}),—נ׳ abs. Zc 11^{7} +4 t.; cstr ψ 27^{4} 90^{17};—**1.** *delightfulness* of י׳: contemplated in temple ψ 27^{4}, shewn in his favour, וִיהִי נֹ׳ אדני ... עָלֵינוּ 90^{17} **2.** name of one of two symbol. staves Zc $11^{7\,10}$. **3.** *pleasantness,* as defining genit.: דַּרְכֵי־נ׳ Pr 3^{17}; אִמְרֵי־נ׳ 15^{26} 16^{24}.

†נַ֫עַם n.pr.m. son of Caleb, 1 Ch 4^{15}; 𝔊 Νοομ, A Νααμ.

†I. נָעִים adj. pleasant, delightful (poet.);—abs. נ׳ Pr 22^{18}+; cstr. נעים 2 S 23^{1}; pl. נְעִמִים ψ 16^{6}, נעימים 2 S 1^{23}, נעימם Pr 23^{8}; f. נְעִמוֹת ψ 16^{11};—**1.** *delightful* הַנֶּאֱהָבִים וְהַנְּ׳ בְּחַיֵּיהֶם 2 S 1^{23} (of Saul and Jonath); of wealth, הוֹן יָקָר וְנָ׳ Pr 24^{4}, words Pr 23^{8}; of acts, etc.: מַה־טּוֹב וּמַה־נּ׳ שֶׁבֶת אַחִים גַּם־יָחַד ψ 133^{1}; singing praises to י׳, 135^{3} 147^{1}; keeping wise teachings Pr 22^{18}, as subst = *delight* יְכַלּוּ יְמֵיהֶם בַּטּוֹב וּשְׁנֵיהֶם בַּנְּעִימִים Jb 36^{11} (of earthly prosperity); of spiritual delights ψ $16^{6\,11}$. **2.** *lovely, beautiful* (physically), Ct 1^{16} (||יָפֶה) —ψ 81^{3} 2 S 23^{1} v. II. נָעִים sub II. נעם.

†I. נַעֲמָה n.pr.f. 1. sister of Tubal Cain Gn 4^{22} 𝔊 Νοεμα, 𝔊L Νοεμμα. **2.** Ammonitess, mother of Rehoboam 1 K 14^{21} 𝔊 Μααχαμ, A Νααμα, 𝔊L Naava = 2 Ch 12^{13}, 𝔊 Νοομμα, 𝔊L Νααμα; also 1 K 14^{31} but prob. gloss (om. 𝔊B, 𝔊L, etc.)

†II **נַעֲמָה n.pr loc** city assigned to Judah in Philist plain Jos 15[41], 𝔊 Νωμαν, A Νωμα, 𝔊L Νομα.

נַעֲמִי v. infr.

נָעֳמִי n pr.f. mother-in-law of Ruth, Ru 1[2.3.8] + 18 t. Ru; 𝔊B Νωεμειν; A Νωεμμειν 1[2], Νοεμμειν v[3], usu. Νοομει(ν); 𝔊L Νοομι.

†I. **[נַעֲמָן] n.[m.]** usu. **pleasantness** (so Thes *amoenitas*), but perh epithet of **Adonis** (so Mo[Phoen. i. 227] Lag[Symm i 468, Semit i. 32] who cp red flower called شقايق النعمان [v. Lane[1578]], i e *wound of Adonis*, whence ἀνεμώνη, cf Ew[Proph i 364] RS[Proph vi n 10] and v. Lewy[Fremdwörter, 49]);—only pl נִטְעֵי נַעֲמָנִים Is 17[10] (𝔊 φύτευμα ἄπιστον) perh = *Adonis-plantations*, or gardens (on double pl v. Ges[§124 q]; and on Ἀδώνιδος κῆποι v. Rochette[Rev Archéol viii. 1851, 105-123] Daremberg et Saglio[Dict des Antiquités (1877) i 73, and reff] WSmith[Dict Antiq (3) i. 25] Fl in Levy[NHWB iv 229])

II **נַעֲמָן** 16 **n pr.m. 1.** son of Benj Gn 46[21], 𝔊 Νοεμ(μ)αν; = grandson of Benj Nu 26[40.40], 𝔊 Νοεμα(νει), 1 Ch 8[4.7] (so 𝔊 Gn 46[21]), 𝔊 in Ch Νοομα, 𝔊L Ναμει, Νααμαν **2.** Aramaean general 2 K 5[1.2.6] + 8 t 2 K 5, 𝔊 Ναιμαν, 𝔊L Νεεμαν

†**נַעֲמִי adj gent.** from n. נַעֲמָן **1,** Nu 26[40], rd doubtless נעמני (so Sam)

†**נַעֲמָתִי adj. gent.** (from unused n pr),—צוֹפַר הַנּ׳ Jb 2[11] (𝔊 ὁ Μειναίων βασιλεύς), 11[1] 20[1] 42[9] (all 𝔊 ὁ Μειναῖος), Hom[Aufsätze 48] prop. מְעוֹנִי

†**[מַנְעַמִּים] n [m.] pl. delicacies, dainties,**—only sf וּבַל־אֶלְחַם בְּמַנְעַמֵּיהֶם ψ 141[4].

II **נעם** (perh. to be assumed as √ of foll, Ne[Marg 10], Ar. نَغَمَ *speak in a low, gentle voice,* نَغْمَة *note, melody;* Syr. ܢܓܡ *rugivit,* ܢܓܡܬܐ *gentle sound, note,* NH נְעִימָה *melody;* Ecclus 45[9] לתת נעימה *to make music,* cf Hiph. 47[9 b marg])

†II **נָעִים adj.** perh **singing, sweetly sounding, musical,**—abs כִּנּוֹר נ׳ ψ 81[3] *sweetly-sounding lyre;* cstr., as subst, נְעִים זְמִרוֹת יִשׂ׳ 2 S 23[1] *Israel's sweet singer of songs* (cf Dr[288, 10] Lohr; 𝔙 *egregius psaltes Israel,* and so Ges Ew al., from I. נעם, *joy of the songs of Isr.* HPS, cf. Klo Kit).

נעץ (√ of foll, NH נָעַץ *prick, stick or thrust in, wedge in,* 𝔗 נְעַץ *id,* NH נַעֲצוּץ fig of *wicked person,* 𝔗 נַעֲצוּצָא = BH)

†**נַעֲצוּץ n.[m.] thorn-bush** (on form cf. Ba[NB 213]),—abs. נ׳ Is 55[13]; pl. נַעֲצוּצִים 7[19].

†I. **[נָעַר] vb. growl** (NH *id cry, bray;* cf. Syr ܢܥܰܪ, Ar. نَعَرَ *make a noise* Lane[2815]; poss As *na'ru, cry, roar* (?) Dl[HWB 439]),—only **Qal** *Pf* 3 pl. נָעֲרוּ כְּגוֹרֵי אֲרָיוֹת Je 51[38] (|| כַּכְּפִרִים יִשְׁאָגוּ)

†II **[נָעַר] vb. shake, shake out or off** (NH נָעַר *shake, stir up,* esp. Pi Niph; 𝔗 נְעֹרֶת *tow* (v. infr), Ar. نَعَرَ, نَغَرَ *boil, be in violent commotion, be very angry*);—**Qal** *Pf.* 1 s נָעַרְתִּי Ne 5[13]; *Pt act.* נֹעֵר Is 33[9.15]; *pass.* Ne 5[13],—*shake out,* to shew emptiness, חָצְנִי נ׳ Ne 5[13] (symbol), נ׳ כַּפָּיו מִתְּמֹךְ בַּשֹּׁחַד Is 33[15]; pt. *shaken out, emptied* נ׳ וָרֵק Ne 5[13] (i e. stripped of possessions), *shake off* (leaves) Is 33[9] (cf. || cl). **Niph.** *Pf* 1 s. נִנְעַרְתִּי כָּאַרְבֶּה ψ 109[23] *I am shaken out like a locust* (fr. fold of a garment; sim. of perishing helplessly); cf. *Impf* 3 mpl. וְיִנָּעֲרוּ רְשָׁעִים מִמֶּנָּה Jb 38[13] to seize the corners of the earth *that wicked men may be shaken out of it;* 1 s אִנָּעֵר Ju 16[20] *I will shake myself* (free? cf. Hithp and GFM). **Pi.** *Impf* 3 ms juss. יְנַעֵר Ne 5[13] *so may* God *shake utterly out* every man from (מִן) his house, etc; וַיְנַעֵר Ex 14[27] *and* י׳ *shook off* the Egypt into (ב) the sea, = *Pf.* נִעֵר ψ 136[15] (also c acc. + ב) **Hithp.** *Imv* fs. הִתְנַעֲרִי מֵעָפָר Is 52[2] *shake thyself* (*free*), etc. (of personif. Zion).

†I. **נֹעַר n.[m.]** usu interpr. as **a shaking, scattering,** abst. for concr. = *scattered ones,* only Zc 11[16], but text corrupt, v. We Now.

†**נְעֹרֶת n.f. tow** (as *shaken off* from the flax when beaten, on form cf. Ba[NB 64]);—in sim פְּתִיל־הַנּ׳ Ju 16[9] *a thread of tow* (snapping from heat), נ׳ Is 1[31] (fig.; as inflammable).

III. **נער** (√ of foll.; meaning unknown)

II. **נַעַר** 239 **n.m. 1. boy, lad, youth 2. retainer** (not in P) (NH as BH; Ph נער Lzb[324]);—נ׳ abs. Gn 37[2]+; cstr. 1 S 2[13]+; sf נַעֲרוֹ Ju 19[3]+, נַעֲרָהּ 2 K 4[24], pl. נְעָרִים 1 S 25[5]+, cstr. נַעֲרֵי Ex 24[5]+, sf נְעָרַי Ne 4[10] 5[10], etc.,—**1.** *boy, lad, youth* (c. 133 t.) **a.** of infant Ex 2[6] (E, 3 months old), to be born Ju 13[5.7.8.12], just born 1 S 4[21], not weaned 1 S 1[22], also Is 8[4], cf 7[16]+. **b.** of lad just weaned 1 S 1[24] (del. 2nd נער, cf further Dr Bu HPS), v[25 27], etc. **c.** =

youth: of young Ishmael Gn 21$^{12f.}$ (E), Isaac 22$^{5.12}$ (E), Joseph Gn 37^{2} (E; 17 years old), Benj. 43^{8} 44$^{22f.}$ (J), sons of Samuel 1 S 2^{17}, of Jesse 1 S 16^{11}; נ׳ קָטֹן *little lad* 1 S 20^{35} 1 K 3^{7} 2 K 5^{14} Is 11^{6}, נ׳ קָטָן 1 K 11^{17}, pl. 2 K 2^{23}. **d.** נ׳ with special stress on youthfulness Ju 8^{20} 1 S 17$^{33.42}$ Ho 11^{1} Is 3^{4} cf. Ec 10^{16} Is 3^{5} 10^{19} Je 1$^{6.7}$ 1 Ch 22^{5} 29^{1} 2 Ch 13^{7} 34^{3}; so in phr. מִנַּ׳ וְעַד זָקֵן Gn 19^{4} (J), Jos 6^{21} (J), Est 3^{13} cf. Ex 10^{9} (E), Dt 28^{50} Is 20^{4} 65^{20} Je 51^{22} La 2^{21} ψ 37^{25} 148^{12} Pr 22^{6}. **e.** of marriageable age Gn 34^{19} (J), warrior Absalom 2 S 18$^{5.12}$+, Zadok 1 Ch 12^{29}, etc. **2.** *servant, retainer* (c. 105 t.): **a.** = personal attendant, household servant, Nu 22^{22} (J), Ju 7$^{10.11}$ 19^{3} 1 S 9$^{3f.}$ 2 K 4$^{12.25}$+oft. **b.** = retainer, follower Gn 14^{24} 1 S 25$^{5f.}$ 2 S 2$^{14f.}$ 1 K 20$^{14f.}$ 2 K 19^{6} = Is 37^{6}, Jb 1$^{15.16.17}$ Ne 4$^{10.17}$+oft.—Zc 11^{16} is corrupt, cf. We Now.—*Note.* נער occurs in Pent. as Kt with Qr perpet. נַעֲרָה q.v.

†נֹעַר **n.m.** youth, early life (rare poet. synon. for נְעוּרִים);—abs. נ׳ Jb 33^{25} (=youthful vigour), 36^{14}, מִנֹּ׳ Pr 29^{21} ψ 88^{16} *from youth up.*

†II. נַעֲרָה **n.f.** girl, damsel;—abs. נ׳ Ju 19^{3} + 22 t., also Qr Gn 24^{14} + 20 t. Gn Dt (נַעֲרָ Kt in Pent. only Dt 22^{19}, v. infr.); pl. abs. נְעָרוֹת 1 S 9^{11}+, cstr. נַעֲרוֹת Est 4^{4}; sf. נַעֲרוֹתָיו Ru 2^{22} 3^{2}, נַעֲרֹתֶיהָ Gn 24^{61} Ex 2^{5}, etc.;—**1.** *girl, damsel;* נ׳ קְטַנָּה *little girl* only 2 K 5^{2}, cf. v^{4}, perh. = young daughters Jb 40^{29}; elsewh. = young woman 1 S 9^{11}; esp. as marriageable, Gn 24$^{14.16.28.55.57}$ 34$^{3.12}$ (all J), Dt 22$^{15.15.16.19.20.21.24.25.26.29}$ 1 K 1$^{3.4}$ Est 2$^{4.7.8.9.12.12.13}$; specif. virgin נ׳ בְּתוּלָה Ju 21^{12} Dt 22$^{23.28}$ 1 K 1^{2} Est 2$^{2.3}$ (cf. Dt 22$^{15b.20}$); נ׳ מְאֹרָשָׂה *betrothed girl* Dt 22$^{25.27}$; young widow Ru 2^{6} 4^{12}; of a concubine Ju 19$^{3.4.5.6.8.9}$, a prostitute Am 2^{7}. **2.** of female attendants, *maids* (alw. pl.), Gn 24^{61} (J), Ex 2^{5} (E), 1 S 25^{42} Pr 9^{3} 27^{27} 31^{15} Est 2$^{9.9}$ 4$^{4.16}$; gleaners Ru 2$^{8.22.23}$ 3^{2}.—*Note.* נער Kt in Pent. as fem. (Qr נַעֲרָ) is prob. not original; it is not found in Sam. Pent., and fpl. נַעֲרֹתֶיהָ occurs Gn Ex; cf. Ges §§ 2 n, 17 c.

†נְעוּרִים **n.[m.] pl.** youth, early life;—abs. נ׳ Is 54^{6} ψ 127^{4}; elsewhere sf. נְעֻרַי 1 S 12^{2}, נְעוּרַי Jb 31^{18}+, נְעֻרֶיךָ 2 S 19^{8}, נְעוּרֶיךָ Pr 5^{18}+, נְעוּרַיִךְ Je 2^{2}+, נְעוּרָיְכִי ψ 103^{5}, נְעוּרֵיהֶן Ez 23^{3}, etc.;—*youth, early life,* esp. in phr. מִנְּ׳ *from one's youth up* Gn 8^{21} (J), 1 S 17^{33} 1 K 18^{12} Je 3^{24} Zc 13^{5} Jb 31^{18} (extreme youth; ‖ מִבֶּטֶן אִמִּי); fig. of Babylon Is 47$^{12.15}$, Moab Je 48^{11}, Judah 22^{21}, cf. ψ 71$^{5.17}$ 129$^{1.2}$; מִנְּ׳ וְעַד־עַתָּה Gn 46^{34} (J), 2 S 19^{8} Ez 4^{14}; מִנְּ׳ וְעַד־הַיּוֹם הַזֶּה 1 S 12^{2} Je 3^{25}; as time in or during which Lv 22^{13} (H), Nu 30$^{4.17}$ (P), La 3^{27} ψ 144^{12}, fig. of Judah and Sam., personif., Ez 23$^{3.8}$; cf. יְמֵי נ׳ (in fig. of Isr.) Ho 2^{17} (‖ יוֹם עֲלוֹתָהּ מֵאֶרֶץ מִצְרָיִם), Ez 16$^{22.43.60}$ 23^{19}; other phr. are: אַלּוּף נ׳ Je 3^{4} *friend of my youth,* cf. Pr 2^{17}, עֲוֺנוֹת נ׳ Jb 13^{26}, חַטֹּאות נ׳ ψ 25^{7}, חֶסֶד נ׳ Je 2^{2}, חֶרְפַּת נ׳ 31^{19}, זִמַּת נ׳ Ez 23^{21}, שְׁדֵי נ׳ v^{21}, בַּעַל נ׳ Jo 1^{8}, and esp. אֵשֶׁת נ׳ Pr 5^{18} Mal 2$^{14.15}$ Is 54^{6} (fig.); בְּנֵי נ׳ ψ 127^{4} sons of (a man's) *youth;* = *youthful vigour* ψ 103^{5}.

†[נְעוּרוֹת] **n.[f.] pl.** id.;—only מִנְּעֻרֹתֵיהֶם Je 32^{30} (fig. of nation).

†II. [נַעֲרָה] **n.pr.loc.** on border of Ephr.:—only c. ה loc., נַעֲרָתָה Jos 16^{7} (𝔊 αἱ κῶμαι αὐτῶν; 𝔊L *id.* + Αναραθα); appar. = נַעֲרָן, q.v. infr.; Νοοραθ lay 5 Rom. miles fr. Jericho Lag Onom. 283, 11 cf. Buhl Geogr. 181.

†III. נַעֲרָה **n.pr.f.** in Judah 1 Ch 4$^{5.6.6}$; 𝔊 Θοαδα, A Νοορα, 𝔊L Νοερα.

†נַעֲרַי **n.pr.m.** one of David's heroes, נ׳ בֶּן־אֶזְבָּי 1 Ch 11^{37}; 𝔊 Νααραι, A Νοορα, 𝔊L Ναραι (= פַּעֲרַי הָאַרְבִּי 2 S 23^{35}).

†נְעַרְיָה **n.pr.m.** **1.** a descendant of David 1 Ch 3$^{22.23}$, 𝔊 Νωαδεια, 𝔊L Νεαριου. **2.** a Simeonite 1 Ch 4^{42}; 𝔊 *id.*, 𝔊L Νααριας (cf. Sinait. n.pr. נערת Cook^{82}).

†נַעֲרָן **n.pr.loc.** in E of Ephr., 1 Ch 7^{28} (𝔊 Νααρναν, A Νααραν, 𝔊L Νοαραν), appar. = [נַעֲרָה] q.v.

נֹף v. מֹף.

†נֶפֶג **n.pr.m.** **1.** a Levite Ex 6^{21} (P), 𝔊 Ναφεκ, F Ναφεγ. **2.** a son of David 2 S 5^{15} (𝔊 *id.*, 𝔊L Ναφεθ), 1 Ch 3^{7} (𝔊 Ναφαθ, A Ναφεγ, 𝔊L Νεεγ), 14^{6} (𝔊 *id.*, א Ναφατ, A Ναφαγ, 𝔊L Ναφεκ).

I, II. נָפָה v. I, II. נוף.

נְפוּסִים, נְפוּשְׁסִים v. נפיסים infr.

†[נָפַח] **vb.** breathe, blow (כור נפוח Ecclus 43^{4} *a furnace blown upon* (heated hot); NH נָפַח, *id.*, 𝔗 נְפַח, Syr. ܢܦܚ; As. *napâḫu, inflame, nappaḫu, smith* Dl HWB 474; Ar. (نَفَحَ and) نَفَخَ *blow;* Eth. ነፍኀ: or ነፍሐ: Di^{712});—**Qal** *Pf.* 3 fs. נָפְחָה Je 15^{9}; וְנָפַחְתִּי Hg 1^{9}; וְנָפַחְתִּי Ez 22^{21};

Impf וַיִּפַּח Gn 2^{7}, *Imv.* fs פְּחִי Ez 37^{9}, *Inf.* (לָ)פַּחַת Ez 22^{20}, *Pt act* נֹפֵחַ Is 54^{16}; *pass* נָפוּחַ Je 1^{13} Jb 41^{12},—*breathe, blow,* וַיִּפַּח בְּאַפָּיו נִשְׁמַת חַיִּים Gn 2^{7} (J); sq בּ also Ez 37^{9} Is 54^{16} and Hg 1^{9} *blow* into it (to scatter it); sq עַל־ לָפַּחַת עָלָיו אֵשׁ Ez 22^{20} *to blow fire upon it* (ore, for melting), so fig Ez 22^{21} *and I will blow upon you with* (בּ) *the fire of my wrath;* נ׳ נַפְשָׁהּ Je 15^{9} *she hath breathed out her life* (of a mother, cf **Hiph.**), abs סִיר נָפוּחַ Je 1^{13} *a blown* (i e well-heated, boiling) *pot,* cf דּוּד נ׳ Jb 41^{12} (sim). **Pu.** *Pf.* אֵשׁ לֹא נֻפָּח Jb 20^{26} *a fire not blown* (by any human breath) So perh. also Nu 21^{30} (reading עַד־נֻפַּח אֵשׁ וגו׳ *until fire was blown* [hot] as far as Medeba), cf. Di. **Hiph.** *Pf* 1 s. נֶפֶשׁ בְּעָלֶיהָ הִפָּחְתִּי Jb 31^{39} (or if) *the life of its* (the land's) *owners I have caused them to breathe out;* והִפַּחְתֶּם אוֹתוֹ Mal 1^{13} *and ye have sniffed at it* (in contempt).

נֹפַח appar **n.pr.loc.** Nu 21^{30} (= נֹבַח?) perhaps נפח (𝔊 προσεξέκαυσαν), v נפח **Pu.**

†[מַפָּח] **n.[m.] breathing out**;—only cstr. מַפַּח נֶפֶשׁ Jb 11^{20} *a breathing out of life* = expiring (cf נפח Jb 31^{39} Je 15^{9})

†מַפֻּחַ **n.m. bellows,**—נָחַר מ׳ Je 6^{29} (fig of vain prophetic labour).

†I תַּפּוּחַ **n.[m.] apple-tree, apple** (from aromatic *scent* (breath), Thes Lag[BN 111, 129] Post (v infr), Ar تُفَّاحٌ is loan-wd Frä[140], on meaning *apple* v Löw[No 109] RS[JPh xiii 65 f] Post[Hast Dict Bib 'Apple'])—**1.** sg תַּפּוּחַ *apple-tree* Jo 1^{12} Ct 2^{3} 8^{5}. **2.** pl תַּפּוּחִים *apples* Ct 2^{5}, רֵיחַ אַפֵּךְ כַּתּ׳ 7^{9}, תַּפּוּחֵי זָהָב Pr 25^{11} (in sim.)

†II תַּפּוּחַ **n.pr.m.** son of Hebron, acc. to 1 Ch 2^{43}, 𝔊 Θαπους, A Θαφφου, 𝔊L Φεθρουθ.

†III. תַּפּוּחַ **n pr.loc. 1.** in lowland of Judah Jos 12^{17} (𝔊 Ταφουτ, A Θαφφου, 𝔊L Θαπφου), 15^{34} (𝔊 Ιλουλωθ, 𝔊L Θαφφουα) **2.** on border between Ephraim and Manasseh Jos 16^{8} (𝔊 Ταφου, 𝔊L Θαπφουε), $17^{8.8}$ (𝔊 Θαφεθ, A Θαφθωθ, 𝔊L Θαφωθ), = עֵין ת׳ v[7] (𝔊 Θαφθωθ, 𝔊L Ναφθωθ), so read also perh 2 K 15^{16} (for MT תִּפְסַח, 𝔊L Th Kmp[Kau] Benz; 𝔊 Θερσα, A Θαιρα, but 𝔊L τὴν Ταφωε). On locality v Buhl[Geogr 174].—Vid also בֵּית תַּפּוּחַ

†נְפִיסִים **n.pr.** Kt, in phr בְּנֵי נ׳ Ezr 2^{50}, Qr נְפוּסִים, of family of returned exiles, 𝔊 Ναφεισων, A Νεφουσειμ, 𝔊L Νεφωσειμ; = נפושסים Ne 7^{52} Kt, Qr נְפִישְׁסִים, 𝔊 Νεφωσασει, etc., 𝔊L Νεφουσειμ;—Kt Ezr and Qr Ne, respectively, are prob to be preferred (cf נָפִישׁ sub נפש), but Ne has mixture of two variants, נפישים, נפיסים.

נְפִישְׁסִים v. foregoing

†נֹפֶךְ **n.[m.]** a precious stone which Tyre gained by trade Ez 27^{16} (where נ׳ doubted by Berthol, queried by Toy[Hpt]), cf 28^{13} (symbol of wealth and honour of king of Tyre); in high priest's breastplate Ex 28^{18} 39^{11}. Perh. = *ruby* or *carbuncle* 𝔊 Joseph. ἄνθραξ, 𝔙 *carbunculus,* cf. Di[Ex] Kau[Ez] Sgfr[Ezek] Co Berthol; 𝔗 AV *emerald.*

נָפַל [433] **vb. fall, lie** (NH = BH, 𝔗 נְפַל, Syr. ܢܦܠ, cf also Ar. نَفَلَ *dedit praedam* (No[ZMG xl (1886). 725] Frä[153 f]), Min נפל *remove* Hom[Sudar Chrest 128]),—**Qal** [366] *Pf.* נ׳ Ju 5^{27}+, 3 fs. נָפְלָה Gn 15^{12}+, etc; *Impf.* יִפֹּל 1 S 14^{45}+, וַיִּפֹּל Ju 4^{16}+; 1 s אֶפֹּל 1 Ch 21^{13} (needless change fr 1 pl נפלה ‖ 2 S 24^{14} We Dr); 3 mpl. יִפְּלוּ Ho 7^{16}+, יִפֹּלוּ Is 3^{25}+, 3 fpl תִּפֹּלְנָה Ez 13^{11} 30^{25}, etc, *Imv.* mpl. נִפְלוּ Ho 10^{8} Je 25^{27}; *Inf abs.* נָפוֹל Est 6^{13}; *cstr* נְפֹל Is 30^{25}+, לִנְפֹּל, Je 51^{49}+; sf נָפְלוֹ 1 S 29^{3}, נָפְלוֹ 2 S 1^{10}, נִפְלָם Je 49^{21} (on these forms cf Ba[NB 104]); *Pt* נֹפֵל Ju 4^{22}+, f נֹפֶלֶת Gn 15^{12}+; pl נֹפְלִים Jos 8^{25}+ (ins. also 1 S 28^{19b} 𝔊 Th We Dr Kit Bu HPS; Klo כרעים), etc;—**1.** *fall*, by accident, וְנָ׳ שָׁמָּה Ex 21^{33} (E) *and there fall into it* (a pit) an ox or an ass, cf. Dt 22^{4} (בַּדֶּרֶךְ, *on the way*), bird עַל־פַּח Am 3^{5}; subj pers, 1 S 4^{18} (fr. seat, מֵעַל), Dt $22^{8.8}$ (fr roof, מִן); oft into (בּ) pit (usu. fig) Pr 26^{27} 28^{10}, also (abs), 22^{14}, Ec 10^{8} ψ 7^{16} 57^{7} (בתוך), cf. 35^{8} 141^{10} (net), also, c. אֶל, Is 24^{18} = Je 48^{44}, fall בְּלֵב יַמִּים Ez 27^{27} (of Tyrian people); abs. 2 S 4^{4} Gn 14^{10} Je 25^{27}; opp קוּם Je 8^{4} cf Ec $4^{10.10}$, c אָחוֹר *fall backward* Gn 49^{17} (poem), c בְּעַד *through* 2 K 1^{2} cf. (of locusts) Jo 2^{8}; +נ׳ עַל־חֶרֶב causing death 1 S $31^{4.5}$ = 1 Ch $10^{4.5}$, +נ׳ עַל־פָּנָיו אַרְצָה 1 S 17^{49} (Goliath); subj rei, 2 K $2^{13.14}$ (מֵעַל), 6^{5} (אֶל־ *into* water), v[6] (abs); c עַל Lv $11^{32.35.37.38}$, אֶל־ v[33]; abs of tent Ju 7^{13} + v[13] (gloss, GFM, Bu); of wall Jos 6^{5} (JE), Je 51^{44}, fig Ez 13^{11} (del. 𝔊 𝔖 Sm Co Berthol), v[12.14], לָאָרֶץ Ez 38^{20}, +תַּחְתֶּיהָ i e. *flat* Jos 6^{20}, נ׳ of bricks Is 9^{9} (in fig), פֶּרֶץ 30^{13}, towers v[25], foundations Je 50^{15}, *wall fell upon*

(עַל) 1 K 20^{30}, so of house Ju 16^{30} Jb 1^{19}, mts. Ho 10^{8}; mt. also abs. Jb 14^{18} (cf. נָבֵל), height Ez 38^{20}; tree Ec 11$^{3.3}$ (ב loc.), cf. Is 10^{34} (בְּ instr., in fig.), Zc 11^{2} (abs.); branches Ez 31^{12} (fig.); a grain Am 9^{9} (אָרֶץ = *to earth*); of dew 2 S 17^{12} (c. עַל), hailstones Ez 13^{11}; blood (אַ֫רְצָה) 1 S 26^{20}; †hair of head (ארצה) 1 S 14^{45} 2 S 14^{11} 1 K 1^{52}; horns of altar Am 3^{14} (לָאָרֶץ); peg Is 22^{25}; fruit עַל־פֶּה Na 3^{12}; crown La 5^{16}; arm from (מִן) shoulder Jb 31^{22}; of sword (appar.) 2 S 20^{8} (but on text v. Comm.); †fire from heaven, abs. 1 K 18^{38} c. מִן Jb 1^{16}†; †hand of י׳ Ez 8^{1} (c. עַל־; but rd. וַתְּהִי 𝔊 Co Berthol); spirit of י׳ Ez 11^{5} (עַל־); of lot (גּוֹרָל) Ez 24^{6} Jon 1^{7} (both c. עַל), 1 Ch 26^{14} (c. לְ; ∥ יָצָא), + Est 3^{7} 𝔊 Ry Wild (עַל); cf. **Hiph. 3**; hence (of share, inheritance) *fall*, be allotted, to (לְ) Ju 18^{1} (ב = *as*: בְּ **I 7 c**; so Nu 34^{2} Ez 47^{14}), ψ 16^{6}, abs. Jos 17^{5}.—On Ez 47$^{22\,b}$ v. **Hiph. 3.**

2. a. Esp. of violent death (c. 96 t.), Ju 5$^{27.27.27}$ (+ שָׁדוּד), 1 S 4^{10} 14^{13} 2 S 11^{17} 21^{9}, 1 K 22^{20} = 2 Ch 18^{9}, etc.; + וַיָּמֹת, etc., 2 S 1^{4} 2$^{23.23}$; נ׳ חָלָל *fall pierced* (fatally) Ju 9^{40} 1 S 17^{52} 31^{1} = 1 Ch 10^{1} +; חַלְלֵי חֶרֶב Ez 35^{8}; cf. בְּתוֹךְ חֲלָלִים 32^{20}; נ׳ תַּחַת הֲרוּגִים Is 10^{4}; נ׳ פְּגָרִים *corpses fall* Je 9^{21} Nu 14^{29} (P), v^{32} (JE); by the sword, בַּחֶרֶב Am 7^{17} Ho 7^{16} 14^{1} Is 3^{25} 2 S 1^{12} Ez 5^{12} 6^{11} Nu 14$^{3.43}$ (JE), (+ בַּדֶּבֶר, בָּרָעָב), etc.; נ׳ לְפִי חָרֶב †Jos 8^{24} (JE), Ju 4^{16}†; בְּיַד *by the hand of* †2 S 21^{22} 24$^{14.14}$ = 1 Ch 21$^{13.13}$, 1 Ch 5^{10} 20^{8}†; נ׳ תַּחַת רגלי *fall under my feet* 2 S 22^{39} = ψ 18^{39}. **b.** fig. = go to ruin, perish, etc. (c. 30 t.); Am 5^{2} 8^{14} +; oft. ∥ כָּשַׁל Is 3^{8} 8^{15} (+ other words), 31^{3} Je 8^{12} 46^{12} 50^{32} ψ 27^{2} Pr 24^{17}; ∥ כָּרַע ψ 20^{9}; fig. of earth Is 24^{20} (opp. קוּם); Haman *falls* before (לִפְנֵי) Mordecai Est 6$^{13.13}$; cf. Is 14^{12} (abs.); peculiar to Pr are נ׳ בְּרִשְׁעָה Pr 11^{5}, בְּרָע 13^{17}, בְּרָעָה 17^{20} 28^{14}. **c.** fig. = experience calamity Mi 7^{8} (opp. קוּם), ψ 37^{24} 145^{14} Pr 24^{16}. **d.** *fall*, of a city Je 51^{8} (∥ וַתִּשָּׁבֵר).

3. a. *Fall prostrate*, Ju 19$^{26.27}$, + אַ֫רְצָה Jb 1^{20}; *fall at full length* (in a faint) וַיִּפֹּל מְלֹא־קוֹמָתוֹ 1 S 28^{20}; *sink down* Nu 24$^{4.16}$ (JE; supernat. influence); of arms of Pharaoh Ez 30^{25} (opp. חָזַק). **b.** *fall = prostrate oneself before* (לִפְנֵי) man Gn 50^{18} (E), 2 S 19^{19} Gn 44^{14} (J; + אַ֫רְצָה); before י׳ 2 Ch 20^{18}; נ׳ אֶל־פָּנָיו אַ֫רְצָה before י׳ or his representative Jos 5^{14} 7^{6} (both JE); also (ארצה om.) Ez 43^{3} 44^{4}; before man 2 S 14^{22}; more oft. נ׳ עַל־פָּנָיו, before man 2 S 9^{6} 1 K 18$^{7.39}$ Ru 2^{10}, before י׳ Gn 17$^{3.17}$ + 6 t. P, Ez 3^{23} 9^{8} 11^{13} 1 Ch 21^{16} Dn 8^{17}; + אַ֫רְצָה, before man 2 S 14^{4}, before י׳ Ju 13^{20}; לְאַפָּיו אַ֫רְצָה 1 S 20^{41}, לְאַפֵּי דָוִד עַל־פָּנֶיהָ 1 S 25^{23}, נ׳ ארצה 2 S 1^{2} (all before man); נ׳ עַל־רַגְלָיו *fall at* one's *feet* 1 S 25^{24} 2 K 4^{37}, לִפְנֵי ר׳ Est 8^{3}. Vid. syn. sub קדד. **c.** *fall upon* (עַל) one's neck, in embrace Gn 33^{4} 46^{29} (both J), 45^{14} (E), עַל־פְּנֵי אָבִיו 50^{1} (J).

4. a. *Fall upon* (עַל) = attack Je 48^{32} (fig.), cf. Is 16^{9}; c. בְּ Jos 11^{7} (D), abs. Jb 1^{15}; נ׳ אִישׁ אֶל־רֵעֵהוּ Je 46^{16}. **b.** †*desert* or *fall away to, go over to*, c. עַל־ 2 K 25$^{11.11}$ = Je 52$^{15.15}$, Je 21^{9} 37^{14} 39^{9} 1 Ch 12$^{20.21.21}$ (van d. H. v$^{19.20.20}$), 2 Ch 15^{9}, c. אֶל־ 2 K 7^{4} Je 37^{13} 38^{19}, abs. 1 S 29^{3} Je 39^{9}. **c.** נ׳ בְּיַד *fall into the hand* (power) *of* Ju 15^{18} La 1^{7}:—cf. also **2. a.** supr.

5. †Fig., of deep sleep, c. עַל Gn 15^{12} (J), 1 S 26^{12} Jb 4^{13} 33^{15}; face, countenance (in displeasure) Gn 4$^{5.6}$ (J); נ׳ לֵב אָדָם עָלָיו 1 S 17^{32} (of *sinking* heart); וַיִּפְּלוּ בְעֵינֵיהֶם Ne 6^{16} *and they were cast down in their* (*own*) *eyes* (cf. Be-Ry, Ryle); †of calamity sq. עַל־ Is 47^{11} Ec 9^{12}; terror, etc., sq. עַל־ Gn 15^{12} (J), Jos 2^{9} (JE), Ex 15^{16} (song), 1 S 11^{7} Jb 13^{11} ψ 55^{5} 105^{38} Est 8^{17} 9$^{2.3}$ Dn 10^{7}; reproach, sq. עַל־ ψ 69^{10}; † = *fail* to be accomplished Jos 21^{43} 23$^{14.14}$ (all D), 1 K 8^{56} 2 K 10^{10} (+ אַ֫רְצָה); = not to be reckoned Nu 6^{12} (P); †of word (דָּבָר) *falling* into (ב) Isr. Is 9^{7}; † = *fall out, turn out, result* Ru 3^{18} (subj. דָּבָר).

6. Other idiomatic uses are: נ׳ לְמִשְׁכָּב *take to one's bed* Ex 21^{18} (E); *settle* Gn 25^{18} (J); = *alight quickly*, מֵעַל הַגָּמָל Gn 24^{64} (J), מֵעַל הַמֶּרְכָּבָה 2 K 5^{21}; *waste away* Nu 5$^{21.22.27}$; = *be born* Is 26^{18} (cf. **Hiph.** v^{19}); = *be offered*, of supplication (לִפְנֵי י׳) Je 36^{7} 37^{20} 42^{2} (cf. **Hiph. 6**); c. מִן = *be inferior to* Jb 12^{3} 13^{2}.

†**7.** = *lie*, of Midianites, etc. (like locusts; ב loc.) Ju 9^{12}; = *lie prostrate*, 1 S 19^{24}; usu. pt. Jos 7^{10} (JE; עַל־פָּנֶיךָ), 1 S 5$^{3.4}$ (לְפָנָיו), Am 9^{11}, עַל־הַמִּטָּה Est 7^{8}; of the dead 1 S 31^{8} = 1 Ch 10^{8} Dt 21^{1} Ez 32^{27} (Co conj. נְפִילִים [cf. Gn 6^{4}], v. also Berthol Toy^{Hpt}); נֹפֵל אַ֫רְצָה מֵת Ju 3^{25} cf. 4^{22} (om. ארצה); פְּגָרִים נ׳ אַ֫רְצָה 2 Ch 20^{24}; cf. also Ez 32$^{22.23.24}$ (del. in v^{22} Hi Co Berthol, in v^{23} Toy^{Hpt}).

Hiph. *Pf.* הִפִּיל 1 S 3^{19} +; 2 ms. sf. הִפַּלְתָּם ψ 73^{18}; 3 pl. הִפִּילוּ Ju 2^{19} +; 1 pl. הִפַּלְנוּ Ne 10^{35}, etc.; *Impf.* יַפִּיל Ex 21^{27}, וַיַּפֵּל Gn 2^{21} +, sf. יַפִּלֵם

ψ 140[11], 3 mpl יַפִּילוּ 2 K 3[25] ψ 22[19], יַבִּילוּן Jb 29[24], etc ; *Imv.* ms. sf הַפִּלָה Jos 13[6], mpl הַפִּילוּ 1 S 14[42], *Inf cstr* לְהַפִּיל 1 S 18[25]+, לנפל Nu 5[22] rd. לנפל (Di Ol[§ 178 c] Sta[§ 114 a. 2] Ko[i. 309] Ges[§ 66. 2 R 1]); *Pt* מַפִּיל 2 K 6[5]+2 t, pl. מַפִּילִים Dn 9[18]; —**1.** *cause to fall*, c. acc, lit. **a.** *fell* tree 2 K 3[19.25] cf 6[5]. **b.** *throw down* wall 2 S 20[15]. **c.** *knock out* tooth Ex 21[27] (E). **d.** *lay prostrate* Dn 25[2] (for bastinado). **e.** *cast* (cedar pillars) into (עַל־) fire Je 22[7]; so (c ב), wicked men ψ 140[11]. **f** *make* sword *drop* from (מִן) hand Ez 30[22] (fig), cf 39[3]. **g.** *cause* stone *to fall* עַל Nu 35[23], flesh ψ 78[28] (בקרב), stars Dn 8[10] (in vision)

2. Of causing death בַּחֶרֶב 2 K 19[7]=Is 37[7], Je 19[7] Ez 32[12] (all י׳ subj), 2 Ch 32[21] (human subj), בְּיַד 1 S 18[25], +חֲלָלִים Ez 6[4] Pr 7[26]; also ψ 106[26] Dn 11[12]=*overthrow*, bring to destruction, ψ 37[14] 73[18] (c לְ), 106[27].

3. Esp. of *casting* lot (גּוֹרָל), Is 34[17] (c. לְ *for*), Ne 10[35] (c עַל+inf), 11[1] (c. inf), 1 Ch 26[14] (c לְ, so rd Kit[Hpt] cf 𝔊𝔙 Be Ot), ψ 22[19] (c עַל), Est 9[24] (c. inf), abs Jon 1[7.7] 1 Ch 24[31] 25[8] 26[13] Est 3[7]; +בתוכנו Pr 1[14] (i e share with us); om גורל 1 S 14[42] (c בֵּין), Jb 6[27] (c עַל); hence הפ׳ = *assign, apportion, by lot*, usu c לְ pers, Jos 13[6] 23[4] (both D), Ez 45[1] 47[22 a]+v[22 b] (rd. יַפִּילוּ 𝔙 𝔗 Hi-Sm Co Berthol), 48[29] (read בְּנַחֲלָה for מנ׳, 𝔊 𝔙 Hi-Sm, etc), ψ 78[55] (cf. **Qal 1** end; and **I 7 c** ב)

4 Fig, *let drop, cause to fail* (cf **Qal 5**), Ju 2[19] Est 6[10], +אַרְצָה 1 S 3[19].

5 *Cause* deep sleep *to fall* (עַל־) Gn 2[21] (J), Pr 19[15] (abs), *make* countenance *fall*, look displeased at (ב), Je 3[12], cf Jb 29[24] (אוֹר פָּנַי obj), *cause* terror, etc, *to fall* (עַל־) Je 15[8].

6. Other idioms are. *bring to life* (prop *drop* young) Is 26[19] (fig.), *present* supplication Je 38[26] 42[9] Dn 9[18.20] (all c. לִפְנֵי),—on both cf **Qal 6.**

Hithp. *throw*, or *prostrate oneself*, **1.** *Inf cstr* התנפל *throw himself upon* (על) Gn 43[18] (J, i e attack) **2.** *Pf.* 1 s הִתְנַפַּלְתִּי Dt 9[25], *Impf.* 1 s וָאֶתְנַפַּל Dt 9[18.25], *Pt* מתנפל Ezr 10[1], —*prostrate oneself* and *lie prostrate*, לִפְנֵי י׳.— **Pil'el.** ונפלל Ez 28[23], rd וְנָפַל Hi-Sm Co Berthol

†נֵפֶל **n.m.**[Jb 3 16] **untimely birth, abortion**,— נֵפֶל abs Jb 3[16] (Baer, Ginsb., > van d. H נפל), נָפֶל Ec 6[3], cstr נֵפֶל אֵשֶׁת ψ 58[9].

†[מַפָּל] **n.m.**[Jb 41. 15] **refuse, hanging parts**; —**1.** *fallings, refuse*, cstr מַפַּל בַּר Am 8[6] *the refuse* of wheat. **2.** pl cstr מַפְּלֵי בְשָׂרוֹ Jb 41[15] *the hanging* (falling, drooping) *parts of his flesh* (of crocodile).

†מַפָּלָה **n.f. a ruin**;—abs. מ׳ of city Is 17[1].

†מַפֵּלָה **n.f. id.**,—abs מ׳ of city Is 23[13] 25[2].

†מַפֶּלֶת **n.f. carcass, ruin, overthrow**;— **1.** *carcass*, of lion, מ׳ cstr. Ju 14[8] **2.** elsewh. sf **a.** *a ruin*, מַפַּלְתּוֹ Ez 31[13] (kg. under fig of tree). **b.** *overthrow*, id v[16] (same fig), מַפַּלְתֵּךְ (kg) 32[10], מַפַּלְתֵּךְ (of Tyre) 26[15.18] 27[27]; מַפַּלְתָּם (of wicked) Pr 29[16]

†נְפִלִים **n.m.pl. giants**, acc to 𝔊 γίγαντες, so 𝔖𝔙; הַנְּפִלִים Gn 6[4] (J), הַנְּפִילִים בְּנֵי עֲנָק מִן־הַנְּפִלִים Nu 13[33] (JE); 𝔊 om. בני וגו׳, and so Di; these words perhaps doublet, but already in Sam, also 𝔙 (etym. dub; cf Aram. נִיפְלָא, נפילא *Orion*; conject. v in Thes Di[ad loc]; Tuch Kn Len[Or i 344 Eng. Tr 345 f], Che[Hbr Lit (1887), 175, 176]; all very precarious).

†I [נָפַץ] **vb. shatter** (NH *id., dash, beat*, As *napâsu, shatter, destroy* Dl[HWB 475], 𝔗 נפע Pa *shatter*, but also נפץ Pa, *id*, Syr ܢܦܨ *shake, break*, so Mand, No[M 240 and ZMG xxxii (1878), 406]); —**Qal** *Inf. abs* וְנָפוֹץ c acc Ju 7[19] *and a shattering* (=*and shattered*) the jars, *Pt pass* עֶצֶב נִבְזֶה נָפוּץ Je 22[28] (fig.) *a vessel to be despised (and) shattered* (cf. Ew Gie Rothstein[Kau]), also *Pt act* נֹפֵץ *shatterer* of the holy people Dn 12[7] (Bev Marti[Kau], rdg (כִּכְלוֹת יַד נֹפֵץ) **Pi.** *dash to pieces: Pf* 3 ms ונפץ consec. ψ 137[9] c acc infants ag (אֶל) rock; 1 s וְנִפַּצְתִּי of י׳ dashing all in pieces with (ב) Babyl as war-club Je 51[20.21 21 22.22.22.23.23.23], sf. וְנִפַּצְתִּים אִישׁ אֶל־אָחִיו 13[14]; *Impf.* 2 ms sf. כִּכְלִי יוֹצֵר תְּנַפְּצֵם ψ 2[9] (i.e. nations); 3 mpl. וְכֵלָיו יְנַפֵּצוּ Je 48[12] (symbol of destroying Moab); *Inf* נַפֵּץ יַד־עַם־קֹדֶשׁ Dn 12[7] *when (they) finish shattering the hand* (fig for *power*) *of the holy people*, but rd poss. נֹפֵץ, v **Qal.** **Pu.** *Pt* fpl מְנֻפָּצוֹת Is 27[9] like chalk-stones *pulverized.*

†נֶפֶץ **n.[m.] driving storm** (lit. *bursting* of clouds, Che[Comm]), נ׳ וָזֶרֶם וְאֶבֶן בָּרָד Is 30[30] (theoph).

†[מַפָּץ] **n.[m.] shattering**,—כְּלִי מַפָּצוֹ Ez 9[2] with *his shattering-weapon* in his hand.

†מַפֵּץ **n.m. war-club** (lit. *a shatterer*),—מַפֵּץ־אַתָּה לִי Je 51^{20} *a war-club art thou to me* (׳י addressing Babylon, cf Gf Gie).

†II. **נָפַץ vb. disperse, be scattered** (oft. taken as secondary √fr. Niph. of פוץ, yet cf. NH נפץ, Qal (Pt.), Pi, *scatter;* Syr. ܢܦܨ *pour out, throw down,* ܬ נְפַץ; Ar نفض *shake* (irreg correspondence of sibilants cf. No$^{L.c.}$), Eth ነፍጸ: *dissipari, aufugere* Di ^{713}),—**Qal** *Pf.* 3 ms. נ׳ הָעָם מֵעָלַי 1 S 13^{11} *the people were scattered from me;* 3 fs. נָפְצָה כָל־הָאָרֶץ Gn 9^{19} (J) thence *dispersed all* (the population of) *the earth;* 3 pl נָפְצוּ גוֹיִם Is 33^3 *nations were scattered; Pt. pass.* fpl. cstr. נְפֻצוֹת יְהוּדָה Is 11^{12} *the dispersed of Judah* he shall collect (‖ נִדְחֵי יִשְׂרָאֵל).

נפשׁ (√of foll, cf. Ar. نَفْس *soul, life, person, living being, blood, desire,* نَفَس *breath, sweet odour,* نَفُسَ *be high in estimation, become avaricious;* III *desire a thing, aspire to it, v. breathe, sigh* As. *napâšu, get breath, be broad, extended; napištu, life,* less frequently *soul, living being, person.* Vbs appar. denom; nouns in all Semitic languages: Ph. נפש, CIS I 86 B 5, Eth. ነፍስ:, in the foll = both *soul, person,* and *tombstone, monument* (as representing person, v. esp Duval Rev Sémit ii (1894), 259 ff.): NH נפש v Levy ZMG xii (1858), 215; O Aram. נפש, Nab. Palm. נפש, v. Lzb 325 Cook 82; Syr ܢܦܫܐ, v. 1 Macc $13^{27.28}$; Sab. נפס Levy-Os ZMG xix (1865) 3.5.290 Mordtm ib xxxii (1878), 202 cf. Lihyan, DHM Epigr Denkm 67, Min. Hom Südarab. Chrest 128)

נֶ֫פֶשׁ 756 **n.f.** Gn 49,6 (so even Gn 2^{19} Nu 31^{28} 1 K 19^2 v Albrecht ZAW xvi (1896), 42 SS) **soul, living being, life, self, person, desire, appetite, emotion, and passion** (Ecclus 3^{18} $4^{1.1.2.2}$ 13^{12} 14^{11});—נ׳ Gn 1^{20}+; נָ֫פֶשׁ Gn 37^{21}+; sf. נַפְשִׁי Gn 12^{13}+; pl. נְפָשׁוֹת Ez 13^{18}+13 t; נפשׂת Ex 12^4 Lv 27^2, *cstr* נַפְשׁוֹת Gn 36^6+4 t, נַפְשֹׁת Lv 21^{11}; נְפָשִׁים Ez 13^{20} (but rd. חָפְשִׁים, v. Co Berthol Toy); sf. נַפְשֹׁתָם 2 S 23^{17}+; נַפְשֹׁתָם Nu 17^3+·—

1. = *that which breathes, the breathing substance or being* = ψυχή, anima, *the soul, the inner being of man.* **a.** disting. fr. בָּשָׂר: מִנֶּפֶשׁ וְעַד בָּשָׂר Is 10^{18}; הנפש עם הַבָּשָׂר Dt 12^{23}; fr. שְׁאֵר Pr 11^{17}; fr בֶּטֶן *body* ψ 31^{10}. **b.** both the inner נפש and the outer בשר are conceived as resting on a common substratum: אַךְ בְּשָׂרוֹ עָלָיו יִכְאָב וְנַפְשׁוֹ עָלָיו תֶּאֱבָל׃ Jb 14^{22} *only his flesh upon him is in pain, and his soul upon him mourneth;* cf. ψ $42^{5.7}$ 131^2 Jb 30^{16} La 3^{20} [v. עַל **1 d**], all poetical (cf. **6 c**). **c.** נ׳ departs at death and returns with life: וַיְהִי בצאת נַפְשָׁהּ כִּי מֵתָה Gn 35^{18} (E) *and it came to pass when her soul was going forth* (*for she died*); נָפְחָה נַפְשָׁהּ Je 15^9 *she breathed out her soul,* cf. 1 K $17^{21.22}$ Jb 11^{20} 31^{39}. **d.** oft desired that the נפש may be delivered: fr. She'ôl ψ 16^{10} 30^4 49^{16} 86^{13} 89^{49} Pr 23^{14}; fr. שַׁחַת, the pit of She'ôl, Is 38^{17} Jb $33^{18.22.28.30}$.

2. The נפש becomes a living being: by God's breathing נשמת חיים into the nostrils of its בשר; of man Gn 2^7 (J); by implication of animals also Gn 2^{19} (J); so ψ $104^{29.30}$ cf. 66^9; man is נֶפֶשׁ חַיָּה, a living, breathing being Gn 2^7 (J); elsewh נפש חיה alw. of animals Gn $1^{20.24.30}$ $9^{12.15.16}$ (all P), Ez 47^9; so נפש החיה Gn 1^{21} 9^{10} (both P), Lv $11^{10.46}$ (H), נפש השרצת Lv 11^{46} (H); נפש כל חי Jb 12^{10}. נפש is frequently used with the verb חיה: †וחיתה נפשׁ Gn 12^{13} 19^{20} (both J), 1 K 20^{32} (E), ψ 119^{175} Je $38^{17.20}$; †חי נַפְשְׁךָ 1 S 1^{26} 17^{55} 20^3 25^{26} 2 S 11^{11} 14^{19} 2 K $2^{2.4.6}$ 4^{30} (all JE), cf †יְחִיֶה נ׳ 1 K 20^{31} (E), Ez 18^{27} ψ 22^{30}; also Gn 19^{19} Is 55^3 Pr 3^{22}.

3. The נֶפֶשׁ (without חיה noun or verb) is specif: **a.** a living being whose life resides in the blood [so in Arab We Skizzen iii 217 G. Jacob Arab Dicht. iv 97] (hence sacrificial use of blood, and its prohib. in other uses; first in D), Dt $12^{23.24}$ *only be sure that thou eat not the blood, for the blood is the living being* (הַדָּם הוּא הַנָּפֶשׁ); *and thou shalt not eat the living being with the flesh* (הַנפש עם הַבָּשָׂר); *thou shalt pour it upon the earth as water;* this is enlarged in H, Lv $17^{10.11.12.14}$ and in P Gn $9^{4.5}$, cf. Je 2^{34}. **b.** a serious attack upon the life is an attack upon this inner living being 2 S 1^9 Je 4^{10} Jon 2^6 ψ 69^2 $124^{4.5}$ Jb 27^3. **c.** נפש is used for life itself 171 t., of animals Pr 12^{10}, and of man Gn 44^{30} (J); נפש תַּחַת נפש *life for life* Ex 21^{23} (E), Lv 24^{18} (H), 1 K $20^{39.42}$ 2 K 10^{24}, נפשנו תחתיכם Jos 2^{14} (J), נפש בנפש Dt 19^{21}; בנפש *for the life of* 2 S 14^7 Jon 1^{14}, שׂם נפש בכף *put life in one's own hand* Ju 12^3 1 S 19^5 28^{21} Jb 13^{14}; חֵרֵף נפשו למות Ju 5^{18} *risked his life to die;* †בנפשׁ *at the risk of life* Nu 17^3 (P), 2 S 23^{17} = 1 Ch $11^{19.19}$, 1 K 2^{23} Pr 7^{23} La 5^9; †בקשׁ נפשׁ Ex 4^{19} (J), 1 S 20^1 $22^{23.23}$ 23^{15} 25^{29} 2 S 4^8 16^{11} 1 K $19^{10.14}$ Je 4^{30} 11^{21} $19^{7.9}$ 21^7 22^{25} $34^{20.21}$ 38^{16} $44^{30.30}$ 46^{26} 49^{37} ψ 35^4 38^{13} 40^{15} 54^5 63^{10} 70^3 86^{14} Pr 29^{10}; †שאל נ׳ 1 K 3^{11} = 2 Ch 1^{11}, 1 K 19^4 = Jon 4^8; †הִכָּה נפשׁ *smite mortally* Gn 37^{21} (J), Dt $19^{6.11}$ Je $40^{14.15}$, †לקח נ׳ 1 K 19^4 Jon 4^3 ψ 31^{14} Pr 1^{19}; †הִצִּיל

נפשׁ מִמָּוֶת *deliver life from death* Jos 2^{13} ψ 33^{19} 56^{14}, †מלט נפשׁ 1 S 19^{11} 2 S 19$^{6.6.6}$ 1 K 1$^{12.12}$ Je 48^{6} 51$^{6.45}$ Ez 33^{5} Am 2$^{14.15}$ ψ 89^{49} 116^{4}, †פדה נ׳ 2 S 4^{9} 1 K 1^{29} ψ 34^{23} 49^{16} 55^{19} 71^{23}, †שׁמר נ׳ ψ 25^{20} 97^{10} Jb 2^{6} Pr 13^{3} 16^{17} 19^{16} 22^{5}.

4. The נפשׁ as the essential of man stands for *the man himself*. **a.** paraphrase for pers pron. esp in poetry and ornate discourse, 70 t; (1) נַפְשִׁי = *me* אל תבא נפשׁי Gn 49^{6} *let me not enter* (poem in J), תָּמֹת נ׳ מות ישׁרים Nu 23^{10} *let me die*, etc (poem); תָּמוֹת נַפְשִׁי Ju 16^{30} (J); אמרה נפשׁי La 3^{24} *I say.* (2) נַפְשְׁךָ = *thee* לְאֻמִּים תַּחַת נַפְשֶׁךָ Is 43^{4} *peoples instead of thee*, אָמְרוּ לְנַפְשֵׁךְ 51^{23}. (3) נַפְשׁוֹ = *he:* נפשׁו בטוב תלין ψ 25^{13} *he will not dwell in good circumstances.* (4) נַפְשֵׁנוּ = *we*· נַפְשֵׁנוּ כצפור נִמְלְטָה מפח יוקשׁים ψ 124^{7}. (5) נַפְשָׁם = *they, them:* נַפְשָׁם בַּשְּׁבִי הָלָכָה Is 46^{2} *they are gone into captivity;* אוי לנפשׁם Is 3^{9} **b.** = reflexive, *self,* 53 t אסר על נפשׁ *bind oneself* Nu 30$^{3.5.6.6.7.8.9.10.11.12}$; לְעַנֹּת נ׳ Nu 30^{14} *to afflict oneself.* (1) נַפְשִׁי = *myself* לא אדע נפשׁי Jb 9^{21} *I know not myself* (2) נַפְשְׁךָ = *thyself*· שׁמר נ׳ Dt 4^{9} *keep thyself* (3) נַפְשׁוֹ = *himself:* אהב כנ׳ 1 S 18$^{1.3}$ 20^{17} *loved as himself.* (4) נַפְשָׁהּ = *herself:* צדקה נ׳ Je 3^{11} *justified herself* (5) נַפְשָׁם = *themselves:* הציל נ׳ *deliver themselves* Is 47^{14} Ez 14$^{14.20}$ (6) נַפְשֹׁתֵיכֶם, נַפְשְׁכֶם = *yourselves:* אַל־תַּשִּׁאוּ נ׳ Je 37^{9} *deceive not yourselves,* also 42^{20} 44^{7}, ענה נ׳ Lv 16$^{29.31}$ 23$^{27.32}$ Nu 29^{7} (P); נשׁמרתם לנ׳ Dt 4^{15} Jos 23^{11} (D). (7) נַפְשׁוֹתֵינוּ = *ourselves:* על נ׳ Je 26^{19} *against ourselves.* **c.** = *person* of man, individual, 144 t., first in D^{2}, esp in H, P, and kindred writers· (1) c אָדָם נ׳ אדם Lv 24^{17} opp. נ׳ בהמה 24^{18} (both H), and so נ׳ אדם *human persons* Nu 31$^{35.40.46}$ (P) 1 Ch 5^{21} Ez 27^{13}. Elsewhere without אדם. נ׳ ברכה Pr 11^{25} *one who blesses;* נ׳ רמיה Pr 19^{15} *idle person;* נ׳ תחת נ׳ *person in place of person,* Jb 16^{4}, כפר על נ׳ Ex 30$^{15.16}$ Nu 15^{28} 31^{50} (all P) Lv 17^{11} (H). †(2) נפשׁ = *person, any one*· Dt 24^{7} 27^{25} Pr 28^{17} Ez 18$^{4.4.4}$ 33^{6}, elsewhere only H P: Lv 2^{1} 4$^{2.27}$ 5$^{1.2.4.15.17.21}$ 7$^{18.20.21.25.27}$ 23$^{29.30.30}$ Nu 5^{6} 15$^{27.30}$ 19^{22} 31$^{19.28}$ 35$^{11.15.30.30}$ Jos 20$^{3.9}$ (all P), Lv 17$^{10.12.15}$ 20$^{6.6}$ 22$^{6.11}$ (all H); נכרתה הנ׳ ההוא מן *that person shall be cut off from* only in Gn 17^{14} Ex 12$^{15.19}$ 31^{14} Lv 7$^{20.21.27}$ Nu 9^{13} 15$^{30.31}$ 19$^{13.20}$ (all P), Lv 19^{8} 22^{3} (both H) †(3) נפשׁ coll for *persons,* in enumerations: Dt 10^{22} Jos 10$^{28.30.32.35.37.37.39}$ 11^{11} (all D^{2}) Je 43^{6} 52$^{29.30.30}$ Ez 22^{25}, elsewhere only Gn 12^{5} 46$^{15.18.22.25.26.26.27.27}$ Ex 1$^{5.5}$ 12^{16} Nu 31$^{35.40}$ (all P). †(4) נְפָשׁוֹת *persons* Gn 36^{6} Ex 12^{4} 16^{16} Nu 19^{18} (all P), Lv 18^{29} 20^{25} 27^{2} (all H), 2 K 12^{5} Pr 11^{30} 14^{25} Ez 13$^{18.18.18.19.19.20.20}$ 17^{17} 18^{4} 22^{27} (נפשׁים 13^{20} v. supr) †(5) נפשׁ = *deceased person,* sts c מת, נֶפֶשׁ מֵת Nu 6^{6} (P), נַפְשׁוֹת מֵת (𝔊 𝔖 נֶפֶשׁ) Lv 21^{11} (H), usu without מת, נפשׁ (ה)אדם Nu 9$^{6.7}$ 19$^{11.13}$ (P), or simply נפשׁ, Lv 19^{28} 21^{1} 22^{4} (all H) Nu 5^{2} 6^{11} 9^{10} (all P); elsewhere only Hag 2^{13}.

5. נפשׁ = *seat of the appetites,* in all periods (46 t)—**a.** hunger: נ׳ רְעֵבָה *hungry soul* ψ 107^{9} Pr 27^{7}, with noun or verb of *satisfy* שׂבע Is 56^{11} 58^{10} Je 50^{19} Ez 7^{19} ψ 63^{6} 107^{9} Pr 13^{25} 27^{7}, מתוק לנ׳ Pr 16^{24} *sweet to the taste.* **b.** thirst· נ׳ עֲיֵפָה *weary soul* Pr 25^{25} Je 31^{25}, נ׳ כארץ עיפה ψ 143^{6}; צמאה נ׳ ψ 42^{3} 63^{2} **c.** appetite in general: אֹיְבַי בְּנ׳ יַקִּיפוּ עָלָיו ψ 17^{9} *my enemies compass me about with greed;* הרחיבה שׁאול נַפְשָׁהּ וּפָעֲרָה פִיהָ Is 5^{14} *She'ôl enlarged her appetite,* etc., cf Hb 2^{5}; Pr 23^{2} בַּעַל נֶפֶשׁ; Ec uses נפשׁ only in the sense of **a, b, c**; the נפשׁ craves, lacks, and is filled with good things: Ec 2^{24} 4^{8} 6$^{2.3.7.9}$ 7^{28}.

6. נ׳ = *seat of emotions and passions* (151 t.)—**a.** desire: †אִוְּתָה נ׳ *soul desires* Dt 12^{20} 14^{26} 1 S 2^{16} 2 S 3^{21} 1 K 11^{37} Jb 23^{13} Pr 13^{4} 21^{10} Mi 7^{1}, תַּאֲוַת נ׳ ψ 10^{3} Is 26^{8}; †אַוַּת נ׳ Dt 12$^{15.20.21}$ 18^{6} 1 S 23^{20} Je 2^{24}; so also לנפשׁ *according to one's desire* Dt 21^{14} ψ 78^{18} Je 34^{16}; כנפשׁ Dt 23^{25}, האח נפשׁנו *ah, our desire* ψ 35^{25}; בנפשׁ *at one's desire* ψ 105^{22} Ez 16^{27}; נ׳ יָצְאָה בְדַבְּרוֹ Ct 5^{6}; †נשׂא נ׳ *lift up the soul, desire* Dt 24^{15} 2 S 14^{14} (rd אלהים, not אלהים), ψ 24^{4} 25^{1} 86^{4} 143^{8} Pr 19^{8} Je 22^{27} 44^{14} Ho 4^{8} †**b.** abhorrence, loathing: נעלה נ׳ *soul abhorreth* Lv 26$^{11.15.30.43}$ (H) Je 14^{19}; וגם נ׳ בחלה בי Zc 11^{8} *and their soul also felt a loathing against me.* **c.** sorrow and distress· †מרי נ׳ *bitter, gloomy, discontented of soul* Ju 18^{25} (E) 2 S 17^{8} Jb 3^{20} Pr 31^{6}; †מר נ׳ 1 S 22^{2} cf. Jb 7^{11} 10^{1} Is 38^{15} Ez 27^{31}; עָגְמָה נ׳ Jb 30^{25} *grieved,* אגמי נ׳ *sad of soul* Is 19^{10}, תבכה נ׳ *my soul shall weep* Je 13^{17}; צרת נ׳ *distress of soul* Gn 42^{21} (E) †**d.** joy: נ׳ תגיל *my soul rejoiceth* ψ 35^{9} Is 61^{10}, שׂמח נ׳ *rejoice the soul* ψ 86^{4}; also ψ 94^{19} 138^{3} Pr 29^{17}. †**e.** love: ידדות נ׳ *my soul loveth* Ct 1^{7} 3$^{1.2.3.4}$; אהבה נ׳ *darling of my soul* Je 12^{7}; דבקה נ׳ ב׳ *his soul clave unto* Gn 34^{3} (J), c. אחרי ψ 63^{9}, חשׁקה נ׳ ב׳ *soul is attached to* Gn 34^{8} (P). **f.** alienation, hatred, revenge: †נ׳ מן חקע *the soul is*

alienated from Je 6[8] Ez 23[17.18]; נקעה נ׳ מן Ez 23[18.22.28]; שׂנאה נ׳ שְׂנֻאֵי נ׳ *hated of soul* 2 S 5[8] (Qr); ψ 11[5] Is 1[14]. **g.** other emotions and feelings: השיב נ׳ *bring back soul* La 1[11.19] (*i.e.* revive, cf c שׁוב 1 K 17[21 f]), hence fig. *refresh, cheer,* v[16] ψ 19[8] Pr 25[13] Ru 4[15]; שׁובב נ׳ ψ 23[3]; מַחְמַל נ׳ *your souls' compassion* Ez 24[21]; קצרה נ׳ *soul was impatient* Nu 21[4] (E), Ju 10[16] 16[16] Zc 11[8], כי אאריך נ׳ *that I should prolong my patience* Jb 6[11]; ידעתם את־נ׳ הגר *ye know the feeling of the stranger* Ex 23[9] (R[D]).

7. נפשׁ is used occasionally for mental acts + לבב (see **10**); poss. also alone, owing to unconscious assimilation by late writers; but most, if not all, exx may be otherwise explained: נפשׁי ידעת מאד ψ 139[14] *my soul knoweth well* (or *I know well;* cf. **4 a**); בלא דעת נ׳ לא טוב Pr 19[2] *that the soul be without knowledge is not good* (but RV[m] *desire without knowledge,* cf. **6 a**); דעה חכמה לנ׳ Pr 24[14] *know wisdom for thy soul* (or *according to thy desire,* cf **6 a**); אל תדמי בנ׳ Est 4[13] *think not in thy soul* (or *in thyself,* cf. **4 b**); כמו שׁער בנ׳ Pr 23[7] *as he reckoneth in his soul* (but RV *in himself,* cf. **4 b**); מה תאמר נ׳ 1 S 20[4] (but AV RV foll. 𝔊 ἐπιθυμεῖ = תְּאַוֶּה; v. **6 a**).

8. נפשׁ for acts of the will is dub.: אם ישׁ (את) נפשׁכם *if it is your purpose* Gn 23[8] (P) 2 K 9[15] (or *if it is your desire,* **6 a**); בחרה נ׳ *my soul chooseth* Jb 7[15], מאנה נ׳ *my soul refuseth* Jb 6[7] ψ 77[3]; חפצה נ׳ *their soul delighteth in* Is 66[3], רצתה נ׳ *my soul delighteth in* Is 42[1]; (all perhaps emotional, **6 b, d, g**).

9. נפשׁ = character is still more dub.: לֹא־יָשְׁרָה נ׳ בוֹ Hb 2[4] *his soul is not right in him* (but 𝔊 οὐκ εὐδοκεῖ ἡ ψυχή μου ἐν αὐτῷ [εὐδοκεῖ = רצתה], v **6**); נַפְשִׁי לֹא מְטֻמָּאָה Ez 4[14] *my soul hath not* (or *I have not,* **4 a**) *been polluted.*

†**10.** נ׳ in D, when used with לבב, is assim. to it, and shares with it the mngs. of **7, 8, 9**; and so in later writers influenced by D (unless we may think that ל׳ is used of intellect, while נ׳ is used of the feelings): thus, בכל לבב ובכל נפשׁ (see לבב): c. דרשׁ Dt 4[29] 2 Ch 15[12]; עשׂה Dt 26[16]; אהב Dt 6[5] 13[4] 30[6]; ידע Jos 23[14], עבד Dt 10[12] 11[13] Jos 22[5], שׁמע בקלו Dt 30[2]; שׁוב אל Dt 30[10] 1 K 8[48] = 2 Ch 6[38], 2 K 23[25]; שׁמר מצות 2 K 23[3] = 2 Ch 34[31]; הלך לפני 1 K 2[4], and Dt 11[18] 1 S 2[35] 1 Ch 22[19] 28[9] Je 32[41] ψ 13[3] Pr 2[10] 24[12]. *Note.*—In three cases is generally found closer approach to supposed radical meaning *breath:*—**a.** שׁמן וקטרת ישׂמח לב ומתק רעהו מעצת נפשׁ Pr 27[9]. Ges (after Doderlein) renders מעצת נ׳ *more than odorous trees,* so later edds., even Buhl; but 𝔙 De SS transp. וּמֶתֶק נ׳ מֵעֲצַת רֵעֵהוּ. 𝔊 Hi Bi ומתקרעה = *the soul is rent asunder by cares.* In any case נפשׁ is ‖ לב, cf. **10**. **b.** נַפְשׁוֹ גֶּחָלִים תְּלַהֵט Jb 41[13] *his breath kindleth coals* (of the crocodile) The piece is one of the latest in the book; primitive meaning hardly in such a passage; context favours ref. to *passion* or *fury;* perhaps sub **6 f**, *his passion* or *fury* kindleth coals. **c.** בָּתֵּי הַנֶּפֶשׁ Is 3[20] *perfume boxes;* mng. evident fr. context; but not necessarily *scent* (*breath*)-*boxes;* may be **6 a**, *boxes of desire,* or **5**, *boxes exciting the sense of smell;* = *smelling* boxes or bottles. No sufficient evid. in BH, therefore, for meaning *breath, odour*—See, for complete study of נֶפֶשׁ (all passages), Br[JBL 1897, 17 ff]

†[נָפַשׁ] **vb.denom.** (cf. Syr. ܢܦܫ *refresh;* ܐܬܢܦܫ, ܐܬܢܦܫ *be refreshed;* Eth ነፍሰ:);—**Niph.** *Impf.* 3 ms יִנָּפֵשׁ Ex 23[12] (E) 2 S 16[14]; וַיִּנָּפַשׁ Ex 31[17] (P);—*take breath, refresh oneself.*

†נָפִישׁ **n.pr.m.** son of Ishmael, acc. to Gn 25[15] (P), = 1 Ch 1[31] (𝔊 Ναφες, 𝔊L Ναφεις); = (Arab) tribe 5[19] (𝔊 Ναφεισαδαιων, A 𝔊L Ναφισαιων).

נֶפֶת v. II. נוף.

†נֹפֶת **n.m.** [Pr 24,13] **flowing honey, honey from the comb** (Ph. נפת CIS[I. 166, 8 b]);—נ׳ abs. Pr 5[3] + 3 t, cstr ψ 19[11];—sweet Pr 24[13] (‖ דְּבַשׁ), cf. 27[7]; fig. of sweet words Pr 5[3], and perh. Ct 4[11] (Bu of kisses; ‖ דְּבַשׁ, חָלָב); in full נ׳ צוּפִים ψ 19[11] *honey of (the) combs* (comp. with מִשְׁפְּטֵי י׳ ‖ דְּבַשׁ).

נַפְתּוּחַ v. פתח.

נַפְתָּלִי, נַפְתּוּלִים v. פתל.

†נַפְתֻּחִים **n.pr.loc.** Gn 10[13] = 1 Ch 1[11] (𝔊 Νεφθαλ(ι)ειμ, but 𝔊L in Ch Νεφθωσειμ); = *p3t3mhi, the northern land,* i.e. Lower Egypt, acc. to Brugsch [Hierogl. WB. Suppl. 633], and esp Erman [ZAW x (1890) 118, 119] rdg פתמחים. Other conj v Di[Gn].

I. [נֵץ] v. II. נצץ. II. נֵץ v. III. נצץ.

†[נָצָא] **vb.** = נָצָה = **fly,** acc Thes Gf al;—only **Qal** *Inf. abs.* (si vera l) נָצֹא תֵּצֵא Je 48[9], but improb; 𝔗 Symm יְצָא cf. Ol[§ 245 h] Gie; > Schwally[ZAW viii (1888), 197] נָצֹה תִּצֶּה, √III. נצה.

†[נָצַב] **vb. Niph.** take one's stand, stand (NH נִצָּב *id.* (rare), הַצָּבָה n. *taking a stand;* Ph. (Pun.) מצבת, מנצבת, נצב *monument* Lzb[325]; Nab. Palm. נצב *set up;* Zinj. *id.*, *statue*, all Lzb[325] Cook[82]; Palm. מצבא *image*, Nab. נצב *id.*, DHM[VOJ viii (1894), 12], cf. Lzb[l.c.]; perhaps As. *naṣâbu* Tel Am, Wkl[TA 24*b]; Aram. נְצַב, نِصَب; Ar. نَصَبَ *set up, erect*, نُصْبٌ *sign, mark, way-mark;* Sab. נצב *cippus* CIS[iv. 23] Sab Denkm[95] DHM[ZMG xxx (1876), 115f.] Derenb[JAs. 1883, Aug.-Sept. 244]; Min. מצב *statue* (=מנצב) Hom[Südar. Chrest. 128]);—**Niph.** *Pf.* 3 fs. נִצְּבָה ψ 45[10], נִצָּבָה Gn 37[7] Pr 8[2]; 2 ms. וְנִצַּבְתָּ Ex 7[15] + 2 t.; 3 pl. נִצְּבוּ 15[8], וְנִצְּבוּ consec. 33[8]; *Pt.* נִצָּב Gn 24[13] +, f. נִצָּבָה Zc 11[16], נִצֶּבֶת 1 S 1[26]; mpl. נִצָּבִים Ex 5[20] +; fpl. נִצָּבוֹת 1 S 1[26];—**1. a.** *station oneself, take one's stand*, for definite purpose, c. עַל loc. (*by, on*) Gn 24[13.43] 28[13] Ex 7[15] 33[21] 34[2] (all J), Ex 17[9] 18[14] (E), Nu 23[6.17] (JE); Am 7[7] 9[1] Pr 8[2]; of י׳ Is 3[13] *taketh his stand to plead;* c. בְּ loc. Ex 5[20] ψ 82[1] (of God), cf. Nu 22[23.31.34]; נ׳ עִמְּכָה 1 S 1[26]; לִפְנֵי י׳ Dt 29[9]; c. פֶּתַח Nu 16[27] (JE), Ju 18[16.17]; abs. La 2[4] (on text v. Löhr). **b.** *stand = be stationed* (by appointment, or in fulfilment of duty), c. עַל pers. (sitting or lying) Gn 45[1] 1 S 4[20] 22[6.7.17]; נ׳ עַל־מִשְׁמַרְתִּי Is 21[8] *stand at my watchman's post* (‖ עֹמֵד); לִימִינְךָ ψ 45[10]; abs. 2 S 13[31]. **c.** *take an upright position, stand*, יָקוּמוּ וְנ׳ Ex 33[8] (E; + פֶּתַח loc.), cf. Gn 37[7] (E; of sheaf); of waters, נ׳ כְּמוֹ־נֵד Ex 15[8] (song). **2.** *be stationed = appointed* over (עַל), 1 S 22[9] Ru 2[5.6]; with Samuel *presiding over* (עַל) *them* 1 S 19[20]. Hence **3.** Pt. as subst. *deputy, prefect* (as *appointed, deputed*), only 1 K 4[5.7] 5[7.30] 9[23] 2 Ch 8[10] (all of Sol.'s officers; so also 2 Ch 8[10] Qr, < Kt נציב), 1 K 22[48] (of Edom). **4.** *stand firm*, fig. כָּל־אָדָם נִצָּב ψ 39[6] *every man*, (even) *the firm-standing*, is wholly vanity (but expression strange, and text dub.); נ׳ בַּשָּׁמָיִם 119[89] (of י׳'s word); *that which stands firm* Zc 11[16] (Isr. under fig. of sheep), but dub.; We GASm leave untranslated; Now prop. הַנַּחֲלָה *the diseased.*

Hiph. *Pf.* הִצִּיב 1 K 16[34]; 2 ms. הִצַּבְתָּ Gn 21[29] ψ 74[17]; 3 mpl. הִצִּיבוּ Je 5[26]; *Impf.* יַצִּיב Jos 6[26], יַצֵּב Dt 32[8] (dub.; poet. for יַ׳ Ew[§ 233a] Di; rhythmical shortening Ges[§ 109 k]; read יַצֵּב Dr Da[Synt. p. 94]), וַיַּצֶּב־ 2 S 18[18]; sf. וַיַּצִּיבֵנִי La 3[12]; *Imv.* fs. הַצִּיבִי Je 31[21]; *Inf. cstr.* הַצִּיב 1 S 13[21] 1 Ch 18[3]; *Pt.* מַצִּיב 1 S 15[12] (but rd. הִצִּיב 𝔊 We Dr Bu Kit HPS);—**1.** *station, set:* c. acc., ewes Gn 21[28.29] (E; לְבַד *apart*), trap Je 5[26]; fig. *set me before thee* (לְפָנֶיךָ) ψ 41[13]; *set me* as a target La 3[12]. **2.** *set up, erect* pillar (מַצֵּבָה) Gn 35[14.20] (E), 2 S 18[18], + אֲשֵׁרִים 2 K 17[10]; altar Gn 33[20] (E), stone-heap 2 S 18[17]; monument (יָד) 1 S 15[12]; city-gates (c. בְּ), Jos 6[26] (JE) = 1 K 16[34]. **3.** *cause to stand erect*, waters, כְּמוֹ־נֵד ψ 78[13] (cf. **Qal** Ex 15[8]). **4.** *fix, establish* boundary (subj. י׳) Dt 32[8] ψ 74[17] Pr 15[15]; dominion (יָד) 1 Ch 18[3] (of king).—1 S 13[21] is dub.; AV *sharpen*, RV *set;* Kit *'gerade machen';* Klo נִצָּב subst., v. infr.; cf. HPS.

Hoph. *Pf.* 3 ms. הֻצַּב Na 2[8] *it is fixed, determined* (Kl Or), but very dub.; perh. n.pr., or epith., of queen, cf. We Now GASm, q.v.; *Pt.* סֻלָּם מֻצָּב אַרְצָה Gn 28[12] (E) *a ladder set up on the earth;* אֵלוֹן מ׳ Ju 9[6], read אֵלוֹן הַמַּצֵּבָה GFM, v. infr.—Cf. also יצב **Hithp.**

†נִצָּב **n.m. 1.** haft, hilt of sword Ju 3[22] (Ar. نِصَابٌ *handle of knife*, 'in wh. the سِيلَان [i.e. the *shank*] is set' Lane[2800]). **2.** prefect, deputy, v. נצב **Niph. 3.**

†I. נְצִיב **n.m.** pillar, prefect, also appar. garrison, post (Ecclus 46[18] ויכנע נציבי צר *and he subdued garrisons, posts, of the foe*);—נ׳ abs. 1 K 4[19]; cstr. 1 S 13[3] + 3 t.; pl. נְצִיבִים 2 S 8[6] + 2 t. + 2 Ch 8[10] Kt, נְצִבִים 2 S 8[14.14]; cstr. נְצִבֵי 1 S 10[5] MT, but rd. נְצִיב 𝔊 𝔖 𝔙 Th We Dr Klo Kit Bu HPS;—**1.** *pillar*, נ׳ מֶלַח Gn 19[26] (J). **2.** *prefect, deputy* 1 K 4[19] (on text cf. Klo Benz), so perh. also 1 S 10[5] (HPS; *pillar* 𝔊 Th Dr Klo Kit), and appar. 13[3.4] (> al. *pillar*); this mng. serves also for 2 S 8[6.14.14] (so Ki; Th HPS *garrison*) 1 Ch 11[16] 18[13] 2 Ch 8[10] (where rd. Kt), 17[2] (Kau *garrison* in 11[16] 17[2]; Ecclus 46[18]—v. supr.—would favour this meaning in other passages).

†II. נְצִיב **n.pr.loc.** in Judah on border of Philist. Jos 15[43]; 𝔊 Νασειβ, A 𝔊L Νεσ(ε)ιβ; v. also Lag BN[95 Anm. *]; mod. *Beit Naṣîb*, c. 8 m. NW. of Hebron Buhl[Geogr. 193].

†מַצָּב **n.m.**[1 S 13, 23] **standing-place, station, garrison;**—מ׳ abs. 1 S 14[15], cstr. מַצַּב Jos 4[3.9] + (Baer in Sm מַצָּב, cf. on 1 S 13[23], but v. Ginsb); sf. מַצָּבְךָ Is 22[19];—**1.** *standing-place* of feet Jos 4[3.9] (JE). **2.** *station, office* Is 22[19] (‖ מַעֲמָד). **3.** *garrison, post*, or *outpost* (of Philistines) 1 S 13[23] 14[1.4.6.11.15] 2 S 23[14]; so rd. also 1 S 14[12] (for MT מַצָּבָה) 𝔊 Th We Bu HPS.

מָצָּב n.[m.] palisade or intrenchment;—only Is 29³ (of siege-works; ‖מְצֻרֹת).

מַצָּבָה n.f. אַנְשֵׁי מ׳ 1 S 14¹² v. מַצָּב.

†מִצָּבָה n.f. guard, watch?—only וְחָנִיתִי לְבֵיתִי מ׳ Zc 9⁸ *and I encamp as watch for my house* (so We Now GASm, but dub.; Kue Sta Marti^Kau GASm rd. מַצָּבָה, but this prob. non-existent, v. supr; MT appar. intends *because of a host* = מִצָּבָא).

†מַצֵּבָה, מַצֶּבֶת n.f. pillar, maṣṣēbā, stump;—abs. מַצֵּבָה Ho 3⁴+, מַצֶּבֶת 2 S 18¹⁸ ᵃ (rd. הַמּ׳ 𝔊 Dr Bu Kit), v¹⁸ ᵇ Is 6¹³, cstr. מַצֵּבַת 2 K 3² 10²⁷, מַצֶּבֶת Gn 35^{14.20}, sf. מַצַּבְתָּהּ Is 6¹³; pl. abs. מַצֵּבוֹת 1 K 14²³, cstr מַצְּבוֹת 2 K 10²⁶, etc;—**1. a.** pillar, as monument, personal memorial 2 S 18^{18 18}. **b.** a stone, set up (שׂים, הציב), and anointed as memorial of divine appearance Gn 28^{18.22} 31¹³ (all E), 35¹⁴ (J); so also 33²⁰ (E), where ins. מ׳, or rd. מ׳ for MT מִזְבֵּחַ (We Di Now^{Arch. ii. 18}), set up (הציב, הרים, שׂים), in token of an agreement 31^{45.51 52.52} (all E), over grave 35^{20.20} (E) **c.** esp. of sacred stones or pillars in connexion with altar, erected (בנה) by Moses Ex 24⁴ (E; 12 pillars), Ho 3⁴ 10^{1 2} Is 19¹⁹, conj also 2 K 12¹⁰ for MT מִזְבֵּחַ Sta^{ZAW v (1885), 296} Now ^{Arch l.c.}, but dub., v Benz^{ad loc}, (usu.+ אֲשֵׁרִים etc.). of Canaanites Ex 23²⁴ (E), 34¹³ (J), Dt 7⁵ 12³, cf מ׳ הַבַּעַל 2 K 3² 10^{26.27}; Tyre, מ׳ עֻזֵּךְ, Ez 26¹¹, of obelisks of Heliopolis in Egypt; condemned for Isr. by Deut code, and Deut. redaction of K: Dt 16²² 1 K 14²³ 17¹⁰ 18⁴ 23¹⁴, 2 Ch 14² 31¹; cf. Mi 5¹² Lv 26¹ (H)—On *maṣṣēbā* v. further Now^{Arch ii 18 f.} Benz^{Arch 380 f.} Dr^{Dt. 16, 21 f.} We ^{Skizzen iii 99, 165} RS^{Sem. i. 184 ff. 437 f; 2d ed 204 ff. 456 f.; K. 50} —Ju 9⁶, v [נָצַב] **Hoph.** **2.** *stock, stump* of tree Is 6¹³ ᵃ (in sim.), so v¹³ ᵇ (fig.; but prob. del. as gloss).

†I. [נָצָה] vb. fly (?);—only **Qal** Pf. 3 pl. (si vera l.) נָצוּ גַּם־נָעוּ La 4¹⁵ (of homeless exiles); text very dub.; rd perh. נָדוּ (cf. Gn 4^{12 14}), so Bu; Lohr (more venturesomely) כי לא ימצאו מָנוֹחַ, Buhl¹³ perhaps כִּי גַם נָגְעוּ.

†נוֹצָה n.f. plumage (cf. poss Ar. نَاصِيَةٌ *hair over forehead, fore-lock* of horse, Lane³⁰³³, v. also As. *na-as kappe*),—of eagle מְלֵא הַנּ׳ Ez 17³ (fig of Nebuch; + אֵבֶר, כָּנָף); also רַב נ׳ v⁷ (fig of kg of Egypt; + כָּנָף); of ostrich נֹצָה Jb 39¹³ (‖ אֶבְרָה + כנף; cf Di Bu). Here belongs prob. also בנֹצָתָהּ Lv 1¹⁶, rd בְּנֹצָתָהּ (Dr-Wh^{SBOT}), בנצתו (Sam), or (אֶת־) נֹצָתוֹ (cf. Di), *its feathers*; of bird for burnt-offering; 𝔊 σὺν τοῖς πτεροῖς, 𝔙 *et plumas*; so AV RVm, > with *its filth* (i e. of the crop) 𝔗^{Onk} 𝔖 Ges Kn Ke Kal Ew RV; meaning without evidence elsewhere.

†II. [נָצָה] vb. **Niph. Hiph.** struggle (NH *id*, Hithp. (Jastrow⁹²⁸); Aram. נְצָא, نْصَا *quarrel*; Ar. نَصَا *apprehendit, arripuit aliquem antiis suis*, Eth. ነጸየ: *vellere, evellere*, are perh. denom. from نَاصِيَةٌ (v. נוצה), so Thes),—**Niph.** recipr. *struggle with each other* · *Impf.* 3 mpl. יִנָּצוּ Ex 21²² (E), Lv 24¹⁰ (H), 2 S 14⁶; יִנָּ׳ יַחְדָּו Dt 25¹¹; *Pt.* נִצִּים Ex 2¹³ (E); all of physical struggle, wrestling, and the like. **Hiph.** *engage in a struggle* against. *Pf* 3 pl. הִצּוּ Nu 26⁹ (עַל); *Inf. cstr* sf. הַצֹּתָם v⁹ (עַל); הַצּוֹתוֹ אֶת ψ 60² (title); only here of *war*, hence Klo's suggestion (cf. Buhl¹³) הַכּוֹתוֹ is plausible (cf. 2 S 8^{3.5.9}).

†II. מַצָּה n.f. strife, contention,—abs. מ׳ Is 58⁴ Pr 13¹⁰ 17¹⁹.—I. מַצָּה v. מצץ.

†[מַצּוּת] n.f. id;—only sf. אַנְשֵׁי מַצֻּתֶךָ Is 41¹² i.e. *the men who strove with thee* (‖ אַנְשֵׁי מִלְחַמְתֶּךָ).

†III. [נָצָה] vb. fall in ruins;—**Qal** *Impf.* 3 fpl. עָרַיִךְ תִּצֶּינָה מאין יושב Je 4⁷ *thy cities shall fall in ruins* (read prob. תִּנָּצֶינָה **Niph.**). **Niph.** *Pt.* pl גַּלִּים נִצִּים *ruined heaps*, i e. ruin-heaps, 2 K 19²⁵ = Is 37²⁶.—On Je 2¹⁵ 9^{9 11} 46¹⁹ v. יצת.

נִצָּה v. נצץ. נֹצָתָהּ Lv 1¹⁶ v נוֹצָה supr.

†I [נָצַח] vb. be pre-eminent, enduring (Ecclus [Pi.] *make brilliant* 43^{5.13} [?] (cf. Oxford ed.^{xxiii}); NH נִצַּח *conquer*, etc.; Ph. נצח, Aram. נְצַח, نْصَح *shine, be illustrious, pre-eminent, victorious*; Ar نَصَحَ *be pure, reliable*; Eth. ነጽሐ: *be pure, innocent*; both classes of meaning prob. derived from *shine, be bright, brilliant*, v. also Dr^{1 S 15, 29}),—**Niph.** *Pt. act* f. נִצַּחַת Je 8⁵ *enduring* (מְשֻׁבָה *apostasy*).

Piel = *act as overseer, superintendent, director*, only Chr. and ψ-titles;—*Inf.* לְנַצֵּחַ 1 Ch 15²¹ + 4 t., pt. לַמְנַצֵּחַ Hb 3¹⁹ ψ 4¹ + 54 t ψψ; *pl.* מְנַצְּחִים 2 Ch 2^{1 17} 34¹³;—**1.** in building temple 2 Ch 2^{1 17} Ezr 3^{8 9}, cf. 2 Ch 34^{12.13}. **2.** in

ministry of house of 'י 1 Ch 23⁴. **3.** in liturgical service of song, על־השׁמינית, over the bass voices, leading them with לְנַצֵּחַ בְּכִנֹּרוֹת 1 Ch 15²¹; in titles of ψψ has prob. sim. meaning, = *musical director* or *choirmaster;* Gk. Vrss. of 2nd cent. A.D., Aq Theod Sym, and so Jer, think of Aram. *victorious*, but no clear explan.; 𝔊 εἰς τὸ τέλος (prob. לָמְנֶצַח) follows ordinary meaning of noun נֵצַח, which may be expl. in eschatological sense as referring to end of age of world after Euseb Theod; or for *full rendering* after De; neither satisfactory. Chr., near in date, gives the clue which is intrinsically prob.: לְ indicates, not assignment (nothing special in these ψψ to suggest it, and assignment of ψψ for such use a matter of course), but that these ψψ were taken by final editor from an older major Psalter known as the Director's Collection, cf. the still earlier collections known as (ל)דוד, (ל)בני קרח, (ל)אסף. The 55 ψψ with למנצח were taken 39 from Davidic, 9 from Korahite, and 5 from Asaphic Psalters; only 2 anonymous. Hb 3 originally belonged to Director's Psalter. This and other Director's ψψ have musical directions in titles. The Director's Psalter was prob. the prayer-book of synagogue of Gk. period, presupposed by our Hab., the collection of the twelve Minor Prophets, the prophetic canon, and Daniel (v. Br^Gen. Intr. 123^).

†I. **נֵצַח** **n.m.**^La 3,18^ **eminence, enduring, everlastingness, perpetuity** (לנצח Ecclus 40¹⁴ as **4** infr.);—נֵצַח 1 S 15²⁹ + 3 t.; נֶצַח Am 1¹¹ + 36 t.; sf. נִצְחִי La 3¹⁸; pl. נְצָחִים 34¹⁰;—**1.** *eminence:* נצח ישׂראל *the Eminence of Israel* ('י) 1 S 15²⁹ (Dr^Sam. 98^ *glory of Israel*); attribute of God 1 Ch 29¹¹ (‖ הוד, תפארת et al.). **2.** *enduring of life*, and so *life* itself as enduring: אָבַד נִצְחִי La 3¹⁸ *my endurance doth vanish* (De *sap* of life, v. II. 'נ). **3.** *endurance in time:* לנ' יְדַבֵּר ψ 74³ *perpetual desolations;* משׁאות נ' Pr 21²⁸ *speaketh continually* (?; v. Toy); עד־נ' ψ 49²⁰ *unto the end* (a long duration), so Jb 34³⁶. **4.** *everlastingness, ever*, usu. לָנֶצַח *for ever*, 2 S 2²⁶ Is 13²⁰ 25⁸ 28²⁸ 33²⁰ 57¹⁶ Je 3⁵ 50³⁹ Am 8⁷ Hb 1⁴ ψ 9^7.19^ 10¹¹ 44²⁴ 49¹⁰ 52⁷ 68¹⁷ 74^1.10.19^ 77⁹ 79⁵ 89⁴⁷ 103⁹ Jb 4²⁰ 14²⁰ 20⁷ 23⁷ 36⁷ La 5²⁰; לנצח נצחים (cf. עולם עולמים) Is 34¹⁰; seldom abbr. נֶצַח Am 1¹¹ (לָנ' 𝔊 We Now GASm), Je 15¹⁸ ψ 13² 16¹¹.

II. **נצח** (√ of foll.; cf. Ar. نَضَحَ, نَضَخَ Lane ^2806, 2807^ *sprinkle;* Ba^ES 52^ cp. Eth. ነዝኀ: *spargere, aspergere* Di ^677^ (rare)).

†II. [**נֵצַח**] **n.m. juice** of grapes, fig. of **blood, gore**;—only sf. נִצְחָם Is 63^3.6^.

†**נְצִיחַ** **n.pr.m.** head of a family of Nethinim Ezr 2⁵⁴ (𝔊 Νασους, A Νεθιε) = Ne 7⁵⁶ 𝔊 Ασεια, A Νεισεια; 𝔊L Νεσια in both.

[**נָצַל**]~212~ **vb.** not in **Qal**; **Pi. strip, plunder; Niph. deliver oneself, be delivered; Hiph. snatch away, deliver** (Ecclus Hiph. Pt. מצלה *delivering* 40^24 b^ (Levi conj. יציל 40^24 a^); NH Hiph. = BH; BAram. Haph. *id.;* Syr. ܢܨܠ *pour out;* Ar. نَصَلَ intrans. *tincturam exuit emisitque* barba, ex cuspide *excidit* sagitta, etc., Kam Frey; Eth. III. ተናጸለ: *evulsum* vel *abruptum excidere e suo loco*, Di^698^);—†**Niph.** *Pf.* 1 pl. נִצַּלְנוּ Je 7¹⁰; *Impf.* יִנָּצֵל Dt 23¹⁶, + 1 s. אִנָּצְלָה ψ 69¹⁵, + 8 t. Impf.; *Inf.* הִנָּצֵל Is 20⁶ + 3 t. —**1.** reflex. *tear oneself away, deliver oneself:* abs. Pr 6³ Ez 14^16.18^ 2 K 19¹¹ = Is 37¹¹; c. מִיַּד Pr 6⁵; מֵעִם... אֶל *escape from—unto* Dt 23¹⁶. **2.** passive, *be torn out or away* מִפִּי הָאֲרִי Am 3¹²; *be delivered*, abs. Gn 32³¹ Je 7¹⁰ ψ 33¹⁶ Mi 4¹⁰; מִפְּנֵי Is 20⁶; מִכַּף Hb 2⁹; מִן ψ 69¹⁵.

†**Pi.** *Pf.* 2 mpl. נִצַּלְתֶּם Ex 3²²; *Impf.* יְנַצֵּל Ez 14¹⁴ + 2 t.;—**1.** *strip off, spoil*, abs. 2 Ch 20²⁵; c. acc. pers. Ex 3²² 12³⁶ (J). **2.** *deliver*, c. acc. נַפְשָׁם Ez 14¹⁴.

Hiph.~190~ *Pf.* הִצִּיל Ex 12²⁷; 2 ms. הִצַּלְתָּ Ex 5²³ + 50 t. Pf.; *Impf.* יַצִּיל 2 K 17³⁹; יַצֵּל Gn 31⁹; + 63 t. Impf.; *Imv.* הַצֵּל Pr 24¹¹; הַצִּילָה ψ 22²¹; sf. הַצִּילֵנִי Gn 32¹² + 24 t. Imv.; *Inf. abs.* הַצֵּל 2 K 18³⁰ + 4 t.; *cstr.* הַצִּיל Gn 37²² + 23 t. Inf.; *Pt.* מַצִּיל Dt 32³⁹ + 16 t. Pt.—†**1.** *take away, snatch away*, e.g. property Gn 31^9.16^ (E) Ho 2¹¹, prey from the mouth of animals 1 S 17³⁵ Am 3¹² Ez 34¹⁰, words of 'י from the mouth ψ 119⁴³; וְאֵין מַצִּיל בֵּינֵיהֶם 2 S 14⁶ *and there was none to tear them apart* (two fighting); וְהִצִּיל עֵינֵנוּ 2 S 20⁶ *and take away our eye* (elude our sight, Ges; Ew We after 𝔊 *cast shadow* over our eye, denom. from צֵל; Bö Th after 𝔖 *tear away* our eye, harm us irretrievably, v. Dr^1 8 26, 2^; HPS *escape from us* [מִמֶּנּוּ, as 𝔊L], cf. Bu [(וְנִצַּל)]). †**2.** *rescue, recover*, e.g. cities Ju 11²⁶; wives and property 1 S 30^8.18.22^. **3.** *deliver from:* **a.** *enemies and troubles*, abs. 1 S 12²¹ Pr 19¹⁹ Is 50² Je 39¹⁷; †אֵין מַצִּיל Ju 18²⁸ Jb 5⁴ 10⁷ ψ 7³ 50²² 71¹¹ Is 5²⁹ 42²² 43¹³ Dn 8⁴⁷ Ho 5¹⁴ Mi 5⁷; c. acc. Gn 18⁸ (E), Ex 5²³ 12²⁷ (J), Dt 23¹⁵ + 39 t.;

†הִצִּיל נַפְשׁוֹ Is 44[20] 47[14] Ez 3[19, 21] 14[20] 33[9]; c. מִן *from* Mi 5[5] + 25 t.; מִיַּד *from the hand* or *power of* Gn 32[12] Ex 2[19] (J) + 57 t.; מִתַּחַת יַד Ex 18[10] (E), †מִכַּף 2 S 14[16] 19[10] 22[1] = ψ 18[1], 2 K 20[6] = Is 38[6], 2 Ch 32[11] Ezr 8[31]. †**b.** *from death* Pr 11[4] 12[6]; ממות Jos 2[13] (J), ψ 33[19] 56[14] Pr 10[2] = 11[4]; מִשְּׁאוֹל ψ 86[13] Pr 23[14]. †**4.** *deliver from sin and guilt* (in late writings), מִכָּל־פְּשָׁעַי ψ 39[9] *from all my transgressions;* מִדָּמִים ψ 51[16] *from bloodguiltiness,* הַצִּילֵנוּ וְכַפֵּר עַל־חַטֹּאתֵינוּ ψ 79[9] *deliver us and cover over all our sins;* prob. also כְּאִמְרָתְךָ הַצִּילֵנִי ψ 119[170].

†**Hoph.** *Pt.* כְּאוּד מֻצָּל מִשְּׂרֵפָה—, מֻצָּל Am 4[11] *as a brand plucked out of the burning;* מֵאֵשׁ Zc 3[2] *from the fire.*

†**Hithp.** וַיִּתְנַצְּלוּ אֶת־עֶדְיָם Ex 33[6] (E) *and they stripped themselves* of their ornaments.

†הַצָּלָה **n.f.** deliverance Est 4[14] (old Sem. Inf. in *ā* acc. to Ba[NB 90], Inf. also Sta[§ 621 c] cf. Ges[§ 85 c] Ko[ii 1. 402]; prob. here by Aram. infl.)

[נִצָּן] v. II. נצץ

†I. [נָצַץ] **vb. shine, sparkle** (NH נִצְנֵץ; akin to Ar. نَاصَ *sparkle, flash,* 𝔗 נְצָא);—**Qal** *Pt.* וְנֹצְצִים כְּעֵין נְחֹשֶׁת Ez 1[7] (of cherubim);—Perles[Anal 46] prop נוציצם *their plumage* (נ׳ ‖ form of נוֹצָה), cf. Ew.

†נִיצוֹץ **n.[m.] spark**;—Is 1[31] (fig.).

†I. [נֵץ] **n.m.** only sf. נִצָּה Gn 40[10], v. foll.

†נִצָּה **n.f. blossom** (perhaps fr. above √, blossom, flower, as *shining* amid leaves),—abs. נ׳ of vine Is 18[5] (‖ פֶּרַח, = *berry-cluster* acc. to Di Kit Che[Hpt] cf. J. Derenb[ZAW v (1885), 301 f., vi (1886), 94 f.]); sf. נִצָּתוֹ Jb 15[33] (of olive); read also נִצָּתָהּ Gn 40[10] (of vine) for MT נִצָּה, cf. Di Holz.

†[נִצָּן] **n.[m.]** id., only pl. נִצָּנִים Ct 2[12].

†[נָצַץ] **vb. denom. bloom, blossom** (NH *id.;* Jewish-Aram. נְצַץ *id*);—**Hiph.** *Pf.* 3 pl. הֵנֵצוּ Ct 6[11] (no dagh., v. Ko[i. 381] Ges[§ 67 8 R. 11]) the pomegranates *have put forth blossoms,* so 7[13]; *Impf* 3 ms. יָנֵאץ Ec 12[5] the almond-tree *wears blossoms.*

II. נצץ (√ of foll.; cf. Ph. n.pr.loc. אי־נצם *isle (coast) of hawks,* Lzb[323, 326]; Syr. ܢܨܐ *hawk;* 𝔗 נַצָּא (cf. Me[Chrest. 241]))

†II. נֵץ **n.m.** a bird of prey, generic name, incl. **hawk** and **falcon** (Tristr[NHB]; *accipiter* Bo Hieroz ii. 266 ff.; ed. Rosenm. iii. 8 ff. cf. Now[Arch i. 116]);—unclean bird, Lv 11[16] (P), Dt 14[15] (varieties, לְמִינֵהוּ); bird of passage Jb 39[26].

†I [נָצַר] **vb. watch, guard, keep** (NH *id, observe;* As. *naṣâru, watch over, protect;* OAram. נצר *protect* Lzb[324] Cook[83]; Palm. in n.pr. Vog[150, 4] Cook[124]; Aram נְטַר, ܢܛܰܪ (cf. Wetzst in De[Job (2)] on 27[18]); Ar نَظَرَ *look at, consider, examine* (نَاطُورٌ, *overseer* is Aram. loan-word Fra[138]); Sab. להנצרהמו *to aid them* Hal[Rev Sém. iv (1896) 71]; Eth. ነጸረ: *spectare, intueri,* etc., Di[701],—cf. also נמר);—**Qal** *Pf.* 3 ms. sf. נְצָרָתַם ψ 119[129]; 1 s. נָצַרְתִּי ψ 119[22.56.100], 3 mpl. נָצָרוּ Pr 22[12]; *Impf* יִצֹּר Pr 3[1], sf. יִצְּרֶנְהוּ (Ges § 58, 4 R.) Dt 32[10], f sf תִּנְצְרֶכָּה Pr 2[11] (Ges § 58, 4 R), 1 s אֶצֹּר ψ 119[69], אֶצְּרָה ψ 119[34.115]; ψ אֶצְּרָה 119[145]; sf. אֶצָּרְךָ Is 42[6] 49[8] (Ges Bo Ew al. from יצר); אֶצֳּרֶנָּה Is 27[3]; 3 mpl. יִצְּרוּ Pr 20[28]; יִנְצֹרוּ Dt 33[9] (on forms v Ges § 66, 2 R 1) + 15 t. Impf.; *Imv* נְצֹר ψ 34[14] + 3 t.; נִצְּרָה ψ 141[3] (d. f. dirim. Ges § 20, 2 b); sf. נִצְּרֶהָ Pr 4[13]; *Inf. abs.* נָצוֹר Na 2[2]; *cstr* נְצֹר Pr 2[8]; *Pt.* נֹצֵר Pr 28[7], נֹצֵר Ex 34[7] + 7 t.; sf. נֹצְרָהּ Is 27[3]; pl. נֹצְרִים 2 K 17[9] 18[8], etc.; *pass* נָצוּר Ez 6[12]; pl. נְצוּרִים Is 65[4] (𝔊 ἐν τοῖς σπηλαίοις, בַּמְּעָרוֹת); cstr. נְצוּרֵי (Kt נצירי only here) Is 49[6]; f. נְצוּרָה Is 1[8] (Di rds. נְצוֹרָה Niph Pt. √צור); cstr נְצֻרַת Pr 7[10]; pl נְצֻרוֹת Is 48[6] (Che rds בְּצֻרוֹת).

1. *Watch, guard, keep,* a vineyard Jb 27[18] (cf. Wetzst in De[Job (2) ad loc]), Is 27[3.3], fig-tree Pr 27[18], fortification Na 2[2], נֹצְרִים *watchmen* Je 31[6]; מִגְדַּל נ׳ *tower of watchmen* 2 K 17[9] 18[8]; in ethical sense of men, guarding the mouth Pr 13[3], the way Pr 16[17], לֵב Pr 4[23]; the tongue מֵרָע ψ 34[14]; c עַל, over the door of the lips ψ 141[3]; of God נֹצֵר הָאָדָם Jb 7[20] (thou) *watcher of men* (iron.).

2. *Guard from dangers, preserve,* c. acc., subj. God or his attributes Dt 32[10] ψ 25[21] 31[24] 40[12] 61[8] Is 26[3] 42[6] 49[8] Pr 2[8] 20[28] 22[12]; נֹצֵר נַפְשׁ Pr 24[12]; c. acc. and מִן *from* which ψ 12[8] 32[7] 64[2] 140[2.5]. In WisdLit subj. is abstr.: חכמה Pr 4[6]; תבונה Pr 2[11]; צדקה Pr 13[6]; נְצוּרֵי יִשְׂרָאֵל Is 49[6] *preserved of Israel.*

3. *Guard with fidelity, keep, observe:* of ׳, נֹצֵר חֶסֶד לָאֲלָפִים Ex 34[7] (J); elsewhere of man observing the covenant Dt 33[9] (poem) ψ 25[10], the divine law ψ 78[7] 105[45] 119[2.22.33.34.56.69.100.115.129.145];

commands of parents Pr 6^{20} 28^{7}; and discipline of Wisdom Pr 3$^{1.21}$ 4^{13} 5^{2}.

4. *Guard, keep secret*, dub: נְצֻרוֹת *secret things* Is 48^{6}, נצורים *secret places* Is 65^{4} (see forms above); נְצֻרַת לֵב *secret, wily minded* Pr 7^{10} (of harlot, so RVm *close*, i e. *secretive*).

5. *Kept close, blockaded*, dub: הַנָּצוּר *the blockaded* (so Ew Hi Co Toy; but Ke Bth Kau *preserved;* Hi Co Bth Toy del. (והנשאר) Ez 6^{12}, עיר נצורה *blockaded city* Is 1^{8} (see form above), נֹצְרִים *blockaders* Je 4^{16} (but 𝔊 *συστροφαί* = צררים i. e *foes*)

נצורים v I. נצר **Qal** *Pt pass.*

†[נָצִיר] **adj. preserved**;—only pl. cstr. נצירי Is 49^{6} Kt, Qr נצוּרי q v. נצר *Pt*

נִצְּרָה ψ 141^{3} v I נצר Qal Imv.

II. **נצר** (√of foll, cf. perh. Ar. نَضُرَ *be fresh, bright, grow green;* Ecclus 40^{15} נוֹצֵר, marg נֵצֶר, *branch*, NH נֵצֶר = BH).

†נֵ֫צֶר **n m. sprout, shoot**, in fig uses:—נ׳ abs Is 11^{1} 14^{19} (sim.); cstr 60^{21} (נ׳ מַטָּעַי), Dn 11^{7} (נ׳ מִשָּׁרָשֶׁיהָ ,מִנ׳ שָׁרָשֶׁיהָ, but 𝔊 Bev 'poss')

†I [נָקַב] **vb. pierce** (NH *id.*, SI$^{11.4}$ הנקבה *the piercing, boring through;* Aram. נְקַב, نقب *id;* נִקְבָא *hole*, etc., Sinait. n.pr.m נקבו Eut$^{441.2}$, נקיבו Eut$^{99.2, 153.2}$ (Lzb$^{325.326}$ Cook^{83}); As *nakbu, depth, spring* of water, Ar نَقَبَ *perforate, pierce, scrutinize*, etc, نَقِيبَة *sagacity*, etc, نَقِيب *leader, chief* (one who *scrutinizes*)), —**Qal** *Pf.* 3 fs sf נְקָבָהּ 2 K 18^{21} Is 36^{6}, 2 ms נָקַבְתָּ Hb 3^{14}, *Impf* יִנְּקָב־ Jb 40^{24}, וַיִּקֹּב 2 K 12^{10}, sf יִקְּבֻהוּ Is 62^{2}, 2 ms תקב Jb 40^{26}; *Imv* ms נָקְבָה Gn 30^{28}, *Pt pass* נָקוּב Hg 1^{6}, pl cstr נְקֻבֵי Am 6^{1},—**1.** *pierce, bore*, c. acc. 2 K 18^{21} = Is 36^{6}, Hb 3^{14} (all in fig), Jb 40$^{24.26}$, c acc cogn + בְּ, וַיִּקֹּב חֹר בְּדַלְתּוֹ 2 K 12^{10} *and he bored a hole in its lid;* צְרוֹר נָקוּב Hg 1^{6} *a bag pierced*, i e. with a hole in it. **2.** *prick off*, designate, wages Gn 30^{28} (J), name Is 62^{2} (י׳ subj; cf. **Niph.**); pt pass *noted, distinguished* Am 6^{1}. **Niph.** *Pf* 3 pl in phr. (אֲשֶׁר) נקבו בשמות *who were pricked off, designated, by name* Nu 1^{17} 1 Ch 12^{32} (v^{31} van d H), 16^{41} 2 Ch 28^{15} 31^{19}, cf Ezr 8^{20}

†I [נֶ֫קֶב] **n.[m.]** term techn. of jeweller's work, prob. some hole or cavity (Hi-Sm Co Berthol, Toy^{Hpt} leaves untransl),—only pl sf. תֻּפֶּיךָ וּנְקָבֶיךָ Ez 28^{13} *thy sockets and thy grooves* (Da), or *thy settings and thy sockets*

†II נֶ֫קֶב **n.pr.loc.** only in אֲדָמִי הַנּ׳ Jos 19^{33} (𝔊 Αρμε καὶ Ναβωκ; A Αρμαι καὶ Νακεβ; 𝔊L Αδεμμη αννεκβ); on border of Naphtali; appar. a *pass* (Ar نَقْب, *road between mountains*)

†נְקֵבָה **n f. female** (*perforata* (Ba$^{NB 166}$); so Thes and most, > another view in Schwally ZAW xi (1891), 181 f, Idiot 67, NH = BH; Aram. נוּקְבָא, נוקבתא, ܢܩܒܬܐ, ܢܩܒܐ);—alw. abs. נ׳ Je 31^{22} + 21 t (all Pent, and all P exc Dt 4^{16}) **1.** *woman* (or female child) Je 31^{22} (opp גֶּבֶר), Gn 1^{27} 5^{2} Lv 12$^{5.7}$ 15^{33} 27$^{4.5.6.7}$ Nu 5^{3} (all opp. זָכָר), Nu 31^{15} **2.** *female animal* Gn 6^{19} 7$^{3.9.16}$ Lv 3$^{1.6}$ (all opp זָכָר), 4$^{28.32}$ 5^{6}.—Dt 4^{16} (opp. זָכָר) may include both women and animals

†I מַקֶּ֫בֶת **n.f. hammer** (by means of which one *drives in* nails and pegs);—abs. מ׳ Ju 4^{21} (+ יָתֵד), elsewhere pl. מַקָּבוֹת 1 K 6^{7} (+ גַּרְזֶן); Is 44^{12} Je 10^{4} (+ מַסְמְרוֹת)—On name *Maccabee* v. Schurer$^{Gesch\ 1\ 158}$

†II מַקֶּ֫בֶת **n.f. hole, excavation**;—only cstr. מ׳ בּוֹר Is 51^{1} (fig), *excavation of a pit*, = quarry (|| צוּר)

†II. [נָקַב] **vb. curse** (perh. akin to I. נקב, perh secondary format. fr. קָבַב, q.v. for forms קַב, יִקֹּב, etc),—**Qal** *Inf.* sf. נָקְבוֹ שֵׁם Lv 24^{16}, *Pt.* נֹקֵב שֵׁם י׳ v^{16} (on text v Di, Gei Urschrift 274 Dalman$^{Adonai\ 44\ f.}$).

I **נקד** (√of foll., NH נָקַד *point, furnish with points*, cf. Syr. ܢܩܕ (very rare) PS^{2453}, n ܢܘܩܕܐ, but also ܢܘܩܙܐ *point, mark*, vbs. perh denom., Ar نَقَطَ *point* or *dot* (letter, word, etc), II. *make specks, spots*, on garment, etc, prob. loan-word Fra^{195}; Di$^{Lex.\ 648}$ cp Eth. ነቀዘ: *be decayed, worm-eaten* (of wood, bread, etc.)).

†נָקֹד **adj. speckled**;—only of sheep and goats, נ׳ Gn 30$^{32.33}$, fpl נקדות v^{35} (all || טָלוּא), mpl נקדים v^{39} (|| *id* + עֲקֻדִּים,—all these J); mpl. also 31$^{8.8}$ and (+ עֲקֻדִּים, בְּרֻדִּים) v$^{10.12}$ (all E).

†[נִקֻּד] **n.[m.]** perh **what is crumbled or easily crumbles, crumb** (cf. נְקֻדָּה),—only pl **1.** *crumbs* כֹּל לֶחֶם צֵידָם יָבֵשׁ הָיָה נִקֻּדִים Jos 9^{5} *all the bread of their provision was dry* (and) *become crumbs* (𝔊 βεβρωμένος[οι]; 𝔙 *in frusta comminuti*), cf. יָבֵשׁ וְהָיָה נ׳ v^{12} (v Di Benn). **2.** appar. a kind of (hard) biscuit or cake 1 K 14^{3} (brought as present; + לֶחֶם, etc.).

†[נְקֻדָּה] **n.f.** point, or drop;—only pl. cstr תּוֹרֵי זָהָב נַעֲשֶׂה־לָּךְ עִם נְקֻדּוֹת הַכָּסֶף Ct 1^{11} rows (strings or chains) of gold will we make for thee, with *points of silver.*

II נקד (√of foll.; cf. Ar. نَقَدٌ *a kind of small sheep* with very abundant wool (Jacob Altarab Bed Leben, 1897, 63), whence نَقَّادٌ *shepherd* of this kind of sheep, נקד perh. MI^{30}; As. *nâḳidu* Dl$^{HWB\ 479}$; cf. NH נוֹקֵד (rare)).

†נֹקֵד **n.m.** sheep-raiser, -dealer, or -tender (Lag$^{NB\ 106}$);—abs. נ׳ only 2 K 3^4 (of Mesha, king of Moab); pl. אֲשֶׁר בַּנֹּקְדִים מִתְּקוֹעַ Am 1^1 (of Amos, v Dr; cf 7^{14}, where read נוקד for בוקר acc. to We Now Dr, not GASm, v. Bu infr.); perh. gloss, cf. Bu$^{Kohut\ Memorial\ 108\ f.}$ Now$^{ad\ loc}$

†נְקוֹדָא **n.pr.m.** head of a family of Nethinim Ezr $2^{48.60}$ = Ne $7^{50.62}$, 𝔊 Νεκωδα, Νεχωδα.

†[נָקָה] **vb.** be empty(?), clean (Ecclus 16^{11b} Niph. *Impf.* ינקה *be unpunished*, so 40^{15} 31^5 = Pr 28^{20}; NH Pi. = BH; Aram. נְקָא Pa. = BH, adj. נְקָא *clean;* Ph. נקי adj. *pure;* Palm. נקא *be clean* (perh.) in n pr. Sachau$^{ZMG\ xxxv\ (1881),\ 735}$ Lzb^{325}; As. *nâḳû, pour out, pour libation, make offering, niḳû, libation, offering;* OAram. נקיה perhaps = נְקִיָּה *libation* (Lzb^{326}), cf. Syr. ܢܩܝܐ Cook^{83}; Syr. ܢܩܐ Pa. *pour out, make a libation;* on the other hand, Ar. نَقِيَ *purus, mundus fuit* Kam Frey; II. *cleanse,* etc, Lane^{3037}.—Orig meaning prob *empty out,* hence *pour* and *be empty, clean*),—**Qal** *Inf. abs.* נָקֹה Je 49^{12} (נָקֹה תִּנָּקֶה, prob. err. for הנקה ת׳, cf. Je 25^{29}).

Niph. *Pf* 3 ms נִקָּה Zc 5^3 + 5 t.; f. נִקָּתָה Nu 5^{28}, נִקָּתָה Is 3^{26}; 2 ms. נִקִּיתָ Gn 24^8; 1 s נִקֵּיתִי Ju 15^3 + 2 t; *Impf* יִנָּקֶה Pr 6^{29} + 6 t.; 2 ms. תִּנָּקֶה Gn 24^{41} + 2 t; pl. תִּנָּקוּ Je $25^{29.29}$; *Imv* הִנָּקִי Nu 5^{19}, *Inf.* הִנָּקֵה Je 25^{29},—**1.** *be cleaned out,* of a plundered city Is 3^{26}, *purged out,* of liars and perjurers Zc $5^{3\ 3}$. **2.** *be clean, free from guilt, innocent,* Je 2^{35} c מִן, מִפֶּשַׁע ψ 19^{14}; מֵעָוֺן Nu 5^{31} (P); מִפְּלִשְׁתִּים *from* (at the hands of) *the Philistines* Ju 15^3. **3.** *be free, exempt from punishment,* abs. Ex 21^{19} (E) Nu 5^{28} (P) 1 S 26^9, לֹא יִנָּקֶה Pr 6^{29} 11^{21} 16^5 17^5 $19^{5\ 9}$ 28^{20} Je $25^{29.29.29}$ 49^{12b}, נָקֹה תִנָּקֶה v^{12a}. **4.** *free, exempt from obligation,* c. מִן, from oaths Gn $24^{8.41}$ (J); מִמֵּי הַמָּרִים from effects of drinking the bitter water Nu 5^{19} (P).

Piel *Pf.* 1 s. נִקֵּיתִי Jo 4^{21} (𝔊 𝔖 נִקַּמְתִּי; so Now SS Buhl); *Impf.* 3 ms. יְנַקֶּה Ex 20^7 + 2 t.; יְנַקֶּה Nu 14^{18} Na 1^3; 2 ms. sf. תְּנַקֵּנִי Jb 9^{28} 10^{14}; תְּנַקֵּהוּ 1 K 2^9; 1 s sf. אֲנַקֶּךָּ Je 30^{11} 46^{28}; *Imv* sf. נַקֵּנִי ψ 19^{13}; *Inf. abs.* נַקֵּה Ex 34^7 + 4 t.;—**1.** *hold innocent, acquit,* Jb 9^{28}; מֵעֲוֺנִי Jb 10^{14}; מִנִּסְתָּרוֹת ψ 19^{13}. **2.** *leave unpunished:* of man, c. acc. 1 K 2^9, elsewhere of God: abs. נַקֵּה לֹא יְנַקֶּה Ex $34^{7\ 7}$ = Nu $14^{18.18}$ (all J) = Na $1^{3.3}$; c. acc. לֹא יְנַקֶּה Ex 20^7 = Dt 5^{11}; נַקֵּה לֹא אֲנַקֶּךָּ Je $30^{11\ 11}$ = $46^{28.28}$, cf. Jo $4^{21\ 21}$ (but v. supr.).

†נָקִי **adj.** clean, free from, exempt;—נ׳ Gn 24^{41} + 31 t; cstr. נְקִי ψ 24^4; pl. נקיים Je 2^{34}, נְקִיִּם Gn 44^{10} + 6 t.,—**1.** *free from guilt, clean, innocent,* ‖ צַדִּיק: נָקִי וְצַדִּיק Ex 23^7 (E), נָקִי *innocent person* Jb 4^7 17^8 $22^{19.30}$ 27^{17} ψ 10^8 15^5 Pr 1^{11}; נקיים Jb 9^{23}; דם נקי *innocent blood,* first used in D, Dt 19^{10} 27^{25} 1 S 19^5 2 K 21^{16} 24^4 ψ 94^2 106^{38} Pr 6^{17} Is 59^7 Je 7^6 22^3 26^{15}; דם הנקי Dt 19^{13} 1 K 24^4 Je 22^{17}, הדם הנקי Dt 21^9, דם נְקִי (מֵעִם ^ +) 2 S 3^{28}; נְקִי כַפַּיִם Je 19^4; אביונים נקיים ψ 24^4, Je 2^{34}. **2.** *free from punishment* Ex 21^{28} (E) 2 S 14^9. **3.** *free, exempt from obligations* Gn 44^{10} (J); from service in war Nu 32^{22} (P; + מִן pers, v. מִן **2 d**), Dt 24^5 1 K 15^{22} (cf Ar نَقِيَ and Wetzst ZMG xxii (1868), 129); c. מִן, from oaths Gn 24^{41} (J) Jos $2^{17\ 19.20}$ (JE)

†נָקִיא **adj.** innocent,—דָּם נָקִיא *innocent blood* Jo 4^{19} Jon 1^{14} (both Kt; Qr נָקִי).

†נִקָּיוֹן **n.[m.]** innocency,—נ׳ ψ 26^6 73^{13}; נִקָּיֹן Ho 8^5; cstr. נִקְיוֹן Am 4^6; נִקְיֹן Gn 20^5;—**1.** *freedom from guilt, innocency:* נ׳ כַּפַּי Gn 20^5 (R^{JE}), ארחץ בנ׳ כַּפָּי ψ 26^6 *I will wash my hands in innocency* = 73^{13}. **2.** *freedom from punishment* Ho 8^5. **3.** in physical sense, נִקְיוֹן שִׁנַּיִם *cleanness of teeth* (without food) Am 4^6 (but read perh after 𝔊 𝔖 𝔗 קֵהָיוֹן *bluntness,* so Lag$^{BN\ 201}$).

†[מְנַקִּיָּה] **n.f.** sacrificial bowl;—pl מְנַקִּיּוֹת Je 52^{19}; מְנַקִּיֹּת Nu 4^7; sf. מְנַקִּיֹּתָיו Ex 25^{29} 37^{16}.

נקט v. קוט

†[נָקַם] **vb.** avenge, take vengeance (Ecclus 46^{1c} להנקם נקמי אויב (Niph. + acc. cogn), נקם n. also 12^6 (cf. Dt 32^{41}), 39^{30} 48^7; NH נָקַם esp. in deriv.; Aram. נקם (rare), ܢܩܡ in der species; Ar. نَقَمَ *take vengeance* (عَلَى *upon*), Lane^{3037}; cf. Eth. ቀየመ: Di^{453} *vindictae studium, ultionis cupido;* As. *iḳḳimu, ven-*

geance, requital, is poss. fr. √אקם Jager $^{BAS\ ii.}$ יא);—**Qal** *Pf* 3 ms sf. נְקָמַנִי 1 S 24^{13}, *Impf.* יקּוֹם Dt 32^{43}; יִקֹּם Jos 10^{13}; 2 ms תקם Lv 19^{18}, *Inf abs* נָקֹם Ex 21^{20}, cstr נקם Ez 24^{8} 25^{12}; *Imv.* נקם Nu 31^{2}; *Pt.* נֹקֵם Na 1^{2} + 3 t., f. נֹקֶמֶת Lv 26^{25},—**1.** *avenge, take vengeance:* **a.** God subj. דַּם עֲבָדָיו יקּוֹם Dt 32^{43} *the blood of his servants he avengeth* (against those who slew them) (+ 1 K 2^{5} 𝔊L Klo), 'נ abs Na 1$^{2.2}$ c ל (agst. Nineveh) Na 1^{2}; נ' נָקָם (agst. Jerus.) Ez 24^{8}; עַל־עֲלִילוֹתָם *on their doings* (his people's) ψ 99^{8}, נ' נקם ברית Lv 26^{25} (H) *the vengeance of the covenant* (against those who break it), נְקָמַנִי, 1 S 24^{13}, c. מִן of pers *from* whom vengeance is taken (cp Je 20^{10}) **b.** *Israel and its leaders against their enemies,* נ' נקמה c. מִן against whom Nu 31^{2} (P), c. acc. יִקֹּם אֹיְבָיו Jos 10^{13} (poem). **c.** Edom against Judah נ' נקם ל Ez 25^{12}. **d.** in administration of justice agst. murder Ex 21^{20} (E). **2.** *entertain revengeful feelings* (opp. אהב) against neighbour forbidden Lv 19^{18} (H).

Niph *Pf* 1 s נִקַּמְתִּי Ju 15^{7} 1 S 14^{24}, 3 mpl. נקמו Ez 25^{12}, *Impf* יִנָּקֵם Ex 21^{20}, 1 s אִנָּקְמָה Ju 16^{28} Is 1^{24}, 3 mpl יִנָּקֵמוּ Ez 25^{15}, *Inf* הִנָּקֵם Je 46^{10} + 2 t, *Imv.* הִנָּקֵם Je 15^{15}, pl הִנָּקְמוּ Je 50^{15} —**1.** *avenge oneself,* **a.** י' subj. c מִן of adversary Is 1^{24} Je 46^{10}, c מִן advers, ל for whom Je 15^{15}; c. ב adversary Je 50^{15}. **b.** of Israel and champions c מִן Ju 16^{28} 1 S 14^{24} Est 8^{13}; c ב Ju 15^{7} 1 S 18^{25}. **c.** of enemies against Israel נ' נקם ב Ez 25^{15}; c. ב Ez 25^{12}. **2.** *suffer vengeance* (of law against murder) Ex 21^{20} (E). **Piel** *Pf.* 1 s. נִקַּמְתִּי 2 K 9^{7} Je 51^{36},—*avenge,* י' subj. נ' דְּמֵי מיד 2 K 9^{7} *blood at hands of;* נ' נִקְמָתֵךְ Je 51^{36} *take vengeance for thee.*

Hoph. *Impf.* יֻקַּם Gn 4^{24} Ex 21^{21}, יֻקָּם Gn 4^{15} *be avenged, vengeance be taken* (for blood).

Hithp. *Impf.* תִּתְנַקֵּם Je 5$^{9.29}$ 9^{8}, *Pt.* מִתְנַקֵּם ψ 8^{3} 44^{17}; *avenge oneself,* י' subj. לא תתנקם נַפְשִׁי ב' Je 5$^{9.29}$ 9^{8}; of Israel's enemies אוֹיֵב וּמִתְנַקֵּם ψ 8^{3} 44^{17}.

† נָקָם **n.m. vengeance,**—נ' Dt 32^{35} + 14 t; cstr נְקַם Lv 26^{25} Ju 16^{28};—**1.** taken by God, abs. Ez 24^{8} ψ 58^{11}; נ' ברית *vengeance of the covenant* Lv 26^{25} (H); יום נקם Is 34^{8} 61^{2} 63^{4}; בגדי נ' Is 59^{17} לִי נָקָם ושלם Dt 32^{35}; לקח נ' Is 47^{3}; נ' יבוא Is 35^{4}, c acc. adversary עשׂה נ' Mi 5^{14}; c. ל advers השיב נ' Dt 32$^{41.43}$. **2.** Samson against Philistines, נקם נ' Ju 16^{28}. **3.** enemies against Judah, abs Ez 25$^{12.15}$; individual enemy יום נ' Pr 6^{34}

† נְקָמָה **n.f. vengeance** (on format. cf. Lag $^{BN\ 143}$);—נ' Je 46^{10} + 3 t; cstr. נִקְמַת Nu 31^{2} + 7 t.; *sf.* נִקְמָתִי Ez 25^{14} + 7 t. sfs.; pl. נְקָמוֹת Ju 11^{36} + 5 t., נְקָמֹת 2 S 22^{48};—**1.** *vengeance* of God, abs. Ez 25^{14}; נקם נ' Je 51^{36}, נקמת יום נ' Je 51^{6}; עת נ' 94^{1}, אֵל נְקָמוֹת ψ 79^{10}; דם Je 46^{10}, נ' יהוה 50$^{15.28}$ 51^{11}; נ' הֵיכָלוֹ 50^{28} 51^{11}; c. ב of adversary, נתן נ' Ez 25$^{14.17}$; עשׂה נ' Ez 25^{17}; c מִן of adversary נתן נ' 2 S 4^{8} עשׂה נ' Ju 11^{36}, נִקְמָתְךָ מֵהֶם Je 11^{20} 20^{12}; c לְ for whom נתן נ' 2 S 22^{48} = ψ 18^{48}. **2.** of Israel and its chiefs נקם נ' מן Nu 31^{2} (P), c. ב', נתן נ' Nu 31^{3} (P); עשׂה נ' ψ 149^{7}. **3.** enemies of Israel abs. La 3^{60}; עשׂה בנקמה Ez 25^{15}; of Jeremiah לקח נ' מן Je 20^{10}.

†[נָקַע] **vb.** be [severed, fig.] **alienated, estranged** (cf Ar. نَقَعَ *split, rend, sacrifice* RS $^{Sem\ i\ 471\ f.,\ 2d\ ed.\ 491}$, Eth. ነቀዐ: *split up, open* (intrans) Di ^{647}, NH נָקַע *cleft,* Syr ܢܩܥ *id*);—**Qal** *Pf* 3 fs. נָקְעָה נַפְשִׁי מֵעָל Ez 23^{18} *my soul was estranged from* her sister (‖ יָקַע), cf. v$^{22.28}$ (both c. מן).

†I [נָקַף] **vb. strike off** (NH *strike, wound,* Aram. נְקַף *id.;* Ar. نَقَفَ *fregit* caput, ut cerebrum appareret; Vulg. Ar. *snap* with the finger (Dozy $^{ii.\ 716}$); As *nakpu* prob = *mutilated;* Eth. ነቀፈ: *peel, flay* Di ^{649}),—**Niph.** *Pf.* 3 ms. וְנִקַּף סִבְכֵי הַיַּעַר consec. Is 10^{34} and the thickets of the forest shall be *struck away* (on sg vb cf. Ges $^{§ 145\ o}$ Da $^{Synt.\ §\ 113\ b}$, or rd. נִקְּפוּ;—form poss. Pi, but cf Di Du Che ^{Hpt}). **Pi.** *Pf.* 3 pl וְאַחַר עוֹרִי נִקְּפוּ־זֹאת Jb 19^{26} *after my skin, which they* (Ges $^{§ 144\ g}$) *have struck off* (alluding to ravages of his disease)—*this!* but text dub.; Bu נִקַּף כְּזֹאת (**Niph.**) *which has been thus struck off.*

† נֹקֶף **n.[m.] striking off,**—only cstr. כְּנֹקֶף זַיִת *as (at) the striking of olive-trees* Is 17^{6} 24^{13} (sim of fewness of people after י''s judgment).

II. [נָקַף] **vb. go around** (intrans.), (Ecclus 45^{9} Hiph. ויקיפהו *surround something with* (2 acc.); Pf. 3 fs. הקיפה 43^{12} (acc. + ב instr.); NH Hiph. הִקִּיף = BH; also = *cling to, be attached, joined to,* and so Aram אַקִּיף (Aph), ܐܩܦ),—**Qal** *Impf* חַגִּים יִנְקֹפוּ Is 29^{1} (fig.) *let feasts go around,* i e. run the round (of the year). **Hiph.** *Pf.* הִקִּיף Jb 19^{6}; 3 fs. הִקִּיפָה Is 15^{8}; 3 pl. הִקִּיפוּ Jb 1^{5} ψ 88^{18}, וְהִקִּיפוּ consec. 2 Ch 23^{7}, sf. הקיפוני ψ 22^{17}; 2 mpl. וְהִקַּפְתֶּם

consec. 2 K 11[8], *Impf.* וַיַּקֵּף La 3[5]; 3 mpl. יַקִּ֫יפוּ ψ 17[9], וַיַּקִּ֫פוּ 2 K 6[14]; 2 mpl. תַּקִּפוּ Lv 19[27]; *Imv.* mpl. sf. הַקִּיפוּהָ ψ 48[13]; *Inf. abs* הַקֵּיף Jos 6[3], הַקֵּף v[11]; *Pt.* pl. מַקִּ(י)פִים 1 K 7[24] 2 Ch 4[3],—**1.** *go around, surround, encompass*: **a.** *go around*, c. acc. of city, Jos 6[3] cf v[11] (acc. om.), ψ 48[13] (all ‖ סָבַב); also (fig.) הִקִּיפָה הַזְּעָקָה אֶת־ Is 15[8] *the cry hath gone about* the border of Moab **b.** *surround, encompass, enclose*, usu. c. עַל־: וַיַּקִּ֫פוּ עַל־הָעִיר 2 K 6[14] *and they closed in upon the city* (beleaguered it); c עַל pers. 2 K 11[8] (+סָבִיב), ψ 17[9] 88[18] (‖ סָבַב), +acc. rei Jb 19[6] *he hath closed his net in upon me*, cf. La 3[5], less oft c. acc. pers. ψ 22[17] (‖ סָבַב), 2 Ch 23[7] (‖ 2 K 11[8]; +סָבִיב), also of inanim. things 1 K 7[24] = 2 Ch 4[3] (both +סָבִיב, ‖ סָבַב) **2.** *make the round*, i.e. *complete the circuit* הִקִּ׳ יְמֵי הַמִּשְׁתֶּה Jb 1[5] when *the days of feasting had completed their circuit.* **3.** *make round, round off* (lit.). לֹא תַקִּ׳ פְּאַת רֹאשְׁכֶם Lv 19[27] (‖ לא תשחית את פאת) (וְזָקָנֶךָ), of heathen rite.

†נִקְפָּה **n.f. encircling rope** (of captive), תַּחַת חֲגוֹרָה נִקְפָּה Is 3[24].

נקק

(√of foll. cf. Eth. ንቅቅ: *rima, fissura*, Di[645]; NH נָקִיק (rare) *cleft of rock*)

†[נָקִיק] **n.m. cleft** of rock;—only cstr.: sg נְקִיק הַסֶּלַע Je 13[4]; pl נְקִיקֵי הַסְּלָעִים Is 7[19] (‖ נַחֲלֵי הַבַּתּוֹת), Je 16[16].

†[נָקַר] **vb. bore, pick, dig** (NH *id*, Aram נְקַר, ܢܩܰܪ *id.*, Ar. نَقَرَ *perforate, bore out, hollow out* Lane[2836]; Eth. ነቈረ: *be one-eyed* Di[645]),—**Qal** *Impf.* 3 mpl. sf. יִקְּרוּהָ Pr 30[17]; *Inf.* נקור 1 S 11[2], both of *boring*, or *picking out* eye (acc.). **Pi.** *Impf.* 2 ms. תְּנַקֵּר Nu 16[14] (JE), 3 mpl. וַיְנַקְּרוּ Ju 16[21] both of *boring out* eyes (acc); *Pf.* 3 ms. נִקַּר Jb 30[17] *he* (or *it*, i.e. the night) *boreth* my bones מֵעָלַי (of effects of elephantiasis; Bu rds נִקַּר) **Pu.** *Pf.* 2 mpl. נֻקַּרְתֶּם Is 51[1] the quarry (fr. wh.) *ye were digged.*

†[נְקָרָה] **n.f. hole, crevice**;—cstr. נִקְרַת הַצּוּר Ex 33[22], pl cstr. נִקְרוֹת הַצֻּרִים Is 2[21] (‖ סְעִפֵי הַסְּלָעִים).

†[נָקַשׁ] **vb. knock, strike**, only in specif. sense of hit, strike or bring down (a bird), and only fig (Ecclus ינקש 41[2a] *striketh* against (ב, marg. ונוקש), so ב נוקש 13[2c]; NH *knock, strike* e.g. the knees, or a door (so Hiph.); Aram. (incl. BAram.) נְקַשׁ *id*, ܢܩܰܫ *fixit, impegit, percussit*, etc. (Ar. نَقَشَ *strike in, carve*, etc, is loan-wd. Fra[194]);—the Heb. vb. appar. means *bring down with a* [certain kind of] *stick*, perh. like a boomerang, v. descript. and illustr in Wilkinson [Manners and Customs of Egypt. (new ed. 1878), ii. 103 f. 109 f.] Erman [Aegypten 323] WMM [Asien u. Europa 123 f.]),—**Qal** *Pt* נוקש ψ 9[17] he (׳י) *striketh down* the wicked (so Hup-Now De Che); Vrss Ol Ew Bae Kau We Buhl [Lex] rd. נוקש, **Niph.** fr. יקש. **Niph.** *Impf* 2 ms. תִּנָּקֵשׁ אַחֲרֵיהֶם Dt 12[30] lest *thou be thrust* (impelled) *after them* **Pi.** *Impf* יְנַקֵּשׁ ψ 109[11] let the creditor *strike* at, *take aim* at (ל); 3 mpl וַיְנַקְשׁוּ 38[13] (abs). **Hithp.** *Pt* מִתְנַקֵּשׁ בנפשי 1 S 28[9] why *art* thou *striking at my life?*

I, II. נֵר, נִר, (ניר) v. נור.

†נֵרְגַל **n.pr.div.** (Ph. נרגל CIS [I. 119. 2])—worshipped by men of Cuth, 2 K 17[30] (v. Schr [COT 2 K 17. 30] Jen [Kosmol 476–490] Muss-Arnolt [JBL xi (1892). 168]).

†נֵרְגַל שַׂרְאֶצֶר **n.pr.m.** (so Baer Ginsb, van d. H. שַׁר־), chief soothsayer (רַב־מָג) in train of Nebuchad. Je 39[3a] (del. Gie, plausibly) v[3b. 13] (cf. Schr [COT ad loc]).

נִרְגָּן v. רגן.

†נֵרְדְּ **n.m. nard**, an odorif. plant fr. India (*via* Persia) (Skr *naladâ*; Pers *nârdîn*; Sab. Ar. transp. رَنْد acc. to DHM [Burgen u. Schlösser 978 (SB xcvii)] v. also Sab. Denkm[82]; Gk. νάρδος [so 𝔊] (through Semites) Lewy [Fremdwörter 40]; cf. Low [No. 316] Lag [M ii 25]);—abs נ׳ Ct 4[14], sf. נִרְדִּי נָתַן רֵיחוֹ 1[12], pl נְרָדִים 4[13].

נֵרִיָּה v. נֵר sub נור.

נָשָׂא

[665] **vb. lift, carry, take** (NH=BH, Ph. נשא *id.* Lzb[326]; As. *našû*, *id.* Dl [HWB 484]; BAram. נְשָׂא (rare), Syr. in ܡܰܣܰܐܬܳܐ *scales*; Palm נשא, נסא n pr. Lzb[326] Cook[81, 83] (cp. נשא *forget*); Ar. نَشَأَ intrans. *rise, be high*, etc, Sab. in n pr, e g. CIS [iv 5. 1]; also נשא vb. Hal [Rev Sém. iv (1896), 69] Min. נשא *take*, Hom [Südar Chrest 128]; Eth. ነሥአ: *suscipere, tollere* Di[635], so O Eth., DHM [Epigr Denkm aus Abess. (1894), 52]);—**Qal** [599] *Pf.* נ׳ Gn 13[6]+, 2 ms נָשָׂאתָ 1 K 2[26]+, נָשָׂאתָה Nu 14[19], sf. נשאתני ψ 102[11]; 2 fs. sf. נשאתים Ez 16[58]; 3 pl. נָשְׂאוּ 2 S 18[28]+, נָשׂוּא ψ 139[20], וְנָשׂוּ consec. Ez 39[26], sf. נְשָׂאוּם 2 Ch 12[11], etc.; *Impf.* 3 ms. יִשָּׂא Gn 32[21]+, וַיִּשָּׂא 13[10]+, sf. יִשָּׂאֵהוּ Dt 32[11]+;

3 mpl. יִשְׂאוּ Ho 4^{8}+, יִשָּׂאוּ Hb 2^{6}+, וַיִּשְׂאוּ Ju 2^{4}+; sf. יִשָּׂאֻנוּ Is 64^{5}; 3 fpl. תִּשֶּׂנָּה Je 9^{17}, וַתִּשֶּׂאנָה Ru 1^{9}, וַתִּשֶּׂנָה Zc 5^{9} Ru 1^{14}; 2 fpl. תִּשֶּׂאינָה Ez 23^{49}, etc.; *Imv.* ms. שָׂא Gn 13^{14}+, נְשָׂא ψ 10^{12}, נְסָה 4^{7}; sf. שָׂאֵהוּ Nu 11^{12} 2 K 4^{19}; fs. שְׂאִי Gn 21^{18}+, etc.; *Inf. abs.* נָשׂוֹא Je 10^{5}, נָשֹׂא Ho 1^{6}+2 t.; cstr. נְשֹׂא Is 1^{14}+2 t., שׂוֹא ψ 89^{10} (rd. perh. שְׁאוֹן *roar* Ri Bi Che, cf. Hi שׂוֹא), usu. שְׂאֵת Gn 4^{7}+; sf. נְשִׂאִי ψ 28^{2}, שְׂאֵתִי Je 15^{15} ψ 89^{51}, etc.; Aramaizing Inf. לְמַשְׂאוֹת Ez 17^{9} (si vera l.; Co Berthol לְיוֹם שְׂאֵת); *Pt. act.* נֹשֵׂא Ex 34^{7}+, f. נֹשֵׂאת 1 K 10^{22}, נֹשֵׂאת Est 2^{15}, etc.; *pass.* cstr. נְשׂוּא Is 3^{3}+, נְשׂוּי ψ 32^{1}, etc.;—**1.** *lift, lift up:* **a.** lit., c. acc. pers. vel rei; the flood lifts ark Gn 7^{17} (J), י׳ lifts standard (נֵס) Is 5^{26} 11^{12}+ (oft. sq. לְ pers.), rod Is 10^{26}, c. עַל *against* v^{24}, נ׳ חֶרֶב אֶל־ Mi 4^{3}=Is 2^{4}, etc.;—esp. *lift* in order to hold, carry away, etc. Gn 21^{18} (E), Ju 9^{48} Am 6^{10} 2 S 2^{32} 4^{4} 1 K 13^{29} 2 K $9^{25.26}$ Ez $3^{12.14}$ 8^{3} 11^{24}+; *lift up* wings to fly Ez $10^{16.19}$ 11^{22}; נ׳ רַגְלָיו וַיֵּלֶךְ† Gn 29^{1} *he lifted up his feet and went; lift up, upon* (עַל) Gn 31^{17} 42^{26} (both E), fig. Jb 31^{36}; נ׳ בְּמֹאזְנַיִם Jb 6^{2} *put* a thing into scale; נ׳ בוֹ אָלָה *put on him* (require of him) *an oath* 1 K 8^{31}=2 Ch 6^{22}, so van d. H., 𝔊; correct MT נָשָׁא (Baer Ginsb), but sense hardly possible; אֶשָּׂא בְשָׂרִי בְשִׁנָּי Jb 13^{14} *I will take up my flesh in my teeth* (fig. for hazarding life). **b.** in many phr., lit. and fig., e.g.: (1) *lift up hand;* against (בְּ) 2 S 18^{28} 20^{21}, c. לְ ψ 106^{26}; אֶל־ (as signal) Is 49^{22}; abs., in display of power ψ 10^{12}; freq. in oath (esp. Ez P; of י׳; usu. sq. inf., oft. + לְ pers.) Ex 6^{8} Nu 14^{30} (both P), Ez $20^{5.5.6.15.23.28.42}$ 36^{7} 44^{12} 47^{14} Ne 9^{15}, + אֶל־שָׁמַיִם Dt 32^{40} *lift hand to heaven;* in prayer (c. אֶל־) ψ 28^{2} La 2^{19}, so (בְּשִׁמְךָ) ψ 63^{5}, abs. 134^{2}, and, remarkably, אֶל־מִצְוֺתֶיךָ 119^{48}; also fig. of the deep (תְּהוֹם) Hb 3^{10}; in blessing Lv 9^{22} (P; c. אֶל). (2) *lift up one's head*=shew boldness, independence Ju 8^{28} Zc 2^{4} Jb 10^{15} ψ 83^{3}; of another=restore to honour Gn $40^{13.20}$ (E), but *lift thy head* from off thee (מֵעָלֶיךָ), v^{19}, by word-play;—+ מִבֵּית כֶּלֶא 2 K 25^{27}=Je 52^{31}; fig. of gates, *lift up your heads* ψ $24^{7.9}$. (3) *lift up one's face, countenance* (פָּנִים), lit., 2 K 9^{32} (אֶל־); sign of good conscience 2 S 2^{22} (אֶל־), abs. Jb 11^{15}; of י׳, sign of favour, נ׳ פָּנָיו אֶל־ Nu 6^{26} (P; form of benediction); cf. נ׳ אוֹר פָּנֶיךָ עַל־ ψ 4^{7}; esp. *lift up face* of another (orig. prob. of one prostrate in humility; opp. הֵשִׁיב פָּנִים *repel*), in various shades of mng.: =grant a request Gn 19^{21} (J; + לַדָּבָר הַזֶּה), 1 S 25^{35} Jb $42^{8.9}$; =be gracious to, Gn 32^{21} (E), Mal $1^{8.9}$; hence phr. נְשׂוּא פָנִים *graciously received, held in honour* †2 K 5^{1} (of Naaman), and, as subst., *honourable, eminent one* Is 3^{3} 9^{14} (but del. as gloss), Jb 22^{8}†; =shew consideration for Dt 28^{50} La 4^{16}; also in bad sense=be unduly influenced by Jb 32^{21}, and, specif.,=shew partiality (towards) Dt 10^{17} (denied of י׳), Lv 19^{15} (H), Mal 2^{9} (בַּתּוֹרָה), Jb $13^{8.10}$ 34^{19} Pr 18^{5} ψ 82^{2} (syn. הִכִּיר פ׳); even נ׳ פְּנֵי כָל־כֹּפֶר Pr 6^{35} i.e. regard any bribe. (4) *lift up eyes*, on high 2 K 19^{22}=Is 37^{23}, cf. ψ 121^{1} (אֶל־); לַשָּׁמַיִם Is 51^{6} (|| הַבִּיטוּ אֶל־); sq. ה loc. Dt 3^{27} 4^{19} cf. Ez $8^{5.5}$; toward (אֶל־) idols Ez $18^{6.12.15}$ 33^{25}, cf. 23^{27}; toward (אֶל־) י׳ ψ 123^{1} (these with implied worship); נ׳ עֵינֶיהָ אֶל־ Gn 39^{7} i.e. she gazed at him with desire; usu. + vb. of seeing (35 t.) Gn $13^{10.14}$ 18^{2}+ (Hex only JE), Is 40^{26} (+ מָרוֹם), 49^{18} 60^{4} (both + סָבִיב), Je 3^{2} (+ עַל־). (5) *lift up voice* (קוֹל), give (loud) utterance Is 52^{8}, of floods ψ 93^{3}, + *and weep* Gn 21^{16} (E) 27^{38} 29^{11} (both J), Ju 2^{4}, + וַתִּשָּׂא וַיִּתְּנוּ אֶת־קוֹלָם וַיִּבְכּוּ Nu 14^{1} (P), + 9 t.; + יָרֹנּוּ Is 24^{14}; + קָרָא Ju 9^{7}; קוֹל om. Is 3^{7} 42^{2}, v^{11} (|| יָרֹנּוּ); also (6) *lift up* (+ vb. of saying, usu. אָמַר), oft. of formal and solemn utterance, נ׳ מָשָׁל Nu $23^{7.18}$ $24^{3.15.20.21.23}$ Jb 27^{1} 29^{1} + עַל Mi 2^{4} Hb 2^{6} Is 14^{4}; וְנָשָׁא־בוֹ אָלָה 1 K 8^{31} *and he shall lift up against him an oath*= 2 Ch 6^{22} (MT וְנָשָׁא v. Baer Ginsb, but sense difficult; read rather וְנָשָׂא); נ׳ עָלָיו הַמַּשָּׂא הַזֶּה 2 K 9^{25}; נ׳ קִינָה + עַל־ Je 7^{29} Ez 26^{17} 27^{2} 28^{12} 32^{2}, + אֶל־ 19^{1} 27^{32}; *lift up* word Am 5^{1} (עַל, + קִינָה); weeping Je 9^{9} (עַל־); lamentation (נְהִי) v^{17} (עַל־), reproach ψ 15^{3} (עַל־). (7) *lift up, take up*= utter: name of י׳, לַשָּׁוְא Ex $20^{7.7}$ = Dt $5^{11.11}$ (Decalogue); cf. ψ 139^{20} (read prob. שְׁמֶךָ Bö Ol Che Kau); בַּל־אֶשָּׂא שְׁמוֹתָם עַל־שְׂפָתָי ψ 16^{4}; נ׳ בְּרִיתִי עֲלֵי־פִיךָ ψ 50^{16}; prob. also נ׳ שֵׁמַע שָׁוְא Ex 23^{1} (E). (8) *lift up* prayer in behalf of (בְּעַד) †2 K 19^{4}=Is 37^{4}, Je 7^{16} 11^{14}. (9) *lift up* soul (נֶפֶשׁ), i.e. direct the desire (נֶפֶשׁ **1 d**) towards (אל) a thing, Dt 24^{15} Pr 19^{18}, אֶל־עֲוֺן Ho 4^{8}, לַשָּׁוְא ψ 24^{4} (cf. **Pi.** and II. מַשָּׂא **2**); אֶל־י׳ ψ 25^{1} 86^{4} 143^{8}, so the heart La 3^{41}. (10) *take up* (incur) sin, iniquity, (only HP) †Ex 28^{43} Nu 18^{22}, c. עַל *for* Lv 19^{17} 22^{9} Nu 18^{32} (cf. also **2 b**). (11) of heart *lifting* one *up*, (inciting), Ex $35^{21.26}$ 36^{2} (all P); of presumption 2 K 14^{10} =2 Ch 25^{19}.—MT appar. requires intrans. or reflex. meaning, *lift oneself up*, in foll., text dub.

in all: Ho 13^{1} rd. perh. נָשִׂיא Oort We cf. Now; Na 1^{5} Now (after Bi) וַתִּשָּׂא (rd. וַתִּשָּׁא ? √שׁאה); ψ 89^{10} rd. שְׁאוֹן Bi Ri Che; Hb 1^{3} יִשָּׂא queried by We Gr Buhl al., cf. Gunkel$^{Schöpfung\ 33}$.

2. *Bear, carry:* **a.** lit., a load or burden (usu. acc.) Gn 37^{25} 44^{1} (both J), 45$^{23.23}$ (E), 1 S 10$^{3.3.3}$ Je 10^{5} 17$^{21.27}$ + very oft.; נֹשֵׂא כֵלִים *armour-bearer* Ju 9^{54} 1 S 14^{1} + oft. S; bearing weapons 1 Ch 5^{18} 12^{24} 2 Ch 14$^{7.7}$; La 3^{27} (נ׳ עֹל fig.), Is 1^{14} (fig., cf **d** infr.); a load of care, responsibility Dt 1$^{9.12}$; *share a burden with* נ׳ אֶת־ Ex 18^{22} (E; no acc.); with בְּ׳, יִשָּׂא בְשִׂיחִי מִשְׁכָּבִי Jb 7^{13} *my bed shall carry at* (help carry) my grief, Nu 11^{17}, *take up and carry* (idolatrous images) Am 5^{26} Is 46^{7}; *bear* ephod, 1 S 2^{28} 14^{3} + v^{18} (𝔊), 22^{18} (v Dr in Hastings$^{Dict.\ 726}$); in triumph Is 8^{4}. **b.** esp *bear* guilt, or punishment Gn 4^{13} (J, עֲוֺנִי), oft. Ez HP: † נ׳ עָוֺן Lv 5$^{1.17}$ 7^{18} Nu 5^{31} 14^{34}, cf. 15^{31} (all P), Lv 17^{16} 19^{8} 20$^{17.19}$ (H) Ez 14^{10} 44^{12} (cf. **Hiph.** Lv 22^{16}); נ׳ חֵטְא Lv 20^{20} 24^{15} (H) Nu 9^{13} (P), cf. Ez 23^{49}, cf. נ׳ כְּלִמָּה 16$^{52.52}$, נ׳ עֹנֶשׁ Pr 19^{19}, נ׳ abs. 9^{12}; נ׳ עָוֺן ... = *be responsible for* Ex 28^{38} Nu 18$^{1.1}$ cf. v^{23}, = *bear guilt* for others Lv 10^{17} 16^{22} (of goat, + אֶל־אֶרֶץ, cstr. praegn.), Nu 30^{16} (all P), Ez 4$^{4.5.6}$, cf נ׳ זְנוּתֵיכֶם Nu 14^{33}; נ׳ חֵטְא Is 53^{12}, cf נ׳ חֳלָיֵנוּ v^{4}; also נ׳ בַּעֲוֺן ... *bear at* (share in), Ez 18$^{19.20.20}$. **c.** *support, sustain,* on (עַל) wings Ex 19^{4} Dt 32^{11} ψ 91^{12} (all fig.); land could not *support* them Gn 13^{6} (J), 36^{7} (P). **d.** *endure* Je 15^{15} 31^{19} Ez 36^{6} Jb 34^{31} ψ 55^{13} 69^{8} 88^{16} Pr 18^{14} 30^{21}, *suffer, bear with, permit* Jb 21^{3}. **e.** *bear, carry,* וַיִּשָּׂא מַשְׂאֹת מֵאֵת פָּנָיו אֲלֵהֶם Gn 43^{34} (J) *and they* (indef.) *carried* portions *from his presence unto them,* *carry* gifts as tribute 2 S 8$^{2.6}$, later, *bring* an offering ψ 96^{8} = 1 Ch 16^{29}, Ez 20^{31} (𝔊 Co בְּרֵאשִׁית; Toy foll. MT) **f.** *carry* = contain, hold: bath to hold $\frac{1}{10}$ homer Ez 45^{11} **g.** *bear* fruit, of tree Hg 2^{19} Jo 2^{22}, fig. Ez 36^{8}, boughs 17^{23} (in fig.), *produce, yield,* of mountains Jb 40^{20} ψ 72^{3} (both c לְ *for*).

3. *Take, take away:* **a.** lit. c. מִן 1 S 17^{34} Nu 16^{15} (unjustly). **b.** *take away, carry off,* Ju 21^{23} 1 K 15^{22} = 2 Ch 16^{6}, 1 K 18^{12} La 5^{13} Mi 2^{2} Je 49^{29} (לְ pers.), Is 40^{24} 41^{16}+; *take away* head (מֵעַל pers.) Gn 40^{19} (v. supr.); *sweep away* = destroy Jb 32^{22} (cf. **Niph. 4**); life 2 S 14^{14}. **c.** *take away,* guilt, iniquity, transgression, etc., i.e. *forgive,* c acc. Gn 50^{17} (E), Ex 32^{32} (E), 10^{17} 34^{7} (J), Nu 14^{18} (JE), 1 S 15^{25} Ho 14^{3} Jb 7^{21} (|| הֶעֱבִיר עָוֺן), ψ 32^{5}; + לְ pers. Mi 7^{18}; לְ pers., acc. om., Gn 18^{26} (J), Nu 14^{19} (JE; || סלח עָוֺן), Ho 1^{6} Is 2^{9} (prob. gloss.), ψ 99^{8}; **c.** לְ of sin Gn 50^{17} Ex 23^{21} (both E), 1 S 25^{28} ψ 25^{18}; נְשֻׂא עָוֺן Is 33^{24}; נְשׂוּי־פֶּשַׁע ψ 32^{1}. [In this sense נ׳ used in E; סלח in D P; both in J; נ׳ also in early proph., S. and Jb, and in earlier and latest ψψ; not in Je K Is^{2} La Chr Dn, which use סלח, v. Br$^{Hex.\ 155}$.] **d.** *take* as wife (usu c. לְ *for*), late: Ezr 9$^{2.12}$ 10^{44} Ne 13^{25} 2 Ch 11^{21} 13^{21} 24^{3} Ru 1^{4}. **e.** *take* an enumeration, usu. c רֹאשׁ *sum* Ex 30^{12} Nu 1$^{2.49}$ 4$^{2.22}$ 26^{2} 32$^{26.49}$ (all P); c מִסְפָּר Nu 3^{40} 1 Ch 27^{23}. **f.** *take and carry away, receive,* Dt 33^{3} 1 K 5^{23} ψ 24^{5}; hence, *obtain* favour (חֵן, חֶסֶד) Est 2$^{9.17}$ (both + לִפְנֵי), 5^{2} (+ בְּעֵינָיו).—לְמַשְׂאוֹת אוֹתָהּ מִשָּׁרָשֶׁיהָ Ez 17^{9} (Co Berthol לְיוֹם שְׂאֵת וגו׳) is usu. rendered *plucking it up* (tearing it away) *by the roots,* but dub.; נ׳ not elsewhere in this sense.

† **Niph.** *Pf* נִשָּׂא Je 51^{9}, וְנִ׳ consec. Ex 25^{28}+; *Impf.* יִנָּשֵׂא Is 40^{4}, 3 mpl. יִנָּשְׂאוּ Ez 1$^{19.20.21}$, יִנָּשֵׂאוּ Je 10^{5}, יִנָּשְׂאוּ Pr 30^{13}; 3 fpl. תִּנָּשֶׂאנָה Is 49^{22}, etc.; *Imv.* הִנָּשֵׂא ψ 7^{7} 94^{2}, mpl. הִנָּשְׂאוּ ψ 24^{7}, *Inf.* הִנָּשֵׂא Ez 1^{19}, sf. הִנָּשְׂאָם Ez 1^{21}, *Pt.* נִשָּׂא Is 2^{2}+, f. נִשָּׂאָה Is 30^{25}, נִשֵּׂאת Zc 5^{7} 1 Ch 14^{2}, etc.,—2 S 19^{43} is dub., and pt (Ol$^{§\ 192c}$ Ko$^{i.\ 632t}$) inexplicable; rd. נִשֹּׂא (Inf abs. **Niph.**) Dr (cf. Th), or מַשְׂאֵת *portion* Gr HPS; > Ba$^{NB\ 90}$ thinks נִשֵּׂאת Inf Niph. with compensative ending;—**1.** *be lifted up,* **a.** lit. Zc 5^{7} Ez 1$^{19.21}$ (both מֵעַל הָאָרֶץ), v$^{19.20.21}$ (all in vision), of valleys Is 40^{4}, of gates ψ 24^{7} + v^{9b} (rd. **Niph.**); of eyelids Pr 30^{13} (*superciliousness*); metaph. of judgment on Babylon *reaching up* to the sky (עַד); pt. = *elevated, exalted* Is 6^{1} (of י׳'s throne, in vision); of lofty hills Is 2^{14} 30^{25} 57^{7}, cf Mi 4^{1} = Is 2^{2} (מִן, *lifted from out* the hills), once of trees 2^{13} (text dub.); gen., Is 2^{12}. **b.** fig., *be exalted,* of kg., 2 Ch 32^{23}, kingdom 1 Ch 14^{2}, servant of י׳ Is 52^{13}, י׳ himself 57^{15}. **2.** refl. *lift oneself up* = *rise up,* of י׳, to display power in judgment: Is 33^{10} ψ 94^{2}. **3.** *be borne, carried* Je 10^{5} Ex 25^{28} (P), Is 49^{22} 66^{12}. **4.** *be taken away, carried off,* 2 K 20^{17} (ה loc.) = Is 39^{6}; *be swept away* (of multitude) Dn 11^{12} (cf. Bev Behrm, Prince, v. also **Qal 3**; Ew Hi as **2**, v. Dr).

† **Pi.** *Pf.* נִשָּׂא 2 S 5^{12}, נִשֵּׂאת (anal of ל״ה) 2 S 19^{43} 1 K 9^{11}, וְנִשָּׂא consec. Am 4^{2}, etc.; *Impf.* 3 ms. sf וַיְנַשְּׂאֵהוּ Est 3^{1}, וַיְנַשְּׂאֵם Is 63^{9}; 3 mpl. sf יְנַשְּׂאוּהוּ Ezr 1^{4}, *Imv.* ms. sf. נַשְּׂאֵם ψ 28^{9}; *Pt.* pl. מְנַשְּׂאִים Je 22^{27} + 2 t;—**1.** *lift up* = exalt,

kingdom 2 S 5^{12} (‖ **Niph.** 1 Ch 14^{2}), pers. Est 5^{11} (עַל), cf 3^{1}, = *support, aid, assist* Ezr 8^{36} Est 9^{3}; c. ב *aid with trees* (supply with) 1 K 9^{11}, so Ezr 1^{4} **2.** fig נ׳ נֶפֶשׁ = desire, long, Je 22^{14} 44^{14}. **3** *carry, bear continuously* Is 63^{9}, ψ 28^{9}. **4.** *take, take away* 2 S 19^{43} (ל *for*; but v. **Niph.** supr), Am 4^{2} (ב instr, We Now וְנִשְּׂאוּ).—

†**Hithp.** *Impf* יִתְנַשָּׂא Nu 23^{24}, 3 fs תִּנַּשֵּׂא 24^{7}, 2 ms תִּתְנַשֵּׂא Ez 29^{15}; 3 mpl. יִנַּשְּׂאוּ Dn 11^{14}, 2 mpl. תִּתְנַשְּׂאוּ Nu 16^{3}, *Inf.* הִתְנַשֵּׂא Ez 17^{14} Pr 30^{32}, *Pt.* מִתְנַשֵּׂא 1 K 1^{5} 1 Ch 29^{11};—*lift oneself up*, like a lion Nu 23^{24} (JE), pt *he who exalts himself* 1 Ch 29^{11} (+ לְכֹל לְרֹאשׁ) as human ruler (Kau), > (sc. אַתָּה) of י׳ as ruler; Ew^{§160e} Ke Be as subst [inf. of Aram. form], *the exaltation*; of a kingdom Nu 24^{7} (JE), cf. Ez 17^{14}; in arrogance 1 K 1^{5} Nu 16^{3} (P, c. עַל־), Ez 29^{15} (c עַל), Pr 30^{32} Dn 11^{14} †**Hiph.** *Pf.* 3 ms. consec. **1.** *cause one to bear* iniquity (2 acc.) וְהִשִּׂיאוּ Lv 22^{16} **2.** appar *cause to bring, have brought*, וְהִשִּׂיאוּ 2 S 17^{13} (c acc rei + אֶל loc), but very dub; Ki Kit Bu וְיָשִׂימוּ, HPS וְהֵבִיאוּ; > We הֵשִׂימוּ.

נִשֵּׂאת 2 S 19^{43} v. נשׂא **Niph.**

†[**נְשׂוּאָה**] **n.f.** what is borne about;—pl sf. נְשֻׂאֹתֵיכֶם עֲמוּסוֹת Is 46^{1}, *your things* (formerly) *borne about* in procession (i e idols) are now loaded on beasts for exile.

I. **נָשִׂיא** ^{128} **n.m.** one lifted up, i e a chief prince;—abs נ׳ Ex 22^{27}+; cstr נְשִׂיא Gn 23^{6}+; pl נְשִׂיאִים Jos 22^{32}+, נְשִׂאִים Ex 34^{31} + 7 t, נְשִׂאִם Gn 17^{20} + 3 t, נְשִׂאִם Ex 35^{27}; cstr. נְשִׂיאֵי Ex 16^{22}+, sf. נְשִׂיאֵי Ez 45^{8}, נְשִׂיאֶיהָ Ez 32^{29}, נְשִׂיאֵיהֶם Nu 17^{21}, נְשִׂיאֵהֶם v^{17}, etc.,—mostly in Isr.. **1.** נ׳ בְּעַמְּךָ of any chief man, Ex 22^{27} (E; human ruler, over ag אֱלֹהִים) **2.** of Solom 1 K 11^{34} Elsewhere only Ez P Chr —**3.** of Abr. Gn 23^{6}, and heads of Ishmaelite tribes 17^{20} 25^{16}. **4.** rulers of the congregation, נְשִׂיאֵי הָעֵדָה Ex 16^{22} Jos $9^{15.18}$ 22^{30}, הַנְּ׳ בָּעֵדָה 34^{31}, cf. 35^{27} Lv 4^{22} Jos $9^{18b.19.21.21}$ 17^{4} $22^{14.14.14.32}$ (all P); esp **5.** tribal chiefs and representatives, acc. to the religious organization of P, Nu $1^{16.44}$ 2^{3} + 57 t. Nu (esp. chaps 2, 7, 34, note נְשִׂיא נְשִׂיאֵי הַלֵּוִי 3^{32}); cf 1 Ch 2^{10} 4^{38} 5^{6} 7^{40} 2 Ch 1^{2}, also 1 K 8^{1} (prob gloss, om. 𝔊 Benz), 2 Ch 5^{2}. **6.** in Ezek. **a.** cf Zedekiah (for מֶלֶךְ, v Bohmer$^{SK\ 1900\ 112\ ff}$), 7^{27} $12^{10.12}$ 21^{30}, + 19^{1} (rd sg 𝔊 Ew Hi Co Berthol Toy) **b.** chief men of Judah 21^{17} 22^{6} $45^{8.9}$. **c.** future Davidic kg 34^{24} 37^{25}, cf. $44^{3.3}$ + 16 t. Ez 45, 46, 48. **d.** foreign princes 26^{16} 27^{21} 30^{13} 32^{29} $38^{2.3}$ $39^{1.18}$. **7.** leader of exiles returning under Cyrus, acc to Ezr 1^{8}. **8.** non-Isr chiefs in P. Gn 34^{2} Nu 25^{18} Jos 13^{21}.

†II. [**נָשִׂיא**] **n.[m.]** rising mist, vapour (Ar. نَشِيءٌ, نَشْءٌ);—only pl. נְשִׂאִים *vapours*, forming clouds, and portending rain, Je 10^{13} = 51^{16}, ψ 135^{7}, נְשִׂיאִים Pr 25^{14}.

†I. **מַשָּׂא** **n m.**$^{ψ\ 38.5}$ **load, burden, lifting, bearing, tribute**;—מ׳ abs. Ne 13^{19}+; cstr. 2 K 5^{17}+, sf מַשָּׂאוֹ Ex 23^{5} + 2 t; מַשַּׂאֲכֶם Dt 1^{12}; מַשָּׂאָם Nu 4^{27} + 2 t.,—**1.** *load, burden* of ass Ex 23^{5} (E), mules 2 K 5^{17}, camels 8^{9}, cf. Is $46^{1.2}$, hanging on a peg Is 22^{25} (fig); forbidden on Sabbath Je $17^{21.22.24.27}$ Ne $13^{15.19}$, fig. of people as burden Nu $11^{11.17}$ (JE), Dt 1^{12}, cf. הָיָה לְמ׳ עַל־ 2 S 15^{33} 19^{36} (אֶל־), also וָאֶהְיֶה עָלַי לְמַשָּׂא Jb 7^{20}; of iniquities ψ 38^{5}.—Ho 8^{10} rd מִשְׁחַ, so 𝔊 We Now GASm. **2.** n. verb, *lifting, uplifting*, only מ׳ נַפְשָׁם Ez 24^{25} *the uplifting of their soul*, i. e. that to which they lift up their soul, their heart's desire **3.** n. verb, *bearing, carrying*, Nu 4^{24} (+ לַעֲבֹד), 2 Ch 20^{25} 35^{3} (בַּכָּתֵף), so prob. 1 Ch $15^{22.22.27}$ (cf. Be Kau, > *singing, uplifting of voice*, e.g Ot), esp. of *responsibility and duty of bearing* sacred vessels (oft. ‖ עֲבֹדָה, פְּקֻדָּה) Nu $4^{15.19.27.27.49}$, עֲבֹדַת מ׳ v^{47}, מִשְׁמֶרֶת מ׳ $v^{31.32}$ **4.** perhaps *what is carried, brought*, i.e. *tribute* כֶּסֶף מ׳ 2 Ch 17^{11} *silver as tribute* (+ מִנְחָה, cf נשׂא **Qal**, others, *silver by the load*, i.e. in great quantity) —I. מַשָּׂא v. supr p 601 b.

†III. **מַשָּׂא** **n.m.**$^{Is\ 14.28}$ **utterance, oracle** (cf. נשׂא **1 b** (6); Gf$^{Je\ 23.33}$),—מ׳ abs. Is 14^{28}+; usu. cstr. 13^{1}+, —of prophetic *utterance*. 2 K 9^{25} Is 14^{28} Ez 12^{10} 2 Ch 24^{27} (c עַל), מ׳ בָּבֶל Is 13^{1}, מ׳ מוֹאָב 15^{1}, cf 17^{1} 19^{1} $21^{1.11}$ 22^{1} 23^{1} 30^{6} Na 1^{1}; מ׳ בַּעְרָב Is 21^{13} is later ins. (Di); מ׳ = *revelation*, הַמ׳ אֲשֶׁר חָזָה חֲבַקּוּק הַנָּבִיא Hb 1^{1}; מ׳ י׳ *utterance of* י׳ Je $23^{33.34.36.38.38.38}$ (cf. 2 K 9^{25}), vid. also $v^{33\,b}$ (rd אַתֶּם הַמַּשָּׂא), with word-play, —sq. וְנָטַשְׁתִּי, $v^{36\,b}$; מ׳ דְּבַר י׳ Zc 9^{1} (+ בְּאֶרֶץ), 12^{1} (+ עַל־יִשְׂרָאֵל), Mal 1^{1} (+ אֶל־יִשׂ׳) —Pr 31^{1} v. I. מַשָּׂא, p 601 supr; in 30^{1} rd מִמַּשָּׂא *from Massa* (Mublau, De), or הַמַּשָּׂאִי (Wild), which however is perhaps not original, but borrowed from 31^{1} (cf. Wild$^{ad\ loc}$ Frankenberg$^{Spr\ p.5}$; corrupt name of Agur's home or tribe, Kau)

†מַשֹּׂא **n.m. lifting up**;—only cstr. מ׳ פָּנִים 2 Ch 19^{7} = *regarding of persons* (partiality, see √**1 a** (3); ‖מִקַּח־שֹׁחַד).

†מַשָּׂאָה **n.f.** the uplifted (cloud);—כֹּבֶד מ׳ Is 30^{27} *weight of uplifted clouds.*

†מַשְׂאֵת **n.f. uprising, utterance, burden, portion** (on format cf. Ol ^{§109a} Sta ^{§272b} Ko $^{ii.1,183}$, Ph. (Pun) has משאת = *payment, tax* v. Lzb ^{326}),—abs. מ׳ Ju 20^{40}+; cstr מַשְׂאַת Gn 43^{34}+, pl abs מַשְׂאֹת Gn 43^{34}, +(prob) מַשְׂאוֹת La 2^{14} (v. infr); cstr מַשְׂאֹת Gn 43^{34},—**1.** *that which rises, uprising, uplifting*: **a.** מ׳ הֶעָשָׁן Ju 20^{38} *uprising of smoke*, cf. (הע׳ om) v^{40}. **b.** in gen. = *signal* Je 6^{1} (= נֵס Gf). **c.** *uplifting* of hands (כַּפַּי) in prayer ψ 141^{2} (‖ תְּפִלָּה). **2.** *utterance, oracle* (= III מַשָּׂא), La 2^{14} (Bu Lohr). **3.** *burden* Zp 3^{18} (of reproach, fig). **4. a.** *portion* (carried to some one), esp from table of king or superior, Gn 43$^{34.34.34}$ (J; on custom v. Di and reff.), 2 S 11^{8}, so rd perh. also 2 S 19^{43} (for MT נִשֵּׂאת) Gr HPS. **b.** perh. also more gen., *present, largess* from a superior Je 40^{5} (+ אֲרֻחָה *food-allowance*), Est 2^{18} (כְּיַד הַמֶּלֶךְ). **c.** exacted or enforced *gift*, from inferior, מ׳ בַר Am 5^{11} (cf Ph. supr; v. also מנחה). **d.** sacred *contribution, tax* מ׳ משֶׁה עֶבֶד (י׳) 2 Ch 24$^{6.9}$ **e.** *offering* to י׳ Ez 20^{40}.

†[שִׂיא] **n.m.** *loftiness*, fig of pride.—אִם־יַעֲלֶה לַשָּׁמַיִם שִׂיאוֹ Jb 20^{6} (of wicked)

†שִׂיאֹן **n.pr.mont.**, i.e. Hermon, הַר שׂ׳ הוּא חֶרְמוֹן Dt 4^{48} (cf. Di Dr).

†שְׂאֵת **n.f. 1. exaltation, dignity. 2. swelling. 3. uprising**;—שׂ׳ abs Gn 4^{7}+, cstr. Lv 13^{28}+; sf שְׂאֵתוֹ Jb 13^{11}+; (מ)שׂתוֹ 41^{17},—**1.** *dignity* Gn 49^{3} (dignity of first-born), ψ 62^{5}, of Chaldeans Hb 1^{7}; of God, *his exaltation, loftiness* Jb 13^{11} 31^{23}. **2.** *swelling*, eruption, בְּעוֹר בְּשָׂר Lv 13^{2} (+בַּהֶרֶת, סַפַּחַת), cf. 14^{56} (+*id*); also 13$^{10.10.19.28}$, שׂ׳ הַנֶּגַע v^{43} (all P). **3.** *uprising*, Jb 41^{17} *at his uprising the mighty are in dread* **4.** Gn 4^{7} is dub;—is there not *acceptance?* 𝔖 𝔙 al.; *forgiveness* 𝔗 Holz al.; *uplifting* of countenance, cheerfulness, Ew De Ke Di Kau.

†[נָשַׂג] **vb.** only **Hiph. reach, overtake** (Ecclus 14^{13} והשׂיגת ידך, 35^{10} ובהשׂגת יד (cf. Schechter on 14^{13}), cf. **3** infr.; ישׂיג מענה 32^{14} *shall obtain an answer*;—**Hiph.** *Pf* 3 ms וְהִשִּׂיג consec. Lv 25^{6}, sf. והשׂיגו consec. Dt 19^{6}; 2 ms. sf. והשׂגתם consec. Gn 44^{4}, etc; *Impf.* יַשִּׂיג Lv 26^{5}, וַיַּשֵּׂג Gn 31^{25}, sf וַיַּשִּׂגֵם Gn 44^{26}, etc.; *Inf. abs.* הַשֵּׂג 1 S 30^{8}; *Pt.* מַשִּׂיג 1 S 14^{26}, sf. מַשִּׂיגֵהוּ Jb 41^{18}, f. מַשֶּׂגֶת Lv 14^{21} 1 Ch 21^{12} (but rd. וְאִם הֱיוֹת as ‖ 2 S 24^{13} We^{Sm} Kit);—**1.** *overtake*, c. acc, oft after רָדַף: **a.** lit. Gn 31^{25} (E), 44$^{4.6}$ (J), Ex 14^{9} (P), 15^{9} (song), Dt 19^{6} Jos 2^{5} (JE), 1 S 30$^{8.8.8}$ 2 S 15^{14} 2 K 25^{5} = Je 39^{5} = 52^{8}, Ho 2^{9}, cf ψ 7^{6} 18^{38} (וָאַשְׁמִידֵם in ‖ 2 S 22^{38}), La 1^{3} (metaph). **b.** fig of battle Ho 10^{9}, sword Je 42^{16}, on 1 Ch 21^{12} v supr; of blessings Dt 28^{2}, curses v$^{15.45}$, predictions Zc 1^{6}, justice Is 59^{9}, wrath of י׳ ψ 69^{25}, iniquities 40^{13}, calamities Jb 27^{20}. **2. a.** *reach, attain to*, Jb 41^{18} (if one) *reach it* (crocodile) with the sword (2 acc), fig. paths of life Pr 2^{19}, joy, etc, Is 35^{10} also 51^{11} (Che ^{Hpt} יְשִׂיגוּם, for MT יַשִּׂיגוּן; Perles $^{Analekten\ 64}$ יִשֹּׂגוּן, fr. שׂגה); of time Gn 47^{9} my days *have not reached* the days... of my fathers, cf. Lv 26$^{5.5}$. **b.** *cause to reach, bring, put*, מַשִּׂיג יָדוֹ אֶל־פִּיו 1 S 14^{26} no one *put his hand to his mouth*, but rd. משיב 𝔊 𝔗 Klo Dr Bu Kit HPS Lohr. **3.** fig הִשִּׂיגָה יָדוֹ *one's hand has reached*, i e. one is able, or has enough, Lv 5^{11} (c. לְ), 14^{21} 25$^{26.49}$; c acc. = *able to secure, get* 14$^{22.30.31.32}$ 27^{8} Nu 6^{21} (all P), Ez 46^{7}; abs. = gain (riches) Lv 25^{47} (H)—Jb 24^{2} v. סוג.

שׂלק v. נשק.

נשׂר (√ of foll; NH נָסַר *saw* (Qal Pi); Aram נְסַר, ܢܣܰܪ *saw*; cf. Eth ወሰረ: *id.*; Ar. مِنْشَارٌ n. *a saw*)

†מַשּׂוֹר **n.m. saw**,—abs. Is 10^{15}.

†I [נָשָׂא] **vb. lend on interest, or usury, be a creditor** (cf Ar نَسَأَ *postpone, delay; sell on credit*, ‖ form of I נָשָׁה, v. Ges^{§75oo});—**Qal** *Pt. act.* נֹשֶׁא (anal. ל״ה) 1 S 22^{2} every man that had *a creditor*; אֲשֶׁר נֹשֵׁא בוֹ Is 24^{2} *against whom is a creditor*, and pl נֹשְׁאִים Ne 5^{7} Kt (נשִׁים Qr, from נָשָׁה), +acc cogn מַשָּׁא **Hiph.** *Impf.* 3 ms. לֹא־יַשִּׁא אוֹיֵב בּוֹ ψ 89^{23} *an enemy shall not act the creditor against him, make exactions of him* (‖ יְעַנֶּנּוּ)—1 K 8^{31} 2 Ch 6^{22} v. נשׂא **Qal 1 b** (5)

†מַשָּׁא **n.m.** $^{Ne\ 5,10}$ **lending on interest, or usury**;—Ne 5^{7} (as acc. cogn.), v^{10}.

†[מַשָּׁאָה] **n.f. loan** (on pledge);—cstr. כִּי תַשֶּׁה בְרֵעֲךָ מַשַּׁאת מְאוּמָה Dt 24^{10}; pl. עֹרְבִים מַשָּׁאוֹת Pr 22^{26} *those pledging* (giving security for) *debts*.

†II **נָשָׁא** vb. only **Niph. Hiph.** beguile, deceive,—(kindred with I שׁוא, from which, however, the forms can hardly be derived (conj We Comp 2. 351)),—**Niph.** *Pf.* 3 pl נִשְּׁאוּ Is 19^{13} the princes *have been beguiled* (‖ נוֹאֲלוּ, הִתְעוּ) **Hiph.** *Pf.* הִשִּׁיא Je 49^{16}, sf הִשִּׁיאַנִי Gn 3^{13}, הִשִּׁיאֻךָ Ob ^{3}, 2 ms הִשֵּׁאתָ Je 4^{10}, 3 pl sf הִשִּׁיאוּךָ Ob ^{7}, *Impf* only juss יַשִּׁיא 2 Ch 32^{15}, so ψ 55^{16} Qr (v infr), יַשִּׁא 2 K 18^{29} Is 36^{14}, sf יַשִּׁאֲךָ 2 K 19^{10} Is 37^{10}, 2 mpl תַּשִּׁאוּ Je 37^{9}, *Inf abs.* הַשֵּׁא Je 4^{10},—*beguile*, usu c acc pers Gn 3^{13} (J, not elsewh Hex), Je 49^{16} Ob $^{3.7}$, אַל־יַשִּׁאֲךָ 2 K 19^{10} *let not thy God beguile thee* = Is 37^{10}, of Hezekiah 2 Ch 32^{15} (cf infr), אַל־תַּשִּׁאוּ נַפְשֹׁתֵיכֶם Je 37^{9} *do not deceive yourselves*, also sq לְ pers. אַל־יַשִּׁא לָכֶם 2 K 18^{29} = Is 36^{14} (= 2 Ch 32^{15}, v supr), Je 29^{8}, הַשֵּׁא הִשֵּׁאתָ לָעָם הַזֶּה 4^{10} *thou hast utterly beguiled this people*, ישימות עָלֵימוֹ ψ 55^{16} Kt appar = *desolations (be) upon them!* (but elsewh only in n pr loc, cf. p. 445 supr), < Qr יַשִּׁיא מָוֶת עָלֵימוֹ Ew Ol Pe De Now Hup, cf 𝔊, *let death (beguile them, i e) come deceitfully upon them!* Brull Che, cf. Bae, conj plausibly יַשִּׁיא מָוֶת יְבַלְּעֵמוֹ.

†[נַשָּׁאוֹן] n.[m.] guile, dissimulation (> acc to Lag BN 196 der fr מַשָּׁא, *lending on usury*), תִּכַּסֶּה שִׂנְאָה בְּמַשָּׁאוֹן Pr 26^{26} *hatred may hide itself with dissimulation*

†מַשּׁוּאוֹת n.f.pl. *deceptions* ψ 73^{18} 74^{3}, but meaning not suitable; read prob מַשּׁוֹאוֹת, v מְשׁוֹאָה sub שׁוא (so Klo Now Hup Bae).

III [נָשָׁא] *forget*, v II. נָשָׁה.

†[נָשַׁב] vb. blow (NH = BH, 𝔗 נְשַׁב (but also נְתַב), Syr ܢܫܰܒ, all *blow*, ‖ form of נָשַׁף),—**Qal** *Pf* 3 fs רוּחַ י׳ נָשְׁבָה בּוֹ Is 40^{7} *the breath of* י׳ *has blown upon it.* **Hiph.** *Impf.* 3 ms יַשֵּׁב רוּחוֹ ψ 147^{18} *he causes* his wind *to blow*, וַיַּשֵּׁב אֹתָם Gn 15^{11} *and he drove them away* (perh orig. *blow away*, drive away by blowing, or by a sound like blowing)

†I **נָשָׁה** vb. lend, become a creditor (cf I נשא),—**Qal** *Pf* 1 s נָשִׁיתִי Je 15^{10}, 3 pl נָשׁוּ v ^{10}, *Pt.* נֹשֶׁה Ex 22^{24} + 4 t, pl. נשים Ne $5^{10\ 11}$ + v ^{7} Qr (Kt נשאים, v. I נשא), sf נוֹשַׁי Is 50^{1};—*lend*, usu c בְּ pers לֹא־נָשִׁיתִי וְלֹא־נָשׁוּ־בִי Je 15^{10} *I have not lent, and they have not lent to me*, Dt 24^{11} Ne 5^{7} (Qr, + acc cogn), v $^{10\ 11}$ (both + acc rei); pt as subst. *creditor, usurer* Ex 22^{24} (E), 2 K 4^{1} Is 24^{2} 50^{1} ψ 109^{11} **Hiph.** *Impf* 3 ms יַשֶּׁה בְּ Dt 15^{2} *who lendeth to* his neighbour, 2 ms תַשֶּׁה בְּ 24^{10} when *thou lendest to* thy neighbour (+ acc cogn)

†[נְשִׁי] n.[m.] debt,—only sf 2 fs נשיכי Kt, נִשְׁיֵךְ Qr 2 K 4^{7} (so Baer; van d. H Ginsb נשיך) *pay* (שַׁלְּמִי) *thy debt*

†[מַשֶּׁה] n.m loan,—only cstr שָׁמוֹט כָּל־בַּעַל מַשֵּׁה יָדוֹ אֲשֶׁר יַשֶּׁה בְּרֵעֵהוּ Dt 15^{2} *every possessor of a loan of his hand shall renounce what he lends to his neighbour* (cf Dr)

†II. [נָשָׁה] vb forget (NH id, As. *nišîtu* perh. *forgottenness* Dl HWB 486, Aram. נְשָׁא (esp. Ithpe, Aph), ܢܫܐ *forget*, Ar. نَسِيَ *forget, neglect*, cf. Eth ረስዐ: *ignoscere, condonare, indulgere* Di 633),—**Qal** *Pf* 1 s וְנָשִׁיתִי אֶתְכֶם נָשֹׁא Je 23^{39} *I will forget you finally* (but 𝔊𝔙𝔖 Che Gie וְנָשָׂאתִי, sq וְנָטַשְׁתִּי as v $^{33\ b}$, v III נשא), נָשִׁיתִי טוֹבָה La 3^{17} *I have forgotten prosperity*, *Impf* 1 s הַאֶשֶּׁה *shall I forget?* i e. overlook, rd by We Mi 6^{10} plausibly for MT הַאִשׁ, *Inf abs* נָשֹׁא (לְ׳ א) Je 23^{39} (v supr). **Niph.** *Impf* 2 ms sf תִנָּשֵׁנִי Is 44^{21} *thou shalt not be forgotten of me*, but dub; Ges § 117e תִשָּׁנִי (Qal), Che Hpt תִּשָּׁנִי (cf. Dt 32^{18}) **Pi.** *Pf* 3 ms. sf נַשַּׁנִי Gn 41^{51} (E) *God hath made me forget* + acc. rei (ַ in 1st syllable only here, infl of מְנַשֶּׁה Ges § 52 m) **Hiph.** *Pf* 3 ms. sf הִשָּׁהּ חָכְמָה Jb 39^{17} *God caused her* (the ostrich) *to forget* wisdom, i e did not endow her with it. *Impf* יַשֶּׁה לְךָ מִן־ Jb 11^{6} Eloah *allows a part of* thy guilt *to be forgotten thee*, i e does not reckon it to thee in full (𝔊 = יִשְׁוֶה לְךָ מֵאֱלוֹהַּ כַּעֲוֹנְךָ [Du] *there is equivalent to thee from Eloah, acc to thine iniquity*, cf. Bi Che Job and Sol, Bu reads נָשָׁה for יַשֶּׁה, Du rejects ver. as gloss)

†נְשִׁיָּה n.f. forgetfulness, oblivion, אֶרֶץ נ׳ ψ 88^{13} (‖ חשׁך), designation of שאול (cf. v $^{11\ 12}$)

†יִשִּׁיָּה, יִשִּׁיָּהוּ† n.pr m. **1.** †יִשִּׁיָּהוּ 1 Ch 12^{7} (van d H v ^{6}) one of David's heroes, 𝔊 Ἰησουνει, A Ἰεσια, 𝔊L Ἰεσσουε **2** יִשִּׁיָּה, a man of Issachar 1 Ch 7^{3}, 𝔊 Εἰσια, Ἰεσια, 𝔊L Ἰωσια (and so in foll). **3.** Levites: **a.** 1 Ch 23^{20} $24^{25\ 26}$. **b.** 1 Ch 24^{21}, 𝔊 Ἰσεια, etc **4.** one of those strange wives Ezr 10^{31}, 𝔊 Ἰεσσ(ε)ια.

†נָשֶׁה n [m.] a vein (or nerve) in the thigh (etym dub.; on format. cf Lag BN 80, Ar نَسًا appar *the portion of the principal*

vein of the leg which is in the thigh, vulg. *sciatic vein*, or (mod.) *sciatic nerve* and even *sciatica*, Lane [3033];—only גִּיד הַנָּשֶׁה Gn 32[33a] *the sinew of the thigh-vein* (or *thigh-nerve*, אֲשֶׁר עַל־כַּף הַיָּרֵךְ), cf. v[33b].—On sacredness of thigh, cf. RS [Sem i. 360; 2nd ed. 380] We [Held (2), 168].

נָשִׁים v. אִשָּׁה p. 61 supr.

† **נָשַׁךְ vb.** bite (NH=BH, but also transp. נָכַשׁ Hiph.); As. *našāku* Dl[HWB 486]; 𝔗 נְכֵית (esp. of snakes); Syr. ܢܟܬ, ܢܟܬ; Eth. ነከሰ: Di[642]; Ba[ZMG xliii (1889), 188] cp. Ar. نَكَثَ, *undo* threads, *untwist* rope, *disintegrate, dissolve*);—**Qal** *Pf.* 3 ms. נָשַׁךְ Nu 21[9], sf. וּנְשָׁכוֹ consec. Am 5[19], וּנְשָׁכָם consec. 9[3]; *Impf.* 3 ms. יִשֹּׁךְ Ec 10[11], יִשָּׁךְ Pr 23[32], sf. יִשְּׁכֶנּוּ Ec 10[8]; *Pt. act.* נֹשֵׁךְ Gn 49[17]; pl. נֹשְׁכִים Mi 3[5], sf. נֹשְׁכֶיךָ Hb 2[7]; *pass.* נָשׁוּךְ Nu 21[8];—*bite*, chiefly of serpent, c. acc., Am 5[19] 9[3] Gn 49[17] (poem in J), Nu 21[8] (pt. pass., abs.), v[9], Ec 10[8] also v[11] (abs.), Pr 23[32] (sim. of wine); fig. of prophets הַנּ׳ בְּשִׁנֵּיהֶם Mi 3[5] *who are biting with their teeth*, and crying, Peace! fig. of oppression, etc., נֹשְׁכֶיךָ Hb 2[7] (with play on sense *thy debtors, those that give thee interest*). **Pi.** *Pf.* 3 pl. וְנִשְּׁכוּ אֶתְכֶם Je 8[17] *and they shall bite you fatally* (fig.); *Impf.* 3 mpl. וַיְנַשְּׁכוּ אֶת־הָעָם Nu 21[6] *and they bit the people fatally* (both of serpents).

† **נֶשֶׁךְ n.[m.]** interest, usury (lit. *something bitten off*);—נ׳ abs. Ex 22[24]+; cstr. Dt 23[20];—c. שִׂים עַל־ Ex 22[24] (E); c. לָקַח מִן Lv 25[36], הֵשִׁיב מִן Ez 18[17], לָקַח 22[12] (no prep.), בְּנֶשֶׁךְ Lv 25[37] *at interest*, so ψ 15[5] Ez 18[8.13]; בְּנ׳ Pr 28[8] *by usury*; as acc. cogn. Dt 23[20.20.20].

† **[נָשַׁךְ] vb. denom.** pay, give interest (cf. Gerber [Verba denom. 89]);—**Qal** *Impf.* 3 ms. יִשַּׁךְ Dt 23[20] interest of anything off which *one giveth interest* (cf. Dr). **Hiph.** *make* one *give interest*; *Impf.* 2 ms. תַשִּׁיךְ Dt 23[20] (+acc. cogn.) v[21.21], all c. לְ pers.

† **נִשְׁכָּה n.f.** chamber (rare ‖ of לִשְׁכָּה, q.v.; cf. W [SG 67]);—abs. נ׳ Ne 13[7], sf. נִשְׁכָּתוֹ Ne 3[30], both rooms of individuals; pl. abs. נְשָׁכוֹת 12[44] (Chr)=treasuries, storehouses.

† **נָשַׁל vb. 1.** intrans. slip or drop off; also trans.: **2.** draw off. **3.** clear away (NH נָשַׁל prob. intrans., Qal not used, but n. נְשִׁילָה *a falling off*, etc.; Pi. Hiph. *cast off, let fall off*, Niph. *be cast off, fall off*; 𝔗 Aph. אַשִּׁיל *cast out* (fr. house); Ar. نَسَلَ *excidit* pluma, etc.; but also trans., avis *mutavit rejecitque* plumas (Frey);—نَسَلَ *celeriter extraxit*, etc., is denom. fr. loan-word acc. to Frä[88]);—**Qal** *Pf.* וְנָשַׁל consec. Dt 7[1]+2 t.; *Impf.* 3 ms. יִשַּׁל Dt 28[40]; *Imv.* ms. שַׁל Ex 3[5] Jos 5[15];—**1.** *slip or drop off*, וְנָשַׁל הַבַּרְזֶל מִן־הָעֵץ Dt 19[5] *and the iron slippeth off from the wood* (i.e. axe-head from helve); יִשַּׁל זֵיתֶךָ Dt 28[40] *thine olives shall drop off* (abs.). **2.** *draw off* sandal fr. (מֵעַל) foot Ex 3[5] (E), Jos 5[15] (JE). **3.** *clear away* nations מִפָּנֶיךָ Dt 7[1.22]. **Pi.** *Impf.* 3 ms. וַיְנַשֵּׁל 2 K 16[6] *he cleared* the Jews *entirely* out of (מִן) Elath.

† **[נָשַׁם] vb.** pant (NH in nn. נְשִׁימָה, נְשָׁמָה, 𝔗 נִשְׁמָתָא, נִשְׁמָא; late Aram. Ithpe.; Syr. ܢܫܡ *breathe, blow*; Ar. نَسَمَ *gently breathe* (of wind), etc.; v. *seek a thing with labour and perseverance* (Lane[3032]); نَسَمَةٌ *a soul*, Lane[ib.]);—*pant*, of the deep and strong breathing of a woman in travail; **Qal** *Impf.* 1 s. אֶשֹּׁם Is 42[14].

† **נְשָׁמָה n.f.** breath;—נ׳ Dt 20[16]+9 t.; cstr. נִשְׁמַת (cf. Lag[BN 82]) Gn 2[7]+10 t.; sf. נִשְׁמָתִי Jb 27[3]; נִשְׁמָתוֹ Jb 34[14]; pl. נְשָׁמוֹת Is 57[16];—**1.** *breath* of God as hot wind kindling a flame Is 30[33]; as destroying wind 2 S 22[16]=ψ 18[16], Jb 4[9]; as cold wind producing ice Jb 37[10]; as creative, giving breath to man Jb 32[8] 33[4]. **2.** *breath of* man 1 K 17[17] Is 42[5] Jb 27[3] Dn 10[7]; breath of life נשמת חיים Gn 2[7] (J); cf. נִשְׁמַת רוּחַ חַיִּים Gn 7[22] (J); as breathed in by God it is God's breath in man Jb 34[14] 36[4]; and is characteristic of man אדם אשר נשמה באפו Is 2[22] *man in whose nostrils is* but *a breath* (late gloss). **3.** syn. נפש כָּל נְשָׁמָה *every breathing thing* Dt 20[16] Jos 11[11.14] 1 K 15[29]; כָּל־הַנְּשָׁמָה Jos 10[40] ψ 150[6]; נְשָׁמוֹת Is 57[16]. **4.** *spirit* of man, ‖ רוּחַ, נֵר י׳ נ׳ אָדָם Pr 20[27] *the spirit of man is a lamp of* י׳.

† **תִּנְשֶׁמֶת n.f.** an animal;—ת׳ Lv 11[18], תִּנְשָׁמֶת Lv 11[30] Dt 14[16]:—**1.** unclean bird, the *ibis, water-hen*, 𝔊 πορφυρίων, (acc. Tristr [NHB 249]); or species of *owl* (Di Bu SS); *pelican* (Ges): Lv 11[18]=Dt 14[16]. **2.** unclean שֶׁרֶץ Lv 11[30], *lizard* (Saad Tristr [NHB 120]), or *chameleon* (Bo [Hieroz. i. 1078 ff.; ed. Rosenm. ii. 503 ff.]), so most; (deriving name from alleged living on air, Plin [NH viii. 51]; but this not applicable to **1**; cf. Lag [BN 130 f.]).

†נָשַׁף **vb. blow** (NH = BH; Chr-Pal-Aram نشف Schwally[Idiot 58], Ar نَسَفَ (vulg) *id* (Dozy[ii 667], on usu mng cf Wetzst[ZPV xiv 7]), ‖ form of נשב, cf Jen[ZA iv (1889) 268]).—**Qal** *Pf* 3 ms נ׳ בָּהֶם Is 40[24] *he hath blown upon them* (of ׳י under fig of wind), 2 ms נָשַׁפְתָּ בְרוּחֲךָ Ex 15[10] (song).

†נֶשֶׁף **n.m. twilight** (prop *twilight-breeze*, cf לְרוּחַ הַיּוֹם Gn 3[8], NH *id.*; ℑ נשׁף, נִשְׁפָּא),—נ׳ abs 1 S 30[17]+, נָשֶׁף Je 13[16], cstr. Is 21[4], sf נִשְׁפּוֹ Jb 3[9],—**1.** *evening twilight* 2 K 7[5.7] (cf לַיְלָה v[12]), opp בקר Is 5[11], time of concealment Jb 24[15] Pr 7[9] (+ עֶרֶב יוֹם, אִישׁוֹן לַיְלָה וַאֲפֵלָה, to emphasize sin that shuns the day); of refreshing Is 21[4] (נ׳ חִשְׁקִי); of stumbling, in dim light Is 59[10] (opp. צָהֳרַיִם), so הָרֵי נָשֶׁף Je 13[16] (both fig), כּוֹכְבֵי נִשְׁפּוֹ Jb 3[9] *the stars of its twilight* (i e of night of Job's birth)—so מֵהַנּ׳ וְעַד־הָעֶרֶב 1 S 30[17] Klo Kit HPS (rd לְהַחֲרִמָם for לְמָחֳרָתָם, We Kit Bu); Th, after Luth, sub **2**, so Buhl[Lex] SS, Lohr allows either. **2** *morning twilight* Jb 7[4] (opp. עֶרֶב), appar also ψ 119[147].

†יַנְשׁוּף and (Is 34[11]) יַנְשׁוֹף **n.[m.]** a bird (with harsh, *strident* note? Bo[Hieroz ii 284, ed Rosenm iii 29], Tristr[NHB 192] think of נֶשֶׁף—i e a *twilight* bird, on format cf Lag[BN 127] Ba[NB 231]),—unclean Lv 11[17] Dt 14[16]; inhabiting deserts Is 34[11]. Prob a kind of *owl* Bo[l c], '*Great Owl*,' Egyptian *Eagle-owl* (*bubo ascalaphus*) Tristr[l c] cf 𝔊ℑ Di Dr-White[Hpt] (Lv), > 𝔊 𝔙 Lv Is *ibis*.

†I נָשַׁק **vb. kiss** (NH *id*, As *našâku*, ℑ נְשַׁק, נַשֵּׁיק, Syr ܢܫܩ, *kiss* (orig *smell* [نَشِقَ] acc to Lag[Nov Psalt Spec 24 f.]) Ar نَسَقَ is *fasten together, arrange in order*, Eth. ነሰቀ: pt. *ordine dispositus, apte sertus* Di[641], poss akin to II. נשק),—**Qal** *Pf* 3 ms נ׳ 1 K 19[18] 2 S 15[5]; 3 fs נָשְׁקָה Pr 7[13]; 3 pl נָשָׁקוּ ψ 85[11], *Impf* יִשַּׁק Gn 41[40], וַיִּשַּׁק 27[27]+, sf יִשָּׁקֵנִי Ct 1[2], 1 s cohort אֶשְּׁקָה־ 1 K 19[20], 3 mpl יִשָּׁקוּן Ho 13[2], etc, *Imv.* שְׁקָה־ Gn 27[26]; *Inf cstr* נְשֹׁק־ 2 S 20[9],—*kiss*, usu c לְ pers Gn 27[26.27] 29[11] 50[1] Ex 4[27] (all J), Gn 48[10] Ex 18[7] (both E), 2 S 15[5] 14[33] 19[40] 20[9] 1 K 19[20] Pr 7[13] Ru 1[9.14]; so of idol-worship 1 K 19[18] (cf We[Skizzen iii 105, Held 109]), cf. וַתִּשַּׁק יָדִי לְפִי Jb 31[27] *and my hand hath kissed my mouth*, rarely c acc pers 1 S 20[41] (אִישׁ אֶת־רֵעֵהוּ), sf pers 1 S 10[1] Ct 1[2] (+ מִנְּשִׁיקוֹת), 8[1], also Gn 33[4] וַיִּשָּׁקֵהוּ (J, Holz E, wd suspicious, Di rejects); עֲגָלִים יִשָּׁ׳ Ho 13[2] *calves do they kiss;* שְׂפָתַיִם יִשָּׁק Pr 24[26] *lips he kisses;* abs. ψ 85[11] (fig, recipr)—עַל־פִּיךָ יִשַּׁק Gn 41[40] is dub, Di 'to thy mouth all my people shall yield' (fit, adapt themselves, cf. Ar. √), so Kau Buhl[Lex], but this meaning uncertain, and text perh. corrupt, v Di Holz). **Pi.** *Impf* 3 ms וַיְנַשֵּׁק Gn 32[1] 45[15], וַיְנַשֶּׁק־ 29[13]; *Imv* mpl נַשְּׁקוּ־ ψ 2[12], *Inf cstr.* נַשֵּׁק Gn 31[28],—*kiss* = **Qal** c לְ pers Gn 29[13] (J), 31[28] 32[1] 45[15] (all E); נַשְּׁקוּ־בַר ψ 2[12] is dub, cf 1 בַּר p 135 a supr **Hiph.** *Pt* מַשִּׁיקוֹת Ez 3[13] of wings of cherubim, *gently touching* each other (c. אֶל־).

†[נְשִׁיקָה] **n.f. kiss**,—only pl cstr. נְשִׁיקוֹת מִנְּשִׁיקוֹת פִּיהוּ Ct 1[2], נְשִׁיקוֹת שׂוֹנֵא Pr 27[6] *kisses of an enemy*.

†II [נָשַׁק] **vb. exact meaning uncertain**; prob either **handle, or be equipped with** (cf. perh Ar. نَسَقَ, etc, sub I נשק),—only **Qal** *Pt* pl cstr נֹשְׁקֵי—נ׳ קֶשֶׁת 1 Ch 12[2] *equipped with the bow*, so 2 Ch 17[17] (+ מָגֵן); נ׳ רוֹמֵי קֶשֶׁת ψ 78[9] is difficult, ר׳ appos of נ׳ acc to Hup-Now Bae al (Ges[§ 130 e]); del רומי as explan. gloss Hup Hi Che Kau; del. ver. as gloss Hup Kau Bae.

†נֶשֶׁק, נֵשֶׁק **n.[m.] equipment, weapons** (coll), **armoury**,—abs. נֵשֶׁק Ez 39[9]+2 t, נֶשֶׁק 1 K 10[25] 2 Ch 9[24], נָשֶׁק 2 K 10[2]+2 t., cstr. נ׳ Is 22[8], נ׳ Jb 20[24],—**1.** *equipment, weapons* 1 K 10[25] 2 K 10[2] Is 22[8] 2 Ch 9[24] Ez 39[9] (gen term, foll by specif), v[10], נ׳ בַּרְזֶל Jb 20[24] (‖ קֶשֶׁת נְחוּשָׁה); יוֹם נָשֶׁק ψ 140[8] i e day of battle, so נ׳ alone Jb 39[21] **2.** appar *armoury* Ne 3[19].

†נֶשֶׁר **n.m.** [Dt 32.11] **griffon-vulture, eagle** (NH *id*, As *našru;* ℑ נִשְׁרָא, Syr ܢܫܪܐ, Ar. نَسْر *vulture* (Lane[2780]), vulg نِسْر, Eth ንስር: Di[641], Sab נסר n pr dei, and ביתן נסר DHM ZMG xxix (1875), 600, xxxvii (1883) 350);—abs נ׳ Ho 8[1]+; נָשֶׁר Dt 28[49]+; pl נְשָׁרִים 2 S 1[23]+, cstr נִשְׁרֵי La 4[19];—sts (perhaps not always) the *griffon-vulture* (Tristr[NHB 172 ff] Dr[Dt 14. 12] Now[Arch i 84] Lane[2780]), Mi 1[16] (bald, in sim), flying swiftly to prey Hb 1[8] Jb 9[26], cf. Pr 30[17] (בְּנֵי־נ׳), unclean Lv 11[13] Dt 14[12], soaring Jb 39[27], also in sim. Pr 23[5] Is 40[31] Ob[4], building nest high Je 49[16] (cf also Jb 39[27]), as swift also 2 S 1[23], esp of Bab and Assyr invader Je 4[13] La 4[19], cf. Ho 8[1] Dt 28[49] Je 48[40] 49[22] (all in comparisons), הַנֶּשֶׁר הַגָּדוֹל Ez 17[3] (fig. of Nebuch), v[7] (fig. of

king of Egypt); leaving no trace of flight Pr 30[19]; as renewing youth (by moulting) ψ 103[5]; as training and supporting its young Ex 19[4] (E), Dt 32[11] (song); פני נ׳ of cherubim in vision Ez 1[10] 10[4].—Only Mi 1[16] seems to compel ref. to vulture (on eating fresh carrion by eagles v. reff. in Di [Lv 11. 13]), and נ׳ may be a more comprehensive word, incl. both vulture and eagle.

†נָשַׁת **vb.** be dry, parched;—**Qal** *Pf.* 3 fs. לְשׁוֹנָם בַּצָּמָא נָשָׁתָּה Is 41[17] (on D. f. affect. v. Ges [§ 20 i]); also fig. נָשְׁתָה גבורתם Je 51[30], *their might is dry*, i.e fails. **Niph.** *Pf.* 3 pl. consec. וְנִשְּׁתוּ־מַיִם מֵהַיָּם Is 19[5] *and water shall be dried up from the sea;* cf *Impf.* יִנָּתְשׁוּ מַיִם Je 18[14], where read prob. יִנָּשְׁתוּ (Gf Gie al.)

†נִשְׁתְּוָן **n.[m.]** letter (usu der. fr. Pers. نُبِشْتن, نُوِشْتن i e. *writing*, Hoffm [ZA ii (1887). 52] yet cf. Meyer [Judenthum 22]),—abs. נ׳ Ezr 4[7] 7[11].

נתב (✓of foll; Ar نَتَبَ *swell forth, become prominent, protuberant*, Lane [2760])

†נָתִיב **n m.** [Jb 28, 7] path, pathway (as *raised*),—abs. נ׳ Jb 18[10]+3 t.; cstr. נתיב ψ 119[35], sf. 3 fs נתיבָהּ Pr 12[28] (si vera l., v infr.; on om of Mappik v Ges [§ 91 e], v infr);—*path* Jb 18[10] (fig), 28[7] 41[24] (track), ψ 78[50] (fig.); נתיב מצותיך ψ 119[35] *the path of thy commands;* דֶּרֶךְ נְתִיבָה אַל־מָוֶת Pr 12[28] *the journey of her pathway is no-death!* (|| בארח צדקה חיים) Ew Be De, v. אַל p. 39 a supr., others rd אֶל־, and either transl נ׳ *by-paths* (Hi Str), or substitute a syn. of 'wickedness' (cf Now Frankenb, Perles [Analekten 67 f.] נתעָבים after Levy [ChWB i. 28 b])

†נְתִיבָה **n.f.** id;—abs נ׳ Is 43[16], sf. נתיבָתִי Jb 30[13] + 2 t, נתיבָתָם Pr 1[15], pl. abs נתיבות Pr 8[2]+; cstr *id.* Jb 38[20]+, sf נתיבֹתַי Jb 19[8] La 3[9], נתיבֹתָיו Jb 24[13], etc;—*path:* **1.** lit הֹלְכֵי נְתִיבוֹת Ju 5[6] *goers on paths,* i e. travellers, Pr 8[2] Is 58[12] (Oort Lag Klo נתיצות but against this Du); *path* through sea Is 43[16] (in fig), of path to house of (personif.) light and darkness Jb 38[20]. **2.** oft || דֶּרֶךְ · **a.** = course of life Jb 19[8] 30[13] La 3[9] ψ 119[105] 142[4], of Isr. Ho 2[8]; of path of God's appointment Is 42[16]. **b.** of moral action, and character: paths of wisdom Pr 3[17], justice 8[20] (|| אֹרַח צְדָקָה); light Jb 24[13], נ׳ עוֹלָם Je 6[16] (|| דֶּרֶךְ הַטּוֹב); path of wicked Pr 1[15], Is 59[8] (crooked), path of adulteress Pr 7[25]; נְתִיבוֹת Je 18[15] is rendered 'by-paths,' by Gf Rothst al; < Gie makes cstr. bef. foll. דֶּרֶךְ לֹא סְלוּלָה.—נתיבָה Pr 12[28] v. נָתִיב.

†[נָתַח] **vb.** only **Pi.** cut up, cut in pieces, divide by joints (Dr [1 S 11, 7]; NH *id*, Pi.; rare);—**Pi.** *Pf* נִתַּח Lv 8[20], וְנִתַּח consec. Lv 1[6. 12], *Impf* 3 ms וַיְנַתַּח 1 K 18[33], sf וַיְנַתְּחֵהוּ 1 S 11[7], וַיְנַתְּחֶהָ Ju 19[29], etc,—*cut up, cut in pieces,* c acc. of animals 1 S 11[7], of woman Ju 20[6] (all these to be sent about as token for assembling warriors, on signif of the practice cf. RS [Sem i. 383, 2nd ed 402]); elsewh. usu.+ לִנְתָחִים, *cut up into pieces,* of woman Ju 19[29], of sacrificial animals 1 K 18[23. 33] (acc. only), Ex 29[17] Lv 1[6 12] 8[20] (all P).

†נֵתַח **n.m.** [Ez 24, 4] piece of a divided carcass (Ecclus נתחים 50 [12 c]);—abs. נ׳ Ez 24[4]; pl נְתָחִים Ju 19[29]+2 t.; sf. נְתָחָיו Ex 29[17 17]+2 t., נְתָחֶיהָ Lv 1[6]+3 t.,—usu pl *pieces:* of meat in a caldron (symbol. of Jerusalem) Ez 24[4. 6] (sg. only v[4 b]), v[6. 6]; of sacrif. animals Ex 29[17 b] Lv 1[8] 8[20 b] 9[13]; elsewh לִנ׳ after vb. נתח (q v.): of woman Ju 19[29]; Ex 29[17 a] Lv 1[6 12] 8[20 a].

†[נָתַךְ] **vb.** pour forth (intrans.), be poured out (NH *id*, Niph. *flow,* Hiph. *melt* (trans.); As. *natâku, flow* Dl [HWB 487] Jager [BAS ii. 292], ℑ Aph *pour out,* esp *melt;* Zinj. ליתכה (Haph.) No [ZMG xlvii (1893), 98] Cook [83]; Syr ܢܬܟ (rare) PS [2480]);—**Qal** *Impf.* 3 fs. תִּתַּךְ Je 42[18] +3 t, וַתִּתַּךְ Je 44[6] Dn 9[11]; 3 mpl וַיִּתְּכוּ Jb 3[24]; —*pour forth,* alw fig, וַיִּתְּ׳ כַּמַּיִם שַׁאֲגֹתָי Jb 3[24] *and my groans have poured forth like water;* usu of divine wrath (חֵמָה) Je 42[18] (c. עַל־ pers.), 44[6] (abs.), 2 Ch 12[7] 34[25] (both c. ב loc. *against*); cf. also Dn 9[11] v[27] (both c עַל־ pers). **Niph.** *Pf.* 3 ms. נִתַּךְ Ex 9[33] + 2 t, 3 fs. נִתְּכָה Na 1[6] 2 Ch 34[21], וְנִתְּכָה consec. Ez 24[11]; 2 mpl. וּנְתַכְתֶּם Ez 22[21]; *Pt* f נִתֶּכֶת Je 7[20],—*be poured,* of rain, נ׳ מַיִם עֲלֵיהֶם אָרְצָה Ex 9[33] (J), cf 2 S 21[10]; *be poured out,* of wrath of י׳ Na 1[6] (abs); Je 7[20] (c אֶל־ loc.), 42[18] (c עַל־ pers.), 2 Ch 34[21] (c. ב pers); *be poured forth* i e melted, annihilated in the midst of (בתוך) the fire of י׳'s fury Ez 22[21] (subj. persons), so 24[11] (subj. impurity, fig of caldron). **Hiph.** *Pf* 3 mpl. הִתִּיכוּ עֲבָדֶיךָ אֶת־הַכֶּסֶף 2 K 22[9] *thy servants have poured out the money* (|| 2 Ch 34[17] infr.); 1 s. וְהִתַּכְתִּי אֶתְכֶם consec. Ez 22[20] *and I will melt you* (fig. of judgment); *Inf cstr* לְהַנְתִּיךְ Ez 22[20] *in order to melt* it (i e. metal in furnace; Co after 𝔊 𝔖 reads

Niph להִנָּתֵךְ *Inf*, so Berthol, cf. Toy), *Impf* 3 mpl וַיִּתִּיכוּ 2 Ch 34[17] (‖ 2 K 22[9] supr.), הֲלֹא כֶּחָלָב תַּתִּיכֵנִי Jb 10[10] *dost* (= didst) *thou not pour me out like milk?* (of beginnings of life) **Hoph.** *Impf.* 2 mpl. כן תֻּתְּכוּ Ez 22[22] *so shall ye be melted* (fig of judgment)

†הִתּוּךְ **n.[m.]** *a melting* (Hophal-format., dissim from הַתּוּךְ, acc to Ba [NB § 102 d]),—cstr כְּהִתּוּךְ כֶּסֶף בְּתוֹךְ כּוּר Ez 22[22] *like a melting of silver in a smelting-pot*

נָתַן [2007] **vb.** give, put, set (Ecclus נתן 44[19] + oft, OHeb נתן־יהו n pr m Lzb[327]; NH = BH, Ph נתן, יתן in n pr. מתנת, etc, Lzb[292, 327], As *nadânu* Dl [HWB 450] (rarely *ittan* Id [ib 488]), Zinj נתן, also in n pr, Lzb[327] Cook[84], Nab Impf ינתן, and n pr, Palm, also n pr. Lzb[l c] Cook[l c], 𝔗 Impf יִתֵּן, Inf מִתַּן; Sab נתן Hal[154], Lih n pr נתנבעל [North-Sem form] DHM [Epigr Denkm 80 No 35], Chr Pal Aram ܢܬܠ (rare) Schwally [Idiot 58], Syr Impf ܢܶܬܶܠ, Inf ܡܶܬܰܠ Lindberg [Vergl Sem Gram 93 f], but Mand נתן No [M 52]),—**Qal**,[1917] *Pf* נ׳ Gn 24[53] +; 2 ms נָתַתָּ Ju 15[18] +, נָתַתָּה Gn 3[12] +, תַּתָּה 2 S 22[41] (defended as vulg form with aphaer of נ׳ by Th Ges [Lgb 139] Ew [§ 195 b] Ko [§ 300] De [ψ 18, 41] al, < txt err for נָתַתָּה (so ‖ ψ 18[41]) Ol [§ 89] Sta [§ 127 b] Ges [§ 19 l] (hesitantly), Klo Bu Lohr HPS, cf Hup-Now [ψ 18, 41]), 2 fs נָתַתְּ Ez 16[33.36], נָתַתִּי v[19], sf נְתַתִּיהוּ v[19], 1 s נָתַתִּי Ju 1[2] +, etc., *Impf* יִתֵּן Gn 43[14] +, וַיִּתֵּן 15[10] +; sf 3 ms. יִתְּנֶנּוּ Lv 5[24] Ec 2[21], 1 s אֶתֵּן Gn 12[7] +, 1 pl נִתֵּן 34[21] +, נִתֶּן־ Ju 16[5], etc, *Imv* ms תֵּן 2 K 4[42] +, תֶּן־ Gn 14[21], תְּנָה 1 S 2[15] +, sf תְּנֵהוּ Ne 1[11] 1 Ch 21[22], תְּנֶנָּה 1 S 21[10], fs תְּנִי Gn 30[14] +, תֵּנִי Is 43[6], mpl תְּנוּ Gn 34[8] +, *Inf. abs* נָתוֹן Dt 15[10] +, נָתֹן Nu 21[2] +, cstr נתן 20[21], תֵּת־ Gn 38[9], לִתֵּתן 1 K 6[19] (but read לָתֵת so Ol [§ 224 d] Ges [§ 67 l] Benz), תתן also 17[14] Kt (Qr תֵּת)— > these forms retained by Ew [§ 238 c] Ko [I 304],—תֵּת Gn 4[12] +, esp. לָתֵת 15[7] +, לָתֶת־ Ju 21[18], לָתֶת־ Ex 5[21] (so Ginsb, van d H. לָתֵת־, cf also Ki in Ko [I 304 f]) +, sf תִּתִּי Gn 29[19] +, תִּתְּךָ Dt 15[10] +, etc, *Pt* נֹתֵן Ju 21[18] +, etc.;—

1. *give*: **a.** = give personally, deliver or hand to, c acc rei + לְ pers 1 S 10[4] 22[10] 2 K 22[10] Lv 5[16] (P) 22[14] (H) Ru 4[7] + oft.; in trade Pr 31[24]; אֶל־ pers Gn 21[14] (E), Je 3[8] Lv 15[14] + oft, explicitly נ׳ בְּיַד Dt 24[1.3] (bill of divorce), c. acc rei alone Ju 5[25] **b.** = *bestow* upon, c acc rei + לְ pers Gn 24[53] (J) 20[16] (E) 1[29] (P) + oft., an understanding heart 1 K 3[9.12], blessing Dt 12[15], mercy 13[18], cf. Je 16[13] 42[12], strength Dt 8[18] ψ 68[36]; the sabbath Ex 16[29] (J) Ez 20[12]; = procure for (לְ) one 1 S 17[10] 1 K 21[7]; יִתֵּן לָכֶם רַחֲמִים לִפְנֵי Gn 43[14] (J) *he will give you compassion in the eyes of* the man (cf also **2 b, 3 b**), give persons 46[18.25] (P), of Levites given to (לְ) Aaron and his sons Nu 3[9] cf. 8[19], to י׳ 8[16] cf 18[6] (all P); esp of י׳'s giving land to Abr. and his descendants Gn 15[18] 26[4] (J) 17[8] (P) Ex 6[8] (P; + מוֹרָשָׁה) + oft (pt in this sense 37 t Dt), + לְרִשְׁתָּהּ Dt 3[18] +; אַל־תִּתֵּן לַנָּשִׁים חֵילֶךָ Pr 31[3], + מִן of source נָתַתִּי מִמֶּנָּה לְךָ בֵּן Gn 17[16] (P), c. acc. alone ψ 61[6] Ec 12[7] (רוּחַ), give something to (לְ) one for (לְ) sthg, in some capacity, אֶת־כָּל־אֶחָיו נ׳ לוֹ לַעֲבָדִים Gn 27[37] +, prob also נ׳ בְּבָרוּתִי רֹאשׁ ψ 69[22] *they gave, as my food, gall* (בְּ essentiae), cf supr בְּ **7 c**, Hup-Now [ad loc], acc + inf נ׳־לִי לֶחֶם לֶאֱכֹל וּבֶגֶד לִלְבֹּשׁ Gn 28[20] (J), cf Ex 16[15] (P), Ne 9[15.20], לֹא נ׳ לָכֶם לֵב לָדַעַת וְעֵינַיִם לִרְאוֹת וְאָזְנַיִם לִשְׁמֹעַ Dt 29[3]. Esp **c.** *give* woman to (לְ) man as (לְ) wife, Gn 29[28] (E), 34[8.12] (J), Jos 15[16.17] (JE), = Ju 1[12.13] +, without 2nd לְ Gn 29[19.19] (E), Gn 38[21] Ex 2[21] (J), Gn 34[9.14.16] (P), Ju 15[2.6] +; c. acc alone, Gn 29[26] (E), 1 S 25[44]. **d.** of (gracious) bestowals of various kinds: *give* = grant, send rain, מְטַר־אַרְצְכֶם Dt 11[14], גִּשְׁמֵיכֶם Lv 26[4] (H), מָטָר עַל־אַרְצְךָ 1 K 8[36], etc, also of sending plague of hail Ex 9[23] (E), send herbage (עֵשֶׂב) in (בְּ) your field for (לְ) your cattle Dt 11[15]; grant a remnant to (לְ) Judah Je 40[11]; וְנָתַתִּי לְךָ אֶת־נַפְשְׁךָ לְשָׁלָל 45[5] *and I will grant thee thy life as spoil;* grant revenge (acc) to (לְ) the king on (מִן) Saul, etc. 2 S 4[8], cf הָאֵל הַנֹּתֵן נְקָמוֹת לִי 2 S 22[48] = ψ 18[48], other gifts Ju 13[18] (בְּיַד), 1 S 1[11] (לְ), Ru 4[13]. **e.** *grant* a request, שְׁאֵלָה 1 S 1[17.27] Est 5[3] ψ 106[15] (+ לְ pers), בַּקָּשָׁה Ezr 7[6], תַּאֲוָה Pr 10[24], (רָשָׁע) מַאֲוַיֵּי ψ 140[9], תִּקְוָה Jb 6[8], יִתֵּן י׳ לָכֶם וּמְצֶאןָ מְנוּחָה Ru 1[9]. משאלת לבך ψ 37[4], cf. Esp †**f.** מִי יִתֵּן *who will give* or *grant*, in expressions of wish = O that (I had! etc., = As. *mannu inamdin* Jager [BAS ii 279]), esp. (9 t) Jb: c. acc. מִי־יִתֵּן עֶרֶב Dt 28[67] cf. v[67], Jb 14[4] ψ 14[7] = 53[7], 55[7] Je 9[1]; c 2 acc. כָּל־עַם י׳ נְבִיאִים Nu 11[29] (JE), lit *who will make all* י׳'s *people prophets?* cf. Je 8[23]; c. acc + כְּ, מִי יִתֶּנְךָ כְּאָח לִי Ct 8[1], cf. Jb 29[2], c. acc. + בְּ, אֶת־הָעָם הַזֶּה בְּיָדִי Ju 9[29] *O that this people were in my charge!* c acc + לְ Jb 31[35], lit. *who will give to me* (לִי) one hearing me? also מִי יִתְּנֵנִי Is 27[4] where sf. appar = לִי, c inf מִי יִתֵּן מוּתֵנוּ Ex 16[3] (P), co

2 S 19^{1}, מִי יִתֵּן אֱלוֹהַּ דַּבֵּר Jb 11^{5}; c. impf תָּבוֹא שְׁאֶלָתִי Jb 6^{8} *O that my request might come to pass!* 14^{13} 31^{31}; impf. + ו 19$^{23.23}$; c. pf. יָדַעְתִּי 23^{3} *O that I knew!* (+ ואמצאהו), c. pf consec. Dt 5^{26}†. **g.** *permit*, c. acc + inf, לֹא־נְתַתִּיךָ לִנְגֹּעַ אֵלֶיהָ Gn 20^{6} (E), cf. 31^{7} (E) Ex 3^{19} (J) Nu 20^{21} 21^{23} (JE) + oft, c. ל pers. + inf 2 Ch 20^{10}; other constructions are: לֹא כֵן נ׳ לְךָ י׳ Dt 18^{14} *not thus hath* י׳ *permitted to thee*, אִם־אֶתֵּן שְׁנַת לְעֵינַי וגו׳ ψ 132^{4} Pr 6^{4}; *give thyself* (ל) *no rest* La 2^{18}, *give him* (ל) *no rest* Is 62^{6}. **h.** = ascribe glory, etc (acc) to (ל) God 1 S 6^{5} Jb 36^{3}, esp imv. Je 13^{16} Ezr 10^{11} ψ 68^{35} cf 115^{1} (so הָבוּ, v. יהב **4**); to man 1 S 18$^{8.8}$; unseemliness (תִּפְלָה) to God Jb 1^{22}. **i.** = apply, devote heart to seek out, acc + inf Ec 1$^{13.17}$ 8$^{9.16}$ Dn 10^{12}, נ׳ לֵב לְ Ec 7^{21} = attend to; conversely אֶת־כָּל־זֶה נָתַתִּי אֶל־לִבִּי Ec 9^{1} = *all this I set before my mind*, 7^{2}; also (with subj diff fr. ind obj) מָה אֱלֹהַי נֹתֵן אֶל־לִבִּי לַעֲשׂוֹת Ne 2^{12} cf. 7^{5} **j.** = employ, devote money (acc) עַל־עֲבֹדַת אהל מועד Ex 30^{16} (P) **k.** *give* offerings, לי׳ Nu 18^{12} (P), תרומת י׳ Ex 30^{15} (P), cf give spoil to (ל) י׳ Dt 20^{14} (י׳ subj); מִיָּדְךָ נָתַנּוּ לָךְ 1 Ch 29^{14}, offering to (ל) idols Ez 6^{13}, esp to Moloch Lv 20$^{2.4}$, to pass through fire to (ל) M 18^{2}, etc. **l** = consecrate, dedicate to (ל) י׳ 1 S 1^{11} Ex 22^{29} (E). **m.** *give* a sign or wonder, acc 1 K 13$^{3.5}$, + ל pers Jos 2^{12} (JE), with reflex. לָכֶם Ex 7^{9} (P), alm = display, exhibit; cf נָתְנוּ הֲדָרֵךְ Ez 27^{10} *they set forth, exhibit* thy splendour; כִּי יִתֵּן בַּכּוֹס עֵינוֹ Pr 23^{31} *when it sheweth its sparkle in the cup.* **n.** = pay, wages (acc., + sf.), נ׳ שְׂכָרִי Gn 30^{18} (E) *he hath paid my hire*, Ex 2^{9} (E) Dt 24^{15}, cf. Is 61^{8}; + ל pers. Je 22^{13}; a price, נ׳ מכרם Nu 20^{19} (JE), וַיִּתֵּן שְׂכָרָהּ Jon 1^{3}, i e paid his fare, passage-money; money (as) price (מחיר) 1 K 21^{2}, cf נ׳ כֶּסֶף הַשָּׂדֶה Gn 23^{13} (P); pay money for (ב) something Dt 14^{26}; wealth for (ב) love Ct 8^{7}; tax or rent, c. acc. rei + ל pers. Gn 47^{24} (J); fine (c. *id*) Ex 21^{32} (E) Dt 22^{29}, acc. om. v^{19}, cf. וְנָתַן בִּפְלִלִים Ex 21^{22} (v. פָּלִיל), v^{19} נ׳ שִׁבְתּוֹ (i e pay for his lost time), v^{30} נ׳ פִּדְיֹן נַפְשׁוֹ (pay redemption-money; all E), cf וְנ׳ אִישׁ כֹּפֶר נַפְשׁוֹ לי׳ 30^{12} (P); pay votive offering (c. acc. + ל) Lv 27^{23} (P); a wager (c acc. + ל) Ju 14$^{12.13}$. **o.** c ב, *give* for (ב) money = sell, תְּנָה־לִּי אֶת־כַּרְמְךָ בכסף 1 K 21^{6}, cf Dt 2^{28} 14^{25} 1 Ch 21^{22},—נ׳ Ez 27 is trading term, but sts. connexion obscure and text dub: *give* wares for (ב) 27^{12} (but rd. prob ךְ for ב 𝔊 𝔖 Co Berthol), v$^{13.16}$ (del. 2nd ב), v$^{17.19.22}$ (cf, further, Co Berthol and esp. Sm); נ׳ הַיֶּלֶד בַּזּוֹנָה Jo 4^{3} (|| מָכַר); ב instr., give בְּגוֹרָל *by lot* Jos 21^{8}. **p.** *give* instead of, exchange for, c. תַּחַת Ex 21^{23} (E) 1 K 21$^{2.6}$ Is 43^{4} 61^{3}, בְּעַד Jb 2^{4}. **q.** give, i e. lend, at interest, כַּסְפּוֹ לֹא נ׳ בְּנֶשֶׁךְ Lv 25^{37} ψ 15^{5}, so (acc om) Ez 18$^{8.13}$. **r.** = commit, entrust to, c acc + אֶל־ pers. Ex 22$^{6.9}$ (E), c. ל pers. Ct 8^{11}, c. בְּיַד Gn 30^{35} 39$^{4.8.22}$ (all J), 2 S 10^{10}. **s.** *give over*, deliver up, c acc Nu 21^{3} (JE) Ju 20^{13} 1 S 11^{12} 2 S 14^{7} 20^{21} 1 K 14^{16} Ho 11^{8} (|| מגן), Mi 5^{2}; נ׳ בָּנָיו פְּלֵיטִם וּבְנֹתָיו בַּשְּׁבִית לְמֶלֶךְ אֱמֹרִי Nu 21^{29} (JE), + ל, נ׳ פ׳ לַמָּוֶת ψ 118^{18}, + לפני Dt 7$^{2.23}$ 31^{5} + (see Dr$^{Dt\ lxxxiii,\ No\ 52}$, and v further **2 b** *ad fin.*); esp נ׳ בְּיַד, c acc, Nu 21^{34} (JE) Jos 2^{24} (JE) Dt 2^{24} + oft **t.** *yield* produce, fruit, etc., esp. of land, ground, Gn 4^{12} (J), Lv 25^{19} 26$^{4.20}$ (all H), Dt 11^{17} Is 55^{10} (+ ל pers) Zc 8^{12} ψ 67^{7} 85^{13} cf Ez 36^{8}, of tree Ez 34^{27} Lv 26$^{4.20}$ (H) ψ 1^{3}, + vine Jo 2^{22}, vine Zc 8^{12}, abs root of righteous *yields*, יִתֵּן Pr 12^{12} acc to De Str (dub; prop to insert פְּרִי), Dy Kau Wild prop. אֵיתָן (as ψ 74^{15}, etc), cf as to sense Ew; other conj. v. Now; cf Nu 20^{8} (P) Zc 8^{12} Ct 1^{12} 2^{13} 7^{14}. **u.** = occasion, produce, שכל טוב יִתֶּן־חֵן Pr 13^{15} cf. 29^{15}, v^{25} חרדת אָדָם יתן מוקש *trembling before man occasioneth a snare* **v.** *requite* to (ל) a man, acc. to (כְּ) character 1 K 8^{39} = 2 Ch 6^{30} Je 17^{10} 32^{19} ψ 28$^{4.4}$; c. ב + עַל־ Ez 7^{9}; c. עַל־ pers. + acc of sin 7$^{3.4.8}$ 23^{49} (cf **2 b**). **w.** = report, mention, וַיִּתֵּן אֶת־מִסְפַּר... אֶל־הַמֶּלֶךְ 2 S 24^{9} *he reported the number unto the king*; וָאֶתְּנָה לוֹ זְמָן Ne 2^{6} *and I mentioned to him a time.* **x.** = utter, usu c. acc. קוֹל, utter a sound, lift up the voice: Je 4^{16} (+ עַל *against*), 22^{20} 48^{34} La 2^{7}, in weeping, וַיִּתֵּן אֶת־קֹלוֹ בבכי Gn 45^{2} (E), וַיִּבְכּוּ Nu 14^{1} (P); + ל pers. Pr 2^{3} (|| לַבִּינָה תִקְרָא); of wisdom Pr 1^{20} 8^{1} (|| קרא); of י׳, esp. in thunder of theoph Am 1^{2} 2 S 22^{14} (|| יַרְעֵם), = ψ 18^{14}, Je 25^{30} Jo 2^{11}, of clouds ψ 77^{18}, the deep Hb 3^{10}; of young lion's roaring Am 3^{4} Je 2^{15}; of birds ψ 104^{12}, קול om, נ׳ דָּוִד... לְהֹדוֹת לי׳ 1 Ch 16^{7}; so of י׳'s voice in thunder, לְקוֹל תִּתּוֹ Je 10^{13} (sc. קולו) *at the sound of his uttering* (his voice) = 51^{16}; נ׳ בקול Je 12^{8} (+ עַל־ *against*), of י׳ ψ 46^{7}, הֵן־יִתֵּן בְּקוֹלוֹ קוֹל עֹז 68^{34}; נ׳ with other words, אֹמֶר v^{12} (of י׳); of confession, (acc + ל pers) Jos 7^{19} (JE) Ezr 10^{11}. **y.** *give* = stretch out, extend, וַיִּתֶּן־יָד Gn 38^{28} (J) *it put out a hand*; וַיִּתֵּן צַמַּרְתּוֹ אֶל־בֵּין עֲבֹתִים

(read עֲבֹות) Ez $31^{10.14}$ *and it stretched its top amid the clouds* **z.** combinations are: יתן וַיִּתֵּנוּ לְמַכֵּהוּ לֶחִי La 3^{30} (humiliation), cf Is 50^{6}, וַיִּתְּנוּ כָתֵף סֹרֶרֶת Zc 7^{11} (of stubbornness), so Ne 9^{29} (|| עָרְפָּם הִקְשׁוּ), also וַיִּתְּנוּ עֹרֶף 2 Ch 29^{6} *gave, i e turned* (their) *back* (on 'י, || וַיַּסֵּבּוּ פְנֵיהֶם מִמִּשְׁכַּן 'י), of compact, תְּנָה אֶת־יָדְךָ 2 K 10^{15} cf v^{15}, so מִצְרַיִם נָתַנּוּ יָד La 5^{6}, of submission, נָתְנָה יָדָהּ Je 50^{15} = *she* (Babyl) *hath surrendered,* תְּנוּ יָד לי' 2 Ch 30^{8} = *submit to* 'י, more explicitly, נ' יָד תַּחַת שְׁלֹמֹה 1 Ch 29^{24}, נ' מָקוֹם לְ Ju 20^{36} *give place to* (retire before), of sexual relation, אֶל־אֵשֶׁת ... לֹא־תִתֵּן שְׁכָבְתְּךָ לְזָרַע Lv 18^{20} (H), וַיִּתֵּן אִישׁ בָּךְ אֶת־שְׁכָבְתּוֹ Nu 5^{20} (P), so (בְּכָל־בְּהֵמָה) Lv 18^{23} (H), cf 20^{15} (H) —יתן is taken impers = 'es giebt,' *there is, there are,* in Jb 37^{10} Pr 10^{24} 13^{10} by De, citing Ew§ 295 d, Now Pr 13, 10 Str Frankenb (in transl, dub in note), Bae Jb in Kau Ges§ 144 b, but improb, Kau Pr Di Jb, so Hi Bu Du (on Jb 37^{10}), reading יִתֵּן, cf. Ko Synt § 324 d β.

2. *Put, set,* nearly = שׂים, and sts || with it: **a.** lit, (esp. oft in Ez P): c acc + עַל־ *on,* ring on hand Gn 41^{42} (E), cf Ez 16^{11}, helmet on head 1 S 17^{38}, also Je 27^{2} 28^{14} (in fig), 1 K $12^{4.9}$ (in fig), 18^{23} (|| שׂים), Ex 12^{7} (acc om), cf. $25^{12.26.30}$ + oft P, c עַל־ = *above* Ex 25^{21} 26^{34} (P), = *for,* נ' גֹּרָלוֹת עַל־ Lv 16^{8} (P), *cast lots for,* = *against* Ez 26^{8}, c אֶל־ *into* ark into cart 1 S 6^{8}, *put* one in the stocks Je 29^{26} (also c עַל־ 20^{2}), in prison 37^{18} 38^{11}, cf Ex 25^{16} 28^{30} (P), *put* water upon (עַל־) sthg *into* (אֶל־) vessel Nu 19^{17}, = *toward* וַיִּתֵּן פְּנֵי הַצֹּאן אֶל־עָקֹד Gn 30^{40} (J, del. Ol Di al); c בְּ, cup into hand Gn 40^{13} (E), cf Ju 7^{16}, also Gn 41^{48} (E), cf 1 K 7^{51}, Gn 1^{17} (P), 9^{13} (P), 2 K 19^{18}, Je 27^{8}, נָתַתִּי שְׂפָתַי בְחִיקֶךָ (in fig), נ' בֶּעָפָר פִּיהוּ La 3^{29} (in fig), נָתַתִּי שִׁפְחָתִי בְּחֵיקֶךָ Gn 16^{5} (J), וְנָתַתָּה בְאָזְנוֹ וּבַדֶּלֶת Dt 15^{17} *and thou shalt put* (the awl) *into his ear and into the door* (pin his ear to the door), put disease into one Dt 7^{15} (|| שִׂים), inflict blemish (מוּם) on (בְּ), Lv $24^{19.20}$, וּכְתֹבֶת קַעֲקַע לֹא תִתְּנוּ בָּכֶם 19^{28}, c לְ + בְּ שֶׂרֶט לָנֶפֶשׁ לֹא תִתְּנוּ בִּבְשַׂרְכֶם v^{28} (all H); c לִפְנֵי *before, in front of, set food before* one, 2 K $4^{43.44}$, cf Zc 3^{9} Ez 3^{20} Ex 30^{6} $40^{5.6}$ (all P); c בֵּין *between,* Ex 30^{18} 40^{17} (P); c לְ מִגְרָעוֹת נ' לַבַּיִת סָבִיב 1 K 6^{6} *he put ledges to the house,* c other preps הָאִשָּׁה אֲשֶׁר נָתַתָּה עִמָּדִי Gn 3^{12} (J), *the woman whom thou hast set at my side,* cf Ex 31^{6} (נ' אִתּוֹ, fig. of association, assistance); c לִקְרַאת Gn 15^{10} (J), *lay* each piece *to meet* its fellow, he set the sea מִכֶּתֶף הַבַּיִת 1 K 7^{39}; c. ה loc. put money שָׁמָּה *into it* 2 K 12^{10}, so of water Ex 30^{18} (P), cf 40^{7} (שָׁם), c. 2 acc נ' אֹתוֹ בֵּית הַכְּלוּא Je 37^{4} cf. v^{15}, *put, place,* abs. Ex 40^{8} (P, || שִׂים, cf. 26^{32}), *set up,* אֶבֶן מַשְׂכִּית בְּ Lv 26^{1} (H, || הָקִים); + לְ + pers, *lay snare for me* ψ 119^{110} (in fig) **b.** fig, in many phr.: c. עַל, *put my spirit upon him* Is 42^{1}, reproach *upon* one Je 23^{40}, blessing on Mt Gerizim, etc., Dt 11^{29}, curses on enemies 30^{7}; impose tax upon Ne 10^{33} cf 2 K 23^{33}; נָתַן הוֹד עַל *put majesty upon* one 1 Ch 29^{25} Dn 11^{21} Nu 27^{20} (P, מֵהוֹד, cf. ψ 21^{6}), so also perh ψ 8^{2} *hast set thy majesty upon* (over) *the heavens,* cf. 𝔊 𝔙 𝔗 (rd נָתַתָּה for תְּנָה, Hup De Pe Bae al; other views v. in Thes Ew Ol Now Che We Du); = *above,* וּנְתָנְךָ עֶלְיוֹן עַל־כָּל־גּוֹיֵי הָאָרֶץ Dt 28^{1} cf. 26^{19}, put (sthg) *over* mouth Mi 3^{5} (i e stop one's mouth, by a gift), = *against* נ' מָצוֹר עַל־ Ez 4^{2} (siege), cf v^{2b}, c אֶל־, וָאֶתְּנָה אֶת־פָּנַי אֶל־ אֲדֹנָי ... לְבַקֵּשׁ Dn 9^{3}, c בְּ, words into mouth Dt 18^{18} Je 1^{9}, cf 1 K 22^{23}, wisdom into heart, or person, 1 K 10^{24} Ex 31^{6} $36^{1.2}$ (all P), cf. ψ 4^{8}, set peace in earth Lv 26^{6} (H), (the idea of) perpetuity (עוֹלָם) in heart Ec 3^{11}; a purpose, וּלְהוֹרֹת נ' בְּלִבּוֹ Ex 35^{34} (P); וְנָתַתִּי אֶת־יָדִי בְּמִצְרַיִם Ex 7^{4} (P), אַל־תִּתֵּן דָּם נָקִי בְּקֶרֶב עַמְּךָ Dt 21^{8}, וַיִּתֵּן חִנּוֹ בְּעֵינֵי Gn 39^{21} (J), *and he put his favour in the eyes of the prison-keeper* (made the keeper favourable to him), cf Ex 3^{21} 11^{3} 12^{36} (all E; cf. also **1 b**, **3 b**), c בְּ pers = *against,* in phr *set my face against,* oppose Ez 14^{8} 15^{7} Lv 17^{10} 20^{6} (both H), c בֵּין, = *put,* i e *make* a covenant *between* Gn 17^{2} (P), cf. Lv 26^{46} (H), נ' אֶרֶץ לִפְנֵיכֶם i e. place at your disposal Dt $1^{8.21}$ cf. 2^{36}, *set* ordinances, etc, before, לִפְנֵי (for observance), 1 K 9^{6} Je 26^{4} 44^{10} Dn 9^{10}; blessings and cursings (for choice) Dt $30^{1.15.19}$, נ' דֶּרֶךְ בְּרֹאשׁ פ' *set* or *place* one's *way upon his head,* i e requite him, Ez 9^{10} 11^{21} 16^{43} 22^{31} cf 17^{19}, also 1 K 8^{32} = 2 Ch 6^{23} + (cf. **1 v**); לָתֵת נִקְמַת י' בְּמִדְיָן Nu 31^{3} *to set the vengeance of* 'י *upon Midian,* נ' בְּ', ψ 50^{20} = *set in,* i.e. *impute to* (usu שׂים בְּ') **c.** *set, appoint,* c. acc + עַל־ *over,* 'י *hath set a king over you* 1 S 12^{13} cf. Gn 41^{41} (E), c. עַל־ *on,* נ' יֹשֵׁב עַל־כִּסְאִי 1 K 1^{48}; c בְּ *in* = over, 1 Ch 12^{9} Ne 13^{4}, c לְ, Nethinim לַעֲבֹדָה Ezr 8^{20}, c acc. alone, idol-priests 2 K 23^{5}, prophet Je 1^{5} (2 acc), leader Nu 14^{4}, one instead of (תַּחַת) another 1 K 2^{35}. **d.** = assign, designate, c לְ: God *hath*

assigned victim-flesh to (ל) you, in order to bear sins of people Lv 10^{17}, cf Nu 18^{8} (both P), cities for (ל) flight of man-slayer Nu 35^{6} (P); נָתַתִּי לָכֶם עַל־הַמִּזְבֵּחַ לְכַפֵּר Lv 17^{11} (H).

3. *Make, constitute,* **a.** c 2 acc, וְנָתַתִּי נְעָרִים שָׂרֵיהֶם Is 3^{4} *and I will make boys their princes,* cf Gn 17^{5} Ex 7^{1} (both P), ψ 18^{33} (> וַיַּתֵּר in ‖ 2 S 22^{33}), 39^{6} 69^{12} 135^{12}, etc, + בין Jos 22^{25} (P); + אֶל־ + pers וְנָתַתִּי אֶת־כָּל־אֹיְבֶיךָ אֵלֶיךָ עֹרֶף Ex 23^{27} (E), *and I will make all thine enemies unto thee a back,* i.e make them shew thee their back, flee from thee, so c. ל ψ 18^{41} = 2 S 22^{41}. **b.** c. acc. + ל, וְנָתַתִּי אֶת־יְרוּשָׁלַםִ לְגַלִּים Je 9^{10} *and I will make Jerusalem into ruin-heaps,* cf. Dt 28^{13} Is 42^{24} Gn 17$^{6.20}$ 48^{4} Nu 5^{21} Jos 17^{3} (all P) + ; נ׳ פ׳ לְרַחֲמִים לִפְנֵי 1 K 8^{50} *make* persons an object of *compassion before* (in the eyes of), so Ne 1^{11} ψ 106^{46} Dn 1^{9} (cf also **1 b, 2 b**); + ל pers. *for* (esp. Je), וּנְתַתִּים לְזַוָעָה לְכֹל מַמְלְכוֹת הָאָרֶץ Je 15^{4} *and I will make them a terror for all kingdoms of the earth,* cf 24^{9} 29^{18} 34^{17}. **c.** c. acc + כְּ, ואת הָאֲרָזִים נ׳ כַּשִּׁקְמִים 1 K 10^{27} *and the cedars he made like the sycomores,* i e. as common, = 2 Ch 1^{15}, cf. 1 K 16^{3} Ez 28^{6} Lv 26^{19} (H), Ru 4^{11}; וַיִּתֵּן אֹתָנוּ כִּמְרַגְּלִים Gn 42^{30} (E), i.e. regarded, treated us as spies, but ins. בְּמִשְׁמָר 𝔊 Ol Di Ball Holz,—אַל־תִּתֵּן אֶת־אֲמָתְךָ לִפְנֵי בַּת בְּלִיַּעַל 1 S 1^{16} difficult, (notwithstanding Jb 3^{24} 4^{19}), rd. prob. כ (HPS), or ל, for לפני **d.** rarely c. acc. alone: וּמִבְּנֵי יִשׂ׳ לֹא נ׳ שְׁלֹמֹה עֶבֶד 1 K 9^{22} *and of the sons of Israel Sol. made no slave,* but rd. prob לְמַס עֹבֵד (as v^{21}; 𝔊A εἰς πρᾶγμα, om. B 𝔊L; cf Klo Benz), וָאֶתֵּן עֲלֵיהֶם קְהִלָּה Ne 5^{7} *and I made* (held) *over their case a* great *assembly, make a decree,* חֹק, ψ 148^{6}; perh also וַתִּתֵּן אֹתֹת בְּפַרְעֹה Ne 9^{10} *and thou didst perform signs* and wonders *against Pharaoh,* etc. (cf שִׂים אוֹתֹת בּ Ex 10^{2} ψ 78^{43}).

Niph. $_{82}$ *Pf* נִתַּן Is 9^{5}+; 3 fs. נִתְּנָה Gn 38^{14}+; 2 mpl וּנְתַתֶּם consec. Lv 26^{25}, 1 pl נִתַּנּוּ Ezr 9^{7}, etc, *Impf* יִנָּתֵן Ex 5^{18}+, יִנָּתֶן לוֹ 2 Ch 2^{13} (Ginsb van d H. יִנָּתֶן־לוֹ), etc.; *Inf. abs.* הִנָּתֹן Je 32^{4} 38^{3}; *cstr.* לְהִנָּתֵן Est 3^{14} 8^{13};—**1.** *be given* to (usu c ל pers.) **a.** = bestowed upon Jos 24^{33} (E), Ez 11^{15} (+ לְמוֹרָשָׁה), 33^{24} (+ *id*), Jb 15^{19}; Ez 16^{34} Nu 26^{62} (P), Is 9^{5}, portion from sacrifice Lv 10^{14} (P), glory Is 35^{2}, birthright 1 Ch 5^{1}, freedom Lv 19^{20} (H) **b.** *given* to one (ל) for wife (ל) Gn 38^{14} (J), 1 S 18^{19} **c.** *provided,* usu. c. ל Ex 5$^{16.18}$ (J); 1 S 25^{27} 2 K 25^{30} = Je 52^{34}, Is 33^{16} Ne 13^{10}; נ׳ מֵרֹעֶה אֶחָד Ec 12^{11} *they are given from one shepherd* (i.e words of wise) acc. to Ew De Hi-Now Ruetschi^{Kau}; Wild underst subj of *compilers* **d.** = entrusted to Je 13^{20} cf. 2 Ch 2^{13}, c. עַל־יָדָם 2 K 22^{7}, בְּיַד 2 Ch 34^{16}. **e.** = give into the power of (usu. c בְּיַד), esp. of city (kg, people) given into the hand of foe 2 K 18^{30} (+ אֶת־ acc.), 19^{10} = Is 36^{15} 37^{10}, Je 21^{10} + 18 t. Je Lv Chr Dn; earth into hand of wicked Jb 9^{24}; in good sense Gn 9^{2} (P); delivered to death (ל), unto lower world (אֶל־), Ez 31^{14}; *given to us* (ל) *for devouring* (ל) 35^{12}, חֶרֶב נ׳ Ez 32^{20} *delivered to the sword* (del. 𝔊𝔖 Co Sgfr^{Kau} Toy); abs, of צָבָא, Dn 8^{12} (al. *was appointed,* v esp. Dr), 11^{6}. **f.** of request, *be granted* to (ל), Est 2^{13} 5^{3} (בַּקָּשָׁה), v^{6} 7^{2} 9^{12} (all שאלה), cf 7^{3} (בבקשה, בשאלה) **g.** = be permitted Est 9^{13} (+ inf). **h.** = be issued, published (of royal decree), abs. Est 3$^{8.14}$ 4^{8} 8$^{13.14}$ 9^{14}; of law given בְּיַד מֹשֶׁה Ne 10^{30}. **i.** = be uttered, נ׳ שְׁאוֹן קוֹלָם Je 51^{55} (of stormers of Babylon). **j.** *be assigned* for (ל), Ez 47^{11}.

2. *Be put, set:* **a.** lit, crown בְּרֹאשׁ Est 6^{8}; of personif. folly נ׳ הַסֶּכֶל בַּמְּרוֹמִים Ec 10^{6}. **b.** in imagery of Ezek נ׳ . . . בְּיַרְכְּתֵי־בוֹר Ez 32^{23}, c את (with) v^{29}, c בתוך v^{25}, vine put (cast) לָאֵשׁ לְאָכְלָה Ez 15^{4} *into the fire for consuming;* fig. of terror נ׳ בארץ 32^{25} **c.** = be made, בֶּן־אָדָם חָצִיר יִנָּתֵן Is 51^{12}. **d.** = be inflicted, of blemish (מוּם) Lv 24^{20} (c בְּ pers)

†**Hoph.** (or **Qal** *pass.* Ges^{§53u}) *Impf.* יֻתַּן 1 K 2^{21} + 5 t + 2 S 21^{6} Qr (Kt ינתן); יֻתַּן 2 S 18^{9},—**1. a.** *be given, bestowed,* abs. Nu 26^{54}; c. ל pers. 2 K 5^{17}, Nu 32^{5} (אֶת־ c. acc.; both P), in exchange for (תַּחַת) Jb 28^{15}. **b.** = *be given* to one (ל) for wife (ל) 1 K 2^{21} (Abishag, אֶת־ c. acc). **c.** = *be given, delivered, up* to (ל) 2 S 21^{6}. **2.** *be put* upon (עַל־) Lv 11^{38} (P), of Absalom וַיֻּתַּן בֵּין הַשָּׁמַיִם וגו׳ 2 S 18^{9}, > וַיִּתָּל (√תלה) 𝔊𝔖 We Dr (?), Klo Kit Bu HPS

נָתָן $_{42}$ **n pr.m.** 𝔊 Ναθαν,—†**1.** a son of David 2 S 5^{14} = 1 Ch 3^{5}, 1 Ch 14^{4}. **2.** the prophet of David's time 2 S 7$^{2.3.4.17}$ = 1 Ch 17$^{1.2.3.15}$, 2 S 12^{1} + 6 t 2 S 12, 1 K 1^{8} + 10 t 1 K 1, 2 Ch 29^{25} ψ 51^{2} (title), דִּבְרֵי נָתָן הַנָּבִיא as name of a book 1 Ch 29^{29} 2 Ch 9^{29}. †**3.** father of one of David's heroes 2 S 23^{36}. †**4.** father of officers of Solomon, 1 K 4$^{5.5}$ (= **2** ?). †**5.** name in Judah: **a.** 1 Ch 2$^{36.36}$. **b.** 11^{38}. †**6.** companion

of Ezra from Babylon Ezr 8^{16}. †**7.** one of those who took strange wives 10^{39}. †**8.** head of a family Zc 12^{12}.

†נְתַן־מֶלֶךְ **n.pr.m.** an official of Judah, Josiah's time 2 K 23^{11}, 𝔊 Ναθαν βασιλέως (τοῦ εὐνούχου), 𝔊L Ναθαν εὐνούχου τοῦ βασιλέως.

†נְתִינִים **n.m.pl.** **Nethinim** (prop. *those given* to the service of the sanctuary, as Levites are called נתונים Nu 3^{9}, $8^{16.19}$),—only 1 Ch 9^{2} (where disting. from priests and Levites) + 16 t. Ezr Ne (oft disting. from priests, Levites and porters; Ezr 8^{17} Kt has הנתונים, Qr הַנְּתִינִים), viz: Ezr $2^{43.58.70}$ = Ne $7^{46.60.72}$ (so Baer, Ginsb; van d H v^{73}), Ezr 7^{7} $8^{17.20}$ (appointment ascribed to David, cf 1 Ch 9^{2}), v^{20} Ne 10^{29} 11^{3}, living on the Ophel 3^{26} 11^{21}, with their own overseers v^{21}, having a house known (in part) by their name 3^{31}.—On נ׳ v. further Bau[Priesterthum 100. 142 f.]

†נְתַנְאֵל **n.pr.m.** (v. Gray[Prop. N 181, 192, 205], on n.pr. of this kind cf RS[Sem i 100 n., 2nd ed 108], Gray[Prop N 264]),—𝔊 Ναθαναηλ,—**1.** a chief of Issachar Nu 1^{8} 2^{5} $7^{18.23}$ 10^{15}. **2.** 4th son of Jesse 1 Ch 2^{14}. **3.** name of priests **a.** 1 Ch 15^{24}. **b.** Ne 12^{21}. **4.** priest's son (who had strange wife) Ezr 10^{22}, perh = Ne 12^{36}. **5.** Levite name **a.** 1 Ch 24^{6}. **b.** 26^{4}. **c.** 2 Ch 35^{9}. **6.** a prince of Jehoshaphat 2 Ch 17^{7}.

†נְתַנְיָה, נְתַנְיָהוּ **n.pr.m.** (cf. Gray[Prop N 294]), 𝔊 Ναθανιας;—**1.** נְתַנְיָהוּ father of Jehudi Je 36^{14}. **2.** נ׳ father of Ishmael Gedaliah's murderer Je 40^{8} 41^{9} = נְתַנְיָה 2 K $25^{23.25}$ Je $40^{14.15}$ 41^{1} + 9 t. Je 41. **3.** נְתַנְיָהוּ Levite name **a.** 2 Ch 17^{8}. **b.** 1 Ch 25^{12} = נְתַנְיָה v^{2}.

†I. מַתָּן **n.m.** [Pr 18.16] **coll. gift(s)**,—abs מ׳ Gn 34^{12} + 2 t., cstr *id* Pr 18^{16} (v. Baer[ad loc] Ges[§ 93 r] Kö[ii. 1, 98]); sf מַתָּנָם Nu 18^{11},—*marriage-gifts* Gn 34^{12} (J, + מֹהַר); *offerings* Nu 18^{11} (P; תרומת מ׳), elsewh gen., *gifts, presents*, Pr 18^{16} 21^{14} (||שֹׁחַד), אִישׁ מַתָּן 19^{6} = *a giver of gifts*.

†II. מַתָּן **n.pr.m.** **1.** priest of Baal at Jerusalem 2 K 11^{18} = 2 Ch 23^{17}, 𝔊 Μαγθαν, Ματθαν, 𝔊L Ματθαν. **2.** father of Shephatiah, in Judah Je 38^{1}, 𝔊 Ναθαν, Μαθθᾶ.

†I. מַתָּנָה **n.f.** gift,—abs מ׳ Nu 18^{6} + 4 t., cstr מַתְּנַת Dt 16^{17}, pl מַתָּנֹת Gn 25^{6} +, cstr מַתְּנֹת Ex 28^{38}, sf מַתְּנֹתֵיכֶם Ez 20^{31} +, etc.;—*gift*, Gn 25^{6} (J) Ez $46^{16.17}$ 2 Ch 21^{3}, offerings to י׳ Ex 28^{38} (מַתְּנֹת קָדְשֵׁיכֶם), Lv 23^{38} (disting. from נֶדֶר and נְדָבָה), 18^{29} (cf מַתָּנָם v^{11};—all P); rejected (idolatrous) offerings Ez $20^{26.31.39}$, אִישׁ כְּמַתְּנַת יָדוֹ Dt 16^{17} *each man acc. to the gift of his hand*, i.e. acc. to his ability, cf לָקַחְתָּ מ׳ בָּאָדָם ψ 68^{19} *thou* (י׳) *hast received gifts among men* (i.e. either tribute gained by battle, cf. Che, or the offerings of those who turn to י׳ Hup-Now, >*gifts consisting of men* JDMich Hgst Bo Ew DeWette), מ׳ used of Levites, as God's *gift* to Aaron and his sons, Nu 18^{6}, whose priesthood is עֲבֹדַת מ׳ v^{7}, i.e. a service which is a gift from God; מַתָּנוֹת לָאֶבְיֹנִים Est 9^{22} *gifts to the poor*, = bribe Pr 15^{27} Ec 7^{7}.

†II. מַתָּנָה **n.pr.loc.** a station of Isr. E. of Jordan Nu $21^{18.19}$ (JE), 𝔊 Μανθαναειν.

מַתְּנַי v. מַתַּנְיָה infr.

†[מַתַּת] **n.f. id.**,—abs. מַתַּת 1 K 13^{7}, cstr מַתַּת Pr 25^{14} + 4 t.,—*gift* = reward 1 K 13^{7}, מַתַּת יָדוֹ *the gift of his hand*, i.e. of his power, what he is able to give Ez $46^{5.11}$ (cf מַתָּנָה and יָד **2**); מ׳ אֱלֹהִים Ec 3^{13} *the gift of God* (of the enjoyment of man), so 5^{18}, מ׳ שָׁקֶר Pr 25^{14} *a gift of falsity*, i.e. one promised and not given.

†מַתַּנְיָה, מַתַּנְיָהוּ **n.pr.m.** (cf. Gray[Prop N 294, No. 82]);—𝔊 Μαθθας, Μανθανιας, Ματθανιας, etc.;—**1.** מַתַּנְיָה, last king of Judah, name changed to Zedekiah 2 K 24^{17}. **2.** מַתַּנְיָהוּ, Levite name. **a.** son of Heman 1 Ch 25^{4}. **b.** Asaphite 1 Ch 25^{16}. **c.** *id*, 2 Ch 29^{13} (Hezekiah's time). **3.** מַתַּנְיָה, Levite name. **a.** Asaphite 1 Ch 9^{15} Ne $11^{17.22}$ $12^{8.35}$, perh = **2 b, c** (but much confusion and uncertainty, e.g. מ׳ is of Hezekiah's time 2 Ch 29^{13}, and 4th generation before Neh., Ne 11^{22} 12^{35}, while contemp. of Zerub 12^{8} and of Neh. 11^{17}). **b.** other Levites: (1) 2 Ch 20^{14}, (2) Ne 12^{25}, (3) 13^{13}. **4.** מַתַּנְיָה, name of several who took strange wives: **a.** Ezr 10^{26}. **b.** v^{27}. **c.** v^{30}. **d.** v^{37}.

†מַתְּנַי **n.pr.m.** (abbrev. fr. foregoing),—𝔊 Μαθ(θ)ανια, Μαθθαναι,—**1.** a priest Ne 12^{19}. **2.** name of two who took strange wives. **a.** Ezr 10^{33}. **b.** v^{37}.

†מַתִּתְיָה, מַתִּתְיָהוּ **n.pr.m.** (cf Gray[Prop. N 294, No 81]),—𝔊 Ματταθιας, etc.,—**1.** a Levitical musician, מַתִּתְיָהוּ 1 Ch $15^{18.21}$ $25^{3.21}$ = מַתִּתְיָה 16^{5}. **2.** מַתִּתְיָה, Levitical name 1 Ch 9^{31}. **3.** מ׳, attendant of Ezra (also Levite?) Ne 8^{4}. **4.** one of those who took strange wives Ezr 10^{43}.

†מַתַּתָּה **n.pr.m.** one of those who took foreign wives Ezr 10^{33}, 𝔊 Αθα, A 𝔊L Μαθθαθ(α).

†[נָתַס] **vb.** tear or break down (=נָתַץ);—**Qal** *Pf* 3 pl נָתְסוּ נְתִיבָתִי Jb 30^{13} *they have broken down my path*, made it impassable (fig).

†[נָתַע] **vb. break, break down, or out;—Niph.** *Pf.* 3 pl. שִׁנֵּי כְפִירִים נִתָּעוּ Jb 4^{10},—Aramaic (?) form, or < textual error for נִתָּצוּ.

†נָתַץ **vb. pull down, break down** (NH Hoph, and deriv; cf. perh Eth. ነሠተ: (with transp and weakening of sibilant), *destruere, demoliri, excidere* Di^{634}),—**Qal** *Pf* 3 ms. נ׳ Ju 6^{30}+, 3 pl. נָֽתְצוּ 2 K 25^{10} Je 52^{14}, etc, *Impf* 3 ms. וַיִּתֹּץ יִתֹּץ Ez 26^{9}+v^{12} (Co, for MT יִתְּצוּ); Ju 9^{45} 2 K 23^{7}; sf. יִתְּצֵנִי Jb 19^{10}, יִתָּצְךָ ψ 52^{7}; 1 s. אתוץ Ju 8^{9}, 3 mpl. וַיִּתְּצוּ 2 K 10$^{27\,27}$; 2 mpl תִּתֹּצוּ Dt 7^{5}, תתצון Ex 34^{13} Ju 2^{2}; וְתִתְּצוּ Is 22^{2}, etc.; *Imv.* נתוץ ψ 58^{7}; *Inf cstr* לנתוץ Je 1^{10} 18^{7}, לִנְתֹּץ 31^{28} (on ה v. Ges$^{§45\,e}$); *Pt. pass* pl. הַנְּתֻצִים Je 33^{4};—**1.** lit. *pull down* a structure (acc) altar Ju 2^{2} 6$^{30\,31.32}$ Ex 34^{13} (J), Dt 7^{5} 2 K 23^{12}, high place (במה) v^{8}, בָּמָה + מזבח v^{15}; מַצֵּבָה 10^{27}; בית הַבַּעַל v^{27} 11^{18} = 2 Ch 23^{17}, cf 2 K 23^{7}; a tower Ju 8$^{9\,17}$, cf Ez 26^{9} (בחרבותיו); (any) house Is 22^{10} Ez 26^{12} Lv 14^{45}, so הַנְּתֻצִים Je 33^{4} (strangely + אֶל, cf. Gf Gie), city-wall Je 39^{8} 2 K 25^{10} = Je 52^{14}, city Ju 9^{45}. **2.** fig **a.** *pull down* a nation, break its power, וְלִנְתוֹשׁ וְלִנ׳ וּלְהַאֲבִיד (וְלַהֲרוֹס) (obj not expressed) Je 1^{10} (so Ecclus 49^{7b}), = 18^{7}, cf. 31^{28}. **b.** an individual, subj God, יִתְּצֵנִי סָבִיב Jb 19^{10}, יִתָּצְךָ ψ 52^{7} **c.** jaw-teeth of lions (metaph.) ψ 58^{7} (*break down, break off*, so only here, but v. נָתַע). **Niph.** *be pulled, broken, down*. *Pf.* 3 pl. נתצו מפני י׳ Je 4^{26} (of cities), so נ׳ מִמֶּנּוּ Na 1^{6} (of rocks) **Pi.** *Pf.* 3 ms נִתַּץ 2 Ch 33^{3}, 3 pl. ונתצו Ez 16^{39} (consec.); 2 mpl. וְנִתַּצְתֶּם Dt 12^{3}, *Impf.* 3 ms. וַיְנַתֵּץ 2 Ch 34^{7}; 3 mpl. וַיְנַתְּצוּ 31^{1}+2 t;—*tear down* (chiefly late): c acc. altars Dt 12^{3}, + בָּמוֹת 2 Ch 31^{1}, + הַחַמָּנִים, etc., 34^{4}, + אֲשֵׁרִים v^{7}, בָּמוֹת alone 33^{3}, רָמֹתַיִךְ Ez 16^{39}, city wall 2 Ch 36^{19}. **Pu.** *be torn down: Pf.* 3 ms. נֻתַּץ Ju 6^{28} (of altar + אֲשֵׁרָה). **Hoph.** (or **Qal** *pass* Ges^{§53u}) *be broken down, broken*, only *Impf.* 3 ms. יֻתָּץ Lv 11^{35} (of תַּנּוּר, v. Dr-White^{Hpt}, and כִּירַיִם, v. supr., p 468 b).

†[נָתַק] **vb. pull, draw, tear away, apart, off** (NH *id*; 𝔗 נְתַק in der. species (rare), *pull off, tear off*, Chr Pal Aram. ܢܬܩ *shake off*, Schwally$^{Idiot\ 56}$; Ar. نَتَقَ *pull off, draw out, shake;* Di^{660} cp Eth ነተተ: ነተቀ: *detrahere*, etc),—**Qal** *Pf* 1 pl. sf וּנְתַקְנוּהוּ consec. Ju 20^{32} (on d. f dirim. v. Ges$^{§20\,h}$); *Impf* 1 s. sf. אֶתְּקֶנְךָּ Je 22^{24} (cf. Ges$^{§58,\,i}$); *Pt. pass.* נָתוּק Lv 22^{24},—**1.** *draw away* warriors from (מִן) city, unto (אֶל־) high road Ju 20^{32}. **2.** *draw* or *pull off* ring from (מִן) finger Je 22^{24} (fig. of rejection of king of Judah by י׳) **3.** *pull, tear away* Lv 22^{24} (pass, of testicles, + כָּרוּת, כָּתוּת, מָעוּךְ). **Niph.** *Pf.* 3 ms. נִתַּק Is 5^{27}; 3 pl. נִתְּקוּ Jos 4^{18} Jb 17^{11}, נִתָּֽקוּ Je 6^{29} 10^{20}; *Impf* 3 ms. יִנָּתֵק Ju 16^{9} + 2 t., 3 mpl וַיִּנָּֽתְקוּ Jos 8^{16}, יִנָּתֵֽקוּ Is 33^{20};—**1.** *be drawn away* from (מִן) city Jos 8^{16} (cf. **Qal 1**); of soles of feet, *be drawn out* (from water) unto (אֶל־) dry ground 4^{18}. **2.** *be torn apart*, or *in two, snapped*. of sandal-thong Is 5^{27}, strand of tow Ju 16^{9} (sim), cord Ec 4^{12}; esp tent-cord (in fig) Is 33^{20} Je 10^{20}, so יִנָּתֵק מֵאָהֳלוֹ מִבְטַחוֹ Jb 18^{14}; metaph. of plans (זִמּוֹת) 17^{11} **3.** *be separated*, in smelting, fig., רָעִים לֹא נִתָּֽקוּ Je 6^{29}. **Pi.** *Pf.* 1 s. נִתַּקְתִּי Je 2^{20}; 3 pl. נִתְּקוּ 5^{5}; *Impf.* 3 ms יְנַתֵּק Ez 17^{9} ψ 107^{14}, וַיְנַתֵּק Ju 16^{9}, sf. וַיְנַתְּקֵם v^{12}; 2 fs תְּנַתֵּקִי Ez 23^{34}; 1 s אֲנַתֵּק Na 1^{13}; 1 pl נְנַתְּקָה cohort. ψ 2^{3}; 2 mpl. תְּנַתֵּֽקוּ Is 58^{6};—**1.** *tear apart, snap*, c acc הַיְתָרִים Ju 16^{9} *the cords*, v^{12} (+ מֵעַל זְרֹעֹתָיו); esp c acc. מוֹסֵרוֹת, *bonds* (fig.) Na 1^{13} Je 2^{20} 5^{5} 30^{8} ψ 2^{3} 107^{14}; obj. מוֹטָה Is 58^{6} (|| פַּתֵּחַ, and הַתֵּר אֲגֻדּוֹת מוֹטָה) **2.** *tear out, up*, obj. roots Ez 17^{9} (in fig); *tear out, away*, obj breasts 23^{34} (in violent fig of Jerus. as drunken woman). **Hiph.** **1.** *Inf cstr.* sf. הַתִּיקֵנוּ *draw away* warriors from (מִן) city Jos 8^{6} (= **Qal 1**). **2.** *Imv.* ms. sf הַתִּקֵם *drag them away* like sheep to slaughter Je 12^{3} (of י׳'s dealing with wicked). **Hoph.** *Pf* (si vera l.) הָנְתְּקוּ מִן־הָעִיר Ju 20^{31} *they were drawn away from the city* (cf. **Niph. 1**), but prob. gloss, v. GFM.

†נֶ֫תֶק **n.m.** $^{Lv\ 13,\ 32}$ scab, an eruption of skin, on head or in beard, causing suspicion of leprosy (lit. *a tearing off*, i e. what one is inclined to scratch or tear away, cf. *scabies* fr. *scabere*, *Kratze* fr *kratzen*, etc, v Di$^{Lv\ 13,\ 30}$),—נ׳ abs. Lv 13$^{30.32.32.33.34.34.35.36.37.37}$; נֶתֶק 14^{54}; נֶגַע הַנֶּתֶק 13$^{31.31}$ (all P)

†I. [נָתַר] **vb. spring or start up,—Qal** *Impf.* וִיִּתַּר מִמְּקוֹמוֹ Jb 37[1] *yea, it* (the heart) *starts up from its place* (‖ יֶחֱרַד) **Pi.** *Inf.* לְנַתֵּר בָּהֵן עַל־הָאָרֶץ Lv 11[21] (P), *to leap with them* (i e its legs) *upon the earth* (of locust) **Hiph** *Impf* וַיַּתֵּר גּוֹיִם Hb 3[6] he (י׳) looked, *and made nations start up*

†II [נָתַר] **vb be free, loose** (? usu. placed sub I, but connexion not obvious; cf also NH Niph *free oneself*, Hiph = BH, perh cp Ar نَتَرَ *rend* a garment, *break* string (of bow), etc), —**Hiph.** *Impf.* 3 ms. juss יַתֵּר Jb 6[9], sf וַיַּתִּירֵהוּ ψ 105[20], *Inf. abs* הַתֵּר Is 58[6], *Pt* מַתִּיר ψ 146[7],—**1.** *unfasten, loosen*, c acc rei, thongs of yoke Is 58[6] (‖ פַּתֵּחַ, תְּנַתֵּקוּ) **2.** *set free, unbind* c acc pers, prisoners ψ 105[20] (‖ וַיְפַתְּחֵהוּ), 146[7], fig יַתֵּר יָדוֹ Jb 6[9] *that he would let loose his hand* and cut me off, —וַיַּתֵּר 2 S 22[33] was poss connected by Mass with תור (v Comm), but rd. וַיִּתֵּן (as ‖ ψ 18[33])

†נֶ֫תֶר **n.[m.] natron, or carbonate of soda,** a mineral alkali (NH = BH; Aram. נִתְרָא, ܢܬܪܐ, cf Gk νίτρον, λίτρον, Lat *nitrum* (v Lexx)),—אִם־תְּכַבְּסִי בַּנֶּתֶר Je 2[22] though thou wash thyself with *natron* (fig; ‖ בֹּרִית; on use of 'nitrum,' for handwashing among Greeks v Meineke [Fragm. Comicorum ii 638]), חֹמֶץ עַל־נָתֶר Pr 25[20] (fig of the incompatible)

†נָתַשׁ **vb. pull or pluck up, root out,** esp in Je and later (Ecclus *Impf* 3 fs תנתש נטע 3[9], NH=BH, ܐ נתש *id*, Syr ܢܬܫ *tear off, away*; Ar. نَتَشَ is loan-wd Fra [137]),—**Qal** *Pf* 3 ms. וְנָתַשׁ consec. 1 K 14[15]; 2 fs. נָתַשְׁתְּ ψ 9[7], etc; *Impf* 3 ms sf. וַיִּתְּשֵׁם Dt 29[27]; 1 s. אֶתּשׁ Je 12[14], אֶתּוֹשׁ 24[6] 42[10]; *Inf. abs* נָתוֹשׁ Je 12[17], *cstr* לִנְתוֹשׁ Je 1[10] 18[7], לִנְתשׁ 31[28] (on תּ v. Ges [§45 g]), sf נָתְשִׁי 12[15], *Pt act* נֹתֵשׁ 45[4], sf. נֹתְשָׁם 12[14],—*pull* or *pluck up*, c acc Asherim Mi 5[13] (מִקִּרְבֶּךָ); esp. of nation, וְנ׳ אֶת־יִשׂ׳ מֵעַל הָאֲדָמָה 1 K 14[15], so Dt 29[27] Je 12[14] 2 Ch 7[20], אֶתּשׁ מִתּוֹכָם Je 12[14], without מֵעַל וגו׳ Je 12[15 17]; opp נָטַע 45[4]; obj om 24[6] 42[10] (both opp. נָטַע); so inf. abs. נָתוֹשׁ וְאַבֵּד 12[17]; inf. cstr. לִנְתוֹשׁ Je 1[10] = 18[7] cf. 31[28] (v. נתץ **Qal 2 a**), once of cities ψ 9[7] עָרִים נ׳ *thou hast uprooted cities* **Niph.** *Impf* 3 ms יִנָּתֵשׁ Je 31[40] *it shall not be rooted up* (‖ יֵהָרֵס, ref. to the city Jerus), 3 fs תִּנָּתֵשׁ Dn 11[4] of kingdom; 3 mpl. יִנָּתְשׁוּ מֵעַל אַדְמָתָם Am 9[15] (of Isr, opp נָטַע)—For יִנָּתְשׁוּ Je 18[14] rd יִנָּשְׁתוּ √ נשת q v. **Hoph.** *Impf.* 3 fs וַתֻּתַּשׁ Ez 19[12] *and she was rooted up* (of Isr., under fig. of vine).

ס

ס, *Samekh*, fifteenth letter, used as numeral 60 in postB Heb.

†סְאָה **n.f.** (v *infr.*) sᵉʾāh, a measure of flour, grain, etc (√ unknown; perh foreign word, NH *id.*, Aram סְאָה, סָאתָא, ܣܐܬܐ, ܣܐܐ, ܣܐܬܐ (Gk. σάτον, Lewy [Fremdwörter 116 f])),—abs סְאָה־ 2 K 7[1.16], וּסְאָה־ v[18] (Baer Ginsb cf Ges [§10 h]), du סָאתַיִם 1 K 18[32] + 3 t., pl סְאִים Gn 18[6] 1 S 25[18],—alw c appos. of thing measured, Gn 18[6] (J), 1 S 25[18] 1 K 18[32] 2 K 7[1 1 16 16 18 18] (where appar. masc, perh. after anal of other measures of capacity, הִין, חֹמֶר, כֹּר, etc, Albrecht [ZAW xvi (1896). 95]),—סַאסְּאָה Is 27[8] v סאסא.—On size of sᵉʾāh = ⅓ ephah, = 12 148 *litres* (= 10 696 qts), v Now [Arch i 203] Benz [Arch. 183].

†[סְאוֹן ?] **n.[m.] sandal, boot of soldier** (prob loan-word from As *šênu, shoe, sandal* (of leather), Dl [HWB 634] Wkl [Tel Amarna, Gloss], whence (denom) *šênu, put on sandals* Dl [l c], cf Aram סֵינָא, ܣܐܢܐ, ܣܝܢܐ, *sandal* (vb denom ܣܐܢ); Eth ሳእን: *sandal*);—prob cstr כָּל־סְאוֹן סֹאֵן Is 9[4] *every boot of one tramping* (abs. Du al.).

†[סָאַן] **vb.** prob. **denom. tread, tramp,**—only **Qal** *Pt* סֹאֵן בְּרַעַשׁ Is 9[4] (v. foregoing).

†[סַאסֵא] **vb. Pilpēl,** whence *Inf.* בְּסַאסְּאָה (MT בסאסאה) Is 27[8] = *by driving her* (it) *away* (conj fr ‖ בְּשַׁלְּחָהּ), acc to Hi Ew Di DuChe [Hpt] Am RV[m], > = בִּסְאָה סְאָה *by the sᵉʾāh, the sᵉʾāh*, i e. (Ges [§123 c, 133 k]) *by exact measure* Vrss (not ܣ), Ges De cf AV RV, which is prob. Rabbin. conceit. (On format cf. מאטא, and v Ges [§55 f] Sta [§112 a Anm 2, 238])

†[סָבָא] **vb. imbibe, drink largely** (NH *id*; Aram. סְבָא *id* (rare), cf. As. *sabû*, *sesame-wine* Dl [HWB],—Ar سَبَأ *wine*, is prob. loan-wd. and سَبَأ *import foreign wine* denom.,

Frä$^{157 f}$);—**Qal** *Impf.* 1 pl. cohort. נִסְבְּאָה Is 56^{12}; *Pt. act.* סֹבֵא Dt 21^{20} Pr 23^{21}; pl. סוֹבְאִים Ez 23^{42} Kt (Qr סָבָאִים, v. infr); cstr. סֹבְאֵי Pr 23^{20}, *pass* סְבוּאִים Na 1^{10},—*imbibe*, c. acc. שֵׁכָר Is 56^{12}; pt. act = subst. *wine-bibber, drunkard* Dt 21^{20} Pr 23^{21} (both + זולל); fully, סֹבְאֵי יַיִן 23^{20} (+ זֹלֲלֵי בָשָׂר); so also Ez 23^{42} Kt (Qr perh. n gent, so 𝔊 AV, v. infr), which rd Sm RV Sgfr^{Kau} Da; Co thinks dittogr. of מוּבָאִים, but perh. the reverse (Toy^{Hpt} om. מוּבָאִים); > Berthol (q v.) מִסְבָּא, other conj v. in Sm; וּכְסָבְאָם סְבוּאִים Na 1^{10} is prob corrupt, pt. pass of person dub, and sense obscure, del both as dittogr. Gunkel$^{ZAW\ xiii\ (1893),\ 235}$ Now, om. in transl We Kau. On Ho 4^{18} v. סֹבֶא.

†[סָבָא] only pl סָבָאִים Ez 23^{42} Qr = *drunkards, wine-bibbers*(?) so Thes al., but v. סְבָאִים.

†[סֹבֶא] **n.m.** $^{Is\ 1,22}$ drink, liquor;—only sf. סָבְאֵךְ Is 1^{22}, סָבְאָם Ho 4^{18} (but v. infr.), Na 1^{10} (but v. סָבָא);—*liquor* (appar. strong, choice) Is 1^{22}, סָר ס׳ Ho 4^{18} *their liquor* (i e their drunkenness) *is gone* Thes Hi Che RV^{m}, but very dub., 𝔊 quite diff. (ἡρέτισεν Χαναναίους), We Gu^{Kau} Now om. in transl.; conj. of Houtsma$^{ThTijdschr\ ix\ (1875),\ 60}$ סֹד סֹבְאִים, *a company of wine-bibbers*, makes good sense.

†סְבָא **n.pr.m.** 1st son of Cush, poet. and late;—Gn 10^{7} (P) (𝔊 Σαβα, as שְׁבָא) = 1 Ch 1^{9} (𝔊 *id*, but B Σαβατ), = nation (or territory) ψ 72^{10} (𝔊 Σαβα, + שְׁבָא, 𝔊 Αραβων), so (+ כּוּשׁ, ‖ מִצְרַיִם) Is 43^{3} (𝔊 Σοηνη); clearly situated in south, most prob. = λιμὴν Σαβά, and Σαβαὶ πόλις εὐμεγέθης, in Adulic gulf on W. coast of Red Sea; v Strabo$^{xvi\ 4.8.10}$ Ptol$^{iv\ 7.7f.}$ Di^{Gn} Bae$^{\psi}$ Du^{Is}; > *Meroe* Jos$^{Ant\ ii\ 10,2}$ al.

†סְבָאִים **n.pl.gent.** S^{e}bā'îm, 𝔊 οἱ Σαβαειμ, A Σεβωειμ; — כּוּשׁ וס׳ אַנְשֵׁי מִדָּה Is 45^{14} (+ כּוּשׁ, ‖ מִצְרַיִם, cf. 43^{3} supr), this perh. intended also by Ez 23^{42} Qr (v. סָבָא), perh. confounding it with שְׁבָא, cf 𝔊.

†סָבַב **vb. turn about, go around, surround** (NH *id.*, Pi Hiph, and deriv; Aram. סוּבְּבָא *rim, border;* Ar. سَبَبٌ *rope,* سَبِيبٌ *lock of hair;* poss. also سَبَّ II. *prepare a means of attaining* sthg. Lane^{1284}),—**Qal** *Pf.* 3 ms. ס׳ Ez 42^{19}+; 1 s. סַבּוֹתִי 1 S 22^{22} (but v. infr), סַבֹּתִי Ec 2^{20} 7^{25}; 3 pl סָבְבוּ Jos 6^{15} + 1 S 14^{21} 2 S 24^{6} (v. infr.), sf סְבָבוּנִי ψ 18^{6}+, סַבּוּנִי 88^{18} + 2 t, סְבָנִי 2 S 22^{6}, 2 mpl וְסַבֹּתֶם consec. Jos 6^{3}, etc.; *Impf.* יָסֹב 1 K 7^{15}+, sf יְסֻבֵּנִי ψ 49^{6}, oftener יִסֹּב 1 S 5^{8}+, וַיִּסֹּב Gn 42^{24}+, 3 mpl. יָסֹבּוּ Jb 16^{13}, וַיָּסֹבּוּ Jos 6^{14}+, 3 fpl. תְּסֻבֶּינָה Gn 37^{7}, etc., *Imv.* ms. סֹב 1 S 22^{18}, fs. סֹבִּי Is 23^{16}, etc; *Inf. cstr.* לִסְבֹב Nu 21^{4}, סֹב Dt 2^{3}; *Pt.* סוֹבֵב 2 K 6^{15}+, הַסֹּבִיב 8^{21} (Ginsb הַסֹּבִיב Kt, הַסֹּבֵב Qr), etc.,—**1.** *turn*, intrans. (Impf of form יִסֹּב in this sense only): **a.** *turn about*, oft. as preliminary to something else 1 S 15$^{12.27}$ (sq. inf), 1 Ch 16^{43} (*id*; וַיָּשָׁב in ‖ 2 S 6^{20}) + 1 S 14^{21} (rd סָבְבוּ גַם for MT סָבִיב וְגַם, 𝔊𝔖𝔙 Th We, etc.), Je 41^{14a} (+ שׁוּב v^{b}, but 𝔊 om. v^{a} cf. Gie), Ec 1$^{6\ 6}$, of door, Pr 26^{14} *turn on* (עַל) *its hinge* (cf Niph. Ez 26^{2}); *turn* (toward one) 1 S 22$^{17.18.18}$ 2 S 18$^{30.30}$ Ct 2^{17} (v. Bu); also c. אֶל־ 2 S 14$^{24.24}$ + 24^{6} (rd. סָבְבוּ for סָבִיב We Dr Bu Kit HPS; Klo יָסֹבּוּ, cf. Lohr), Ez 42^{19} Ec 1^{6}, אֶל־אַחֲרַי 2 K 9$^{18.19}$; of cup of י׳, *it shall come round unto* (עַל־, with hostile implic.; עָבַר עַל La 4^{21}) Hb 2^{16}; of Jordan, turn לְאָחוֹר ψ 114$^{3.5}$; *turn about* from (מֵעַל) Gn 42^{24}, (מִן) 1 S 18^{11}, + אֶל־ 17^{30}; so of inheritance Nu 36^{7} it *shall not go about from* (מִן) *tribe to* (אֶל־) *tribe*, also v^{9} (ל for אֶל־), cf. (abs) וַתִּסֹּב הַמְּלוּכָה וַתְּהִי לְאָחִי 1 K 2^{15} (cf. **Hiph. 1 b**); = *be brought round*, c acc loc. 1 S 5^{8} (of ark). **b.** *turn* = *change*, only Zc 14^{10} (of land, changed like [כ, i.e *into*] a plain), cf. **Hiph. 1 c.** **c.** fig *turn* (in a new direction) to do something (inf) Ec 2^{20} 7^{25}.—ψ 71^{21} is dub; Bae reads וְתָשֹׁב for וְתִסֹּב after 𝔊𝔖𝔙; Hup-Now Che al sub **a.** supr.: *turn, comfort me.*—Jb 10^{8} rd. אַחַר תְּסֹב for MT יחד סביב De al. **2. a.** *march*, or *walk, around*, c acc (city) Jos 6$^{3.4.7.14.15.15}$ (all JE), ψ 48^{13}; poss. also נָסֹב 1 S 16^{11} (of marching about altar? so HPS; *turn* to do something else Th), but cf. תסוב Ecclus 32^{1} *sit about* a table (v. Schechter$^{BS\ p.\ 66}$, and cf. מֵסַב), or rd. נשב Weir in Dr Kit Bu Lohr (perh.). **b.** *go partly round, circle about, skirt*, c. acc. (land) Nu 21^{4} (JE) Ju 11^{18}, also Dt 2$^{1.3}$; of rivers Gn 2$^{11.13}$. **c.** *make a round*, or *circuit, go about to*, c. acc. loc. 1 S 7^{16}; *go about in* (בְּ) 2 Ch 17^{9}, cf. also (c. בְּ) 23^{2} Ct 3^{2} 5^{7} Ec 12^{5}, so c acc. Is 23^{16}; = *make a circuitous march* 2 K 3^{9} (c. acc. דֶּרֶךְ).—Vid. also 2 S 5^{23} 1 Ch 14^{14} **Hiph. 2 a.** **d.** *surround, encompass*, abs. Gn 37^{7} (E); c. acc. Jb 40^{22}; with hostile purpose, 2 K 6^{15} Ec 9^{14} (both of siege), cf. 2 K 3^{25}; acc om. Ju 16^{2}, cf. 2 S 18^{15}; c. acc. rei + עַל־ pers. Ju 20^{5}, c. עַל־ pers. alone Jb 16^{13} 2 Ch

18^{31}, c אֶל־ pers 2 K 8^{21}=2 Ch 21^{9}, oft fig in poetry, c. acc Ho 7^{2} 2 S 22^{6}=ψ 18^{6}, ψ 22$^{13.17}$ 49^{6} 88^{18} 118$^{10.11.11.12}$; so also ψ 17^{11} (Kt סבבוני, Qr סְבָבוּנוּ, on text v esp Hup-Now), lit of cord *surrounding* (measuring circumf of), c acc. 1 K 7^{15} = Je 52^{21}, 1 K 7^{23} = 2 Ch 4^{2}, of ornaments, etc, *surrounding* something (acc) 1 K 7^{24} 2 Ch 4^{3}, *surround* one *with* something (2 acc) 1 K 5^{17} ψ 109^{3}, acc + בּ instr Ho 12^{1}, לְעֹכֶל ס׳ 2 Ch 33^{14} (i e build a wall around it) — 1 S 22^{22} rd חַבֹתִי (√חוב), 𝔊 𝔖 Th We Dr Kit Bu Lohr HPS

Niph. *Pf* 3 ms. נָסַב Jos 15^{3}+, 3 fs נָסַבָּה Ez 26^{2} (Ges^{§67t} St^{§410b} Kö$^{i\ 342}$), וְנָסְבָה 41^{7} (but rd. ונוסבה Ew Sm Co Toy^{Hpt}, cf Berthol), 3 pl נָסַבּוּ Gn 19^{4}+, *Impf* 3 mpl יִסַּבּוּ Ez 1^{9}+5 t, — **1. a.** *turn oneself* against (עַל־), *close round* upon (עַל) Gn 19^{4} (J) Jos 7^{9} (JE), c acc Ju 19^{22} **b.** *turn round* (from a direct course), of wheels Ez 1$^{9.12.17}$ 10$^{11.11}$, also v^{16} (but dub, Co ישבו, Toy^{Hpt} *leave*, Symm ἀπελείποντο), נָסַבָּה אֵלַי Ez 26^{2} of Jerus under fig of door (Sm Co Berthol Toy^{Hpt}) **c.** esp of boundary (Hex only P) *turn round* from (מִן), toward (לְ) Nu 34^{4}, +ה loc Jos 18^{14}, c מִן+ה loc + אֶל־ 15^{10}, c מִן alone Nu 34^{5}, c. ה loc. alone Je 31^{39} Jos 15^{3} 16^{6}, *circle about, skirt*, c. acc Jos 19^{14} **2.** pass *be turned over* to (לְ), into the power of, Je 6^{12}

Pi. *Inf cstr.* סַבֵּב אֶת־פְּנֵי הַדָּבָר 2 S 14^{20} *to change, transform, the aspect of the matter*

Po'. *Impf* 3 ms sf. יְסֹבְבֶנְהוּ, יסבבני Jon 2$^{4.6}$, Dt 32^{10}, יְסוֹבְבֶנְוּ ψ 32^{10}; 3 fs תסובב Je 31^{22}, etc, —*encompass, surround* (poet. and chiefly late) — **1.** *encompass* (with protection), c acc Dt 32^{10} (י׳ subj), c 2 acc חֶסֶד יסובבנו ψ 32^{10}, cf v^{7} (but 2nd obj here dub), similarly נקבה תסובב גָּבֶר Je 31^{22} i e *either shall protect* (so most) or (Che, cf Gf) the woman (fig. of Isr), instead of holding aloof (הַבַּת הַשּׁוֹבֵבָה v^{22}), will, in the new future which י׳ creates, with affection *press round* her divine husband **2.** *come about, assemble round* (acc pers י׳) ψ 7^{8}. **3.** *march* or *go about*, city (acc) ψ 55^{11} 59$^{7.15}$; altar (in solemn procession) 26^{6}, *go about* in (בְּ) city Ct 3^{2}. **4.** *enclose, envelop*, c acc pers. Jon 2$^{4.6}$ (of waters)

Hiph. *Pf.* 3 ms הֵסֵב 2 K 16^{18}+, 2 ms הֲסִבֹּתָ 1 K 18^{37}, 3 pl הֵסַבּוּ 1 S 5$^{9.10}$, etc.; *Impf.* 3 ms. וַיַּסֵּב Ex 13^{18}+, sf וַיְסִבֵּנִי Ez 47^{2}, 3 mpl וַיַּסֵּבּוּ Ju 18^{23}+2 t, 1 pl נָסֵב 2 Ch 14^{6}, cohort נָסֵבָּה 1 Ch 13^{3}; *Imv.* ms הָסֵב 2 S 5^{23} 1 Ch 14^{14} (but v. infr), fs הָסֵבִּי Ct 6^{5}, *Inf cstr.* הָסֵב 2 S 3^{12} 1 Ch 12^{23}; *Pt* מסב Je 21^{4}, perh also pl sf מְסִבַּי ψ 140^{10} (Ginsb), — **1. a.** *turn* (trans), *cause to turn* · *turn* face (acc) Ju 18^{23} 1 K 8^{14}=2 Ch 6^{3} (all = *turn toward*); = *turn round* face 1 K 21^{4}, + אֶל־הַקִּיר 2 K 20^{2}=Is 38^{2}; + מִן Ez 7^{22} (subj י׳), 2 Ch 29^{6} (of neglect), 35^{22} (of avoiding battle), *turn away* eyes from (מִן), Ct 6^{5}, *turn* (back), *change* heart 1 K 18^{37} (recall from apostasy, + אֲחֹרַנִּית), Ezr 6^{22} (+ עַל־), *turn back, reverse* (weapons) Je 21^{4} **b.** *bring over* (i e to allegiance), c acc + אֶל־ pers, 2 S 3^{12} 1 Ch 12^{24} (van d H. v^{23}), of י׳, *turn over* kingdom to (לְ) 1 Ch 10^{14} (cf **Qal 1 a**, 1 K 2^{15}) **c.** *turn into*, of changing name, 2 acc 2 K 23^{34}=2 Ch 36^{4}, 2 K 24^{17} **d.** = *bring round*, c. acc 1 S 5$^{8.9}$; + מִן 2 S 20^{12}, + אֶל־ 1 S 5^{10} 1 Ch 13^{3}, + acc loc. 2 K 16^{18} (sense obscure). **2. a** *cause to go around*. of carrying ark around city (2 acc.) Jos 6^{11} (JE, but **Qal** 𝔊 𝔖 𝔙), *lead round*, i.e. by a round-about way, acc pers. + acc דֶּרֶךְ Ex 13^{18} (E) Ez 47^{2}; c acc. + inf. of purpose 2 Ch 13^{13}, acc om, *lead round* toward (אֶל־) 2 S 5^{23}, away from (מֵעַל־) ‖ 1 Ch 14^{14} (where, however, perh. read as S, so Be Ot, and, in both, סב for הָסֵב Dr Kit$^{Kau\ Hpt}$ Bu HPS Lohr). **b.** *surround* with (acc) wall, 2 Ch 14^{6} (acc of city om) **c.** perh also *encompass* (as foe), מְסִבַּי ψ 140^{10} *those encompassing me* (others sub מֵסַב intr)

Hoph. *Impf* 3 ms. יוּסַב Is 28^{27}, *Pt.* fpl. cstr מֻסַבֹּת Ex 28^{11} 39^{6}, מוּסַבֹּת v^{13} Nu 32^{38} (v infr); מוּסַבּוֹת Ez 41^{24}, —**1.** *be turned*, of cart wheel, c עַל־ *upon, over*; מוּסַבּוֹת דְּלָתוֹת Ez 41^{24} pt appar as gerundive, *that can be turned, movable* (Ges^{§116e}, Co rds צלעות מ׳, cf. Toy^{Hpt}); מוּס׳ שֵׁם Nu 32^{38} *turned* (i e changed) *as to name*, but gloss, v. Di. **2.** *surrounded*, i.e. *set*, of jewels (pt cstr) Ex 28^{11} 39$^{6.13}$ (all P)

†סִבָּה **n.f.** turn of affairs, — only abs הָיְתָה סִבָּה מֵעִם י׳ 1 K 12^{15} *it was a turn* (an ordering) from י׳ (=נסבה q v, in ‖ 2 Ch 10^{15})

סָבִיב$_{336}$ **subst.**, used mostly as **adv.** and **prep.**, circuit, round about:—cstr סְבִיב + Am 3^{11}, pl. cstr סביבי + Je 32^{44} 33^{13}, sf. סְבִיבֶיךָ etc. (10 t), much oftener סְבִיבוֹת Ex 7^{24}+22 t., -תֶיךָ, סְבִיבוֹתַי, etc., Dt 17^{14}, etc. (48 t) —**1.** in *sg*. —**a.** as **subst.** 1 Ch 11^{8} מִן־הַמִּלּוֹא וְעַד־הַסָּבִיב and to *the parts round about* **b.** as **adv. acc.** סָבִיב (in) *a circuit*, i e. *round about*, Gn 23^{17}

בְּכָל־גְּבֻלוֹ סָבִיב Ex 19^{12} 25$^{11.24.25}$, Lv 1$^{5.11}$ עַל הַמִּזְבֵּחַ סָבִיב, Ju 20^{29} 1 K 3^{1} 5^{11} ψ 3^{7} אֲשֶׁר ס׳ שָׁתוּ עָלָי, 12^{9} 34^{8} + oft.; sometimes doubled, for the sake of emphasis, 2 Ch 4^{3}, Ez 8^{10} עַל הַקִּיר ס׳ ס׳, 37^{2} 40^{5} and oft. in Ez 40–43. **c.** as **prep.:** (*a*) †Am 3^{11} צַר וּסְבִיב הָאָרֶץ *distress,* and that *in the circuit of* (=*round about*) the land (but rd. prob. with 𝔖 יְסֹבֵב *will encircle*). (*b*) סָבִיב לְ׳ Ex 16^{13} 40^{33} Nu 1$^{50.53}$ 2^{2} Ju 7^{21} 1 K 6^{5} 18$^{32.35}$ Ez 41$^{10.16}$ Jb 19^{12} ψ 34^{8} 78^{28} 125$^{2.2}$ יְ׳ סָבִיב לְעַמּוֹ, 128^{3} Ct 3^{7} Na 3^{8}. (*c*) strangely, סָבִיב אֶת † 1 K 6^{5} (om. 𝔊), Ez 43^{17}. **d.** מִסָּבִיב$_{42}$, *from round about, from every side,* Ez 16$^{33.37}$ 23^{22} 37^{21}, but usu. (מִן **1 c**)=*on every side,* Je 4^{17} הָיוּ עָלֶיהָ מִסָּבִיב, Is 42^{25} וַתְּלַהֲטֵהוּ מִ׳, Jo 4$^{11.12}$; מָגוֹר מִסָּבִיב† terror *on every side!* Je 6^{25} 20$^{3.10}$ 46^{5} 49^{29} ψ 31^{14}, cf. La 2^{22}; esp. in the Deut. phrases אֹיְבִים מ׳, or הֵנִיחַ מ׳ (sts. in combin.), as Dt 12^{10} והניח לכם מכל־אויביכם מ׳, 25^{19} Jos 21^{42} וַיָּנַח יְ׳ לָהֶם מ׳, 23^{1} Ju 2^{14} 8^{34} 1 S 12^{11} +; מִסָּבִיב לְ *from round about,* †Nu 16$^{24.27}$. —On 1 S 14^{21} 2 S 24^{6} Jb 10^{8} v. סָבַב.

2. In *plur.*:—**a.** †סְבִיבִים: (*a*) in masc. sense, *those round about,* ψ 76^{12} כָּל־סְבִיבָיו יֹבִילוּ שַׁי, 89^{8} Je 48$^{17.39}$. (*b*) in neuter sense, *the parts round about,* Je 49^{5} מִכָּל־סְבִיבָיִךְ, בִּסְבִיבֵי ירושלם 32^{44} 33^{13}; 21^{14} וְאָכְלָה כָּל־סְבִיבֶיהָ, 46^{14}; with the force of a **prep.,** ψ 50^{3} וסביביו נשערה מאד, 97^{2} La 1^{17}. **b.** סְבִיבוֹת: (*a*) as **subst.** (α) *circuits,* Ec 1^{6} ועל סביבותיו שָׁב הָרוּחַ; (β) *the parts round about,* Nu 22^{4} ילחכו הקהל את־כל־סְבִיבֹתֵינוּ, Je 17^{26} 50^{32} (cf. 21^{14} supr.); with ref. to their inhabitants, ψ 44^{14} = 79^{4} לעג וקלס לסב׳, Ez 16^{57} 28^{24} Dn 9^{16}. (*b*) with the force of a **prep.** Ex 7^{24} סְבִיבֹת הַיְאֹר lit. (in) *the circuits of* the Nile = *round about* the Nile, Nu 11$^{24.31.32}$ 35^{2} סְבִיבֹתֵיהֶם, Ju 7^{18} 1 S 26$^{5.7}$ 2 K 6^{17} סביבֹת אלישע, ψ 18^{12} 27^{6} עַל אֹיְבַי סביבותי, etc.; oft. idiom. preceded by אשר, as Gn 35^{5} הערים אשר סביבותיהם 41^{48} Lv 25^{44} Nu 16^{34} Dt 6^{14} 13^{8} 17^{14} 21^{2} +. In the same sense מִסְּבִיבוֹתָם †Ez 28^{26}.

†מֵסַב **n.**[**m.**] **that which surrounds,** or **is round**;—**1. a.** pl. *surrounding places,* מְסִבֵּי יְרוּשָׁ׳ 2 K 23^{5} *places round about Jerus.* **b.** as adv. מֵסַב *round about* 1 K 6^{29}; fpl. מְסִבּוֹת *on all sides, in all directions,* Jb 37^{12} (of cloud Di < of lightning Bu Du). **2.** sf. מְסִבּוֹ Ct 1^{12} dub.: *round table* Ew De; *cushion, divan* Bae Kau; cf. on all these Bu.—מְסִבַּי ψ 140^{10} v. סבב **Hiph.**

†[מוּסָב] **n.m. encompassing, surrounding** (?);—only cstr. מוּסַב הַבַּיִת Ez 41^{7} *the encompassing of the house,* but mng. wholly obscure; *מוּסָף *enlargement* Ew Berthol Toy^{Hpt} after 𝔊; Co del. clause as dittogr.

†נְסִבָּה **n.f.** turn of affairs;—abs. 2 Ch 10^{15} (=סִבָּה q.v., ‖ 1 K 12^{15}).

†[סָבַךְ] **vb. interweave** (‖ form to שׂבך q.v.);—**Qal** *Pt. pass.* pl. סִירִים סְבֻכִים Na 1^{10} *interwoven* (entangled) *thorns* (cf. Da); Gunkel ZAW xiii (1893). 235 prop. (after 𝔊 𝔗 Vollers) כְּסוּחִים i.e. *cut off, away* (Is 33^{12}) cf. Now; text very dub. **Pu.** *Impf.* 3 mpl. עַל־גַּל שָׁרָשָׁיו יְסֻבָּכוּ Jb 8^{17} *are interwoven* (in a tangled mass).

†סְבַךְ **n.**[**m.**] **thicket**;—abs. (נֶאֱחַז) בַּסְּבַךְ Gn 22^{13} (so Ginsb; Baer בִּסְבַךְ, van d. H. בַּסְּבַךְ) a ram *caught in the thicket* by its horns; pl. cstr. סִבְכֵי הַיַּעַר Is 9^{17} *thickets of the forest,* 10^{34}.

†[סְבֹךְ] **n.**[**m.**] id.;—cstr. בִּסְבָךְ־עֵץ ψ 74^{5} *in the thicket of trees;* sf. מִסֻּבְּכוֹ Je 4^{7} (abode of lion; on בְּ v. Ges^{§20h}; on ـ Kö$^{II. 1. 512}$).

†סִבְּכַי **n.pr.m.** a captain of David; 𝔊 Σοβοχαι, etc.; 2 S 21^{18} = 1 Ch 20^{4}, 1 Ch 11^{29} + ‖ 2 S 23^{27} where rd. ס׳ for MT מְבֻנַּי Th We Dr Klo Bu Kit Löhr cf. HPS (B ἐκ τῶν υἱῶν, but 𝔊L Σαβενι); also 1 Ch 27^{11}.

†[סָבַל] **vb. bear a heavy load** (NH *id.*; Ar. סְבַל, ܣܰܒܶܠ *id.*; cf. also sub זבל p. 259 b supr.);—**Qal** *Pf.* 3 ms. sf. סְבָלָם Is 53^{4}; 1 pl. סְבָלְנוּ La 5^{7};—*Impf.* 3 ms. יִסְבֹּל Is 53^{11}; 1 s. אֶסְבֹּל 46^{4}; 3 mpl. sf. יִסְבְּלֻהוּ 46^{7}; *Inf. cstr.* לִסְבֹּל Gn 49^{15};—*bear* a load, וַיֵּט שִׁכְמוֹ לִסְבֹּל Gn 49^{15} (poem in J; of Issachar under fig. of ass); of carrying an idol Is 46^{7}; of יְ׳ carrying Isr. v$^{4.4}$; servant of יְ׳ carrying load of pain 53^{4} and guilt v^{11}; Isr. bearing iniquities of fathers La 5^{7}. **Pu.** *Pt.* pl. מְסֻבָּלִים *laden,* ψ 144^{14} (i.e. pregnant Ges Hi Ew Hup-Now Che al.; perh. better, token of abundant harvest, so many, v. esp. Bae). **Hithp.** *Impf.* וְיִסְתַּבֵּל הֶחָגָב Ec 12^{5} *drag oneself along,* as a burden (v. חָגָב).

†סֵבֶל **n.**[**m.**] **load, burden**;—abs. Ne 4^{11} ψ 81^{7} (enforced burden); cstr. *id.,*=*burdensome labour* (of *corvée*) 1 K 11^{28}.—Vid. also סַבָּל.

†[סֹבֶל] **n.m.**$^{Is\ 10.27}$ **burden** (always fig. of burden of tyranny);—only sf. סֻבֳּלוֹ, Is 10^{27}

(v reff. on סִבְּכוֹ, [סְבֹךְ]), ס׳ על 9³ 14²⁵ (in all conceived as burden resting on shoulders)

†סַבָּל n [m.] burden-bearer, (late),—only abs ס׳ coll Ne 4⁴ 2 Ch 2¹ ¹⁷, mpl abs סַבָּלִים 2 Ch 34¹³,—נשׂא סַבָּל 1 K 5²⁹ is certainly wrong; 𝔊 αἴροντες ἄρσιν, 𝔙 qui onera portabant, hence prob נֹשֵׂא סֹבֶל, > אִישׁ סַבָּל, as ‖ 2 Ch 2¹

†[סְבָלָה] n.f. burden;—pl. cstr. סִבְלֹת מִצְרַיִם Ex 6⁶ (P), of the heavy labours imposed on Isr by Egypt, v⁷, sf סִבְלֹתֵיכֶם 5⁴ (J), סִבְלֹתָם 1¹¹ 5⁵ (both J), 2¹¹ (E), (cf. ψ 81⁷, סֵבֶל).

†סִבֹּלֶת n.f. prob ear of wheat, etc., only Ju 12⁶ dial form of II שִׁבֹּלֶת q.v (> = late wd שִׁבֹּלֶת tide, flood), cf Marquardt[ZAW viii (1888), 151 ff] but also GFM Bu

†סִבְרַיִם n pr.loc. city between the border of Damascus and that of Hamath Ez 47¹⁶, identif by v Kasteren[Revue Bibl Internat 1895, 23 ff] with Khirbet Sanbariye on the river Hâsbânî, SW. of Hermon, cf Buhl[Geogr 67 238], but this appar too far SW., 𝔊 Σεβραμ, A Σεφραμ A city Šabara'in is named in Bab Chron.[1 28] (Schr[KB ii 276]), but location not given

†סְבָא, סַבְתָּה n.pr.gent. 3rd 'son' of Cush acc to Gn 10⁷ (ה‍ָ—), = 1 Ch 1⁹ (א‍ָ—), identif with Σαββαθα [Periplus maris Erythr.[27]], Σαυβαθα Ptol[vi 7 38], or Σαβατα [Strabo[xvi 42]], Sabota [Plin[NH vi § 1.8, xii 63]], old commercial city of S Arabia, by Tuch Ku, but this = Sab שבות (not ס׳) Levy-Os[ZMG xix (1865), 253, xx (1866), 273], cf Hal[JAs 7, iv 525], Glaser[Skizze ii 252 f] prop Σαφθα (Ptol[vi 7 30]), near W. shore of Pers Gulf, 𝔊 Σαβαθα, Σαβατα, Σεβαθα. All uncertain conjectures

†סַבְתְּכָא n.pr.gent. 5th 'son' of Cush acc to Gn 10⁷ = 1 Ch 1⁹ (ה‍ָ— acc. to Baer, א‍ָ—, as Gn, van d. H. Ginsb), location quite unknown, 𝔖 Σαβακαθα, Σεβεκαθα

†[סָגַד] vb. prostrate oneself in worship (only Is 44, 46) (perh Aram loan-word in Heb, cf No[ZMG xli (1887) 719], Aram סגד, ܣܓܕ, so OAram. סגד, ܣܓܕ (Sachau) Lzb[328], Eth. ሰገደ: all id, Ar سَجَدَ be lowly, submissive, prostrate oneself in prayer, etc, مَسْجِد mosque, Nab מסגדא shrine (?) Lzb[152.328], Syr ܣܓܕܬܐ = Ar, cf We[Skizzen iii 165; Held 141]),—**Qal** *Impf* 3 ms יִסְגּוֹד לוֹ Is 44¹⁷ Kt he prostrateth himself to it (an idol; Qr יִסְגָּד־לוֹ; + יִשְׁתַּחוּ, יִתְפַּלֵּל), v¹⁵ וַיִּסְגָּד־לָמוֹ (‖וַיִּשְׁתַּחוּ), 1 s. אֶסְגּוֹד לְבוּל עֵץ v¹⁹; 3 mpl. יִסְגְּדוּ אַף־יִשְׁתַּחֲווּ 46⁶ (abs)—Cf. BAram סגד.

סוּג, סִגִים, סגים v. סִיג sub I סוג

סגל (√of foll; cf NH סְגוּלָּה as BH, סגל acquire property, Aram. סְגוּלָא, ܣܓܘܠܐ, bunch of grapes, As. sugullâtê, herds; also Ar سَجْل [a full bucket, bucketful], share, portion)

†סְגֻלָּה n.f. possession, property (on format. v Ba[NB § 95 b] Ko[ii 1 168]),—abs ס׳ Ex 19⁵ + 5 t, cstr. סְגֻלַּת Ec 2⁸, sf סְגֻלָּתוֹ ψ 135⁴,—**1.** valued property, peculiar treasure, which ׳׳ has chosen (בחר) and taken to himself, always of people of Israel, first Ex 19⁵ (E, 𝔊 λαὸς περιούσιος = Tit 2¹⁴, 1 Pet 2⁹ λαὸς εἰς περιποίησιν = περιποίησις Eph 1¹⁴ cf. Br[MP 102, MA 52, 235]), then עם ס׳ Dt 7⁶ 14² 26¹⁸; later ס׳ alone, Mal 3¹⁷ ψ 135⁴ **2.** treasure (very late), of kings 1 Ch 29³ (gold and silver), Ec 2⁸

†[סָגָן, סֶגֶן] n.m. prefect, ruler (loan-word fr As šaknu, prefect of conquered city or province (√šakânu, set, appoint) Dl[HWB 659], cf Schr[COT ii 41 25], appar = NH סְגָן, סֶגֶן, Aram סגנא a superior (not high) priest, Mand אשנאנדא WBrandt[Mand. Schriften 169] a candidate for priesthood; cf Jen in Brandt[ib.], hence perh Gk ζωγάνης, cf Lewy[Fremdw 129]),—only pl סְגָנִים Ez 23⁶ + 14 t, sf סְגָנֶיהָ Je 51⁵⁷ + v²⁸ (where rd prob סְגָנָיו 𝔊 Gie),—**1.** prefects of Assyr and Bab Ez 23⁶ ¹²·²³ Je 51²³·⁵⁷ (all + פַּחוֹת), Is 41²⁵, of king of Medes Je 51²⁸ (+ פַּחוֹת). **2.** petty rulers, officials of Judah (only Ne Ezr in sources). disting from חֹרִים nobles Ne 2¹⁶ 4⁸ ¹³ 5⁷ 7⁵, alone, 2¹⁶ 12⁴⁰ 13¹¹, + יְהוּדִים 5¹⁷ (v. also 2¹⁶), + שָׂרִים Ezr 9². Cf BAram סְגַן

I. סָגַר vb. shut, close (NH id, Aram סְגַר, ܣܓܪ id.; Zinj מסגרת prison Lzb[328], Ph סגר Pi. or Hiph deliver over; poss Eth ሰጋሪ: (prison) guard Pra[BAS i 371]),—**Qal** *Pf* 3 ms ס׳ Gn 19⁶ +, 3 pl סָגְרוּ 2 Ch 29⁷, סָגְרוּ ψ 17¹⁰ (cf. Baer's n, Ges[§ 20 c] Ko[ii 1, 633 Anm]), סָגְרוּ Gn 19¹⁰ Jos 2⁷, *Impf* יִסְגֹּר Jb 12¹⁴ Mal 1¹⁰, 1 pl cohort. נִסְגְּרָה Ne 6¹⁰, etc, *Imv* ms. סְגֹר ψ 35³ Is 26²⁰ (וּסְגֹר Baer Ginsb), mpl. סִגְרוּ 2 K 6³², *Inf cstr.* לִסְגּוֹר Jos 2⁵, *Pt act* סֹגֵר Is 22²², f. סֹגֶרֶת Jos 6¹ (but v. infr), *pass* סָגוּר 1 K 6²⁰ + 12 t.;—**1.** shut door (דֶּלֶת) Gn 19¹⁰ (J) 2 K 6³² Mal 1¹⁰ Ne 6¹⁰ 2 Ch 28²⁴ 29⁷; gate (שַׁעַר) Jos 2⁷ (JE) Ez 46¹²,

cf. 44$^{1.2.2}$ 46^{1}, וַיְהִי הַשּׁ׳ לִסְגֹּר Jos 2^{5} (JE), also (שַׁעַר om.) Jos 6^{1} (si vera l.; סֹגֶרֶת dittogr. acc. to Buhl$^{Lex 13}$); door after one (אַחֲרֵי), on leaving room Gn 19^{6} (J); upon, behind, oneself, from within (בְּעַד q.v.) 2 K 4$^{4.5.33}$ Is 26^{20} (fig.), also (דֶּלֶת om.) Ju 9^{51} 2 K 4^{21}; c. בְּעַד + דֶּלֶת upon one left inside Ju 3^{23}, and (דֶּלֶת om.) Gn 7^{16} (J); fig. ס׳ בְּעַד רַחְמָהּ 1 S 1^{6}, cf. ס׳ דַּלְתֵי בִטְנִי Jb 3^{10}, רַחְמָהּ v^{6}; abs. *shut* (opp. פָּתַח) Is 22$^{22.22}$; metaph. חֶלְבָּמוֹ ס׳ ψ 17^{10} *their fat* (i.e. gross, unreceptive heart) *they have closed.* **2. a.** *close* in upon (בְּעַד) Ju 3^{22} (fat upon blade of sword), so poss. also וַיִּסְגֹּר בָּשָׂר תַּחְתֶּנָּה Gn 2^{21} (J) *and flesh closed in,* in place of it (usu. and he closed flesh, i.e. closed the gap with flesh); ס׳ עֲלֵיהֶם הַמִּדְבָּר Ex 14^{3} *the wilderness hath closed in upon them;* obj. om., יִסְגֹּר עַל־אִישׁ Jb 12^{14} *he closeth in upon a man,* fig. of imprisonment. **b.** *close up* breach (פֶּרֶץ) [in wall] of city 1 K 11^{27}; poss. *close* up [path] (si vera l.) ψ 35^{3} Vrss Ol De Bae; JDMich DeW Ew Hup-Now Che take סְגֹר here as weapon, usu. *battle-axe* [Gk. σάγαρις] of Massagetae Herod$^{1.215}$ cf. Lag$^{Ges. Abh. 203}$, also Egypt. *sagartá* (loan-word) Bondi^{55}; both improb., text prob. corrupt; Schwally$^{ZAW xi (1891), 258}$ reads חָגֹר > Hal$^{Rev. Sém. iii (1894), 47}$ עֶזְרָה (cf. ψ 59^{5}). **3.** *Pt. pass., closed up = closely joined* with tight seal, Jb 41^{7} (of scales of crocodile). **4.** elsewhere only *Pt. pass.* in זָהָב סָגוּר (gold *shut up,* and so *prized, rare, fine* ?), only of temple adornment and utensils 1 K 6$^{20.21}$ 7$^{49.50}$ 10^{21} = 1 Ch 9^{20}, 1 Ch 4$^{20.22}$; perh. read סָגוּר (abbrev. for ז׳ ס׳) Jb 28^{15} (for MT סְגוֹר, so Hoffm Bu Du): cf. As. *ḫurâṣu sakru,* Dl$^{HWB 499}$.

Niph. *Pf.* 3 ms. נִסְגַּר 1 S 23^{7}; *Impf.* 3 ms. יִסָּגֵר Ez 46^{2}; 3 fs. juss. תִּסָּגֵר Nu 12^{14}, וַתִּסָּגֵר v^{15}; 3 mpl. יִסָּגֵרוּ Is 45^{1} 60^{11}, וַיִּסָּגְרוּ Ne 13^{19}; *Imv.* ms. הִסָּגֵר Ez 3^{24};—**1.** subj. pers. *be shut up* [in city] 1 S 23^{7}, מִחוּץ לַמַּחֲנֶה Nu 12$^{14.15}$ (E); בְּתוֹךְ בֵּית Ez 3^{24}. **2.** *be shut, closed,* of city gates Ez 46^{2} Is 45^{1} 60^{11} and (דלתות) Ne 13^{19}.

Pi. *Pf.* 3 ms. סִגַּר 1 S 26^{8} 2 S 18^{28}; sf. סִגְּרַנִי 1 S 24^{19}; *Impf.* 3 ms. sf. יְסַגֶּרְךָ 1 S 17^{46};—*deliver up* to (leave no other opening for one, shut one up to), cf. [מָגַן], מִגֵּן, p. 171 b supr.), only S: c. acc. pers. + בְּיַד 1 S 17^{46} 24^{19} 26^{8}; בְּיַד om. 2 S 18^{28} (v. also **Hiph.**).

Pu. *Pf.* 3 ms. סֻגַּר Is 24^{10}; 3 pl. סֻגְּרוּ Je 13^{19}, וְסֻגְּרוּ consec. Is 24^{22}; *Pt.* f. מְסֻגֶּרֶת Jos 6^{1};—*be shut up:* **1.** of cities Je 13^{19} (opp. פָּתַח), of beleaguered city Jos 6^{1} (JE), of houses Is 24^{10} (+ מִבּוֹא). **2.** of prisoners עַל־מַסְגֵּר Is 24^{22} = *down into* a dungeon. **3.** of doors Ec 12^{4}.

Hiph. *Pf.* 3 ms. הִסְגִּיר Lv 14^{46} +; 2 ms. sf. הִסְגַּרְתַּנִי ψ 31^{9}; 1 s. וְהִסְגַּרְתִּי Am 6^{8}, etc.; *Impf.* 3 ms. יַסְגִּיר Jb 11^{10}, וַיַּסְגֵּר ψ 78$^{48.62}$; 2 ms. תַּסְגִּיר Dt 23^{16}, juss. תַּסְגֵּר Ob^{14}, etc.; *Inf. cstr.* הַסְגִּיר Am 1^{6}, sf. הַסְגִּירוֹ 1 S 23^{20}, הַסְגִּירָם Am 1^{9};—**1.** *deliver up* to (cf. **Pi.**), c. acc. pers. + בְּיַד 1 S 23$^{11.12.20}$ 30^{15} Jos 20^{5} (D) ψ 31^{9}; + לְ Am 1^{9} ψ 78$^{50.62}$, and (acc. pers. om.) Am 1^{6}; + אֶל־ Dt 23^{16} Jb 16^{11}; c. acc. of animal + לְ ψ 78^{48}; c. acc. pers. alone Dt 32^{30} Ob^{14}, acc. om. 1 S 23^{12}; c. acc. urb. alone Am 6^{8}. **2.** *shut up* (late; chiefly Lv 13, 14, P): **a.** c. acc. pers. Lv 13$^{5.11.21.26}$ cf. v$^{4.31.33}$, so (abs.) = *imprison* Jb 11^{10}; c. acc. rei Lv 13^{54} cf. v^{50}. **b.** c. acc. הַבַּיִת Lv 14^{38} and (indef. subj.) v^{46}.

†סְגוֹר **n.[m.]** enclosure, encasement;—cstr. סְגוֹר לִבָּם Ho 13^{8} *the encasement of their heart* (*pericardium;* i.e. their vitals).—סְגוֹר Jb 28^{15} must = *fine gold,* si vera l., but v. סגר, **Qal** ad fin.; סְגֹר ψ 35^{3} v. *id.*, **Qal 2 b.**

†סוּגַר **n.[m.]** cage, prison (poss. loan-word from As. *šigaru, cage* (Ba$^{NB 22}$); NH סוּגַר *dog-collar* or *chain* = Syr. ܣܘܓܪܐ (*clog of*) *dog-collar;* whence Ar. سَاجُور *dog-collar* (as loan-word), Frä^{114} Prä$^{BAS i. 372}$);—וַיִּתְּנֻהוּ בַסּוּגַר Ez 19^{9} *and they put him into a cage.*

†מַסְגֵּר **n.[m.]** **1.** locksmith, smith. **2.** dungeon:—alw. abs.: **1.** coll. *smiths,* וְכָל־הֶחָרָשׁ וְהַמַּ׳ 2 K 24^{14} cf. v^{16}, Je 24^{1} 29^{2}. **2.** *dungeon* Is 24^{22} (cf. סגר **Pu.**); fig. of exile 42^{7} (הוֹצִיא מִמַּ׳); הוֹצִיאָה מִמַּ׳ נַפְשִׁי ψ 142^{8}.

†מִסְגֶּרֶת **n.f.** **1.** border, rim. **2.** fastness;—abs. מ׳ Ex 25^{27} 37^{14}; cstr. מ׳ 25^{25} 37^{12}; sf. מִסְגַּרְתּוֹ 25^{25} 37^{12}; pl. abs. מִסְגְּרוֹת 1 K 7^{28} +; sf. מִסְגְּרֹתֶיהָ v$^{35.36}$, etc.;—**1.** *border, rim* (enclosure), of sacred table in tabern. Ex 25$^{25.25.27}$ = 37$^{12.12.14}$; of bases of the sea, in temple 1 K 7$^{28.29.31.32.35.36}$ (cf. Benz), also 2 K 16^{17}. **2.** *fastness,* וְיַחְרְגוּ מִמִּ׳ ψ 18^{46} = 2 S 22^{46} (v. חרג) *and they shall come quaking out of their fastnesses,* so Mi 7^{17} (יִרְגְּזוּ, like reptiles), all of nations, in awe of י׳.

II. סגר (√ of foll.; cf. appar. Ar. سَجَرَ *fill with water* Lane^{1308}, سَاجِرٌ torrent *that fills everything* Id$^{ib.}$; Syr. ܣܓܪܐ *imber vehemens,* and Sam. אַסְגָר, cf. Gei$^{Nachgel. Schr. iv. 186}$).

†סַגְרִיר **n.[m.]** **steady, persistent rain** (on format. cf. Ba[NB 215]);—abs. יוֹם ס׳ Pr 27[15] *a day of steady rain, rainy day.*

†סַד **n.[m.]** **stocks,** for confining feet of culprits (prob. loan-word fr. Aram. סַדָּנָא, סַדָּא, ܣܕܐ; NH סַד, pl. סַדִּין); = Lat. *nervus*, Gk. ποδοκάκη;—abs. שִׂים בַּסַּד רַגְלָיִם Jb 13[27] (𝔊 κώλυμα), 33[11] (𝔖 ξύλον); (cf. syn. מַהְפֶּכֶת, and Gk. equiv. there cited).

סְדֹם[39] **n.pr.loc. Sodom,** important Canaanitish city named (usu.) with Gomorrha (עֲמֹרָה, q.v.);—𝔊 Σόδομα (inflected Σοδόμων, Σοδόμοις):—ס׳ (on format. cf. Lag[BN 54]), Gn 13[10.12.13] + 7 t. Gn 18, 19, + סְדֹמָה (ה loc.) Gn 10[19] 18[22] 19[1] (all J), + 8 t. Gn 14; fr. 8th cent. onwards, used as illustrating י׳'s judgments, Am 4[11] Is 1[9] 13[19] Dt 29[22] Je 49[18] 50[40] Zp 2[9] La 4[6]; as proverbial for open sin Is 3[9] Je 23[14], so metaph. קְצִינֵי ס׳ Is 1[10] (i.e. rulers as corrupt as in Sodom), גֶּפֶן ס׳ Dt 32[32] (i.e. wickedness like Sodom's); Judah cp. with ס׳ to her disadvantage Ez 16[46.48.49.53.55.56]. Site prob. at S. end of Dead Sea, where are now *Jebel Usdum* (SW.), and *Zoar* (SE.) cf. Di[Gn 19, 20 ff.] Rob[BR ii. 187 ff.] GASm[Geogr. 505 ff.] Blankenhorn[ZPV xix (1896). 53 ff.] Bd[Pal. 3. 146] Buhl[Geogr. 117, 271, 274]. Vid. also שִׂדִּים.

†סָדִין **n.[m.]** **linen wrapper** (perh. foreign word; cf. As. *sudinnu* Dl[HWB 490], a garment; NH סָדִין, 𝔗 סְדִינָא, Syr. ܣܕܝܢܐ, ܣܘܕܢܐ (rare) Mk 15[46]; > cf. Ar. سَدِينٌ, سِدْنٌ *veil, saddle-cover* (v. Lane[1335]), or ܣܘܕܪܐ, Gk. [and 𝔊] σινδών, cf. Frä[48] Lewy[Fremdw. 85]);—abs. ס׳ Pr 31[24]; pl. סְדִינִים Ju 14[12.13] Is 3[23];—*wrapper* or rectangular piece of fine *linen*, worn as outer, or (at night) as sole garment (cf. GFM[Ju 14, 12]), + חֲלִפֹת בְּגָדִים Ju 14[12.13], in list of women's finery Is 3[23], made and sold by the capable woman Pr 31[24].

סדר (√of foll.; cf. As. *sadâru, arrange in order, sidru, sidirtu, row, battle-line;* NH סָדַר *arrange, order,* Aram. סְדַר, ܣܕܪ, all c. deriv.).

†[סֵדֶר] **n.[m.]** **arrangement, order** (on vocaliz. cf. As. *sidru, sidirtu*, and Ba[NB § 77 c]);—only pl. לֹא סְדָרִים Jb 10[22] = *disorder, confusion,* of the dark underworld.

†[שְׂדֵרָה] **n.f. 1. row, rank** of soldiers in line. **2.** architectural term. (prob. for סְדֵרָה, v. supr. and cf. Ba[§ 92 a]);—only pl. abs. שְׂדֵרוֹת 2 K 11[8] 2 Ch 23[14], רֹת- 1 K 6[9] 2 K 11[15];—**1.** *rows, ranks,* 2 K 11[8], and v[15] = 2 Ch 23[14] (where thought to be gloss by Benz, on account of מִבֵּית, *within*). **2.** term. techn. of building, גֵּבִים וּשְׂדֵרֹת בָּאֲרָזִים 1 K 6[9], meaning unknown.

†[מִסְדְּרוֹן] **n.[m.]** **porch, colonnade**? (*place of a row* (of pillars)?);—only c. ה loc.: וַיֵּצֵא אֵהוּד הַמִּסְדְּרוֹנָה Ju 3[23] precise meaning dub., cf. GFM.

סהר (√of foll. = *be round*?; cf. NH סַהַר *a round place; As. sîru, enclosing wall;* also Ph. סהרו **n.pr.loc.**).

†סַהַר **n.[m.]** **roundness**;—אַגַּן הַסּ׳ Ct 7[3] *a bowl of roundness* = a round bowl (in sim.).

†סֹהַר **n.[m.]** **roundness** (?);—only in בֵּית הַסּ׳ Gn 39[20.20.21.22.23] (all J), 40[3.5] (R[J]), *the round house* (name of a prison: but ס׳ perh. an Egypt. word Hebraized, cf. Dr in Hastings[DB ii. 768 n.] and Eb[Äg. M. 318 f.]).

†סוֹא **n.pr.m.** (𝔊 Σηγωρ, A Σωα, 𝔊L Αδραμελεχ τὸν Αἰθίοπα τὸν κατοικοῦντα ἐν Αἰγύπτῳ (!); Jos[Ant. ix. 14, 1] Σωαν; 𝔙 *Sua;* all acc.), called מֶלֶךְ מִצְרַיִם 2 K 17[4], with whom Hoshea had intrigue; poss. = *Šab-'-ê*, or *Sib-'-ê* mentioned by Sargon (KB[ii. 54, l. 25, 26] COT[ad loc.]) as a ruler (appar.) under *Pir'u* king of *Muṣuri;* hence Schr[COT l. c.] prop. to rd. סֶוֶא, and, further, identif. *Šab-'-ê* = סֶוֶא with *Šabaku*, founder of 25th (Ethiop.) dynasty, cf. Wied[Äg. Gesch. 583 f.]; very uncertain is Wkl's conj. of סוא = *Sib-'-ê* as general of kg. *Pir'u* of *Muṣri* in N Arab. (Wkl[MVG 1898, 3 ff.]).

I. [**סוּג**, seldom **שׂוּג**] **vb. move away, backslide** (ש׳ erron.; Ar. (سوج), سَاجَ *go and come* Lane[1459], سَوْجَانٌ *abitus et adventus* Frey (Ḳam));—**Qal** *Pf.* 3 ms. סָג ψ 53[4]; *Impf.* 1 pl. נָסוֹג ψ 80[19]; *Pt. act.* cstr. סוּג Pr 14[14] (Ba[NB § 124 e] Ges[§§ 50 f, 72 p]);—*backslide, prove recreant to* י׳, c. מִן ψ 80[19]; so abs. 53[4]; סוּג לֵב Pr 14[14] *a backslider in heart.* **Niph.** *Pf.* 3 ms. נָסוֹג ψ 44[19], נָשׂוֹג 2 S 1[20] (שׂ for ס); 1 s. נְסוּגֹתִי Is 50[5]; 3 pl. נָסֹגוּ Is 42[17] Je 38[22]; *Impf.* 3 ms. יִסַּג Mi 2[6] (Ges[§ 72 dd], but v. infr.); 3 mpl. יִסֹּגוּ ψ 35[4] + 3 t., וַיִּסֹּגוּ ψ 78[57]; *Inf. abs.* נָסוֹג Is 59[13]; *Pt.* pl. נְסוֹגִים Zp 1[6] Je 46[5];—**1.** refl. *turn oneself away, turn back:* **a.** lit. of Jonathan's bow 2 S 1[22], c. מִן (v. HPS). **b.** fig. = prove faithless (as **Qal**): (1) of human friends, נס׳ אָחוֹר Je 38[22] (abs.); usu. (2) נס׳ מֵאַחֲרֵי י׳ Zp 1[6] cf. Is 59[13]; so abs. ψ 78[57] (+ בָּגַד), c. אָחוֹר Is 50[5] (‖ מָרִיתִי), ψ 44[19]

(נָטָה מִן ‖).—לֹא יִסַּג כְּלִמּוֹת Mi 2^{6} could mean *reproaches do not depart,* i.e. cease (Hi-St Che GASm Now RV); Now prop. also (emending foll. v.) *shall not disgrace depart from Jacob's house?* Buhl$^{Lex\,13}$ conj., plausibly, יַשִּׂיג (√נשׂג) *disgrace shall not overtake* us. **2.** *be turned* or *driven back, be repulsed,* of י׳'s foes: + אָחוֹר Je 46^{5} Is 42^{17} ψ 35^{4} 40^{15} = 70^{3}, 129^{5}. **Hiph. 1.** usu. of *displacing, moving back* a boundary mark (גְּבוּל), *Impf.* 2 ms. תַּסִּיג Dt 19^{14}, juss. תַּסֵּג Pr 22^{28} 23^{10}; 3 mpl. יַשִּׂיגוּ Jb 24^{2} (שׂ for ס); *Pt.* מַסִּיג ג׳ Dt 27^{17}, מַסִּיגֵי ג׳ Ho 5^{10}. **2.** *remove, carry away,* valuables, to rescue them, juss., 2 ms. תַּסֵּג Mi 6^{14} si vera l. (on synt. v. Dr$^{\S\,152,\,1.\,2;\;155\,Obs.}$). **Hoph.** *Pf.* 3 ms. וְהֻסַּג אָחוֹר מִשְׁפָּט Is 59^{14} *and justice is driven back* (צְדָקָה מֵרָחוֹק ‖ תַּעֲמֹד).

סוּג Ez 22^{18} v. following.

†סִיג, שִׂיג **n.[m.]** **1.** **a moving back** or **away; 2. dross** (*what is removed* from metal);—abs. סִיג Ez 22^{18} Qr (סוּג Kt), שִׂיג 1 K 18^{27} (שׂ for ס, but v. infr.); pl. סִיגִים (van d. H. סִגִּים) Is 1^{22} + 3 t.; סִגִּים Ez 22^{18} + 2 t.; sf. סִיגַיִךְ Is 1^{25};—**1.** *a moving back, away:* שִׂיג לוֹ 1 K 18^{27} *there is a moving back to him* = *he has moved back, away* (prob. of temporary withdrawal, diff. from דֶּרֶךְ *journey*). **2.** *dross,* usu. of silver Pr 25^{4} (מִכֶּסֶף), 26^{23} (כֶּסֶף ס׳), so (fig. of Isr.) Is 1^{22} cf. v^{25}, Ez 22^{18b} (בְּתוֹךְ סִיגִים כֶּסֶף MT, כ׳ ס׳ 𝔊 Co Berthol;—Co del. ס׳, not so Berthol Toy), cf. $v^{18a.\,19}$; indef. ψ 119^{119}.

† II. [שׂוּג, סוּג] **vb. fence about** (Aram. word; ܣܳܓ, ܣܝܳܓ *sepsit, circumsepsit, clausit,* ܣܝܳܓܳܐ *sepes,* cf. 𝔗 סִיג Pa. *fence about,* סְיָיגָא *fence;* NH סוג *fence about;* Ar. سِيَاجٌ *enclosure made with thorns,* etc., *around grape-vines,* etc. Lane^{1460}, سَوَّجَ II. *make a* (سِيَاج);—only **Qal** *Pt. pass.* f. בִּטְנֵךְ עֲרֵמַת חִטִּים סוּגָה בַּשּׁוֹשַׁנִּים Ct 7^{3} *thy body a heap of wheat fenced about with lilies* (cf. esp. De Bu). **Pilp.** intens. *Impf.* 2 fs. תְּשַׂגְשֵׂגִי Is 17^{11} *thou dost fence it carefully about* (> *make it grow,* as if שׂנה=שׂוג, AE Ki Brd Du).

סוד (√of foll.; perh. kindred with יסד (cf. יסד **Niph.**), v. Kö$^{II.\,1,\,49}$; Ecclus 42^{12} Hithp. הִסְתַּיֵּד (marg. הסתיד) *converse,* is perh. denom.; Syr. ܣܘܳܕܳܐ, ܣܰܘܶܕ *friendly, confidential speech,* ὁμιλία, ܐܶܣܬܰܘܰܕ = ὁμιλεῖν; Sab. מסוד *place of speaker, oracle,* Hom$^{ZMG\,xlvi\,(1892),\,529}$, who finds connexion with سَيِّدٌ *lord, chief* (and سَادَ *be lord*), properly *speaker;* NH=BH).

†סוֹד **n.[m.]** council, counsel;—ס׳ abs. Pr 11^{13} +; cstr. Je 6^{11} +; sf. סוֹדִי Je 23^{22} Jb 19^{19}; סוֹדוֹ Am 3^{7} Pr 3^{32}; סֹדָם Gn 49^{6};—**1.** *council,* in familiar conversation;—**a.** *divan* or *circle* of familiar friends, ס׳ בַּחוּרִים Je 6^{11}, ס׳ משׂחקים 15^{17}; מְתֵי סוֹדִי Jb 19^{19} *men of my intimate circle;* עמד בסוד (י׳) Je $23^{18.\,22}$ *in the intimate circle of* י׳; בסוד אלוה Jb 15^{8}; in bad sense, ס׳ מְרֵעִים ψ 64^{3}. **b.** *assembly, company,* ס׳ יְשָׁרִים ψ 111^{1} (‖ עֵדָה); ס׳ קדשׁים ψ 89^{8} (of angels); in סוֹד עמי Ez 13^{9}; bad sense, בסוד בא Gn 49^{6} (‖ קהל). **2.** *counsel,* taken by those in familiar conversation: **a.** *counsel* itself, מחשׁבות באין סוד Pr 15^{22} *thoughts without counsel;* of intimate friendship, ψ 55^{15} נַמְתִּיק סוֹד; in bad sense, of crafty plotting 83^{4} יַעֲרִימוּ סוֹד. **b.** *secret counsel,* which may be revealed (גלה), Am 3^{7} Pr 11^{13} 20^{19} 25^{9}. **c.** *familiar converse* with God, *intimacy,* ס׳ י׳ ליראיו ψ 25^{14} *intimacy with* י׳ *have those who fear him* (‖ ברית), את־ישׁרים סודו Pr 3^{32} *with the upright is his intimacy;* here also Jb 29^{4} (si vera l.) Di De al.; Siegf Du cf. Buhl^{Lex} בְּסֹךְ *when Eloah sheltered* my tent.

†סוֹדִי **n. pr. m.** a Zebulunite Nu 13^{10} (=*סוֹדְיָה *intimacy of Yah*);—𝔊 Σουδ(ε)ι.—Vid. also בְּסוֹדְיָה p. 126 supr.

סוה (√of foll.; cf. Ph. סוית *curtain, veil?* Bloch^{46} Lzb^{328}).

†[סוּת] **n.[m.]** vesture (NH, but dub.; v. Levy$^{s.v.}$);—sf. 3 ms. סוּתֹה Gn 49^{11} (poem in J; ‖ לְבֻשׁוֹ).

†מַסְוֶה **n.[m.]** veil;—abs. מ׳ עַל־פָּנָיו Ex 34^{33} cf. $v^{34.\,35}$ (P).

סוח (√ of following; = סחה q.v.).

†סוּחָה **n.f.** offal;—abs. in sim. נִבְלָתָם כַּסּוּחָה בְּקֶרֶב חוּצוֹת Is 5^{25}.

†סוּחַ **n.pr.m.** an Asherite 1 Ch 7^{36}; 𝔊 Σουχι, A 𝔊L Σουε.

†סֹטַי, סוֹטַי **n.pr.m.**; בְּנֵי־סֹטַי among returned captives Ezr 2^{55} = בְּנֵי סוֹטַי Ne 7^{57}; 𝔊 Σατει, Σουτει, 𝔊L Σωται.

†I. [סוּךְ, סִיךְ] **vb.** pour in anointing, anoint (NH Aram. סוּךְ *anoint*);—**Qal** *Pf.* 2 fs. וְסַכְתְּ consec. Ru 3^{3}; 1 s. סַכְתִּי Dn 10^{3};

Impf. 2 ms. תָּסוּךְ Dt 28[40] Mi 6[15], 2 fs תָּסוּכִי 2 S 14[2], 1 s sf וָאֲסֻכֵךְ Ez 16[9], 3 mpl sf וַיְסֻכוּם 2 Ch 28[15], also (prob) 3 ms. וַיָּסֶךְ 2 S 12[20] (Ges[§ 73 f]), *Inf abs* סוּךְ Dn 10[3], appar *Impf pass* is יִיסָךְ rd. יוּסָךְ Sam, cf Ko[i. 436] (and not **Hoph.**, cf. Ges[l c]),—*anoint*, in the toilet, oft. after washing; usu **1.** refl *anoint oneself*, 2 S 12[20], Ru 3[3], סוּךְ לֹא־סָכְתִּי Dn 10[3], + שֶׁמֶן as acc. mat. 2 S 14[2] Mi 6[15] Dt 28[40] **2.** act, *anoint* another Ez 16[9] (בַּשָּׁמֶן), 2 Ch 28[15] **3.** pass, *be poured*, Ex 30[32] (P, subj the sacred oil).

†אָסוּךְ **n.[m.] flask** (*for pouring, anointing*);—appar cstr. אָ׳ שָׁמֶן 2 K 4[2], cf Ko[ii 1. 139, 401, 494], yet form unusual and text dub, Gi סֶךְ, or מַסֵּכָה, Klo פַּךְ.

†II [סוּךְ, סִיךְ] **vb. hedge, or fence about, shut in** (‖ form of שׂוּךְ, prob not connected with Ar شَوْكٌ, Eth. ሦክ: *thorns*, poss cf Syr ܣܳܟ *finish*, Pa ܣܰܝܶܟ *finish, conclude, comprehend*, and Ar سَكَّ *close, close up, stop, stop up, lock up*, Lane[1386]),—**Qal** (al **Hiph**, but cf שׂוּךְ) *Impf* 3 ms וַיָּסֶךְ אֱלוֹהַּ בַּעֲדוֹ Jb 3[23], c acc + ב instr. וַיָּסֶךְ בִּדְלָתַיִם יָם 38[8] *and (who) shut in the sea with doors?* (Bi Bu וּמִי סָךְ, Me מִי סָךְ)

†מְסוּכָה **n f. hedge** (‖ form of מְשֻׂכָּה q v sub שׂוּךְ),—only in fig יָשָׁר מִמְּסוּכָה Mi 7[4], rd יְשָׁרָם מְס׳ (‖ טוֹבָם כְּחֵדֶק), *their most upright one is a hedge* (an obstruction)

†[סוֹן, < סְוֵן], סְוֵנֵה **n. pr. loc. Syene**, city on S border of Egypt, toward Ethiopia, only in phr מִמִּגְדֹּל ס׳ (וְעַד־גְּבוּל כּוּשׁ) Ez 29[10] cf 30[6], rd prob סְוֵנָה or < סְוֵנֶה (Copt *Suan*), c ה loc (JDMich Sm Co Berthol) = Egypt *Sun*, Copt *Suan*, mod أَسْوَان, *Aswân*; 𝔊 ἕως Συηνης; rd prob. סְוֵן also 30[16] (for MT סִין q v.) 𝔊 Συηνη — See further Jos[BJ iv 10, 5] Strabo[xxxii 817-820], Brugsch[Geogr Inscr 1 155, Reisober aus Aegypt 247] Bd Egypt[4 324 f] Budge[Nile 284].

†סְוֵנִים **adj. gent. pl. Syenites**, so (or סְוֵנִים) rd prob. for סִינִים (q v.) Is 49[12]

†I. סוּס **n.[m] swallow or swift** (*cypselus*, Tristr[FFP 52 ff]) (𝔗 סוּסְיָא Is 38[14]),—as twittering Is 38[14] (in sim), 𝔊 χελιδων, 𝔙 *pullus hirundinis*, so Je 8[7] Kt (Qr סִיס wrongly, perhaps to distinguish from foll, so Gie), 𝔊 *id*, 𝔙 *hirundo*

II. סוּס[138] **n.m.**[Ex 15, 1] **horse** (NH סוּסָה, סוּס, Aram. סוּסְיָא, ܣܘܣܝܐ, Mand סוּסִיא, Sin *id*, Lzb[328]; As *sisû* (*sîsû*?) Dl[HWB 506], Tel Am. *su-u[su]* Wkl[TA 101 24], prob. foreign word cf. No[M 147] Erman[Aegypten 649, Eng tr 490]),—ס׳ abs. 1 K 20[20] +, cstr. Ex 15[19] +, pl סוּסִים Gn 47[17] +, סֻסִים 2 S 15[1]; cstr. סוּסֵי 2 K 2[11], sf סוּסַי 1 K 22[4] 2 K 3[7], סוּסֶיךָ Mi 5[9] + 4 t, סוּסָיו Is 5[28] +, סוּסֵיכֶם Am 4[10], סוּסֵיהֶם Jos 11[6] +,—*horse* **1.** non-Isr.; *chariot-horses* of Canaanites Ju 5[22] (cf. v[28] 4[3 13]; ס׳ coll, as oft), עִקְּבֵי ס׳, Jos 11[4 6 9] (JE); *horses* as property of Egyptians Gn 47[17] Ex 9[3] (both J), cf Zc 14[15], merchandise of Tyre Ez 27[14], *chariot-horses* of Egypt [cf Hom[II Ix 384]], Ex 14[9 23] (P), 15[1 21] (poem), v[19] (P, on all v Di), Dt 11[4] Is 31[1 3] Je 46[4 9] Ez 17[15], of Aram 1 K 20[1] + 11 t. K (1 K 20[20] *ridden*, for flight), Assyr. Is 5[28] + 3 t, Chaldeans Je 4[13] + 6 t., other nations Na 3[2] Je 50[42] + 5 t, as ridden 1 K 20[20] (v. supr), Je 8[23] Ez 38[4 15] + 13 t (late) **2.** in Isr.; chariot-horses of Absalom 2 S 15[1], esp of Sol., and later, 1 K 5[6.8] 10[25.28.29], and ‖ Chr; 18[5] and (as war-equipment) 22[4] 2 K 3[7] 9[33] 10[2] Pr 21[31]; סוּסֵי אֵשׁ 2 K 2[11] (Elijah), cf. 6[17], consecr. to sun 2 K 23[11] (cf RS[Sem 275, 2nd ed 293]); sign of luxury and apostasy Am 4[10] Ho 1[7] 14[4] Is 2[7] Mi 5[9] Zc 9[10], cf Dt 17[6.16], but v Zc 14[20]; in vision Zc 6[2.2.3.3 6]; ridden 2 K 9[18 19] 18[23] = Is 36[8], Am 2[15] + 4 t Is Je, in vision Zc 1[8.8], שַׁעַר הַס׳ Je 31[40] Ne 3[28], cf 2 K 11[16] = 2 Ch 23[15]; property of returned exiles Ezr 2[66] = Ne 7[68] van d H (om Mass Baer Ginsb q v); description of horse Jb 39[19]; in various sim and fig Am 6[12] Je 5[8] 8[6] 12[5] Ez 23[20] Is 63[13] Jo 2[4] Pr 27[3] ψ 32[9] 147[10] **3.** *chariot-horses* of י׳ Hb 3[15] (fig of clouds), cf. Zc 10[3] —Cf also חֲצַר סוּסִים, and פָּרָשׁ, רֶכֶשׁ.

†[סוּסָה] **n.f mare**;—c. sf. סֻסָתִי Ct 1[9].—Cf. also חֲצַר סוּסָה.

†סוּסִי **n.pr.m.** (Gray[Prop. N 92]),—a Manassite Nu 13[11], 𝔊 Σουσ(ε)ι,—but text dub Nes[Eg 209] Di[ad loc] (cf Gray[l c])

†[סוּף] **vb. come to an end, cease** (𝔗 סוּף, Syr (ܣܳܦ) ܣܳܦ, *cease, stop* (oft), 𝔗 סוֹפָא, Syr ܣܰܘܦܳܐ, NH סוֹף *end*);—**Qal** *Pf* 3 pl סָפוּ ψ 73[19], וְסָפוּ consec. Am 3[15], *Impf* 3 ms יָסוּף Est 9[28], 3 mpl. יָסֻפוּ Is 66[17],—*come to an end* Am 3[15] Is 66[17] ψ 73[19] (+ תַּמּוּ), וְזִכְרָם לֹא־יָסוּף מִזַּרְעָם Est 9[28]. **Hiph.** *make an end of*, only (if text correct) *Impf.* 1 s (+ Inf. abs. אָסֹף, chosen for assonance, v. אסף), cohort. = juss. in form, אָסֹף אָסֵף Zp 1[2], אָסֵף v[3.3], אָסֹף אֲסִיפֵם Je 8[13] (on these forms v Gf Bo[§ 988, 1] Ko[i 445, 466]); but rd. perhaps, for אָסֵף, אֶאֱסֹף, We Buhl[Lex 13], or אָסֹף,

Ges[§§ 72 aa, 113 w n 3] Now[Zp 1,2], and in Je אָסֹף אסִפם Ges[1 o] (against Gie v. Hi)

† סוֹף **n.m.**[Ec 7,2] **end**, late synon of קֵץ;—ס׳ abs Ec 3[11], cstr. 2 Ch 20[16] + 2 t.; sf. סֹפוֹ Jo 2[20];—*end* of wady 2 Ch 20[16], of invading swarm Jo 2[20], of God's work מֵראשׁ וְעַד־סוֹף Ec 3[11], death as *end* of all men 7[2]; = *conclusion, sum* of instruction 12[13]. Cf. BAram.

† I. סוּפָה **n f. storm-wind** (that *makes an end*?),—abs. ס׳ Is 5[28]+, סוּפָתָה Ho 8[7] (Ges[§90 f]), sf. סוּפָתֶךָ ψ 83[16], pl. סוּפוֹת Is 21[1],—*storm-wind*, ס׳ בְּסַעַר בְּיוֹם Am 1[14], Na 1[3] (‖ שְׂעָרָה), Is 17[13] (‖ רוּחַ), Jb 37[9] Is 21[1], as driving chaff Jb 21[18] (vb גָּנַב; in sim), sim. of rushing chariots Is 5[28] 66[15] Je 4[13], of ruin Pr 1[27] cf. 10[25]; symbol. of י׳'s judgments, רוּחַ יִזְרָעוּ וְס׳ יִקְצֹרוּ Ho 8[7], ψ 83[16] (‖ סַעַר), Jb 27[20] (vb גָּנַב), Is 29[6] (+ סְעָרָה).

† I. סוּף **n.m.**[Jon 2,6] **reeds, rushes** (coll) (prob. loan-word from Egypt *twfi, reeds*, Steindorff [BAS i. 603] Erman [ZMG xlvi (1892), 122]; Semitic acc to WMM [As. u. Eur 101]);—**1.** *rushes*, in Nile Ex 2[3.5] (E); קָנֶה וָסוּף Is 19[6] (of Egypt) **2.** usu. in combin יַם־סוּף prob = *sea of rushes* or *reeds* (> *sea of* (city) *Suph*), which Gk. incl. in wider name θάλασσα ἐρυθρά, **Red Sea** (cf Di [Ex 13, 18] and esp. WMM [As u. Eur 42 f], who expl as name orig given to upper end of Gulf of Suez, extending into Bitter Lakes, shallow and marshy, whence *reeds* (prob. also reddish colour)),—name applied only to arms of Red Sea; most oft. **a.** to *Gulf of Suez* Ex 10[19] Jos 2[10] (both J), Ex 13[18] 15[4.22] 23[31] (all E), Dt 11[4] Jos 4[23] (D), Nu 33[10 11] (P), elsewh. late Ne 9[9] ψ 106[7.9.22] 136[13 15] **b.** sts to *Gulf of Akaba* 1 K 9[26], and דֶּרֶךְ יַם־סוּף Nu 21[4] (E), prob. also 14[25] (E), Dt 1[40] 2[1]; perh. Ju 11[16] Je 49[21], poss rd. מִיַּם־סוּף for מוֹל ס׳ Dt 1[1] (v. infr.).

† II. סוּף **n.pr.loc.** (si vera l.) named in defining loc. of Deut law-giving Dt 1[1] (מוֹל סוּף, where מוֹל by dissimil for מוּל); but read perh. מִיַּם סוּף (𝔊 πλησίον τῆς ἐρυθρᾶς, 𝔊L + θαλάσσης, 𝔙 *contra mare rubrum*), v. I. סוּף

† II. סוּפָה **n.pr.loc.** E. of Jordan;—only in phr. וָהֵב בְּס׳ in ancient poet. fragment Nu 21[14], Tristr[Moab 50] cp. *Sûfieh* (صافيه), SE. oasis of Dead Sea, but ס = ص is most improb.

סוּר and (Ho 9[12]) [שׂוּר][300] **vb. turn aside** (NH Hiph. *cause to turn aside*, or *apostatize;* Tel Am. *sûru*, n. *rebel* Wkl[Gloss]),—**Qal**[161] *Pf.* 3 ms סָר Ex 3[4]+, 3 fs. סָ֫רָה 1 S 16[14]+; 1 s. סַרְתִּי ψ 119[102]; 3 pl סָ֫רוּ Dt 9[12]+; 2 mpl. סַרְתֶּם v[16]+, etc , *Impf* 3 ms יָסוּר Gn 49[10]+, וַיָּ֫סַר Ju 4[18]+; 3 fs. תָּסוּר 1 S 6[3]+, 1 s. cohort. אָסֻ֫רָה Ex 3[3]; 3 mpl. יָסֻ֫רוּ Ex 25[15]+, etc ; *Imv.* ms. סוּר 2 S 2[22]+, etc., *Inf. abs* סוֹר Dn 9[5], סָר v[11]; *cstr.* סוּר Is 7[17]+; sf שׂוּרִי Ho 9[12] (Ges[§ 6 k] Now); *Pt.* סָר Jb 1[1]+; f. cstr. סָרַת Pr 11[22]; mpl. cstr. סָרֵי Je 6[28] (or from סרר, or שָׂר); *pass.* f. סוּרָה Is 49[21], c. intrans. meaning (Ges[§ 50 f] Kö[ii 1, 137]), pl. sf. סוּרַי Je 17[13] Qr; and cstr. סוּרֵי 2[21],—**1.** *turn aside*, out of one's course 1 S 6[12] Dt 2[27], *from following*, מֵאַחֲרֵי pers 2 S 2[21 22], abs. v[23], *from attacking*, מֵעַל 2 Ch 20[10]; *turn in unto* (for shelter, refuge, etc.), c אֶל־, Gn 19[2.3] (J) Ju 4[18 18 18] 19[11 12] 2 K 4[11], c. לְ Ju 20[8], c שָׁם 18[3] 19[15], שָׁ֫מָּה 18[15] 2 K 4[8] (+ inf), v[10]; c הֵ֫נָּה Pr 9[4.16] (in fig); for purpose implied Ex 3[3] (J) Ru 4[1.1], or expr. by inf. Ex 3[4] (J) Ju 14[8] Je 15[5] (in fig.); esp. fig *turn aside* from right path, from י׳, his commands, etc, usu. c. מִן Ex 32[8] (J) Ju 2[17] Dt 9[12] + 7 t D, Pr 13[14] + 5 t Pr, + 10 t. elsewhere, + 2 Ch 8[15] (ins. מִן); c. מֵאַחֲרֵי 1 S 12[20] + 4 t; c. מֵעַל Je 32[40] Ez 6[9], יָמִין + מִן etc. Dt 5[29] 17[11] 2 K 22[2] = 2 Ch 34[2], abs (sts = *revolt*) ψ 14[3] Je 5[23] Dt 11[16] 17[17] (subj לְבָב), וְסוּרַי Je 17[13] Qr (> יסורי Kt) read prob. וְסוּרֶיךָ *those revolting from thee* (Ew Gie), סוּרֵי הַגֶּפֶן נָכְרִיָּה Je 2[21] *degenerate* (shoots) *of the foreign vine* (fig); סָרַת טָעַם Pr 11[22] a woman *turning aside as to discretion*, shewing lack of it, also from wrong path, sins (of Jerob), etc, c. מִן 2 K 3[3] 14[24] + 7 t. 2 K, c. מֵעַל 2 K 10[31] 15[18], c מֵאַחֲרֵי 2 K 10[29]; סָר מֵרָע (pt) Jb 1[1.8] 2[3] also Is 59[15]; סוּר מֵרָע (inf. and imv.) Jb 28[28] Pr 3[7] 13[19] 16[6.17] ψ 34[15] 37[27]. **2.** *depart*, usu. c מִן, of frogs Ex 8[7], flies v[25] (both J), sword 2 S 12[10]; sceptre from Judah Gn 49[10] (poem in J) י׳'s hand 1 S 6[3], his kindness 2 S 7[15] (MT, but rd אָסִיר 𝔊𝔖𝔙 ‖ 1 Ch 17[13] Th We Dr Klo Bu Kit HPS), his wrath Ez 16[42] (but del. Co Siegf Toy), *depart from way* = get out of the way, cease to obstruct Is 30[11], etc.; c. מִתּוֹךְ 1 S 15[6.6]; c. מֵעַל Is 7[17] Ju 16[19] Nu 12[10], etc; of י׳ *departing*, מִן pers, Ho 9[12], מֵעַל Ju 16[20] 1 S 28[15], מֵעִם 1 S 18[12]; God, c. מִן Jb 21[14] 22[17], c. מֵעַל 1 S 28[15], רוּחַ י׳, c. מֵעִם 1 S 16[14]; evil spirit, c. מֵעַל v[23]; abs. *depart* [from Babyl.] Is 52[11 11]; = *avoid* contact La 4[15 15.15]; of wicked Jb 15[30] *he shall not depart out of* (מִנִּי) *darkness*, i.e shall not avoid it, escape it; pt. pass. *made to depart, thrust away*, of Isr. under fig. of wife Is 49[21] (> act., acc. to Ba[NB § 124 c]). **3.** of life-

less things = *be removed*, oppressor's yoke, c מֵעַל Is 14^{25} cf. v^{29} 10^{27}, staves from (מִן) ark Ex 25^{15}; abs. iniquity Is 6^{7}, esp of בָּמוֹת 1 K 15^{14} 22^{44} 2 K 12^{4} 14^{4} $15^{4.35}$ 2 Ch 15^{17} 20^{33}. **4.** =*come to an end*, Am 6^{7} Is 11^{13}—For סָר אֶל־ 1 S 22^{14} read שַׂר עַל־ 𝔊 Th Dr Klo Bu Kit Lohr HPS, in 15^{32} Th HPS del סָר (after 𝔊 𝔙 𝔖) as dittogr, סָר סָבְאָם Ho 4^{18} v סבא, Ho 7^{14} rd. יָסוּרוּ for יָסוֹרוּ (√סרר q v), Je 6^{28}, it is uncertain whether סָרֵי (סוררים) belongs here, *revolters among the rebellious*, or sub סרר, or even = שָׂרֵי *princes, chiefs* (cf 1 S 22^{14})

†**Pôlēl** *Pf* 3 ms סורר דְּרָכַי La 3^{11} *he turned aside my ways* (my steps)

Hiph.$_{133}$ *Pf* 3 ms הסיר 2 K 18^{4}+, 2 ms. וַהֲסִרֹתָ consec (Dr §110(5) Obs) 1 K 3^{11}, 1 s. הֲסִירֹתִי 2 K 23^{27}+, וַהֲסִרֹתִי 1 S 17^{46}+, 3 pl הֵסִירוּ 2 Ch 30^{14}, etc, *Impf* 3 ms יָסִיר Is 3^{18}+, juss. יָסֵר Ex 8^{4}+, וַיָּסַר Gn 8^{13}+, sf וַיְסִרֵהוּ 1 S 18^{13}, יָסִירוּ 1 K 15^{13}, יסירֶנָּה Lv 3^{4}+, 3 mpl. יָסִירוּ Is 5^{23}+, etc, *Imv* ms הָסֵר 1 K 20^{24}+, הָסִיר Ez 21^{31} (rd הָסֵר,הָסִיר), fs הָסִירִי 1 S 1^{14}, etc; *Inf. abs* הָסֵר Gn 30^{32}+, *cstr* הָסִיר 2 K 6^{32}+, etc; *Pt* מסיר Is 3^{1} + 3 t,—**1.** *cause to* (turn aside,) *depart*, common word for *remove, take away* c מִן, Ex $8^{4.27}$ 33^{23} (all J), 23^{25} (E) Dt 7^{15} 1 S 28^{3} Jos 7^{13} (J) Ju 10^{16} Is 3^{1} ψ 18^{23} (+∥ 2 S 22^{23}, rd אָסִיר מִמֶּנִּי De Hup-Now HPS), shoulder from burden ψ 81^{7}; מסיר אָזְנוֹ משׁמע Pr 28^{9}, +oft, +Jb33^{17} (ins. מִן 𝔊 Ew Di De Hi Bu al), c מֵעַל, *take off* ring Gn 41^{42} (E) Est 3^{10}, also 8^{2} (abs), garments Gn $38^{14.19}$ (J) Dt 21^{13} Zc 3^{4} 1 S 17^{39} (armour), also Ex 34^{34} (P, abs) and Ez26^{16} (Co ins מֵעַל), *take off* head, מֵעַל 1 S 17^{46}, abs 2 S 4^{7} 16^{9} 2 K 16^{32}, c מֵעַל also oft. fig (*from upon* = from resting on, or burdening), plagues Ex 8^{4} 10^{17} (J), cf Nu 21^{7} (E), also 1 S 1^{14} Am 5^{23} 1 K 2^{31}; reproach 1 S 17^{26} Is 25^{8}, c מֵעִם = from one's presence 1 S 18^{13}, also of י׳ removing his kindness 1 Ch 16^{13}+∥ 2 S 7^{15} (v **Qal 2**), c מֵעַל פָּנָיו, of י׳ removing Isr. 2 K $17^{18.23}$ 23^{27} 24^{3} Je 32^{31}, abs. 2 K 23^{27}, oft. abs, Gn 8^{13} *Noah removed the covering*; remove = *depose* c מִן 1 K 15^{13} = 2 Ch 15^{16} (v מִן **7 b** (*b*)), abs 2 Ch 36^{3}, cf Ju 9^{29} Jb 34^{20}, remove בָּמוֹת, etc, 2 K 18^{4}, v^{22} = Is 36^{7} = 2 Ch 32^{12}, 2 K 23^{19} 2 Ch 30^{14} 14^{2}, cf 14^{4} 17^{6} (both c מִן), = *put away* strange gods, etc, Gn 35^{2} Jos $24^{14.23}$ (all E), 1 S 7^{4}, c מִתּוֹךְ v^{3} Is 58^{9}, once c לְ, מסיר שָׂפָה לנאמנים Jb 12^{20}. **2.** rarer uses are *put aside* = leave undone Jos 11^{15} (D), *retract* words Is 31^{2} (of י׳), *reject* prayer ψ 66^{20}, *abolish* sacrifice Dn 11^{31}, *turn* one *away* מֵאַחֲרֵי, i e from following Dt 7^{4}, c. אֶל־ pers, *remove the ark unto* 2 S 6^{10} = 1 Ch 13^{13}.

†**Hoph.** *Pf.* 3 ms הוּסַר Lv 4^{31} Dn 12^{11}; *Impf* 3 ms יוּסַר Lv 4^{35}; *Pt* מוּסָר Is 17^{1}; pl. מוּסָרים 1 S 21^{7} (but final ם prob dittogr. before מ We Dr Klo Kit HPS),—*be taken away, removed*. c מִן Lv 4^{35}, מִלִּפְנֵי י׳ v^{31}, מֵעַל 1 S 21^{7}, מוּסָר מֵעִיר Is 17^{1} *Damascus is removed from* being *a city*, abs *be abolished* Dn 12^{11} (cf 11^{31} Hiph)

I סוּר **adj. verb.** properly *Pt* of סור q.v

†II סוּר **n pr.** of a temple-gate,—שַׁעַר ס׳ 2 K 11^{6} (>∥ 2 Ch 23^{5} שַׁעַר הַיְסוֹד, v. יְסוֹד), but del ver. as gloss We$^{Bleek, Einl 4, 258}$ Kmp^{Kau} Benz.

†סָרָה **n.f. a turning aside, defection, apostasy, withdrawal**,—alw. abs ס׳,—**1.** *defection*, used appar of any moral or legal offence Dt 19^{16}, so prob Is59^{13} (+דברי שֶׁקֶר, עֹשֶׁק) **2.** *apostasy*, Dt 13^{6} Is 1^{5} 31^{6} Je 28^{16} 29^{32}. **3.** בִּלְתִּי סָרָה *non-withdrawal* Is 14^{6} (cf. vb, v^{25} Am 6^{7})

סִרָה v. בּוֹר הַסִּ׳ p 92 supr. יסור, only in יסורי Je 17^{13} Kt, but v. Qr סור **Qal** *Pt*

†[סוּת] **vb. Hiph.** *incite, allure, instigate* (NH Hiph, *id*),—**Hiph.** *Pf.* 3 ms. sf הֱסִיתְךָ 1 S 26^{19}, הֱסִיתְךָ Jb 36^{16}, 3 fs הֵסַתָּה 1 K 21^{25} (Ges §72 w Kö I. 460), 3 pl sf הסיתוך Je 38^{22} (Ges §72 ee), *Impf* 3 ms יָסִית 2 K 18^{32}+2 t, but also וַיָּסֶת 2 S 24^{1} 1 Ch 21^{1}, sf יְסִיתְךָ Dt 13^{7} Jb 36^{18}, etc; *Pt* מַסִּית Je 43^{3} 2 Ch 32^{11},—**1. a.** *incite* to make a request (c. acc. pers + inf) Ju 1^{14} (on text v GFM) = Jos 15^{18} **b.** *allure* וַיְסִיתֵם מִמֶּנּוּ 2 Ch 18^{31} *and God allured them away from him* (si vera l, del cl as gloss Be Kit), so also Jb 36^{16} acc to De Hi Bu al, *he allureth thee* out *of the mouth of distress*, but Di Du *freedom hath seduced thee*, for meaning *seduce, entice*, cf also v^{18}. **2** *instigate*, in bad sense, c. acc pers, + בְּ *against*, 1 S 26^{19} 2 S 24^{1} Je 43^{3} Jb 2^{3}, c. acc pers alone 1 K 21^{25} 2 K 18^{32} = Is 36^{18}, cf 2 Ch 32^{15}, Dt 13^{7} Je 38^{22}, + inf. 1 Ch 21^{1} 2 Ch 18^{2} 32^{11}.

סוּת **n.** v סוה

†[סָחַב] **vb. drag** (*Impf* consec. 1 s. ואסחב MI^{18}, sf. ואסחבה Ib$^{12.13}$, Ph. סחב Lzb^{328}; Ar سَحَبَ, Eth ሰሐበ:),—**Qal** *Pf* 1 pl וְסָחַבְנוּ consec 2 S 17^{13}, *Impf.* 3 ms sf יִסְחָבוּם Je 49^{20} 50^{45}, *Inf. abs* סָחוֹב Je 22^{19}, *cstr* לִסְחֹב Je 15^{3};—*drag*, a city עַד־הַנַּחַל 2 S 17^{13}, corpses Je 15^{3}

22[4], captives, under fig. of sheep dragged off by wild beast 49[20] = 50[45] (𝔊 pass, whence Schwally Gie suppose a **Niph.** יִסָּחֲבוּ).

†סְחָבָה **n.f.** rag, clout (stuff *pulled* or *dragged about*, > Lag[BN 143] √ سَحَبَ, شَحُبَ *become altered for the worse*);—only pl. סְחָבוֹת Je 38[11 12] (both + מְלָחִים).

†[סָחָה] **vb.** scrape (Ar. سَحَا (سحو, and سحى Lane[1322]) *scrape off, clear away*; cf. Talm. סְחִיתָא, סְחוּתָא *refuse*, 𝔗 סְחִיתָא *dirt, dung*);—only **Pi.** **scrape clean, scour**, *Pf* 1 s. consec. וסחיתי עֲפָרָהּ מִמֶּנָּה Ez 26[4] *and I will scrape clean her dust from her*

† סְחִי n.[m.] offscouring;—ס׳ וּמָאוֹס תְּשִׂימֵנוּ La 3[45].

†סָחִישׁ n.[m.] grain that shoots up of itself in 2nd year (√unknown);—‖ סָפִיחַ, 2 K 19[29] (= שָׁחִיס ‖ Is 37[30]); on use of this for food, cf. Strabo[xi. 4, 3] (of Albanians).

†[סָחַף] **vb.** prostrate (NH סחף, Aram סְחַף, ܣܚܦ (for ἐδαφίζω, Lk 19[42]), As. *saḫâpu*, *throw down, overwhelm*),—**Qal** *Pf.* מָטָר סֹחֵף Pr 28[3] *a prostrating rain* (beating down grain), ואין לָחֶם *and* (so) *there is no bread.* **Niph.** *Pf* 3 ms נסחף אַבִּירֶיךָ Je 46[15] *why are thy mighty ones* (or, *why is thy bull*, i.e Apis, Hi Ew Gf) *prostrated?* but rd. perh נָס חַף אַבִּירְךָ לֹא עָמַד (𝔊 Mich Gie Co) *why hath Apis fled, thy bull doth not stand?*

†[סָחַר] **vb.** go around, about, travel about in (NH *id*, *go about as merchant, pedlar*, perh denom. from סוחר (Jastr), Syr. ܣܚܪ *go about as beggar, be beggar* PS[2593] (rare), esp. ChrPalAram v. Schwally[Idiot. 61 f.]; As. *saḫâru*, *turn, surround*, Tel Am. *return* Wkl[TA Glos], 𝔗 *surround* (oft.), and deriv, Ar سَخِرَ is *mock at, deride*),—**Qal** *Pf.* 3 pl סָחֲרוּ Je 14[18], *Impf.* 3 mpl. יִסְחֲרוּ Gn 34[21]; 2 mpl. תסחרו Gn 42[34], *Imv* mpl. sf. סְחָרוּהָ Gn 34[10], *Pt.* סחר Gn 23[16], סוחר Pr 31[14]; cstr. סחר Is 23[2]; fs. sf. סחרתך Ez 27[12 16.18] + סחרתיך v[15] (v. infr), mpl. סֹחֲרִים Gn 37[28] + 2 t.; cstr סֹחֲרֵי 1 K 10[28] + 3 t.; sf. סחריך Is 47[15], ־רַיִךְ Ez 27[21], ־רֶיהָ Is 23[8],—**1.** *go about, to and fro* (i e go about one's affairs, carry on one's business) *in*, c acc. אֶרֶץ Gn 42[34] (E), 34[10.21] (P); c. אל־ארץ Je 14[18], but dub., 𝔊 Gf Hi Or Co[Hpt] Rothst[Kau] *journey unto a land which* they have not known. **2.** *Pt.* = subst. *a trafficker, trader* (who *goes about* with wares, etc.) Gn 23[16] (P), 37[28] (E), Is 23[2.8] 47[15] 1 K 10[28] = 2 Ch 1[16], Ez 27[21 21.36] 38[13], + תָּרִים 2 Ch 9[14], f, of a city or country, Ez 27[12 16 18]; also in v[15] rd. סֹחֲרֹתַיִךְ for MT (ידך) סחרת Sm Co Berthol Toy. **Pilp.** *Pf.* 3 ms. לִבִּי סְחַרְחַר ψ 38[11] (Ges[§ 55 e]) *my heart palpitates* (+ עֲזָבַנִי כֹחִי).

†[סַחַר] **n.m.**[Pr 3, 14] traffic, gain;—cstr. סְחַר Is 23[3] + 2 t; sf. סַחְרָהּ Pr 3[14] + 3 t;—*traffic*, i.e. *gain* from traffic, Is 23[3 18] (+ אֶתְנַנָּהּ), v[18] 45[14] Pr 3[14] 31[18].

†[סחֹרָה] **n.f.** merchandise;—cstr. סְחֹרַת Ez 27[15], but v. סחר *Pt.*

†סֹחֵרָה **n.f.** buckler,—ψ 91[4] (+ צִנָּה; fig of י׳'s faithfulness)

†[מִסְחָר] **n.m.** appar. **merchandise**;—cstr. מִסְחַר הָרֹכְלִים 1 K 10[15], but text prob. crpt, Klo prop. מִסַּחַר, so Buhl[Lex 13]; ‖ 2 Ch 9[14] has הַסֹּחֲרִים, and so Benz here (for both wds. of MT).

†[סֹחֶרֶת] **n.f.** a stone used (with marble) in paving (cf. As. *sаḫru*, a precious stone, Dl[HWB 495]),—סֹחָרֶת Est 1[6].

[סֵט], סֵטִים v. שׂוּט sub שׁוּט. סִיג v. סוג.

†סִיוָן **n.pr.** of 3rd month, **Siwān** = May–June (loan-word from As-Bab *Simânu*, cf Schr[COT Ne 1, 1] Muss-Arnolt[JBL xi (1892), 82 ff.]; Palm. סיון Lzb[328] Cook[84]),—בַּחֹדֶשׁ הַשְּׁלִישִׁי הוּא־חֹדֶשׁ ס׳ Est 8[9].

סִיחוֹן, סִיחֹן [35] **n.pr.m.** Sihon (on format cf. Lag[BN 196]);—סיחון Nu 21[27] + 18 t., סיחן v[21] + 17 t.;—king of Amorites, Nu 21[21] + 7 t. Nu 21 (JE), 32[33] (R) Dt 1[4] + 10 t Dt, Ju 2[10] + 4 t Ju (D) + 13[21 21 27] (P), 11[19.20.20 21] Je 48[45] 1 K 4[19] Ne 9[22] ψ 135[11] 136[19]. 𝔊 Σηων, 𝔊L Σιων.

†I. סִין **n.pr.loc.** Sin, i e *Pelusium*, E. frontier city of Egypt (Egypt. *'Imt* = *clay*, of which סִין is transl (cf. Aram. סְיָן *clay*), acc. to Steindorff[BAS i 599], who cp. Πηλούσιον (πηλός = *dirt, mud*), cf. Brugsch[Dict. Géogr 1081 ff]),—Ez 30[15] (𝔊 Σαιν acc), + v[16], but here Co Toy rd. plausibly סְוֵן, i e. סְוֵן = Syene (v [סְוֵן], סְוֵנֵה), 𝔊 Συηνη—On Pelusium v. Bd[Egypt 4 (1898), 169].

†II. סִין **n.pr.loc.** wilderness between Elim and Sinai, מִדְבַּר־סִין, acc. to P, Ex 16[1] 17[1] Nu 33[11 12], 𝔊 Σειν, A𝔊L Σιν; cf. Eb[GS 2, 156 ff.] and esp. Di[Ex 16, 1].

†סִינַי n.pr.mont. Sinai,—name of mt. of law-giving in J and esp. P (חֹרֵב in E and esp. D) Ju 5⁵ ψ 68⁹ Dt 33² (poem), also Ex 16¹ (P), usu. הַר־סִינַי (סִינַי Lv 7³⁸ +), rarely J, Ex 19²⁰·²³ and perh. 34²·⁴, elsewh. mostly P, 24¹⁶ 31¹⁸ 34²⁹·³² Lv 7³⁸ 25¹ 27³⁴ and 26⁴⁶ (H), Nu 3¹ 28⁶, also Ne 9¹³, מִדְבַּר סִינַי (סִינָי Nu 1¹⁹ +), Ex 19¹·² Lv 7³⁸ Nu 1¹·¹⁹ 3⁴·¹⁴ 9¹·⁵ 10¹² 26⁶⁴ 33¹⁵·¹⁶ (all P),—in view of these facts, and of E's use of חרב (q.v.), it is prob that Ex 19¹¹·¹⁸ (in E passages) are from R.—𝔊 Σ(ε)ινα Identif. dub; local tradition names *Jebel Musa*, mt. at S. end of peninsular between the two arms of Red Sea, so Rob^BR i 90 ff, esp 119–122 cf Stanley^Sinai and Pal 42 f. al, specif its N spur, *Ras Safsâfeh*, but Lepsius^Briefe 345 ff 416 ff Eb^GS esp 392 ff al. advocate *Serbal*, NW from *Jebel Musa* (on trad, cf Eb^ib 413 ff), v. discussion Di^Ex 19, 1. Against both is the working of Egypt mines in the penins as late as the 19th dyn (v Eb^GS 135. 146 ff, 149, etc), involving presence of soldiers there. This, and connex with Midian (cf also Ju 5⁵), have led to search for Sinai further NE, near head of Gulf of Akaba, or even in Seir, so Say^Monuments 263 ff, cf. GFM^Ju 5, 5. 6, 1 and *Yakut*, cited by Id^179 n 4, also v. Gall^Altisr Kultst. 12, on sanctity of mt v further RS^Sem i. 110 f 2nd ed 117 f Sm^Rel Gesch 30

†סִינִי adj.gent. only c art = subst. Gn 10¹⁷ = 1 Ch 1¹⁵ a Canaanite people, in north, 𝔊 τὸν Ἀσενναῖον, cf city *Siânu*, 'on shore of sea,' in As inscr Dl^Pa 282, Σινναν (acc.) in possession of those holding Lebanon Strabo^xvi 2 8 (v Di^Gn)

†סִינִים adj.gent pl. = subst., אֶרֶץ ס׳ Is 49¹², identif with *Chinese* by Thes^948–950 De Che ^Comm al, but see v Richthofen^China i 436 f, 504, rev. by Yule^Acad xiii 339, Di Du; T de Lacouperie ^BOR i 45 ff 183 ff, who thinks of *Šina*, at foot of Hindu Kush, but unlikely, rd prob סְוֵנִים (or סְוֵנִים), so Che^Intr Is. 275, and Hpt, cf already JDMich.

סִים Je 8⁷ Qr v. I סוּס.

סִיסְרָא₂₁ n.pr.m. (GFM^Ju 4, 2, PAOS xix (1898), 160 cp. Hittite names in *-sira*),—**1.** general of Jabin, king of Hazor Ju 4²+12 t Ju 4; appar himself king 5²⁰·²⁶·²⁸·³⁰, cf 1 S 12⁹ ψ 83¹⁰,—on ס׳ v GFM^Ju, 107 ff PAOS l c, 𝔊 Σ(ε)ισαρα. †**2.** בְּנֵי־סִיסְרָא, returned exiles, Ezr 2⁵³ = Ne 7⁵⁵, 𝔊 Σεισαραθ, Σισαρα, etc

†סִיעָא, סִיעֲהָא n.pr m. בְּנֵי־סִיעָא returned exiles Ne 7⁴⁷ = בְּנֵי־סִיעֲהָא Ezr 2⁴⁴, 𝔊 Ne Ασουια, ℵ Ιασουια, A Σιαια, 𝔊L Ιωσιου; 𝔊 Ezr Σωηλ, A Ασαα, 𝔊L Ιωσια.

†I סִיר n.m.^Je 1, 13 et f.^2 K 4, 38 pot (probably foreign wd. (Egypt.?), Ar. زِيرٌ a large water-jar Lane^1276 is perh loan-wd, on Gk. deriv. σιρός, σίρινος, v. Lewy^Fremdw 107),—ס׳ abs 2 K 4³⁸ +, cstr Ex 16³ +; pl סִירֹת 38³, סִירוֹת 1 K 7⁴⁵ +; sf סִירֹתָיו Ex 27³, סִירֹתֵיכֶם ψ 58¹⁰,—*pot*: **1. a.** household utensil for boiling 2 K 4³⁸·³⁹·⁴⁰·⁴¹·⁴¹, ס׳ הַבָּשָׂר Ex 16³ (P), Zc 14²¹, ס׳ נָפוּחַ Je 1¹³ (cf. נפח, in vision), symbol. of Jerus Ez 11³·⁷·¹¹ 24³·⁶; fig also ψ 58¹⁰ (cf Che), in sim. Mi 3³ Jb 41²³ Ec 7⁶. **b.** ס׳ רַחְצִי ψ 60¹⁰ *my washing-pot*, 108¹⁰. **2.** *pots* used in sanctuary, Ex 27³ 38³ (both P), 1 K 7⁴⁰ (rd סִירוֹת for MT כִּיֹּרוֹת, so Codd of 𝔖 𝔊 𝔙 Th Ke Klo Kmp Benz), v⁴⁵ = 2 Ch 4¹¹·¹⁶, 2 K 25¹⁴ = Je 52¹⁸, also Je 52¹⁹ 2 Ch 35¹³ Zc 14²⁰.—Here belongs prob. סִרָה in בּוֹר הַסִּרָה, v. p 92 b

†II [סִיר] n.[m.] thorn, hook (𝔖id, cf. סירים in Sab. n pr Hom^ZMG xlvi (1892), 532),—**1.** pl. סִירִים, *thorns*, sign of desolation Is 34¹³, a barrier Ho 2⁸, on Na 1¹⁰ v [סָבַךְ], כְּקוֹל הַס׳ תַּחַת הַסִּיר Ec 7⁶ *as the sound of thorns* (crackling as they burn) *under the pot.* **2.** pl סִירוֹת *hooks* Am 4² (cf. דּוּגָה sub דגה, || צִנּוֹת, on relation of meanings v. חוֹחַ, צֵן).

סכך סַךְ, [סֹךְ], סֻכָּה, סֻכּוֹת v. II סכך

†סִכּוּת n.pr.div. Am 5²⁶ read prob. *סַכּוּת, = As. *Sakkut* (epithet of Adar-Ninip = Saturn), Schr^SK 1874, 332, COT Am 5, 26, cf Tiele^Gesch 528 Bae^Bel 239 Rogers^Ency Bib. 749 (Vrss Thes al = סֻכָּה, סֻכּוֹת).

†סֻכּוֹת בְּנוֹת n.pr div. 2 K 17³⁰, As.-Bab. deity, worshipped by Babylonians in Samaria; text of name corrupt; Schr^COT ad loc (after H. Rawlinson) prop *Zîr-bânit*, or *Zarpanituv*, wife of *Marduk* (cf Hpt^Andover Rev., May 1884 Muss-Arnolt^JBL xi (1892), 167), rejecting *Sakkut-binûtu* = Marduk Dl^Par 215, Jen^ZA iv 352 makes בנות = *banîtu*, epithet of Ištar; all doubtful.

†סֻכִּיִּים n.pr.m pl. a people in army of Shishak acc. to 2 Ch 12³ (between לוּבִים and כּוּשִׁים); 𝔊 Τρωγλοδυται, so 𝔙; 𝔊L Σουχιειμ.

†I. [סָכַךְ] vb. overshadow, screen, cover (|| √ to I שׂכך (which is prob. orig., cf. Ar. شَكَّ, and Fra⁹⁰), NH הסיך *cover*, and perh. סכך *roof over*);—**Qal** *Pf* only 2 ms. סַכֹּתָה Ex 40³, סַכֹּתָה La 3⁴³·⁴⁴, סַכּוֹתָה ψ 140⁸, *Impf.* 3 mpl. וַיָּסֹכּוּ 1 K 8⁷, sf. יְסֻכֻּהוּ Jb 40²²; *Pt. act.* סוֹכֵךְ

Ez $28^{14.16}$, pl. סֹכְכִים Ex 25^{20} + 2 t.;—**1.** *screen, cover*, usu. c. עַל־ of thing covered, 1 K 8^{7} 1 Ch 28^{18}; + acc. of covering Ex 40^{3} (P); + בְּ of covering 25^{20} 37^{9} (both P); c. לְ of thing covered ψ 140^{8}; so (+ בְּ instr.) ס׳ בֶּעָנָן לָךְ La 3^{44} *thou hast screened thyself with the clouds;* c. acc. Jb 40^{22} *lotus-trees, as its shade, screen it;* abs. Ez $28^{14.16}$ (difficult, text prob. corrupt, Co Toy del. as gloss). **2.** reflex. *cover oneself* ס׳ בָאַף La 3^{43} *thou hast covered* (clothed, panoplied) *thyself with anger* (si vera l.; cf. v^{44} *supr.*). **Hiph.** *Impf.* 3 ms. וְיָסֵךְ יָסֶךְ לָךְ ψ 91^{4}, וַיָּסֶךְ Ex 40^{1} + 2 t.; 2 ms. תָּסֵךְ ψ 5^{12}; *Inf. cstr.* הָסֵךְ 1 S 24^{4}; *Pt.* מֵסִיךְ Ju 3^{24} (Ges ^{§67v});—*screen, cover*, **1.** specif. c. אֶת־רַגְלָיו, i.e. with long garments, euphemism for evacuating the bowels, from posture assumed, so inf. Ju 3^{24}, pt. 1 S 24^{4} (cf. NH הֵסִיךְ, and v. GFM, HPS). **2.** elsewhere Impf., as **Qal** (expl. as Qal Ba$^{ZMG\ xliii\ (1889).\ 178}$), c. עַל־ Ex 40^{21}, of protection ψ 5^{12}; c. לְ pers. + בְּ instr. 91^{4} (of protection). **Pilp.** סִכְסֵךְ, denom., v. sub III. שׂכך.

†מָסָךְ n.[m.] covering, screen;—abs. מ׳ 2 S 17^{19} + 11 t.; cstr. מָסַךְ Is 22^{8} + 12 t.;—**1.** *covering*, large cloth spread (פרשׂ) over well to hide persons within 2 S 17^{19}; fig. of protection, or of eye-screen, וַיְגַל אֵת־מ׳ יְהוּדָה Is 22^{8}; *screen*, of cloud ψ 105^{39} (פרשׂ). **2.** name given (in P) to each of three *screens*, of tabern.: **a.** at gate (שַׁעַר) of court Ex 27^{16} 35^{17} 38^{18} 39^{40} $40^{8.33}$ Nu 3^{26} (פֶּתַח), 4^{26}. **b.** at entrance (פֶּתַח) of tent Ex $26^{36.37}$ 35^{15} 36^{37} 39^{38} $40^{5.28}$ Nu $3^{25.31}$ 4^{25}. **c.** פָּרֹכֶת הַמּ׳ (v. פ׳), dividing off the Most Holy Place within the tent, Ex 35^{12} 39^{34} 40^{21} Nu 4^{5}.

†[מְסֻכָה] n.f. that with which one is covered, covering;—sf. מְסֻכָתֶךָ Ez 28^{13} (so Baer Ginsb; van d. H. מְסַכּ׳) *all precious stones were thy covering* (= *thou wast covered* with them);—the tradition is strong in favour of *Raphē*, but sense favours deriv. from סכך.

†[מוּסָךְ] n.m. architect. term (si vera l.) of some *covered* structure, otherwise unknown; —only cstr. מוּסַךְ־הַשַּׁבָּת 2 K 16^{18} Qr (Kt מיסך i.e. מֵיסַךְ);—𝔊 τὸν θεμέλιον τῆς καθέδρας, i.e. מוּסַד הַשֶּׁבֶת?

†II. [סָכַךְ] vb. weave together (‖ form of II. שָׂכַךְ; NH Hiph. הֵסִיךְ *weave*, סוּכָּה, *booth*); —**Qal** *Pf.* 2 ms. sf. תְּסֻכֵּנִי ψ 139^{13} *thou didst weave me together* in my mother's womb.

†[סֹךְ] n.[m.] throng (prop. *an interwoven mass*);—אֶעֱבֹר בַּסָּךְ ψ 42^{5} *I used to pass along in the throng*, so most; but word dub.

†[סֹךְ] n.[m.] thicket, covert, lair;—only sf. סֻכּוֹ Je 25^{38} *lair* of י׳, under fig. of lion (but Gie סֻכּוֹ cf. 4^{7}), סֻכֹּה ψ 10^{9} of lion (sim. of wicked; Bae סֻכָּה; Lag Che We סֻכּוֹ); סֻכּוֹ 76^{3} *his covert* (of י׳ under fig. of lion; ‖ מְעוֹנָתוֹ); for סֻכֹּה *in his covert* ψ 27^{5} Qr rd. perh., with Kt סֻכָּה *a booth* (Ol Hup-Now Bae cf. 31^{21}).

†סֻכָּה n.f. thicket, booth (prop. of *interwoven* boughs cf. Ne 8^{15});—abs. ס׳ Is 1^{8} +; cstr. סֻכַּת Am 9^{11}; sf. סֻכָּתוֹ Jb 36^{29} ψ 18^{12}, and so rd. ‖ 2 S 22^{12} (for MT סֻכּוֹת; De Hup-Now HPS); usu. pl. סֻכֹּת Gn 33^{17} +; סֻכּוֹת 2 S 11^{11} +; —**1.** *thicket*, lurking-place of lions Jb 38^{40} (cf. [סֹךְ] **1**). **2.** *booth*, rude or temporary shelter, for cattle Gn 33^{17} (J; distinct fr. בַּיִת), but also for warriors in the field 2 S 11^{11} 1 K $20^{12.16}$; for watchers in vineyards Is 1^{8} (sim.) Jb 27^{18} (sim. of frailty), for man's shelter from sun Jon 4^{5}, cf. (fig.) Is 4^{6} ψ 31^{21}, prob. also 27^{5} (v. [סֹךְ]); poet. of fallen house (dynasty) of David Am 9^{11}; of clouds as (temporary) enclosure (AV 'pavilion') of י׳ in storm ψ 18^{12} = 2 S 22^{12} Jb 36^{29}. **3.** specif. of *booths*, made of boughs, in which people lived at harvest-feast Lv $23^{42.42.43}$ (H), Ne $8^{14.15.16.17.17}$, hence called חַג הַסֻּכּוֹת Dt $16^{13.16}$ 31^{10} Lv 23^{34} (P), Zc $14^{16.18.19}$ 2 Ch 8^{13} Ezr 3^{4}.

סֻכּוֹת $_{18}$ **n.pr.loc.**;—**1.** סֻכֹּתָה (ה loc.) Gn $33^{17.17}$ (J; expl. from Jacob's making *booths*), elsewhere סֻכּוֹת;—city E. of Jordan Ju 8^{5} + 6 t. Ju 8, Jos 13^{27} (P); prob. also 1 K 7^{46} = 2 Ch 4^{17} (reading מַעְבְּרַת אֲדָמָה *ford of Adamah* GFM $^{Ju\ 7,\ 22}$ cf. Buhl$^{Geogr.\ 206}$ Benz$^{1\ K\ 7,\ 46}$); עֵמֶק ס׳ ψ 60^{8} = 108^{8} is Jordan-valley near *Succôth;* on identif. cf. GFM$^{Ju\ 8,\ 5}$ Buhl$^{Geogr.\ 260}$ GASm$^{Geogr.\ 585}$, and reff.; acc. to Talm. *Dêr 'alla*, 1 m. N. of Jabbok Nbr$^{Géogr.\ du\ Talm.\ 248}$, so S. Merrill$^{East\ of\ Jordan\ 385\ ff.}$; 𝔊 Σοκχωθ (Σκηναί Gn 33 cf. ψψ). †**2.** סֻכֹּתָה (ה loc.) Ex 12^{37}, elsewh. סֻכֹּת;—first station of Isr. at Exodus, Ex 12^{37} 13^{20} Nu $33^{5.6}$ (all P); = Egypt. *Thku(t)* WMM$^{As.\ u.\ Eur.\ 70}$, *Thkw* Steindorff$^{BAS\ i.\ 603}$; on site v. Naville$^{Pithom\ (1885),\ esp.\ pp.\ 6.\ 23\ f.}$ Guthe$^{ZPV\ viii\ (1885),\ 219\ f.}$; 𝔊 Σοκχωθ.

†סֹכֵךְ n.[m.] protector;—term. techn. of structure shielding stormers of city (Lat. *testudo*) הַסֹּ׳ Na 2^{6}; 𝔊 τὰς προφυλακὰς αὐτῶν.

†סְכָכָה **n.pr loc.** in wilderness of Judah Jos 15[61], A Σοχοχα, 𝔊 L Σχοχα Site unknown

†[סָכַל] **vb.** be foolish, or a fool, usu. in moral or spiritual sense (Syr ܣܟܠ, Aph *act foolishly*, ܣܟܠܐ *foolish*, etc, 𝔗 סכל der species, *act foolishly;* סִכְלָא *fool*, ChrPalAram ܣܟܠ, Aph = ἁμαρτάνω, also deriv Schwally[Idiot 62], As. *saklu*, perh. *foolish*, Dl[HWB 498], Aram ܣܟܠ, סכל *know, be intelligent, cause to understand*, etc (der. species), cf שׂכל; Me[Chrest Targ] derives both these opp mngs fr Ar شَكْل *form, likeness* Gerber[178] thinks Heb vb denom),—**Piel** *Impf* יְסַכֵּל Is 44[25], *Imv.* סַכֶּל־נָא 2 S 15[31], *make foolish, turn into foolishness* **Niph.** *Pf* 2 ms נִסְכַּלְתָּ 2 Ch 16[9], נִסְכָּלְתָּ 1 S 13[13]; 1 s נִסְכַּלְתִּי 2 S 24[10] = 1 Ch 21[8], *act or do foolishly* **Hiph.** *Pf* 2 ms הִסְכַּלְתָּ Gn 31[28] (E), 1 s. הִסְכַּלְתִּי 1 S 26[21], *do foolishly, play the fool*

†סָכָל **n.m.** fool (on format cf Lag[BN 48]),—Je 5[21] Ec 2[19] 7[17] 10[3.3.14], pl adj סְכָלִים Je 4[22]

†סֶכֶל **n.m.** folly,—Ec 10[6]

†סִכְלוּת, שִׂכְלוּת **n.f.** folly,—ס׳ Ec 2[3 12 13] 7[25] 10[1 13], ש׳ Ec 1[17] (ש erroneously for ס).

†I [סָכַן] **vb.** be of use or service, benefit (Tel Am *sakânu, care for* (c prep *ana*) Zim[ZA vi 248] Wkl[TA Gloss.], Ph סכן *prefect* Lzb[329]; cf perh Tel Am *zukini* as loan-word Wkl[1 c]),—**Qal** *Impf* 3 ms only Jb יִסְכָּן 22[2], ־ן 15[3], יִסְכָּן־ 22[2] + 2 t; *Pt.* סֹכֵן Is 22[15]; f סֹכֶנֶת 1 K 1[2.4], —**1.** *be of use* or *service*, only pt ס׳ וּתְהִי לוֹ 1 K 1[2] *and let her become servitress to him*, so v[4] (+ וַתְּשָׁרְתֵהוּ), סכן Is 22[15] = *servitor, steward.* **2.** *benefit, profit*, abs. Jb 15[3], c לְ pers 22[2] 35[3], עָלֵי pers. 22[2], c. acc 34[9] (or abs *gain benefit*, גבר subj). **Hiph.** *Pf* 1 s הִסְכַּנְתִּי Nu 22[30], 2 ms הִסְכַּנְתָּה ψ 139[3], *Imv.* הַסְכֶּן־נָא Jb 22[21], *Inf abs* הַסְכֵּן Nu 22[30],—*be used, wont*, strictly *exhibit use*, or *habit*, הַהַסְכֵּן הִסְכַּנְתִּי לַעֲשׂוֹת לְךָ כֹּה Nu 22[30] (J) *have I ever shewn the habit of doing thus to thee?* hence *shew harmony with* (עִם) one Jb 22[21], *be familiar with, know intimately* (subj י׳) ψ 139[3] (c acc דְּרָכַי)

†מִסְכְּנוֹת **n.f.pl.** supply, storage (Dl[Pr 186]),—עָרֵי (הַ)מ׳ Ex 1[11] (J), 1 K 9[19] = 2 Ch 8[6], 2 Ch 8[4] 17[12], מ׳ ע׳ 16[4] prob corrupt (Be al, v. עִיר); מ׳ alone 32[28] *storage-places, magazines*

II. [סָכַן] **vb.** incur danger (late) (NH *id.* Pi *endanger*, Hiph. *be endangered*, סַכָּנָה *danger*, etc, Aram סְכַן *id*, cf. Levy[NHWB iii 526 &] De[iiL und Koheleth 203, Eng Trans. 194]),—**Niph.** *Impf* 3 ms יִסָּכֶן־בָּם Ec 10[9] he that cleaveth (logs of) wood *endangers himself by them.*

†III [סָכַן] **vb.** (so most) be poor, but v infr,—**Pu.** *Pt* הַמְסֻכָּן תְּרוּמָה Is 40[20] usu., *he who is impoverished in respect to offering*, but very dub, v. conject in Du (against him Di-Kit) Skinner Zim[ZA ix 111] Che[Heb. Hpt] —מִסְכֵּן *poor*, מִסְכֵּנֻת *poverty*, v. p. 587

[סכסך] v sub IV. שׂכך

†I [סָכַר] **vb.** shut up, stop up (Aram. סְכַר, ܣܟܪ *shut up, stop up, dam up;* Ar. سَكَرَ *fill, stop up, dam* (river), etc, also *close, stop up* door, Lane[1390], As. *sikêru, dam up*, ii. 2. *stop ears;* cf. *sikkuru, bolt* Dl[HWB 499], appar. kindr. with סגר,—hence Egypt *t'akar, barrier*, Bondi[83]),—**Niph.** *Impf* 3 ms יִסָּכֵר פִּי וגו׳ ψ 63[12] *the mouth* of liars *shall be stopped*, 3 mpl. וַיִּסָּכְרוּ Gn 8[2] (P) *and* the springs of the deep etc, *were shut up* **Pi** *Pf* וְסִכַּרְתִּי אֶת־מִצְרַיִם בְּיַד Is 19[4] *and I will shut up* (*deliver*) *Egypt into the hand of*, etc (cf סגר, מגן)

†II. [סָכַר] **vb.** hire (= שָׂכַר; ס erroneously for שׂ),—only **Qal** *Pt* pl. וְסֹכְרִים Ezr 4[5] *and hiring* against (עַל) them agents.

†[סָכַת] **vb.** be silent (Ar. سَكَتَ *id*, Lane[1399]; Sam ࠎࠊࠕ *pay attention*, cf Thes, Ar = also *be quiet* (in gen), = Syr. ܫܟܬ, a differentiated ✓?),—**Hiph.** declar. *shew silence* *Imv* ms הַסְכֵּת Dt 27[9] *keep silence* and listen (cf. נסכת Ecclus 13[23]).

סַל v סלל

†סִלָּא word in (unintelligible) design loc. בֵּית מִלֹּא הַיֹּרֵד ס׳ 2 K 12[21], Th conj. מְסִלָּה *highway*, Klo בְּמוֹרַד מִלֹּא other conj. in Benz.

†[סָלָא] **vb.** weigh (Ar سَلَأَ *pay promptly* Lane[1398], cf Sab סלא *consecrate, devote* Hom[ZMG xlvi (1892), 531, Süd-Arab Chrest 124]),—only **Pu.** *Pt.* הַמְסֻלָּאִים בַּפָּז La 4[2] *they who were weighed against gold*, reckoned of such value—Cf. also II סלה.

†[סָלַד] **vb.** very dubious, perh. spring (NH *start* or *spring back*, as hand from fire; v Levy),—**Pi.** *Impf* 1 s. וַאֲסַלְּדָה Jb 6[10] *and I would spring* (for joy) in (my) anguish.

†סֶ֫לֶד **n.pr.m.** in Judah 1 Ch $2^{30.30}$, 𝔊 Σαλαδ, 𝔊L Σαλεδ.

†I. [סָלָה] **vb. make light of, toss aside** (cf. As. *salû, throw off, shake off* (yoke) Dl[600]; Ar. سلو, سَلَا is *be forgetful, neglectful* Lane[1417]; Aram. סְלָא *despise*, ܣܠܐ *reject*);—**Qal** *Pf.* 2 ms. סָלִיתָ ψ 119^{118} *thou dost make light of* all those that err from thy statutes.—Cf. also סִלּוֹן infr. **Pi.** intens. *Pf.* 3 ms. סִלָּה La 1^{15} Adonay *hath flouted at* my mighty ones.

†II. [סָלָה] **vb. weigh, balance** (‖ form of סָלָא q.v.);—**Pu.** *Impf.* 3 fs. לֹא־תְסֻלֶּה בְּכֶתֶם Jb 28^{16} *it cannot be weighed against* (estimated in) *gold* of Ophir, cf. v^{19}.

סֶ֫לָה v. סלל.

†סַלּוּ **n.pr.m.** a priest, Zerub.'s time, acc. to Ne 12^{7} (𝔊L Σαλουια), = סַלָּי v^{20} (𝔊L Σαλουαι; om. BA in both).

†סָלוּא **n.pr.m.** a Simeonite Nu 25^{14}, 𝔊 Σαλμων, A Σαλω, 𝔊L Σαλωμ.

†סַלּוּא **n.pr.m.** a post-exil. Benjamite 1 Ch 9^{7} (𝔊 Σαλωμ, A Σαλω) = סַלָּא Ne 11^{7} (𝔊 Σηλω, 𝔊L Σαμαα).

†[סַלּוֹן], סִלּוֹן **n.m. brier** (√unknown);—סִלּוֹן מַמְאִיר Ez 28^{24} *a pricking brier* (fig. of national distress; ‖ קוֹץ מַכְאִב); pl. סַלּוֹנִים 2^{6} (+ סָרָבִים; Co [after Vrss] Berthol [not Toy] rd. סֹרְבִים וְסֹלִים (אותך) *resisting and despising thee;* סֹלִ׳ is then *Pt.* from I. סלה).

†סַלַּי **n.pr.m. 1.** Ne 12^{20} = סַלּוּ q.v. **2.** סַלַּי a Benjamite Ne 11^{8}, 𝔊 Σηλε(ε)ι.

†[סָלַח] **vb. forgive, pardon** (𝔗 סְלַח *id.*, NH סְלִיחָה *forgiveness*);—**Qal** *Pf.* 2 ms. סָלַחְתָּ Ex 34^{9} + 9 t., סָלָ֑חְתָּ La 3^{42} + 2 t.; 1 s. סָלַחְתִּי Nu 14^{20} + 2 t.; *Impf.* 3 ms. יִסְלַח 30^{6} + 4 t.; 1 s. אֶסְלַח Je 31^{34} + 3 t. + 5^{7} Qr (Kt אֶסְלוֹחַ); *Imv.* סְלַח Nu 14^{19} Am 7^{2}; סְלָ֑חָה Dn 9^{19}; *Inf.* סְלֹחַ Dt 29^{19} 2 K 24^{4}; סְלוֹחַ Is 55^{7}; *Pt. act.* סֹלֵחַ ψ 103^{3};—*forgive, pardon,* always of God: abs. Nu 14^{20} (J), 1 K $8^{30.39}$ = 2 Ch $6^{21.30}$, 2 K 24^{4} Is 55^{7} Am 7^{2} La 3^{42} Dn 9^{19}; c. לְ, of the sin Ex 34^{9} Nu 14^{19} (both J), Je 31^{34} 33^{8} 36^{3} ψ 25^{11} 103^{3} 1 K $8^{34.36}$ = 2 Ch $6^{25.27}$, 2 Ch 7^{14}; + לְ, of sinner Dt 29^{19} 1 K 8^{50} = 2 Ch 6^{39}, 2 K $5^{18.18}$ Je $5^{1.7}$ 50^{20}, and in law, Nu $30^{6.9.13}$ (P). **Niph.** *Pf.* 3 ms. נִסְלַח, c. לְ, term. techn. in code of P, *it shall be forgiven him* לוֹ Lv $4^{26.31.35}$ $5^{10.13.16.18.26}$ 19^{22} Nu 15^{28}; *them* לָהֶם Lv 4^{20} Nu 15^{25}; לְכָל־עֲדַת וגו׳ v^{26}.

†סַלָּח **adj. ready to forgive, forgiving;**—אַתָּה אֲדֹנָי טוֹב וְס׳ ψ 86^{5} thou Lord art *kind and forgiving.*

†סְלִיחָה **n.f. forgiveness** (late; on format. v. Kö $^{ii.1,197}$);—ס׳ ψ 130^{4}; pl. abstr. intens. *abundant forgiveness,* סְלִיחוֹת Ne 9^{17}, סְלִחוֹת Dn 9^{9}.

†סַלְכָה **n.pr.loc.** city on E. border of Bashan, Dt 3^{10} Jos 12^{5} 13^{11} (all D), 1 Ch 5^{11}; = Nab. צלחד (Lzb[358] Cook[101]), mod. *Ṣalḫad, Ṣarḫad,* on S. spur of *Jebel Hauran,* c. 63 m. due E. of Jordan; cf. Buhl[Geogr. 252] Dr[Dt 3.10]; 𝔊 Σελχα, Ελχα, etc. (Σ lost often after ἕως).

†I. [סָלַל] **vb. lift up, cast up** (NH סִלְסֵל *esteem highly,* סִלְסוּל *loftiness, distinction;* סוּלָּם *ladder;* 𝔗 סוּלְּמָא *id.;* MI[26] מסלת *highway;* Ph. סלמת *stair* (?) Lzb[329]; As. *sellu, sillu,* perh. *breast-works* Dl[HWB 501]; Ar. سَلَّ is *draw out, forth* Lane[1395] = שָׁלַל, but سُلَّم *ladder* (a loan-wd. acc. to Schwally[ZMG liii (1899), 197]), cf. סֻלָּם; v. also *tṛry, siege-wall,* Egypt. loan-word from סֹלְלָה acc. to WMM[As. u. Eur. 101]);—**Qal** *Impf.* וַיָּסֹלּוּ Jb 19^{12} 30^{12}; *Imv.* mpl. סֹלּוּ Is 57^{14} + 4 t.; sf. סָלּוּהָ Je 50^{26} (cf. סָלָּה); *Pt. pass.* סְלוּלָה Je 18^{15}; סְלֻלָה Pr 15^{19};—**1.** *cast up a highway:* ס׳ מְסִלָּה Is $62^{10.10}$, without obj. Is $57^{14.14}$, דֶּרֶךְ לֹא סְלוּלָה Je 18^{15}; fig. of path of upright Pr 15^{19}. **2.** *cast up a way:* דֶּרֶךְ, c. עַל *against,* Jb 19^{12} (of besieger, in fig.), ארח Jb 30^{12} (of besetting foe); Bab. as a heap of garbage Je 50^{26}. **3.** *lift up* (a song) ψ 68^{5}, c. לְ pers. (‖ זַמְּרוּ, שִׁירוּ; most as **1**). **Pilp.** *Imv.* sf. סַלְסְלֶהָ Pr 4^{8} *exalt her* (i.e. Wisdom), i.e. (cf. Toy) *esteem highly, prize.* **Hithp.** *Pt.* מִסְתּוֹלֵל Ex 9^{17} (J) *exalt oneself,* c. בְּ *against* (denom. from סֹלְלָה acc. to Gerber[52]); cf. Ecclus 39^{24} 40^{28}.

†סֶ֫לָה **vb. lift up** (voices in ברוך לעולם), or **exalt** (לעולם י׳) (*Imv.* of סלל (cf. Pr 4^{8} ψ 68^{5}; הִגָּיוֹן סלה 9^{17}, v. הִגּ׳), properly סֹ֫לָּה, סֶ֫לָּה poss. Qr = נֶצַח, Hexapla σελ; but cf. הֶרֶה Ew[554] Kö[ii.1,539]; 𝔊 Sym Theod διάψαλμα, expl. Suidas μέλους ἐναλλαγή; Theodoret Hippolytus μέλους μεταβολή (cf. Hexapla Hb 3^{3} μεταβολὴ διαψάλ-

ματος, Syr. Hexapla Aq. עוניתא in 5 ψψ, Field in ψ 38^{12}); 𝔊 adds *διάψαλμα*, e g 2^{2} 34^{11} 94^{15}, after final editing of Heb Psalter, so Psalms of Sol 17^{31} 18^{10} on same principles as in MT, used therefore with full knowledge that it indicated some kind of interruption or change in the regular rendering סלה is used in שמונה עשרה after Benedictions 3, 18, and after other early Jewish prayers, shewing knowledge, c 100 A D, Aq gives *ἀεί* (Theod also ψ 9^{17}); Sexta *διαπαντός* (except 20^{4} *εἰς τέλος*), Quinta *εἰς τοὺς αἰῶνας*, Jer *semper*, 𝔗 usu לעלמא, לעלמין, but 39^{6} לחיי עלמא, 44^{9} לעלמי עלמין, 48^{9} עד עלמי עלמין, 49^{14} לעלמא דאתי; uniform tradition best expl by closing contents of the Benedictions, מהעולם ועד העולם So Jer classes *sela* with *amen* and *salom*; and Jacob of Edessa in Bar Hebr 10^{1} cp. Christian *Amen* of the people after *Gloria*),—this interpr agrees with usage 71 t in 39 ψψ, 3 t Hb 3 (taken from Minor Psalter למנצח, v נצח), it occurs at end of 3^{9} 24^{10} 46^{12} (om 𝔊), 9^{21} (𝔊 combines 9 and 10); elsewh. at close of strophe, $3^{3.5}$ $4^{3.5}$ 7^{6} 9^{17} 24^{6} $32^{4.5.7}$ $39^{6.12}$ $46^{4.8}$ 47^{5} 48^{9} 49^{13} (so rd MT v^{14} by error) v^{16} 50^{6} $52^{5.7}$ 54^{5} $59^{6.14}$ 61^{5} $62^{5.9}$ $66^{4.7.15}$ 67^{5} 68^{20} $76^{4.10}$ $77^{4.10.16}$ 81^{8} 82^{2} 83^{9} $84^{5.9}$ $88^{8.11}$ $89^{38.46}$ $140^{4.6.9}$ 143^{6}, or where citations have been made, 44^{9} 55^{8} 57^{7} 60^{6} 67^{2} $68^{8.33}$ 89^{5} Hb $3^{3.9}$, or where extracts might be made for liturgical purposes, 20^{4} 21^{3} 55^{20} 75^{4} 85^{3} $87^{3.6}$ 89^{49}, so 57^{3} (𝔊 for MT v^{4}) Hb 3^{13}—Of ψψ c סלה, 23 used in Elohistic Psalter, 28 in Director's Psalter, 39 in final editing of Psalter These editors found it in earlier Psalters Davidic Psalter uses 20 of them, so few in proportion that it is not characteristic of this Psalter; but Korahite 9 (out of 12), and Asaph 7 + 80^{8} [𝔊] (prob 8 out of 12), appar it came into use in time of these editors In Director's Psalter musical terms are added to 19 of the 28 it uses (and only to ten others, of which some could hardly use סלה), ψψ with סלה all (except 61, 81) name the kind of ψ in title 3 מִכְתָּם, 7 מַשְׂכִּיל, 10 שִׁיר, 26 (27) others מִזְמוֹר, Hb 3 תְּפִלָּה, ׳ס is esp frequent with שִׁיר and מַשְׂכִּיל, terms associated with musical rendering It prob came into use in late Persian period in connexion with ψψ used with musical accompaniment in public worship, to indicate place of benedictions. It was not added by later editors to other psalms, but was revived in first century B C, and continued in use for some time (v. Jacob[ZAW xvi (1896), 129 f.] Br[JBL 1899] EGBriggs[Am J Sem Lang Oct 1899, 1 ff]).

†**סֹלְלָה** **n.f. mound**,—׳ס 2 S 20^{15} + 7 t.; סוֹלְלָה Dn 11^{15}, pl. סללות Je 32^{24} 33^{4}.—שָׁפַךְ ס׳ עַל־הָעִיר *cast up mound against the city*, besieging it, 2 K 19^{32} = Is 37^{33}, Je 6^{6} Ez 4^{2} 26^{8}; c. אֶל 2 S 20^{15} (error for עַל); without על העיר Ez 17^{17} 21^{27} Dn 11^{15}, without vb. Je 32^{24} 33^{4}

†**סֻלָּם** **n.m. ladder**;—Gn 28^{12} (E).

†**מְסִלָּה** **n f. highway**;—׳מ Is 11^{16} + 12 t; cstr. מְסִלַּת Is 7^{3} + 3 t; sf. מסלתו Jo 2^{8}, pl. מסלות Is 33^{8} + 5 t., sf מְסִלֹּתַי Is 49^{11}; מסלותם Ju 5^{20} Is 59^{7},—*raised way, highway, public road* (never of street in city) Nu 20^{19} Ju $20^{31.32.45}$ 21^{19} 1 S 6^{12} 2 S $20^{12.12.13}$ 2 K 18^{17} = Is 36^{2}, 1 Ch $26^{16.18}$ Is 7^{3} 11^{16} 19^{23} 33^{8} 49^{11} 59^{7} Je 31^{21}, ישר מ׳ Is 40^{3}, סלל מ׳ Is 62^{10}. in a fig. sense, of the courses of the stars Ju 5^{20}, the march of locusts Jo 2^{8}, the conduct of the upright Pr 16^{17}, of the ascents to Zion in the mind of the pious ψ 84^{6} (𝔊 Bae rds מַעֲלוֹת)—In 2 Ch 9^{11} מסלות is error for מִסְעָד(וֹת) of ‖ 1 K 10^{12}

†**מַסְלוּל** **n.m. highway**,—Is 35^{8} (foll ודרך corrupt, 𝔊 *ὁδὸς καθαρά*).

II **סלל** (√of foll, cf. NH סלסל *plait, curl* hair, NH סַל, 𝔗 סַלָּא, Talm סילְתָא, Syr. ܣܠܐ, Chr Pal Aram. ܣܠܐ, all = *basket*; Ar. سَلّ, سَلَّة prob. loan-wd Fra[75 f], cf Schwally[Idiot 63])

†**סַל** **n.m.**[Gn 40, 16] **basket**,—׳ס abs. Gn 40^{17} +; cstr Ex 29^{23} +; pl סַלִּים Gn 40^{18}; cstr. סַלֵּי v^{16};—*basket* Gn $40^{16.17.17.18}$ (E), Ju 6^{19}, Ex $29^{3.3.23.32}$ Lv $8^{2.26.31}$ Nu $6^{15.17.19}$.

†[**סַלְסִלָּה**] **n.[f.] basket** acc. to 𝔊𝔙 AV RV, but prob. **shoot, branch** Ew Hi Gf Gie al, only pl. abs. הָשֵׁב יָדְךָ (rd. prob. יָד) כְּבוֹצֵר עַל־סַלְסִלּוֹת Je 6^{9}.

סלע (√of foll; cf. Ar. سَلَعَ *cleave, split*, سَلْعٌ *cleft, fissure*, Lane[1406], hence סֶלַע *split, jagged cliff, crag*, oft. *isolated* (split off) *rock* (cf. Wetzst[De Is 3, 696–707, and esp. ZAW iii (1883), 273]), then of smaller fragments, NH סֶלַע *rock, stone*, also *scale* (of serpent), *weight* (in trade); Aram. סלעא specif. *weight* for coin; Nab. סלע, a coin Lzb[329] Cook[85])

I. **סֶלַע**$_{61}$ **n.m.**[Ju 6, 20] **crag, cliff**, synon. צוּר;—abs ׳ס Ju 6^{20} +, סָלַע Nu 20^{10} +; cstr. סֶלַע 1 S

23^{23}; sf. סַלְעִי 2 S 22^{2}+, סַלְעוֹ Is 31^{9}; pl. סְלָעִים Is 2^{21}+;—**1.** lit. *cliff, crag* Ju 6^{20} Is 2^{21} 7^{19} Am 6^{12} Nu $20^{8.8.10.10.11}$ (cf. Ne 9^{15} ψ 78^{16}, and contr. the צור of Ex 17^{6}), Nu 24^{21} Dt 32^{13} (not elsewh Hex), + 10 t., שֵׁן הַסּ׳ 1 S $14^{4.4}$ *tooth of the crag,* i.e. sharp crag, so Jb 39^{28}, excav. in cliff as place of burial Is 22^{16}, abode of wild animals, יַעֲלֵי־ס׳ v^{1}, cf. ψ 104^{18} Pr 30^{26}, of birds Jb 39^{28} Ct 2^{14} (in fig.), cf. Je 48^{28}, so of Edom Ob^{3} = Je 49^{16}; cf. (Nu 24^{21} *supr.* and) Is 42^{11}; particular cliffs are: ס׳ עֵיטָם Ju $15^{8.11}$ cf. v^{13}, ס׳ (הָ)רִמּוֹן $20^{45.47.47}$ 21^{13} ס׳ הַמַּחְלְקוֹת 1 S 23^{28} cf. v^{25}; v. also II סֶלַע. †**2.** fig., esp סַלְעִי of י׳ (only ψψ), ψ 18^{3} = 2 S 22^{2}, ψ 31^{4} 42^{10} 71^{3}, of As god Is 31^{9} (prob; cf. צור Dt $32^{31.37}$); צֵל ס׳ כָּבֵד Is 32^{2} (sim. of protecting care); fig. of security ψ 40^{3} (feet on cliff), מְצָדוֹת סְלָעִים מִשְׂגַּבּוֹ Is 33^{16}, symb. of obstinacy חִזְּקוּ פְנֵיהֶם מִסּ׳ Je 5^{3}; צְחִיחַ ס׳ (*bare cliff,* lit *glare of* [*the*] *cliff*), in fig of openness, flagrancy Ez $24^{7.8}$, of razed city $26^{4.14}$ (only here Ez); in fig of fall of Bab. Je 51^{25}.

†II. סֶלַע **n.pr loc** in Edom, הַסּ׳ Ju 1^{36} (del ס, cf. GFM), הַסּ׳ captured in war 2 K 14^{7} (and called יָקְתְאֵל); מִסּ׳ Is 16^{1}; site dub; old identif. with *Petra* denied, plausibly, by Buhl ^{Edom} GFM$^{Ju 1.36}$ (who thinks of an actual *cliff*), but held Benz$^{2 K 14.7}$ Bd$^{Pal (1898), 206}$; 𝔊 (ἡ) πέτρα

†סָלְעָם **n.m.** an edible, winged, **locust** (NH *id.*; *swallower, consumer,* cf 𝔗 סַלְעֵם *swallow up, destroy;* Ar. سَلْعَفَ vb. *swallow,* Ko$^{II 1. 404}$);—Lv 11^{22} (+ אַרְבֶּה, חַרגֹּל, חָגָב).

סָלַף **vb. twist, pervert, overturn** (𝔗 סְלַף *twist* (rare); Ar سَلَفَ is *pass, pass away, come to naught* Lane$^{1407 f}$),—**Pi.** *Impf* 3 ms יְסַלֵּף Jb 12^{19} + 2 t., וַיְסַלֵּף Pr 22^{12}; 3 fs. תְּסַלֵּף Pr 13^{6} 19^{3}; *Pt* מְסַלֵּף Pr 21^{12},—**1.** *pervert,* Ex 23^{8} (E) a bribe *perverteth* the case (cause, דִּבְרֵי) of righteous, = Dt 16^{19}. **2.** *subvert, turn upside down, ruin* (only WisdLt) c acc. pers. Jb 12^{19} Pr 13^{6} (opp. תִּצֹּר), 21^{12}; אִוֶּלֶת אָדָם תּ׳ דַּרְכּוֹ 19^{3} *a man's folly subverteth his way,* וַיְסַלֵּף דִּבְרֵי בֹגֵד 22^{12} *and he* (י׳) *subverteth the affairs of a treacherous* man.

†סֶלֶף **n m.**$^{Pr 11.3 Qr}$ crookedness, crooked dealing:—ס׳ abs Pr 15^{4} (of tongue); cstr. ס׳ בּוֹגְדִים 11^{3}.

†[סָלַק] **vb. ascend** (loan-word from Aram סְלֵק, ܣܠܶܩ, Palm סלק *id.,* Lzb^{329} Cook^{85}, NH סלק Pi. *remove;* Ar. سَلِقَ *ascend,* Lane^{1410} (also loan-word?)),—only **Qal** *Impf.* 1 s אֶסַּק ψ 139^{8} *if I ascend to heaven* (שָׁמַיִם), thou art there (on form, = *אֶסְלַק, v Ges$^{§ 66 e}$ Ko$^{I. 301}$ Kau$^{§ 44}$).

סֹלֶת $_{53}$ **n.f.**$^{Lv 2.5}$ (cf. on gender Albrecht $^{ZAW xvi (1896), 106}$) **fine flour** (𝔊 σεμίδαλις, 𝔙 simila) (NH *id*; Aram. סוּלְתָא; Ar. سُلْتٌ *a kind of barley without husks* Lane^{1401}; As. *sillatu,* or *šillatu,* a kind of grain (?) Meissner-Rost$^{BAS III. 361}$; also *ṭultà, ṭuruṭ, flour,* as loan-word in Egypt, Bondi^{84} WMM$^{As. u. Eur 101}$),—abs ס׳ Gn 18^{6}+, cstr. ס׳ Ex 29^{2}+; sf סָלְתָּהּ Lv 2^{2},—*fine flour,* used in king's household 1 K 5^{2} (‖ קֶמַח), for honoured guests קֶמַח ס׳ Gn 18^{6} (J), a *seʾāh* of it sold for a shekel in time of scarcity 2 K $7^{1.16.18}$ (v. Benz); luxurious food Ez $16^{13.19}$ (of Jerus under fig. of woman); elsewh. only in offerings Ez 46^{14} 1 Ch 9^{29} 23^{29}, and P; ס׳ חִטִּים Ex 29^{2}, ס׳ v^{40}, Lv 2^{1} + 13 t. Lv., Nu 6^{15} + 26 t Nu.

סַם v. סמם.

†סַמְגַּר נְבוֹ **n.pr.m.** an officer of Nebuchad. acc to MT Je 39^{3} = (assumed) *Šumgir Nabu* (Schr^{COT}), but prob. text. err, Gie (plausibly) takes סמגר as crpt dittogr of רב מג, and joins נבו to foll., נְבוּשַׁזְבָּן = נבושרסכים, cf. v^{13} and 𝔊 Σαμαγωθ (Σαμαγαδ, Σαμαγαρ, etc.) καὶ Ναβουσαχαρ.

†[סְמָדַר ?], also סְמָדַר, כְּמָדַר **n.m.**$^{Ct 7.13}$ blossom of grape (just at flowering Duval$^{REJ xiv (1887), 227 ff.}$ NH *id*; Aram. סמדר, ܣܡܳܕܪܳܐ, Mand סימאדרא No$^{M. 128}$),—alw. abs. ס׳, only Ct: הַגְּפָנִים סְמָדַר 2^{13} *the vines are* (all) *blossom;* כְּרָמִים סְמָדַר v^{15} (on bold predicate cf. Ges$^{§ 141 d}$); פִּתַּח הַסְּמָדַר 7^{13} *the blossom has opened* (its buds).

סָמַךְ $_{48}$ **vb. lean, lay, rest, support** (NH *id.;* Ph in n pr. Lzb$^{317.329}$, Aram סְמַךְ, ܣܡܰܟ; also Eth. (ሰመከ:) አስመከ: *cause to lean upon,* etc. Di^{335}; Ar. سَمَكَ is *be high, ascend, raise, uplift,* سَمْكٌ *roof*);—**Qal** $_{41}$ *Pf.* 3 ms. ס׳ Dt 34^{9} Ez 24^{2}, וְסָמַךְ consec. Am 5^{19}+; 3 fs סָמָכָה ψ 88^{8}, sf סְמָכַתְהוּ Is 59^{16}, סְמָכָתְנִי 63^{5}, etc; *Impf.* 3 ms. וַיִּסְמֹךְ Lv 8^{14} Nu 27^{23}, sf. יִסְמְכֵנִי ψ 3^{6}, etc; *Imv.* ms. sf. סָמְכֵנִי ψ 119^{116}; *Pt act.* סוֹמֵךְ Is 63^{5} + 3 t; pl. cstr. סֹמְכֵי Ez 30^{6} ψ 54^{6}; *pass.* סָמוּךְ Is 26^{3} ψ 112^{8}; pl. סְמוּכִים 111^{8},—**1. a.** *lean* or *lay* hand upon (עַל־): Am 5^{19}; elsewh. in sacred rite: on head of sacrif. victim, as those who share in sacrif., Ex $29^{10.15.19}$ Lv 1^{4} + 12 t. Lv, Nu 8^{12} (all P), 2 Ch 29^{23}; so of Levites,

presented to י׳ Nu 8[10] (P), on head of blasphemer Lv 24[14] (P, as witnesses of his guilt); on head of Joshua in consecration (Moses subj) Nu 27[18.23] Dt 34[9] (all P) **b.** intrans ψ 88[8] thy wrath *hath rested* upon me (עָלַי), also סָמַךְ מֶלֶךְ־בָּבֶל אֶל־ Ez 24[2] *hath leaned against, rested his weight upon*, Jerusalem, i.e. invested (Toy), begun the siege of it †**2.** *support, uphold, sustain*, only fig c. 2 acc Gn 27[37] (J) with corn and must *have I sustained him*, provided sustenance for him, cf (of י׳) ψ 51[14], *uphold* Egypt Ez 30[6], abs Is 63[5], esp of י׳ *upholding, sustaining* Is 59[16] 63[5] ψ 3[6] 37[17.24] 54[6] (on ב *essentiae* v Ges[§119i], ב supr **7 a**), 119[116] 145[14], so pt pass ψ 111[8] *they are sustained*, i.e. maintained (י׳'s commands), סָמוּךְ לִבּוֹ 112[8] *his heart is sustained*, firm, and so יֵצֶר ס׳ Is 26[3]

†**Niph.** *Pf* 1 s נִסְמַכְתִּי ψ 71[6], 3 pl נִסְמָכוּ Is 48[2], *Impf* יִסָּמֵךְ 2 K 18[21] Is 36[6], וַיִּסָּמֵךְ Ju 16[29], 3 mpl וַיִּסָּמְכוּ 2 Ch 32[8], — reflex *support*, or *brace oneself*, also c. עַל־. Ju 16[29] *and he braced himself* against (upon) them (the pillars), 2 K 18[21] (if) a man *support himself* on it (Egypt as a cracked reed) = Is 36[6], on cheering words 2 Ch 32[8]; on God Is 48[2] ψ 71[6]

†**Pi.** *Imv* mpl sf + ב instr סַמְּכוּנִי Ct 2[5] *sustain* (refresh, revive) *me with raisin-cakes*

†סְמַכְיָהוּ **n.pr.m.** (cf Gray[Prop N 294, No 89], = י׳ *hath sustained*), — Korahite name 1 Ch 26[7]; 𝔊 Σαβχια, A 𝔊L Σαμαχια(ς)

†יִסְמַכְיָהוּ **n.pr.m.** (י׳ *sustaineth*, but perh. rd סמ׳ as foreg Gray[Prop. N 291 No 60]), — Levite name 2 Ch 31[13], 𝔊 Σαμαχ(ε)ια

†סֶמֶל **n.m.** [Ez 8, 5] perh orig. n.pr. div., then gen *image, statue* (Ph. סמל *id*, f סמלת, Lzb[151, 329], also פנסמלת Id[329], Bau[Rel 1 88] understands ס׳ to be design of foreign god), — abs הַס׳ 2 Ch 33[7.15], סֶמֶל Dt 4[16], cstr. סֵמֶל Ez 8[3.5], — *image, figure* of anything, פֶּסֶל תְּמוּנַת כָּל־ס׳ Dt 4[16], *id. l-image* פסל הַס׳ 2 Ch 33[7] and (פסל om.) v[15], סֵמֶל הַקִּנְאָה Ez 8[3] *the statue of jealousy*, i.e. that rouses י׳'s jealousy, = v[5]

סמם (√ of foll, meaning dub, if akin to Ar سَمَّ *smell* Lane[1593], مَشْمُوم *any fragrant plant* Id[1594], then ס must be for שׁ; in that case ס׳ perh loan-word in Heb, NH *id*, *spice, drug* (Ecclus ש׳ 38[4 m]), Aram סַמָּא *id*, ܣܡܐ *drug, pigment*, Ar. سُمّ *poison* is appar loan-word Fra[262]).

†[סַם] [16] **n.m.** *spice*, used in incense, — only pl abs סַמִּים, and only P Ch; Ex 30[34.34], elsewh. קְטֹרֶת (הַ)סַּמִּים *incense of spices* 25[6] + 8 t Ex, Lv 4[7] 16[12] Nu 4[16] 2 Ch 2[3] 13[11]

†סמן **vb.** whence **Niph.** *Pt* נִסְמָן Is 28[25] (si vera l.) barley *in an appointed place*, or *a determined portion* (cf Ges Hi De al.), but נ׳ lacking in 𝔊 and plausibly taken as dittogr. for כֻּסֶּמֶת by We[Prol 417, Gesch Isr 1 409] Che[Comm and Hpt] Du, cf Brd Gu[Kau]

†סמר **vb** *bristle up* (Lag[BN 108] cp Ar. شَمَّرَ *contract*, in that case ס׳ for שׁ׳), — **Qal** *Pf.* 3 ms ס׳ מִפַּחְדְּךָ בְשָׂרִי ψ 119[120] *from fear of thee did my flesh bristle up*, 'creep' **Pi.** *Impf* תְּסַמֵּר שַׂעֲרַת בְּשָׂרִי Jb 4[15].

†סָמָר **adj.** *bristling, rough*, — יֶלֶק ס׳ Je 51[27] *bristling locust*, perh with allusion to horn-like sheaths enclosing wings of the pupa, v Dr[Joel and Amos, 88] (on format. cf. Lag[BN 60])

†[מַסְמֵר] **n.m** [Ec 12, 11] *nail* (connexion with above √ dub, 𝔗 מַסְמְרָא, ChrPalAram ܡܣܡܪܐ Schwally[63 122], NH vb. סמר *nail on* or *up*; Ar مِسْمَار is perh loan-word Fra[89]); — pl abs. מַסְמְרִים Is 41[7], מסמרים 1 Ch 22[3] (of iron, on — v. Ges[§85 f]), also מַסְמְרוֹת Je 10[4] (+ מַקָּבוֹת), מַשְׂמְרוֹת נְטוּעִים, Ec 12[11] (sim.; + דָּרְבֹנוֹת), and מסמרות 2 Ch 3[9] (of gold)

†סְנָאָה appar. **n.pr.m.** בני ס׳ Ezr 2[35] = Ne 7[38], בְּנֵי הַס׳ Ne 3[3]; 𝔊 Σαανα, Σαναυα(τ), etc, 𝔊L Σεννaa; Mey[Judenth 150, 154] rds סְנִאָה (ס׳ for שׂ׳, cf שְׂנוּאָה) = *sons of the hated* (rejected) *woman*, i.e. the poorer classes of Jerusalem.

†סַנְבַלַּט (so Baer, van d H. Ginsb סַנְבַלָּט) **n.pr.m.** leader of Samaritan opponents of Nehemiah · Ne 2[10.19] 3[33] 4[1] 6[1.2.5.12.14] 13[28]; (Bab, = *Sin-uballit, Sin gave life* Schr[COT Ne 2, 10])

†סְנֶה **n.m.** [Ex 3, 2] a thorny bush, perh **blackberry bush** (cf. Low[No 219], *rubus fruticosus* Linn; Aram סַנְיָא, ܣܢܝܐ *thorn-bush*, As *sinû*, Meissner[ZA vi 293] *blackberry bush* (M thinks Aram ס׳ loan-word from this); Ar سَنَا *senna*, Lane[1449]), — abs ס׳ Ex 3[2.2.4], סְנֶה v[2.3] (all E) Dt 33[16] (akin to E).

†סֶנֶּה **n.pr.rup.** (= *thorny*, cf. GASm[Geogr 250 n.] HPS[ad loc.]), — a cliff opp the cliff called בּוֹצֵץ, 1 S 14[4] (Ginsb as here, Baer סֶנֶּה, van d H. סְנֶה), 𝔊 Σεννααρ.

†**סְנוּאָה** **n.pr.m.** (but v. סְנָאָה);—בֶּן־הַסּ׳ Ne 11^{9} (𝔊 Ασαυα, 𝔊L Ασεννα), בֶּן־הַסְּנֻאָה 1 Ch 9^{7} (𝔊 Ασυα, Α Ασανουα, 𝔊L Σαουα).

†**סַנְוֵרִים** **n.[m.] pl. intens.** vel **abstr.** (Sta$^{§ 324 b}$) **sudden blindness** (etym. dub.; der. fr. נור highly improb., whether *antiphr.* Wetzst $^{\psi\psi 4, 886}$ Kö$^{ii. 1, 404}$, or fr. *dazzling*, cf. 'flimmern' Hoffm$^{ZAW ii (1882), 68}$; but also view of Hal$^{REJ xi. 66}$ deriv. fr. √סנר *cover with a skin*, i.e. *produce film over*, lacks demonstration; at present we must be content with assuming quadrilit. √, Thes Sta$^{§ 243}$);—הִכּוּ בַּסּ׳ Gn 19^{11} (J) *they smote* the men *with sudden blindness*, cf. 2 K 6$^{18.18}$ (all cases miraculous, and in K temporary).

†**סַנְחֵרִיב** **n.pr.m. Sennacherib** (=*Sin-aḫê-irba, Sin multiplied brothers*, Schr$^{COT 2 K 18, 13}$);—son of Sargon and father of Esarhaddon, king of Assyria (B.C. 705–681; cf. Tiele $^{Gesch. 285 ff.}$); 2 K 18^{13} 19$^{16.20.36}$=Is 36^{1} 37$^{17.21.37}$ 2 Ch 32$^{1.2.9.10.22}$ (all as above, exc. סַנְחֵרֵב 2 K 19^{20}); 𝔊 Σενναχηρειμ, 𝔊L Σενναχειρειμ; Σεναχήριβος Jos $^{Ant. x. 1 ff.}$; Σαναχάριβον (acc.) Herodot.$^{ii. 141}$.

סַנָּה v. קִרְיַת־סַנָּה.

סַנְסַנָּה **n.pr.loc.** in S. Judah;—Jos 15^{31}, 𝔊 Σεθεννακ, Α Σανσαννα, 𝔊L Σεεvακ; prob.= חֲצַר סוּסָה 19^{5}, חֲצַר־סוּסִים 1 Ch 4^{31}; conj. on loc. (near Gaza), v. in Di$^{ad loc.}$ Buhl$^{Geogr. 183}$ and reff. (*Simsum*, NE. of Gaza, cp. by J. Schwarz$^{Das heilig. Land (1852), 72}$ van d. Velde$^{Mem, 346}$, is too far north).

†[**סַנְסִנִּים**] **n.[m.]pl. fruit-stalk** of date (Löw$^{p. 119}$) (Aram. loan-word fr. ܣܢܣܢܐ PS^{2617} *racemus dactylorum*, cf. As. *sissinnu*, part of the date-palm Dl^{507});—sf. אֹחֲזָה בְּסַנְסִנָּיו Ct 7^{9}.

†**סְנַפִּיר** **n.[m.] fin** (NH *id.*; quadrilit. acc. to Sta$^{§ 243}$; Fl in Levy$^{NHWB iii. 725 a}$ cp. Aram. סַמְפּוּרִין *points, nails*, and der. this fr. סְמַר vb. *nail*, with infixed פ (Levy$^{ChWB ii. 570 b}$));—Lv 11$^{9.10.12}$=Dt 14$^{9.10}$.

†**סָס** **n.m. moth** (𝔗 סָסָא, Syr. ܣܣܐ; As. *sâsu*, Dl$^{HWB 506}$; Ar. سُوسٌ, سُوسَةٌ; Eth. ፀፀ: Thes Lag$^{Armen. Stud. § 2262}$ cp. Armen. *zez*=Gk. σής, wh. is der. fr. סָס by Bo$^{Hieroz. iii. 514}$ Lewy$^{Fremdw. 16 f.}$);—וְכַצֶּמֶר יֹאכְלֵם סָס Is 51^{8}.

†**סִסְמַי** **n.pr.m.** name in Judah (on Ph. n. pr. div. (י)ססמ v. Lzb^{330} Ren in CIS$^{i. No. 95, 3, al.}$ Bae$^{Rel. 64 f.}$ Kit$^{1 Ch 2, 40}$);—ס׳ 1 Ch 2$^{40 b}$, סִסְמָי v$^{40 a}$; 𝔊 Σοσομαι, 𝔊L Σασαμει.

†**סָעַד** **vb. support, sustain, stay** (NH *id.*, esp. *take a meal*; Aram. סְעַד *support, stay*; Zinj. סעד *strengthen* Lzb^{330}, *support*, perh. *feed* Cook^{85}; ChrPalAram. n. ܣܥܕܘܢܐ *aid*, Schwally $^{Idiot. 64}$; Ar. سَعَدَ, سَعِدَ III, IV. *aid, assist*, Lane^{1360}, سَاعِدٌ *forearm* Id^{1362}; Sab. סעד DHM $^{Südar. Alt. p. 16}$);—**Qal** *Pf.* 3 ms. וְסָעַד consec. Pr 20^{28}; *Impf.* 3 ms. יִסְעָד; 3 fs. sf. תִּסְעָדֵנִי ψ 18^{36}, rd. also in ‖ 2 S 22^{36}, etc.; *Imv.* ms. סְעָד Ju 19^{5} (on ‗ prob. ŏ, by err., v. Kö$^{i. 261 f.}$ GFM$^{ad loc.}$), סְעָד־נָא v^{8} (cf. *id.*), וּסְעָדָה 1 K 13^{7}; sf. סְעָדֵנִי ψ 119^{117}; *Inf. cstr.* sf. וּלְסַעֲדָהּ Is 9^{6};—*support, sustain*, alw. fig.: **1.** *sustain, stay*, the heart (cf. לֵבָב **8**, לֵב **8**), with food Gn 18^{5} (J), Ju 19^{5} (c. 2 acc.), v^{8}, ψ 104^{15}; obj. om. 1 K 13^{7}. **2. a.** *support* throne (subj. kg.) Pr 20^{28}, coming ruler Is 9^{6}. **b.** *support, uphold* c. acc. pers. (subj. י׳, his hand etc.) ψ 18^{36} + ‖ 2 S 22^{36} (v *supr.*), ψ 20^{3} 41^{4} 94^{18} 119^{117}.

† **מִסְעָד** **n.[m.] support**;—abs. מ׳ 1 K 10^{12}; precise meaning unintelligible.

†[**סָעָה**] **vb.** (dub.) **rush**, of storm-wind (cf. Ar. سَعَى (and سعو), *go quickly, run, be energetic*; Syr. ܣܥܐ *make an attack upon*);—**Qal** *Pt.* fs. מֵרוּחַ סֹעָה ψ 55^{9} *from rushing wind* (and) from tempest (סַעַר); Hup (not Now) Gr Dy סוּפָה or סְעָרָה.

סעף (√of foll.; appar.=*cleave, divide*; cf. perh. Ar. سَعِفَ, of hand, *become cracked around nails* etc., Lane^{1364}, سَعَفٌ *palm-branches with leaves on them*, Id^{1365}; Ba$^{ES 56}$ GFM$^{Ju 15, 8}$ cp. شُعْبَةٌ *cleft*, (*forked*) *branch*, cf. Buhl$^{Lex 13}$).

†[**סָעִיף**] **n.[m.] 1. cleft. 2. branch**;—**1.** *cleft* of a crag, cstr. סְעִיף סֶלַע Ju 15$^{8.11}$; pl. cstr. וּבִסְעִפֵי הַסְּלָעִים Is 2^{21}; סְעִיפֵי הַסּ׳ 57^{5}. **2.** *branches, boughs*, pl. cstr. סְעִפֶּיהָ פֹּרִיָּה Is 17^{6} (so divide, Hi Kn Di Dr$^{Sm xxx}$ Du al.) *the boughs of the fruit-tree*; sf. סְעִיפֶיהָ 27^{10} (of ruined city; cf. קְצִירָהּ v^{11}).

†[**סְעַפָּה**] **n.f. bough, branch**;—pl. sf. סְעַפֹּתָיו Ez 31$^{6.8}$ (of king under fig. of cedar).

†I. [**סֵעֵף**] **vb. Pi. denom. lop off boughs**;—*Pt.* מְסָעֵף פֻּארָה Is 10^{33} י׳ . . . *shall lop off* (the) crown of branches.

†**סַרְעַפָּה** **n.f. bough** (with infixed ר, cf. Ges$^{§ 85 w}$, as transition-cons. Kö$^{ii. 1, 472}$; cf. BAram., Kau$^{§ 62}$ F. Selle$^{De Aramaismis Lib. Ezech. 17}$);—pl. sf.

סַרְעַפֹּתָיו Ez 31[6] (of Pharaoh under fig. of tree, cf Co Berthol Toy)

† II [סֵעֵף] (Kö[II 106]) **adj. divided, half-hearted**;—pl abs as subst, in religious sense, סֵעֲפִים שָׂנֵאתִי ψ 119[113] *half-hearted ones do I hate.*

† [סְעִפָּה] **n.f. division, divided opinion**;—pl abs עַל־שְׁתֵּי הַסְּעִפִּים 1 K 18[21] how long are ye limping *on the two divided opinions* (as on unequal legs; 𝔊 ταῖς ἰγνύαις seems an attempt to interpret the fig.; acc to Albrecht[ZAW xvi (1896) 7] ס׳ really = *legs*)

† [סָעַר] **vb. storm, rage** (Ecclus סער Hiph. 47[17] *move tempestuously*, סְעָרָה *storm-wind* 43[17] 48[9], NH Pi *stir up, blow*, סְעָרָה *storm-wind*, = II. שַׂעַר, but relation obscure, As *šâru, wind*, favours originality of ׳ש, but this only late in Heb., and for ׳ס Fra[189] cp. Ar سَعَرَ *kindle fire, excite, inflame, be vehemently hungry and thirsty, be mad, insane*, etc Lane[1363]),—**Qal** *Impf* 3 mpl. fig, יִסְעֲרוּ Hb 3[14] *they* [my foes] *storm along* to scatter me; *Pt act* סֹעֵר Jon 1[11] the sea *was growing* more and more *stormy*, so v[13] (+ עֲלֵיהֶם), f. סֹעֲרָה Is 54[11] *storm-tossed* (fig of Jerusalem) **Niph.** *Impf* 3 ms וַיִּסָּעֵר 2 K 6[11] and the heart of the king .. *was enraged* because of (עַל־) this thing **Pi.** *Impf* 1 s sf וְאֵסָעֲרֵם עַל־ Zc 7[14] (on form v. Ges[§ 23 h 52 n]) *and storm them away* (hurl them by a storm-wind) *upon* the nations. **Po** *Impf* 3 ms כְּמֹץ יְסֹעֵר Ho 13[3] shall be *like chaff* (which) *is storm-driven* from a threshing-floor

† סַעַר **n.m.**[Je 23, 19] **tempest**,—abs. ׳ס Am 1[14] + 5 t; סֹעַר ψ 55[9]; pl sf סַעֲרֶךָ 83[16],—*tempest*, esp fig of passionate acts of men, מֵרוּחַ סֹעָה מִסַּעַר ψ 55[9] (׳מס here awkward, without ו), of י׳'s wrath Je 23[19] (ס׳ מתחולל), cf. 25[32] 30[23]; *tempest* as instr. of י׳'s wrath, ψ 83[16] (‖ סוּפָה), v. also בְּסַעַר בְּיוֹם סוּפָה Am 1[14] and Jo 1[4 12]

† סְעָרָה **n.f. tempest, storm-wind**,—abs. סְעָרָה Is 29[6] + (so also 2 K 2[11] Ginsb; Baer בַּסְּעָרָה); cstr סַעֲרַת Je 23[19] 30[23], pl סְעָרוֹת Ez 13[11 13], cstr סַעֲרוֹת Zc 9[14],—*tempest, storm-wind*, as instr of י׳'s wrath, Is 29[6] (+ סוּפָה), cf. 40[24] 41[16], also רוּחַ סְעָרוֹת Ez 13[11 13] (against nation under fig of wall), *storm-wind* of Elijah's translation 2 K 2[1 11], of theophany Ez 1[4] (רוּחַ סְעָרָה), Jb 38[1] 40[6], and סַעֲרוֹת תֵּימָן Zc 9[14]; סַעֲרַת י׳ as fig. of י׳'s wrath Je 23[19] 30[23], of ordinary tempests only in late ψψ· רוּחַ סְעָרָה 107[25] 148[8], ׳ס opp דְּמָמָה 107[29].

I, II, III. סַף v. ספף.

ספא (√ of foll, cf NH ספי, סָפָא *give to eat*, 𝔗 סְפֵי *id.*; perh. Palm. ספא *feed, nourish*, Lzb[330] Cook[85]).

† מִסְפּוֹא **n.m.**[Gn 24, 25] **fodder**;—alw. abs ׳מ, Gn 24[25], elsewhere obj of נָתַן v[32] 43[24] (all J) 42[27] (E) Ju 19[19].

† [סָפַד] **vb. wail, lament** (NH *id.*, 𝔗 סְפַד, ChrPalAram ܣܦܕ *id*, Schwally[Idiot 64]; As. [*sapâdu*], *sipdu*, *sipittu*, *mourning* Dl[HWB 507]; cf Amhar ሰቀፈ: *dirge* Pia[ZMG xxiv (1861), 762]),—**Qal** *Pf* 3 fs. וְסָפְדָה consec. Zc 12[12], 3 pl. וְסָפְדוּ consec 1 K 14[13] Zc 12[10], *Impf* 3 fs וַתִּסְפֹּד 2 S 11[26], 2 ms תספד Ez 24[16], 1 s cohort אֶסְפְּדָה Mi 1[8], 3 mpl יִסְפְּדוּ Je 6[16] +, etc; *Imv.* mpl ספדו 2 S 3[31] + 2 t, fpl סְפֹדְנָה Je 49[3]; *Inf abs* סָפוֹד Zc 7[5], cstr סְפוֹד Ec 3[4], לִסְפֹּד Gn 23[2] 1 K 13[29], לִסְפּוֹד Je 16[5]; *Pt. act* pl. ספדים Is 32[12], סֹ׳ Ec 12[5],—*wail, lament* (with loud cries, etc, v. Mi 1[8], and cf. Dr[Am 6. 16]), esp. for dead, c. לְ, 1 S 25[1] 28[3] 1 K 14[13.18] Gn 23[2] (P) Je 16[6] 22[18.18] 34[5], cf וְאַל־תֵּלֵךְ לִסְפּוֹד וְאַל־תָּנֹד לָהֶם 16[5], c עַל־ *over* 2 S 1[12] 11[26] 1 K 13[30], cf Zc 12[10] (see v[12] infr.), c לִפְנֵי i e marching *before* (bier) 2 S 3[31] (v. Dr), c acc cogn Gn 50[10] (J); abs 1 K 13[29] Ez 24[16] cf v[23] Ec 3[4] (opp. רקד; cf ψ 30[12]), and pt. as subst Ec 12[5] *wailers;* also, with idea of guilt on part of those wailing, Zc 12[12] (cf v[10] supr), over calamity, judgment, c עַל־ Mi 1[8], abs Je 4[8] (both + הֵילִיל), 49[3] and (with fasting) Zc 7[5] Jo 1[13]—עַל־שָׁדַיִם ספדים עַל־שְׂדֵי־חֶמֶד וגו׳ Is 32[12] is dub, Thes Ew De Che al. *upon the breasts smiting* (?) *for the fields*, etc, but rd prob. שָׂדַיִם (ים—, ־וֹת) Ges[Comm] (q v) Buhl[Lex 13] Skinner al.. *over the fields wailing, over the delightful fields*, etc **Niph.** *Impf* 3 mpl לֹא יִסָּפְדוּ Je 16[4] *they shall not be bewailed*, so 25[33].

מִסְפֵּד **n.m.**[Gn 50, 10] **wailing**;—abs ׳מ Am 5[16] + 11 t.; cstr. מִסְפַּד Mi 1[11] + 2 t; sf. מִסְפְּדִי ψ 30[12],—*wailing:* **1.** for dead, Gn 50[10] (J; as acc cogn), Zc 12[10] (c עַל־; cf. v[11 11] infr.). **2.** for calamity experienced Am 5[16 16] (‖ אֵבֶל), v[17] Mi 1[8] (מ׳ כַּתַּנִּים ‖ אבל), v[11] Je 48[38] Ez 27[31], anticipated Je 6[26] Est 4[3]. **3.** in contrition Is 22[12] (+ בכי), Jo 2[12] (+ בכי, צום), cf. Zc 12[11 11]. **4.** in gen, ψ 30[12] (opp מָחוֹל, cf. Ec 3[4]).

†[סָפָה] **vb. sweep or snatch away, catch up** (NH ספי, סָפָא *collect* (rare), 𝔗 סְפֵי (rare), Syr. ܣܦܐ *collect, pick up;* Ar. سَفَا of wind, *raise dust and carry it away* Lane 1377);—**Qal 1.** intrans.: *Pf.* 3 fs. סָפְתָה Je 12[4] *be snatched away* (rd poss. סָפָה [סוּף]). **2.** trans.. *Impf.* 3 fs תִּסְפֶּה Is 7[20] *sweep away* beard, 2 ms תִּסְפֶּה Gn 18[23.24] *sweep away* indiscriminately (good and bad); *Inf. cstr* סְפוֹת Dt 29[18] *to snatch away* the moist with the dry (proverb. expression, cf. Dr), sf לִסְפּוֹתָהּ ψ 40[15] *to snatch it away* (i.e. my life).—וְסָפוּ Am 3[15] v. סוּף. **Niph.** *Pf* 3 ms. ונספה consec 1 S 26[10]; *Impf.* 2 ms. תִּסָּפֶה Gn 19[15.17]; 1 s. אֶסָּפֶה 1 S 27[1]; 2 mpl. תִּסָּפוּ Nu 16[26], תִּסָּפוּ 1 S 12[25]; *Pt.* נִסְפֶּה Is 13[15] Pr 13[23] (1 Ch 21[12] v infr.);—**1.** *be swept away, destroyed,* Gn 19[15] (בַּעֲוֺן הָעִיר *by reason of the iniquity of the city*), v[17] (both J), Nu 16[26] (JE) 1 S 12[25] 26[10] (in battle), + בְּיַד of agent 1 S 27[1]; cf וְיֵשׁ נִסְפֶּה בְּלֹא מִשְׁפָּט Pr 13[23] *and there is that is swept away for lack of justice.*—1 Ch 21[12] rd. נוֹסָף (as ‖ 2 S 24[13], v. נוס). **2.** *be caught up, captured,* Is 13[15] (‖ נִמְצָא). **Hiph.** *Impf.* 1 s אַסְפֶּה עָלֵימוֹ רָעוֹת Dt 32[23] *I will catch up against them calamities,* but read אֹסְפָה *I will gather* (√ אסף), or < אֹסִפָה (Di Dr Buhl[Lex 13]) *I will add,* i.e. *multiply* (√ יסף; v. Ges[§ 69 h. note]).

† I. [סָפַח] **vb. join, attach to;**—**Qal** *Imv* ms sf. סְפָחֵנִי נָא אֶל־וגו׳ 1 S 2[36] *attach me, pray, to* one of the priest's offices. **Niph.** *Pf* 3 pl. וְנִסְפְּחוּ עַל־ consec. Is 14[1] *and they shall attach themselves to* the house of Jacob (‖ נִלְוָה). **Pi.** *Pt.* מְסַפֵּחַ חֲמָתְךָ Hb 2[15] *joining* (to it?) *thy fury,* but read prob. מִסַּף (ח dittogr.) *from the goblet of thy fury* (so We Gr Now GASm Da) **Pu.** *Impf* 3 mpl. יְסֻפָּחוּ Jb 30[7] *are joined together, hold themselves together* (yet rd. perh. Niph. יִסָּפְחוּ Bu). **Hithp.** *Inf cstr.* מֵהִסְתַּפֵּחַ 1 S 26[19] they have driven me out *from joining myself* with (בְּ) the inheritance of י׳.

II. ספח (√ of foll; appar. *pour out;* cf. Ar. سَفَحَ *pour out, shed* (blood; Qor 6[146]); NH סָפַח of river, *cast out* alluvial soil, make new land)

† I. [סָפִיחַ] **n.[m.]** outpouring (?),—pl. sf. תִּשְׁטֹף־סְפִיחֶיהָ עֲפַר הָאָרֶץ Jb 14[19] (si vera l.) *its outpourings sweep away the dust of the earth,* so most, but dub.; Bu prop. *סְחִיפָה, cf. מָטָר סֹחֵף Pr 28[3].

† II. סָפִיחַ **n.[m.] growth from spilled kernels** ((kernels) *poured out,* accidentally, in harvesting, acc. to most; Buhl[Lex 13] al. think of *additional* growth, √ I. ספח);—it is what springs up of itself in second year, and serves as food when no grain could be sown: abs ס׳ 2 K 19[29]=Is 37[30]; cstr. סְפִיחַ קְצִירְךָ Lv 25[5]; sf. תִקְצְרוּ אֶת־סְפִיחֶיהָ v[11].

† מִשְׂפָּח **n.[m.]** prob. outpouring (of blood), **bloodshed** (שׂ subst for ס; word chosen for assonance with מִשְׁפָּט),—abs., וַיְקַו לְמִשְׁפָּט וְהִנֵּה מ׳ Is 5[7] *and he waited for justice and lo! bloodshed,* so Ges Hi Ew Di Gu Du Che[Comm] Che[Hpt] (dub)

III ספח (√ of foll, meaning dubious).

† סַפַּחַת **n.f. eruption, scab,** either malignant or harmless;—abs. שְׂאֵת אוֹ ס׳ אוֹ בַהֶרֶת Lv 13[2] cf. 14[56].

† מִסְפַּחַת **n.f.** id.;—abs. Lv 13[6.7.8].

† שִׂפַּח **vb. Pi. denom. cause a scab upon, smite with scab** (שׂ subst for ס);—וְשִׂפַּח אֲדֹנָי קָדְקֹד וגו׳ (consec.) Is 3[17] *and Adonay shall smite with scab the crown of* the daughters of Zion.

† [מִסְפָּחָה] **n.f. long veil** (prop *sheathing?*) covering whole person, pl. abs. וְעֹשׂוֹת הַמִּסְפָּחוֹת עַל־רֹאשׁ Ez 13[18], sf מִסְפְּחֹתֵיכֶם v[21].

ספי v. ספף.

† סַפִּיר **n.[m.] sapphire,** perh. also **lapis lazuli** (cf Di[Ex 24, 10] Now[Arch. i 131]) (NH *id,* and סַפִּירִינוֹן; 𝔗 סַפִּירִינָא; 𝔖 ܣܦܝܠܐ; loan-word from Skr. *çanipriya* acc. to Lag[Ges. Abh 72] Lewy[Fremdw 56] cf. Gk. *σάπφειρος*),—abs ס׳ Ex 24[10]+8 t.; pl. סַפִּירִים Is 54[11] Ct 5[14];—with other jewels as ornaments of prince Ez 28[13]; in high priest's breastplate Ex 28[18] 39[11]; found in mines Jb 28[6], costly Jb 28[16] cf. Is 54[11]; taking high polish La 4[7] (in fig.); שֵׁן מְעֻלֶּפֶת סַפִּירִים Ct 5[14] *ivory covered with sapphires* (in fig); *lapis lazuli,* acc to Hi Bu Du al. in Jb 28[6] (עַפְרֹת זָהָב לוֹ being understood of sparkling crystals of iron pyrites in this), but v. Di; *lapis lazuli* may be intended in לִבְנַת הַסּ׳ Ex 24[10] (J) *pavement of sapphire* (in theoph.), cf. אֶבֶן־ס׳ Ez 1[26] 10[1].

† סֵפֶל **n.[m.] bowl** (√ unknown; perhaps foreign word; As. *saplu, bowl, basin* (Dl[HWB 508] Schr[COT 2 K 9, 2]) [occurs as object of tribute or

plunder]; NH = BH; 𝔗 סִיפְּלָא *bowl, basin,* ChrPalAram. ܣܦܠܐ (wash-)*basin* Schwally Idiot. 64; Ar. سِفْلٌ *bowl, jar* Fl[Levy NHWB iii. 320; Kl. Schr. ii. 556 f.] is perh. loan-word Frä[67 f.]);—abs. מְלֹא הַסּ׳ Ju 6[38]; for drinking, cstr. סֵפֶל אַדִּירִים 5[25] *a bowl of* (fit for) *nobles, huge bowl* (GFM).

†[סָפַן], once, erron., [שׂ׳] **vb. cover, cover in, panel** (NH סָפַן is *respect, care for;* Ph. מספנת *roof,* Lzb[330]; Aram. סְפַן Ithpe. *be covered, overlaid;* As. *sapânu* (sts. *šapânu!*), *cover, overwhelm* Dl[508]; *sapannu, concealment, obscurity, depth* (of sea); Eth. ሰፈነ: *invalescere, percrebescere, praevalere,* Di[406]);—**Qal** *Impf.* 3 ms. וַיִּסְפֹּן אֶת־הַבַּיִת גֵּבִים 1 K 6[9] *and he covered in the house with beams* (?); *Inf. abs.* סָפוּן בָּאָרֶז Je 22[14] (rdg. with JDMich Hi Gf Or Gie Co, חַלּוֹנָיו סָפוּן, for MT חַלּוֹנָי וְסָפוּן, cf. Dr[Sm xxx]) *covering* (it) *in, panelling* (it) with cedar; *Pt. pass.* סָפוּן בָּאָרֶז 1 K 7[7], סָפֻן בָּאָרֶז v[3]; pl. בְּבָתֵּיכֶם סְפוּנִים Hg 1[4] *in your panelled houses.*—סָפוּן strangely = *reserved, laid up,* Dt 33[21], and = *hidden* v[19] שְׂפֻנֵי טְמוּנֵי חוֹל (only here with שׂ; both in sense of צָפוּן [rd. this?], cf. Dr).

†סִפֻּן **n.[m.] ceiling**;—abs. הַסּ׳ 1 K 6[15].

†סְפִינָה **n.f. vessel, ship** (*covered in, overlaid,* with sheathing, deck, etc.; Aram. ܣܦܝܢܬܐ; on Ar. سَفِينَةٌ as loan-word v. Frä[216]);—only יַרְכְּתֵי הַסּ׳ Jon 1[5].

ספף (√of foll., meaning unknown).

†I. סַף **n.m. basin, goblet** (NH סַף; Ph. סף (Inscr. of Tyre [(1), 5, 6]) Schröd [ZMG xxxix (1885), 317 f.] Cl-Gann [Annales du Musée Guimet x. 511 = Recueil d'arch. orient. (1886), 89] Hal [RÉJ xii. 107] Bloch; but Lzb[330] *door-sill*);—ס׳ abs. *basin* Ex 12[22.22] (J; containing blood of passover lamb); cstr. סַף־רַעַל Zc 12[2] *goblet of reeling* (intoxicating, fig.), prob. also Hb 2[15], where rd. מִסַּף חֲמָתְךָ *from the goblet of thy fury* (for MT מְסַפֵּחַ ח׳, v. I. ספח); pl. abs. סִפּוֹת 2 S 17[28] *basins* for ordinary use; הַסִּפִּים Je 52[19], הַסִּפּוֹת 1 K 7[50] and cstr. סִפּוֹת כֶּסֶף 2 K 12[14], of temple utensils.

II. סַף[24] **n.m.**[Am 9, 1] **threshold, sill** (NH *id.;* Ph. v. Lzb I. סַף; Aram. סִפָּא, ܣܦܐ, Ar. *sippu* Dl[509], all *id.*);—abs. ס׳ 2 K 12[10] +, also הַסָּף Ju 19[27] + 3 t. (Baer Ginsb), הַסָּף 2 K 25[8]; sf. סִפִּי Ez 43[8], סִפָּם v[8]; pl. סִפִּים Am 9[1] Is 6[4] + 6 t. Ez Ch;—*threshold, sill* Ju 19[27] Am 9[1] Is 6[4] Ez 41[16.16] 43[8.8] 2 Ch 3[7], ס׳ הַבַּיִת 1 K 14[17], ס׳ הַשַּׁעַר Ez 40[6.7], cf. v[6 b]; שֹׁמֵר הַסַּף = *door-keeper,* an important temple official, Je 35[4], so שֹׁמְרֵי הַסּ׳ 2 K 12[10] (priests), 22[4] = 2 Ch 34[9] (Levites!), 2 K 23[4] 25[18] = Je 52[24]; in Persia, of palace Est 2[21] 6[2]; of tabern. שֹׁ׳ הַסִּפִּים 1 Ch 9[19]; שֹׁעֲרֵי הַסּ׳ 2 Ch 23[4] (Levites), שֹׁעֲרִים בַּסּ׳ 1 Ch 9[22]; coll. חֹרֶב בַּסַּף Zp 2[14] *desolation in the thresholds.*

†[ספף] **vb. denom. Hithpô'. stand at, or guard, the threshold**;—*Inf. cstr.* בָּחַרְתִּי הִסְתּוֹפֵף בְּבֵית אֱלֹהַי ψ 84[11] *I choose standing at the threshold in the house of my God.*

†III. סַף, סִפַּי **n.pr.m.** a Philistine, 2 S 21[18] (𝔊 τὸν Σεφ(ε); 𝔊L τοὺς ἐπισυνηγμένους), = סִפַּי 1 Ch 20[4] (𝔊 τὸν Σαφουτ, A Σεφφι, 𝔊L Σαπφι).

†סָפַק, [שָׂפַק], **vb. slap, clap** (NH Pi. *id.;* Ar. سَفَقَ *slap* (face), *strike* (hands) Lane[1373]);—**Qal** *Pf.* 3 ms. וְסָפַק consec. Je 48[26], sf. סְפָקָם Jb 34[26]; 1 s. סָפַקְתִּי Je 31[19]; 3 pl. סָפְקוּ La 2[15]; *Impf.* 3 ms. יִשְׂפֹּק (שׂ subst. for ס) Jb 27[23], יִסְפּוֹק 34[37], וַיִּסְפֹּק Nu 24[10]; *Imv.* ms. סְפֹק Ez 21[17];—**1.** *slap,* sq. עַל־יָרֵךְ *on the thigh,* in remorse and sorrow Je 31[19] Ez 21[17]; c. כַּפַּיִם *clap* one's *hands* Nu 24[10] (in anger), c. עַל *at,* La 2[15] Jb 27[23] (in mockery); כ׳ om. Jb 34[37] (in presumptuousness, against God). **2.** *slap, chastise,* c. acc. pers. Jb 34[26] (subj. God). **3.** *splash* וְס׳ מוֹאָב בְּקִיאוֹ Je 48[26] *and Moab shall splash* (fall with a splash) *into his vomit,* > Thes Buhl[Lex 13] *empty himself* (?), *throw up* (cf. Syr. ܣܦܩ Pa.). **Hiph.** *Impf.* 3 mpl. וּבְיַלְדֵי נָכְרִים יַשְׂפִּיקוּ Is 2[6] (rd. perh. וּבִידֵי Hi Du Che, *and into the hands of foreigners they clap,* lit. *cause to clap,* sc. their hands; > 𝔊 𝔖 from I. שׂפק q.v., *they abound in, have a sufficiency of*).

†[שֶׂפֶק] **n.[m.]** doubtful word; **hand-clapping, i.e. mockery** (?) (cf. vb. Jb 27[23]);—כִּי־חֵמָה פֶּן־יְסִיתְךָ בְשׂ׳ שָׂפֶק Jb 36[18] in difficult cl. *because* there is *passion,* (beware) *lest it incite thee to mockery,* Bae[Kau] Da (but הסית בְּ = *incite against,* hence Bu reads לְשָׂפֶק); De is not clear; others (as Di): *lest it* (passion) *excite thee at the chastisement* (v. √**2**; cf. Thes); Du reads מִשְּׂפֶק לְחֵמָה lest *chastisement* incite thee *to wrath.*—On Jb 20[22] (edd.) v. שֵׂפֶק.

סֵפֶר[185] **n.m.**[Is 29, 11] **missive, document, writing, book** (prob. ancient loan-word from As. *šipru, missive, message* Dl[HWB 683], Tel Am. *šipru, šipirtu, id.* Wkl[TA Gloss.]; √*šapâru, send, send message* or *letter* Dl[HWB 683], Wkl[l. c.], whence also

šâpiru, writer, and (perh) *ruler, šapirûtu, rule;* v. Hom$^{Aufsätze (1892) 34}$ Buhl$^{Lex 13}$; perh cf Ar سَفَرَ *go forth to journey,* II. *send on a journey* Lane^{1370}; NH סֵפֶר = BH; so Aram סִיפְרָא, ܣܶܦܪܳܐ; ChrPal Aram. ܣܦܪܐ Schwally$^{Idiot. 64}$; Ar. سِفْرٌ);—ס׳ abs. 2 S 11^{14}+; cstr. Ex 24^{7}+; sf סִפְרִי Ex 32^{33}, סִפְרְךָ v^{33} ψ 139^{16}; pl. סְפָרִים 1 K 21^{8}+;—†**1.** *missive*: **a.** *letter* of instruction, *written order, commission,* or *request,* usu fr. king, 2 S 11$^{14.15}$ 1 K 21$^{8.8.9.11}$ 2 K 5$^{5.6.6.7}$ 10$^{1.2.6.7}$, 19^{14} = Is 37^{14} cf 2 Ch 32^{17}, 2 K 20^{12} = Is 39^{1}; = *written decree* for publication Est 1^{22} 3^{13} 8^{5} 9$^{20.25.30}$ (= אִגֶּרֶת v$^{26.29}$, vid. p 8 b supra), cf. וַיִּשְׁלַח סְפָרִים בְּיַד הָרָצִים בַּסּוּסִים רֹכְבֵי הָרֶכֶשׁ 8^{10};—[כָּתַב ס׳ 2 S 11^{14} 1 K 21^{8} 2 K 10$^{1.6}$ 2 Ch 32^{17}, כָּתַב בַּס׳ (of specif contents) 2 S 11^{15} 1 K 21$^{9.11}$; קָרָא אֶת־הַס׳ 2 K 5^{7} *read the letter*]—**b.** fr prophet Je 29^{1}, other influential persons v$^{25.29}$†. †**2.** *legal document,* ס׳ כְּרִיתֻת *certificate of divorce* Dt 24$^{1.3}$ and (fig) Je 3^{8} Is 50^{1}; ס׳ הַמִּקְנָה *deed of purchase* Je 32$^{11.12}$ (del. art.), v$^{12.14.16}$, cf בַּס׳ v^{10}, הַסְּפָרִים v^{14} (si vera l; del. 𝔊 Gie cf. Gf), סֵפֶר v$^{16 b.44}$; ס׳ = *indictment* Jb 31^{35} (obj of כָּתַב; כָּתַב בּ׳ = *sign* Je 32$^{10.12.44}$). **3.** *book,* or *scroll,* in which something is written to preserve it for future use Ex 17^{14} (E), Jos 18^{9} (JE), 1 S 10^{25} Is 30^{8} Jb 19^{23}+; in form of roll, cf. וְנָגֹלּוּ כַסֵּפֶר הַשָּׁמַיִם Is 34^{4}, הַס׳ הֶחָתוּם 29$^{11.12}$ (v. Je 36, etc, infr), partic.: **a.** *book of prophecies* Je 25^{13} 30^{2}+6 t. Je 36, Dn 12^{4}; ס׳ חֲזוֹן נַחוּם Na 1^{1}; סֵפֶר ׳ Is 34^{4}; so מְגִלַּת סֵפֶר Je 36$^{2.4}$ (= מְגִלָּה v^{6}+6 t.; with many columns, דְּלָתוֹת v^{23}), Ez 2^{9}, cf. ψ 40^{8}. **b.** *geneal. register,* ס׳ תּוֹלְדוֹת Gn 5^{1} (P), ס׳ הַיַּחַשׂ Ne 7^{5}. **c.** *law-book,* †ס׳ הַבְּרִית Ex 24^{7} (E), 2 K 23^{2} = 2 Ch 34^{30}, 2 K 23^{21}; †ס׳ הַתּוֹרָה Dt 28^{61} 29^{20} 30^{10} 31^{26} Jos 1^{8} 8^{34} (all D), 2 K 22^{8} = 2 Ch 34^{15}, 2 K 22^{11} Ne 8^{3}; †ס׳ תּוֹרַת אֱלֹהִים Jos 24^{26} (E), Ne 8^{8} (rdg. ס׳ תּוֹרַת, so 𝔊, cf. Talm$^{Nedarim 37 b}$), v^{18} 9^{3}; †ס׳ תּוֹרַת ׳ 2 Ch 17^{9} 34^{14}, †ס׳ תּוֹרַת מֹשֶׁה Jos 8^{31} 23^{6} (both D), 2 K 14^{6} Ne 8^{1}; †ס׳ מֹשֶׁה 2 Ch 25^{4} 35^{12} Ne 13^{1}. **d.** *book* of poems, ס׳ מִלְחֲמֹת ׳ Nu 21^{14} (JE), ס׳ הַיָּשָׁר Jos 10^{13} (JE), 2 S 1^{18}. **e.** *book* concerned with kings, ס׳ דִּבְרֵי שְׁלֹמֹה 1 K 11^{41}, and esp. ס׳ דִּבְרֵי הַיָּמִים לְמַלְכֵי וגו׳ 1 K 14$^{19.29}$+31 t. K (18 t. of Isr., 15 t. of Judah), cf. Est 10^{2} (of Media and Pers.); also ס׳ דִּבְרֵי הַיָּמִים לַמֶּלֶךְ דָּוִיד 1 Ch 27^{24} (rdg. ס׳ for מִסְפָּר, 𝔊 Kit^{Hpt});—ס׳ מַלְכֵי יִשְׂרָאֵל 2 Ch 16^{11}, ס׳ הַמְּלָכִים לִיהוּדָה וְיִשְׂרָאֵל 27^{7} ס׳ מ׳ יִשׂ׳ וִיהוּדָה 25^{26} 28^{26} 32^{32}; יְהוּדָה וְיִשׂ׳ 35^{27} 36^{8}; ס׳ מ׳ יִשׂ׳ 1 Ch 9^{1} 2 Ch 20^{34}; מִדְרַשׁ ס׳ הַמְּלָכִים 24^{27}, also ס׳ דִּבְרֵי הַיָּמִים Ne 12^{23} Est 2^{23}; ס׳ הַזִּכְרֹנוֹת דִּבְרֵי הַיָּמִים Est 6^{1}. **f.** once בַּסְּפָרִים Dn 9^{2} *by means of the Scriptures* (canonical books) cf Ew Meinh Bev Marti^{Kau}. **g.** God's *record-book,* ψ 139^{16}, ס׳ זִכָּרוֹן Mal 3^{16}; God's register of living, Ex 32$^{32.33}$ (E), ס׳ חַיִּים ψ 69^{29}; הַס׳ Dn 12^{1} (citizens of Mess. kingdom) **4.** ס׳ = *book-learning,* esp. *writing:* יָדַע (הַ)סֵּפֶר Is 29$^{11.12.12}$ (of ability to read), so לְלַמְּדָם סֵפֶר וּלְשׁוֹן כַּשְׂדִּים Dn 1^{4} *to teach them the writing and speech of the Chaldeans* (on constr. v Ges$^{§ 128 a}$), more gen. הַשְׂכֵּיל בְּכָל־ס׳ וְחָכְמָה v^{17}.—[סֵפֶר *book* is joined with vbs. thus: it is written (יִכָּתֵב) Mal 3^{16}; a thing is written בַּס׳ Ex 17^{14}+20 t., עַל־ס׳ 2 S 1^{18}+50 t. (+Je 36^{32}, בַּדְּיוֹ *with ink* v^{18}), דָּרַשׁ מֵעַל ס׳ †Je 30^{2} 51^{60}; conversely אֶל־ס׳ Is 34^{16}, שָׁמַע מֵעַל ס׳ Je 36^{11}; v. also †בַּס׳ וְיֻחַקוּ Jb 19^{23} *inscribe in a book,* †עַל־ס׳ חֻקָּהּ Is 30^{8} (‖ כָּתְבָהּ עַל־לוּחַ); †מָחָה מס׳ *blot out of a book* Ex 32$^{32.33}$ ψ 69^{29}; †קָרָא אֶת־הַס׳ Je 51^{63} *read the book,* scroll, but usu. †קָרָא בס׳ 36$^{8.10.13}$ Ne 8$^{8.18}$ 9^{3} 13^{1}]—in ס׳, קִרְיַת ס׳, v. ק׳.

†[סִפְרָה] **n.f.** book;—sf. הֲלֹא בְּסִפְרָתֶךָ ψ 56^{9} (cf סֵפֶר **3 g**); del. as gloss Bi Che Hup-Now Du.—Cf also [סְפֹרָה] infr.

סָפַר$_{107}$ **vb. count, Pi. recount, relate** (prob. ancient denom. from סֵפֶר; NH = BH; Eth. ሰፈረ: *measure* Di^{404}),—**Qal**$_{27}$ *Pf* 3 ms ס׳ 2 S 24^{10}, 2 ms. סָפַרְתָּה ψ 56^{9}, וְסָפַרְתָּ Lv 25^{8}, etc.; *Impf.* יִסְפֹּר ψ 87^{6}+Jb 38^{37} where read prob. יְסַפֵּר (Bu) for MT יִסְפּוֹר, יְסַפֵּר Jb 31^{4}, וַיִּסְפֹּר 2 Ch 2^{16}, sf. וַיִּסְפְּרֵם Ezr 1^{8}; 2 ms תִּסְפֹּר Jb 39^{2}, תִּסְפּוֹר 14^{16}, תִּסְפָּר־ Dt 16^{9}, etc; *Imv.* ms. סְפֹר Gn 15^{5}; mpl. סִפְרוּ 1 Ch 21^{2} ψ 48^{13}; *Inf. cstr.* לִסְפֹּר Gn 15^{5}+2 t.; *Pt.* סֹפֵר Is 33$^{18.18}$ (v. also סֹפֵר **n.** infr);—**1.** *count* things, to learn their number, c. acc., Gn 15$^{5.5}$ (J) 2 S 24^{10}+10 t. (+acc. cogn. 2 Ch 2^{16}); acc. om. Gn 41^{49} (E); + לְ (dat. comm. vel eth), Lv 15$^{13.28}$ 23^{15} 25^{8} (all PH), Dt 16^{9} Ez 44^{26} Ezr 1^{8} ψ 87^{6} Is 33^{18} (abs), v^{18} (but text suspicious, conjj in Du Che^{Hpt}). **2.** *number* = *take account of,* carefully observe and consider, *reckon:* צְעָדַי תִּסְפּוֹר Jb 14^{16} *of my steps thou takest account,* so 31^{4}; v. also 38^{37} (cf. supr.), נֹדִי סָפַרְתָּה ψ 56^{9} *my wandering hast thou reckoned,* taken into account (Che reads סְפַרְתִּי after 𝔊).

†**Niph.** *Impf* 3 ms. יִסָּפֵר Ho 2^{1}+4 t.; 3 mpl. יִסָּפְרוּ 1 K 8^{5} 2 Ch 5^{6}, וַיִּסָּפְרוּ 1 Ch 23^{3};—

be counted, numbered, usu. c. neg., to indicate multitude, לֹא יִסָּ׳ מֵרֹב Gn 16[10] (J) *it is not to be counted, for multitude*, so 32[13] (J), 1 K 3[8] (‖ לֹא יִמָּנֶה), 8[5] (+ *id.*), 2 Ch 5[6] (+ *id.*); cf. Ho 2[1] (+ לֹא־יִמַּד), Je 33[22] (‖ לֹא יִמַּד); positively, only וַיִּסָּפְרוּ הַלְוִיִּם 1 Ch 23[3].

Pi. 67 *Pf.* 1 s. סִפַּ֫רְתִּי ψ 119[26], סִפַּרְתִּי v[13]; 3 pl. סִפְּרוּ Ju 6[13] + 3 t.; *Impf.* 3 ms. יְסַפֵּר Jb 38[37] +, 1 s. אֲסַפֵּר ψ 22[18] +; cohort. אֲסַפֵּ֫רָה Jb 15[7]; 1 pl. וּנְסַפֶּר־ Ex 10[2], etc.; *Imv.* סַפֵּר Is 43[26], etc.; *Inf. cstr.* (לְ)סַפֵּר ψ 50[16] + 5 t.; *Pt.* מְסַפֵּר Ju 7[13] 2 K 8[5]; pl. מְסַפְּרִים ψ 19[2] 78[4];—*recount, rehearse, declare*: **1.** *recount* something (acc.), to (לְ pers.) Ju 6[13] 7[13] Gn 24[66] (J), 1 S 11[5] + 18 t. (of *rehearsing* glorious deeds of י׳ ψ 44[2] 73[28] 78[3.4] 79[13]); c. acc. + בְּ loc. Ez 12[16], elsewhere of rehearsing name or praise of י׳ Ex 9[16] (J) ψ 9[15] 96[3] = 1 Ch 16[24], ψ 102[22] Je 51[10]; c. acc. alone ψ 9[2] 19[2] 119[13] (+ בְּ instr.), 145[6] + 8 t. ψψ + Is 43[21], all of rehearsing praise of י׳; cf. עָצְמוּ מִסַּפֵּר ψ 40[6] *they are too great to rehearse*, c. acc. also Je 23[28.32] Jb 15[17] 28[27] ψ 119[26]; acc. om. Is 43[26], c. לְ pers. Gn 40[8] (E) + 6 t., c. אֶל־ pers. Gn 37[10] (E), c. בְּאָזְנֵי Ex 10[2]; c. כְּמוֹ (q. v.) ψ 73[15]; c. אֶל־ *concerning* ψ 2[7], cf. 69[27] (𝔊 𝔖 Ew Ol Gr Bi Che Bae *add*; in that case read יְסַפּוּ); c. עַל־ *concerning*, + לְ pers. Jo 1[3]. **2.** appar., in weakened sense, *talk* ψ 59[13], 64[6] (c. לְ *concerning*), 73[15] (c. כְּמוֹ). **3.** *count exactly, accurately*, אֲסַפֵּר כָּל־עַצְמוֹתָי ψ 22[18] *I can count exactly all my bones* (in wasted body).—ψ 40[6] v. sub **1**, Jb 38[37] read יִסְפֹּר.

†**Pu.** *be recounted, related, rehearsed*: *Pf.* 3 ms. סֻפַּר לְ Is 52[15]; *Impf.* 3 ms. יְסֻפַּר לְ Jb 37[20] (cl. as subj.), + לְ *concerning* ψ 22[31]; c. בְּ loc. 88[12]; abs. יְסֻפָּר Hb 1[5].

†סֹפֵר, סוֹפֵר **n.m.** ψ 45, 2 **enumerator, muster-officer, secretary, scribe** (prop. pt. of סָפַר; Aram. סָפְרָא, ܣܳܦܪܳܐ *id.*, cf. ܣܰܦܪܳܐ *doctus, literatus*; OAram. ספרא *id.*, Lzb[330] Cook[85]; Ph. ספר Lzb[330]);—abs. סֹפֵר Ju 5[14] +, סוֹפֵר 2 S 8[17] +; cstr. סֹפֵר 2 K 12[11] + 2 t., + Je 52[25] (Gie GFM rd. הַסּ׳ as ‖ 2 K 25[19]); pl. סֹפְרִים 1 K 4[3] Je 8[8], סוֹ׳ 1 Ch 2[55] 34[13]; cstr. סֹפְרֵי Est 3[12] 8[9];—**1. a.** *enumerator, muster-officer*, in description of leaders of Isr. מֹשְׁכִים בְּשֵׁבֶט ס׳ Ju 5[14]. **b.** king's official = *secretary* 2 S 8[17] = 20[25] = 1 Ch 18[16], 2 K 18[18.37] = Is 36[3.22]; Sol. had two 1 K 4[3] (in all these disting. from מַזְכִּיר); also 2 K 19[2] = Is 37[2], Je 36[10.12], cf. לִשְׁכַּת הַסּ׳ v[12.20.21], בֵּית הַסּ׳ 37[15.20]; acting as treasurer and paymaster 2 K 12[11] = 2 Ch 24[11],—cf. Zadok Ne 13[13];—2 K 22[3.8.9.10.12] = 2 Ch 34[15.18.20]; 1 Ch 24[6] (Levite); הַסּ׳ שַׂר הַצָּבָא 2 K 25[19] = Je 52[25] (si vera l. in K) implies military authority (but שַׂר הַצּ׳ perh. gloss GFM Ju 5, 14); Ew Sta al. read (as Je) *scribe of general*. **c.** in Persia, *secretaries* who wrote out (king's) decrees, acc. to Est 3[12] 8[9]. **d.** 2 Ch 26[11] uses ס׳ for muster-officer; 1 Ch 2[55] mentions families of סוֹפְרִים; 2 Ch 34[13] knows ס׳ as Levites; ס׳ 1 Ch 27[32] = *man of learning*. **2.** professional class of *learned men*, '*scribes*,' able to read and write Je 36[26.32]; with writing implements, עֵט ס׳ מָהִיר ψ 45[2], קֶסֶת הַסּ׳ Ez 9[2.3], תַּעַר הַסּ׳ Je 36[23]; esp. *learned* in the law, and assuming to issue its precepts, עֵט שֶׁקֶר סֹפְרִים 8[8]. **3.** specif. of Ezra, at once priest (כֹּהֵן) and learned in the law (סֹפֵר), Ezr 7[11], ס׳ דִּבְרֵי מִצְוֹת י׳ v[11] [cf. Aram. v[12.21]], ס׳ מָהִיר בְּתוֹרַת מֹשֶׁה v[6]; Ne 8[1.4.9.13] 12[26.36].

†I. סְפָר **n.[m.]** **enumeration, census** (late; on format. cf. Lag[BN 175]);—abs. ס׳, sq. אֲשֶׁר as acc. cogn. with סָפַר 2 Ch 2[16].

†II. [סְפָר] **n.pr.loc.** in S. Arabia;—only c. ה loc. סְפָ֫רָה Gn 10[30], 𝔊 Σωφηρα; usu. indentif. with *Ṭafâr* (ظفار, pronounced إِسْفَار, إِشْفَار acc. to Thes), ancient city of Ḥimyarite kings (Ptol. Σαπφαρ μητρόπολις v. Sprenger[Alte Geogr. Arab. § 301 et pass.]), so Thes Tuch[Comm. Gen. 2, 212], but dub. Glaser[Skizze ii. 437], ס = צ improb. Di[ad loc.] Lag[BN 61].

†[סְפֹרָה] **n.f.** number;—pl. abs. לֹא יָדַעְתִּי סְפֹרוֹת ψ 71[15] *I know not* (*the*) *numbers* (of י׳'s acts of righteousness and deliverance, i.e. they are *innumerable*; cf. 𝔗 Symm.); > Du (after 𝔊 B[ab] א 𝔖 𝔙) reads סְפָרוֹת (cf. סִפְרָה supr.).

I. מִסְפָּר 133 **n.m.** 1 Ch 27, 24 **number, tale**;—abs. מ׳ Gn 34[30] +; cstr. מִסְפַּר Ex 16[16] +; sf. מִסְפַּרְכֶם Nu 14[29], מִסְפָּרָם Ju 21[23] +; pl. cstr. מִסְפְּרֵי 1 Ch 12[23];—**1. a.** *number*, Ju 7[6] *the number of those lapping*, מִס׳ לַכּוֹכָבִים ψ 147[4], + oft. (37 t. PH); לֹא עָלָה הַמִּסְפָּר בְּמִסְפַּר דִּבְרֵי וגו׳ 1 Ch 27[24] (read בְּסֵפֶר) *the number did not come up into* (was not recorded in) *the book of the daily doings*, etc.; redund. after num., †2 S 21[20] *twenty-four* (*in*) *number*; אֵין מ׳ *it was* (*they were*) *innumerable* Gn 41[49] (E), c. לְ Ju 6[5] 7[12] 1 Ch 22[16] 2 Ch 12[3], לִתְבוּנָתוֹ אֵין מ׳ ψ 147[5] (of י׳); abs. Je 2[32] Jb 21[33] Ct 6[8]; †עַד־אֵין מ׳ = *id.*, Jb 5[9] 9[10] ψ 40[13], וְאֵין מ׳ Je 46[23]; לְאֵין מ׳ †1 Ch 22[4]; וְאֵין לָהֶם מ׳ †ψ 104[25] 105[34] Jo 1[6]; הֲיֵשׁ מ׳ לִגְדוּדָיו Jb 25[3] *can his bands be numbered?* without אֵין = *numerable*,

i.e. *few*, וִיהִי מְתָיו מ׳ Dt 33^{6} but *let his men be few*, יָמִים מ׳ Nu 9^{20}, מ׳ alone Is 10^{19}, usu. in combin., מְתֵי מ׳ = *a few men* Gn 34^{30} (J), Dt 4^{27} Je 44^{28} 1 Ch 16^{19} ψ 105^{12}, אַנְשֵׁי מ׳ Ez 12^{16}; so שְׁנוֹת מ׳ Jb 16^{22}; adv. phr. מִסְפַּר יְמֵי חַיֵּיהֶם Ec 2^{3} = *during all their lives*, cf. 5^{17} 6^{12}; = *appointed* (normal) *number*, מ׳ יָמֶיךָ אֲמַלֵּא Ex 23^{26} (E). **b.** c. prep. בְּ: בְּמ׳ מְעַט בְּמ׳ Ez 5^{3} *few in number*; בְּמ׳ *by* (exact) *count, tale* 2 S 2^{15} Dt 25^{2} 1 Ch 9$^{28.28}$, so prob. Ez 20^{37} rd. בְּמִסְפָּר 𝔊 Toy for MT מָסֹרֶת; *in* (prescribed) *number* Nu 29^{18} + 6 t. Nu 29 (P), Ezr 3^{4}; = *acc. to* (proportioned to) *the number of* Lv 25$^{15.15}$ + oft.; לְמ׳ *acc. to number* Ju 21^{23} Jos 4$^{5.8}$ (JE) Nu 14^{29} (P) Ez 4^{5} 1 Ch 27^{1}; כְּמ׳ = *id.*, 1 K 18^{31} Nu 15$^{12.12}$ (P); so מ׳ alone (adv. acc.) Ex 16^{16} (P) Jb 1^{5} Je 2^{28} 11^{13}.—Nu 23^{10b} rd. מִי סָפַר, cf. v^{a}, so 𝔊 Di So[Kau]. †**2.** *recounting, relation*, מִסְפַּר הַחֲלוֹם Ju 7^{15} *the recounting of the dream.*

†II. מִסְפָּר **n.pr.m.** a returned exile Ezr 2^{2} (𝔊 Μαλσαρ, A 𝔊L Μασφαρ), = מִסְפֶּרֶת Ne 7^{7} (𝔊 Μασφεραν, ℵ Μασφαραδ, A Μασσφαραθ, 𝔊L Μασφαρ).

מִסְפֶּרֶת v. foregoing.

†סֹפֶרֶת **n.pr.m.** in בְּנֵי־הַסּ׳ Ezr 2^{55} a family of returned exiles (𝔊 Ασεφηραθ, A Ασεφοραθ, 𝔊L Ασωφερεθ) = בְּנֵי־ס׳ Ne 7^{57} (𝔊 Σαφαραθ(ι), 𝔊L Ασοφερεθ).

†[סְפָרֵד?], סְפָרַד **n.pr.loc.** Ob^{20} 𝔊 Εφραθα, Q^{a} Σαφαραδ; loc. dub.; Spieg[APK 242] Nö[ZMG xxxiii (1879), 323] Che[Founders 312] Say[Monuments 483] al. cp. *Sparda* in Asia Minor (= *Sardis?* Behistun[i, 15] Persep. I^{12} NR[a 28]); Schr[COT ad loc. (cf. KGF 116 ff.)] Dl[Par 249], cf. GASm[12 Proph. ii. 176], cp. *Šaparda* in SW. Media (time of Sargon); a *Saparda* also NE. from Nineveh (Esarhaddon's time), cf. Knudtzon[Ass. Gebete, Nos. 8, 11, 30].

†סְפַרְוַיִם **n.pr.loc.** city conquered by king of Assyr.;—ס׳ 2 K 17^{24} 18^{34} = סְפַרְוָיִם Is 36^{19}, עִיר סְפַרְוָיִם 2 K 19^{13} = Is 37^{13}; סְפַרְוַיִם also 2 K 17^{31b} Qr (Kt. ספרים); 𝔊 Σεπφαρουαιν, Επφαρουαιμ, etc., 𝔊L Σεπφαρειμ;—usu. identif. with *Sippara* (on a canal), between Bagdad and Babyl., a city in two parts, *Sipp. of Šamaš* (mod. *Abbu Habba*), and *Sipp. of Anunitu(m)*, on opp. side of canal, hence du. ס׳ = *the two Sipparas*, Schr[COT 2 K 17, 24], cf. Dl[Par 209–212] Tiele[Gesch. 88]; this recently disputed, in view of mention with Hamath and other northern cities (2 K 17^{24} and esp. 18^{34}), v. Hal[ZA ii. 401 ff.] Di[Is 36, 19] Wkl[Alttest. Unters. 101] Benz[2 K 17, 24] al., who cp. *Šabara'in*, city conquered by Šalmanašarid IV (Wkl in Schr[KB ii. 276]); but this by no means certain.

†[סְפַרְוִי] **adj. gent.** of **Sepharvaim**, only pl. c. art. = subst., הַסְפַרְוִים 2 K 17^{31a}.

†[סָקַל] **vb.** **stone, put to death by stoning, also (Pi.) free from stones** (appears like denom., but noun unknown; NH סְקִילָא *execution by stoning*);—**Qal** *Pf.* 2 ms. sf. וּסְקַלְתּוֹ consec. Dt 13^{11}; 3 mpl. sf. וּסְקָלֻנִי consec. Ex 17^{4}; 2 mpl. וּסְקַלְתֶּם consec. Dt 22^{24}, etc.; *Impf.* 3 mpl. יִסְקְלוּ Jos 7^{25}, sf. יִסְקְלֻהוּ 1 K 21^{13}, etc.; *Imv.* mpl. sf. סִקְלֻהוּ 1 K 21^{10}; *Inf. abs.* סָקוֹל Ex 19^{13} 21^{28}; *cstr.* sf. סָקְלוֹ 1 S 30^{6};—*pelt with stones, stone to death*, (as penalty) c. acc. pers. vel animal., Ex 8^{22} 17^{4} (both JE) 1 S 30^{6} 1 K 21^{10}, abs. Ex 19^{3} 21^{28} (JE); c. acc. pers. + בְּ instr. בָּאֲבָנִים Dt 13^{11} 17^{5} 22$^{21.24}$ Jos 7^{25} 1 K 21^{13}. **Niph.** *Impf.* 3 ms. יִסָּקֵל *be stoned to death* Ez 19^{13} 21$^{28.29.32}$ (JE). **Pi.** *Impf.* 3 ms. יְסַקֵּל 2 S 16$^{6.13}$, sf. יְסַקְּלֵהוּ Is 5^{2}; *Imv.* mpl. סַקְּלוּ Is 62^{10};—**1.** *stone, pelt with stones*, c. acc. pers. + בָּאֲבָנִים 2 S 16^{6}, acc. om. v^{13} (‖ עִפַּר בֶּעָפָר). **2.** *free* vineyard (acc.) *from stones* (Ges[§ 52 h]) Is 5^{2}; so also 2 S 4^{6}, reading pt. f. מְסַקְּלָה חִטִּים lo, the portress *was cleansing wheat from stones* (for MT לֹקְחֵי ח׳), so We Dr Bu Kit Löhr HPS, after 𝔊; (>rdg. however mostly סֹלֶקֶת, **Qal** *Pt.*); סַקְּלוּ מֵאֶבֶן Is 62^{10} *free* (highway) *fr. stones.* **Pu.** *Pf.* סֻקַּל *be stoned to death* 1 K 21$^{14.15}$.—Not in HP; these and other writings (exc. above) use syn. רגם, cf. Br[Hex 73].

סַר v. סרר.

†[סָרָב] **n.m.** **rebel?** acc. to Thes al. (prob. Aram. loan-word, cf. Aram. ܣܪܒ *contradict, chatter, prattle, tell lies*; Pa. סָרֵב and NH Pi. סֵרֵב = BH; cf. סרב Ecclus 41^{2d} *loving contradiction*);—pl. abs. (i.e. סָרָבִים וְסַלּוֹנִים אוֹתָךְ (אִתָּךְ)) Ez 2^{6} *rebelles et quasi spinae sunt erga te* Thes; Vrss rd. ptcp., Co Berthol סֹרְבִים וְסֹלִים *resisting and despising* thee (cf. סַלּוֹן); AV RV *briers and thorns*, cf. Ew Hi-Sm Siegf[Kau] Da Toy.

†סַרְגּוֹן **n.pr.m.** **Sargon** (As. *Šargânu*, and (prob. by pop. etymol.) *Šarrukênu* = *firm, faithful, king*, v. reff. infr.);—king of Assyria B.C. 722–705, conqueror of Samaria, father of

Sennacherib, only Is 20^{1} (𝔊 Αρνα, Aq Theod Σαραγᾶ, Symm Σαργων [Q^{mg}]), Ptol^{Canon} Ἀρκεάνου (genit.), cf Schr$^{COT\ ad\ loc.}$ Tiele$^{Gesch\ 236\ ff}$.

סרד (√of foll, Thes. cp. Syr ܣܪܕ *be frightened*)

†**סֶ֫רֶד** **n.pr.m.** son of Zebulun,—Gn 46^{14} (𝔊 Σερέδ, 𝔊L Σεδεκ), Nu 26^{26} (𝔊 Σαρεδ)

†**סַרְדִּי** **adj.gent.** of foregoing, only c art הַסּ׳ as n coll, Nu 26^{26}.

סָרָה v סור

סִרָה v בּוֹר הַסִּרָה supr p. 92 b

†[**סָרַח**] **vb. go free, be unrestrained, overrun, exceed** (NH סָרוּחַ *overhanging, flapping;* Ar سَرَحَ of camels, etc, *pasture where they please,* also *send forth* to pasture; II. *let* a wife *go free; let down* the hair, سُرُحٌ *easy*—NH סָרַח, Aram ܣܪܚ usu = *corrupt, sin*),—**Qal** *Impf* 3 fs. תִּסְרַח Ex 26^{12}, *Pt. act* f. סֹרַחַת Ez 17^{6}, *pass* סָרוּחַ (cf. Kö$^{II\ 1.137}$ Ges$^{§50\ f}$ Ba$^{NB\ 180}$) Ex 26^{13}, pl. סְרֻחִים Am 6^{7}, סרחים v^{4}, cstr סרוּחֵי Ez 23^{15},—**1.** *go free, be unrestrained.* וּסְרֻחִים עַל־עַרְשׂוֹתָם Am 6^{4} i e. prob. = *and are sprawling* upon their couches (in contempt. hyperbole), מִרְזַח ס׳ v^{7} *the revelry of sprawlers;* pt. act of *overrunning, spreading* vine Ez 17^{6} **2.** of *overhanging* stuffs (prop. *overrunning, exceeding, extended beyond limits*) תִּסְרַח עַל אֲחֹרֵי הַמִּשְׁכָּן Ex 26^{12} (P) *it shall overrun (overhang),* over the back of the tabern, so יִהְיֶה סָרוּחַ v^{13}, עַל־צִדֵּי הַמּ׳ סְרוּחֵי טְבוּלִים Ez 23^{15} *overhung of turbans,* extended with respect to turbans, = with pendant turbans (cf [טבול]). **Niph.** *Pf.* 3 fs נִסְרְחָה חָכְמָתָם Je 49^{7} usu. *is their wisdom let loose* (i e. *dismissed, gone*)? (‖ הַאֵין עוֹד חָכְמָה בתימן אָבְדָה עֵצָה מִבָּנִים), but No$^{Expos\ May,\ 1897,\ 363}$ *is corrupt* (cf NH, and esp Aram.)

†**סֶ֫רַח** **n.m. excess**,—ס׳ הָעֹדֵף Ex 26^{12} (P) *the excess* (sc of tent-covering), *which remains over*

†[**סִרְיוֹן**] **n** [**m.**] **armour** (‖form of שִׁרְיוֹן q v),—sf יִתְעַל בְּסִרְיֹנוֹ Je 51^{3} *let him raise himself in his armour,* pl לִבְשׁוּ הַסִּרְיֹנוֹת 46^{4}

סָרִיס 45 **n.m.** eunuch (NH *id*, 𝔗 סְרִיסָא, Syr ܣܪܝܣܐ (all c vb denom = *emasculate*), OAram סרסא Lzb^{331} Cook^{86}, Ar سَرِيسٌ, سَرِيسٌ (vb سَرِسَ *be impotent*), Kam Frey (not Lane); prob. foreign word; acc to Jen$^{ZA\ vii\ 174}$ = As. *ša rêši (rîši), he who is the head, chief,* cf. Brock$^{Lex\ 239\ b}$ Dl$^{HWB\ 694}$ (*ša-riš?*), Zim$^{ZMG\ liii\ 1899,\ 116}$; *eunuch* being specialized meaning, in any case Ar. is Aram loan-word),—abs. ס׳ 1 K 22^{9} + 7 t.; cstr. סְרִיס Gn 37^{36} + 3 t; pl סָרִיסִים 2 K 9^{32} + 17 t.; cstr סְרִיסֵי Gn 40^{7} + 4 t., sf סָרִיסָיו Gn 40^{2} + 4 t., סָרִיסֶיהָ Est 4^{4},—*eunuch,* of Pharaoh Gn 37^{36} 40^{27} (all E), married 39^{1} (R^{JE}); of Isr. kings 1 S 8^{15} (predict.), 1 K 22^{9} = 2 Ch 18^{8}, 2 K 8^{6} 9^{32} (all of N Isr); 1 Ch 28^{1} (in David's time), 2 K 23^{11} 24$^{12.15}$ cf Je 29^{2}, also 34^{19} 38^{7} 41^{16} (all in Judah; so likewise) 2 K 25^{19} (military officer) = Je 52^{25}, of Bab kings 2 K 20^{18} = Is 39^{7} (predict), ascribed to Nebuch. in Dn, רַב סָרִיסָיו Dn 1^{3}, שַׂר הַסָּרִיסִים v$^{7.8.9.10.11.18}$, to king of Persia in Est, 1$^{10.12.15}$ + 9 t. Est, promises made to eunuchs Is 56$^{3.4}$. (Term never used in lawcodes; on contrary cf. exclusion of פְּצוּעַ דַּכָּא, and כְּרוּת שָׁפְכָה Dt 23^{2} [v Dr$^{ad\ loc}$], also מְרוֹחַ אָשֶׁךְ Lv 21^{20}.)—רַב־סָרִיס is title of high military officer 2 K 18^{17} (As.), Je 39$^{3.13}$ (Bab)—Vid. further, Thes Smith^{DB} Art '*Eunuch,*' Di$^{Gn\ 39\ 1}$ Dr Dt$^{23.1}$.

I. [**סֶ֫רֶן**] 21 **n.m. tyrant, lord** (Philist loan-word),—pl abs. הַסְּרָנִים Ju 16^{30} + 2 t; cstr. סַרְנֵי Ju 3^{3} + 16 t; sf. סַרְנֵיכֶם 1 S 6^{4},—only of *tyrants, lords* of the Philistines, five in no Ju 3^{3} Jos 13^{3} (D), 1 S 6$^{16.18}$ cf. v^{4}, i.e appar., one ruling each of the five cities (named 1 S 6^{17}); without the numeral Ju 16^{5} + 6 t Ju 16, 1 S 5^{8} + 7 t. 1 S, + 1 Ch 12^{20} (Baer Ginsb, v^{19} van d H).

†II [**סֶ֫רֶן**] **n.**[**m.**] **axle** (Aram. ܣܪܢܐ; √unknown);—סַרְנֵי נְחֹשֶׁת 1 K 7^{30} *axles of brass* (𝔊 τὰ προσέχοντα, 𝔙 *axes*)

[**סַרְעַפָּה**] v. סעף. **סרף** v. שׂרף

†**סִרְפַּד** **n.**[**m.**] a desert-plant, contrasted with הֲדַס, *myrtle* תַּחַת הַסּ׳ יַעֲלֶה הֲדַס Is 55^{13}; not clearly identif., 𝔊 κόνυζα, 𝔖 ܚܪܘܓܐ, 𝔙 *urtica.*

†**סָרַר** **vb. be stubborn, rebellious** (usu. towards י׳) (NH *id*, (rare); As *sarâru*),—**Qal** *Pf.* 3 ms ס׳ יִשְׂרָאֵל Ho 4^{16} *Isr. is stubborn;* *Pt act* בֵּן סוֹרֵר וּמוֹרֶה Dt 21^{18}, cf. v^{20}, בָּנִים סוֹרְרִים Is 30^{1}, עַם סוֹרֵר 65^{2}, דּוֹר ס׳ וּמֹרֶה ψ 78^{8} (all of Isr), לֵב ס׳ וּמוֹרֶה Je 5^{23}, פָּרָה סֹרֵרָה Ho 4^{16} (sim. of Isr, v. supr); as pred. שָׂרֵיהֶם סוֹרְרִים Ho 9^{15} cf Is 1^{23}, סָרֵי סוֹרְרִים Je 6^{28} *revolters among the rebellious* (? cf. סור **Qal** ad

fin., and סַר infr); of loose woman הֹמִיָּה הִיא וְסֹרָרֶת Pr 7^{11}; as subst. = *the stubborn*, ψ 66^{7} 68$^{7.19}$; fs וַיִּתְּנוּ כָתֵף סוֹרֶרֶת Ne 9^{29} *and they presented a stubborn shoulder* (of Isr.) = Zc 7^{11} (סֹרָרֶת).

†סַר adj. **stubborn, resentful, sullen, implacable**;—סַר וְזָעֵף 1 K 20^{43} 21^{4}; f. מַה־זֶּה רוּחֲךָ סָרָה v^{5} why then *is thy spirit sullen?* poss. also pl cstr. סָרֵי סוֹרְרִים Je 6^{28} *revolters (stubborn ones)* among, etc (v. supr. and סור **Qal** ad fin).

†סתו Kt, סְתָיו Qr **n.m. winter** (loan-wd. fr. Aram., cf. Syr. ܣܬܘܐ, 𝔗 סִיתְוָא; Ar. شِتَاءٌ Lane^{1504}, prob orig. שׁ', cf. Schwally$^{Idiot. 64}$; on ו as old nominat. ending (ס' for *šutayu*) cf. Lag$^{BN\ 190\ Anm}$),—הַסְּתָו עָבָר Ct 2^{11}.

†סָתַם **vb. stop up, shut up, keep close** (NH *id*; 𝔗 סְתַם *id.*; Syr. ܣܬܡ (ܣܛܡ) very rare); Ar. سَدَمَ *close* door Lane^{1334}, and سَطَمَ Kam Frey, are perh loan-words),—**Qal** *Pf.* 3 ms ס' 2 Ch 32^{30}; *Impf.* 2 mpl. תִּסְתֹּמוּ 2 K 3^{19}; 3 mpl יִסְתְּמוּ v^{25}, וַיִּסְתְּמוּ 2 Ch 32^{4}, *Imv.* ms. סְתֹם Dn 8^{26} 12^{4}; *Inf cstr.* לִסְתּוֹם 2 Ch 32^{3}; *Pt pass.* סָתוּם Ez 28^{3}, סָתֻם ψ 51^{8}, pl. סְתֻמִים Dn 12^{9};—**1.** *stop up* springs of water 2 K 3$^{19.25}$ 2 Ch 32$^{3.4}$, cf. v^{30}. **2.** *shut up, keep close,* prophetic words Dn 8^{26} 12$^{4.9}$; בְסָתֻם ψ 51^{8} *in* (the) *closed* (chamber of the breast, ‖ טֻחוֹת).—כָּל־סָתוּם Ez 28^{3} usu. no *secret* is too dark for thee, but doubtful (v II. עמם); 𝔊 σοφοί, Co חַרְטֻמִּים < Toy חֲכָמִים, or Berthol. קֹסְמִים. **Niph.** *Inf. cstr.* לְהִסָּתֵם Ne 4^{1} the breaches [in the walls] had begun *to be stopped up.* **Pi.** *Pf.* 3 pl. sf סִתְּמוּם Gn 26^{15}; *Impf.* 3 mpl sf. וַיְסַתְּמוּם v^{18}, both of *stopping* wells *quite up* (R^{JE})

†סָתַר **vb. hide, conceal** (NH *id*, der. species; 𝔗 סְתַר Pa Ithpa., Syr. ܣܬܪ Pe Pt. pass, chiefly Pa. Ithpa., *id*; Ar. سَتَرَ *veil, conceal, hide,* Lane^{1304}; Eth. ሰተረ: (rare) Di^{364});—**Niph.** *Pf.* 3 ms. נִסְתַּר Pr 27^{12} + 22^{3} Qr (Kt וְנִסְתָּר); 2 ms. נִסְתַּרְתָּ 1 S 20^{19}; 1 pl. נִסְתָּרְנוּ Is 28^{15}, etc; *Impf.* 3 ms. יִסָּתֵר Ho 13^{14} +; 1 s אֶסָּתֵר Gn 4^{14} +; 3 mpl יִסָּתְרוּ Am 9^{3}; 1 pl. נִסָּתֵר Gn 31^{49}, etc; *Imv.* ms. הִסָּתֵר Je 36^{19}; *Inf. cstr.* לְהִסָּתֶר שָׁם Jb 34^{22}; *Pt.* נִסְתָּר ψ 19^{7}, pl. נִסְתָּרִים Dt 7^{20}; fpl נִסְתָּרֹת Dt 29^{28}, -וֹת ψ 19^{13};—**1.** *hide oneself*, c בְּ loc., 1 S 20$^{5.24}$ 1 K 17^{3} Je 23^{24}, so (fig) Is 28^{15}, c. שָׁם 1 S 20^{19} Jb 34^{22}; abs. Je 36^{19} Pr 22^{3} 27^{12} 28^{28} ψ 89^{47}; c. מִפְּנֵי pers. Dt 7^{20} Jb 13^{20}, c. מִן pers. ψ 55^{13}. **2.** *be hid, concealed*, esp fig. of escaping God's notice, c. מִפְּנֵי pers Gn 4^{14} (J), מִלְּפָנַי Je 16^{17}, מִנֶּגֶד עֵינַי Am 9^{3}, מֵעֵינַי Is 65^{16} Ho 13^{14} (subj. נֹחַם, i.e. I will not repent, change my purpose of judgment), מִן ψ 38^{10} Is 40^{27}; fr. heat of sun ψ 19^{7} (i.e. it penetrates everywhere); fr. birds Jb 28^{21} (of place of wisdom); recipr. נס' איש מרעהו Gn 31^{49} (J) when *we are hidden each from the other* (i.e separated); abs Nu 5^{13} Jb 3^{23} (*whose way is hid* sc from himself), Zp 2^{3} (i e. escape י''s judgment); pt. *hidden, secret things*, in gen. Dt 29^{28}, of sins ψ 19^{13}.

Pi. *Imv* fs. סַתְּרִי Is 16^{3} *carefully hide* (i e *shelter*) the outcasts (Moab speaks to Zion).

Pu. *Pt.* fs. אַהֲבָה מְסֻתָּרֶת Pr 27^{5} *love carefully concealed.*

Hithp. *Impf.* 3 fs. תִּסְתַּתָּר Is 29^{14}; *Pt.* מסתתר 1 S 23^{19} + 3 t.,—*hide oneself carefully*, of David's taking refuge with (עם) Ziphites 1 S 23^{19} = ψ 54^{2} (title), in (ב) a hill 1 S 26^{1}; אֵל מ' Is 45^{15} *a God that completely hides himself.*

Hiph. *Pf* 3 ms. הסתיר ψ 10^{11} 22^{25}; 2 ms. הִסְתַּרְתָּ ψ 30^{8} Is 64^{6}, etc., *Impf.* 3 ms. יַסְתִּיר 1 S 20^{2}, וַיַּסְתֵּר Ex 3^{6} Jb 3^{10}, sf. יַסְתִּרֵנִי ψ 27^{5}, וַיַּסְתִּרֵם Je 36^{26}; 3 fs. sf וַתַּסְתִּירֵהוּ 2 Ch 22^{11}; 1 s. וָאַסְתִּר Ez 39$^{23.24}$, etc; *Imv.* ms. הַסְתֵּר ψ 51^{11}; *Inf abs* הַסְתֵּר Dt 31^{18} Is 57^{17}; *cstr.* הַסְתֵּר Pr 25^{2} (v. Ko$^{i.\ 223}$ and reff; yet cf inf. abs. אָכֹל v^{27}), לַסְתִּר Is 29^{15} (Ges$^{§53\ q}$), *Pt.* מַסְתִּיר Is 8^{17};—*conceal, hide:* **1.** a person from (מִפְּנֵי) enemy 2 K 11^{2} = 2 Ch 22^{11}; subj י', c. מִן ψ 64^{3}, abs. Je 36^{26}; *hide* anything from (מִן) one 1 S 20^{2}, a thing, in gen, Pr 25^{2}; anything (fr. י', מִן in ‖ cl) Is 29^{15}; in gen. = *shelter* a person Jb 14^{13}, c בְּ loc. (subj. י') ψ 17^{8} 27^{5} 31^{21} (all metaph); toil (עָמָל), מֵעֵינָי Jb 3^{10}; commands fr, מִן pers. (subj. י') ψ 119^{19}; *hide* one as arrow in quiver Is 49^{2}. **2.** esp. *hide* the face: **a.** lit., of Moses Ex 3^{6} (E), usu. fig: **b.** subj. י', c מִן, i.e. be not observant of sin ψ 51^{11}, abs. ψ 10^{11}; more oft. **c.** י' *hides* his face from (מִן pers), i e. withdraws his favour, Mi 3^{4} Is 8^{17} 54^{8} 64^{6} Dt 31^{17} 32^{20} Je 33^{5} Ez 39$^{23.24.29}$ ψ 13^{2} 22^{25} 27^{9} 69^{18} 88^{15} 102^{3} 143^{7}; abs. Dt 31^{18} Jb 13^{24} 34^{29} ψ 30^{8} cf. 104^{29}, 44^{25}; פָּנִים om. Is 57^{17}; cf. Is 59^{2} your sins *have hidden* (his) *face* from (מִן) you; of hiding one's face from (מִן) shame, i.e. avoiding it Is 50^{6} (of servant of י').

†סֵתֶר **n.[m.] covering, hiding-place, secrecy,**—abs ס׳ Ju 3^{19}+, סָ֑תֶר 2 S 12^{12} Pr 25^{23}, סָ֫תֶר ψ 139^{15}; cstr. סֵתֶר 1 S 25^{20}+; sf. סִתְרוֹ ψ 18^{12} (ms also ∥ 2 S 22^{12} 𝔊𝔖 Th Bu HPS), סִתְרִי ψ 119^{114}, pl סְתָרִים Pr 9^{17},—**1.** *covering, cover,* בס׳ הָהָר 1 S 25^{20} *under cover of the mt*, concealed by it; of clouds as covering for י׳ (shutting out his view) Jb 22^{14}, of darkness (i.e dark clouds) as י׳'s *hiding-place* (in theoph) ψ 18^{12} (= 2 S 22^{12} v. supr), so ס׳ רַעַם 81^{8} *hiding-place of thunder*, of adulterer ס׳ פָּנִים יָשִׂים Jb 24^{15} i e disguiseth himself **2. a.** *hiding-place*, 1 S 19^{2} Is 28^{17} ס׳ הַמַּדְרֵגָה Ct 2^{14} (in fig, ∥ חַגְוֵי הַסֶּלַע), of hippopot. Jb 40^{21}, fig. of Isr as shelter to Moab c מִפְּנֵי Is 16^{4}, of ideal Israelite, as ס׳ זֶרֶם 32^{2}, esp of י׳ as *shelter*: ס׳ אָהֳלוֹ ψ 27^{5}, ס׳ פָּנֶיךָ 31^{21}, ס׳ כְּנָפֶיךָ 61^{5}, ס׳ עֶלְיוֹן 91^{1}, אַתָּה ס׳ לִי 32^{7} cf 119^{114}. **b.** *secret place*, of womb ψ 139^{15} (∥ תַּחְתִּיּוֹת אָ֑רֶץ) **3.** *secrecy*: דְּבַר־ס׳ Ju 3^{19} *a matter of secrecy*, secret matter; pl. abstr. intens לֶחֶם סְתָרִים Pr 9^{17} *bread of utter secrecy* (i e. gained stealthily, ∥ מַיִם גְּנוּבִים); לְשׁוֹן סָ֑תֶר 25^{23} *tongue of secrecy*, i e slanderous, elsewhere בַּסֵּ׳ *in secrecy, secretly* Dt 13^{7} $27^{15.24}$ 28^{57} 2 S 12^{12} Je 37^{17} 38^{16} 40^{15} Is 45^{19} 48^{16} Jb 13^{10} 31^{27} Pr 21^{14} ψ 101^{5}

†סִתְרָה **n.f. shelter, protection,** יְהִי עֲלֵיכֶם ס׳ Dt 32^{38} (rd. perh יהיו, cf. Dr) *let them* (the strange gods) *be over you as a shelter.*

†סְתוּר **n.pr.m.** a spy, from Asher;—Nu 13^{13}, 𝔊 Σαθουρ, 𝔊L Θασουρ.

†סִתְרִי **n.pr.m.** a Levite;—Ex 6^{22}, 𝔊 Σεγρει, A Σεθρει, 𝔊L Σετρι.

†מִסְתּוֹר **n.[m.] place of shelter;** abs מִסְתּוֹר מִזֶּרֶם Is 4^{6} (fig. of י׳'s protection, cf. סֵתֶר Is 32^{2})

†מִסְתָּר **n.[m.] secret place, hiding-place,**—abs מ׳ ψ 10^{9} Hb 3^{14}, usu. pl. מִסְתָּרִים Je 13^{17} + 6 t; sf מִסְתָּרָיו Je 49^{10},—**1.** *secret place(s)*, concealed from view, Je 13^{17}; where treasures are stored Is 45^{3}. **2.** *hiding-place(s)* **a.** for protection Je 23^{24} 49^{10}. **b.** for perpetration of crime, esp. murder. ψ 10^{8} (∥ מַאְרָב), sim of lion v ^{9} 17^{12}, cf Hb 3^{14}, ψ 64^{5}, of י׳ lying in wait La 3^{10} (as a lion).

†מַסְתֵּר **n.[m.] hiding, act of hiding;**—cstr וּכְמַסְתֵּר פָּנִים מִמֶּנּוּ Is 53^{3} *and like a hiding of face from him* i e like one before whom the face is hidden (e g. a leper, cf. Che^Hpt).

ע

ע, *'Ayin*, sixteenth letter, used as numeral 70 in postB Heb

עבב (√ of foll, cf Ko ii 1.40, meaning unknown)

†I. עָב, [עָב] **n.m.** archit. term, meaning unknown, **projecting roof** is conjectured (Sm Co Berthol); others **landing** (Da), AV RV *thick beam* or *plank*, RVm *threshold*, Benz Kit Toy leave untranslated, in any case a structure of wood,—abs וְעָמֻדִים וְעָב 1 K 7^{6}, appar cstr. וְעָב הָעֵץ אֶל־פְּנֵי הָאוּלָם מֵהַחוּץ Ez 41^{25}, pl (si vera l) הָעֻבִּים v ^{26}.

II עָב v. עוב

עָבַד 290 **vb. work, serve** (OAram עבד *do, make*, esp Nab Palm (oft), Lzb 331 f Cook 86, so 𝔗 עֲבַד, Syr ܥܒܰܕ (very oft), but also OAram Ph עבד *slave, vassal* (and in many n pr.), 𝔗 עַבְדָּא, Syr. ܥܰܒܕܳܐ *id*; As *abdu*, *id* (rare); NH עָבַד *serve, perform acts of worship* (c acc. cogn.), and deriv, Ar عَبَدَ *worship, obey* (God); cf. We Skizzen iii. 165, Held 141, ii. *enslave*; عَبْد *slave, worshipper*; Sab עבד *id*. DHM Südar Alt. p 18, Gerber Verb Denom 14 ff thinks *be slave, serve* (Qal) and *enslave* (Hiph) are denom, cf also No ZMG xl (1886). 741);—**Qal** 272 *Pf.* 3 ms ע׳ Ez 29^{18}+; sf. עֲבָדוֹ Mal 3^{18}+, 3 mpl עָבְדוּ Dt 7^{4}, עֲבָדוּ Nu 4^{26}, +64 t Pf., *Impf* 3 ms יַעֲבֹד Gn 25^{23}+; sf יַעַבְדֵנִי Ex 4^{23}; יַעַבְדֶנּוּ ψ 22^{31} 2 K 10^{18}, 3 mpl יַעַבְדוּ Dt 12^{30}+; יַעַבְדוּ Gn 15^{14} (Dr §103) Jb 36^{11}; 2 mpl תַּעַבְדוּן Ex 3^{12}, תַּעֲבֹדוּן Jos 24^{15}, +99t. Impf.; (נֶעֶבְדֵם, תָעָבְדֵם v **Hoph.**), *Imv.* עֲבֹד 1 S 26^{19}, sf עָבְדֵהוּ 1 Ch 28^{9}; עִבְדוּ Ex 5^{18}+15 t; עִבְדוּ Ez 20^{39}, sf עִבְדֻהוּ 1 S 7^{3}, *Inf. cstr* עֲבֹד Mal 3^{14}+, עֲבֹד Je $34^{9.10}$, sf עָבְדוֹ Je 27^{8}+, etc.; *Pt.* עֹבֵד Gn 4^{2}+, pl. עֹבְדִים Nu 18^{21}+; cstr. עֹבְדֵי ψ 97^{7}+, sf עֲבָדָיו 2 K 10^{19}, עֹבְדֵיהֶם Zc 2^{13},

—†**1.** *labour, work, do work:* abs. Ex 20^{9}=34^{21}=Dt 5^{13} (4th word); Ex 5^{18} (E) Ec 5^{11}; c. acc. rei, *till* the ground Gn 2^{5} 3^{23} $4^{2.12}$ (J), 2 S 9^{10} Is 30^{24} Je 27^{11} Zc 13^{5} Pr 12^{11} 28^{19}; obj. om. Dt 15^{19} Ez 48^{19}; vineyard Dt 28^{39}; garden Gn 2^{15} (J); עֹבְדֵי פִּשְׁתִּים Is 19^{9} *workers in flax;* עֹבְדֵ(י) הָעִיר Ez $48^{18.19}$ *labourers of the city;* ע׳ עֲבֹדָתוֹ Is 28^{21} *work his work* (only here of God, ‖ עשׂה מַעֲשֵׂהוּ); ע׳ עבדה על Ez 29^{18} *serve a military service against.* †**2.** *work for another, serve him by labour:* abs. Ex 21^{2} (E); c. acc. pers. Gn 29^{15} 31^{6} Ex 21^{6} (E) Dt $15^{12.18}$ Mal 3^{17} Je 34^{14}, king his people 1 K 12^{7}; subj. animals Je 27^{6} Jb 39^{9}; c. acc. pers. et rei Gn $30^{26.26.29}$ (J); c. לְ pers. 2 S 16^{19}; עִם Gn $29^{25.30}$ (E) Lv 25^{40} (P); עִמָּדִי Gn 29^{27} (E); לִפְנֵי 2 S $16^{19.19}$; c. בְּ of price Gn $29^{18.20.25}$ 31^{41} (E) Ho 12^{13} Ez 29^{20}; c. בְּ pers. *work by means of another, use him as slave,* Ex 1^{14} Lv $25^{39.46}$ (P) Je 22^{13} $34^{9.10}$. **3.** *serve as subjects:* usu. c. acc., their own chiefs or kings Ju $9^{28.28.38}$ 1 S 11^{1} 1 K 5^{1}+; other kings, by tribute ψ 18^{44}=2 S 22^{44}, Je 27^{7} 28^{14} 2 K 25^{24}+, other nations 2 S 10^{19} Je 40^{9} Zc 2^{13}+, kings other kings 2 K 18^{7}+, c. לְ, 1 S $4^{9.9}$; †מַס עֹבֵד Gn 49^{15} (J) Jos 16^{10} 1 K 9^{21} (see מַס); †c. בְּ pers., *work with,* i.e. use as subjects, impose tribute upon, Je 25^{14} 27^{7} 30^{8} Ez 34^{27}. **4.** *serve* God: **a.** c. acc. י׳, Ex 3^{12} 4^{23} $7^{16.26}$ (JE), ψ 22^{31} Jb 21^{15} Mal 3^{14}+; c. acc. pers. et rei Ex 10^{26} (E); acc. pers. om., Je 2^{20} (rd. אֶעֱבוֹד Kt), עבד זבח ומנחה Is 19^{21} *serve with peace-offering and grain-offering;* עבד עֲבֹדָה Ex 13^{5} (of מַצֹּת). **b.** other gods, c. acc. א׳ †Dt 7^{16} $12^{2.30}$†; אלהים אחרים 7^{4} 8^{19} 11^{16} $13^{7.14}$ 17^{3} $28^{14.36.64}$ 29^{25} 30^{17} 31^{20} Jos 23^{16} $24^{2.16}$ Ju 2^{19} 10^{13} 1 S 8^{8} 26^{19} 1 K $9^{6.9}$ 2 K 17^{35} 2 Ch $7^{19.22}$ Je 11^{10} 13^{10} $16^{11.13}$ 22^{9} 25^{6} 35^{15} (all D and Je); אֱלֹהֵי הַגּוֹיִם Dt 29^{17}; זָרִים Je 5^{19}; †כל צבא השמים† Dt 4^{19} 2 K 21^{3} 2 Ch 33^{3} Je 8^{2}; †הבעל(ים)† Ju 2^{11} 3^{7} $10^{6.10}$ 1 S 12^{10} 1 K 16^{31} 22^{54} 2 K $10^{18.18.19.19.21.22.23.23}$ 17^{16}; †אלהי נֵכָר† Jos 24^{20} Je 5^{19}; †(הַ)גִּלּוּלִים† 2 K 17^{12} $21^{21.21}$ Ez 20^{39}; †האשרים† 2 Ch 24^{18}; עצבים ψ 106^{36}; †פסיל(ים)† 2 Ch 33^{22} 2 K 17^{41}; פסל ψ 97^{7}; c. לְ, †לבעל Ju 2^{13}; †לאלהים אחרים† Je 44^{3}. **5.** *serve* י׳ *with Levitical service* (all P; cf. RS [Sem i. 69]): c. acc. עבד עֲבֹדָה (v. עֲבֹדָה) Nu $3^{7.8}$ $4^{23.30.47}$ 7^{5} $8^{11.19.22.26}$ 16^{9} $18^{6.21.23}$ Jos 22^{27}; acc. om. Nu $4^{24.26.37.41}$ 8^{15} (but Sam 𝔊 עבדה), v^{25} 18^{7}.

†**Niph.** *Pf.* 3 ms. נֶעֱבַד Ec 5^{8}; 2 mpl. נֶעֱבַדְתֶּם Ez 36^{9}; *Impf.* 3 ms. יֵעָבֵד Dt 21^{4}; 3 fs. תֵּעָבֵד Ez 36^{34};—**1.** *be tilled,* of land Dt 21^{4} Ez $36^{9.34}$. **2.** Ec 5^{8} מֶלֶךְ לְשָׂדֶה נֶעֱבָד dub.: a king for (devoted to) the *cultivated* field (Hi); a king *that maketh himself servant* to the field (devoted to agriculture), De: v. Comm., esp. De.

†**Pual** *Pf.* 3 ms. עֻבַּד Dt 21^{3} Is 14^{3}; pass. of **Qal**, c. בְּ: impers. Dt 21^{3} of a calf with which *it has not been worked;* hard *service* with which it *was worked with captives* Is 14^{3}.

†**Hiph.** *Pf.* 3 ms. הֶעֱבִיר Ez 29^{18}; 2 ms. sf. הֶעֱבַדְתַּנִי Is 43^{24}, הֶעֱבַדְתִּיךָ v^{23}, וְהַעֲבַדְתִּיךָ Je 17^{4}; *Impf.* 3 ms. וַיַּעֲבֵד 2 Ch 34^{33}; 3 mpl. יַעֲבִדוּ Ex 1^{13}; *Inf. cstr.* הַעֲבִד 2 Ch 2^{17}; *Pt.* pl. מַעֲבִדִים Ex 6^{5};—**1.** *compel to labour* as slaves Ex 1^{13} 6^{5} (P) 2 Ch 2^{17}, + Gn 47^{21} (reading הֶעֱבִיד לַעֲבָדִים), 2 S 12^{31} (reading וְהֶעֱבִיד, + בְּ *at;* on both these v. עבר **Hiph.** ad fin.); *cause to serve,* of army's service against, c. acc. + אל (על) Ez 29^{18}; *cause to labour, weary,* c. בְּ of means Is $43^{23.24}$ (perh. play on meanings **2, 3**). **2.** *make to serve as subjects,* c. 2 acc. Je 17^{4}, + Je 15^{14} (rd. וְהַעֲבַדְתִּיךָ, v. עבר **Hiph.** ad fin.). **3.** *cause to serve* God 2 Ch 34^{33}.

Hoph. *Impf.* 2 ms. sf. תָּעָבְדֵם Ex 20^{5}= Dt 5^{9}, Ex 23^{24}; 1 pl. sf. נָעָבְדֵם Dt 13^{3} (Kö [i. 259] Sta [§ 549 g] Thes; < Nes [Marg. 12 f.] Qal anom. pointed (cf. W [AG. ed. 2, i. 62 n.] Fl [Kl. Schr. i. 98]); Ges [§ 60, R. 1] Dr Qal falsely pointed as Hoph.);—*be led* or *enticed to serve* other gods Ex 20^{5} = Dt 5^{9} Ex 23^{24} Dt 13^{3}.

I. עֶבֶד [799] **n.m. slave, servant** (on format. Lag [BN 77]);—ע׳ Gn 9^{25}+, עָבֶד 44^{10}+; sf. עַבְדִּי 26^{24}+; עַבְדְּךָ 19^{19}+; עַבְדֶּךָ 18^{3}+; pl. עֲבָדִים 9^{25}+, עַבְדֵי 21^{25}+; sf. עֲבָדַי Lv 25^{42}+, עַבְדֵיכֶם Jos 9^{11}+, etc.;—**1.** *slave, servant* of household Gn $39^{17.19}$ 41^{12} 50^{2} Ex 21^{2}+; *man-servant,* ‖ אמה Ex 20^{10} Lv 25^{6} Dt 5^{14} Jb 31^{13}+; ‖ שפחה Gn 12^{16} 32^{6} Je 34^{11} Is 14^{2}+; + אדון Dt 23^{16} Is 24^{2} Mal 1^{6}+; מִקְנַת כֶּסֶף Ex 12^{44} or יְלִיד בַּיִת Je 2^{14}; עֶבֶד עֲבָדִים *servant of servants, humblest servant,* Gn 9^{25}; † בֵּית עֲבָדִים *house of slaves,* esp. Israel in Egypt Ex $13^{3.14}$ (D?) Dt 5^{6} 6^{12} 7^{8} 8^{14} $13^{6.11}$ Jos 24^{17} Ju 6^{8} Je 34^{13} Mi 6^{4}; †וזכרת כי עבד היית ב(ארץ) מצרים *and thou shalt remember that thou wast a slave in* (the land of) *Egypt* Dt 5^{15} 15^{15} 16^{12} $24^{18.22}$; king of Babylon is slave to י׳ Je 25^{9} 27^{6} 43^{10}; the borrower to the lender Pr 22^{7}; fig. of beast Jb 40^{28}; of things Gn 47^{19}.

2. *Subjects,* of chief Gn $26^{15.19.25.32}$ 27^{37} $32^{17.17}$+; of king 21^{25} Ex $7^{28.29}$ 1 K 9^{27} Dt 29^{1}+; vassal kings 2 S 10^{19}; tributary nations $8^{2.6.14}$ =1 Ch $18^{2.6.13}$; specif. officers of king 1 S 19^{1} 21^{8} 2 S 11^{13} Pr 14^{35}+; עַבְדֵי פַרְעֹה Gn 40^{20} 41^{10}; ע׳ הַמֶּלֶךְ 1 K 1^{47} Est ... ע׳ שָׁאוּל 1 S 16^{17} 18^{22} 28^{7};

3^{5}+; עֶבֶד הַמֶּלֶךְ 2 K 22^{12} = 2 Ch 34^{20} (a court official); opp. שַׂר Pr 19^{10} Ec 10^{7}; מֶלֶךְ Pr 30^{22}; ambassadors Nu 22^{18} 2 S 10^{2}; soldiers of army 1 S 17^{8} 25^{10} 2 S 2^{12}, + officers of army 1 S 29^{3} 1 K 11^{26} 2 K 25^{8} Is 36^{9}.

3. *Servants, worshippers,* of God: † עַבְדֵי יהוה 2 K 9^{7} 10^{23} Is 54^{17}, cf. Gn 50^{17} Is 56^{6}; עֲבָדָיו Dt 32^{36} = ψ 135^{14}, Is 65^{15} 66^{14} ψ 34^{23} 69^{37} Ne 2^{20}; ‖ עַמּוֹ ψ 105^{25} cf. Dt 32^{43}; עֲבָדַי Is $65^{8.9.13.13.13.14}$; עֲבָדֶיךָ 1 K 8^{23} Is 63^{17} (‖ שִׁבְטֵי נחלתך), ψ 89^{51} $90^{13.16}$ $102^{15.29}$ 119^{91}, $79^{2.10}$ (‖ חֲסִידֶיךָ); delivered from Egypt Lv $25^{42.55.55}$ 26^{13} (P); עַבְדְּךָ ψ 119^{125} 143^{2}, ‖ בֶּן־אֲמָתֶךָ 86^{16} $116^{16.16}$; specif. angels Jb 4^{18}; and ancient worthies, patriarchs Ex 32^{13} (J) Dt 9^{27}; Abraham Gn 26^{24} (J) ψ $105^{6.42}$; Isaac Gn 24^{14} (J); Jacob, Israel Ez 28^{25} 37^{25} 1 Ch 16^{13}; Moses †Ex 14^{31} Jos 18^{7} (J) Nu $12^{7.8}$ (E) Dt 34^{5} (?) Jos $1^{1.2.7.13.15}$ $8^{31.33}$ 9^{24} $11^{12.15}$ $12^{6.6}$ 13^{8} 14^{7} $22^{2.4.5}$ (all D), 1 K $8^{53.56}$ 2 K 18^{12} 21^{8} 1 Ch 6^{34} 2 Ch 1^{3} $24^{6.9}$ Ne 1^{8} 9^{14} 10^{30} ψ 105^{26} Mal 3^{22} Dn 9^{11}; Joshua † Jos 24^{29} (E) Ju 2^{8}; Caleb † Nu 14^{24} (J); Job † Jb 1^{8} 2^{3} $42^{7.8.8.8}$; David 2 S 3^{18} $7^{5.8.26}$ + 27 t.; Hezekiah † 2 Ch 32^{16}; Zerubbabel † Hag 2^{23}; Eliakim † Is 22^{20}.—The צֶמַח Zc 3^{8} cf. 6^{12} is also servant of י׳ as Messianic builder of temple (see Br[MP 442 ff.]).

†**4.** *Servant* of י׳, in a special sense: of Levitical singers using benedictions in temple ψ 113^{1} 134^{1} 135^{1}; usu. of prophets, עֲבָדַי הַנְּבִיאִים *my servants the prophets* 2 K 9^{7} 17^{13} Je 7^{25} 26^{5} 29^{19} 35^{15} 44^{4} Ez 38^{17} Zc 1^{6}; עֲבָדָיו הַנְּבִיאִים 2 K 17^{23} 21^{10} 24^{2} Je 25^{4} Am 3^{7} Dn 9^{10}; עֲבָדֶיךָ הנביאים Ezr 9^{11} Dn 9^{6}; specif. Ahia 1 K 14^{18} 15^{29}; Elijah 2 K 9^{36} 10^{10}; Jonah 2 K 14^{25}; Isaiah Is 20^{3}; עַבְדּוֹ, ‖ מלאכיו 44^{26}; as one calling to fear י׳ 50^{10}.

†**5.** Israel as a people is *servant* of י׳: יִשְׂרָאֵל Is $41^{8.9}$ $44^{21.21}$ 49^{3} ψ 136^{22}; יעקב Is $44^{1.2}$ 45^{4} 48^{20} Je 30^{10} $46^{27.28}$; עַבְדִּי = עֶבֶד יהוה ‖ מַלְאָכִי, as having a mission to the nations Is $42^{19.19}$; and chosen as witness of י׳ 43^{10}. But there is also an ideal servant chosen and endowed with the divine Spirit to be a covenant of Israel and a light of the nations Is 42^{1} (cf. v^{2-6}); formed to bring back Jacob, raise up the tribes, and become salvation to the end of the earth $49^{5.6.7}$; bearing the sins of all as a lamb and a trespass-offering, and yet prospering and justifying many as interposing martyr 52^{13} 53^{11}: many understand of ideal Israel, contr. with the actual; al. of personif. ‖ with Zion the wife and mother, disting. from unworthy Israel as Zion from her apostate children; al. of ideal prophetic writer; al. of ideal prophetic person; al. (esp. in Is 53) of an actual proph. known to writer and his readers; [in any case it is Messianic, v. Mt $8^{16.17}$ 12^{16-21} Lk 4^{17-22} Phil 2^{5-11}]; see De[Is ii. 174] Da[Expos. 1884, 358 ff.] Di Du Che al. on Is 42, 53, Dr[Is 168 ff.] Br[MP 345 ff.], also Gie[Beitr. 146 ff.] Berthol[Is 53].

6. In polite address of equals or superiors the Hebrews used עַבְדְּךָ *thy servant* = 1 pers. sing., *I*, Gn 18^{3} 1 S $20^{7.8.8}$ 2 K 8^{13} +; עֲבָדֶיךָ *thy servants* = *we* Gn 42^{11} Is 36^{11}; also עַבְדּוֹ *his servant* = *I*, 1 S $26^{18.19}$ 2 S 14^{22} 24^{21} +; also in addressing God, esp. in prayer Ex 4^{10} Nu 11^{11} Ju 15^{18} 1 S $3^{9.10}$ 25^{39} 2 S 24^{10} ψ $19^{12.14}$ 27^{9} 31^{17} 35^{27} 69^{18} 109^{28} 143^{2} +.

7. Phrases are: † (היה) עבד, c. לְ pers., *become servant to* Gn $9^{26.27}$ $44^{10.16.17.33}$ $47^{19.25}$ (J) Dt 6^{21} 15^{17} 2 S 8^{14} 2 K 17^{3} 24^{1} 1 Ch $18^{2.6.13}$ 2 Ch 10^{7} Pr 11^{29} 12^{9} 22^{7}; † היה לעבד, c. לְ pers., Gn 44^{9} (J) 50^{18} (E) 1 S 8^{17} $17^{9.9}$ 27^{12} 2 S $8^{2.6}$ Je 34^{16}; † כבשׁ לעבדים 2 Ch 28^{10} Ne 5^{5} Je 34^{11}; לקח לע׳ Gn 43^{18} (J) 2 K 4^{1} Jb 40^{28}.

† II. עֶבֶד **n.pr.m.** (*servant* of God = עַבְדְּאֵל); —**1.** father of Gaal Ju $9^{26.28.30.31.35}$ (GFM, after Hollenb[ThLz 1891, 371] [cf. Bu[ib. 1892, 63]] עֶבֶד, as 𝔊L; v. also Gray[Prop. N. 184, 272]); 𝔊 Ιωβηλ, A 𝔊L Αβεδ. **2.** a companion of Ezra Ezr 8^{6}; 𝔊 Ωβηθ, 𝔊L Αμιναδαβ. — For list of Ar. names beginning with عبد v. Nö[ZMG xli (1887), 724 ff.], cf. also Id[ib. xlii (1888), 486] We[Heid. 2, 2 ff.]

† [עֲבַד] **n.m.** work (late; Aram. form); pl. sf. עֲבָדֵיהֶם Ec 9^{1} (cf. Syr. ܥܒܕܐ).

† עוֹבֵד, עֹבֵד **n.pr.m.** (*worshipper*; cf. Sab. עבד Os[22] and DHM[ZMG xxxvii (1883), 14]; —**1.** son of Boaz and Ruth Ru 4^{17}, v^{21} = 1 Ch 2^{12}, Ru 4^{22} (only here עֹבֵד) = 1 Ch 2^{12}, 𝔊 Ωβηδ. **2.** names in Judah, 𝔊 Ωβηδ: **a.** 1 Ch $2^{37.38}$. **b.** 2 Ch 23^{1}. **3.** a mighty man of David 1 Ch 11^{47}, 𝔊 Ιωβηθ, A Ιωβηδ. **4.** a doorkeeper 1 Ch 26^{7}, 𝔊 Ωβηδ.

† עֹבֵד אֱדֹם, and (2 Ch 25^{24}) ע׳ אֱדוֹם **n.pr.m.** (*servant of* (god) *Edom*, cf. עבד אדם CIS[No. 295]; Dr[Sm 206, 293] and reff., RS[Sem i. 43; 2nd ed. 42] and reff., HPS[286, 10]; but Bae[Rel 10] *servant of man*, אֱדֹם = אָדָם, which is thought possible by Nö[ZMG xlii (1888), 470] Buhl[Edomiter 49]); —**1.** the Gittite who harboured the ark 2 S $6^{10.11.11.12.12}$ = 1 Ch $13^{13.14.14}$, 1 Ch 15^{25}; 𝔊 Αβεδδαρα, 𝔊L Αβεδδαδαν. **2.** (= **1** ?) one of the chief Levitical singers and doorkeepers 1 Ch $15^{18.21.24}$ $16^{5.38.38}$ $26^{4.8.8.15}$; 𝔊 Αβαεδωμ, Αβδεδωμ, etc., 𝔊L Αβεδδομ. **3.** the family of the same 2 Ch 25^{24} (not in ‖ 2 K 14^{14}).

†עֶבֶד מֶ֫לֶךְ **n.pr.m.** (= *servant of the king*, or < *of* (god) *Melek*, cf. Gray$^{Prop. N. 117, 147 ff.}$);—Eth. official of Zedekiah Je 38$^{7.8.10.11.12}$ 39^{16}; 𝔊 Αβδεμελεχ.

†עֲבֵד נְגוֹ **n.pr.m.** (*servant of* (God) *Nebo*, נגו being corrupt (intent. or unintent.) for נבו (q.v.), COT$^{Dn 1,7}$ Bev$^{Dn 1,7}$);—Babylonian name of Azariah, one of the three companions of Daniel Dn 1^{7} (v. also BAram); 𝔊 Theod Αβδεναγω.

†עַבְדָּא **n.pr.m.** (*servant of* י׳ (= עֹבַדְיָה 1 Ch 9^{16} = Ne 11^{17}), but form dub., v. 𝔊);—**1.** father of Adoniram 1 K 4^{6}; 𝔊 Εφρα, A Αβαω, 𝔊L Εδραμ. **2.** a Levite Ne 11^{17}; 𝔊 Ωβηβ, A Ιωβηβ, 𝔊L Αβδιας.

†עַבְדְּאֵל **n.pr.m.** (*servant of Ēl*, cf. עַבְדִּיאֵל) name in Judah Je 36^{26}; 𝔊 Εσ(δ)ριηλ.

†עֲבֹדָה, and (Chr) עֲבוֹדָה$_{145}$ **n.f. labour, service** (on format. v. Lag$^{BN 179}$ Ba$^{NB 61}$);—ע׳ Ex 1^{14} + 41 t.; cstr. עֲבֹדַת 30^{16} + 43 t.; sf. עֲבֹדָתִי Gn 30^{26} + 33 t. sfs.; in Chr עֲבוֹדָה 1 Ch 28^{14} + 7 t.; cstr. עֲבוֹדַת 6^{33} + 13 t.; sf. עֲבוֹדָתִי 2 Ch 12^{8}; עֲבוֹדָתָם 1 Ch 6^{17} 2 Ch 31^{16};—**1.** †*labour, work*, ψ 104^{23}; in the field Ex 1^{14} 1 Ch 27^{26}, prob. Ne 10^{38} (עָרֵי ע׳), ψ 104^{14} (עֵשֶׂב לע׳); in fine linen 1 Ch 4^{21}; in erection of tabernacle Ex 35^{24} 36$^{1.3.5}$ 39^{42} (P); in repairing temple 2 Ch 34$^{13.13}$; כל מלאכת עבדה לא תעשׂו *ye shall do no laborious work* Lv 23$^{7.8.21.25.35.36}$ Nu 28$^{18.25.26}$ 29$^{1.12.35}$ (P); fig. of man, ע׳ הַצְּדָקָה Is 32^{17} (‖ מַעֲשֵׂה הצ׳); of God's work of judgment Is 28$^{21.21}$. †**2.** *labour of servant or slave:* of Jacob for Laban Gn 29^{27} 30^{26} (JE); ע׳ עֶבֶד of bondservant Lv 25^{39} (P); of the Nethinim Ezr 8^{20}; *service* of things, vessels of tabernacle and temple Nu 4$^{26.32}$ (P) 1 Ch 9^{28} 28$^{14.14.15}$. †**3.** *labour, service of captives or subjects:* of Israel in Egypt Ex 1^{14} 2$^{23.23}$ (P), 5^{11} (E), 6^{6} (P); כבד(ה) הע׳ 5^{9} (E) Ne 5^{18}; ע׳ קשׁה Ex 1^{14} 6^{9} (P) Dt 26^{6} 1 K 12^{4} = 2 Ch 10^{4}, Is 14^{3}; מֵרֹב ע׳ La 1^{3}; ע׳ ממלכות 2 Ch 12^{8}; ע׳ המלך 1 Ch 26^{30}; ע׳ אדניהם Ne 3^{5}; military service Ez 29$^{18.18}$. **4.** *service* of God, in P Chr Ez: by people Jos 22^{27} (P) 2 Ch 12^{8}, feast of passover Ex 12$^{25.26}$ 2 Ch 35$^{10.16}$, unleavened bread Ex 13^{5}; Levites and priests Nu 4$^{19.49}$ 8^{11} 1 Ch 24$^{3.19}$ 2 Ch 8^{14} 31^{16}; ע׳ מתנה Nu 18^{7}; Levites Ex 38^{21} Nu 4$^{24.27.27.28.33.47.47}$ 7$^{7.8}$ 8^{26} 18^{21} 1 Ch 6^{17} 2 Ch 31^{2}; c. בְּאֹהֶל מוֹעֵד v$^{4.23.31.33.35.39.43}$ 8$^{19.22}$ 18^{31}; אֹהֶל מוֹעֵד Ex 30^{16} Nu 4^{30} 7^{5} 8^{24} 18$^{4.6.21.23}$, cf. Ex 35^{21} Nu 7^{5}; (ה)מִשְׁכָּן Ex 39$^{32.40}$ Nu 3$^{7.8}$ 16^{9} 1 Ch 6^{33}, cf. Ex 27^{19} Nu 3^{36} 1 Ch 23^{26}; ע׳ הַקֹּדֶשׁ Nu 7^{9}, cf. 3^{31}; of its court v^{26}; more specif. ע׳ בית י׳ (ה)אלהים 1 Ch 23$^{24.28.32}$ 25^{6} 28$^{13.13.21.21}$ 29^{7} 2 Ch 29^{35} 31^{21} 35^{2} Ne 10^{33}; ע׳ צבא הע׳ 8^{25}; ע׳ משׂא 4^{47}; מלאכת ע׳ בית האלהים 1 Ch 9^{13} 28^{20} 2 Ch 24^{12}; מעשׂה ע׳ 1 Ch 23^{28}; its service Ez 44^{14} 1 Ch 9^{19}; specif. service of Levit. singers 25$^{1.1}$, and doorkeepers 26^{8} 2 Ch 35^{15}.

†עֲבֻדָּה **n.f. service** (on format. v. Lag$^{BN 151}$);—of household servants as a body, ‖ cattle, etc., Gn 26^{14} (J) Jb 1^{3}.

†עַבְדּוֹן **n.pr.** I. **n.pr.m. 1.** a judge Ju 12$^{13.15}$, 𝔊 Αβδων, A 𝔊L Λαβδω(μ); (Ew cp. בְּדָן 1 S 12^{11}, but read בָּרָק, v. בְּדָן supr.). **2.** a Benjamite 1 Ch 8^{23}, 𝔊 Αβαδων, A 𝔊L Αβδων. **3.** son of Jehiel a Gibeonite 1 Ch 8^{30} 9^{36}; 𝔊 Αβαλων, Σαβαδων, A Αβδων, Σαβδων, 𝔊L Αβδων. **4.** son of Micah 2 Ch 34^{20}, 𝔊 Αβδοδομ, A 𝔊L Αβδων (= עַכְבּוֹר 2 K 22^{12}). II. **n.pr.loc.** Levitical city in Asher Jos 21^{30} 1 Ch 6^{59}, 𝔊 Δαββων, Αβαραν, A 𝔊L Αβδων (20 Codd. rd. עַבְדֹּן Jos 19^{28} for עֶבְרֹן), *'Abde*, Guérin$^{Gal 2, 37}$ cf. Buhl$^{Geogr. 230}$.

†[עַבְדוּת] **n.f. servitude, bondage**;—sf. עַבְדֻתֵנוּ Ez 9$^{8.9}$; עַבְדֻתָם Ne 9^{17} (cf. Syr. ܥܒܕܘܬܐ).

†עַבְדִּי **n.pr.m.** (= עֹבַדְיָה *servant of Yah*; v. however, Gray$^{Prop. N. 149 ff.}$ and cf. OAram. עבדו, Nab. Palm. עבדי Lzb$^{333, 334}$ Cook^{87});—**1.** a Levite 1 Ch 6^{29} 2 Ch 29^{12}; 𝔊 Αβδ(ε)ι, 𝔊L 1 Ch Αβδια. **2.** one with a foreign wife Ezr 10^{26}; 𝔊 Αβδε(ι)α.

†עַבְדִּיאֵל **n.pr.m.** (*servant of Ēl*; on this and foll. cf. Ph. עבדאלם, Nab. עבדאלהא, Sin. עבדאלהי, etc., Lzb^{332} Cook^{87}; Sab. עבדלת = [עבדאלת] Hal^{168} DHM$^{ZMG xxxvii (1883), 16}$; v. also Gray$^{Prop. N. 309, No. 53}$);—a Gadite 1 Ch 5^{15}; 𝔊 Αβδεηλ, A 𝔊L Αβδιηλ.

†עֹבַדְיָה, עֹבַדְיָ֫הוּ **n.pr.m.** (*servant of Yah*, cf. Gray$^{Prop. N. 295, No. 90}$; also Ph. עבדבעל, Palm. עבדבל, OAram. עבדהדד Lzb^{333}, OHeb. עבדיהו Id.^{334});—I. עֹבַדְיָ֫הוּ: **1.** chief of Ahab's household 1 K 18$^{3.3.4.5.6.7.16}$, 𝔊 Αβδ(ε)ιου. **2.** father of one of the chiefs of Zebulun 1 Ch 27^{19}, 𝔊 Αβδ(ε)ιου (genit.). **3.** a Levite overseer in time of Josiah 2 Ch 34^{12}, 𝔊 Αβδ(ε)ια, A 𝔊L Αβδιας. II. עֹבַדְיָה: **1.** the prophet Ob^{1}, 𝔊 Οβδ(ε)ιου (genit.), Αβδ(ε)ιου. **2.** a descendant of David 1 Ch 3^{21}, 𝔊 Αβδεια, 𝔊L Οβδιας. **3.** chief of tribe of Issachar 1 Ch 7^{3}, 𝔊 Μειβδεια, A Οβδια, 𝔊L Αβδια. **4.** a Benjamite 1 Ch

8^{33} 9^{44}, 𝔊 Αβδ(ε)ια. **5.** a Levite 1 Ch 9^{16} (‖ עַבְדָּא Ne 11^{17}), 𝔊 Αβδεια, A Οβδια, 𝔊L Αβια. **6.** a Gadite chief 1 Ch 12^{9}, 𝔊 Αβδ(ε)ια. **7.** a prince in time of Jehoshaphat 2 Ch 17^{7}, 𝔊 Αβ(δ)ιαν. **8.** priestly companion of Ezra Ezr 8^{9} Ne 10^{6}, 𝔊 Αδεια, Αβ(α)δ(ε)ια, 𝔊L Αβδιου, Αβιας **9.** a doorkeeper Ne 12^{25}, א Οβδιας, 𝔊L Αβδιας

†[מַעְבָּד] **n.[m.]** work (late form, BAram מַעְבַד);—pl sf מַעְבָּדֵיהֶם Jb 34^{25}

†**עָבָה** **vb. be thick, fat, gross** (NH Pi עִבָּה *make thick*, and deriv; Syr ܥܒܐ *swell up*, pt. pass *swollen, thick, dense, stupid*, and many deriv, Ar غَبِىَ *be dense, stupid*, أَغْبَى *dense foliage*, Eth **ዐበየ:** *be great* Di^{985});—**Qal** *Pf* 3 ms. קָטָנִּי עָ׳ מִמָּתְנֵי אָבִי 1 K 12^{10} *my little finger is thicker* (stouter) than, etc, = 2 Ch 10^{10}; *be thick, gross*, of rebell. Isr under fig of highly fed beast, 2 ms שָׁמַנְתָּ עָבִיתָ כָּשִׂיתָ Dt 32^{15}.

†**עֳבִי** **n.[m.]** thickness;—cstr. עֳ׳ גַּבֵּי מָגִנָּיו Jb 15^{26} *the thickness* (stoutness) *of the bosses* of his shields (in fig); sf. עָבְיוֹ *its thickness*, of the molten sea 1 K 7^{26} = 2 Ch 4^{5}; of pillar Je 52^{21}—2 Ch 4^{17} v foll—Under עבה belongs perh. also בעב הֶעָנָן Ex 19^{9} (rd. בַּעֲבִי ?) in *the thickness* of the clouds, cf. Bu$^{Th\ Lz\ 1892(3),\ 63}$ Ko$^{ii\ 1\ 86}$.

†**מַעֲבֶה** **n.[m.]** si vera l, thickness, compactness,—בְּמַעֲבֵה הָאֲדָמָה 1 K 7^{46} *in the compactness of the soil*, i.e *clayey ground* or *clay mould* = 2 Ch 4^{17} (where MT בַּעֲבִי ה׳); but read doubtless in both בְּמַעְבְּרֹת אֲדָמָה *at the ford of Adamah*, v. GFM$^{Ju\ 7,\ 22}$ Benz^{K}.

עֲבוֹת v עבת.

עבט (perh √ of foll; cf As *ubbutu'* (ii of אבט [= עבט?]) *be pledged* Dl^{HWB6}, Aram. (Talm) עֲבִיטָה *pledge*, עֲבַט Ithpe. *be taken in pledge*; but We$^{Jo\ 2,\ 7}$ thinks עבוט Aram loan-word, and cp Ar. ضَبَطَ *hold, keep, guard*).

†**עֲבוֹט** **n.[m.]** pledge, article pledged as security for debt,—abs עָ׳ Dt $24^{11\ 13}$, sf. עֲבֹטוֹ v^{10} (as acc. cogn.), v^{12}.

†**עַבְטִיט** **n.[m.] intens. weight of pledges, heavy debts,**—abs מַכְבִּיד עָלָיו עָ׳ Hb 2^{6}.

†[**עָבַט**] **vb. denom. take or give a pledge**,—**Qal** *Inf cstr* לַעֲבֹט Dt 24^{10} *to take possession of a thing pledged* (c. acc. cogn), *Impf* 2 ms *give a pledge* תַּעֲבֹט Dt 15^{6} (i e *borrow*) **Hiph.** *Pf.* 2 ms. וְהַעֲבַטְתָּ גּוֹיִם רַבִּים v^{6} *and thou shalt cause many nations to give pledges* (i e. lend to them); *Impf* 3 ms. sf. + *Inf abs.* הַעֲבֵט תַּעֲבִיטֶנּוּ v^{8} *thou shalt surely lend to him* (lit. as above). **Pi.** *Impf* יְעַבְּטוּן Jo 2^{7} hardly makes sense (*lend on pledge = interchange?*), most rd. יעבתון; יְעַוְּתוּן We, cf Now Dr GASm, Gr יִטּוּן

עבל (√of foll, cf poss Ar عَبُلَ *be bulky, stout*; Pun. n.pr. עבל Lzb^{335}).

†**עוֹבָל**, **I.** **עֵיבָל** **n. pr. gent.** Arabian people, descended from Joktan acc to Gn 10^{28} (𝔊L Γαιβαλ), = עֵיבָל 1 Ch 1^{22} (𝔊L Ηβηλ). On loc. cf. Glaser$^{Skizze\ ii\ 426}$.

I **עֵיבָל** v עוֹבָל supr

†**II.** **עֵיבָל** **n.pr.m. vel gent.** name in Edom, Gn 36^{23} (𝔊 Γαιβηλ), = 1 Ch 1^{40} (𝔊 Γαιβηλ, A Γαοβηλ, 𝔊L Ουβαλ); acc to Glaser$^{Skizze\ ii.\ 426}$ poss. = foregoing (cp. with name of (god) *Bēl*, Wkl$^{Gesch\ Isr\ 120,\ Altest\ Unters\ 117\ f.}$)

†**III.** **עֵיבָל** **n pr. mont.** Ebal, the mt of cursing, N. of Shechem (Nabulus), and opp. Mt. Gerizim (mt. of blessing, S. of Shechem), Dt 11^{29}, also Jos $8^{30.33}$ (D); 𝔊 Γαιβαλ (connex with above √dub; on בל = *Bēl*, cf Gray$^{Prop\ N.\ 124\ n,\ and\ reff}$);—on Ebal v Rob$^{BR\ ii\ 275\ ff.}$ GASm$^{Geogr\ Ch\ vi}$ Di$^{Dt\ 11,\ 29}$ Dr^{ib} Bd$^{Pal\ (1898),\ 237}$.

עבץ (√of foll; meaning unknown)

†**יַעְבֵּץ** **n.pr. 1. m. Jabez**, a man of the Calebites, 1 Ch $4^{9\ 9\ 10}$ (where interpr. as akin to עצב; on position of this family cf Mey$^{Judenthum\ 118}$), 𝔊 Ιγαβης, A Ιαγβης, Γαβης, GL Ιαβιης, Ιαβηλ, Ιαβεις. **2. loc.** in Judah, appar near Bethlehem 1 Ch 2^{55} (cf v^{54}), 𝔊 Γαμες, A Γαβης, 𝔊L Ιαβις

עָבַר 548 **vb. pass over, through, by, pass on** (NH = BH, Zinj עבר Haph Lzb^{336} Cook^{88}, perh also Nab עבר Id^{ib}, 𝔗 עֲבַר, Syr ܥܒܪ *id.*; As *ebêru, id* Dl$^{HWB\ 10}$, and deriv.; Ar. عَبَرَ *id*, and deriv; Sab עבר = Heb. עָבַר **1.** Mordt$^{Sab\ Denkm\ 49}$; עברת *passage, march through* DHM$^{ZMG\ xxix\ (1875),\ 614}$ also *bank* or *neighbourhood of a stream* Sab Denkm^{49}),—**Qal**$_{465}$ *Pf.* 3 ms. עָ׳ Gn 15^{17}+, sf עֲבָרוֹ Je 23^{9}, 1 s. עָבַרְתִּי 1 S 15^{24}+; 2 mpl עֲבַרְתֶּם Gn 18^{5}+, 1 pl עָבַרְנוּ Jos 24^{17}+, etc, *Impf* 3 ms יַעֲבֹר Am 8^{5}+, יַעֲבָר־ Gn 33^{14}+, sf 3 ms יַעַבְרֶנּוּ Is 33^{21} 35^{8}, יַעַבְרֻנְהוּ Je 5^{22}, וַיַּעֲבֹר Gn 12^{6}+, 1 s אֶעֱבֹר Am 5^{17}+, cohort. אֶעְבְּרָה

Nu 21[22]+, אֶעְבְּרָה Nu 20[19] Ju 12[5], etc.; *Imv.* ms. עֲבֹר Ex 17[5]+; fs עִבְרִי Mi 1[11]+2 t.; עִבְרִי Is 23[12], mpl. עִבְרוּ Am 6[2]+; *Inf abs.* עָבוֹר 2 S 17[16]; *cstr* עֲבֹר Am 7[8]+, לַעֲבָר־ 1 K 18[6]+Na 2[1] Qr (Kt לעבור); sf. עָבְרִי Ex 33[22] Dt 4[21], etc; *Pt.* עֹבֵר Ju 8[4]+, etc.;—**1.** *pass over:* **a.** = *cross* (stream, wady, sea, etc.), (1) c. acc. Gn 31[21] (E), 32[11] (J), Jos 3[14 17] 4[1] (all JE), Dt 2[14] (D), Nu 32[29] (P), 2 S 17[20.22.24] Is 16[8], + 37 t., + Gn 32[23] (E; acc. מַעֲבַר), וְעָבְרָה הָעֲבָרָה לַעֲבִיר 2 S 19[19] (rd. וַיַּעַבְרוּ We Dr Kit Lohr, *and they crossed the ford,* or וְעָבְרוּ frequent., HPS; > 𝔊 Klo Bu וַיַּעַבְדוּ הָעֲבֹדָה *and they performed the service*); also c. acc. + acc. loc. 1 S 13[7], + ה loc. Dt 4[26] 31[13] 32[47]. (2) acc. om Ju 3[28] 2 S 17[16.16]+32 t, + עֹבֵר Ju 8[4] (rd וַיַּעֲבֹר Vrss, or del. as gloss GFM Bu), 2 S 15[23 a] (where rd. עֹמֵד for MT עֹבֵר We Dr Bu Kit Lohr HPS, but del. עֹבְרִים, plausibly, Klo HPS); c. אֶל־ †Nu 32[7] (JE), Dt 27[2] (D), Jos 4[13] 22[19] (both P), c. אֶל־עֵבֶר Dt 30[13], c. הָעֵבֶר 1 S 26[13]; c. ה loc. †Dt 3[21] 4[14] 6[1] 11[8.11] 34[4] Is 23[6], c acc loc. †Is 23[12] Je 2[10] Nu 32[32] (P) †**b.** *cross* border, boundary, c. acc. Nu 20[17 b] 21[22 b] (both JE), + אֶל־ 1 S 27[2], of invasion, acc. om., c. אֶל־ Ju 11[32] 12[3] 1 S 14[1.6.8], c. ה loc. 2 K 8[21], abs 2 Ch 21[9]. **c.** *cross over* (sc. intervening space) against (עַל־) 1 S 14[4], unto 2 S 24[20] (rd. אֶל־ for עַל־ Bu HPS, cf. 𝔊L), so perh. also Is 45[14] (עַל; rd. אֵל?), c. acc. of goal Am 5[5] 6[2]. †**d.** *pass, march over* (sc. bodies of captives), Is 51[23.23] †**e.** = *overflow,* fig, Is 23[10], abs. of invasion (like a flood) Is 8[8], hence Dn 11[10.40], Na 1[8] (cf. **4 c**); of evil thoughts ψ 73[7]; cf. עָבְרוּ דִבְרֵי־רָע Je 5[28] *they overflow with evil matters* †**f.** *pass, go, over,* of waves, over one's head, usu c עַל־ Is 54[9] ψ 42[8] 88[17] 124[4.5] (all fig), Jon 2[4], c. acc ψ 38[5], cf. Je 23[9] *over whom wine hath gone* (= overcome with wine). †**g.** of razor *passing over* head, c. עַל Nu 6[5]; fig. of time *passing over* one, c. עַל־ 1 Ch 29[30] (cf BAram. חלף על Dn 4[13]+). †**h.** *pass over upon* (עַל־), in weakened sense, nearly = come or light upon; of spirit Nu 5[14 14.30]; abs + מֵאֵת 1 K 22[24] = 2 Ch 18[23], c עַל־ also *light upon* in chastisement or judgment, Ho 10[11] Jb 13[13], cf Na 3[19]; Dt 24[5] *no affair shall pass over upon* (עַל־) *him,* i.e no duty be laid upon him. †**i.** *overstep, transgress,* c. acc. of covenant, command, etc. (usu divine), Nu 14[41] Jos 7[11 15] (all JE), Dt 17[2] 26[13] Jos 23[16] (all D), Ju 2[20] 1 S 15[24] Ho 6[7] 8[1] 2 K 18[12] Je 34[18] Is 24[5] ψ 148[6] 2 Ch 24[20] Dn 9[11]; command of earthly king Est 3[3], abs. ψ 17[3]. †**j.** *pass over = overlook, forgive* עַל־פֶּשַׁע Mi 7[18] (+ לְ pers.), Pr 19[11]; c. לְ pers. only, Am 7[8] 8[2].

†**2.** *Pass beyond,* c acc. 1 S 14[23] (of battle), Je 5[22 22] (of sea); + אֶל Gn 31[52.52] (E); *pass a little beyond* כִּמְעַט מֵהָרֹאשׁ עְ׳ מְעַט 2 S 16[1], כִּמְעַט שֶׁעָבַרְתִּי מֵהֶם Ct 3[4], c. acc. of God's command (פֶּה), Pr 8[29] (of sea), Nu 22[18] = 24[13] (JE); acc. om. Jb 14[5] ψ 104[9].

3. *Pass through, traverse,* usu. **a.** c. בְּ of land, city, etc.: Nu 22[21] (E), 20[21] Jos 18[9] (JE), Ex 12[12] (P), 1 S 9[4.4.4.4] 2 S 20[14] (+ ה loc.), + 31 t; c. בְּתוֹךְ †Ez 9[4] Jb 15[19]; c. בְּקֶרֶב of camp, nation(s) †Jos 1[11] 3[2] (D), 24[17] (E), Am 5[17] Dt 29[15]; c acc. †Dt 2[18] 29[15] Ju 11[29.29] Is 10[29] Jb 14[5], abs. Ex 12[23] (J), Nu 20[19.20] (JE), Dt 2[28] Mi 5[7] La 3[44] Ez 14[15] 33[28]; † opp. שׁוּב, *pass through* and return, go to and fro, Ex 32[27] (E; מִשַּׁעַר לָשַׁעַר ב׳), pt. abs. *those going to and fro* Ez 35[7] Zc 7[14] 9[8]. †**b.** c. בְּ of river 2 S 19[19]+15[23] (but rd. עֹמֵד We Dr Bu al.), of sea Zc 10[11], cf. Is 43[2] ψ 66[6], c בְּתוֹךְ Nu 33[8] (P), Ne 9[11]; c. בְּ of gates Is 62[10 10]; cf. עֹבְרֵי בְּעֵמֶק ψ 84[7] (Ges[§130 a]). **c.** pt. abs. הָעֹבְרִים *the passers-through* Ez 39[11 a], rd. prob הָעֲבָרִים (JDMich Hi Co Berthol), v[11 b] (Co rds. אֶת־הַגַּיְא; Toy del as gloss), v[14] (del 𝔊𝔖 Co Toy Berthol). †**d.** *pass through* between (בֵּין) parts of victim, in covenant Gn 15[7] (J), Je 34[18 19]. **e.** *traverse* c. acc. of expanse of water Is 33[21] (of ship).

4. a. *pass along* by (עַל־), Gn 18[5] (J; not סָרְתֶם אֶל־ Ball after 𝔊), 1 K 9[8] Je 18[16]+14 t.; c. עַל־פָּנָיו †Ex 34[6] (J); c. acc. †Gn 32[32] Ju 3[26] (on other possibilities v. GFM), 2 K 6[9]; abs. *pass by* Ex 33[22.22] (J), 2 K 4[8]+15 t., + (of wind) Jb 37[21] Pr 10[25] and (of waters, = *flow past*) Hb 3[10] (cf. Jb 6[15]), Jb 11[16], hence מוֹר עֹבֵר Ct 5[5 13] *flowing myrrh* (liquid, opp hard = מ׳ דְּרוֹר Ex 30[23]), pt = *passer-by* Mi 2[8] Ez 5[14] 36[34] 39[15] + 6 t. (Pr 26[10] v. Toy), + עֹבֵר אֹרַח Is 33[8], + עֹבְרֵי דֶרֶךְ †La 1[12] 2[15] Jb 21[29] Pr 9[15] ψ 80[13] 89[42]; *pass by = overtake and pass* c. acc. †2 S 18[23]. **b.** *pass by,* בְּ rei, ψ 103[16] (of wind) **c.** *sweep by,* of scourge (fig.) Is 28[15 18.19] (cf. מַעֲבָר **3**) **d.** *be past, over,* of time, etc, Am 8[5] 1 K 18[29] Gn 50[4] Ct 2[11]+7 t. **e.** *pass along* (from hand to hand), only pt. שֶׁקֶל כֶּסֶף עֹבֵר לַסֹּחֵר Gn 23[16] i.e. *current* money *of the merchant* (or, money *passing over to* merchant? Bu[Th Lz 1892 (3), 63]); כֶּסֶף עֹבֵר 2 K 12[5].

5. *Pass on, go on:* **a.** abs. Gn 18^{5} (J), Nu 22^{26} (E), Ju 12^{1} + 20 t., + Ju 11^{29} 18^{13} Jos 10^{29} (D; all c. acc. of goal + מִן), Gn 18^{3} (J; c. מֵעַל pers.); also c. אֶל־ pers. vel rei, *proceed unto* 1 K 19^{19} 2 K 4^{8} Ne 2^{14}, c. עַל־ pers. (rd. אֶל־ ?) La 4^{21}; c. מִן Ru 2^{8}, *out of the city* 2 S 15^{24}; c. ה loc. Ju 12^{1} 2 S 19^{41}, c. ה loc. + מִן Jos 10$^{31.34}$ (D); ע׳ מֵעִיר לָעִיר בארץ 2 Ch 30^{10}; abs. 2 S 19^{41} *all the people of Judah proceeding with the king* (rd. עֹבְרִים for ויעברו, v. **Hiph.** ad fin.). †**b.** specif. of boundary-line, *pass on*, c. ה loc. Nu 34$^{4.4}$ Jos 15$^{3.4}$ 16^{6} (om. אותו 𝔊𝔙 cf. Benn^{Hpt} Steuern); + מִן 19^{13} + אֶל־ + מִן 18^{13}; c. לְ + מִן 15^{6}; c. אֶל־ 15$^{7.10}$ 16^{2} 18$^{18.19}$; c. acc. loc. 15$^{3.10.11}$ (all P, exc. Jos 16^{2} JE). **c.** c. לִפְנֵי *pass on before, go in advance of* Gn 32^{17} Ex 17^{5} (both E), Gn 32^{22} 33$^{3.14}$ (all J), Dt 9^{3} + 7 t., + Dt 3$^{18.28}$ 31$^{3.3}$ Jos 1^{14} (all D) where ref. may be to *crossing* in advance of; c. עַל־פְּנֵי 2 S 15^{18} so v$^{23\,b}$ (reading עַל־פָּנָיו 𝔊L We Dr Klo Bu Kit HPS). †**d.** *pass on* as far as (עַד), Ju 19^{12}, + מִן v^{18}; c. אַחֲרֵי *after* 2 S 20^{13}; תַּעֲבָר־כּוֹס עַל La 4^{21} *pass on unto* (cf. תִּסּוֹב Hb 2^{16}). †**e.** *pass on* into (בְּ), Jos 3^{11} (+ לִפְנֵי), 4^{7} (both JE), cf. Ju 9^{26} Jb 33^{28}, so also ע׳ בִּבְרִית י׳ Dt 29^{11} *enter into a covenant with* י׳; (Klo rds. וַיַּעֲבֹר בַּבּ׳ also 2 K 23^{3} for MT ויעמד). †**f.** *pass on* away from (מֵאֵת) Dt 2^{8} (+ ה loc.). †**g.** *pass on* in order, for counting 2 S 2^{15}, עַל־יְדֵי מוֹנֶה Je 33^{13}, עֹבֵר עַל־הַפְּקֻדִים Ex 30$^{13.14}$ 38^{26}, also *pass on* under (תַּחַת) rod Lv 27^{32} (for counting; all P; cf. **Hiph. 3 d**). †**h.** *pass along, travel* c. acc. of way Is 35^{8} cf. 51^{10}; עֹבֵר אָרְחוֹת יַמִּים ψ 8^{9}; c. בְּ of way Jos 3^{4} Pr 4^{15} 7^{8}. **i.** *pass on, advance*, abs., ψ 48^{5} (Ol We *pass away, perish*), Mi 2^{13a} (acc. loc.).

†**6.** *Pass away:* **a.** *emigrate*, leave one's territory or city Mi 1^{11}. **b.** vanish, of chaff, Is 29^{5} cf. Je 13^{24}, shadow ψ 144^{4}, brooks Jb 6^{15} (all in sim.), Ct 5^{6}. **c.** = cease to exist, perish Na 1^{12} Jb 30^{15} 33^{18} (בְּ instr.), 36^{12} (*id.*), 34^{20} ψ 37^{36} (but rd. ואעבר *and I passed by*, cf. **4 a**), cf. Is 31^{9} (סלעו subj.), מֵאֱלֹהֵי מִשְׁפָּטִי יַעֲבוֹר 40^{27} *pass away from.* **d.** = become invalid, obsolete, of law, decree, Est 1^{19} 9^{27}, also v^{28} (+ מִתּוֹךְ הַיְּהוּדִים). **e.** c. מִן of hands ψ 81^{7} (i.e. they were freed from). **f.** = *be alienated, pass into other hands* Ez 48^{14} (rdg. Kt; > Qr **Hiph.**).—Je 2^{20} rd. אֶעֱבוֹד Kt (not אֶעֱבוֹר Qr); וָאֶתֵּן לָהֶם יַעַבְרוּם 8^{13} *and I gave to them that which they transgress* 𝔖𝔙𝔗 Aq Symm Ew, *those that shall pass over them* Hi Gf Ke RVm, *those that shall consume, devour them* Rothst^{Kau} (rdg. יְבַעֲרוּם) but all very dub.; 𝔊 Co del.; 11^{15} rd. Hiph. q.v.; מִנֹּגַהּ נֶגְדּוֹ עָבָיו עָבְרוּ ψ 18^{13} is difficult; perhaps best, as Che Kit^{Kau} Löhr, *out of the brightness before him issued forth* hailstones, etc. (del. עָבָיו); > ∥ 2 S 22^{13} בָּעֲרוּ and so here Bu HPS cf. Woods$^{Hbr\,1887,\,262}$, *his clouds burned* with hailstones, etc.; rd. rather עברו in 2 S.

†**Niph.** *Impf.* 3 ms. נַחַל אֲשֶׁר לֹא יֵעָבֵר Ez 47^{5} *a stream which cannot be forded.*

Pi. 1. *Pf.* 3 ms. שׁוֹרוֹ עִבַּר Jb 21^{10} *his bull impregnateth* (cf. NH) abs. (prop. *causeth to pass over*, sc. *semen*). **2.** *Impf.* 3 ms. וַיְעַבֵּר בְּ׳ 1 K 6^{21} *he made to pass across* with chains of gold.—**Hithp.** v. [עָבַר] infr.

†**Hiph.** *Pf.* 3 ms. הֶעֱבִיר 2 S 12^{13} +; 2 ms. הֶעֱבַרְתָּ Jos 7^{7} (Ges$^{§\,63\,p}$), וְהַעֲבַרְתָּ Ez 5^{1} +; 1 s. הֶעֱבַרְתִּי Zc 3^{4}, וְהַעֲבַרְתִּי Ez 20^{37} + Je 15^{14} (but rd. והעבדתי 𝔊𝔖𝔗 Codd Ew Hi Gf Gie), etc.; *Impf.* 3 ms. וַיַּעֲבֵר Gn 8^{1} +, וַיַּעֲבֶר־ 2 Ch 36^{22} = Ezr 1^{1}, sf. וַיַּעֲבִרֵנִי Ez 46^{21} +, etc.; *Imv.* ms. הַעֲבֵר ψ 119^{37} + 2 t., הַעֲבֶר־ 2 S 24^{10} = 1 Ch 21^{8}; mpl. sf. הַעֲבִירוּנִי 2 Ch 35^{23}; *Inf. abs.* הַעֲבִיר Jos 7^{7} (rd. prob. הֶעֱבִיר); *cstr.* הַעֲבִיר 2 S 3^{10} +, לַעֲבִיר 2 S 19^{19} (Ges$^{§\,53\,q}$), etc.; *Pt.* מַעֲבִיר Dt 18^{10} Dn 11^{20}, pl. מַעֲבִרִים 1 S 2^{24} (v. infr.);—**1.** *cause to pass over, bring over:* **a.** *cause* one *to cross* river, c. 2 acc., Gn 32^{24} (J), Nu 32^{5} Jos 7^{7} (both JE), 2 S 19$^{16.42}$; acc. of river om. Gn 32^{24} (J), Jos 4^{3} 7^{7} (+ Inf. abs.; both JE), 4^{8} (JE; + אֶל־), 2 S 2^{8} (+ acc. loc.). **b.** *cause* something *to pass over* (עַל־): razor (acc.) Nu 8^{7} (P), cf. Ez 5^{1} (where Co rds. sf. of razor), wind Gn 8^{1} (P). **c.** *make over* to (לְ), acc. of inheritance Nu 27$^{7.8}$ (P); of *making over, dedicating,* something to (לְ) deity Ex 13^{12} (JE; = קִדֵּשׁ). Esp. **d.** *devote* children to (לְ) heathen god Je 32^{35} Ez 23^{37} (+ לְאָכְלָה), Lv 18^{21} (H), cf. Ez 16^{21}; + בָּאֵשׁ *by fire* 2 K 23^{10}; c. acc. alone *devote* Ez 20^{26}; c. acc. + בָּאֵשׁ alone, *devote by fire* Dt 18^{10} 2 K 16^{3} 17^{7} 21^{6} = 2 Ch 33^{6}, Ez 20^{31} (on the practice cf. Now$^{Arch.\,ii.\,205\,f.}$ Benz$^{Arch.\,433\,f.}$ Toy$^{Ez\,16,\,20;\,20,\,26}$ GFM$^{JBL\,xvi\,(1897),\,161\,ff.}$).

2. a. *cause to pass through*, c. acc. + בְּ Ez 14^{15} 47$^{3.4}$ + v^{4} (where ins. בְּ, cf. Co Berthol Toy), Nu 31$^{23.23}$ (P); c. acc. + בְּתוֹךְ ψ 136^{14}; c. acc. pers. alone 78^{13}, + אֶל־ Ez 46^{21}, + עַד־אֲשֶׁר Ne 2^{7}; c. acc. of (sound of) שׁוֹפָר Lv 25^{9} (H), + בְּ v^{9} (P); c. acc. קוֹל = *proclamation*, + בְּ Ex 36^{6} (P), 2 Ch 30^{5} 36^{22} = Ezr 1^{1}, Ezr 10^{7} (+ לְ pers.), Ne 8^{15}. **b.** *let pass through*, c. acc. + בְּ pers. Dt 2^{30}.

3. a. *cause to pass by*, c. acc. + עַל־, Ez 37^{2}

(+ סָבִיב סָבִיב), + עַל־פְּנֵי Ex 33^{19} (J), + לִפְנֵי 1 S 16$^{8.10}$ and (לפני om.) v^{9}. **b.** *let pass by*, c. acc. מוֹעֵד Je 46^{17} *he hath let the set time pass by* (in mocking appell. of Pharaoh). **c.** *cause* arrow *to pass beyond* one 1 S 20^{36}. **d.** *cause to pass* under rod, for counting, Ez 20^{37} (cf **Qal 5 g**).

4. *Cause to pass away, take away*, kingdom (acc) + מִן pers. 2 S 3^{10}, cf. Est 8^{2}, + מֵעַל Jon 3^{6} (of putting off garment); c. acc. of sin 2 S 12^{13} 24^{10} = 1 Ch 21^{8}, Jb 7^{21}, + מֵעַל pers Zc 3^{4} Je 11^{15} (rdg. יַעֲבִרוּ מֵעַל Ew Gf Gie), *put away* evil things (acc) from (מִן), 1 K 15^{12} cf. ‖ 2 Ch 15^{8}, Zc 13^{2} Ec 11^{10}, c. acc alone ψ 119^{39} Est 8^{3}; also *take me away* (sf) 2 Ch 35^{23} (c. מִן) v^{24}, *turn away* eyes (acc) + מִן ψ 119^{37}.—Gn 47^{21} rd. הֶעֱבִיד לַעֲבָדִים Sam 𝔊 𝔙 Ol Kn Di Kau Holz; Je 15^{14} rd. וְהַעֲבַדְתִּיךָ 𝔊 𝔗 Codd Gie; 2 S 12^{31} rd. וְהֶעֱבִיד Hoffm ZAW ii (1882), 53 f. Gr Klo Bu Kit HPS, cf Dr Lohr, 2 S 19^{41} (for ויעברו Kt, הֶעֱבִרוּ Qr) rd. עֹבְרִים 𝔊 We Bu Löhr HPS, וַיַּעֲבִרוּ Kit (v. **Qal 5 a**); Ez 48^{14} rd **Qal** (so Kt; v. **Qal 6 e**); מַעֲבִרִים עַם־י׳ 1 S 2^{24} not good is the report which I hear *the people of* ׳י *spreading* (cf. **2**), so Ew Th We Dr Kit Lohr RVm, but order of words difficult, > (ye) *make the people of* ׳י *transgress* 𝔙 AV RV; text dub.; מַעֲבִיר נוֹגֵשׂ Dn 11^{20} *one causing an exactor to pass through* Ew al. RV, Bev prop. נוגש מ׳ *an exactor causing to pass away* the glory, etc.

I. עֵ֫בֶר $_{91}$ **n.m.** $^{1\ S\ 14,\ 40}$ **region across** or **beyond, side** (on format cf. Ba$^{NB\ 144}$, cf. esp. As *êbru, êbirtu, id*, *êbirtan*, adv. *beyond*);—ע׳ abs. 1 S 14^{4} +; cstr. Jos 24^{4} +; sf עֶבְרוֹ Is 47^{15}, pl. cstr. עֶבְרֵי Is 7^{20} Je 48^{28} (si vera l, v. infr.); sf. עֲבָרָיו 1 K 5^{4} Je 49^{32} (read probably עֶבְרֵיהֶם, so Vrss), עֶבְרֵיהֶם Ex 32^{15},—**1.** *region across* or *beyond* anything (usu wady, river, or sea), mostly c. prep: בְּעֵבֶר אַרְנוֹן Nu 21^{13} (JE) Ju 11^{18}, cf. Je 25^{22}; אֶל־ע׳ הַיָּם Dt 30^{13b}, מֵעֵבֶר לַיָּם v^{13a} *beyond the sea;* מֵע׳ לְנַהֲרֵי־כוּשׁ Is 18^{1}, cf. עַד־מֵע׳ 1 K 4^{12} (מִן *on the side of, on*, v. מִן **1 c**; so usu. c. ע׳), but also (rarely) מֵע׳ *from the other side of* Zp 3^{10} Jb 1^{19} 2 Ch 20^{2}, abs. הָע׳ 1 S 26^{13} *to the other side* (sc. of a ravine; after וַיַּעֲבֹר), בְּעֵבֶר הָעֵמֶק 1 S 31^{7}, read perh בְּעָרֵי הָע׳, so Klo Bu HPS; בְּעֶבְרֵי פִי־פָחַת Je 48^{28} *beyond the mouth of a chasm* is dub; Gie prop. בְּחֹרֵי כֵּפֵּי בַתַּת *in the rock-holes of the precipices;* esp. (chiefly Hex, 37 t.) ע׳ הַיַּרְדֵּן (30 t.), or (less oft, Jos 13^{32} + 13 t.), לְיַרְדֵּן יְרֵחוֹ, לַיַּרְדֵּן (only c. מֵע׳), of either E. Jordan (36 t.) or W. Jordan land (9 t.) acc. to standpoint of speaker or writer: **A.** E Jordan (fr. standpoint of writer) Gn 50$^{10.11}$ (J) Jos 17^{5} (JE) Dt 1$^{1.5}$ 4$^{41.46.47.49}$ Jos 1^{14} 12^{1} 13^{8} (D), Nu 22^{1} 32^{19} 34^{15} Jos 13$^{27.32}$ 14^{3} 20^{8} (P), Ju 7^{25} 10^{8} 1 S 31^{7} Is 8^{23} 1 Ch 6^{63} 12^{37}; fr. standpoint of speaker, Jos 7^{7} (JE), 24^{8} (E), 1^{15} 2^{10} 9^{10} 18^{7} 22^{4} (D), Ju 5^{17}; in Nu 35^{14} (Moses speaks) it is *land opp* to Can., cf. Nu 32^{32}; in Dt 3^{8} (Moses speaks) writer (D) ascribes his own standpoint to Moses, (oft further topogr. note is added, e g מִזְרָחָה Dt 4^{49} +, מִזְרַח הַשֶּׁמֶשׁ Jos 1^{15} +, etc); אֶל־עֵבֶר בְּנֵי יִשְׂר׳ Jos 22^{11} *toward the region opposite the sons of Israel* appar also refers to E. side (v. Steuernagel on text) **B.** W. Jordan (9 t.), from standpoint of speaker Dt 3$^{20.25}$ (Moses), also 11^{30} (but here + מְבוֹא הַשֶּׁמֶשׁ, and in all foll. some special designation of *West*), + יָ֫מָּה Jos 5^{1} (D, from standpoint of those just crossed), 12^{7} (*opposite* East v$^{1-6}$), 22^{7} (*id*; Kt מעבר, Qr בְּעֵבֶר), cf. 9^{1} (as 5^{1}); + וָהָ֫לְאָה Nu 32^{19a} (*opposite* East v^{b}), in 1 Ch 26^{30} מע׳ לַיַּר׳ מַעְרָבָה ע׳ seems = *side* (v. infr.). Also בְּע׳ הַנָּהָר *beyond the river* (Euphrates) Jos 24$^{2.14.15}$ (E; Kt Qr מֵע׳), מֵע׳ 2 S 10^{16} = 1 Ch 19^{16} *beyond*, and 1 K 14^{15} *to the other side of* (v. מִן **1 c**), מֵע׳ *from beyond* the river only Jos 24^{3} (E), in all these = beyond the Euphr. *eastward*, from standpoint of those west of Euphr, so pl. בְּעֶבְרֵי הַנּ׳ Is 7^{20}; poss also ע׳ alone (si vera l) in the difficult passage Nu 24^{24}; ע׳ הַנָּהָר = *region beyond the river* (Euphr) westward (from standpoint of those in Babylonia or Persia) Ne 2$^{7.9}$ 3^{7} Ezr 8^{36}, also 1 K 5$^{4.4}$ (written in Bab.; cf BAram. עֲבַר, and Dr$^{Intr\ (6)\ 504}$)

2. (Opposite) *side, side*. מֵע׳ הַלָּז 1 S 14^{1} *on yonder side* seems transition to this meaning; מֵהָע׳ מִזֶּה twice, v^{4} = *on one side, on the other side*, so לְע׳ אֶחָד twice v^{40}; even מִשְּׁנֵי עֶבְרֵיהֶם Ex 32^{15} (E) *on their two sides* (i e. of tablets); אֶל־ע׳ הָאֵפוֹד בָּיְתָה Ex 28^{26} (P) *toward the inner side of the ephod;* in 1 K 7$^{20.30}$ ע׳ appar. = *at the side of* or *opposite*, but the archit. details are obscure; מִכָּל־עֲבָרָיו מִסָּבִיב 1 K 5^{4} *on all sides of him*, round about, מִכָּל־עֲבָרָיו Je 49^{32} (rd. עֶבְרֵיהֶם Vrss Gie) *from all sides of them* (all directions, = מִכָּל־סְבִיבָיִךְ v^{5}), אֶל־עֵבֶר פָּנָיו יֵלֵכוּ *to the side of their faces* (i e in front, straight forward) *they* (always) *went* Ez 1$^{9.12}$ 10^{22}, cf. עַל־ע׳ פָּנֶיהָ Ex 25^{37} to give light *upon the space in front of it*, אִישׁ לְעֶבְרוֹ תָּעוּ Is 47^{15} *they wander away each in his own direction* (regardless of thee).—On 1 Ch 26^{30} v. supr.

†II עֵ֫בֶר **n.pr.m. Eber** (perh eponym of *Hebrews*, form inferred from עִבְרִי, cf. reff. there),—**1** 'son' of Shelah, and 'grandson' of Arpachshad Gn 10^{24} (J) = 1 Ch 1^{18}, Gn 11$^{14\,15}$ (P), 'father' of Peleg and Joktan 10^{25} (J, with esp ref to Joktan v$^{26\,ff}$, i e to Arabians) = 1 Ch 1^{19} (cf. v$^{20\,ff}$), of Peleg specif Gn 11$^{16\,17}$ (P, with esp ref to Abr v$^{26\,f}$) cf 1 Ch 1^{25} (see v$^{27\,f}$), in Gn 10^{21} (J) Shem is called אֲבִי כָּל־בְּנֵי־עֵבֶר, 𝔊 Εβερ —ע׳ Nu 24^{24} perh (si vera l) belongs not here (= עברים *Hebrews*, 𝔊 Ἐβραίους, so Thes), but sub I עֵבֶר = the (land) beyond (the river), ‖ אַשּׁוּר, so Di Kau. **2.** a Gadite chief 1 Ch 5^{13}, 𝔊 Ωβηδ, 𝔊L Εβερ **3.** Benjamite names. **a.** 1 Ch 8^{12}, 𝔊 Ωβηδ, 𝔊L Αβερ. **b.** 1 Ch 8^{22} (עבר van d H Ginsb, עֶבֶד Baer), 𝔊 Ωβδη, A Ωβηδ, 𝔊L Αβερ **4.** a priest Ne 12^{20} 𝔊L Αβεδ

†I עִבְרִי **adj.** et **n. gent. Hebrew**, either **a.** put into the mouth of foreigners (Egypt. and Philist), or **b.** used to distinguish Isr. from foreigners (= *one from beyond, from the other side*, i e prob (in Heb trad) *from beyond the Euphrates* (cf Jos 24$^{2\,3}$ E), but poss. in fact (if name given in Canaan) *from beyond the Jordan;* cf. Ges^{§2b} Sta^{§1b} Ko$^{i\,18\,ff}$ We$^{Isr\,u.\,Jüd\,Gesch\,7}$ Kau$^{'Eber\,and\,Hebräer}$ in Ri$^{HWB\,332,\,600}$—On connexion of ע׳ (in wide sense) with *Ḥabiri* (Tel Am) v. Wkl$^{Gesch\,Isr\,17\,ff}$, $^{Sem.\,Studies\,in\,Mem.\,of\,Kohut,\,606\,ff}$ EMey$^{Aegyptiaca\,[Ebers],\,75}$ cf Glaser$^{MVG\,1897,\,255\,ff.}$ Ko$^{Exp.\,Times\,xi.\,238}$, opp Jastr$^{JBL\,xi\,(1892),\,118\,ff}$ Say$^{Monuments\,188,\,333}$ WMM$^{As\,u\,Eur\,396}$),—ms ע׳ Gn 39^{14}+, fs עבריה Dt 15^{12} Je 34^{9}; mpl. עברים Gn 43^{32}+, עבריים Ex 3^{18}, fpl עבריֹּת Ex 1^{15} + 2 t, ־יֹּת 1^{16}; word not in P, —**1. adj. a.** איש עברי Gn 39^{14} cf. v^{17} (both J), 41^{12} (E) **b.** איש עברי Ex 2^{11} cf v^{13} 21^{2} (all E), Dt 15^{12} Je 34$^{9\,14}$; f. Dt 15^{12} Je 34^{9}. **2. n. a.** Ex 1$^{16\,19}$ 2^{7} (all f) 2^{6} (all E), 1 S 4$^{6\,9}$ 13^{19} 14^{11} 29^{3} **b.** Gn 40^{15} Ex 1^{15} (f; both E), 1 S 13^{3} 14^{21}, Gn 43^{32} (J), esp in אֱלֹהֵי הָעִבְרִים Ex 3^{18} 5^{3} 7^{16} 9$^{1\,13}$ 10^{3} (all J), sg. only אַבְרָם הָע׳ Gn 14^{13}, ע׳ אָנֹכִי Jon 1^{9} —𝔊 Ἑβραῖος, Ἑβραία, Gn 14^{13} τῷ περάτῃ. —1 S 13^{7} read prob for ועברים וגו׳, וְעָבְרוּ מַעְבְּרוֹת הַיַּרְדֵּן (We), or, better, וַיַּעַבְרוּ Dr Kit Lohr, > וְעַם רַב Klo Bu HPS.

†II עִבְרִי **n.pr.m.** Levite name, 1 Ch 24^{27}, 𝔊 Αβαι, A Ωβδι, 𝔊L Αβαρια.

†עֲבָרָה **n.f. ford**, rare synon of מַעֲבָר, מַעְבָּרָה,—abs הָע׳ 2 S 19^{19} *and they crossed the ford* (v עבר **Qal 1 a**), pl cstr עַבְרוֹת הַמִּדְבָּר 2 S 15^{28} Kt (Qr עַרְבוֹת), so 17^{16} van d. H. (but Baer Ginsb עַרְבוֹת Kt also), עֲב׳ preferable (so Th We Dr Bu Kit Lohr HPS), *the fords of the desert* (HPS 17^{16} n pr.).

†עֶבְרָה **n f. overflow, arrogance, fury**;—abs ע׳ Is 13^{9}+, cstr עֶבְרַת Zp 1^{18}+; sf. עֶבְרָתִי Is 10^{6}+, etc; pl עֲבָרוֹת Jb 21^{30}, cstr. עַבְרוֹת ψ 7^{7} Jb 40^{11};—**1.** *overflow, excess, outburst*, ע׳ זָדוֹן Pr 21^{24} *excess of insolence;* עַבְרוֹת אַפֶּךָ Jb 40^{11} *outbursts of thine anger.* **2.** *arrogance*, of Moab Is 16^{6} (+ גָּאוֹן, גַּאֲוָה), hence Je 48^{30} (+ *id* v^{29}). **3.** *overflowing rage, fury:* **a.** of men, Gn 49^{7} (poem in J), Am 1^{11} (both ‖ אַף), Is 14^{6} Pr 14^{35}, שֵׁבֶט עֶבְרָתוֹ 22^{8} (i.e. rod wielded by him in fury, v. also La 3^{1} infr.), עַבְרוֹת צוֹרְרָי ψ 7^{7} *the outbursts of fury of my foes* **b.** of י׳ Ho 5^{10} 13^{11} (‖ אַף), Hb 3^{8} (‖ *id.*), Is 9^{18} La 2^{2} ψ 90$^{9\,11}$, + חֲרוֹן אַף Is 13^{9}, ‖ *id.* v^{13} ψ 78^{49} (+ וָזַעַם), 85^{4}, אֵשׁ עֶבְרָתִי Ez 21^{36} (‖ זַעַם), 22^{31} (‖ *id.*), v^{21} 38^{19}; שֵׁבֶט עֶבְרָתוֹ La 3^{1} (cf. Pr 22^{8} supr); עַם עֶבְרָתִי Is 10^{6} (i e obj of my rage), cf דּוֹר עֶבְרָתוֹ Je 7^{29}; יוֹם עֶבְרַת י׳ Zp 1^{18} *day of* י׳*'s fury* (coming judgment), so Ez 7^{19} (del. Co Berthol, after 𝔊, as gloss from Zp); so יוֹם עֶבְרָה Zp 1^{15} Pr 11^{4}, יוֹם עֲבָרוֹת Jb 21^{30}, cf. עֶבְרָה Pr 11^{23}

†[עָבַר] **vb. denom. Hithp. be arrogant, infuriate oneself**,—*Pf.* 3 ms הִתְעַבֵּר ψ 78^{62}; 2 ms הִתְעַבַּרְתָּ 89^{39}; *Impf* 3 ms וַיִּתְעַבֵּר Dt 3^{26}, וַיִּתְעַבַּר ψ 78$^{21.59}$, *Pt.* מתעבר Pr 14^{16} 26^{17}; sf מִתְעַבְּרוֹ 20^{2},—**1.** *be arrogant*, Pr 14^{16} (opp יָרֵא). **2. a.** *put oneself in a fury, become furious*, c. בְּ pers Dt 3^{26} ψ 78^{62}, c עִם pers. 89^{39}; abs 78$^{21.59}$ (all of God), of man, c עַל rei Pr 26^{17}. **b.** *incite one to fury for oneself* Pr 20^{2} (si vera l., cf. De Ges$^{§54\,f}$)

†עֲבָרִים **n.pr.loc. 'Abarîm** (prop *regions beyond* river or sea);—usu הַר הָע׳ Nu 27^{12} Dt 32^{49} (= הַר־נְבוֹ, both P), and הָרֵי הָע׳ 33^{47} (לִפְנֵי נְבוֹ), v^{48} (P); alone only צַעֲקִי מֵעֲבָרִים Je 22^{20}, the mountainous district in NW. Moab, just NE of Dead Sea, GASm$^{Geogr\,548\,and\,EBi}$ Buhl$^{Geogr\,122}$; 𝔊 Αβαρειμ (-ειν), but τὸ ἐν τῷ πέραν Nu 33^{47}, εἰς τὸ πέραν τῆς θαλάσσης Je 22^{20} —Vid. also sub עִיִּים

עֶבְרֹן **n.pr.loc.** Jos 19^{28} (𝔊 Ελβων, A 𝔊L Αχραν), read probably עַבְדֹּן q.v.

†עַבְרֹנָה **n pr.loc.** a station of Israelites in wilderness, one march from Ezion-geber, on Gulf of Akaba Nu 33$^{34.35}$ (P); 𝔊 (Σ)εβρωνα.

†I. [עָבוּר] **n.[m.] produce, yield** (cf. As. *ebûru, id*, Dl$^{HWB\ 11}$; Syr. ܥܒܘܪܐ *corn*);—cstr. עֲבוּר הָאָרֶץ Jos $5^{11.12}$ (P).

II. [עָבוּר] **n.** only in בַּעֲבוּר, בַּעֲבֻר (Gn $27^{10.31}$), **prep.** and **conj.** *for the sake of, on account of, in order that* (perh. orig *for the produce* or *gain of*), sf. בַּעֲבוּרִי, 1 S 23^{10}, etc.;—**1. as prep.: a.** Gn 3^{17} ארורה האדמה בעבורך *for* thy *sake*, 8^{21} בעבור האדם *for* man's *sake*, 12^{13} לְמַעַן יִיטַב־לִי בַעֲבוּרֵךְ, v^{16} $18^{26.29}$ 26^{24}, Ex 9^{16} 13^{8} ב׳ זה, 1 S 12^{22} 2 S 5^{12} 6^{12} 7^{21} $9^{1.7}$ Am 2^{6} 8^{6} ב׳ זאת, ב׳ נַעֲלָיִם, ואביון ב׳ נַעֲלָיִם, Mi 2^{10} ב׳ טָמְאָה *on account of* uncleanness, ψ 106^{32} 132^{10}, etc.; 2 S 12^{21} ב׳ הַיֶּלֶד חַי *because of* the child, (being) alive (=while he was alive), Je 14^{4} ב׳ הָאֲדָמָה חַתָּה *on account of* the ground, (which) is dismayed, Jb 20^{2} וּבַעֲבוּר חוּשִׁי בִי rd. ובי׳ זאת, or וּבַעֲבוּרָהּ. **†b.** sq. inf (cf לְמַעַן), *in order to*, Ex 9^{16} ב׳ הַרְאֹתְךָ אֶת־כֹּחִי, 1 S 1^{6} 2 S 10^{3} ב׳ חֲקֹר אֶת־הָעִיר, 18^{18}: so לְבַעֲבוּר Ex 20^{20} 2 S 14^{20} 17^{14}; בעבור לְ 1 Ch 19^{3} (‖ 2 S 10^{3}, no לְ) **†2.** as **conj.** Gn 27^{10} ב׳ אֲשֶׁר יְבָרֶכְךָ; without אשר, Gn 21^{30} ב׳ תִּהְיֶה לִּי לְעֵדָה *in order that* it may be a witness for me, 27^{4} ב׳ תְּבָרֶכְךָ נַפְשִׁי, v$^{19.31}$ 46^{34} Ex 9^{14} 19^{9} 20^{20} ψ 105^{45}.

†[מַעֲבָר] **n.[m.] ford, pass, passing**;—only cstr.: **1.** מַעֲבַר יַבֹּק Gn 32^{23} (J) *the ford of* (the) *Jabbok* **2.** *pass*, מַעֲבַר מִכְמָשׂ 1 S 13^{23} *the pass of M.* **3.** *passing, sweep*, כֹּל־מַעֲבַר מַטֵּה Is 30^{32} *every sweep of the rod* (עָבַר **4 c**).

†מַעְבָּרָה **n.f. ford, pass, passage**,—abs. מ׳ Is 10^{29}; pl. מַעְבָּרוֹת Is 16^{2} Je 51^{32}, מַעְבָּרוֹת abs Jos 2^{7} 1 S 14^{4}, cstr Ju 3^{28}+2 t.;—**1.** *ford*, only pl. Jos 2^{7} (JE), Ju 3^{28} $12^{5.6}$ Is 16^{2}; so also 1 S 13^{7} (for MT עָבְרוּ) We Dr Kit Lohr; + מַעֲבֶרֶת 1 K 7^{46} = 2 Ch 4^{17}, v. סֻכּוֹת. **2.** *pass* (wady, ravine), 1 S 14^{4} Is 10^{29} **3.** *passage* in defensive works of Bab Je 51^{32}.

†[עָבַשׁ] **vb. shrivel** (cf. Ar. عَبَسَ *contract* (esp face), *frown*),—**Qal** *Pf.* 3 mpl. עָבְשׁוּ פְרֻדוֹת Jo 1^{17} *the grains have shrivelled* (cf. Dr Now).

†[עָבַת] **vb. Pi. wind, weave** (cf. derivatives);—*Impf.* 3 mpl. sf. וַיְעַבְּתוּהָ Mi 7^{3} *and* (*so*) *they wind it* (or *weave it*; i e. mischief); so Hi Che GASm, but dub.; Ew rds. עָבַת = *twist, pervert* (cp. Jo 2^{7}, but v. עבט), We וַיְעַוְּתוּהָ = *id.*, cf. Now (?), Dr

†עָבֹת **adj.** having **interwoven** foliage, **leafy**;—עֵץ עָבֹת *leafy trees* Ez 20^{28} Ne 8^{15}; עֵץ עָבֹת Lv 23^{40} (H); f. אֵלָה עֲבֻתָּה Ez 6^{13} *a leafy terebinth*.—עבות 2 S 23^{4} ψ 77^{18} v. II. עָב sub עוב.

†עֲבֹת **n.m.**$^{Ju\ 15\ 13+}$ et **f.**$^{Ju\ 15.14+}$ **(twisted) cord, rope; cordage; interwoven foliage** (?); —abs ע׳ Ex 28^{14}+2 t.; cstr. עֲבוֹת Is 5^{18} ψ 129^{4}, sf. 3 ms. עֲבֹתוֹ Jb 39^{10}, 3 mpl. עֲבֹתֵימוֹ ψ 2^{3}; pl. עֲבֹתִים Ju 15^{13}+, עֲבֹתֹת Ex 28^{14}+, etc,—**1.** *cord, rope*: **a.** as fetter, Ju $15^{13.14}$ $16^{11.12}$ Ez 3^{25} 4^{8}. Jb 39^{10} (of wild ox), so also prob ψ 118^{27} *bind the festal victim* (חַג) *with cords* Ew Ol De Hup-Now Dr al; > *with branches* Che, cf. Bae Du, fig. of authority ψ 2^{3} (‖ מוֹסְרוֹתֵימוֹ), 129^{4}. **b.** עֲבוֹת הָעֲגָלָה Is 5^{18} i e with which a cart is drawn (in sim.; ‖ חַבְלֵי הַשָּׁוְא); fig. עבתות אַהֲבָה Ho 11^{4} *with the cords of love*, of י׳'s drawing Isr. (‖ חַבְלֵי אָדָם) **c.** *cordage, cord*, of (twisted) golden chains on high priest's breast-piece (all P) · מַעֲשֵׂה עֲבֹת, *cordage-work* Ex $28^{14.22}$ 39^{15}, שַׁרְשְׁרֹת הָעֲבֹתֹת 28^{14} *the chains of cords* (cordlike chains); שְׁתֵּי (הָ)עֲבֹתֹת *the two cords* v$^{24.25}$ $39^{17.18}$. **2.** *interwoven foliage* (?) in phr. (עַל־)בֵּין עֲבֹתִים of top of a vine Ez 19^{11} (*clouds* Ew Hi-Sm Toy, rd. then עָבוֹת); of cedar, $31^{3.10.14}$, but in these certainly *clouds*, so 𝔊 Ew Hi-Sm Co al.

עֹג v. עוג.

†[עָגַב] **vb. have inordinate affection, lust** (cf. Ar. عَجِبَ *wonder, admire*, عَجِيبٌ *beloved*; and (on sens. obsc. in NH) Levy$^{NHWB\ III\ 616}$);—**Qal** *Pf* 3 fs עָגְבָה Ez $23^{7.9.12}$; *Impf.* 3 fs וַתַּעְגַּב v^{5}, + v^{16} Kt (Qr וַתַּעְגְּבָה), וַתַּעְגְּבָה v^{20} (Ew $\S 191 e$ Ol$\S 228 b$), *Pt.* pl. עֹגְבִים Je 4^{30};—*lust* after (עַל־), only in fig. of relations of Samaria and Jerus. (personif.) with foreigners Ez $23^{5.9.12.16.20}$, so c. acc. v^{7}; pt. as subst. *paramours* Je 4^{30}.

†[עֶגֶב] **n.[m.]** (**sensuous**) **love** (on form cf. Lag$^{BN\ 143}$),—only pl intens. שִׁיר עֲגָבִים Ez 33^{32} thou art to them as a *love-song*.—For עֲגָבִים v^{31} rd. כְּזָבִים 𝔊 𝔖 Co Berthol Toy.

†[עֲגָבָה] **n.f. lustfulness**;—sf. עַגְבָתָהּ Ez 23^{11} (of personif. Jerus.; ‖ תַּזְנוּתֶיהָ).

†עוּגָב **n.m.** a **musical instr.** (poss. from above √, because of *sensuous* or *appealing* tones);—Gn 4^{21} (J; +כִּנּוֹר), Jb 21^{12} (‖ כִּנּוֹר, תֹּף), ψ 150^{4} (+ מִנִּים), sf. עֻגָבִי Jb 30^{31} (‖ כִּנֹּרִי);—acc. to 𝔗 a reed-pipe or flute (אַבּוּבָא), 𝔙 a *Pan's*

pipe (*organon*, made up of several reeds together); Now$^{Arch\ 1\ 277}$ Benz$^{Arch\ 276}$ think of *bag-pipe* (=סומפּניה Dn 3$^{5\ 10.15}$), cf also in We$^{Eng\ Tr\ 219}$, >a stringed instr 𝔊𝔖 (Gn 4^{21})

עוג v עֻגָה

עגל (√of foll., cf NH עָגַל Niph *be rounded*, Pi *roll* a thing, etc., Aram Pa ܥܰܓܶܠ *roll* a thing, and deriv., 𝔗 עגולא, עִגּוּלָא *rolled* cake, עִגּוּלָא *shield*, בְּעִגָּלָא, Syr ܒܥܓܠ, *in swiftness, swiftly*, Ar عَجِلَ *hasten, be swift*, cf Lag$^{BN\ 31,\ 143}$)

† **עֵגֶל** n.m.$^{Ex\ 32,\ 24}$ **calf** (as *rolling* or *circling* about? cf כַּר fr כָּרַר; NH *id*, Ph (Pu) עגל *id* Lzb^{336}, עגילו Palm. n pr *id* Cook^{89}, Aram. עִגְלָא, עֶגְלְתָא, ܥܶܓܠܳܐ, ܥܶܓܠܬܳܐ, *id*; As [*agalu*], pl *agalê* prob *calves* Dl$^{HWB\ 16}$ (cf against this Jen$^{Kosmol.\ 110}$, but v also Jager$^{BAS\ II\ 2,\ 286}$), Ar عِجْلٌ *id*; Eth ዕጐል: ዕጐልት:, cf also Hom$^{NS\ 226}$),—ע׳ abs. Ex 32^{19}+, cstr. 1 S 28^{24}+; sf. עֶגְלְךָ Ho 8^{5}, pl עֲגָלִים Ho 13^{2}+, cstr עֶגְלֵי 1 K 12^{28}+,—*calf*, Is 11^{6} 27^{10} in sim of leaping mts. ψ 29^{6}; in sim of foot-sole of cherubim Ez 1^{7}, ע׳ מַרְבֵּק i e a *stall*-fed (fatted) *calf*, 1 S 28^{24}, in sim Je 46^{21} Mal 3^{20}, cf ע׳ מִתּוֹךְ מַרְבֵּק Am 6^{4}; ע׳ לֹא לֻמָּד Je 31^{18} *an untrained calf*, עֶגְלֵי עַמִּים ψ 68^{31} *calves of peoples*, i e peoples like calves, so most, perh rd בַּעֲלֵי עמ׳ Matthes Che Gunkel$^{Schöpf\ 66\ f}$ cf Bae; *calf* as sacrif victim Mi 6^{6} Lv 9$^{2.3.8}$ (P), cut in two, in ratifying covenant Je 34$^{18.19}$ (cf עֶגְלָה Gn 15^{9}); elsewh. *image* of calf made at Horeb, ע׳ מַסֵּכָה Ex 32$^{4.8}$ Dt 9^{16} Ne 9^{18}, ע׳ alone Ex 32$^{19.20.24.35}$ Dt 9^{21} ψ 106^{19}, two set up by Jerob I in N. Isr., 1 K 12$^{28.32}$ 2 K 10^{29} 17^{16} 2 Ch 11^{15} 13^{8}, cf Ho 8$^{5.6}$ (ע׳ שֹׁמְרוֹן, עגלך), 13^{2}, also 10^{5} (v I עֶגְלָה ad fin)

† I **עֶגְלָה** n.f. **heifer**,—abs ע׳ Gn 15^{9}+, cstr. עֶגְלַת Is 7^{21}+, sf עֶגְלָתִי Ju 14^{18}, pl cstr. עֶגְלוֹת Ho 10^{5} (but v infr),—*heifer*, Is 7^{21}, used in ploughing Ju 14^{18} (fig), threshing Je 50^{11} (ע׳ דָשָׁא, in sim, v דוש, read perh. דָשָׁה), fig of stateliness etc. Je 46^{20}, ע׳ מְלֻמָּדָה Ho 10^{11} *a trained heifer* (sim of Ephr), used for sacrif 1 S 16^{2} (עֶגְלַת בָּקָר), cut in two for ratifying covenant Gn 15^{9} (J, ע׳ מְשֻׁלֶּשֶׁת, cf עגל Je 34$^{18.19}$), in cleansing city from blood-guiltiness Dt 21^{3} (ע׳ בָּקָר), v$^{4.6}$, once of *calves* worshipped in N Isr. Ho 10^{5} (where read prob עגל, so 𝔊 We Now GASm, cf Che, v also the foll. sfs ms)

† II. **עֶגְלָה** n.pr.f. wife of David (on sense *heifer* cf. רָחֵל, לֵאָה, v also Gray$^{Prop\ N\ 92,\ No\ 27}$);—2 S 3^{5} (𝔊 Αιγαλ, A Αιγας, 𝔊L Αγλα) = 1 Ch 3^{3} (𝔊 Αλα, A Αγλα, 𝔊L Εγλα)

† **עֶגְלַת** n.pr.loc.,—ע׳ שְׁלִשִׁיָּה (the) *third Eglath* Is 15^{5} (𝔊 δάμαλις τριετής) Je 48^{34} (𝔊 ἀγγελίαν Σαλασεια), near Zoar and S. border of Moab.

† **עָגֹל**, **עָגוֹל** adj. round,—abs עָגֹל 1 K 7^{23} + 2 t, עָגוֹל 10^{19} 2 Ch 4^{2}; fpl עֲגֻלּוֹת 1 K 7^{31},—*round* 1 K 7$^{31.31}$ (opp מְרֻבָּעוֹת), 10^{19}, ע׳ סָבִיב *round in circuit* (perimeter) 7^{23} = 2 Ch 4^{2}, 1 K 7^{35}.

† **עֲגָלָה** n.f. **cart** (from *rolling* of wheels; NH *id*, Ph (Pu.) עגלת (?) Lzb^{336}; Aram עֲגַלְתָא, ܥܓܠܬܐ; Sem. loan-word in Egypt. *āgarθa* Bondi^{38}, *'agolt* Erman$^{Egypt\ 491}$; cf. also Wilkinson$^{Anc\ Egypt.\ (1878),\ i\ 223-241,\ esp\ 235,\ also\ 249}$ (illustr. vehicles drawn by cattle, cf 1 S 6^{7} Nu 7^{3})),—abs. ע׳ 1 S 6^{7}+, sf עֶגְלָתוֹ Is 28^{28}; pl עֲגָלוֹת Gn 45^{19}+; cstr. עֶגְלֹת Nu 7^{3},—*cart*, used for transporting persons and things Gn 45$^{19.21.27}$ 46^{5} (E), 1 S 6$^{7.7.8.10.11.14.14}$, 2 S 6$^{3.3}$ = 1 Ch 13$^{7.7}$, Nu 7^{3} (ע׳ צָב *covered carts*), v$^{3.6.7.8}$ (P), in sim Am 2^{13}, עֲבוֹת הָע׳ Is 5^{18} *cart-rope*, אוֹפַן ע׳ 28^{27} of (*threshing-*) *wagon* (cf. Dr$^{Am\ p\ 228}$), גַּלְגַּל ע׳ v^{28} *id*, —ע׳ = *war-chariots* only ψ 46^{10} (Du *transport-wagons*)

† **עָגִיל** n. [m.] hoop, ring;—abs ע׳ Nu 31^{50} prob. *ear-ring* (+ טַבַּעַת, etc.), pl. עֲגִילִים עַל־ אָזְנָיִךְ Ez 16^{12} (+ נֶזֶם עַל־אַפֵּךְ *nose-ring*)

עֶגְלוֹן $_{13}$ n.pr. (cf Gray$^{Prop.\ N\ 92,\ No\ 27}$),—† **1. m.** a king of Moab, Ju 3$^{12.14.15.17.17}$, 𝔊 Εγλωμ. **2. loc.** Jos 10$^{3.5.23.37}$ 12^{12} 15^{34}, c. ה loc 10^{34}, עֶגְלוֹנָה v^{36}, 𝔊 Οδολλαμ Jos 10, Αιλαμ 12^{12}, A Εγλωμ, 𝔊L Εγλων, and so 15^{39}, site *'Aǧlân*, N. of *Tel-el-Ḥesy*, Buhl$^{Geogr\ 192}$.

עֶגְלַיִם Ez 47^{10} in עֵין ע׳ q v.

† **מַעְגָּל** n m. $^{ψ\ 65\ 12}$ **1. entrenchment**; **2. track**,—abs מ׳ 1 S 26^{5}+, c ה loc. הַמַּעְגָּלָה 17^{20}, cstr מַעְגַּל Pr 5^{26}+; pl. cstr מַעְגְּלֵי ψ 23^{3} Pr 4^{11}, sf. מַעְגָּלֶיךָ ψ 65^{12}, elsewh. מַעְגְּלוֹתֶיךָ, מַעְגְּלֹתָיו 17^{8}, —תָיהָ Pr 5^{21}, 2^{12} 5^{6}, —תָם 2^{15} Is 59^{8},—**1.** *circumvallation, entrenchment* 1 S 17^{20} 26$^{5.7}$. **2.** *track* (prop *wagon*-track), only fig · **a.** in fig. of snares of wicked ψ 140^{6}. **b.** = course of action, or life, מ׳ רַגְלְךָ Pr 4^{26}, מ׳ 5^{21} (|| דַּרְכֵי־אִישׁ); specif good, right, מ׳ צֶדֶק ψ 23^{3}, מ׳ יֹשֶׁר Pr 4^{11}, מ׳ צַדִּיק Is 26^{7}, מ׳ טוֹב 2^{9}, bad sense Pr 2$^{15.18}$ 5^{6}

Is 59[8]; *tracks of* ′י are those approved by him ψ 17[5]; or those traversed by him, מַעְגָּלֶיךָ יִרְעֲפוּן דָּשֶׁן 65[12] fig. of richly-laden cart dropping its contents in its track.

†[עָגַם] **vb. be grieved** (NH *id.*; Aram. עֲגַם, and ܥܓܡ (in Lexx.) *id.*; cf. perh. also As. *agâmu, be vexed* Dl[HWB 16] (rare; cited under אנם));—**Qal** *Pf.* 3 fs. אִם־לֹא . . . עָגְמָה נַפְשִׁי לָאֶבְיוֹן Jb 30[25] *was not my soul grieved for the poor?* (‖ בָּכִיתִי).

† [עָגַן] **vb. Niph. shut oneself in or off** (NH *id.*, Pt. pass. *restrained* (esp. from marriage), also עוֹגִין *anchor;* 𝔗 עֲגַן *be imprisoned*);—*Impf.* 2 fpl. תֵּעָגֵנָה לְבִלְתִּי הֱיוֹת לְאִישׁ Ru 1[13] *would ye shut yourselves off, so as not to belong to a man?*

עגר (√of foll., meaning dubious; conject. in Meier [WurzelWB 38] Lag [BN 59]; on Gk. ἄγορ cf. Lewy[Fremdw. 8]).

†עָגוּר **n.[m.]** appar. understood by Mass. as name of a bird; very uncertain; **crane** acc. to Saad. (Is), but note of crane not suitable (Tristr[NHB 239 f.]);—כְּסוּס עָגוּר וְתוֹר וְסוּס וְעָגוּר Je 8[7]; Is 38[14] (but here gloss Klo Brd Di Dn Che[Hpt]); Thes and (in Je) Hi Gf Gie del. ו and take ′ע as adj. of סוּס=*twittering* or the like; Thes assumes transpos. fr. נער, Eth. **ወወለ**: *cry*.

I, II, III. עַד v. I. עדה. עֵד v. עוד.

עֹד v. עוד. עִדֹּא v. עדד.

עדד (√of foll.; cf. Ar. عَدَّ *count, reckon,* عِدَّةٌ *number, period;* Aram. עִדָּנָא *time*).

†[עִדָּה] **n.f. menstruation,** so Vrss (prop. *time, period*);—pl. abs. בֶּגֶד עִדִּים Is 64[5] i.e. stained garment (fig. of best deeds of guilty people; ‖ טָמֵא).

†עִדּוֹ, עִדֹּא, עִדּוֹא, עִדּוֹא **n.pr.m. Iddo**;—**1.** father of an officer of Sol. עִדֹּא 1 K 4[14]; 𝔊 Αχελ, A Σαδωκ, 𝔊L Αχιαβ. **2.** grandfather of prophet Zechariah עִדּוֹ Zc 1[1], עִדּוֹא v[7]; 𝔊 Αδδω. **3.** a Levite עִדּוֹ 1 Ch 6[6]; 𝔊 Αδει, 𝔊L Αδδω. **4.** a priestly name עִדּוֹא van d. H. Ginsb (Baer עִדּוֹ) Ne 12[4]; 𝔊א etc. Αδαιας; also עדיא v[16] Kt (עִדְיָא?), Qr עִדּוֹא; 𝔊א τῷ Αδδαι, 𝔊L τῷ Αδαια. **5.** a seer עִדּוֹ הַחֹזֶה 2 Ch 12[15] = עִדּוֹ הַנָּבִיא 2 Ch 13[22]; 𝔊 Αδ(δ)ω; = יֶעְדּוֹ 2 Ch 9[29], Ιωηλ(δ).

עֹדֵד v. עוד.

†I. **עָדָה** **vb. pass on, advance** (Ar. عَدَا (عدو) *pass by,* also *run* = Eth. **ዐደወ**: *pass by;* Aram. עדי *go along, go by* (oft. for Heb. עָבַר), Aph. *remove;* Syr. ܥܕܐ *pass by, come,* c. ܥܠ *fall upon*);—**Qal** *Pf.* 3 ms. עָדָה Jb 28[8] the fierce lion *hath not advanced* upon it (sc. the way). **Hiph.** *Pt.* מַעֲדֶה בֶּגֶד Pr 25[20] *removing a garment* (cf. Gn 38[19] 𝔗, Jon 3[6] Heb. and 𝔗).

†I. עַד and וָעֶד (so alw.) **n.m. perpetuity** (=*advancing* time, cf. As. *adû, time, at the present time*);—**1.** of *past time:* מִנִּי עַד Jb 20[4]; הררי עד Hb 3[6] *ancient mountains* (cf. עולם **1**). **2.** of *future time,* לָעַד (usu. לָעַד) *for ever:* **a.** during lifetime, of king ψ 21[7] Pr 29[14]; of others ψ 9[19] 22[27] 61[9] Pr 12[19]. **b.** of things, לָעַד בַּצּוּר יֵחָצְבוּן Jb 19[24]. **c.** *of continuous existence,* of nations, נִבְרֶכֶת עַד (of Babylon, cf. עולם **2 c**) Is 47[7] (yet v. III. עַד **II 3**); anger, לעד Am 1[11]; elsewh. עֲדֵי עַד ψ 83[18] 92[8] Is 26[4] 65[18]. **d.** of divine existence, שֹׁכֵן עַד Is 57[15]; attributes, לָעַד ψ 111[3.10] 112[3.9]; residence in Zion, עֲדֵי עַד 132[14]; law of God, לָעַד 19[10]; promise as to dynasty of David, לָעַד 89[30]; עֲדֵי עַד 132[12]; inheritance of land, לָעַד 37[29]; continuous relations between God and his people 1 Ch 28[9] Is 64[8] Mi 7[18] לָעַד. **e.** phrases (see עולם **2 m**): (לְ)עוֹלָם וָעֶד ψ 9[6] 10[16] 21[5] 45[7.18] 48[15] 52[10] 104[5] 119[44] 145[1.2.21] Ex 15[18] Mi 4[5] Dn 12[3]; לָעַד לְעוֹלָם ψ 111[8] 148[6]; עַד־עוֹלְמֵי עַד Is 45[17].—Is 30[8] rd. (עַד־עוֹלָם) לְעֵד *for a witness* (𝔖 𝔙 𝔗 Ges Ew Di Che Du) for MT לָעַד.

†II. עַד **n.[m.] booty, prey** (upon which one *advances, falls*);—יֹאכַל עַד Gn 49[27] *devour prey* (‖ שָׁלָל); עַד שָׁלָל מַרְבֶּה Is 33[23] *prey of great spoil;* קוּמִי לְעַד Zp 3[8] (of God) my *rising up to the prey* (Br[MP]); אֲבִי עַד Is 9[5] *father* (i.e. *distributor*) *of booty* (Hi Kn Kue Br[MP] Du Che[Hpt]; > Ges Ew Di al. *everlasting father*).

III. עַד, in poetry עֲדֵי (+Nu 24[20.24] ψ 104[23] 147[6] Jb 7[4] 20[5], and in עֲדֵי עַד Is 26[4] 65[18] ψ 83[18] 92[8] 132[12.14]: cf. אֱלֵי, עֲלֵי), **prep. as far as, even to, up to, until, while** (Aram. עַד, ܥܕܡܐ; Sab. עד, עדי, Mordtm[ZMG xxx (1876), 27]; DHM[xxxvii (1883), 414], As. *adi* Dl[§ 81 a] (Ar. عَدَا is *except*); perh. akin to عَدَا *pass on, advance to,* Kö[ii. 304, 309]: עֲדֵי prob. from ground-form *ʿădăy,* Ol[428, 431] Kö[ii. 309 ff.]; but Lag[Sym. ii. 101–3, Mitth. i. 231 f.], as plur. like אַחֲרֵי);—with sf. עָדַי Nu 23[18]+, עָדֶיךָ Mi 4[8]+, etc., עֲדֵיכֶם +Jb 32[12]; 2 K 9[18] עַד־הֵם occurs;

—*as far as, even to* (differing from אֶל, in that the limit is *included*, as in Ar. حَتَّى Fl Kl Schr i. 402 f). **I. prep. 1** of *space*.—**a.** Gn 11[31] ויבאו עד חרן *as far as* Haran, 12[6] 13[3.12] + oft, Is 8[8] עד צואר יגיע, 15[4] עד יהץ נשמע קולם, 25[12] 26[5] באו מים עד נפש, 69[2] אמונתך עד שחקים ψ 36[6] (cf Jon 2[6] Mi 1[9] Je 4[10.18]), 90[3] תָּשֵׁב אנוש עד דַּכָּא, Jb 11[7], etc, pregn. ψ 118[27] אִסְרוּ חַג עד וגו׳ *bind* (and lead) *up to* ..; Is 57[9] עד מרחוק *even to* afar (מן **1 c**), with the goal a *person*, Ex 22[8] עד עָדֶיךָ כָּל־בָּשָׂר 65[3] ψ 1 S 9[9], האלהים יָבֹא דבר שניהם, Is 45[24] Jb 4[5], יָבֹא, Ho 14[2] שוב עד י׳ *al* (v שׁוּב, stronger than שׁוּב אל־י׳), poet Nu 24[20] ואחריתו עֲדֵי אבד shall be *even unto* destruction, shall issue in destruction, v[24]; rarely with verbs of *attending*, עד הֶאֱזִין + Nu 23[18], התבונן עד + Jb 32[12] 38[18] (usu אֶל) Before another prep., 1 S 7[11] עד מתחת ל׳, 1 K 4[12] עד מֵעֵבֶר ל׳, עד מעל Ez 41[20], עד אֱלֵיהֶם Est 4[2], and even (si vera l) עד לפני 2 K 9[20] cf עד נֶגֶד Ne 3[16.26], עד נֹכַח Ju 19[10] +.

b. In the combin מִן ... עַד(וְ), as Gn 10[19] מצידון *from* Sidon ... עד עַזָּה *as far as* Gaza + oft (v מן **5 a**), and idiom, not of actual space, but of *classes of objects*, to express the idea of *both* .. *and*, as Gn 19[4] מִנַּעַר וְעַד זָקֵן *from* young *to* old (inclusively) = *both* young *and* old (v. מן **5 b**); without מִן, *even to* = *including*, Lv 11[42] Nu 8[4] *even to* (i e. including) its base and its flowers, cf 1 S 18[4].

2. Of *time*: **a.** (*a*) *even to, until* Gn 8[5] *even to* the 10th month, Ex 12[6] *unto* the 14th day, etc, v[15.18], etc; עד היום *unto this day*, Gn 19[37.38], עד היום הזה 26[33] 32[33], both + oft; עד יום sq inf. Ex 40[37] Jos 6[10] Ju 18[30], עד בקר *till* morning, Ex 12[10] + (15 t), עד הבקר 16[23] + (11 t), so עד (ה)ערב Ex 18[13.14] +, poet עֲדֵי ערב ψ 104[23], עד עולם Gn 13[15] + oft, עד שֶׁבַע פְּעָמִים 2 K 4[35], עד דור וָדוֹר Is 13[20], v. also בְּלִי, and בִּלְתִּי, *ad fin* And sq another prep, Lv 23[16] עד מִמָּחֳרַת הַשַּׁבָּת, Ne 13[9] עד אַחַר הַשַּׁבָּת With the force of *against*, Ju 6[31] יוּמַת עד הַבֹּקֶר; cf (*b*) *end*. (*b*) sq inf, both of past time, as Gn 8[7] 32[35] עד עֲלוֹת הַשָּׁחַר, 33[3] 34[5], and esp. of future time, as 3[19] עד שׁוּבְךָ *until* thy returning, 19[22] 27[44] Dt 7[20.23] 20[20] 22[2] 28[20.22],—both + oft; cf עד תֻּמָּם Ju 3[25] +; עד תם... Lv 25[29] + 10t., עד בוש Dt 2[15] +; עד כַּלֵּה + 2 K 13[17.19] Ezr 9[14]; עד כַּלּוֹתָ(ם) 1 S 15[18] Je 9[15] +, עד אוֹר הַבֹּקֶר, Ju 16[2] +; also in עד השמדך אתם Dt 7[24] (cf. 28[48] Jos 11[14] 1 K 15[29] 2 K 3[25] 10[17] 24[20] [|| Je 52[3] השליכו]; on the anom ה׳, v Dr, rd prob. הַ׳), and most prob. (cf Ko iii 583) in עד בִּלְתִּי השאיר לו (לָהֶם) שָׂרִיד Dt 3[3] (v. Dr), + 5 t (v supr. p. 117), rd prob. הַשְׁאִיר.

With the force of *towards the end of, against*, esp. in עד בֹּא(ם), Gn 43[25] Ex 22[25] Nu 10[21] והקימו את המשכן עד באם used to set up the tab *against* their coming, 2 K 16[11], Ez 33[22], cf. 2 S 17[22] Ellipt. Ju 16[2] עד אוֹר הַבֹּקֶר וַהֲרַגְנֻהוּ (wait) *till* the morning dawn, and we slay him! (GFM; Dr[§ 115]). (*c*) with various adverbs of time (q v), as עד הֵנָּה, עד מָתַי, עַד־מָה, עד אָנָה, עד עַתָּה, עד כֵּן, עד כה, cf עד כַּמֶּה פְעָמִים (v מָה **4 b**) (*d*) to suggest also *degree* (cf **3**), עד אין מָקוֹם *until* there is no place Is 5[8], עד אֵין מספר + ψ 40[13] Jb 5[9] 9[10]; cf. Lv 26[18] ואם־עד־אלה and if *even up to these things*, even the end of all these punishments, you do not hearken to me.

b. *During* (rare; prop. *as far as* the limit indicated, including the time previous, cf ἕως: so oft Aram עַד, حتى, *while*), 2 K 9[22] what is peace עד זנוני איזבל *during*, etc? Jb 20[5] עֲדֵי רָגַע *during* a moment, sq. inf. Ju 3[26] עד הִתְמַהְמְהָם *during* their delaying, Ex 33[22] Jb 7[19] עד בִּלְעִי רֻקִּי Jon 4[2].

3. Of *degree*, to suggest a higher or the highest; as עד מְאֹד *even to* muchness, i e. exceedingly (v. מאד), עד מְהֵרָה *even to* haste + ψ 147[15]; Est 5[6] וּמַה־בַּקָּשָׁתֵךְ עַד־חֲצִי הַמַּלְכוּת וְתֵעָשׂ, v[3] 7[2]. See also עד ל, below. With a neg, to express *not even as much as*, Dt 2[5] לא אתן לכם מארצם עד מדרך כַּף רָגֶל, and with אֶחָד, + Ex 9[7] לֹא מֵת ... עַד־אֶחָד, simil. 14[28] Ju 4[16] 2 S 17[22] (rd אֶחָד for אַחַד: v Dr) Sts almost = Lat. *adeo*, 1 S 2[5] (si vera l.) עד עֲקָרָה ילדה שבעה *even to* the barren, she hath borne seven, i e *even* the barren hath, etc, Jb 25[5] הֵן עַד־יָרֵחַ ולא יאהיל, Hg 2[19]. In comparisons, *to the degree of, even like* (rare), Na 1[10] עד סירים סְבֻכִים (text dub.) entangled *even like* thorns, 1 Ch 4[27] לא הרבו עד בני יהודה did not multiply *to the degree of* (i e. *like*), etc Cf. 2 S 23[19] עד הַשְּׁלֹשָׁה לֹא בָא did not *attain* (in prowess) *unto* the three.

II. Conj. 1. *until*:—**a.** עד אֲשֶׁר *until that*: (*a*) with pf., of *past time*, Ex 32[20] ויטחן עד אשר דק (Dt 9[21]), Dt 2[14] עד אשר עָבַרְנוּ, Jos 3[17] 8[26] Ju 4[24] 1 K 10[7] (2 Ch 9[6]), 2 K 17[20.23] 21[16]; with suggestion of *degree*, 1 S 30[4] (sq. אין), 1 K 17[17]; rarely of *future* time (the 'future perfect,' Dr[§ 17]), 2 S 17[13] (of degree), Ez 34[21]. So עד שֶׁ־ (oft. in NH; v. שֶׁ), + Ju 5[7] Ct 3[4.4], + Gn 26[13] עד כִּי־גָדֵל מְאֹד, 41[49] 2 S 23[10] עד כִּי

2 Ch 26^{15}; and (of future time) עַד אֲשֶׁר אִם †Gn 28^{15} Nu 32^{17} Is 6^{11}. (*b*) with impf., usu. of *future* time, Gn 27^{44} עַד אֲשֶׁר תָּשׁוּב חֲמַת אָחִיךָ, 29^{8} Ex 23^{30} 24^{14} Lv 22^{4} Nu 11^{20} 20^{17} 1 S 22^{3} Ho 5^{15}+; rarely of *past* time, Jon 4^{5} עד אשר יראה *till he should* see, Ec 2^{3}. So (of the future) עַד שֶׁ- †Ct $2^{7.17}$ 3^{5} 4^{6} 8^{4} ψ 123^{2}; and עַד כִּי †Gn 49^{10} עַד כִּי־יָבֹא שִׁילֹה.

b. עַד alone, *until:* (*a*) with pf., of *past* time, Jos 2^{22} 4^{23} עַד־עָבְרֵנוּ, 1 S 20^{41} עַד דָּוִד הִגְדִּיל, 2 S 21^{10} 1 K 11^{16} Ez 28^{15}; of the *future* (rare), 2 K 7^{3} עַד מַתְנוּ, Ez 39^{15} Dn 11^{36} עַד כָּלָה זַעַם. So עַד אִם (of the fut.), †Gn $24^{19.33}$ Is 30^{17} Ru 2^{21}. (*b*) with impf., of *future* time, 1 S 1^{22} (ellipt.: cf. Ju 16^{2}, **I 2 a** (*b*) *end*), Is 22^{14} 26^{20} 32^{15} $62^{1.7}$ ψ 57^{2} 71^{18} Jb 27^{5}+; of the *past* (rare), Ex 15^{16} עד יעבור עמך, v^{16} Jos 10^{13} (poet.) עַד יִקֹּם גּוֹי אֹיְבָיו, ψ 73^{17}.—N.B. In poetry, עַד is sts. used to mark not an absolute close, but an epoch, or turning-point, in the fut., as ψ 110^{1} (v. De) עַד אָשִׁית אֹיְבֶיךָ הֲדֹם לְרַגְלֶיךָ, Ho 10^{12} Jb 14^{6} (but v. **3**); after a neg. cl., Gn 49^{10} Nu 23^{24} Is 42^{4} ψ 71^{18} 112^{8} Jb 8^{21} (but rd. prob. with Ew Hi Di Du *al.* עֹד he will *yet*, etc., understanding v^{20} as present, not future).

2. *While* (rare: cf. **I 2 b**):—**a.** with pf., 1 S 14^{19} עַד דִּבֶּר שָׁאוּל *while* Saul spake. **b.** with impf., ψ 141^{10} יַחַד אָנֹכִי עַד אֶעֱבוֹר *while I* at the same time pass by. **c.** with ptcp., Jb 1^{18} עַד זֶה מְדַבֵּר (but rd. prob. עֹד, as v$^{16.17}$), Ne 7^{3}. **d.** עַד שֶׁ- (without vb.) †Ct 1^{12}. So עַד לֹא *while not*=*ere yet* (of past time) †Pr 8^{26} עד לא עשה ארץ (so עַד לָא, ܥܕ ܠܐ, oft., e.g. Gn 24^{15} 𝔗, Mt 1^{18}); and עד אשר לא (of the fut.) †Ec $12^{1.2.6}$ (cf. Talm. עַד דְּלָא, Mishn. עַד שֶׁלֹּא).

3. Of degree, *to the point that, so that even* (rare), Is 47^{7} Thou saidst, I shall be for ever a lady, עַד לֹא שַׂמְתְּ אֵלֶּה עַל לִבֵּךְ *to the point that* (going so far in thy pride that) thou didst not, etc. (but Hi Che Du *al.* join גְּבֶרֶת עַד I shall be for ever, a lady *perpetually;* v. 1. עַד); Jb 14^{6} (Di De Bu Du) *to the point that* he may enjoy, etc., Is 22^{14} (Du). In Jos 17^{14} עַד אֲשֶׁר עַד כֹּה בֵּרְכַנִי י׳, rd. עַל אֲשֶׁר *because* that (Ges Buhl; cf. Di).

†**III.** עַד לְ, a strengthened form for עַד, found chiefly in Ch Ezr, and occurring in most of the above senses. Thus **1.** of *space:* עַד לְבוֹא חֲמָת Jos 13^{5} Ju 3^{3} 1 Ch 13^{5}, עד ל׳ מִדְבָּרָה 5^{9}, עד ל׳ מצרים 2 Ch 26^{8}; עַד לְמִזְרַח הַגַּיְא 1 Ch 4^{39}, עַד לְמִצָּד 12^{17}; עַד לְנֶגֶר 2 Ch 14^{12}; עַד לְשָׁמַיִם 2 Ch 28^{9} Ezr 9^{6}.

2. Of *time:* עד לעולם 1 Ch 23^{25} 28^{7}; עד לְמֵרָחוֹק 2 Ch 26^{15} Ezr 3^{13}; Ezr 9^{4} עד למנחת הערב; עַד לַדָּבָר הַזֶּה Ezr 10^{14} prob. *during* (Keil: Ges Be *with regard to*, strengthened for לְ); sq. inf. עַד לַעֲלוֹת הַמִּנְחָה 1 K 18^{29}; עַד לְכַלּוֹת 1 Ch 28^{20} 2 Ch 29^{28}; עַד לְכַלֵּה 2 Ch 24^{10} 31^{1}; עד להשחית 26^{16}; עַד לָמוּת 32^{24} (‖ 2 K 20^{1} לָמוּת alone); Ezr 10^{14} עד להשיב.

3. Of *degree:* עַד לְמַחֲנֶה גָדוֹל *even unto* (till there was) a great camp, 1 Ch 12^{23}; עַד לְמַעְלָה =*exceedingly* 2 Ch 16^{12} 17^{12} 26^{8}; עַד לִמְאֹד 2 Ch 16^{14}; עַד לְשִׂמְחָה 29^{30}; עַד לָרֹב 31^{30}; עַד לְאֵין מַרְפֵּא 36^{16}.

†עֲדֶנָּה Ec 4^{2} Baer Ginsb (al. עֲדֶנָּה), abbrev. עֲדֶן Ec 4^{3} (from עַד־הֵנָּה, עַד־הֵן; cf. NH עֲדַיִן, e.g. Ned. 9^{10}), **adv. hitherto, still.**

†II. עָדָה **vb. ornament, deck oneself** (Aram. in deriv. עִידּוּת, *ornament;* cf. perh. עֲדִיתָא, *scurf, scab;* Ar. عَدْوَى *mange, scab*, etc. [as sheathing, or excrescence?], also عِدَّى, *broad stone* for covering grave, etc., Lane 1979);—**Qal** *Pf.* 2 fs. וְעָדִית Ez 23^{40}; *Impf.* 3 fs. תַּעְדֶּה Is 61^{10}, וַתַּעַד Ho 2^{15}; 2 fs. תַּעְדִּי Je 4^{30} 31^{4}, וַתַּעְדִּי Ez 16^{13}; 1 s. sf. וָאֶעְדֵּךְ v^{11}; *Imv.* ms. עֲדֵה־נָא Jb 40^{10};—*ornament;* usu. **1. a.** reflex., *deck oneself* with, c. acc. of (woman's) ornaments, of bride Is 61^{10} (sim.; cf. הִלְבִּישׁ v^{a}); fig. of Isr. Ho 2^{15} Je 31^{4}; Jerus. Je 4^{30} (c. acc. cogn.; ‖ לָבַשׁ), Ez 16^{13} (מַלְבּוּשֵׁךְ in ‖ clause), 23^{40} (c. acc. cogn.). **b.** metaph., עֲדֵה־נָא גָאוֹן וגו׳ Jb 40^{10} *deck now thyself* [Job] *with majesty.* **2.** c. 2 acc., וָאֶעְדֵּךְ עֶדִי Ez 16^{11} *and I decked thee* [Jerus.] *with finery* (? rd. **Hiph.** וָאַ׳).

†עָדָה **n.pr.f.** (*ornament;* or (Ar. غُدْوَةٌ, غَدْوَةٌ) *morning*) 𝔊 Αδ(δ)α;—wife, **1.** of Lamech Gn $4^{19.20.23}$ (J). **2.** of Esau $36^{2.4.10.12.16}$ (P^{R}).

†עֲדִי **n.[m.] coll. ornaments** (with which one is *decked*);—ע׳ abs. Is 49^{18}, עֶדִי Ez 16^{11} 23^{40}; cstr. 2 S 1^{24}+; sf. עֶדְיוֹ Ex 33^{4}+, עֶדְיְךָ Ex 33^{5}, etc.;—*ornaments:* **1.** of women 2 S 1^{24} (ע׳ זָהָב), Je 2^{32}; of Jerus. under fig. of woman 4^{30} (ע׳ זָהָב), Ez 16^{11} 23^{40} (all acc. cogn. c. עָדָה), Is 49^{18} (sim.).—עֲדִי עֲדָיִים Ez 16^{7}, rd. prob. עַד עִדִּים *unto menstruation* (maturity), JDMich Co Berthol (rdg. בְּעֵת עִד׳), Toy. עֶדְיֵךְ ψ 103^{5} [sf. ref. to נַפְשִׁי] is dub., 𝔊 τ. ἐπιθυμίαν σου [rdg. אַוָּתֵךְ? this usu. c.

[נֶפֶשׁ], *thine age, prime* (cf I. עַד) JDMich Thes, conject in Hup-Now Che Du. **2.** of men Ex 33[4.5.6] (JE) **3.** in gen, as feeding pride Ez 7[20] (צבי עדיו, sf. ref to silver and gold, v[19]). **4** *trappings* of horse ψ 32[9] (De Hup, cf Du), si vera l, but prob corrupt, Che (after v Ortenb) לבלם עד יובל אליך must be curbed *till he can be brought*, etc.

†עֲדִיאֵל **n.pr.m.** (*an ornament is Ēl*; cf Sab n. pr עדאל Hal[51,2]),—**1.** a Simeonite 1 Ch 4[36], 𝔊A Εδιηλ, 𝔊L Αδαηλ. **2** a priest 9[12], 𝔊 Αδιηλ. **3.** father of officer, David's time 27[25], 𝔊 Ωδιηλ —Cf Gray[Prop. N 225, 231].

†עֲדָיָה(וּ) **n.pr.m.** (*'י has decked himself*);— **1** עֲדָיָהוּ father of a Judaean captain 2 Ch 23[1], 𝔊 Αζεια, A Αδαια, 𝔊L Αδαιου (genit). Elsewhere עֲדָיָה **2.** grandfather of Josiah 2 K 22[1], 𝔊 Εδεινα, A Ιεδιδα, 𝔊L Οζιου (genit). **3** a Levite 1 Ch 6[26], 𝔊 Αζεια, A 𝔊L Αδ(α)ια. **4.** a Benjamite 8[21], 𝔊 Αβια, A Αλαια, 𝔊L Αδαια **5.** a priest 9[12] Ne 11[12], 𝔊 Αδαια(ς). **6.** two with foreign wives: **a.** Ezr 10[29], 𝔊 Αδα, 𝔊L Αδαιας. **b.** v[39], 𝔊 Αδαια, 𝔊L Αδδαιας. **7.** a Judahite Ne 11[5], 𝔊 Οζ(ε)ια, 𝔊L Αδαια

†עֲדִיתַיִם **n pr loc.** town of Judah in the שְׁפֵלָה Jos 15[36], 𝔊A Αδιαθαειμ, 𝔊L Αγεθθαιμ

I. עֵדָה v יעד. II III עֵדָה v עוד

[עֲדָה], עדו(א) v עדד. עדות עֵדֻת v. עוד.

עֲדִי, עֲדִיאֵל, עֲדָיָה(וּ) v II עדה.

עדיא v עדוא עדים v עֲדָה

עֲדִיתַיִם v עדה.

I עדל (√ of foll, poss. = Ar عَدَلَ *act equitably* (so Thes), or As *edlu, hero*)

†עַדְלַי **n.pr.m.** 1 Ch 27[29], 𝔊 Αδαι, 𝔊L Αδλι.

II עדל (√ of foll; cf Ar عَدَلَ *turn aside*, whence עֲדֻלָּם = *retreat, refuge*, so Lag[BN 54], cf. Dr[Sm p 293] Buhl[Geogr 97])

†עֲדֻלָּם **n.pr.loc.** old Canaanite city,-𝔊 Οδολλαμ, with king Jos 12[15] (D), in the שְׁפֵלָה 15[35] (P, 𝔊L Αδυλαμ), cf Mi 1[15] Ne 11[30], (re-) built by Rehob acc to 2 Ch 11[7] (Οδολαμ), מְעָרַת ע' (rd מְצֻדַת, מצדת, v מְעָרָה sub I ערר) 1 S 22[1] 2 S 23[13] 1 Ch 11[15], site prob *'Îd-el-Mîye* (*'Aid el-Ma*), c. 13 miles WSW from Bethlehem, v GASm[Geogr 229] Buhl[Geogr 193] and reff

†עֲדֻלָּמִי **adj gent.** Adullamite,—איש ע' Gn 38[1], הָע' as subst. v[12 20]

I. עדן (√ of foll, cf. Ar. عَدَنَ *mollities, languor*, etc, Frey (Kam); Palm עדנא (good) *fortune* Cook[89], NH עידון *luxuriousness*).

†I [עֵדֶן] **n [m.] luxury, dainty, delight,**—pl abs עֲדָנִים *luxuries* 2 S 1[24] si vera l. (rd. perh סְדִינִים [v. סָדִין] Klo Gr HPS), pl sf. Je 51[34] he hath filled his belly מֵעֲדָנָי *from my dainties* (fig. of Nebuchad's plunder; Gie reads מֵעֲדָנַי), 𝔗 Gf Rothst join with foll: *from my dainties hath he thrust me forth*; fig of *delights* of worshipping 'י, ψ 36[9] נַחַל עֲדָנֶיךָ ‖ (דֶשֶׁן בֵּיתֶךָ)

†[עָדַן] **vb.denom. Hithp. luxuriate** (NH Pi *delight* (act), so Syr (ܥܕܢ),—*Impf.* 3 mpl. וַיִּתְעַדְּנוּ בְּטוּבְךָ Ne 9[25] *and they luxuriated in thy great goodness* (+ וַיֹּאכְלוּ וַיִּשְׂבְּעוּ וַיַּשְׁמִינוּ).

†II עֵדֶן **n.pr.m.** Levite name 2 Ch 29[12] (𝔊 Ιω(α)δαν), 31[15] (𝔊 Οδομ, 𝔊L Ιαδαν).

†עַדְנָא **n.pr m. 1.** man with foreign wife Ezr 10[30] (Ginsb, עֲדְנָה van d. H. Baer), 𝔊 Αιδαινε, 𝔊L Εδνα **2** Ne 12[5], 𝔊א Αδανας, 𝔊L Εδνας.

†עֶדְנָה **n.f delight**,—Gn 18[12] (sexual).

†עַדְנָה **n.pr.m. 1.** a prince of Judah 2 Ch 17[14], 𝔊 Εδνα(α)ς. **2.** a Manassite 1 Ch 12[21], prob. (rdg. 'ע, with Codd., for עַדְנַח, van d H. עַדְנַח, 𝔊 Εδνα) —Vid also עַדְנָא.

†I [עָדִין] **adj. voluptuous**,—fs עֲדִינָה as subst Is 47[8], of Bab personified, (thou) *voluptuous one*.—עדינו העצנו 2 S 23[8], read עוֹרֵר אֶת־ חֲנִיתוֹ, ‖ 1 Ch 11[11] Th We Dr, cf Ginsb[note].

†II עָדִין **n.pr.m. 1.** in בְּנֵי ע', returned exiles Ezr 2[15] = Ne 7[20], Ezr 8[6], 𝔊 Αδ(δ)ιν, Ηδ(ε)ιν, etc **2.** a chief Ne 10[17], 𝔊 Ηδ(ε)ιν, Αδειν.

†עֲדִינָא **n.pr.m.** Reubenite captain, David's time, acc to 1 Ch 11[42], 𝔊 Αδ(ε)ινα.

†[מַעֲדָן] **n.[m.] dainty** (food), **delight**;—only pl, —מַעֲדַנֵּי מֶלֶךְ Gn 49[20] (poem) *royal dainties*, הָאֹכְלִים לְמַעֲדַנִּים La 4[5] those who ate (*acc to dainties*) *daintily*, more gen. וְיִתֵּן מַעֲדַנִּים לְנַפְשֶׁךָ Pr 29[17] he shall give *delight* to thy soul (‖ וִינִיחֶךָ)—מַעֲדַנּוֹת, v. p 588, also sub ענד.

II. עדן (√ of foll, cf. perh. As. *edinu*, *plain* (in word-lists), Schr[COT Gn 2, 8], Dl[Pa 79 f.]; other views v. Di[Gn 2, 8])

† III. עֵ֫דֶן **n.pr.terr.** (prob. associated by Heb with I. עֵדֶן),—district in which lay garden of י׳, home of Adam and Eve: וַיִּטַּע גַּן־בְּעֵדֶן Gn 2[8], river יֹצֵא מֵע׳ v[10], קִדְמַת־ע׳ 4[16], גַּן־ע׳ 2[15] 3[23.24] (all 𝔊 Εδεμ), cf. כְּגַן־ע׳ Ez 36[35] Jo 2[3] and כְּע׳ Is 51[3] (‖ כְּגַן־י׳), all sim. of fertility; ע׳ גַּן־אלהים Ez 28[13], עֲצֵי ע׳ אֲשֶׁר בְּגַן הָאֱלֹהִים 31[9], עֲצֵי ע׳ v[16.18.18] (𝔊 Ez Jo ἡ τρυφή; Is παράδεισος).

† עֵ֫דֶן **n.pr. (? urb. et) terr.** conquered by Assyria (prob = IV. עֶדֶן; pointed עֵדֶן, to differentiate from III ע׳, cf WMM[As u. Eur 291]);—בְּנֵי־ע׳ 2 K 19[12] (𝔊 υἱοὺς Ἔδεμ) = Is 37[12] (in Telassar), ע׳ alone Ez 27[23] (+ חָרָן וְכַנֵּה), prob. = (Bit-)Adini on Middle Euphrates Schr[COT 2 K 19,12] Dl[Pa 263 f] — בֵּית ע׳, v p. 112

עֵדֶן, עֲדֶ֫נָה v עַד prep. sub I. עדה

עַדְנָח v. עַדְנָה sub I עדן.

עֲדַעְדָּה v. II עֲרוֹעֵר sub II. ערר.

† [עָדַף] **vb. remain over, be in excess,** syn. of סרח q v., only Pt (NH id., Aram. עֲדִיף superior (to), Ar عَدَفَ be profuse, IV let down veil, or curtain, etc, عَدَفٌ plentifulness),—**Qal** *Pt* סֶרַח הָעֹדֵף Ex 26[12] *the surplus* (of curtains) *that remains over,* so f. הָעֹדֶפֶת v[12], and הָעֹדֵף as subst v[13] *the excess* in (ב) length; הָעֹדֵף = *the surplus* of food Ex 16[23], of price of field Lv 25[27]; הָעֹדְפִים עַל־ *those over and above,* Nu 3[46.49], cf v[48] (no עַל־) **Hiph.** *Pf* 3 ms הֶעְדִּיף Ex 16[18] *have a surplus* (of manna; opp. הֶחְסִיר).

† I [עָדַר] **vb.** prob (si vera l) **help** (Aram loan-word, Syr. ܥܕܰܪ, 𝔗 עֲדַר (rare) = Heb. עזר q.v, > Thes, assuming mng. *arrange, order*),—**Qal** *Inf. cstr* לַעְדֹּר I Ch 12[34] (Baer Ginsb; van d H v[33], this mng also 𝔊 𝔙); but < Codd. לַעֲזֹר (cf v[18.22.23], van d. H. v[17.21.22]), so Kau Buhl, *Pt* pl cstr עֹדְרֵי מַעֲרָכָה v[39] (van d. H. v[38]), rd. עֹרְכֵי (q v v[34]) 𝔊 Kau; see ערך.

† עַדְרִיאֵל **n.pr.m.** son-in-law of Saul (appar. Aram. name, *my help is God* = Heb. עזריאל q v; so Ne[Am Jour Sem. Lang. xiii (1897), 173] HPS cf Gray[Prop N 309], cf. OAram. יעדראל ClGann [JAs. 1883, Fev Mar, 139, No 13]);—I S 18[19] (𝔊A Ἰηλ, 𝔊L Εδριηλ), 2 S 21[8] (𝔊 Σερει, A Εσδρι, 𝔊L Εζρι).

† II [עָדַר] **vb. hoe** (NH *id.*; so Ar. (in Syria) عَدَرَ, مِعْدُور *pick, hoe,* Cuche (معدور also Dozy[ii. 101b]); cf Fl[Kl Schr ii 629]),—**Niph.** *Impf.* 3 ms. לֹא יֵעָדֵר Is 5[6] *it* (the vineyard) *shall not be hoed* (‖ יִזָּמֵר); 3 mpl בַּמַּעְדֵּר יֵעָדֵרוּן 7[25] which *used to be hoed with the hoe* (subj הֶהָרִים).

† מַעְדֵּר **n.[m.]** hoe Is 7[25], v foregoing.

† III. [עָדַר] **vb. Niph. be lacking, fail** (Ar. عَدِرَ *remain or lag behind*),—**Niph.** *Pf*, all c לֹא, 3 ms נֶעְדַּר לָהֶם I S 30[19] not anything *was lacking to them*, נֶעְדָּר none *was lacking* 2 S 17[22] Is 40[26]; of י׳, Zp 3[5] *he doth not fail;* 3 fs נֶעְדָּרָה Is 34[16] no wild beast *is lacking. Pt.* f. נֶעְדֶּרֶת Is 59[15] truth has become *lacking* **Pi.** *Impf.* 3 mpl. לֹא יְעַדְּרוּ דָּבָר I K 5[7] *they left nothing lacking*

† I. עֵ֫דֶר **n.m.**[Gn 29,2] **flock, herd** (NH *id.;* Aram עֶדְרָא, on 𝔊 Γαδερ Gn 35[16] (= 𝔖 v[21]) v. Lag[BN 76 f.], who assigns ע׳ therefore, plausibly, to III עדר (عدر), as *lagging, loitering*);—ע׳ abs Gn 32[17.17] +, cstr. Ct 4[1] +; sf עֶדְרוֹ Is 40[11] +; pl. עֲדָרִים Gn 29[2] +, cstr עֶדְרֵי Mi 5[7] +, etc.,— **1.** *flock:* **a.** of sheep, ע׳ צֹאן Gn 29[2] (J), Mi 5[7], ע׳ הַצֹּ׳ Jo 1[18], cf. Gn 29[2.3.8] 30[4] (all J), I S 17[34] Je 51[23] Mal 1[14]; ‖ צֹאן Ez 34[12] (sim), Pr 27[23]; ע׳ הָרְחֵלִים Ct 6[6] = 4[2] (ins. prob הָר׳), בהמה + 2 Ch 32[28]; sign of desolation Is 17[2] 32[14] (מרעה ע׳), Zp 2[14] Je 6[3], of peace 31[24], in sim. also Mi 2[12] Je 31[10] ψ 78[52], fig. of Isr. Is 40[11] Je 13[20] (‖ צאן), ע׳ יהוה v[17], so עֶדְרוֹ Zc 10[3]. **b.** of goats, ע׳ הָעִזִּים Ct 4[1] 6[5] **c.** undefined Ju 5[16] Jb 24[2] Ct 1[7] **2.** *herds, flocks and herds.* **a.** incl. sheep, cattle, etc, Gn 32[17.17.17.17.20] (cf. v[14]; all E) **b.** specif. ע׳ בָּקָר Jo 1[18].—מִגְדַּל־עֵדֶר v p. 154 supr.

† II. עֵ֫דֶר **n.pr.m.** (cf. Nab n pr עדרו = Ar. عَدَرٌ Lzb[337]),—a Levite I Ch 23[23] 24[30], 𝔊 Αιδαθ, Ηλα, A 𝔊L Εδερ

† III. עֵ֫דֶר **n.pr.loc.** in extreme S of Judah Jos 15[21], site unknown; 𝔊 Αρα, A Εδραι, 𝔊L Εβερ.

† [עֵ֫דֶר] **n.pr.m.** a Benjamite, עֵ֫דֶר I Ch 8[15]; 𝔊 Ωδηδ, A Ωδερ, 𝔊L Αδαρ.

† [עֲדָשָׁה] **n f. lentile** (NH עֲדָשָׁה *id.;* Low No 140, Ar. عَدَسٌ; on formation v. Lag[BN 60]);—pl. עֲדָשִׁים growing 2 S 23[11]; art. of food, 2 S 17[28] Ez 4[9], נְזִיד ע׳ Gn 25[34] (J) *pottage of lentiles.*

עַוָּא v עִוָּה.

עוב (√ of foll.; cf. Ar. غيب, عَابَ *be absent, hidden,* of sun, *set;* غَابَةٌ *hidden place, thicket, wood,* so Syr. ܥܒܐ; hence *obscuring clouds,* cf NH עָב, Aram עֵיבָא *cloud(s)*).

II. **עָב** $_{33}$ **n.m.**$^{Is 19,1}$ and (1 K 18^{44} Ko$^{Synt 163}$) **f.** **dark cloud, cloud-mass, thicket**,—ע׳ abs 1 K 18^{44}+, cstr Is 18^{4} Pr 16^{15}; pl עָבִים Ju 5^{4}+, עָבוֹת 2 S 23^{4} ψ 77^{18}, cstr עָבֵי 2 S 22^{12} ψ 18^{12}, sf עָבָיו ψ 18^{13} (but prob. del, v עבר **Qal** ad fin),—**1.** *dark cloud* **a.** rain-cloud Ju 5^{4} Is 5^{6} 1 K 18$^{44.45}$+9 t. **b.** as high Is 14^{14} Jb 20^{6}, +Ez 19^{11} 31$^{3.10.14}$ (rdg עָבוֹת, v. עבת) **c.** chariot of י׳ Is 19^{1} ψ 104^{3}, covering his eyes Jb 22^{14} **d.** casting shadow Is 25^{5}, cf 2 S 23^{4} **e.** as swift Is 60^{8}, and transient 44^{22} Jb 30^{15} (all sim) **f.** disposed by God Jb 36^{29} 37^{16} **g.** ע׳ טַל Is 18^{4} *cloud of dew, dew-mist* (sim) **2.** (cloud-) *mass*, ע׳ שְׁחָקִים 2 S 22^{12} *masses of clouds* (enwrapping י׳)=ψ 18^{12} (v^{13} v supr) **3.** *thicket* as refuge Je 4^{29} (perh under Aram influence) — עָב Ex 19^{9} v עָבִי sub עבה I עָב v p 713 supr

†[**עִיב**] **vb. denom Hiph.** becloud, *Impf* 3 ms יָעִיב בְּאַפּוֹ אֲדֹנָי אֶת־בַּת־צִיּוֹן La 2^{1} (Bu הֵעִיב)

עוג (√of foll, cf NH *id draw a circle*, עוּגָה (circular) *ditch*, Aram עוּגִית *id*; Ar عَوِجَ *be crooked, curved, bent*, عَاجٌ *elephant's tusk, tortoise-shell*)

†**עֻגָה** **n.f.** disc or cake of bread,—abs. ע׳ Ho 7^{8} 1 K 17^{13}, cstr. עֻגַת 19^{6} Ez 4^{12}, pl. עֻגוֹת Gn 18^{6} Nu 11^{8}, cstr עֻגֹת Ex 12^{39},—*bread-cake*, made of קֶמַח סֹלֶת Gn 18^{6} (J), of קֶמַח 1 K 17^{13}, of manna Nu 11^{8} (JE, vb בשׁל), of barley Ez 4^{12} (sim), unleavened, עֻגֹת מַצּוֹת Ex 12^{39} (E, vb אָפָה), ע׳ רְצָפִים 1 K 19^{6} *cake of hot-stones*, i e baked on them; metaph ע׳ בְּלִי הֲפוּכָה Ho 7^{8} Ephr is *a cake not turned* (i. e burnt, ruined). —On ע׳ v Benz$^{Arch. 85f}$ Now$^{Arch I. 111}$ Kennedy$^{Ency Bib BREAD}$ and synonyms, Ib^{CAKE}.

†[**עוּג**] **vb. denom.** bake (a cake; lit. *make a cake of*),—**Qal** *Impf* 2 ms sf 3 fs. תְּעֻגֶנָּה (so Baer Ginsb, > van d H תְּעֻגֶנָה) *thou shalt bake it* (on form v Ko$^{I 496f}$ Ges$^{§ 58k}$) Ez 4^{12}.

†**מָעוֹג** **n.[m.]** cake,—abs 1 K 17^{12}, לַעֲגֵי מ׳ ψ 35^{16} *mockers of* (for) *a cake*, i. e. buffoons, but 𝔊 Che al rd. לָעֲגוּ (לַעֲגֵי) לַעַג

†**עוֹג** and (1 K 4^{19}) **עֹג** **n pr.m.** (orig n pr div acc to RS$^{Sem I 91 2nd ed 93}$),—**Og**, giant king of Bashan (i e, peculiarly, of a country, v RS$^{l.c}$), usu + סִיחוֹן (q v), Nu 21^{33} (JE), 32^{33} (P), Dt 1^{4} 3$^{1.3.4.10.11.13}$ 4^{47} 29^{6} 31^{4} Jos 2^{10} 9^{10} 12^{4} 13$^{12.30.31}$ (prob all D), 1 K 4^{19} Ne 9^{22} ψ 135^{11} 136^{20}; 𝔊 Ωγ (Γωγ B Dt 3^{1} 4^{47})

עֻגָב, עוּגָב v ענב

† [**עוּד**] **vb.** prob. return, go about, repeat, do again (Ar. عود, عَادَ *return, do again*, IV. *restore*, also *say again, iterate*, عَادَةٌ *habit*; Eth ዐዶ: *turn about, surround*, ዐውድ: *circuit, circle*; Syr Pa ܥܰܝܶܕ *accustom*, Ethpe. Aph. *be accustomed*, ܥܝܳܕܳܐ *usage, ceremony*, ܥܐܕܳܐ *festival* (Brock), whence Ar عِيدٌ *id*, as loan-word, Fra^{276}, Palm. עידא *usage* Lzb^{337} Cook^{90}; NH עֵד, and esp עֵדוּת = BH, also עִיד *festival*, 𝔗 עִידָא, cf. prob As. Shaph *uš-id, he solemnly affirmed* Dl$^{HWB 32}$),—only intens **Pi.** *surround* (cf Eth), *Pf* 3 ms sf עִוְּדֻנִי ψ 119^{61} (cf סְבָבוּנִי 18^{6}) **Pōʿēl**, *restore, relieve* (cf Ar IV), *Impf* 3 ms. יְעוֹדֵד, c acc pers ψ 146^{9} (|| שָׁמַר, opp עוּת), 147^{6} (opp הִשְׁפִּיל) **Hithpōl.** *be restored, Impf* 1 pl. וַנִּתְעוֹדָד ψ 20^{9} (+קוּם, opp נָפַל; 𝔊 ἀνωρθώθημεν).

עוֹד and (14 t · Fr$^{MM 236}$) עֹד, **subst. a going round, continuance**, but used mostly as **adv. acc. still, yet, again, besides**: with sf. עוֹדֶנִּי (with appar. verbal form, like אֵינֶנִּי. Ol$^{§ 221}$ Sta$^{§ 352 b}$ Ko$^{II 444, III 360}$ Ges$^{§ 100.5}$), +Dt 31^{27} Jos 14^{11} 1 S 20^{14}, עוֹדִי +Gn 48^{15} ψ 104^{33} 139^{18} 146^{2}; עוֹדְךָ Gn 46^{30}+4 t., f עוֹדָךְ +1 K 1^{14}; עוֹדֶנּוּ Gn 18^{22}+20 t. (never עוֹדוֹ), עוֹדֶנָּה +1 K 1^{22}, עוֹדָה +Is 28^{4}; עוֹדָם +Ex 4^{18} Est 6^{14}, 3 fpl עוֹדֵינָה +La 4^{17} Kt (Qr 1 pl. עוֹדֵינוּ); there occur also עוֹד אֲנִי +2 S 14^{32} Dn 9$^{20.21}$, and עוֹד הֵם +Is 65^{24}.— **1.** as *adv*: **a.** (*a*) expressing *continuance, persistence*, usu of the past or present, *still, yet*, Gn 18^{22} וְאַבְרָהָם עוֹדֶנּוּ עֹמֵד and A, he was *still* standing before י׳ (note oft. so עוֹדֶנּוּ after cas pend., 44^{14} 1 S 13^{7} 1 K 12^{2} Je 33^{1} 2 Ch 34^{3}), 29^{7} הֵן עוֹד הַיּוֹם גָּדוֹל the day is *still* high, 31^{14} 43^{7} הַעוֹד אֲבִיכֶם חַי, v^{27} 45^{3} Ex 4^{18} 9^{2} Nu 19^{13} Ju 6^{24} 8^{20} 1 K 20^{32} הַעוֹדֶנּוּ חַי; 2 S 14^{32} (but Ko$^{III 658}$ עַד), 18^{14}, Is 5^{25} וְעוֹד יָדוֹ נְטוּיָה; 10^{32} עוֹד הַיּוֹם בְּנֹב לַעֲמֹד *still* to-day (such is his haste) will he tarry in Nob, 1 K 22^{44} עוֹד הָעָם מְזַבְּחִים the people were *still* sacrificing, etc (so 2 K 12^{4}+); 2 S 1^{9} כִּי־כָל־עוֹד נַפְשִׁי בִּי, Jb 27^{3} (v. כֹּל **1 f**); Mi 6^{10} (v הֲ **1 b** *end*, and Ke; but also We Now); La 4^{17} the sf. is anticipatory, either of *eyes* (Kt) or *our* (Qr 𝔊), poet. for עוֹד עֵינֵינוּ כָּלוֹת, but Dys Lohr *al.* rd עַד מָה for ע׳, Bi^{1} Wild simply עוֹד. 2 Ch 14^{6} rd. either עוֹדֶנּוּ (sf. 1 pl antic of לְפָנֵינוּ), or עוֹד. Twice, peculiarly, עוֹד לֹא *still not* (Germ. *noch nicht*) i e *not yet* (in class Heb. טֶרֶם), Je 40^{5} וְעוֹדֶנּוּ לֹא יָשׁוּב, 2 Ch 20^{33} וְעוֹד הָעָם לֹא הֵכִינוּ לְבָבָם (the vb. fin. on acc of לֹא) Sq. וְ, Nu 11^{33} הַבָּשָׂר עוֹדֶנּוּ בֵּין שִׁנֵּיהֶם . . . וְאַף י׳ חָרָה בָעָם the flesh was *still* between their teeth . ., *and* (=*when*) etc.,

(cf. ψ 78[30 f.] Jb 8[12]); and oft. in the phr. עוֹדֶנּוּ (עוֹדָם וגו׳) מְדַבֵּר (מְדַבְּרִים) he (they, etc.) was (were) *still* speaking, *and* (=*when*) etc., Gn 29[9] עודנו מְדַבֵּר עמם ורחל באה, 1 K 1[22.42] 2 K 6[33] Est 6[14] Dn 9[20.21], so ... עוֹד זֶה Jb 1[16.17] (+v[18] for עַד): and of the future, 1 K 1[14] Is 65[24] (עוֹד הֵם מְדַבְּרִים ואני אשמע); cf. Ex 9[17].

(*b*) Expressing *addition* or *repetition, still, yet, more,* Gn 7[4] כי לימים עוד שבעה after *yet* seven days, 8[10.12] 29[27.30] עוד שבע שנים אחרות, 45[6] 2 K 6[33] Is 1[5] Hb 2[3] כִּי עוֹד חָזוֹן לַמּוֹעֵד (cf. Dn 10[14] 11[2.27.35]), Je 13[27] אַחֲרֵי מָתַי עוֹד after how long *still?* with stress on the idea of *continuance,* Gn 46[29] וַיֵּבְךְּ עַל צַוָּארָיו עוֹד *still going on* (AV. *a good while*), Ru 1[14], ψ 84[5] עוד יהללוך they will be *still praising* thee, Jb 34[23]; with עוֹד prefixed for emph., Ex 11[1] עוד נגע אחד אביא על פ׳, Is 49[20] 56[8] עוֹד אֲקַבֵּץ וגו׳, Ez 8[13.15] ψ 42[6] 92[15]+; in the phr. עוֹד מְעַט sq. pf. consec., †Ex 17[4] עוד מעט וּסְקָלֻנִי *yet* a little, *and* they will stone me, Ho 1[4] Je 51[33], cf. ψ 37[10], Is 10[25] 29[17]; simil. Jon 3[4] (cf. בְּעוֹד Is 21[16]), 2 Ch 10[5] (but see 𝔊 and ‖ 1 K 12[5]); לֹא ... עוֹד *no more,* both of the past, as Ex 2[3] Jos 5[1.12] 1 K 10[5], and of the fut., as Gn 17[5] לֹא יִקָּרֵא עוד שמך א׳, 32[29] Dt 31[2] Is 2[4] 30[20] 62[4] Je 3[16]+oft., עוֹד ... לֹא Gn 8[22]; so with אֵין Is 23[10] Je 10[20] 48[2] ψ 74[9] *al.*

b. When the continuance is limited by its nature to a single occurrence, עוֹד becomes= *again,* Gn 4[25] 9[11] לֹא יִכָּרֵת כל בשר עוד, 18[29] וַיֹּסֶף עוֹד לְדַבֵּר and he added *still* to speak, i.e. he spake yet *again* (so oft. with יָסַף; v. √), 24[20] וַתָּרָץ עוֹד and she ran *again,* 29[33] וַתַּהַר עוד, 35[9] 37[9] Ex 3[15] 4[6] Dt 3[26] 1 S 10[22]+oft.; with עוֹד prefixed, Ho 12[10] Je 31[4.5.23] 32[15] 33[12.13]; לֹא ... עוֹד *not again, no more,* Dt 13[17] 34[10].

c. *Still, moreover, besides* (not in temporal sense); Gn 19[12] עוֹד מִי לְךָ פֹה whom hast thou here *besides?* 43[6] הַעוֹד לָכֶם אָח Am 6[10]; 1 S 10[22] הֲבָא עוֹד הֲלֹם אִישׁ is there *still* a man come hither? (sc. besides ourselves: but 𝔊 We al. הֲבָא הֲלֹם הָאִישׁ), 16[11] עוֹד שָׁאַר הַקָּטָן, 18[8] ועוד לו אך המלוכה, 1 K 22[7.8] 2 K 4[6] אֵין עוֹד כֶּלִי, Is 5[4] Je 36[32] Ez 20[27] 23[38] 36[37] Pr 9[9] Ec 12[9] 1 Ch 29[3] 2 Ch 17[6]+; וְאֵין עוֹד and there is none *besides,* †Dt 4[39] (cf. v[35]), 1 K 8[60] Is 45[5.6.14.18.22] (cf. v[21]), 46[9] Jo 2[27]; אֲנִי וְאַפְסִי עוֹד †Is 47[8.10] Zp 2[15].

2. With prefixes:—†**a.** בְּעוֹד, lit. *in the continuance of ...,* i.e. (*a*) *while yet:* Gn 25[6] בְּעוֹדֶנּוּ חַי *while* he was *yet alive,* Dt 31[27] 2 S 12[22] בְּעוֹד הַיֶּלֶד חַי, Is 28[4] ψ 39[2] Jb 29[5]; בְּעוֹדִי alone, =*so long as I live,* ψ 104[33] 146[2] (‖ בְּחַיַּי); 2 S 3[35] בעוד היום, Je 15[9] בעוד יומם, Pr 31[15]. (*b*) *within yet,* usu. of time, Gn 40[13] בְּעוֹד שְׁלֹשֶׁת יָמִים יִשָּׂא וגו׳ *within yet* three days, etc., v[19] Jos 1[11] Is 7[8] 21[16] בְּעוֹד שָׁנָה (sq. pf. cons.), Je 28[3.11] Am 4[7]; but also of distance, Gn 48[7] בְּעוֹד כִּבְרַת ארץ לבוא אפרתה (cf. 35[16] ויהי עוד וגו׳); cf. SI[2] ובעוד שלש אמה להן[נֶּקֶב]. **b.** †מֵעוֹד, lit. *from the continuance of ...,* only in the phr. מֵעוֹדִי (מֵעוֹדְךָ) עד היום הזה *ever since I was* (*thou wast*) unto this day, Gn 48[15] Nu 22[30].

†**עֹדֵד, עוֹדֵד** n.pr.m. (*restorer*);—𝔊 Ωδηδ, Αδαδ: **1.** עֲזַרְיָהוּ בֶן־עו׳ 2 Ch 15[1], so read also v[8] (MT עֹדֵד alone). **2.** עֹדֵד a prophet 2 Ch 28[9].

עֵד [69] **n.m.**[Dt 17,6] witness (prob. fr. *reiterating,* hence *emphatically affirming*);—ע׳ abs. Gn 31[48]+, cstr. Ex 20[16]+; sf. עֵדִי Jb 16[19]; pl. עֵדִים Nu 35[30]+, cstr. עֵדֵי ψ 27[12] 35[11]; sf. עֵדַי Is 43[10.12], etc.;—†**1.** *witness, testimony, evidence,* of things: heap of stones Gn 31[44.48.52] (JE), torn animal Ex 22[12] (E), song of Moses Dt 31[19.21] (J), law-book v[26] (D), witness of י׳ against Israel; altar E. of Jordan, c. בֵּין, Jos 22[27.28.34] (P), cf. Is 19[20]; Job's evil condition Jb 16[8]; the moon ψ 89[38]. **2.** *witness,* a person: †**a.** God, in heaven for Job Jb 16[19]; on earth, for Samuel 1 S 12[5.5]+v[6] 𝔊 Th and most, Jeremiah Je 42[5]; see also 1 S 20[12] (ins. עֵד bef. י׳ 𝔖 Dr Bu Kit Löhr HPS); against persons Je 29[23] Mal 3[5], nations Mi 1[2]; between (בֵּין) persons Gn 31[50] (E). **b.** Davidic dyn., to nations Is 55[4]. **c.** *witnesses,* of transfer of property Je 32[10.12.25.44], betrothal Ru 4[9.10.11]; usu. of testimony in court, and in civil and social relations, c. בְּ against, Nu 5[13] Jos 24[22] 1 S 12[5]+, c. קום *rise up against* ψ 27[12] 35[11]; †עָנָה עֵד שֶׁקֶר בְּ *answer* (in court) *as a false witness against* Ex 20[16]=עֵד שָׁוְא Dt 5[17], Pr 25[18]; †לְפִי עֵדִים Nu 35[30] (P); †עַל־פִּי עֵד(ים) Dt 17[6.6] *at the mouth of witnesses,* so 19[15.15].—*False witness* is ע׳ שֶׁקֶר Ex 20[16] Dt 19[18.18] ψ 27[12] Pr 6[19] 14[5]; ע׳ שְׁקָרִים 12[17] 19[5.9]; ע׳ כְּזָבִים 21[28]; ע׳ בְּלִיַּעַל 19[28]; ע׳ חָמָס *witness of* (i.e. supporting) *violence* Ex 23[1] (E) Dt 19[16] ψ 35[11]. *Faithful witness* is ע׳ אֱמוּנִים Pr 14[5]; ע׳ אֱמֶת Je 42[5] Pr 14[25].

†II. **עֵדָה** n.f. testimony, witness, of things (only E);—Gn 21[30] 31[52] Jos 24[27.27] (J uses עֵד for feminine things).—I. עֵדָה v. יעד.

†[**עוּד**] **vb. denom.** (Gerber [42 f.]) bear witness;—**Qal** *Impf.* 1 s. sf. אֲעִידֵךְ La 2[13] Kt;

< **Hiph.** Qr Bu. **Hiph.** *Pf* 3 ms. העיד 2 K 17^{15} Mal 2^{14}, הָעֵדֹתָה, הָעֵד Gn 43^{3}; 2 ms. הַעִידֹתָ Ne 9^{34}, Ex 19^{23}, 1 s הַעִידֹתִי Dt 4^{26} Je 42^{19}, 3 mpl. הֵעִידוּ Ne 9^{26}, etc, *Impf* וַיָּעַד 2 K 17^{13} Zc 3^{6}; 3 fs sf וַתְּעִידֵנִי Jb 29^{11} + 15 t Impf.; *Inf. abs.* הָעֵד Gn 43^{3} + 4 t, *Imv* הָעֵד Ex 19^{21} + 2 t Imv *Pt* מֵעִיד Dt 32^{46}—**1.** *testify, bear witness*, c. sf against one 1 K 21$^{10.13}$, in favour of Jb 29^{11} La 2^{13} (Qr), c. בין Mal 2^{14} **2.** *cause to testify, take as witness*, c. acc pers. Is 8^{2} Je 32$^{10.25.44}$, *call as witness, invoke*, c acc את השמים ואת הארץ + ב *against* Dt 4^{26} 30^{19} 31^{28} **3.** *protest, affirm solemnly, warn* subj men, abs Je 6^{10} Ne 13^{15}, c ב pers Gn 43$^{3.3}$ (J) Ex 19^{21} (E) 1 S 8^{9} 1 K 2^{42} 2 Ch 24^{19} Ne 9^{26} 13^{21} Je 42^{19} Am 3^{13}; *exhort solemnly, admonish, charge*, 'י subj, c ב pers, Ex 19^{23} (J) Dt 8^{19} 2 K 17^{13} Ne 9$^{29.30}$ Je 11$^{7.7.7}$ Zc 3^{6} ψ 50^{7} 81^{9}, *enjoin solemnly*, c. ב pers + acc rei עדות 2 K 17^{15} Ne 9^{34}, דברים Dt 32^{46}. **Hoph.** *Pf* 3 ms והוּעַד consec Ex 21^{29} (E) impers *and protest be entered*, c ב pers.

†III [עֵדָה] **n.f.** only *pl* MT **testimonies** (always of laws as divine testimonies or solemn charges),—pl abs עדת Dt 4^{45} 6^{20}, sf (of 'י), עדתי ψ 132^{12} (Ges^{§91n}), עדֹתָיו Dt 6^{17} ψ 25^{10} 99^{7} 119^{2}, עדותיו 78^{56}, עדתיך 93^{5} 119$^{22.24.46.59.79.95.119.125.138.146.152.167.168}$ (MT pointing artificial, der prob fr עֵדוּת, reading עדת for עדת, or regarding עדת as contr from עדות, pl of עדות [Sta^{§320b} SS Buhl], v. also Dr$^{Dt\ 4.45}$, Dt 4^{45} 6$^{17.20}$ are redactional)

†עֵדוּת$_{19}$ and עֵדֻת$_{27}$ **n.f. testimony**,—'ע abs Ex 16^{34} +, cstr ψ 19^{8} +; pl sf עֵדְוֹתֶיךָ 119^{14} +, עדותיו Je 44^{23} + 4 t,—**1.** *testimony* of the Ten Words on the tables as a solemn divine charge, לֻחֹת הע' Ex 31^{18} 32^{15} 34^{29} (P), הע' 25$^{16.21}$ 40^{20} (P), ark as containing tables, ארון הע' 25^{22} 26$^{33.34}$ 30$^{6.26}$ 39^{35} 40$^{3.5.21}$ Nu 4^{5} 7^{89} (all P), Jos 4^{16} (JE, Kue הברית [ag him Di], so Benn Steuernag), הארן לע' Ex 31^{7} (P), abbrev. לפני הע' 16^{34} 30^{36} Nu 17$^{19.25}$ (P), על הע' Ex 27^{21} (= הע' Lv 24^{3}), 30^{6} Lv 16^{13} (P), tabernacle as containing ark of testimony, משכן הע' *tabernacle of the testimony* Ex 38^{21} Nu 1$^{50.53.53}$ 10^{11} (P), so אהל הע' 9^{15} 17$^{22.23}$ 18^{2} (P) 2 Ch 24^{6}. **2.** the code of law in gen (late), as a *testimony* of God · ψ 19^{8} 119^{88} 122^{4}, ‖ תּוֹרָה 78^{5}, ‖ חק 81^{6}. In titles, עַל־שׁוֹשַׁן ע' ψ 60^{1}, אֶל־שֹׁשַׁנִּים ע' 80^{1} = melody whose first line cp law as testimony to a choice flower. Special laws of the code are denoted by pl; + חֻקּוֹת etc 1 K 2^{3} 2 K 23^{3} = 2 Ch 34^{31} (+ חקים etc.), Je 44^{23}, חֻקִּים etc 1 Ch 29^{19}, מצות Ne 9^{34}, pl of contents of covenant 2 K 17^{15}, pl. elsewh. ψ 119$^{14.31.36.99.111.129.144.157}$ Vid. also III [עֵדָה].—For הָעֵדוּת 2 K 11^{12} = 2 Ch 23^{11} rd prob הַצְּעָדוֹת (cf. 2 S 1^{10} We al).

†תְּעוּדָה **n.f. testimony, attestation**,—**1.** *testimony*, prophet *injunction*, ‖ תורה Is 8$^{16.20}$ **2.** *attestation*, Ru 4^{7} (> *fixed usage* Buhl^{Lex})

†I [עָוָה] **vb. bend, twist** (so Ar. عَوَى),—**Niph.** *Pf* 1 s נַעֲוֵיתִי Is 21^{3} ψ 38^{7}; *Pt* cstr נַעֲוֵה Pr 12^{8}, f cstr נַעֲוַת 1 S 20^{30} (but rd נַעֲרַת 𝔊 We Dr SS Bu HPS),—*be bent, bowed down, twisted*, ‖ שחה ψ 38^{7}, ‖ נבהל Is 21^{3}, נַעֲוֵה לב Pr 12^{8} *one perverted of mind* **Pi.** *Pf.* 3 ms עִוָּה, subj 'י— La 3^{9} my paths *hath he twisted*, ועי' Is 24^{1} *its surface will he distort* (‖ בּוֹקֵק הָאָרֶץ) **Hiph.** *Pf* 1 s. יָשָׁר הֶעֱוֵיתִי Jb 33^{27} *the right have I perverted* (‖ חָטָא), so 3 pl הֶעֱווּ אֶת־דַּרְכָּם Je 3^{21}.

†I עַוָּה **n.f. distortion, ruin**,—עַוָּה עַוָּה עַוָּה אֲשִׂימֶנָּה Ez 21^{32} (cf. √**Pi.** Is 24^{1}).

†עִוְעִים **n.pl. abstr. distorting, warping** (for *עִוְעֻיִם),—רוּחַ עועים Is 19^{14} *temper of distorting*, i e *warped* judgment

†עִי **n [m.] ruin, heap of ruins**;—'ע abs Jb 30^{24}, cstr Mi 1^{6}, pl עִיִּין (Aram. form) 3^{12}, but עִיִּים in the quotation Je 26^{18}, and ψ 79^{1}

†מְעִי **n.[m.] ruin** (si vera l.),—וְהָיְתָה מְעִי מַפָּלָה consec Is 17^{1} *Damascus shall become a ruinous heap* (but del. 'מ 𝔊 Lag Che SS Buhl).

II. עוה (√ of foll, cf Ar عَوَى *err from the way*, Eth ዐየየ: *err*, distinct from I עוה, cf Lag$^{M\ I\ 236f}$ Dr$^{18\ 20,30}$ Gerber^{90})

†עָוֹן **n.m.**$^{Is\ 22,14}$ **iniquity, guilt, or punishment of iniquity**,—'ע abs Ex 21^{43} +; עָוֹן 2 K 7^{9} ψ 51^{7}, cstr עון Gn 15^{16} +, עון 1 Ch 21^{8}; sf עוני Gn 4^{13} + (2 S 16^{12} read בְּעָנְיִי), עונך Ho 9^{7} +; עֲוֹנֵבִי ψ 103^{3}, עֲוֹנָהּ Nu 15^{31} (Ges^{§91e}), etc; pl. עֲוֹנוֹת abs ψ 130^{3} +, cstr. Jb 13^{26} +, עֹנֹת abs ψ 65^{4}, cstr. Lv 16^{21} +, sf. עֲוֹנֹתֶיךָ Is 43^{24}, עֲוֹנֹתֵיכֶם Nu 14^{34} +, etc; also עוניך Ez 28^{18}, עונינו Is 64^{6} +, etc (SS doubt all these);—**1.** *iniquity*, Jb 15^{5} 20^{27} Je 11^{10} 14^{7} 16^{17} La 2^{14} Ez 7^{13}; ‖ חטאת 1 S 20^{1} Jb 13^{23} Is 5^{18} 43^{24} 59^{2} Je 5^{25} 16^{10} La 4$^{6.13}$ Dn 9^{16} Ho 4^{8} 13^{12}; ‖ פשע Jb 14^{17} 31^{33} ψ 107^{17} Is 50^{1} 53^{5}; ‖ אשמה Ezr 9$^{6.7.13}$; רעה Jb 22^{5} Ho 7^{1}. **a.** ע' נעורי Jb 13^{26} *iniquities of my youth*; ע' חֶרֶב 19^{29} *iniquities* calling *for the sword*; ע' פלילי(ם) 31$^{11.28}$ *iniquity for* (to be punished by) *judges*; בשל בע' שתי עונתם Ho 10^{10} (so rd. Vrss Hi al.),

stumble by iniquity Ho 5[5] 14[2]; cf. מִכְשׁוֹל ע׳ Ez 7[19] 14[3.4.7] 18[30] 44[12]; לכל־עון Dt 19[15], אשתמרה מע׳ 2 S 22[24] = ψ 18[24]; עָוֹן אֲשֶׁר־חֵטְא Ho 12[9]. **b.** *iniquity* as recognized, ידע ע׳ 1 S 3[13] Is 59[12] Je 3[13] 14[20]; confessed, התודה ע׳ Lv 16[21] 26[40.40] (P), Ne 9[2], הגיד ע׳ ψ 38[19], לא כסה ע׳ 32[5]; brought to remembrance, הזכיר ע׳ Nu 5[15] (P) 1 K 17[18] Ez 21[28.29] 29[16], causing shame, יִכָּלְמוּ מע׳ Ez 43[10]; turned from, שוב מע׳ Dn 9[13], cf השיב מע׳ Mal 2[6]. **c.** (1) phrases of punishment: פקד ע׳ על Ex 20[5] = Dt 5[9], Ex 34[7] Nu 14[18] (J), Lv 18[25] (H) 2 S 3[8] Is 13[11] 26[21] Je 25[12] 36[31] Am 3[2], without על, La 4[22], פקד ע׳ ב ψ 89[33]; Jb 11[6] v. II. [נשא]; יסר על ע׳ ψ 39[12] *chastise for iniquity;* שַׁתָּ ע׳ לנגדך 90[8] *set our iniquities before thee,* נמל כע׳ 103[10], שמר ע׳ 130[3]; שלם ע׳ Is 65[7.7] Je 16[18] 32[18]; מַטְבֵּחַ בע׳ Is 14[21], (2) of forgiveness or removal: העביר ע׳ 2 S 24[10] = 1 Ch 21[8], Jb 7[21] Zc 3[4], משתי ע׳ 3[9], סלח לע׳ Ex 34[9] Nu 14[19] (J), ψ 25[11] 103[3] Je 31[34] 33[8] 36[3]; נשא ע׳ Ex 34[7] Nu 14[18] (J), ψ 32[5] 85[3] Is 33[24] Ho 14[3] Mi 7[18], סר ע׳ Is 6[7], יכבוש ע׳ Mi 7[19]; (3) of covering over, כסה על ע׳ Ne 3[37], כפר ע׳ ψ 78[38] Pr 16[6] Is 22[14] 27[9] Dn 9[24], כפר על ע׳ Je 18[23], יתכפר ע׳ 1 S 3[14], (4) of cleansing from. כבס מע׳ ψ 51[4]; מחה ע׳ v[11], טהר מע׳ Je 33[8] Ez 36[33]; (5) of imputing, reckoning to one חשב ע׳ ל 2 S 19[20] ψ 32[2], זכר ע׳ (ל) 79[8] Is 64[8] Je 14[10] Ho 8[13] 9[9], יִזָּכֵר ע׳ ψ 109[14], בקש (ל)ע׳ Jb 10[6] Je 50[20]; (6) פדה מע׳ ψ 130[8] *ransom from iniquity.*

2. *Guilt of iniquity* (not always easy to disting from **1**, SS give more, Buhl fewer, sub **2**),—‖ תועבות Ez 36[31], ‖ דם Is 59[3]; ‖ חמס Ez 9[9], ע׳ פעור Jos 22[17] (P), ע׳ סדם Ez 16[49]; ע׳ בצעו Is 57[17]; שְׁנֵי עונם Ez 4[4], נִכְתָּם עֲוֹנֵךְ לְפָנַי Je 2[22] *the guilt of thine iniquity is marked before me;* מצא ע׳ Gn 44[16] (E) ψ 36[3]. **a.** ע׳ בְּ · *guilt of iniquity upon one* Nu 15[31] (P) 1 S 20[8] 2 S 14[32]; לא ע׳ לִי Jb 33[9] (‖ זַךְ), בלי־עון ψ 59[5] *without my guilt.* **b.** *guilt*, as great, increased. רב עָוֹן Je 13[22] 30[14.15] Ez 28[18] Ho 9[7], לֹא־שָׁלֵם ע׳ Gn 15[16] (J); ע׳ השיגוני ψ 38[5], ע׳ עָבְרוּ ראשי 40[13]; ע׳ עקבי יסובני 49[6]; ע׳ גברו מני 65[4], עַם כֶּבֶד ע׳ Is 1[4]; בע׳ נלקח Ez 33[6]. **c.** as a condition, בע׳ · c. חוללתי *was I brought forth* ψ 51[7]; c. גָּוַע *expire* Jos 22[20] (P), c מות *die* Je 31[30] Ez 3[18.19] 18[17.18] 33[8.9].

3. *Consequence of, or punishment for, iniquity* (SS include most of these under **2**, and do not recognize **3**; Buhl thinks this meaning rare, giving only Gn 4[13] Is 5[18]),—אם יִקְּרֵךְ ע׳ בדבר הזה 1 S 28[10] *no punishment shall happen unto thee for,* etc; נשא ע׳ *bear the punishment for iniquity* of others Ex 28[38] Lv 10[17] (*take away* ע׳ Di Now[ii 233 n]) 16[22] Nu 30[16] (P), Ez 4[4.5.6]; בע׳ 18[19.20.20]; one's own, Ex 28[43] Lv 5[1.17] 7[18] 17[16] 19[8] 20[17.19] 22[16] Nu 5[31] 14[34] 18[1.1.23] (P), Ez 14[10] 44[10.12], גדול ע׳ מנשוא Gn 4[13] (J) *my punishment is greater than I can bear,* נִרְצָה עֲוֹנָהּ Is 40[2] *her punishment is accepted,* cf רצה ע׳ Lv 26[41.43] (H); ומצאנו ע׳ 2 K 7[9] *punishment will overtake us;* תנה ע׳ על ע׳ ψ 69[28] *add punishment to their punishment;* ע׳ הוא יסבל Is 53[11] *the consequences of their iniquities he shall bear,* cf ע׳ סָבָלְנוּ La 5[7], הפגיע בו ע׳ Is 53[6]; נִקָּה מע׳ *freed from punishment* Nu 5[31] (P) Jb 10[14]; בי אני העון 1 S 25[24] *on me the punishment;* עלי הע׳ 2 S 14[9], בע׳ c. various vbs.. Gn 19[15] (J) Lv 26[39.39] (H) ψ 31[11] 106[43] Je 51[6] Ez 4[17] 7[16] 24[23] 39[23]; עת ע׳ קץ 21[30.34] 35[5], see also: Pr 5[22] (‖ חַבְלֵי חטאת), Is 30[13] 64[5.6] La 4[22] Ez 4[4] 14[10.10] 32[27].

† [עָוָה] **vb. denom.** (Gerber[90]) commit iniquity, do wrong (Aram עוי *commit sin,* עֲוָיָא *sin,* cf Levy[NHWB iii 626]),—**Qal** (late) *Pf* 3 fs. עָוְתָה Est 1[16] *she hath done wrong* (c. על); 1 pl. עָוִינוּ Dn 9[5] *we have committed iniquity* (‖ חָטָא) **Hiph.** *commit iniquity,*—*Pf* 3 ms. הֶעֱוָה 2 S 19[20], 1 s. הֶעֱוֵיתִי 24[17] (‖ חָטָא), 1 pl. הֶעֱוִינוּ 1 K 8[47] = 2 Ch 6[37], ψ 106[6] (all ‖ חָטָא), *Inf. abs* הַעֲוֵה Je 9[4], *cstr.* sf. הַעֲוֹתוֹ 2 S 7[14]—Jb 33[27] v I עָוָה.

† II עַוָּה, עִוָּה **n.pr.loc.** city conquered by Assyrians;—עַוָּה 2 K 17[24] (van d. H. עַוָּא) = עִוָּה 18[34] 19[13] = Is 37[13], 𝔊 Αια(ν), Αυα, and (2 K 19[13]) Ουδου, A Αυτα, 𝔊L Αιυαγ, etc; site in N. Syria Wkl[Altest Unters. 102 f.] Benz, Sachau[ZA xii (1897), 48] prop. *Emma* (Tab. Pent.) = Ἴμμα Ptol[v 15, 15], mod. *'Imm* betw Antioch and Aleppo.—I. עַוָּה v. sub I. עוה.

† [עַוִּי] **adj.gent.** only pl הָעַוִּים as subst, inhab of II עַוָּה 2 K 17[31] (another עַוִּים infr.).

עוז **n.** v. עֹז sub עזז

† [עוּז], עוֹז **vb.** take or seek refuge (Ar. عوذ, عَاذَ *take refuge, seek protection,* مَعَاذٌ *a refuge*);—**Qal** *Inf. cstr.* לָעוֹז במעוז Is 30[2] (‖ לַחְסוֹת בְּ). **Hiph.** *bring into safety,* Pf. 3 mpl. הֵעִיזוּ Is 10[31], obj. om, and so *Imv* mpl. הָעִיזוּ Je 4[6], הָעִזוּ מִקֶּרֶב 6[1]; c. acc, ms. הָעֵז Ex 9[19].

† מָעוֹז **n.m.**[Ju 6, 26] place or means of safety, protection (MT sfs. as if from עזז, but prob. erron., cf Buhl[Lex 13] Ges[§ 85 k]);—מ׳ abs. Ju 6[26] +, cstr. Is 30[2] +; sf. מָעוּזִּי 2 S 22[33] (but rd. הַמְאַזְּרֵנִי as ‖ ψ 18[33]), מָעוּזִּי ψ 31[3] +, מָעֻזִּי Is 27[5] +, מָעוּזּוֹ ψ 52[9] +, מָעֻזָּה Dn 11[10], etc. (rd prob מְעוּזִּי, etc.), pl. מָעֻזִּים v[38.39], sf. מָעֻזְנֶיהָ Is 23[11], read מָעֻזֶּיהָ (Ges § 20 c Che[Heb Hpt] al.; del d f. in all, v. supr.);—

1. lit *place of safety* Ju 6^{26}, hence (c collat idea of *strength*, as if fr עזז) = *fastness* Is $23^{11.14}$ (in v^{14} Che$^{Heb. Hpt}$ prop. מְחוֹזְכֶם *your city*), Ez 24^{25} 30^{15} Dn $11^{7.10.19}$, הַמִּקְדָּשׁ הַמ׳ v^{31}, מבצרי מָעֻזִּים v^{39}, מ׳ הַיָּם i e *harbour* Is 23^4, but del Ol Du Che^{Hpt}, מ׳ מֵאוֹיֵב Na 3^{11}; cf עָרֵי מ׳ Is 17^9. **2. a.** fig, of God (י׳) as *refuge* Na 1^7 ψ 27^1 31^5 37^{39} 52^9 Is $25^{4.4}$ Jo 4^{16}, י׳ עֻזִּי וּמָעֻזִּי וּמְנוּסִי Je 16^{19}, מ׳ יְשׁוּעוֹת מְשִׁיחוֹ ψ 28^8 (|| עֹז), so צוּר מ׳ ψ 31^3, אֱלֹהֵי מ׳ 43^2, also יַחֲזֵק בְּמָעֻזִּי Is 27^5 *let him lay hold of my refuge* (me as refuge), cf מ׳ לָחֶם דֶּרֶךְ י׳ חֶדְוַת י׳ הִיא מָעֻזְּכֶם Ne 8^{10}, Pr 10^{29}. **b.** of a heathen god, אֱלֹהַּ מָעֻזִּים Dn 11^{38} (rd מְחוֹזִים *cities* Che$^{Is 23, 1, Heb Hpt}$) **3.** fig of human *protection*, מ׳ פַּרְעֹה Is $30^{2.3}$ (both || צֵל), אֶפְרַיִם מ׳ רֹאשִׁי ψ 60^9 = 108^9, i e. my helmet; also (of angel) Dn 11^1 (|| מַחֲזִיק)

עויל v II עוּל.

† **עַוִּים** **n.pr. 1. gent.** הָע׳ people on SW coast of Mediterr before the כַּפְתֹּרִים (q v) came Dt 2^{23}, and remaining thereafter Jos 13^3 (D^2), 𝔊 Ευαιοι. **2. loc.** הָע׳ city in Benj Jos 18^{23} (= הָעַי ?), 𝔊 Αιειν, Αυειμ —Vid also [עַיִּי] supr.

† **עֲוִית** **n pr.loc.** in Edom Gn 36^{35} = Qr 1 Ch 1^{46} (Kt עיות); 𝔊 Γεθθαιμ, but 𝔊L 1 Ch 1^{46} Ευιθ

† I. [**עוּל**] **vb. give suck** (Ar. عَالَ, عيل, *give suck* (while pregnant), cf Aram ܥܘܠܐ *foetus, sucking child*, ܥܝܠܐ *foal*, so Eth ዐዋል: Talm עִילָה),—**Qal** *Pt* fpl עָלוֹת *giving suck*, of cows 1 S $6^{7.10}$, ewes ψ 78^{71} and (fig of returning exiles) Is 40^{11}, of both Gn 33^{13} (J).

† **עוּל** **n m. sucking child, suckling,**— cstr עוּל יָמִים Is 65^{20} *a suckling of days*, i.e a few days old, sf עוּלָהּ 49^{15} (|| בֶּן־בִּטְנָהּ).

II **עול** (√of foll, cf Ar عول, عَالَ *feed, nourish*, v Wetzst in De$^{Jb 16, 11}$).

† I [**עֲוִיל**] **n m. young boy,**—pl עֲוִילִים Jb 19^{18}, sf עֲוִילֵיהֶם 21^{11} —II עֲוִיל sub III. עול

III. **עול** (√of foll, cf Ar عول, عَالَ *deviate from* (right course); Aram ܥܘܠ Aph. *act unjustly*, and many deriv, עַוְלָא *unrighteousness*, Eth ዐለወ: *pervert, corrupt*)

† **עָוֶל** **n m. injustice, unrighteousness** (opp צְדָקָה),—ע׳ Lv 19^{15}+, cstr. עֶוֶל Ez 28^{18} (van d H עָוֶל, but v Baer Ginsb), sf עַוְלוֹ 18^{26} 33^{13},—עשה עול Lv $19^{15.35}$ (H) Dt 25^{16} Ez 3^{20} $18^{24.26.26}$ $33^{13.13.15.18}$, הִתְעִיבוּ ע׳ ,פֹּעַל ע׳ Jb 34^{32}; ψ 53^2 (|| עֲלִילָה 14^2), שְׁפַט ע׳ 82^2; אִישׁ ע׳ Pr 29^{27}; מצא ע׳ ב Je 2^5, ע׳ בְּכַפַּי ψ 7^4; read prob. also בְּעֶוֶל Ez 28^{15} (for MT עולתה), מַע׳ יָשִׁיב יָדוֹ 18^8, רְכֻלָּתְךָ 28^{18}, of God, אֵין עָוֶל (|| אֱמוּנָה) Dt 32^4; חָלִלָה מֵעָ׳ Jb 34^{10}.

† **עִוֵּל** **vb. denom.** (Gerber^{21}) **act wrongfully,**—**Pi.** *Impf.* 3 ms. יְעַוֵּל Is 26^{10} (opp. נכחות), *Pt* מְעַוֵּל ψ 71^4 (+ חוֹמֵץ, || רָשָׁע)

† **עַוְלָה** **n f.**$^{Jb 11 14}$ (? **m** Mal 2^6 Ko$^{ii\ 2.453, §345d}$ Ez 28^{15} [עולתה, but ע׳ only here Ez, error for עול] questioned by SS, v Albrecht$^{ZAW\ xvi\ (1896), 117}$) **injustice, unrighteousness, wrong,**—ע׳ ψ 37^1 + 24 t, + 1. עוֹלָה Is 61^8 (rd prob עַוְלָה), עוֹלָתָה ψ 125^3 92^{16} (Qr) + 2 t., עֹלָתָה v^{16} (Kt) Jb 5^{16}, pl עוֹלוֹת ψ 58^3 64^7,—**1.** *violent deeds of injustice*, בְּנֵי עַוְלָה 2 S 3^{34} 7^{10} = 1 Ch 17^9, בֶּן־ע׳ ψ 89^{23}, cf. בְּנֵי עַלְוָה Ho 10^9 (rd עַוְלָה Now), אִישׁ מִרְמָה וְע׳ ψ 43^1, בְּע׳ Is 61^8; || דָּם Mi 3^{10} Hb 2^{11}, עֹשֵׂה ע׳ ψ 37^1 Zp $3^{5.13}$, פֹּעַל ע׳ ψ 58^3 119^3 Jb 36^{23}; שָׁלַח בְּע׳ יְדֵיהֶם ψ 125^3 **2** *injustice* of speech. דִּבֶּר ע׳ בִּלְשׁוֹנִי ע׳, Is 59^3, לְשׁוֹנְכֶם ע׳ תֶּהְגֶּה Jb 13^7 27^4; ע׳ קָפְצָה פִּיהָ Jb 6^{30}, ע׳ לֹא נִמְצָא בִשְׂפָתָיו Mal 2^6, ψ 107^{42} Jb 5^{16}. **3.** *injustice*, in general, ψ 64^7 Jb 6^{29} 11^{14} 15^{16} 22^{23} 24^{20}, + 36^{33} (for MT עולה) acc. to 𝔊 Di Bu Du al, Pr 22^8 Ho 10^{13}, of God, לֹא ע׳ בּוֹ ψ 92^{16}, אֵין עִם י׳ ע׳ 2 Ch 19^7

† II. **עֲוִיל** **n.m.** unjust one, Jb 16^{11} (v foll.).

† **עַוָּל** **n.m. unjust, unrighteous one**;— esp. of oppressive ruler Zp 3^5 Jb 18^{18} 27^7 (|| רָשָׁע), 29^{17} 31^3 (|| פֹּעֲלֵי אָוֶן); prob also 16^{11} (for MT עֲוִיל, so Di, || רְשָׁעִים)

I [**עֹלָה**] v. II. עול. II. **עוֹלָה** v עלה.

עוֹלָל, עוֹלֵל v II. עלל **עוֹלָם** v. עלם.

† [**עוּן**] **vb. dwell** (prob; √of foll; Ar. عَانَ, عون, is *support*, *help*, v. esp Fl$^{Kl\ Schr\ i\ 87\ ff}$),—**Qal** *Pf* 3 fs. consec. וְעָנָה (rd וְעָנוּ ?) Is 13^{22} *and* jackals *shall dwell*, etc. (on agreement v Ges^{§145k}, || שכן v^{21}), so 𝔊 Buhl, Che$^{Heb. Hpt\ 124}$ וְשָׁכְנוּ; > 𝔊𝔗𝔖 al √IV. ענה.—ψ 87^7 v מַעְיָן.

† I **מָעוֹן** **n.[m.] dwelling, habitation**;— abs מ׳ ψ 71^3+, cstr. מְעוֹן Je 25^{30}+, sf. מְעוֹנְךָ ψ 91^9, etc,—**1.** *lair* of jackals Je 9^{10} 10^{22} 49^{33} 51^{37} (all of desolated cities), מ׳ אֲרָיוֹת Na 2^{12} (|| מִרְעֶה, fig of Nineveh). **2.** *dwelling* of י׳·

a. in heaven מ׳ קָדְשְׁךָ Dt 26^{15} cf. Je 25^{30} (|| מָרוֹם), Zc 2^{17} ψ 68^{6} 2 Ch 30^{27}. **b.** in temple מ׳ בֵּיתֶךָ ψ 26^{8}, מְעוֹנוֹ 2 Ch 36^{15} (only here alone). **3.** fig. of י׳ as abode of his people, צוּר מ׳ ψ 71^{3}, מ׳ alone 90^{1} 91^{9}.—מ׳ 1 S 2$^{29.32}$ is unintellig. (v. Comm.), poss rd. מְעוֹיֵן (*eyeing* [enviously], v עין denom.) Klo HPS, cf 𝔊 Bu. מעונה Zp 3^{7} is difficult in context, 𝔊 We Now rd. מֵעֵינֶיהָ (cf. Jos 9^{23} 2 S 3^{29}).

†II. מָעוֹן **n.pr. 1. loc.** in Judah Jos 15^{55} (P), 1 S 25^{2} (𝔊 Μααν, Μαων), now *Ma'în* (Buhl Geogr. 163 and reff.), 8 miles S of Hebron; hence מִדְבַּר מ׳ 23$^{24.25}$ 25, so rd. also 25^{1} (for MT פארן) 𝔊 Th We Dr Bu Klo Kit Lohr; cf. **2. m.** in Judah 1 Ch 2$^{45.45}$, 𝔊 Μεων, Μαων. **3. gent.** Ju 10^{12} named with Sidonians and Amalek as ancient foes of Isr.; poss. intended by writer as = מְעוּנִים q v. p. 589 supr., many read מדין (𝔊^{BA} 𝔊L Μαδιαμ); v. GFM —בֵּית בַּעַל מְעוֹן v. מָעוֹן p. 111 supr.; 1 Ch 4^{41} v. מְעוּנִים p. 589.

†מְעוֹנָה **n.f.** id;—**1.** *den, lair* of wild beasts: of כפיר, מְעֹנָתוֹ Am 3^{4}, so pl abs. מְעוֹנוֹת Jb 38^{40} (|| סֻכָּה), sf מְעוֹנֹתָם ψ 104^{22}; cstr. מְעֹנוֹת אֲרָיוֹת Ct 4^{8}, מְעֹנֹתָיו Na 2^{13} (|| חֹרָיו; of אַרְיֵה, fig. of Nineveh); of חַיָּה in gen, בִּמְעוֹנֹתֶיהָ תִשְׁכֹּן Jb 37^{8} (|| אֶרֶב); so appar. fig. of men, hunted by י׳, מְעוֹנוֹתֵינוּ Je 21^{13}, fig also of י׳ dwelling in temple, sg sf., מְעוֹנָתוֹ בְצִיּוֹן ψ 76^{3} (|| סֻכּוֹ). **2.** fig מְעֹנָה אֱלֹהֵי קֶדֶם Dt 33^{27} *the ancient God is a dwelling-place* (for his people, cf 1. מָעוֹן **3**)

†מְעוֹנֹתַי **n.pr.m.** name in Judah 1 Ch 4^{14}, 𝔊 Μα(ω)ναθει.

†[עוֹנָה] Qr, [עִינָה] Kt **n.f.** only sf Ho 10^{10}: Qr pl. עוֹנֹתָם Baer, sg עוֹנָתָם Ginsb, > עינֹתָם Kt; but rd עֲוֹנֹתָם, v עָוֹן **1 a.** p. 730.

עוֹן Kt 1 S 18^{9} v עין.

עוֹעִים v. sub I עוה.

†I. עוּף **vb. fly** (NH *id*, (rare) *flicker, flutter*, עוֹף *fowl*, Aram. עוּפָא, ܥܘܦܐ *id.*; Eth. ፀፈ: *id*; Ar. عَوْفٌ *augury*, from birds (cf. We Heid. 2. 202), *fortune*, عاف، عيف *practice augury*, عَائِف *augur*; also عوف، عاف *fly about*, of birds);—**Qal** *Pf.* 3 mpl וְעָפוּ consec. Is 11^{14}; *Impf.* 3 ms. יָעוּף Jb 20^{8} ψ 91^{5} + Pr 23^{5b} Qr (> Kt ועוף [van d.H.], or יָעִיף [Ginsb]); וַיָּעֹף 2 S 22^{11} = ψ 18^{11}, Na 3^{16}, וַיָּעָף Is 6^{6}; 3 fs (הֲ)תָעוּף Pr 23^{5a} Kt (v. infr.), 3 fpl. תְּעוּפֶינָה Is 60^{8}, etc.; *Inf. cstr.* עוּף Jb 5^{7} Pr 26^{2}; *Pt.* fs. עָפָה Zc 5$^{1.2}$; pl. עָפוֹת Is 31^{5};—**1. a.** *fly*, of birds Dt 4^{17}, specif. of swallow (in sim.) Pr 26^{2} (|| נוּד); of seraph Is 6^{6} (cf. **Pōl.**), י׳ riding (רכב) on cherub 2 S 22^{11} = ψ 18^{11}; roll (in vision) Zc 5$^{1.2}$, arrow ψ 91^{5}, of swift army Is 11^{14} (under fig of bird, sq. בְּכָתֵף) Hb 1^{8} (sim of vulture), fig. of ships (like cloud, or doves) Is 60^{8}; בְּנֵי־רֶשֶׁף יַגְבִּיהוּ עוּף Jb 5^{7} *make high to fly*, i e make their flight high, soar aloft (sim of irresistible tendency) **b.** *hover* (protectingly) Is 31^{5} (birds, sim. of י׳; on sense cf. Dt 32^{11}). **2.** *fly away*, to a distance, ψ 55^{7} (fig.; || אַרְחִיק נְדֹד v^{8}); = vanish, of locusts Na 3^{16} (fig.); כְּנֶשֶׁר יָעוּף הַשָּׁמַיִם Pr 23^{5b} (Qr) sim. of riches (v. Toy); of wicked Jb 20^{8} (כַּחֲלוֹם), end of life, in gen., וַנָּעֻפָה ψ 90^{10} —הֲתָעוּף Pr 23^{5a} Kt, *do thine eyes fly* (*light*) upon it? (הֲתָעִיף **Hiph.** Qr *dost thou cause thine eyes to fly*, etc.?) is difficult, and line perhaps not original (v. Toy) **Pōl. 1.** *fly about, to and fro; Impf.* 3 ms. יְעוֹפֵף of birds Gn 1^{20} (P); seraphim Is 6^{2}; *Pt.* שָׂרָף מְעוֹפֵף *flying* fiery serpent Is 14^{29} 30^{6}. **2.** *cause to fly to and fro, brandish, Inf. cstr.* sf. בְּעוֹפְפִי חַרְבִּי Ez 32^{10} *when I brandish my sword* before them. **Hithpōʻl.** *Impf* 3 ms. כָּעוֹף יִתְעוֹפֵף כְּבוֹדָם Ho 9^{11} *like a bird their glory shall fly away* **Hiph.** *Impf.* 2 ms. Qr, v. **Qal** ad fin.

עוֹף $_{70}$ **n.m.** Gn 40, 17 **coll. flying creatures, fowl, insects**;—ע׳ abs Gn 1^{20}+, cstr. v^{21}+; —**1.** *fowl, birds*, Gn 40$^{17.19}$ (E), 7^{8} (J), 1$^{20.22}$ (P), 1 K 5^{13}+; esp. (38 t.) עוֹף הַשָּׁמַיִם *fowl of the sky*, Gn 2$^{19.20}$ (J), 1$^{26.28.30}$ (P), Ho 2^{20} Ec 10^{20}+, carrion birds 1 S 17$^{44.46}$ 2 S 21^{10} 1 K 14^{11}+ 11 t.; כִּכְלוּב מָלֵא ע׳ Je 5^{27}; ע׳ נוֹדֵד Is 16^{2}, ע׳ הָרִים ψ 50^{11}; redundantly ע׳ כָּנָף *fowl of wing* Gn 1^{21} (P), ψ 78^{27} (for food); for food also Lv 7^{26} (P), 17^{13} 20^{25} (both H), cf Lv 11$^{13.46}$ (H, clean and unclean); for offering Gn 8^{20} (J; הָע׳ הַטָּהוֹר), Lv 1^{14} (P). **2.** *winged insects* (clean and unclean) שֶׁרֶץ הָע׳ הַהֹלֵךְ עַל־אַרְבַּע Lv 11$^{20.21}$ (H), שֶׁ׳ הָע׳ Dt 14^{19}, so prob. הָע׳ alone v^{20}; שֶׁ׳ הָע׳ אֲשֶׁר־לוֹ אַרְבַּע רַגְלַיִם Lv 11^{23} (H).

†[עַפְעַף] **n.m.** Je 9, 17 **eyelid** (NH *id.*; from *fluttering*?), —only du. cstr. (v. infr.) and sf. עַפְעַפֵּי Jb 16^{16} ψ 132^{4}, עַפְעַפֶּיךָ Pr 4^{25} 6^{4}, etc.;— *eyelids*, usu. nearly = *eyes* (6 t. || עֵינַיִם), as weeping, עַפְעַפֵּינוּ Je 9^{17}; closed in sleep ψ 132^{4} Pr 6^{4}, cf. of צַלְמָוֶת Jb 16^{16}; looking Pr 4^{25} cf ψ 11^{4} (of י׳, testing men); used seductively by wanton women Pr 6^{25}; raised, in arrogance

(*'superciliousness'*) 30[13], fig עַפְעַפֵּי־שָׁחַר Jb 3[9] *eyelids of dawn*, break of dawn, 41[10] (sim)

†II [עוּף], I [עִיף] **vb. be dark**,—only **Qal** *Impf* 2 ms. תָּעֻפָה Jb 11[17] (though) *it be dark*, but rd. prob תְּעֻפָה, subst, v infr

†I עֵיפָה **n.f. darkness**,—עשה שַׁחַר עיפה Am 4[13], אֶרֶץ עֵפָתָה Jb 10[22] (Ges [§ 90 f], ‖ צַלְמָוֶת)

†II עֵיפָה **n.pr. 1. gent.** 'son' of Midian Gn 25[4] (J) = 1 Ch 1[33], cf Is 60[6], 𝔊 Γαφερ, Γεφαρ, Γαιφα(ρ) **2. m** name in Judah 1 Ch 2[47], 𝔊 Γαιφα **3 f** concubine of Caleb 1 Ch 2[46], 𝔊 Γαιφαηλ, A Γαιφα ἡ, 𝔊L Γαιφα

†מוּעָף **n.[m.]** gloom,—Is 8[23]

†[מָעוּף] **n.[m.]** id,—cstr מעוף צוקה Is 8[22] (‖ חֲשֵׁכָה), Che [Hpt] rds מוּעָף

†תְּעֻפָה **n f.** id,—so rd prob. for תָּעֻפָה Jb 11[17] (opp בֹּקֶר)

†עוֹפַי Kt, עֵיפַי Qr **n.pr.m.** a Netophathite, Je 40[8], 𝔊 Ιωφε, Ωφε, Ωφετ

†[עוּץ] **vb. counsel, plan** (Aram *id*; ‖ form of יעץ);—only **Qal** *Imv* mpl. עֻצוּ Ju 19[30] (GFM rds עֵצָה, but v Bu), Is 8[10] c acc cogn עֵצָה. (Sta [ThLz 1894 Apr 28, 235] der עֻצוּ fr יעץ)

†עוּץ **n.pr. 1. m. a.** (eldest) 'son' of Aram Gn 10[23] (P), = 'son' of Shem 1 Ch 1[17], 𝔊 Ως, 𝔊L Ch Ουζ. **b.** eldest 'son' of Nahor Gn 22[21] (J), A Ωξ, 𝔊L Ωζ. **c** Edomite name Gn 36[28] = 1 Ch 1[42], 𝔊 Ως, 𝔊L Ους. **2 loc** (= **1. a, b,** poss also **c**), מַלְכֵי אֶרֶץ הָעוּץ Je 25[20] (𝔊 om), בארץ־עוץ Jb 1[1] (home of Job), 𝔊 Αυσιτις, La 4[21] (del עוץ 𝔊 cf. Bu and reff.); on Uz as vague name for E country v. esp. Bu [11 f], Dl [Pa 259 ZKF ii 87 ff.] puts in Hauran, or N (NE) therefrom, = As *Ussu*, but dub With name עוץ RS [K 261] cp Ar n pr div عَوْص, so We [Held 2, 146], against this No [ZMG xl (1886), 183 f.], but v reply RS [Sem i 43]

†יְעוּץ **n.pr.m.** Benjamite name 1 Ch 8[10], 𝔊 Ιδως, A Ιεους, 𝔊L Ιωας

†[עוּק] **vb** dub (if correct, Aram form (cf עוק, ܥܳܩ) for צוק *press*, so Thes al),—only **Hiph.** *Impf* 3 fs תָּעִיק Am 2[13], *Pt.* מֵעִיק v[13], but read prob תָּפִיק, מפיק *totter, cause tottering* Hi We Now Dr

†[עָקָה] **n.f. pressure** (si vera l, Aram word, 𝔗 עָקְתָא, Syr ܥܳܩܬܳܐ),—only cstr מִפְּנֵי עָקַת רָשָׁע ψ 55[4] *because of the pressure of the wicked*; > rd צַעֲקַת (‖ קוֹל; Ol al), which means *cry for help*

†מוּעָקָה **n.f. compression, distress** (si vera l, Aram word, = מצוקה);—שַׂמְתָּ מ׳ בְמָתְנֵינוּ ψ 66[11], 𝔊 θλίψεις, 𝔙 *tribulationes*; but word dub.

†[עִוֵּר] **vb. Pi. make blind, blind** (orig. meaning of √ dub.; Thes עור = *dig* (Ar. غَارٌ etc. *cave*), Hal [REJ xi, 67] cp עור *skin*, whence *blindness* as cataract,—Aram adj עַוִּיר, ܥܰܘܺܝܪܳܐ *blind*, Pa עַוַּר, ܥܰܘܰܪ = Heb Pi; Ar. عَوِرَ *be one-eyed*, Eth. ዐወረ: *be blind* Di [995]),—**Pi.** *Pf* 3 ms עִוֵּר 2 K 25[7], c עֵינֵי *put out the eyes of* = Je 39[7] = 52[11], *Impf.* 3 ms יְעַוֵּר fig, Ex 23[8] (E) a bribe *blindeth*, c. acc pers. (Sam 𝔊 ins עיני), Dt 16[19], c. עיני

†עִוֵּר **adj. blind**,—only abs. ע׳ Ex 4[11]+, pl. עִוְרִים 2 S 5[6]+, f עִוְרוֹת Is 42[7], (c art הָעִוֵּר Dt 28[29], elsewh הַע׳ Baer Ginsb, van d H. לָעִוֵּר Jb 29[15], הָעִוְרִים 2 S 5[6.8] Is 42[18]),—*blind*, usu. as subst. = *the blind* **1.** lit, physically *blind*. **a** of men Ex 4[11] (J, opp. פִּקֵּחַ), 2 S 5[6.8.8] Lv 19[14] (H), Dt 27[18] Je 31[8] Jb 29[15]; in sim Dt 28[29] Zp 1[17] Is 59[10], cf La 4[14] (appos); as adj. attribute איש ע׳ Lv 21[18] (H). **b.** of sacrif. animal Dt 15[21] Mal 1[8]. **2.** fig, **a** of the helpless, groping Is 29[18] 35[5] 42[16] ψ 146[8], as adj attribute, עֵינַיִם עִוְרוֹת Is 42[7]. **b.** of the dull, unreceptive, Is 42[18 19 19 19] (but v[19c] rd. חרשׁ q v), as adj attrib. עם עור 43[8]; as predicate 56[10]

†עִוָּרוֹן **n [m.] blindness**,—only in phr (subj י׳), *smite* (הִכָּה) *with blindness*. fig. of 'blind incapacity' (Dr) בע׳ Dt 28[28]; of smiting horses בע׳ Zc 12[4], i e with *blind staggers*, making them helplessly wild

†עַוֶּרֶת **n.f.** id,—of sacrif animals, abstr. for concr, Lv 22[22] (H)

†I [עוּר] **vb. rouse oneself, awake** (NH *id*; Aram עור, ܥܳܪ, Ar. عَارَ, عير, v. עִיר, עיר, عير, عَارَ is *be jealous*, cf Syr ܚܣܳܐ *hate, revenge*),—**Qal** *Impf* 3 ms sf. יְעוּרֶנּוּ Jb 41[2] Baer Ginsb, and Qr van d H, but Kt יעירנו (Hiph), Bab. Mass (v Baer [p 58]), so Ginsb [marg] van d H, rd. thus, or יְעוֹרְרֶנּוּ (Pōʿl) Bu, > contr form of Pōʿl. Ges [§ 72 cc] Di, cf Sta [§ 484 a], *Imv* ms עוּרָה ψ 7[7]+, fs. עוּרִי Ju 5[12 12]+3t., עוּרִי Ju 5[12 12]+5t (for rhythm); *Pt* עָר Ct 5[2] + Mal 2[12] (read prob. עֵד We Now GASm, cf 𝔊 ἕως = עַד),—*rouse oneself* to activity, of Deborah Ju 5[12 12 12 12]; of י׳ ψ 7[7] (‖ קוּמָה, הִנָּשֵׂא), 59[5] (sq inf), 44[24] (opp. יָשֵׁן), of י׳'s arm Is 51[9 9.9], of oneself ψ 57[9], of Zion Is 52[1 1], of stone (idol)

Hb 2[19], sword Zc 13[7] (+ עַל *against*), wind Ct 4[16], harp and lyre ψ 57[9] = 108[3]; לִבִּי עֵר Ct 5[2] *my heart waketh* (opp יָשֵׁן) —Jb 41[2] Mal 2[12] v. supr. **Niph.** *Pf* 3 ms. נֵעוֹר Zc 2[17]; *Impf* 3 ms. יֵעוֹר Je 6[22] Zc 4[1]; 3 mpl יֵעֹרוּ Je 50[41] Jb 14[12], יֵעוֹרוּ Jo 4[12],—*be roused* Zc 4[1] (fr. [מִן] sleep, in sim.), so Jb 14[12] (sleep of death, ‖ יָקוּם, יָקִיצוּ), *be incited* to activity, c. מִן loc.: of ׳י Zc 2[17], of nation Je 6[22], kings 50[41], whirlwind 25[32]; abs. of nations Jo 4[12]. **Pōʿl.** *Pf* 3 ms עוֹרֵר 2 S 23[18]+, ׳וְע consec. Is 10[26], 1 s וְעוֹרַרְתִּי Zc 9[13], sf. עוֹרַרְתִּיךָ Ct 8[5]; *Impf.* 3 fs תְּעוֹרֵר Pr 10[12], 2 mpl. תעוררו Ct 2[7] 3[5], תְּעֹרְרוּ 8[4] (fem. subj Ges[§144a]); *Imv* ms. עוֹרְרָה ψ 80[3]; *Inf* עֹרֵר Jb 3[8],—*rouse, incite* to activity, c. acc. pers Zc 9[13] (+ עַל *against*), acc. רפאים Is 14[9] (subj. שאול v. Ges[§145t]); ׳ע הָעֲתִידִים עֹרֵר לִוְיָתָן Jb 3[8], (of ׳י) ψ 80[3] אֶת־גְּבוּרָתֶךָ; esp *rouse, excite* love Ct 2[7] 3[5] 8[4] (all ‖ תָּעִירוּ; fem subj. v. Ges[§144a]); עוֹרַרְתִּיךָ 8[5] is dubious, of exciting love De, arousing from slumber Bu, so, reading עוֹרַרְתִּיךְ, Siegf; שִׂנְאָה תְּע׳ מְדָנִים Pr 10[12] *hatred stirreth up strifes;* c. acc. of weapon 2 S 23[18] *rouse, awaken*, i.e *wield, brandish* (+ עַל *against*), so read also v[8] (v. חֲנִית **1**) = 1 Ch 11[11.20], so Is 10[26].—Is 23[13] v עֹרֵר. **Pilp.** *Impf* 3 mpl זַעֲקַת־שֶׁבֶר יְעֹעֵרוּ Is 15[5], usu. expl as = יְעַרְעֵרוּ (wh. some rd.), *rouse* (i.e *raise?*) *a cry of destruction*, Ges[Comm. Thes] De Di Du Ges[§72cc] Ko[i.500, ii.497]; Pilp not elsewhere, very dub.; rd. perh. יְעוֹרְרוּ; Lag[Proph. Chald. II] Che Gu[Kau] SS rd יָרִיעוּ *shout*, but improb. with זַעֲקַת. **Hithpōʿl.** *Pf* וְהִתְעֹרַרְתִּי כִּי consec Jb 31[29] *and I was* (joyfully) *excited, triumphant*, that (‖ אִם־שָׂמַח), so perh. *Impf.* 3 ms. Jb 17[8], rdg וְחָנֵף עַל־נָקִי יִתְעֹרָר Me Di Beer (MT וְנָקִי עַל־חָנֵף יִתְע׳, i.e *be excited with displeasure*), *rouse oneself* to activity, *Pt.* מִתְעוֹרֵר לְהַחֲזִיק בָּךְ Is 64[6]. **Hiph.** *Pf* 3 ms הֵעִיר Is 41[2]+; 1 s. הַעִירֹתִי Is 41[25] (v. Ko[i.500] Ges[§72x]), sf. הַעִירֹתִהוּ 45[13]; *Impf* 3 ms. יָעִיר Dt 32[11]+, וְיָעֵר Dn 11[25], וַיָּעַר Hg 1[14]+, sf וַיְעִירֵנִי Zc 4[1], etc.; *Imv* ms. הָעִירָה ψ 35[23], mpl. הָעִירוּ Jo 4[9], *Inf* בָּעִיר (= בְּהָעִיר) ψ 73[20] (Ges[§53q]), *Pt* מֵעִיר Is 13[17]+, sf. מְעִירָם Jo 4[7];—**1.** *rouse*, c sf. Zc 4[1] (as if from sleep, v **Qal**); *rouse, stir up*, to activity, כְּנֶשֶׁר יָעִיר קִנּוֹ Dt 32[11]; c acc. pers., or equiv., expressed or implied, esp. subj ׳י: Is 45[13]; c. מִן loc. 41[2.25] Jo 4[7]; + עַל *against* Is 13[17], cf. Je 50[9] 51[1] Ez 23[22], ׳הֵעִיר אֶת־רוּחַ פּ Je 51[11] Hg 1[14] 1 Ch 5[26] 2 Ch 21[16] (+ עַל *against*), 36[22] = Ezr 1[1], cf. v[5]; ׳י subj also in foll.: יָעִיר קִנְאָה Is 42[13], יָעִיר 50[4] (+ לִי אֹזֶן); human subj., c. acc. pers. Jo 4[9], Dn 11[2] (+ את in conflict *with*, 𝔅 deW Meinh Behrm, cf Bev. who thinks יעיר לקראת יערך poss); perh. also, obj. crocodile Jb 41[2] (rdg. יְעִירֶנּוּ v. **Qal**); וְיָעֵר כֹּחוֹ וּלְבָבוֹ Dn 11[25] (+ עַל *against*); esp. of *rousing* love Ct 2[7] 3[5] 8[4] (all ‖ **Pōʿl.** q v), fig. אָעִירָה שָּׁחַר ψ 57[9] *I will arouse the dawn* (‖ Imv. **Qal** q.v.), pt. abs = *stirring up* (a fire) Ho 7[4] (si vera l.; cf. Ges[§120b]; but text dubious cf. We Now GASm). **2.** declarative or exhibitive sense, *act in an aroused manner, awake*, הָעִירָה וְהָקִיצָה לְמִשְׁפָּטִי ψ 35[23], cf Jb 8[6] (+ עַל *over=for;* both subj ׳י), abs ψ 73[20].

†I. עִיר **n.[m.]** **excitement**;—of terror, ע׳ וּבֶהָלוֹת Je 15[8], of rage (si vera l.), לֹא אָבוֹא בְּעִיר Ho 11[9], but St prop לְבָעֵר cf. We Oort Now GASm—בָּעִיר ψ 73[20] v. עור **Hiph.**—II, III עיר v. p 746 infr.

†עֵר **n.pr.m.** Hp (cf עור Qal Pt);—**1.** eldest son of Judah Gn 38[3.6] = 1 Ch 2[3.3], Gn 38[7] 46[12.12] Nu 26[19.19]. **2.** son of Judah's son Shelah 1 Ch 4[21]. —Vid. also **Qal** *Pt.* עֵר supr.

†I. עֵרִי **n.pr.m.** a son of Gad Gn 46[16] Nu 26[16], Αηδις, Αδδει.

II. עֵרִי **adj.gent.** of I עֵרִי, c. art as subst. coll. הָעֵרִי Nu 26[16], Αδδει.

†עֵרָן **n.pr.m.** (si vera l) an Ephraimite Nu 26[36], but עדן Sam Ginsb[marg], 𝔊 Εδεν.

†עֵרָנִי **adj.gent.** of עֵרָן, c art. as subst. coll. Nu 26[36], עדני Sam Ginsb[marg], 𝔊 Εδενει.

†יָעוּר Kt, יָעִיר Qr, **n.pr.m.** father of Elhanan the giant-slayer 1 Ch 20[5] (Ιαειρ) + ‖ 2 S 21[19] (where read יעיר for יַעְרֵי, and del. ארגים, v. Th We Dr Bu Kit HPS).

†II. [עוּר] **vb. be exposed, bare** (akin to עָרָה, ערר; Ar عَوْرَةٌ = *pudenda*);—**Niph.** *Impf.* 3 fs. עֶרְיָה תֵעוֹר קַשְׁתֶּךָ Hb 3[9] *into nakedness* (i.e utterly) *is thy bow laid bare*, made ready; We prop. עוֹרֵר תְּעוֹרֵר (cf. 2 S 23[18], I. עור **Pōʿl.**), and so Now [from √ערר, *lay bare*] *thou layest*, etc

†[מָעוֹר] **n[.m.] nakedness, pudendum**,—only pl. sf. מְעוֹרֵיהֶם Hb 2[15].

†עֵירֹם, עֵרֹם **adj.** and **n.[m.]** **1. naked**; **2. nakedness** (√עור Ew[423,426] Ges[§85.1] Sta[§§295, 327a], > √ערם (not Heb. in this sense) Ba[NB §27c] Ko[ii.84,120]),—abs. עֵירֹם Gn 3[10.11] + 4 t, עֵרֹם Ez 16[7] + 2 t. Ez; pl. עֵירֻמִּים Gn 3[7];—**1. adj.** *naked*

Gn 3$^{7.10.11}$ (all pred.); as subst. concr. Ez 18$^{7.16}$. **2. n.abstr.** *nakedness* Dt 28^{48}; ע׳ וְעֶרְיָה *nakedness and bareness* (=naked and bare, of personified Jerusalem), Ez 16$^{7.22.39}$ 22^{29}.

†עָרֹם, עָרוֹם **adj.** naked (perh. secondary form from עֵירֹם Ew §163c Sta §327a; or from √עָרָה, q.v.);—abs. עָרוֹם Am 2^{16}+8 t., עָרֹם 1 S 19^{24}+3 t.; f. עֲרֻמָּה Ho 2^{5}; pl. עֲרוּמִּים Gn 2^{25} Jb 22^{6};—*naked* Gn 2^{25} (J) 1 S 19^{14} Ho 2^{5}; adverb. (Ges §118n) c. הָלַךְ Is 20$^{2.3.4}$ Mi 1^{8}, cf. Am 2^{16} Jb 24$^{7.10}$; =subst. concr. Is 58^{7} Jb 22^{6}; = without possessions Jb 1$^{21.21}$=Ec 5^{14}; of She'ôl, open before י׳ Jb 26^{6}.

†[מַעֲרֹם, Kö ii. 1. 121] **n.m. naked thing**;—pl. abstr. sf. מַעֲרֻמֵּיהֶם 2 Ch 28^{15} *their nakedness* (denom. fr. foreg. Sta §273a; > √ערם Ba NB §166b).

III. עור (√of foll.; meaning unknown).

עוֹר 99 **n.m.** Jb 7,5 **skin** (NH *id.*; Ph. ערת Lzb 346);—ע׳ abs. Gn 3^{21}+, cstr. Ex 34^{29}+; sf. עֹרוֹ 29^{14}+, עוֹרוֹ Je 13^{23}, עֹרָהּ Nu 19^{5}, etc.; pl. cstr. עֹרֹת Gn 27^{16}+, עוֹרֹת Ex 39^{34}, sf. עֹרֹתָם Lv 16^{27};—*skin*: **1.** of men (55 t.), שִׂמְלָתוֹ לְעֹרוֹ Ex 22^{26} (E), ע׳ פָּנָיו 34$^{29.30}$ cf. v^{35} (all P); (dark) skin of Cushite Je 13^{23}; v. also Ez 37$^{6.8}$ La 3^{8} Jb 7^{5} 10^{11}+; in hyperb. Mi 3$^{2.3}$; עוֹר שִׁנָּי Jb 19^{20b} *the skin of my teeth*, i.e. gums (si vera l.); also Lv 13^{2}+33 t. Lv 13 (P), in tests for leprosy (v. esp. ע׳־בְּשָׂרוֹ v$^{2.2.3.4.11}$, cf. v$^{3.38.39.43}$); עוֹר בְּעַד עוֹר Jb 2^{4} *skin in behalf of, for, skin*, appar. proverb. phrase of barter, = everything has its price (on varieties of interpr. v. Comm.). **2.** *hide* of animals (44 t.), alw.—exc. Jb 40^{31}—after skinning: Gn 27^{16} (J); of sacrif. victims Ex 29^{14} Lv 4^{11}+5 t. (all P); prepared for use (by some process of tanning, cf. Now Arch. i. 242), sts. = *leather*: material of garments Gn 3^{21} (J), girdle 2 K 1^{8}, any article Lv 11^{32} 13^{48ff} Nu 31^{20} (P); covering of tabern. Ex 25$^{5.5}$+10 t. Ex 26, 35, 36, 39, of ark, sacred utensils, etc., Nu 4^{6}+5 t. Nu 4.

עורים Is 30^{6} v. עַיִר.

†[עוּשׁ] **vb.** si vera l., **lend aid, come to help** (Ar. غَاثَ IV. *aid, succour*; Sab. עוה n. *help*, Sab Denkm 91; Nab. Sin. עות in n.pr. Lzb 337 Cook 90);—**Qal** *Imv.* mpl. עוּשׁוּ וָבֹאוּ Jo 4^{11} but dub.; Gr Dr, plausibly, חוּשׁוּ; Che Expos., Nov. 1897, 365 נֹשׁוּ (√נגש); עוּרוּ We Now.

†יְעוּשׁ (also Kt יעיש) **n.pr.m.** (prob. *he comes to help*, Nö ZMG xl (1886), 168; =Ar. n.pr.div. يَغُوثُ, We Skizzen iii, 171; Heid. 2, 146 RS K 218 (cf. Sem i. 43) Nö l.c., yet against this 𝔊 Ιεους (i.e. ع; not Ιαγους, غ), and יְ (not יַ), Lag M ii. 77; BN 133 Buhl Edom. 48 f.);—**1.** son of Esau Gn 36$^{5.14}$ (both Kt יעיש), v^{18} 1 Ch 1^{35}. **2.** Benjamites: **a.** 1 Ch 7^{10} (Kt יעיש). **b.** 1 Ch 8^{39}. **3.** a Levite 1 Ch 23$^{10.11}$. **4.** son of Rehoboam 2 Ch 11^{19}.—יוֹעָשׁ v. supr., p. 222 b.

†[עָוַת] **vb. be bent, crooked** (NH *id.*, Pi. Nithp.; Aram. עַוֵּית Pa.; cf. ܥܘܬ, ܥܘܿܬ *deceive* PS 3008);—**Pi.** *Pf.* 3 ms. sf. עִוְּתָנִי Jb 19^{6}, עִוְּתוֹ Ec 7^{13}; 3 pl. sf. עִוְּתוּנִי ψ 119^{78}; *Impf.* 3 ms. יְעַוֵּת ψ 146^{9} Jb 8^{3}, יְעַוֵּת־ v^{3}; *Inf.* לְעַוֵּת Am 8^{5} La 3^{22};—**1. a.** *make crooked* = falsify, scales Am 8^{5}; *pervert* justice (צֶדֶק, מִשְׁפָּט) Jb 8$^{3.3}$ 34^{12} (all God subj.); c. acc. pers. *subvert* (i.e. deprive of justice), לְעַוֵּת אָדָם בְּרִיבוֹ La 3^{36}, cf. ψ 119^{78}; so עִוְּתָנִי Jb 19^{6} (י׳ subj.). **2.** *bend, make crooked*, דֶּרֶךְ רְשָׁעִים ψ 146^{9} (י׳ subj.); in gen. Ec 7^{13} (God subj.; opp. תִּקֵּן). **Pu.** *Pt.* מְעֻוָּת Ec 1^{15} *what is bent* (opp. תִּקֵּן). **Hithp.** *Pf.* 3 pl. consec. וְהִתְעַוְּתוּ Ec 12^{3} *and* the strong men *bend themselves*.

†[עַוָּתָה] **n.f. subversion,** i.e. **deprivation of justice**;—sf. עַוָּתָתִי La 3^{59} (opp. מִשְׁפָּטִי).

†עוּת **vb.** very dub.; only in לָדַעַת לָעוּת אֶת־יָעֵף דָּבָר Is 50^{4} usu. *to help*, so Ges Del Di Ry Kau al., but in that case an Aramaism (Aram. *עות = Ar. غاث, q.v. sub עוּשׁ); text prob. corrupt, 𝔊 Oort Th T 1891, 469 לְעִתּוֹ, and del. אֶת־יָעֵף; Klo Che Comm. לִרְעוֹת '*teach, edify*,' Gr לַעֲנוֹת, Che Hpt. לְהַחֲיוֹת.

†עוּתַי **n.pr.m. 1.** name in Judah 1 Ch 9^{4}, Γωθει (= עֲתָיָה Ne 11^{4}). **2.** Ezr 8^{14}, Ουθι.

עַז, עֹז, עָזָא v. עזז. עֵז v. ענז.

†עֲזָאזֵל **n.[m.] entire removal** (redupl. intens. (Ges §30n. Sta §124a), abstr., √[עזל] = Ar. عزل *remove*, v. Bähr Symb. ii. 668 Win ii. 659 ff. Me in Schenkel BL. i. 256; > most, n.pr. of spirit haunting desert, Thes Di Dr Hastings, DB [a fallen angel, Lv 16^{8ff} being late, acc. to Che ZAW xv (1895), 153 ff., Ency. Bib., who der. fr. עזז־אל; cf. Benz Ency. Bib.], as in Jewish angelology, where prob. based on interpret. of Lv 16^{8ff}; name not elsewhere);—ע׳ Lv 16$^{8.10.10.26}$ in ritual of Day of Atonement, =*entire removal* of sin and guilt from sacred places into desert on back of goat, symb. of entire forgiveness.

I. עָזַב 213 **vb. leave, forsake, loose** (NH *id.* (rare); Ar. عَزَبَ *be remote, absent, depart*, As. *ezêbu, leave*, Shaph. *ušezib, rescue*, cf. BAram. שֵׁיזִב;—Eth. ዐፀበ: *widowed* Di 973);—**Qal** *Pf.* 3 ms. ע׳ Gn 24^{27}+, sf. עֲזָבַנִי Is 49^{14} ψ 38^{11};

3 fs. עָזְבָה Ez 23^{8}; 1 s. sf. עֲזַבְתִּיךְ Is 54^{7}; 2 fpl. עֲזַבְתֶּן Ex 2^{20}, etc.; *Impf.* 3 ms. יַעֲזֹב Is 55^{7} +, יַעֲזָב־ Gn 2^{24}, sf. 1 s. וַיַּעַזְבֵנִי 1 S 30^{13}, etc.; *Imv.* עֲזֹב ψ 37^{8}, עָזְבָה Je 49^{11}, עִזְבוּ Je 48^{28} Pr 9^{6}, etc.; *Inf. abs.* עָזוֹב Je 14^{5}, עָזֹב Ex 23^{5}; *cstr.* עֲזֹב Gn 44^{22} +, sf. עָזְבֵךְ Je 2^{17} +, etc.; *Pt. act.* עֹזֵב Pr 10^{17} +, cstr. עֹזְבֵי (Ges § 90 l); f. cstr. עֹזֶבֶת Pr 2^{17} etc.; *pass.* עָזוּב Dt 32^{36} +, etc.;—†**1.** *leave*, c. acc. (on order of meanings cf. Nö ZMG. xl (1886), 726): **a.** = *depart from*, acc. pers. Gn 44$^{22.22}$ (J), 2 K 2$^{2.4.6}$ 4^{30} Nu 10^{31} (P), Ru 1^{16} Je 9^{1} (‖ הָלַךְ מֵאֵת); acc. loc. 1 K 8^{6} Je 25^{38} (י׳ as lion leaving lair); c. מִן loc. intrans. (strangely) Je 18^{14} (of snow). **b.** *leave behind*, acc. pers. Ex 2^{20} (J), 2 S 15^{16} (+ inf.), Ez 24^{21}; acc. rei + בְּיַד Gn 39$^{12.13}$, + אֶצְלִי v$^{15.18}$ (all J); + בְּ loc. 50^{8} (J); acc. pers. et rei Ex 9^{21} (J). **c.** *leave* in the presence of (לִפְנֵי) 1 Ch 16^{37} (לְ of accus., cf. לְ **3 b** supr.), 2 Ch 28^{14}. **d.** *leave in safety*, וְאָנָה תַּעַזְבוּ כְבוֹדְכֶם Is 10^{3}. **e.** *leave* in a given condition, situation, ע׳ אֹתוֹ בְּמַחֲלָיִים 2 Ch 24^{25} *they left him in* great *suffering*; c. adv. acc. Ez 23^{29}; a city פְּתוּחָה Jos 8^{17}. **f.** *leave undisturbed, let alone* Ru 2^{16}. **g.** *leave* unexercised, Gn 24^{27} pregn. *he hath not left his kindness and his faithfulness from* (being) *with* (מֵעִם) *my master*; so ע׳ חַסְדּוֹ אֶת־ Ru 2^{20} (both of י׳); ע׳ חֵמָה ψ 37^{8} (‖ הֶרֶף מֵאַף). **h.** *leave* in the hand of, entrust to, acc. rei + בְּיַד Gn 39^{6} (J), + אֶל־ Jb 39^{11} (‖ בָּטַח בְּ), + עַל־ ψ 10^{14} (acc. om., *his cause*).—So also poss. (c. לְ) Ne 3^{34} (reading לֵאלֹהִים for MT לָהֶם), but text prob. otherwise corrupt. **i.** *leave* to (לְ) one (unaided), וְחָדַלְתָּ מֵעֲזֹב לוֹ Ex 23^{5a} (E) *thou shalt refrain from leaving* it (sc. the affair) *to him*; cf. תַּעֲזֹב לָאָרֶץ בֵּיצֶיהָ Jb 39^{14} (of ostrich). **j.** *leave over, remaining*, acc. pers. Jos 2^{21} (JE); acc. rei + לְ pers. Lv 19^{10} 23^{22} (H), Mal 3^{19}. **k.** *leave* = have nothing to do with Pr 9^{6}. **2.** *leave, abandon, forsake*: †**a.** *abandon*, acc. rei: (1) land, house, city, tent, etc., 1 S 31^{7} = 1 Ch 10^{7}, 2 K 7^{7} Je 9^{18} 48^{28} 51^{9} 2 Ch 11^{14}, Is 17^{9} (+ מִפְּנֵי of enemy); pt. pass. of cities v^{2} Je 4^{29} Zp 2^{4}, cf. עֲזוּבָה Is 17^{9} pt. = subst. = *deserted region*. (2) oxen 1 K 19^{20}, idol-images (+ שָׁם) 2 S 5^{21} = 1 Ch 14^{12}, flock Zc 11^{17}; pt. pass. of eggs Is 10^{14}. †**b.** *forsake*, (1) human subj. and obj.: Gn 2^{24} (J; a man his parents), 1 S 30^{13} Jos 22^{3} (D), Je 49^{11} ψ 27^{10} (parent a child), Pr 2^{17} (wife her husband, אַלּוּף), cf. אִשָּׁה עֲזוּבָה Is 54^{6}, and ע׳ of personif. Zion Is 60^{15} 62^{4}. (2) an animal its young Je 14^{5} (obj. om.). †**c.** = neglect, Levite Dt 12^{19} 14^{27}, poor Jb 20^{19}. **d.** esp. (1) fig. of *forsaking* God (י׳), apostatizing, Ju 10^{10} Dt 28^{20} 31^{16} Je 1^{16} + 38 t. (oft. Je and later); + Jon 2^{9} (obj. חַסְדָּם, i.e. God, v. חֶסֶד **II**); c. לְ + inf. only אֶת־י׳ עָזְבוּ לִשְׁמֹר Ho 4^{10} (Oort We Now doubt לִשְׁמֹר). (2) obj. י׳'s law, commands, covenant, etc., Dt 29^{24} 1 K 19$^{10.14}$ + 14 t.; house of י׳ 2 Ch 24^{18} Ne 10^{40}. †(3) *forsake*, fail to follow, obey advice, instruction, wisdom, reproof: 1 K 12$^{8.13}$ = 2 Ch 10$^{8.13}$ Pr 2^{13} 4$^{2.6}$ 10^{17} 15^{10} 27^{10}. †(4) but also of *forsaking* idols Ez 20^{8}, sins of various kinds 23^{8} Is 55^{7} Pr 28^{13} (obj. om.; + מוֹדֶה *confess*); הַמַּשָּׁא *usury* Ne 5^{10}. **e.** of God's *forsaking, abandoning* men: Dt 31^{17} Is 42^{16} 49^{14} 54^{7} 2 Ch 12^{5} Ezr 9^{9} ψ 9^{11} 22^{2} + 8 t. ψψ; + בְּיַד Ne 9^{28} ψ 37^{33}; ψ 16^{10} *thou wilt not abandon my soul* לִשְׁאוֹל; of temporary abandonment 2 Ch 32^{31} (+ inf. of purpose); etc. (34 t. in all); + Je 12^{7} (י׳ abandoning his house). †**f.** of God's *leaving*, i.e. ceasing to regard, the earth, thus giving impunity to crime, Ez 8^{12} 9^{9}. †**g.** of strength (כֹּחַ) *forsaking* one ψ 38^{11}, courage (לֵב) 40^{13}, kindness and faithfulness (חֶסֶד וֶאֱמֶת) Pr 3^{3}. †**3.** *let loose, set free, let go* עָזֹב תַּעֲזֹב עִמּוֹ Ex 23^{5b} (E) *thou shalt by all means free* it (sc. the beast) *with him*, (aid him to set it free; on sense, cf. Dt 22^{4}; DHM sub II. עזב); עָצוּר וְעָזוּב *shut up and freed*, proverb. phr., = all classes of people Dt 32^{36} 1 K 14^{10} 21^{21} 2 K 9^{8} 14^{26} (exact meaning dub.; prob. either = bond and free, or [v. RS Sem i. 437, 2nd ed. 456] under taboo and free from it); *let go* Jb 20^{13} (c. acc. of wickedness as morsel in mouth); *let loose* my complaint Jb 10^{1} (עָלַי *apud me*, cf. עַל **II 1 d**); אֶעֶזְבָה פָנַי Jb 9^{27} *I will loosen, relax, my face*, (cf. Thes De Me Stu Di Buhl Lex Bu; > *abandon my* [gloomy] *countenance* AV RV SS Bae Kau Du). †**Niph.** *Pf.* 3 ms. נֶעֱזַב Ne 13^{11}; 3 fs. נֶעֱזָבָה Is 62^{12}; *Impf.* 3 fs. תֵּעָזֵב Is 7^{16} Lv 26^{43}, תֵּעָזַב Jb 18^{4}; 3 mpl. יֵעָזְבוּ Is 18^{6}; *Pt.* נֶעֱזָב Is 27^{10} ψ 37^{25}; fpl. נֶעֱזָבוֹת Ez 36^{4};—**1.** *be left to* (לְ), i.e. to the possession of, Is 18^{6}. **2.** *be forsaken*, of house of God Ne 13^{11}, a city Ez 36^{4} Is 27^{10} (‖ מְשֻׁלָּח), 62^{12}; the earth Jb 18^{4}, land Is 7^{16}, Lv 26^{43} (+ מִן of exiles); of man ψ 37^{25}. †**Pu.** (or **Qal pass.**, v. Ges § 52 e) *be deserted*, of city: *Pf.* 3 ms. הֲמוֹן עִיר עֻזָּב Is 32^{14} (‖ נֻטָּשׁ); 3 fs. עֻזְּבָה Je 49^{25}.

†I. עֲזוּבָה **n.f. forsakenness, desolation**;—וְרַבָּה הָע׳ בְּקֶרֶב הָאָרֶץ Is 6^{12}.—17^{9} v. √**2 a.**

†II. עֲזוּבָה **n.pr.f. 1.** Αζαεβα, Αζουβα, mother of Jehoshaphat 1 K 22[42] = 2 Ch 20[31]. **2.** (Γ)αζουβα, wife of Caleb 1 Ch 2[18.19].

†[עִזָּבוֹן] **n.[m.]** only pl. **wares** (as *left* in the purchaser's hand; cf. As. *uzub(b)u*, a specif. *payment*);—sf. 2 fs. עִזְבוֹנַיִךְ Ez 27[27.33], -נָיִךְ v[12] + 4 t.;—*wares*, only Ez 27 (oft. ‖ מַעֲרָב q.v. sub ערב); בַּרְזֶל בְּדִיל וְעוֹפֶרֶת נָתְנוּ ע׳ Ez 27[12] *iron, tin and lead they furnished as thy wares;* similarly v[14.22]; also v[16] (MT בְּע׳, but prob. del בְּ); בְּע׳ נָתְנוּ v[19] *at the price of (in exchange for) thy wares they furnished*, etc.; הוֹנֵךְ וְע׳ (as subj. of sentence) v[27]; בְּצֵאת ע׳ מִיַּמִּים v[33] *when thy wares came forth*, etc.

† II. [עָזַב] **vb. restore, repair** (?) (cf. perhaps Sab. עדב *restore*, Sab Denkm[90] DHM Öster. Monatsschr. f. d. Orient 1885, 226; also NH מַעֲזִיבָה *restoration, erection* Levy NHWB iii. 186, Ar. معزب *building-stone* Kremer Beitr. ii. 18);—**Qal** *Impf.* 3 mpl. וַיַּעַזְבוּ Ne 3[8] *and they repaired* (?) Jerus. as far as the broad wall; > *paved* Gu ZPV viii (1885), 282 f., or fr. √ I. עזב (see views in Be Ryle).

עֲזוּבָה, עַזְגָּד, עַזְבּוּק, עַזָּה v. עזז.

†עַזָּה **n.pr.loc. Gaza,** Γαζα (As. *Ḫazzutu*, etc., COT i. 97 Dl Pa 290, TelAm *Ḫazati, Azzati* Wkl[38*]; Egypt. *Gadatu* WMM As. u. Eur. 87, 96, 159, 392; 𝔊 Γαζα, so Jos Ant. xiii. 5, 5, etc.; Herod. ii. 159; iii. 5 Κάδυτις);—Philistine city (mod. غَزَّة, Ghazze, Razze), c. Lat. 31° 3′ N, Long. 34° 28′ E, c. 50 miles WSW. from Jerus., near the sea (Rob BR ii. 36 ff. GASm Geogr. 181 ff. Buhl Geogr. 190 f.), Ju 16[1.21] (both עַזָּתָה), southernmost of the famous five cities, Gn 10[19] (J), Ju 6[4] 1 K 5[4] 2 K 18[8], cf. Dt 2[23] Jos 10[41] (D); also 11[22] (D), 15[47] (P), Ju 1[18] 1 S 6[17] Am 1[6.7] Zp 2[4] Je 25[20] 47[1.5] Zc 9[5.5];—On commercial importance v. DHM B und S 989 Gatt ZPV vii (1884), 1 ff., 293 ff.; viii (1885), 69 ff., 179 ff..—For עַזָּה 1 Ch 7[28] van d. H., read עַיָּה Baer Ginsb (q. v.), Be Oettli Kau Kit Hpt.; v. עַי.

†עַזָּתִי **adj.gent.** of foreg., c. art. as subst. coll. Jos 13[3] (D); pl. לָעַזָּתִים Ju 16[2].

†[עָזַז] **vb. be strong** (NH *id.*, Hiph., esp. in bad sense, and esp. deriv. עַז; Ph. עז *strength*, also in n.pr. Lzb[338]; Aram. عَزّ *be mighty, strong*, cf. OAram. Nab. Palm. n.pr. עזיזו Lzb 338 Cook[90]; Ar. عَزَّ *be mighty, strong*, Eth. **ዐዘዘ:** *id.;* As. *ezêzu, be furious, ezzu, fierce*);—**Qal** *Impf.* 3 ms. יָעֹז ψ 9[20] 52[9], יָעוֹז Dn 11[12]; 3 fs. תָּעֹז ψ 89[14] Ec 7[19], וַתָּעָז Ju 3[10] 6[2]; *Imv.* ms. עוּזָּה ψ 68[29] (but v. infr.); *Inf. cstr.* עֲזוֹז Pr 8[28];—*be strong, prevail,* וַתָּעָז יָדוֹ עַל־ Ju 3[10] *and his hand prevailed against,* so 6[2]; אַל־יָעֹז אֱנוֹשׁ ψ 9[20], Dn 11[12]; abs. תָּעֹז יָדְךָ ψ 89[14] (of י׳); of appar. strength of wicked 52[9]; בַּעֲזוֹז עִינוֹת תְּהוֹם Pr 8[28] *when the fountains of the deep grew strong,* i. e. firm, fixed; but Oort Bi Toy rd. בְּעַזְּזוֹ *when he made firm, fixed fast* (‖ בְּאַמְּצוֹ); עוּזָּה אֱלֹהִים ψ 68[29] Che Bae al. *shew thyself strong, O God,* who, etc., cf. Kö i. 363; < עֹז הָא׳ *the might, O God,* wh., etc., Hup Du; הַחָכְמָה תָּעֹז לֶחָכָם Ec 7[19] *wisdom is strong for the wise.*—לָעוֹז Is 30[2] v. עוז. **Hiph.** *Pf.* 3 ms. הֵעֵז אִישׁ רָשָׁע בְּפָנָיו Pr 21[29] *a wicked man maketh firm* (*sheweth boldness*) *with his face;* so 3 fs. הֵעֵזָּה פָנֶיהָ 7[13] (Ges § 67 dd Kö i. 372) *she maketh bold her face.*

†עַז **adj. strong, mighty, fierce;**—ע׳ abs. Nu 13[28] + 2 t., עָז Ju 14[18], עָז Am 5[9] + 4 t.; עַז cstr. Dt 28[50] Dn 8[23]; f. עַזָּה Ex 14[21] + 2 t.; pl. עַזִּים Ez 7[24] + 3 t.; f. עַזּוֹת Pr 18[23]; cstr. עַזֵּי Is 56[11];—*strong, mighty,* wind Ex 14[21] (J); border Nu 21[24] (JE), but rd. prob. יַעְזֵר (𝔊 Di al.) *Ya'zer was t. border;* of people Pr 30[25] (fig. of ants), מַיִם עַזִּים Is 43[16] (‖ הַיָּם), Ne 9[11]; of love Ct 8[6];=subst. *the mighty* Am 5[9] Ez 7[24] + Pr 24[5] (of physical force; rdg. טוֹב מֵעַז or the like 𝔊𝔖𝔗 Kmp Kau Wild Toy); *formidable, fierce,* of lion Ju 14[18], so (=subst.) v[14], of king Is 19[4] (‖ אֲדֹנִים קָשֶׁה), of people Nu 13[28] (JE), Is 25[3] (‖ עָרִיצִים); of enemy 2 S 22[18] = ψ 18[18], so as subst. ψ 59[4]; עַז פָּנִים Dt 28[50] *fierce of countenance,* Dn 8[23], so perh. = *impudent* Ec 8[1] (rdg. עַז for עֹז q.v.); of anger (אַף) Gn 49[7] (poem in J), wrath (חֵמָה) Pr 21[14]; הַכְּלָבִים עַזֵּי־נֶפֶשׁ Is 56[11] *dogs fierce of appetite* (‖ לֹא יָדְעוּ שָׂבְעָה); fpl. as adv. accus. יַעֲנֶה עַזּוֹת Pr 18[23] the rich *answereth fiercely.*

†עֹז, and (rarely) עוֹז **n.m. strength, might;**—abs. ע׳ Ju 9[51] +, עוֹז ψ 84[6] +, עָז־ Is 26[1], once עָז Gn 49[3]; cstr. עֹז Mi 5[3] +, עָז־ ψ 28[8]; sf. עֻזִּי Ex 15[2] + 2 t., עֻזִּי ψ 28[7] +; עֻזְּךָ 21[2] + 2 t., 66[3] +; sf. 1 pl. עֻזֵּנוּ 81[2]; 3 mpl. עֻזָּמוֹ 89[18], etc.;—*strength, might* (usu. poet., 44 t. ψψ): **1.** material and physical, מִגְדַּל־עֹז Ju 9[51], and fig. (of י׳), ψ 61[4] Pr 18[10], מַחְסִי־עֹז ψ 71[7], cf. עִיר עָז־לָנוּ Is 26[1], עֹז מִבְטֶחָה קִרְיַת־עֻזּוֹ Pr 18[19] (sim.), 10[15] = 18[11] (fig.); Pr 21[22] (of a city, read poss. מעוז Toy); צוּר עֻזִּי ψ 62[8] (fig.); מְרוֹם עֻזָּהּ Je 51[53] (of Bab.), מַצְּבוֹת עֻזֵּךְ Ez 26[11] (of Tyre), cf. ψ 30[8] (rdg. לְהַרְרֵי־עֹז 𝔗 Hup Che Kau We; but no obj. for vb.; Gie in Bae prop. הֶעֱמַדְתִּי for הֶעֱמַדְתָּה); רְקִיעַ עֻזּוֹ ψ 150[1] *his*

mighty firmament (De Hup Kau al.; Ki AV RV Che *the f. of his power*, where his power dwells); בְּכָל־עֹז *with all* one's *might* 2 S 6[14] = 1 Ch 13[8], + 2 Ch 30[21] (where so read, for MT כְּלֵי עֹז, Kau Kit cf. Be Oettli); בְּעוֹז Pr 31[17 25]; abstr. for concr. Ju 5[21] si vera l., but prob. crpt., cf. GFM Bu, of crocodile Jb 41[14], קוֹל עֹז ψ 68[34] *a mighty voice*; זְרוֹעַ עֻזּוֹ = *his mighty arm* (fig. of י׳) Is 62[8], cf 51[9] ψ 89[11] Jb 26[2], גֶּשֶׁם מִטְרוֹת עֻזּוֹ Jb 37[6]; מַטֵּה־עֹז, fig of political power Je 48[17] (|| מַקֵּל תִּפְאָרָה), Ez 19[11 12 14] (vine-branches, in fig.), ψ 110[2]. **2.** personal, social, and political: **a.** Am 3[11], גְּאוֹן ע׳ Lv 26[19] (H), Ez 24[21] 30[6 18] 33[28] **b.** bestowed by י׳, 1 S 2[10] (song), ψ 29[11] 68[36] 86[16] 138[3], עוֹז־לוֹ בָךְ 84[6] 138[3], so (implic.) of Zion Is 52[1] **c.** of י׳ as strength of his servants Mi 5[3] Is 49[5] ψ 81[2] 84[6], also Ex 15[2] (|| יְשׁוּעָה) = Is 12[2] = ψ 118[14], cf. Is 45[24], עֹז יְשׁוּעָתִי ψ 140[8], תִּפְאֶרֶת עֻזָּמוֹ 89[18]; sts as their stronghold, for defence Je 16[19] (+ מָעֻזִּי), ψ 28[7] (+ מָגִנִּי), v[8] (|| מָעוֹז), 46[2] (+ מַחְסֶה), 59[10] (rdg עֻזִּי, v Comm. and Ginsb[marg]; || מִשְׂגַּבִּי), v[18] (|| *id.*), cf. Pr 14[26] (|| מַחְסֶה), v. also sub **1**.—Pr 24[5] v. עָז. **3.** *might* of י׳ (esp. ψψ). **a.** as essential attribute Hb 3[4] Jb 12[16] ψ 62[12] 63[3] 68[35] 93[1] 96[6] = 1 Ch 16[27]; עֹז מֶלֶךְ ψ 99[4] (title of י׳). **b.** theme of ascription in praise ψ 29[1] (c. הָבוּ) = 96[7] = 1 Ch 16[28], ψ 59[17] (c שִׁיר), 68[35] (c. נָתַן) **c.** exerted for his people and against his foes Ex 15[13] (song), ψ 21[2] (|| יְשׁוּעָה), v[14] 66[3] 68[29] + v[29] (rdg עֹז for עוּזָּה, v. עזז), 74[13] 77[15] 78[26] 105[4] = 1 Ch 16[11], Ezr 8[22] (+ אַפּוֹ), cf עֹז אַפֶּךָ ψ 90[11]. **d.** manifested in connex. with the ark, אֲרוֹן עֻזֶּךָ 2 Ch 6[41] = ψ 132[8], עֹז = ark 78[61]. **4.** עֹז פָּנָיו = *boldness, impudence* Ec 8[1], changed by wisdom, De Wild al; < rd עֹז פ׳ *he who is impudent* 𝔊 Siegf (cf. עזז **Hiph.**) **5.** = *stronghold* (cf. **2 c**): ψ 8[3] *out of the mouth of babes . . . thou hast founded strength, or a stronghold* (for thy defence, cf. v[b]), so Ew De Hup Kau Sch Che Dr, cf. Du, > *praise* Vrss Bae.—מָעֵת v עֵת.

† עֱזוּז **n.[m.]** strength, might, fierceness = עֹז;—cstr ע׳ מִלְחָמָה Is 42[25] *fierceness of battle* (fr י׳, + חֲמַת אַפּוֹ), ע׳ נוֹרְאֹתֶיךָ ψ 145[6]; sf עֱזוּזוֹ וְנִפְלְאֹתָיו 78[4].

† עִזּוּז **adj.** mighty, powerful,—of an army Is 43[17], of י׳ ψ 24[8].

† עָזָז **n.pr.m.** Reubenite name 1 Ch 5[8], Οζουζ, 𝔊L Ιωαζαζ (Ginsb[marg] עָזָז, עֻזָּז, עוּז, cf. Baer[100])

† עֻזָּא **n.pr.m.** Οζα, Αζα: **1.** driver of the ark 2 S 6[3] = עֻזָּה v[6.7.8] = עֻזָּא 1 Ch 13[7 9 10 11]. **2.** in בְּגַן־עֻזָּא burial-place of Manasseh and Amon 2 K 21[18.26] (ע׳ perh = עֻזִּיָּה, cf Sta[G i. 569, ii 679] Kit). **3.** Benjamite name 1 Ch 8[7]. **4.** head of family of returned exiles Ezr 2[49] = Ne 7[51].

† עֻזָּה **n.pr.m.** **1.** Levite name 1 Ch 6[14], Οζ(ι)α, Αζα **2.** v. עֻזָּא.

† עֲזִיזָא **n.pr.m.** one with foreign wife Ezr 10[27], Οζει(α), Αζιζα.

† עֲזַזְיָהוּ **n.pr.m.** (י׳ *is mighty*);—Οζ(ε)ιας (= עֻזִּיָּהוּ): **1.** Levite names: **a.** 1 Ch 15[21] (del. Kit). **b.** 2 Ch 31[13] (? Kit). **2.** a Benjamite 1 Ch 27[20] (Kit עֻזִּיָּהוּ; v also Gray[Prop. N 295]).

† עֻזִּיאֵל **n.pr.m.** (*my strength is Ēl*),—Οζ(ε)ιηλ: **1.** Levites: **a.** Ex 6[18.22] Lv 10[4] Nu 3[19.30] 1 Ch 5[28] 6[3] 15[10] 23[12.20] 24[24]. **b.** 1 Ch 25[4] (= עֲזַרְאֵל v[18]), 𝔊[B] Αζαραηλ. **c.** 2 Ch 29[14]. **2.** Simeonite 1 Ch 4[42]. **3.** Benjamite 1 Ch 7[7]. **4.** repairer of wall Ne 3[8].—Vid יַעֲזִיאֵל.

† עָזִּיאֵלִי **adj. gent.** of foregoing, c. art. as subst coll. Nu 3[27] (Ginsb[marg] הָעֻזִּי׳), לָעֻזִּ׳ 1 Ch 26[23].

† עֻזִּיָּהוּ, עֻזִּיָּה **n.pr.m.** (*my strength is* י׳; cf. OHeb. עזיו Lzb[338]),—**1.** Οζειας, but also Αζαριας. king of Judah = עֲזַרְיָהוּ: **a.** עֻזִּיָּהוּ 2 K 15[32.34] 2 Ch 26[1.3.8.9 11 14 18.18.19.21 22 23] 27[2] Is 1[1] 6[1] 7[1]. **b.** עֻזִּיָּה 2 K 15[13.30] Ho 1[1] Am 1[1] Zc 14[5]. **2.** עֻזִּיָּהוּ father of an officer of David 1 Ch 27[25]. **3.** עֻזִּיָּה Levite name 1 Ch 6[9]. **4.** *id*. priest with foreign wife Ezr 10[21] **5.** *id*. name in Judah Ne 11[4] (also v[5] 𝔊 for חזיה)—Vid also יַעֲזִיָּהוּ.

† עֻזִּיָּא **n.pr.m.** (= foregoing; cf. Gray[Prop. N 295]);—hero of David 1 Ch 11[44], Οζεια(ς).

† עֻזִּי **n.pr.m.** Οζει: **1.** Levites **a.** 1 Ch 5[31.32] 6[36] Ezr 7[4]. **b.** Ne 11[22]. **c.** priestly name Ne 12[19.42]. **2.** name in Issachar 1 Ch 7[2.3]. **3.** Benjamite name 1 Ch 7[7] 9[8].

† (וְ)יַעֲזִיאֵל **n.pr.m.** Οζειηλ, Levite name 1 Ch 15[18] = (וְ)עֲזִיאֵל v[20], both prob. err. for עֻזִּיאֵל Gray[Prop. N 210, 224, 307, 309].

† יַעֲזִיָּהוּ **n.pr.m.** Οζεια(ς), Levite name 1 Ch 24[26.27], perhaps for עֻזִּיָּהוּ Gray[Prop. N 291].

† עַזְבּוּק **n.pr.m.** father of one Nehemiah, a wall-builder Ne 3[16], Αζαβουχ, 𝔊L Εζδουκ.

† עַזְגָּד **n.pr.m.** Ασγαδ, Αζγαδ (*Gad is mighty*; Gray[Prop. N 145]);—**1. a.** head of family returning with Zerub Ezr 2[12] = Ne 7[17]. **b.** returning with Ezra Ezr 8[12]. **2.** one of those sealed Ne 10[16].

†I עַזְמָ֫וֶת **n.pr.m** A𝔊Lusu Αζμωθ, Ασμωθ: **1. a.** one of David's heroes 2 S 23^{31} 1 Ch 11^{33}, B Ασβωθ **b.** father of two of David's men 1 Ch 12^{3} **c.** officer of David 1 Ch 27^{25} **2.** Benjamite name 1 Ch 8^{36} 9^{42}, B Σαλμω, Γαβαωθ.

†II עַזְמָ֫וֶת **n pr loc.** v בית־ע׳ p 112 supr.

†עַזָּן **n pr.m.** Οζα, Οζα, in Issachar Nu 34^{26}.

†עָזְנִיָּה **n f.** (unclean) bird of prey, appar akin to vulture (Now$^{\text{Arch I 84, 116}}$), named + נשר, פרס Dt 14^{12} Lv 11^{13} (H), = *osprey* Tristr$^{\text{NHB 184}}$ Dr$^{\text{Dt 14, 12}}$ (others *vulture* Di$^{\text{Lv 11, 13}}$) (√ unknown; conject. v in Di, perhaps foreign word)

†[עָזַק] **vb. dig about** (NH *id*, also *surround, enclose*, Aram עִזְקְתָא, ܥܙܩܬܐ, *ring*, Ar عَزَقَ *cleave* or *furrow the earth* with implement مِعْزَقَة, Eth ዐዘቅት: *well, cistern*),—**Pi** *Impf* 3 ms sf וַיְעַזְּקֵהוּ Is 5^{2} (intens.) *and he dug it carefully about*

†עֲזֵקָה **n.pr.loc.** Αζηκα, in the Shephelah of Judah, near שוכה, Jos 10$^{10\,11}$ (JE), 15^{35} (P), 1 S 17^{1} Je 34^{7} 2 Ch 11^{9} Ne 11^{30}, not identified.

I [עָזַר] $_{82}$ **vb. help, succour** (NH *n* עֶזְרָה *help*, Ph in deriv and cpds Lzb$^{338\,f.}$, Ar عَذَرَ *excuse, exculpate*, also *aid*, Aram ܥܕܪ *help*, Palm עדר, rarely עזר Lzb^{338} Cook$^{89\,90}$),—**Qal** *Pf* 3 ms sf. עֲזָרָ֫נִי ψ 118^{13}, עֲזָרְךָ 1 Ch 12^{19}, 3 pl sf עֲזָרֻם 1 Ch 12^{20}, etc.; *Impf* 3 ms יַעֲזֹר Is 50$^{7\,9}$, sf יַעְזְרֶךָּ Is 44^{2}, 3 mpl יַעְזֹרוּ Is 30^{7} 41^{6}, וַיַּעְזְרוּ 1 K 1^{7}, sf יַעְזְרֻנִי ψ 119^{175}, etc, *Imv* ms sf. עָזְרֵנִי ψ 109^{26} 119^{86} + Jos 10^{4} Kt, mpl sf עִזְרוּנִי Qr, etc, *Inf cstr* לַעְזֹר 1 Ch 22^{17}, לַעְזוֹר 18^{5}, לַעְזֹר Jos 10^{33} + 5 t., לַעְזוֹר 2 Ch 25^{8} + 2 S 18^{3} Qr (> Kt לַעְזִיר **Hiph.**), sf לעזרני 1 Ch 12^{17} + 2 t, etc., *Pt. act* עֹזֵר 1 K 20^{16}+, etc, *pass* עָזוּר Is 31^{3},—*help*, c acc pers 1 K 20^{16} Jos 1^{14} (D), Is 41^{6} + 2 Ch 28^{23} (rdg עוזרים Ges$^{\S\,53\,o}$, for MT מַעְזִרִים, appar. **Hiph.**, subj false gods); c. acc loc (city) Jos 10^{33} (D), esp c sf pers Jos 10$^{4\,6}$ (+ הושיע, both JE), 1 Ch 12$^{18\,20\,23}$ (van d H v$^{17\,19.22}$), 2 Ch 32^{3} Ezr 8^{22} (+ מִן of enemy), 10^{15} Dn 10^{13} (subj Michael), subj oft God (י׳), c acc pers ψ 10^{14} 1 Ch 15^{26}, usu. sf Gn 49^{25} (poem in J), 1 S 7^{12} Is 41$^{10\,13\,14}$ + 12 t + 2 Ch 26^{7} (c על *against*), ψ 37^{40} (+ פלט), 46^{6} (sf of city), 109^{26} (‖ הושיע), subj. false gods Dt 32^{8} 2 Ch 28^{23}, c לְ pers 2 S 8^{5} + 1 Ch 18^{5} + 4 t + 2 S 18^{3} (rd Qr לַעְזוֹר, or לעזור ? cf HPS), subj י׳ Is 50$^{7\,9}$; c. עִם pers 1 Ch 12^{22} (van d. H. v^{21}; + על *against*); c. אַחֲרֵי pers (constr. praegn) 1 K 1^{7}, c בְּ pers. against whom 2 Ch 20^{23} (+ inf); c לְ . . . בֵּין, of י׳, 2 Ch 14^{10}, abs Is 30^{7} 2 Ch 26^{13} (+ על *against*), 28^{16}, ע׳ לְרָעָה Zc 1^{15} *they helped, with evil result*; י׳ subj, 2 Ch 25^{8} (opp. הַכְשִׁיל), also pt. c. sf Ez 30^{8} + 3 t.; c לְ pers. 2 K 14^{26} + 5 t, of י׳ ψ 30^{11} 54^{6}, abs Is 31^{3} 63^{5} Je 47^{4} ψ 22^{12} 107^{12}, cstr עֹזְרֵי הַמִּלְחָמָה 1 Ch 12^{1}, עֹזְרֵי רָהַב Jb 9^{13} (v רַהַב); Pt. pass. abs as subst *he who is helped* Is 31^{3} †**Niph.** *Pf* וְנֶעֱזָ֫רְתִּי ψ 28^{7} *I am helped* (sc by י׳); *Impf* 3 mpl. וַיֵּעָזְרוּ 1 Ch 5^{20} (sc *id*; + על *against*), c n cogn. יֵעָזְרוּ עֵזֶר מְעָט Dn 11^{34}; *Inf cstr.* הפליא להעזר 2 Ch 26^{15} *he was wonderfully helped* (lit. *made wonderful to be helped*). †**Hiph.** dub *Inf. cstr* 2 S 18^{3} Kt, *Pt* pl. מַעְזְרִים 2 Ch 28^{23}, v **Qal.**

†I עֵ֫זֶר **n.m.** $^{\psi\,121,1}$ **help, succour**;—ע׳ abs. Gn 2^{18}+, sf. עֶזְרִי Ex 18^{4}, עזרה Ez 12^{14}, etc;— **1.** *help, succour* Is 30^{5} (‖ הוֹעִיל, opp בֹּשֶׁת, חֶרְפָּה), Dn 11^{34}, fr י׳ ψ 20^{3} 121$^{1\,2}$ 124^{8}, in 89^{20} rd נֵזֶר for ע׳ Dy Gr Kau (עז Bi Che), cf Hup, מָגֵן עֶזְרֶךָ Dt 33^{29} (= י׳) **2.** concr = *one who helps* (cf. 1 עֶזְרָה **2**) (ב essent, בע׳ v. ב **I 7 b**, Ges$^{\S\,119\,h\,1}$) Gn 2$^{18.20}$ (J) + Ho 13^{9} (rd מי בע׳ Che We Gu^{Kau} Now), coll (without ב) Ez 12^{14} (si vera l, Co עֹזְרָיו), esp of י׳ ע׳ מִצָּרָיו Dt 33^{7} (poem), מָגֵן + ע׳ ψ 33^{20} 115$^{9\,10\,11}$, + מְפַלֵּט 70^{6}, בע׳ (v supr.) Ex 18^{4} (E), Dt 33^{26} (poem), ψ 146^{4}

†II עֵ֫זֶר **n.pr.m.** (Ph and OHeb. עזר Lzb^{338});—**1.** a wall-builder Ne 3^{19}, Αζουρ **2.** name in Judah 1 Ch 4^{4}, Αζηρ, Εζερ **3.** hero of David 1 Ch 12^{10} (van d H. v^{9}), Αζερ, etc

†עֵ֫זֶר **n.pr.m.** **1.** Ephraimite 1 Ch 7^{21}, Εζερ. **2.** עֶזֶר, a priest, Ne 12^{42}, Ιεζουρ.

†עֶזְרָא **n.pr m.** Εσρας, Εσδρας, Εζδρας, **1. Ezra** Ezr 7$^{1\,10}$ 10$^{1\,2.\,5.\,6}$ Ne 8^{6}; called (ה)ספר Ezr 7^{6} Ne 8$^{1\,4\,5\,13}$ 12^{36}, הַכֹּהֵן Ezr 10$^{10\,16}$ Ne 8$^{2.9}$, both Ezr 7^{11} Ne 12^{26}. **2.** priest with Zerub Ne 12$^{1\,13}$ **3.** Ne 12^{33}.

†I. עֶזְרָה, עֶזְרַת, עֶזְרָ֫תָה **n.f. help, succour, assistance**;—abs ע׳ Is 10^{3}+, עֶזְרָת ψ 60^{13} 108^{13} (Ges$^{\S\,80\,g}$), עֶזְרָ֫תָה ψ 63^{8} + 2 t; cstr. עֶזְרַת Is 31^{2}+, sf. עֶזְרָתִי ψ 22^{20}+, etc,—**1.** *help, succour* Is 10^{3} 20^{6} (+ לְהִנָּצֵל), 31^{1} Je 37^{7} La 4^{17} Jb 6^{13} 2 Ch 28^{21}, ע׳ פֹּעֲלֵי אָוֶן Is 31^{2} *help from*, etc; ע׳ י׳ Ju 5$^{23.23}$ *help of* (for) י׳; from

'י ψ 22^{20} 38^{23} 40^{14} (‖ לְהַצִּילֵנִי), 70^{2} (‖ *id.*), 71^{12}, + מִצַּר 60^{13} (‖ תְּשׁוּעָה) = 108^{13} **2.** concr., embodied *help, one who helps* (cf 1. עֵזֶר **2**): **a.** coll. Jb 31^{21} *when I saw my help* (assistance, support) in the gate, בע׳ (v. 1. עֵזֶר **2**) Na 3^{9}. **b.** of 'י ψ 27^{9} 40^{18} (+ מְפַלֵּט), 46^{2} (‖ מַחֲסֶה, עֹז), 44^{27} 63^{8} 94^{17}; בְּע׳ 35^{2}.

†II. עֶזְרָה **n.pr.m.** Εσρει, Ιεζραα, in Judah 1 Ch 4^{17}.

†עָזוּר and (once) עַזֻּר **n.pr.m.** Αζωρ, Εζερ, Ιαζερ· **1.** father of Hananiah Je 28^{1}. **2.** עַזֻּר Ez 11^{1}. **3.** a chief of people Ne 10^{18}.

†עֲזַרְאֵל **n.pr.m.** (*Ēl hath helped*),— Οζριηλ, Εζριηλ, etc: **1.** warrior of David 1 Ch 12^{7} (van d H. v^{6}). **2.** Levite musician 1 Ch 25^{18} (= עֻזִּיאֵל v^{4}), B Αζαρια, A Εζριηλ **3.** a Danite 1 Ch 27^{22}, Αζαραηλ, Εζριηλ. **4.** one with foreign wife Ezr 10^{41}. **5.** priestly name: **a.** Ne 11^{13}. **b.** 12^{36}

†עזריאל **n.pr.m.** (*my help is Ēl*),— Εσ(δ)ριηλ, etc **1.** Je 36^{26}. **2.** a Manassite 1 Ch 5^{24}. **3.** name in Naphtali 27^{19}

†עֲזַרְיָהוּ, עֲזַרְיָה **n.pr.m.** (*'י hath helped*), **Azariah** (OHeb עזריהו, Ph. עזרבעל, OAram. הדדעזר, הדעדר, Lzb $^{338\ 253}$ Cook ^{42}),—Αζαριας: **1.** king of Judah (As. *Azriyâ'u* COT $^{2\,K\,15,1}$ Jager $^{BAS\,I\,468}$) עֲזַרְיָהוּ 2 K $15^{6.8}$; עזריה 14^{21} $15^{1.7\ 17\ 23.27}$ 1 Ch 3^{12} (v עֻזִּיָּה) **2.** ־יָהוּ officer of Sol 1 K 4^{5}. **3.** *id.* prophet 2 Ch 15^{1}. **4.** sons of Jehosh: **a.** *id*, 2 Ch 21^{2} **b.** ־יָה v^{2}. **5.** priests: **a.** ־יָהוּ 1 K 4^{2} = ־יָה 1 Ch $5^{36.37}$ Ezr 7^{3} **b.** ־יָה 1 Ch $5^{35.36}$ **c.** *id*, 1 Ch $5^{39\ 40}$ 9^{11} Ezr 7^{1} **d.** *id.*, Ne 10^{3} **e.** ־יָהוּ 2 Ch $31^{10\ 13}$, = ־יָה $26^{17.20}$ **6.** Levites, ־יָהוּ **a.** 2 Ch 29^{12}. **b.** v^{12}. ־יָה **c.** 1 Ch 6^{21}. **d.** Ne 8^{7}. **7.** ־יָהוּ a temple captain 2 Ch 23^{1a} (van d H ־יָה cf. Ginsb ^{marg}), v^{1b}. **8.** ־יָה wall-builder Ne $3^{23.24}$ **9.** ־יָה one with Zerub. 7^{7} (שְׂרָיָה ‖ Ezr 2^{2}) **10.** ־יָה 12^{33} **11.** ־יָהוּ Ephraimite 2 Ch 28^{12}. **12.** ־יָה name in Judah **a.** son of Ethan (!) 1 Ch 2^{8} **b.** $v^{38.39}$.—For עֲזַרְיָהוּ 2 Ch 22^{6} rd. אֲחַזְיָה cf. v^{7}.

†עָזְרִי **n.pr.m.** 1 Ch 27^{26}, Εσδρει, Εζραι.

†עַזְרִיקָם **n.pr.m.** Εζρεικαν, Εζρικαμ, etc.. **1.** descendant of David 1 Ch 3^{23} **2.** prince in Judah 2 Ch 28^{7} **3.** Benjamite 1 Ch 8^{38} 9^{44}. **4.** Levite 9^{14} Ne 11^{15}.

†יַעְזֵר and (1 Ch 6^{66} 26^{31}) יַעְזֵיר **n.pr.loc.** Ιαζηρ, E. of Jordan (**Qal** *Impf.* in — acc to Ba $^{NB\,104}$),—oft + Heshbon and other important towns, Nu 21^{32} + v^{24} (v. עַז) 32^{1} (אֶרֶץ יַע׳), $v^{3.35}$ (all JE), 2 S 24^{5}, Jos 13^{25} (P), 21^{39} (Ginsb, v^{37} van d. H. Baer; P); with vineyards Is $16^{8\,9}$ = Je $48^{32.32}$ (where del. יָם before יַע׳ 𝔊 Hi Gf Gie Rothst). Site dub., cf. Buhl $^{Geogr\ 264}$.

II. עזר (√of foll; connexion with I ע׳ dub; cf Sab. מעדר, 'Einfassung' Sab Denkm ^{97}; NH עֲזָרָה *temple-court*, 𝔗 עֲזַרְתָּא).

†עֲזָרָה **n.f.** appar. enclosure;—abs. ע׳. **1.** *ledge surrounding* Ezekiel's altar; הָע׳ הַגְּדוֹלָה below ,43^{14} Ez הָע׳ הַקְּטַנָּה = הַתַּחְתּוֹנָה v^{14}, הָע׳ alone $v^{17\ 20}$ 45^{19} (v. Comm). **2.** outer *court* of temple, הָע׳ הַגְּדֹלָה 2 Ch 4^{9}; with doors v^{9}, 6^{13} (v. 1. חָצֵר **3 b**, and on ע׳ in Herod's temple Now $^{Arch\ II\ 78\,ff}$).

עַזָּתִי v. sub עַזָּה

†עֵט **n.m.** $^{Je\,8,8}$ **stylus** (√dub, Ko $^{II\ 1,83}$ (after older authorities) cp. Ar عوط, غاط *sink, penetrate*);—ע׳ only cstr.: **1.** of iron, for use on stone or metal Je 17^{1} (בצפרן שָׁמִיר *with diamond-point*), Jb 19^{24} (v also חֶרֶט). **2.** prob = reed-pen (used on roll, cf Je $36^{2\ 23}$ etc), ע׳ שֶׁקֶר ספרים Je 8^{8}, fig., לְשׁוֹנִי ע׳ סוֹפֵר מָהִיר ψ 45^{1} (cf. Now $^{Arch\ I\ 290}$ Benz $^{Arch\ 290}$).

†I עָטָה **vb. wrap oneself, enwrap, envelop oneself** (Ar. غطا *cover, conceal*; Aram. ܥܛܐ *extinguish, destroy*; As *eṭû, be dark, eṭûtu, darkness*),—**Qal** *Pf* 3 ms. ועע׳ (consec) Je 43^{12}; 3 pl וְעָטוּ (consec.) Mi 3^{7}, *Impf.* 3 ms. יַעְטֶה Lv 13^{45} + 2 t, וַיַּעַט Is 59^{17}; 2 ms תַּעְטֶה Ez 24^{17}; 3 mpl יַעֲטוּ (Baer יַע׳) ψ 71^{13} 109^{29}; 2 mpl תַעְטוּ Ez 24^{22}; *Pt. act.* עֹטֶה 1 S 28^{14} ψ 104^{2}; fs. עֹטְיָה Ct 1^{7},—**1.** *wrap, envelop* oneself *with* sthg. (acc., like לבש): והוא עֹטֶה מעיל 1 S 28^{14} an old man ascending, *and he is enwrapped in a robe*; so יַע׳ הָרֹעֶה בגדו Je 43^{12} (sim), and וע׳ אֶת־אֶרֶץ מצרים v^{12} *he will wrap himself in the land of Egypt* (use it as a robe, fig, of Nebuchadnezzar; so completely will it be in his power, Gf); so fig of 'י, וַיַּעַט כַּמְּעִיל קִנְאָה Is 59^{17} (‖ לָבַשׁ), ע׳־אור כַּשַּׂלְמָה ψ 104^{2}; of men, יַע׳ כְּבֶגֶד 109^{19} (sim ‖ לָבַשׁ v^{18}), יַע׳ v^{29} (‖ *id*), וְיַע׳ כַּמְּעִיל בָּשְׁתָּם חֶרְפָּה וגו׳ 71^{13}, c עַל of part covered, in phrase וְעָטוּ עַל־שָׂפָם Mi 3^{7} *they shall envelop themselves upon their beard* (cover the beard, sign of mourning or shame Che Now Benz $^{Arch.\ 165}$ Now $^{Arch\ I\ 193}$), so Ez $24^{17\ 22}$ and (of leper) Lv 13^{45} (P);

pt. f עֹטְיָה Ct 1^7 as subst, *one wrapping* (a veil about her), i e a mourner; > a harlot (cf Gn 38^{14}), but rd perh טֹעְיָה *wandering woman*, v. טעה — וַיַּעַט etc, v also עיט; מַעֲטֶה, v. מרט **Hiph.** *Pf* 2 ms הֶעֱטִיתָ עָלָיו בּוּשָׁה ψ 89^{46} (of י׳) *thou hast wrapped shame upon him* (enwrapped him in shame); *Impf* 3 ms. בְּרָכוֹת יַעְטֶה מוֹרֶה ψ 84^7 *early rain enwrappeth* (it, עֵמֶק הַבָּכָא v^6) *with blessings* (𝔊 δώσει, as if from Ar. عطو, عَطَا, III, IV *give*, cf Ne[Mars 41]), read prob also יַעְטֵנִי Is 61^{10} (for MT יְעָטָנִי, v יעט) *with a robe of rightness he enveloppeth me*, so Brd Di Ry[Kau] Du, > **Qal** *Pf* עָטָנִי Klo Che[Hpt].

†[מַעֲטֶה] **n.[m.]** **wrap, mantle**, — only cstr fig מַעֲטֵה תְהִלָּה Is 61^3 *a mantle of praise*

†II [עָטָה] **vb. grasp** (Ar عطو, عَطَا, I, VII *take with hands*); — **Qal** *Inf abs* + *Pt act* sf ועֹטְךָ עָטֹה Is 22^{17} *he shall grasp thee forcibly*, cf Ges[Comm] Hi Ew De Che[Comm] Di Gu Kau, > Thes RobGes Buhl[Lex (13)] fr I עטה (*he shall wrap, roll thee tight together*) for this vb. not trans

†עֲטַלֵּף **n.[m.]** **bat** (quadrilit, Ges[§ 85 w] Sta[§ 243, 8], NH *id*, Ph. οθολαβαδ Ges[Mon Ph 391], Lewy[Fremdw 17] cp ἀττέλεβος, name of a locust in N. Africa Herod[iv 172]), — ע׳ abs. Lv 11^{19} (H), = Dt 14^{18} (unclean creature), pl. עֲטַלֵּפִים Is 2^{20}.

עטן (√of foll, NH עָטַן *put* olives into vat or press, or in vessel, Ar عَطَنَ *put skin into tan*)

†[עֲטִין] **n.[m.]** prob **pail, bucket** (NH מַעְטָן *vessel for olives*), — עֲטִינָיו מָלְאוּ חָלָב Jb 21^{24} *his pails are full of milk*

†I [עָטַף] **vb. turn aside** (Syr. ܥܛܦ *turn, return*, Ar عَطَفَ *incline, bend*), — **Qal** *Impf* 3 ms יַעְטֹף *turn aside* (so Ew Di De Bae Kau al), Jb 23^9 *he turneth aside* to the right (יָמִין ‖ שְׂמֹאול בַּעֲשֹׂתוֹ), rd prob 1 s. אֶעְטֹף Me Bu Du, *I turn . . and do not see him* (and ‖ שׂ׳ בְּבַקְּשׁוֹ)

†II [עָטַף] **vb envelop oneself** (Aramaism) (NH *id*, Aram עֲטַף, ܥܛܦ, Eth. ዐጠፈ: *covered*, also n *web, texture*), — **Qal** *Impf* 3 ms. יַעֲטָף־ ψ 73^6, 3 mpl יַעַטְפוּ 65^{14}, — *envelop oneself* ψ 65^{14} *the valleys cover themselves with corn* (‖ לָבְשׁוּ), יַע׳־שִׁית חָמָס לָמוֹ 73^6 *they put on for themselves* (each) *a garb of violence*.

†[מַעֲטָפָה] **n.f.** **overtunic** (so Ar. مِعْطَف, Aram ܡܥܛܦܐ, ܥܛܦܐ), — pl abs מַעֲטָפוֹת Is 3^{22}.

†III [עָטַף] **vb. be feeble, faint** (Ba[ES 27] cp Ar عَطِبَ *perish, flag*), — **Qal** *Impf* 3 ms. יַעֲטֹף ψ 102^1, יַעֲטוֹף Is 57^{16}; *Inf cstr.* עֲטֹף ψ 61^3, *Pt. pass.* (Ges[§ 50 f]) pl עֲטֻפִים Gn 30^{42}, עֲטוּפִים La 2^{19}; — lit *be feeble* Gn 30^{42} (J; opp קְשֻׁרִים), הָעֲטוּפִים בְּרָעָב La 2^{19}, fig רוּחַ מִלְּפָנַי יַע׳ Is 57^{16} *the spirit would faint before me* (י׳), בַּעֲטֹף לִבִּי ψ 61^3, 101^2 (title) **Niph.** *Inf cstr* בֵּעָטֵף עוֹלֵל La 2^{11} *when infants faint* (for בהע׳, but read perh. בַּעֲטֹף **Qal**, so Buhl) **Hiph.** *Inf. cstr.* בְּהַעֲטִיף הַצֹּאן Gn 30^{42} when the flock *shewed feebleness* **Hithp.** *Impf* 3 fs תִּתְעַטֵּף ψ 77^4, וַתִּתְ׳ 143^4, תִּתְעַטָּף 107^5, *Inf cstr* הִתְעַטֵּף 142^4 Jon 2^8, sf הִתְעַטְּפָם La 2^{12}, — *faint, faint away*, La 2^{12} (כֶּחָלָל *like the wounded*), subj. רוּחַ ψ 77^4 142^4 (+ עָלַי, v. על **II 1 d**), 143^4 (+ *id*); subj. נֶפֶשׁ Jon 2^8 (+ *id*), ψ 107^5 (+ בָּהֶם)

†[עָטַר] **vb. surround** (NH *id*, and deriv; Ph. עטרת *wreath*, עטר Pi denom *crown* Lzb[339]; Aram עֲטַר, As *etêru, spare, rescue*), — **Qal** *Impf* 2 ms sf כַּצִּנָּה רָצוֹן תַּעְטְרֶנּוּ ψ 5^{13} *as with a shield, with favour wilt thou surround him*, *Pt* pl. עֹטְרִים אֶל־דָּוִד 1 S 23^{26} Saul and his men *were surrounding* (closing in) *upon David*.

†1 עֲטָרָה **n.f. crown, wreath**, — abs. ע׳ Ez 21^{31} Ct 3^{11}, cstr עֲטֶרֶת 2 S 12^{30} + 17 t; pl עֲטָרוֹת Zc 6^{11} Jb 31^{36}, עֲטֶרֶת Zc 6^{14}, — *crown*: **1** of idol-image (*Milcom*, 𝔊 We Klo Dr Kit Lohr HPS) 2 S 12^{30} = 1 Ch 20^2; golden, ע׳ פָּז ψ 21^4, ע׳ תִּפְאַרְתְּכֶם of king and queen, Je 13^{18} *the crown of your splendour*; cf Ez 21^{31}, wedding-crown Ct 3^{11}. **2.** ע׳ זָהָב Est 8^{15} (of Mordecai), of silver and gold Zc $6^{11.14}$; ע׳ תפארת *crown of splendour*, on personif. Jerus Ez 16^{12} (in allegory), Jerus and Samaria 23^{42}, ע׳ as appos (= sim) Jb 31^{36} **3.** fig. of honour, etc, Jb 19^9 (‖ כְּבוֹדִי) La 5^{16}, אֵשֶׁת חַיִל ע׳ בַּעְלָהּ Pr 12^4, cf. 14^{24} 17^6; ע׳ תִּפְאֶרֶת 16^{31} (of שֵׂיבָה), gift of wisdom 4^9; fig of Jerus Is 62^3 (‖ צְנִיף מְלוּכָה), cf. $28^{1.3}$ fig of Samaria; fig. of י׳, ע׳ צְבִי ע׳ גֵּאוּת v^5 (‖ צְפִירַת תִּפְאָרָה)

†II. עֲטָרָה **n.pr.f.** 1 Ch 2^{26}, Ατάρα.

†[עָטַר] **vb.denom. crown**, — **Pi.** *Pf.* 3 fs. שֶׁעִטְּרָה לוֹ Ct 3^{11} *with which* his mother *crowned him* (v. I. עֲטָרָה **1**), elsewh fig. 2 ms. עִטַּרְתָּ שְׁנַת טוֹבָתֶךָ ψ 65^{12} *thou* (י׳) *hast crowned the year of*

thy goodness; Impf. 2 ms sf. וְכָבוֹד וְהָדָר תְּעַטְּרֵהוּ 8^{6}; *Pt.* sf. הַמְעַטְּרֵכִי חֶסֶד וְרַחֲמִים 103^{4} (of 'י) **Hiph.** *Pt* f. צֹר הַמַּעֲטִירָה Is 23^{8} usu. *Tyre the crown-bestower* (Ges Ew De Che^{Comm} Di Du Gu^{Kau} Skinner), but dub.; < *the crown-wearer* Hi Gr (after 𝔊), so Ren Che^{Hpt} (rdg. הַמְעֻטָּרָה).

†עֲטָרוֹת and (Nu 32^{34}) עֲטָרֹת **n.pr.loc.** Αταρωθ, etc.: **1.** E. of Jordan (MI$^{10.11}$),—**a.** Nu 32^{3} (+ דִּיבֹן, etc.)—mod *Attarûs*, c. 8 miles NNW. from Dibon—built by Gad Nu 32^{34} (+ 'ד, ערער, and also) **b.** עַטְרֹת שׁוֹפָן v^{35} (Sam. ע' שפים, v. Di; site unknown) **2.** W. of Jordan, conject. as to sites v. in Di Buhl$^{Geogr\ 172}$: **a.** on border between Ephr and Benj Jos 16^{2}, = עַטְרוֹת אַדָּר v^{5} 18^{13} **b.** on E. border of Ephr. Jos 16^{7}. **c.** עטרות בית יואב 1 Ch 2^{54} in Judah, a 'son' of Salma (+ Bethlehem, al)

עטשׁ (√ of foll., NH עָטַשׁ *sneeze*, Aram ܥܛܫ in deriv. n.; Ar عَطَسَ *id*, Eth. [ዐጥሰ:], ዐጥስ:, ዐጥስ: *sneezing*)

†[עֲטִישָׁה] **n.f.** sneezing,—pl sf עֲטִישֹׁתָיו Jb 41^{10}, v. I. הלל (Bi Siegf Bu Du rd sg)

עַי, עַיָּת, עַיָּה, n pr.loc. Αγγαι (Gn), Γαι. **1.** old Canaanit. city, 'ע alw. c. art. (הָעַי) Gn 13^{3}+), near Bethel to the SE (exact site unknown, cf. Di$^{Jos\ 7.2}$ Buhl$^{Geogr\ 177}$), Gn 12^{8} (J), 13^{3} (J), Jos $7^{2.2.3.4.5}$ $8^{1\ 1\ 2.3}$ + 18 t Jos 8 (+ Qr $v^{12.16}$, but improb., Kt עיר, cf. Di), 9^{3} $10^{1.2}$ (all JE), 12^{9} (D), Ezr 2^{28} = Ne 7^{32}, = עַיָּת Is 10^{28}; עַיָּה (so Baer Ginsb, > עַיָּא van d. H.) Ne 11^{31}, so rd also (for עַזָּה q v. ad fin) 1 Ch 7^{28}. **2.** E Jordan city Je 49^{3} (+ חֶשְׁבּוֹן), but rd. עָר *city* (?) Gf Rothst^{Kau} Co (הָעִיר ?)

עִי v. I. עוה. עַיָּא v עַי עַיִב v. עוב.

עַיְבָל v. עֵיבָל sub עבל. עַיָּה v. עַי

†עִיּוֹן **n.pr.loc.** Αιν, in Naphtali;—1 K 15^{20} = 2 Ch 16^{4}, 2 K 15^{29} (on 2 S 24^{6} v. דָּן p 193 a supr). Perh = *Tell Dibbin*, on the plateau *Merj 'ayyûn* (Buhl$^{Geogr\ 11\ 110}$), between the Lîtânî and the Hâsbânî (Id$^{ib\ 237\ f.}$).

עיות Kt v עוית.

†[עִיט] **vb.** **scream, shriek** (Ar عيط, عَاطَ II. *scream, scold*, عِيَاط *screaming, scolding*, Frey Dozy$^{ii.\ 193}$, Syr ܥܝܛܐ *anger, reviling*);—only **Qal** *Impf* 3 ms וַיָּעַט בָּהֶם 1 S 25^{14} *and he screamed at them* (of Nabal).

†עַיִט **n.m.** $^{Je\ 12.19}$ bird(s) of prey (from *scream*),—abs. 'ע Gn 15^{11}+, עָיִט Jb 28^{7}, c. art. (perh) הָע' Je 12^{9b} (cf. Gie; הַע' interrog. v^{a}), cstr. עֵיט Is 18^{6} Ez 39^{4},—usu. coll. Gn 15^{11} (JE), Is 18^{6} Jb 28^{7}, עֵיט הָרִים Is 18^{6}, עֵיט צִפּוֹר כָּל־כָּנָף Ez 39^{4}; fig. of foes of Judah Je 12^{9b}; of single bird v^{9a} (fig of Judah), Is 46^{11} (fig of invader, ‖ אִישׁ עֲצָתִי).

†[עִיט] **vb.denom.** dart greedily (like a bird of prey),—**Qal** *Impf.* 3 ms. וַיַּ֫עַט Qr (Kt erron. ויעש) 1 S 14^{32} *and* the people *darted greedily* upon the spoil (אֶל־הַשָּׁלָל), so 2 ms. וַתַּ֫עַט 15^{19} (on forms v. Ges$^{\S 72\ ff}$)

†עֵיטָם **n.pr.loc.** (perh animal-name, fr. עַיִט, cf Gray$^{Prop\ Names\ 93}$),—**1.** Ηιταμ, 𝔊L Ιταμ, a cliff, סְעִיף סֶלַע ע' Ju $15^{8.11}$ perh. near town עֵיטָם, v foll., but at *'Arâk Isma'în* near edge of Shephelah, WSW. fr. Jerus. acc. to Schick ZPV x (1887), 143 ff. **2.** Αιταν[μ], etc., city fortified by Rehob 2 Ch 11^{6}, between Bethlehem and Tekoa, = *'Ain'Atân* c. 2 miles SSW. from B, Buhl$^{Geogr\ 92}$ GFM$^{Ju\ 15,8}$, near Ûrtâs Rob$^{BR\ I\ 477}$, clan in Judah 1 Ch 4^{3}. **3.** Αιταν[μ], in Simeon 1 Ch 4^{32} (Be [not Oettli Kau Kit] rds. עֶתֶר fr Jos 15^{42}).

†עִיִּים **n.pr.loc.** Γαι, etc. (as if 'עִ): **1.** station of Isr. on E. border of Moab, before דִּיבֹן גָּד Nu 33^{45}, = עִיֵּי הָעֲבָרִים v^{44} 21^{11} (all P; 𝔊 ignores הָעֲבָרִים). **2.** city in Judah Jos 15^{29} (P).

עילום v. עוֹלָם sub עלם

†עִילַי **n.pr.m.** one of David's heroes 1 Ch 11^{29}, Ηλει, Ηλα (= צַלְמוֹן 2 S 23^{28})

†I. עֵילָם **n.pr.gent. et terr.** **Elam,** Αιλαμ, Ἐλαμεῖται, well-known country and people NE. of Lower Tigris (As. *Elamtu* Dl$^{Pa\ 320\ ff.}$ COT$^{Gn\ 10,22}$),—as early invaders of Palestine Gn $14^{1.9}$, allies of Assyr. Is 22^{6}; foe of Babylon 21^{2}; abode of dispersed Israelites 11^{11}; prophesied against Je $49^{34.35.36.38}$ (Qr, Kt עולם), $v^{37.38.39}$ Ez 32^{24}, cf. כָּל־מַלְכֵי ע' Je 25^{25}; called 'son' of Shem Gn 10^{22} (P) = 1 Ch 1^{17}; purely local designation ע' הַמְּדִינָה Dn 8^{2}.

†II. עֵילָם **n.pr.m.** Ηλαμ, Αιλαμ: **1.** heads of families of returned exiles. **a.** Ezr 2^{7} = Ne 7^{12}. **b.** Ezr 2^{31} = Ne 7^{34}. **c.** Ezr 8^{7} 10^{2} (Qr; Kt עולם), v^{26}. **2.** a chief of people Ne 10^{15}. **3.** name in Benjamin 1 Ch 8^{24}. **4.** Levite name 1 Ch 26^{3}. **5.** a priest Ne 12^{42}.

†[עֲיָם] **n.[m.]** dub., poss. **glow** (Ar. غيم, غَامَ to *thirst*, غَيْمَةٌ *thirst, internal heat*), si vera l. (so Du; on form cf. Nö ZMG xxxvii (1883), 526);—cstr. בַּעְיָם רוּחוֹ Is 11[15], rd. perh. בְּעֹצֶם (so appar. Vrss) Thes Luzz Krochm Che Gu Kau Gr Perles Anal. 52.

I. עַיִן 859 **n.f.** Gn 3.7 and (Zc 3[9] 4[10] Albr ZAW xvi (1896), 75) **m. eye** (ancient Sem. word; √ and relation to II. ע׳ unknown; NH *id.*; Ph. ען; 𝔗 עֵינָא, עַיְנָא; Palm. עינא, Zinj. sf. עיני, עינך; Syr. ܥܰܝܢܳܐ; As. *ênu, enu*, TelAm. sf. *inaya* and (appar. Can. gloss) *ḫinaya*; Ar. عَيْنٌ; Eth. ዐይን:);—abs. ע׳ Ex 21[24]+, cstr. עֵין v[26]+; sf. עֵינִי Gn 44[21]+ (2 S 16[12] rd. עָנְיִי Vrss Comm.), עֵינְךָ Dt 7[16]+, עֵינֵנוּ ψ 35[21] (2 S 20[6] v. נצל Hiph.); sf. 3 mpl. עֵינָם Is 13[18] (Zc 5[6] rd. עֲוֺנָם 𝔊 We Gr Now), עֵינֵמוֹ ψ 73[7] (but rd. עֲוֺנָמוֹ v. Comm.); usu. du. עֵינַיִם Gn 20[16]+, עֵינָיִם Is 3[16]+, esp. cstr. עֵינֵי Gn 3[7]+, עֵנֵי Is 3[8]; sf. עֵינַי Gn 31[10]+, עֵינֶיךָ Ju 6[17]+, etc. (Ho 10[10] rd. עֲוֺנֹתָם cf. 𝔊 𝔙 Che We Gr Now);—*eye*: **1.** lit. as physical organ, **a.** of man Ex 21[6.6.6](E), Gn 3[6](J)+, Lv 21[20] 24[20.20] 26[16](H; very rarely P, e.g. Dt 34[4.7]), 2 K 4[34.34]+; once שְׁתֵּי עֵינַי Ju 16[28]. **b.** anthropomorph. of י׳ ψ 33[18] 34[16]+. **c.** of idols ψ 115[5] 135[16]. **d.** of beasts Gn 30[41](J), Jb 40[24](hippop., si vera l., but prob. crpt. Di Siegf Bu Du where see conj.), 41[10] (crocod.); bird Jb 28[7] 39[29] Pr 1[17]. †**e.** in wheels Ez 1[18] cf. 10[12]; on stone Zc 3[9] (all in visions). **f.** subj. of ראה *see* Gn 45[12.12](E), +(oft. Dt), c. חזה ψ 11[4]; men *see* בְּעֵ׳ Dt 3[27] 2 K 7[12]+; esp. נָשָׂא ע׳ + ראה Gn 13[10.14](J)+; cf. לְכָל־מַרְאֵה עֵינֵי הַכֹּהֵן Lv 13[12] = *as far as the priest can see*, מַרְאֵה ע׳ Dt 28[34] *what is seen by the eyes* = v[67] Ec 6[9]. **g.** as affected by sleep, v. שֵׁנָה sub [יָשֵׁן]. **h.** as weeping, מְקוֹר דִּמְעָה ע׳ Je 8[23], נִגְּרָה ע׳ La 3[49], דָּלְפָה ע׳ Jb 16[20]; v. also Je 31[16] ψ 116[8], and ירד **Qal 3 c.** **i.** as growing dim, v. I. כָּהָה, חָשַׁךְ **3**; c. כָּבֵד Gn 48[10] (E), קוּם 1 S 4[15] 1 K 14[4], שָׁעַע Is 32[3] 6[10] (Hiph.); c. כָּלָה *pine, languish*, v. כ׳ **Qal 2 b, Pi. 2 b**, c. דָּאַב ψ 88[10], עָשֵׁשׁ 6[8] 31[10], דָּלַל Is 38[14]. †**j.** c. פָּקַח *open*, after sleep Jb 27[19], sleep of death 2 K 4[35]; = *keep awake* Pr 20[13] (opp. שֵׁנָה); of new power of vision Gn 3[5.7] (J), given by God 21[19] (E), 2 K 6[17.17]; so (c. וַיְגַל) Nu 22[31] (JE); = *give sight to* blind 2 K 6[20.20] Is 35[5] 42[7] ψ 146[8]; of God (י׳) opening his eyes, פְּקַח ע׳ 2 K 19[16] = Is 37[17], Dn 9[18], + עַל־ Je 32[19] Zc 12[4] Jb 14[3]; c. פָּתַח, + אֶל־ 1 K 8[29] = 2 Ch 6[20], 1 K 8[52] Ne 1[6], + לְ v[40] 7[15]; + inf. Ne 1[6].—Nu 24[3.15] v. שׁתם. **k.** אוֹר ע׳ etc., = *revive*, v. אור **vb. Qal, Hiph.; noun, 10.** †**l.** קָרַץ ע׳ = *wink* ψ 35[19] Pr 10[10], קְ׳ בְּעֵ׳ 6[13]. †**m.** רָזַם ע׳ Jb 15[12] i.e. *roll* (in anger). †**n.** לָטַשׁ ע׳ לְ׳ Jb 16[9] *whet eyes against* = 'look daggers at.' **o.** *put out* eye, v. עִוֵּר, נקר. **p.** as feature of beauty, יְפֵה ע׳ Dt 16[12]; cf. Ct 4[9] 7[5], ע׳ יוֹנִים 1[15] 4[1] and 5[12] (כְּיוֹנִים); on other hand, ע׳ לֵאָה רַכּוֹת Gn 29[17](E); וַתָּשֶׂם בַּפּוּךְ ע׳ †2 K 9[30] (v. פּוּךְ), cf. Je 4[30], כָּחַל ע׳ Ez 23[40] *paint the eyes*†. **q.** *apple of the eye*, v. אִישׁוֹן, [בָּבָה], בַּת **6**. **r.** גַּבֹּת ע׳ Lv 14[9] *eyebrows*. **s.** חַכְלִילִי ע׳ מִיַּיִן Gn 49[12], חַכְלִלוּת ע׳ Pr 23[29] (v. ח׳); מְאוֹר ע׳ Pr 15[30], v. Toy.

2. a. eyes as shewing mental qualities: arrogance גַּבְהוּת ע׳ Is 2[11], ע׳ גְבֹהִים 5[15], גְּבַה־ע׳ ψ 101[5], תִּפְאֶרֶת רוּם ע׳ Is 10[12]; c. רוּם also ψ 18[28] (so read also ∥ 2 S 22[28] Hup HPS), 131[1] Pr 6[17] 21[4]; humility, שַׁח ע׳ Jb 22[29]; mockery, ע׳ תִּלְעַג לְ Pr 30[17]; cf. רָעָה ע׳ בְּ Dt 15[9] (grudging), 28[54.56] (*id.*); esp. ע׳ אַל־תָּחֹס (עַל) *not have pity on* Dt 7[16] + 4 t. Dt, Ez 5[11] + 8 t. Ez, Is 13[18], also Gn 45[20] (E; = not regret); cf. נֹחַם יִסָּתֵר מֵעֵ׳ Ho 13[14]. **b.** מַחְמַד ע׳ Ez 24[16] *desire of the eyes*, so v[21.25]; שִׁקּוּצֵי ע׳ 20[7] *abominations of the eyes*, so v[8].—ψ 73[7] v. חֵלֶב.

3. Fig. of mental and spiritual faculties, acts and states: **a.** תִּפָּקַחְנָה ע׳ Gn 3[5.7](J) Is 42[7], גְּלוּי ע׳ Nu 24[4.16] (JE); also טַח מֵרְאוֹת ע׳ Is 44[18]; ע׳ אֶל־י׳ ψ 123[2] (see v[2.2] for origin of fig.), +; of י׳, 33[18] (i.e. his favour) 34[16] (*id.*)+. **b.** ע׳ הַזֹּנוֹת Ez 6[9]; תִּשְׂבַּע ע׳ Ec 1[8] 4[8]; שָׁאֲלוּ ע׳ 2[10]; לְנֹכַח יַבִּיטוּ ע׳ Pr 4[25]; טוֹב־ע׳ 22[9] = *bountiful*, רַע עָיִן 23[6] = *niggardly one*, so 28[22]; eye as avenue of temptation Jb 31[1.7]; שִׁית ע׳ ψ 17[11] = design. **c.** esp. בְּעֵינֵי, c. adj. and intrans. verbs, *in the view, opinion, of* Gn 16[4.5] (J), 21[11.12] (E), 34[18] (P), + oft.; c. act. vb. 2 S 10[3] = 1 Ch 19[3], Est 1[17] 3[6]; הַטּוֹב בְּעֵ׳ Gn 16[6] 19[14] (J), +, i.e. what one pleases, Nu 36[6] (P) whom they please; הַיָּשָׁר בְּעֵ׳ Dt 12[8.25]+, הַטּוֹב וְהַיָּשָׁר בְּעֵ׳ v[28] Jos 9[25] (D), הָרַע בְּעֵ׳ Ju 2[11] 3[7] Dt 4[25] + esp. D and K (R^D); so לְנֶגֶד עֵינָיו 2 S 22[25] = ψ 18[25]; אַחֲרֵי עֵינֵיכֶם Nu 15[39] = acc. to your wish, fancy (+ לְבַבְכֶם). **d.** נֶעְלַם מֵעֵ׳ Lv 4[13] i.e. hid from knowledge of, so Nu 5[13] (both P), Jb 28[21]; מֵעֵ׳ Nu 15[24] (P) *without the knowledge of;* אַעְלִים ע׳ מִן Is 1[15] = disregard, pay no attention; cf. Lv 20[4] (H) Ez 22[26]; without מִן, abs., Pr 28[27]; אַעְלִים ע׳ בּוֹ (i.e. כֹּפֶר) 1 S 12[3] (נעלים *sandals* + ענו בי 𝔊 Th We Kit, cf. Ecclus xlvi. 19; Bu HPS ins. ענו בי); וַיַּסְתֵּר עָמָל מֵעֵ׳ Jb 3[10]; נִסְתְּרוּ מֵעֵ׳ Is 65[16]; הַשֹּׁחַד יְעַוֵּר ע׳ Dt 16[19], cf. כְּסוּת ע׳ Gn 20[16] (E).

4. Transferred mngs.: **a.** visible *surface* of earth Ex 10[5.15] (J) Nu 22[5.11] (JE). **b.** *appearance* Lv 13[5] (P; rdg. בְּעֵינוֹ Di Kau Dr-Wh), v[37]

(P, rdg *id*), v^{55} (P) Nu 11^{17} (JE), so appar. dual 1 S 16^{7} **c.** *gleam, sparkle* (of metal, jewels, etc.) Ez 1$^{4\,7\,16.22\,27}$ 8^{2} 10^{9} Dn 10^{6}, of wine Pr 23^{31}.

5. Other phrases are · ע׳ תַּחַת ע׳ Ex 21^{24} (E)=Lv 24^{20}(H), =ע׳ בע׳ Dt 19^{21}, all=*an eye for an eye*, ע׳ בע׳=*eye to eye*, Nu 14^{14} (P) Is 52^{8} (fig), cf וע׳ אֶת־ע׳ תראֶינָה Je 32^{4} 34^{3}, esp לְעֵינֵי *in the presence of, in full view of* Gn 42^{24}(E) 47^{19}(J) Ex 4^{30}(J) Nu 19^{5}(P), + oft; of business transaction Je 32$^{12\,12}$ Gn 23$^{11\,18}$(P); so נֶגֶד ע׳ Jo 1^{16}, לְנֶגֶד ע׳ Jb 4^{16}, and even בע׳ 1 S 21^{14} Ezr 3^{12}, ע׳ נִגְרַזְתִּי מִנֶּגֶד ψ 31^{23}; בין ע׳=*on the forehead* Ex 13$^{9\,16}$ (JE) Dt 6^{8} 11^{18} 14^{1} Dn 8$^{5\,21}$

†[עָיַן] **vb. denom.** eye (enviously), look (askance) **at**,—**Qal** *Pt* (or **Pô'ēl**, מ om, v. Dr), c acc. עֹיֵן 1 S 18^{9} Qr (Kt עון).

†II עַ֫יִן **n.f. spring** (of water) (connexion with I ע׳ dub; NH *id*, Ph ען, As. *ênu, înu*, Ar. عَيْنٌ, Eth. ዐይን፡; Palm עינא, 𝔗 עֵינָא, עַיְינָא, Syr. ܥܝܢܐ),—abs ע׳ 1 S 29^{1}+, עָיִן Gn 49^{22}+, הָעַ֫יְנָה 24$^{16.45}$, cstr עין v^{13}+; pl עֵינֹת Dt 8^{7}, ת-ִ 2 Ch 32^{3}, cstr עינות Ex 15^{27}=Nu 33^{9}, עְינוֹת Pr 8^{28} (Ges $^{§ 93 v}$),—*spring* Gn 16^{7} 24$^{16.29\,30.42.45}$ (all J) 49^{22} (poem in J), 1 S 29^{1}, עין הַמַּיִם Gn 16^{7} 24$^{13.43}$ (J), cf Ex 15^{27} (J) Nu 33^{9} (P), נַחֲלֵי מַיִם ע׳ וּתְהֹמֹת Dt 8^{7}, מימי הָעֲיָנוֹת 2 Ch 32^{3}, ע׳ תהום Pr 8^{28} (i.e of the sea), fig עין יַעֲקֹב Dt 33^{28} (poem), i e Jacob's descendants Particular springs are: **a.** ע׳ חרד Ju 7^{1} (on loc. cf GFM) **b.** ע׳ הַקּוֹרֵא (*partridge-spring*) Ju 15^{19} (cf *id*) **c.** ע׳ רגל near Jerus (early sanctuary RS$^{\text{Sem I 157, 2nd ed 172}}$) 2 S 17^{17} cf 1 K 1^{9}, on border of Judah Jos 15^{7}, and Benj 18^{16} **d.** ע׳ הַתַּנִּין (*dragon-spring*) Ne 2^{13} (=**c**? so RS$^{\text{l.c.}}$)—On שַׁעַר הָעַיִן Ne 2^{14} 3^{15} 12^{37} v. שַׁעַר.

†III. עַ֫יִן **n.pr.loc. 1.** לְעַ֫יִן, on NE. border of Can. Nu 34^{11}, 𝔊 ἐπὶ πηγάς. **2. a.** in Negeb of Judah Jos 15^{32} (+וְרִמּוֹן), Levit city 21^{16} (but 𝔊^{B} Ασα rd עָשָׁן, as 1 Ch 6^{44}), appar = **b.** 19^{7} (+ר׳, assigned to Simeon), עַ֫יִן ר׳ 1 Ch 4^{32} (id prob. וְעַיִן ר׳); prob. mod. *Umm er-Ramāmīn*, c. 18 miles SW from Hebron, Buhl$^{\text{Geogr 183}}$.—Vid. עין רמון

†עין גֶּ֫דִי **n.pr loc.** Εγγαδδει, etc.;—מְצָדֹת ע׳ 1 S 23^{29}, מדבר ע׳ 24^{1}, כַּרְמֵי ע׳ Ct 1^{14}, עין גֶּדִי חַצְצוֹן תָּמָר=ע׳ (q.v) acc. to 2 Ch 20^{2}, עין גֶּדִי Ez 47^{10}, mod. *'Ain ğidî*, on W shore of Dead Sea, GASm$^{\text{Geogr 269 f., 512}}$ Buhl$^{\text{Geogr 41, 164 f}}$

†עין גַּנִּים **n.pr.loc. 1.** in the Shephelah of Judah Jos 15^{34}, perh. *Umm-ğîna*, c. 1 mile S. of W. from Bethshemesh Cl-Gann Buhl$^{\text{Geogr 194 f}}$. **2** in Issachar 19^{21} (A Ηνγαννιμ), Levit city 21^{29} (πηγὴν γραμμάτων); hence by txt err. עָנֵם 1 Ch 6^{58}, *Gennin*, near SE end of plain of Jezreel, c 15 m. NNE fr Samaria, Buhl$^{\text{Geogr 202}}$

†עֵין־דֹּר **n.pr.loc.** in Manasseh Jos 17^{11} (JE; om 𝔊),=ע׳ דור 1 S 28^{7} (Αελδωρ, 𝔊L Αενδωρ), ע׳־דֹאר ψ 83^{11} (Gr ע׳ חָרוֹד), Αενδωρ, *Endûr*, c 14 miles NNE from foregoing.

†עין חַדָּה **n.pr.loc.** in Issachar Jos 19^{21}, Αιμαρεκ, A Ηναδδα, 𝔊L Αναδδα

†עין חָצוֹר **n.pr.loc.** in Naphtali Jos 19^{37}, πηγὴ Ασορ

†עין משְׁפָּט **n.pr.loc.** Gn 14^{7} = קָדֵשׁ (בַּרְנֵעַ) q v. (𝔊 τὴν πηγὴν τῆς κρίσεως; on signif. of name cf. RS$^{\text{Sem I. 165, 2nd ed. 181}}$).

†עין עֶגְלַיִם **n.pr.loc.** on Dead Sea Ez 47^{10}, Εναγαλειμ.

עין רִמּוֹן **n.pr.loc.** in post-exil. Judah Ne 11^{29} (A (εν)Ρεμμων), prob = III עַיִן **2** q v. and רִמּוֹן Zc 14^{10}.

†עין שֶׁ֫מֶשׁ **n.pr.loc.** on border betw Judah Jos 15^{7} (πηγῆς ἡλίου) and Benj 18^{17} (πηγὴν Βαιθσαμυς, 𝔊L [πη]γὴν Σαμες), conj in Buhl$^{\text{Geogr 98}}$.

עין תַּפּוּחַ **n.pr loc.** v III. תַּפּוּחַ sub נפח

†עֵינַ֫יִם **n.pr.loc.** (on form v Ges$^{§ 88 c}$),—Gn 38$^{14.21}$ (J), Αιναν = following

†עֵינָם **n.pr loc.** in the Shephelah of Judah, הָע׳ Jos 15^{34} (Μαιανει, A 𝔊L Ηναειμ) = עֵינַיִם.

†עֵינָן **n.pr.m.** Αιναν, name in Naphtali Nu 1^{15} 2^{29} 7$^{78.83}$ 10^{27}—Vid also חֲצַר עינון.

עֵינוֹן v. חֲצַר עינון.

†עֲנִים **n.pr.loc.** in hill-country of Judah Jos 15^{50}, Αισαμ, Ανειμ[S], perh *Ghuwain*, c 17 miles W. of S. from Hebron, Buhl$^{\text{Geogr 163 f}}$

†מַעְיָן **n.m.**$^{\text{Pr 8, 24}}$ **spring**;—abs. מ׳ ψ 74^{15}+; cstr מַעְיַן 2 K 3^{25}+, מַעְיְנוֹ ψ 114^{8} (Ges$^{§ 90 n}$); sf. מַעְיָנוֹ Ho 13^{15}, pl מַעְיָנִים Is 41^{18}+, מַעְיָנוֹת ψ 104^{10}, cstr מַעְינוֹת Gn 7^{11}+, מַעְיְנֵי 1 K 18^{5} 2 K 3^{19}, מַעְיְנֵי Is 12^{3}; sf. מַעְיָנַי ψ 87^{7} (but v. infr), מַעְיְנֹתֶיךָ Pr 5^{16},—*spring*, cstr before מַיִם 1 K 18^{5} 2 K 3$^{19\,25}$, Jos 15^{9} 18^{15} (both P), ψ 114^{8},

cf. Pr 8²⁴, מַע׳ alone Is 41¹⁸ Lv 11³⁶ (P), ψ 74¹⁵ 104¹⁰ 2 Ch 32⁴, cf Jo 4¹⁸ (in eschatol picture), in sim Pr 25²⁶, מ׳ תהום Gn 7¹¹ 8² (cf Pr 8²⁸), fig of source of happiness, enjoyment Ho 13¹⁵ (מקורו ‖) ψ 84⁷ Pr 5¹⁶ (of wife, v Toy), cf מ׳ חָתוּם Ct 4¹², מ׳ גַּנִּים v¹⁵, also ψ 87⁷ (si vera l, so De Che Du, Hup Bae We rd form of מָעוֹן *dwelling*), מ׳ הַיְשׁוּעָה Is 12³

I [עִיף] = II עוף q v for עִיפָה, עֵיפַי etc

†II [עִיף] **vb** be faint (cf Syr ܥܳܐܶܦ 3, PS²⁸³⁰, ‖ form of יעף q v, occurrences dub).— **Qal** *Pf* 3 fs עָיְפָה נַפְשִׁי לְ Je 4³¹ (? rd עָיְפָה), *Impf* 3 ms וַיָּעַף Ju 4²¹ (< וַיָּעַף GFM Bu), 1 S 14²⁸ (del We Bu Kit Loh, emend HPS), v³¹ (rd וַיִּיעַף [√יעף] Buhl HPS), 2 S 21¹⁵ (corrupt, HPS, for Philist name We Dr Bu Kit)

†עָיֵף **adj.** faint, weary,—ע׳ abs Gn 25²⁹ +, f עֲיֵפָה Je 31²⁵ +, pl עֲיֵפִים Ju 8⁴ +,—fr exertion and hunger Gn 25²⁹·³⁰ (J), Ju 8⁴·⁵ Dt 25¹⁸ (+יָגֵעַ), cf Is 5²⁷, הָנִיחוּ לֶע׳ 28¹² (fig), 2 S 16¹⁴ (si vera l, n pr loc needed, cf We Dr HPS), +רָעֵב, צָמֵא 17²⁹, specif from thirst Is 29⁸ (sim), Jb 22⁷, נפש ע׳ Pr 25²⁵ and (fig) Je 31²⁵ (‖ דָּאֲבָה), hence אֶרֶץ צִיָּה וְעָיֵף ψ 63² (fig, on masc v Ko Synt § 334 f), cf 143⁶ (sim), Is 32² (opp. צֵל, in sim), ע׳ sc beast 46¹ —Vid also foregoing.

I עִיר v sub I עור

II עִיר ₁₀₉₂ **n.f.**^Gn 10 12^ (Albrecht ZAW xvi 49 f) city, town (√unkn, NH *id*, ? Ph ער Lzb³⁴⁵, Sab ער *fortified height* (cf **3**) Pra ZMG xxvi (1872) 437, ערן, עהרן *city* CIS iv pp 94, 95, 173), —ע׳ abs. Gn 4¹⁷ +, cstr 24¹⁰ +, הָעִירָה 1 K 14¹² + 7 t, sf עִירִי 2 S 19³⁸ + 2 t, etc, pl. עָרִים Is 6¹¹ +, עֲיָרִים Ju 10⁴ (txt. err, or word-play, cf GFM), cstr עָרֵי Gn 19²⁹ +, sf עָרַי Zc 1¹⁷, עָרֵיכֶם Is 1⁷ +, etc,— **1.** *city, town*, abode of men Gn 4¹⁷ (J) and oft; נדלָה 10¹² (J), +, or קְטַנָּה Ec 9¹⁴ (cf Gn 19²⁰), esp **a** fortified עָרִים בְּצֻרוֹת 2 S 20⁶ +, etc, v בָּצַר, מִבְצָר, עיר מִבְצַר־צֹר Jos 19²⁹ (P) *fortified city (of) Tyre*, ע׳ מָצוֹר ψ 31²² +, etc, v מָצוֹר, מצוּרָה sub צור (Mi 7¹² v מָצוֹר p 596 a), ע׳ עֻדַּלְנוּ Is 26¹, ע׳ דְּלָתַיִם וּבְרִיחַ 1 S 23⁷; עָרֵי מָעֻזּוֹ 17⁹, ע׳ חוֹמָה Lv 25²⁹, cf v³⁰ (P), 1 K 4¹³, on Ho 10¹⁴ v 1 עַם **2 b** (1 S 9¹⁴ rd הַשַּׁעַר 𝔊 We Dr al.) **b.** ע׳ הַפְּרָזוֹת opp עָרֵי הַפּ׳ Dt 3⁵, כֹּפֶר הַפְּרָזִי 1 S 6¹⁸, Est 9¹⁹, disting fr dependencies חֲצֵרִים Jos 13²³ + oft P. **c.** עָרֶיהָ are dependent towns Jos 13¹⁷ (P), Je 19¹⁵. †**d.** עָרֵי הַמַּמְלָכָה Jos 10² (JE) *royal cities* (i.e with a king, cf Tel Am *al šarri*), so sg 1 S 27⁵, opp עָרֵי הַשָּׂדֶה v⁵ *rural towns;* ע׳ הַמְּלוּכָה 2 S 12²⁶ (but rd. ע׳ הַמַּיִם We Bu Kit Loh HPS, v. **2** infr) †**e.** עָרֵי מִסְכְּנוֹת Ex 1¹¹ *storage-cities*, so 1 K 9¹⁹ = 2 Ch 8⁶, 2 Ch 8⁴ 17¹²; for מ׳ ע׳ נַפְתָּלִי 16⁴ rd prob כִנֲרוֹת עַל־וגו׳ (as 1 K 15²⁰, Be Kit Buhl), cf ע׳ הָרֶכֶב 1 K 9¹⁹ 10²⁶ = 2 Ch 8⁶ 9²⁵, 2 Ch 1¹⁴, ע׳ הַפָּרָשִׁים 1 K 9¹⁹ = 2 Ch 8⁶ †**f.** ע׳ (הַ)מִּקְלָט (P) *asylum-cities* Nu 35¹¹ ¹³ ¹⁴ Jos 20², cf Nu 35²⁵ ²⁶·²⁷ ²⁸·³², ע׳ לְמִקְלָט v¹²; ע׳ מִקְלַט הָרֹצֵחַ Jos 21¹³ + 4 t. 21. **g.** ע׳(הָ)אֱלֹהִים = Jerus ψ 46⁵ 87³, cf 48²·⁹, ע׳ י׳ Is 60¹⁴ ψ 101⁸; ע׳ י׳ צְבָאוֹת 48⁹. **h.** *city* = inhabitants 1 S 4¹³ 5¹² Is 22² Ru 1¹⁹, so 2 S 20²² (rdg הָעִיר for MT הָעָם) 𝔊 We Dr al (cf also foll) **i.** combinations are ע׳ רכלים Ez 17⁴ *city of merchants;* ע׳ מוֹשָׁב ψ 107⁴·⁷·³⁶ *city for dwelling;* esp. of character or condition: †ע׳ הַצֶּדֶק Is 1²⁶, †ע׳ הָאֱמֶת Zc 8³, †ע׳ הַקֹּדֶשׁ Is 48² 52¹ Ne 11¹·¹⁸, cf Dn 9²⁴, all of Jerus, עָרֵי קָדְשְׁךָ Je 5¹⁷ of Judaean cities, of foreign cities, הָע׳ ע׳ תהלָּה Je 49²⁵, הַהֹלֵלָה Ez 26¹⁷, הָע׳ הָעַלִּיזָה Zp 2¹⁵, of Jerus also הָע׳ הַיּוֹנָה Zp 3¹ *oppressive city*, ע׳ (הַ)דָּמִים *bloody city* Ez 22² 24⁶·⁹ and (of Nineveh) Na 3¹ **2.** of fortress in a city esp. עִיר דָּוִד 2 S 5⁷·⁹ 6¹⁰ + oft (v דָּוִד), ע׳ בֵּית הַבַּעַל 2 K 10²⁵ (crpt, Klo prop דביר for ע׳, cf Kmp Benz Kit), ע׳ הַמַּיִם 2 S 12²⁷ (so rd also v²⁶, see **1 d**) **3.** appar fortified place, of any size, בְּכָל־עָרֵיהֶם מִמִּגְדַּל נוֹצְרִים עַד עִיר מִבְצָר 2 K 17⁹ = 18⁸; cf Nu 13⁹ (P, but on comp of ver. see Di), perh. also ע׳ עֲמָלֵק 1 S 15⁵ (HPS) —Ho 7⁴ v I. עור **Hiph.**

עִיר הַהֶרֶס v. הרס

†עִיר־הַמֶּלַח **n.pr.loc.** (*city of salt*) in desert of Judah, Jos 15⁶² (P, + En-gedi), πόλεις Σαδων (A 𝔊L [τῶν] ἁλῶν), site unknown.

עִיר נָחָשׁ as **n.pr.m.** v II נָחָשׁ

†עִיר שֶׁמֶשׁ **n.pr.loc.** (*city of the sun(-god)*), assigned to Dan Jos 19⁴¹ (P), = בֵּית שׁ׳ q v; πόλεις Σαμμαυς, A 𝔊L πόλις Σαμες.

עִיר הַתְּמָרִים (*city of palms*) = יְרִיחוֹ q.v.

†III. עִיר **n.pr.m.** in בני ע׳ 1 Ch 7¹², txt. dub, v Be Kau

עיר (√of foll, cf Ar عَارَ, عير *go away, go hither and thither, escape through sprightliness*, whence عَيْرٌ *ass*, esp *wild ass* De Jb (2), 149 Hom NS 121-127)

†עַ֫יִר **n.m.**[Gn 32, 16] **male ass** (young and vigorous);—pl. עֲיָרִים Gn 32[16] (E); sf. עִירֹה 49[11] (poem; ‖ בְּנִי אֲתֹנוֹ); cstr. עַיִר פֶּרֶא (Ges[§ 131 c N. 2], or appos. Kö[Synt. § 333 a] Di al.) Jb 11[12] *wild ass's colt;* pl. עֲיָרִים, for riding Ju 10[4a] (v[4b] see II. עִיר), 12[14], sg. abs. עַיִר Zc 9[9]; עֲיָרִים for carrying Is 30[6] Qr (Kt עורים), עֲיָרִם for tillage v[24].

†עִירָא **n.pr.m.** (v. Sab. n.pr.m. עיר Hal [159]);—**1.** כֹּהֵן (q.v. **1**) of David 2 S 20[26]; on poss. ident. with **2 b** v. Th Klo HPS, opp. We Dr; Ειρας, 𝔊L Ιωδαε. **2.** heroes of David (Ειρας, etc., 𝔊L Ιδαε, Οιαδ, etc.): **a.** 2 S 23[26] = 1 Ch 11[28], 1 Ch 27[9]. **b.** 2 S 23[38] = 1 Ch 11[40].

†עִירָד **n.pr.m.** a Cainite Gn 4[18.18] Γαιδαδ.

†עִירוּ **n.pr.m.** in Judah 1 Ch 4[15], Ηρ(α).

†עִירִי **n.pr.m.** Benjamite 1 Ch 7[7], Ουρ(ε)ι.

†עִירָם **n.pr.m.** in Edom Gn 36[43] = 1 Ch 1[54], Ζαφω(ε)ιν (A Gn Ηραμ).

עֵירֹם v. II. עור.

†עַ֫יִשׁ **n.f.** a constellation, perh. **Great Bear** (cf. esp. Di) (point perh. עָיִשׁ (v. Bu and reff.), cf. Syr. ܥܝܘܬܐ PS[2866], ܥܝܘܬܐ Brock., name of a star);—וְעַ׳ עַל־בָּנֶיהָ Jb 38[32] = עָשׁ 9[9] (both + כְּסִיל, כִּימָה etc.).

עַיָּת **n.pr.loc.** v. עַי.

†עַכְבּוֹר, עַכְבֹּר **n.pr.m.** (*mouse*, cf. עַכְבָּר, v. Gray[Prop. N. 93]; עכבר OH and Ph. as n.pr. Lzb [340] (cf. also on simil. Lat. n.pr. Cl-Gann[JAs 1883, Fev.-Mar. 128]));—𝔊 Αχοβωρ: **1.** Edomite Gn 36[38.39] (P) = עַכְבּוֹר 1 Ch 1[49] (Baer Ginsb). **2.** courtier of Josiah 2 K 22[12.14], perh. also Je 26[22] 36[12] (cf. Gie and Ency. Bib.).

†עַכְבָּר **n.m.**[1 S 6, 4] **mouse** (NH *id.;* Aram. עַכְבְּרָא; Syr. (in Lexx) ܥܘܟܒܪܐ, ܥܒܪܐ (PS[22]); Ar. عكابر pl. *mares murum* Frey (Kam), cf. also Hom[AS 338]; Ar. of *jerboa* RS[K 302]; v. Tristr [NHB 122] FFP[10 ff.]);—abs. הָעַ׳ unclean Lv 11[29] (H), Is 66[17] (cf. RS[Sem i. 275, 2nd ed. 293]); pl. cstr. עַכְבְּרֵי (ה)זָהָב 1 S 6[4.11.18]; sf. צַלְמֵי עַכְבְּרֵיכֶם v[5].

†עַכָּבִישׁ **n.m.** spider (𝔗 עַכְּבִיתָא, עכובִיתָא; whence Ar. عنكبوت as loan-wd.; NH עַכְשׁוּב prob. *tarantula*, acc. to Levy[NHWB iii. 648]);—בֵּית עַ׳ Jb 8[14] i. e. web, so prob. 27[18] (rdg. עַ׳ for MT עָשׁ); cf. קוּרֵי עַ׳ Is 59[5] *filaments of a spider.*

†עַכּוֹ **n.pr.loc.** Ακχω, **Acco**, in Asher, Ju 1[31], + Jos 19[30] (P), rdg. עַ׳ for MT עֻמָּה, Di Kau Benn Ency. Bib., after 𝔊 Codd.; a seaport N. of Carmel (= Acre, Ptolemais), mod. *'Akka*, cf. Buhl[Geogr. 228] (Egypt. *'A-ka*, 'Ακη WMM[As. u. Eur. 181]; As. *Akkû*, COT[Gloss], TelAm. *Ak-ka*).

עכן (√of foll.; meaning unknown).

†עָכָן **n.pr.m.** man of Judah;—Jos 7[1] (P), v[18.19.20.24] (JE), 22[20] (P); = עָכָר 1 Ch 2[7] (fr. עָכוֹר Jos 7[26], v. also עָכָר); Αχαρ, Αχαν.

†יַעְכָּן **n.pr.m.** Gadite 1 Ch 5[13], Χιμα, Ιαχᾶ.

עכס (√of foll.; Ar. عَكَسَ is *reverse, tie backward*, whence عِكَاس *hopple*, of camel).

†[עֶ֫כֶס] **n.[m.]** **anklet, bangle;**—pl. abs. הָעֲכָסִים Is 3[18] *bangles, anklets* (as ornaments); for sg. abs. עַ׳ Pr 7[22] read עֵגֶל Toy.

†[עָכַס] **vb. denom. Pi. shake bangles,** rattle, tinkle;—*Impf.* 3 fpl. וּבְרַגְלֵיהֶם תְּעַכַּסְנָה Is 3[16] *and with their feet they rattle their bangles.*

†עַכְסָה **n.pr.f.** daughter of Caleb Jos 15[16.17] (JE) = Ju 1[12.13], 1 Ch 2[49], Ασχα, Αχσα, Αζα, Οξα.

†**עָכַר** **vb.** stir up, disturb, trouble (NH *id., make turbid;* Ar. عَكِرَ *be turbid*);—**Qal** *Pf.* 3 ms. עַ׳ 1 S 14[29]; 2 ms. sf. עֲכַרְתָּנִי Jos 7[25], etc.; *Impf.* 3 ms. sf. יַעְכָּרְךָ v[25]; *Pt.* עֹכֵר 1 K 18[17] + 3 t., עוֹכֵר 1 Ch 2[7]; pl. sf. עֹכְרַי Ju 11[35];—*disturb, trouble*, c. acc. pers. Gn 34[30] (J), Jos 6[18] 7[25.25] (all JE; v[25b] subj. י׳), Ju 11[35]; cf. Pr 11[17] (opp. גֹּמֵל), v[29] 15[27] (opp. חָיָה); עַ׳ יִשְׂרָאֵל 1 K 18[17.18] 1 Ch 2[7] (cf. Jos 7[18] etc., supr.); עַ׳ אֶת־הָאָרֶץ 1 S 14[29]. **Niph.** *Pf.* 3 ms. וּכְאֵבִי נֶעְכָּר ψ 39[3] *my pain was stirred up;* *Pt.* f. נֶעְכֶּרֶת Pr 15[6] usu. as n. abstr. *disturbance, calamity*, but < read וּתְבוּאַת רָשָׁע נִכְרַת[ה] *the income of the wicked is cut off* (Toy).

†עָכוֹר **n.[m.]** **disturbance, trouble,** only in עֵמֶק עַ׳ *valley of trouble*, W. or SW. from Jericho Jos 7[24.26] (JE; name explained), on border of Judah 15[7] (P), cf. Ho 2[17] Is 65[10]; on identif. cf. esp. Di[Jos 7, 24] Buhl[Geogr. 98]; Εμεκαχωρ, φάραγξ (or κοίλας) Αχωρ.

עָכָר **n.pr.m.** v. עָכָן.

†עָכְרָן **n.pr.m.** name in Asher Nu 1[13] 2[27] 7[72.77] 10[26]; Εχραν.

†עַכְשׁוּב **n.m.** usu. **asp, viper** (so 𝔊 𝔙; perh. conject. fr. sense and ‖ נָחָשׁ), but perh. =

(? crpt for) עַכָּבִישׁ **spider** (q.v.; cf. ℑ ad loc),—חֲמַת ע׳ ψ 140⁴ *a viper's (? spider's) venom* is under their lips (v. esp Che and reff).

עַל v. עלה. עַל v. III עלל.

†עֻלָּא **n.pr.m.** in Asher 1 Ch 7³⁹, Ωλα.

עַלְבוֹן only in אֲבִי־עַלְבוֹן q.v. p. 3 b supr.

עלג (√ of foll., cf. לעג, and v. esp Lag M iii 29 ff No ZMG xli (1887), 718 f., who cites Mand אלגא).

†[עִלֵּג] **adj.** **speaking inarticulately**,—pl. לשׁן עלגים Is 32⁴ (𝔊 ψελλίζουσαι, Lag l.c.).

עָלָה 890 **vb.** **go up, ascend, climb** (NH id., MI³³(?), Ph עלה, As *elû*, Ar. عَلَا, ℑ and Syr in der species; cf. perh. Eth. ዐለለ: (for ዐለወ: ዐልዐለ: Di⁵⁴). Sab עלי = عَلِيَ DHM ZMG xxxvii 415, cf. עלוהו = عُلُوٌّ Sab Denkm⁹¹),—**Qal** *Pf.* 3 ms. ע׳ Gn 19¹⁵+, 3 fs. עָלְתָה 40¹⁰+, עָלָתָה Je 14² 1 S 1²², 2 ms. עָלִיתָ Gn 49⁴+, etc.; *Impf.* 3 ms. יַעֲלֶה 2⁶+, יַּעַל 44³³+, וַיַּעַל 13¹+, sf. יַעַלֶנָּה Is 35⁹, etc., *Inf. abs.* עָלֹה Gn 46⁴+2 t.; cstr. עֲלוֹת 32²⁵+, etc., *Imv.* עֲלֵה 35¹+, fs. עֲלִי Nu 21¹⁷+, pl. עֲלוּ Gn 44¹⁷+, *Pt.* עֹלֶה 38¹³+; עוֹלָה Is 24¹⁸+, pl. עֹלִים Gn 28¹²+, etc.,—**1.** of persons, *go up, ascend*, in local relations **a.** from low place to high, c. מִן, ממצרים Gn 45²⁵ (E)+6 t., מארץ מצרים Ex 13¹⁸ (E)+3 t.; †מִבָּבֶל Ezr 7⁶ 8¹, מן הירדן Jos 4¹⁶ ¹⁷ ¹⁹ (P), מ(ן־ה)מדבר Ct 3⁶ 8⁵ etc. **b.** out of a place, c. מִן, מן הארץ 1 S 28¹³, מ(תוך) הַפַּחַת Is 24¹⁸ Je 48⁴⁴ מִהַבּאר 2 S 17²¹. **c.** c. acc. of place whither: a city ביתאל Gn 35¹ ³ (E), באר שׁבע 26²³ (J); a mountain ההר Nu 13¹⁷ (JE) Dt 1²⁴+, etc., a bed Gn 49⁴ (J) 2 K 1⁴ ¹⁶, gate Ru 4¹, (הַ)שָּׁמַיִם Dt 30¹² 2 K 2¹¹ Am 9²+4 t., c. אֶל־, אל (ה)הר Ex 19²³ 34²·⁴ (J) 24¹⁵ ¹⁸ (P)+5 t. P, אֶל־הַמָּקוֹם Dt 17⁸, אל ירושׁלם Ezr 7⁷, Is 2³ = Mi 4² (אל הר), c. acc. loc. + אל־י׳ (v. **2 b**) Je 31⁶, of going up to Jerusalem (from a distance), etc., c. לְ *to*, לירושׁלם Ezr 1³ (from Babylon), לבית 1 S 25³⁵, etc., c. עַד *unto*, עד־נחל Nu 32⁹ (J), †c. בְּ, בְּאַחַת עָרֵי 2 S 2¹ (constr. praegn.), בבעל פרצים 1 Ch 14¹¹ (del. בְּ), בַּגִּלְגָּל Ju 1³. **d.** to sacred places, Ex 34²⁴, c. acc. †בית יהוה, from palace 2 K 19¹⁴ 20⁵ ⁸ 23² 2 Ch 29²⁰ 34³⁰ Is 37¹⁴ 38²² Je 26¹⁰; c. אֶל, אל הר האלהים Ex 24¹³ (E); בַּמָּה 1 S 9¹³ ¹⁴ ¹⁹, בבית י׳ 1 S 1⁷ (בְּ dittogr.), בהר יהוה ψ 24³. **e.** c. acc. דֶּרֶךְ *by the way to* † Nu 21³³ (E) Dt 3¹ Ju 8¹¹ 1 S 6⁹ 2 K 3⁸, מעלה Je 48⁵, חוֹמָה Jo 2⁷. **f.** *ascend, climb*, c. בְּ *by*, a ladder Gn 28¹² (E), Ez 40⁶·²²·⁴⁹, etc.; c. עַל *upon*, altar by (בְּ) steps, of priest, Ex 20²⁶ (Gi; van d. H. v²⁶, E) the roof Jos 2⁸ Ju 9⁵¹, bed ψ 132³, עַל־יָדָיו *on his hands* 1 S 14¹³; על במתי עב Is 14¹⁴ (|| ממעל לכוכבי אל), etc. **2.** *go up*, in personal relations **a.** *to meet* or *visit*, c. אֶל pers., Gn 44¹⁷ ²⁴ ³⁴ 45⁹ (J) Jos 10⁴ ⁶ (all with implication of *ascent*), Dt 25⁷ (to gate of city), +, c. †על pers., Gn 38¹² (+ ה loc., up *to Timnah*); לקראת 46²⁹ (J) Ju 6³⁵ 2 K 1³ ⁶ ⁷. †**b.** *go up* unto (אֶל) God, on a height, אל האלהים Ex 19³ (E) 1 S 10³; אל יהוה Ex 24¹ (E) 19²⁴ 32³⁰ (J) Ju 21⁵·⁵·⁸ (to war), אֵלַי Ex 24¹² (E) Dt 10¹, unto Deborah Ju 4⁵. **c.** *go up*, in war, c. אֶל *against* Nu 13³¹ (E) Ju 1¹ 12³ 1 S 7⁷ Is 36¹⁰ (= עַל 2 K 18²⁵)+, oftener c. עַל, 1 S 14¹⁰ Ju 6³ 15¹⁰ 18⁹ 1 K 14²⁵+; c. לַצָּבָא + על Jos 22¹²·³³ (P), c. בְּ, Is 7⁶ Je 48¹⁸, c. לְ, Hb 3¹⁶, + למלחמה Ju 20¹⁸ + 3 t., + במלחמה 1 S 29⁹, וַתַּעַל (ה)מלחמה 1 K 22³⁵ = 2 Ch 18³⁴. **d.** *go up after*, c. אחרי = *follow* 1 S 25¹³ 1 K 1³⁵·⁴⁰. **e.** *go up, depart*, c. מעל (q.v.) 1 S 6²⁰ Gn 17²² 35¹³ (P)+, subj. כבוד י׳ Ez 11²³·²⁴; = *withdraw, retreat*, 1 K 15¹⁹ 2 K 12¹⁹ Je 21², abs. 2 S 23⁹, and so read || 1 Ch 11¹³ (v. Dr Sm). †**3.** of animals, *go* or *come up*: abs. frogs Ex 7²⁸ (J) 8² (P), quails Ex 16¹³ (P), lion Is 35⁹; fox Ne 3³⁵, *rise up, fly up*, eagle Is 40³¹ Je 49²²; c. מִן, cattle out of water Gn 41² ³·¹⁸ ¹⁹ Ct 4² 6⁶, lion מִגְּאוֹן הַיַּרְדֵּן Je 49¹⁹ = 50⁴⁴, מִסֻּבְּכוֹ Je 4⁷, from prey Gn 49⁹ (J), *climb up* into (בְּ) houses, locusts Jo 2⁹, frogs, on (בְּ) persons Ex 7²⁹ (J); c. עַל, of cattle, sexually Gn 31¹⁰·¹² (E); locusts upon the land Ex 10¹² ¹⁴ (E) Jo 1⁶. †**4.** of vegetation, *spring up, grow, shoot forth*: trees Is 55¹³ ¹³ Ez 47¹², קִיקָיוֹן Jon 4⁶, grass Dt 29²² Am 7¹, ears of grain Gn 41⁵ ²² (E), also Gn 40¹⁰ (E) Is 5⁶ 32¹³ cf. sim. 53², Ho 10⁸ Pr 26⁹, ע׳ כֻּלּוֹ קִמְּשֹׂנִים Pr 24³¹ *all of it grown up with thorns*, Is 34¹³; fig. קֶרֶן Dn 8³·⁸. **5.** of natural phenom., *go up, rise*: dew, Ex 16¹⁴, i.e. disappear (P), אד ע׳ מִן־הָאָרֶץ Gn 2⁶ (J), cloud 1 K 18⁴⁴ Je 4¹³, ע׳ הַשַּׁחַר dawn, etc. Gn 19¹⁵ (JE) Ju 19²⁵ 1 S 9²⁶+; smoke Gn 19²⁸ Ex 19¹⁸ (J) Ju 20⁴⁰+, fire 6²¹, flame 13²⁰; stench Is 34³ Jo 2²⁰, incense Ez 8¹¹, well Nu 21¹⁷ (E), waters Je 47²; Nile Je 46⁷·⁸ Am 8⁸ 9⁵; c. עַל, of overflow Is 8⁷+. †**6.** of inanimate things (instead of passive construction), abs., shock of grain (to גֹּרֶן) Jb 5²⁶; of בָּשָׂר (covering bones in Ezek.'s vision) Ez 37⁸; c. עַל, of garments upon the body Lv 19¹⁹ (P) Ez 44¹⁷; razor on head Ju 13⁵ 16¹⁷ 1 S 1¹¹, yoke upon oxen

Nu 19[2] (P) 1 S 6[7]; lot upon an animal Lv 16[9.10] (P); c. ב, weight in balance ψ 62[10]; entry in (ב) a book 1 Ch 27[24], =*be offered* (of sacrif.) 1 K 18[29] 2 K 3[20] Is 60[7]; אֲרוּכָה (q v.) in healing, Je 8[22], fig. 2 Ch 24[13] Ne 4[1] **7.** of thoughts, ע׳ על לב 2 K 12[5] Is 65[17] + 5 t, ע׳ על לבב Je 51[50] Ez 38[10], ע׳ על רוּחַ 14[7]; ע׳ אל לב 20[32]; of anger 2 S 11[20] 2 Ch 36[16] (ב pers) + 3 t, temper Ec 10[4] (עָלֶיךָ) **8.** *come up* before God, arrogance, בְאָזְנָיו 2 K 19[28] = Is 37[29], cry, אֶל־א׳ Ex 2[23] (P), c. acc. 1 S 5[12], abs. Je 14[2], tumult ψ 74[23]; of evil Jon 1[2] (לְפָנָי). †**9.** *go up, extend,* of boundary, c. מן *whence*, + acc, אֶל, ל and even ב *whither* Jos 15[3.6.8] 18[12.12] + (all P) †**10.** *excel. thou excellest* (על) *them* Pr 31[29]; *be superior to* יעלה עליך מעלה מעלה Dt 28[43]—עוֹלָה Jb 36[33] is difficult, cf Comm., and v. עַוְלָה.

†**Niph.** *Pf* 3 ms. נַעֲלָה Nu 10[11] +; 2 ms. נַעֲלֵיתָ ψ 97[9]; *Impf.* יֵעָלֶה Ex 40[37], etc; *Inf. cstr.* העלות Nu 9[17] +, etc; *Imv* mpl הֵעָלוּ 16[24];—**1. a.** *be brought up:* מבבל לירושלם Ezr 1[11]. **b.** *be taken up,* וַתֵּעָלוּ על שפת לשון Ez 36[3] (Ko[1 553]; talked about) **c.** (1) pass., *be taken up, away,* of (pillar of) cloud, sq מֵעַל of tabern. Ex 40[36] Nu 9[17] 10[11] (P), abs. Ex 40[37.37] Nu 9[21.21.22] (P), of the glory from upon the cherubim Ez 9[3], (2) reflex, *take oneself away from, get up from:* מסביב Nu 16[24]; מעל v[27]; of a besieging army Je 37[5.11] **2.** reflex: *take oneself away* מאחרי pers, from following after, 2 S 2[27]. **3.** *be exalted,* of God ψ 47[10]; c. על, *over* all gods 97[9].

Hiph. *Pf.* הֶעֱלָה Nu 8[3] +, העלה Hb 1[15] (Ges [§ 63 p]); sf הֶעֶלְךָ Ne 9[18], הֶעֱלָנוּ Ex 32[1] + 2 t., 3 fs. וְהֶעֱלָתָה 1 S 2[19] consec; sf הֶעֱלָתַם Jos 2[6]; 2 ms הֶעֱלִיתָ Ex 33[1] +; וְהַעֲלִיתָ consec Dt 27[6] +; הֶעֱלִיתָ Ex 32[7]; וְהַעֲלִיתָ consec 40[4]; 2 mpl. sf. הֶעֱלִיתֻנוּ Nu 20[5] 21[5], etc.; *Impf.* יַעֲלֶה Lv 17[8] +; וַיַּעַל 2 S 24[22], וַיַּעֲלֶה, Je 10[13]; וַיַּעַל Gn 8[20] +, sf. יַעֲלֵם Dt 28[61], etc.; *Inf. abs.* הַעֲלֵה Ez 23[46], cstr. הַעֲלוֹת 1 Ch 23[31] +, etc.; *Imv* הַעַל Ex 33[12] + 2 t; fs הַעֲלִי 1 S 28[8.11] +, etc.; *Pt* מַעֲלֶה 7[10] +; cstr. מַעֲלֵה Lv 11[4] +; sf. מַעַלְךָ Dt 20[1] ψ 81[11]; f. מעלה Lv 11[26]; cstr. מַעֲלַת Lv 11[3.6] Dt 14[6], etc;—**1.** *bring up* persons: **a.** from a place, c. מן. מן הַסֶּלַע Ju 15[13]; ממצרים Ex 17[3] (E) + 3 t E, + 8 t.; מארץ מצרים Ex 32[1] (J) + 5 t. J, + Lv 11[45] (P), Dt 20[1] Jos 24[17] (E), + 13 t; מארץ צפון Je 16[15] = 23[8]. **b.** (1) out of a place, c. מִן הַבּוֹר + מִן Gn 37[28] (E) ψ 40[3] Je 38[10.13]; משחת Jon 2[7]; מקברות Ez 37[12.13], מִן־שְׁאוֹל ψ 30[4], etc., (2) c. ב *by means of*, בַּחֲרָמִי Ez 32[3] (Hb 1[15] v. **3** infr.). **c.** c. acc. of place whither, Nu 20[25] (P) 22[41] (E) Jos 2[6] 7[24] (J) Ezr 4[2]; c אֶל: אֶל־הָעֲלִיָּה 1 K 17[19], השמים 2 K 2[1]; c ל· לבית 2 Ch 8[11]. **d.** *cause to ascend, climb:* על המרכבה 1 K 20[33] (אֶל 2 K 10[15] prob. error), על־המגדלות 2 Ch 32[5] (𝔊 *built towers thereon*, i e. ע׳ עָלָיו), מעל לחומה Ne 12[31] vid. על **IV 2 e.** †**2.** in personal relations **a.** *bring up*, c. אל, 1 S 19[15] 2 K 10[15] 25[6] Je 39[5] 52[9]; c. ל, 1 S 28[8.11.11] **b.** in war, c. על *against* 2 Ch 36[17] Je 50[9] Ez 16[40] 23[46] 26[3]. **c.** *take away* (from life) ψ 102[25] Jb 36[20]. †**3.** *bring up* animals, c. על, frogs על הארץ Ex 8[1.3] (P); *bring up* horses to a charge Je 51[27], cf. Na 3[3], *draw up* men, under fig. of fish (בְּחַכָּה) Hb 1[15]; *train*, young lion Ez 19[3], of cattle, מעלה גֵרָה, i e. *chewing the cud* Lv 11[3.4.4.5.6.26] Dt 14[6.7.7] **4.** *cause to ascend:* c. acc rei, smoke מן העיר Ju 20[38]; stench באף Am 4[10], etc.; *bring waters* upon, על Is 8[7]; *bring up* from (מן loc.) 2 S 6[2.12] 1 K 8[1] Gn 50[25] (JE), +; c. אֶל loc., Ju 16[3] 1 Ch 15[3.12], c. acc. loc. 2 Ch 2[15]; c. אל pers. 1 S 6[21], c. לְ pers. Ju 16[8] 1 S 2[19]; c. על, *bring* sickness *upon* Dt 28[61], הע׳ עפר על ראש† *throw dust on the head* Jos 7[6] La 2[10] Ez 27[30]; *clothe* sackcloth *upon* Am 8[10]; flesh upon Ez 37[6]; *put* ornaments *on* 2 S 1[24], cf. also 1 K 10[16.17] = 2 Ch 9[15.16], 2 Ch 3[5.14]; הע׳ נר *light lamp* (make flame go up; Thes al of *raising* lamp upon the lamp-stand) Ex 25[37] 27[20] + 6 t P; *bring up* new flesh (heal; v. אֲרוּכָה) Je 30[17] 33[6]. †**5.** mentally: הע׳ גלולים על לב Ez 14[3], אל לב v[7], i.e. make object of thought, *rouse, stir up*, c. acc. אַף, *anger* Pr 15[1], cf. Ez 24[8]. †**6.** הע׳ מנחה ל׳ 2 K 17[4] *offer* a present, *bring up* tithe to (ל) Ne 10[39]; הע׳ מַס *raise a levy* 1 K 5[27] 9[15], למס v[21] 2 Ch 8[8]. †**7.** *exalt:* ψ 137[6] *if I exalt not Jerus. above* (על) *my chief joy;* אנכי אַעַלְךָ גם־(ם)עלה Gn 46[4] (E) *I will exalt thee exceedingly* (cf. **Qal 10;** מ lost in MT, after ם; Di and most *bring up*) **8.** *cause to ascend* (in flame; Thes al. to go up on altar), *offer* sacrifice, usu. עֹלָה, either alone or foll. by other sacrif. העלה עלות Ex 24[5] (E) 32[6] (J) Lv 17[8] (H) Dt 12[13.14] + (see עֹלָה), seldom: קטרת† Ex 30[9] (P), cf. ψ 66[15], מנחה† Is 57[6] 66[3], also prob 1 K 18[29.36] 2 K 3[20] (>**Qal**), פר(ים) Nu 23[2.4.14.30] (E) ψ 51[21]; הטוב בעיניו 2 S 24[22]; הע׳ ליהוה Ju 13[16]; abs 2 Ch 8[13] 29[29]; הע׳ לעולה† Gn 22[2.13] (E); c. acc. loc מַעֲלָה בָמָה Je 48[35]; מזבח(ה) Lv 14[20] (P) Is 60[7] (>**Qal**); c. לְ loc. 2 Ch 29[27]; c. בְּ loc. Gn 8[20] (J) Nu 23[2.4.14.30] (E); עַל־הַחֹמָה 2 K 3[27]; usu. על loc, על הַצּוּר Ju 13[19], הע׳ על מזבח 1 K

12$^{32.33.33}$ 2 K 16^{12} 2 Ch 1^{6} 29^{21} 1 S 2^{28}, פרים על ψ 51^{21}, elsewh העׄ׳ עלות על מזבח Ex 40^{29} (P) Jos 22^{23} 1 K 3^{4} 9^{25} 2 Ch 1^{6} 35^{16} Ezr 3^{2} Ez 43^{18}, העׄ׳ עלות ליהוה על מז׳ Dt 27^{6} Jos 8^{31} 1 Ch 16^{40} 2 Ch 8^{12} Ezr 3^{3}

†**Hoph.** *Pf*,—**1.** *be carried away*, 3 fs הֹעֲלָתָה Na 2^{8} **2.** *be taken up* into, *inserted* in, 3 ms. הֹעֲלָה 2 Ch 20^{34} (על כפר) (pass of **Qal 6**) **3.** 3 ms *be offered*, of פר Ju 6^{28} (על המזבח)

†**Hithp.** *lift oneself* *Impf* 3 ms אֶל־יִתְעַל Je 51^{3} *against* (him that) *lifts himself*, but corrupt; either rd אַל־, *let him not*, etc (𝔖𝔗𝔙 Hi Gf Gie Rothst), or del אל (𝔊 Co$^{Hpt.}$)

†עָלֶה **n.m.** leaf, leafage (v עלה **Qal 4**),— ע׳ Lv 26^{36}+, cstr עלה Gn 3^{7} 8^{11}, sf עָלֵהוּ Je 17^{8}+, pl cstr עלֵי Ne 8^{15}+, sf עָלֶהָ Is 1^{30},— *leaf, leafage*, of various trees Gn 3^{7} 8^{11} Ne 8^{15} $^{15.15.15.15}$, green Je 17^{8}, flourishing Pr 11^{28}; but usu fading Is 1^{30} 34^{4} 64^{5} Je 8^{13} Ez 47^{12} ψ 1^{3}, *driven leaf* Lv 26^{36} Jb 13^{25}, עלה לתרופה *leaf for healing* Ez 47^{12}

†עֱלִי **n.[m.]** pestle (as *rising* before the blow),—Pr 27^{22}

עֵלִי **n.pr.m.** Eli, priest at Shiloh 1 S 1^{3} (+v^{3} 𝔊 Th Klo HPS), v$^{9.12}$+28 t 1–4+14^{3} 1 K 2^{27}; Ηλει

I עֹלָה$_{286}$ **n.f.** whole burnt-offering (*that which goes up* (√**6**) to heaven (al on altar)),— ע׳ Gn 22^{3}+141 t, עוֹלָה Nu 28^{37}+33 t, cstr עֹלַת Ex 29^{42}+27 t, עוֹלַת Nu 28^{24}+2 t, sf. עוֹלָתְךָ ψ 20^{4}, etc, pl עֹלוֹת Jos 8^{31}+42 t, עלֹת Gn 8^{20} +3 t, עוֹלֹת Dt 27^{6}, עולות Am 5^{22}+, sf עולותיכם Je 6^{20}+, etc,—the *whole burnt-offering* (beast or fowl) is entirely consumed and goes up in the flame of the altar to God expressing the ascent of the soul in worship. All of the victim is laid on the altar except the hide and such parts as could not be washed clean If beast the ע׳ must be a male without blemish Lv 1$^{3.10}$ 22$^{18.19}$, of herd or flock; if of flock, either sheep or goat, if fowl, either turtle-dove or young pigeon Lv 1^{14}, the latter usu offered by the poor † 5^{7} 12^{8} 14^{22} 15$^{14.16.29.30}$ Nu 6$^{10.11}$. A lamb was offered by individuals Lv 12^{6} Nu 6^{14}, and by the nation at the עמר offering Lv 23^{12}, and daily at the עֹלַת הַבֹּקֶר 9^{17} Nu 28^{23} 2 K 16^{15} Ez 46^{13}, and at morning and evening עלה תמיד Nu 28^{3}, †עֹלַת (הַ)תָּמִיד Ex 29^{42} Nu 28$^{6.10.15.23.24.31}$ 29$^{6.11.16.19.22.25.28.31.34.38}$ Ezr 3^{5} Ne 10^{34} Ez 46^{15}. These were doubled at the עלת שַׁבָּת Nu 28^{10} A ram was offered by Aaron and his sons †Ex 29^{18} Lv 8^{18} 9^{2} 16$^{3.5}$; but a young bullock was of greater value Nu 15$^{8.24}$ 2 S 24^{22}= 1 Ch 21^{23}, at consecration of Levites Nu 8^{12}, so calves Mi 6^{6}, on great occasions bullocks+rams Nu 23$^{1-6.14.15}$, bullocks+rams +lambs Is 1^{11}, one of each kind offered by tribal chiefs Nu 7$^{15.21.27.33.39.45.51.57.63.69.75.81.87}$. In ritual of (ה)חדש עֹלַת Nu 28^{14} 29^{6} and at מצות and Pentecost 2 bullocks, 1 ram, and 7 lambs were added to daily offering Nu 28$^{11.19.27}$; at offering of new bread at Pentecost 1 bullock, 2 rams, and 7 lambs Lv 23^{18}, on the 1st and 10th of the 7th month and at עצרת 1 bullock, 1 ram, and 7 lambs, in addition to the offerings of new moon Nu 29$^{2.8.36}$, the system culminated in 70 bullocks, 14 rams, 98 lambs for the 7 days of Tabernacles 29^{13ff} Acc. to Ezek the prince was to offer on each of 7 days of מצות 7 bullocks and 7 rams Ez 45^{23}, and on Sabbath 6 lambs and 1 ram 46^{4}. At the reconsecration of temple 70 bullocks, 100 rams, and 200 lambs were offered 2 Ch 29^{32}, and at the return of exiles 12 bullocks, 96 rams, and 77 lambs Ezr 8^{35} In early times whole burnt-offerings of children were sometimes made, e g Jephthah's daughter Ju 11^{31}; Isaac proposed as, Gn 22^{2} but ram substituted v^{13}, made to other gods 2 K 3^{27} Je 19^{5}+. The ע׳ was anciently made on any altar used for worship, but in P confined to †מזבח הָעֹלָה Ex 30^{28} 31^{9} 35^{16} 38^{1} 40^{6} $^{10.29}$ Lv 4$^{7.10.18.25.25.30.34}$ 1 Ch 6^{34} 16^{40} 21$^{26.29}$ 2 Ch 29^{18} (not in other lit.); מזבח לעלה Jos 22^{29} 1 Ch 22^{1}. The offerer imposed his hands on head of animal, then slaughtered it Lv 1$^{4.5}$, †שחט ע׳ 4$^{24.33}$ 6^{18} 7^{2} 9^{12} 14$^{13.19.31}$ Ez 40$^{39.42}$ 44^{11}, and flayed it †הפשיט ע׳ Lv 1^{6} 2 Ch 29^{34} The priest washed the pieces Ez 40^{38}; arranged them on the altar above the wood Lv 6^{5}, the fire devoured them v$^{2-6}$ 9^{24} 1 K 18^{38} 2 Ch 7^{1}, they went up in the flame ריח ניחח ליהוה (ל) Lv 1$^{9.13.17}$ 8^{21} Nu 28^{13}; לְרָצוֹן, according to character of offerer Is 56^{7} Je 6^{20}, see also ψ 20^{4} 40^{7} 51^{18} 1 S 15^{22}.

Phrases. †העלה ע׳ Gn 8^{20} Ex 32^{6} (J) 24^{5} (E) 30^{9} 40^{29} Lv 14^{20} 17^{8} (P) Dt 12$^{13.14}$ 27^{6} Jos 8^{31} 22^{23} Ju 6^{26} 20^{26} 21^{4} 1 S 6$^{14.15}$ 7$^{9.10}$ 10^{8} 13$^{9.10.12}$ 2 S 6$^{17.18}$ 24$^{24.25}$ 1 K 3$^{4.15}$ 9^{25} 10^{5} 2 K 3^{27} 1 Ch 16$^{2.40}$ 21$^{24.26}$ 23^{31} 29^{21} 2 Ch 1^{6} 8^{12} 9^{4} 23^{18} 24^{14} 29$^{7.27}$ 35$^{14.16}$ Ezr 3$^{2.3.6}$ Jb 1^{5} 42^{8} ψ 66^{15} Je 14^{12} 33^{18} Ez 43$^{18.24}$ Am 5^{22} (cf העלה **9**); †זבח ע׳ Ex 20^{24} (E), עשה לע׳ Lv 23^{12} Nu 6^{11} 15^{24} 29^{39}; †עָשָׂה ע׳ Lv 5^{10} 9$^{7.22}$ 15$^{15.30}$ 16$^{24.24}$ Nu 6^{16} 8^{12} 15$^{3.8}$ 29^{2} Dt 12^{27} Ju 13^{16} 1 K 8^{64} 2 K 5^{17} 10$^{24.25}$ 2 Ch 7^{7} Ez 43^{27} 45$^{17.23}$ 46^{2} $^{12.12.13}$, †הקריב ע׳ Lv 7^{8} 9^{16} 10^{19} 23^{37} Nu 28$^{3.11}$ $^{19.27}$ 29$^{8.13.36}$ 1 Ch 16^{1} Ezr 8^{35} Ez 46^{4}; הקריב לע׳

Lv 22^{18} Nu 6^{14}; +† ע׳ הביא Dt 12$^{6.11}$ 2 Ch 29$^{31.32}$ 30^{15} Is 43^{23} Je 17^{26}; +† הקטיר ע׳ 2 K 16$^{13.15}$ 2 Ch 13^{11} —עֹלָתָה, עולות v. also עוֹלָה sub I. עול.

†II. [עֲלָה] **n.f. ascent, stairway,** עלותו Ez 40^{26} Kt, עלוֹתָיו Qr; rd. prob. מַעֲלֹתו (𝔊 Co SS לו, Toy עלתו).

†[עִלִּי] **adj. upper**;—fs. עלית Ju 1^{15}; pl. עִלִּיּוֹת Jos 15^{19} (opp תַּחְתִּית, תַּחְתִּיּוֹת)

†עֲלִיָּה **n.f.** (c adj masc Je 22^{14}, cf. Albrecht ZAW xvi (1896). 83 Ko$^{Synt. § 251 k}$) **roof-chamber** (NH *id.*, 𝔗 עִלִּיתָא, Syr ܥܠܝܬܐ (whence Ar. عِلِّيَّة *dining-room* as loan-wd Fra$^{20 f}$); Sab עלית DHM$^{Epigr\ Denkm\ 27}$);—chamber on roof, cool and secluded: abs ע׳ Ju 3$^{23.24.25}$ (cf Nes$^{Marg\ 13}$), 1 K 17$^{19.23}$ 2 K 4^{11}; cstr. עֲלִיַּת הַמְּקֵרָה Ju 3^{20}, ע׳־קִיר 2 K 4^{10} *roof-chamber with walls* (permanent); ע׳ הַשַּׁעַר 2 S 19^{1}, i.e. over the gateway; ע׳ הַפִּנָּה Ne 3$^{31.32}$ i.e. at a corner of the wall, ע׳ אָחָז 2 K 23^{12} (prob. built by A), sf. עֲלִיָּתוֹ 1^{2} (belonging to Ahaziah);—2 Ch 9^{4} rd עֹלָתוֹ (cf ‖ 1 K 10^{5}); pl abs. עֲלִיּוֹת מְרֻוָּחִים Je 22^{14} *spacious roof-chambers*, in Sol.'s temple acc. to 2 Ch 3^{9}, so sf. עֲלִיֹּתָיו 1 Ch 28^{11}, more gen. עֲלִיּוֹתָיו Je 22^{13}, י׳'s chambers in sky ψ 104^{3}, containing rain, v^{13}.

I. עֶלְיוֹן$_{22}$ **adj. 1.** high,—ms. ע׳ Dt 26^{19} 28^{1} 1 K 9^{8} († rdg הַבַּיִת הַזֶּה הָע׳ as 𝔊𝔏 Benz) = 2 Ch 7^{21}, of י׳ ψ 97^{9}. **2.** *upper* Bethhoron, ע׳ Jos 16^{5}, העליון 1 Ch 7^{24} 2 Ch 8^{5}, *the upper* (opp lower), of house Ne 3^{25}, cf. 2 K 15^{35} 2 Ch 23^{20} + 5 t, + Gn 40^{17} (*uppermost* basket); fs. הָעֶלְיוֹנָה *the upper* pool 2 K 18^{17} = Is 36^{2}, Is 7^{3}; *the highest* side-chamber (צֵלָע) Ez 41^{7}, fpl הָעֶלְיוֹנֹת 42^{5} *the upper* chambers (לְשָׁכוֹת) **3.** of Davidic king exalted above monarchs ψ 89^{28} (cf. Dt 28^{1}, supr).

†II. עֶלְיוֹן **n.m. Highest, Most High** (prob = foreg),—**1.** name of God Nu 24^{16} Dt 32^{8} ψ 18^{14} = 2 S 22^{14} ψ 9^{3} 21^{8} 46^{5} 50^{14} 73^{11} 77^{11} 78^{17} 83^{19} 87^{5} 91$^{1.9}$ 92^{2} 107^{11} Is 14^{14} La 3$^{35.38}$; with other divine names אל עליון Gn 14$^{18.19.20.22}$ (v Di) ψ 78^{35}, יהוה עליון ψ 7^{18} 47^{3}; אלהים עליון ψ 57^{3} 78^{56} **2.** of rulers, either monarchs or angel-princes, בְּנֵי עֶלְיוֹן = אלהים ψ 82^{6}.

†מֹעַל **n.[m.]** lifting,—בְּמֹעַל יְדֵיהֶם Ne 8^{6}.

מַעֲלֶה$_{19}$ **n.m.**$^{Is\ 15.5}$ **ascent**;—מ׳ Ne 12^{37}; cstr. מַעֲלֵה Jos 10^{10} + 14 t, מַעֲלָו Ez 40$^{31.34.37}$; **1.** *ascent* of hill or mt · to a city 1 S 9^{11}, to the royal sepulchres (in Jerus.) 2 Ch 32^{33}; מ׳ הַזֵּיתִים 2 S 15^{30} (v. זַיִת **3**); מ׳ עַקְרַבִּים = *Scorpion-pass*, on S border of Pal., Ju 1^{36} Nu 34^{4} Jos 15^{3} (both P), i e. prob the *Nakb es-safâ* SW from Dead Sea Buhl$^{Geogr\ 16.66}$ Di and GFM ad loc, and reff; oft def by n pr loc. מ׳ אֲדֻמִּים 15^{7} 18^{17}, S. of valley of Achor, between Jerusalem and Jericho, cf. mod *Tel'at ed-dâm* Buhl$^{Geogr\ 98}$; v also בית חורן, I. גּוּר, II. לוּחִית, חֶרֶס, II. ציץ **2** of stairs Ez 40$^{31.34.37}$; to a wall Ne 12^{37}, מַעֲלֵה הַלְוִיִּם Ne 9^{4}.

מַעַל$_{140}$ **subst., higher part,** only in **adv.** and **prep.** phrases, **above, upwards** (Ph מעל, v. sub מַטָּה p 641: abbrev. from מַעְלָה; cf. מַעַן in לְמַעַן from עָנָה: Ko$^{ii.\ 116}$) —+**1.** מִמַּעַל = *above* (v. מן **1 c**): **a.** as *adv.* Am 2^{9} וָאַשְׁמִיד פִּרְיוֹ מִמַּעַל his fruit *above* (opp. שָׁרָשָׁיו מִתָּחַת), Jb 18^{16}; 1 K 7$^{3.20.29}$, oft. in the phr הַשָּׁמַיִם מִמַּעַל Dt 4^{39} 5^{8} (= Ex 20^{4}), Jos 2^{11} 1 K 8^{23} Is 45^{8} Je 4^{28}; cf. אֱלוֹהַּ מ׳ Jb 3^{4} 31^{2}, שְׁחָקִים מ׳ ψ 78^{23} Pr 8^{28}, אֵל מ׳ 31^{28}. **b.** מִמַּעַל לְ, as *prep.* (מן **1 c**), *on the top of, above,* Gn 22^{9} ממעל לָעֵצִים *above* the wood, Ex 28^{27} = 39^{20}, Lv 11^{21} כְּרָעַיִם מִמַּעַל לְרַגְלָיו, Is 6^{2} שְׂרָפִים עֹמְדִים מִמַּעַל לוֹ, 14^{13} Je 43^{10} Ez 1^{26} Dn 12$^{6.7}$; = *on higher ground than,* Je 35^{4}, fig Je 52^{32} (‖ 2 K 25^{28} מעל)

2. With ־ָה *loc.* מַעְלָה, מָ֫עְלָה, *upwards* (opp. מַטָּה p. 641): +**a.** fig Dt 28^{43} יַעֲלֶה עָלֶיךָ מַעְלָה מָּ֫עְלָה *upwards, upwards,* i e. *higher and higher* (opp מַטָּה מָּטָּה) +**b.** וָמָ֫עְלָה (*a*) of direction in *space,* Ju 1^{36} מֵהַסֶּלַע וָמָ֫עְלָה from the rock *and upwards* (cf. Bu), 1 K 7^{31} (corrupt: v. Sta VB Benz), 1 S 9^{2} = 10^{23} משכמו וָמַעְלָה from his shoulder *and upwards.* so ולמ׳, +Ez 1^{27} ממראה מָתְנָיו וּלְמַעְלָה, 8^{2} 43^{15}. (*b*) of direction in *time,* or age —(*α*) מִבֶּן עֶשְׂרִים שָׁנָה וָמָעְלָה Ex 30^{14} Nu 1^{3} + 19 t P, מבן חדש וָמ׳ Nu 3$^{15.22}$ + 6 t. P, simil 4^{3} 8^{24} + 7 t P, elsewhere only 1 Ch 23$^{3.24}$ Ezr 3^{8}, and with וּלְמַעְלָה + 1 Ch 23^{17} 2 Ch 31$^{16.17}$; מִכֹּל חגר חֲגֹרָה וָמ׳ 2 K 3^{21}; and לְמִבֶּן +2 Ch 25^{5}. וָמ׳. +(*β*) מהיום ההוא וָמ׳ from that day *and onwards,* 1 S 16^{13} 30^{25}. +(*γ*) מן היום הזה וָמ׳ from this day *and upwards* (i.e. *and back*), Hg 2$^{15.18}$. +**c.** לְמַ֫עְלָה *upwards,* more common than מ׳ alone (**a**) (*α*) Ex 25^{20} (= 37^{9}) פֹּרְשֵׂי כְנָפַיִם לְמ׳, Ju 7^{13} ויהפכהו לְמ׳ overthrew it *upwards,* i.e turned it downside up, Is 7^{11} או הַגְבֵּהַּ לְמ׳ or make it (the request) high *upwards,* 8^{21} וּפָנָה לְמ׳, 37^{31} (2 K 19^{30}) ועשה פרי לְמ׳ (cf. Am 2^{9}, **1 a**), Ez 41$^{7\ a.\ \beta}$ (v$^{a.a}$ *bis* לְמ׳ לְמ׳)

=*higher and higher*), ψ 74^{5}; fig. וְהָיִיתָ רַק לְמ׳ Dt 28^{13} (cf. **a**), Pr 15^{24} אֹרַח חַיִּים לְמ׳ (opp. שְׁאוֹל :מָטָּה), cf. Ec 3^{21}; sq. a noun, Ezr 9^{6} לְמ׳ רֹאשׁ *over* the head, sq. מֵעַל (cf. *Aboth* 2^{1} לְמַעְלָה מִן)= *above*, 2 Ch 34^{4}: v. also **b** *a*, *b a*. (*b*) metaph. =*exceedingly*, only in Chr, 1 Ch 14^{2} 22^{5} the house must be built to J. לְהַגְדִּיל לְמ׳ so as to shew greatness *exceedingly*, 23^{17} וּבְנֵי ר׳ רָבוּ לְמ׳, 29^{3} (sq. מִן; =*over and above* . . .), v^{25} 2 Ch 1^{1} וַיְגַדְּלֵהוּ לְמ׳, 20^{19}; עַד לְמַ֫עְלָה, 16^{12} 17^{12} 26^{8}. †**d.** מִלְמַ֫עְלָה (v. מִן **9 a**); adv., *above* (the more usual *prose* syn. of מִמַּעַל): Gn 6^{16} אֶל־אַמָּה תְּכַלֶּנָּה מ׳, 7^{20} 15 cubits מ׳ (i.e. above the mountain-tops), Ex 25^{21} (40^{20}) וְנָתַתָּ֫ה אֶת־הַכַּפֹּרֶת על הארון מ׳ upon the ark *above*, 26^{14} (36^{19} 40^{19} Nu 4^{25}) a covering of skins on the tent מ׳ *above*, 39^{31} Nu 4^{6}, 1 K 7^{11} 7^{25} 8^{7} (2 Ch 4^{4} 5^{8}), Je 31^{37} אִם יִמַּדּוּ שָׁמַיִם מ׳ (cf. **1 a**), Ez 1^{11} פְּרֻדוֹת מ׳ separate *above*, v$^{22.26}$ 10^{19} 11^{22} 37^{8}; *from above*, Jos $3^{13.16}$ הַמַּיִם הַיֹּרְדִים מ׳.

†I. [מַעֲלָה] **n.f. what comes up**;—pl. cstr. מַעֲלוֹת רוּחֲכֶם Ez 11^{5}, i.e. your thoughts.

II. מַעֲלָה$_{46}$ **n.f. step, stair**;—מ׳ Ezr 7^{9} 1 Ch 17^{17}; pl. מַעֲלוֹת Is 38^{8}+, sf. מַעֲלֹתָו Am 9^{6}, etc.;—**1.** *step, stair* of temple Ez 40^{6}+5 t. 40, and temple porch 40^{49}; of altar Ex 20^{26} (E) (forbidden, cf. RS$^{\text{OTJC xii, n. 1; 2nd ed. 358}}$) Ez 43^{17} (prescribed); of house 2 K 9^{13}, of throne 1 K $10^{19.20}$ 2 Ch $9^{18.19}$; to the city of David Ne 3^{15} 12^{37}. **2.** *steps* (forming sun-dial, cf. Di^{Is}) 2 K $20^{9.9.10.10.11.11.11}$ = Is $38^{8.8.8.8.8.8}$. **3.** *stories* of heaven Am 9^{6}. **4.** *ascent* מִבָּבֶל Ezr 7^{9}. **5.** שִׁיר (לְ)הַמַּעֲלוֹת *song of ascents*, to the three great pilgrim feasts, i.e. to be sung on way up to Jerusalem, titles of ψψ 120–134+84^{6} We al.—כְּתוֹר האדם המעלה 1 Ch 17^{17} is crpt., v. Comm.$^{\text{ad loc.}}$ (and on ‖ 2 S 7^{19}).

†I. תְּעָלָה **n.f. water-course**;—ת׳ Je 30^{13}+; cstr. תְּעָלַת Is 7^{3}+2 t.; pl. sf. תְּעָלֹתֶיהָ Ez 31^{4};—**1. a.** *water-course*, conducted for irrigation Ez 31^{4}; hence poet., channel for rain Jb 38^{25}. **b.** *conduit*, 2 K 18^{17} = Is 36^{2}, Is 7^{3}, cf. 2 K 20^{20}. **c.** *trench*, 1 K $18^{32.35.38}$.

†II. תְּעָלָה **n.f. healing** (of new flesh and skin forming over wound);—(fig.) Je 30^{13} 46^{11}.

עַל, עָל (cf. Kö$^{\text{ii. 261 f.}}$) **I. subst. height** (poet.) †Ho 7^{16} יָשׁוּבוּ לֹא עָל they return (but) not *up*wards (i.e. not God-wards), 11^{7} וְאֶל־עַל יִקְרָאֻהוּ they (the prophets) call it (the people) *up*wards, (but) none striveth to rise; as adv. accus., 2 S 23^{1} the man הֻקַם עָל (that) is raised up *on high*. With מִן, מֵעַל, (הַ)שׁמים מֵעָל+ (the) heavens *above* Gn 27^{39} 49^{25} ψ 50^{4} (opp. מִתַּחַת Ex 20^{4}. In prose מִמַּעַל).

II. As **prep. upon,** and hence **on the ground of, according to, on account of, on behalf of, concerning, beside, in addition to, together with, beyond, above, over, by, on to, towards, to, against** (SI$^{4.6}$; Moab. Aram. *id.*; Ph. על, and עלת; Palm. Nab. על; Sab. עלי, Ar. عَلَى);—abbrev. from עֲלֵי (cf. אֱלֵי, עֲדֵי), which is preserved in poetry, Gn $49^{17.17.22.22}$ Nu $24^{6.6}$ Dt $32^{2.2}$ Is 18^{4} Je 8^{18} Mi 5^{6} La 4^{5} 1 K 20^{41} Qr, Jb 7^{1} Qr+10 t. ψ, 3 t. Pr, 15 t. Jb; with sf. עָלַי; עָלֶיךָ, עָלַיִךְ (+ψ 116^{7} the Aramaizing form עָלָיְכִי); עָלָיו, +1 S 2^{10} עָלָו, עָלֶיהָ; 1 pl. עָלֵינוּ; 2 mpl. עֲלֵיכֶם, +Ex 12^{13} עֲלֵכֶם, 2 fpl. עֲלֵיכֶן +Ez 23^{49}; 3 mpl. עֲלֵיהֶם, 13 t. in Pent. עֲלֵהֶם Gn 45^{15}, etc. (Kö$^{\text{ii. 305}}$), poet. עָלֵ֫ימוֹ Dt 22^{23}+11 t. ψ, Jb (perh. sts. sg., Ges$^{\text{§ 103 f, N.}}$); 3 fpl. עֲלֵיהֶן, +Lv $3^{4.10.15}$ עֲלֵהֶן (on the appar. *plur.* form of עֲלֵי, עָלַי, etc., v. Kö$^{\text{ii. 309 ff.}}$, and cf. sub עד).

1. Upon, of the substratum *upon* which an object in any way rests, or *on* which an action is performed; as עַל־הארץ *upon* the earth Gn $1^{11.26}$ 7^{6}, etc., ψ 110^{6} על ארץ רבה *over* a wide country; על האדמה *upon* the ground Ex 20^{12} +oft., Am 7^{12} עַל אֲדָמָה טְמֵאָה, Is 14^{2} על אדמת י׳, ψ 137^{4} עַל אַדְמַת נֵכָר (אֲדָמָה being properly *ground, soil*, is construed regularly with על, באדמה being very rare), more definitely על פני האדמה Gn 6^{1} Nu 12^{3}+oft.; על מקום Lv 14^{28} Je 45^{5} (uncommon: usu. בְּ); Dt 17^{20} Is 9^{6} עַל מַמְלַכְתּוֹ *upon* his realm, 2 Ch 1^{1}; עַל בָּתֵּיהֶם very strangely Ho 11^{11} (rd. וַהֲשִׁבֹתִים with 𝔊: v. **7 c** *a β*); constantly after such vbs. as נוח, ישׁב, רכב, etc., Gn 8^{4} Ex 11^{5}; כתב על to write (idiom.) *on* a book or other surface, Jos 10^{13}, etc.; יצא על go forth *over* Gn 41^{45} Zc 5^{3} ψ 81^{6}; with בָּטַח, נִסְמַךְ, נִשְׁעַן (fig.), to lean or trust *upon:* Gn 3^{14} to go עַל גְּחֹנְךָ *upon* thy belly, 32^{32} to limp עַל יְרֵכוֹ *upon* his thigh, 1 S 14^{13} Ez 37^{10}; Ju 15^{8} to smite שׁוֹק עַל יָרֵךְ leg *upon* thigh, i.e. so that the scattered limbs fall one upon another, Am 3^{15}. And with ref. not to a horizontal surface but to a *side*, Lv 1^{5}+ זָרַק עַל to pour *against* the altar, 1 K $6^{5.18}$ to build *against* the temple, Jos 10^{27}, etc. Fig. Ex 23^{13} let it not be heard עַל פִּיךָ *upon* thy mouth (in our idiom, *upon thy lips*, as Pr 22^{18}), ψ 15^{3} לֹא רָגַל עַל לְשֹׁנוֹ he slandereth not (i.e. prepares

not slander) *upon* his tongue, 2 S 23^{2} וּמִלָּתוֹ עַל לְשׁוֹנִי, Pr $16^{23.27}$ 31^{26} Ec 5^{1}; cf. נָשָׂא עַל שְׂפָתַיִם or עַל פֶּה ψ 16^{4} 50^{16}; Ez 36^{3b}.

Specially **a.**—(*a*) of *clothing*, etc., which any one wears, Gn 37^{23} the tunic אשר עליו which was *upon* him, Jos 9^{5} 1 K 11^{30} Ru 3^{15}+; Gn 24^{30} 38^{30} 2 S 13^{18}, of a sword 20^{8} Ct 3^{8}; so הָיָה עַל Lv 16^{4} Dt 22^{5} Ez 44^{18} 1 Ch 15^{27} 18^{7} (‖ 2 S 8^{7} אֶל: see p. 41 a); cf. לֹא יַעֲלֶה עָלֶיךָ Lv 19^{19} Ez 44^{17}, and with הֶעֱלָה, below, **7 b.**

(*b*) With verbs of *covering* or *protecting*, even though the cover or veil be not *over* or *above* the thing covered, but *around* or *before* it ('upon' referred to a *side*): v. סָכַךְ, כָּסָה, גָּנַן, עָטָה; Ne 2^{8} יד אלהי הטובה עלי, cf. v^{18} Ezr $7^{6.9}$ $8^{18.22.31}$; Ex 27^{21} the veil that is *over* (i.e. *before*) the testimony, 1 S 25^{16} חוֹמָה הָיוּ עָלֵינוּ they were a wall *about* us; סָגַר עַל to shut *in* (or *down*) *upon* Ex 14^{3} Jb 12^{14}; Ez 13^{5} Jb 13^{27} 26^{9} 36^{30} he spreadeth his light עָלָיו *about* him.

b. Of what rests heavily *upon* a person, or is a burden to him, Is 1^{14} הָיוּ עָלַי לָטֹרַח they are a cumbrance *upon* me, Jb 7^{20} I am a burden עָלַי *upon* myself, 2 S 15^{33} (cf. with אֶל 19^{36}); כָּבֵד עַל to be heavy *upon* Ex 5^{9} al. (v. כָּבֵד); of sin, calamity, etc. Is 53^{5} Ez 33^{10} ψ 88^{8} Jb 21^{9} 2 Ch 15^{5} 28^{13} Ec 6^{1} 8^{6} (cf. **5 a β**); Lv 7^{20} וְטֻמְאָתוֹ עָלָיו 22^{3}: idiomatically, Gn 48^{7} מֵתָה עָלַי רָחֵל Rachel died *upon* me (i.e. to my sorrow), 33^{13} וְהַבָּקָר עָלוֹת עָלָי are giving suck *upon* me (i.e. as a care to me), Nu 11^{13} יִבְכּוּ עָלַי they weep *upon* me (vexing me), Ju $14^{16.17}$ 19^{2} (v. Be), 1 S 21^{16} to play the mad man *upon* me, Je 12^{11}.

c. Of a duty, payment, care, etc., imposed *upon* a person, or devolving *on* him, as שָׂם עַל to lay *upon* Ex 5^{8} $21^{22.30}$ (שִׁית), 22^{24}, cf. Gn 47^{26} 2 Ch 35^{25}; with other verbs, Jb 38^{10} Dt 24^{5} 26^{6} 2 K 15^{20} 18^{14} 23^{33} Ne $10^{33.35}$ Est 1^{8} $9^{21.27.31}$; with צִוָּה enjoin *upon* Gn 2^{16}+ oft., כתב prescribe *to* 2 K 22^{13} ψ 40^{8}, נטשׁ cast *upon* 1 S 17^{20} (v^{22} על יד), נתן על יד (fig.) Gn 42^{37} 2 K 12^{12} 22^{5}, cf. 1 K 14^{27}, עזב ψ 10^{14}, גלל 37^{5}, השליך 55^{23}, פקד Jb 34^{13} al.; Gn 30^{28} נָקְבָה שְׂכָרְךָ עָלַי fix thy wages *upon* me (*name* thy wages *to* me), 34^{12} הַרְבּוּ עָלַי מְאֹד מֹהַר וּמַתָּן multiply *upon* me, etc., 2 S 19^{39} (pregn.) whatsoever thou choosest (and layest) *upon* me; without a verb, Ju 19^{20} רַק כָּל־מַחְסֹרְךָ עָלָי only let all thy wants be *upon* me, Ezr 10^{4} ψ 56^{13} עָלַי נְדָרֶיךָ thy vows are *upon* me (i.e. I owe them: cf. Nu $30^{7.9.15}$), Pr 7^{14} זִבְחֵי שְׁלָמִים עָלָי peace-offerings were *upon* me (=were due from me); perh. ψ 62^{1} 77^{1} (to the charge of); with an inf. 2 S 18^{11} וְעָלַי לָתֵת and it would have been *incumbent on* me to give, etc., 1 K 4^{7} Ezr 10^{12} (accents [Baer], RV^{m}), Ne 13^{13}, cf. Zc 12^{2} (Ew RV^{m}); Nu 7^{9} (P) the service of . . . was *upon* them, Ez 45^{17}, so especially late 1 Ch $9^{27.33}$ 23^{31} 2 Ch 2^{3} לעולם זאת על ישראל, 8^{15} 24^{9} Ezr 7^{11} Ne 11^{23}; Is 9^{5} and the government is *upon* his shoulder (cf. 22^{22}), 2 Ch 25^{3}; ψ 7^{11} מָגִנִּי עַל־א׳ my shield rests *upon* God (he has undertaken my defence), 62^{8} עַל־אלהים יִשְׁעִי וּכְבוֹדִי.

d. עַל is used idiom. to give pathos to the expression of an emotion, by emphasizing the person who is its subject, and who, as it were, feels it acting *upon* him: ψ 42^{6} why art thou cast down, O my soul, וַתֶּהֱמִי עָלָי and disquieted *upon me?* v^{7} my soul *upon me* is cast down, v^{12} 43^{5} La 3^{20}; ψ 131^{2} כַּגָּמֻל עָלַי אִמּוֹ כַּגָּמֻל עָלַי נַפְשִׁי is my soul *upon me;* 142^{4} בְּהִתְעַטֵּף עָלַי רוּחִי when my spirit faints *upon me,* 143^{4} Jon 2^{8}; Je 8^{18} עָלַי לִבִּי דַוָּי: my heart *upon me* is sick, Jb $14^{22.22}$ (cf. Di), Hos 11^{8} נהפך עלי לבי my heart is turned (altered) *upon me,* 1 S 17^{32} 25^{36} Ne 5^{7} וַיִּמָּלֵךְ לִבִּי עָלַי and my heart took counsel *upon me:* cf. ψ 42^{5} I will pour out my soul *upon me,* Jb 30^{16}; 10^{1} אעזבה עלי שׂיחי I will let loose my complaint *upon me.* (Thes *apud me, mecum.* The rend. '*within* me' alters entirely the point of view of the Heb. expression, and is incorrect.) Denoting with some emph. the subj. of an experience, Jb 30^{2} עלימו אבד כָּלַח, Dn 2^{1} his sleep נִהְיְתָה עָלָיו was done with *upon* him (cf. Aram. 6^{19} נַדַּת עֲלוֹהִי), 10^{8} וְהוֹדִי נֶהְפַּךְ עָלַי (cf. 5^{9} 7^{28}): also, rather differently, Lv 18^{18b} Je 49^{20} אִם לֹא יַשִּׁים עֲלֵיהֶם נְוֵהֶם, Mi 7^{13} ψ 90^{17b}; ψ 7^{9} acc. to my perfectness *upon* me, Ez 18^{20}; 22^{3} 2 Ch 36^{8}.

e. חָיָה עַל to live *upon* (as upon a foundation or support; cf. Is 3^{1}, and ζῆν ἐπί τινος), Dt 8^{3} עַל־הַלֶּחֶם, Is 38^{16} (cf. Hi), Gn 27^{40} על חרבך תחיה *upon* (=*by*) thy sword thou shalt live (cf. Kazwini $^{ii. 17}$ *ap.* Tuch), Ez 33^{19}, cf. v^{26}.

f. Of the *ground*, or *basis*, *on* which a thing is done, as Gn 24^{9} עַל הדבר הזה, Lv 7^{12} if he offers it עַל תּוֹדָה *on the ground of* a thanksgiving, Nu 6^{21} עַל נִזְרוֹ, v^{b} Ez 16^{15} 28^{17} Dn 8^{25} 9^{18} על צדקותינו, עַל שִׂכְלוֹ (with عَلَى this use is extended so as to denote explicitly *on condition of*). Hence (*a*) the basis being conceived as

regulative, עַל comes to denote the *norm* or *standard* (cf Germ '*auf* die Art', W$^{AG\ ii.\ §59\ i}$) the transition may be seen in a passage like Ex 24^{8} the covenant which ׳י made with you *on the basis of* (עַל), or *in agreement with*, all these words (cf עַל פִּי 34^{27}), Nu 35^{24} עַל המשפטים האלה, Dt 17^{11} Je 30^{18} the palace shall sit (i.e be inhabited v. ישׁב) עַל מִשְׁפָּטוֹ *in accordance with* its manner, ψ 94^{20} who frames mischief עֲלֵי־חק *in accordance with* a law, . . . עַל פִּי *acc to* the mouth (i e command, Gn 45^{21} + oft, evidence Dt 17^{6} 19^{15}, sentence 21^{5}) of . ; . . . עַל שֵׁם *acc to* the name of (mostly with *call, be called*) Gn 48^{6} Ex 28^{21} 2 S 18^{18}+, cf 1 Ch 23^{14}, Ex 6^{26} 12^{51} עַל צִבְאֹתָם *acc to* their hosts (usu לְ), Nu 1^{18} עַל מִשְׁפְּחֹתָם (usu לְ), v^{52} 2$^{2.34}$ 7^{3} (‖ לְ), Dt 18^{8} (prob); עַל יְדֵי *acc. to* the hands (direction) of Je 5^{31} 33^{13} *al* (v p 391 b), ψ 110^{4} עַל דִּבְרָתִי מ׳ *after* the manner of M, Pr 25^{11} (prob) a word spoken עַל אָפְנָיו *in accordance with* its circumstances = appositely, of the tune *acc to* which a song is to be sung (RV. *set* to) ψ 6^{1} (1 Ch 15^{21}), 8^{1} 9^{1} 12^{1} 45^{1} 46^{1} (1 Ch 15^{20}) עַל־עֲלָמוֹת (perh, however, *in the manner of* maidens = for 'sopranos'), 53^{1} 56^{1} 60^{1} 69^{1} 81^{1} 84^{1} 88^{1} (cf in Syr. ܥܰܠ ܩܳܠܳܐ)

(*b*) The basis being conceived as involving the *ground*, עַל denotes the cause or reason, *on account of, because of*, Gn 20^{3} lo thou shalt die עַל הָאִשָּׁה *on account* of the woman, 21^{12} 26$^{7.9}$ 27^{41} 42^{21} Lv 4$^{3.28}$ 5^{18} 19^{17} 26$^{18.24.28}$ Dt 9^{18} 24^{16} fathers shall not be put to death עַל־בָּנִים *on account of* children, 31^{18} Jos 9^{20} Je 1^{16} 5^{9} Ez 18^{26} עליהם (‖ 33^{18} בָּהֶם), Pr 28^{21} ψ 39^{12} 50^{8} + oft, ψ 44^{23} עָלֶיךָ הֹרַגְנוּ *on thy account* are we slain all the day, 69^{8} Je 15^{15}, in the phrases עַל זֶה and עַל זֹאת ,עַל אוֹדוֹת ,דבר . . . *on* this *account*, עַל מָה *on* what *account?* עַל־כֵּן = *therefore* (v אוֹדָה ,דָּבָר, etc); before an inf., as Ex 17^{7} וְעַל נַסֹּתָם את־י׳ and *on account* of their trying ׳י, Am 1^{3} עַל דּוּשָׁם *on account of* their threshing = because they threshed, v$^{6\ 9\ 11\ 13}$, etc, Je 2^{35} עַל אָמְרֵךְ *because of* thy saying, 9^{12} 16^{18}+, and as a conj both with and without אֲשֶׁר or כִּי (v infr. **III**). And so often of the ground or cause of fear, grief, delight, or other emotions, e g Ex 18^{9} 32^{14} (נִחַם *repent* · so oft), 1 S 4^{13} 30^{6} 2 S 1^{26} 3^{8} 1 K 21^{4} 2 K 6^{11} Je 10^{19} Am 6^{6}

(*c*) Somewhat more strongly, *on behalf of, for the sake of*, Gn 19^{17} escape עַל נַפְשֶׁךָ *for* thy life, Ju 9^{17} 2 K 10^{3} נִלְחַם עַל (usu לְ); 1 K 2^{18} I will speak *on thy behalf* to the king, v^{19} (2 K 4^{13} לְ); Est 4^{16}, 4^{8} 7^{7}, 8^{11} 9^{16} Dn 12^{1} עמד עַל stand up (in late Heb) *on behalf of*, התפלל עַל intercede *for* (usu. בעד) Jb 42^{8} Ne 1^{6} 2 Ch 30^{18}, 29^{21} Ezr 8^{35}, and very often with כפר (q v) make atonement *for* (Not very common with other verbs)

(*d*) Sometimes it acquires almost a final force, *for*; Ex 12^{4} 29^{36} 30^{16} Dt 27^{13} there shall stand עַל־הַקְּלָלָה (‖ v^{12} לְבָרֵךְ), ψ 89^{48} עַל־מַה־שָּׁוְא בָּרָאתָ כָל־בְּנֵי־אָדָם *unto* what vanity hast thou created, etc! Pr 29$^{5\ b}$ 2 Ch 23^{18} Ec 3^{17}

(*e*) Of a *condition*, or *attendant circumstances* (rare, so عَلَى, W$^{AG\ ii\ §59\ e}$): ψ 50^{5} עֲלֵי זָבַח: *upon, with* sacrifice, 92^{4} עֲלֵי עָשׂוֹר וגו׳ *with* a ten-stringed instr, *with* a harp, *with* sounding music on a lyre; עַל רִיב *upon occasion of* a lawsuit Ex 23^{2} Ez 44^{24}, עַל יוֹם טוֹב 1 S 25^{8} (cf عَلَى حِينِ *at a time of* Qor 28^{14}), Ne 12^{22} (l rd עַד BeRy), Is 18^{4} כחם צח עֲלֵי אור *at time* of sunshine, 64^{11} עַל אֵלֶּה, Je 8^{18} עֲלֵי יָגוֹן *at time of* sorrow, 16^{7} (but Gie עַל אָבֵל *to*): with abstr. substs. to form a periphr for adverbs, Lv 5^{22} and swear עַל שָׁקֶר *upon* falseness = falsely, Je 6^{14} = 8^{11} to heal a wound עַל נְקַלָּה *lightly, easily*, ψ 31^{24} עַל יֶתֶר = *abundantly*, Is 60^{7} עַל רָצוֹן = *acceptably* (cf عَلَى لَذَّةٍ = *with* delight)

(*f*) It hence acquires the force of *in spite of, notwithstanding* (so عَلَى, W$^{AG\ ii\ §59\ h}$), Jb 10^{7} עַל דַּעְתְּךָ *in spite of* thy knowing, 34^{6} עַל מִשְׁפָּטִי *notwithstanding* my right I am to be a liar (Di De Da RV: otherwise Hi RV^{m}) Cf below, **III c** *b*

(*g*) *Upon, concerning*, with vbs of speaking, as דִּבֶּר Ju 9^{3} 1 K 5^{13}, אָמַר Je 16^{3} 27^{19} (‖ אֶל) 33^{4}, hearing Gn 41^{15} שָׁמַעְתִּי עָלֶיךָ I have heard *concerning* thee, saying, etc, 1 K 10^{6} Is 37^{9} (‖ 2 K 19^{9} אֶל), disputing Gn 26^{21}, telling 1 S 27^{11} Jo 1^{3}, commanding 2 S 14^{8} 1 K 11^{10}, being vexed 21^{4} 2 K 6^{11}, crying 8^{5}, confessing ψ 32^{5} Ne 1^{6}, of the object of a prophecy or vision 1 K 22^{8} Is 1^{1} 2^{1}, and often with similar verbs.

(*h*) In a somewhat weaker sense, *in the matter of, as regards*, Gn 41^{32} וְעַל הִשָּׁנוֹת הַחֲלוֹם, Ex 22^{8} Ru 4^{7} Lv 5$^{22.26}$ Dn 9$^{14\ b}$ Ne 9^{33}, חָטָא עַל Lv 4^{14} (‖ v^{23} בָּהּ, cogn. acc v^{28}), 5^{5} Nu 6^{11} Ne 13^{26}, עַל־דְּבַר . . . *in the matter of*, Nu 25^{18} 31^{16}

2. It expresses *excess* (synon. מִן q.v); Gn 48^{22} I give thee שְׁכֶם אַחַד עַל אַחֶיךָ one shoulder (ridge) *above* thy brethren, Ex 16^{5} מִשְׁנֶה עַל double *above* or *beyond*, Nu 3^{46} Dt 25^{3} stripes עַל־אֵלֶּה *beyond* these, Jos 3^{15} Jordan מָלֵא עַל was full *over* all its banks (cf. 4^{18} Is 8^{7b} עלה, הלך על), ψ 138^{2} Ec 1^{16} Dn 1^{20} עֶשֶׂר יָדוֹת עַל ten times *above* (cf. in Aram 3^{19}, and عَلَى Qor 37^{153}), Ezr 1^{6} עַל+לְבַד=*beside* (v. בַּד); ψ 16^{2} (si vera l) טוֹבָתִי בַּל עָלֶיךָ my welfare is not *beyond* thee, i e. does not lie outside thee. —Of *time*, Lv 15^{25} if she has an issue עַל נִדָּתָהּ *beyond* her time of impurity (cf. Is 32^{10}, **4 b**).

3. It denotes *elevation* or *pre-eminence*, as עליון על high (fig) *above*, Dt 26^{19} *al.*, 28^{43} יעלה עליך will go up *above* thee, cf Pr 31^{29}, ψ 57$^{6.12}$ be thou exalted *above* the heavens, 89^{8} 95^{3} 96^{4}, etc, Ne 9^{5}, with words (q v.) such as נבר, גדל, חזק, נשא (Ni Pi. Hithp.), עזז, and esp. those denoting rule or superintendence, as מלך, הפקיד, so with שִׁית, היה, נתן, Gn 41$^{33.40.43}$, שׂם 1 S 18^{5}; with מָלַךְ, שַׂר, פָּקִיד, etc., Gn 41^{34} Ex 1^{11} 18^{21}, etc., abs 2 S 8^{16} Joab was על־הצבא *over* the host, 20$^{23b\ 24}$ 1 K 4$^{4-6}$ 5^{30}; Nu 10^{14ff} 1 Ch 9$^{23.26ff}$ 27^{25ff} 2 Ch 30^{17} 31^{12}, אֲשֶׁר עַל בֵּיתוֹ of Joseph's steward Gn 43$^{16.19}$ 44$^{1.4}$; and in the official titles אֲשֶׁר עַל־הַבַּיִת=the Governor of the Palace Is 22^{15} al (v. בַּיִת **6**), אֲשֶׁר עַל־הַמַּס the overseer of the forced labour 1 K 12^{18}; אשר עַל־הָעִיר the governor of the city 2 K 10^{5}, אשר על המלחמה v^{22}.

4. It expresses *addition* (cf. ἐπί in Gk, e g ἐπὶ τούτοις), viz **a.** introducing the complement of a verb, as with יָסַף to add *upon* or *to*, ψ 61^{7}+oft (v. יָסַף), שִׁית to put *to* Gn 30^{40}, נִלְוָה to be joined *to* Nu 18$^{2.4}$ Is 14^{1} (also c. אֶל), נָפַל to fall *to*, i.e. desert to, Je 21^{9}+, עבר to pass *over to* Ex 30$^{13.14}$ Is 45^{14} (cf. 60^{5}), also Hb 2^{16} תסב כוס על La 4^{21}, Est 4^{7}; נֶחְשַׁב to be reckoned *to* Lv 25^{31} 2 S 4^{2}, היה על Nu 36^{12}, ψ 69^{28} תְּנָה עָוֹן עַל עֲוֹנָם, Is 56^{8} עוֹד אֲקַבֵּץ עָלָיו I will yet gather (others) *unto* him.

b. Used absol, as Gn 28^{9} he took Mahalath עַל נָשָׁיו *in addition to* his (other) wives, 31^{50} (cf אל Lv 18^{18}), Nu 31^{8} עַל חַלְלֵיהֶם *in addition to* their slain (‖ Jos 13^{22} אֶל), Dt 23^{14} Ez 16$^{37.43}$ 25^{10}; Is 32^{10} יָמִים עַל שָׁנָה days *upon, in addition to*, a year, 2 Ch 31^{15} יָמִים עַל יָמִים, Ez 7^{26} הֹוָה עַל הוָֹה (‖ אל), Je 4^{20} (if נקרא=*be proclaimed*), Jb 16^{14} יִפְרְצֵנִי פֶרֶץ עַל־פְּנֵי־פָרֶץ (cf Lag$^{M\ III\ 112}$; also Il 14^{130} ἕλκος ἐφ' ἕλκει, Odyss. 7^{120f}, Qor 31^{13}). So often in laws of P (cf **c**), Lv 7^{12} he shall offer עַל־זֶבַח הַתּוֹדָה *in addition to* the sacrifice of thanksgiving, etc., v^{13b} Nu 6^{20} 15^{9} 28$^{10.15.24}$ (cf מִלְּבַד v^{31} 29^{6}), 35^{6}; Ez 16^{43} (Hi Sm RV: cf. 44^{7} אל).

c. Hence by an easy transition it denotes *together with, with*, Ex 35^{22} men *together with* (על) women, Jb 38^{32} ועיש עַל־בָּנֶיהָ תַנְחֵם and the Bear *with* her children, wilt thou lead them? 1 K 15^{20} Je 3^{18} the house of Isr. *with* the house of Judah, Mi 5^{2} (Ca Ke Kue; but al. as **7 c** *a*), Gn 32^{12} lest he come and smite me, אֵם עַל בָּנִים the mother *with* the children (cf Ho 10^{14} Dt 22^{6}); and as a techn. term in the regulations for sacrifice, esp. with אכל, Ex 12^{8} עַל־מְרֹרִים יֹאכְלֻהוּ *together with* bitter herbs they shall eat it, v^{9} his head *with* (על) his legs, etc., Nu 9^{11} Dt 16^{3} לֹא־תֹאכַל עָלָיו חָמֵץ (cf. Ex 23^{18} 34^{25}), v^{3}, in the phrase אכל על הדם to eat *with* the blood 1 S 14$^{32.33}$ (v^{34} אל), Lv 19^{26} Ez 33^{25} (cf. in Gk e.g. ἐπὶ τῷ σίτῳ πίνειν ὕδωρ); see also Lv 2$^{2.16}$ 3^{4} (so v$^{10.15}$ 4^{9} 7^{4}), 4^{11} 7$^{13.a.30}$ 10^{15} 14^{31} 23$^{18.20}$ Nu 6^{17} 19^{5}; 1 Ch 7^{4}.

5. It expresses the idea of being suspended, or extended, *over* anything, without however being in contact with it, above, over: Gn 1^{20} let fowl fly *over* the earth, 19^{23} השמש יצא על had come forth *upon* the earth (cf. זרח על Ex 22^{2}+; בא על go down [set] *upon* Dt 24^{15} Mi 3^{6}; Jb 25^{3}), Nu 10^{34} 14^{14} and thy cloud stood עליהם *over* them, Dt 28^{23} the heavens על־ראשך *above* thy head, Is 4^{5} 60^{12} Zp 2^{11} Zc 9^{14} ψ 7^{8} *over* it return thou on high, Jb 29^{3} בהלו נֵרוֹ עֲלֵי ראשי (cf. דעך על be extinguished *over*, 18^{6}), Ct 2^{4} his banner *over* me: fig. of protection Dt 32^{38} ψ 68^{35}: with vbs. of motion (expressed or implied), נשקף על to incline *over* 1 S 13^{18}+, נטה ידו על Ex 14^{16} Is 23^{11}+ (cf. ψ 21^{12}), הניף על to swing *over* Is 11^{15} 19^{16}; השמיע על to proclaim *over* Je 4^{16} Am 3^{9}, cf. Nu 10^{10} 2 Ch 13^{12}, נקרא שם על a name to be called *over* 2 S 12^{28}+ (v. קרא)

6. From the sense of *inclining* or *impending over*, על comes to denote *contiguity* or *proximity*, Engl. *by* (or sts. *on*):—**a.** in designating localities, esp those beside water, Gn 14^{6} עַל־הַמִּדְבָּר *by* the wilderness, 16^{7} עַל עֵין הַמַּיִם *by* the spring of water, 24$^{13.30}$ 29^{2} three flocks lying עָלֶיהָ *by* it (the well), 41^{1} Nu 3^{29} 13^{29} עַל־הַיָּם *by* the sea, 22^{5} 24^{6} gardens עֲלֵי נָהָר

Dt 3^{12} 33^{8} Ju 5^{19} 7^{1} 1 S 1^{9} על מזוזת היכל י׳ (Ez 46^{2}), 4^{1} 2 K 2^{7} and they stood על־הירדן *by* the Jordan, 25^{4} Is 19^{7} 38^{20} ψ 1^{3} planted *by* water-courses, Je 17$^{2.8}$ Jb 30^{4} 31^{9} על פתח *by* the entrance, Pr 14^{19}, + oft, על הדרך *by* the way Gn 38^{21} 1 S 24^{4}, Ez 48^{21} ff על גבולו *adjoining* his border, עבר על to pass *by* a place 1 K 9^{8} Je 18^{16} +, fig עבר על פשע to pass *by* transgression, i e. to overlook it, Mi 7^{18} al · על ימין . . . *on* the right of . ψ 110^{5} +, . . . על יָד, . . . על יֶרֶךְ, . . . על כֶּתֶף *on* the side of. (see these words) less freq (exc as **c**) with ref to persons, Nu 2^{5} והחנים עָלָיו and those encamping *next* him, v$^{12.20.27}$ 6^{9} וכי ימות מת עליו, 2 K 11^{11} *by* the king round about (cf Nu 3^{26} supr.), עבר על פ׳ Gn 18^{5} 2 K 4^{9} +.

b. 2 S 9$^{7.10}$ to eat bread על שֻׁלְחַן פ׳ *at* any one's table, Ex 16^{3} when we sat על־סיר הַבָּשָׂר, 1 S 20^{24} Kt to sit על־הַלֶּחֶם *at* meat; 25^{13} 30^{24} to remain על־הַכֵּלִים; Pr 23^{30} to tarry long על־היין *at* (or *over*) the wine, Jb 39^{9} עַל־אֲבוּסֶךָ: *at* thy crib: cf. הַיּוֹשֵׁב עַל הַמִּשְׁפָּט Is 28^{6}.

c. Idiomatically, with עָמַד and נִצַּב to stand *by* (lit *over*,—orig no doubt with ref to one supposed to be seated), Gn 18^{2} three men נִצָּבִים עָלָיו standing *by* him, v^{8} and he עמד עליו standing *by* him under the tree, 24^{30} *by* the camels, 28^{13} 1 S 4^{20} 2 S 1^{9} 12^{17} 20$^{11.12}$ Am 7^{7}, esp of persons standing *about* a superior, as servants or courtiers, Gn 45^{1} Ju 3^{19} 1 S 22$^{6.7.17}$, of persons surrounding a judge Ex 18$^{13.14}$, of י׳'s heavenly ministers, 1 K 22^{19} (cf. Is 6^{2} ממעל לו), Zc 4^{14}, and with התיצב 6^{5} Jb 1^{6} 2^{1}, also of one standing *by* (prop leaning *over*) an altar or sacrifice Nu 23$^{3.6}$ 1 K 13^{1} (cf **7 b**) Am 9^{1}, of an Ashērah *by* an altar Ju 6$^{25.28}$ (cf. אצל Dt 16^{21})

7. In connexion with verbs of *motion* (actual or fig) —**a.** of motion from a higher place downwards, *down upon*: thus (*a*) המטיר על to rain *upon* Gn 2^{5} 19^{24}, ירד על, 15^{11}, יצק על to pour *upon* Gn 28^{18}, נפל על צוארי פ׳ Gn 33^{4}, שׂם, 17$^{3.17}$ נפל על כניו to fall *on* his (own) face על to put *upon*, 21^{14} 22$^{6.9}$ 24^{47} (v^{22} Sam Di), נתן על כף to place *on* the hand of . . 40$^{11.21}$, השליך על 2 S 20^{12}, etc, cf Jb 29^{22} ועלימו תטף מִלָּתִי, Mi 3^{5} Na 3^{12}

(*b*) In diff fig connexions, as of sleep falling *upon* one, Gn 2^{21} 15^{12}, of fear 9^{2} 1 S 11^{7} (v אֵימָה, חֲרָדָה, פַּחַד), of good or bad fortune, esp the latter, coming *upon* one, as with בוא and הביא, Gn 27^{12} Dt 28^{2} (in good sense), v^{15}, Je 5^{12} 19^{3} (רעה, as oft), of retribution, reproach, the Divine wrath, etc, with diff verbs (הביא, נתן, ירד, חול, היה, etc), as Gn 20^{9} Nu 12^{11} חטאה; Gn 42^{36} עָלַי הָיוּ כֻלָּנָה *upon me* are they all; Nu 18^{5} + (היה קֶצֶף על), Dt 19^{10} דם (cf אל 2 S 21^{2} 𝔊 We Dr), Ju 9^{24} 1 K 2^{32} 2 S 16^{8} Ho 12^{15}; 2 S 3^{29}, 15^{14}, 1 S 11^{2} חרפה, Je 14^{16}; 26^{15} דם נקי (אל ‖), Jon 1^{14}; Ez 7$^{3.4.8}$ 23^{49} 36^{29}, ψ 7^{17} 94$^{2.23}$ 109^{5} וישימו עלי רעה תחת טובה (*lay* upon me: but Hu וישיבו, Pr 17^{13}), 140^{11}, שָׁפַךְ חֵמָה על Ez 7^{8} + oft, without a verb, Gn 16^{5} חֲמָסִי עָלֶיךָ my wrong be *upon* thee, Je 51^{35} (אל ‖); Gn 27^{13} עלי קללתך, 38^{29} (accents, RV^{m}), 2 S 1^{16} דמיך על ראשך, 14^{9} עָלַי הֶעָוֹן; Is 24^{17} Je 48^{43}; 50^{27}; Ez 13^{3} . . . הוי על; ψ 55^{16} Kt, of a blessing, Ex 32^{29} ψ 3^{9}, a curse Dt 30^{7}, mercies (prob conceived spec. as descending *from heaven*) ψ 33^{22} 86^{13} 90^{17} 103^{17} (with גבר be mighty *over* or *upon*, v^{11} 117^{2}), 116^{12} 145^{9} Ezr 3^{11}, שלום ψ 125^{5} 128^{6} 1 Ch 22^{9}.

(*c*) Introducing the object *upon* which an action, or emotion, esp if accompanied by a gesture, is conceived as being directed (but with some of these words, esp when they refer to an *event*, rather than a person, as Ex 18^{9}, על is to be explained from **1 f** *b*) Thus with verbs denoting the manifestation of joy or grief, as שׂוּשׂ to rejoice *over*, התפאר, התענג, שמח, גיל, שחק, אבל, ספד, שמם, בכה Ju 11^{37} +, נשׂא קינה (משל) to take up a lament, or proverb, *over* (see these words), prob also in הִנָּבֵא על prophecy *over* Ez 11^{4} 13^{17} +, with רִחַם, חָמַל, חוס, to shew compassion *on* (cf 1 K 3^{26} [Gn 43^{30} אל], Ct 5^{4} [Je 31^{20} ל]), with שמר, שקד, הֵעִיר (Jb 8^{6}) to guard or watch *over*, with יעץ to counsel *upon* Is 14^{26} +, חשב to devise (usu in bad sense, Je 29^{11} in good), דִּבֶּר (רעה Je 11^{17} +, טובה 18^{20} 32^{42}), הקים דָּבָר Je 29^{10} Of more distinctly phys acts, with בכה to weep *on* Gn 45$^{14.15}$ +, שׁרק *to hiss*, ספק or תקע כף *to clap the hand*, הִכָּה כף Ez 22^{13} (אל ‖), Is 5^{30} to growl *over*, 31^{4} Ez 36^{2} Jb 30^{5}, התוַדָּה to confess *over* (the goat), Lv 16^{21}, Ex 30^{10a} (prob.); Dt 21^{6}, Jb 6^{27} 40^{30}

b. From a lower place upwards, *up upon*, *up to*, as עלה על to go up *upon*. Ex 20^{26} 1 S 2^{28} 1 K 12^{33b} 2 K 16^{12b} 2 Ch 1^{6} (an *altar*, i.e. to a ledge beside it; cf 2 K 23^{9}, and ירד Lv 9^{22} 1 K 1^{53}), Ju 9^{51} Is 14^{14} 40^{9}, etc, to come up *upon* (in diff connexions) Ex 10^{12} Lv 16^{9} (fig), 19^{19} 1 S 1^{11} 6^{7} 1 K 10$^{16.17}$, fig עלה על לב Is 65^{17} +

(v. לבב ,לב, **3 d**); in Hiph. 1 K 20^{33} וַיַּעֲלֵהוּ עַל הַמֶּרְכָּבָה, Am 8^{10} (cf. **1 a** *a*), 2 S 1^{24} Ez 37^{6} ψ 137^{6} (fig.), 2 Ch 3$^{5.14}$ (= *ornamented with*); Dt 28^{61} (cf. Ex 15$^{26\,b}$); 2 Ch 20^{34} the history of Jehu which הֹעֲלָה עַל *was brought up upon* (i.e. inserted in) the book of, etc. (cf. 32^{32}; and כתב על supr. **1**); cf. נטה יד על־השמים *up to* heaven Ex 9^{22} 10^{21}; 17^{16}.

c. Expressing direction *towards* (not common, exc. in sense *against*: v. infr.)—(*a*) with verbs of motion, properly of a person (or thing) moving to another so as either to stand *above*, or rest *upon*, it (cf. Pusey$^{Min.\,Pr.\,333}$), Ex 34^{12} הארץ אשר אתה בא עליה (simil., of a land, or place, 18^{23} Nu 11^{12} 1 K 2^{26} עֲנָתֹת לֵךְ עַל־שָׂדֶיךָ, Ez 32^{9} Je 3$^{18\,b}$ 16^{13} 22^{26}, and after שׁוּב or הֵשִׁיב 16^{15} 22^{27} 23^{3} 24^{6} [but אֶל 27^{22} 30^{3} *al.*], Ez 29^{14}; Gn 40^{13} וֶהֱשִׁיבְךָ עַל־כַּנֶּךָ, 41^{13}; 30^{33} כִּי תָבוֹא עַל שְׂכָרִי *to view* my hire; בא על נפש מֵת to enter in *upon* or *beside* a corpse; בא על אשה Gn 19^{31} Dt 25^{5} (usu. אל); Jos 3^{16} מַיִם יֹרְדִים עַל יָם, Ez 47^{8} 1 K 18^{12} יִשָּׂאֲךָ עַל־אֲשֶׁר לֹא־אֵדָע, ψ 19^{7}; 2 K 16^{12}; 2 Ch 20^{24}; Is 53^{1} *upon* whom (coming from above) was י׳'s arm revealed? 62^{10} הרימו נֵס על העמים *over towards* (but 49^{22} אל): but often it is dub. if this force is perceptible; and in gen. על in such cases seems to be used merely as a syn.—perh. as a slightly more graphic syn.—of אֶל (cf. p. 41); in the later language, also, it may be due partly to the infl. of Aram., which does not use אֶל; thus (*a*) with a *personal* obj., with *assemble* or *be assembled*, Ex 32^{1} 2 S 17^{11} 1 K 8^{5} 11^{24} 2 K 22^{20} (2 Ch 34^{28} and usu. אל), 2 Ch 13^{7}, עלה Gn 38^{12} Jos 2^{8} 1 S 14^{10} (v$^{9.12}$ אל), עבר 1 S 14^{4} (v^{1} אל), בא 2 S 15^{4} (v. Dr) 1 Ch 12$^{23\,f.}$, יצא 2 K 24^{12}, הוליך 25^{20}, נגע Ju 20$^{34.41}$ (cf. Is 6^{7} Je 1^{9}), נס Is 10^{3}, הלך 22^{15} (אל . . . על), נשא 30^{6}, שלח 2 K 18^{27} (על . . . אל . . . על: ‖ Is 36^{12} אל . . . אל . . . על), Je 26^{15} 29^{31} 1 Ch 13^{2} 2 Ch 28^{16} 30^{1} 32$^{9.31}$ 36^{15} Ne 6^{3}, נגשׁ Ez 9^{6}, שׁב, הֹשיב Ne 4^{6} Ml 3^{24} (v. *c*), sq. על י׳ 2 Ch 15^{4} 30^{9}, התיצב 2 Ch 11^{13}; letters going על פ׳ Ne 2^{7} 6$^{17\,a}$ (v^{b} אל). (*β*) of *places*, Gn 24^{49} 2 S 2^{19}+ על ימין *to* the right; with הלך 1 S 2^{11} 1 K 20^{43} על־ביתו (21^{4} אל), 2 S 15^{20} ואני הולך על אשר אני הולך, Je 1^{7} Ez 1^{20} (v^{12} אל), הוליך 1 K 1^{38} (v^{33} אל), נהר Mi 4^{1} (‖ Is 2^{2} אל), Je 31^{12} (אל . . . על), נגשׁ Ez 44^{13} (‖ אל), עלה 1 S 24^{23} 2 S 19^{1} 1 K 6^{8} (‖ אל), Ez 41^{7}, בא Je 14^{3} 51^{51}, (על הר) הביא Is 66^{20} (56^{7} אל), ירד Je 36^{12}, נתן Pr 21^{1}, הסיר 2 S 6^{10} (‖ 1 Ch 13^{13} אל), הִטָּה Is 29^{12} (v^{11} אל) Mi 1^{14} 3^{5} Gn 42^{37}, שׁב, הֹשיב, Nu 33^{7} Je 11^{10} (fig., על עֲוֹנֹת), ψ 35^{13} Jb 34^{15} (Gn 3^{19} אל), Pr 26^{11} Ec 1^{6}, 1 K 17$^{21.22}$ (cf. 1 S 30^{12} אל), השתחוה Lv 26^{1} (prob.), Is 60^{14}; pregn. Is 24^{22} אֻסְּפוּ עַל בּוֹר be collected (and delivered) *into* a dungeon: cf. חוּשׁ על Jb 31^{5} (fig.), also to requite עַל־חֵיק Is 65$^{6.7\,Kt.}$ (Je 32^{18} ψ 79^{12} אל). After נראה *appear*, ψ 90^{16} (אל . . . על). And *as far as, unto* (nearly = עַד) Gn 49^{13} וְיַרְכָתוֹ עַל צִידֹן, Jos 2^{7} 18^{13} 19^{12} Je 31^{39} Ez 47^{18} 48$^{21.28}$ ψ 48^{11} 1 Ch 5^{16}.

(*b*) With אמר say *to*, 2 K 22^{8} Je 18^{11} (אל . . . על), 22^{6} 23$^{2.35}$ (על . . . אל), 36^{29} 44^{20} (אל . . . על), דבר 1 S 1^{13} (Gn 24^{45} אל), 1 K 9^{5} Ho 12^{11} Je 6^{10} 10^{1} 11^{2} (אל . . . על), speak *to* 25^{2} (על . . . אל), 26^{2}, cf. Est 1^{17}, היה דבר י׳ Je 25^{1} 1 Ch 22^{8} cf. 11^{10}, ענה 2 S 19^{43}, קרא Is 34^{14} 2 Ch 32^{18}, שִׁוַּע ψ 18^{42}, הֵרַע 1 K 17^{20}, שָׁר ,שֹׁרֵר *sing* Pr 25^{20} Jb 33^{27}, החליק Pr 29^{5} (ψ 36^{3} אל), התפלל 1 S 1^{10}, כתב 2 Ch 30^{1} Ezr 4^{7} Est 8^{8}, שׁמע 2 K 20^{13} (= Is 39^{2}), 22^{13} Je 23^{16} 26^{5} 35^{18} Hg 1^{12}; v. also השׂכיל, התבונן, הבין, האזין, הקשיב.

(*c*) Expressing (or implying) the direction of the mind, 2 S 14^{1} לב המלך על אבשלם; Mal 3^{24} Ezr 6^{22}; Ct 7^{11} וְעָלַי תְּשׁוּקָתוֹ (Gn 3^{16} 4^{7} אל); שָׂם לִבּוֹ על Jb 1^{8} (2^{3} אל), 1 S 25^{25} (אל . . . על); Je 22^{17} thy eyes and thy heart are only (set) *upon* (על) . . ., 1 Ch 12^{17} 1 K 1^{20} 2 Ch 20^{12} כִּי עָלֶיךָ עֵינֵינוּ (elsewhere אל), 1 K 2^{15} עָלַי שָׂמוּ פניהם, ψ 146^{5} שִׂבְרוֹ על י׳; Is 10^{25} וְאַפִּי עַל־תַּבְלִיתָם be (directed) *towards* their destruction, Je 32^{31} (Gf Ew: cf. RV); cf. שׁעה על look *to* (trustfully) Is 17^{7} 31^{1}. (The uses *a*, *b*, *c* are all exceptional: אל would be regularly employed.)

(*d*) With the force of *over* and *towards* (cf. **5** and **7 a** *b, end*): ψ 65^{5} נוֹרָא עֲלִילָה עַל; to shine, etc. *on*, ψ 31^{17} הָאִירָה פָנֶיךָ עַל (Nu 6^{25} אל); רָאָה עַל Ex 5^{21}; הוֹפִיעַ עַל Jb 10^{3}; וְשַׂמְתִּי עֵינַי עַל Am 9^{4}+ (cf. Jb 14^{3} 24^{3} 34^{21}); הִשְׁקִיף עַל look out *over* ψ 14^{2}+.

d. In a hostile sense, *upon, against*: so very often, after every kind of verb expressing or implying attack, as בא Gn 34$^{25.27}$, נֶאֶסַף v^{30}, קצף to be angry 40^{2}, לון to murmur Ex 15^{24}, עמד stand up Lv 19^{16}+, קָם rise up Dt 19^{11} Am 7^{9}, נלחם Dt 20^{10}, חנה 1 S 11^{1} ψ 27^{3}, עלה 2 K 17^{3}, חרה אף Zc 10^{3} (usu. בְּ), שׁפך סללה Is 37^{33}, צוּר besiege Dt 20^{12}, חשׁב to devise Gn 50^{20} Je 11^{19}, דִּבֶּר Dt 13^{6}+, etc.: add Jb 16$^{4.4.9.10.13}$ 19^{12} 21^{27} 30^{12}, etc.; היה על 2 S 11^{23} Nu 31^{3}: הִנְנִי עָלַיִךְ (v. אֶל **4**); note also Ju 9^{31} 20^{5}: without a verb

Is 9^{20}; Ju 16^{12} פלשתים עליך the Philistines are *upon* thee, 20^{9} עָלֶיהָ בְּגוֹרָל Against it by lot!

8. By writers of the silver age, על is sts. used with the force of a *dative*, 1 Ch 13^{2} אִם עֲלֵיכֶם טוֹב (in classical Heb. בְּעֵינֵיכֶם) if it seems good *to* you, אִם עַל הַמֶּלֶךְ טוֹב + Ne $2^{5.7}$ Est 1^{19} 3^{9} $5^{4.8}$ 7^{3} 8^{5} 9^{13} (cf. in Aram. Ezr 5^{17} 7^{18}); שָׁפַר עַל ψ 16^{6} (cf. in Aram. Dn 4^{24}); עָרֵב עַל ψ 104^{34} (elsewhere לְ); בְּאִשׁ עַל רַע עַל Ec 2^{17} (v. De; cf. Dn 6^{15}): comp. Jb 22^{2} סָכַן עַל be profitable *to*, 33^{23}; also גָּמַל עַל (in both good and bad sense: v. גמל), Ne 5^{19} עשׂה על, 9^{30} משך על prolong (mercy) *to;* הִטָּה חֶסֶד עַל Ezr 7^{28} 9^{9} (Gn 39^{21} אל): 1 S 20^{8} rd. prob. עם for על. Cf. Mish. חביב על, dear *to;* סני על hateful *to;* Syr. ܫܦܝܪ ܥܠ, ܡܩܒܠܐ ܥܠ, pleasant, acceptable *to*.—Comp. in gen. the uses of عَلَى, W AG ii. § 59.

9. With other particles:—עַל אַחֲרֵי Ez 41^{15}; עַל בֵּין Ez 19^{11} (cf. אל $31^{10.14}$); עַל לִפְנֵי Ez 40^{15}; עַל מֵעַל Ez 41^{17} (txt. dub.), v^{20}; עַל עֵבֶר Ex 25^{37} (cf. אל Ez $1^{9.12}$); עַל־כָּכָה Est 9^{26} (v. p. 462).—On פָּנִים ,פֶּה ,יָד, v. עַל־פְּנֵי ,עַל פִּי ,עַל־יְדֵי ,עַל־יַד.

III. As **conj.**: **a.** עַל אֲשֶׁר *because that* ... (cf. above, **II 1 f** *b*), Ex 32^{35} and י׳ plagued the people *because* על אשר עשׂו they had made, etc., Nu 20^{24} Dt 29^{24} (in answer to על מה: so 1 K 9^{9} Je 16^{11} 22^{9}), $32^{51.51}$ 1 S 24^{6} 2 S 3^{30} 6^{8} 8^{10} 12^{6} ψ 119^{49} +.

b. עַל כִּי similar in meaning, but less frequent: † Dt 31^{17} Ju 3^{12} Je 4^{28} Mal 2^{14} ψ 139^{14}.

c. על alone: (*a*) *because*, † Gn 31^{20} (E) עַל בְּלִי הִגִּיד, ψ 119^{136} עַל לֹא. (*b*) *notwithstanding that* (above, **1 f** *f*), *although*, † Is 53^{9} עַל לֹא חָמָס עָשָׂה *although* he did no violence, Jb 16^{17} עַל לֹא חָמָס בְּכַפָּי.

IV. Compounds:—**1.** with כְּ (rare and late), **a.** *as concerning, as upon* † ψ 119^{14} כְּעַל כָּל־הוֹן, 2 Ch 32^{19}. **b.** (pleon. for כְּ), † Is 59^{18} כְּעַל גְּמֻלוֹת כְּעַל יְשַׁלֵּם *the like of* their deeds is *the like of* (that which) he will repay (כְּעַל repeated on the anal. of כְּ Nu 15^{15} Ho 4^{9}: v. כְּ) = *according to* their deeds is (that which) he will repay, Is 63^{7} *according to.*

2. מֵעַל$_{304}$ **from upon, from over, from by**—used with much delicacy of application in many different connexions, corresponding mostly with the different senses of על. Thus **a.** *from upon* idiomatically, when removal, motion, etc., from a *surface* is involved, as מעל פני האדמה ,מעל האדמה *from upon* (the face of) the ground, usu. with expel, destroy, perish, etc. Gn 4^{14} 6^{7} 7^{4} Ex 32^{12} Dt 6^{15} $28^{21.63}$ + oft. esp. Je and compiler of K; to be lifted up מעל הארץ Gn 7^{17} Ez $1^{19.21}$ +, to return or be dried (of water) מעל הארץ Gn $8^{3.7.11.13}$; to roll a stone מֵעַל פִּי הַבְּאֵר 29^{3}; of the cloud departing מֵעַל האהל Nu 9^{17} 12^{10}, cf. Ne 9^{19}; to rise up מֵעַל הַכִּסֵּא Ju 3^{20} 1 K 2^{4}, מֵעַל מִשְׁכָּבוֹ 2 S 11^{2}; to alight מֵעַל הַגָּמָל (נָפַל) Gn 24^{64} (cf. Jos 15^{18} צנח, 1 S 25^{23} ירד), מֵעַל הַמֶּרְכָּבָה Ju 4^{15} 2 K 5^{21} (נפל); to take מֵעַל רֹאשׁ Gn 40^{19} 2 S 12^{30}, מֵעַל הַמִּזְבֵּחַ Lv 16^{12} Nu 17^{11} Is 6^{6}; to see מֵעַל הַגָּג 2 S 11^{2}; to shoot מֵעַל הַחוֹמָה $v^{20.24}$; to speak מֵעַל הַכַּפֹּרֶת Ex 25^{22} Nu 7^{89}; to cast down מֵעַל יָדָיִם Dt 9^{17} Lv 8^{28} (כַּפַּיִם); to break, remove, etc., a yoke מעל שׁכמך (צואר) Gn 27^{40} Is 10^{27} Je $28^{10.11}$; to wipe tears מֵעַל כָּל־פָּנִים Is 25^{8}; to take a bandage מעל עיניו 1 K 20^{41} (cf. על v^{38}); often of putting off a garment or ornament, as Gn $38^{14.19}$ הוֹרֵד עֶדְיְךָ מֵעָלֶיךָ, Ex 33^{5} וַתָּסַר צְעִיפָהּ מֵעָלֶיהָ, a sandal Ex 3^{5} Jos 5^{15}, a ring מֵעַל יָדוֹ Gn 41^{42}; to seek (דרשׁ), or hear, words מֵעַל הַסֵּפֶר Is 34^{16} Je 36^{11} (cf. כתב על ספר above); pregn. with בָּלָה to wear away (and fall) *from off*, Dt 8^{4} 29^{4}, cf. of the bones or skin in disease Jb 30^{17} עֲצָמַי נִקַּר מֵעָלָי are pierced (and drop) *from off* me, v^{30} עוֹרִי שָׁחַר מעלי is black (and falls) *from off* me; fig. 1 S 1^{14} הָסִירִי יֵינֵךְ מֵעָלָיִךְ remove thy wine *from off* thee; Nu 14^{9} סָר צִלָּם מֵעֲלֵיהֶם; Ju $16^{19.20}$ י׳ סר מעליו (with allusion to the hair, as the seat of Samson's strength), 1 S 16^{23} (cf. על in v^{16}).

b. Of relief from a burden or trouble: as of a plague, stroke, rod, etc., removed *from* (resting) *on* one, Ex 10^{17} וְיָסֵר מֵעָלַי אֶת־הַמָּוֶת הַזֶּה, Nu 21^{7} 25^{8} וַתֵּעָצַר הַמַּגֵּפָה מֵעַל ישׂר׳ (2 S $24^{21.25}$), ψ 39^{11} הָסֵר מֵעָלַי נִגְעֶךָ, Jb 9^{34} 13^{21} Jo 2^{20}; of reproach Jos 5^{9} Is 25^{8} ψ 119^{22}, iniquity Ez 18^{31} Zc 3^{4}, bloodguiltiness, 1 K 2^{31}, wrath Ju 8^{3} Nu 25^{11} Pr 24^{18}, murmurings Nu $17^{21.25}$; הָקֵל מֵעַל to lighten *from upon* one Ex 18^{22} +; Am 5^{23} הָסֵר מֵעָלַי הֲמוֹן שִׁירֶיךָ; pregn. Jon $1^{11.12}$ that the sea יִשְׁתֹּק מֵעָלֵינוּ may be calm *from off* us; to remove, etc., מֵעַל פְּנֵי (v. פָּנִים); 1 S 6^{20} to whom shall he go up מֵעָלֵינוּ—not merely 'from us,' but—*from upon us* (relieving us of his presence), so often of an army retiring from a country or raising a siege, 2 S 10^{14} וַיָּשָׁב יוֹאָב מֵעַל בְּנֵי עַמּוֹן,

20^{21} וְאֵלְכָה מֵעַל הָעִיר, v^{22} 2 K 3^{27} 18^{14}, esp. with עָלָה, נַעֲלָה, 1 K 15^{19} Je 21^{2} $37^{5.11}$ +; 2 S 19^{10} David fled מעל אבשלום *from* Absalom (whom his presence had encumbered), Ne 13^{28} וָאַבְרִיחֵהוּ מֵעָלָי, cf. Gn 13^{11} 25^{6} Nu 20^{21} וַיֵּט ישׂר׳ מֵעָלָיו, 2 Ch 20^{10}; Ex 10^{28} לֵךְ מֵעָלָי (contemptuously; be no more obnoxious to me), similarly 2 S 13^{17} שלחו־נא את־זאת מעלי (Amnon of Tamar).

c. *From beside* (cf. על **6 c**), in different *nuances:* Gn 17^{22} God went up מעל אברהם *from beside* A., 35^{13}; 18^{3} אל נא תעבר מעל עבדך (cf. על v^{5}), 42^{24} Nu $16^{26.27}$; 1 K 1^{53} to come down מֵעַל הַמִּזְבֵּחַ (cf. על 13^{1}; **6 c** and **7 b**); *from attendance on* Gn 45^{1} (cf. על *ib.*), Ju 3^{19} וַיֵּצְאוּ מֵעָלָיו כָּל־הָעֹמְדִים עָלָיו 1 S 17^{15} (v. Dr), 2 S 13^{9}, cf. 1 S $13^{8.11}$ 2 K 25^{5} (Je 36^{21} rd. עַל, מ being dittogr.), cf. 2 Ch 35^{15}; *from attachment to,* רָחַק מֵעַל י׳ Je 2^{5} Ez 11^{15} 44^{10}, cf. 8^{6}, סָר מֵעַל י׳ Je 32^{40} Ez 6^{9}, תָּעָה מֵעַל י׳ Ez $44^{10.15}$, cf. 14^{5} Dt 13^{11}; also סָר מֵעַל חַטֹּאות 2 K 10^{31} 15^{18} (usu. מֵחַטֹּאות), cf. Ez 14^{6} 23^{18}; *from companionship with,* Jb 19^{13} אַחַי מֵעָלַי הִרְחִיק; *from accompanying protectingly* 1 S 28^{15} וֵאלֹהִים סָר מֵעָלַי, v^{16} (cf. על ψ 110^{5}; and v. Dr); *from adhesion to* 2 K 17^{21} קָרַע ישׂראל מֵעַל בֵּית דָּוִד, Is 7^{17} 56^{3} יַבְדִּילַנִי י׳ מֵעַל עַמּוֹ, Hos 9^{1} זָנִיתָ מֵעַל אֱלֹהֶיךָ.

d. In late Heb., = על *above:* 2 K 25^{28} נָתַן כִּסְאוֹ מֵעַל כִּסֵּא וגו׳ (|| Je 52^{32} more class. מִמַּעַל לְ), Est 3^{1} ψ 108^{5} גדול מעל שמים (|| 57^{11} עד), 148^{4} Ec 5^{7} גָּבֹהַּ מֵעַל גָּבֹהַּ שֹׁמֵר, Ne 3^{28} 8^{5} 2 Ch 34^{4} לְמַעְלָה מֵעֲלֵיהֶם on high *above* them; Ez $41^{17.20}$.—Pr 14^{14} rd. with De Now Str וּמִמַּעֲלָלָיו.

e. מֵעַל לְ (chiefly late, and pleon. for עַל, or else = the more class. syn. מִמַּעַל לְ): (*a*) Gn 1^{7} מֵעַל לָרָקִיעַ (Ez 1^{26} מִמַּעַל לְ), Ez 1^{25} (txt. dub.; v. Comm.), 1 S 17^{39} Jon 4^{6} Mal 1^{5} *upon, over* the border (territory) of Israel (so Köhl Ke: but Hi Ew We *beyond*), 2 Ch 13^{4} *upon* mount Zemaraim, 24^{20}. (*b*) *beside* 2 Ch 26^{19} מֵעַל לְמִזְבַּח הַקְּטֹרֶת; Ne $12^{31.31.37.38.38.39}$ dub.: BeRy (in all) *off the side of* (מִן **6**) = *at a little distance from;* Ke in $v^{31.38a}$ *upon,* in $v^{37.38b.39}$ *by the side of* (*an … vorüber*).

†I. עַלְוָה transp. fr. עַוְלָה (q.v.) Ho 10^{9}.

†II. עַלְוָה **n.pr.m.** in Edom Gn 36^{40} (P) = 1 Ch 1^{51} Qr (Kt עליה), 𝔊 Γωλα; 𝔊L[Chr] Αλουα.

†עַלְוָן **n.pr.m.** in Edom Gn 36^{23} (P), 𝔊 Γωλων, Γωλαμ = 1 Ch 1^{40} Qr (Kt עלין), 𝔊 Σωλαμ, Α Ιωλαμ, 𝔊L Αλουαν.

†[עָלַז] **vb.** exult (|| form of עלץ q.v.; cf. Ph. n.pr.m. נבעלז);—**Qal** *Impf.* 3 ms. יַעֲלֹז ψ 96^{12}; 1 s. וְאֶעְלֹז Je 15^{17}; אֶעֱלֹזָה ψ 60^{8} 108^{8}; 3 mpl. יַעְלְזוּ 149^{5}, יַעֲלֹזוּ Je 51^{39} ψ 94^{3}, etc.; *Imv.* fs. עִלְזִי Zp 3^{14}; mpl. עִלְזוּ ψ 68^{5}; *Inf. cstr.* לַעֲלוֹז Is 23^{12};—*exult, triumph* Is 23^{12} Je 15^{17}; of Isr.'s foes 2 S 1^{20} Je 50^{11} (|| שׂמח), of wicked ψ 94^{3} Je 11^{15}; of Isr. Zp 3^{14} (+ שִׂמְחִי), בְּי׳ אֶע׳ Hb 3^{18} *in* י׳ *will I exult* (|| אָגִילָה), ψ 149^{5}; ע׳ לְפָנָיו 68^{5}; subj. לִבִּי 28^{7}, כִּלְיוֹתָי Pr 23^{16}; fig. of field ψ 96^{12} (|| רִנֵּן); of י׳ ψ 60^{8} = 108^{8}.

†עָלֵז **adj.** exultant, jubilant; as **n.** Is 5^{14}.

†[עַלִּיז] **adj.** exultant, jubilant (on form cf. Lag[BN 110]);—fs. עַלִּיזָה *jubilant city* Is 22^{2} (|| עִיר הוֹמִיָּה), 32^{13}, cf. Zp 2^{15} and (*city* om.) Is 23^{7}; of pers., pl. שְׁאוֹן עַלִּיזִים 24^{8}; cstr. עַלִּיזֵי גַּאֲוָתִי 13^{3}, cf. Zp 3^{11}, v. גַּאֲוָה.

†עֲלָטָה **n.f.** thick darkness (NH עֲלָטָה (rare); acc. to Ba[ES 5] transp. fr. Ar. غَطَلَ [*be cloudy*]; غَيْطَلَةٌ *darkness*);—abs. ע׳, attending sunset Gn 15^{17} (c. vb. masc.; Albr[ZAW xv (1895), 325] Kö[Synt. § 350 e] rd. הָיְתָה); בָּע׳ Ez 12^{7} (|| בָּעֶרֶב), $v^{6.12}$.

עֵלִי, עֱלִי, עִלִּי, עֲלִיָּה, עֶלְיוֹן v. עלה.

עֲלֵי v. עַל. עֲלִיָּה, עַלְיָן v. עלוה, עלון.

†I. [עָלַל] **vb.** **Po'ēl,** act severely (toward) (NH *id.*, *deal with* (rare), and deriv.; Ar. عَلَّ *do a thing* (drink, beat, give) *a second time,* II. *divert, occupy,* V. *divert, occupy oneself with* (food, a woman, etc.); Syr. ܥܠܬܐ *cause, occasion, affair*);—*act severely,* alw. c. לְ pers.: *Pf.* 2 ms. עוֹלַלְתָּ לִי La 1^{22} *as thou hast acted severely to me* (in punishment, subj. י׳); לְמִי ע׳ 2^{20} *to whom hast thou acted thus severely?* 3 fs. עֵינִי עוֹלְלָה לְנַפְשִׁי 3^{51} *my eye deals severely with me,* i.e. gives me pain (?; text dub.; cf. Perles[Anal. 18] Bu). *Imv.* ms. עוֹלֵל לָמוֹ La 1^{22} *deal severely with them.*—Vid. also ע׳ **denom.** infr. **Pō'al** *Pf.* 3 ms. מַכְאֹבִי אֲשֶׁר עוֹלַל לִי La 1^{12} *my pain which is severely dealt out to me.* **Hithpa.** *Pf.* **1.** *busy, divert oneself* with (cf. Ar. V.), alw. c. בְּ pers.: 1 s. אֵת־אֲשֶׁר הִתְעַלַּלְתִּי בְּ׳ Ex 10^{2} (J) *how I* [י׳] *have made a toy of* Egypt; esp. *deal wantonly, ruthlessly* with (בְּ pers.): 3 ms. הִתְעַלֵּל 1 S 6^{6}; 2 fs. הִתְעַלַּלְתְּ Nu 22^{29} (JE; Balaam's ass); 3 pl. וְהִתְעַלְּלוּ consec. 1 S 31^{4} = 1 Ch 10^{4}, Je 38^{19}; *Impf.* 3 mpl. וַיִּתְעַלְּלוּ־בָהּ Ju 19^{25} (of abusing a woman;

(וַיֵּדְעוּ אִתָּהּ ‖) **Hithpō'.** *Inf. cstr* לְהִתְעוֹלֵל עֲלִלוֹת ψ 141⁴ *to practise practices* in wickedness (perhaps denom.)

†עוֹלֵלוֹת **n.f. pl. intens. gleaning** (*going over a second time*),—*gleaning* (of grapes and olives, לֶקֶט of grain), always fig. of remnant abs. ע׳ Is 17⁶ (‖ כְּנֹקֶף זַיִת), 24¹³ (sim., ‖ *id.*, + בָּצִיר), Je 49⁹ (cf. בֹּצְרִים ·י) = Ob⁵ (*id.*), cstr. עֹלְלֹת בָּצִיר Mi 7¹, fig. of warlike achievement עֹלְלוֹת אֶפְרַיִם Ju 8² (opp. בְּצִיר)

†[עָלַל] **vb. denom.** **Pō'. glean** (grapes or olives, לקט of grain),—*Impf.* 2 ms. תְּעוֹלֵל Lv 19¹⁰ (obj. כַּרְמְךָ ‖ תְלַקֵּט), Dt 24²¹ (abs., + אַחֲרֶיךָ), 3 mpl. fig. (+ *Inf. abs.*) עוֹלֵל יְעוֹלְלוּ כַגֶּפֶן שְׁאֵרִית יִשְׂרָאֵל Je 6⁹, וַיְעֹלְלֻהוּ Ju 20⁴⁵ *they made a gleaning of them* (i.e. smote the fugitives)

†עֲלִילָה **n.f. wantonness, deed**,—abs. ע׳ ψ 14¹ 66⁵, elsewh. pl. עֲלִלוֹת 1 S 2³ ψ 141⁴, cstr. עֲלִילֹת Dt 22¹⁴ ¹⁷; sf. עֲלִילוֹתָם ψ 77¹³, עֲלִילוֹתֶיךָ Zp 3⁷ +, etc.,—**1.** *wantonness*, ע׳ דְּבָרִים Dt 22¹⁴ ¹⁷ *wantonness of words*, i.e. baseless charges (cf. Dr, esp. Di) **2.** *deed* **a.** in gen., of men 1 S 2³. **b.** of י׳ (only ψψ) ψ 9¹² = 105¹ = Is 12⁴ = 1 Ch 16⁸, ψ 77¹³ (‖ פָּעָלֶךָ), 78¹¹ (‖ נפלאותיו), 103⁷, נוֹרָא ע׳ עַל 66⁵ *he is terrible in deed toward*, etc. **c.** usu. *practices* = *evil deeds* (esp. Ez 8 t.) Ez 14²² ²³ 20⁴³ 24¹⁴ 36¹⁷ ¹⁹ (all ‖ דֶּרֶךְ), fully ע׳ הַנִּשְׁחָתוֹת 20⁴⁴ (‖ ד׳ הָרָעִים), הִשְׁחִיתוּ כֹּל ע׳ Zp 3¹¹, 21²⁹ Zp 3¹¹, v⁷

†עֲלִילִיָּה **n.f.** (Kö^{ii. 1. 204}) **deed**;—of י׳, רַב הָעֲ׳ Je 32¹⁹ (‖ גְּדֹל הָעֵצָה), but rd. prob. הָעֲלִילָה

[מַעֲלָל]₄₁ **n.m.**^{Ne 9. 35} **deed, practice**,—only pl. מַעֲלָלִים 1 S 25³, cstr. מַעַלְלֵי ψ 77¹² 78⁷, sf. מַעֲלָלֶיךָ Dt 28²⁰, מַעֲלָלָיו Ho 4⁹ +, מַעַלְלֵיכֶם Is 1¹⁶ +, מַעַלְלֵיהֶם 3¹⁰ +, etc.,—**1.** usu. (esp. Je 17 t.) bad *practices* of men, רַע מַעֲלָלִים 1 S 25³ he was *evil in his practices*, Ju 2¹⁹ (‖ דֶּרֶךְ), Ho 5⁴ 7² Is 3⁸ Je 11¹⁸ ψ 106²⁹ ³⁹ (‖ מַעֲשֵׂיהֶם), מ׳ הָרָעִים Ne 9³⁵, רֹעַ מ׳ *the evil of your* (their, etc.) *practices* Ho 9¹⁵ Is 1¹⁶ Je 4⁴ 21¹² (sf. 3 mpl. Kt, 2 mpl. Qr), +, מ׳ הָרָעִים Zc 1⁴ Qr (+ ד׳ הָרָעִים, Kt מעליליהם), מ׳ אשר לא טובים Ez 36³¹ (+ *id.*), הֵרֵעוּ מ׳ Mi 3⁴, פְּרִי מ׳, i.e. their consequences, Is 3¹⁰ Je 17¹⁰ 21¹⁴ 32¹⁹ (+ דֶּרֶךְ) **2.** *deeds* of י׳ ψ 77¹², of אל 78⁷, cf. Mi 2⁷. **3.** *acts*, in gen., of youth Pr 20¹¹ (‖ פָּעֳלוֹ)

[מעליל], מעליליהם Zc 1⁴ Kt, v. foreg. **1.**

†תַּעֲלוּלִים **n.m. pl. abstr. wantonness, caprice**,—ת׳ יִמְשְׁלוּ בָם Is 3⁴ *caprice shall rule over them*, sf. תַּעֲלֻלֵיהֶם 66⁴ *their wanton dealing*, i.e. that inflicted on them

II עלל (√ of foll., poss. = I. עלל (Kö^{ii. 1, 106}) whence child as *capricious, mischievous*, but dub., > foll. fr. עול; in either case orig. meaning quite forgotten, prob. distinct √, meaning unknown)

†עוֹלֵל, עוֹלָל **n.m.**^{La 2, 19} **child**,—abs. עולל 1 S 15³ +, עוֹלָל Je 6¹¹ 9²⁰, usu. pl. עוללים ψ 8³, עללים Jb 3¹⁶, עוֹלָלִים La 4⁴ Jo 2¹⁶, cstr. עוללי La 2²⁰, sf. עוֹלָלֶיהָ Mi 2⁹ +, עֹלָלַיִךְ ψ 137⁹, עולליהם 2 K 8¹² +, etc.,—*child* Mi 2⁹ La 2¹⁹ ²⁰ 4⁴, + יונק (sts. disting. from men and women), 1 S 15³ 22¹⁹ ψ 8³ Je 44⁷ La 2¹¹ Jo 2¹⁶, ‖ בַּחוּרִים Je 6¹¹ 9²⁰, ‖ בָּנִים ψ 17¹⁴ (heirs of father); dashed in pieces (רטשׁ) by foe 2 K 8¹² Ho 14¹ Na 3¹⁰ Is 13¹⁶, cf. ψ 137⁹ (נפץ), taken captive La 1⁵, stillborn Jb 3¹⁶.

†[עָלַל] **vb. denom. act** or **play the child**,—only **Pō'.** *Pt* עַמִּי נֹגְשָׂיו מְעוֹלֵל Is 3¹² *my people—its ruler is acting the child.*

†III [עָלַל] **vb. insert, thrust in** (Ar. عَلَّ, whence عُلّ *yoke*, cf. OAram עלל, 𝔗 עלל, Syr. ܥܰܠ, all *enter*),—only **Pō'.** *Pf.* 1 s. עֹלַלְתִּי בֶעָפָר קַרְנִי Jb 16¹⁵ fig. of humiliation.

†עֹל₃₉ **n.m.**^{1 K 12, 4} **yoke**,—ע׳ abs. Ho 11⁴ +, cstr. Is 9³ +; sf. עֻלְּךָ Je 2²⁰ Is 47⁶, עֻלּוֹ Gn 27⁴⁰ +, עֻלָּם 1 K 12¹¹, etc.,—*yoke*, for cattle, עָלָה עליהם ע׳ 1 S 6⁷, cf. Nu 19² (P), מָשְׁכָה בעֹ׳ Dt 21³, usu. fig. of servitude 1 K 12⁴ ¹⁰ ¹¹ ¹¹ ¹⁴ ¹⁴ = 2 Ch 10⁴ ¹⁰ ¹¹ ¹¹ ¹⁴, נָתַן ע׳ עַל 1 K 12⁴ ⁹ = 2 Ch 10⁴ ⁹; וּנְתַן ע׳ עַל־זָקֵן הכבדת ע׳ Dt 28⁴⁸, so Je 28¹⁴, בַּרְזֶל עַל־צַוָּארֶךָ Is 47⁶, also נָתַן (הביא) את־צַוָּארוֹ בעל Je 27⁸ ¹¹ ¹², שָׁבַר ע׳ *break the yoke* Je 2²⁰ 5⁵ 28² ⁴ ¹¹ 30⁸ (+ מֵעַל צ׳), so מֹטֹת ע׳ Lv 26¹³ (H), Ez 34²⁷ (v. מוֹטָה), פָּרַק ע׳ Gn 27⁴⁰ (J; + מעל צ׳), החת ע׳ Is 9³, cf. הרים ע׳ Ho 11⁴, also יָסוּר ע׳ מעל צ׳ Is 10²⁷, and 14²⁵, fig. of transgressions La 1¹⁴, del ע׳ 𝔊 𝔙 Lohr Bu, but read עַל vᵇ (v. *id.*), of hardship, נָשָׂא ע׳ 3²⁷.

†עֲלִיל appar. **n.** [**m.**], only כֶּסֶף צָרוּף בַּעֲ׳ לָאָרֶץ ψ 12⁷, usu. (after 𝔗 כּוּרָא) *furnace, crucible* (Hup. fr. III עלל; De al. *workshop*, fr. I. עלל), but wholly dub., NH *openly* Levy^{NHWB iii. 654}; Che Du del as gloss; cf. discussion Che Expos. T viii 236, 336 Ne^{lb 267, 379}.

†I. [עָלַם] **vb.** conceal (NH *id.*, der. spec),—**Qal** *Pt. pass.* עֲלֻמֵנוּ ψ 90^{8} as subst *our secret*, i e. hidden sin (‖ עֲוֹנֹת). **Niph.** *Pf. be concealed*, of wisdom, 3 fs נֶעֶלְמָה מֵעֵינֵי Jb 28^{21}; of a fact or condition, נֶעְלַם 2 Ch 9^{2}, וְנ׳ consec Lv 5$^{2.3.4}$ (all c. מִן pers), וְנ׳ מֵעֵינֵי Lv 4^{13} Nu 5^{13} (all P); *Pt.* **1.** נֶעְלָם *concealed*, c הָיָה in periphrastic conjug. 1 K 10^{3} (מִן pers); abs כָּל־נֶעְלָם Ec 12^{14}. **2.** fs. תְּהִי נַעֲלָמָה Na 3^{11} *mayest thou become obscured* (as to the senses, fig. for *swoon*), but very doubtful, read perhaps תעלפה? [Dr] **3** pl נַעֲלָמִים ψ 26^{4} *those who conceal themselves*, i e their thoughts, *dissemblers* (‖ מְתֵי שָׁוְא) **Hiph.** *Pf.* 3 ms הֶעְלִים 2 K 4^{27}, 3 pl העלימו Ez 22^{26}, *Impf* 2 ms. תַּעְלִים ψ 10^{1}, תַּעְלֵם La 3^{56}; 3 mpl יַעְלִימוּ Lv 20^{4}, etc, *Inf abs* הַעְלֵם v^{4}, *Pt.* מַעְלִים Jb 42^{3} Pr 28^{27},—*conceal, hide*, c מִן pers. 2 K 4^{27} (‖ לֹא הִגִּיד לִי); usu. *hide* the eyes from (מִן), i e. *disregard* Is 1^{15} Ez 22^{26}, הַעְלֵם יַע׳ וגו׳ Lv 20^{4}, מִן om Pr 28^{27}, *hide* the eyes by (בְּ) a bribe 1 S 12^{3} (i e. pervert justice, but v I. עַיִן **3 d**); *hide* (cover) the ear La 3^{56} (turn a deaf ear), *hide* (obscure) counsel (עֵצָה) Jb 42^{3}; לָמָה תַּע׳ ψ 10^{1} *why dost thou* [י׳] *hide*, sc. thine eyes (so most), or *practise concealment* (=hide thyself)? **Hithp.** *Pf.* 2 ms consec וְהִתְעַלַּמְתָּ מֵהֶם Dt 22$^{1.4}$ *and thou hide thyself completely from them* (utterly neglect to aid), so *Inf. cstr.* (מהם om) לְהִתְעַלֵּם v^{3}, so also *Impf* c מִן, תִּתְעַלַּם ψ 55^{2}, תִּתְעַלָּם Is 58^{7}, once lit יִתְעַלֶּם־שָׁלֶג Jb 6^{16} wherein *snow hides itself*

†תַּעֲלֻמָה **n.f** hidden thing, secret (so, c. הּ, van d. H Bu, ה- Baer Ginsb),—ת׳ *what is hidden* Jb 28^{11}, pl. cstr. תַּעֲלֻמוֹת חָכְמָה Jb 11^{6} *secrets of wisdom*, ת׳ לֵב ψ 44^{22}.

†עַלְמוֹן **n.pr.loc.** (cf. Sab. n pr. עלמן Hal^{192});—priestly city in Benj Jos 21^{18} (P), 𝔊 Γαμαλα, A Αλμων, 𝔊L Ελμων; = עָלֶמֶת in ‖ 1 Ch 6^{45} (𝔊 Γαλεμεθ, 𝔊L Αλαμωθ); mod *'Almît*, c 1 hour NE of Jerusalem, v. Buhl$^{Geogr\ 175}$.

†עַלְמֹן דִּבְלָתָיְמָה **n pr.loc.** in Moab, Nu 33$^{46.47}$ (P), 𝔊 Γελμων Δεβλαθαιμ; = בֵּית ד׳ q.v.

עַל־מוּת, עֲלָמוֹת etc., v. עַלְמָה sub II. עלם.

†עָלֶמֶת **1. n.pr.m.** a Benjamite 1 Ch 8^{36} 9^{42}, עָלָמֶת 7^{8}; 𝔊 Σαλαμαιθ, Γαλεμαθ, Αλαμωθ, etc. **2. n.pr.loc.** (= עַלְמוֹן q v.) 1 Ch 6^{45} Baer Ginsb (van d H. עָלֶמֶת)

†יַעְלָם **n.pr.m.** Edomite Gn 36$^{5.14.18}$ = 1 Ch 1^{35}, Ιεγλομ.

II עלם (√ of foll., perh. orig *be mature* (sexually), Aram עֲלַם *be strong*, ܐܬܥܠܡ *rejuvenate* (certainly denom.), Ar. عَلِمَ *be lustful* (*id.*), cf. Sab. עלם, עלמן *young man* CIS$^{iv\ pp\ 30,42}$, Ar غُلَام *id.*; Ph עלמת *girl*, Nab Palm. עלם, עלים *slave*, Palm. fpl. *harlots*; 𝔗 עוּלֵימָא, עוּלֵימְתָא, Syr ܥܠܝܡܐ, ܥܠܝܡܬܐ *young man, young woman*)

†עֶלֶם **n m.** young man,—ע׳ abs 1 S 20^{22}, הָעֶלֶם 17^{56}; ע׳ prob. also v^{42} 16^{12} (for MT עִם) Gr Krenkel$^{ZAW\ ii\ (1882),\ 309}$ Bu HPS.

†עַלְמָה **n.f.** young woman (ripe sexually; maid or newly married),—ע׳ Gn 24^{43} (J), Ex 2^{8} (E), Pr 30^{19} Is 7^{14}; pl עֲלָמוֹת ψ 68^{26} Ct 1^{3} 6^{8}; עַל־עֲלָמוֹת *to* (the voice of) *young women*, either lit, or of soprano or falsetto of boys · 1 Ch 15^{20} ψ 9^{1} (rd עַל־עֲלָמוֹת לַבֵּן [for עַל־מוּת לַבֵּן], '*voce virginea a pueris* decantandum,' Thes), 46^{1} 48^{15} (rd עַל־עֲלָמוֹת [for עַל־מוּת], tr. prob to 49^{1}).

†[עֲלוּמִים] **n.pl.abstr.** youth, youthful vigour,—only sf עֲלוּמָיו Jb 20^{11} Qr (Kt עֲלֻמוֹ), עֲלוּמָיו ψ 89^{46} Jb 33^{25}, עֲלוּמַיִךְ Is 54^{4}

III. עלם (√ of foll, meaning dub; cf. NH עוֹלָם (chiefly *world, age*), MI$^{7.10}$ עלם, Ph. *id.*, Aram. עָלְמָא, ܥܠܡܐ, Nab עלם, Palm. עלמא; Ar عَالَمٌ *creation, world*, etc; Eth ዓለም: *aevum, saeculum*, etc; acc to Thes al from I. עלם *the hidden*, cf. Ko$^{ii\ 1,\ 87}$, Lag$^{BN\ 115}$ cp quadril. عَيْلَمٌ *primitive waters*; Ew^{177e} cp Eth. ዑለተ: *time* [√ ועל Di^{923}]; Ba$^{ZMG\ xliv\ (1890),\ 685}$ cp As *ullâti, ullâ* [*ullânu, remote time*], cf. Dl$^{HWB\ 65}$ Jen$^{ZA\ vii}$).

עוֹלָם$_{439}$ **n.m.** long duration, antiquity, futurity,—ע׳ Gn 9^{12} + 405 t, עֹלָם 3^{22} + 19 t, עילום 2 Ch 33^{7}, rd prob עוֹלָם (for other explan. v note in Kit^{Hpt}); sf עֹלָמוֹ Ec 12^{5}; pl. עוֹלָמִים Is 26^{4} + 7 t, עֹלָמִים ψ 145^{13} + 2 t.; cstr. עוֹלְמֵי Is 45^{17};—†**1.** of past time: **a.** *ancient time*: יְמֵי ע׳ *days of old* Is 63$^{9.11}$ Am 9^{11} Mi 5^{1} 7^{14} Mal 3^{4}; יְמוֹת ע׳ Dt 32^{7}, עַם ע׳ Is 44^{7} *ancient people*; גּוֹי מֵע׳ Je 5^{15}, חָרְבוֹת ע׳ *old waste places* Is 58^{12} 61^{4}, cf Ez 26^{20b}, פִּתְחֵי ע׳ *ancient gates* ψ 24$^{7.9}$, אֹרַח ע׳ Jb 22^{15}, נְתִבוֹת ע׳ Je 6^{16}; שְׁבִילֵי ע׳ 18^{15}; גְּבוּל ע׳ Pr 22^{28} 23^{10}, בָּמוֹת ע׳ Ez 36^{2}; מִן (מֵ)ע׳ *from of old* Is 64^{3} Je 2^{20} Jo 2^{2}, of the fathers Jos 24^{2}, the prophets Je 28^{8}, the ancient נְפִלִים

Gn 6^{4}, (Ez 32^{27} 𝔊 Co for מֵעֲרֵלִים, but 1 S 27^{8} read מטלם for מעולם We Dr HPS), בהם ע׳ *long in them* Is 64^{4} (text dub) **b.** מתי ע׳ *the long dead* ψ 143^{3} La 3^{6}, so עם ע׳ Ez 26^{20} **c.** of God, מע׳ former acts Is 46^{9}, as redeemer Is 63^{16}, of love ψ 25^{6}, judgment 119^{52}, dominion Is 63^{19}, long silence 42^{14} 57^{11}, his wisdom personif Pr 8^{23}, his existence ψ 93^{2} **d** of things גבעות ע׳ *ancient hills* Gn 49^{26} (J), Hb 3^{6} (|| הררי־עד), Dt 33^{15} (|| הררי קדם). **e** pl שנות עולמים ψ 77^{6} *years of ancient times*, דורות עולמים Is 51^{9}, לעלמים Ec 1^{10} *in olden times* **2 a** indef *futurity*, c prep. *for ever, always* (sts = *during the lifetime*); עבד עולם *slave for ever* Dt 15^{17} 1 S 27^{12} Jb 40^{28}, עָבַד לע׳ *serve for ever* Ex 21^{6} (E), Lv 25^{46}, עד ע׳ 1 S 1^{22}, גְּאֻלַּת ע׳ Lv 25^{32} *redemption at any time*, הֲרַת ע׳ Je 20^{17} *ever pregnant* (womb), כלמת ע׳ v^{11} of persecutors of Jeremiah, חרפת ע׳ 23^{40}, שַׁלְוֵי ע׳ ψ 73^{12} *alway at ease*, יחי לע׳ (יחיה) *may the king live alway* 1 K 1^{31} Ne 2^{3}, cf אֹרֶךְ יָמִים עולם ועד ψ 21^{5}, ישב עולם לפני אלהים 61^{8}, so of the pious, לע׳ לא ימוט 15^{5}, בל ימוט Pr 10^{30}, cf ψ 30^{7}, other phr ψ 37$^{27.28}$ 41^{13} 55^{23} 61^{8} 73^{26} 121^{8} Pr 10^{25}; אשירה ע׳ ψ 89^{2} *I will sing for ever* (as long as I live), cf 52^{10} 115^{18} 145$^{1.2}$, הודה לע׳ 30^{13} 44^{9} 52^{11} 79^{13}, other emotions and activities continuous through life 5^{12} 31^{2} = 71^{1}, 75^{10} 86^{12} 119$^{44.93.98.111.112}$ Mi 4^{5}, cf לע׳ 2^{9} **b.** = *continuous existence*, (1) of things the earth, הָאָרֶץ לעולם עֹמָדֶת Ec 1^{4}; other phr: ψ 78^{69} 104^{5}, heavens and contents 148^{6}, ruined cities Is 25^{2} 32^{14} Ez 26^{21} 27^{36} 28^{19}, ruined lands Je 18^{16} 25$^{9.12}$ 49$^{13.33}$ 51$^{26.62}$ Ez 35^{9} Zp 2^{9}, לעד עד ע׳ Is 30^{8} *for a witness for ever*, in a book; (2) of nations לעולם אהיה 47^{7} (Babylon loqu), cf ψ 81^{16} Ob^{10}, ישב לע׳ of Judah Jo 4^{20}, (3) families ψ 49^{12} Is 14^{20}, the dynasty of Saul 1 S 13^{13}, house of Eli 2^{30}, (4) national relations. איבת ע׳ *continual enmity* Ez 25^{15} 35^{5}, of exclusion from קהל י׳, עד ע׳ Dt 23^{4} = Ne 13^{1}; various relations Is 32^{17} 34^{10}, חרפת ע׳ *perpetual reproach* ψ 78^{66}, of dynasty of David 2 S 3^{28} 12^{10} 1 K 2^{33}, families v^{33} 2 K 5^{27} ψ 106^{31} Je 35^{6} **c** of divine existence אל עולם Gn 21^{33} (J), אלהי ע׳ Is 40^{28}, חי אנכי לע׳ Dt 32^{40}, חי הע׳ Dn 12^{7}, of divine name, זה שמי לע׳ Ex 3^{15} (E), cf. 2 Ch 33^{7} (v supr), blessing and praise of it 2 S 7^{26} = 1 Ch 17^{24}, ψ 72^{19} 135^{13}, of י׳ himself 89^{53}; attributes, אהבה Je 31^{3} 1 K 10^{9}, חסד Is 54^{8} ψ 89^{2} 138^{8}, לע׳ חַסְדּוֹ 1 Ch 26$^{34.41}$ 2 Ch 5^{13} 7$^{3.6}$ 20^{21} Ezr 3^{11} ψ 100^{5} 106^{1} 107^{1} 118$^{1.2.3.4.29}$ 136^{1} + 25 t, Je 33^{11}; כבוד ψ 104^{31}, אמת 117^{2} 146^{6}, צדק 119^{142}, עצה 33^{11}, reign Ex 15^{18} (E), ψ 10^{16} 66^{7} 92^{9} 146^{10} Je 10^{10} Mi 4^{7}, ישב יהוה לע׳ ψ 9^{8} 29^{10} 102^{13} La 5^{19}; presence in Zion 1 Ch 23^{25} Is 33^{14} 60$^{19.20}$ Ez 37^{28} 43$^{7.9}$, his salvation Is 51$^{6.8}$, זרעת ע׳ Dt 33^{27} *everlasting arms*; כל אשר יעשה האלהים יהיה לע׳ Ec 3^{14} **d.** of God's covenant בְּרִית ע׳ *everlasting covenant* Gn 9^{16} 17$^{7.13.19}$ Ex 31^{16} Lv 24^{8} Nu 18^{19} (all P), 2 S 23^{5} 1 Ch 16^{17} = ψ 105^{10}, Is 24^{5} 55^{3} 61^{8} Je 32^{40} 50^{5} Ez 16^{60} 37^{26}, covenant with Noah, לדרת ע׳ Gn 9^{12} (P), God remembers it 1 Ch 16^{15} = ψ 105^{8}, ψ 111^{5}, will not break it, לע׳ Ju 2^{1}, אות ע׳ Ex 31^{17} (P), אות עד ע׳ Dt 28^{46}. **e.** of God's laws: דבר(ים) Is 59^{21} ψ 119^{89}, משפט 119^{160}, עדות v$^{144.152}$, חק ע׳ Ex 29^{28} 30^{21} (E), Lv 6$^{11.15}$ 7^{34} 10^{15} 24^{9} Nu 18$^{8.11.19}$ (P), also Je 5^{22} (of bounds of sea), חק עד ע׳ Ex 12^{24} (J), חֻקַּת ע׳ v$^{14.17}$ 27^{21} 28^{43} 29^{9} Lv 3^{17} 7^{36} 10^{9} 16$^{29.31.34}$ 17^{7} 23$^{14.21.31.41}$ 24$^{3.8}$ Nu 10^{8} 15^{15} 18^{23} 19$^{10.21}$ (P) (most of these in fact specif. Jewish and temporary); temple to bear God's name, עד ע׳ 1 K 9^{3} = 2 Ch 7^{16}, לע׳ 2 K 21^{7} 2 Ch 33^{4}, consecrated לע׳ 30^{8}, its ceremonies לע׳ 2^{3}, Levit. priesthood, לשרתו עד ע׳ 1 Ch 15^{2}, Aaronic priesthood, לברך בשמי עד ע׳ 23$^{13.13}$ **f.** of God's promises: his word, יקום לע׳ Is 40^{8}, promised dynasty of David, עד (ה)ע׳ 2 S 7$^{13.16.16.25}$ = 1 Ch 17$^{12.14.14.23}$, ψ 18^{51} = 2 S 22^{51}, 1 K 2$^{33.45}$ 1 Ch 22^{10} ψ 89^{5}, לע׳ 1 K 9^{5} 1 Ch 28$^{4.7}$ 2 Ch 13^{5} ψ 89$^{29.37}$ 2 S 7$^{29.29}$ = 1 Ch 17$^{27.27}$, of holy land 1 Ch 28^{8}, אֲחֻזַּת ע׳ Gn 17^{8} 48^{4} Lv 25^{34} (P), given לע׳ Ex 32^{13} (J) 2 Ch 20^{7}, עד ע׳ Gn 13^{15}, inherited לע׳ Is 60^{21} ψ 37^{18}, עד ע׳ Is 34^{17}, dwelt in עד ע׳ Ez 37^{25}, other blessings, לע׳ Dt 5^{26} Ho 2^{21}, עד ע׳ Dt 12^{28} 2 S 7^{24} = 1 Ch 17^{22}, ψ 133^{3}, שמחת ע׳ Is 35^{10} 51^{11} 61^{7}, דֶּרֶךְ ע׳ ψ 139^{24}, שם ע׳ Is 56^{5} 63^{12}, אות ע׳ 55^{13}, גאון ע׳ 60^{15}, Jerus to abide לע׳ Je 17^{25} ψ 125^{1}, cf Je 31^{40}, עד ע׳ ψ 48^{9}. **g.** of relations between God and his people, לע׳ 1 Ch 29^{18} ψ 45^{18} 85^{6} 103^{9} 145^{21} Is 57^{16} Je 3$^{5.12}$ La 3^{31} Jo 2$^{26.27}$, עד (ה)ע׳ ψ 28^{9} Mal 1^{4} **h.** of Messianic dynasty and king (ל)ע׳ ψ 110^{4}, having divine throne 45^{7}, name endures 72^{17}, established 89^{38}, God blesses him 45^{3}, of his reign, מעתה ועד ע׳ Is 9^{6}. **i.** = *indefinite, unending future* live לע׳ Gn 3^{22} Jb 7^{16}, הנביאים הלע׳ יחיו Zc 1^{5} *the prophets, can they live for ever?* cf חדל לע׳ ψ 49^{9}, c neg *never* Ezr 9^{12} Pr 27^{24}. **j.** after death. שְׁנַת ע׳ Je 51$^{39.57}$, בית ע׳ Ec 12^{5}, חַיֵּי ע׳ Dn 12^{2}, דראון ע׳ v^{2}, also v^{3} Jon 2^{7} Ec 2^{16} 9^{6}. **k.** = *age (duration) of the world* את העלם נתן בלבם Ec 3^{11} *the age of the world he hath set*, etc (cf esp NH; others **i**) **l.** pl intens *everlastingness, eternity*: תשועת עולמים Is 45^{17}, צדק עלמים Dn 9^{24}, צור עולמים

Is 26⁴ (RVm *rock of ages*); מלכות כל עלמים ψ 145[13]; also 61[5] 77[8] 1 K 8[13] = 2 Ch 6[2]. **m.** special phr.: (מן) מ(ה)עולם (ו)עד (ה)עולם *from everlasting to everlasting*, of ׳י ψ 90[2], ׳חסד י 103[17]; benedictions 1 Ch 16[36] = ψ 106[48], Ne 9[5] 1 Ch 29[10] ψ 41[14]; the land given למן עולם ועד עולם Je 7[7] 25[5]; מעתה ועד עולם *from now and for ever* ψ 115[18] 121[8] (i.e. as long as one lives); of people's hope in God 131[3]; dynasty of David Is 9[6]; of God's acts, words, etc. Mi 4[7] Is 59[21] ψ 125[2], cf. 113[2];—v. further I. עַד p. 723.

עֵילוֹם v. עוֹלָם. **עֲלָמוֹת** v. עַלְמָה, II. עלם.

עַל־מוּת לַבֵּן, עַל־מוּת v. עַלְמָה, II. עלם.

†[**עָלַס**] **vb.** rejoice (‖ with עָלַז, עָלַץ, q.v.; NH עֲלִיסָה *rejoicing* (once Levy[NHWB III. 657]));—**Qal** *Impf.* 3 ms. יַעֲלֹס Jb 20[18] *he shall* not *rejoice.* **Niph.** *Pf.* 3 fs. נֶעֱלָסָה Jb 39[13] (of ostrich's wing) = *flap joyously.* **Hithp.** *Impf.* 1 pl. cohort. נִתְעַלְּסָה Pr 7[18] *let us delight ourselves* in (ב) love.

†[**עָלַע**] **vb.** assumed as √ of **Pi.** *Impf.* 3 mpl. יְעַלְעוּ־דָם Jb 39[30] *they drink* (?) *blood*, but rd. prob. יְלַעְלְעוּ (√ I. לוע) Thes Ol De Me Di al.

†[**עָלַף**] **vb.** cover (NH *id., cover, faint;* Ar. عَلَفَ *smear*, II. *cover*, غِلَافٌ *sheath;* As. *elpitu, pining, exhaustion*);—**Pu.** *Pt.* f. *covered, encrusted*, cstr. מְעֻלֶּפֶת Ct 5[14] his belly of ivory *encrusted with* sapphires. *Pf.* 3 pl. בָּנַיִךְ עֻלְּפוּ Is 51[20] *thy sons are enshrouded, enwrapped*, i. e. their senses obscured = *have swooned away;* so also Ez 31[15], rdg. 3 fs. עֻלְּפָה for subst. עַלְפֶּה (Kö[II. 1. 118]), all the trees *have fainted* for (עַל) him (so 𝔊𝔖𝔙 Hi Co al.). **Hithp.** *enwrap oneself, Impf.* 3 fs. וַתִּתְעַלָּף Gn 38[14] (J); = *swoon away*, 3 ms. וַיִּתְעַלָּף Jon 4[8]; 3 fpl. תִּתְעַלַּפְנָה Am 8[13].

עַלְפֶּה Ez 31[15] v. foregoing.

†**עָלַץ** **vb.** rejoice, exult (NH *id.* (rare); Hiph. Impf. יעליצו Ecclus 40[20]; As. *elêṣu, exult;* Sab. מעלץ *joys* CIS[iv. No. 197, l. 5. 7]; v. also עלז, עלס);—**Qal** *Pf.* 3 ms. ׳עָ׳ לִבִּי בַּי 1 S 2[1] *my heart exulteth in* ׳י; *Impf.* 3 ms. יַעֲלֹץ הַשָּׂדֶה 1 Ch 16[32] *the field exulteth;* cf. 3 fs. תַּעֲלֹץ קִרְיָה Pr 11[10] (‖ רנן); 1 s. אֶעֶלְצָה בָּךְ ψ 9[3] (i.e. in ׳י; + שׂמח, ‖ זמר); 3 mpl. יַעְלְצוּ בְךָ ψ 5[12] (in ׳י; ‖ רנן, שׂמח); יַעַלְצוּ לִפְנֵי אֱלֹהִים 68[4] (+ שׂמח ‖ שׂישׂ); + לִי 25[2] *exult at me; Inf. cstr.* בַּעֲלֹץ Pr 28[12] *when* the righteous *exult.*

†[**עֲלִיצוּת**] **n.f.** exultation;—sf. עֲלִיצֻתָם כְּמוֹ לֶאֱכֹל עָנִי Hb 3[14] *their exultation was as it were to devour the poor.*

עלק (√ of foll.; cf. Ar. عَلِقَ *hang, be suspended, cleave, adhere;* عَلَقٌ *leech;* n. unit. عَلَقَةٌ; As. *ilkitu*, of some inferior animal (word-list); Syr. ܥܠܘܩܐ, etc., 𝔗 עֲלוּקָא all *leech*).

†**עֲלוּקָה** **n.f.** leech (perh. Aram. loan-wd.; > vampyre-like demon, Ew al. = Ar. *'Aulak* We[Heid. 2, 149], or name of sage, as some Rabb.; v. discussion De Toy);—לַעֲ׳ שְׁתֵּי בָנוֹת Pr 30[15].

עֲלָתָה Jb 5[16] etc., v. עַוְלָה sub עול.

I, II. **עַם**, **עִם** v. sub I. עמם.

עָמַד [520] take one's stand, stand (NH *id.;* Ph. עמד; As. *emêdu, stand, set up;* Ar. عَمَدَ *prop up, support*, and deriv.; Eth. ዐምድ: *pillar;* 𝔗 עַמּוּדָא *pillar*, Syr. ܥܡܘܕܐ, Palm. עמודא, cf. also n.pr. תימעמד; Sab. עמד *pillar*, acc. to CIS[iv. 91] (or other deriv. fr. √ עמד DHM ZMG xxxvii (1883), 5), pl. אעמדן *pillars* DHM[Epigr. Denkm. aus Abess. 80]);—**Qal** [435] *Pf.* ׳עָ Gn 19[27] +, 3 fs. עָמְדָה 2 K 13[6] +, etc.; *Impf.* יַעֲמֹד Ex 21[21], יַעֲמוֹד Na 1[6] +, יַעֲמָד־ 1 S 16[22] +; 1 s. אֶעֱמֹדָה Hb 2[1], וָאֶעֱמֹד 2 S 1[10]; 3 mpl. יַעַמְדוּ Je 32[14] +, וַיַּעַמְדוּ Ez 1[21] +, 2 mpl. וַתַּעַמְדוּן Dt 4[11], etc.; *Imv.* עֲמֹד 1 S 9[27] +, עֲמָד־ 2 S 1[9]; fs. עִמְדִי Is 47[12] Je 48[19], etc.; *Inf. abs.* עָמֹד Est 9[16]; *cstr.* עֲמֹד Ex 18[23] +, sf. עָמְדִי Je 18[20], עָמְדְךָ Ob[11], etc.; *Pt.* עֹמֵד Is 3[13] +, f. עֹמֶדֶת Hg 2[5] +, etc.;—**1. a.** *take one's stand*, and (esp. pt.) *stand, be in a standing attitude:* c. עַל *by*, 1 S 26[13] 2 S 2[25] 2 K 2[7] +, so pt. Gn 18[8] (J), 41[1.17] (E) +, עַל *on*, Ex 3[5] (E), Dt 27[12] +; c. ב loc. Ex 32[26] Nu 22[24.26] (all JE), +; c. אֶל loc. 1 K 20[38] (+ לְ pers.), Je 48[19] Ez 21[26] 27[29]; c. אֶל pers. 1 S 17[51] 2 K 5[25]; c. אֵצֶל Gn 41[3] (E), Ez 9[2] 10[6] Ne 8[4]; c. לִפְנֵי Gn 18[22] 1 K 3[16] 8[22] +; before ׳י, for intercession Gn 19[27] (J), Dt 4[10] Je 15[1] 18[20], etc.; *take one's stand* and do a thing 1 S 17[8] 1 K 8[55] 2 K 18[28] = Is 36[13] +; sq. inf. 1 K 8[11] = 2 Ch 5[14] +. **b.** *stand forth* (to speak, etc.) 2 K 10[9] +. **c.** *take a stand* against (עַל), in opposition to, Ju 6[31] Ezr 10[15] (but *stand* over, = have charge of, acc. to Kue[Ges. Abh. 247 f.]) 2 Ch 26[18]; cf. עַל־דַּם Lv 19[16] (H) *against the blood of*, i. e. seek one's blood, life; c. יַחַד Is 50[8] *together*, i. e. against each other. **d.** *present* oneself before (לִפְנֵי) Gn 43[15] (J), Ex 9[10] (E), Nu 27[2.21] (P), 1 S 16[21] +; before ׳י (in sanctuary) Dt 19[17] Je 7[10]

cf 18^{20} Lv 9^{5} (P), so in heaven 1 K 22^{21} = 2 Ch 18^{20}, c ב loc of child at birth Ho 13^{13}, in palace (as retainer, courtier) Dn 1^{4}. **e.** c לִפְנֵי *attend upon, be(come) servant of* 1 S 16^{22} (v Dr), 1 K 1^{2}+; servant of י׳ 1 K 17^{1} 18^{15} 2 K 3^{14} 5^{16} Je 15^{19}; priests (לְשָׁרְתוֹ) לפני י׳ Dt 10^{8} Ju 20^{28} Ez 44^{15} 2 Ch 29^{11}, of Levites, *stand* before congreg. for menial duties Ez 44^{11} Nu 16^{9} (P) **f.** *stand* afar מרחוק Ex 20$^{18.21}$ (E), Is 59^{14} ψ 38^{12}, בר׳ ψ 10^{1}, מִנֶּגֶד מר׳ 2 K 2^{7}, *stand* aloof, מנגד Ob^{11} ψ 38^{12} **g.** *stand* (silent) Jb 32^{16}. **h.** *stand* (appealingly) Jb 30^{20} (but rd עָמַדְתָּ, of God, Me Hi Du) **i** *stand*, subj רגל Zc 14^{4} (על loc), ψ 122^{2} (ב loc) so 26^{12} (fig) **j.** *stand*, of water, עַל־הָרִים ψ 104^{6} Vid also preps עִם, מִמַּעַל, עַל, אֵצֶל, אֶל, etc **2. a** *stand still, stop,* cease moving, of moon Jos 10^{13} (JE, ‖ וידם), sun v^{13}, both, Hb 3^{11}, of pers 1 S 9^{27} (opp עָבַר), 2 S 2^{28} (opp. רָדַף), עִמְדוּ עֲמֹדוּ Na 2^{9}+, *stop* flowing (of oil) 2 K 4^{6}, *remain standing*, c. תַּחְתֵּינוּ Ju 7^{21} 1 S 14^{9} etc, of eruption in skin = remain unchanged Lv 13$^{23.28}$, so (without ת׳) 13$^{5.37}$ (all P) **b.** = be inactive 2 Ch 20^{17} (opp הִתְיַצְּבוּ + לְהִלָּחֵם). **c** = be attentive Jb 37^{14} **d** *stop, cease* doing a thing 2 K 13^{18}, c מִן Gn 29^{35} 30^{9} (both J), Jo 1^{15} **3. a.** *tarry, delay* Gn 45^{9} (E), Jos 10^{19} (JE, opp רָדַף), 1 S 20^{38} (opp חוּשָׁה, מְהֵרָה), + **b.** *remain*, c ב loc 2 K 15^{20} Dt 10^{10}, c עִמָּדִי Dt 5^{28} (opp שׁוּב), + inf. purpose Est 7^{7} **c.** *continue, abide* Je 32^{14} Is 66^{22} ψ 102^{27} (opp. אָבַד), = dwell Ex 8^{18} (J, על loc); לָעַד ψ 19^{10} 111$^{3.10}$ 112$^{3.9}$, לְעוֹלָם ψ 33^{11} Ec 1^{4}, בתוך Hg 2^{5}, of plan = be established ψ 33^{11} (earlier קוּם, as Is 14^{24}), so Est 3^{4} Dn 11^{17b}, = maintain itself (earlier קום Jos 2^{11}) Ec 2^{9}, לא יַעֲמָד־בִּי כֹחַ Dn 10^{17} **d** *endure* Ex 18^{23} (E), Ez 22^{14} (‖ חָזַק) **e.** *be steadfast* Dt 25^{8} Ru 2^{7} **f.** *persist* Ec 8^{3} **4.** *make a stand, hold one's ground*, Am 2^{15} 2 K 10^{4} Mal 3^{2}+; c לִפְנֵי Ju 2^{14} 2 K 10^{4}+, בפני Jos 10^{8} 21^{44} (Gins, van d H Baer v^{42}), 23^{9} (all D), c עַל, for one's life Est 8^{11} 9^{16} **5.** *stand upright* **a.** *remain standing* 2 K 13^{6}, of head 6^{31} *remain upright* upon him (עָלָיו), of house (fig of endurance) Jb 8^{15}, Pr 12^{7}. **b.** *stand up*, opp sit, Ne 8^{5} Jb 29^{8} (+קום), opp. lie prostrate Ez 2^{1} (עַל־רַגְלֶיךָ), so 37^{10} (*id*), Dn 10^{11}, v^{11} (עַל־עָמְדֶךָ) Est 8^{4}, of revival after death Dn 12^{13} (late for קום) **c.** *stand up, rise*, of water Jos 3^{13} (+ appos נֵד אֶחָד), v^{16} (+ קָמוּ + *id*, both JE). **d.** *be erect, upright* of boards Ex 26^{15} 36^{20} (P) **+6. a.** *arise, appear, come on the scene* (=קום, late) Ezr 2^{63} = Ne 7^{65}, ψ 106^{30} (cf Ecclus 47$^{1.12}$), esp Dn 8$^{22.22.23}$ 11$^{2.3.4}$ 12^{1}, cf. 11^{1} (כַּנּוֹ), v$^{20.21}$ (עַל־כַּנּוֹ), c תַּחַת *instead of* Ec 4^{15}, of war 1 Ch 20^{4}, deliverance Est 4^{14}. **b.** *stand forth, appear* = come into being Is 48^{13} ψ 33^{9} 119^{90} **c** *rise up* as foe (earlier קום Am 7^{9} Gn 4^{8}), c עַל *against* 1 Ch 21^{1} 2 Ch 20^{23} Dn 8^{25} 11^{14}, c לְנֶגְדִּי *against* 10^{13}. **7.** rare usages are: **a.** ע׳ אֶת־ *stand with*, as attendant, servitor Gn 45^{1} (E), Nu 1^{5} (P) **b.** *take one's stand* in covenant, בַּבְּרִית 2 K 23^{3}. **c** *stand* עַל־חרב Ez 33^{26} (resort to the sword) **d.** *stand* בסוד י׳ Je 23$^{18.22}$ (v סוד) **e** *be appointed* Ezr 10^{14}. **f** *stand* before (לפני) beast Lv 18^{23} (carnal intercourse) **g.** *grow flat, insipid* (Gie), taste of wine Je 48^{11} (fig. of Moab), or *remain unchanged* (so most, in that case cf **3 b**)—עָמְדִי Dn 11^{1b} is err pt., rd prob עָמַדְתִּי, or עָמַד (מִיכָאֵל subj.), join then to 10^{21} and del 11^{1a}, so Bev Behrm Marti^{Kau}.

Hiph $_{83}$ (cf Dr$^{Intr (6) 535}$) *Pf.* 3 ms. הֶעֱמִיד 1 K 12^{32}+, 2 ms הֶעֱמַדְתָּה ψ 30^{8}, וְהֶעֱמַדְתָּ Nu 3^{6}+, etc, *Impf* יַעֲמִיד Pr 29^{4}+, וַיַּעֲמֵד 2 K 8^{1}+, 3 fs. sf וַתַּעֲמִדֵנִי Ez 2^{2} 3^{24}, 1 pl וַנַּעֲמִיד Ne 4^{3}, etc, *Imv* הַעֲמֵד Is 21^{6}, sf הַעֲמִידֶהָ Ez 24^{11}, *Inf abs.* הַעֲמֵיד Ne 7^{3}, *cstr* הַעֲמִיד 1 K 15^{4}+, *Pt* מַעֲמִיד 2 Ch 18^{34} (but v. **Hoph**),—**1.** *station, set*, c. acc Ju 16^{25} (בין), for duty Nu 11^{24} (E, סְבִיבֹת), 1 K 12^{32} (ב loc) 2 Ch 19^{5} (*id*), Ne 13^{11} (עַל־עָמְדָם), Is 21^{6}+ (Ne 4^{7a} read perhaps **Qal**, so Perles$^{Anal 65}$), c. על *against* Ne 4^{3} **2.** *cause to stand firm* ψ 18^{34} = 2 S 22^{34} (c על loc), *maintain* (opp overthrow) Ex 9^{16} (J), 1 K 15^{4}, cf Pr 29^{4} **3** *cause to stand up, set up, erect*, c acc. + עַל־רַגְלַי Ez 2^{2} 3^{24}, so עַל־עָמְדִי Dn 8^{18}, temple Ezr 2^{68} (על loc), cf 2 Ch 24^{13} (על loc., of repairs); esp doors Ne 3^{1}+7 t. Ne; Asherim 2 Ch 33^{19}, cf 25^{14} **4.** + לִפְנֵי *present* one *before* king Gn 47^{7} (P), י׳ (in sanctuary) Lv 14^{11}+3 t. P, + (of goat) Lv 16^{7}, priest Lv 27^{8}+4 t P, + (of beast) Lv 27^{11} **5** *appoint* Ne 7^{3} 1 Ch 15^{17}+ (late), c על *over* Ne 13^{9}+, c inf. purpose 6^{7}+, c. 2 acc 1 Ch 15^{16}, = assign (land) to (ל) 2 Ch 33^{8} (‖ 2 K 21^{8} נָתַן), *appoint* courses of priests 8^{14} 31^{2}, cf Ne 13^{30}, *ordain* commandments, על pers Ne 10^{33}, cf. 2 Ch 30^{5}; *establish* עַד־הָעוֹלָם 1 Ch 17^{14} (ב loc), cf 2 Ch 9^{8} ψ 148^{6}; c acc of covenant ψ 105^{10} = 1 Ch 16^{17} (ל pers + ל rei); c חָזוֹן *vision* Dn 11^{14} (= fulfil, earlier הקים). **+6.** other meanings **a.** ע׳ אֶת־פָּנָיו 2 K 8^{11} *have a fixed look* **b.** c acc ב + רַגְלַי loc ψ 31^{9} (fig). **c.** *make to stand* (in a covt, v ‖ 2 K 23^{3}) 2 Ch 34^{32} **d.** *restore* waste places Ezr 9^{9} **e.** + לְפָנֶיהָ Est 4^{5}, i e *make servant to*. **f** *cause* wind *to arise*

ψ 107^{25}. **g.** = *raise* an army Dn 11$^{11.13}$.—2 Ch 18^{34} v. **Hoph.**; ψ 30^{8} v. עֹז; Ez 29^{7} v. מָעַד

† **Hoph.** *Impf.* 3 ms יָעֳמַד Lv 16^{10} *be presented* (of goat) + לִפְנֵי י׳, *Pt* הָיָה מָעֳמָד 1 K 22^{35} *he was caused to stand,* i.e. propped up, in (ב) his chariot, so rd. also ‖ 2 Ch 18^{34} (as 𝔊), for MT מַעֲמִיד.—On *Pf* הֶעֱמַדְתִּי v. עז ψ 30^{8}.

† [עֹמֶד] **n.[m.]** **standing-place**;—only sf. after prep: וַיָּקוּמוּ עַל־עָמְדָם Ne 9^{3} *they stood up in their place* (later equiv. of תַּחְתָּם), 8^{7} (no vb); c. עָמַד 2 Ch 30^{16} 35^{10}, ע׳ עַל־עָמְדוֹ 34^{31}, וָאַעֲמִדֵם עַל־עָמְדָם Ne 13^{11}, so עַל־עָמְדִי Dn 8^{18}, עֲמֹד עַל־עָמְדֶךָ 10^{11}, v^{17} וַיָּבֹא אֵצֶל עָמְדִי.

† [עֶמְדָּה] **n.f.** **standing-ground**,—sf. יִקַּח מִכֶּם עֶמְדָּתוֹ Mi 1^{11}, text dub. v. Now.

עַמּוּד, עַמֻּד$_{110}$ **n.m.**$^{1 K 7^{15}}$ **pillar, column**,—עמוד abs. 1 K 7^{15}+, cstr. Ex 13^{21}+; עַמֻּד abs. Je 52^{21}, cstr. Nu 14^{14}, sf. עמודו 2 Ch 23^{13}, pl. עמודים 1 K 7^{16}+, less oft. עַמֻּ׳ v^{21}+, cstr. עמודי Ex 26^{32}+, less oft. עַמֻּ׳ 38^{17}+; sf. עמודיו Ex 36^{38}+, עַמֻּדָיו 27^{10}+, etc.,—**1.** *pillar,* supporting house Ju 16$^{25.26.29}$; *pillars* in tabern. Ex 27$^{10.11.17}$ 36^{38} Nu 3^{37}+27 t. Ex Nu (P), + עמודי שטים *pillars of acacia* wood Ex 26$^{32.37}$ 36^{36}, *pillars* in Sol.'s palace 1 K 7$^{2.3.6}$, אוּלָם הָע׳ v^{6}, עמודי אֲרָזִים v^{2} *pillars of cedar* (P); in Ezek.'s temple Ez 42$^{6.6}$, ע׳ שֵׁשׁ Est 1^{6} (in palace), Ct 5^{15} (sim.). **2.** two bronze pillars—1 K 7^{15} 2 K 25^{13} = Je 52^{17}—before temple 1 K 7$^{15.15}$+ 14 t. 1 K 7, +2 K 25$^{16.17.17}$ = Je 52$^{20.21.21}$, Je 27^{19} 1 Ch 18^{8} 2 Ch 3$^{15.17}$+5 t. Ch., perh. one of these was הָע׳ by which king stood in temple 2 K 11^{14} = 2 Ch 23^{13}, 2 K 23^{3}; > ע׳ here = *standing-place, platform* Thes al., two pillars bef. Ezek.'s temple Ez 40^{49}. **3.** *columns, uprights,* of silver Ct 3^{10} (litter). **4.** ע׳ עָשָׁן Ju 20^{40} *column of smoke*: ע׳ (הֶ)עָנָן Ex 13$^{21.22}$ (J)+6 t. JE, hence Ne 9$^{12.19}$ ψ 99^{7}; ‖ ע׳ (הָ)אֵשׁ Ex 13$^{21.22}$ (J), Nu 14^{14} (JE), Ne 9$^{12.19}$; ע׳ אֵשׁ וְעָנָן Ex 14^{24} (J), all of the theoph. at time of Exodus. **5. a.** ע׳ בַּרְזֶל Je 1^{18} (fig. of proph.). **b.** poet. of pillars of earth Jb 9^{6} ψ 75^{4}, of heaven Jb 26^{11}. **c.** of wisdom's house Pr 9^{1}.

† [מַעֲמָד] **n.[m.]** **office, function, service**,—**1.** *station, office, post* מַעֲמָדְךָ Is 22^{19} (‖ מַצָּבְךָ), עַל־מַעֲמָדָם 2 Ch 35^{15} *at their post*. **2.** *office, function* 1 Ch 23^{28}. **3.** *service,* prob. specif. *waiting* at table (strictly *mode of standing*), cstr. מַעֲמַד מְשָׁרְתָיו 1 K 10^{5} = 2 Ch 9^{4}.

† מָעֳמָד **n.[m.]** **standing-ground, foothold** ψ 69^{3} (in fig.)

עַבְדִּי v. עם infr. sub עמם

עמה (√ of foll.; cf. As. *emû, be united, associated; emûtu, family, family connexion;* NH עָמִית = BH (rare))

† [עָמִית] **n.m.**$^{Lv 18.20}$ **associate, fellow, relation** (perh. orig. f. abstr. *association,* cf. פֶּחָה),—alw. sf.: גֶּבֶר עֲמִיתִי Zc 13^{7} *a man* (who is) *my fellow;* elsewhere only Lv: עֲמִיתוֹ 5$^{21.21}$; recipr. אִישׁ בַּעֲמִיתוֹ 19^{11} 24^{19}, cf. 25^{17}, עֲמִיתְךָ 18^{20}, עֲמִיתֶךָ 19$^{15.17}$ 25$^{14.14.15}$.

עַמִּיאֵל and similar n.pr. v. sub I. עמם.

† **עָמַל** **vb. labour, toil** (NH *id.*; Ar. عَمِلَ *labour, make,* Sab. עמל *work* (? n. or vb) CIS$^{iv \, No \, 250}$, Aram. עֲמַל, ܥܡܠ; Zinj. עמל; As. *nimelu, gain, possession*),—**Qal** *Pf.* 3 ms. ע׳ Ec 2^{21}; 3 fs עָמְלָה Pr 16^{26}; 2 ms עָמַלְתָּ Jon 4^{10}, 1 s. עָמַלְתִּי Ec 2^{11}+2 t., 3 pl. עָמְלוּ ψ 127^{1}; *Impf.* 3 ms. יַעֲמֹל Ec 1^{3}+3 t.,—*labour* (very late) in building ψ 127^{1}, tillage, c. ב Jon 4^{10}, gen., c. ב Ec 2^{21}, c. ל Pr 16^{26} Ec 5^{15}, c. ל+ inf. 8^{17}; עֲמָלוֹ שֶׁיַּעֲמֹל 1^{3} 5^{17}, cf. 2$^{11.19.20}$.

† I. עָמָל **n.m.**$^{Jb 4.8}$ **f.**$^{Ec 10.15}$ (against Albr$^{ZAW \, xvi}$ (1896) 113, v. Kö$^{Synt \, \S 249 m}$) **trouble, labour, toil** (on this form as abstr. v. Lag$^{BN \, 143}$ Ba$^{NB \, 105}$),—ע׳ Nu 23^{21}+, cstr. עֲמַל Ju 10^{16}+; sf. עֲמָלִי Gn 41^{51}+, etc.,—**1.** *trouble* (‖ *sorrow*): one's own suffering, עָמָל וְיָגוֹן Je 20^{18}; ע׳ וָכַעַס ψ 10^{14}; עָנְיִי וַע׳ Dt 26^{7} ψ 25^{18}, ע׳ וָאָוֶן 90^{10}; ‖ אָוֶן Nu 23^{21} Jb 5^{6}, ‖ שָׁוְא Jb 7^{3}; ע׳ נַפְשׁוֹ Is 53^{11}, ע׳ בְעֵינָי ψ 73^{16}; אדם לְע׳ 16^{2}, מְנַחֲמֵי ע׳ Jb 3^{10}; וַיַּסְתֵּר ע׳ מֵעֵינָי 5^{7}; יוּלָּד ψ 73^{5}; בע׳ אנוש אינמו Jb 11^{16}, שׁכח ע׳ נַשֵּׁנִי ע׳ Gn 41^{51} (E); ע׳ לא זכר Pr 31^{7}; תקצר נפשו בע׳ Ju 10^{16}. **2.** *trouble, mischief,* as done to others. ‖ שֹׁד Pr 24^{2}; יֹצֵר ע׳ ψ 94^{20}; ע׳ וָאָוֶן ψ 7^{17} יָשׁוּב ע׳ בראשו 10^{7}; ‖ רָע Hb 1^{13}; און וע׳ 55^{11}; ‖ אָוֶן Is 10^{1} 59^{4} Hb 1^{3} ψ 7^{15} Jb 4^{8} 15^{35}, עֲמַל שְׂפָתֵימוֹ ψ 140^{10} *mischief of their lips.* **3.** *toil, labour* (late in Heb.): Ec 2$^{10.10.21.24}$ 3^{13} 4$^{4.6.8.9}$ 5$^{14.18}$ 6^{7} 8^{15} 10^{15}, c. עָמַל (q. v.) 1^{3} 2$^{11.19.20}$ 5^{17}, 9^{9}, ע׳ אֲשֶׁר עָמַל 2$^{18.22}$; ע׳ שֶׁאֲנִי (שהוא) עָמֵל, = fruit of labour, ע׳ לְאֻמִּים יִירָשׁוּ ψ 105^{44}, וַיַּכְנַע בעמ׳ לִבָּם 107^{12} *he humbled their mind by toil*

† II. עָמָל **n.pr.m.** name in Asher 1 Ch 7^{35}, 𝔊 Αμια, 𝔊^{L} Αλαμ.

†I. **עָמֵל n.m.** [Pr 16.26] **labourer, sufferer**,—'ע Pr 16[26] + 2 t, pl עֲמֵלִים Ju 5[26],—**1.** *labourer, workman* Ju 5[26] Pr 16[26] **2.** *sufferer,* Jb 3[20] (|| מָרֵי נָפֶשׁ), 20[22]

†II **עָמֵל adj. verb** toiling, only Ec, as pred,—Ec 2[18.22] 3[9] 4[8] 9[9]

עֲמָלֵק [39] **n pr.gent** **Amalek** (on ‒ָ‒ v Lag [BN 162] Ba[NB 160]),—ancient people Nu 24[20.20], S of Canaan—in Negeb 13[29] (all JE), fierce and warlike Bedawin (cf GASm[Geogr 282] GFM[Ju 6, 3.33]), foes of Isr during Exodus Ex 17[8] + 6 t. Ex 17 (E), Dt 25[17 19], later marauders in Isr. territory Ju 3[13] 6[3.33] 7[12] 10[12], defeated by Saul 1 S 14[48] 15[2] + 9 t 1 S 14, 28[18], and by David 30[18] (cf **adj. gent.** infr), 2 S 8[12] = 1 Ch 18[11], cf ψ 83[8], also 'הָעֲ 2 S 1[1] (where read עֲמָלֵק or הָעֲמָלֵקִי, v. Comm), 'ע 1 Ch 4[43], as grandson of Esau Gn 36[12] (P) = 1 Ch 1[36], Gn 36[16]; appar connected with Ephr territory Ju 5[14] (cf 12[15] infr, yet GFM conj עֵמֶק)—On Amalek v No[Amalekites (1864)], Ency Bi s v

†**עֲמָלֵקִי adj gent.** 1 S 30[13] 2 S 1[13], also (as pred) v[8], coll = (*the*) *Amalekites* 1 S 15[6 15] 30[1], elsewh c art. 'הָעֲ Nu 14[25.43.45] (J, all + הַכְּנַעֲנִי), 1 S 27[8], 'שְׂדֵה הָעֲ Gn 14[7], 'הַר הָעֲ Ju 12[15] (in Ephraim), rd 'הָעֲ also Ju 1[16] (for הָעָם) Bu GFM, > עֲמָלֵק Hollenb Mey Kit[Kau], on 2 S 1[1] v foreg

† I **עָמַם vb.** (√ of foll cf Ar عَمَّ *be comprehensive, include,* عَمٌّ *company,* also *paternal uncle,* perhaps As *ummanu, people,* Sab עם either (*a*) *people,* or (*b*) *paternal uncle* CIS[iv p 20], pl sf אעממהו = (*b*) Mordtm[Himj Inschr 45 70], also often in n pr CIS[iv No 5,1 99,7] etc, Prat[Neue Beitr 25] Hom[Chrest. 12, 133, A und A 6] We[GGN 1893, 480])

I **עַם, עָם** [1810] **n.m.** [Gn 11,6] (v infr) **people** (NH id, *plebeian, common man,* 𝔗 עַמָּא *people,* pl *peoples, tribes,* etc, Syr ܥܰܡܳܐ; Ar عَمّ v supr, orig mng prob *those united, connected, related,* cf We[GGN 1893, 480]),—abs עַם Gn 11[6] +, עָם Ju 9[36] +, הָעָם Jos 8[11] +, cstr עַם Nu 21[29] +; sf עַמִּי Ex 3[7] +, עַמְּךָ 22[27] +, etc, pl עַמִּים Is 2[3] +, עֲמָמִים (cf BAram) Ne 9[22], cstr עַמֵּי 1 K 8[43] +, עַמְמֵי Ne 9[24], pl c sf v II עַם,—(Thes cites foll as **f.** וְחָטָאת עַמֶּךָ Ex 5[16] [but corrupt and unintellig, read perh 'וְחָטָאתָ לְעַ, so 𝔊 𝔖 Di], Ju 18[7] [but יֹשֶׁבֶת must agree with lost word *city,* or the like, v GFM], Je 8[5] [but read שׁוֹבֵב for שׁוֹבֵבָה Gie]),—**1.** *a people, nation* (sts || גּוֹי), n. coll (sg Ex 21[8] Jos 17[14 15 17] 2 S 17[29] + oft, or pl Ex 20[15] 24[2] Je 5[31] + oft, or both in same clause Ex 1[20] 2 S 13[24]) עַם אֶחָד = all mankind Gn 11[6] (J), peoples in gen. 27[29] (J, || לְאֻמִּים), Ex 19[5] (E), Dt 2[25] 4[6] + oft Dt, Ne 13[24] + oft, קְהַל עַמִּים Gn 28[3] (P) *an assembly* (multitude) *of peoples,* 48[4] (P), Ez 23[24] 32[3] (+ רַבִּים), one's own people Je 46[16] ψ 45[11] Ru 1[10 15 16 16] + (on עַמִּי נָדִיב Ct 6[12] v esp. Bu); particular peoples, Egypt Gn 41[40] (E), Ex 1[22] (E), Ne 9[10] +, עַם־אֲרָם Am 1[5], עַם־כְּמוֹשׁ (i e Moab) Nu 21[29] (JE), Je 48[46], but esp Isr Ex 1[20] (E) + oft, 'עַם־בְּנֵי יִשׂ v[9] (J); called 'עַ יהוה Nu 11[29] (E), 1 S 2[24] +, and (by 'י) עַמִּי Ex 3[7] 5[1] (J) + oft. (all periods), עַם־הָאֱלֹהִים קְהַל עַם־הַקָּהָל Ju 20[2], Lv 16[33] (P), קְהַל עָם ψ 107[32], esp. הָעָם הַזֶּה (oft. in contempt or disgust) Nu 11[1 12 13] +; fig of ants Pr 30[25], the *shaphan* v[26], locusts Jo 2[2], cf. לְעָם לְצִיִּים ψ 74[14] (where rd לְעַם צִיִּים Hup-Now) —On Ju 1[16] v עֲמָלֵקִי **2.** = smaller units, e g **a.** inhab of a city Gn 19[4] (J), 1 S 9[12 13] Je 29[16.25] 2 Ch 31[4] + (Je 8[5] del 'יְרוּשׁ 𝔊 Gie Co Rothst). **b.** inhab of a locality Je 37[12] [appar not = tribe, Dt 33[3] rd עַמּוֹ 𝔊 Di Dr, Ho 10[14] Ju 5[8 14] rd בְּעָרֶיךָ We Now; v sub **d**] **c.** retainers, followers Gn 14[16] 32[8] 33[15] 35[6] Ju 3[18] 8[5] 2 S 15[17] Je 41[13 14] +. **d.** people bearing arms 1 S 11[11] 1 K 20[10] +, 'עַ כָּבֵד Nu 20[20] (JE), i e. a powerful force, עַם הַצָּבָא Nu 31[32] (P), 'עַ הַמִּלְחָמָה Jos 8[1.3 11] 10[7] 11[7] (all JE), so prob Ju 5[8] *a* (fighting) *band;* perh also v[14] (rd sg ? v GFM Bu) **3.** = common people Je 21[7] 22[4], Lv 4[27] (opp ruler v[22]), Ne 5[1] (opp יְהוּדִים), 7[5] (opp rulers) **4.** *people* in gen, *persons* Gn 50[20] (E), so appar 'כָּל־הָעָם אֲשֶׁר וגו Ex 33[16] (J), Nu 11[34] (J), Jos 5[5.5] (D), Ju 9[36] (as sg), v[37] (as pl), Je 36[9], persons labouring 1 K 9[23], superior persons Jb 12[2] (iron.), עַם עוֹלָם Ez 26[20] *people of long ago* (now in Sheʾôl) **5.** phrases are **a.** בְּנֵי עַמִּי (עַמְּךָ, עַמִּי, עַמָּהּ) *members of one's people, compatriots, fellow-countrymen,* etc Nu 22[5] (E), Gn 23[11] (P) Lv 19[18] (H), Ju 14[16 17] Ez 33[2 12] + **b** בְּנֵי הָעָם = *common people* (v 3) 2 K 23[6] Je 26[23] +; *people* in gen שַׁעַר בְּנֵי הָעָם Je 17[19] i e *public gate* 2 Ch 35[5 12] **c.** עַם הָאָרֶץ *the people* at large, as a body 2 K 11[14 18 19.20] 15[5] 16[15] 21[24 24] +, Je 37[2] 44[21] Lv 20[2] (H), Gn 23[7 12 13] (P), common people Je 34[19], cf. 'דַּלַּת עַ' הָא 2 K 24[14], disting from prince Ez 45[22] 46[9], from priests Hg 2[4] Zc 7[5], = Canaanites Nu 14[9] (JE), cf עַמֵּי הָאָרֶץ 1 Ch 5[25], mixed post-exil population Ezr 4[4]. **d.** עַמֵּי הָאָרֶץ usu. *peoples of the earth* Jos 4[24] (D), 2 Ch 32[19] +; of heathen peoples about and in Pal after exile Ezr 10[2.11]; traders Ne 10[31], עַמֵּי הָאֲרָצוֹת 9[30] 10[29] 2 Ch 32[13]. **e.** מִשְׁפְּחוֹת עַמִּים ψ 96[7] = 1 Ch 16[28] (cf. ψ 22[28]).

f. בַּת־עַמִּי = people personif. Is 22^{4} Je 4^{11} + 7 t Je + 6^{14} (van d. H., om. בַּת Baer Gi), La 2^{11} 3^{48} 4$^{3.6.10}$; בְּתוּלַת בַּת־עַמִּי Je 14^{17}. **g.** designations of Isr. are: עַם־קָדוֹשׁ Dt 7^{6} + 3 t, ע׳ קְדוֹשִׁים Dn 8^{24}, ע׳ (ה)קֹּדֶשׁ Is 62^{12} 63^{18} Dn 12^{7}; ע׳ סְגֻלָּה Dt 7^{6} 14^{2} 26^{18}. **h.** of foreign (non-Isr) peoples: ע׳ נָכְרִי Ex 21^{8} (E), ע׳ אַחֵר Dt 28^{32}, and esp. from language, ע׳ עִמְקֵי שָׂפָה Ez 3^{5} cf. v^{6}, כִּלְשׁוֹן עַם וָעָם Ne 13^{24} cf Est 1$^{22.22}$ 3^{12}, ע׳ לֹעֵז ψ 114^{1}. **i.** עַם עַמִּי עֶבְרָתִי Is 10^{6}, ע׳ חֶרְמִי 34^{11}, ע׳ מִבְחָרָיו Dn 11^{15}, עַם תּוֹעֵבוֹת הָאֵלֶּה Ezr 9^{14}; לֹא עַם בִּינוֹת Is 27^{11} —For עַם־עוֹלָם Is 44^{7} read (מִי הִשְׁמִי)ע מֵעוֹלָם (אֹתִיּוֹת) Oort Du Kit Che^{Hpt} cf Perles$^{Anal\ 40,64}$.

עִם **prep** **with** (Aram. עִם, ܥܡ, Sab עם DHM$^{Epigr\ Denkm\ 12}$ Hom$^{Chrest\ 51}$, cf Ar مَعْ, مَعَ (but v. Prat$^{BAS.\ i\ 26}$)), sf עִמִּי$_{46}$ and עִמָּדִי$_{45}$ (prob akin to Ar. عِنْدَ *side*, عِنْدَ *beside*: cf √ענד), without difference of meaning (עִמִּי in Pent. Gn 31^{31} 39$^{7.12.14}$ Ex 33^{12} Lv 26$^{21.23.27.40}$ [H] Nu 22^{19}; Jos–K. 13 t; ψ 42^{9} 86^{17} Jb 10^{17} Ru 1^{11} Est 7^{8}, in Dn 7 t., Ezr Ne Ch 11 t עִמָּדִי in Pent Gn [JE] 14 t, Ex 17^{2} Lv 25^{23} Dt 5^{28} 32$^{34.39}$, Ju S 7 t.; ψ 23^{4} 50^{11} 55^{19} 101^{6}, Jb 14 t., Ru 1^{8}); עִמְּךָ, עִמָּכָה + 1 S 1^{26}, עִמָּךְ; עִמּוֹ, עִמָּהּ; עִמָּנוּ, עִמָּכֶם; עִמָּם$_{27}$ (Gn 18^{16}, etc. Gn–K 20 t.; Ne 13^{25}; not Ezr Ch), and עִמָּהֶם$_{23}$ (chiefly late: Nu 22^{12} Dt 29^{16} (v^{24} עִמָּם), Jon 1^{3} Jb 1^{4}, and 19 t. Ne Ezr Ch):—**1.** of fellowship and companionship (Lat *cum*), as Gn 13^{1} וְלוֹט עִמּוֹ and Lot *with* him, 18^{16} 19^{30} 24^{54} הוּא וְהָאֲנָשִׁים אֲשֶׁר עִמּוֹ, וְכָל יִשְׂרָאֵל עִמּוֹ Jos 7^{24} *al.*, + oft. Peculiar to Ch Ezr are clauses introd. by . . . וְעִמָּהֶם 1 Ch 12^{34} 13^{2} 15^{18}+, Ezr 8$^{13.14}$ (Aram 5^{2})+, so . . . וְעִמּוֹ 1 Ch 12^{28} 2 Ch 17$^{14-18}$ 26^{17} Ezr 8$^{3-12.33}$. Coupling substantives, *together with*, chiefly in poetry. Dt 12^{23} לֹא תֹאכַל הַנֶּפֶשׁ עִם הַבָּשָׂר, Jos 11^{21} Ju 16^{3} Ec 7^{11}; 2 S 1^{24} שָׁנִי עִם עֲדָנִים, Dt 32^{14} עִם חֵלֶב כָּרִים, v$^{14.24.25}$ Am 4^{10} Is 25^{11} 34^{7} Je 6^{11} 51^{40} Na 3^{12} ψ 66^{15} אֶעֱשֶׂה בָקָר עִם עַתּוּדִים, 81^{3} 83^{8} 87^{4} 89^{14} 104^{25}+, Ct 1^{11} 4$^{13.13}$ כְּפָרִים עִם נְרָדִים, v$^{14.14}$ 5$^{1.1.1}$. Unusually, Est 9^{25} אָמַר עִם הַסֵּפֶר he ordered *in conjunction with* writing, in a written order. Poet or late uses: ψ 42^{9} וּבַלַּיְלָה שִׁירֹה עִמִּי, ψ 89^{22} אֲשֶׁר יָדִי תִּכּוֹן עִמּוֹ, v^{25}; in Jb of the companionship of sufferings or prosperity, 6^{4} חִצֵּי שַׁדַּי עִמָּדִי, 17^{2} אִם לֹא הֲתֻלִים עִמָּדִי, 29^{6} וְצוּר יָצוּק עִמָּדִי פַּלְגֵי שָׁמֶן, v^{20} כְּבוֹדִי חָדָשׁ עִמָּדִי, 2 Ch 14^{5} וְאֵין עִמּוֹ מִלְחָמָה, 16^{19} יֵשׁ עִמְּךָ מִלְחָמוֹת, 28^{10} עִמָּכֶם אֲשָׁמוֹת. Hence, in partic. **a.** of *aid*, Ex 23^{5} Dt 22^{4}, 1 Ch 12^{19}, esp. of God, Gn 21^{22} אֱלֹהִים עִמְּךָ, 26^{3} וְאֶהְיֶה עִמְּךָ, v^{33} 31$^{3.5}$ Ex 3^{12} Jos 1^{5} Is 8^{10} כִּי עִמָּנוּ אֵל ψ 23^{4} 46$^{8.12}$ Jb 29^{5} + oft. (cf. אֵת, Gn 39$^{2.3.21.23}$ Is 43^{5}+): so הִתְחַזֵּק עִם 1 Ch 11^{10} 2 Ch 16^{9} Dn 10^{21}, עָזַר עִם 1 Ch 12^{21}, כִּי גַם יָדָם עִם דָּוִד 1 S 22^{17}, 2 S 3^{12} 1 Ch 4^{10} (cf. Ex 23^{1}, and II. אֵת **1 a**). *With the help of* (= Gk σύν), 1 S 14^{45} כִּי עִם אֱלֹהִים עָשָׂה הַיּוֹם הַזֶּה, Dn 11^{39} (rare).

b. Of actions done jointly *with* another, as יָרַשׁ עִם inherit *with*, Gn 21^{10}, כָּרַת בְּרִית עִם 26^{28} + oft., חָלַק (חִלֵּק) עִם to share *with* Jos 22^{8} Is 53^{12}+; cf. Dt 10^{9} חֵלֶק וְנַחֲלָה עִם אֶחָיו, 18^{1}

c. If the common action be of the nature of a contest or combat, עִם is *with* in the sense of *against*. so often with נִלְחַם *to fight*, נִשְׁפַּט *to dispute*, נֶאֱבַק *to wrestle*, רִיב *to strive* (see these verbs), Gn 26^{20} 30^{8} 32^{29}; בָּא בְמִשְׁפָּט עִם to enter into judgment *with* Is 3^{14}+, Jb 14^{3} (הֵבִיא), רִיב לי׳ עִם Hos 4^{1}+; hence, without a verb expressing the idea explicitly, ψ 94^{16} מִי יָקוּם לִי עִם מְרֵעִים *in the struggle with* evil-doers? v^{b} 55^{19} כִּי בְרַבִּים הָיוּ עִמָּדִי for as many are they *in combat with* me, Jb 9^{14} אֶבְחֲרָה דְבָרַי עִמּוֹ *in the contest with* him, 10$^{17\ b}$ 16^{21}, perhaps צָדַק עִם 9^{2} 25^{4} (cf. **4 b** *end*)

d. Of dealing *with* a person, or of the relation in which one stands *with*, or *towards*, another: as עָשָׂה חֶסֶד עִם to do kindness *with* Gn 24^{12} + oft (in 1 pers observe that in this phr. עִמָּדִי, not עִמִּי, is regul. used, Gn 19^{19} 20^{13} 40^{14} 1 S 20^{14} 2 S 10^{2} [‖ 1 Ch 19^{2} עִמִּי: here only], *al.*), עָשָׂה טוֹב עִם Gn 26^{29}+, v. also 20^{9} 31^{29} Dt 33^{21} Ju 15^{3} Jb 10^{12} 13^{20} 42^{8} ψ 86^{17} (cf אִתְּכֶם Dt 1^{30} 10^{21}; and Aram Dn 3^{32}), 119^{124} 126^{2} (1 S 12^{24}), Jb 33^{29}; הֵיטִיב עִם Gn 32$^{10.13}$+, הֵרַע עִם 31^{7}; רָצָה עִם be well pleased *with* ψ 50^{18} Jb 34^{9}, דִּבֶּר עִם to speak *with* (subj usu. God) Ex 19^{9}+ (v. דִּבֶּר **3 e**), hence דָּבָר עִם Ju 18$^{7.28}$ 2 S 3^{17} 1 K 1^{7} Jb 15^{11} דָּבָר לָאַט עִמָּךְ a word (spoken) gently *with* thee, cf 11^{5} וְיִפְתַּח שְׂפָתָיו עִמָּךְ; יֵאָמֵן עִם 2 Ch 1^{9} and with adj. תָּמִים עִם perfect *with* (i e *toward*) Dt 18^{13} ψ 18^{24}, שָׁלֵם עִם 1 K 8^{61}+, cf. וְלִבָּם לֹא נָכוֹן עִמּוֹ ψ 78^{37}, 2 S 21^{4} 23^{5} 1 K 3^{6} (עִמָּךְ), Mi 6^{8} הַצְנֵעַ לֶכֶת עִם אֱלֹהֶיךָ, ψ 73^{22} *toward* thee, 1 Ch 19^{6} Hos 12^{1} (?); also הָלַךְ קֶרִי עִם Lv 26$^{21.27}$ (7 t.), מַמְרִים הֱיִיתֶם עִם Dt 9$^{7.24}$ 31^{27}, 2 Ch 16^{10} 26^{19} ψ 85^{6} Jb 10$^{17\ a}$.

e. Of a common lot, Gn 18^{23} הַאַף תִּסְפֶּה צַדִּיק עִם רָשָׁע *together with* the wicked, v^{25} Jb 3$^{14.15}$ Is 38^{11} ψ 26^{9} אַל תֶּאֱסֹף עִם חַטָּאִים נַפְשִׁי, v^{b} 28$^{3.3}$, 69^{29} Jb 30^{1} 1 Ch 24^{5}; hence *like*, ψ 73^{5} וְעִם אָדָם לֹא יְנֻגָּעוּ *with* (i e. *like*) men (in general),

106[6] חטאנו עם אבותינו, Ec 2[16] ואיך ימות הֶחָכָם עם הכסיל i e *like* the fool

f. Of equality or resemblance generally (poet), Jb 9[26] חָלְפוּ עם אֳנִיּוֹת אֵבֶה they pass by *with*, i e as swiftly as, skiffs of reed, 37[18] תרקיע עמו i e *like* him, 40[15] אשר עשיתי עמך, so נמשל עם ψ 28[1] 143[7], נֶחְשַׁב עם 88[5]

†**g** Of *time*, = *as long as*, ψ 72[5] ייראוך עם שמשׁ *as long as* the sun *endureth* (cf Aram Dn 3[33] 4[31], also Ovid *Am* 1 15, 16 *cum* sole et luna semper Aratus erit), *at the time of* (?) 2 Ch 21[19] (but rd perh מחליו), and c inf (late), Ezr 1[11] עם הֵעָלוֹת הַגּוֹלָה (cf ἅμα τῷ sq inf Ju 3[21] 9[33], also עם Ecclus 40[14])

2. Of a locality, *close to, beside* · † Gn 25[11] וישב יצחק עם באר לחי ראי *beside* the well of, etc , 35[4] תַּחַת הָאֵלָה אשר עם שכם (so, after אשר, Jos 7[2] Ju 9[6] 18[22] 2 S 13[23]), Jos 19[46] (?), Ju 18[3] הֵמָּה עם בית מיכה (so 19[11] 2 S 20[8]), 1 S 10[2] 2 S 6[7] וַיָּמָת שָׁם עם אֲרוֹן הא׳, 19[38] 24[16] 1 K 1[9] 1 Ch 13[14] *by* the house of O , in its own house (v Be), 21[15] (2 S 24[16]), 26[16] (cf את **2**). By a *person*, Dt 5[28] ואתה עמד פה עמדי *by me*, 1 S 1[26] הַנִּצֶּבֶת עִמְּכָה +, of one living *near* another, Ex 22[24] Lv 25[35.36.39 47]

3. Of persons, עם is spec. **a.** *in the house or family* or *service of* (*apud, chez*) Gn 23[4] גר ותושב עמך (fig of י׳ Lv 25[23] ψ 39[13]), 27[44] 29[14] וַיֵּשֶׁב עמו, v[25] עבדתי עמך I have served *with* thee (so v[30], cf Dt 15[16]), 31[38] Lv 25[6.40 40.50.53] Dt 22[2] 23[17] Ju 17[10] 2 S 19[34] 1 K 11[22], cf 1 S 2[21] עם י׳ i e at his sanctuary

b *In the possession of* (Lat *penes*) Gn 24[25] straw, etc , is עִמָּנוּ, 31[32] Dt 17[19] והיתה עמו *with him, at his side*, 29[16] Jb 28[14] וְיָם אָמַר אין עִמָּדִי, = *stored up with*, Dt 32[34] כָּמֻס עִמָּדִי, Jb 27[13] (but rd here prob מאל, cf 20[29]), of ethical or mental attributes, 1 S 25[25] וּנְבָלָה עמו, Jb 12[13] עִמּוֹ חָכְמָה וּגְבוּרָה, v[16] 25[2] ψ 130[7] 2 Ch 19[3.7] Cf fig ψ 36[10] כי עמך מקור חיים

c. *In the custody* or *care of*, 1 S 9[23] שים עמך, 22[23] כי משמרת אתה עמדי, cf Jb 17[3] עָרְבֵנִי עִמָּךְ be surety for me *with thyself*

d. *Beside* = *except*, Dt 32[39] אין אלהים עִמָּדִי, ψ 73[25] ועמך לא חפצתי בארץ and *beside thee* I delight not (in aught that is) upon earth (al *in comparison of* thee, **1 f**), 2 Ch 14[10] ואין עמך לַעְזֹר there is none *beside thee* to help, 20[6], perh Hos 9[8] (Hi Ke; but very dub , v Comm) Cf את **1 b**

e. *With* = *friendly with*, Gn 31[2] כי איננו עמי (אל v 5 *towards*), 2 K 10[15] לְבָבִי עם לְבָבְךָ, Pr 23[7] ולבו בל עמך

4. Idiom of a *thought* or *purpose* present *with* one —†**a** עם לבב פ׳, esp in Dt and the later Deut style, Dt 8[5] וְיָדַעְתָּ עם לְבָבֶךָ thou shalt know *with* thy heart, 15[9] פן יהיה דבר עם לבבך בליעל a wicked thought *with* thy heart, Jos 14[7] I brought back word כאשר עם לבבי, ויהי עם לבב פ׳, esp of a purpose, 1 K 8[17] היה עם לבב דוד לבנות וגו׳ i e it was David's *purpose* to build, etc , v[18 18] 1 K 10[2] (= 2 Ch 6[7 8.8] 9[1]), 1 Ch 22[7] 28[2] (both based on 1 K 8[17], etc), 2 Ch 1[11] 24[4] 29[10], rather differently, to *muse* or *talk with* one's heart, ψ 77[7] Ec 1[16]

†**b.** עם alone, = in one's *consciousness*, whether of knowledge or memory or purpose (cf את **3 b**, عِنْدَ W[AG ii § 60]). Nu 14[24] עֵקֶב הָיְתָה רוּחַ אַחֶרֶת עמו i e operating in his mind, 1 K 11[11] יען אשר היתה זאת עמך, 1 Ch 28[12] the pattern of all אשר היה בָרוּחַ עמו that was in spirit (i e mentally) *with* him, ψ 50[11] וְזִיז שָׂדַי עִמָּדִי is *with* me (i e is known to me, ‖ידעתי), prob also 73[23] 139[18] (= in thy thought and care); Jb 9[35] לא כן אנכי עמדי not so am I *with myself* (my consciousness—or conscience—does not tell me that I need dread him), 10[13] ידעתי כי זאת עמך i e. that this was thy purpose (‖ אֵלֶּה צָפַנְתָּ בִלְבָבֶךָ), 15[9] ולא עמנו הוא and is not *with us* (= in our knowledge , ‖ ולא נֵדַע), 23[10] כי ידע דרך עמדי the way *of which I am conscious* (De; Ew Di the way *attending* me, my usual way), v[14] וְכָהֵנָּה רַבּוֹת עמו i e he has many such purposes, 27[11] אֲשֶׁר עִם שַׁדַּי לֹא אֲכַחֵד i.e. his purposes or principles of action Also sts *in the judgment* or *estimation of*, 1 S 2[26] טוֹב עם, 2 S 6[22] נכבד עם, perh צָדַק עם Jb 9[2] 25[4] (Ges Bu, but Ew as **1 c**, Hi De *beside in comparison of*).

†**5** Metaph *together with* = *in spite of, notwithstanding* Ne 5[18] ועם זֶה (cf مَعَ W[AG ii § 67], in Heb ב is the more usual syn) —In 1 S 16[12] אַדְמוֹנִי עם יפה עינים (cf 17[42] עם יפה מַרְאֶה), if text correct, יפה must be a neuter subst., *with* beauty of eyes, but rd prob (Gr Bu) עֶלֶם *a youth* (17[56] 20[22]) for עם (v HPS, Che[Expos T x 521] אַדְמֹנִי עֶצֶם, cf La 4[7])

מעם[72] *from with* or *beside* (= παρά with a gen : cf. מאת) hence **a.** after verbs of departing, taking, removing, etc , Gn 13[14] אַחֲרֵי הִפָּרֶד לוֹט מעמו, 26[16] לֵךְ מֵעִמָּנוּ, 1 S 10[2] 14[17] מי הלך מעמנו, 2 S 1[2], 1 S 16[14] ורוח י׳ סרה מעם שאול, 18[12], 2 K 2[9] בטרם אֶלָּקַח מעמך, 2 S 15[28] עד בוא דָּבָר מֵעִמָּכֶם, of heart turning מעם י׳ Dt 29[17] 1 K 11[9], after שאל *to ask*, Ex 22[13] Dt 10[12] מה י׳

דרשׁ ,שׁאַל מֵעִמְּךָ 1 S 1^{17} 20^{28} (Niph.), Is 7^{11}+; דרשׁ *to require*, Dt 18^{19} 23^{22}, 1 K 14^{5} (*to inquire*); יצא מעם פרעה *from* (being) *with* Ph. Ex $8^{8.25.26}$ 9^{33}+: cf. 2 S 3^{26}, 1 S 18^{13} ויסירהו שׁאול מעמו, and מֵעִם פְּנֵי Gn 44^{29} Jb 1^{12}. †Sq. a word denoting a place, Gn 48^{12} וַיּוֹצֵא יוֹסֵף אֹתָם מֵעִם בִּרְכָּיו, Ex 21^{14} מֵעִם מִזְבְּחִי (cf. 1 S 2^{33}), Ju 9^{37} מֵעִם טַבּוּר הארץ, 1 S 20^{34} מֵעִם הַשֻּׁלְחָן; Jb 28^{4} מֵעִם גָּר *away from, far from* (si vera l)

†**b.** Gn 24^{27} אשׁר לא עזב חסדו מעם אֲדֹנִי (cf. with הכרית 1 S 20^{15}, הסיר 2 S 7^{15} 1 Ch 17^{13} (‖ 2 S 7^{15} מִן), הפיר ψ 89^{34}); Ru 4^{10} לֹא־יִכָּרֵת שׁם מעם

†**c.** *From the possession*, or *custody*, *of* (cf. עִם **3 b, c**): so with גזל Gn 31^{31}, ערב *to take in pledge* 44^{32}, גנב Ex 22^{11}, יצא (subj. a slave; cf. עם **3 a**) Lv 25^{41} Dt 15^{16} (cf with שִׁלַּח חָפְשִׁי Dt $15^{12.13.18}$ Je 34^{14}, הִצִּיל Dt 23^{16}), לקח 2 S 3^{15}, קנה 24^{21}.

†**d.** Expressing *origination* or *authorship*: 1 S 20^{7} כִּי כָלְתָה הָרָעָה מעמו, v $^{9.33}$ (cf. מאת Est 7^{17}), esp of י׳ (cf מֵאֵת **c**), Gn 41^{32} נָכוֹן הַדָּבָר מֵעִם הא׳ *is established from*, on the part of, God, 1 K 2^{33} שָׁלוֹם . . . מעם י׳, 12^{15} (2 Ch 10^{15}) כִּי הָיְתָה סִבָּה מעם י׳, Is 8^{18} signs and portents מעם י׳, 28^{29} גם זאת מעם י׳ יצאה, 29^{6} ψ 121^{2} עֶזְרִי מעם י׳, Ru 2^{12}. And of a judgment proceeding *from* any one: 2 S 3^{28} נקי מעם י׳ = *pronounced* guiltless *by* י׳, Jb 34^{33} הֲמֵעִמְּךָ *at thy judgment* shall he requite? (cf. מִן **2 d** *end*).

†עִמָּנוּאֵל **n.pr.m.** **Immanuēl** (*with us is God*),—ע׳ Is 7^{14} van d H Baer, עִמָּנוּ אֵל Gi;—name of child, symbolizing presence of י׳ to deliver his people (on interpret v. Comm.)—עִמָּנוּ אֵל $8^{8.10}$ is declaration of trust and confidence, *with us is God!* (cf ψ $46^{8.12}$); v. עם

† II [עַם] **n.**[**m.**] **kinsman** (on father's side) (Ar عَمّ *paternal uncle*, etc., v. I. עמם; cf. perh TelAm. *ammu*, *kinsmen* (?); on Nab עם *ancestor* cf Lzb ^{161,490}; v also esp. Nes $^{Eg\ 187}$, ZAW xvi (1896) 322 f Krenkel $^{ib.\ viii\ (1888),\ 280-84}$); — sf. עַמִּי in בֶּן־עַמִּי (q.v), and n pr sqq.; elsewhere pl. sf. עַמֶּיךָ Nu 27^{13} 31^{2} (Lv 19^{16} read עמך 𝔊 Sam),+ (poss) עַמְּמָיךְ Ju 5^{14}; עַמָּיו Gn 25^{8}+ 15 t., עַמֶּיהָ 17^{14}+3 t.; read עַמַּי (for MT עַמִּי, I עַם; cf Krenkel $^{l.c\ 281}$) Gn 49^{29} and perh Ju 14^{3} (cf. Lv 21^{14}), acc. to Buhl Kit also 2 K 4^{13};—*father's kinsmen*: וַיֵּאָסֶף אֶל־עַמָּיו Gn 25^{8} (of joining kinsmen in Sheʾôl), so v^{17} 35^{29} 49^{33} Nu 20^{24} Dt 32^{50}, cf. Gn 49^{29} (v. supr), Nu 27^{13} 31^{2} Dt 32^{50} (all P); וְנִכְרְתָה הַנֶּפֶשׁ מֵעַמֶּיהָ Gn 17^{4} (severed from living kinsmen), so Lv $7^{20.21.25.27}$ 19^{8} 23^{29} Nu 9^{13}, מִקֶּרֶב עַמֶּיהָ Ex 31^{14}, cf. $30^{33.38}$ Lv 17^{9} (all PH); מֵעַמָּיו יִקַּח אִשָּׁה 21^{14} (H), and perh. Ju 14^{3} (sim. I עַם: [־ָה, ־ֵם] מִקֶּרֶב עַמּוֹ Lv $17^{4.10}$ 18^{29}+); other combin Ju 5^{14} (si vera l, read perh. בַּעֲמֶקָךְ, v. I. עם **2 d**), Lv $21^{1.4.15}$ (H), Ez 18^{18} and (perh) 2 K 4^{13}.—בֶּן־עַמִּי (v. p. 122 b) perh = *son of my kinsman*; on n pr. c. עם v. Gray $^{Prop.\ N\ 41\ ff}$.

† I. [עֻמָּה] **n.f. juxtaposition**, but only in st. c. with force of a **prep. close by, side by side with, parallel to, agreeing with, corresponding to**,—st. c. עֻמַּת, exc. Ec 5^{15} always c. לְ, sf. לְעֻמָּתִי, once pl. cstr. לְעֻמּוֹת Ez 45^{7},—**a.** *close by, side by side with*: Ex 25^{27} (37^{14}), 28^{27} (39^{20}), Lv 3^{9} לְעֻמַּת הֶעָצֶה יְסִירֶנָּה shall take it away *close by* the backbone; esp. of what is *parallel*, Ez 42^{7} the wall *alongside of* the chambers; of the contiguous portions in Ezek.'s division of the land, *alongside of* each other, Ez $45^{6.7}$ $48^{13.18.18.21}$; of movement in parallel lines, 2 S 16^{13} Shimei was going along לְעֻמָּתוֹ *parallel with* him, v^{13} Ez 1^{20} וְהָאוֹפַנִּים יִנָּשְׂאוּ לְעֻמָּתָם, v^{21} 3^{13} 10^{19} 11^{22}; 3^{8} נָתַתִּי פָנֶיךָ חֲזָקִים לְעֻמַּת פְּנֵיהֶם *by the side of* their face (which, as antagonism is implied, = *against*, RV), v^{8}. **b.** *agreeing with, corresponding to* (a common result of juxtaposition), Ex 38^{18} a screen five cubits high לעמת קלעי החצר *agreeing with* (RV *answerable unto*) the hangings of the court (in height), Ez 40^{18}; prob. also 1 Ch 26^{16} Ne 12^{24} משׁמר לְ׳ משׁמר ward *corresponding to* ward **c.** *correspondingly to*, 1 Ch 24^{31} they also cast lots לְעֻמַּת אֲחֵיהֶם *correspondingly to* their brethren, v^{b} the head, *correspondingly to* his younger brother, 26^{12} to these . . . belonged charges *correspondingly to* (in common with) their brethren. **d.** before a sentence (Ges ^{§155a}), 1 Ch 25^{8} (strangely) לְעֻמַּת כַּקָּטֹן כַּגָּדוֹל (v. Ke) *correspondingly to* (the principle) *of*, as the small so the great, Ec 5^{15} כָּל־עֻמַּת שֶׁבָּא *quite exactly as* he came, so shall he go (but Lambert REJ xxxi 47, Rahlfs $^{Th\ Lit.-z\ 1896,\ 587}$ כְּלְעֻמַּת). **e.** מִלְּעֻמַּת (v. מִן **1 c, 9 a**) 1 K 7^{20} *close beside*.

† II עֻמָּה **n.pr.loc.** Jos 19^{30}, v. עַכּוֹ.

עַמּוֹן$_{106}$ **n.pr.gent. Ammon**, 𝔊 Αμμαν, Αμμων (As. *Bît Ammanu* COT $^{Gloss.}$);—always (except 1 S 11^{11} [where however 𝔊 rds. בְּנֵי ע׳], ψ 83^{8}, which have ע׳ alone) בני עמון, connected by J with בֶּן־עַמִּי son of Lot Gn 19^{38} (and meaning of name doubtless sought herein by J; cf. II עַם); people apparently akin to Isr., but usu.

hostile, dwelling E. of Jordan, NE. of Moab, between Arnon and Jabbok: Nu 21$^{24.24}$ (JE), Dt 2$^{19.19.37}$ 3$^{11.16}$ Jos 12^{2} 13^{10} (D), v^{25} (P), Ju 3^{13} 10^{6} + 25 t. Ju 10–12, 1 S 11^{11} 12^{12} 14^{47} 2 S 8^{12} 10^{1} + 14 t. 2 S 10–12, 17^{27} 1 K 11$^{7.33}$ 2 K 23^{13} 24^{2} 1 Ch 18^{11} + 20 t. Ch, Am 1^{13} Is 11^{14} Je 9^{25} + 9 t. Je, Zp 2$^{8.9}$ Ez 21$^{25.33}$ + 5 t. Ez 25, Dn 11^{41}. —Vid. Che^{Ammon} in Ency. Bib.

† עַמֹּנִי, עַמּוֹנִי **adj. gent. Ammonite**;—abs. ms. עַמּוֹנִי as subst. Dt 23^{4} *an Ammonite* (generic), so עַמֹּנִי Ne 13^{1}; הָעַמּוֹנִי of individual 1 S 11$^{1.2}$ 2 S 23^{37} = 1 Ch 11^{39}, Ne 2^{19}, so הָעַמֹּנִי 2^{10} 3^{35}; fs. הָעַמֹּנִית 1 K 14^{21} = 2 Ch 12^{13}, 1 K 14^{31}, so הָעַמּוֹנִית 2 Ch 24^{26}; הָעַמֹּנִי as subst. coll. Ezr 9^{1}; mpl. as subst. עַמֹּנִים 1 K 11^{5}, הָעַ׳ Dt 2^{20} Ne 4^{1}, הָעַמּו׳ 2 Ch 26^{8} (on 20^{1} v. מְעוּנִים); fpl. as adj. עַמֳּנִיֹּת 1 K 11^{1}, so Ne 13^{23} Qr, Kt עמוניות.

† עַמִּיאֵל **n.pr.m.** (*my kinsman is God*, Gray$^{Prop. N. 254}$);—𝔊* Αμ(με)ιηλ: **1.** E. Jordan name 2 S 9$^{4.5}$ 17^{27}. **2.** a Danite Nu 13^{12} (P). **3.** David's father-in-law 1 Ch 3^{5} (= אֱלִיעָם 2 S 11^{3}). **4.** son of Obed Edom 1 Ch 26^{5}.

† עַמִּיהוּד **n.pr.m.** (*my kinsman is majesty*);—𝔊 (Σ)εμιουδ, Αμιουδ, etc.: **1.** a Geshurite 2 S 13^{37} Qr (> Kt עַמִּיחוּר, cf. Dr al., Gray$^{Prop. N. 43}$). **2.** an Ephraimite Nu 1^{10} 2^{18} 7$^{48.53}$ 10^{22} (all P), 1 Ch 7^{26}. **3.** a Simeonite Nu 34^{20}. **4.** a Naphtalite Nu 34^{28}. **5.** a Judahite 1 Ch 9^{4}.

† עַמִּיזָבָד **n.pr.m.** (*my kinsman hath bestowed*; cf. זְבַדְיָה, זַבְדִּיאֵל, יְהוֹזָבָד, אֶלְזָבָד, זָבָד, and, esp. on Palm. equiv., v. Gray$^{Prop. N. 223 f.}$ also Lzb^{265} Cook$^{46 f.}$);—son of Benaiah 1 Ch 27^{6}, 𝔊 Λαιβαζαθ, A Αμιραζαθ, 𝔊L Αμειναζαβαδ.

עמיחור 2 S 13^{37} Kt v. עַמִּיהוּד.

† עַמִּינָדָב **n.pr.m.** (*my kinsman is noble*);—𝔊 Αμ(ε)ιναδαβ: **1.** Aaron's father-in-law Ex 6^{23} Nu 1^{7} 2^{3} 7$^{12.17}$ 10^{14} (all P), Ru 4$^{19.20}$ 1 Ch 2$^{10.10}$. **2.** Levites: **a.** 1 Ch 6^{7}. **b.** 15$^{10.11}$.

† עַמִּישַׁדָּי **n.pr.m.** (*my kinsman is Shaddai*);—a Danite Nu 1^{12} 2^{25} 7$^{66.71}$ 10^{25}, 𝔊 Αμ(ε)ισαδαι, 𝔊L Αμισαδε.

† II. [עָמַם] **vb. darken, dim** (NH *id.*; Ar. غَمَّ *cover, veil, conceal*; 𝔗 עֲמַם *grow dark*);—**Qal** *Pf.* 3 pl. sf. עֲמָמֻהוּ Ez 31^{8} dub., but prob. (as Thes) cedars *did* not *eclipse him*; עֲמָמוּךָ 28^{3} no secret *do they hold dark* (= is held dark) for thee (Ges$^{§ 117 x}$). **Hoph.** *Impf.* 3 ms. יוּעַם זָהָב La 4^{1} (fig.) *how is the gold dimmed!* cf. Bu.

עַמְמֵי, עֲמָמִים v. I. עַם supr.

עִמָּנוּאֵל v. sub עִם supr.

†[עָמַשׂ ?, עָמַס] **vb. 1.** load. **2.** carry a load (NH *id.*; Ph. עמס *carry*; cf. poss. Ar. عَمِسَ *gravis et obscurus fuit dies* (Frey));—**Qal** *Impf.* 3 ms. וַיַּעֲמֹס Gn 44^{13}, יַעֲמָס־ ψ 68^{20}; *Pt. act.* עֹמְסִים Ne 13^{15}; עֹמְשִׂים 4^{11} (but v. infr.); sf. עֹמְסֶיהָ Zc 12^{3}; *pass.* עֲמֻסִים Is 46^{3}, עֲמוּסוֹת v^{1};—**1.** *load* (obj. om.) upon (עַל) ass Gn 44^{13} (E), Ne 13^{15}; so abs. 4^{11}, lit., si vera l. (v. Be-Ry Ryle); but rd. prob. חֲמֻשִׁים Ry^{Kau}. **2.** *carry a load* ψ 68^{20} (י׳, for (ל) his people), *carry as a load* Zc 12^{3} (fig.), pass. Is 46^{1} (lit.), v^{3} (fig.).

† עָמוֹס **n.pr.m. Amos** the prophet;—Am 1^{1} 7$^{8.10.11.12.14}$ 8^{2}, 𝔊 Αμως.

† עֲמַסְיָה **n.pr.m.** name in Judah 2 Ch 17^{16}, 𝔊 Μασαιας, 𝔊L Αμασιας (cf. Ph. אשמנעמס, בעלעמס CIS$^{I. 139, 169, 719}$, v. also Gray$^{Prop. N. 296 f.}$).

† מַעֲמָסָה **n.f. load, burden**;—אֶבֶן מ׳ Zc 12^{3} *a stone of burden* = heavy stone, hard to lift.

† עַמְעָד **n.pr.loc.** in Asher, Jos 19^{26}, 𝔊 Αμιηλ, A Αμαδ, 𝔊L Αλφααδ.

†[עָמֹק, Lag$^{BN 28}$] **vb. be deep** (NH in deriv.; Ar. عَمُقَ; Eth. ዐመቀ: prob. As. [*emêḳu*] III. 2 *implore* (earnestly; 'from *bottom* of one's soul'), *emûḳu, might, nîmeḳu, wisdom* (? as unfathomable); 𝔗 in deriv.; Syr. in der. spec.);—**Qal** *Pf.* 3 mpl. עָמְקוּ ψ 92^{6} (of י׳'s designs; cf. As. supr.). **Hiph.** *make deep*: *Pf.* 3 ms. (symbol.) הֶעְמִיק הִרְחִב Is 30^{33} (sc. Tophet; van d. H. הֶעְמִק, and so in foll.); 3 mpl. הֶעְמִיקוּ Ho 5^{2} the pit of Shittim (?) *have they made deep* (reading שַׁחַת הַשִּׁטִּים We Now, cf. Che Gu^{Kau}); הֶעְמִיקוּ סָרָה Is 31^{6} (fig.) *they have made deep* (*their*) *apostasy*; sq. vb., with adverbial force הֶעְ׳ שִׁחֵתוּ Ho 9^{9} = *they are in the depth of corruption* (v. שׁחת); *Imv.* mpl. הַעְמִיקוּ (Ges$^{§ 63 o}$), sq. inf. Je 49$^{8.30}$ *make deep to dwell* (of hiding, so most; > Gie *take an abject seat*, as 13^{18} 48^{18}); *Pt.* הַמַּעֲמִיקִים לַסְתִּר Is 29^{15} *they who deeply hide* fr. י׳ (their) counsel; *Inf. abs.* הַעֲמֵק Is 7^{11} = Imv. *make deep* (ask a sign in the depths of She'ôl, reading שְׁאָלָה; opp. הַגְבֵּהַ).

עֵמֶק $_{70}$ **n.m.**$^{Mi 1,4}$ **vale** (prop. *deepening, depth*, v. GASm$^{Geogr. 384 f. 654 f.}$; cf. נַחַל, גַּיְא, בִּקְעָה);—ע׳ abs. Jos 8^{13}+, cstr. Gn 14^{17}+; sf. עִמְקֵךְ Je

49^{4}, עֲמָקָם 47^{5} (but v. infr.); pl עֲמָקִים Mi 1^{4}, sf. עֲמָקַיִךְ Is 22^{7};—*vale, valley, lowland*, opp הֶהָרִים Mi 1^{4}, amid mts., e g. about Jerus. Is 22^{7} Je 31^{40}, so perh. ע׳ שָׁוֵה Gn 14^{17} = ע׳ הַמֶּלֶךְ v^{17} 2 S 18^{18}, cf. ע׳ חֶבְרוֹן Gn 37^{14} (J), ע׳ בגבעון Is 28^{21}, Jos 8^{13} (JE), ע׳ הָאֵלָה 1 S 17$^{2.19}$ 21^{10} (perh. *Wady es-Sant*, in Shephelah, W. of Bethlehem, GASm$^{Geogr\ 226}$), ע׳ אֲשֶׁר לְבֵית רְחוֹב Ju 18^{28} in extreme north; in Moab Je 48^{8}(‖[opp ?] מִישׁוֹר); or wider, e. g. Ju 5^{15} (scene of Sisera's defeat; rd. perh ע׳ also for עֲמָלֵק v^{14} GFM), ע׳ יִזְרְעֶאל Ju 6^{33} Ho 1^{5} Jos 17^{16} (JE), cf. Ju 7$^{1.8.12}$ 1 S 31^{7} = 1 Ch 10^{7}, these all perh. narrow ends of plain (cf. GASm$^{l.c}$), but v. 1 K 20^{28} (opp. הֶהָרִים; ‖ מִישׁוֹר v^{23}; = *open country*, cf. Aphek v^{26}); of Jordan-valley Jos 13$^{19.27}$ (P); of maritime plain (opp. הָהָר) Ju 1$^{19.34}$; fit for chariots, so also אֶרֶץ הָע׳ Jos 17^{16} (P), cf. Jb 39^{21}, יֹשֶׁבֶת הָע׳ Je 21^{13}, cf Nu 14^{25} (v. Gie Di); cultivated 1 S 6^{13} Je 49$^{4.4}$ Jb 39^{10}, fertile 1 Ch 27^{29} ψ 65^{14} Ct 2^{1}, v. also עָכוֹר, סֻכּוֹת, יְהוֹשָׁפָט, חָרוּץ II, בְּרָכָה, בָּכָא, אַיָּלוֹן, בֵּית הָע׳, שֵׁדִים, רְפָאִים, קְצִיץ v p 112 a —For עֲמָקָם Je 47^{5} rd. עֲנָקִם *Anakim* 𝔊 Thes Hi Gf Gie Co Rothst; so also (more dub) 1 Ch 12^{16} (van d. H. v^{15}) Gf Gie, where otherwise הָע׳ = *people of valleys*

†עֹמֶק n.[m.] depth,—abs Pr 25^{3}; pl. cstr. עִמְקֵי שְׁאוֹל 9^{18} (Ko$^{ii\ 1,\ 32}$).

†[עָמֵק] adj. deep, unfathomable,—pl. cstr. עִמְקֵי שָׂפָה (Ges$^{§93\,ll}$) i. e *unintelligible of speech* Is 33^{19} Ez 3$^{5.6}$—Pr 9^{18} v עֵמֶק.

עָמֹק$_{17}$ adj. deep (cf Ba$^{NB\,§\,23\,b}$);—**1.** ע׳ lit. Lv 13^{3} + 6 t Lv 13, f עֲמֻקָּה of cup Ez 23^{32}, trench Pr 22^{14} 23^{27} (all 3 in sim); ע׳ משׁאול Jb 11^{8} (fig); pl. מַיִם עֲמֻקִּים (sim) Pr 18^{4} 20^{5}. **2.** = *unsearchable* עָמֹק ψ 64^{7} Ec 7$^{24.24}$; pl. עֲמֻקּוֹת (Baer עֲמוּקוֹת, van d. H עֲמֻקּוֹת) Jb 12^{22}.

†עֲמוֹק n.pr.m. a priest Ne 12$^{7.20}$, Αμουκ

†מַעֲמַקִּים n.m.pl. depths,—abs. מ׳ ψ 130^{1} (fig); cstr. lit מַעֲמַקֵּי־יָם Is 51^{10}; fig מ׳ מַיִם Ez 27^{34} (fall of Tyre), ψ 69$^{3.15}$ (distress).

I. עָמַר (√ of foll; mng. dub., perh. related to Ar. عَمَرَ *be abundant* (of water), *surpass, overtop;* NH עוֹמֶר, עָמִיר = BH, 𝔗 עוּמְרָא, עֲמִירָא = BH I עֹמֶר)

†I. עֹמֶר n.m.$^{Lv\ 23,\ 11}$ sheaf (*swath*, row of fallen grain, Wetzst$^{Z\ f.\ Ethnol\ 1873,\ 273\ (Syr\ Dreschtafel)}$, ag. him Vogelstein$^{Landwirthschaft\ in\ Pal\ 61}$ who trans. *heap of sheaves*);—ע׳ abs Dt 24^{19} Lv 23$^{11.12.15}$, cstr. v^{10}; fig of food (abs) Jb 24^{10}, pl. עֳמָרִים lit Ru 2$^{7.15}$.

†II. עֹמֶר n.m.$^{Ex\ 16,\ 22}$ omer (cf. Ar غُمَر *small drinking cup* or *bowl;* relation to I ע׳ obscure);—a measure, only Ex 16,—the measure itself v$^{18.32.33}$; amount measured v$^{16.22}$, = $\frac{1}{10}$ ephah v^{36}; 𝔊 γόμορ.

†עָמִיר n.[m.] swath, row of fallen grain (*hay*, as Mishn, acc to Vogelstein$^{l.c\ 74f}$ (who is then compelled to rd. עֹמֶר Mi 4^{12}), cf. Syr. ܥܡܝܪܐ *grass*, Schwally$^{Idiot.\ 69}$),—Am 2^{13} (on cart), Je 9^{21} (falling behind reaper), Mi 4^{12} (brought to threshing-floor), Zc 12^{6} (inflammable).

†[עמר] vb. Pi. denom. bind sheaves (NH *id*, so 𝔗 ψ 129,7, cf. Chr Pal Aram. Schwally$^{Idiot.\ 69}$), —*Pt.* מְעַמֵּר ψ 129^{7} (in sim; ‖ קוֹצֵר).

†II [עָמַר] vb. Hithp. deal tyrannically with (ב) (Ar. غَمَرَ *cherish enmity, rancour, malice*, III. *plunge* into a conflict, غِمْرٌ *rancour, malice*);—*Pf* 3 ms וְהִתְעַמֶּר consec. Dt 24^{7}, *Impf* 2 ms. תתעמר 21^{14}.

†עֲמֹרָה$_{19}$ n.pr.loc. Gomorrah, Γομορρα (ר = غ; √ II. עמר acc to Lag$^{BN\ 54}$);—alw c. סְדֹם q v, Gn 10^{19} + 8 t Gn, in sim. Am 4^{11} Is 1^{9} 13^{19} Dt 29^{22} Je 49^{18} 50^{40} Zp 2^{9}, cf Dt 32^{32}; fig of iniquity Is 1^{10} Je 23^{14}.

III. עמר (√ of foll, cf Ar. عَمِرَ, عَمَرَ *live, live long;* also *worship;* n pr. عُمَرُ etc; RS$^{K\ 264}$ prop. mng. *worshipper*, עָמְרִי *worshipper of* י׳ (cf. We$^{Skizzen\ iii\ 165}$), against him No$^{ZMG\ xl\ (1886),\ 185}$, who cp meaning *live*, عَمْرٌ, عُمْرٌ, *life*).

עָמְרִי$_{18}$ n.pr.m. **1.** Omri, king of Israel (MI$^{4.5.7}$ עמרי; in As. *Humri* COT^{Gloss}),—1 K 16^{16} + 11 t. 1 K 16, 2 K 8^{26} = 2 Ch 22^{2}, Mi 6^{16}, 𝔊 (Z)αμβρ(ε)ι. **2. a.** name in Benj. 1 Ch 7^{8}. **b.** in Judah 9^{4}. **c.** in Issachar 27^{18}.

עַמְרָם$_{14}$ n.pr.m. (√ עמר No$^{ZMG\ xl\ (1886),\ 185}$; poss עַם + רָם Thes, cf Gray$^{Prop.\ N\ 45,\ 47,\ 51}$);—**1.** father of Moses Ex 6$^{18.20.20}$ + 4 t. P, 1 Ch 5$^{28.29}$ + 4 t Ch; Αμ(β)ραμ[ν]. **2.** Ezr 10^{34}.

†עַמְרָמִי adj. gent. of **1**, c art. as n.coll. Nu 3^{27} 1 Ch 26^{23}.

עמשׂ v. עמס

עֲמָשָׂא$_{16}$ n.pr.m. (cf עמס, עמשׂ? or read עֲמִשַׁי (II. עַם + יִשַׁי), We$^{Isr\ u.\ Jüd.\ Gesch\ 24}$, cf Gray

$^{\text{Prop N 44,323}}$),—**1.** Absalom's general 2 S $17^{25.26}$ 19^{14}+8 t 2 S 20, 1 K $2^{5.32}$ 1 Ch 2^{17} ^{17}, 𝔊 Αμεσσ(α)ει, 𝔊L Αμεσσα. **2.** Ephraimite 2 Ch 28^{12}

†עֲמָשַׁי **n.pr.m.** (cf foreg.),—**1.** warrior of David 1 Ch 12^{19} (van d. H v^{18}), Αμασαι, perh = אֲבִישַׁי (2 S 23^{18}). **2.** Levites **a.** 1 Ch $6^{10.20}$ (עֲמָשָׂי). **b.** 2 Ch 29^{12}. **c.** priest 1 Ch 15^{24}

†עֲמַשְׁסַי **n.pr.m.** (prob. textual error for foreg, Ol $^{\S 277i}$, cf Thes^{1044}),—a priest Ne 11^{13}, Αμασεια [-σαι], = מַעְשַׂי 1 Ch 9^{12} (Μαασαια [-σει])

ענב (√of foll, cf NH עֲנָב = BH; Ar عِنَب id; Sab אנעב *vineyards* SabDenkm^{47}, Mordtm$^{\text{ZMG xli (1887), 309, 364}}$, 𝔗 עִנְּבָא; perh. also As *inbu, fruit* (and not = אב q v.), cf Hom$^{\text{A und A 94}}$)

†עֵנָב **n.m.**$^{\text{Gn 40, 11}}$ **grape(s)** (on formation cf Lag$^{\text{BN 183}}$),—ע׳ abs Dt 32^{14} (coll), elsewhere pl. עֲנָבִים Gn 40^{10}+; cstr ענבי (Ges $^{\S 20b}$) Lv 25^{5} Dt 32^{32}; sf. עֲנָבָמוֹ v^{32},—*grapes* Gn $40^{10\ 11}$ (E), Am 9^{13} (all as yielding juice for drink), Ho 9^{10} (sim), Is $5^{2\ 4}$ (parable), Je 8^{13} Ne 13^{15} Lv 25^{5} (H); ע׳ מִשְׁרַת Nu 6^{3} (P), poet דַּם־ע׳ Gn 49^{11} Dt 32^{14}; ע׳ בכורי Nu 13^{20}, ע׳ אֶשְׁכּוֹל v^{23} (JE); eaten Dt 23^{25}, so ע׳ לַחִים וִיבֵשִׁים Nu 6^{3}; ע׳ אֲשִׁישֵׁי Ho 3^{1} *raisin-cakes;* ע׳ רוֹשׁ Dt 32^{32} *grapes of poison*

†עֲנָב **n.pr.loc.** in hill-country of Judah Jos 11^{21} 15^{50}, Αναβ(ωθ), Ανωβ[ν], mod. *'Anab,* 18½ miles SW. from Hebron, Buhl$^{\text{Geogr 164}}$.

†עֲנוּב **n.pr m.** 1 Ch 4^{8}, Εννων, 𝔊L Ανωβ

†[עָנַג, Lag$^{\text{BN 31}}$] **vb. be soft, delicate, dainty** (NH id Pi *make soft, pliable, live* or *spend in enjoyment,* Ar. غَنِجَ *use amorous behaviour, affect langour*),—**Pu.** *Pt.* f. הַמְעֻנָּגָה Je 6^{2} *daintily bred,* fig. of Jerusalem. **Hithp. 1.** *be of dainty habit, Inf cstr.* הִתְעַנֵּג Dt 28^{56} (woman, ‖ רַךְ). **2.** *take exquisite delight, Pf* 3 pl. והתענגו consec ψ 37^{11} (עַל rei); 2 mpl וְהִתְעַנַּגְתֶּם consec. Is 66^{11} (מִן rei); *Impf* 3 ms יִתְעַנָּג Jb 27^{10}, 2 ms תִּתְעַנַּג Is 58^{14}, תתענג Jb 22^{26} (all c. [עַל־י׳] [שַׁדַּי]); 3 fs. תִּתְעַנַּג Is 55^{2} (ב rei), *Imv* ms. הִתְעַנַּג עַל־י׳ ψ 37^{4} **3.** c עַל, in bad sense, *make merry over, make sport of,* *Impf.* 2 mpl. עַל־מִי תִּתְעַנָּגוּ Is 57^{4}.

†עֹנֶג **n.**[**m.**] **daintiness, exquisite delight,**—הֵיכְלֵי ע׳ Is 13^{22}, וְקָרָאתָ לַשַּׁבָּת ע׳ 58^{13}

†עָנֹג **adj. dainty,**—הָע׳ Dt 28^{54} man; הָעֲנֻגָּה v^{56} woman, Is 47^{1} (Bab personif); all ‖ [רַכ[ה.

†תַּעֲנוּג **n.**[**m**] **daintiness, luxury, exquisite delight,**—**1.** *luxury* ת׳ Pr 19^{10}, elsewhere pl; cstr תַּעֲנֻגוֹת Ec 2^{8} **2.** sf. בְּנֵי תַּעֲנוּגָיִךְ Mi 1^{16} *thy dainty sons,* בֵּית תַּעֲנֻגֶיהָ 2^{9} *her* (their) *dainty house(s),* > of tender love (rdg. בָּנֶיהָ 2^{9}) We Now. **3.** *delight* of love, pl abs בַּתַּעֲנוּגִים Ct 7^{7} (Perles$^{\text{Anal 22f}}$ conj בַּת עַמִּינָדָב).

†[עָנַד] **vb.** bind around, upon (cf. Ar. عَنَدَ *turn aside* fr. way; Syr. ܥܢܕ *defecit, defuit;* cf also עֲמָדִי (for עמי)),—**Qal** *Impf* 1 s. אֶעֶנְדֶנּוּ לִי Jb 31^{36} (obj. garland, in fig.); *Imv* sf. עָנְדֵם Pr 6^{21} (fig; ‖ קָשַׁר)

†מַעֲדַנּוֹת **n.f.pl. bonds, bands;** so appar. הַתְקַשֵּׁר מ׳ כִּימָה Jb 38^{31} (by metath. or err from √ענד, v. Di Bu)—1 S 15^{32} v. מ׳ p 588 supr.

I **עָנָה** ^{316} **vb. answer, respond** (NH *id.,* *respond, make response;* 𝔗 עֲנָא, Syr. ܥܢܐ; OAram. Palm ענה, cf Ar عنى, عَنَا *intend* by saying);—**Qal** *Pf* 3 ms ע׳ Mi 6^{5}+, sf עָנָנִי 1 S 28^{15}+, עָנָךְ Is 30^{19} Je 23^{37}, עָנָהוּ 1 S 9^{17}+; 1 s עָנִיתִי Ho 14^{9}, etc; *Impf* 3 ms. יַעֲנֶה Gn 41^{16}+, וַיַּעַן Am 7^{14}+, sf. יַעֲנֵנִי Jb 20^{3}+, etc, *Imv.* עֲנֵה Mi 6^{3} Pr 26^{5} etc; *Inf. cstr* עֲנוֹת Gn 45^{3}+ [2 S 22^{36} v. עָנָוָה], *Pt* עֹנֶה Ju 19^{28}+, etc.;—**1.** *answer, respond to* sthg said, actual or implied, Ju 8^{8} 1 S 4^{20} Jb 9^{15}+, esp **a.** of men, c. acc. pers Gn 45^{3} (E), Ju 5^{29} 2 K 18^{36} = Is 36^{21} Jb 5^{1} + very oft. (c 110 t), specif. *be responsive,* i.e. *answer kindly,* grant request 1 K 12^{7} (sf. pers.); = *be amenable, docile* (toward י׳) Ho 2^{17} (of Isr. in fig.); seldom and late, c. acc. of thing replied to, Jb 32^{12} 33^{13} (De Di Bu), 40^{2}. **b.** of God answering (graciously). usu. c. acc pers.; by oracle 1 S 14^{37} $28^{6\ 15}$+, fig. Hb 2^{11}; by deed 1 S 7^{9} 1 K $18^{37\ 37}$, cf. בָּאֵשׁ v^{24} 1 Ch 21^{26}, and esp. Ho $2^{23.24}$ 14^{9}, v also Mi 3^{4} Is 41^{17} 49^{8} Je 33^{3} Jb 12^{4}+, esp ψψ, e g 3^{5} 4^{2} 20^{2}+33 t, etc (in all c. 77 t). **c.** rarely c acc, or cl, of answer: אלהים יַעֲ׳ אֶת־שְׁלוֹם פַּרְעֹה Gn 41^{16}, Jb 15^{2} Pr 18^{23}; Ne 8^{6} they *responded, Amen!* 2 S 19^{43} *they made reply against* Isr (c. עַל *against,* only here), + quoted answer, c. acc pers. + answer 1 S 20^{28} *Jonathan answered Saul, David asked leave,* etc., c. 2 acc. (c. 20 t.) 2 K 18^{36} = Is 36^{21}, Jb 23^{5}+; so = *grant, vouchsafe to,* נוֹרָאוֹת תַּעֲנֵנוּ ψ 65^{6} *terrible things dost thou* [י׳] *vouchsafe to us.* **d.** oft. + אָמַר Gn 18^{27} Abr *answered and said,* Ex 4^{1} (J), 19^{8} (E), Jb 4^{1} 6^{1} etc.; + אָמַר אֶל־ Gn 27^{39}+16 t.; + א׳ לְ v^{37}+8 t; ע׳ + acc. pers. + אמר, 1 S 9^{8} *he answered Saul and said,* + 23 t. (in all c. 130 t.); seldom + לֵאמֹר + Nu 32^{31} (P),

ע׳ + acc. pers. + לא׳ Gn 23⁶ ¹⁰·¹⁴ (P), 41¹⁶ 42²² (E), Jos 1¹⁶ (D) †. **e.** seldom + דבר Jos 22²¹ (P), 2 K 1¹⁰ ¹¹ ¹²; ע׳ + acc. pers. + ד׳ Gn 34¹³ (P). **2. a.** *respond* to an occasion, speak in view of circumstances: 1 S 9¹⁷ (acc. pers. + quot.), Ju 18¹⁴ (+ אָמַר), Nu 11²⁸ (JE, + *id.*), 2 K 1¹¹ (+ *id.*), + 19 t. **b.** fig. יַעֲנֶה אֶת־הַכֹּל Ec 10¹⁹ money *meets all demands.* **†3. a.** specif. *respond* as a witness, *testify*, so perh. pt עֹנֶה (abs.) Mal 2¹² (in good sense), c. בְּ pers. = *in the case of* = *for* Gn 30³³; usu. *against*, 1 S 12³ 2 S 1¹⁶ Is 3⁹ 59¹² Mi 6³ Je 14⁷ Nu 35³⁰ (P), Ru 1²¹ (> Be *be occupied with*, II. ענה; Vrss Luth Kit^Kau ענה *humiliate*); c. בְּפָנָיו Ho 5⁵ 7¹⁰ Jb 16⁸, c. לְפָנָיו Dt 31²¹ (+ לְעֵד *as witness*); c. בְּ pers. + acc. of charge, סָרָה 19¹⁶, of false witness עֵד־שֶׁקֶר v¹⁸, שֶׁקֶר Ex 20¹⁶ (Ginsb v¹³), ‖ Dt 5¹⁷, Pr 25¹⁸. abs. (bad implic.) Ex 23² (E, עַל *concerning*) **b.** less oft. *make response* as one accused (*respondent*) Jb 9¹⁴ ¹⁵. **†Niph. 1.** *make answer*, subj ׳י, c. לְ pers., *Pf.* 1 s. נַעֲנֵיתִי Ez 14⁴; *Pt.* נַעֲנֶה v⁷ (**Qal** not in Ez). **2.** *be answered*: *Impf.* 3 ms. יֵעָנֶה, **a.** Jb 11² (subj. words) **b.** of man = *receive answer* Pr 21¹³, so 1 s. אֵעָנֶה Jb 19⁷. **†Hiph.** *Pt.* מַעֲנֶה בשמחת לבו Ec 5¹⁹, wholly dub.; Hi (God) *causes* (all things) *to respond in the joy of his heart*; De *answers to the joy*, etc; de Jong Wild *occupies him* (II. עָנָה) *with the joy*, etc.

†[עֹנָה] **n.f.** cohabitation (NH עוֹנָה *time*, also = BH; poss *response* or *correspondence*, *commerce*, from above √; or else euphemist., specific *time*, SS (cf Ba^ES17, from √أنى), Thes from עון *dwell*),—sf. עֹנָתָהּ Ex 21¹⁰ (E) i.e. her marriage rights—Ho 10¹⁰ v. עָוֹן.

עֵת ²⁹⁷ **n.f.** ^Am 5.13 and (seldom, mostly late) **m.** ^Ezr 10.14 **time** (NH *id*, Ph עת; As. *inu*, *ittu*, *time*; Talm. עִנְתָּא; clearly fr. a √ענה, but doubtful whether I. ע׳);—abs. ע׳ Ho 10¹² +, cstr. ע׳ Gn 24¹¹ +, עֶת־ Lv 15²⁵ + 5 t.; sf. עִתּוֹ Ho 2¹¹ +, etc.; pl, late, עִתִּים 1 Ch 12³² +, sf. עִתֶּיךָ Is 33⁶; עִתּוֹת ψ 9¹⁰ 10¹, sf עִתֹּתַי 31¹⁶;—ע׳ only twice P, once H;—**1.** *time* of an event, etc.: **a.** usu. (213 t.) c. prep.: c. בְּ (142 t.), esp בָּע׳ הַהוּא Gn 21²² (E) *in that time*, 38¹ (J), Nu 22⁴ (E), Dt 1⁹ + 14 t. Dt; בָּע׳ הַהִיא Jos 5² Am 5¹³ Dn 12¹¹ + (69 t., not in P); בָּע׳ הַזֹּאת Est 4¹⁴, בְּעִתִּים הָהֵם 2 Ch 15⁵ Dn 11¹⁴; בְּכָל־עֵת *at all times* Ex 18²² ²⁶ (E), Lv 16² (P) ψ 34² +, = *continually* Pr 8³⁰, בְּכָל־עֵת אֲשֶׁר Est 5¹³ *as long as* I see Mordecai; c. לְ (31 t.; cf לְ **6**, p 516 supr.), 2 S 11¹ + *at the time*, but Ez 12²⁷ *for distant times*, cf. לָעֵת כָּזֹאת Est 4¹⁴, etc; c. כְּ (21 t.; cf. כְּ **1 a**, p. 453 supr.), † מָחָר כָּע׳ הַזֹּאת Jos 11⁶ (JE) *tomorrow about this time*, usu. כָּע׳ מָחָר (Ko^Synt. 401 e) Ex 9¹⁸ (J), 1 S 9¹⁶ (cf. Dr), 20¹² 1 K 19² 20⁶ 2 K 7¹ ¹⁸ 10⁶ †; כָּעֵת חַיָּה v. p. 312; † כָּעֵת הָרִאשׁוֹן Is 8²³ *at the former time*; כָּעֵת alone Nu 23²³ (JE) *at this time* = *now* (prob., cf. Di), Ju 13²³ 21²² †, etc.; c. מִן (8 t.), מִן הָעֵת הַהִיא Ne 13²¹, etc.; c. עַד (12 t.), מֵעֵת עַד־עֵת עַד־הָע׳ הַהִיא Ne 6¹ *up to that time*, Ez 4¹⁰ ¹¹, etc (5 t. Dn); c. אֶל־, מֵעֵת אֶל־עֵת 1 Ch 9²⁵. **b.** oft. cstr. defined by n. foll.: בְּעֵת צָהֳרַיִם Je 20¹⁶, לְעֵת (הָ)עֶרֶב 2 S 11² Gn 8¹¹ 24¹¹ (both J), Is 17¹⁴ Zc 14⁷, עַד־עֵת הָעֶרֶב Jos 8²⁹ (JE), כְּעֵת מִנְחָה Dn 9²¹, redundantly לְעֵת־יוֹם בְּיוֹם 1 Ch 12²², ע׳ זִקְנָה עֶרֶב Je 50¹⁶ 51³³, ע׳ הַזָּמִיר Ct 2¹², ע׳ (הַ)קָּצִיר לְע׳ פָּנֶיךָ Je 18²³ = 1 K 11⁴ 15²³ ψ 71⁹, בְּע׳ אָסְפְּךָ ψ 21¹⁰ (of anger), לְעִתּוֹת בַּצָּרָה 9¹⁰ 10¹ *at times of destitution* (v. בַּצָּרָה), etc. **c.** sq. inf לְע׳ בּוֹא הַשֶּׁמֶשׁ Jos 10²⁷ (JE), 2 Ch 18³⁴, בְּע׳ קָרְאָם Je 11¹⁴ (rd בְּעֵת also v^b, Gie), etc. **d.** sq. cl. c. vb. fin. (poet. or late) Dt 32³⁵ Jb 6¹⁷ 2 Ch 20²² 24¹¹ 29²⁷ + (cf. **2 c**). **2. a.** = *usual time*: לְע׳ צֵאת 2 S 11¹ *at the time of* kings' *going forth* = 1 Ch 20¹; בְּעֵת יַחֵם Gn 31¹⁰; עֵת לֶדֶת Jb 39¹·². **b.** *proper*, *suitable time*: rain בְּעִתּוֹ Dt 11¹⁴ Je 5²⁴ +, cf. Lv 26⁴ (H), also ψ 1³ 104²⁷ 145¹⁵ Pr 15²³ Is 60²² Ec 3¹¹; הַעֵת לָקַחַת, ע׳ שָׁלוֹם v⁸, עֵת מִלְחָמָה v⁸; sq inf Ho 10¹², 2 K 5²⁶ *is it a time to take money?* Hg 1⁴, עֵת־בֵּית ׳י לְהִבָּנוֹת v² (v⁴ read עֵת בָּא Hi We Now al.); עֵת לַעֲשׂוֹת ψ 119¹²⁶, cf. Ec 3²⁻⁸ (26 t.); abs כִּי עֵת Ho 13¹³ (Hi We al; Gu^Kau gives עֵת, > Now כָּעֵת); abs c. neg. Jb 22¹⁶ Ec 7¹⁷; hence (late) יוֹדְעֵי בִינָה לָעִתִּים 1 Ch 12³³, יֹדְעֵי הָעִתִּים Est 1¹³ i.e. astrologers, etc. **c.** *appointed time*, בְּעֵת תֵּת וגו׳ 1 S 18¹⁹ *at the appointed time of giving*, Ez 7⁷ ¹² Is 13²², ע׳ פְּקֻדָּתָם Je 8¹² 10¹⁵ = 51¹⁸, 46²¹ 50²⁷ cf. (c. vb fin.) 6¹⁵ 49⁸ 50³¹, ע׳ אַרְצוֹ Je 27⁷, ע׳ גּוֹיִם Ez 30³, לְעִתִּים מְזֻמָּנִים Ezr 10¹⁴ Ne 10³⁵ cf 13³¹; עַד־ע׳ מוֹעֵד 2 S 24¹⁵, ψ 103¹⁴ (‖ מוֹעֵד), etc.; cf עֵת וּמִשְׁפָּט Ec 8⁵·⁶ (for *time of judgment*), עִתּוֹ 9¹²; esp. לְעֵת קֵץ Dn 8¹⁷ cf. 11³⁵ ⁴⁰ 12⁴·⁹, בְּע׳ עֲוֹן קֵץ Ez 21³⁰·³⁴ cf. 35⁵, לְקֵץ הָעִתִּים Dn 11¹³. **d.** as uncertain עֵת וָפֶגַע Ec 9¹¹. **3.** = *experiences, fortunes*, pl אֱמוּנַת עִתֶּיךָ Is 33⁶, ψ 31¹⁶; הָעִתִּים אֲשֶׁר עָבְרוּ עָלָיו 1 Ch 29³⁰. **†4.** *occurrence, occasion* (= פַּעַם), רַבּוֹת עִתִּים Ne 9²⁸ *great numbers of times* (= very often).

†[עֵת] קָצִין **n.pr.loc.** on border of Zebulun, only c. ה loc., עִתָּה ק׳ Jos 19¹³; site unknown.

עַתָּה ⁴³⁵ (also Ez 23⁴³ ψ 74⁶ עת Kt, Qr עַתָּה), **עָתָּה** Gn 32⁵ +, **adv.** of time, now (prop. acc.

of [ʿint], עת (Ko$^{ii\ 260}$), *at the time*, in partic of the present time, i e *now*, cf Germ *zur Zeit*, Ar. اَلْآنَ *at the time*, i e *now*),—*now* · **1. a.** Gn 12^{19} ועתה הנה אשתך and *now*, behold thy wife, 22^{12} כי עתה ידעתי *now* I know (so Ex 18^{11} Ju 17^{13} 1 K 17^{24} [עַתָּה זה], ψ 20^{7}), 26$^{22.29}$ 27^{36} 31$^{13.28}$, etc, Ex 5^{5} הן רבים עתה עם הארץ; whether in opp to past time, as Gn 32^{11} Jos 14^{11} כְּכֹחִי אָז וּכְכֹחִי עָתָּה, Ju 11^{8} 1 K 12^{4} Is 1^{21} ועתה מרצחים, 16^{14} Ho 2^{9} כי טוב לי אָז מֵעָתָּה, 13^{2}, Jb 30^{1}+, or to future, as Nu 24^{17} אֶרְאֶנּוּ ולא עתה, Ju 8^{6} הֲכַף ... עַתָּה־בְיָדֶךָ זבח וג׳, 1 S 2^{16} כי עַתָּה תתן; = *after all* Nu 22^{38} Ju 8^{2}, = *now at last* 2 S 24^{16} 1 K 19^{4} 2 K 19^{25} Ho 7^{2} Je 4^{12}, and in the phr. מעתה ועד עולם †Is 9^{6} 59^{21} Mi 4^{7} (v. infr), ψ 113^{2} 115^{18} 121^{8} 125^{2} 131^{3} **b.** of the imminent or impending future Gn 19^{9} עַתָּה נָרַע לְךָ מֵהֶם, 29^{32} כי עתה יאהבני אישי, v^{34} Ex 6^{1} עתה תראה, Nu 11^{23} 22^{4} 2 S 20^{6} Is 33^{10} (ψ 12^{6}), 43^{19} 49^{19} Am 6^{7} לכן עתה יִגְלוּ, Is 49^{19} Mi 7$^{4.10}$ Dn 10^{20}, and esp *ἀσυνδέτως* in Hos, introducing a punishment, Ho 4^{16} 5^{7} 8$^{8.13}$ עתה ירעם י׳ וגו׳ (Je 14^{10}), 10^{2} **c.** of a time *ideally* present (= *then*, from our point of view) Is 29^{22} לא עתה יבוש יעקב, v^{b} Ho 10^{3} Mi 4$^{9.10.11.14}$ 5^{3} **d.** describing a present state = *as things are* 1 S 8^{5} thou art old, etc, עתה שִׂימָה לנו מלך, 9^{6} 13^{12} 14^{30} 25^{7b} 27^{1} *now* I shall be swept away one day, etc, 2 K 18$^{20.25}$ Jb 6^{21} 14^{16} 16^{7} **e.** with an Imv, as an encouragement, implying that the time has come for the exhortation or advice to be followed, Gn 31^{13} עתה קום צא, Ex 18^{19} עתה שְׁמַע בקולי, Nu 22^{11} Dt 2^{13} Is 30^{8}.

2. Phrases **a.** עַתָּה זה (זה **4 h**) † 1 K 17^{24} 2 K 5^{22}. **b.** ועתה and, *now*, or *now*, therefore (ו **4**), drawing a conclusion, esp (cf **1 e**) a practical one, from what has been stated. Gn 3^{22} *and now* (since man has once been disobedient), lest he put forth his hand, etc, 20$^{7.23}$ וְעַתָּה הִשָּׁבְעָה לִי הֵנָּה, 27$^{3.8}$ ועתה בני שמע בקולי, 30^{30} 31$^{16.44}$ 37^{20}+oft, Is 5$^{3.5}$ 36^{8} ψ 2^{10}, Gn 11^{6} ועתה לא־יִבָּצֵר מהם וגו׳, 31^{30} 45^{8} 2 S 19^{11} ψ 39^{8} ועתה מַה־קִּוִּיתִי אֲדֹנָי, Is 52^{5} **c.** ועתה הנה stating the ground on which some conclusion or action is to be based, Ex 3^{9} Jo 14$^{10.10}$ 1 S 12^{2} 24^{21} 1 K 1^{18} Je 40^{4} (with ועתה usu repeated after the הנה-clause) †**d.** גם עתה Gn 44^{10} 1 S 12^{16} 1 K 14^{14} Jo 2^{12} Jb 16^{19}. †**e.** מֵעַתָּה *from now, henceforth*, Je 3^{4} Is 48^{6} Dn 10^{17} (acc to some, here = from *just now*), 2 Ch 16^{9}, מעתה ועד עולם, v supr **1 a** *end* **f.** עַד־עַתָּה *until now*, Gn 32^{5} וָאֵחַר עַד־ע׳, Dt 12^{9} לא באתם עד ע׳ אל הנחלה (opp to the fut), 2 K 13^{23}, esp. after clause with מִן, 46^{34} מִנְּעוּרֵינוּ וְעַד־ע׳ (2 S 19^{8} Ez 4^{14}), Ex 9^{18} 2 K 8^{6} Ru 2^{7} **g.** כי עַתָּה *for in this case*, in our idiom, *for then* (עתה pointing to a condition assumed as a possible contingency, cf Dr$^{\S 141,142}$), †(*a*) Ex 9^{15} כי עתה שלחתי וגו׳ for *then* (if the intention expressed in v^{14} had not existed) *I should have* put forth my hand, etc, Nu 22^{29} כי עתה הֲרַגְתִּיךְ, 1 S 13^{13} Jb 3^{13}; sq impf Jb 6^{3} for *then* (if it were weighed, v^{2}) it would be heavier, etc, 13^{19} *for then* would I be silent and die; (*b*) after a protasis, *surely then* Gn 31^{42}+ (see כי **1 d b**, p 472)—*Note.* Read כְּמוֹ עֵת (𝔊𝔙) *as now*, for כמו עת Ez 16^{57}, עֵת נִשְׁבֶּרֶת (𝔊𝔖𝔙) *now art thou broken!* for עת נשברת Ez 27^{34}, and prob עֵת בָּא (Hi We Ko Now, cf 𝔊𝔖) for עת־בא Hg 1^{2}, also עַתָּה for אַתָּה 1 K 1^{20}, and אַתָּה for עַתָּה v^{18b} 2 S 18^{3}.

†**עַתַּי** **n.pr.m.** (I)εθθει **1.** of Judah 1 Ch 2^{35} (עַתָּי), v^{36}. **2.** of Gad 12^{11}. **3.** 2 Ch 11^{20}

†**עִתִּי** **adj. timely, ready** (Gk. ὡραῖος),—איש ע׳ Lv 16^{21} *a man who is in readiness*

יַעַן$_{96}$ prop **subst., purpose, intention, but** always used as **prep.** or **conj., on account of, because** (for יַעֲנֶה, of the form יִצְהָר, etc, Sta §259 Ko$^{ii\ 403}$, cf عَنَى *mean, intend*)—**1. as prep.,** rarely with a subst, †Ez 5^{9} יַעַן תועבותיכם, Hg 1^{9} יַעַן מֶה, v^{9} יַעַן בֵּיתִי, with a ptcp. Ez 36^{13} יען אמרים *because of men saying* to you (but rd prob אָמְרָם, Co Toy Berthol); freq with inf. c, 1 K 21^{20} יַעַן הִתְמַכֶּרְךָ *on account of* thy having sold thyself, Am 5^{11} Is 30^{12} 37^{29} (= 2 K 19^{28}) יַעַן הִתְרַגֶּזְךָ אֵלַי, Je 5^{14} 7^{13} 23^{38} 48^{7}, and oft (c 18 t) in Ezek, as 5^{7} (rd יַעַן הֲמָרְתְכֶם), 13$^{8.22}$ 25$^{3.6.8.12}$.

2. As **conj** **a.** יַעַן אֲשֶׁר (32 t), usu with pf, as Gn 22^{16} יען אשר עשית זאת *because that* thou hast done this, Dt 1^{36} (Jos 14^{9}), Ju 2^{20} 1 S 30^{22} 1 K 3^{11} 8^{18} Je 19^{4} 25^{8} 29^{23} (not Is)+; with impf. (in frequent. sense) Ez 44^{12} †**b.** יַעַן כִּי, Nu 11^{20} יַעַן כִּי מְאַסְתֶּם אֶת־י׳, 1 K 13^{21} 21^{29} Is 3^{16} 7^{5} 8^{6} 29^{13} **c.** יַעַן alone (23 t), with pf Nu 20^{12} יַעַן לא הֶאֱמַנְתֶּם בי, 1 S 15^{23} 1 K 14^{13} 20^{42} 2 K 22^{19} Ho 8^{1} Is 61^{1} 65^{12} 66^{4}, with impf. (freq) †Ez 34^{21}; of the fut. †Ez 12^{12} *because* he shall not see, etc, (but 𝔊 Co Kau Berthol לְמַעַן אשר לא יִרְאֶה לָעַיִן). usu. the vb follows immediately, but Ezek sometimes puts the obj first for emph, 5^{11} יַעַן אֶת־מִקְדָּשִׁי טִמֵּאת, 20$^{16.24}$ 36^{6}, cf 34^{21}.

†**3.** **יַעַן וּבְיַעַן**, q. d. *because and by the cause* (that), sq. perf., Lv 26[43] (H) יען וביען בְּמִשְׁפָּטַי מָאָסוּ, Ez 13[10]; יַעַן בְּיַעַן sq. inf., Ez 36[3]. (In all, reckoning יען (ו)ביען once each, 93 t., of which 20 are in 1–2 K, 11 in Je, 38 in Ez; and only 9 in Gn–2 S.)

†**מַעֲנֶה** **n.m.**[Pr 15, 1] **answer, response;**—abs. מ׳־רַךְ Pr 15[1] *a gentle answer;* cstr. מַעֲנֵה פִּיו v[23], cf. מ׳ לָשׁוֹן 16[1] (i.e. ability to answer); מ׳ אֱלֹהִים Mi 3[7] i.e. *response* for guidance; abs. also Pr 29[19] *response*=obedience; Jb 32[3.5] *reply,* refutation; sf. לַמַּעֲנֵהוּ 16[4]=for its purpose, that for which it *answers* (v. Toy).

[**מַ֫עַן**] **subst.** purpose, intent, only with לְ, in **לְמַ֫עַן**[271] **prep.** and **conj.** for the sake of, on account of, to the intent or in order that (abbrev. from מַעֲנֶה: cf. מַ֫עַל; Kö[ii. 116]);—with sf. לְמַעַנְךָ, לְמַעֲנִי, and לְמַעַנְכֶם;—**1. prep.**:—**a.** Gn 18[24] wilt thou . . . not spare the place למען חמשים הצדיקים *for the sake of* the 50 righteous? Dt 30[6] לְ׳ חַיֶּיךָ *for thy life's sake,* 1 K 8[41] the foreigner who comes from afar לְ׳ שְׁמֶךָ, Is 43[14] לְמַעַנְכֶם שִׁלַּחְתִּי בָבֶלָה, 45[4] 62[1] 63[17] לְ׳ עבדיך, 65[8] Ez 36[22.22] Jb 18[4] ψ 122[8.9]; לְ׳ ציון; לְמַעַן דָּוִד (עַבְדִּי ד׳), i.e. for the sake of David's memory, and the promises given to him, † 1 K 11[12.13.32.34] 15[4] 2 K 8[19] 19[34] (=Is 37[35]), 20[6] (all D[2]); לְמַעֲנִי (of י׳) *for my own sake,* i.e. to vindicate my name, † 2 K 19[34] (=Is 37[35]), 20[6] Is 43[25] 48[11] לְמַעֲנִי לְמַעֲנִי אֶעֱשֶׂה, so לְמַעַנְךָ Dn 9[19], לְ׳ אֲדֹנָי v[17]; י׳ is said (or entreated) to act לְמַעַן שְׁמוֹ (שְׁמִי, שִׁמְךָ), i.e. to maintain his reputation, or character, †ψ 23[3] 25[11] 31[4] 79[9] 106[8] 109[21] 143[11] Je 14[7.21] Ez 20[9.14.22.44] Is 48[9]; simil. לְ׳ חַסְדֶּךָ (i.e. to maintain it consistently) †ψ 6[5] 44[27], לְ׳ טוּבְךָ + 25[7], לְ׳ צִדְקוֹ †Is 42[21].

b. *In view of, on account of* (but not expressing causation distinctly, like מִן **2 f,** or מִפְּנֵי), Dt 3[26] ויתעבר י׳ בי לְמַעַנְכֶם *on your account,* 1 K 11[39] לְ׳ זאת *in view of this,* לְ׳ שׁוֹרְרָי *on account of* my watchful foes, †ψ 5[9] 27[11], לְ׳ צוררים ψ 8[3], simil. 69[19]; 48[12] (97[8]) ישמח הר ציון . . . לְ׳ משפטיך *in view of* thy judgments.

c. Sq. inf. Gn 18[19] לְמַעַן הָבִיא י׳ *for the purpose of* J.'s bringing=*to the intent that* J. *might* bring, 37[22] לְ׳ הַצִּיל *in order to* rescue, 50[20] Ex 1[11] 9[16] 10[1], etc., Dt 2[30] 6[23], etc., 2 K 10[19], Je 7[10.18] 11[5] 50[34] (on הִרְגִּיעַ, v. עַד **2 a** *b*), Ez 14[5] 21[15] 22[6], etc., 36[5] (v. p. 176), + oft. (Kö[iii. 585 f.]). Once, pleon., לְמַעַן לָמוּג לֵב Ez 21[20] (cf. בַּעֲבוּר לְ 1 Ch 19[3]; but rd. prob. הָמוֹג).

2. Conj. (sq. impf.):—**a.** לְמַעַן אֲשֶׁר Gn 18[19] I have known him לְ׳ אשר יְצַוֶּה *to the end that* he might command, etc., Dt 27[3] Jos 3[4] 2 S 13[5] Je 42[6]; more oft. **b.** without אשר, as Gn 12[13] לְמַעַן יִיטַב לִי, 27[25] Ex 4[5] לְ׳ יאמינו, 8[6.18] 9[29] 10[2] Is 5[19] 23[16] ψ 9[15] 30[13] 48[14] + oft. (Kö[iii. 571]).

c. Sq. לֹא: (*a*) לְ׳ אשר לא †Nu 17[5] Dt 20[18] Ez 31[14] 36[30] 46[18]; (*b*) לְ׳ לֹא †Ez 14[11] 19[9] 25[10] 26[20] Zech 12[7] ψ 119[11.80] 125[3] (Kö[iii. 574]. Less common than לְבִלְתִּי or מִן with inf., or פֶּן־).

Note 1.—לְמַעַן is always *in order that,* never merely *so that* (ἐκβατικῶς); but sts., in rhetorical passages, the issue of a line of action, though really undesigned, is represented by it ironically as if it were designed: Dt 29[18] (v. Dr) וְהִתְבָּרֵךְ בִּלְבָבוֹ . . . לְ׳ סְפוֹת וגו׳ and he congratulate himself . . . *in order to* sweep away the moistened with the dry (i.e. to destroy all together), Is 30[1] 44[9] בל יראו ובל ידעו לְ׳ יֵבֹשׁוּ *in order that they may be* put to shame, Je 7[18] 27[10.15] 32[29] Ho 8[4] לְ׳ בֹּשֶׁת פְּנֵיהֶם v[19], לְ׳ הַכְעִיסֵנִי their silver, etc., they have made into idols לְ׳ יִכָּרֵת *in order that* it may be cut off (of course, not the *real* purpose of the idolatry), Am 2[7] Mi 6[16]: cf. ψ 51[6] (v. Comm.) *in order that* thou mightest be just when thou judgest (*sc.* by manifesting thy justice in judgment on my sin). Cf. لِ Qor 28[7] (Fl[Kl. Schr. i. 397 f.]).

Note 2.—In Jos 4[24] for the anom. לְ׳ יְרָאתֶם, rd. inf. לְ׳ יִרְאָתָם *in order that they* might fear (Dr[§ 14 Obs.]): Neh 6[13] לְמַעַן שָׂכוּר הוּא לְמַעַן אִירָא (si vera l.) the first לְ׳ points forwards, *to this intent* was he hired, *to the intent that* I should be afraid.—On Pr 16[4], v. מַעֲנֶה.

†II. [**עָנָה**] **vb. be occupied, busied with** (ב), only Ec (perh. Aram. loan-word; Syr. ܥܢܐ *be occupied with,* ܥܢܝܢܐ *occupation, affair;* cf. Ar. عنى, عَنَا *concern one,* also *be occupied* by; Ecclus 42[8 marg.]);—**Qal** *Inf.* עֲנוֹת Ec 1[13] 3[10].

†**עִנְיָן** **n.m.**[Ec 1, 13] **occupation, task,** only Ec (Aram. loan-word Lag[BN 205]; common in NH);—ע׳ abs. Ec 2[26] 3[10] 5[2] 8[16]; sf. כַּעַס עִנְיָנוֹ 2[23] *his task is* (sheer) *vexation;* עִנְיַן רָע 1[13] *an evil* (worthless) *task,* so 4[8] (Mass. עִנְיַן as if cstr., v. Baer[1, 13] but Kö[ii. 1, 99]), and, in weakened sense, 5[13] *a bad business, bad affair.*

†**מַעֲנָה** **n.f. place for task** (?), **specif. field for ploughing**,—pl. sf לְמַעֲנוֹתָם ψ 129^{3} Kt *they have extended their ploughing-grounds* (Qr מַעֲנִיתָם), sg מַעֲנָה only 1 S 14^{14}, where text corrupt and meaning dub. v. Comm

מַעֲנִית ψ 129^{3} Qr v foregoing

†III. [**עָנָה**] **vb be bowed down, afflicted** (NH *id*, MI Pi ויענו l^{5}, אענו l^{6}, As *enû*, *thwart, frustrate, do violence to*, Ar. عَنَا, عنو, *be lowly, submissive*, v Rahlfs עָנִי und עָנָו in d Psalmen (1892), 67 ff, 𝔗 עַנִּי Pa *oppress;* Syr Ethpe *humble oneself*, and deriv);—**Qal** *Pf* 1 s עָנִיתִי ψ 116^{10}, *Impf* 3 ms יַעֲנֶה Is 25^{5} 31^{4}, etc;—**1.** *be put down* or *become low*, of song of triumph Is 25^{5} (others as **Hiph.** *he putteth down*, ‖ תַּכְנִיעַ) **2.** *be depressed, downcast* Is 31^{4} (of lion, ‖ יֵחָת). **3.** *be afflicted* ψ 116^{10} 119^{67} Zc 10^{2} **Niph.** *Pf* 1 s נַעֲנֵיתִי ψ 119^{107}, *Inf cstr* לַעֲנֹת (perh. rd. as Qal Ges$^{§ 51 l}$) Ex 10^{3}, *Pt* נַעֲנֶה Is 53^{7}, fs נַעֲנָה 58^{10},—**1.** *humble oneself* מִפְּנֵי Ex 10^{3} **2.** *be afflicted* ψ 119^{107} Is 53^{7} 58^{10} **Piel.** *Pf* 3 ms עִנָּה Dt 22^{24} + 5 t; 2 ms עִנִּיתָ ψ 88^{8}, 1 s עִנֵּיתִי ψ 35^{13}, sf. וְעִנִּתְךָ consec Na 1^{12}, etc; *Impf.* יְעַנֶּה Jb 37^{23}, etc.; *Imv* עַנּוּ Ju 19^{24}, *Inf. abs* עַנֵּה Ex 22^{22}, *cstr.* עַנּוֹת Is 58^{5}+, etc; *Pt* pl sf מְעַנַּיִךְ Is 60^{14} Zp 3^{19},—**1.** *humble, mishandle, afflict*: individual Gn 16^{6} 31^{50} (J) Ex 22$^{21.22.22}$ (E) Jb 30^{11}; by imprisonment and bonds Ju 16$^{5.6.19}$ ψ 105^{18}; a nation by war or in bondage Gn 15^{13} (J) Ex 1$^{11.12}$ Nu 24$^{24.24}$ (E) Dt 26^{6} 1 S 12^{8} (inserting וַיְעַנּוּם מִצְרַיִם, so 𝔊 Dr Bu Kit HPS [cf Th We]), 2 S 7^{10} 2 K 17^{20} ψ 94^{5} Is 60^{14} Zp 3^{19}, dynasty of David ψ 89^{23}. **2.** *humble*, a woman by cohabit, Gn 34^{2} (J) Dt 21^{14} 22$^{24.29}$ Ju 19^{24} 20^{5} 2 S 13$^{12.14.22.32}$ Ez 22$^{10.11}$ La 5^{11} **3.** *afflict* as a discipline (God agent) Dt 8$^{2.3.16}$ 1 K 11^{39} ψ 88^{8} 90^{15} 119^{75} Is 64^{11} Na 1$^{12.12}$ La 3^{33}. **4.** *humble, weaken*, obj כֹּחַ ψ 102^{24}, מִשְׁפָּט Jb 37^{23} (cf. Talm. עִנָּה דִין), נֶפֶשׁ *oneself*, by fasting Lv 16$^{29.31}$ 23$^{27.32}$ Nu 29^{7} (P) ψ 35^{13} Is 58$^{3.5}$; by an oath Nu 30^{14} (P) **Pu** *Pf* 1 s עֻנֵּיתִי ψ 119^{71}; *Impf* 3 fs. תְּעֻנֶּה Lv 23^{29}, *Inf cstr* sf עֻנּוֹתוֹ ψ 132^{1}; *Pt.* מְעֻנֶּה Is 53^{4};—**1.** *be afflicted*, in discipline by God ψ 119^{71} 132^{1} Is 53^{4} **2.** *be humbled* by fasting Lv 23^{29} (P). **Hiph.** *Impf* 2 ms. sf תַּעֲנֵם 1 K 8^{35} = 2 Ch 6^{26} *afflict*, in discipline. **Hithp.** *Pf.* 3 ms הִתְעַנָּה 1 K 2^{26}, 2 ms הִתְעַנִּיתָ v^{26}, *Impf.* 3 mpl יִתְעַנּוּ ψ 107^{17}, *Imv* הִתְעַנִּי Gn 16^{9}, *Inf. cstr* הִתְעַנּוֹת Ez 8^{21} Dn 10^{12},—**1.** *humble oneself* (c תַּחַת יָדֶיהָ) Gn 16^{9} (J) **2.** *be afflicted*, by men 1 K 2$^{26.26}$, by God in discipline ψ 107^{17}. **3.** *humble oneself* in fasting Ezr 8^{21} Dn 10^{12}.

†**עָנָו** (?, Lag$^{BN 48}$) **n.m. poor, afflicted, humble, meek**,—עָנָו Nu 12^{3} (Kt; Qr עָנָיו is to ensure the ָ acc. to Di Ko$^{ii. 1 76}$), elsewh pl. עֲנָוִים Is 29^{19} + 11 t. + Kt עֲנָוִים Is 32^{7} ψ 9^{19} (Qr עֲנִיִּים); Qr עֲנָוִים ψ 9^{13} 10^{12} Pr 3^{34} 14^{21} 16^{19} (Kt עניים), cstr. עַנְוֵי Zp 2^{3} + 2 t, + Kt ענוי (Qr עֲנִיֵּי) Am 8^{4} (so Jb 24^{4} van d H.; but עֲנִיֵּי Kt and Qr Baer Ginsb)—these forms shew confusion with עָנִי, which is perh only another form of עָנָו (otherwise Rahlfs$^{op cit. 62 f.}$ Dr$^{'Poor'}$ in Hastings^{DB}, עָנָו = *humble, meek*, עָנִי = pass. *humbled, afflicted*);—**1.** *poor, needy* Pr 14^{21} (Qr). **2.** *poor and weak*, oppressed by rich and powerful Am 2^{7} Is 29^{19} 32^{7} (Kt), ענוי (ה)ארץ ψ 76^{10} Is 11^{4} Zp 2^{3} Am 8^{4} (Kt), Jb 24^{4}. **3.** *poor, weak and afflicted* Israel (usu. rendered *meek*) ψ 10^{17} 22^{27} 25$^{9.9}$ 34^{3} 37^{11} 69^{33} (עני **3**, also in all these ψψ), 147^{6} 149^{4} Is 61^{1} (‖ נשברי לב, cf. 66^{2} עני **3**), ψ 9^{19} (Kt) v^{13} 10^{12} (Qr). **4.** *humble, lowly, meek* Nu 12^{3} (Moses); Pr 3^{34} 16^{19} (both Qr)

†**עֲנָוָה** **n.f. humility**;—ע׳ Pr 15^{33} + 3 t; עַנְוָה־ (contr. because of Maqqeph, see Br^{MP}) ψ 45^{5}, עַנְוַתְךָ ψ 18^{36} (= עֲנֹתְךָ 2 S 22^{36} v. I ענה; rd עֶזְרָתְךָ Ol We),—**1.** *humility, meekness* ψ 45^{5} (dub), Pr 15^{33} 18^{12} 22^{4} Zp 2^{3} (prob gloss, v. We Now). **2.** *condescension* ψ 18^{36} (dub, v. supr).

†**עֱנוּת** **n.f. affliction**,—ψ 22^{25}; Che$^{JBL xv (1896), 198}$ prop. צַעֲקַת *cry* [cf. 𝔊𝔙𝔗], (צ dropped out after ץ).

†**עָנִי** **adj. poor, afflicted, humble**;—ע׳ Dt 24^{12} + 51 t.; pl. עֲנִיִּים Is 3^{15} + 6 t., cstr. עֲנִיֵּי Is 10^{2} + 4 t (v. also Kt and Qr sub עָנָו supr.); sf. עֲנִיֶּיךָ ψ 72^{2} 74^{19}, עֲנִיֶּךָ Dt 15^{11}, עֲנִיָּו Is 49^{13}; fs. עֲנִיָּה Is 51^{21} 54^{11} (+ Is 10^{30} MT, but rd. עֲנִיהָ, v. I. ענה),—**1.** *poor, needy*, ‖ אביון Dt 15^{11} 24$^{14.15}$ Pr 31^{20}, ‖ יתום Jb 24^{9} Ex 22^{24} (E), Dt 24^{12}, having right to gleanings Lv 19^{10} 23^{22} (H); יְמֵי ע׳ Pr 15^{15}, cf Pr 14^{21} (Kt). **2.** *poor and weak*, oppressed by the rich and powerful Is 3$^{14.15}$ 32^{7} (Qr), 58^{7} 29^{12} 36$^{6.15}$ Pr 30^{14} Ec 6^{8} Ez 18^{17} Zc 7^{10} Jb 24^{4}, also Am 8^{4} (Qr), ‖ דל Jb 34^{28} Pr 22^{22}, עֲנִיֵּי עַמִּי Is 10^{2}, עני ואביון Jb 24^{14} Pr 31^{9} Je 22^{16} Ez 16^{49} 18^{12} 22^{29}. **3.** *poor, weak, afflicted* Israel, or *pious* in Israel *afflicted* by wicked nations or the wicked in Israel itself ψ 10$^{2.9.9}$ 14^{6} (dub, cf. ψ 53^{6}) 102^{1} (or n.pr), Is 14^{32} Hb 3^{14}, of Zion, עֲנִיָּה Is 51^{21} 54^{11}; ψ 12^{6} שֹׁד ע׳, 25^{16} יחיד וע׳, עני ואביון 35^{10} 37^{14} 40^{18} = 70^{6}, 74^{21} 86^{1} 109$^{16.22}$, pl Is 41^{17}; עני וְכוֹאֵב ψ 69^{30}; ע׳ וָרָשׁ 82^{3}; עֲנוֹת ע׳

22[25], ע׳ נֶ־תֶ֫ 88[16], ‖ דל Is 26[6] Zp 3[12]; ע׳ וּגְבַה־רוּחַ Is 66[2];—Zc 11[7 11] v. 11. כְּנַעֲנִי;—God does not forget them ψ 9[13 19] 10[12] (Kt) 74[19], but has compassion on them Is 49[13], saves ψ 34[7], delivers 35[10], and bestows various favours 68[11] 140[13], the king also judges 72[2.4], and delivers 72[12]. **4.** *humble, lowly,* Zc 9[9] (victorious king); opp. לֵצִים Pr 3[34] (Kt); opp. גאים 16[19] (Kt), עם עני opp. עינים רמות ψ 18[28] = 2 S 22[28].

†עֳנִי **n.m.** affliction, poverty;—ע׳ Ex 3[7] +; עָנְיִ Dt 16[3] +, ψ עָוֹנִי 107[41], עוני 2 S 16[12] (Kt, but rd. עָנְיִי; >Qr בעיני(ו)); sf. עָנְיִי Gn 31[42] +, עָנְיֵךְ 16[11], etc.,—**1.** *affliction,* Jb 36[15.21] ψ 44[25] 88[10] 107[41] 119[50.92] La 1[3] 3[19], ארץ ע׳ Gn 41[52] (E); ימי ע׳ Jb 30[16.27] La 1[7], כור ע׳ Is 48[10]; חַבְלֵי ע׳ Jb 36[8]; אֲסִירֵי ע׳ ψ 107[10], בני ע׳ Pr 31[5]; ראה ע׳ Gn 31[42] (E), Ex 3[7] 4[31] (J), Dt 26[7] 2 K 14[26] Ne 9[9] Jb 10[15] ψ 9[14] 25[18] 31[8] 119[153] La 1[9] 3[1], ins also before עמי 1 S 9[16 b] 𝔊 Th We Dr Kit Bu HPS; ראה בע׳ Gn 29[32] (J), 1 S 1[11] 2 S 16[12] (v. supr.); שמע ע׳ Gn 16[11] (J); העלה מע׳ Ex 3[17] (J); לחם עני Dt 16[3]. **2.** *poverty,* בְּעָנְיִי הכינותי זהב 1 Ch 22[14].

†[תַּעֲנִית] **n.f.** humiliation, by fasting (cf. √**Pi. Hithp.**; NH ת׳ = *fasting*), sf. תַּעֲנִיתִי Ezr 9[5].

†IV עָנָה **vb.** sing (Ar غَنَّى *sing, chant,* غِنَآء *singing, chanting,* etc.; Syr. ܥܢܐ *sing responsively,* ܥܘܢܝܬܐ *hymn, refrain;* poss. As. *enû, resound* (?); Egypt. *anni* is loan-word acc. to Bondi[80]);—**Qal** *Pf* 3 ms. וְעָנוּ consec. Je 51[14]; *Impf.* 3 ms. יַעֲנֶה Je 25[30], 3 fs. וַתַּעַן Ex 15[21]; 3 fpl. וַתַּעֲנֶינָה 1 S 18[7], etc., *Imv.* ענו Nu 21[17] ψ 147[7]; *Inf. cstr.* עֲנוֹת Ex 32[18.18];—*sing, utter tunefully,* Ex 15[21] (E) *and Miriam sang to* (ל) *them;* of uttering shout (הידד), as in vintage Je 25[30] (subj. ע׳, + אֶל־ pers), in attack 51[14] (+ עַל־ pers); (חֲלוּשָׁה) קול עֲנוֹת גבורה Ex 32[18.18] (E); c. ל rei vel pers. laudat. Nu 21[17] (JE; well); ψ 147[7] (ל; ‖ זַמְּרוּ), Ezr 3[11]; + אָמַר 1 S 18[7] *the women sang, and said;* יַעֲנוּ בַמְּחֹלוֹת לֵאמֹר 21[12] 29[5]; c acc. rei laudat. ψ 119[172] (cf. ‖ v[171])—Is 14[22] v. עַן. **Pi.** intens: *Imv* ענו־לָהּ Is 27[2] *sing sweetly of it; Inf.* קול עַנּוֹת Ex 32[18] (E) *the sound of distinct singing;* cf. לְעַנּוֹת ψ 88[1].

עֲנָה [12] **n.pr.m.** Horites:—**1.** Gn 36[2] (read הַחֹרִי for הַחִוִּי v. Di) v[14.18.20.25.25.29] = 1 Ch 1[38.41] **2.** ('nephew' of **1**) Gn 36[24.24] = 1 Ch 1[40].—Ανα, A(ι)να(ν) (cf. n pr m. עַן, Safa, Hal[JAs 7. x 374]).

ענו Kt v. עָנִי. ענוק v. I. עֲנָק.

ענז (√ of foll.; Ko[ii. 1, 38] cp. Ar. عَنَزَ *turn aside,* whence [fr. movements] عَنْزٌ *goat,* cf. As. *enzu;* Syr. ܥܙܐ, cstr ܥܙܬ; also ܥܙܝܐ; ܥܙܝܝܐ *goat-herd;* Ph Palm. עז; NH עז (rare)).

עֵז [74] **n.f.** [Gn 15, 9] she-goat;—abs. ע׳ Gn 15[9] + 6 t.; pl עִזִּים 27[9] + 65 t.; sf. עִזֶּיךָ 31[38];—†**1.** as property Gn 30[32.33.35] (J), 31[15.38] (E), 1 S 25[2]. **2.** as food: גְּדִיֵי (גדי) עִזִּים *kid(s) of she-goats* Gn 27[9.16] (J) + 7 t., שְׂעִיר עִזִּים 37[31] (J) *a buck of goats, he-goat,* שֵׂה עִזִּים Dt 14[4] *a(n individual) goat;* cf. Lv 7[23] (P; fat forbidden); also חֲלֵב ע׳ Pr 27[27] *goats' milk.* **3.** as sacrificial victim, chiefly P: **a.** in gen. Lv 22[27] (H), Nu 15[11]. †**b.** in ברית Gn 15[9] (JE; cf. v[18]). †**c.** פֶּסַח Ex 12[5] (שֶׂה), בְּנֵי עִזִּים 2 Ch 35[7]. †**d.** עֹלָה Lv 22[19] (H), 1[10] Nu 28[30] (שְׂעִיר ע׳). †**e.** זֶבַח שְׁלָמִים Lv 3[12] 17[3] (H; cf. v[5]), אִשֶּׁה Nu 18[17] (בְּכוֹר ע׳). **f.** חַטָּאת, שְׂעִיר ע׳ Ez 43[22] 45[23] Lv 4[23] + 3 t Lv, Nu 7[16] + 19 t. Nu; שְׂעִירַת עִזִּים *a single she-goat* Lv 4[28] 5[6]; צְפִירֵי עִזִּים 2 Ch 29[21] *he-goats* **4.** עִזִּים = *goats' hair,* as material 1 S 19[13.16] Ex 25[4] + 6 t. P (35[26] obj. of טָווּ). †**5.** in sim. חֲשִׂפֵי עִזִּים 1 K 20[27] (v. [חָשִׂיף]); כְּעֵדֶר הָע׳ Ct 4[1] 6[5], of flowing, undulating hair. †**6.** צְפִיר הָע׳ Dn 8[5.8] *he-goat* in vision.

†עֻנִּי **n.pr.m.** Levites:—**1.** 1 Ch 15[18.20], Ωνει, 𝔊L Αναιας. **2.** Ne 12[9] Qr (Kt ענו), Ιανα(ι).

†עֲנָיָה **n.pr.m.** Ne 8[4] 10[23], Ανανια(ς).

עָנִיר v. עָנִי sub III. ענה עֲנִים v. p. 745.

עִנְיָן v. II [ענה] עֵנָם v. עֵין גַּנִּים.

†עֲנָמִים **n.pr.gent.** in (or near) Egypt Gn 10[13] = 1 Ch 1[11], Αινεμαμειμ, Αινεμετιειμ, etc; form dub and locality unknown, v. conj. in Di.

†עֲנַמֶּלֶךְ **n.pr.div.** of סְפַרְוִים (q v) 2 K 17[31], Ανημελεχ (om. 𝔊L), = As. *Anu-malik* acc. to Schr[COT ad loc.], but dub, v. Kit[ad loc] and reff., Che[Expos. Times, June, 1898, 429] rds. ענומלך, and ins. also 2 K 19[37] (bef. אלהיו); cf. also Hal cited sub עֲנָת.

I. ענן (√ of foll., perh. orig. *cover,* as Sab. ظلل = ענן (Heb. צלל), DHM[Epigr Denkm. 36 f.]; or < Ar. عَنَّ *appear, present oneself,* specif. *intervene as an obstacle* (Lane; cf. Lag[BN 103]), hence عَنَانٌ *clouds,* as *intervening,* and so *obstructing;* cf. NH עָנָן *cloud* = BH (rare), vb denom. Pi. עִנֵּן as BH; 𝔗 עֲנָנָא, Syr. ܥܢܢܐ *clouds*).

I. עָנָן [87] **n.m.** [Ex 19, 16] cloud-mass, cloud;—(ה)ע׳ abs Ex 19[9] +; cstr. עֲנַן Ho 6[4] +; sf. עֲנָנְךָ

Nu 14[14], עֲנָנוֹ Jb 26[9] 37[15], pl עֲנָנִים Je 4[13],—**1.** *cloud-mass:* **a.** esp of theophanic cloud (58 t.), chiefly at Exodus in JE (less oft P), usu עמוד הע׳ Ex 13[21 22] + (v. עמוד), but also ע׳ alone Ex 34[5] cf. 14[20] (J), Nu 10[34] 11[25] 14[14] (all JE); עב־הע׳ Ex 19[9], ע׳ כָּבֵד v[16] (E), ע׳ in P Ex 16[10] 24[15] + 23 t; also Dt 1[33] 4[11] 5[19], ψ 78[14] 105[39], in temple 1 K 8[10 11] = 2 Ch 5[13 14], cf Ez 1[4] 10[3.4], hence in gen ψ 97[2], as symbol of protection Is 4[5], as a barrier La 3[44]; cf הע׳ אֲבַק רַגְלָיו Na 1[3] **b.** of rain-bow cloud Gn 9[13 14 14 16] (P), Ez 1[28] (sim) **c.** עֲנַן־בֹּקֶר Ho 6[4] 13[3] (sim of transitoriness, on phenom in Pal v Chaplin[PEQ. 1883, 19]), cf. Is 44[22] Jb 7[9] (both id), sim of invasion Ez 38[9 16], pl Je 4[13]. **d.** poet in various connex Jb 26[8.9] 38[9], c אור as thunder-cloud 37[11 15]. **e.** symbol of gloom Ez 30[18] 32[7], יוֹם ע׳ וַעֲרָפֶל Zp 1[15] Ez 34[12] Jo 2[2], cf Ez 30[3] (all of day of י׳) **†2.** ע׳ קְטֹרֶת Lv 16[13] (P) *cloud of incense*, so Ez 8[11] (del ע׳ 𝔊 Co Berthol, not Toy)

†[עָנַן] vb. denom. Pi. *Inf cstr* sf c acc. cogn בְּעַנְנִי ע׳ עַל־הָאָרֶץ Gn 9[14] (P) *when I bring clouds*, etc

†עֲנָנָה n.f. cloud (Ges[§ 122 t]) Jb 3[5]

†II [עָנַן] vb. Pō῾ practise soothsaying (prob denom, but orig meaning dub, connex with I עָנָן (De[1s 2.6]) now gen abandoned, Low [ZMG xxxi (1877) 539] cp עַיִן *eye*, so We[Skizzen iii 148] (but v infr), RS[JPhil xiv (1885) 119 f] cp Ar غَنَّة *nasal twang, hum of insects*, whence diviners as *crooning*, Ew Gerber[31] of diviner as interpreting *hum* of insects, *whisper* of leaves, etc, We[Heid 2,204] now cp عَنَّ *appear*, i e *dealers in phenomena*),—*Pf.* 3 ms consec. ועונן 2 K 21[6] = 2 Ch 33[6], *Impf* 2 mpl. ולא תעוֹנֵנוּ Lv 19[26] (H), *Pt.* as subst. מְעוֹנֵן Dt 18[10] (forbidden), pl מְעוֹנְנִים v[14], מעו׳ Mi 5[11], אלון מעוננים Ju 9[37] (v I אֵלָה, seat of an oracle, cf. RS[Sem i 179 2nd ed 196]); also (without מ, cf. Sta[§ 233] Ko[i 349]) עננים Is 2[6], sf עֹנְנֵיכֶם Je 27[9], fs in בני עֹנְנָה Is 57[3] *sons of a soothsaying woman*, fig of apostates —Vid. כשף, II [נָחַשׁ], [קָסַם]

†II. עָנָן n.pr.m. Ne 10[27], Ηναμ, Η(ι)ναν (cf. n pr m. Sab ענן SabDenkm[30], Palm ענני).

†עֲנָנִי n pr.m. 1 Ch 3[24], Ανανι, Ανανι(ας)

†עֲנָנְיָה n pr. 1. m. Ne 3[23], Ανανια(ς) **2. loc.** Ne 11[32], Ανανια, Ανια, perh mod. *Beit Ḥanîna*, c 4 miles NNW from Jerusalem, cf Buhl[Geogr 167].

ענף (√of foll; meaning unknown, NH עָנָף = BH, 𝔗 עַנְפָּא (both rare), Syr ܥܢܦܐ)

†עָנָף n.[m.] branch(es), bough(s);—usu. sg coll, abs ע׳ *branches* of vine Ez 17[8], pl only sf עֲנָפֶיהָ ψ 80[11] (both in fig), *boughs* of tree, cstr עֲנַף Lv 23[40], sf. (as if from *עֶנֶף Ko[ii 1, 74]) ענפכם Ez 36[8]; sg abs (in fig) Mal 3[19], of cedar Ez 17[23] 31[3].

†[עָנֵף] adj. full of branches;—fs. עֲנֵפָה Ez 19[10] (of vine, in fig).

ענק (√of foll, mng. dub; cf. Ar. عُنُق, عَنَق *neck*, 𝔗 עוּנְקָא; also עִינְקָא *necklace*, Syr. ܥܢܩܐ, Eth ዐንቅ: *gem*, vbs denom. in Ar, Eth., NH)

†I. עֲנָק n.[m.] neck, only in **epith. gent.** בני הָעֲנָק *long-necked* (tall) *men*, early giant people about Hebron and in Philistia, Εναχ, Εναχ, Jos 15[14] (JE) = Ju 1[20], without art. Nu 13[33] (JE), Dt 9[2]; also ילִידֵי הָע׳ Nu 13[22.28] Jos 15[14] (all JE); called also עֲנָקִים *long-necks*, Ενακειμ, Jos 14[12 15] (JE), 11[21 22] (D), Dt 2[10 11 21] + Je 47[5] (rd עֲנָקִים for MT עמקם), and perh 1 Ch 12[16] (v. עֵמֶק *ad fin.*); בני עֲנָקִים 1[28] (𝔊 γίγαντες, cf. Nu 13[33]), 9[2]; עֲנָק later (erron.) as eponym. ancestor of Anakim Jos 15[13] = עֲנוֹק 21[11] (both P)—Vid esp. Mey ZAW i (1881), 139 GFM[Ju 1. 10 20] Che[Ency Bib Anak].

†II עֲנָק n.m.[Ct 4.9] **necklace, neck-pendant** (Aramaism acc. to Lag[BN 175]);—abs. ע׳ Ct 4[9] appar. part of necklace, perh. *neck-pendant*, pl עֲנָקוֹת Ju 8[26] (ornament of camels), עֲנָקִים Pr 1[9] (of youth, in fig)

†[עָנַק] vb. denom. serve as necklace,—**Qal** 3 fs sf עֲנָקַתְמוֹ ψ 73[6] pride *is necklace for them*. **Hiph.** *Impf.* and *Inf abs* הַעֲנֵיק תַּעֲנִיק לוֹ Dt 15[14] *thou shalt make a rich necklace for him* fr thy flock, etc, fig for *richly load him*.

†עָנֵר n.pr. 1. appar. **m.** ally of Abram Gn 14[13.24], Αυναν, cf אֶשְׁכֹּל, מַמְרֵא. **2. loc.** in Manasseh 1 Ch 6[55] Αμαρ, 𝔊L Ανηρ

ענש (√of foll, mng. dub; cf (as denom) Ph. Niph נענ[ש] *be fined* CIS[i 165, 20], Palm. ענושותא *treasurership*, v. also NH עוֹנֶשׁ *punishment*, עָנַשׁ *punish* (in general))

†עֹנֶשׁ n.[m.] indemnity, fine;—וַיִּתֶּן־ע׳ עַל־הָאָרֶץ 2 K 23[33], of individual נשא ע׳ Pr 19[19].

†[עָנַשׁ] vb. denom. (Gerber[61 f]) fine, mulct,—**Qal** *Pf* consec וְעָנְשׁוּ Dt 22[19] (2 acc.), *Impf* וַיַּעֲנֹשׁ 2 Ch 36[3] (2 acc; ‖ 2 K 23[33] supr), *Inf cstr* עֲנוֹשׁ Pr 17[26] (לְ pers), = *punish* (in gen) עָנַשׁ־ 21[11], *Pt pass* עֲנוּשִׁים Am 2[8] *those fined*,

mulcted **Niph.** *Impf.* + **Qal** *Inf. abs.* עָנוֹשׁ יֵעָנֵשׁ Ex 21[22] (E) *he shall be strictly fined;* more gen. *Pf.* נֶעֱנָשׁוּ Pr 22[3] *be mulcted, punished* = 27[12].

† עֲנָת **n.pr.m.** father of Shamgar Ju 3[31] 5[6], Αναθ (Δειναχ, Κεναθ);—v. also בֵּית עֲנוֹת, ב׳ עֲנָת (cf. Tel Am. n pr *Anati*, Wkl [125, 43]; As. n pr deae *Anatu* (Jastr[Rel Bab. 163], hence) in Syria and Ph —also Egypt—ענת (Muss-Arnolt[JBL xi (1892), 80] Pietschmann[Phön 149 f.] Hal[JAs 7, x (1877), 774, xiii (1879), 208]))

† עֲנָתוֹת and (1 K 2[26]) עֲנָתֹת **n.pr.** Αναθωθ, **1. loc.** (cf. goddess *Anat*, ref sub foregoing); —Is 10[30] 1 K 2[26] Je 1[1] 11[21 23] 32[7.8.9] Jos 21[18] (P), 1 Ch 6[45] Ezr 2[23] = Ne 7[27], Ne 11[32]; mod. *ʿAnâtâ*, c 3 miles NNE from Jerusalem, cf. Buhl[Geogr 175] GASm[Geogr 315]. **2. m. a.** 1 Ch 7[8]. **b.** Ne 10[20].

† עַנְּתֹתִי **adj. gent.** of foreg.;—הָע׳ Je 29[27] 1 Ch 12[3] 2 S 23[27] = הָעֲנְּתוֹתִי 1 Ch 11[28] 27[12].

† עַנְתֹתִיָּה **n. pr. m.** Benjamite 1 Ch 8[24], Ανωθαιθ, Αναθωθ(ι)α

† [עָסַס] **vb. press, crush,** by treading, **tread down** (NH עסיסית *crushed* wheat; cf. Ar عَسَّ *go the rounds,* [*tramp*], *prowl;* Syr. ܥܣ *explore,* v. Brockelmann), —**Qal** *Pf.* 2 mpl. fig. וְעַסּוֹתֶם רְשָׁעִים Mal 3[21] (consec.)

† עָסִיס **n.m.**[Jo 1. 5] **sweet wine** (prop *pressed out* juice);—abs ע׳ Am 9[13] (v Dr and reff.), Jo 1[5] 4[18]; in sim. Is 49[26]; cstr. עֲסִיס רִמֹּנִי Ct 8[2].

† עפאים Kt, עֳפָיִים Qr **n.[m.]pl. foliage** (cf. Ges[§ 93 x]; Aram. loan-word, ﬡ עֶפְיָא *foliage,* Syr. ܥܦܝܐ *flower, branch*),—ψ 104[12]

† I. עָפַל **vb. swell** (?; so Thes; inferred fr. deriv.; Ar. عَفَلٌ is a *tumour* in the vulva or anus, عَفِلَ appar. denom. (cf II. עֹפֶל) v As. *uplu,* prob. *tumour* (Dl[HWB 7] *ublu,* but v. Jen[Th Lz 1895, 250])),—**Pu.** *Pf.* 3 fs. עֻפְּלָה Hb 2[4] acc to MT (subj. נַפְשׁוֹ, cf. GASm), but subst. needed, Brd[SK 1889, 121] הַמְעֻלָּף, We Now הָעַוָּל, cf. Gu[Kau].—**Hiph.** v. II עפל

† I. עֹפֶל **n.[m.] mound, hill,** only as acropolis,—ע׳ abs 2 K 5[24] +, cstr. Mi 4[8];—fortified mound or hill within city, of Jerus. (cf. Rob[BR I 267] Gu[ZPV v (1882), 328]) Mi 4[8] Is 32[14]; S end of eastern hill Ne 3[26] 11[21] 2 Ch 33[14] חוֹמַת הָע׳ Ne 3[27] 2 Ch 27[3] (cf. חמת העפל in קרחה MI[21 22]); of Samaria 2 K 5[24].

† II. [עֹפֶל] **n.m.**[1 S 6. 4] **tumour;**—only pl. Kt (בְּ)עֳפָלִים Dt 28[27] 1 S 5[6.9 12]; cstr. עָפְלֵי 6[4]; sf עָפְלֵיכֶם v[5]; Qr in all (ב)טחרים, טְחֹרֵי, טְחֹרֵיכֶם, v. [טְחוֹר].

† II. [עָפַל] **vb. perhaps be heedless** (Ar. غَفَلَ *be heedless, neglectful, inadvertent*);—**Hiph.** *shew heedlessness, Impf.* 3 mpl. וַיַּעְפִּלוּ לַעֲלוֹת Nu 14[44] (JE) *they shewed heedlessness in going up* (went up heedlessly), so de Dieu, cited (and allowed) by Di Buhl[Lex]; > Thes al. *shewed presumption* (I עפל, this sense dub.).

† עָפְנִי **n.pr.loc.** in Benj, הָע׳ Jos 18[24], ⓖL Αφνη.

עפעף v עוף.

I. עפר (√of foll; mng dub, cf Ar. عَفَرٌ *dust,* As *epru, epiru,* Tel Am. *ḫaparu* and *aparu* (Canaan. glosses); ﬡ עַפְרָא, Syr. ܥܦܪܐ; NH עָפָר = BH)

† עָפָר **n.m.**[Lv 14. 42] **dry earth, dust;**—abs ע׳ Gn 2[7] +, cstr עֲפַר Gn 13[16] +; sf. עֲפָרֵךְ Ez 26[12], עֲפָרוֹ Dt 9[21], etc.; pl. cstr עַפְרוֹת Jb 28[6] Pr 8[26], —**1.** lit: **a.** *dry, loose earth,* thrown (in malice) 2 S 16[13] (‖אֲבָנִים), וַיַּעֲלוּ ע׳ עַל־רֹאשׁ Jos 7[6] (JE; sign of grief), so Ez 27[30] La 2[10], and (c. זָרַק) Jb 2[12]; loose earth (on surface of ground) 1 K 18[38] Am 2[7] Mi 1[10] Is 34[7.9] Lv 17[13] (H) Ez 24[7] (in fig.), Nu 5[17] Jb 14[19] 38[38] 39[14], Gn 26[15] (R), made into siege works Hb 1[10], of sand-storm Dt 28[24] (+ אָבָק); as serpent's food, token of punishment and humiliation, Gn 3[14] (J) Is 65[25] (cf. Mi 7[17] **2 e** infr.), זֹחֲלֵי ע׳ Dt 32[24] (poem; cf. **2 e**). **b.** specif as material of human body Gn 2[7] 3[19] (J), Ec 3[20], cf. Jb 4[19] 8[19] ψ 103[14], to which it returns (שׁוּב אֶל־) Gn 3[19] Jb 10[9] ψ 104[29] Ec 3[20]; so (c. עַל) Jb 34[15] Ec 12[7]. **c.** = surface of ground Ex 8[12.13 13] (P; ע׳ הָאָרֶץ), Jb 19[25] Is 25[12] 26[5] (both ‖אֶרֶץ), surface of (whole) earth Jb 41[25], מְחִלּוֹת ע׳ Is 2[19] (for hiding), so ע׳ alone v[10], cf חֹרֵי ע׳ Jb 30[6]; = *soil,* Jb 5[6] 14[8]. **d.** *powder* of anything pulverized Dt 9[21.21] (cf. דַּק ‖Ex 32[20]), 2 K 23[6.6.12 15], so in sim 2 S 22[43] = ψ 18[43], hence = ashes v[4] Nu 19[17]. **e.** *debris,* of ruined city 1 K 20[10] Ez 26[4.12] Ne 3[34] 4[4] ψ 102[15]. The foll. are late. **f.** earth of the grave: לֶעָ׳ אֶשְׁכָּב Jb 7[21], so (c. עַל) 20[11] 21[26], cf 17[16], יוֹרְדֵי ע׳ ψ 22[30], שֹׁכְנֵי ע׳ Is 26[19], יְשֵׁנֵי אַדְמַת־ע׳ Dn 12[2]; עֲפַר־מָוֶת ψ 22[16], ע׳ in fig. ψ 30[10]. **g.** *mortar* (i. e. dried mud) for plastering houses Lv 14[41 42.45] (P). **h.** (iron-) *ore* Jb 28[2]; עַפְרֹת זָהָב v[6] *gold-dust* (but v. סַפִּיר) **i.** material of earth Is 40[12], cf. רֹאשׁ עַפְרוֹת תֵּבֵל Pr 8[26] *the first of the earth-*

particles of the world. **2.** fig.: **a.** of abundance Gn 13$^{16.16}$ 28^{14} (all J) 2 Ch 1^{9} Jb 27^{16} ψ 78^{27} (‖חוֹל יַמִּים), cf. עֲפַר יַעֲקֹב Nu 23^{10} (JE); with added idea of commonness, worthlessness Zp 1^{17} Zc 9^{3}. **b.** of worthlessness (alone) Jb 22^{24}. **c.** sim. of the scattered, dispersed 2 K 13^{7}; כֶּע׳ Is 41^{2} (so van d. H. Ginsb; Baer כֶּע׳; on meaning v. Du Che, rdg. תְּשִׂימֵם for יִתֵּן). **d.** of self-abasement Gn 18^{27} (+ אֵפֶר), וְנִחַמְתִּי עַל־ע׳ Jb 42^{6}, יִתֵּן בֶּע׳ פִּיהוּ La 3^{29}. **e.** of humiliation (sitting or lying in dust) Is 47^{1} cf. 29$^{4.4}$, Jb 16^{15} 40^{13} ψ 7^{6} 44^{26} 119^{25}, sim. Jb 30^{19}; licking dust ψ 72^{9} Is 49^{23} Mi 7^{17}, cf. TelAm. *tikalu ipra* (of enemies, v. Wkl$^{Altor. Forsch. iii. 291}$; also of serpent **1 a** supr.); of ׳י raising from the dust 1 S 2^{8} = ψ 113^{7}, 1 K 16^{2}; of lifting oneself Is 52^{2}.

† [עִפֵּר] **vb. denom. Pi.** וְעִפַּר בֶּעָפָר 2 S 16^{13} *and kept dusting* (him) *with dust* (throwing [lumps of] dry earth at him).

II. **עפר** (√of foll.; cf. Ar. غُفْرٌ *young of mountain-goat*, NH עוֹפֶר *young* of animals).

† **עֹפֶר** **n.m.**$^{Ct 4, 5}$ **young hart, stag**;—cstr. ע׳ הָאַיָּלִים (‖צְבִי) Ct 2$^{9.17}$ 8^{14}; pl. abs. עֳפָרִים תְּאוֹמֵי צְבִיָּה 4^{5} 7^{4} (all in sim.).

† **עֵפֶר** **n.pr.m.** Αφερ, etc.;—**1.** 'son' of Midian Gn 25^{4} = 1 Ch 1^{33} (𝔊L Γοφερ). **2.** in Judah 1 Ch 4^{17} (A Γαφερ). **3.** in Manasseh 5^{24}.

עַפְרָה v. בֵּית לְע׳ p. 112 supr.

† **עָפְרָה** **n.pr. 1. loc.: a.** in Benj. Jos 18^{23} (P), Αφαρ, etc.; 1 S 13^{7} Γοφερα; prob. = עֶפְרוֹן **2** and אֶפְרַיִם **6**; perh. mod. *eṭ-Ṭayyibeh*, c. 4 miles NE. from Bethel, cf. GASm$^{Geogr. 252}$ Buhl$^{Geogr. 177}$. **b.** in Manasseh, Εφραθα: Ju 6^{11} 8^{27}; cstr. עָפְרַת אֲבִי הָעֶזְרִי 6^{24}, but עָפְרָה וגו׳ 8^{32}; c. ה loc. עָפְרָתָה Ju 9^{5}. **2. m.** in Judah 1 Ch 4^{14}, Γοφερα, 𝔊L Εφραθ.

† **עֶפְרוֹן** **n.pr.** Εφρων:—**1. m.** Hittite, Abr.'s time, acc. to Gn 23$^{8.10.10.13.16.17}$ 49^{29}, עֶפְרֹן 23^{6} 25^{9} 49^{30} 50^{13} (all P). **2. loc.** 2 Ch 13^{19} Kt (עֶפְרַיִן Qr), cf. עָפְרָה **1 a.** **3. mont.** הַר־ע׳, on N. border of Judah Jos 15^{9}.

עֶפְרַיִן 2 Ch 13^{19} Qr v. עֶפְרוֹן **2.**

† **עֹפֶרֶת** **n.m.**$^{Je 6, 29 (si vera l. Qr)}$ **lead** (√dub.; prob. foreign word; cf. 𝔗 אֲבָרָא *lead*, Syr. ܐܒܪܐ, and (as Aram. loan-word) Ar. آنُكٌ [v. Dozy], Frä ^{152}; perh. also As. *abaru*, a metal, *magnesite* acc. to Hilpr$^{Assyriaca i (1894). 80 ff.}$ Hpt$^{ib. 83}$);—כִּכַּר ע׳ Zc 5^{7} *a round weight* (disc) *of lead*, אֶבֶן־הָעֹ׳ v^{8}; with other metals (v. בְּדִיל): עֹ׳ Ez 22$^{18.20}$ 27^{12}, הָעֹפָרֶת Nu 31^{22} (P); עֹפֶ׳ also Jb 19^{24} (with which chiselled letters are filled acc. to Di and most; Bu rds. בְּע׳ *in* [a tablet of] *lead*); also (as flux) Je 6^{29} (rdg. Qr; so Gf Co; emend. Gie); עֹ׳ in sim. Ex 15^{10} (song).

עֵפָתָה v. עֵיפָה sub II. עוּף. **עֵץ** v. II. עצה.

†I. **[עָצַב]** **vb. hurt, pain, grieve** (NH Nithp. and in deriv.; 𝔗 עֲצַב *be in pain* (rare); Eth. **ዐጸበ፡** *be hard, difficult;* Lag$^{BN 50, cf. 201}$ cp. Ar. غَضِبَ *be angry*, but dub.);—**Qal** *Pf.* 3 ms. sf. עֲצָבוֹ 1 K 1^{6} his father *had* not *pained him* (𝔊 Klo Gr עֲצָרוֹ, but v. Benz); ins. עצב (with other words) 2 S 13^{21} 𝔊 Ew Th We Kit Bu HPS; *Inf. cstr.* sf. לְבִלְתִּי עָצְבִּי 1 Ch 4^{10} *that* it (רָעָה) *may not pain me; Pt. pass.* cstr. עֲצוּבַת רוּחַ Is 54^{6} *hurt in spirit* (of Zion under fig. of deserted wife). **Niph.** *Pf.* 3 ms. נֶעְצַב 1 S 20^{34} *be pained* for (אֶל pers.; del. 𝔊 HPS); נֶעֱצַב 2 S 19^{3} the king *is in pain* (is grieving) for (עַל pers.); *Impf.* 3 ms. יֵעָצֵב 1 S 20^{3} lest *he be pained;* + בָּהֶם instr. Ec 10^{9} *shall be hurt* by them (i. e. אֲבָנִים; only here of physical pain); 2 mpl. תֵּעָצְבוּ Gn 45^{5} *be* not *grieved* (+ יִחַר; sq. כִּי *that* ye sold me), cf. Ne 8$^{10.11}$ (abs.) *do not grieve.* **Pi.** *Pf.* 3 pl. עִצְּבוּ c. acc. Is 63^{10} *they vexed* his holy spirit (+ מָרוּ); *Impf.* 3 mpl. דְּבָרַי יְעַצֵּבוּ ψ 56^{6} *my affairs they vex* (Thes al.), but improb., < Che בְּדָבָר יְע׳ *with speech they vex* (me). **Hiph.** *Impf.* 3 mpl. sf. יַעֲצִיבוּהוּ ψ 78^{40} *they used to cause him* [׳י] *pain.* **Hithp.** *Impf.* 3 ms. וַיִּתְעַצֵּב אֶל־לִבּוֹ Gn 6^{6} *and he was vexed to his heart* (of ׳י; ‖ וַיִּנָּחֶם); 3 mpl. וַיִּתְעַצְּבוּ Gn 34^{7} (+ וַיִּחַר, sq. clause with כִּי).

† **I. עֶצֶב** **n.[m.] pain, hurt, toil**;—**1.** ע׳ *pain* Gn 3^{16} (of travail), Pr 10^{22}. **2.** *hurt* (of mind), דְּבַר־ע׳ Pr 15^{1} *a word that hurts* (opp. מַעֲנֶה־רַךְ). **3.** *toil* Pr 14^{23}; pl. לֶחֶם הָעֲצָבִים ψ 127^{2} *bread of* (gained by) *toils;* sf. עֲצָבֶיךָ Pr 5^{10}.

† **I. עֹצֶב** **n.[m.]** pain;—ע׳ 1 Ch 4^{9} (of travail); דֶּרֶךְ־ע׳ ψ 139^{24} *hurtful way* (of any wicked habit; > 𝔗 Thes *way of idolatry;* II. עֹצֶב); sf. עָצְבְּךָ Is 14^{3} of the *pain* of exile.

† [עָצֵב, > עַצָּב] **n.[m.]** toiler (prop. *sufferer;* less well עֶצֶב *toil* Thes Kö$^{ii. 1, 29}$ al.);—pl. sf. עַצְּבֵיכֶם תִּנְגֹּשׂוּ Is 58^{3} (d. f. dirim. Ges$^{§ 20 h}$) *your toilers ye drive on;* Klo Che עֲבֹט בְּיֶדְכֶם (cf. Vrss in part) *money lent on pledge* ye exact.

† [עַצֶּ֫בֶת] **n.f. hurt, injury, pain;**—עַצָּ֑בֶת Pr 10^{10} he that winketh with the eye causeth *hurt* (stirs up strife, etc.); cstr. עַצֶּבֶת־לֵב *pain of heart* 15^{13} (opp. לֵב שָׂמֵחַ); pl. sf. עַצְּבֹתָ֑י Jb 9^{28} *my pains,* to rd. perh. also 7^{15} (for MT עַצְמוֹתָי), עַצְּבוֹתָם ψ 16^{4} (due to idolatry; > *idols* 𝔗 𝔙 We al); מְחַבֵּשׁ לְע׳ 147^{3} *binding up their hurts.*

† עִצָּבוֹן **n.[m.] pain, toil,**—ע׳ abs Gn 3^{17} *toil;* cstr. עִצְּבוֹן יָדֵינוּ 5^{29} (both of agriculture); sf. עִצְּבוֹנֵךְ 3^{16} (of travail; all J)

† מַעֲצֵבָה **n.f. place of pain** (> simply *pain*);—לְמ׳ תִּשְׁכָּבוּן Is 50^{11} *in* (constr. praegn.) *a place of pain shall ye lie down.*

† II [עָצַב] **vb. Pi. shape, fashion** (NH Pi *stretch* child *into shape;* Buhl^{Lex} cp. عَصَبَ *cut, cut off* [whence idea of *carving, fashioning*]),—**Pi.** *Pf.* יָדֶיךָ עִצְּבוּנִי וַיַּעֲשׂוּנִי Jb 10^{8} *thy hands shaped me,* etc. **Hiph.** *Inf. cstr.* לְהַעֲצִבָה Je 44^{19}, but rd ־בָהּ, *to fashion her,* i e. make images of her (poss. denom. from עָצָב)

† II. עֶ֫צֶב **n.m. vessel** (as *fashioned*);—ע׳ נִבְזֶה וגו׳ Je 22^{28} *a vessel despised,* etc. (fig. of Coniah = Jehoiachin)

† II. [עֹ֫צֶב] **n.m. idol,**—sf. עָצְבִּי Is 48^{5}.

† [עָצָב] **n.[m.] idol,**—always pl. עֲצַבִּים (Ges$^{§93\,ee}$). Ho 4^{17} 8^{4} (כַּסְפָּם וּזְהָבָם), 13^{2} (כַּסְפָּם ‖ מַסֵּכָה), 14^{9} Zc 13^{2} 2 Ch 24^{18} (+ אֲשֵׁרִים), cstr. עֲצַבֵּי ψ 106^{38} 135^{15} (כֶּסֶף וְזָהָב); sf. עֲצַבֶּיהָ Is 10^{11} (‖ אֱלִילֶיהָ), Je 50^{2} (‖ גִלּוּלֶיהָ), Mi 1^{7}; עֲצַבֵּיהֶם 1 S 31^{9} = 1 Ch 10^{9}, 2 S 5^{21} (but read אֱלֹהֵיהֶם as ‖ 1 Ch 14^{12}, so 𝔊 We Dr al), Is 46^{1} ψ 106^{36} 115^{4} (כֶּסֶף וְזָהָב).

עצד (√ of foll.; cf. Ar. عَضَدَ *lop trees with a* مِعْضَد, a kind of *reaping-hook;* Eth. ዐፀደ: *reap,* መዐፀድ:, መዐፀድ: *sickle;* NH מַעֲצָד *axe* (smaller than כַּשִּׁיל Levy$^{NHWB\ II.\ 423}$).

† מַעֲצָד **n.[m.] axe;**—Je 10^{3}; in Is 44^{12} prob. del (so Du Che^{Hpt} Skinner).

† I [עָצָה] **vb. shut** (Ar. (و et ى) عَصَا IV *shut* eyes, Eth ዐፀወ: *shut* door);—**Qal** *Pt. act.* עֹצֶה עֵינָיו Pr 16^{30} *he that shuts his eyes* (SS cp. עצם [Is 29^{10}], which Gr reads)

II. **עצה** (√ of foll.; meaning dub.; cf. Sab. עצם *wood* DHM$^{ZMG\ xxxvii\ (1883),\ 341,\ 412}$, Ar. عِضَةٌ, orig. عِضَهَةٌ nom. unit. of عِضَاهٌ *large, thorny trees* (v. Lane; also No$^{GGA\ 1862,\ 544;\ ZMG\ xxxii\ (1878),\ 406}$ Lag$^{BN\ 158\ f}$), Eth. ዕፅ: *tree, wood;* As. *iṣ(ṣ)u,* Ph. עץ *wood;* NH = BH; Aram. אָע (init. א by dissim.); Ba$^{NB\ §2,\ c\ 1}$ thinks originally bilit.).

עֵץ$_{329}$ **n.m.** $^{Gn\ 2,\ 9}$ **tree, trees, wood;**—ע׳ abs. Gn 3^{3}+, cstr. 3^{24}+, עֵ֫ץ 2^{16}+; sf. עֵצְךָ Dt 28^{42}, etc., pl עֵצִים Ju 9^{8}+, cstr עֲצֵי Is 7^{2}+, sf עֵצָיךְ Dt 29^{10}, עֵצֵינוּ La 5^{4}, etc.,—**1.** (c. 150 t.) **a.** a standing *tree* Gn 18$^{4.8}$ (J)+, Ex 15^{25} (J; of shrub?), Je 17^{18} = ψ 1^{3} (sim.); to be felled Dt 19^{5} 2 K 6^{6}; הָעֵצִים (appar. incl vine and bramble) in allegory Ju 9^{8} + 6 t. Ju 9; עֵץ הַחַיִּים + Gn 2^{9} 3$^{22.24}$ (J), cf ע׳ חַיִּים, fig of source of (life and) happiness + Pr 3^{18} 11^{30} 13^{12} 15^{4}; ע׳ הַדַּעַת טוֹב וָרָע Gn 2$^{9.16}$ (J); עֲצֵי (ה)יַּעַר Is 7^{2} (sim.), 44^{14} Ez 15^{2}+; עֲצֵי הַשָּׂדֶה Is 55^{12} Ez 17^{24} (fig.), +; עֲצֵי לְבָנוֹן 2 Ch 2^{7}; עֲצֵי־מַיִם + Ez 31^{14}; עֲצֵי י׳ + ψ 104^{16}; עֲצֵי עֵדֶן + Ez 31$^{9.16.18.18}$; עֲצֵי לְבוֹנָה Ct 4^{14}; of vine עֵץ הַגֶּפֶן + Ez 15$^{2.6}$; תַּחַת כָּל־עֵץ רַעֲנָן place of illicit worship + Dt 12^{2} Je 2^{20} 3$^{6.13}$ 1 K 14^{23} 2 K 16^{4} 17^{10} Ez 6^{13} Is 57^{5} 2 Ch 28^{4}, cf. עַל־עֵץ רַעֲנָן Je 17^{2}; כָּל־עֵץ עָבֹת Ez 20^{28}. **b.** coll *trees,* עֵץ־הַגָּן Gn 2^{16} 3$^{1.2.8}$ (all J); usu. later, ע׳ 1$^{12.29.29}$ (P), +; עֵץ פְּרִי *fruit*-bearing *trees* Gn 1^{11} (P), ψ 148^{9}, cf. Ec 2^{5}, פְּרִי עֵץ Ex 10^{15} (J), Ez 36^{30} Lv 23^{40} (H), cf. Jo 2^{22}; עֵץ־מַאֲכָל Dt 20^{20} Lv 19^{23} (H), Ez 47^{12} Ne 9^{25}; עֵץ־שֶׁמֶן Hg 2^{19} *olive trees,* עֵץ שֶׁמֶן Ne 8^{15}, עֵץ הַזַּיִת Is 41^{19}; סְבַךְ־עֵץ ψ 74^{5} *thicket of trees;* עֵץ הַשָּׂדֶה Ex 9^{25} (J), +; עֵץ הַיַּעַר + Ez 15^{6}, cf. Is 10^{19} 44^{23}; כִּימֵי הָעֵץ Is 65^{22} (sim. of great age). **c.** pl. of *trees* felled for building, 1 K 5$^{20.32}$ (+ אֲבָנִים); עֲצֵי בְרוֹשִׁים 2 S 5^{11} = 1 Ch 14^{1} + 7 t.; עֲצֵי אֲרָזִים 1 K 5$^{22.24}$ 9^{11}; עֲצֵי אַלְמֻגִּים (אַלְג׳), v אַלְג׳ p. 38 supr. **2.** (c. 175 t.; c. 120 t. pl, to denote *pieces* [or articles] *of wood*) **a.** *wood,* as material; for building, 2 K 12^{13} (+ אַבְנֵי מַחְצֵב), 22^{6} = 2 Ch 34^{11} (both + *id*), Ne 2^{8}+; עֲצֵי שֶׁמֶן 1 K 6$^{23.31.33}$ cf. v^{32}; עֲצֵי־גֹפֶר Gn 6^{14} (Noah's ark), עֲצֵי שִׁטִּים Ex 25$^{5.10}$ + 20 t. Ex (of tabern. and its furniture; all P) Dt 10^{3}; מִגְדַּל־עֵץ Ne 8^{4}; מוֹטֹת עֵץ Je 28^{13} (in fig; opp. מ׳ בַּרְזֶל); כְּלִי־עֵץ *article of wood* Lv 11^{32} 15^{12} Nu 31^{20}, cf 35^{18} (all P). Hence **b.** עֵצִים = *articles of wood* Ex 7^{19} (P; ‖ אֲבָנִים), 1 Ch 29^{2}; so עֲצֵי בְרוֹשִׁים 2 S 6^{5} (but v. ברושׁ *ad fin.*); specif. הָעֵץ = helve of axe Dt 19^{5}; עֵץ חֲנִית(וֹ) 1 S 17^{7} Qr (Kt חץ) = 1 Ch 20^{5}, 2 S 21^{19} 23^{7}; עֲצֵי הָעֲגָלָה 1 S 6^{14} (i e. wood of which cart was made), עֲצֵי הָאֲשֵׁרָה Ju 6^{26}, esp. *timbers* of a house Zc 5^{4} Hb 2^{11} Lv 14^{45}, of a city 1 K 15^{22} = 2 Ch 16^{6}, Ez 26^{12}; עֵץ of *pole* on which bodies of slain (criminals and others) were exposed (perhaps orig. *tree*) Gn 40^{19} (E), Jos 8$^{29.29}$ 10$^{26.26.27}$ (all JE),

Dt 21$^{22.23}$, late (in Pers.) used for executing criminals (? by hanging = *gallows*), תָּלָה עַל־עֵץ Est 2^{23} + 8 t. Est **†c.** of idols, עֵץ וָאֶבֶן Dt 4^{28} 28$^{36.64}$ 29^{16} 2 K 19^{18} = Is 37^{19}, Ez 20^{32}, cf Je 2^{27} 3^{9} Hb 2^{19}; so עֵץ alone Ho 4^{12} Is 40^{20}, cf 44^{19} 45^{20}, אֲשֵׁרָה כָּל־עֵץ Dt 16^{21} **d.** (fire-)*wood* Jos 9$^{23.27}$ (J), v^{21} (P), Dt 19^{5} Is 30^{33}+, rd. עצים also Ez 24^{5} (for MT עצמים) Bo Ew Sm Co Berthol Toy, esp for sacrifices 1 K 18$^{23.23}$+, Gn 22$^{7.9.9}$ Lv 1^{7} + 6 t Lv (all P), 2 S 24^{22} ‖ 1 Ch 21^{23}, +; עֲצֵי עוֹלָה Gn 22$^{3.6}$ (P). **e.** עֵץ (הָ)אֶרֶז *cedar-wood*, used in purifications Lv 14$^{4.6.49.51.52}$ Nu 19^{6} (all P) **f.** פִּשְׁתֵּי הָעֵץ Jos 2^{6} *woody-flax*, i e. flax on the stalk — Je 10^{8} Gie prop הֶבֶל מֹעֲצָתוֹ for MT הֲבָלִים עֵץ הוּא — מֹאֶסֶת כָּל־עֵץ Ez 21^{15} is dub, Sm prop מָאַסְתְּ כָּל־עֵץ, Co מֹאֲסֵי כָּל־עֵז, Berthol וּמֹאֵסֶף כָּל־עֵז, Siegf^{Kau} Toy leave untranslated.

†II. עֵצָה **n.f. coll. trees** Je 6^{6}, but rd עֵצָהּ (עֵץ c sf 3 fs), so Orient. Codd. 𝔊 𝔖 𝔙 𝔗 Hi Gf Gie — I. עצה v. sub יָעַץ.

III עצה (√ of foll, meaning dub, cf As *eṣên-ṣêri, eṣên of the back*, prob. *spine*, Ar عَصًا *os cruris*, Lane^{2069c} *bone of the shank*, عُصْعُص *os caudae coccygisve*)

†עָצֶה **n.[m.]** either spine or os sacrum, bone close to fat-tail, הֶעָ׳ Lv 3^{9}

IV עצה (√ of foll, Lag$^{BN 157}$ cp. عَضَاةٌ *a land abounding with the trees called* عَضًا)

†עֶצְיוֹן גֶּבֶר **n pr.loc.** usu. Γασιων [Γεσ] Γαβερ, near Elath at head of Gulf of Akaba 1 K 9^{26} = 2 Ch 8^{17}, עֶ׳ גָּבֶר 1 K 22^{49} = 2 Ch 20^{36}, עֶצְיֹן גָּבֶר Dt 2^{8} Nu 33$^{35.36}$ (P)

†[עָצַל] **vb Niph.** be sluggish (NH in der species, and deriv, cf Ar عَطِلَ III *stick fast in coitu*, Lane^{2086}, Syr ܥܛܠ *be stupid*), —*Impf* 2 mpl אַל־תֵּעָצְלוּ לָלֶכֶת Ju 18^{9} *be not sluggish in going.*

עָצֵל$_{14}$ **adj.** sluggish, lazy, — alw ׳עָ abs, — אִישׁ עָ׳ Pr 24^{30}, elsewhere subst *sluggard* Pr 6$^{6.9}$ + 10 t. Pr + הֶעָ׳ 10^{26}

†עַצְלָה **n.f.** sluggishness, — עָ׳ Pr 19^{15}, du intens עֲצַלְתַּיִם Ec 10^{18} *double* (i e. great) *sluggishness* (so Thes De al, rd then perhaps עֲצַלְתַּיִם, > fr. עָצֵל *a sluggish pair*, i.e. hands Ew al), but improb, ‖ שִׁפְלוּת יָדַיִם, whence Bi conj עַצְלוּת, Siegf עַצְלַת יָדַיִם

†עַצְלוּת **n.f.** id; — לֶחֶם עַ׳ Pr 31^{27}.

†I [עָצַם, cf. Lag$^{BN 31}$], עָצַם **vb. be vast, mighty, numerous** (NH Nithp *contend strenuously*, and in deriv.; Ph in עצמת *mighty deeds*, עצמם *bones*, Ar عَظُمَ *be great* in bone, or anything, عَظْم *bones*, Eth ዐፀም: *id*; Aram עַטְמָא, ܥܛܡܐ *thigh*), — **Qal** *Pf.* 3 ms עָצַם consec Dn 8^{24} 11^{23}, 2 ms עָצַמְתָּ Gn 26^{16}, 3 pl עָצְמוּ Is 31^{1}+, עָצֵמוּ ψ 38^{20}, *Impf* 3 mpl. וַיַּעַצְמוּ Ex 1$^{7.20}$, *Inf cstr* עָצְמַת Is 47^{9}, sf. עָצְמוֹ Dn 8^{8}, — **1.** *be mighty*, Gn 26^{16} (J, c מִן comp), Dn 8$^{8.24}$ 11^{23} **2.** *be numerous*, ‖ רַבּוּ etc, Is 31^{1}, בְּעָצְמַת חֲבָרַיִךְ מְאֹד 47^{9}, Je 5^{6} 30$^{14.15}$ Ex 1^{7} (P), v^{20} (J), ψ 38^{20} 69^{5}, c מִן comp Je 15^{8} ψ 40$^{6.13}$, alone 139^{17}. **Hiph.** *make strong*, *Impf* 3 ms sf. וַיַּעֲצִמֵהוּ ψ 105^{24} + מִן comp.

†עֹצֶם **n [m.]** might, bones, — **1.** *might*, cstr עֹ׳ יָדִי Dt 8^{17}, עֹ׳ יָדְךָ Jb 30^{21}; sf עָצְמָה Na 3^{9} (Ges$^{§ 91 e}$), + בעֹ׳ רוּחוֹ Is 11^{15} (Thes al; for MT בַּעְיָם ר׳) **2.** *bones* (coll) sf. עָצְמִי ψ 139^{15} = *my frame*

†עָצְמָה **n.f.** might, — Is 40^{29} (‖ כֹּחַ)

I. עֶצֶם$_{125}$ **n f.**$^{ψ 35,10}$ (c pron masc. Ez 37$^{5.6}$ etc, cf. Albr$^{ZAW xvi (1896), 73}$) **bone, substance, self**, — abs עֶ׳ Gn 2^{23}+, עָצֶם Pr 15^{30} 16^{24}, cstr. עֶצֶם Ex 24^{10}+, sf. עַצְמִי Jb 19^{20}+, etc.; pl. עֲצָמוֹת 2 K 23^{16}+, cstr. עַצְמוֹת Jos 24^{32}+; sf. עַצְמֹתַי Jb 4^{14}+, etc.; also עֲצָמִים Ez 24^{4}+, sf. עֲצָמַי Gn 2^{23}+, etc, — **1.** *bone*: **a.** of living pers Mi 3$^{2.3}$ (hyperb.), Jb 10^{11} 19^{20} La 4^{8} ψ 102^{6} Ec 11^{5}+, fig of close relationship †עֶצֶם מֵעֲצָמַי Gn 2^{23}, cf. 29^{14} (both J), Ju 9^{2} 2 S 5^{1} = 1 Ch 11^{1}, 2 S 19$^{13.14}$ (all + בָּשָׂר) **b.** עֶ׳ + בָּשָׂר = *body*, Jb 2^{5}; pl = *bodily frame* Je 20^{9} (sim.), *limbs, members*, לַעֲצָמֶיהָ Ju 9^{29} i e. *limb by limb* (GFM); as seat of vigour Jb 20^{11}, etc. **c.** (poet) as seat of disease and pain Jb 30$^{17.30}$ and (esp. of personif Isr) ψ 22^{15} 31^{11} 102^{4} La 1^{13} Hb 3^{16}+ **d.** pl as representing entire person = one's whole being, (esp of personif Isr) ψ 6^{3} (‖ נַפְשִׁי v^{4}), 35^{10} (‖ נפשׁ v^{9}), Is 66^{14}; of individ. (incl physical and moral) Pr 3^{8} 14^{30} 15^{30} 16^{24}. **e.** sg = *external body* La 4^{7} Ew Th al., but dub; Bi Bu *bones* (= branches) of coral (פנינים), Lohr עוֹרָם *their skin* **f** esp of dead Nu 19$^{16.18}$ (P), Ez 37^{1}+, oft. (pl) = *remains* Am 6^{10} Gn 50^{25} Ex 13$^{19.19}$ Jos 24^{32} (all E)+. **2.** *bone* of animal Ex 12^{46} Nu 9^{12} (both P), Ez 24$^{4.5}$ (symbol); of (living) hippopot. Jb 40^{18}. **†3.** sg. *substance, self* (cf גֶּרֶם **3**) כְּעֶ׳ הַשָּׁמַיִם Ex 24^{10} (JE),

like the substance of the sky = the sky itself; בְּעֶ׳ תֻּמּוֹ Jb 21^{23} i.e. full prosperity; esp. אֶת־ע׳ בְּעֶ׳ הַיּוֹם הַזֶּה Ez 24^{2} *this selfsame day*, בְּעֶ׳ וגו׳ 24^{2} 40^{1} Gn 7^{13} $17^{23.26}$ Ex $12^{17.41.51}$ Lv $23^{21.28.29.30}$ Dt 32^{48} Jos 5^{11} (all P), עַד־ע׳ וגו׳ Ez 2^{3} Lv 23^{14} (P), Jos 10^{27} (R).—Ez 24^{5a} rd. הָעֵצִים (Bö Ew al.); v^{10} del. הָעֲצָמוֹת (Co Toy); Jb 7^{15} rd. מֵעַצְּבוֹתַי (Reiske Me Bu Du al.); ψ 53^{6} rd. perh. מֵעֲצַת (cf. ‖ ψ 14^{6} Bae; v. Hup Che al.); 69^{5} rd. מֵעַצְמוֹתַי (for MT מַצְמִיתַי), 𝔖 Ol Che Bae al.

†II. עֶצֶם **n.pr.loc.** Ασομ, etc., in Negeb of Judah, עֶצֶם Jos 15^{29}, Simeon 19^{3} 1 Ch 4^{29} (עָצֶם).

עָצוּם **adj. mighty, numerous**;—ע׳ Gn 18^{18}+, pl. עֲצוּמִים Is 8^{7}+, עֲצֻמִים Mi 4^{3}+; sf. עֲצוּמָיו ψ 10^{10};—**1.** *mighty*, esp. of people, *strong* in numbers (oft. ‖ גָּדוֹל, רַב) Gn 18^{18} Ex 1^{9} + 3 t. JE; Dt 4^{38} + 6 t. D, Mi $4^{3.7}$ Zc 8^{22} Is 60^{22} (opp. צָעִיר), of locusts Jo 1^{6} $2^{2.5}$, cf. v^{11}; so of חַיִל Dn 11^{25}; עַם לֹא עָצוּם, i.e. feeble Pr 30^{26} (of the שָׁפָן); less oft. of individ. מְלָכִים ע׳ ψ 135^{10}; of waters Is 8^{7}; ע׳ alone Pr 18^{18} *the mighty*, Dn 8^{24}; ψ 10^{10} *his mighty ones* (i.e. claws, of lion, so Ew De Che Bae al.). **2.** *numerous, countless* (all ‖ רַב): Am 5^{12} ψ 35^{18}; as subst. = *many* Is 53^{12} Pr 7^{26}.—Is 41^{21} v. עֲצֻמָה sub III. עצם.

†[תַּעֲצֻמָה] **n.f. might**;—pl. intens. עֹז וְתַעֲצֻמוֹת ψ 68^{36} *strength and abundant might*.

†עַצְמוֹן **n.pr.loc.** Ασε(λ)μωνα, on extreme S. border of Canaan, Nu 34^{5}, c. ה loc. עַצְמֹנָה v^{4}, עַצְמוֹנָה Jos 15^{4}.

†II. [עָצַם] **vb. shut the eyes** (NH Hiph.; poss. connex. with Syr. ܥܡܨ = *id.*, Ar. غَمَّضَ, غَمَضَ IV (on ض = ܨ v. Nö ZMG xxxii (1878), 406); NH עִמֵּץ *close* eyes of dead; cf. Ba ES 5 f.);—**Qal** *Pt.* וְעֹצֵם עֵינָיו מֵן Is 33^{15} *shutteth his eyes from seeing*. **Pi.** *Impf.* 3 ms. וַיְעַצֵּם אֶת־עֵינֵיכֶם Is 29^{10} *he hath tightly shut your eyes* (cf. I. עצה).

III. עצם (√ of foll., si vera l.; cf. Ar. عَصَمَ *defend, protect*, عِصْمَةٌ *defence*, v. Du and cf. Thes; > De Di al. *your mighty things*, strong arguments (fr. עָצוּם, sub I. עצם, which foll. perhaps imitates in vocalization)).

†[עֲצֻמָה] **n.f. defence**;—pl. sf. עֲצֻמוֹתֵיכֶם (so Baer Ginsb; van d. H. עַצְמ׳) Is 41^{21} *bring forward your defences*, defensive arguments (Che Hpt עַצְּבוֹתֵיכֶם *your idols*, after Gr, [so Lo Klo explain עצמ׳, as *mightiest aid*, I. עצם]).

(ה)עצני 2 S 23^{8}, v. 1. עֲדִין sub I. עדן.

עָצַר **vb. restrain, retain** (NH *id.*; cf. prob. As. *eṣêru*, *retain, restrain*, Dl HWB 122 Jäger BAS i. 483 Zehnpfund ib. 500; Eth. ዐጸረ: *press*, Ar. عَصَرَ; 𝔗 עֲצַר, Syr. ܥܨܰܪ *id.*);—**Qal** *Pf.* 3 ms. ע׳ Gn 20^{18}+, sf. עֲצָרַנִי 16^{2}; 1 s. עָצַרְתִּי Dn $10^{8.16}$, etc.; *Impf.* 3 ms. יַעְצֹר 1 S 9^{17}+, יַעֲצָר־ 2 Ch 2^{5}; sf. יַעַצָרְכָה 1 K 18^{44}, etc.; *Inf. abs.* עָצֹר Gn 20^{18}, *cstr.* לַעְצֹר 2 Ch 22^{9}, וַעְצֹר Jb 4^{2} (Ges §28 b); *Pt. pass.* עָצוּר Je 33^{1}+, etc.;—**1.** *restrain*, c. acc. pers. Gn 16^{2} (J; + מִן, i.e. prevent), עָצֹר עָצַר בְּעַד כָּל־רֶחֶם 20^{18} (E), cf. abs. Is 66^{9} (opp. מוֹלִיד); sq. inf. 2 K 4^{24}; c. acc. pers. alone 1 K 18^{44} *hinder, stop*; c. acc. of sky (hindering rain) Dt 11^{17} 2 Ch 7^{13}; pt. pass. abs. *shut up*, or *hindered* (for reasons not given) Je 36^{5} Ne 6^{10} (? by a vow, or by ceremonial uncleanness, cf. RS Sem i. 436 f., 2nd ed. 455 f.); = *shut up* (c. בְּ, in prison) 2 K 17^{4}, pt. pass. Je 33^{1} 39^{15}, fig. 20^{9}; on עָצוּר וְעָזוּב (5 t.), v. I. עזב; עֲצֻרָה לָנוּ 1 S 21^{6} women have been *kept away* with ref. to us (cf. RS l.c.); עָצוּר מִפְּנֵי 1 Ch 12^{1} *kept away from before* Saul; = *detain*, c. acc. Ju $13^{15.16}$; in Jb c. בְּ, ע׳ בְּמִלִּין 4^{2}, cf. 29^{9}, so בַּמַּיִם 12^{5}; ע׳ בְּעַמִּי 1 S 9^{17} is *rule over*, etc. (si vera l.); ins. also (with other words) 10^{1} 𝔊 We Dr al. **2.** (late) *retain*, c. acc. כֹּחַ 2 Ch 13^{20} 22^{9} Dn $10^{8.16}$ 11^{6}; + inf. = *be able to* 1 Ch 29^{14} 2 Ch 2^{5}; om. כֹּחַ 14^{10} (+ עִמְּךָ), 20^{37} (+ inf.). †**Niph.** *be restrained, stayed*, of plague: Pf. 3 fs. נֶעֶצָרָה Nu 17^{15}; *Impf.* 3 fs. וַתֵּעָצַר 2 S 24^{21} = 1 Ch 21^{22}, וַתֵּעָצַר Nu 17^{13} 25^{8} (P) 2 S 24^{25} ψ 106^{30}; *be shut up* (of sky), *Inf. cstr.* בְּהֵעָצֵר 1 K 8^{35} = 2 Ch 6^{26}; *be under restraint* or *detention Pt.* נֶעְצָר 1 S 21^{8} + לִפְנֵי י׳ (? i.e. kept by a vow, cf. HPS and Ne 6^{10} supr.).

†עֶצֶר **n.[m.] restraint** (?), only יוֹרֵשׁ ע׳ Ju 18^{7} *a possessor of restraint*, i.e. ruler, but 𝔊 𝔙 *wealth*, so Thes al., text very dub., cf. GFM; Bu conj. that ע׳ combines readings אֹצֶר and עֹשֶׁר.

†עֹצֶר **n.[m.] restraint, coercion**;—ע׳ abs.: מֵעֹ׳ וּמִמִּשְׁפָּט Is 53^{8} *from* (as a result of) *coercion and judgment* he was taken off; cstr. ע׳ רָעָה ψ 107^{39}; ע׳ רֶחֶם Pr 30^{16} *restraint of womb*, barrenness (so ψ 107^{39} Perles Anal. 85).

†עֲצָרָה, עֲצֶרֶת **n.f. assembly** (? as *confined, held in*);—abs. עֲצָרָה Is 1^{13} + 2 t.; עֲצֶרֶת Dt 16^{8} + 3 t., עֲצֶרֶת 2 Ch 7^{9}; cstr. עֲצֶרֶת Je 9^{1}; pl. sf. עַצְּרֹתֵיכֶם Am 5^{21};—**1.** sacred *assembly*, rejected by י׳, Is 1^{13} and (at Bethel, etc.) Am 5^{21}; for Baal 2 K 10^{20}; Dt 16^{8} (last day of Maṣṣoth), Lv 23^{36} (P), Nu 29^{35} (P), Ne 8^{18} (all of day after

feast of booths), cf 2 Ch 7^{9} [NH of feast of weeks, 𝔗 עֲצַרְתָּא Jos$^{Ant. iii 10,6}$ Ἀσάρθα]; occasional, Jo 1^{14} 2^{15}. **2.** *assemblage, company* (in gen), ע׳ בגדים Je 9^{1} *an assemblage of deceivers* (Gi עֵרָה, Che חֶבְרַת).

†**מַעְצוֹר n.[m.]** restraint, hindrance;—מ׳ 1 S 14^{6} sq inf, ׳י has no *hindrance* in delivering.

†**מַעְצָר n.[m.]** restraint, control;—מ׳ Pr 25^{28} a man whose spirit is without *control*.

עקב (√of foll, meaning dub.: Thes assumes *be protuberant*, whence both עָקֵב *heel*, and II עָקֹב *hilly*)

†I **עָקֵב n.m.** heel, footprint, hinder-part (Arab عَقِبٌ *heel*, fig *end* (of a month), عِقْبَةٌ *mark, sign, trace*, Aram. עִקְבָא, ܥܩܒܐ *heel, footprint*, fig. *trace, mark* (cf. Wsd 2^{4} 𝔖, Ecclus 13^{26} 𝔊𝔖), also *end, extremity*),—ע׳ abs Gn 3^{15}+, cstr עֲקֵב 25^{26}, pl. cstr. עִקְּבֵי Ct 1^{8}, עִקְּבֵי Gn 49^{17} Ju 5^{22}, עקבות ψ 77^{20} 89^{52}, etc.;—**a.** *heel*, of man, Gn 25^{26} וְיָדוֹ אֹחֶזֶת בַּעֲקֵב אָחִיו, as obj. of attack from behind, 3^{15} וְאַתָּה תְּשׁוּפֶנּוּ עָקֵב, Jb 18^{9} יֹאחֵז בְּעָ׳ פָּח, Je 13^{22} נֶחְמְסוּ עֲקֵבָיִךְ are treated violently, i e. are rudely exposed (|| נִגְלוּ שׁוּלַיִךְ), as instrument of attack, ψ 41^{10} הִגְדִּיל עָלַי עָ׳ hath *made great the heel against me*, i e given me insidiously a great fall (fig. for, taken some cruel advantage of me, cf ὑποσκελίζω); of an animal, Gn 49^{17} הַנֹּשֵׁךְ עִקְּבֵי סוּס, Ju 5^{22}. **b.** *mark of heel, footprint*, Ct 1^{8} צְאִי־לָךְ בְּעִקְבֵי הַצֹּאן, ψ 56^{7} יִשְׁמְרוּ עֲקֵבַי they mark my *footprints*, i e. watch me insidiously wherever I go, 89^{52} אֲשֶׁר חֵרְפוּ עִקְּבוֹת מְשִׁיחֶךָ i e. followed him mockingly, of ׳י (fig) ψ 77^{20} עִקְּבוֹתֶיךָ לֹא נֹדָעוּ thy *footprints* were not known (the waters closing over them) **c.** *hinder-part, rear* (of a troop of men), Gn 49^{19} וְהוּא יָגֻד עָקֵב: (rd עֲקֵבָם: אָשֵׁר) he will troop on *their rear*, Jos 8^{13} עֲקֵבוֹ (cf Di).

†**עָקַב vb.** follow at the heel, fig. assail insidiously, circumvent, overreach (denom from עָקֵב, cf Ar. عَقَبَ *follow* (at the heel), *succeed*, III *bring consequence on*, i e *punish*, Qor 22^{43}, IV *make to follow*, i. e. *reward* or *punish*, عَاقِبَةٌ *end, final lot* 6^{11}, *reward* 6^{136}, ܥܩܒ *hold back* (rare), *follow*, Pa *investigate, search out*. Eth ዐቀበ: is *keep, guard*),—**Qal** *Pf* 3 ms Ho 12^{4} בַּבֶּטֶן עָקַב אֶת־אָחִיו he *attacked* his brother *at the heel* (cf Gn 25^{26} sub עָקֵב), *Impf* 3 ms Gn 27^{36} הֲכִי קָרָא שְׁמוֹ יַעֲקֹב וַיַּעְקְבֵנִי זֶה פַעֲמַיִם and he hath *overreached* me now twice; + *Inf. abs* Je 9^{3} כָּל־אָח עָקוֹב יַעְקֹב surely *overreacheth* (|| רָכִיל יַהֲלֹךְ). [𝔊 πτερνίζω, to attack *with* the heel; but this dub In 'supplant,' also, the fig is a different one.] **Pi.** Jb 37^{4} וְלֹא יְעַקְּבֵם, dub.; poss *attack at the heel* (cf. זנב), hence fig *hold back*; more prob. rd. וְלֹא יְעַכְּבֵם *holdeth* them not *back* (sc. בְּרָקָיו his lightnings), when his voice is heard, from עכב *to hold back* (common in NH, 𝔗 עֲכַב)

†II **עָקֵב adj. verb.** overreacher, ψ 49^{6} עֲוֹן עֲקֵבַי יְסֻבֵּנִי i e. of those who would take some insidious advantage of me

†I. **עָקֹב adj. 1.** insidious, deceitful, Je 17^{9} עָקֹב הַלֵּב מִכֹּל **2.** foot-tracked (denom. from I. עָקֵב) Ho 6^{8} גִּלְעָד קִרְיַת פֹּעֲלֵי אָוֶן עֲקֻבָּה מִדָּם.

†II **עָקֹב adj.** steep, hilly (v. √; cf عَقَبَةٌ *difficult mountain path*, Qor 90^{11}, ዐቀብ: *hill*),—Is 40^{4} וְהָיָה הֶעָקֹב לְמִישׁוֹר let the *steep ground* (Ch) become a plain (|| הָרְכָסִים) Cf Ecclus 6^{20}.

†**עָקְבָה n.f.** insidiousness, 2 K 10^{19} וְיֵהוּא עָשָׂה בְעָ׳.

†**עֵקֶב n.[m.]** consequence, usu. as **adv. acc.** as a consequence of, because (that), also reward, end (v sub עָקֵב; and cf عَقِبٌ *heel*, fig *consequence, result*),—**1.** Is 5^{23} מַצְדִּיקֵי רָשָׁע עֵקֶב שֹׁחַד (adv. acc) *in consequence of* a bribe, ψ 40^{16} (= 70^{4}) עַל עֵקֶב בָּשְׁתָּם (pleon.) *according to the consequence of* their shame, i e. *in consequence of* the disgrace falling upon them. Hence as **conj.** עֵקֶב אֲשֶׁר *as a consequence of* (the fact) *that, because*, Gn 22^{18} ע׳ אֲשֶׁר שָׁמַעְתָּ בְּקֹלִי, 26^{5} 2 S 12^{6}, so עֵקֶב כִּי 2 S 12^{10} Am 4^{12} ע׳ כִּי זֹאת אֶעֱשֶׂה לָּךְ; עֵקֶב alone, Nu 14^{24}, and (sq. impf) Dt 7^{12} ע׳ תִּשְׁמְעוּן *in consequence of* your hearkening, etc, 8^{20} **2.** *consequence* = *gain, reward*, ψ 19^{12} בְּשָׁמְרָם עֵקֶב רָב, Pr 22^{4} עֵקֶב עֲנָוָה (וְ)יִרְאַת ׳י עֹשֶׁר וגו׳. **3.** *end* (of time), adv. acc., ψ 119^{33} וְאֶצְּרֶנָּה ע׳ *to the end*, v^{112} לְעוֹלָם ע׳ (cf. Ecclus 16^{3}, 𝔗 עִקְבָא (rare))

†**עַקּוּב n.pr.m.** 𝔊B usu. (Ι)ακουν[μ], A 𝔊L Ακ(κ)ουβ —**1.** descendant of David 1 Ch 3^{24}. **2.** heads of post-exilic families. **a.** Ezr 2^{42} = Ne 7^{45} **b.** Ezr 2^{45} (si vera l). **3.** Levites: **a.** 1 Ch 9^{17}. **b.** Ne 8^{7} **c.** Ne 11^{19} 12^{25}.

יַעֲקֹב, **יַעֲקוֹב** $_{344}$, $_{5}$ **n.pr.m.** et **gent.** **Jacob**, Ιακωβ, son of Isaac and Rebekah, father of tribes of Isr (expl fr עָקֵב *heel* Gn 25^{26} Ho 12^{4}, i e *supplanter*; cp. with עָקַב *overreach* Gn 27^{36}, *one closely following* acc. to Lag$^{BN\ 127}$, connexion

with Pal city (?) called in Egyptian *Y'kb'ara* (i.e. יַעֲקֹב־אֵל) is obscure, cf. Mey$^{ZAW\ vi\ 1ff}$ WMM $^{As\ u\ Eur\ 162ff}$ Jen$^{ZA\ x\ (1895-6),\ 347ff.}$; v. also Bab. n.pr.m. *Ya'kubilu*, Pinches in Hom$^{AHT\ 61,96,112}$, hence OT יַעֲקֹב perhaps orig. יעקבאל or the like, cf. Palm n pr. (עתעקב, בלעקב),—יַעֲקוֹב Je 30^{18}+3 t. Je, Lv 26^{42}; יַעֲקֹב 215 t. Hex. (chiefly JE; 180 t. Gn, once Lv, etc.), 34 t. ψ, 42 t. Is (27 t. 40–66), etc ,—**1.** as **n.pr.m.** Gn 25^{26}+205 t. (+אַבְרָהָם, יִצְחָק 19 t), also 'בית יע of people (v. בַּיִת **5 d** (γ)), 'עֵין יַע (v. בֵּן **1 j** (β)), 'זֶרַע יַע (v. זֶרַע **4 f**), (v. עַיִן), etc. **2.** as **n.pr.gent.** (c. 100 t.; poet. and proph) Nu $24^{5.19}$ Dt 32^{9} ψ 44^{5} Is 10^{21} 17^{4} Je 10^{25} 30^{7}+, ‖ יִשְׂרָאֵל Nu 23^{7} Dt 33^{10} Is 14^{1} ψ 14^{7}+c 35 t., specif. of N. Isr Am $7^{2.5}$ Ho 12^{13} (+10^{11} 12^{3} prob , v. Now), Mi $1^{5.5}$ Is 9^{7}, of Judah Mi $3^{1.8}$ Ob ^{10} Is 65^{9} Mal 2^{12}+ al post-exilic, 'נְאוֹן יַע v 'גְּאוֹן יַע, +'אל יע ψ 146^{5}, 'אֱלֹהֵי יַע ψ 114^{7}+; 'אֱלֹהֵי יַע 2 S 23^{1} Is 2^{3}=Mi 4^{2}+9 t. ψψ, +ψ 24^{6} ('א׳ יַע for MT 'יַע alone), so 𝔊 𝔖 𝔙 Ew Ol Hup Bae We Che al ; read 'א׳ יַע also prob 2 S 23^{3} (for 'א׳ יִשׂ ‖ 'צוּר יִשׂ) 𝔙 HPS; 'קְדוֹשׁ יַע Is 29^{23} (‖ 'א׳ יִשׂ), 'מֶלֶךְ יַע 41^{21} (‖ יהוה).—On יַעֲקֹב v. esp. Dr *'Jacob'* in Hastings$^{Dict\ Bib\ ii\ 526ff}$.

†יַעֲקֹבָה **n.pr.m.** Simeonite 1 Ch 4^{36} Ιωκαβα, A Ιακαβα, 𝔊L Ιεκεβα.

†I [עָקַד] **vb.** bind (NH *id.*, *bind bent limbs together*, Ar. عَقَدَ *tie, tie fast;* Eth. ዐቀደ: Syr. ܥܩܕ and esp. ܥܩܰܕ *bend, twist*, 𝔗 עֲקַד as NH, also *kneel*, cf Chr. Pal , Schwally$^{Idiot\ 71}$); —**Qal** *Impf.* וַיַּעֲקֹד אֶת־יִצְחָק Gn 22^{9}.

עֵקֶד **n.[m.]** ? binding, cf בֵּית עֵ׳ הָרֹעִים

II. עקד (√ of foll , usu. identif. with I, whence עָקֹד *striped with bands*, but dubious ; Lag$^{BN\ 31}$ vocalizes √ עקר).

†עָקֹד **adj.** striped, streaked ;—of Jacob's goats and sheep ; as subst 'ע Gn 30^{40} (coll), pl. עֲקֻדִּים $31^{8.8}$; pl as attrib $30^{35.39}$, pred. $31^{10.12}$.

†[עָקָה] **n.f.** ψ 55^{4} v. עוק p. 734.

עקה (√ of foll ; cf. Ar عَقَا *hinder*).

†מַעֲקֶה **n.[m.]** parapet ;—Dt 22^{8}.

†[עָקַל] **vb.** bend, twist (NH esp. in deriv , 𝔗 in deriv., Syr. ܥܩܠ *twist*, in der spec ; Ar عَقَلَ *bind* camel's folded fore-shank and arm together) ;—**Pu.** *be bent out of shape, crooked*, *Pt.* fig. מִשְׁפָּט מְעֻקָּל Hb 1^{4} *crooked justice.*

†[עֲקַלְקַל] **adj. intens.** crooked ; — fpl. אֳרָחוֹת עֲקַלְקַלּוֹת Ju 5^{6} i.e roundabout paths (GFM); sf. עֲקַלְקַלּוֹתָם ψ 125^{5} *their crookednesses.*

†עֲקַלָּתוֹן **adj.** crooked (acc to Sm$^{ZAW\ iv\ 213}$ constellation *Draco*),—'לִוְיָתָן נָחָשׁ ע Is 27^{1}.

†עַקָן **n.pr.m.** in Edom ; —'יַע Gn 36^{27}, (Ι)ουκαμ, = יַעֲקָן 1 Ch 1^{42}, Ωυαν, Ιαακαν, etc. (v. Lag$^{BN\ 84\ Anm.**}$, also בְּנֵי־יַעֲקָן and 'בְּאֵרֹת בְּ׳ יע)

עקר (√ of foll.; mng. dub.; cf. Aram. עִקְּרָא, ܥܶܩܳܪܳܐ *root ;* Eth. ዐቀር: *medicine ;* Ar. vb. appar. denom. عَقَّرَ *extirpate*, 𝔗 עֲקַר *id* , NH עִקֵּר=BH).

† I עֵקֶר **n.m.** offshoot, member (? from *root*),—cstr. 'מִשְׁפַּחַת גֵּר ע Lv 25^{47} *a member of a sojourner's family*

†[עָקַר] **vb. denom.** pluck or root up ;—**Qal** *Inf. cstr* לַעֲקוֹר c. acc Ec 3^{2} (opp נָטַע). **Niph.** *Impf.* 3 fs עֶקְרוֹן תֵּעָקֵר Zp 2^{4} (word-play).

†עקר **vb. Pi. denom.** (from עִקָּר or other like word=(*root-sinew*), *hamstring*);—**ham-string** horses (on Arab funeral usage, with camel and horse v. We$^{Heid\ 2,\ 161}$): *Pf.* 3 ms 'ע Jos 11^{9}, *Impf* 3 ms. וַיְעַקֵּר 2 S 8^{4}=1 Ch 18^{4}, 2 ms תְּעַקֵּר Jos 11^{6} all c. acc., *Pf.* 3 mpl. עִקְּרוּ שׁוֹר Gn 49^{6} *they hamstrung an ox.*

†עָקָר **adj.** barren;—'ע of male Dt 7^{14}, עֲקָרָה of female v^{14} (mankind and beasts), Ex 23^{26} (E; female); elsewhere of women Gn 11^{30} 25^{21} 29^{31} (all J), Ju $13^{2.3}$ 1 S 2^{5} Jb 24^{21} ψ 113^{9} (עֲקֶרֶת cstr); of personif. Zion Is 54^{1}.

†II. עֵקֶר **n.pr.m.** in Judah 1 Ch 2^{27}, Ακορ, Ικαρ.

†עַקְרָב **n.m.** scorpion (appar. quadrilit.; NH *id* ; As *akrabu*, Eth ዐቅረብ: ; Ar. عَقْرَبٌ ; 𝔗 עֲקַרְבָּא);—abs עַקְרָב Dt 8^{15} (coll.; of wilderness), pl. עַקְרַבִּים Ez 2^{6} (fig. of enemies); 'יִסַּר בָּע 1 K $12^{11.14}$=2 Ch $10^{11.14}$, i e. scourges with points, stings —Vid. also מַעֲלֵה עַקְרַבִּים.

עֶקְרוֹן $_{22}$ **n.pr.loc.** Ekrôn, Ακκαρων (in As *Amkarruna* COT^{Gloss}, Dl$^{Pa\ 289}$ who prop. עַקְּרוֹן); —Philistine city, one of the famous five, Am 1^{8} Jos 13^{3} (D)+4 t. Jos (P), Ju 1^{18} 1 S $5^{10.10}$+5 t. 1 S ; 2 K $1^{2.3.6.16}$ Je 25^{20} Zp 2^{4} Zc $9^{5.7}$; mod. *'Âkir* Rob$^{BR\ i\ 227ff}$ GASm$^{Geogr\ 193}$ Buhl$^{Geogr\ 187f.}$

†עֶקְרוֹנִי **adj. gent.** of foregoing, c. art.= subst the *Ekrônite* Jos 13^{3} (D), pl הָעֶקְרֹנִים 1 S 5^{10}.

† [עָקַשׁ] **vb. twist** (NH *id.* (rare)),—**Niph.** *Pt* cstr נעקשׁ דְּרָכַיִם Pr 28[18] *one crooked in ways* (< pl, cf Toy) **Pi.** *Pf* 3 pl עקשׁו לָהֶם Is 59[8] *their paths they have twisted* *Impf* 3 mpl יְעַקֵּשׁוּ Mi 3[9] all that is straight *they make crooked*, *Pt* מְעַקֵּשׁ דרכיו Pr 10[9] (cf **Niph**) **Hiph.** *Impf* וַיַּעְקְשֵׁנִי Jb 9[20] (Ges§53n) *he hath declared me crooked*, devious (in life)

† I עִקֵּשׁ **adj. twisted, perverted**,—abs דור ע׳ ופתלתל Dt 32[5] *a generation twisted and crooked*, לֵבָב ע׳ ψ 101[4], as n m (of one devious in life) *the perverted* 2 S 22[27] = ψ 18[27], Pr 22[5], of things 8[8], cstr ע׳ דְּרָכִים 28[6], ע׳ שְׂפָתָיו 19[1], עקשׁ־לב 17[20], pl אָרחתיהם עקשׁים 2[15] *whose ways are twisted*, cstr עקשׁי־לב 11[20]

† II עִקֵּשׁ **n pr m.** a Tekoan 2 S 23[26] = 1 Ch 11[28], 1 Ch 27[9], Εισκα, Εκκις, etc.

† עִקְּשׁוּת **n.f crookedness**—cstr ע׳ פה *crookedness of mouth* Pr 4[24] 6[12] (cf עקשׁ 19[1])

† [מַעֲקָשׁ] **n.[m.] twisted, crooked place**,—pl מַעֲקַשִּׁים Is 42[16] (opp מישׁור).

† I עָר **n pr loc.** in Moab, S of Arnon (Ηρ Nu 21[15], elsewhere chiefly Αροηρ);—ע׳ Nu 21[15] Dt 2[9.18.29], עָר מוֹאָב Nu 21[28] Is 15[1],—usually interpreted as capital *city* (עָר = עִיר) of Moab (DHM ZMG xxxvii (1883) 398 cp Sab ער *fortified height*, cf Mordtm Him Inschr 29 Hal Ét. Sab 159, so Ar اَلْعُرّ, dial. of Yemen); Buhl Geogr 269 f thinks name of *district* S. of Arnon

† II עָר **n.m.** only 2 t · עָרֶךָ 1 S 28[16] (v. Di), rd צָרֶךָ *thine adversary* Klo HPS (al as altern. with foll) > עִם רֵעֶךָ 𝔊 𝔖 𝔗 Th Bu Kit (?) al.; עָרֶיךָ ψ 139[20] is very dub; Hup עָלֶיךָ, Ol Che al שָׂנְאֶךָ, Bae leaves untranslated.

ער v. I. עור

I. ערב (√of foll; prob *עָרַב *mix*; NH עָרַב *mix*, so 𝔗 Pa. (oft), Syr. ܥܪܰܒ *mix* (rarely, in der forms), ܥܘܪܳܒܳܐ *mixture*)

† I עֵרֶב **n.m.** Ex 12, 38 **mixture, mixed company**,—heterogeneous body attached to a people, to Israel Ex 12[38] (E), Ne 13[3]; to Egyptians Je 25[20] (𝔅 joins to v[19], so Gie); to Chaldeans 50[37]; in Je 25[24] del. ואת . . . . הָעֶרֶב as doublet (so Gie, cf. 𝔊), in 1 K 10[15] rd עֲרָב (as ‖ 2 Ch 9[14], so Benz Kit al), Ez 30[5] rd. prob *id.* (Co).

II עֵרֶב **n.[m.] woof** (as *mixed*, interwoven, with warp);—Lv 13[48] + 8 t. 13 (all opp. שְׁתִי *warp*), cf GFM PAOS 1889, clxxviii.

עָרֹב **n.m.** Ex 8, 20 prob **swarm** (*mixture*, from incessant, involved motion; Lag BN 112 doubts);—of plague of stinging flies, coming in a *swarm* (v. Di Ex) Ex 8[17.17] + 5 t 8 (J), ψ 78[45] 105[31].

† II עָרַב **vb. take on pledge, give in pledge, exchange** (NH *go surety for* (rare); Ph. ערב *surety*, OAram ערבא *pledge*; 𝔗 עֲרַב, Syr. ܥܪܰܒ, *go surety for*; usu. identified with I. ערב—*mix, exchange, pledge*—but quite uncertain; cf. Buhl Lex Lag BN 203),—**Qal** *Pf* 3 ms. ע׳ Gn 44[32] + 4 t; 2 ms. עָרַבְתָּ Pr 6[1]; *Impf.* 1 s sf. אֶעֶרְבֶנּוּ Gn 43[9], *Imv.* ערב ψ 119[122], sf. עָרְבֵנִי Is 38[14], so Jb 17[3] (but v infr.), *Inf. cstr.* לַעֲרֹב Ez 27[9]; *Pt.* ערב Pr 17[18], etc,—**1.** c. acc. pers. *take on pledge*, i e. *go surety for* the safety of, Gn 43[9] (J), 44[32] (J, + מֵעִם pers.), for the debts of Pr 11[15] 20[16] 27[13], of God Is 38[14] *go surety for me*, ψ 119[122], so Jb 17[3] (si vera l., v. עֶרְבֹן); acc. pers om, ע׳ לְ Pr 6[1] *go surety to* one (in behalf of another, ‖ תָּקַע לַזָּר כַּפֶּךָ), c. acc. rei Pr 22[26] (‖ תֹּקְעֵי־כָף). **2.** *give in pledge*, c acc. rei Ne 5[3] (i e mortgage), fig ע׳ אֶת־לִבּוֹ Je 30[21] so ע׳ עֲרֻבָּה לִפְנֵי רֵעֵהוּ Pr 17[18] (‖ תֹּקֵעַ כָּף). **3.** *exchange* (in trade), c acc. cogn מַעֲרָבֵךְ Ez 27[9.27]. **Hithp 1.** recipr. *Imv* הִתְעָרֶב נָא אֶת־אֲדֹנִי 2 K 18[23] *exchange pledges* (make a bargain) *with my lord* = Is 36[8]. **2. a.** *have fellowship* with, בְּ pers, *Pf* 3 pl. התערבו Ezr 9[2], *Impf.* 3 mpl וַיִּתְעָרְבוּ ψ 106[35], 2 ms תִּתְעָרָב c לְ pers. Pr 20[19], c עם pers 24[21]. **b.** *share in*, בְּ rei, 3 ms. יִתְעָרַב Pr 14[10] in his joy no other *shares*.

† עֲרֻבָּה **n.f. thing exchanged, pledge, token**,—sf. עֲרֻבָּתָם 1 S 17[18] = *a token from them*, i. e. response, token of welfare, Th Dr al., abs as acc cogn. ע׳ עָרַב Pr 17[18] *give a pledge*

† עֵרָבוֹן **n. [m.] pledge**;—נָתַן ע׳ *give a pledge* Gn 38[17.18], לָקַח ע׳ v[20] (all J), *receive* (back) *a pledge* (when condition is fulfilled)—Jb 17[3] rd perh. ערבני (for MT עָרְבֵנִי), as obj. of שִׂימָה *set my pledge* (*a surety for me*), so Beer Bu al.

† I [מַעֲרָב] **n.m.** usu **coll. articles of exchange, merchandise** (only of Tyre, Ez 27),—sf. מַעֲרָבֵךְ v[13.17.19.25.27a.34], as acc. cogn. c עָרַב v[9.27], pl sf. מַעֲרָבַיִךְ v[33] perh *thy* (diverse) *wares* (DHM VOJ viii (1894), 4 prop, ingeniously, meaning *imports*, deriving fr. V. ערב *enter*, but improb)

†[תַּעֲרֻבָה] **n.f. pledge**;—only pl. in phr. בְּנֵי הַתַּעֲרֻבוֹת 2 K 14[14] i. e. *hostages* = 2 Ch 25[24].

†III. [עָרֵב] **vb. be sweet, pleasing** (NH *id.* (rare); Hiph. Impf. יעריבו Ecclus 40[21]; 𝔗 עָרִיב adj. *pleasant, sweet*);—**Qal** *Pf.* 3 fs. עָרְבָה Je 31[26] my sleep *was sweet* to me (לִי), וְע׳ שְׁנָתְךָ consec. Pr 3[24]; of offering לא ע׳ לי׳ Mal 3[4]; 2 fs. עָרַבְתְּ Ez 16[37] c. עַל pers., to whom *thou wast pleasing*; 3 pl. לֹא עָרְבוּ לִי Je 6[20] (of sacrif.); *Impf.* 3 ms. יֶעֱרַב עָלָיו שִׂיחִי ψ 104[34] *let my meditation be pleasing unto him!* 3 fs. תֶּעֱרַב לְ Pr 13[19] (of realized wish); 3 mpl. לֹא יֶעֶרְבוּ לוֹ Ho 9[4] (of sacrifice; but Kue Che We GASm Now read יַעַרְכוּ).

†עָרֵב **adj. sweet, pleasant**;—ע׳ לָאִישׁ לֶחֶם שָׁקֶר Pr 20[17]; קוֹלֵךְ ע׳ Ct 2[14].

IV. ערב (√of foll.; poss. *be arid;* Thes cp. Eth. ዐበረ: *be arid, sterile*, so Baentsch[Die Wüste (1883). 17], but dub.; Syr. ܥܪܒܐ = BH; Ar. العَرَبَة n.pr. of depression S. of Dead Sea).

†עֲרָב **n.[m.] desert-plateau, steppe** (cf. Che[Intr. Is. 129]);—בַּעֲרָב בַּעְרַב (si vera l.) Is 21[13.13] *in the steppe* (of what we know as N. Arabia); but in v[b] Vrss Lo Che Gu[Kau] al. בָּעֶרֶב *in the evening*.

†עֲרָבִי **n. gent.** of foregoing, steppe-dweller;—Is 13[20]; כַּעֲרָבִי בַּמִּדְבָּר Je 3[2].

†עֲרָב **n.pr. gent. coll. steppe-dwellers** of N. Arabia (Wetzst[ZVölkerpsych. vii. 463 f.]; extended later (so Herod[ii. 11] etc.) to whole peninsula, cf. Ar. العَرَبُ *the Arabs*, Bedûwy *the people*, Doughty[Arab. Deserta, i. 224]; Sab. ערבן, ערב, אערב CIS[iv. p. 123], As. *Aribu, Arubu, Arabi*, people in N. Arabia, Dl[Pa 295 f. 304 f.] COT[Je 25, 24]; also *Urbi* Dl[Pa 305 f.] of nomad 'Arab' tribes);—מַלְכֵי ע׳ הַשֹּׁכְנִים בַּמִּדְבָּר Je 25[24] (v. I. עֶרֶב), 2 Ch 9[14] + ‖ 1 K 10[15] (v. *id.*); ע׳ also Ez 27[21] + 30[5] (v. *id.*); v. esp. Nö[Arabia] in Ency. Bib.

†עֲרָבִי **adj. gent. Arabian** (in strictly ethnographic sense, Nö[l. c.]);—הָע׳ as subst. Ne 2[19] Geshem *the Arabian*, so 6[1]; pl. הָעַרְבִים Ne 4[1] 2 Ch 21[16] 22[1]; also (written as NH) הערביים 26[7] (Qr הָעַרְבִים), and even הָעַרְבִיאִים 17[11].

I. עֲרָבָה[61] **n.f. desert-plain, steppe**;—abs. ע׳ 2 S 4[7] +, sf. עַרְבָתָהּ Is 51[3]; pl. עֲרָבוֹת Je 5[6] ψ 68[5], cstr. עַרְבוֹת 2 K 25[5] +, עַרְבֹת Je 52[8];—**1.** earliest use: **a.** arid steppe W. of Dead Sea (in S. Judah) 1 S 23[24], also Ez 47[8] Is 51[3], whence name יָם הָע׳ Jos 3[16] (JE ‖ יָם הַמֶּלַח), also 2 K 14[25] Dt 4[49], and (‖ *id.*) 3[17] Jos 12[3] (D); נַחַל הָעֲרָבָה Am 6[14] must be E. of Dead Sea, si vera l., but rd. prob. נַחַל נ׳ מִצְרַיִם v. **b.** Jordan-valley W. of river + adjacent plain; near ford (opp. Jericho) 2 S 2[29], cf. Jos 8[14] (JE); also Dt 11[30] 2 K 25[4] = Je 39[4] = 52[7];—2 S 15[28] 17[16] v. עֲבָרָה. **c.** Jordan-valley E. of river 2 S 4[7]. **2.** in D: **a.** esp. of E. Jordan plain Dt 1[1] (prob.) Jos 12[1.3], E. half of Jordan-valley Dt 3[17] 4[49]; of entire Jordan-valley (between כִּנֶּרֶת and Dead Sea, mod. *El-Ghôr, the Depression*) Dt 1[7] Jos 11[2.16]; W. Jordan plain only Jos 12[8]; depression S. of Dead Sea (mod. *Wady el-'Arabah*) Dt 2[8]. **3.** in P always pl. cstr. עַרְבוֹת מוֹאָב (E. Jordan) Nu 22[1] + 11 t. (v. מוֹאָב); ע׳ יְרֵחוֹ (W. Jordan) Jos 4[13] 5[10], also 2 K 25[5] = Je 39[5] = 52[8]. **4.** appar. N. Arabian desert Is 40[3] 41[19]. **5.** in gen. *the steppe* (oft. ‖ מִדְבָּר), Je 17[6] 50[12] Is 33[9] 35[1.6] Jb 24[5] 39[6] ψ 68[5]; זְאֵב עֲרָבוֹת Je 5[6] (fig. of invader); cf. description of Exodus אֶרֶץ עֲרָבָה וְשׁוּחָה Je 2[6]; in sim., of a *plain*, of future land of Judah Zc 14[10].—Vid. Dr[Dt 1. 1 and reff.] Buhl[Geogr. 111].

בֵּית הָעֲרָבָה v. עַרְבָתִי.

V. ערב (√of foll.; cf. As. *erêbu, enter, go in; erêb šamši, sunset;* Ar. غَرَبَ *set* (distinct fr. غَرَبَ *depart*, = Sab. ערב *withdraw*, acc. to DHM[Epigr. Denkm. 27]), غَرْبٌ *place of sunset, west;* Sab. מערבם, מערבי [not ע׳!] *west, western*, CIS[iv. p. 199] DHM[l. c.]; Eth. ዐረበ: *set* (of heavenly bodies), so Syr. ܥܪܒ; ܡܥܪܒܐ *evening* (Lag[BN 64 f.]); Zinj. מערב *west;* NH עֶרֶב = BH. Hence also Εὐρώπη, *Europe*, Lewy[Fremdw. 139]).

עֶרֶב[131] **n.[m.** 1 S 20[5] del. הַשְּׁלִשִׁית v. We Dr al.] **(sun)set, evening**;—abs. ע׳ 2 K 2[16] +, עָרֶב Ex 12[18] +; cstr. עֶרֶב Pr 7[9]; du. עַרְבַּיִם Ex 30[8] + 4 t., -בַּיִם 12[16] + 5 t. (all P);—**1. a.** *evening*, orig. sun*set*, and hence perh. לְעֵת ע׳ *at the time of* sunset †Gn 8[11] (J), 24[11] (J; ‖ לְעֵת צֵאת הַשֹּׁאֲבֹת), 2 S 11[2] Is 17[14] and (of the day of י׳) Zc 14[7], עֵת הָע׳ Jos 8[29] (JE)†; usu. ע׳ alone = *time of sunset, evening:* בָּע׳ *in the evening* Gn 19[1] (J), 29[23] (E), Ex 12[18] (P), Dt 16[6] (+ כְּבוֹא שֶׁמֶשׁ), 1 K 22[35] (cf. ‖ 2 Ch 18[34] where + לְעֵת בּוֹא הַשָּׁמֶשׁ) + 20 t. + בָּע׳(־)בָּע׳ 2 Ch 13[11.11] = *every evening;* לָע׳ *at evening* only late: †1 Ch 16[40] 23[30] 2 Ch 2[3] Ezr 3[3] ψ 59[7.15] 90[6] Ec 11[6]†; לִפְנוֹת ע׳ *at the turn of evening* †Gn 24[63] (J), Dt 23[12]; ע׳ as adv. acc. Ec 16[6] (P), ψ 55[18]; as marking duration of impurity, in phr. עַד־הָע׳ Lv 11[24] + 30 t. P + Lv 22[6] (H); of Day of Atonement מֵע׳

†[עֲרוּגָה] **n.f. garden terrace or bed**;—cstr. עֲרוּגַת הַבֹּשֶׂם Ct 5[13] *bed of balsam* (sim); pl cstr. עֲרֻגוֹת הַבּ׳ 6[2], ע׳ מַטָּעָהּ Ez 17[7] i e. where the vine was planted, עֲרֻגֹת צִמְחָהּ v[10] (all fig).

† I עֲרָד **n.pr.loc.** Can. city in the Negeb, Αραδ (Egypt *'a-ru-dâ* WMM[As. u Eur 168. 170]),—Ju 1[16], מֶלֶךְ־ע׳ Nu 21[1] (JE) = 33[40], Jos 12[14] (D, Α(ι)ραθ, A 𝔊L Αδερ), prob. mod. *Tel Arad*, 16½ miles S. of Hebron, cf GFM[Ju 1.16] Buhl[Geogr 182]

† II עֲרָד **n.pr.m.** Benjamite 1 Ch 8[15], Ωρηρ, A Αρωδ, 𝔊L Αραδ.

†[עָרָה] **vb. be naked, bare** (Ar. عَرِيَ *be naked*; Pi ערה [Pi.] *lay bare* (cf Bloch Lzb), As *ûru*, *nakedness*, also *desert waste* (cf [עָרָה] infr) Jager[BAS II 282] and reff; NH עֶרְוָה = BH, 𝔗 עירִיתָא; Syr. ܥܰܪܛܳܐ in Lexx),—**Pi.** *Pf.* 3 ms עֵרָה Is 22[6] Zp 2[14], *Impf* 3 ms. יְעָרֶה Is 3[17], 3 fs וַתְּעַר Gn 24[20]; 2 ms juss תְּעַר ψ 141[8], 3 mpl. וַיְעָרוּ 2 Ch 24[11]; *Imv* mpl. עָרוּ ψ 137[7], *Inf. abs.* עָרוֹת Hb 3[13] (Ges[§ 75 n]),—**1.** *lay bare* Is 3[17] 22[6] Zp 2[14] (indef subj.), of laying foundations bare, i.e. tearing down walls, etc Hb 3[13] (yet on text v. Now), abs. עָרוּ עָרוּ ψ 137[7]. **2.** *lay bare* by removing contents, *empty*, water-jar Gn 24[20] (J; + אֶל loc.), chest 2 Ch 24[11]. **3.** *pour out*, אַל־תְּעַר נַפְשִׁי ψ 141[8] (i e. slay) **Hiph.** *Pf.* 3 ms. הֶעֱרָה: **1.** *make naked*, of sexual offences Lv 20[18.19] (both ‖ גִּלָּה). **2.** *pour out*, הֶע׳ לַמָּוֶת נַפְשׁוֹ Is 53[12] (fig. for *slay*, cf. **Qal 3**) **Niph.** pass of **Hiph. 2**: 3 ms. יֵעָרֶה עָלֵינוּ רוּחַ Is 32[15] (fig.) until *there be poured upon us a spirit* from on high **Hithp. 1.** *Impf.* 2 fs תִּתְעָרִי La 4[21] *thou shalt make thyself naked* (of Edom under fig of drunken woman). **2.** *Pt* מִתְעָרֶה ψ 37[35] usu *pouring himself*, i e. *spreading himself out* like a tree (Bae doubts; Du מִתְעַלֶּה *lifting himself up*, cf. 𝔊).

†[עָרָה] **n.f. bare place**;—pl עָרוֹת Is 19[7] (si vera interpr.; > 𝔊 ἄχ(ε)ι, Ki Saad *reeds*).

עֶרְוָה[54] **n.f. nakedness, pudenda**;—abs ע׳ Ex 28[42] Lv 18[6], usu. cstr עֶרְוַת Gn 9[22]+, sf. ערותך Ex 20[23] (Ginsb), Lv 18[10]; עֶרְוָתֵךְ Is 47[3]+; תוֹ- Lv 20[17], תָהּ- 18[7]+; sf 3 fpl. עֶרְוָתָן v[9.10],—**1.** *pudenda*, of man, רָאָה ע׳ implying shameful exposure Gn 9[22.23] (J); mostly of woman: fig. of Jerus. (c. רָאָה) La 1[8] Ez 16[37]; usu. c גלה: lit תִּגָּלֶה ע׳ i e be exposed to view Ex 20[23] (Ginsb; van d H v[26], E), so, as shameful punishment,

עַד־ע׳ 23[32] (P) **b.** du in phrase (only P) בֵּין הָעַרְבַּיִם *between the two evenings*, i e prob. between sunset and dark (v Thes [various views fully given], otherwise Di[Ex 12.6], on form as poss. only expanded pl v Ges[§ 88 c]), †Ex 12[6] 16[12] 29[39.41] 30[8] Lv 23[5] Nu 9[3.5.11] 28[4.8]† **c.** other phrases are: צִלְלֵי ע׳ Je 6[4] (dist fr. צָהֳרַיִם and לַיְלָה v[5]), מִנְחַת (הָ)ע׳ †2 K 16[15] Ezr 9[4.5] ψ 141[2] Dn 9[21]†, זְאֵבֵי ע׳ v I זְאֵב, for all combin with בֹּקֶר *morning*, v ב׳ **1 d, e.** **2** (late poet.) = *night*, עֶרֶב Jb 7[4], cf. בְּנֶשֶׁף בְּעֶרֶב יוֹם Pr 7[9] (‖ בְּאִישׁוֹן לַיְלָה וַאֲפֵלָה)

†[עָרַב] **vb. denom.** become evening, grow dark (?),—**Qal** *Inf. cstr.* רָפָה הַיּוֹם לַעֲרוֹב Ju 19[9], but rd prob נָטָה הַיּוֹם לַעֲרֹב 𝔊L GFM; *Pf* 3 fs fig עָרְבָה Is 24[11] all joy *has grown dark*, but rd עָבְרָה *has passed away* Lo Gr Perles[Anal 91] Che[Hpt] al. **Hiph.** *Inf abs* הַשְׁכֵּם וְהַעֲרֵב 1 S 17[16] *doing it* at morning and *at evening.*

† II מַעֲרָב **n.[m.]** west (late) (place of sun*set*);—מַעֲרָבָה (= -ָבָה, cf. De Ges[§ 91 e]) Is 45[6] *from its setting-place* (opp. מִמִּזְרַח־שֶׁמֶשׁ); מַעֲרָב opp מִזְרָח also 43[5] 59[19] ψ 103[12] 107[3], so לַמּ׳ *westward* 1 Ch 7[28] 12[16] (van d. H. v[15]), 26[16.18]; מ׳ opp מוֹצָא ψ 75[7]; מִן־הַמַּעֲרָב (alone) Dn 8[5], c. ה loc מַעֲרָבָה 1 Ch 26[30] *westward*, sq לְ = *to the west of* 2 Ch 32[30] 33[14], ממ׳ לַגִּבְעָה Ju 20[33] acc. to 𝔊 (not B) 𝔙 Be GFM al (v [מַעֲרֶה]).

VI עָרַב (√of foll.; cf Ar غَرِبَ *be black*, غُرَابٌ *crow* (raven, rook, etc); As *âribu*, *êribu*; Aram ܥܽܘܪܒܳܐ, עוּרְבָא, all *crow*, *raven*).

†עֹרֵב **n m.**[Lv 11.15] **raven**,—הָעֹ׳ Gn 8[7] (J), Lv 11[15] (H) = Dt 14[14] Jb 38[41]; כָּעוֹרֵב Ct 5[11] black *as the raven*; בְּנֵי עֹרֵב ψ 147[9] *young ravens*; pl abs הָעֹרְבִים 1 K 17[4.6], cstr עֹרְבֵי־נַחַל Pr 30[17].

† II [עֲרָבָה] **n.[f.] poplar** (*populus Euphratica* = Ar غَرَبٌ We in De[Gn (4). 568] Kersten ZPV II 209 De[Is (4) 44, 4] Low[p 300 Anm]; NH עֲרָבָה; √obscure),—pl. abs עֲרָבִים עַל־יִבְלֵי־מָיִם Is 44[4], cf. ψ 137[2], cstr. עַרְבֵי־נָחַל Lv 23[40] (H), Jb 40[22]; נַחַל־הָעֲרָבִים Is 15[7] (a wady in Moab, identification dub, v conjectures in Buhl[Geogr 124]).

†[עָרַג] **vb.** long for (cf Ar. عَرَجَ *ascend*, II. *bend*, *incline* toward (على); عَرِيجٌ *high*, *elevated*; Eth. ዐረገ: *ascend*, NH עֲרוּגָה = BH),—**Qal** *Impf* 3 fs. תַּעֲרֹג ψ 42[2] (of stag, c. עַל rei in sim), c אֶל, *of longing for God* v[2] (subj נַפְשִׁי), so תַּעֲרוֹג Jo 1[20] (of beasts, craving water)

fig. of Egypt Is 20^{4} (gloss acc. to Du Che Di-Kit), Bab 47^{3}, of Jerus Ez 16^{37} 23$^{10.29}$ (עֶרְוַת זְנוּנַיִךְ; all three obj. of act vb.), chiefly euphem. for cohabit., גִּלָּה ע׳ Lv 18^{6}+ (v. גלה **Pi. 1 a**); fig of Jerus. (vb. pass) Ez 16^{36}; רָאָה ע׳ in same meaning Lv 20$^{17\,17}$ (H; of both sexes); ע׳ also 18$^{8\,10\,16}$ (H); כִּסָּה ע׳ *cover nakedness* Gn 9^{23} (J), Ex 28^{42} (P; בְּשַׂר ע׳), Ho 2^{11} (fig. of Isr.), Ez 16^{8} (of Jerus); reviling words are לְבֹשֶׁת ע׳ אִמֶּךָ 1 S 20^{30} (cf Doughty$^{\text{Arab Deserta I 269}}$). **2.** עֶרְוַת דָּבָר *nakedness of a thing*, i.e. prob. *indecency, improper behaviour* Dt 23^{15} 24^{1} (v. Dr). **3.** fig. ע׳ הָאָרֶץ Gn 42$^{9.12}$ (E), i.e its exposed, undefended parts (Ar. عَوْرَةٌ).

† **עֶרְיָה** n.f. **nakedness**;—alw abs. ע׳;—ע׳־בֹשֶׁת Mi 1^{11} (in) *nakedness*, (in) *shame* (fig of town Shaphir); of Jerus. ערם וע׳ Ez 16^{7}+3 t. (v עירם sub II. עור); of bow Hb 3^{9} (v. II. עור).

† [**מַעֲרָה**], **מַעַר** n.[m.] **bare, naked place** (hence Μαραθών, Marathon, acc to Lewy$^{\text{Fremdw 144}}$),—**1.** *bare place*, or *space*. cstr. מִמַּעֲרֵה־גָבַע Ju 20^{33} *bare* (open) *space* of Geba' (si vera l.; but v II. מַעֲרָב); כְּמַעַר־אִישׁ 1 K 7^{36} *according to the clear space on each* (plate, v. לוּחַ). **2.** sf מַעְרֵךְ Na 3^{5} fig. of Nineveh (*pudenda* exposed in shameful punishment; cf עֶרְוָה).

† **מַעֲרָת** n. pr. loc. in Judah Jos 15^{59}, Μαγαρωθ, A 𝔊L Μα(α)ρωθ.

† **תַּעַר** n.m. $^{\text{ψ 52,4}}$ and (Is 7^{20}) **f. razor, sheath**,—**1. a.** *razor*, abs יְגַלַּח בְּת׳ Is 7^{20} (fig.); subj of לֹא יַעֲבֹר עַל־רֹאשׁ Nu 6^{5}, obj. of הֶעֱבִיר עַל־ 8^{7} (P), cf. cstr. ת׳ הַגַּלָּבִים Ez 5^{1}; abs. כְּת׳ מְלֻטָּשׁ ψ 52^{4} (sim of tongue). **b.** cstr. ת׳ הַסֹּפֵר Je 36^{23} =*penknife*. **2.** *sheath*, always sf. of sword: בְּתַעְרָהּ 2 S 20^{8}; of drawing sword, שָׁלַף מִת׳ 1 S 17^{51}, הוֹצִיא מִת׳ Ez 21$^{8.10}$, תֵּצֵא מִת׳ v^{9}, of sheathing, הָשֵׁב אֶל־תַּעְרָהּ Je 47^{6}, הָאָסְפִי אֶל־תַּעְרֵךְ Ez 21^{35}.

† **עָרוֹד** n.[m.] **wild ass** (prob. Aram. loan-word (=Heb. פֶּרֶא), 𝔗 עֲרָדָא, ערודא, Syr. ܥܪܳܕܳܐ; Mand. אראדא, cf. Hom$^{\text{NS 133}}$),—Jb 39^{5}.

† **עָרַךְ** vb. **arrange or set in order** (NH *id*; also *roll* dough, 𝔗 עֲרַךְ *id.*; Ph. ערכת CIS$^{\text{No. 132, 4}}$ *valuation*, Bloch, but dub; Ar. عَرَكَ III *contend* in battle, مَعْرَكٌ, مَعْرَكَةٌ *battle-ground*),—**Qal** *Pf.* 3 ms. ע׳ Jb 32^{14} 2 Ch 13^{3}, וְע׳ consec. Lv 1^{12} 6^{5}; עָרַכְתִּי Nu 23^{4}+, etc, *Impf.* 3 ms. יַעֲרֹךְ Ex 27^{21}+, etc; *Imv.* עֶרְכָה Jb 33^{5}, ערכו Je 46^{3} 50^{14}, *Inf. abs.* עָרֹךְ Is 21^{5}; *cstr* עֲרֹךְ Ju 20^{22}+; *Pt. act* pl ערכים Is 65^{11}, etc; *pass.* עָרוּךְ Je 6^{23}+, cstr. עֲרוּךְ Jo 2^{5}, etc.;—not in D;—**1. a.** *arrange in order*, seven altars Nu 23^{4}, i.e. I have built seven altars *in a row* (cf. בנה v^{1}), flax-stalks Jos 2^{6} (both JE); esp. **b.** *set* or *lay in order*, as wood Gn 22^{9} (E), 1 K 18^{33}, cf. Tophet Is 30^{33}, Lv 1^{7}; offerings Lv 1$^{8\,12}$ 6^{5}; lamp(s) Ex 27^{21} Lv 24$^{3.4}$ (all P), lamp (fig. of dynasty) ψ 132^{17}; 'shew'-bread Ex 40$^{4.23}$ (upon [על] sacred שֻׁלְחָן; both c. acc cogn), Lv 24^{8} (P). **c.** in common life (cf RS$^{\text{Sem I 183 f., 2nd ed 200 f.}}$), *arrange* a table (i.e. dishes in order upon it), שֻׁלְחָן Is 21^{5} Pr 9^{2} (fig. of wisdom), Ez 23^{41} (of Jerus. in fig), ψ 23^{5} 78^{19} (fig.; subj God); in idolatr. worship Is 65^{11} **d.** *arrange* a battle, i e draw up in battle order, ע׳ מִלְחָמָה Ju 20^{22} 1 S 17^{8} 2 S 10^{8}=1 Ch 19^{9}, 1 Ch 12^{37} (van d. H. v^{36}), 2 Ch 14^{9}, עֹרְכֵי מלחמה 1 Ch 12$^{34.36}$ (van d H. v$^{33.35}$), עֲרוּךְ מ׳ Jo 2^{5}; + אֵת *with*, i.e *against* Ju 20^{20} Gn 14^{8}, עִם 2 Ch 13^{3}; + לִקְרַאת 1 S 17^{2} 1 Ch 19$^{17\,b}$, ע׳ מַעֲרָכָה לִקְרַאת 1 S 17^{21}; עָרוּךְ כְּאִישׁ לַמִּלְחָמָה Je 6^{23} 50^{42}; obj om. Ju 20$^{22.33}$, + לִקְרַאת 1 S 4^{2} 2 S 10$^{9.10}$=1 Ch 19$^{10.11}$, 2 S 10^{17}, + אֶל *against* Ju 20^{30} Je 50^{14} 1 Ch 19$^{17\,a}$, לְ *against* Je 50^{9},—Jb 6^{4} read יַעַבְרוּנִי Di Bu Du. **e.** *arrange* weapons of army *in order* for battle Je 46^{3}, 1 Ch 12^{9} (van d. H. v^{8}). **f.** *arrange* words (מִלִּין) Jb 32^{14} (+ אֶל *against*), so (obj om.) 33^{5} (+ לְפָנַי), 37^{19} ψ 5^{4} (prob, > of arranging a sacrifice), cf. *recount* things *in order*, יַעַרְכֶהָ לִי Is 44^{7} **g.** *state in order, set forth* a legal case Jb 13^{18} 23^{4}, so prob. (obj. om) of God ψ 50^{21} (+ לְעֵינֶיךָ), and (pass. of בְּרִית) 2 S 23^{5} (cf Dr).—הֲיַעֲרֹךְ שׁוּעֲךָ Jb 36^{19} is difficult: Di *will he set thy cry* (שׁוּעֲךָ) *in order?* Bi (for לֹא) הֲיַעֲרָךְ שׁ׳ לוֹ *shall thy cry be set in order unto him?* (sense good, although **Niph.** not found); v. al. in Di. **2. a.** *compare* (as result of arranging in order): מַה־דְּמוּת תַּעַרְכוּ־לוֹ Is 40^{18} *what likeness will ye compare to him?* אֵין עֲרֹךְ אֵלֶיךָ ψ 40^{6}. **b.** intrans. *be comparable*, c לְ, ψ 89^{7} (‖ דָּמָה), c. sf. of thing compared Jb 28$^{17\,19}$.

עֵרֶךְ$_{33}$ n.m. $^{\text{Lv 27, 25}}$ **order, row, estimate**,—cstr. ע׳ Ju 17^{10} Ex 40^{23}; sf. עֶרְכִּי ψ 55^{14}, עֶרְכְּךָ Lv 5^{15}+, etc.;—**1.** *order, row*, ע׳ בְּגָדִים Ju 17^{10} *a* (complete) *suit of clothes* (laid out in order), 𝔊^{B} στολὴν ἱματίων; ע׳ לֶחֶם Ex 40^{23} i e. loaves arranged in a row, so ע׳ alone v^{4} (P), עֶרְכּוֹ Jb 41^{4} *his symmetry* (v. חִין sub חנן). **2.** *estimate, valuation*, made by ordering, classifying: איש

כערכו 2 K 23[35]; in 12[a] read עֶרְכּךָ (for MT עובר) *money of a man's valuation* 𝔊 Benz Kit, and prob del כ׳ עֶרֶךְ נ׳) כֶּסֶף נַפְשׁוֹת עֶרְכּוֹ Kit) as gloss (Sta[ZAW v (1885), 288 f]), כערכי ψ 55[14] a man *acc to my valuation*, fig for *my equal*, elsewhere P, of priest's valuation of trespass-offering Lv 5[15 18 25], vows, and redemption-money 27[2.3.3.4] + 17 t 27 (כסף ערכך v[15 19], מִכְסַת הָעֶרְכְּךָ v[23] [del הָ], cf v[23b] [del *id*]), Nu 18[16].—Jb 28[13] read דַּרְכָּהּ 𝔊 Di al

†[עָרַךְ] **vb. denom. Hiph. value** (for taxation), **tax** (from ערך **2**),—*Pf* 3 ms. הֶעֱרִיךְ אֶת־הָאָרֶץ 2 K 23[35]; in P, וְהֶעֱ׳ consec, c acc pers Lv 27[8 12] c sf v[14], *Impf* יַעֲרִיךְ v[14], sf יַעֲרִיכֶנּוּ v[8]

†[מַעֲרָךְ] **n.[m.] arrangement**,—pl cstr מַעַרְכֵי־לֵב Pr 16[1] to man belong *arrangements* (plans) *of the mind* (cf לב **3**)

†מַעֲרָכָה **n.f. row, rank, battle-line**,—**1. a.** מ׳ *battle-line* 1 S 4[2 12 16 16], וַיָּרָץ הַמּ׳ 17[22] *and he ran to the battle-line*, so v[23] (on ref here to Isr's line cf HPS), עֹרְכֵי מ׳, v[21], מ׳ לִקְרַאת מ׳ 1 Ch 12[39] (van d H. v[34]), nearly=battle הַחַיִל הַיֹּצֵא אֶל־הַמּ׳ 1 S 17[20] **b.** pl *ranks*=army, cstr מַעַרְכוֹת יִשׂ׳ 1 S 17[10.45], מַעַרְכֶת יִשׂ׳ v[8], מ׳ אֱלֹהִים חַיִּים v[26 36], מ׳ פלשתים 23[3] and 17[23] Qr, so 𝔊[A] (v om B) 𝔙 𝔗; sg 𝔊L 𝔖 (>Kt מערות) **2** נֵרוֹת הַמַּעֲרָכָה Ex 39[37] *lamps of the row*, i.e. arranged in a row.

†מַעֲרֶכֶת **n.f row, line**,—only of the rows of 'shew'-bread, abs. מ׳ Lv 24[7], מַעֲרֶכֶת v[6] (P), elsewh Chr לֶחֶם הַמּ׳ 1 Ch 9[32] 23[29] Ne 10[34], שֻׁלְחַן הַמּ׳ 2 Ch 29[18], cf. 1 Ch 28[16], cstr מַעֲרֶכֶת לֶחֶם 2 Ch 13[11] *the row of bread*, so מ׳ תָּמִיד 2[3] *the row of continuity*, bread continually present in rows; pl abs שְׁתַּיִם מַעֲרָכוֹת Lv 24[6].

ערל (√of foll., meaning dub.; cf Ar غُرْلَةٌ *foreskin*, Aram עוּרְלְתָא, ܥܘܪܠܬܐ, NH=BH, also Egypt *karnatha* Brugsch[AZ 1876, 128] Krall[SB der Wiener Ak. hist-phil Cl cxvi (1888) 650 f])

†עָרְלָה [16] **n f foreskin**,—ע׳ Gn 34[14] Je 9[24], cstr. עָרְלַת Ex 4[25] Dt 10[16], etc, pl הָעֲרָלוֹת (not ע׳) Jos 5[3] (Kö[ii 1, 181]), cstr עָרְלוֹת Je 4[4]+2 t, עָרְלֹתֵיהֶם 1 S 18[27],—*foreskin* 1 S 18[25.27] 2 S 3[14], cf גִּבְעַת הָעֲרָלוֹת Jos 5[3] *hill of the foreskins*, near Gilgal, of circumcision, כרת ע׳ Ex 4[25] (J), בשר ע׳ Gn 17[11]+5 t P (v II מול), אִישׁ אֲשֶׁר לוֹ ע׳ Gn 34[14] (P), i e one uncircumcised, cf Je 9[24], fig. of fruit trees, עָרְלָתוֹ Lv 19[23] (P; v. [עָרַל]), fig. of heart, ע׳ לבב Dt 10[16] Je 4[4].

†[עָרַל] **vb. denom. count as foreskin**, i e. as uncircumcised;—**Qal** *Pf* 2 mpl, c acc. cogn וַעֲרַלְתֶּם עָרְלָתוֹ Lv 19[23] *ye shall regard* its fruit *as uncircumcised*, and not eat it (for three years) (>SS *remove its foreskin* (its fruit), as 𝔙, cf. 𝔊 περικαθαριεῖτε τὴν ἀκαθαρσίαν αὐτοῦ). **Niph.** *Imv* הֵעָרֵל Hb 2[16] *be counted uncircumcised*, i e be object of mockery; but dub., read probably הֵרָעֵל *reel* (𝔊 𝔖 We Now Buhl[Lex]).

†עָרֵל [35] **adj. having foreskin**, i.e. **uncircumcised**,—ע׳ Ex 12[48]+5 t; cstr עֲרַל Ez 44[9 9]; עֲרַל Ex 6[12 30], f. עֲרֵלָה Je 6[10], pl עֲרֵלִים Lv 19[23] +20 t, cstr עַרְלֵי Je 9[25]+2 t;—*uncircumcised person* Ex 12[48] Jos 5[7] (P), Philistines Ju 14[3] 15[18] 1 S 14[6] 17[26.36] 31[4] 2 S 1[20] 1 Ch 10[4], of other nations Is 52[1] Je 9[25], esp. as slain Ez 28[10] 31[18] 32[19]+9 t. 32, in v[27] rd מעולם so Hi and most (v. on meaning Toy[31, 18]), עָרֵל זָכָר *uncircumcised male* Gn 17[14] (P); ע׳ בָּשָׂר Ez 44[7 9] *uncircumcised of flesh;* fig of fruit trees Lv 19[23] (cf. [עָרַל] supr), ע׳ שְׂפָתַיִם fig. of incapacity to speak Ex 6[12.30], of character, ע׳ לב Je 9[25] Ez 44[7 9], cf. לְבָבָם הֶעָרֵל Lv 26[41] (P), עֲרֵלָה אָזְנָם Je 6[10] *their ear is uncircumcised* (unreceptive).

ערם, עָרֹם, עָרוֹם v II עור.

†I. [עָרַם] **vb. Niph. be heaped up** (cf. Sab אערמהו, pl of [ערם] *dam*, so Ar. عَرِمٌ, cf. DHM[ZMG xxx (1876), 676 VOJ i 25] who cp. BH עֲרֵמָה, Ar. عَرَمَة (which Fra[135] thinks Aram loan-word), cf ܚܪܡ Pa. *heap up;* >Wetzst[Zeitschr für Ethnol 1873, 279 (Syr Dreschtafel)] who cp عَرَمَ *strip* [whence עַרְמוֹן infr], and thinks עֲרֵמָה=*bare heap*);—*Pf* 3 pl נֶעֶרְמוּ מַיִם Ex 15[8].

†עֲרֵמָה **n.f. heap**,—abs ע׳ Ru 3[7], cstr. עֲרֵמַת Hg 2[16] Ct 7[3], pl. עֲרֵמוֹת abs. Ne 13[15]+, cstr 3[34], abs עֲרֵמִים Je 50[26],—*heap* of rubbish (עָפָר) Ne 3[34]; ע׳=ruin-heap Je 50[26]; =grain-heap (of threshed grain, عَرَمَةٌ unthreshed, acc to Wetzst[l c.]), Hg 2[16] Ne 13[15] Ru 3[7], ע׳ חטים Ct 7[3], of grain and fruit 2 Ch 31[6.6.7 8.9].

II ערם (√of foll.; cf Ar عَرَمَ *strip* flesh from bone (to eat it), *strip* leaves from trees (said of camels), عُرَامٌ *bark* of tree (stripped off))

†עַרְמוֹן **n.[m.] plane-tree** (as *stripped* of bark),—ע׳ Gn 30[37] (J), pl עַרְמֹנִים Ez 31[8]

מַעֲרֻמֵּיהֶם 2 Ch 28[15] v sub II עור.

†[**עָרַם**] Lag[BN 31] **vb. be shrewd, crafty** (NH *id.*, Hiph; Ar. عَرِمَ, عَرُمَ, عَرَمَ *be ill-natured, cross;* 𝔗 adj. עֲרִים *shrewd*, Syr. ܥܪܝܡ *id*, and vb. in der. spec. (Pe. in Lexx)),—**Qal** *Inf. abs* in עָרֹם יַעְרִם 1 S 23[22] *he is exceedingly crafty* **Hiph.** *Impf be crafty*, 3 ms יַעְרִם 1 S 23[22]; *be* or *become shrewd* יַעְרִם Pr 15[5] 19[25], all these **Qal** Impf in —ִ acc to Ba[ZMG xliii (1889), 180] so Ges[§ 63 n] Buhl[Lex], but perh rd יַעֲרֹם as **Qal**; true **Hiph.** in 3 mpl. יַעֲרִימוּ סוֹד ψ 83[4] *they make crafty* (their) *counsel* against thy people.

†[**עֹרֶם**] **n.[m.] craftiness**,—sf. בְּעָרְמָם Jb 5[13] (possibly from עָרְמָה Ges[§ 91 e] al.).

†**עָרְמָה** **n.f. craftiness, prudence**;—**1.** בע׳ *craftily* Ex 21[14] (E), Jos 9[4] (JE) **2.** ע׳ in Pr, in good sense, *prudence* Pr 1[4] 8[5.12].

†**עָרוּם** **adj. crafty, shrewd, sensible**;—**1.** *crafty*, ע׳ as pred., of serpent Gn 3[1], pl as subst. מַחְשְׁבוֹת עֲרוּמִים Jb 5[12], ע׳ לְשׁוֹן 15[5]. **2.** in Pr, in good sense (opp. פֶּתִי, כְּסִיל, אֱוִיל); as attrib. אָדָם עָרוּם Pr 12[23] *a shrewd* or *sensible man*, ע׳ as subst = *id*, v[16] 13[16], so ע׳ חָכְמַת v[8], = *prudent man* 14[15] 22[3] 27[12], pl. עֲרוּמִים 14[18].

עֵרָן, עֵרָנִי v. sub I. עור.

ערס (√of foll).

†[**עֲרִיסָה**] **n.f.** meaning dub, usu. **coarse meal**; 𝔊 AV RV **dough**, so Toy (with ?) (NH עֲרָסָן *barley-meal*, Syr ܥܪܣܢܐ (in Lexx) *hulled barley*, or (cf Lag[GGN 1889, 301 f.]) *wheat*); > Sm[Ez] Co[Ez] **kneading-trough** (so NH עֲרִיסָה Jastr; appar. secondary, עֲרִיסָה also [*bed*], *cradle*, v ערש),—only ר׳ עֲרִיסֹתֵינוּ, רֵאשִׁית עֲרִיסֹתֵיכֶם Ez 44[30], Ne 10[38], ר׳ עֲרִסֹתֵיכֶם Nu 15[20.21] (P).

עֲרֹעֵר, עֲרֹעֵר, עֲרוֹעֵר, עַרְעָר, עֲרֹעֵר v. II ערר

I **ערף** (√of foll; meaning dub., NH עוֹרֶף = BH, Ar عُرْفٌ *mane* of horse, also part of *neck* where hair grows, etc).

†**עֹרֶף** **n.m.**[Dt 31, 27] **back of neck, neck**;—ע׳ abs. Jos 7[12]+, cstr Gn 49[8]+, sf. עָרְפִּי Jb 16[12], עָרְפְּךָ Dt 31[27], etc.,—**1.** *back of neck* of fleeing foe יָדְךָ בע׳ וגו׳ Gn 49[8] (poem in J), cf וְאָחַז בְּעָרְפִּי Jb 16[12] (fig); Ex 23[27] (E), ψ 18[41] = 2 S 22[41]; *turn* (פָּנָה, הָפַךְ) *one's back before* (לִפְנֵי) a foe Jos 7[8.12] (JE), abs. Je 48[39]; fig. of apostasy פָּנָה ע׳ אל Je 2[27] 32[33] (opp פָּנָה פָנִים) abs. וַיִּתְּנוּ ע׳ 2 Ch 29[6]; of י׳'s disfavour ע׳ וְלֹא פָנִים אֶרְאֵם Je 18[17] *with the back and not the face will I look at them.* **2.** fig. in קְשֵׁה־ע׳ *stiff of neck*, i.e. *obstinate*, of Isr. Ex 32[9] 33[3.5] 34[9] (all JE), Dt 9[6.13]; עָרְפְּךָ הַקָּשֶׁה Dt 31[27]; with vb. הִקְשָׁה ע׳ i.e. be obstinate, intractable 10[16] Je 7[26] 17[23] 19[15] 2 K 17[14.14] Ne 9[16.17.29] 2 Ch 30[8]; cf. גִּיד בַּרְזֶל ע׳ Is 48[4] (|| קָשֶׁה אָתָּה); הקשה ע׳ of individual 2 Ch 36[13] Pr 29[1]. **3.** of bird: nip its head ממול ערפו Lv 5[8] (P).

†[**עָרַף**] **vb. denom. break the neck of an animal**;—**Qal** *Pf* 2 ms sf וַעֲרַפְתּוֹ consec. Ex 13[13] 34[20] (JE), 3 pl. וְעָרְפוּ־שָׁם אֶת־הָעֶגְלָה consec. Dt 21[4]; *Pt. act.* עוֹרֵף כֶּלֶב Is 66[3]; *pass.* הָעֶגְלָה הָעֲרוּפָה Dt 21[6]; *Impf* 3 ms. יַעֲרֹף Ho 10[2] fig. of breaking down altars.

†**עָרְפָּה** **n.pr.f.** sister-in-law of Ruth, Ru 1[4.14], Ορφα

†II [**עָרַף**] **vb. drip, drop** (cf Ar. عَرَفَ *lade out water with the hand* (as with ladle), cf Ph. ערפת *portico* (whence rain *drips*) v. Hoffm[Abh d. GGW xxxvi, May, 1889, 32 f]; cf. also Ar غُرْفَةٌ *upper-room*, מערף ענן Ecclus 43[22] *the dropping of a cloud*, As. *irpu*, *irpitu*, *cloud(s)*),—**Qal** *Impf.* 3 mpl. שָׁמָיו יַעַרְפוּ־טָל Dt 33[28] *his heavens drop dew*; fig., of speech, intrans, יַעֲרֹף כַּמָּטָר לִקְחִי 32[2] *let my teaching drop like the rain* (|| תִּזַּל כַּטַּל אִמְרָתִי).—Cf. רָעַף.

†[**עָרִיף**] **n.[m.]** cloud,—pl. sf. בַּעֲרִיפֶיהָ Is 5[30] (Perles[JQ 1899 689] prop בְּעַד יָפְיָהּ, referring sf to ארץ, and cp. ψ 139[11]).

†**עֲרָפֶל** **n m. cloud, heavy cloud** (perh. fr. above √ + ל afform; NH = BH; Syr. ܥܪܦܠܐ; 𝔗 עֲרָפִילָא, Mand ארפילא No[M 126, 128]; on vocaliz. v. Ba[NB 160] and against him Schwally[ZAW x (1890), 178] who prop. עֲרֹפֶל);—ע׳ in which God dwells Ex 20[18] (Gi, van d H. v[21]), 1 K 8[12] = 2 Ch 6[1]; + עָנָן Dt 4[11] (also חֹשֶׁךְ), 5[19] ψ 97[2]; Jb 22[13] v. בְּעַד; ע׳ תַּחַת רַגְלָיו 2 S 22[10] = ψ 18[10]; as swaddling-bands of sea Jb 38[9], fig of misery Is 60[2] (|| חֹשֶׁךְ); of י׳'s judgment Je 13[16] (|| צַלְמָוֶת), as a past day יוֹם עָנָן וַע׳ Ez 34[12] = (of future day of י׳) Zp 1[15] (|| יוֹם חֹשֶׁךְ וַאֲפֵלָה) = Jo 2[2] (|| *id*)

†[**עָרַץ**] **vb. cause to tremble, tremble** (in terror, or awe) (cf Ar. عَرَصَ *quiver, flicker;* Syr ܥܪܨ *come upon suddenly* or *violently*, PS s v. *passim;* cf Egypt. *'u-ra-ḏau(t)*, *they terrified* (= ערצו) WMM[As. u Eur. 76]);—**Qal** *Impf.* 2 ms

תַּעֲרֹץ Dt 7^{21}+; 2 fs. תַּעֲרוֹצִי Is 47^{12}; 1 s. אֶעֱרוֹץ Jb 31^{34}, etc.; *Inf. cstr.* עֲרֹץ Is 2^{19}+;—**1.** *cause to tremble* (i.e. strike with awe) c. acc. הָאָרֶץ Is $2^{19.21}$ (subj. ′י; ins. prob. also v^{10}); הֶעָלֶה נִדָּף תַּעֲ′ Jb 13^{25} *wilt thou strike with awe the driven leaf?* abs. *cause trembling = inspire awe* Is 47^{12} (of Bab.), ψ 10^{18}. **2.** intrans. *tremble, feel dread* (D), Dt 1^{29} 7^{21} 20^{3} 31^{6} Jos 1^{9}; c. acc. Jb 31^{34} because *I stood in awe of* the great multitude. **Niph.** *Pt.* אֵל נַעֲרָץ ψ 89^{8} *El, terrible* in the company of the holy ones (‖נוֹרָא). **Hiph. 1.** *regard,* or *treat, with awe, as awful:* 2 mpl. וְלֹא תַעֲרִיצוּ Is 8^{12} (acc. מוֹרָאוֹ); 3 mpl. יַעֲרִיצוּ 29^{23} acc. אֶת־אֱלֹהֵי יִשׂ′. **2.** *inspire with awe* (cf. **Qal 2**);—*Pt.* sf. הוּא מַעֲרִצְכֶם Is 8^{13} *he shall be your awe-inspirer.*

†[עָרוּץ] **adj. dreadful** (prop. Pt. pass.) cstr. בַּעֲרוּץ נְחָלִים Jb 30^{6} *in the* (most) *dreadful of ravines.*

†עָרִיץ **adj. awe-inspiring, terror-striking**;—ע′ of ′י, כְּגִבּוֹר עָרִיץ Je 20^{11}; pl. as subst. עָרִיצִים, in bad sense of formidable adversaries, personal, Je 15^{21} (‖רָעִים), Jb 6^{23} (‖צָר), and national, ψ 54^{5} (‖זָרִים), = עֲדַת ע′ 86^{14} (‖זֵדִים), הֲמוֹן ע′ Is 29^{5} (‖זָרַיִךְ); esp. of Chaldeans Is 13^{11}, cstr. עָרִיצֵי גוֹיִם *most terrifying of the nations* Ez 28^{7} (‖זָרִים) 30^{11} 31^{12} (‖זָרִים), 32^{12}; so (prob.) sg. עָרִיץ Is 49^{25} (rd. ע′ also for צַדִּיק v^{24}, so Lo Ew Che Gr al.); without specif. ref. גּוֹיִם עָרִיצִים Is 25^{3} *awe-inspiring nations* (Du Che take ע′ as subst.), רוּחַ ע′ v^{4} (del. as gloss Di al.), זְמִיר ע′ v^{5} (del. verse as gloss Du Che); late, of wicked in gen., as *ruthless* רָאִיתִי רָשָׁע ע′ ψ 37^{35} *I have seen a wicked man ruthless;* as subst., Is 29^{20} (‖לֵץ), Jb 15^{20} (‖רשע), pl. 27^{13} (‖*id.*), Pr 11^{16}; rd. also עָרִיצ(ים) Is 11^{4} (for MT אֶרֶץ), so Che Br^{MP} Du Gr al. (‖רָשָׁע).

†מַעֲרָצָה **n.f. awful shock, crash**;—Is 10^{33}, of ′י's lopping off (tree-)crown (fig.).

†[עָרַק] **vb. gnaw** (Ar. عَرَقَ *id.;* Syr. ܥܪܩ Pa.);—**Qal** *Pt.* pl. הָעֹרְקִים צִיָּה Jb 30^{3} *they who gnaw the dry* (ground; fig. of scanty subsistence); sf. עֹרְקַי v^{17} *my gnawing* (pains) do not sleep.

†עַרְקִי **adj. gent.** Arkite, inhabitant of city ʿ*Arka* (As. *Arḳa* COT$^{Gloss.}$ Dl$^{Pa\ 282}$, Tel Am. *Irḳat(a)*, Egypt. *Arḳantu*, cf. As. n.gent. *Irḳanatai* COT$^{Gloss.}$, Ency. Bib.$^{I.\ 310}$);—only הָע′ as n.coll. Gn 10^{17}, τὸν Ἀρουκαῖον, = 1 Ch 1^{15}, A *id.*, 𝔊L τὸν Αρακει: mod. ʿ*Arḳa*, near Mediterranean, c. 60 miles N. of Beirut (cf. Ency. Bib.$^{l.c.}$).

I. ערר (√ of foll.; on this [and not עור] v. Nö$^{ZMG\ xxxii\ (1878).\ 404}$ Lag$^{Symm.\ ii.\ 91\ f.}$; cf. Palm. מערתא *sepulchre*).

מְעָרָה$_{40}$ **n.f. cave**;—abs. מ′ Gn 19^{30}+; cstr. מְעָרַת 23^{19}+; pl. מְעָרוֹת Ju 6^{2}+, cstr. *id.* Is 2^{19};—*cave*, esp. as place of sojourn or refuge Gn 19^{30} (J), 1 S $24^{3.3.7.8.10}$ (Ginsb; $v^{4.8.9.11}$ van d.H. Baer), 1 K $19^{1.13}$, Ez 33^{27} Jos 10^{16} (מ′ בַּמַּקֵּדָה)+ 7 t. Jos 10, Ju 6^{2} 1 S 13^{6} 1 K $18^{4.13}$, cf. ψ 57^{1} 142^{1}; מְעָרוֹת צֻרִים Is 2^{19}, hence מ′ פָּרִצִים Je 7^{11} *robbers' cave;* Is 32^{14} *den* (of wild beasts);—מ′ עֲדֻלָּם 1 S 22^{1} 2 S 23^{13}, whence in ‖ 1 Ch 11^{15}, rd. prob. מְצֻדַת ע′ or מְצֻדַת We, cf. Dr, Bu Kit HPS;—as burial place, מ′ הַמַּכְפֵּלָה Gn 23^{9}+ (v. מַכְפֵּלָה) = מ′ alone $23^{11.17.20}$ $49^{29.32}$ (all P). מ′ אֲשֶׁר לַצִּידֹנִים Jos 13^{4} (D), cave-region in Lebanon E. of Sidon, mod. *Mughâr Ğezzîn*, acc. to most, but dub.; perhaps, rather, near Tyre Buhl$^{MDPV\ 1895,\ 55}$.

†II. [עָרַר] **vb. strip oneself** (‖ form of ערה, II. עור);—**Qal** *Imv.* עֹרָה Is 32^{11} (‖פְּשֹׁטָה; acc. to Ges$^{§\ 110k}$ Hi De al. ms. with fpl. subj.; acc. to Ew$^{§\ 226a}$ Du Di al. fpl., shortened from ערנה etc.). **Pōʿ.** *Pf.* 3 pl. עֹרְרוּ אַרְמְנוֹתֶיהָ Is 23^{13} *they have laid bare* (the foundations of) *her palaces*, i.e. destroyed them; so **Pilp.** *Inf. abs.* + **Hithpalp.** *Impf.* 3 fs. עַרְעֵר תִּתְעַרְעַר Je 51^{58} *be laid utterly bare*, cf. ערה **Pi. 1.**

†עֲרִירִי **adj. stripped,** specif. **childless**;—ע′ Gn 15^{2} (JE), Je 22^{30}; pl. עֲרִירִים Lv $20^{20.21}$ (H).

†עַרְעָר **adj. stripped, destitute**;—הָע′ as subst. ψ 102^{18} *the prayer of the destitute.*—Je 17^{6} v. עֲרוֹעֵר.

†I. עֲרוֹעֵר **n.[m.]** prob. a tree or bush; **juniper?** (Ar. عَرْعَرٌ *juniper* (or *cypress?* v. Lane), so Tristr$^{NHB\ 358}$ Rob$^{BR\ ii.\ 124}$; on format. v. Lag$^{BN\ 162}$ Ba$^{NB\ 160}$);—עֲרוֹעֵר בַּמִּדְבָּר Je 48^{6}, + 17^{6}, where rd. prob. עֲרֹעֵר בָּעֲרָבָה (for MT עַרְעָר; > Gf al. conversely, rd. עַרְעָר 48^{6}).

†II. עֲרֹעֵר$_{1}$, עֲרוֹעֵר$_{5}$, עֲרֹעֵר$_{10}$, **n.pr.loc.** Αροηρ, MI^{26} ערער;—**1.** city on N. bank of Arnon, S. limit of E. Jordan Isr., עֲרֹעֵר Nu 32^{34} (JE), Dt 2^{36} 3^{12} 4^{48} Jos 12^{2} (D) 2 K 10^{33} 1 Ch 5^{8}; עֲרוֹעֵר Jos 13^{9} (D), v^{16} (P), 2 S 24^{5}; Moabitish Je 48^{19} (cf. MI^{26}); once עַרְעֵר Ju 11^{26}; mod. ʿ*Arʿâir* Buhl

Geogr ^{269}, Tristr$^{Moab\ 129\ ff.}$ **2.** city near Rabbah in Ammon, עֲרֹעֵר Ju 11^{33}, עֲרוֹ' Jos 13^{25} (P), site unknown. **3.** city in S. Judah, עֲרֹעֵר 1 S 30^{28} (𝔊 Αροηρ + Αμμαδει, latter orig. acc. to We, indicating form ערערה; 𝔊L Ραγουηλ); + Jos 15^{22} rdg. ע' (or עַרְעָרָה) for MT עַדְעָדָה, 𝔊^{B} Αρουηλ, We^{1830,28} (cf. Dr HPS), Di$^{ad\ loc.}$ Benn Steuern; poss. *ʽAr‘âra* c 9 miles S. of E. from Beersheba, but cf. Buhl$^{Geogr\ 183}$.—Is 17^{2} rd. עָרֶיהָ עֲדֵי עַד 𝔊 Lo Lag$^{Sem\ i\ 30}$ Che Buhl^{Lex} al. (for MT עָרֵי עֲרֹעֵר).—Vid. also Che$^{Ency\ Bib.\ 317}$.

†עֲרֹעֵרִי **adj. gent.** of foreg, הָעֲ' 1 Ch 11^{44}.

עָרַשׂ (√of foll, cf Ar عَرْشٌ *booth, shed, throne*, عَرِيشٌ grape-*trellis*, woman's (camel-) *saddle;* Eth. ዐረሰ: *booth* (? also ዐራት: *bed*); As. *iršu, bed, couch;* NH עֲרִיסָה *cradle*, 𝔗 עַרְסָא, Syr. ܥܪܣܐ, Palm. ערשא; the common idea is appar. that of a *wooden structure, frame*, cf. No$^{ZMG\ xl\ (1886).\ 737}$).

†עֶרֶשׂ **n.f.**$^{Jb\ 7,13}$ couch, divan;—cstr. ע' Dt 3^{11}+; abs. עָרֶשׂ Am 3^{12}; sf. ערשי Jb 7^{13}+, etc; pl. sf ערשותם Am 6^{4},—*couch, divan*, Am 3^{12} 6^{4} (‖מטות), + 2 S 17^{28} (rd. ערשת משכב Klo Ne^{Marg} ^{18} HPS, cf. 𝔊); for lying at night Jb 7^{13} ψ 6^{7} (‖מִטָּה), Pr 7^{16}, עֶרֶשׂ יְצוּעָי ψ 132^{3} *the couch of* (consisting in) *my bed;* couch of sickness ψ 41^{4}, marriage couch Ct 1^{16}; perhaps transf. to sarcophagus, as last couch ערשו עֶרֶשׂ בַּרְזֶל Dt 3^{11} (v. Dr).

עָרַשׁ (√of foll., meaning unknown).

†יַעֲרֶשְׁיָה **n. pr. m.** Benjamite 1 Ch 8^{27}, Ιασαραια, A Ιαρασια, 𝔊L Ιερσια.

עָשַׁב (√of foll., mng. dub; cf. As. *ešēbu* [*bear fruit*], II 1, causat (Dl$^{Pr\ 87}$), *išbu*, perh. = H; Ar. عَشِبَ is *be dry*, but عُشْبٌ *fresh, juicy herbage*, NH = BH, cf. 𝔗 עִסְבָּא, Syr. ܥܣܒܐ, Palm עשביא).

†עֵשֶׂב **n.m.**$^{Gn\ 1,11}$ **herb, herbage**;—ע' abs. Dt 11^{15}+; cstr. Gn 2^{5}+; sf עֶשְׂבָּם Is 42^{15}, pl. cstr. עִשְּׂבוֹת (d f dirim.) Pr 27^{25},—*herb, herbage*, in oldest use oft gen. (therefore incl. grass [דֶּשֶׁא]) ע' הַשָּׂדֶה · Ex 9^{22} (E), Gn 2^{5} (+ שִׂיחַ) Ex 9^{25} (+ עֵץ), 10^{15} (+ *id;* all J) Am 7^{2}, so ע' הָאָרֶץ Ex 10^{12} (E), + פְּרִי הָעֵץ v^{15} (J), whence ψ 105^{35}; appar. gen also in ע' הארץ Jb 5^{25} ψ 72^{16}, ע' alone 92^{8}, ע' כָל־הַשָּׂדֶה Je 12^{4}, ע' alone Dt 32^{2} (‖דֶּשֶׁא), Is 42^{15} ψ 102$^{5.12}$, and Dt 29^{22} Mi 5^{6} Pr 19^{12}; hence ע' as food for cattle Dt 11^{15} ψ 106^{20} cf. Je 14^{6} Zc 10^{1}; עִשְּׂבוֹת הָרִים Pr 27^{25} (‖דֶּשֶׁא, חָצִיר); but as human food (hence excluding דֶּשֶׁא) ע' הַשָּׂדֶה Gn 3^{18} (J); esp. P Gn 1^{29} (+ עֵץ), יֶרֶק ע' v^{30} 9^{3}, hence ע' ψ 104^{14} (‖חָצִיר for cattle); ע' disting fr דֶּשֶׁא, עֵץ also Gn 1$^{11.12}$, ע' שָׂדֶה + דֶּשֶׁא, חָצִיר 2 K 19^{26} + Is 37^{27}.

I. **עָשָׂה**$_{2622}$ **vb. do, make** (NH = BH; MI$^{23.26}$ עשתי, l.$^{8.9}$ ואעש, l.^{24} Imv עשו; OH n.pr. עשיו, אלעשה, מעשיהו; not Aram., and not certainly found in S Sem. lang.; on Sab. v. esp. DHM$^{SB\ Berl\ Ak.\ 1886,\ 849}$);—**Qal**$_{2524}$ *Pf* 3 ms. Gn 3^{1}+, sf עָשָׂהוּ Ho 8^{6}+; 3 fs. עָשְׂתָה Dt 22^{21}+, וְעָשְׂתָה consec. Lv 25^{21}; 2 ms. עָשִׂיתָ Gn 3^{14}+, etc; *Impf.* 3 ms. יַעֲשֶׂה Gn 18^{25}+, וַיַּעֲשֶׂה 1 K 16^{25} + 3 t., וַיַּעַשׂ Is 5^{2}+; יַעֲשֶׂה Is 64^{3}, 2 ms. תַּעֲשֶׂה 1 S 10^{8}, תעשׂה Gn 26^{29} Jos 7^{9}, juss (c. אַל) תַּעַשׂ Gn 22^{12}+, תעשׂה 2 S 13^{12} Je 40^{16} Qr (Kt תַּעַשׂ); 1 s אֶעֱשֶׂה Gn 2^{18}+, וָאֶעֱשֶׂה Ez 20^{14} Dn 8^{27}, וָאַעַשׂ Dt 10^{3} + 4 t. Ez; etc.; *Imv.* ms עֲשֵׂה Ju 10^{15}+; fs. עֲשִׂי Je 6^{26}+, etc; *Inf. abs.* עָשֹׂה 44^{17}+, עָשׂוֹ 7^{5} + 2 t. (4^{18} van d. H. עָשׂוֹ), cstr עֲשׂוֹת Gn 2^{4}+, עֲשֹׂה 50^{20} + 2 t., עֲשׂוֹ 31^{28}, sf. עֲשֹׂתוֹ 41^{32}+, עֲשֹׂהוּ + Ex 18^{18}, etc.; *Pt act.* עֹשֶׂה Is 5^{4}+, sf. הָעֹשׂוֹ Jb 40^{19} (but v. infr.); pl. עֹשִׂים Gn 24^{49}+; sf עֹשָׂי Jb 35^{10} (yet v. Ges$^{§124\ k}$), etc., *pass.* עָשׂוּי Ex 3^{16}+, הֶעָשׂוּ Jb 41^{25} (Ges$^{§75\ k}$), f. עֲשׂוּיָה Ez 21^{20}+, etc.;—**I. 1.** *do* (1560+t.): **a.** (1) c. acc. act. Gn 3^{14} (J) 20^{10} (E) + oft.; *do* right in eyes of י' 2 K 12^{3} 14^{3}+, evil 8$^{18.27}$+ (cf. 1 עין **3 c**); *do* God's commands, statutes, etc., Dt 16^{12} 30^{8}, Nu 15^{39} (P); ע' חַיִל 1 S 14^{48}+ *do might*, i.e. mightily, valiantly; Pr 31^{29} *do efficiency*, i e. efficiently, = commit (offence) Lv 20^{13} (H), Dt 20^{18}; sq מִן part, וְעָשָׂה מֵאַחַת מֵהֵנָּה Lv 4^{2} *and shall do a single one of them* (things prohibited; v. מִן **3 b** (*d*)), cf וְעָשׂוּ אַחַת מִכָּל־מִצְוֹת י' v$^{13.22}$ 5^{17} (all P); *do* = *perform* a work, c acc. cogn. מַעֲשֶׂה Ex 18^{20} 23^{12} (E), also (י' subj) Dt 11^{7} Dn 9^{14} Ec 3^{11}; c acc. מְלָאכָה Gn 2$^{2.2}$ (J), Ex 20$^{9.10}$ = Dt 9^{13} (10 Words); c. acc. דְּרָכֶיךָ + Is 58^{13}; ע' מְלוּכָה עַל 1 K 21^{7} = *exercise sovereignty over;* of י' performing signs (אתת) Jos 24^{17} (E), Nu 14$^{11.22}$ (JE), Dt 11^{3}, so Moses Ex 4^{17} and (מֹפְתִים) v^{21}. (2) *do* something to one (לְ pers) Gn 20^{9} (E), Ju 9^{56}+; c. עַל reflex. Je 26^{19} *do evil against ourselves;* esp. י' subj, c. לְ, *do* good to Ex 18^{9} (E), 2 K 8^{66}, or evil Gn 42^{28} (E); in phr. *so may God do to me*, etc. 1 S 3^{17} 2 K 6^{31} + (v. יסף **Hiph. 1**). (3) *do* something for one (לְ pers) Gn 30^{31} 1 K 11^{8}+, dir. obj om 1 S 20^{4}; + לְ rei Ju 21$^{7.16}$ *what shall*

we do for them, for wives? c. על pers Ne 5^{19}, c dat eth. (ל) 1 S 10^{7}, c ל, of י׳ doing kindness for 1 S 22^{3}; executing vengeance for Ju 11^{36} (+ מן of enemy), י׳ doing a sign (אות) for †Ju 6^{17} (elsewhere נָתַן אות ל), cf עשה־עמי אות לטובה ψ 86^{17}. (4) do something (in relation or intercourse) with (את pers), י׳ subj. Dt 1^{30} *all that he did with you,* 10^{21} (cf ψ 86^{17} supr), human subj. 2 Ch 24^{24} (obj. שְׁפָטִים), Ru 2^{11}. (5) seldom c ב, usu of executing judgment upon 1 S 28^{18} Is 48^{14}, more gen Est 1^{15} *what shall we do with the queen?* also, subj י׳, Ez 25^{11} 28^{26} ψ 149$^{7.9}$ Nu 33^{4} (on false gods), in good sense, ע׳ חֲסָדִים ב׳ Ne 13^{14} (6) of י׳ *doing* the justice (משׁפט) of any one, i e maintaining his cause 1 K 8$^{45.49}$ ψ 9^{5} (7) c adv *do thus,* כֹּה, Jos 6^{14} (JE), *acc. to,* כ, Gn 6^{22} (P), 18^{21} (J), 1 K 2^{6}, *acc as,* כַּאֲשֶׁר Gn 27^{19} (J), Ex 1^{17} (E) +; c. ב of manner, Ju 9^{16a}, Ez 8^{18} 25^{15}. **b.** *work* for (ל rei) Gn 30^{30} (J), c ל pers. 1 S 14^{6} Ez 29^{20} (for י׳), *work* in (ב) gold or other material 1 K 7^{14} 2 Ch 2$^{6.13}$ Ex 31$^{4.5}$ 35^{32} (all P), c בָּהּ (i e בְּעַבְדָה) Ex 5^{9} (J) *in toil, work* with (עם) God 1 S 14^{45}, so prob of God's working with (את) Moses and Aaron 1 S 12^{6} (usu. *appoint*), c אֶת *with* (of pers in whose company, in whose field) Ru 2$^{19.19}$ (gleaning), work בחפץ כַּפֶּיהָ Pr 31^{13}, without prep Ex 36^{1} Ne 3^{28}. **2.** *deal* with, c עם, 2 Ch 2^{2} Dn 1^{13} (כַּאֲשֶׁר *acc. as*), c את, Ez 20^{44} ψ 109^{21}, Ez 22^{14} Zp 3^{19} (perh; Gr Now ins כָּלָה, v **II 1 g**), + כ Je 21^{2}, + ב of manner Ez 23$^{25.29}$, c ל pers + ב 25^{12}, c ב pers, Je 18^{23} Dn 11^{7}, + כ *acc to* Ne 9^{24} Est 3^{11}. **3.** oft. in phr., *do* kindness (חֶסֶד) with: c. עם (עִמָּדִי) Gn 19^{19} 24$^{12.14}$ (J), Ju 1^{24} 8^{35} 1 S 15^{6} 2 S 2^{5} 10^{2} = 1 Ch 19^{2} +, c. עַל, 1 S 20^{8} (but rd עם Vrss We Dr al.), abs, ψ 109^{16}, obj. אֱמֶת + חֶסֶד, c. עם, Jos 2^{14} (JE) Ju 9^{19} 2 S 2^{6}, c. את *with,* Gn 24^{49} 32^{11} 47^{29} (all J), c. ל, Ex 20^{6} = Dt 5^{10}, 2 S 22^{51} = ψ 18^{51}, so ע׳ טוב, c עם, Gn 26^{29} (J), cf Ju 8^{35} 9^{16}, c את *with,* 1 S 24^{19} 2 S 2^{6} **4.** abs *act, act with effect,* esp of י׳, 1 K 8$^{32.39}$ Je 14^{7} Ez 20$^{9.14.22}$ ψ 22^{32} 37^{5} 52^{11} Dn 9^{19}; of men 2 Ch 31^{21} Dn 8$^{12.24}$ 11$^{28.30.32}$, c ל pers Ez 31^{11}.

II 1. *make* (670+t) **a.** c obj concr, ark Gn 8^{6}, altar 13^{4}, idols Ju 18$^{24.31}$ +, etc. **b.** oft of God's making (creating) Gn 3^{1} (J), 1$^{7.16.25}$ (P), Ne 9^{6} Jb 9^{9} Pr 8^{26} 2 Ch 2^{11} ψ 95^{5} +, making man ψ 100^{3} 119^{73} (made by God's hands), in the womb Jb 31$^{15.15}$, making, constituting, nation Dt 26^{19} 32$^{6.15}$; pt sf עשׂהו *his Maker* Is 17^{7} Pr 14^{31} 17^{5} (הָעֹשׂו Jb 40^{19} is improb, most rd הֶעָשׂוּ, with various interpr of foll words), עֹשֵׂךְ Is 51^{13}, עֹשֵׂנִי Jb 32^{22} (Ginsb; v^{22} van d. H. Baer), עֹשֵׂנוּ ψ 95^{6}; so appar pt. pl עֹשָׂי Jb 35^{10}, עֹשַׂיִךְ Is 54^{5} (Ges^{§124k} expl. as sg). **c.** *make* something, c ל reflex, *make for thee* Ex 20^{4} Dt 9^{12} 10^{1} +, for (ל) another 1 S 2^{19} 2 S 7^{11} 1 K 2^{24} +, obj מִשְׁתֶּה *banquet* Gn 40^{20} Est 5^{4}, also (no ל) Gn 29^{22} (E) Ju 14^{10} Est 5$^{5.12}$ and (fig., י׳ subj) Is 25^{6}; c. ל rei, Dt 22^{8}, c ל of animal Gn 33^{17} (J) **d.** *make* a name (שׁם) for oneself (ל) 2 S 7^{9} 1 Ch 17^{8}, also (no ל) 2 S 8^{13}, a new heart for oneself (ל) Ez 18^{31} **e.** *make* war with (את) Gn 14^{2} Jos 11^{18} (D); c. עם, Dt 20$^{12.20}$ 1 Ch 5$^{10.19}$; abs 1 Ch 22^{8}, c ל reflex Pr 24^{6}, pt. עשׂה מלחמה 2 Ch 11^{1} 26$^{11.13}$, *make* peace, c ל pers Jos 9^{15} (J), ע׳ אתי בְרָכָה 2 K 18^{31} *make an agreement with me* **f** c ב, ע׳ פֶּרֶץ ב׳ י׳ Ju 21^{15} *brought a catastrophe upon* (cf פרץ) **g.** c 2 acc., *make* something out of (acc mater) Ex 25^{18} 28^{13} 37$^{17.24}$ Ct 3^{10} Dt 10^{3}+, *make* something into something (Ges^{§117ii}) Ho 8^{4} Gn 27^{9} Ju 17^{4} Nu 11^{8} 17^{3} ψ 104^{4}, *make* something כָּלָה, i e utterly destroy it Na 1^{8} Zp 1^{18} Ez 20^{17} Ne 9^{31}; c. pt pass. as 2nd acc Ex 38^{7} *they made it* נבוב לֻחת *hollow with boards,* 39^{9}; but also c acc + ל, Ho 2^{10} gold they made into (ל) the Baal, Ju 8^{27} Ex 27^{3} (P), Dt 9^{14} Je 37^{15} Ez 4^{9} Is 44$^{17.19}$, *make* something for (ל pers), + מן of material Ct 3^{9}. **2.** *produce, yield*: of grain, yielding meal Ho 8$^{7.7}$, vineyard, grapes Is 5$^{2.2.4.4.10}$, tree, fruit 2 K 19^{30} = Is 37^{31}, Ho 9^{16} Je 12^{2} 17^{8} Ez 17^{23} (all fig), Gn 1$^{11.12}$ (P), branches Jb 14^{9} and (fig) Ez 17^{8}; land, fruit Lv 25^{21} cf. Hb 3^{17}, abs. Gn 41^{47}; of seed Is 5^{10}, vine, shoots Ez 17^{6} (fig.), of cows, *yielding* milk Is 7^{22}, hippop producing fat Jb 15^{27} **3.** *prepare,* esp. of dressing and cooking food, Gn 18$^{7.8}$ Ju 6^{19} 13^{5} 1 S 25^{18} (pass), 2 S 12$^{4.4}$ Gn 27$^{14.17.31}$ 2 S 13$^{5.7}$ 1 K 17^{12} Ex 12^{39} (+ ל reflex.), a bullock for sacrifice (v. infr.) 1 K 18$^{23.25.26}$, כלי גולה Ez 12^{3} (+ ל reflex), a chamber Ne 13^{7}, *prepare* to build (+ ל pers and inf). **4.** *make* offering, e. g עוֹלָה Ju 13^{16} Je 33^{18} Lv 16^{24}, עולה וָזבח 2 K 5^{17} (+ ל dei), הַחַטָּאת Lv 14^{19}, אִשֶּׁה Nu 15$^{3.14}$, various offerings 1 K 8^{64} Lv 9^{22} Ez 45^{17} 46^{2} +; + לי׳ *to* י׳ Lv 17^{9} +; also c acc of thing sacrificed (perh. orig. *prepare* or *provide,* v supr) Ez 43$^{25.25}$ 46^{15} Lv 14^{30} 15$^{15.30}$ 16^{9} Nu 6$^{11.17}$ ψ 66^{15} (+ ל dei) +, abs = *offer sacrifice* Ex 10^{25} (E + לי׳), to (ל) heathen gods 2 K 17^{32} **5.** *attend to, put in order:* pare (the nails) Dt 21^{12}, wash (feet) 2 S 19^{25}; trim (beard) v^{25} (cf. Fr. *faire la barbe,* Ger *die Haare machen*). **6.** *observe, celebrate,* religious festival, e g. pass-

over Ex 12[48] Nu 9[4.6.13] Jos 5[10], also (+ 'לי) Ex 12[48] Nu 9[10.14] (all P), Dt 16[1]+; sabbath Ex 31[16] Dt 5[15]; feast of weeks 16[10], booths 16[13], Purim Est 9[21.27], etc. **7.** *acquire* property of various kinds (cf. 'make money') Gn 12[5] 31[1] (J), Is 15[7] Je 17[11] 48[36] Dt 8[18] Ez 22[13] 28[4.4] 38[12] 2 Ch 32[29] Ec 2[8]; + ל reflex. Dt 8[17] 2 S 15[1] 1 K 1[5]; of fruits from vineyards, etc. ψ 107[37]. **8.** *appoint* priests 1 K 12[31] 13[33] 2 Ch 2[17] (all + מִן source), a feast 1 K 12[32.33] (+ ל pers.); *ordain* a sacrifice Nu 28[6], a festal day ψ 118[24]; *institute*, אוֹב וְיִדְּעֹנִי *ghost and familiar spirit* 2 K 21[6] = 2 Ch 33[6] (cf. Dr[Dt 18.11]). **9.** *bring about*, of 'י's effecting a deliverance Ex 14[13] (לָכֶם), 1 S 11[13] 2 S 23[10] (ins. also ‖ 1 Ch 11[13] Dr), v[12], *cause*, sq cl. c. שֶׁ Ec 3[14] **10.** *use*, עָ' לִמְלַאכְתּוֹ 1 S 8[16], pass. Ex 38[24] **11.** *spend, pass*, days of life Ec 6[12].

Niph.[97] *Pf.* 3 ms. נַעֲשָׂה Ju 16[11]+; 3 fs נַעַשְׂתָה 2 S 17[23]+, etc., *Impf* 3 ms יֵעָשֶׂה Gn 29[26]+, 3 fs. c. ו subord וְתֵעָשׂ Est 5[6] 7[2] 9[12] (Ges § 109 f), etc., *Inf cstr.* הֵעָשׂוֹת Est 9[1.14], etc; *Pt.* נַעֲשֶׂה Ne 5[18], etc.,—**1.** *be done* (pass of **Qal I 1**) **a.** subj מְלָאכָה Ju 16[11] (c ב instr), Ne 6[16] (c מֵאֵת אֱלֹהִים), v[9] Ex 12[16]+4 t., subj om Ez 44[14], indef. Est 4[1], c כֵּן 9[14], *be done*, כַּתּוֹרָה Ezr 10[3]; *be committed*, of offence, Dt 13[15] Nu 15[24] Ec 4[1]+ 3 t; c neg *not* (yet) *done*, i e future Is 46[10], *be accomplished, performed, fulfilled* Ez 12[25.28] Dn 11[36] Est 5[5] 7[2] 9[12]; *be executed, carried out*, of sentence Ec 8[11], decree Est 9[1], *be followed*, of counsel 2 S 17[23], nearly = *occur* Ec 1[9.9.13] 9[3.6], subj מַעֲשֶׂה 1[14] 2[17] 4[3] 8[9.17], subj הֶבֶל v[14], עִנְיָן v[16] **b.** *Impf.* c. neg., *is (are) not done*, not acc. to usage, of flagrant offences Gn 20[9] (E), 29[26] (c. כֵּן), 34[7] (both J), 2 S 13[12] (כֵּן); hence (P) *not to be done*, forbidden by 'י Lv 4[2.13.22.27] 5[17]. **c.** *be done to*, c. ל of animal 1 S 11[7] (כֹּה); ל pers. Ex 2[4] (E) 21[31] (E; כַּמִּשְׁפָּט), Is 3[11] Je 5[13] (כֹּה), Lv 24[19] (H; כֵּן), Nu 15[34] (P)+8 t, *be done for*, ל pers. Ju 11[37] Est 6[3], עִם pers v[3]; ל rei Nu 15[11] (כָּכָה). **d.** *be done* upon, against (ב) Dn 9[12]. †**2.** (pass of **Qal II**) **a.** *be made*, of concr. things 1 K 10[20] = 2 Ch 9[19] (throne), Je 3[16] (ark), 2 K 12[14] Ez 43[18] Ex 25[31] Nu 4[26] (P); c acc. mat Lv 2[7]. **b.** *be produced* from (מִן) vine Nu 6[4]. **c.** *be prepared*, of food Ex 12[16] Lv 6[14] 7[9] (all P), Ne 5[18.18]. **d.** *be offered*, מִנְחָה Lv 2[8.11], kid Nu 28[15.24]. **e.** *be observed*, passover 2 K 23[22.23] (ל dei) = 2 Ch 35[18.19]; Purim Est 9[28]. **f.** *be used* Lv 7[24] (P), + ל rei 13[51] (P) Ez 15[5.5]

†**Pu.** *Pf.* 1 s. עֻשֵּׂיתִי ψ 139[15] *I was made.*

עֲשָׂהאֵל[18] **n.pr.m.** Ασαηλ, 𝔊L Ασσαηλ (on this and foll cf. אֶלְעָשָׂה),—**1.** brother of Joab and Abishai 2 S 2[18.18]+7 t 2, + 3[27.30] 23[24] 1 Ch 2[16] 11[26] 27[7]. **2.** Levites: **a.** 2 Ch 17[8] (Ιασειηλ, Ασιηλ). **b.** 31[13]. **3.** post-exil. name Ezr 10[15].

†**עֲשִׂיאֵל** **n.pr.m.** Simeonite 1 Ch 4[35], Ασιηλ.

†**עֲשָׂיָה** **n.pr.m.** Ασαιας, etc.; 𝔊L in Kgs. Αζαριας;—**1.** servant of Josiah 2 K 22[12.14] = 2 Ch 34[20]. **2.** Simeonite 1 Ch 4[36]. **3.** Levites: **a.** 6[15] 15[6.11]. **b.** 9[5]

†(ו)יעשו Kt, (ו)יַעֲשָׂי Qr, **n.pr.m.** one with foreign wife Ezr 10[37], 𝔊 καὶ ἐποίησαν.

†**יַעֲשִׂיאֵל** **n.pr.m.** **1.** hero of David 1 Ch 11[47], (Ι)εσσιηλ. **2.** Benjamite ruler 27[21], Ασειηρ, 𝔊L Ιασσιηλ.

מַעֲשֶׂה[233] **n.m.**[Gn 20.9] deed, work,—abs. מ' Gn 44[15]+, cstr. מַעֲשֵׂה Is 5[12]+; sf. מַעֲשֵׂהוּ Ju 13[12]+, etc.; pl. מַעֲשִׂים Gn 20[9]+; cstr מַעֲשֵׂי Je 1[16]+; sf מַעֲשָׂיו 1 S 19[4] (or sg, so Dr)+, etc,—oft. acc cogn. c. עשׂה;—**1. a.** (1) *deed, thing done* by man Nu 16[28] (JE), 1 K 13[11] Is 26[12],—1 S 20[19] is obscure; (2) implic. evil Gn 44[15] (J), Ex 23[24] (E), Ne 6[14]+8 t., + sg. coll. *doing(s)* Mi 6[16] Lv 18[3.3] (H), 2 Ch 17[4], מ' יְדֵיהֶם La 3[64] Hg 2[14], Jb 33[17] (rdg. מִמַּעֲשֵׂהוּ 𝔊 Di Siegf Bu), Ez 16[30] (*behaviour*); explic מַעֲשֵׂינוּ הָרָעִים Ezr 9[13] cf. Ec 4[3] 8[11.14], מַעֲשֵׂי־אָוֶן Is 59[6]; specif. of idolatr. practices, מ' יְדֵיכֶם sg. Dt 31[29] Je 25[6.7] 32[30], pl. 44[8], cf. sg 1 K 16[7] 2 K 22[17] = 2 Ch 34[25]; (3) implic. right, praiseworthy 1 S 19[4] 2 K 23[19] Jon 3[10] Pr 31[31], of duty in gen הַמּ' אֲשֶׁר יַעֲשׂוּן Ex 18[20] (E) = *what they are to do*; explic. Ec 4[4] 8[14]; (4) as basis of judgment (good or bad) Is 66[18] ψ 33[15] 62[13] Ec 12[14], מ' יְדֵיהֶם Je 25[14]. **b.** (1) *work, labour*, husbandry Ex 23[16] (E), Gn 5[29] (J), Ju 19[16], מ' יְדֵיכֶם Hg 2[17]; enforced labour of Isr. in Egypt Ex 5[4.13] (J); in gen. 23[12] (E); also of product of labour 23[16], cf. Is 65[22] Ec 5[5]; שֵׁשֶׁת יְמֵי הַמּ' Ez 46[1] *the six working-days;* of religious work, מ' עֲבֹדַת בֵּית הָא' 1 Ch 23[28], cf. מ' 2 Ch 31[21]; (2) *business, pursuit*, Gn 46[33] 47[3] (J), Ju 13[12] 1 S 25[2] Is 54[16]; in gen., *occupation* Is 29[15] Ec 2[4.11] 3[17.22] 8[9] 9[7.10]; (3) *undertaking, enterprise* Is 19[14.15] Dt 15[10], מ' יָדְךָ Dt 2[7]+ 5 t. Dt, 2 Ch 32[30] Jb 1[10] ψ 28[4], מ' יָדֵינוּ ψ 90[17.17]; (4) *achievement* Je 48[7] Est 10[2]; (5) in weakened sense, מַעֲשֶׂיךָ Pr 16[3] *thine affairs;* nearly = *occurrences* Ec 1[14] (pl), 2[17] 8[17] (sg.) **c.** *deed(s), work(s)* of 'י, esp in deliverance and in judgment, Ju 2[7.10] Jos 24[31] (D), ψ 33[4]+21 t., + מ' יָדָיו

etc. Is 5[12] ψ 28[5] 92[5] + 4 t.; מ׳ הָאֱלֹהִים in gen. Ec 7[13] 8[17] 11[5] cf. 3[11]. **2. a.** (1) *work, thing made*, by man, מ׳ אֹפֶה Gn 40[17] (E) *baker's work;* מ׳ יְדֵי יוֹצֵר La 4[2]; oft. of furnishings of tabern., מ׳ אֹרֵג, מ׳ חֹשֵׁב Ex 26[1] + 7 t., מ׳ רֹקֵם 26[36] + 5 t., 28[32] + 2 t., מ׳ חָרָשׁ 28[11], cf. מ׳ יְדֵי אָמָּן Ct 7[2]; of holy oil, etc. מ׳ רֹקֵחַ Ex 30[25] + 2 t. (ins. רֹקֵחַ perh. also 2 Ch 16[14]); hence מ׳ = *work of art* Is 3[24] (of coiffure), cf. כְּלִי מ׳ Nu 31[51]; sq. n. of material, pattern, etc., מ׳ עִזִּים v[20] (i.e. goats' hair), v. also Ex 27[4] 28[14] +; in temple, מ׳ שְׂבָכָה 1 K 7[17], מ׳ שׁוֹשַׁן v[19], etc.; מ׳ צַעֲצֻעִים 2 Ch 3[10], cf. מ׳ הַחֲבִתִּים 1 Ch 9[31] *the work of* (consisting in) *bread-wafers;* = *materials* of (prepared for) הָעוֹלָה 2 Ch 4[6]; in theoph. מ׳ לִבְנַת הַסַּפִּיר Ex 24[10] (J); מ׳ of ships 2 Ch 20[37]; in gen. Is 29[16]; Ez 27[16.18] = *thy manufactures, wares;* מַעֲשַׂי ψ 45[2] = *my verses* (ποίημα, *poem*); (2) *workmanship* Ez 1[16.16] (v[16a] del. Co Toy) 1 K 7[8] Ex 28[8] + 11 t.; (3) מ׳ יְדֵי אָדָם of idols (contemptuously) Dt 4[28] 2 K 19[18] = Is 37[19] = 2 Ch 32[19], ψ 115[4] 135[15], cf. Is 2[8] (מ׳ יָדָיו), Ho 14[4] Mi 5[12] Je 1[16]; so (יְדֵי) מ׳ חָרָשׁ Dt 27[15] Je 10[3.9], cf. Ho 13[2]; מ׳ חֲכָמִים Je 10[9]; מ׳ תַּעְתֻּעִים v[15] 51[18]; appar. also מַעֲשֵׂיהֶם Is 41[29] cf. 57[12] Ez 6[6]; מ׳ יָדָיו of altars Is 17[8]. **b.** *work* (made by) God Ex 32[16] (E); esp. (poet. and late), of created things, ψ 103[22] 104[24] + 4 t. ψ; מ׳ יָדֶיךָ 8[4], מ׳ אֶצְבְּעֹתֶיךָ 102[26] (both of heavens), cf. 19[2] (heavenly bodies), 8[7] (animals); of man Jb 14[15] 34[19], cf. לָדַעַת כָּל־אַנְשֵׁי מַעֲשֵׂהוּ 37[7] (but rd. prob. אנשים 𝔙 Ol Di al.); of a nation Is 19[25] 60[21] 64[7]; of weights Pr 16[11] (but rd. perh. הַמֶּלֶךְ for י׳ Gr Toy). **c.** *product* of olive-tree, מ׳ זַיִת Hb 3[17]; fig. *product of righteousness* Is 32[17].

†מַעֲשֵׂיָהוּ, מַעֲשֵׂיָה, -יָה n.pr.m. (*work of* י׳; cf. n. pr. מעשיהו on Isr. seal, Cl-Gann, v. Lzb[315]);—Μα(α)σσαια(ς), etc., 𝔊[B] Ezr 10[21] Μασαηλ:—**1.** priest, Je.'s time, מַעֲשֵׂיָה Je 21[1] 29[25] 37[3]; perh. 35[4] (-יָהוּ). **2.** 29[21]. מַעֲשֵׂיָהוּ **3.** Levites: **a.** 1 Ch 15[18.20]. **b.** 2 Ch 23[1]. **4.** officials: **a.** 26[11]. **b.** 34[8]. **5.** son of Ahaz 28[7]. **6.** Levite 1 Ch 6[25] rdg. מַעֲשֵׂיָה for MT בַּעֲשֵׂיָה q.v., cf. Kit. מַעֲשֵׂיָה of various post-exil. men: **7.** Ne 3[23] (Μαδασηλ, A Μαασιου). **8. a.** 8[4.7]. **b.** 10[26]. **c.** 11[5]. **d.** v[7]. **e.** 12[41]. **f.** v[42]. **9. a.** Ezr 10[18]. **b.** v[21] (Μασαηλ, Μασειας). **c.** v[22]. **d.** v[30]. **10.** מַעְשַׂי (van d. H. מַעֲשַׂי) Μα(α)σαι(α), a priest 1 Ch 9[12].

†II. [עָשָׂה] **vb. Pi. press, squeeze** (NH עִשָּׂה Pi. *compel;* 𝔗 עַסִּי Pa. *crush, gnash* (teeth); cf. Ar. غَشِيَ *compress* a woman);—*Pf.* 3 pl. עִשּׂוּ דַּדֵּי בְּתוּלֶיהָ Ez 23[3.8] (unchaste act); *Inf. cstr.* בַּעֲשׂוֹת . . . דַּדַּיִךְ v[21] rd. Pi. בְּעַשּׂוֹת (Ew Co Toy, al.).

עֵשָׂו [97] **n.pr.m. Esau**, Ησαυ;—*Esau*, elder son of Isaac Gn 25[25.26] + 7 t. 25, 26[34] 27[1] + 24 t. 27, 28, 32[4] + 15 t. 32, 33, 35, Jos 24[4.4] Mal 1[2.3] 1 Ch 1[34]; identif. with אֱדוֹם Gn 36[1.8.19], ancestor of Edomites v[9.43], cf. 1 Ch 1[35]; dwelling in Mt. Seir Gn 36[8] (25 t. in all, Gn 36) Dt 2[5] Jos 24[4]; בְּנֵי עֵשָׂו = Edomites Dt 2[4.8.12.22.29]; עֵשָׂו = Edom Je 49[8] Ob[6], בֵּית עֵשָׂו v[18.18], הַר עֵשָׂו v[8.9.19.21].

† [עָשַׂק] **vb. Hithp. contend** (perh. orig. *cling* to (in strife), cf. Ar. عَشِقَ *cling* with love (Lag[BN 143]); Syr. ܥܫܩ, Ethpa. *be difficult* (i.e. *indignant, hostile*); NH עָסַק, 𝔗 עֲסַק, *busy oneself*, NH עֵסֶק *business, occupation*);—*Pf.* 3 pl. הִתְעַשְּׂקוּ עִמּוֹ Gn 26[20] *they contended with him.*

†עֵשֶׂק **n.pr.font.** in SW. Pal. Gn 26[20] (expl. as *contention*);—locality unknown, 𝔊 Ἀδικία.

עשׂר (√ of foll.; appar. *gather, unite*, cf. Ar. عَشِيرٌ *kinsman*, عَشِيرَةٌ *tribe*, مَعْشَرٌ *assembly;* hence *ten* = *collection, union*).

עֶשֶׂר, עֲשָׂרָה [176] **n.m.** and **f. ten** (NH = BH; perh. MI[33] עשׂר; Ph. עשר, עסר, עשרת, etc.; Ar. عَشْرٌ, عَشَرَةٌ; Sab. עשר SabDenkm[No. 11 b, 1.5.6] עשרת and cpds. Hom[Chrest. 48]; Eth. ዐሥሩ: ዐሠርቱ:; As. *ešertu;* 𝔗 עֲסַר, עֶשֶׂר, עַסְרָא, עֲשָׂרָא; Syr. ܥܣܪ, ܥܣܪܐ; Nab. עשר, all = *ten;* Palm. עשרתא *the Ten* (rulers));—**m.** (c. **n.f.**) עֶשֶׂר 2 S 15[16] + 53 t. (abs. and cstr. usu. indistinguishable); עֲשַׂר 1 K 7[43] 1 Ch 6[46]; **f.** (c. **n.m.**): abs. עֲשָׂרָה Gn 24[10] + 69 t.; cstr. (prob.) עֲשֶׂרֶת 1 S 17[18] + 46 t.; f.pl. עֲשָׂרֹת Ex 18[21] + 2 t.;—on pl. עֶשְׂרִים, 20, v. infr.;—†**1.** *a ten*, only f.pl. *tens* in phr. שָׂרֵי ע׳ *captains of tens* Ex 18[21.25] (E), Dt 1[15]. **2.** *ten*, enumerating pers. or things, usually without other num.: **a.** עֶשֶׂר bef. n.f.pl., Gn 45[23] + 43 t.; after n. †1 K 7[27.43] + late passages Jos 15[57] 21[5.26] (all P), 1 Ch 6[46] 2 Ch 4[7]; bef. בָּאַמָּה = *ten cubits* †1 K 6[3.25.26] 7[23.24]. **b.** עֲשָׂרָה bef. n.m.pl., Gn 45[23] + 25 t. (incl. ע׳ אֲלָפִים = 10,000 2 S 18[3] 2 K 24[14] Kt, עֲשֶׂרֶת Qr); bef. n. coll. בָּקָר 1 K 5[3], רֶכֶב 2 K 13[7]; also ע׳ לֶחֶם הַזֶּה 1 S 17[17] *these ten loaves*, cf. 1 K 14[3]; ע׳ אֶלֶף Ez 45[1] rd. עֶשְׂרִים א׳ 𝔊 Hi Co Berthol Toy; after n.m.pl. †Gn 32[16.16] 43[3] (all E), Jos 17[5] (JE), Nu 29[23] (P), 1 K 7[43] 2 Ch 4[6.8] Dn 1[12.14.15] +; after n. coll. צאן 2 Ch 30[24]; n. om., sc. *men*, †Gn 18[32] (J) Am 5[3] Ezr 8[4]; sc. *shekels* (weight) Gn 24[22] (J) Nu 7[14] + 13 t. Nu 7

(עֲ' זָהָב); עֲ' כֶּסֶף (sc. *shekels*, value) 2 S 18^{11}; sc. *measures* (of grain) Hg 2^{16}; c. art. *the ten* Gn 18^{32} (J; sc. *men*), Ne 11^{1} (*id.*=*every ten*); as pred. Ex 27$^{12.12}$=38$^{12.12}$ (all P)†. **c.** עֲשֶׂרֶת bef. n.m.pl. Ex 34^{28}+18 t., + כַּעֲשֶׂרֶת הַיָּמִים 1 S 25^{38} (on art. cf. Weir in Dr, but dub.; prob. om., so 𝔊 We Bu), + עֲ' אֲלָפִים =10,000 Ju 1^{4}+26 t.; n. om. עֲ' כֶּסֶף (sc. *shekels*) Ju 17^{10}. †**3.** rarely + other num.: **a.** עֶשֶׂר after larger num., מֵאָה וְעֶ' שָׁנִים Gn 50$^{22.26}$ Jos 24^{29} (all E), Ju 2^{8}. **b.** עֲ' before larger num. עֶשֶׂר שָׁנִים וּתְשַׁע מֵאוֹת שָׁנָה Gn 5^{14} (P). **c.** עֲשָׂרָה after larger num., מֵאָה וַעֲשָׂרָה הַזְּכָרִים Ezr 8^{12}, cf. (n. preceding) 1^{10}. **d.** עֲשָׂרָה after smaller num., שִׁבְעָה שְׁקָלִים וַעֲשָׂרָה הַכָּסֶף Je 32^{9}=*seventeen shekels;* before smaller num. + n. sg. עֲשָׂרָה וַחֲמִשָּׁה שֶׁקֶל Ez 45^{12}, but rd. חֲמִשִּׁים, joining עֲשָׂרָה to preceding, 𝔊^{A} Hi Co al.

עָשָׂר 203, עֶשְׂרֵה 144 **n.** ten, only after units to make num. 11–19, both cardinal and ordinal; עֶשְׂרֵה c. **n.f.**, עָשָׂר c. **n.m.**, thus: **1.** *eleven:* **a.** אַחַד עָשָׂר (c. n.m.) Gn 32^{23}+2 t. **b.** אַחַת עֶשְׂרֵה (c. n.f.) 2 K 23^{36}+7 t.; also = *eleventh* 1 K 6^{38} 2 K 9^{29}. **c.** עַשְׁתֵּי עָשָׂר (c. n.m.) Nu 29^{20}; ord. Dt 1^{3}+7 t. **d.** עַשְׁתֵּי עֶשְׂרֵה (c. n.f.) Ex 26^{7}+4 t.; ord. Je 1^{3}+4 t. **2.** *twelve:* **a.** שְׁנֵי(ם) עָשָׂר (c. n.m.) Gn 35^{22}+80 t.; ord. 1 K 19^{19}+12 t. **b.** שְׁתֵּי(ם) עֶשְׂרֵה (c. n.f.) Ex 24^{4}+31 t.; ord. 2 K 8^{25}+6 t. **3.** *thirteen:* **a.** שְׁלֹשָׁה עָשָׂר (c. n.m.) Nu 29^{14}+2 t.; ord. Est 3^{12}+7 t. **b.** שְׁלֹשׁ עֶשְׂרֵה (c. n.f.) 1 K 7^{1}+9 t.; ord. Gn 14^{4}+2 t. **4.** *fourteen:* **a.** אַרְבָּעָה עָשָׂר Gn 46^{22}+13 t.; ord. Ex 12^{6}+17 t. **b.** אַרְבַּע עֶשְׂרֵה Gn 31^{41}+5 t.; ord. 2 K 18^{13}+3 t. **5.** *fifteen:* **a.** חֲמִשָּׁה עָשָׂר Ho 3^{2}+3 t.; ord. Ex 16^{1}+14 t. †**b.** חֲמֵשֶׁת עָשָׂר Ju 8^{10} 2 S 19^{18}. **c.** חֲמֵשׁ עֶשְׂרֵה 2 K 14^{17}+9 t.; ord. †2 K 14^{23} 2 Ch 15^{10}.—Vid. also עֶשֶׂר **2 d.** **6.** *sixteen:* **a.** שִׁשָּׁה עָשָׂר Ex 26^{25}+6 t.; ord. 1 Ch 24^{14}+2 t. **b.** שֵׁשׁ עֶשְׂרֵה Gn 46^{18}+13 t. **7.** *seventeen:* **a.** שִׁבְעָה עָשָׂר 1 Ch 7^{11}+2 t.; ord. Gn 7^{11}+3 t. **b.** שְׁבַע עֶשְׂרֵה Gn 37^{2}+4 t.; ord. 1 K 22^{52} 2 K 16^{1}.—Vid. also עֶשֶׂר **3 d.** **8.** *eighteen:* **a.** שְׁמֹנָה (שְׁמֹנַת) עָשָׂר Gn 14^{4}+10 t.; ord. †1 Ch 24^{15} 25^{25}. **b.** שְׁמֹנֶה עֶשְׂרֵה Ju 3^{14}+6 t.; ord. 1 K 15^{1}+8 t. †**9.** *nineteen:* **a.** תִּשְׁעָה עָשָׂר 2 S 2^{30}; ord. 1 Ch 24^{16} 25^{26}. **b.** תְּשַׁע עֶשְׂרֵה Gn 11^{25} Jos 19^{38}; ord. 2 K 25^{8}=Je 52^{12}.

These num. usually take sg. of the nouns most often used, אִישׁ, יוֹם, שָׁנָה, חֹדֶשׁ, cf. (sts.) אַמָּה, etc.; otherwise pl.; rarely (late usage) they follow noun, which is then usu. pl., e.g. Nu 29^{30} Jos 15^{51} (P), Ezr 8$^{35.35}$ Est 3^{13} 8^{5}, etc. (even שָׁנִים שְׁתֵּים עֶשְׂרֵה Na 5^{14}), but שָׁנָה precedes ordinal 1 K 6^{38}, שְׁנַת 15^{1}+8 t., so יוֹם (c. ord.) 2 Ch 29^{17}+5 t. Est 9; also יוֹם and שָׁנָה (שְׁנַת) both precede and foll. ordinal Nu 7$^{72.78}$ 2 K 8^{25} 9^{29} 14^{23} 16^{1} Je 32^{1} 2 K 25^{8}=Je 52^{12}.—Vid. also Kö$^{ii. 1, 211 ff.}$ Da$^{Synt. § 37 a, also R. 1, 2}$ Ges$^{§§ 92 d, e, 134}$, and esp. Herner$^{Synt. d. Zahlwörter im AT (1893)}$; on form in ה◌ֵ (prob for י◌ֵ), Ol$^{§ 110}$ Kö$^{ii. 1, 427}$ W$^{SG 138}$.

†[עָשַׂר] **vb. denom.** take the tenth of, tithe;—**Qal** *Impf.* 3 ms. יַעְשֹׂר 1 S 8$^{15.17}$ (c. acc. of thing tithed). **Pi.** *Impf.* + *Inf. abs. give a tenth of*, c. acc. rei: 2 ms. עַשֵּׂר תְּעַשֵּׂר Dt 14^{22}; 1 s. עַשֵּׂר אֲעַשְּׂרֶנּוּ לָךְ Gn 28^{22} (P); *Pt. taking the tenth*, הַמְעַשְּׂרִים Ne 10^{38}. **Hiph.** (so usu. expl.) *Inf.* לַעְשֵׂר Dt 26^{12} c. acc. cogn. i.e. *taking, reckoning, tithe*, but Inf. cstr. with ◌ַ improb., < rd. לְעַשֵּׂר **Pi.**; בַּעְשֵׂר Ne 10^{39} abs., i.e. *receiving tithes*, but read prob. בַּעְשֹׂר **Qal** (on anom. points, see Ges$^{§ 53 k}$ Dr$^{Dt 26, 12}$).

† עָשׂוֹר, and (Ex 12^{3}) עָשֹׂר **n.** [**m.**] a ten, decade;—**1.** usu. of days: **a.** *a period of ten days* Gn 24^{55} (J). **b.** in phr., בֶּעָשׂוֹר (עָשֹׂר) לַחֹדֶשׁ *on the tenth day of the month* Lv 25^{9} (H), Ez 20^{1} 24^{1} 40^{1} Ex 12^{3} Lv 16^{29} 23^{27} Nu 29^{7} Jos 4^{19} (all P), 2 K 25^{1}=Je 52^{4}, Je 52^{12} (*seventh day* in ‖ 2 K 25^{8}). **2.** of strings of instr.: נֵבֶל עָ' *harp, a ten*(-stringed one) ψ 33^{2} 144^{9}; עָ' alone ψ 92^{4} upon *a ten*(-stringed instrument).

עֶשְׂרִים 315 **n. pl. indecl.** (a) twenty (ancient pl. of עֶשֶׂר Prä$^{BAS i. 376}$; NH=BH; Ar. عِشْرُونَ; As. *ešrâ;* Sab. עשרי Hom$^{Chrest. 48}$; Eth. ዕሥራ: Aram. עשרין, ܥܣܪܝܢ; Nab. (עשרין);—**I.** as cardinal: **1.** without other num.: **a.** usu. sq. n.s. (esp. שָׁנָה, אִישׁ, אַמָּה, etc.) Gn 31^{38} 1 S 14^{14} Ex 38^{18}+64 t., + עֶשְׂרִים אֶלֶף 20,000 1 Ch 18^{4}+7 t. + Ez 45^{1} (rdg. עֶשְׂרִים אֶלֶף, v. עֶשֶׂר **2 b**). **b.** sq. n.pl. 2 S 3^{20} Ex 36$^{23.24.25}$+4 t. †**c.** sq. n.s. coll. 1 K 5^{3}. **d.** n.pl. precedes Gn 32$^{15.15.16}$ 2 Ch 3^{3}+6 t. **e.** n. om. Gn 18$^{31.31}$ (הָעֶ'), 1 K 6^{2}+6 t., as pred. Ex 27$^{10.10.11.11}$+4 t. †**f.** + בָּאַמָּה Zc 5^{2}. **2.** + other num.: **a.** c. units, usu. 20 + (c. וְ) unit + n.s. Ju 10$^{2.3}$ 1 K 14^{20}+58 t. (incl. 20 + 1 × 1000, etc., 27 t.); n. om. Jos 15^{32}+2 t. pred.; less oft. unit + 20 + n.s. Gn 11^{24} Ex 38^{24} Nu 8^{24} (all P) + 27 t.; unit + 20 + בָּאַמָּה Ez 40^{21} Ex 26^{2} 36^{9} (both P). **b.** 20 + unit + n.pl. Nu 7^{88} (P), 1 Ch 2^{22}+3 t. Chr. †**c.** n.pl. + 20 + unit Jos 19^{30} 1 Ch 12^{29} (van d. H. v^{28}). **d.** c. hundreds, 20 usu. foll.; sq. n.s. 1 K 9^{14} Gn 6^{3} Dt 31^{2}+7 t.; n. om. 2 Ch 3^{4} Ezr 2^{32}=Ne 7^{35}; 20 + 100 (n. om.)

Nu 7^{86}. **e** n.pl. + 100 + 20 1 Ch $15^{5.6}$;—cf. further מֵאָה. **II.** as ordinal: **1.** 20 alone, בִּשְׁנַת ע׳ *in the twentieth year* 1 K 15^{9} + 4 t.; n. om. Nu 10^{11} + 3 t. **2. a.** 20 + unit + ns. Ez 29^{17} 40^{1}. **b.** ns. + 20 + unit Hg 1^{15} 2 Ch 7^{10} +; ns. + unit + 20 Ex 12^{8}; בִּשְׁנַת + 20 + unit 1 K 16^{10}, etc.—Vid. reff. sub עֶשֶׂר.

עֲשִׂירִי $_{20}$ **m.**, עֲשִׂירִיָּה, and עֲשִׂירִית $_{8}$ **f. adj. num. ord.** tenth;—**1.** דּוֹר עֲשִׂירִי Dt $23^{3.4}$; בַּיּוֹם הָע׳ Nu 7^{66} (P); הַחֹדֶשׁ הָע׳ Gn 8^{5} (P) Ez 24^{1} + 5 t.; בַּחֹדֶשׁ הָעֲשִׂרִי Je 39^{1}; ח׳ om. הָעֲשִׂירִי Gn 8^{5}(P), בָּעֲשִׂרִי Ez 29^{1} 33^{21}; other nouns om. הָעֲשִׂירִי 1 Ch 12^{13} 25^{17} 27^{13}, הָעֲשִׂרִי 24^{11}; בַּשָּׁנָה הָעֲשִׂרִית Ez 29^{1}, בַּשׁ׳ הָעֲשִׂרִית Je 32^{1}. **2.** as subst. *a tenth part:* f. abs. עֲשִׂרִיָּה Is 6^{13}; f. cstr. עֲשִׂירִית הָאֵיפָה Nu 28^{5}, עֲשִׂרִית Ex 16^{36}, עֲשִׂירִת Lv 5^{11} 6^{13} Nu 5^{15}; עֲשִׂירִת הַחֹמֶר Ez 45^{11}; m. abs. הָעֲשִׂירִי Lv 27^{32} *the tithe* (i.e. of cattle, etc.).

עִשָּׂרוֹן $_{33}$ **n.m.** $^{Lv\ 14,\ 10}$ **tenth part** (of ephah; cf. 𝔊 δέκατον τοῦ οἰφί Nu 15^{4}, and עֲשִׂירִית הָאֵיפָה 28^{5}; i.e. = עֹמֶר, v. further Benz $^{Arch.\ 182}$ Now $^{Arch.\ i.\ 203}$);—abs. ע׳ Lv 14^{21} +, עִשָּׂרֹן Ex 29^{40} Nu 28^{13}; pl. עֶשְׂרֹנִים Nu 28^{9} +;—only P (H), as measure of סֹלֶת used in meal-offering Ex 29^{40} Lv 14^{10} + 3 t. Lv (H only 23^{17}); Nu 15^{4} + 26 t. Nu, incl. distributive עִשָּׂר(ו)ן עִשָּׂרוֹן 28^{13} + 4 t.

†מַעֲשֵׂר **n.m.** $^{Nu\ 18,\ 28}$ **tenth part, tithe**;—abs. מ׳ Nu 18^{26} +; cstr. מַעְשַׂר Lv 27^{30} +, מַעְשַׂר Ne 10^{39} (bef. הַמַּעֲשֵׂר); sf. מַעְשְׂרוֹ Lv 27^{31}; pl. abs. מַעַשְׂרוֹת Ne 12^{44}; sf. מַעְשְׂרֹתֵיכֶם Am 4^{4} + 3 t.;—**1.** *tenth part* of homer Ez 45^{11}, of bath v^{14}. **2.** *tithe, payment of tenth part:* c. מִן rei Gn 14^{20} Nu 18^{26}; usu. cstr. bef. n. rei Dt 12^{17} $14^{23.28}$ 26^{12} Lv $27^{30.32}$ 2 Ch $31^{5.6.6}$ Ne $10^{38.39}$ $13^{5.12}$; abs. Nu $18^{21.26.26}$ Mal $3^{8.10}$ 2 Ch 31^{12} Ne 10^{39} 12^{44}; שְׁנַת הַמ׳ Dt 26^{12} *the year of the tithe* (i.e. of tithing); c. genit. pers. paying tithe Am 4^{4} Dt $12^{6.11}$ Lv 27^{31} Nu $18^{24.28}$.—Cf. RS $^{Sem.\ i.\ 228\ ff.;\ 2nd\ ed.\ 245\ ff.;\ Proph.\ Lect.\ ii.\ N.}$ Now $^{Arch.\ i.\ 313;\ ii.\ 257\ f.}$ Benz $^{Arch.\ 309,\ 460\ f.}$ Dr $^{Dt.\ 168\ ff.}$

I. עָשׁ Jb 9^{9} prob. error for עַיִשׁ, v. עַיִשׁ.

II. עָשׁ v. עשׁשׁ.

†עַשְׁוָת **n.pr.m.** in Asher 1 Ch 7^{33}, Ασειθ, Ασουαθ.

עשׁן (√of foll.; cf. Ar. عَشَنَ *ascend*, Lag $^{BN\ 61}$ (plausibly); v. عُثَانٌ, عَثَنَ *smoke;* also Syr. ܬܢܢܐ (Nö ^{§116}), ܬܢܢܐ, from √ *ܬܢܢ acc. to Hoffm $^{LCB\ 1882,\ 320}$; vb. denom. in Ar. NH).

†I. עָשָׁן **n.m.** $^{Ex\ 19,\ 18}$ **smoke**;—abs. ע׳ Ju 20^{38} +, cstr. עֲשַׁן Jos $8^{20.21}$, עֶשֶׁן Ex 19^{18}; sf. עֲשָׁנוֹ Ex 19^{18}, עֲשָׁנָהּ Is 34^{10};—**1. a.** of burning city Jos $8^{20.21}$ Ju $20^{38.40}$, cf. Na 2^{14}; heralding a foe Is 14^{31}. **b.** in fig. of destruction of Isr. Is 9^{17}, Edom 34^{10}. **c.** sim. of dust-cloud Ct 3^{6}; of transitoriness Ho 13^{3} Is 51^{6} ψ 37^{20} (rdg. כֶּעָ׳, as 𝔊 𝔖 𝔙), 68^{3} 102^{4}; sim. of the unpleasant, Pr 10^{26}. **d.** breath of crocodile Jb 41^{12}. **2. a.** attending theoph., תַּנּוּר ע׳ Gn 15^{17}; of mt. Ex 19^{18}, cf. sim. כְּע׳ הַכִּבְשָׁן v^{18}; Is 6^{4}, also 4^{5} Jo 3^{3}. **b.** of God's anger, ע׳ בְּאַפּוֹ 2 S 22^{9} = ψ 18^{9}; so prob. also Is 65^{5}.

†עָשַׁן **vb. denom. smoke, be wroth**;—**Qal 1. a.** *smoke, Pf.* 3 ms. ע׳ of mt. Ex 19^{18}, so *Impf.* 3 mpl. יֶעֱשָׁנוּ (at touch of י׳) ψ 104^{32} 144^{5}. **b.** fig., 3 ms. יֶעְשַׁן אַף־י׳, c. ב *against,* Dt 29^{19} ψ 74^{1}. Hence **2.** subj. pers., *fume,* i.e. *be wroth, Pf.* 2 ms. עָשַׁנְתָּ בּ׳ ψ 80^{5}.

†עָשֵׁן **adj.** smoking;—ע׳ of mt. Ex 20^{18} (Gi v^{15}); pl. הָאוּדִים הָעֲשֵׁנִים Is 7^{4} *the smoking firebrands* (dying out; in fig.).

†II. עָשָׁן **n.pr.loc.** in Shephelah of Judah Jos 15^{42}, in Simeon acc. to 19^{7} 1 Ch 4^{32}, Levit. city 6^{44}; Ασαν, etc.; = בּוֹר עָשָׁן, q.v. p. 92 supr.

†**עָשַׁק** **vb. oppress, wrong, extort** (𝔗 עֲשַׁק = BH, so OAram. עשק; Syr. ܥܫܩ *accuse, slander;* As. adj. *ešḳu, strong;* Ar. عَسَقَ *roughness, injustice*);—**Qal** *Pf.* ע׳ Lv 5^{21} Ez 18^{18}; 2 ms. sf. עֲשַׁקְתָּנוּ 1 S 12^{4}, etc.; *Impf.* 3 ms. sf. יַעַשְׁקֻנִי ψ 119^{122}; 2 ms. תַּעֲשֹׁק Lv 19^{13} +, etc.; *Inf. cstr.* עֲשֹׁק Ho 12^{8}, sf. עָשְׁקָם 1 Ch 16^{21} ψ 105^{14}; *Pt. act.* עֹשֵׁק Pr 14^{31} +, fpl. הָעֹשְׁקוֹת Am 4^{1}, etc.; *pass.* עָשׁוּק Dt 28^{29} +, etc.;—**1.** *oppress, wrong* (oft. by extortion, ∥ גָּזַל), c. acc. pers. 1 S $12^{3.4}$ Mi 2^{2} Lv 5^{21} 19^{13}; esp. the poor and helpless Am 4^{1} Dt 24^{14} Je 7^{6} Ez 22^{29} Zc 7^{10} Pr 14^{31} 22^{16} 28^{3} Ec 4^{1}; also c. acc. cogn. ע׳ עֹשֶׁק (ו)גָזֵל גָּזֵל Ez 18^{18} *practise extortion,* 22^{29}, *take by extortion* Lv 5^{23} and (c. acc. rei) Mal 3^{5}; abs. Ho 12^{8} *practise extortion;* Jb 10^{3} *deal tyrannically* (of God); pt. *oppressor, extortioner* Je 21^{12} ψ 72^{4} Ec 4^{1}; pt. pass. as subst. *the oppressed* ψ 103^{6} 146^{7}. **2.** *oppress* a nation Is 52^{4}, cf. ψ 105^{14} = 1 Ch 16^{21}, ψ 119^{122}, pt. act. *oppressor* v^{121}, pt. pass. *oppressed* Je 50^{33}, in predict. ע׳ וְגָזוּל Dt 28^{29}, ע׳ וְרָצוּץ v^{33} Ho 5^{11}. **3.** dub. are: יַעֲשֹׁק נָהָר Jb 40^{23} *a river oppresses* him, i.e. rushes violently upon him (sc. the hippopot.; Du יָשֹׁק, fr. שׁוּק; >Gunk Bu יִשְׁקַע *falls, sinks*); עָשֻׁק בְּדַם נָפֶשׁ

Pr 28[17] *oppressed* (? *burdened*) with the blood of a person **Pu.** *Pt.* f. הַמְעֻשָּׁקָה Is 23[12] *crushed* (of conquered Sidon under fig. of woman).

†עֹשֶׁק **n.m.**[Ec 7, 7] **oppression, extortion;**—ע׳ abs Je 6[6]+, cstr ψ 119[134] Ec 5[7],—**1.** Je 6[6] 22[17] Ez 22[7 12] ψ 73[8]; c genit. subj. 119[134], obj. Ec 5[7]; as acc. cogn. c. עָשַׁק (q.v.) Ez 18[18] 22[29]. **2.** national *oppression*, Is 54[14]. **3.** concr, *gain of extortion* ψ 62[11], so perh. Ec 7[7]; as acc cogn. Lv 5[23] (‖ גָּזֵל)—Is 30[12] 59[13] rd. עִקֵּשׁ Lag Gr al.

†עֵשֶׁק **n.pr.m.** Benjamite 1 Ch 8[39], Ασηλ, Ασεκ.

†עָשְׁקָה **n.f.** oppression, distress;—עָשְׁקָה־לִּי Is 38[14] (cf Ges[§ 9 v. 48 i]) *oppression to me!* = I am oppressed, distressed.

†עָשׁוֹק **n.**[**m.**] **oppressor, extortioner;**—Je 22[3] (= עשק 21[12])

†עֲשׁוּקִים **n.pl.abstr.** oppression, extortion,—ע׳ Am 3[9] Jb 35[9], עֲשֻׁקִים Ec 4[1].

†[מַעֲשַׁקָּה] **n.f.** extortionate act;—pl. abs רַב מַעֲשַׁקּוֹת Pr 28[16] *great in extortions*, בֶּצַע מ׳ Is 33[15] *gain of extortions*

†[עָשַׁר] **vb.** be or become rich (NH in der. spec, and deriv., Aram. עֲתַר, ܥܬܰܪ; cf Ar. عَثَرَ *abound with herbage*, عَثَرٌ *abundance*, of herbage, goods, etc),—**Qal** *Pf* 1 s. עָשַׁרְתִּי Ho 12[9] *I have become rich*, *Impf.* 3 ms. יַעֲשִׁר Jb 15[29] *he shall* not *be rich*—1 K 22[49] rd. עָשָׂה. **Hiph. 1.** *make rich*, c. acc. pers.: *Pf.* 1 s. הֶעֱשַׁרְתִּי Gn 14[23], 2 fs הֶעֱשַׁרְתְּ Ez 27[33] (of personif. Tyre; + ברב הוניך); *Impf* 3 ms sf. יַעְשְׁרֶנּוּ (Ges[§ 53 n]), + acc cogn עֹשֶׁר, 2 ms sf. רַבַּת תַּעְשְׁרֶנָּה ψ 65[10] *thou dost greatly enrich it* (the land); obj. om. 3 fs תַּעֲשִׁיר Pr 10[22], so *Pt* מַעֲשִׁיר 1 S 2[7] ׳י *maketh rich* (opp. מוריש). **2.** *gain riches*, abs.: *Impf.* 3 ms יַעֲשִׁר ψ 49[17], יַעֲשִׁיר Pr 21[17] Dn 11[2] (+ acc. cogn. עשר); 3 fs. תַּעֲשִׁיר Pr 10[4]; 1 s. וָאַעְשִׁר Zc 11[5] (Gi Kt; van d H Baer וְאַעְשִׁר), 3 mpl וַיַּעֲשִׁירוּ Je 5[27], *Inf. cstr* לְהַעֲשִׁיר Pr 23[4] 28[20] **Hithp.** *Pt* מִתְעַשֵּׁר Pr 13[7] *one enriching himself.*

עֹשֶׁר[37] **n.m.**[1 S 17, 25] riches,—ע׳ abs. Gn 31[16]+ 27 t, cstr Est 1[4]; sf עָשְׁרוֹ Je 9[22]+5 t., עָשְׁרָם ψ 49[7] Pr 14[24], + (or ‖) כָּבוֹד 1 K 3[13] Pr 3[16]+9 t., עָשָׂה ע׳ Je 17[11], cf. Eng. 'make money.'

עָשִׁיר[23] **adj.** et **n.** rich;—abs. ע׳ Ex 30[15]+ 19 t., pl. abs. עֲשִׁירִים Ec 10[6]; cstr עֲשִׁירֵי ψ 45[13]; sf. עֲשִׁירֶיהָ Mi 6[12],—**adj. m.** 2 S 12[1.4] (opp. רָאשׁ), Ru 3[10] (opp דַּל); usu **n.m.** *the rich*, opp. דַּל, Pr 10[15]+3 t.; opp. רָשׁ 2 S 12[2] Pr 14[20]+4 t.; opp אֶבְיוֹן ψ 49[3], alone Je 9[22] Mi 6[12]+5 t, + עֲשִׁירֵי עָם ψ 45[13]; ע׳ Is 53[9] is prob. crpt, cf. ‖ רְשָׁעִים; Bo Ry Di-Kit עֹשֵׂי רָע; Krochm Gr Che[Hpt] conj. רְשָׁעִים for ע׳, and פֹּשְׁעִים for ר׳.

†[עָשֵׁשׁ] **vb.** waste away (cf As *ašašu, moth;* Ar عُثّ *moth*(-worm), عَثَّ *eat* (of moth; ? denom.); acc. to De[ψ 6, 8] al. עשש is denom from עָשׁ, prop. *be moth-eaten*, but improb),—**Qal** *Pf* 3 fs. עָשְׁשָׁה מִכַּעַס עֵינִי ψ 6[8] *my eye is wasted from grief*, = 31[10] (בְּכַעַס; + בִּטְנִי, נַפְשִׁי); 3 pl עָשֵׁשׁוּ עֲצָמַי v[11].

†**II. עָשׁ n.m.**[Is 50, 9] moth (as *waster, consumer*);—ע׳ abs, Ho 5[12] (‖ רָקָב), Is 50[9] 51[8], in sim. ψ 39[12]; כְּבֶגֶד אֲכָלוֹ עָשׁ Jb 13[28]; symbol of fragility Jb 4[19].—27[10] read prob. עַכָּבִישׁ q.v.

†**I** [עָשַׁת] **vb.** be smooth or shiny (?), si vera l (cf. עֶשֶׁת),—only **Qal** *Pf.* 3 pl. שָׁמְנוּ עָשְׁתוּ Je 5[28] (fig.) *they have grown fat, they are smooth* (or *shine*, from fat); doubtful word, Thes conj עָשְׁרוּ *have grown rich* (cf. 𝔊 𝔖 𝔗), so Gie (but וַיַּעֲשִׁירוּ precedes, v[27]).

†עֶשֶׁת **n.**[**m.**] plate (as *smooth, shiny?* NH *id*, *lump* or *bar* of metal);—cstr. ע׳ שֵׁן Ct 5[14] *a plate of ivory* (Low in Buhl[Lex] Bu)

†עָשׁוֹת **adj.** smooth?—only בַּרְזֶל ע׳ Ez 27[19] as merchandise of Tyre; Co עָשׁוּת, i.e. pt. pass, from √עשת *forge*, or *work skilfully*, Toy *iron skilfully wrought;* all dubious

†**II.** [עָשַׁת] **vb. Hithp.** think (Aramaism: BAram Pt. עֲשִׁית, 𝔗 אִתְעַשַּׁת);—**Hithp.** *Impf.* 3 ms. יִתְעַשֵּׁת א׳ לָנוּ Jon 1[6] perhaps *God will give a thought to us* (cf חָשַׁב ψ 40[18]).

†עֶשְׁתּוּת (van d. H וּת-) **n.f.** thought;—cstr. ע׳ שַׁאֲנָן Jb 12[5] (וּת- would be pl., fr. *עֶשֶׁת).

†[עֶשְׁתֹּנָה] **n.f.** id (Aram: 𝔗 עֶשְׁתּוֹנָא, cstr. עשתוני Ecclus 3[21]),—pl. sf. אָבְדוּ עֶשְׁתֹּנֹתָיו ψ 146[4].

†עַשְׁתֵּי[19] **n.num.** one (As *ištên, one; išten ešrit, eleven;* Dl[§ 75], TelAm. [*iš*-]*tit, first time;* v. Gie[ZAW i (1881), 226] Ges[§ 97 e] Ko[ii. 1, 212] and reff.);—only + עָשָׂר, עֶשְׂרֵה (q. v.) = *eleven, eleventh*, Je 1[3] 39[2] = 52[5] = 2 K 25[2], Ez 26[1] 40[49] Zc 1[7] Ex 26[7.8] 36[14 15] Nu 7[72] 29[20] (all P), Dt 1[3] 1 Ch 12[13] 24[12] 25[18] 27[14].

†עַשְׁתֹּרֶת **n pr.deae.** '**Aštōreth**, < '**Aštart**, '**Aštéreth** (v infr.) (MI[17] עשתר כמש; Ph. עשתרת (+oft in n pr), n pr. עבד עשתר Cook[Acad. Jan 18, 1896] Sab n pr dei עַתְּתַר v. esp Os[ZMG xx (1866), 279 f.] DHM[ib xxxvii (1883), 376] Fell[Sab Götternamen ZMG liv (1900), 231 ff esp 237 ff]; As *Ištar*, OAram. Palm. עתר (=עַתְּתַר) in n pr, in Egypt. *'astirati* WMM[As. u Eur 313], Gk Ἀστάρτη; on other Gk equivalents (e g. Ἀφροδίτη) cf Lewy[Fremdw 148, 186 f. 250]), —— prob artificial, to suggest בשת, orig. ־תֶּרֶת, ־תַּרְתּ, cf *Ištar*, Αστάρτη, etc, 'ע 1 K 11[5] + 2 t, pl ־תָּרוֹת Ju 2[13] + 3 t. + ־רת 1 S 7[4]; 1 S 31[10] rd prob sg (Dr al), —*'Aštart*, *'Ašteretħ* (Αστάρτη, pl Ασταρται, but Ju 10[6] 1 S 7[4] Ασταρωθ), ancient Sem. goddess (with male counterpart in Moab, Sab and appar Ph), Phoenician deity, עשתרת אֱלֹהֵי צדנים 1 K 11[5, 33], 'ע' שִׁקֻּץ צ 2 K 23[13]; so prob 'בית ע 1 S 31[10] (rdg sg, v. esp Dr), elsewhere pl, of various local goddesses, called עַשְׁתָּרוֹת (cf As *ilâni u ištarat* = *gods and Ištars* (i e goddesses), usu + (בעל(ים, as Canaanitish deities Ju 2[13] 10[6] 1 S 7[4] 12[10], ‖ אֱלֹהֵי הַנֵּכָר 7[3] — Vid esp. Dr[Ashtoreth] in Hast[DB], on *Ištar* Jastr[Rel. Bab pass esp 202 f], on *'Athtar* Bae[Rel 117 f.], on Ph *'Aštart* Pietschm[Gesch Phön 184 f], on *'Ashtoreth* Barton[JBL x (1891), 73 ff] GFM[Ency Bib]

I עַשְׁתָּרוֹת v. foregoing.

†II [עַשְׁתָּרוֹת] **n.pl.f.** only cstr in phr. עַשְׁתְּרֹ(ו)ת צֹאנֶךָ Dt 7[13] 28[4. 18. 51] (all ‖ שְׁגַר אֲלָפֶיךָ) usu interpr either as **a.** = *ewes* (Thes) or as **b.** = *young* (cf. *veneres gregis*, in either case with ref to *'Aštart* as goddess of fecundity; RS[Sem 1 292, 457 f., 2nd ed 310, 476 f.], adopting **b**, thinks one type of 'Ašt in Canaan had form of sheep, so Dr[Dt 7, 13]), cf. also عَثَرِى as name of land fertilized by dew and rain We[Skizzen iii 170].

†III עַשְׁתָּרוֹת **n.pr.loc.** Ασταρωθ, etc, E. of Jordan (name from worship of diff forms of 'Aštart, in Egypt. *'astiratu*, as E. Jordan loc WMM[As u Eur 162, 313]; cf TelAm n pr.loc *Aštarti*), —in Bashan (near Edrei) Dt 1[4] (־רת), Jos 12[4] 13[12 31] (all + אֶדְרֶעִי), 9[10] 1 Ch 6[56] = עשתרה (בית עַשְׁתְּרָה i e) בְּעֶשְׁתְּרָה Jos 21[27]; also עַשְׁתְּרֹת קַרְנַיִם Gn 14[5] (𝔊 Ασταρωθ Καρναιν, cf GFM[JBL xvi (1897), 156 f.] who expl name as *'Ashtereth of the two-peaked mt*); cf further, קַרְנַיִם Am 6[13], —site prob. either *Tel 'Aštara*, 21 miles E. of Sea of Galilee, or *Muzeirib*, 8 miles further S; poss both occur in OT, cf esp Dr[Ashtaroth] in Hast[DB] Di[Gn 14. 5] Buhl[Geogr 248 ff] GASm[Ency Bib 335 f]

†עַשְׁתְּרָתִי **adj. gent.** of foreg. 'הָעֶ 1 Ch 11[44].

עֵת v. I. ענה.

†I. [עָתַד] **vb. be ready** (NH adj עָתִיד *future* (as prepared), Ar. عَتُدَ *be ready, prepared* (also *great, bulky*), Syr. ܥܬܰܕ, 𝔗 in der. spec and deriv), —**Pi.** *Imv.* ms. sf. וְעַתְּדָהּ Pr 24[27] *and make it ready* i e. thy work (‖ הָכֵן). **Hithp.** *Pf* 3 pl הִתְעַתְּדוּ לְגַלִּים Jb 15[28] which [houses] *were prepared* (destined) *for* (i e. to be) *heaps* of ruin.

†עָתִיד, [עָתוּד] **adj. ready, prepared**;— **1.** abs עָתִיד לְכִידוֹר Jb 15[24] a king *ready for the onset*, pl עֲתִדִים לַיּוֹם Est 3[14] *ready for the day*, so 8[13] Qr (Kt עתודים) **2.** *ready* = skilled הָעֲתִידִים עֹרֵר Jb 3[8] *those skilled in rousing* Leviathan. **3.** *prepared* = impending (cf NH = *future*), fpl וְחָשׁ עֲתִדֹת Dt 32[35] *the impending things are hastening* (‖ קָרוֹב יוֹם אֵידָם). **4** *prepared* = stored up, ועתידתיהם Is 10[13] Kt (Qr וַעֲתוּדֹתֵיהֶם, to differentiate it from above) *and their stores* have I plundered.

[עַתּוּד] 29 **n.m.**[Gn 31. 10] **he-goat** (NH = BH; As. *atudû*; Ar. عَتُودٌ *young he-goat*, relation to above √ not clear, Thes *well-developed*, cp. Ar عَتَدٌ *horse fit for running* (cf. √ mng. *great*, i.e. perh *full-grown*); acc. to Hom[NS 247 f] animal *ready* to fight), —only pl. עַתּוּדִים Is 1[11] + 13 t; עַתֻּדִים Gn 31[10] + 13 t; cstr עַתּוּדֵי Is 34[6]; —as property Gn 31[10 12] Ez 27[21] Pr 27[26], food Dt 32[14]; as leaders of flock Je 50[8] (sim.), hence fig. of princes and chief men Is 14[9] Ez 34[17], v. also infr, as sacrif. victims Is 1[11] Nu 7[17] + 12 t. Nu 7, ψ 66[15] and (iron) 50[9 13]; fig of people and princes in 'י's great sacrifice Is 34[6] Je 51[40] (sim), Ez 39[18], and (idea of sacrif. dropped) Zc 10[3].

עַתָּה, עַתַּי, עתי v. עת sub I. ענה.

†עֲתָיָה **n.pr.m.** Ne 11[4], Αθεα, 𝔊L Αθαραοθας (very dub), = עוּתַי 1 Ch 9[4]

†עֲתָךְ **n.pr.loc.** in Judah 1 S 30[30] 𝔊A Αθαγ, 𝔊L Ναγεβ; HPS prop עֶרֶד; v. עָתָר.

עתל (√ of foll; perh = As *atâlu*, *grow great*, cf. *etellu*, *great, exalted*, so Che[Expos Times, vii 484, 568, viii 48])

†עֲתַלְיָה(וּ), עֲתַלְיָה **n.pr.f. et m.** (יְ *is exalted*), —**1. f.** Athaliah, daughter of Ahab and Jezebel, mother of Ahaziah king of Judah,

Γοθολια: יְהוֹ- 2 K 8[26] 11[2.20] = 2 Ch 22[2.10.11] 23[12.13.21] 24[7]; יָה- 2 K 11[1.3.13.14] 2 Ch 22[12]. **2. m. a.** 1 Ch 8[26] Ογοθολια. **b.** Ezr 8[7] Αθελει, A Αθλια; 𝔊L Γοθονίου (genit.). **c.** עַתְלַי one with foreign wife Ezr 10[28], Θαλι, A Οθαλι.

†[**עָתַם**] **vb.** dub.; **Niph.** *Pf.* 3 ms. נֶעְתַּם אֶרֶץ Is 9[18] (غَتَمَ is *be clogged in speech*, غَتْمٌ *suffocating heat*, مَغْتُومٌ *burned by heat*; hence Thes *scorched*, but derived sense dub.; v. RS[JPhil. xiii. 61 f.]);—read perhaps נִצְּתָה (√יצת) *is burned up*, cf. RS[l.c.], Krochm Kit Che[Hpt]. *

†**עָתְנִי** **n.pr.m.** Levite 1 Ch 26[7], Γοονει, (Γ)οθνι.

†**עָתְנִיאֵל** **n.pr.m.** son of Ḳenaz, a hero in Isr., Γοθονιηλ, Jos 15[17] Ju 1[13] 3[9.11] 1 Ch 4[13.13]; name of family 27[15].

†[**עָתַק**] **vb. move, proceed, advance** (NH Hiph.; As. *etêḳu* as H., also trans. *bring, move*; Ar. عَتَقَ, عَتُقَ *precede, pass forth, become free, grow old*; Aram. ܥܬܩ, עֲתֵק *grow old*, Palm. adj. עתק *old*);—**Qal** *Pf.* 3 fs. עָתְקָה ψ 6[8], 3 pl. עָתְקוּ Jb 21[7]; *Impf.* 3 ms. יֶעְתַּק Jb 14[18] 18[4];—**1.** *move* וְצוּר יֶעְ׳ מִמְּקֹמוֹ Jb 14[18], so 18[4]. **2.** *advance* (in years; Aramaic sense) 21[7] (‖יִחְיוּ); hence = grow old and weak ψ 6[8] (of eye, ‖עָשְׁשָׁה). **Hiph.** *Pf.* 3 pl. הֶעְתִּיקוּ Jb 32[15] (Gi; van d. H. Baer v[15]), Pr 25[1]; *Impf.* 3 ms. וַיַּעְתֵּק Gn 12[8] 26[22]; *Pt.* מַעְתִּיק Jb 9[5];—**1.** *move forward* (sc. tent) = proceed Gn 12[8] (מִשָּׁם, ה loc.), 26[22] (מִשָּׁם); so fig. Jb 32[15] (v. supr.) words *have moved away* from them (מֵהֶם), but v. prob. gloss (Bu al.). **2.** Jb 9[5] *he who removeth mountains*. **3.** very late Pr 25[1] *transcribe* (*remove* from one book or roll to another; 𝔊 ἐξεγράψαντο, 𝔙 *transtulerunt*; so in mediaeval Heb.: Zunz[ZMG xxv (1871), 447 f. = Ges. Schr. iii. 66 f]).

†**עָתָק** **adj. forward, arrogant** (of speech) (Thes *free* (v. Ar.), *unrestrained*);—1 S 2[3] ψ 31[19] 94[4]; so also 75[6] (cf. צַוָּאר).

†**עָתֵק** **adj.** Thes (*ancient* and so) **valuable**; < **advanced, eminent, surpassing** (cf. عتيق *preceding*, hence *surpassing, choice* Lane [1947]);—הוֹן עָ׳ Pr 8[18] *eminent wealth*.

†**עָתִיק** **adj. eminent, surpassing, choice** (v. עָתֵק);—מְכַסֶּה עָ׳ Is 23[18] *choice attire*.

†[**עַתִּיק**] **adj.** removed, old;—**1.** *removed*, עַתִּיקֵי מִשָּׁדָיִם Is 28[9] i.e. weaned (‖ גְּמוּלֵי מֵחָלָב; on cstr. v. Ges[§ 130 a]). **2.** *old, ancient* (Aramaism: עַתִּיק, ܥܬܝܩ, *old*), הַדְּבָרִים עַתִּיקִים 1 Ch 4[22].

†I. [**עָתַר**] **vb. pray, supplicate** (always to God) (cf. Ar. عَتَرَ *slaughter for sacrifice* De[Gn (4) 381] We[Skizzen iii. 115, 166; Held. (2), 118, 142]; RS[Sem i. 210 f.; 2nd ed., 227 f.]);—**Qal** *Impf.* 3 ms. וַיֶּעְתַּר לי׳ Gn 25[21], אֶל־י׳ Ex 8[26] 10[18] Ju 13[8]; יֶעְתַּר אֶל־אֱלוֹהַּ Jb 33[26]. **Niph.** *be supplicated, entreated* (and grant entreaty; always of God), usu. c. לְ of worshipper (v. לְ **5 d**): *Pf.* 3 ms. consec. וְנֶעְתַּר לָהֶם Is 19[22]; *Impf.* 3 ms. וַיֵּעָתֶר לוֹ Gn 25[21] 2 Ch 33[13], וַיֵּעָתֵר לָנוּ Ezr 8[23]; c. לָאָרֶץ *for the land* 2 S 21[14] 24[25]; *Inf. abs.* וְנַעְתּוֹר לָהֶם 1 Ch 5[20]; *cstr.* (as subst.) הֵעָתֶר־לוֹ 2 Ch 33[19]. **Hiph.** = **Qal**, *make supplication*, c. לְ, אֶל: *Pf.* וְהַעְתַּרְתִּי אֶל־י׳ Ex 8[25]; *Impf.* 2 ms. תַּעְתִּיר אֵלָיו Jb 22[27]; *Imv.* mpl. הַעְתִּירוּ אֶל־י׳ Ex 8[4] 9[28], לי׳ 10[17]; also c. לְ pers. *in behalf of* whom, *Impf.* 1 s. אַעְתִּיר לְךָ Ex 8[5], so *Imv.* הַעְתִּירוּ, c. בַּעֲדִי v[24].

†I. [**עָתָר**] **n.[m.] suppliant, worshipper** (? ; so usu., but dub.);—only pl. sf. עֲתָרַי Zp 3[10].

†II. [**עָתַר**] **vb. be abundant**, si vera l. (as Aram. loan-word; עֲתַר, ܥܬܪ, *be rich* = Heb. עָשַׁר);—**Niph.** *Pt.* fpl. נַעְתָּרוֹת Pr 27[6] (of enemy's kisses; De *excessive*; opp. נֶאֱמָנִים); Toy prop. נֶעְקָשׁוֹת, or נַעֲוֹת, *crooked, hypocritical*. **Hiph.** *Pf.* 2 mpl. הַעְתַּרְתֶּם עָלַי דִּבְרֵיכֶם Ez 35[13] *ye have multiplied against me your words* (‖ וְהִגְדַּלְתֶּם עָלַי בְּפִיכֶם), del. as gloss Co after 𝔊, Toy reads sg., and thinks verb due to Aramaizing scribe.

†**עֲתֶרֶת** **n.f.** abundance (Aramaism, si vera l.);—cstr. Je 33[6] I will reveal to them *abundance* of peace, etc. (corrupt acc. to Gie Buhl[Lex]; Vrss. render variously).

†**עֶתֶר** **n.pr.loc.** (√dub.);—in Judah Jos 15[42] (Ιθακ; A𝔊L Αθερ), in Simeon 19[7] (Ιεθερ; in both sq. עָשָׁן); perhaps = עֲתָךְ q.v.; perhaps (Conder[Survey iii. 261]) *'Atr*, c. 2 miles NW. of *Beit Jibrin* (cf. GASm[Geogr. Map]).

III. **עתר** (√of following).

†II. [**עָתָר**] **n.[m.] odour** (si vera l.) (so Vrss.);—cstr. עֲתַר Ez 8[11], of incense.

פ, ף

פ, פּ, ף, *Pê*, seventeenth letter; used as numeral 80 in postB. Hebrew.

פֹּא v. פֹּה.

† [**פָּאָה**] **vb.** perh. (si vera l.) **cleave in pieces** (Ar. فَأَى (فأو, فأى) *cleave, split* (head, bowl, etc.); Sab. פאי DHM$^{\text{ZMG xxx (1876), 701 f.}}$);—**Hiph.** *Impf.* 1 s. sf. אַפְאֵיהֶם Dt 32^{26} *I* [י׳] *will cleave them in pieces* (poss. point אֶפְ׳, i.e. **Qal**; on other views v. Dr; rd. perh. אֲפִיצֵם 𝔊 Gr).

פֵּאָה 86 **n.f. corner, side** (*part cut off*, 'Abschnitt,' acc. to Schröter in Me$^{\text{Archiv. i. 461}}$ Ba$^{\text{ZMG xli (1887), 615}}$ Buhl^{Lex}, but perh. bilit., Nö$^{\text{M. 485}}$ Sta$^{\text{§185}}$, and not fr. √פאה; cf. Ar. فِئَةٌ *company*, etc. (Nö$^{\text{l.c.}}$); As. *pâtu, side, edge, border*, v. esp. Meissn$^{\text{Suppl. 74}}$; NH=BH, Aram. פָּאתָא, ܦܐܬܐ);—abs. פ׳ Je 9^{25}+4 t.; cstr. פְּאַת Am 3^{12}+77 t.; pl. abs. פֵּאֹת Ex 25^{26} 37^{23}; du. cstr. פַּאֲתֵי Nu 24^{17} (but read prob. פְּאַת as ‖ Je 48^{45});—†**1.** *corner* of divan Am 3^{12}; table Ex 25^{26} 37^{23}; field Lv 19^{9} 23^{22} (H); land (prob.) וַתַּחְלְקֵם לְפֵאָה Ne 9^{22}, i.e. into every corner; פ׳ רֹאשְׁכֶם Lv 19^{27} (i.e. *your temples*), פ׳ זְקָנֶךָ v^{27} cf. 21^{5} (all H); קְצוּצֵי פֵאָה *those clipped on the temples* Je 9^{25} 25^{23} 49^{32} (epith. of Arab. tribes, Herod.$^{\text{iii. 8}}$ WMM$^{\text{As. u. Eur. 140 f.}}$ We$^{\text{Skizzen iii. 119; Heid. 2, 198}}$); *temples of Moab* (under fig. of man) Nu 24^{17} (JE) Je 48^{45}. **2.** *side*: **a.** usu. of Ezekiel's temple, the tabern., the holy city and the land, or its subdivisions (only Ez 41–48 [47 t.] and P [26 t.]): in plur. פְּאַת קָדִימָה(ה) *East side* Ez 47^{18}+17 t. Ez, =פ׳ קֵדְמָה Ex 27^{13}+3 t. P and Ez 45^{7} (v. Co Toy); פ׳ צָפוֹן(ה) *North side* Ez 47^{15} Ex 26^{20}+9 t.; פ׳ נֶגֶב (נֶגְבָּה) *South side* Ez $47^{19.19}$ Ex 27^{9}+8 t.; פ׳ יָם (יָמָּה) *West side* Ez 45^{7} Ex 27^{12}+21 t. + פ׳ דֶּרֶךְ הַיָּם Ez 41^{12} (also פ׳ קָדִים הַיָּם 48^{1}); abs. only לִפְאַת הָאֶחָת Ex 27^{9}. **b.** פְּאַת פָּנָיו Lv 13^{41} *side* (border) *of his face* (forehead and temples; P).

פאם v. פימה.

†I. [**פָּאַר**] **vb. Pi. beautify, glorify**;—*Pf.* 3 ms. sf. פֵּאֲרָךְ (obj. Isr.) Is 55^{5} 60^{9}; c. acc. of temple; *Impf.* 1 s. אֲפָאֵר 60^{7}; *Inf. cstr.* פָּאֵר v^{13} Ezr 7^{27}; so יְפָאֵר עֲנָוִים בִּישׁוּעָה ψ 149^{4}. **Hithp. 1.** *glorify oneself*, c. עַל pers.: =boast, *Impf.* 3 ms. יִתְפָּאֵר Ju 7^{2} Is 10^{15}; as polite address to king, *Imv.* ms. הִתְפָּאֵר Ex 8^{5} (J), *assume the honour over me* (to decide) *when*, etc. **2.** *get glory to oneself, be glorified, by means of* (בְּ), of י׳, בְּיִשְׂרָאֵל יִתְפָּאָר Is 44^{23}, so 1 s. אֶתְפָּאָר 49^{3}; of people [by י׳], *Inf. cstr.* לְהִתְפָּאֵר 60^{21} 61^{3}.

† **פְּאֵר** **n.m.** $^{\text{Ez 44, 18}}$ **head-dress, turban** (? orig. *ornament*);—abs. פ׳ of bridegroom Is 61^{10}, sign of joy v^{3} (opp. mourning, and so) פְּאֵרְךָ Ez 24^{17}, pl. sf. פְּאֵרֵכֶם v^{23} (worn by men of position); of priests פַּאֲרֵי פִשְׁתִּים Ez 44^{18}, פ׳ הַמִּגְבָּעֹת שֵׁשׁ Ex 39^{28} (P); pl. abs. פְּאֵרִים Is 3^{20} (of luxurious women).

†**תִּפְאָרָה** **n.f. beauty, glory**;—ת׳ Is 28^{5} Je 48^{17}; elsewh. abs. and cstr. תִּפְאֶרֶת Is 3^{18}+20 t.; תִּפְאֶרֶת Pr 28^{12}+6 t.; sf. תִּפְאַרְתִּי Is 46^{13}+20 t. sf.;—**1.** *beauty, finery* Is 3^{18}; of garments 52^{1}; jewels Ez $16^{17.39}$ 23^{26}, cf. 2 Ch 3^{6}; flock Je 13^{20}; a man Is 44^{13}; city of Samaria $28^{1.4}$; diadem v^{5}. **2.** *glory*: **a.** of rank: apparel of h.p. Ex $28^{2.40}$ (P); עֲטֶרֶת ת׳ *crown of glory* Pr 4^{9} 16^{31} Is 62^{3} Je 13^{18} Ez 16^{12} 23^{42}; greatness of monarch Est 1^{4}; house of David and inhabitants of Jerus. Zc $12^{7.7}$. **b.** of renown לְשֵׁם ולת׳ Dt 26^{19} 1 Ch 22^{5} Je 13^{11} 33^{9}. **c.** attribute of י׳ ψ 71^{8} 1 Ch 29^{11}; שֵׁם ת׳ Is 63^{14} 1 Ch 29^{13}; ת׳ עֹז ψ 89^{18}; זְרוֹעַ ת׳ Is 63^{12}; hence ת׳ in י׳'s sanctuary ψ 96^{6}, בֵּית תִּפְאַרְתִּי Is 60^{7} cf. 63^{15} (of heavenly temple), 64^{10}; ת׳ as י׳'s gift to Isr. 46^{13} cf. 60^{19} (also ψ 89^{18} supr.); of future fruit of land 4^{2}; design. of ark of י׳ ψ 78^{61}. **3. a.** *honour* of nation Isr. La 2^{1}. **b.** *glorying, boasting*, of individ., Is 20^{5} Pr 17^{6} 19^{11} 20^{29} 28^{12}; warrior Ju 4^{9}; monarchs Is 10^{12}; nations Is 13^{19} Ez 24^{25}, מַקֵּל ת׳ *rod (sceptre) of glorying* Je 48^{17} (others **1**).

II. **פאר** (doubtful √).

† [**פֹּארָה**] **n.f. bough**;—pl., all in fig.: of vine, abs. פֹּארוֹת Ez 17^{6} (Baer פֹּראֹת); of cedar, sf. פֹּארֹתָו 31^{5} (Kt; ־ָיו Qr); פֹּארֹתָיו v^{6}, פֹּארֹתָיו v$^{8.12.13}$.

†**פארה** Kt., **פֻּארָה** Qr **n.f.coll. boughs** Is 10^{33} (van d. H. Baer פֻּארָה).

† [**פֵּאֵר**] **vb. denom. Pi. go over the boughs**;—*Impf.* 2 ms. תְּפָאֵר Dt 24^{20} *thou shalt* not *go over the boughs* after thee (i.e. glean).

†**פָּארוּר** **n.[m.]** mng. dub.; only קִבְּצוּ פ׳ Na 2^{11} Jo 2^{6}; Thes, all faces *gather a glow* (*glow* with dread, fr. assumed √פאר), so We

Now; AE Hi al. *gather in* (their) *beauty* (√I. פאר; grow pale); Vrss AV *gather blackness* (fr. פָּרוּר *a pot!*), v. Dr; all very uncertain.

†פָּארָן **n.pr.loc.** Paran, Φαραν (cf. n.pr. פארן Sin. Inscr.);—usu. מִדְבַּר פ׳ home of Ishmael Gn 21[21] (E), traversed by Isr. in Exodus Nu 12[16] (E), 10[12] 13[3.26] (all P); it lay NE. fr. (the traditional) Sinai, with Gulf of Akaba and the 'Arabah as its E. border; in the same region was הַר פ׳ Dt 33[2] Hb 3[3],—perh. coast-range of mts. along W. shore of Gulf of Akaba; פ׳ alone 1 K 11[18.18] (betw. Midian and Egypt); Dt 1[1] (loc. dub.).—1 S 25[1] v. ıı. מָעוֹן sub עון.—Vid. Rob[BR i. 177 f.] Palmer[Desert of Exodus, 284 ff.], Di Dr[Dt].

פגג (√of foll.; mng. dub.; NH פַּגָּה *unripe fig*, pl. פַּגִּין; so Syr. ܦܰܓܳܐ in Lexx; Ar. فِجّ *unripe fruit;* ܬ פַּגָּא *unripe grape;* cf. Post in Hastings[DB. 'Fig'] Tristr[NHB 352] Löw[p. 391]).

†[פַּגָּה] **n.f.** (cf. NH) early fig;—pl. sf. פַּגֶּיהָ Ct 2[13].

פגל (√of foll.; mng. dub.; Ar. فَجُلَ (فَجِلَ) is *be thick and soft, flaccid;* NH פִּגּוּל =BH, cf. Levy[NHWB s.v.]).

†פִּגּוּל **n.m.**[Lv 7, 18] foul thing, refuse, but only as term. techn. of unclean sacrificial flesh;—it is פ׳ if eaten on third day Lv 7[18] (P), 19[7] (H); cf. בְּשַׂר פ׳ Ez 4[14] (undefined); pl. מְרַק פִּגֻּלִים Is 65[4] *broth of refuse things* (Kt פרק), RS[Sem i. 325, 2nd ed. 343] thinks of flesh with the blood; Du[ad loc.] of mice and other unclean animals.

†**פגע** **vb.** meet, encounter, reach (NH *id.;* Aram. פְּגַע, ܦܓܰܥ; poss. akin to Ar. فَجَأَ, فَجِئَ *happen to, light upon;* فَجَعَ is *pain, afflict*);—**Qal** *Pf.* 3 ms. פ׳ 1 K 2[32]+, sf. וּפְגָעוֹ consec. Am 5[19], etc.; *Impf.* 3 ms. וַיִּפְגַּע Gn 28[11]+; 1 pl. נִפְגַּע Jb 21[15], etc.; *Imv.* ms. פְּגַע Ju 8[21]+; mpl. פִּגְעוּ Gn 23[8]; *Inf. cstr.* לִפְגֹּעַ 1 S 22[17], sf. פִּגְעוֹ Nu 35[19.21];—**1.** *meet, light upon*, c. acc. pers. 1 S 10[5] Ex 5[20] (J), c. sf. pers. Am 5[19]; פ׳ שׁוֹר Ex 23[4]; c. בְּ pers. Gn 32[2] (E), Nu 35[19.21] (P); c. בְּ loc. Gn 28[11] (E). **2.** *meet*, with kindness, c. acc. pers. Is 64[4] (subj. י׳), so 47[3] acc. to Ew De Di al.; Che[Hpt] אֶפְגַּע (reading, with Du, אמר for אָדָם). **3.** *encounter* with hostility, *fall upon* c. בְּ pers. Jos 2[16] (JE), Ju 8[21] 15[12] 18[25] 1 S 22[17.18.18] 2 S 1[15] 1 K 2[25.29.31.32.34.46] Ru 2[22]; of God, c. acc. (sf.), +בְּ instr. Ex 5[3]. **4.** *encounter* with request, *entreat*, c. בְּ pers. Je 7[16] Jb 21[15], sq. cl. Je 27[18] Ru 1[16], +לְ pers. on whose behalf Gn 23[8]. **5.** *strike, touch*, of boundary, c. בְּ loc. Jos 16[7] 19[11.22.26.27.34.34], cf. 17[10]; c. אֶל loc. 19[11]. **Hiph. 1.** *cause to light upon*, *Pf.* 3 ms. הִפְגִּיעַ c. acc. rei +בְּ pers. Is 53[6]. **2.** *cause one* (acc.) *to entreat* 1 s. הִפְגַּעְתִּי (בְּ pers.) Je 15[11] (otherwise Gie; Co del. v. as gloss). **3.** *make entreaty*, 3 pl. הִפְגִּעוּ Je 36[25] c. בְּ pers.; more gen. *interpose*, *Impf.* 3 ms. יַפְגִּיעַ Is 53[12], c. לְ pers. in whose behalf; *Pt.* מַפְגִּיעַ 59[16] *one interposing.* **4.** *make attack*, only *Pt.* Jb 36[32] *assailant*, but Ol Bu Du al. מִפְגָּע *mark.*

†פֶּגַע **n.m.** occurrence, chance;—abs. פ׳ 1 K 5[18] evil *occurrence;* Ec 9[11] time and *chance.*

†מִפְגָּע **n.[m.]** thing hit, mark;—לָמָּה שַׂמְתַּנִי לְמִ׳ לָךְ Jb 7[20] (cf. also פגע **Hiph. 1**).

†פַּגְעִיאֵל **n.m.** Asherite, Φαγαιηλ, -εηλ;—Nu 1[13] 2[27] 7[72.77] 10[26].

†[פָּגַר] **vb. Pi.** be exhausted, faint (ܬ פְּגַר der. spec. *tear down, destroy;* As. *pagru, body, corpse;* NH פֶּגֶר=BH; Aram. פִּגְרָא, ܦܓܪܳܐ; Palm. פגר; Mand. פאגרא Nö[M § 89]);—*Pf.* 3 pl. פִּגְּרוּ מִן *they were too faint* to go, etc. 1 S 30[10.21].

†פֶּגֶר **n.m.**[Is 14, 19] corpse, carcass;—abs. פ׳ Is 14[19]+, פָּגֶר Na 3[3]; cstr. פֶּגֶר 1 S 17[46]; pl. פְּגָרִים 2 K 19[35]+; cstr. פִּגְרֵי Je 33[5]; sf. פִּגְרֵיכֶם Lv 26[30]+, etc.;—**1.** of men, sg. Is 14[19]; usu. pl. 34[3] 66[24] Je 31[40] 33[5] 41[9] Ez 6[5] 43[7.9] Lv 26[30] Nu 14[29.32.33] 2 Ch 20[24],—v[25] rd. prob. בְּגָדִים, so 𝔊 (?), 𝔙 Be Krochm Kau Kit;—פְּגָרִים מֵתִים 2 K 19[35]= Is 37[36]; sg. coll. 1 S 17[46], רַב־הַפָּגֶר Am 8[3], כֹּבֶד־פ׳ Na 3[3]; fig. of idols פִּגְרֵי גִּלּוּלֵיכֶם Lv 26[30]. **2.** of animals Gn 15[11].

†[פָּגַשׁ] **vb.** meet, encounter (syn. פָּגַע);—**Qal** *Pf.* 1 s. פָּגָשְׁתִּי Gn 33[8]; 3 pl. consec. וּפָגְשׁוּ Is 34[14]; *Impf.* 3 ms. sf. יִפְגָּשְׁךָ Gn 32[18] (Gi; Baer יְפָגֶשְׁךָ; van d. H. יִפְגָּשְׁךָ), וַיִּפְגְּשֵׁהוּ Ex 4[24.27]; 3 fs. וַתִּפְגֹּשׁ 1 S 25[20] (rd. prob. וַתִּפְגַּשׁ Ges[§ 47 k], cf. van d. H), etc.; *Inf. abs.* פָּגוֹשׁ Pr 17[12]; *cstr.* פְּגֹשׁ Je 41[6];—*meet*, c. acc. Gn 33[8] 1 S 25[20] Is 34[14] Je 41[6], so c. sf. Gn 32[18] Ex 4[24.27] 2 S 2[13]; *meet, encounter*, of bear, c. בְּ pers. Pr 17[12], of י׳ (like a bear) Ho 13[8] (c. sf. pers.). **Niph.** *meet together, each other*, *Pf.* 3 pl. נִפְגָּשׁוּ Pr 22[2] 29[13], fig. of חֶסֶד וֶאֱמֶת ψ 85[11]. **Pi.** intens. *Impf.* 3 mpl. יְפַגְּשׁוּ חֹשֶׁךְ Jb 5[14] *they keep encountering darkness* in the daytime.

†**פָּדָה** **vb.** ransom (NH in deriv.; Ph. in n.pr.; As. *padû, id.*, Ar. فَدَى; Eth. ፈደየ:; Min. פדית *redeemed* or *purchased land* Mordt $^{Beitr. 23}$);—**Qal** *Pf.* 3 ms. פָּדָה Lv 27^{27}+; sf. פְּדָךְ Jb 5^{20}; 2 ms. פָּדִיתָ Dt 9^{26}+, etc.; *Impf.* יִפְדֶּה ψ 49^{8}+, etc.; *Imv.* פְּדֵה ψ 25^{22}; sf. פְּדֵנִי ψ 26^{11} +3 t.; *Inf. abs.* פָּדֹה Nu 18^{15} ψ 49^{8}; *cstr.* לִפְדּוֹת 2 S 7^{23}=1 Ch 17^{2}; *Pt. act.* פּוֹדֶה ψ 34^{23}; sf. פֹּדְךָ Dt 13^{6}; *pass.* pl. cstr. פְּדוּיֵי Is 35^{10} 51^{11} Nu 3^{49}; also abs. פְּדוּיִם Nu 3^{51} (Qr; Kt פדים), cstr. פְּדוּיֵי v^{46}; sf. פְּדוּיָו Nu 18^{16} (all n. abstr. acc. to Di Kö $^{ii. 1, 138}$, v. פְּדִיִּם, פְּדוּיִם infr.);—*ransom:* **1.** for an assessed price Ex 13$^{13.15}$ 34^{20} (J), Lv 27^{27} Nu 3$^{46.48.49.51}$ 18$^{15.16.17}$ (P). **2.** fr. violence and death 1 S 14^{45} Jb 6^{23} ψ 49^{8}. **3.** God subj. (underlying thought of payment): **a.** fr. Egypt, c. מִן, מִבֵּית עֲבָדִים Dt 7^{8} 13^{6} Mi 6^{4}; מִנִּי־צָר ψ 78^{42}; ממצרים 2 S 7^{23} (but del. פָּדִיתָ Gei $^{Urschr. 288}$ We Dr al.)=1 Ch 17^{21}; מִשָּׁם Dt 24^{18}; abs. Dt 9^{26} 15^{15} 21^{8} Ne 1^{10}. **b.** from exile, Je 31^{11} Zc 10^{8}; פְּדוּיֵי י׳ יְשֻׁבוּן Is 35^{10}=51^{11}. **c.** in gen. Ho 7^{13}; מִכֹּל צָרוֹתָיו ψ 25^{22}; מִכֹּל עֲוֹנוֹתָיו ψ 130^{8}. **d.** c. acc. individ. ψ 26^{11} 31^{6} 44^{27} 69^{19}; Abraham Is 29^{22}; פ׳ מֵעֲבֹר בַּשָּׁחַת; 1 K 1^{29} מכל צרה 2 S 4^{9}+; 71^{23} נפש ψ 34^{23} Jb 33^{28}; מִקְּרָב־לִי ψ 55^{19}; מִמָּוֶת Jb 5^{20}; מיד שאול ψ 49^{16} Ho 13^{14}; מֵעֹשֶׁק אָדָם ψ 119^{134}; מִכַּף עָרִיצִים Je 15^{21}. **Niph.** *Pf.* 3 fs. (+**Hoph.** *Inf. abs.*) הָפְדֵּה לֹא נִפְדָּתָה Lv 19^{20} *she hath not been at all ransomed* (from bondage); *Impf.* יִפָּדֶה Lv 27^{29} (from ban); 3 fs. צִיּוֹן בְּמִשְׁפָּט תִּפָּדֶה Is 1^{27}. **Hiph.** *Pf.* 3 ms. sf. וְהֶפְדָּהּ Ex 21^{8} *he shall let her be ransomed.* **Hiph.** *Inf. abs.* v. **Niph.**

†**פְּדוּיִם** **n.[m.]pl.abstr.** ransom;—so rd. perh. Nu 3^{49} for MT פִּדְיוֹם, Sam. פדוים; cstr. פְּדוּיֵי v^{48}; for other poss. cases v. **Qal** *Pt. pass.*

†**פָּדוֹן** **n.pr.m.** (*ransom;* cf. Ph. פדי) head of family of Nethinim Ezr 2^{44} Ne 7^{47}; Φαδων.

†**פְּדוּת** **n.f.** ransom; פ׳ ψ 111^{9}+2 t.; פְּדֻת Ex 8^{19};—fr. exile Is 50^{2}; fr. iniquities ψ 130^{7}; in gen. ψ 111^{9}, וְשַׂמְתִּי פְדֻת בֵּין עַמִּי וּבֵין עַמֶּךָ Ex 8^{19} *I will set a ransom* (distinguishing) *between my people and thy people* 𝔗, but improb. and text dub.; 𝔊𝔖𝔙 *set a distinction* (rdg. what?).

†**פִּדְיוֹם** **n.m.** ransom;—Nu 3^{49}, rd. prob. פְּדוּיִם (so Sam.); פְּדִיִּם v^{51} Kt (Qr פְּדוּיִם);—v. פדה **Qal** *Pt. pass.*, and פְּדוּיִם supr.

†**פִּדְיוֹן** **n.m.** id.;—פ׳ נַפְשׁוֹ Ex 21^{30} (E), ψ 49^{9}.

†**פְּדָהאֵל** **n.pr.m.** (*Ēl hath ransomed;* cf. Ph. בעלפדה; As. *Pudu-ilu, Padi-ilu* COT$^{Gloss.}$);—prince of Naphtali Nu 34^{28}; Φαδαηλ.

†**פְּדָהצוּר** **n.pr.m.** (*the Rock hath ransomed*) Manassite, Nu 1^{10} 2^{20} 7$^{54.59}$ 10^{23} Φαδασσουρ.

†**פְּדָיָה, פְּדָיָהוּ** **n.pr.m.** (י׳ *hath ransomed;* in late As. *Padâma*, Hilpr $^{Univ. Pa. Exp. ix. 27, 68}$);—פְּדָיָה: **1.** father-in-law of Josiah 2 K 23^{36}, but 𝔊 Εδειλ (𝔊L Ιερεμιας, fr. v^{31}). **2.** father of Zerub. 1 Ch 3$^{18.19}$. **3. a.** Ne 3^{25}. **b.** 8^{4}. **4.** Benjamite Ne 11^{7}. **5.** Levite Ne 13^{13}. **6.** פְּדָיָהוּ, Manassite 1 Ch 27^{20}—𝔊 (exc. **1**) Φα(λ)δαιας, etc.

פַּדָּן **n.pr.loc.** (?*garden, field;* cf. 𝔗 פַּדְנָא *yoke, span of oxen;* Syr. ܦܕܢܐ *yoke,* whence, as loan-wd. Ar. فَدَّانٌ Frä^{129}; As. *padanu,* =*road,* and also *garden,* etc. (in word-lists, v. KAT$^{2, 612}$); also Nö$^{Aram.}$ in Ency. Bib.);—פ׳ Gn 48^{7}, abbrev. fr. פַּדַּן־אֲרָם (?=*garden, field of* [*in*] *Aram;* conj. by many that שְׂדֵה אֲרָם Ho 12^{13} is Heb. transl., cf. Di $^{Gn 25, 20}$) 25^{20}+5 t.; פַּדֶּנָה א׳ 28$^{2f.}$ (v. אֲרָם **b**; all P); 𝔊 Μεσοποταμία (Συρίας); perh. *Paddânâ,* near Haran (and *Tel Faddān* of Arab. geogr.), v. Nö$^{l.c.}$

†[**פָּדַע**] **vb.** dub., only *Imv.* ms. sf. פְּדָעֵהוּ Jb 33^{24} a mng. like *deliver him* needed, Codd. Bu Du פְּרָעֵהוּ; < rd. פְּדֵהוּ (פדה) Ew Di SS.

†[**פֶּדֶר**] **n.[m.]** suet, of עֹלָה (so Vrss NH: √ unknown);—abs. פֶּדֶר Lv 1^{8} 8^{20}; sf. פִּדְרוֹ 1^{12}.

פֶּה **n.m.** $^{Jos 9, 2}$ mouth (prob. bilit. [פי, פו] Sta$^{§ 182}$; NH=BH; Ph. לפי *acc. to;* As. *pû, mouth;* Ar. فَمٌ ,فُوهٌ ,فَاهٌ ,فِيهٌ; Eth. አፍ:; Syr. ܠܦܘܡ *acc. to;* but also Ar. فَمٌ ,فُمٌ ,فِمٌ, BAram. פֻּם, 𝔗 פּוּמָא; Syr. ܦܘܡܐ; Mand. פומא Nö $^{M §87}$);—abs. פ׳ Ex 4^{10}+, cstr. פִּי Is 1^{20}+; sf. 1 s. פִּי Gn 45^{12}+, 2 ms. פִּיךָ 41^{40}+, 3 ms. פִּיו 25^{28}+, פִּיהוּ Ex 4^{15}+, 3 mpl. פִּיהֶם Ju 7^{6}+, פִּימוֹ ψ 17^{10}+2 t., etc.; pl. פֵּיוֹת Pr 5^{4}, (שְׁנֵי) פִּיּוֹת Ju 3^{16}, פִּיפִיּוֹת Is 41^{15} ψ 149^{6}; פִּים 1 S 13^{21} (corrupt, v. Dr al.);—**1. a.** *mouth,* of man, organ of eating and drinking Gn 25^{28} Ju 7^{6} 1 S 14$^{26.27}$ Ne 9^{20} Pr 19^{24}=26^{15}+; fig. as finding things sweet Jb 20^{12} ψ 119^{103}; fig. of earth Gn 4^{11}, swallowing Korah, etc. Nu 16$^{30.32}$ 26^{10} Dt 11^{6}; fig. also of She'ôl, וּפָעֲרָה פִיהָ Is 5^{14}, cf. ψ 69^{16}. **b.** external organ, וַיָּשֶׂם פִּיו עַל־פִּיו 2 K 4^{34} Pr 30^{20}; of kissing 1 K 19^{18} Ct 1^{2}; וַתִּשַּׁק יָדִי לְפִי Jb 31^{27}; cf. phr. שִׂים יָד עַל־פֶּה (of keeping silence) Ju 18^{19} Mi 7^{16} Jb 21^{5}, cf. 29^{9} 40^{4} Pr 30^{32}; of mocking triumph הִרְחִיב פ׳ עַל ψ 35^{21}; פָּעֲרוּ עָלַי בְּפִיהֶם Jb 16^{10}; Is 57^{4}, also רָחַב פִּי עַל 1 S 2^{1}. **c.** of י׳ in theoph., sending out fire 2 S 22^{9}=ψ 18^{9}. **2. a.** much

oftener, as organ of speech, of man: פ׳ speaks Gn 45[12] 2 S 1[16] Is 9[16] Jb 9[20] 15[5.6] ψ 37[30]+; speak בְּמוֹ־פִי Jb 19[16]; open פ׳, אֶל־י״ Ju 11[35.36], abs. Jb 3[1] 33[2]+; shut פ׳ (be silent) Is 52[15], cf. חָשַׂךְ פ׳ Jb 7[11], and (of iniquity, personif.) קָפְצָה פ׳ Jb 5[16] ψ 107[42]; guard פ׳, Pr 13[3] (נֹצֵר), 21[23] (שֹׁמֵר), cf. שְׁמֹר פִּתְחֵי פ׳ Mi 7[5], also ψ 39[2] (v שׁמר), words, etc, are in (בְּ) mouth 2 S 17[5] 18[25] Dt 30[14] 1 K 17[24], שׂוּם דְּבָרִים בְּפ׳ 2 S 14[3.19] Ex 4[15], also (God subj) Nu 22[38] 23[12.16]+, of utterance יָצָא מִפּ׳ Ju 11[36] Nu 30[3] 32[24] Jos 6[10]+, depart fr mouth (cease to be mentioned) מוּשׁ מִפּ׳ Jos 1[8] Is 59[21], cf. נִכְרְתָה מִפּ׳ Je 7[28], לֹא יִשָּׁמַע עַל־פִּיךָ Ex 23[13], אִמְרֵי פ׳ Dt 32[1] *words of my mouth*, so Jb 8[2] ψ 19[15] 54[4], דִּבְרֵי פ׳ ψ 36[4] Ec 10[12], of agency, בְּפ׳ *by the mouth of* 2 Ch 36[21.22] = מִפּ׳ Ezr 1[1], דִּבֶּר פִּיו עִם־פִּיו Je 32[4] *speak mouth to mouth* = 34[3], פ׳ = *speech, sayings* Is 29[13] ψ 49[14] Ec 10[13]; כְּבַד פ׳ Ex 4[10] *heavy of speech* (not eloquent); אֶהְיֶה עִם־פ׳ v[12.15], i.e. aid thee in speaking, יִהְיֶה־לְּךָ לְפ׳ v[16] *he shall be mouth for thee;* מִפִּיו יִקְרָא אֵלַי Je 36[18], i e. dictate, כָּתַב מִפּ׳ v. כָּתַב **1 b** (3), bad qualities ascribed to it, עִקְּשׁוּת פ׳ Pr 4[24] 6[12], פִּי תַהְפֻּכוֹת 8[13], פֶּה חָלָק 26[28], אַל־תַּגְדֵּל פ׳ Ob[12], cf Mi 6[12] Ez 35[13]. **b.** as laughing Jb 8[21] ψ 126[2], panting 119[131]. **c.** of God; his mouth speaks Is 1[20] 40[5] Je 9[11]+, he speaks בְּפ׳ 1 K 8[15.24], wd. proceeds מִפּ׳ Dt 8[3] Is 45[23]+; פֶּה אֶל־פֶּה אֲדַבֶּר בּוֹ Nu 12[8]; he creates בְּרוּחַ פִּיו ψ 33[6], he executes judgment בְּשֵׁבֶט פִּיו Is 11[4], esp = *command:* עָבַר אֶת־פִּי י״ 1 S 15[24] Nu 14[41], cf 22[18] Pr 8[29], מָרָה (אֶת־) פ׳ 1 S 12[14.15] Nu 20[24] 1 K 13[21]+, cf. **6 d.** **d.** of idols, ψ 115[5] 136[16.17]. **e.** of musical instr = sound Am 6[5] (cf **6 d**) **3.** of animals: bird Gn 8[11] (carrying), Is 10[14] (chirping); ass Nu 22[28] (speaking); bear, lion 1 S 17[35] (seizing), Am 3[12] (id), hippop. Jb 40[23] (drinking), crocod. 41[11.13] (breathing flame); also of human foes, under fig. of ravenous beasts ψ 22[22] Ez 21[27] 34[10]; פָּצָה פ׳ עַל ψ 22[14] La 2[16] 3[46], hence of *edge* of sword, חֶרֶב פִּיּוֹת Pr 5[4] *a sword with edges* (in sim), = ח׳ פִּיפִיּוֹת ψ 149[6], cf. Ju 3[16], v also **6 c** (2), infr., בַּעַל פִּיפִיּוֹת Is 41[15], of מוֹרַג. **4.** *mouth* = opening, orifice; of well Gn 29[2.3.8.10]; cave Jos 10[18.22.27]; ravine, abyss Je 48[28] (si vera l, cf. Gie), also of Sheʼôl ψ 141[7]; of a sack Gn 42[27] 43[12.21] 44[1.2.8]; ephah Zc 5[8], high-priest's robe Ex 28[32] +5t, cf. prob ψ 133[2], tunic Jb 30[18]; of a round opening also 1 K 7[31 31 31] (on text and meaning v. Benz Kit); of *mouth* of Nile Is 19[7] (others *brink*); gate of city Pr 8[3] (but rd. perhaps לִפְנֵי, v. Toy). **5. a.** *extremity, end* פֶּה לָפֶה *from end to end*, of a temple 2 K 10[21]; city 21[16], מִפֶּה אֶל־פֶּה of land Ezr 9[11] **b.** = portion, פִּי שְׁנַיִם +Dt 21[17] 2 K 2[9] Zc 13[8]. **6.** with preps:— **a.** אֶל פִּי, v. infr. **d**(2). **b.** כְּפִי. (*a*) *acc. to the command of,* 1 Ch 12[23], (*b*) *acc to the mouth of,* i e. *in proportion to* (cf. As *ki-i pi-i*, Dl[HWB 524]), †Ex 16[21] they gathered it אִישׁ כְּפִי אָכְלוֹ each *in proportion to* his eating (v[16.18] לְפִי), Lv 25[52] כְּפִי שָׁנָיו *acc. to* the number of his years (cf. v[16] לְפִי); Nu 6[21] אִישׁ כְּפִי עֲבֹדָתוֹ 7[5] (so 2 Ch 31[2]), 7[7.8] 35[8] (all P); Jb 33[6] הֵן־אֲנִי כְפִיךָ לָאֵל I am *in the proportion of* thee as regards God, i e. I stand towards God even as thou dost. As **conj.,** כְּפִי אֲשֶׁר, +Ml 2[9] כְּפִי אֲשֶׁר אֵינְכֶם שֹׁמְרִים אֶת־דְּרָכַי *acc as* ye do not keep, etc, and without אשׁר Zc 2[4] כפי אישׁ־לא נָשָׂא ראשׁו *in such proportion that* none did lift up his head (but We Now אֲשֶׁר for אִישׁ, that it, Judah, did not, etc) **c.** לְפִי, nearly i q. כפי (v. לְ **5 i b**), but more common (cf Aram לפום, ܠܦܘܡ). (1) +Gn 47[12] לְפִי הַטָּף, Ex 12[4] ye shall compute אִישׁ לְפִי אָכְלוֹ each *acc. to* his eating (acc. to the quantity which his family will consume), 16[16.18] Lv 25[16] לְפִי רֹב הַשָּׁנִים, v[16.51] 27[16] לְפִי זַרְעוֹ, Nu 26[54] Jos 18[4] 1 K 17[1] except לְפִי דְבָרִי, Ho 10[12] (לִצְדָקָה ‖) קִצְרוּ לְפִי חֶסֶד, Pr 12[8] 27[21] sq. inf. Nu 9[17] לְפִי הֵעָלוֹת הֶעָנָן = *acc as* the cloud was lifted up, Je 29[10]. (2) in the phr. לְפִי חֶרֶב *acc to the mouth*, or *measure*, of the sword, i e. as the sword devours, without quarter, Gn 34[26] Ex 17[13] Nu 21[24]+oft. **d.** עַל פִּי · (1) *acc to* (עַל **1 f a**) *the mouth of*, i e (*a*) the command of, Gn 41[40] 45[21] Ex 17[1] 38[21] Nu 3[16.39] +(esp P), 2 K 23[35], (*β*) the evidence or sentence of, Dt 17[6] עַל־פִּי עֵד אֶחָד, 19[15] 21[5] (on עַל־פִּי הַגּוֹרָל Am 6[5], v. **2 e** supr) (2) *acc. to the measure of, in accordance with,* † Gn 43[7] we told him עַל פִּי הדברים האלה *acc to* these words (i e. the questions Joseph asked), Ex 34[27] *in accordance with* these words, Lv 27[8] עַל־פִּי אֲשֶׁר תַּשִּׂיג יַד הַנֹּדֵר *acc to* what the hand of the vower can reach to, v[18] (cf לְפִי 25[16.51]), Dt 17[10.11] 2 S 13[32] (but v שׂוּמָה), Pr 22[6] חֲנֹךְ לַנַּעַר עַל פִּי דַרְכּוֹ. In the same sense אֶל פִּי, †Jos 15[13] 17[4] 21[3].

פֹּה[82], and (Ez 40–41, 23 out of 35 t) **פוֹ**, also †Jb 38[11b] **פֹּא**, **adv.loc. here, hither** (prob from the same demonst. √ found in ف *so, then* (oft. in apod), אֵפוֹא, אַף: cf. Ko[ii.1, 247 f, 245, 331 f]).—**1.** *here:* **a.** Gn 19[12] עֹד מִי־לְךָ פֹה whom hast thou still *here?* 22[5] שְׁבוּ לָכֶם פֹּה,

40[15] Nu 22[8] 32[16] Dt 5[28] 12[8] Ju 4[20] הֲיֵשׁ פֹּה אִישׁ, 2 K 3[11], etc, asked in some surprise, Ju 18[3] מַה־לְּךָ פֹה = what is thy business *here?* simil. †1 K 19[9.13] Is 22[16] 52[5] עַתָּה מַה־לִּי־פֹה Cf. the syn כֹּה, בָּזֶה. **2.** **b.** עַד־פֹּה †Jb 38[11]. **c.** מִפֹּה or מִכּוֹ, only Ez 40–41, and always (exc 40[12a], where it must be supplied with 𝔊 𝔖) repeated, *on this side ... on that side* (cf מִזֶּה . . . מִזֶּה), Ez 40[10.10.12b.21.21], etc. **d.** with the interrog אֵי, אֵיפֹה *where?* v p 33 †**2.** after a verb of motion, *hither*, 1 S 16[11] עַד־בֹּאוֹ פֹה, Ezr 4[2]

†**פּוּאָה**, **פֻּוָּה** **n.pr.m.** in Issachar, Φουα, etc,—פּוּאָה Ju 10[1] (v GFM), 1 Ch 7[1], פֻּוָּה Gn 46[13] Nu 26[23]

†**פּוּנִי** **adj.gent.** of פֻּוָּה, c art Nu 26[23], rd. פֻּוִּי? or (Φουαι) פֻּוִּי?—𝔊 L Φουλαϊ

†[**פּוּג**] **vb. grow numb** (Ar. فاج *grow cool*, Syr ܦܳܓ *be cold*, 𝔗 פּוּג *cease, be helpless*, NH *id vanish*).—**Qal** *Impf* 3 ms וַיָּפָג לִבּוֹ Gn 45[26], 3 fs תָּפוּג ψ 77[3] of hand (si vera l., v נגר), i e drop helpless; Hb 1[4] of תּוֹרָה, i e be ineffective **Niph.** *Pf* 1 s נְפוּגוֹתִי וְנִדְכֵּיתִי ψ 38[9] *I am benumbed and crushed* (fig); rd. prob also אָפוּנָה ψ 88[16] (for MT ἅπ λεγ אָפוּנָה), Ol Hup Dy Gr Che אָפוּגָה.

†**פּוּגַת** (Ges[§80f]) **n.f. benumbing** (fig), **cessation**,—אַל־תִּתְּנִי פ׳ לָךְ La 2[18] *grant thyself no benumbing* (id prob פוגת)

†[**הֲפִיגָה**] **n.f. id.**,—pl מֵאֵין הֲפֻגוֹת La 3[49] (of weeping, form very strange, id. prob פֻּגוֹת),

†[**פּוּחַ**] **vb. breathe, blow** (NH פּוּחַ *blow out*, Ar (فوح), فاح = Heb, so Aram. פּוּחַ, ܦܳܚ),—**Qal** *Impf* 3 ms. יָפוּחַ הַיּוֹם Ct 2[17] 4[6] until *the day breathes*, i e grows cool **Hiph.** *Impf* 3 ms יָפִיחַ ψ 10[5]+, יָפֵחַ Pr 14[25], וְיָפֵחַ Hb 2[3], etc, *Imv* fs הָפִיחִי Ct 4[16],—**1.** *cause* garden (acc) *to exhale* (sc. odours) Ct 4[16] **2. a.** *puff, snort*, against, בְּ pers, ψ 10[5]. **b.** עַל pers, Ez 21[36] with the fire of my wrath *will I blow against thee* **c.** *excite, inflame* city Pr 29[8] **d.** c לוֹ ψ 12[6] *puff*, =*pant for it* (so most, Thes Hi al *against whom men puff*, Bae אַבִּיעַ לוֹ *I will shine forth to him*), לַקֵּץ Hb 2[3] the vision *panteth* (hasteth) *towards the end* (so most) **3.** *breathe out, utter*, כְּזָבִים Pr 6[19] 14[5.25] 19[5.9], אֱמוּנָה 12[17].

†**פִּיחַ** **n.[m.]** **soot**, 𝔊 αἰθάλη (?*wafted* about),—cstr. פ׳ (הַ)כִּבְשָׁן Ex 9[8.10] (P) *furnace-soot*

†**פּוּט** **n pr.gent.** prob. **Libyans**, or **Lib. tribe**, usu named with African peoples: Na 3[9] Je 46[9] Ez 27[10] 30[5] 38[5] (𝔊 usu Λίβυες); Gn 10[6] (P) = 1 Ch 1[8] (Φουδ), +Is 66[19] (for MT פּוּל, 𝔊 Φουδ),—vid Di[Gn 10.6] Jen[ZA x 325 ff].

†**פּוּטִיאֵל** **n.pr m.** Eleazar's father-in-law Ex 6[25], Φουτιηλ

†**פּוֹטִיפַר** **n.pr.m.** Joseph's master (abbrev fr foll),—Gn 37[36] (E), 39[1] (R[J]), Πετεφρης, etc

†**פּוֹטִי פֶרַע** **n.pr.m.** priest of On, Joseph's father-in-law (Egypt *P'-di-p'-R'*, i e *he whom the Ra gave*, v. Sethe[De aleph prosthetico in ling aeg (1892) 31]; Di in Hastings[DB]),—Gn 41[45.50] (E), 46[20] (P), Πετεφρης, A Πετρεφης.

†**פּוּךְ** **n.[m.]** **antimony, stibium** (NH = BH, cf poss Ar فكّ *open, separate*, Syr. ܦܽܘܟ *pulverize*; but פּוּךְ perh foreign word),—black mineral powder, for increasing brilliance of eyes by darkening edges of lids; וַתָּשֶׂם בַּפּ׳ עֵינֶיהָ 2 K 9[30], תִּקְרְעִי וגו׳ Je 4[30]; (on practice in Arab v. We[GGN, 1893, 443], in Egypt, Lane[Mod Egypt. ed 5. i 45 f]), fig Is 54[11] of dark cement setting off precious stones (but We[DLZ, Aug 2. 1890] Che[Hpt] al. rd. נֹפֶךְ q v.), אַבְנֵי פ׳ 1 Ch 29[2] are perh. stones of brilliant hue of antimony —Cf n pr. קֶרֶן הַפּוּךְ, and כָּחַל

†**פּוֹל** **n [m.] coll. beans** (NH = BH, Ar. فُول, Eth. ፋል: 𝔗 פּוֹלָא);—2 S 17[28] Ez 4[9], 𝔊 κύαμος

†**פּוּל** **n.pr.m.** = תִּגְלַת פִּלְאֶסֶר (q v) (As *Pulu*, Babylonian name of TP, Schr[SBAk 1887, 592; KB ii 287 cf 277] Tiele[Gesch 264 f], cf (through Pers trad., EMey[Entstehung 96]) Πῶρος, Canon of Ptol. KAT[2, 490]), 2 K 15[19.19] 1 Ch 5[26], Φουα[λ]—Is 66[19], v פּוּט.

†[**פּוּן**] **vb.** (?); only אָפוּנָה ψ 88[16]; rd prob. אָפוּגָה, v. פּוּג, אָפוּנָה.

פּוּנֶה 2 Ch 25[23] v פָּנָה פּוּנִי v. פּוּאָה.

†**פּוּנֹן** **n.pr.loc.** 2nd station of Isr fr. Hor Nu 33[42.43], Φ(ε)ινω, betw Petra and Zoar, famous for mines, Gk Φινων, Φαινων Euseb[Onom ed Lag 299, 85], v also Ritter[Erdkunde Asien xiv 125 ff] Seetzen[Reise iii, 17] (*Kálaát Phenân*), perh. = Edom n pr m. פִּינֹן q v.

†**פּוּעָה** **n.pr.f.** a midwife Ex 1[15], Φουα.

†I [**פּוּץ**] **vb. be dispersed, scattered** (NH = BH, perh akin to Ar فضّ *break asunder, scatter*),—**Qal** *Impf.* 3 mpl יָפוּצוּ ψ 68[2], יָפֻצוּ Ez 48[16]+, 3 fpl וַתְּפוּצֶינָה Ez 34[5]+, וַתְּפוּצֶינָה Zc 13[7], etc, *Imv.* mpl. פֻּצוּ 1 S 14[34], *Pt.*

pass. pl. sf. פּוּצַי Zp 3^{10} (v infr.),—*be dispersed, disperse,* בָּעָם 1 S 14^{34}; *be scattered,* of enemies 1 S 11^{11} Nu 10^{35} ψ 68^{2}; of Isr. (among nations) under fig. of flock Ez $34^{5.6}$ Zc 13^{7}, בַּת־פּוּצַי Zp 3^{10} is prob. crpt., and $v^{9.10}$ gloss v. Schwally ZAW x (1890) 203 Now Da; of besieging army 2 S 20^{22} (מֵעַל הָעִיר); people from (מִן) possessions Ez 46^{18}; men (from Babel) Gn 11^{4} (עַל loc.). **Niph.** *Pf* 3 fs נָפוֹצָה Je 10^{21}, 3 pl נָפֹצוּ Gn 10^{18}+, 2 mpl נפצתם Ez 11^{17}+, etc; *Pt.* f נְפוֹצֶת 2 S 18^{8} Qr (> Kt נפוצות) cf. Dr al, pl נְפֹצִים 1 K 22^{17}, נפוצים 2 Ch 18^{16},—**1.** *be scattered,* of army 2 K 25^{5} (מֵעַל pers.) = Je 52^{8}, 1 K 22^{17} (אֶל loc) = 2 Ch 18^{16} (עַל), cf. Je 40^{15} (abs); of dispersed Isr. c. בְּ loc. Ez 11^{17} $20^{34.41}$ 28^{25}, as flock Je 10^{21} Ez 34^{6} (עַל loc), v^{12} (שָׁם); Egyptians 29^{13} (שָׁמָּה); of battle *scattered* over country by defeat 2 S 18^{8} **2.** *be spread abroad,* of peoples Gn 10^{18}.

Hiph. *Pf.* 3 ms consec והפיץ Dt 4^{27}+, 1 s consec. וַהֲפִיצוֹתִי Ez 22^{15}, etc.; *Impf* 3 ms. יָפִיץ Jb 37^{11}, וַיָּפֶץ Gn 11^{8}+, etc.; *Imv* ms. הָפֵץ Jb 40^{11}; *Inf cstr* לְהָפִיץ Ez 20^{23}, etc;—**1.** trans. *scatter*: **a.** c acc pers. Gn $11^{8.9}$ (עַל loc), Is 41^{16} Hb 3^{14}, c בְּ Gn 49^{7}; Isr. among (בְּ) nations Dt 4^{27} 28^{64} Je 9^{15} Ez 11^{16} 12^{15} 20^{23} 22^{15} 36^{19} Ne 1^{8}; c שָׁמ(ה) Dt 30^{3} Je 30^{11}, c. אֶל loc Ez 34^{21}; abs Je 13^{24} 18^{17}, under fig of flock Je $23^{1.2}$, Gr rds. אֲפִיצֵם also Dt 32^{26} (v. [פאה]); Egyptians (c בְּ) Ez 29^{12} $30^{23.26}$, inhab of earth Is 24^{1}. **b.** c. acc. rei, arrows (fig for lightnings) 2 S 22^{15} = ψ 18^{15}, ψ 144^{6}; cloud Jb 37^{11}, הָפֵץ עֶבְרוֹת אַפֶּךָ 40^{11} (i e. lightnings?); seed Is 28^{25}. **c.** וֶהֱפִיצֻהוּ Jb 18^{11} *and drive him* (si vera l, vid. conj in Bu) **2.** intrans, *scatter,* c בְּ loc Ex 5^{12}, c מֵעַל pers 1 S 13^{8}, of wind Jb 38^{24} (עַל loc).

†מֵפִיץ **n.m. scatterer, disperser**;—Na 2^{2} (si vera l), but rd. perh מַפֵּץ *club, hammer* JD Mich We Now; so also Pr 25^{18}, cf. Toy.

†[תְּפוֹצָה] assumed as sg. of **n.f.pl.** sf. ותפוצותיכם Je 25^{34} (so van d. H) *your dispersions* (𝔙 al), but Baer Gi ־תִיכֶם, expl. as **vb. Tiph.** 1 s. Thes al, so (rdg הֲפִיצוֹתִיכֶם) Hi Gf Ko I 471, word corrupt; Gi ונפצתם, Gie ונפצתיכם

†II פּוּץ **vb. flow, overflow** (Ar فَاضَ *flow,* cf Ba ES 60),—**Qal** *Impf.* 3 mpl. יָפוּצוּ Pr 5^{16} of springs, fig for sources of pleasure, 3 fpl. תְּפוּצֶנָה עָרַי מִטּוֹב Zc 1^{17} *my cities shall overflow with good*

†I [פּוּק] **vb. reel, totter**;—**Qal** *Pf.* 3 pl. פָּקוּ פְּלִילִיָּה Is 28^{7} *they reel* (drunken, in giving) *judgment* (‖ שָׁגוּ, תָּעוּ, etc); rd. prob. also *Impf* 3 fs תָּפוּק Am 2^{13} *tottereth* (v. עוק) **Hiph.** *Impf* **1.** *totter.* 3 ms יָפִיק Je 10^{4} (of idol) **2.** rd prob also *Pt* מֵפִיק Am 2^{13} *cause tottering* (v עוק).

†פּוּקָה **n.f. tottering, staggering**;—fig for qualm of conscience 1 S 25^{31} (+ מכשול לב, v. Dr).

†פִּיק, פֵּק **n.[m.]** id lit,—פק ברכים Na 2^{11} *tottering of knees* (so Baer Gi, פִּיק van d. H)

†II. פּוּק **vb. Hiph. bring out, furnish, promote** (NH *id*; appar akin to Aram נפק *go forth,* Aph *bring forth, produce*);—**1.** *produce, furnish*: *Impf.* (juss) ותפק לָרָעֵב Is 58^{10} c נַפְשֶׁךָ (rd perh לַחְמְךָ v Che Hpt), *Pt* מפיקים ψ 144^{13} (v זַן) מִזַּן אֶל־זַן **2.** *bring out, elicit, obtain,* c acc., יָפִיק Pr 3^{13}, + מִן pers, וַיָּפֶק 8^{35} 18^{22} (all ‖ מצא), 12^{2}. **3.** ψ 140^{9} זְמָמוֹ אַל־תָּפֵק *his device do not promote*

†פּוּר **n.m. lot** (NH = BH, perh As loan-word fr. *puru, buru, stone* Jen ZA x 339 f. and in Wild Est p 173 f),—expl by הַגּוֹרָל Est 3^{7} 9^{24}; שֵׁם הַפּוּר v^{26} explains name of feast פּוּרִים v^{26}, יְמֵי הַפֻּרִים *days of Purim* $v^{28.31}$; דברי הפ׳ v^{29}, אִגֶּרֶת הַפּ׳ v^{32}—Vid. on *Purim* esp Now Arch ii 194 ff and reff.

I פּוּר (√ of foll; poss *foam,* cf Ar. (فور), فَارَ, *boil, ferment,* Syr. ܦܘܪ, Ethpe, of anger)

†פּוּרָה **n.f wine-press**;—פ׳ דָּרַכְתִּי Is 63^{3} (v דָּרַךְ 3), disting. fr יֶקֶב, and perh. part of it, Hg 2^{16} (rdg מפ׳, so Sm Now; usu *measure* of juice from one filling of the פ׳, v Ke)

†פָּרוּר **n.[m.]** pot (Thes fr *boiling,* dub; otherwise Ko II 1, 161),—*pot* (earthen? v פרור Ecclus 13^{2}, Gk. χύτρα, opp λέβης, Syr. ܩܘܩܐ, ܩܘܩܐ ܕܦܚܪܐ *jar of the potter,* opp ܠܒܝܬܐ), for boiling Nu 11^{8} (JE), 1 S 2^{14}. cf. Ju 6^{19} (𝔊 χύτρα, κύθρα)

II פּוּר v. II פרר.

†פּוֹרָתָא **n.pr.m.** son of Haman Est 9^{8}, Φαραδαθα, Βαρδαθα.

†I [פּוּשׁ] **vb.** appar **spring about, Qal** *Pf.* 3 pl consec. וּפָשׁוּ פָּרָשָׁיו Hb 1^{8} (but prob. del ופשו as dittogr. v. Now); 2 mpl. consec. וּפִשְׁתֶּם Mal 3^{20}, *Impf.* 2 mpl. תָּפוּשׁוּ Je 50^{11} Qr (so 𝔊; > Kt תפושי), in both, sim. of gambolling calves.

†II. [פּוּשׁ] **vb. Niph. be scattered**;—3 pl. נָפֹשׁוּ עַמְּךָ עַל־הֶהָרִים Na 3^{18} (rd. prob נָפֹצוּ).

†פּוּתִי **adj.gent.** c art הַפּ׳ 1 Ch 2^{53}, a family in Judah, Μιφαθειμ, A Ηφιθειν, 𝔊L Αφφουθι.

פַּז v. I פזז.

†I [פָּזַז] vb. **Hoph.** be refined (?) (dub √),—*Pt* זָהָב מוּפָז 1 K 10[18] *refined gold* (si vera l., 𝔊 δόκιμος, ‖ 2 Ch 9[17] טָהוֹר)

†פַּז n.m ψ 19 11 refined, pure gold (Talm פִּיזָא, 𝔗 כֵּיפָא)—עֲטֶרֶת פָּז ψ 21[4], in compar of value or beauty La 4[2], אַדְנֵי־פ׳ Ct 5[15]; ‖ (or +) כֶּתֶם זהב Jb 28[17] (כְּלִי־פ׳), ψ 19[11] (רָב +), 119[127], ‖ Is 13[12], cf כֶּתֶם פּ׳ Ct 5[11], + חָרוּץ Pr 8[19]

†II [פָּזַז] vb be supple, agile (Talm (rare) פזיזא *hasty*, Ar فَزَّ *be frightened, excited*, Syr (Lexx.) ܦܙ *leap*, ܦܙܝܙܐ *agile*, etc),—**Qal** *Impf* 3 mpl וַיָּפֹזּוּ Gn 49[24], of arms **Pi.** *shew agility, leap* (in dance), *Pt* מְפַזֵּז וּמְכַרְכֵּר 2 S 6[16].

†[פָּזַר] vb. scatter (usually regarded as secondary form of בזר q v, NH *id* Pi (opp כִּנֵּס=כנס), Niph, Ar فَزَرَ *rend, slit*, also *separate, disperse*),—**Qal** *Pt pass* f שֶׂה פְזוּרָה Je 50[17] *a scattered sheep* is Israel (i e driven off, isolated) **Niph.** *Pf* 3 pl נִפְזְרוּ ψ 141[7] our bones *are scattered* לְפִי שְׁאוֹל. **Pi.** *Pf* 3 ms פִּזַּר ψ 53[6] 112[9], etc, *Impf* 3 ms יְפַזֵּר 147[16], 2 fs וַתְּפַזְּרִי Je 3[13], *Pt* מְפַזֵּר Pr 11[24],—*scatter* ψ 89[11] 53[6] 147[16] (all subj ׳י), Jo 4[2], obj דְּרָכַיִךְ Je 3[13], of Isr running hither and thither to strange gods, abs of spending money ψ 112[9] (alms), Pr 11[24] **Pu** *Pt* מְפֻזָּר Est 3[8] *scattered*, of Isr

פחח v פַּח I, II

†פָּחַד vb. dread, be in dread, in awe (NH Hithp (rare), Ecclus 41[12] Imv. פחד על *fear for*, 𝔗 פַּחְדָא n),—**Qal** *Pf* 3 ms פָּחַד ψ 119[161], פ׳ consec Is 19[16] 60[5], 1 s פָּחַדְתִּי Jb 3[25], etc, *Impf* 3 ms יִפְחַד Is 19[17]; 2 ms. תִּפְחַד Dt 28[67] +, etc,—**1.** *be in dread*, abs Dt 28[66] Is 12[2] 33[14] 44[8.11] ψ 78[53] Pr 3[24], לֹא פ׳ Je 36[24] sign of callousness, c acc cogn פָּחַד Dt 28[67] Jb 3[25] ψ 14[5]=53[6], c מִן pers Is 19[17] Jb 23[15] ψ 27[1] (‖ יָרֵא), cf 119[161], and (c מִפְּנֵי) Is 19[16], c עַל rei Je 33[9] (+ רָגְזוּ), c אֶל, pregn, *turn in dread* to each other Je 36[16], submitting to ׳י Ho 3[5] Mi 7[17] (‖ יָרֵא) **2.** *be in awe* (at ׳י's favour), abs, Is 60[5] **Pi** *be in great dread*, *Impf* 2 ms וַתְּפַחֵד Is 51[13], c מִפְּנֵי rei, *Pt* abs מְפַחֵד Pr 28[14] *deeply dreading* (sc sin) **Hiph.** *Pf* 3 ms הִפְחִיד Jb 4[14] *filled* my bones *with dread*

1 פַּחַד 49 n m. 18 11 7 dread,—פ׳ abs. Gn 31[42] +, cstr 1 S 11[7] +, sf פַּחְדְּךָ Dt 2[25] ψ 119[120], פַּחְדּוֹ Jb 13[11] 1 Ch 14[17], etc, pl פְּחָדִים Jb 15[21].—**1.** *dread*, פ׳ י׳, i e before ׳י, oft (not alw.) terrifying, unfitting for action, † Is 2[10.19.21] 1 S 11[7] 2 Ch 14[13] 17[10], so פ׳ אֱלֹהִים + 20[29], c sf. Jb 13[11] ψ 119[120] *trembleth for dread of thee*, c genit. obj Isr., † Dt 2[25] (‖ יִרְאָה), 11[25] (‖ מוֹרָא), ψ 105[38] Est 8[17] 9[2], פ׳ אוֹיֵב + ψ 64[2], of individual † 1 Ch 14[17] Est 9[3], c genit obj rei Pr 1[33], abs, in gen, Ex 15[16] (song, ‖ אֵימָתָה), Jb 4[14] (‖ רְעָדָה), Je 30[5] (‖ קוֹל חֲרָדָה +), as acc. cogn c פָּחַד ψ 14[5] + (v. פָּחַד); c genit. subj † Pr 1[26.27] (both ‖ אֵיד) Dt 28[67]. **2.** = *object of dread* † ψ 31[12] 36[2], פ׳ אֵלִי Jb 31[23]; פַּחַד פְּחַדְתִּי † Jb 3[25], מִקּוֹל הַפַּחַד † Is 24[18] *sound of the disaster*, for מִפְּנֵי הַפּ׳ of orig. Je 48[44], but קוֹל פְּחָדִים † Jb 15[21] = a sound of terrors, פ׳ בתאם 22[10] Pr 3[25]. **3.** as design dei † פ׳ יִצְחָק Gn 31[42] (‖ אֱלֹהֵי אַבְרָהָם), so v[53] (‖ *id.*; both E).

†[פַּחְדָּה] n.f. dread, religious awe, sf. לֹא פַּחְדָּתִי אֵלַיִךְ Je 2[19] no *awe of me* (came) *unto thee*.

†II. [פַּחַד] n.[m.] thigh (prob loan-word (through Aram, otherwise ז=د) from Ar. فَخِذ *thigh* and (cf We[GGN, 1893, 479]) *sub-tribe*, Palm פחד *tribe*),—גִּידֵי פַחֲדוֹ Jb 40[17] Kt *the sinews of his thigh* (Qr פַּחֲדָיו), of hippopotamus

פֶּחָה 28 n.m. 2 K 18, 24 governor (loan-word fr. As *paḫâti* [abbrev from *bel paḫâti*], *lord of a district*, cf. perh OAram פחי *governor*),—abs. הַפ׳ Ne 5[14], cstr פַּחַת Hg 1[1] +, פַּחַת 2[21]; sf. פֶּחָ֑ךָ Mal 1[8], פֶּחָם Ne 5[14] (but read prob. פֶּחָה), pl abs. פַּחוֹת 1 K 20[24] +; cstr פַּחוֹת 10[15] = 2 Ch 9[14], פַּחֲוֹת Ezr 8[36] +; sf. פַּחוֹתֶיהָ Je 51[28.57],—as Assyr. captains 2 K 18[24] = Is 36[9] (< del פ׳, cf Sta[ZAW vi (1886), 182] al), cf. Ez 23[6.12], of Babylon Je 51[23.57], and Bab allies Ez 23[23], of Media Je 51[28], Pers *governor* of עֵבֶר הַנָּהָר, i. e in Pal, Hg 1[1.14] 2[2.21] Ne 2[7.9] + 8 t; Pers *satraps* in gen. Est 3[12] 8[9] 9[3]; applied (by late writer) to Sol's *governors* 1 K 10[15] = 2 Ch 9[14], Benhadad's *captains* 1 K 20[24] (del v, Sta al)—Cf. BAram.

†[פָּחַז] vb be wanton, reckless (NH *id* (rare), Ar. فَخَزَ *be haughty, boastful, reckless*; 𝔗 פְּחַז, Syr. ܦܚܙ *be lascivious*, in der spec and deriv.),—**Qal** *Pt* אֲנָשִׁים רֵיקִים וּפֹחֲזִים Ju 9[4], of prophets Zp 3[4] *extravagant* (‖ אַנְשֵׁי בֹּגְדוֹת)

†פַּחַז n.[m.] wantonness, recklessness, unbridled license,—Gn 49[4], abstr for concr. (+ כַּמַּיִם *like* [boiling, or overflowing] *water*)

†[פַּחֲזוּת] n.f. recklessness, extravagance,—sf. ־תָם Je 23[32] of prophets

פחח (√of foll; meaning dub.; cf. Aram. פַּחָא, ‏فَخّ‎, whence (Fra[119]) Ar. ‏فَخّ‎ as loan-word).

†I. **פַּח** **n.m.**[+124,7] **bird-trap** (cf. Wilkinson Egyptians (1874) ii, 103, 109 f. Dr[Am 3, 5] Hoffm[ZAW iii (1883), 101]);—פ׳ abs Ho 5[1]+, פָּח Je 48[44]+; cstr. פַּח Ho 9[8]+, pl. פַּחִים Je 18[22]+;—**1.** lit. יַעֲלֶה פ׳ Am 3[5b] (as metaph, v[a] del. פ׳), Pr 7[23] Ec 9[12] (c. אָחוּז, both in sim.). **2.** usually fig. (sts. ‖ רֶשֶׁת, מוֹקֵשׁ, צַמִּים) **a.** of calamities and plots, פ׳ יָקוּשׁ Ho 9[8], cf. ψ 91[3] 124[7], פ׳ alone Je 48[43] = Is 24[17], Jb 22[10] ψ 124[7] Pr 22[5], טָמַן פ׳ לְ Je 18[22] ψ 140[6] 142[4], נָתַן פ׳ לְ 119[110], יָקַשׁ פ׳ לְ 141[9]; יֹאחֵז בְּעָקֵב פ׳ Jb 18[9]; יִלָּכֵד בַּפ׳ Je 48[44] = Is 24[18] **b.** = source or agent of calamity Ho 5[1] Jos 23[13] (D), Is 8[14] ψ 69[23]. —ψ 11[6] v. פֶּחָם.

†[**פָּחַח**] **vb. Hiph. denom.** **ensnare**; *Inf. abs* הָפֵחַ בְּלָם Is 42[22], c. בְּ loc. *an ensnaring* [i.e. men have ensnared] *them all in*, etc.

†II. [**פַּח**] **n.[m.]** **plate of metal**; pl. רִקֻּעֵי פַחִים Nu 17[3], cstr וַיְרַקְּעוּ אֶת־פַּחֵי הַזָּהָב Ex 39[3].

פחם (√of foll; cf prob. Ar ‏فَحُمَ‎ *be black*, NH פֶּחָם *id.* (in der. spec.), פֶּחָם = BH, Ar. ‏فَحْم‎ *charcoal*, As *pêntu* (= *pêmtu) glowing *coal*; Syr ‏ܦܚܡܐ‎ in Lexx).

†**פֶּחָם** **n.[m.]** **coal** (coll); abs. פ׳, as inflammable, פ׳ לְגֶחָלִים Pr 26[21] (*charcoal for embers*, Toy); of glowing coal Is 44[12], אֵשׁ פ׳ 54[16]; ψ 11[6] for MT פַּחִים אֵשׁ read פַּחֵם אֵשׁ (or פַּחֲמֵי) *coals of fire* (‖ גָּפְרִית), so Ew al.

פחת (√of foll.; cf. Ar ‏فَحَتَ‎ *cut off*, VII. *be perforated* (of roof); Syr ‏ܦܚܬ‎ Pa. *pierce, break through*, ‏ܦܚܬܐ‎ *pit, chasm*; NH פָּחַת *dig, hollow out*, also *diminish*)

†**פַּחַת** **n.m.**[2 S 18, 17] (in 17[9] rd. בְּאַחַד) **pit**,—פ׳ abs. Je 48[43]+, בַּפַּחַת v[28], pl. פְּחָתִים 2 S 17[9]; —*pit*, 2 S 17[9] 18[17] Je 48[28] (Gie qu. text); fig. of calamity פַּחַד וָפ׳ וָפָח Je 48[43] cf v[44.44] = Is 24[17] cf. v[13.18] and La 3[47].

†**פְּחֶתֶת** **n.f.** **a boring or eating out**,—Lv 13[55], of leprous decay in garment

†**פַּחַת מוֹאָב** **n.pr.m.** post-exil. name,—בְּנֵי־פ׳ מ׳ Ne 3[11] (Φααβ[θ]μωαβ, ⅁L Ερωμαθ), בְּנֵי־פ׳ מ׳ Ezr 2[6] = Ne 7[11], Ezr 8[4] (all Φααθμωαβ, etc), 10[30], פ׳ מ׳ Ne 10[15] (both Φααδ[θ]μωαβ, etc.).

†**פִּטְדָה** **n.f.** (**m.** acc. to Albr[ZAW xvi (1896), 108]) **topaz** or **chrysolite** (acc. to ⅁ τοπάζιον, 𝔙 *topazius*, etc.; prob. foreign word, cf. Skr. *pîta* (prop *yellow*)),—named with other precious stones Ez 28[13] Ex 28[17] = 39[10], cstr. פִּטְדַת־כּוּשׁ Jb 28[19]—Vid. Plin[NH xxxvii 8 (32)], Houghton in Sm DB, Topaz Ri[HWB, Edelstein].

†**פַּטִּישׁ** **n.m.**[Je 50, 23] **forge-hammer**;—(NH = BH; Aram. loan-word acc. to Fra[85], and so Ar. ‏فِطِّيس‎ (cf. Ar. trad. in Lane), v 𝔗 פַּטִּישָׁא; but Lag[BN 103] cp. ‏فِنْطِيسَة‎ *swine's snout*, Syr. ‏ܦܛܝܣܐ‎ *flat-nosed*),—פ׳ abs Is 41[7] Je 23[29]; cstr. 50[23] fig of Bab. as destroyer.

†**פָּטַר** **vb.** **separate, remove, set free** (NH *depart, set free*, Niph. also *die*; Ph. פטר CIS[102a, 2] *depart* (*die?*); As. *patâru*, *split, break through*, *ipṭiru*, *ransom*, Tel Am. *escape, set free* (perh Canaanit), Ar. ‏فَطَرَ‎ *cleave, split*, also *create*, Eth ፈጠረ: *create, fabricate*; Aram. פְּטַר, ‏ܦܛܪ‎; *withdraw, depart*),—**Qal** *Pf.* 3 ms. פ׳ 2 Ch 23[8]; *Impf.* 3 ms. וַיִּפְטַר 1 S 19[10], *Pt act* פּוֹטֵר Pr 17[14]; *pass* פְּטוּרִים 1 Ch 9[33] Qr (Kt פטירים); cstr. פְּטוּרֵי 1 K 6[18.29.32], פְּטֻרֵי v[35],—**1.** intrans *remove* oneself, specif. *escape* 1 S 19[10] (מִפְּנֵי, cf. Dr). **2.** trans *set free* fr. duty 2 Ch 23[8] (acc pers.), so pass 1 Ch 9[33] Qr (Kt פטירים adj or Aram. pt, same mng); פ׳ מַיִם Pr 17[14] *set free, let out*; pass. פְּטוּרֵי צִצִּים term. techn of ornament in temple, dub, usually *out-spread* (garlands) *of flowers* 1 K 6[18.29.32.35]. **Hiph.** *Impf.* 3 ms. יַפְטִירוּ בְשָׂפָה ψ 22[8] *they separate with the lip*, i e. open mouth wide (insultingly).

†**פֶּטֶר** **n.[m.]** **that which separates, first opens**;—cstr., פ׳ רֶחֶם i.e. firstborn, of man and beast, Ez 20[26] Ex 13[12.15] 34[19] Nu 18[15]; appos בְּכוֹר Ex 13[2] Nu 3[12], רֶחֶם om. Ex 13[12.13] 34[19.20].

†[**פִּטְרָה**] **n.f.** id, פִּטְרַת כָּל־רֶחֶם Nu 8[16].

פטיר 1 Ch 9[33] Kt v. פטר **2.**

פֶּה v **פי**.

†**פִּי־בֶסֶת** **n.pr.loc.** in Egypt (*Pabast*, Eb GS 495, or *Per-Bastet*, Griffith[Hastings DB iii 874], '*House of Bast(et)*' orig *Pĕr-wbaste* acc. to Steind[BAS i 350], cf. Naville[Bubastis 44, 46, 48, 54], Gk. Βούβαστις (Herod.), Βούβαστος (Diod. Sic.));—Ez 30[17] ⅁ Βουβάστου (genit.), mod. *Tel-Basṭa*, near Zakazik, c 30 miles NNE. fr. Cairo.—Vid Herod.[ii. 59 f. 67, 137 f. 166] Diod.[xvi 49 51] Naville[l.c.] Trans Vict Inst, xxiii. 157 ff.

†**פִּי הַחִירֹת** **n.pr.loc.** on E. border of Egypt, Ex 14[2.9] (⅁ ἡ ἔπαυλις), Nu 33[7] (Ε(π)ιρωθ) + v[8] (read מִפִּי ה׳ Sam 𝔖 𝔙 𝔗, or מִפְּנֵי פִּי ה׳, for MT מִפְּנֵי ה׳, cf. Di). Site unknown

פוד, פיד (√of foll; cf Ar فود, فَادَ *die*, فند, فَادَ *pass away, be exhausted* (of property)).

†**פִּיד** **n.[m.]** ruin, disaster,—abs. Jb 12⁵, cstr 31[29] Pr 24[22], sf פִּידוֹ Jb 30[24] + 21[20] (for כִּידוֹ).

פיות, פִּיּוֹת v. פֶּה **פִּיחַ** v פוח

†**פִּיכֹל** **n.pr.m.** captain of Abimelech of Gerar Gn 21[22.32] 26[26], Φικολ, 𝔊L Φιχολ.

פִּילֶגֶשׁ v. פִּלֶּגֶשׁ.

פִּים, perh < **פאם** (√of foll, cf Ar فَأَمَ *fill*, II *make wide*, IV *become full* (of fat), hence (Thes al) foll, by syncope of א, cf Ges§19k)

†**פִּימָה** **n f** superabundance (of fat);—פ׳ Jb 15[27] (‖ חֶלְבּוֹ)

פִּינְחָס[25] **n.pr.m.** (Egypt. *Pe-nehasi, the negro*, acc to Lauth[Moses (1868) 71 ZMG xxv (1871) 139 f] cf Nes[Eg 112, AJSL xiii (1897) 174] Baen[Ex 6 25], yet v Di),—**1.** grandson of Aaron, Φ(ε)ινεες, Ex 6[25] Nu 25⁷ + 16 t †**2.** son of Eli 1 S 1³ (†פִּנְחָס), 2[34] 4[4 11 17 19] 14³

†**פִּינֹן** **n.pr.m.** Edomite Gn 36[41] 1 Ch 1[52], Φινες, Φινων, Φινα,—cf. פּוּנֹן

פִּיפִיּוֹת v פֶּה **פִּיק** v I פוק

†**פִּישׁוֹן** **n.pr.fl.** (Thes sub פּוּשׁ, cf esp Nes[Marg 5], but dub),—one of the rivers of Eden Gn 2[11], Φ(ε)ισων, (on theories of identif v Comm, also reff. sub גִּיחוֹן)

†**פִּיתוֹן** **n.pr.m.** descendant of Saul 1 Ch 8[35] = פִּיתֹן 9[41], Φιθων, Φαιθων, 𝔊L Φιθωθ

פכך (√of foll, cf NH פַּךְ *flask*. also פִּכְפֵּךְ *trickle*, denom, or < onomatop)

†**פַּךְ** **n.m**[2 K 9.1] **vial, flask**,—cstr פַּךְ הַשֶּׁמֶן, for anointing, 1 S 10¹ 2 K 9[1.3]

†**פָּכָה** **vb Pi. trickle**, perh denom,—*Pt* pl מַיִם מְפַכִּים מִן Ez 47² *water trickling on* the south side

†**פֹּכֶרֶת הַצְּבָיִים** **n.pr.m.** (*bindress* [Aram, perh *binder* (fem of office)] of *the gazelles*),—head of post-exilic family, בְּנֵי פ׳ הַ׳ Ezr 2[57] = Ne 7[59] (הַצְּבָיִים), υἱοὶ Φασραθ υἱοὶ Ασεβωειν (Φακαραθ, Σαβαειμ, etc).

פלא (√of foll, *separate* from the ordinary, *distinguish* acc to Thes Gerber[212], cf פלה)

†**פֶּלֶא** **n.m.** wonder (NH *id*, as *unusual, extraordinary*),—פ׳ Ex 15[11] + 6 t; sf. פִּלְאֲךָ ψ 89⁶; פִּלְאֶךָ 77[12] 88[13], pl פְּלָאִים La 1⁹; fpl. פְּלָאוֹת ψ 119[129] Dn 12⁶,—**1.** *wonder*: extraordinary, hard to be understood, God's dealings with His people Is 29[14]; the testimonies of the Law ψ 119[129], פֶּלֶא יוֹעֵץ Is 9⁵ *marvel of a counsellor* (Baer פֶּלֶא), *wonderful counsellor* (of Mess. king), pl. as adv acc וַתֵּרֶד פ׳ La 1⁹ *she* (Jerus.) *hath come down marvellously* **2.** *wonder*: of God's acts of judgment and redemption ψ 77[12] 88[13] 89⁶; עֹשֵׂה פ׳ Ex 15[11] Is 25¹ ψ 77[15] 78[12] 88[11], of extraord trials קֵץ הַפ׳ Dn 12⁶.

[פָּלָא][71] **vb. denom. Niph** etc., **be surpassing, extraordinary** (cf. Gerber[212]),—**Niph** *Pf* 3 fs. נִפְלְאַתָה (Ges§§75 ...) ψ 118[23] נִפְלָאת, 2 S 1[26] (Kö[1 610 L 614] Ges§75oo), 3 pl. נִפְלְאוּ Pr 30[18]; *Impf* יִפָּלֵא Dt 17⁸ + 6 t, *Pt* mpl נִפְלָאִים ψ 139[14], fs נִפְלֵאת Dt 30[11], pl נִפְלָאוֹת Jos 3⁵ +, sf נִפְלְאֹתַי Ex 3[20], etc,—†**1.** *be beyond one's power, difficult* to do, לַעֲשׂוֹת 2 S 13², בְּעֵינֵי פ׳ Zc 8[6.6], c מִן pers *too difficult for* Dt 30[11], for י׳ Gn 18[14] (J) Je 32[17 27] †**2.** *be difficult* to understand, c מִן pers *too difficult for* ψ 131¹ Pr 30[18] Jb 42³, to decide Dt 17⁸ Esp †**3.** **a.** *be extraordinary, wonderful*, 2 S 1[26] ψ 119[18]; of God's acts, בְּעֵינֵינוּ נ׳ 118[23], cf 139[14]. **b.** *Pt.* as subst *marvellous things* Jb 37[14] (acts of God), Dn 11[36] (presumptuous words), as adv *wondrously* Jb 37⁵ Dn 8[24]. **4.** נִפְלָאוֹת = *wonderful acts* of י׳ in judgment and redemption, Ex 3[20] (J) Ju 6[13] Je 21² 1 Ch 16[9.24] ψ 9² 26⁷ + 15 t. ψψ; also עָשָׂה נ׳ Ex 34[10] Jos 3⁵ (J) Jb 5⁹ = 9[10], + 9 t. Chi ψψ, הַרְאָה נ׳ Mi 7[15] ψ 78[11]. †**Pi.** *Inf.* cstr לְפַלֵּא נֶדֶר *make a special votive offering*, Lv 22[21] Nu 15[3.8] (P) **Hiph.** *Pf* 3 ms. הִפְלִיא ψ 31[22] 2 Ch 26[15], הִפְלָא Is 28[29], וְהִפְלָא consec. Dt 28[59] (Ges§75oo), *Impf.* יַפְלִא Lv 27² Nu 6², *Inf abs* הַפְלֵא Is 29[14] 2 Ch 2⁸, cstr הַפְלִיא Is 29[14] Jo 2[26]; *Pt* מַפְלִא Ju 13[19],—**1.** *do a hard or difficult thing*, הִפ׳ (לִנְדֹּר) נֶדֶר *make a hard vow* Lv 27² Nu 6² (cf. **Pi.**) **2.** *make wonderful, do wondrously*: of God, הִפ׳ מַכּוֹת *make plagues wonderful* (exceptional), Dt 28[59], הִפ׳ עֵצָה Is 28[29] *make counsel wondrous*, 29[14] *do wonderfully with people*, + הַפְלֵא וָפֶלֶא; עָשָׂה עִמָּכֶם לְהַ׳ Jo 2[26] *dealt with you doing wondrously*; הִפ׳ חַסְדּוֹ לִי ψ 31[22], הִפ׳ לְהֵעָזֵר 2 Ch 26[15] *did marvellously in receiving help*, of the temple גָּדוֹל וְהַפְלֵא 2 Ch 2⁸ (Kö[Synt. § 318 e]) **3.** of God, מַפְלִא לַעֲשׂוֹת Ju 13[19] *working wonders in doing*. †**Hithp.** *Impf* תִּתְפַּלָּא בִי Jb 10[16] *thou dost shew thyself marvellous* (act inexplicably) *against me*

†פַּלּוּא **n.pr.m.** (DHM Epigr Denkm. 8. 1 cp. Lihy. n pr. פלה),—son of Reuben Gn 46^9 Ex 6^{14} Nu $26^{5.8}$ 1 Ch 5^3, Φαλλου(ς), etc; v. also פֶּלֶת.

†פַּלֻּאִי **adj. gent.** of foregoing, c. art. as n. coll., Nu 26^5.

[פָּלִא] v following

†[פִּלְאִי] **adj. wonderful, incomprehensible**;—**m.** פלאי (i e פִּלְאִי) Kt, Ju 13^{18} (name of מַלְאַךְ י׳, > Qr (פֶּלִ(א)י), **f.** פליאה דַּעַת מִמֶּנִּי (i e. פְּלִיאָה) ψ 139^6 God's knowledge; > Qr פְּלִאָיה

†פְּלָאיָה **n.pr.m.** Ne 8^7 10^{11}, 𝔊L Φαλαιας.

†פְּלָיָה **n.pr.m.** (late As *Pi-liâma* Hilpr Univ. Pa. Exp. ix. 66),—1 Ch 3^{24}, Φαρα, Φαλαια, Φαδια.

†[מִפְלָאָה] **n.f. wondrous work** (si vera l.);—pl. cstr. מִפְלְאוֹת Jb 37^{16} (of providence, but read probably נפלאות Bu SS, cf. Di).

†[פָּלַג] **vb. split, divide** (NH chiefly in secondary meanings and deriv, Ar فَلَجَ *divide, split*; Aram פְּלַג, ܦܠܓ *divide*; Eth ፈለግ: *ravine, stream*; As. *palgu, canal*),—**Niph.** *Pf.* 3 fs נִפְלְגָה Gn 10^{25} the earth *was divided.* **Pi. 1.** *Pf* 3 ms פִּלַּג Jb 38^{25} *cleave* a channel for rain **2.** *Imv* ms פַּלַּג (Ges §52 n) ψ 55^{10} *divide* their speech (their counsels).

†I פֶּלֶג **n.m.** ψ 65, 10 (cleft) **channel, (artif.) canal**,—usu pl. פְּלָגִים Is 30^{25} (+ יִבְלֵי־מָיִם), cstr פַּלְגֵי־מָיִם ψ 1^3, sim Is 32^2 Pr 21^1, metaph. 5^{16}, of tears La 3^{48} ψ 119^{136}; פְּלָגָיו ψ 46^5 (i e. irrigating canals fr. river, metaph). פַּלְגֵי־שָׁמֶן Jb 29^6 (fig of prosperity), sg פֶּלֶג אֱלֹהִים ψ 65^{10}, poet of channel for rain (cf. Jb 38^{25})

†II פֶּלֶג **n.pr.m.** son of Eber, Φαλεκ, 𝔊L Φαλεγ Gn 10^{25} $11^{17.18.19}$ 1 Ch $1^{19.25}$, פָּלֶג Gn 11^{16}

†[פְּלַגָּה] **n.f. 1. stream. 2. division**,—pl. פְּלַגּוֹת **1.** *streams* Jb 20^{17}. **2.** *divisions, sections* of tribe, פ׳ cstr. Ju $5^{15.16}$ (read perhaps פְּלֻגּוֹת, v. following), > *streams.*

†[פְּלֻגָּה] **n.f. division** (= מַחֲלֹקֶת q.v.), of priests, for service,—pl. cstr. פְּלֻגּוֹת 2 Ch 35^5.

†[מִפְלַגָּה] **n.f.** id; pl abs. מִפְלַגּוֹת 2 Ch 35^{12}.

פִּילֶגֶשׁ, פִּלֶגֶשׁ ₃₇ **n.f. concubine** (NH *id.*, 𝔗 Jer פִּלַּקְתָּא (פַּלְקְתָא), perhaps influenced by Gk. παλλακή, παλλακίς (prop *young girl*), Lat *pellex*; orig. Gk. word acc. to Sta G i 380, cf also Lewy Fremdw 66 f.; on poss. Hittite origin v Jen ZMG xlviii (1894). 468 ff);—פ׳ abs. 2 S 3^7, cstr 21^{11}, פִּי׳ abs. Gn 36^{12} Ju 19^1, cstr Gn 35^{22} + 4 t.; sf. פִּילַגְשׁוֹ 22^{24} +, -שׁהּ Ju 19^{24}; -שׁי 20^4 + 2 t.; pl פִּלַגְשִׁים 2 S 5^{13} + 2 t, פִּי׳ Gn 25^6 + 5 t.; cstr פִּלַגְשֵׁי 2 S $16^{21.22}$; sf. פִּילַגְשָׁיו 2 Ch 11^{21}, פִּלַגְשֶׁיךָ 2 S 19^6, פִּלַגְשֵׁיהֶם Ez 23^{20};—**1.** *concubine* Gn 22^{24} 25^6 35^{22} 36^{12} Ju 8^{31} 19^1 + 10 t Ju 19, 20, 2 S 3^7 + 7 t. 2 S, 1 K 11^3 1 Ch 1^{32} + 6 t. Ch, Est 2^{14} Ct $6^{8.9}$ **2.** either = *paramour* (perhaps contempt., ὁ πάλλαξ = *youth*), or < *concubinage* Ez 23^{20} (fig. of Jerusalem doting on Babylon).

†[פְּלָדָה] **n.f.** usu. **iron, steel** (origin dub; *steel* in Ar. is فُولَاذ, فَالُوذ, but Vulg. Ar. بُولَاد, Syr ܦܘܠܕ (in Lexx); loan-wd fr. Pers پولاد acc. to Lag Ges. Abh 75, cf No ZMG xxx (1876), 768, but uncertain, cf. Now and reff);—pl. [abs!] בְּאֵשׁ־פְּלָדֹת הָרֶכֶב Na 2^4 < כְּאֵשׁ פלדת וגו׳ We Now, *like fire the steel* (fittings) *of the chariots.*

†פִּלְדָּשׁ **n.pr.m.** Nahorite Gn 22^{22}, Φαλδας.

†[פָּלָה] **vb. Niph.** be separated, distinct (‖ form of פלא q.v., cf Ar فَلَا, فلو *separate from sucking, wean*; Eth. ፈለየ: *separate, distinguish*);—**1.** *Pf* 1 pl consec. וְנִפְלִינוּ Ex 33^{16} *and we shall be distinct*, c. מִן pers **2.** 1 s נִפְלֵיתִי ψ 139^{14} *I am wonderful* (viz. in bodily stature etc), < Vrss Hup-Now Bae We ־תָ *thou* [י׳] *art wonderful* (פלא **3**). **Hiph.** *Pf* 3 ms. הִפְלָה ψ 4^4, וה׳ consec. Ex 9^4; 1 s. וְהִפְלֵיתִי consec. 8^{18}, *Impf* 3 ms. יַפְלֶה 11^7; *Imv.* ms. הַפְלֵה ψ 17^7,—of י׳, *make separate*, c. acc Ex 8^{18} (by treating differently); *set apart* ψ 4^4, but perh. read חֶסֶד לִי (for MT חָסִיד לוֹ), *hath made wonderful* (his) *kindness to me* (Dy Gi Che We Du [Bae 'perh.']), so 17^7 (cf. 31^{22}); *distinguish* between, בֵּין rei, Ex 9^4, בֵּין pers. 11^7.

†I. פְּלֹנִי **pron. a certain one**; Gk. ὁ, ἡ δεῖνα (acc to Thes from above √, through an unused noun פֶּלֶן, prop *one defined, a particular one*: NH *id*; Aram ܦܠܢ, f. ܦܠܢܝܬܐ; Arab فُلَان W AG i §353 R. c, voc فُلُ Siegf ZWTh xxvii 355; As *pulpul* Hpt BAS i. 114), always joined with אַלְמֹנִי (prop. *one not mentioned*) in the sense of 'ein *gewisser* verschwiegener' (Ew §106 c. 2 Sta §150 b), '*a certain* unnamed *one*,' i e. *such a one*; Ru 4^1 שְׁבָה־פֹּה פְּלֹנִי אַלְמֹנִי sit down here, *such a one* (Gk. ὦ οὗτος; Ar. يَا فُلُ); in the phr. מְקוֹם פ׳ א׳ the place of *such a one* = *such and such* a place, 1 S 21^3

2 K 6⁵ From פ׳ א׳ arose by contraction (or conflation, Perles^Anal 82) פַּלְמֹנִי + Dn 8¹³ . . ויאמר לַפ׳ הַמְדַבֵּר to *that certain one* who spake —II פלני v p 813

†[פָּלַח] **vb. cleave** (Ar فلح *cleave*, Aram פלח (usu). ܦܠܚ, are *till, work, serve* [=עָבַד]), —**Qal** *Pt* פֹּלֵחַ ψ 141⁷ of *cleaving*, ploughing, (בקע‖) בָּאָרֶץ **Pi.** *Impf* **1** *cleave open, through*, 3 ms יְפַלַּח of piercing kidneys Jb 16¹³, liver Pr 7²³ (both fig), וַיְפַלַּח אֶל 2 K 4³⁹ of cutting up (fruit) into pot **2** *cause to cleave open*, 3 fpl יַלְדֵיהֶן תְּפַלַּחְנָה Jb 39³ of animals bringing forth young, rd perh תְּפַלֵּטְנָה (21¹⁰).

†פֶּלַח **n.f.**^Jb 41 16 **cleavage, mill-stone** (mill *cleft* betw the stones? cf GFM^Ju, ܦ (פַּלְחָא),— פ׳ abs Jb 41¹⁶, elsewh cstr ,—**1. a.** *mill-stone*, פ׳ רֶכֶב *mill-stone of riding*, i e upper stone, wh is turned (cf רָכַב), Ju 9⁵³ 2 S 11²¹, פ׳ תַּחְתִּית Jb 41¹⁶ *lower mill-stone* (sim of hardness) **b.** פ׳ דבלה 1 S 30¹² *a cake of figs* (from shape?) **2.** *cleavage, split*, hence *slice* פ׳ הָרִמּוֹן Ct 4³ =6⁷ sim of human temple (from colour, cf. Wetzst in De^Comm Excurs A)

†פִּלְחָא (Baer פִּלְחָה) **n.pr.m.** post-exilic name Ne 10²⁵, Φαδαεις, 𝔊L Φαλλαει

†[פָּלַט] **vb. escape** (NH *id.;* Ph in n pr ; Ar فلت iv *escape*, Vulg Ar فلط, OAram פלט Pa *rescue*, ܦ פַּלֵּט, Syr ܦܠܛ),—**Qal** *Pf* 3 pl consec וּפָלְטוּ Ez 7¹⁶ *and* (if) escapers of them *escape* **Pi** causat *Impf.* 3 ms. sf יְפַלְּטֵם, 2 ms תְּפַלֵּט Mi 6¹⁴, etc , *Imv* ms. פַּלְּטָה ψ 17¹³, etc , *Pt* sf מְפַלְטִי 18³+,—**1.** *bring into security* Mi 6¹⁴, esp of ׳י, *deliver*, c acc pers, ψ 22⁵ ⁹ 31² 37⁴⁰ 71² (+הציל),82⁴ 91¹⁴, +מִן *from* 2 S 22⁴⁴ =ψ 18⁴⁴, ψ 18⁴⁹ (מוציא ‖ 2 S 22⁴⁹), 17¹³ 37⁴⁰ 43¹ 71⁴, pt c sf, *my deliverer* 2 S 22²=ψ 18³, ψ 40¹⁸ 70⁶ 144². **2.** *cause to escape, cast forth*, of cow calving Jb 21¹⁰ (cf [פָּלַט] **Hiph.**, also ܦ *vomit* out, and so ܦܠܛ) **3.** appar intrans *be delivered*, c מִן Jb 23⁷, but dub., Bu **Qal** ('perh '), 𝔊 Du read מִשְׁפָּטִי as obj (but elsewhere ׳י subj of **Pi**) **Hiph.** *bring into security, Impf* 3 ms יַפְלִיט Is 5²⁹ of Assyria, under fig. of lion, carrying off prey (opp הִצִּיל), 2 ms תַּפְלִיט Mi 6¹⁴ (cf **Pi. 1**)

†פֶּלֶט **n.pr.m. 1** 1 Ch 2⁴⁷, Φαλεκ[γ, τ] **2.** 1 Ch 12³, Ιωφαλητ, Φαλετ, etc —Vid בֵּית פֶּלֶט

I פַּלְטִי **adj. gent.** v בֵּית פֶּלֶט.

†פַּלֵּט **n.[m.] deliverance** (si vera l., prop. Inf of foregoing),—רָנֵּי פ׳ ψ 32⁷ *shouts of deliverance* (dub , v Comm), עַל־אָוֶן פַּלֶּט־לָמוֹ 56⁸, read פַּלֶּס־ (Ew Hup al) *for* (their) *iniquity weigh* to them (retribution), or עַל־אָוֶן אֵין פַּלֶּט־ Bae

†פָּלִיט **n m.**^Am 9,1 **escaped one, fugitive;**— פ׳ abs 2 K 9¹⁵+; pl cstr. פְּלִיטֵי Ju 12⁴+, sf פְּלִיטָיו Ob¹⁴, etc.,—Am 9¹ 2 K 9¹⁵ Gn 14¹³ Ez 24²⁶·²⁷ 33²¹ (+מִן loc), v²², שָׂרִיד וּפ׳ Jos 8²² Je 42¹⁷, פ׳ וְשָׂרִיד 44¹⁴ La 2²², c. genit subj Ju 12⁵ *fugitives of Ephr* (del. in v⁴, see GFM), so c. sf Ez 6⁹ 7¹⁶ Ob¹⁴; c. genit. obj , *escaped of*, i.e. *from* Is 45²⁰, so פְּלִיטֵי חֶרֶב Je 44²⁸ Ez 6⁸.

†[פָּלֵיט] **n.m.** id.,—pl פְּלֵיטִם Nu 21²⁹ (as appos , or adj), ־ִים Is 66¹⁹, פְּלֵטִים Je 44¹⁴, +מִן *from* 50²⁸ 51⁵⁰.

†פְּלֵיטָה **n.f. escape** (on form cf. Ba^NB 144, 166),—abs פ׳ Gn 32⁹+, פְּלֵטָה Ex 10⁵+; cstr. פְּלֵיטַת 2 K 19³⁰+,—**1.** *escape, deliverance* Gn 45⁷ (E) Je 25³⁵ **2.** elsewh prob alw *escaped remnant* . **a.** of green things (fr. locusts) Ex 10⁵ (J) Jo 2³ **b.** of pers. Gn 32⁹ (J) Ju 21¹⁷ Is 15⁹ Je 50²⁹ 1 Ch 4⁴³ 2 Ch 12⁷ 20²⁴ 30⁶ Ezr 9⁸ Dn 11⁴², +מִסְּנִי 2 S 15¹⁴ **c.** specif of *those* of Judah *escaped* fr. Assyr 2 K 19³⁰·³¹ (+מִן) = Is 37³¹·³², cf Is 10²⁰, fr. Bab Ne 1² Ezr 9¹³ ¹⁴ ¹⁵, cf Ez 14²², after ׳י's future judgment Is 4² Ob¹⁷ Jo 3⁵.

†II. פַּלְטִי **n.pr.m.** Φαλτει (perh. abbrev fr. פַּלְטִיאֵל);—**1.** Benjamite Nu 13⁹ **2.** second husband of Michal 1 S 25⁴⁴ (=פַּלְטִיאֵל 2 S 3¹⁵).

†פִּלְטַי **n.pr.m.** priest Ne 12¹⁷, Φεληπει, etc.

†פַּלְטִיאֵל **n. pr. m.** Φαλτ(ε)ιηλ · **1.** Nu 34²⁶. **2.** 2 S 3¹⁵ (=פַּלְטִי 1 S 25⁴⁴), 𝔊L Φαλτιου

†פְּלַטְיָהוּ, פְּלַטְיָה **n.pr.m.** Φαλτιας, Φαλεττι(α), etc —**1.** ־ְיָהוּ, a prince of people Ez 11¹ ¹³ **2.** ־ְיָה, grandson of Zerub 1 Ch 3²¹, perh =Ne 10²³ **3.** ־ְיָה, Simeonite 1 Ch 4⁴².

†יַפְלֵט **n.pr.m.** Asherite (on form cf Ba^NB 144, 166),—1 Ch 7³²·³³, also v³² (Gi יַפְלֵט), Ιφαμηλ, Αφαληκ, etc , Α Ιαφαλητ.

†יַפְלֵטִי **adj. gent.** c art as n coll. הַיּ׳ *the Japhlites* Jos 16³, family or clan on SW border of Ephraim; Απταλειμ, Α Ιεφαλθι, 𝔊L Ιεφλητι

†מִפְלָט **n.[m.] escape** (Hup Bae) **or place of escape** (We Du),—ψ 55⁹ si vera l , 𝔊 Che מְפַלֵּט *deliverer*

פְּלִיָּה, פְּלִי v. פלא.

פלך (√of foll.; cf. Ar. فَلَكَ II. *be round* (esp. *hemispherical*), فَلْكَةٌ *whirl* of spindle, so As. *pilakku*; NH = BH; 𝔗 פֶּלֶךְ *circuit, district*; As. also *pilku, district*).

†פֶּ֫לֶךְ **n.[m.]** **1. whirl of spindle. 2.** district (prop. *circle, circuit*);—abs. 'פ 2 S 3[29], פָּ֑לֶךְ Pr 31[19]; cstr. פֶּלֶךְ Ne 3[9]+; sf. פִּלְכּוֹ v[17];—**1.** *whirl of spindle*, 2 S 3[29] (prob., v. Dr), Pr 31[19] (‖ כִּישׁוֹר). **2.** *district*, Ne 3[9.12.14.15.16.17.17.18].

[פָּלַל]$_{84}$ **vb.** prob. intervene, interpose (hence both *arbitrate, judge,* and *intercede, pray,* cf. Dr[1 S 2.25]; NH פלל (rare), נתפלל, *pray*, פִּילּוּל *act of prayer*, פְּלִילָה *judicial matter*;—otherwise We[Heid. (2), 126] who conj. der. for הִתְפַּלֵּל from Ar. فَلَّ *notch edge* (of sword, etc.), i.e. *cut oneself* in worship);—†**Pi.** *mediate, judge*: *Pf.* 3 ms. consec., *arbitrate*, sf. וּפִלְלוֹ 1 S 2[25] (but read prob. 3 pl. וּפִלְלוּ We Dr al., word-play with 'יִתְפ foll.); 2 fs. פִּלַּלְתְּ Ez 16[52] *mediate for* (ל pers.) viz., through thine own sins; 1 s. פִּלָּ֑לְתִּי Gn 48[11] (E; poss. denom. from פליל) *I did* not *judge* (have the opinion, expect) to see, etc.; *Impf.* 3 ms. וַיְפַלֵּל ψ 106[30] (abs.) *he interposed* (by slaying offender). **Hithp.**$_{80}$ *Pf.* 3 ms. הִתְפַּלֵּל 1 K 8[42]; 1 s. הִתְפַּלָּ֫לְתִּי 1 S 1[27], etc.; *Impf.* יִתְפַּלֵּל ψ 32[6]+; יִתְפַּלֶּל־ 1 S 2[25]; 1 s. אֶתְפַּלָּ֑ל ψ 5[3], etc.; *Imv.* הִתְפַּלֵּל Nu 21[7]+, etc.; *Inf. cstr.* הִתְפַּלֵּל Ez 10[1]+, etc.; *Pt.* מִתְפַּלֵּל Je 42[4]+, etc.;—**1.** specif. *intercede* (with 'י), c. בעד, *on behalf of* Gn 20[7] Nu 21[7] (E) Dt 9[20] 1 S 12[23] + 6 t.; c. לְ, 1 S 2[25]; אֶל־יהוה Nu 11[2] 21[7] (JE) Dt 9[26]; c. אל־יהוה + בעד 1 S 7[5] Je 29[7] + 4 t.; אל־האלהים Gn 20[17] (E); c. על *for* 2 Ch 30[18] Jb 42[8] (late). **2.** gen. *pray*, c. אֶל, unto idol Is 44[17] 45[20]; unto Israel v[14]; 'בּוֹא אל־מקדשׁ להתפ 16[12]. **3.** *pray* (to 'י), abs. 1 K 8[33] 2 K 6[17] Ezr 10[1] Dn 9[20] 2 Ch 6[24] 7[1.14], c. אֶל־י״ 1 S 1[26] 8[6] 2 K 4[33] 6[18] 20[2] = Is 38[2] = 2 Ch 32[24], + 10 t.; 'הִתְפּ' תפלה אֶל־י 2 S 7[27] 1 K 8[54]; על יהוה 1 S 1[10] (rd. אֶל); לִפְנֵי 1 S 1[12] 1 K 8[28] + 5 t.; c. לְ Dn 9[4]; c. אֶל of thing prayed for 1 S 1[27]; c. אֶל *against* 2 K 19[20] = Is 37[21] (read עַל); על־זאת *because of this* 2 Ch 32[20] ψ 32[6]; c. אֶל loc.: אֶל־הַמָּקוֹם 1 K 8[29.30.35] = 2 Ch 6[20.21.26]; אֶל־הַבַּיִת 1 K 8[42] = 2 Ch 6[32]; c. acc. דֶּרֶךְ הָעִיר 1 K 8[44] = 2 Ch 6[34]; דֶּרֶךְ אַרְצָם 1 K 8[48] = 2 Ch 6[38]. **4.** of *poetical, liturgical* prayer, abs. 1 S 2[1], c. אֶל Jon 2[2].

תְּפִלָּה$_{77}$ **n.f.** prayer;—'ת Is 1[15]+, cstr. תְּפִלַּת ψ 80[5]+; sf. תְּפִלָּתִי 4[2]+, etc.; pl. תְּפִלּוֹת 72[20];—**1. a.** *prayer*, 1 K 8[38] = 2 Ch 6[29], Is 1[15] ψ 35[13] 80[5]+. **b.** *pray a prayer*, 'הִתְפּ' ת 2 S 7[27] 1 K 8[54] (cf. v[28.29] = 2 Ch 6[19.20]); 'דִּבֶּר בַּתּ Dn 9[21]; specif. of intercession, 'נשׂא ת, c. בְּעַד *in behalf of* 2 K 19[4] = Is 37[4] Je 7[16] 11[14]. **c.** 'ת אֶל־אֱלֹהִים 2 Ch 33[18], לְאֵל ψ 42[9], cf. 69[14]; c. vb. + לפני 88[3] 141[2]; 'ת תְּקַדְּמֶךָּ 88[14]. **d.** 'בית ת Is 56[7.7] *house of prayer* (temple); c. vb. + 'אֶל־י + אל־היכל Jon 2[8]; c. vb. + למעון קדשׁו 2 Ch 30[27]. **e.** *hear prayer* is 'שׁמע (אֶת־) ת 1 K 8[45.49] = 2 Ch 6[35.39], 1 K 9[3] ψ 4[2] 39[13] + 9 t.; 'שׁמע אֶל־ת 1 K 8[28.29] = 2 Ch 6[19.20], Ne 1[6] Dn 9[17]; 'פנה אל ת 1 K 8[28] = 2 Ch 6[19], ψ 102[18]; הַקְשִׁיבָה (אֶל) Ne 1[11], cf. 'אָזְנֶיךָ קַשֻּׁבוֹת לת 2 Ch 6[40] 7[15], ψ 61[2]; 'הִקְשִׁיב בְּקוֹל ת 66[19]; 'הַאֲזִינָה ת 17[1] 55[2] 86[6]; 'לקח ת 6[10]; cf. 66[20] 102[18b]. **2.** in ψ-titles, poetic, liturgical prayer ψ 17[1] 86[1] 90[1] 102[1] 142[1] Hb 3[1]; of Davidic Psalter, תפלות דוד ψ 72[20].

†פָּלָל **n.pr.m.** a wall-builder Ne 3[25], Φαλαλ, א Φαλακ, A Φαλαξ, 𝔊L Φαλλη.

†[פָּלִיל] **n.m.** judge; pl. פְּלִילִים Dt 32[31] our enemies being *judges, umpires*; 'עָוֹן פ Jb 31[11], rd. 'עָוֹן פ acc. to Di Siegf, cf. De; < עָוֹן פְּלִילִי as v[28], so Bu Du; בִּפְלִלִים Ex 21[22], rd. perh. בַּנְּפָלִים *for the abortion* Bu[ZAW xi (1891). 107], cf. also Di-Ry.

†פְּלִילָה **n.f.** office of judge or umpire;—'עשׂי פ (Qr עֲשׂוּ) Is 16[3] *do an umpire's office*.

†פְּלִילִי **adj.** for a judge, calling for judgment;—'עָוֹן פ Jb 31[28] (on v[11] see פָּלִיל; Kue[Ond. (2) 161] reads עָוֹן פְּלִילִים in both v[11] and v[28]).

†פְּלִילִיָּה **n.f.** the giving a decision;—'פ Is 28[7] (of priests).

†פְּלַלְיָה **n.pr.m.** ('י *hath interposed*);—priest Ne 11[12], Φαλ(λ)αλια(ς).

†אֱפְלָל **n.pr.m.** in Judah 1 Ch 2[37.37], Αφαμηλ, etc., 𝔊L Ελφαελ.

פַּלְמֹנִי v. I. פְּלֹנִי sub פלה.

†II. פַּלּוֹנִי, פְּלֹנִי **adj. gent.** erron.: c. art. הַפְּלוֹנִי 1 Ch 11[27] 27[10] read הַפַּלְטִי as 2 S 23[26] (v. בֵּית פֶּלֶט); הַפְּלֹנִי 1 Ch 11[36] read הַגִּלֹנִי, as 2 S 23[34].—I. פְּלֹנִי v. פלה.

פלס, פלשׁ (√of foll.; *? be even, balance*).

†פֶּ֫לֶס **n.[m.]** balance, scale;—lit. Pr 16[11], fig. Is 40[11] (in both ‖ מֹאזְנַיִם).

†[פִּלֵּס] **vb. Pi. denom. weigh, make level** (Ph. פלס Pi. *make level* (?) in n.pr.);—*Impf.* 3 ms. יְפַלֵּס ψ 78[20]; 2 mpl. תְּפַלֵּסוּן ψ 58[3] (v. infr.), etc.; *Imv.* ms. פַּלֵּס Pr 4[26]; *Pt.* מְפַלֵּס 5[11];—**1.** *weigh out* חֲמַס יְדֵיכֶם תְּפ׳ ψ 58[3] (fig.; but read perh. חָמָס יְדֵיכֶם תְּפַלֵּסְנָה *violence do your hands weigh out*, so 𝔊 𝔖 𝔗 Bae Kau We). **2.** *make level*, smooth (cf. Gerber[32]), c. acc. of path (fig.), מַעְגָּל Pr 4[26] 5[21] Is 26[7], נָתִיב ψ 78[50], אֹרַח Pr 5[6].

†[מִפְלָשׂ] **n.[m.] swaying, poising**;—מִפְלְשֵׂי־עָב Jb 37[16]; Bu (plausibly) מִפְרְשֵׂי, as 36[29].

†[פָּלַץ] **vb. Hithp. shudder**;—*Impf.* 3 mpl. יִתְפַּלָּצוּן Jb 9[6] its (earth's) pillars *shudder*.

†פַּלָּצוּת **n.f. shuddering**;—פ׳ abs. Jb 21[6] Is 21[4] Ez 7[18] ψ 55[6].

†מִפְלֶצֶת **n.f. horrid thing** (thing *to shudder at*);—עָשְׂתָה מ׳ לָאֲשֵׁרָה 1 K 15[13] (of some abominable object of idolatry, not precisely known), so sf. מִפְלַצְתָּהּ v[13] = 2 Ch 15[16.16].

†[תִּפְלֶצֶת] **n.f. shuddering, horror**;—sf. תִּפְלַצְתְּךָ Je 49[16] *horror at thee!* (exclam.); not quite certain, v. Gie.

פלשׂ v. פלס.

†[פָּלַשׁ] **vb. Hithp.** act of mourning, poss. roll in (dust, etc.; weakened fr. *burrow into*) (NH Pi. *break open*, or *through*; As. *palâšu, dig a hole*; Syr. ܦܠܫ *dig* or *break through*; but connexion dub., Vrss mostly *besprinkle oneself*, Aq *roll oneself*);—*Pf.* 1 s. עָפָר הִתְפַּלָּשְׁתִּי Mi 1[10] Kt (Qr *Imv.* -פַּלָּשִׁי, others mpl. -פַּלָּשׁוּ); *Impf.* 3 mpl. בָּאֵפֶר יִתְפַּלָּשׁוּ Ez 27[30], so *Imv.* fs. הִתְפַּלְּשִׁי בָאֵפֶר Je 6[26] (cf. Mi 1[10] Qr); abs., mpl. הִתְפַּלְּשׁוּ 25[34].

†פְּלֶשֶׁת **n.pr.terr. Philistia**, poet. and late;—(יֹשְׁבֵי) פְּלָשֶׁת Ex 15[14] (Φυλιστιειμ; elsewh. (οἱ) ἀλλόφυλοι), Jo 4[4], elsewhere פְּלֶשֶׁת Is 14[29.31] ψ 60[10] = 108[10], 83[8] 87[4]; As. *Palastu, Pilistu*, COT[Gn 10, 14] Dl[Pa 288 f.] Gk. Παλαιστίνη Herod.[ii. 104, 106, vii. 89] Jos[Ant. i. 6, 2] (also Φυλιστίνου); v. Rel[Pal. 73 f.]

פְּלִשְׁתִּי [288] **adj.gent. Philistine**, (οἱ) Φυλιστιειμ, and (not in Hex) (ὁ) ἀλλόφυλος, (οἱ) ἀλλόφυλοι;—only as subst.: הַפּ׳ *the Philistine* (Goliath) slain by David 1 S 17[8] + 27 t. 17, 18[6] 19[5] 21[10] 22[10]; one slain by Abishai 2 S 21[17]; elsewhere pl. *the Philistines* [255], usu. פְּלִשְׁתִּים without art., rarely הַפּ׳ 1 S 4[7] 7[13] + (esp. c. prep. בַּפּ׳ v[13] +, and then perh. due to punctuators), Gn 10[14] = 1 Ch 1[12], Gn 26[14.15.18] Ju 3[31] + 33 t. Ju, 1 S 4[1.1] + 118 t. 1 S, 2 S 1[20] + 28 t. 2 S, +; אֶרֶץ פ׳ Gn 21[32.34] + 12 t.; שְׂדֵה פ׳ 1 S 6[1] 27[7.11]; מֶלֶךְ פ׳ Gn 26[1.8]; שָׂרֵי פ׳ 1 S 18[30] + 5 t.; סַרְנֵי פ׳ Jos 13[3] Ju 3[3] + 13 t.; יָם פ׳ Ex 23[31]; אֱלֹהֵי פ׳ Ju 10[6].—Cf. כַּפְתּוֹר, II. כְּרֵתִי. On Philistines v. also WMM[As. u. Eur. 387 f.] Evans[Cretan Pictographs, 100 ff.] Schwally[ZWT xxxiv. 103 f., 255]

†פֶּלֶת **n. pr. m. 1.** Reubenite Nu 16[1], Φαλεθ[κ]; rd. prob. פַּלּוּא (q. v.) so Gf Dr al. **2.** Judahite 1 Ch 2[33], Θαλεθ, Φαλεθ[ατ].

†פְּלֵתִי **adj.gent.** from unknown n.pr.; only c. art. as n. coll. with הַכְּרֵתִי (q.v.) of David's guard 2 S 8[18] 15[18] 20[7.23] 1 K 1[38.44] 1 Ch 18[17].

פֶּן־ [133] (alw. with Makkeph) **conj.** (averting, or deprecating), **lest** (origin dub.: Thes Kö[ii. 334] from פָּנָה, prop. subst. cstr. in accus. *for the aversion of*; but פָּנָה is intrans.: Nö[M. 474] cps. the enclitic particle פוּן in 𝔗, *then*, ἄν, 'etwa,' thinking that a part. with the mng. 'es möchte etwa,' spoken in a tone of alarm, might readily acquire a deprecatory force);—*lest*: **1.** with *impf.* Gn 3[3] ye shall not eat thereof ... פֶּן־תְּמֻתוּן *lest* ye die, 11[4] let us build a city פֶּן־נָפוּץ *lest* we be scattered, 19[15.17.19] 38[23] 45[11] Ex 1[10] 23[29.33] etc., 2 K 10[23] (sq. יֵשׁ), Is 6[10] 27[3] 28[22] 48[5.7] ψ 2[12] 7[3] etc.; oft. after הִשָּׁמֶר־לְךָ *take heed to thyself* Gn 24[6] 31[24], and esp. in Dt, as 4[9.23] 6[12] 8[11] al.; after a vb. of fearing Gn 32[12], and once, even, of swearing Ju 15[12]; deprecating pathetically, Gn 44[34] how shall I go up, etc.? *lest* I look upon the evil that will befal my father. Once, unusually, preceding the principal clause, Pr 5[6] אֹרַח חַיִּים פֶּן־תְּפַלֵּס *lest* she should make level the path of life, her ways are unstable, etc. (Ew Be Now; v. also Toy). Note esp. **a.** the idiom כִּי אָמַר (אָמַרְתִּי) פֶּן־ *for he (I) said, Lest* ..., implying always that some precaution has been taken to avert the dreaded contingency, †Gn 26[9] for I said, Lest I die on account of her (to obviate which, Isaac had called Rebecca his sister), 31[31] 38[11] 42[4] Ex 13[17] Nu 16[34] 1 S 13[19] 27[11] (לֵאמֹר), ψ 38[17]; with כי אמר implied Gn 26[7]; cf., with an aposiop., 3[22] and now, *lest* he put forth his hand, etc. (implying that measures are taken to prevent this, see v[23]): cf. Tob 8[9]. **b.** פֶּן־ at the beg. of a sentence, with a dissuasive force, (Beware) *lest*: †Is 36[18] פֶּן־יַסִּית אֶתְכֶם חזקיהו (beware) *lest* Hezekiah deceive you, Dt 29[17.17] (sq. יֵשׁ), Je 51[46] Jb 32[13] 36[18]. **2.** with

Pf, the result feared being conceived as having possibly already taken place; †2 S 20^{6} pursue after him, פֶּן־מָצָא לוֹ . . . והציל *lest he have found* him fenced cities, etc. (but the tense of והציל makes יִמְצָא prob., Dr^{Sm} Bu Ko$^{iii\ 486}$), 2 K 2^{16} פֶּן־נְשָׂאוֹ רוּחַ י׳ וַיַּשְׁלִכֵהוּ וגו׳,

†[פַּנַּג] **n.[m.]** unknown word, appar. some kind of food, חִטֵּי מִנִּית ופ׳ וּדְבַשׁ וגו׳ Ez 27^{17}; Vrss conject, Co prop וּדוֹנַג, so Hoffm$^{Ph.\ Inschr\ 15}$ Krae Berthol ('perhaps')

פָּנָה$_{133}$ **vb.** turn (NH *id.*; Syr. ܦܢܐ, ܐ פְּנָא, Eth ፈነወ: Ar فني *pass away, banish*; cf Sab. פנה (variously) e g CIS$^{iv\ Nos\ 1\ 37.40}$, As. *pânu*, *face*, Ph פנם, MI$^{13.18}$ לפני, sf מפני 1^{19});—**Qal**$_{117}$ *Pf* 3 ms. פ׳ Je 6^{4}+, 2 ms פָּנִיתָ 2 S 9^{8}, etc; *Impf.* 3 ms יפנה 1 S 13^{17}+, וַיִּפֶן Ex 2^{12}+, 3 fs. וַתֵּפֶן 1 K 10^{13}, 1 s וָאֵפֶן Dt 9^{15} 10^{5}, 1 pl וַנֵּפֶן 2^{1}+, etc; *Imv* ms פנה ψ 25^{16}+, etc; *Inf abs.* פָּנֹה Hg 1^{9}, cstr. לפנות Gn 24^{63}+, etc, *Pt.* פנה Dt 29^{17}+, etc,—**1.** †**a.** *turn* toward, אֶל pers, lit, Ju 6^{14} Is 13^{14}=Je 50^{16}, Jb 21^{5} (i.e. attentively), cf. of branches Ez 17^{6} (in allegory); c עַל of direction Gn 24^{49}; fig c. אל־י׳ (in worship), Is 45^{22}, other gods Ho 3^{1} Dt 31$^{18.20}$ Lv 19^{4}; for help Lv 19^{31} 20^{6} Jb 5^{1}; אֶל־אָוֶן 36^{21}; c acc הַמָּקוֹם אֲשֶׁר יִפְנֶה Ez 10^{11}, c ה loc 1 K 17^{3} Dt 2^{3} (+לָכֶם dat eth), Ct 6^{1}; c דֶּרֶךְ 1 S 13$^{18.18}$ Jb 24^{18}, אֶל־ד׳ Ju 20^{42} 1 S 13^{17}, fig לְדַרְכּוֹ Is 53^{6} 56^{11}, c. acc בְּכֹל אֲשֶׁר־יִפְנֶה 1 S 14^{47}, so, + שָׁם, fig. 1 K 2^{3}, i.e whatever thou undertakest, אֶל־כָּל־אֲשֶׁר יִפְנֶה Pr 17^{8}. †**b.** *turn* from, מִן loc. Gn 18^{22}, fig, of heart, c מֵעִם י׳ Dt 29^{17}, abs =*turn away* 30^{17}, in phr. פ׳ עֹרֶף *turn* (with) *the back* (cf ראה עֹרֶף Je 18^{17}), + לִפְנֵי, Jos 7^{12} (of flight), fig, + אֶל־י׳, Je 2^{27} 32^{33}. **c.** *turn* and do a thing, lit. (esp. + vb. of motion) Nu 21^{33} Dt 1$^{7.24}$ Ju 18^{21} 1 K 10^{13} + 17 t.; to do a thing (inf.) †Ec 2^{12}. †**d.** *turn, decline*, of day Je 6^{4}, days of life ψ 90^{9}. †**e.** *turn toward, approach*, of evening, לִפְנוֹת עֶרֶב Gn 24^{63} Dt 23^{12}, of morning, לפ׳ (הַ)בֹּקֶר Ex 14^{27} Ju 19^{26} ψ 46^{6} (fig) †**2. a.** *turn and look, look*, lit., אֶל pers Nu 12^{10} 2 Ch 20^{24} 26^{20}, וַיִּפֶן כֹּה וָכֹה Ex 2^{12}, c לְמַעְלָה Is 8^{21}; abs *look* (back) 2 Ch 13^{14}, c. אַחֲרֵי *look behind one* (and see, or say), Jos 8^{20} Ju 20^{40} 2 S 1^{7} 2^{20} 2 K 2^{24}, *look after* another Ez 29^{16} (fig for seek alliance with); c. אֶל of direction Ex 16^{10} Nu 17^{7}. **b.** of inanimate things, *face*, c. אֶל loc. Jos 15^{7}, usu of facing points of compass, c. ה loc 1 K 7$^{25.25\ 25.25}$=2 Ch 4$^{4.4\ 4.4}$, Jos 15^{2} Ez 8^{3} 46^{19}, but also c קָדִים 43^{17} 44^{1} 46$^{1.12}$ 47^{2}, cf. 43^{1}. **c.** esp. fig *look* at, אֶל־ pers., *regard*, (1) graciously 2 S 9^{8}; of י׳ Ez 36^{9} Lv 26^{9} 2 K 13^{23} ψ 40^{5}, + חָנַן 25^{16} 69^{17} 86^{16} 119^{132}; c. אֶל־תְּפִלָּה 1 K 8^{28}=2 Ch 6^{19}, ψ 102^{18}, אֶל־מִנְחָה Nu 16^{15} Mal 2^{13}; (2) sternly, אֶל־קְשִׁי הָעָם Dt 9^{27}. **d.** *look* for (אֶל rei)=expect Hg 1^{9}. **e.** fig. *look at* (ב rei)=consider Ec 2^{11}.—2 Ch 25^{23} v. פִּנָּה. †**Pi.** *Pf.* 3 ms. פִּנָּה Zp 3^{15}, etc; *Imv* mpl פַּנּוּ Is 40^{3}+ 2 t.,—*turn away, put out of the way*, c. acc. pers. Zp 3^{15} (‖ הסיר); hence *make clear*, c. acc הַבַּיִת, i.e. clear away things scattered about, make orderly, Germ. 'aufraumen,' Gn 24^{31}; *empty* it Lv 14^{36}, fig, c acc. דֶּרֶךְ *make clear*, free from obstacles, Is 40^{3} 57^{14} 62^{10} Mal 3^{1}; acc. om. *clear away* (ground) before it, i e. to plant it ψ 80^{10} (fig). †**Hiph.** (esp Je) *Pf.* 3 ms. הִפְנָה Je 48^{39}, 3 fs. הִפְנְתָה 49^{24}, etc.; *Impf* וַיֶּפֶן Ju 15^{4}; *Inf cstr* sf. הַפְנֹתוֹ 1 S 10^{9}, *Pt* מַפְנֶה Na 2^{9},—**1.** *turn*, c acc וַיֶּפֶן זָנָב אֶל־זָנָב Ju 15^{4}, עֹרֶף Je 48^{39} (cf. הפך Jos 7^{8}), שִׁכְמוֹ לָלֶכֶת 1 S 10^{9}. **2.** *make a turn, shew* (signs of) *turning*, + נָסוּ Je 46^{21}, לָנוּס 49^{24}; opp. נָסוּ 46^{5}, cf Na 2^{9}, + אֶל pers 47^{3}. †**Hoph.** *Imv.* mpl הָפְנוּ Je 49^{8} (Ges$^{§46\ a,\ N}$) *be ye turned back!* (in flight, + נָסוּ); *Pt.* מָפְנֶה צָפוֹנָה Ez 9^{2} the gate . . . *which is faced northward* (cf. **Qal 2 b**)

[פָּנֶה], pl. פָּנִים$_{2183}$ **n.m.**$^{Pr\ 25\ 23}$ and (Ez 21^{21} =*edge*; on 2 S 10^{9} v infr.) **f. face**, also **faces** (as *turned* toward one),—pl. abs. פָּנִים Gn 32^{31}+, cstr. פְּנֵי 2 S 14^{32}+; sf 1 s פָּנַי Gn 43^{3}+; 3 ms פָּנָיו Gn 4^{5}+, פָּנֵימוֹ ψ 11^{7} (Ko$^{ii.\ 1,\ 446}$), 2 mpl. פְּנֵיכֶם Gn 40^{7}+, etc.,—usu c. vb. pl, Gn 4$^{5.6}$ Ex 33^{14}+; c. vb. sg. La 4^{16} (through influence of intervening י׳, Ges$^{§145\ a}$), Pr 15^{14} (but read פִּי, as Qr, v פה),—**I. 1.** *face, faces* (Je 30^{6} Ez 27^{35}+, cf. 1^{6} 10$^{14.21}$ etc.): **a.** lit, of man Gn 43^{31} 2 S 19^{5} 1 K 19^{13} Lv 13^{41} Dn 8^{18} 10$^{9.15}$+; עוֹר פ׳ Ex 35$^{29.30.35}$, pale (from alarm) Is 29^{22} Je 30^{6}, flushed Is 13^{8} Ez 21^{3}, cf Na 2^{11} Jo 2^{6}; tearful Is 25^{8} Jb 16^{16}, sad, פ׳ רעים Gn 40^{7}, cf. Ne 2$^{2.3}$, also רֹעַ פ׳ Ec 7^{3} i e. sadness; פ׳ יֵיטִב Pr 15^{13} *maketh glad the face*, נָפְלוּ פָנֶיךָ Gn 4$^{5.6}$ why is *thy face fallen* (in displeasure), cf. 1 S 1^{18} (rdg. הִבִּילָה, or נָפְלוּ, נָפְלָה); covered with shame Ez 7^{18}, whence fig of confusion, discomfiture Je 51^{51} ψ 69^{8} 83^{17}, etc **b.** of י׳ Ex 33^{20}, cf. v^{23}. **c.** פָּנִים אֶל־פָּנִים *face to face*, of seeing (God) Gn 32^{31}, cf. Ju 6^{22}, knowing Dt 34^{10}, judging Ez 20^{35}, speaking Ex 33^{11}, and so פ׳ בְּפ׳ Dt 5^{4}; נִתְרָאֶה פָנִים 2 K 14^{8} *see each other* (in the) *face*=meet each other

in battle, cf v^{11} = 2 Ch 25$^{17.21}$. **d.** of relations with ׳י הרים פ׳ Ezr 9^{6}, in worship (v also נשׂא), in spiritual sense Je 2^{27} 32^{33} (פָּנָה אֵלַי עֹרֶף) נָתַן אֶת־פ׳ לדרוש ׳י 2 Ch 20^{3}, (ולא פָנים הַבָּנִים קְשֵׁי פָנִים Ez 2^{4}. **e.** of ׳י אֶל־אֲדֹנָי Dn 9^{3}, פני ׳י בעשׂי himself, לא יָסִיר פָּנִים מִכֶּם 2 Ch 30^{9}, רָע ψ 34^{17}, גַּעֲרַת פָּנֶיךָ 80^{17} —Vid further sub **7.** **2** **a** = *presence, person*, of ׳י Ex 33$^{14.15}$, בפָנָיו Dt 4^{37}, מַלְאַךְ פָּנָיו Is 63^{9}, לֶחֶם הַפָּנִים v לֶחֶם; of ׳י's angry presence La 4^{16} ψ 21^{10}, of Absalom 2 S 17^{11}, in weakened sense, nearly = sf (cf נפשׁ **4 a**), Pr 7^{15} †**b** c ראה technically, *see* one's *face*, i e appear before one, in one's presence before a man Gn 32^{21} (+ 3 other uses of ׳פ), (God, c יראה pointed as **Niph.**, v **II 2**), esp as privilege, = have access to, man of rank Gn 43$^{3.5}$ 44$^{23.26}$, king Ex 10$^{28.28}$ cf v^{29} (all J), 2 S 14$^{24.24.28.32}$ cf 3$^{13.13}$, ראי פני הַמֶּלֶךְ 2 K 25^{19} = Je 52^{25}, Est 1^{14}, implying favour of person seen, man Gn 33^{10} (J), God v^{10}, cf Jb 33^{26} (Hiph.), and, c חזה, ψ 11^{7} 17^{15} **3** *face* of seraphim Is 6^{2}, cherubim Ex 25$^{20.20}$ = 37$^{9.9}$, Ez 1$^{8.11}$ 2 Ch 3^{13} +. **4.** *face* of animals, פני הַצֹּאן Gn 30^{40}, פ׳ אַרְיֵה וּפ׳ שׁוֹר וּפ׳ נֶשֶׁר Ez 1^{10} (in descr. of cherubim), cf 10^{14}, פ׳ אַרְיֵה also 1 Ch 12^{8} (fig.), פ׳־כפיר Ez 41^{19}, כתחי פ׳ Jb 41^{6} of crocodile **5** *face* (= *surface*) of ground (הָאֲדָמָה) Gn 2^{6} 4^{14} 7^{4} ψ 104^{30} +, so פ׳ הָאָרֶץ Gn 1^{29} 7^{3} 8^{9} 11$^{4.8.9}$ 19^{28} Is 24^{1}, פ׳ תבל Is 14^{21} 27^{6}, of a field Pr 24^{31}, פ׳ תהום Gn 1^{2} Jb 38^{30}, פ׳ הַמַּיִם Gn 7^{18} פ׳ רקיע הַשָּׁמַיִם 1^{20}, פ׳־כסה Jb 26^{9} i.e of God's throne (but Bu reads כֶּסֶה *fullmoon*), פ׳ הַלּוֹט Is 25^{7} v [לוט], פ׳ לבושׁו Jb 41^{5} *the expanse of his* [the crocodile's] *coat*, *front* (esp Ezek), of house Ez 41^{14} 47^{1}, פ׳ הַקֹּדֶשׁ 41^{21}, of gate 40$^{6.20.22}$ 42^{15} 43^{4}, of chamber 40$^{44.44.45.46}$, of pot (סיר) Je 1^{13}, פ׳ הַמִּלְחָמָה 2 S 10^{9} *battle-front* = 1 Ch 19^{10} (vb. agrees with הַמ׳ in gender, Ges^{§146a}), = *van* of locust-army Jo 2^{20} (opp. ספו); *front*, i e *edge*, of sword Ez 21^{21}, of axe Ec 10^{10}, = condition, state of a thing, as denoted by its *appearance*, of flock Pr 27^{23}; פ׳ הַדָּבָר 2 S 14^{20} *the appearance* (situation, attitude) *of the affair* **6.** as **adv.loc.** מִפָּנִים וּמֵאָחוֹר 2 S 10^{9} *before and behind* = פ׳ וא׳ 1 Ch 19^{10}, also Ez 2^{10} 2 Ch 13^{14}, פְּנֵי *toward* Ct 7^{5}, also *in front* (to the East?) *of* 2 Ch 20^{16} (v לפני **d** infr), לְפָנִים *forward* Je 7^{24} (opp לאחור), מִלְּפָנִים 1 K 6^{29} v. פְּנִימָה; **adv. temp** לְפָנִים *formerly* Dt 2$^{12.20}$ Jos 11^{10} Ju 1$^{10.11.13}$ + 12 t, מִלְּפָנִים Is 41^{26} *from beforetime* (‖ מראשׁ) **7.** for other phrases see אור **vb. Hiph. 5**; אור **n. 10**, בושׁ **Hiph.**, בקשׁ **Pi. 3**; בֹּשֶׁת **1**, p 102, [הַכָּרָה], p 648, הָדַר **2**, זָעַם **Niph.**, זָעַף **1**; חָבַשׁ **1 a**, I חָרָה, I חָוַר; חָזַק **Pi. 5**; II חלה; IV. חמר, חָפָה, טָחַן, יָעַר **Hoph.**; ישׁוּעָה **3**, p 447, כון **Hiph. 3**; כֹּפֶר **1**, p 497, כָּסָה **Pi. 1, 2**, מָאוֹר, p. 22, מַ־מָה p 169; מוּל 1, מַשָּׂא, p 673; [נָבַט] **Hiph. 3**, נגד **1, 2 c**; נָשָׂא, נכח, נָכַר **Hiph.**, נָפַל **3 b**, and **Hiph. 5**; **1 b** (3), נָתַן **2 b**, סָבַב **Hiph 1 a**, סָתַר **Hiph. 2**, עָבַר 1 **2**, עָז, עָזַז **Hiph.**, עָמַד **Hiph. 6 a**, עֻמָּה II, [צָרַב], [קָדַם] **Pi.**, שׂים, שׁוּב **Hiph.**; שִׁית, II שָׁנָה **Pi.**; תֹּפֶת

II. פני, with prepositions :—**1.** אֶל־פני **a.** *to the presence of*, Ex 23^{17} pregn יֵרָאֶה . . . אֶל־פני הָאָדֹן shall appear (coming) to *the presence of* (= before) ׳י (‖ 34^{23} אֶת־פני הָא׳), c. יָצָא = *to confront* 2 Ch 19^{2}. **b.** *to the front of*, after a vb of motion, Lv 6^{7} הַקְרֵב אתה . . . אל־פני הַמִּזְבֵּחַ, 9^{5} 16^{2} Nu 17^{8} 20^{10}. **c.** *towards* or *on the front of* (אֶל = עַל · see p 41), Ez 41$^{4.12.15.25}$ 42$^{2.3.7.10.13}$ 45^{7} 48^{21}. **d.** *on to the surface of*, Lv 14^{53} ושִׁלַּח . . . אל־פני הַשָּׂדֶה, Ez 16^{5}.

†**2.** את־פני *close by* (II. את) *the face* or *front of* hence **a.** *in the presence of*, 1 S 2^{11} אֶת־פ׳ עֵלִי 1 K 12^{6} who stood את־פ׳ שְׁלֹמֹה (cf לפני 10^{8}), Est 1^{10} Pr 17^{24}, pregn. (nisi וַיְּנַחֵם leg, 𝔖 𝔗 We Dr al) 1 S 22^{4} Spec את־פני ׳י Gn 19^{13} (1 S 2^{17}), v^{27} 1 S 2^{18}, and with נראה of the appearance of all males at the three annual חַגִּים, Ex 34^{23} v^{24}, יֵרָאֶה כָל־זְכוּרְךָ את־פ׳ הָאָדֹן Dt 16^{16} (cf. Dr), 31^{11} 1 S 1^{22} (‖ אל־פ׳ ׳י Ex 23^{17}), so פְּנֵי alone Ex 23^{15} = 34^{20} (ולא יֵרָאוּ פָנַי ריקם), Is 1^{12}, פָּנֶיךָ ψ 42^{3} (acc to many, as Ges^{Thes} Di$^{Ex\ 23,15}$ Che$^{Is\ 1,12,\ crit\ n.}$, the vb in all these passages was originally **Qal**, afterwards pointed as **Niph.** to avoid the expression *see the face of* ׳י), אֶת־פָּנֶיךָ *in thy presence* ψ 16^{10} 21^{7} 140^{14}. **b.** *in front of*, Gn 33^{18} לִפְנֵי ׳י את־פ׳ פָּרֹכֶת הַקֹּדֶשׁ, Lv 4^{6} וַיִּחַן את־פ׳ הָעִיר, v^{17} —מאת פני *from before*, v. II את **4 a.**

3. בפני · †(*a*) *in the face of*, mostly in partic. phrases, with hostile import. thus, with יָרַק *to spit* Nu 12^{14} Dt 25^{9}; התיצב *to make a stand* Dt 7^{24} 11^{25}, and עמד Jos 10^{8}, לא יַעֲמֹד אישׁ בפָנֶיךָ 21^{42} 23^{9}; עָנָה *to answer* (give evidence) *against*, Ho 5^{5} וענה גאון ישׂראל בפניו, 7^{10} Jb 16^{8}, וְנָקֹטּוּ בפניהֶם = feel loathing *against* their own selves, Ez 6^{9}, so 20^{43} 36^{31}. †(*b*) *in front of*, Ez 42^{12}.

4. לפני, prop. *at the face* or *front of*, the most general word for *in the presence of*, *before*: as Gn 18^{22} עֹמֵד לפני אַבְרָהָם, Ex 4^{21} 11^{10} 2 S 2^{14} Pr 17^{18} + oft, after a vb of motion, Gn 47^{2} וַיַּצִּגֵם לִפְנֵי פ׳ and set them *before* Ph., 27^{20} כי הִקְרָה ׳י

לפני lit. made (it) to meet *before* me (cf. 24^{12}), Ex 29^{10} Pr 18^{16} etc. In partic.,

a. With the implication of (*a*) *under the eye* or *oversight of*, Dt 25^{2} 1 S 3^{1}. (*b*) *under the eye and regard of*, Gn 17^{18} לוּ יִשְׁמָעֵאל יִחְיֶה לְפָנֶיךָ, Ho 6^{2} Is 53^{2} ψ 61^{8}; cf. Je 30^{20} 31^{36} Is 66^{22} ψ 102^{29}: also 1 S 2^{28} 2 S 19^{14}. (*c*) fig. for *in* (or *into*) *the full* (mental) *view of*, Gn 6^{13} קֵץ כָּל־בָּשָׂר בָּא לְפָנַי is come in *before me*, La 1^{22} תָּבֹא כָל־רָעָתָם לְפָנֶיךָ, Jon 1^{2} עָלְתָה רָעָתָם לְפָנָי (cf. אֶל Gn 18^{21} Ex 2^{23}), Is 65^{6} כְּתוּבָה לְפָנָי, Je 2^{22} נִכְתָּם עֲוֹנֵךְ לְפָנַי (cf. נֶגְדִּי Is 47^{12}). (*d*) *openly before*, 1 S 12^{2} הִתְהַלַּכְתִּי לִפְנֵיכֶם, and with collat. idea of deserving (and receiving) regard 2^{35}, esp. לפני י׳ Gn 17^{1} al. (v. p. 236^{a}). (*e*) *in presence of* the moon or sun, ψ 72$^{5.17}$, i.e. as long as they endure. (*f*) *free before, at the disposal of*, Gn 13^{9} הֲלֹא כָל־הָאָרֶץ לְפָנֶיךָ (cf. 20^{15} 34^{10} 47^{6} Je 40^{4} 2 Ch 14^{6}), 24^{51} Ct 8^{12}. (*g*) *in the sight* (estimation) *of*, Gn 7^{1} thee have I seen to be just *before* me, 10^{9} a mighty hunter *before* י׳, Dt 24^{4} תּוֹעֵבָה לִ׳ י׳, v^{13} צְדָקָה לִ׳ י׳, 1 S 20^{1b} אָרוּר לִ׳ י׳ Jos 6^{26} 1 S 26^{19}, לְרָצוֹן לִ׳ י׳ acceptable *before* י׳, Lv 1^{3}+, ψ 19^{15}; 2 K 5^{1} a great man לִפְנֵי אֲדֹנָיו, Pr 14^{12} ψ 143^{2}; וַיִּיטַב לִ׳ (late syn. of earlier בְּעֵינֵי) +Ne 2$^{5.6}$ Est 5^{14}; טוֹב לִ׳ Ec 2^{26} 7^{26}; cf. also נָתַן לְרַחֲמִים לִפְנֵי, v. רַחֲמִים. (*h*) לִפְנֵי י׳, spec. of acts done with a solemn sense of י׳'s presence, often, but not always, at a sanctuary: Gn 27^{7} that I may eat and bless thee *before* י׳, before I die, Ex 18^{12} to eat bread *before* God, Dt 1^{45} ye wept *before* י׳, 6^{25} 12^{7} (to eat, so v^{18} 14$^{23.26}$ 15^{20}), v^{12} (rejoice, so v^{18} 27^{7} Is 9^{2}), Jos 18^{6} 24^{1} Ju 11^{11} 20$^{23.26}$ 21^{2} 1 S 7^{6} 10^{19} 11^{15} 12^{7} 15^{33} 23^{18} 2 S 5^{3} 7^{18} 21^{9}; and constantly in P, as Ex 16$^{9.33.34}$ Lv 1$^{5.11}$ 3$^{1.7}$ etc.; of residents in Jerus. Is 23^{18}. So in הָלַךְ לִ׳ י׳ 1 K 2^{4} al. (v. p. 234^{b} **c**).

b. In other phrases:—(*a*) עָמַד לִפְנֵי *to stand before*, i.e. *wait upon, be in attendance on*, Dt 1^{38} al. (v. עָמַד **1 e**). Simil. הָיָה לִפְנֵי 1 S 19^{7} (cf. 29^{8}), 2 K 5^{2}; עָבַד לִ׳ 2 S 16^{19}. (*b*) הִשְׁתַּחֲוָה לִפְנֵי *to bow down before* Gn 23^{12} Dt 26^{10} 2 K 18^{22} al. (v. sub שָׁחָה; also נָפַל **3 b**): so with הִתְפַּלֵּל *to pray* 1 S 1^{12}+; cf. הלך לפני 1 K 12^{30} 1 Ch 21^{30}. (*c*) *to be smitten* (נִגַּף) *before* a foe; v. נָגַף Niph. [contrast נוּס מִפְּנֵי: infr. **6 a**]. So with נָפַל 1 S 14^{13}; נָתַן (in helplessness or flight), esp. in Dt, as 1$^{8.21}$ 7$^{2.23}$ Jos 10^{12} 11^{6}+(Dr$^{Dt\ lxxxii}$): cf. Ju 4^{15} 2 S 5^{20} Is 45^{1} Je 1^{17}. (*d*) עָמַד לִפְנֵי *to stand* (make a stand) *before* (not quite so strong as ע׳ בִּפְנֵי, supr. **3**), Ex 9^{11} Ju 2^{14} 2 K 10^{4} Je 49^{19} ψ 76^{8} 147^{17} Na 1^{6}; so with הִתְיַצֵּב Dt 9^{2} Jos 1^{5} Jb 41^{2}, קוּם Jos 7$^{12.13}$. (*e*) in hostile sense (rare), יָצָא לִפְנֵי go forth *to face* 1 Ch 14^{8} 2 Ch 14^{9}. (*f*) שִׂים (נָתַן) לִפְנֵי, of food, to set or place *before*, Gn 18^{8} 24^{33}+. (*g*) נָתַן לִפְנֵי to *set before*, i.e. propound for acceptance or choice, usu. of laws (esp. Dt Je), Dt 4^{8} 11$^{26.32}$ 30$^{1.15.19}$ 1 K 9^{6} (D^{2}), Je 9^{12} 21^{8} 26^{4} 44^{10} Dn 9^{10}, cf. Ez 23^{24} (place at disposal of): so with שִׂים Ex 19^{7} 21^{1}.

c. With reference to *position:* (*a*) *in front of, before*, esp. with vbs. of motion (with which נֶגֶד is hardly used), Gn 32^{21} בַּמִּנְחָה הַהֹלֶכֶת לְפָנָי that goeth *before* me, 33^{14} the cattle אֲשֶׁר לְפָנַי, Ex 17^{5} 23^{20} etc.; in the description of a march or procession, Ex 13$^{21.22}$ Nu 10^{33} Is 52^{12} 58^{8}+; 2 S 3^{31} and wail *before* Abner (before his bier); of flocks before a shepherd Gn 32^{18}; of captives or booty driven before a conqueror 1 S 30^{20} (rd. וַיִּנְהֲגוּ לְפָנָיו We Dr), Is 8^{4} 40^{10}=62^{11} וּפְעֻלָּתוֹ לְפָנָיו his recompence (i.e. his newly-recovered people, regarded as his prize of war) *before* him, Am 9^{4} La 1$^{5.6}$. (*b*) of a leader, etc.=*at the head of*, Dt 10^{11} Ju 9^{39} 1 S 8^{20} Mi 1^{13} al.; cf. בא ויצא לפני (העם) Nu 27^{17} 1 S 18$^{13.16}$ 2 Ch 1^{10}; Ec 4^{16} *before* whom (at whose head) he was. (*c*) denoting superiority, *before, above*, Gn 48^{20} וַיָּשֶׂם את־אפרים לפני מנשה, Jb 34^{19}.

d. Of *places* (not very common): Ex 14^{2} *before* Pi-haḥiroth . . ., *before* Baal-ẓephon, Nu 33^{7b}, Gn 23^{17} אשר לִ׳ מַמְרֵא (usu. על פני מ׳: v. **7 a** *d*), 1 Ch 19^{7} Ne 8$^{1.3}$; *before* the temple, veil, altar, etc., Ex 16^{34}+ לִ׳ הָעֵדֻת, 30^{6}+ לִ׳ הַפָּרֹכֶת, 40$^{5.6}$ Nu 3^{38} 7^{10} al. (all P), 1 K 6^{21} 7^{49}+.

e. Of time, *before:* Am 1^{1} לפני הָרָעַשׁ *before* the earthquake, Gn 29^{26} 30^{30} לְפָנָי *before* me (i.e. before I came to thee), Ex 10^{14} לפניו לא היה כן *before* it there was not the like, Nu 13^{22} 1 K 16$^{25.30}$ מִכֹּל אֲשֶׁר לְפָנָיו, Is 43^{10} 48^{7} Pr 8^{25} Jb 15^{7} etc. Sq. inf., Gn 13^{10} לִפְנֵי שַׁחֵת י׳ *before* י׳'s destroying, etc., 27^{7} לִפְנֵי מוֹתִי, 36^{31} 1 S 9^{15}+. Once, in late Heb., לִפְנֵי מִזֶּה *before* this Ne 13^{4}.

f. *In the manner of, like* (rare and dub.), 1 S 1^{16} אַל־תִּתֵּן אֶת־אֲמָתְךָ לִפְנֵי בַּת־בְּלִיָּעַל *like* a worthless woman, Jb 3^{24} *like* my food, 4^{19} they are crushed *like* the moth (cf. Lat. *pro*).

5. מִלִּפְנֵי$_{_{27}}$ *from before:*—**a.** *from the presence of* (properly, from a position *before* a person or object: to be distinguished from מִפְּנֵי; v. **6**): (*a*) Gn 41^{46} ויצא יוסף מִלִּפְנֵי פ׳ *from before* Ph., 47^{10} 2 K 5^{27} 6^{32}+; מלִ׳ י׳ Gn 4^{6} Cain went forth *from before* י׳, Jon 1$^{3.10}$; spec. of the sanctuary, Lv 9^{24} ותצא אש מלפני י׳ (so 10^{2}), קֶצֶף Nu 17^{11} (cf. 2 Ch 19^{2}), with לָקַח etc. Lv 16^{12} Nu 17^{24} 20^{9}, 1 S 21^{7} the shew-bread that was removed *from before* י׳; *from before* a place 1 K 8^{54} Ezr 10^{6}

2 Ch 1[13] (*b*) of taking, etc, *from before* a person, Gn 23[4] to bury my dead *from before* me, v[8] Ex 36[3] Dt 17[18] וכתב לו משנה התורה הזאת מל׳ הכהנים *from* (the copy) *before* the priests, 28[31] נָזִל מלפניך. (*c*) with בקש Est 4[8] [cf מִן קֳדָם Dn 2[18]], and to express the idea of *proceeding* from a person, Est 1[19] [cf Dn 2[15]], Ec 10[5], 1 Ch 29[12] הָעשֶׁר והכבוד מלפניך (cf Acts 3[19]); ψ 17[2] מלפניך יצא משפטי (*d*) of cutting off, etc, *from before* לא־יִכָּרֵת לך איש לפני (cf לפני **a** *b*, *c*), Lv 22[3] 1 K 8[25] ׳י אַל־תַּשְׁלִיכֵנִי מִלְּפָנֶי, Je 31[36] 33[18] Is 48[19] ψ 51[13] מלפניך (cf **8 a**), Je 16[17] לא נִסְתְּרוּ מִלְּפָנַי, 18[23] Ne 3[37]. (*e*) of expelling *from before* an invader, Ex 23[28] Dt 9[4] 11[23] 31[3] + (but much less common than מפני)

†**b.** (Chiefly late) to express the *source* or *cause*, with the force of the ל weakened, in cases where the earlier language would have used מפני with vbs of fearing, 1 S 18[12] Ec 3[14] 8[12.13], 1 Ch 16[30] חִילוּ מלְּפָנָיו [|| ψ 96[9] מפניו], ψ 114[7], Est 7[6], 2 Ch 32[7] (+מפני); failing, etc, Is 57[16] ψ 97[5], being humbled, 1 K 21[29] (+מפני), 2 Ch 32[12.13] 34[27] [|| 2 K 22[19] מפני], 36[12], crying for help 1 S 8[18] [cf מפני Ex 3[7]], singing 1 Ch 16[33] [|| ψ 96[13] לפני], fleeing, 19[18] [|| 2 S 10[18] מפני] †**c.** of time, once, = לִפְנֵי Ec 1[10] —With the later usages of מל׳, cf מִן קֳדָם in BAram and 𝔗 (Dr Sm lxx-lxxi lxxiii), v also Ko[ii 320]

6. מפני *from the face* or *presence of*, *from before*, Ex 14[19] וַיִּסַּע עמוד הענן מפניהם removed *from before* them, Is 30[11] Ho 11[2], so **a.** (oft with suggestion of causation (v מן **2 d, e, f**), *because of*, *for fear of* [so AV RV Ju 9[21] 1 S 21[11] 23[26] Je 35[11.11] 37[11] 41[9] 50[16]]) after vbs of hiding Gn 3[8] 4[14] Is 2[10] (cf v[19.21]), and esp of escaping, Ju 9[21] (Thes 'bene 𝔅 *ob metum A*'), 1 S 18[11] 19[10] 23[26], or fleeing, Ex 4[3] 14[25] 1 S 17[24] + oft (v נוס and בָּרַח), and expelling, destroying, etc Ex 23[30] אֲגָרְשֶׁנּוּ מִפָּנֶיךָ I will expel them *from before* thee, 34[11.24] אוריש גוים מִפָּנֶיךָ (v הוריש), Lv 18[24] Dt 8[20] Am 2[9] ψ 89[24] + oft (as though clearing the way for Israel, for Israel's sake cf Is 63[12] בוקע מַיִם מפניהם, Jos 2[10] 4[23]) Pregn Is 17[9] כַּעֲזוּבַת . . . אשר עזבו מפני בני ישׂר׳ which they forsook (fleeing) *from before*, etc **b.** implying causation more distinctly, ψ 9[4] יאבדו מפניך perish *from before* thee or *at thy presence*, Dt 7[20] very oft with vbs of fearing, as חיל, יגר, גור, ירא, ערץ, פחד, קוץ Ex 9[30] Nu 22[3] Dt 1[17] Je 5[22] etc (mostly when the object inspiring fear is a person: when it is a thing, מן alone is preferred, but see Dt 5[5] 9[19]), of being alarmed or dismayed Gn 45[3] Jos 2[9] Je 1[17] Jb 23[15], etc, of humbling oneself Ex 10[3] Ju 11[33] +, with other words, to indicate the *external ground* of an action or effect, as הַס מִפָּנָיו be silent *at* (i e. *because of*) his presence Zp 1[7] Hb 2[20], Ju 5[5] the mts. flowed מפני י׳ *at the presence of* ׳י, Is 63[19] Je 4[26] Na 1[5], ψ 68[3] as wax melteth מפני אש; Dt 20[19], Is 19[1], 26[17] כן היינו מפניך so were we *through thy presence* (more than לפניך,—implying that their state was *due to* ׳י); קום מפני to rise up *at the presence of* Gn 31[35] Lv 19[32] (N.B In **a, b,** freq rendered *before* in AV RV, and so confused with לפני, but the מן retains always its full force in the Heb) **c.** of the *cause*, whether nearer or more remote (*a*) Gn 6[13] מָלְאָה הָאָרֶץ חָמָס מפניהם *because of* them (i. e. occasioned by them), 27[4] I loathe my life *because of* the daughters of Heth, 36[7] the land could not support them *because of* their cattle, 41[31] 47[13] Ex 3[7] their cry *by reason of* their taskmasters, 8[20] תִּשָּׁחֵת הָאָרֶץ מפני הֶעָרֹב, 9[11] Jos 2[11] 23[3] Ju 2[18] 6[6] 1 K 5[17] 8[11] + oft; Is 10[27] (RVm), Je 15[17] ψ 38[4.6], etc, Je 4[4] + מִפְּנֵי רֹעַ מַעַלְלֵיכֶם *by reason of* the evil of your doings, 7[12] 9[6] 13[17] 14[16] 23[9] + oft (*b*) stating the reason for which a thing is *not* done (Lat. *prae*), 1 K 8[11] Jb 37[19]. †(*c*) with אֲשֶׁר as a **conj.**, twice, *because that*, Ex 19[18] Je 44[23]—Nu 33[8] v פי הַחִירֹת

7 עַל־פְּנֵי (cf Ph על פנ, עלת פנ, Lzb[352]) has different meanings according to the different senses of the noun and the prep —

a. From the sense of *face* or *front*: (*a*) *in front of* (more definite and distinct than לפני) ψ 18[43] as dust *before* the wind (cf לפני 35[5] 83[14] +), Gn 32[22] the present passed on עַל־פָּנָיו *in front of* him, Ex 33[19] אעביר כל־טובי על־פניך, 2 S 15[18.23] (read על־פניו. v. Dr), Jb 4[15], = *in the sight of*, Lv 10[3] ועל־פני כל העם אכבד, Je 6[7] עַל־פָּנַי תָּמִיד חֳלִי וּמַכָּה, 13[26] (cf Na 3[5]), ψ 9[20] יִשָּׁפְטוּ גוים אם־לא על־פניך *before* thee defiantly, Jb 1[11] על־פניך יְבָרֲכֶךָּ will renounce thee *to thy face*, 6[28] ועל־פניכם אם אֲכַזֵּב, 21[31], to die *in the presence of* any one (= in his lifetime) † Gn 11[28] Nu 3[4] (*b*) *before*, to the exclusion of another, i e. *in preference to*, Dt 21[16], and perh (Ew §217 h) Ex 20[3] (Dt 5[7]) לא יהיה לך אלהים אחרים על־פני (Thes al. as c) (*c*) *in addition to*, Jb 16[14] פֶּרֶץ עַל־פְּנֵי־פָרֶץ יִפְרְצֵנִי. (*d*) of localities, *in front of*, mostly (but not always v. GFM[Ju., p 351]) = *east of*, 1 K 6[3] the porch *in front of*, etc, v[3] 7[6] 8[8] 2 Ch 3[17] Ez 42[8], Gn 16[12] על־פני כל־אחיו ישכן (cf. 25[18b]), perh (Di al.) with collateral idea of defiance; עַל־פ׳ מַמְרֵא 23[19] (50[13]), Ex 16[14], oft in . . . אשר על־פני Gn 25[9] (49[30]), מצרים v[18a] (Jos 13[3] 1 S 15[7]), Nu 21[11] 33[7.8], ירחו Dt 32[49] (34[1]), Jos 13[3.25] 15[8] (18[16]), 17[7] 18[14] 19[11] Ju 16[3] 1 S 24[3] (prob), 26[1.3] 2 S 2[24] 1 K

11^{7} (the Mt. of Olives, E. of Jerus.; so 2 K 23^{13} Zc 14^{4}), 17$^{3.5}$.—Gn 1^{20} let fowl fly על־פני רקיע השמים *in front of* the firmament of heaven, viz. as looked up to from below, i. e. between the firmament and the earth. (*e*) with vbs. implying direction, *over towards*, Gn 18^{16} וישקף על־פני סדם, 19^{28}; Nu 21^{20} (23^{28}) נשקפה על־פני הישימן *overlooking;* to sprinkle *against the front of* Lv 16^{14}; in a hostile sense (rare), Na 2^{2} עָלָה מֵפִיץ עַל־פָּנַיִךְ, ψ 21^{13} Ez 32^{10}.

b. From the sense of *surface*, Gn 1^{2} על־פני תהום *upon the face* of the deep, Ex 16^{14} על־פ׳ המדבר: oft. in the phrases על־פני (כל) הארץ Gn 1^{29} 7^{3}+, and (more freq.) על־פני האדמה *on the face* of the ground 6^{1} 7^{23} etc.; על פני השדה Lv 17^{5} Nu 19^{16} 1 S 14^{25}+; after vbs. of motion, 11^{4} lest we be scattered *over the face* of all the earth, v$^{8.9}$ Ex 32^{20} Lv 14^{7} (v^{53} אל), Is 18^{2} 19^{8} Am 5^{8} Ez 32^{4} Jb 5^{10}+.

8. מֵעַל־פְּנֵי: **a.** *from before the face of*, Gn 23^{3} Abraham rose up מֵעַל פְּנֵי מֵתוֹ *from before* his dead, i.e. from mourning before or beside it; מֵעַל פני (פניו)+ *from before my* (*his*) *face*, oft. in K Je of the rejection of Isr. or the temple, as with שִׁלַּח 1 K 9^{7} (‖ 2 Ch 7^{20} השליך), Je 15^{1}, השליך 2 K 13^{23} 24^{20} (Je 52^{3}), Je 7^{15}, נטשׁ Je 23^{39}, הסיר 2 K 17$^{18.23}$ 23^{27} 24^{3} Je 32^{31}. **b.** *from off the surface of*, oft. in the phrase מֵעַל פְּנֵי הָאֲדָמָה, with verbs of cutting off, removing, expelling, etc., †Gn 4^{14} 6^{7} 7^{4} 8^{8} Ex 32^{12} Dt 6^{15} 1 S 20^{15} 1 K 9^{7} 13^{34} Am 9^{8} Je 28^{16} Zp 1$^{2.3}$.

†פְּנִ֫ימָה **adv.** (ה loc.) **1. towards the** (**in-**) **side. 2. within** (lit. *faceward*, fr. point of view of one entering by opposite door);—of a building, usu. temple: **1.** after vb. of motion Lv 10^{18} 2 Ch 29^{18}, and (after הִגִּיד) 2 K 7^{11}, also לִפ׳ Ez 41^{3} 2 Ch 29^{16}. **2.** פ׳ 1 K 6^{18}, also לִפ׳ v^{30}, so read also v^{29} (for MT מִלִּפְנִים, v. Kmp^{Kau} Kit Benz), Ez 40$^{16.16}$, also ψ 45^{14} MT, i.e. within the house, but Krochm Gr Che al. (plausibly) פְּנִינִים, q.v.; מִפּ׳ 1 K 6$^{19.21}$=2 Ch 3^{4}.

פְּנִימִי$_{32}$ **adj. inner**;—פ׳ 1 K 6^{27}+; f. פְּנִימִית v^{36}+; mpl. פְּנִימִים 1 Ch 28^{11}; fpl. פְּנִימִיּוֹת 2 Ch 4^{22};—alw. c. art., and alw. of parts of building, usu. temple: 1 K 6^{27} 7^{12}+; esp. Ez 8$^{3.16}$ 10^{3}+ 21 t. 40–46; as subst. בַּפְּנִימִי 41^{17} *on the inside* (but dub., v. Co al.); אֶל־הַפְּנִימִית 42^{4} *toward the inside* (del. 𝔊 𝔖 Co Toy al.).

לִפְנַי 1 K 6^{17}, Ew^{§164a} Ke as adj., *anterior*, but rd., with 𝔊, לִפְנֵי הַדְּבִיר Th Sta Kit al.

†פְּנוּאֵל **n.pr.** (*face of God*, cf. GFM Ju 8, 8; late As. *Panîli* Hilpr$^{Univ. Pa. Exp. ix. 68}$);—Φανουηλ, but in Gn εἶδος (τοῦ) Θεοῦ: **1. loc.** E. of Jordan, near Jabboḳ Gn 32^{32} Ju 8$^{8.8.9.17}$ 1 K 12^{25}=פְּנִיאֵל Gn 32^{31}: site unknown; v. esp. Paine$^{Bib. Sac. 1878, 481 ff.}$ **2. m. a.** in Judah 1 Ch 4^{4}. **b.** in Benjamin 1 Ch 8^{25} Qr (Kt פניאל).

יְפֻנֶּה$_{16}$ **n.pr.m.** (on form cf. Lag$^{BN 134}$);—**1.** father of Caleb Nu 13^{6} 14^{6} Jos 14$^{6.13}$ 1 Ch 4^{15}+ 10 t., Ιεφοννη. **2.** Asherite 1 Ch 7^{38}, Ιφινα, A Ιεφιηλ, 𝔊L Ιεφοννη.

פִּנְחָס v. פִּינְחָס. פְּנִיאֵל, פְּנוּאֵל v. פנה.

פניים v. פְּנִינִים. פָּנִים, etc., v. פנה.

פנן (√of foll.; appar. ‖ form of פנה).

פִּנָּה$_{28}$ **n.f. corner**;—abs. פ׳ 2 K 14^{13}+, cstr. פִּנַּת Je 31^{40}+; sf. פִּנָּתָהּ Jb 38^{9}, פִּנָּהּ Pr 7^{8} (Ges ^{§91e}); pl. abs. פִּנּוֹת Zp 1^{16} 2 Ch 26^{15}, פִּנִּים Zc 14^{10}; cstr. פִּנּוֹת 1 K 7^{34}+, etc.;—**1. a.** *corner*, of square objects 1 K 7^{34}+v^{30} (rd. פִּנֹּתָיו for פַּעֲמֹתָיו, cf. Kit), Ex 27^{2} 38^{2} Ez 43^{20}, 45^{19}; of house Jb 1^{19}, roof Pr 7^{12} 21^{9}=25^{24}; אֶבֶן פִּנָּה Je 51^{26} i.e. a corner-stone; אֶבֶן פ׳ of earth Jb 38^{9}; cf. (fig.) ψ 118^{22}, and (אבן om.) Is 28^{16}; פ׳=street-*corner* 2 Ch 28^{24}. **b.** specif. of wall of Jerus., Ne 3^{24} (in SE.), v$^{31.32}$ (NE.); שַׁעַר הַפּ׳ 2 K 14^{13}+‖ 2 Ch 25^{23} 𝔊 𝔖 𝔗 and most (for MT (ש׳ הַפּוֹנֶה), + (v. שַׁעַר); הַפִּנּוֹת appar. with battlements 2 Ch 26^{15}; of cities in gen. הַפּ׳ הַגְּבֹהוֹת Zp 1^{16}; of the nations 3^{6}. **2.** fig. of chief, ruler as *corner* (support or defence), Ju 20^{2} 1 S 14^{38} Is 19^{13} (rd. perhaps pl.); Zc 10^{4} (+ יָתֵד q.v.).

†פְּנִינִים **n.**[**f.**]**pl. corals** (? as *branching*, cf. Ar. فَنَنٌ *branch* of tree; so Mich Thes al.; >*pearls* Bo$^{Hieroz. 601}$ Di^{Jb} after Ra al.);—פ׳ fig. of value Pr 20^{15}; usu. מִפּ׳, comp. Jb 28^{18} Pr 3^{15} (Kt מפניים), 8^{11} 31^{10} (all of value), La 4^{7} (of red colour); + ψ 45^{14} (perh.; for פְּנִימָה, q. v.).

†פְּנִנָּה **n.pr.f.** (prop. sg. of foregoing ?) wife of Elkanah 1 S 1$^{2.2.4}$, Φεννανα.

†[פִּנֵּק] **vb. Pi. indulge, pamper** (NH Pi.; cf. Ecclus 14^{16}; Ar. فَنَّقَ II.; Aram. פנק, ܦܢܩ Pa.);—Pt. מְפַנֵּק Pr 29^{21} *one pampering* a servant.

[פַּס] v. פסס. אֶפֶס ד׳ פַּס דַּמִּים v. ד׳.

†**פסג** **vb. Pi.** dub.; if correct, **pass between** (NH Pi. *split, cut off*, also=BH; 𝔗 פְּסַג *cut in two*);—*Imv.* mpl. פַּסְּגוּ ψ 48^{14} *pass between* her palaces; Gr Che פַּקְּדוּ; Du conj. 'possibly' פִּסְעוּ *step*, cp. [NH פָּסַע] Aram. פְּסַע *step*, cf. [פָּשַׂע].

†**פִּסְגָּה n.pr mont. Pisgah** (prob *cleft*, fr a natural feature of mt, Di Dt 3 17),—alw 'הַפּ: ראש הַפּ' Nu 21^{20} 23^{14} Dt 3^{27} 34^{1}, אַשְׁדֹּת הַפּ' 3^{17} 4^{49} Jos 12^{3} 13^{20}, mt in Moab, on NE shore of Dead Sea, exact loc unknown (cf *Fešḥa* as a cliff on NW shore, v Di Nu 21,20), Φασγα Dt 3^{17} +, τ. λαξευτήν 4^{49}, Λελαξευμένου Nu 21^{20} +

[פִּסָּה] v פסס

†I **פָּסַח vb. pass or spring over**,—**Qal** *Pf.* 3 ms 'פ Ex 12^{27}, 'וּפ consec v^{23} (J), 1 s וּפָסַחְתִּי v^{13} (P), all c עַל, of 'י *passing over* (sparing) houses of Isr; *Inf abs* פָּסוֹחַ Is 31^{5} *a passing over* (sc. עַל־יְרוּשָׁלָםִ)

†**פֶּסַח n.m. passover** (usu (Thes and most) from I פסח, with reference to Ex 12^{13} etc, Reuss Gesch AT § 58 *passing over* into new year, Schaefer Pasah Mazzoth (1900) 316 cp As *pašāḫu, soothe, placate* [deity], < *be soothed*, Pi trans, Jen ZA iv (1889) 275 Zim Bab Rel i (1896) Gloss. ii (1899) 92, Schwally Idiot 124 fr II פסח, of sacred dance),—abs 'פ Ex 12^{11} +, פָּסַח v^{21} +, pl פְּסָחִים 2 Ch 30^{17} + 3 t,—**1.** *sacrifice of passover*, involving communion-meal, hence a species of peace-offering (cf זבח **II. 2**), זֶבַח פ' הוּא לי' Ex 12^{27} (J), cf v^{11} (P); זָבַח פ' Dt 16$^{2.5.6}$, אכל הפ' 2 Ch 30^{18}, the special feature lay in the application of blood to homes to consecrate them, cf sim Bab rite of purification Zim ib ii 126-7. **2.** *the animal victim of the passover* שחט פ' Ex 12^{21} (J) 2 Ch 30^{15} 35$^{1.6.11}$ Ez 6^{20}, cf 2 Ch 30^{17}; בשל הפ' באש 2 Ch 35^{13}, לַפְּסָחִים 2 Ch 35$^{7.8.9}$ [Passover animals (cf Br Hex 206) were צאן *flock* Ex 12^{21} (J), שֶׂה v$^{3.4.5}$, incl. כֶּבֶשׂ and עֵז v^{5} (P), צֹאן וּבקר Dt 16^{2}; large numbers of all these (שֶׂה not used) in Josiah's passover, acc to 2 Ch 35$^{7.8.9}$, but evident mingling of whole burnt-offerings for the passover with special passover victim] **3.** *festival of the passover* חג הפ' Ex 34^{25} (J), 'פ(ה) Lv 23^{5} Nu 28^{16} 33^{3} Jos 5^{11} (P) Ez 45^{21}; חֻקַּת הפ' Ex 12^{43} Nu 9$^{12.14}$ (P), עשה פ' Ex 12^{48} Nu 9$^{2.4.5.6.10.13.14}$ Jos 5^{10} (P) Dt 16^{1} 2 K 23$^{21.22.23}$ 2 Ch 30$^{1.2.5}$ 35$^{1.16.17.18.18.19}$ Ezr 6^{19}; it was held in month הָאָבִיב Dt 16^{1}, בָּעֶרֶב v^{6}, on 14th day Jos 5^{10} (P), of 1st month Ez 45^{21}; בין הערבים (Ex 12^{6}) Lv 23^{5} Nu 9^{5} (P); if impossible at that time, then on 14th of 2nd month Nu 9$^{10.12}$. [No ref to פֶּסַח in E, J subordinates it to מַצּוֹת (the great feast of JE), in D it predom. over מצות; P makes it first in importance (Br Hex 195 f)]

†**תִּפְסַח n.pr.loc.** on Euphrates (prob *ford* (though Lag BN 131 doubts), Lewy Fremdw 146 cp Λάμψακος (on Bosphorus), expl as לְפֶּסַח);—1 K 5^{4}, NE limit of Sol.'s dominion; = Gk Θαψακος Xen Anab. i. 4 etc, identif. with *Kal'at Dibse*, at the great easterly bend of the river, c Lat. 35° 55′ N, Long 38° 20′ E, JPPeters Nation, May 23, 1889, Nippur i 96 ff

†II **[פָּסַח] vb. limp** (Thes sub I. 'פ, but dub, Ar فَسَخَ is *dislocate;* acc. to Gerber 73 II 'פ is denom. fr פסח [and this sub I 'פ?]),—**Qal** *Pt* pl פֹּסְחִים עַל־שְׁתֵּי הַסְּעִפִּים 1 K 18^{21} fig (v. [סְעִפָּה]) **Niph.** *Impf.* 3 ms וַיִּפֹּל וַיִּפָּסֵחַ 2 S 4^{4} *and he fell and was made limping* (lame) **Pi.** *Impf* 3 mpl וַיְפַסְּחוּ עַל־הַמִּזְבֵּחַ 1 K 18^{26} *they went limping* (along by the altar), i e. prob in their dance, v Kit Pietschm Phön 220 (Gr ויפסעו [= וַיִּפְשְׂעוּ] *stepped*).

†**פָּסֵחַ n.pr.m.** (*limper*),—**1.** in Judah 1 Ch 4^{12}, Βεσσηε, Φεσση, etc **2.** head of post-ex family Ezr 2^{49} = Ne 7^{51}, Φισον, etc, 𝔊L Φασσα **3.** father of wall-builder Ne 3^{6}, Φασεκ, Φεσσε

†**פִּסֵּחַ adj. lame**,—abs. 'פ 2 S 9^{13} +; pl פִּסְחִים 5^{6} +,—as attrib Lv 21^{18} (+ עִוֵּר); pred. 2 S 19^{27}, 9^{13} פ' שתי רַגְלָיו *lame as to both his feet;* cf also (of animal) Dt 15^{21} (+ עִוֵּר), as subst. 2 S 5$^{6.8.8}$ Je 31^{8} Mal 1$^{8.13}$ Jb 29^{15} (all + עִוֵּר), also Is 33^{23} 35^{6} Pr 26^{7}

†**פָּסַךְ** (van d H פָּסֵךְ) **n.pr.m.** Asherite 1 Ch 7^{33}, Βαισηχι, A Φεσηχι, 𝔊L Φασεχ

†**פָּסַל vb. hew, hew into shape** (NH Pi. *hew off* boughs, Aram. פְּסַל, ܦܣܠ = BH; Nab. פסלא *stone-cutter*),—**Qal** *Pf.* 3 ms. sf. פְּסָלוֹ Hb 2^{18}, *Impf.* 3 ms וַיִּפְסֹל Ex 34^{4}, etc, *Imv.* ms פְּסָל־ Ex 34^{1} Dt 10^{1},—*hew out* stone tablets Ex 34$^{1.4}$ Dt 10$^{1.3}$; building-stones 1 K 5^{32}; c cogn acc (sf referring to פֶּסֶל) Hb 2^{18}.

פֶּסֶל n.m. Hb 2, 18 **idol, image**,—abs 'פ Ju 17^{3} +, פָּסֶל Is 42^{17}, cstr. פֶּסֶל Ju 18^{31} +, sf פִּסְלִי Is 48^{5}, etc; pl supplied by פְּסִילִים, v. foll.;—*idol*, as likeness of man or animal Ex 20^{4} = Dt 5^{8}, Dt 4$^{16.23.25}$, also 27^{15} 2 K 21^{7} 2 Ch 33^{7} Is 42^{17} 44^{9} 48^{5} Na 1^{14} Hb 2^{18} (of wood or stone, cf. v^{19}); of metal Ju 17$^{3.4}$ + 6 t 18 (cf. GFM), Is 40^{19} 44^{10} (c נָסַךְ), Je 10^{14} 51^{17} (c. צורף); of wood Is 40^{20} 44$^{15.17}$ 45^{20}.

[פָּסִיל] n.m. Dt 7, 25 id;—pl (פֶּסֶל serving as sg) פסילים Ju 3^{19} +; פסלים Ho 11^{2} +; cstr. פְּסִילֵי Je 51^{47} +, sf פְּסִילֶיךָ Mi 5^{12}, etc.,—*idols*, Ho 11^{2} Is 10^{10} + 10 t., + (of wood, c. שָׂרַף) Dt

7[5.25], so (c. נֵרַע) 12[3], of stone Is 21[9] (c. שִׁבֵּר), Ju 3[19.26] (cf GFM), stone or metal Mi 1[7] 2 Ch 34[7] (כִּתַּת), cf. v[3.4]; (sheathed with) silver Is 30[22].

I **פסס** (√of foll.; perh. cp פשה *spread;* cf. Ph. (Pu) פס *tablet;* Aram. פַּסָּא, ܦܣܐ, = BH)

† **[פַּס] n.[m.] flat of hand or foot** (palm, sole),—only כְּתֹנֶת פַּסִּים tunic reaching to palms and soles (v כ׳) Gn 37[3.23.32] 2 S 13[18.19] (cf. Dr).

† **[פִּסָּה] n.f.** dub, if correct, prob **abundance, plenty** (√ prop *spread out*);—cstr. פִּסַּת בַּר ψ 72[16], Lag Gr Che al read שִׁפְעַת.

† II **[פָּסַס] vb. disappear, vanish** (si vera l, cf As *pasâsu, do away, blot out* (esp sins)),—**Qal** *Pf.* 3 pl. פַּסּוּ מִן ψ 12[2] the faithful *have vanished* (Che Dr) *from* (among) .. men; Lag[Proph. Chald xlvi] Gr We Du read אָפֵס (Is 16[4]).

† **פִּסְפָּה n.pr.m.** Asherite 1 Ch 7[38], Φασφα(ι)

† **[פָּעָה] vb. groan** (onomatop. acc to Thes; NH Hiph. *bleat,* so Ar دعى، نعى Dozy; Aram. פְּעָא, ܦܥܐ *bleat*),—*Impf* 1 s. כַּיּוֹלֵדָה אֶפְעֶה Is 42[14] (of י׳ straining himself to deliver Isr, + [נשׁם] אשׁם, [אֶשְׁאַף]—[אֶפַע] Is 41[24], v. p. 67

† **אֶפְעֶה n.[m.]** a kind of **viper** (Thes 'a flando et sibilando,' cf Ar أفعى *viper,* Eth አፍዖት: *id*),—א׳ Is 30[6] 59[5], לְשׁוֹן א׳ Jb 20[16].

† **פָּעוּ, פָּעִי n pr.loc.** in Edom, פָּעוּ Gn 36[39] = פָּעִי 1 Ch 1[50]; Φογωρ, 𝔊L Ch Φαουα

פָּעַל[57] **vb. do, make** (poet. for עָשָׂה) (NH פּוֹעֵל *workman,* cf. JAram; Ph. פעל = BH (oft), Ar فَعَلَ *id;* OAram. פעל; Syr. in der. spec. and deriv);—**Qal** *Pf.* 3 ms Dt 32[27]+, פָּעַל אֵל Nu 23[23], 2 ms פָּעַלְתָּ Ex 15[17]+, etc., *Impf.* 3 ms יִפְעַל Jb 22[17]+; 2 ms. תִּפְעָל־ 35[6], etc, *Inf cstr* לִפְעָלָם Jb 37[12] (v infr.), *Pt act.* פֹּעֵל ψ 15[2]+, pl cstr. פֹּעֲלֵי 5[6]+, etc;—**1.** *do.* **a.** of God, c acc (abstr.) Nu 23[23] Dt 32[27] Jb 33[29], יְשׁוּעוֹת ψ 74[12], + לְ pers. ψ 31[20] 68[29] Is 26[12] Jb 22[17]; c. acc. cogn פֹּעַל ψ 44[2] Hb 1[5]; acc. om Is 43[13], cf. 41[4] **b.** of men, c acc. ψ 11[3] Jb 11[8], + לְ pers (God) 7[20], + בְּ pers. (God) 35[6]; esp. of doing evil, שֶׁקֶר Ho 7[1], עָוֶל Jb 34[32], עוֹלָה 36[23] ψ 58[3] 119[3], אָוֶן Pr 30[20], esp פֹּעֲלֵי אָוֶן Ho 6[8] Is 31[2] Jb 31[3] 34[8.22] ψ 5[6] + 15 t. ψ, Pr 10[29] 21[15], פֹּעֲלֵי רָע Mi 2[1], rarely of doing right, c acc. מִשְׁפָּטוֹ Zp 2[3], צֶדֶק ψ 15[2]. **c.** of clouds, c. acc. Jb 37[12] (disregarding ֿ). **2.** *make.* **a.** of God, c acc. concr. Ex 15[17]; + לְ rei Pr 16[4], לְ of 2nd obj. ψ 7[14]; פֹּעֲלִי Jb 36[3] *my Maker* **b.** of man, c. acc. concr. Is 44[12.15], acc om. 44[12] ψ 7[14].—Is 1[31] v פֹּעַל.

פֹּעַל[37] **n.m.**[Pr 20.11] **doing, deed, work** (poet. and late, nearly = מַעֲשֶׂה),—פ׳ abs. Hb 1[5] ψ 44[2], cstr. Dt 33[11]+, sf. פָּעֳלוֹ 32[4]+, פֹּעֲלוֹ Is 1[31] (Kö[II 1,35,493] Ges[§93q], v. infr.), Je 22[13], פָּעָלְכֶם Is 41[24], etc; pl פְּעָלִים 2 S 23[20] 1 Ch 11[22];—**1.** *deed, thing done* · **a.** of God, פָּעֳלוֹ his work in providence Dt 32[4] Is 5[12] Jb 36[24]; in deliverance ψ 44[2] (as acc cogn.), 77[13]+5 t., in judgment 64[10] 95[9], as acc cogn Hb 1[5] **b.** of false gods Is 41[24] **c.** of men, daily toil Jb 24[5] ψ 104[23]; specif. act Ru 2[12], פ׳ יָדָיו of sacrificing Dt 33[11]; pl of *achievements* 2 S 23[20] = 1 Ch 11[22]; action as having moral quality Jb 34[11] Pr 20[11] 24[12.29], evil implied Je 25[14] 50[29] Jb 36[9] ψ 28[4], פ׳ כַּפָּיו 9[17]; פ׳ חָמָס Is 59[6], good action Pr 21[8] **2.** *work, thing made:* **a.** by hands of God Is 45[9.11] (of men) **b.** by man Is 1[31] (i e prob. his idol Ges Che[Comm] Di al, > read פֹּעֲלוֹ Lag[Sem i. 5] Sta[ZAW iii (1883). 12 f]). **3.** *wages of work* Je 22[13] Jb 7[2] **4.** *acquisition* of treasures Pr 21[6].

† **[פְּעֻלָּה] n.f. work, recompence** (poet. and late),—cstr. פְּעֻלַּת Lv 19[13]+, sf. פְּעֻלָּתִי Is 49[4], etc., pl. cstr פְּעֻלּוֹת ψ 17[4], ־לֹת 28[5];—**1.** *work.* **a.** pl. *deeds of* י׳ ψ 28[5]. **b.** of men, ψ 17[4] (pl.), toil, suffering Je 31[16], good action 2 Ch 15[7], wicked Is 65[7], פ׳ שָׁקֶר Pr 11[18]. **2.** *wages* (as earned by work) Lv 19[13] Pr 10[16] (‖ תְּבוּאָה), Ez 29[20], *reward* (from י׳) Is 49[4] 61[8]; prob fig. of people won back by י׳ in warfare 40[10] 62[11] (‖ שָׂכָר), of punishment, ψ 109[20].

† **פְּעֻלְּתַי n.pr.m.** Levite 1 Ch 26[5], Ιαφθοσλααθι, A Φολλαθι, 𝔊L Φελλαθι

† **[מִפְעָל] n.[m.] work, thing made** (by י׳),—pl. sf. מִפְעָלָיו Pr 8[22].

† **[מִפְעָלָה] n.[f.] deed** (of י׳);—pl. cstr. מִפְעֲלוֹת י׳ ψ 46[9], מ׳ אֱלֹהִים 66[5].

† **[פָּעַם] vb. thrust, impel** (prob orig. *strike, hit,* v deriv, and Ph. פעם *foot*),—**Qal** *Inf cstr.* sf לְפַעֲמוֹ Ju 13[25] the spirit of י׳ began *to impel him.* **Niph.** *be disturbed, Pf.* 1 s. נִפְעַמְתִּי ψ 77[5], *Impf.* 3 fs. וַתִּפָּעֶם רוּחוֹ Gn 41[8] Dn 2[3]; so **Hithp.** *Impf.* 3 fs. וַתִּתְפָּעֶם רוּחוֹ Dn 2[1].

פַּעַם[118] **n.f.**[Ez 6,28] (masc. only Ju 16[28] [text suspicious, v GFM Albr[ZAW xvi (1896). 76] Kö[Synt. § 248 m]], 2 S 23[8] [< Qr fem.], 1 K 7[30] [crpt, v. infr.]) **beat,**

foot, anvil, occurrence;—abs. פ׳ Gn 2^{23}+; פַּעַם 46^{30}+; du. פַּעֲמַיִם Gn 27^{36}+, etc.; pl. פְּעָמִים 33^{3}+; also (concr.) ‹ str. פַּעֲמֵי Ju 5^{28}+; sf. פְּעָמַי ψ 57^{7} 119^{133}, etc.; פַּעֲמֹתָיו (only **1 c**) Ex 25^{12} + 2 t.;—**1. a.** poet., *hoof-beat* Ju 5^{28}; late, of human *footfall, footstep*, fig. ψ 17^{5} (‖ אֲשֻׁרַי), 119^{133}; וְיָשֵׂם לְדֶרֶךְ פְּעָמָיו 85^{14}. **b.** *foot*, fig., 57^{7} 58^{11} 74^{3} 140^{5} Pr 29^{5}; lit. Is 26^{6} (‖ רֶגֶל), Ct 7^{2}; בְּכַף פ׳ 2 K 19^{24} = Is 37^{25}. **c.** *foot*, of ark Ex 25^{12} 37^{3} (P).—פַּעֲמֹתָיו 1 K 7^{30} read פִּנֹּתָיו (cf. v^{34}). **2.** = *anvil* (struck by hammer) Is 41^{7}. **3.** *occurrence, time* (orig. *stroke, beat*): **a.** פ׳ אַחַת [אֶחָת] *one time, once* Jos $6^{3.11.14}$ (JE), 10^{42} (D) + 3 t. + 2 S 23^{8} Qr (> Kt אחד); פַּעֲמַיִם *twice* Gn 41^{32} + 6 t.; פ׳ Na 1^{9} *second time;* אַרְבַּע פ׳ Ne 6^{4} *four times;* חָמֵשׁ אוֹ שֵׁשׁ פ׳ 2 K 13^{19}, cf. פ׳ חֲמִישִׁית Ne 6^{5}; also c. שֶׁבַע, שָׁלשׁ, q.v.; (זֶה) עֶשֶׂר פ׳ Nu 14^{22} (JE) Ne 4^{6} Jb 19^{3}, all indef. = over and over; indef. also פַּעַם וּשְׁתַּיִם Ne 13^{20} *once and* [i.e. or] *twice;* פַּעֲמַיִם שָׁלוֹשׁ Jb 33^{29} *twice* (or) *thrice;* אֶלֶף פ׳ 2 S 24^{3} = 1 Ch 21^{3}, מֵאָה פְּעָמִים Dt 1^{11}; פ׳ רַבּוֹת ψ 106^{43} Ec 7^{22}; עַד־כַּמֶּה פְעָמִים 1 K 22^{16} = 2 Ch 18^{15}. **b.** כְּפַעַם־בְּפַעַם *as time on time*, i.e. as formerly, as usual, Nu 24^{1} (E) Ju 16^{20} $20^{30.31}$ 1 S 3^{10} (cf. Dr) 20^{25}. **c.** (גַּם) בַּפַּעַם הַזֹּאת *at this repetition* (this time) also Ex 8^{28} 9^{14} (J) + 3 t.; גַּם בַּפ׳ הַהוּא Dt 9^{19} 10^{10}. **d.** הַפַּעַם (Hex only J): (1) = *this once* Gn 18^{32}, אַךְ הַפ׳ Ex 10^{17} Ju 6^{39}, רַק־הַפ׳ v^{39}, אַךְ הַפ׳ הַזֶּה 16^{28} (הַזֶּה dub., v. supr.); (2) = *now at length* Gn 2^{23} $29^{34.35}$ 30^{20} 46^{30} Ju 15^{3} 16^{18}, cf. also Ex 9^{27} *now at length* (it is clear that) *I have sinned.* **e.** פַּעַם . . . פַּעַם Pr 7^{12} *now . . . now, at one time . . . at another.*

† פַּעֲמֹן **n.[m.]** **bell**, on high-p.'s robe (from its *stroke, beat*);—פ׳ abs. Ex $39^{26.26}$; cstr. פ׳ זָהָב $28^{34.34}$; pl. הַפַּעֲמֹנִים 39^{25}, cstr. פַּעֲמֹנֵי זָהָב 28^{33} 39^{25}.

צָפְנַת פ׳ v. פַּעְנֵחַ.

† [פָּעַר] **vb. open wide** (the mouth) (NH rarely = BH, usu. *open* bowels, go to stool; cf. JAram. פְּעַר; Ar. فَغَرَ and Syr. ܦܥܪ = BH, ܦܥܪܐ *chasm*);—**Qal** *Pf.* of voracious greed, fig. 3 fs. וּפָעֲרָה פִיהָ Is 5^{14} (of Sheʾôl), 3 pl. פָּעֲרוּ עָלַי בְּפִיהֶם (Ges $^{§ 119q}$) Jb 16^{10}; of eager desire (good sense), פִּיהֶם פָּעֲרוּ 29^{23}, פִּי־פָעַרְתִּי ψ 119^{131}.

† פַּעֲרַי **n.pr.m.** 2 S 23^{35} (cf. Ph. n.pr.m. פער) = נַעֲרַי q.v.

† פְּעוֹר **n.pr.** Φογωρ: **1. mont.** in Moab (appar. from some √פער);—Nu 23^{28} cf. (בֵּית פ׳, בַּעַל פ׳ and reff.; also) Buhl $^{Geogr. 122}$ Dr $^{Dt 3, 29}$; [𝔊 Jos $15^{59a[60]}$ gives a Φαγωρ with Bethlehem; v. also 𝔊 for פְּעִי, פָּעוּ]. **2. dei** (appar.) Nu $25^{18.18}$ (cf. בַּעַל פ׳ $v^{3.5}$), 31^{16} Jos 22^{17}.

† [פָּצָה] **vb. part, open** (Ar. فَصَى I, II. *separate, remove;* Aram. פְּצָא esp. *set free,* ܦܨܐ Pa. *set free*);—**Qal** *Pf.* 3 fs. פָּצְתָה Gn 4^{11}+, 2 ms. פָּצִיתָ Ju 11^{36}, etc.; *Impf.* 3 ms. יִפְצֶה Jb 35^{16}; *Imv.* ms. פְּצֵה Ez 2^{8}, sf. פְּצֵנִי ψ $144^{7.11}$; *Pt.* פֹּצֶה Is 10^{14}, פוֹ׳ ψ 144^{10};—**1.** *open* mouth: **a.** to swallow, fig. of ground, הָאֲדָמָה Gn 4^{11} (J), Nu 16^{30} (JE), הָאָרֶץ Dt 11^{6}; of enemies, + עַל pers. La 2^{16} 3^{46} ψ 22^{14}; lit. Ez 2^{8}. **b.** to speak Ju $11^{35.36}$ (utter a vow, + אֶל־י׳); Jb 35^{16}; hence = *utter,* אֲשֶׁר פָּצוּ שְׂפָתָי ψ 66^{14}; of bird chirping פֹּצֶה פֶה Is 10^{14} (in fig.). **2.** *snatch away, set free* (Aram. loan-word), only ψ 144, + הִצִּיל c. מִן $v^{7.11}$; פ׳ c. מִן v^{10}.

† פָּצַח **vb. cause to break or burst forth, break forth with** (cf. Ar. فَضَحَ *break, crush;* Eth. ፈጸሐ: *shatter;* Syr. ܦܨܚ is *be joyous, hilarious*);—**Qal** *Pf.* 3 pl. פָּצְחוּ רִנָּה Is 14^{7} *they have broken forth with joyous shout; Impf.* יִפְצְחוּ רִנָּה 55^{12} (of mts.); *Imv.* fs. פִּצְחִי רִנָּה 54^{1} (of Zion); mpl. פִּצְחוּ ר׳ 44^{23} 49^{13} Qr (> Kt יפצחו; of mts.); abs. פִּצְחוּ Is 52^{9} ψ 98^{4} (both + רַנְּנוּ). **Pi.** *break* bones *in pieces: Pf.* 3 pl. פִּצֵּחוּ Mi 3^{3}.

† [פָּצַל] **vb. Pi. peel** (NH Pi. *split, divide;* so Ar. فَصَلَ, JAram. (Talm.) פְּצַל, Syr. ܦܨܠ; akin to בצל q.v.);—*Pf.* 3 ms. פִּצֵּל Gn 30^{38} (obj. rods); *Impf.* 3 ms. וַיְפַצֵּל v^{37} (c. acc. cogn.).

† [פְּצָלָה] **n.f.pl. peeled spot or stripe**;—pl. פְּצָלוֹת לְבָנוֹת Gn 30^{37} (as acc. cogn.).

† [פָּצַם] **vb. split open** (Ar. فَصَمَ *crack;* 𝔗 פְּצַם Je 22^{14}, *cut out*, make, window);—**Qal** *Pf.* 2 ms. sf. of earth, פְּצַמְתָּהּ ψ 60^{4} (subj. God).

† [פָּצַע] **vb. bruise, wound by bruising** (NH *split, bruise;* Ar. فَصَعَ *squeeze* a ripe date, *rub;* Aram. פְּצַע *split*);—**Qal** *Pf.* 3 pl. sf. הִכּוּנִי פְצָעוּנִי Ct 5^{7}; *Inf. abs.* הַכֵּה וּפָצֹעַ 1 K 20^{37} *a smiting and a bruising* (him); *Pt. pass.* cstr. פְּצוּעַ־דַּכָּה Dt 23^{2} *one wounded by crushing.*

† פֶּצַע **n.m.** $^{Pr 27, 6}$ **bruise, wound**;—abs. פ׳ Ex 21^{25} Is 1^{6} (fig.), Pr 20^{30}, פָּצַע Ex 21^{25}; sf. פְּצָעַי Gn 4^{23}; pl. פְּצָעִים Pr 23^{29}; fig. also cstr. פִּצְעֵי 27^{6} and sf. פְּצָעָי Jb 9^{17}.

† [פָּצַץ] **vb. break** (Ar. فَضَّ *break, break asunder;* Nab. פצין *break asunder;* Syr. ܦܨ

crush);—**Pō'.** *Impf* 3 ms. יְפֹצֵץ סָלַע Je 23[29] a hammer which *shatters rock.* **Pilp.** *Impf.* 3 ms. sf. וַיְפַצְפְּצֵנִי Jb 16[12] *he* [God] *dashed me in pieces* (fig)

† פִּצֵּץ only הַפּ׳ **n.pr.m.** priestly name 1 Ch 24[15]; τῷ Φεταια, A Αφεσση, 𝔊L Αφεσσει

בֵּצֵץ v. בית פַּצֵּץ p. 112.

† [פָּצַר] **vb. push, press** (perh. related, by transp, to Ar. فَرَضَ *appoint, prescribe,* As. *parsu, command,* cf. Ba[ZMG xliii (1889), 188]);—**Qal** *Impf.* 3 ms. וַיִּפְצַר־ Gn 19[3]+, 3 mpl. וַיִּפְצְרוּ v[9] 2 K 2[17],—*push, press,* upon (בְּ pers) physically Gn 19[9]; =*urge* v[3] 33[11] Ju 19[7] 2 K 2[17], + inf 5[16]; read also prob וַיִּפְצַר־בּוֹ 2 S 13[25.27] 2 K 5[23] (for וַיִּפְרָץ), וַיִּפְצְרוּ־בוֹ 1 S 28[23] (for וַיִּפְרְצוּ־), Tanchum (cf. The), Weir in Dr[1 S 28, 23] Kit[id] Bu HPS Lohr. **Hiph.** *Inf abs.* הַפְצַר 1 S 15[23] *to display pushing* (i. e. arrogance, presumption; ‖ מֶרִי, cf. Dr)

† פְּצִירָה appar. **n.f.** fr. √פצר, 1 S 13[21]; dub, prob. incurably crpt., AV *file* fr. 𝔗𝔖 Rabb, Ke *bluntness;* both lack philol. ground, v. esp. Dr.

פֵּק v. פיק.

פָּקַד [303] **vb. attend to, visit, muster, appoint** (NH *id, visit, enjoin;* Ph. פקד *attend to, provide;* As. *pakâdu* = BH; Ar فَقَدَ *lose, miss;* also (Dozy) *give heed, attention, to;* Eth. ፈቀደ: *visit, muster, desire, need,* etc., Nab. פקד *command* (Cook), so 𝔗 פַּקֵּד Pa., Syr. ܦܩܕ, also *visit*),—**Qal**[234] *Pf* 3 ms פ׳ Ex 4[31]+; 1 s. פָּקַדְתִּי 3[16]+, etc., *Impf.* 3 ms יפקד Gn 50[24]+, etc; *Imv.* ms. פְּקֹד Nu 3[15]+, etc, *Inf. abs.* פָּקֹד Gn 50[24]+; *cstr.* לִפְקֹד 2 S 24[4]+, etc, *Pt. act* פֹּקֵד Ex 20[5]+; *pass* (הַ)פְּקֻדִים 30[14]+, cstr. פְּקוּדֵי Nu 31[14]+, etc.,—**A. 1. a.** *pay attention to, observe* (with care, practical interest), of י׳ c. acc. pers + rei Ex 3[16] (J), c. acc. pers. 4[31] (J; ‖ רָאָה), ψ 8[5] (with providence, cf פְּקֻדָּה Jb 10[12], ‖ זָכַר); c acc rei 1 S 15[2] ψ 80[15] (‖ רָאָה, הבּיט), La 4[22] (‖ גִּלָּה עַל), יִזְכֹּר עֲוֺנָם וְיִפְקֹד חַטֹּאתָם Ho 8[13] = 9[9] = Je 14[10], 1 S 17[18] *observe thy brothers as to well-being* (לְשָׁלוֹם, i e see how they fare) **b.** *attend to,* in act, *see to,* c. acc pers. 2 K 9[34]; acc. of sheep Je 23[2] (in fig); cf. Zc 10[3b] 11[16]. **c.** *seek* (with interest, desire), seek י׳ Is 26[16]; in bad sense, *look about for* Ez 23[21]. Hence **d.** *seek in vain, need, miss, lack* (cf. **Niph.**, and Ar. Eth. supr), c. acc pers. 1 S 20[6] Is 34[16], rei 1 S 25[15] Je 3[16]. **2.** specif *visit,* c acc., for different purposes: with (בְּ) a present Ju 15[1]; esp. of י׳, *visit graciously* Gn 21[1] 50[24.25] = Ex 13[19] (all E), Is 23[17] Je 15[15] (‖ זָכַר), 27[22] 29[10] ψ 8[5] (‖ זָכַר) 65[10]+; בִּישׁוּעָתֶךָ 106[4] (‖ זָכַר); *visit* to search, test, acc. pers Jb 7[18] (‖ בָּחַן), ψ 17[3] (‖ *id,* obj om.), abs Jb 31[14]; to punish Je 6[15] 49[8] 50[31] ψ 59[6], acc. pers om. Ex 32[34a] Is 26[14], c עַל rei (of sin) Je 5[9.29] 9[8] (here + בְּ pers.); acc. rei ψ 89[33], abs, of י׳'s anger Jb 35[15]. **3.** c. עַל pers, *visit upon,* י׳ subj, + acc rei (of sin) Am 3[2.14] Ho 1[4] 2[15] Ex 20[5] 34[7] Dt 5[9]+10 t.; acc. rei om., =*punish* Is 10[12] Je 9[24] 11[22] 13[21]+10 t. Je, +8 t.; + בְּ rei Ho 12[3] Je 21[14]; + cl of sin Ho 4[14]; c אֶל pers. Je 50[18.18], אֶל + עַל 46[25]; indef subj. c. עַל of vineyard = *injure* Is 27[3]. **4.** *pass in review, muster* (nearly = *number*), c acc., 1 S 11[8] 13[15] 2 S 24[2.4]+11 t. + Nu 1[3.19.44.49]+16 t. Nu (P); acc. om. 1 S 14[17.17] Nu 3[42]; obj. נָוֶה Jb 5[24]; esp pt. pass, persons or things *mustered* (*numbered*), Ex 30[12.13.14] 38[25.26] Nu 1[21.22]+67 t. Nu, + 1 Ch 23[24]. **B.** *appoint:* **1.** c. acc. pers + אִתָּם Gn 40[4], + עַל pers. over whom Je 15[3] 51[27] Nu 27[16], + אֶל (for עַל) Je 49[19] = 50[44], c. acc. pers alone Nu 3[10], + בְּרֹאשׁ הָעָם Dt 20[9]; *pt pass* pl *appointed ones, officers,* of (fighting) host Nu 31[14.48] 2 K 11[15] 2 Ch 23[14]. **2.** c acc. rei, *appoint, assign,* + עַל pers to whom, Nu 4[27] (on text v Di); c. acc rei only, v[32]; cf Jb 34[13] 36[23]; *lay upon* (עַל pers) *as a charge,* Zp 3[7] (rdg מֵעֵינֶיהָ, 𝔊 We Now, for מְעוֹנָהּ); + inf. 2 Ch 36[23] = Ezr 1[2], =*deposit,* c. acc. rei + בְּ loc, 2 K 5[24] (cf פִּקָּדוֹן). †**Niph.** *Pf.* 3 ms נִפְקַד 1 S 25[7]+; 2 ms. וְנִפְקַדְתָּ 20[18], *Impf* 3 ms. יִפָּקֵד v[18]+, etc; *Inf.* הִפָּקֵד *abs* 1 K 20[39], *cstr* Ju 21[3],—**1.** *be* (*sought,* i e. *needed*) *missed, lacking* 1 S 20[18]+ v[19] (𝔊, for MT תֵּרֵד, We Dr al), 25[7] 1 K 20[39] (+ inf abs), 2 K 10[19.19] Je 23[4] (Gr Gie conj. יִפָּחֲדוּ), + מִן part Ju 21[3] 1 S 25[21] 2 S 2[30] Nu 31[49]; of seat 1 S 20[18], place v[25.27] (i e *be empty*) **2.** *be visited* (graciously) Ez 38[8] Is 24[22], cf. 29[6] (בְּ accomp; v Di) **3.** *be visited upon,* עַל pers, Nu 16[29] (subj פְּקֻדָּה), בַּל יִפּ׳ רָע Pr 19[23] *evil shall not be visited* (sc. upon him; rd. perh. שֶׁבֶר עָלָיו for שָׂבֵעַ יָלִין v. Toy). **4.** *be appointed* Ne 7[1], + עַל 12[44]. †**Pi.** (intens) *muster* a host, *Pt.* מְפַקֵּד Is 13[4] (of י׳). †**Pu.** *be passed in review, Pf.* 3 ms. פֻּקַּד Ex 38[21]; *be caused to miss,* deprived of, 1 s. פֻּקַּדְתִּי Is 38[10] c. acc. rei. †**Hithp.** *be mustered, Pf.* 3 pl. הִתְפָּקְדוּ Ju 20[15.17], *Impf.* 3 ms. וַיִּתְפָּקֵד 21[9]; 3 mpl. 20[15] (on form v. Ges[§54.1]) †**Hothp.** *id, Pf.* 3 pl. הָתְפָּקְדוּ 1 K 20[27] Nu 1[47] 2[33] 26[62] (Ges[l.c.]). **Hiph.**[29] *Pf.* 3 ms. הִפְקִיד Gn 39[5]+, 2 ms sf. הִפְקַדְתּוֹ 1 S 29[4], etc.; *Impf.* 3 ms. יַפְקִיד Is 10[28], etc; *Imv* ms הַפְקֵד Nu 1[50] ψ 109[6], etc,—**1.** c acc. pers, *set* (*over*), *make overseer,* 2 K 25[23], + עַל Gn 39[4] Je 1[10] Nu 1[50]+8 t., fig,

acc of punishment, Lv 26[16], + ב Je 40[5] + 3 t., + ב and על Gn 39[5], + ל 1 K 11[28], + אֲשֶׁר שָׁם 1 S 29[4] *where thou hast stationed him*, ins. also v[10] 𝔊 The We Dr al; + אתו Je 40[7], cf 41[10] **2.** c acc rei (implic), **a.** *commit, entrust* (cf פִּקָּדוֹן), בְּיָדְךָ + רוּחִי ψ 31[6] עַל־יַד פ׳ 1 K 14[27] = 2 Ch 12[10], c acc **b.** *deposit*, c acc rei + ב loc Je 36[20], + ל loc Is 10[28], acc pers (Jer as prisoner) + ב loc Je 37[21] †**Hoph. 1.** *be visited* in punishment, *Pf* 3 ms הָפְקַד Je 6[6] (impers; but 𝔊 ψευδής, read הַשֶּׁקֶר JDMich, הַפֶּרֶק Gie). **2.** *be deposited*, אתו Lv 5[23] (subj הַפִּקָּדוֹן) **3** *be made overseer*, *Pt.* (הַ)מֻּפְקָדִים, c בית 2 K 22[9] 12[12] Qr (Kt הבקדים), בבית י׳ 22[5] (Qr del ב), 2 Ch 34[10], c על pers 2 Ch 34[12], abs v[17].

פְּקֻדָּה[32] **n.f. oversight, mustering, visitation, store,**—abs. פ׳ Ho 9[7] 1 Ch 23[11], cstr פְּקֻדַּת Nu 3[32] +, sf פְּקֻדָּתוֹ 109[8], etc, pl פְּקֻדֹּ(ו)ת Je 52[11] +,—**1.** *visitation*. **a.** = punishment Ho 9[7] Is 10[3] Mi 7[4] Ez 9[1] Nu 16[29] (P), esp in (עֵת, שְׁנַת) פְּקֻדָּתָם Je 8[12] 10[15] + 6 t Je (cf עֵת c פָּקַד 6[15] 49[8] 50[31]), בֵּית הַפְּ׳ = prison 52[11] **b.** gracious visitation, providence Jb 10[12] **2. a.** *oversight, charge* Nu 4[16] (P), also 3[36] (P, redund), 1 Ch 26[30], = *office* 2 Ch 23[18] **b** *overseer* (abstr. for concr), 2 K 11[18] Ez 44[11] (c. אֶל rei), Nu 3[32] (P), coll = magistracy Is 60[17] (Lag[BN 151]), cf 2 Ch 24[11] **c.** *class of officers* 1 Ch 23[11] 24[3.19] **d.** *charge* = thing entrusted Nu 4[16] (P) **3.** *mustering* 2 Ch 17[14] 26[11] **4** *store* things laid up, Is 15[7] ψ 109[8] (perh, Hup We[Skizzen vi 184] al *office*)

†[פְּקוּדִים] **n.pl.** [**m.**] **abstr. musterings,** i e **expenses,**—cstr פְּקוּדֵי Ex 38[21] (v Di)

†פָּקִיד **n m. commissioner, deputy, overseer,**—abs פ׳ Je 20[1] +; cstr. פְּקִיד 2 Ch 24[11] Ne 11[22], sf פְּקִידוֹ Ju 9[28], pl פְּקִדִים Gn 41[34] Je 29[26], פְּקִידִים 2 Ch 31[13] Est 2[3],—*commissioner*, for special duty Gn 41[34] (E), Est 2[3]; permanent *deputy* of king Ju 9[28], of priest 2 Ch 24[11], of Levites 31[13], *overseer, one in charge* of men, c עַל of soldiers 2 K 25[19] = Je 52[25], Benjamites Ne 11[9], priests v[14], abs, without עַל, Je 29[26] (of priest in temple, reading פָּקִיד Viss Gie), cf 20[1] (v נָגִיד **3**), c. sf of Levites Ne 11[22], singers 12[42]

†פְּקִדֻת **n.f** oversight,—בַּעַל פ׳ Je 37[13] *sentinel*

[פִּקּוּד][24] **n m.**[ψ 19 9] **precept** (of י׳, prop. *thing appointed, charge*, cf √**B 2**), in ψψ (cf. Syr ܦܘܩܕܢܐ, ܦܘܩܕܐ),—only pl cstr פִּקּוּדֵי י׳ ψ 19[9], and sf פִּקּוּדָיו 111[7], פִּקֻּדָיו 103[18]; elsewh פִּקּוּדֶיךָ 119[15 27] + 10 t 119 + v[128] (for MT בְּקוּדֵי כֹל, 𝔊𝔙 and most), פִּקֻּדֶיךָ v[4 45] + 6 t 119

†פִּקָּדוֹן **n.m.**[Lv 5. 23] **deposit, store** (cf. √**Qal B2, Hiph 2**),—פ׳ abs, of grain stored against famine Gn 41[36], thing left in trust Lv 5[21 23].

†מִפְקָד **n** [**m.**] **muster, appointment, appointed place,**—abs מ׳ only in שַׁעַר הַמּ׳ Ne 3[31], v 1. שַׁעַר, cstr מִפְקַד. **1.** *muster* of people 2 S 24[9] = 1 Ch 21[5]. **2.** *appointment* of (by) Hezekiah 2 Ch 31[13]. **3.** *appointed place* of (in) temple Ez 43[21] (Krae *watch, guard-house*, Ko[ii 1 93] conj מוקד)

†פְּקוֹד **n.pr. gent. et terr.** a people in Bab army Ez 23[23] (Φακουκ, A και Φουδ), יֹשְׁבֵי פ׳ Je 50[21], = As *Pukûdu*, tribe in SE Babylonia, bordering Elam Wkl[Sargon i 241] Schr[COT Je] Dl[Pa 240 f.]

†פָּקַח **vb. open eyes and (once) ears** (NH *id*, *open* (and remove) rubbish heap, sq עַל *look to, attend to*, Ar. فَقَحَ *blossom*, II *open eyes*, JAram פְּקַח *open eyes*, etc, Syr ܦܩܚ *blossom*),—**Qal** *Pf* 3 ms פ׳ Jb 27[19], 2 ms פָּקַחְתָּ 14[3], *Impf* 3 ms. וַיִּפְקַח Gn 21[19] +, 1 s. אֶפְקַח Zc 12[4], *Imv* ms פְּקַח 2 K 6[17] +, so Dn 9[18] Qr (Kt פקחה), *Inf abs* פָּקוֹחַ Is 42[20], cstr לִפְקֹחַ v[7], *Pt act.* פֹּקֵחַ ψ 146[8], *pass* fpl פְּקֻחוֹת Je 32[19],—**1.** *open* eyes **a.** one's own 2 K 4[35] Jb 27[19] Pr 20[13], 2 K 19[16] = Is 37[17] Dn 9[18], + עַל Je 32[19] Zc 12[4] Jb 14[3]. **b.** eyes of others Gn 21[19] 2 K 6[17 17 20 20] Is 42[7] ψ 146[8],—for details v. עַיִן **1 j.** **2.** *open* ears = hear Is 42[20] (without understanding, fig of Isr) **Niph.** *Pf.* 3 pl. consec וְנִפְקְחוּ Gn 3[5], *Impf* 3 fpl תִּפָּקַחְנָה Is 35[5], וַתִּ׳ Gn 3[7],—*be opened*, of eyes; fig, so as to know good and evil Gn 3[5 7], opp. blindness (fig) Is 35[5].

†פִּקֵּחַ **adj. seeing,**—פ׳ Ex 4[11] (opp. עִוֵּר); pl פִּקְחִים, fig, 23[8] *clear-sighted ones* (cf. [עִוֵּר])

†פְּקַח־קוֹחַ, rd פְּקַחְקוֹחַ **n.** [**m.**] **opening** (of eyes, cf Comm, Ges[§ 85 n], prop *wide*, or *complete, opening*),—לַאֲסוּרִים Is 61[1], fig of freeing fr. dark prison, but 𝔊 Che[Hpt] read לְעִוְרִים, cf Di-Kit.

†פֶּקַח **n.pr.m.** usurping king of Israel, Φακεε (*opening* (? of eyes), or cf. Syr. ܦܩܚܐ *flower*, cf. n pr m פקח, פקחי, on old Isr seals; in As *Pakaḥa* (acc) Schr[COT 2 K 15, 30]);—2 K 15[25 27 29 30.31 32 37] 16[1.5] Is 7[1] 2 Ch 28[6].

†פְּקַחְיָה **n.pr.m.** king of Israel (י׳ *hath opened* the eyes),—2 K 15[22 23 26], Φακεσιας, Φακειας.

פקע (√of foll., mng. dub.; NH פָּקַע *split, spring off;* cf. 𝔗 Ithpe, Syr. ܦܩܥ *burst, crash,* NH פְּקַעַת is *ball, roll,* פקיע *wick,* הפקיע denom.; Ar. فقع is *be yellow,* also *break wind,* II. *crack* finger-joints, etc, Ecclus 46[17] פקע *crash;* 𝔗 פקע *roll noisily;* Syr. ܦܩܥܐ *crash, crack*)

†פְּקָעִים **n.m.**[1 K 7, 24] **pl.** carved wood or metal ornaments, either **ball-, knob-shaped** (Low p 332 f) or **gourd-shaped** (so most; cf. foll; Syr ܦܩܘܥܐ *flowers* [Lexx]),—1 K 6[18] 7[24.24].

†פַּקֻּעֹת **n.[f.] pl. gourds** (*wild cucumbers, citrullus colocynthis,* with purgative properties, acc. to Post[Hastings DB ii 250] De[Ri HWB 278 f] 𝔊 κολοκυνθίς; > *momordica* (or *ecballium*) *elaterium,* which is not a *vine;* cf Syr ܦܩܘܥܬܐ, fruit of *colocynthis* (or the similar *cucumis prophetarum*), Low[l.c.] Brock),—cstr פ׳ שָׂדֶה 2 K 4[39].

פַּר v. פרר

I. **פרא** v. **Hiph.** *Impf.* יַפְרִיא sub פרה.

II **פרא** (√of foll, Jen[Cosmol 110] cp. Talm פרא *run,* Ar فَرَأ, فَرَأٌ *wild ass,* Hom[NS 123]; As. *parû, mule* (*wild ass* is *purîmu*))

†פֶּ֫רֶא **n.m.**[Jb 39, 5] (**m.** et **f.** Je 2[24], but **f.** prob. erron., cf. Ko[Synt 157] Albr[ZAW xvi (1896) 68]) **wild ass** (prob. from swiftness),—פ׳ abs. Ho 8[9]+ (so Je 2[24] Gi, van d. H. Baer פֶּרָה), cstr. Gn 16[12]; pl. פְּרָאִים Je 14[6]+,—*wild ass* Je 14[6] Jb 6[5] 39[5] Is 32[14] ψ 104[11]; עַיִר פ׳ Jb 11[12] *wild ass's colt;* פ׳ אָדָם Gn 16[12] (J) *a wild ass of a man* (Ishmael as a free nomad), fig. of wilfulness Ho 8[9] (v. I בָּדָד); of lust Je 2[24] (i e Israel's love of idolatry), of poor desert-dwellers Jb 24[5].

†פִּרְאָם **n.pr.m.** Canaanite king of Jarmuth Jos 10[3], Φειδων, 𝔊L Φεδαμ, A Φερααμ.

פֹּארָה v פארת פַּרְבָּר v. [פַּרְוָר]

†I. [**פָּרַד**] **vb.** divide (NH *id, divide, separate,* so Syr. in der. spec and deriv, Ar. فرد *be single, sole,* also (Dozy) *unfold, unroll*),—**Qal** *Pt. pass.* fpl פְּרֻדוֹת Ez 1[11] *divided,* i e. spread, of wings. **Niph.** *Pf* 3 pl. נפרדו Gn 10[5.32], נִפְרָדוּ 2 S 1[23], *Impf.* יִפָּרֵד Gn 2[10] Pr 19[4], etc, *Imv* ms הִפָּרֶד נָא Gn 13[9]; *Inf cstr.* הִפָּרֵד לוֹט v[14]; *Pt.* נפרד Ju 4[11] Pr 18[1], נפרדים Ne 4[13];—**1.** *divide, separate* (intrans), Gn 2[10] (of river, *dividing* into branches), of one man *separating* from another, c. מֵעַל 13[9 11], מעם v[14] (all J), from others, מִן Ju 4[11]; recipr Gn 25[23] (J; of sons of Rebekah representing nations, c. מִמֵּעַיִךְ in constr. praegn. [Ges[§ 119 ff]], i.e divided (hostile) from birth); abs. Pr 18[1], of peoples separating from (מִן) parent stock 10[5.32] (P) **2.** *be divided, separated,* 2 S 1[23] Ne 4[13]; of loss of friendship Pr 19[4] **Pi.** *Impf.* 3 ms יְפָרֵדוּ Ho 4[14] *make a separation,* i e go apart (in company with [עִם] harlots, cf. RS[Sem 1 435, 2nd ed 455]). **Pu.** *Pt. divided,* עַם . . . מְפֻזָּר וּמְפֹרָד בֵּין הָעַמִּים Est 3[8]. **Hiph.** *Pf.* 3 ms. הִפְרִיד Gn 30[40]; *Impf.* יַפְרִיד Ru 1[17] Pr 18[18], 3 mpl. וַיַּפְרִדוּ 2 K 2[11]; *Inf cstr* sf. בְּהַפְרִידוֹ Dt 32[8], *Pt* מַפְרִיד Pr 16[28] 17[9],—**1.** *divide, separate* Gn 30[40] (JE) Dt 32[8], of separating friends Pr 16[28] 17[9]. **2.** *make a division, separation,* between (בֵּין), 2 K 2[11] Ru 1[17]; of parting disputants (c. בין) Pr 18[18]. **Hithp.** *Pf.* 3 pl. והתפרדו ψ 22[15]; *Impf.* יִתְפָּרְדוּ 92[10], -רָדוּ Jb 4[11] 41[9];—*be divided, separated, from each other;* of scales of crocodile (c. neg.) Jb 41[9], of bones, = be loosened at the joint, ψ 22[15] (fig. of helplessness); = be dispersed Jb 4[11] ψ 92[10]

†[פְּרֻדָה] **n.f. grain** of seed (?) (prop, si vera l, the *separated;* cf. Syr ܦܪܕܐ, ܦܪܕܬܐ, Talm. פְּרִידָא, *pebble, berry*),—only pl. פְּרֻדוֹת Jo 1[17]

†פְּרוּדָא **n.pr.m.** post-exil name Ezr 2[55] (Φαδουρα), = פְּרִידָא Ne 7[57] (Φερειδα, 𝔊L as Ezr)

II. **פרד** (√of foll, cf. Syr. ܦܪܕ *flee, flee away,* so 𝔗 der spec., NH פֶּרֶד = BH)

†פֶּ֫רֶד **n.m.**[2 S 18, 9] **mule,**—פ׳ abs. 2 S 18[9 9 9]+, sf פרדו 13[29], pl פְּרָדִים 1 K 10[25]+; פרדיהם Ezr 2[66] = Ne 7[68] (van d H, Gi Baer in marg.),—*mule,* ridden by princes 2 S 13[29], in battle 18[9.9.9], cf (later, + horses, etc) Zc 14[15] Is 66[20], royal gift 1 K 10[25] = 2 Ch 9[24], royal property 1 K 18[5], in trade of Tyre Ez 27[14]; beast of burden, מַשָּׂא צֶמֶד פְּרָדִים 2 K 5[17] *the load of a pair of mules,* of earth, 1 Ch 12[40]; property of returning exiles Ezr 2[66] = Ne 7[68]; as refractory ψ 32[9] (in sim.)

†פִּרְדָּה **n f. she-mule;**—פ׳ ridden by king 1 K 1[33], cstr. פִּרְדַּת הַמֶּלֶךְ v[38.44].

†פַּרְדֵּס **n.[m.] preserve, park** (loan-word from Zend *pairi-daêza, enclosure,* Spieg Haug in Ew[Jahrb v 162 f], cf. Spieg[Avesta i 293], Pers. پالیز, *pâlêz* Lag[Ges Abh 75, 221], Kurd. *parês* No[ZMG xxxvi (1882), 182]; hence Arm. *partêz* Lag[Arm Stud. § 1873], late As. *pardisu* Meissn[ZA vi 290], Ar فِرْدَوْس, Gk. παράδεισος; cf also Dl[Pa 95 ff] Di[Gn 2, 8]);—הַפ׳ Ne 2[8] (containing trees); cstr. פַּרְדֵּס רִמּוֹנִים Ct 4[13] (fruit-trees and costly plants), pl. פַּרְדֵּסִים Ec 2[5] (+ גַּנּוֹת).

† [פָּרָה] **vb. bear fruit, be fruitful** (NH = BH **1**, פרי = BH, Ph פר *fruit*, Eth ፈረየ: ፈሪየ: *blossom, bear fruit*, As *pir'u*, *posterity*, cf. also פֵּירָא ℑ, Syr ܦܐܪܐ *fruit*, and Ba^ZMG xli (1887), 604),— **Qal** *Pf* 3 pl פָּרוּ Ex 1^7, 1 pl consec וּפָרִינוּ Gn 26^22, etc, *Impf* 3 ms. יִפְרֶה Is 11^1, etc, *Imv* ms פרה Gn 35^11, mpl פרו 1^22+, *Pt act* פֹּרֶה Dt 29^17, f פֹּרִיָּה Ez 19^10 Is 17^6, פֹּרָת (Ges^§80g, for *פֹּרַיְתּ Lag^BN 81) Gn 49^22.22,—**1.** of men and animals, Ex 23^30 (E) Gn 26^22 (J), esp + רבה Je 3^16 23^3 Ez 36^11 Gn 35^11 47^27 (P), and שָׁרַץ (P) Gn 8^17 9^7 Ex 1^7, פרו ורבו ומלאו וגו׳ Gn 1^22.28 9^1. **2.** of vine, גֶּפֶן פֹּרִיָּה Is 32^12 *fruitful vine*, so ψ 128^3 (sim of wife); cf (in fig of Isr) Ez 19^10; in Mess prediction Is 11^1 a shoot from his [Jesse's] roots *shall bear fruit*; c acc שֹׁרֶשׁ פֹּ׳ ראשׁ fig, Dt 29^17 *a root bearing gall* (as its fruit), יִפְרוּ יֶשַׁע Is 45^8 is dub, read perh 3 fs תפר *let earth be fruitful in salvation* (Oort al), *Pt* f, as subst, הַפֹּרִיָּה *the fruit-bearer*, poet. for tree, Is 17^6 (cf [סָעִיף] **2**), so בֵּן פֹּרָת Gn 49^22.22 Joseph is *son of a fruit-bearer*, i e a fruitful bough **Hiph. 1.** *cause to bear fruit*, **2.** *make fruitful*, subj ׳י, c acc of man or people **1.** *Pf* 3 ms. sf. הִפְרַנִי Gn 41^52 (E) **2.** in P, והפרתי Gn 17^6.20 (-ריתי), + הרבה Lv 26^9 (H), *Impf* 3 ms juss יַפְרְךָ וְיַרְבֶּךָ Gn 28^3, ויפר ψ 105^24, *Pt* הנני מַפְרְךָ והרביתך Gn 48^4. **3.** *shew fruitfulness, bear fruit* (Ges^§53c d r) *Impf.* 3 ms יַפְרִיא Ho 13^15 (as if from פרא)

פְּרִי 119 **n.m.** Ho 14,9 **fruit**,—abs פ׳ Ho 9^16+, פֶּרִי Je 12^12+, esp cstr פרי Gn 4^3+, sf פִּרְיִי Pr 8^19, פִּרְיֵךְ Ho 14^9, פריו Gn 3^6+, פִּרְיְכֶם Ez 36^8, פִּרְיָהּ ψ 21^11, פִּרְיָמוֹ La 2^20+, פִּרְיָם Am 9^14, פריהם Je 29^28, פִּרְיָהּ v^5, etc,—**1.** פְּרִי הָאֲדָמָה Gn 4^3 (J), *fruit of the ground*, of produce in gen, so Dt 7^13 + 9 t Dt + 3 t, פ׳ הָאָרֶץ Nu 13^20.26.27 (JE) + 5 t, cf Ez 25^4, *fruit* of vineyard 2 K 19^29 = Is 37^30, Zc 8^12 Is 65^21 Ct 8^11.12, in fig Ho 10^11 + 5 t + Ez 17^14 (but del. 𝔊 Co al), esp פ׳ הָעֵץ Gn 3^2.3.6 Ex 10^15 (all J) + 21 t, also, in fig, Am 2^9 Ho 9^16 + 4 t + Ez 17^23 (read פֹּארָה *branches* Co al), of gardens Am 9^14 Je 29^5.28, fig. Ct 4^12.16, עֵץ פְּרִי is *fruit-tree* Gn 1^11 ψ 148^9, cf Ec 2^5, עֵץ פְּרִי ψ 107^34, פְּרִי תְבוּאָה v^37 *fruit of* (consisting in) *a crop*, ψ 72^16 is dub, Che Du interpr as **2**, Bae prop יפרו **2.** = *offspring: fruit* of womb (בֶּטֶן) Gn 30^2 Dt 7^13 + 9 t, cf. La 2^20 ψ 21^11, of cattle (בהמה) Dt 28^4.11.51 30^9, of serpent, fig of power conquering Philistia Is 14^29. **3.** fig of *fruit* of actions, i.e their consequences good Is 3^10 ψ 58^12; bad Ho 10^13 Pr 1^31 Mi 7^13, of thoughts Je 6^19; of result of removing sin Is 27^9, result of labour (*fruit* of hands) Pr 31^16.31, product of works of ׳י ψ 104^13, of wisdom Pr 8^19, פ׳ צְדָקָה Am 6^12, cf פ׳ צַדִּיק Pr 11^30 (r d. צדק 𝔊 Hi Toy), of doings (i e course of life, or character) Je 17^10 21^14 32^19, פ׳ פִּי־אִישׁ i e speech Pr 12^14 13^2 18^20, *fruit* of arrogance Is 10^12 is arrogant speech; *fruit* of tongue Pr 18^21 = consequences of speech

פֶּרֶא v פרא פָּרָה v III פרר פֹּרָה I, II

[פָּרָה], פרות Is 2^20 v. [חֲפַרְפָּרָה] p 344

† פָּרָה **n.pr.m.** Ju 7^10.11, Φαρα

† פַּרְוַיִם **n.pr.loc.** זְהַב פ׳ 2 Ch 3^6, Φαρουαιμ, in Arabia? Sprenger^Al's Geogr Ar 54 f identif. with *Farwa* in Yemen, Gl^Skizze ii 347 (less prob) with *Sâk el Farwain* in Yemama (Nejd)

† [פַּרְוָר] **n.** [**m.**] structure (colonnade?) attached to W. side of Solomon's temple, pl פַּרְוָרִים 2 K 23^11, appar same word in sg פַּרְבָּר 1 Ch 26^18.18 (all c. art) (Thes cp Pers فرور *open kiosk, summer-house* (lit *light-bearer*), whence perhaps פ׳ as loan-word, cf Mishn פַּרְוָר, פַּרְוָאר, פַּרְוָרָא ℑ *suburb* (made up of *villas*, *summer-houses* Thes), פ׳ then post-ex. insertion in 2 K 23^11, cf further Dr in Hastings^DB)

† [פְּרָז or פָּרָז] **n.** [**m.**] פְּרָזָו Hb 3^14, text and meaning dub, *warriors* (𝔙ℑ) or *leaders* (𝔊 δυναστῶν, cf. 𝔖 Thes We) would suit context.

פרז (√of foll, cf Ar فرز *remove, separate*, فرز *depressed ground between hills*, NH הפריז *extend* border, *exceed* limit, פְּרוֹז = BH פְּרָזִי)

† [פְּרָזָה] **n.f open region, hamlet**,—only pl פְּרָזוֹת אֶרֶץ פ׳ Ez 38^11 *a land of hamlets* (opp חומה, etc), פ׳ תשב יְרוּשָׁלַםִ Zc 2^8 *as open regions shall Jerusalem sit* (יָשַׁב **4**), עָרֵי הַפּ׳ Est 9^19 (opp. שׁוּשַׁן v^18), perh. Ju 5^7 (פ׳ for פְּרָזוֹן, cf. 𝔖ℑGFM).

† פְּרָזִי **n.** [**m.**] **hamlet-dweller**,—coll. c. art כפר הַפּ׳ 1 S 6^18 (opp עיר מבצר), עָרֵי הַפּ׳ Dt 3^5 (opp עָרִים בְּצֻרֹת חוֹמָה וגו׳), pl הַפְּרָזִים Est 9^19 Qr (Kt הפרוזים)

† פְּרָזוֹן **n.** [**m.**] dub, פ׳ Ju 5^7, sf פרזונו v^11 (Lag^BN 119), poss coll. *rural population, rustics*, Bachm Bu (the latter as gen obj after צדקת *righteous acts to the peasants*), > 𝔊 Thes Be *leaders* and *leadership* (cf. [פְּרָז]); text very uncertain, on v^7 see [פְּרָזָה] supr

פְּרִזִּי[23] **adj.gent.** Perizzite (poss., but not certainly, connected with above √),—only הַפּ׳ as n pr coll. ὁ (οἱ) Φερεζαῖος (-αῖοι), of ancient inhab of Canaan, + הַכְּנַעֲנִי [q v.] Gn 13[7] 34[30] (J), Ju 1[4.5]; also in list of peoples dispossessed by Israel Gn 15[20] Ex 3[8] + 17 t.

† I. **פָּרַח** **vb.** bud, sprout, shoot (NH Hiph. = BH **Hiph. 2**; Ecclus פרח **Qal** = *flourish*, **Hiph.** causat., 49[10] 40[19], Ar. فَرَخَ II *hatch*, also *sprout*, فَرْخٌ *young* of bird (v אֶפְרֹחַ infr), *twig, sprout*; As *pirḫu*, n *sprout*;—on mng. cf. GFM JBL x (1891), 67),—**Qal** *Pf* 3 ms פ׳ Ez 7[10] +, etc., *Impf.* 3 ms יִפְרַח Ho 14[6] +, 3 fpl תפרחנה Is 66[14], etc; *Inf abs.* פָּרֹחַ 35[2], cstr. בפרח ψ 92[8], *Pt* f פֹּרַחַת Gn 40[10],—*bud, sprout, send out shoots*, of vine Gn 40[10] (E), Ho 14[8] (sim), Ct 6[11] 7[13], fig-tree Hb 3[17] (< 𝔊 We Now תִפְרַח); rods Nu 17[20.23]; metaph. of restored Isr. Ho 14[6] Is 27[6], cf. of bones Is 66[14] (כַּדֶּשֶׁא), of righteous ψ 72[7] 92[13] Pr 11[28]; of wicked (כמוֹ עֵשֶׂב) ψ 92[8], also of steppe (עֲרָבָה) Is 35[1], פָּרֹחַ תפרח v[2], fig of judgment Ho 10[4] (כָּראשׁ; but on text v. Now), of זָדוֹן (q.v p 268) Ez 7[10]. **Hiph.** *Pf* 1 s הפרחתי Ez 17[24], *Impf* יַפְרִחַ Jb 14[9], etc;—**1.** *cause to bud* or *sprout*, c acc. עֵץ Ez 17[24], זֶרַע Is 17[11], both fig. **2.** *shew buds, sprouts*, of tree Jb 14[9], fig of righteous ψ 92[14]; = flourish, of אֹהֶל יְשָׁרִים, Pr 14[11] (all **Qal** in — acc. to Ba ZMG xliii (1889), 180 f.).

† **פֶּרַח** **n.m.** Na 1,4 bud, sprout,—abs. פ׳ Is 18[5] +, פָּרַח Ex 25[33] 37[19], cstr. פרח Na 1[4] +; sf. פִּרְחָהּ Nu 8[4], פִּרְחָם Is 5[24], pl sf. פְּרָחֶיהָ Ex 25[31] +,—*bud*, Is 5[24], of vine 18[5] (both fig.), Nu 17[23], פ׳ לְבָנוֹן Na 1[4] *the sprout of Lebanon* (i e of its cedars), of bud-shaped ornament in temple 1 K 7[26] (פ׳ שׁוֹשָׁן) v[49] = 2 Ch 4[5] (פ׳ שׁוֹשַׁנָּה) v[21], in tabern Ex 25[31.33 33.34] 37[17 19 19 20] Nu 8[4].

† **פִּרְחָח** **n.m. coll.** brood (? as *offshoot, offspring*),—פ׳ Jb 30[12], i.e. the wretched crowd.

† [**אֶפְרֹחַ**] **n.m** Jb 39 30 young one, pl. young ones, young, of birds (Eth **አፍርኅት**: *id*);—אֶפְרֹחִים Dt 22[6.6], sf. אפרחו Jb 39[30], אֶפְרֹחֶיהָ ψ 84[4].

† II **פָּרַח** **vb.** break out, of leprosy and like eruptions (in P) (usu taken as = I. פ׳, but dub, NH *id*, also *decay, ferment* Vogelst Landwirthschaft 22; Syr. ܦܪܰܚ *spread*, of leprosy, etc; NS ܦܘܪܚܵܐ *leprous spots*);—**Qal** *Pf.* 3 ms. פ׳ Lv 13[39] (of בֹּהַק), ופ׳ consec 14[43] (of נֶגַע); of צָרַעַת, 3 fs. פָּרְחָה 13[20 25], also *Impf* 3 fs. + *Inf. abs.* פָּרוֹחַ תִּפְרַח v[12], and *Pt.* f. פֹּרַחַת v[42]; of שְׁחִין *Pt.* m. פֹּרֵחַ Ex 9[9 10].

† III. [**פָּרַח**] **vb.** fly, Aramaism, si vera l. (NH *id*, esp *fly away*; Aram. פְּרַח, ܦܪܰܚ *fly*; ܦܪܵܚܬܵܐ *insect, bird*),—**Qal** *Pt.* fpl. לְפֹרְחוֹת Ez 13[20.20] *for* (like?) *flying things*, i. e birds, but del. 𝔊 𝔖 Hi Siegf in v[a] (where prob. ins. from v[b]); Co Toy Berthol Krae in v[a b].

† **פָּרוּחַ** **n.pr.m.** in Issachar 1 K 4[17], 𝔊 Φουασουδ, A Φαρρου, 𝔊L Βαρσαουχ.

† [**פָּרַט**] **vb.** very dub, **Qal** *Pt.* pl. הַפֹּרְטִים עַל־פִּי הַנָּבֶל Am 6[5] (NH *break off, divide*, so Syr. ܦܪܰܛ; NH פְּרוּטָה, Aram פְּרִיטָא, *small coin, change*, hence) AW RaAEKi *divide* words into parts (in singing), AV *chant*; and Thes *scatter* (cf. פֶּרֶט) empty words, poss. also would be *stammer* (of broken speech; said contemptuously)·—(Ar. فَرَطَ is *precede, act hastily*, IV *act extravagantly, talk immoderately* (v. further Dr Am 236), hence) AW (as altern.) *improvise carelessly, idly*.

† **פֶּרֶט** **n.[m.]** the broken off, i e fallen grapes;—cstr. פ׳ כַּרְמְךָ Lv 19[10].

פרי v. **פרה**

I. **פרך** (√of foll; NH פָּרַךְ *rub, chafe, crumble*, As. *parâku*, *display violence*, Ar. فَرَكَ *rub and press*, also *hate violently*; Aram. פְּרַךְ, ܦܪܰܟ *rub, crumble*)

† **פֶּרֶךְ** **n.[m.]** harshness, severity,—in phr. בפ׳ Lv 25[53], בְּפָרֶךְ v[43 46] (H P), Ez 34[4] (all c רדה *rule harshly*); Ex 1[13] (c. וַיַּעֲבִדוּ), v[14] (c עֲבֹדָה, both P)

II **פרך** (√of foll., cf. As *parâku*, *bar, shut off*, *parakku*, *apartment, shrine*; Syr. ܦܪܟܐ *shrine* (v RS JPhil 13, 283); v. also Muss-Arnolt JBL xi (1892) 77 Ko ii 1 201).

פָּרֹכֶת[25] **n.f.** curtain, before Most Holy Place, in tabern (P) (prop *that which habitually shuts off*, i.e *parrâku (Lag BN 88) Ko ii. 1, 201);—פ׳ abs. Ex 26[31] + 17 t. P; cstr. פ׳ הַמָּסָךְ Ex 35[12] 39[34] 40[21] Nu 4[5], פ׳ הַקֹּדֶשׁ Lv 4[6], פ׳ הָעֵדֻת 24[3]; in temple 2 Ch 3[14].

† [**פָּרַם**] **vb.** tear, rend garment (NH = BH; Ar. فَرَمَ *chop up* onions, etc. (Landberg Prov 421); Syr. ܦܪܰܡ *cut, rend*);—always c בְּגָדִים:

Qal *Impf* 3 ms יפרם Lv 21[10] (H), 2 mpl תִּפְרֹמוּ 10[6] (P), *Pt pass.* pl פְּרֻמִים 13[45] (P)

† פַּרְמַשְׁתָּא **n.pr.m** son of Haman Est 9[9], Μαρμασιμ(ν)α

† פַּרְנָךְ **n. pr. m.** of Zebulun Nu 34[25], Φαρ(α)ναχ

פָּרַס [28] **n pr.terr. Persia,** Περσῶν (genit.), Dn 11[2] τῇ Περσίδι (𝔊 et Θ), 2 Ch 36[20] Μήδων (OPers *Pârsa, Persian, Persia,* Spieg[APK 231], NPers پارس, فارس, Ar (فارِسُ),—פ׳ 2 Ch 36[22]+, פָּרָס v[20]+,—in late lit, 2 Ch 36[20], v[22 22 23]=Ezr 1[1 1 2], Dn 10[1]+11 t Ezr Dn+(c מָדַי) Est 1[3 14 18 19] 10[2] Dn 8[20], פ׳ Ez 27[10] 38[5] is doubted by Toy (who, 27[10], rds כּוּשׁ, after Gr), but Krae defends

† פַּרְסִי **adj. gent.** Persian,—הַפּ׳ Ne 12[22].

† [פָּרַס, erron פָּרַשׂ No[ZA I 417]] **vb. break** in two, divide (NH in der forms; As *parâsu, divide, hinder,* Ar فَرَسَ *break* neck, etc; Syr ܦܪܣܬܐ *hoof,* 𝔗 פַּרְסְתָא (v פַּרְסָה infr.), cf. No[ZA I 417f]),—**Qal** *Pf.* 3 pl וּפָרֵשׂוּ Mi 3[3] *they have broken up* bones, as in kettle (? rd Impf וַיִּפְרְשׂוּ No[l c]), *Inf abs* פָּרֹס לָרָעֵב לַחְמֶךָ Is 58[7] *a breaking for the hungry thy bread,* so *Impf.* 3 mpl. יִפְרְסוּ יפ׳ לָהֶם אֵל־אֵבֶל Je 16[7] (לחם) om, but read לֶחֶם לָהֶם Gie, cf. [in part] 𝔊 𝔙 Gf), *Pt.* פֹּרֵשׂ לָהֶם La 4[4] (acc לֶחֶם om) **Hiph.** *Pf* 3 fs הִפְרִיסָה Lv 11[6], etc, *Impf* 3 ms יַפְרִיס v[4], *Pt* מַפְרִיס v[4]+, מַפְרֶסֶת v[4]+, etc,—**1.** c acc. פַּרְסָה *divide hoof,* i. e. have divided hoof (>denom *have hoofs*), Dt 14[6.7 8] and ‖ Lv 11[3.4 5.6 7], so also Lv 11[26], מַפְרִיסֵי הַפּ׳ Dt 14[7]=מַפְרִסֵי הַפּ׳ Lv 11[4] (H) **2** pt. abs denom ψ 69[32] *having hoofs* (+ מַקְרִן).

† פֶּרֶס **n.[m.]** a bird of prey, perh **bearded vulture** (*gypaetus barbatus*), 'ossifrage' (Tristr[NHB 171 FFP 94], from *tearing* its prey),—forbidden as food Dt 14[12]=Lv 11[13] (H)

פַּרְסָה [21] **n.f hoof** (prob orig *divided* hoof, cf No[ZA I (1891) 417], later of any hoof (v **2** infr), even Aram of foot-sole of dove 𝔗[Onk Gn 8.9], and of men (Je 47[3]+), cf No[l c]),—פ׳ abs Ex 10[26]+, pl פְּרָס(וֹ)ת Dt 14[6] Lv 11[3], cstr. *id* Is 5[28]+, sf פַּרְסֹתֶיךָ Mi 4[13], פַּרְסֵיהֶן Zc 11[16],—**1.** of ruminants Ex 10[26] (E, meton for animal itself), Mi 4[13] (fig of Zion), Ez 32[13] Zc 11[16] (fig), esp שֶׁסַע (שְׁתֵּי פ׳) Dt 14[6]=Lv 11[3], Lv 11[7], and c פָּרַס **Hiph.** (q v.) v[3]+10 t Lv 11 Dt 14 **2.** of horses (not *divided*) Is 5[28] Ez 26[11] (so 𝔗 𝔖), Je 47[3]

I פרע (√of foll; cf perh Ar. فَرَعَ *overtop, fig excel;* فَرْعٌ *noble, eminent man,* Sab. פרע *be lofty* Os[ZMG xix (1865). 178f], פרע *highest part* SabDenkm[90], fig. *best,* DHM[ib., 32f] CIS[iv No 2.1.13], esp of *offering* DHM[ZMG xxxvii (1883), 341 ff] (cf Ar فَرَعٌ *firstling offered to gods*)).

I פֶּרַע **n.[m.]** leader (?),—pl. abs בִּפְרֹעַ פְּרָעוֹת Ju 5[2] *for the leading of the leaders* (𝔊[A] Be Bu al, but uncertain, 𝔊[B] Symm, cf We[Isr u Jud Gesch (2), 97], Held (2), 123] al, *for the loosing of locks* [II. פֶּרַע], in vow of war, on these and other views v esp GFM[ad loc], conj also by Lambert[REJ xxiv 140] Grimme[ZMG l (1896), 572] Che[JQ July 1899 561] [reading בָּרְכוּ]), cstr. מֵרֹאשׁ פַּרְעוֹת אוֹיֵב Dt 32[42] *from the head of leaders of the foe* 𝔊 DiSteuern al, Kn Ke Dr al *from the long-haired heads of the foe.*

† [פָּרַע] **vb. denom act as leader, lead** (?);—only Inf cstr. בִּפְרֹעַ Ju 5[2], v supr.

† פִּרְעָתוֹן **n pr.loc.** in Ephr. (? = *height;* cf. Sab n pr יהפרע *he makes lofty* Os[l c]);—Ju 12[15], Φαραθωμ, A 𝔊L Φρααθων, perh mod *Far'atâ,* c 6 miles WSW. from Nablus, cf Buhl[Geogr 206] (GASm[Geogr 355] prop top of *Wady Farah* NE from Nablus)

† פִּרְעָתוֹנִי **adj.gent** of foregoing, Ju 12[13 15], 1 Ch 27[14] cf פִּרְעָתֹנִי 2 S 23[30]=1 Ch 11[31].

II פרע (√of foll, cf Syr ܦܪܥ *sprout;* As *pir'u, sprout, progeny, pirtu, hair of head;* late Ar فَرْعٌ *sprout* (Schroeter in Me[Archiv I. 176] Dozy[II 256]), فَرْعٌ *long hair* of woman,—on this and foll √ v Schulthess[Hom Wurz 56] No[ZMG liv (1900), 154])

† II פֶּרַע **n.[m.] long hair of head, locks,**—פ׳ abs Ez 44[20]; cstr פ׳ שְׂעַר רֹאשׁוֹ Nu 6[5] (P)—Ju 5[2] Dt 32[42], v I פֶּרַע

† III פָּרַע **vb. let go, let alone** (NH *id* unbind (hair), *uncover;* Ar. فَرَغَ *be empty, vacant, unoccupied* (c من rei), Syr. ܦܪܥ *uncover,* 𝔗 פרע =NH);—**Qal** *Pf* 3 ms consec וּפָרַע Nu 5[18], sf. פְּרָעֹה (Ges[§ 7b, c]) Ex 32[25]; *Impf.* 3 ms יִפְרַע Lv 21[10], etc.; *Imv* ms. sf פְּרָעֵהוּ Pr 4[15], *Inf cstr.* פְּרֹעַ Ju 5[2], *Pt act* פּוֹרֵעַ Pr 13[18] 15[32], *pass.* פָּרֻעַ Lv 13[45], פָּרֻעַ Ez 32[25],—**1.** *let go, let loose,* people, i e remove restraint from them, Ex 32[25.25] (E); cf Jb 15[4] Che[JQ July 1897 577] (תִּפְרַע for תִּגְרַע); *unbind* head (by removing turban, sign of mourning) Lv 10[6] 21[10] (forbidden to priests);

also 13^{45} (leper), Nu 5^{18} (woman; all c. ראשׁ; v Now$^{Arch\ II\ 114}$; >denom. from פֶּרַע Gerber^{18} al.) **2.** *let alone*=avoid Pr 4^{15}, =neglect 1^{25} 8^{33} 13^{18} 15^{32}; abs =refrain Ez 24^{14}.—Ju 5^{2} v. I. פֶּרַע. **Niph.** *Impf* 3 ms יִפָּרַע עָם Pr 29^{18} *the people is let loose,* lacks restraint. **Hiph.** *Pf* 3 ms. הִפְרִיעַ 2 Ch 28^{19}; *Impf* 2 mpl. תַּפְרִיעוּ Ex 5^{4},—**1.** *cause* people *to refrain,* מִמַּעֲשָׂיו Ex 5^{4}. **2.** *shew lack of restraint* 2 Ch 28^{19}.

פַּרְעֹה$_{275}$ **n.m.** Pharaoh, Φαραω, title of Egyptian kings (Egypt. *pr-'o, great house,* of royal court, and (in new kingdom) of king Griffith$^{Hastings\ DB}$ Mey$^{Gesch\ Alt\ I\ 59}$ Steind$^{BAS\ I.\ 343}$, in As *pir'u* acc. to most, cf COT^{Gloss} Steind$^{l\ c}$, but v Wkl$^{MVAG.\ 1898.\ 3f}$),—פ׳ Gn 12$^{15.15.15.17}$ + 212 t Hex (mostly JE, rarely DP), 1 S 2^{27} 6^{6} 1 K 3^{1} + 19 t K, Is 19$^{11.11}$ + 3 t, Je 25^{19} + 10 t, Ez 17^{17} + 12 t, Ne 9^{10} 1 Ch 4^{18} 2 Ch 8^{11} ψ 135^{9} 136^{15} Ct 1^{9}, + מֶלֶךְ מִצְרַיִם (not early) Je 25^{19} 46^{17} Dt 7^{8} 11^{3} Ez 29$^{2.3}$ 30$^{21.22}$ 31^{2} 1 K 3^{1} 9^{16} 11^{18} 2 K 17^{7} 18^{21} = Is 36^{6}, Gn 41^{46} (E), Ex 6$^{11.13.27.29}$ 14^{8} (all P); c n.pr פ׳ נכה Je 44^{30}, פ׳ חָפְרַע 46^{2} 2 K 23$^{29.33.34.35}$

† I פַּרְעֹשׁ **n.m.** flea (As *puršu'û, paršu'û,* on transp of, v Hom$^{A\ u.\ A\ I\ 21}$),—fig of insignificance 1 S 24^{15}; 26^{20} נַפְשִׁי 𝔊 Th We Dr al

† II. פַּרְעֹשׁ **n.pr.m.** Φορος, Φαρες, etc (flea, cf Gray$^{Prop.\ N\ 94}$),—**1.** head of post-ex family Ezr 2^{3} = Ne 7^{8}, Ezr 8^{3} 10^{25} Ne 3^{25}. **2.** Ne 10^{15}.

† פַּרְפַּר **n.pr.flum.** near Damascus 2 K 5^{12}, (A)φαρφαρ; A Φαρφαρα, perh mod. *'Awaj,* S. of Damascus Rob$^{BR\ III.\ 447\ f}$.

† I פָּרַץ **vb.** break through (NH *id*, JAram פְּרַץ *id.*, perh As. *paràşu* (v Dl^{HWB}), Ar فَرَصَ *cut, slit,* also *hit*),—**Qal** *Pf.* 3 ms פָּרַץ 2 S 5^{20}+, 2 ms sf. פְּרַצְתָּנוּ ψ 60^{3}, etc., *Impf.* 3 ms יִפְרֹץ Ex 1^{12} 19^{22}, יִפְרָץ־ v^{24}, וַיִּפְרֹץ Gn 30^{30}+, etc; *Inf abs.* פָּרוֹץ Is 5^{5}; cstr. פְּרֹץ 2 Ch 31^{5}, פרוץ Ec 3^{3}; *Pt. act* פֹּרֵץ Mi 2^{13} Ec 10^{8}, *pass* fs פְּרוּצָה 2 Ch 32^{5} Pr 25^{28}, mpl פְּרֻצִים Ne 4^{1}, +הֵם פְּרוּצִים 2^{13} Qr (>Kt המפרוצים),—*break through*· **1.** *break* or *burst out,* from womb Gn 38^{29} (J, c acc. cogn.); from enclosure Mi 2^{13}. **2.** *break through, down* (from without), c. acc. גָּדֵר Is 5^{5} ψ 80^{13} 89^{41} Ec 10^{8}; חוֹמָה Ne 3^{35} 2 Ch 26^{6}, cf. pt. pass Ne 2^{13} 2 Ch 32^{5}; c בְּחוֹמָה = *make a breach in* 2 K 14^{13} = 2 Ch 25^{23}; עִיר פְּרוּצָה Pr 25^{28}, abs., opp. בָּנָה Ec 3^{3}; הַפֹּרֵץ Mi 2^{13}; הַפְּרוּצִים Ne 4^{1} *the part broken down* **3.** *break into,* c acc. בֵּית י׳ 2 Ch 24^{7}. **4.** *break open,* a mining shaft Jb 28^{4}. **5.** *break up, break in pieces,* c. acc. מַעֲשֶׂיךָ 2 Ch 20^{37} (וַיִּשָּׁבְרוּ אֳנִיּוֹת ‖). **6.** *break out* (violently) *upon,* of י׳ in sudden judgment, c. acc pers. 2 S 5^{20} = 1 Ch 14^{11}, ψ 60^{3}; c. בְּ pers Ex 19$^{22.24}$ (J), 1 Ch 15^{13}, so of plague ψ 106^{29}, of י׳, c acc. cogn. פֶּרֶץ + בְּ pers 2 S 6^{8} = 1 Ch 13^{11}; c. acc. cogn. + sf. Jb 16^{14}. **7.** *use violence,* abs Ho 4^{2}. **8.** *break over* [limits], *increase,* וַיִּפְרֹץ לָרֹב Gn 30^{30} (J), 1 Ch 4^{38}, + ה loc. Gn 28^{14} (J); abs. 30^{43} (J), Ex 1^{12} (J, + רָבָה), Ho 4^{10} Is 54^{3}, פָּרַץ בָּאָרֶץ Jb 1^{10}. **9.** *burst open,* intrans, of wine-vats Pr 3^{10} (c. acc. mat. תִּירוֹשׁ) **10.** *spread,* i e. become known, of הַדָּבָר 2 Ch 31^{5}.—1 Ch 13^{2} is prob. corrupt, v. Kau, who (after SS) conj נֶחֱרָצָה; פ׳ in 2 Ch 11^{23} is appar *distribute* (c מִן partit.), but dubious —1 S 28^{23} 2 S 13$^{25.27}$ 2 K 5^{23} v. פצר. **Niph.** *Pt.* אֵין חָזוֹן נִפְרָץ 1 S 3^{1} *no vision spread abroad* (i.e. general, or frequent, cf. **Qal 10**, ‖ דְּבַר י׳ הָיָה יָקָר), but text dubious **Pu.** *Pt* f. מְפֹרֶצֶת Ne 1^{3} (of wall) **Hithp.** *Pt* pl הַמִּתְפָּרְצִים 1 S 25^{10} slaves *who break away,* each from (מִפְּנֵי) his master.

† I פֶּרֶץ **n.m.**$^{Jb\ 30,\ 14}$ **bursting forth, breach;** abs פ׳ Ju 21^{15}+, פָּרֶץ Gn 38^{29}+, cstr פֶּרֶץ 2 S 5^{20}+, pl פְּרָצִים Am 4^{3}+, פְּרָצוֹת Ez 13^{5}, sf פִּרְצֵיהֶן Am 9^{11} (פִּרְצֶיהָ We Now),—**1.** *bursting forth, outburst,* of water 2 S 5^{20} = 1 Ch 14^{11}, fr womb Gn 38^{29} (J) **2.** *breach* in wall Am 4^{3} 1 K 11^{27} Ne 6^{1} ψ 144^{14}, Jb 30^{14}, so (c. גָּדַר, i.e repair) Am 9^{11} Is 58^{12}, fig of effort to avert calamity, עָלָה בַּפְּרָצוֹת Ez 13^{5} (‖ גָּדַר), עָמַד בַּפֶּרֶץ 22^{30} (‖ id.), cf. ψ 106^{23}, by instruction and (esp) intercession. **3.** *broken wall,* פ׳ נֹפֵל Is 30^{13}. **4.** fig of *outburst* of י׳'s wrath, acc. cogn c. פָּרַץ 2 S 6^{8} = 1 Ch 13^{11}, Jb 16^{14} (פֶּרֶץ עַל־פְּנֵי־פָרֶץ), עָשָׂה פ׳ בְּ Ju 21^{15}.

† II. פֶּרֶץ **n pr. 1. m.** son of Judah and Tamar, Φαρες;—פ׳ Gn 46^{12} +, פָּרֶץ 38^{29} + 3 t.;—Gn 38^{29} 46$^{12.12}$ Nu 26$^{20.21}$ Ru 4$^{12.18.18}$ 1 Ch 2$^{4.5}$ 4^{1} 9^{4} 27^{3} Ne 11$^{4.6}$. **2. loc.** in **a.** פ׳ עֻזָּה near Jerus. 2 S 6^{8} = 2 Ch 13^{11} **b.** הַר פְּרָצִים Is 28^{21}, perh.= בַּעַל פ׳ q v. p 128.—Cf. רִמֹּן פֶּרֶץ.

† פַּרְצִי **adj. gent.** of II פֶּרֶץ **1,** c. art. as n coll. Nu 26^{20}.

† פָּרִיץ **n.m.** violent one (robber, murderer),—פ׳ שֹׁפֵךְ דָּם Ez 18^{10}; אָרְחוֹת פ׳ ψ 17^{4}; pl. פָּרִיצִים Ez 7^{22}, מְעָרַת פָּרִצִים Je 7^{11}, cstr. בְּנֵי פָּרִיצֵי עַמְּךָ Dn 11^{14}; of wild beast, פְּרִיץ חַיּוֹת Is 35^{9}.

II. פרץ (√ of foll., cf. Ar فَرَضَ *notch, make mark by notching;* فُرْضَة *gap* by which boats ascend, unload, or are stationed; فِرَاضٌ *mouth* of river or inlet).

†[מִפְרָץ] **n.[m.]** **landing-place** — וְעַל מִפְרָצָיו יִשְׁכּוֹן Ju 5[17] (cf GFM)

†[פָּרַק] **vb. tear apart, away** (NH *remove* (load, etc), Pi *separate, take to pieces*, Ar فَرَقَ *split, divide*, 𝔗 פְּרַק esp *redeem, rescue*, Syr. ܦܪܩ *withdraw* (intrans), also *remove, rescue*; Eth ፈረቀ: *set free*) —**Qal** *Pf.* 2 ms וּפָרַקְתָּ Gn 27[40], *Impf* 3 ms sf וַיִּפְרְקֵנוּ ψ 136[24], *Pt. act* פֹּרֵק La 5[8] ψ 7[3] *tear away* yoke from off (מֵעַל) neck Gn 27[40] (J), *snatch* from (מִן) foes, = *rescue* (Aram) La 5[8] ψ 136[24], so abs ψ 7[3] (prefixing אֵין(ו), 𝔊 𝔖 Che Du We), > Hup Bae al. *snatch away* as prey **Pi.** *Impf* 3 ms יְפָרֵק Zc 11[16] *he shall tear off* their hoofs, *Imv* mpl פָּרְקוּ Ex 32[2] (E) *tear off* the golden ear-rings, *Pt* מְפָרֵק 1 K 19[11] a great wind *rending* mts (‖ מְשַׁבֵּר) **Hithp.** *tear off* (for, i e from, oneself Ges[§ 54 f]), *Impf* 3 mpl וַיִּתְפָּרְקוּ Ex 32[3] (E), c acc אֶת־נִזְמֵי הַזָּהָב, *Imv* mpl הִתְפָּרְקוּ v[24] (E; obj om); pass *be broken off*, *Pf* 3 pl הִתְפָּרְקוּ Ez 19[12] (branches)

†פֶּרֶק **n.[m.]** **1.** **parting of ways**, Ob[14] **2.** **plunder** (as *snatched away*), Na 3[1]

†[פָּרָק] **n.[m.]** **fragment**;—cstr פְּרַק פִּגֻּלִים Is 65[4] Kt, but read מְרַק, v מָרָק

†[מַפְרֶקֶת] **n.f.** **neck** (*dividing* head from body),—sf וַתִּשָּׁבֵר מַפְרַקְתּוֹ 1 S 4[18]

†I [פָּרַר] **vb. Hiph.** **break, frustrate** (NH Pi *crumble*, JAram. פְּרַר, As *parâru*, *destroy*, II *shatter*, Lihy והפרו *destroy*, DHM Epigr Denkm No 21 7), —*Pf* 3 ms הֵפֵר Is 33[8] +, הֵפַר Gn 17[14] Nu 15[31], also metaplastic form הֵפִיר Ez 17[19] ψ 33[10] (Ges[§ 67 v]), 2 ms וְהֵפַרְתָּה 2 S 15[34], etc, *Impf* 3 ms יָפֵר Nu 30[13] +, וַיָּפֶר Ne 4[9], etc, also 1 s. אָפִיר ψ 89[34] (Ges[l c]), *Imv* ms הָפֵר 2 Ch 16[3] ψ 85[5], הָפֵרָה 1 K 15[19]; *Inf abs* הָפֵר Pr 15[22] +, cstr לְהָפֵר 2 S 17[14] +, לְהָפִיר Zc 11[10], sf לְהַפְרְכֶם Lv 26[15] (Ges[§ 67 dd]), *Pt* מֵפֵר Is 44[25] Jb 5[12],—**1.** *break, violate*, esp c. acc בְּרִית **a.** of יהוה Ju 2[1] Je 14[21] Lv 26[44] Zc 11[10]. **b.** of men violating covenant with יהוה Je 11[10] 31[32] Dt 31[16.20] Lv 26[15] Ez 44[7] Gn 17[14] Is 24[5], cf Je 33[20]. **c.** of men breaking compact, league (with men), Is 33[8] 1 K 15[19] = 2 Ch 16[3], Ez 17[15.16.18.19]. **d.** of destroying the אַחֲוָה between Judah and Israel Zc 11[14] **e.** of breaking יהוה's מִצְוָה Nu 15[31] Ezr 9[14], תּוֹרָה ψ 119[126] **2.** *frustrate, make ineffectual*. **a.** counsel (עֵצָה) 2 S 15[34] 17[14] Ezr 4[5], יהוה subj. Ne 4[9] ψ 33[10], of man frustrating יהוה's counsel Is 14[27], so, c. acc מִשְׁפָּט Jb 40[8], c acc מַחְשְׁבוֹת in gen, of men Pr 15[22], יהוה subj Jb 5[12], so, c. acc. אֹתוֹת Is 44[25] **b.** *make* vow (נֶדֶר) *ineffectual*, *annul* it Ne 30[9.14] (opp הֵקִים), v[13], also (Impf + Inf abs) v[13.16] **c.** of annulling (godly) fear Jb 15[4], חַסְדִּי לֹא אָפִיר מֵעִמּוֹ ψ 89[34] **d.** prob אָסִיר Ol Che Bae al, הָפֵר כַּעַסְךָ 85[5] (rd הָסֵר 𝔊 Bi Che). **d.** וְתָפֵר הָאֲבִיּוֹנָה Ec 12[5] is dub. De Wild al *fails* (to excite [? < וְתֻפַר **Hoph.** *is made ineffectual*]), Ew *bursts* (Siegf וְתִפָּר), but caper-berry not dehiscent (Post Flora of Syr 106 ff M'Lean-Dyer Ency Bib 696) Post Letter July 26, 1901 *breaks up* (by shrivelling), fig of failing sexual power; Aq from פרה *bear fruit* (cf GFM JBL x (1891) 60), Perles Anal 30 ותפרח **Hoph.** *Impf* **1.** *be frustrated*, 3 fs וְתֻפַר Is 8[10] (of עֵצָה) **2.** *be broken*, of covenant, 3 fs. תֻּפַר Je 33[21], וַתֻּפַר Zc 11[11], so Is 28[18] (read ותפר for וְכֻפַּר, v כ׳) **Pilp.** *Impf* 3 ms sf וַיְפַרְפְּרֵנִי Jb 16[12] *he hath shattered me*

†II [פָּרַר] **vb** **split, divide** (so ψ 74[13] seems to require [but √פור SS is possible], cf. Ar فَرْفَرَ *split, tear, rend*, perh = I; > Buhl Lex *shake, quake*, citing Ar فَرْفَرَ *shake*, Aram. אִתְפַּרְפַּר, ܦܪܦܪ, cf NH (בִּרְפֵּר),—**Qal** *Inf abs* + **Hithpō**. *Pf* 3 fs פּוֹר הִתְפּוֹרְרָה אֶרֶץ Is 24[19] *split* or *cracked through is the earth* (Che Heb Hpt פרוק התפרקה) **Pō'ēl** *Pf* 2 ms פּוֹרַרְתָּ ψ 74[13] *thou* [יהוה] *didst divide* the sea

III. פרר (√of foll., cf. NH פָּרָה, פַּר = BH, Ar فَرَارٌ *young* of ewe, cow, or goat; Syr. ܦܪܐܠܐ *ewe* (cf No ZMG xl (1886), 731), and so As. *parru*, acc. to Jen and Zim ZA III 202)

פַּר[132] **n.m** Gn 32, 16 **young bull, steer**,—abs. פ׳ Nu 7[15] +, פָּר ψ 50[9], alw הַפָּר 1 S 1[25] +, cstr. פַּר (הַ)חַטָּאת Ex 29[36] +; pl פָּרִים Gn 32[16] +, sf פָּרֶיהָ Je 50[27], —*steer* [v esp פַּר בֶּן־בָּקָר Lv 4[3] + 6 t, פ׳ אֶחָד ב׳־ב׳ Ex 29[1] + 12 t Nu 7, cf 8[8], פ׳ ב׳־ב׳ אֶחָד Nu 15[24] + 3 t, cf Ez 43[23] 45[18] 46[6]; pl. פָּרִים בני־ב׳ Nu 28[11] + 4 t., v. בָּקָר, בֵּן] **1.** as gift Gn 32[16] (E), fig of fierce enemies ψ 22[13]. **2** elsewh as sacrificial victims **a.** in peace-offering Ex 24[5] (E, Covenant Code), 1 S 1[24] (rd. פַּר for פָּרִים 𝔊 𝔖 Th We Dr al), v[25] Nu 7[88] (P), 2 Ch 30[24.24]. **b.** burnt-offering Ju 6[25.26] (on text cf GFM), v[26.28] 1 K 18[23.23.23.25.26.33], Ez 43[23] + 5 t. Ez, Nu 7[15.21] + 46 t Nu (P), 1 Ch 15[26] 29[21] Ezr 8[35] Jb 42[8] ψ 50[9] 51[21], Lv 23[18] (gloss, Dr-Wh) **c.** sin-offering Ez 43[19] + 5 t Ez, Ex 29[1.3.10.10.11.12.14.36] cf 2 Ch 13[9] 29[21], Lv 4[3.4.4.4] + 25 t. Lv (P), Nu 8[8]; —both **b.** and **c.** Nu 8[12]. **d.** more gen. Is 1[11] ψ 69[32] **e.** fig פָּרִים שְׂפָתֵינוּ Ho 14[3] we will pay (as with) *bullocks, our lips*, but read פְּרִי 𝔊 We

Now, cf. Che **f.** of princes and warriors slain by ׳י, under fig. of sacrifice Is 34^{7} Je 50^{27} Ez 39^{18}

I **פָּרָה** $_{26}$ **n.f. heifer, cow**;—abs פ׳ Is 11^{7}+; sf. פָּרָתוֹ Jb 21^{10}; pl. פָּרוֹת Gn 32^{16}+, פָּרֹת 41^{26}, cstr פָּרוֹת Am 4^{1};—as gift Gn 32^{16}; in Pharaoh's dream 41$^{2.3.3}$+8 t. 41, drawing cart 1 S 6$^{7\ 12\ 14}$ + פ׳ עָלוֹת v$^{7\ 10}$ *cows giving suck,* milch cows, פ׳ calving Jb 21^{10}, grazing Is 11^{7}; פ׳ אֲדֻמָּה *red heifer* Nu 19^{2}, cf. v$^{5\ 6\ 9\ 10}$, sim. of stubbornness Ho 4^{16}; פָּרוֹת הַבָּשָׁן Am 4^{1}, fig. of luxurious women.

†II. **פָּרָה** **n.pr.loc.** in Benj., הַפּ׳ Jos 18^{23}, Φαρα, Αφρα

†**פָּרַשׂ** **vb. spread out, spread** (NH *id.*, Ar فَرَشَ, ‎𝔗 פְּרַס (rare), Syr. ܦܪܣ, cf. As *parašu, fly* (dei spec, prop. *spread* [wings]); v. also No$^{ZA\ 1\ 417}$),—**Qal** *Pf.* 3 ms פ׳ La 1^{10}+; 2 ms וּפָרַשְׂתָּ Jb 11^{13} Ru 3^{9}, etc., *Impf.* 3 ms. יִפְרֹשׂ Dt 32^{11}+; 3 fs. וַתִּפְרֹשׂ 2 S 17^{19}, etc; *Pt. act* פּוֹרֵשׂ Pr 29^{5}, etc.; *pass.* פָּרֻשׂ Jo 2^{2}, fs פְּרוּשָׂה Ho 5^{1}, pl פְּרֻשׂוֹת 1 K 8^{54},—**1.** *spread out* a garment (שִׂמְלָה) Ju 8^{25}, + לִפְנֵי pers. Dt 22^{17},—wings 32^{11} 1 K 6^{27} (rd. כַּנְפֵיהֶם 𝔊 Sta Kmp Kit Benz), + עַל Je 49^{22} (fig.), + אֶל 48^{40} 1 K 8^{7}=2 Ch 5^{8} (עַל), + לְ Jb 39^{26}, לְמַעְלָה Ex 25^{20} 37^{9}; wings om. 1 Ch 28^{18} and perhaps 2 Ch 3^{13} (del כַּנְפֵי Be), of ׳י, פ׳ עָלָיו אוֹרוֹ Jb 36^{30}, *spread out* writing, לִפְנֵי pers. 2 K 19^{14}=Is 37^{14}, Ez 2^{10}, sail Is 33^{23}; fishing-net, מִכְמֶרֶת Is 19^{8} (עַל loc); net (רֶשֶׁת) as snare, fig. Ho 5^{1} (עַל loc), ψ 140^{6}, לְרַגְלַי La 1^{13}, c. עַל pers. Ho 7^{12} (of ׳י), Ez 12^{13}=17^{20}, 19^{8} 32^{3}, עַל־פְּעָמָיו Pr 29^{5}, פ׳ כַּפַּיִם in prayer, + אֶל Ex 9$^{29.33}$ (J), 1 K 8^{38}=2 Ch 6^{29}, Ezr 9^{5} Jb 11^{13}, + לְ ψ 44^{21}, + הַשָּׁמַיִם 1 K 8^{22}=2 Ch 6^{13} (הַשָּׁמָיְמָה), 1 K 8^{54}, no complem 2 Ch 6^{12}; of almsgiving, כַּפָּהּ פָּרְשָׂה לֶעָנִי Pr 31^{20}, פ׳ יָד, c עַל rei, La 1^{10} of enemy's greed (si vera l, v. Bu); *spread out*=display וּכְסִיל יִפְרֹשׂ אִוֶּלֶת Pr 13^{16}. **2.** *spread* covering over 2 S 17^{19} (עַל־פְּנֵי + מָסָךְ rei), הַמִּכְבָּר over (עַל) face of another 2 K 8^{15}, כָּנָף *skirt,* עַל pers. Ru 3^{9} Ez 16^{8} (fig. of ׳י); בֶּגֶד c. עַל rei Nu 4$^{7.8.11\ 13}$, c. מִלְמַעְלָה v^{6}, כִּסּוּי c עַל rei v^{14}; אֶת־הָאֹהֶל, c. עַל־הַמִּשְׁכָּן Ex 40^{19}, שַׁחַר פָּרֻשׂ עַל־הֶהָרִים Jo 2^{2}; of ׳י, פ׳ עָנָן לְמָסָךְ ψ 105^{39}—Mi 3^{3} La 4^{4} v. פָּרַס. **Niph.** *Impf* 3 mpl. יִפָּרֵשׂוּ Ez 17^{21} *they shall be scattered* לְכָל־רוּחַ; 34^{12} read prob *Pt* צֹאן נִפְרָשׁוֹת (for ־שׁוֹת, Ha Krae; on emend. of context v. esp Toy Krae) **Pi.** *Pf.* 3 ms. consec. וּפֵרַשׂ Is 25^{11}, etc.; *Impf.* 3 ms יְפָרֵשׂ v^{11}, 3 fs. תְּפָרֵשׂ Je 4^{31}; *Inf cstr.* פָּרֵשׂ ψ 68^{15}, sf. פָּרִשְׂכֶם Is 1^{15},—**1.** *spread out:* **a.** c acc כַּפַּיִם in prayer Is 1^{15} Je 4^{31}, so c יָדַיִם ψ 143^{6} (אֶל־י׳), and of ׳י entreating people Is 65^{2} (אֶל); פ׳ צִיּוֹן בְּיָדֶיהָ La 1^{17} **b.** *spread out* hands as in swimming Is 25^{11}, and (יָדַיִם om) v^{11}. **2.**=*scatter,* (?) subj ׳י, c acc. pers Zc 2^{10} (𝔊 We Now קִבַּצְתִּי מִן, yet v. GASm); ψ 68^{15}, in doubtful connexion.

†[**מִפְרָשׂ**] **n.[m.] spreading out, thing spread**,—sf. מִפְרָשֵׂךְ Ez 27^{7} *thy spread* (canvas, as sail, cf vb Is 33^{23}); pl cstr מִפְרְשֵׂי עָב Jb 36^{29}, so perhaps 37^{16} (for מִפְלְשֵׂי)

†**פַּרְשֵׁז** (Baer, ־שֵׁז van d H. Gi), *Inf. abs* **Pi'lēl** (Ges^{§56}) from פָּרַשׂ (si vera l), פ׳ עָלָיו עֲנָנוֹ Jb 26^{9} *a spreading his cloud upon it* (but Bu Du al. read פָּרַשׂ ,פֵּרַשׂ, or פֵּרֵשׂ)

†I. [**פָּרַשׁ**] **vb. make distinct, declare** (NH *separate oneself,* Pi. *separate, explain,* so Aram. פָּרֵשׁ, esp Pa.; Syr. ܦܪܫ *separate, distinguish, explain,* cf. Mand, No$^{M\ 221}$),—**Qal** *Inf. cstr* לִפְרֹשׁ לָהֶם עַל־פִּי י׳ Lv 24^{12} (P) *to declare distinctly to them.* **Niph.** *Pt.* נִפְרָשׁוֹת Ez 34^{12} read prob. ־שׂוֹת, v. פרשׂ. **Pu.** *Pf.* 3 ms. פֹּרַשׁ Nu 15^{34} (P) what should be done to him *had* not *been distinctly declared; Pt.* מְפֹרָשׁ Ne 8^{8} *made distinct* (cf BAram Ezr 4^{18}), v. Be-Ry Ko$^{Einl\ 99}$, >*interpreted,* Ke al, Berliner$^{T\ Onk\ ii\ 74}$.

†[**פָּרָשָׁה**] **n.f. exact statement**;—cstr. פָּרָשַׁת הַכֶּסֶף Est 4^{7}, פ׳ גְּדֻלַּת מָרְדֳּכַי 10^{2}.

†II. [**פָּרַשׁ**] **vb. Hiph. pierce, sting** (?) (cf. As *paruššu, staff* (which pierces), Aram. פַּרְשָׁא, ܦܪܫܐ (in Lexx) *ox-goad*);—*Impf.* 3 ms. יַפְרִשׁ Pr 23^{32} (כְּנָחָשׁ יִשָּׁךְ ‖ כְּצִפְעֹנִי), of wine

III. **פרשׁ** (√ of foll, cf Aram פְּרַת Pa. (rare) *cause to break* or *burst forth* (a serpent its brood), פַּרְתָּא *dung;* Syr. ܦܪܬ Pa. *rip open,* ܦܪܬܐ =1 פֶּרֶשׁ, Ar. فَرَثَ iv *rip open* stomach, *and scatter* contents (cf vii), فَرْثٌ=1. פֶּרֶשׁ).

†I. **פֶּרֶשׁ** **n.[m.] fæcal matter** found in intestines of victim,—פ׳ abs Mal 2^{3}; cstr. v^{3}, sf. פִּרְשׁוֹ Ex 29^{14} Lv 4^{11} 8^{17}; פִּרְשָׁהּ Nu 19^{5}; פִּרְשָׁם Lv 16^{27} (all P).

†II. **פֶּרֶשׁ** **n.pr.m.** Manassite 1 Ch 7^{16}, A 𝔊L Φαρες.

IV **פרשׁ** (√of foll.; mng. dub.; against Lag$^{BN\ 50}$ (*horse,* one that *breaks* the ground, Ar. فَرَسٌ) v Fra^{94}, cf. also No$^{ZMG\ xl\ (1886).737}$).

†II [פָּרָשׁ] **n.[m.]** **horse, steed** (less common synon of סוּס (> explained away by Schwally ZAW viii (1888) 191), Ar فَرَس *horse, mare* (oft), so Eth ፈረስ፡, cf Sab פרס *horse*, Mordtm Him Inschr 70), — pl. פָּרָשִׁים (erron for *פְּרָשִׁים Kö ii 1 89) Ez 27^{14}+, sf פָּרָשָׁיו Is 28^{28} 1 S 8^{11}, — *steeds* Ez 27^{14} (+ סוּסִים, פְּרָדִים), from Togarmah; sim of swiftness Jo 2^4 (‖ סוּסִים); prob also Is 28^{28} Je 46^4 (‖ סוּסִים, cf Gf Gie), and perhaps 1 S 8^{11} וְשָׂם לוֹ בְּמֶרְכַּבְתּוֹ וּבְפָרָשָׁיו וְרָצוּ וגו׳ (kg subj)

†II פָּרָשׁ **n.m.** Ne 3.3 **horseman** (i e. *parrāš, cf. Ges § 84 b, Ar فَارِس, Eth. ፈረስ፡; Aram פָּרָשׁ, ܦܪܫܐ),—abs. פ׳ Na 3^3 Je 4^{29}, also פָּרָשׁ Ez 26^{10} (as if cstr Kö Synt § 337 s), pl פָּרָשִׁים Gn 50^9+; sf פָּרָשָׁיו Ex 14^9+,—*horseman*, usu pl, esp + רכב *chariotry*. Egyptian Gn 50^9 (J), Jos 24^6 (E), Ex $14^{9.17.18.23.26.28}$ (all P), 15^{19} (song), Is 31^1 2 K 18^{24} = Is 36^9, 2 Ch 12^3 cf 16^8, Philistine 1 S 13^5 2 S 1^6 (del בַּעֲלֵי 𝔊 We Dr Bu HPS), Aramæan 2 S 10^{18} (but read prob אִישׁ, cf ‖ 1 Ch 19^{18}, We Dr al), and (+ אִישׁ רַגְלִי) 2 S 8^4 = 1 Ch 18^4, cf 1 Ch 19^6, also עַל־סוּס וּפָרָשִׁים 1 K 20^{20} (si vera l), Isr, of Adonijah 1 K 1^5 (+ רֶכֶב, חֲמִשִּׁים אִישׁ רָצִים), Solomon + רֶכֶב $9^{19.22}$ $10^{26.26}$ = 2 Ch $8^{6.9}$ $1^{14.14}$, prob also 1 K 5^6 (+ סוּסִים לְמֶרְכָּבוֹ) = 2 Ch 9^{25} (+ סוּסִים וּמֶרְכָּבוֹת), Jehoahaz 2 K 13^7 (+ רֶכֶב, + רַגְלִי), fig of Elijah 2 K 2^{12}, of Elisha 13^{14}, + סוּסִים Ho 1^7, Assyrian Is $22^{6.7}$ (+ רכב), cf Na 3^3, פ׳ רֹכְבֵי סוּסִים Ez $23^{6.12}$; Babylonian Hb $1^{8.8}$ Je 4^{29} (+ רֹמֵה קֶשֶׁת), Ez 26^7 (+ רֶכֶב, סוּס), v^{10} (+ גַּלְגַּל וָרֶכֶב), Scythian (Gog) 38^4 (+ סוּסִים), Persian Is $21^{7.9}$ (צֶמֶד פ׳), Ne 2^9 Ezr 8^{22}, of king of north Dn 11^{40} (+ רכב)

†פַּרְשֶׁגֶן **n m. copy** (loan-word from Persian through Aram, v BAram),—cstr פ׳ הַנִּשְׁתְּוָן Ezr 7^{11}, cf פַּתְשֶׁגֶן

†פַּרְשְׁדֹנָה **n.[m.]** only וַיֵּצֵא הַפּ׳ Ju 3^{22}, read perh פֶּרֶשׁ *fæces* (𝔙 𝔗 Nö Untersuch 180 Bu GFM).

פַּרְשֵׁז v פרשׁז sub פרשׁ

†פַּרְשַׁנְדָּתָא **n.pr.m.** a son of Haman Est 9^7, Φαρσαν και Νεσταιν, Φαρσανεσταν, etc

†פְּרָת **n.pr. flum Euphrates**, Ευφρατης (As. *Purattu* Dl Pa 169 ff, whence OPers *Ufrâtu*, Spieg APK 211),—the greatest river of W Asia, פ׳ Gn 2^{14}, נְהַר פ׳ 15^{18} (both secondary phrases in J), נהר פ׳ also 2 S 8^3 (Qr, v נָהָר), Je $46^{2.6.10}$ Dt 1^7 11^{24} Jos 1^4 (D), 2 K 23^{29} 24^7 1 Ch 5^9 18^3, נהר om Je $13^{4.5.6.7}$ (where Ew Hi Marti, after Schick ZPV iii 11, think of some other פָּרָה, but Gf Gie and most defend *Euphrates*), 51^{63} 2 Ch 35^{20} (cf Gn 2^{14} supr); name not certainly attested before D Je, on earlier הַנָּהָר for this river v נ׳.

פְּרָת Gn 42^{22} v [פָּרָה]

†פַּרְתְּמִים **n.m pl. nobles** (loan-word from OPers *fratama, first*, Spieg APK 232, cf Skr *prathama*; Lag Arm Stud § 2289),—הַפּ׳ Est 1^3 6^9 Dn 1^3.

פָּשָׂה **vb spread**, intrans (NH פָּסָה *id*; Ar فَشَا (فشو) *be divulged, spread, be extensive*),—**Qal** *Pf* 3 ms פ׳ Lv 13^5+, 3 fs. פָּשְׂתָה v^8, פָּשָׂתָה v^{24}, *Impf* 3 ms יִפְשֶׂה v^{35}, 3 fs תִּפְשֶׂה v^7+; *Inf. abs* פָּשֹׂה v^7+,—only Lv 13, 14, of leprosy and like eruptions: c בַּבֶּגֶד, בָּעוֹר, etc, Lv 13^5+7 t 13, $14^{39.44.48}$ + בָּעוֹר (תפ׳) פָּשׂה יִפְשֶׂה $13^{7.22.27.35}$, abs $v^{23.32.53}$

†[פָּשַׂע] **vb. step, march** (NH פָּסַע; Aram פְּסַע, ܦܣܰܥ),—**Qal** *Impf* 1 s. אֶפְשְׂעָה (Ges § 10 h) Is 27^4, c. ב *against*

†פֶּשַׂע **n [m.] step**, כְּפ׳ בֵּינִי וּבֵין הַמָּוֶת 1 S 20^3.

†מִפְשָׂעָה **n.f. stepping-region of body, hip or buttock**, עַד־הַמִּ׳ 1 Ch 19^4 (= שְׁתוֹתֵיהֶם ‖ 2 S 10^4)

†[פָּשַׂק] **vb. part, open wide** (NH פָּסַק, Aram. פְּסַק, ܦܣܰܩ, all *cut, sever, cleave*),—**Qal** *Pt* פֹּשֵׂק שְׂפָתָיו Pr 13^3 i.e one talkative. **Pi.** *Impf.* 2 fs וַתְּפַשְּׂקִי אֶת־רַגְלַיִךְ Ez 16^{25} (c. ל pers; sensu obsc)

†פַּשׁ **n.[m.]** Jb 35^{15} si vera l from √פשׁשׁ (cf Ar فَسِيس *weak* in mind or body, فَسْفَاس *very stupid*),—i.e folly, but read פֶּשַׁע (𝔊 Theod Symm 𝔙 Di Bae Kau Du).

†[פָּשַׁח] **vb. Pi. tear in pieces** (NH פִּשַּׁח; Aram. פַּשַּׁח 1 S 15^{33} (Agag), ܦܰܫܰܚ, ܦܫܰܚ),—*Impf.* 3 ms. sf וַיְפַשְּׁחֵנִי La 3^{11} (of lion, in fig).

†פַּשְׁחוּר **n.pr.m.** Πασχωρ, Φα(δα)σσουρ, etc: **1.** Je $20^{1.2.3.3.6}$. **2.** 21^1 38^{1b} Ne 11^{12}, cf 1 Ch 9^{12} **3.** Ne 10^4 **4.** father of one Gedaliah Je 38^{1a} **5.** head of post-exil. family Ezr 2^{38} = Ne 7^{41}, Ezr 10^{22}. Cf. Mey Entstehung 169 f.

†פָּשַׁט **vb. strip off, make a dash, raid** (cf As *pašâtu, expunge, obliterate*, NH פָּשַׁט, Aram פְּשַׁט, ܦܫܰܛ, are *stretch out, extend, make plain*, so Ar بَسَطَ),—**Qal** *Pf.* 3 ms פ׳ Ho 7^1+, 2 ms וּפָשַׁטְתָּ Ju 9^{33}, etc.; *Impf* 3 ms וַיִּפְשֹׁט 1 S 19^{24}; 3 mpl יִפְשְׁטוּ Ez 26^1, etc., *Imv* ms. פְּשֹׁטָה Is 32^{11},

Pt. pl. פֹּשְׁטִים Ne 4^{17};—**1.** *strip off, put off,* one's garment (acc.) 1 S 19^{24} Ez 26^{16} 44^{19} Lv 6^{4} (opp. לָבַשׁ), 16^{23} (*id.;* both P), Ne 4^{17} Ct 5^{3}; acc. om. Is 32^{11}; of locusts Na 3^{16} *stripping off* (sheaths of wings, cf. Da Dr$^{Am. 85}$). **2.** *put off* (one's shelter), i.e. *make a dash* (from a sheltered place), c. אֶל Ju 20^{37}, abs. 9^{44}; esp. of marauding foray, Ho 7^{1}, c. עַל *against* Ju $9^{33.44}$ 1 S 23^{27} 30^{14} (ins. עַל cf. 𝔊 We Dr al.), Jb 1^{17}, c. אֶל 1 S 27^{8} 30^{1}, c. בְּ 1 Ch $14^{9.13}$ 2 Ch 25^{13} 28^{18}; in 1 S 27^{10} rd. אֶן (for אֶל־), We Dr al. **Pi.** *Inf. cstr.* לְפַשֵּׁט, c. acc. pers. 1 S 31^{8} *to strip the slain* = 1 Ch 10^{8}; abs. *only to strip* (sc. the slain) 2 S 23^{10} (ins. also ‖ 1 Ch 11^{13} Dr). **Hiph.** *Pf.* 3 ms. הִפְשִׁיט Jb 19^{9}; 3 mpl. sf. וְהִפְשִׁיטוּךְ Ez 23^{26}, etc.; *Impf.* 3 ms. וַיַּפְשֵׁט Nu 20^{28}; 1 s. sf. אַפְשִׁיטֶנָּה Ho 2^{5}; 2 mpl. תַּפְשִׁיטוּן Mi 2^{8}, etc.; *Imv.* הַפְשֵׁט Nu 20^{26}; *Inf. cstr.* הַפְשִׁיט 2 Ch 29^{34}; *Pt.* pl. מַפְשִׁיטִים 35^{11};—**1.** *strip* one *of* garment (2 acc.) Gn 37^{23} (E), Nu $20^{26.28}$ (opp. הִלְבִּישׁ), Ez 16^{39} 23^{26}; c. acc. pers. alone 1 Ch 10^{9}; Ho 2^{5} *strip* her (sf.) naked (עֲרֻמָּה). **2.** *strip off,* acc. כֵּלָיו 1 S 31^{9}, clothing Jb 22^{6}; c. acc. אֶדֶר + מִמּוּל Mi 2^{8}; c. acc. עוֹר + מֵעַל 3^{3}, cf. (acc. כְּבוֹדִי) Jb 19^{9}. **3.** *flay,* c. acc. הָעֹלָה Lv 1^{6} 2 Ch 29^{34}; acc. om. 35^{11}. **Hithp.** *Impf.* 3 ms. וַיִּתְפַּשֵּׁט 1 S 18^{4} *he stripped himself of* his garment (acc.).

† פָּשַׁע vb. rebel, transgress (NH *id.;* Syr. ܦܫܥ is *be terrified,* ܦܫܝܥܐ *tepid, insipid*);—**Qal** *Pf.* 3 ms. פ׳ 2 K 3^{7}+, 2 fs. פָּשַׁעַתְּ Zp 3^{11}; פָּשַׁעַתְּ Je 3^{13}, etc.; *Impf.* יִפְשַׁע Pr 28^{21} + 8 t. Impf.; *Imv.* mpl. פִּשְׁעוּ Am 4^{4}; *Inf. abs.* פָּשֹׁעַ Is 59^{13}; cstr. פְּשֹׁעַ Am 4^{4} Ez 10^{13}; *Pt.* פֹּשֵׁעַ Is 48^{8}; פֹּשְׁעִים Is 1^{28}+, etc.;—**1.** *rebel, revolt,* of nations, c. בְּ *against,* 1 K 12^{19} 2 K 1^{1} $3^{5.7}$ 2 Ch 10^{19}; abs. 2 K 8^{22}, מִתַּחַת יַד $v^{20.22}$ 2 Ch $21^{8.10.10}$; פָּשְׁעוּ בִי Is 1^{2} (Isr. under fig. of י׳'s sons). **2.** *transgress* against God, abs. Is 1^{28} 46^{8} 48^{8} $53^{12.12}$ Ho 14^{10} Am $4^{4.4}$ La 3^{42} Dn 8^{23} ψ 37^{38} 51^{15}, *for* (עַל) *a bit of bread* Pr 28^{21}; עַל בַּדָּבָר הַזֶּה Ezr 10^{13} *in this thing;* פ׳ ב׳ תּוֹרָתִי Ho 8^{1}; elsewhere c. בְּ *against* God: Is 43^{27} 59^{13} 66^{24} Je $2^{8.29}$ 3^{13} 33^{8} Ez 2^{3} 20^{38} Ho 7^{13}; עלילות אשר פ׳ב פשעים אשר פ׳ב 1 K 8^{50} Ez 18^{31}; Zp 3^{11}. **Niph.** *Pf.* 3 ms. אָח נִפְשָׁע (van d. H. *Pt.* נִפְשָׁע) *a brother* (who has been) *offended* Pr 18^{19}, but very dubious, cf. Toy.

† פֶּשַׁע n.m.$^{ψ 13, 14}$ **transgression;**—abs. פ׳ Ex 22^{8}+, פָּשַׁע Pr 10^{19}+; cstr. פֶּשַׁע Gn 50^{17}+; sf. פִּשְׁעִי Gn 31^{36} + 14 t. sfs.; pl. פְּשָׁעִים Pr 10^{12}; cstr. פִּשְׁעֵי Am 1^{3}+, etc.;—**1.** *transgression* against individuals Gn 31^{36} $50^{17.17}$ Ex 22^{8} (E), 1 S 24^{12} 25^{28} Pr 10^{19} 17^{19} 28^{24} $29^{6.16.22}$; פ׳ שְׂפָתַיִם 12^{13}; על כל־פשעים תְּכַסֶּה אַהֲבָה 10^{12}, cf. 17^{9} 19^{11} 28^{13}. **2.** of nation, against nation: Am $1^{3.6.9.11.13}$ 2^{1}; of land Pr 28^{2}. Elsewh. **3.** against God: **a.** in gen., ‖ חטאת Is 58^{1} 59^{12} Mi $1^{5.5.13}$ 3^{8} Am 5^{12}; ‖ עון Ez 21^{29} ψ 107^{17}; עשה פ׳ Ez $18^{22.28}$; ביום פ׳ 33^{12}; רַבּוּ פ׳ Is 59^{12} Jb 35^{6} Je 5^{6} (?); יֹסִיף על חטאתו פ׳ Jb 34^{37} *he addeth transgression unto his sin;* יִלְדֵי פ׳ Is 57^{4}; personified as evil spirit, נאם פשע ψ 36^{2}. **b.** as recognized by sinner; he knows it ψ 51^{5}, makes known concerning it to י׳ 32^{5}, does not cover it (כסה) Jb 31^{33}; turns from it Is 59^{20} Ez 18^{30}; casts it away from him Ez 18^{31}. **c.** God deals with it: by visiting it (פקד) Am 3^{14} ψ 89^{33}, dealing with one according to it, עשה כ Ez 39^{24}, making it known to sinner Jb 13^{23} 36^{9}; punishing in various ways: מִפ׳ *because of* it Is $53^{5.8}$; c. עַל, *acc. to* it Am $2^{4.6}$ La $1^{5.22}$; *for* it, c. ב Is 50^{1}; על פ׳ La 1^{14} *yoke of transgression;* personified, וַיְשַׁלְּחֵם בְּיַד פ׳ Jb 8^{4}; he does not grant forgiveness to it, לא נשא ל׳ Ex 23^{21} Jos 24^{19} (E). **d.** God forgives (נשא) it Ex 34^{7} Nu 14^{18} (J), Jb 7^{21}, cf. ψ 32^{1}; pardons (סלח) 1 K 8^{50}; passes over (עבר על, cf. Pr 19^{11}) Mi 7^{18}; removes (הרחיק) ψ 103^{12}; covers over (כפר) 65^{4};—cf. (of priest) וְכִפֶּר עַל־הַקֹּדֶשׁ מִפּ׳ Lv 16^{16}, and confession of פ׳ over (על) goat v^{21};—God blots out (מחה) Is 43^{25} 44^{22} ψ 51^{3}; ומפ׳ אַל־תִּזְכֹּר 25^{7}; delivers from, הציל מן 39^{9}.—Jb 35^{15} read פֶּשַׁע for פַּשׁ q.v. **4.** *guilt of transgression* (cf. עון **2**), בְּלִי פ׳ *without* (guilt of) transgression Jb 33^{9} 34^{6}; לא פ׳ ψ 59^{4}; עלינו פ׳ Ez 33^{10}; כבד עליה פ׳ Is 24^{20}; בְּרֹב פ׳ ψ 5^{11}; נקיתי מפ׳ 19^{14}; יִטַּמְּאוּ בְּכָל־פ׳ *defile themselves with all (the guilt of) their transgressions* Ez 14^{11} 37^{23}; חָתֻם בִּצְרוֹר פ׳ Jb 14^{17}. **5.** *punishment for transgression,* Dn $8^{12.13}$ 9^{24}, cf. עון **3**. **6.** *offering for transgression,* האתן בכורי פשעי Mi 6^{7} *shall I give my first-born as an offering for my transgression* (cf. חטאת **4**).

†פֵּשֶׁר n.[m.] solution, interpretation (loan-word from Aram. פִּשְׁרָא);—cstr. פ׳ Ec 8^{1}.

†[פֵּשֶׁת] n.[m.] flax, linen (✓dub.; NH פִּשְׁתָּן, Pun. Φοιστ; Löw$^{p. 233}$);—sf. פִּשְׁתִּי Ho $2^{7.11}$; elsewhere pl. פִּשְׁתִּים Ju 15^{14}+, cstr. פִּשְׁתֵּי Jos 2^{6};—**1.** *flax,* after gathering, פִּשְׁתֵּי הָעֵץ Jos 2^{6} (JE, v. עֵץ **2 f**); inflammable Ju 15^{14} (sim.); as natural product (+ צֶמֶר) Ho $2^{7.11}$; as material, פְּתִיל פ׳ Ez 40^{3}; of various garments Je 13^{1} Ez $44^{17.18.18}$, + צֶמֶר Dt 22^{11} Lv $13^{47.48.52.59}$ (P), cf. Pr 31^{13}; עֹבְדֵי פ׳ שְׂרִיקוֹת Is 19^{9} (v. [שָׂרִיק]).

†פִּשְׁתָּה n.f. flax;—פ׳: 1. growing Ex 9[31.31] (J). 2. =wick Is 42[3] 43[17] (in sim.).

פַּת v. פתת.

†[פֹּת] n.[f.] pl. הַפֹּתוֹת לְדַלְתוֹת הַבַּיִת 1 K 7[50] i.e. prob. the *sockets* above and below, in which the door-pivots turned (performing office of mod. hinges); sg. sf. פָּתְהֵן Is 3[17] (Ges §91f), prob., si vera l., *their secret parts, cardo femina* (so Thes and most); but read perh. חָרְפָּתְהֵן Bachm SK. 1894, 650 Kit (in Di) Marti; > פַּאֲתְהֵן Sta ZAW vi (1886), 336, cf. 𝔙 Di.

פְּתָאִים v. I. פֶּתִי sub I. פתה.

פִּתְאֹם v. פֶּתַע.

†[פַּת־בַּג] (read always [פַּתְבַּג]) n.[m.] portion (of food) for king, delicacies (Pers. loan-word, cf. Skr. *prati-bhâga*, Zend [*pati-baga*; whence] Gk. translit. *ποτίβαζις*, Syr. ܦܛܒܓܐ; Gildem ZKM iv. 213 f. Lag Ges. Abh. 73 Bev Dn Dr Dn);—cstr. פַּת־בַּג הַמֶּלֶךְ Dn 1[5.8.13.15], sf. פַּת־בָּגָם v[16], אֲכָלַי פַּת־בָּגוֹ 11[26].

†פִּתְגָּם n.m. edict, decree (Pers. loan-wd., OPers. *patigâma* (*patigam, come to, arrive*), NPers. *paigâm, message*; v. Gildem ZKM iv. 214 Mey Entstehung 23; Aram. פִּתְגָּמָא, ܦܬܓܡܐ, *word, command*, B Aram. = BH);—cstr. פ׳ הַמֶּלֶךְ Est 1[20]; c. genit. obj. פ׳ מַעֲשֵׂה הָרָעָה Ec 8[11] (appar. f., cf. De; but Hi Albr ZAW xvi (1896), 115 read נַעֲשָׂה for נַעֲשָׂה).

[פָּתָה] vb. be spacious, wide, open (Aram. פְּתָא *be spacious*, ܦܬܐ *be spacious, abundant*; cf. Ar. فَتُوَ, فَتِيَ *be youthful, in prime of life*, فَتًى *young man, one in prime of life* (development of various meanings from √ not wholly clear, cf. Nö ZMG xl (1886), 735));—Qal *Pt.* פֹּתֶה Pr 20[19] poss. *one open* as to lips, but v. פָּתָה denom. infr. Hiph. *Impf.* 3 ms. juss. יַפְתְּ א׳ לְיֶפֶת Gn 9[27] *may God make wide for Japhet* (give him an extensive inheritance).—*Pf.* poss. Pr 24[28] (reading וְהִפְתִּיתָ בִשְׂפָתֶיךָ, *make wide with* (open wide) *thy lips*, for MT וַהֲפִתִּיתָ בִּשׂ׳, so SS; but cf. פָּתָה denom. Pi.).

†פֶּתִי [for פֶּתִי Lag BN 52 Ba ZMG xlii (1888), 353; NB 320] adj. simple, poss. as open-minded;—פֶּתִי Pr 9[4]+, פֶּתִי ψ 19[8]+; pl. פְּתָאִים (Ges §93x) 116[6]+6 t. Pr; פְּתָיִים 119[130] Pr 22[3]; פְּתָיִם 1[22.32];—*simple*, as subst. concr.: open to the instruction of wisdom or folly, Pr 9[4.16]; believing every word 14[15]; lacking עָרְמָה 1[4] 8[5] 19[25]; needing בִּין ψ 119[130], חכמה 19[8] Pr 21[11]; in good sense, שמר פתאים י׳ ψ 116[6] *preserveth the simple-minded;* but usu. tendency to bad sense; פתי love פתאים Pr 1[22]; inherit אִוֶּלֶת 14[18], are easily enticed, misled and go back 1[32] 7[7] 9[6] 22[3]=27[12]; they need atonement Ez 45[20] (‖ שׁגה).

†[פְּתִי] n.f. simplicity (i.e. lack of wisdom), עַד־מָתַי פְּתָיִם תְּאֵהֲבוּ־פֶתִי Pr 1[22].

†פְּתַיּוּת n.f. id. Pr 9[13] (Toy conj. מְפַתָּה).

†[פָּתָה] vb. denom. be simple (NH Pi. *entice*);—Qal *Impf.* 3 ms. יִפְתֶּה Dt 11[16]; וַיִּפְתְּ Jb 31[27]; *Pt.* פֹּתֶה Jb 5[2] Pr 20[19]; f. פּוֹתָה Ho 7[11];—1. *be open-minded* (?), *simple* Jb 5[2]; יוֹנָה פוֹתָה Ho 7[11] *silly dove;* פֹּתֶה שְׂפָתָיו Pr 20[19] *one foolish as to his lips* (most, *openeth wide his lips*). 2. *be enticed, deceived* Dt 11[16] Jb 31[27]. Niph. *Pf.* 3 ms. נִפְתָּה Jb 31[9]; *Impf.* 1 s. וָאֶפָּת Je 20[7];—*be deceived* Je 20[7]; c. עַל *enticed unto* Jb 31[9]. Piel *Pf.* 2 ms. פִּתִּיתָ Pr 24[28]; sf. פִּתִּיתַנִי Je 20[7]; 1 s. פִּתֵּיתִי Ez 14[9]; *Impf.* 3 ms. יְפַתֶּה Ex 22[15]+, etc.; *Imv.* פַּתִּי Ju 14[15] 16[5]; *Inf. cstr.* sf. פַּתֹּתְךָ 2 S 3[25]; *Pt.* sf. מְפַתֶּיהָ (Ges §93ss) Ho 2[16];—1. *persuade*, woman Ho 2[16] (fig., י׳ subj.), *seduce*, virgin Ex 22[15]; *entice*, husband Ju 14[15] 16[5]; a man to sin Pr 1[10] 16[29]. 2. *deceive*, 2 S 3[25] Pr 24[28] (yet cf. √ Hiph. supr.); subj. י׳, obj. proph., Je 20[7] Ez 14[9], cf. 1 K 22[20.21.22]=2 Ch 18[19.20.21]; obj. י׳, ψ 78[36]. Pual *Impf.* 3 ms. יְפֻתֶּה: 1. *be persuaded*, Pr 25[15]. 2. *be deceived*, Je 20[10]; by י׳, Ez 14[9].

†יֶפֶת n.pr.m. third son of Noah, Ἰαφεθ;—יֶפֶת: יַפְתְּ א׳ לְיֶפֶת Gn 9[27] (J), 7[13], 10[2] (P) = 1 Ch 1[4], Gn 9[23] 10[21] (J); יָפֶת 9[18] (J), 5[32] 6[10] 10[1] (P), 1 Ch 1[5].

†פְּתוּאֵל n.pr.m. father of prophet Joel Jo 1[1] (𝔊 Βαθουηλ, i.e. בְּתוּאֵל).

†פְּתוֹר n.pr.loc. home of Balaam;—c. ה loc. פְּתוֹרָה Nu 22[5], Φαθουρα, A Βαθουρα; פ׳ אֲרַם נַהֲרַיִם Dt 23[5], but om. פ׳ 𝔊;—cf. As. *Pitru* (on W. bank of upper Euphr.) Schr KGF 220; COT Nu 22, 5 Dl Pa 269 Dr Hastings DB; Eg. *Pe-d-ru* WMM As. u. Eur. 291.

[פְּתוֹת] v. פתת.

†I. פָּתַח vb. open (NH *id.*; Ph. פתח; As. *pitû, patû*; Sab. פתח Os ZMG xix (1865), 197; Ar. فَتَحَ; Eth. ፈትሐ፡; Aram. פְּתַח, ܦܬܚ; Nab. Palm. פתח);—Qal *Pf.* 3 ms. פ׳ 2 K 15[16]+, etc.; *Impf.* 3 ms. יִפְתַּח Ex 21[33]+; 3 mpl. sf. יִפְתָּחוּם Ne 13[19], etc.; *Imv.* ms. פְּתַח 2 K 13[17]+; fs. פִּתְחִי

Ct 5^{2}; mpl. פִּתְחוּ Jos 10^{22}+; *Inf. abs.* פָּתֹחַ Dt 15^{8}+; cstr. לִפְתֹּחַ Ez 21^{27}+; *Pt. act.* פֹּתֵחַ Ju 3^{25}+, *pass.* פָּתוּחַ Je 5^{16}+, etc.;—*open* sack, שַׂק, Gn 42^{27} (E), אַמְתַּחַת 43^{21} 44^{11} (J), skin-bottle (נאוד) Ju 4^{19}, hamper (תֵּבָה) Ex 2^{6} (E), pit (בּוֹר) 21^{33} (E; i.e. uncover it), mouth (פִּי) of cave Jos 10^{22} (JE), grave Ez $37^{12.13}$ (to bring forth dead), cf. (in fig.) Je 5^{16} ψ 5^{10}; כְּלִי פָּתוּחַ Nu 19^{15} (P) *open vessel*, door (דֶּלֶת; sts. opp. סָגַר) Ju 3^{25} + v^{25} (obj. om.), 19^{27} 1 S 3^{15} 2 K $9^{3.10}$ 2 Ch 29^{3} Jb 31^{32} (c. לְ pers.); fig. of Leb. Zc 11^{1}, דַּלְתֵי שָׁמַיִם ψ 78^{23} (of י׳, sending rain), ד׳ = city-gates Ne 13^{19} Is 45^{1} (‖ שְׁעָרִים; י׳ subj, c. לְפָנָיו), ד׳ om Ct $5^{2.5.6}$; gate (שַׁעַר), of land Na 3^{13} (Inf. abs. + Impf. **Niph.** q v.), cf. Ez 25^{9}, שַׁעַר of temple (-court) Ez 46^{12} (c. לְ pers.), ψ 118^{19} (*id*), city Is 26^{2}, obj om. Dt 20^{11} 2 K 15^{16}; window, חַלּוֹן, 2 K $13^{17.17}$, אֲרֻבּוֹת הַשָּׁמַיִם (by י׳ sending rain) Gn 8^{6} (J), Mal 3^{10}, city Je 13^{19}, עִיר פְּתוּחָה Jos 8^{17} (JE); abs. פ׳ וְלֹא סגר Is $22^{22.22}$;—14^{17} is dubious, Gr Perles[Anal 28.42] Kit (in Di) read לַאֲסִירָיו לֹא־פ׳ בֵּית־הַכֶּלֶא; > Bu Che Marti אֲסִירָיו לֹא פתח אִישׁ לְבֵיתוֹ; storehouse, armoury Gn 41^{56} Je 50^{25} (of י׳), Je 50^{26} (for destruction), fig. of sky, for rain Dt 28^{12} (c. לְ pers.; of י׳), cf. *open* בַּר, expose for sale, Am 8^{5}; *open* womb, i.e. grant offspring Gn 29^{31} 30^{22} (J); *open* mouth (פֶּה) to cry, speak Ez 21^{27} Jb 3^{1} Dn 10^{16}, hence = speak Is $53^{7.7}$ Jb 33^{2} ψ 39^{10} 78^{2} (בְּמָשָׁל), 109^{2} (c. עַל pers), Pr 24^{7} 31^{8} (c. לְ pers), v$^{9.26}$ (בְּחָכְמָה); ψ 49^{5} either *utter, declare, propound* riddle, or *open up, expound;* have power of speech ψ 38^{14}, of י׳ giving power of (prophetic) speech Ez 3^{27} 33^{22}, giving speech to ass Nu 22^{28} (J); *open* mouth, to eat Ez 3^{2}, of earth, to swallow up, Nu 16^{32} 26^{10}, cf. (פֶּה om.) ψ 106^{17}; *open* lips, to speak Jb 11^{5} (c עִם pers), 32^{20} (Gi v^{21}); of י׳ opening man's lips ψ 51^{17}, man's ear Is 50^{5} (As. *uznâ puttû*); of eyes only pt. pass., c אֶל 1 K 8^{29} = 2 Ch 6^{20}, 1 K 8^{52} Ne 1^{6}, c. לְ 2 Ch 6^{40} (by zeugma), 7^{15} (all of י׳'s favour); *open* hand, in giving Dt $15^{8.11}$ (c. לְ pers., + inf. abs.), of י׳ ψ 104^{28} 145^{16}; book Ne $8^{5.5}$, letter 6^{5}; *open* river (channel) Is 41^{18} (of י׳), rock, letting out water, ψ 105^{41} (*id*); *open* sword, = draw it Ez 21^{33} ψ 37^{14}; of root שָׁרְשִׁי פָתוּחַ אֱלֵי־מָיִם Jb 29^{19}, i.e. with no obstacle intervening.—תִּפְתַּח אֶרֶץ Is 45^{8} is dub.; verb not elsewhere intrans.; Du Che[Hpt] Marti prop. רַחְמָהּ as obj.; Gr Kit (in Di) read תִּפָּתַח. **Niph.** *Pf* 3 ms נִפְתַּח Is 5^{27}, etc.; *Impf.* 3 ms. יִפָּתַח Ez 24^{27}, יִפָּתֵחַ 44^{2}+, etc.; *Inf. cstr.* הִפָּתַח Is 51^{14}; *Pt.* נִפְתָּח Zc 13^{1};—*be opened*, of girdle Is 5^{27} (i.e. loosened), cf. of captive 51^{14}, and, of calamity, Je 1^{14} *be let loose* (c. עַל pers); gates Na 2^{7} 3^{13} (of land, *thrown open* to (לְ) enemy), Ez 44^{2} $46^{1.1}$ Ne 7^{3}; impers. of man shut in by God Jb 12^{14}; of windows of heaven Gn 7^{11} (P), cf. Is 24^{18} (of future destruction), the heavens themselves Ez 1^{1} (for visions); fountain Zc 13^{1}; wine(-skin, c neg) Jb 32^{19}, mouth, in speech 24^{27} 33^{22}; ears Is 35^{5}. **Pi.** *Pf.* 3 ms. פִּתַּח Jb 30^{11}+, פִּתֵּחַ 12^{18}+, etc, *Impf.* 3 ms. יְפַתַּח Is 28^{24}, 1 s. אֲפַתֵּחַ Is 45^{1}, etc; *Inf abs* פַּתֵּחַ Is 58^{6}; cstr, *id* ψ 102^{21}; *Pt* מְפַתֵּחַ 1 K 20^{11};—*loose*: **1.** *free*, i e. ungird, camels Gn 24^{32} (J): loins of kings Is 45^{1} (i.e. disarm them); *set free*, c sf. pers ψ 105^{20}, Je 40^{4} (c. מִן), c. acc. בְּנֵי תְמוּתָה ψ 102^{21}. **2.** *loosen* (and remove) sack-cloth Is 20^{2} (c מֵעַל), ψ 30^{12}, armour 1 K 20^{11} (obj. om., opp. חָגַר); bonds Jb 12^{18} ψ 116^{16}, cf Is 58^{6} Jb 39^{5}, cord 30^{11} 38^{31}; *loosen* ground Is 28^{24} (in tillage; cf. Vogelst[Landwirthschaft 38], As. *puttû*) **3.** *open* gates Is 60^{11}, doors Jb 41^{6} (fig. of crocodile's jaws), ear Is 48^{8} (rd. prob either פִּתַּחְתִּי, פָּתַחְתִּי [𝔊 Du Marti], or נִפְתְּחָה [Gr Che Kit in Di]; buds Ct 7^{13} (of blossom; obj om.; or intrans, as sts Ar. فَتَّحَ, v Dozy). **Hithp.** *Imv.* mpl. התפתחו Is 52^{2} Kt < Qr fs הִתְפַּתְּחִי (so 𝔊; of personif. Jerus) *loosen thee* (Ges[§54 f]) *the fetters of thy neck*

פֶּתַח [164] **n.m.**[Ez 8.8] (**f.** 2 S 17^{9} but We reads אַחַד for אַחַת, and so Albr[ZAW xvi (1896). 86]) opening, doorway, entrance;—abs פ׳ Gn 4^{7}+, פָּתַח 19^{11}+, הַפֶּתְחָה v^{6}; cstr. פֶּתַח 18^{1}+; sf. פִּתְחוֹ Pr 17^{19}, פִּתְחָהּ Ez 40^{38}; pl פְּתָחִים 1 K 7^{5} Pr 8^{3}; cstr. פִּתְחֵי ψ 24^{7}+; sf פְּתָחַי Pr 8^{34}, etc;—*doorway* of nomad's tent, פ׳ הָאֹהֶל Gn $18^{1.2.10}$ (J), Ex $33^{8.10}$ (E), Nu 11^{10} 16^{27} (JE), Ju 4^{20}, cf. (without הָאֹהֶל) Gn 4^{7} (in fig.), Jb $31^{9.34}$; of sacred tent, פ׳ הָאֹהֶל Ex $33^{9.10}$ Nu 12^{5} (E), 26^{36} 36^{37} 39^{38} (P), Dt 31^{15}, usu (P) פ׳ אֹהֶל מוֹעֵד Ex 29^{4} + 6 t. Ex + $40^{6.29}$ (פ׳ מִשְׁכַּן אֹהֶל מ׳), Lv 1^{3} + 22 t. Lv, Nu 3^{25} + 11 t. Nu, Jos 19^{51} 1 S 2^{22}, cf. 1 Ch 9^{21}; פ׳ הַמִּשְׁכָּן Ex 35^{15}, cf. $40^{5.28}$ (all P); of court Nu 3^{26} cf. 4^{26} and (of temple) Ez 8^{7}; *doorway* of (private) house Gn $19^{6.11.11}$ + 22 t., cf. Ct 7^{14}; in Pr 17^{19} Frankenb Toy rd. פִּיו for פִּתְחוֹ; of temple 1 K 6^{33} Ez 8^{16}, so פ׳ הַבַּיִת Ez 47^{1} 2 Ch 4^{22}; פ׳ הַדְּבִיר 1 K 6^{31}, פ׳ הַצֵּלָע v^{8} Ez 41^{11} cf. v$^{11.11}$; pl 1 K 7^{5}; various doorways in Ezek.'s temple Ez $40^{13.13}$ + 13 t. 40–42 (v. also infr.); doorway of ark Gn 6^{16} (P); of tower Ju 9^{52}; in wall Ez 8^{8}; *opening* (mouth) of cave 1 K 19^{13}; פ׳ הַשַּׁעַר *opening*, i.e.

doorway, of gate Ez 40^{11}, of city פ׳ שַׁעַר הָעִיר, i e. the outer aperture of the gate Jos 8^{29} 20^{4} Ju 9$^{35.44}$ Je 1^{15} (pl), cf. 19^{8} 1 K 22^{10}=2 Ch 18^{9}, 2 K 23^{8} Pr 1^{21}; so פ׳ הַשַּׁעַר Ju 9^{40} 2 S 10^{8} 11^{23} 2 K 7^{3} 10^{8}, and (of farm or village) Ju 18$^{16.17}$, so פ׳ הָעִיר 1 K 17^{10} 1 Ch 19^{9} (=2 S 10^{8} supr.), cf. Gn 38^{14}, pl of city gates themselves (poet.) Is 3^{26} (personif), פ׳ נדיבים 13^{2}; ψ 24$^{7.9}$ פִּתְחֵי עוֹלָם (שְׁעָרִים ||), cf. fig שמר פִּתְחֵי־פִיךָ Mi 7^{5}, also פ׳ שַׁעַר בֵּית י׳ Je 36^{10} Ez 8^{14} 10^{19} cf. 8^{3} 11^{1} 40^{4} 46^{3}, פ׳ ש׳ י׳ Je 26^{10}, פְּתָחֶיהָ Mi 5^{5} of *entrances* to a country, fig. פ׳ תִּקְוָה Ho 2^{17} *doorway of hope*

†**פֵּתַח** **n m. opening, unfolding**,—cstr. פ׳ דְּבָרֶיךָ יָאִיר ψ 119^{130}, so 𝔊 and most; > Symm Jer Bae פְּתַח (=*thy words as a doorway*).

†**פִּתְחוֹן** **n.[m.] opening**,—cstr. פִּתְחוֹן פֶּה *opening of mouth* in speech or song Ez 16^{63} 29^{21}.

†**[פְּתִיחָה]** **n.[f.] drawn sword**;—pl פתחות ψ 55^{22} (fig of words; cf Ez 21^{33} ψ 37^{14}).

†**פְּתַחְיָה** **n.pr.m. 1.** priest 1 Ch 24^{16}, Εζεκηλ, Φεθεια, etc **2.** Levite Ezr 10^{23} Ne 9^{5}, Φαθαια, Φεθεια(ς), etc. **3.** Judahite Ne 11^{24}, Παθαια, Φαθαια.

†**יִפְתָּח** **n.pr. 1. m. Jephthah**, Ιεφθαε (*he* [God] *openeth*),—Ju 11^{1}+26 t. 11, 12, 1 S 12^{11}. **2. loc.** in the שְׁפֵלָה Jos 15^{43} (P), A 𝔊L Ιεφθα

†**יִפְתַּח־אֵל** **n.pr.loc.** (*God openeth*; cf. Sab n pr.m. יפתחאל Hal^{148,1}),—in גֵּי יִפ׳ (Γαιφαηλ, Γαι και Φθαιηλ, A 𝔊L Γαι (Ι)εφθαηλ), valley betw. Zebulun and Asher Jos 19$^{14.27}$ (P), prob. near *Jêfât* (*Jotapata*), and perhaps upper part of *Wady ʿAbellîn*, v. Buhl$^{Geogr\ 109,223}$.

†**[מִפְתָּח]** **n.[m.] opening, utterance**,—cstr. מִפְתַּח שְׂפָתַי Pr 8^{6} i e that with which my lips open.

†**מַפְתֵּחַ** **n.m. key** (*opening instrument*);—abs מ׳ Ju 3^{25} 1 Ch 9^{27}; cstr. Is 22^{22} (fig.).

†**נֶפְתּוֹחַ** **n.pr.loc.** Μαφθω, Ναφθω, in מֵי נ׳ Jos 15^{9} 18^{15} (P), on border of Judah and Benj.; usu. identif with spring *Liftâ*, near Jerus. to the NW, v. Buhl$^{Geogr\ 101}$. נַפְתָּחִים v. p 661.

I, II. **פְּתִי, פְּתָיוּת** v. sub פתה

†II. **[פָּתַח]** **vb. Pi. engrave** (NH Pi id, פִּתּוּחַ = BH, and so 𝔗, As. *patâhu, bore, penetrate*; cf perh. Ar. فَتْخَةٌ, فَتَخَةٌ *ring* (cf Frä^{252}));—*Pf.* 3 ms. פִּתַּח 2 Ch 3^{7}, etc., *Impf.* 3 ms. וַיְפַתַּח 1 K 7^{36}; 2 ms. תְּפַתַּח Ex 28^{11}; *Inf. cstr* לְפַתֵּחַ 2 Ch 2$^{6.13}$; *Pt* מְפַתֵּחַ Zc 3^{9},—*engrave*, c.acc. + עַל, on metal 1 K 7^{36} 2 Ch 3^{7} Ex 28^{36} (acc. cogn. פִּתּוּחֵי חוֹתָם), on stone v^{9}; c. acc. אבן + acc. cogn v^{11} (all P); c. acc. cogn. only, Zc 3^{9} (on stone), and, in gen, 2 Ch 2$^{6.13}$. **Pu.** *Pt* fpl מְפֻתָּחֹת פִּתּוּחֵי חוֹתָם Ex 39^{6} (P) *stones engraved with the engravings of a signet.*

†**פִּתּוּחַ** **n.m. engraving**;—abs. פ׳ 2 Ch 2^{13}; sf. פִּתֻּחָהּ Zc 3^{9}, elsewhere pl פִּתּוּחִים 2 Ch 2^{6}, etc.;—on (wood overlaid with) metal, פִּתּוּחֵי מִקְלְעוֹת כְּרוּבִים 1 K 6^{29} (see v$^{21.22}$), in temple, so ψ 74^{6}, on stone Zc 3^{9}, esp פִּתּוּחֵי חֹתָם Ex 28$^{11.21.36}$ 39$^{6.14.30}$; in gen. 2 Ch 2$^{6.13}$.

†**פְּתִיגִיל** **n.[m.] rich robe(?)** (prob foreign word),—abs פ׳ Is 3^{24}, 𝔊 χιτὼν μεσοπόρφυρος, 𝔙 *fascia pectoralis*.

†**[פָּתַל]** **vb. twist** (NH Pi and deriv.; Ar. فَتَلَ; Eth ፈተለ:, Aram פְּתַל, chiefly deriv, in fig. senses, Syr ܦܬܠ);—**Niph.** *Pf.* 1 s. נִפְתַּלְתִּי עִם Gn 30^{8} *I have wrestled* (lit. twisted myself) *with*; *Pt* עֲצַת נִפְתָּלִים Jb 5^{13} *the plan of the tortuous*; נִפְתָּל וְעִקֵּשׁ Pr 8^{8} anything *tortuous and twisted.* **Hithp.** *Impf* 2 ms. עִם־עִקֵּשׁ תִּתְפַּתָּל ψ 18^{27} *with the twisted thou dost deal tortuously* = 2 S 22^{27} (so rd for imposs תִּתַּפָּל).

†**פָּתִיל** **n.m.**$^{Ju\ 16,9}$ **cord, thread** (*twisted*);—abs. פ׳ Nu 19^{15}, cstr. פְּתִיל Ju 16^{9}+, sf. פְּתִילְךָ Gn 38^{18}, pl. פְּתִילִים v^{25}, פְּתִלִם Ex 39^{3};—*cord* (from which seal was hung) Gn 38$^{18.25}$ (J), פ׳ נְעֹרֶת Ju 16^{9} (sim), פ׳ פִּשְׁתִּים Ez 40^{3} (as measuring line); פ׳ תְּכֵלֶת, for fastening, Ex 28$^{28.37}$ 39$^{21.31}$ Nu 15^{38}, cf. פְּתִיל alone 19^{15} (perh. gloss, v Di); *threads* (of gold) in ephod Ex 39^{3} (all P).

†**פְּתַלְתֹּל** **adj. tortuous**;—דּוֹר עִקֵּשׁ וּפ׳ Dt 32^{5}.

†**[נַפְתּוּלִים]** **n.[m.] pl. wrestlings** (cf. √ **Niph.** *Pf*),—cstr נַפְתּוּלֵי א׳ Gn 30^{8} *wrestlings of God*, i.e mighty wrestlings.

נַפְתָּלִי^{51} **n.pr.m. et trib. Naphtali**, Νεφθαλει(μ), etc (interpr. as *my wrestling* Gn 30^{8}; perhaps orig *crafty, cunning one*),—**1.** second son of Jacob and Bilhah Gn 30^{8} (J), 35^{25} 46^{24} (P), 1 Ch 2^{2}, cf. Gn 49^{21} (poem). **2.** as a tribe of Isr.. **a.** Ju 1^{33} 4^{10} 5^{18} Dt 33$^{23.23}$+, so (Hex, only P) בְּנֵי נ׳ Ju 4^{6} Nu 1^{42}+6 t, מַטֵּה נ׳ Nu 2^{29} 1 K 7^{14} +5 t, מַטֵּה בְנֵי נ׳ Nu 10^{27} 34^{28} Jos 19^{39}, שַׁעַר נ׳

Ez 48^{34} (in new Jerus.); אֶרֶץ נ׳ 1 K 15^{20} 2 K 15^{29}, cf. Is 8^{23}; קֶדֶשׁ נ׳ Ju 4^{6}; הַר נ׳ Jos 20^{7}; גְּבוּל נ׳ Ez 48^{4}, יָמָּה נ׳ v^{3}, עָרֵי נ׳ 2 Ch 16^{4}. **b.** as territorial name Dt 34^{2} (JE) 1 K 4^{15} 1 Ch 12^{41} (van d. H. v^{40}), 2 Ch 34^{6}; Ju 6^{35} 7^{23} might be **a** or **b**.

†פִּתֹם **n.pr.loc.** Pithom, Π(ε)ιθω, A Πιθωμ (Egypt. *Patum, Per-Atum, house of* (god) *Atum*) one of the עָרֵי מִסְכְּנוֹת built by Isr. for Pharaoh Ex 1^{11}; identif by Naville with *Tel el-Maskhûta*, near E. end of Wady Tumilat, Naville[Pithom, 1885] Di-Ry[ad loc] Di[SBAk, 1886, 889 ff.] Bad[Egypt (4), 159].

פתן (√of foll; mng dub; Hilpr[Bab. Exped Univ Pennsylv ix (1896), 53], cp As *patânu, 'protect,'* whence two foll, 'serpent' as *protector*, and 'threshold' as *asylum;* plausible, but exact meaning of *patânu* still uncertain).

†פֶּתֶן **n.m.**[ψ 68, 5] a venomous serpent, perh cobra (פתן Ecclus 39^{30}; Aram. פִּתְנָא, ܦܬܢܐ, whence perh. Ar. بَتَن);—only poet.: pl רֹאשׁ פְּתָנִים Dt 32^{33} (‖ חֲמַת תַּנִּינִם), Jb 20^{16}, מְרֹרַת פ׳ v^{14}; sg. פֶּתֶן ψ 91^{13} (‖ תַּנִּין), פ׳ חֵרֵשׁ 58^{5}, חֻר פָּתֶן Is 11^{8}.

†מִפְתָּן **n.[m.]** threshold (cf. NH פָּתִין *cross-beam;* ? Ar فَيْتَن *carpenter*);—abs. מ׳ 1 S 5^{4} Zp 1^{9}; cstr. מִפְתַּן דָּגוֹן 1 S 5^{5}, מ׳ הַבַּיִת Ez 9^{3} $10^{4.18}$ 47^{1}, מ׳ הַשַּׁעַר 46^{2}.

†פֶּתַע **subst.** suddenness (√unknown: cf. As. *ina pitti, ina pittimma, in suddenness, instantly,* Dl[HWB 553]):—Nu 35^{22} וְאִם־בְּפֶתַע ... הֲדָפוֹ if he have thrust him *in suddenness*, before he is aware what he has done (i.e. accidentally); + פִּתְאֹם Nu 6^{9}, וכי ימות מת עליו בפתע פתאם i.e. very suddenly; לְפֶתַע *according to* (לְ, p. 516b) *suddenness*, Is 29^{5} והיה לפתע פתאם = *at an instant*, suddenly, 30^{13} אשׁר פתאם לפתע יבוא שִׁבְרָהּ. As adv. acc., *suddenly*, Pr 6^{15} (= 29^{1}) פֶּתַע יִשָּׁבֵר, Hb 2^{7}.

†פִּתְאֹם, once ψ 64^{8} (v. Baer) פִּתְאוֹם **subst.** suddenness, usu. as **adv. acc.** suddenly (from פֶּתַע, with the term ם- (cf. שִׁלְשֹׁם), and with ע weakened to א: Sta[§ 296] Ko[II. 255 f.] Ba[NB § 216 b]),—Nu 12^{4} ויאמר י׳ פ׳ אל־משׁה, Jos 10^{9} 11^{7}; esp. of calamity, invasion, etc., coming *suddenly*, Is 47^{11} 48^{3} Je 4^{20} פ׳ שֻׁדְּדוּ אֹהָלַי, 6^{26} 15^{8} 18^{22} 51^{8} ψ 64^{5} פ׳ יֹרֻהוּ ולא יִירָאוּ, v^{8} Jb 5^{3} 9^{23} Ec 9^{12} Pr 6^{15} 24^{22}; also 7^{22} Mal 3^{1}; thrice with פֶּתַע (q.v.). As a gen. †Pr 3^{25} אל־תירא מפחד פ׳ of the terror of *suddenness*, i.e. the *sudden* terror, Jb 22^{10}; and with בְּ, *in suddenness*, †2 Ch 29^{36} בפ׳ היה הדבר.

†פָּתַר **vb.** interpret (dream), only Gn 40, 41 (NH *id.*, JAram. פְּתַר; appar = Aram. פְּשַׁר, ܦܫܰܪ, *dissolve*, fig. *solve, interpret*, cf. פֵּשֶׁר);—**Qal** *Pf.* 3 ms. פָּתַר, c. לְ pers. Gn 40^{22} 41^{13}; abs. פֹּתֵר 40^{16} 41^{12}, c. acc. rei: *Impf* 3 ms וַיִּפְתָּר־לָנוּ 41^{12}, *Inf. cstr.* לִפְתֹּר 41^{15}; *Pt act.* פֹּתֵר 40^{8} 41^{15}, פֹּ׳ 41^{8}.

†פִּתְרוֹן [Ko[II. 1, 184]] **n.m.** interpretation (of a dream), only Gn 40, 41,—cstr. פִּתְרוֹן Gn 40^{5} 41^{11}; sf. פִּתְרֹנוֹ $40^{12.18}$, pl. פִּתְרֹנִים v^{8}.

†פַּתְרוֹס **n.pr.terr.** = Upper Egypt, Παθουρης, Φαθουρης, etc. (Egypt *p(ĕ)-tĕ-res, south land*, in As. *Paturisi*, Erman[ZAW x (1890), 118 f.] Steind[BAS i 344] WMM[Hastings DB]; also (on As) Schr[KGF 283 f.] Dl[Pa 310]);—alw. in connexion with מִצְרַיִם, etc: Is 11^{11} Je 44^{15} Ez 30^{14}, אֶרֶץ פ׳ Je 44^{1} Ez 29^{14}; מִפַּתְרֹס prop. also ψ 68^{31} (for מִתְרַפֵּס) Ne[JBL x (1891), 152] (plausibly), cf. Che[ib. xi (1892), 125] Kau[ψψ crit. n.].

†פַּתְרֻסִים **adj. gent. pl.** of foregoing, as subst Gn 10^{14} = 1 Ch 1^{12}.

†פַּתְשֶׁגֶן **n.m.** copy (= פַּרְשֶׁגֶן q.v.);—cstr פ׳ (הַ)כְּתָב Est 3^{14} 4^{8} 8^{13}.

†[פָּתַת] **vb.** break up, crumble (NH *id.;* Ar. فَتَّ, Eth ፈተተ:; Syr. ܦܰܬ);—**Qal** *Inf. abs.* of bread of מִנְחָה. פָּתוֹת אֹתָהּ פִּתִּים Lv 2^{6}.

†פַּת **n.f.**[Pr 17, 1] fragment, bit, morsel of bread;—abs. פ׳ חֲרֵבָה Pr 17^{1} *a dry morsel;* cstr. פַּת־לֶחֶם Gn 18^{5} Ju 19^{5} 1 S 2^{36} 28^{22} 1 K 17^{11} Pr 28^{21}; sf פִּתִּי Jb 31^{17}, פִּתְּךָ Pr 23^{8}, פִּתֵּךְ Ru 2^{14}, פִּתּוֹ 2 S 12^{3}; pl פִּתִּים Lv 2^{6} 6^{14}; in sim. ψ 147^{17}.

†[פָּתוֹת] **n.[m.]** id;—pl. cstr. פְּתוֹתֵי לֶחֶם Ez 13^{19}.

צ

צ, ץ, *Ṣādê*, eighteenth letter; used as numeral 90 in post B.Hebrew

[צָאָה], צֹאָה, [צֹאִי] v. צוא.

†**צֶאֱלִים n.m.pl.** a kind of **lotus** (*Rhamnus* (more exactly *Zizyphus*), *Lotus* [Linn], *thorny lotus* (not sacred *Nymphaea Lotus*), Saad ضَال, cf. AW De[Job 2], Syr ܥܠܐ, v Löw[P 275]),—Jb 40[21 22]

צאן (√of foll., Dl[Pr 87 f. HWB] cp As. *sênu*, adj, *good, docile*, Thes (cf Lag[BN 136]) cp יָצָא [as πρόβατον from προβαίνω], As *ṣênu*=BH צאן, and so NH *id*, MI[31] צאן, Ar. ضَأْن *id.*, TelAm *ṣunu* is Canaanitish acc. to Zim[ZA vi (1891) 156], Aram עָנָא, ܥܢܐ, and perhaps Palm. ענא).

צֹאן [273] **n. coll. f.** [Gn 30, 36] (poss. **m.** v[39 a]+, Kö[Synt §247 e], but dub, v[39 b] c vb. fpl, as usually, in 1 S 15[14] join הַזֶּה with קוֹל; v. further Albr [ZAW xv (1895), 316 ff]) **small cattle, sheep and goats, flock, flocks**,—צ׳ abs Gn 4[2]+, cstr. 29[9]+, sf צאנו 4[4]+, צאננו Ex 10[9], צאונו ψ 144[13], as pl צֹאנֵינוּ Ne 10[37] van d H Gi (not Baer; very late, si vera l), etc.;—**1.** lit **a.** *small cattle*, usu of sheep and goats in one flock (Rob[BR i 477]) Gn 30[31 32]+, sheep specified also 21[28] (כבשת הצ׳), 31[38] (אילי צ׳)+; sheep only 1 S 25[2] (+עזים), goats specified Gn 27[9] Je 50[8], צ׳ as yielding (1) animals for food Am 6[4] (כָּרִים), 1 S 14[32] 2 S 12[4] Ne 5[18]+, צ׳ מַאֲכָל ψ 44[12] (in sim.); (2) wool Gn 31[19]+ (v [נָזַז], נז), (3) milk, חֲלֵב צ׳ Dt 32[14] (? goats' milk, cf Pr 27[27]); (4) sacrif victims Gn 4[4] (J), Lv 1[2 10] 3[6] Nu 15[3] (all P), 22[40] (E), Dt 12[6 17 21]+oft; so צאן קָדָשִׁים Ez 36[38 a], cf בכורי בקרינו וצאנינו Ne 10[37]; in gen. as property (oft +בָּקָר, etc) Gn 12[16] 13[5] 24[35] Jb 1[3] 42[12]+oft (v. also ii [עַשְׁתָּרוֹת]), gift Gn 20[14] 21[27] 38[17] (goat), Dt 15[14] 2 Ch 17[11], booty 1 S 15[9 15]+. **b.** צ׳ sts of a definite number of animals (i e as pl. of שֶׂה, etc) two Is 7[21], four Ex 21[37] (larger numbers v 1 S 25[2.5 18] Nu 31[32.36] Ne 5[18] Jb 1[3] 42[12] supr)—Vid also בן **7 b**, מִרְבַּץ, מִכְלָה, גְּדֵרָה, שַׁעַר, רֹעֶה, כֶּלֶב; עֵדֶר, נָוֶה **2.** sim of multitude Ez 36[37.38], cf ψ 107[41]; of children Jb 21[11]; of dead, with death as shepherd ψ 49[15]; of (shepherdless) Isr Nu 27[17] 1 K 22[17]=2 Ch 18[16], Zc 10[2] 13[7], wandering in sin Is 53[6]; of Isr led by י׳ ψ 77[21] 78[52] 80[2], cf Zc 9[16] (on text v We Now); Ez 34[12], of Isr. in distress, כצ׳ מבחה ψ 44[23], cf (of wicked) צ׳ לטבחה Je 12[3]; of scattered Bab. Is 13[14] **3.** metaph. of multitude, צ׳ אָדָם Ez 36[38], of Isr. 2 S 24[17]=1 Ch 21[17], Je 23[1 2.3] Ez 24[5], and esp sustained fig 34[2.3]+17 t 34, also Zc 11[7 17], צ׳ אבדות Je 50[6], צ׳ תִּפְאַרְתֵּךְ 13[20], of Isr. under י׳'s care, (—י׳, ـِ) צ׳ מַרְעִיתֶךָ ψ 74[1] 79[13] 100[3] Ez 34[31], also צ׳ יָדוֹ ψ 95[7] (|| עם־ מַרְעִיתוֹ; rd perh. עם ידו, צ׳ מרעיתו, so Che al), צ׳ נַחֲלָתֶךָ Mi 7[14], also in combinations: אדירי הצ׳ Je 25[34 35.36], עֲנִיֵּי הַצ׳ Zc 11[4.7] (cf. ψ 44[23]), צ׳ הַהֲרֵגָה v[7 11] (all of Isr), of Edom צעירי הַצ׳ Je 49[20] 50[45].

†**צַאֲנָן n.pr.loc.** Mi 1[11] Σεννααρ [ν], perh.=צְנָן in the Shephelah of Judah Jos 15[37], Σεννα(μ)

[צֶאֱצָא] v יצא i, ii צב v i, ii צבב

†**[צָבָא]** **vb. wage war, serve** (Sab. צֹבא *wage war with*, also n *army, campaign* Hom[Chrest 125] CIS[iv 299 l 2] DHM[VOJ i 28]; Eth. ፀብአ: (>ጸብአ:) *wage war*, As *ṣâbu, man, soldier*; No[ZMG xl (1886) 726] al cp (on account of Sab. Eth צ) Ar ضَبَأَ *conceal oneself*, hence *lie in wait*; this is phonetically suitable, but better in mng would be صَبَأَ *go* or *come forth* (against one), etc, so Thes Lag[BN 21], Fra[232] cp صَبِيّ *young man*),—**Qal** *Pf.* 3 mpl. צָבְאוּ Ex 38[8] Zc 14[12], *Impf* 3 mpl יִצְבְּאוּ Nu 31[7], *Inf. cstr.* לצבא Is 31[4], לִצְבֹא Nu 4[23] 8[24], *Pt* pl צֹבְאִים Nu 31[42] Is 29[7 8], sf צֹבֶיהָ Is 29[7] (Ges[§75 oo]; Di צָרֶיהָ); fpl. צבאת Ex 38[8], צֹבְאוֹת 1 S 2[22],—**1.** *wage war, fight*, c עַל *against*, Nu 31[7] (P) Is 29[7 8] 31[4] Zc 14[12], c sf. Is 29[7] (?), abs Nu 31[42] (P). **2.** *serve* at sacred tent, Levites, c. acc. צָבָא Nu 4[23] 8[24] (P); women Ex 38[8 8] (P) 1 S 2[22]. **Hiph.** *Pt.* הַמַּצְבִּא את־עם וגו׳ 2 K 25[19]=Je 52[25] *muster*.

צָבָא [485] **n.m.** [2 Ch 26, 9] (poss. **f.** Is 40[2] Dn 8[12], but v. Albr[ZAW xv (1895), 319], Bev[Dn]) **army, war, warfare**,—abs צ׳ Nu 1[3]+ (מִצָּבָה Zc 9[8] v. p 663 a), cstr צבא Nu 10[15]+; sf צבאי Jb 14[14]; צְבָאֲךָ Ju 8[9] 9[29]; צְבָאָיו ψ 103[21] 148[2] (Kt צבאו; so read prob. in both), etc, pl צְבָאוֹת Nu 20[9]+278 t.; cstr. צבאות Ex 12[41]+2 t, sf צְבָאֹתַי 7[4], צבאתם 6[26]+, etc.,—**1.** *army, host* **a.** organized for war Ju 8[6] 9[29] (J) Is 34[2] Je 51[3] 2 Ch 28[9], צְבָאוֹ *his host* Nu 2[4.6]+10 t 2 (P), לצבאתם 1[3.52] 2[3.9]+11 t 2, 10, 33[1] (P), צ׳ ישראל 31[48] (P), אַלְפֵי הצ׳ 2 Ch 25[7]; חיל (ה)צ׳ 1 Ch 20[1] 2 Ch 26[13]; גְּדוּדֵי צ׳

1 Ch 7^{4}; כל־הצבא 2 S 3^{23} 10^{7} 1 Ch 19^{8} 2 Ch 26^{14}; שַׂר (ה)צ׳ *captain of* (the) *host* Gn 21$^{22.32}$ (E) 26^{26} (J) Ju 4$^{2.7}$ 1 S 12^{9} + 21 t.; שָׂרֵי (ה)צבא 1 K 1^{25} (but rd. שַׂר), 1 Ch 25^{1} 26^{26} 2 Ch 33^{11}; שָׂרִים בצ׳ 1 Ch 12^{22}; שָׂרֵי (ה)צבאות Dt 20^{9} 1 K 2^{5} 1 Ch 27^{3}; עַל (ה)צ׳ ψ 68^{13}; מַלְכֵי צבאות 1 Ch 12^{14}; רָאשֵׁי הצ׳ *over the host* (as captain) Nu 10$^{14.15}$ + 10 t Nu 10 (P), 2 S 8^{16} = 1 Ch 18^{15}, 2 S 17^{25} 1 K 2^{32} 4^{4}; אֶל־ כל הצ׳ 2 S 20^{23} (אל for על); עַל־צִבְאֹתָם Ex 6^{26} 12^{51} (P); הוציא צבאות *lead out armies* Ex 7^{4} 12^{17} (P); יצא צ׳ *army goes forth* (to war) Ex 12^{41} 1 Ch 7^{11}; לֹא תֵצֵא בצבאותינו ψ 44^{10}, of י׳ going *with our armies* = 60^{12} = 108^{12}; fig. of great number, צבא רב 68^{12}.—On חֲלִיפוֹת וְצָבָא Jb 10^{17} v. Di; Bu prop. תַּחֲלִף צְבָאֲ(ךָ) i.e. *thou dost renew* (*thine*) *army* against me. **b.** *host* (organized body) of angels (cf Lu 2^{13}), (כל) צבא השמים *all the host of heaven* 1 K 22^{19} = 2 Ch 18^{18}, Ne 9^{6}; כל צבאיו ψ 103^{21} 148^{2}, צבא הַמָּרוֹם Is 24^{21} *host of the high* (angel-princes; ‖ earthly monarchs); צבא השמים Dn 8^{10}, הצבא v^{10} (al. v^{b} fig. of Israel); שר צ׳ י׳ *captain of the host of* י׳ Jos 5$^{14.15}$ (theophanic angel); שר הצבא Dn 8^{11} (angel-prince of Israel, others, God). **c.** of sun, moon and stars, כל צבא השמים Dt 4^{19} 17^{3} 2 K 17^{16} 21$^{3.5}$ = 2 Ch 33$^{3.5}$, 2 K 23$^{4.5}$ Je 8^{2} 19^{13} (all as objects of worship), Is 34^{4}, צ׳ השמים Je 33^{22} Zp 1^{5}, כל צבאם Ne 9^{6} ψ 33^{6} Is 34^{4} 45^{12}; צבאם Is 40^{26}.—Je 3^{19} v. I צְבִי. **d.** of the entire creation, כל צבאם Gn 2^{1}. **2.** *war, warfare, service:* יָצָא צָבָא *go out to war* Nu 1$^{3.20}$ + 12 t. Nu 1, 26^{2} (P) 1 Ch 5^{18} 7^{11} 12$^{33.36}$ 2 Ch 25^{5} 26^{11}; יצא בצ׳ Nu 31^{36} (P) Dt 24^{5}; יצא לצ׳ Nu 31$^{27.28}$ (P); עלה לצ׳ *go up to war* Jos 22$^{12.33}$ (P); בא מצ׳ *come from war* Nu 31^{14} 2 Ch 28^{12}; התיחשׂם לצ׳ 1 S 28^{1}; קבץ לצ׳ שלח לצ׳ Nu 31$^{4.6.6}$ (P), בצ׳ 1 Ch 7^{40}; צ׳ תִּנְתֵן Dn 8^{12}, אַנְשֵׁי (ה)צ׳ *men of war* Nu 31$^{21.53}$ (P) 1 Ch 12^{8}, cf. עם הצ׳ Nu 31^{32} (P); v. also II. חלץ; גבורי חֵיל לצ׳ 1 Ch 12^{25}; כלי צ׳ 1 Ch 12^{37} *instruments of war*. **3.** *service:* **a.** of Levites in sacred places Nu 4$^{3.23.30.35.39.43}$ 8$^{24.25}$; קֹדֶשׁ וְצָבָא Dn 8^{13} (al. as v^{11}, **1 b**). **b.** of *hard service* of troubled life Jb 7^{1} 14^{14} Is 40^{2} Dn 10^{1}. **4.** צְבָאוֹת, in name of י׳ as God of war, prob first in time of warlike David (some connect with sacred ark, but ark older), explained יהוה צבאות אֱלֹהֵי מערכות ישראל 1 S 17^{45} י׳ *Sebaoth God of the battle array of Israel* (the thought of angels and stars as army of God is later); **a.** earliest form c. art.: ^ אֱלֹהֵי הַצְּבָאוֹת Am 3^{13} 6^{14} 9^{5} (אֱלֹהֵי om by error, cf We), Ho 12^{6}. **b.** without art, definite by usage, י׳ אֱלֹהֵי צְבָאוֹת 2 S 5^{10} Am 5$^{14.15.16}$ 6^{8} 1 K 19$^{10.14}$ Je 5^{14} 15^{16} ψ 89^{9},

Je 35^{17} 38^{17} 44^{7} 1 S 7^{27} י׳ אֱלֹהֵי צְבָאוֹת אֱלֹהֵי יִשְׂרָאֵל = 1 Ch 17^{24}, Is 21^{10} 37^{16}; 1st אֱלֹהֵי om. Je 7$^{3.21}$ + 30 t. Je; Zp 2^{9}, י׳ אלהים צ׳ אלהי ישראל ψ 59^{6} (אלהים variant of י׳); י׳ א׳ צ׳ שְׁמוֹ ,י׳ *God of hosts his name* Am 4^{13} 5^{27}, later reduced to י׳ צ׳ שְׁמוֹ Is 47^{4} 48^{2} 51^{15} 54^{5} Je 10^{16} 31^{35} + 6 t Je. **c.** as n pr. *Sebaoth:* י׳ צבאות, י׳ *Sebaoth* (*Lord of hosts*, Vrss, owing to Qr אֲדֹנָי, but this never cstr. אֲדֹנֵי; al. ^ *of hosts*, but < names in appos., since י׳ is n pr.; צ׳ for earlier אלהי צ׳; cf. Σαβαωθ Ja 5^{4} Rom 9^{29}): 1 S 1$^{3.11}$ 4^{4} 15^{2} 17^{45} 2 S 6$^{2.18}$ 7$^{8.26}$ 1 K 18^{15} 2 K 3^{14} 19^{31} 1 Ch 11^{9} 17^{7} ψ 24^{10} + 6 t ψψ, Mi 4^{4} Na 2^{14} 3^{5} Hb 2^{13} Zp 2^{10} Is 1^{9} 2^{12} 5$^{7.9.16.24}$ + 35 t. Is 6–39, Is^{2} only 44^{6} 45^{13}, Je 6$^{6.9}$ 8^{3} 9$^{6.16}$ + 26 t. Je, Hg 1$^{2.5}$ + 12 t Hg, Zc 1$^{3.3.3.4}$ + 40 t. Zc 1–8, 9^{15} + 8 t 10–14, Mal 1$^{4.6.8}$ + 21 t Mal; האדון י׳ צ׳ Is 1^{24} + 4 t. Is (incl 10^{16} Baer Gi > van d H. אֲדֹנָי for י׳); אֲדֹנָי י׳ צ׳ 3^{15} + (on these phr. v. אדן **1, 6**); י׳ אלהים צ׳ (א׳ later Qr for orig. י׳) ψ 80$^{8.15}$, י׳ אלהים צ׳ (earlier י׳ + later [inserted] א׳) ψ 80$^{5.20}$ 84^{9}.—Cf. Driver Hastings DB (1900), Lord of Hosts and reff., Löhr Amos (Beihefte zur ZAW iv (1900), 38-67).

צְבָאוֹת ,צְבָאִים ,צְבָאוֹת v. further I, II. צְבִי.

צְבָאִים v. צְבִיִּם

I. **צבב** (√ of foll.; cf As. *ṣumbu* (=**ṣubbu*), *cart;* 𝔗 צִיבָא *low, covered wagon*).

†I. צָב **n.[m.]** litter;—abs. צ׳, in עֶגְלֹת צָב Nu 7^{3}, prob. *litter-wagons*, i e wagons covered, like palanquin; pl צַבִּים Is 66^{20} *litters* (on Vrss cf. Di^{Nu})

II. **צבב** (√ of foll., cf. Ar. ضَبّ *cleave to ground*, NH צָב = BH, Syr ܨܒܐ in Lexx, Ar. ضَبّ is a large lizard, v. esp Seetzen Reisen iii. 436 ff.).

†II. צָב **n.[m.]** lizard, as unclean, Lv 11^{29}.

†צֹבֵבָה **n.pr.m.** in Judah, הַצּ׳ 1 Ch 4^{8}, Σαβαθα, A Σωβηβα, 𝔊L Σαβηβα.

†I. [צָבָה] **vb. swell, swell up** (NH id);—**Qal** *Pf* 3 fs. consec. וְצָבְתָה Nu 5^{27}; appar. **Hiph.** *Inf. cstr.* לַצְבּוֹת v^{22}, < read **Qal** לִצְבּוֹת Di Ol$^{§ 78 e}$ Sta$^{§ 114 a, 2}$; both of adulteress' belly.— צְבִיָּה Is 29^{7} v. צבא.

†[צָבֶה] **adj. swelling, swollen**;—f. צָבָה Nu 5^{21} (as foregoing).

II **צבה** (√ of foll.; meaning dub.; Dl$^{Pr 150}$ Buhl al. cp Ar. صبا *lean, incline* (esp. III.), fig. *incline* toward (الى), *yearn* for, As. *ṣabû*, Aram. צְבָא, ܨܒܐ, all *desire*, etc.)

†I צְבִי **n.m.** [381.19] **beauty, honour**;—abs צ׳ 2 S 1[19]+, צְבִ֑י Dn 8[9]; cstr צבי Is 13[19]+; pl cstr צבאות Je 3[19] (so 𝔗 Ki Thes Hi Gf Ol[§145b] Kö[II.1.584] al, > fr צבא 𝔙 Gie al),—**1. a.** *beauty, decoration*, צ׳ עדיו, of silver and gold Ez 7[20], of products of soil Is 4[2] (predict.). **b.** elsewhere in fig. of drunkard's chaplet, צ׳ תִפְאַרְתּוֹ Is 28[1.4] (fig. of Samaria), עֲטֶרֶת צ׳ v[5] (of י׳); הַצּ׳ 2 S 1[19] (Saul and Jonathan); גְּאוֹן כָּל־צ׳, of Tyre Is 23[9], צ׳ מַמְלָכוֹת 13[19] (of Bab); of land of Isr. (Judah), נַחֲלַת צְבִי צִבְאוֹת צבי היא לְכָל־הָאֲרָצוֹת Ez 20[6.15], גּוֹיִם Je 3[19] (v supr) *heritage of the beauty of beauties of the nations*, i.e. most beauteous heritage, הַצּ׳ esp of Jerus and temple Dn 8[9] (Bev), cf אֶרֶץ הַצּ׳ 11[16.41] (v Dr), הַר צ׳־קֹדֶשׁ v[45] (i.e. temple-hill), of cities of Moab, צ׳ אֶרֶץ Ez 25[9]. **2.** = *honour*, צ׳ לַצַּדִּיק Is 24[16]—Ez 26[20] rd וְנָתַתִּי צבי for וְנָתַתִּי צבי, so 𝔊 Co Berthol Toy Krae al.

III צבה (√ of foll; NH צְבִיָּה, צבי = BH, so As *sabîtu*, Ar ظَبْى, Aram. טַבְיָא, ܛܒܝܐ)

†II צְבִי **n.m.** [Is 13.14] **gazelle**;—צ׳ abs Dt 12[15]+; pl צְבָאִים 2 S 2[18], צְבָיִם 1 Ch 12[9] (Gi Baer, van d H v[8]), צְבָאוֹת Ct 2[7] 3[5],—*gazelle*, allowed as food Dt 14[5], cf 12[15.22] (although not for sacrif, Dr, all + אַיָּל), so 15[22] (+ אַיָּל, יַחְמוּר, etc), v. 1 K 5[3], sim of swiftness 2 S 2[18] 1 Ch 12[9] v supr, Pr 6[5], of grace and beauty Ct 2[9.17] 8[14] (cf. Jacob Arab Dichter iv 20 f), hence used in adjuration 2[7] 3[5] (+ אילות), צ׳ מֻדָּח Is 13[14], sim of fugitives.

†I. צְבִיָּה **n.f.** id.,—תָּאֳמֵי צ׳ Ct 4[5] = 7[4]

†צִבְיָא **n.pr.m.** in Benjamin 1 Ch 8[9], Ιεβια, A Σεβια, 𝔊L Σαβια.

†צִבְיָה **n.pr.f.** (= צְבִיָּה *gazelle*, cf. Sta §192b),—mother of Jehoash of Judah 2 K 12[2], Αβια = 2 Ch 24[1], Αβια, 𝔊L Σαβια.

†צְבֹיִים **n.pr.loc.** near Sodom, Gn 14[2.8] Dt 29[22] = צבים Gn 10[19] = צְבֹאִים Ho 11[8] Kt (צְבוֹיִם Qr), Σεβωειμ

†[צָבַט] **vb.** reach, hold out, to (לְ pers) (prop *grasp, hold*, so NH (rare), בית הַצְּבִיטָה *handle* (of jug); Ar ضَبَطَ *hold firmly, seize*; Eth ፀበጠ: *grasp firmly*),—**Qal** *Impf.* 3 ms וַיִּצְבָּט־לָהּ Ru 2[14] (acc rei)

I. צבע (√ of foll, NH צָבַע *dye*, As. *sibûtum*, *ṣubâtu*, *dyed stuff* (v Zehnpf[BAS I 519]); Ar صَبَغَ, Aram צְבַע, ܨܒܥ, all *dip, dye*).

†צֶ֫בַע **n.** [m.] **dye, dyed stuff**;—cstr. צ׳ רִקְמָתַיִם Ju 5[30] (perhaps del צ׳, cf GFM); pl. צְבָעִים שְׁלַל *booty of dyed stuffs* v[30.30].

†צָבוּעַ **adj.** coloured, variegated (prop pt. pass),—עַיִט צ׳ Je 12[9] *a variegated bird of prey*.

II צבע (√ of foll.; cf. Ar صَبَعَ *point* Lag[BN 20 21], إِصْبَع, *finger*, Sab. אצבע DHM[ZMG xxxvii (1883) 375]; Eth. አጽባዕት: NH = BH; Aram אֶצְבְּעָא, ܨܒܥܐ, Mand. צבאתא Nö[M 36], Dl[Pr 171] Kö[II 1,96] cp. As. *sibû* II. *surround firmly*)

אֶצְבַּע [31] **n.f.** [Lv 14.6] **finger**,—א׳ abs. Is 58[9], cstr Ex 8[15]+, sf אֶצְבָּעוֹ Lv 4[6]+; pl אֶצְבָּעוֹת Je 52[21], cstr אֶצְבְּעֹת 2 S 21[20]+, etc,—**1.** *finger*, esp **a.** *forefinger*, of priest, applying blood (P), Ex 29[12] Lv 4[6.17.25] + 8 t; applying oil 14[16.16.27]. **b.** שְׁלַח א׳ of any one Is 58[9], sign of contempt. **c.** of God, as writing Ex 31[18] (E) Dt 9[10], = *act* of God Ex 8[15] (J) **d.** pl of all the fingers 2 S 21[20a], fingers in gen Is 2[8] 17[8] 59[3] ψ 144[1], Pr 7[3] Ct 5[5]; of י׳ ψ 8[4]; מֹרֶה בא׳ Pr 6[13] (of contempt. gesture); as measure of thickness, Je 52[21] *four fingers*. **2.** *toes* אצבעת רגליו 2 S 21[20b], lit *fingers of his feet*, cf. א׳ ‖ 1 Ch 20[6] = fingers and toes

III צבע (perhaps √ of foll, cf Ar. ضبع *limp* (so Lag[BN 20]), whence ضَبُعٌ *hyena*, Syr. ܦܥܐ *id*, NH צָבוֹעַ)

†צִבְעוֹן **n.pr.m.** a Horite (*hyena*, RS[K 219], Gray[Prop. N 95] and reff),—Gn 36[2.14.20] (in these gloss acc. to Di Holz), v[24.24.29] 1 Ch 1[38.40], Σεβεγων

†צְבֹעִים **n.pr.loc.** in Benj,—גֵּי הַצּ׳ (perh. *valley of hyenas*, so Thes, cf Lag[BN 38] Gray[l.c.]);—1 S 13[18] (acc. to Buhl[Geogr 98] = *Wady el-Kelt*, between Jerus and Jericho), Σαμειν, 𝔊L Σαβαιν, cf. צ׳ Ne 11[34], A Σεβοειμ, 𝔊L Σεβωειν.

†[צָבַר] **vb.** heap up (NH *id.*; Aram. צְבַר, Syr. ܨܒܪ is *prate, chatter, rave*; Ar. صَبَرَ is *collect, bind together*; cf. further Dozy),—**Qal** *Impf.* 3 ms. יִצְבֹּר Gn 41[35] ψ 39[7]; 3 fs. וַתִּצְבָּר־ Zc 9[3], etc,—*heap up*, in great quantity: c acc corn Gn 41[35.49] (E), dead frogs Ex 8[10] (J), dust Hb 1[10], silver like dust Zc 9[3] Jb 27[16], cf (obj om) ψ 39[7].

†[צִבּוּר] **n.m.** heap,—only pl שְׁנֵי צִבֻּרִים 2 K 10[8] *two heaps* (of heads)

צבת (√ of foll.; NH צָבַת *bind, unite*; As *ṣabâtu, grasp, take*; Talm צבת *join*, and der).

† צְבָתִים **n.[m.]pl. bundles** of grain Ru 2^{16} (Vogelst$^{\text{Landwirthschaft 61}}$ *swaths* [grasped and] lifted for binding).

צדד (√ of foll.; cf. Ar. صَدَّ *turn away*, then *shun, alienate;* NH BAram. צַד = BH; Ar. صَدَدٌ *vicinity,* صَدَدَ *in front of, in the vicinity of;* Aram. צַיד, ܨܶܝܕ *by, apud*).

† צַד **n.m.**$^{\text{Ex 25, 32}}$ **side;**—צַד abs. Ez 34^{21} Is 60^{4}, cstr. 2 S 2^{16} +; sf. צִדּוֹ Gn 6^{16} +, etc.; for צִדָּה 1 S 20^{20} rd. צִדָּה (or צִדּוֹ; cf. Dr, > צִדָּה); pl. צִדִּים Ju 2^{3}, rd. prob. צְנִינִים as Nu 33^{55} Jos 23^{13}; cstr. צִדֵּי Ex 26^{13}, etc.;—*side*, of man 2 S 2^{16} Nu 33^{55} (H) Jos 23^{13} (D), Ju 2^{3} (prob. rd. context as Nu 33^{55} GFM; Dl$^{\text{Pr 75}}$ cp. As. *ṣaddu, snare, trap*); of one lying Ez 4$^{4.6.9}$, מִצִּדְּךָ אֶל־צִדֶּךָ v^{8} *turn from side to side;* children carried עַל־צ׳ (i.e. prob. on hip) Is 60^{4} 66^{12}; of cattle Ez 34^{21} (in fig.); of things 1 S 20^{20} (cf. Dr), Gn 6^{16} Ex 25$^{32.32.32}$ = 37$^{18.18.18}$, 26^{13} 30^{4} = 37^{27}, Dt 31^{26} (all P); מִצַּד *at the side of,* c. gen. pers. 1 S 20^{25} Ru 2^{14}, so מִצִּדְּךָ ψ 91^{7}; c. gen. loc. Jos 3^{16} 12^{9}, מִצַּד הָהָר 2 S 13^{34}; מִצַּד הָהָר מִזֶּה 1 S 23$^{26\text{bis}}$ *on this side* of the hill and on *that side;* c. sf. rei מִצִּדּוֹ 1 S 6^{8}.

† [צְדָד, צְדָדָה] **n.pr.loc.** on N. border of Canaan, c. ה loc., צְדָדָה Nu 34^{8} (Σαραδακ, Sam. צרדה), Ez 47^{15} (Σεδδαμμα), rd. prob. צְרָדָה; perh. *Khirbet Ṣerādā*, N. of Abil, E. of *Merj ʿAjûn* toward Hermon (lat. c. 33° 25′ N., long. c. 35° 35′ E.), so van Kasteren$^{\text{Rev. Bibl., 1895, 30}}$, cf. Buhl$^{\text{Geogr. 67}}$.

† צִדִּים **n.pr.loc.** in Naphtali, הַצ׳ Jos 19^{35} (𝔊 τῶν Τυρίων).

† I. **צָדָה** **vb. lie in wait** (NH *id.*, rare; cf. (si vera l.) BAram. צְדָא Dn 3^{14});—**Qal** *Pf.* 3 ms. צ׳ Ex 21^{13} (E; abs.); *Pt.* c. acc. וְאַתָּה צֹדֶה אֶת־נַפְשִׁי לְקַחְתָּהּ 1 S 24^{11} (Gi; v^{12} van d. H. Baer).

† צְדִיָּה **n.f. lying-in-wait;**—(בִ)צ׳ Nu 35$^{20.22}$ i.e. with malicious intent (P).

† II. [**צָדָה**] **vb. lay waste** (NH *id.* (rare), Aram. צְדָא, ܨܕܳܐ, ܨܕܺܝ *id.*);—**Niph.** *Pf.* 3 pl. נִצְדּוּ עָרֵיהֶם Zp 3^{6} *their cities are laid waste.*

צֵדָה v. צֵידָה, sub II. צוד. צִדֹנִי v. צִידֹנִית.

צדק (√ of foll.; NH, Aram. in deriv.; cf. Ar. صَدَقَ *speak the truth* (also صَدْقٌ *hard, even, straight, perfect*); Sab. צדק *just*, epith. of king Mordtm$^{\text{ZMG xxx (1876), 37}}$ Hom$^{\text{Chrest. 125}}$; usu. *excellent* DHM$^{\text{ZMG xxix (1875), 595, 599}}$ CIS$^{\text{iv. p. 176}}$; also verb *favour, endow* (one with something) CIS$^{\text{iv. No. 198, 1.4}}$ DHM$^{\text{l.c.}}$ Mordtm$^{\text{Him. Inschr. 70 f.}}$; Ph. צדק adj. *just, right*, TelAm (Can.) *ṣaduk, innocent;* OAram. צדק n. *righteousness, loyalty*, Nab. אצדק adj. *authorized*, Palm. זדקתא εὐσεβής; Saho *sadak, be true, clear* Reinisch$^{\text{Saho Spr. (1890) 312}}$; Eth. ጻድቅ: *be just, righteous*, so NH צדק Pi. Hiph., Aram. צַדֵּיק, ܙܕܺܝܩ; cf. Kau$^{\text{Deriv. d. St. צדק (1881)}}$ HPS$^{\text{צדק etc. Presb. Rev., 1882, 165 ff.}}$ Gerber$^{\text{206 ff.}}$).

† צֶדֶק **n.m.** $^{\text{Is 1, 21}}$ **rightness, righteousness;**—צ׳ Lv 19^{36} + 87 t.; צִדְקִי Is 41^{10} + 8 t., etc.;—**1.** *what is right, just, normal; rightness, justness,* of weights and measures, אֶבֶן שְׁלֵמָה וָצֶדֶק אֵיפָה Dt 25^{15} *a perfect and a just weight, ephah;* מֹאזְנֵי צ׳; אַבְנֵי צ׳, אֵיפַת צ׳, הִין צ׳, בַּת צ׳ Lv 19^{36} (H) Jb 31^{6} Ez 45^{10}; מַעְגְּלֵי צ׳ *right paths* ψ 23^{3}; זִבְחֵי צ׳ *right peace-offerings* Dt 33^{19} ψ 4^{6} 51^{21}. **2.** *righteousness*, in government: **a.** of judges, rulers, kings, שפט בצ׳ Lv 19^{15} (H); שפט צ׳ Dt 1^{16} Pr 31^{9}; משפט צ׳ Dt 16^{18}; רדף צ׳ v^{20}; חוֹקֵק צ׳ Pr 8^{15}; מלך לצ׳ Is 32^{1}; דבר צ׳ ψ 58^{2}; also Pr 25^{5} ψ 94^{15} Ec 5^{7}. **b.** of law, as מִשְׁפָּטִים Is 58^{2} ψ 119$^{7.62.75.106.160}$ (𝔊, but MT מִשְׁפַּט), v^{164}; as עֵדוֹת v$^{138.144}$; as מִצְוֹת v^{172}. **c.** of Davidic king, Messiah Is 11$^{4.5}$ 16^{5} ψ 45^{5}, דין בצ׳ 72^{2}. **d.** of Jerus., as seat of just government, עִיר הַצֶּדֶק Is 1^{26} *city of righteousness;* נְוֵה צ׳ Je 31^{23} 50^{7} (poss. these reflect an orig. god צֶדֶק, v. מַלְכִּי צֶדֶק); צ׳ יָלִין בָּהּ Is 1^{21} *righteousness used to lodge in her;* cf. מְקוֹם הצ׳ Ec 3^{16} *the place of righteousness.* **e.** of God's attribute as sovereign Jb 36^{3}, husband of Israel Ho 2^{21}; צ׳ his personif. agent ψ 85$^{11.12.14}$, foundation of his throne 89^{15} = 97^{2}; in his government ψ 9^{9} 65^{6} 96^{13} = 98^{9}, promise Is 45^{19}, administration of justice Jb 8^{3} Je 11^{20} ψ 7^{18} 48^{11} 50^{6} = 97^{6}, vindication of his people 9^{5} 35$^{24.28}$; raising up Cyrus Is 45^{13}, calling his servant 42^{6}; אֱלֹהֵי צִדְקִי ψ 4^{2} God *of my righteousness* (who vindicates me); his צ׳ is everlasting 119^{142}. **3.** *righteousness, justice,* in a case or cause Jb 6^{29} 8^{6} 29^{14} ψ 35^{27} Is 59^{4}; God שפט בצ׳ ψ 7^{9} *judges according to righteousness;* גמל כצ׳ 18^{21}; השיב כצ׳ v^{25}; שמע צ׳ 17^{1}; הוציא צ׳ 37^{6}. **4.** *rightness,* in speech, דבר צ׳ ψ 52^{5} (opp. שֶׁקֶר); יַגִּיד צ׳ Pr 12^{17}; בצ׳ כל אמרי פי 8^{8}; שִׂפְתֵי צ׳ 16^{13}. **5.** *righteousness*, as ethically right Jb 35^{2} ψ 17^{15} 45^{8} Pr 1^{3} 2^{9} Ec 7^{15} Je 22^{13} Ez 3^{20} Ho 10^{12} (read פְּרִי צ׳, so 𝔊 We Now); פעל צ׳ עלמים Dn 9^{24}; עשה צ׳ Is 64^{4} ψ 119^{121}; למד צ׳ 15^{2}; Is 26$^{9.10}$; בקש צ׳ Zp 2^{3}; רדף צ׳ Is 51^{1}; ידע צ׳ v^{7}. **6.** *righteousness* as vindicated,

justification in controversy with enemies and troubles, *deliverance, victory, prosperity*: **a.** of God as covenant-keeping, in redemption, בִּימִין צִדְקִי Is 41^{10}, ∥ יֶשַׁע 45^{8} 51^{5}, cf. 42^{21}; בשׂר צ׳ ψ 40^{10}; אִמְרַת צ׳ 119^{123}. **b.** in name יהוה צִדְקֵנוּ, of Messianic king (vindicating people's cause and giving victory) Je 23^{6}; of city 33^{16}. **c.** of people as enjoying צ׳ of salvation, ∥ יְשׁוּעָה Is 62^{1}; ∥ כָּבוֹד 58^{8} 62^{2}; כהנים יִלְבְּשׁוּ צ׳ ψ 132^{9}; שַׁעֲרֵי צ׳ 118^{19}; אֵילֵי הצ׳ Is 61^{3}. **d.** of Cyrus, צ׳ יִקְרָאֵהוּ לְרַגְלוֹ Is 41^{2} (who) *in victory calleth him at every step* (Che^{Hpt} *on whose steps attends victory*, so Di Du).

צְדָקָה$_{157}$ **n.f.** righteousness;—abs. צ׳ Gn 15^{6} + 81 t.; cstr. צִדְקַת Dt 33^{21} + 5 t.; sf. צִדְקָתִי Gn 30^{33} +, etc.; pl. צְדָקוֹת Is 33^{15} + 3 t.; cstr. צִדְקוֹת Ju 5^{11} +; sf. צִדְקֹתֶיךָ Dn 9^{16}, etc.;—**1.** *righteousness*, in government: **a.** of judge, ruler, king: ∥ משׁפט Is 5^{7} 9^{6} Am 5^{7} 6^{12}; משׁפט וצ׳ עשׂה 2 S 8^{15}, *D. executed justice and righteousness* = 1 Ch 18^{14}, cf. 1 K 10^{9} = 2 Ch 9^{8}, Je 22$^{3.15}$ 33^{15} Ez 45^{9}; בצ׳ יִכּוֹן כִּסֵּא Pr 16^{12}, cf. Is 54^{14}; מַעֲשֵׂה הצ׳, עֲבֹדַת הצ׳ Is 32^{17}, cf. v^{16}; נֹגְשַׂיִךְ צ׳ Is 60^{17}. **b.** of law, ∥ מִשְׁפָּטִים, צִדְקַת י׳ Dt 33^{21}. **c.** of Davidic king, Messiah, ∥ משׁפט, ψ 72$^{1.3}$ Is 9^{6} Je 23^{5} 33^{15}. **2.** God's attribute as sovereign ψ 36^{7} 71^{19}; in government, עשׂה משׁפט וצ׳ 99^{4} Je 9^{23}; administering justice Jb 37^{23}; punishment Is 1^{27} 5^{16} 10^{22} 28^{17} Dn 9^{7}; vindication of his people Mi 7^{9}. **3.** *righteousness*, in a case or cause, בצדקתי החזקתי Jb 27^{6} *on my righteousness I hold fast*; מה ישׁ לי עוד צ׳ 2 S 19^{29} *what right have I yet?* of God's judgments, הגיד צ׳ Is 57^{12} (iron.); השׁיב צ׳ 1 S 26^{23} Jb 33^{26}; השׁיב כצ׳, 2 S 22^{25}, גמל v^{21}, נתן 1 K 8^{32} = 2 Ch 6^{23}. **4.** *righteousness* = *truthfulness*, באמת ובצ׳ Is 48^{1} Zc 8^{8}; in word Is 45^{23} 63^{1}, oath Je 4^{2}. **5.** *righteousness*, as ethically right: Gn 30^{33} (J) Dt 6^{25} Is 33^{5} 41^{18} Ez 14$^{14.20}$ Pr 10^{2} 11$^{4.5.18.19}$ + 17 t., + צִדְקַת (ה)צַדִּיק(ים) Is 5^{23} Ez 18^{20} 33^{12}; צ׳ ישׁרים Pr 11^{6}; אֹרַח צ׳ 8^{20} 12^{28}; דֶּרֶךְ צ׳ 16^{31}; עשׂה צ׳ *do righteousness* ψ 106^{3} Is 56^{1} 58^{2} Ez 18^{22}; עשׂה משׁפט וצ׳ Ez 18^{5} + 6 t. Ez; עשׂה צ׳ ומשׁפט Gn 18^{19} (J) Pr 21^{3}; רדף צ׳ Pr 15^{9} 21^{21}; הלך באמת ובצ׳ 1 K 3^{6}; חשׁב לו (ל)צ׳ Gn 15^{6} (JE) *imputed to him* (*for*) *righteousness*, ψ 106^{31}; צ׳ וָחֶסֶד Pr 21$^{21.21}$ (del. 𝔊^{AB} Toy). **6.** *righteousness* as vindicated, *justification, salvation*, etc. (cf. צֶדֶק **6**): **a.** of God, ∥ יֶשַׁע, תְּשׁוּעָה, יְשׁוּעָה Is 45^{8} 46^{13} 51^{6} + 7 t. Is^{2}; ∥ בְּרָכָה ψ 24^{5}; ∥ נַחֲלָה Is 54^{17}; ∥ חֶסֶד ψ 36^{11} 103^{17}; שֶׁמֶשׁ צ׳ Mal 3^{20} *sun of righteousness* (with healing); בְּצ׳, י׳ delivers, guides, exalts his people ψ 5^{9} 31^{2} 71^{2} 89^{17} 119^{40} 143$^{1.11}$; אַל־יָבֹאוּ בְּצִדְקָתֶךָ 69^{28} (of wicked); as acc. after verbs of declaring, etc., his *saving* (*delivering*) *righteousness* 22^{32} 40^{11} 51^{16} 71$^{15.16.24}$ 98^{2} 145^{7}; also יִוָּדַע צ׳ 88^{13}; צ׳ עֹמֶדֶת לָעַד *his righteousness endureth* for ever 111^{3} cf. 119^{142}. **b.** of people, = *prosperity*, ∥ עשׁר, הון Pr 8^{18}; מוֹרֶה לצ׳ *early rain for prosperity* Jo 2^{23}. **7.** pl. *righteous acts*: **a.** of God Ju 5$^{11.11}$ 1 S 12^{7} Mi 6^{5}; vindication of right ψ 103^{6}; redemptive Is 45^{24} Dn 9^{16}. **b.** of man's moral conduct Is 64^{5} Je 51^{10}, also prob. Ez 3^{20} 18^{24} 33^{13} (Kt sg.) ψ 11^{7} (? gloss), Dn 9^{18}; as adv. acc., הֹלֵךְ צְדָקוֹת Is 33^{15}.

†[צָדֵק, צָדֹק] **vb. denom.** be just, righteous;—**Qal** *Pf.* 3 fs. צָדְקָה Gn 38^{26}; 2 ms. צָדַקְתָּ Jb 33^{12} 35^{7}, etc.; *Impf.* 3 ms. יִצְדַּק Jb 9^{2}+; יִצְדָּק Jb 4^{17} 11^{2}; 3 fpl. תִּצְדַּקְנָה Ez 16^{52} (𝔊 Co תְּצַדְּקִין, not Berthol Toy Krae), etc.;—**1.** *have a just cause, be in the right*, Jb 9$^{15.20}$ 13^{18} 34^{5}; in complaint Jb 33^{12}; c. מִן pers. Gn 38^{26} (J; of Tamar). **2.** *be justified*, in one's plea Jb 11^{2}; c. עִם (man with God) 9^{2} 25^{4}; בי׳ Is 45^{25}; by witnesses 43^{9}; by acquittal ψ 143^{2} Is 43^{26}; by condemnation of opponent Jb 40^{8}. **3.** *be just*: of God, in his government, in charging with sin ψ 51^{6}; of מִשְׁפְּטֵי־י׳ 19^{10}. **4.** *be just, righteous*, in conduct and character: of men Jb 10^{15} 15^{14} 22^{3} 35^{7}, c. מִן comp., Jb 4^{17} (more than God; Dr *at God's hand*, מִן **2 d**), Ez 16^{52} (< 𝔊 Co **Pi.**). **Niph.** *Pf.* 3 ms. וְנִצְדַּק קֹדֶשׁ consec. Dn 8^{14} *the holy place shall be put right*, in a right condition (Marti^{Kau} Buhl SS; Bev Dr Marti$^{Comm.}$ *be justified*, its cause vindicated). **Pi.** *Pf.* 3 fs. צִדְּקָה Je 3^{11}; *Impf.* 2 fs. תְּצַדְּקִי Ez 16^{51}; *Inf. cstr.* sf. צַדֶּקְךָ Jb 33^{32}; צַדֶּקְתֵּךְ (Ges §52 p) Ez 16^{52}; צַדְּקוֹ Jb 32^{2};—*justify*: עַל צַדְּקוֹ נַפְשׁוֹ מֵאֱלֹהִים Jb 32^{2} *because he justified himself rather than God* (cf. **Qal 1**); *make to appear righteous* Je 3^{11} Ez 16$^{51.52}$ (all c. מִן comp.); חָפַצְתִּי צַדְּקֶךָ Jb 33^{32} *I desire to justify thee* (in thy plea, cf. **Qal 2**). **Hiph.** *Pf.* 1 s. sf. הִצְדַּקְתִּיו 2 S 15^{4}; 3 mpl. הִצְדִּיקוּ Dt 25^{1}; *Impf.* 3 ms. יַצְדִּיק Is 53^{11}; 1 s. אַצְדִּיק Ex 23^{7} Jb 27^{5}; *Inf. cstr.* הַצְדִּיק 1 K 8^{32} = 2 Ch 6^{23}; *Imv.* mpl. הַצְדִּיקוּ ψ 82^{3}; *Pt.* מַצְדִּיק Pr 17^{15}, etc.;—**1.** *do justice*, in administering law 2 S 15^{4} ψ 82^{3}. **2.** *declare righteous, justify*, c. acc. (ה)צַדִּיק Dt 25^{1} 1 K 8^{32} = 2 Ch 6^{23}; רָשָׁע Ex 23^{7} (E) Is 5^{23} Pr 17^{15}; *justify* accusers, by recognizing charge as just Jb 27^{5}. **3.** *justify, vindicate the cause of, save*, c. acc., Is 50^{8} (of God), c. לְ of obj. Is 53^{11} (of servant

of ׳י). **4.** *make righteous, turn to righteousness*, Dn 12³, cf. Aboth 5²⁶·²⁷ Bev. **Hithp.** *Impf.* 1 pl נִצְטַדָּק Gn 44¹⁶ (J) how *shall we justify ourselves*, clear ourselves from suspicion?

צַדִּיק ₂₀₆ **adj. just, righteous**;—abs. צ׳ Gn 6⁹+; pl. צַדִּיקִים Ex 23⁸+, etc.;—**1.** *just, righteous*, in government: **a.** of Davidic king 2 S 23³; צֶמַח Je 23⁵ Zc 9⁹ (‖ *victorious*). **b.** of judges, Ez 23⁴⁵ Pr 29² (v. Toy; Kau questions this meaning in all these). **c.** of law, מִשְׁפָּטִים צ׳ Dt 4⁸. **d.** of God Dt 32⁴ ψ 119¹³⁷ 129⁴ Jb 34¹⁷, opp Pharaoh Ex 9²⁷ (J); in discrimination Je 12¹ Zp 3⁵ ψ 7¹⁰ ¹² 11⁷; condemnation 2 Ch 12⁶ Dn 9¹⁴ La 1¹⁸ Ezr 9¹⁵ Ne 9³³; redemption Is 45²¹ ψ 116⁵; keeping promises Ne 9⁸; in all his ways ψ 145¹⁷. **2.** *just* in one's cause, *right:* Ex 23⁷·⁸ (E) Dt 16¹⁹ 25¹ 1 K 8³²=2 Ch 6²³, Is 5²³ 29²¹ Jb 32¹ 36⁷ Pr 17¹⁵·²⁶ 18⁵ ¹⁷ 24²⁴ Am 2⁶ 5¹² Hb 1⁴ ¹³; right in law, not under penalty 2 S 4¹¹ 1 K 2³²; innocent of specif. offence 2 K 10⁹; c. מִן comp. 1 S 24¹⁸. **3.** *just, righteous*, in conduct and character: **a.** towards God Gn 7¹ 18²³·²⁴·²⁴·²⁵·²⁵·²⁶·²⁸ (J) 20⁴ (E), Hb 2⁴ Mal 3¹⁸. **b.** in gen, ethically: ψ 5¹³ 7¹⁰ 11³·⁵+21 t. ψψ (+infr), Pr 2²⁰ 3³³ 4¹⁸ 9⁹+56 t. Pr, Ec 3¹⁷+7 t. Ec, Is 3¹⁰ 57¹ ¹ Je 20¹² La 4¹³ Ez 3²⁰·²¹·²¹+12 t. Ez, Ho 14¹⁰, ‖ תמים Gn 6⁹ (P) Jb 12⁴, ‖ נָקִי Jb 17⁹ 22¹⁹ 27¹⁷ ψ 94²¹; ‖ יִשְׁרֵי לֵב ψ 32¹¹ 64¹¹ 97¹¹ **4.** *righteous*, as justified and vindicated by ׳י, esp. servant of ׳י Is 53¹¹, so his people, usu. pl. Is 60²¹ ψ 33¹+ 8 t. ψψ (v. also supr.); אָהֳלֵי צ׳ 118¹⁵ *tents of the righteous;* דֶּרֶךְ צ׳ 1⁶, עֲדַת צ׳ v⁵, גּוֹרַל צ׳ 125³, v⁶; sg. coll 34²⁰·²² 75¹¹ Is 24¹⁶ 26⁷ ⁷; גּוֹי צַדִּיק v² (‖ שֹׁמֵר אֱמֻנִים). **5.** *right, correct*, Is 41²⁶ (cf. אֱמֶת 43⁹); *lawful* שְׁבִי צ׳ 49²⁴ EV, but rd עָרִיץ.

צָדוֹק, and (1 K 1²⁶) צָדֹק ₅₄ **n.pr.m.** (*just, righteous;* cf. Sab n. pr. צדק CIS^iv, No 287, 1 2 11 16 etc, DHM^Hof Museum, No 32),—Σαδωκ, Σαδδουκ (cf. Lag^BN 225 ff):—**1.**₄₈ priests: **a.** David's time 2 S 8¹⁷=1 Ch 18¹⁶, 2 S 15²⁴·²⁵+23 t. S K Ch, +(Sol.'s time) 1 K 2³⁵=1 Ch 29²², 1 K 4²·⁴, ancestor of בְּנֵי צָדוֹק Ez 40⁴⁶ 44¹⁵ 48¹¹, זֶרַע צ׳ 43¹⁹, בֵּית צ׳ 2 Ch 31¹⁰; descendant of Eleazar 1 Ch 5³⁴·³⁴+5 t. Ch. **b.** 1 Ch 5³⁸·³⁸, poss=**c.** 1 Ch 9¹¹ Ne 11¹¹. **†2.** father-in-law of Uzziah 2 K 15³³ =2 Ch 27¹¹ **†3.** two wall-builders: **a.** Ne 3⁴. **b.** v²⁹, perh.=**c.** 10²², and **d.** צ׳ הַסּוֹפֵר 13¹³.

צִדְקִיָּהוּ ₅₆, ־יָה ₇ **n.pr m.** (׳י *is righteousness*, cf. Sab. צדקאל DHM^Ib., on No 32),—Σεδεκια(ς): **1.** last king of Judah, מַתַּנְיָה, changed to צ׳: ־יָּהוּ 2 K 24¹⁷ ¹⁸·²⁰ 25² ⁷ ⁷=2 Ch 36¹⁰·¹¹, 1 Ch 3¹⁵ Je 1³ 21¹ ³·⁷+37 t. Je; ־יָה +Je 27¹² 28¹ 29³ 49³⁴. **†2.** false prophets: **a.** under Ahab, ־יָּהוּ 1 K 22²⁴=2 Ch 18¹⁰·²³; ־יָה 1 K 22¹¹. **b.** ־יָּהוּ Jerem.'s time, Je 29²¹ ²². **†3.** ־יָּהוּ prince, Jerem.'s time, Je 36¹². **†4.** ־יָה, priest, Nehem.'s time, Ne 10² (𝔊L Σεχενιας). **†5.** ־יָה, son of Jehoiachin, acc. to 1 Ch 3¹⁶, but prob. gloss, Be SS, cf. Kit.

†[צָהֹב, צָהַב, cf. Lag^BN 31] **vb. gleam** (NH *id* (of face, bronze, etc); Ar. صَهُبَ *be red*),—**Hoph.** *Pt.* נְחֹשֶׁת מֻצְהָב Ezr 8²⁷ *polished bronze* (so NH and—appar. Hebraism—𝔗 2 Ch 4¹⁶).

†צָהֹב **adj. gleaming, yellow** (of hair);— שֵׂעָר צ׳ Lv 13³⁰·³²·³⁶ (opp. שֵׂ׳ שָׁחֹר v³¹ ³⁷).

†I [צָהַל] **vb. neigh, cry shrilly** (Ar. صَهَلَ *neigh*, Syr. ܨܗܠ *id.;* 𝔗 Est 8¹⁵=BH);— **Qal** *Pf.* 3 fs. צָהֲלָה Est 8¹⁵; 3 pl צָהֲלוּ Is 24¹⁴; *Impf* 3 mpl. יִצְהָלוּ Je 5⁸; 2 fs. תצהלי 50¹¹ Kt, Qr 2 mpl. תִּצְהֲלוּ and so Vrss; *Imv.* fs. צַהֲלִי Is 10³⁰+; mpl. צַהֲלוּ Je 31⁷;—**1.** *neigh*, of men under fig. of stallions, c. אֶל *unto* (in desire) Je 5⁸, of profligate Judaeans; abs 50¹¹ of arrogant Chaldeans. **2.** *cry shrilly*, in distress Is 10³⁰ (c. adv. acc. קוֹלֵךְ); usu joy, praise (‖ רָנַן) 12⁶ 54¹, c. בְּ *at, over*, Je 31⁷ Is 24¹⁴, + שָׂמְחָה Est 8¹⁵.

†[מִצְהָלָה] **n.f. neighing**,—pl. cstr. קוֹל מִצְהֲלוֹת אַבִּירָיו Je 8¹⁶ (‖ נַחְרַת סוּסָיו); sf מִצְהֲלוֹתַיִךְ 13²⁷ of idolatrous Judah, under fig. of mare desiring stallion (‖ זִמַּת זְנוּתֵךְ, נִאֻפַיִךְ).

†II. [צָהַל] **vb. Hiph. make shining** (NH *id.*(rare); ‖ form of צהר, denom fr. צהרים); —*Inf cstr.* לְהַצְהִיל פָּנִים מִשָּׁמֶן ψ 104¹⁵.

צהר (√of foll; cf. Ar. ظَهَرَ *appear, mount*, ظَهْر *back*, ظَهِيرَة *midday;* As. *ṣêru* (TelAm. *zu'ru*, etc.), *back;* Aram טִיהֲרָא, ܛܗܪܐ, MI¹⁵ הצהרם, *midday*, Lag^BN 129; >Ko^ii 1, 93 (cf. Thes)=*shine*, ‖ זהר, NH Hiph. (rare), for this is in Aram צהר (rare)); הִצְהִיר Ecclus 43³ is denom from צהרים.

†1. [צֹהַר] **n.[m.]** only pl. צָהֳרַיִם **midday, noon**, Dt 28²⁹+, צָהֳרָיִם Gn 43¹⁶+ (when sun *mounts* its highest; on form as expanded pl. (not du) v. Ges^§ 88 c and reff);—usu. **1.** *noon* as a specif. time of day, 1 K 18²⁷; esp. בַּצּ׳ *at noon* Gn 43¹⁶·²⁵ Am 8⁹ 1 K 18²⁷ 20¹⁶ Ct 1⁷ (resting-time for flock), Je 6⁴ (opp. evening); בְּעֵת צ׳ Je 20¹⁶ (dist fr. morning) as time of supposed security Je 15⁸ Zp 2⁴; also מֵהַבֹּקֶר וְעַד הַצּ׳ 1 K 18²⁶,

עד־הצ׳ 2 K 4^{20}; without ב, as adv, צ׳ as time of prayer ψ 55^{18} (+ ערב, בקר), as time of wasting קֶטֶב 91^{6}, משׁכב הצ׳ 2 S 4^{5} *noonday repose* **2.** *noon*, as bright, sim of happiness, blessing, Is 58^{10} (opp אֲפֵלָה), ψ 37^{6} (‖ כָּאוֹר); cf Jb 11^{17} (Ges § 124 e), v. also בתוך הצ׳ Is 16^{3} (opp. צִלֵּךְ); בַּצ׳ Dt 28^{29} Is 59^{10} Jb 5^{14}

†II צֹהַר **n f** prob roof (cf Ar As TelAm *back*; > Thes Di al. *light*, window),—צ׳ תַּעֲשֶׂה לַתֵּבָה Gn 6^{16}

†I. יִצְהָר **n.**[**m**] **fresh oil** (newly *appeared*, cf 'Ausbruch' Lag BN 129 Kö II 1 93, > Thes al. that which *shines*),—abs. יצ׳ Ho 2^{10} +, sf יִצְהָרְךָ Dt 7^{13} +,—*fresh oil*, as product of land, in unmanufactured state, usu. + דָּגָן, תירושׁ etc., rich possession, gift of י׳ Ho $2^{10.24}$ Je 31^{12} Dt 7^{13} 11^{14} Jo $2^{19.24}$, so חלב יצ׳ Nu 18^{12}; Dt 28^{51} Hg 1^{11} 2 Ch 32^{28} Ne 5^{11}, tithed Dt 12^{17} 14^{23}, firstfruits for priest 18^{4} Ne 10^{38} cf v^{40} 13^{5} (tithe for Levites), v^{12}, for priest and Levite 2 Ch 31^{5}; זית יצ׳ 2 K 18^{32} *oil-olive*, i.e oil-yielding olive-trees, cf יצ׳ alone Jo 1^{10}; יִצ׳ as *anointing oil* only in בני היצ׳ Zc 4^{14}, i.e. anointed ones.

†[צָהַר] **vb.denom.** fr foreg., **Hiph. press out oil**,—*Impf.* 3 mpl יַצְהִירוּ Jb 24^{11}

†II יִצְהָר **n.pr.m.** Ισ(σ)αάρ: Levite, son of Kohath Ex $6^{18.21}$ Nu 3^{19} 16^{1} 1 Ch 5^{28} $6^{3.23}$ $23^{12.18}$.

†יִצְהָרִי **adj.gent.** of foreg, c. art. as subst. coll הַיִּצ׳ Nu 3^{27} 1 Ch 24^{22} $26^{23.29}$.

צַו v. צוה

צוא (√of foll; cf. Syr. ܨܘܐ *be foul*, Eth. ጸአ:, prob. also Ar وَضِي *be polluted*; Dl Pr 160 Kö II 1 162 cp also As *si'*, *destroy*, *ruin*; NH צוֹאָה = BH, Aram צָאתָא, ܨܐܬܐ, *filth*)

†[צֵאָה] **n.f. filth, specif. human excrement**,—sf. צֵאָתֶךָ Dt 23^{14}, cstr בְּגֶלְלֵי צֵאת הָאָדָם Ez 4^{12} (as fuel, cf. [גָּל] p 165 supr.).

†צֹאָה **n. f. filth**;—abs צ׳ Is 28^{8} (of drunkards' vomit, cf קִיא); צ׳ fig of iniquity, cstr. צֹאַת Is 4^{4}, sf צֹאָתוֹ Pr 30^{12}, specif of human *excrement* (= [צֵאָה]) sf צֹאָתָם 2 K 18^{27} = Is 36^{12} (both Qr, Kt חר(א)יהם, cf [חֶרֶא] p 351 supr.).

†[צֹאִי] **adj. filthy**,—pl צוֹאִים Zc 3^{3}, צאים v^{4} (both of garments)

צַוָּאר v. I. צור

†צוֹבָא, צוֹבָה **n.pr.terr.** Σουβα, rarely Σωβα(λ): an Aramaean kingdom, time of (Saul and) David אֲרַם צוֹבָא 2 S $10^{6.8}$ (elsewhere צוֹבָה), ψ אֲרַם צוֹבָה 60^{2} (title), הֲדַדְעֶזֶר מֶלֶךְ צ׳ 2 S $8^{3.5.12}$ = 1 Ch $18^{3.5}$, 1 K 11^{23} 1 Ch 18^{9}; צ׳ also 19^{6}; חֲמַת צ׳ 2 Ch 8^{3}; orig. home of one of David's heroes 2 S 23^{36} (perh. rd. also for n pr.m. מִבְחָר ‖ 1 Ch 11^{38}, cf Dr); מַלְכֵי צ׳ 1 S 14^{47} (only here in Saul's time), No ARAM. in Ency Bib., cf ZMG xxv (1871), 113 ff. places between Hamath and Damascus (about *Hums*, Emesa), and so Dl Pa 279 f, who cp. As. city *Subitu*, cf. Schr COT 288 f.

†I **צוּד** **vb. hunt** (NH *id* (rare), מְצוּדָה = BH, As. *ṣâdu*, *hunt*, so Ar. (صيد), صَادَ, Aram. צוּד, צֵיד, (ܨܝܕ) ܨܳܕ, OAram צידא *hunting*),—**Qal** *Pf.* 3 pl. צָדוּ La 4^{18}, sf. צָדוּנִי 3^{52}, וְצָדוּם consec. Je 16^{16}, *Impf.* 3 ms. יָצוּד Lv 17^{13}, etc, *Imv* ms. צוּדָה Gn 27^{3}; *Inf. abs.* צוד La 3^{52}; *cstr.* לָצוּד Gn 27^{5}; *Pt.* הַצָּד v^{33},—*hunt*, c. acc. 1 צַיִד Gn 27^{3} Qr (> Kt צידה), $v^{5.33}$ (all J), צֵיד חַיָּה Lv 17^{13} (H), טֶרֶף Jb 38^{39}; c acc pers. Mi 7^{2} (+ חֵרֶם, instr.), Je 16^{16} (+ מֵעַל), Jb 10^{16}, צוֹד צָדוּנִי כַּצִּפּוֹר La 3^{52}, subj. evil ψ 140^{12}; c acc נֶפֶשׁ יְקָרָה Pr 6^{26}.—Ho 9^{13} rd prob. לָצוּד (or לְצַיִד), for MT לְצוֹר, v. צֹר **Pōʿl.** *hunt* (keenly, eagerly?), *Impf.* 2 fpl. תְּצוֹדֵדְנָה Ez 13^{18}; *Inf cstr* לצודד v^{18}, *Pt* fpl מצודדות $v^{20.20}$, all c. acc. נפשׁות (of magic arts, necromancy, etc).

†I. צַיִד **n.m. hunting, game**;—abs. צ׳ Gn 10^{9} +, צָיִד 27^{3} (Qr; > Kt צידה), Ne 13^{15}, cstr. ציד Gn 27^{25}, sf צידי v^{19}, etc,—**1.** *hunting* Gn 27^{30}, גבר־צ׳ $10^{9.9}$, ידע צ׳ 25^{27} (all J). **2.** *game* hunted and taken (cf. Ba NB 161), Gn 25^{28} 27^{3} (v. supr) $v^{5.7.19.25.31.33}$ (all J), cf Pr 12^{27}; צֵיד חַיָּה אוֹ עוֹף Lv 17^{13} (H).

†[צַיָּד] **n.m. hunter**,—pl. צַיָּדִים Je 16^{16}.

†מָצוֹד, מְצָד **n.f.** Je 48, 41 **fastness, stronghold** (prop. *hunting-place*?),—abs. מְצָד 1 Ch 11^{7} 12^{16}, מצד 12^{8}; pl. abs. מְצָדוֹת 1 S 23^{14} +, cstr. *id.* v^{29} (Gi, 24^{1} van d. H. Baer), Is 33^{16};—**1.** *mountain-fastness* Ju 6^{2} 1 S $23^{14.19.29}$ (v. supr.), Ez 33^{27} 1 Ch $12^{8.16}$; מְצָדוֹת סְלָעִים Is 33^{16}. **2.** more gen., *stronghold* Je 48^{41} 51^{30} Ez 19^{9} (Baer Gi, van d. H. מְצָדוֹת *id.* [II. מצודה] Ew Hi-Sm Da al; *nets* [I מְצוּדָה] Krae, del. Co Oort Toy); citadel of Jerusalem 1 Ch 11^{7}.

†I [מָצוֹד] **n.m.** in pl, dub, usu. **siege-works**,—מְצוֹדִים גדלים Ec 9^{14}, but read מְצוּרִים Wkl Altor Forsch iv 353, v. מָצוֹר **2**, p. 849 a

†II [מָצוֹד] **n.**[**m.**] **hunting implement**, specif. net (cf Syr ܡܨܝܕܬܐ, ܬ מְצָדְתָּא, *net*),—

only fig.: cstr. מְצוֹד רָעִים Pr 12^{12} (but text dub., v. conj in Toy); sf. מְצוּדוֹ Jb 19^{6} (of God as Job's hunter); pl. מְצוֹדִים וַחֲרָמִים לִבָּהּ Ec 7^{26} (of woman)

†I. **מְצוֹדָה** **n.f. net**;—מ׳ Ec 9^{12} for fish (in sim.),—pl. Ez 19^{9} v. מָצָד supr.

†I. **מְצוּדָה** **n.f. net, prey**,—abs. מ׳ Ez 13^{21} ψ 66^{11}; sf. מְצוּדָתִי Ez 12^{13} 17^{20},—**1.** *net*, in fig of י׳'s judgment, Ez 12^{13} 17^{20} (both ‖ רֶשֶׁת), ψ 66^{11}. **2.** *prey* Ez 13^{21} (fig.)

†II. **[מְצוּדָה]** **n.f. fastness, stronghold**,—sf. מְצֻדָתָהּ Is 29^{7} (of Ariel),—pl Ez 19^{9} v. מָצָד.

†II. **מְצוּדָה** **n.f. fastness, stronghold**;—abs. מ׳ 1 S 22^{4}+, מְצֻדָה 2 S 5^{9}, cstr. מְצֻדַת v^{7}; sf. מְצוּדָתִי ψ 18^{3}+, מְצֻדָתִי 2 S 22^{2}; pl מצודות ψ 31^{3},—*fastness* of David, 1 S 22$^{4.5}$ 24^{23} (Gi v^{22}) 2 S 5^{17} 23^{14} = 1 Ch 11^{16}, rd. also מְצֻדַת עֲדֻלָּם 1 S 22^{1} 2 S 23^{13} 1 Ch 11^{15}, for MT מְעָרַת (v מְעָרָה p 792 b); of Jerus., מְצֻדַת צִיּוֹן 2 S 5^{7} = 1 Ch 11^{5}, cf. 2 S 5^{9}; home of eagle Jb 39^{28} (+שֶׁן־סֶלַע); elsewhere fig. of י׳ ψ 18^{3} = 2 S 22^{2}, ψ 31^{4} 71^{3} (all + סַלְעִי), 91^{2} (+ מַחְסִי), 144^{2} (+ חַסְדִּי), but this dub, Krochm Gr Che חסני, Dy חִזְקִי, Du סַלְעִי; poss. is מַחְסִי); also בית מְצוּדוֹת 31^{3}.

II. **צוד** (√ of foll; relation to I. צוד dub.; cf. As. *ṣîditu*, Ar. زاد (و), Aram זְוָדָה, ܙܘܕܐ, Palm. זוד, all *provisions* (esp for journey); in Thes = I. צוד; on *game* as early food of nomads v. RS$^{Sem. i\ 205,\ 2nd\ ed\ 222f.}$ cf. Doughty$^{Arab.\ Des.\ i.\ 70,\ 326,\ 562}$; ז (Ar Aram) is then secondary).

†II. **[צַיִד]** **n.[m.] provision, food**,—abs צֵיד Ne 13^{15}, sf. צֵידוֹ Jb 38^{41}, etc.;—*provision* taken on journey Jos 9^{14}, לֶחֶם צֵידָם v^{5} (both JE); more gen. (late), *food, food-supply*, Ne 13^{15} ψ 132^{15}, of raven Jb 38^{41}.—I. צַיִד v. צוד.

†**צֵידָה** **n.f. id.**;—abs צ׳ Jos 9^{11} + 2 t., צֵדָה Gn 42^{25} + 5 t.;—*provision* for journey, march, Gn 42^{25} 45^{21} Ex 12^{39} (all E), Jos 1^{11} (D), 9^{11} (JE), Ju 7^{8} (text dub. cf. GFM), 20^{10} 1 S 22^{10}, *supply of food* ψ 78^{25}—Gn 27^{3} v. I. צַיִד, sub צוד.

†**[צִיֵּד]** **vb. denom. Hithp. supply oneself with provisions, take as one's provision**;—*Pf.* 1 pl. הִצְטַיַּדְנוּ Jos 9^{12} this bread *we took as our provision*; *Impf* 3 mpl וַיִּצְטַיָּדוּ v^{4} (so rd. for MT וַיִּצְטַיָּרוּ, Codd Vrss Thes al), abs.

[צָוָה]$_{485}$ **vb. Pi. lay charge (upon), give charge (to), charge, command, order** (Ba ZMG xli (1887). 641 Gerber^{124} cp Ar وَصَّى *combine*, II. *enjoin*, IV. *charge*; وَصِيَّة *injunction, command*; Thes cp Syr. ܙܘܐ, *erect*, ܙܘܝܐ, *stone-heap*, Ar. صُوَّة *guide-stone*, cf. Schulth^{87}; Gerber makes Heb vb denom. fr. מִצְוָה, but vb is much earlier);—*Pf.* 3 ms. צִוָּה Gn 6^{22}+, sf. צִוַּנִי Dt 4^{5}+; צִוְּךָ Dt 4^{23}+; צִוָּהוּ Gn 7^{5}+, etc.; 1 s. צִוִּיתִי Ex 29^{35} + 29 t., צֻוֵּיתִי Lv 8^{31} + 4 t, etc; *Impf.* 3 ms. יְצַוֶּה Gn 18^{19} + 8 t; יְצַו Dt 28^{8}; וַיְצַו Gn 2^{16}+; sf וַיְצַוֵּךְ 1 Ch 22^{12}, etc.; 1 s. וָאֲצַוֶּה Ezr 8^{17} Qr (> Kt ואוצאה), 3 mpl. וַיְצַוּוּ Gn 50^{16}+, etc; *Inf. cstr.* צַוּוֹת 2 S 18^{5}+, etc; *Imv* ms. צַוֵּה Jos 4^{16} + 2 t.; צַו Lv 6^{2} + 9 t; mpl. צַוּוּ Jos 1^{11} 4^{3}; *Pt* מְצַוֶּה Nu 32^{25}+; cstr. מְצַוֵּה Is 55^{4}, etc., f. מְצַוָּה Gn 27^{8};—**1. a.** *lay charge upon*, c עַל pers., Gn 2^{16} (J) 28^{6} (P) 1 K 2^{43} 11^{11} Am 2^{12} Je 35^{6} + 6 t; עַל rei, עַל הֶעָבִים אֲצַוֶּה מֵהַמְטִיר Is 5^{6}, cf. Jb 36^{32}, צ׳ עַל־חָגָב 2 Ch 7^{13}. **b.** *give charge to, command to* c. לְ pers. Ex 1^{22} (E) 1 S 20^{29} 1 Ch 22^{17} Is 13^{3} Jer 32^{23} ψ 105^{8} תורה צ׳ לָנוּ משֶׁה Dt 33^{4}, cf. Ne 9^{14}, צַו לְבֵיתֶךָ 2 K 20^{1} *give charge to thy household* (in preparation for death) = Is 38^{1} (cf. NH, B.Bath^{151b}, צַוָּאָה '*verbal will*' Id^{147a}). **c.** *give charge unto*, c. אֶל pers. Ex 16^{34} (P), 1 K 11^{10}; וַיְצַו אֶל־בֵּיתוֹ 2 S 17^{23} (cf b). **d.** *give charge over, appoint*, c. acc. pers. + עַל rei, Ne 7^{2} 1 Ch 22^{12}, צ׳ (לִהְיוֹת) נָגִיד עַל *appoint* one (to be) ruler over 2 S 6^{21} 1 K 1^{35}; c לנגיד 1 S 13^{14} 25^{30}, שֹׁפְטִים על 2 S 7^{11} = 1 Ch 17^{10}; c. inf. (no עַל), לרעות עמי 2 S 7^{7} = 1 Ch 17^{6}; וְצִוִּיתָה אֹתוֹ לְעֵינֵיהֶם Nu 27^{19} (P) *and thou shalt install him in their sight*, cf. v^{23} (P). **e.** *give* one *charge, command* (oft עַל *concerning*), Gn 12^{20} (J), Nu 8^{22} (P), 2 S 14^{8} 18^{5} Je 7^{22} 39^{11} Is 45^{12} (AV RV Che Ry^{Kau}, > Ges Ew Di Du al as **d**), 10^{6} (al. *against*), Na 1^{14} (al. *id*); c. לְ Nu 9^{8} 32^{28} (P), ψ 91^{11} La 1^{17} Est 3^{2}, c. אֶל Is 23^{11} Je 47^{7}. **2.** *charge, command*: **a.** c. acc. pers. + rei, oft., esp. of the law: Deut. phrases are אשר אנכי מצוך Ex 34^{11} (J), Dt 4^{40} 6$^{2.6}$ + 18 t. Dt, cf. 15^{15}; אשר אנכי מצוה אתכם Dt 4$^{2.2}$ + 9 t. Dt; הַדֶּרֶךְ† אשר צ׳ Dt 13^{6} Ex 32^{8} (E) Dt 5^{30} 9$^{12.16}$ 11^{28} 31^{29}. **b.** c. acc. pers. + obj clause, e.g., Inf. Gn 50^{2}+; ו consec. Pf. 18^{19} (J), Nu 35^{2} (P); ו consec. Impf. 2 S 4^{12} 1 K 2^{46}; weak ו c. Impf. Ex 27^{20} (P) Jos 4^{16}; Imv. Jos 1^{9} 1 S 18^{22}. **c.** acc, pers, acc. rei om, Ex 18^{23} (E) Gn 49^{33} (P)+; obj given after לֵאמֹר Gn 26^{11} 32$^{18.20}$ Lv 6^{2}+; וַיֹּאמֶר, etc, Gn 28^{1} 49^{29}+. **d.** acc rei, acc. pers. om, צ׳ לעולם בריתו ψ 111^{9}; זֶה הַדָּבָר† אֲשֶׁר צ׳ י׳, Ex 16$^{16.32}$ 35^{4} Lv 8^{5} 9^{6} 17^{2} Nu 30^{2} 36^{6} (P), obj. cl., Lv 8^{34} (P), 13^{54} (P); Gn 42^{25}

(E), 1 K 5^{20}, Ju 4^{6} **e.** abs. Gn 50^{16} (E), La 3^{37}. **3.** *charge, command*, acc pers in phr כַּאֲשֶׁר צ׳ Ex 23^{15} (E) Gn 7^{9} (P)+, ככל אשר צ׳ Gn 7^{5} (J) Ex 29^{35} (P)+, כאשר צ׳ י׳ מֹשֶׁה Ex 12$^{28.50}$ 39$^{1.5}$ +37 t P, ככל אשר צ׳ י׳ משה 39$^{32.42}$+5 t. P, †לכל אשר צ׳ Jos 1^{18} 22^{2} Je 35^{8}, acc pers. om ככל אשר צ׳ Ex 7^{10} Nu 32^{25} (P)+; כאשר צ׳ 2 K 11^{9}=2 Ch 23^{8}+, †לכל אשר צ׳ Ex 36^{1} (P). †**4.** *charge*, with command to others, *commission*, **a.** acc pers + אֶל pers. (sts + acc rei) Ex 6^{13} 25^{22} Lv 27^{34} (P) Dt 1^{3} Je 27^{4} Est 4^{10}, acc. pers om Gn 50^{16} (E) Est 3^{12} 8^{9} **b.** בְּיַד of agent, + אֶל, Nu 15^{23} 36^{13} (P), אֶל om. Lv 8^{36} (P), Ezr 9^{11} Ne 8^{14} **c.** acc pers + עַל for אל Ezr 8^{17} 1 Ch 22^{13} Mal 3^{22} Est 4^{5} **d.** c acc rei, וצ׳ ברכתי ל Lv 25^{21} (P) *and I will command my blessing to you*, c אתך Dt 28^{8}, cf ψ 133^{3}, צ׳ חסדו 42^{9}, חֶרֶב, נָחָשׁ Am 9$^{3.4}$ בֹּקֶר Jb 38^{12} †**5.** *command, appoint, ordain*, of divine act in creation Is 45^{12} ψ 33^{9} 148^{5}, providence 2 S 17^{14} Am 6^{11} 9^{9} Jb 37^{12} ψ 78^{23} Is 34^{16}, redemption ψ 7^{7} 44^{5} 68^{29} 71^{3}, so of idol Is 48^{5} (|| עשה) †**Pu.** *Pf* 3 ms. צֻוָּה Nu 3^{16} 36^{2}, 2 ms צֻוֵּיתָה Gn 45^{19}, etc, *Impf* 3 ms יְצֻוֶּה Ex 34^{34},—*be commanded*, i e receive command, subj pers, Gn 45^{19} (E), c בּ by whom Nu 36^{2} (P), אשר צ׳ Ex 34^{34} (P), כִּי־כֵן צ׳ Lv 8^{35} 10^{13} (P), כאשר צ׳ Nu 3^{16} (P) Ez 12^{7} 24^{18} 37^{7}

†צִיּוּן **n m. sign-post, monument** (NH *id.* (צִיֵּן Pi denom), prob from √ in orig physical sense, v. esp Ar. صُوَّة, صَوَّان, Syr ܨܘܝܐ, cf Schulth$^{Hom\ Wurz\ 57}$ Ko$^{ii\ 1.154}$, > √ צין Buhl),—abs. צ׳, grave-stone 2 K 23^{17}, sign-post Ez 39^{15}; guide-posts, pl צִיֻּנִים Je 31^{21} (|| תַּמְרוּרִים)

מִצְוָה$_{181}$ **n.f. commandment**;—מ׳ Pr 6^{23}+; cstr מִצְוַת Jos 22^{3}+, sf מִצְוָתְךָ Dt 26^{13} ψ 119^{96}; מִצְוָתוֹ Nu 15^{31}; pl מצות abs. Lv 26^{14}+ (מִצְוֹת Ne 9^{14}), cstr. 4^{2}+, sf. מִצְוֹתַי Gn 26^{5}+, etc,—not used before D and Je; in Je only of man's commands, not Ez nor Minor Proph, exc. Mal;—**1.** *commandment*, of man: king, 1 K 2^{43} 2 K 18^{36}=Is 36^{21}, 2 Ch 8^{15}+14 t., מ׳ אב Je 35$^{14.16.18}$ Pr 6^{20}, מ׳ אנשים Is 29^{13}, pl. only Je 35^{18} Pr 10^{8} Ne 10^{33}, המצוה, *the order* (title of property) Je 32^{11} **2.** of God. **a.** sg *the commandment*, code of law. 2 Ch 8^{13} Ezr 10^{3} ψ 19^{9}; esp of D שמר המ׳ Dt 8$^{1.2}$+5 t. D, עשה המ׳ Dt 6^{25} 15^{5}, (ה)מ׳ אשר צוה Dt 26^{13} 30^{11} 31^{5}; סור מן המ׳ Dt 17^{20}, מ׳ הפר Nu 15^{31} (P); || תּוֹרָה Ex 24^{12} (R^{D}) Jos 22^{5} (D) 2 Ch 14^{3} 31^{21}, + משפטים, חקים Dt 5^{28} 6^{1}+. **b.** pl of *commands* of D and later codes c. 2 pl. (*ye shall, shall not*; Br$^{Hex\ new\ ed.,\ 246\ ff}$), Lv 4^{2}+5 t. P, Is 48^{18}+25 t. (late, esp ψ 119, 20 t), שמר מ׳ Ex 20^{6} (R) Lv 22^{31} (H) Dt 4^{2}+10 t D, 1 K 14^{8} 2 K 18^{6}+5 t.; עשה מ׳ Lv 26^{14} (H)+5 t; שמע מ׳ Dt 11^{13}+4 t; עבר מ׳ Dt 26^{13} 2 Ch 24^{20}; המ׳ אשר צוה Lv 27^{34} (H), עזב מ׳ 1 K 18^{18} 2 K 17^{16} Ezr 9^{10}, הפר מ׳ Ezr 9^{14}, in combinations, esp by Redactors and late writers; order various (1) with חֻקִּים Ex 15^{26} (R^{D}) Dt 4^{40} Ezr 7^{11}+, משפטים+ח׳ Dt 26^{17} 1 K 8^{58} Ne 1^{7} 10^{30}; תורות, משפטים+ Ne 9^{13}; תורה+ Ne 9^{14}, עדות+ Dt 6^{17} 1 Ch 29^{19} 2 Ch 34^{31}. (2) with חֻקּוֹת Lv 26^{3} (H) Dt 6^{2} 10^{13}+9 t, משפטים+ח׳ Lv 26^{15} Dt 8^{11} 11^{1} 30^{16} 1 K 6^{12}, תורה+משפטים ψ 89^{32}, עדות, משפטים+ 1 K 2^{3}; תורות+ Gn 26^{5} (R^{D}), עדות+ 2 K 23^{3}. (3) with משפטים Nu 36^{13} (P) 1 Ch 28^{7} Ne 9^{29} Dn 9^{5}; with תורות Ex 16^{28} (R), with עדות Ne 9^{34}. **c.** of special *commands* of God 1 S 13^{13} 1 K 13^{21} 2 Ch 29^{25} Ne 13^{5} Mal 2$^{1.4}$ Jb 23^{12} **3.** *commandment*, sg, of code of wisdom Pr 19^{16}, || תורה 6^{23}, || דבר 13^{13}; pl of special commands 2^{1} 3^{1} 4^{4} 7$^{1.2}$.

†צַו appar **n.[m.]**, dub word,—in הָלַךְ אַחֲרֵי־צָו Ho 5^{11} usu. *command, ordinance*; < 𝔊𝔖 Che Now GASm שָׁוְא, elsewh only צַו לָצָו צַו לָצָו (|| קַו לָקָו קַו לָקָו), Is 28^{10} in mocking mimicry of Is.'s words, and, v^{13}, of the unintelligible speech of י׳'s foreign agents of judgment; Ges Che^{Comm} al (cf AV RV) render *command upon command*; Ew Di (carpenter's) *rule* (+ קַו = *line and rule*), fr √ צָוָה (whence צִיּוּן); Du Che^{Hpt} explain as mocking sounds without sense.

†[צָוַח] **vb. cry aloud** (NH *id*; so As. *ṣâḫu* (?), Ar. (صِيحَ), صَاحَ, Aram. צְוַח, ܨܘܚ; Eth. ጸውዐ: *call*),—**Qal** *Impf.* 3 mpl. יִצְוָחוּ Is 42^{11} (in joy, || יָרֹנּוּ).

†צְוָחָה **n.f. outcry**,—in distress, grief, abs. צ׳ ψ 144^{14}; cstr צִוְחַת Je 14^{2}, sf צִוְחָתֵךְ 46^{12}; abs also Is 24^{11} (c. עַל *for, because of*).

צול (√ of foll, cf *miswal* (in Syria), a stone-lined hollow, or basin, for washing grain, Wetzst$^{Siebe\ ZPV\ xiv\ (1891),\ 3}$).

†צוּלָה **n.f. ocean-deep**,—Is 44^{27}.

†[מְצוּלָה], מְצוֹלָה **n.f. depth, deep**;—abs מְצוּלָה Jb 41^{23}+, pl abs. מְצוֹלֹת Ex 15^{5} Ne 9^{11}, מְצֻלוֹת ψ 88^{7}, cstr. מְצוּלוֹת Zc 10^{11}, מצלות Mi 7^{19} ψ 68^{23},—*depth*, pl מ׳ יָם *depths of the sea* Mi 7^{19} ψ 68^{23}, abs Ex 15^{5} (of Red Sea) Ne 9^{11}

(*id.*); fig. of deep distress ψ 88[7] (‖ בּוֹר תַּחְתִּיּוֹת); מְ׳ יְאֹר Zc 10[11] (i.e. of Nile); sg. = *the deep sea, deep,* ψ 107[24] Jon 2[4] Jb 41[23] (in hyperb. descript. of crocodile); *depth* of marsh, swamp, בִּיוַן מְ׳ ψ 69[3] *in mire of (the) depth,* fig. of distress (‖ מַעֲמַקֵּי־מַיִם), cf. מְ׳ alone v[16] (‖ בְּאֵר).

†מְצֻלָה **n.f.** dub. word: Zc 1[8] the myrtles which are בַּמְּ׳, appar. some locality about Jerus., called *the basin, hollow;* GASm *glen* or *valley-bottom;* poss. is מְצִלָּה < מְצֻלָה, *shadow* (III. צלל).

†[צוּם] **vb. abstain from food, fast** (NH *id.;* Ar. صَامَ (صوم), Eth. ጾመ: Aram. צוּם, ܨܳܡ);—**Qal** *Pf.* 2 ms. צַמְתָּ 2 S 12[21]; 2 mpl. צַמְתֶּם Zc 7[5], sf. צַמְתֻּנִי v[5]; *Impf.* 3 ms. וַיָּצָם 2 S 12[16], וַיָּצוֹם 1 K 21[27]; 1 s. אָצוּם Est 4[16], etc.; *Imv.* mpl. צוּמוּ v[16]; *Inf. abs.* צוֹם Zc 7[5]; *Pt.* צָם 2 S 12[23] Ne 1[4];—*fast,* in mourning the dead 1 S 31[13] = 1 Ch 10[12], 2 S 1[12]; in worship (contrition, intercession, etc.) Ju 20[26] 1 S 7[6] 2 S 12[16] (c. acc. cogn. צוֹם; ‖ בִּקֵּשׁ), v[23] and (+ בָּכָה), v[21.22] (q.v. for explanation), Je 14[12] Zc 7[5] (+ סָפוֹד), הֲצוֹם צַמְתֻּנִי v[5] (Ges §117 x) *was it at all unto me* [לִי] *that ye fasted?* וָאֱהִי צָם Ne 1[4] (periphr. conj.; + מִתְפַּלֵּל), cf. Ezr 8[23] (+ בִּקֵּשׁ), Est 4[16] (c. עַל pers. *for* whom), v[16], Is 58[3] (‖ עִנִּינוּ נַפְשֵׁנוּ), v[4] (c. לְ rei), v[4]; once in disappointment and vexation 1 K 21[27].

†צוֹם **n.m.**[Is 58,5] **fasting, fast;**—צ׳ abs. 2 S 12[16]+, cstr. Zc 8[19] (4 t.); sf. צֹמְכֶם Is 58[3]; pl. צוֹמוֹת Est 9[31];—*fast,* as acc. cogn. 2 S 12[16]; public observance 1 K 21[9.12] 2 Ch 20[3] Ezr 8[21] Je 36[9] Jon 3[5] (all obj. of קָרָא *proclaim*), cf. Jo 1[14] 2[15] (both obj. of קִדְּשׁוּ); יוֹם צוֹם Je 36[6], יוֹם צֹמְכֶם Is 58[3], cf. v[5] (‖ יוֹם עַנּוֹת אָדָם נַפְשׁוֹ), v[5.6]; of periodic fasts Zc 8[19.19.19.19] Est 9[31]; act or state of fasting, נֶאֶסְפוּ בְצ׳ וּבְשַׂקִּים Ne 9[1] cf. Jo 2[12] Dn 9[3] Est 4[3]; עִנֵּיתִי בַצ׳ נַפְשִׁי ψ 35[13] cf. 69[11] (on וָאֶבְכֶּה v. Che Bae); causing physical weakness 109[24].

צוע (√ of foll.; cf. Ar. صَاغَ *form, fashion*).

†צַעֲצֻעִים **n.[m.]pl. things formed, images;** מַעֲשֵׂה צ׳ 2 Ch 3[10] *image work* (of cherubim).

†[צוּף] **vb. flow, overflow,** [**float**] (NH *id.;* so Aram. טוּף, ܛܳܦ;—Ar. طَوْفٌ *skin-raft* is loan-wd. Frä[220]);—**Qal** *Pf.* 3 pl. צָפוּ־מַיִם עַל־רֹאשִׁי La 3[54] (fig.). **Hiph. 1.** *Pf. cause to flow over,* הֵצִיף אֶת־מֵי יַם־סוּף עַל־פְּנֵיהֶם Dt 11[4]. **2.** *cause to float: Impf.* 3 ms. וַיָּצֶף הַבַּרְזֶל 2 K 6[6].

†I. צוּף **n.m.** (**honey-**)**comb** (as *exuding* honey);—only fig.: cstr. צוּף־דְּבַשׁ Pr 16[24]; pl. צוּפִים ψ 19[11] (+ נֹפֶת ‖ דְּבַשׁ), 𝔊 κηρίον, κηρία, 𝔙 *favus.*

†II. צוּף **n.m.** Ephr. ancestor of Elkanah and Samuel, בֶּן־צ׳ 1 S 1[1] (ἐν Νασειβ, 𝔊L υἱοῦ Σωφ), 1 Ch 6[20] Qr 𝔊 𝔙 (Kt צִיף); appar. = צוֹפַי v[11] (Levite), Σουφ(ει): hence prob. אֶרֶץ צוּף 1 S 9[5] (in Benj., τὴν (γῆν) Σ(ε)ιφ(α)).

†צוּפִי **adj.gent. Ṣuphite;**—so read prob. for צוֹפִים 1 S 1[1] (We Klo Dr and most mod., after 𝔊 Σ(ε)ιφα, A Σωφιμ).

†[צָפָה] **n.f. out-flow;**—sf. צָפָתֵךְ Ez 32[6] *thine outflow* (flowing blood), Co Bthl Toy Krae.

צוֹפַי = II. צוּף. צוֹפִים v. צוּפִי.

†I. [צוּץ, צִיץ] **vb. 1. blossom. 2. shine, sparkle** (perh. orig. meaning of √, but connex. of **1, 2.** dub.) (NH *id.* Hiph., fig. senses, צִיץ n. = BH);—**Qal** *Pf.* **1.** 3 ms. צָץ הַמַּטֶּה Ez 7[10] (fig.; ‖ פָּרַח הַזָּדוֹן); *Impf.* 3 ms. יָצִיץ ψ 90[6] (of grass, ‖ חָצִיר), 103[15] (man under fig. of flower), fig. יָצִיץ וּפָרַח יִשְׂ׳ Is 27[6]; 3 mpl. יָצִיצוּ ψ 72[16], וַיָּצִיצוּ 92[8] (‖ פָּרַח; both fig. of men =) *flourish.* **2.** *shine, gleam:* of crown (נֵזֶר) ψ 132[18]. **Hiph.** *Impf.* 3 ms. וַיָּצֵץ צִיץ Nu 17[23] *it put forth blossoms* (of rod; — perhaps from ‖ וַיֹּצֵא פֶרַח).

†I. צִיץ **n.m.**[Is 28,1] **1. blossom, flower. 2. shining thing;**—צ׳ abs. Is 42[7]+, cstr. v[6]+; pl. צִצִּים 1 K 6[18] + 3 t. 6 (on form v. Kö[II.1,60]);—**1.** *blossom, flower,* Nu 17[23] (P; of Aaron's rod); (fig. of man Is 40[7.8] (both נָבֵל צ׳; ‖ חָצִיר), cf. sim. צִיץ הַשָּׂדֶה v[6] (‖ *id.*), ψ 103[15], and צ׳ alone Jb 14[2]; צ׳ נֹבֵל Is 28[1] (fig. of Samaria), so prob. also v[4] (for MT צִיצַת נ׳; so Marti); פְּטוּרֵי צִצִּים, as ornaments of temple 1 K 6[18.29.32.35]. **2.** *shining thing,* plate of gold, constituting the diadem on front of high priest's mitre, Lv 8[9] Ex 28[36] 39[30] (all P).—II, III. צִיץ, v. p. 851 infr.

צִיצַת Is 28[4], v. I. צִיץ supr.

†II. [צוּץ] **vb. Hiph. gaze, peep** (NH Hiph. *gaze* (rare); Aram. צִיץ *gaze*);—*Pt.* מֵצִיץ מִן־הַחֲרַכִּים Ct 2[9] (v. ח׳, p. 355).

†I. [צוּק] **vb. Hiph. constrain, bring into straits, press upon** (NH צוּק *be distressed* (rare), Hiph. = BH; Ar. ضَاقَ (ى) *be narrow, tight,* so Eth. ጸበቀ; Aram. עִיק, ܥܳܩ; ChrPal. ܥܘܩ);—*Pf.* 3 fs. הֱצִיקָה Ju 16[16], sf. הֱצִיקַתְהוּ 14[17], כִּי־ Jb 32[18] (Gi v[19]); 1 s. וַהֲצִיקוֹתִי consec. Is 29[2]; *Impf.* 3 ms. יָצִיק Dt 28[53] + 2 t.; 3 mpl. יְצִיקוּ Je 19[9]; *Pt.* מֵצִיק Is 51[13.13], pl. מְצִיקִים 29[7];—*bring into straits,* by importunity c. לְ pers. Ju 16[16]; c. sf. pers. 14[17]; *constrain* (to speak) Jb 32[18]

(sf pers.); elsewhere of *bringing into straits* a city or people, c ל, Is $29^{2.7}$, so 7^{6} (reading ונציקנה for MT ונקיצנה), Thes Che Du Gi Marti, cf formula בְּמָצוֹר וּבְמָצוֹק אֲשֶׁר יָצִ׳ ל Dt $28^{53.55.57}$ Je 19^{9}, pt abs הַמֵּצִיק Is $51^{13.13}$ *the oppressor.*

†צוֹק **n.[m.]** si vera l, **constraint, distress**;—וּבְצוֹק הָעִתִּים Dn 9^{25} usu *in distressful times,* Gr וּבקין וגו׳ (so 𝔊 [v^{27}] 𝔖), as beginning of v^{26}, omitting ו in ואחרי (cf Bev Marti)

†צוּקָה **n.f. pressure, distress**;—national Is 8^{22} (+צָרָה), cf אֶרֶץ צָרָה וצ׳ 30^{6}; personal צָרָה וצ׳ Pr 1^{27}.

†II מוּצָק, מוּצָק **n.[m.] constraint, distress**,—abs מוּצָק Is 8^{23} *distress,* abs. also מוּצָק Jb 36^{16}, of distress as *constraint* (opp. רֹחַב); רחב מַיִם בְּמוּצָק 37^{10}, lit. *in constraint* (i e frozen) —I מוּצָק v יצק

†מָצוֹק **n.[m.] straitness, straits, stress**,—alw abs מ׳,—כָּל־אִישׁ מ׳ 1 S 22^{2} *every man of straits* (in straits), בְּמָצוֹר וּבמ׳ Dt $28^{53.55.57}$ Je 19^{9} (all of national *straits*), צַר־וּמ׳ מְצָאוּנִי ψ 119^{143}; perh rd מָצוֹק also 32^{6}, for מצא רק, cf Du Br.

†מְצוּקָה **n.f.** id,—abs. יוֹם צַר וּמ׳ Jb 15^{24}; צָרָה וּמ׳ Zp 1^{15}, pl sf., of י׳ delivering מִמְּצוּקוֹתַי ψ 25^{17}, מִמְּצוּקוֹתֵיהֶם etc, $107^{6.13.19.28}$.

†II. [צוּק] **vb. pour out, melt** (‖ יצק),—**Qal** *Pf* 3 pl (acc. to Thes al) צָקוּן Is 26^{16}, but v infr, *Impf* 3 ms וְאֶבֶן יָצוּק נְחוּשָׁה Jb 28^{2} (rd perh. יָצוּקוּ, v. Bu) *and stone* (ore, *men*) *melt it into copper;* צוּר יָצוּק עִמָּדִי פַּלְגֵי־שָׁמֶן Jb 29^{6} *the rock used to pour out beside me streams of oil* —Is 26^{16} (as above) must mean *they poured out* (uttered) a whisper (לַחַשׁ, i.e. prayer); but form most improb; Koppe Gr Di Du al. prop. צקון לַחַשׁ (from assumed צָקוֹן, I. צוק)=*constraint of* (like that of) *magic;* <Houb Kit צָעֲקוּ בְלַחַץ, or Che^{Hpt} צָעַקְנוּ מִלַּחַץ כִּי מוּסָרְךָ לָנוּ וגו׳.

†[מָצוּק] **n.m. molten support, pillar**,—pl. cstr מְצֻקֵי אֶרֶץ 1 S 2^{8} *the supports of the earth* are י׳'s,—מָצוּק 14^{5} ('as a pillar,' 'steep,' etc.) is difficult (cf HPS), del with 𝔊 Th Dr Bu.

I. צור (√ of foll, cf. possibly Ar صَارَ (و) *cause to incline, lean,* NH=BH (rare), so Aram. ܨܘܪܐ (cf. $Ko^{ii\ 1,90}$), צַוְּרָא)

†צַוָּאר **n.m.**$^{41.6}$ **neck, back of neck**,—abs. צ׳ Is 8^{8}+, cstr צַוַּאר Je 28^{10}+3 t 28, sf צַוָּארִי La 1^{14}, צַוָּרָם Ne 3^{5}, etc, pl. cstr צַוְּארֵי Ju 8^{21}+, sf. צַוָּארָיו Gn 27^{16}+, צוּארֵיכֶם Je 27^{12}, +צַוְּארֹתֵיכֶם Mi 2^{3},—**1.** *neck,* esp. *back of neck,* of man, wearing chain as ornament Gn 41^{42}(E), so of woman Ct 1^{10}, cf. Ju 5^{30} (rd. perh צַוָּארַי for ־רֵי), elsewh in Gn usu. pl intens, of individual, נָפַל עַל־צ׳ 45^{14} (E), 46^{29} 33^{4} (Qr, Kt sg), so בָּכָה עַל־צ׳ 45^{14} 46^{29} (all J), חֶלְקַת צַוָּארָיו 27^{16} *smooth part of neck* (J), neck of beautiful woman Ct 4^{4} 7^{5}; neck as pressed by foot of conqueror Jos $10^{24.24}$ (JE); place of yoke Gn 27^{40} (sg; J), Dt 28^{48} Is 10^{27} Je $27^{2.8.11.12}$ $28^{10.11.12.14}$ 30^{8}, of transgressions as yoke La 1^{14}, place of bonds Is 52^{2}; of bearing load, Ne 3^{5} (fig), hence calamity as burden Mi 2^{3}; neck as smitten with sword Ez 21^{34}, עַד־צ׳ as measurement of height (depth; in fig) Is 8^{8} 30^{8} Hb 3^{13}, בצ׳ עָתָק fig. ψ 75^{6} speak not with *arrogant neck* (si vera l.; but rd. perh. בְּצוּר *against the Rock,* 𝔊 κατὰ τοῦ θεοῦ, Bae Hup-Now Che Kau); of wicked, rushing against God Jb 15^{26}—עַל־צַוָּארֵנוּ נרדפנו La 5^{5} is dubious; Matthes Lohr Bae עַל עֹל־וגו׳, Bu עַל צַו׳, and הֻרְדָּפְנוּ or יְהֹדפנו for נִר׳ **2.** *neck* of animals, camels (wearing ornaments) Ju $8^{21.26}$; heifer Ho 10^{11} (i.e. place of yoke, in fig. of Ephr.); horse Jb 39^{19}, crocodile 41^{14}.

†[צַוְּרוֹן] **n.[m.] pl. necklace**,—sf אַחַד עֲנָק מִצַּוְּרֹנָיִךְ Ct 4^{9}.

II צור **vb. confine, bind, besiege** (NH *id., wrap* (rare); Aram. צוּר *besiege, beleaguer*);—**Qal** *Pf.* 2 ms וְצַרְתָּ Dt 14^{25}, etc; *Impf.* 3 ms וַיָּצַר 1 K 20^{1}+, 2 ms תָּצוּר Dt 20^{19}, etc; *Imv.* fs. צוּרִי Is 21^{2} (after עֲלִי $Ko^{i\ 444}$, cf. $Ges^{§72s}$); *Inf cstr.* לָצוּר 1 S 23^{8}, *Pt* pl צָרִים 1 K 15^{27}+;—**1.** *confine, secure* (‖ I. צרר), acc rei + בְּ of receptacle Dt 14^{25} 2 K 5^{23} Ez 5^{3}, complem om. 2 K 12^{11}, **2.** *shut in, besiege,* c עַל of city 2 S 11^{1} 1 K 15^{27} 16^{17} 20^{1} 2 K $6^{24.25}$ 17^{5} 18^{9} 24^{11} Is 29^{3} (+acc. of siege-works), Je 32^{2} 37^{5} 39^{1} Dt 20^{12} Ez 4^{3} Dn 1^{1}; c. עַל pers. (within city) 2 S 20^{15} 2 K 16^{5} Je $21^{4.9}$, c אֶל of city (for עַל) Dt 20^{19}, c. אֶל pers 1 S 23^{8}; c. את of city only 1 Ch 20^{1} (‖ 2 S 11^{1} supr); abs Is 21^{2}.—הִנָּם צָרִים אֶת־הָעִיר עָלֶיךָ Ju 9^{31} is corrupt; $Frankenb^{Richterbuch\ 28}$ Bu GFM^{Hpt} Now מְעִרִים *inciting* against. **3.** *shut up, enclose:* נָצוּר עָלֶיהָ לוּחַ אָרֶז Ct 8^{9} (עַל of maid [under fig. of door] + acc mater, cf. Is 29^{3} supr.); c. sf. pers. ψ 139^{5} (fig., י׳ subj).

†מָצוֹר **n.[m.] siege-enclosure, siege, entrenchment**,—alw. מ׳ abs, exc. cstr. מְצוֹר Ez 4^{7}, sf. מְצוּרֵךְ v^{8};—**1.** *siege* מ׳ שָׂם עָלֵינוּ Mi 4^{14} *he hath*

laid siege to us, cf. וְנָתַתָּה עָלֶיהָ מ׳ Ez 4[2], בּוֹא בַּמּ׳ is *come into a state of siege* Dt 20[19] 2 K 24[10] 25[2] Je 52[5], cf. וְהָיְתָה בַּמּ׳ Ez 4[3]; יוֹשֶׁבֶת בַּמּ׳ Je 10[17]; מְצוֹר יְרוּ׳ Ez 4[7] *siege of Jerus.*, but also מ׳ עַל־יְרוּ׳ Zc 12[2]; יְמֵי מ׳ of duration of siege Ez 4[8] 5[2]; מֵי מ׳ Na 3[14] *water for a siege;* in phr בְּמ׳ וּבְמָצוֹק *in the siege and stress* Dt 28[53.55.57] Je 19[9]. **2.** *enclosure*, i.e. *siege-works* Dt 20[20]; late=*rampart* Zc 9[3], עִיר מ׳ *entrenched city* ψ 31[22] (al. *besieged*), 60[11] (‖ 108[11] ע׳ מִבְצָר), cf 2 Ch 8[5]; עָרִים לְמ׳ 11[5], יֹשְׁבִים בְּמ׳ בִּירוּשָׁלָם 32[10]; מ׳ Hb 2[1] acc. to most (‖ מִשְׁמַרְתּ); but We der. fr. נצר, i.e *watch-tower*, Now conj. מִצְפֶּה (cf וַאֲצַפֶּה foll.); >Buhl conj. מְצָד.—מ׳ **n.pr.terr.** v. p 566.

†מְצוּרָה **n.f. siege-works, rampart**,—abs. מ׳ Na 2[2] 2 Ch 14[5], pl. מְצוּרוֹת 2 Ch 11[11]+, מְצֻרֹת Is 29[3], etc,—**1.** *siege-works* Is 29[3]. **2.** *rampart* נָצוֹר מ׳ Na 2[2] *guard the rampart!* (‖ צַפֵּה דֶרֶךְ; We Now der. fr נצר, i e. *keep watch!*), 2 Ch 11[11], עָרֵי מְצוּרָה 14[5] *fortified* cities, so עָרֵי (הַ)מְּצוּרוֹת v[10.23] 12[4] 21[3].

†III. [צוּר] **vb. shew hostility to, treat as foe** (c. acc. pers) (akin to II. צרר, to which SS assign the forms, but cf. Ar. ضَارَ (ى) *act unjustly*, also *defraud;* Syr ܥܪܬܐ, *rival wife*),—**Qal** *Pf.* 1 s. וְצַרְתִּי אֶת־צֹרְרֶיךָ Ex 23[22] (subj. י׳; ‖ וְאָיַבְתִּי אֶת־אֹיְבֶיךָ); *Impf* 2 ms. אַל־תָּצַר אֶת־מוֹאָב Dt 2[9], 2 mpl. sf. אַל־תְּצֻרֵם v[19], *Pt.* הַצָּרִים אוֹתָם Est 8[11].

†IV. [צוּר] **vb. fashion, delineate** (NH *id*, so Aram. צוּר, ܨܘܪ, ܨܪ; ܨܘܪܬܐ *picture*, Sab. צור, pl צורת Hom[Chrest 125] Mordtm[Him. Inschr. 14 15]; Ar. صُورَة is loan-word acc. to Fra[272]);—*Pf.* 2 ms וְצַרְתָּ Ez 43[11] (for MT צוּרַת) acc. to 𝔊 We Sm Co Toy Berthol Krae, *and thou shalt delineate* the house (cf. הַגֵּד v[10], הוֹדַע וּכְתֹב v[11]); *Impf.* 3 ms. וַיָּצַר אֹתוֹ בַּחֶרֶט Ex 32[4] (E) *and fashioned it* [the gold] *with a graving-tool;* וַיָּצַר אֶת־שְׁנֵי הָעַמּוּדִים 1 K 7[15] (+acc mater.), rd. וַיִּצֹק (יצק), so 𝔊 SS Kit Benz cf. Th; 1 s sf. אצורך Je 1[5] Kt, v. יצר.

†[צוּרָה] **n.f. form, fashion**,—cstr. צוּרַת Ez 43[11] v. foreg.; sf. צוּרָתוֹ v[11] (𝔊 מְצֻוֹתָיו, so Co, or תּוֹרֹתָיו, so Berthol Krae; Toy as MT); so also Kt v[11 11] (Qr pl. sf. צוּרֹתָיו) 2nd of these del. as dittogr all moderns, 1st rd. as Kt Co Berthol, as Qr Toy; sg. sf. צוּרָם (Ges[§ 91 e] Ko[ii 1, 440]) ψ 49[15] Qr (Kt צירם) *their form* (of the dead).

†I. [צִיר] **n.m. image**;—pl. צִירִים Is 45[16]=*idols;* sg. sf. צירם ψ 49[5] Kt *their form* (v. צוּרָה).

V. צוּר (√of foll., ‖ III. צרר; cf SI[3.4] צר, *rock*, Aram. טוּרָא, ܛܘܪܐ *hill*, so Palm. pl טוריא).

†I צוּר **n.m.**[Jb 29,6] **rock, cliff**;—צ׳ abs. Ex 17[6]+, cstr. Dt 8[15]+; sf. צוּרִי 2 S 22[3], etc; pl צֻרִים Nu 23[9]+, צוּרוֹת Jb 28[10], cstr צוּרֵי 1 S 24[3] (Gi v[2]),—**1. a.** *rocky wall, cliff*, Ex 17[6.6] (E), Dt 8[15] (צ׳ הַחַלָּמִישׁ), Is 48[21 21] ψ 78[15.20] 105[41] 114[8] (‖ חַלָּמִישׁ); בּוֹא בַצּ׳ Is 2[10], בִּמְעָרוֹת צֻרִים v[19], בְּנִקְרוֹת הַצּ׳ v[21], cf. Ex 33[21.22] (JE); yielding honey (from its clefts) ψ 81[17] (cf. Dt 32[13]; Dy Perles[Anal 34] We rd צוּף); as look-out Nu 23[9] (JE), home of goats 1 S 24[3] (Gi v[2]), snow-covered Je 18[14]; bearing (olives for) oil Dt 32[13] (חַלְמִישׁ צ׳), Jb 29[6]; resort of homeless 24[8], pierced by miners 28[10], cf. perh. שִׁית בְּצ׳ נְחָלִים אוֹפִיר 22[24] *deposit* (thy) gold *in the rock* of the wadys (most sub צר *pebble*); as quarry, fig. of Abr. as ancestor of Isr. Is 51[1]; place of security 1 Ch 11[15], צ׳ הַמִּישֹׁר Je 21[13] (of city), fig. ψ 27[5] 61[3]; symb. of firmness Na 1[6] Jb 14[18] 18[4]; enduring material 19[24]. **b.** *rock* with flat surface 2 S 21[10] Pr 30[19]. **c.** *block of stone, boulder* Ju 6[21] 13[19] (as altar), cf. צוּר מִכְשׁוֹל Is 8[14] (‖ אֶבֶן נֶגֶף). **d.** *rock* with specif name, צ׳ עוֹרֵב Ju 7[25] Is 10[26]. **2. a.** fig. of God (33 t.) as support and defence of his people (oft. ‖ אֱלֹהִים, י׳, etc), צ׳ מָעֻזֵּךְ Is 17[10], צ׳ מָעוֹז ψ 31[3], צ׳ עֻזִּי 62[8], צ׳ מָעוֹן 71[3], צ׳ יְשֻׁעָתוֹ Dt 32[15] cf 2 S 22[47 b] (but del., v. ‖ ψ 18[47]), ψ 89[27] 95[1], צ׳ יְשׁוּעָתִי 62[3.7], צ׳ מַחְסִי 94[22], צ׳ יִשְׂרָאֵל Is 30[29] 2 S 23[3] (personif.), צוּרִי ψ 18[3.47] =2 S 22[3.47 a], ψ 19[15] 28[1] 92[16] 144[1], צ׳ לְבָבִי 73[26], צוּרֵנוּ Dt 32[31], צוּרָם v[30] ψ 78[35]; c. בְּ essent. בְּיָהּ י׳ צ׳ עוֹלָמִים Is 26[4] (cf. ψ 62[8], v. ב **I. 7 c**); as **n.pr. dei** (*the*) *Rock* Dt 32[4 18] (צ׳ יְלָדְךָ), v[37] Hb 1[12], + (perh) ψ 75[6] (rd. בַּצּוּר, v. צַוָּאר; v. also פְּדָהצוּר). **b.** of a heathen god Dt 32[31], cf. Is 44[8], מִי צוּר מִבַּלְעֲדֵי א׳ 2 S 22[32] ‖ ψ 18[32], cf. 1 S 2[2].—Vid. also בית צור and חֶלְקַת הַצֻּרִים.—ψ 89[44] v. צר sub III צרר, 49[15] v. צוּרָה sub III. צור.

† II. צוּר **n.pr.m.** Σουρ (*Rock*);—**1.** a prince of Midian Nu 25[15] 31[8] Jos 13[21]. **2.** Gibeonite 1 Ch 8[30] 9[36].

†צוּרִיאֵל **n.pr.m.** (*my rock is El*);—a Levite Nu 3[35], Σουριηλ.

†צוּרִישַׁדָּי **n.pr.m.** Σουρ(ε)ισαδαι[ε] (*my rock is Shadday*),—a Simeonite Nu 1[6] 2[12] 7[36.41] 10[19].

צֹאר v צוּרנים צַוָּר v צר Tyre צוֹר

[צות] **Hiph.** Is 27[4] v יצת

צִיחָא v. צִחָא צחח v צַח

צחה (√of foll, Ar صَحَا (و) *be cloudless*, so Eth ጸሐወ: Aram צְחָא, צְחִי *be thirsty*).

†[צחה] **adj intens.** parched (cf Ges [§84bc]),—cstr. צחה צָמָא Is 5[13] *parched with thirst*.

†[צָחַח] **vb.** be dazzling (ℑ צחצח *polish*; Syr ܨܚ *be scorched*, Aph *declare in writing* (make clear), ܨܚܝܚܐ *clarus, lucidus, fulgidus*, صَحْصَحَانٌ, صَحْصَحٌ, *smooth, plain*),—**Qal** *Pf* 3 pl. צַחוּ מֵחָלָב La 4[7] (|| זַכּוּ מִשֶּׁלֶג), *they are more dazzling* (i e. *whiter*) *than milk* (of effeminate skin)

†צַח **adj.** dazzling, glowing, clear,—חֹם צַח Is 18[4] *glowing heat*; רוּחַ צַח Je 4[11] *glowing wind*; דודי צח ואדום Ct 5[10] *my beloved is dazzling* (*white*) *and ruddy* (cf La 4[7]); fpl לְדַבֵּר צחות Is 32[4] *to speak clear* (words), *clearly*.

† [צְחִיחַ] **n.[m.]** shining, glaring, surface cstr צחיח סלע i e a smooth, bare, rock Ez 24[7.8] 26[4.14], pl בַּצְּחִיחִים Ne 4[7] Qr (Kt בַּצְחִחִיִּם), *in glaring, bare places* (?)

†צְחִיחָה **n f.** scorched land,—צ׳ ψ 68[7].

†[צַחְצָחָה] **n.[f.]** scorched region,—pl. צחצחות Is 58[11]

צחן (√of foll, NH צַחֲנָה=BH, Aram צַחֲנְתָא *stinking fluid*, ܨܚܢܐ, سَخِن *foul*).

†[צַחֲנָה] **n.f.** stench;—sf צַחֲנָתוֹ Jo 2[20] (|| בָּאְשׁוֹ)—Cf עפר צחנה Ecclus 11[12].

†[צָחַק] **vb.** laugh (Ar. ضَحِكَ, *laugh*, Syr. ܓܚܟ, cf Ba[ES 34], v also שׂחק);—**Qal** *Pf.* 3 fs צָחֲקָה Gn 18[13], etc.; *Impf* 3 ms. יִצְחַק־ Gn 21[6], וַיִּצְחָק 17[17], 3 fs וַתִּצְחַק 18[12],—*laugh*, Gn 18[12.13.15.15] (J), 17[17] (P), c ל *at, concerning*, 21[6]. **Pi.** *Impf* וַיְצַחֵק Ju 16[25], *Inf cstr.* לְצַחֵק Ex 32[6], (בִּי) לְצַחֶק בָּנוּ Gn 39[14.17], *Pt* מְצַחֵק Gn 19[14] 26[8], מְצַחֵק 21[9],—**1.** *jest* Gn 19[14] (J) **2.** *sport, play* Gn 21[9] (E) Ex 32[6] (J), *make sport for* Ju 16[25] (לִפְנֵי || וִישַׂחֶק־לָנוּ), *toy with* (אֶת), of conjugal caresses Gn 26[8] (cf Doughty[Arab. Des. i 231]), *make a toy of*, c ב, 39[14.17] (all J).

†צְחֹק **n.[m.]** laughter,—צחק עָשָׂה לִי א׳ Gn 21[6] (E) *laughter hath God caused for me*; =*laughing-stock*, תִּהְיֶה לִצְ׳ וּלְלַעַג Ez 23[32] (del. 𝔊[B] Hi Co Berthol Siegf Krae; not Toy)

יִצְחָק[108], יִשְׂחָק[4], **n.pr.m.** Ισαακ **Isaac**, son of Abr and Sarah (*he laugheth*, cf. play upon name Gn 18[12f] (J), 21[6] (E), 17[17.19] (P); 26[8] (J));—יִצְחָק Gn 21[3.4.5] (E) +, 24[62.63.67] (J) +, 17[19.21] (P) +, (80 t Gn, 9 t. Ex, 7 t. Dt), Lv 26[42] Nu 32[11] Jos 24[3.4], 1 K 18[36] 2 Ch 13[23] 1 Ch 1[28.34.34] 16[16] 29[18] 2 Ch 30[6], †יִשְׂחָק Je 33[26] ψ 105[9], and (=Israel) בָּמוֹת יִשְׂחָק Am 7[9], בֵּית יִשְׂחָק v[16].

צחר (√of foll; cf Ar صَحِرَ XI. *dry up, become yellow* [parched by sun], صُحْرَة *reddish-gray colour* (v. Mull[Königsb Stud i 6]))

†[צָחֹר] **n.[m.]** reddish-gray, tawny;—צֶמֶר צָחַר Ez 27[18] *wool of reddish-gray, tawny wool*, or (Hi-Sm Krae), *of* land *Sachar* (si vera l, Co del. צחר as dittogr.)

†[צָחֹר] **adj.** tawny,—fpl. אֲתֹנוֹת צְחֹרוֹת Ju 5[10].

†צֹחַר **n.pr.m.** **1.** father of Ephron the Hittite Gn 23[8] 25[9], Σααρ **2.** son of Simeon Gn 46[10] Ex 6[15], Σααρ **3.** name in Judah 1 Ch 4[7] Qr (וְצֹחַר; Kt יצחר), Σααρ, 𝔊L Εισαρ.

יִצְחָר 1 Ch 4[7] Kt, v. foregoing.

†I צִי **n.m.**[Is 33, 21] ship (loan-word from Egypt. *t'aï*, acc to Bondi[56], cf. Erman[ZMG xlvi (1892) 123] DHM[VOJ viii 7, 165]),—abs. צִי אַדִּיר Is 33[21] *a majestic ship*; pl. צִים Nu 24[24] (JE), Ez 30[9] (בַּצִּ׳, but 𝔊 σπεύδοντες, cf. 𝔖, whence Co Berthol אֲצִים)

†II. [צִי] **n.m.**[Je 50, 39] a wild beast, prop either **desert-dweller** (denom. from צִיָּה, so most), or **crier, yelper** (√*צוה=ضوى [*yelp*, Dozy], Ba[NB 188], cf Ew[§146 e note]),—in any case a specif. animal, but not certainly identif.; Bo[Hieroz i, lib 3, § 14], cp Ar. ضَيْوَن *wild cat*;—pl. צִיִּים Is 13[21] (f. אִיִּים v[22]), 23[13] 34[14] (+אִיִּים), Je 50[39] (*id*; all betokening desolation); לְעַם לַצִּ׳ ψ 74[14] (rd. לְעַמְלְצֵי יָם Hup-Now Bae); appar. of people 72[9], but prob. corrupt, Ol conj צָרִים (|| אֹיְבָיו), and so most moderns

צִיבָא and (2 S 16[4]) צִבָא[16] **n.pr.m.** Σ(ε)ιβα: servant of Saul's house, 2 S 9[2.2] + 14 t 9, 16, 19.

†צִידוֹן and (Gn 10[15.19] 49[13]) צִידֹן **n.pr.loc.** **Sidôn**, Σιδων, ancient Phoenician city, on coast N. of Tyre (in As *Sidun(n)u*, COT[Gloss], TelAm. *Ṣiduna*, Ph. צדן, OAram. צידן; in Egypt. *Di-(d)u-na*, WMM[As u Eur 184]),—'first-born' of

Canaan Gn 10[15] = 1 Ch 1[13]; northern limit of Canaanite Gn 10[19], cf. 49[13]; defined as צ׳ רַבָּה Jos 11[8] (so 19[28] infr.); also Ju 1[31] 10[6] (אֱלֹהֵי צ׳), 18[28] 1 K 17[9]; named with Tyre Jos 19[28] (cf. v[29]), 2 S 24[6] (cf. v[7]), Is 23[2.4] and בתולת בַּת־צ׳ v[12] (cf. v[5], etc.), Je 25[22] 27[3] 47[4] Ez 27[8] 28[21.22] (cf v[2.12]), Zc 9[2] Jo 4[4] —Vid. Pietsch[Phöniz. 54 ff] Prutz[Aus Phönicien (1876), 98 ff] Rob[BR ii 473 ff] de Luynes[Voyage à la Mer Morte i 18 ff., and Pl vi-xi] Bd[Pal 3 (1898), 313 ff.].

† צִידֹנִי **adj. gent.** of foregoing;—צ׳ Ju 3[3] Ez 32[30]; elsewhere pl. צִידֹנִים Dt 3[9]+, צִידוֹנִים Ju 10[12], צִדֹנִים 18[7]+3 t., fpl. צִדֹנִיּת 1 K 11[1],—as subst.=*Sidonians*, coll c. art. Ez 32[30] Ju 3[3]; in earlier lit appar.=*Phoenicians* Dt 3[9] Jos 13[4.6] Ju 3[3] 10[12] 18[7.7] 1 K 5[20] (=Tyre v[15]), 16[31] (if, [Jos[Ant. viii 13, 1]] Ethb was king of Tyre also), Ez 32[30]; also עַשְׁתֹּרֶת אֱלֹהֵי צ׳ 1 K 11[5.33], cf. 2 K 23[13]; named with Tyrians 1 Ch 22[4] Ezr 3[7].

צוה, ציה (√of foll.; Ar. صَوِيَ *be parched*, so Aram צְוָא, צְוֵי (not 𝔗), ܨܘܐ (chiefly in Lexx)).

† צִיָּה **n.f. dryness, drought**,—abs. צ׳ Ho 2[5]+; pl. צִיּוֹת ψ 105[41],—*drought* Jb 24[19] (‖ חֹם); elsewh. of land (oft ‖ עֲרָבָה, מִדְבָּר, etc.) אֶרֶץ צ׳ *land of drought, desert* Ho 2[5] (sim.), Je 2[6] 50[12] (fig), 51[43] Is 41[18] 53[2] (in sim.), ψ 107[35]; + צָמֵא Ez 19[13] (fig.), + שְׁמָמָה Jo 2[20], + עָיֵף ψ 63[2] (fig); צ׳=*desert* Is 35[1] Zp 2[13] Jb 30[3] ψ 78[17]; pl. 105[41].

† צָיוֹן **n.[m.] dryness, parched ground** (on format v. Lag[BN 204]);—בְּצ׳, כְּחֹרֶב בצ׳ Is 25[5], 32[2] (‖ אֶרֶץ עֲיֵפָה; both in sim).

צִיּוֹן [154] **n.pr.loc.** Σ(ε)ιων; **Ṣiyyôn, Zion** (Syr. ܨܗܝܘܢ, older form, acc. to Lag[BN 84, cf. 198]);—צ׳ 2 S 5[7]+; צִיּוֹנָה Je 4[6];—stronghold (of Jebusites), מְצֻדַת צ׳ captured by David, and made his residence 2 S 5[7]=1 Ch 11[5] (both + היא עִיר דָּוִד), on S part of E. hill of Jerusalem, distinct from site of temple 1 K 8[1]=2 Ch 5[2] (both מֵעִיר ד׳ היא צ׳), not elsewh. in narrative, but often in poets and proph.: as name of Jerus, from political point of view (sts.=inhabitants), Am 6[1] (‖ הַר־שֹׁמְרוֹן), ‖ יְרוּשָׁלִַם Mi 3[10.12]=Je 26[18], Is 4[3] 30[19] 40[9] 41[27] 52[1] 62[1] 64[9] Zp 3[16] Zc 1[14.17] ψ 51[20] and (בַּת־צ׳) Is 52[2] Mi 4[8] (‖ בַּת־יְרוּשׁ׳), La 2[13] (‖ *id*), also (יוֹשֶׁבֶת צ׳) Je 51[35]; =Jerus. also Is 14[32] 33[5]+, so esp. in phr. בנות צ׳ Is 3[16.17] 4[4] Ct 3[11], בְּנֵי צ׳ La 4[2] Jo 2[23] ψ 149[2] (‖ יִשְׂרָאֵל), cf Zc 9[13], יַלְדָה צ׳ אֶת־בָּנֶיהָ Is 66[8], and even הַר־צ׳ 2 K 19[31]=Is 37[32] (both ‖ יְרוּשׁ׳), Is 29[8] (‖ אֲרִיאֵל v[7]), Ob[17.21] ψ 48[12] (‖ בְּנוֹת יְהוּדָה), 125[1], so also הַר־בַּת צ׳ Is 16[1] and 10[32] Qr (Kt בית · ‖ גִּבְעַת־יְרוּשׁ׳); cf מְרוֹם־צ׳ Je 31[12]; in foll. הַר־צ׳ might refer to temple-hill Is 10[12] (+ יְרוּשׁ׳), 31[4] (+ גִּבְעָתָהּ=יְרוּשׁ׳ v[5]), La 5[18] Jo 3[5] (+ יְרוּשׁ׳), specif. of Jerus as abode of י׳ and place of his worship Am 1[2] Is 31[9] Zc 8[3] Mi 4[2] =Is 2[3], Jo 4[16] ψ 102[22] 135[21] 147[12] (all ‖ יְרוּשׁ׳), 76[3] (‖ שָׁלֵם); partic. of sanctuary 20[3] (‖ קֹדֶשׁ), 14[7]=53[7]+; of Jerus. הַר־צ׳ ψ 48[3] (‖ קִרְיַת מֶלֶךְ רָב), 78[68] (‖ שֵׁבֶט יְהוּדָה), Is 24[23] (‖ יְרוּשׁ׳), etc.; הַרְרֵי צ׳ in same sense † ψ 133[3]; particularly of sanctuary Is 4[5] and (‖ הַר־קָדְשִׁי) Jo 2[1] 4[17], הַר צ׳ קָדְשִׁי ψ 2[6] is seat of king —Vid. also הַר־צ׳, בַּת־צ׳, יֹשֶׁבֶת צ׳, sub יָשַׁב, הַר, בַּת.

צִיּוֹן v. ציה. **צִיּוּן** v. צוה.

† צִיחָא **n.pr.m.** an overseer of Nethinim Ne 11[21], who are called בְּנֵי צִיחָא Ezr 2[43]=בְּנֵי צִחָא Ne 7[46]; Σηα, Σιααν, Σιαλ, Σουλαι, etc.

צִיִּים, צִים v. I, II. צִי. **צִין** **n.pr.loc.** v. צִן.

צִינֹק v. צנק. **צִיעֹר** v. צער.

צִיף v. II. צוף. **I. צִיץ, צִיצָה** v. I. [צוץ]

† II. צִיץ **n.[m.]** meaning dubious; only in תְּנוּ־צִיץ לְמוֹאָב Je 48[9] usu. (after AV Ra Ki al) *wings* (coll.) (cf. Aram. צִיץ *wing, fin*, Thes Gf al); cf. Perles[Anal. 46], who reads נוֹצִין (wing-) *feathers* (as in Aram); 𝔊 σημεῖα, whence Gie *sign-post*, rdg. צִיּוּן,—or נֵס,—(indicating flight).

† III. צִיץ **n.pr.loc.** in מַעֲלֵה הַצִּ׳ 2 Ch 20[16]; ה perh. radical, cf. *Wady Ḥaṣâṣâ*, and plateau *Ḥaṣâṣâ*, N. of Engedi, Buhl[Geogr 97]; 𝔊 Ασαε, 𝔊L τῆς ἐξοχῆς Ασισα.

† צִיצִת **n.f. tassel, lock** (√dub.; NH *id.*, so 𝔗 צִיצִיתָא, Syr. ܨܝܨܝܬܐ; cf. Ar. نَاصِيَةٌ *hair on forehead*),—צ׳ abs. Nu 15[38.39] *tassel* on flowing ends (כְּנָפֵי) of garments, cstr. צ׳ הַכָּנָף v[38] (v. Kennedy[Hast. DB ii. 69, Fringes]); צ׳ רֹאשִׁי Ez 8[3] *lock* of hair on forehead.

צִיקְלַג v. צִקְלַג.

I **צִיר** (√of foll.; cf. صَارَ (ى) *become, attain to, go*; perh Sab. (Min.) ציר (*cause to become*), *form* Hom[Chrest. 123]);—on Hithp. Jos 9[4] v. ציד.

† II **צִיר** **n.m.**[Pr 25, 13] **envoy, messenger**;—צ׳ abs. Je 49[14]+, cstr. Pr 13[17]; pl. צִירִים Is 18[2]; sf צִירַיִךְ 57[9];—*envoy*, from Cush Is 18[2], from apostate Isr. 57[9]; from י׳ Je 49[14]=Ob[1]; *messenger* in gen. צִיר אֱמוּנִים Pr 13[17], צ׳ נֶאֱמָן 25[13].—1. צִיר v. III. צור.

II. **ציר** (√ of foll.; ? *turn, revolve;* NH ציר *pivot* (of door), *hinge*, so Ar. صَائِرٌ (cf. سَيَّارٌ, Dozy[I. 712 b]); perh. As. *ṣirru;* Aram. צִירְתָּא, ܨܝܪܐ).

† III. [**צִיר**] **n.[m.] pivot** (of door), **hinge**;—sf. הַדֶּלֶת תִּסּוֹב עַל־צִירָהּ Pr 26[14] (in ‖ of sluggard).

† IV. [**צִיר**] **n.[m.] pang** (prop. *writhing*);—pl. צִירִים Is 13[8] 21[3]; cstr. צִירֵי 21[3]; sf. צִירַי Dn 10[16], צִרֶיהָ 1 S 4[19];—*pangs* of childbirth 1 S 4[19], so (sim.) Is 21[3]; and, of terror, 13[8] (+חֲבָלִים), 21[3]; in gen., of physical effects of mental distress Dn 10[16].

צֵל, צָלָה v. III. צלל.

† [**צָלָה**] **vb. roast flesh** (NH *id.;* so Ar. صَلَا (ى), Eth. ጸለወ:);—**Qal** *Impf.* 3 ms. יִצְלֶה צָלִי Is 44[16] *he roasteth a roast;* 1 s. אֶצְלֶה בָשָׂר v[19]; *Inf. cstr.* לִצְלוֹת 1 S 2[15] give flesh (בָּשָׂר) *to roast.*

† **צָלִי** **adj. et n.m. roasted, roast**;—cstr. (as adj.) צְלִי־אֵשׁ (P) of flesh (בָּשָׂר) Ex 12[8.9] (opp. מְבֻשָּׁל בַּמָּיִם); abs. as subst. cogn. Is 44[16] v. [צָלָה].

† I. [**צָלַח**] **vb. rush**;—(Thes al. cp. ℭ צְלַח, Syr. ܨܠܚ, *cleave, penetrate,* then *advance,* v. foll.);—**Qal** *Pf.* 3 fs. וְצָלְחָה consec. 1 S 10[6]; 3 pl. וְצָלְחוּ 2 S 19[18]; *Impf.* 3 ms. יִצְלַח Am 5[6] (v. infr.), 3 fs. וַתִּצְלַח Ju 14[6]+;—*rush,* וְצ׳ הַיַּרְדֵּן 2 S 19[18] *they rushed into the Jordan* (dub., v. Dr HPS), יִצ׳ כָּאֵשׁ בֵּית יוֹסֵף Am 5[6] lest *he rush like fire upon the house of Joseph* (or *O house,* etc. GASm; Now conj. יַצִּית בָּאֵשׁ); esp. of sudden possession by (אֱלֹהִים) רוּחַ י׳, c. עַל pers. Ju 14[6] the Spirit ... *rushed upon* him, so v[19] 15[14] 1 S 10[6.10] 11[6]; c. אֶל pers. 16[13] and (of רוּחַ א׳ רָעָה) 18[10].

† II. [**צָלַח, צָלֵחַ**] **vb. advance, prosper** (NH *id.;* Ph. Pi. causat. in n.pr.; Ar. صَلَحَ *be in good condition,* cf. Sab. הצלח Sab Denkm[93]; Aram. צְלַח, ܨܠܚ *prosper*);—**Qal** *Pf.* 3 fs. צָלְחָה Je 12[1]; *Impf.* 3 ms. יִצְלַח Je 13[7]+, etc.; *Imv.* ms. צְלַח;—*prosper,* of way of wicked Je 12[1], cf. Nu 14[41] Is 53[10] 54[17] Ez 17[9.10] Dn 11[27]; c. לְ rei, = *be good for* anything Je 13[7.10] Ez 15[4]; subj. pers., abs., Je 22[30.30] Ez 17[15], ψ 45[5] *be successful!* וַתִּצְלְחִי לִמְלוּכָה Ez 16[13] *and thou didst prosper to royalty* (dub.; del. 𝔊 Co Toy; > Sta ZAW vi (1886). 337 f. Krae לִמְלָאכָה i.e. harlotry). **Hiph.** *Pf.* 3 ms. הִצְלִיחַ Gn 24[21], 2 ms. וְהִצְלַחְתָּ 1 Ch 22[11], etc.; *Impf.* 3 ms. יַצְלִיחַ Ne 2[20]+, וַיַּצְלַח 1 Ch 29[23] 2 Ch 32[30], etc.; *Imv.* ms. הַצְלַח 1 K 22[12]+, הַצְלִיחָה Ne 1[11], ־ָה ψ 118[25], etc.; *Pt.* מַצְלִיחַ Gn 24[42]+;—**1.** *make prosperous, bring to successful issue,* of י׳, c. acc. of man's way (דֶּרֶךְ), Gn 24[21.40.42.56] (J), c. acc. rei Gn 39[3.23] (J), c. acc. pers. 2 Ch 26[5], c. לְ pers. Ne 1[11] 2[20]; abs. *send success* ψ 118[25]; human subj. c. acc. דֶּרֶךְ Dt 28[29] Jos 1[8] (D), Is 48[15] ψ 37[7], so prob. 1[3] (al. sub **2**), 2 Ch 7[11]; c. acc. מִרְמָה Dn 8[25]. **2.** *shew, experience, prosperity,* of men 1 K 22[12.15] = 2 Ch 18[11.14], Je 2[37] (+לְ pers. in ref. to whom) 5[28] 32[5] 1 Ch 22[11.13] 29[23] 2 Ch 13[12] 14[6] 20[20] 24[20] 31[21] 32[30] (בְּכָל־מַעֲשֵׂהוּ), Pr 28[13] Dn 8[12] (of horn), v[24] 11[36]; אִישׁ מַצְלִיחַ Gn 39[2] (J) *a prosperous man;* subj. דֶּרֶךְ Ju 18[5] (cf. ψ 1[3] supr.), י׳'s word Is 55[11].

III. **צלח** (√ of foll.; NH צְלֹחִית = BH; cf. Aram. צְלוֹחִיתָא, ܨܠܘܚܝܬܐ (in Lexx) *flat dish;* Eth. ጸሕል: Amhar. ጸጕሕ: ጸሕ: (v. Prä[Amh. Spr. § 65 c]); Ar. صَحْنٌ, all *bowl, dish;* v. Frä[63.170]).

† [**צַלַּחַת**] **n.[f.] pot for cooking**;—pl. צְלָחוֹת 2 Ch 35[13] (+דְּוָדִים, סִירוֹת).

† **צַלַּחַת** **n.f. dish**;—2 K 21[13] (sim.), צַלַּחַת Pr 19[24] 26[15] (v. טמן).

† **צְלֹחִית** **n.f.** cstr. כ;—צ׳ חֲדָשָׁה 2 K 2[20].

צָלִי v. צלה.

† I. [**צָלַל**] **vb. tingle, quiver** (NH צִלְצֵל *whirr* (rare); Ar. صَلْصَلَ, صَلَّ; ℭ צְלַל; Syr. ܨܠ);—*Pf.* 3 pl. צָלְלוּ Hb 3[16]; *Impf.* 3 fpl. תְּצִלֶּינָה 1 S 3[11], תְּצִלֶּנָה (Ges[§ 67 g]) 2 K 21[12] Je 19[3];—*tingle,* of ears, at horrid sound 1 S 3[11] 2 K 21[12] Je 19[3] (all of dreadful news); of lips, *quiver* in terror Hb 3[16].

I. [**צְלָצַל**] **n.[m.] whirring, buzzing**;—cstr. אֶרֶץ צִלְצַל כְּנָפָיִם Is 18[1] *land of buzzing of* (insects') *wings* (so prob.; other views v. in Di).

† II. [**צִלְצַל**] **n.[m.] spear** (fr. *whizzing*);—cstr. צִלְצַל דָּגִים Jb 40[31] *fish-spear, harpoon.*

† **צְלָצַל** **n.m.** a **whirring locust** (cf. As. *ṣarṣaru,* Ar. صَرْصَرٌ, Syr. ܨܪܨܘܪܐ, ܨܪܨܪܐ; Lag Ges. Abh. 145, N. 9);—Dt 28[42] (devouring; not identif.; Tr[NHB 313]).

† **צֶלְצְלִים** **n.m.pl.** musical instr. of percussion, **cymbals** (with *clashing* sound; NH צִלְצַל, Aram. צִלְצְלִין, ܨܠܨܠܐ);—צ׳ 2 S 6[5] (+מְנַעַנְעִים, q. v.; ‖ 1 Ch 13[8] מְצִלְתַּיִם); cstr. צִלְצְלֵי־שָׁמַע

ψ 150[5], צ׳ תְּרוּעָה v[5];—cf. Now[Arch. i. 273 f.] Benz Arch. 277 We[Skiz Tr 232].

†[מְצִלָּה] n.f. bell (fr. *tinkling*);—pl. cstr. מְצִלּוֹת הַסּוּס Zc 14[20].

†מְצִלְתַּיִם n.f.du. cymbals (appar. later equiv. of צֶלְצְלִים where v. reff),—מ׳ 1 Ch 13[8] (‖ 2 S 6[5] v. צֶלְצְלִים), 15[19] 16[5.42] 25[6] 2 Ch 5[12.13] 29[25] Ezr 3[10] Ne 12[27], ־תַּיִם 1 Ch 15[16.28] 25[1].

†II. [צָלַל] vb. sink, be submerged (NH *id*; As *ṣalâlu, sink down, sink to rest*, II. *launch* (Hpt[Prol Assyr. Gr iiii, BAS i. 127; Ball, Gen 83]), Eth. ጸለለ: *float*, cf. Nes[Mar x]: Aram. צְלַל, ܨܠ, are *filter, clarify*);—**Qal** *Pf.* 3 pl. צָלְלוּ כַּעוֹפֶרֶת בְּמַיִם Ex 15[10].

†III. [צָלַל] vb. be or grow dark (cf. Ar. ظَلَّ *be black*, ظِلّ *shade*; Eth. ጸለለ: *be dark*; As. *ṣillu, shade, ṣalâlu*, Pi. *roof over*, so Sab. טלל [II], טלת *ceiling, roof*, Hom[Chrest. 125], cf. Palm תטלילא; OAram. טלל *overshadow*, Aram. טְלָלָא, ܛܠܠܐ *shadow*),—**Qal** *Pf* 3 pl. צָלְלוּ שַׁעֲרֵי יר׳ Ne 13[19] *the gates of Jerusalem grew dark*, i e. evening came on. **Hiph.** *Pt.* חֹרֶשׁ מֵצַל Ez 31[3] *a shadowing wood* (but del. 𝔊 Co Toy Krae).

†צֵל n.m.[ψ 144,4] shadow;—צ׳ abs. 2 K 20[9]+, cstr. Gn 19[8]+; sf. צִלְּךָ ψ 121[5], צִלּוֹ Ez 31[6]+, also צִלְלוֹ Jb 40[22], etc.; pl. צְלָלִים Ct 2[17] 4[6]; cstr. צִלְלֵי Je 6[4];—**1.** *shadow* on dial 2 K 20[9.10.10.11] ‖ Is 38[8]; צִלְלֵי־עָרֶב Je 6[4], cf. Ct 2[17] 4[6], of mt. Ju 9[36]. **2.** *shadow, shade*, as protection (fr. sun)· of branches, Ju 9[15] (in allegory), Ho 4[13] Jb 40[22] Jon 4[5.6] and (in fig.) Ho 14[8] Ez 17[23] 31[6.12.17] ψ 80[11] Ct 2[3] (of refreshment, delight); of rock Is 32[2] (sim); צ׳ קֹרָתִי Gn 19[8] *shadow of my roof;* of cloud Is 25[4] and (fig of י׳'s protection) 4[6] 25[4], so prob. 16[3]; צ׳ כְּנָפֶיךָ *shadow of thy wings*, fig. of י׳'s protection ψ 17[8] 36[8] 57[2] 63[8]; *shade*, in gen, Jb 7[2], fig. of י׳ ψ 121[5]; hence = *protection, defence*, of city (wall) Je 48[45]; of י׳ Nu 14[9] (JE), ψ 91[1] (v. also n.pr. בְּצַלְאֵל), cf. צֵל יָדוֹ Is 49[2] (covering prophet, under fig. of sword), 51[16] (covering people); of human ally Is 30[2.3], of king La 4[20]; also of wisdom Ec 7[12], money v[12].—בְצִלָּהּ Is 34[15] appar. ref. to קִפּוֹז, but improb.; rd. perh בֵּיצֶיהָ *her eggs* Du Che[Hpt] (Che[Heb Hpt] transp. וּבָקְעָה וְדָגְרָה). **3.** *shadow* as symb. of transitoriness of life Jb 8[9] 14[2] ψ 144[4] (כְּצֵל עוֹבֵר), Ec 6[12] 8[13]; כְּצֵל נָטוּי of an individ. life near its end ψ 102[12], so כְּצֵל כִּנְטוֹתוֹ 109[23]; in sim. of emaciated members, וִיצֻרַי כַּצֵּל Jb 17[7].

†צִלָּה n.pr.f. wife of Lam. Gn 4[19.22.23], Σελλα

†צִלְּתַי n.pr.m. (Thes expl. as צִלַּת יָהּ);—**1.** Benj, 1 Ch 8[20], Σελαθ(ε)ι. **2.** צִלְּתַי, Manassite, 1 Ch 12[21] (van d.H. v[20]), Σεμαθει, Σιλαθα, etc.

†צַלְמָוֶת n. [m.] death-shadow, deep shadow, poet. (prob. = צֵל + מָוֶת, 𝔊 (usu.) σκιὰ θανάτου, cf 𝔖 𝔙, so Thes Schwally[Leben n d Tode, 194], v. esp. No[ZAW xvii (1897), 183 ff.]; Ew Br and most mod. (after older comm) rd צַלְמוּת *darkness, deep darkness*, cp. Ar. ظَلِمَ IV, As. [*ṣalâmu*], Eth. ጸለመ: *be black, dark*);—*death-shadow*, oft. ‖ חֹשֶׁךְ, לַיְלָה, etc., and opp. בֹּקֶר, אוֹר. **1.** = *deep shadow, darkness* (cf אַרְזֵי אֵל, הַרְרֵי אֵל). Am 5[8] Jb 3[5] 12[22] 24[17 a] 28[3] 34[22]; of eyes heavy with weeping 16[16]; בַּלְהוֹת צ׳ 24[17 b] *terrors of the darkness*. **2.** fig **a.** of distress Je 13[16] ψ 107[10.14]; אֶרֶץ צ׳ Is 9[1]. **b.** of extreme danger Je 2[6] ψ 23[4] 44[20]. **3.** characterizing world of the dead, אֶרֶץ חֹשֶׁךְ וצ׳ Jb 10[21], כְּמוֹ אֹפֶל צ׳ v[22] (text dub., v. Bu Du); שַׁעֲרֵי צ׳ 38[17] (𝔊 πυλωροὶ δὲ ᾅδου; ‖ שַׁעֲרֵי־מָוֶת)

צֵל v. צִלְלוֹ ,צְלָלִים ,צִלְלֵי

†הַצְלֶלְפּוֹנִי n.pr.f. in Judah (*give shade, thou that turnest to me!*) 1 Ch 4[3], Εσηλεββων, etc

IV צלל (√ of foll, meaning dub.; Eth. መጽለት: is *unleavened bread* (Di[1267] as *pure*, unfermented, cf ܨܠ sub II. צלל), more prob. would be designation of shape).

†צְלוּל Kt, צְלִיל Qr n.m. cake, round loaf;—צ׳ לֶחֶם שְׂעֹרִים Ju 7[13] (cf. GFM).

צלם (√ of foll, No[ZMG xl (1886) 733 f.] cp. Ar. صَلَمَ, *cut off* (e g. an ear, a nose),—NH צֶלֶם = BH, so As. *ṣalmu*, Sab. צלם Gildemeister[ZMG xxiv (1870), 180] CIS[iv. no. 2, l. 4], Aram. צַלְמָא, ܨܠܡܐ, OAram. צלמא, so Nab. Palm. (also צלמתא of woman's statue)).

†צֶלֶם n.m.[Ez 16, 17] image (something *cut out*, cf פֶּסֶל; No 'Schnitzbild');—צ׳ abs. ψ 39[7], cstr. Gn 1[27]+; sf. צַלְמוֹ v[27] 5[3], צַלְמֵנוּ 1[26], צַלְמָם ψ 73[20]; pl cstr צַלְמֵי 1 S 6[5.5]+, sf. צְלָמָיו 2 K 11[18] 2 Ch 23[17], צַלְמֵיכֶם Am 5[26];—**1.** *images* of tumours and mice (of gold) 1 S 6[5.5.11]; esp. of heathen gods Am 5[26] (text dub; del. We as gloss, cf. GASm Dr), 2 K 11[18] = 2 Ch 23[17] (both c. vb. שִׁבֵּר), Ez 7[20], so צ׳ זָכָר 16[17] (i.e. in male form, acc. to fig. of harlotry for idolatry); צַלְמֵי מַסֵּכֹתָם Nu 33[52] *their molten images;* of painted pictures of men Ez 23[14]. **2.** *image, likeness*, of resem-

blance, (רָאָה) בצ׳ עָשָׂה, of God's making man in his own image, Gn 1^{26} (כִּדְמוּתֵנוּ ||), v$^{27.27}$ 9^{6}, כְּצ׳ 5^{3} (בדמותו ||, all P) **3.** fig. = *mere, empty, image, semblance,* בְּצ׳ ψ 39^{7} *as* (ב essentiae) *a* (mere) *semblance man walks about;* צַלְמָם תבזה 73^{20} *thou wilt despise their semblance.*

†I. **צַלְמוֹן** **n pr.mont.** **1.** הַר־צ׳ Ju 9^{48} near Shechem, not identif, cf. GFM, Buhl$^{Geogr\ 100}$, Ερμων (erron) **2.** snow-capped mt. ψ 68^{15}, prob E of Jordan (in Hauran acc. to Wetzst, cf Buhl$^{Geogr\ 115}$), Σελμων

†II **צַלְמוֹן** **n.pr.m.** a hero of David 2 S 23^{28} (= עִילַי 1 Ch 11^{29}), (Σ)ελλω, 𝔊L Ελιμαν.

צַלְמָוֶת v. III. צלל.

†**צַלְמֹנָה** **n.pr.loc.** station of Isr. in wilderness Nu 33$^{41.42}$, Σελμωνα.

צַלְמֻנָּע$_{12}$ **n.pr.m.** a king of Midian, + זֶבַח, Ju 8^{5} + 10 t. Ju 8, ψ 83^{12}, Σελμανα, Σαλμ

I **צלע** (√of foll; cf. Ar ضَلَعَ, *decline, deviate,* ضَلِعٌ *curved;* NH צֶלַע = BH, so Ar. ضِلَعٌ, As *sêlu,* BAram. עִילְעָא ,עֲלַע, Syr ܐܠܥܐ)

צֵלָע$_{41}$ **n.f.** (m. 1 K 6^{34}, and appar. Ex 26^{20}) rib, side;—abs צ׳ Gn 2^{22} +, cstr. צֶלַע Ex 26^{26} +, also צְלַע 2 S 16^{13}, sf צַלְעוֹ Ex 25^{12} +, pl. צְלָעִים 1 K 6^{34}, צְלָעוֹת v^{5} +; cstr. צַלְעֹת Ez 41^{26} +; sf. צַלְעֹתָיו Gn 2^{21} +;—**1.** *rib* of man Gn 2$^{21.22}$ (J) **2.** *rib* of hill, i e ridge, or terrace 2 S 16^{13}. **3.** *side-chambers* or *cells* (enclosing temple like ribs) 1 K 6$^{5.8}$ (rd הַצ׳ for היצוע, v [יָצִיעַ]), 7^{3}, so of Ezek's temple Ez 41^{5} + 10 t. 41 (on text v. Co Toy Krae) **4.** *ribs* of cedar and fir, i e *planks, boards* (pl), of temple wall 1 K 6$^{15.16}$, floor v^{15} **5.** *leaves* of door v^{34}. **6.** (in P) *side,* of ark (אָרוֹן) Ex 25$^{12.12.14}$ = 37$^{3.3.5}$; of tabern. (מִשְׁכָּן) 26^{20} (|| פְּאָה v^{18}), v$^{26.27.27}$ = 36$^{2\cdot}$ (|| פ׳ v^{23}), v$^{31.32}$, 26$^{35.35}$, of altar 27^{7} = 38^{7}, 30^{4} = 37^{27}.— Je 20^{10} Jb 18^{12} v. צֶלַע sub II. צלע.

†**צֵלַע** **n pr.loc.** in Benj Jos 18^{28}, A 𝔊L Σελα[(ε)λαφ], burial-place of Saul 2 S 21^{14} (צֶלַע), ἐν τῇ πλευρᾷ, poss = TelAm *Zilu,* so Zim$^{ZA\ vi\ 258}$ Jastr$^{JBL\ xi\ (1892)\ 106}$ (Wkl, however, thinks of סלע)

†II **[צָלַע]** **vb.** limp (Ar ظَلَعَ, Aram סלע Aph),—**Qal** *Pt* צֹלֵעַ עַל־יְרֵכוֹ Gn 32^{32} (J, of Jacob), f הַצֹּלֵעָה as subst, of personif Judah as flock [צאן] Mi 4$^{6.7}$ Zp 3^{19}.

†**צֶלַע** **n.[m.]** limping, stumbling;—fig. of calamity, abs. לְצ׳ ψ 38^{18} *I am ready* (נָכוֹן) *for stumbling* (and falling); sf. בְּצַלְעִי ψ 35^{15} *at my stumbling,* שֹׁמְרֵי צ׳ Je 20^{10} *watchers of my stumbling,* איד נָכוֹן לְצַלְעוֹ Jb 18^{12} *ruin is ready for his stumbling.*—Vid. also צֶלַע cstr.

†**צָלָף** **n.pr.m.** (NH *caper-plant*),—father of a wall-builder Ne 3^{30}, Σελε(φ), etc

†**צְלָפְחָד** **n.pr.m.** of Manasseh, Nu 26$^{33.33}$ 27$^{1.7}$ 36$^{2.6.10.11}$ Jos 17^{3} 1 Ch 7$^{15.15}$, Σαλπααδ, etc.

†**צֶלְצַח** **n.pr.loc.** in Benj 1 S 10^{2} (si vera l.; prob crpt. (Dr); HPS conj מִצֶּלַע, cf 2 S 21^{14}).

I, II. **[צִלְצַל]**, **צְלָצַל**, **צֶלְצְלִים** v. I. צלל.

†**צֶלֶק** **n.pr.m.** Ammonite hero of David 2 S 23^{37} = 1 Ch 11^{39}, Ελιε, Σελ(λ)η(κ), Σαλααδ, etc.

צִלְּתַי v. III צלל

†**[צָמֵא]** **vb.** be thirsty (NH = BH (rare); so Ar ظَمِئَ, Eth. ጽምአ: As *sûmu, thirst,* etc);—**Qal** *Pf.* 3 fs. צָמְאָה ψ 42^{3} 63^{2}; 2 fs וְצָמֵת consec. Ru 2^{9} (Ges$^{§\ 75\ qq}$); 1 s. צָמֵתִי Ju 4^{19} (Ges $^{§\ 74\ k}$), 3 pl. צָמֵאוּ Is 28^{21}, *Impf.* 3 ms. וַיִּצְמָא Ex 17^{3} Ju 15^{18}, 3 mpl יִצְמָאוּ Is 49^{10}, וַיִּצ׳ Jb 24^{11}; 2 mpl תִּצְמָאוּ Is 65^{13};—*be thirsty* Ju 4^{19} 15^{18} Ru 2^{9} Is 48^{21} 49^{10} (|| יִרְעָבוּ), 65^{13} (|| תִּרְעָבוּ) Jb 24^{11}; c לְ rei, Ex 17^{3} (E); fig צָמְאָה נַפְשִׁי לֵאלֹהִים ψ 42^{3} *my soul thirsteth for God,* cf. 63^{2}.

†**צָמָא** **n.[m.]** thirst;—abs. צ׳ Ex 17^{3} +, sf. צְמָאִי ψ 69^{22}, etc.,—Ex 17^{3} (E), Ju 15^{18} Ho 2^{5} Am 8^{13} La 4^{4} Ne 9^{20} ψ 69^{22}, || רָעָב Is 5^{13} (van d. H צְמֵה), Dt 28^{48} Ne 9^{15} 2 Ch 32^{11}, of wild asses ψ 104^{11}, of fish וְתָמֹת בַּצ׳ Is 50^{2}, but rd. perh. (or וּבְהֶמְתָּם בַּצָּמָא (בַּצְמָאָה Gunk$^{Schöpf\ 96}$ Che ^{Hpt}Marti (cf Is 44^{7} sub foll); fig of grief of exile Is 41^{17}, cf. אֶרֶץ צִיָּה וְצָמָא Ez 19^{13}, c. לְ, *thirst for* water Am 8^{11} — בַּצ׳ Je 48^{18} is prob. corrupt; read perhaps לָאָרֶץ (Gie), or בֶּעָפָר.

†**צָמֵא** **adj.** thirsty,—abs. צ׳ Is 21^{14} +; fs. צְמֵאָה Dt 29^{18}, pl צְמֵאִים ψ 107^{5};—*thirsty,* usu. + (or ||) רָעֵב. 2 S 17^{29} Pr 25^{21} ψ 107^{5}, as subst. *thirsty one* Is 29^{8} 32^{6}; so also 21^{14}, and (fig of thirst for י׳'s favour) 55^{1}; צָמֵא 44^{3} = *thirsty land* (Gunk i e prop צְמֵאָה); הָרָוָה אֶת־הַצְּמֵאָה Dt 29^{18} *the watered* (plant, herbage) *with the thirsty,* fig of *entire* people

†**צִמְאָה** **n.f.** parched condition;—Je 2^{25} spare thy throat מִצ׳, *from being parched* (in fig.).

†צִמָּאוֹן n.[m.] thirsty ground;—abs. 'צ Dt 8[15] Is 35[7] ψ 107[33].

†[צָמַד] vb. bind, join (Ar. ضَمَدَ bind, wind, specif. of girl with two lovers We[GGN 1893, 470]; fasten (cattle) to yoke Dozy, ضِمَاد yoke, Id; As. samâdu, bind, harness, so Eth. ፀመደ: and III. be attached, attach oneself, specif. be (religiously) devoted, Aram. צְמַד, ܨܡܕ, bind);—Niph. Impf. 3 ms וַיִּצָּמֶד Nu 25[3], 3 mpl וַיִּצָּמְדוּ ψ 106[28]; Pt pl. נִצְמָדִים Nu 25[5], join, attach, oneself to (ל) Baal Peor, i.e. adopt his worship Nu 25[3.5] (JE), whence ψ 106[28]. Pu. Pt. f. מְצֻמֶּדֶת 2 S 20[8] a sword bound upon (עַל) his loins. Hiph. Impf. 3 fs. תַּצְמִיד מִרְמָה ψ 50[19] thy tongue combineth (fitteth together, frameth) deceit (> denom. fr. צֶמֶד Gerber[170])

†צֶמֶד n.m.[1K 19, 19] couple, pair;—'צ cstr. Ju 19[3]+; sf צמדו Je 51[23]; pl. צְמָדִים 1 K 19[19] 2 K 9[25] (but v infr); cstr. צמדי Is 5[10] (Ges[§ 93m]);—1. couple, pair, usu of animals, צ׳ חֲמֹרִים Ju 19[3.10] 2 S 16[1], (הַ)בָּקָר 'צ span of oxen 1 S 11[7] 1 K 19[21], pl. of more than one span v[19] (ploughing), Jb 1[3] 42[12]; צֶמֶד פְּרָדִים 2 K 5[17]; צ׳ פָּרָשִׁים Is 21[7.9] a pair of horsemen, pl also of one pair of riders 2 K 9[25] (but rd. prob. צֶמֶד, so Kit), 'צ alone = span (of oxen) Je 51[23]. 2. a measure of land (only square measure in OT) like acre; orig appar. what a span can plough (in a day; v. Now[Arch. i 202] Benz[Arch. 208], cf. mod. faddan, = what can be ploughed in a season Schumacher[ZPV xii (1889), 163 f., Across Jordan 22], or in a day Bergheim[PEQ 1894, 192], Ency. Bib[Acre]), צ׳ שָׂדֶה 1 S 14[14] (on text v. Dr HPS), צִמְדֵּי־כֶרֶם Is 5[10].

†I צָמִיד n.m.[Gn 24, 22] bracelet (bound on wrist);—abs. 'צ Nu 31[50], pl. צמידים Gn 24[22]+,—bracelet Gn 24[22.30.47] (J), Nu 31[50] (P); in fig. Ez 16[11] 23[42].

†II. צָמִיד n.[m.] cover, of vessel, Nu 19[15].

צַמָּה v. צמם.

†צָמַח vb. sprout, spring up (NH id, so 𝔗 צְמַח; Syr ܨܡܚ spring or shine forth, ܨܶܡܚܳܐ shining, also sprout; Ph. צמח posterity);—Qal Pf 3 ms. צָמַח־בּוֹ Lv 13[37]; 3 pl. וְצָמְחוּ consec. Is 44[4]; Impf 3 ms. יצמח Jb 5[6], 3 fpl. תִּצְמַחְנָה Is 42[9], etc, Pt. צֹמֵחַ Ex 10[5], צוֹמֵחַ Ec 2[6]; fpl. צֹמחות Gn 41[6.23],—sprout, spring up: 1. of plants, trees, etc. Gn 2[5] Ex 10[5] (both J), Gn 41[6.23] (E), Ez 17[6] (in fig), once (late) יַעַר צוֹמֵחַ עֵצִים Ec 2[6] wood sprouting with trees (full of growing trees), fig. of future ruler (v. צֶמַח) Zc 6[12], posterity Is 44[4], cf Jb 8[19], trouble (עָמָל) 5[6], truth (אֱמֶת) ψ 85[12], restoration (אֲרֻכָתְךָ) Is 58[8], future events Is 42[9]. 2. of hair Lv 13[37] (P; cf. Pi.) Pi. grow abundantly, always of hair;—Pf 3 ms. צִמֵּחַ Ez 16[7] (in fig.): Impf. 3 ms. יְצַמַּח 2 S 10[5] = 1 Ch 19[5] (of beard); Inf. cstr. לְצַמֵּחַ Ju 16[22] (Samson's hair). Hiph. Pf. 3 ms. sf וְהִצְמִיחָהּ Is 55[10]; Impf. 3 ms יַצְמִיחַ 2 S 23[5] Is 61[11], וַיַּצְמַח Gn 2[9], etc., Inf. cstr. לְהַצְמִיחַ Jb 38[27], Pt. מַצְמִיחַ ψ 104[14] 147[8];—1. cause to grow, c. acc. of plant, subj. ׳י Gn 2[9] ψ 104[14], cf. Jb 38[27], c. 2 acc. ψ 147[8] who causeth mts. to sprout grass; fig., obj. צֶמַח צְדָקָה Je 33[15]; horn (קֶרֶן) of Isr Ez 29[21], of David ψ 132[17], righteousness, etc. Is 61[11 b], cf also 2 S 23[5] (if interrog, v. Dr Bu, otherwise HPS); subj. ground Gn 3[18] cf Is 61[11 a] (sim.), Dt 29[22] (obj om); also (fig) Is 45[8] (cf. Di Kit). 2. of rain, cause the earth to sprout (abs.), Is 55[10].

†צֶמַח n.m.[Je 23, 5] sprout, growth;—abs. 'צ Ho 8[7]+, צֶמַח Zc 3[8]; cstr. צֶמַח Gn 19[25]+; sf. צִמְחָהּ Ez 17[9]+;—1. coll sprouting, growth, צ׳ הָאֲדָמָה Gn 19[25] (J), צ׳ הַשָּׂדֶה Ez 16[7] (sim.), cf. Is 61[11] ψ 65[11]; so צ׳ יהוה Is 4[2], 'צ abs Ho 8[7]; growth (= foliage) of vine, טַרְפֵּי צ׳ Ez 17[9]. 2. process of growth, of vine, עֲרֻגוֹת צִמְחָהּ Ez 17[10] = the beds where it grew. 3. future ruler, under fig. of sprout from Davidic tree (cf. ψ 132[17] (הַקְמֹתִי לְדָוִד צ׳ צַדִּיק Je 23[5] a righteous sprout, shoot, = אַצְמִיחַ לְדָוִד צ׳ צְדָקָה 33[15]; hence (as n.pr.) עַבְדִּי צ׳ Ze 3[8], of Zerub. אִישׁ צ׳ שְׁמוֹ 6[12].

צַמִּים v. צמם. צְמִיתֻת v צמת.

צמם (✓of foll.; cf. Ar. ضَمَّ draw together, or ضِمَام bandage (a wound), be compact; NH צִמְצֵם press; 𝔗[Jer] Palp. Ithpalp. veil (? denom.)).

†צַמָּה n.f. woman's veil; sf. צַמָּתֵךְ;—Is 47[2] Ct 4[1.3] 6[7].

†צַמִּים n.m. doubtful word, usu. snare, trap (fr ‖ פַּח Jb 18[9]),—וְשָׁאַף צ׳ חֵילָם Jb 5[5] and a snare snappeth at his wealth (so Bu Bev[JPhil. xxvi. 304 f.]; Vrss Di Du and most mod צְמֵאִים, or צָמֵא, the thirsty, sometimes with change of וְשָׁאַף), 18[9] (‖ פַּח; Che[JQ ix (1897) 578] צִירִים pangs, cf. Is 13[8]).

†[צָמַק] vb. dry up, shrivel (NH id; 𝔗[J] Nu 6[3] צִמּוּקִין, for יבשים);—Qal Pt. act. pl שָׁדַיִם צֹמְקִים Ho 9[14] shrivelling breasts (of women; ‖ רֶחֶם מַשְׁכִּיל).

†[צִמּוּק] **n.m.**[1 S 30, 12] **bunch of raisins** (*dried grapes*);—pl. צִמֻּקִים 1 S 25[18] 30[12], צִמּוּקִים 2 S 16[1] 1 Ch 12[41] (van d. H. v[40]).

צמר (√of foll.; NH צֶמֶר = BH; Eth. **ፀምር**: Aram. עַמְרָא, ܥܡܪܐ; Palm. עמרא).

†**צֶמֶר** **n.m.**[Ez 44, 17] **wool**;—abs. 'צ Is 1[18], צָמֶר Lv 13[48]; cstr. צֶמֶר Ez 27[18] (v. infr.); sf. צַמְרִי Ho 2[7.11];—*wool* (usu. c. (פִּשְׁתִּ(ים *flax, linen*): in natural state גִּזַּת הַצ' Ju 6[37], אֵילִים צ' 2 K 3[4] (but constr. difficult, and 'צ perhaps gloss); Ho 2[7.11] (as gift of value); white Is 1[18] (sim.; ‖ שֶׁלֶג), sim. of snow ψ 147[16] (from white flakes); *white* (?) *wool* as merchandise Ez 27[18] (צ' צָחַר, but on text v. צָחַר), Pr 31[12]; prey of moth Is 51[8] (sim.); made up into garments Dt 22[11], בֶּגֶד צ' Lv 13[47.59] cf. v[48.52]; בֶּגֶד om. Ez 34[3] 44[17].

†**צַמֶּרֶת** **n.f.** tree-top (poss. from *woolly*, feathery, appearance);—'צ cstr., of cedar (in fig.) Ez 17[3.22], so sf. צַמַּרְתּוֹ 31[3.10]; of tall trees in gen., צַמַּרְתָּם v[14].

†**צְמָרִי** **adj. gent.** c. art. as subst. coll. (people of the city called *Ṣimirra* by As., COT[Gn] Dl[Pa 281 f.], Egypt. *D̲a-(m)-ma-ra* WMM [As. u. Eur. 187]; Tel Am. *Ṣumur* acc. to Zim[ZPV xiii (1890), 145] Jastr[JBL xii (1893), 63]; Gk. τὰ Σίμυρα, etc., e. g. Strabo[xvi. 2, 12], >Wkl[MVG 1896, 203 f., cf. Tel Am. 40*] thinks 'צ, Σίμυρα, = As. *Zimarra*, distinct from *Ṣimirra-Ṣumur*);—הַצ' Gn 10[18] = 1 Ch 1[16], 𝔊 τὸν Σαμαραῖον; Ez 27[11] Co rds. וּצְמָרִים for וְנֶפְדִים (q.v.); Toy Krae retain 'וְצ;—cf. mod. *Ṣumra*, N. of Tripoli and S. of Ruad (Arvad), v. Pietschm [Phön. 39] Bäd[Pal. 3 (1898), 407].

†**צְמָרַיִם** **n.pr.loc.** **1.** in Benj. Jos 18[22], Σαρα, A Σεμριμ, 𝔊L Σαμαρειμ, perh. *Es-samra*, N. of Jericho Buhl[Geogr. 180]. **2.** הַר־צ' mt. in Ephraim 2 Ch 13[4], Σομορων, unknown.

†[**צָמַת**] **vb. put an end to, exterminate,** poet. and (in **Qal, Pi.**) hyperb. (prop. *compress*, NH *id.*, *press together*; Ar. صَمَتَ is *be silent*, II, IV. *make speechless, silence*; Syr. ܨܡܬ *be silent* (in Lexx));—**Qal** *Pf.* 3 pl. צָמְתוּ . . . חַיָּי La 3[53] *they have put an end to my life* (Bu conj. **Pi.**). **Niph.** *be ended, annihilated*; *Pf.* 1 s. נִצְמַתִּי מִפְּנֵי־חֹשֶׁךְ Jb 23[17] *I am* [not] *annihilated because of* (the) *darkness*; 3 pl. נִצְמָתוּ Jb 6[17] (of dried-up brooks). **Pi.** *Pf.* 3 fs. sf. צִמְּתַתְנִי ψ 119[139] קִנְאָתִי *hath put an end to me* (it is so intense). **Pi'lēl** *Pf.* 3 pl. sf. צִמְּתֻתוּנִי (but rd. צִמְּתוּנִי Ges[§ 55 d], or צִמְּתֻתְנִי Hi [Ges[§ 145 k]]; cf. Bae) ψ 88[17] thine alarms *have annihilated me*. **Hiph.** *Pf.* 2 ms. הִצְמַתָּה ψ 73[27]; *Impf.* 3 ms. sf. יַצְמִיתֵם ψ 94[23.23]; 2 ms. תַּצְמִית ψ 143[12], etc.; *Imv.* ms. sf. הַצְמִיתֵם ψ 54[7]; *Pt.* pl. sf. מַצְמִיתַי ψ 69[5];—*exterminate, annihilate*, c. acc. pers., subj. Psalmist ψ 18[41] = 2 S 22[41] (read as in ψ), 101[5.8]; his foes ψ 69[5]; ' 54[7] 73[27] 94[23.23] 143[12].

†**צְמִיתֻת** **n.f.** completion, finality, only in phr. 'לַצ, 'לִצ = *in perpetuity*, of alienation of land; לִצְמִיתֻת Lv 25[23], לַצְמִתֻת v[30] (P).

†**צִן** **n.pr.loc.** Σ(ε)ιν; name of wilderness S. of Canaan, where lay Kadesh Barnea, c. ה loc. צִנָה Nu 34[4] (where Lag[BN 47] חצן), Jos 15[3] (van d. H. צִנָּה in Jos); elsewh. מִדְבַּר־צִן Nu 13[21] 20[1] 27[14.14] 33[36] 34[3] Dt 32[51] Jos 15[1] (all P).

[צֵן], I, II, III. צִנָּה, v. I, II, III. צנן.

†**צֹנֶה**, [צֹנֶא] [**n.m.**] **flocks** (‖ form of צֹאן q.v.);—abs. צֹנֶה ψ 8[8]; sf. צֹנַאֲכֶם Nu 32[24] (JE).

†[**צָנַח**] **vb. descend** (meaning inferred fr. context);—**Qal** *Impf.* 3 fs. וַתִּצְנַח מֵעַל הַחֲמוֹר Ju 1[14] = Jos 15[18] *and she descended* (alighted) *from the ass*; וַתִּ' בָּאָרֶץ Ju 4[21] *and it* (the tent-peg) *went down into the ground*.

†[**צָנַם**] **vb. dry up, harden** (cf. Aram. צִנְמָא, צוּנְמָא, ܨܘܢܡܐ, *stone*);—**Qal** *Pt. pass.* fpl. צְנֻמוֹת Gn 41[23] (E) of ears of grain.

I. **צנן** (√of foll.; meaning obscure).

†[**צֵן**] **n.**[**m.**] **thorn? barb?**;—pl. צִנִּים Pr 22[5] (+ פַּחִים); וְאֶל־מִצִּנִּים Jb 5[5] *from* (behind) *thorns* (a protecting thorn hedge, so Di), but very dub.; Che[JQ July, 1897, 576] del. as doublet of צַמִּים; Bev[JPhil. xxvi. 305] prop. וְאֹנָם צִנִּים [*and as to their wealth, barbs* (? barbed spears) *take* it].

†I. [**צִנָּה**] **n. f.** appar. **hook**, or **barb** (of fishing-spear ?);—pl. צִנּוֹת Am 4[2] (‖ סִירוֹת דּוּגָה).

†[**צָנִין**] **n.**[**m.**] **thorn, prick**;—pl. צְנִינִם Nu 33[55] (P; ‖ שִׂכִּים), צְנִנִים Jos 23[13] (D; both fig.).

II. **צנן** (√of foll.; NH צִנֵּן *be cold*, so JAram. צְנַן; 𝔗 צִינְתָא *cold*).

†II. [**צִנָּה**] **n.f.** coolness;—cstr. צִנַּת־שֶׁלֶג Pr 25[13] *coolness of snow* (צינת רוח צפון Ecclus 43[20]).

III. **צנן** (√of foll.; Thes (so Di[Lex]) cp. Ar. صَانَ *preserve, keep*, Eth. **ጸወነ**: *protect*, but dub.).

†III. **צִנָּה** **n.f.** large shield (*covering* whole body);—abs. צ׳ 1 S 17^{7}+; pl. צִנּוֹת 2 Ch 11^{12}; —*shield*, larger than מָגֵן 1 K 10$^{16.16}$ (cf. v^{17})= 2 Ch 9$^{15.15}$; נֹשֵׂא (הַ)צִּנָּה 1 S 17$^{7.41}$ (הָאִישׁ נ׳ הַצ׳), 2 Ch 14^{7}, נֹשְׂאֵי צ׳ 1 Ch 12^{25} (van d H. v^{24}); ערכו מָגֵן וְצִנָּה Je 46^{3}, cf. עֹרְכֵי צ׳ 1 Ch 12^{9} (van d. H. v^{8}); אֹחֲזֵי רֹמַח וְצ׳ 2 Ch 25^{5}; הַחֲזֵק מָגֵן וְצ׳ ψ 35^{2}, הֵקִים עָלַיִךְ צ׳ Ez 26^{8}; + מָגֵן also 23^{24} 38^{4} 39^{9}; צ׳ 1 Ch 12^{35} (van d. H. v^{34}) 2 Ch 11^{12}; sim. of י׳'s favour ψ 5^{13}; fig. of י׳'s faithfulness 91^{4}.

†**צִנְצֶנֶת** **n.f.** jar, or like receptacle (so Vrss and context; perh. from above √; > *basket* = ℭ Talm. צַנָּא);—Ex 16^{33} (P).

צָנָן v. צַאֲנָן.

†[**צָנַע**] **vb.** be modest, humble (perhaps prop. *be retired*, NH Hiph. *keep close, reserve, preserve*, so ℭ אַצְנַע; צניע *retiring, modest*),—**Hiph.** *Inf.abs.* הַצְנֵעַ לֶכֶת Mi 6^{8} *a making humble to walk* = shewing a humble walk (with God).

†[**צָנוּעַ**] **adj.** modest (on format. cf. Ba $^{NB § 31 d}$),—pl. צְנוּעִים Pr 11^{2} (v. Toy; opp. זָדוֹן).

†[**צָנַף**] **vb.** wrap, or wind up, together (cf. Ar. صَنِفَةٌ *hem* of garment, ℭ^{J} צִנְפָּא *skirt* (=כָּנָף); מַצְנְפָא, مَصْنَفَةٌ *turban*, ChrPal ܨܢܦܐ *tassel*);—**Qal** *Impf.* 3 ms. יִצְנֹף Lv 16^{4} *he shall wind* (his head) with (ב) the turban (מִצְנֶפֶת q.v.); sf., + *Inf. abs* and acc. cogn. צָנוֹף יִצְנָפְךָ צְנֵפָה Is 22^{18} *he will wind thee entirely up* (with) *a winding* (under fig. of ball, to be driven far off, in exile) —צנוף Is 62^{3} v. following.

†**צָנִיף** **n.m.**$^{Zc 3, 5}$ turban;—abs צ׳ Zc 3$^{5.5}$ (for h priest) and (fig of righteousness) Jb 29^{14}; cstr. צְנִיף מְלוּכָה Is 62^{3} Qr *royal turban* (Kt צנוף); pl הַצְּנִיפוֹת Is 3^{23} (of women's turbans)

†**צְנֵפָה** **n.f.** winding,—Is 22^{18}, v. [צנף].

†**מִצְנֶפֶת** **n.f.** turban of high priest,—abs. מ׳ Ez 21^{31}, מִצְנֶפֶת Ex 28^{37} 29^{6}; cstr. מִצְנֶפֶת Lv 16^{4};—*turban* of linen Ex 28$^{4.37.37.39}$ 29$^{6.6}$ 39$^{28.31}$ Lv 8$^{9.9}$ 16^{4}; sign of royalty Ez 21^{31}.

צנק (√of foll; cf. Sam. חצנק *shut up* or *in*, and perh. Eth ጸፈቀ: *hedge about*, Pra$^{BAS I. 374}$; cf. also Ar. زَنَقَ *bind, restrain, straighten*, Syr. ܙܢܩ (in Lexx; usu *throw*))

†**צִינֹק** **n.[m.]** pillory;—Je 29^{26} (‖ מַהְפֶּכֶת).

צנר (√of foll; NH צִנּוֹר = BH (also *hinge-socket*), and so ℭ צִינוֹרָא (rare)).

†**צִנּוֹר** **n.m.** pipe, spout, conduit (so NH);—abs. וְיִגַּע בַּצִּנּוֹר 2 S 5^{8} (i e., si vera l., of Jerus, but very dubious, cf. Dr HPS); pl. sf. קוֹל צִנּוֹרֶיךָ ψ 42^{8} *the sound of thy* (water-) *spouts* fig, of sluices of heaven opened, cf. אֲרֻבָּה, פֶּלֶג.

†**צַנְתְּרוֹת** **n. m. pl.** cstr. pipes feeding lamps with oil Zc 4^{12} (in vision) (formation by inserting ת acc. to Bo$^{§ 300 b}$ Ko$^{ii 1, 201}$).

†[**צָעַד**] **vb.** step, march (NH *id.* (rare); Ar. صَعِدَ *ascend*);—**Qal** *Pf.* 3 fs. צָעֲדָה Gn 49^{22} (but on text v. infr.); 3 pl צָעֲדוּ 2 S 6^{13}, *Impf.* 3 ms. יִצְעַד Pr 7^{8}, etc.; *Inf. cstr.* sf בְּצַעְדְּךָ Ju 5^{4}, בְּצַעְדְּךָ ψ 68^{8},—*step, march*, of י׳ Ju 5^{4} ψ 68^{8} (c. ב loc.), Hb 3^{12} (c. acc. אֶרֶץ); rd. prob. also צֹעֵד Is 63^{1} (for MT צֹעֶה, v. צעה); of men, c. acc. cogn. צְעָדִים 2 S 6^{13} *they had gone six steps*; c. acc. דֶּרֶךְ *step* a certain way Pr 7^{8}; of idols, לֹא יִצְעָדוּ Je 10^{5}.—בָּנוֹת צָעֲדָה עֲלֵי־שׁוּר Gn 49^{22} is dubious: usu (its) *daughters* (twigs of bough) *have climbed* over the wall (on sg. vb. v. Ges$^{§ 145 k}$, others think ָה old fpl. ending, e. g. No$^{ZMG xxxviii (1884), 411}$ JPPeters$^{Hbr iii (1887), 111; v (1888), 199}$; conject. emend. of text v. in Ball^{Hpt} Holz). **Hiph.** *Impf.* 3 fs. sf. וַתַּצְעִדֵהוּ Jb 18^{14} *and it* (an unseen power Di; disease Du, rdg. וְיַצ׳) *makes him march*, c. ל pers.

†[**צַעַד**] **n.m.**$^{2 S 6, 13}$ step, pace;—abs. צַעַד Pr 30^{29}, sf. צַעֲדוֹ Je 10^{3} Pr 6^{9}, etc.; pl cstr. צַעֲדֵי Jb 18^{7}; sf. צְעָדַי Jb 31^{4}, etc;—**1.** lit. *step, pace*, 2 S 6^{13}, תַּרְחִיב צַעֲדִי תַחְתָּנִי 2 S 22^{37} = ψ 18^{37}, i.e. givest me firm footing, מֵיטִיבֵי צ׳ Pr 30^{29} = *making a good step*, stately in march; La 4^{18} (‖ לֶכֶת). **2.** *step, steps*, in fig of course of life, fortune: sg. לֹא יֵצַר צ׳ Pr 4^{12}; ‖ דֶּרֶךְ Je 10^{23} Pr 16^{9}; pl. Jb 14^{16} 31^{4} 34^{21}, צַעֲדֵי אוֹנוֹ 18^{7} (cf. Pr 4^{12} supr.); מִסְפַּר־צְעָדַי אַגִּידֶנּוּ 31^{37}; of harlot Pr 5^{5} fig., שְׁאוֹל צְעָדֶיהָ יִתְמֹכוּ.

†I. **צְעָדָה** **n.f.** marching;—קוֹל צ׳ 2 S 5^{24} *the sound of marching* = 1 Ch 14^{15}.

[**מִצְעָד**] **n.[m.]** step;—pl. sf. בְּמִצְעָדָיו Dn 11^{43} i. e. at his heels, in his train; cstr, fig of course of life, מִצְעֲדֵי־גֶבֶר ψ 37^{23} (‖ דַּרְכּוֹ), Pr 20^{24}.

II. **צעד** (√of foll.; meaning unknown).

†II. [**צְעָדָה**] **n.f.** armlet, band clasping upper arm (so SS al.; most *step-chain*, from I. צעד);—pl. הַצְּעָדוֹת Is 3^{20} (ladies' finery); read הַצ׳ also 2 K 11^{12} (for MT הָעֵדוּת) We$^{Bl. Einl. 4, 253 = Comp. (2), 361}$ Kmp SS Kit Benz.

†אֶצְעָדָה **n.f.** id.,—abs. א׳ Nu 31[50] (+צָמִיד *bracelet*); אֶצְעָדָה אֲשֶׁר עַל־זְרֹעוֹ 2 S 1[10] (read הַצְּעָדָה We Dr Bu HPS, cf. 2 K 11[12] supr.)

†[צָעָה] **vb. stoop, bend, incline** (Ar. صَعَا (و, ى) *incline, lean*, cf. also صَغِىَ),—**Qal** *Pt.* **1.** צֹעֶה Is 51[14] *one stooping* (under a burden), 63[1] *bending* (forward or backward, fr. abundant strength), but read prob. צֹעֵד *marching* (Lo Gr Che Du Di-Kit al.); f. אַתְּ צֹעָה זֹנָה Je 2[20] (in sensu obscoeno). **2.** trans. (= **Pi.** q.v.) pl. צֹעִים Je 48[12] *men inclining, tipping* a vessel, to empty it. **Pi.** *Pf.* 3 pl. sf. וְצֵעֻהוּ Je 48[12] I will send tippers *and they shall tip him over* (Moab, under fig. of vessel).

†[צָעַן] **vb. wander, travel** (Ar. ظَعَنَ *journey, go away*, prob. connected with As. *ṣênu*, Eth ጸዐነ:, Aram טְעַן, Palm טען, all *load* (beast, etc.) = Heb טָעַן † Gn 45[17], Aram. טְעַן, ܛܥܰܢ also *bear, carry*),—**Qal** *Impf.* 3 ms. יִצְעַן Is 33[20] *travel*, i.e. be removed, of tent (+ יִסַּע).

†צֹעַן **n.pr.loc.** Τανις: **Tanis**, in Egypt (Egypt *Ḏaʿnĕ(t)* Steind[BAS 600], in As *Ṣiʾinu*, *Ṣaʾanu* Ib[id 596 ff] Dl[Pa 315]), it was built 7 years after Hebron acc. to Nu 13[22], Is 19[11, 13] 30[4] Ez 30[14] ψ 78[12, 43], mod. *Ṣân*, in NW. part of Delta, v. also Eb[GS 512 ff] Bd[Lower Eg 3 (1885), 223] Petrie[Tanis (1885)]

†צַעֲנַנִּים **n.pr.loc.** only c. בְּ, pointed as prep., and so most (but בּ perh. radical, v. GFM), on border of Naphtali, near Ḳedesh;—בצ׳ Jos 19[33] (Βεσεμιειν, Σεενανιμ, etc.) + Ju 4[11] Qr (Kt בצענים), 𝔊 πλεονεκτούντων (√בָּצַע), ἀναπαυομένων

צעף (√of foll., cf. Ar ضَعَّفَ III. *make double*, ضِعْف *double*, Eth ፀዐፈ: *fold, double*, so Aram עוּף, ܥܘܦ, ܥܳܦ̈ܐ *double* (for צָעִיף =), cf. 𝔗 עִיפָא for Heb צָעִיף (prop. *a double* or *folded thing*); v. esp. Lag[Sem i 23 ff])

†צָעִיף **n. [m.] wrapper, shawl, or veil**;—abs. צ׳ Gn 24[65] 38[14], sf. צְעִיפָהּ v[19] (all J).

צַעֲצֻעִים v. צוע.

†צָעַק **vb. cry, cry out, call** (‖ זָעַק, NH *id.*; Ar صَعِقَ, perhaps orig. *sound as thunder*, cf. صَاعِقَة *thunderbolt*, صَعِق *bellow* (of bull)),—**Qal** *Pf.* 3 ms. צ׳ 1 K 20[39] La 2[18], 3 fs צָעֲקָה Dt 22[24] +, etc.; *Impf.* יִצְעַק Ex 23[22] +, etc.; *Imv.* fs צַעֲקִי Je 22[20], וְּצַעֲקִי v[20], fpl צְעַקְנָה 49[3], *Inf. abs* צָעֹק Ex 22[22], cstr לִצְעֹק 2 K 8[3], *Pt.* fs abs צֹעֶקֶת 2 K 8[5]; mpl. צֹעֲקִים Gn 4[10] Ex 5[8];—**1.** *cry, cry out*, for help, usu. c. אֶל pers.,—**a.** unto man Gn 41[55] (E; + לְ rei), Nu 11[2] (JE), 1 K 20[39] 2 K 6[26] 8[3] (+ אֶל rei), v[5] (+ עַל rei); sq. אמר Ex 5[15] (J), 2 K 4[1] and (אֶל pers. om.) Ex 5[8] (J), 2 K 4[40] 6[5]. **b.** esp. unto י׳. Gn 4[10] Ex 8[8] (+ עַל־דְּבַר rei), 14[10, 15] 15[25] 17[4] 22[22] (צָעֹק יִצְעַק), v[26] Nu 12[13] 20[16] Jos 24[7] (all JE), Ju 4[3] 10[12] Dt 26[7] Is 19[20] (+ מִפְּנֵי rei), La 2[18] Ne 9[27] ψ 107[6, 28]; קוֹלִי נֶגְדֶּךָ 77[2], cf. 34[18]; c. לְי׳ 2 Ch 13[14], וְאֶצְעֲקָה אֶל־א׳ ψ 88[2]. **c.** *cry* unto (אֶל) idol Is 46[7]. **2.** abs. *cry, cry out*, in distress, need;—Gn 27[34] (J; c. acc. cogn.), Dt 22[24, 27] Is 33[7] (‖ בָּכָה), 65[14] (‖ הֵילִיל), opp. רָנַן; c. מִן rei), Je 22[20, 20] (‖ נָתַן קוֹל), 49[3] (‖ הֵילִיל), Jb 35[12], c. obj. חָמָס Jb 19[7] (‖ אֲשַׁוַּע). **3.** *make outcry, clamour*, Is 42[2] (+ יִשָּׂא, יַשְׁמִיעַ קוֹלוֹ). **Niph.** *be summoned* (i.e. to arms), abs.; *Impf.* 3 ms. וַיִּצָּעֵק Ju 7[23, 24] 12[1], so 3 mpl. וַיִּצָּעֲקוּ 10[17] 2 K 3[21], sq. אַחֲרֵי שָׁאוּל + acc. loc. 1 S 13[4]. **Pi.** *Pt.* מְצַעֵק *cry aloud*, in grief, 2 K 2[12]. **Hiph.** *call together* וַיַּצְעֵק אֶת־הָעָם אֶל־י׳ הַמִּצְפָּה 1 S 10[17].

†צְעָקָה **n.f. cry, outcry** (older form of זְעָקָה),—abs. צ׳ Gn 27[34] +; cstr. צַעֲקַת Ex 3[9] +; sf. צַעֲקָתוֹ 1 S 9[16] +, etc.;—**1.** *outcry* against (Sodom) Gn 18[21] 19[13] (both J). **2.** *cry of distress*, esp. as *heard* by י׳ Ex 3[7] (J), 22[22] (E), cf. Is 5[7] Jb 27[9] 34[28] ψ 9[13], צ׳ בָּאָה אֵלַי Ex 3[9] (E), 1 S 9[16], cf. Jb 34[28]; צ׳ גְּדֹלָה Ex 11[6] 12[30] (both J), Ne 5[1]; as acc. cogn. Gn 27[34] (J); קוֹל צ׳ 1 S 4[14] Je 25[36] (‖ יְלָלָה), Zp 1[10] (‖ *id.*, + שֶׁבֶר גָּדוֹל), Je 48[3] (‖ שֹׁד וָשֶׁבֶר גָּדוֹל), cf. 49[21], צַעֲקַת שֶׁבֶר 48[5] (‖ בְּכִי)

†[צָעַר] **vb. be, or grow, insignificant** (‖ זער; NH *id.*, As. *ṣeḫêru*, *be small*, Ar صَغُرَ *id.*; Syr. ܙܥܰܪ *be insignificant, despicable*; 𝔗 צְעַר trans. *despise, revile*),—**Qal** *Impf.* (opp. כָּבֵד), 3 mpl. יִצְעָרוּ Jb 14[21], יִצְעָרוּ Je 30[19]; *Pt.* as subst. הַצֹּעֲרִים Zc 13[7] (i.e. sheep, in fig., cf. Now).

†צֹעַר, צוֹעַר, צֹעַר **n.pr.loc. Zoar** (understood as *insignificance*, cf. Gn 19[20]),—Σηγωρ, 𝔊L Σιγωρ, but Gn 13[10] Je 48[34] Ζογορ(α); on 𝔊 cf. further Lag[BN 54 f.]. city at SE. end of Dead Sea, צֹעַר Gn 13[10] 14[2, 8] (both = בֶּלַע), Dt 34[3] Is 15[5] Je 48[34], צוֹעַר Gn 19[22, 30, 30], c. ה loc., צֹעֲרָה v[23] + Je 48[4] (for MT צעוריה), 𝔊 Ζογορα, JDMich Ew Gf Gie al.—Cf. Buhl[Geogr 271, 274] GASm[Geogr 506 f. 678 (App.)].

†I. צָעִיר **adj.** little, insignificant, young;—abs. צָעִיר Gn 25²³+; f. צְעִירָה Gn 19³¹+; צְעִרָה 1 S 9²¹, mpl. צְעִירִים Jb 30¹; sf. צְעִירֶיהָ Je 48⁴ Qr (Kt צעוריה; but v. צָעַר); צְעִירֵיהֶם Je 14³ (Kt צעוריהם), etc.;—**1. a.** *little*, with idea of *insignificance* Ju 6¹⁵ (‖ הַדַּל), cf. 1 S 9²¹ (‖ קְטַנֵּי), Mi 5¹ ψ 68²⁸ Is 60²² (opp. גוי עצום), of horn in vision Dn 8⁹, rd. prob. אחרת צעירה for אחת מִצְּעִירָה, cf. Bev Dr; צְעִירֵי הַצֹּאן Je 49²⁰ 50⁴⁵ (fig. of helpless captives). **b.** *insignificant, mean*, ψ 119¹⁴¹ (‖ נִבְזֶה), Je 14³ (as subst.); on Je 48⁴ v. צָעַר. **2.** more oft. of age, *young* (usu. c. art. the *younger, youngest*, as subst.), of son (brother), opp הַבְּכוֹר Gn 43³³ 48¹⁴ (both J), Jos 6²⁶ 1 K 16³⁴, opp. רַב Gn 25²³ (J), cf. צ׳ אני לְיָמִים ואתם יְשִׁישִׁים Jb 32⁶; of daughter (sister), opp. הַבְּכִירָה Gn 19³¹·³⁴·³⁵·³⁸ (J) 29²⁶ (E);—here belongs also צְעִירִים מִמֶּנִּי לימים Jb 30¹, si vera l.; GHBWr Siegf Bu del ממני לימים; 𝔊 ἐλάχιστοι; put then under **1 b.**

†II. [צָעִיר] **n.pr.loc.** prob. on border of Edom, צָעִירָה 2 K 8²¹, εἰς Σειωρ (𝔊L ἐκ Σιωρ).

†[צְעִירָה] **n.f.** youth;—sf. בִּצְעִרָתוֹ Gn 43³³ (J; opp. כִּבְכֹרָתוֹ).—On adj צעירה v foregoing; צעוריה Je 48⁴, צעוריהם Je 14³, v. צָעִיר, צָעַר.

†צוּעָר **n.pr.m.** Σωγαρ, in Issachar (*little one*);—alw. in נְתַנְאֵל בֶּן־צ׳ Nu 1⁸ 2⁵ 7¹⁸·²³ 10¹⁵.

†צִיעֹר **n.pr.loc.** Σωρθ, A𝔊L Σιωρ, Jos 15⁵⁴, prob. *Ṣâ'ir*, 5 m. NNE fr. Hebron, Buhl[Geogr 158].

†I מִצְעָר **n.m.** a small thing (‖ מְעָר),—**1.** abs. מ׳ *a small thing*, of city Gn 19²⁰·²⁰ (J); of Job's fortunes, רֵאשִׁיתְךָ מ׳ Jb 8⁷ (opp. יִשְׂגֶּה מְאֹד); cstr. מִצְעַר אֲנָשִׁים 2 Ch 24²⁴ *a few men;* of time לַמּ׳ Is 63¹⁸ *for the* [*a*] *little while*.—ψ 42⁷ v. II מ׳.

†II מִצְעָר **n.pr.mont.** near Hermon, הַר מ׳ ψ 42⁷ *mt* (of) *Miṣ'ar* (perh. orig. *littleness*), not identified; so De Now Du Dr GASm[Geogr 477], others *mt of littleness, little mt.*, so 𝔊 𝔙 Hi Che Bae We al. (interpr. then usu. of Zion)

†צָפַד **vb.** draw together, contract (NH *id*, trans., Ar صَفَدَ *bind fast, shackle*, cf. Nö[ZMG 46] who cp. Mand. סאפאדים *fetters*),—**Qal** *Pf.* 3 ms. צ׳ La 4⁸ their skin *contracteth, shrivelleth*, upon (עַל) their bones.

צָפָה Ez 32⁶ v. צוּף.

I [צָפָה]₃₇ **vb.** look out or about, spy, keep watch (NH *id*, Pi. *hope;* Eth. ሰፈወ: III *hope*);—**Qal**₂₈ *Impf.* 3 ms. juss. יִצֶף י׳ בֵּינִי וּבֵינֶךָ Gn 31⁴⁹ (J) *may* י׳ *keep watch between me and thee* (that the covenant be kept=עֵד א׳ v⁵⁰); 3 fpl. עֵינָיו בַּגּוֹיִם תִּצְפֶּינָה ψ 66⁷ *his eyes keep watch upon the nations; Pt. act.* צוֹפֶה רָשָׁע לַצַּדִּיק ψ 37³² *a wicked man spieth upon the righteous;* Ct 7⁵ the town *which looketh* toward (פְּנֵי) Damascus; f. צוֹפִיָּה Pr 31²⁷ *she keepeth watch* of (c. acc.); pl. עֵינֵי י׳ צֹפוֹת רָעִים וטוֹבִים Pr 15³; elsewh as subst. *watchman*, abs. צֹפֶה 2 S 13³⁴+; pl. צֹפִים 1 S 14¹⁶+, sf. צֹפָיו Is 56¹⁰ Qr (Kt צפו), צֹפַיִךְ Is 52⁸,—1 S 14¹⁶ 2 S 13³⁴+8 t SK, Ez 33²·⁶·⁶ Is 52⁸, so in שׂדה צפים Nu 23¹⁴ (JE); fig of prophets Ho 9⁸ Je 6¹⁷ Ez 3¹⁷ 33⁷ Is 56¹⁰,—צוֹפִים 1 S 1¹ v. צוֹפַי; *Pt. pass.* צָפוּ (Codd. and Qr צָפוּי), Jb 15²² *spied out* (and brought) *to* (אֱלֵי) the sword (Ew Bi Perles[Anal. 29] צָפוּן cf. Di Bu). †**Pi.** *Pf.* 1 pl. צִפִּינוּ La 4¹⁷, *Impf.* 1 s. אֲצַפֶּה Mi 7⁷+; *Imv* ms. צַפֵּה Na 2², fs. צַפִּי Je 48¹⁹; *Pt.* מְצַפֶּה 1 S 4¹³, Is 21⁶; pl. sf. מְצַפַּיִךְ Mi 7⁴;—*watch* (*closely*), אֶל־דֶּרֶךְ Je 48¹⁹, צ׳־דֶרֶךְ Na 2², + אֶל of person expected La 4¹⁷, fig בְּי׳ אֲצַפֶּה Mi 7⁷; abs. lit. 1 S 4¹³; fig Hb 2¹ *I will look forth*, to see (לִרְאוֹת) what he will say; ψ 5⁴ *I will look out* (expectantly); pt as n = *watchman* Is 21⁶ Mi 7⁴.

†צְפִי, צְפוֹ **n.pr.m.** Σωφαρ: in Edom (? *gaze, gazing*),—צְפוֹ Gn 36¹¹·¹⁵+v⁴³ (ins. prob. after עירם; cf. Lag[Sept. Stud. ii 10, i. 178, 37, i. 270] Nes[Mar 12]) = צְפִי 1 Ch 1³⁶

צְפוֹן, צְפוֹנִי v. צפן.

†[צְפִיָּה] **n.f.** outlook-post (?),—sf. בְּצִפִּיָּתֵנוּ צִפִּינוּ La 4¹⁷ (Ba[NB 139]; Bi [for both] בְּצַפּוּתֵנוּ).

†צִפְיוֹן **n.pr.m.** Σαφων: son of Gad (? *gaze*),—Gn 46¹⁶, = צְפוֹן Nu 26¹⁵ (v. בַּעַל צ׳)

†I. צְפוֹנִי **adj. gent.** of צפון (v foregoing); c. art as subst coll Nu 26¹⁵.—II. צ׳ v. צָפַן.

†I מִצְפֶּה **n.m. 1.** watch-tower, Is 21⁸. **2.** outlook-point, 2 Ch 20²⁴ on high ground.

†II. מִצְפֶּה **n.pr.loc. 1.** הַמּ׳ in Shephelah of Judah Jos 15³⁸, Μασ(σ)ηφα. **2.** מִצְפֵּה־מוֹאָב 1 S 22³, Μασσηφα **3.** מִצְפֵּה גִלְעָד Ju 11²⁹·²⁹ (ἡ σκοπιά) prob. = רָמַת הַמּ׳ Jos 13²⁶ Μασ(ση)φα and perh. מצפה **2.**—Jos 11⁸ 18²⁶ v. מִצְפָּה **3, 4.**

מִצְפָּה₃₈ **n.pr.loc.** (prop. *outlook-point* or *-height*, c. art (exc. Ho 5¹));—†**1.** in Gilead, expl. as name given to Laban's cairn, N. of Jabbok

Gn 31^{49} (on text v. Ball Holz, 𝔊 ἡ ὅρασις). †2. prob S of Jabbok, Ju 10^{17} (ἡ σκοπιά), 11$^{11.34}$ (Μασσηφα, so 𝔊L 10^{17}), Ho 5^{1} (ἡ σκοπιά); appar. = ii מִצְפֶּה 3, Buhl$^{Geogr\ 262}$ (-פֶּה, -פָה, seem to interchange); site unknown; v. conj. in Buhl$^{l.c.}$, cf. GASm$^{Geogr\ 586}$. †3. near Hermon, אֶרֶץ הַמּ׳ Jos 11^{3}, Μασευμαν, Μασσηφα(θ), = בִּקְעַת־מִצְפֶּה v^{8}, Μασσωχ, Μασσηφα, v. Buhl$^{Geogr\ 240}$. 4. old sacred place in Benj, Μασσηφα, etc.,—הַמּ׳ Ju 20^{1}+, הַמִּצְפָּ֫תָה 1 S 7^{5}+;—Ju 20$^{1.3}$ 21$^{1.5.8}$ 1 S 7^{6} + 7 t. 1 S 7, 10, 1 K 15^{22} = 2 Ch 16^{6}, 2 K 25$^{23.25}$ Je 40^{10} + 12 t. 40, 41, Ne 3$^{7.15.19}$, = הַמִּצְפָּה Jos 18^{26},—mod. *Nabî Samwîl*, 5 miles NW of Jerusalem, v. Buhl$^{Geogr\ 167f}$.

II. [צָפָה]$_{47}$ **vb. lay out, lay over** (NH Pi = BH),—**Qal** *Inf. abs.* צָפֹה הַצָּפִית Is 21^{5} *they lay out the rug!* or the like, so most moderns, v. צָפִית. **Pi.** *overlay, plate. Pf.* 3 ms צִפָּה 1 K 6^{15}+; 2 ms צִפִּיתָ Ex 25^{11}+; *Impf.* 3 ms וַיְצַף 1 K 6^{20}+, sf וַיְצַפֵּהוּ v^{20}+; 2 ms תְּצַפֶּה Ex 29^{29}, 3 mpl וַיְצַפּוּ 2 Ch 3^{10}, etc.;—*overlay*, esp. *plate* sthg *with* metal (gold, bronze), usu. 2 acc. 1 K 6$^{20.20}$ + 6 t. 1 K 6, + 10^{18}, ∥ 2 Ch 3$^{4.10}$ 4^{9} 9^{17}, Ex 25$^{11.13}$ + 21 t. Ex 25–38 (all P), *overlay, stud with* precious stones, 2 acc. 2 Ch 3^{6}, also *plate*, acc. mater. om., 1 K 6^{15} 2 K 18^{16} Ex 25^{11} 38^{28}; acc. dir. obj. om. 1 K 6$^{32.35}$, c. acc. + בְּ mater. v^{15} *overlaid the floor of the house with timbers*. †**Pu.** *Pt.* מְצֻפֶּה Pr 26^{23} impure silver (Toy) *laid over* (עַל) a sherd; pl. מְצֻפִּים זָהָב Ex 26^{32}, pillars *overlaid with gold*.

†צִפּוּי **n.[m.]** metal **plating**,—of idols Is 30^{22}, capitals Ex 38$^{17.19}$, altar Nu 17$^{3.4}$.

†צָפִית **n.f. rug, carpet** (*laid out*);—צָפֹה הַצָּפִית Is 21^{5}, so now most, v. esp. Che$^{Intr\ Is.\ 126}$; > *watch, outlook* (I צפה), Ges De al.

†צֶ֫פֶת **n.f.** appar. **plated capital** of pillar 2 Ch 3^{15}.

צפח (√ of foll.; cf. Ar. صَفَّحَ II *make wide, broad;* صَفِيحَة *anything broad* (stone, plank, sheathing, plating), Syr. ܨܦܝܚܐ *plating;* also Eth. ሰፍሐ: *spread out, extend;* Sab. (Lih.) הצפחת, אצפחת, *platform*, DHM$^{Epigr\ Denkm\ 84.86}$, but (transp.) Ar. صَحْفَة, *wide bowl*, cf. Fra^{63})

†צַפַּ֫חַת **n.f.** jar, jug, of flat or broad shape,—abs. צַפַּ֫חַת 1 K 17^{12}, cstr. צַפַּ֫חַת 1 S 26^{11}+,—*jar* or *jug* for water 1 S 26$^{11.12.16}$ 1 K 19^{6}, for oil 1 K 17$^{12.14.16}$ (on masc. verb חָסֵר v. Ew^{§317c}, but prob. rd. חָסֵרָה SS Albr$^{ZAW\ xvi\ (1896),\ 89}$, cf. v^{14}).

†צַפִּיחִת **n.f. flat cake, wafer;**—Ex 16^{31}.

†צוֹפַח **n.pr.m.** in Asher, 1 Ch 7^{35}, צוֹפַח v^{36}, Σωχαθ, Σωφας[ρ], 𝔊L Σουφα.

צְפִי, צְפִיָּה, צִפְיוֹן v. I. צפה.

צָפִית v. II. צפה

†צָפַן **vb. hide, treasure up** (NH *id.;* TelAm *ṣapânu, set*, of sun),—**Qal** *Pf.* 3 ms צ׳ Pr 27^{16}. 2 ms צָפַנְתָּ Jb 10^{13}+, etc.; *Impf.* יִצְפֹּן Jb 21^{19} + Pr 2^{7} Qr (Kt וצפן), sf יִצְפְּנֵנִי ψ 27^{5}, etc.; *Pt. act.* pl. sf. צֹפְנֶיהָ Pr 27^{16}, *pass.* צָפוּן Pr. 13^{22}+, ψ 17^{14} Kt; f. צְפוּנָה Ho 13^{12}, etc.;—**1.** trans. *hide*, c. acc. pers. Ex 2^{2} (E), Jos 2^{4} (JE), of *hiding* a quarrelsome woman, like hiding wind Pr 27$^{16.16}$ (si vera l., cf. Toy), of י׳'s *hiding* his servants (from evil) ψ 27^{5} 31^{21}: = *treasure up* a thing, Pr 10^{14}, + אִתָּךְ *with thyself*, in thine own keeping 2^{1} = 7^{1}, in (בְּ) the heart Jb 10^{13} (subj. י׳, of secret purposes), ψ 119^{11}, cf. Jb 23^{12}, + לְ pers. Pr 13^{22} Ct 7^{14}, subj. י׳ Jb 21^{19} *reserve* penalty; blessings ψ 31^{20} Pr 2^{7}; + מִן Jb 17^{4} *thou* [God] *hast treasured up* their heart *away from* understanding, kept it therefrom; pass., of sin Ho 13^{12} (abs.; ∥ צָרוּר); read poss. צָפוּן for צֹפֶה Jb 15^{22} *treasured up* for (אֱלֵי) the sword (v. I צפה); צָפוּן = *treasured, cherished place* (i.e. Jerusalem) Ez 7^{22}, = *treasure* ψ 17^{14} Qr (Kt צפינך, v. צָפִין), Jb 20^{26} (on dub. text v. Bu); pl. of י׳'s *treasured ones*, his saints ψ 83^{4}. **2.** intrans. *lie hid, lurk*, abs. ψ 56^{7}, c. לְ pers. Pr 1$^{11.18}$ and (of eyes of wicked) ψ 10^{8}. **Niph.** *Pf.* 3 ms נִצְפַּן Je 16^{17} *be hidden* from before (מִנֶּגֶד) י׳'s eyes (∥ נִסְתְּרוּ); 3 pl. נִצְפְּנוּ Jb 24^{1} + מִשַּׁדַּי *stored up on the part of Shadday, stored up* for (לְ) one 15^{20}. **Hiph.** *hide*, = **Qal**: *Impf.* 2 ms sf תַּצְפִּנֵנִי Jb 14^{13}, c. בְּ loc.; 3 mpl יַצְפִּינוּ ψ 56^{7} Kt (but < Qr v. **Qal**); *Inf. cstr.* sf הַצְּפִינוֹ (Ges^{§20b}) Ex 2^{3} *to hide him*.

†[צָפִין] **n.[m.] treasure;**—sf. צְפִינְךָ ψ 17^{14} Kt < צְפוּנְךָ Qr, v. צפן pt. pass.

I. צָפוֹן$_{153}$ **n.f.**$^{Is\ 43.6}$ north (as the *hidden, dark;* cf. Thes Lewy$^{Fremdw\ 188f.}$, perh. Ph. צפל *north*),—abs. צ׳ Je 26^{26}+, צָפֹ֫נָה *northward* Gn 13^{14}+, oftener צָפ֫וֹנָה Je 3^{12}+, also צָפֹן = צָפ֫וֹנָה Je 1^{13}+ (after preps. and st. cstr.; cf. Ges^{§90e}), cstr. מִצְּפוֹן לְ Jos 8^{11}+, also מִצָּפוֹן 19^{14} Gi (cf. Benn; van d H Baer מִצְּ׳), מִצְּפ֫וֹנָה לְ Ju 21^{19}; (צ׳ occurs oftenest in Ez [46 t.], Jos [25 t.], Je [25 t.], Dn [9 t.]);—*north* (opp. S., E., W.)

Gn 13[14] 28[14] (both J), Ex 27[11] (P), +; פְּאַת צ׳ *north side* Ex 26[20] Jos 15[5]+ (v. פֵּאָה); so צֶלַע צ׳ Ex 26[35], עַל־יֶרֶךְ הַמִּזְבֵּחַ צָפוֹנָה cf רוּחַ הַצ׳ Ez 42[17], 2 K 16[14]; גְּבוּל צ׳ Nu 34[7.9] *north boundary;* יַרְכְּתֵי צ׳ *remote parts of north* Is 14[13] (as divine abode), Ez 38[6.15]+ (v. [יַרְכָּה]), שַׁעַר הַצ׳ Ez 40[35]+, פָּתַח צ׳ 42[2]; רוּחַ צ׳ Pr 25[23] *north wind,* and so צ׳ alone Ct 4[16]; *toward the north* is צָפוֹנָה Jos 13[3]+ (v. also supr.), and אֶל־צָפוֹן Ec 1[6], אֶל־הַצ׳ Ez 42[1], דֶּרֶךְ הַצָּפוֹן v[20], לַצָּפוֹן 40[23], ד׳ צָפוֹנָה 8[14], אֶל־הַצָּפוֹנָה 8[5.5]+, etc.; esp. (in Je Ez etc) of quarter whence invaders were to come, e g. Assyr. Is 14[31], cf Zp 2[13], Babylonians Je 6[1.22] 15[12] 46[20.24] (עַם־צ׳), 47[2], Ez 26[7], Cyrus against Bab Is 41[25], cf Je 50[3.9.41] 51[48]; more vaguely, Je 1[14.15] (מַמְלְכוֹת צ׳), 4[6] 10[22] 13[20] 25[9.26] (מַלְכֵי הַצ׳), of Gog's host Ez 38[6.15] 39[2]; נְסִיכֵי צ׳ 32[30] (appar. of nearer [Aramæan?] princes); אֶרֶץ צ׳ Je 31[8] is region of Carchemish, but Zc 2[10] 6[6.8.8] of Babylon, מֵאֶרֶץ צ׳ (sts.+other countries) the exiles and dispersed are to return Je 3[18] 16[15]=23[8], 31[8], cf. Is 43[6] 49[12]; מֶלֶךְ הַצ׳ Dn 11[6.7.8.11.13.15.40] denotes successive Seleucidae

†II. צְפוֹנִי **adj.** from foregoing, northern (so most);—c. art. as **n.m.** northern one, northerner, invader from north Jo 2[20] (of locust-swarm, cf We Now Dr, GASm[Proph. ii. 397])—I. צְפוֹנִי v. צִפְיוֹן sub I. צפה.

†II. צָפוֹן **n.pr.loc.** on E bank of Jordan, in tribe of Gad, צ׳ Jos 13[27] (Σαφαν[ων]), צָפוֹנָה Ju 12[1] (Βοῤῥᾶν, 𝔊L Σεφηνα); acc. to Talm.=mod. *Amateh,* N of Jabbok, GFM Buhl[Geogr 259] (who doubts); *Saphuna* appears Tel Am Wkl[No. 174].

צָפוֹן, in בַּעַל צְפוֹן (q v.), perhaps n.pr.dei, Bae[Rel. 22] No[ZMG xlii (1888), 473] Gray[Prop. N 134].

†צְפַנְיָה(וּ) **n.pr.m.** Σοφονιας (*י hath treasured;* OHeb. צפניהו, Ph. צפנבעל),—**1.** priest, -יָה Je 21[1] 29[25.29] 52[24]=-יָהוּ 2 K 25[18] (𝔊L Σαφανιας), Je 37[3]. Elsewhere -יָה. **2.** the prophet Zp 1[1]. **3.** a Judæan Zc 6[10.14]. **4.** ancestor of Heman 1 Ch 6[21] (Σαφανιας; =אוּרִיאֵל v[9]).

†[מַצְפּוֹן] **n.[m.]** hidden treasure, treasure,—sf. מַצְפֻּנָיו Ob[6] *his treasures.*

†צָפְנַת פַּעְנֵחַ **n.pr.m.** (<vocaliz. *Ṣapnĕtĕph 'ônḥ,* i.e. *the god speaks and he lives,* Egypt *D(d)-pnt(r)-ĕf-'nḥ* (*Dĕ-pnutĕ-ef-'ônḥ*), v. Steind[ZS 1889, 41 f; 1892, 50 ff], so Eb[Smith DB (2) 1796 b] Brugsch, v. Dr[Hast. ii. 775a n.], Crum[ib. i. 665 b] Griffith [ib. iii 819 b]);—Egypt. name given to Joseph Gn 41[45], Ψονθομφανηχ, 𝔊L Ψομ´.

I. צפע (√of following; meaning dub, perh. *hiss,* onomatop, so Thes, NH צִפְעוֹן=BH)

†צֶפַע **n.m.** a (poisonous) serpent (from *hissing?*);—Is 14[29]; usu. taken as=following

†צִפְעֹנִי **n.m.** *id;*—abs צ׳ Is 11[8] (|| פֶּתֶן), בֵּיצֵי צ׳ 59[5], כְּצִפְעֹנִי Pr 23[32] (sim, || נָחָשׁ), pl. צִפְעֹנִים Je 8[17] (app נְחָשִׁים), identif. dub., Tristr[NHB 276] ('poss.') *daboia xanthina,* a venomous viper, but vipers do not lay eggs Furrer[Bi HWB 2, 1423]; Furrer proposes *ailurophis vivax.*

II. צפע (√of foll; cf. Ar. صَفَعَ *cacavit,* صَفْعٌ, Eth. ጸፍዕ: *excrement*)

†[צָפִיעַ] **n [m.]** dung of cattle;—pl. cstr צְפִיעֵי הַבָּקָר Ez 4[15] Qr (opp. גֶּלְלֵי הָאָדָם), so Co Toy al, >Kt צפועי

III. צפע (√of foll; meaning unknown).

†[צְפִיעָה] **n.f.** dub; appar, fr. context, offshoot;—pl. הַצְּפִיעוֹת Is 22[24] (fig, || הַצֶּאֱצָאִים).

†[צִפְצֵף] **vb. Pilp.** chirp, peep (onomatop; NH Pilp. *id,* JAram צַפְצֵף *chirp;* Ar. صُفْصُفٌ *sparrow,* etc),—*Impf* 3 fs. תְּצַפְצֵף Is 29[4], 1 s. אֲצַפְצֵף 38[14], *Pt* מְצַפְצֵף 10[14], pl. הַמְצַפְצְפִים 8[19];—*chirp, peep:* **1.** of birds Is 10[14] (fig. of conquered peoples), of mourning, כְּסוּס . . . אֲצַ׳ 38[14] (|| אֶהְגֶּה כַּיּוֹנָה) **2.** of spirits, ghosts Is 8[19] (+ הַמְּהַגִּים), מֵעָפָר אִמְרָתֵךְ תְּצַ׳ 29[4] (like a spirit's).

†צַפְצָפָה **n.f.** a kind of willow (?onomatop., from *rustling;* NH *id,* Ar صَفْصَافٌ);—Ez 17[5].

†I. [צָפַר] **vb.** dub,—*Impf.* 3 ms. יָשֹׁב וְיִצְפֹּר מֵהַר הַגִּלְעָד Ju 7[3] *let him return and* (Vrss) *let him depart,* AV *depart early* (as Ki, fr. Aram צפרא, صَفَرَ *morning,* improb.), wholly uncertain; Gr וַיַּעֲבֹר, on difficulty of מֵהַר הַגּ׳ v גִּלְעָד **2**, and GFM, who conj. וַיִּצְרְפֵם גִּדְעוֹן and so *Gideon put them to the test* (cf. v[4]), so Bu Now (cf. Dr[Hast. ii. 176 n]).

II. צפר (√of foll., cf. Ar صَفَرَ *peep, twitter, whistle* (usu of bird; onomatop.); As. *ṣapâru* is *cry, howl;* NH צִפּוֹר=BH, so Ph. צפר, 𝔗 צִפַּר, Syr ܨܶܦܪܳܐ, Mand ציפאר, ציפרא No[M § 102]; also Ar. عُصْفُورٌ *sparrow,* etc., and (perh.) As *iṣṣuru, bird*).

1. צִפּוֹר, צִפֹּר[40] **n.f.**[Am 3.5] (**m.** ψ 102[8], cf Kö[Synt. § 252 a], so 104[17], yet cf. Albr[ZAW xvi (1896), 71]), **bird,**—abs. צִפּוֹר Ho 11[11]+15 t, צִפֹּר Gn 15[10]+

11 t, cstr צפור Dt 4^{17} + 5 t., צפר ψ 8^{9}; pl. צִפֳּרִים Lv 14^{4} + 5 t, —**1.** single *bird*, Am 3^{5} Ho 11^{11} (sim, ‖ יוֹנָה), La 3^{52} Jb 40^{29} ψ 102^{8} 124^{7} Pr 6^{5} 7^{23} 26^{2} 27^{8} (all sim), Lv 14^{5} + 10 t. Lv 14, כָּל־צ׳ קן־צ׳ כְּנָף Dt 4^{17}, כָּל־צ׳ טהוֹרָה 14^{11} (כל distrib.), 22^{6} *bird's nest*, קול הַצ׳ Ec 12^{4}, pl Is 31^{5} (sim), Ne 5^{18} Lv 14^{4} (שתי צִפֳּרִים, in purif, cf We^Held 2 171^ RS^Sem 1 402 2nd ed 422^), v^{49} (*id*), ψ 104^{17} Ec 9^{12}. **2.** less oft coll, either def. Gn 15^{10} (two), or indef ψ 11^{1} (fig), צפר שָׁמַיִם 8^{9}, esp צ׳ (כָּל־)כָּנָף Ez 39^{17} ψ 148^{10}, כל צ׳ כָּל־כָּנָף 17^{23} Gn 7^{14}, also redund. c. עִיט, עִיט צ׳ כָּל־כָּנָף Ez 39^{4} *birds of prey of all kinds*

†II צִפּוֹר **n.pr m.** father of Balak, king of Moab (*bird*; perh. specif *sparrow*, cf. Gray ^Prop N 94^, Palm n pr.m. צפרא), —צ׳ Nu $22^{2.4.16}$ Jos 24^{9} Ju 11^{25}, צפר Nu 22^{10} 23^{18}, Σεπφωρ.

†צִפֹּרָה **n.pr.f.** wife of Moses (*bird*), —Ex 2^{21} 4^{25} 18^{2}, Σεπφωρα (cf Lag^BN 90 Anm.^)

III. צפר (√of following; cf Ar صَفَرَ *plait, braid*, Eth ፀፈረ: *id.*; NH צפירה = *rim* of basket)

†צְפִירָה **n.f.** plait, chaplet,—abs. צ׳ Ez 7^{7}, צפרה v^{10}, cstr צְפִירַת Is 28^{5};—*chaplet, coronet, diadem*, צ׳ תִּפְאָרָה Is 28^{5} (fig. of ׳י, ‖ עֲטֶרֶת צְבִי)— צ׳ Ez $7^{7.10}$ is dub; AV *morning* (as Ki, fr Aram) is unsuitable; most (after AW دَوْر) *doom, fate* (as *coming round* upon one, cf RV Da Toy), but v Dr^Hast II 176a^; *diadem* is possible v^{10} (‖ הַמַּטֶּה); of royal house of Judah Co Berthol; or of Jerus Krae), but not v^{7}, conj in Co Berthol Krae.

IV. צפר (√of foll., mng. dub, NH = BH, so Ar ظُفْر, ظُفُر, Eth ጽፍር:, As. *supru*; Aram טְפַר, טוּפְרָא, ܛܦܪܐ, all *nail*)

†צִפֹּרֶן **n.[m.]** nail (of finger), stylus-point,—cstr צ׳ Je 17^{1}, pl sf. צִפָּרְנֶיהָ Dt 21^{12},— **1.** *finger-nail* Dt 21^{12} (cf. RS^K 178, Sem 1 407 2nd ed 428^ We^Held 2 171^) **2.** transf, בצ׳ שָׁמִיר Je 17^{1} *with a point of diamond* (cf. Plin^NH 37, 4^)

V. צפר (√of foll, cf Aram. צְפִירָא, ܨܦܝܪܐ = צָפִיר; perh. cp Ar صَفَرَ *leap* (but ز = ص ?))

†צָפִיר **n m.** he-goat (late),—abs צ׳ Dn $8^{5.21}$, cstr. צפיר הָעִזִּים $v^{5.8}$ (all in vision, symbol. of Alex.), pl cstr (lit) צְפִירֵי עִזִּים 2 Ch 29^{21}, צפירי חַטָּאת Ezr 8^{35} *he-goats for a sin-offering*

†צֹפַר and (Jb 2^{11}) צוֹפַר **n.pr.m.** Job's third friend, צ׳ הַנַּעֲמָתִי Jb 2^{11} 11^{1} 20^{1} 42^{9}, Σωφαρ.

†צְפַרְדֵּעַ **n.f.** ^Ex 8, 2^ (cf. also Albr ^ZAW xv (1896), 322^ Ges^§ 13c, 14c^) frogs (Ar ضِفْدَع, etc., Aram. עוּרדְעָנַיָּא, אוּרְדְּעָא, ܐܘܪܕܥܐ);—*frogs*, coll Ex 8^{2} ψ 78^{45}, pl. צפרדעים Ex $7^{27.28.29}$ $8^{1.3.4.5.7.8.9}$ ψ 105^{30}.

צֶפֶת v. II צפה.

†צְפַת **n.pr.loc.** Σεφεκ[ρ]. Canaanite city Ju 1^{17} = חָרְמָה q v., identif. by many (v. esp Palmer ^Desert of Exod. 374 ff^) with *Sebaita* (c Lat. 30° 54′ N., Long 34° 40′ E), by Rob^BR II 181^ with pass *es-Ṣûfâh*, further E.; against both v GFM.

†צְפָתָה **n.pr.loc** in Judah (van d. H. צְפָתָה, so Kit), בגיא צ׳ לְמָרֵשָׁה 2 Ch 14^{9}; 𝔊 κατὰ βορρᾶν, whence Hi al. prop. צָפֹנָה, so Buhl^Lex^.

צִצִּים v. I. צִיץ sub I צוץ.

צִקּוֹן Is 26^{16} v. II צוק

†צִקְלַג and (1 Ch $12^{1.21}$ צִיק׳) **n. pr. loc.** (צִקְלַג 1 S 27^{6} +, צִקְלָג 2 S 2^{1}, צִיקְלָג 1 Ch 12^{1}),— assigned to Judah Jos 15^{31}, to Simeon 19^{5}; Philistine city given to David 1 S $27^{6.6}$ $30^{1.1.1.14.26}$ 2 S 1^{1} 4^{10} 1 Ch 4^{30} $12^{1.21}$ (van d. H. v^{20}); Σεκελακ, Σικελαγ, etc.; usually identified with *Zuheilikah*, 19 miles SW. from Bêt Jibrin, 11 miles ESE from Gaza (cf. Buhl^Geogr 185^).

†[צִקָּלוֹן] **n.[m.]** doubtful word,—sf כַּרְמֶל בְּצִקְלֹנוֹ 2 K 4^{42} 𝔖 𝔗 *garment*; 𝔊 om, but A βακελλεθ, Arm. *bakelaθ*, whence Lag^Armen. Stud. § 333, M 1 212^ reads (plausibly) בְּקִלְעוֹ *in his wallet*, Ar. قَلْعَة, قَلْعَة, and so 𝔙 *pera*.

I, II, III, IV. צַר, II צֹר, v. I, II, III. צרר.

†צֵר **n.pr.loc.** in Naphtali, Jos 19^{35}; Τυρος.

†I. צֹר, צוֹר **n.pr.loc.** Τυρος · Tyre, famous Phoenician city (Ph צר; As *Surru*, so TelAm, Egypt *Ḏa-(i)ra*, *Ḏa-ru* WMM^As u Eur 185^);— צר 2 S 24^{7} + 32 t, צוֹר 1 K 5^{15} + 8 t. (Gi);—city of Hiram, friend of David and Sol. 2 S 5^{11} 1 K 5^{15} $9^{11.12}$ 1 Ch 14^{1} 2 Ch $2^{2.10}$; of artif. Hiram 1 K 7^{13}; בַּת־צֹר ψ 45^{13} of city personif. (another view in Che), צ׳. also in name of Ph. fortress, מִבְצַר־צ׳ 2 S 24^{7}, עִיר מ׳ צ׳ Jos 19^{29} (P), threatened by proph. Am $1^{9.10}$ and (with esp ref. to commercial greatness) Is 23^{1} (מַשָּׂא צֹר), $v^{5.8.15.15.17}$ Je 25^{22} (מַלְכֵי־צֹר), 27^{3} (מֶלֶךְ צֹר), 47^{4} Ez $26^{2.3.4.7.15}$ $27^{2.3.3.8.32}$, 28^{2} (נגיד צֹר), v^{12} (מֶלֶךְ צוֹר); besieged by Nebuch. $29^{18.18}$, cf. Zc $9^{2.3}$ Jo 4^{4} ψ 83^{8} (יֹשְׁבֵי צ׳); of Tyrians as proselytes ψ 87^{4} (predict);—לְצוֹר Ho 9^{13} is prob. corrupt, read לְצוּד or לְצַיִד 𝔊 We GASm,

cf. Now.—'צ oft. + צִידוֹן q. v.;—see, on Tyre, Pietschm Phön. 50 ff. Rob BR ii. 461 ff. de Luynes Voyage à la Mer Morte (1874) i. 28 ff., and Pl. xiii-xviii Bd Pal. 3 (1898), 307 ff.—

II. צֹר (*flint, knife*) v. III. צרר.

†צֹרִי **adj. gent. Tyrian**;—אִישׁ צ' 1 K 7[14] = 2 Ch 2[13]; pl. as subst. הַצֹּרִים *the Tyrians* 1 Ch 22[4] Ezr 3[7] (both + הַצִּידֹנִים), Ne 13[16].

†[צָרַב] **vb. burn, scorch** (As. *ṣarâbu, burn*; Frä ZA iii. 52 Ba ES 32 cp. Ar. ضرم *be kindled, blaze*; cf. also זרב);—**Niph.** *Pf.* 3 pl. consec. וְנִצְרְבוּ Ez 21[3] all faces *shall be scorched.*

†[צָרָב] **adj. burning, scorching** (= *צָרֵב Thes al.);—כְּאֵשׁ צָרָבֶת Pr 16[27] (sim. of words).

†צָרֶבֶת **n.f. scab, scar,** of a sore (lit. *a burning, scorching*);—cstr. צָרֶבֶת הַשְּׁחִין הִוא Lv 13[23]; צ' הַמִּכְוָה הִוא v[28].

†צְרֵדָה **n.pr.loc.** home of Jerob. 1 K 11[26], Σαρειρα, A Σαριδα; v. [צְרֵרָה] צָרְתָן.

צְרֵדָתָה 2 Ch 4[17] v. צָרְתָן.

I, II. צָרָה v. I, II. צרר.

צרה (√ of foll.; cf. Ar. ضرا (و, ى) of vein, *run blood, bleed*, ضرو an odorif. tree, or its gum, cf. Hom A. und A. i. 4, Sab. צרו SabDenkm 83; (Syr. ܨܪܘܐ *fructus pini*, etc. is loan-word); NH = BH; as to form cp. Gk. στύραξ (hardly ‖ in meaning, Lag M. i. 234, 384, v. Ency. Bib. infr.), cf. Lewy Fremdw. 41).

†צֳרִי and (Gn 37[25]) (וּ)צְרִי **n.[m.]** a kind of **balsam,** as merchandise Gn 37[25] (J), Ez 27[17], gift Gn 43[11] (J), medicament Je 8[22] 46[11] 51[8] (for national disaster, in fig.);—ThDyer-M'Lean in Ency. Bib. Balm think a resin, like (not necess. =) gum of mastic-tree, *pistacia lentiscus* (otherwise Post Hastings DB).

†צְרִי **n.pr.m.** a musician, 1 Ch 25[3] (Σ)ουρ(ε)ι, = יִצְרִי (q.v.) v[11] (Ιεσδρει, 𝔊L Ασειρηλα).

†צְרוּיָה **n.pr.f.** Σαρουια: mother of Abishai, Joab and Asahel;—'צ 1 S 26[6] +, צְרֻיָה 2 S 14[1] 16[10] 23[37];—acc. to 1 Ch 2[16]* she was David's sister; called אֵם יוֹאָב 2 S 17[25]; elsewh. after cstr. בֶּן־ (בְּנֵי): בֶּן־צ' of Abishai 1 S 26[6] 2 S 16[9] 18[2] 19[22] 21[17] 1 Ch 18[12]; of Joab 2 S 2[13] 8[16] = 1 Ch 18[15], 2 S 14[1] 23[18] and v[37] = 1 Ch 11[39], 1 K 1[7] 2[5.22] 1 Ch 11[6] 26[28] 27[24]; pl. of all three 2 S 2[18] 1 Ch 2[16]; Abishai and Joab 2 S 3[39] 16[10] 19[23].

†I. **צָרַח** **vb. cry, roar** (NH *id., cry* (of raven); As. *ṣarâḫu, cry aloud*, Ar. صرخ, Eth. ጸርሐ: 𝔗 צְרַח Aph. (of bear), Syr. ܨܪܚ esp. Aph. and deriv.);—**Qal** *Pt. act.* מַר צֹרֵחַ שָׁם גִּבּוֹר Zp 1[14] *bitterly roareth there a hero*, but abrupt in context and improb.; Gr (in part after 𝔖) conj. קוֹל י' יִצְרַח כַּגִּבּוֹר (cf. **Hiph.**). **Hiph.** *Impf.* 3 ms. יַצְרִיחַ Is 42[13] *utter a roar* (of י', going to battle; ‖ יָרִיעַ).

II. **צרח** (√ of foll.; cf. Ar. ضرح *dig a* ضريح, also *cleave* the ground, *rend open*; ضريح *sepulchral chamber* (with niches for bodies); Nab. צריחה (cf. Nö in Eut Nab. Inschr. 55 Dr Sm. 76)).

†צְרִיחַ **n.[m.]** perh. **excavation, underground chamber**;—'צ abs. Ju 9[49], cstr. v[46]; pl. צְרִחִים 1 S 13[6];—used as hiding-places 1 S 13[6] (+ בֹּרוֹת, סְלָעִים, חֲוָחִים, מְעָרוֹת); as refuge Ju 9[46] (where connected with shrine), v[49] (Vrss *stronghold*; on uncertainty of meaning v. GFM).

צֹרִי v. I. צֹר. צְרִי, צֳרִי, צְרִיָּה v. צרה.

צרך (√ of foll.; NH צָרַךְ *have need of*; Ar. ضرك *be needy*, so Aram. צְרַךְ, ܨܪܟ (צ, ܨ = ض!); ChrPal. ܨܘܪܟܐ χρεία).

†[צֹרֶךְ] **n.[m.]** need (Aram.);—sf. כְּכָל־צָרְכֶּךָ 2 Ch 2[15] *according to all thy need*, cf. Ecclus 8[9] + often.

צרע (√ of foll.; cf. perh. Ar. صرع *throw down, prostrate*; Sab. צרע *humble oneself*, DHM Hofm. No. 6, l. 8 Mordtm Him. Inschr. 71; vbs. denom. in NH 𝔗).

צָרַעַת 35 **n.f. leprosy**;—abs. 'צ Dt 24[8] +, צָרָעַת Lv 13[2] +; cstr. צָרַעַת 2 K 5[27] +; sf. צָרַעְתּוֹ 2 K 5[3.6.7];—*leprosy* 2 K 5[3.6.7.27] 2 Ch 26[19]; elsewhere only in laws: נֶגַע צ' Dt 24[8], and Lv 13, 14 (P; 29 t.): תּוֹרַת הַצ' 14[57]; specif. of **a.** human disease (as above) נֶגַע צ' Lv 13[2] + 8 t.; without 'נ 13[8] + 10 t. **b.** *leprosy* in a garment 13[47.49.51.52.59] (תּוֹרַת נֶגַע צ' בֶּגֶד). **c.** in house 14[34] (נֶגַע צ'), v[44]; house or garment v[55].—Exact meaning of **b.** and **c.** dub., perh. some fungus or mould; v. esp. Di Dr-Wh Baen.

†[צָרַע] **vb.denom.,** only in pass., **be struck with leprosy, leprous**;—**Qal** *Pt. pass.* אִישׁ צָרוּעַ Lv 13[44]; elsewh. as subst., = *leper*, v[45] 14[3] Nu 5[2] (all P), Lv 22[4] (H). **Pu.** *Pt.* מְצֹרָע 2 S 3[29] +, מְצוֹרָע 2 Ch 26[20]; pl. מְצֹרָעִים 2 K 7[3.8];

f. מְצֹרַ֫עַת Ex 4⁶+, מְצֹרָ֫עַת Nu 12[10],—*leprous*, of hand Ex 4⁶ (J), of pers Nu 12[10 10] (E), 2 K 5[27] 2 Ch 26[20], אֲנָשִׁים מְצֹרָעִים 2 K 7³, as subst = *leper* 2 S 3[29] 2 K 5[1 11] 7⁸ 15⁵=2 Ch 26[21a], 2 Ch 26[21b, 23], תּוֹרַת הַמְּצֹרָע Lv 14².

†צִרְעָה **n.f coll. hornets** (? as *wounding, prostrating*, NH=BH),—allies of Isr ,—הַצּ׳ Ex 23[28] Jos 24[12] (both E), Dt 7[20].

†צְרוּעָה **n.f.** mother of Jeroboam 1 K 11[26], 𝔊^A Σαρουα

†צָרְעָה **n.pr.loc.** Σαραα, etc. (cf also Lag [BN 84]), in the Shephelah of Judah (Tel Am. *Sarḫa*, named with *Aialuna*, Ajalon),—Jos 15[33], but assigned to Dan 19[41], Ju 13[2 25] 16[31] 18[2.8 11] 2 Ch 11[10] Ne 11[29], mod *Sar'a*, 15 miles W from Jerus, cf GASm[Geogr 218] Buhl[Geogr 19].

†צָרְעִי v foll.

†צָרְעָתִי **adj. gent.** c art as n coll הַצּ׳ 1 Ch 2[53] 4²=הַצָּרְעִי 2[54]

†צָרַף **vb. smelt, refine, test** (NH id, Ph מצרף *smelter*; As *ṣurrupu, refined, ṣarpu, silver, naṣraptu, crucible*, Ar. صَرْفٌ is *pure, unmixed* (esp of wine), very doubtful is Sab צרף *silver, money*, cf Mordtm[Him Inschr pp 14, 29] CIS[iv, No. 291 l. 1]), —**Qal** *Pf* 3 ms צ׳ Je 6[29], sf צְרָפַתְהוּ ψ 105[19], 2 ms sf. צְרַפְתָּנִי ψ 17³, etc., *Impf* 1 s אֶצְרֹף Is 1[25], sf. אֶצְרְפֶנּוּ Ju 7⁴, *Imv.* ms. צרופה ψ 26² Kt, צָרְפָה Qr; *Inf abs* צָרוֹף Je 6[29]; *cstr.* לִצְרוֹף Dn 11[35], etc, *Pt. act* sf. צוֹרְפָם Je 9⁶, etc; *pass* צָרוּף ψ 12⁷, etc.;—**1.** *smelt, refine*: Je 6[29.29] *in vain hath he smelted continually* (inf. abs., fig. of purifying people), so *smelt away* Is 1[25] (acc. of dross; fig.), of silver Zc 13⁹ ψ 66[10], כֶּסֶף צָרוּף בַּעֲלִיל 12⁷ (all sim); of אִמְרַת י׳ ψ 18[31]=2 S 22[31], ψ 119[140] Pr 30⁵ (אִמְרַת אֱלוֹהַּ); *refine* (men, by trials) Dn 11[35] (+לְבָרֵר, לְלַבֵּן) **2.** *test* Ju 7⁴ *I will test them* (the warriors) *for thee* (י׳ subj),—perh also v⁵ (v I צפר); more gen., of י׳'s *testing, trying* (the hearts of) men (oft ‖ בָּחַן) Je 9⁶ Is 48[10] Zc 13⁹ ψ 26² 66[10] **3.** *test* (and prove true) a man (subj י׳'s saying) ψ 105[19] **4.** *Pt act.* as **n.** *smelter, refiner*, hence=*goldsmith* Ju 17⁴ Je 10[9 14] 51[17] Is 40[19 19] (but perhaps del v^b, cf. Du Che Marti), 41⁷ 46⁶ Pr 25⁴; as a guild Ne 3[8.32] **Niph.** *Impf* 3 mpl יִצָּרְפוּ Dn 12[10] many *shall be refined* (by suffering; + יִתְבָּרְרוּ, יִתְלַבְּנוּ) **Pi.** *Pt* מְצָרֵף as **n.** *a refiner*, כְּאֵשׁ מ׳ Mal 3² (sim of י׳), cf. מְ׳ alone v³ (+מְטַהֵר כֶּסֶף).

†צֹרְפִי **n. [m.] coll. goldsmiths**;—only בֶּן־הַצֹּ׳ Ne 3[31] i e. *belonging to the goldsmiths*, a member of their guild

†צָרְפַת **n.pr.loc.** Σαρεπτα on coast S of Sidon (? *smelting*-place, on strange form cf. Lag[BN 84], As. *Ṣariptu* Dl[Pa 284] COT[1 K 17, 9], Egypt. *Da-ira-pu-ti* WMM[As u Eur 184]), — צ׳ Ob[20]; צָרְפָ֫תָה 1 K 17[9 10] (so Gi, -פָ֫תָה van d. H. Baer); mod *Sarfend* Rob[BR ii 474 ff] Pietschm[Phön. 58 f].

†מַצְרֵף **n.[m.] crucible** (prop. *place* or *instrument of refining*); מ׳ לַכֶּסֶף וכוּר לַזָּהָב Pr 17³ 27[21]

†I. צָרַר **vb. bind, tie up, be restricted, narrow, scant, cramped** (NH id.; Ar صَرَّ *bind, tie up*; so Aram. צְרַר, ܨܪ),—**A.** trans.: **Qal** *Pf.* 3 ms. צָרַר Ho 4[19] Pr 30⁴, *Imv* צוֹר Is 8[16], *Inf. cstr.* צרוֹר Pr 26⁸ (?), *Pt act* צרר Jb 26⁸; *pass.* צָרוּר Ho 13[12], f צְרוּרָה 1 S 25[29], fpl. צְרֻרֹת Ex 12[34] 2 S 20³;—*bind* or *tie up*, of kneading-troughs Ex 12[34] (E), fig. of a life preserved by י׳, נֶפֶשׁ צְרוּרָה בִּצְרוֹר הַחַיִּים 1 S 25[29]; of preserving prophetic teaching Is 8[16], of retention of guilt Ho 13[12]; of י׳'s *binding* waters in (a garment of) cloud Pr 30⁴ Jb 26⁸; =*shut up* 2 S 20³,—צָרַר רוּחַ אוֹתָהּ בִּכְנָפֶיהָ Ho 4[19] (si vera l) pregn., *the wind hath wrapped her up in its wings*, to carry her off; כִּצְרוֹר אֶבֶן Pr 26⁸ *like the tying up of a stone*, but unintellig. in context (v. Toy) **Pu.** *Pt* pl מְצֹרָרִים Jos 9⁴ *tied up* (mended by tying), of old wine-skins. **B.** intrans.. **Qal** *Pf.* 3 fs. צָ֫רָה Is 28[20], *Impf.* 3 ms יֵצַר Pr 4[12], יֵ֫צֶר לוֹ Jb 20[22], וַיֵּ֫צֶר Gn 32⁸+, etc.;—*be scant, cramped, in straits*, of scanty bed-covering Is 28[20] (in fig); of land too small for (מִן) its people Is 49[19]+Jos 19[47] (for וַיֵּצֵא) Dr[Expos. Jan 1887 59] Benn, cf. 𝔊; of steps = *be cramped*, or impeded, Pr 4[12] Jb 18⁷ (both in fig.); esp. impers. c. לְ pers, וַיֵּ֫צֶר לוֹ Gn 32⁸ *and it was narrow for him*=he was in straits, distress, so Ju 2[15] 2 S 13² Jb 20[22], also 3 fs. וַתֵּ֫צֶר לְ Ju 10⁹ 1 S 30⁶ (v Dr). **Hiph.** *Pf* 3 ms. וְהֵצַר Dt 28[52.52] consec; 1 s וַהֲצֵרֹתִי Je 10[18] Zp 1[17]; *Impf.* 3 ms יָצֶר־לוֹ 1 K 8[37]=2 Ch 6[28], וַיָּ֫צֶר 2 Ch 28[20]; 3 mpl. וַיָּצֵרוּ Ne 9[27]; *Inf. cstr.* הָצֵר 2 Ch 28[22] 33[12];—*make narrow* for, *press hard* upon, *cause distress* to, c. לְ pers, Je 10[18] (subj. י׳), Zp 1[17] (subj. id.), Dt 28[52.52] 1 K 8[37]=2 Ch 6[28], Ne 9[27] (all subj foe), 2 Ch 28[20] (subj. TP); indef subj 2 Ch 28[22] (but rd. כִּי אִם לְצָרָה לוֹ, and join to v[21], opp. לְעֶזְרָה לוֹ, 𝔊 Kit Buhl[Lex]), 33[12].

†I. צַר **adj.** **narrow, tight**;—abs. צ׳ 2 K 6[1]+; צָר Nu 22[26]+; f. צָרָה Pr 23[27],—*narrow*, צָר מִמֶּנּוּ 2 K 6[1] *too narrow for us*, cf מָקוֹם צָר Nu 22[26], צַר־לִי הַמָּקוֹם Is 49[20] (of land of Judah after exile); בְּאֵר צָרָה Pr 23[27] (fig of harlot; i.e. rescue difficult; ‖ שׁוּחָה עֲמֻקָּה); כַּנָּהָר צָר Is 59[19] *like a contracted* (and hence swift, powerful) *river* (sim. of י׳; Klo נְהַר מָצוֹר, Che[Hpt] נ׳ מצר, both 'of Egypt'), סְגוּר חוֹתָם צָר Jb 41[7] (of scaly back of crocodile), usu. closely joined (as) *with tight seal* (𝔊 Me Bi Hoffm Bu Du חותם צר *with seal of flint*, but why specify material?); ביום צָרָה צַר כֹּחֶכָה Pr 24[10] *thy strength* will be *narrow*, limited (si vera l, cf. Toy).

†II צַר **n.[m.]** **straits, distress**;—abs. צ׳ Jb 15[24]+, also c. art. בַּצַּר Ho 5[15]+, צָר ψ 4[2]+;—*straits, distress* Is 5[30] Jb 15[24] ψ 32[7] 60[13] 108[13] 119[143]; עֵת־צ׳ Jb 38[23], cf. בַּצַּר Is 26[16], צַר־וּמָצוֹק ψ 4[2]; צ׳־רוּחִי Jb 7[11] *distress of my spirit*, לֶחֶם צָר Is 30[20], לֹא צָר Is 63[9] usu *he* (י׳) *had distress* (rdg לוֹ Qr), but 𝔊 οὐ πρέσβυς, Du Che[Hpt] al. לֹא צִר, *no messenger* and (or) angel, (but) his own face, etc. Instead of sf. directly appended, לְ sf. is used (only after בּ): בַּצַּר־לִי *in my distress* ψ 18[7] = 2 S 22[7], ψ 66[14], so ביום צַר־לִי 59[17] 102[3], בַּצַּר לְךָ Dt 4[30] (prob orig. meant as בְּצַר, or בצר [inf], Dr, so) בַּצַּר־לוֹ Is 25[4] 2 Ch 15[4], בַּצַּר לָהֶם Ho 5[15] ψ 107[6.13.19.28], also (after רָאָה) 106[44].—צַר־ 1 S 2[32] is corrupt, cf. Dr.

I צָרָה n.f. id.;—abs. צ׳ 1 S 26[24]+, צָרָתָה ψ 120[1] (Ges[§90g]); cstr צָרַת Gn 42[21]; sf צָרָתִי 35[3]+, צָרַתְכֶם Ju 10[14], etc; pl. צָרוֹת abs. Is 65[16]+, sf. צָרֹתֵיכֶם 1 S 10[19], etc;—*straits, distress*, Gn 42[21] (E), 1 S 26[24] 2 S 4[9] 1 K 1[29] Is 8[22] Jb 5[19] 27[9]; esp. ψψ (24 t), e.g. 22[12] 25[17] (v. רחב), v[22] 31[8] 34[17.18], specif of travail, צָרָה וַחֲבָלִים Je 49[24] (sim.), cf 4[31] (Gie צְוָחָה, after 𝔊); צָרַת נַפְשׁוֹ Gn 42[21] (E), ביום צָרָתִי 35[3] (E), ψ 77[3] 86[7], cf. 2 K 19[3] = Is 37[3], ψ 20[2] 50[15] Pr 24[10] 25[19] Je 16[19] Ob[12.14] Na 1[7] Hb 3[16], יום צ׳ וּמְצוּקָה Zp 1[15]; בְּעֵת־צָרַתְכֶם Ju 10[14], cf. Ne 9[27] ψ 37[39] Is 33[2] Je 14[8] 15[11] 30[7] Dn 12[1], also בְּצָרָה ψ 81[8], בְּצָרָה 91[15] Ne 9[37], בְּצָרוֹת ψ 46[2], etc.; צָרָה וְצוּקָה ψ 71[20], רָעוֹת וְצָרוֹת Dt 31[17.21] cf 1 S 10[19] בְּצָרָתָה לִי Pr 1[27], אֶרֶץ צ׳ וְצ׳ Is 30[6]; c. לְ (poet), צָרָה לִי ψ 120[1] *in my distress*, מִצָּרָה לִי Jon 2[3].—צָרָה Zc 10[11], rd. מִצְרַיִם [or מָצוֹר] We Now GASm; צָרָה Klo[ThLZ. 1879, 566] Sta[ZAW i (1881), 22], ψ 9[10] 10[1] v. בַּצָּרָה.

†[צָרַר] **vb. denom.** **Hiph.** **suffer distress** (specif. of travail, cf Je 4[31] 49[24]);—*Pt.* לֵב אִשָּׁה מְצֵרָה (in sim.) Je 48[41] 49[22].

†I. צְרוֹר **n.m.**[Hg 1.6] **bundle, parcel, pouch, bag** (prop. *a binding*, i.e. sthg. bound up);—צ׳ abs. Am 9[9]+, cstr. Gn 42[35]+; pl. cstr. צְרֹרוֹת v[35];—*bundle* or *pouch* (purse) of money 42[35.35] (E), Pr 7[20]; צ׳ הַמֹּר Ct 1[13] (fig. of lover); צְרוּרָה בצ׳ הַחַיִּים 1 S 25[29] (fig; v. I צרר); חָתֻם בצ׳ פִּשְׁעִי Jb 14[17] (i.e. hidden, forgotten Hi Bu al.; >al. *treasured up*), צ׳ נָקוּב Hg 1[6] (v. I. נקב).

†מֵצַר **n.[m.]** **straits, distress**,—abs. מִן־הַמֵּצַר קָרָאתִי ψ 118[5]; pl. הַמְּצָרִים La 1[3] *the distresses*, of conquered Judah; cstr מְצָרֵי שְׁאוֹל ψ 116[3] *the straits* of Sheol, i.e. the worst possible (‖ חֶבְלֵי־מָוֶת).

† II. צָרַר **vb.** **shew hostility toward, vex** (NH צַר *foe*, Ar ضَرَّ *harm, damage*, Sab. צר *war, foe* Mordtm[Him Inschr 60.71] SabDenkm[24] CIS[iv 174, 1.6] Hom[Chrest 125]; Eth. ፀረረ: *be hostile*, in der. spec and deriv.; As. *ṣarâru*, *be hostile*, *ṣarru*, *foe*; Ar ضَرَّة, As. *ṣirritu*, Syr. ܥܪܬܐ, all = *rival-wife*, so (? Heb infl) 𝔗 צָרָא 1 S 1[6], v. esp. Lag Deceased Wife's Sister, GGN 1882 No 13, = ML 125 ff Dr[1 S 1, 6]),—**Qal** *Pf* 3 pl. וּצָרְרוּ Nu 33[55] consec, sf. צְרָרוּנִי ψ 129[1.2], *Impf.* 3 ms יָצֹר Is 11[13], *Inf abs* צָרוֹר Nu 25[17]; *Pt act* צֹרֵר 10[9], pl. sf. צֹרְרַי ψ 31[12]+, etc;—*shew hostility toward, treat with enmity, vex, harass*, c. acc. pers Is 11[13] Nu 10[9] 25[17], once c לְ pers v[18], also pt. as subst. (cstr or c sf.) *vexer, harasser*, Am 5[12] Is 11[13] Ex 23[22] (E), ψ 6[8] 7[5.7] 8[3] 10[5] 23[5] 31[12] 42[11] 69[20] 74[4.23] 143[12] Est 3[10] 8[1] 9[10.24].—Lv 18[18] v. [צָרַר] sub II. צָרָה, infr.

III. צַר **n.m.**[Nu 10, 9] **adversary, foe**;—abs צַר Am 3[11]+, even c art. הַצַּר Nu 10[9], but also הַצָּר Est 7[4]; צָר Zc 8[10]+, pl. צָרִים La 1[7]; cstr. צָרֵי Ezr 4[1] + Is 9[10] (but read prob צָרוֹ or צָרָיו, cf. Di-Kit Che[Hpt]; al שָׂרֵי), Je 48[5] (del. 𝔊 Hi Gie), Ez 30[16] (but 𝔊 Sm וְנִפְצוּ, so Berthol; Co וְנִפְרְצוּ, so Toy; Krae יָעוּף), sf. צָרַי ψ 3[2], צָרֵיהֶם Ez 39[23], צָרֵימוֹ Dt 32[27], etc.;—*adversary, foe*, Am 3[11] Gn 14[20] Nu 10[9] (P), 24[8] (JE) Dt 32[27] 33[7] Jos 5[13] (JE), 2 S 24[13] Is 9[10] (v supr), Zc 8[10] Ezr 4[1] Ne 4[5] Est 7[6] (אִישׁ צַר ואויב), + 21 t., + ψ 3[2] 13[5] 27[2] 78[42], + 13 t. ψψ, + (of י׳'s foes) 78[66] 97[3]; + (of י׳'s foes) also Is 1[24] 26[11] 59[18] 64[1] Je 46[10] Na 1[2] Dt 32[41.43] Jb 19[11].—Je 48[5] Ez 30[16] v. supr.

†II. [צָרָה] **n.f.** **vexer, rival-wife** (v. reff. sub √; also Ecclus 37[11]);—sf. צָרָתָהּ 1 S 1[6].

†[צָרַר] **vb. denom.** **make a rival-wife**;—**Qal** *Inf. cstr.* לִצְרֹר Lv 18[18] *to make* [her] *a rival-wife* (Lag[GGN, 1882, 406] Dr-Wh[Lv] Baen[Lv]).

III **צרר** (√of foll, cf Ar. طَرَّ *be sharp* (? denom), طُرَرٌ طِرٌّ *sharp-edged hard stone,* As *ṣurtu,* appar. *knife* RJHarper$^{BAS\ II\ 436}$, Syr ܛܪܢܳܐ *rock, stone, flint*)

†IV **צַר** **n.[m.]** hard pebble, flint,—כַּצַּר Is 5^{28} (sim. of horses' hoofs; read perhaps כַּצֹּר)

†II **צֹר** **n.[m.]** id,—צ׳ used as knife Ex 4^{25}, in comp, כְּשָׁמִיר חָזָק מִצֹּר Ez 3^{9}; pl. חַרְבוֹת צֻרִים Jos 5$^{2.3}$ *knives of flint*—צוּר חַרְבּוֹ ψ 89^{44} is dub, צ׳ usu taken as=צֹר, and then either *flint of his sword* (i e sword sharp as flint, Bae), or *edge* (like flint) *of his sword* (most), We leaves untransl, חֶלְקַת הַצֻּרִים v I חֶלְקָה—Jb 22^{24} v. I צוּר sub V צור I צֹר v p 862.

†II **צְרוֹר** **n.m.** pebble,—צ׳ 2 S 17^{13}, also Am 9^{9} (where perhaps fig for grain of wheat, in metaph of winnowed Isr, cf Dr Now al, >pebble retained in sieve Preuschen$^{ZAW\ xv\ (1895),\ 24}$, cf. on custom Wetzst$^{ZPV\ xiv\ (1891),\ 2f}$).

†III. **צְרוֹר** **n.pr.m.** grandfather of Ḳish 1 S 9^{1}, Αρεδ, 𝔊L Σαρα.

†[**צְרֵרָה**] **n.pr.loc.** צְרֵרָתָה Ju 7^{22} (Γαραγαθα, 𝔊L καὶ ἦν συνηγμένη), usu thought corrupt for צְרֵדָתָה, and in any case prob =צָרְתָן, q.v. (GFM).

†**צֶרֶת** **n.pr.m.** in Judah 1 Ch 4^{7}, Αρεθ, A Σαρεθ, 𝔊L Σαρηθ.

†**צֶרֶת הַשַּׁחַר** **n.pr.loc.** assigned to Reuben Jos 13^{19}, Σεραδα και Σειων, 𝔊L Σαρθ; cf. mod. *es-Sara,* on spur of Mt. *'Attârûs,* E of Dead Sea Buhl$^{Geogr\ 268}$

†**צָרְתָן** **n.pr.loc.** in Jordan valley, near ford, Buhl$^{Geogr\ 181}$, exact site unknown; Jos 3^{16} (Καθιαιρειν, 𝔊L Καριαθιαρειμ), 1 K 7^{46} (Σειρα, 𝔊L Σαρθαν)=צְרֵדָתָה 2 Ch 4^{17} (Αναμε [i.e. ἀνὰ μέσον] σιρδαθαι; Σα(ρι)δαθα; is Chr right?); צָרְתָנָה 1 K 4^{12} (Σεσαθαν, 𝔊L Σαρθαν)—cf צְרֵרָתָה Ju 7^{22}, appar same place; identity with צְרֵדָה 1 K 11^{26} is usually assumed, but not proven.

ק

ק, *Ḳôph,* 19th letter;=100 in post B. Heb

[קא] v קיא קָאם v קום.

†**קָאַת, קָאָת** **n.[f.]** a bird, usu. pelican (cf 𝔊 Lv Dt ψ, 𝔙 ψ (der by Thes from [קוא], קיא (v Ko$^{II\ 1,\ 171}$, and, on ת, Ges^{§80g}), as *throwing up* food from its crop for its young), but sea-fowl improb in ψ Is, NH קָאַת, 𝔗 קָאתָא *id.*), —abs הַקָּאַת Lv 11^{18}=Dt 14^{17}, as unclean, קָאַת (van d H Gi; Baer קָאָת) Is 34^{11} Zp 2^{14}, as inhabiting ruins, cstr קְאַת מִדְבָּר ψ 102^{7}, sim. of loneliness

קַב v. I קבב

I. **קבב** (√of foll; cf Ar. قُبَّةٌ *arch, dome* (hence '*al-cove*'), *vaulted tent,* esp *tent of honour* Goldziher$^{ZMG\ xlvii\ (1893)\ 74f}$ Jacob$^{Beduinenleben\ (2)\ 86,\ 245}$, Syr. ܩܒܳܐ *vault, dome,* ܩܘܒܬܳܐ *id, vaulted tent* PS$^{3466\ b}$; so NH קוּבָּה, specif. *lupanar;* 𝔗 קוּבְתָא *vault* (esp *vaulted* heavens), perh also As. *kabâbu, shield*)

†**קַב** **n.[m.]** ḳab (NH *id;* Syr ܩܰܒܳܐ; Talm. קַבָּא;—a measure of capacity, BH only dry measure, רֹבַע הַקַּב 2 K 6^{25} ¼ *kab,* on size of קַב =4 לֹג = ⅙ סְאָה = 1/18 הִין = c 2 litres v. Now Arch I 202f Benz$^{Arch\ 182}$.

†**קֻבָּה** **n.f.** large vaulted tent;—abs. Nu 25^{8} (P) Ke al. Zimri's *princely tent,* >Thes al. *large tent* used as *lupanar* (cf. NH)

†II. [**קָבַב**] **vb. utter a curse against, curse** (cf [ב]יקו Ecclus 41^{7}),—**Qal** *curse,* c acc, usu pers: *Pf* 3 ms sf. קַבֹּה (Ges^{§58d}) Nu 23^{8}, 2 ms. sf consec וְקַבֹּתוֹ v^{27}, *Impf.* 3 ms. וַיִּקֹּב (Ges^{§67g}) Lv 24^{11} (c acc אֶת־הַשֵּׁם); 2 ms. sf תִקָּבֶנּוּ Nu 23^{25} (+Inf abs); 1 s. אֶקֹּב v^{8} (obj. om), וָאֶקּוֹב נָוֵהוּ Jb 5^{3} (prob corrupt; 𝔊 Du rd. וַיִּרְקַב, cf. Me Bi Siegf Beer, וַיִּפָּקֵד Bu, וַיִּקַּב Che JQ July 1897, 575; וַיִּבֹּלְ Bev$^{JPhil\ xxvi\ 308}$ (cf. Is 24^{13} Je 51^{2} Na 2^{3})), 3 mpl sf יִקְּבֻהוּ Jb 3^{8} Pr 11^{26} 24^{24}; *Imv.* ms. קָבָה־לִּי (Ges^{§67o} Ko$^{I\ 329e}$) Nu 22$^{11.17}$, sf. 3 ms. וְקָבְנוֹ־לִי (Ges^{§67o}) 23^{13} (all JE; all +לִי as dat comm, so also v^{27} vid *Pf* supr); *Inf. abs* קֹב v^{25} (+Impf.); *Inf. cstr* לָקֹב v^{11} 24^{10}.

קבה (√of foll (cf. Dl$^{Pr\ 113}$ Ko$^{II\ 1,\ 185}$): Ar. قِبَةٌ *echinus,* i e *stomachi pars pelliculata;* Syr. ܩܒܳܐ is *collect, contain,* water, ܡܩܒܝܳܐ (ܩܒܳܐ) *cistern;* Eth. ቀበወ: *have dropsy;* NH קֵבָה=BH)

קֵבָה, sf. קֵבָתָהּ (Kö[l.c.] cf. Ges[§10h]) **n.f.** **stomach, belly**;—**1.** abs. הַקּ׳ of sacrificial victim, assigned to priest Dt 18[3], 𝔊 τὸ ἤνυστρον, i.e. *fourth stomach* of ruminants (cf. Dr), 𝔙 *ventriculum*. **2.** sf. of woman, appar. more gen., *belly* Nu 25[8] (P).

†[קִבֵּל] **vb. Pi. receive, take** (late) (Aram. loan-word (and in Aram. denom.) Gerber[32], cf. Aram. (לְ)קֳבֵיל *in front*, ܩܘܒܠ ܠܩܒܠ *opposite*, BAram. לָקֳבֵל *before*, OAram. Palm. לקבל *over against*, Nab. *id.*, *in view of*; also Sab. לקבל *in view of* CIS[iv, No. 79, ll. 2.4.5.8], As. *ḳablu*, *encounter*; verbs are: Sab. קבל *accept*, DHM[ZMG xxix (1875), 615; xxx (1876), 672]; Ar. قَبِلَ *be in front, opposite*, قَبَّلَ *accept, admit*; Eth. ቀበለ:, esp. III. 2, *go to meet, accept*; NH קִבֵּל *accuse*, Pi.=BH; Aram. קַבֵּל, ܩܰܒܶܠ *receive*);—*Pf.* 3 ms. קִבֵּל Est 4[4] + (9[27] Qr קִבְּלוּ); 3 pl. קִבְּלוּ Ezr 8[30]; *Impf.* 3 ms. sf. וַיְקַבְּלֵם 1 Ch 12[19] (v[18] van d. H.); 3 mpl. וַיְקַבְּלוּ 2 Ch 29[16.22]; 1 pl. נְקַבֵּל Jb 2[10.10]; *Imv.* ms. קַבֵּל Pr 19[20], קַבֵּל־ 1 Ch 21[11];—**1.** *take*, c. acc. rei 2 Ch 29[22] Ezr 8[30]; acc. om. 2 Ch 29[16], + לְ reflex. = choose 1 Ch 21[11]; *receive*, c. acc. pers. 12[19] (van d. H. v[18]). **2.** *accept*, c. acc. rei Jb 2[10.10]; ק׳ מוּסָר Pr 19[20]; acc. om. Est 4[4]. **3.** *accept, assume*, an obligation, sq. cl., Est 9[23], sq. inf. v[27] (+ עַל reflex.). **Hiph.** *Pt.* fpl. מַקְבִּילֹת *shew oppositeness*, i.e. correspond, one to (אֶל) another Ex 26[5] 36[12] (both P).

†[קֹבֶל] **n.[m.]** **1.** **something in front**, spec. an **attacking-engine** (cf. قُبُل *front*; ܩܘܒܠܐ, *advance* to attack, so הקביל Ecclus 12[5]), Ez 26[9] מְחִי קָבָלּוֹ the stroke of his *attacking-engine* (on the form *ḳobollô*, from קֹבֶל for *ḳŭbŭl*, see Ol[§169] Kö[ii. 88 f.]; and cf. קְטַנִּי from קֹטֶן for *ḳŭṭŭn*, קָרְבְּכֶם, קָטָבְךָ; and on the בְּ, Ges[§93q]). **2.** cstr. קָבָל־עָם (*ḳobol*) 2 K 15[10], explained formerly as *before* the people, i.e. publicly (cf. BAram קֳבֵל *before*); but the Aram. is surprising, and הָעָם needed: rd. בְּיִבְלְעָם *in Ibleam*, with 𝔊L (confirming earlier conj. of Gr[G ii. 1. 99] Sta[G i. 575]), Dr Klo Benz Kit al.

†קָבַע **vb.** dub., perhaps **rob** (syn. גזל, so Rabb. (rare), v. De[Pr 22, 23]);—**Qal** *Pf.* 3 ms. consec. וְקָבַע Pr 22[23], subj. י׳, c. acc. pers. + rei; c. acc. pers. alone 1 pl. בַּמֶּה קְבַעֲנוּךָ Mal 3[8] (obj. י׳); *Impf.* 3 ms. הֲיִקְבַּע אָדָם אֱלֹהִים v[8]; *Pt. act.* אַתֶּם קֹבְעִים אֹתִי v[8.9]; sf. קֹבְעֵיהֶם Pr 22[23] *those robbing them*.—In Mal 𝔊 We עָקַב *circumvent*.

†קֻבַּעַת **n.f. cup** (perhaps loan-word from As. [*ḳabu'tu*], pl. *ḳabûâtê*, prob. *cups, goblets*; cf. Ar. قُبَعَةٌ *flower-cup, calyx*);—cstr. ק׳ כּוֹס הַתַּרְעֵלָה Is 51[17] cf. v[22] (both fig., and כּוֹס in both prob. explanatory gloss, v. Comm.).

קָבַץ[127] **vb. gather, collect** (syn. אָסַף) (Ar. قَبَضَ *grasp, seize*; Sab. קבץ *harvest*, in דק׳, attrib. of ʿAttar, acc. to Fell[ZMG liv (1900), 237 f.]; Eth. ቀበጸ: is *fail, despair*; NH קִבֵּץ=BH);—†**Qal** *Pf.* 3 ms. ק׳ 1 K 20[1]; *Impf.* 3 ms. יִקְבָּץ־ ψ 41[7], וַיִּקְבֹּץ Gn 41[48]+, etc.; *Imv.* ms. קְבֹץ 1 K 18[19], mpl. קִבְצוּ 1 S 7[5]+; *Inf. cstr.* sf. לְקָבְצִי Zp 3[8]; *Pt. act.* קֹבֵץ Ez 22[19] Pr 13[11]; *pass.* pl. קְבוּצִים Ne 5[16];—*gather, collect*: **1.** c. acc. rei, grain Gn 41[35.48] (E), booty Dt 13[17] (+ אֶל loc.), money 2 Ch 24[5] (+ מִן pers.), so Ez 16[31] (Gr Toy Krae, rdg. לְקַבֵּץ fr. לְקַלֵּס, cf. 𝔊 𝔖 Symm); acc. om. קֹבֵץ Pr 13[11] *one gathering* by degrees; fig. לִבּוֹ יִקְבָּץ־אָוֶן לוֹ ψ 41[7] *his heart gathereth wickedness to itself*. **2.** usu. c. acc. pers. *gather, assemble*, + ה loc. 1 S 7[5] 29[1] (for battle); + אֶל loc. 1 K 18[20] Ezr 8[15] Est 2[3]; + אֶל pers. 2 S 3[21] Hb 2[5] (in fig.; ‖ אָסַף); + עַל (= אֶל) pers. 1 K 11[24]; + אֶל pers. et loc. 1 K 18[19] 2 Ch 32[6]; + מִן loc. 2 Ch 23[2], cf. Ezr 7[28]; acc. pers. alone 1 K 22[6] = 2 Ch 18[5], 2 K 10[18], Ne 7[5] (+ inf. purpose), Jo 2[16] (‖ אָסַף), 2 Ch 15[9] 24[5] 25[5]; pass. c. עַל + שָׁם of work Ne 5[16]; for י׳'s judgment Zp 3[8] (‖ אָסַף), Ez 22[20] cf. v[19] (+ אֶל־תּוֹךְ; fig. of metals into furnace); specif. for war, battle, Ju 12[4] 1 S 28[1] 2 S 2[30] 1 K 20[1] 2 K 6[24]; + לַצָּבָא 1 S 28[1] (29[1] v. supr.). †**Niph.** *Pf.* 3 pl. נִקְבְּצוּ Jos 10[6]+, etc.; *Impf.* 2 ms. תִּקָּבֵץ Ez 29[5]; 3 mpl. וַיִּקָּבְצוּ 1 S 7[6]+, etc.; *Imv.* mpl. הִקָּבְצוּ Gn 49[2]+; *Inf. cstr.* הִקָּבֵץ Ezr 10[7]+; *Pt.* pl. נִקְבָּצִים Je 40[15], sf. נִקְבָּצָיו Is 56[8];—**1.** intrans. *assemble, gather* 1 S 25[1] Gn 49[2] Is 45[20] 48[14] 49[18] 60[4] Jo 4[11] 2 Ch 20[4] (+ inf. purpose) 32[4]; for war 1 S 28[4] Jos 10[6] (c. אֶל *against*); c. ה loc. 1 S 7[6], acc. loc. Ezr 10[7.9] 2 Ch 15[10]; c. אֶל pers. *unto* Je 40[15] 1 Ch 13[2] Ezr 10[1] Ne 4[14], cf. 2 Ch 13[7] (עַל for אֶל); אֶל pers. + ה loc. 1 Ch 11[1]; c. יַחְדָּו Ho 2[2] Is 43[9] (‖ אָסַף), ψ 102[23]; of birds and beasts Is 34[15] (c. שָׁם), Ez 39[17]. **2.** pass. *be gathered* Is 60[7] (of flocks, + לְ pers.), Est 2[8] (+ אֶל loc.), v[19]; pt. c. sf. pers. Is 56[8]; Ez 29[5] (‖ אסף) rd. תִּקָּבֵר Hi (not Sm) Co Berthol Toy Krae. **Pi.** 51

Pf. 3 ms sf וקבצך Dt 30[3] consec, קִבַּצְתִּם Mi 4[12] ψ 107[3], קִבַּצָן Is 34[16], 3 fs קִבָּצָה Mi 1[7], etc; *Impf* יְקַבֵּץ Is 11[12] 40[11], etc; *Imv.* ms. sf קַבְּצֵנוּ 1 Ch 16[35], ψ 106[47], *Inf. abs.* קַבֵּץ Mi 2[12]; *cstr.* קַבֵּץ Is 66[18] etc, *Pt.* מְקַבֵּץ Na 3[18]+, etc,—*gather together* **1.** usu of י׳ *gathering* his dispersed people (acc), sts. under fig of flock: Mi 2[12]+inf abs (|| אָסֹף), 4[6] Zp 3[19 20] Je 31[10] Zc 10[8] Is 54[7] 56[8a], cf also 40[11], c acc + מִן loc Dt 30[3 4] Je 23[3] 29[14] 31[8] 32[37] Ez 11[17]+6 t Ez+ 37[21] (מִסָּבִיב), Is 11[12] 43[5] Zc 10[10] Ne 1[9] ψ 106[47], cf || 1 Ch 16[35], ψ 107[3], acc + עַל pers Is 56[8b] (cf **Niph.** *Pt*), = (*gather* and) restrain Ho 8[10] (c acc alone), of י׳ *gathering* dispersed Egyptians, acc + מִן loc Ez 29[13], *gathering* the nations (acc) for judgment Mi 4[12] Is 66[18] Jo 4[2]; *gathering* lovers of Jerus. (under fig of harlot) Ez 16[37.37] (עַל + מִסָּבִיב pers *against*), *gathering* beasts into Edom Is 34[15] **2.** men subj: מצרים תקבצם מף תְּקַבְּרֵם Ho 9[6] (cf Ez 29[5] **Niph.**, supr), Ne 13[11], c acc rei Mi 1[7] (+ מִן), Is 22[9] 62[9] Pr 28[8], אֵין מְקַבֵּץ *none that gathereth* Is 13[14] (acc om), Na 3[18] (*id*), Je 49[5] (sq לַנֹּדֵד, cf **3** ל ad fin). **3** perh (*gather* and so) *take away* (= אָסַף **4**), Na 2[11] Jo 2[6], v פָּארוּר **Pu.** *Pt* מְקֻבֶּצֶת Ez 38[8] (c מִן) of land (for people) of Isr †**Hithp.** *gather together* (intrans), *be gathered together* *Pf* 3 pl הִתְקַבְּצוּ Ju 9[47] 1 S 7[7] (+ ה loc), *Impf* 3 mpl. וַיִּתְקַבְּצוּ 1 S 8[4] 22[2] (+ אֶל pers), יִתְקַ׳ Is 44[11], for battle, war, *Imv.* mpl. הִתְקַבְּצוּ Je 49[14], *Impf* also Jos 9[2] (c. יַחְדָּו, + inf. purpose), + אַחֲרֵי pers 2 S 2[25]

†[קִבּוּץ] **n.m.** (si vera l) **heap**,—pl sf. קִבּוּצַיִךְ Is 57[13] *thy heaps* (of idols); but read perh שִׁקּוּצַיִךְ Weir in Che, Che[Hpt] Kit-Di Marti.

†[קְבֻצָה] **n.f. a gathering**;—cstr. קְבֻצַת כֶּסֶף . . . אֶל־תּוֹךְ כּוּר Ez 22[20] (after קֹבֵץ אֶתְכֶם, sq. אֶקְבֹּץ)

†קַבְצְאֵל, [יְקַבְצְאֵל] **n. pr. loc.** in S of Judah (*gathering of Ēl*, or *Ēl gathereth*, cf Sab, of *ʿAttar*, sub √supr),—ק׳ Jos 15[21] 2 S 23[20] = 1 Ch 11[22], Καβ(ε)σεηλ, etc; וּבִיקַבְ׳ Ne 11[25], 𝔊L Καβσεηλ

†קִבְצַיִם **n.pr.loc.** (Theis *two heaps*),—Levite city in Ephr Jos 21[22] (𝔊B om, A Καβσαειμ, 𝔊L Καβσειμ), = יָקְמְעָם [q v sub קום] 1 Ch 6[53]

קָבַר $_{133}$ **vb. bury** (NH *id*; Ph. קבר, *bury*, קבר *tomb*, Ar. قَبَرَ, As. *kibiru*, Aram. קְבַר, ܩܒܰܪ, Nab קבר, all *bury*, Palm. Nab. קברא *tomb*, so Sab קבר Hom[Chrest 126], Lihy. קבר *bury*, DHM[Epigr Denkm. No. 35, 2, 3], cf. (הם)מקבר *burial-place* CIS[iv, No 20, 1 2 4]);—**Qal** $_{88}$ *Pf.* 3 ms. ק׳ Gn 23[19], 2 ms sf. consec וּקְבַרְתַּנִי 47[30], etc; *Impf.* 3 ms וַיִּקְבֹּר Dt 34[6] 2 K 21[26], etc, *Imv.* קְבֹר Gn 23[6]+, etc, *Inf abs* קָבוֹר Dt 21[23]; *cstr.* לִקְבּוֹר Je 19[11]+, etc; *Pt act* קֹבֵר 2 K 9[10]+, etc; *pass* קָבוּר 1 K 13[31], pl קְבֻרִים Ec 8[10] *bury*, acc. pers, bones, etc., usu. c בְּ loc, 2 S 2[32] 1 K 13[31.31] Gn 23[6] Jos 24[30.32 32] Ju 2[9]+33 t; c בֵּיתוֹ loc. 2 Ch 33[20] (בְּגַן־בֵּיתוֹ || 2 K 21[18], also בְּבֵיתוֹ 1 S 25[1] 1 K 2[34]); c שָׁם Nu 11[34], תַּחַת 1 S 31[13] = 1 Ch 10[12], pregn c. אֶל loc Gn 23[19] 25[9] Ez 39[11]; אֶל־אֲבֹתַי Gn 49[29], cf. עִם־אֲבוֹתָיו 2 K 12[22] 15[7] 2 Ch 25[28] 26[23] (v also **Niph.**, and תָּבוֹא אֶל־אֲבֹתֶיךָ Gn 15[15]), c שָׁמָּה Gn 23[13] 49[31 31 31] 50[5]; c acc. pers. alone 2 S 2[4.5]+22 t; + מִלְּפָנַי Gn 23[4 8], pass. Ec 8[10], acc. om 2 K 9[10]+3 t.+ (c בְּ) 2 S 4[12]. **Niph.** $_{39}$ *Impf* 3 ms יִקָּבֵר Je 22[19], etc;—*be buried* Gn 15[15] Je 8[2] 16[4.6] 25[33] (+ אסף), so rd perh Ez 29[5] for תִקָּבֵץ (+ *id.*), קְבוּרַת חֲמוֹר יִקָּ׳ Je 22[19], usu. c בְּ loc Gn 35[19] Ju 8[32] + 6 t Ju, 2 S 17[23] 1 K 2[10.34] + 16 t K Ch (+ עִם־מַלְכֵי יִשׂרָ׳ 1 K 14[31] 15[24]+6 t.; עִם־אֲבוֹתָיו 2 K 13[13] 14[16]), c שָׁם Nu 20[1]+3 t, c תַּחַת, מִתַּחַת Gn 35[8] †**Pi.** *bury* (in masses), c acc *Impf.* 3 fs sf תְּקַבְּרֵם Ho 9[6], *Inf. cstr.* לְקַבֵּר 1 K 11[15]; *Pt* pl מְקַבְּרִים Nu 33[4] Ez 39[14]; as n. intens, of office, *burier*, sg. מְקַבֵּר Je 14[16], pl הַמְ׳ Ez 39[15]. †**Pu.** *Pf.* 3 ms שָׁמָּה קֻבַּר אַבְרָהָם Gn 25[10]

קֶבֶר $_{67}$ **n.m.** [1 K 13, 31] **grave, sepulchre**;—abs. ק׳ Gn 23[4]+, קָבֶר 1 K 14[13]+; cstr. קֶבֶר Ju 8[32]+; sf. קִבְרִי Gn 50[5], etc, pl קְבָרִים Ex 14[11]+, cstr. קִבְרֵי Je 26[23]+, sf. קִבְרֵיהֶם 8[1]; also קְבָרוֹת Jb 21[32], cstr קִבְרוֹת Ne 2[3]+, sf קִבְרֹתָיו Ez 32[22] 2 Ch 16[14], etc,—*grave, sepulchre*, Ju 8[32] 2 S 2[32] 1 K 13[22]+; אֲחֻזַּת ק׳ Gn 23[4.9.20] 49[30] 50[13], hewn out (חָצַב) Is 22[16 16]; מִבֶּטֶן לַקֶּבֶר אוּבָל Jb 10[19]; fig וַתְּהִי־לִי אִמִּי קִ׳ Je 20[17], שֹׁכְבֵי ק׳ ψ 88[6] the slain *lying in grave*; הַיֹּשְׁבִים בַּקְּבָרִים Is 65[4] *they who sit in the tombs* (occult rite, prob in necromancy, etc, cf Che and RS[Sem i 180 ff; 2nd ed. 197 ff]), קֶבֶר בְּנֵי הָעָם 2 K 23[6] i e burial-place of common people, so קִבְרֵי בְּנֵי הָעָם Je 26[23]; pl. intens Jb 17[1], also of stately (royal) sepulchre 2 K 22[20] = 2 Ch 34[28], Ne 3[16] 2 Ch 16[14] cf 35[24]; Jb 21[32]; conceived as in lower world Ez 32[22.23 25.26], || אֲבַדּוֹן ψ 88[12]; ψ 49[12] rd קִרְבָּם for קִבְרָם Vrss and most; ק׳ פָּתוּחַ sim. of quiver Je 5[16]; fig. ק׳ פּ׳ גְּרוֹנָם ψ 5[10], of exile Ez 37[12.12 13.13].

†קִבְרוֹת הַתַּאֲוָה **n.pr.loc.** Μνήματα (τῆς) ἐπιθυμίας: a station in wilderness (*the graves of desire*, cf. Nu 11^{34} and תַּאֲוָה p. 16 supr.);—Nu 11$^{34.35}$, קִבְרֹת הַתּ׳ 33$^{16.17}$ Dt 9^{22}.

†[קְבֻרָה], and (4 t.) קְבוּרָה **n.f. grave, burial**;—abs. קְבוּרָה Is 14^{20} + 2 t.; cstr. קְבוּרַת Je 22^{19}, קְבֻרַת Gn 35^{20} +; sf. קְבֻרָתוֹ Dt 34^{6} +;—**1.** *grave* Gn 35$^{20.20}$ 47^{30} Dt 34^{6} 1 S 10^{2} 2 K 9^{28} 21^{26} 23^{30} Ez 32$^{23.24}$; שְׂדֵה הַקּ׳ 2 Ch 26^{23}. **2.** *burial*, Is 14^{20} Ec 6^{3}; קְבוּרַת חֲמוֹר Je 22^{19}.

קָבְתָה v. קֵבָה.

†I. [קָדַד] **vb. bow down** (As. (including TelAm.) *kadâdu, bow down*); — **Qal** *Impf.* 3 ms. וַיִּקֹּד Gn 24^{26} +, etc.;—usu. + וַיִּשְׁתַּחוּ etc.; in worship of י׳ Gn 24$^{26.48}$ Ex 4^{31} 12^{27} 34^{8} Nu 22^{31} 2 Ch 20^{18} 29^{30} Ne 8^{6}; homage to man of rank Gn 43^{28}, king 1 S 24^{9} (Gi v^{8}), 28^{14} 1 K 1$^{16.31}$; to י׳ + king 1 Ch 29^{20}.

II. קדד (√of foll.; mng. dub.; NH קָדְקֹד = BH; As. *kakkadu* = קָדְקֹד; cf. JAram.).

†קָדְקֹד **n.[m.] head, crown of head**;—קּ׳ abs. Dt 33^{20} Je 2^{16}, cstr. Is 3^{17} +; sf. קָדְקֳדוֹ 2 S 14^{25} Jb 2^{7}; קָדְקֳדֶךָ Dt 28^{35};—esp. poet. Gn 49^{26} = Dt 33^{16}, ψ 7^{17}, קּ׳ שֵׂעָר 68^{22} *hairy crown* or *scalp* (all ‖ רֹאשׁ), Is 3^{17} Je 2^{16} 48^{45} (‖ פֵּאָה), so rd. also Nu 24^{17} for וְקַרְקַר (‖ *id.*), v. Ew Di Pat al., Dt 33^{20}; in prose only מִכַּף רַגְלְ וְעַד־קּ׳ Dt 28^{35} 2 S 14^{25} Jb 2^{7}.

†קִדָּה **n.f.** a spice, usu. **cassia** (𝔊 𝔙 𝔗 cf. Di^{Ex}; √dub.; perh. foreign word);—merchandise Ez 27^{19}; ingredient of sacred oil Ex 30^{24} (P):—cf. Dioscor.$^{\text{De Mater. Med. i. 12}}$ (κασσία = ἡ κιττώ), Theophr$^{\text{Hist. Plant. ix. 5}}$ Plin$^{\text{NH xii. 19 (42 ff.)}}$; v. also Schröd$^{\text{Ph. Spr. 126}}$ Lewy$^{\text{Fremdw. 36}}$.

†[קָדַח] **vb. be kindled, kindle** (NH *id.*, also *bore*, Aram. קְדַח, ܩܕܚ *bore, kindle;* Ar. قَدَحَ *strike fire* (with flint, etc.); Ph. מקדח is *lamp-lighter* (in temple) acc. to CIS$^{\text{i. No. 352, l. 3}}$);—**Qal 1.** *be kindled: Pf.* 3 fs. אֵשׁ קָדְחָה בְאַפִּי Dt 32^{22} Je 15^{14} 17^{4} (rdg. קָדְחָה for קְדַחְתֶּם), all of י׳'s wrath. **2.** act. *kindle; Inf. cstr.* כִּקְדֹחַ אֵשׁ הֲמָסִים Is 64^{1} (v. [הָמָס]); *Pt.* קֹדְחֵי אֵשׁ 50^{11}.

†קַדַּחַת **n.f. fever**;—Dt 28^{22} Lv 26^{16}.

†אֶקְדָּח **n.[m.]** perh. **fiery glow, sparkle**; אַבְנֵי אֶקְדָּח Is 54^{12} i.e. carbuncles (?);—𝔊 λίθους κρυστάλλου, 𝔙 *lapides sculptos*, Aq Theod Sym.

קדם (√of foll.; *be before, in front,* cf. As. *ḳudmu, front, former time;* Ar. قَدَمَ *precede* (so Eth. ቀደመ:), iv, v. *be bold and foremost in attack* (קֶדֶם **1 a**); Sab. קדם *begin* Hom$^{\text{Chrest. 126}}$, *march forth, advance,* CIS$^{\text{iv, No. 79, l. 9}}$ Sab Denkm$^{\text{No. 9, l. 2.4.6.7.8.9}}$, (הו)קדמ *front* CIS$^{\text{iv, No. 276, l. 2}}$; Ph. כקדם *as formerly* (?); OAram. קדם *before,* so Palm. Nab.; BAram. 𝔗 קֳדָם *before;* Syr. ܩܕܡ *precede;* NH קָדַם *be in front*).

†קֶדֶם **n.[m.] front, east, aforetime**;—abs. קּ׳ Dt 33^{27} +, קֵדְמָה Ju 8^{10} +; cstr. קֶדֶם Pr 8^{22}; once pl. cstr. קַדְמֵי v^{23};—**1.** loc. **a.** *front,* מִקּ׳ Is 9^{11} *from the front* (i.e. East), *in front* (opp. מֵאָחוֹר), אָחוֹר וָקּ׳ ψ 139^{5} *behind and before;* קּ׳ אֶהֱלֹךְ Jb 23^{8} *I go forward* (opp. אָחוֹר). **b.** *East:* הַר־הַקּ׳ Gn 10^{30} (J) *mount of the East;* בְּנֵי־קּ׳ = dwellers in the E., tribes E. or NE. of Canaan Gn 29^{1} (E), Ju 6$^{3.33}$ 7^{12} 8^{10} 1 K 5^{10} Is 11^{14} Je 49^{28} Ez 25$^{4.10}$ Jb 1^{3}; הַרְרֵי קּ׳ Nu 23^{7}, v. Di Sachau$^{\text{Reise (1883), 159 ff. 165 ff.}}$ Dr in Hast.^{PETHOR}; אֶרֶץ קּ׳ Gn 25^{6} (J); מָלְאוּ מִקֶּדֶם Is 2^{6} *they are full from the E.* (ins. prob. מִקְסָם, קֶסֶם, or < קֹסְמִים before מִקּ׳, cf. Lo De Du Che^{Hpt} Di-Kit); elsewh. מִקּ׳ = *eastward:* (1) *in the E.* Gn 2^{8}; (2) *on the E.* (side) 12^{8} (J) Zc 14^{4}; מִקּ׳ לְ *on the E. of* Gn 3^{24} (J), 12^{8} (J), Nu 34^{11} (P), Jos 7^{2} (JE), Ju 8^{11} Ez 11^{23} Jon 4^{5}; (3) *eastward,* c. vb. of motion Gn 11^{2} 13^{11} (both J). **2.** temp., *ancient time, aforetime:* **a.** הַרְרֵי קּ׳ Dt 33^{15} *ancient mts.,* cf. אֱלֹהֵי קּ׳ v^{27}, בִּימֵי קּ׳ Is 19^{11}, בִּשְׁמֵי שְׁמֵי־קּ׳ ψ 68^{34}. **b.** מַלְכֵי־קּ׳ ψ 44^{2} *in ancient days;* cf. מִימֵי קּ׳ *from of old* Is 23^{7} Mi 7^{20} La 1^{7} 2^{17}, Is 37^{26} = לְמִימֵי קּ׳ 2 K 19^{25} (v. מִן **9 b** (2)); כִּימֵי קּ׳ Is 51^{9} Je 46^{26}; יַרְחֵי קּ׳ Jb 29^{2} *months of old.* **c.** מִקּ׳ *from of old* Mi 5^{1} Is 45^{21} 46^{10} Hb 1^{12} Ne 12^{46} ψ 74^{12} 77^{12}; מִנִּי־קּ׳ 78^{2} *springing out of, derived from, ancient times* (cf. Dr); יָמִים מִקּ׳ 77^{6} 143^{5} *days from of old.* **d.** קּ׳ alone, as adv. *anciently, of old* ψ 74^{2} 119^{152}; כְּקּ׳ Je 30^{20} La 5^{21}; יֹשֵׁב קּ׳ ψ 55^{20} *he that sitteth* (enthroned from) *of old.* **e.** *beginning,* מִקַּדְמֵי־אָרֶץ Pr 8^{23} *from the beginnings of the earth;* קּ׳ מִפְעָלָיו Pr 8^{22} *the beginning of his works* (‖ רֵאשִׁית).

†[קָדַם] **vb. Pi. denom.** (Gerber ^{130}) **come or be in front, meet**;—*Pf.* 1 s. קִדַּמְתִּי Jon 4^{2} ψ 119^{147}; 3 pl. קִדְּמוּ Dt 23^{5} +, etc.; *Impf.* 3 ms. sf. יְקַדְּמֵנִי ψ 59^{11}; 3 fs. sf. תְּקַדְּמֶךָּ ψ 88^{14}; 1 s. אֲקַדֵּם Mi 6^{6}; *Imv.* ms. קַדְּמָה ψ 17^{13};—**1. a.** *meet, confront* (with hostility) c. acc. pers. 2 S 22$^{6.19}$ = ψ 18$^{6.19}$, Jb 30^{27}, c. acc. פָּנָיו ψ 17^{13}; of hostile approach to city (acc.) 2 K 19^{32} = Is 37^{33}

(+adv acc) **b.** *come to meet* one (acc) as friend, with (ב) sthg. Is 21^{14} Dt 23^{5} Ne 13^{2}, so, as worshippers (acc of 'י), Mi 6^{6}, c acc pers. + rei ψ 21^{4}, so 59^{11} Kt 𝔊 𝔙 (acc. pers. alone Qr), acc. pers alone ψ 79^{8}, acc 'י 88^{14}, acc. פָּנָיו (of 'י) 95^{2}, cf. חֶסֶד וֶאֱמֶת יְקַדְּמוּ פָנֶיךָ 89^{15} (viz, to join themselves to thee) **c.** *meet, receive,* acc pers, Jb 3^{12}. **2. a.** *go before, in front* ψ 68^{26} **b.** *be in front,* 1 S 20^{25} (rd וַיִּקָּדֵם for וַיָּקָם) 𝔊 Ew Th We Dr al **3.** *be beforehand,* c. ב temp ψ 119^{147}, + inf cstr. Jon 4^{2}, *anticipate, forestall,* c acc. rei ψ 119^{148}. **Hiph. 1.** *Impf* 3 fs תַּקְדִּים (We Now GASm תקדם) Am 9^{10} *calamity . . . shall not come in front about us* (בַּעֲדֵינוּ) **2.** *Pf* 3 ms sf הקדימני Jb 41^{3} who *has anticipated me* [God]? 𝔊 Me Bi Bu *confronted me* (rdg וַיִּשְׁלָם for foll ואשלם), Du יְקַדְּמֶנּוּ *confronted him* (the crocodile)

†[קֵ֫דְם], c. ה loc I קֵ֫דְמָה **adv** eastward, to, toward, the E,—Gn 25^{6} (J), Lv 1^{16} 16^{14} Nu 34$^{3\,11\,15}$ Jos 19$^{12\,13}$ (all P), 1 K 7^{39} = 2 Ch 4^{10}, 1 K 17^{3} 2 K 13^{17} Ez 8$^{16\,16}$, + N, S, W, Gn 13^{14} 28^{14} (both J), Nu 2^{3} 3^{38} 10^{5} (N, W, in 𝔊), 34^{10} (all P), also as **n** after פְּאַת = *E. side,* Ex 27^{13} 38^{13} (both P), + W Ez 45^{7} (del Co, rd קֶדֶם Berthol Toy Krae), + N, S, W, Nu 35^{5} Jos 18^{20} so גבול ק' 15^{5} (all P)

†[קַדְמָה] **n.f.** antiquity, former state,— **1.** *antiquity, beginning,* sf קַדְמָתָהּ Is 23^{7} (of Tyre) **2.** *former state,* sf קַדְמָתָן Ez 16$^{55.55}$, קַדְמַתְכֶן v^{55}, pl sf קַדְמוֹתֵיכֶם 36^{11}. **3.** cstr sg = **conj** *before* (temp, Aram) שֶׁקַּדְמַת שָׁלַף ψ 129^{6}

†[קִדְמָה] **n f.** front, East,—only cstr. קִדְמַת as prep. **1.** *in front of, over against* (cf. No$^{ZMG\ xxxiii\ (1879)\ 532}$), Gn 2^{14} (i e from standpoint of writer, really, on geogr grounds, = W of; yet v. Di$^{ed\ 6}$), 4^{16} (both J) **2** *on the E of,* Ez 39^{11}; 1 S 13^{5} may be either.

†II. קֵדְמָה **n.pr.m.** Κεδ(ε)μα, son of Ishmael Gn 25^{15} = 1 Ch 1^{31}.—I. ק' v [קֶדֶם]

קָדִים$_{69}$ **n.m.**$^{Ho\,13,15}$ **East, east wind,**—abs ק' Gn 41^{6}+, c. ה loc. קָדִימָה Ez 11^{1}+, קָדִ֫מָה 48^{4}+,—†**1.** (apart from Ez) *East,* esp רוּחַ (הַ)ק' *wind of the East, east wind,* oft as violent and scorching, from desert on SE, = Ar. *sirocco* (شرقية *eastern*), cf Dr$^{Am\ 4\ 9}$. Ex 10$^{13\,13}$ (JE), 14^{21} (J), Je 18^{17} (sim), Jon 4^{8} ψ 48^{8}; also ק' (רוּחַ om) = *east wind* Gn 41$^{6.23.27}$ (E), Ho 12^{2} 13^{15} Is 27^{8} Jb 15^{2} 27^{21} 38^{24} ψ 78^{26}.—קָדִימָה Hb 1^{9} is dub, usu *eastward,* i.e *forward,* but text prob. corrupt, cf. We Now Da, GASm prop מְקָרִים (v also [מְגַמָּה] p 169 supr) **2.** in Ez (52 t). **a.** *East* רוּחַ הַק' *east wind* 17^{10} 19^{12} 27^{26}; *east side* 42^{16} (+N, S, W), שַׁעַר הַק' 40^{44} (+N, S); פְּאַת ק' 47^{18}, + W 48$^{6.7.8}$, cf. v^{1} (פ' ק') מִפְּ' ק' וְעַד פ' יָמָּה, הַיָּם, but rd. 𝔊 Co Toy al.), + N, S, W, v^{16}, דֶּרֶךְ הַק' i e *toward the E.* 40^{10} + 7 t, לַק' 43^{2}, מִדּ' הַק' 40^{23} *eastward* (+N) 41^{14}, מֵהַק' 42^{9} *on the East* **b** קָדִימָה = *East:* פְּאַת 45^{7} 48^{21} (+W); דֶּרֶךְ הַק' 40^{6}; נְבוּל קָדִימָה קָדִימָה 47^{18}, + W 48^{1} + 8 t, + N, S, W, v^{32}. **c.** as adv. קָדִ֫ימָה *eastward* 11^{1} 44^{1} 47^{1}; + W 45^{7} (del. Berthol Krae), 48^{18}, + N, S, W, v$^{10.17}$; also (הַ)קָּדִים *eastward* 40^{19} 43^{17} 46$^{1\,12}$ 47$^{1.3}$, + N v^{2}

†קְדוּמִים **n.[m.] pl.** only (נַחַל) ק' Ju 5^{21}, meaning dub; 𝔊^{A} n pr. Καδησειμ, 𝔊L Καδημειμ; 𝔊^{B} ἀρχαίων, so 𝔗, AV *ancient* river (lit. *of antiquity*), Bachm al, Be al *of attack* (cf. קָדַם **1 a**), v. further GFM Bu Now Cook$^{Ency\ Bib\ 2683}$.

†[קַדְמוֹן] **adj.** eastern; — fs. הַגְּלִילָה הַקַּדְמוֹנָה Ez 47^{8} *the eastern circuit*

†I קַדְמֹנִי **adj.** former, eastern (on format. v Lag$^{BN\ 105}$ Ba$^{NB,\ §\ 227\ d}$); — abs. ק' 1 S 24^{14} (Gi v^{13}), Jo 2^{20}; -מוֹנִי Ez 10^{19}+, mpl. קַדְמֹנִים Jb 18^{20}, -מוֹנִים Ez 38^{17}, fpl קַדְמֹנִיּוֹת Is 43^{18} Mal 3^{4};— **1.** *former, ancient,* יָמִים ק' Ez 38^{17} *former days;* שָׁנִים ק' Mal 3^{4} (|| יְמֵי עוֹלָם) fpl as n., *former things* Is 43^{18} (|| רִאשֹׁנוֹת), ms as n coll מְשַׁל הַקַּדְמֹנִי 1 S 24^{14} *a proverb of the ancients* **2.** *eastern:* of שַׁעַר Ez 10^{19} 11^{1}, יָם (i e. Dead Sea) 47^{18} and (opp הַיָּם הָאַחֲרוֹן) Zc 14^{8} Jo 2^{20}, mpl. as n. *Easterns, those of the E.* (opp W) Jb 18^{20} (so Ew De Hi Di Bae Du, Vrss *earlier* and later, so Da al. [both future], Bu *former* generations [now in Sheʾôl], and future).

†II קַדְמֹנִי **adj.gent.** c. art הַק', as n.pr coll. (*Easterners*),—Gn 15^{19} *the Kadmonites* (in list of peoples), τοὺς Κελμωναίους, 𝔊L Κεδμωναίους.

†קְדֵמוֹת **n pr.loc.** in Reuben (Moab) Κεδ(α)μωθ, Καδημωθ, etc; Jos 13^{18}, -מוֹת 21^{37} 1 Ch 6^{64}; hence מִדְבַּר קדמות Dt 2^{26} of contiguous desert; —ק' lay N of upper Arnon; not identified; Buhl$^{Geogr\ 268}$ conj *Umm-er-rasâs,* c 10 m. ENE. from Dibon (cf. Tristr$^{Moab\ 140\ ff}$ Bd$^{Pal.\ 3\ (1898),\ 177}$).

†קַדְמִיאֵל **n.pr.m.** Καδμιηλ, 𝔊L Κεδμιηλ; Levite name (*Ēl is the ancient one;* cf. Sab. אלקדם DHM$^{ZMG\ xxxvii\ (1883),\ 374}$);—Ezr 2^{40} = Ne 7^{43}, Ezr 3^{9} Ne 9$^{4.5}$ 10^{10} 12$^{8.24}$.

קָדְקֹד v. II. קדד.

†קָדַר **vb. be dark** (*dull-coloured*, cf. Ar. قَذِرَ *be dirty* (on ذ = ד v. No[ZMG xl (1886), 729]); NH Hiph. (of face) *shew gloom*; 𝔗ᴶ קְדַר *be dark*),—**Qal** *Pf.* consec וְקָדַר Mi 3^{6}; 1 s. קָדַרְתִּי Je 8^{21}, etc., *Pt.* קֹדֵר ψ 35^{14}+; pl. קֹדְרִים Jb 5^{11} 6^{16};—*be dark*, of sky Je 4^{28} (leaden-coloured, as with clouds, v Hithp), of sun and moon Jo 2^{10} 4^{15}; fig of lack of revelation from י׳, וְקָ׳ עֲלֵיהֶם הַיּוֹם Mi 3^{6}; of turbid stream Jb 6^{16}; fig. of mourning (prob *be squalid*, of neglected person and dress of mourner, cf. 2 S 19^{25}) Je 8^{21} 14^{2} (לָאָרֶץ, metaph of gates); Jb 5^{11} 30^{28} (בְּלֹא חַמָּה), ψ 35^{14} 38^{7} 42^{10} 43^{2}. **Hiph. 1.** *darken*: *Pf.* 1 s. consec. וְהִקְדַּרְתִּי Ez 32^{7} (obj. stars), cf. *Impf* 1 s. sf אַקְדִּירִם עָלֶיךָ 32^{8}. **2.** *cause to mourn* וָאַקְדִּר עָלָיו לְבָנוֹן 31^{15}. **Hithp.** *Pf.* 3 pl וְהַשָּׁמַיִם הִתְקַדְּרוּ עָבִים 1 K 18^{45} *and the heavens grew dark with clouds.*

†קַדְרוּת **n.f. darkness, gloom**,—אַלְבִּישׁ שָׁמַיִם ק׳ Is 50^{3} (cf. √, Je 4^{28} 1 K 18^{45}; ‖ שַׂק).

†קְדֹרַנִּית **adv. as mourners**;—Mal 3^{14}.

†קֵדָר **n.pr.gent.** (*swarthy? black*-tented?), Κηδαρ: **1.** tribe of nomads in Arab. desert Is 21^{16} 42^{11} (c vb. fem), 60^{7}, Je 2^{10} $49^{28.28}$ Ez 27^{21}; בְּנֵי־ק׳ Is 21^{17}, אָהֳלֵי ק׳ ψ 120^{5} Ct 1^{5} (made of black goat-skins Jacob[Beduinenleben (2), 41] or black woven stuff Doughty[Arab Des. i 224 f], sim. of swarthy hue). **2.** ancestor of **1**, son of Ishmael, Gn 25^{13} = 1 Ch 1^{29}—Cf. As. *Ḳidru* COT[Gn 25, 13], Plin[NH v 11 (12)] *Cedrei*; also Sab tribe-name קדר Hal[623] (cf. DHM[ZMG xxxvii (1883), 14]).

†קִדְרוֹן **n.pr.** of wady just E. of Jerusalem (Thes. *turbidus*);—נַחַל ק׳ 2 S 15^{23} 1 K 2^{37}; usu. as place for refuse 1 K 15^{13} = 2 Ch 15^{16}, 2 K $23^{6.6.12}$ 2 Ch 29^{16} 30^{14}, Je 31^{40}, so שַׁדְמוֹת ק׳ 2 K 23^{4}; Κεδρων; cf. Rob[Phys. Geogr 87 ff] Buhl[Geogr 93] Bd[Pal. 3 (1896), 94].

קדשׁ (√of foll.; poss. orig. idea of *separation, withdrawal* (Baud[Studien, ii] No[LCB Mar 22, 1879, 361] RS[Sem. i. 140, 2nd ed 150]); NH = BH; Ph. קדש *holy*, מקדש *sanctuary*; As. *kadâšu* ii. 1, *cleanse* (Meissn[Suppl. 84]), also *ḳadištu*, *hierodule* consecrated to Ištar (cf. AJerem[Izdubar 59 f.]); Ar قُدْس n pr.mont. (No[l. c.] RS[Proph v N 9]); in Ar. otherwise under infl. of Heb., so Eth; cf. 𝔗 קדש in der. spec. and deriv., Syr. ܩܰܕܶܫ *consecrate*, etc; Palm. קדש *id*; Aram. קְדָשָׁא, ܩܕܫܐ (ear- or nose-) *ring*, (orig. *holy* thing, No[l. c.]);—on whole subj. v. Baud No RS (reff. above), also HPS[Presb Rev. 1881, 588 ff.]; diff. fr. חרם v. GFM[Ju. p. 36]).

קֹדֶשׁ 469 **n.m. apartness, sacredness** (opp. חֹל Lv 10^{10} + 4 t. Ez);—abs. ק׳ Ex 3^{5} +; קוֹדֶשׁ Dn 11^{30}; cstr. קֹדֶשׁ Ex 30^{36} +; sf. קָדְשִׁי Lv 20^{3} +, etc.; pl קֳדָשִׁים Ex 29^{37} +, הַקֳּדָשִׁים 26^{33} +; cstr. קָדְשֵׁי Lv 22^{15} +; sf. קָדָשַׁי Ez 22^{8} + 3 t, קָדָשֶׁיךָ †Dt 12^{26}, קֳדָשָׁיו, Nu 5^{10} 2 K 12^{19}, קֳדָשָׁיו †2 Ch 15^{18}, etc.;—**1.** *apartness, sacredness, holiness*, of God: **a.** of divine activity, syn. majesty, בַּקֹּדֶשׁ (of victory), Ex 15^{11} (song) ψ 68^{18} 77^{14}; זְרוֹעַ ק׳ *holy arm* Is 52^{10} ψ 98^{1}. **b.** to attest his word as inviolable נשבע בק׳ Am 4^{2} ψ 89^{36}; cf דִּבְרֵי ק׳ Je 23^{9}, דְּבַר ק׳ ψ 105^{42}. **c.** of his name as sacred, inviolable, separate from all defilement, etc.: שֵׁם קָדְשִׁי Lv 20^{3} $22^{2.32}$ (P), Am 2^{7} 1 Ch $16^{10.35}$ 29^{16} + 9 t. Ez, 5 t. ψψ; זֵכֶר ק׳ ψ 30^{5} = 97^{12}; and so **d.** רוּחַ קָדְשׁוֹ *his holy Spirit* Is $63^{10.11}$, cf. ψ 51^{13}. **2.** of places set apart as sacred by God's presence: †**a.** heavenly abode; מעון ק׳ Dt 26^{15} Je 25^{30} Zc 2^{17} 2 Ch 30^{27} ψ 68^{6}; היכל ק׳ Mi 1^{2} Hb 2^{20} Jon $2^{5.8}$ ψ 11^{4}, מרום ק׳ ψ 102^{20}; זְבוּל ק׳ Is 63^{15}; שְׁמֵי ק׳ ψ 20^{7} כסא ק׳ 47^{9}; בקדשו 150^{1}. †**b.** on earth: אַדְמַת ק׳ Ex 3^{5} (E), cf. Jos 5^{15} (JE) 2 Ch 8^{11}; הַר ק׳ אלהים Ez 28^{14} (cf. p. 249 b). **c.** (only P and Ch) the tabernacle and its courts Ex 40^{9} Nu 3^{28} +; tabernacle by itself Ex 38^{24} Lv 10^{4} +; court Lv $10^{17.18}$ + (so קדש הקדשים †Nu 18^{10}); the outer room (specific designation, הַקּ׳) Ex 26^{33} 28^{29} +; inner room Lv 4^{6} 16^{2} +, but specif. design. קדש הקדשים Ex $26^{33.34}$ 1 Ch 6^{34}, שֶׁקֶל הקּ׳ *shekel of the sanctuary* Ex 30^{13} + 24 t. P. **d.** the temple and its precincts 2 Ch 29^{7} Dn 8^{13} +; שָׂרֵי ק׳ Is 43^{28} 1 Ch 24^{5}, דבר בְּקָדְשׁוֹ ψ 60^{8} = 108^{8} (oracle; al. *by his holiness*, as נשבעתי בקדשי 89^{36}), temple by itself 2 Ch 29^{5}; †בית (ה)ק׳ Is 64^{10} 1 Ch 29^{3}; †היכל קדשך ψ 5^{8} = 138^{2}, 79^{1}; הַקּ׳ outer room 1 K 8^{10} = 2 Ch 5^{11}; courts of priests Ez 42^{14} $44^{27.27}$; †חצרות קדשי Is 62^{9}; inner room Ez $41^{21.23}$, specif. †דביר קדשך ψ 28^{2}; †קדש הקדשים 1 K 6^{16} 7^{50} 8^{6} 2 Ch $3^{8.10}$ 4^{22} 5^{7} Ez 41^{4}; †לִשְׁכֹת הַקּ׳ Ez 42^{13} 44^{19} 46^{19} (v. לִשְׁכָּה **1 c**). †**e.** Jerus. and its hills. מקום קדשו Ezr 9^{8}, עיר הק׳ Is 48^{2} 52^{1} Ne $11^{1.18}$, ע׳ קדשך Dn 9^{24}, הר (ה)ק׳ Is 11^{9} + 6 t. Is$^{2.3}$, Je 31^{23} Ez 20^{40} Jo 2^{1} 4^{17} Ob^{16} Zp 3^{11} Zc 8^{3} Dn $9^{16.20}$ 11^{45} + 6 t. ψψ; גְּבוּל ק׳ ψ 78^{54}, הַרְרֵי ק׳ 87^{1} prob. also 110^{3}, ק׳ of city and suburbs in Mess. future Je 31^{40} Jo 4^{17}. Cf. **f.** (ה)קדש of Zion Ob^{17} ψ 20^{3} 24^{3} 63^{3} 68^{25}, ק׳ קדשים

Ez 43^{12}, נוה ק׳ Ex 15^{13} of Zion (or Shiloh). **g.** of holy land Zp 3^{4}, עָרֵי קדשך, אדמת הק׳ Zc 2^{16}, Is 64^{9}, future portion of priests ק׳ Ez 45^{1} + 11 t Ez, קדש קדשים Ez 45^{3} 48^{12}, of Levites קדש Ez 48^{14}. **3.** things consecrated at sacred places **a.** furniture of tabern †קדש (ה)קדשים Ex $30^{10.29}$ Nu $4^{4.19}$, altar of burnt-offering Ex 29^{37} 40^{10} Dn 9^{24}, ארון הק׳ 2 Ch 35^{3} **b.** sacrifices of animals Nu 18^{17} Ez 36^{38} 2 Ch 29^{33}, sacrificial food Lv 21^{22b} Nu 5^{9} +, †קדש (ה)קדשים Lv $2^{3.10}$ $6^{10.18.22}$ $7^{1.6}$ $10^{12.17}$ 14^{13} Nu $18^{9.9}$ (all P), Ez $42^{13.13}$ 2 Ch 31^{14} Ezr 2^{63} = Ne 7^{65}, tithe was קדש Lv 27^{30} +, also first loaves of new harvest Lv 23^{20}, fruit of trees of 4th year Lv 19^{24} **c** any consecrated thing ‖ vows Dt 12^{26} Pr 20^{25} +, house Lv 27^{14}, field Lv $27^{21.23}$, treasures consecrated to treasury of tabern or temple Jos 6^{19} (E) 1 K 7^{51} +, consecrated things in gen. Ex 28^{38} (P), Ez 20^{40} 22^{8} +, these may be †קדש (ה)קדשים Ez 44^{13}, so חֵרֶם Lv 27^{28} **d.** anointing oil of priest Ex $30^{25.25}$ + 5 t (P), ψ 89^{21}, incense Ex $30^{35.37}$, ק׳ קדשים v ^{36}; shew-bread 1 S 21^{5}, קדש (ה)ק׳ Lv 24^{9} cf 21^{22a} (P), foretold of common articles, ק׳ לי׳ Zc $14^{20.21}$. On ק׳ הקדשים v also Di $^{Ex\ 26.33\ Lv\ 21\ 22}$ We $^{Comp\ 160\ f.}$ Dr $^{Dn\ 9\ 24}$ **4.** persons sacred by connex with sacred places. **a.** priests Lv 21^{6} 2 Ch 23^{6} 31^{18} Ezr 8^{28}, garments of priesthood Ex $28^{2.4}$ + 7 t Ex, Lv $16^{4.32}$ Ez 42^{14}, specif. of h priest כתנת ק׳ Lv 16^{4}, נֵזֶר הק׳ Ex 29^{6} 39^{30} Lv 8^{9}, inscription on head piece קדש ליהוה Ex 28^{36} 39^{30} **b.** of Israel, קדש לי׳ Je 2^{3}, היתה עם קדשך ψ 114^{2}, עם (ה)קדש Is 62^{12} Dn 12^{7}, ψ לקדשו Is 63^{18}, זֶרַע (ה)קדש Is 6^{13} Ezr 9^{2}, אַנְשֵׁי קדש Ex 22^{30} (R), and so spoil for their use Is 23^{18}, holy adornment הַדְרַת ק׳ 1 Ch 16^{29} 2 Ch 20^{21} ψ 29^{2} 96^{9}, הַדְרֵי ק׳ ψ 110^{3} (but rd הררי see **2 e**; הָדָר **1**); covt between God and his people ברית ק׳ Dn $11^{28.30.30}$. **5.** times consecrated to worship שבת Ex 16^{23} $31^{14.15}$ 35^{2} (P) Ne 9^{14}, of שבת also יום ק׳ Is 58^{13}, disting. fr שבת Ne 10^{32}; יובל Lv 25^{12} (P), assembly called at stated times for worship מקרא(י) ק׳ Ex $12^{16.16}$ + 17 t Lv 23 Nu 28 (all P). †**6.** of things and persons ceremonially cleansed, and so separated as sacred; things 1 S 21^{6}, flesh Je 11^{15} Mal 2^{11}, priests cleanse thus, 1 Ch $23^{13.28}$, בין (ה)קדש להל Ez 22^{26} 42^{20} 44^{23}, בין הק׳ ובין החל Lv 10^{10}; דֶּרֶךְ הק׳ Is 35^{8} way of the clean, ψ שָׁאוּ יְדֵכֶם ק׳ 134^{2}; ψ לְבֵיתְךָ נַאֲוָה־ק׳ 93^{5}.—*Note:* מרבבת קֹדֶשׁ Dt 33^{2} is lit *from myriads of sacredness, sacred myriads;* but ‖ suggests n pr loc, 𝔊 σὺν μυριά σιν Καδής, < מִמְּרִבַת קָדֵשׁ *from Meribah Kadesh* Di Buhl Steuern, or (מִן om.) *to M. Kadesh* We $^{Prol\ 364,\ 3rd\ ed\ 359,\ Hist.\ 344}$, v. קָדֵשׁ and Dr ^{Dt}.

†קָדוֹשׁ **adj. sacred, holy;**—abs ק׳ Ex 19^{6} +; קָדֹשׁ Ex 29^{31} +, cstr. קדוש Is 1^{4} +, קְדשׁ Is 49^{7} + 2 t, sf קְדֹשִׁי Hb 1^{12}; קדושׁוֹ Is 10^{17} 49^{7} קְדוֹשְׁכֶם Is 43^{15}, pl. קְדוֹשִׁים Ho 12^{1} + 2 t, קְדֹשִׁים Lv 11^{44} + 16 t., sf. קדשָׁיו Dt 33^{3} ψ 34^{10}, קְדשָׂו Jb 15^{15},—**1.** of God, as separate, apart, and so *sacred, holy*· **a.** exalted on theophanic throne Is $6^{3.3.3}$, ψ 22^{4}, heavenly throne Is 57^{15}, in victory 5^{16} 1 S 2^{2} ψ 99^{3} (‖נורא), v $^{5.9}$, ק׳ ונוֹרָא שְׁמוֹ 111^{9}. **b.** separate from human infirmity, impurity, and sin· Jos 24^{19} (E), 1 S 6^{20} Hb 1^{12}, קדוש אני כי קדוש Lv $11^{44.45}$ 19^{2} 20^{26} 21^{8} (H), ק׳ בישראל Ez 39^{7} **c.** קָדוֹשׁ בקרבך Ho 11^{9}, קְדוֹשׁ יִשְׂרָאֵל = divine name (originating fr *trisagion,* Is 6^{3}) Is 1^{4} $5^{19.24}$ 10^{20} 12^{6} 17^{7} 29^{19} $30^{11.12.15}$ 31^{1}, Is^{2} $41^{14.16.20}$ $43^{3.14}$ 45^{11} 47^{4} 48^{17} 49^{7} 54^{5} 55^{5} $60^{9.14}$ elsewhere only 2 K 19^{22} = Is 37^{23}, Je 50^{29} 51^{5} ψ 71^{22} 78^{41} 89^{19}; ק׳ יעקב Is 29^{23}, קְדוֹשׁוֹ 10^{17} 49^{7}, קדוֹשְׁכֶם 43^{15}, קָדוֹשׁ 40^{25} Hb 3^{3} Jb 6^{10}, pl. intens. קד(ו)שים Ho 12^{1} Pr 9^{10} 30^{3}. **2. a.** of place, *sacred, holy,* chambers of priests Ez 42^{13}, camp of Isr Dt 23^{15}, + מָרוֹם of heaven Is 57^{15} (but of י׳ Du Ry, and [rdg בק׳ *as holy,* ב essent.] Klo Che Marti); in foll (oft defect.) pointing dub, rd. prob קֹדֶשׁ **2**: מק(ו)ם ק׳ of the court of tabernacle, Ex 29^{31} Lv $6^{9.19.20}$ 7^{6} 10^{13} 16^{24} 24^{9} (P), of Jerusalem Ec 8^{10}, ק׳ מִשְׁכְּנֵי עליון ψ 46^{5}; ק׳ הֵיכָלֶךָ 65^{5} **b.** persons: priests Lv $21^{7.8}$ Nu $16^{5.7}$ (P), Aaron ψ 106^{16}, Levites 2 Ch 35^{3}, prophet 2 K 4^{9}, Nazirite Nu $6^{5.8}$ (P), Isr. גוֹי ק׳ Ex 19^{6} (E), עם ק׳ Dt 7^{6} $14^{2.21}$ 26^{19} 28^{9}, כָּל־הָעֵדָה Nu 16^{3} (P); remnant in Jerus. Is 4^{3}, קדשים *sacred* Lv $11^{44.45}$ 19^{2} $20^{7.26}$ 21^{6} Nu 15^{40}, קדשים *sacred ones, saints* Dt 33^{3} (song), ψ 16^{3} 34^{10} Dn 8^{24} **c.** angels, ψ $89^{6.8}$ Jb 5^{1} 15^{15} Zc 14^{5} Dn $8^{13.13}$. **d.** מים קדשים Nu 5^{17} *holy water* **e** time הַיּוֹם ק׳ (לי׳) Ne $8^{9.10.11}$; קדוש י׳ Is 58^{13}, of Sabbath —(Cf. BAram. קַדִּישׁ).

†קָדַשׁ **vb. denom. be set apart, consecrated** (Gerber $^{238\ ff}$);—**Qal** *Pf.* 3 ms ק׳ Ex 29^{21}, sf קְדַשְׁתִּיךָ Is 65^{5}, 3 mpl קָדֵשׁוּ Nu 17^{2}; *Impf* 3 ms. יִקְדַּשׁ 1 S 21^{6}; יִקְדָּשׁ Ex 29^{37} +, etc; —**1.** *be set apart, consecrated,* hallowed, of shew-bread 1 S 21^{6} (dub. passage, but cf esp. RS $^{Sem\ 1\ 436,\ 2nd\ ed.\ 455}$ [also Dr $^{Sm\ 293}$], who prop. יְקַדֵּשׁ); Aaron and his sons by blood Ex 29^{21} (P), other persons Is 65^{5} (Di, but **Pi.** Ges RS $^{Sem.\ 1\ 431,\ 2nd\ ed.\ 451}$ Che Du Buhl) **2.** *be hallowed,* by contact with sacred things, and so tabooed from

profane use, or forfeited to sanctuary Ex 29[37] 30[29] Lv 6[11.20] Nu 17[2.3] (P), Hg 2[12]. **3.** *consecrated, tabooed* (supr.) Dt 22[9] (law against mixtures). **Niph.** *Pf.* 3 ms נִקְדַּשׁ Is 5[16] Ex 29[43], etc.; *Impf.* 3 ms וַיִּקָּדֵשׁ Nu 20[13], 1 s. אֶקָּדֵשׁ Lv 10[3]; *Inf cstr.* sf. הִקָּֽדְשִׁי Ez 36[23] 38[16];—**1.** *shew oneself sacred, majestic:* c. בְּ pers., + לְעֵינֵי Ez 20[41] 28[25] 36[23] 38[16] 39[27]; c. בְּ Is 5[16] Ez 28[22], cf. Nu 20[13] (P). **2.** *be honoured* or *treated as sacred* ‖ נכבד Lv 10[3] (P); opp. חִלֵּל שֵׁם Lv 22[32] (P). **3.** *be consecrated, dedicated,* by כבוד י׳ Ex 29[43] (P). **Pi.** *Pf.* 3 ms. קִדַּשׁ Nu 6[11] 1 K 8[64], etc; *Impf.* 3 ms יְקַדֵּשׁ Gn 2[3]+, etc.; *Imv.* ms. קַדֵּשׁ Jos 7[13]; קַדֶּשׁ־ Ex 13[2], etc.; *Inf. cstr.* קַדֵּשׁ Ex 29[1]+, etc.; *Pt.* מְקַדֵּשׁ Ex 37[28], sf. מְקַדִּשְׁכֶם Ex 31[13]+, etc;—**1.** *set apart as sacred, consecrate, dedicate:* **a.** places: Sinai Ex 19[23] (J), altar, etc., Ex 29[36.37] 30[29] (P), tabern., etc Ex 40[9 10 11] Lv 8[10.11 15] Nu 7[1] (P); tent of meeting Ex 29[44] (P); place of sacrifice 1 K 8[64] = 2 Ch 7[7]; gate Ne 3[1];—Ez 7[24] v. מִקְדָּשׁ infr. **b.** wave-offering Ex 29[27] (P) **c.** persons: priests Ex 28[3.41] 29[1.33.44] 30[30] 40[13] Lv 8[12.30]; firstborn Ex 13[2] (P); keepers of ark 1 S 7[1]. †**d.** 7th day (by God) Gn 2[3] Ex 20[11] (P). **2.** *observe as holy, keep sacred:* feasts, Sabbath Ex 20[8] = Dt 5[12] (Decal.), Je 17[22.24.27] Ez 20[20] 44[24] Ne 13[22]; fast Jo 1[14] 2[15], year of Jubilee Lv 25[10] (P); so עצרה לבעל 2 K 10[20]. **3.** *honour as sacred, hallow:* **a.** God Dt 32[51], his name Ez 36[23]. **b.** priest Lv 21[8] (H). **4.** *consecrate* by purification: **a.** places, house of י׳ 2 Ch 29[5.17 17], altar מִטֻּמְאֹת, Lv 16[19]. **b.** people העם Jos 7[13] (J), Ez 44[19] 46[20]; by washing Ex 19[10 14] (E), קהל for fast Jo 2[16]; Nazirite Nu 6[11] (P), sons of Job Jb 1[5]; family for sacrif. 1 S 16[5]. **c.** war, or warriors, fr. custom of opening campaign by sacrifice, ק׳ מִלְחָמָה (עַל) Je 6[4] Jo 4[9] Mi 3[5]; Je 22[7] 51[27 28]. **d.** of God, keeping his people pure and sacred: אני יהוה מְקַדֵּשׁ Ex 31[13] Lv 20[8] 21[8 15.23] 22[9 16.32] (H), Ez 20[12] 37[28]. **Pu.** *Pt.* מְקֻדָּשׁ Ez 48[11], etc,—*consecrated, dedicated:* priests 2 Ch 26[18] Ez 48[11] (rd. pl.), things 2 Ch 31[6], feasts Ezr 3[5], warriors Is 13[3]. **Hiph.** *Pf.* 3 ms. הִקְדִּישׁ Zp 1[7]+, etc; *Impf.* יַקְדִּישׁ Lv 27[16]+4 t, יַקְדִּשׁ Lv 27[14], etc; *Imv.* sf. הַקְדִּשֵׁם Je 12[3], *Inf abs.* הַקְדֵּשׁ Ju 17[3]; *cstr.* הַקְדִּישׁ 2 Ch 2[3]+, etc.; *Pt* מַקְדִּישׁ Lv 27[15]+, etc **1.** *set apart, devote, consecrate:* **a.** places, temple 2 Ch 2[3], city Jos 20[7] (P). **b.** things Ex 28[38] Lv 22[2.3] (P) 2 K 12[19] 1 Ch 23[13] 26[26.27 28.28] Ne 12[47 47]; money Ju 17[3.3]; spoil 2 S 8[11 11] = 1 Ch 18[11], field Lv 27[16 17 18.19.22] (H); house Lv 27[14 15] (H), firstlings Dt 15[19] (D) Lv 27[26] (H). **c.** of God. *consecrate* temple 1 K 9[3.7] = 2 Ch 7[16.20], 2 Ch 30[8] 36[14]; prophet Je 1[5]; firstborn Nu 3[13] 8[17] (P); devote wicked (as sheep) for sacrifice Je 12[3]. **2.** *regard,* or *treat, as sacred, hallow:* God Is 8[13] 29[23.23], + לְעֵינֵי pers. Nu 20[12] 27[14]. **3.** *consecrate* by purification: vessels 2 Ch 29[19]; persons for passover 30[17]; guests for sacrif. feast Zp 1[7] (God subj). **Hithp.** *Pf.* 1 s הִתְקַדִּשְׁתִּי Ez 38[23], 2 mpl. (consec.) וְהִתְקַדִּשְׁתֶּם Lv 11[44] 20[7], 3 pl. הִתְקַדָּשׁוּ 2 Ch 5[11] 30[17], etc.; *Impf.* 3 ms. יִתְקַדְּשׁוּ 2 Ch 29[34]+; יִתְקַדָּשׁוּ Ex 19[22], *Imv.* mpl. הִתְקַדְּשׁוּ Nu 11[18]+; הִתְקַדָּשׁוּ Jos 3[5]; *Inf cstr.* הִתְקַדֵּשׁ 2 Ch 29[34]; הִתְקַדֵּשׁ Is 30[29]; *Pt.* fs. מִתְקַדֶּשֶׁת 2 S 11[4]; pl. מִתְקַדְּשִׁים Is 66[17];—**1.** *keep oneself apart* from unclean things Lv 11[44] 20[7] (P). **2.** of God, *cause himself to be hallowed,* לְעֵינֵי גוֹיִם Ez 38[23]. **3.** *be observed as holy,* of feast Is 30[29]. **4.** *consecrate oneself* by purification, of priests and Levites Ex 19[22] (J), 1 Ch 15[12 14] 2 Ch 5[11] 29[5.15 34.34] 30[3.15.24] 31[18] 35[6]; of people Nu 11[18] Jos 3[5] 7[13] (J) 1 S 16[5] 2 Ch 30[17] Is 66[17]; woman 2 S 11[4] *she having (just) purified herself* מִטֻּמְאָתָהּ RS[K.276] Dr HPS.

†I. קָדֵשׁ **n.m.** temple-prostitute (man) (cf RS[Proph. ii. N 19], and v. As. sub √);—ק׳ Dt 23[18]; coll. 1 K 14[24] 22[47]; pl קְדֵשִׁים 15[12] 2 K 23[7] Jb 36[14]; also f. קְדֵשָׁה (woman) Dt 23[18]; pl. קְדֵשׁוֹת Ho 4[14]; = *harlot,* fs Gn 38[21 21.22] (J).

†קֶדֶשׁ **n.pr.loc.** (*sanctuary*) Κάδης: **1.** in Galilee Jos 20[7] 21[32] (P), 1 Ch 6[61]; Naphtali Jos 19[37] (P), ק׳ נַפְתָּלִי Ju 4[6]; = קֶדֶשׁ alone Jos 12[22] (D; with king); Ju 4[9 10] + v[11] (where poss. different place on sea of Galilee, v GFM[Ju 117. 119]), also 2 K 15[29]; TelAm. *Kidši*, Eg. *Ḳdše* WMM[As. u. Eur 173, 217]; mod *Kades*, NW. of Lake Huleh; v. Rob[BR iii. 366 ff] Survey[WP i 226 ff] Buhl[Geogr 235 f]. **2.** Κέδες: city of refuge in Issachar 1 Ch 6[57] = קִשְׁיוֹן Jos 21[28], poss. *Tel Abu Kudeis* [Survey[WP i. 69]], c. 2 miles SE from *Lejjun* (*Megiddo*) cf. Buhl[Geogr 209] **3.** Κάδης: in S. Judah; Jos 15[23] (P) (= II. קָדֵשׁ **1**? if so, then Mass. distinction from קֶדֶשׁ in N. was here neglected)

†II. קָדֵשׁ **n.pr.loc.** (*sacred;* but perh orig. קֶדֶשׁ, and pointing artif. to disting. fr. ק׳ in N);—**1.** Κάδης: in S of Judah Gn 16[14] (J), 20[1] (E), in מִדְבַּר פָּארָן Nu 13[26] (P), specif. מ׳ צִן 20[1] 33[36], cf מ׳ קָדֵשׁ ψ 29[8]; on W. border of Edom Nu 20[16] (E), 33[37] (P), cf. 20[14] (E), v[22] (P), Ju 11[16 17] (hence Rob[BR ii 175, 194] sought it at *'Ain Weibeh,* in W. of Arabah); long abode of Isr. during Exod. Dt 1[46], מֵי מְרִיבַת ק׳ Nu 27[14] (cf. 20[1-13]), Dt 32[51] (P), Ez 47[19] (rd. מְרִיבַת), 48[28], cf. Dt 33[2]

(v. קָדֵשׁ ad fin.); cf. עֵין מִשְׁפָּט Gn 14[7]; = ק׳ בַּרְנֵעַ (meaning of ב׳ unknown; 𝔊 K. (τοῦ) Βαρνη);—Nu 32[8] (J), Dt 1[2.19] 2[14] 9[23] Jos 10[41] 14[6] (D), Nu 34[4] Jos 15[3] (P);—mod. *'Ain Ḳadîs* (*Ḳudais*, قُدَيْس), c. 50 miles S. of Beersheba, JRowlands (1842) v. GWilliams[Holy City, 464 f.], and especially HCTrumbull (1881) [Kadesh Barnea, 238–321]. **2.** Hittite capital on the Orontes, N. of Damascus, towards Hamath (Eg. *Ḳdš, Ḳdšụ, Ḳdšẹ̄*, WMM [As. u. Eur. 213 ff.]);—2 S 24[6] 𝔊L We Dr Kit Bu Löhr, rdg. אֶרֶץ הַחִתִּים קָדֵשָׁה for MT א׳ תַּחְתִּים חָדְשִׁי (קָדֵשָׁה הַחִתִּים already Hi[Gesch. Isr. i. 29]; קָדֵשָׁה Th, Klo, of קֶדֶשׁ in Napht.); HPS doubts.

מִקְדָּשׁ 74 **n.m.** [Am 7.9] **sacred place, sanctuary**;—מ׳ Ex 25[8]+; מִקְּדָשׁ 15[17] (Ges[§20h] Kö [ii. 1, 471]); cstr. מִקְדַּשׁ Lv 16[33]+; sf. מִקְדָּשִׁי Lv 20[3]+, etc., מִקְדָּשׁוֹ Nu 18[29] (Kö[ii. 1, 97]); pl. מִקְדָּשִׁים Ez 21[7], cstr. מִקְדְּשֵׁי Je 51[51] + 2 t.; sf. מִקְדָּשַׁי Lv 21[23]; מִקְדְּשֵׁיהֶם Ez 7[24] (on anomalous pointing v. Ew [§215a] Hi-Sm; but prob. **Pi.** *Pt.* was in mind, Ges[§93oo Anm.]; < rd. מְקַדְשֵׁיהֶם); etc.;—**1.** old Isr. *sanctuaries*: of י׳ at Shechem Jos 24[26] (E); prob. also Ex 15[17] (i.e. Shiloh); pl. of sanct. to be destroyed by י׳ Lv 26[31] (H); מִקְדְּשֵׁי יִשׂ׳ in N. Isr. Am 7[9]; מִקְדַּשׁ־מֶלֶךְ v[13] (Bethel). **2.** of the nations: Moab Is 16[12] pl. of Tyre Ez 28[18] (Co Toy [not Berthol Krae] read קָדְשְׁךָ *thy sanctity*). **3.** tabernacle and its precincts Ex 25[8] (P)+; מִקְדַּשׁ הַקֹּדֶשׁ Lv 16[33], pl. 21[23]. **4.** temple and precincts 1 Ch 22[19] Is 63[18] ψ 74[7]+; בֵּית מִקְדָּשִׁים 2 Ch 36[17], מקדש הבית Ez 48[21], מְכוֹן מ׳ Dn 8[11]; pl. of many sacred places in and about the temple, מִקְדְּשֵׁי בית י׳ Je 51[51]; מִקְדְּשֵׁי אֵל ψ 73[17]. Doubtful are: מִמִּקְדָּשֶׁיךָ ψ 68[36] (𝔊 ἐν τοῖς ὁσίοις αὐτοῦ; 𝔙 *de sanctuario*; SS מִקְדָּשְׁךָ); מִקְדָּשִׁים Ez 21[7] (𝔊 Co Berthol Buhl מִקְדָּשָׁם; Toy Krae מִקְדָּשָׁהּ; ‖ יְרוּשָׁלַםִ); וּמִקְדָּשׁ לַמִּקְדָּשׁ Ez 45[4 b] (Co, after 𝔊, לְבָתִּים וּלְמִגְרָשִׁים] Toy ;[לְבָתֵּי] מִפְקַד לְקָדְשָׁם, cf. Krae לְמִגְרָשׁ). **5.** י׳ will become לְמ׳ for his people Ez 11[16] (Br[MP 268]), so appar. Is 8[14] (but gloss Du Che[Hpt] Marti; Lag[Sem. i. 16] מִקְשׁ i.e. *stumbling-block* [he cp. Syr. ܢܩܫ *strike*]). **6.** of י׳'s future sanct., מ׳ בתוכם לעולם Ez 37[26.28].—(מִכָּל־חֶלְבּוֹ) אֶת־מִקְדְּשׁוֹ (מִמֶּנּוּ) Nu 18[29] *even the hallowed part thereof* AV RV, but this not the meaning of מ׳; Ew[§255c] assumes מִקְדָּשׁ* in this sense; < rd. קָדְשׁוֹ (v. קֹדֶשׁ **3 d**), מ being dittogr.

†**[קָהָה]** **vb.** be blunt, dull (NH *id.*; Aram. קְהָא, ܩܗܐ);— **Qal** *Impf.* 3 fpl. תִּקְהֶינָה Je 31[29.30] Ez 18[2] (all of teeth). **Pi.** in sense of **Qal**: *Pf.* 3 ms. קֵהָה Ec 10[10] *if the iron be blunt.*

†**[קִהָיוֹן]** **n.[m.]** **bluntness** (Lag[BN 201]);—rd. perh. cstr. קִהְיוֹן Am 4[6] (for נִקְיוֹן; v. נִקָּיוֹן).

קהל (√ of following; cf. Sab. קהלת ,קהל *assembly, congregation* DHM[ZMG xxx (1876), 685] Hom [Chrest. 127]; Saho *kahal, come together, assemble* Reinisch[Saho Spr. 210]; Syr. ܩܗܠ *assemble*, ChrPal. ܩܗܠܐ, λαός; NH Hiph. = BH; Lag[BN 51] cp. Ar. قَهَّلَ *rebuke*, and conj. קָהָל = 'Rügegericht').

קָהָל 123 **n.m.** [Ez 38.15] **assembly, convocation, congregation**;—abs. ק׳ Je 31[8]+; cstr. קְהַל Ex 12[6]+; sf. קְהָלֶךָ Ez 38[13], etc.; pl. sf. קְהָלֶיךָ Ez 38[7];—**1.** *assembly* specially convoked: †**a.** for evil counsel, ‖ סוד Gn 49[6] (poem); ק׳ מרעים ψ 26[5]; for civil affairs Pr 5[14] (v. Toy), 26[26] Jb 30[28] (Di *publice*). **b.** for war or invasion, Nu 22[4] (E), Ju 20[2] 21[5.8] 1 S 17[47] Ez 16[40] 38[7] (pl. only here), + 8 t. Ez; ק׳ גדול (‖ חיל רב) Ez 38[15]; ק׳ רב (‖ חיל גדול) 17[17] 38[4]; ק׳ גוים Je 50[9]; ק׳ עמים Ez 23[24] 32[3]. **c.** *company* of returning exiles, Je 31[8] Ezr 2[64] = Ne 7[66]. **d.** for religious purposes, to hear words of י׳ at Horeb Dt 5[19], ביום הק׳ Dt 9[10] 10[4] (gloss, not in 𝔊), 18[16]; word of Jer. Je 26[17] 44[15]; for feasts, fasts and worship 2 Ch 20[5] 30[25.25] Ne 5[13] Jo 2[16] ψ 107[32]; ק׳ רב 22[26] + 4 t.; ק׳ לרב מְאֹד . . . וַיֵּאָסְפוּ 2 Ch 30[13]; ק׳ גדול 1 K 8[65] = 2 Ch 7[8]; בתוך (ה)ק׳ 2 Ch 20[14] ψ 22[23]. **2.** *congregation*, as organized body: **a.** of Isr.: בא בק׳ (י׳) Mi 2[5] Nu 16[3] 20[4] (P), 1 Ch 28[8]; ק׳ יהוה Dt 23[2.3.3.4.4.9] Ne 13[1] La 1[10]; כל ק׳ ישראל Dt 31[30] Jos 8[35] (D) Lv 16[17] (P) 1 K 8[14.14.22.55] = 2 Ch 6[3.3.12.13], 1 K 12[3] 1 Ch 13[2]; כל ק׳ עדת ישראל Ex 12[6] (𝔊 rds. בני before יִשׂ׳), Nu 14[5] (P; 𝔊 συναγωγή; MT prob. conflation); כל עם הק׳ Lv 16[33]; כל הק׳ Ex 16[3] (P) 1 Ch 13[4] + 12 t. Ch; הק׳ Lv 4[13.14.21] + 8 t. Nu (P), 8 t. 2 Ch. **b.** restored community in Jerus. Ezr 10[12.14] Ne 8[2.17]; ק׳ הַגּוֹלָה Ezr 10[8]; later the better part of it, ק׳ חסידים ψ 149[1]. **c.** of angels, ק׳ קדשים ψ 89[6]. **d.** more gen.: *company*, assembled multitude, ק׳ גוים Gn 35[11] (P), ק׳ עמים Gn 28[3] 48[4] (P), ק׳ רפאים Pr 21[16].

†**[קָהַל]** **vb. denom.** (Gerber[107 f.]) **assemble** as a קָהָל;—**Niph.** *Pf.* 3 mpl. נִקְהֲלוּ Est 9[2]+ 3 t.; *Impf.* 3 ms. וַיִּקָּהֵל Ex 32[1] Je 26[9]; 3 mpl. וַיִּקָּהֲלוּ 2 S 20[14] Qr (Kt ויקלהו, cf. HPS), etc.; *Inf.* cstr. הִקָּהֵל Nu 17[7] Est 8[11]; *Pt.* pl. נִקְהָלִים Ez 38[7];—*assemble as a* קָהָל: **1. a.** for conflict or war 2 S 20[14] (Qr; v. supr.), Est 8[11] 9[2.15.16.18]; c. עַל pers. Ez 38[7], acc. loc. Jos 22[12] Ju 20[1]. **b.** rebellion, c. עַל pers. Nu 16[3] 17[7] 20[2] (P), poss.

also Ex 32^{1} (J; most, *unto* Aaron). **2.** for religious purpose: to erect tent of meeting, acc. loc. Jos 18^{1} (P); hear word of י׳, c. אֶל loc. Lv 8^{4} (P), בְּ loc. + אֶל pers. Je 26^{9}; for festival, אֶל pers. 1 K 8^{2} = 2 Ch 5^{3}; לְ loc. 2 Ch 20^{26}. **Hiph.** *Pf.* 2 ms. הִקְהַלְתָּ Ez 38^{13}, וְהִקְהַלְתָּ Nu 8^{9}; 3 mpl. הִקְהִילוּ 1^{18}; *Impf.* 3 ms. יַקְהִיל Jb 11^{10}; אָז יַקְהֵל 1 K 8^{1} = יַקְהִיל 2 Ch 5^{2}; וַיַּקְהֵל Ex 35^{1} + (**Qal** *Impf.* in *i* acc. to Ba$^{NB\ p.\ 147}$); pl. וַיַּקְהִלוּ Nu 20^{10}; *Imv.* ms. הַקְהֵל Lv 8^{3} +, etc.; *Inf. cstr.* הַקְהִיל Nu 10^{7};—*summon an assembly:* **1. a.** for judgment Jb 11^{10}. **b.** for war 1 K 12^{21} = 2 Ch 11^{1}, Ez 38^{13}. **2.** for *religious purposes:* c. acc. אֶת־הַקָּהָל Nu 10^{7}, + אֶל loc. 20^{10}, c. acc. (כָּל־)הָעֵדָה Ex 35^{1} Nu 1^{18} 8^{9} 20^{8} (P), + אֶל loc. Lv 8^{3} Nu 16^{19} (P); c. acc. הָעָם Dt 4^{10} 31^{12}; כָּל־יִשְׂרָאֵל 1 Ch 13^{5} 15^{3}; elders of tribes Dt 31^{28}, of Isr. 1 K 8^{1} = 2 Ch 5^{2}; princes of Isr. 1 Ch 28^{1}.

†קְהִלָּה **n.f.** **assembly, congregation**;—abs. ק׳ Ne 5^{7}; cstr. קְהִלַּת Dt 33^{4} (poem).

†קֹהֶלֶת, (†קוֹהֶלֶת Ec 12^{8}) **n.m.**$^{Ec\ 1,2}$ collector (of sentences), or (AV RV) **preacher** (*concionator* Jer.: ἐκκλησιαστής 𝔊 (member of an ἐκκλησία); fem. either of office, Ges^{§122r} De Now Che, cf. סֹפֶרֶת Ezr 2^{55}; خَلِيفَة, *Khalif;* Germ. *Majestät, Excellenz;* or as in Ar. with intensive force, one realizing the idea in its completeness (cf. جَمَّاعَة *great collector,* بَاقِرَة *deep investigator* (formed like קֹהֶלֶת), W$^{AG\ i.\ §233\ R.\ c}$ v. Dr$^{Intr.\ 466}$; RVm *great orator*): hence either *convener,* or *great collector* (of sentences), cf. בַּעֲלֵי אֲסֻפּוֹת Ec 12^{11}, בקשׁ ק׳ למצא דברי חפץ v^{10} (but Kö$^{Einl.\ 428}$ Dr$^{l.c.}$ al. *speaker in assembly,* Plumptre *debater*));—ק׳ a king in Jerus., son of David, prob. = Sol., the pseudonym of book of Ec.: Ec 1^{1}, v^{2} (appos. of אֲנִי), called חכם 12^{9}, cf. v^{10}; אמר ק׳ 1^{2}, אמר הק׳ 12^{8} + 7^{27} for MT אמרה ק׳.

†קְהֵלָתָה **n.pr.** (*assembly*) station of Isr. in wilderness Nu $33^{22.23}$ (P); 𝔊 Μακελλαθ.

†[מַקְהֵל] **n.[m.]** **assembly, for worship,** pl.: poss. **choirs,** מַקְהֵלִים ψ 26^{12}, מַקְהֲלוֹת 68^{27}.

†מַקְהֵלֹת **n.pr.loc.** (*place of assembly*);—station of Isr. in Exod. Nu $33^{25.26}$ (P); 𝔊 Μακηλωθ.

קְהָת$_{30}$ **n.pr.m.** Κααθ: son of Levi Gn 46^{11} Ex 6^{16} Nu 3^{17} 1 Ch 5^{27} 6^{1} 23^{6}, cf. Ex 6^{18} Nu 26^{58} and בֶּן־ק׳ Nu 16^{1} 1 Ch 6^{23}; בְּנֵי ק׳ Ex 6^{18} + 4 t. Ch; as a division of Levites Nu $3^{19.29}$ + 9 t.; מִשְׁפְּחוֹת ב׳ ק׳ Jos $21^{20.26}$ 1 Ch 6^{51}, מִשְׁפַּחַת לִבְ׳ ק׳ v^{55}.—Van d. H. has קְהָת Nu 3^{19} + 7 t.

†קְהָתִי **adj. gent.** of foreg., c. art. הַקּ׳ as subst. coll.: מִשְׁפַּחַת (-וֹת) הַקּ׳ Nu 26^{57} + 8 t.; בְּנֵי הַקּ׳ Nu 4^{34} 1 Ch 6^{18} 2 Ch 29^{12}; pl. הַקְּהָתִים Nu 10^{21} and בְּנֵי הַקּ׳ 2 Ch 20^{19} 34^{12}.—Van d. H. has הַקְּהָתִי(ם) Nu 3^{27} 10^{21} + 6 t.

I. קַו only in קַו לָקָו Is $28^{10.10.13.13}$, mimicry of Isaiah's words, perh. senseless, v. צַו p. 846.

II. קַו v. I. קוה.

†קוֹבַע **n.[m.]** **helmet** (word of peculiar form, and dub. √; prob. foreign word; cf. Eth. ቆብዕ: *turban, tiara, cowl,* so Syr. ܩܘܒܥܐ; 𝔗 קוּבְעָא *turban*);—abs. ק׳ Ez 23^{24}; cstr. קוֹבַע נְחשֶׁת 1 S 17^{38}.—Cf. also כּוֹבַע.

קוא only in מִקְוֵא v. II. מִקְוֶה sub II. קוה.

†קְוֵה, or קוֵא **n.pr.terr.** Kuë in Cilicia (cf. KAT$^{2.\ 257}$); מִקְוֵה *from Kuë,* for MT מִקְוֵה 1 K $10^{28.28}$ and ‖ מִקְוֵא 2 Ch $1^{16.16}$; so Wkl$^{Alttest.\ Unters.\ 173}$ Gr Benz Kit, cf. 𝔊 ἐκ Θεκουε (also ἐκ Κωα Field$^{Hexapla\ I.\ 616}$), 𝔙 *de Coa,* Κωδ Lag$^{Onom.\ 273}$, Jer *Coa* Id.$^{ibid.\ 111}$.

†I. [קָוָה] **vb. wait for** (prob. orig. *twist, stretch,* then of *tension* of enduring, waiting: As. *ḳu'û* II, 1. *wait, ḳû, cord;* Ar. قَوِيَ *be strong,* قُوَّة *strength,* also *strand* of rope; Syr. ܩܘܐ *endure, remain, await,* ܩܘ̈ܐ *threads,* so 𝔗 קוּרִין spider's *threads, web*);—**Qal** *Pt.* pl. *those waiting for* (י׳): cstr. קֹוֵי י׳ ψ 37^{9}; so Is 40^{31} van d. H., and Kt Baer Gi (Qr קֹוֵי); sf. קֹוָי 49^{23}, קֹוֶיךָ ψ 25^{3} 69^{7}; קֹוָיו La 3^{25} Qr (Kt קוו, i.e. קֹוו). **Pi.** *Pf.* 3 fs. קִוְּתָה ψ 130^{5}; 1 s. קִוִּיתִי Gn 49^{18} + 5 t., קִוִּיתִי Is 5^{4}, וְק׳ consec. 8^{17}; sf. קִוִּיתִיךָ ψ 25^{21}; 3 pl. קִוּוּ ψ 56^{7} +, etc.; *Impf.* יְקַוֶּה Mi 5^{6} Jb 7^{2}, juss. יְקַו Jb 3^{9}, וַיְקַו Is $5^{2.7}$, etc.; *Imv.* ms. קַוֵּה Ho 12^{7} +; *Inf. abs.* קַוֺּה ψ 40^{2}, קַוֵּה Je 8^{15} 14^{19};—**1.** *wait, or look eagerly, for,* c. לְ rei Is 5^{7} $59^{9.11}$ Je 8^{15}, 13^{16} 14^{19} Jb 3^{9} 6^{19}; לִישׁוּעָתְךָ Gn 49^{18}; c. acc. rei La 2^{16} (sf.), Jb 7^{2} 30^{26} ψ 39^{8}; obj. rei om. Is 64^{2}; sq. inf. Is $5^{2.4}$ ψ 69^{21}; abs. Jb 17^{13}; c. acc. י׳ Is 26^{8} (sf.), ψ $25^{5.21}$ (sf.), 40^{2} (+ inf. abs.), 130^{5}, acc. om. v^{5}, acc. שִׁמְךָ ψ 52^{11} (but rd. prob. אֲחַוֶּה, Hi Che Bae al., v. III. חוה); c. לְ of י׳ Is 8^{17} $25^{9.9}$ 33^{2} 60^{9} (but rd. prob. צִיִּים יִקָּווּ *ships shall gather* (II. קוה), so Du Che^{Hpt} Di-Kit Marti, cf. Skinner (also Luzz Gei Oort), Je 14^{22} Pr 20^{22}; c. אֶל־אֱלֹהִים Ho 12^{7}, אֶל־י׳ Is 51^{5} ψ $27^{14.14}$ 37^{34}. **2.** *lie in wait for,* sq. נַפְשִׁי ψ 56^{7}; sq. לְ pers. ψ 119^{95} (+ inf. purpose). **3.** *wait* (linger) *for* c. לְ of man Mi 5^{6} (‖ יְיַחֵל).

†II. קַו **n.m** $^{Zc\ 1,16}$ **line** (cf. Ko$^{ii\ 1,40\ Anm.\ 2}$),—abs קו Ez 47^{3}+Zc 1^{16} Qr (Kt קוה), קָו Is 34^{17}+; cstr קַו 2 K 21^{13}+,—*measuring-line* (ק׳ מִדָּה Je 31^{39}) 1 K 7^{23} (Qr, Kt קוה, v infr.)=2 Ch 4^{2}, Ez 47^{3}, for marking off a possession in land Is 34^{17} (fig), esp נָטָה ק׳ עַל, in building, Jb 38^{5} (fig of earth), Zc 1^{16} (יִבָּנֶה ‖ ; יִנָּטֶה), so יָצָא ק׳ Je 31^{39} (Qr; Kt קוה), נָטָה ק׳ of designing idol Is 44^{13}, marking off for destruction, נָטָה ק׳ עַל 2 K 21^{13} Is 34^{11} (קרתהו), וְשַׂמְתִּי נ׳ ק׳ La 2^{8}; so מִשְׁפָּט לְקָו Is 28^{17}.—קַוָּם ψ 19^{5} (AV *their line*, fig. of their domain) rd prob קֹלָם *their sound*, Capp Ol Che and now most. Is 18$^{2.7}$ v קוקו infr; 28$^{10.13}$ v I. קַו.

†קוה **n.m.** Kt=II קַו Qr, abs (קָוֶה, or קָוָה) Zc 1^{16}, cstr. (קְוֵה, or קוה) 1 K 7^{23} Je 31^{39}.

†קוקו (or קַוְקַו, קוֹקָו) **n.[m.] might(?)**,—so read (acc. to most) for קַו־קָו, in phrase גּוֹי ק׳ Is 18$^{2.7}$ i e *a mighty nation* (cf Ar قُوَّة *strength*; v. (on redupl) Ges$^{§\ 123\ e}$); > RV '*meting out*' conquered lands, lit 'of line, line' (II קַו).

†I. מִקְוֶה **n.[m.]** hope,—abs. מ׳ 1 Ch 29^{15} Ezr 10^{2}, cstr in phr מִקְוֵה יִשְׂרָאֵל, epithet of י׳, Je 14^{8} 17^{13}, cf. 50^{7}.

†I [תִּקְוָה] **n.f. cord** (cf √*ad init*),—cstr תִּקְוַת (חוּט) הַשָּׁנִי Jos 2$^{18.21}$.

†II תִּקְוָה$_{34}$ **n.f. hope**,—abs ת׳ Ho 2^{17}+, cstr. תִּקְוַת Jb 8^{13}+, sf תִּקְוָתִי 6^{8}+, etc,—**1.** *hope*, Je 31^{17} La 3^{29} Jb 5^{16} 7^{6} 11$^{18.20}$ 14$^{7.19}$ 17^{15a} 19^{10} ψ 62^{6} Pr 19^{18} 26^{12} 29^{20} Ru 1^{12}, פֶּתַח ת׳ Ho 2^{17}, אֲסִירֵי הַתּ׳ Zc 9^{12} (i e. with hope of deliverance) **2** =ground of hope Jb 4^{6} ψ 71^{5} (cf. 62^{6}) **3** *things hoped for, outcome*, Ez 19^{5} 37^{11} Jb 6^{8} 8^{13} 17^{15b} (but rd. טוֹבָתִי 𝔊 Me Bi Siegf Beer Bu Du), 27^{8} ψ 9^{19} Pr 10^{28} 11$^{7.23}$ 23^{18} 24^{14} (del Toy as gloss); אַחֲרִית וְת׳ Je 29^{11} (i e. by hendyadis, the hoped-for future)

†III תָּקְוָה **n pr.m.** (*hope*, cf. Lag$^{BN\ 131}$);—**1.** father-in-law of Huldah 2 K 22^{14}, Θεκουαν, A 𝔊L Θεκ(κ)ουε (=תוקהת 2 Ch 34^{22} Kt [Qr תָּקְהַת], Καθουαλ, A Θακουαθ, 𝔊L Θεκωε) **2.** post-ex name Ezr 10^{15}, Ελκεια, A 𝔊L Θεκουε.

†II [קָוָה] **vb. collect** (NH Hiph. *collect*),—**Niph.** *be collected*, *Pf* 3 pl וְנִקְווּ consec. Je 3^{17} (of nations), *Impf* 3 mpl. יִקָּווּ Gn 1^{9} (P, of waters; both c. אֶל loc), so prob of ships (c. לְ pers) Is 60^{9} (for MT יְקַוּוּ), v. I קוה **Pi. 1.**

†II. [מִקְוֶה] **n.[m.] collection, collected mass** (P),—cstr. מִקְוֵה Gn 1^{10} (מִקְוֶה also v^{9}, for מָקוֹם, acc. to 𝔊 Ball), Ex 7^{19} Lv 11^{36}, all of water. —מ׳ 1 K 10$^{28.28}$ = מִקְוֵא 2 Ch 1^{16} (*company* of merchants; *drove* of horses), v. קֹוֶה.

†מִקְוָה **n.f. reservoir**;—Is 22^{11}.

פְּקַח־קוֹחַ v. קוֹחַ.

†[קוּט] **vb. feel a loathing** (‖ form of קוּץ q v.),—**Qal** *Impf.* 1 s. אָקוּט בְּדוֹר ψ 95^{10} *I felt a loathing at* the generation **Niph.** *Pf.* 2 mpl. consec. וּנְקֹטֹתֶם בִּפְנֵיכֶם Ez 20^{43} *ye shall feel loathing against your faces* (at yourselves), c. בְּ rei, so 36^{31} (עַל rei); metapl. (as if from קטט) 3 pl consec וְנָקֹטּוּ בִּפְנֵיהֶם Ez 6^{9} (אֶל rei, for עַל, +לְ rei, for which Co בְּ, Krae בְּ or עַל); also 3 fs. נָקְטָה נַפְשִׁי בְּ Jb 10^{1} (as if from *נקט; on both forms v. Ges$^{§\ 67\ dd,\ 72\ dd}$). **Hithpō'l.** *id.* *Impf.* 1 s. אֶתְקוֹטָט בְּ ψ 139^{21} (We אֶתְקוֹמָם), abs. וָאֶתְקוֹטָטָה 119^{158}.—Ez 16^{47} v קָט, Jb 8^{14} v. foll.

†[קוּט] dub **vb intrans.**, assumed mng. **break, snap** (supposed to be akin to Ar. قَطَّ *cut, cut off, pare, trim* [whence Buhl assumes √קטט]), to account for יָקוֹט Jb 8^{14}, either as **Qal** *Impf* 3 ms. whose hope *snappeth*, or as **n.[m]**=*fragile thing* (‖ בֵּית עַכָּבִישׁ, cf Di Bu); prob. crpt, Du Beer rd. קוּרִים, Bu conj קְרֵי קַיִט [Aramaism for ק׳ קַיִץ]

קוֹל

(√of foll; As *kâlu*, *speak*, *call*, *cry* (TelAm. *lament*), *kûlu*, *speech*; Ar (و)قَالَ *say*, قَوْلٌ *word*, Eth. ቃል: *sound*, *voice*, and so Aram. קָלָא, ܩܳܠܳܐ, Ph קל *voice*, so NPun. קאל, sf. קולא; Sl^{2} *sound, voice*, NH קוֹל *noise*, בַּת קוֹל=*echo*).

קוֹל (sts., c pref et suff, קֹל)$_{506}$ **n.m.** $^{Gn\ 39,14}$ **sound, voice**;—abs קוֹל Gn 4^{10}+ (הַקֹּל 27^{22} 45^{16}), cstr קוֹל 3^{8}+ (וְקֹל Ex 19^{16}, לְקֹל 4$^{8.8}$), sf. קוֹלִי 1 S 26^{17}+, קוֹלְךָ Ju 18^{25}+, etc (קֹלִי Gn 22^{18}, קֹלֶךָ Ex 3^{18}, etc.); pl. (usu. of thunder) קֹלֹת Ex 9^{23}+4 t, קוֹלֹת 20^{18} (Gi v^{15}), קֹלוֹת 1 S 2^{17}+5 t,—**1.** *sound*: esp **a.** of human voice Jos 6^{10} 2 K 7^{10}, in speech Gn 27$^{22.22}$ 1 S 1^{13} 24^{17} 26$^{17.17}$; recognized (הִכִּיר) v^{17} Je 18^{3}; יְפֵה ק׳ Ez 33^{32} *pleasant of voice*, cf. Ct 2$^{14.14}$ 8^{13}, in singing Ex 32^{18} 2 S 19^{36} Is 52^{8}, calling Ju 9^{7}, shouting Ex 32^{17} 1 S 4$^{6.6}$ 1 K 1^{40} Ezr 3^{13}, rejoicing Je 7$^{34.34.34.34}$=16^{9} 25^{10} 33^{11}, praise ψ 66^{8} 26^{7} Jo 2^{10}, laughter Je 30^{19}, weeping Gn 21^{16} Ju 2^{4} 1 S 11^{4} Ru 1$^{9.14}$ Ezr 3^{13}, outcry Gn 39$^{15.18}$ 1 S 4^{14} Je 8^{19}, distress, lament Je 9^{18} Ez 27^{30} Zc 11^{3} ψ 102^{6},

supplication ψ $28^{2.6}$ 31^{23} 86^{6}; adv. ק׳ אֶחָד *with one voice* Ex 24^{3} 2 Ch 5^{13}, ק׳ גָּדוֹל *loud voice* 2 S 15^{23}+ (cf. בְּק׳ ג׳ Gn 39^{14} 1 S 28^{12}+), ק׳ רָם †Dt 27^{14}, נָשָׂא ק׳ Gn 21^{16} + (v. נשׂא **1 b** (5)), הֵרִים ק׳ 39^{15} + (v. רום **Hiph.**); on ק׳ as independ. nom., sq. subj. + vb. of calling ψ 3^{5} 27^{7} 142^{2} v. Ges$^{§ 144 m}$. **b.** of י׳ Gn $3^{8.10}$ Is 6^{8} Ex 19^{19} 1 K 19^{13} Mi 6^{9} Ez 10^{5} (cf. also **2 b**) +; adv. ק׳ גָּדוֹל Dt 5^{19} Ez 9^{1}; ק׳ דְּמָמָה דַקָּה 1 K 19^{12}. **c.** of seraph Is 6^{4}. **d.** of angel Dn 8^{16} (ק׳ דְּבָרָיו ק׳ אָדָם i.e. in human speech, cf. Bev); $10^{6.9.9}$. **e.** of animals: bleating of sheep 1 S 15^{14}, lowing of cattle v^{14} Je 9^{9}, neighing of horses 8^{16}, roaring of lion Am 3^{4} Je 2^{15}+, hissing of serpent 46^{22} (in sim.), singing of birds Na 2^{8} Zp 2^{14} ψ 104^{12} Ct 2^{12} Ec 12^{4}. **f.** exclamation, at beginning of cl., *a sound of* . . . ! = *hark!* Gn 4^{10} Is 13^{4} 40^{3} 52^{8} Je 4^{15} 10^{22} 50^{28} Ct 2^{8} 5^{2} (Ges$^{§ 146 b}$). **2.** *sound:* **a.** of instrument, esp. ק׳ (הַ)שֹּׁפָר Ex 9^{16} 20^{18} (Gi v^{15}) Am 2^{2} 1 K 1^{41}+, חֲצֹצְרוֹת וגו׳ 2 Ch 5^{13}, כִּנּוֹר Ez 26^{13}, עוּגָב Jb 21^{12}; of פַּעֲמֹנִים on high priest's robe Ex 28^{35}. **b.** thunder-clap or peal (cf. Dr 1 S 12^{17}), קוֹל י׳ (or קוֹלוֹ) Am 1^{2} Is $30^{30.31}$ Je 10^{13} = 51^{16}, Jo 2^{11} 4^{16} ψ 18^{14} = 2 S 22^{14}, ψ $29^{3-5.7-9}$ 46^{7} Jb 37^{4} (cf 1 S 7^{10} ψ $77^{18.19}$ 104^{7}), so esp. pl. abs. (v. supr.) †Ex $9^{23.28.29.33.34}$ 19^{16} 20^{18} (Gi v^{15}), 1 S 7^{10} $12^{17.18}$ Jb 28^{26} = 38^{25}. **c.** קוֹל רַגְלֶיהָ 1 K 14^{6} cf 2 K 6^{32}, and (prob.) Gn 3^{8}; also ק׳ (הַ)צְּעָדָה 2 S 5^{24} = 1 Ch 14^{15}; of runners 2 K 11^{13} 2 Ch 23^{12}. **d.** stamping of hoofs Je 47^{3} Ez 26^{10} (+ chariots, etc.), cf. 1 K 1^{41}. **e.** of chariots Na 3^{2} Jo 2^{5}, wheels Ez 3^{13}; whip Na 3^{2}. **f.** of sea, and great waters Hb 3^{10} Ez 1^{24} 43^{2} ψ $93^{3.4}$, cf. Je 50^{42} (in sim.); ק׳ צִנּוֹרֶיךָ ψ 42^{8}. **g.** earthquake Ez 37^{7}. **h.** a fall Je 49^{21} Ez 26^{15} 31^{16}. **i.** of a multitude 1 S 4^{14} Is 13^{4} Ez 23^{42}. **j.** din of war Ex 32^{17} Je $50^{22.46}$ 51^{55} La 2^{7}. **k.** of wings Ez 1^{24} 3^{13} 10^{5}. **l.** flame Jo 2^{5}; crackling of thorns Ec 7^{6}; rustling of leaves Lv 26^{36}. **m.** millstones Je 25^{10} Ec 12^{4}. **3.** of articulate speech, thing said. **a.** (1) oft. of human advice, command, entreaty Gn 3^{17} 4^{23} Ex 3^{18} $4^{1.9}$ Dt 1^{45} $21^{18.18.20}$ 1 S 2^{25} $8^{7.9}$ 2 S 12^{18}; ק׳ דבריכם Dt 1^{34} 5^{25}; even of written words 2 K 10^{6}; so also ק׳ הָאֹת Ex $4^{8.8}$ *voice* (teaching) *of the sign.* (2) of a report Gn 45^{16} Ec 10^{20}. (3) of a proclamation Ex 36^{6} (P), 2 Ch 24^{9} 30^{5} 36^{22} = Ezr 1^{1}, Ezr 10^{7} Ne 8^{15}. (4) ק׳ אָלָה Lv 5^{1} *utterance of adjuration* **b.** oft. (esp Dt Je) of words of י׳ Gn 22^{18} 26^{5} Ex 5^{2} 15^{26} 19^{5} Dt 8^{20} 9^{23} $13^{5.19}$+, Ju $2^{2.20}$ 6^{10} 1 S $12^{14.15}$ $15^{1.19.20.22}$ Je $3^{13.25}$ 7^{23}+; of מַלְאַךְ י׳ Ex $23^{21.22}$.—קֹל Je 3^{9} v. sub קלל.

†**קוֹלָיָה** n.pr.m. (*voice of* י׳);—**1.** father of proph. Ahab Je 29^{21}. **2.** Benjamite Ne 11^{7}; Κωδια, A Κωλεια, 𝔊L Κολεια. Prob. also **3.** Levite Ezr 10^{23}, MT קְלִיטָא but 𝔊 Κωλεια, A Κωλαιι (cf. Gray$^{Prop. N\ 297}$).

קוּם$_{628}$ **vb. arise, stand up, stand;**—(NH in der. spec. and deriv., Ph. Hiph. Pt and מקם *place;* Ar. قَامَ (و) *stand, rise,* Eth. ቆመ: *stand, stop;* Sab. מקם, *place,* Hom$^{Chrest. 127}$; Aram. קוּם, ܩܳܡ = BH, so OAram. Nab. קום; Palm Aph. אקים *erect* statue; cf. prob. As. *kumu* (*k* = כ), *place, dwelling, kum, kêmu, in place of,* and perh. *kaiamânu, enduring, constant* (v. כיון); Thes cp. also Sam. ࠒࠅࠌ, *live,* cf. esp. 𝔗 Pa),— **Qal**$_{460}$ *Pf* 3 ms. קָם 1 S 17^{48}+, וְקָאם consec. Ho 10^{14} (Ges$^{§ 72 p}$); 2 ms קַמְתָּ 2 S 12^{21}, etc.; *Impf.* 3 ms. יָקוּם Ex 21^{19}, juss. יָקֹם Gn 27^{31}, וַיָּקָם Jb 22^{28} (Ges$^{§ 109 h}$ Dr$^{§ 102 (3)}$); וַיָּקָם (לָךְ) Gn 4^{8}+, etc.; *Imv.* ms. קוּם Gn 13^{17}+, fpl. קֹמְנָה Is 32^{9}, etc.; *Inf. abs.* קוֹם Je 44^{29}, *cstr.* קוּם Am 5^{2}+, etc; *Pt.* fs. קָמָה Mi 7^{6}, mpl. קָמִים 2 S 18^{31}+, הַקּוֹמִים 2 K 16^{17} (Ges$^{§ 72 p}$), etc.;— **1.** *arise.* מִתַּחְתָּיו Ex 10^{23} (E). Specif: **a.** after lying down (sleep, sickness, mourning, etc.), 1 S $3^{6.8}$ 2 S 12^{21} Ex 21^{19} Gn $19^{33.35}$ 31^{17} Ru 3^{14} Ec 12^{4}+50 t.; fr lying dead, וַיָּקָם עַל־רַגְלָיו 2 K 13^{21}, cf. Jb 14^{12} Is $26^{14.19}$ ψ 88^{11}; after falling Am 5^{2} 8^{14} Je 8^{4} 25^{27}+4 t. (chiefly fig.), after being smitten, wounded, etc. ψ 18^{39} ‖ 2 S 22^{39}, Is 27^{9} (of Asherim, etc.), 43^{17}+4 t.; from sitting, reclining, esp. at meals Gn 25^{34} 1 S 1^{9} 20^{34} (מֵעִם הַשֻּׁלְחָן; v^{25} see קֶדֶם), Est 7^{7} (+ אֶל in constr. praegn.), but also Ju 3^{20} (מֵעַל), 2 S $2^{14.14.15}$, Jon 3^{6} (מִכִּסְאוֹ), + 11 t., + (*arise* = stand up, in respect), Gn 19^{1} (+ לִקְרָאתָם), 31^{35} (מִפָּנֶיךָ), Lv 19^{32} (מִפְּנֵי), Is 49^{7} Jb 29^{8}; + וַיִּשְׁתַּחוּ 2 K 2^{19}, cf. Gn 23^{7} Ex 33^{10} 1 S 20^{41} 25^{41},—(v. also **e**), from kneeling (מִן, + מִלִּפְנֵי loc.) 1 K 8^{54}, fr. obeisance 1 S 24^{42} Est 8^{4}; from bending over (עַל) dead Gn 23^{3} (P). **b.** out of (מִן) a condition, state, Ezr 9^{5}. **c.** of bear *rising* עַל pers., 1 S 17^{35}. **d.** *arise* (+ stand) Ex 33^{8} ψ 20^{9} (fig of success, prosperity), Jb 24^{22} (*id.*), +, of sheaf Gn 37^{7}; of waters Jos 3^{16} (נֵד־אֶחָד). **e.** constr. praegn. *arise* (and stand) for a purpose Nu 11^{32} (E); *over,* עַל pers., 2 S 12^{17}. **f.** *arise* as prelim. to formal speech Ju 20^{8} Mi 6^{1} Je 1^{17} 1 Ch 28^{2} (עַל־רַגְלָיו), Pr 31^{28} Jb 30^{28}+5 t; to testify (against) Dt $19^{15.16}$ (both בְּ pers.), ψ 27^{12} 35^{11}, cf. also וַיָּקָם בִּי Jb 16^{8} (of כַּחַשׁ q.v.; Bu כַּעַשׂ); to vindicate Jb 19^{25} (עַל־עָפָר); to rd. aloud Ne 9^{3} (עַל־עָמְדָם); to bless people 2 Ch 30^{27} (priests). **g.** to listen to God's

word Nu 23^{18} Is 32^{9}, to praise God 2 Ch 20^{19} Ne 9$^{4.5}$. **h.** of noise, tumult Ho 10^{14}; of light Jb 25^{3} (עַל pers) **2.** *arise,* in hostile sense (oft with idea of suddenness), c. עַל pers. Dt 19^{11} (out of ambush), 22^{26} Ju 9^{18} 20^{5} ψ 27^{3} (of war), Ob^{1} (לַמִּלְחָמָה), + 11 t, + Jb 30^{12} (acc to Bu, rdg עָלַי for עַל־יָמִין), + (of י׳) Am 7^{9} (ב instr), Is 14^{22} 31^{2}, c אֶל pers Gn 4^{8} 1 S 22^{13} 24^{8} (Gi v^{7}), c ב pers. Mi 7^{6} ψ 27^{12} (false witness), Mi 7^{6}, c עִם pers ψ 94^{16} (||יתיצב), v. esp. pt c. sf = *those rising up against me* (thee, etc.) Ex 15^{7} 32^{25} Dt 33^{11} + 8 t + ψ 109^{28} (rd. קָמַי יֵבֹשׁוּ 𝔊𝔙 Bae We Du, cf Hup Dr), c מִן *from, out of* Jos 8$^{7.19}$ Ju 9$^{35.43}$ 20^{33}, = *revolt* Nu 16^{2} (לִפְנֵי pers), 2 K 12^{21} 2 Ch 13^{6}, cf Hb 2^{7}. **3.** *arise,* abs, = become powerful Pr 28$^{12.28}$ **4.** *arise* = come on the scene, appear, of leader, prophet, king Ju 5$^{7.7}$ 10$^{1.3}$ Dt 13^{2} 34^{10} Ex 1^{8} 2 K 23^{25}; of years of famine Gn 41^{30}, c אַחֲרֵי pers Dt 29^{21} Ju 2^{10} 1 K 3^{12}, c תַּחַת, *in place of,* 1 K 8^{20} = 2 Ch 6^{10}, Nu 32^{14}, c עַל־מַמְלֶכֶת 2 Ch 21^{4}, c מִן Nu 24^{17} (sceptre out of Isr), of calamity, Na 1^{9} Pr 24^{22}, מִצָּהֳרַיִם יָקוּם חָלֶד Jb 11^{17} i e to shine upon thee **5.** *arise* for, i e. to become, c ל rei, ביום קומי לעד Zp 3^{8} (read לְעֵד, *for a witness,* 𝔊𝔖 We Now GASm cf. Da), הֶחָמָס קָם לְמַטֵּה־רֶשַׁע Ez 7^{11} (but dub.; Co Berthol Krae קָמַל) **6. a.** *arise* for action, esp of י׳ arising [from his throne], + inf Is 2$^{19.21}$, for judgment ψ 76^{10} (לַמִּשְׁפָּט), Jb 31^{14}; oft. Imv. Nu 10^{35} Je 2^{27} ψ 3^{8} + 8 t ψψ + 2 Ch 6^{41} (c. לנוחך), ψ 132^{8} (c למנוחתך), Impf Is 28^{21} + 4 t., Imv. also of men, *arise! up!* i.e act! Ju 4^{14} Ezr 10^{4}, of idols Je 2^{28}, Impf of the tongue (personified) Is 54^{17} (אתך למשפט) **b.** *arise* (out of inaction), introducing some specific deed Gn 21^{18} Ex 32^{1} Ju 5^{12} 8$^{20.21}$ Je 49^{14} (לַמִּלְחָמָה), Ob^{1} (קומו ונקומה עָלֶיהָ לַמִּלְחָמָה), + 37 t. **c.** esp. *arise* = start, make a move, to go somewhere, Gn 13^{17} 19$^{14.15}$ 1 S 9^{3} Jon 1^{3} (in flight), 3^{3} + 110 t **7.** *stand* esp fig **a.** = *maintain oneself* Jos 7$^{12.13}$ (JE; לִפְנֵי pers), Am 7$^{2.5}$ Na 1^{6} La 1^{14} ψ 1^{5} 24^{3} Jb 41^{18} (of sword), of courage (רוח) Jos 2^{11} (D, באיש, + לִפְנֵי pers). **b.** = *be established, confirmed,* of kingdom 1 S 24^{21} (בְּיָדְךָ, Gi v^{20}); of purchase Lv 27^{19}, c ל pers *be assured to* 25^{30} Gn 23$^{17.20}$ (all P) **c.** *stand, endure* 1 S 13^{14} Jb 8^{15} (||עָמַד), 15^{29}. **d.** = *be fixed,* of price, Lv 27$^{14.17}$. **e.** = *be valid,* of vows, Nu 30$^{5.6}$ + 6 t Nu 30 + v^{10} (c עַל pers., all P) **f** = *be proven* Dt 19^{15}. **g.** = *be fulfilled* Je 44^{29} (impf. + inf abs.; עַל pers.), Jb 22^{28} (ל pers), of י׳'s purpose Je 51^{29} (עַל pers.), Is 14^{24} Pr 19^{21}, cf. Je 44^{28} Is 40^{8} 46^{10}; of human plans, *succeed* Is 7^{7} 8^{10} 28^{18} Pr 15^{22}. **h.** *persist,* עַל־נְדִיבוֹת יָקוּם Is 32^{8} lit *on noble things doth he take his stand.* **i.** יָקוּם עַל־שֵׁם אָחִיו Dt 25^{6} *he shall stand upon the name of his dead brother,* represent him **j.** of eyes, = *be set, fixed,* without vision 1 S 4^{15} 1 K 14^{4} (עין **1 i**).

†**Pi.** *Pf* 3 ms. קִיַּם Est 9$^{31.32}$, 3 pl. קִיְּמוּ v$^{27.31}$, *Impf* 1 s וַאֲקַיֵּמָה ψ 119^{106}, *Imv* ms sf. קַיְּמֵנִי v^{28}; *Inf cstr* לְקַיֵּם Ez 13^{6} +;—late (Aram.) **1.** *fulfil,* Ez 13^{6} ψ 119^{106}. **2. a.** *confirm, ratify,* Ru 4^{7}. **b.** *confirm, establish,* of י׳ ψ 119^{28} (c. sf. acc) **c.** *impose,* an obligation, עַל pers. Est 9$^{21.31b}$, עַל reflex v$^{27.31c}$, c acc. rei v$^{29.31a.32}$. †**Pōʿl.** *raise up Impf* 2 ms. תְּקוֹמֵם Is 58^{12}, 1 s אֲקוֹמֵם 44^{26}, 3 mpl יְקוֹמֵמוּ 61^{4} (all of rebuilding),—יְקוֹמֵם Mi 2^{8}, rd תְּקוּמוּ We Now, or קָמִים GASm Buhl

†**Hithpōʿl.** *raise oneself,* = *rise up: Pt.* fs. מִתְקוֹמָמָה Jb 20^{27} (ל pers *against*); ms. sf מִתְקוֹמְמִי 27^{7} *one rising up against me* (|| אֹיְבִי), pl abs. מִתְקוֹמְמִים ψ 17^{7}, sf מִתְקֹמְמַי 59^{2}; v also 139^{21}, reading וּבְמִתְקוֹמְמֶיךָ (for MT וּבִתְק׳ || מְשַׂנְאֶיךָ); see also קוט

Hiph. 146 *Pf* 3 ms. הֵקִים Jos 4^{9} +; 2 ms. וַהֲקֵמֹתָ Ex 26^{30} Dt 27^{2}, 1 s. הקימתי 1 S 15^{13}, הֲקִמֹתִי Gn 9^{17} +, etc, *Impf* 3 ms. יָקִים Dt 18^{15} +; juss. יָקֵם 1 S 1^{23} +, וַיָּקֶם Ju 2^{16} +, 2 fpl. תְּקִימֶנָה Je 44^{25}, etc, *Imv.* ms הָקֵם 2 S 7^{25} +, etc; *Inf abs.* הָקִים Je 44^{25}, הָקֵם Dt 22^{4} Ju 7^{19}, cstr הָקִים 2 S 3^{10} +, etc; *Pt* מֵקִים Am 6^{14} +, etc,—†**1.** *cause to arise, raise.* **a** the prostrate (acc pers vel rei) 2 S 12^{17} (מִן־הָאָרֶץ), Dt 22^{4} (הָקֵם תָּקִים עִמּוֹ), ψ 41^{11} Ec 4$^{10.10}$, fig Am 5^{2} 9$^{11.11}$ Ho 6^{2} Is 49^{8} 1 S 2^{8} = ψ 113^{7} (|| הרים), Jb 4^{4}, Je 50^{32}. **b.** from throne (מִן) Is 14^{9} **c.** *lift up* shield (צִנָּה) against (עַל) Ez 26^{8}. **d.** fig. *raise* (to dignity, power) Is 49^{6}. **2.** †**a.** *raise, set up,* stones Jos 4^{9} (JE; בתוך loc), v^{20} (JE, ב loc), 24^{26} (E; תַּחַת, שָׁם loc), Dt 27^{2}; pillars 1 K 7$^{21.21.21}$ || 2 Ch 3^{17} Ex 40^{18} (P); פֶּסֶל, מַצֵּבָה Ju 18^{30} (ל reflex.), Lv 26^{1} Dt 16^{22}; throne, fig, 2 S 3^{10}, king Dt 28^{36} (both c. עַל *over*). **b.** *erect, build:* Is 23^{13} Ex 26^{30}, heap of stones over (עַל) Jos 7^{26} 8^{29}, altar 2 S 24^{18} (לי׳) || 1 Ch 21^{18} (*id.*), 1 K 16^{32} (לבעל), 2 K 21^{3} (*id.*) = 2 Ch 33^{3} (לבעלים), curtains Je 10^{20} (of Judah's tent, in fig); tabern., etc, Ex 40$^{2.18.33}$ + 4 t. Nu; *erect* against (עַל) Is 29^{3}. †**c.** fig of setting up law ψ 78^{5} (עֵדוּת; || שׂים). †**3.** *raise up* = bring on the scene: c acc., sons in place of (תַּחַת) fathers Jos 5^{7}, אַחֲרֶיךָ 2 S 7^{12} = 1 Ch 17^{11}, 1 K 15^{4}; *raise up* זֶרַע לְאָחִיךָ Gn 38^{8} (J); judges Ju 2$^{16.18}$

(לָהֶם), cf. 3$^{9.15}$ (both ל pers.); king Je 30^{9}, צֶמַח צַדִּיק 23^{5}, prophet Je 29^{15} Dt 18$^{15.18}$, priest 1 S 2^{35} (all ל pers.); shepherds, etc. Mi 5^{5} (עַל *against*), Zc 11^{16}; לְהָקִים לְאָחִיו שֵׁם Dt 25^{7}; plant of name Ez 34^{29} (ל pers.); evil (רָעָה) 2 S 12^{11} (עַל *against*). †**4. a.** *raise up*=rouse, stir up (lion, in fig.) Gn 49^{9} (poem)=Nu 24^{9} (JE). **b.** *instigate*, c. acc. pers.+עַל *against* Am 6^{14} 1 S 22^{8}; +ל pers. 1 K 11$^{14.23}$; c. acc. alone Hb 1^{6}. †**5.** *raise up*=constitute, הֲקִים־אֹתְךָ . . . לוֹ לְעָם Dt 29^{12} cf. 28^{9} Jb 16^{12}; וָאָקִים מִבְּנֵיכֶם לִנְבִיאִים Am 2^{11}; יָקֵם סְעָרָה לִדְמָמָה ψ 107^{29} (cf. **Qal 5**). **6.** *cause to stand:* †**a.** *set, station*, sentinels Ju 7^{19} (הָקֵם הֵקִים), Je 51^{12}, cf. 6^{17} (עַל pers.), 23^{4} Ez 34^{23}; *set* feet on (עַל) rock ψ 40^{3}. †**b.** *cause to hold one's ground* ψ 89^{44} (בַּמִּלְחָמָה). †**c.** *establish* throne 2 Ch 7^{18}, כָּל־אַפְסֵי־אָרֶץ Pr 30^{4}. †**d.** *establish* (make, ratify) covenant, of י׳, c. אֵת (prep.) pers. Gn 6^{18} 9$^{9.11}$ 17$^{19.21}$ Ex 6^{4} (all P), Ez 16^{62}; c. בֵּין . . . בֵּין Gn 9^{17} 17^{7} (both P); c. ל pers. Ez 16^{60}. †**e.** = *make binding*, a vow Nu 30$^{14.15.15}$. **f.** = *carry out, give effect to* (Dr $^{Sm. 1, 23}$), oath, covenant, vow, word, plan, command, of man 1 S 15$^{11.13}$+6 t.; of י׳ Gn 26^{3} Lv 26^{9} 1 S 1^{23} 1 K 6^{12} Dt 8^{18} Je 23^{20}+18 t. †**g.** לְהָקִים שֵׁם־הַמֵּת עַל־נַחֲלָתוֹ Ru 4$^{5.10}$ *to cause the dead man's name to stand upon his inheritance* (cf. **Qal 7 i**). †**Hoph.** *Pf.* 3 ms. הֻקַם עָל 2 S 23^{1} *be raised up* (on הֻקַּם van d. H., v. Dr); הוּקַם *be set up* Ex 40^{17} (of tabern.); הוּקַם אֶת־דִּבְרֵי פ׳ Je 35^{14} *be held upright* (Ges $^{§ 121 a}$), i.e. observed, obeyed.

קוֹמָה, קֹמָה $_{45}$ **n.f. height**;—abs. קוֹמָה Ex 38^{18}+, קֹמָה 27^{18}; cstr. קוֹמַת 1 K 6^{26}+; sf. קוֹמָתוֹ 7^{23}+, קֹמָתוֹ Ex 25^{10}+, etc.;—**1.** *height*, of pers., *stature* 1 S 16^{7} Ez 13^{18} Ct 7^{8}; מְלֹא־קוֹמָתוֹ 1 S 28^{20} *his full length.* **2.** of tree 2 K 19^{23}= Is 37^{24}; in fig. Is 10^{33} Ez 31$^{3.5.10.14}$; of vine (fig.) Ez 19^{11} and שִׁפְלַת ק׳ 17^{6} *low of height.* **3.** of artificial structures: temple, its parts, furnishings, etc., 1 K 6^{2}+12 t. 1 K 6, 7, 2 K 25$^{17.17}$= Je 52$^{21.22}$, 2 Ch 4$^{1.2}$ 6^{13}; a wall Ez 40^{5}; tabern. and furnishings Ex 25$^{10.23}$+8 t. Ex (all P); Noah's ark Gn 6^{15} (P).

†קָמָה **n.f. standing grain**;—abs. ק׳ Ex 22^{5}+; cstr. קָמַת Dt 23$^{26.26}$; pl. cstr. קָמוֹת Ju 15^{5};—*standing grain* (mature) Ex 22^{5} (E), Dt 16^{9} 23$^{26.26}$ Ju 15$^{5.5}$ Is 17^{5}; לִפְנֵי ק׳ 2 K 19^{26}=Is 37^{27} (i.e. before maturity); in fig. Ho 8^{7}.—Cf. Vogelst $^{Landwirthsch. 51}$

†[קִים] **n.m. adversary** (prop. *uprising, insurgent* [Kö $^{II. 1, 60}$], cf. √**Qal 2**);—sf. קִימָנוּ (Kö $^{II. 1, 442}$) Jb 22^{20}, but prob. corrupt; Ges $^{§ 91 f}$, Du קָמֵ(י)נוּ (Pt. sf.) Me Bu יְקָמָם, Perles $^{Anal. 59}$ קִנְיָנָם.

†[קִימָה] **n.f. rising up**;—sf. קִימָתָם La 3^{63} (opp. שִׁבְתָּם).

†קָמוֹן **n.pr.loc.** Ju 10^{5}, Ραμνων, A Ραμμω (𝔊L Καλκων); in Gilead Jos $^{Ant. v. 7, 6}$ (Καμων); prob.=Καμουν of Polyb $^{v. 70, 12}$ (named next after Πελλα); Buhl $^{Geogr. 256}$ thinks of *Ḳumêm, Ḳamm* (Schumacher $^{Northern\ Ajlûn\ 137 f.}$), between Jarmuk and Jabbok, W. of *Irbid*.

†קוֹמְמִיּוּת **n.f. uprightness**;—only as adv. Lv 26^{13} made you go *upright*, i.e. as freemen.

אֲלְקוּם v. supr. p. 39.

†יְקוּם **n.[m.] substance, existence** כָּל־הַיְקוּם = *all that subsists* Gn 7$^{4.23}$ (man and animal), in more limited sense Dt 11^{6}.

†יָקִים **n.pr.m.** (*he lifteth up;* cf. Sab. n.pr. יהקם Hal ^{151});—Ιακειμ, A (24^{12}) Ελιακειμ: **1.** Benjamite 1 Ch 8^{19}. **2.** Levite 24^{12}.

†תְּקוּמָה **n.f. standing, power to stand** (cf. √**Qal 7 a**);—abs. ת׳ Lv 26^{37} (c. לִפְנֵי pers.).

†[תְּקוֹמֵם], וּבִתְקוֹמְמֶיךָ ψ 139^{21}, v. √, **Hithpōʿl.**

מָקוֹם, מָקֹם (Ex 29^{31}, etc.) $_{399}$ **n.m.** $^{Gn 19, 13}$ (but v. infr.), **standing-place, place**;—abs. מ׳ Ex 21^{13}+; cstr. מְקוֹם Gn 12^{6}+ (oft. before אֲשֶׁר 39^{20}+); sf. מְקוֹמוֹ 1 S 3^{2}+, מְקֹמוֹ Gn 18^{33}+, etc.; pl. usu. מְקֹמוֹת Ju 19^{13}+, מְקוֹמוֹת 1 S 7^{16} Je 29^{14}, ־מֹת 2 S 17^{9}+2 t.; sf. מְקוֹמֹתֵיכֶם Am 4^{6}, etc. [appar. **f.** (not Gn 18^{24}, where עִיר is in mind, but) Jb 20^{9} (emend. v. Comm.), and Codd. (either Kt or Qr) Ju 19^{13} 2 S 17$^{9.12}$; mostly expl. away by Albr $^{ZAW\ xvi\ (1896), 63}$];—**1. a.** *standing-place* Ex 3^{5} (E), Jos 5^{15} Ex 33^{21} Nu 23$^{13.27}$ (all JE), Gn 19^{27} (J), Jos 3^{3} (D), of מַצֵּבוֹת, etc., 2 K 23^{14}, of ark (place where it is set, stands) 1 K 8^{7} = 2 Ch 5^{8}, earth Is 13^{13} Jb 9^{6}, rock Jb 14^{18} 18^{4}; cf. 38$^{12.19}$. **b.** *station*, where soldiers are placed Jos 8^{19} (JE), Ju 20$^{33.33}$; *post* in battle 2 S 11^{16}. **c.** *post, office* 1 K 20^{24} Ec 10^{4}. **2. a.** *place* where a thing belongs Gn 29^{3} (J), Jos 4^{18} (JE), 1 S 5^{3} Is 46^{7} Jb 6^{17} 37^{1} (of the heart), Ec 1^{5}; esp. of ark 1 S 5^{11}+9 t.; of pers.=destination Ju 11^{19}. **b.** esp. (1) *place of human abode* Gn 13^{14} 20^{13} Ju 7^{7} 1 S 2^{20}+42 t., + מְקוֹם אָהֳלֵךְ Is 54^{2}. (2) of י׳'s abode Ho 5^{15}, in heaven

Mi 1[3] Is 26[21] 1 K 8[30] = 2 Ch 6[21]. (3) lair of lion (fig.) Je 4[7]. **3.** *place* = **a.** *city* Gn 18[24.26] 20[11] Dt 21[19] (‖ עיר) 2 K 18[25] + 39 t. (1 S 7[16] המקדשים ‭𝔊‬, cf. We HPS). **b.** of land Canaan Ex 23[20] 1 S 12[8] Je 16[2.3] (‖ ארץ) + 17 t. (12 t. Je), Philistia 1 S 14[46], Egypt Je 44[29], appos מְדִינָה Est 4[3], = עיר + מדינה 8[17]. **c.** plot, parcel, of ground Is 7[23], מקום הַגֹּרֶן 1 Ch 21[22], cf. v[25] 2 Ch 3[1]. **d.** land, region Nu 20[5] 32[1]; Che (privately) prop בִּמְקֹם בְּקָעוֹת ψ 84[7] (for בעמק הַבָּכָא, cf. Is 41[18]). **4.** in gen., *place, locality, spot* Gn 28[16.17] Ju 2[5] Am 4[6] Ne 4[6.7.14] + (221 t. in all); מקום פלני אלמני *place of such a one* † 1 S 21[3] 2 K 6[8]; בְּכָל־הַמָּקוֹם אֲשֶׁר Ex 20[24] (E, Gi v[21]) *in all places that*, בְּכָל־מ׳ Nu 18[31] = *anywhere*, cf. Dt 12[13]; = *everywhere* Pr 15[3] Mal 1[11], cf. Am 8[3], מ׳ צַר Nu 22[26] *narrow place*; מ׳ Ne 2[14] (passable) *place*; in partic. *place* at banquet † 1 S 9[22] 20[25.27], sleeping-*place*, couch, † 1 S 3[2.9] Ru 4[10], מְקוֹם הַחֵצִי 1 S 20[37] i.e. where arrow fell, = haunt, lurking-place 1 S 23[22] 2 S 17[9.12], מקום תַּנִּים ψ 44[20] *place of jackals*, i.e. desert, מ׳ הַמֻּנָּח Ez 41[11 b] *place of the uncovered space*, portion (cf. הַמֻּנָּח alone v[11 a]), מ׳ הַשֶּׁבֶת of seat of Sol.'s throne 1 K 10[19] = 2 Ch 9[18], מ׳ אֶחָד where waters were collected Gn 1[9] (𝔊 Ball מִקְוֶה), ψ 104[8]; destination of dead Ec 3[20] 6[6], מ׳ = resting-*place* Jb 16[18]; מ׳ נֶאֱמָן *sure place*, for a peg (securely fastened) Is 22[23.25] (fig., cf. Ezr 9[8]), of places, spots, on the body: leprous spot † 2 K 5[11]; מ׳ הַשְּׁחִין † Lv 13[19] *place of the boil*, esp. of shrine, sanctuary (cf. We[187.16]), מקום שְׁכֶם Gn 12[6] (J, v. Di Holz), so of Bethel Gn 13[3] (J), v[4] (J, מְקוֹם הַמִּזְבֵּחַ), 28[19] (J), v[11.11.11] (E), 22[3.4.9.14] (E), +, of idolatrous shrines Dt 12[2.3] Ez 6[13] 2 Ch 33[19], esp. of temple הַמ׳ אֲשֶׁר יִבְחַר (י׳ אלהיכם בו) Dt 12[5.14] 14[23.24] 15[20] 16[2.6] 17[8] 18[6] + 13 t. Dt + Jos 9[27] (D), Ne 1[9], מ׳ י׳ 1 K 8[29.29.30.35] = 2 Ch 6[20.20.21.26] Je 27[22] +, מ׳ שֵׁם־י׳ צְבָאוֹת הַר־צִיּוֹן Is 18[7], מְ׳ מִקְדָּשִׁי Ez 43[7], מְ׳ מִקְדָּשֵׁנוּ Je 17[12], מ׳ כִּסְאִי Is 60[3], מ׳ קָדְשׁוֹ † Ezr 9[8] ψ 24[3], etc., of tabern. מ׳ הַקֹּדֶשׁ Lv 10[17] 14[13], מְ׳ קָדוֹשׁ in or about tabern., Ex 29[31] Lv 6[9.19.20] + (all P), מ׳ קָדוֹשׁ Ec 8[10]. Note esp. † מקום before rel. cl., c. אֲשֶׁר Gn 39[20] 40[3] Ez 6[13] Est 4[3] 8[17], c. שׁ Ec 1[7] 3[16], rel. om. Jb 18[21], also בִּמְ׳ אֲשֶׁר Ho 2[1] 2 S 15[21] 1 K 21[19] Je 22[12] Ez 21[35] Ne 4[14] Lv 4[24.33] 6[18] 7[2] 14[13] Nu 9[17] (Ges § 130 c). † **5. a.** *space, room*, Gn 24[23.25.31] (J), Is 5[8] cf. 28[8], Je 7[32] 19[11]. **b.** *space, distance*, between (בין) 1 S 26[13]. † **6.** *region, quarter, direction* Ez 10[11]; מִמָּ׳ אַחֵר Est 4[14] *from another quarter*, source. † **7.** peculiar uses are, **a.** נָתַן מ׳ לְ Ju 20[36] *give place* (yield ground) *to*. Perh. **b.** בִּמְ׳ אֲשֶׁר יֵאָמֵר Ho 2[1] *instead of* its being said (cf. תַּחַת); מְקוֹם נְהָרִים Is 33[21] *instead of* rivers (i.e. a substitute for them). — מְקוֹמָהּ Na 1[8] (‖ אֹיְבָיו) rd. בְּקָמָיו We, מִתְקוֹמְמָו Buhl[ZAW v (1885). 181], or בק׳ מְקָמָיו Now (all = *his adversaries*, cf. GASm).

† **יְקַמְיָה** **n.pr.m.** in Judah (= יָקֻם יָהּ acc. to Ol[§ 277 h. 2]); — **1.** 1 Ch 2[41.41], Ιεχεμιας, A Ιεκομιας, 𝔊L Ιακεμιας. **2.** 3[18], Ιεκενια, 𝔊L Ιεκεμια.

† **יְקַמְעָם** **n.pr.m.** (= יָקֻם עָם acc. to Ol[§ 277 f], meaning then *may kinsman establish*, cf. Gray[Prop. N. 46 f. 59]), — a Levite 1 Ch 23[19] 24[23], Ιεκεμιας, Ιοκομ (24[23]), etc., 𝔊L Ιακαμιας.

† **יָקְמְעָם** **n.pr.loc.** (perh. = יקמעם i.e. יָקֻם עָם Ol[§ 277 k. 3], = *let the people be established?* cf. Gray[Prop. N. 218]), — in N. Isr. 1 K 4[12], Λουκαμ, 𝔊L Ουκαμ; poss. = mod. *Tel Kaimûn*, N. of Megiddo, Buhl[Geogr. 210], city of refuge in Ephr. 1 Ch 6[53] (= קִבְצַיִם [q. v.] Jos 21[22]), Ικααμ, Ιεκμααν, etc.

קוֹנֵן v. קין.

† **קוֹעַ** **n.pr.gent.** named with Bab., Chald., Assyr., פְּקוֹד וְשׁוֹעַ וְקוֹעַ Ez 23[23] *Šôa and Ḳôa*; identif. by Dl[Pa 235] with As. *Sutû, Kutû* (abbrev. *Su* (? v. שׁוֹעַ) and [by infer.] *Ku*), E. of Tigris, on border of Elam and Media; cf. COT[Ez 23, 23] Dr[Hast III KOA], but קוע = *Kutû* now doubted by Wkl[Altor. Forsch. II 2 (1899), 54].

† [**קוֹף**] **n.[m.]** **ape**, so Vrss, 𝔊 πιθηκοι (om. 𝔊[B] in K) (foreign word; prob. = Skr. *kapi, id.*; Egypt. as loan-word *gôfe* WMM[As. u. Eur. 95], *gi'f* Erman[ZMG xlvi (1892), 121], Gk. κῆβος, κῆπος is of Eg. orig. acc. to Lewy[Fremdw. 6]), — pl. קֹפִים 1 K 10[22] = קופים 2 Ch 9[21], brought to Sol. [from SE.] by Phoenician fleet, cf. Ar. prov. '*donum regionis Jemen simiae sunt*,' Freytag[Provv. III 3160].

קוף (√ of foll., appar. = II. נקף, *go around*)

† [**תְּקוּפָה**] **n.f.** **coming round, circuit**; — cstr. תְּקוּפַת הַשָּׁנָה Ex 34[22] (JE), adv., *at the circuit* (completion) *of the year*, so לִתְ׳ הַשָּׁנָה 2 Ch 24[23]; = pl. cstr. לִתְקֻפוֹת הַיָּמִים 1 S 1[20]; sg. sf. of finished *circuit* of sun ψ 19[7] (opp. מוֹצָאוֹ; cf. of moon, בתקופתו Ecclus 43[7]).

† I [**קוּץ**] **vb.** **feel a loathing, abhorrence, sickening dread** (‖ √ of קוּם; 𝔗 קוּץ *id.*; for connex. of meanings cf. Aram. קְנַס *loathe*, ܩܢܛ *fear*), — **Qal** *Pf.* 3 fs. קָצָה Nu 21[5]; 1 s. קַצְתִּי Gn 27[46], *Impf.* 3 ms. וַיָּקָץ Nu 22[3] 1 K 11[25] (but v. infr.), 2 ms. juss. תָּקֹץ Pr 3[11]; 1 s. וָאָקֻץ Lv

20²³; 3 mpl וַיָּקֻצוּ Ex 1¹²; *Pt.* קָץ Is 7¹⁶,—**1.** *feel a loathing* at, *abhor*, c. בְּ rei Nu 21⁵ (JE), Gn 27⁴⁶ (P), Pr 3¹¹ (‖ מָאַס); c בְּ pers. Lv 20²³ (H; subj. 'י), so 1 K 11²⁵, but Kit (after 𝔊, cf. 𝔖) prop. וַיָּצֶק (√ צוק **Hiph.** *distress*). **2.** *feel a sickening dread*, c. מִפְּנֵי pers Ex 1¹² (J), Nu 22³ (E), Is 7¹⁶. **Hiph.** *Impf.* 1 pl sf. נְקִיצֶנָּה Is 7⁶ (sf of Judah) *let us cause her sickening dread*, but weak, rd. נְצִיקֶנָּה (√צוק) Thes Che Du Gr Marti.—Other **Hiph.** forms v. קִיץ.

II קוץ (√of foll; cf perh NH, 𝔗, קוץ *cut off*; NH קוֹץ=BH).

†I קוֹץ **n.m.** Ez 28, 24 **thornbush, thorn**;—abs. 'ק Gn 3¹⁸+; pl קֹצִים Ex 22⁵+, קוֹצִים Is 33¹²+; cstr קוֹצֵי Ju 8⁷ ¹⁶,—**1.** *thornbush*, +דַּרְדַּר (q v) Gn 3¹⁸ (J), Ho 10⁸; +שָׁמִיר Is 32¹³; + בַּרְקָנִים (q.v.), קֹ׳ הַמִּדְבָּר Ju 8⁷ ¹⁶, 'ק alone Ex 22⁵ (E), כְּאֵשׁ קוֹצִים ψ 118¹² (sim. of foes); in various fig, Is 33¹² Je 4³ 12¹³. **2.** *thorn*, fig, Ez 28²⁴ (c. מַכְאִב, v. כאב; ‖ סִלּוֹן q v); sim כְּקֹ׳ מֻנָד 2 S 23⁶ (Perles Anal 53 conj. מֹץ, but v. also נוד **Hoph.**).

†II. קוֹץ **n.pr.m.** **1.** name in Judah 1 Ch 4⁸, Κωε, Κως. **2.** 'הַקּ. priest 1 Ch 24¹⁰, Κως, A 𝔊L Ακκως; Ezr 2⁶¹=Ne 7⁶³, Ne 3⁴ ²¹, Ακ(κ)ους, -ως.

†[קְוֻצּוֹת] **n.f.pl.** **locks of hair** (√obscure; NH *id*; Syr. ܩܘܨܬܐ, ܩܘܨܬܐ PS³⁵⁵⁶, Ar. قُصَّةٌ *hair over forehead*);—sf. קְוֻצּוֹתַי Ct 5², -תָיו v¹¹.

†I [קוּר] **vb. bore, dig** (Ar. قَارَ (و) *cut a round hole in, scoop out*);—**Qal** *Pf.* 1 s. קַרְתִּי 2 K 19²⁴ *I have dug* (sc. a well)=Is 37²⁵ (Meinh conj. כָּרִתִי).—**Hiph., Pilp.,** v. I, II. קרר.

†מָקוֹר **n.m.** Ze 13, 1 **spring, fountain** (app. orig. *well*),—abs 'מ Zc 13¹ Pr 25²⁶; cstr. מְקוֹר Je 2¹³+, מְקֹר Lv 12⁷ 20¹⁸; sf. מְקוֹרוֹ Ho 13¹⁵, etc;—**1.** *spring* of water. **a.** fig., of 'י, מְ׳ מַיִם מ׳ חַיִּים Je 2¹³ 17¹³, cf מְ׳ חַיִּים ψ 36¹⁰; מְ׳ חַיִּים (more gen), Pr 10¹¹ 13¹⁴ 14²⁷ 16²²+18⁴ (so rd. for מְ׳ חָכְמָה 𝔊 Heb Codd Toy) **b.** fig of purification Ez 13¹. **c.** מְקוֹר מָשְׁחָת Pr 25²⁶ (fig.; + מַעְיָן). **d.** fig of source of life and vigour Ho 13¹⁵ Je 51³⁶; of a nation's orig. source, stock ψ 68²⁷ (Kay Che, of temple); source of joy Pr 5¹⁸ (fig. of wife; ‖ אֵשֶׁת) **2.** fig. of eye, מְקוֹר דִּמְעָה, Je 8²³. **3.** *source* of menstruous blood, מְ׳ דָּמֶיהָ Lv 20¹⁸, so מְקֹרָהּ v¹⁸ (H) **4.** =*flow* of blood after child-birth מְ׳ דָּמֶיהָ 12⁷ (P)

II. קוּר (√of foll.; cf. Ar. قَارَ (و) v. *turn, twist* (of serpent), قُورٌ a kind of *rope*).

†[קוּר] **n.m.** Is 59, 6 **thread, film**;—pl. cstr. קוּרֵי עַכָּבִישׁ Is 59⁵ they weave *spider-threads*, fig. of machinations of wicked, so sf. קוּרֵיהֶם v⁶.

קוֹרֵא v. קרא. קוֹרָה v. קרה

†[קוֹשׁ] **vb. lay bait or lure** (‖ √of יקשׁ);—**Qal** *Impf.* 3 mpl. יְקֹשׁוּן Is 29²¹, c לְ pers. (fig).

†קוּשָׁיָהוּ **n.pr.m.** (form dub.; Kit Hpt 'קִישׁ, cf. 6²⁹ and 𝔊, Pei ZAW xvii (1897). 348 finds here a god *Ḳûs*, but very precarious);—Levite, 1 Ch 15¹⁷, (υἱὸς) Κ(ε)ισαίου, =קִישִׁי 6²⁹, Κεισαι[ν], 𝔊L Κουσει.

קַח, קֵח, קַחַת etc., v. לקח.

†קַט Ez 16⁴⁷ (כִּמְעַט קָ׳), dub, Ki *only* (Ar. قَطْ); del. 𝔊 𝔖 Thes Hi Co Berthol, Toy זֹאת, Perles Anal 30 קָטֹן; Krae conj. כְּרֵאשׁ עַסְפַּת, for כִּמְעַט קָט.

קטב (√of foll.; cf 𝔗 קְטַב *cut off* (rare); in Ar. قَطَبَ *id.*, ط said to be for ص, v. Lane).

†קֶטֶב, [קֹטֶב] **n.m.** Dt 32, 24 **destruction**;—of pestilence, abs 'ק Dt 32²⁴ (‖ רֶשֶׁף), ψ 91⁶ (‖ דֶּבֶר), so sf. (of She'ôl) קָטָבְךָ (Ges § 93 q) Ho 13¹⁴ (‖ of דְּבָרֶיךָ, מָוֶת); more gen., שַׁעַר קֶטֶב Is 28².

†[קָטַל] **vb. slay** (poet. and late) (Ar. قَتَلَ, Eth. ቀተለ: Sab קתל Hom Chrest 126, all *slay* (orig. form with ת; changed later, after ק); Aram. קְטַל, ܩܛܠ; OAram. קטל, כטל, קתל);—**Qal** *Impf.* c. acc. pers, 3 ms. יִקְטָל־ Jb 24¹⁴; sf., subj. God, יִקְטְלֵנִי 13¹⁵, of God also 2 ms. תִּקְטֹל ψ 139¹⁹.

†[קֶטֶל] **n.[m.] slaughter,**—מִקֶּטֶל MT Ob⁹, but join to v¹⁰ (then מִקֶּטֶל), 𝔊 We Now GASm.

†[קָטֹן, Lag BN 26 31] **vb. be small, insignificant** (NH Hiph and deriv.; JAram. in deriv., Syr. ܩܛܢ; OAram. קטין *insignificant*; Ar. قَطِينٌ *parum edens*; Eth. ቀጥነ: *be thin*, chiefly in deriv.; prob also As *kuṭtinnu, small, younger*, Zehnpf BAS i. 505 (otherwise Dl HWB 323); Meissn Suppl. *katânu, be short* (of hair), cf. Bez ZA viii. 141 f);—**Qal** *Pf.* 1 s קָטֹנְתִּי Gn 32¹¹, c. מִן comp., *I am too insignificant for* all the kindnesses; *Impf.* 3 fs. וַתִּקְטַן זֹאת בְּעֵינֶיךָ 2 S 7¹⁹=1 Ch 17¹⁷. **Hiph.** lit. *Inf cstr.* לְהַקְטִין Am 8⁵ *making* ephah *small*.

†I. קָטָן **adj. small, young, unimportant,**—abs. 'ק Gn 9²⁴+, sf. קְטַנָּם (Ko ii 1, 74) Je 6¹³+;

fs. קְטַנָּה Gn 29[16]+; mpl. קְטַנִּים 2 K 18[24]+; cstr. קְטַנֵּי 1 S 9[21] (v. Dr; We conj. ־ַּי, old cstr., cf. HPS), Pr 30[24]; fpl. קְטַנּוֹת Ez 16[61]+;—**1.** *small:* esp. **a.** of children, youth=*young*, Gn 44[20] (J) 2 S 9[12] 1 K 11[17] 2 K 2[23] 5[2], of sister Ct 8[8]; =*younger*, of two children (oft. opp. גדול), Gn 9[24] 27[15.42] (all J), 29[16.18] (E), 1 S 14[49] (f.; opp. הַבְּכִירָה); of *younger* sister Ju 15[2], so (fig.) Ez 16[46] and (+מִן comp.) v[61]; brother 1 Ch 24[31]; הַקּ׳ *youngest* son (of several) 1 S 16[11] 17[14]; +גָּדוֹל = *young and old* (v. קָטֹן **1**) Je 16[6] cf. 2 Ch 31[15] 34[30]. **b.** of things: utterance Nu 22[18] (E), weight Dt 25[13.14], vessels 2 Ch 36[18], animals ψ 104[25] (all opp. גדול); cf. also 2 S 12[3] 1 K 2[20] 17[13] 18[44] 2 K 4[10] Ez 43[14] (opp. גדול), Pr 30[24] Ct 2[15], + prob. Ez 46[22] (v. II. [קָטַר]); כְּלֵי הַקָּטָן Is 22[24] the vessels *of small size* (fig.). **2.** *small:* **a.** with added idea of weakness, pers. 2 K 18[24]=Is 36[9], city Ec 9[14]. **b.**=*insignificant*, (1) tribe 1 S 9[21]; (2) pers. (+גדול;=all persons) Je 6[13] 31[34] Jon 3[5] ψ 115[13] Est 1[5.20], cf. 1 Ch 12[14] (van d. H. v[13]); (3) in gen., יוֹם קְטַנּוֹת Zc 4[10] *day of small things.*—Vid. also קָטֹן.

†II. קָטָן **n.pr.m.** (*the small*);—הַקּ׳, post-ex. name Ezr 8[12], Ακ(κ)αταν.

קָטֹן [54] **adj. small, insignificant**;—abs. ק׳ 1 S 2[19]+; cstr. קְטֹן 2 Ch 21[17];—f., pl. and sf. supplied by קָטָן;—**1.** *small:* esp. **a.** of youth =*young*, נַעַר ק׳ 1 S 20[35] 1 K 3[7] 2 K 5[14] Is 11[6]; =*younger* of two brothers, Gn 48[19] (E) Ju 1[13] 3[9] (+מִן comp.); הַקּ׳ *youngest* brother Gn 42[13]+ 10 t. Gn (JE), son Ju 9[5] 2 Ch 22[1], so קְטֹן בָּנָיו 21[17]; +גדול = *young and old* (v. קָטָן **1**), i.e. everybody Gn 19[11] (J), 1 S 5[9] 30[2]+ (of pers. and things) v[19]. **b.** of things 1 S 2[19] 1 K 8[64] (+מִן comp.), Am 6[11] Is 54[7]; opp. גָּדוֹל 1 S 22[15] 25[36] Gn 1[16] (P). **2.** = *unimportant*, things, Ex 18[22.26] (E), 1 S 20[2] (all opp. גדול); pers.,=*feeble* Am 7[2.5]; =*insignificant* Je 49[15] Ob[2] (both ‖ בָּזוּי), Is 60[22] (‖ צָעִיר) ק׳ בְּעֵינֶיךָ 1 S 15[17]; esp.+גָּדוֹל= low and high,= everybody, Dt 1[17] 1 K 22[31]= 2 Ch 18[30], Je 8[10] Jb 3[19], +8 t.—Vid. also קָטָן.

†[קֹטֶן] **n.m. little (finger)**;—sf. קָטָנִּי (=קְטַנִּי van d. H. in Ch; cf. Kö ii. 69 Ges § 93 q), 1 K 12[10]=2 Ch 10[10].

[קָטַף] **vb. pluck off** (twigs, etc.), or out (NH=BH; Ar. قَطَفَ *pluck* grapes; 𝔗 קְטַף, Syr. ܩܛܦ; cf. As. *ḳaṭâpu*, appar. *pluck off*);—**Qal** *Pf.* 3 ms. קָטַף Ez 17[4] *he* [i.e. eagle, in fig.] *plucked off* twigs; 2 ms. וְקָטַפְתָּ Dt 23[26] (ears of grain, בְּיָדֶךָ); *Impf.* 1 s. אֶקְטֹף Ez 17[22] (subj. י׳; acc.+מִן *from*); *Pt.* mpl. הַקֹּטְפִים Jb 30[4] *they who pluck out* the mallow. **Niph.** *Impf.* 3 ms. יִקָּטֵף Jb 8[12] *it is* not *plucked off.*

I. קטר (√of foll.; cf. As. *ḳutru* (with ת) *smoke*; Talm. 𝔗 קִיטְרָא, קוּטְרָא (thick) *smoke*; Ar. قُتَارٌ *smoke* (said of fire); usu. *exhale odour* (esp. of roast meat); As. *ḳutrinnu*, *incense-offering*; Sab. מקטר *censer* CIS iv. nos. 26, l. 6; 30, l. 4; Eth. ቀተረ: *incense*; Egypt. *ḳatalθa* Bondi 74 ff., *karatuṭ* WMM As. u. Eur. 97 = קְטֹרֶת, קְטֹרוֹת; NH [קָטַר] *smoke* (said of incense)).

†קִיטוֹר (Lag BN 182) **n.m. thick smoke**;—קִיטֹר Gn 19[28.28] (J), ־טוֹר ψ 119[83]; 148[8] (fig. of clouds in thunderstorm; Vrss. appar. קֶרַח, cf. Du).

†קְטוּרָה **n.m. smoke of sacrifice**;—abs. Dt 33[10] (E; Di al. of *incense*).

†קְטוּרָה **n.pr.f.** a wife of Abraham, after Sarah's death, Gn 25[1.4] 1 Ch 1[32.33]; Χεττουρα.

קְטֹרֶת [60] **n.f. smoke, odour of (burning) sacrifice, incense**;—ק׳ abs. Ex 30[1]+; cstr. 25[6]+; sf. קְטָרְתִּי Ez 16[18] 23[41];—**1.** *sweet smoke of sacrifice*, ‖ מנחה Is 1[13] ψ 141[2], ק׳ אֵילִים 66[15], לְהַקְטִיר ק׳ 1 S 2[28] (?). **2.** *incense*, ק׳ (ה)סמים Ex 25[6] 30[7] 31[11] 40[27]+9 t.; ק׳ תמיד Ex 30[8], ק׳ רֹקַח v[35], הק׳ alone v[37] Lv 16[13] Nu 16[35] 17[12]; so ק׳ 16[7.17.18] 17[5.11] 2 Ch 29[7], ק׳ זָרָה Ex 30[9], ענן הק׳ Lv 16[13] Ez 8[11], also of אש זרה Lv 10[1] (illegal worship); in offering of the princes Nu 7[14]+ 11 t. 7, cf. v[86]. Altar of incense is מזבח מקטר ק׳ Ex 30[1], מ׳ הזהב לק׳ 1 Ch 28[18], מ׳ הק׳ זהב Ex 40[5], מ׳ ק׳ הסמים Lv 4[7], מ׳ הק׳ Ex 30[27]+6 t. **3.** *perfume*, ‖ שֶׁמֶן Ez 16[18] 23[41] Pr 27[9].

[קָטַר] [115] **vb. denom. Pi. Hiph. make sacrifices smoke**, send them up in smoke (prop. *produce* קְטֹרֶת, v. Sta ZAW vi (1886), 298 f.);—**Pi.** [42] *Pf.* 3 mpl. קִטְּרוּ Je 19[13]+, קִטַּרְתֶּם Je 44[21.23]; *Impf.* 3 ms. יְקַטֵּר Hb 1[16]+; 3 mpl. יְקַטְּרוּן Ho 11[2], etc.; *Inf. abs.* קַטֵּר 1 S 2[16]+; *cstr.* Je 11[13]+, *Pt.* pl. מְקַטְּרִים Is 65[3]+, etc.;—*make sacrifices smoke*, offer them by burning: to י׳, 1 S 2[16] (where prob. rd. יַקְטִירוּן [and so v[15]] Sta l.c. 299): elsewhere to other gods or in illegal worship, Je 44[23]; c.acc. קִטֵּר (but see this, infr.) Je 44[21] (here [and al. in some other passages] of *incense*), תּוֹדָה Am 4[5]; place is usu. c. בְּ, e.g. עוֹד הָעָם מְזַבְּחִים וּמְקַטְּרִים בַּבָּמוֹת 2 K 17[11] 23[5]; בַּבָּמוֹת 1 K 22[44] 2 K 12[4] 14[4] 15[4.35] (R), cf. 2 K

16^{4} = 2 Ch 28^{4} (cf. RS$^{Sem. I 471, 2nd ed 490}$); הַבּ׳ אֲשֶׁר קִטְּרוּ שָׁמָּה 2 K 23^{8}; c. עַל e g. על הגבעות Ho 4^{13}, על ההרים Je 19^{13} 32^{29}, על הלבנים Is 65^{3}, על גג(ו)ת v^{7}, c. לְ of deity, Ho 11^{2} Je 1^{16} + 14 t Je (+ 19^{13} 32^{29} supr.), Hb 1^{16} 2 K 22^{17} 23^{5} 2 Ch 25^{14} 28^{25} 34^{25} Qr (> Kt **Hiph.**), to the brazen serpent 2 K 18^{4}. **Pu.** *Pt.* מְקֻטֶּרֶת מֹר וגו׳ Ct 3^{6} *fumigated with myrrh*, etc (Aq 𝔙 Schlottm מִקְטֶרֶת). **Hiph.** *Pf* 3 ms הִקְטִיר Lv 9^{10}+, 2 ms. הִקְטַרְתָּ Ex 29$^{13. 18. 25}$, etc.; *Impf.* 3 ms. יַקְטִיר Lv 4^{26} 16^{25}, וַיַּקְטֵר Ex 40^{27}+, etc. *Imv* ms. הַקְטֵר 2 K 16^{15}, *Inf abs* הַקְטֵיר 1 K 9^{25}; *cstr.* לְהַקְטִיר Ex 30^{20}+; *Pt* מַקְטִיר Je 33^{18}+, etc. **1.** *make sacrifices smoke*, usu **a.** in worship of י׳: abs 1 K 12^{33} 13^{1} 2 Ch 29^{11}, c. acc חלב Lv 17^{6} Nu 18^{17} 1 S 2$^{15. 16}$, עלת 2 K 16$^{13. 15}$ 2 Ch 13^{11}, אשה Ex 30^{20} Lv 2^{11} Nu 18^{17}, מנחה Je 33^{18}, ראש, etc, Lv 8^{20} אַזְכָּרָה Lv 2^{16}, חלבי השלמים Lv 6^{5}; קטרת 1 S 2^{28}, on 1 K 9^{25} v. Klo Benz, place is על מזבח Lv 4^{10} + 5 t, הַמִּזְבֵּחָה Ex 29$^{13. 18. 25}$ + 23 t. Lv, Nu 5^{26} (all P), c. הַמִּזְבֵּחַ (acc.) Lv 6^{8}, בַּבָּמוֹת 1 K 3^{3}; בגיא בן הנם 2 Ch 28^{3}. **b.** less oft in worship of other gods, לאלהיהן (gods of Sol.'s wives) 1 K 11^{8}, לאלהיו (of Moab) Je 48^{35}, להם (Baalim) Ho 2^{15}, — 2 Ch 34^{25} rd. Qr **Qal**. **2.** *cause incense to smoke, offer incense* abs. 2 Ch 2^{3} 26$^{18. 18. 19}$, c עַל of altar 2 Ch 26^{16} Ex 30^{7} 40^{27}, c acc יַקְטִירֶנָּה 30$^{7. 8}$, קטרת סמים 30^{7} 40^{27} 2 Ch 2^{3}, קטרת תמיד Ex 30^{8}, הק׳ קטרת Nu 17^{5} 2 Ch 29^{7} **3.** *make smoke* upon (עַל) both altars (of burnt-offering and of incense) 1 Ch 6^{34}, cf. also 23^{13}. **Hoph.** *be made to smoke* as a sacrifice: *Impf* 3 fs תָּקְטָר Lv 6^{15}, *Pt* מֻקְטָר Mal 1^{11} (Ew Ke al [Ges §121 b], We Now rd. מ׳ לִשְׁמִי מִנְחָה; but v. מֻקְטָר).

† קְטֹרֶת (Ol §182 e) **n.f.** incense;—Je 44^{21} (on gender v Albr$^{ZAW xvi (1896), 100}$, who reads אתה for אתם, and so Rothst^{Kau} Gie; Gie also קְטֹרֶת)

† [מִקְטָר, מְקַטֵּר] **n.m.** place of sacrificial smoke;—cstr. מִזְבֵּחַ מִקְטַר קְטֹרֶת Ex 30^{1} *altar, place of offering incense* (SS Kau Buhl^{13} al n. act. *burning*).

† מֻקְטָר **n.m.** incense;—abs. מ׳ Mal 1^{11} (Thes Hi Marti^{Kau} GASm Ko$^{iii, §307}$).

† מִקְטֶרֶת **n.f.** censer,—מ׳ abs. 2 Ch 26^{19}, sf. מִקְטַרְתּוֹ Ez 8^{11}.

† [מְקַטְּרָה] **n.f.** incense-altar;—pl. abs. מְקַטְּרוֹת 2 Ch 30^{14}.

† II. [קָטַר] **vb.** dubious word; si vera l. appar. = shut in, enclose (𝔗 קְטַר, Syr ܩܛܪ bind, ܩܶܛܪܳܐ chain);—**Qal** *Pt. pass.* pl. חֲצֵרוֹת קְטֻרוֹת Ez 46^{22} *enclosed courts* (cf. interpr. in Levy^{NHWB}, and ܚܨܪ̈ܐ ܩܛܝܪ̈ܐ PS^{3589}), but rd. prob. קְטַנּוֹת *small*, 𝔊 𝔖 Co Toy Berthol Krae.

† קִטְרוֹן **n.pr.loc.** in Zebulun Ju 1^{30}, Κεδρων, A Χεβρων; = קַטָּת Jos 19^{15}? site unknown.

† קַטָּת **n.pr.loc.** in Zebulun Jos 19^{15}, Καταναθ, A Κατταθ, 𝔊L Κοτταθ,—v קִטְרוֹן.

† [קִיא No$^{ZMG xxxvii (1883), 539}$] **vb.** vomit up, spue out, disgorge (NH *id.*, Hiph; As *ḳâ'u*, *spit* Meissn$^{Suppl 83}$, Ar. قَآءَ *vomit*, Eth. [ቀየአ:] ቂአ: *vomit*),—**Qal** *Pt* f. קָאָה Lv 18^{28}, but read prob. קָאָה, *Pf* 3 fs. (Di Baen); *Impf.* (**Qal** or **Hiph.**) 3 ms וַיָּקֵא Jon 2^{11}, sf. וְיָקִאֶנּוּ Jb 20^{15}, 3 fs. תָּקִיא Lv 18^{28} 20^{22}, וַתָּקִא 18^{25}; 2 ms. sf תְּקִיאֶנָּה Pr 23^{8}, **Hiph.** *Pf.* sf. consec. וַהֲקֵאתוֹ 25^{16}; all *vomit up*—c. acc., lit. Pr 23^{8} 25^{16} Jon 2^{11}, fig. of land casting out inhab Lv 18$^{25. 28. 28}$ 20^{22} (all H); of *disgorging* riches Jb 20^{15}.

† [קֵא] **n.[m.]** what is vomited up, vomit (v Ba$^{NB 79}$);—sf. קֵאוֹ Pr 26^{11} (of dog).

† קִיא **n.m.** id. (v. Ba$^{NB 80}$),—abs. ק׳ Is 28^{8}; sf. קִיאוֹ Is 19^{14} (sim.), fig. Je 48^{26} (of Moab)

† [קָיָה] **vb.** vomit (si vera l. = קיא, Ges$^{§76 h}$ Ko$^{ii 1, 586}$),—**Qal** *Imv.* mpl. וּקְיוּ Je 25^{27} Qr (Kt וקוו), be drunken *and vomit* (? err for וְקִיאוּ).

קִיטוֹר v. קטר. קִימָה, קִים v. קום.

קִימוֹשׁ v. קמש.

קין (✓ of foll; cf. Ar. قَانَ *fit together, fabricate* (*make artificially*), *forge* (cf. Wetzst$^{Syr. Dreschtafel (1873) 297}$), whence قَيْنٌ *worker in iron*, As. *kinai* (Meissn$^{ZA viii (1893), 82}$), 𝔗 קֵינָאָה, Syr. ܩܝܢܝܐ, Palm. קיניא (pl.) *metal-worker*, cf. BH תּוּבַל קַיִן; also Ar قَيْنَةٌ *slave-girl*, and *woman-singer, lute-player* (fr. skill); cf. Eth. ቀኔ: *song, singing*, Syr ܩܝܢܬܐ, *hymn, elegy;* Ar. vb. iv Dozy; NH קִינָה = BH; cf. also Bu$^{ZAW ii (1882), 28}$).

† I. [קַיִן] **n.[m.]** spear 𝔊 and most;—sf. קֵינוֹ 2 S 21^{16}; < rd. קוֹבָעוֹ (cf. 1 S 17^{38}) Klo Bu HPS al.

† II. קַיִן **n.pr.** **1.** gent. (v. Sta$^{GI 131 f.}$ Mey$^{Entstehung 113}$; cf. Ar. n.pr.fam. قَيْن, Nab. Sin. n pr.m. et. f. קינו; tribe of *smiths?*);—tribe of Moses' father-in-law Ju 4^{11} (cf. קֵינִי 1^{16}), Καινα, 𝔊L Κειν; akin to Midian (Nu 10^{29} P), settled among Amal. in S. of Canaan (v. קֵינִי);

prophesied against by Balaam Nu 24^{22} (קַיִן; JE);—v. also קֵינִי. **2. loc.** הַקַּיִן, in S. Judah (a settlement of II. ק׳ **1**?);—Jos 15^{57}, [Ζακαν]αειμ, A [Ζανω] Ακειμ, 𝔊L [Ζανου] Ακεν; poss. = *Yûḳîn* SE. from Hebron [Rob[BR ii. 86]] (v. Buhl[Geogr. 162 f.] who, however, cp. קִינָה v^{22}).

† I. קִינָה **n.pr.loc.** in S. Judah (a settlement of II. קַיִן **1**?), Jos 15^{22}, Ικαμ, A 𝔊L Κ(ε)ινα.

† III. קַיִן **n.pr.m. Cain**, Καιν, eldest son of Adam and Eve (expl. Gn 4^1 fr. קָנָה *acquire;* but in fact = II. ק׳, as *heros eponymos*, acc. to We[Comp. 11] Sta[G 285 ff.] Bu[Urg. 193] Holz[Gn 50 f.] esp. Sta[ZAW xiv (1894), 250 ff.; xv (1895), 157 ff.], Che[Ency. Bib. Cain]);—ק׳ Gn $4^{1.2.3.5.5.8.8.9.13.15.15.16.17}$, קָיִן v$^{6.24.25}$ (all J).

† קֵינִי **adj.gent.** of II. קַיִן **1** (q.v.), חֶבֶר הַקּ׳ (dwelling in N. Isr.), ὁ Κειναῖος, Ju $4^{11.17.17}$ 5^{24} (against WMM Jen, who ref. ק׳ here to city *Kîn* near Megiddo, mentioned by Egypt., v. esp. Bu Now on 4^{11}); rd. prob. also חֹבָב הַקּ׳ 1^{16} (for בְּנֵי ק׳; so Bu GFM; 𝔊 οἱ υἱοὶ Ιωθορ τοῦ Κειναίου); elsewhere as **n. gent. coll.** הַקּ׳ settled among Amal., Nu 24^{21} (JE; v. II. קַיִן **1**), 1 S 15^6—= קֵינִי v^6 (We Bu Kit קַיִן, HPS הַקֵּינִי);—הַקּ׳ also 27^{10} 30^{29} (B 𝔊L Κενεζ(ε)ι = קְנִזִּי; A Κηνει, Κειναῖος); Gn 15^{19} (list of peoples; R);—הַקֵּינִים 1 Ch 2^{55} (Κ(ε)ιναῖοι), related to Rechabites.

† קֵינָן **n.pr.m.** a Sethite (Sab. n. pr. dei קינן CIS[iv. no. 8. 1. 2]);—Gn $5^{9.10.12.13.14}$ 1 Ch 1^2, Καιναν.

† II. קִינָה **n.f. elegy, dirge**;—abs. ק׳ 2 S 1^{17}+; pl. קִינִים Ez 2^{10} (but rd. קינה Co—not Berthol Toy Krae), קִינוֹת 2 Ch 35^{25}; sf. קִינוֹתֵיהֶם v^{25};—*elegy, dirge* 2 S 1^{17} Ez $19^{14.14}$ 32^{16}, pl. 2 Ch 35^{25}; sg. ‖ אֵבֶל Am 8^{10}, ‖ הֶגֶה וָהִי Ez 2^{10}, נשׂא ק׳ Je 7^{29}, c. עַל *for*, Am 5^1 Je 9^9 Ez 26^{17} 27^2 28^{12} 32^2; c. אֶל Ez 19^1 27^{32}; לִמֵּד ק׳ Je 9^{19} (‖ נְהִי); pl. as collection of written dirges 2 Ch 35^{25}.—Bu[ZAW ii (1882), 1 ff., cf. iii (1883), 299 ff.] thinks *Kina* rhythm always 3 + 2 tone-beats, but book La (Heb. קִינוֹת) is in all parts pentam., 3 + 2 varying sts. with 2 + 3, yet always 5 in line, with caesura; of other קִינוֹת, Am 5^2 Ez $19^{2\,ff.}$ $26^{17\,b\,ff.}$ are pent., 2 S $1^{19\,ff.}$ $3^{33\,f.}$ tetr., Ez $27^{3\,ff.}$ $28^{12\,ff.}$ $32^{2\,ff.}$ hex.; v. Br[Gen. Intr. 379 ff.].

† [קִינֵן] **vb. denom. Pōʿl.** chant a קִינָה;—*Pf.* 3 pl. consec. וְקוֹנְנוּ Ez 27^{32} (עַל pers.), sf. (cogn.) וְקוֹנְנוּהָ 32^{16}; *Impf.* 3 ms. וַיְקֹנֵן 2 S 1^{17} (c. acc. cogn. + עַל pers.), cf. (עַל pers. only), 2 Ch 35^{25} and (אֶל pers.) 2 S 3^{33}; 3 fpl. תְּקוֹנֵנָּה c. acc. cogn., Ez 32^{16}, + עַל pers. v^{16}; *Pt.* as subst. Je 9^{16} (professional) *wailing women.*

† I. [קִיץ] **vb. Hiph. awake** (‖ form of יקץ; NH in Hiph. (rare));—*Pf.* 3 ms. הֵקִיץ 2 K 4^{31} Ez 7^6; 2 ms. וַהֲקִיצוֹתָ consec. Pr 6^{22}, etc.; *Impf.* 1 s. אָקִיץ Pr 23^{35}; 3 mpl. יָקִיצוּ Je 51^{39}+; *Imv.* ms. הָקִיצָה Hb 2^{19}+; mpl. הָקִיצוּ Is 26^{19} Jo 1^5; *Inf. cstr.* הָקִיץ ψ 17^{15} 73^{20}; *Pt.* מֵקִיץ 1 S 26^{12};—*shew signs of waking, awake:* **1.** from sleep, **a.** 1 S 26^{12} Is $29^{8.8}$ ψ 3^6 73^{20} 139^{18} Pr 6^{22} (doubtful line, v. Toy). **b.** of י׳ ψ 44^{24} *awake* [fr. sleep] to activity, so 35^{23} (c. לְ rei), 59^6 (c. inf. purpose). **c.** fr. ecstatic sleep of proph. Je 31^{26}. **2.** fr. sleep of death, c. neg. 2 K 4^{31} Je $51^{39.57}$ Jb 14^{12}; of resurrection Is 26^{19} Dn 12^2. **3.** from stupor (of drunkenness) Jo 1^5 Pr 23^{35}. **4.** of inanimate thing Hb 2^{19}; cf. בָּא הַקֵּץ הֵקִיץ אֵלָיִךְ Ez 7^6 *the end cometh, it hath awaked unto thee* (Co del. הֵקִיץ, but the word-play favours it).—ψ 17^{15} is put by Thes Ol Hup Du al. sub **1 a**; Ew De Che sub **2**; We sub **1 b**; Calv Now: from night of distress and helplessness, and so Bae (psalmist representing Isr.).

II. קיץ (√ of foll.; usu. taken as = I. קִיץ, but connex. not clear; cf. Ar. قَيْظٌ *vehement heat of summer, late summer* (We[Skizzen iii. 90]), قَاظَ *be vehemently hot;* Sab. קים *summer* Mordtm[Him. Inschr. 71]; NH קַיִץ = BH, so 𝔗 קַיְטָא, Syr. ܩܲܝܛܵܐ; OAram. (Zinj.) כיצא *summer*).

† קַיִץ **n.m.**[Je 8. 20] **summer, summer-fruit** (cf. Gk. θέρος in both meanings);—abs. ק׳ Gn 8^{22}+; קָיִץ Am 3^{15}+; sf. קֵיצֵךְ Is 16^9 Je 48^{32};—**1.** *summer*-season, opp. חֹרֶף Gn 8^{22} (J), Am 3^{15} Zc 14^8 ψ 74^{17}; ‖ קָצִיר Je 8^{20} Pr 6^8 10^5 26^1, also (without קָצִיר) 30^{25}; as fruit harvest Is 28^4; time of drought ψ 32^4 (fig.). **2.** *summer-fruit* 2 S $16^{1.2}$ Am $8^{1.2}$ Je $40^{10.12}$ also, ‖ בָּצִיר, 48^{32} Mi 7^1 (in sim.), but ‖ קציר Is 16^9 (assim. to ק of קַיִץ; rd. prob. בציר).

קִיצוֹן v. קצץ.

† קִיקָיוֹן **n.m.**[Jon 4. 6] a plant (cf. As. *kukkânîtum* (כ) a garden-plant, Dl[HWB 327]);—usu. **ricinus** (R. *communis*, Linn. = *castor-oil tree;* cf. Dioscor.[iv. 164] κίκι (Egypt.) = κρότων [*castor-oil tree*]; Talm. שֶׁמֶן קִיק; v. esp. Löw[p. 353 f.]); perh. < **bottle-gourd** (𝔊 κολόκυνθα; i.e. *cucurbita lagenaria*, a vine growing and withering rapidly, Post in Hastings[DB ii. 250]);—Jon $4^{6.6.7.9.10}$.

קִיקָלוֹן v. קלל.

I. קִיר$_{74}$ **n.m.**$^{\psi 62,4}$ wall (√unknown);—abs. ק׳ Nu 22^{25}+, קִר Is 22^5; cstr. קִיר 1 K 6^5+; pl. קִירוֹת 1 K 6^{15}+, cstr. *id.*, v^5+; sf. קִירֹתָיו Ex 30^3+, etc.;—*wall*, esp. as flat surface: **1.** usu. of house or chamber: **a.** inner surface, Am 5^{19} 1 S 18^{11}+9 t., +(of temple) 1 K 6^{15a}+ v^{15b} (but rd. קוֹרוֹת *beams*, with 𝔊 The Kit Benz), $v^{16.27.27}$+6 t. †**b.** outer surface, 2 K 9^{33} Ez 33^{30} Is 59^{10} (in sim.); so זֶרֶם קִיר Is 25^4 (but Lo Kn Gr Di Du Che^{Hpt} al. rd. קֹר; JP Peters $^{\text{JBL xi (1892), 46}}$ prop. בָּרָד [as 28^2]); of temple 1 K $6^{5.5.6}$, cf. Ez $41^{6.6}$. †**c.** both inner and outer $v^{17.20.25}$. †**d.** indeterminate, $12^{5.7.12}$ 23^{14}. †**e.** thickness specified, Ez $41^{5.9.12.13}$ (of Ezekiel's temple). †**f.** as enclosing, 2 K 4^{10} (of עֲלִיָּה, q.v.); as separating Ez 43^8. †**2.** *wall* of (temple-)court Ez $8^{7.8.8}$ (in vision); of vineyard Nu $22^{25.25}$ (J), of city 35^4 (P), cf. ק׳ הַחוֹמָה Jos 2^{15} (JE) *the* (inner) *surface of the wall.* †**3.** more gen., 1 K 5^{13}, and (in phr. מַשְׁתִּין בְּקִיר) 1 S $25^{22.34}$ 1 K 14^{10} 16^{11} 21^{21} 2 K 9^8; in fig. Ez $13^{12.14}$ (appar. fem., but city Jerus. prob. in mind, cf. Albr$^{\text{ZAW xvi (1896), 85}}$ Kö$^{\text{ii. 2, 175}}$), $v^{15.15}$ (‖ חַיִץ v^{10}), ק׳ נָטוּי ψ 62^4; ק׳ אֶבֶן 2 S 5^{11} = ק׳ 1 Ch 14^1, cf. Hb 2^{11} (fig.); קִיר בַּרְזֶל Ez 4^3 (symbol.).—Is 22^5 is dub.: usu. *wall* (so even Du Che^{Hpt} Marti), but ref. not clear; Ew Che$^{\text{Comm.}}$ III. קִיר; Klo Brd Wkl$^{\text{Alttest. Unters. 177}}$ קוֹעַ, so WMM$^{\text{Hast. DB Kir}}$, but v. Dr$^{\text{ib. Koa}}$. †**4.** of flat side of altar Ez 41^{22} Ex 30^3 37^{26} Lv 1^{15} 5^9 (all P). †**5.** קִירוֹת לִבִּי Je 4^{19} *walls of my heart* (as seat of pain).

†II. קִיר in **n.pr.loc.** of Moabite cities (cf. קר = *city* MI$^{11.12.24}$, pl. קרן l.^{29});—𝔊 usu. om., or reads τὸ τεῖχος;—**1.** ק׳ מוֹאָב Is 15^1, poss. *Rabba*, S. of Arnon, v. Buhl$^{\text{Geogr. 270}}$. **2.** ק׳ חֶרֶשׂ Je $48^{31.36}$, ק׳ חָרֶשׂ Is 16^{11} = ק׳ חֲרֶשֶׂת Is 16^7, 2 K 3^{25} (Gi ק׳ חֲרָשֶׂת), perh. *Kerak*, S. of Rabba, v. Buhl$^{\text{ib.}}$, and cp. (on Kerak) Palmer$^{\text{Des. of Ex. ii. 472}}$ Dowling$^{\text{PEQ. Oct. 1896, 327}}$, esp. Mauss in de Luynes Voyage à la Mer Morte (1864), ii. 106 ff., iii (Atlas, ad fin.), 13 pl.

†III. קִיר **n.pr.terr. et gent.** ק׳ orig. house of Aram Am 9^7; קִירָה as place of exile Am 1^5 2 K 16^9 (𝔊 τὴν πόλιν); קִיר as people in As. army Is 22^6 (v^5 vid. I. קִיר ad fin.).—Location dub., v. conspectus of older views Dr$^{\text{Am 1, 5}}$; plausible is some tribe in S. Babylonia, E. of Tigris Wkl AT Unters. 178, cf. Hal$^{\text{REJ xi. 60}}$;—WMM$^{\text{Hast. DB Kir}}$ everywhere del., or em. קוֹעַ, but v. I. קִיר **3.**

קִירֹס = קֵרֹס.

†קִישׁ **n.pr.m.** (prob. *קַיִשׁ, Ar. قَيْس, Aram. קישא, Nö$^{\text{ZMG xl (1886), 167}}$; orig. n.pr.dei as Ar. قيس, wh. now only in n.pr. pers. We$^{\text{Heid. 2. 67}}$);—K(ε)ις: **1.** father of Saul 1 S $9^{1.3.3}$ $10^{11.21}$ 14^{51} 2 S 21^{14} 1 Ch $8^{30.33}$ (where read אֲבִינֵר, Be Kau Kit), v^{33} = $9^{36.39}$ (read as above), v^{39} 12^1 26^{28}. **2.** Levites: **a.** 1 Ch $23^{21.22}$ $24^{29.29}$. **b.** 2 Ch 29^{12}. **3.** ancestor of Mordecai Est 2^5 (Κεισαίου).

†קִישׁוֹן **n.pr.** of wady running NW. through plain of Megiddo (Esdraelon), K(ε)ισων (*stream of* (god) *Kish* RS$^{\text{Sem. i. 155; 2nd ed. 170}}$);—alw. נַחַל ק׳ Ju $4^{7.13}$ $5^{21.21}$ ψ 83^{10}, also 1 K 18^{40}; mod. *Nahr-el-Mukaṭṭa'*; v. Buhl$^{\text{Geogr. 106, 209}}$, GASm$^{\text{Geogr. 382}}$.

קִישִׁי v. קוּשָׁיָהוּ sub קוש.

קַל, קַל v. קלל. (קֹל *voice*, v. קול).

קלה 2 S 20^{14} Kt, v. קהל.

†I. [קָלָה] **vb.** roast, parch (NH קָלָה *id.* (rare), קָלִי = BH; As. *kalû*, II. 1, III. 1 *burn, consume* Meissn$^{\text{Suppl. 84}}$; Sab. קלאתם *conflagratio, aestus* Os$^{\text{4. 1. 19. 20}}$ CIS$^{\text{iv. No. 74, 1. 20}}$; Ar. قَلَى *fry* or *roast* wheat; Eth. ቀለወ፡ ቀለየ፡ *burn, fry*, so 𝔗 קְלָא, Syr. ܩܠܐ);—**Qal** *Pf.* 3 ms. sf. קָלָם בָּאֵשׁ Je 29^{22} (acc. pers.) *he roasted them with fire; Pt. pass.* אָבִיב קָלוּי בָּאֵשׁ Lv 2^{14} (P) grain *parched* with fire; so קָלוּי alone, as common food, Jos 5^{11} (P), v. קָלִי. **Niph.** *Pt.* נִקְלֶה as n. ψ 38^8 my loins are filled *with burning* (Vrss Bae *with contempt*, II. קלה).

†קָלִי **n.m.**$^{\text{1 S 17, 17}}$ parched grain, a common food (Rob$^{\text{BR ii. 50}}$ Anderlind$^{\text{ZPV ix. 3}}$);—abs. ק׳ 1 S 25^{18} 2 S 17^{28a} + v^{28b} (but dittogr., del. 𝔊 𝔖 and Comm.), Lv 23^{14} (P), Ru 2^{14}; = קָלִיא 1 S 17^{17}.

†II. [קָלָה] **vb. Niph.** be lightly esteemed, dishonoured (‖ form of קלל; cf. NH קָלוֹן, 𝔗 קְלָנָא, *disgrace, shame*);—*Pf.* 3 ms. consec. וְנִקְלָה Is 16^{14} Dt 25^3; *Pt.* נִקְלֶה Is 3^5+2 t.;—*be lightly esteemed*, held of little account, Is 16^{14} (glory of Moab); אִישׁ רָשׁ וְנִקְלֶה 1 S 18^{23}; so (Pt. as subst.) Is 3^5 (opp. נִכְבָּד), Pr 12^9 (opp. מִתְכַּבֵּד); more positively, *be dishonoured*, degraded, Dt 25^3 (לְעֵינֶיךָ). **Hiph.** *treat with contempt, dishonour*, *Pt.* מַקְלֶה אָבִיו וגו׳ Dt 27^{16} *one dishonouring* [i.e. opp. כַּבֵּד of 5th Command].

†קָלוֹן **n.m.**$^{\text{Pr 11, 2}}$ ignominy, dishonour;—abs. ק׳ Ho 4^7+; cstr. קְלוֹן Is 22^{18}; sf. קְלוֹנֵךְ Je 13^{26}+;—**1.** of national *ignominy* Ho $4^{7.18}$ (dub. line, v. Che Now), Je 46^{12} (rd. prob. קוֹלֵךְ, so 𝔊

Gie Co^{Hpt}), Hb 2^{16} ψ 83^{17}; of nation under fig. of woman, = pudenda, Je 13^{26} Na 3^{5} (‖ מַעֲרֵךְ). **2.** personal *dishonour, disgrace*, of Shebna, as *disgrace* to his lord's house Is 22^{18} (opp. כְּבוֹדֶךָ); individ., Jb 10^{15} Pr 3^{35} (opp. כָּבוֹד), 6^{33} 9^{7} 11^{2} 12^{16} 13^{18} (opp. יְכֻבָּד), 18^{3} 22^{10}.

† קַלַּחַת **n.f.** caldron (Erman$^{ZMG\ xlvi\ (1892),\ 121}$ cp. Egypt. *krḥt, pot*, cf. OCopt. *ǵalaḥt* Lag$^{BN\ 88}$, wh. has come back as loan-wd. WMM$^{As.\ u.\ Eur.\ 94}$);—abs. ק׳ 1 S 2^{14} (+ כִּיּוֹר, דּוּד, פָּרוּר); קַלַּחַת Mi 3^{3} (‖ סִיר).

I. קלט (√ of foll.; NH קָלַט *take up, in, harbour*, so 𝔗 קְלַט; Ba$^{ES\ 36}$ cp. Ar. قَلْتٌ reservoir with ת, cf. קטל, קטן).

† מִקְלָט **n.[m.]** refuge, asylum (P Ch);—עָרֵי מ׳ *asylum-cities* Nu $35^{11.13.14}$, עָרֵי הַמּ׳ Nu 35^{6} Jos 20^{2}, so 1 Ch $6^{42.52}$ (but rd. עִיר הַמּ׳, acc. to ‖ Jos $21^{13.21}$, so Be Kau Kit), לְמ׳ (after הָיָה) Nu $35^{12.15}$ Jos 20^{3}; cstr. in phr. עִיר מִקְלַט הָרֹצֵחַ Jos $21^{13.21.27.32.38}$ (Gi; v^{38} van d. H. Baer); sf. of refugee, עִיר מִקְלָטוֹ Nu $35^{25.26.27.28.32}$.

† II. [קָלַט] **vb.** be stunted (? = I. ק׳; prop. *be drawn in?* cf. Ar. قُلَاطٌ *very short*);—**Qal** *Pt. pass.* שָׂרוּעַ וְקָלוּט Lv 22^{23} sacrif. animal, overgrown or *stunted*.

† קְלִיטָא **n.pr.m.** Levite, Ne 8^{7} 10^{11} (𝔊^{L} in both Καλλιτας) Ezr 10^{23} (where called also קֵלָיָה, v. קוֹלָיָה), Κωλιευ, A Κωλιτας, 𝔊^{L} as Ne.

קְלִי(א) v. I. קלה. קָלִי v. קלל. קֵלָיָה v. קְלִיטָא.

[קָלַל]$_{82}$ **vb. be slight, swift, trifling** (prob. orig. *be light*; NH [קָלַל], קַל, קָלַל = BH; As. *ḳalâlu* II. *despise, dishonour*; so Tel Am (appar. Canaanism); Ar. قَلَّ *be small, scanty*; Sab. קללם *scanty* Hal$^{143.8\ f.}$ (cf. Fell$^{ZMG\ liv\ (1900),\ 246}$); Eth. ቀለለ: *be light, small, easy*; II. *despise*; 𝔗 קְלַל, Syr. ܩܰܠ, = BH; also (v. **Pilp.**, etc.) Ar. قَلْقَلَ *shake*, ቈልቈለ: *vibrate, whirl* (of sword), ቀልቀለ: v. *be shaken*;—Schwally$^{ZAW\ xi\ (1891),\ 170\ ff.}$ thinks *shake* original, v. מַקֵּל);—† **Qal** *Pf.* 2 ms. קַלּוֹתָ Na 1^{14}; 1 s. קַלֹּתִי Jb 40^{4}; 3 pl. קַלּוּ Gn 8^{11}+; *Impf.* 3 fs. וַתֵּקַל 16^{4}; 1 s. וָאֵקַל v^{5}; 3 mpl. יֵקַלּוּ 1 S 2^{30};—**1.** *be slight*, of water, *be abated*, fr. off (מֵעַל) earth Gn $8^{8.11}$ (J). **2.** *be swift*, c. מִן comp., of warriors 2 S 1^{23}, horses Je 4^{13} Hb 1^{8}; one's days Jb 7^{6} 9^{25}. **3.** *trifling*, i.e. of little account, of pers., Gn $16^{4.5}$ (J; both c. בְּעֵינֶיהָ); 1 S 2^{30} (opp. אֲכַבֵּד). † **Niph.** *Pf.* 3 ms. נָקַל (Ges$^{§\ 67\ t}$) 2 K 20^{10}+, וְנָקַל consec. 2 K 3^{18}; נָקֵל Pr 14^{6}; 1 s. consec. וּנְקַלֹּתִי 2 S 6^{22}; *Impf.* 3 mpl. יִקַּלּוּ Is 30^{16}; *Pt.* f. (עַל־)נְקַלָּה Je 6^{14} + 2 t.;—**1.** *shew oneself swift* Is 30^{16} (‖ עַל־קַל נִרְכָּב). **2.** *appear trifling*, 1 S 18^{23} (בְּעֵינֵיכֶם; Inf. subj., cf. Dr), c. מִן comp. *be too trifling* Is 49^{6}, esp. of sin 1 K 16^{31} (Inf. subj.), and (c. מִן comp.) Ez 8^{17}; *easy* 2 K 3^{18} (בְּעֵינֵי), 20^{10} (c. Inf.), Pr 14^{6}; *Pt.* (as subst.) c. עַל in adv. phr. עַל־נְקַלָּה *lightly* i.e. superficially, Je 6^{14} 8^{11}. **3.** *be lightly esteemed* 2 S 6^{22} (‖ שָׁפָל; opp. אִכָּבֵדָה).

Pi.$_{40}$ *Pf.* 3 ms. קִלֵּל 2 S 19^{22}+, etc.; *Impf.* יְקַלֵּל Lv 20^{9}+, etc.; *Imv.* ms. קַלֵּל 2 S 16^{10}; *Inf. cstr.* קַלֵּל Gn 8^{21} Jos 24^{9}, etc.; *Pt.* מְקַלֵּל Ex 21^{17}+; sf. כֻּלֹּה מקללוני Je 15^{10}, rd. מְקַלְלוּנִי! (Baer); err. for כֻּלְּהֶם קִלְלוּנִי JDMich Gf Gie Du al., etc.;—*curse* (prop. *make contemptible*): **1.** c. acc. pers. homin. Ex 21^{17} (E), Gn 12^{3} (J), Lv 19^{14} (H), Ju 9^{27} 2 S 16^{9} + 16 t.; קִלְלַנִי קְלָלָה 1 K 2^{8}; obj. om. 2 S $16^{5.7.10.11.13}$ ψ 62^{5} 109^{28} (opp. בֵּרַךְ); acc. pers. + בְּ of oath 1 S 17^{43} 2 K 2^{24}; c. בְּ of oath alone Is 8^{21}. **2.** c. acc. dei Ex 22^{27} (E), Lv 24^{15} (H), 1 S 3^{13} (rdg. אֱלֹהִים for לָהֶם, 𝔊 Comm.), + (obj. om.) Lv $24^{11.14.23}$. **3.** c. acc. rei Gn 8^{21} (׳י subj.), Jb 3^{1}. † **Pu.** *Impf.* 3 ms. יְקֻלָּל Is 65^{20} *be cursed* by death; 3 fs. תְּקֻלַּל Jb 24^{18} their portion *is cursed*; *Pt.* pl. sf. מְקֻלָּלָיו ψ 37^{22} *those cursed by him* (opp. מְבֹרָכָיו). † **Hiph.** *Pf.* 3 ms. הֵקַל Is 8^{23}; 2 ms. sf. הֱקִלֹּתַנִי 2 S 19^{44} (van d. H. הֲ-); 3 pl. הֵקַלּוּ Ez 22^{7}; *Impf.* 3 ms. יָקֵל 1 S 6^{5}; *Imv.* ms. הָקֵל Ex 18^{22}+; *Inf. cstr. id.*, Is 23^{9} Jon 1^{5};—**1.** *make light, lighten*, יָקֵל אֶת־יָדוֹ מֵעֲלֵיכֶם 1 S 6^{5} *he will lighten his hand from upon you*; c. מֵעַל pers. alone, *make light from upon* one, lighten one's burden Ex 18^{22} (E), Jon 1^{5} 1 K 12^{10} = 2 Ch 10^{10}; + מִן partit. 1 K $12^{4.9}$ = 2 Ch $10^{4.9}$. **2.** *treat with contempt*, acc. pers. 2 S 19^{44} Is 23^{9} Ez 22^{7}; dir. caus. *bring contempt, dishonour* Is 8^{23} (opp. הִכְבִּיד). † **Pilp.** *Pf.* 3 ms. **1.** *shake* קִלְקַל בַּחִצִּים Ez 21^{26} (in divination). **2.** (peculiarly) *whet* Ec 10^{10} (prop. move quickly to and fro). † **Hithpalp.** reflex. of **1**: *Pf.* 3 pl. הִתְקַלְקָלוּ Je 4^{24} hills *shook themselves*, shook.

קַל **adj. light, swift, fleet**;—ms. ק׳ Am 2^{15}+, קַל v^{14}; fs. קַלָּה Je 2^{23}; pl. קַלִּים Is 18^{2}+;—קַל בְּרַגְלָיו *light with his feet* Am 2^{15} 2 S 2^{18}; ק׳

alone, *swift*, messengers Is 18[2], pursuers La 4[19] (מִן comp.), camel Je 2[23], cloud Is 19[1]; of swift vanishing of wicked Jb 24[18] (Bu קַל for קַל הוּא), as subst Am 2[14] Je 46[6] Ec 9[11], = *swift* (horse) Is 30[16]; קַל as adv., *swiftly* (+ מְהֵרָה) Is 5[26] Jo 4[4].

†קַל **n.[m.]** lightness, frivolity (so Vrss Ki Gie; Gf thinks = קָלוֹן; > = *voice*);—מִקֹּל זְנוּתָהּ Je 3[9].—קֹל *voice*, v. קול

†קָלָל **adj.** burnished (tr *light, quick* movement of rubbing?);—נְחֹשֶׁת ק׳ *burnished brass* Ez 1[7] Dn 10[6] (so most, Co, Ez, קלות, in prefixing כַּנְפֵיהֶם fr v[8]; Dn then follows crpt. Ez.

קְלָלָה[33] **n.f.** curse;—abs. ק׳ Gn 27[12]+; cstr. קִלְלַת Ju 9[57]+; sf קִלְלָתְךָ Gn 27[13], קִלְלָתוֹ 2 S 16[12] (van d. H. Kt קללתי, so We Dr Lohr); pl קְלָלוֹת Dt 28[15.45],—*curse*, Gn 27[12 13](J), oft opp. בְּרָכָה, Dt 11[26.28] 23[6] = Ne 13[2], + 8 t. Dt, Jos 8[34] (D), Ju 9[57] ψ 109[17 18] Pr 27[14], קִלְלַת חִנָּם Pr 26[2] *a groundless curse*, cf. 2 S 16[12], קְלָלָה נִמְרֶצֶת 1 K 2[8] *a grievous curse*, = a formula of cursing Je 29[22], = *object of curse*, קִלְלַת אֱלֹהִים תָּלוּי Dt 21[23], שַׁמָּה וּקְלָלָה 2 K 22[19], cf. Je 24[9] 25[18] + 6 t. Je, Zc 8[13].

†קַלַּי **n.pr.m.** priest Ne 12[20], 𝔊L Καλμει.

†קְלֹקֵל **adj.** contemptible, worthless (cf Ol[§189 f] Ba[NB 160]),—בַּלֶּחֶם הַקּ׳ Nu 21[5] (JE)

†קִיקָלוֹן **n. [m]** disgrace,—Hb 2[16], si vera l intens. Ol[§182 c] Ko[II 130, 497], but dub (v We Now GASm)

†[קָלַס] **vb.** mock, scoff (Ecclus 11[4] תקלס, text by Adler[JQ xii (1900), 470]),—**Pi.** *Inf cstr.* לְקַלֵּס אֶתְנָן Ez 16[31] *to scoff at hire* (of Jerusalem under fig of harlot), but 𝔊 𝔖 Symm *collect*, rd. לְקַבֵּץ Gr Toy Krae (or לְלַקֵּט, Co) **Hithp.** *mock, deride*, c ב pers, *Impf.* 3 ms. יִתְקַלָּס Hb 1[10], 3 mpl. יִתְקַלְּסוּ Ez 22[5], יִתְ׳ 2 K 2[23].

†קֶלֶס **n.[m.]** derision, i e, object of it, ‖ חֶרְפָּה;—Je 20[8], + לַעַג ψ 44[14] 79[4].

†קַלָּסָה **n.f.** id, ‖ *id*;—Ez 22[4].

†I [קָלַע] **vb.** sling, hurl forth (Thes cp. Ar. قَلِقَ *sit insecurely* (v also Fra[224], Socin in Buhl[Lex 13]), *waver*, whence قِلْعٌ *sail* (loan-wd. Fra[l c]), JAram קִלְעָא *id*, BH NH קֶלַע *curtain*; thence *hurl, sling*; but this perh. denom. (Socin[l c]) fr. قُلَاعَة *loosened clod*, cf Syr. ܩܠܥܐ *id.* (No in Fra[l c]); Ar. مِقْلَاع *sling*, Eth. ሞቀፀ: *id.*, 𝔗 קְלַע vb *sling*, Syr n ܩܠܥܐ *sling*),—**Qal** *Pt* קֹלֵעַ בָּאֶבֶן אֶל־ Ju 20[16] *one slinging (with) a stone at* a hair; קוֹ׳ c acc. pers Je 10[18] *I will sling forth* the inhabitants **Pi.** *Impf.* 3 ms וַיְקַלַּע 1 S 17[49] *and he slang* (sc. the stone), sf יְקַלְּעֶנָּה 25[29] *he shall sling away* (life of enemy).

†I. קֶלַע **n [m.]** sling,—abs ק׳ 1 S 17[50], כַּף הַקָּלַע 25[29] *hollow of the sling* (fig), sf. קַלְעוֹ 17[40], אַבְנֵי־קֶלַע Jb 41[20] *sling-stones*, so א׳ קְלָעִים 2 Ch 26[14]; א׳־קֶלַע Zc 9[15] is difficult: Marti[Kau] כְּא׳־ק׳; We Now בני ק׳ *sons of* —— ?

†[קַלָּע] **n.m.** slinger;—pl. קַלָּעִים 2 K 3[25].

II [קֶלַע][15] **n.[m.]** curtain, hanging (P),—pl abs. קְלָעִים Ex 27[9] + 7 t. Ex; cstr. קַלְעֵי 35[17] + 4 t Ex, Nu 3[26] 4[26].—1 K 6[34 b] read צְלָעִים.

†II. קָלַע **vb.** carve;—**Qal** *Pf.* 3 ms ק׳ c. 2 acc., *carve walls with*, 1 K 6[29]; c. acc cogn. + עַל v[32], c. acc. of thing carved v[35].

†מִקְלַעַת **n.f.** carving;—cstr. מ׳ 1 K 6[18], pl. abs מִקְלָעוֹת 7[31]; cstr. מִקְלְעוֹת (after קָלַע) 6[29.32].

קלקל v קלל.

†קִלְּשׁוֹן doubtful word, in phrase וְלִשְׁלֹשׁ ק׳ 1 S 13[21] (poss. would be *fine point*, cf Aram. קלש *be thin*, hence ש׳ ק׳ *tridens*, E V. *forks*, but against anal, v. esp Dr)

קָמָה v קום

†קְמוּאֵל **n.pr.m.** Καμουηλ **1.** son of Nahor Gn 22[21]. **2.** Ephraimite Nu 34[24]. **3.** Levite 1 Ch 27[17] (B Σαμουηλ, A Καμ, 𝔊L Κεμ.).

קָמוֹן v. קום.

קמח (✓ of foll.; As. *kamû*, perh *crush, grind*, *kêmu* (= *kemû*?), *flour*; NH = BH, so 𝔗 קִמְחָא, Syr ܩܡܚܐ; Vulg. Ar. قمح *wheat*; Eth. ቀምሕ: *produce, fruit, vegetables*; cf. Egypt. *kamāh*, Bondi[77], *kmḥ*, a kind of bread, Erman[ZMG xlvi (1892) 120])

†קֶמַח **n.[m.]** flour, meal;—abs. ק׳ 1 S 1[24]+, קָמַח Is 47[2]; cstr קֶמַח Nu 5[15];—Ju 6[19] (material for unleavened cakes), 1 S 1[24] 28[24] 2 K 4[41]; defined by סֹלֶת (q v.) Gn 18[6], disting. fr. סֹלֶת 1 K 5[2]; of barley (שְׂעֹרִים) Nu 5[15] (P), but 2 S 17[28] + קָלִי, שְׂעֹרִים, חִטִּים; + other articles of

food 1 Ch 12[41] (van d H. v[40]); kept in a כַּד 1 K 17[12 14.16]; made by grinding Is 47[2]; צֶמַח בְּלִי יַעֲשֶׂה ק׳ Ho 8[7].

†[קָמַט] **vb. seize** (NH *id*, *seize, grasp, press together*, Ar. قَمَطَ *bind together*, Aram קמט = BH, ܩܡܛ *seize, compress*),—**Qal** *Impf* 2 ms sf וַתִּקְמְטֵנִי Jb 16[8] *and thou didst seize me.* **Pu.** *be snatched* (untimely) *Pf* 3 pl קֻמְּטוּ Jb 22[16].

†[קָמַל] **vb. be decayed** (Syr ܩܡܠ *be mouldy, decay*),—**Qal** *Pf.* 3 ms. קָמֵל Is 33[9] *Lebanon mouldereth*, 3 pl קָמֵלוּ 19[6] (of קָנֶה וָסוּף).

†קָמַץ **vb. enclose with the hand, grasp** (NH *id* = BH, 𝔗 קְמַץ; As *kimṣu, kinṣu*, is a part of the body occurring in pairs, Meissn [Suppl 84]),—**Qal** *Pf* 3 ms consec וְקָמַץ Lv 2[2] 5[12] (both c acc. מְלֹא קֻמְצוֹ + מִן of source), Nu 5[26] (c. acc + מִן of source, all P)

†[קֹמֶץ] **n.[m.] closed hand, fist**,—sf מְלֹא קֻמְצוֹ *his fist-full* Lv 2[2] 5[12], take up בְּק׳ 6[8] *in his fist* (all P), pl לִקְמָצִים Gn 41[47] the earth yielded *by handfuls* (i e abundantly, E, acc to most, P, Ball Holz, who questions text)

קמשׁ (√of following; meaning unknown)

†קִמּוֹשׁ **n.m.** [Ho 9. 6] **coll. thistles or nettles** (𝔊 ἄκανθαι, cf K1, 𝔙 *urtica*);—abs ק׳, sign of desolation, Ho 9[6] (> van d H קִימֹשׁ, cf. Baer De [Complut Var 23], || חוֹחַ), Is 34[13] (+ חוֹחַ, סִירִים), pl. (c ־ ins, Thes No [M 169 Anm 3] Low [194 Anm]) קִמְּשֹׂנִים Pr 24[31] (> van d H קִמְּשׁוֹנִים, || חֲרֻלִּים).

קֵן v קנן

קנא (√of foll., Ar. قَنَأَ *become intensely red* (or *black*), with dye, NH קִנְאָה *jealousy*, Syr ܩܢܐ *lividus fuit*, ܩܢܐܢܐ *zeal, envy* (rare), vb denom NH קִנֵּא, Aram קַנֵּא, Eth ቀንአ: all *be jealous, zealous*)

†קִנְאָה **n.f. ardour, zeal, jealousy** (from colour produced in face by deep emotion),—abs ק׳ Nu 5[14]+, cstr קִנְאַת Is 9[6], sf. קִנְאָתִי Nu 25[11]+, etc, pl. קְנָאֹת Nu 5[15 18.25.29],—**1.** *ardour of jealousy* of husband Pr 6[34] 27[4]; רוּחַ ק׳ *jealous disposition* Nu 5[14 14 30] (P), offering for jealousy, מנחת ק׳ v[15 18 25] (P), תורת הק׳ v[29] (P); of *rivalry* Ec 4[4] 9[6], Ephr against Judah Is 11[13]; *ardent love*, || אהבה Ct 8[6] **2.** ardour of *zeal*: **a.** of men for God Nu 25[11 11] (P) 2 K 10[16], for the house of י׳ ψ 69[10]. **b.** of God for his people, esp. in battle Is 42[13] 63[15] Zc 1[14] 8[2]; מְעִיל ק׳ Is 59[17], ק׳ י׳ תעשה זאת 9[6] 37[32] = 2 K 19[31] **3.** ardour of *anger*: **a.** of men against adversaries ψ 119[139] Jb 5[2] (|| כעשׂ), Pr 14[30] (opp. לֵב מַרְפֵּא). **b.** of God against men, || חֵמָה Ez 5[13] 16[38.42] 23[25] 36[6], || עֶבְרָה 38[19], || אַף Dt 29[19] Ez 35[11], + אֵשׁ Is 26[11] Ez 36[5] Zp 1[18] 3[8] ψ 79[5]; סֶמֶל הַקּ׳ הַמַּקְנֶה Ez 8[3] *the anger-image provoking to anger*; ס׳ הק׳ alone v[5].

†[קָנָא] **vb. denom. Pi. be jealous, zealous** (Gerber[131]),—*Pf.* 3 ms קִנֵּא Nu 25[13]+; 1 s. קִנֵּאתִי Zc 1[14]+ etc; *Impf* יְקַנֵּא Is 11[13] Pr 23[17], etc, *Inf. abs* קַנֹּא 1 K 19[10 14]; *cstr* sf קַנְאוֹ Nu 25[11], קַנֹּאתוֹ 2 S 21[2]; *Pt* מְקַנֵּא Nu 11[29],—**1.** *be jealous of*, c acc. אֶת־אִשְׁתּוֹ Nu 5[14 14.30] (P), in rivalry Is 11[13] **2.** *be envious of*, c בְּ pers., Gn 30[1] (E), 37[11] (J) ψ 37[1] 73[3] Pr 3[31] 23[17] 24[1 19]; c acc pers Gn 26[14] (J), Ez 31[9]; c. לְ pers. ψ 106[16]. **3.** *be zealous* for: **a** of man, c. לְ pers Nu 11[29] (J), 2 S 21[2]; for God Nu 25[13] (P), 1 K 19[10.14]; קנאה ק׳ Nu 25[11] (P). **b.** of God, לשם קָדשׁי Ez 39[25], לְאַרְצוֹ Jo 2[18], לירוש׳ Zc 1[14], לְצִיּוֹן Zc 8[2.2]. **4.** *excite to jealous anger*, c. בְּ instr. Dt 32[21 a] (dub; probably הִקְנִאוּנִי; cf v[16.21 b]), 1 K 14[22]. **Hiph.** *provoke to jealous anger*. *Impf.* 3 mpl sf יַקְנִאֻהוּ Dt 32[16], יַקְנִיאוּהוּ ψ 78[58] (|| וַיַּכְעִיסוּהוּ); 1 s. אַקְנִיאֵם Dt 32[21 b]; *Pt* metapl. מַקְנֶה Ez 8[3] (Ges[§ 75 q], del. Co)

†קַנָּא **adj. jealous**;—only of God: אֵל קַנָּא Ex 20[5] (J) = Dt 5[9] (as punishing those who hate him), Ex 34[14] (J), Dt 4[24] 6[15] (demanding exclusive service), קַנָּא שְׁמוֹ Ex 34[14] (J).

†קַנּוֹא **adj.** id.,—אֵל קַנּוֹא Jos 24[19] (E) (cf. Dt 6[15] supr.), Nah 1[2] (|| נֹקֵם).

I. קָנָה [84] **vb. get, acquire** (NH = BH; Ph. (Pun) מקנא, *property* [in cattle]; As. *kanû*, *gain, acquire*, Meissn [Suppl 85], Ar. قَنَا (و, ى) *acquire, procure*, Sab. קני *acquire, possess*, CIS [iv. no 89, 5.6], קני n. *property* Id [ib. no 3 8 29 3], Eth. ቀነየ: *acquire, subjugate*; Aram. קְנָא, ܩܢܐ, *acquire*);—**Qal** [81] *Pf.* 3 ms ק׳ Gn 25[10]+; sf. קָנְךָ Dt 32[6], קָנָהוּ Lv 27[24]; 3 fs. קָנְתָה ψ 78[54]; 2 ms. קָנִיתָ Ex 15[16]+, etc., *Impf.* 3 ms. יִקְנֶה Lv 22[11]+, וַיִּקֶן Gn 33[19]+, etc.; *Imv.* ms. קְנֵה Gn 47[19]+, *Inf. abs.* קָנֹה Lv 25[14] 1 Ch 21[24], קָנוֹ 2 S 24[24]; *cstr.* קְנֹה Pr 16[16], קְנוֹת Pr 16[16]+, etc., *Pt.* קֹנֶה Dt 28[68], קוֹנָה Pr 15[32]+, etc.;—†**1.** *get, acquire* (all poet.): **a.** of God as originating, creating, קנה שָׁמַיִם וָאָרֶץ Gn 14[19.22], Dt 32[6] (Isr.),

ψ 139[13] (כִּלְיֹתָי); Pr 8[22] (חכמה q.v.). **b.** of God as victoriously redeeming his people Ex 15[16] Is 11[11] ψ 74[2] (|| גָּאַל); obj. הַר־זֶה 78[54]. **c.** of Eve, acquiring קָנִיתִי אֶת־י׳ (i e. *with the help of*), Gn 4[1] (J). **d.** of acquiring wisdom, knowledge (only Pi): Pr 1[5] 4[5.5.7.7] 15[32] 16[16.16] 17[16] 18[15] 19[8] 23[23]. **2.** elsewhere *buy* Ex 21[2] (E), Gn 47[22] (J), 50[13] (P), Lv 27[24] (H), Dt 28[68] Is 24[2] Je 13[1] Ez 7[12] Pr 20[14]+; קֹנֶה *owner*, as purchaser Lv 25[30] (P) Is 1[3] Zc 11[5]+. **Niph.** *be bought*: *Pf.* 3 ms. נִקְנָה Je 32[43], *Impf* 3 mpl. יִקָּנוּ v[15]. **Hiph.** *Pf* 3 ms. sf. אָדָם הִקְנַנִי Zc 13[5]; AV makes denom. of מִקְנֶה *cattle*; Thes RV Marti[Kau] Buhl *caused* (one) *to purchase me*, i.e. *made me a bondman*; < We Now GASm read אֲדָמָה קִנְיָנִי.—*Pt.* מַקְנֶה v קנא.

†קִנְיָן **n.[m.]** **thing got or acquired, acquisition** (Aramaism, Lag[BN 205]); abs. ק׳ Ez 38[12.13], cstr קִנְיַן Lv 22[11], sf. קִנְיָנְךָ Pr 4[7]+, etc.;—**1.** *thing acquired* by purchase קִנְיַן כַּסְפּוֹ Lv 22[11] (H; cf מִקְנָה); of property Gn 34[23] 36[6] Jos 14[4] (all P), Ez 38[12.13] (in all disting fr. מִקְנֶה cattle); || בַּיִת ψ 105[21]; מקנה קנינו Gn 31[18] (P; prob. doublet, 𝔊 om), בְּכָל־קִנְיָנְךָ קְנֵה בִינָה Pr 4[7] *with* (or *at the price of*) *all that thou hast acquired, get understanding*. **2.** more gen: coll. *creatures* 𝔊 κτίσις ψ 104[24] (cf. √1 a).

מִקְנֶה[76] **n.m.**[Ex 10,26] **cattle**;—abs. מ׳ Gn 46[32]+; cstr. מקנה Gn 13[7]+, sf. מִקְנֵהוּ Gn 3[18]+, מִקְנֶךָ Is 30[23] (Ges[§93ss]), etc; pl. sf. (but v. Ko[II 112f]) מִקְנַי Ex 17[3]+, מִקְנֵיכֶם Gn 47[16]+, etc;—**1.** *cattle* in gen., including cows, sheep, horses, asses, camels (any or all of them), as purchasable domestic animals, Gn 47[16.16.17.17] Ex 9[3]+ (J), 10[26] (E), Dt 3[19] (not in P), Jb 1[3] ψ 78[48] Je 9[9] 1 Ch 5[21]+; so prob. ישב אֹהֶל ומקנה Gn 4[20] (J) of nomads, מקנה הַבְּהֵמָה Gn 47[18] (J) **2.** specif. of cows, sheep, and goats in herds and flocks Gn 13[2] (J), 31[9] (E), v[18] 36[7] 46[6] Nu 32[1] (all P), Is 30[23]+; אַנְשֵׁי מ׳ Gn 46[32.34] (J), שָׂרֵי מ׳ Gn 47[6] (P), cf 1 Ch 28[1], רֹעֵי מ׳ Gn 13[7.7] (J); disting. from בְּהֵמָה Nu 31[9] (P), 32[26] 2 K 3[17], fr. קנין Jos 14[4] (P) Ez 38[12.13]; from both Gn 34[23] 36[6] (P); מ׳ צאן ובקר 2 Ch 32[29] Ec 2[7], מ׳ צאן ומ׳ בקר Gn 26[14] 47[17] מ׳ בקר וצאן (J); sheep only Gn 29[7] (J) Nu 32[16] (E).—מִקְנֵה הַשָּׂדֶה Gn 49[32] (P) rd מִקְנַת; מִקְנֶה אַף עַל עוֹלֶה Jb 36[33] rd מַקְנֶה (**Hiph.** *Pt*), or מְקַנֶּה (**Pi.** *Pt*) metapl. fr. קנא, Hi Bö Di Du; 1 S 30[20] del. הַמּ׳ 𝔊 We Dr al, v esp HPS.

†מִקְנָה **n.f.** **purchase**,—abs. מ׳ Gn 23[18]+; cstr. מִקְנַת Gn 17[12]+; sf. מִקְנָתוֹ Lv 25[16]+;—**1.** *purchase*, מִקְנַת כֶּסֶף Gn 17[12.13.23.27] Ex 12[44] (all P); סֵפֶר הַמּ׳ *document of purchase* Je 32[11.12.12.14.16]. **2.** *purchase-price*, Lv 25[16.16.51] 27[22] (P). **3.** *possession* (gained by purchase), לְמִקְנָה Gn 23[18] (P)

†מִקְנֵיָהוּ **n.pr.m.** (*possession of* י׳),—Levit. musician 1 Ch 15[18.21], Μακ(κ)ελλ(ει)α, Μακενια(ς), Μακκανια(ς).

II. קנה (√of foll; cf. As. *kanû*, *reed*; Ar. قَنَاة *spear-shaft*; Eth. ቀኖት፡ *goad*; NH קָנֶה, Aram. קַנְיָא, ܩܢܝܐ, all = BH Hence Gk. κάννα, κάνης, also κάνεον *basket* (Lewy[Fremdw 99]), Lat. *canna*).

קָנֶה[62] **n.m.**[Gn 41,5] **stalk, reed**;—abs. ק׳ 1 K 14[15]+; cstr. קְנֵה Ez 40[3]+; sf קָנֶהָ Ex 25[31] 37[17] = קָנָהּ (Ges[§91e]) Jb 31[22]; pl. קָנִים Ex 25[32]+, cstr. קְנֵי 37[18]+; sf. קְנֹתָם 25[36] 37[22];—†**1.** *stalk* of grain Gn 41[5.22] (E). †**2.** *water-plant, reed*, 1 K 14[15] Is 19[6] (+ סוּף), 35[7] (+ גֹּמֶא), coll., חַיַּת ק׳ ψ 68[31] *beasts of* (*the*) *reeds* (dwelling among them), cf. בְּסֵתֶר ק׳ וּבִצָּה Jb 40[21]; מִשְׁעֶנֶת הַקּ׳ הָרָצוּץ 2 K 18[21] = Is 36[6], מִשׁ׳ ק׳ Ez 29[6], all fig. of weak support; cf. ק׳ רָצוּץ Is 42[3] (spared by עבד י׳). †**3.** *calamus*, aromatic reed, ק׳ הַטּוֹב Je 6[20] (Ges[§126w]), ק׳־בֹּשֶׂם Ex 30[23] (P); ק׳ alone Ez 27[19] Is 43[24] Ct 4[14]. **4.** derived meanings: †**a.** *measuring-rod*, קנה הַמִּדָּה Ez 40[3.5] (6 cubits long, v. אַמָּה) 42[16.16.17.18.19]. **b.** unit of measure, *reed* (of 6 cubits, as As *kanû*) Ez 40[5.5] + 10 t. 40, 42, + מְלוֹ הַקּ׳ 41[8] *full reed* (emphat) †**c.** *beam* of scales, for scales themselves Is 46[6]. †**d.** *shaft* of lamp-stand Ex 25[31] = 37[17] (P). **e.** *branches* thereof, Ex 25[32.32.32] = 37[18.18.18] + 16 t. 25, 37 (all P). †**f.** *shoulder-joint*, Jb 31[22] (|| שְׁכֶם).

†קָנָה **n.pr.** **1.** of wady between Ephr. and Manass, נַחַל ק׳ Jos 16[8] 17[9] (both P), Κα(ρα)να, Καναι, etc.; identif. by Rob[BR iii 135] with *Wady Kânah*, S. and SW. of Nablûs, cf Buhl[Geogr 101, 104]. **2. loc.** in Asher, 19[28], Καν(θ)α(ν), etc.; prob *Ḳâna*, SE. fr. Tyre Rob[BR ii. 455f] Buhl[229], Egypt. *Ka'nô* WMM[As u. Eur 181], and perhaps Tel Am. *Kanû*.

†קְנַז **n.pr.m.** in Edom, Κενεζ: son of Eliphaz Gn 36[11] = 1 Ch 1[36], Gn 36[15] cf v[42] = 1 Ch 1[53], and father of Othniel Jos 15[17] Ju 1[13] 3[9.11] (v. Di[Gn] Bu[RS 9, Comm Ju 1, 13] GFM[Ju 1, 13ff] Mey[Entstehung 115 f.]).

†קְנִזִּי **adj. gent.**, c. art. הַקּ׳, of Caleb Nu 32[12] Jos 14[6.14] (all JE); as n coll. Gn 15[19] (in list; appar. S Canaanitish people).

קֵנִי v. קַיִן.

†קִנָּמוֹן **n.m. cinnamon** (prob. foreign wd., coming with the thing from remote E., cf. M'Lean-ThDyer[Ency. Bib. s.v.]; cp. with Malay *kainamanis* by Röd[Thes. Add. 111], *kāyū mānīs* Lewy[Fremdw. 37], but only *kāyu, wood*, given by Scott[Mal. Words in Eng. JAOS xvii, xviii (1896, 1897)]; Gk. κιννάμωον from Heb. (against Lag[BN 199]));—fragrant bark used as spice: abs. ק׳ Pr 7[17] Ct 4[14]; cstr. קִנְּמָן־בֶּשֶׂם Ex 30[23] (P) *cinnamon of sweet odour*.—Vid. also Houghton-Tr[Smith DB s.v.] Post[Hastings DB s.v.].

קנן (√of foll.; mng.? NH קֵן *nest*, As. *ḳinnu, ḳannu, nest, family;* Aram. קִנָּא, ܩܢܐ *nest*).

קֵן **n.m.**[Dt 22, 6] **nest**;—abs. ק׳ Is 10[14]+; cstr. קַן־ Dt 22[6]; sf. קִנּוֹ 32[11]+, etc.; pl. קִנִּים Gn 6[14];—**1.** *nest*, of bird Dt 22[6] Jb 39[27]; in sim. Is 10[14] Pr 27[8], of *nestlings* Dt 32[11] Is 16[2] (קֵן מְשֻׁלָּח), perhaps also עִם־קִנִּי Jb 29[18], but difficult, Che[JQ July, 1897, 578] prop. זָקֵן or בְּזִקְנִי (cf. 𝔊); *nest* on high, of rock-dwellings Nu 24[21] (JE) Je 49[16] Ob[4]; fig. of Chaldeans' secure abode Hb 2[9]; temple as secure home for Isr. ψ 84[4] (fig. of swallow). **2.** *cells*, like nests, in Noah's ark Gn 6[14] (P; read prob. קִנִּים קִנִּים, so Lag Ol Bu[Urg. 255] Di Holz Gunk).

†[קָנַן] **vb. denom. Pi. make a nest, nest**;—*Pf.* 3 fs. קִנְּנָה Is 34[15]; 3 pl. קִנְּנוּ Ez 31[6] (in fig.); *Impf.* 3 ms. יְקַנֵּנוּ ψ 104[17]; 3 fs. תְּקַנֵּן Je 48[28] (sim.). **Pu.** *Pt.* fs. מקננתי (Ges[§ 90 l]) Je 22[23] Kt (Qr מְקֻנַּנְתְּ; cf. Ges[§ 80 d]) (thou) *who art nested* in the cedars (fig.).

קנץ (√of foll., si vera l.; cf. Ar. قَنَصَ *catch, capture, ensnare*).

†[קֶנֶץ] **n.[m.] snare, net** (si vera l.);—pl. cstr. (Ges[§ 130 a]) עַד־אָנָה תְּשִׂימוּן קִנְצֵי לְמִלִּין Jb 18[2] *how long will ye lay snares for words* (catch at words, talk without knowledge)? so Castle JDMich and most, but sense strange; Vrss transl. *end*, so Thes al. (expl. קנצי [very dub.] as Aram.), rd. then קֵץ (with sg. vb., after 𝔊), Me Bi Siegf Du, and del. עַד־אָנָה Du.

†קְנָת **n.pr.loc.** Κααθ, Κα(α)ναθ, E. of Jordan Nu 32[42] (JE) 1 Ch 2[23]; perh. *Ḳanawat* on W. slope of Hauran mountains (Buhl[Geogr. 252]).

קסם (√of foll.; appar. orig. *divide, assign* (deity), Ar. قَسَمَ *divide, distribute*, x. *get a part allotted to oneself*, especially by drawing lots [with headless arrows] at a sanctuary (cf. esp. Ez 21[26.27]); IV. أَقْسَمَ *swear;* v. also Eth. ቀሰመ: IV. *use divination*, so 𝔗 קְסַם, Syr. ܩܣܡ; קִיסְמָא *divination;* see esp. RS[JPhil. xiii (1885), 276 ff.], We[Skizzen iii. 127 f. 167; Heid. 2. 132 ff.] Dr[Dt 18, 10]).

†קֶסֶם **n.[m.] divination**;—abs. ק׳ Nu 23[23]+, קָסֶם Ez 21[26]; cstr. קְסַם 13[6]; pl. קְסָמִים Dt 18[10]+;—**1.** of the nations: Balaam, Nu 23[23] (poem in JE; ‖ נַחַשׁ; c. ב *against;* as acc. cogn. לִקְסָם־ק׳ Ez 21[26]; ק׳ as instr. of divination בִּימִינוֹ v[27]; so of elders of Moab and Midian, קְסָמִים בְּיָדָם, Nu 22[7] (E).—Is 2[6] v. [קֹסֵם]. **2.** of false proph. ק׳ כָּזָב Ez 13[6] (but v. [קָסַם]); ק׳ as acc. cogn. Ez 13[23] (< Co Berthol Krae כָּזָב as v[9] 21[34] 22[28]); ק׳ אֱלִיל (so Gf for MT וֶאֱלִיל) Je 14[14] (all ‖ חזה שוא or שקר); קֹסֵם קְסָמִים prohibited Dt 18[10] 2 K 17[17]; reprobated 1 S 15[23] (poem; ‖ תרפים). **3.** in good sense ק׳ עַל שִׂפְתֵי מֶלֶךְ Pr 16[10] (king's lips as oracle).

†[קָסַם] **vb.denom. practise divination**;—**Qal** *Impf.* 3 mpl. יִקְסְמוּ 2 K 17[17], יִקְסֹמוּ Mi 3[11]; 2 fs. תִּקְסַמְנָה Ez 13[23]; *Imv.* fs. קָסֳמִי 1 S 28[8] Qr (Kt קסומי); *Inf. cstr.* קְסֹם Mi 3[6] (Buhl קְסֹם), קְסָם־ Ez 21[26.34] קְסוֹם־ Ez 21[28] (read קֶסֶם Co Buhl), esp. *Pt.* קֹסֵם Dt 18[10] Is 3[2], etc.;—**1.** of diviners of the nations, Balaam, Jos 13[22] (D), Philist. 1 S 6[2] (‖ כהנים), Bab. Is 44[25] (‖ חכמים) Ez 21[26] cf. ק׳ שׁוא Ez 21[28] (but rd. קֶסֶם), + Is 2[6] (ins. prob. קְסָמִים > קֶסֶם, or מִקֶּסֶם; v. קֶדֶם **1 b**); of Can. necromancers בָּאוֹב 1 S 28[8]; ‖ מְעֹנְנִים Dt 18[14]; of Ammonites ק׳ כָּזָב Ez 21[34] (+ לְ pers.). **2.** false proph. of Isr. ‖ חזה Mi 3[6] (? קְסֹם; ‖ חזון), v[7]; Is 3[2] (+ נביא; cf. v[3]), ‖ נביאים Je 27[9] 29[8], ק׳ : חזה שוא ‖ בְּכֶסֶף Mi 3[11], ‖ חזה שקר Zc 10[2]; ‖ חזה שוא קֶסֶם Ez 13[23] (but v. קֶסֶם), ק׳ כָּזָב Ez 13[9] 22[28], + 13[6] (rd. וְקָסְמוּ, or [Co Berthol] inf. abs. וְקָסֹם, Vrss, Toy). **3.** ק׳ קְסָמִים prohibited Dt 18[10] 2 K 17[17].

†[מִקְסָם] **n.[m.] divination**; cstr. מִקְסַם חָלָק Ez 12[24] (‖ חזון שוא); מִקְסַם כָּזָב Ez 13[7] (‖ מחזה שוא).

†[קָסַס] **vb. Pō'. strip off** (so context requires; verb otherwise unknown);—*Impf.* 3 ms. וְאֶת־פִּרְיָהּ יְקוֹסֵס Ez 17[9] *and its fruit shall he not strip off?*

קֶסֶת v. קשׁה.

קְעִילָה[18] **n.pr.loc.** Κεειλα: in Judah, toward Philistines, ק׳ 1 S 23[1] + 13 t. 23 (קְעִלָה, v[3.13]); Jos 15[44] (P), cf. 2 Ch 4[19] (geneal. scheme); post-ex. פֶּלֶךְ קְעִילָה Ne 3[17.18]; mod. *Kīlā*, c. 8 m. NW. from Hebron, GASm[Geogr. 230] Buhl[Geogr. 193]; cf. TelAm. *Ḳilti* Wkl[No. 165, 11, 18, etc.].

קעקע (√of foll.; NH קִעְקַע usu. *pull, tear* (or *cut*) *down, off*, Levy[NHWB] Ecclus 10[15] (cf. Frä[ZAW xxi (1901), 102]); also, as to Lv 19[28], *incise*, appar. reduplicated fr. a √קוע (Thes) or קעע).

†**קַעֲקַע** **n.[m.] incision, imprintment, tattoo**; Lv 19[28] (H), v. כְּתֹבֶת (RS[Sem. 1. 316; 2nd ed. 324]).

קער (√of foll.; cf. Ar. قَعُرَ *be deep*, of well, قَعَّرَ *come to bottom* of well, vessel, also *make* well *deep*; II. *hollow out* (Dozy); قَعِيرٌ *deep*, of well, bowl; Nab. קער *hollow* or *carve out* (Sachau SB Ak. 1896, 1057); Syr. ܡܩܥܪܐ, *calyx, acorn-cup, well*; Bondi[60] cp. Egypt. *māqaār, bottom part* of oven).

קְעָרָה 17 **n.f. dish, platter** (P) (NH *id.*);—abs. ק׳ Nu 7[85]; cstr. קַעֲרַת־כֶּסֶף Nu 7[13] + 11 t. 7; pl. cstr. קַעֲרֹת כֶּסֶף 7[84], all of dedication gifts; as utensils in tabern. pl. abs. קְעָרֹת 4[7], sf. קְעָרֹתָיו Ex 25[29] 37[16].

†[**שְׁקַעֲרוּרָה**] **n.f. depression, hollow** (on format. v. Ges[§ 55 i]);—pl. שְׁקַעֲרוּרֹת Lv 14[37] in wall.

†[**קָפָא**] **vb. thicken, condense, congeal** (cf. Syr. ܩܦܐ *heap up, collect*);—**Qal** *Pf.* 3 pl. קָפְאוּ תְהֹמֹת Ex 15[8] (song) *the deeps were condensed*, became firm walls; *Impf.* יקפאון Zc 14[6] Kt (i.e. יִקְפָּאוּן [poss. is also יִקָּפְאוּן **Niph.**]) Thes al. glorious(?) ones [stars] *shall contract* (dwindle), but rd. Qr וְקִפָּאוֹן v. foll. *Pt.* הַקֹּפְאִים עַל־שִׁמְרֵיהֶם Zp 1[12] the men *who are thickening on their lees* (easy-going men, under figure of undisturbed wine). **Hiph.** *Impf.* 2 ms. sf. תַּקְפִּיאֵנִי Jb 10[10] *didst thou not curdle me* like cheese (of formation of foetus)?

†**קִפָּאוֹן** **n.[m.] congelation**;—Zc 14[6] Qr [> Kt v. √**Qal** *Impf.*], so 𝔊 𝔖 Symm We Now (with other change, but see GASm), v. יָקָר.

†[**קָפַד**] **vb. Pi. gather together, roll up** (Ar. قَفَدَ *wind* turban *snugly*; Aram. קְפַד, ܩܦܕ, Ithpe. *be drawn in, together*; also קוּפְדָא, ܩܘܦܕܐ, *porcupine*; so Ar. (د) قُنْفُذٌ (cf. Lag[BN 182]), Eth. ቀንፋዝ);—*Pf.* 1 s. קִפַּדְתִּי Is 38[12] *I have rolled up*, like a weaver, my life (i.e. finished it; Buhl[Lex 13] תָּ- [of י׳], but 3 ms. foll. of י׳).

†**קִפֹּד** **n.[m.] porcupine** (fr. *rolling* itself *together*; 𝔊 ἐχῖνοι (alw. pl.), 𝔙 *ericius*, Bo[Hieroz. iii. cap. 36] Post[Hastings DB BITTERN]; > (from context) *bittern* Tr[NHB 243] Hi Che Gu[Kau]; v. discussion by M'Lean-Shipley[Ency. Bib. BITTERN]);—ק׳ as haunting desolate places, Is 14[23] Zp 2[14], קִפּוֹד Is 34[11].

†[**קְפָדָה**] **n.[f.**, Albr[ZAW xvi (1896), 116] cf. Sta[§ 308a]] **shuddering** (cf. ܩܦܕ, of skin, = סָמַר ψ 119[20], v. Thes);—abs. קְפָדָה־בָא Ez 7[25] (read בָּאָה Co Krae, and on tone v. Ges[§ 29 e]).

קפז (√of foll.; cf. Ar. قَفَزَ *leap, spring*; so 𝔗 קְפַז (rare), v. Syr. ܩܦܙ *id.*, ܩܦܘܙܐ *weasel*).

†**קִפּוֹז** **n.f. arrow-snake** (Ar. قِفَّازٌ, so Bo Hieroz. Pars post. iii. cap. 11 (citing Avicenna[ii. 139, 16], cf. Thes Lag[BN 89]), and most moderns; cf. Dozy[ii. 383] PS 1375 ad fin.; = ἀκοντίας Aelian[Hist. Anim. vi. 18, viii. 13], called ק׳ as *leaping* from trees on passers-by; but ag. this v. Houghton[Acad. Apr. 24, 1886, 292 f.] (arrow-snake does not incubate) Post[Hast. DB iii. 637] who conj. an owl (as AV));—Is 34[15], token of desolation.

†**קָפַץ** **vb. draw together, shut** (NH = BH; Ar. قَفَصَ *collect, conjoin, tie*; Syr. ܩܦܨ *draw together, contract, withdraw* (cf. Nö[M 47; ZMG xxxiii (1879), 516]); 𝔗 קְפַץ *hasten* (double oneself up in running), Pi. *hop, spring*);—**Qal** *Pf.* 3 ms. ק׳ ψ 77[10], etc.; *Impf.* 2 ms. תִקְפֹּץ Dt 15[7]; 3 mpl. יִקְפְּצוּ Is 52[15];—*shut* hand Dt 15[7] (c. מִן *away from*, so as not to lend; opp. פתח v[8]); mouth, in astonishment Is 52[15], in abject silence Jb 5[16] ψ 107[42]; fig. ק׳ רַחֲמָיו 77[10] *shut up his compassion.* **Niph.** *Impf.* 3 ms. יִקָּפְצוּן Jb 24[24] si vera l., *they draw themselves together*, of contraction in death (cf. Di Bu; Ol יִקָּבְצוּן *are gathered in*). **Pi.** *Pt.* מְקַפֵּץ עַל־הַגְּבָעוֹת Ct 2[8] *springing* (i.e. making repeated contractions of body, in taking leaps) *upon the hills* (‖ מְדַלֵּג).

קֵץ v. קצץ.

[**קָצַב**] **vb. cut off, shear** (?) (NH קָצַב *decide, determine*, **Pi.** *chop* meat; Palm. קצבא *butcher*, so Syr. ܩܨܒܐ, JAram. קַצָּבָא, and Ar. قَصَّابٌ as loan-word Frä[258]; Ar. قَضَبَ also is *cut off* a branch);—**Qal** *Impf.* 3 ms. וַיִּקְצָב־עֵץ 2 K 6[6] *he cut off a stick*; *Pt. pass.* fpl. עֵדֶר הַקְּצוּבוֹת Ct 4[2] *a flock of* (sheep) *that are shorn* (?).

†**קֶצֶב** **n.m.**[1 K 6, 25] **1. cut, shape**; **2. extremity**;—**1.** ק׳ abs., *shape* of cherubim 1 K 6[25] (+ מִדָּה), of bases 7[37] (+ *id.*). **2.** *extremity*, pl. cstr. קִצְבֵי הָרִים Jon 2[7] *the extremities* (bottoms) *of* (the) *mountains* (= קצבי הרים Ecclus 16[19]).

† I. [**קָצָה**] **vb. cut off** (NH *id.*, *separate*, Ph. קצה *cut off, exterminate*; Aram. קְצָא, ܩܨܐ *break off* (e.g. bread); Ar. قَصَا *be remote*, قُصْيَا *remote extremity*);—**Qal** *Inf.* קְצוֹת עַמִּים Hb 2[10] *cutting off* many *peoples*; Vrss קְצוֹתָ (√קצץ);

Gr Now conj הַצִּיקוֹת **Pi.** *Inf. cstr.* לְקַצּוֹת בּ 2 K 10[32] *to cut off in Israel*, read prob. לְקַצֹּף *to be angry with*, 𝔗 Hi Che[Crit n Is 14 6 (in Comm.)] Kmp[Kau] Kit Benz, 𝔙 Gr לְקֹץ, *Pt.* מְקַצֶּה רַגְלַיִם Pr 26[6] (fig) **Hiph.** *Pf* 3 pl. הקצו Lv 14[41], acc. *dust*; *Inf cstr* הקצות v[43], acc *house*, in both appar = קָצַע *scrape, scrape off* (q v, v[41 a]), and so prob read, viz הִקְצִעוּ, הַקְצִיעַ, RS[JPhil xvi (1888) 72] Dr-Wh Di-Ry Baen

קָצֶה[† 93] **n.[m.]** end, extremity, only sg.. abs ק׳ Gn 19[4]+3 t; cstr קצה Ju 6[21]+, sf קָצֵהוּ Gn 47[21]+4 t, (מִ)קְּצֵיהֶם Ez 33[2] (sg, Ges § 93 ss), pl. (cstr) supplied by קצות, v. foll;— **1.** *end*, of staff Ju 6[21], rod 1 S 14[27.43], curtains Ex 26[5]=36[12] (P, cf קָצָה), of conduit Is 7[3], river, = *mouth* v[18] (prob.), Jos 15[5.5] 18[19], of field Gn 23[9], valley Jos 15[8], tribe v[21], sea v[2] Nu 34[3] (all P); of territory (גבול) Nu 20[16] (JE, just *without*), 22[36] (E, just *within*), cf Ez 25[9] (al. sub **3**), מק׳ גבול־מצרים ועד־קצהו Gn 47[21] (J), cf מִן־הַק׳ אֶל־הַק׳ Ex 26[28]=36[33] (of side of tabern), מקצה צָפוֹנָה Ez 48[1] *at the northern extremity*, cf מק׳ תֵּימָן Jos 15[1] (P); of earth, מק׳ (הָ)אָרֶץ Is 5[26] 43[6] Dt 28[49] (all ‖ מֵרָחוֹק), Is 42[10]+4 t, + phr מק׳ (הָ)אָרֶץ ועד־ק׳ הָאָרֶץ Dt 13[8] 28[64] Je 25[33], of land 12[12] (cf Is 26[15]), of earth, abbrev. אֶל־ק׳ עד־ק׳ הָא׳ 25[31] Is 48[20] 49[6] ψ 46[10], בק׳ תבל בק׳־אֶרֶץ Pr 17[24], הָא׳ Is 62[11], of earth, ψ 19[5], מק׳ הַשָּׁמַיִם Is 13[5] (‖ מֵאֶרֶץ מֶרְחָק), ψ 19[7] לְמִק׳ הַשׁ׳ בק׳ הַשׁ׳ Dt 30[4]=Ne 1[9], (‖ עַל־קְצוֹתָם) ועד־ק׳ הַשׁ׳ Dt 4[32] **2.** *border, outskirts*, of city 1 S 9[27] 14[2] Jos 4[19] 18[15], camp Nu 11[1] (JE), esp to one approaching Ju 7[17.19] 2 K 7[5.8], so of armed force Ju 7[11], people Nu 22[41] (E), 23[13] (JE, emphat אֶפֶס ק׳, opp כֻּלּוֹ), mt Ex 19[12] (E), Jos 18[16] (JE), see also 3[8] (D), v[15] (JE), Ex 13[20] = Nu 33[6], Ex 16[35] Nu 33[37] Jos 13[27] (all P), Ru 3[7] †**3.** condensed term for what is included within extremities, = the whole. מק׳ אֶחָיו Gn 47[2] (J), cf. Ez 33[2], abs. מקצה Gn 19[4] (J) = in (its) entirety; = on all sides, Je 51[31]+50[26] (מִקָּצֶה for מקץ, Gie), so מִקָּצֵהוּ Is 56[11] Di, but om מק׳ 𝔊 Du Che Marti. **4.** מקצה *at the end of* a certain time Jos 9[16] (JE), 2 S 24[8]+8 t

†**קָצָה** **n.f. et** (pl) **m.**[Ex 25,18] end (pl. 4 t. **f.** [c. num masc], Albr[ZAW xvi (1896), 93] changes gender of num. in all, or regards as irregular agreement in gender (Ges § 97 c), otherwise Kö[ii 1, 61, 176]), —abs. ק׳ Ex 25[19]+, pl cstr קְצוֹת 1 K 12[31]+, sf קְצוֹתָיו Ex 27[4]+ (so also Ex 37[8] 39[4] Qr; Kt קצוותו, cf. קְצָת infr.), etc;—**1.** *end*, sg. of כַּפֹּרֶת in tabern. Ex 25[19.19]=37[8.8], of curtain 26[4]=36[11]; elsewh. pl., ק׳ הַכַּפֹּרֶת 25[18]=37[7], cf. 25[19]=37[8]; of ephod 28[7]=39[4], breast-plate 28[23.24.26]=39[16.17.19], chains 28[25]=39[18], grating 27[4] (appar = *corners*); *tips* of wings 1 K 6[24.24]; of vine Ez 15[4], ק׳ הָאָרֶץ *ends of the earth* Is 40[28] 41[5.9] Jb 28[24], אַרְבַּע ק׳ הַשָּׁמַיִם Je 49[36], cf ψ 19[7]; ק׳ דְּרָכָיו Jb 26[14], i.e the mere edge, minute part, of his doings. **2.** מִקְצוֹת הָעָם = *from the whole of* (fr among) *the people*, 1 K 12[31] 13[33], cf Ju 18[2] 2 K 17[32] (v. also Ecclus 16[17], and קָצָה **3**)

†**קָצֶה** (Baer קְצָה) **n.[m.]** end (on—Ba[NB § 12 a], and [on ה] Kö[ii 1, 64]),—only אֵין ק׳, usu. + לְ, *no end to* (of), Is 2[7.7] Na 2[10] 3[3]; abs אין קצה v[9].

†[**קָצוּ**] **n.[m.]** end, boundary (on form Kö[ii 1, 61]),—only pl cstr. קַצְוֵי־אֶרֶץ *ends of the earth* ψ 48[11] 65[6], *boundaries of the land* Is 26[15].

†**קְצָת** **n f.** end (Lag[BN 10] Ges[§ 95 n]),—cstr. ק׳ Ne 7[69] (Gi Baer, v[70] van d. H) +; sf. קְצָתָם Dn 1[5]; pl. abs קצות Ex 38[5] ψ 65[9] (+ perh. קצוותו Ex 37[8] 39[4] Kt. v. קָצָה, Kö[ii 1, 61] der. these pl. forms fr [קָצוּ]);—**1.** *end*, of *corners* of grating Ex 38[5] (‖ קצותיו 27[4]), cf. Ex 37[8] 39[4] supr (all P); *ends* of earth ψ 65[9] **2.** מִקְצָת (some) *from the end of, some of* (מִן **3 b**) Ne 7[69] (so NH), Dn 1[2]. **3.** מִק׳ *at the end of* a certain time Dn 1[5.15.18].

II **קצה** (√of foll (Ol[§ 215 b] Kö[ii 1, 405]), cf. Ar قَضَى *decide judicially, decree*, قَاضٍ *Kadi*)

†**קָצִין** **n.m.**[Dn 11,18] chief, ruler (prop *decider*, cf Dr[Dn 11 8]),—abs. ק׳ Ju 11[6]+, cstr קצין Is 3[7], pl cstr קציני Is 1[10]+; sf קְצִינַיִךְ Is 22[3],—**1.** *chief, commander* in war Jos 10[24] (JE), Ju 11[6.11] (‖ ראש), Dn 11[18]. **2.** *dictator*, Is 3[6.7]. **3.** more gen., *ruler*, man in authority, Is 1[10] 22[3] Mi 3[1.9]; of ants, אין ק׳ Pr 6[7] (+ שֹׁטֵר, מֹשֵׁל)— Pr 25[15] read probably קֶצֶף (Toy)

קְצוֹת v. קְצָת

קצח (√of foll; mng unknown; NH קֶצַח = BH; Ar. قَرْحٌ, قِرْحٌ *seeds used for seasoning*)

†**קֶצַח** **n.m.**[Is 28,27] black cumin (*Nigella sativa* Linn; 𝔊 μελάνθιον, 𝔙 *gith*, *id*; cf Tr[NHB 444, Smith DB 2nd ed Fitches] Post[Hastings DB Id]),— plant with small black acrid seeds, used as condiment abs. ק׳ Is 28[25.27.27].

I **קָצַע** **vb. scrape, scrape off** (NH *id*, also קְצִיעָה = BH, 𝔗 קְצִיעֲתָא, Ar. قُفَاعٌ *fine dust*), —**Hiph.** *id. Impf.* 3 ms אֶת־הַבַּיִת יַקְצִעַ Lv 14[41].

†I. [קְצִיעָה] **n.f.** cassia, a *powdered* bark, like cinnamon (hence Gk. κασία, Lat. *casia*, Lewy[Fremdw. 37]);—pl. קְצִיעוֹת (מֹר וַאֲהָלוֹת) ψ 45[9] (Che now קְצִיעוֹת תרצק *are shed*, v. in [Ency. Bib. CASSIA, n.]).

†II. קְצִיעָה **n.pr.f.** (*cassia*, fr. fragrance);—Job's second daughter Jb 42[14], Κασ(σ)ιαν (acc.).

†[מַקְצֻעָה] **n.[f.]** scraping tool, used in fashioning idols;—pl. בַּמַּקְצֻעוֹת Is 44[13].

†II. קצע (√ of foll.; cf. Aram. קְטַע, ܩܨܰܥ *cut off*, also Ar. قطع *break off* (if for قطع, RS[JPhil. xvi. 74]), مقطع *place where something is cut off* or *ends abruptly* RS[infr.]; Sab. קצע appar. *cut off*, or the like, Sab Denkm[91]).

מִקְצֹעַ **n.m.**[Ez 46. 21] place of corner-structure, (inner) corner-buttress (as (place of) *cutting off* of an inner angle if √ rightly expl.; v. RS[l. c. 71–81]);—abs. מ׳ Ne 3[19]+, -צוֹעַ Ne 3[20]+; cstr. -צַע Ez 46[21.21]; pl. abs. מִקְצֹעֹת Ex 26[24] 36[29], cstr. -עוֹת Ez 46[22], מִקְצוֹעֵי v[21], also מְקֻצָּעֹת Ex 26[23] 36[28] Di (not **Pu.** *Pt.* fr. קצע Thes Buhl[Lex 13] al.), but rd. prob. מִקְצֹעֹת, so SS Baen; sf. מִקְצְעוֹתָיו Ez 41[22];—*corner-post* of altar Ez 41[22], tabern. Ex 26[23.24]=36[28.29]; (inner) *buttress-place* of court, where the small corner-courts were, Ez 46[21.21.21.22]; of inner (rock-?) *buttress* at NE. corner of wall of Jerus., הַמּ׳, nearly=n.pr., Ne 3[19.20.25], also (disting. fr. פִּנָּה) v[24] 2 Ch 26[9].

קָצַע **vb. denom. Hoph.** *Pt.* מְהֻקְצָעוֹת (Ew [§ 192 d] Ol[§ 78 c] Ges[§ 53 q. a.]) Ez 46[22] *cornered? set in corners?* del. with 𝔐 (cf. Ol) 𝔊𝔖𝔙 Hi Kö[i. 1, 204] Co Berthol Toy Krae.—Ex 26[23] 36[28] v. מִקְצֹעַ.

†I. קָצַף **vb.** be wroth (NH *id.*, Hiph. *make wrathful* (rare); Syr. ܩܦܰܣ *be wrathful*, also *be anxious, fearful*);—**Qal** *Pf.* 3 ms. ק׳ Gn 41[10]+, etc.; *Impf.* 3 ms. יִקְצֹף Lv 10[6]+, etc.; *Inf. cstr.* קְצֹף Is 54[9]; *Pt.* קֹצֵף Zc 1[15];—*be wroth:* **1.** of God; abs. Dt 1[34] Is 57[16.17.17] 64[4.8] Zc 1[15]; c. עַל *against*, Lv 10[6] Nu 16[22] (P), Dt 9[19] Is 47[6] 54[9] La 5[22] Zc 1[2.15] Ec 5[5]; c. אֶל Jos 22[18] (P). **2.** of man; abs. Est 1[12] 2[21] 2 K 5[11]; c. עַל Gn 40[2] 41[10] (E), Ex 16[20] Lv 10[16] Nu 31[14] (P), Je 37[15] 1 S 29[4] 2 K 13[19]. **Hiph.** *Pf.* 2 ms. הִקְצַפְתָּ Dt 9[7]; 2 mpl. הִקְצַפְתֶּם v[8]; *Impf.* 3 mpl. יַקְצִיפוּ ψ 106[32]; *Inf. cstr.* הַקְצִיף Zc 8[14]; *Pt.* pl. מַקְצִפִים Dt 9[22];—*provoke to wrath*, c. acc. י׳ Dt 9[7.8.22] Zc 8[14]; so (acc. om.) ψ 106[32]. **Hithp.** *put oneself in a rage: Pf.* 3 ms. consec. וְהִתְקַצַּף Is 8[21], of hard-pressed people.

†I. קֶצֶף **n.m.**[2 K 3. 27] wrath;—abs. ק׳ Nu 1[53]+; קָצֶף Jos 22[20]+; cstr. קֶצֶף Je 50[13]+; sf. קִצְפִּי Is 60[10]; קִצְפְּךָ ψ 38[2], קִצְפֶּךָ 102[11], קִצְפּוֹ Je 10[10];—**1.** of God: abs. Nu 17[11] (P), Dt 29[27] Is 60[10] Je 10[10] 21[5] 32[37] 50[13] ψ 38[2] 102[11] Zc 7[12]; c. עַל *against* Nu 1[53] 18[5] Jos 9[20] 22[20] (P), 2 K 3[27] 1 Ch 27[24] 2 Ch 19[2.10] 24[18] 29[8] 32[25.26] Is 34[2] Zc 1[2.15]; ק׳ בְּשֶׁצֶף Is 54[8]. **2.** of man (late), Est 1[18] Ec 5[16].—Ho 10[7] v. II. קֶצֶף.

II. קצף (√ of foll.; Ar. قَصَفَ *break, snap off*).

†קְצָפָה **n.f.** a snapping or splintering (on abstr. formation v. Ba[NB 87]);—Jo 1[7] (of fig-tree; ‖ שַׁמָּה).

†II. קֶצֶף **n.[m.]** prob. splinter;—only קְק׳ עַל־פְּנֵי־מָיִם Ho 10[7] (sim. of helpless king).

[קָצַץ] **vb.** cut off (NH *id.*, also קֵץ *end;* As. *kaṣâṣu*, *hew off, cut off, kiṣṣatu, boundary-stone*, Belser[BAS ii. 120, 189], cf. Hilpr[Assyriaca i. 12]; Ar. قَصّ *cut, clip, cut off;* Aram. קְצַץ, ܩܰܨ *cut off*, קִיצָא, ܩܶܨܳܐ *end*);—**Qal** *Pf.* 2 ms. consec. וְקַצֹּתָה Dt 25[12] (acc. כַּפָּהּ); *Pt. pass.* pl. cstr. קְצוּצֵי פֵאָה Je 9[25] 25[23] 49[32] (v. פֵּאָה **1**). **Pi.** *Pf.* 3 ms. קִצֵּץ ψ 129[4], וְק׳ consec. Ex 39[3] ψ 46[10], קִצַּץ 2 K 18[16]; *Impf.* וַיְקַצֵּץ 16[17]+, etc.;—*cut* or *hew off*, thumbs, toes, Ju 1[6], hands and feet 2 S 4[12]; *cut in two*, spear (חֲנִית) ψ 46[10], threads Ex 39[3] (P), cords ψ 129[4] (fig.); *cut in pieces*, vessels (of gold) 2 K 24[13] 2 Ch 28[24]; bases (הַמְּכֹנוֹת) 2 K 16[17] (so Kit Benz, transposing הַמִּסְגְּרוֹת), doors 2 K 18[16] (both, for the sake of metal sheathing). **Pu.** *Pt.* pl. מְקֻצָּצִים Ju 1[7] *hewn off* (as v[6] supr.).

קֵץ[68] **n.m.**[Ez 7, 6] end;—ק׳ abs. Am 8[2]+, cstr. Gn 4[3]+, עֶת־ Dn 8[17]; sf. קִצּוֹ Is 37[24]+, קִצָּהּ ‖ 2 K 19[23], etc.;—**1.** *end*, usu. of time, esp. in phr. מִקֵּץ *at the end of* a definite time Gn 8[6] (J), 41[1] (E), 16[3] (P)+15 t., + מִקֵּץ הֱיוֹת Est 2[12]; indef. Gn 4[3] (J) 1 K 17[7] Je 13[6]; so (late) לְקֵץ of indef. time 2 Ch 18[2] Ne 13[6] Dn 11[6.13]; defin. כְּעֵת צֵאת הַקּ׳ לְיָמִים שְׁנַיִם 2 Ch 21[19]; *end* of life, of a people Am 8[2] Ez 7[2.2.3.6.6] Je 51[13] La 4[18.18], cf. (of all flesh) Gn 6[13] (P); of individ. Jb 6[11] ψ 39[5] (‖ מִדַּת יָמַי), Dn 9[26 a] 11[45]; in eschatol. sense, עֵת עֲוֹן קֵץ *time of final punishment* (Toy) Ez 21[30.34] 35[5]; לַקֵּץ Hb 2[3] *to the end;* esp. Dn, of time of Antiochus' persecution, foll. by A.'s death, עֵת קֵץ *time of the end* 8[17] 11[35.40] 12[4.9], ק׳ מוֹעֵד 8[19]; cf. ק׳ הַיָּמִין 12[13], ק׳ alone 9[26 b] 12[13]; *end*, cessation, abs. לַמּוֹעֵד ק׳ 11[27]; ק׳ הַפְּלָאוֹת 12[6], of words Jb 16[3], darkness 28[3],

perfection ψ 119^{96}, אין ק׳ *no end*, of peace Is 9^{6}, iniquities Jb 22^{5}, toil Ec 4^{8}, עשות ספרים 12^{12}. **2.** *end*, in space, מלה קצה 2 K 19^{23} *its remotest lodging-place* = Is 37^{24} (v מָלוֹן p 533); אין ק׳, of multitude Ec 4^{16} —Je 50^{26} v קָצֶה **3**

†קְצִיץ **n.pr.loc.** (fr above √?),—only in עֵמֶק ק׳ in Benj, Jos 18^{21}, Αμεκασεις, etc

†[קִיצוֹן] **adj. at the end, outermost,**—fs קִיצֹנָה, of curtain (יריעה) Ex 26$^{4.10a}$ = 36$^{11.17a}$, ins also prob 26^{10b} = 36^{17b} so Kit (in Di) Baen

†[קָצַר], I קָצַר (Ges^{§46c} Sta$^{§384.2}$) **vb. be short** (NH קָצַר *short*, קצר *shorten*, Ar قَصَّرَ *shorten*, قَصُرَ *be short*, c عَنْ *come short of*; JAram קְצַר *be short*),—**Qal** *Pf.* 3 ms קָצַר Is 28^{20} Mi 2^{7} (SS קָצֵר fr adj. קָצֵר), 3 fs קָצְרָה Is 50^{2} 59^{1}, *Impf* 3 fs תקצר Jb 21^{4}+, 3 fpl תקצרנה Pr 10^{27}, *Inf abs* קָצוֹר Is 50^{2}; *Pt. pass* fpl קצרות Ez 42^{5},—*be short*, of bed Is 28^{20} (fig), of לִשְׁכוֹת Ez 42^{5}; esp (fig.) of יַד י׳, i.e. be ineffective, powerless Nu 11^{23} (JE), c מִן comp Is 50^{2} (+ inf. abs), 59^{1}, c נֶפֶשׁ, רוּחַ, = *be impatient* (opp [אָרַךְ] **Hiph. 1** (c)) וַתִּק׳ נֶפֶשׁ הָעָם Nu 21^{4b} (JE), of utter discouragement, cf. (of רוּחַ) Jb 21^{4}, וַתִּק׳ נַפְשׁוֹ Ju 16^{16} i.e he was worn out (by importunity), so of proph (representing י׳) Zc 11^{8} (ב pers) reach limit of patience with, endurance of, of י׳ Ju 10^{16} (ב rei), ק׳ רוּחַ י׳ Mi 2^{7} (v supr), ק׳ of time †Pr 10^{27} (years of wicked) **Pi.** *shorten Pf* 3 ms קִצַּר יָמַי ψ 102^{24} **Hiph.** *id*, *Pf* 3 ms הִקְצַרְתָּ יְמֵי וגו׳ ψ 89^{46}.

†[קָצֵר] **adj. short,**—in phr. קצרי־יד 2 K 19^{26} *short of hand*, feeble, = Is 37^{27}, fig קְצַר אַפַּיִם Pr 14^{17} = *impatient*, so קְצַר רוּחַ v^{29} (opp אֶרֶךְ אַפַּיִם); of time קְצַר יָמִים †Jb 14^{1} *short-lived*

†קֹצֶר **n.[m.] shortness,**—cstr. ק׳ רוּחַ Ex 6^{9} (P) = *impatience*

†II [קָצַר] **vb. reap, harvest** (NH *id*, also קָצִיר *harvest*, cf As *kaṣâru*, *join together, collect*, v Dl$^{Pr 106f}$ Zehnpf$^{BAS i. 503}$ (not Syr. ܩܨܪ *bind*, Eth ቈጸረ: [ቀጸረ:] *constringere*, v. No$^{ZMG xl (1886), 735}$)),—**Qal** *Pf* 3 pl קָצְרוּ Je 12^{13}, etc; *Impf* 3 ms יקצור Is 17^{5} Ec 11^{4} + Pr 22^{8} Kt (Qr יִקְצָר־), 3 mpl יִקְצֹרוּן Ru 2^{9}, etc, *Imv.* mpl קִצְרוּ Ho 10^{12}+; *Inf cstr* לקצר 1 S 8^{12}+; sf. קְצָרְךָ Lv 23^{22}, קְצָרְכֶם 19^{9} 23^{22}, *Pt.* קוֹצֵר Je 9^{21}+, etc.:—*reap*, c acc of crop acc cogn קָצִיר 1 S 6^{13} 8^{12} (+ חָרַשׁ), Lv 19^{9} 23$^{10.22}$ (all H) Dt 24^{19}; acc of grain Is 17^{5} (fig, ‖ אָסַף), Jb 24^{6} (Qr; Kt vid **Hiph.**), cf Lv 25^{5} (H), v^{11} (P; + זָרַע), so (obj. om) 2 K 19^{29} = Is 37^{30}, Mi 6^{15} (opp. זָרַע), Lv 19^{9b} 23^{22b} Ru 2^{9} Ec 11^{4} (+ זָרַע), obj קצים Je 12^{13} (opp זָרַע); *Pt* = *reaper* Am 9^{13} (+ חוֹרשׁ), Je 9^{21} (sim), ψ 129^{7} (‖ מעמר), + Is 17^{5} (for קָצִיר, so Buhl$^{Lex 13}$ Marti), pl 2 K 4^{18} Ru 2$^{3.4.5.6.7.14}$, fig of reaping fruits of righteousness Ho 10^{12} (+ זָרַע), of evil Ho 8^{7} (both + זָרַע), 10^{13} (+ חָרַשׁ), Jb 4^{8} (+ חָרַשׁ, זָרַע), Pr 22^{8}, ψ 126^{5} they that sow (זָרַע) in tears *shall reap* in joy. **Hiph.** *Impf.* יקצירו Jb 24^{6} Kt (< Qr יִקְצוֹרוּ, v. supr.).

†I קָצִיר **n.m.**$^{Je 8.20}$ **harvesting, harvest** (cf. Lag$^{BN 173}$),—abs. ק׳ Gn 45^{6}+, cstr. קְצִיר Ju 15^{1}+; sf קְצִירְךָ Lv 19^{9}+, etc.;—*harvest*: **1.** process of *harvesting*, Gn 45^{6} (E; + חָרִישׁ), Ru 2^{23}. **2.** *what is reaped, harvested, crop*, spec. of grain: Gn 8^{22} (+ זֶרַע; J), Is 17^{11} (fig; cf. נוד; ‖ זֶרַע), ק׳ יאר, 23^{3} (‖ *id*.) i.e. exported grain of Egypt; ק׳ חטים Ex 34^{22} (JE), ins also 2 S 24^{15} (𝔊 Th We Dr al), לֶקֶט ק׳ Lv 19^{9b} 23^{22b}; ק׳ as eaten Je 5^{17} Jb 5^{5} (but rd here קֹצְרוֹ 𝔊 Me Bu al, cf Bev$^{JPhil xxvi. 304}$); as acc cogn. c קָצַר 1 S 8^{12} Dt 24^{19} Lv 19^{9a} 23$^{10.10.22a}$ ספיח ק׳ Lv 25^{5} (all H), ק׳ חטים 1 S 6^{13}, of ripe grain Is 1^{11} (ק׳ שָׂדֶה), 4^{13} (בְּשַׁל ק׳); fig of punishment Ho 6^{11}, of vintage Is 16^{9} (‖ קַיִץ, rd. prob בָּצִיר as ‖ Je 48^{32}, Buhl$^{Lex 13}$). **3** *time of harvest*, Ex 34^{21} (+ חָרִישׁ; JE), 2 S 21^{10} (23^{13} rd. הַצּוּר as ‖ 1 Ch 11^{15}, so 𝔊L Th We and most), Is 9^{2} (sim), 18^{5} (fig.), Je 5^{24}, ‖ קַיִץ 8^{20} Pr 6^{8} 10^{5} 26^{1} (sim.), opp חֹרֶף 20^{4}, ימי ק׳ Jos 3^{15} (JE), 2 S 21^{9a}, יום ק׳ Pr 25^{13} (sim), עֵת(הַ)ק׳ Je 50^{16} 51^{33} (fig), of *wheat-harvest*, ימי ק׳ חטים Gn 30^{14} (J), Ju 15^{1}, without ימי Ru 2^{21b}, הֲלוֹא ק׳־ח׳ הַיּוֹם 1 S 12^{17}, *barley harvest*, ק׳ (הַ)שערים 2 S 21^{9b} Ru 1^{22} 2^{23a}, חֹם קָצִיר Is 18^{4}, חַג הַק׳ Ex 23^{16} (E) On harvest in Pal. v Vogelst$^{Landwirthsch. 57ff}$ Hayman$^{Smith DB AGRICULTURE}$. —Is 17^{5} rd קֹצֵר, v. קָצַר.

†II קָצִיר **n.m.**$^{Is 27.11}$ usually coll, **boughs, branches** (connex with above √ dub.),—abs. ק׳ Jb 14^{9}, sf. קצירי Jb 29^{19} (in fig; ‖ שֹׁרֶשׁ), קצירו 18^{16} (fig, ‖ *id*); קְצִירָהּ Is 27^{11}; pl. sf. קְצִירֶיהָ ψ 80^{12}.

קְצָת v. I. קצה.

קַר, קָר v. I. קרר. קִר v I. קיר.

I קָרָא^{734} **vb. call, proclaim, read** (NH *id*, *read aloud, read*, Ph. קרא *call*, Ar. قَرَأَ *read aloud, recite* (the 'Ḳor'ān'), القرآن *the Kor'ān*, Aram קְרָא, ܩܪܐ *call*, etc, so OAram.

קרא, Nab. *id*, Palm. *id*, (קרה);—**Qal** ₆₅₃ *Pf.* ק׳ Gn 11[9]+, 3 fs. consec. וְקָרָאת Is 7[14] (Ges §74 g); 2 ms. קָרָאתָ Ju 12[1]+, etc.; *Impf.* 3 ms. יִקְרָא Gn 2[19]+; sf. יִקְרָאוֹ Je 23[6], -אֵהוּ Is 41[2]+, 1 s. אֶקְרָא Dt 32[3]+, וָאֶקְרָאֶה 1 S 28[15] (Ges §48 d Nes Marg 15); 3 fpl. וַתִּקְרֶאןָ, וַתִּקְרֶאנָה Ru 4[17 17], Nu 25[2]; 2 fpl. תִּקְרֶאנָה Ru 1[20.21], etc.; *Imv.* ms. קְרָא Ju 7[3]+, sf. קְרָאֻנִי ψ 50[15], etc; *Inf. cstr.* קְרֹא 1 S 3[8]+, קְרֹאות (Baer -את) Ju 8[1] (Ges §74 h); sf. קָרְאִי ψ 4[2]+, etc; *Pt. act.* קֹרֵא Am 5[8]+, קֹרֵא Je 1[15]+; pl. קֹרְאִים ψ 99[6] (Ges §§74 i. 75 oo); *pass.* קָרוּא Est 5[12], pl קְרוּאִים 1 S 9[22] Ez 23[23], קְרֻאִים 1 S 9[13]+; cstr. קְרוּאֵי Nu 1[16] Qr (Kt קריאי), 26[9] Kt (Qr קְרִיאֵי, v. קָרִיא),—**1. a.** *call, cry, utter a loud sound,* Ju 9[7] 2 S 18[25] (in v[28] read וַיִּקְרַב We, confirmed by 𝔊L, so Dr and all recent Comm), Je 4[5] Dn 8[16] (all + אמר), 2 K 7[11] (on text v. Kit Benz), Is 6[4]; for help Gn 39[15 18] (J); of pleading in court Is 59[4] (ב of manner); explicitly בקול גָּדוֹל Gn 39[14] (J), 1 K 18[27 28] 2 K 18[28]=Is 36[13]=2 Ch 32[18], קול גָּדוֹל Ez 9[1] (+באזני), c. אַחֲרֵי pers. 1 S 20[37] (+ אָמַר), 24[8] (Gi; v[9] van d. H. Baer, + לאמר), Je 12[6] **b.** *call, cry,* obj. in orat. recta Ju 7[20] 1 S 3[4] (rd. שְׁמוּאֵל שמואל; 𝔊 Th We Dr Kit Bu HPS), v[6] (cf. 𝔊), v[8] (agst. accents), v[10] (v. שמואל), 20[38] 2 S 20[16] 2 K 11[14] Je 20[8] Lv 13[45], = utter, speak Je 36[18]; of command Gn 45[1] (E) **2. a.** *call unto* some one: אל pers. (oft. + אָמַר; sts. c. מן loc), Gn 3[9] 19[5] Ex 3[4] Is 6[3]+ oft., c. עַל (for אֶל) of satyrs Is 34[14] (so Vrss Ges Che^Comm al. > recent Comm from II קָרָא or קָרָה which (in Qal) alw. take accus), unto (אֶל) י׳ (God), in praise †ψ 66[17] 1 Ch 4[10], usu. for help, Ju 15[18] 1 S 12[17 18] Ho 7[7] ψ 3[5] 4[4]+, + עַל pers. *against* Dt 15[9] 24[15]; to (ל) י׳ (God) †Jb 14[14] ψ 57[3] 141[1]; to (ל) a servant (for service) 2 K 4[36] Jb 19[16], so (אֶל) 2 S 1[15], *call* to (ל) one Je 3[4] (+ orat. rect), La 4[15] (*id*), Pr 2[3] (לַבִּינָה); subj. י׳ Mi 6[9] Je 35[17]. **b.** *cry* for help, abs, (poet. and late) Zc 7[13] Is 58[9] 65[24] Jb 5[1] 9[16] Pr 21[13] ψ 4[2] 20[10]+ 10 t. ψψ (147[9] of young ravens); באזני Ez 8[18]. **c.** ק׳ בשם י׳ *call with name of* י׳ (i.e. use it in invocation): Gn 4[26] 12[8] 2 K 5[11] Je 10[25]=ψ 79[6]+ 16 t. (1 K 18[24] of specif appeal to י׳ to display his power), + Is 65[1] (v. **Pu.**), with name of Baal †1 K 18[24.25.26]. **d.** late, c. acc. dei Is 43[22] ψ 14[4]+ 4 t. ψψ; abs. ψ 116[2]. **3.** *proclaim:* **a.** c. acc. rei procl Am 4[5] Gn 41[43] Dt 15[2] Je 31[6] Lv 25[10]+; ק׳ צוֹם *proclaim a fast* 1 K 21[9 12] Je 36[9]+, ק׳ מוֹעֲדֵי י׳ Lv 23[2.4]; ק׳ sq. orat rect. Ex 34[6], etc.; sq ל pers. Je 34[8.15.17 17] Is 61[1], עַל pers. (*against, concerning*) 1 K 13[4 32] Je 49[29] La 1[15]; *proclaim* peace to (ל pers.) Ju 21[13]; cf. ק׳ אֵלֶיהָ לְשָׁלוֹם Dt 20[10]; ק׳ c. acc. cogn. מִקְרָא Is 1[13], הַקְּרִיאָה Jon 3[2] (+ אֶל) **b.** ק׳ שם י׳ Dt 32[3] ψ 99[6]; so (earlier) ק׳ בְּשֵׁם י׳ Ex 33[19] 34[5] (JE); cf. ק׳ בשם יַעֲקֹב Is 44[5] (but read יִקָּרֵא, Lo Che and most). **c.** ק׳ בש׳ עֲלֵי ψ 49[12] *proclaim (with) name over* landed estates, claim possession (Hup Bae); *proclaim* one's own name Ru 4[11] = become famous; pt. pass. *proclaimed*, i e. renowned Ez 23[23]. **d.** abs. *make proclamation* (sts + לֵאמֹר, אָמַר) Ju 7[3] Je 2[2] (בְּאָזְנֵי) Zc 1[14 17] Jon 3[4] Is 40[2.6]+, c. עַל *concerning* Ne 6[7], *against* 1 K 13[2] Jon 1[2]. †**4. a.** *read aloud,* oft. בְּאָזְנֵי, less oft. לִפְנֵי, c. ב of roll, book Je 36[6.8 14] Ne 8[3.8] 9[3] 2 Ch 34[18], + acc of words Je 36[8 10]; obj. om. Ex 24[7] (E) Je 36[15], c. acc. of roll, book v[13.21] 51[63] 2 K 22[10] 2 Ch 34[24], of letter (סֵפֶר), writing 2 K 5[7] Is 29[11 12] Je 29[29], columns of manuscript Je 36[23]; c. acc. of words Jos 8[34.35] Je 36[6] 51[61] 2 K 23[2]=2 Ch 34[30], cf. Dt 31[11] **b.** *read,* to oneself, in (ב) a roll, book, Dt 17[19] Ne 8[18], so of vision written on tablets Hb 2[2]; c acc. of letter (סֵפֶר) 2 K 19[14] = Is 37[14], book 2 K 22[8]; abs Is 34[16]. **c.** *read,* for hear read, 2 K 22[16]. **5.** *summon:* usu. **a.** c. ל pers. Gn 12[18] 20[8.9] Nu 22[5 20.37] Ju 8[1] 1 S 3[5.6.8.8]+ oft. (c. 100 t), + ל reflex. 1 K 1[28.32], + אֶל loc. Ex 19[20], + אֶל pers 2 S 9[2], + inf. purpose Jos 24[9] Ju 12[1] 14[15] 1 S 28[15], + מִן loc. Ho 11[1] Ju 4[6]; + בְּשִׁמְךָ Is 45[4] *summon* by thy name; specif. *summon* = *invite* (esp. to feast) Ex 34[15] Ju 14[15] (+ inf purpose) 1 S 16[3] (+ בַּזָּבַח, rd. prob. לַזּ׳ v. HPS), v[5] (+ לַזּ׳), 1 K 19[26]+ (c. 17 t). **b.** c. אֶל pers. Ex 10[24] Jos 4[4] 10[24] 1 K 13[21]+ (c. 20 t.); אֶל pers. + ל pers. (diff persons in same relation) Ex 8[21] Je 42[8], = *call for* (demand to see), c. אֶל pers. 2 K 18[18]; c ל rei = demand, require Pr 18[6] cf. 27[16] (prob. corrupt, v. Toy). **c.** c. acc. pers. Gn 41[8.14] Ex 2[7] (+ ל pers.), v[7] Am 5[16] (+ אֶל rei), Is 13[3] (ל rei), 1 S 3[16] 22[11]+ (c. 33 t.), ins וַיִּקְרָא in this sense also 2 S 15[12] 𝔊L We Dr and most; + inf. purpose Nu 24[10], ק׳ מִמִּזְרַח עַיִט Is 46[11]; in weakened sense (to bring response, or bring pers. near) Ct 5[6], specif. *invite*, 1 S 9[24] (but corrupt, v. esp. HPS), 1 K 1[9] (also + ל, MT), v[10] 12[20] (+ אֶל loc.), Dt 33[19] (acc. loc); אֲנִי קָרוּא לָהּ Est 5[12], pt. pass. elsewh. pl., *invited ones, guests* 1 S 9[13.22] 2 S 15[11] 1 K 1[41 49] Zp 1[7] Pr 9[18]; *invite* or *summon* (acc. pers) for help, succour, Ho 7[11]; usu. obj י׳ (poet. and late) Je 29[12] 2 S 22[4.7] = ψ 18[4 7] Is 55[6] La 3[57] Jb 27[10] ψ 50[15] 86[5]+ 8 t. ψψ, acc שם י׳ La 3[55]; acc. חכמה Pr 1[28] **d.** abs. *call, summon* Am 7[4] (+ ל rei), Is 22[12] (*id.*), 1 S 3[5.6]

Zc 7[13], subj 'י (God) Is 52[2] 65[12] 66[4] Jb 13[22] 14[15], קְרוּאֵי הָעֵדָה Nu 1[17] Qr (Kt קְרִיאֵי), 26[9] Kt (Qr קְרִיאֵי) **e.** *call and commission, appoint*, acc pers, Is 48[15] 49[1], + בשם *by name, specifically*, Ex 31[2] 35[30] Is 43[1] 45[3] **f.** *call and endow* (with privilege) Is 51[2] 54[6] 55[5]. **6.** *call = name*. **a.** (early and most common usage), *call* one's name (שם) so and so, 2 acc of pers Gn 3[20] 4[25 26] 5[2.3.29] + 34 t Gn, Ex 2[10 22] Ho 1[4 6.9] Is 7[14] 8[3] 9[5] + 10 t (Je 46[17] read קראו שם 𝔊 Gie al.); of places, etc, Gn 4[17] 11[9] + 17 t Gn, Ju 1[17 26] 2[5] 15[19] 18[29] + 21 t. **b.** c acc. of appellation only, Ez 39[11] **c.** acc. pers vel loc. + acc appell. Ho 2[18] Dt 3[14] Je 23[6] Is 58[5] Nu 32[41] **d.** acc pers. + cl ψ 89[27]. **e.** = *give name to*, acc appell + ל pers. (loc, vel rei) (1) pers Ho 2[18] Gn 35[18] 1 S 4[21] Je 3[19] 30[17] 33[16] + 9 t., (2) loc, vel rei, Ju 18[12] 2 S 2[16] 5[9] 6[8] Jos 22[34] (name lost, 𝔖 Heb Codd ins עד, cf Di Steuern), Gn 1[5.s.8] 2[19 19] Ex 33[7] + 30 t. + Jb 17[14] (ל + sentence incl name). **f.** c בשם + ל Is 40[26], cf 65[15] (שם אַחֵר), ψ 147[4] (שמות), Ru 4[17] (לאמר + שם), Gn 2[20] 26[18 18] (all c שם). **g** c ל rei + על־שם 2 S 18[18] **h.** *call by* (ב) names the names (acc) of cities Nu 32[38], *call* to (ל) city, + appell, + בשמו v[42] **i** *call* cities (acc.) בשם, i e specify them, Jos 21[9] 1 Ch 6[50] (בשמות) †**Niph.** *Pf.* 3 ms נִקְרָא Je 4[20] +, 1 s נקראתי Est 4[11], etc; *Impf* 3 ms יִקָּרֵא Gn 2[23] +, וַיִּקָּרֵא Ez 20[29] +, etc; *Pt* נִקְרָא Is 43[7] Je 44[26], pl נקראים Is 48[1] Est 6[1], — **1.** reflex, מֵעִיר הַקֹּדֶשׁ נִקְ׳ Is 48[2] *from the holy city they call themselves.* **2.** pass. *be called* **a.** *be proclaimed* (cf. **Qal 3**), of שם י׳ Je 44[26] (בפה instr), of man's name = be famous Ru 4[14], = be announced Je 4[20] **b.** *be read aloud* (cf. **Qal 4**) impers c ב of book, + באזני Ne 13[1], subj records Est 6[1] (לפני). **c.** *be summoned* (cf **Qal 5**) · Is 31[4] (על *against*); Est 3[12] 4[11 11] 8[9], + בשם, i.e specifically, 2[14]. **d.** *be named* (cf **Qal 6**) (1) appell. subj + ל pers Gn 2[23] *to her shall be called 'woman,'* 1 S 9[9] Is 32[5] 62[4 12] Pr 16[21], + ל loc. 2 S 18[18] Is 1[26] 35[8] Je 19[6]. (2) וְנִקְרָא שְׁמוֹ וגו׳ Dt 25[10], so Gn 35[10] Dn 10[1] Ez 20[29] (of place); אֶת־שִׁמְךָ Ez 20[29]. (3) ונקראה יְרוּשׁ׳ וגו׳ Zc 8[3], so of land Dt 3[13], temple Is 56[7]. (4) esp נִקְרָא שֵׁם י׳ עַל, denoting ownership, of pers. Je 15[16], people Dt 28[10] Je 14[9] Am 9[12] Is 63[19] 2 Ch 7[14], ark 2 S 6[2] (del. 2nd שם 𝔊 We Dr al), = 1 Ch 13[6] (adding עָלָיו Oettli Kau, > Kit[Hpt] שְׁמוֹ שָׁם), temple 1 K 8[43] = 2 Ch 6[33], Je 7[10 11 14.30] 32[34] 34[15], city Je 25[29] Dn 9[18], city + people v[19]; so name of man 2 S 12[28], as given to his wife Is 4[1]. (5) be called על שם, i.e reckoned to, Gn 48[6] Is 54[5] 61[6]; עַל־שְׁבָם 1 Ch 23[14], cf Ezr 2[61] = Ne 7[63] (6) *be called* בשם Is 43[7] 48[1]. (7) בְּיִצְחָק יִקָּ׳ לְךָ זָרַע Gn 21[12], i e in (through) יצ׳ shall seed be reckoned to thee, וְיִקָּרֵא בָהֶם שְׁמִי 48[16] *through them shall my name be called*, i e. perpetuated (8) *be named* = mentioned, of pers Is 14[20]. (9) subj שם Ec 6[10], i e. thing is known †**Pu.** (Ez and Is[2]) *Pf* 3 ms קֹרָא *be called*, subj appell + ל pers vel rei = *be named*, Is 48[8] Ez 10[13] (קו׳); וְקֹרָא consec Is 58[12] 61[3] 62[2] (שם חָדָשׁ); גוי לא קרא בשמי 65[1] (< קָרָא or קרא [**Qal 2 c**], Vrss Lo Ew Che Di al); *be called and privileged* (cf. **Qal 5 f**), *Pt* יִשׂ׳ מְקֹרָאִי 48[12].

†I. קֹרֵא **n.m.** [Je 17,11] usu. **partridge** (fr. *calling*; v Gray in FFP[123] Post[Hastings DB s v] Tristr[Moab 129 144 f], otherwise Bo[Hieroz Pt 2, 81 ff, ed. Rosenm vol II 632 ff]), — 1 S 26[20] Je 17[11], cf. עֵין הַקּוֹ׳ Ju 15[19].

†II קוֹרֵא **n. pr. m.** Κωρηβ, Κωρη, etc.; Levites: **1.** 1 Ch 9[19] 26[1] (קֹרֵא). **2.** 2 Ch 31[4].

†[קָרִיא] **adj.** called, summoned; — pl. cstr as subst, קריאי מועד Nu 16[2] *the summoned ones of assembly*, term. techn for representatives, councillors, so קריאי הָעֵדָה 1[16] Kt (Qr קרואי), 26[9] Qr (Kt קרואי! cf. √**Qal 5 d**).

†קְרִיאָה **n.f.** proclamation; — Jon 3[2].

מִקְרָא[23] **n.m.** [Ex 12,16] convocation, convoking, reading, — מ׳ abs Is 1[13] Ne 8[8], cstr Ex 12[16] +; pl cstr מִקְרָאֵי Lv 23[2] +, sf. מִקְרָאֶהָ (Ges[§ 91 k]) Is 4[5], — **1.** *convocation, sacred assembly* Is 1[13] (after קרא), 4[5]; usu explicitly מ׳ קֹדֶשׁ, term techn in P for religious gathering on Sabbath and certain sacred days, Ex 12[16.16] + 14 t Lv 23 Nu 28, 29, + (pl.) Lv 23[2.4 37]. **2.** (n verbi, as Aram. Inf, Ges[§ 45 e cf 115 d]) *convoking*, מ׳ הָעֵדָה Nu 10[2]. **3.** *reading* Ne 8[8].

II [קָרָא][137] **vb. encounter, befall** (‖ form of קָרָה q v; Sl[4] לקרת *to meet, opposite*; Ar. قَرَا, *put part to part*; Min. קרא *set opposite*, Hom Chrest[127]), — **Qal**[131] *Pf*[5] 3 ms sf. קְרָאַנִי Je 13[22] Jb 4[2]; 3 fs. קָרָאת Dt 31[29] Je 44[23], etc.; *Impf*[4] 3 ms. יִקְרָא Gn 49[1], sf. יִקְרָאֵנוּ Gn 42[4], 3 fpl. וַתִּקְרֶאנָה Lv 10[19], Ex 1[10] rd. 3 fs sf תִּקְרָאֵנוּ (Sam Vrss Di Ges[§ 47 k] So[Kau] Baen), *Inf cstr*[121] לִקְרַאת (Ges[§ 19 k] Ol[§ 137]), Gn 15[10] +, etc; *Pt* fpl sf קֹרְאֹתַיִךְ Is 51[19], — **1.** *meet, encounter*, only inf. cstr. לִקְרַאת oft = prep. *toward, against* (Ko[ii 1 317]), almost always c. acc. pers, after vb of motion, Is 7[3] Gn 19[1] 24[17] Ju 4[18.22] 1 K 2[8] +; in war, battle,

Ju 7^{24} $20^{25.31}$ 1 S 4^{1} 1 K 20^{27}+, after עָרַךְ 2 S $10^{9.10.17}$+, ψ 35^{3} v. I. סגר **2 b**; לְחַזֵּק לִבָּם לִקְ׳ הַמִּלְחָמָה Jos 11^{20} *to harden their heart to encounter the war* with Isr; after הִנֵּה (without vb. of motion), †1 S 10^{10} 2 S 15^{32} 16^{1} 1 K 18^{7} Pr 7^{10}; in constr. prægn. וַיִּשְׂמַח לִקְ׳ Ju 19^{3} *he rejoiced to meet him*, + 1 S 6^{13} (𝔊 We Dr al.), חרד לִקְ׳ 1 S 16^{4} 21^{2}; so c. שׁאג Ju 14^{5}, הריע 15^{14}, מצא 2 K 10^{15}, נצב Ex 5^{20} 7^{15} Nu 22^{34}, etc; redund. יִקָּרֶה י׳ לִקְ׳ Nu 23^{3}; implic. of *helping*, Is 21^{14} ψ 59^{5} (fig.); לִקְ׳ נְחָשִׁים Nu 24^{1} he did not go *to encounter* (in expectation of) *signs of divination*; in metaph. Is 14^{9}, לִקְ׳ אֱלֹהֶיךָ Am 4^{12}. **2.** fig. *befall* c. acc pers, bad sense Gn $42^{4.38}$ Dt 31^{29} Je 13^{22} 44^{23} Is 51^{19} Jb 4^{14} Lv 10^{19}; of war Ex 1^{10} (v. supr.); in gen., Gn 49^{1}. **Niph.** *meet unexpectedly; Pf.* 3 ms. נִקְרָא, c. עַל pers. Ex 5^{3}; *Impf.* 3 ms. וַיִּקָּרֵא, c. לִפְנֵי pers. 2 S 18^{9}; *Pf.* 20^{1}, c. שָׁם, *chanced to be there; Impf* of bird's nest Dt 22^{6} (לְפָנֶיךָ); *Inf abs.* נִקְרֹא v. קרה. **Hiph.** *Impf.* 2 ms. וַתַּקְרֵא Je 32^{23} *thou didst cause* all this evil *to befall* them (acc. pers. et rei).

[קְרָאת], לִקְרַאת *to meet*, v II. קרא.

I. **[קָרַב], קָרֵב** $_{279}$ **vb. come near, approach** (NH *approach, be offered*, As *karâbu, approach*, Ar. قَرُبَ, قَرِبَ *be near, approach*; so Eth. ቀረበ: Sab. קרב *approach* a woman (sexually, v. **1 a** infr.), DHM[Hofmus No. 6. l. 2], but also gen. רחק וקרב ד *he who is far and he who is near* CIS[iv. no. 95. 7. 8] cf. SabDenkm[No 12. 9. 10]; Aram. קְרֵב, ܩܪܶܒ, *approach*; also, = *oblation*, Sab. קרבן DHM[ZMG xxx (1876). 672] Ar. قُرْبَان, OAram. קרבן, 𝔗 קוּרְבָּנָא, Syr. ܩܘܪܒܢܐ; cf. As. *kurbannu* (כ), Dl[HWB 591]),—**Qal** $_{93}$ *Pf.* 3 ms. קְ׳ Gn 20^{4}+; 3 fs קָרְבָה Zp 3^{2}, etc., *Impf.* 3 ms יִקְרַב Gn 37^{18}+etc.; *Imv.* ms. קְרַב 2 S 20^{16}+, קָרְבָה ψ 69^{19}; mpl קִרְבוּ Ex 16^{9}, *Inf abs* קָרוֹב Ec 4^{17} De Siegf Ol §249c Sta §642c Kö[i 175], *cstr.* קְרֹב ψ 27^{2} 32^{9}, לְקָרְבָה Ex 36^{2}, etc.;—*approach*. **1. a.** c. אֶל pers. (27 t.) Gn 37^{18} Nu 18^{4} Mal 3^{5} (+לַמִּשְׁפָּט), Jon 1^{6}+; in kindness 1 K 2^{7}, of י׳ to help ψ 69^{19}, for war, battle, Ex 14^{20} Ju 20^{24}; unto God †1 S 14^{36} (+הֲלֹום), Zp 3^{2}, י׳ †Ez 44^{15} Is 48^{16}; *approach* sexually, of man, †Gn 20^{4} Is 8^{3} Dt 22^{14} Lv $18^{6.14.19}$ (H) Ez 18^{6}; of woman †Lv 20^{16} (אֶל of beast); קְ׳ אֵלֶיךָ Is 65^{5} = *keep to thyself* (‖ אַל־תִּגַּשׁ־בִּי); c. עַל pers., in hostility, ψ 27^{2} (+inf. purpose), so prob. מִקְּרָב־לִי ψ 55^{19} *that none may approach me* (קְ׳ inf. cstr, so Che Bae Dr, > n. = *battle*). **b.** אֶל loc. Ex 32^{19} Dt 2^{37} 20^{10} Jos 8^{5} Pr 5^{8}; אֶל rei Jos 3^{4} Ez 42^{14} 44^{16} Lv 22^{3} (H), Ex 36^{2}+5 t. P; עַל־הַמִּזְבֵּחַ 2 K 16^{12}; אֶל־הַמִּלְחָמָה Dt 20^{2}. †**c.** לִפְנֵי pers. (י׳) Ex 16^{9} Lv 16^{1} ψ 119^{169} (of cry); before men Nu 9^{6} Jos 17^{4}. †**d.** מוּל gent. Dt 2^{19} †**e.** בְּ loc Ju 19^{13} ψ 91^{10} (of evil). †**f.** לְ loc. Jb 33^{22}, adv. loc. הֲלֹם Ex 3^{5}, הֵנָּה Is 57^{3} (cf. **g**, 2 S 20^{16}). †**g.** *draw near* for a purpose, c. Inf. 1 S 17^{48} 2 S 15^{5} Dt 25^{11} Ex 12^{48} Lv 21^{17} Nu 17^{5} Is 34^{1} Ec 4^{17}, + (Inf. om.) Lv 21^{18}; c. וְ subord. 2 S 20^{16} (+עַד־הֵנָּה); c לַמִּשְׁפָּט Is 41^{1} (cf. **a.** Mal 3^{5}); + Imv. Dt 5^{24} Jos 10^{24} Lv 10^{4}, + Impf. Jos 10^{24} Lv 10^{5}. **h.** abs (15 t.) Jos $7^{14.14.14}$ (technically of approach to sanctuary, for trial by lot), Is 5^{19} (of י׳'s counsel), 41^{5}+, La 3^{57} (of י׳, to help); וַתִּקְ׳ הַמִּלְחָמָה 1 K 20^{29} i e. the battle was joined; of calamities Ez 9^{1}, קְ׳ קִצֵּנוּ La 4^{18}. †**2.** of time, *draw near*, Gn 27^{41} Dt 15^{9} Ez 12^{23}; spec. קְ׳ יְמֵי פ׳ לָמוּת Gn 47^{29} Dt 31^{14} 1 K 2^{1}. †**Niph.** *Pf.* 3 ms. consec. וְנִקְרַב אֶל־הָאֱלֹהִים Ex 22^{7} *he shall be brought unto God* (at the sanctuary), also (abs., reflex.) 2 mpl. consec. וְנִקְרַבְתֶּם Jos 7^{14} (cf. **Qal 1 h**). †**Pi.** *Pf.* 1 s קֵרַבְתִּי Is 46^{13}; 3 pl. קֵרְבוּ Ho 7^{6} (v. infr.), Ez 36^{8}; *Impf* 2 ms. וּתְקָרֵב ψ 65^{5}, 1 s sf אֲקָרְבֶנּוּ Jb 31^{37}; *Imv.* ms. קָרֵב Ez 37^{17}; mpl. קָרְבוּ Is 41^{21};—*cause to approach, bring near:* **1.** in space, acc rei + אֶל Ez 37^{17}; = *receive*, acc. pers. Jb 31^{37} (Thes Du; most *approach majestically, march up to*), acc. om. ψ 65^{5}; קְ׳ רִיבְכֶם Is 41^{21} *bring on your suit!* **2.** in time, קְ׳ צִדְקָתִי Is 46^{13} (of י׳), קְ׳ לָבוֹא Ez 36^{8} *they have brought near to come, brought their coming near*, it is at hand (cf. **Hiph.** Gn 12^{11})—Ho 7^{6} rd. בָּעַר for קֵרְבוּ (קרבו) RS Proph. iv, N 19), cf. 𝔊 Now **Hiph.** $_{177}$ *Pf.* 3 ms. הִקְרִיב Gn 12^{11}+, -רִב Nu 7^{19}; 2 ms. וְהִקְרַבְתָּ Ex 29^{3}+, etc.; *Impf.* 3 ms יַקְרִיב Ez 44^{27}+, -רֵב 46^{4}; וַיַּקְרֵב Ju 3^{17}+; 1 pl. וַנַּקְרֵב Nu 31^{50}, etc; *Imv.* ms. הַקְרֵב Nu 3^{6}+, etc.; *Inf. abs.* הַקְרֵב Lv 6^{7}, cstr. הַקְרִיב Ju 3^{18}+, etc; *Pt.* מַקְרִיב Lv 3^{1}+, etc.;—**1. a.** *bring near, bring, present*, c. acc. rei, Ju 5^{25} (+בְּסֵפֶל), cf. Ex 29^{3} (+בְּסַל); tribute ψ 72^{10}; מִנְחָה Ju 3^{17} (+ לְ pers), v^{18}; cf. (לְ pers.) Mal 1^{8}; שָׂדֶה בְּשָׂדֶה יַקְ׳ Is 5^{8} i e. *join, incorporate*; pregn., c. מִן loc. 2 K 16^{14} (v. RS Sem. I 466 ff., 2nd ed 486 ff.); acc. of case, affair, †Dt 1^{17} (+ אֶל pers), Nu 27^{5} (+ לִפְנֵי י׳); c. acc. pers.: + אֶל pers. Nu 15^{33} 25^{6} Jos 8^{23}, + אֶל reflex.

Ex 28^{1}, + אֶת (prep) reflex. Nu 18^{2}; abs., of pers, *make an approach* Ex 14^{10} **b.** of time, וַתַּקְרִיבִי Gn 12^{11}; הִקְרִיב לָבוֹא Is 26^{17}, תַּקְרִיב לָלֶדֶת Ez 22^{4} **2.** as term. techn. (c 158 t.), chiefly in Ez HP, *bring near*, of presenting, dedicating, or offering to י׳ †**a.** c. acc pers, (1) Aaron and his sons, and Levites, sts c אֶל, לִפְנֵי, pers or loc, Ex $29^{4.8}$ $40^{12.14}$ Lv 3^{6} 7^{35} $8^{6.13.24}$ Nu $8^{9.10}$ $16^{5.9.10}$, cf (of prince, subj י׳) Je 30^{21}, (2) for selection by lot Jos $7^{16.17.17.18}$ 1 S $10^{20.21}$, (3) for ordeal of מֵי הַמָּרִים Nu 5^{16}. **b** usually (c 142 t) c acc of offering, with or without further complement (לִפְנֵי י׳, אֶל, לְי׳, loc, rarely אֶל, לְ, of priest, etc) (1) animal-offering Lv $3^{7.12}$ $8^{18.22}$ (all + סָמַךְ of offerer), Ex 29^{10} Lv 1^{15} $4^{3.14}$+, etc, (2) זֶבַח Lv 7^{16}, עֹלָה Nu $29^{13.36}$, אִשֶּׁה Lv $3^{3.14}$ $23^{8.25}$+; †(3) blood Lv 1^{5} (+וְזָרְקוּ), 7^{33} 9^{9}, (4) מִנְחָה Lv 2^{8} 6^{7} 7^{12} 23^{16} Nu 5^{25} 6^{16} 15^{9}, לֶחֶם אֱלֹהָיו Lv $21^{6.8.17.21}$, etc; (5) incense Nu 16^{35}, censer v^{17} $17^{3.4}$, אֵשׁ זָרָה Lv 10^{1} Nu 3^{4} 26^{61}, (6) esp c acc cogn קָרְבָּן Lv $1^{2.2.14}$ $2^{1.4}$ 22^{18} Nu $7^{10.11}$ 31^{50} + (c 33 t), (7) acc. om. 2 Ch 35^{12}. **c.** abs *make an offering* Nu $7^{2.18}$

†קָרֵב **adj. vb. approaching**,—abs קָ׳ 1 S 17^{41}+, pl קְרֵבִים Ez 40^{46} 45^{4},—*approaching*. **1.** as pred, אַתֶּם קְרֵבִים 1 S 17^{41} הָלוֹךְ וְקָ׳ אֶל־דָּוִד, לַמִּלְחָמָה Dt 20^{3}, abs הָלוֹךְ וְקָ׳ 2 S 18^{25}, c art as subst, 1 K 5^{7} (+אֶל־שֻׁלְחַן), Nu $17^{28.28}$ (+ אֶל־ מִשְׁכַּן י׳) **2.** c art, *approaching* י׳, temple or tabern, for service, c לְשָׁרֵת Ez 40^{46} (+ אֶל־י׳), 45^{4}, abs הַזָּר הַקָּ׳ Nu 1^{51} $3^{10.38}$ 18^{7}

†קְרָב **n.[m.] battle, war** (hostile *approach*; Aramaism = ܩܪܳܒܳܐ, קְרָב, cf Lag$^{BN 175}$),—abs קְ׳ Zc 14^{3}+, pl קְרָבוֹת ψ 68^{31},—מִלְחָמָה ‖ Jb 38^{23} ψ 144^{1}, יוֹם קְ׳ Zc 14^{3} ψ 78^{9}, כְּלֵי קְ׳ Ec 9^{18}, *his heart was war* ψ 55^{22} (v^{19} v √ **Qal 1 a**), pl ψ 68^{31} peoples that delight in *battles*.—2 S 17^{11} read בְּקִרְבָּם 𝔊 𝔖 𝔙 Th Dr and most

†[קִרְבָה Lag$^{BN 82}$Ko$^{I 174}$] **n.f. approach**;—cstr in phr קִרְבַת אֱלֹהִים *approach to God* (Che Intr Is 325) Is 58^{2} ψ 73^{28}.

†קָרֹב, קָרוֹב$_{78}$ **adj. near**,—abs קָרֹב Ex 12^{4}+, וֹב- 2 S 19^{43}+; pl קְרוֹבִים 1 K 8^{59}, קְרֹבִים Is 33^{13}+, fpl קְרֹבוֹת Ez 22^{5}, etc.,—*near* (oft. opp רָחוֹק) **1.** of city Gn 19^{20} (+לָנוּס שָׁמָּה), Je 48^{24}, הַקָּ׳ Dt 21^{3} *the nearest* (+אֶל), cf (of elders) v^{6}, of land 1 K 8^{46} = 2 Ch 6^{36}, road Ex 13^{17}, =contiguous, כֶּרֶם 1 K 21^{2} (+ אֵצֶל בֵּיתִי)

2. of pers: **a.** + אֶל pers. Gn 45^{10} Dt 13^{8} 22^{2} Jos 9^{16} 1 Ch 12^{41} (van d H v^{40}), הַקָּ׳ אֶל Ex 12^{4} *the nearest to*; c. sf קְרֹבוֹ Ex 32^{27}, i e *his neighbour*. **b.** abs. (opp. or + רָחוֹק, oft = *near and far*, i e all without distinction), Ez 6^{12} Is 57^{19} Pr 27^{10}, pl Is 33^{13} Je 25^{26} Dn 9^{7} Est 9^{20} Ez 22^{5}; קְ׳ of distress, personif, ψ 22^{12}.—Ez $23^{5.12}$ Co Berthol read קְרוּאִים *famous*; Toy רַבִּים (cf. Je 39^{13}), Hpt in Toy Krae conj קְרוּדִים (As *kurâdu, warrior*) **c** of near relationship, + אֶל pers. 2 S 19^{43} Lv $21^{2.3}$ 25^{25} (all H), Nu 27^{11} (P), לְ pers Ne 13^{4} Ru 2^{20}, + מִן comp. 3^{12}; of intimacy, ψ 15^{3} (רֵעֵהוּ ‖) קְרוֹבִי, Jb 19^{14} (מְיֻדָּעַי ‖), ψ 38^{12} קְרֹבוֹ (אֹהֲבַי וְרֵעַי ‖); *near*, in office, Est 1^{14} **d.** *near* to י׳, ψ עַם קְרֹבוֹ ψ 148^{14} (Rie Bae קְרֹבָיו *the people of those near him*) **e.** *near* to י׳ in ceremon. function, c אֶל Ez 43^{19}, c לְ 42^{13}, sf. Lv 10^{3} **f.** of God (י׳), + אֶל pers Dt 4^{7} 30^{14}, לְ pers ψ 34^{19} 145^{18}, abs Je 12^{2} Is 50^{8} 55^{6} ψ 119^{151}; אֱלֹהֵי מִקָּרֹב Je 23^{23} *a God from near by* (opp. אֱ׳ מֵרָחוֹק), קְ׳ of צִדְקִי Is 51^{5}, יֶשַׁע י׳ ψ 85^{10} (+ לְ pers);—קְ׳ שְׁמֶךָ ψ 75^{2}, read קֹרְאֵי בְשִׁ׳ Dy Che Gr Dr, cf Bae 𝔊 𝔖 Du **g.** of word, + אֶל pers. Dt 30^{14}, prayer, + אֶל־י׳ 1 K 8^{59}. **3.** of time: קָ׳ יוֹם אֵידָם Dt 32^{35}, esp of יוֹם י׳ Zp $1^{7.14.14}$ Ez 30^{3} (perh. del as 𝔊 Co Krae), v^{3} Is 13^{6} Ob ^{15} Jo 1^{15} 2^{1} 4^{14}, cf. Ez 7^{7}, + inf. קָ׳ אֵיד־מוֹאָב לָבוֹא Je 48^{16}, cf. Is 13^{22} 56^{1}; מְחִתָּה קְ׳ Pr 10^{14} *imminent ruin*, מִקָּרוֹב Dt 32^{17} *recently*, so Ez 11^{3} 𝔊 𝔙 Co Siegf Berthol (for MT + בִּקְרוֹב); Ez 7^{8} *soon*, Jb 20^{5} *of the briefest*—אוֹר קָ׳ מִפְּנֵי חֹשֶׁךְ Jb 17^{12} is dub., Thes (my) *light is near to* (prope abest a, as Ar. قَرُبَ مِن, but not proven in Heb) *darkness*; Di *light* (they say) *is near* (breaking away) *from darkness*, will soon leave it behind, Bu אוֹר קָרוֹב פְּנֵי־חֹשֶׁךְ *the light of their intimate friend shall not* (?) *grow dark*.

קָרְבָּן$_{T\,80}$ **n.m.**$^{Lv\,6,\,13}$ **offering, oblation** (As. *kurbannu*, id, appar alw. with בּ, Dl$^{HWB\,591}$),—abs קָ׳ Lv 1^{2}+, cstr קָרְבַּן 2^{1}+, sf קָרְבָּנִי Nu 28^{2}, pl sf. קָרְבְּנֵיהֶם Lv 7^{38},—*offering, oblation*, gen. term for all kinds of offering (only Ez Lv Nu [HP]). animal Lv $1^{2.3.10}$+, vegetable $2^{1.1.3}$+, articles of gold Nu 31^{50}, silver 7^{13}+, etc, as acc. cogn after הִקְרִיב Lv $1^{2.2}$ 3^{14} Nu 6^{14}+ (v. √ **Hiph. 2 b** (5)), cstr. קָ׳ מִנְחָה Lv $2^{1.4.13}$, קָ׳ רֵאשִׁית v^{12}, קָ׳ אִשֶּׁה 22^{27}, קָ׳ י׳ Nu $9^{7.13}$ (cf. 31^{50})

†[קֻרְבָּן] **n [m.] offering**,—cstr קֻרְבַּן הָעֵצִים *wood-offering* for second temple Ne 10^{35} 13^{31}.

II. **קרב** (√of foll.; cf. As. *kirbu, midst;* NH [קֶרֶב] pl. *entrails* (rare); MI^{23,24} בקרב *in the midst of* the city; perh. also Ar. قَلْبٌ *heart*).

קֶ֫רֶב $_{227}$ **n.[m.] inward part, midst**;—ק׳ abs. Ex 29^{13} + (only **3**); cstr. Gn 45^{6} +; sf. קִרְבִּי Jos 9^{7} +, 3 fpl. קִרְבֶּ֫נָה Gn 41^{21}, -בֶּ֫נָה v^{21} (Ges$^{§91\,f.}$ Kö$^{ii.1,488\,N.1}$), etc.; pl. only (sf.) קְרָבַי ψ 103^{1};—usu. c. prep. (בְּק׳ 143 t., מִק׳ 43 t.);—**1.** †**a.** *inward part* of human body, physical sense, בְּק׳ *within* one's body Gn 25^{22} (J), cf. 18^{12} (J), 1 S 25^{37} Je 23^{9} Jb 20^{14} (‖ בְּמֵעָיו), cf. Is 19^{1} (of nation personif.); *into* his body ψ 109^{18} (sim.); as seat of life (ו)תָּשָׁב נֶפֶשׁ־הַיֶּ֫לֶד עַל־קִרְבּוֹ 1 K 17$^{21.22}$, cf. (of idol) Hb 2^{19} (v. also **2**). †**b.** = belly, of kine אֶל־ק׳ Gn 41$^{21.21}$. **c.** of city (בְּק׳ *within it,* מִק׳ etc.) Gn 18^{24} Ju 18^{7} Am 3^{9} + 18 t. cf. Is 25^{11}; בְּק׳ חוצות Is 5^{25}. **d.** of house ψ 101$^{2.7}$; temple 48^{10}; בְּק׳ מוֹעֲדֶ֑ךָ 74^{4}. **e.** of land (earth) Gn 45^{6} 48^{16} Am 2^{3} Is 5^{8} 24^{13} (‖ בְּתוֹךְ הָעַמִּים), + 10 t. (בְּק׳, מִק׳). **f.** of a number of pers., בְּק׳ *in the midst, among,* מִק׳ *from among:* esp. (1) people (96 t.; 80 t. as sg. coll., 15 t. pl.), Am 7^{8} Gn 24^{3} Ex 23^{25} Dt 31^{17} Je 46^{21} 1 S 4^{3} Jos 7^{12} Ju 10^{16} +, בְּק׳ יִשׂ׳ Dt 17^{10} +, בְּק׳ מִק׳ גּוֹי Dt 4^{34}, etc. בֵּית יִשׂ׳ Am 7^{10}; בְּק׳ הַכְּנַעֲנִי + Ju 1$^{32.33}$ 3^{5}, (2) הַמַּחֲנֶה (מִק׳) בְּק׳ Jos 1^{11} Nu 14^{44} + 6 t. †(3) בְּק׳ אֶחָיו Dt 18^{2} 1 S 16^{13}, and (מִק׳) Dt 17^{15} 18^{18}. †(4) מִק׳ עַמֶּיהָ Ex 31^{14} (II. עַם). (5) בְּק׳ אֹיְבֶיךָ ψ 110^{2}, cf. (of wicked) 55^{16}; בְּק׳ חֲכָמִים Pr 15^{31}. (6) בְּק׳ אֱלֹהִים יִשְׁפֹּט ψ 82^{1}. (7) בְּק׳ הַמִּלְחָמָה 1 K 20^{39} *into the midst of the battle,* the thick of the fight; בְּק׳ צָרָה ψ 138^{7}. †(8) of nations, בְּק׳ הַגּוֹיִם Dt 29^{15}, מִק׳ הָעַמִּים La 3^{45}, cf. Jos 24^{17} Mi 5$^{6.7}$. **g.** מִק׳ חוקך ψ 74^{11} (Qr חֵיקְךָ) thy hand *fr. within thy bosom,* (anthrop. of י׳; v. I. כלה **Pi. 2 c**). †**h.** of a period of time, בְּק׳ שָׁנִים Hb 3$^{2.2}$. †**2.** of inward part of man; **a.** as seat of thought and emotion: בְּק׳ 1 K 3^{28} Je 4^{14} 9^{7} Pr 26^{24} ψ 62^{5} 94^{19}; ‖ בְּלֵב Pr 14^{33}, עַל־לֵב Je 31^{33}; seat of לֵב ψ 39^{4} 55^{5} 109^{22} La 1^{20}; of רוּחַ Ez 11^{19} 36$^{26.27}$ Zc 12^{1} Is 26^{9} ψ 51^{12}, cf. Is 19$^{3.14}$; בְּק׳ לִבִּי ψ 36^{2} (rd. לִבּוֹ Vrss Hup Now Che Bae al.). **b.** as faculty of thought and emotion, subj. (no prep.) Is 16^{11} (‖ מֵעַי), ψ 64^{7} (‖ לֵב) 5^{10}; כָּל־קְרָבַי 103^{1} (only here pl.; ‖ נַפְשִׁי).—49^{12} rd. קִבְרָם 𝔊 𝔖 𝔗, or קְבָרִם, Ew Gr Ol Bi Che Bae al. (for קִרְבָּם). †**3.** term. techn. in P of *entrails* of sacrificial animals (Di$^{Lv\,1,9}$ Dr-Wh$^{Lv,\,pl.\,facing\,p.\,4}$), Ex 12^{9} 29$^{13.17.22}$ Lv 1$^{9.13}$ 3$^{3.3.9.9.14.14}$ 4$^{8.8.11}$ 7^{3} 8$^{16.21.25}$ 9^{14}.

†[**קַרְדֹּם**] **n.[m.] axe** (√unknown; cf. NH קַרְדּוֹם *double hoe,* one side of which could split wood, Vogelst$^{Landwirthsch.\,37}$; Ar. قَدُّومٌ, قَدُوم *adze* is loan-wd. acc. to Frä^{84});—sf. קַרְדֻּמּוֹ 1 S 13^{20} + Ju 9^{48} (so prob. rd. for הַקַּרְדֻּמּוֹת, A 𝔊L *τ. ἀξίνην,* GFM Bu Now); pl. קַרְדֻּמִּים 1 S 13^{21}, קַרְדֻּמּוֹת Je 46^{22} ψ 74^{5}.

קָרָה *cold,* v. קרר.

†[**קָרָה**] **vb. encounter, meet, befall** (‖ II. קָרָא; NH קָרָה *meet* (rare), קֶרִי *misfortune,* specif. (nocturnal) *pollution,* and so Aram. קִרְיוּתָא, ܩܶܪܝܳܐ; Ar. قَرَا (و) is *go, seek earnestly,* قَرَى *receive hospitably* as guest; Eth. II. 3, **አቀረየ፡** *present, offer as sacrifice*);—**Qal** *Pf.* 3 ms. sf. קָרְךָ Dt 25^{18}, (ו)קָרָהוּ Gn 44^{29} +; *Impf.* 3 ms. יִקְרֶה Ec 9^{11} + Dn 10^{14} Kt (Qr יִקְרָא), וַיִּ֫קֶר Ru 2^{3}, sf. יִקְרְךָ Nu 11^{23}, יִקְּרְךָ 1 S 28^{10} (d. f. dirim.); *Pt.* fpl. קֹרֹת Gn 42^{29};—**1.** *encounter, meet,* acc. pers. Dt 25^{18}, cf. (acc. rei) וַיִּקֶר מִקְרֶהָ חֶלְקַת וגו׳ Ru 2^{3} *her chance lighted upon a field,* etc. **2.** *befall,* acc. pers., subj. evil Gn 44^{29} (J), 1 S 28^{10}, י׳'s word Nu 11^{23} (JE), indef. Gn 42^{29} (J) Is 41^{22} (abs.) Est 4^{7} 6^{13} Dn 10^{14} (לְ pers.); עֵת וָפֶגַע יִק׳ אֶת־כֻּלָּם Ec 9^{11}; subj. מִקְרֶה 2^{14}, cf. v^{15}. **Niph.** *Pf.* 3 ms. נִקְרָה Ex 3^{18}; 1 s. נִקְרֵיתִי 2 S 1^{6}; *Impf.* 3 ms. יִקָּרֶה Nu 23^{3}, וַיִּקָּר v$^{4.16}$; 1 s. אִקָּרֶה v^{15};—**1.** *encounter, meet* without pre-arrangement, usu. of י׳ (God): c. עַל pers. Ex 3^{18} (J), אֶל pers. Nu 23$^{4.16}$; יִק׳ י׳ לִקְרָאתִי v^{3} (all JE); obj. י׳ (om.) v^{15}. **2.** *chance to be present,* בְּ loc., 2 S 1^{6} (+ Inf. abs. נִקְרֹא). **Hiph. 1.** of י׳, *cause* (the right thing, good fortune) *to occur,* c. לִפְנֵי pers.; *Pf.* 3 ms. הִקְרָה Gn 27^{20}; *Imv.* ms. הַקְרֵה 24^{12} (both J). **2.** of Israel, *Pf.* 2 mpl. consec. וְהִקְרִיתֶם לָכֶם עָרִים Nu 35^{11} ye shall (*cause* cities *to occur* rightly *for yourselves,* i. e.) *select* cities *as suitable.*

†[**קָרֶה**] **n.[m.] chance, accident**;—cstr. מִקְּרֵה לָ֫יְלָה Dt 23^{11} *by reason of the chance of the night* (i.e. nocturnal pollution, cf. Lv 15^{16}).

†[**קְרִי**] **n.[m.] opposition, contrariness**;—only (בְּ)קֶרִי in Lv 26, as adv. modifier of הָלַךְ (in fig. sense), + עִם pers., of Isr.'s relation to י׳: תֵּלְכוּ עִמִּי קֶרִי Lv 26^{21} *if ye walk with me contrariwise,* so v^{23}, בְּקֶרִי v$^{27.40}$; י׳ subj., וְהָלַכְתִּי עִמָּכֶם בְּקֶרִי v^{24}, so v^{41} and (בַּחֲמַת ק׳ *in wrath of opposition*) v^{28}.

†**מִקְרֶה** **n.m.**$^{1\,S\,6,9}$ **accident, chance, fortune**;—abs. מ׳ 1 S 6^{9} +; cstr. מִקְרֵה Ec 2^{15} (so

read also 3[19 19] with 𝔊 Ruet[Esu] Wild, for MT מִקְרָה);—**1.** *accident, chance,* 1 S 6[9] 20[26], c קָרָה Ru 2[3] (v. ק׳ **1**). **2.** in Ec, *fortune, fate,* מ׳ אֶחָד יִקְרֶה אֶת־כֻּלָּם Ec 2[14] cf v[15], 3[19 19 19] 9[2.3]

†קוֹרָה **n.f. rafter, beam** (prop a thing *meeting*, fitting into, another),—sf. קֹרָתִי Gn 19[8] (J)=*my roof-tree*, pl קֹרוֹת *rafters*, abs 2 Ch 3[7], cstr. ‖ 1 K 6[15b] (reading קוֹרוֹת הַסִּפֻּן 𝔊 Th Kit Benz, for MT קִירוֹת), + 7[7b] (reading הַקּוֹרוֹת for הַקַּרְקַע, v ק׳), Ct 1[17] (‖ רחיטנו Kt, רָהִיטֵנוּ Qr); more gen *beam*, sg abs קוֹרָה 2 K 6[2.5].

†[קָרָה] **vb. denom Pi. lay the beams of, furnish with beams,**—c. acc of the building *Pf* 3 pl sf קֵרוּהוּ Ne 3[3.6]; *Inf cstr* לְקָרוֹת Ne 2[8] 2 Ch 34[11], *Pt* הַמְקָרֶה ψ 104[3] (fig.)

†מְקָרֶה **n.[m.] beam-work**;—Ec 10[18]

†קִרְיָה **n.f. town, city** (syn. of עִיר, chiefly poet., and in the higher style; perhaps from above √ as *meeting*-place of men; cf n pr loc. MI[13] קרית, l[10] קריתן; JAram. קִרְיָה),—abs. ק׳ Is 1[21]+; cstr. קִרְיַת Nu 21[28]+,—**1.** in gen. Dt 2[36] 3[4] **2.** of specif. towns, Ho 6[8] (גִּלְעָד, 𝔊[Codd] Γαλγαλα, cf Now), קִרְיַת סִיחֹן Nu 21[28], Damascus, ק׳ מְשׂוֹשִׂי Je 49[25] (‖ עִיר תְּהִלָּה), esp of Jerus Mi 4[10] Is 29[1] 33[20], ק׳ רחבות La 2[11], ק׳ מֶלֶךְ רָב ψ 48[3], city for inhab. 1 K 1[41.45], ק׳ נֶאֱמָנָה Is 1[21 26] (‖ עִיר הַצֶּדֶק), ק׳ עַלִּיזָה 22[2] (‖ עִיר הוֹמִיָּה), 32[13] **3.** in Is 24–26 coll., i.e. denoting various, representative, cities, ק׳ תֹהוּ 24[10], ק׳ בְּצוּרָה 25[2], ק׳ גּוֹיִם עָרִיצִים v[3], ק׳ נִשְׂגָּבָה 26[5], so prob Hb 2[8.17] **4.** indef., Hb 2[12] (‖ עִיר); Pr 29[8], ק׳ עֹז 18[19] *a city of strength*, so ק׳ עֻזּוֹ 10[15] (in fig.)=18[11] (*id.*),=inhab., 11[10], הֲמוֹן ק׳ Jb 39[7].

קִרְיַת יְעָרִים v קִרְיַת.

†קִרְיָתַיִם **n.pr loc.** Καριαθαιμ (perh. *double city* (du.), yet in gen on ־ַיִם in n.pr.loc v. Ges[§ 88 c]),—**1.** in Moab (MI[10]) Je 48[1] (־תָיִם), v[23], so קִרְיָתָ֫יְמָה Ez 25[9] Qr (Kt קריתמה), Reubenite city acc. to Nu 32[37] (־תָיִם) Jos 13[9]; שָׁוֵה קִרְיָתַיִם Gn 14[5] *plain of Kiryathaim* (v. שָׁוֵה), mod *Kurêyât*, c 1¼ m SE from (Mt.) 'Aṭṭarus (עֲטָרוֹת), and 6⅔ m NNW. from Dibon, GASm[Geogr 567 f] Buhl[Geogr 267]. **2** Levit city in Naphtali 1 Ch 6[61], = קַרְתָּן ‖ Jos 21[32] (Θεμμων, 𝔊L Καρθαν).

†קִרְיַת אַרְבַּע **n.pr.loc.** older name of Hebron; πόλις Αρβο(κ), Καρ(ι)αθαρβοκ, etc. (prob. =*fourfold city* (otherwise Jos 14[15] 15[13] 21[11]), v. esp GFM);—Jos 14[15] (JED), Ju 1[10b] (ק׳ אַרְבַּע), also Gn 23[2] Jos 15[13.54] 20[7] 21[11] (all P); ק׳ הָא׳ Gn 35[27] (P) Ne 11[25].—Vid חֶבְרוֹן.

†קִרְיַת בַּעַל v. קִרְיַת יְעָרִים.

†קִרְיַת חֻצוֹת **n.pr.loc.** in Moab, πόλεις ἐπαύλεων, Nu 22[39], site unknown.

†קִרְיַת יְעָרִים **n.pr.loc.** πόλ(ε)ις Ιαρειμ[ν], Καριαθιαρειμ, etc. (*city of forests*),—city of the Gibeonites Jos 9[17], assigned to Judah Jos 15[60] cf Ju 18[12 12], on border of Benj. Jos 15[9] (הַר יְעָרִים v[10], 𝔊 πόλιν Ιαρειν, v יְעָרִים), 18[14], assigned to Benj. v[28] (יְעָרִים om by text. err before עָרִים, v 𝔊), near Beth Shemesh 1 S 6[21], long the abode of ark 7[1 2] 1 Ch 13[5 6] 2 Ch 1[4]; named in genealogical list 1 Ch 2[50.52.53], named also Ne 7[29] = ק׳ עָרִים Ezr 2[25] (read יְעָרִים), c art. ק׳ הַיְּעָרִים Je 26[20], abbreviated (in poet.) (שְׂדֵי) יַעַר ψ 132[6], called also קִרְיַת־בַּעַל (ΚαριαθΒααλ) Jos 15[60] 18[14]+v[15] (where read for ק׳ יְעָרִים, so 𝔊 Di Benn Steuern); this abbrev into בַּעֲלָה, 15[9 10] [(Ιε)Βααλ], also v[11 29], and מִבַּעֲלֵי יְהוּדָה 2 S 6[2] (rd. בַּעַל יְהֹ׳, or בַּעֲלַת יְהֹ׳), בַּעֲלָתָה ‖ 1 Ch 13[6] (v. on these II בַּעֲלָה) Identif. uncertain; Rob[BR ii 11] conj *Kiryat el-'Enab*, 8 m+W of Jerusalem (cf Καριαθιαρειμ Lag[Onom. 271]); *'Erma* (Henderson[Pal 85, 112, 210] Conder[Survey Mem iii 43 ff]), cf. GASm[Geogr 225 f.] Buhl[Geogr. 166 f.].

קִרְיַת־סַנָּה v. foll.   ק׳ עָרִים v. foreg.

†קִרְיַת־סֵפֶר **n.pr.loc.** πόλις (τῶν) γραμμάτων, +(𝔊[B] Ju 1[11]) Καριασσωφαρ: ancient name of דְּבִיר (v II ד׳ **2 c**) (perh ק׳־סֵפֶר *scribe-town*, cf. 𝔊 supr., also 𝔖 and Egyptian *Ba'-tiṭu-pa-ṭrạ*, *house of scribe*, WMM[As. u. Eur 174] Buhl[Geogr 274], cf. GFM[Ju]),—Jos 15[15 16] Ju 1[11 12], another name is ק׳־סַנָּה Jos 15[49] (but 𝔊 πόλις γραμμάτων, hence rd. perh ק׳־סֵפֶר, so Steuern), in S Judah; on site (prob *Dhoheriye*, 5 h SW. from Hebron) v II. דְּבִיר **2 c** and Buhl[Geogr 164].

†[קֶרֶת] **n.f. town, city** (late poet.) (cf. Ph. קרת חדשת n pr loc in Cyprus, also=*Carthage*, and perhaps *Cirta*, *Tigranocerta*, cp. Thes);—always קָרֶת,—of Job's city, Jb 29[7]; indef. Pr 8[3] 9[3 14]; city as a corporate body of men 11[11].

†קַרְתָּה **n.pr.loc.** Καδης, Καριθα, etc: Levit. city in Zebulun Jos 21[34], site unknown

קַרְתָּן v. קִרְיָתַיִם **2**.

†קְרִיּוֹת **n.pr.loc.** (formed as pl. intens. fr. קִרְיָה?);—**1.** in Judah Jos 15[25] (αἱ πόλεις; whence, as supposed, Judas אִישׁ קְרִיּוֹת), perh. *Ḳaryatên*, c. 12 m. S. of Hebron, Buhl[Geogr. 182]. **2.** in Moab, Καριωθ, αἱ πόλεις; MI[13] קרית: Je 48[24], הַקּ׳ v[41] Am 2[2]; perh. = Ραββαθ Μωαβ = Μοαβ = Αρεοπολις (Euseb., v. Lag[Onom. 277, 60 al.]), mod. *Rabba*, c. 11 m. S. of Arnon, cf. Buhl[Geogr. 270].

†I. קָרַח **vb. make bald, or a baldness,** usu. (by mourners) for the dead, cf. RS[Sem. 1. 306, 2nd ed. 324] (Arab. parallels) (NH *id.* Hiph. *shew baldness*; Ar. قَرَحَ *wound, make sores,* قُرْحَة *whiteness in face* of horse (but قَرِعَ *be bald,* أَقْرَعُ *bald*); Eth. ቀረሐ: *make bald* (rare); Aram. קְרַח, ܩܪܰܚ, chiefly deriv. (and der. meanings); cf. Sin. n.pr.m. קרחה, קרחו; MI[3.21.24.25] n.pr.loc. קרחה);—**Qal** *Impf.* 3 mpl. יִקְרְחוּ קָרְחָה בְּרֹאשָׁם Lv 21[5] Qr (> Kt יקרחה; ‖ יְגַלֵּחוּ; cf. Dt 14[1]); *Imv.* fs. קָרְחִי וָגֹזִּי עַל Mi 1[16] *make a baldness . . . for.* **Niph.** *Impf.* 3 ms. יִקָּרֵחַ לָהֶם Je 16[6] men *shall* not *make themselves bald for them.* **Hiph.** *Pf.* 3 pl. consec. וְהִקְרִיחוּ אֵלַיִךְ קָרְחָה Ez 27[31] *and they shall make a baldness* (cf. **Qal**) *for thee.* **Hoph.** *Pt.* כָּל־רֹאשׁ מֻקְרָח Ez 29[18] *every head made bald* (by carrying load).

†קֵרֵחַ **adj. bald**;—Lv 13[40] (distinct fr. גִּבֵּחַ v[41]); **n.m.** 2 K 2[23.23].

†קָרְחָה **n.f. baldness, bald spot,** made as sign of mourning;—abs. ק׳ Is 3[24] +; sf. קָרְחָתֵךְ Mi 1[16];—*bald spot,* עַל־כָּל־רֹאשׁ Am 8[10], בְּכָל־ר׳ Is 15[2] Ez 7[18]; ק׳ בְּרֹאשׁ Lv 21[5] (acc. cogn.); בֵּין עֵינֵיכֶם Dt 14[1]; ק׳ כַּנֶּשֶׁר Mi 1[16]; כָּל־רֹאשׁ ק׳ Je 48[37]; opp. מַעֲשֶׂה מִקְשֶׁה Is 3[24]; also Je 47[5] and (acc. cogn.) Ez 27[31].

†קָרַחַת **n.f. baldness of head**;—abs. ק׳ Lv 13[42a]; sf. קָרַחְתּוֹ v[42] +;—*baldness of head* (alw. opp. גַּבַּחַת *baldness of forehead*), Lv 13[42.42.43.55].

קָרֵחַ[14] **n.pr.m.** in Judah (*bald one*);—2 K 25[23], Καρηθ, 𝔊L Καρηε; Je 40[8] + 12 t. Je, Καρηε.

קֹרַח[37] **n.pr.m.** Κορε (baldness?);—**1.** Edomite name: **a.** Gn 36[5.14.18] 1 Ch 1[35]. **b.** Gn 36[16] (not Sam.; prob. gloss fr. v[18] Di Kau Ball al.; Holz hesitates). **2.** Levite, rebel ag. Moses, Nu 16[1] + 10 t. 16, 17, 26[9.10] 27[3]; in geneal. lists Ex 6[21.24] 1 Ch 6[7.22]; בְּנֵי־ק׳ 9[19]; בְּנֵי־ק׳ Nu 26[11]; esp. לִבְנֵי־ק׳ as company of ψ-collectors (or singers), in titles: ψ 42[1] 44[1] 45[1] 46[1] 47[1] 48[1] 49[1] 84[1] 85[1] 87[1] 88[1]. **3.** a 'son' of Hebron, i.e. Judahite clan 1 Ch 2[43] Κορεε, etc.

†קָרְחִי **adj.gent.** of קֹרַח **2**; alw. c. art.; 1 Ch 9[31]; as subst. coll. Ex 6[24] Nu 26[58]; pl. הַקָּרְחִים 1 Ch 9[19] 12[7] (van d. H. v[6]), 26[1]; בְּנֵי הַקָּרְחִי v[19]; בְּנֵי הַקָּרְחִים 2 Ch 20[19].

II. קרח (√ of foll.; meaning unknown).

†קֶרַח **n.m.**[Jb 38, 29] **frost, ice**;—abs. ק׳ Gn 31[40] +, קָרַח Jb 6[16] +; sf. קַרְחוֹ ψ 147[17];—**1.** *frost* of night (opp. חֹרֶב of day), Gn 31[40] (E), Je 36[30]. **2.** *ice,* Jb 6[16] 37[10] 38[29] (‖ כְּפֹר *hoar-frost*), מַשְׁלִיךְ ק׳ כְּפִתִּים ψ 147[17] (Hup al. think of hail, but v. Bae; ‖ קָרָה *cold,* שֶׁלֶג, כְּפוֹר v[16]); probably also כְּעֵין ק׳ Ez 1[22] (so Krae; most *crystal,* after 𝔊).

קְרִי, קִרְיָה, קִרְיַת, קְרִיּוֹת, etc., v. קרה.

†[קָרַם] **vb. spread or lay something over** (NH *id. form a crust,* so Hiph. יקרים על Ecclus 43[20]; Aram. קְרַם, ܩܪܰܡ, *incrust, overlay*);—**Qal** *Pf.* 1 s. וְקָרַמְתִּי עֲלֵיכֶם עוֹר Ez 37[6] *I will spread skin over you* (i.e. the dry bones); *Impf.* 3 ms. וַיִּקְרַם עֲלֵיהֶם עוֹר v[8] (so Gi van d. H.; Baer וַיִּקְרֹם, of which conflicting explan. Ges[§§ 9 u, 29 l]), indef. subj. instead of pass.; but rd. **Niph.** וַיִּקָּרֵם 𝔖 (cf. 𝔙) Co Berthol Toy Krae.

קרן (√ of foll.; mng. dub.; cf. As. *ḳarnu,* Ar. قَرْنٌ, Eth. ቀርን: NH קֶרֶן, Ph. קרן, Aram. קַרְנָא, ܩܰܪܢܳܐ, all *horn;* Sab. קרן *spur* of mt. (?) Hom[Chrest. 127]; v. also Ar. قَرْنٌ *part of man's head where horns are in beasts,* قُرْنَةٌ *corner, extremity,* of anything Frey, *horn* of uterus, Lane).

קֶרֶן[75] **n.f.**[Je 48, 25] **horn**;—abs. ק׳ Is 5[1] +, קָרֶן ψ 75[5]; cstr. קֶרֶן Jos 6[5] +; sf. קַרְנִי 1 S 2[1] ψ 92[11], etc.; du. קַרְנַיִם Hb 3[4], קְרָנַיִם Dn 8[3.6], ־נַיִם v[3.20]; cstr. קַרְנֵי 1 K 22[11] +, sf. קַרְנָיו Gn 22[13] Dt 33[17], קְרָנָיו Dn 8[7], קַרְנֵיכֶם Ez 34[21]; pl. (usu. in der. senses) קְרָנוֹת Ez 43[15] +; cstr. קַרְנֹת Ex 29[12] +, sf. קַרְנֹתָיו 27[2] +, etc.;—*horn:* †**1. a.** of ram (אַיִל) Gn 22[13], so in Daniel's vision Dn 8[3.3.6.7.20], and (of goat) v[5.8.9.21]; of oppressors in Isr. (under fig. of rams) Ez 34[21], so of nations Zc 2[2.4.4.4]; of רְאֵם Dt 33[17] ψ 22[22] (both fig., cf. 92[11]); of Zion under fig. of threshing-ox Mi 4[13]; ק׳ בַּרְזֶל 1 K 22[11] = 2 Ch 18[10] (symbol.); seen in Zech.'s vision Zc 2[1]. **b.** used as oil-flask 1 S 16[1.13] 1 K 1[39] (cf. קֶרֶן הַפּוּךְ infr.). **c.** ק׳ הַיּוֹבֵל, as wind-instr. Jos 6[5] (cf. שׁוֹפָר). **d.** קַרְנוֹת שֵׁן Ez 27[15] (from curved shape of tusks). †**2.** fig., of pers., symbol of strength Dt 33[17], ק׳ יִשְׁעִי 2 S 22[3] =

ψ 18^{3} (of ׳י as deliverer), others sub **3** or **4**, esp as lifted up (רום, as of a lordly animal, cf Dr$^{1 S 2.1}$), denoting increase of might, dignity 1 S 2$^{1.10}$ La 2^{17} ψ 75^{11} 89$^{18.25}$ 92^{11} 112^{9}, so perh 1 Ch 25^{5} (v Kau, >Be *blow loudly* [cf. **1 c**]), ψ 148^{14} (subj ׳י) + לְעַמּוֹ; also haughtiness, arrogance 75$^{5.6}$, opp גָּדַע ק׳ *hew off horns*, i e. reduce, humiliate, La 2^{3} ψ 75^{11}, pass Je 48^{25}, so ועללתי בעָפָר קַרְנִי Jb 16^{15}, אַצְמִיחַ ק׳ לבית יש׳ Ez 29^{21} is appar of restoration of might (as ψ 148^{14} supr, c. וַיָּרֶם), but ψ 132^{17} אַצְ׳ ק׳ לְדָוִד of raising up individual ruler of Davidic line **3.** of altar, horn-like projections at corners (26 t), Am 3^{14} Je 17^{1} Ez 43$^{15.20}$ ψ 118^{27} Ex 27^{2} + 8 t Ex, Lv 4$^{7.18}$ + 6 t Lv (all P), as sanctuary, refuge 1 K 1$^{50.51}$ 2^{28}. †**4.** *hill* (so in Ar, *peak, isolated hill*, cf Ges) Is 5^{1} †**5.** קַרְנַיִם מִיָּדוֹ לוֹ Hb 3^{4} *rays at his side(s) had he* (of lightning-flashes in theoph, cf. Now Da) —Am 6^{13} v. קַרְנַיִם n.pr loc.

†קָרַן **vb. Qal denom.** of קֶרֶן **5, send out rays**,—*Pf* 3 ms. קָרַן עור פָּנָיו Ex 34$^{29.30.35}$ (P). **Hiph. denom.** of קֶרֶן **1 a, display** (grow) **horns** (be fully developed), *Pt* פָּר מַקְרִן מַפְרִיס ψ 69^{32}.

†קֶרֶן הַפּוּךְ **n.pr.f.** (*horn of antimony*, i e *beautifier*, v פּוּךְ),—Job's third daughter Jb 42^{14}.

†קַרְנַיִם **n.pr.loc.** conquered by Isr Am 6^{13} (so Gr We Now GASm, cf also לֹא דָבָר p. 520 supr; 𝔊 and most sub קֶרֶן **2**); prob in Bashan, =Καρναιν 1 Macc 5$^{43.44}$, Καρνιον 2 Macc 12^{21}, also in עשתרות ק׳ Gn 14^{5} (v III. עַשְׁתָּרוֹת p. 800 supr.).

†[קָרַס] **vb. bend down, stoop, crouch** (intrans) (cf. perh Ar. قُرْصٌ *disc, round cake*, cp NH קַרְסוֹל, קַרְצוֹל, 𝔗 קַרְסוּלָא, קַרְצוּלָא all *ankle*),—**Qal** *Pf.* 3 pl קָרְסוּ Is 46^{2}, *Pt* קֹרֵס v^{1} (both + כָּרַע), of vanquished gods of Babylon

†[קֶרֶס] **n [m] hook,** on edge of curtains of tabern, matching the loops (לֻלָאֹת, v. [לוּלִי]); pl קְרָסִים Ex 26$^{6.11}$=36$^{13.18}$, 26^{33}; cstr. קַרְסֵי זָהָב v^{6}=36^{13}, ק׳ נחשׁת 26^{11}=36^{18}, sf קְרָסָיו 35^{11}=39^{33}.

†[קַרְסֹל] **n.** [**f.** Albr$^{ZAW\ xvi\ (1896).\ 77}$] **ankle** (cf. 𝔊 𝔙 2 S 22^{37}, =קרס+ל v. Kö$^{II\ 1,121}$; pl. sf. קַרְסֻלָּי 2 S 22^{37}=ψ 18^{37})

†קֵרֹס **n.pr.m.** post-ex, Ezr 2^{44}, Καδης, A Κηραος, =קֵירֹס Ne 7^{47}, Κειρα(ς), 𝔊L (both) Κορες.

קָרַע$_{63}$ **vb. tear** (NH *id*; Ar. قَرَعَ *strike* head, bell, etc, *beat* drum, *box* ear, *gnash* teeth (Frey Dozy), also *impugn, censure*),—**Qal** *Pf.* 3 ms ק׳ 1 S 15^{28}+, etc, *Impf* 3 ms. וַיִּקְרַע Gn 37^{29}+, 1 s sf אֶקְרָעֶנָּה 1 K 11^{12}, etc., *Imv.* mpl. קִרְעוּ 2 S 3^{31} Jo 2^{13}; *Inf. abs* קָרֹעַ 1 K 11^{11}; cstr. לִקְרוֹעַ Ec 3^{7}, sf קָרְעִי Ezr 9^{5}; *Pt act.* קֹרֵעַ 1 K 11^{31}; *pass* קָרוּעַ 2 S 15^{32}, etc;—*tear, rend*. **1. a.** usu. (39 t.) of *rending* garment in (1) sign of grief, distress: בֶּגֶד (29 t) Gn 37$^{29.34}$ 44^{13} 2 S 13^{19}+, ק׳ לְבַבְכֶם וְאַל ב׳ Jo 2^{13}, ק׳ ב׳ לִשְׁנַיִם קְרָעִים 2 K 2^{12}, pt. pass ק׳ בְּגָדָיו 2 S 1^{2}, cstr קְרֻעֵי ב׳ *torn of garments* (pers *with torn garments*) 2 S 13^{31} (but read קָרְעוּ ב׳ 𝔊 𝔙 Th We al), 2 K 18^{37}=Is 36^{22}, Je 41^{5}; מְעִיל + Jb 1^{20} 2^{12} Ezr 9^{3} (+בֶּגֶד), כְּתֹנֶת 2 S 13^{19}, קָרוּעַ כֻּתָּנְתּוֹ 2 S 15^{32} (Ges$^{§ 121\ d}$), שִׂמְלֹת +Gn 37^{34} 44^{13} Jos 7^{6}, pt pass †מַדָּיו קְרֻעִים 1 S 4^{12}; †(2) as symbolic act, ק׳ שַׂלְמָה שְׁנֵים עָשָׂר קְרָעִים 1 K 11^{30}, †(3) abs עֵת לִקְרוֹעַ וְעֵת לִתְפּוֹר Ec 3^{7} **b.** *tear* away or out. veils Ez 13^{21}, fillets from (מֵעַל) arms v^{20}, mark of leprosy out of (מִן) garment Lv 13^{56}. †**2.** *tear away* sovereignty (under fig. of garment), subj ׳י, מֵעַל pers 1 S 15^{28} 1 K 11^{11}, also מִיַּד 1 S 28^{17} 1 K 11$^{12.31}$, מִן 14^{8}, abs. 11^{13}; c. acc יש׳ + מֵעַל 2 K 17^{21}. †**3.** *tear, rend asunder* **a.** book with (בְּ) knife Je 36^{23}. **b.** =*make wide, large*, eyes, with (בְּ) stibium Je 4^{30}, windows, וְק׳ לוֹ חַלּוֹנָ[י] 22^{14} **c.** *rend open* heavens, and descend, of ׳י, Is 63^{19}. †**4.** *tear, rend*, of wild beasts: ׳י as fierce bear Ho 13^{8} (obj. סְגוֹר לִבָּם); fig. of human foes ψ 35^{15} (acc. pers. om), so Hup al, but (fr. context) Ol Bae We al *malign, rail* (cf. Ar. supr), >Gr al. קָרְאוּ. †**Niph.** *be rent*, of garment (מְעִיל), *Impf.* 3 ms. וַיִּקָּרַע 1 S 15^{27}, יִקָּרֵעַ Ex 28^{32} 39^{23}, *be rent, split asunder*, of altar 1 K 13$^{3.5}$.

†[קֶרַע] **n.m.**$^{1\ K\ 11.\ 30}$ **torn piece of garment, rag**,—pl קְרָעִים 1 K 11^{30} he tore it into twelve *pieces*, v^{31} 2 K 2^{12}, *rags* Pr 23^{21} (sign of poverty).

†[קָרַץ] **vb. nip, pinch** (NH קָרַץ *cut* dough, *compress* lips, קֶרֶץ *piece of bread*, As *karâṣu, nip off, gnaw*, Ar. قَرَصَ *pinch*, Eth. ቀረጸ: *incise*, Syr. ܩܪܨܐ *nail* [v. also BAram], cf. Fr^{Aram});—**Qal** *Impf* 3 mpl יִקְרְצוּ־עָיִן ψ 35^{19} *let them* not *pinch the eye*, i e wink maliciously, so *Pt act.* קֹרֵץ ע׳ Pr 10^{10}, ק׳ בְּעֵינָו 6^{13}; also ק׳ שְׂפָתָיו 16^{30} *pinching his lips* (i e. compressing, as NH, or biting, gnawing, cf. As). **Pu.** *Pf.* 1 s מֵחֹמֶר קֹרַצְתִּי Jb 33^{6} *from clay I was nipped off* (cf As *ṭiṭa iktarıṣ, he nipped off clay*, to form Eabani).

†קָ֫רֶץ **n.m.** dub. word, appar. nipping, concr. nipper usu. interpr. (since Hi) of a nipping or stinging insect (cf. Aram. קְרוּצָא, Ar. قَارِصٌ *biting insect*); e.g. *gadfly* (cf. Thes$^{\text{Add. 111}}$), fig. of Nebuchadr. ק׳ מִצָּפוֹן בָּא Je 46^{20} *a gadfly cometh from the north;* 𝔊 (Aq Symm) *stimulator*, i.e. קֹרֵץ; Thes al., more gen., *excidium.*

†I. קַרְקַע **n.[m.]** floor (prob. redupl. fr. a √קרר, or קור; NH *id., ground,* so 𝔗 קַרְקְעָא, קַרְקְעִיתָא; appar. = As. *kakkaru, ground, earth,* Ar. قَرْقَرٌ *terra aequabilis mollisque;* cf. Kö$^{\text{II. 1, 91}}$);—abs. ק׳ 1 K 6^{16} 7^{7a}, קַרְקַ֑ע v^{7b} (v. infr.); cstr. קַרְקַע Nu 5^{17}+;—*floor* of temple 1 K $6^{15.15.16.30}$ 7^{7a}; v^{7b} read prob. הַקּוֹרוֹת *rafters* (cf. 6^{15} and קוֹרָה) 𝔖 𝔙 Th Sta Kmp^{Kau} Benz; (*earth*)*-floor* of tabern. Nu 5^{17}; קַרְקַע הַיָּם Am 9^{3} *the floor,* bottom *of the sea.*

†II. קַרְקַע **n.pr.loc.** (*floor*);—c. art. + ה loc., הַקַּרְקָ֫עָה Jos 15^{3}, on extreme S. border of Judah; τὴν κατὰ δυσμὰς Καδης.

†קַרְקֹר **n.pr.loc.** E. of Jordan, Ju 8^{10}, site unknown; Καρκαρ.

קַרְקַר Nu 24^{17} read קָדְקֹד q.v.

†I. [קָרַר] **vb.** be cold (Ar. قَرَّ *be cold,* so Eth. ቀረረ: Syr. ܩܪ; 𝔗 Ithpa. is *cool oneself* (rare); Levy cp. also NH Nithp. נִתְקָרֵר *grow calm* [i.e. cool]);—**Hiph.** *make* or *keep cool: Pf.* 3 fs. הֵקֵ֫רָה, fig., Je 6^{7b} Jerus. *keepeth* her wickedness *cool,* fresh; *Inf. cstr.* metapl. הָקִיר (Ges^{§67v}) v^{7a}, of בּוֹר *keeping* water *cool* (sim.).

†קַר **adj.** cool;—cstr. (fig.) וְקַר־רוּחַ Pr 17^{27} (Kt) *cool of spirit,* i.e. calm, self-possessed (Qr יְקַר); pl. קָרִים of water Je 18^{14} Pr 25^{25}.

†קֹר **n.[m.]** cold;—abs. Gn 8^{22} (חֹם).

†קָרָה **n.f.** id.;—abs. בְּיוֹם ק׳ Na 3^{17} *a day of coldness,* cold day, so Pr 25^{20}; ק׳ alone, *cold* of night Jb 24^{7}; in gen., due to winds 37^{9} (מְזָרִים v. זרה **Pi.**; yet Voigt Bu, attractively, מִמְּזָוִים (cf. ψ 144^{13}) *out of storehouses* [|| חֶדֶר]); לִפְנֵי קָרָתוֹ מִי יַעֲמֹד ψ 147^{17}, + pl. Zc 14^{6} (rd. וְקִרֹות, v. יָקָר).

†מְקֵרָה **n.f.** coolness;—abs. מ׳ of chamber: עֲלִיַּת הַמּ׳ Ju 3^{20} = חֲדַר הַמּ׳ v^{24}.

†II. [קָרַר] **vb. Pilp.** tear down (?) (NH קִרְקֵר *tear down* wall);—only *Pt.* מְקַרְקַר קִר Is 22^{5} usu. (men are) *tearing down wall(s),* but v. I. קִיר **3** *ad fin.*

קרשׁ (√of foll.; cf. NH קָרַשׁ *be(come) firm, solid,* קֶרֶשׁ *board* (rare)).

קֶ֫רֶשׁ **n.m.**$^{\text{Ex 26.16}}$ **board, boards**;—abs. ק׳ Ex 26^{18}+, קָ֑רֶשׁ v^{20}+; sf. קְרָשַׁיִךְ Ez 27^{6}; pl. קְרָשִׁים v^{15}+; cstr. קַרְשֵׁי v^{26}+; sf. קְרָשָׁיו 35^{11}+;—†**1.** coll. *boards,* of deck Ez 27^{6} (of Tyre under fig. of ship). **2.** *board* of tabern. Ex $26^{15.16.16}$+45 t. 26–40; Nu 3^{36} 4^{31} (all P).

קֶ֫רֶת v. קרה.

קשׂה (√of foll., meaning dub.; cf. Ar. قَشْوَةٌ *basket of palm-leaves;* Eth. ቀሡት: *urn, jar;* NH קַסְוָה = BH קשׂוה, cf. 𝔗 קַסְוָתָא, or קסתות; Talm. קִיסְטָא, קִסְט a measure, Syr. ܩܣܛܐ *jar,* (ט after ק), Nö$^{\text{SB Ak. 1882, 1179}}$ Frä$^{\text{63, 205}}$ Brock$^{\text{s.v.}}$).

†[קַשְׂוָה, Kö$^{\text{II. 1, 165}}$] **n.f.** a kind of jug, jar, utensil of tabern. and (Ch) temple;—pl. קְשָׂוֹת Ex 37^{16} 1 Ch 28^{17}; cstr. קְשׂוֹת הַנָּ֑סֶךְ Nu 4^{7} *jars of the drink-offering;* sf. (of table) Ex 25^{29}.

†קֶ֫סֶת (for קֶשֶׂת) **n.[f.]** pot (for ink), inkhorn;—cstr. ק׳ הַסֹּפֵר Ez $9^{2.3}$, abs. הַקֶּ֫סֶת v^{11}.

קשׂט (√of foll.; meaning dub.).

†קְשִׂיטָה **n.f.** unit of (unknown) value, perh. weight: Gn 33^{19} || Jos 24^{32} (both E), Jb 42^{11}.

קשׂשׂ (√of following; NH קַשְׂקֶשֶׂת *scale;* cf. Ar. قَشَّ *skim off fat,* IV. *scale off* (Berggren), اقشّ *be healed from small-pox,* etc. (Muḥîṭ; i.e. scale off), cf. قَشَّ *get well* from leanness, Frey (Ḳam Golius); also *sweep* (up débris) Dozy$^{\text{II. 347}}$).

†קַשְׂקֶ֫שֶׂת **n.f.** scale of fish, etc.;—of water-animals having סְנַפִּיר וְק׳ *fin and scale* Dt $14^{9.10}$ = Lv $11^{9.10.12}$; pl. קַשְׂקַשִּׂים, of scale-armour 1 S 17^{5}; pl. sf. קַשְׂקְשֹׂתֶיךָ Ez $29^{4.4}$ (of Pharaoh under fig. of crocodile).

קַשׂ v. קשׂשׂ.

קשׁא (√of foll.; cf. Ar. قِثَّاءٌ, Eth. ቍስያ: NH קִשּׁוּת, Pun. κισσου Löw$^{\text{p. 408}}$, all *cucumber(s)* (Löw$^{\text{p. 330}}$), so prob. As. *kiššû;* cf. Syr. ܩܛܘܬܐ *id.* (Lexx), 𝔗$^{\text{Jer. I.}}$ Nu 11^{5} pl. קַטִּיָּיא (ט for ת after ק); Gk. σίκυος, σικύη Lag$^{\text{Arm. Stud. § 1975; M ii. 356}}$ Lewy$^{\text{Fremdw. 30}}$).

†[קִשֻּׁאָה, Löw$^{\text{p. 330}}$] **n.f.** cucumber;—pl. קִשֻּׁאִים Nu 11^{5}.

†II. מִקְשָׁה **n.f. place, field, of cucumbers,** Is 1^{8}; so Je 10^{5} Gf Gie al. (cf. Baruch 6^{70}).

[קָשַׁב] vb. incline, attend, of ears;—†**Qal** *Impf.* 3 fpl. תִּקְשַׁבְנָה Is 32³ (subj. אזנים) **Hiph.** *Pf.* 3 ms הִקְשִׁיב Je 23¹⁸ ψ 66¹⁹, etc; *Impf* 3 ms יַקְשִׁב Is 42²³, etc, *Imv.* ms. הַקְשֵׁב Jb 33³¹, esp. הַקְשִׁיבָה ψ 5³+, etc; *Inf cstr.* הַקְשִׁיב 1 S 15²²+; *Pt* מַקְשִׁיב Pr 1²⁴+, pl מַקְשִׁיבִים Ct 8¹³,—*give attention* (sts. + שָׁמַע); abs Ho 5¹ 1 S 15²² Is 10³⁰ 28²³ 34¹ 49¹ Mi 1²+12 t.; + אֶל pers Je 18¹⁹ Zc 1⁴ Is 51⁴ (|| הַאֲזִינוּ), לְ pers. ψ 55³; + אֶל rei Je 18¹⁸ Ne 9³⁴ ψ 142⁷, עַל rei Je 6¹⁹ Pr 17⁴ 29¹², לְ rei Je 6¹⁷ Is 48¹⁸ Pr 4²⁰ 5¹ 7²⁴ ψ 5³ Ct 8¹³, בְּ rei ψ 66¹⁹ 86⁶, also c acc rei Je 23¹⁸ Jb 13⁶ ψ 17¹ 61²; acc cogn Is 21⁷, appar = *cause to attend*, c. acc אָזְנְךָ Pr 2² (+ לְ rei), ψ 10¹⁷, but usage would be so late and rare that אָזְנְךָ is prob subj rei (Ges § 144 m Da Synt. § 109, R. 3).

†קֶשֶׁב n.m. attentiveness,—קָשֶׁב, as sign of life 2 K 4³¹, of a living deity 1 K 18²⁹; as acc cogn והקשיב קֶשֶׁב רַב־קָשֶׁב Is 21⁷ *he shall attend an attentiveness* (give close attention),—*abundance of attentiveness* (cf. 63⁷ ψ 145⁷)

†[קַשָּׁב] adj. attentive;—fs תְּהִי נָא אָזְנְךָ קַשֶּׁבֶת Ne 1⁶, + אֶל rei v¹¹

†[קַשֻּׁב] adj. id,—fpl קַשֻּׁבוֹת, of אָזְנַיִם, 2 Ch 6⁴⁰ 7¹⁵ ψ 130², all + לְ rei

I [קָשָׁה] vb. be hard, severe, fierce (NH קָשָׁה *be severe*, Ar قَسَا (ى) *be hard, dry*, III *endure, struggle against, severity*, Aram קְשָׁא, فَسَا *be hard, difficult*, JAram קְשִׁי, קַשְׁיָה, קְשֵׁי adj *hard*),—**Qal** *Pf* 3 fs קָשְׁתָה 1 S 5⁷, קָשָׁתָה Gn 49⁷, *Impf* 3 ms יִקְשֶׁה Dt 1¹⁷ 15¹⁸, וַיִּקֶשׁ 2 S 19⁴⁴,—**1** *be hard, difficult* Dt 1¹⁷ (of a legal case, מִן compar) **2.** *be hard, severe*, ק׳ יָדוֹ עָלֵינוּ 1 S 5⁷ (of י׳, in judgment), יק׳ בעינך Dt 15¹⁸ *it shall not be hard in thine eyes* (seem a severe trial, an injustice); of wrath Gn 49⁷ (poem in J, || עַז); of fierce words 2 S 19⁴⁴. **Niph.** *Pt* נקשה Is 8²¹ *hardly bestead, hard pressed* **Pi.** *Impf* 3 fs וַתְּקַשׁ בלדתה Gn 35¹⁶ (E) *she made hard in her bearing* (had severe labour). **Hiph.** *Pf* 3 ms הקשה Ex 13¹⁵+, etc, *Impf* 3 ms וַיֶּקֶשׁ 2 Ch 36¹³, 3 mpl וַיַּקְשׁוּ Je 7²⁶+, etc., *Inf. cstr* sf. בהקשתה Gn 35¹⁷, *Pt* מַקְשֶׁה Pr 28¹⁴ 29¹, —**1.** *make difficult, difficulty*. הִקְשָׁה לשלחנו Ex 13¹⁵ Pharaoh *made difficulty about sending us away*, of travail Gn 35¹⁷ (E, as **Pi.**), הִקְשִׁיתָ לשאול 2 K 2¹⁰ *thou hast made hard to ask*, asked a hard thing **2.** *make severe, burdensome*, yoke imposed by king 1 K 12⁴ = 2 Ch 10⁴. **3.** **a.** *make hard, stiff, stubborn*, fig of obstinacy: וַיַּקְשׁוּ אֶת־עָרְפָּם 2 K 17¹⁴ *they stiffened their neck*, so Je 7²⁶ 17²³ 19¹⁵ Dt 10¹⁶ 2 Ch 30⁸ 36¹³ Ne 9¹⁶·¹⁷·²⁹ Pr 29¹; אַל־תַּקְשׁוּ לְבַבְכֶם ψ 95⁸, cf. Pr 28¹⁴, subj י׳, אַקְשֶׁה אֶת־לֵב פ׳ Ex 7³ (P), acc. את־רוחו Dt 2³⁰. **b.** *shew stubbornness* Jb 9⁴ (c. אֶל pers [י׳])

†קָשֶׁה adj. hard, severe;—abs. ק׳ Ex 18²⁶+; cstr 32⁹+; fs. קָשָׁה Dt 26⁶+, cstr. קְשַׁת 1 S 1¹⁵; mpl קָשִׁים 2 S 3³⁹; cstr קְשֵׁי Ez 2⁴ 3⁷, fpl. קָשׁוֹת Gn 42⁷·³⁰,—**1.** *hard, difficult*, of a legal question (דָּבָר) Ex 18²⁶ (E) **2. a.** *severe*, of battle 2 S 2¹⁷, wind Is 27⁸, servitude (עֲבֹדָה) 1 K 12⁴ = 2 Ch 10⁴, Dt 26⁶ Is 14³ Ex 1¹⁴ 6⁹ (both P); as n.coll הִרְאִיתָ עַמְּךָ קָשָׁה ψ 60⁵ *thou hast made thy people see severe things*, קשה יום Jb 30²⁵ i.e one whose time (life) is hard, so 1 S 1¹⁵ (reading קשת יום for ק׳ רוּחַ, 𝔊 Th We Dr al); *severe, rough*, of lord (אֲדֹנִים) Is 19⁴, cf. 2 S 3³⁹ (c. מן comp. [מִמֶּנּוּ ? v. HPS]); הָלוֹךְ וְקָשָׁה עַל־ Ju 4²⁴ the hand of the sons of Israel went on *being more and more severe* upon Jabin; *fierce, relentless*, of י׳'s sword Is 27¹ (in fig), *rough, rude* 1 S 25³, *severe things*, of language Gn 42⁷·³⁰ (E, c. דבר), 1 S 20¹⁰ 1 K 12¹³ = 2 Ch 10¹³ (all c. עָנָה), ואנכי שָׁלוּחַ אליך קָשָׁה 1 K 14⁶ *I am commissioned with a severe (message) unto thee* (Ges § 121 d N 2 Da Synt §§ 75 (d) 80), חָזוּת קָשָׁה Is 21². **b.** *fierce, intense, vehement*, of קִנְאָה Ct 8⁶ (|| עַזָּה, cf Gn 49⁷). **3.** עַם־קְשֵׁה־עֹרֶף *a people stiff of neck, stubborn*, Ex 32⁹ 33³·⁵ 34⁹ (all JE), Dt 9⁶·¹³; עָרְפְּךָ הַקָּשֶׁה 31²⁷; cf דַּרְכָּם הַקָּשָׁה Ju 2¹⁹; קְשֵׁי פָנִים Ez 2⁴ (+ חִזְקֵי־לֵב), קְשֵׁי־לֵב 3⁷ (+ חִזְקֵי־מֵצַח); ק׳ alone = *stubborn* Is 48⁴.

†קְשִׁי n [m.] stubbornness,—cstr. Dt 9²⁷.

†קִשְׁיוֹן n pr.loc. Levit city in Issachar, Jos 19²⁰ 21²⁸ (in || 1 Ch 6⁵⁷ קֶדֶשׁ q v.); Κεισων, 𝔊L Κεσιων, A Κεσ', Κισ'.

II. קשה (√of foll. mng dub; Thes *decorticavit*, = Ar. قَشَا, then *tornavit*, but ش = שׁ ?).

†מִקְשֶׁה n.[m.] an artistic hair arrangement; ? turner's work, Is 3²⁴, so most

†I. מִקְשָׁה n f. perhaps hammered work, only of metals (orig *turner's work* ?),—abs. מ׳, of cherubim in tabern. Ex 25¹⁸ 37⁷, lampstand 25³¹·³⁶ 37¹⁷·²² Nu 8⁴·⁴, clarions 10².—II. מ׳ v קשא

†[קָשַׁח] **vb. Hiph. 1. make hard. 2. treat hardly** (Ar. قسح *be hard, firm, tough;* Sab. קסח *hardness, severity, cruelty,* SabDenkm ^{51}),—**1.** *make hard, stubborn, Impf.* 2 ms תַּקְשִׁיחַ (subj. ^), c. acc. לֵב Is 63^{17} (+מִיִּרְאָתֶךָ). **2.** *treat hardly, roughly* (of ostrich), *Pf.* 3 ms. הִקְשִׁיחַ Jb 39^{16} (c. acc. בָּנֶיהָ; rd. 3 fs. הִקְשִׁיחָה Hi Siegf Du); <(Di) *Inf. abs* (Ges $^{§113\,x}$) הַקְשִׁיחַ Ew, or *Impf.* 3 fs. תַּקְשִׁיחַ Hirz Bae^{Kau} Bu.

†קֹשֶׁט **n.[m.?] bow;**—ψ 60^{6}, Aram. form of קֶשֶׁת, q.v. (ט for ת after ק).

קשט (√of foll.; cf. Palm. קשט *succeed;* Aram. קְשׁוֹט, קֻשְׁטָא *right, truth;* Syr ܩܘܫܛܐ *id*, ChrPalAram. ܩܫܛ *true,* Mand. כשט *be true,* v. Schwally$^{Idiot.86}$; Ar قِسْط *equity, justice* is loan-word (v. Fra^{206})).

†קֹשְׁטְ **n.m. truth;**—Pr 22^{21} (acc to Toy Aram. gloss to foll. אִמְרֵי אֱמֶת).

קְשִׁי, קָשׁוֹן, v. I קשה.

†קָשַׁר **vb. bind, league together, conspire** (NH *id, bind, join,* קֶשֶׁר *knot;* ܬ קְטַר, Syr. ܩܛܰܪ *bind* (ט for ת after ק) No$^{ZMG\,xl\,734}$, who cp also ('perh') Ar. قَسَرَ *force* to do a thing, Eth ቀጸረ: *bind*);—**Qal** *Pf* 3 ms. קָשַׁר Am 7^{10} 1 K 16^{16}; 2 ms. sf וּקְשַׁרְתָּם consec Dt 6^{8}, etc.; *Impf* 3 ms. וַיִּקְשֹׁר 1 K 15^{27}+, וַיִּקְשָׁר־ 2 K 15^{30}, etc.; *Imv.* ms. sf קָשְׁרֵם Pr 3^{3}+; *Pt. act* pl. קֹשְׁרִים 2 S 15^{31}+; *pass* fs. קְשׁוּרָה Gn 44^{30} Pr 22^{15}, pl. קְשֻׁרִים Gn 30^{42};—**1.** *bind*: **a.** lit., c acc. rei + עַל Gn 38^{28} (J), Je 51^{63}, + בְּ, Jos $2^{18.21}$ (JE); *bind, confine,* c. acc. רֵים Jb 39^{10} (+בְּתֶלֶם), acc. of crocod. 40^{29} **b.** fig., c acc. + עַל Dt 6^{8} 11^{18} Pr 3^{3} 6^{21} 7^{3} (all of religious and moral precepts); c בְּ, נַפְשׁוֹ קְשׁוּרָה בְנַפְשׁוֹ Gn 44^{30} *his life is bound up with his* [viz the boy's] *life* (J; of strong affection); אִוֶּלֶת ק׳ בְלֶב־נַעַר Pr 22^{15} **c.** pt pass. *vigorous* (prop. well-*knit;* opp. עֲטֻפִים) Gn 30^{42} (J) **2.** *league together, conspire:* c. עַל pers. *against* 1 S $22^{8.13}$ Am 7^{10} 1 K 15^{27} 16^{9} 2 K 10^{9} $15^{10.25}$, $21^{23.24}$ = 2 Ch $33^{24.25}$, 2 Ch 24^{21}; c. acc. cogn. קֶשֶׁר, 1 K 16^{20} 2 K 12^{21} 15^{15}, + עַל pers. 14^{19} = 2 Ch 25^{27}, 2 K 15^{30}; abs. 1 K 16^{16} Ne 4^{2} (+inf. purpose); c עִם, *together with,* 2 S 15^{31}. **Niph.** *Pf.* 3 fs. נִקְשְׁרָה 1 S 18^{1} *the life of Jonathan was bound up with the life of D.* (**Qal 1 b**); *Impf* 3 fs. וַתִּקָּשֵׁר כָּל־הַחוֹמָה Ne 3^{38} *all the wall was joined together* (the circuit complete). **Pi.** *Impf.* **1.** *bind on* (as ornament), 2 fs. sf. וּתְקַשְּׁרִים Is 49^{18} (fig.; ∥ תִּלְבָּשִׁי). **2.** *bind fast,* 2 ms. (הַ)תְקַשֵּׁר מַעֲדַנּוֹת כִּימָה Jb 38^{31} *canst thou bind fast the bands of the Pleiades?* **Pu.** *Pt* הַצֹּאן הַמְקֻשָּׁרוֹת Gn 30^{41} (J), = **Qal 1 c. Hithp.** *conspire: Pf.* 3 pl. הִתְקַשְּׁרוּ עַל־ 2 Ch 24^{25} (∥ 2 K 12^{21} **Qal 2**), *Impf.* 3 ms. וַיִּתְקַשֵּׁר אֶל־ 2 K 9^{14}; *Pt.* pl. הַמִּתְקַשְּׁרִים עָלָיו 2 Ch 24^{26}.

†קֶשֶׁר **n.m.** $^{2\,S\,15.12}$ **conspiracy;**—abs. ק׳ 2 S 15^{12}+, קָשֶׁר 2 K 11^{14}+; cstr. קֶשֶׁר Ez 22^{25} (but v. infr); sf. קִשְׁרוֹ 1 K 16^{20} 2 K 15^{15},—*conspiracy* 2 S 15^{12}; as acc. cogn. c. קָשַׁר 1 K 16^{20} 2 K 12^{21} 14^{19} = 2 Ch 25^{27}, 2 K $15^{15.30}$, וַיִּמָּצֵא 2 K 17^{4}, נִמְצָא ק׳ בְּאִישׁ וגו׳ Je 11^{9}; as exclam. 2 K $11^{14.14}$ = 2 Ch $23^{13.13}$, Is $8^{12.12}$ (Gr Lag Che^{Comm} Gu^{Kau} al. קֹדֶשׁ or קָדוֹשׁ), קֶשֶׁר נְבִיאֶיהָ Ez 22^{25}, < rd אֲשֶׁר נְשִׂיאֶיהָ Co Toy Krae al. (after 𝔊)

†קִשֻּׁרִים **n.[m.] pl. bands, sashes,** or other woman's ornament that is *bound on:*—abs. ק׳ Is 3^{20}, sf קִשֻּׁרֶיהָ Je 2^{32} (∥ עֶדְיָהּ, cf. √**Pi.** Is 49^{18}).

I **קשׁשׁ** (√of foll; cf. ܬ קְשַׁשׁ *be old* (orig. *be dried up?*), Syr. ܩܫ *be old;* J Aram. קְשִׁישׁ *old;* Palm. קשישא name of office, perh. *elder;* NH קַשׁ *stubble, straw* (Low$^{p.160}$), so Syr. ܩܶܫܳܐ, ܬ קַשָּׁא (Ex 15^{7} Is 40^{24}), Ar. قَشّ is loan-word Fra^{137}).

†קַשׁ **n.m.** $^{Na\,1\,10}$ **stubble, chaff;**—abs ק׳ Ex 5^{12}+, קַשׁ־ 15^{7},—lit. as acc. cogn. לְקֹשֵׁשׁ ק׳ לַתֶּבֶן Ex 5^{12} (J); in sim, as inflammable, 15^{7} Is 5^{24} 47^{14} Na 1^{10} Jo 2^{5}, so in metaph Is 33^{11} Ob ^{18} Mal 3^{19}; in sim., as driven by wind Is 40^{24} 41^{2} Je 13^{24} ψ 83^{14}; fig. of the worthless Jb 13^{25}, of harmless trifles $41^{20.21}$.

†[קָשַׁשׁ] **vb. denom. Pō'. gather stubble;**—*Pf.* 3 pl. consec. וְקֹשְׁשׁוּ Ex 5^{7}; *Inf. cstr.* לְקֹשֵׁשׁ v^{12}, *Pt.* מְקֹשֵׁשׁ Nu $15^{32.33}$, f. מְקֹשֶׁשֶׁת 1 K $17^{10.12}$,—*gather stubble,* c acc cogn קַשׁ Ex 5^{12} (לַתֶּבֶן); also c acc. תֶּבֶן v^{7} (both J); c. acc. עֵצִים as firewood Nu $15^{32.33}$ (P), 1 K $17^{10.12}$.

†II [קָשַׁשׁ] doubtful **vb.,** only **Qal** *Imv.* + **Hithpō'.** *Imv*, הִתְקוֹשְׁשׁוּ וָקוֹשּׁוּ Zp 2^{1}; AV RV *gather yourselves together, yea gather together,* from foregoing (cf. Vrss), but this only denom. in specif. mng. *gather stubble, sticks,* etc.; read prob. with Gi Bu$^{SK\,1893,396}$ al. הִתְבּוֹשְׁשׁוּ וָבוֹשׁוּ..

†קֶשֶׁת **n.f.** $^{Gn\,9.14}$ (appar. **m.** 2 S 1^{22} but v. Albr$^{ZAW\,xvi\,(1896)\,91}$) **bow** (orig. √perh. קוש, mng. unknown; NH *id.;* As *kaštu;* Eth. ቀስት:

Ar. قَوْسٌ, pl قِسِيٌّ ,قُسِيٌّ, etc.; 𝔗 קַשְׁתָּא and (ט for ת after ק) קוּשְׁטָא (rare), all *bow*, קַשָּׁתָא *bowman*, Syr ܩܫܬܐ *bow*, ܩܫܬܐ *bowman*; OAram קשת *bow*, Mand כשטא (Fi a[206]), Palm קשטא *bowman*),—abs ק׳ Ho 1[7]+, קֶשֶׁת Je 46[9]+, cstr. קֶשֶׁת Ho 1[5]+, sf קַשְׁתִּי Gn 48[22]+, etc, pl abs. קְשָׁתוֹת 2 Ch 26[14]+, sf קַשְׁתֹתָיו (Ges§ 20 h) Is 5[28], קַשְׁתֹתָיו Je 51[56] ψ 37[15], קַשְּׁתֹתֵיהֶם Ne 4[7] (קַשְׁתֹתָם etc, van d H [exc ψ 37[15]]),—**1.** *bow* **a.** for hunting Gn 27[3] (J, + תְּלִי) **b** battle + (or ‖) חרב, Gn 48[22] Jos 24[12] (both E), Ho 1[7] 2[20] 1 S 18[4] (+ חֲגֹרוֹ), 2 S 1[22] 2 K 6[22] Is 41[2] Ne 4[7] (+ רָמְחֵיהֶם), Zc 9[13] (fig of Judah as י׳'s bow), ψ 37[15] (fig), 44[7] (+ or ‖ חֶרֶב also infr), + (or ‖) חצים Is 7[24] 2 K 13[15] [16] Ez 39[3.9] 1 Ch 12[2a]; cf רשפי ק׳ ψ 76[4]=arrow (+ מָגֵן וְחֶרֶב) so ק׳ בֵּן Jb 41[20] (cf La 3[13] Jb 5[7]); + חֲנִית ψ 46[10], + כידון Je 6[23] 50[42], + various weapons Ne 4[10] 2 Ch 26[14], alone Is 13[18] (context corrupt), 22[3] Je 51[56] Hb 3[9] (of י׳ as *warrior*); ק׳ מִלְחָמָה Zc 9[10] 10[4], in sim כְּק׳ רְמִיָּה *like a bow of deception* Ho 7[16] ψ 78[57] (i e. one that misses its aim, al. *slack bow*) **c.** ק׳ coll = *bow(-men), archers* Is 21[17]. **d** phrases are. הַמּוֹרִים אֲנָשִׁים בַּקּ׳ 1 S 31[3] *archers, bowmen* (but dub., Dr Kit Lohr tr., א׳ הַמ׳, We Bu del. א׳, as ‖ 1 Ch 10[3], HPS Now del. א׳ בַקּ׳), הַמּוֹרִים בַּקּ׳ 1 Ch 10[3]; מְטַחֲוֵי ק׳ Gn 21[16] (v. [טָחָה]), רמה ק׳ Je 4[29], cf. perh. Gn 21[20] v. קַשָּׁת; נשקי ק׳ ‖ (v. II. נָשַׁק) 1 Ch 12[2b] 2 Ch 17[17], רוֹמֵי ק׳ ‖ נוֹ׳ ψ 78[9], תפש הַקּ׳ Am 2[15] *one grasping the bow*, (v Je 46[9] infr) v also מִלֵּא יָדוֹ בַקּ׳ 2 K 9[24], דָּרַךְ ק׳ 13[16], הִרְכִּיב יָדְךָ עַל־הַקּ׳ *bend* (lit. *tread) the bow*, Is 5[28] (pt. pass), 21[15] (*id.*, ‖ חֶרֶב), Je 50[14.29] 51[3] 1 Ch 5[18] 8[40] 2 Ch 14[7]; ψ 37[14] (‖ חֶרֶב), in fig 11[2] (‖ חֵץ), and, of God, La 2[4] 3[12] ψ 7[13] (‖ חֶרֶב), תפשי דֹּרְכֵי ק׳ Je 46[9]; cf. (fig) וַיַּדְרְכוּ אֶת־לְשׁוֹנָם קַשְׁתָּם Je 9[2]; also וְנִחֲתָה ק׳ נְחוּשָׁה ψ 18[35]=2 S 22[35] (rd ונחתה for ונחת); מָשַׁךְ בַּקּ׳ *draw the bow* 1 K 22[34] = 2 Ch 18[33], Is 66[19]. **e.** *bow* (passing over into) fig. of *might*, Gn 49[24] (poem), 1 S 2[4] Ho 1[5] Je 49[35] Jb 29[20] (cf. ψ 37[15], **b.** supr). **f.** ק׳ נְחוּשָׁה fig. of divine judgment Jb 20[24] (‖ נשק בַּרְזֶל) **2.** *rainbow* · כְּמַרְאֵה הַקּ׳ אֲשֶׁר יִהְיֶה בֶעָנָן בְּיוֹם הַגֶּשֶׁם Ez 1[28], Gn 9[13 14.16] (P) — וַיֹּאמֶר לְלַמֵּד בְּנֵי־יְהוּדָה קָשֶׁת 2 S 1[18] is corrupt; 𝔊 al om; We Now think misplaced gloss on v[6], v further HPS.

† קַשָּׁת n.m. bowman (si vera l.);—וַיְהִי רֹבֶה ק׳ Gn 21[20] *and he became, growing up, a bowman*, but ר׳ then superfluous (om 𝔊), after וַיִּגְדַּל v[8], Kn Di רבה קֶשֶׁת (= רמה ק׳ Je 4[29], which Ball reads here), cf. Holz Gunk.

ר

ר *Rêš*, 20th letter, = 200 in post B. Heb

רָאָה Dt 14[13] textual error, v דָּאָה.

רָאָה [1313] **vb. see** (NH *id.*, MI[4] ואראה, הראני l[7], cf רית *spectacle* l[12], Sab. ראי *see, expect*, DHM ZMG xxix (1875) 236, 209, Ar. رَأَى *see*, so Eth ርእየ: 𝔗 ריוא, רו human *appearance, features*, etc (cf Heb רֳאִי **2**)),—**Qal** [1141] *Pf.* 3 ms. ר׳ Gn 29[10]+, sf רָאֲךָ consec Ex 4[14], רָאָהוּ 2 K 2[12]+, 3 fs רָאֲתָה Gn 38[14], sf רָאָתְךָ Jb 42[5], 2 ms רָאִיתָ Gn 20[10]+, etc, *Impf* 3 ms יִרְאֶה 22[8]+, juss יֵרֶא Gn 41[33] (Baer Gi, Ges§ 75 p. hh Kö I 561, van d. H יֵרָא), יֵרֶא Ex 5[21]+, וַיַּרְא Gn 18[2]+ (1 S 19[20] read pl 𝔊 Comm, i e וַיִּרְאוּ Dr Sm lxiii), sf. יִרְאֵנִי Ex 33[20], וַיִּרְאֵנִי 2 S 1[7], 3 fs תִּרְאֶה Lv 20[17] Jb 33[28], juss. תֵּרֶא Mi 7[10] Zc 9[5] (Baer Gi, cf Ges Kö supr, van d H. תֵּרָא), וַתֵּרֶא Gn 3[6]+, 1 s. אֶרְאֶה 21[16]+, וָאֵרֶא 31[10]+, etc, *Imv* ראה 27[27]+, etc, *Inf. abs.* רָאֹה Ex 3[7]+, רָאוֹ Gn 26[28] Is 6[9], cstr. ראה Gn 48[11], ראות Ex 10[28]+, רְאוֹת Ez 28[17], etc; *Pt act* רֹאֶה Gn 13[15]+, etc; *pass* רְאוּיוֹת (Baer Gi; van d. H רְאֻיוֹת)·—**1. a.** *see*, subj. עַיִן, עֵינַיִם, c. acc pers Is 6[5] 30[20] Je 42[2]+5 t Jb Pr, subj. pers, c. acc pers. Gn 12[12 14]+ (מִי רָאָהוּ 1 S 23[22], rd. הַמְּהֵרָה 𝔊 Th We al. [not HPS]), ראי 16[13] (pt sf, cf בְּאֵר לַחַי רֹאִי v[14], p 91 supr); acc of God 32[31] (פָּנִים אֶל־פָּנִים), acc pers. om. 18[2] 19[1]+; c acc. פְּנֵי 31[2] 46[30] 48[11] Ex 33[20], opp. את־אֲחֹרָי v[23]; c. acc פני specif. of having access to man of rank Gn 43[3.5]+ (v [פָּנֶה] **2 b**) **b.** *see*, c acc rei: subj עַיִן, עֵינַיִם Jos 24[7] (E) 1 S 24[11] (van d H Baer; v[10] Gi), Dt 3[21]+5 t Dt, +, וְעֵינָיו אֶת־עֵינָיו תִרְאֶינָה Je 32[4], cf. 34[3]; acc om 2 S 24[3] Dt 21[7]+9 t. (לִרְאוֹת 1 S 6[13] rd. לִקְרָאתוֹ 𝔊 We Dr Kit Bu HPS Now); subj. pers. Gn 13[15] 31[12] + very oft., c acc cogn מַרְאֶה Ex 3[3]+7 t, מַרְאָה Dn 10[7.7.8], חָזוֹן 8[15], חֶזְיֹנוֹת Jo 3[1], hence *see* abs =

receive revelation, Is 30[10] (‖ חזה), cf. Ez 13[3] and v. 1. רֹאֶה; c. acc. עֶרְוָה, v. עׄ, p. 788 f.; *see* war, i.e. see it impending Ex 13[17] (E); רׄ אֶת־הַקּוֹלֹת 20[18] (Gi v[15]); וְאֶת־הַלַּפִּידִים Ec 7[11] רֹאֵי הַשָּׁמֶשׁ *those who see the sun*=living men; acc. rei om. Ex 22[9] 2 S 13[5]+, לֹא יָדְעוּ וָאֶרְאֶה בֶּחָזוֹן Dn 8[2.2] (abs.); מְקוֹם רֹאִים Ne 4[5]; וְלֹא יִרְאוּ עֵינֵי רֹאִים Is 32[3], Jb 34[26]; c. adv. or adv. phr. instead of acc. rei: כָּהֵנָּה Gn 41[19] cf. Is 66[8], Ez 1[27.27], כַּאֲשֶׁר 2 K 2[19] 2 Ch 29[8] 30[7] Jb 4[8] Ez 16[50] Dn 1[13], כֵּן ψ 48[6]. **2.** *see*, sq. acc.+cl. or phr. of closer design.: (1) +epex. cl. c. כִּי, acc. pers. Gn 6[2] *saw* them *that they were fair*, 12[4] (both J), Ex 2[2] 32[25] (both E), 1 K 11[28], acc. of face+*id.* Gn 31[5] (E), Ex 34[35] (P); acc. rei Gn 49[15] (poem), Is 22[9] Gn 1[4] (P), Ec 2[24] 4[4] and prob. 2 K 14[26] (rdg. כִּי מַר הוּא); (2) רׄ כָּל־הַבָּא עָלָיו וְעָמָד 2 S 20[12]; (3)+adj. (incl. pt.), acc. pers. Gn 7[1] (J), Am 9[1] 2 S 18[10] +39 t. (Je 46[5] del. רׄ 𝔊 Gie), +acc. אֲשֶׁר Ex 14[13.13] (J); acc. rei, †Ex 23[5] 33[10] (both E), Dt 22[4] Ez 33[3.6] Dn 1[10] 8[4.6.7]; †(4)+מָה, acc. rei Nu 13[18] (JE), Hg 2[3]; †(5)+prep. phr., acc. pers. Ex 5[19] (J), Zc 4[10] Ec 10[7] Est 5[9]; acc. rei +בִּכְבוֹדוֹ Hg 2[3], +ב pers. Je 23[13.14], +כ pers. Ju 9[36], כ rei 2 S 18[27]; (6) acc. pers.+adv. acc. +כ pers. Je 30[6]. **3.** *see*, so as to learn to know: c. acc. pers. Dt 33[9] (‖ יָדַע, הִכִּיר); c. acc. rei Dt 1[19.31] 11[2] Jb 11[11] (‖ יָדַע), ψ 16[10] 49[10];=have experience of, Je 5[12] 14[13] 20[18] 42[14] Zp 3[15] ψ 89[49] Ec 5[17], שֵׁנָה בְּעֵינָיו אֵינֶנּוּ רֹאֶה Ec 8[16]; מָה רָאִיתָ Gn 20[10] i.e. *what hast thou encountered, that ...?* Bacher[ZAW xix (1899), 345 ff.; Terminol. 177 f.] **4.** abs. *see*, *have* (power of) *vision*, Gn 27[1] (J), 48[10] (E), 1 S 3[2] 4[15] 1 K 14[4], miraculous 2 K 6[17.17.20.20]; denied of idols Dt 4[28] ψ 115[5] 135[16]; fig. of spiritual vision Is 6[10] 29[18] 42[18] 44[18] Je 5[21] Dt 29[3] Ez 12[2.2] ψ 40[13] 69[24]; עַיִן רֹאָה Pr 20[12].—1 S 14[27] rd. Qr v. אור. **5.** *see*=perceive: **a.** sq. cl. c. כִּי, Ex 3[4] 8[11] Gn 1[10.12]+oft. (1 S 23[15] rd. וַיִּרָא *and he feared* We Dr Kit Bu HPS Now); om. כִּי (late) †La 1[10] ψ 49[11] Ec 3[16]; sq. מָה of indirect question Gn 2[19] (J), 37[20] (E), Ju 9[48] Dt 32[20] Je 7[17] 33[24] Ez 8[6] Jon 4[5]+; בַּמֶּה Ju 16[5] cf. 1 S 14[38], כַּמָּה Zc 2[6] ψ 35[17]; sq. מִי of indirect question 1 S 14[17] Is 40[26] La 2[20] (+הַבִּיטָה); sq. אַי 1 S 26[16], אֵיכֹה 2 K 6[13], אֵיפֹה Je 3[2]; sq. cl. c. הֲ *whether*, Gn 8[8] 18[21] Nu 11[23] (all J), Ex 4[18] (E), ψ 14[2] 53[3] Ct 6[11b] Est 3[4], אִם *whether* Je 30[6] La 1[12] ψ 139[24] Ct 7[13], אֲשֶׁר *that* or *how* 1 S 18[15], אַי Ec 2[3], שֶׁ *that* v[13], שֶׁ 3[18]. **b.** c. acc. צָרַת נַפְשׁוֹ Gn 42[21] (i.e. saw it by outward signs), cf. Ho 5[13]. [*Note*, under **5** (rarely in other cases, and only S K Je), †Imv.+ידע Imv.: דְּעִי וּרְאִי 1 S 24[12] 2 S 24[13] 1 K 20[22]; דַּע וּרְאֵה 1 S 25[17] Je 2[19]; דְּעוּ וּרְאוּ 1 S 12[17] 14[38] 23[22] 1 K 20[7] 2 K 5[7]; in reverse order, רְאוּ וּדְעוּ 1 S 23[23] Je 5[1].] **6.** *look at, see*, by direct volition: **a.** subj. men, c. acc. rei, Gn 9[22.23] (J), 42[9.12] (E), Lv 13[3.15]+; c. acc. of land=reconnoitre Jos 2[1]; *look at* sun, etc., for worship †Dt 4[19] Jb 31[26]; =inspect 1 K 9[12] Lv 14[36.36]; c. acc. pers. Nu 24[20.21] (JE), Ex 2[25] Lv 13[3.5] (all P), 1 S 9[16]+, (1 S 19[15] HPS prop. אֶל־בֵּית for לִרְאוֹת); c. prep. רׄ אַחֲרֵי רֹאִי Gn 16[13] (J) *I have looked after one seeing me* (interpr. v. Di). **b.** subj. God, c. acc. rei Gn 9[16] (P); =inspect 11[5] (J); *look at* with favour, acc. pers. Jb 37[24] ψ 138[6]; so perh. fig., subj. man, *regard*, c. acc. אָוֶן ψ 66[18] (Hup-Now; Che Bae Dr al. *intend*); *look* with pleasure (acc. om., +מִן *by reason of, as a fruit of*) Is 53[11] (si vera l.; ins. acc. אור 𝔊 Houb Klo Du Che[Hpt] Kit [perh.], with Hiph. יַרְאֶה 𝔊 Du Che[Hpt], rescues from travail his soul, *makes it see light*). **c.** without acc., *look, take a look*, etc. (of man and God; oft.+וְ)הִנֵּה), Gn 8[13] 18[2] Ex 3[2] Lv 13[8] La 3[50] (מִן loc.), Gn 13[14] (מִן loc.+ה loc.), Dt 3[27] Ez 40[4] 44[5] (all בְּעֵינֶיךָ), +oft.; peculiarly, מִמֶּנִּי תִרְאוּ וְכֵן תַּעֲשׂוּ Ju 7[17] (cf. GFM). **d.** *look after, see after, learn about*, c. acc. rei Gn 37[14] (J), c. acc. pers.=visit (go to *see*) 1 S 15[35] 20[29] 2 S 13[5.6] 2 K 8[29]=2 Ch 22[6], 2 K 9[16], cf. Ez 20[28], עַיִן רֹאִי Jb 7[8] (Di Bu al.). **e.** *observe, watch*, abs., 1 S 6[9.16] 17[28] Ec 8[16] (‖ ידע). **f.** *look upon*=endure to see, c. acc. rei Hb 1[13] (‖ הַבִּיט). **g.** *look out, find out*, acc. pers. 2 K 9[2], Gn 41[33] (E), +ל pers. 1 S 16[17]; *select*, acc. pers.+מִן *from among* 2 K 10[3], +ב among+ל pers. 1 S 16[1]; *provide, furnish*, c. acc. rei Dt 33[21] (poem), +ל pers. Gn 22[8] (E), cf. abs. יׄ יִרְאֶה as n.pr.loc.=יׄ *seeth* v[14a] (E; ? read יֵרָאֶה, cf. v[b], **Niph.** and Di); רְאֻיוֹת Est 2[9] *looked out*=suitable (as oft. NH). **h.** *look at*=concern oneself about, acc. rei (+בְּיָדוֹ) Gn 39[23] (J). **7.** of mental observation: **a.** *Imv. see! observe! consider!* exclam. (nearly =הִנֵּה), sq. cl.: Gn 27[27] 31[50] *see! God is witness* 39[14] 41[41] Ex 4[21] Dt 1[8]+; sq. nom. independ. 2 S 24[22] (‖ 1 Ch 21[23] sq. cl.). **b.** *look at*, i.e. inquire into, a matter, acc. rei om., of יׄ, 1 S 24[16] (Gi v[15]). **c.** *give attention to*, acc. rei, Je 2[31], abs. *give attention!* 2 S 13[28] 2 K 6[32] Ex 25[40] ψ 45[11]; *take heed to*, acc. rei, 1 K 12[16]=2 Ch 10[16]; abs. *take heed!* Ex 10[10], +פֶּן 2 K 10[23]. **d.** *discern*, לִבִּי רׄ חָכְמָה Ec 1[16], רׄ טוֹב 3[13]. **e.** *distinguish*, c. בֵּין...לְ of pers. Mal 3[18]. **f.** *consider, reflect*, Ec 7[14] (sq. cl. orat. rect.). †**8. a.** c. ב, lit., *look into*, hence *look at* with interest (Germ.

'sich vertiefen in') (1) *gaze at* 1 S 6^{19} (on context v. We Dr HPS), so as to become acquainted with Gn 34^{1} (P); so as to find out Ec 3^{22}, *inspect* liver (for omens) Ez 21^{26}; somewhat weakened = *behold* Jb 3^{9} 2 Ch 7^{3} ψ 64^{9}. (2) *look at* with kindness, helpfulness, of ׳י, בְּעֳנִי Gn 29^{32} 1 S 1^{11} (+inf. abs), 2 S 16^{12}, בַּצַּר ψ 106^{44}. (3) upon a spectacle causing anger Ex 2^{11} (E), grief Gn 21^{16} (E), 44^{34} Nu 11^{15} (both J), 2 K 22^{20} (subj עֵינַיִם) = 2 Ch 34^{28}, Est $8^{6.6}$, abhorrence Is 66^{24} (4) *gaze at* with apprehension Ec 11^{4}. (5) with joy, pleasure, 2 K 10^{16} Mi 7^{9} Je 29^{32} Is 52^{8} (עַיִן בְּעַיִן, cf **Niph.** Nu 14^{14}), Jb 20^{17} 33^{28} ψ 54^{9} 106^{5} 128^{5} Ct 3^{11} 6^{11a} Ec 2^{1}. (6) esp with exultation, triumph = *feast eyes upon*, sts *gloat over* (fallen enemies), Ju 16^{27} Mi 7^{10} Ez 28^{17} Ob $^{12.13}$ ψ 22^{18} 112^{8} 118^{7}. **b.** c אֶל pers. Is 17^{7} (subj עֵינַיִם, ‖ שָׁעָה עַל), עַל pers. Ex 5^{21} (J), ר׳ עַל־הָאָבְנָיִם Ex 1^{16} v [אבן] and Comm, also Spiegelb ZA xiv (June 1900), 269 ff. **c** c לְ, מִי 1 S 16^{7}, הָאָדָם יִר׳ לָעֵינַיִם וַיהוה יִר׳ לַלֵּבָב וּרְאִיתַנִי כתור הָאָדָם ψ 64^{6}.—Corrupt is יִרְאֶה־לָּמוֹ 1 Ch 17^{17} (and ‖ וזאת תּוֹרַת הָאָדָם 2 S 7^{19}), read וַתַּרְאֵנִי (with other changes) We Dr Kau Bu HPS Now, Ez 12^{12} read prob **Niph.** 𝔊 Hi Co Krae; Mi 6^{9} read prob. יִרְאָה cf. Now GASm **Niph.** *Pf* 3 ms נִרְאָה Gn 48^{3}+, etc., *Impf.* 3 ms. יֵרָאֶה Gn 22^{14}+, juss. יֵרָא Ex 34^{3} Lv 9^{6}, וַיֵּרָא Gn 12^{7}+, 1 s וָאֵרָא Ex 6^{3}, etc; *Imv.* ms. הֵרָאֵה 1 K 18^{1}, *Inf cstr* לְהֵרָאוֹת 1 S 17^{17}+, לֵרָאוֹת Is 1^{12}+ 2 t., הֵרָאֹה Ju 13^{21} 1 S 3^{21}, etc.;—**1.** *appear*, esp **a.** of ׳י (God) c אֶל pers. Gn $12^{7.7}$+6 t. J, Gn 35^{1} (E), v^{9} 48^{3} Ex 6^{3} (בְּ essent., באל שַׁדַּי), Lv 9^{4} (all P), 1 K 3^{5} $9^{2.2}$ = 2 Ch 7^{12}, 1 K 11^{9}, c. לְ pers Je 31^{3} 2 Ch 1^{7} 3^{1} (ins ׳י 𝔊 Kau Kit); abs Gn 22^{14} in the mt where ׳י *appeareth* (prob., Di Sta $^{G I\ 450}$ Dr $^{Hast\ DB\ ii\ 563}$, E), Nu 14^{14} (JE; עַיִן בְּעַיִן, v. Is 52^{8} **Qal 8 a** (5)), Lv 16^{2} (P, בְּ loc. + עַל), 1 S 3^{21} (בְּ loc), 2 S 22^{11} (עַל־כַּנְפֵי־רוּחַ; ‖ וַיֵּרָא < ψ 18^{11}), +5 t, of מַלְאַךְ ׳י, c. אֶל pers Ex 3^{2} (E), Ju 13^{21}, of כבוד ׳י; c. אֶל pers Lv $9^{6.23}$ Nu 14^{10} (בְּ loc), 16^{19} 20^{6} (all P), Ju 6^{12} 13^{3}, עַל pers. Is 60^{2}, abs Ex 16^{10} (בְּ loc), Nu 17^{7} (both P) **b.** *appear*, of man, = *present oneself*. c אֶל pers Gn 46^{29} (J), Ju 13^{10} 1 K $18^{2.15}$ Lv $13^{7.7.19}$, אֶל of God ψ 84^{8} (בְּ loc), אֶל־פְּנֵי הָאָדֹן Ex 23^{17} (E); abs Is 16^{12} (del as dittogr Lo Du Che ^{Hpt} Marti al), esp. (Mass) sq אֶת־פְּנֵי) of ׳י, rendered *appear before* ׳י so וְנִרְאָה 1 S 1^{22}, יֵרָאֶה Ex 34^{23} (JE), Dt 16^{16}, וְאֵרָאֶה ψ 42^{3}, יֵרָאוּ Ex 23^{15} (E), 34^{20} (JE), Dt 16^{16}, לֵרָאוֹת Ex 34^{24} (JE), Dt 31^{11} Is 1^{12}, read prob. in all **Qal** (v [פָּנֶה] II **2**).

c. *appear*, of things: late (Hex only P), abs. Gn 1^{9} 8^{5}, c. בְּ loc 9^{14} Lv $13^{14.57}$; elsewhere poet. ψ 18^{16} = 2 S 22^{16}, ψ 90^{16} Pr 27^{25} (of דֶּשֶׁא), Ct 2^{12} (בְּ loc; of blossoms); subj. מַרְאֵיהֶם Dn 1^{15} (+adj. pred.), v^{13} (+לְפָנֶיךָ); subj חָזוֹן, c. אֶל pers Dn $8^{1.1}$; subj. כְּנֶגַע Lv 14^{35} (c לְ pers) **2.** *be seen*: **a.** subj rei, 1 K 10^{12} = 2 Ch 9^{11} (where כֵּהֶם subj) Ez 19^{11}, of sins 21^{29} (‖ הִגָּלוֹת), subj כָּאֶבֶן קְוֹאת Ju 19^{30}, כאבן etc. Ez 10^{1}. **b.** subj. pers. 2 S 17^{17} (+לָבוֹא) *be seen to come* **c.** *be seen* = occur 2 K 23^{24} (בְּ loc.); = exist, + לְ pers. Ex $13^{7.7}$ (JE), Dt 16^{4}, cf Ez 10^{8}; = be present, + בְּ loc. Ju 5^{8} Ex 34^{3} (JE) **3.** *be visible*, Ex 33^{23} (JE; subj ׳י's face), אֵין אֶבֶן נִרְאָה 1 K 6^{18}, $8^{8.8}$ = 2 Ch $5^{9.9}$, Je 13^{26} Is 47^{3}. †**Pu.** *Pf.* 3 pl עַצְמֹתָיו לֹא רֻאּוּ Jb 33^{21} (Baer Gi; d. f. Ki Ko $^{I\ 41.563}$, Mappik Ges ^{§14d}, van d H רֻאוּ), appar. *his bones are not seen, detected;* De *which were* (formerly) *not seen;* Di *are insignificant* ('unscheinbar'), so Bae, prob. corrupt, Bu נָאווּ, Du del as doublet. †**Hithp.** recipr. *look at each other* *Impf* 2 mpl לָמָּה תִּתְרָאוּ Gn 42^{1} (E); techn. 3 mpl. וַיִּתְרָאוּ פָנִים 2 K 14^{11} = 2 Ch 25^{21} *and they looked each other in the face*, i e. met in combat, so 1 pl. נִתְרָאֶה פ׳ 2 K 14^{8} = 2 Ch 25^{17}, cf. (perhaps) 2 K 23^{29}, where Wkl Benz conj. כְּהִתְרָאוֹת אתו (or **Niph.** כהראות אתו) for MT כראתו אתו **Hiph.**$_{62}$ *Pf* 3 ms הֶרְאָה Gn 41^{28}+, sf. הֶרְאַנִי Am 7^{1}+, הֶרְאַנִי Ez 11^{25}, הֶרְאָנוּ Dt 5^{21} Ju 13^{23}, הֶרְאֲךָ Dt 4^{36}, 1 s. וְהִרְאִיתִי Na 3^{5} (Ges ^{§53p}), sf הֶרְאִיתִיךָ Dt 34^{4}, הראיתים Is 39^{4} cf. ‖ 2 K 20^{15}, etc.; *Impf* 3 ms. יַרְאֶה Is 30^{30}, וַיַּרְא 2 K 11^{4}, sf יַרְאֵנִי Nu 23^{3} ψ 59^{11}; 1 s sf אַרְאֶךָּ Gn 12^{1}+, etc; *Imv* ms. sf הַרְאֵנִי Ex 33^{18}, etc.; *Inf cstr* הַרְאוֹת Dt 3^{24}+, sf הַרְאֹתְכָה Ez 40^{4}, לְרַאֹתְכֶם Dt 1^{33}, etc., *Pt* מַרְאֶה Ex 25^{9} Ez 40^{4},—**1. a.** *cause* one *to see* something, *shew* (1) subj man, c. acc. pers + rei, Nu 13^{26b} (JE), Ju $1^{24.25}$ 2 K $20^{13.15}$ = Is $39^{2.4}$+4 t, acc rei om Ez 40^{4} Est 4^{8}, acc. refl נַפְשׁוֹ + acc rei Ec 2^{24}, מִי יַרְאֵנוּ טוֹב ψ 4^{7}, acc. pers. om, = *exhibit* Est 1^{4}; c. 2 acc. pers. Ju 4^{22} 2 K 11^{4}. (2) especially subj ׳י (God), c. acc. pers + rei, Gn 12^{1} Ex 9^{16} (both J), Gn 41^{28} 48^{11} (both E), Ex 33^{18} Dt 34^{1b} (both JE), Dt 3^{24} 4^{36} 5^{21} Jos 5^{6} (D), Ex 25^{9} (P), Ju 13^{23}+5 t + (of revelation to prophets) Nu 23^{3} (JE), Je 38^{21} Ez 11^{25}, also, c acc. rei cogn, Nu 8^{4} (P), acc. rei om. Dt 34^{4} (JE), acc. pers om = *exhibit*, Is 30^{30}; of visions, ׳י subj, c acc. pers. + כֹּה Am $7^{1.4.7}$ 8^{1}, + כַּאֲשֶׁר Ex 27^{8} (P), c acc. pers only = *cause to see* [a vision] Je 24^{1}; c. 2 acc. pers. + appos. 2 K 8^{13}, acc pers + cl. c כִּי v^{10}. (3) subj. angel, acc pers

+rei, of revelation to prophet Zc 2³ 3¹; acc. pers. + cl. c. מָה Zc 1⁹. **b.** *cause to experience* something, c. acc. pers. + rei, subj. 'י, Hb 1³ ψ 60⁵ 71²⁰ 85⁸. †**2.** *cause to look intently at, to behold*, c. acc. pers. + בּ rei (cf. **Qal 8**), subj. 'י: **a.** *cause to gaze at*, with joy ψ 50²³ 91¹⁶. **b.** in exultation, *cause to feast one's eyes upon*, fallen enemies ψ 59¹¹ (cf. MI⁷). **c.** in weakened sense, *cause to behold* Dt 1³³ (cf. Dr). †**Hoph. 1.** *be caused to see, be shewn: Pf.* 2 ms. הָרְאֵיתָ, subj. man, acc. rei, Ex 26³⁰ (P; בּ loc.); so *Pt.* מָרְאֶה 25⁴⁰ (P; בּ loc.); sq. inf. אַתָּה הָרְאֵתָ לָדַעַת כִּי Dt 4³⁵. **2.** *be exhibited to*, subj. rei, acc. pers., *Pf.* 3 ms. consec. וְהָרְאָה אֶת־הַכֹּהֵן Lv 13⁴⁹ (P).

†[רָאֶה] **adj. seeing**, assumed by Thes al. to explain cstr. וּרְאֵה עָנְיִי Jb 10¹⁵, but improb.; Mass. appar. intended *Imv.* (unsuitable); Ew al. וְרָאֵה; Di Bu Du (after Lag Gei) רְוֵה עָנְיִי *drenched* (i.e. sated) *with affliction*.

†I. **רֹאֶה n.[m.]** seer, c. art. 'הָר (exc. 2 S 15²⁷);—old name for נָבִיא 1 S 9⁹ᵇ, used of Sam. v⁹ᵃ·¹¹·¹⁸·¹⁹ and (as archaism) 1 Ch 9²² 26²⁸ 29²⁹; of חֲנָנִי 2 Ch 16⁷·¹⁰; הֲרוֹאֶה appar. of Zadok 2 S 15²⁷, but crpt. (conj. in We Dr); pl. (c. prep.) לָרֹאִים Is 30¹⁰ *the seers*, as a class.

†II. **רֹאֶה n.[m.]** prophetic **vision** 'שָׁגוּ בָּר Is 28⁷ *they reel in* (their) *vision* (‖ פָּקוּ פְּלִילִיָּה).

†III. **רֹאֶה n.pr.m.** 1 Ch 2⁵², v. רְאָיָה infr.

†רַאֲוָה Ez 28¹⁷ v. √**Qal** *Inf.*, and **8 a** (6).

†**רְאוּת n.f. look**;—cstr. רְאוּת עֵינָיו Ec 5¹⁰ Qr (Kt ראית).

†**רְאִי n.m. mirror**;—'כִּר מוּצָק Jb 37¹⁸ (sim.).

†**רֳאִי n.[m.] looking, seeing, sight**;—**1.** *seeing*, 'אֵל ר Gn 16¹³ᵃ *a God of seeing* (= who sees). **2.** *appearance* (= מַרְאֶה), טוֹב רֹאִי 1 S 16¹²; מֵרֹאִי Jb 33²¹ *without* (healthy, fair) *appearance*. **3.** *sight*, (warning-) *spectacle*, כְּרֹאִי Na 3⁶.—'ר Gn 16¹³ᵇ Jb 7⁸ is **Qal** *Pt.* sf.

ראית v. רְאוּת.

†I. **מַרְאָה n.f. vision**, as means of revelation: 'מ abs. Nu 12⁶ (E), 1 S 3¹⁵ Dn 10¹⁶, as acc. cogn. v⁷·⁷·⁸; appar. pl. abs. מַרְאוֹת Ez 43³, but rd. כְּמַרְאֵה הָרֶכֶב 𝔊 Co Berthol Siegf Krae, or del. Toy Krae (as altern.); cstr. מַרְאוֹת הַלַּיְלָה Gn 46² (E), מַרְאוֹת אֱלֹהִים Ez 1¹ 8³ 40².

†II. [מַרְאָה] **n.f. mirror** (so Vrss; as *place*, or *instrument, of seeing* (oneself));—pl. cstr. מַרְאֹת הַצֹּבְאֹת Ex 38⁸ (P) *the mirrors of the serving-women* (v. Di).

מַרְאֶה ₁₀₂ **n.m.** ^Ex 3, 3^ **sight, appearance, vision**;—'מ abs. Gn 12¹¹+; cstr. מַרְאֵה Dt 28³⁴+; sf. מַרְאֵהוּ Jo 2⁴+, מַרְאֶהָ Lv 13⁴+; appar. pl. cstr. מַרְאֵי Ec 11⁹ (Kö^ii. 1. 112^), sf. (prob. in fact sg. Ges ⁹³ˢˢ) מַרְאֵיךְ Ct 2¹⁴·¹⁴, מַרְאֵיהֶן Na 2⁵+, etc.;—**1.** †**a.** *sight, phenomenon, spectacle* Ex 3³ (J). **b.** *appearance* 'נֶחְמָד לְמ Gn 2⁹ (J) *desirable in appearance*, 'גָּדוֹל לְמ Jos 22¹⁰; *appearance* of man (or woman), Ju 13⁶·⁶ (angel), Is 52¹⁴ (servant of 'י), Ct 5¹⁵ Dn 8¹⁵ 10¹⁸; = outward person (opp. inner man) 1 S 16⁷; visible form Ct 2¹⁴·¹⁴ Dn 1¹³·¹³·¹⁵; 'בְּמ Nu 12⁸ (E; so rd. Sam 𝔊 𝔖 𝔗 Di, for MT וּמַרְאֶה), i.e. in personal presence (< Ew Pat^Hpt^ (לֹא בְמ'); כְּמַרְאֵה סוּסִים מַרְאֵהוּ Jo 2⁴; of crocod. Jb 41²; 'מ' כְּבוֹד י Ex 24¹⁷ (P), 'מ' הַנֶּגַע Lv 13³, מ'־אֵשׁ Nu 9¹⁵·¹⁶, מ' בָּרָק Dn 10⁶+; esp. Ez *appearance* pers. vel rei (27 t., sts. redundant), 1⁵·¹³·²⁶ 8² 10¹+, מִמַּ' מָתְנָיו 1²⁷·²⁷ 8² (‖ מִמַּתְנָיו); of beauty וִיפֵה מַרְאֶה *fair of appearance* Gn 39⁶ (J; + יְפֵה־תֹאַר), cf. 1 S 17⁴² (rd. עֶלֶם [q.v.] for עִם); fem. (אִשָּׁה) יְפַת־מ' Gn 12¹¹ (J), 29¹⁷ (E; יְפַת תֹּאַר+), 2 S 14²⁷; of kine יְפוֹת (ה)מ' Gn 41²·⁴ (E), opp. רָעוֹת (ה)מ' v³·⁴, רַע מַרְאֵיהֶן v²¹ (all E); of women also טֹבַת מ' Gn 24¹⁶ 26⁷ (both J), 2 S 11² Est 1¹¹ 2³·⁷, טוֹבוֹת מ' 2²; of boys טוֹבֵי מ' Dn 1⁴, cf. 'מ alone in לֹא־מ' וְנֶחְמְדֵהוּ (of suffering servant of 'י) Is 53²; אִישׁ מ' 2 S 23²¹ (but rd. as ‖ 1 Ch 11²³ אִישׁ מִדָּה We Dr al.). †**c.** *appearance, sight, vision* Nu 8⁴ (P). †**2.** in gen. *what is seen*, מ' עֵינָיו Is 11³ i.e. what his outward eyes see (cf. 1 S 16⁷ **1 b**), לְמ' עֵינֶיהָ Ez 23¹⁶, מ' עֵינֶיךָ אֲשֶׁר תִּרְאֶה Dt 28³⁴·⁶⁷, לְכָל־מ' עֵינֵי הַכֹּהֵן Lv 13¹² (P). †**3.** specif. *a* (supernat.) *vision* (in Ez Dn; oft. acc. cogn. c. ראה): Ez 8⁴ 11²⁴ 43³·³·³, rd. also מַרְאֵה הָרֶכֶב v³ (for מַרְאוֹת v. I. מַרְאָה supr.); 'בַּמ 11²⁴; Dn 8¹⁶·²⁷ 9²³ 10¹; 'מ הָעֶרֶב וְהַבֹּקֶר 8²⁶. †**4.** *sight, vision* = power of seeing (and enjoying), late: מ' עֵינַיִם Ec 6⁹, הַלֵּךְ בְּדַרְכֵי לִבְּךָ וּבְמַרְאֵי עֵינֶיךָ 11⁹.

†**יְרִאִיָּיה n.pr.m.** (rd. יְרִאִיָּה; 'י *seeth*);—officer, Jeremiah's time, Je 37¹³·¹⁴, Σαρουια(ς).

†**רְאָיָה n.pr.m.** ('י *hath seen*);—**1.** Judaite 1 Ch 4² (Ραδα, A Ρεια, 𝔊L Ρεαα), = III. הָרֹאֶה 2⁵² (crpt.; Αιω, A Αραα). **2.** Reubenite 1 Ch 5⁵, Ρηχα, 𝔊L Ραια. **3.** post-ex. name Ezr 2⁴⁷ (Ρεηλ, A 𝔊L Ραια) = Ne 7⁵⁰ (Ραια, A 𝔊L Ρααια).

רְאוּבֵן 71 **n.pr.m.** **Reuben**, Ρουβην[ιν] (*behold a son!* but Gn 29[32] makes = רָאָה בְּעָנְיִי(!); Jos Ant. i. 19, 7 al. Ρουβηλος, 𝔖 ܪܘܒܝܠ, ר׳ then perh. = Ar. رِئْبَال, *lion*, cf. Di);—**1.** eldest son of Jacob and Leah Gn 29[32] 30[14] + 11 t. Gn, Ex 1[2] 1 Ch 2[1]; as head of family or clan Ex 6[14.14] Nu 1[20] 26[5] (all P), 1 Ch 5[1.3], cf. בְּנֵי אֱלִיאָב בֶּן־רְא׳ Dt 11[6]. **2.** as name of clan or tribe Ju 5[15.16] Dt 27[13] Jos 18[7] (+ גָּד; both D), Dt 33[6] (poem), Ez 48[6.7.31] Nu 1[5] (P); so מַטֵּה ר׳ Nu 1[21] 13[4] Jos 20[8] 21[7] (all P), 1 Ch 6[48.63], מַחֲנֵה ר׳ Nu 2[10.16] 10[18] (all P); בְּנֵי ר׳, as tribe, Nu 16[1b] 32[37] (both JE), 2[10] 7[30] 26[5] Jos 13[23.23] (all P), also (+ Gad and oft. Manasseh) Nu 32[1.2.6.25] (JE), Jos 4[12] (D), Nu 32[29.31.33] Jos 22[9] + 11 t. 22 (all P), cf. 1 Ch 5[18]; בֶּן־ר׳ as tribe Jos 15[6] 18[7] (both P), מַטֵּה בְנֵי־ר׳ 13[15] (P).

†**רְאוּבֵנִי** **adj. gent.** of foreg.; of individ. 1 Ch 11[42a]; c. art. as subst. coll. הָרְאוּבֵנִי Nu 26[7] 34[14] (both P), Jos 13[8] (D; + הַגָּדִי), 2 K 10[33] (+ *id.* + הַמְנַשִּׁי), 1 Ch 12[38] (van d. H. v[37]; + הַגָּדִי + חֲצִי שֵׁבֶט מְנַשֶּׁה), 26[32] (*id.*); לָרְאוּבֵנִי 1 Ch 5[6] 27[16], + וְלַגָּדִי + (+ sts. חֲצִי שֵׁבֶט מ׳) Dt 3[12.16] 29[7] Jos 1[12] 12[6] 22[1] (all D), 1 Ch 5[26], cf. Dt 4[43].

רְאִית, רְאָיָה, רְאִי, רֳאִי, ראות v. ראה.

רְאֵים v. רְאֵם. **ראישׁון** v. רִאשׁוֹן.

†**[רָאַם]** **vb.** (Mass Thes al.) **rise** (si vera l., ‖ form of רום);—**Qal** *Pf.* 3 fs. רָאֲמָה Zc 14[10], but < rd. רָאמָה = רָמָה (√ רום), Ges §72p.

†**רְאֵם** **n.m.** Jb 39, 10 **wild ox** (As. *rêmu* Dl HWB 603 (ראם), Houghton TSBA v (1877). 336 ff., and illustr. bef. p. 33 Schr KGF 135 ff., 530 Hom NS 257 ff., 410, 436 f. Dr Dt 33, 17; on strength and ferocity, Plin NH viii. 21; Aram. רְאֵמָא, רֵימָא, רֵימָנָא, ܪܐܡܐ (Lag BN 58); Ar. رِئْم is *white antelope*, antilope leucoryx; 𝔊 (erron.) μονοκέρως (Is 34[7] ἁδροί), 𝔙 *unicornis*, and (oftener) *rhinoceros*);—abs. ר׳ Nu 23[22] +, רֵים ψ 92[11], רְאֵים Jb 39[9.10]; pl. רְאֵמִים Is 34[7] ψ 29[6], רֵמִים 22[22] (v. Baer);—*wild ox*, as fierce and strong Jb 39[9.10]; sim. of strength of Isr., כְּתוֹעֲפֹת ר׳ לוֹ Nu 23[22] = 24[8] (JE), וַתָּרֶם כִּרְאֵים קַרְנִי ψ 92[11]; so fig. of Joseph, קַרְנֵי ר׳ קַרְנָיו Dt 33[17]; fig. of princes of Edom Is 34[7] (+ פָּרִים עִם אַבִּירִים); of powerful foes, מִקַּרְנֵי רֵמִים ψ 22[22]; in sim. of skipping, leaping, בֶּן־רְאֵמִים ψ 29[6] (‖ עֵגֶל).

†**רְאוּמָה** **n.pr.f.** concubine of Nahor Gn 22[24] (J); A Ρεηρα, 𝔊L Ρεημα.

†I. **רָאמוֹת** **n.[f.pl.]** usu. **corals** (so Ki; *black corals* Thes (פְּנִינִים = *red corals*); cf. Ar. رَأْمَة, *sea-shell*, We Held. 2. 153);—as costly Jb 28[18], as merchandise, רָאמֹת Ez 27[16];—רָאמוֹת לֶאֱוִיל חָכְמוֹת Pr 24[7], reading and sense dub., v. Toy.

II. **רָאמוֹת, רָאמַת, רְאֵמָה** v. רום, II. רמה.

רָאשׁ *poor*, **רֵאשׁ** *poverty*, v. רושׁ.

I. **רֹאשׁ** 599 **n.m.** Lv 13, 45 **head** (common Sem. word; earliest form *ra'š, Ar. رَأْس, Sab. ראס Prä ZMG xxix (1875). 425 Mordtm Him. Inschr. 31; Eth. ርእስ: Amh. ራስ: hence (*a* heightened) As. *rêšu* (rarely *râšu*), Aram. רֵישָׁא (Egypt. Aram. ראש Cooke North-Sem. Inscr. 404), ܪܫܐ, mod. (*Ma'lûla*) *raïša*, Huart JAs xii (1878). 491 Duval id. xiii (1879). 464; Palm. רשא, Lzb 366, cf. BH רִישׁוֹן, רֵאשִׁית; fr. *ra'š, also BH *רָאשׁ, ראשׁ (Lag Symm. i. 113), Tel Am. *rušu(nu)* Wkl 189, 18 (gloss to *kakkadunu*), NH = BH; SI[6] ראש, Ph. רש, ראש (in n.pr.), Pun. *rus* (in n.pr. loc.) Schröd Ph. Spr. 133, ראשת *choicest, chief;* on MI[20] (sf.) רשה, l.[28] [ר]ש, cf. Sm. u. So[14] Nö LCB Jan. 8, 1887, 60);—ר׳ abs. Gn 3[15] +, cstr. 40[20] +; sf. רֹאשִׁי v[16] +, etc.; pl. רָאשִׁים (for *רְאָשִׁים Nö GGA 1884, 1019) Ex 18[25] +; cstr. רָאשֵׁי Ho 7[13] + [מְרַאֲשֹׁתַי 1 S 26[12] v. מְרַאֲשׁוֹת infr.]; sf. רָאשֵׁינוּ 1 Ch 12[19], רָאשֵׁיכֶם Is 29[10] +, etc.;—**1. a.** (c. 230 t.) *head*, of human being; man Gn 40[16.17] + oft., לְר׳ גֶּבֶר Ju 5[30] *for the head of a man*, i.e. *for each man, per capita;* woman 2 K 9[30] Dt 21[12] Nu 5[18] Est 2[17]; boy 2 K 4[19.19] Gn 48[14.14] +; of ׳י, under fig. of armed man ψ 60[9] = 108[9]; of idol 1 S 5[4]; of gates, personif. ψ 24[7.9]. **b.** *head*, of animals: of serpent Gn 3[15], dog 2 S 3[8], ass 2 K 6[25], of הַחַיָּה in Ez 1[22] cf. v[22.26], of הַכְּרֻבִים 10[1] cf. v[11]; of sea-monsters, לִוְיָתָן Jb 40[31] ψ 74[14], תַּנִּינִים v[13]; esp. of animals for sacrifice Ex 12[9] 29[15.19] Lv 1[4.8.12.15] 3[2.8] + 18 t. P; in phr. ר׳ וְזָנָב Is 9[13] (fig. of noble and commoner) cf. v[14] 19[15], so (fig. of relative dignity, power, influence) Dt 28[13.44]. **2. a.** *top* (88 t.): of mt., הַר, Gn 8[5] Ex 19[20.20] 24[17] 34[2] + 34 t.; hill, גִּבְעָה, Ex 17[9.10] (E), 2 S 8[25]; ר׳ מְרוֹמִים Pr 8[2] + 1[21] Toy (for MT הֹמִיּוֹת), ר׳ גֵּיא שְׁמָנִים Is 28[1.4]; of rocks, צֻרִים, Nu 23[9] (JE), crag, סֶלַע, 2 Ch 25[12.12]; tower Gn 11[4] (J), stronghold Ju 6[26], ladder Gn 28[12] (E), tree 2 S 5[24] = 1 Ch 14[15], bough Is 17[6] cf. Ez 17[4.22], mast (?; חִבֵּל) Pr 23[34] (otherwise Toy); of ears of grain, שִׁבֹּלֶת Jb 24[24], of stone Gn 28[18] (E), bed, מִטָּה, 47[31] (J), throne, ר׳ עָגוֹל לְכִסֵּה 1 K 10[19], tabern., or its wall, Ex 26[24] = 36[29] (P); pillar (= capital) 1 K 7[16.17] + 13 t., מְכוֹנָה v[35.35], lampstand Zc 4[2.2], h.p.'s robe, מְעִיל, Ex 28[32] (P), ר׳ פִּנָּה ψ 118[22] *top of* (the)

corner, i.e most conspicuous stone (fig.); =*tip*, *end*, of staves 1 K 8^{8} = 2 Ch 5^{9}, of sceptre Est 5^{2}. **b.** *height* of stars Jb 22^{12} (‖ גֹּבַהּ שָׁמַיִם). **3.**$_{171}$ **a.** *head* = *chief* (man) Ju 10^{18} 11$^{8.9.11}$ Ex 18^{25} (E), Nu 1^{16} (P), Dt 1^{15} Ho 2^{2} Mi 3^{1} + oft; appar. combined with idea of *first* in a series 1 Ch 12^{10} (van d. H. v^{9}, series of 11); of God 2 Ch 13^{12}. †**b.** =*chief* (city) Jos 11^{10} (D), cf. (of city and king) Is 7$^{8.8.9.9}$. †**c.** *chief* nation Je 31^{7}. †**d.** =*chief* (place, position) 1 S 9^{22} 1 K 21$^{9.12}$ Dt 20^{9} 1 Ch 4^{42} (cf. also **5**). **e.** כֹּהֵן הָרֹאשׁ *chief priest* 2 K 25^{18} = Je 52^{24}, 2 Ch 19^{11} 24^{11} 26^{20}, הַכֹּהֵן ראשׁ 1 Ch 27^{5}, הַכּ׳ הָר׳ 2 Ch 31^{10} Ezr 7^{5}; ר׳ alone 2 Ch 24^{6}, רָאשֵׁי הַכֹּהֲנִים Ne 12^{7}. **f.** esp =*head* of a family (P Chr); רָאשֵׁי בֵית (rare ראשׁ) אֲבוֹתָ(ם) Ex 6^{14} Nu 7^{2} 17^{18} Jos 22^{14} 1 Ch 5^{24} 7$^{7.9}$; ר׳ לְבֵית אֲבֹתָיו Nu 1^{4}, cf 1 Ch v^{40}; ר׳ בֵּית הָאָבוֹת 5$^{15.24}$ 7^{2} 9^{13} 24^{4}; ר׳ אֻמּוֹת בֵּית־אָב Nu 25^{15}; ר׳ אֲבוֹת הָעֵדָה 31^{26} cf 32^{28} Jos 14^{1} 21^{1}; ר׳ אֲבוֹת הַלְוִיִּם Ex 6^{25} Jos 21^{1}; ר׳ (הָ)אָבוֹת לַלְוִיִּם 1 Ch 9$^{33.34}$ 15^{12}, cf Nu 36^{1} Jos 19^{51} 1 Ch 8$^{6.13}$ 23$^{9.24}$ + 10 t. Chr.; abs. ר׳ (הָ)אָבוֹת 1 Ch 8$^{10.28}$ 9^{9} 26^{32} 27^{1} 2 Ch 1^{2} + 8 t. Ezr Ne (Chr); ר׳ אֲבֹתֵיהֶם Ezr 8^{1}, רָאשִׁים לָאָבוֹת Ne 11^{13}; so also ר׳ alone 1 Ch 5$^{7.12}$ 7^{3} 8^{28} +; appar combined with idea of *first* in a series 23^{8} (series of 3), v^{11} (of 4), v^{19} (of 3), v^{20} (of 2). †**4. a.** *head*=*front*, leader's place Mi 2^{13} 2 Ch 20^{27}, cf. Am 6^{7}. **b.** of time, *beginning*, of night-watch Ju 7^{19} La 2^{19}, abs. מֵרֹאשׁ *from the beginning* Is 40^{21} 41$^{4.26}$ (‖ מִלְּפָנִים), 48^{16} Pr 8^{23} (‖ מֵעוֹלָם), Ec 3^{11} (‖ עַד־סוֹף), *first* of months Ex 12^{2} (‖ ראשׁוֹן), Nu 10^{10} 28^{11} (all P); בָּרֹאשׁ 1 Ch 16^{7} *at first*. **c.** of things, river-*heads* Gn 2^{10} (J); ר׳ עַפְרוֹת תֵּבֵל Pr 8^{26}. **5.** *chief, choicest, best*, of spices, (בשמ(ים, Ez 27^{22} Ex 30^{23} (P), Ct 4^{14}; ר׳ שִׂמְחָתִי ψ 137^{6} *the choicest of my joy* †**6.** *head*=*division* of army, *company, band*. Ju 7$^{16.20}$ 9$^{34.37.43.44.44}$ 1 S 11^{11} 13$^{17.17.18.18}$ Jb 1^{17}. **7.** =*sum*, esp. in phr. נָשָׂא אֶת־ר׳ בְּנֵי־יִשׂ׳ Ex 30^{12} *take the sum of, enumerate*, cf Nu 1$^{2.49}$ 4$^{2.22}$ 26^{2} 31$^{26.49}$; בראשׁוֹ Lv 5^{24} *in its sum*, i.e. in full, so Nu 5^{7} (all P); of י׳'s thoughts ψ 139^{17}; cf ראשׁ דְּבָרְךָ אֱמֶת 119^{160}. **8.** other phr are: נָשָׂא אֶת־ראשׁ פ׳ v נָשָׂא **Qal 1 b** (2), יָרוּם ראשִׁי עַל־אֹיְבַי ψ 27^{6}, י׳ מֵרִים ראשִׁי 3^{4} (ψ 110^{7} 140^{10} v רום); *shake the head*, v נוע **Hiph.**, cf. יָנִיד בראשׁוֹ Je 8^{16}, מנוד ראשׁ ψ 44^{15}; נָתַן דֶּרֶךְ בְּרֹאשׁ, i e. requite, v. נתן **Qal 2 b** ad fin, יָשׁוּב גְּמֻלְךָ בר׳ Ob^{15}, cf. ψ 7^{17} 1 K 2^{33} (sub דָּם **2 i**), and (c. עַל־ר׳) Est 9^{25}, השיב רָעָה בראשׁ Ju 9^{57} 1 S 25^{39} 1 K 2^{44}, cf. Jo 4$^{4.7}$; 1 K 2^{32} (sub דָּם **2 i**), cf. Ne 3^{36} (אֶל־ראשָׁם), v. also 2 S 3^{29} sub I חול **3**, see, further, דָּם **2 i**; Dn 1^{10} v. חוב **Pi.**

†[רֵאשָׁה] **n.f.** beginning-time, early time;—pl. sf רֵאשֹׁתֵיכֶם Ez 36^{11} (cf. ראשׁ **4 b**)

†רֹאשָׁה **n.f.** top;—appos. הָאֶבֶן הָר׳ Zc 4^{7} i e. the topmost stone.

ראשׁוֹן$_{182}$ **adj.** former, first, chief (*i* heightened fr. orig. *a*, v. √),—abs ר׳ Ho 2^{19} +, -שֹׁן Ex 12^{15} +, רִישׁוֹן Jb 8^{8}, cstr. רִאשׁוֹן Jb 15^{7} Qr (Kt ראישון, and so always Cod. Sam. Pent, v. Ko$^{\text{II. 1, 225 a}}$); f רִאשֹׁנָה Ju 20^{37} + (Jos 21^{10} Kt ראישנה, v. supr); mpl. ראשֹׁנים Ex 34^{1} +, fpl. רִאשֹׁנוֹת Is 41^{22} +, etc;—**1.** *former* **a.** in time, *former* of two Gn 25^{25} (J), 41^{20} (E), Dt 10$^{1.2.3.4.10}$ 24^{4}, cf. Ho 2^{9}, Lv 4^{21} 9^{15} (both P), Ju 20^{39} 2 K 1^{14} Hg 2$^{3.9}$ Ezr 3^{12} +, more gen. *former, previous*, Nu 21^{26} (JE), Mi 4^{8} 2 K 17$^{34.40}$ Zc 1^{4} 7$^{7.12}$ 8^{11} Ne 5^{15} Ec 1 7^{10} ψ 79^{8} +; כָּעֵת הָר׳ Is 8^{23}; דברי דויד הָר׳ †1 Ch 29^{29} *the doings of David, the former* and the latter (הָאַחֲרֹנִים), cf. †2 Ch 9^{29} 12^{15} 16^{11} 20^{34} 25^{26} 26^{22} 28^{26} 35^{27}; *early* days of harvest 2 S 21^{9}, ראשׁנים as subst, *former persons*, ancestors, men of old, Dt 19^{14} Lv 26^{45} (H), Ec 1^{11} (opp אַחֲרֹנִים); (הָ)ראשֹׁנוֹת as subst. the *former things*, i e past events Is 41^{22} 43$^{9.18}$ 46^{9} 48^{3}, earlier predictions 42^{9} **b.** loc, *foremost*, of two 2 S 18^{27}. **2.** *first*: **a.** in time, הַמַּכָּה הָר׳ 1 S 14^{14} *the first slaughter* (prelim. to general carnage); וְלֹא־הָיָה דְבָרִי ר׳ 2 S 19^{44} *was not my word first?* ר׳ in appos with pers subj †2 S 19^{21} I am come *as first*, cf perh. Is 41^{27} (ins. אָמַרְתִּי Ges De < read הִגַּדְתִּים for הִנֵּה הִנָּם, Che^{Hpt} Kit^{Di}), and הָר׳ Je 50^{17} (opp. הָאַחֲרוֹן), Is 43^{27}; ר׳ abs, *first* of mankind Jb 15^{17}; abs of י׳, *I* (am the) *first* Is 41^{4} (+ אֶת־אַחֲרֹנִים), + אַחֲרוֹן 44^{6} 48^{12}; abs. of time, מראשׁון Je 17^{12} *from the beginning*; esp *first* of a def. series (sts. opp אַחֲרוֹן), *first* day of feast Dt 16^{4} Ex 12$^{16.15.16}$ + 5 t. P (H), Ne 8^{18}; usu. *first* month (חֹדֶשׁ) Ex 40$^{2.17}$ Lv 23^{5} + 6 t. P, 1 Ch 12^{16} (van d. H. v^{15}) + 10 t. Ch Ezr, Est 3^{7} Dn 10^{4}, חֹדֶשׁ om Gn 8^{13} Ex 12$^{2.18}$ Nu 9^{5} (all P) Ez 29^{17} 30^{20} 45$^{18.21}$, so Jo 2^{23}, but rd. כְּבָרִאשׁוֹנָה (**3 a**) 𝔊 𝔖 We Now and Dr **b.** *first* in degree, *chief*: יַד הַשָּׂרִים ... ראשׁוֹנָה Ezr 9^{2} *the hand of the princes* . . has been *first* in this trespass; 1 Ch 18^{17} Dn 10^{13} (cf Est 1^{14} infr). †**3. a.** fem. c prep as adv. phr.. (1) of time, בָּרִאשֹׁנָה Gn 13^{4} (J), =*before, formerly*, so Jos 8$^{5.6}$ (JE), 2 S 7^{10} 20^{18} Je 7^{12} Is 52^{4}, לָר׳ =*before, formerly*, Gn 28^{19} (J), Ju 18^{29}; so כבָּר׳ *as formerly* Ju 20^{32} 1 K 13^{6} Is 1^{26} Je 33$^{7.11}$, = כָּר׳ Dt 9^{18} Dn 11^{29} (opp. כָּאַחֲרוֹנָה); בָּר׳ =*at first*, first of all, Dt 13^{10} 17^{7}

Nu 10[13] (P) Jos 8[33] (D), 1 K 17[13] 20[9] Zc 12[7] Pr 20[21] (opp. אַחֲרִיתָהּ), 1 Ch 11[6.6] 17[9] Ne 7[5]; לְמַבָּרִאשׁוֹנָה 1 Ch 15[13] (=לְמַה־בָּר׳) *for what was at first*, etc. (מָה **1 e**); (2) loc., בָּר׳, i.e. *at the head* of an army 1 K 20[17], a procession Nu 10[14] (P), cf. Is 60[9]. **b.** רִאשֹׁנָה alone as adv.: (1) of time, *first* Gn 38[28] (J), 1 K 18[25] Je 16[18] Lv 5[8] Nu 2[9] Jos 21[10] (all P), Is 65[7] (Ew De Che Di Du Skinner, >adj. Ges Hi Kn); (2) of place Gn 33[2] (J); (3) of degree, rank, Est 1[14].

† [רִאשֹׁנִי] **adj. first**;—fs. הַשָּׁנָה הָרִאשֹׁנִית Je 25[1] *the first year;* but rd. ־נָה, Gie Du Kö[ii. 1, 225].

רַאֲשׁוֹת 1 S 26[12] v. מְרַאֲשׁוֹת infr.

† רֵאשִׁית **n.f. beginning, chief** (for *רָאשִׁית Nö[GGA 1884, 1019], cf. Holz[Hex 465]; Syr. ܪܫܝܬܐ);—abs. ר׳ Dt 33[21] +, cstr. ר׳ Gn 10[10] +, רֵשִׁית Dt 11[12]; sf. רֵאשִׁיתוֹ Ec 7[8], רֵאשִׁתוֹ Jb 42[12], etc.;—**1. a.** *beginning*, of kingdom Gn 10[10] (J), year Dt 11[12], reign Je 26[1] 27[1] 28[1] 49[34]; =first phase, step, or element in course of events Is 46[10] (opp. אַחֲרִית); of a thing (דָּבָר) Ec 7[8] (opp. *id.*); of sin Mi 1[13], strife Pr 17[14], wisdom ψ 111[10], knowledge Pr 1[7]; *thy beginning* Jb 8[7] = thine early life, so *his beginning* 42[12] (both opp. אַחֲרִית); ר׳ before cl., בְּר׳ בָּרָא א׳ Gn 1[1] *in the beginning when God created* (>abs. *in the beginning God created*); ר׳ אוֹנִי 49[3] (poem) *beginning* (first product) *of my manly vigour* (‖ כֹּחִי, בְּכֹרִי), so Dt 21[17] ψ 78[51] (both ‖ בְּכוֹר), 105[36]; cf. ר׳ דַּרְכֵי אֵל Jb 40[19] (of hippopot.), ר׳ דַּרְכּוֹ Pr 8[22] (of wisdom); =first season (of a tree) Ho 9[10]; ר׳ גּוֹיִם Nu 24[20] (JE), *first, earliest, of nations.* **b.** *first* of fruits Ex 23[19] (E), 34[26] (JE), Dt 26[2.10] Ez 44[30a], of harvest Lv 23[10] (H), grain Dt 18[4] 2 Ch 31[5], dough Nu 15[20.21] (P), Ez 44[30b] Ne 10[38], wool Dt 18[4]; of כָּל־תְּבוּאָתֶךָ Pr 3[9]; Israel is ר׳ תְּבוּאָתֹה Je 2[3] (i.e. of י׳'s increase); ר׳ =*first-fruits* Lv 2[12] (P), Nu 18[12] (P), Ne 12[44]; ר׳ הָאָרֶץ Ez 48[14]. **2.** *first, chief,* Am 6[1]; ר׳ גְּבוּרָתָם Je 49[35] (of bows); so appar. ר׳ בְּנֵי עַמּוֹן Dn 11[41], i.e. the principal part of them (Buhl Marti conj. שְׁאֵרִית, after 𝔖); ר׳ מַשְׂאוֹתֵיכֶם Ez 20[40], i.e. your chief oblations; ר׳ שְׁמָנִים Am 6[6], i.e. choice oils; =choice part, of land Dt 33[21], offering 1 S 2[29], הַחֵרֶם 15[21]; abs. *chief thing* Pr 4[7] (of wisdom).

מָרֵשָׁה, מָרֵאשָׁה **n.pr.loc.** v. p. 601.

† [מְרַאֲשׁוֹת] **n.[f.]pl. denom. place at the head, head-place**;—only sf. מְרַאֲשֹׁתָיו as adv. *at his head-place* (of one lying down) Gn 28[11.18] (E), 1 S 19[13.16] 1 K 19[6]; so Qr 1 S 26[7.11.16] (Kt מראשתו); in v[12] read מִמְּרַאֲשֹׁתָיו 𝔊 We Dr HPS, for MT מְרַאֲשֹׁתֵי שָׁאוּל; מַרְאֲשׁוֹתֵיכֶם Je 13[18] (*head-tires* AV[m] RV), rd. מֵרָאשֵׁיכֶם, *from your heads,* 𝔊 𝔖 𝔙 Gie Buhl Co[Hpt] (cf., already, Thes).

† II. רֹאשׁ and (†Dt 32[32]) רוֹשׁ **n.m.**[Dt 32, 33] a bitter and poisonous herb, then **venom**, alw. fig.;—**1.** a bitter and poisonous herb, + (or ‖) לַעֲנָה Dt 29[17] La 3[19], so (מֵי רֹאשׁ) מֵי ר׳ Je 9[14] 23[15]; (without מֵי) 8[14]; עִנְּבֵי־רוֹשׁ Dt 32[32] (‖ מְרֹרֹת); ר׳ alone ψ 69[22]; וּפָרַח כָּרֹאשׁ La 3[5]; רֹאשׁ וּתְלָאָה Ho 10[4]; הֲפַכְתֶּם לְר׳ מִשְׁפָּט Am 6[12]. **2.** *venom*, of serpents, ר׳ פְּתָנִים Dt 32[33] Jb 20[16].

† III. רֹאשׁ **n.m.** son of Benj.;—Gn 46[21], *Pws.*

† IV. רֹאשׁ **n.pr.gent. Rôsh** (so 𝔊 and most; >*chief* Ew Sm al. (𝔙 *principem capitis Mosoch*);—only in phr. גּוֹג (אֶרֶץ מָגוֹג) נְשִׂיא רֹאשׁ מֶשֶׁךְ וְתֻבָל Ez 38[2.3] 39[1], *Pws*; not identified.

I, II. רַב, רֹב v. I. רבב. III. רַב v. II. רבב.

רָב v. ריב.

† I. [רָבַב] **vb. be or become, many, much** (NH רַב esp. *lord, master,* רַבִּי *my master, teacher;* MI[5] adj. pl. רבן; Ph. רב, f. רבת; As. [*rabâbu*], *rabbu;* Ar. رَبَّ *rear, increase* (act.; رُبّ *thick juice,* cf. NH רְבָב *grease,* is thought by Buhl al. to indicate original mng. *be thick*), رَبّ *lord, owner, master;* Sab. רב esp. in n.pr., רבאל, רבשמסם, רבבם, etc., CIS[iv. nos. 285, 3; 286, 1; 287, 12], etc.; Liḥy. רבה *its lord* DHM[Epigr. Denkm. Ar. 232]; Eth. ረበበ: *expand, spread* (intrans.); Aram. רַב, ܪܒ *great, chief,* so OAram. Nab. Palm. רב, Lzb[366] Cook[107]);—**Qal** *Pf.* 3 fs. consec. וְרַבָּה Ex 23[29] Is 6[12], רַבָּה Gn 18[20] (Ho 9[7] rd. וְרַב הַמַּשְׂטֵמָה for MT וְרַבָּה מ׳ 𝔊 We Now); elsewh. only 3 pl. רַבּוּ 1 S 25[10] +, רָבּוּ Je 46[23] + 2 t. [other forms supplied by רבה q.v.]; *Inf. cstr.* רֹב Gn 6[1] Jos 9[13] Lv 25[16] רֹב (‖ מְעֹט), sf. רֻבְּכֶם Dt 7[7], and perh. רֻבָּם Ho 4[7] (cf. infr.);—**1.** *be* (*become*) *many,* pers. Gn 6[1] (J) Ex 23[29] (E; v. supr.), 1 S 25[10] Ho 4[7] (perh.), Is 66[16] ψ 3[2] 25[19] 38[20] Ec 5[10], + מִן comp. Je 46[23] Dt 7[7] ψ 69[5]; of things Is 22[9] ψ 4[8] 104[24], years Lv 25[16] (P), sins Je 5[6] 14[7] Is 59[12] Jb 35[6]. **2.** *become great,* Gn 18[20] (J), Is 6[12]; *be long,* of journey, Jos 9[13].—**Pu.** v. [רָבַב] **denom.**

I. רַב[429] **adj. much, many, great**;—ms. abs. ר׳ Gn 24[25] +, רָב Gn 33[9] +, also רָב 2 Ch 20[2], רָב 28[8], רָב Ezr 10[13], etc.; cstr. רַב Ex 34[6] +; fs. רַבָּה Nu 11[33] +; cstr. רַבַּת Ez 22[5] +, רַבָּתִי (Ges[§ 90 k 1]) La 1[1.1]; mpl. abs. רַבִּים Ex 23[2.2] +, cstr. v. II. רַב;

fpl. abs. רַבּוֹת Gn 30^{43}+;—[often both as pred. and as attrib.; as attrib. preceding n. (infl. of usage for numerals? Kö $^{Synt. §334a}$ Ges ^{§132b}): רַב Is 63^{7} ψ 145^{7} (but read prob. רָב־, רֹב; in Is 21^{7} ר׳ is pred.), רַבִּים Je 16^{16} ψ 32^{10} 89^{51} (on context Bö ^{NÄ} Bae, also Hup), Pr 7^{26} 1 Ch 28^{5}, רַבּוֹת Ne 9^{28} Pr 31^{29}];—**1.** (oft. opp. מְעַט) **a.** (1) *much:* of substances, gold 1 K 10^{2} ψ 19^{11}, silver (money) 2 K 12^{11} = 2 Ch 24^{11}, bronze 1 Ch 18^{8}, wine Est 1^{7}; of other quantities, e.g. spoil 2 S 3^{22}, property 2 Ch 32^{29}, seed Dt 28^{38}, etc.; רַב שֶׁיִּהְיוּ Ec 6^{3b} *be it much that* his days *amount to;* (2) esp. of collectives, *numerous,* עַם־רַב Jos 11^{4} 2 S 13^{34}, עֲבֻדָּה רַבָּה Gn 26^{14} Jb 1^{3}, מִקְנֶה רַב Dt 3^{19}+, etc. **b.** pl. *many:* pers. Ex 5^{5} Ju 8^{30} 9^{40} 1 K 4^{20} 11^{1}+, things Gn 30^{43} Am 5^{12} Dt 31^{17}+; n. om. רַבּוֹת Dn 11^{41} (sc. lands; rd. רִבֹּת *myriads* Kmp Bev Behrm Marti Prince); יָמִים רַבִּים *many days* (a long time) Gn 21^{34} 37^{34}+28 t., שָׁנִים רַבּוֹת Ne 9^{30} Ec 6^{3a}, אִם עוֹד רַבּוֹת בַּשָּׁנִים Lv 25^{51}; רַבּוֹת פְּעָמִים Ne 9^{28} *many times* (v. supr.) = עִתִּים רַבּוֹת ψ 106^{43} Ec 7^{22}; מַכָּה רַבָּה Dt 25^{3} *many blows;* מַיִם רַבִּים *many waters* Nu 20^{11} 24^{7}+27 t., cf. Is 8^{7}; etc. **c.** רַב as subst. coll. pers. Ex 19^{21}, also (opp. מְעַט) 1 S 14^{6} Nu 13^{18} $26^{54.56}$ 33^{54} 35^{8}; so רַבַּת (Ges ^{§130a}) 2 Ch $30^{17.18}$, and (rei; = *much*) Ez 24^{12}; רַב cstr. before abstr. (= רֹב) Is 21^{7} 63^{7} ψ 145^{7}; esp. pl. רַבִּים of pers. Ex $23^{2.2}$+37 t. +בַּת־רַבִּים Ct 7^{5} (v. p. 123). †**d.** cstr. = *abounding in,* רַב־בְּרָכוֹת Pr 28^{20}, רַב־חֶסֶד (v. חֶסֶד **3**), רַב־כֹּחַ ψ 147^{5}, רַב־מַאֲרוֹת Pr 28^{27}, רַב־נוֹצָה Je 32^{19}, רַב־הָעֲלִילִיָּה 17^{7}, הַמְּהוּמָה Ez 22^{5}, רַב־פְּעָלִים 2 S 23^{20} = 1 Ch 11^{22}, רַב־פָּשַׁע Pr 29^{22}, רַב־תְּבוּנָה 14^{29}; רַבַּת אוֹצָרֹת Je 51^{13}, רַבַּת בָּנִים 1 S 2^{5}, רַבָּתִי עָם La 1^{1} (Ges ^{§90l}). †**e.** +מִן comp. = *more numerous than* Ex 1^{9} Nu 22^{15} Jos 10^{11} Ju 16^{30} 2 K 6^{16} Is 54^{1} 1 Ch 24^{4} 2 Ch 32^{7} Dn 11^{13}; sq. inf., *too many to* Gn 36^{7} Ju 7^{2} (cf. v^{4}); vid. also foll. †**f.** רַב = *abundant, enough* Gn 24^{25} 33^{9}; as exclam. *enough!* Gn 45^{28} 2 S 24^{16} = 1 Ch 21^{15}, 1 K 19^{4}, so (+מִן inf.) Ex 9^{28} (מִן **6 d**); רַב־לָךְ (with implication of excess) Dt 3^{26} (let it) *suffice thee!* so רַב־לָכֶם Ez 45^{9}, also Nu $16^{3.7}$ = ye assume too much! +inf. *it is enough for you to* Dt 1^{6} 2^{3} (i.e. you have done it enough), so +מִן inf. 1 K 12^{28}, מִן subst. Ez 44^{6}. †**g.** as adv. *much, exceedingly* (only ψψ), רַב ψ 123^{3}, רָב ψ 18^{15} (Hup De Che al.; HPS $^{2 S 22.15}$ conj. רָמָה; om. ‖ 2 S 22^{15}); רַבָּה ψ 62^{3} 78^{15} 89^{8} (𝔊 Bae רַב הוּא); רַבַּת (Aramaism, cf. Syr. ܪܰܒܳܐܺܝܬ, ܪܰܒܰܬ, Nö ^{§155A} W $^{SG 135}$) ψ 65^{10} 120^{6} (= long enough), 123^{4} $129^{1.2}$. **2.** less oft. *great:* **a.** of space 1 S 26^{13}, the deep Am 7^{4} Gn 7^{11} Is 51^{10} ψ 36^{7} (fig.), city La 1^{1} (רַבָּתִי בַגּוֹיִם Ges ^{§90l}),—v. also צִידוֹן, חֲמָת;—plague Nu 11^{33}, empire Est 1^{20}, goodness ψ 31^{20}, wickedness Gn 6^{5}, etc. **b.** specif. *strong* (opp. אֵין כֹּחַ) 2 Ch 14^{10}; רַב לְהוֹשִׁיעַ Is 63^{1}; so רַבִּים as subst. Is 53^{12} (‖ עֲצוּמִים). †**c.** *major natu* Gn 25^{23} (opp. צָעִיר); רַבִּים as subst. *grandævi,* Jb 32^{9}. †**d.** +מִן comp. *greater than* Dt $7^{1.17}$ 9^{14} 20^{1}; *too great for* Jos 19^{9} 1 K 19^{7}.—Pr 26^{10} is hopelessly corrupt, v. Toy.

II. רַב $_{49}$ **n.m. chief** (As.-Bab. influence, cf. *rab* Dl $^{HWB 609b}$; BAram. רַב);—cstr. ר׳ Je 39^{9}+; pl. cstr. רַבֵּי 39^{13} 41^{1} (but v. infr.);—esp. רַב־טַבָּחִים *chief of guardsmen* (v. טַבָּח), only as title of Bab. officer Je $39^{9.10}$+15 t. Je, 7 t. ‖ 2 K 25 (cf. שַׂר הַטּ׳ in Gn [JE]); also †רַב הַחֹבֵל Jon 1^{6} *chief of the sailors,* i.e. captain; †in gen. כָּל־רַב בֵּיתוֹ Est 1^{8}, †רַב־סָרִיסָיו Dn 1^{3} (v. סָרִיס), and so רַבֵּי מֶלֶךְ בָּבֶל Je 39^{13}, רַבֵּי הַמֶּלֶךְ 41^{1} (late gloss; om. 𝔊 and ‖ 2 K 25^{25}, so Hi Gf Gie). †The foll. titles of As.-Bab. officers are prob. loan-words in Heb.: רַב־מָג Je $39^{3.13}$ usu. *chief soothsayer* (v. מָג), but = *rab-mugi* [? *chief of princes*] Pinches $^{Hast. DB. Rab-mag}$; רַב־סָרִיס (cf. OAram. [Nineveh] רב סרס Lzb ^{366}), 2 K 18^{17} (As.; not in ‖ Is 36^{2}), Je $39^{3.13}$ (Bab.), usu. *chief eunuch,* but = *rabû-ša-rêši, chief of the heads* (the principal men) Wkl $^{Unters. z. altor. Gesch., 1889, Excurs. v, p. 138}$ (actually found as *rubû-ša-ri-ešu* Pinches $^{Acad. June 25, 1892, 618}$), Pinches $^{Hast. DB. Rab-saris}$; רַב־שָׁקֵה (van d. H. רַבְשָׁקֵה) *chief of the officers* (?) (so prob. As. *rab-ŠAḲ; šaḳû = high one;* COT $^{2 K 18.17}$ KB $^{ii. 23}$ Dl $^{HWB 685a}$ Tiele $^{Bab.-As. Gesch. 497.513}$ Pinches $^{Hast. DB. iv. 191}$), 2 K $18^{17.19.26.27.28.37}$ $19^{4.8}$ = Is $36^{2.4.11.12.13.22}$ $37^{4.8}$.

†רַבָּה **n.pr.loc. Rabba** (prop. *great* or *populous,* sc. city);—**1.** capital of Ammonites: explicitly, רַבַּת בְּנֵי עַמּוֹן 2 S $12^{26.27}$ 17^{27} Dt 3^{11} Je 49^{2} Ez 21^{25}; רַבָּה alone 2 S 11^{1} ‖ 1 Ch $20^{1.1}$, Am 1^{14} Je 49^{3} Ez 25^{5} Jos 13^{25} (P); c. ה loc. רַבָּתָה 2 S 12^{29}; in Gk. period *Philadelphia,* Lag $^{Onom. 215, 94; 219, 82}$ (but Ραββαταμανα Polyb $^{v. 71. 4}$), mod. *'Ammân,* 13½ m. NE. from Heshbon, 28½ m. E. of Jordan; cf. Buhl $^{Geogr. 260}$;—𝔊 Ραββαθ, Ραββα. **2.** הָרַבָּה, city in Judah Jos 15^{60} (P), site unknown;—𝔊 Σωθηβα, A 𝔊L Αρεββα.

רֹב $_{151}$ **n.m.** $^{Jb 11.2}$ **multitude, abundance, greatness;**—abs. ר׳ Gn 16^{10}+, רוֹב 1 Ch 4^{38} 2 Ch 31^{10}+ Jb 33^{19} Qr (Kt רִיב); cstr. רֹב Ex 15^{7} +(רֹב־ Jb 37^{23} Baer Gi), רָב־ Jb 23^{6}+; 2 K 19^{23} and pl. cstr. רֻבֵּי Ho 8^{12} v. infr.;—**1.** *multitude*

(c. 125 t.): of pers. Ho 10^{13} Pr 14^{28} 20^{6} Est 10^{3}+; of things Is 1^{11} 47^{12} Ez 27^{18} Lv 27^{16} Pr 10^{19} Jb 11^{2}+; = *great quantity, abundance* Gn 27^{28} Ho 9^{7} + oft. (2 K 19^{23} Qr [= Is 37^{24} Kt], > Kt רכב; 2 Ch 24^{27} Kt ורב, > Qr יִרֶב), + (of time) רֹב שָׁנִים Jb 32^{7} (Gi; v^{7} van d. H., Baer), בְּרֹב יָמִים Ec 11^{1}; = *whole number* (of bones) Jb 4^{14} 33^{19} (Qr; Kt ריב); esp. לָרֹב *in respect of, for, multitude,* in sim., like sand, stars, etc., Jos 11^{4} (JE), 1 S 13^{5} 2 S 17^{11} + 10 t.; = *abundantly,* c. vb. (= הַרְבֵּה) Gn 30^{30} (J), 48^{16} (E), 1 K $1^{19.25}$ 10^{10}; usu. late Ne 9^{25} Jb 26^{3} Zc 14^{14} 1 Ch 4^{30} 2 Ch 9^{9} (‖ הַרְבֵּה 1 K 10^{10}) + 23 t. Ch; as pred. c. הָיָה 1 Ch 22^{14}; = *in great numbers,* 2 Ch $30^{5.24}$; nearly = adj. (c. subst.; = רַב) 9^{1} (‖ רַב 1 K 10^{2}), 16^{8} 24^{24} 30^{13}; מֵרֹב *from multitude of,* Dt 7^{7} 28^{47} + 14 t.; abs. *from (for) mult.* 1 K 7^{47}, Gn 16^{10} 32^{13} (J), 1 K 3^{8} 8^{5} = 2 Ch 5^{6}. **2.** *greatness* (c. 26 t.): רֹב חַסְדֶּךָ Ne 13^{22} ψ 5^{8} 69^{14}, cf. 106^{45}, מֵר׳ שִׂיחִי 1 S 1^{16}, ר׳ כֹּחַ Is 63^{1} Jb 23^{6} 30^{18} ψ 33^{16}, etc.; read רֹב prob. also (for רַב) Is 63^{7} ψ 145^{7}; = *length* of journey (cf. vb. Jos 9^{13}) בְּרֹב דַּרְכֵּךְ Is 57^{10}; Ho 8^{12} Qr רֻבֵּי תּוֹרָתִי = *greatnesses* [great things], or *numerous things,* of my law, but form dubious, read perhaps רֹב תּוֹרָתִי (sub **1**), so We (cf. 𝔊); Gr al. דְּבָרַי; > Kt רבו, v. רִבּוֹ.—Lv 25^{16} Dt 7^{7} Ho 4^{7}, v. √.

†רְבָבָה **n. f.** **multitude, myriad, ten thousand** (Kö $^{ii. 1, 221}$);—abs. ר׳ Gn 24^{60}+; sf. רִבְבָתוֹ Kt 1 S 18^{7} + 2 t. (Qr רִבְבֹתָיו); pl. abs. רְבָבוֹת 1 S 18^{8}; cstr. רִבְבוֹת Mi 6^{7}+, רְבָבוֹת Dt 33^{17}; sf. v. supr. Qr;—*myriad,* 10,000: of great number of pers., indef. Gn 24^{60} (J; אַלְפֵי רְבָבָה *thousands of myriads*), Dt 33^{2} (poem; מֵרִבְבֹת קֹדֶשׁ, but v. קֹדֶשׁ, ad fin.), ψ 3^{7} Ct 5^{10}; רִבְבוֹת אַלְפֵי יִשׂ׳ Nu 10^{36}, cf. Dt 33^{17} (poem);—רְבָבָה Ez 16^{7} rd. רֹבִי 𝔊 Co Berthol Krae;—more precisely: (100, 1000), 10,000, Ju 20^{10}; opp. 2, Dt 32^{30} (poem), opp. 100, Lv 26^{8} (H), opp. 1000, 1 S $18^{7.8}$ 21^{12} 29^{5} ψ 91^{7}; so of things, Mi 6^{7}.

†רִבּוֹ, רִבּוֹא **n. f.** $^{Ezr 2, 64}$ **ten thousand, myriad** (later (Aramaizing) synonym of foregoing; perh. for Aram. רִבּוֹ(ת), Kö $^{ii. 1, 221 f.}$, but Palm. רבו Lzb ^{367});—abs. רִבּוֹ 1 Ch $29^{7.7}$ Jon 4^{11} (? cstr.), + cstr. Ho 8^{12} Kt (v. infr.); רִבּוֹא Ezr 2^{64} = Ne 7^{66}, Ne 7^{71} (van d. H. v^{72}); du. רִבֹּתַיִם ψ 68^{18}; pl. רִבּוֹת Ne 7^{70} (van d. H. v^{71}), רִבֹּאוֹת Ezr 2^{69} Dn 11^{12};—*ten thousand;* of pers., 4 × 10,000 + 2000 + 3 × 100 + 60 Ezr 2^{64} = Ne 7^{66}; 12 × 10,000 + n. Jon 4^{11}; indef. Dn 11^{12} *he shall cast down myriads;* rd. רִבּוֹת also v^{41} (for MT רַבּוֹת) Kmp Bev Behrm Marti Prince; of things, esp. units of value, n. + 10,000 1 Ch 29^{7}, n. + 6 × 10,000 + 1000 Ezr 2^{69} ‖ n. + 2 × 10,000 Ne $7^{70.71}$ (v. supr.); 10,000 + 8 × 1000 + n. 1 Ch 29^{7}; indef. רֶכֶב אֱלֹהִים רִבֹּתַיִם ψ 68^{18} (‖ אלפים);—רִבּוֹ תּוֹרָתִי Ho 8^{12} (Kt; 10,000 [precepts] *of my instruction*) would be only early instance, v. רֹב.

†רַבִּית **n. pr. loc.** in Issachar;—הָר׳ Jos 19^{20}; mod. *Râbâ,* c. 13 m. NE. from Nablûs, cf. Buhl $^{Geogr. 204}$;—𝔊 Δαβειρων, A 𝔊L Ραββωθ.

†רְבִיבִים **n. m.** $^{Je 3, 3}$ **pl. copious showers,** causing fertility;—ר׳ Dt 32^{2} + 3 t., רְבִבִים Je 14^{22}, רְבִבִם 3^{3};—*copious showers,* Je 3^{3} (+ מַלְקוֹשׁ), 14^{22} (‖ מְנַשְּׁמִים), ר׳ ψ 65^{11}; sim., of penetrating, pervasive infl. of prophetic words Dt 32^{2} (‖ שְׂעִירִם, also מָטָר, טַל), of Jacob Mi 5^{6} (‖ טַל), of future king ψ 72^{6} (‖ מָטָר).

יָרָבְעָם $_{104}$ **n. pr. m.** **Jeroboam,** Ιεροβοαμ (prob. = יָרֹב + עָם *the people increaseth* Thes Kit $^{1 K 11, 26}$ al.; cf. also Gray $^{Prop. N. 59; Ency. Bib. i. 139 f.}$; > √ ריב *the people contendeth,* or (*the god*) *'Amm contendeth* Nbr $^{Stud. Bib. i. 225}$, cf. Che $^{JQ. July, 1899, 559; Ency. Bib.}$);—**1.** $_{90}$ (K Ch), leader of revolt of N. Isr. (10th cent.), and first king 1 K 11^{26} $12^{2.2.20}$, etc., ‖ 2 Ch $10^{2.2.3.12}$, etc., 1 K $13^{1.4.33}$+; (specif. יר׳ בֶּן־נְבָט 1 K 11^{26} + 23 t.); in later times (under Deut. infl.) as sinful and author of Isr.'s sin 1 K 15^{30} $16^{2.7.19.26.31}$ + 15 t. †**2.** son of Jehoash of N. Isr. (8th cent.) and 13th king 2 K 13^{13} $14^{16.23.27.28.29}$ $15^{1.8}$ Ho 1^{1} Am 1^{1} $7^{9.10.11}$; prob. also 1 Ch 5^{17}.

†II. [רָבַב] **vb. shoot;**—**Qal** *Pf.* 3 pl. וָרֹבּוּ (Ges $^{§ 67 m}$) Gn 49^{23} abs. (בַּעֲלֵי חִצִּים in ‖ l.; Sam. וַיְרִיבֻהוּ, so perh. 𝔊 ἐλοιδόρουν).—רָב חִצָּיו ψ 18^{15} (in ‖ l.), v. I. רַב **1 g.**

†III. [רַב] **n. m. archer;**—pl. רַבִּים Je 50^{29} (‖ דֹּרְכֵי קֶשֶׁת; Gie רֹבִים, II. רבה), sf. רַבָּיו Jb 16^{13} (in fig.; Bö al. רֹבָיו; Vrss. Ew al. *his missiles*).

I. רבד (√ of foll.; cf. Ar. رَبَدَ *confine, tie.*)

†רָבִיד **n. [m.]** **chain, ornament for neck;**—abs. ר׳ Ez 16^{11}; cstr. רְבִד הַזָּהָב Gn 41^{42} (E).

†II. [רָבַד] **vb. be-spread, deck** (cf. Ar. رَبَدَ v. *shew patches of colour, become clouded* (of sky); NH רֹבֶד *pavement, paved terrace,* 𝔗 רוּבְדָא *pavement*);—**Qal** *Pf.* 1 s. מַרְבַדִּים רָבַדְתִּי עַרְשִׂי Pr 7^{16} *with spreads* (coverlets) *have I bespread my couch;* read also *Impf.* 3 ms. וַיִּרְבְּדוּ לְשָׁאוּל 1 S 9^{25} 𝔊 Th We Dr al. (for MT וַיְדַבֵּר עִם שׁ׳), obj. om.

†[מַרְבָד]† **n.[m.] spread, coverlet**,—only pl. abs. מַרְבַדִּים (Ko$^{ii. 1, 97, 471}$) Pr 7^{16} 31^{22}.

I [רָבָה]$_{225}$ **vb. be, or become, much, many, great** (NH *id.*; As. *rabû, be great, grow*, Ar رَبَا, Aram רְבָא, ܪܒܳܐ, all *grow, increase*),—†**Qal**$_{59}$ *Pf.* 3 fs רָבְתָה 1 S 14^{30}, 2 ms. וְרָבִיתָ consec. Dt 30^{16}; 3 pl רָבוּ Ezr 9^{6}+, etc.; *Impf.* 3 ms יִרְבֶּה Dt 8^{13}+, juss יֶרֶב Gn 1^{22}+ 2 Ch 24^{27} Qr (<ורב Kt, v רב 1), וַיִּרֶב Ex 1^{20}, 3 fs. תִּרְבֶּה Dt 7^{22} Dn 12^{4}, וַתֵּרֶב Gn 43^{34} 1 K 5^{10}; 3 mpl. יִרְבּוּ Dt 11^{21}+, יִרְבְּיוּן ψ 139^{18}, יִרְבְּיֻן Dt 8^{13}, etc, *Imv* ms ורבה Gn 35^{11}, *Inf. cstr.* רבות Ex 11^{9}+;—*Pt.* רֹבֶה v. II רבה;—**1.** *become many, numerous*. **a.** of a people, Ex $1^{10\ 12}$ (J), v^{20} (E), Dt 6^{3} 8^{1} 30^{16} Zc 10^{8} 1 Ch 5^{23}; רָבוּ לְמָעְלָה 23^{17}, esp + פרה *be fruitful and multiply* Je 3^{16} 23^{3} (fig of flock), Gn $47^{27\,b}$ (P), Ex 1^{7} (P), ψ 107^{38}, also (of man and beast) Ez 36^{11}, of children Jb 27^{14}, ברבות צ׳ צדיקים Pr 28^{28}, Pr 29^{2} (Toy רדות *rule*, ‖ משל), בר׳ רשׁעים v^{16} (Toy *id.*) **b.** of animals Dt 7^{22} (+ עַל pers.), 8^{13} 1 Ch 5^{9}; + פרה Gn 1^{22} 8^{17} (both P; cf Ez 36^{11} supr) **c.** of things Dt $8^{13.13}$ Ez 31^{5} Ex 11^{9} (P), Ec 5^{10}, of sins Ezr 9^{6} (+ לְמָעְלָה), Pr 29^{16}; + מִן comp. ψ 16^{4} 139^{18}; of days Gn 38^{12} (J), Dt 11^{21} 1 S 7^{2} Pr 9^{11}, years of life 4^{10}; of waters Gn 7^{17} (J), v^{18} (P) **2. a.** *be great* (1) of things, Gn 43^{34} (J, + מִן comp), 1 S 14^{30}, of way=*be long* Dt 19^{6} and (מִן comp pers) 14^{24} *be too long for;* of wisdom 1 K 5^{10} (מִן comp.). (2) of pers, ירבה אֱלֹהִים מֵאֱנוֹשׁ Jb 33^{12} i e. is too great for (De al); has loftier, nobler thoughts (Di Bu), but no ‖. **b.** *grow great* (Aramaism)· (1) of pers.,=grow up Ez 16^{7} (+ גָּדַל), Jb 39^{4} (2) of glory ψ 49^{17}, knowledge Dn 12^{4}.—2 Ch 24^{27} v. supr. †**Pi.**$_{4}$ *make large, increase;*—*Imv.* ms רַבֵּה צְבָאֲךָ Ju 9^{29} *enlarge thy host; Pf.* 2 ms. רבית במחיריהם ψ 44^{13} *thou hast* not *made great with their price* (set a high price, so Ew De Che al), or *increased* (sc thy wealth) *by their price* (Hup Bae), = *bring up, rear* (children) La 2^{22} (+ טפח), whelps Ez 19^{2} (in fig) **Hiph.**$_{162}$ *Pf.* 3 ms הרבה Ho 8^{11}+, sf. והרבך consec. Dt 30^{5}; 2 ms הרבית Is 9^{2}+, 1 s. הרביתי Ho 2^{10}+, etc.; *Impf* ירבה 12^{2}+, וַיֶּרֶב 2 S 18^{8} La 2^{5}, etc; *Imv.* ms הַרְבֵּה Ez 24^{10}, הֶרֶב Ju 20^{38}+ ψ 51^{4} Qr (הרבה Kt, Inf abs), etc, fs. הַרְבִּי Is 23^{16}, mpl. הַרְבּוּ Am 4^{4} Gn 34^{12}, *Inf abs* הרבה 15^{1}+, הַרְבֵּה (Ba$^{NB\ 90,\ 91}$) 3^{16} 16^{10} 22^{17}; *cstr.* הַרְבּוֹת Dt 28^{63}+ (2 S 14^{11} Kt הרבית; Am 4^{9} Pr 25^{27} v. infr.); *Pt.* מַרְבֶּה Ex 16^{17}+, cstr. מַרְבֵּה Lv 11^{42}, etc.;—**1.** *make much*, or *many* · **a.** obj pers. (or a people), *multiply, increase* Gn 16^{10} 17^{20} Is 9^{2}+; Ez 36^{10} (+ עַל pers.), v^{11} (man and beast, + *id*), Dt 30^{5} (+ מִן comp. pers.), + פרה Hiph. Gn 28^{3} 48^{4} (both P); הִרְבָּה כּוֹשֵׁל Je 46^{16} = *he made many stumble;* = *have many* 1 Ch 7^{4} 8^{40} 23^{11}. **b.** obj animals Dt $17^{16.16}$ (cf. Ez 36^{11} supr). **c.** obj. things Ho 2^{10} $8^{11\ 14}$ Gn 3^{16}+, הַרְבּוּ עָלַי מְאֹד מֹהַר וּמַתָּן 34^{12}; opp. המעים Lv 26^{16} Nu 26^{54} 33^{54}; obj. words Ec 10^{14} (v Jb 34^{37} sub **2**), cf. Is 1^{15} Jb 40^{27}, הַרְבִּי שִׁיר Is 23^{16}, obj days Jb 29^{18} (like sand), = *use many* (medicines) Je 46^{11}; *have many* (feet) Lv 11^{42}, *bring abundantly* 2 Ch 31^{5}; *yield abundantly* Ne 9^{37}; c. ל of obj Ho 10^{1} (ל **3 a**); obj om. Hb 2^{6} Pr 22^{16}, also (opp. מעט [usu. Hiph.]) Ex $16^{17\ 18}$ 30^{15} Nu 35^{8} (all P), Pr 13^{11}. †**d.** (1) sq. inf., *make much to do, do much in respect of*, = do much, abundantly greatly, often, etc (Dr$^{161,\ 1(2)}$): הַרְבּוּ לִפְשֹׁעַ Am 4^{4} = *transgress greatly*, so Ezr 10^{13}, cf 2 K 21^{6} = 2 Ch 33^{6}, further, Is 55^{7} Ex 36^{5} 2 Ch 36^{14} ψ 78^{38}, also 2 S 14^{11} (Kt מהרבית, Qr מֵהַרְבַּת, rd prob. מהרבות Dr$^{ref.}$ Ges$^{§75\,ff}$ Th-Lohr); + מִן comp 18^{8}, 1 S 1^{12} = *pray a long time;* Ju 20^{38} del. הֶרֶב as dittogr of הארב Be Bu GFM. (2) sq. vb. fin. (Dr^{8m} Ges$^{§120\,g}$), אַל־תַּרְבּוּ תְדַבְּרוּ 1 S 2^{3} i.e *talk not so much*, cf. ψ 51^{4}. **e.** the Inf abs (Ol$^{§191\,b}$ Ko$^{ii\ 1\ 555}$ Ges$^{§75\,ff}$) is used. (1) הַרְבָּה אַרְבֶּה *I will greatly increase* Gn 3^{16} 16^{10} 22^{17} (all J, Ges$^{§113\,n}$); (2) וְהַרְבֵּה carrying on inf cstr Ez 21^{20}; (3) הַרְבֵּה as adv. (c. vbs. and [Ec 7^{16}] adj), *greatly, exceedingly*, etc, esp. ה׳ מאד Gn 41^{49} (E), 1 S 26^{21} 2 S 12^{30} = 1 Ch 20^{2}, Jos 13^{1} (D), 2 K 21^{16} Ne 2^{2}, perh also 1 K 5^{9} 10^{10} (both c. נָתַן), v^{11} (c. הביא), Je 40^{12} (c אָסַף), 2 Ch 14^{12} (c נָשָׂא); הַרְבֵּה alone 2 K 10^{18} (opp מְעַט), Ne 3^{33} Ec 1^{16} 5^{19} $7^{16\ 17}$ ψ 51^{4} Kt (Qr הֶרֶב Imv.), (4) as adj. attrib. (Ko$^{Synt\ §318\,e}$), ה׳ מְאֹד Dt 3^{5} Jos 22^{8} (D; ‖ בְרב־מאד), 2 S 8^{8} (רַבָּה מְאֹד in ‖ 1 Ch 18^{8}), 12^{2} Is 30^{33} 2 Ch 32^{27}, so הַרְבֵּה alone Ne $4^{4\ 13}$ (+ רְחָבָה), Ezr 10^{1} (preceding n; cf. 1 רַב), Ec 2^{7} $5^{6\ 16}$ (rdg כעס as n., Ew De Hi-Now al), 6^{11} 9^{18} $11^{8\,a}$ $12^{9\ 12\ 12}$, הַרְבּוֹת alone Pr 25^{27} (Toy reads הַרְבֵּה); הַרְבֵּה מְאֹד as pred. Gn 15^{1} (J; Sam. אַרְבֶּה), Ec $11^{8\,b}$ ψ 130^{7} (adv. Bae); (5) הַרְבֵּה as n. concr. (Ko$^{Synt.\ §318\,a}$) 2 S 1^{4} Je 42^{2} (-בָּה van d. H.), c מִן comp., 2 Ch 25^{9} Jon 4^{11}; as obj. (or adv.), opp מְעָט Hg $1^{6\,9}$ Ec 5^{11}; late in adv phr. (מְאֹד) לְהַרְבֵּה †Ne 5^{18} 2 Ch 11^{12} 16^{8}; הַרְבּוֹת as n Am 4^{9} (rd prob. הֶחֱרַבְתִּי We Now). †**2.** *make great*, obj. pers. 2 S 22^{36} = ψ 18^{36};

enlarge border 1 Ch 4^{10}, perhaps also Jb 34^{37} *make words great*, presumptuous, against God (לאל; so Buhl^{Lex}; most *make many words*, **1 c**).

†אַרְבֶּה **n.m.** $^{Ex\ 10\ 19}$ a kind of locust (usu interp as *the multitudinous*, but Dl$^{HWB\ 126}$ as = As *âribu, êribu, éribû, locust-swarm*, from ארב *devastate*),—alw abs א׳(הָ),—usu. coll *locust-swarm*, in sim of swarm of invaders Ju 6^{5}7^{12}, oft appar the common species (‖ other species, cf לְמִינוֹ Lv 11^{22}): Je 46^{23} Na 3^{15} (sim of multitude, ‖ יֶלֶק); as destructive Ex 10$^{4.12.13.14.14.19a}$ (all J), ψ 105^{34} (‖ יֶלֶק), Dt 28^{38} (vb. חסל), 1 K 8^{37} = 2 Ch 6^{28}, ψ 78^{46} (all + חָסִיל), Jo 1$^{4.4}$ (‖ חָסִיל, יֶלֶק, גָּזָם), 2^{25} (‖ *id*), as disappearing suddenly (sim.) Na 3^{17} (‖ גּוֹב גּוֹבַי); as edible Lv 11^{22} (H, ‖ סָלְעָם, חָגָב, חַרְגֹּל), as well organized Pr 30^{27} (cf. Jo 2$^{7.8}$), of single locust, א׳ אֶחָד Ex 10^{19b} (J), as leaping (sim) Jb 39^{20}, as shaken out of garment (sim) ψ 109^{23} (v. II. נָעַר)—Cf. Dr$^{Jo\ 82\ ff}$

†מַרְבֶּה **n.**[**m**] **1. abundance**,—abs מ׳ Is 33^{23}, as adv, *in abundance* **2. increase**(?), cstr. לְמַרְבֵּה (sic) 9^{6} *for the increase* of the dominion (take לם as dittogr. of foregoing, and read רַבָּה, 𝔊 Gr Che Kit Buhl^{Lex} Marti, Du לְמַרְבֵּה, in view of following לְשָׁלוֹם)

†מַרְבָּה **n f. much**,—only מ׳ לְהָכִיל Ez 23^{32} *much to contain*, i e which contains much, but read מַרְבָּה Hiph. Pt Hi-Sm Co Berthol Krae (v √ **Hiph. 1 d** (1)).

†מַרְבִּית **n.f. increase, great number, greatness**,—מ׳ abs Lv 25^{37}, cstr 1 S 2^{33} + 2 t, sf מַרְבִּיתָם 1 Ch 12^{30} (van d H v^{29}),—**1.** *increase*, concr **a.** of family 1 S 2^{33} **b.** *increment, interest, usury*, Lv 25^{37} (H, of food-stuffs, ‖ נֶשֶׁךְ, of money, מ׳ of money Egypt Aram, opp ראשׁ *principal*, Cooke$^{North\ Sem\ Inscr\ 404}$) **2** *great number*: of people 2 Ch 30^{18}, c sf.=the greater part of them, 1 Ch 12^{30} (v. supr). **3.** *greatness*, of wisdom 2 Ch 9^{6}.

†תַּרְבּוּת **n.f. increase, brood**;—cstr. in phr. ת׳ אֲנָשִׁים חַטָּאִים Nu 32^{14} *a brood* (contempt) *of sinful men* (cf מַרְבִּית 1 S 2^{33}).

†תַּרְבִּית **n.f. increment, interest, usury** (= מַרְבִּית **1 b**, cf. (on both) Ar رَبَا IV *take usury*, رِبًا *interest, usury*, Syr. ܪܶܒܺܝܬܳܐ; Saalschutz $^{Mos\ Recht\ (ii\ 1848),\ 820}$ Hoelemann$^{Letzte\ Bibelstud\ (1866)\ 297\ f}$ Dr$^{Lv\ 25\ 36}$ Benn$^{Hast\ DB\ Debt}$),—alw abs ת׳: + נֶשֶׁךְ Lv 25^{36} (H), Ez 18^{17} 22^{12} Pr 28^{8}, ‖ *id* Ez 18$^{8.13}$.

†II [רָבָה] **vb. shoot** (cf. II. רָבַב, I. רָמָה),—only **Qal** *Pt* רֹבֵה קַשָּׁת Gn 21^{20} < רבה קַשָּׁת, Kn Di al, but read prob. רמה ק׳ Ol Ball, *one shooting* the bow.

רבב I v רְבִיבִים, רְבִית, רִבּוֹ(א), רַבָּה

†[רָבַךְ] **vb. mix, stir** (Ar. رَبَكَ *mix, mingle*, NH רביכה, 𝔗 רְבִיכָא [for BH מֻרְבֶּכֶת], (dough) *mixed*, or *stirred*),—**Hoph.** *Pt* f. as term. techn in sacrif, alw. of סֹלֶת *well mixed*, מֻרְבֶּכֶת Lv 6^{14} 7^{12}, הַמֻּרְבֶּכֶת 1 Ch 23^{29}

†רִבְלָה **n.pr.loc. 1.** ר׳ in land of Hamath 2 K 23^{33} 25^{21} = Je 52^{27}, Je 39^{5}; c. ה loc, רִבְלָתָה 2 K 25$^{6.20}$ = Je 52^{26}, also ('in land of Hamath') Je 39^{5} 52^{9}; בְּרִבְלָתָה v^{10}; read רִבְלָתָה also Ez 6^{14} (for MT דִּבְ׳, v. [דִּבְלָה]); 𝔊 usu. Δεβλαθα (also Ez 6^{14}), mod. *Ribla* on Orontes, Rob$^{BR\ ii.\ 507.\ iii\ 545\ ff.}$ Bd$^{Pal\ 3.\ 400}$. **2.** הָרִבְלָה (מִשְּׁפָם) Nu 34^{11}, on NE border of land of Isr, certainly not so far N. as **1**, but site unknown, 𝔊 ἀπὸ Σεπφαμαρ Βηλα, whence Di al conj. הַרְבֵּלָה, but not *Harmel*, 8 m SW from ר׳ **1** (Wetzst$^{ZAW\ iii\ (1883)\ 274\ f}$), see Dr$^{Hast\ DB}$

רַב v. II רב. רַב־סָרִיס, רַב־מָג

I רבע (√ of following, v [רָבַע], רֶבַע, רֹבַע etc, infr, also in ling. cogn).

I אַרְבַּע, אַרְבָּעָה $_{916}$ **n.m.** et **f. four** (NH = BH; MI^{8} ארבען = 40, Ph ארבע Pun ארבעת, *four*; so As *arba'u* (rarely *irba'*), *irbitti*, Ar. أَرْبَعَةٌ, أَرْبَعٌ; Sab ארבעת CIS$^{iv,\ no\ 332\ 2}$ Hom $^{Chrest\ 47}$, Eth. አርባዕ: አርባዕቱ: Aram אַרְבַּע, אַרְבְּעָה, ܐܰܪܒܰܥ, ܐܰܪܒܥܳܐ, Nab ארבע, Palm. ארבע, ארבעא, Lzb^{367});—**m** $_{148}$ (c **n.f.**) אַרְבַּע (abs. vel cstr) Ex 21^{37} +; also אַרְבַּע Lv 11^{20} +; note (Baer Gi) Jos 21^{18} + 6 t. Jos 21 (van d H. אַרְבַּע); in Pr 30^{18} read **f.** with Qr; **f.** (c **n.m.**) abs. אַרְבָּעָה Gn 2^{10} + 125 t + Pr 30^{18} (v. supr.), cstr. אַרְבַּעַת 1 S 4^{2} + 29 t, incl. Ez 7^{2} (but rd **m.** Kt), sf. אַרְבַּעְתָּם Ez 1^{8} + 5 t Ez, אַרְבַּעְתָּן 1$^{10.10}$ (but rd. prob תָּם-, Krae), v$^{16.18}$; du אַרְבַּעְתַּיִם 2 S 12^{6}, v. **1 d**, pl אַרְבָּעִים = 40, v infr,—*four* (in Hex. 108 t, chiefly P, 98 t, Ez 52 t, Ch 47 t.):—**1.** without other num: **a.** אַרְבַּע (1) before n fpl Je 15^{3} Ex 25^{12} (P) + 101 t, incl א׳ אַמּוֹת Dt 3^{11} + 5 t (but also + א׳ בָּאַמָּה *four* (*in*) *cubit*(*s*) Ex 26$^{2.8}$ 36^{9} 1 K 7$^{27.27.38}$), and א׳ מֵאוֹת = 400 Gn 11^{13} + 55 t (2) א׳ bef. du רַגְלַיִם Lv 11^{23}, רַגְלָיו Ex 25^{26}. †(3) bef collective, א׳ צֹאן Ex 21^{37} (E); א׳ רִבּוֹא = 40,000 Ezr 2^{64} = Ne 7^{66}. †(4) rare

and late, after n.fpl. א׳ עָרִים Jos 19[7] (P); after n. fs. cstr. בִּשְׁנַת א׳ לְ 1 K 22[41] Zc 7[1] 2 Ch 3[2].—קִרְיַת א׳, v. this, and II. אַרְבַּע infr. †(5) n om Ez 43[15 b] Pr 30[15 18] (Kt, v. supr.), v[21] Dn 8[8.22]; עַל־אַרְבַּע (sc. רגלים)=*on all fours* Lv 11[20.21 27.42]. **b.** אַרְבָּעָה (1) bef. n. mpl. Gn 2[10] (J), 14[9] Ex 25[26] + 21 t., + יָמִים (ו)א׳ חֳדָשִׁים Ju 19[2] 1 S 27[7]; also א׳ א׳ פָּנִים distrib. Ez 10[21]. †(2) late, after n. mpl. 1 Ch 23[10]. (3) n om., Am 1[3.6.9] + 15 t, +(as pred. of n. mpl) †Ex 27[16 16] 38[19 19]; also בָּא׳, (sc. יוֹם) †Zc 7[1]=ordinal, *on the fourth* (day). **c.** אַרְבַּעַת (1) bef. n. mpl. Ju 11[40] 1 K 7[32] + 11 t (not Ez 7[2], v. supr.), +א׳ אֲלָפִים=4000, 1 S 4[2] + 14 t †(2) bef. coll. הַבָּקָר Nu 7[7]. †(3) n. om. 2 S 21[22]. †(4) c. sf., after n. pl, =*the four of them*, Ez 1[8.10 10.10] + 6 t Ez, Dn 1[17] *these boys, the four of them.* **d.** du. אַרְבַּעְתָּיִם 2 S 12[6] =*four-fold* Ges[§88 b] Kö[II 1.227], but read שִׁבְעָתַיִם 𝔊 Th We Klo Dr Kmp Bu HPS. **2.** with other num.: **a.** (1) אַרְבַּע עֶשְׂרֵה=*14*, (α) before n. fs, א׳ ע׳ שָׁנָה Gn 31[41], +(as ordinal,=*14th*) 14[5] 2 K 18[13]=Is 36[1], Ez 40[1]. (β) after n fpl. א׳ ע׳ עָרִים Jos 15[36] + 8 t., א׳ ע׳ נָשִׁים 2 Ch 13[21]. (2) אַרְבָּעָה עָשָׂר = *14*, (α) before n. ms. Nu 17[14] (14 × 1000), Jb 42[12]; esp. (as ord) א׳ ע׳ יוֹם *14th day* Ex 12[6.18] + 7 t (β) bef n mpl Nu 29[15]. (γ) after n. mpl. Nu 29[13.17] + 6 t. (δ) after n. ms. Est 9[15.19.21], all=*14th* (ε) א׳ ע׳ pred. of נפש Gn 46[22]. (ζ) א׳ ע׳=*14th* (sc. day) Lv 23[5] 2 Ch 30[15] + 6 t. **b.** 20 + (ו) 4 + n. s 1 K 15[33] 1 Ch 23[4] + 13 t. 1 Ch 27; +n pl. †Nu 7[88], n. om. 2 S 21[20], pred. ‖ 1 Ch 20[6], Ne 7[23]; 4 + 20 + n. s. Nu 25[9]; =*24th*, יום ע׳ וא׳ Hg 1[15 15] Zc 1[7] Ne 9[1] Dn 10[4], יום om. Hg 2[10.20], and (א׳ וע׳) 1 Ch 24[18] 25[31]†. **c.** other tens + 4, 1 Ch 7[7] 5[18] (+n. s), Ezr 2[15] + 7 t.; 4 + tens + שָׁנָה Gn 11[16], +אֶלֶף 1000 Nu 1[27 29] 2[4 6] 26[25.43] —Vid Kö[II.1 §106].

†II. אַרְבַּע **n.pr.m.** (called הָאָדָם הַגָּדוֹל בָּעֲנָקִים Jos 14[15], אֲבִי הָעֲנָק 15[13] cf. 21[11]), inferred (erron) from n.pr.loc קִרְיַת א׳ (q. v.).

אַרְבָּעִים [136] **n.pl. indecl. a forty**,—**1.** sine num. al.: **a.** usu. appos bef. n, esp שָׁנָה, יוֹם (sing). אַרְבָּעִים שָׁנָה Ju 3[11] 1 S 4[18] Am 2[10] 5[25] + 29 t.; א׳ יוֹם Gn 7[17] 1 K 19[8] Jon 3[4] + 6 t, א׳ יוֹם וְא׳ לַיְלָה Gn 7[4.12] Ex 24[18] + 7 t.; also א׳ בַּת †1 K 7[38], א׳ גָּמָל †2 K 8[9], א׳ אַמָּה †Ez 41[2] and (אַמָּה om.) 46[22], but א׳ בָּאַמָּה †1 K 6[17] (v. אַמָּה); א׳ אֶלֶף Nu 1[33] 2[19] 26[18] Jos 4[13] Ju 5[8] 2 S 10[18] 1 K 5[6] 1 Ch 12[37] (van d H. v[36]), 19[18] (v. also infr), rarely sq n.pl, א׳ בָּנִים Ju 12[14], א׳ אֲדָנִים Ex 26[19.21] 36[24.26] (P).—(As round no. Gn 7[17] Ju 3[11] 5[31] 8[28] 1 S 4[18] +) **b.** after n. pl, א׳ פָּרוֹת Gn 32[16] (E), א׳ שְׁקָלִים Ne 5[15]. **c.** n om Gn 18[29], הָא׳ v[29]; א׳ יַכֶּנּוּ Dt 25[3] *forty (blows) may he smite him.* **2.** c. num. al.: **a.** before unit, + n. s, 40 + 1 שָׁנָה 1 K 14[21] 15[10], 2 K 14[23], 40 + 2 שָׁנָה 2 Ch 22[2], אִישׁ 2 K 10[14], עִיר Nu 35[6], אֶלֶף Ju 12[6], 40 + 5 שָׁנָה Jos 14[10] (JE), etc (12 t.); +n pl. יְלָדִים 2 K 2[24], after n. pl. הָעַמּוּדִים + 40 + 5 1 K 7[3]; n. om 40 + 5 Gn 18[28], cf Ezr 2[24]=Ne 7[28]. **b.** after unit, 9 + 40 שָׁנָה Lv 25[8] (H); 1 + 40 אֶלֶף Nu 1[41] 2[28], etc. (9 t Nu, P) **c.** c. hundreds, 40 שָׁנָה + 800 שָׁנָה Gn 5[13] (P); 100 + 40 שָׁנָה Jb 42[16]; +units, 7 שָׁנִים + 40 + 100 שָׁנָה Gn 47[28] (P); but (Ezr Ne, mostly pred., without n.), 900 + 40 + 5 Ezr 2[8], cf. v[25] Ne 7[62], and (א׳ without וְ) 600, 40 + 2 Ezr 2[10], v. also ‖ Ne 7[15], Ezr 2[34]=Ne 7[36], Ezr 2[66]=Ne 7[68] (ver. om Baer Gi), Ne 7[13.29.44]; 1000, 200, 40 + 7 Ezr 2[38]=Ne 7[41]; n.pl 200 + 40 + 5 Ne 7[67], n pl. 200, 40 + 2 11[13]; also n. s. נֶפֶשׁ 700, 40 + 5 Je 52[30]. **3.** as ordinal, בְּא׳ שָׁנָה Dt 1[3] *in the fortieth year;* also בִּשְׁנַת הָא׳ Nu 33[38] 1 Ch 26[31]; בִּשְׁנַת א׳ וְאַחַת 2 Ch 16[13] *in the forty-first year.*

†[רָבַע] **vb.denom.**, only *Pt. pass* **squared, square,**—**Qal** *Pt. pass.* רָבוּעַ *square,* of altar Ex 27[1] 30[2] 37[25] 38[1], cf Ez 43[16]; breastplate 30[2] 39[9]; pl רְבֻעִים, of doorways, etc. [on text v. Kit Benz] 1 K 7[5]; fs רְבֻעָה as subst.=*a square* Ez 41[21] (acc. Co Toy, om מְזוּזַת, and joining ר׳ to v[20]; Krae reads מְזוּזֹת רְבֻעֹת, cf. 1 K 6[33], רְבִיעִי **2**). **Pu.** *Pt. square,* מְרֻבָּע Ez 45[2], of piece of land, fs מְרֻבַּעַת 40[47], of court, fpl מְרֻבָּעוֹת 1 K 7[31] (opp. עֲגֻלּוֹת), of borders of bases (cf. Sab. רבעתם, a kind of square building, Sab-Denkm[31])

†I רֹבַע **n.m.**[Ez 1.8] **1. fourth part. 2.** pl. **four sides;**—**1.** ר׳ cstr, *fourth part,* of shekel 1 S 9[8], cf hin Ex 29[40]. **2.** in Ez, pl. sf. *four sides* (אַרְבַּעַת always preceding): רִבְעָיו Ez 43[16], רִבְעֶיהָ v[17]; רִבְעֵיהֶם 1[8] 10[11], -הֶן 1[17].

†רֶבַע **n.**[m.] **fourth part,**—ר׳ cstr.; of Israel Nu 23[10]; of a kab 2 K 6[25].

†רְבִיעִי **m.**, רְבִיעִית **f., adj. num. ordin. fourth,**—**m.** רְבִיעִי Gn 2[14] + 29 t, רְבִעִי 1 Ch 24[8] 26[11], pl. רביעים 2 K 15[12], רבעים 10[30]; **f.** abs. רביעית 1 K 6[1] + 3 t., רביעת Lv 19[24], רבעית 1 K 6[37] + 6 t + 1 K 6[33] (v. infr.), cstr. רְבִיעִית Nu 15[5], רבעת Ex 29[40] + 4 t., רבעית Nu 15[4] + 2 t.;—*fourth,* usu. הָר׳: **1. m.** Gn 2[14] 15[16] (JE), also (esp. of days, months, sons, etc) Gn 1[19] Ex 28[20] 39[13] Nu 7[30] 29[23] Jos 19[17] (all P), Ju 19[5] Je 39[2] 52[6] 1 Ch 27[7 b] 2 Ch 20[26] Ezr 8[33]; n. om. 2 S 3[4]=

1 Ch 3^{2}, 1 Ch 2^{14} 3^{15} 8^{2} 12^{10} 23^{19} 24$^{8.23}$ 25^{11} 26$^{2.4.11}$ 27$^{7.4}$ Ezr 10^{14} Dn 11^{2}, sc חֹדֶשׁ Ez 1^{1} Zc 8^{19}, pl. in בני רב(י)עים *sons of fourth (ones)*, i.e to the fourth generation, 2 K 10^{30} 15^{12} (cf [רבע], and [OAram Nērab] בני רבע Cook^{107}) **2. f.** of years, 1 K 6$^{1.37}$ 2 K 18^{9} Je 25^{1} 28^{1} 36^{1} 45^{1} 46^{2} 51^{59} Zc 6^{3} Lv 19^{24} (H), מאת רבעית 1 K 6^{33}, rd מְזֻזוֹת רְבִעוֹת 𝔊 𝔙 Th Sta Kmp Kit Benz Bur **3.** רביעית Ez 48^{20} *four square* (rd poss רבוּעָה) **4.** רב(י)ע(י)ת as n = *fourth part*, cstr, ר׳ הַהִין Lv 23^{13} (H), Ex 29^{40} Nu 15$^{4.5}$ 28$^{5.7.14}$, ר׳ הַיּוֹם Ne 9^{3a}, so abs (הַיּוֹם om) v^{3b}

† [רִבֵּעַ] **adj. pertaining to the fourth** (in a series),—pl in phr עַל־שִׁלֵּשִׁים וְעַל־רִבֵּעִים, i e those belonging to the 3rd and 4th generations, Ex 20^{5} (E) = Dt 5^{9}, Ex 34^{17} (J), Nu 14^{18} (JE), cf **1** supr.

† II [רָבַע] **vb. lie stretched out, lie down** (Aram form of רָבַץ (q v.), NH רבע usu. of copulation, chiefly unnatural, yet cf also Sab רבע *abide, encamp, settle*, DHM$^{ZMG\ xxix\ (1875),\ 623}$, Ar رَبَعَ *abide, dwell*)—**Qal** only *Inf:* sf. רִבְעִי ψ 139^{3} *my lying down* (for repose, opp אָרְחִי); elsewh (H) for copulation (woman with beast) לְרִבְעָה אֹתָהּ Lv 20^{16}, but read אֹתָהּ (sf of beast) Dr-Wh Ko$^{Synt\ 226e}$, cf Bae Berthol (and Dr$^{28\ 13,14}$); לְרִבְעָה 18^{23}, rd לְרִבְעָה (compl. om, v *id*) **Hiph.** *Impf* 2 ms בהמתך לא תַרְבִּיעַ כִּלְאַיִם Lv 19^{19} (H) *thy cattle thou shalt not cause to* (let) *lie down* (i.e breed) in *two kinds*.

† II רֶבַע **n.m.** a king of Midian Nu 31^{8} Jos 13^{21}, Ροβοκ, Ροβε(κ).

† רָבַץ **vb. stretch oneself out, lie down, lie stretched out** (NH = BH, As *rabāṣu*, *lie, dwell*, *rubṣu* (in word-lists), *stall*, also *womb* (cf II רבע supr), Ar. رَبَضَ *lie down on the breast, stretch oneself out*, مَرابِض, Sab מרבצן CIS$^{iv\ no\ 5\ 2}$, 𝔗 רבע *lie stretched out*, Syr ܪܒܥ, ChrPal ܪܒܥ *recline at meals*, Schwally$^{Idiot\ 87}$),—**Qal** *Pf* 3 ms ר׳ Gn 49^{9}, 3 fs consec וְרָבְצָה Dt 29^{19}, רָבְצָה Ez 19^{2}, etc, *Impf* 3 ms יִרְבַּץ Is 11^{6} 27^{10}, 3 fs וַתִּרְבַּץ Nu 22^{27}, 3 mpl. יִרְבְּצוּ 11^{7}, יִרְבָּצוּ 14^{30}, יִרְבָּצוּן Zp 2^{7} ψ 104^{22}, 3 fpl תִּרְבַּצְנָה Ez 34^{14}; *Pt* רֹבֵץ Ex 23^{5} + 3 t; f. רֹבֶצֶת Gn 49^{25} + 2 t, mpl רֹבְצִים 29^{2},—*lie down, lie:* of domestic animals, ass Ex 23^{5} (E, under heavy burden), Nu 22^{27} (Je, in obstructed path), Gn 49^{14} (at ease, poet, in sim), sheep, in repose, 29^{2} (J), Is 17^{2} Zp 2^{14}, fig of people Ez 34^{14}, calf, in repose Is 27^{10}, of wild beasts, lion, in lair, Gn 49^{9} (poem in J; fig.), ψ 104^{22}; = make lair, abode Ez 19^{2} (fig.), so of צִיִּים Is 13^{21}, תַּנִּין Ez 29^{3} (fig); leopard (with kid) Is 11^{6}, cf v^{7}; = brood, of mother-bird Dt 22^{6} (עַל־הָאֶפְרֹחִים), of man, in repose Is 14^{30} Jb 11^{19}, cf. Zp 2^{7} 3^{13} (fig of flock perhaps impl, cf. Ez 34^{14} supr.); of the deep, רֹבֶצֶת תָּחַת Gn 49^{25} Dt 33^{13}, fig of curse Dt 29^{19} (ב pers), of sin, לַפֶּתַח חַטָּאת רֹבֵץ Gn 4^{7} *at the door sin makes its lair* **Hiph.** *Impf.* 3 ms sf יַרְבִּיצֵנִי ψ 23^{2}, 2 ms. תַּרְבִּיץ Ct 1^{7}, etc, *Pt.* מַרְבִּיץ Is 54^{11}, pl מַרְבִּצִים Je 33^{12},—*cause to lie down*, or *lie*, acc of flock (for repose) Je 33^{12}, also (fig) ψ 23^{2} Ez 34^{15}, acc of flock om Is 13^{10} Ct 1^{7}, of *laying* stones Is 54^{11}

† רֵבֶץ **n [m] (place of) lying down, resting- or dwelling-place**,—cstr ר׳ בָּקָר Is 65^{10} (|| נוה צאן); sf רִבְצָהּ בנוה תַּנִּים 35^{7} (cf. Ges$^{§ 145m}$, but Du רָבְצָה, sc flock); רִבְצָם Je 50^{6} (people as sheep), of man, רִבְצוֹ Pr 24^{15} (|| נוה צַדִּיק)

† מַרְבֵּץ **n. [m.]** id,—of wild beasts, מ׳ לַחַיָּה Zp 2^{15} (sign of desolation, || שַׁמָּה); of flock, cstr. מַרְבַּץ־צֹאן Ez 25^{5} (|| נוה גְמַלִּים)

רבק (√of following; cf Ar رَبَقَ *tie fast;* 𝔗 רִיבְקָא *stall*)

† מַרְבֵּק **n. [m.] stall** (lit *tying-place*),—עֲגָלִים מִתּוֹךְ מ׳ Am 6^{4} *calves out of the stall* (where they were fattened), עֵגֶל־מ׳ 1 S 28^{24} i.e. a stall-fed, fatted, calf, so עֶגְלֵי מ׳ Mal 3^{20} (sim. of prosperity), Je 46^{21} (sim. of well-fed and arrogant mercenaries)

רִבְקָה 30 **n. pr. f. Rebekah,** daughter of Bethuel and wife of Isaac, Gn 22^{23} 24^{15} + 24 t. 24, 25, 26, 27, 28^{5} 29^{12} 35^{8} 49^{31},—𝔊 Ρεβεκκα.

רַב־שָׁקֵה v II. רַב sub רבב.

רגב (√of following)

† [רֶגֶב] **n.m. clod of earth,**—pl. רְגָבִים יְדֻבָּקוּ Jb 38^{38} *clods are joined together*, cstr. רִגְבֵי נָחַל 21^{33} *clods of* (the) *wady*.

† אַרְגָּב **n.m. heap, mound** (prob);—so read 1 S 20^{19} (for אבן), v^{41} (for נגב), 𝔊 (αργαβ, εργαβ), Th We Klo Dr Kit Bu HPS.

† אַרְגֹּב **n.pr. 1. loc.** (*heap*, or *region of clods*, '*glebe*' GASm$^{G\ 551}$),—always חֶבֶל א׳ Dt 3$^{4.14}$ 1 K 4^{13}, ח׳ הָא׳ Dt 3^{13}, = *measured region of Argōb*, some well-defined district of Bashan (appar identif with חַוֹּת יָאִיר Dt 3^{14} [where ח׳ י׳

in Bashan, so Jos 13[30]], but this a harmonistic correction; ח׳ י׳ in fact in Gilead [Nu 32[41] Ju 10[4]], and disting. from אַרְגֹּב 1 K 4[13] cf. Dt 3[13]); exact loc. dubious, GASm[l.c.] and esp. Dr[Dt 3, 4]; Buhl[Geogr. 18] thinks of *Ṣuwet*, S. of Upper Yarmuk, a border district between Bashan and Gilead.—Αργοβ; 1 K 4[13] Ερεβαταμ, 𝔊L Ραγαβαν, A Εργαβ. **2. m.** 2 K 15[25], Αργοβ; dub.; v. Klo Kit Benz Bur.

†**רָגַז** **vb. be agitated, quiver, quake, be excited, perturbed** (Ph. Iph. (+ Inf. abs. Qal) *disquiet, disturb*, Inscr. Tabn.[4.6.7]; NH Hiph. *provoke to wrath*; رجز *tremble* (with rage, fear, Dozy); v, viii, *rumble* (of thunder, Frey), رُجَازٌ *a trembling disease* (of camels), etc.; Aram. רְגַז *tremble, rage*, ܪܓܙ *be enraged*; Zinj. רגז *wrath*, Lzb[367]);—**Qal** *Pf.* 3 ms. consec. וְרָגַז Pr 29[9], 3 fs. רָגְזָה Is 14[9] +, etc.; *Impf.* 3 ms. יִרְגַּז 2 S 7[10] 1 Ch 17[9], 2 fs. וַתִּרְגְּזִי Ez 16[43] (but v. infr.); 3 mpl. יִרְגָּזוּן Hb 3[7], יִרְגָּזוּן Ex 15[14], etc.; *Imv.* ms. רְגָזָה (Ges[§ 48 i]) Is 32[11], mpl. רִגְזוּ ψ 4[5];—*quake*, subj. אֶרֶץ 1 S 14[15] Am 8[8] (עַל rei), ψ 77[19] (+ רָעַשׁ), Jo 2[10] (לְפָנָיו of locusts; ‖ רעשׁ), Pr 30[21] (תַּחַת pers.); subj. מוֹסְדֵי הָרִים ψ 18[8] (‖ רעשׁ), = 2 S 22[8] (מוֹסְדוֹת הַשָּׁמַיִם; ‖ *id.*); הֶהָרִים Is 5[25]; תְּהֹמוֹת ψ 77[17]; of tent-curtains Hb 3[7] (fig. of terror of tent-dwellers); of people, in dread, c. מִפְּנֵי pers. Dt 2[25] (‖ חול), Is 64[1]; c. עַל rei Je 33[9] (+ פָּחַד); abs., Ex 15[14] (‖ חִיל אָחַז וגו׳), ψ 99[1] Jo 2[1]; pregn. = *come quivering* Mi 7[17] (מִן loc.); of pers., in fear, awe, Gn 45[24] (בְּ loc.), Is 32[11] (‖ חָרַד), v[10] ψ 4[5], Hb 3[16] (תַּחְתַּי), cf. of בִּטְנִי Hb 3[16]; of Israel, = *be disquieted*, 2 S 7[10] = 1 Ch 17[9]; *be excited, perturbed*, of pers. 2 S 19[1] (by grief; cf. Dr), שְׁאוֹל Is 14[9] (surprise; לְ pers.); in rage, c. לְ *at*, Ez 16[43] (of Jerus. personif.; but rd. **Hiph.** (i.e. *didst enrage me*) 𝔊𝔖𝔙𝔗 Hi Sm Co Berthol Toy Krae); prob. also וְר׳ וְשָׂחַק Pr 29[9]; of י׳ Is 28[21]. **Hiph.** *Pf.* 3 ms. הִרְגִּיז Is 23[11]; 2 ms. sf. הִרְגַּזְתָּנִי 1 S 28[15]; *Impf.* 1 s. אַרְגִּיז Is 13[13]; *Inf. cstr.* הַרְגִּיז (Ges[§ 53 l]) Je 50[34]; *Pt.* מַרְגִּיז Is 14[16] Jb 9[6], pl. cstr. מַרְגִּיזֵי 12[6];—*cause to quake, disquiet, enrage: cause* earth *to quake* Is 14[16] (fig.; ‖ רעשׁ), Jb 9[6] *shake earth* מִמְּקוֹמָהּ; heavens Is 13[13] (‖ רעשׁ); kingdoms 23[11]; *cause disquiet*, c. לְ pers., Je 50[34] (‖ רגע); = disturb 1 S 28[15] (cf. Ph. תרגזן, Inscr. Tabn.[4] Dr[Sm xxviii]); = enrage, provoke, מַרְגִּיזֵי אֵל Jb 12[6]; so also prob. Ez 16[43] (rdg. תַּרְגִּזִי לִי), v. **Qal** ad fin. **Hithp.** *excite oneself*, only *Inf. cstr.* sf. הִתְרַגֶּזְךָ אֵלַי *thine exciting thyself* (to rage) against me, 2 K 19[27.28] = Is 37[28.29].

†**רֹגֶז** **n. m.** [Jb 3, 26] **agitation, excitement, raging**;—ר׳ abs. Hb 3[2] +, cstr. Jb 37[2]; sf. רָגְזְךָ Is 14[3];—*raging* Jb 3[17]; *disquiet, turmoil* Is 14[3] Jb 3[26] 14[1]; *raging, wrath* Hb 3[2]; ר׳ קֹלוֹ Jb 37[2] *rumbling of his voice* (i.e. thunder); of *excitement* of warhorse, בְּרַעַשׁ וְרֹגֶז 39[24].

†**רׇגְזָה** **n.f. a quivering, quaking**;—ר׳ Ez 12[18] (‖ רַעַשׁ).

†**רַגָּז** **adj. quivering, quaking**;—לֵב ר׳ Dt 28[65] *a quaking heart.*

†**אַרְגָּז** **n.m. box, chest,** or like receptacle (cf. Ar. رِجَازَةٌ *a kind of* (camel-)*vehicle for women*, also *a garment containing stones*, etc., as balance, makeweight (at side of *haudaj*); from above √, as *swaying*? Syr. ܪܓܙܐ *sack*, Talm. אַרְגָּז *chest, coffin*);—הָא׳ 1 S 6[8.11.15], cf. HPS.

רֶגֶל [v. 247] **n.f.** [Dt 8, 4] (on sf. m. Ct 5[3] v. Kö[Synt. § 14] Albr[ZAW (xvi, 1896, 76) xv (1895), 316 f.]), **foot** (NH *id.*; Ar. رِجْلٌ *leg, foot*; Aram. רַגְלָא, ܪܶܓܠܳܐ *foot*; Palm. sf. רגלה Lzb[368]; transp. Zinj. (pl. cstr.) לגרי Id[ib.], Mand. לינרא Nö[M 102]; cf. Eth. ሰረገላ: *vehicle* Di[347]);—abs. ר׳ Ex 21[24] +, רָגֶל v[24] +; cstr. רֶגֶל Nu 22[25] +; sf. רַגְלִי Gn 30[30] +, etc.; du. רַגְלַיִם Is 28[3] +, רַגְלָיִם 2 S 4[4] +; cstr. רַגְלֵי Gn 24[32] +; sf. רַגְלַי Nu 20[19] +, רַגְלֶיךָ Ex 3[5] +, etc.; pl. רְגָלִים 23[14] + 3 t. (v. **2** infr.);—**1.** *foot*: **a.** human, Gn 18[4] 19[2] + 10 t. of washing feet (רחץ); Ex 3[5] 4[25] + oft.; in fig. Dt 32[35] 1 S 2[9] Je 2[25] Jb 12[5] + oft.; ר׳ גַּאֲוָה ψ 36[12] *foot of pride*; הֲדֹם לְר׳ 110[1]; מִכַּף ר׳ + ר׳ כַּף *sole of foot* Dt 2[5] 11[24] 28[56.65] + 6 t., וְעַד ראשׁ Is 1[6], cf. (וְעַד קדקד) 2 S 14[25] Dt 28[35] Jb 2[7]; also ר׳ מֵרֹאשׁ וְעַד Lv 13[12]; שָׁרְשֵׁי ר׳ Jb 13[27], v. שֹׁרֶשׁ; ר׳ אֶצְבְּעוֹת 2 S 21[20] = *toes*, בֹּהֶן ר׳ = *great toe* Ju 1[6.7] Ex 29[20] + 6 t. Lv; ר׳ = *leg* 1 S 17[6] (v. also **f.** ad fin.). †**b.** anthrop. of God, Ex 24[10] 2 S 22[10] = ψ 18[10], Na 1[3] Hb 3[5] Is 60[13] Zc 14[4]; כַּפּוֹת ר׳ Ez 43[7]; הֲדֹם ר׳ Is 66[1] La 2[1] 1 Ch 28[2] ψ 99[5] 132[7]. †**c.** of seraphim Is 6[2], Ezekiel's חַיּוֹת Ez 1[7.7] and (כַּף ר׳) v[7], cherubim 2 Ch 3[13]; idols ψ 115[7]. **d.** of animals: dove, כַּף ר׳ Gn 8[9] (J); שֶׁרֶץ עוֹף Lv 11[21.23], שֶׁרֶץ v[42]; calf, כַּף ר׳ Ez 1[7] (in sim.), בְּהֵמָה 29[11]; Pharaoh under fig. of תַּנִּים 32[2]; prob. of beast also Jb 39[15], indef. Is 28[3] (in fig.). **e.** of table Ex 25[26] 37[13] (P). **f.** phrases: †לְר׳ (לְ **5 i**) *acc. to the pace of* Gn 33[14.14] (J; as fast as cattle, children, can go); *at one's guidance* Dt 33[3]; *at one's foot*, i.e. at every step Gn 30[30] (J), Is 41[2], cf. Jb 18[11] (v. I. [פוץ] **Hiph.**); הלך לְר׳ 1 S 25[42], i.e. went where

she went, cf. 2 S 15$^{15.17.18}$; † בְּרַ׳ *on* one's *feet*, on foot, Nu 20^{19} (JE), Dt 2^{28} Ju 4$^{15.17}$ ψ 66^{6}, שְׁלַח בְּרַ׳ Ju 5^{15} (v. שׁלח), cf. Jb 18^{8} (and רַגְלֵי שִׁלְּחוּ 30^{12}); (הָעָם, הַיְקוּם, הַבְּהֵמָה) אֲשֶׁר בְּרַ׳, i.e. which follow one, hence obey or belong to one, Ex 11^{8} (J), Ju 4^{10} 8^{5} 1 K 20^{10} Dt 11^{6} 2 K 3^{9}, הַמִּתְהַלְּכִים בְּרַ׳ 1 S 25^{27}; נָשָׂא רַ׳ †Gn 29^{1} (E) = set out, but יָרִים אֶת־רַ׳ †41^{44} (E) *lift the foot*, i.e. make a movement, do anything; †euphemism מֵסִיךְ אֶת־רַ׳ Ju 3^{24}, cf. 1 S 24^{3} (Gi; van d. H. Baer v^{4}; v. I. [סָכַךְ] **Hiph.**); וַתְּפַשְּׂקִי אֶת־רַ׳ לְ Ez 16^{25} (v. פשׂק); הַיּוֹצֵאת מִבֵּין רַ׳ Dt 28^{57} (v. יצא **1 h**); מֵימֵי רַ׳ Qr 2 K 18^{27} = Is 36^{12} (Kt שיניהם; v. מַיִם **3**); שְׂעַר הָרַ׳ Is 7^{20}, i.e. hair of the private parts. †**2.** pl. only in phr. שָׁלֹשׁ רְגָלִים *three times* (feet, paces, cf. פַּעַם) Ex 23^{14} (E), Nu 22$^{28.32.33}$ (J).

†רָגַל **vb. denom. foot it, go about**;—**Qal** *go about* (maliciously, *as slanderer*; cf. Ar. مَشَّاءٌ and سَاعٍ *slanderer*, from √√ مَشَى *walk along*, سَعَى *walk quickly*), *slander*, *Pf.* 3 ms. לֹא־רָ׳ עַל־לְשֹׁנוֹ ψ 15^{3} *he takes no slander upon his tongue* (‖ דֹּבֵר אֱמֶת v^{2}). **Pi.** *Impf.* 3 ms. וַיְרַגֵּל 2 S 19^{28}, 3 mpl. וַיְרַגְּלוּ Dt 1^{24} Jos 7^{2}; *Imv.* mpl. רַגְּלוּ Jos 7^{2}; *Inf. cstr.* לְרַגֵּל Nu 21^{32} + 5 t.; sf. לְרַגְּלָהּ 2 S 10^{3}; *Pt.* pl. מְרַגְּלִים Gn 42^{9} + 11 t.;—**1.** *slander* (cf. **Qal**), וַיְרַ׳ בְּעַבְדְּךָ אֶל 2 S 19^{28}. **2.** *go about as explorer, spy*, c. acc. loc. Nu 21^{32} Jos 6^{25} 7$^{2.2}$ 14^{7} (all JE), Ju 18^{2} (‖ חָקַר), v$^{14.17}$ 2 S 10^{3} (‖ חָקַר), 1 Ch 19^{3}, so also pt. Gn 42^{30} (E), Jos 6^{22} (JE); pt., acc. om., as adj., אֲנָשִׁים מְרַגְּלִים Jos 2^{1}, cf. 6^{23} (both JE); as subst., *spies* 1 S 26^{4} 2 S 15^{10}, and so perh. (as pred.) Gn 42$^{9.11.14.16.31.34}$ (all E). **Tiph.** *Pf.* 1 s. תִּרְגַּלְתִּי לְאֶפְרַיִם Ho 11^{3} *I taught* Ephr. *to walk* (si vera l.; v. Ges$^{§55 h}$).

רֹגֵל (*treader, fuller* (cf. כבס), so Thes SS al.) v. עֵין רֹ׳, II. עַיִן **c**.

†רַגְלִי **adj. on foot**;—אִישׁ רַ׳ (after num.) *footmen*, esp. foot-soldiers, Ju 20^{2} 2 S 8^{4} = 1 Ch 18^{4}, 1 Ch 19^{18} (פָּרָשִׁים in ‖ 2 S 10^{18}); elsewhere רַ׳ as subst., usu. coll., of Isr. at Exod. Ex 12^{37} Nu 11^{21} (both JE); = foot-soldiery 1 S 4^{10} 15^{4} 2 S 10^{6} 1 K 20^{29} 2 K 13^{7}; n.pl. רַגְלִים *footmen, men on foot* Je 12^{5} (opp. הַסּוּסִים).

†[מַרְגְּלוֹת] **n.**[**f.**] **pl. denom. place of the feet, feet** (cf. [מְרַאֲשׁוֹת] sub I. ראשׁ);—sf. מַרְגְּלֹתָיו *place of his feet* Ru 3$^{4.7}$; adv. = *at his feet* v^{8} + v^{14} Qr (Kt מרגלתו); = *his feet* Dn 10^{6} (opp. זְרֹעֹתָיו).

†רֹגְלִים **n.pr.loc.** (place of *fullers*, v. רֹגֵל supr.);—in Gilead, 2 S 17^{27} 19^{32}; unknown; 𝔊 Ρωγελ(λ)ειμ, 𝔊L Ρακαβειν.

†[רָגַם] **vb. stone, kill by stoning** (denom.? cf. סקל; or orig. = *throw, hurl*? NH רָגַם *throw at* (rare); Ar. رَجَمَ *throw stones at, stone*, also (from accompaniment of stone-throwing) *revile, curse*, cf. Eth. ረገመ: *curse*, We$^{Held. 2. 111, 250}$; Aram. רְגַם, ܪܓܡ *stone*);—**Qal** *Pf.* 3 pl. consec. וְרָגְמוּ Lv 24^{14} + 2 t., sf. וּרְגָמֻהוּ Dt 21^{21}; *Impf.* 3 mpl. יִרְגְּמוּ Lv 20$^{16.27}$, וַיִּרְ׳ Jos 7^{25} + 4 t.; sf. יִרְגְּמֻהוּ Lv 20^{2}, וַיִּרְ׳ 2 Ch 24^{21}; *Inf. abs.* רָגוֹם Lv 24^{16} Nu 15^{35}; *cstr.* לִרְגּוֹם 14^{10};—*stone*, c. acc. pers. + בָּאֲבָנִים Dt 21^{21} (D), Nu 14^{10} 15$^{35.36}$ (P), + בָּאֶבֶן Ez 16^{40} Lv 20$^{2.27}$ (H); + acc. אֶבֶן Jos 7^{25} (JE), Lv 24^{23} (P), 2 Ch 24^{21}; c. ב pers. + acc. אֶבֶן 1 K 12^{18} = 2 Ch 10^{18}; c. עַל pers. + acc. אֶבֶן Ez 23^{47}; c. acc. pers. alone Lv 24^{14} (P); c. ב pers. alone, רָגוֹם יִרְגְּמוּ־בוֹ v^{16} (P).—Syn. סקל q.v.

†[רִגְמָה] **n.f. heap** (of stones, then) **crowd** (of people; si vera l.);—sf. רִגְמָתָם ψ 68^{28}, but read probably רִגְשָׁתָם, v. [רִגְשָׁה].

†מַרְגֵּמָה **n.f. sling** (?; implement of *hurling* stone? so 𝔊 al.; Thes al. *stone-heap*);—כִּצְרוֹר אֶבֶן בְּמַ׳ Pr 26^{8}, v. esp. Toy.

†רֶגֶם **n.pr.m.** (Thes cp. Ar. رَجْم *friend*; v. also Sab. רגם Hal^{63,4});—1 Ch 2^{47}, Ραγεμ, Ρεγεμ, 𝔊L Ρεγμα.

†רֶגֶם מֶלֶךְ **n.pr.m.** exilic, Zc 7^{2}; Αρβεσεερ ὁ βασιλεύς.

†רָגַן **vb. murmur, whisper** (NH *id.*; 𝔗 Ithpe. *backbite, slander*);—**1.** *murmur* (rebelliously): **Qal** *Pt.* pl. רוֹגְנִים Is 29^{24} *murmurers*; **Niph.** *Impf.* 3 mpl. וַיֵּרָגְנוּ ψ 106^{25} *and they murmured* in their tents, so 2 mpl. וַתֵּרָגְנוּ Dt 1^{27}. **2.** *whisper* (maliciously), *backbite, slander*: **Niph.** *Pt.* נִרְגָּן *backbiter* Pr 16^{28} 18^{8} 26$^{20.22}$.

†I. רָגַע **vb. disturb** (NH Hiph. *move to and fro*; perh. transp. from Ar. رَعَجَ *disturb*, Ba$^{ES 8}$);—**Qal** *Pf.* Jb 26^{12} בְּכֹחוֹ רָגַע הַיָּם; *Pt. cstr.* (Ges$^{65 d, 116 g, z}$), Je 31^{35} = Is 51^{15} רֹגַע הַיָּם וַיֶּהֱמוּ גַלָּיו. **Hiph.** denom. from רֶגַע *make a twinkling*, only 1 s. Impf. cohort. וְעַד אַרְגִּיעָה לְשׁוֹן שָׁקֶר and *while I would twinkle* (= *only for a moment*: cf. Jb 20^{5}) is the false tongue (opp. תִּכּוֹן לָעַד), Pr 12^{19} (cf. De); and כִּי אַרְגִּיעָה

אַרְגִּיעָה מֵעָלֶיהָ *I will twinkle and* (=I will *in a moment*, Ges § 120 g; cf. Hi) chase them away from it, Je 49[19]=50[44]. (Ba § 86 as subst.=רֶגַע, of the very rare type *'aqtîl;* ה- as Ges § 90 f.)

†רֶ֫גַע **n.m.** a moment (NH *id.*; 𝔗 רינעא Ec 9[12]: prob. properly a *movement*, i. e. *twinkling*, of the eye; cf. *momentum*, i. e. *movimentum*);—abs. רֶגַע ,ר׳ Nu 16[21]+, pl. רְגָעִים;—**a.** ψ 30[6] ר׳ בְּאַפּוֹ a *moment* (passes) in his anger (opp. חיים ברצונו); Is 54[7] בְּר׳ קָטֹן during *a little moment.* **b.** usu. in adv. phrases:—(*a*) as adv. acc., (*a*) Ex 33[5] ר׳ אֶחָד *for one moment,* so ר׳ alone Is 54[8]; repeated Je 18[7.9] רֶגַע . . . רֶגַע *at one moment . . . at another moment;* (*β*) *in a moment, suddenly,* ψ 6[11] יָשֻׁבוּ יֵבֹשׁוּ רָ֑גַע, Je 4[20] Is 47[9] Jb 34[20]. (*b*) בְּרֶגַע *in a moment* Jb 21[13] וּבר׳ שְׁאוֹל יֵחָ֑תּוּ (of a quick and painless death; but see 34[20] ψ 73[19]: Hoffm Buhl Beer Bu Du [cf. 𝔊 ἐν ἀναπαύσει, 𝔗 בְּמַרְגּוֹעָא] take רֶגַע (or rd. רֹגַע) as subst. [√ II. רגע] *in tranquillity,* of a peaceful death). So (*c*) כְּר׳ Nu 16[21]=17[10] וַאֲכַלֶּה אֹתָם כְּרָגַע, ψ 73[19]. (*d*) כְּמוֹ ר׳ La 4[6]. (*e*) עֲדֵי רָ֑גַע while *a moment* lasts Jb 20[5]. (*f*) כִּמְעַט ר׳ *like* the littleness of *a moment*=*for* a little *moment* Is 26[20] Ezr 9[8]. (*g*) pl. לִרְגָעִים *by moments, at every moment,* Is 27[3] Ez 26[16] וְחָרְדוּ לִר׳ (so 32[10]), Jb 7[18] (|| לִבְקָרִים).

†II. רָגַע **vb. be at rest, repose** (prob.= Ar. رَجَعَ *return,* prop. *return to rest,* after wanderings, etc.);—**Niph.** *Imv.* 2 fs. Je 47[6] (of sword) be gathered into thy scabbard, הֵרָגְעִי וָדֹמִּי *repose,* and be still. **Hiph. a.** trans. *give rest to;*—*Inf. cstr.* Je 31[2] הָלוֹךְ לְהַרְגִּיעוֹ I will go to *give him* (Isr.) *rest,* 50[34] לְמַעַן הִרְגִּיעַ את־הארץ (on ה׳, v. Ges § 53 l Dr Dt 7, 24; read prob. הַ׳); Is 51[4] ומשפטי לאור עמים אַרְגִּיעַ usu. I will *cause* my judgment (religion) *to repose* as, etc. (i. e. I will establish it; cf. שִׂים 42[4]); but metaph. strange: hence Bachm Che Marti (joining to v[5]) צִדְקִי (<אֲקָרֵב 46[13]) אַרְגִּיעַ אַקְרִיב *in a moment* (I. רגע Hiph.) will I bring near, etc., Du הִרְגִּיעַ קָרֵב, Oort Ry Kit כְּרֶגַע קָרֵב (cf. 𝔊 ἐγγίζει ταχύ). **b.** intrans. *rest, repose,* Dt 28[65] ובגוים ההם לא תַרְגִּיעַ, Is 34[14] שָׁם הִרְגִּיעָה לִּילִית. So Ecclus 36[31].

†רָגֵעַ **adj.** restful, quiet, ψ 35[20] וְעַל רִגְעֵי־ אֶרֶץ דִּבְרֵי מִרְמוֹת יַחֲשֹׁבוּן, of the peaceful worshippers of י׳.

†מַרְגּוֹעַ **n.[m.]** rest (poet.), Je 6[16] וּמִצְאוּ מ׳ לְנַפְשְׁכֶם.

†מַרְגֵּעָה **n.f.** rest, repose (poet.), Is 28[12] אֲשֶׁר אָמַר זֹאת הַמ׳ || הַמְּנוּחָה) וְלֹא אָבוּא שְׁמוֹעַ).

†III. רָגַע **vb.** harden (Eth. ረገዐ: *coagulate, congeal:* poss. a special development of √ رَجَعَ, v. II. ר׳);—Jb 7[5] עוֹרִי רָגַע וַיִּמָּאֵס my skin *hardens,* and (then) runs again (II. מָאַס), of the ulcers in elephantiasis.

†[רָגַשׁ] **vb.** be in tumult or commotion (Ar. جَشَّ, *make a vehement noise;* BAram. Aram. רְגַשׁ, ܪܓܫ *be disturbed, in tumult* (𝔗 Ithp. often for הָמָה, as ψ 46[6], שָׁאָה Is 17[12 f]; ܪܓܘܫܝܐ for הָמוֹן *ibid.*); but Syr. usu. *perceive,* so NH Hiph., but Hithp. *fall stormily upon*);—**Qal** *Pf.* 3 pl. ψ 2[1] רָגְשׁוּ why do the nations *throng tumultuously?*

†[רֶ֫גֶשׁ] **n.[m.]** throng;—ψ 55[15] נְהַלֵּךְ בְּרָגֶשׁ used to walk *in the throng* (cf. הָמוֹן 42[5], also to בית אלהים).

†[רִגְשָׁה] **n.f.** throng;—cstr. רִגְשַׁת פֹּעֲלֵי אָ֑וֶן ψ 64[3]; so (of worshippers, cf. רֶגֶשׁ) 68[28], reading רִגְשָׁתָם for רִגְמָתָם, Hup Pe Bi Che Bae Dr.

†[רָדַד] **vb.** beat out, fig. beat down, subdue (NH Pi. *stamp* or *beat down, make flat, spread out;* 𝔗 רְדַד *beat out;* cf. prob. Ar. رَدَّ *repel, reject* (Nö M 75); As. *radâdu* is *pursue* (rare));—**Qal,** fig., *beat down: Inf. cstr.* לְרַד לְפָנָיו גּוֹיִם Is 45[1]; *Pt. act.* הָרוֹדֵד עַמִּי תַחְתָּי ψ 144[2];—so also *Impf.* יָרֹד Is 41[2] acc. Ew al. (for MT יַרְדְּ, v. I. רדה **Hiph.**).—Ju 19[11] rd. יָרַד. **Hiph.** lit. *beat out: Impf.* 3 ms. וַיָּרֶד עַל־הַכְּרוּבִים . . . אֶת־הַזָּהָב 1 K 6[32] *and beat out the gold upon the cherubim* (covered them with beaten gold).

†[רְדִיד] **n. [m.]** wide wrapper, or large veil (𝔗 Jer רְדִידָא (esp. for Heb. צָעִיף); Syr. ܪܕܝܕܐ, appar. *veil;* Ar. رِدَاءٌ, is *wrapper*);—sf. רְדִידִי Ct 5[7]; pl. הָרְדִידִים Is 3[23] (in list of women's finery).

†רַדַּי **n.pr.m.** fifth son of Jesse, acc. to 1 Ch 2[14]; Ζαδδαι, A Ραδδαι, 𝔊L Ρεδαι.

†I. [רָדָה] **vb.** have dominion, rule, dominate (NH רָדָה, 𝔗 Jon רְדָא, *chastise;* Ar. رَدَى *tread, trample;* Syr. ܪܕܐ *chastise,* also (and so As. *radû*) *go, flow*);—**Qal** *Pf.* 3 pl. consec. וְרָדוּ Is 14[2] Lv 26[17]; 2 mpl. רְדִיתֶם Ez 34[4]; *Impf.* 3 ms. sf. יִרְדֶּנּוּ Lv 25[53], וַיִּרְדֶּנָּה La 1[13], juss. וְיֵרְדְּ Nu 24[19] ψ 72[8]; 2 ms. תִּרְדֶּה Lv 25[43.46], etc.; *Imv.*

ms רדה ψ 110²; mpl רדו Gn 1²⁸ (Jo 4¹³ v. ירד), *Inf cstr* רדות Ez 29¹⁵, *Pt* רֹדֶה 1 K 5⁴ Is 14⁶; sf רדם ψ 68²⁸, pl רֹדִים 1 K 5³⁰ + 2 t,—*have dominion, rule,* over, usu c ב pers vel pop 1 K 5⁴·³⁰ 9²³ = 2 Ch 8¹⁰, Is 14² Lv 25⁴³·⁴⁶·⁵³ 26¹⁷ Ez 29¹⁵ Ne 9²⁸ ψ 49¹⁵, ב of fish, etc, Gn 1²⁶·²⁸, בקרב ψ 110², c acc pers Ez 34⁴ Is 14⁶ (perh + acc cogn, v [מִרְדָּה] infr), acc om Nu 24¹⁹ (מִיַּעֲקֹב), Je 5³¹ (+ עַל־יְדֵיהֶם, v. יָד 5 h (2), vid also ingenious conj sub II רדה, but < Gr יורו *teach*), ψ 72⁸, for וַיִּרְדֶּנָּה La 1¹³ *and it* (the fire) *prevailed against them* (my bones), read perh יָרְדָה into my bones *it descended* (Bu)—רדם ψ 68²⁸ is dub; Grill Hup-Now Che Du קדם יָרַד Ju 5¹³ ¹³ v יָרַד. **Hiph.** *Impf* 3 ms ומלכים ירד Is 41² *and kings he causeth* (him) *to dominate,* but apoc. form strange, read יָרֹד (√ רדד q v) Ew Di Du, יַחֲרִד 𝔊 Klo Che

†[מִרְדָּה] **n.f. dominion**;—as acc cogn מרדת בלי חָשָׂךְ Is 14⁶, cstr. bef cl (Ges § 130 d; so most for MT מֻרְדָּף q v sub רדף)

† II **רָדָה** **vb. scrape out** (NH *id*, *scrape* or *draw off, out* (bread from oven)),—**Qal** *Pf* 3 ms ר׳ הַדְּבַשׁ Ju 14⁹ᵇ out of the carcass *he scraped the honey* (v GFM), sf וַיִּרְדֵּהוּ אֶל־כַּפָּיו v⁹ᵃ *he scraped it out into his palms;* Buhl Lex Du also ר׳ עַל־יְדֵיהֶם Je 5³¹, sc gifts, money, fig for making gain (most I רדה q v.)

רַדַּי **n.pr.** v רדד.

†[רָדַם] **vb. Niph. be in, or fall into, heavy sleep** (NH *id*, cf Ar رَدَمَ *stop up* (door, gap, etc), whence perh *be deaf* (stopped up) to sounds, etc),—*Pf.* 3 ms נִרְדַּם Ju 4²¹, 1 s נרדמתי Dn 8¹⁸, *Impf* 3 ms וַיֵּרָדַם Jon 1⁵, *Pt* נִרְדָּם Pr 10⁵ + 3 t.,—*be* or *fall fast asleep* Ju 4²¹ Jon 1⁵ (after וַיִּשְׁכַּב), v⁶ (pt, Ges § 120 b Da Synt. § 70 (a)), pt as subst נִרְדָּם בַּקָּצִיר Pr 10⁵, of sleep of death ψ 76⁷, stunning effect of awe and dread Dn 8¹⁸ 10⁹ (both + אַרְצָה [וּפָנַי] עַל־פָּנַי)

†תַּרְדֵּמָה **n.f. deep sleep**,—abs ת׳ Gn 2²¹ +, cstr תַּרְדֵּמַת 1 S 26¹²,—*deep sleep,* usu c עַל + נָפַל pers, and usu by supernat agency. ת׳ נָפְלָה עַל וַיַּפֵּל י״ א׳ ת׳ עַל Gn 2²¹ (J, 𝔊 ἔκστασις), 15¹² (J, 𝔊 *id*), Jb 4¹³ = 33¹⁵ (𝔊 [δεινὸς] φόβος), so תַּרְדֵּמַת י״ 1 S 26¹² (𝔊 θάμβος), result of slothfulness (עַל and pers om) Pr 19¹⁵, fig for insensibility of spirit, ת׳ רוּחַ י״ עֲלֵיכֶם נָסַךְ Is 29¹⁰.

†רֹדָן **n. pr. loc.** vel **gent Rhodes, Rhodians,** so read, בני ר׳, Ez 27¹⁵ (for MT בְּנֵי דְדָן, v ד׳ 1), 𝔊 Sta Co Berthol Toy Krae.

†רוֹדָנִים **n.pr.gent.pl. Rhodians,**—1 Ch 1⁷, Ῥόδιοι, and so ‖ Gn 10⁴ (for דֹּדָנִים q.v.)

רָדַף ₁₄₁ **vb. pursue, chase, persecute** (NH *id*, Aram רְדַף, ܪܕܰܦ; Ar. رَدَفَ, Sab רדף *id*, SabDenkm No 7.1 2),—**Qal** ₁₂₈ *Pf* 3 ms ר׳ Ju 4¹⁶ +; 1 s. וְרָדַפְתִּי Je 29¹⁸, etc., *Impf* ירדף Dt 19⁶ +, יִרַדֹּף ψ 7⁶ (appar. to give choice of Qal or Pi, Ki JHMich Bae al; Ges § 63 n expl as developed from יִרְדֹּף, cf Ol § 236 a, and, further, Kö i 160), sf יִרְדָּפְךָ Ez 35⁶·⁶, etc, *Imv.* ms רדף Gn 44⁴ +, sf. רָדְפֵהוּ ψ 34¹⁵, mpl רִדְפוּ Ju 3²⁸ +, *Inf cstr.* לרדף Jos 8¹⁶ +, מרדף 1 S 23²⁸ 2 S 18¹⁶, sf רָדְפִי ψ 38²¹ Qr, רדופי Kt, etc, *Pt* רדף Ju 4²² +, pl רדפים 8⁴ +;—**1. a.** *pursue* (sts. + השיג), lit c אַחֲרֵי pers, in order to overtake Gn 44⁴ (J), 2 K 5²¹, esp with hostile purpose Gn 31²³ (+ הדביק), 35⁵ Jos 24⁶ (all E), 2⁵ ⁷ ⁷ 8¹⁶ ¹⁶·¹⁷ 10¹⁹ (JE), Dt 11⁴ 19⁶ Jos 20⁵ (all D), Ex 14⁴·⁸·⁹ (P), Ju 1⁶ 2 S 20⁶·⁷ ¹⁰ ¹³ 2 K 9²⁷ + 17 t, + 2 K 25⁵ (אַחַר), + Ju 4¹⁶ (אַחֲרֵי הָרֶכֶב), + אַחֲרֵי רִדְפוּ Ju 3²⁸ = *follow me* (as leader; but this meaning not elsewhere, rd רְדוּ 𝔊 Kit GFM) **b.** lit, c acc. pers, *put to flight, chase* (defeated foe; sts c. השיג) Am 1¹¹ Ho 8³ Dt 32³⁰ (poem; ‖ הניס), 28²²·⁴⁵ Jos 23¹⁰ (D), Lv 26⁸·⁸ (H), וְרָדַף אֹתָם קוֹל עָלֶה נִדָּף v³⁶ᵃ (H), Jos 7⁵ 8²⁴ 10¹⁰ 11⁸ (all JE), Gn 14¹⁵ Dt 1⁴⁴ Ju 4²² Is 41³ + 13 t + Ju 7²³ (rd אֶת־ for אֶל־, 𝔊 𝔙 𝔗 GFM Bu Now). †**c.** lit., acc om Ju 8⁴ 1 S 30⁸ (+ השיג), v¹⁰ Gn 14¹⁴ Ex 14²³ (P), 15⁹ (poem; + השיג), Lv 26³⁶ᵇ·³⁷ (H), Pr 28¹; esp pt. pl הָר׳ *the pursuers* Jos 2¹⁶ ¹⁶ ²²·²² Ne 9¹¹ Is 30¹⁶, so הָרֹדֵף Jos 8²⁰ La 1⁶. †**d.** *chase, hunt,* partridge (קרא) 1 S 26²⁰ (in sim., ‖ בקש) †**e.** *pursue,* in fig, Je 20¹¹ La 4¹⁹, רדפו ותפשוהו ψ 71¹¹, cf La 1³, ψ 7⁶ (+ השיג, v supr), esp subj י״, *pursue* (fig. of punishment, judgment), c. acc pers. Je 29¹⁸ (בַּחֶרֶב), La 3⁴³ and (בְּאַף) v⁶⁶, ψ 83¹⁶ (בסערך), אֶת־קַשׁ יָבֵשׁ תרדף Jb 13²⁵ (‖ תַעֲרֹץ), רֹדְפָם, of מַלְאַךְ י״, ψ 35⁶. †**f.** fig *persecute, harass,* c. acc pers Dt 30⁷ Jb 19²² (כמו־אל), ψ 69²⁷ 109¹⁶ 119⁸⁶ ¹⁶¹, c acc נַפְשִׁי 143³, c. acc. נדבתי תרדף Jb 30¹⁵ (but subj obscure, read perh תֵּרָדֵף Bu; Du תִּנְדֹּף), c ל pers Jb 19²⁸, pt. as subst Je 15¹⁵ 17¹⁸ ψ 7² 31¹⁶ (‖ אֹיְבַי, We מְרַדְּפַי for מרדפי), 35³ 119⁸⁴ ¹⁵⁷ (+ צָרַי), 142⁷ †**g.** *pursue, dog,* subj דָּם, c acc pers. Ez 35⁶·⁶ (del vᵃ 𝔊 Co Toy Krae), in good sense, *attend closely upon,* טוֹב וָחֶסֶד ירדפוני ψ 23⁶. †**2.** fig *follow after, aim to secure* in bad sense, c. acc שַׁלְמֹנִים Is 1²³, שֵׁכָר 5¹¹, ר׳ קָדִים Ho 12², רֹדְפֵי זִמָּה ψ 119¹⁵⁰, good

sense, c. inf. לָדַעַת אֶת־י״ Ho 6³, c. acc. צֶדֶק Dt 16²⁰ Is 51¹ (|| מְבַקְשֵׁי י״), צְדָקָה וָחֶסֶד Pr 21²¹, שָׁלוֹם ψ 34¹⁵ (|| בַּקֵּשׁ), טוֹב 38²¹. †**Niph.** pass.: *Pf.* 1 pl. עַל־צַוָּארֵנוּ נִרְדָּפְנוּ La 5⁵ *upon our neck* (i.e. closely) *we are pursued* (improb., cf. Bu); perh. *Impf.* 3 fs. תֵּרָדֵף Jb 30¹⁵ Bu (for תִּרְדֹּף); *Pt.* א׳ יְבַקֵּשׁ אֶת־נִרְדָּף Ec 3¹⁵ *God seeketh the pursued* (i.e. what has disappeared, is past, but dub.). †**Pi.** *Pf.* 3 fs. consec. וְרִדְּפָה Ho 2⁹; *Impf.* 3 ms. יְרַדֶּף־ Na 1⁸ (ψ 7⁶ v. **Qal**); 3 fs. תְּרַדֵּף Pr 13²¹; *Pt.* מְרַדֵּף 11¹⁹ +;—*pursue ardently*, c. acc. pers. Ho 2⁹ (in fig.); fig. also וְאֹיְבָיו יְר׳ חֹשֶׁךְ Na 1⁸ (Gunk ZAW xiii (1893), 230, plausibly, יֶהְדֹּף), cf. Pr 13²¹; elsewhere pt., in Pr: *aim (eagerly) to secure*, c. acc. רָעָה 11¹⁹, רֵיקִים 12¹¹ 28¹⁹, אֲמָרִים 19⁷ (mng. dub., v. Toy); in good sense, צְדָקָה 15⁹. †**Pu.** *Pf.* 3 ms. consec. וְרֻדַּף כְּמֹץ הָרִים Is 17¹³ *it shall be chased away like chaff of the mountains* (|| וְנָס). †**Hiph.** *Pf.* 3 ms. sf. הִרְדִּיפֻהוּ Ju 20⁴³ usu. *they chased him* (Benj., coll.), but strange after כִּתְּרוּ *surrounded* (still stranger after כתתו or כרתו ⅏), and why Hiph.? GFM conj. dittogr. of הִדְרִיכֻהוּ foll.; the reverse conjectured by Bu Now.

†מִרְדָּף **n.[m.]** persecution (si vera l.) (formed like **Hoph.** *Pt.*);—Is 14⁶, but 𝔗 Thes and most מִרְדַּת q.v.

†[רָהַב] **vb.** act stormily, boisterously, arrogantly (Ecclus 13⁸, NH *id.*, Hiph. *make proud* (rare), 𝔗 רְהַב *be arrogant*; As. *ra'âbu*, *storm at* (angrily); Ar. رَهِبَ *be alarmed, frightened*; Syr. ܪܗܒ, Pe. Pt. *trembling, hastening*, Aph. *terrify, hasten*);—**Qal** *Impf.* 3 mpl. יִרְהֲבוּ הַנַּעַר בַּזָּקֵן Is 3⁵ (|| וְנִגַּשׂ) *storm against* (⅏ προσκόψει); *Imv.* רְהַב רֵעֶ(י)ךָ Pr 6³ *beset, importune, thy friend* (Perles Anal. 61 conj. רְהַן *give surety*, cf. NH הרהין). **Hiph.** *Pf.* 3 mpl. sf. הִרְהִיבֻנִי Ct 6⁵, of eyes, dub.: *alarm me* Hi Ew Bu, *awe me* Gi, *disturb, confuse me*, Oettli Dr Intr. 419 (446) Buhl; *Impf.* 2 ms. sf. תַּרְהִבֵנִי ψ 138³ (subj. י׳), Buhl Bae Dr *thou makest me proud, bold* (Thes De Che denom. of רֹהַב).

†[רָהָב] **adj.** proud, defiant (si vera l.);—pl. אֶל־רְהָבִים ψ 40⁵ *unto the proud;* but read prob. הבלים (cf. ⅏ ματαιότητας).

†[רֹהַב] **n.[m.]** Thes al. pride, i.e. obj. of pride;—sf. רָהְבָּם ψ 90¹⁰ (cf. ἡ ἀλαζονία τοῦ βίου 1 Jn 2¹⁶); < ⅏ 𝔙 *their width, extent* (רָחְבָּם).

†רַהַב **n.[m.]** lit. storm, arrogance, but only as names, v. infr.;—abs. ר׳ Is 30⁷, רָהַב Jb 9¹³+;—**1.** mythical sea monster (cf. Barton JAOS xv. 1 (1891), 22 f.): עֹזְרֵי ר׳ Jb 9¹³; || יָם 26¹² ψ 89¹¹; || תַּנִּין Is 51⁹. **2.** emblemat. name of Egypt, רַהַב וּבָבֶל ψ 87⁴; || מצרים Is 30⁷.

מַרְהֵבָה **n.f.** boisterous, raging, behaviour;—Is 14⁴; so read (for MT מַדְהֵבָה) Thes and most, after ⅏; || נגשׂ (cf. 3⁵).

רהג (√of foll.; Ar. رَهَجٌ is *raise* (dust, a tumult, conflict, etc.), Lane).

†רָהֲגָה Qr, רוהגה Kt, **n.pr.m.** in Asher 1 Ch 7³⁴; A Ογα, ⅏L Ραγους.

†[רָהָה] **vb.** dub., appar. fear;—**Qal** *Impf.* 2 mpl. אַל־תִּפְחֲדוּ וְאַל־תִּרְהוּ Is 44⁸; Thes תִּרְהוּ, but no √ ירה; Ew Brd Buhl Lex 13 תִּירְאוּ (יָרֵא); > Lag Gr Che Hpt תִּרְהֲבוּ (in Syr. sense).

I. רהט (√of foll., prob. *collect, gather*, cf. Ar. رَهْطٌ, I, VIII. *be collected, congregated*, cf. Nö ZA xii. 186; 𝔗 רָטְיָא = רְהָטִים, Gn 30³⁸·⁴¹ Ex 2¹⁶; Syr. ܪܗܛܐ is appar. *conduit*, also *reservoir* (?); As. *râṭu*, *vessel* for water, provisions, etc.).

†I. [רַהַט] **n.[m.]** trough (where water is *collected*?);—for watering cattle;—pl. רְהָטִים Gn 30³⁸·⁴¹ Ex 2¹⁶ (all J).

II. רהט (√of two foll.; perhaps Aram. רְהַט = רוץ *run, flow*).

II. [רַהַט] **n.[m.]** dub., Thes and most lock of hair (? fr. *flowing* down);—pl. רְהָטִים Ct 7⁶.

†[רָהִיט] **n.m. coll.** rafters? boards? (as strips *running* between beams? so Bu conj.; cf. Syr. ܪܗܛܐ *boards* (?), Nö in Bu);—sf. רָהִיטֵנוּ Ct 1¹⁷ Qr (Kt רחיטנו; Codd. רח׳ Baer p. 46 Kö ii. 1, 149), || קָרוֹת.

רוב v. רב sub רבב. [רוּב] v. ריב.

†רוד **vb.** wander restlessly, roam (cf. Ar. رَادَ (و) *go to and fro* [Nö ZMG xxxvii (1883), 539], Eth. ሮደ: *run upon, invade, attack*);—**Qal** *Pf.* 3 ms. עֹד רָד עִם אֵל Ho 12¹, fig., crpt., ⅏ appar. עַתָּ יְדָעָם, We עֵדֶר דַּעַת *lacks knowledge*, Now עֹד יְדָעָם יָדַע, Bewer JBL xxi (1902), 108 f. עֹד יְדָעָם; 1 pl. רַדְנוּ Je 2³¹ fig. of Isr.; read וְרָדַתִּי perh. Ju 11³⁷ lit., v. ירד 1 g. **Hiph.** *shew restlessness*: *Impf.* 2 ms. כַּאֲשֶׁר תָּרִיד Gn 27⁴⁰ (dub. Nö l. c. 540); 1 s. אָרִיד בְּשִׂיחִי ψ 55³ *I shew restlessness* (?) *in my murmuring.*

†[מָרוּד, $Ko^{ii.1,127f}$] **n.[m.] restlessness, straying** (?),—sf. עָנְיִי וּמְרוּדִי La 3^{19}; pl. sf יְמֵי עָנְיָהּ וּמְרוּדֶיהָ La 1^{7} (rd prob מְרוּדָהּ $No^{ZMG\ xxxvii\ (1883).\ 539}$); pl וַעֲנִיִּים מְרוּדִים Is 58^{7}, usu concr. *the wandering* (homeless) *poor* (Di thinks old Qal pass. Pt; Che^{Comm} rds Hoph מוּרָדִים, $Buhl^{Lex}$ Hiph. מְרִידִים, $Ko^{ii.1,129}$ takes MT as abstr. for concr. [appos of 'עֲ], so Du Che^{Hpt} ['עֲ gloss], read perhaps pt. מְרִים (מ dittogr)).

†[רָוָה] **vb. be saturated, drink one's fill** (NH in der. spec., Ar رَوِيَ; Eth. ረወየ: Aram. רְוִי, ܪܘܐ),—**Qal** *Pf* 3 fs consec וְרָוְתָה חַרְבִּי Je 46^{10}, fig of sword (‖ אָכְלָה, שָׂבְעָה); *Impf* 3 mpl יִרְוְיֻן מִדֶּשֶׁן בֵּיתֶךָ ψ 36^{9} ($Ges^{\S 75u}$) fig of men (‖ תַשְׁקֵם), 1 pl נִרְוֶה דֹדִים Pr 7^{18} *we will take our fill of love* (‖ נִתְעַלְּסָה). **Pi.** *Pf* 3 fs רִוְּתָה Is 34^{5}, 'וְר consec v^{7}; 1 s. consec. וְרִוֵּיתִי Je 31^{14}, *Impf* 1 s. sf. אֲרַיָּוֶךְ Is 16^{9} (read prob אֲרַוֵּךְ $Margolis^{Am\ J\ Sem\ Lang.\ Oct\ 1902.\ 48}$, vid. also $Ko^{i.589f}$, > אֲרַיָּוֶךְ $Sta^{\S 634e}$ $Ges^{\S 75dd}$), 3 mpl sf. יְרַוֻּךָ Pr 5^{19}, *Inf abs* רַוֵּה ψ 65^{11} ($Ges^{\S 113s}$);—**1.** intens. *be intoxicated, drunk* Is 34^{5}, fig of sword, + מִדָּם v^{7}, of land (‖ יְדֻשָּׁן). **2.** causat., *drench, water abundantly*, c acc. תְּלָמֶיהָ (subj. 'י); Is 16^{9} c. acc pers + דִּמְעָתִי material, *saturate* (fig.), *sate*, דַּדֶּיהָ, sexually, (‖ שׂבע) Je 31^{14} ור' נֶפֶשׁ הַכֹּהֲנִים דָּשֶׁן Pr 5^{19} **Hiph.** *Pf.* 3 ms. הִרְוָה Is 55^{10}, sf הִרְוַנִי La 3^{15}, 2 ms sf. הִרְוִיתָנִי Is 43^{24}; 1 s. הִרְוֵיתִי Je 31^{25}, *Pt* מַרְוֶה Pr 11^{25},—*saturate, water*, c. acc אֶרֶץ Is 55^{10} (subj. גֶּשֶׁם, שֶׁלֶג); *cause to drink* (fig.), c acc pers et rei (הִשְׂבִּיעַנִי ‖) La 3^{15} (לַעֲנָה), c. acc. pers only (נֶפֶשׁ) Je 31^{25} (מִלֵּאתִי ‖), abs. Pr 11^{25}, of Isr satisfying 'י, חֵלֶב זְבָחִים Is 43^{24}. **Hoph.** *Impf.* (וְיָרְוֶה) יוֹרֶא Pr 11^{25} v. Toy and ירא p 432.

†רִי **n.[m.] moisture** (for * רוֶי $Sta^{\S 117e}$, or * רִוְי $Ko^{ii.1,64}$, cf. II. כִּי),—abs אַף־בְּרִי יַטְרִיחַ עָב Jb 37^{11}

†רָוֶה **adj watered**,—ms. 'ר, of garden גַּן (in sim) Je 31^{12} Is 58^{11}, fs הָרָוָה Dt 29^{18} (opp הַצְּמֵאָה, appar of herbage, in proverb expression for *everything*), perhaps also cstr רְוֵה Jb 10^{15} = *sated* with affliction (for רְאֵה), v [רָאֶה]

†רְוָיָה **n.f. saturation** ($Lag^{BN\ 51,\ 150}$),—abs כּוֹסִי ר' ψ 23^{5} (fig.), i.e. is well-filled $Ges^{\S 141c}$, in gen לָר' 66^{12}, but Vrss and most mod. לִרְוָחָה *to* (a place of) *relief*

רוהגה v. רָהֲגָּה sub רהג.

רוח (✓ of foll.; prob. *breathe, blow* (v. $Gerber^{46}$); cf. Syr ܪܘܚ *breathe*; Ar. رَاحَ *be windy*, Eth ረወሐ: *flabello ventilare, ventulum facere*, Ar رِيحٌ *breath, wind, spirit*, رُوحٌ *soul, spirit*, NH רוּחַ, Aram רוּחָא, ܪܘܚܐ *wind, breath, spirit*; also NH רֵיחַ, Aram רֵיחָא, ܪܝܚܐ, all *odour*; NH רֵיחַ, רוּחַ (usu Hiph.), 𝔗 Syr Aph, all *smell*)

רוּחַ $_{378}$ **n.f.** $^{Gn\ 41\ 8}$ (less oft **m.** $^{Ex\ 10,\ 13+}$) **breath, wind, spirit**;—abs 'ר Gn 8^{1}+, רוּחָה Je 52^{23}; cstr. רוּחַ Gn 6^{17}+; sf רוּחִי v^{3}+, רוּחֲךָ ψ 104^{30}+, etc.; pl רוּחוֹת v^{4}+, רֻחוֹת Je 49^{36}, רוּחֹת Nu 16^{22} 26^{16} (v $Br^{Hex\ in\ O\ T,\ JBL\ xix\ (1900),\ 132\ ff}$, full statement of all passages);—†**1.** *breath* of mouth or nostrils (33 t.). **a.** רוּחַ פִּיו Jb 15^{30} *breath of his mouth*, cf 19^{17}, רוּחַ אַפֵּינוּ La 4^{20} (fig of king), of idols לֹא רוּחַ בָּם Je 10^{14} = 51^{17}, Hb 2^{19} ψ 135^{17}; cf Jb 9^{18}. **b.** as mere breath. cf. **2 e.** לְרוּחַ אִמְרֵי Jb 16^{3} i.e. windy words, דִּבְרֵי־רוּחַ Jb 6^{26}, הַנְּבִיאִים יִהְיוּ לְרוּחַ נוֹאָשׁ Je 5^{13}. **c.** as word of command. (1) of God: (נעשׂו) בְּרוּחַ פִּיו כָּל־ צְבָאָם ψ 33^{6}, cf Is 34^{16} (‖ פֶּה), (2) of Messianic king בְּרוּחַ שְׂפָתָיו יָמִית רָשָׁע Is 11^{4} **d.** as hard breathing through the nostrils in anger: (1) of God: מֵרוּחַ אַפּוֹ יִכְלוּ Jb 4^{9} Ex 15^{8} (poem), 2 S 22^{16} = ψ 18^{16}, Is 30^{28} 59^{19}, (2) of man. רוּחַ עָרִיצִים Is 25^{4}. **e.** as sign and symbol of life: רוּחַ חַיִּים *breath of life* Gn 6^{17} 7^{15} (P); נִשְׁמַת רוּחַ חַיִּים בְּאַפָּיו Gn 7^{22} (P), Ez 37^{5}, cf. $v^{6.8.9\ 9.10.14}$ (*breath* or *spirit*), Ec 3^{19}. **2.** *wind* (117 t). **a.** *wind* of heaven: Gn 8^{1} (P) Ex 15^{10} (E) Nu 11^{31} (J) 1 K 18^{45}+, Je 10^{13}, thence 51^{16} ψ 135^{7}, רוּחַ י' Ho 13^{15} Is 40^{7}, cf Jb 26^{13} (Di Bu); †רוּחַ (הַ)קָּדִים *east wind* Ex $10^{13.13}$ 14^{21} (J) ψ 48^{8} Je 18^{17} Ez 17^{10} 19^{12} 27^{26} Jon 4^{8}, †ר' צָפוֹן *north wind* Pr 25^{23}; †ר' יָם *sea wind* (west wind) Ex 10^{19} (J); †ר' הַיּוֹם *day wind*, evening wind Gn 3^{8} (J, cf Ct 2^{17} 4^{6}), †אַרְבַּע רוּחוֹת *four winds* Je 49^{36} Ez 37^{9} (quarters?) Dn 8^{8} 11^{4} (fig. quarters, cf. **b**), Zc 2^{10} 6^{5}; רוּחַ סְעָרָה *storm wind* ψ 107^{25} 148^{8} Ez 1^{4} (ר' סְעָרוֹת), $13^{11.13}$; רוּחַ סֹעָה *rushing wind* ψ 55^{9} (read poss סערה Hup), בַּעְיָם רוּחוֹ Is 11^{15} (read בְּעֹצֶם ר', v עָיָם, עצם), etc; wind personif. כַּנְפֵי רוּחַ 2 S 22^{11} = ψ 18^{11}, 104^{3}, cf Ho 4^{19} ψ 104^{4}. **b.** *quarter* (of wind), *side*: רוּחַ הַקָּדִים Ez 42^{16} *east side*; רוּחַ הַצָּפוֹן v^{17} *north side*; רוּחַ הַדָּרוֹם v^{18} *south side*; רוּחַ הַיָּם v^{19} *west side*; אַרְבַּע רוּחוֹת v^{20} 1 Ch 9^{24} *four sides*; רוּחָה Je 52^{23} *on the sides* **c.** *breath of air*. רוּחַ לֹא יָבֹא בֵינֵיהֶם Jb 41^{8}. שָׁאֲפוּ רוּחַ כַּתַּנִּים Je 14^{6}; **d.** *air, gas*, from womb (dub). כְּמוֹ

רוּחֲכֶם אֵשׁ תֹּאכַלְכֶם Is 26^{18} (Di, e); יָלַדְנוּ רוּחַ (RV breath) Is 33^{11} (Du, **3 c**). **e.** *vain, empty thing:* רוּחַ חַיָּי Jb 7^{7} *my life is wind;* דַּעַת רוּחַ 15^{2}; רוּחַ וָתֹהוּ נִסְכֵּיהֶם Is 41^{29}; רְעוּת רוּחַ *striving for wind* Ec 1^{14} $2^{11.17.26}$ $4^{4.6}$ 6^{9}; cf. 1^{17} 4^{16} 5^{15}. †**3.** *spirit*, as that which breathes quickly *in animation or agitation = temper, disposition* (76 t.; so, distinctively, as compared with נֶפֶשׁ and לֵבָב): **a.** *spirit, animation, vivacity, vigour:* לֹא הָיָה בָהּ עוֹד רוּחַ 1 K 10^{5} = 2 Ch 9^{4}; מַה־זֶּה רוּחֲךָ סָרָה 1 K 21^{5}; וַתְּחִי רוּחַ Gn 45^{27} (E); וַתָּשָׁב רוּחוֹ Ju 15^{19} 1 S 30^{12}. **b.** *courage:* לֹא הָיָה בָם עוֹד ר׳ Jos 5^{1}; יִבְצֹר ר׳ נְגִידִים ψ 76^{13}; וְנָבְקָה ר׳ מִצְרַיִם Is 19^{3}; תתעטף רוּחִי ψ 77^{4} 142^{4} 143^{4}; לֹא קָמָה עוֹד ר׳ Jos 2^{11}; ר׳־אִישׁ יְכַלְכֵּל מַחֲלֵהוּ Pr 18^{14}. **c.** *temper*, esp. *anger:* אָז רוּחַ רָעָה בֵּין וגו׳ Ju 9^{23}; רָפְתָה רוּחָם 8^{3}; מֹשֵׁל בְּרוּחוֹ Pr 16^{32}, cf. 25^{28} 29^{11} Jb 15^{13}; הֵנִיחוּ אֶת־רוּחִי Zc 6^{8}; Ec 7^{9} 10^{4}. **d.** *impatience* or *patience:* קֹצֶר רוּחַ Ex 6^{9} (P) *impatience*, hastiness of temper, cf. (of ׳י) Mi 2^{7}; קְצַר־רוּחַ Pr 14^{29} (‖ אֶרֶךְ אַפַּיִם); הֱצִיקַתְנִי רוּחַ בִּטְנִי Jb 32^{18} (Du *breath;* Di Bu *divine spirit*, cf. v^{8}); אִם מַדּוּעַ לֹא־תִקְצַר רוּחִי Jb 21^{4}; הֲקָצַר רוּחַ י׳ Mi 2^{7}; אֶרֶךְ ר׳ Ec 7^{8}. **e.** *spirit, disposition*, as troubled, bitter, or discontented; וַתִּפָּעֶם רוּח(ו) (*his*) *spirit was troubled* Gn 41^{8} (E) Dn 2^{3}, cf. v^{1}; מֹרַת רוּחַ Gn 26^{35} (P) *bitterness of spirit;* עֲצוּבַת ר׳ Is 54^{6}, cf. Ez 3^{14} Jb 6^{4}. **f.** as crushed: וְכִהֲתָה כָל־רוּחַ Ez 21^{12}, cf. Is 61^{3} Pr $15^{4.13}$ 17^{22} 18^{14} ψ 143^{7}. **g.** *disposition* of various kinds, oft. *unaccountable and uncontrollable impulse:* הֵעִיר אֶת־רוּחַ 1 Ch $5^{26.26}$ 2 Ch 21^{16} 36^{22} Ezr $1^{1.5}$ Je 51^{11} Hg $1^{14.14.14}$; הִנְנִי נֹ(וֹ)תֵן בּוֹ רוּחַ 2 K 19^{7} = Is 37^{7}; Nu 14^{24} (J; v. עִם **4 b**), Mal $2^{15.15.16}$ Dt 2^{30}; רוּחַ קִנְאָה *jealous disposition* Nu $5^{14.14.30}$ (P); רוּחַ זְנוּנִים Ho 4^{12} 5^{4}; רוּחַ עִוְעִים Is 19^{14}; רוּחַ מִשְׁפָּט 28^{6}; אִישׁ אֲשֶׁר רוּחַ אֱלֹהִים בּוֹ (administrative) Gn 41^{38} (E); קַר רוּחַ אִישׁ תְּבוּנָה Pr 17^{27}. **h.** *prophetic spirit:* יְהוֹשֻׁעַ אִישׁ אֲשֶׁר רוּחַ בּוֹ Nu 27^{18} (P; or **g**, as Gn 41^{38}); רוּחַ אֵלִיָּהוּ עַל־אֱלִישָׁע 2 K 2^{15}, cf. v^{9}; רוּחַ תַּרְדֵּמָה *spirit of deep sleep* (ecstatic, cf. Gn 2^{21} 15^{12}, but Di al. **g**, as Is 19^{14}) Is 29^{10}; Mi 2^{11}; רוּחַ הַטֻּמְאָה Zc 13^{2} (of lying proph.), cf. Ez 13^{3}. †**4.** *spirit* of the living, breathing being, dwelling in the בָּשָׂר of men and animals, ‖ נֶפֶשׁ (25 t.): **a.** gift and creation of God: יֹצֵר רוּחַ אָדָם בְּקִרְבּוֹ Zc 12^{1}; רוּחַ אֱלוֹהַּ בְּאַפִּי Jb 27^{3}, cf. Is 42^{5}. **b.** God preserves it: פְּקֻדָּתְךָ שָׁמְרָה רוּחִי Jb 10^{12}, cf. 12^{10}; אֱלֹהֵי הָרוּחֹת לְכָל בָּשָׂר Nu 16^{22} 27^{16} (P); תֹּכֵן רוּחוֹת Pr 16^{2}. **c.** it is therefore God's spirit: Gn 6^{3} (J; v. דִּין ad fin.). **d.** it departs at death: ψ 78^{39} (Dr *a wind* that passeth *away* **2 e**); חַיֵּי רוּחִי Is 38^{16} (Di *principle of life*), ψ 146^{4}; esp. $104^{29.30}$ Jb 17^{1} 34^{14} (cf. v^{15}), Is 57^{16} Ec $8^{8.8}$ (*wind* Wild); אֵינְךָ יוֹדֵעַ מַה־דֶּרֶךְ הָרוּחַ Ec 11^{5}, cf. 3^{21}; over ag. הָרוּחַ תָּשׁוּב אֶל־הָאֱלֹהִים אֲשֶׁר נְתָנָהּ 12^{7}; בְּיָדְךָ אַפְקִיד רוּחִי ψ 31^{6}. **e.** disembodied being (dub., Di Du *breath of wind*): וְרוּחַ עַל־פָּנַי יַחֲלֹף Jb 4^{15}. †**5.** *spirit* as seat of emotion = נֶפֶשׁ: **a.** *desire* (poss. **3 g**), Is 26^{9} (‖ נֶפֶשׁ). **b.** *sorrow, trouble* (prob. **3 e**), Jb 7^{11} (‖ נֶפֶשׁ).—1 S 1^{15} v. קָשֶׁה. †**6.** occasionally (and late) = seat or organ of mental acts, ‖ לֵב, or synon. with it: רוּחַ חָכְמָה Ex 28^{3} Dt 34^{9} (both P; prob. **3 g**); תֹּעֵי רוּחַ Is 29^{24}, cf. Jb 20^{3} (Hi Bu Du *wind* of Job's words), ψ 77^{7} (𝔊 Sym 𝔖 Jer troubled *disposition*); רוּחַ יהוה Is 40^{13}; come into *mind* Ez 11^{5}, 20^{32} (cf. לֵב Is 65^{17} Je 3^{16}+); 1 Ch 28^{12}. †**7.** rarely of the will; also = לֵב: רוּחַ נָכוֹן ψ 51^{12} (= לֵב נָכוֹן $57^{8.8}$+); רוּחַ נְדִיבָה v^{14}; נָדְבָה רוּחוֹ Ex 35^{21} (P; cf. נְדִיב לֵב Ex $35^{5.22}$ (P) 2 Ch 29^{31}). †**8.** רוּחַ esp. of moral character; also = לֵב: רוּחַ חֲדָשָׁה Ez 11^{19} 18^{31} 36^{26}; רוּחִי v^{27} Is 59^{21} (רוּחִי, ‖ דְּבָרַי; but prob. prophetic spirit **9 b**); לֵב חָדָשׁ Ez 18^{31} 36^{26}; נְכֵה רוּחַ Is 66^{2}; דַּכְּאֵי רוּחַ ψ 34^{19} (cf. לֵב נִדְכָּאִים Is 57^{15}); מִשֵּׁבֶר רוּחַ Is 65^{14} (cf. **3 f**); רוּחַ נִשְׁבָּרָה ψ 51^{19} (‖ לֵב נִשְׁבָּר, cf. נִשְׁבְּרֵי לֵב 34^{19} Is 61^{1}); ψ 32^{2} Pr 11^{13} 16^{18} ψ 78^{8} Ec 7^{8} (cf. גְּבַהּ לֵב Pr 16^{5}); שְׁפַל רוּחַ Pr 16^{19} 29^{23} Is 57^{15}; רוּחַ שְׁפָלִים v^{15} (cf. **3 f**). †**9.** *spirit of God* (94 t.; not D or Je or any Deut. writer; conception of its activity in inspiring prophecy prob. discredited from abuse by false prophets, v. נבא, נביא): **a.** as inspiring ecstatic state of prophecy, Nu $11^{17.25.25.26.29}$ (J), 1 S $10^{6.10}$ (cf. v^{5}), $19^{20.23}$; as inciting to deeds of frenzy, in the ecstatic state; hence conceived as ר׳ אֱלֹהִים רָעָה 1 S $16^{15.15.16}$, = ר׳ רָעָה מֵאֵת ^ v^{14} = צלח ר׳ א׳ רָעָה 18^{10} (other narrative) = ר׳ י׳ רָעָה 19^{9}; ר׳ א׳ 16^{23} = רוּחַ הָרָעָה v^{23}, cf. הָרוּחַ 1 K 22^{21} = ר׳ שֶׁקֶר $v^{22.23}$ = 2 Ch $18^{20.21.22}$ = רוּחַ י׳ 1 K 22^{24} = 2 Ch 18^{23}; cf. also (in earlier prophets) אִישׁ הָרוּחַ, i.e. one possessed by the spirit in the ecstatic state, ‖ הַנָּבִיא Ho 9^{7}; רוּחַ י׳ Mi 3^{8} (‖ כֹּחַ) is prob. gloss (We Now); וְלֹא רוּחִי Is 30^{1}; רוּחַ dealing with Ezek.: Ez 2^{2} $3^{12.14.24}$ 8^{3} $11^{1.5.24}$ (Co gloss), 37^{1} 43^{5} (all implying ecstatic state of vision), cf. Elijah 1 K 18^{12} 2 K 2^{16}. **b.** *spirit* as impelling proph. to utter instruction or warning (higher and later conception): transition prob. Nu 24^{2} 2 S 23^{2} 1 Ch 12^{18}; elsewhere in Ch.: 2 Ch 15^{1} 20^{14} 24^{20}; distinctly in Is^{2}, 48^{16}, cf. 61^{1}; so of ancient

prophets, Zc 7^{12} Ne 9^{30}, cf., of future prophetic gift, Jo $3^{1.2}$. **c.** imparting warlike energy, and executive and administrative power: (1) to מְלָכִים, מוֹשִׁיעִים, שֹׁפְטִים, of ancient Isr.: וַתְּהִי רוּחַ י׳ עַל Ju 3^{10} 11^{29}, cf. 6^{34} 13^{25} $14^{6.19}$ 15^{14} 1 S 11^{6} $16^{13.14}$; so also עַד יֵעָרֶה עָלֵינוּ רוּחַ מִמָּרוֹם Is 32^{15}; (2) resting upon Messianic king: Is $11^{2.2.2}$; upon servant of י׳, 42^{1}. **d.** late, as endowing men with various gifts: technical skill Ex 31^{3} 35^{31} (P); understanding Jb 32^{8} (‖ נִשְׁמַת שַׁדַּי); poured out by divine wisdom Pr 1^{23}. **e.** as energy of life: רוּחַ אֱלֹהִים מְרַחֶפֶת עַל־פְּנֵי הַמָּיִם Gn 1^{2} (P); רוּחַ אֵל עָשָׂתְנִי Jb 33^{4} (‖ נִשְׁמַת שַׁדַּי); as vital power, opp. בָּשָׂר: Is 31^{3}; in cherubic chariot: Ez 1^{12}, cf. v$^{20.21}$ 10^{17}; reviving Israel Ez 39^{29} Zc 12^{10} Is 44^{3}. **f.** = ancient angel of the presence and later Shekina: ר׳ קָדְשׁוֹ Is $63^{10.11}$ = ר׳ י׳ v^{14} (= מַלְאַךְ פָּנָיו v^{9}), cf. ψ 106^{33}; so also ר׳ קָדְשְׁךָ ψ 51^{13} (in national prayer), cf. Ne 9^{20} ψ 143^{10}; proph. of restoration conceive of the divine spirit as standing in their midst and about to fulfil all divine promises: רוּחִי עֹמֶדֶת בְּתוֹכְכֶם Hg 2^{5}, Zc 4^{6}; this conception culminates in רוּחַ = divine Presence, and as such omnipresent, ψ 139^{7} (‖ פָּנֶיךָ; cf. v^{8}).

רֵיחַ $_{58}$ **n.m.** $^{Je\ 48,11}$ **scent, odour** (prop. *breath*);—abs. Ct 2^{13}+, usu. cstr. Gn 8^{21}+; sf. רֵיחוֹ Je 48^{11} Ct 1^{12}, רֵיחֵנוּ Ex 5^{21};—**1.** *scent, odour*, of plants and fields Gn 27^{27} (JE) Ct 1^{12} 2^{3} 4^{11} 7^{14} Ho 14^{7}, of ointments Ct 1^{3} 4^{10}, of pers. and garments Gn $27^{27.27}$ (JE) Ct 4^{11} 7^{9}, of water Jb 14^{9}; fig. of influence, reputation Ex 5^{21} (J) Je 48^{11}. **2.** term. techn., רֵיחַ נִיחֹחַ *odour of soothing* (to God), tranquillizing odour (of ascending sacrifices, v. נִיחֹחַ) Gn 8^{21} (J), elsewh. Ez 6^{13} 16^{19} $20^{28.41}$ and P: Ex $29^{18.25.41}$ Lv 1^{9}+ 16 t. Lv, Nu 15^{3}+ 17 t. Nu.

†[רִיחַ] **vb. denom. Hiph.** (?), **smell, perceive odour**;—*Impf.* 3 ms. יָרִיחַ Jb 39^{25}, יָרַח 1 S 26^{19}+ 2 t.; וַיָּרַח Gn 8^{21}; 3 mpl. יְרִיחוּן ψ 115^{6}, יְרִיחֻן Dt 4^{28}, etc.; *Inf. cstr.* הָרִיחַ Ex 30^{38}, etc.;—*smell*, c. acc. Gn 8^{21} 27^{27} (JE), 1 S 26^{19}; abs. Dt 4^{28} ψ 115^{6}; metaph. בַּהֲרִיחוֹ אֵשׁ Ju 16^{9}, יָרִיחַ מִלְחָמָה Jb 39^{25} the horse *scenteth battle*; c. בְּ Ex 30^{38} Lv 26^{31} (both P); metaph. = *delight in* Am 5^{21} Is 11^{3} (prob. dittogr. Br $^{MP\ 202}$).

†רָוַח **vb. be wide, spacious** (NH *id.*, *extend* (intrans.), רֶוַח *wide space*; Ar. رَوِحَ *be wide* (between thighs), and deriv.; cf. perhaps Eth. ርኅወ: *make open, open* (der. spec.; Di ^{293}); Aram. רְוַח *be wide* (usu. fig. as Heb.), ܪܘܚ, ܪܘܰܚ *be wide, enlarged*);—**Qal** *Pf.* 3 ms. ר׳, sq. לְ pers. 1 S 16^{23} fig. there *was enlargement, relief*, for Saul; *Impf.* 3 ms. יִרְוַח לִי Jb 32^{20} that *there may be relief* for me. **Pu.** *Pt.* pl. מְרֻוָּחִים Je 22^{14} *spacious* (of rooms; ‖ בֵּית מִדּוֹת).

†רֶוַח **n.m. 1. space, interval** Gn 32^{17} (E; בֵּין ... וּבֵין). **2. respite, relief,** Est 4^{14}.

†רְוָחָה **n.f. respite, relief**;—abs. ר׳ Ex 8^{11} (J); sf. רַוְחָתִי La 3^{56} (Ew Löhr Bu $^{Comm.}$ צַוְחָתִי *my outcry*; then del. שַׁוְעָתִי as gloss); rd. לִרְוָחָה also for MT לָרְוָיָה ψ 66^{12} (v. sub רוה).

רְוָיָה v. רוה.

†רוּם **vb. be high, exalted, rise** (OHeb., Ph., OAram., Palm., all in n.pr.; Sab. in רים epith. dei et regis Fell $^{ZMG\ liv\ (1900),\ 25\ f.}$ also in n.pr. Mordtm $^{ib.\ xxx\ (1876),\ 36}$ SabDenkm $^{No.\ 14,\ 1.1}$; Ar. رَامَ *be high*, dial. of Oman (Jayakar $^{JA\ xxi.\ 813,\ 875}$) and Zanzibar (Prä $^{ZMG\ xxxiv\ (1880),\ 218}$); Eth. in deriv.; Aram. רָם, ܪܳܡ (very often in der. spec. and deriv.));—**Qal** *Pf.* 3 ms. consec. וְרָם Dt 8^{14}+; 3 fs. רָמָה 1 S 2^{1}+; וְרָאֲמָה Zc 14^{10} v. ראם; 3 pl. רָמוּ Pr 30^{13} ψ 131^{1}, רָמּוּ Jb 22^{12} (Baer Gi; Ges $^{§\ 20\ i}$); *Impf.* יָרוּם Is 30^{18}+, juss. יָרֹם Nu 24^{7}, וַיָּרָם Ho 13^{6} Ez 10^{4} [וַיָּרֻם Ex 16^{20} v. רמם]; 3 mpl. יְרֻמוּן Is 49^{11}, etc.; *Imv.* ms. רוּמָה ψ 21^{14}+; *Inf. cstr.* רוּם Dt 17^{20} Ez 10^{16}, כְּרֻם ψ 12^{9} [Bae conj. כְּרָם], sf. רוּמָם Ez 10^{17} (Ges $^{§\ 72\ q}$); *Pt.* רָם Is 6^{1}+, pl. רָמִים 2^{13}+, cstr. רָמֵי 10^{33}, etc.;—**1. a.** *be high*, lit. rock (in fig.) ψ 61^{3} (מִן comp.); *be (set on) high*, רָמּוּ Jb 22^{12} (of stars), esp. pt., = adj., in gen. Is 2^{12} (+ גֵּאֶה), of mts. v^{14} Dt 12^{2}, hill Ez 6^{13} 20^{28} 34^{6}, throne Is 6^{1}, trees = *tall* 2^{13} Ez 17^{22}, cf. (in fig.) Is 10^{33} (רָמֵי הַקּוֹמָה); human stature Dt 1^{28} (מִן comp.), $2^{10.21}$ 9^{2}; רָמִים ψ 78^{69} *heights* (of heaven; ‖ אֶרֶץ); רָמִים of inhab. of heavens Jb 21^{22}. **b.** esp. of י׳, רָם וְנִשָּׂא Is 57^{15}, cf. ψ 138^{6}, + עַל־כָּל־הָעַמִּים 99^{2}, גּוֹיִם 113^{4}. **2.** *be raised, uplifted*: **a.** of highway Is 49^{11} (*made high*, put in order); voice, Dt 27^{14} (pt. = adj.) *uplifted*. **b.** fig.: of hand, symbol of might, Dt 32^{27}, + עַל pers. Mi 5^{8}; of Isr. in Exodus בְּיָד רָמָה Ex 14^{8} Nu 33^{3} (both P); of י׳'s hand Is 26^{11} ψ 89^{14} (‖ תָּעֹז); fig. of presumption Nu 15^{30} (P); זְרוֹעַ רָמָה of might Jb 38^{15}; of eyes, fig. of arrogance Pr 6^{17} 30^{13} ψ 131^{1} (‖ גָּבַהּ לִבִּי), so 18^{28}, but ‖ 2 S 22^{28} of pers.; of heart, fig. of reckless elation, Ho 13^{6} Dt 8^{14} Ez 31^{10} (‖ גָּבַהְתָּ, בְּגָבְהוֹ, בְּקוֹמָה) Dn 11^{12}, + מִן pers. Dt 17^{20}; of horn, fig.

of triumph 1 S 2^{1} (song), ψ 89^{25} (v^{18} see **Hiph.**), 112^{9}, so head 27^{6} (+ עַל pers.), 140^{9} (join ירומו to v^{10}, but read יָרִימוּ Che, cf. Hup-Now). **c.** of pers., *be exalted* (in fig.), king Nu 24^{7} (JE; + מִן comp.; ‖ תִּנַּשֵּׂא); of God (י׳, i.e. shew his exaltation) Is 30^{18} 2 S 22^{47} = ψ 18^{47}, ψ 21^{14} 46$^{11.11}$, + עַל־(הַ)שָּׁמַיִם 57$^{6.12}$ 108^{6}; עֶבֶד י׳ Is 52^{13}, י׳'s people ψ 89^{17}; rebellious 66^{7} (Qr; Kt Hiph.: *shew exaltation*); worthlessness (personif.) ψ 12^{9}; of city Pr 11^{11}. **3.** *be lifted, rise,* of ark, מֵעַל־הארץ Gn 7^{17} (J), so of cherubim Ez 10^{16}, cf. v^{17}; כְּבוֹד י׳ v^{4} (מֵעַל הַכְּרוּב).—Pr 24^{7} v. I. ראמות p. 910b. **Pōlēl** *Pf.* 3 fs. sf. רֹמְמָתְהוּ Ez 31^{4}; 1 s. רוֹמַמְתִּי Is 1^{2} 23^{4}; *Impf.* 3 ms. יְרוֹמֵם Ho 11^{7}, sf. יְרוֹמְמֵנִי ψ 27^{5}, וִירוֹמִמְךָ 37^{34}; 1 s. sf. וַאֲרֹמְמֶנְהוּ Ex 15^{2} (Ges §58 i), etc. (אֲרוֹמֵם v. **Hithpō'l.**); *Imv.* mpl. רוֹמְמוּ ψ 99$^{5.9}$; *Inf. cstr.* לְרוֹמֵם Ezr 9^{9}; *Pt.* מְרוֹמֵם 1 S 2^{7}, sf. מְרוֹמְמִי ψ 9^{14}, f. רוֹמֵמָה ψ 118^{16} (מ om., Hup-Now Bae; cf. Kö I. 454);—**1. a.** *raise, rear,* children Is 1^{2} 23^{4} (both ‖ גִּדֵּל). **b.** *cause* tree *to grow,* subj. תְּהוֹם Ez 31^{4} (‖ גִּדֵּל). **c.** *rear, erect,* temple Ezr 9^{9}. **2.** *lift up:* **a.** in fig., acc. pers., subj. י׳ ψ 27^{5} (+ בְּצוּר); + מִן comp. 2 S 22^{49} = ψ 18^{49}, + מִן *from* 9^{14}; acc. om. Ho 11^{7} (si vera l., cf. We Now). **b.** *raise* waves of sea, subj. wind, ψ 107^{25}. **c.** *exalt,* acc. pers., subj. י׳ Jb 17^{4} (read perh. תְּרֹמֵם, so Bu, cf. Di), ψ 37^{34} (+ לָרֶשֶׁת אָרֶץ); acc. om. 1 S 2^{7} ψ 118^{16} (in victory); subj. wisdom, acc. pers. Pr 4^{8}, cf. צְדָקָה תְּרוֹמֵם־גּוֹי 14^{34}. **3.** *exalt, extol,* acc. י׳, ψ 30^{2}, ‖ אוֹדֶה Is 25^{1} ψ 118^{28}, ‖ הִשְׁתַּחֲווּ 99$^{5.9}$, ‖ הַלֵּל 107^{32}, ‖ בֵּרֵךְ 145^{1}, ‖ אַנְוֵהוּ Ex 15^{2}; acc. שֵׁם י׳ ψ 34^{4} (‖ גִּדֵּל). **Pōʻlal** *Impf.* 3 fpl. תְּרוֹמַמְנָה ψ 75^{11} *be lifted up,* of horns (cf. **Qal 2 b**); *Pf.* 3 ms. וְרוֹמַם 66^{17} *and he was extolled* (so Ki al.; but v. רוֹמָם infr.); *Pt.* מְרוֹמָם Ne 9^{5} *extolled,* of י׳'s name (cf. **Pōlēl 3**), + עַל־כָּל־בְּרָכָה וג׳. **Hiph.** *Pf.* 3 ms. הֵרִים 1 K 11^{27} +; 2 ms. הֲרִימוֹתָ 2 K 19^{22} ψ 89^{43}, וַהֲרֵמֹתָ Nu 31^{28}; 2 mpl. consec. וַהֲרֵמֹתֶם 18^{26}, etc.; *Impf.* 3 ms. יָרִים Gn 41^{44} +, juss. יָרֵם Nu 17^{2} 1 S 2^{10}, וַיָּרֶם Ex 7^{20} +, sf. וַיְרִימֶהָ Gn 31^{45}, etc.; *Imv.* ms. הָרֵם Ex 14^{16} Is 58^{1}, הָרִימָה ψ 74^{3}, etc.; *Inf. cstr.* הָרִים Is 10^{15} +, sf. הֲרִימִי Gn 39^{18}, etc.; *Pt.* מֵרִים Ex 35^{24} +, etc.;—**1. a.** (1) *raise, lift,* c. acc., hand Ex 17^{11} (E), Nu 20^{11} (P), + אֶל־י׳ (in oath) Gn 14^{22} cf. (אֶל־הַשָּׁמַיִם) Dn 12^{7}, + בּ pers. *against* 1 K 11$^{26.27}$; feet, פְּעָמִים ψ 74^{3}, i.e. run (+ לְ dir.); hand or foot Gn 41^{44} (E), i.e. make any movement (hyperb.); head ψ 110^{7} (As. *ullû rêšu* Dl HWB 62 a), cf. יָרִימוּ 140^{9} (so rd., v. **Qal 2 b**); face, אֶל־י׳ Ezr 9^{6}; hand of another, subj. י׳, fig. of giving strength to, ψ 89^{43}, so head 3^{4}; c. acc. of rod Is 10^{15} Ex 14^{16} (P), הָרִים בַּמַּטֶּה 7^{20} (E); rod subj., c. acc. rei Is 10^{15}. (2) *raise* poor אֶבְיוֹן, c. מִן loc. 1 S 2^{8} ψ 113^{7}. **b.** *lift up* voice Gn 39$^{15.18}$ (J; both + קָרָא), Is 40$^{9.9}$ (acc. om.), 58^{1} Ezr 3^{12}; + בִּתְרוּעָה Ez 21^{27}, בַּחֲצֹצְרוֹת 2 Ch 5^{13}; + לְ pers. Is 13^{2}, לָעָב Jb 38^{34}, + עַל pers. *against* 2 K 19^{22} = Is 37^{23}; הָרִים בְּקוֹל 1 Ch 15^{16}. **c.** (take into one's hand and) *lift, take up,* stone Jos 4^{5} (JE; עַל־שִׁכְמוֹ), leg (of sacrif. meal) 1 S 9^{24}, mantle 2 K 2^{13}, axe 6^{7} (acc. om.), yoke Ho 11^{4} (עַל־לְחֵיהֶם), censers Nu 17^{2} (P; + מִבֵּין), ashes Lv 6^{3}. **d.** *set up, erect,* stone as מַצֵּבָה Gn 31^{45} (E); standard, + אֶל of people Is 49^{22}, עַל 62^{10}. **e.** *set on high,* throne, מִמַּעַל לְכוֹכְבֵי אֵל Is 14^{13}; nest (subj. נֶשֶׁר) Jb 39^{27}. **f.** *lift up, exalt,* c. acc. pers., subj. י׳ 1 K 14^{7} 16^{2} ψ 89^{20} (all c. מִן), ψ 75^{8} (opp. יַשְׁפִּיל); subj. קָלוֹן Pr 3^{35}, cf. 14^{29}; c. acc. קֶרֶן, in both good and bad sense (cf. **Qal 2 b**) 1 S 2^{10} La 2^{17} (לְמָרוֹם), ψ 89^{18} (Kt; Qr **Qal**), 92^{11} 148^{14} ψ 75$^{5.6}$; but 1 Ch 25^{5} *sound the horn;* inf. = *exaltation* ψ 75^{7}; 66^{7} v. **Qal 2 c.** **2.** *lift up* and take away, *remove,* c. acc. הָעֲטָרָה Ez 21^{31} (‖ הָסִיר); acc. rei + מִן loc. Is 57^{14}, Lv 2^{9} 4$^{8.19}$ 6^{8}; = do away with, גְּרֻשֹׁתֵיכֶם Ez 45^{9} (מֵעַל of people), הַתָּמִיד Dn 8^{11} (Kt; Qr **Hoph.**); = set apart, מֶכֶס Nu 31^{28} (מִן pers.). **3.** *lift off and present, contribute, offer:* **a.** to י׳, c. acc. cogn. תְּרוּמָה, Ez 45^{13} 48$^{8.20}$ Nu 15$^{20.20}$ (P), Ex 35^{24} (P); + לי׳ Ez 45^{1} 48^{9} Nu 15^{19} 18$^{19.24}$ 31^{52}; תְּרוּמַת י׳ 18^{26} (+ מִן rei), v$^{28.29}$ (all P); ת׳ בֵּית־א׳ Ezr 8^{25}. **b.** c. acc. rei, + לי׳ Lv 22^{15}. **c.** *contribute,* acc. rei, לְ pers. (for sacrif.), 2 Ch 30$^{24.24}$ 35$^{7.8}$ (acc. om.), v^{9}. **Hoph.** *Pf.* 3 ms. הוּרַם Ex 29^{27}, הֻרַם Dn 8^{11} Qr (Kt **Hiph.**); *Impf.* 3 ms. יוּרַם Lv 4^{10};—*be taken off* from (מִן) Lv 4^{10} (P), cf. Ex 29^{27} (P; ‖ הוּנַף); *be abolished* Dn 8^{11} Qr (cf. **Hiph. 2**); Bev (after 𝔊) ins. *Pt.* מוּרָם after הַתָּמִיד v^{13}. **Hithpō'l.** *Impf.* 3 ms. וְיִתְרוֹמֵם וְיִתְגַּדֵּל עַל־כָּל־אֵל Dn 11^{36} *and he shall exalt and magnify himself above,* etc.; 1 s. (ת assim.) אֲרוֹמֵם Is 33^{10} (Ges §54 c Kö I. 454) *I will raise myself* (+ אֶנָּשֵׂא, אָקוּם).

†רוּם, רֹם, רָם **n.[m.] height, haughtiness** (prop. inf.);—abs. ר׳, **1.** *height, loftiness,* שָׁמַיִם לָר׳ וָאָרֶץ לָעֹמֶק Pr 25^{3}; cstr. רוּם עֵינַיִם fig. of *haughtiness* Is 10^{12} (‖ גֹּדֶל לֵבָב), Pr 21^{4} (‖ רְחַב־לֵב); so רָם לִבּוֹ Je 48^{29} (‖ גָּבְהוֹ, גְּאוֹן, גַּאֲוָה); then alone: **2.** *haughtiness,* רוּם אֲנָשִׁים Is 2$^{11.17}$ (both ‖ גַּבְהוּת).

†רוֹם **adv. on high,** of direction (cf. מָרוֹם 2) רוֹם יָדֵיהוּ נָשָׂא Hb 3^{10} (subj. תְּהוֹם).

†רוּמָה **n.pr.loc.** מִן־ר׳ 2 K 23^{36}; (ἐκ) Κρουμα, A Ρυμα, 𝔊L Λοβεννα; poss = [אֲרוּמָה] Ju 9^{41} (q. l. perh. also v^{31}, see GFM), yet cf Kit Benz.

†רוֹמָה **adv. haughtily,** לא תלכו ר׳ Mi 2^{3}.

†I רָם **n.pr.m. 1. a.** an ancestor of David, Ru 4$^{19.19}$, brother of Jerachmeel 1 Ch 2$^{9.10}$ **b.** son of J 1 Ch 2$^{25.27}$—Αρραν, Ραμ, etc. **2.** name of Elihu's family, Jb 32^{2} (Ραμ[α], Αραμ), dub., cf Bu.

†I. רָמָה **n.f. height, high-place,**—abs ר׳ as term techn (cf בָּמָה), = *shrine* (for illicit worship) Ez 16^{25}, ‖ גַּב v$^{24.31.39}$, so perh 1 S 22^{6}, but rd prob בָּמָה, 𝔊 Βαμα (A Ραμμα), HPS.

II רָמָה **n.pr.loc.** usu c art הָר׳ **the Height, Rama,** הָרָמָה (exc Je 31^{15} Ne 11^{33}) **1.** in Benj, on border of Ephr, Ho 5^{8} 1 K 15$^{17.21.22}$ = 2 Ch 16$^{1.5.6}$, Ju 4^{5} 19^{3} Is 10^{29} Je 31^{15} 40^{1} Jos 18^{25} (P), Ezr 2^{26} = Ne 7^{30}, prob also Ne 11^{33}, 𝔊 usu Ραμα, mod *er-Râm*, 5 miles N of Jerus, Buhl$^{Geogr\ 172}$. **2.** in hill-country of Ephr (= **1**?), home of Samuel 1 S 1^{19} 2^{11} 7^{17} 8^{4} 15^{34} 16^{13} 19$^{18.22a}$ (all c. ה loc, הָרָמָתָה), v$^{19.22b.23.23}$ 20^{1} 25^{1} 28^{3}, = הָרָמָתַיִם 1^{1} (v צופי), 𝔊 Αρμαθαιμ, Ραμα, perhaps (if distinct from **1**) = *Beit-Rima*, 13 miles ENE. of Lydda (GASm$^{Geogr\ 254}$ Buhl$^{Geogr\ 170}$), or *Râm-allah*, 3 m SW. of Bethel (Ew$^{Hist.\ ii\ 421}$ al.) [cf also Ἀριμαθαία Mt 27^{57} +] **3.** in Asher Jos 19^{29} (P), Ραμα, perh *Râmiye*, c. 12 miles E. of Ladder of Tyre Rob$^{BR\ iii\ 79}$ Buhl$^{Geogr\ 231}$ **4.** in Naphtali, Jos 19^{36} (P), Αραηλ, A 𝔊L Ραμα; mod. *Râmeh*, c 8 miles WSW of Safed Buhl$^{Geogr\ 222}$. **5** (בְ)רָמָה 2 K 8^{29} = 2 Ch 22^{6} (Ρεμμωθ, Ραμωθ; 𝔊L Ραμαθ Γαλ), v רָמוֹת **1**—Vid. Dr$^{Hast.\ DB\ Ramah}$.

†רָמָתִי **adj. gent.** (of what Rama?), c art. הָר׳ 1 Ch 27^{27}, ὁ ἐκ Ραηλ; A ὁ Ῥαμαθαῖος.

רָ(א)מַת **n.pr.loc.** cstr, in combin.: **1.** רָמַת לֶחִי Ju 15^{17}, v II לחי p. 534. **2.** רָמַת הַמִּצְפֶּה Jos 13^{26} (P), in Gilead, on N. border of Gad, Αραβωθ [A Ραμωθ, 𝔊L Ραμεθ] κατὰ τὴν Μασ(ση)φα, = II מצפה **3**, on (dub) identif. cf GASm$^{Geogr\ 586f}$ Buhl$^{Geogr\ 262}$ **3.** רָאמַת נֶגֶב Jos 19^{8} (P), Βαμεθ [A 𝔊L Ιαμεθ] κατὰ λίβα (= בַּעֲלַת־בְּאֵר v^{8}, q v p 128), prob = רָמוֹת־נֶגֶב 1 S 30^{27}, Ραμα νότου, site dub, v. Dr$^{Hast\ DB\ Ramah}$.

רָ(א)מוֹת$_{26}$ **n.pr 1. loc. Heights, Ramoth,**—**a** in Gilead, רָמֹת בַּגִּלְעָד Jos 21^{38} (Gi, van d H Baer v^{36}, P), רָאמוֹת בַּגּ׳ (of Gad) Dt 4^{43} 1 Ch 6^{65}, רָאמֹת בַּגּ׳ Jos 20^{8} (P), Ραμωθ [Jos 20^{8} Αρημωθ] ἐν (τῇ) Γαλααδ, usu. רָמֹת ג׳ (Ρεμμαθ [Ιρεμαθ, Ραμωθ, Ραμα(θ)] Γαλ, etc) 1 K 4^{13} + 19t. K Ch (v. גלעד **1 d**); = II. רָמָה **5**, q.v.; site dub.; Onom (Lag$^{287\ 91}$) 15 m. W. of Philadelphia [Jer Ib.$^{145\ 31}$ says E!], hence Di$^{Gn\ 31\ 54}$ Buhl$^{G\ 261f.}$ conj. *el-Jal'aud*, c. 17 Eng m NW. of Phil., and 3 m. S of Yabbok, SMerrill$^{E\ of\ Jordan,\ 284\ ff.,\ Hast\ DB\ Ramoth\ G}$ conj (on gen grounds) *Jerash*, c 28 m N of Phil., GASm$^{G\ 586}$ some place just S of Yarmuk, cf GACooke in Di$^{Dt\ Add.\ xviii\ f.}$, q v. esp. against *es-Salṭ* (Seetzen al) †**b.** רָמוֹת־נֶגֶב 1 S 30^{27}, v. רָ(א)מַת **3** †**c.** רָאמוֹת, Levit city in Issachar 1 Ch 6^{58} (Δαβωρ, 𝔊L Ραμωθ), prob = רֶמֶת Jos 19^{21} (P, Ρεμμας, A Ραμαθ), and יַרְמוּת **2**, Jos 21^{29}, q v. p 438 (v also Di$^{Jos\ 19.21}$) **2. m.** רָ(ו)מוֹת Ezr 10^{29} Qr (Kt ירמות) v ירימות **5 c**, p 438.

רָמָתַיִם **n pr.loc.** הָר׳ 1 S 1^{1}, v. II. רָמָה **2**

†[רָמוּת] **n.f. height, lofty stature,**—sf. רָמוּתֶךָ Ez 32^{5}.

†רוֹמָם **n.[m.] extolling, praise;**—= *song of praise* (to י׳) ψ 66^{17}, so read with van d. H., cf Thes Hup-Now Che Bae Buhl^{Lex}; > Ki Baer Gi vb **Pō'lal,** רוֹמַם, pl cstr רוֹמְמוֹת אל 149^{6}.

†[רוֹמֵמוּת] **n.f. uplifting, arising;**—sf. מֵרוֹמְמֻתֶךָ Is 33^{3} *at thine arising.*

†רוֹמַמְתִּי עֶזֶר as **n.pr.m.** (*I have made lofty help;* cf. גִּדַּלְתִּי and reff),—son of Heman 1 Ch 25^{4}, ר׳ עֶזֶר v^{3}.

רֶמֶת v. רָ(א)מוֹת **1 c.**

†מָרוֹם **n.m.**$^{Ec\ 10.6}$ **height** (poet.);—abs. מ׳ Mi 6^{6} +; cstr. מְרוֹם 2 K 19^{23} +; pl מְרוֹמִים Is 33^{16} +, cstr מְרוֹמֵי Ju 5^{18}, sf. מְרוֹמָיו Jb 25^{2};—**1.** *height, elevation* (concr), *elevated place:* מְרוֹמֵי שָׂדֶה Jb 5^{18}, בראשׁ מרֹמים Pr 8^{2}, מרום שבתו Ob^{3} (cf Now), מְרוֹם גבעה in ‖ Je 49^{16}; מ׳ הָרִים *top of mts* 2 K 19^{23} = Is 37^{24a}, מ׳ קצו v^{24b}, מ׳ עֶנָה Je 51^{53} (of Bab); specif. of Zion, הַר מ׳ Je 17^{12}, מ׳ ציון 31^{12}, בהר מ׳ ישׂראל Ez 17^{23} 20^{40}, בְּהָרֵי מ׳ יִשׂ׳ 34^{14}, indef., Hb 2^{9} (in fig), לָשׂוּם שְׁפָלִים לְמ׳ Jb 5^{11}, בַּמְּרוֹמִים רַבִּים Ec 10^{6} (of high office, rank, opp. שָׁפֵל), ישׁבי מָרוֹם Is 26^{5}, i e in (supposed) security, cf. מְרוֹמִים יִשְׁכֹּן 33^{16} (‖ מְצָדוֹת סְלָעִים), בַּמ׳ לַמ׳ *on high* (Germ *in die Höhe*) ψ 75^{6}, so בַּמּ׳ Jb 39^{18}, adv = *in a high place* Is 22^{16}. **2.** מ׳ alone = *height* of heaven. אֱלֹהֵי מָרוֹם Mi 6^{6}; 2 S 22^{17} = ψ 18^{17}, Is 24$^{21.21}$ 32^{15} 57^{15} 58^{4} La 1^{13} ψ 7^{8} 68^{19} 71^{19} 93^{4} 144^{7}, pl. Jb 25^{2}; ‖ שָׁמַיִם, מ׳ קָדְשׁוֹ ψ 102^{20}, מְרוֹמִים Jb 16^{19} ψ 148^{1}, ‖ מְעוֹן קָדְשׁוֹ Je 25^{30}, ‖ מֵעָל Jb 31^{2} (pl), opp מוֹסְדֵי אֶרֶץ Is 24^{18},

as pred. of ׳י ψ 92^{9} cf. 10^{5}; as adv. (i.e. in heaven) Is 33^{5}; לַמּ׳ *towards heaven* Is 38^{14} 40^{26}, 37^{23} = 2 K 19^{22}; מִמּ׳ in fig. ψ 73^{8} they speak (as if) *from the sky*, from heaven (i.e. so arrogantly) **3.** מ׳ adv. fig, = *proudly* ψ 56^{3} (so Gei Hup-Now al., cf. Che, but dub.), Bae *in high station;* Du reads מָרוֹם (יוֹם to v^{4}; as dittogr.?). **4.** fig. of nobles (coll.) מרום עַם־הָאָרֶץ Is 24^{4}.

תְּרוּמָה **n.f.** contribution, offering, for sacred uses (not certain before Dt.; chiefly Ez P and late) (prop. something *lifted off, separated*); —abs. ת׳ Ez 45^{13}+, cstr. תְּרוּמַת Ex 30^{14}+; sf. תְּרוּמָתִי 25^{2}, ־מַתְכֶם Nu 18^{27}, ־מָתָם Ex 29^{28}; pl. תְּרוּמוֹת Nu 12^{44} Pr 29^{4}, ־מֹת 2 S 1^{21} Nu 18^{19}; sf. תְּרוּמֹתָי v^{8}, etc.;—**1.** earliest use: contrib. of products of soil for ׳י, תְּרוּמַת יֶדְכֶם Dt 12$^{6.11}$, cf. v^{17}, also Ez 20^{40} Nu 15$^{19.20.21}$ **2.** contrib. for prince, in Ezekiel's scheme: Ez 45$^{13\ 16}$ **3.** tract of land to be set apart for temple, and for use of priests and Levites, in Ezek.'s scheme: Ez 45^{1} 48$^{8.9.20a.21b}$; called ת׳ הַקֹּדֶשׁ 45$^{6.7\ 7}$ 48$^{10\ 18.\ 18.20b.21a.21c}$; ת׳ הָאָרֶץ קֹדֶשׁ קָדָשִׁים v^{12}. **4.** contrib. to ׳י, set apart for priests, Ez 44^{30} Lv 22^{12} Nu 5^{9} 18$^{8\ 11\ 19}$ 2 Ch 31$^{10\ 12\ 14}$; specif: **a.** of cakes and cereals Lv 7^{14} Ne 10$^{38.40}$ (also for Levites), 12^{44} (*id.*), 13^{5}; cf. וּשְׂדֵי תְּרוּמֹת 2 S 1^{21}, i.e. (si vera l.) fields yielding sacred imposts, but very dub.; 𝔊L ὄρη θανάτου, cf. We; JPPet$^{JBL\ xii\ (1893),\ 64}$ prop. שְׂדוֹת הַמָּוֶת ה׳ ,ש׳ (הָרֵי) מָוֶת as gloss; HPS > Sta וּשְׂדֵי עֲרֻמּוֹת; v. also Dr. **b.** of animal sacrif., the thigh, שׁוֹק הַת׳ Ex 29^{27} Lv 7^{34} 10$^{14.15}$ Nu 6^{20}. **c.** priests' share of Levites' tithe, Nu 18$^{26.27.28.28\ 29}$. **d.** of booty Nu 31$^{29.41\ 52}$. **e.** tithe for Levites 18^{24}. **5.** materials for tabern., sacred garments, etc, Ex 25$^{2.2.3}$ 35$^{5.5.21.24.24}$ 36$^{3.6}$; for temple Ezr 8^{25} **6.** half-shekel for maintaining service of sanctuary Ex 30$^{13\ 14\ 15}$. **7.** late, *contribution*, in gen., אִישׁ תְּרוּמוֹת Pr 29^{4} *a man of contributions*, i.e demanding them, = man of exactions —ת׳ Is 40^{20} of idol-image (si vera l.), so still Di-Kit; rd perh. תְּמוּנָה 𝔊 (ὁμοίωμα v^{19}) Du; other conj in Che^{Hpt}, v. also III. [סָכַן].—Vbs. c. ת׳ are: הֵרִים Ez 45^{1} + 14 t., הביא Dt 12^{6} + 9 t, נָתַן Ez 44^{30} + 9 t., לָקַח Ex 25$^{2.2}$ + 4 t, הִקְרִיב Lv 7^{14} Nu 5^{9}.—Vid Dr$^{Dt\ 12,6,\ Hast.\ DB\ iii\ 588}$.

†תְּרוּמִיָּה **n.f. denom. what belongs to a contribution, attendant or secondary contribution, subdivision** (on form v. Kö$^{ii\ 1,\ 204}$; strictly adj (used as subst), Ges$^{§\ 86\ h}$);—ת׳ מִתְּרוּמַת הָאָרֶץ Ez 48^{12}, of strip of land for priests in Ezekiel's scheme (but rd. prob. תְּרוּמָה)

†[רוּן] **vb. overcome** (cf. Ar. رَانَ (ى), c. على or ب pers, *overcome*, e g. of wine);—assumed in Heb. by Thes (after 𝔊) and most mod. to explain **Hithpō.** *Pt.* כְּגִבּוֹר מִתְרוֹנֵן מִיָּיִן ψ 78^{65} *like a hero overcome by wine* (cf. ‖ v^{a}); AV RV De Che al. *shout* (√רנן), cf. 𝔗; so Hup-Now, with altern. conj מִתְעוֹרֵר, and this sense more suitable (cf. Luzzatto$^{Il\ Pentateuco\ iii\ (1874),\ 162\ (Lv\ 21\ 7)}$ Perles^{79})—Pr 29^{6} v. רנן, רוץ.

†[רוּעַ] **vb. Hiph.**$_{40}$ **1. raise a shout. 2. give a blast with clarion or horn** (NH *id*, Hiph; Thes cp. Ar. رَغَا *utter a grumbling cry*);—*Pf.* 3 mpl. הֵרִיעוּ Ju 15^{14} Ezr 3^{11}, הרעוּ 1 S 17^{20}, etc.; *Impf.* 3 ms. יָרִיעַ Is 42^{13} ψ 41^{12}, וַיָּרַע Jos 6^{20}, etc.; *Imv* fs. הָרִיעִי Zc 9^{9}; mpl. הָרִיעוּ Jos 6^{10}+; *Inf. cstr.* הָרִיעַ 2 Ch 13$^{12.15}$; *Pt.* pl. מְרִיעִים Ezr 3^{13};—**1.** *shout a war-cry*, or *alarm of battle*, Jos 6$^{10.\ 10\ 10\ 16\ 20}$ Ju 7^{21} 1 S 17^{52} Is 42^{13} 2 Ch 13$^{15\ 15}$, הריע תְּרוּעָה Jos 6$^{5.20}$; לקראת Ju 15^{14}; בַּמִּלְחָמָה 1 S 17^{20}. **2.** *sound a signal for war* or *march*: c. חֲצֹצְרוֹת Nu 10$^{7.9}$ (P); ‖ תקע שׁוֹפָר Ho 5^{8}, cf. Jo 2^{1}; c. עַל *against* 2 Ch 13^{12}; so also prob Jb 30^{5} (against a thief). **3.** *shout in triumph* over enemies: c. עַל, Je 50^{15} ψ 41^{12}; abs. Zp 3^{14} (‖ רנן). **4.** *shout in applause:* abs. 1 S 10^{24} Zc 9^{9}, cf (of angels) Jb 38^{7}. **5.** *shout* with religious impulse: הרי׳ תְּרוּעָה 1 S 4^{5} Ezr 3$^{11\ 13}$; so in public worship with music and sacrifice, c. לְ, to God ψ 47^{2} 66^{1} 81^{2} 95$^{1\ 2}$ 98^{4} 100^{1}, לִפְנֵי 98^{6}; in joy, תַּחְתִּיּוֹת אָרֶץ Is 44^{23} (‖ רָנּוּ שָׁמַיִם) **6.** *cry out in distress*, Is 15^{4} (but Du Bu יָרִיעוּ *tremble*), לָמָּה תָרִיעִי רֵעַ Mi 4^{9} (of Zion under fig. of woman, but perh. read למה תֵּרוֹעִי רע *why art thou broken all to pieces?* as Pr 11^{15}) **Pōʿlal.** *Impf.* 3 ms. impers. לֹא יְרֹעָע Is 16^{10} *a shout shall not be uttered* (of joy in harvest; ‖ יְרֻנָּן) **Hithpōʿl.** *Impf* 1 s. אֶתְרוֹעָע ψ 108^{10}, 3 mpl. יִתְרוֹעֲעוּ 65^{14}; *Imv.* fs. הִתְרוֹעֲעִי 60^{10};—**1.** *shout in triumph:* c. עַל ψ 60^{10} (subj Phil; iron.) ‖ 108^{10} (subj ׳י) **2.** *shout for joy*, ψ 65^{14} (meadows, valleys; ‖ שִׁיר).

†I. רֵעַ **n.verb. shouting, roar, but dub.**;—קוֹל הָעָם בְּרֵעֹה Ex 32^{17} (E) *sound of the people as they shouted* (read Inf. cstr. בְּרֵעֹה for בְּהָרִיעוֹ, cf. √**5**), יַגִּיד עָלָיו רֵעוֹ Jb 36^{33} *the roar thereof telleth of him* (< רַעְמוֹ *his thunder*, so Bu); לָמָּה תָרִיעִי רֵעַ Mi 4^{9} *why criest thou out with a crying?* i.e. so loudly (but v. √**6**).—II. III רֵעַ v. רעה.

†תְּרוּעָה **n.f. shout or blast of war, alarm, or joy**;—ת׳ Lv 23^{24}+; cstr. תְּרוּעַת Je 4^{19}+;—

1. *alarm* of war, *war-cry*, Jos 6$^{5.20}$ Je 20^{16} Ez 21^{27} Am 1^{14} 2^{2} Zp 1^{16} Jb 39^{25}; ת׳ מִלְחָמָה Je 4^{19} 49^{2}; ת׳ מֶלֶךְ *battle-cry of king* Nu 23^{21} (poem in JE). **2.** *blast* for march: תקע ת׳ Nu 10$^{5.6.6}$(P; with חֲצֹצְרוֹת; hence) חֲצֹצְרוֹת הַתּ׳ Nu 31^{6}(P) 2 Ch 13^{12}; on day of atonement שׁוֹפַר ת׳ Lv 25^{9}(H); 1st of mo. (בַּחֹדֶשׁ הַשְּׁבִיעִי בְּאֶחָד לַחֹדֶשׁ) 23^{24}(P; זִכְרוֹן ת׳), יוֹם ת׳ Nu 29^{1}(P); gen. צִלְצְלֵי ת׳ ψ 150^{5}. **3.** *shout of joy* with religious impulse, 1 S 4$^{5.6.6}$ 2 S 6^{15} = 1 Ch 15^{28}, 2 Ch 15^{14} Ezr 3$^{11.12.13}$; קוֹל ת׳ הַשִּׂמְחָה Ezr 3^{13}; in public worship gen. Jb 33^{26}; esp. + musical service ψ 33^{3} 47^{6}; זִבְחֵי ת׳ 27^{6}, יֹדְעֵי ת׳ 89^{16}. **4.** *shout of joy*, in gen. Jb 8^{21} (‖ שְׂחוֹק).

רוף (√ of foll.; = רפא).

†תְּרוּפָה **n.f.** healing;—Ez 47^{12}.

†רוּץ **vb.** run (NH *id.* (rare); Eth. ሮጸ: Zinj. *Pf.* 1 s. רצת; = Aram. רְהַט, ܪܗܛ (W$^{86.47}$); cf. As. *râṣu, be helpful* (i.e. *run* to help?));—**Qal** *Pf.* 3 ms. רָץ Gn 18^{7}; 2 ms. רַצְתָּה Je 12^{5}, etc.; *Impf.* יָרוּץ Hb 2^{2}+, יָרֻץ Jb 16^{14}, וַיָּרָץ Gn 18^{2}+, וַיָּרָץ 2 S 18^{21}; 1 s. sf. ארוצם Je 50^{44} Kt (but < Qr Hiph., v. infr.), etc. [v. also רצץ]; *Imv.* ms. רוּץ 2 S 18^{23} 2 K 4^{26}, רֻץ 1 S 20^{36} Zc 2^{8}; *Inf. cstr.* לָרוּץ 1 S 20^{6}+; *Pt.* רָץ 2 S 18^{22}+, pl. רָצִים 1 S 22^{17}+, רָצִין 2 K 11^{13} (Ges^{§87e});—**1.** *run*, c. אֶל loc. Gn 18^{7} 24^{20} (both J), Nu 17^{12}(P), אֶל pers. Gn 24^{29} (J; + ה loc.), 1 S 3^{5} Is 55^{5} (fig.), with hostility, *against*, Jb 15^{26} (fig.), so goat against ram Dn 8^{6}, עַל pers., *against* Jb 16^{14}; ה loc. also Jos 7^{22}, לְבֵיתוֹ Hg 1^{9}, לָרַע Is 59^{7} Pr 1^{16}; acc. loc. 1 S 20^{6} 17$^{22.48}$ (+ לִקְרַאת); ב loc. *on* (ב II. **2**), of horses Am 6^{12}, locusts Jo 2^{9}; *into* Pr 18^{10} (fig.); מִן loc. 1 S 4^{12}, so MT 2 K 23^{12} (= *he went quickly thence*, but text perh. corrupt, v. Kit Benz, and cf. **Hiph.** infr.); אַחֲרֵי pers. 2 S 18^{22} 1 K 19^{20} 2 K 5$^{20.21}$ Ct 1^{4}, עַד pers. 2 K 4^{22}; לִפְנֵי pers. 2 S 15^{1} 1 K 1^{5} (both of royal escort, *out-runners*), 18^{46} (+ עַד loc.), לִפְנֵי rei 1 S 8^{11}; אֵת pers. accomp. Je 12^{5}; c. acc. of way, אֹרַח ψ 19^{6}, דֶּרֶךְ 2 S 18^{23} ψ 119^{32} (fig.); as prelim., + inf. לִקְרַאת *run to meet* Gn 18^{2} 24^{17} 29^{13} 33^{4} (all J), 2 K 4^{26} Je 51^{31}, + vb. fin. Gn 24^{28} 29^{12} (both J), Nu 11^{27} Jos 8^{19} (both JE), Ju 7^{21} 13^{10} 1 S 10^{23} 17^{51} 2 S 18^{19} ψ 59^{5}; as imv. + imv. 1 S 20^{36} Zc 2^{8}; abs. 1 S 20^{36} Is 40^{31} 2 Ch 23^{12} (v. **2 a**), Pr 4^{12} 6^{18} (of feet), of locusts Jo 2$^{4.7}$; specif., *run* as messenger 2 S 18$^{21.22.23.23.24.26.26}$, fig. of prophet's activity Je 23^{21}, of י׳'s word ψ 147^{15}; fig. of reading smoothly, יָרוּץ קוֹרֵא בוֹ Hb 2^{2}.—ψ 18^{30} = 2 S 22^{30} read אָרֻץ (for אָרוּץ, אָרֻץ), √רצץ Ew Ol Che Bae al. **2.** *Pt.* as subst.: **a.** pl. הָרָצִים *the runners* (prop. *out-runners*, as royal escort, cf. vb. 2 S 15^{1} 1 K 1^{5}; then) of royal body-guard 1 S 22^{17} 1 K 14$^{27.28.28}$ = 2 Ch 12$^{10.11.28}$, 2 K 10$^{25.25}$ 11$^{4.6.11.19.19}$.—הָרָצִין (הָעָם) v^{13} is gloss (Kit Benz; whence [easier] הָעָם הָרָצִים 2 Ch 23^{12} v. **1**).—Pr 29^{6} for יָרֻן Pinsk Toy favour יָרוּץ. **b.** *runner* = (royal messenger, post, late), רָץ Je 51$^{31.31}$ (‖ מַגִּיד), cf. Jb 9^{25} (as swift); הָרָצִים 2 Ch 30$^{6.10}$ Est 3$^{13.15}$, riders הָר׳ רֹכְבֵי הָרֶכֶשׁ 8^{10}, הָר׳ בַּסּוּסִים v^{14}. **Pōʿlēl** *Impf.* 3 mpl. יְרוֹצֵצוּ Na 2^{5} *they run swiftly, dart* (like lightning; of chariots). **Hiph.** *cause to run*: **1.** *bring*, or *move, quickly*, *Impf.* 3 mpl. sf. וַיְרִיצֻהוּ מִן loc. Gn 41^{14} (E), rd. perh. also 3 ms. וַיָּרֶץ 2 K 23^{12} (acc. om.; for MT וַיָּרָץ v. **Qal**); ל pers., acc. rei om. וַיְרִיצוּ 2 Ch 35^{13}; *Imv.* ms. הָרֵץ 1 S 17^{17} (+ acc. loc., ל pers.); *Impf.* 3 fs. תָּרִיץ יָדָיו לֵאלֹהִים ψ 68^{32} *quickly stretch out* hands, (viz. with offerings). **2.** c. מֵעַל = *drive away from*, 1 s., sf. 3 ms., אֲרִיצֶנּוּ Je 49^{19}, so read prob. also in ‖ 50^{44} (Qr אֲרִיצֵם, > Kt ארוצם).

†מֵרוֹץ **n.[m.]** running, race;—abs. Ec 9^{11}.

†I. [מְרוּצָה] **n.f. 1.** running. **2.** course (of life):—**1.** *running, mode, style, of running*, cstr. מְרוּצַת 2 S 18^{27}, מְרֻצַת v^{27}. **2.** *course* (of life), sf. מְרוּצָתָם Je 8^{6} (Qr; > Kt pl. מרצותם), 23^{10}.—II. מְרוּצָה Je 22^{17} v. sub רצץ.

רוֹשׁ *poison*, Dt 32^{32}, v. II. ראשׁ.

[רוּשׁ or רִישׁ]$_{24}$ **vb.** be in want, poor (related to ירשׁ [cf. **Qal 3, Niph. Hiph. 3**]? so Thes);—**Qal** *Pf.* 3 pl. כְּפִירִים רָשׁוּ וְרָעֵבוּ ψ 34^{11} *young lions are in want and hunger*; elsewhere *Pt.* רָשׁ 1 S 18^{23} + 16 t., רָאשׁ 2 S 12^{1} + 2 t.; pl. רָשִׁים Pr 22^{7}, רָאשִׁים 13^{23};—(oft. opp. עָשִׁיר): as adj. 1 S 18^{23} 2 S 12$^{1.4}$ Pr 28^{3} Ec 4^{14}; as subst. = *poor man (men)*, 2 S 12^{3} ψ 82^{3} Ec 5^{7}, esp. Pr 10^{4} 13$^{8.23}$ + 12 t. Pr. **Hithpōʿlēl** *Pt.* מִתְרוֹשֵׁשׁ Pr 13^{7} *one impoverishing himself* (opp. מִתְעַשֵּׁר; cf. Pôʿl. רוֹשֵׁשׁ Ecclus 11^{12} 13^{5}).—Je 5^{17} Mal 1^{4} v. רשׁשׁ.

†רֵישׁ, רִישׁ, רֵאשׁ **n.m.** poverty, only Pr;—רִישׁ 28^{19}, sf. רִישׁוֹ 31^{7}; רֵישׁ 13^{18}, sf. רֵישֶׁךָ 24^{34} (‖ מַחְסֹרֶיךָ), רֵישָׁם 10^{15} (opp. עָשִׁיר); רֵאשׁ 30^{8} (opp. עֹשֶׁר), sf. רֵאשֶׁךָ 6^{11} (= 24^{34}, ‖ *id.*).

רוּת **n.pr.f.** v. sub רעה.

†רָזָה **vb.** be or grow lean (Ar. رَزِئَ *grow thin and weak*);—**Qal** *Pf.* 3 ms. רָזָה Zp 2^{11} obj. false gods, appar. *make lean* (𝔙 *attenuavit*; 𝔊

is ἐξολεθρεύσει), but sense strange, < רָזָה (v. Ar. supr.), yet even this very doubtful. **Niph.** *be made lean*, *Impf.* 3 ms. מִשְׁמַן בְּשָׂרוֹ יֵרָזֶה Is 17^{4}.

†[רָזֶה] **adj.** lean (on formation cf. Lag $^{BN 49}$);—fs. רָזָה, Ez 24^{20} (of שֶׂה; opp. בְּרִיָּה), of land, = barren, Nu 13^{20} (JE; opp. שְׁמֵנָה).

†רָזִי **n.[m.]** leanness, wasting;—רָזִי־לִי Is $24^{16.16}$ *to me, wasting!* (opp. צְבִי).

†I. רָזוֹן **n.[m.]** leanness, wasting, scantness;—abs. ר׳: **1.** *leanness* Is 10^{16} (fig.; opp. מִשְׁמַנָּיו). **2.** *wasting*, i.e. wasting disease, ψ 106^{15} (cf. Bae). **3.** אֵיפַת ר׳ Mi 6^{10} *ephah of scantness*, scant measure.—II. רָזוֹן v. רזן.

רזח (*? cry out*, cf. Talm. מִרְזָח *bewailed*).

†מַרְזֵחַ **n.m.** $^{Am 6.7}$ cry (𝔗 מַרְזְחָא *mourning-feast*; Ph. מרזח a rel. festival (> usu. a month), cf. Palm., ClGann Littm, v. GACooke $^{Inscr. 95. 121 f. 303}$ and reff.; Lzb $^{Ephem. i. 47 f. 343 f.}$);—**1.** *mourning cry* (or *feast?* Talm. מַרְזְחָא), abs. בֵּית מ׳ Je 16^{5} i.e. house of mourning (‖ נוד, ספד). **2.** *cry of revelry*, cstr. מִרְזַח סְרוּחִים Am 6^{7}.

רָזִי v. רזה.

†[רָזַם] **vb.** wink, flash (of eyes) (transp. [text. err.?] for Ar. رَمَزَ, Aram. רְמַז, ܪܡܙ; so NH רָמַז (rare), רֶמֶז *sign, intimation*);—**Qal** *Impf.* 3 mpl. וּמַה־יִּרְזְמוּן עֵינֶיךָ Jb 15^{12} (Codd. ירמזון) *why do thine eyes flash* (in wrath)? but possibly read יְרוּמוּן (Pr 6^{17} 30^{13}, etc., cf. Bu).

†[רָזַן, ? earlier רָזוֹן, so Lag $^{BN 31}$] **vb.** be weighty, judicious, commanding (Ar. رَزُنَ *be weighty, grave, firm of judgment*; NH רוֹזֵן = BH, so רוזנים Ecclus 44^{4});—only **Qal** *Pt.* pl. as subst., *rulers, potentates*, ‖ מְלָכִים: רֹזְנִים Ju 5^{3} Hb 1^{10}, ר׳ ψ 2^{2} Pr 8^{15} 31^{4}, ‖ שֹׁפְטֵי אֶרֶץ Is 40^{23}.

†II. רָזוֹן **n.m.** potentate;—abs. ר׳ Pr 14^{28} (‖ מֶלֶךְ).—I. רָזוֹן v. sub רזה supr.

†רְזוֹן **n.pr.m.** founder of kingdom of Damascus, Solomon's time, 1 K 11^{23}; 𝔊 (v^{14}) Εσρωμ [A v^{23} Ραζων]; identified with חֶזְיוֹן 15^{18} by Th Klo (reading חזרון), but cf. Kit Benz.

†רָחַב [? also רָחֵב, so Lag $^{BN 31}$; cf. also Id $^{ib. 52 f.}$] **vb.** be, or grow, wide, large (NH in der. spec. (rare) and deriv.; Ar. رَحُبَ, Eth. ረሐበ: Sab. in epith. dei Fell $^{ZMG liv (1900), 249}$, and n.pr. CIS $^{iv, no. 1, 3}$ etc.; As. in *rêbitu*, *open place*; Aram. רְחַב in deriv.);—**Qal** *Pf.* 3 ms. ר׳ פִּי 1 S 2^{1}, + עַל *against* (i.e. to devour, in fig.; cf. **Hiph.**); consec. וּפָחַד וְר׳ לְבָבֵךְ Is 60^{5} *be widened*, *enlarged*, relieved, and expanded with joy (cf. **Hiph. 2**); 3 fs. וְרָחֲבָה וְנָסְבָה Ez 41^{7} prob. err., Co וְהָרֹחַב נוֹסָף, Toy רָחֲבָה וְנוֹסְפָה, Krae וַיֹּסִפוּ רָחֲבוּ [וְ]. **Niph.** *Pt.* as adj. כַּר נִרְחָב Is 30^{23} *a broad, roomy, pasture.* **Hiph.** *Pf.* 3 ms. הִרְחִיב Gn 26^{22} Hb 2^{5}, הִרְחִב Is 30^{33}; 2 ms. הִרְחַבְתָּ ψ 4^{2}, etc.; *Impf.* 3 ms. יַרְחִיב Dt 12^{20}+, etc.; *Imv.* ms. הַרְחֶב־ ψ 81^{11} (cf. also 25^{17} infr.); fs. הַרְחִיבִי Is 54^{2}, הַרְחִבִי Mi 1^{16}; *Inf. cstr.* הַרְחִיב Am 1^{13}; *Pt.* מַרְחִיב Dt 33^{20};—**1.** *make large*, c. acc. baldness Mi 1^{16} (sign of mourning), fun. pile Is 30^{33} (acc. om.; + הֶעְמִיק); *make wide*, acc. couch Is 57^{8} (fig.). **2.** *enlarge* limit of territory (גְּבוּל) Am 1^{13} Ex 34^{24} (J), Dt 12^{20} 19^{8}, so מַר׳ גָּד 33^{20}, cf. הַר׳ מְקוֹם אָהֳלֵךְ Is 54^{2} (fig.); also abs. + לְ pers., הִר׳ י׳ לָנוּ Gn 26^{22} (J), and (fig. of deliverance), בַּצָּר הִר׳ לִי ψ 4^{2}; מַתָּן אָדָם יַר׳ לוֹ Pr 18^{16} *a man's gift makes room for him*, gives access to patron; of י׳'s *enlarging* the heart (לִבִּי) ψ 119^{32} (cf. **Qal**); צָרוֹת לְבָבִי הִרְחִיבוּ ψ 25^{17} rd. prob. (with most) מ׳ Imv. הַרְחֵ(י)ב וּמ׳ (Bae הַרְחִיבוּ, *alarm*, cf. Ct 6^{5}); c. acc. צַעֲדִי *my step, stride* ψ 18^{37} = 2 S 22^{37} (i.e. givest me firm footing and vigorous step, cf. צַעַד **2**); *enlarge* mouth, open it wide, c. עַל pers. *against* Is 57^{4} ψ 35^{21} (cf. **Qal**); without עַל, as a young bird to receive food, fig., ψ 81^{11}; הִר׳ שְׁאוֹל נַפְשָׁהּ Is 5^{14} (‖ פָּעֲרָה פִיהָ; נֶפֶשׁ **5 c**), cf. Hb 2^{5}.

†רַחַב **n.[m., not f.** Jb 36^{16} Albr $^{ZAW xvi (1896), 94}$ Di Bu] breadth, broad expanse;—abs. ר׳ Jb 36^{16} (opp. צַר); pl. cstr. intens. רַחֲבֵי־אָרֶץ 38^{18} *the broad expanse of earth.*

רֹחַב $_{101}$ **n.[m.]** breadth, width;—ר׳ abs. Ez 42^{2}+, cstr. 1 K 6^{3}+; sf. רָחְבּוֹ Ex 25^{10}+, ־בָּהּ Gn 6^{15}+, רָחְבָּן Ez 42^{11};—*breadth*, of land, + אֶרֶץ = whole extent, expanse, Gn 13^{17} (J), so ר׳ alone Is 8^{8}; ר׳ מַיִם Jb 37^{10}; fig. ר׳ לֵב *largeness of understanding* (like sand of sea-shore) 1 K 5^{9}; *breadth*, = thickness, of wall גֶּדֶר Ez 42^{10}; elsewh. only in measurements *width, breadth* (Dt 3^{11}, K 10 t., Ez 54 t., Zc 2^{6} 5^{2}, P 23 t., Ch 6 t.; ‖ אֹרֶךְ 1 K 7^{6} + 63 t., + קוֹמָה 6^{2} + 14 t., + גֹּבַהּ + Ez 40^{42} 2 Ch 3^{4}; ‖ קוֹמָה alone † 1 K 7^{27} Ez 40^{5}): of buildings, etc., 1 K $6^{2.3.3.6.6.6}$+, Ez $41^{1.1.1.5.7}$+, altar Ex 27^{1} = 38^{1}, ark, תֵּבָה, Gn 6^{15}, אָרוֹן Ex 25^{10} = 37^{1}, etc.; of area, the עֶרֶשׂ of Og Dt 3^{11}, the תְּרוּמָה of land Ez $45^{1.3.5.6}$+, of court Ex $27^{12.13.18}$; of city Zc 2^{6}; of roll 5^{2}; of curtain Ex $26^{2.8}$+,

etc.; cf wall (קִיר),=*thickness*. Ex 41[9.12] (cf. 42[10] supr.); cf doorway 40[11] 41[11], etc.

I. רָחָב adj. wide, broad;—abs. ר׳ Jb 30[14]; cstr. רְחַב Pr 21[4]+; f.s. רְחָבָה Ex 3[8]+; cstr. רַחֲבַת Gn 34[21]+; mpl. cstr. רַחֲבֵי Is 33[21],—*wide, broad, spacious*, of land Ex 3[8] (J), Ne 9[35], רְחָבָה יָדַיִם, etc., Gn 34[21]+6 t., v. יָד 3 d; ר׳ מִמְּךָ Jb 11[9] of greatness of God. ‖ (אֲרֻכָּה מֵאֶרֶץ): בַּמֶּרְחָבָה as subst. ψ 119[45] *in a wide, roomy, space* (fig.); ר׳ מִתַּחְתֶּיהָ Jb 36[16] (sim.); of cup Ez 23[32] (in fig; ‖ הָעֲמֻקָּה); of wall (=*thick*) Je 51[58]; specif. in Jerusalem (as n.pr.) הַחוֹמָה הָר׳ Ne 3[8] 12[38]; fig. *extensive*, of work, undertaking, הַמְּלָאכָה, Ne 4[13] (‖ הַרְבֵּה); of ׳י's commandment ψ 119[96] (i.e. unlimited, measureless); רְחַב לֵבָב 101[5] i.e. *exultant, arrogant* (‖ גְּבַהּ עֵינַיִם). so ר׳ לֵב Pr 21[4] (‖ רוּם עֵינַיִם); רְחַב נֶפֶשׁ Pr 28[25] i.e. *greedy* (cf. רחב אִוֶּלֶת Ecclus 47[23c], in play on רְחַבְעָם).

†II. רָחָב n.pr.f. harlot in Jericho;—Jos 2[1.3] 6[17.23.25] (all JE); Ρααβ (so Heb 11[31] Jas 2[25], but Mt 1[5] Ραχαβ).

†I. רְחוֹב n.f.[Da 9,25] [not m. Zc 8[5] Albr[ZAW xv (1895), 11] cf. Ges[§ 122, 3 R]] broad open place, plaza (Lag[BN 124] Ba[NB 8c]);—ר׳ abs. Gn 19[2]+, cstr. Ju 19[15]+, רְחֹב v[15] 2 S 21[12]; sf. רְחֹבָהּ Dt 13[17] ψ 55[12]; pl. abs. רְחֹבוֹת Am 5[16]+, cstr. *id* Zc 8[4]+ (v. also רְחֹבוֹת n.pr., infr.); sf. רְחֹבֹתֶיהָ Is 15[3]+, etc.;—*broad open place* in city (usu. near gate, Ne 8[1.3.16.16] 2 Ch 32[6] Jb 29[7]; ‖ חוּץ Je 5[1]+8 t., דְּרָכִים Pr 26[13], שְׁוָקִים Ct 3[2]), for various private and public uses Gn 19[2] (J), Ju 19[15.17.20] Dt 13[17] 2 S 21[12] Je 5[1] Ez 16[24.31] Ne 8[16.16] Is 59[14] ψ 55[12] Jb 29[7], essential part of city Dn 9[25]; for lamentations Am 5[16] Is 15[3] Je 48[38], ר׳ הָעִיר אֲשֶׁר לִפְנֵי שַׁעַר הַמֶּלֶךְ Est 4[6] (cf. v[11]), cf. Je 9[20] 49[26] 50[30] La 2[11.12], ψ 144[14], assemblies 2 Ch 29[4] 32[6] Ezr 10[9] (ר׳ בֵּית הָא׳), Ne 8[1.3], proclamations Est 6[9.11], speeches Pr 1[20]; social life Zc 8[4.5] La 4[18] Pr 5[16] 7[12], cf. 22[13] 26[13], Ct 3[2]; ר׳ in Na 2[5] is appar. outside city (cf. As. *rêbit Nînâ*, etc.).

†II. רְחוֹב, רְחֹב n.pr. Ρααβ, Ροωβ, etc.. 1. (cf. Lag[BN 84]) loc. a. towards Hamath, רְחֹב 2 S 10[8] (𝔊L Βαιθρααβ), רְחֹב Nu 13[21] (P);=בֵּית ר׳ q.v. p. 112 (also 𝔊 1 Ch 19[6] Βαιθεωρ, 𝔊L Βαιθροωβι). b. רְחֹב in Asher (1) Jos 19[28] (P), (2) [perh.= (1)], v[30] (P), Ju 1[31], Levit. city Jos 21[31] (P)= 1 Ch 6[60], Egypt. *Rahubu*, N. of Kishon, WMM As. u. Eur. 153. 2. m. a. Aram name, רְחֹב 2 S 8[3.12] b. post-exilic Levite, רְחוֹב Ne 10[12].

†רְחֹבוֹת n.pr. loc. 1. רְחֹבֹת עִיר near Nineveh Gn 10[11] (J), τὴν Ροωβωθ[θ] πόλιν; Dl Par 261 cf. As. *rêbit Nînâ*, but v. COT[Gn 10, 11]. 2. רְחֹבוֹת, name of well Gn 26[22] (J), Εὐρυχωρία (cf. interpr. v[22]); Palmer[Desert 334 f.] identif. with er-Ruhaibeh (in Wady R.) c. 45 m. SW. of Hebron, N. of lat. 31°. 3. ר׳ הַנָּהָר, home of a king of Edom Gn 36[37] (P)=1 Ch 1[48], Ροωβωθ τῆς παρὰ ποταμόν, P. τοῦ ποταμοῦ (i.e. on Euphrates? here improb.; conj. in Di Holz Wkl[Gesch. Isr. i. 192]).

†(רְחַבְיָהוּ) רְחַבְיָה n.pr.m. son of Eliezer and grandson of Moses: רְחַבְיָה 1 Ch 23[17.17] (Ρααβια) =רְחַבְיָהוּ 26[25] (Ρα(α)βιας, 𝔊L Αβια), appar. also 24[21.21] (Ρααβια, Αβια).

רְחַבְעָם n.pr.m. Rehoboam (word-play on רחב Ecclus 47[23c]);—king of Judah, son of Solomon; Ροβοαμ: 1 K 11[43] 12[1.3.6]+16 t. 1 K 12, 14, +15[6] ‖ 2 Ch 9[31] 10[1.3.6]+21 t. 2 Ch 10, 11, 12, +13[7]; also 1 Ch 3[10].

†מֶרְחָב n.[m.] broad, roomy, place;—abs. מ׳, of pasture Ho 4[16] (in sim); fig. of freedom from distress and anxiety 2 S 22[20]=ψ 18[20], ψ 31[9] 118[5] (MT cstr. in בַּמֶּרְחַבְיָהּ *spacious place of Yah*, i.e. extraordinarily spacious, < מֶרְחַב יָהּ, יָהּ being subj. of vb.); pl. cstr. מֶרְחֲבֵי־אֶרֶץ Hb 1[6] *expanses of the earth*.

רחה (√of foll.; mng. unknown; NH=BH; Ar. رَحًى *handmill* (cf Wetzst Bab. xiv xiv (1891), 4); Aram. רֵחְיָא, ܪܚܝܐ; Lag[BN 167] Ba[NB 8, 21]).

†[רֵחֶה] n.[m.], only du. רֵחַיִם (hand-)mill (prob.=*two mill-stones*);—ר׳ abs., common household utensil, turned by maids, Ex 11[5] (הָרֵחָיִם; J), female slaves Is 47[2] (c. טָחַן, q.v.); ר׳ טָחַן בָּר Nu 11[8] (J); ר׳ וָרָכֶב Dt 24[6] (v. רכב); קוֹל ר׳ as sound of family life Je 25[10].

רְחִיטֵנוּ Ct 1[17] Kt, v. [רָהִיט] sub רהט.

רֵחַיִם v. רחה.

רחל (√of foll.; mng ?; cf. NH רָחֵל (pl. —ים, —וֹת), Ar. رَخِلٌ, رِخْلٌ, Aram. רַחְלָא, all *ewe*; cf. perh. As. *laḫru* (transp.; vid. on לָהַל)).

†I. רָחֵל n.f.[Is 53, 7] ewe;—abs. ר׳ Is 53[7] (in sim., ‖ שֶׂה), pl. רְחֵלִים Gn 32[15] (E; + עִזִּים, אֵילִים), Ct 6[6] (in sim.), sf רְחֵלֶיךָ וְעִזֶּיךָ Gn 31[38] (E).

II רָחֵל n.pr.f. (*ewe*, RS[K 219]);—Rachel, Ραχηλ, daughter of Laban and wife of Jacob: Gn 29[6.9.10.11.12.16.17.18.20.25.28.29.30]+36 t. Gn (JE 37 t., P 6 t.),

+ קִבְרַת(־)ר׳ 35^{20} (JE), 1 S 10^{2} (cf. אֶפְרָתָה **1**, p. 68; on site vid. Dr$^{Hast\ DB\ RACHEL}$); ר׳ (in fig.) Je 31^{15}; ר׳ Ru 4^{11} (in sim.).

I. רחם (√of foll.; orig. meaning dub.; Thes *be soft*, so Gerber^{126}, cp. Ar. رَخُمَ *be soft, gentle* (but ح orig. cons.?), Dl$^{HWB\ 610b}$ *be wide;* cf. As. *rîmu, rêmu*, Ar. رَحِم, NH רֶחֶם, Aram. רַחְמָא, ܪܚܡܐ, all *womb;* MI^{17} רחמת *female captives;* vbs. (connexion with רֶחֶם not wholly clear, cf. No$^{ZMG\ xl\ (1886),\ 151\ f.}$, v. רַחֲמִים): As. *râmu, love, compassionate*, Ar. رَحِمَ *have compassion*, also رَحِمَ *be inclined toward, affectionate to* (= رحم acc. to Ar. authorities, v. Lane); Sab. epith.dei רחמנן *Compassionate* (= Ar. الرَّحْمٰن), CIS$^{iv.\ no.\ 6,\ 2}$ Fell$^{ZMG\ liv\ (1900),\ 252}$ who cp. epith. רחם *id.;* cf. NH רִחֵם Pi.; Thes cp. Eth. ምሕረ: (transp.) *have compassion*, but v. Prät$^{BAS\ i.\ 22}$ and reff.; Aram. רְחֵם, ܪܚܡ, Palm. רחם, all *love* (common); Nab. Palm. רחם *friend*).

†רֶחֶם, רַחַם n.m.$^{Ho\ 9.\ 14}$ womb (f. Je 20^{17}, unless הָרַת a noun, cf. Albr$^{ZAW\ xvi.\ 81}$ SS);—abs. ר׳ Gn 20^{18}+, רַחַם Ju 5^{30}, רָחֶם Je 20^{17}+, רָחֶם Gn 49^{25}+; cstr. רֶחֶם Nu 12^{12} Jb 3^{11}; sf. רַחְמָהּ Gn 29^{31}+, רַחְמָהּ Je 20^{17} (Ges$^{§ 91\ e}$; >f. abs. Kö$^{ii.\ 1,\ 153}$); du. רַחֲמָתַיִם Ju 5^{30};—**1.** *womb*, Gn 49^{25} (J) Je 20^{17} Jb 24^{20}; מֵרֶחֶם i.e. from birth Je 20^{17} ψ 22^{11} 58^{4} Jb 3^{11} (מִנִּי), Is 46^{3}, fig. ψ 110^{3}; בְּרֶחֶם Jb 31^{15}; יצא מֵר׳ *go forth from womb* in birth Je 1^{5} 20^{18} Jb 38^{8}, cf. 10^{18}; מֵר׳ אֵם Nu 12^{12} (E); פתח ר׳ *open the womb*, in order to childbirth Gn 29^{31} 30^{22} (JE); כָּל־פֶּטֶר רחם *all that first opens womb* (of men and animals) Ex $13^{12.15}$ 34^{19} (J) Nu 18^{15} (P) Ez 20^{26}; פטר ר׳ Nu 3^{12} (P), פִּטְרַת כל ר׳ Nu 8^{16}; פטר כל ר׳ Ex 13^{2} (P); on the other hand, ר׳ מַשְׁכִּיל Ho 9^{14} *miscarrying womb;* עֹצֶר ר׳ Pr 30^{16} *restraint* (i.e. barrenness) *of womb* (so ψ 107^{39} Perles$^{Anal.\ 86}$); עָצַר בְּעַד ר׳ (of God) Gn 20^{18} (E); סָגַר ר׳ (בְּעַד) 1 S $1^{5.6}$, preventing childbirth. **2.** *womb-man, woman-slave:* רַחַם רַחֲמָתַיִם Ju 5^{30} *a woman, two women.*

†רַחֲמִים n.m.$^{2\ S\ 24.\ 14}$ abs. pl. intens. compassion (acc. to many denom. from רֶחֶם, orig. *brotherhood, brotherly feeling*, of those born from same womb, v. Nö$^{ZMG\ xl\ (1886),\ 153\ (yet\ v.\ 730)}$ We$^{GGN\ 1893,\ 475}$ Gerber^{126}, or *motherly feeling* Kö$^{ii.\ 1,\ 31}$);—abs. ר׳ Gn 43^{14}+; cstr. רַחֲמֵי Pr 12^{10}; sf. רַחֲמָיו La 3^{22} (Baer Gi; van d. H. Qr, Kt רחמו), 2 S 24^{14} Qr (>Kt רחמו), etc.;—**1.** *compassion:* usu. of God Is $63^{7.15}$ ψ 77^{10} 79^{8} 119^{77} Zc 1^{16} Dn 9^{9} Ne 9^{28}, c. רבים 2 S 24^{14} = 1 Ch 21^{13}, Ne $9^{19.27.31}$ ψ 119^{156} Dn 9^{18}; גדולים Is 54^{7}; ‖ חסד ψ 40^{12} 103^{4} Ho 2^{21} Je 16^{5}; חסדים ψ 25^{6}; כרב רחמיך ψ 51^{3} 69^{17}, c. על rei 145^{9}; נתן ר׳ ל Dt 13^{18} Je 42^{12}; לא כלו ר׳ La 3^{22}. **2.** of man, Am 1^{11} Pr 12^{10}; עשה ר׳ Zc 7^{9}; נָתַן לפ׳ ר׳ לִפְנֵי Gn 43^{14} (R); נתן לר׳ לִפְנֵי 1 K 8^{50} Ne 1^{11} Dn 1^{9} ψ 106^{46}, cf. 2 Ch 30^{9}; שׂם ר׳ ל Is 47^{6}; נִכְמְרוּ ר׳ אל Gn 43^{30} (J), c. על 2 K 3^{26}.

†[רָחַם] vb. denom. love. **Pi.** have compassion;—**Qal** *Impf.* 1 s. sf. אֶרְחָמְךָ ψ 18^{2} *I love thee* (perhaps gloss; v. not in ‖ 2 S 22^{2}; Hi Ch SS Gerber read אֲרוֹמִמְךָ). **Pi.** *Pf.* 3 ms. רִחַם ψ 103^{13}+; sf. וְרִחַמְךָ consec. Dt 13^{18}, etc.; *Impf.* 3 ms. יְרַחֵם Is 9^{16}+; sf. יְרַחֲמֶנּוּ Is 55^{7}, etc.; *Inf. abs.* רַחֵם Je 31^{20} Hb 3^{2}; cstr. רַחֵם Is 49^{15} ψ 103^{13}; sf. רַחֶמְכֶם Is 30^{18}; *Pt.* מְרַחֵם ψ 116^{5}, etc.;—*have compassion, compassionate;*—**1.** usu. of God: c. acc. of his people, Ex $33^{19.19}$ (J) Dt 13^{18} 30^{3} 2 K 13^{23} Is 9^{16} 14^{1} 27^{11} 30^{18} $49^{10.13}$ $54^{8.10}$ 55^{7} 60^{10} Je 12^{15} 30^{18} $31^{20.20}$ 33^{26} Ez 39^{25} Ho $1^{6.7}$ $2^{6.25}$ Mi 7^{19} Zc 1^{12} 10^{6} ψ 102^{14}; c. עַל 103^{13}; abs. Je 13^{14} Hb 3^{2} ψ 116^{5} La 3^{32}. **2.** of man, usu. a conqueror: c. acc. 1 K 8^{50} Je 42^{12}; abs. 6^{23} 21^{7} 50^{42}; elsewhere of children, c. acc. Is 13^{18} 49^{15}; c. עַל ψ 103^{13}. **Pu.** *Pf.* 3 fs. רֻחָמָה Ho 2^{25} (Ges$^{§ 52\ a\ n}$ Kö$^{i.\ 270}$);—*Impf.* 3 ms. יְרֻחָם Ho 14^{4}; יְרֻחָם Pr 28^{13}; *be shewn compassion, compassionated:* of orphans Ho 14^{4}; children of Israel wife of Yahweh 2^{25} (cf. לֹא ר׳ $1^{6.8}$, p. 520); penitent sinner Pr 28^{13}.

†רַחוּם adj. compassionate;—always of God: אֵל רַחוּם Dt 4^{31}, ר׳ וְחַנּוּן Ex 34^{6} (J) = ψ 86^{15} 103^{8}; later חַנּוּן ור׳ 2 Ch 30^{9} Ne $9^{17.31}$ Jo 2^{13} Jon 4^{2} ψ 111^{4} 112^{4} 145^{8}; והוא ר׳ 78^{38}.

†[רַחֲמָנִי] adj. id.;—pl. f. נָשִׁים רַחֲמָנִיּוֹת La 4^{10} *compassionate women.*

†רַחַם n.pr.m. (*girl*(-like)?);—in Judah, 1 Ch 2^{44}; Ραεμ, A Ραμ', ⅁L Ρααμ.

רֻחָמָה in לֹא ר׳ n.pr.f., v. p. 520.

†רְחוּם, רְחֻם n. pr. m. (*compassion*, or *softness, gentleness?*);—post-exilic name: **1.** with Zerub.: **a.** רְחוּם Ezr 2^{2}, A Ιρεουμ', ⅁L Ναουμ (= נַחוּם ‖ Ne 7^{7}). **b.** priest, רְחֻם Ne 12^{3} Ρεουμ (= חָרִם v.^{15}, cf. 7^{42} = Ezr 2^{39}, Ezr 10^{21}, v. חָרִם 3 a). **2.** רְחוּם, with Neh.: **a.** Levite Ne 3^{17}, Βαουθ, ℵA⅁L Ραουμ. **b.** Ne 10^{26}, Ρα[ε]ουμ.

†**יְרֹחָם** **n.pr.m.** (*may he be compassionated*, cf. Lag[BN 134]),—**1.** father of Elkanah, grandf. of Sam., Ephraimite 1 S 1[1] (Ιερεμε[ι]ηλ, A Ιεροαμ), Levite 1 Ch 6[12.19] (Ιδαερ, Ηααλ; A Ιεροβοαμ, Ιερεαμ, 𝔊L Ιεραμαηλ) **2.** Benjamites **a.** 1 Ch 8[27] Ιρααμ, etc. (appar = יְרֵמוֹת v[14]). **b.** 9[8], 𝔊 *id* (= **a**?) **3.** priests. **a** 1 Ch 9[12], Ι(ε)ρααμ, etc **b.** Ne 11[12], Ι(ε)ροαμ **4.** father of a hero of David 1 Ch 12[8] (van d H ע[7]), Ρααμ, A 𝔊L Ιεροαμ. **5.** Danite 1 Ch 27[22], Ιωραμ (𝔊L as **4**). **6.** father of a captain with Jehoiada, 2 Ch 23[1], Ιωραμ

†**יְרַחְמְאֵל** **n pr m** (*may Ēl have compassion*) Ιεραμεηλ, etc,—**1.** name in Judah 1 Ch 2[9.25.26.27.33.42] (cf. **adj. gent** foll). **2.** son of king Jehoiakim Je 36[26] **3.** Levite, 1 Ch 24[29]

†**יְרַחְמְאֵלִי** **adj.gent** (earlier than foregoing; as tribal name bef n pr m [For radical view of relations of יר׳, (with many text emendations), v. Che[Ency Bib Jerahmeel]]),—הַיר׳ as subst. coll, נגב הַיר׳ 1 S 27[10] *the Negeb of the Yeraḥmeelites* (in S Judah), (νότον) Ιεσμεγα, A Ισραμηλει, 𝔊L Αερμων, עָרֵי הַיר׳ 30[29], τοῦ Ισραηλ, A Ιεραμηλει (cf. **1** supr., and Gray[Prop. N 214, 265, 307])

II **רחם** (√of foll; cf. Ar رَخَمٌ *vulture*; n unit رَخَمَةٌ)

†**רָחָם** **n.[m.]** **carrion-vulture**;—abs הָרׇ׳ Lv 11[18] (Sam רחמה; so perh read) = הָרָחָמָה ‖ Dt 14[17] (on accent v Dr, cf. Ges[§ 90 f])

†**רָחָמָה** **n [m]** id, Dt 14[17], v foregoing.

רחן (appar √of foll, meaning dubious)

†**תַּרְחֲנָה** **n.pr.** [**m.? f.?**] child of Caleb 1 Ch 2[48], Θαραμ, A Θαρχνα, 𝔊L Θαρααvα

†I [**רָחַף**] **vb. grow soft, relax** (cf Ar رَخُفَ *be soft*),—**Qal** *Pf* 3 pl רָחֲפוּ Je 23[9] (bones of one appalled)

†II **רָחַף** **vb. Pi. hover** (NH *id*, cf Grunbaum[ZMG xxxix (1885) 607], Syr Pa ܪܰܚܶܦ *move gently*, also *cherish*, and *brood*, cf Thes[s v], connexion with I ר׳ dub),—**Pi.** *Impf* 3 ms יְרַחֵף עַל Dt 32[11] (poem) of vulture *hovering* over young, *Pt* רוּחַ א׳ מְרַחֶפֶת עַל־פְּנֵי הַמָּיִם Gn 1[2] (P), *hovering* over face of waters, or perh (v Syr) *brooding* (and fertilizing), so Jer[Quaest. in Gen ed Lag 4] (reading '*marahaefeth*'), cf Dr Gunk

רָחַץ[72] **vb. wash, wash off, away, bathe** (NH = BH; Ar رَحَضَ (also of garments), Eth. ረሐፀ:, ሐፀፀ: *sweat*; cf. As. *raḥâṣu*, *overflow, flood* (on ḥ = ح v. Nö[ZMG xl (1886) 727])),—**Qal**[72] *Pf.* 3 ms ר׳ Is 4[4]+, etc; *Impf* 3 ms יִרְחַץ Dt 23[12]+etc, *Imv* ms. רחץ 2 S 11[8] 2 K 5[13]; mpl רַחֲצוּ Gn 18[4]+, *Inf cstr.* רחץ Gn 24[32]+, לִרְחֹצָה Ex 30[18]+; *Pt* fs רֹחֶצֶת 2 S 11[2], fpl. רֹחֲצוֹת Ct 5[12],—**1.** trans *wash* (with water), c acc feet (רגלים, בַּמַּיִם oft expr.), Gn 18[4] 19[2] 24[32] 43[24] (all J), Ju 19[21] 1 S 25[41] 2 S 11[8] Ct 5[3]; יר׳ פְּעָמָיו בְּדַם הָרָשָׁע ψ 58[11] (fig of righteous, at י׳'s vengeance); c acc hands (יָדַיִם) Dt 21[6] (+ עַל over, in ceremonial, to express innocence), hence fig. אֶר׳ כַּפַּי בְּנִקָּיוֹן ψ 26[6] 73[13], hands and feet Ex 30[19] (+ מִן of laver), v[21] 40[31] (+ מִן *id.*; all P); c. acc. face (פָּנָיו) Gn 43[31] (J); c acc pers. Ez 16[9] Ex 29[4] 40[12] Lv 8[6] (all P), acc בְּשָׂרוֹ (oft ‖ כבס of garments), Lv 14[9] 15[13] + 9 t P (H); c acc. of parts of sacrificial victim Ex 29[17] Lv 1[9.13] 8[21] 9[14], *wash off, away*, c acc. of filth Is 4[4] (fig). **2.** intrans *wash, bathe* (oneself) Ex 2[5] (E), 2 S 11[2] 12[20] 1 K 22[38] 2 K 5[10.12.13] Is 1[16] Ez 23[40] (+ לְ pers for whom), Ru 3[3] Lv 14[8] + 14 t. P (oft. ‖ כבס), + בְּ of laver 2 Ch 4[6.6]; of eyes, *bathed* in milk (בֶּחָלָב) Ct 5[12] (fig), Jb 29[6] (fig), v. הָלִיךְ. †**Pu.** *Pf.* 3 ms. רֻחָץ Pr 30[12] *be washed* (+ מִן of filth, fig.); 2 fs. בַּמַּיִם לֹא רֻחַצְתְּ Ez 16[4] (in fig). †**Hithp.** *Pf.* 1 s הִתְרָחַצְתִּי במו שלג Jb 9[30] if *I washed myself in snow* (fig.).

†[**רַחַץ**] **n.[m.]** **washing**, fig,—only sf. in סִיר רַחְצִי ψ 60[10] Moab is *my wash-pot* = 108[10].

†**רַחְצָה** **n.f.** **id.**, lit,—עָלוּ מִן־הָר׳, of sheep, Ct 4[2] 6[6] (in sim.)

†**רָחַק** **vb. be, or become, far, distant** (NH = BH; As esp. adj *rûḳu*, *far*, cf. Ar. رَحِيقٌ *choice wine* (i.e. from a distance) Fra[158]; Eth. ርሕቀ: *be far*, Sab רחק CIS[iv. nos. 95, 98]; Aram. רְחֵק, רחיק, and (oft in der spec and deriv) ܪܚܩ),—**Qal** *Pf* 3 ms ר׳ Is 59[9] La 1[16], etc.; *Impf* 3 ms. ירחק Dt 12[21]+, etc; *Imv.* fs. רַחֲקִי Is 54[14], mpl. רַחֲקוּ Ez 11[15] < *Pf* רָחֲקוּ Ra Hi Sm Co Toy Krae, *Inf cstr* רחק ψ 103[12] Ec 3[5], לְרָחֳקָה Ez 8[6],—*be far, distant* c. מִן pers, of place Dt 12[21] 14[24], of pers, = neglect, abandon, Pr 19[7], esp in ψψ, of י׳, ψ 22[12.20] (מִן pers. om.), 35[22] 38[22] 71[12]; of utter absence, or non-existence La 1[16], cf Is 49[19] (abs), subj justice Is 59[9] (opp השׂיג), cf. v[11] (‖ אַיִן), subj blessing ψ 109[17], subj עֲצַת רְשָׁעִים Jb 21[16] 22[18], c. מֵעַל pers. (י׳), of Isr (fig) Je 2[5], cf Ez 44[10], = *far from* (land of) י׳ 11[15] (v. supr., Krae ins. אֶרֶץ), c. מֵעַל loc Ez 8[6] (of י׳),

מן loc. (E. from W.) ψ 103^{12}; c. מן rei (fig.): תּוֹרָתְךָ 119^{150} (opp קרב); מֵיֶשַׁע Jb 5^{4}, מֵעֹשֶׁק Is 54^{14}, cf Pr 22^{5}; =*wholly abstain from* Ex 23^{7} (E), so (מן inf) Ec 3^{5}; abs of י׳'s righteousness, with ref. to time Is 46^{13} (|| אחר; opp קרב)—יִרְחַק־חֹק Mi 7^{11} *boundary shall become distant*, i.e territory be enlarged (? crpt., cf. We Now), ירחק חֶבֶל הַכֶּסֶף Kt Ec 12^{6} *be removed?* Qr יֵרָתֵק *be joined?* 𝔊 ἀνατραπῇ, 𝔙 *rumpatur*, cf. 𝔖, rd. prob. יִנָּתֵק Pfannk Thes Ew De Siegf Buhl[Lex]. **Pi.** *Pf.* 3 ms רִחַק Is 6^{12}, of י׳, *send far away*, acc pers, of people, לִבּוֹ ר׳ 29^{13}, c. מן of י׳; 2 ms. רִחַקְתָּ 26^{15} *thou hast far extended* (c. acc.) all the ends (boundaries) of the land, *Impf.* 3 mpl יְרַחֲקוּ אֶת־זְנוּתָם Ez 43^{9}. **Hiph.** *Pf.* 3 ms. הרחיק Jb 19^{13} ψ 103^{12}, 1 s sf. הִרְחַקְתִּים Ez 11^{16}, etc; *Impf.* 3 ms. sf. יַרְחִיקֶנָּה Pr 22^{15}, 2 ms תַּרְחִיק Jb 22^{23}, etc, *Imv.* ms. הַרְחֵק Pr 4^{24} + 2 t, הַרְחֵק Jb 13^{21}, sf. הַרְחִיקֵהוּ 11^{14}; *Inf. abs* הַרְחֵק Gn 21^{16}+, *cstr.* הַרְחִיק Je 27^{10}, sf. הַרְחִיקָם Jo 4^{6};—**1.** dir. caus. *make*, or *exhibit, distance, be gone far*, subj pers.: Gn 44^{4} (J), c. מן loc. Jos 8^{4} (JE), Ju 18^{22}, sq inf. cstr. הַרְחֵק לֹא תַרְ׳ לָלֶכֶת Ex 8^{24} (J), cf. ψ 55^{8}, Inf. abs. as adv. = *at a distance* Gn 21^{16} (E), c. מן loc. Ex 33^{7} (E), Jos 3^{16} (JE; הַר׳ מאד מן, Qr; > Kt ב for מן). **2.** indir. caus. *remove, put far away*, c acc. pers + מֵעַל of land Je 27^{10}, cf. Jo 4^{6}, + מֵעַל pers. Jb 19^{13} and (acc. הַצְּפוֹנִי) Jo 2^{20}, + מן pers. ψ $88^{9.19}$; + בְּגוֹיִם Ez 11^{16}, c. acc. כַּף + מֵעַל pers Jb 13^{21}, c. acc. דֶּרֶךְ + *id.* Pr 5^{8}; c. acc. of sin + מן pers 4^{24} Jb 11^{14} (מן pers. om); Pr 22^{15} 30^{8} ψ 103^{12}; + מן loc Jb 22^{23}.

† [רָחֵק] **adj. verb. removing, departing**;—pl sf., as subst., רְחֵקֶיךָ ψ 73^{27} *those departing from thee* (i.e. from י׳).

† רָחֹק, רָחוֹק **adj. distant, far, et n.m.**[Jos 3,4] **distance** (Lag[BN 31]);—abs רָחֹק Ex 2^{4}+, רָחוֹק Ez 6^{12}+; fs. רחֹקה Dt 30^{11}+, רחוקה Jos 9^{6}+, mpl. רחקים Dt 13^{8}+, etc, fpl. abs רְחֹקוֹת Je 48^{24}+, etc.,—oft. opp קָרוֹב: **1. adj. a.** of space: *distant*, land Jos $9^{6.9}$ (+ מְאֹד), Dt 29^{21} 1 K $8^{41.46}$ = 2 Ch $6^{32.36}$, 2 K 20^{14} = Is 39^{3}, אִיִּים ר׳ Is 66^{19} + perh. ψ 65^{6} (Che We read אִיִּם for יָם; Weir in Che גוים; MT makes ר׳ = *distant ones*, people), c. מן pers, of peoples Jos 9^{22} (JE), Ju 18^{7}, persons Ez 22^{5} Ne 4^{13} Pr 15^{29} (י׳, fig.), cf Je 12^{2} (*id*), cities Dt 20^{15}, so (מן loc.) Ju 18^{28}; abs of people Jo 4^{8}, persons Is 33^{13} 57^{19} Je 25^{26} Ez 6^{12} Zc 6^{15} Pr 27^{10} Dn 9^{7} Est 9^{20}, cities Je 48^{24}, trees ψ 56^{1} (title; v יוֹנָה *ad fin*, p 401), of *distant* journey Nu 9^{10} (P); fig, רָחוֹק pred. (indef.) Ec 7^{24}, of י׳'s מִצְוָה Dt 30^{11}; c. מן pers. (i.e. absent from, lacking to), of salvation ψ 119^{155}, wisdom Ec 7^{23}, of pers. c. מן of act or quality Is 46^{12} ψ 22^{2}, of price, c. מן comp. = *far beyond* Pr 31^{10}. **b.** of time: לְעִתִּים רחוקות Ez 12^{27}. **2. n.m.** always sing.. **a.** of space: *distance* Jos 3^{4} (D), elsewhere c. prep.: (1) מֵר׳ *from a distance*, c verbs implying motion, physical or mental: look Gn 24^{4} (E) 37^{18} (J) Jb 2^{12} 36^{25}; bring Dt 28^{49} Is 43^{6} 60^{9}, cf. Je 46^{27}; come Is 49^{12} 60^{4} Hb 1^{8}, hear Is 49^{1}; smell Jb 39^{25}, remember Je 51^{50}; understand ψ 139^{2}; prob. also worship Ex 24^{1} (J), (2) מֵר׳ *at a distance* (מן **1 c**) Ex 2^{4} (E), $20^{18.21}$ (E, Gi v[15 18]), 1 S 26^{13} 2 K 2^{7} Is 5^{26} 59^{14} ψ 38^{12}, cf. אֱלֹהֵי מֵר׳ Je 23^{23} *a God afar off* (on cstr. cf. Ges[§ 130a]; < read אלהים ר׳ Gie, cf. 𝔊); (3) לְמֵר׳ *to a distance* (מן **1 c**) Is 22^{3} 23^{7} Pr 7^{19}, (4) בְּר׳ *at a distance* ψ 10^{1}; עַד־ר׳ *to a distance* Mi 4^{3}; also c two prepp.: (5) לְמֵר׳ *from* (מן **9 b**), Jb 36^{3} 39^{29}; (6) עַד־מֵר׳ (III. עַד **I. 1 a**) *to a distance* Is 57^{9} + Ne 12^{43} van d H. (עד om. Baer Gi); even (7) עַד־לְמֵר׳ (עַד III) 2 Ch 26^{15} Ezr 3^{13} **b.** of time, מֵר׳ *long ago* Is 22^{11}, c. noun = *ancient, of long standing* 25^{1}, לְמֵר׳ *long ago* 2 K 19^{25} = Is 37^{26}; *from afar* 2 S 7^{19} = 1 Ch 17^{17}.

† מֶרְחָק **n.m. distant place, distance**;—abs. מ׳ Is 10^{3}+, מֶרְחָק ψ 138^{6}; pl מֶרְחַקִּים Zc 10^{9}, מֶר׳ Is 33^{17} Je 8^{19}, cstr. מֶרְחַקֵּי Is 8^{9},—*distant place, far country* Is 8^{9} Zc 10^{9}; often c אֶרֶץ. א׳ (ה)מֶרְחָק *land of distance*, distant land Is 13^{5} 46^{11} Je 4^{16} 6^{20} Pr 25^{25}, so c pl א׳ מרחקים Je 8^{19}, *land of distances*, i.e. of wide extent, Is 33^{17}; ממ׳ *from far* Is 10^{3} 30^{27} Je 5^{15} Ez 23^{40} Pr 31^{14}; fig ψ 138^{6}; ממ׳ *at a distance* Je 31^{10}, *to a distance* Is 17^{13} — בֵּית הַמ׳ v. p 112

† רָחַשׁ **vb. keep moving, stir** (NH *stir, move*, esp of lips in speech, also, in expl. of מרחשת, of *stewing, boiling*, Aram. רְחַשׁ, ܪܚܫ, *creep, move, flutter*, ܪܚܫܐ *reptile*);—**Qal** *Pf.* 3 ms. ר׳ לִבִּי דָּבָר טוֹב ψ 45^{2} *is astir.*

† מַרְחֶשֶׁת **n.f. stew-pan, sauce-pan** (so NH, v esp Levy[NHWB III 69b], and cf. NH רָחוּשׁ Id ib iv 443a),—מִנְחַת מ׳ Lv 2^{7}, 7^{9} כָּל־[מִנְחָה] נַעֲשָׂה בַמּ׳.

† רַחַת **n.[f.] winnowing-shovel**, or the like (√ unknown, Thes fr רוח = *ventilabrum*, cf No[ZMG xl (1886) 723], Wetzst in De[Is (2). 709] fr. רחה = رَخُوَ *be soft, loose, friable*, etc., cf. Kö[II. 1. 177]; NH = BH, Ar. رَحْتٌ is prob. loan-wd. No[l.c.]),—זֹרֶה בָר׳ וּבַמִּזְרֶה Is 30^{24}.

†[רָטֹב, רָטַב Lag[BN 31]] **vb. be moist** (NH *id*, As. *raṭâbu*, II. *moisten;* Ar. رَطِبَ, Eth. ረጠበ: Aram. רְטַב, رطب, all *be moist*);—**Qal** *Impf* 3 ms מִזֶּרֶם הָרִים יִרְטָבוּ Jb 24[8].

†רָטֹב **adj. moist, juicy, fresh**,—ר׳ הוּא לִפְנֵי־שָׁמֶשׁ Jb 8[16]

†[רָטָה] **vb.** (dub.) **wring out** (NH=BH (si vera l, v Levy[NHWB iv 444] and reff)),—**Qal** *Impf* 3 ms. sf יִרְטֵנִי Jb 16[11] upon the hands of wicked men *he wrings me out*, but read prob יָרַט ‚√ יר׳ (Di Bu Du al), q v

רטט (Aram רטט *tremble*, rare, der. spec).

†רֶטֶט **n.[m.] trembling, panic** (Ba[NB § 20 a] Ko[ii 1 42]),—abs ר׳ הֶחֱזִיקָה Je 49[24] *she hath seized panic*, but < החזיקה (Gie), *panic hath seized her.*

†רֻטֲפַשׁ **vb. quadril. intrans. grow fresh** (Ges[§ 56], si vera l, transp. טרפש [expanded from טָפַשׁ *be wide, loose, delicate*, cf. esp As. *tapâšu*, *be fat*, Zim[BP 99 A] Fra[ZA III. 54]], cf Talm טַרְפְּשָׁא *fatty membrane*, Syr. ܛܰܪܦܶܫܳܐ PS[1527] *thin flesh*, Ar طَرْفَشَ *be convalescent;* but ר׳ perh. not orig),—*Pf* pass. רֻטֲפַשׁ בְּשָׂרוֹ מִנֹּעַר Jb 33[25] *his flesh hath grown fresher than*, etc.; rd. perh טפש Altschuller[ZAW vi (1886). 212], יטפש Bi Bu cf Du

†[רָטַשׁ] **vb. Pi. dash in pieces** (cf. 𝔗 רְטַשׁ **cast away, reject**; but possibly akin to לָטַשׁ),—**Pi.** *Impf* 2 ms תְּרַטֵּשׁ 2 K 8[12] their children *thou wilt dash in pieces;* 3 fpl. קְשָׁתוֹת נְעָרִים תְּרַטַּשְׁנָה Is 13[18], but prob. crpt., Du conj. נְעָרוֹת תְּרַטַּשְׁנָה, cf Che **Pu.** *Pf* 3 fs. אֵם עַל־בָּנִים רֻטָּשָׁה Ho 10[14], *Impf* 3 mpl יְרֻטְּשׁוּ Is 13[16] Na 3[10], יְרֻטָּשׁוּ Ho 14[1], all of children

רי v. רוה

†רִיב [No[ZMG xxxvii (1883). 530. 534] Ges[§ 73 b]] **vb. strive, contend** (cf Ar رَابَ (ى) *agitate* (the mind), رَيْبٌ *disquiet*, cf. also Syr ܐܰܘ *cry, shout*, Aph also *quarrel noisily*, ܐܽܘܟܳܐ *shouting, clamour* (v. No[1 c]); on Sab n pr. ריב=Ar. رِيَاب v. DHM[ib 14]),—**Qal** *Pf* 3 ms רָב Ju 11[25] 1 S 25[39], 2 ms רַבְתָּ La 3[58], רִיבוֹתָ Jb 33[13], etc; *Impf* 3 ms יָרִיב Ju 6[31] +, juss יָרֵב Ho 4[4] 1 S 24[16], וַיָּרֶב Ju 6[31 32] (לוֹ(בוֹ, וַיָּרֶב Gn 31[36] +; 2 ms. תרוב Pr 3[30] Kt, תָּרִיב Qr, 3 mpl יְרִיבֻן Ex 21[18], etc, *Imv.* ms רִיב Mi 6[1] Pr 25[9], רִיבָה ψ 35[1] +, mpl. רִיבוּ Is 1[17] Ho 2[4], *Inf. abs* רוֹב Ju 11[25], רָב Jb 40[2], רִיב Je 50[34] (Ges[§ 73 d] Ko[i 509] Ba[NB 80]), *cstr.* רִיב Is 3[13] Jb 9[3] + Ju 21[22] Qr (Kt רוב), רָב Am 7[4] Pr 25[8]; *Pt.* רָב Is 19[20] +,—*strive:* **1.** involving bodily struggle Ex 21[18] (sc one with another; E); public hostilities, יָדָיו רָב לוֹ Dt 33[7] (with) *his hands he strove for it*, c עִם of Israel, הֲרוֹב רָב Ju 11[25] (|| נִלְחַם) **2.** with words, c. בְּ pers. Gn 31[36] (E), Ex 17[2a] (J) Ju 6[32], so (in fig) Ho 2[4] cf. v[4]; oft =*quarrel*, c. עִם pers., Gn 26[20] Ex 17[2b] Nu 20[3] (all J), Ne 13[25]; subj God Jb 9[3] 13[19] 23[6]; also 40[2] (עִם of God, on inf abs. v Ges[§ 113 ee]), in gen. Pr 3[30], c. את pers Ju 8[1] Ne 5[7] 13[11 17], subj. י׳ Is 49[25] (cf 1 יָרִיב infr.), ψ 35[1] (|| לְחַם), אֶת of י׳ Is 45[9] (pt. *one striving*), Nu 20[13] (P), c. עַל rei Gn 26[21 22]; abs =*find fault* Ho 4[4] (|| הוֹכִיחַ). Esp **3.** *conduct a* (legal) *case, suit*, usu. fig., י׳ subj; Is 3[13] (|| דִּין), 57[16] (|| קָצַף), ψ 103[9] (נָטַר [|| אַף]), cf קֹרֵא לָרִב בָּאֵשׁ Am 7[4]; c. acc. pers. with whom (unfriendly sense), Jb 10[2] Is 27[8]; c. acc. cogn רִיב in good sense, =take one's part, 1 S 24[16] (Gi; v[16] van d. H Baer; || שָׁפַט), Mi 7[9] Je 50[34] (רִיב יָרִיב אֶת־רִיבָם, inf. cstr.=inf. abs, v. supr), 51[36] (|| נקם), La 3[58] Pr 22[23] ψ 43[1] (+ מַגֵּר, || שָׁפַט), 119[154] (+ גָּאַל), also 74[22] (God, his own cause); + מִיַּד pers. against whom 1 S 25[39] (of vengeance), + את pers against whom Pr 23[11], so (without acc. cogn) Is 50[8] Je 2[9.9], cf. אֶת־הֶהָרִים Mi 6[1] (II את **1 c**; 𝔊 πρός, whence We Now אֶל־ *in the presence of*, but on רִיב אֶל v. **4**); ר׳=*plead*, c. לְ pers for whom Ju 6[31.31.31] Jb 13[8], c acc. pers. for whom Is 1[17], of God 51[22], cf. Dt 33[8] (obscure, v. Dr); of human disputes Pr 25[8], רִיבְךָ רִיב אֶת־רֵעֶךָ v[9]. **4.** =*make complaint*, c. אֶל pers. unto and against whom Ju 21[22] Je 2[29] 12[1] Jb 33[13]. **Hiph.** *Pt.* sf מריבו 1 S 2[10] Kt (Qr מְרִיבָיו), i e (those) *displaying contention against him* (י׳), cf pl cstr וְעַמְּךָ כִּמְרִיבֵי כֹהֵן Ho 4[4], obscure; RS[Proph 406] מָרוּ בִי *thy people have rebelled against me, O priest!* BeckWü We GASm וְעַמִּי כִּכְמָרָיו הַכֹּהֵן (הַכֹּ׳ as voc., and [by some] joined to v[5]); Hermann[SK. 1879. 516] עַמְּךָ מְרִיבַי הַכֹּ׳, cf Oort (רִיבִי), Ruben[Crit. Rem ad loc] וְעַמִּי כְּמוֹךָ הַכֹּ׳, so Now.—וַיָּרֶב 1 S 15[5] v. ארב **Hiph.**

רִיב [62] **n.m.**[Is 1. 23] **strife, dispute**;—abs ר׳ Gn 13[7] +, רִב Ex 23[2] +; cstr. רִיב 17[7] +, sf. רִיבִי 1 S 24[16] +, רִבְכֶם Jb 31[13] (or inf.?), etc; pl. רִיבֹת Dt 17[8], cstr רִיבֵי 2 S 22[44] + 2 t, רִבוֹת Jb 13[6];—*strife, quarrel.* †**1.** in words, Ex 17[7] (J), Dt 1[12], about pasturage Gn 13[7] (J, =מְרִיבָה v[8]), in gen. Pr 15[18] 17[14] 20[3] 26[17 21] 30[33], + מָדוֹן Hb 1[3], so וּבְחִיר ר׳ Pr 17[1], fig ר׳ עֲצָמָיו Jb 33[19] Kt (Qr רוֹב, i.e. רב q. v); ר׳ לְשֹׁנוֹת ψ 31[21], cf. Is 58[4] Pr 18[6];

א׳ ר׳ Je 15[10] (+ (א׳ מָדוֹן). †**2.** of public hostilities 2 S 22[44] = ψ 18[44], cf. אִישׁ רִיב Ju 12[2], אַנְשֵׁי רִיבֶךָ Is 41[11]; ‖ חָמָס ψ 55[10]. **3.** ₃₁ esp. *dispute, controversy, case at law:* Ex 23[2.3.6] (E), Dt 21[5] (+ (נֶגַע), 25[1] 2 S 15[2.4] (‖ מִשְׁפָּט), + 10 t., + (of י׳) Ho 4[1] 12[3] Mi 6[2.2] Je 25[31] Ez 44[24] La 3[36]; as acc. cogn., *case, cause* Mi 7[9] Je 50[34] + 8 t. (v. √ **3**), דִּבְרֵי רִיבֹת + 1 S 25[39], רִיב חֶרְפָּתִי + 1 S 25[39], רִיבֵי נַפְשִׁי La 3[58]; Dt 17[8] *matters of controversy;* ר׳ 19[17] *dispute* as to guilt; אִישׁ רִיבִי Jb 31[35] = *accuser.* †**4.** *plea* · Pr 18[17], רִבוֹת שְׂפָתַי Jb 13[6] *pleadings of my lips.*

†**רִיבַי n.pr.m.** in Benj, 2 S 23[29] (Ρειβα, Ερειβα) = 1 Ch 11[31] (Ρεβει, Ρηβαι, Ριβαι, etc.); cf. יְרִיבַי.

†**יָרֵב n.m. epith.** of Assyrian king (prop, si vera l., vb = *let him contend,* or (one who) *contends*),—only מֶלֶךְ י׳ Ho 5[13] 10[6], i e. TP. III; WMM [ZAW xvii (1897), 335] prop. מַלְכִּי רָב (י- old nom. termin.) = As *šarru rabbu;* Che [Expos., Nov 1897 364] מֶלֶךְ רַב; Che [Ency Bib. Jareb] conj מֶלֶךְ עַרְבִי, *Arabian king,* cf., further, Comm., Schr [COT ad loc.] J A Selbie [Hastings DB, Jareb] and reff.

†I. [**יָרִיב**] **n.[m.] opponent, adversary** (Ges [§ 85d]);—sf. (of Zion), יְרִיבֵךְ Is 49[25] (𝔊 רִיבֵךְ, so Du), cf. pl. sf. יְרִיבַי ψ 35[1] (‖ לֹחֲמָי); of personal opponent, יְרִיבָי Je 18[19] (𝔊 רִיבִי, so Gie)

†II. **יָרִיב n.pr.m.** (*he contendeth* or *taketh* (our) *part, conducteth* (our) *case;* cf. Sab. ירב Hal [615]),—**1.** son of Simeon 1 Ch 4[24], Ιαρειν [μ, β], = יָכִין **1**, v. sub כון. **2.** post-ex. names, Ιαρειμ [β], etc.: **a.** Ezr 8[16], perhaps = **b.** 10[18].

† [**יְרִיבַי**] **n.pr.m.** a hero of David (OAram. יריבי CIS [ii 70 (biling)] ‖ As *Iribai*);—c. ו, וִירִיבַי 1 Ch 11[46], Ιαριβει, 𝔊L Ιαρειβ

† I. **מְרִיבָה n.f. strife, contention**;—abs. מ׳, of quarrel between herdsmen Gn 13[8] (J); cstr. מְרִיבַת הָעֵדָה, of people's strife with Moses at Kadesh Nu 27[14] (P), cf. II. מ׳ **2.**

† II. **מְרִיבָה n.pr.loc.** (*place of strife*);—**1.** at Rephidim, מַסָּה וּמ׳ Ex 17[7] (J), Λοιδόρησις. **2.** at Kadesh, esp in מֵי מְרִיבָה *water of M.* (𝔊 ὕδωρ ἀντιλογίας) Dt 33[8] Nu 20[13] (P) ψ 81[8] 106[32], also (𝔊 ὕδωρ τῆς λοιδορίας, 𝔊L as above) Nu 20[24] (P); מ׳ cstr. in מֵי מְרִיבַת קָדֵשׁ (𝔊 ὕδωρ ἀντιλογίας [ἐν] Καδης) Nu 27[14] Dt 32[51] (both P), and (𝔊 ὕδωρ Βαριμωθ Καδης) Ez 48[28]; so מֵי מְרִיבוֹת ק׳ 47[19] (𝔊 ὕδωρ Μαριμωθ Καδης), Dt 33[2] v. *ad fin.;* מְרִיבָה alone, only ψ 95[8] (παραπικρασμός; ‖ יוֹם מַסָּה).

יְרֻבַּעַל ₁₄ **n.pr.m.** name given to Gideon (acc. to Ju 6[32], where expl. as *let Baal contend* (cf. Dr [§ 84, 4] Kö [ii 1. 467]); Impf. ירוב not elsewhere [yet תרוב Pr 3[30] Kt, and Inf. cstr. רוב Ju 21[22] Kt], hence We [Sm 31] expl. as = יְרוּבַעַל, √ ירה, cf. יְרִיאֵל, יְרוּאֵל (p. 436 b), so GFM [Ju] Bu [Ju] Now [Ju]),—Ju 6[32] 7[1] 8[29.35] 9[1] + 8 t. 9 (הַבַּ֫עַל- 9[24.57]), 1 S 12[11]; = יְרֻבֶּ֫שֶׁת + 2 S 11[21] (v. בֹּשֶׁת **2**, sub בושׁ); Ιεροβααλ (usu., so 𝔊L 1 S 12[11] 2 S 11[21], where 𝔊B Ιεροβοαμ).—יָרָבְעָם, v. רבב.

† **יְרֻבֶּ֫שֶׁת** 2 S 11[21] v. foregoing.

† **מְרִיב בַּ֫עַל n.pr.m.** (*Baal is* (our, my, his) *advocate* (?), cf. Nes [Eg 120] Dr [§ 84, 4]; but Gray [Prop. N 201] thinks מרי בעל orig. form = *hero of Baal*),—**1.** son of Jonathan 1 Ch 8[34], מ׳ בַּ֫עַל v[34] 9[40] = מְרִי־בַ֫עַל (err. ?) v[40] = מְפִיבֹ֫שֶׁת (later change, v. בֹּשֶׁת sub בושׁ) 2 S 4[4] 9[6.6 10 11 12 12.13] 16[1.4] 19[25.31] 21[7], מְפִבֹ֫שֶׁת 16[25] (called בֶּן־שָׁאוּל); 𝔊 in 2 S Μεμφιβοσθε, in 1 Ch (usu) Μεριβααλ; 𝔊L Μεμφιβααλ in 2 S (exc. 4[1.2] etc., where not in 𝔥). **2.** מְפִבֹ֫שֶׁת son of Saul and Rispah, acc. to 2 S 21[8], 𝔊 (incl. 𝔊L) Μεμφιβοσθε.

רִיחַ, רֵיחַ v. רוח. **רִים** v. רְאֵם.

[**רִיעַ**] v. II רֵעַ sub רעה. **רִיעַ** v. רוע.

ריף (√of following; meaning unknown).

† [**רִיפָה**] **n.[f.]** dub.; some grain or fruit (such as was spread out to dry (2 S), and also pounded (Pr); 𝔙 [2 S] *as if drying barley-groats,* 𝔊L παλάθας, *cakes of preserved fruit,* cf preparation of 'apricot-cheese' Wetzst [ZPV xiv 2] Nes [Marg 18], who cites also Almkvist [Kl Beitr zur Lexicogr des Vulg Ar Actes, 419]),—pl. abs. רִפוֹת 2 S 17[19], רִיפוֹת Pr 27[22].

† **רִיפַת n. pr. gent.** 'son' of Gomer (of Japhet);—Gn 10[3] (P, > ‖ 1 Ch 1[6] דִּיפַת q.v.); Joseph. makes = Paphlagonians; Bo Lag [Ges. Abh. 255] cp river Ῥῆβας (Arrian [Peripl 12, 3]) = *Rhebas* (Plin [NH vi 4]), on Thracian Bosphorus, but v. Di.

† [**רִיק**] **vb. Hiph. make empty, empty out** (Ar. رَاقَ (ى) *pour out, forth,* intrans. (of water, blood, etc.), Aram. ריק *empty, pour,* ܪܩ in deriv.; As. *rêku, empty*),—*Pf.* 1 s. הֲרִיקֹתִי Lv 26[33] Mal 3[10]; 3 pl. הֵרִיקוּ Ez 28[7] 30[11], *Impf.* 3 ms יָרִיק Hb 1[17], וַיָּ֫רֶק Gn 14[14] (but v. infr.); *Imv.* ms הָרֵק ψ 35[3]; *Inf cstr.* הָרִיק Is 32[6]; *Pt.* pl. מְרִיקִים Gn 42[35] Zc 4[12];—**1.** *empty* vessels Gn 42[35] (E) Je 48[12]; *keep empty,* לְהָרִיק נֶפֶשׁ רָעֵב

Is 32^{6} (i.e. keep hungry). **2.** *pour out* or *down*, rain Mal 3^{10} Ec 11^{3}, oil Zc 4^{12}. **3.** *empty out* (i.e. *draw*) sword (cf. As. *kakkê ittabbaku* [pass.], Dl$^{HWB\ 689b}$) Ex 15^{9} (poem), Lv 26^{33} (H), Ez 5$^{2.12}$ 12^{14} 28^{7} 30^{11}; prob. also Hb 1^{17} (חרבו for חרמו Gie We Now); of lance ψ 35^{3}; cf. (si vera l.) וירק חניכיו Gn 14^{14} (R) *led forth*, < Sam. וַיָּדֶק (Aram. דוּק Aph. *look*) i.e. *mustered* 𝔊 cf. Di al., ויפקד Ball.—In ψ 18^{43} 𝔊 𝔖 Hup-Now Bae rd. אֲדִקֵּם; so ‖ 2 S 22^{43} MT; but De Dr < אֲרִיקֵם (v. דקק). **Hoph.** *be emptied out* from vessel: *Pf.* 3 ms. הוּרַק Je 48^{11}; *Impf.* 2 ms. תּוּרַק Ct 1^{3} (al. 3 fs.; of ointment, in sim.); cf. also Am 6^{6}, where Oort מוּרָקֵי for מִזְרְקֵי.

†[רִיק], רֵק **adj.** empty, vain;—m. abs. רֵק Gn 37^{24} + 2 t.; f. רֵקָה Ez 24^{11} Is 29^{8}; mpl. רֵ(י)קִים Ju 7^{16}+; fpl. רֵקוֹת Gn 41^{27};—**1.** *empty*, of vessels 2 K 4^{3} Ju 7^{16} Ez 24^{11} + (prob.) Je 14^{3} (רֵיקִם for רֵיקָם), 51^{34} (רִיק for רֵיק); of pit Gn 37^{24} (J), lap Ne 5^{13}, ears of grain Gn 41^{27} (E; דַּקּוֹת v$^{6.7.23.24}$); רֵקָה נַפְשׁוֹ Is 29^{8} (cf. 32^{6} √ **1**). **2.** *empty, idle, worthless*, ethically; אנשים ריקים *worthless fellows* Ju 9^{4} 11^{3} 2 Ch 13^{7}, so הָרֵקִים alone (as subst.) 2 S 6^{20}; מְרַדֵּף רֵיקִים Pr 12^{11} AV RV of persons; < *vain, unprofitable things*, 28^{19} (v. Toy); דָּבָר ר׳ מִן Dt 32^{47} (D) *a thing too empty* (of significance) for you; + (prob.) ψ 4^{3} (רֵיק for MT רִיק) *love an empty thing* (‖ כזב), of abortive course of action.

†רִיק **n.[m.]** emptiness, vanity;—chiefly in adv. phr. לָרִיק Is 49^{4} Jb 39^{16} *in vain* (of labour without benefit), so לָר׳ Lv 26$^{16.20}$ (H), Is 65^{23}; and as adv. acc. רִיק Is 30^{7} ψ 73^{13}, prob. also 2^{1} (most = *empty scheme* as רֵיק **2**) cf. ψ 4^{3} (rd. prob. רֵיק); בְּדֵי רִיק Je 51^{58} = Hb 2^{13}.—Je 51^{34} v. רֵק **1**.

†רֵיקָם **adv.** emptily, vainly;—**1.** *in empty condition, empty* = with empty hands; c. vb. of sending Gn 31^{42} (E), Dt 15^{13} 1 S 6^{3} Jb 22^{9}; of going forth Ex 3^{21}, returning Ru 1^{21} 3^{17}; = without an offering, לֹא יֵרָאוּ פָנַי ר׳ Ex 23^{15} (E) = 34^{20} (J), more fully Dt 16^{16} (cf. [פָּנֶה] II. **2**, ראה **Niph. 1 b**). **2.** *in vain, without effect*: c. שׁוּב 2 S 1^{22} (poem), Is 55^{11} Je 14^{3} (but v. רֵק **1**), 50^{9}; prob. also צוֹרְרַי ר׳ ψ 7^{5} *those who were my adversaries in vain* (without success); הַבּוֹגְדִים ר׳ 25^{3} that *deal treacherously in vain* (in both most *without cause*).

†[רִיר] **vb.** flow (like slime);—(Aram. רִירָא, ܪܝܪܐ *saliva, spittle*; cf. Ar. رَالَ *slaver, slobber*);—**Qal** *Pf.* 3 ms. רָר בְּשָׂרוֹ אֶת־זוֹבוֹ Lv 15^{3} *his flesh* (בָּשָׂר **3**) *flows with his issue*.

†רִיר **n.m.** slimy juice, spittle;—cstr. בְּרִיר חַלָּמוּת Jb 6^{6} *in the juice of* ח׳ (al. *slime of yolk*, i.e. white of egg); sf. רִירוֹ 1 S 21^{14} *his spittle*.

רִישׁ, רֵישׁ v. רוש. רִישׁוֹן v. ראשון.

רַךְ, רֹךְ v. רכך.

†רָכַב **vb.** mount and ride, ride (NH = BH; As. *rakâbu*, Ar. رَكِبَ, Aram. רְכֵב, ܪܟܒ, all *id.*; cf. Zinj. רכב *war-chariot*, n.pr. div. רכבאל (Cook^{108}); Sab. רכבהו = *his rider* Mordtm Him. Inschr. 25 (of horse; but *his trappings* CIS$^{iv,\ no.\ 306,\ 5}$); Eth. ረከበ: is *attain, acquire*);—**Qal** *Pf.* 3 ms. ר׳ Est 6^{8}; 2 ms. רָכַבְתָּ Nu 22^{30}; 3 pl. רָכְבוּ 1 S 30^{17}; *Impf.* 3 ms. יִרְכַּב Lv 15^{9}, etc.; *Imv.* ms. רְכַב ψ 45^{5}; *Inf. cstr.* לִרְכֹּב 2 S 16^{2} 2 K 4^{24}; *Pt. act.* רֹכֵב abs. Nu 22^{22}+, cstr. Am 2^{15}; sf. רֹכְבוֹ Gn 49^{17}+; fs. abs. רֹכֶבֶת 1 S 25^{20}; mpl. רֹכְבִים Ju 10^{4}+, etc.;—**1.** *mount, mount and sit*, or *ride*, c. עַל of camel Gn 24^{61} (J), 1 S 30^{17}, of ass (חֲמוֹר) 1 S 25^{42} 25^{20} 2 S 16^{2} (עַל obj. om.), 19^{27} 1 K 13^{13}, of mule (פֶּרֶד) 2 S 13^{29}; abs. of mounting (and riding in) chariot 1 K 18^{45} 2 K 9^{16}. **2.** *ride, be riding*, c. עַל of mule (פֶּרֶד) 2 S 18^{9}, of ass, אָתוֹן Nu 22^{22} (J), so (עַל obj. om.) 2 K 4^{24}, of חֲמוֹר Zc 9^{9}, of horse Zc 1^{8}; c. עַל־מֶרְכָּב (v. מ׳) Lv 15^{9}; c. בְּ of animal (בְּהֵמָה) Ne 2^{12}; בְּ of chariotry and horses Je 17^{25} = 22^{4}; abs. (perh. in chariot) ψ 45^{5} *ride on! ride* (habitually) c. עַל of אָתוֹן Nu 22^{30} (J), of עֲיָרִים Ju 10^{4} 12^{14}, of סוּס Ho 14^{4} (fig. of alliance with Egypt), Je 6^{23} 50^{42} Est 6^{8}, Hb 3^{8} (fig. of י׳; poss. add sf. ref. to יָם, cf. Dt 33^{26}), עַל־קַל (‖ סוּס) Is 30^{16}; of י׳, עַל־כְּרוּב 2 S 22^{11} = ψ 18^{11}, עַל־עָב קַל Is 19^{1}, c. acc. שָׁמַיִם *ride through* Dt 33^{26}, but also c. בְּ loc. *in, through*, ψ 68$^{5.34}$. **3.** pt. רֹכֵב etc., as subst., *rider*: רֹכְבֵי אֲתֹנוֹת Ju 5^{10}; ר׳ (ה)סוּס Am 2^{15} 2 K 9$^{18.19}$ Ez 23^{23} 38^{15} Zc 10^{5}, so (appos. פָּרָשִׁים) Ez 23$^{6.12}$; sf. of סוס Gn 49^{17} Ex 15$^{1.21}$ Je 51^{21a} Zc 12^{4} Jb 39^{18} Hg 2^{22b}; עַל of סוס 2 K 18^{23} = Is 36^{8}; רֹכְבֵי רֶכֶשׁ Est 8$^{10.14}$; sf. of chariot Je 51^{21b} Hg 2^{22}. **Hiph.** *Pf.* 2 ms. הִרְכַּבְתָּ ψ 66^{12}, etc.; *Impf.* 3 ms. וַיַּרְכֵּב Gn 41^{43} 2 K 13^{16}, sf. יַרְכִּבֵהוּ Dt 32^{13}, etc.; *Imv.* ms. הַרְכֵּב 2 K 13^{16};—**1.** *cause to* (*mount and*) *ride*: c. acc. pers. + עַל of חֲמוֹר Ex 4^{20} (J), of פִּרְדָּה 1 K 1$^{33.38.44}$, of סוס Est 6^{9}, cf. (עַל־סוּס om.) v^{11}; c. acc. pers. + בְּ of chariot Gn 41^{43} (E), 2 K 10^{16}; בְּ of chariot om. 2 K 9^{28} 23^{30} = (c. עַל־רֶכֶב) 2 Ch 35^{24}; fig. Jb 30^{22} (sc. on the wind); c. acc. rei + אֶל־עֲגָלָה 2 S 6^{3} = 1 Ch 13^{7}; fig., c. acc. pers. + עַל loc. (על־במותי ארץ) Dt 32^{13} so Is 58^{14}, +

לְרֹאשֵׁנוּ ψ 66[12] *over our heads*. **2.** *cause to draw* (plough, etc) Ho 10[11], obj Ephr. under fig. of heifer. **3.** fig. (עַל־הַקֶּשֶׁת) הַרְכֵּב יָדְךָ 2 K 13[16 16] *cause hand to ride upon* (grasp) *bow*.

רֶכֶב 120 **n.m.**[2 K 13.7] [even Na 2[5], where read מַרְאֵיהֶם (for הֵן-) We Now Albr[ZAW xvi (1896), 90]] **chariotry, chariot, mill-stone**, appar. also **riders** (cf. Lag[BN 151]);—abs. ר׳ Gn 50[9]+, רָכֶב 2 S 8[4]+; cstr. רֶכֶב Ex 14[9]+; sf רִכְבִּי Ju 4[7]+, רִכְבּוֹ 2 K 5[9]+, רִכְבָּה Na 2[14], pl cstr. רִכְבֵי Ct 1[9],—Ho 10[13] v. infr.,—**1.** 109 coll *chariotry, chariots* [sts. of specific no 2 K 13[7] 2 S 8[4] Ex 14[7] etc., often + פָּרָשִׁים, (סוּס(ים)], esp. war-chariots: in Egypt Ex 14[7] (J), Jos 24[6] (E)+; early Canaan Jos 11[4] Ju 4[7 13] 5[28] (not sg, ‖ מַרְכְּבוֹתָיו) +, called ר׳ בַּרְזֶל (i e. iron-bound, or studded, cf. GFM Ju 1.19 and reff), †Jos 17[16 18] Ju 1[19] 4[3 13]†; Philist., acc. to 1 S 13[5] 2 S 1[6]; Aram 8[4] 10[18]+; Judah and Israel (from David's time, cf. 8[4]) 1 K 9[19 22] 10[26]+, read also בְּרִכְבְּךָ Ho 10[13] (for בְּדַרְכְּךָ) 𝔊[A] We Now GASm, Assyria 2 K 19[23] = Is 37[24], Na 2[4 5 14] (to be burnt; made mainly of wood); Babyl. Je 47[3] (on title v[1], see Gf Gie), 50[37] 51[21] Ez 23[24]+, etc.; for dignity and display 1 K 1[5] 2 K 5[9] Je 17[25] 22[4] Is 66[20], cf. Gn 50[9] (J), (cf. also 1 K 9[19.22] 10[26], etc.), fig. of Elijah, ר׳ יִשְׂרָאֵל וּפָרָשָׁיו 2 K 2[12], of Elisha 13[14], רֶכֶב אֵשׁ 2 K 2[11] *chariotry of fire* (at Elijah's translation); ר׳ אל ψ 68[18] *chariots of Ēl*, i.e his heavenly host, cf vision 2 K 6[17], and also 7[6]; ר׳ meton. for chariot-*horses* 2 S 8[4] = 1 Ch 18[4]. †**2.** of single chariot 1 K 22[35.38] 2 K 9[21 21 24] 10[16] 2 Ch 35[24], prob. also Ex 14[6], pl רִכְבֵי פַרְעֹה Ct 1[9]. †**3.** *upper millstone* (as *riding* on the lower) Dt 24[6] Ju 9[53] 2 S 11[21]. **4.** appar. = *riders* (coll.), *troop* (of riders): שְׁנֵי רֶכֶב סוּסִים 2 K 7[14] *two riders of horses, horsemen* (or *two chariots drawn by horses*?); in foll. text dub. ר׳ צֶמֶד פָּרָשִׁים ר׳ חֲמוֹר ר׳ גָמָל Is 21[7] *riders*, viz *a pair of horsemen, ass-riders, camel-riders*; cf ר׳ איש צמד פָּרָשִׁים v[9] i.e. *men riding, a pair of horsemen*, בְּר׳ אָדָם פָּרָשִׁים 22[6] *with riders* (consisting of) *men, horsemen*, but use of אָדָם very improb.; attractive is *with chariotry of* (drawn by) *steeds* (א׳ as gloss) Du Che[Hpt] Di-Kit but פ׳ hardly *steeds* here (cf. פ׳ *horsemen*, v[7]), read perhaps simply בְּר׳ וּפ׳.

†רִכְבָּה **n.f.** act of riding;—לְר׳ Ez 27[20].

†רַכָּב **n.m. 1.** charioteer, רַכָּבוֹ 1 K 22[34] = הָרַכָּב 2 Ch 18[33]. **2.** horseman, הָרַכָּב 2 K 9[17] (= רֹכֵב (ה)סוּס v[18 19]).

†[רְכוּב] **n.[m.]** chariot (Ba[NB 85]);—sf. הַשָּׂם עָבִים רְכוּבוֹ ψ 104[3] (of י׳).

†רֵכָב **n.pr.m.** (*band of riders*? cf. Ar. رِكَابٌ *camels used in journeying*),—**1.** Ρηχαβ: **a.** in יְהוֹנָדָב בֶּן־ר׳ (Jehu's time, v. יְהוֹ׳) 2 K 10[15.23], whose descendants [or, the members of whose society, RS[K 15], yet v. No[ZMG xl (1886), 171]] were contemp. with Jerem., Je 35[6.8 14 16 19]; 1 Ch 2[55] הַקִּינִים (v. קֵינִי) are said to be descended fr. *Hammath*, אֲבִי בֵית־רֵכָב.—On the asceticism of diff. tribes cf. Diod[xix 94] (Nabataeans), Palmer[Desert 432] (*Kheibari* Jews in Arabia); v. also Berthol[Stellung Isr. und Fremden 80]. **b.** (perh. = **a**, so EMey[Entstehung 147]) in מַלְכִּיָּה בֶן־ר׳ Ne 3[14]. **2.** in Benjamin, 2 S 4[2] (Ρηχαβ), v[5.6.9] (Ρεκχα; A 𝔊L Ρηχαβ in all).

†[רֵכָבִי] **adj. gent.** of רֵכָב **1,** only pl הָרֵכָבִים as subst., in בֵּית הָר׳ Je 35[2.3 18], בְּנֵי בֵית־הָר׳ v[5], Αρχαβειν, Ραχαβειν, etc.

†מֶרְכָּב **n.m.**[Lv 15.9] **chariot, riding-seat** (prop *riding-place*),—**1.** *chariot* (= foll.), sf סוּסִים לְמֶרְכָּבוֹ 1 K 5[6] **2.** abs. מ׳, prob *saddle* Lv 15[9] (P) **3.** מֶרְכָּבוֹ *seat* of litter Ct 3[10].

†מֶרְכָּבָה **n.f.** chariot;—abs. מ׳ Ju 4[15]+, cstr. מִרְכֶּבֶת †Gn 41[43]; sf מֶרְכַּבְתּוֹ 46[29]+; pl. מַרְכָּבוֹת Zc 6[1]+; cstr. מַרְכְּבוֹת 2 K 23[11]+, ־בֹת Ex 15[4], sf. מַרְכְּבֹתֶיךָ Mi 5[10] Hb 3[8], etc.;—*chariot* (oft. ‖ (סוּס(ים), 1 S 8[11] פָּרָשִׁים): esp. war-chariot, Egypt., Ex 14[25] (J), 15[4] (song), 2 Ch 14[8]; from *Muṣri* in N. Syr. (acc to Wkl, v מצרים *ad fin.*, cf. Kit[1 K 10.28] Benz[ib.]) 1 K 10[29] = 2 Ch 1[17]; Can., Jos 11[6 9] (JE), Ju 4[15] (‖ רֶכֶב), 5[28] (‖ *id.*); Assyr., Is 2[7] Na 3[2]; foe from north Je 4[13], nations in gen. Hg 2[22]; Isr. and Jud. 1 K 20[33] 22[35] = 2 Ch 18[34], 2 K 9[27] 10[15] 2 Ch 35[24] Mi 5[10]; fig. of י׳'s chariots Is 66[15] Hb 3[8], cf (in vision) Zc 6[1 2.2.3.3]; מ׳ for dignity and display Gn 41[43] (E), 46[29] (J), 1 S 8[11 11] 2 S 15[1] 2 K 5[21.26], מַרְכְּבוֹת כְּבוֹדֶךָ Is 22[18] (iron.); used in flight 1 K 12[18] = 2 Ch 10[18], Mi 1[13]; מַרְכְּבוֹת הַשֶּׁמֶשׁ 2 K 23[11] (idolatrous); הַמ׳ הַכְּרוּבִים (read מִרְכֶּבֶת הַכ׳, 𝔊 Benz) 1 Ch 28[18] (on this conception of cherubim in temple v. Benz); מ׳ in similes · כְּמַעֲשֵׂה אוֹפַן הַמ׳ 1 K 7[33], כְּקוֹל מ׳ Jo 2[5], on the obscure מַר׳ עַמִּי נָדִיב Ct 6[12] *chariots of my people, a prince* (?) v. esp. Bu

†רֵכָה **n.pr.loc.** in Judah;—1 Ch 4[12], Ρηχαβ.

†[רָכַךְ] **vb. be tender, weak, soft** (Ar. رَقَّ, Aram. רְכַךְ (in der spec. and deriv.), رَكَّ, *id*),—**Qal** *Pf.* 3 ms. רַךְ 2 K 22[19] 2 Ch 34[27];

3 pl. רַכּוּ ψ 55^{22}; *Impf.* יֵרַךְ (Ges[§ 67 p]) Is 7^4+;—**1.** *be tender, weak,* of heart: **a.** *be timid, fearful,* ‖ יָרֵא, Is 7^4 Je 51^{46} Dt 20^3. **b.** *be softened, penitent,* ‖ כָּנַע Niph., 2 K 22^{19} = 2 Ch 34^{27}. **2.** *be soft,* of treacherous words ψ 55^{22} (c. מִן comp.; ‖ II. חָלַק). **Pu.** *Pf.* 3 fs. רֻכְּכָה Is 1^6 *it has* not *been softened,* mollified, with oil (of wound, סֻכָּה). **Hiph.** *Pf.* 3 ms. וְאֵל הֵרַךְ לִבִּי Jb 23^{16} (Ges[§ 67 v]), causat. of **Qal 1 a.**

† **רַךְ adj. tender, delicate, soft**;—ר׳ abs. Gn 18^7+, cstr. *Dt* 20^8 *2 Ch* 13^7; *fs.* רַכָּה Dt 28^{56}+; mpl. רַכִּים Gn 33^{13}; fpl. abs. רַכּוֹת 29^{17} Jb 40^{27};—**1.** *tender* of flesh Gn 18^7 (J; בֶּן־בָּקָר); *tender, delicate,* esp. in body, of children 33^{13} (J), cf. (implying weakness of undeveloped character) 2 S 3^{39}, נַעַר וָרָךְ 1 Ch 22^5 29^1, (וְיָחִיד) רַךְ Pr 4^3 ('of tender age,' Toy, q.v.); of man (+ עָנֹג; i.e. delicately nurtured) Dt 28^{54}, so of woman v^{56} (+ עֲנֻגָּה), so, fig. of Bab., Is 47^1 (+*id.*); רַךְ as subst. = *tender* (twig) Ez 17^{22} (in fig.); *delicate, weak,* of eyes Gn 29^{17} (E). **2.** רַךְ (ה)לֵבָב *weak of heart,* timid, Dt 20^8 (+ יָרֵא), 2 Ch 13^7 (נַעַר). **3.** *soft,* of words, abs. רַכּוֹת Jb 40^{27} = subst., mild, gentle words (‖ תַּחֲנוּנִים); מַעֲנֶה רַךְ Pr 15^1 (opp. דְּבַר עֶצֶב), לָשׁוֹן רַכָּה 25^{15}.

† **רֹךְ n.[m.] tenderness, delicacy**;—of delicately-nurtured woman, מֵהִתְעַנֵּג וּמֵרֹךְ Dt 28^{56}.

† **מֹרֶךְ n.[m.] weakness** (Kö[II. 1, 98]);—Lv 26^{36} *I will send* מ׳ *into* (ב) *your heart* (i.e. make you timid, fearful, cf. √ **1 a,** רַךְ **2**).

† **[רָכַל] vb. prob. go about,** from one to another (for trade or gossip) (? connected with רגל; cf. Ar. رَكَلَ *kick* a horse, to make him go [? prop. *use the foot,* cf. رِجل ?]; NH רוֹכֵל, Aram. רוֹכְלָא, ܪܘܟܠܐ *trader,* NH רְכִילוּת *slander* [cf. مَاشٍ *calumniator,* fr. مَشَى *go about,* Qor 2^{19} al.]);—**Qal** *Pt.* רֹכֵל רוֹכֵל Ct 3^6; fs. cstr. רֹכֶלֶת Ez 27^3, sf. רֹכַלְתֵּךְ $v^{20.23}$; mpl. רֹכְלִים 1 K 10^{15}+, etc.;—as subst. = *trafficker, trader:* usu. pl., Na 3^{16} Ez 17^4 (עִיר ר׳), $27^{13.15.17.22.22.23a}$ (< del. Toy Krae), v^{24} Ne $3^{31.32}$ 13^{20} (+ מֹכְרֵי כָל־מִמְכָּר), מִסְחַר הָר׳ 1 K 10^{15} (text dub.; cf. מ׳, p. 695); sg. fig. of Tyre, רֹכֶלֶת הָעַמִּים אֶל־אִיִּים רַבִּים Ez 27^3, of a people $v^{20.23b}$ (pl. Mez[Harran 34] Krae, v. also כִּלְמַד); sg. of pers. only אַבְקַת רוֹכֵל Ct 3^6.

† **[רְכֻלָּה] n.f. 1. traffic**;—sf. רְכֻלָּתְךָ Ez $28^{5.16.18}$. **2. merchandise,** רְכֻלָּתֵךְ 26^{12}.

† **רָכָל n.pr.loc.** (*trader?*);—in S. of Judah בְּרָכָל 1 S 30^{29}, 𝔊 ἐν Καρμήλῳ [A Ραχηλ], rd. prob. בְּכַרְמֶל We Dr Bu Kit HPS; v. II. כ׳ **2.**

† **רָכִיל n.[m.] slander, > tale-bearer, informer**;—always ר׳ abs.;—הֹלֵךְ ר׳ יַהֲלֹךְ Je 9^3, Lv 19^{16} (H), הוֹלֵךְ ר׳ Pr 11^{13} 20^{19}, all of going about *in slander,* as slanderer (Ges[§ 118 q]); הֹלְכֵי ר׳ Je 6^{28} *goers of slander* (slanderous persons) (cf. הָלַךְ, p. 231 f.); אַנְשֵׁי ר׳ Ez 22^9 *men of slander,* informers.

† **[מַרְכֹּלֶת] n.f.** prob. **place of trade, market-place**;—sf. בְּמַרְכֻלְתֵּךְ Ez 27^{24} *in thy market-place* (Thes Buhl[Lex] Hi-Sm Krae al.; > בָּם רְכֻלָּתֵךְ 𝔗 Co Berthol, cf. Toy).

† **[רָכַס] vb. bind** (As. *rakâsu, id.*; NH *found, lay foundation* (rare); Ar. رَكَسَ *bind with* رِكَاسٌ [rope tying camel's head to forefoot] (Frey); but usu. *turn over, reverse* (Lane));—**Qal** *Impf.* 3 mpl. יִרְכְּסוּ (P) Ex 28^{28}, וַיִּרְכְּסוּ 39^{21}, *bind* חֹשֶׁן by (מִן) its rings to (אֶל) rings of ephod.

† **[רֶכֶס] n.[m.]** dub.; perh. *roughness* (of ground; ? lit. *binding, knot*); or bound up, impeded, i.e. *the impassable;* or mountain-*chain* (v. Thes);—pl. הָרְכָסִים Is 40^4 (‖ הֶעָקֹב; opp. בִּקְעָה).

† **[רֹכֶס] n.[m.]** dub., Thes Hup-Now *snare,* or *band* (Dr *banding together*), or (most) *league, conspiracy* (RV *plottings*); Ol reads deriv. of רכל = *slander,* so (רְכִלֵי) Che Du; Bae despairs;—pl. cstr. רֻכְסֵי־אִישׁ ψ 31^{21} (‖ רִיב לְשֹׁנוֹת).

† **רָכַשׁ vb. collect, gather property,** vb. only P (rare) (Mand. רכש *gather,* Norberg[Lexid. 231]; As. *rukûšu, property* (Hpt[Hbr iii. 110] *riding anim.*); Aram. רְכָשָׁא, ܪܟܫܐ = BH רְכֻשׁ);—**Qal** *Pf.* 3 ms. ר׳, acc. קִנְיָן, Gn 31^{18b} 36^6; elsewhere c. acc. cogn. רְכוּשׁ: רָכַשׁ אֲשֶׁר רָכָשׁ 31^{18a}, 3 pl. רָכָשׁוּ 46^6, רָכָשׁוּ 12^5.

† **רֶכֶשׁ n.m.**[Est 8, 10] **coll. steeds** (connex. with √ dub.);—abs. ר׳ Mi 1^{13}+, רָכֶשׁ 1 K 5^8;—+ סוּסִים 1 K 5^8, harnessed to chariot Mi 1^{13}, ridden Est 8^{10} (+ סוּסִים; defined as בְּנֵי הָרַמָּכִים), v^{14}.

† **רְכֻשׁ, רְכוּשׁ n.m.**[Gn 13, 6] **property, goods**;—abs. רְכוּשׁ Nu 16^{32}+, רְכֻשׁ Gn $14^{16.21}$; cstr. רְכוּשׁ 2 Ch 35^7, רְכֻשׁ Gn 14^{11}; sf. רְכֻשׁוֹ v^{12}+, רְכוּשָׁם 12^5+, etc.;—*property, goods,* PRChr Dn Gn 14: **1.** gen. term for movable possessions of all kinds (oft. specif. incl. cattle), Gn 12^5 15^{14} Nu 16^{32} 1 Ch 27^{31} 28^1 2 Ch 31^3 32^{29} Ezr 8^{21} 10^8. **2.** used specif. of cattle, flocks, etc. Gn 13^6 31^{18} 36^7 Nu 35^3 2 Ch 35^7. **3.** of stores, utensils, etc. Gn 46^6 Ezr $1^{4.6}$, as camp-baggage Dn 11^{13}, esp. as booty Gn $14^{11.12.16.16.21}$ 2 Ch 20^{25} $21^{14.17}$ Dn $11^{24.28}$.

I, II. רָם ,רָם v. רום. רם v. רְאֵם.

†I. רָמָה vb. cast, shoot (As. *ramû, throw, lay;* Ar. رَمَى *throw, shoot;* Eth. ረመየ: *strike, aim a blow at;* Aram רְמָא, ܪܡܐ *cast, throw*),—**Qal** *Pf* 3 ms. ר׳, subj. י׳ Ex $15^{1.21}$ (song), c. acc. +בַּיָּם; *Pt* רֹמֵה קֶשֶׁת Je 4^{29} coll. (or read רֹמֵי) *bow-shooters, bowmen,* pl. cstr. נוֹשְׁקֵי רוֹמֵי־ק׳ ψ 78^{9} (v. II. נשק); cf. רבה Gn 21^{20} (v. II. רבה, קַשָּׁת)

†II. [רָמָה] vb. **Pi.** beguile, deal treacherously with (NH in deriv.; 𝔗 רמא Pa.; Buhl^{Lex} cp. Ar. رَمَى VI *be sluggish, backward* (of wound), *become putrid, corrupt*);—*Pf.* 3 ms. רִמָּה Pr 26^{19}, sf. רִמָּנִי 2 S 19^{27}; 2 ms. sf רִמִּיתָנִי Gn 29^{25} 1 S 28^{12}; 2 fs sf. רִמִּיתִנִי 19^{17}, etc.; *Inf. cstr.* sf. לְרַמּוֹתֵנִי 1 Ch 12^{18} (van d. H. v^{17});—*beguile, deceive, mislead,* acc. pers, Gn 29^{25} (E), Jos 9^{22} (JE), 1 S 28^{12} 2 S 19^{27} Pr 26^{19}; *deal treacherously with, betray,* acc. pers., 1 S 19^{17} La 1^{19}, + לְצָרַי 1 Ch 12^{17}.

†I. רְמִיָּה n.f. deceit, treachery,—always abs. ר׳,—*deceit, treachery:* esp. of speech, pred. of לָשׁוֹן Mi 6^{12} (‖ שֶׁקֶר), appos of לָשׁוֹן (or read לָשׁוֹן) ψ 120^{2} (‖ שְׂפַת שֶׁקֶר), v^{3}; of man, עֹשֵׂה ר׳ 52^{4} *that workest treachery,* 101^{7} (‖ דֹּבֵר שְׁקָרִים), also Jb 13^{7} 27^{4} (both ‖ עַוְלָה); *deception* ψ 32^{2} (‖ עָוֹן); in phr קֶשֶׁת ר׳ *treacherous bow* (sim.) Ho 7^{16} ψ 78^{57} (failing him who trusts to it)

†I מִרְמָה n.f. deceit, treachery;—abs מ׳ Am 8^{5}+, pl. abs מִרְמוֹת ψ 10^{7}+;—*deceit,* of balances, מֹאזְנֵי מ׳ i e *deceptive balances* Am 8^{5} (‖ שֶׁקֶר), Ho 12^{8} Pr 11^{1} (opp. אֶבֶן שְׁלֵמָה), 20^{23}, אַבְנֵי מ׳ Mi 6^{11} (v. [מאזן] p. 24); esp *treachery, craftiness,* 2 K 9^{23}, בְּמ׳ *treacherously,* Gn 27^{35} (J), and (of crafty speech) 34^{13} (P); שִׂפְתֵי מ׳ ψ 17^{1} i.e. *treacherous lips,* לְשׁוֹן מ׳ 52^{6}, פִּי מ׳ 109^{2} נִשְׁבַּע לְמ׳ ψ 24^{4}, דברי מרמות 35^{20}, (לְשׁוֹן שֶׁקֶר ‖) (‖ לַשָּׁוְא), cf. Is 53^{9} (‖ חָמָס); also Ho 12^{1} (‖ כַּחַשׁ), Je 5^{27} $9^{5.6.7}$ Zp 1^{9} (+ חָמָס), ψ 10^{7} (+ תֹּךְ ‖ עָמָל), 34^{14} 36^{4} (+ אָוֶן), 38^{13} 59^{19} 55^{12} (+ תֹּךְ), Jb 15^{35} 31^{5} (‖ שָׁוְא), Pr 12^{20} 14^{8} 26^{24} Dn 8^{25}; opp. מִשְׁפָּט Pr 12^{5}, + עֵד שְׁקָרִים v^{17}, + יָפִיחַ כְּזָבִים 14^{25} (Hi Wild Toy read מְדַמֶּה for מרמה, but II. דמה not elsewhere Pi); אִישׁ דָּמִים וּמ׳ ψ 5^{7} (‖ דֹּבְרֵי כָזָב), cf 55^{24}, אִישׁ מ׳ וְעַוְלָה 43^{1}, יַעֲשֶׂה מ׳ Dn 11^{23}.—II. מִרְמָה n pr. v. p 599.

†תַּרְמָה in בְּת׳ Ju 9^{31} si vera l *in treachery, treacherously,* but form strange and meaning unsuitable; read poss. (בָּ)אֲרוּמָה n.pr.loc. (q.v.), cf. v^{41} and GFM.

תרמות Je 14^{14} Kt, v. foll.

†תַּרְמִית n.f. deceitfulness;—abs. לְשׁוֹן תּ׳ Zp 3^{13} (‖ כָּזָב, עַוְלָה), תַּרְמִת Je 8^{5}; cstr. תַּרְמִית לִבָּם 14^{14} Qr (> Kt תרבות), תַּרְמִת לִבָּם 23^{26} (‖ שֶׁקֶר); sf. שֶׁקֶר תַּרְמִיתָם ψ 119^{118} (where 𝔊 𝔖 𝔙 al. תַּרְעִיתָם Aram. *their thought*)

III. רמה (√ of foll.; connex. with II ר׳ dub.; cf. As *ramû, grow loose;* II. *loosen*).

†II. רְמִיָּה n.f. laxness, slackness;—alw. abs. ר׳;—כַּף ר׳ Pr 10^{4} *slack* (negligent, idle) *hand* (opp. יַד חָרוּצִים); ר׳ alone = *slackness* (abstr. for concr. = one who is slack) 12^{24} (‖ *id.*), v^{27} (v. חרך); נֶפֶשׁ ר׳ 19^{15} (‖ עַצְלָה); as adv. עֹשֶׂה מְלֶאכֶת י׳ רְמִיָּה Je 48^{10}

יִרְמְיָה(וּ)$_{147}$ n.pr.m. (י׳ *looseneth,* sc. the womb? cf. As *ša kirimmaša rummû, whose womb is loosened* Dl$^{HWB\ 623}$),—**1.**$_{134}$ proph., son of Ḥilkiah, of priestly family in ʿAnathôth: יִרְמְיָהוּ Je $1^{1.11}$ 29^{27} $36^{1.4.4}$ + 116 t. Je, + 2 Ch 35^{25} $36^{12.21.22}$ (יר׳ הַנָּבִיא) Je 21^{2} + oft); ־יָה Je 27^{1} $28^{5.6.10.11.12.15}$ 29^{1} Ezr 1^{1} Dn 9^{2}; Ἱερεμίας. †**2.** יִרְמְיָהוּ, of Libnah, father of Josiah's wife, 2 K 23^{31} 24^{18} = Je 52^{1}, Ἱερεμίας. †**3.** ־יָהוּ Gadite, David's time 1 Ch 12^{13}, Ιερμεια, 𝔊L Ιεραμαου. The foll. all ־יָה, 𝔊 Ἱερεμία(ς), Ἱερμία(ς), etc.: †**4.** Manassite 1 Ch 5^{24}. †**5.** Benjamite 12^{4}. †**6.** Gadite 12^{10}. †**7. a.** priestly name: Ne $12^{1.12}$. **b.** Ne 10^{3}, perhaps = 12^{34}.

†רַמְיָה n.pr.m. (prop. י׳ *hath loosened*?);—one with foreign wife Ezr 10^{25}, Ραμιά(ς).

I, II. רָמָה v. רום. רִמָּה v. II. רמם.

†I. רִמּוֹן n.m.$^{Je\ 52,\ 23}$ pomegranate (foreign word of doubtful origin, cf. Low$^{No.\ 310}$ Hom$^{A.\ u.\ A.\ 97\ ff}$; Aram. רִימּוֹנָא, רוּמָנָא, ܪܘܡܢܐ, Mand רומאנא No$^{M.\ 123}$; Ar. رُمَّان (Aram. loan-word, Fra^{142}), Eth. ሮማን:);—abs. ר׳ 1 S 14^{2}+, רִמֹּן Ex $39^{26.26}$; sf רִמֹּנִי Ct 8^{2}; pl. רִמּוֹנִים 1 K 7^{20}+, etc,—*pomegranate*: **1.** tree 1 S 14^{2}, oft. + גֶּפֶן, תְּאֵנָה, etc., Nu 20^{5} (JE), Dt 8^{8} Hg 2^{19} Jo 1^{12} Ct 4^{13} 6^{11} 7^{13}. **2.** fruit Nu 13^{23} (JE; + עֲנָבִים, תְּאֵנִים), עֲסִיס ר׳ Ct 8^{2}, פֶּלַח הָר׳ (in sim.) 4^{3} 6^{7}. **3.** ornaments in temple, shaped like pomegranates (cf. رُمَّانة in mod. Syria = *epaulet,* Almkvist$^{Kl.\ Beiträge\ zur\ Lexicogr.\ etc.}$ Nes$^{Marg\ 12}$), 1 K 7^{18} (on text cf. Sta$^{ZAW\ III\ (1883),\ 154\ f.}$ Kit Benz), $v^{20.42.42}$

‖ 2 Ch 3^{16} $4^{13.13}$ 2 K 25^{17} = Je 52^{22}, Je $52^{22.23.23}$, so in tabernacle, Ex $28^{33.34.34}$ $39^{24.25.25.26.26}$.

† II רִמּוֹן **n.pr dei,** in Aram. (OAram רמן in n pr Lzb[369] Cook[108], As *Rammânu*, god of wind, rain and storm (Schr[COT 2 K 5, 18] Zim[KAT 3 442 ff.] Muss-Arnolt[JBL xi (1892) 172] Jastr[Rel Bab. 156 ff.]), Sab רמן (CIS[iv no. 140, 209] H. Derenb in Kohut-Studies[120 ff.]), etym dub, √רעם *thunder* Schr; √*ramâmu, roar* Dl[HWB 624] and most, = I רמון Hom[A. u A 93]),— בית ר׳ 2 K 5^{18}, בית רמון $v^{18.18}$, Ρεμμαν[θ],—v. also הֲדַדְרִמּוֹן p 213, טַבְרִמּוֹן p 372

† III רִמּוֹן **n.pr.m.** in Benj, 2 S $4^{2.5.9}$, Ρεμμων

† IV רִמּוֹן **n pr loc. 1.** in סֶלַע הָרִמּוֹן *cliff of R* Ju $20^{45.47}$, ס׳ רמון v^{47} 21^{13}, Ρεμμων, = mod cliff *Rammôn*, E from Bethel, Buhl[G 100], cf. GFM[Ju 20, 45] **2.** in S Judah, עין ור׳ Jos 15^{32}; עין ר׳ 19^{7} (both P), 1 Ch 4^{32}, = ר׳ Zc 14^{10}, Ρεμμων[θ], etc, v III עין 2, p 745, and עין רמון. **3.** in Zebulun Jos 19^{13} (Ρεμμωνα(μ)), = רמונו 1 Ch 6^{62} (Ρεμμων), + Jos 21^{35} (rd רִמֹּנָה for דמנה, Di Benn Steuern), mod *Rummâne*, c 6 miles E of N. from Nazareth (Buhl[G 221])

† רִמֹּן פֶּרֶץ **n.pr.loc.** station of Israel in wilderness, Nu $33^{19.20}$ (P), Ρεμμων, Ραμμων

רִמּוֹנוֹ 1 Ch 6^{62} see IV רמון **3.**

רָמוֹת, [רָמוּת] v רום

† רֹמַח **n.[m.] spear, lance** (etym. unknown, Aram. רוּמְחָא, ܪܘܡܚܐ, Ar رُمْح, Eth ርምሕ:),—oft + חרב, צנה, מָגֵן, קשת, etc,— abs ר׳ Ju 5^{8} Nu 25^{7} (P), Ez 39^{9} 1 Ch $12^{9.25}$ (van d H $v^{8.24}$), 2 Ch 14^{7} 25^{5}, pl רְמָחִים 1 K 18^{28} Je 46^{4} Jo 4^{10} Ne $4^{10.15}$ 2 Ch 11^{12} 26^{14}, sf. רָמְחֵיהֶם Ne 4^{7}

הָרַמִּים 2 Ch 22^{5}, err for הָאֲרַמִּים, v. אֲרָם.

רַמְיָה, I, II רְמִיָּה v II. רמה.

† [רַמָּךְ] **n.[f]** exact meaning dub (cf. Syr ܪܡܟܐ *herd*, foreign wd, Pahlavi *ramak*, NPers رمه *herd* of sheep, horses, etc, Thes[1291] Vullers[ii 52], in NH *mule* born of mare and he-ass),— בני הָרַמָּכִים Est 8^{10} usu *sons of the (royal) mares*, said of הָרֶכֶשׁ.

רמל (in foll cpd., Thes cp Ar رَمَّلَ *adorn with gems*, OHeb רמליהו Lzb[369])

† רְמַלְיָהוּ **n.pr.m.** father of Pekah, king of Israel, בן־ר׳ 2 K $15^{25.27.30.32.37}$ $16^{1.5}$ Is 7^{1} 2 Ch 28^{6}, contempt (פקח om) Is $7^{4.5.9}$ 8^{6}, υἱὸς Ῥομελίου.

† I [רָמַם] **vb. be exalted** (‖form (acc. to Mas) of רום);—**Qal** *Pf.* 3 pl. רוֹמּוּ מְעַט וְאֵינֶנּוּ Jb 24^{24} (perhaps pass. form Ges[§ 67 m] Bu; Du רֹמּוּ);— *Pt* רמם v רום **Pô'l** **Niph.** *Impf* 1 s. אֵרוֹמָם Is 33^{10} (‖אֶנָּשֵׂא), **Hithpô'l.** fr. רום Kö[i 454] Ges[§ 54 c]), 3 mpl וַיֵּרֹמּוּ Ez 10^{15} (of cherubim), יֵרֹמּוּ v^{17}, וַיֵּרוֹמּוּ v^{19}, *Imv* mpl הֵרֹמּוּ מתוך הָעֵדָה Nu 17^{10} (P)

II רמם (√of following, cf Ar رَمَّ *grow rotten, decay*)

† רִמָּה **n.f. worm** (cause and sign of *decay*),— abs ר׳ Ex 16^{24} (P), Is 14^{11} (‖תולעה), Jb 7^{5} 17^{14} 21^{26} 24^{20} all indic corruption, feeding on dead, etc, hyperb of insignificant man 25^{6} (‖תולעה)

† [רָמַם] **vb. denom. be wormy,**—*Impf* 3 ms (c acc. result, Ges[§ 121 d R]) וַיָּרֻם תולעים Ex 16^{20} (Ges[§ 67 n], + וַיִּבְאַשׁ).

רֹמַמְתִּי עֶזֶר v. sub רום.

† רָמַס **vb. trample** (NH *id*; JAram רְמַס; cf perh Syr. ܦܡܣ, Ar. رَمَسَ *kick* (Ba[ES 33] Kö[ii 196]), رَمَسَ is *bury, and conceal grave*),—**Qal** *Pf* 3 ms consec. ור׳ Mi 5^{7}, *Impf* 3 ms. ירמס Ez 26^{11} ψ 7^{6}, יִרְמָס־ Is 41^{25}, sf וַיִּרְמְסֶנָּה 2 K 9^{33}, etc.; *Imv* fs רְמֹסִי Na 3^{14}, *Inf cstr* רמס Is 1^{12}; *Pt* רֹמֵס Is 16^{4},—*trample*, of men, c acc. חֲצֵרָי Is 1^{12}, טִיט 41^{25} (in sim), cf ר׳ בַּחֹמֶר Na 3^{14}, acc מִרְעֶה Ez 34^{18} (in fig), *trample down*, acc pers, anim, vel rei, 2 K $7^{17.20}$, so (by horses' hoofs) 9^{33}, יר׳ לָאָרֶץ חַיָּי, ψ 7^{6}, 91^{13} (‖תדרך), subj י׳ Is 63^{13} (fig.; + דָּרַךְ), subj רֶגֶל Is 26^{6}, subj beast 2 K 14^{9} (allegory) = 2 Ch 25^{18}, Dn 8^{7} (vision), of horn, v^{10}, abs. of lion, ור׳ וְטָרַף Mi 5^{7} (sim), pt. as subst coll *tramplers* (i e. devastators) Is 16^{4}. **Niph.** *be trampled, Impf* 3 fpl בְּרַגְלַיִם תֵּרָמַסְנָה Is 28^{3} (on subj cf. Di Du Che[Hpt] Kö[i 183])

† מִרְמָס **n.[m.] trampling-place, trampling,**—abs מ׳ Mi 7^{10} +, מִרְמַס (Kö[ii 1, 96]) Is 10^{6}; cstr מִרְמַס 7^{25} Ez 34^{19},—**1** *trampling-place*, מ׳ שֶׂה Is 7^{25} (‖ מִשְׁלַח), מ׳ רַגְלֵיכֶם Ez 34^{19} (fig.) **2.** *trampling*, וְהָיָה לְמ׳ Is 5^{5} *it shall become a trampling*, be trampled down, so Mi 7^{10}, Is 28^{18} והייתם לו למרמס, cf 10^{6} Dn 8^{13}.

† רָמַשׂ **vb. creep, move lightly, move about** (chiefly P) (Ar رَمَسَ *touch gently* (Kam Frey), NH רְמָשִׂים *creeping things* (rare)),— **Qal** *Impf* 3 fs תרמשׂ Gn 9^{2} + 2 t.; *Pt.* רֹמֵשׂ 1^{26} +, fs רֹמֶשֶׂת Lv 11^{46} + 2 t;—**1.** subj ground,

כֹּל אֲשֶׁר תִּ׳ הָאֲדָמָה *all with which the ground creeps* (teems), i.e. all creeping things, Lv 20[25] (H), Gn 9[2] (P). **2.** elsewhere subj animal: **a.** *creep*, עַל־הָאָרֶץ Dt 4[18] Gn 7[8] (P), עַל־הָאֲדָמָה Lv 11[44] (H), Gn 1[30] (P); הָרֶמֶשׂ הָרֹמֵשׂ עַל־הָאֲדָמָה Ez 38[20], עַל־הָאָרֶץ Gn 1[26] 7[14] 8[17] (all P) **b.** *move lightly, glide about*, of water animals, כָּל־נֶפֶשׁ הַחַיָּה הָרֹמֶשֶׂת (בַּמַּיִם) Lv 11[46] (H), Gn 1[21] (P), cf. ψ 69[35]. **c.** in gen. *move about*, of all land-animals, עַל־הָאָרֶץ Gn 1[28] 7[21] 8[19] (all P); specif. of wild beasts prowling at night ψ 104[20].

†רֶ֫מֶשׂ **n.m.** Ez 38,20 **coll. creeping things, moving things**,—ר׳ abs. 1 K 5[13]+, cstr. Ho 2[20]+;—**1.** *creeping things* (disting. from בְּהֵמָה, חַיָּה, עוֹף, צִפּוֹר, דָּג) Ho 2[20] 1 K 5[13] Ez 8[10] 38[20] Gn 1[24.25.26] 6[7.20] 7[14.23] 8[17.19] (all P), Hb 1[14] (in sim) ψ 148[10]. **2.** of sea animals, *gliding things*, ψ 104[25]. **3.** *moving things*, of all animals Gn 9[3] (P).—Cf. Dr[Hast. DB Creeping Things].

רָמֹת, רָמָתִי, רָמָתַיִם v. רום.

רֹן, I, II. רִנָּה v. רנן.

†[רָנָה] **vb. rattle** (onomatop.?),—**Qal** *Impf.* 3 fs תִּרְנֶה Jb 39[23] the quiver *rattleth*.

†[רָנַן] **vb. give a ringing cry** (onomatop.? cf. Ar. رَنَّ *cry aloud*, also *twang* (of bowstring), NH Pi *murmur, complain*, cf. JAram (not 𝔗)),—**Qal** *Impf.* 3 ms. יָרֹן (Ges§67 q) Pr 29[6] (but rd. perhaps יָרוּץ, Pinsk Toy, v. רוץ **2**); 3 fs. תָּרֹן Is 35[6], 3 mpl. יָרֹנּוּ 24[14]+, וַיָּרֹ׳ Lv 9[24], 3 fpl תָּרֹנָּה Pr 1[20] 8[3]; *Imv.* fs. רָנִּי Is 54[1]+, רֹנִּי 12[6]; mpl רָנּוּ Je 31[7]+; *Inf. cstr* בְּרָן־ Jb 38[7],—*give a ringing cry*. **1.** in joy, exultation, ‖ צָהַל Je 31[7] (ר׳ שִׂמְחָה), Is 12[6] 24[14] (‖ נָשָׂא קוֹל), 54[1] (+ פָּצַח) ‖ הֵרִיעַ Zp 3[14] (+ עלז, שמח), Is 44[23] Jb 38[7]; (רִנָּה); ‖ שָׂמַח Zc 2[14] ψ 35[27] Pr 29[6] (v. supr.); ‖ גִּיל Is 49[13] (+ הֵרִים רִנָּה), ‖ צָוַח 42[11]; opp. צָעַק (*cry* in distress) 65[14] (מִן of cause), Lv 9[24] Is 35[6] (subj לָשׁוֹן).—Is 61[7] is corrupt; read perh וָרֹק *and spitting*, Klo Che[Hpt]. **2.** in distress, La 2[19]. **3.** *cry aloud*, in summons, exhortation (of wisdom) Pr 1[20] (‖ נָתַן קוֹל), 8[3]. **Pi.** *Pf.* 3 pl. consec. וְרִנְּנוּ Je 31[12] 51[48]; *Impf.* 3 fs. תְּרַנֵּן ψ 51[16], 3 mpl. יְרַנְּנוּ 84[3]+, יְרַנֵּנוּ 5[12]+; 3 fpl תְּרַנֵּנָּה 71[23] (van d. H תְּרַנֶּנָּה), etc.; *Imv.* mpl. רַנְּנוּ Is 52[9]+; *Inf. abs* רַנֵּן ψ 132[16], *cstr id.* Is 35[2],—*give a ringing cry*, in joy, exultation, esp in praise to י׳, Je 31[12] 51[48] Is 26[19] 35[2] (+ גִּילַת, v. גִּילָה), 52[8] (‖ נָשָׂא קוֹל), v[9] (+ פָּצַח), elsewh. only ψψ: ψ 5[12] (‖ עָלַץ, שָׂמַח), 67[5] 90[14] 92[5] (c. בְּ rei; all ‖ שׂ׳ alone); 149[5] (‖ עָלַז); 98[4] (‖ הֵרִיעַ; + פָּצַח, זִמֵּר), 132[9] 145[7], רַנֵּן יְרַנֵּנוּ 132[16]; c. acc. of theme 51[16] 59[17] (‖ שִׁיר); בִּי׳ 33[1], בְּ rei 20[6] 63[8] 89[13], c. לִי׳ 95[1] (‖ הֵרִיעַ), אֶל־אֵל 84[3], לִפְנֵי י׳ (מִ) 96[12] (‖ עָלַז) = 1 Ch 16[33] (‖ עָלַץ), ψ 98[8]; subj שְׂפָתַיִם 71[23] (‖ זִמֵּר) **Pu.** *Impf.* 3 ms. impers לֹא יְרֻנָּן Is 16[10] *no ringing cry shall be given* (‖ יְרֹעָע). **Hiph.** *Impf.* *cause to ring out* for joy, 1 s. לֵב אַלְמָנָה אַרְנִן Jb 29[13], 2 ms. מוֹצָאֵי בֹקֶר וָעֶרֶב תַּרְנִין ψ 65[9], *Imv.* mpl הַרְנִינוּ *ring out a cry* of joy ψ 32[11] (‖ שמח, גיל), לֵי׳ 81[2] (‖ הריע); c. acc. of theme, עַמּוֹ Dt 32[43] (v. Dr; cf. **Pi.**)—**Hithpo'l.** ψ 78[65] cf רון.

†[רֹן] **n.[m.] ringing cry**; pl cstr רָנֵּי פַלֵּט ψ 32[7].

†רְנָנָה **n.f.** id.,—ר׳ abs, of joy Jb 3[7] ψ 100[2] (‖ שִׂמְחָה), pl שִׂפְתֵי רְנָנוֹת 63[6]; exultation, sg. cstr. רִנְנַת רְשָׁעִים Jb 20[5] (‖ שִׂמְחָה).

†I. רִנָּה **n.f. ringing cry**,—abs ר׳ Je 7[16]+; sf. רִנָּתִי ψ 17[1]+, רִנָּתָם Je 14[12]+;—*ringing cry*: **1.** in entreaty, supplication, to י׳, 1 K 8[28] = 2 Ch 6[19], Je 7[16] 11[14] ψ 17[1] 61[2] 88[3] (all + תְּפִלָּה), 106[44] 119[169] 142[7] Je 14[12]. **2.** in proclamation 1 K 22[36]. **3.** in joy, esp. praise to י׳, + שִׂמְחָה Is 35[10] 51[11] (+ שָׂשׂוֹן); + תְּהִלָּה 2 Ch 20[22], + שָׂשׂוֹן ψ 105[43], + תּוֹדָה 107[22], + עלז Pr 11[10]; ‖ שְׂחוֹק ψ 126[2]; opp. בְּכִי, etc. 30[6] 126[6], cf. v[5]; קוֹל ר׳ Is 48[20] ψ 42[5] (+ תּוֹדָה), 47[2] 118[15] (+ יְשׁוּעָה); פָּצַח ר׳ Is 14[7] 44[23] 49[13] 54[1] 55[12]; of י׳'s joy over Zion Zp 3[17],—בָּאֳנִיּוֹת רִנָּתָם Is 43[14] *in the ships of their ringing cry*, in which they exulted, but dub.; Hi Ew בָּאֲנִיּוֹת (bring down) *into mourning their* ר׳; cf. Kit-Di Du Che[Hpt] Marti.

†II. רִנָּה **n pr.m.** in Judah 1 Ch 4[20]; Ava, A Ραννων, 𝔊L Ρεννα

†רְנָנִים **n.[m.] pl. bird of piercing cries**, i e ostrich, acc. to 𝔙 Bo Di and most, כְּנַף ר׳ Jb 39[13], but read prob יְעֵנִים Hoffm Bu Du (as La 4[3] Qr), v. [יָעֵן]

†רִסָּה **n.pr.loc.** station in wilderness, Nu 33[21.22]; Δεσσα, A Ρεσσα, 𝔊L Δρεσσα.

רסן (√of following; cf. Ar. رَسَنَ (Fra[100 f.]) = רֶסֶן; 𝔗 רִסְנָא (rare), cf Dalm[WB]).

†I רֶ֫סֶן **n m.** Is 30,28. **1. halter; 2. jaw**(?);—**1.** abs ר׳ ψ 32[9] restraining mouth of horse or ass (+ מֶתֶג), fig of ר׳ עַל־לְחָיֵי עַמִּים שָׂם י׳ Is 30[28]; ר׳ מִפָּנַי שִׁלֵּחוּ Jb 30[11], i.e. threw off restraint.

2. sf. כֶּפֶל רִסְנוֹ Jb 41^{5} *the double of his jaw*, his double jaws (of croc.), si vera l.; connexion of mngs. strange, ‖ פְּנֵי לְבוּשׁוֹ, whence GHBWright Du conj. סִרְיֹנוֹ.

†II. רֶסֶן **n.pr.loc.** in Assyria, near Nineveh Gn 10^{12}; Δασεμ (prob.=*rêš êni, head of spring*; cf. Dl$^{Pa\ 261}$ COT$^{Gn\ 10,\ 12}$).

†I. [רָסַס] **vb. moisten** (so Aram. רְסַס, ܪܣܣ; Ar. رَشَّ (! ش) *sprinkle*);—**Qal** *Inf. cstr.* שֶׁמֶן לָרֹס אֶת־הַסֹּלֶת Ez 46^{14}.

†I. [רָסִיס] **n.[m.] drop** (of dew);—pl. cstr. רְסִיסֵי לָיְלָה Ct 5^{2} (‖ טַל).

II. רסס (√of foll.; NH רָסַס Pi. *break, crush*; so Mand. רסס Norberg$^{Lexid.\ 232}$, JAram. רְסַס; cf. Ar. رَسَّ *well stopped up with stones* Hoffm$^{ZAW\ iii\ (1883),\ 115}$).

†II. [רָסִיס] **n.[m.] fragment**;—pl. רְסִיסִים, of houses destroyed Am 6^{11} (‖ בְּקִעִים).

רֵעַ, רֵעַ v. I. רעע. I. רַע v. רוע.

II, III. רֵעַ v. II. רעה.

†רָעֵב **vb. be hungry** (NH *id.* Hiph. and deriv.; As. *rûbatu, hunger*; Ar. رَغِبَ *be roomy, voracious*, رَغِبَ *desire vehemently*; Eth. ረኀበ: *be hungry*);—**Qal** *Pf.* 3 ms. ר׳ Is 9^{19} 44^{12}; 3 pl. רָעֵבוּ ψ 34^{11}; *Impf.* 3 ms. יִרְעַב Is 8^{21}, 1 pl. נִרְעָב Je 42^{14}, etc.;—*be hungry* Is 8^{21} Gn 41^{55} (E; of land, =have famine), Je 42^{14} (לַלֶּחֶם), Is 49^{10} (‖ צמא), 65^{13} (‖ *id.*; opp. אכל), ψ 50^{12} *if I should be hungry* (of י׳), Pr 6^{30} 19^{15}. **Hiph.** *allow* one *to hunger*, subj. י׳: *Impf.* 3 ms. וַיַּרְעִבֶךָ Dt 8^{3} (opp. וַיַּאֲכִלְךָ), יַרְעִיב נֶפֶשׁ Pr 10^{3}.

רָעָב$_{101}$ **n.m.**$^{Gn\ 26,1}$ **famine, hunger**;—abs. ר׳ Gn 12^{10}+; sf. רְעָבָם Ne 9^{15}; **1.** *famine* (in land, nation or city), Gn 12^{10} 26^{1} 41$^{30.31}$ Ex 16^{3} 2 S 21^{1} 24^{13}=2 K 4^{38} 6^{25}+; שְׁנַת ר׳, שְׁנֵי (הָ)ר׳ Gn 41$^{27.30.36}$, v^{50}, but also שֶׁבַע [שָׁלוֹשׁ] שָׁנִים ר׳ 2 S 24^{13} (on gender v. Albr$^{ZAW\ xvi\ (1896),\ 103}$)=1 Ch 21^{12}; c. חזק (*be*) *severe* Gn 41$^{56.57}$ 1 K 18^{2} 25^{3}=Je 52^{6}, חזק על Gn 47^{20}; c. כָּבֵד 12^{10} 47$^{4.13}$; ר׳ גָּדוֹל 2 K 6^{25}; וְלַעֲפוֹת ר׳ La 5^{10}; מְזֵי ר׳ Dt 32^{24}+ Is 5^{13} (v. [מָזֶה]), תַּחֲלוּאֵי ר׳ Je 14^{18}, חַלְלֵי ר׳ La 5^{10}, אַסְפֵי ר׳ Ez 34^{29}; חִצֵּי הָר׳ 5^{16}; as scourge of י׳ (+ דֶּבֶר, חֶרֶב, etc.; esp. Je Ez), Je 5^{12} 11^{22} 14^{12} 21$^{7.9}$ Ez 5^{2} 6$^{11.12}$+, etc.; fig. of lack of י׳'s word Am 8^{11}. **2.** *hunger*, of individual Je 32^{9} Dt 28^{48} (+ צָמָא, etc.), 2 Ch 32^{11} (+*id.*).

†רָעֵב **adj. hungry**;—abs. ר׳ 2 S 17^{29}+; fs. רְעֵבָה ψ 107^{9} Pr 27^{7}; mpl. רְעֵבִים 1 S 2^{5}+;—*hungry* (sts. + צָמֵא, עָיֵף), 2 S 17^{29} 2 K 7^{12} Is 8^{21} Pr 25^{21} ψ 107^{5}; נֶפֶשׁ רְעֵבָה v^{9} Pr 27^{7}; as subst. sg. *a hungry man* Is 29^{8} 32^{6} 58$^{7.10}$ Ez 18$^{7.16}$ Jb 5^{5} (Bev$^{JPhil.\ xxvi.\ 304}$ prop. רָעֵב, cf. Ez 7^{15}) 22^{7}, pl. 1 S 2^{5}(opp. שְׂבֵעִים בַּלֶּחֶם), Jb 24^{10}(‖ עָרוֹם), ψ 107^{36} 146^{7}; יְהִי־רָעֵב אֹנוֹ Jb 18^{12}(fig.) *his strength grows hungry*, i.e. fails (𝔙 Ew Di al.); 𝔖 De Bu Du (reading אֵידוֹ) al. *his trouble grows hungry* (i.e. ravenous for him), but ר׳ never elsewhere in this sense.

†רְעָבוֹן **n.[m.] hunger, lack of food, famine**;—cstr. רַעֲבוֹן בָּתֵּיכֶם Gn 42$^{19.33}$(E); abs. בִּימֵי רְעָבוֹן ψ 37^{19}.

†[רָעַד] **vb. tremble, quake** (NH *id.*, Hiph. *shake* (rare), רְעָדָה *a trembling, shaking*; Ar. رَعَدَ *thunder* (said of sky), VIII. *tremble, quiver*; Eth. ርዕደ: *tremble*; JAram. רְעַד *tremble, shake*);—**Qal** *Impf.* 3 fs. וַתִּרְעָד ψ 104^{32} and it (the earth) *trembleth* at the gaze of י׳, in theoph. **Hiph.** *Pt.* עָמַדְתִּי מַרְעִיד Dn 10^{11} *I stood trembling*; pl. מַרְעִידִים Ezr 10^{9}, c. יָשַׁב.

†רַעַד **n.m. trembling**;—יִרְאָה וָר׳ יָבֹא בִי ψ 55^{6}; יֹאחֲזֵמוֹ רָעַד Ex 15^{15}.

†רְעָדָה **n.f. id.**; subj. of אֲחָזָה Is 33^{14} ψ 48^{7}; ‖ יִרְאָה 2^{11}; ‖ פַּחַד Jb 4^{14}.

I. רָעָה$_{167}$ **vb. pasture, tend, graze** (As. *rê'û*, vb. *pasture*, n. *ruler*, TelAm. *ruḫi* (as Canaanism) Wkl$^{No.\ 181,\ 11}$; Ar. رَعَى, Eth. ረዐየ: Aram. רְעָא, ܪܥܐ, all=BH);—**Qal** *Pf.* 3 ms. consec. וְרָעָה Mi 5^{3}+, 1 s. sf. consec. וּרְעִיתִים Ez 34^{13}, 3 pl. sf. consec. וְרָעוּם Je 23^{4}, etc.; *Impf.* 3 ms. יִרְעֶה Is 27^{10}+, juss. יֵרַע Jb 20^{26}, sf. יִרְעֶנָּה ψ 80^{14}, וַיִּרְעֵם ψ 78^{72} (וַיַּר׳ **Hiph.** van d. H.), etc.; *Imv.* ms. רְעֵה Mi 7^{14}+, sf. רְעֵם ψ 28^{9}; fs. רְעִי Ct 1^{8}; mpl. רְעוּ Gn 29^{7}; *Inf. cstr.* לִרְעוֹת 37^{12}+, etc.; *Pt.* רֹעֶה 30^{36}+, sf. רֹעִי ψ 23^{1}+; fs. רֹעָה Gn 29^{9} Pr 25^{19}, etc.;—**1.** trans. **a.** *pasture, tend* (*pascere*), lit., c. acc. צאן Gn 30$^{31.36}$ 37^{12} (all J), Ex 3^{1} (E), 1 S 17^{15} 25^{16} Is 61^{5}, acc. of asses Gn 36^{24} (P), kids Ct 1^{8}; acc. (צאן) om. Gn 29^{7} 37^{13} (ב loc.) v^{16} (all J), Ct 1^{7} (‖ הִרְבִּיץ), Jb 24^{2} (𝔊 Me Siegf Bu (וְרֹעוּ);—metaph. גֹּרֶן וָיֶקֶב לֹא יִרְעֵם Ho 9^{2}, but rd. יֵדָעֵם 𝔊 We Now GASm; מָוֶת יִרְעֵם ψ 49^{15}. **b.** fig. of י׳, acc. pers., Gn 48^{15} (E) God, who *shepherded* me; c. acc. of people, as flock Ho 4^{16} Is 40^{11} Mi 7^{14} (בְּשִׁבְטֶךָ), Ez 34^{13} (pregn., c. אֶל loc.), v$^{14.15}$ (+ הִרְבִּיץ), v^{16} ψ 28^{9}. **c.** fig. of ruler, and

teacher, acc. of people, as flock, 2 S 5[2] = 1 Ch 11[2], 2 S 7[7] = 1 Ch 17[6], ψ 78[72] Je 3[15] 23[2.4] Ez 34[2.3.8.10.23.23] Zc 11[4.7.7.9]; of teaching, שִׂפְתֵי צַדִּיק יִרְעוּ רַבִּים Pr 10[21]; c. ב of people ψ 78[71]; abs. Mi 5[3]; c. acc. pers. reflex. *pastured* (fed, enriched) *themselves* Ez 34[2.8.10]. **d.** esp. pt. רֹעֶה, etc., as subst. = *shepherd, herdsman:* (1) lit., רֹעֵה צֹאן Gn 4[2] 46[32.34] 47[3] (all J), רֹעֶה בַּצּ׳ 37[2] (E), 1 S 16[11] 17[34]; רֹעֵי מִקְנֵה Gn 13[7.7] (J); (ה)ר׳ alone, sg. Am 3[12] + 7 t. (all in sim.); רֹעָה *shepherdess,* Gn 29[9] (J); כְּלִי רֹעֶה אֱוִלִי Zc 11[15] (v. כְּלִי **2 c**), as symbol; pl. (הָ)רֹעִים Am 1[2] Ex 2[17.19] (J), 1 S 21[8] (אַבִּיר הָר׳; Gr Dr Bu Kit Löhr א׳ הָרָצִים; 𝔊 Lag BN 45 HPS אֹבִיל הָעֲיָרִים, but cf. We) + 8 t. + Is 31[4] (sim.), 38[12] (rd. רֹעִים for רֹעִי Perles[29] Du Che Hpt cf. Di), cf. (sf.) Gn 13[8.8] (J); כְּלִי הָרֹעִים 1 S 17[40] (v. כְּלִי **3**);—בֵּית־עֵקֶד הָרֹעִים, v. p. 112. (2) fig. of ruler (as oft. As.; cf. Gk. (Homer) ποιμένα λαῶν), abs. sg. Je 17[16] Zc 10[2] 11[16] 13[7b] + 8 t. Je Ez; sf. of י׳, רֹעִי Is 44[28] (of Cyrus), Zc 13[7a.17] (rd. רֹעִי הָאֱוִלִי We Now GASm); abs. pl. Is 56[11] Je 2[8] 3[15] Mi 5[4] Zc 10[3] 11[5.8] + 18 t. Je Ez 34, + (of Assyrian leaders) Na 3[18]; רֹעֵי יִשׂ׳ Ez 34[2]; רֹעֵי צֹאנוֹ Is 63[11] (but rd. רֹעֵה [of Moses] 𝔊 𝔗 Di Du al.). (3) epith. of י׳: רֹעִי ψ 23[1], רֹעֵה יִשׂ׳ 80[2], רֹעֶה אֶבֶן יִשׂ׳ Gn 49[24] (poem in J; rd. cstr. רֹעֵה, cf. Comm.); מֵרֹעֶה אֶחָד Ec 12[11] DeWild, < *president* of assembly of sages Siegf SS. **2.** intrans. *feed, graze:* **a.** lit. of cows, sheep, etc.: c. ב loc. Gn 41[2.18] (E), 1 Ch 27[29]; c. acc. of pasture Is 30[23]; c. עַל loc. Zp 2[7] (עַל־הַיָּם for MT עֲלֵיהֶם, v. Now); אֶל־מוּל loc. Ex 34[3] (J); abs. Is 5[17] 11[7] (|| רבץ; but v. II. רעה infr.) 27[10] (|| *id.*), 65[25] Jon 3[7] Jb 1[14]. **b.** fig. of idolater, Is 44[20] *he feedeth on ashes* (acc.); cf. Ho 12[2] Ephr. *feedeth on wind* (acc.); פִּי כְסִילִים יִר׳ אִוֶּלֶת Pr 15[14] (so Vrss Qr; Kt פני for פי) *the mouth of fools feeds on folly* (Toy; Buhl √ II. רעה, Gerber[162] sub III. רעה); in Ct, c. ב loc., fig. of lover Ct 2[16] 6[2.3]; of breasts (like gazelles) 4[5]. **c.** fig., of Isr. as flock Is 14[30] (|| רבץ), rd. (בְּכָרַי(—) *in my pasture(s),* for MT בְּכוֹרֵי, Koppe Ew Di Du (otherwise Che Hpt, cf. Marti); Zp 3[13] (|| *id.*); c. עַל־דְּרָכִים Is 49[9]; c. acc. of pasture-land Je 50[19] Mi 7[14] Ez 34[14b] (+ אֶל loc.), v[18.19]; hence *crop, strip,* i.e. devastate, of conqueror, c. acc. of land Mi 5[5], cf. אֶת־יָדוֹ Je 6[3]; so יִרְעוּךְ קָדְקֹד 2[16]; acc. of Isr. under fig. of vine (subj. foes, as beasts) ψ 80[14]. **d.** subj. wind, c. acc. pers. Je 22[22], i.e. drive them away; subj. fire, c. acc. rei, יֵרַע Jb 20[26], but read perh. יֵרָע, **Niph.** (Ol Di Hoffm Siegf Bu; otherwise Du). —רֹעֶה עֲקָרָה 24[21] is difficult; Bu הֵרַע for ר׳; more radical conj. in Du. **Niph.** poss. Jb 20[26], v. **2 d** supr. **Hiph.** ψ 78[72] van d. H., v. **1 c** supr.

רֹעֶה *shepherd,* רֹעָה *shepherdess,* v. √ **1 d.**

†רְעִי **n.** [**m.**] pasture;—עֶשְׂרִים בָּקָר ר׳ 1 K 5[3] *twenty cattle* (fr.) *pasture* (v. Ges § 131 e; Kit בְּקַר).

רֹעִי Is 38[12] Zc 11[17], v. √ **1 d** (1), (2).

†מִרְעֶה **n.m.** Ez 34.14 **pasturage, pasture**;—abs. מ׳ Gn 47[4] +; cstr. מִרְעֵה Is 34[14]; sf. מִרְעֵהוּ Jb 39[8], מִרְעֵיכֶם Ez 34[18];—*pasturage,* לְצֹאן Gn 47[4] (J), cf. 1 Ch 4[39.41], also Is 32[14]; מ׳ שָׁמֵן וָטוֹב v[40], cf. (fig.) Ez 34[14.14.18a]; of cattle Jo 1[18], stag La 1[6]; = *pasture,* of wild ass Jb 39[8]; of כְּפִירִים Na 2[12] (but read מְעָרָה *cave,* for מרעה, We Now, || מָעוֹן); יֶתֶר מִרְעֵיכֶם Ez 34[18b] (fig.).

†[מַרְעִית] **n.f. pasturing, shepherding, pasturage** (alw. fig.);—sf. מַרְעִיתִי Je 23[1] Ez 34[31], מַרְעִיתֶךָ ψ 74[1] 79[13], etc.;—**1.** *pasturing, shepherding,* צֹאן מַרְעִיתִי, of Isr. as flock of י׳, Je 23[1] Ez 34[31], cf. ψ 74[1] 79[13] 100[3] + 95[7] (rd. צ׳ מ׳ וְעַם יָדוֹ, cf. Hup-Now Che). **2.** *pasturage,* Ho 13[6] (Now כְּמַרְעוֹתָם), Is 49[9] Je 25[36]. **3.** by meton. = *flock* Je 10[21].

†II. [רָעָה] **vb. prob. associate with** (cf. Schulthess[69 ff.] but also Nö ZMG liv (1900), 154 f.; As. *ru'a, rutlu, neighbour, fellow* (m. et f.; cf. Jäger BAS i. 483, 486); so Bed. رَاعِي, راعيها, *master, owner,* Wallin ZMG v (1851). 9 Jayakar JA xxi. 851; Eth. መርዓ: *marriage;* Ar. رَعْوَة, Eth. አርዑት: *yoke;* NH רֵעוּת *friendship* is fr. BH רֵעַ);—**Qal** *Imv.* ms. וּרְעֵה אֱמוּנָה ψ 37[3] *cherish faithfulness* (Hup-Now RV Che Du Dr); > *feed securely* (Bae; I. רעה; *feed on* (his) *faithfulness* Am RV); *Pt.* רֹעֶה כְסִילִים Pr 13[20] *one associating with fools,* so ר׳ זוֹלְלִים 28[7], ר׳ זוֹנוֹת 29[3] (Thes al. think these fig. fr. I. רעה, v. **2 b**). **Hithp.** 2 ms. אַל־תִּתְרַע אֶת־בַּעַל אָף Pr 22[24] *do not make companionship with a bad-tempered man;* perhaps also 3 fpl. תִּתְרָעֶינָה Is 11[7] (Lag Or. i. 21; Deceased Wife's Sister 399 Brd Du Che Hpt) cow and bear *shall be each other's companions;* + *Inf. cstr.* הִתְרָעֵת Pr 18[24] (Toy, for MT הִתְרֹעֵעַ) there are [יֵשׁ for אִישׁ] friends (merely) *to be companions* (v. II. רעע *ad fin.*).

II. רֵעַ [187] **n.m.** Pr 17.17 **friend, companion, fellow**;—ר׳ abs. 2 S 13[3] +, cstr. 1 Ch 27[33]; sf. רֵעִי Jb 31[9] +, רֵעֲךָ Dt 5[17] +, רֵעֶךָ Ex 2[13] +, also רֵעֶיךָ 2 S 12[11] (sg.; Ges § 93 ss), רֵעֵהוּ (Ges § 84a l) Gn 11[3] + 114 t., רֵעוֹ Je 6[21], רֵעָהּ 3[20]; pl. רֵעִים Je 3[1] +, cstr. רֵעֵי Jb 2[11]; sf. רֵעָיו 32[3], רֵעֵהוּ (Ges § 91 k) 42[10]

1 S 30^{26}, etc ,—**1.** *friend, intimate,* Gn 38$^{12.20}$(J), 1 S 30^{26} 2 S 13^{3} 1 K 16^{11} (𝔊om); רֵעֲךָ אֲשֶׁר כְּנַפְשְׁךָ Dt 13^{7}, מתֹק רעהו Pr 27^{9} (txt dub , v Toy), Mi 7^{5} (|| אַלּוּף), Je 9^{3} (|| אָח), 19^{9} La 1^{2} (+ אֹהֲבֶיהָ), ψ 35^{14} (|| אָח) + 3 t ψψ, esp. Jb 2^{11} 6^{14} + 8 t Jb, Pr 17^{17} 18^{24} + 8 t Pr (12^{26} v. מרע infr), Ct 5^{1} (|| דודים), associates Zc 3^{8}, term. techn רֵ׳ הַמֶּלֶךְ 1 Ch 27^{33} (v רֵעֶה), cf 2 S 16$^{17.17}$, of lover Ct 5^{16} (|| דודי), husband Je 3^{20}, paramours Ho 3^{1} Je 3^{1}, metaph. רֵעַ לִבְנוֹת יַעֲנָה Jb 30^{29} (|| אָח לְתַנִּים) **2.** in weaker sense, *fellow, fellow-citizen,* even *another person,* with whom one stands in recipr relations, Ex 2^{13} 20$^{16.17.17.17}$(Gi v$^{13.14.14.14}$) = Dt 5$^{17.18.18.18}$, Ex 21^{14} 22$^{7.8.10.}$... (all E), Lv 19$^{13.16.18}$ 20^{10} (all H), Dt 4^{42} 15$^{2.2}$ + 11 t Dt, Jos 20^{5} (D), Ju 7^{14} Je 9^{7} 22^{13} 29^{23} Ez 18$^{6.11.15}$ 22$^{11.12}$ Hb 2^{15} Jb 16^{21} Ru 4^{7} ψ 15^{3} 28^{3} 101^{5} Pr 3$^{28.29}$ 6^{1} (|| זָר) + 18 t Pr; שְׁכֵן ורעו Je 6^{21}, 1 S 15^{28} *hath given* (the kingdom) *to thy fellow,* = another than thou, so 28^{17} 2 S 12^{11}; so also איש . . . רעהו *a* (given, certain) *man* over against *his fellow* (diff. fr **3**) Ex 21$^{18.35}$ 22$^{6.9.13}$ 33^{11} (all E), Dt 19^{11} 22^{26} Ju 7^{13} 1 K 8^{31} 20^{35} Je 7^{5} 1 Ch 6^{22} Ru 3^{14} Ec 4^{4}, similarly שָׂעִיר אֶל־רֵעֵהוּ Is 34^{14}. **3.** in recipr phr איש . . . רעהו Gn 11^{3} they said *one* to *another* (איש distrib), *each* the speech of *the other* v^{7}, absent *one* from *the other* 31^{49}, cf 43^{33} (all J), Ex 11^{2} 18$^{7.16}$ 32^{27} (all E), Ju 6^{29} 7^{22} 10^{18} 2 S 2$^{16.16}$ + 4 t. 1 S, 2 K 3^{23} 7$^{3.9}$ 2 Ch 20^{23} Is 3^{5}(|| איש באיש), 13^{8} 19^{2} (|| איש באחיו), 41^{6} Je 5^{8} + 11 t Je, Ez 33^{26} Zc 3^{10} + 6 t. Zc (11^{6} read רעהו Sta$^{ZAW\ i\ (1881),\ 26}$), Mal 3^{16} Jon 1^{7}; so of things Gn 15^{10} (J) —ı רע v. רוע.

†רֵעֶה **n m. friend** (cf Sta^{§184} Lag$^{BN\ 156}$ Ba^{§12a}),—cstr in term techn רֵעֵה הַמֶּלֶךְ (Ges^{§93ll} Ko$^{ii\ 1,78\ f}$) 1 K 4^{5} (= רֵעַ 1 Ch 27^{33}), cf. רֵעֶה דָוִד 2 S 15^{37} 16^{16}, ins. also 15^{32} (cf. v^{37}) 𝔊 We Dr al ; in simple sense Pr 27^{10} Kt (Qr רֵעַ; cf. Ko$^{l\ c}$).

†[רָעָה] **vb. denom. Pi. be a special friend,**—*Pf* 3 ms מֵרֵעֵהוּ אֲשֶׁר רֵעָה לוֹ Ju 14^{20} his comrade who *had been 'best man'* (GFM) to him.

†[רֵעָה] **n.f. companion, attendant ,**—of maidens, pl sf רֵעוֹתַי Ju 11^{37} Qr (> Kt רעיתי), רֵעוֹתֶיהָ v^{38} ψ 45^{15}

†[רַעְיָה] **n.f. companion ;**—of beloved bride, sf. רַעְיָתִי Ct 1$^{9.15}$ 2$^{2.10.13}$ 4$^{1.7}$ 5^{2} 6^{4}, so of attendant maidens Ju 11^{37} Kt, but v. foregoing

†ı רְעוּת **n.f. fellow (-woman),**—sf in recipr phr. אִשָּׁה מֵאֵת רְעוּתָהּ Ex 11^{2} (E) *each from her fellow* (|| איש מאת רעהו, cf ıı רֵעַ **3**); cf. Je 9^{19}, of birds of prey (דַּיּוֹת) Is 34^{15} cf. v^{16}, people under fig. of sheep Zc 11^{9}, רְעוּתָהּ Est 1^{19} = *another than she* (cf 1 S 15^{28} ıı רֵעַ **2**).

†רוּת **n.pr.f. Ruth** (for רעות, i e *friendship,* Syr ܪܥܘܬ, Thes Lag$^{BN\ 84,\ 156.\ Or\ ii\ 41}$ Ko$^{ii\ 1,\ 481}$),—Moabitess, ancestress of David, Ru 1$^{4.14.16.22}$ 2$^{2.8.21.22}$ 3^{9} 4$^{5.10.13}$; Ρουθ

†רְעוּ **n.pr.m.** (prop. name of a god, Duval $^{ZA\ vi\ 126}$ Mez$^{Harran\ 21}$, cf. Hom$^{A\ u\ A\ ii\ 208}$),—son of Peleg : Gn 11$^{18.19.20.21}$ (P), 1 Ch 1^{25}, Ραγαυ.

†רְעוּאֵל **n.pr.m.** Ραγουηλ· **1.** Moses' father-in-law Ex 2^{18} (J, 𝔊L Ιοθορ), Nu 10^{29} (JE), elsewhere יתרו q.v. **2.** Edomite Gn 36$^{4.10.13.17.17}$ (P), || 1 Ch 1$^{35.37}$. **3.** Gadite Nu 2^{14}, v דְּעוּאֵל p 396. **4.** Benjamite 1 Ch 9^{8}.

†רֵעִי **n.pr.m.** (cf Palm n pr. רעי *friendly*(?) Cook^{109}),—courtier of David (si vera l) 1 K 1^{8}; Ρησει, 𝔊L οἱ ἑταῖροι αὐτοῦ.

†[מֵרֵעַ] **n.m. friend, companion** (strange formation; orig. dub , Wetzst$^{Syr\ Dreschtafel,\ Z\ Ethnol.\ 1873,\ 289}$ cp مرياع *miryâ'*, name of bell-wether among Syr. nomads (prop [inseparable] *companion*), and der. fr. *ריע, prop. *closely joined;* cf. Gerber$^{97.162}$);—sf מֵרֵעֵהוּ Gn 26^{26} +, מֵרֵעֵהוּ Pr 19^{7}, מֵרֵעֲךָ Ju 15^{2}, pl. מרעים 14^{11},—*companion, confidential friend,* Gn 26^{26} (J , cf רֵעֶה); of bridegroom's escort 14^{11}, 'best man' (GFM) v^{20} 15$^{2.6}$; more gen. *friends* (|| אחים) 2 S 3^{8} Pr 19^{7}; 12^{26} is dub , Dod Hi De al מרעהו, Toy conj. poss (יָסֵר) מֵרָעָה, v. further תור

III רָעָה (Aram רְעָא, ܪܥܐ, *take pleasure* (in), *desire,* = Ar. رضى [Heb רָצָה], whence Aram. רְעוּתָא *desire,* רַעְיָנָא, רַעְיוֹנָא, ܪܶܥܝܳܢܳܐ, *opinion, thought, disposition,* and following late and Aram words in Heb, cf. No$^{ZMG\ liv\ (1900),\ 153}$; > De Siegf$^{Qoh\ 13}$ al from I. רעה **2 b**, cf Ho 12^{2}, and Ar. رَعَى *watch, regard, respect* (Lane) [Ba$^{WU\ 46\ f}$ Kau$^{Aramaismen\ 82\ f.}$ derive foll from I. רעה = *observe, attend to,* specif. *tend sheep,* also *aim at, purpose*])

†III. [רֵעַ] **n.[m.] purpose, aim ;**—sf. רֵעִי ψ 139^{2} (of man), pl sf רֵעֶיךָ v^{17} (of Ēl).

†II רְעוּת **n.f. longing, striving ,**—cstr., 4^{6} עָמָל ור׳ רוּחַ הבל ור׳ רוּחַ Ec 1^{14} 2$^{11.17.26}$ 4^{4} 6^{9},

†רַעְיוֹן **n.[m.]** id ,—cstr., רַעְיוֹן רוּחַ Ec 1^{17}, 2^{22} בְּכָל־עֲמָלוֹ וּבר׳ לִבּוֹ 4^{16} הֶבֶל ור׳ רוּחַ (cf. foreg),

רָעָה v ıı רעע.

†[רָעַל] **vb. quiver, shake, reel** (Aram. רְעַל, ܪܥܠ, *quiver, shake, tremble;* Ar. رَعَلَ, *the hanging part* of a sheep's split ear, also (Frey) a kind of *veil* of which a part hangs down in front, أَرْعَلُ *dangling;* Lihy. has n pr. רעל DHM[Epigr Denkm. Ar 38]),—**Hoph.** *Pf.* 3 pl הָרְעָלוּ הַבְּרוֹשִׁים Na 2[4] *are made to quiver.* Vid. also [עָרַל]

†רַעַל **n.[m.]** reeling,—only סַף־ר׳ Zc 12[2] *goblet of reeling* (fig. of Jerusalem).

†[רְעָלָה] **n.[f.]** prob. **veil** (cf Ar. supr.);—pl. הָרְעָלוֹת Is 3[19], in list of finery.

מַרְעֵלָה v. p. 599.

†תַּרְעֵלָה **n.f. reeling** (cf. רַעַל),—כּוֹס הַתּ׳ Is 51[17.22]; יֵין תּ׳ ψ 60[5] drink *reeling as wine.*

†רְעֵלָיָה **n. pr. m.** companion of Zerub., Ezr 2[2] (Ρεελια, 𝔊L Δεμίου), = רַעַמְיָה Ne 7[7] (Naαμια, א Δαεμια, 𝔊L Δαιμίας, A Ρεελμα).

רעם (√ of foll., prob. onomatop.; Gerber[47] prop. *move violently* as orig. meaning, but ref. to thunderous *sound* everywhere, exc. Ez 27[35] where text dub., v. infr., cf. Aram. רַעַם, רְעִים n. *thunder,* רְעֵם vb *thunder;* esp. Aph. Ithpa. *utter* (loud) *complaints;* ܪܥܡܐ, ܐܪܥܡ n. *thunder,* ܪܥܡ vb. *thunder, lament,* cf. NH רָעַם Hiph *thunder,* Hithp. *complain;* Eth. ረዐም: n. *thunder,* As. *rimu, id.;* Ar. رَغِمَ *vex, dislike,* etc)

†רַעַם **n.[m.]** thunder;—ascribed to י׳: ר׳ abs. Is 29[6], בְּסֵתֶר רַעַם ψ 81[8] (Baer Gi; i.e thunder-cloud); sf. קוֹל רַעַמְךָ 77[19] 104[7]; cstr. רַעַם גְּבוּרֹתָו Jb 26[14] (fig of י׳'s display of might; opp שֶׁמֶץ), fig of captains, ר׳ שָׂרִים 39[25], i.e. thunderous shouting (+ תְּרוּעָה).

†[רָעַם] **vb. denom. thunder;—Qal** *make the sound of thunder, thunder: Impf.* 3 ms. יִרְעַם *let* the sea *thunder* (in praise, ‖ יָגֵל, שׂמח, עלז, הריע, מחא כף, רנן) ψ 96[11] = 1 Ch 16[32], ψ 98[7].—*Pf.* 3 pl. רָעֲמוּ פָּנִים Ez 27[35] is dub.: *faces tremble* (Toy *are convulsed*), or *they tremble* (cf Hi-Sm Krae; AV RV *are troubled*) *in face,* lacks etym. support (otherwise Gerber[47], but v. √ supr.); 𝔊 𝔖 Co דָּמְעוּ פְּנֵיהֶם. **Hiph.** (Gerber[47]) *thunder, cause thunder;—Pf.* 3 ms הִרְעִים ψ 29[3]; *Impf* 3 ms. יַרְעֵם (on — v. Ko[i 210]) ψ 18[14]+; וַיַּרְעֵם 1 S 7[10]; 2 ms. תַּרְעֵם Jb 40[9]; 1 S 1[6] v. infr;—*thunder,* of י׳ (God) 2[10] 7[10] (both c. עַל pers. *against* whom), ψ 18[14] = 2 S 22[14], ψ 29[3] Jb 37[4.5], cf. 40[9].—הַרְּעִמָהּ 1 S 1[6] is appar. *Inf cstr. sf.* (Ges[§ 20 b; 22 s]), but not understood by 𝔊 and dub· AV RV *to make her fret,* cf. Aram. *utter* (loud) *complaints* (Weir in Dr[Sm 291]); perhaps corrupt HPS.

רַעְמָא v. II. רַעְמָה.

†I. רַעְמָה (Gi[Intr 127 f.]) **n.f. vibration?** **quivering mane?** of horse's neck: Jb 39[19] *hast thou clothed his neck* (*with*) ר׳? so most, but very uncertain.

†II. רַעְמָה, רַעְמָא (Gi[Intr 124 ff]) **n. pr. m.** 'son' of Cush, ־ָה Gn 10[7] = ־ָא 1 Ch 1[9] (Baer, v. his note; van d. H. Gi ־ָה v[b]), Ρεγχμα, Ρεγμα, ־ָה as trading people Ez 27[22], Ραμα, Ραγμα Identified by many with city Ῥεγ(α)μα (Ptol[vi. 7, 14]), Ῥηγμα (Steph. Byz), in SE. Arabia, on Pers. Gulf (so even DHM[ZMG xxx (1876), 122] Glas Skizze ii 251, 325), but this is رجمة in inscr. (Glas[ib. 252]); < Sab. רעמת near *Me'in* in SW. Arabia (Hom Südar Chr 131 Hal[835, 11], cf. DHM[l. c.]), perh. = Ῥαμμανῖται of Strabo[xvi. 4. 24], v. Di[Gn 10, 7].

רַעַמְיָה (? *thunder of* י׳) Ne 7[7] v. רְעֵלָיָה.

†רַעְמְסֵס **n.pr.loc.** Ex 1[11] (J), = רַעְמְסֵס Gn 47[11] Ex 12[37] Nu 33[3.5] (all P), **Rameses,** city in Egypt; Ραμεσ(σ)η; built by King Rameses II (hence its name; the king used Israelitish *corvée* acc. to Ex 1[11]), near *Tel el-Maskhuta* (Pithom), but not certainly identified, v. פתם and reff; אֶרֶץ ר׳ Gn 47[11] of district round.

†[רָעַן] **vb.** only **Pa'lel be or grow luxuriant, fresh, green;**—*Pf.* 3 fs. רַעֲנָנָה (De[Hiob]) Jb 15[32] (of branch, in fig.).

†רַעֲנָן **adj. luxuriant, fresh;**—m. ר׳ Dt 12[2]+; f. רַעֲנָנָה Ct 1[16]; mpl רַעֲנַנִּים ψ 92[15];—*luxuriant,* of trees: ברוש Ho 14[9], זית ψ 52[10] (both sim), Je 11[16] (fig.); sim also, כְּאֶזְרָח ר׳ ψ 37[35] (but rd. כְּאֶרֶז הַלְּבָנוֹן 𝔊 𝔖 and most); esp in phrase תַּחַת כָּל־עֵץ ר׳ place of idolatrous rites, Dt 12[2] 1 K 14[23] 2 K 16[4] = 2 Ch 28[4], 2 K 17[10] Je 2[20] 3[6.13] Is 57[5] Ez 6[13], עַל־עֵץ ר׳ Je 17[2] (si vera l.); leaf v[8] (fig); leafy couch Ct 1[16]; *fresh,* oil ψ 92[11]; *fresh, flourishing,* pers. (fig., as trees) v[15] (+ דְּשֵׁנִים).

I. **רעע** (√ of foll; orig meaning dub).

†רַע **n.[m.]** badness, evil;—ר׳ abs. Gn 41[19] + 4 t. Je; cstr. Ho 9[15] + 13 t;—**1.** *badness, bad quality,* of cattle Gn 41[19] (E), figs Je 24[2.3.8] 29[17]. **2.** *wilfulness,* רֹעַ לְבָב 1 S 17[28] (Gerber[161] makes **2** and **4** [inf. of] vb.). **3.** ethical, *evil, badness,* only in phr.: רֹעַ מַעֲלָלִים *evil of doings*

Dt 28^{29} Is 1^{16} Je 4^{4} 21^{12} 23$^{2.22}$ 25^{5} 26^{3} 44^{22} Ho 9^{15} ψ 28^{4} (cf רַע מעללים 1 S 25^{3}). **4.** *sadness*, ר׳ לב Ec 7^{3}, ר׳ פָּנִים Ne 2^{2} (cf [רָעַע] **2**)

I רַע$_{228}$ **adj.** bad, evil (distinction from n., and vb Pf 3 ms, is sts not easy, and opinions differ);—ms רַע Gn 6^{5}+; רָע 31^{24}+, pl רָעִים 13^{13}+, cstr רָעֵי Ez 7^{24} (del Co); fs רָעָה Gn 37^{2}+37 t (this form usu noun), pl. רָעוֹת 28^{8} +14 t., רָעֹת 41^{27} (18 t noun),—†**1.** *bad, disagreeable, malignant*. of a woman, רָעָה בעיני Ex 21^{8} (E, perhaps, with changed accent, vb 3 fs רָ֫עָה) *disagreeable, unpleasing in the eyes of*, pl Gn 28^{8} (P), of poisonous herb 2 K 4^{41}, malignant boils Dt 28^{35} Jb 2^{7}, diseases Dt 7^{15} 28^{59} 2 Ch 21^{19} Ec 6^{2}, deadly sword ψ 144^{10}, arrows Ez 5^{16}, severe judgments 14^{21}, wonders Dt 6^{22}, מַלְאֲכֵי רָעִים ψ 78^{49} = fierce messengers (of God, Ew § 287 a Ges § 130 e), wild beasts Gn 37$^{20.33}$ (JE) Lv 26^{6} (H) Ez 5^{17} 14$^{15.21}$ 34^{25}, unclean thing Dt 23^{10}. †**2.** *bad, unpleasant*, giving pain, unhappiness, misery. ימים רעים *evil days* (of trial and hardship) Gn 47^{9} (P) Pr 15^{15}, ענין רע Ec 1^{13} 5^{13}; עִנְיָן 4^{8}, cf. 2^{17} 9^{3}, הַמַּעֲשֶׂה הָרָע 4^{3}, הדבר הרע *evil report* Ex 33^{4} (J), so דִבָּה רָעָה Gn 37^{2} (JE) Nu 14^{37} (P), שם רע Dt 22$^{14.19}$ Ne 6^{13}, שְׁמוּעָה רָעָה Je 49^{23} ψ 112^{7}, of things painful discipline Pr 15^{10}, evil occurrence 1 K 5^{18}, *evil*(-bringing) *net* Ec 9^{12}, instruments Is 32^{7} כל הדבר הרע Jos 23^{15} (D) *all evil* (injurious) *things;* רַע it is *bad, harmful* Is 3^{11} Je 2^{19}, of speech, דבר, רע או טוב Gn 24^{50} (J) in prov., speak *bad or good* = anything at all, מטוב עד רע 31$^{24.29}$ (E), לְמֵרַע ועד טוב 2 S 13^{22}, of the divine spirit as producing an ecstatic state of frenzy and violence 1 S 16$^{14.15.16.23}$ 18^{10} 19^{9} (see רוּחַ **9**). †**3.** *evil, displeasing* עָשָׂה רָע בעיני סַרְנֵי פלשתים 1 S 29^{7} †**4.** *bad of its kind*, land Nu 13^{19} (J), place 20^{5} (JE), waters 2 K 2^{19}, figs Je 24$^{2.3.3.8}$, kine Gn 41$^{3.4.19.20.21.27}$ (E), מום רע Dt 15^{21}, cf 17^{1}. †**5.** *bad*, i e of low value Lv 27$^{10.10.12.14.33}$ (H), cf Mal 1$^{8.8}$, רַע רַע יֹאמַר הַקּוֹנֶה Pr 20$^{14.14}$. †**6.** רָעֵי + מִן comp, *worse than*, 2 S 19^{8}, as superl, רָעֵי גוים Ez 7^{24} *worst of nations* (del. Co) †**7.** *sad, unhappy* · לֵב־רָע *sad heart* (cf. opp טוב, יטב) Pr 25^{20}, of face Gn 40^{7} (E) Ne 2^{2}, רע לְפָנָיו v^{1}. †**8.** חָשַׁב מַחֲשֶׁבֶת (ה)רָעָה *devise evil* (hurtful) *device* Ez 38^{10} Est 9^{25}. †**9** *bad, unkind*, vicious in disposition or temper ולב־רָע *when the mind is vicious*, harmful Pr 26^{23}, רַע עָיִן *one evil of eye* Pr 23^{6} 28^{22}; רוּחַ רָעָה Ju 9^{23} *bad temper*.

10. ethically *bad, evil, wicked:* †**a.** in gen., אם טוב ואם רע Ec 12^{14} *whether good or bad.* †**b.** of persons, איש רע 1 S 30^{22}, אדם רע ψ 140^{2}; המן הרע הזה Est 7^{6} *this wicked Haman*, so רָע = *evil man* ψ 10^{15}, Jb 21^{30} Pr 11^{21} 12^{13} 24^{20}, רָעִים = *evil men* Gn 13^{13} (J) Je 6^{29} 15^{21} Ez 30^{12} Jb 35^{12} Pr 4^{14} 12^{12} 14^{19} 15^{3}, רָעוֹת *evil women* Je 2^{33}, שכנים רעים 12^{14} *evil neighbours;* of הַדּוֹר Dt 1^{35}, הָעָם Je 13^{10}, הָעֵדָה Nu 14$^{27.35}$ (P), המשפחה Je 8^{3}, רע בעיני י׳ *wicked* in the eyes of י׳ Gn 38^{7} (JE) = 1 Ch 2^{3}, עָשָׂה הָרַע בעיני י׳ Nu 32^{13} (R) Dt 4^{25} 9^{18} 17^{2} 31^{29} Ju 2^{11} + 48 t, + (c. sf of God) 2 K 21^{15} Is 65^{12} 66^{4} Je 7^{30} 32^{30} ψ 51^{6} 2 S 12^{9}, prob also Je 18^{10} (read הָרַע for הָרָעָה). **c.** of thoughts, יֵצֶר Gn 6^{5} 8^{21} (J), הַלֵּב הָרָע Je 3^{17} 7^{24} 11^{8} 16^{12} 18^{12}, words, רעות Pr 15^{26} **d.** *deeds, actions*, עשׂה (כ)דבר הרע Dt 13^{12} 17^{5} 19^{20} Ne 13^{17}, דברים הרעות Je 3^{5}, דבר רע ψ 64^{6} 141^{4} Ec 8$^{3.5}$; דֶּרֶךְ 1 S 2^{23} 2 K 17^{11}, 1 K 13^{33} Je 18^{11} 23^{22} + 11 t, דרכים 2 K 17^{13} 2 Ch 7^{14} Ez 20^{44} 33^{11} 36^{31} Zc 1^{4}, מעשׂינו Ezr 9^{13}; מעללים Zc 1^{4} Ne 9^{35} (cf. רֹעַ **4**); (ה)תועבות (ה)רעות Ez 6^{11} 8^{9} (del. Co), מרוצתם Je 23^{10}, בצע רע Hb 2^{9}, כי רָעוֹת במגוּרָם ψ 55^{16} *for evil deeds are in their dwelling.*

II רַע$_{126}$ **n.m.** $^{Jb\ 30,\ 26}$ **evil, distress, misery, injury, calamity**,—abs רַע Nu 11^{1}+, בְּרָע Ex 5^{19}+, רָע Gn 48^{16}+,—†**1.** *evil, distress, adversity*. יָרֵא רַע *fear evil* ψ 23^{4} Zp 3^{15}; בורא רָע Is 45^{7} (of God), הביא רע 31^{2}; מתאננים רַע Nu 11^{1} (J) *murmuring respecting distress* (see Di); אם טוב ואם רע Je 42^{6} *whether prosperity or adversity*, יום רע Am 6^{3} *day of calamity;* יְמֵי רע ψ 49^{6} 94^{13}, כי טוב קויתי ויבא רע Jb 30^{26}; בְּרָע *in adversity* Ex 5^{19} (E) ψ 10^{6}, יפל בְּרָע Pr 13^{17}, בכל־רע Pr 5^{14}, אֶרְאֶה בְרָע Gn 44^{34} (J), מכל רע Gn 48^{16} (E) ψ 121^{7}; v. also Mi 1^{12} ψ 140^{12} Jb 5^{19} 31^{29} Pr 12^{21} 19^{23}. †**2.** *evil, injury, wrong* · עשׂה רע + עִם pers Gn 31^{29} (E); ל pers Je 39^{12}, as obj of חשׁב Ho 7^{15}, חרשׁ Pr 6^{14} 12^{20} 14^{22}, השׁיב ψ 54^{7}, גמל 7^{5} Pr 31^{12}, בקשׁ 71^{13}, שׁלם 20^{22}, אמר ψ 41^{6}, דבר 109^{20}, דבר בְּרָע 73^{8} *speak about injury*, לא יתנבא טוב כִּי אם רָע 1 K 22$^{8.18}$ = 2 Ch (18^{7} לְרָעָה), לְרָע 18^{17}, לרע *for harm, injury* Is 59^{7} Je 7^{6} 25^{7} ψ 56^{6} Pr 1^{16} 21^{12} Ec 8^{9}, רַע ירוֹע Pr 11^{15} (but rd רע Gr SS, v. Toy). **3.** ethical *evil*, Dt 30^{15} 2 S 14^{17} Is 5^{20} Am 5^{14} Mi 7^{3} + 10 t.; עשׂה רע 2 K 21^{9} 2 Ch 12^{14} 33^{9} Ne 9^{28} + 8 t.; פעלי רע Mi 2^{1}, אהב רע 3^{2} (Qr), ψ 52^{5}; שׂנא רע Am 5^{15} ψ 97^{10} Pr 8^{13}; מאס ברע ψ 36^{5}, מאס רע Is 7$^{15.16}$, בער הרע מן *consume evil from* Dt 13^{6} + 8 t. Dt,

לֹא יְגֻרְךָ רָע ψ 5^{5} (adj.=*evil man* Hup De al.); סר מֵרָע ידע טוב ורע Gn 2$^{9.17}$ 3$^{5.22}$ (all J), Dt 1^{39}; Is 59^{15} ψ 34^{15} 37^{27} Pr 3^{7} + 8 t.; כי ברע הוא Ex 32^{22} (J) *he is set on evil;* רע מעללים ,7^{10} ψ רע רשעים 1 S 25^{3}, cf. Mi 3^{4} (v. רֹעַ **3**); דִּבְרֵי רָע *deeds of evil* Je 5^{28}; תַּהְפֻּכוֹת רָע Pr 2^{14}; ψ 119^{101} אֹרַח רע; עֲצַת רע Ez 11^{2}; מַחְשְׁבוֹת רע Pr 15^{26}; אִישׁ רע 29^{6}; אַנְשֵׁי רע 28^{5}; אֵשֶׁת רע 6^{24} (but rd. רֵעַ Gr Bi Toy).

רָעָה $_{310}$ **n.f. evil, misery, distress, injury**;—abs. ר׳ Gn 26^{29}+; cstr. רָעַת 6^{5}+; sf. רָעָתִי ψ 35^{4}+; רָעָתְךָ 1 K 2^{44}+; רָעָתֵכִי Je 11^{15} (txt. dub.); רָעַתְכֶם 1 S 12^{17}, etc.; pl. רָעוֹת Dt 31^{17}+; רָעֹת Je 44^{9} Ex 23^{2}; sf. רָעוֹתֵיכֶם 1 S 10^{19}+, etc.;—**1.** *evil, misery, distress:* פַּחַד רָעָה Pr 1^{33}, באה (ה)רעה Ez 7$^{5.6}$; c. עַל Is 47^{11} (read באה for (בא), Je 5^{12} + 5 t.; c. אֶל Je 2^{3} 51^{60}; †הביא רעה Je 4^{6} 1 K 21^{29}; + אֶל 2 S 17^{14} + 8 t. K Je; + עַל 1 K 9^{9} = 2 Ch 7^{22}, Je 19^{3} + 6 t. Je + 8 t.; + אֶל et עַל Je 19^{15} 36^{31}; יום רעה 17$^{17.18}$ + 5 t.; יְמֵי הרעה †Ec 12^{1} (i.e., spring days, fatal to old people, Wetzst in De $^{Koh. 447}$); רָעוֹת *evils* Dt 31$^{17.17.21}$ (JE), 32^{23} (poem), ψ 34^{20} 40^{13} 88^{4}; עֵת רָעָה Am 5^{13} Je 2$^{27.28}$ + 5 t.; †ראה ברעה Nu 11^{15} (JE) Ob^{13} Est 8^{6}; †ראה רעה Je 44^{17} ψ 90^{15} Pr 22^{3} = 27^{12}; †יפול ברעה 17^{20} 28^{14}; †בְּרָעָה Gn 44^{29} (J) Pr 14^{32} 24^{16} Ne 1^{3} 1 Ch 7^{23} ψ 107^{26}; ברעותיכם 141^{5}; נִחַם עַל רָעָה Ex 32$^{12.14}$ (J) Je 8^{6} + 6 t.; c. אֶל 2 S 24^{16} Je 26$^{3.13.19}$ 42^{10}. **2.** *evil, injury, wrong:* †עשׂה רעה 2 S 12^{18} Je 26^{19} 41^{11}; c. עִם Gn 26^{29} (J) Ju 15^{3} 2 S 13^{16}; c. את Ju 11^{27}; c. ל 1 S 6^{9} 1 K 2^{44} + 4 t.; c. אֶל Je 44^{7}; obj. of vbs. חשׁב Gn 50^{20} (E) Je 36^{3} 48^{2} + 7 t.; †חרשׁ 1 S 23^{9} Pr 3^{29}; הֵשִׁיב Gn 50^{15} (E) Ju 9$^{56.57}$ + 4 t.; †גמל Gn 50^{17} (E) 1 S 24$^{18(17)}$ Is 3^{9} Pr 3^{30}; בקשׁ Nu 35^{23} (P) 1 S 24$^{10(9)}$ 25^{26} + 4 t.; †שׁלם Gn 44^{4} (J) Je 18^{20} 51^{24} ψ 35^{12} 38^{21}; לְרָעָה *for harm* Gn 31^{52} Ex 23^{2} (E) Dt 29^{20} Ju 2^{15} 2 S 18^{32} Je 21^{10} + 8 t. Je, Am 9^{4} Zc 1^{15} Pr 6^{18} Ec 5^{12}; בְּרָעָתֶךָ 2 S 16^{8} *in thy mischief;* בְּרָעָה Ex 32^{12} (J) *for mischief;* רָעָה רַבָּה Ec 2^{21}; רָעָה חולה Ec 5$^{12.15}$. **3.** ethical *evil,* 1 S 12$^{17.19}$ 24^{12} 26^{18} Is 47^{10} Je 2^{19} + 13 t. Je, + 18 t., + foll.: עָשָׂה (הָ)רָעָה Gn 39^{9} Dt 31^{18} (J) + 5 t. + Je 18^{10} (Kt, but Qr רע); שׁוּב מרעה Ec 8^{11}; מַעֲשֵׂה רעה אהב רעה Mi 3^{2} (Kt); Je 18^{8} 23^{14} 44^{5}; בִּעֵר רעה מ׳ Ju 20^{13} (v. 11. רע **3**); מפני רָעַת רעתכם Ho 10^{15}; מִפְּנֵי רָעָה Je 7^{12} 44^{3}; מֵר׳ ψ 107^{34} 1^{16} 32^{32} 33^{5}; על כל ר׳ Je 11^{17}; בגלל ר׳ Je 12^{4}; אַנְשֵׁי רָעָה Pr 24^{1}.

[רָעַע] $_{93}$ **vb. denom.** be evil, bad;— †**Qal** *Pf.* 3 ms. רַע Nu 22^{34} + 3 t., רָע 1 K 11^{10}; 3 fs. רָעָה Dt 15^{9} (Ex 21^{8} v. 1. רַע); *Impf.* 3 ms. יֵרַע (Ges ^{§67p}) Gn 21^{12}+; 3 fs. תֵּרַע Dt 28$^{54.56}$; 3 mpl. יֵרְעוּ Ne 2^{3};—**1.** *be displeasing:* רַע בְּעֵינֵי Nu 11^{10} 22^{34} (J), Jos 24^{15} (E), Je 40^{4} Pr 24^{18} (c. ו consec.) impf. יֵרַע בְּעֵינֵי Gn 21$^{11.12}$ (E), 48^{17} (J), 1 S 8^{6} 18^{8} 2 S 11^{25}; later, וַיֵּרַע אֶל Jon 4^{1} or וירע לְ Ne 2^{10} (intensified by רָעָה גְדוֹלָה), וַיֵּרַע לִי מְאֹד 13^{8}. **2.** *be sad:* ירע לבב Dt 15^{10} 1 S 1^{8}; יֵרְעוּ פָּנֶי Ne 2^{3}. **3.** *be injurious, evil:* וַיֵּרַע לְ ψ 106^{32} *it went ill with* Moses, pers. subj. 2 S 20^{6}; רָעָה עַיִן *be grudging,* c. ב pers., Dt 15^{9} 28$^{54.56}$. **4.** *be evil, wicked,* ethically: וַיֵּרַע בְּעֵינֵי י׳ Gn 38^{10} (J) 2 S 11^{27} Is 59^{15}; בְּעֵינֵי אֱלֹהִים 1 Ch 21^{7}. †**Niph.** *suffer hurt:* *Impf.* 3 ms. יֵרוֹעַ (רע) Pr 11^{15} 13^{20}. **Hiph.** $_{70}$ *Pf.* 3 ms. הֵרַע Ex 5^{23}+; 2 ms. הֲרֵעוֹתָ 1 K 17^{20}, etc.; *Impf.* 3 ms. יָרֵעַ Zp 1^{12}, וַיָּרַע 1 K 16^{25}; 2 ms. תָּרַע ψ 44^{3}+, etc.; *Inf. abs.* הָרֵעַ 1 S 12^{25} 1 Ch 21^{17}; *cstr.* הָרַע Gn 31^{7} + 8 t., הָרֵעַ Is 1^{16} + 4 t.; *Pt.* מֵרַע Is 9^{16} Pr 17^{4}; pl. מְרֵעִים Is 1^{4}+;—**1.** *do an injury, hurt:* abs. Gn 44^{5} (J), Is 11^{9} = 65^{25}, Je 31^{28} Pr 4^{16} 24^{8}; opp. היטיב Is 41^{23} Je 10^{5} Zp 1^{12} (all in prov. phr. = do anything at all, cf. רַע **2**); הרע לְ Gn 19^{9} 43^{6} Ex 5$^{22.23}$ Nu 11^{11} (J) 20^{15} Jos 24^{20} (E) + 5 t.; c. acc. pers. Nu 16^{15} (J) + 4 t.; c. בְּ, 1 Ch 16^{22} = ψ 105^{15} (c. לְ), Je 25^{29} ψ 74^{3}; c. עִמָּדִי Gn 31^{7} (E); c. עַל 1 K 17^{20} *bring evil upon;* swear לְהָרַע, = to one's hurt, ψ 15^{4} Lv 5^{4} (P); Pt. = subst. לְבָבָם לְמֵרָע Dn 11^{27} (shall be) *for mischief.* **2.** *do evil, wickedly:* abs. Gn 19^{7} (J) 1 S 12$^{25.25}$ + 6 t.; opp. היטיב Je 4^{22} 13^{23}; c. מִן comp., 1 K 14^{9} 16^{25} 2 K 21^{11} Je 7^{26} 16^{12}; c. acc. הֵרֵעוּ מַעַלְלֵיהֶם Mi 3^{4}, cf. 1 S 25^{3}; *Pt.* מֵרַע *evil doer,* Is 9^{16} Pr 17^{4}; pl. Je 20^{13} 23^{14} ψ 27^{2} + 7 t.; זֶרַע מ׳ Is 1^{4} 14^{20}; בית מ׳ 31^{2}; עֲדַת מ׳ ψ 22^{17}; קְהַל מ׳ 26^{5}; סוֹד מ׳ 64^{3}.

†**II. [רָעַע]** **vb. break** (Aram. loan-word = Heb. רָצַץ q. v.);—**Qal** *Pf.* 3 pl. רָעוּ Je 11^{16}; *Impf.* 3 ms. יָרֹעַ Je 15^{12} Jb 34^{24}, 2 ms. sf. תְּרֹעֵם ψ 2^{9} (but v. infr.); *Inf. abs.* רֹעָה Is 24^{19} (del. ה as dittogr. and read רֹעַ, v. **Hithpō**.); *Pt.* f. רֹעָה (? for רֹעָעָה) Pr 25^{19}:—**1.** trans. הֲיָרֹעַ בַּרְזֶל *can one break iron, iron out of the north?* בַּרְזֶל וגו׳ Je 15^{12} cf. יָרֹעַ כַּבִּירִים Jb 34^{24}; תְּרֹעֵם בְּשֵׁבֶט בַּרְזֶל ψ 2^{9} (but rd. תִּרְעֵם, v. I. רעה, 𝔊 𝔖 𝔙 Hup-Now al.). **2.** intrans. *break = be broken,* of branches Je 11^{16} (in fig.; Gf Or al.; > Hi Gie *are in a sad state,* √I. רעע); שֵׁן רֹעָה Pr 25^{19} *a broken tooth* (ר׳ = רֹעָעָה ?; Frankenb **Niph.** *Pt.* נִרְעָה, cf. Toy, but Niph. not elsewhere; Vrss רָעָה *bad*).—רֹעוּ Is 8^{9} read דְּעוּ (𝔊 Lo Che al.,

הָאֲוִינוּ ||). **Hithpō'.** *Pf.* 3 fs. + **Qal** *Inf. abs.* (v. supr.) רֹעַ הִתְרֹעֲעָה [הָ]ארץ Is 24[19] *the earth is broken asunder* (|| מוֹט הִתְמוֹטְטָה, פּוֹר הִתְפּוֹרְרָה); also *Inf. cstr.* לְהִתְרוֹעֵעַ Pr 18[24] *will be broken in pieces* (Ges § 114 i), *ruined*, De al., but < read לְהִתְרָעוֹת Vrss Toy al., v. II. רעה Hithp. (see, however, Dr Expos. Times xi (1899-1900). 230 f.).

†[רָעַף] **vb. trickle, drip,** synon. of נזל, II. ערף (cf. Ar. رَعَفَ *flow* (of blood), *bleed* (of the nose));—**Qal** *Impf.* 3 mpl. יִרְעֲפוּ, of clouds Jb 36[28] (c. עֲלֵי pers.; || יִזְּלוּ), c. acc. mat. טַל Pr 3[20]; fig. וּמַעְגָּלֶיךָ יִרְעֲפוּן דָּשֶׁן ψ 65[12] (i.e. fertilizing rain); subj. of moistened ground, נְאוֹת מִדְבָּר, v[13]. **Hiph.** *Imv.* mpl. הַרְעִיפוּ Is 45[8] *trickle*, O heavens, from above (fig.: || יִזְּלוּ צֶדֶק).

†[רָעַץ] **vb. shatter** (Aram. רְעַץ *smite, shatter*; cf. perh. TelAm. *raḫâṣu*, Wkl TelAm. 128, 31; 137, 32);—*Impf.* 3 fs. יְמִינְךָ י׳ תִּרְעַץ אוֹיֵב Ex 15[6]; 3 m. pl. וַיִּרְעֲצוּ Ju 10[8], acc. pers. (of men; || וַיְרֹצְצוּ).

†[רָעַשׁ] **vb. quake, shake,** intr. (NH = BH, so Aram. ܪܥܫ (rare), and (once) רְעַשׁ *toss, rage* (of sea); Ar. رَعَسَ, usu. رَعَشَ, رَعِشَ (loan-word ?), *tremble, quiver, quake*; cf. perhaps As. *rêšu, exult*);—**Qal** *Pf.* 3 fs. רָעֲשָׁה Je 8[16] 49[21], רָעָ֑שָׁה Ju 5[4] ψ 68[9]; 3 pl. רָעֲשׁוּ Jo 2[10] +, etc. *Impf.* 3 ms. יִרְעַשׁ ψ 72[16], 3 fpl. תִּרְעַשְׁנָה Ez 26[10], etc.; *Pt.* pl. רֹעֲשִׁים Je 4[24];—*quake, shake*, of earth Ju 5[4] = ψ 68[9], 2 S 22[8] (|| רגז) = ψ 18[8] (|| *id.*), ψ 77[19] (+ רגז), also Is 13[13] (c. מִמְּקוֹמוֹ + עַל־כֵּן, pregn.; || רָגַז), Je 51[29]; c. מִן caus. Je 8[16] 10[10] 49[21]; of מוֹסְדֵי אָרֶץ Is 24[18]; of heavens Jo 2[10] (לְפָנָיו caus.; || רָגַז); heavens and earth 4[16]; mts. Je 4[24] Na 1[5] (מִן pers. caus.), ψ 46[4] (ב caus.); walls Ez 26[10] (מִן caus.); אִיִּים v[15] (id.); מִגְרָשׁוֹת 27[28] (ל caus.); הַסִּפִּים Am 9[1]; all living things Ez 38[20] (מִפָּנַי caus.); of waving grain ψ 72[16]. **Niph.** נִרְעֲשָׁה הָאָרֶץ Je 50[46] *is made to quake* (מִקּוֹל). **Hiph.** *Pf.* 2 ms. הִרְעַשְׁתָּה ψ 60[4]; 1 s. הִרְעַשְׁתִּי Ez 31[16]; וְהִר׳ consec. Hg 2[7]; *Impf.* 2 ms. sf. 3 ms. (הֲ)תַרְעִישֶׁנּוּ Jb 39[20]; *Pt.* מַרְעִישׁ Is 14[16] + 2 t.;—**1.** *cause to quake*, subj. י׳, c. acc. of heavens, earth, nations, etc., Hg 2[6.7.21], cf. ψ 60[4]; nations + מִקּוֹל Ez 31[16]; subj. man, c. acc. of kingdoms Is 14[16] (|| מַרְגִּיז). **2.** *cause* (horse) *to spring, leap* (like locust), man subj., Jb 39[20].

†רַעַשׁ **n.m.** Je 10,22 **quaking, shaking**;—ר׳ abs. 1 K 19[11] +, cstr. Na 3[2] Jb 41[21];—**1.** specif. *earthquake*, Am 1[1] Zc 14[5] 1 K 19[11.11.12]; fig. of י׳'s judgment Is 29[6] Ez 38[19]; cf. (in vision) קוֹל ר׳ גָּדוֹל 3[12.13]; prob. also 37[7] (𝔊 Thes Co Krae; > *rustling, rattling*, Hi-Sm Toy); hence hyperbol. of shaking of earth by tramping of warriors Is 9[4], by war-chariots Je 47[3], cf. 10[22], or wheels Na 3[2], by war-horse('s hoofs) Jb 39[24] (+ רֹגֶז). **2.** *quaking, trembling*, of pers. Ez 12[18]. **3.** *shaking, quivering*, of dart Jb 41[21] (al. *rushing sound*).

†רָפָא **vb. heal** (NH in deriv.; Ph. רפא, Syr. ܐܣܐ *heal*; on Aram. n.pr. cpd. with רפא v. Nö ZMG xl (1886). 723 Lzb 369; Sab. n.pr. אלרפא Langer 1, 1 DHM ZMG xxxvii (1883). 326; Ar. رَفَا (and رَفَأَ) *darn, mend, repair, pacify*; Eth. ረፍአ: *stitch together, mend*; cf. Küchenmeister ZWiss. Th. xxx (1887), 257 ff.);—**Qal** *Pf.* 3 ms. consec. וְר׳ Is 6[10], sf. וּרְפָאָם 19[22], 1 s. sf. consec. וּרְפָאתִיו 57[19], etc.; *Impf.* 3 ms. יִרְפָּא 2 K 20[8] +, sf. יִרְפָּאֵנוּ Ho 6[1], 1 s. אֶרְפָּא Ho 14[5] +, אֶרְפָּה (Ges § 75 pp) Je 3[22]; 3 fpl. תִּרְפֶּינָה (Id ib. qq) Jb 5[18], etc.; *Imv.* ms. רְפָא Nu 12[13], רְפָה (Id ib. pp) ψ 60[4], רְפָאָה 41[5], etc.; *Inf. abs.* רָפוֹא Is 19[22]; *cstr.* לִרְפֹּא Ho 5[13], etc.; *Pt.* רֹפֵא 2 K 20[5] +, etc.;—*heal*: **1.** lit., **a.** of God, c. acc. pers. Gn 20[17] (E), ψ 107[20] (sf.), c. ל pers. Nu 12[13] (JE) 2 K 20[5.8]. **b.** of men, abs. Ec 3[3] (opp. הרג); pt. as subst. *healer, physician*, Gn 50[2.2] (J) 2 Ch 16[12]. **2.** fig., *heal* hurts of nation, involving י׳'s (restored) favour (and, often, forgiveness): **a.** subj. י׳, c. sf. pers., Ho 6[1] 11[3] (yet cf. We Now), Ex 15[26] (J), Is 19[22b] 57[18.19] Je 33[6] ψ 30[3], cf. 6[3]; c. acc. עַם 2 Ch 30[20], c. acc. אֶרֶץ 2 Ch 7[14]; c. ל of nation Ho 7[1], and (indef. subj.) Is 6[10] (lest) *one heal them* (= pass., *they be healed*); c. acc. of hurt, מַחַץ מַכָּתוֹ 30[26], שְׁבָרִים (of land) ψ 60[4], so מְשׁוּבָה Ho 14[5] Je 3[22] (incl. the *consequences* of backsliding); c. ל of hurt ψ 103[3]; acc. nation (personif.) + מִן of hurt Je 30[17] *I will heal thee of thy wounds* (|| אֶרְפָּאֵךְ); abs. Is 19[22a] (opp. נגף), Dt 32[39] (opp. מחץ); pt. as subst. *healer, physician* Je 8[22]. **b.** human subj., c. ל of nation, Ho 5[13], cf. La 2[13]. **3. a.** fig., *heal* individ. distresses, c. sf. pers. Je 17[14], c. acc. נַפְשִׁי = *me* ψ 41[5], c. ל pers., לִשְׁבוּרֵי לֵב ψ 147[3] (i.e. longing exiles, cf. Is 61[1]); abs. Jb 5[18] (opp. מחץ); pt. as subst. Jb 13[4]. **Niph.** *Pf.* 3 ms. נִרְפָּא Lv 13[37] +, 3 fs. נִרְפְּתָה (Ges § 75 qq) Je 51[9]; 3 pl. וְנִרְפְּאוּ consec. Ez 47[8]; *Impf.* 2 ms. תֵּרָפֵא Je 51[8]; 3 mpl. יֵרָפְאוּ Ez 47[9.11], וַיֵּרָפוּ (Ges l.c.) 2 K 2[22], etc.; *Inf. cstr.* הֵרָפֵא Je 15[18] +, הֵרָפֵה (Id ib.) Je 19[11];—*be healed*: **1.** lit., of pers. 1 S 6[3]; + acc. of disease Dt 28[27.35]; subj. disease Lv 13[18.37] 14[3.48]; of (bad) water

2 K 2^{22}, salt waters (prediction), i e. be made fresh, Ez $47^{8.9\,11}$; of (broken) pottery, i.e. be made whole, Je 19^{11} (in sim) **2.** fig, *be healed:* **a.** of national hurts, subj. city Je $51^{8.9}$, involving forgiveness and י׳'s blessing, impers. c. לְ of people, נִרְפָּא־לָנוּ Is 53^{5} i e. *healing has come to us.* **b.** of personal distress, subj pers. Je 17^{14}, subj. the distress 15^{18}. **Pi.** *Pf.* 1 s. רִפֵּאתִי 2 K 2^{21}; 2 mpl. רִפֵּאתֶם Ez 34^{4}; 1 pl רִפִּאנוּ Je 51^{9}, *Impf.* 3 ms יְרַפֵּא Ex 21^{19} Zc 11^{16}, וַיְרַפֵּא 1 K 18^{30}; 3 mpl. וַיְרַפְּאוּ Je 6^{14}, וַיְרַפּוּ (Ges §75 qq) 8^{11}, *Inf. abs.* רַפֵּא Ex 21^{19},—*have healed, heal,* usu. human subj: **1.** lit., רַפֵּא יְרַפֵּא Ex 21^{19} *he shall have (him) well healed;* c acc. of altar, =*repair,* 1 K 18^{30}; c לְ of water (subj. י׳) 2 K 2^{21}. **2.** fig. of healing national defects and hurts, acc pers, Ez 34^{14} Zc 11^{16}; *work at healing, treat* (acc of hurt) Je 6^{14} 8^{11} (both עַל־נְקַלָּה, v. [קָלַל] **Niph. 2**), 51^{9}. **Hithp.** *Inf. cstr* of purpose, לְהִתְרַפֵּא, lit, *in order to get healed,* + מִן of wounds 2 K 8^{29} = 9^{15}, so ‖ 2 Ch 22^{6} (rd. with 𝔊 מִן for כִּי, cf. Be Kau Benz)

† I. רָפָא **n.pr.m.** in Benj., 1 Ch 8^{2}, Ραφη[α]—II. רָפָא v. רפה—Vid. also בֵּית ר׳ p. 112.

I, II. רְפָאִים v. sub רפה.

† I. רָפָה **n.pr.m.** in Saul's line 1 Ch 8^{37}, Ραφαι(α), 𝔊L Αραχα; v רָפָיָה.—II ר׳ v. רפה.

† רָפוּא **n.pr.m.** in Benj, Nu 13^{9}, Ραφου[αν].

† [רְפֻאָה] **n.f.** remedy, medicine;—pl abs. רְפֻאוֹת Ez 30^{21} Je 30^{13}, ־וֹת 46^{11} (all fig).

† רִפְאוּת **n.f.** healing;—ר׳ abs. Pr 3^{8} (fig.).

† רְפָאֵל **n.pr.m.** Levite, 1 Ch 26^{7}, Ραφαηλ.

† רְפָיָה **n.pr.m.** **1.** in David's family 1 Ch 3^{21}, Ραφαλ, A 𝔊L Ραφαια **2.** in Simeon, 4^{42}, Ραφαια(ς) **3.** in Issachar, 7^{2}, Ραφαρα, A 𝔊L Ραφαια. **4.** descendant of Saul 9^{43}, Ραφαια, 𝔊L Αραχα (= רָפָה 8^{37}) **5.** post-ex. name Ne 3^{9}, Ραφαια(ς).

† יִרְפְּאֵל **n.pr.loc.** in Benj, Jos 18^{27}, A 𝔊L Ιερφ(α)ηλ; unknown

† מַרְפֵּא, מַרְפֵּה **n.m.** Ec 10 4 healing, cure, health (usu fig);—abs. מַרְפֵּא Je 14^{19} +, מַרְפֵּה 8^{15}, cstr. מַרְפֵּא Pr 15^{4},—**1.** *healing, cure,* of national woes, Je 8^{15} 14^{19b} (‖ שָׁלוֹם), 36^{6} (+ אֲרֻכָה); esp אֵין לָנוּ מ׳ Je 14^{19a} *there is no cure for us,* עַד לְאֵין מ׳ 2 Ch 36^{16}. **2.** fig of pers, *health, profit,* Pr 4^{22} (‖ חַיִּים), 12^{18} 13^{17} 16^{24}; with spiritual implic. Mal 3^{20}; אֵין מ׳ Pr 6^{15} = 29^{1}; לֵב מ׳ 14^{30} *a mind of health* (healthy, composed, mind), cf. מ׳ alone = *composure* Ec 10^{4}; מ׳ לָשׁוֹן 15^{4} *healing of the tongue,* = a soothing tongue (Toy) **3.** lit, of disease, לְאֵין מ׳ 2 Ch 21^{18}

† [רָפַד] **vb. spread** (As. *rapâdu, stretch oneself;* Ar. رَفَدَ *prop up, support, aid, give,* cf. **Pi.** infr; Sab רפדת pl. *protection, guard,* CIS iv, no. 40, 3, cf. ארפד *terraces* DHM Hofmus),—**Qal** *Impf* 3 ms. יִרְפַּד Jb 41^{22} *he* (the crocodile) *spreadeth a threshing-sledge upon the mud* (leaves marks upon it from his scales) **Pi.** *Pf* 1 s. of couch (fig.) רִפַּדְתִּי יְצוּעָי Jb 17^{13}; then (*spread out* any support, hence) *Imv.* mpl sf. רַפְּדוּנִי Ct 2^{5} *support me* with apples (‖ סַמְּכוּנִי).

† [רְפִידָה] **n.f.** perh **support** (cf Ar. supr.), i e. back, or arm, of palanquin; sf רְפִידָתוֹ Ct 3^{10}, 𝔊 ἀνάκλιτον, 𝔙 *reclinatorium.*

† רְפִידִים **n.pr.loc.** station of Isr. at Exodus (in P), Ex 17^{1} 19^{2}; רפידם 17^{8} Nu $33^{14\,15}$, Ραφιδειν. —אַרְפַּד v. p 75.

† רָפָה **vb. sink, relax** (NH *id.*, so Aram. רפא (der. spec), Zinj. רפה Aph, ܪܦܐ; Ar رَفَاهَة *an easy life* is perhaps akin);—**Qal** *Pf* 3 ms. Ju 19^{9} (yet v infr.); 3 fs. רָפְתָה Ju 8^{3} Je 49^{24}, etc.; *Impf.* 3 ms. יִרְפֶּה Is 5^{24}, וַיִּרֶף Ex 4^{26} (v. infr.), etc;—**1.** *sink down,* of hay in flame Is 5^{24}; *sink, decline,* of day Ju 19^{9} (si vera l; 𝔊L κέκλικεν, GFM נָטָה [but how expl. the difficult רפה?]). Usu **2.** *sink, drop* (of wings, v. **Pi.**), of hands, c מִן Ne 6^{9} *their hands will drop from the work* (in fear); elsewh abs fig = *lose heart, energy,* 2 S 4^{1} Is 13^{7} Je 6^{24} 50^{43} Ez 7^{17} 21^{12} Zp 3^{16}, יָדַיִם om. Je 49^{24}. **3.** *sink, relax, abate,* of temper Ju 8^{3} (+ מֵעַל pers.) **4.** *relax, withdraw,* subj י׳, מִן pers. Ex 4^{26} (J), i e. let one alone (but rd. perh. וַיֶּרֶף, v. **Hiph.**). **Niph.** *Pt.* pl. נִרְפִּים *idle* Ex $5^{8\,17}$ (J). **Pi.** *Pf.* 3 ms. רִפָּה Jb 12^{21}; *Impf.* 3 fpl תְּרַפֶּינָה Ez $1^{24.25}$; *Pt.* מְרַפֵּא (Ges §75 rr) Je 38^{4}, pl. מְרַפִּים Ezr 4^{4};—causat. *let* wings *drop* Ez $1^{24.25}$ (rd. **Qal,** כנפיהם subj, 𝔊 Co Toy Krae al., who del in v^{25}); loosen and *let drop,* girdle of mighty, fig. for *weaken* them Jb 12^{21}; c acc hands, fig for *enfeeble, dishearten* Je 38^{4} Ezr 4^{4}. **Hiph.** *Impf.,* 3 ms. sf. יַרְפְּךָ Dt 4^{31} +; juss 2 ms. תֶּרֶף Jos 10^{6} +, etc.; *Imv.* ms. הַרְפֵּה Ju 11^{37} 2 K 4^{27}, הֶרֶף Dt 9^{14} +; mpl. הַרְפּוּ ψ 46^{11}; —causat., **1.** *let drop,* the hand 2 S 24^{16} = 1 Ch 21^{15}; fig., + מִן pers, = *abandon,* Jos 10^{6} (JE);

perh. also (יָד om.)=*relax, refrain* Ex 4^{26} (rdg. יִרֶף, v. **Qal**); acc. rei,=*abandon, forsake*, Ne 6^{3}, so (subj. ׳י) ψ 138^{8}; subj. ׳י, c. acc. pers., Dt 4^{31} $31^{6.8}$ Jos 1^{5} (D), 1 Ch 28^{20}. **2.** *let go*, sf. pers., Ct 3^{4} (opp. אחז); fig., acc. (om.) מוּסָר, Pr 4^{13} (opp. החזיק), צְדָקָה Jb 27^{6} (opp. *id.*). **3.** *refrain*, c. מִן pers., =*let* one *alone* Ju 11^{37} Dt 9^{14}, מִן of anger ψ 37^{8}; c. לְ pers. 1 S 11^{3} 2 K 4^{27}; acc. pers. Jb 7^{19}; abs. *let alone*, i.e. do nothing, be quiet, 1 S 15^{16} ψ 46^{11} (cf. Weir in $Dr^{1 S 15,16}$).—Je 3^{22} Jb 5^{18} ψ 60^{4} v. רָפָא. **Hithp.** *Pf.* 2 ms. הִתְרַפִּיתָ Pr 24^{10} *hast shewn thyself slack*; *Pt.* מִתְרַפֶּה 18^{9} *one shewing himself slack*, pl. מִתְרַפִּים Jos 18^{3}.—Vid. also רָפָא *heal*.

†רָפֶה **adj. slack**;—abs. ׳ר, of people, Nu 13^{18} (J); cstr. רְפֵה יָדַיִם 2 S 17^{2}, i.e. weak (|| יָגֵעַ); fpl. יָדַיִם רָפוֹת, fig. of discouragement and fear Is 35^{3} Jb 4^{3}. Cf. √**Qal 2.**

†[רִפָּיוֹן $Ges^{§ 85u}$, or רִפְיוֹן $Sta^{§ 296 d}$ cf. $Kö^{ii. 154}$] **n.[m.] sinking**;—cstr. רִפְיוֹן יָדַיִם Je 47^{3} *sinking of hands*, fig. of helpless terror.

†ii. רָפָה, ii. רָפָא as **n.pr.m.**, alw. c. art. **Hā-Rāphā** (perh. der. fr. n.pr.gent. ii. רְפָאִים, q.v.);—הָרָפָה 2 S $21^{16.18}$, c. prep. לְהָ׳ $v^{20.22}$= לְהָרָפָא 1 Ch $20^{6.8}$;—only as parent, בִּילִידֵי הָר׳ 2 S $21^{16.18}$ (=מִילִידֵי הָרְפָאִים 1 Ch 20^{4}); יֻלַּד לְהָר׳ $v^{20.22}$ || 1 Ch $20^{6.8}$.—i. רָפָה v. sub רָפָא.

†i. רְפָאִים **n.m.** $^{Jb 26, 5}$ **pl. shades, ghosts** (by most connected with above √, as *sunken, powerless, ones*, $Sta^{G. i. 420}$; Ph. רפאם);—Wisd. Lit. and late, name of dead in Sheʾôl, c. art. הָר׳ Jb 26^{5}, elsewhere nearly= n.pr.: ׳ר Is 14^{9} (in Sheʾôl), 26^{4} (|| מֵתִים), ψ 88^{11} (|| *id.*), Pr 2^{18} (|| מָוֶת), 9^{18} (in עִמְקֵי שְׁאוֹל), קְהַל רְפָאִים 21^{16}; of righteous Isr. Is 26^{19} *earth shall cast forth* ׳ר (|| מֵתֶיךָ).

†ii. רְפָאִים **n.pr.gent.** old race of giants (perh.=i. ׳ר, as extinct and *powerless;* v. esp. WRS in $Dr^{Dt 2, 11}$; or as shadowy, vaguely known, $Schwally^{ZAW xviii (1898), 127 ff.}$ v. also $Sta^{l.c.}$);—ancient inhab. of Canaan [W. of Jordan ?], Gn 15^{20} Jos 17^{15} (JE), cf. 1 Ch 20^{4} (v. ii. רָפָה supr.); hence עֵמֶק ר׳, plain S. of Jerus. 2 S $5^{18.22}$ 23^{13} 1 Ch 11^{15} 14^{9} Is 17^{5} Jos 15^{8} 18^{16} (P); ׳ר E. of Jordan Dt 2^{11} (|| עֲנָקִים; tall, cf. v^{10}), v^{20} (|| *id.*; tall;= Zamzummim); in Bashan, Gn 14^{5}, Og the last of them Dt 3^{11} (of huge size), Jos 12^{4} 13^{12} (D); אֶרֶץ ר׳ Dt 2^{20} 3^{13}. 𝔊 Ραφαειν[μ]; οἱ γίγαντες Gn 14^{5}+ 4 t.; τῶν Τιτάνων 2 S $5^{18.22}$+ (𝔊L) 23^{13}.

רְפוֹת v. רִיפָה sub ריף.

†רֶפַח **n.pr.m.** in Ephr., 1 Ch 7^{25}, Ραφη[α].

רְפָיָה **n.pr.m.** v. sub רפא. רִפְיוֹן v. רפה.

†רָפַשׂ, רָפַס **vb. stamp, tread, foul by stamping, treading** (NH רָפַס *tread*, Syr. ܪܦܣ; cf. Ar. رَفَسَ *kick*);—**Qal** *Impf.* 2 ms. וַתִּרְפֹּס Ez 32^{2}, c. acc. rivers; 2 mpl. תִּרְפֹּשׂוּן 34^{18}. **Niph.** *Pt.* מַעְיָן נִרְפָּשׂ Pr 25^{26} *a fountain befouled.* **Hithp.** (*stamp oneself down*, then fig.), *Imv.* ms. הִתְרַפֵּס Pr 6^{3} *humble thyself*, become a suppliant (RV^{m} Toy *bestir thyself*, as conject.); *Pt.* מִתְרַפֵּס בְּרַצֵּי כָסֶף ψ 68^{31} *stamping, trampling, down pieces of silver* (?), obscure and prob. crpt., see conjj. in Bae al. and פַּתְרֹס supr., ad fin.

†[מִרְפָּשׂ] **n.[m.]** (water) befouled (by trampling);—cstr. מִרְפַּשׂ רַגְלֵיכֶם Ez 34^{19}.

†[רַפְסֹדָה] **n.[f.] raft** (etym. dub.; NH once רַפְסוֹדוֹת *bench* or *stool* on which feet rest);—pl. רַפְסֹדוֹת 2 Ch 2^{15} (late || for דֹּבְרוֹת 1 K 5^{23}).

†[רָפַף] **vb. Pō. shake, rock** (Aram. רְפַף, ܪܦ *move gently;* Ar. رَفَّ *quiver, flash, throb;* also NH רִפְרֵף *flutter*, Ar. رَفْرَفَ *flutter, flap wings*);—*Impf.* 3 mpl. עַמּוּדֵי שָׁמַיִם יְרוֹפָפוּ Jb 26^{11}.

†[רָפַק] **vb. Hithp. support oneself, lean** (Eth. ረፈቀ: *reclinare, accumbere* ad mensam; cf. Ar. رَفَقَ *be gentle, bind camel's arm to prevent going quickly;* مِرْفَق, NH מַרְפֵּק, J Aram. מַרְפְּקָא, *elbow*);—*Pt.* f. מִתְרַפֶּקֶת Ct 8^{5} (c. עַל pers.).

רפשׂ v. רפס.

רפשׁ (√of foll.; NH רֶפֶשׁ = BH; $Schulthess^{71 f.}$ cp. Ar. رَفَثَ *talk* or *act obscenely*, and a Syr. ܪܦܬܐ *slag, refuse* (not in PS Brock al.)).

†רֶפֶשׁ **n.[m.] mire**;—Is 57^{20} (+ מַיִם).

†[רֶפֶת] **n.[m.]** appar. **stable, stall** (NH *id.*; √dub.; Thes fr. רפף, cf. Ar. رَفْت *enclosure for sheep and goats*, but no satisfactory meaning of רפף known);—pl. רְפָתִים Hb 3^{17} (for cattle).

רָץ v. רוץ. [רָץ] v. רצץ.

†[רָצָא] **vb.** si vera l., || form of רוץ *run*, *Inf. abs.* רָצוֹא Ez 1^{14}, but rd. יָצוֹא (יָצְאוּ) Hi-Sm Co Toy, cf. Krae Berthol al.; 𝔊 om. verse and most mod. think interpol.—Vid. also רצה.

†[רָצַד] **vb. Pi.** watch stealthily, or with envious hostility (Ar. رَصَدَ *watch* or *wait* (oft. *lie*

in wait) for; ירצד Ecclus 14^{22} *observe stealthily,* so once Aram. רְצַד Levy[NHWB iv. 464]);—only *Impf.* 2 mpl. תְּרַצְּדוּן ψ 68^{17} (fig. of mts., c. acc.).

† **רָצָה** **vb.** **be pleased with, accept favourably** (NH *id., will, be willing;* Ar. رَضِيَ (orig. و) *be well pleased with,* Nö[ZMG liv (1900), 155]; Sab. רצו *favour* CIS[iv. no. 77, 9 al.], cf. Hom[Südar. Chrest. 123]; רצים *good, acceptable,* CIS[iv. no. 73, 9, al.], of a coin, *good,* Id[ib. no. 21, 5]; Aram. רְעָא, رعا *have pleasure in,* cf. II. רָעָה supr.);—**Qal** *Pf.* 3 ms. ר׳ Ec 9^7; sf. רָצָם Je 14^{10}; 1 s. וְרָצָאתִי Ez 43^{27} consec. (metapl. Ges[§ 75 rr]; Aramaism, Krae; but Co וְרָצִיתִי), etc.; *Impf.* 3 ms. יִרְצֶה ψ 147^{10}+, sf. יִרְצְךָ Mal 1^8; 3 fs. juss. תִּרֶץ Lv 26^{43}; 3 fpl. תִּרְצֶנָה Pr 23^{26} Kt (< Qr תִּצֹּרְנָה, √נצר, cf. Toy), etc.; *Imv.* רְצֵה ψ 40^{14} 119^{108}; *Inf. cstr.* רְצוֹת Pr 16^7 ψ 77^8, etc.; *Pt.* רוֹצֶה 147^{11} 149^4, sf. רֹצָם Je 14^{12}; pass. רָצוּי Est 10^3, cstr. רְצוּי Dt 33^{24};—**1.** *be pleased with, favourable to:* **a.** of God, c. acc. pers. Is 42^1 ψ 44^4 147^{11} Jb 33^{26}; c. acc. rei ψ 85^2 1 Ch 29^{17} Pr 16^7 Ec 9^7; c. ב pers. ψ 149^4; ב rei 147^{10} Hg 1^8; abs. ψ 77^8. **b.** of men: c. acc. pers., subj. father Mal 1^8, ‖ אהב Pr 3^{12}; of brother Gn 33^{10} (JE), monarch 2 Ch 10^7; c. acc. rei ψ 62^5 102^{15} Jb 14^6 Pr 23^{26} (but v. supr.); c. בְּ rei 1 Ch 29^3 ψ 49^{14}; עִם pers. Jb 34^9 ψ 50^{18}; pt. pass. רְצוּי *favoured, acceptable to* Dt 33^{24} (poem), Est 10^3. **2.** *accept:* of God, c. acc. pers., sacrificing, 2 S 24^{23} Ho 8^{13} Je $14^{10.12}$ Ez $20^{40.41}$ 43^{27}; c. acc. of sacrifice Dt 33^{11} Mal $1^{10.13}$ ψ 51^{18} 119^{108}; c. בְּ of sacrifice Mi 6^7; abs. Am 5^{22}. **3.** *be pleased:* **a.** *determined,* c. inf. ψ 40^{14}. **b.** c. ב pers. 1 Ch 28^4. **4.** *make acceptable, satisfy* (by paying off debt), subj. land, paying off its sabbaths (Di Dr al. *accept,* be satisfied with [in payment]) Lv $26^{34.43}$ 2 Ch 36^{21}, c. acc. of guilt incurred (עָוֹן) Lv $26^{41.43}$ (< point all these as **Hiph.**, so SS Gerber). **Niph.** *Pf.* 3 ms. נִרְצָה Lv 1^4 Is 40^2; *Impf.* 3 ms. יֵרָצֶה Lv 7^{18}+, etc.;—**1.** pass. of **Qal 2**, *be accepted,* of sacrifices, c. לְ pers., Lv 1^4 22^{25}; c. לְ of sacrifice $22^{23.27}$; abs. 7^{18} 19^7. **2.** pass. of **Qal 4**: נִרְצָה עֲוֹנָהּ Is 40^2 *her punishment is accepted* (as satisfactory). **Pi.** *Impf.* 3 mpl. יְרַצּוּ Jb 20^{10}, c. acc. דַּלִּים *seek the favour of the poor* (but Bu SS Gerber from רצץ). **Hiph.** *Pf.* 3 fs. וְהִרְצָת (Ges[§ 75 m]) consec. Lv 26^{34} *the land shall pay off her sabbaths* (acc.), cf. **Qal 4.** **Hithp.** *Impf.* 3 ms. יִתְרַצֶּה 1 S 29^4 with what *shall he make himself acceptable unto* (אֶל) his lord? + 3 mpl. יִתְרַצּוּ Ho 4^{10} 𝔊 We Now (for MT יפרצו) *they shall* not *have delight.*

† **רָצוֹן** **n.[m.]** **goodwill, favour, acceptance, will;**—abs. ר׳ Dt 33^{23}+; cstr. רְצוֹן ψ 145^{19}+; sf. רְצוֹנִי Is 60^{10}, רְצֹנוֹ Dn 8^4+, etc.;—**1.** *goodwill, favour:* **a.** of God, Dt 33^{16} Is 60^{10} ψ 5^{13} $30^{6.8}$ 51^{20} 89^{18} 106^4 Pr 8^{35} 12^2 18^{22}; עֵת ר׳ Is 49^8 ψ 69^{14}; יוֹם ר׳ Is 58^5; שְׁנַת־ר׳ Is 61^2; ‖ בְּרָכָה Dt 33^{23}; opp. תּוֹעֵבָה Pr $11^{1.20}$ 12^{22} 15^8. **b.** of men: in gen. Pr 10^{32} 11^{27} 14^9; of kings v[35] $16^{13.15}$ 19^{12}. **2.** *acceptance,* of persons, offering sacrifice, לרצון לפני יהוה Ex 28^{38} (P); c. לְ pers. *for acceptance for him before* י׳; c. sf. pers. לרצנו Lv 1^3; abbrev. לְרָצוֹן לָכֶם 22^{20}, לרצנכם 19^5 $22^{19.29}$ 23^{11}, לרצון 22^{21} Is 56^7 Je 6^{20} ψ 19^{15} (of words; cf. Ho 14^3); על רצון Is 60^7 (read לְ, so Codd., v. Gi, also Du), רצון Mal 2^{13}. **3.** *will, desire, pleasure:* **a.** of God, עשׂה ר׳ *do* his *will* Ezr 10^{11} ψ 40^9 103^{21} 143^{10}. **b.** of man, עשׂה כרצונו *do according to his will,* exactly as he pleased, Dn 8^4 $11^{3.16.36}$ Ne 9^{24} Est 1^8 9^5, cf. Ne 9^{37}; *desire* ψ $145^{16.19}$ 2 Ch 15^{15}; = self-will Gn 49^6 (poem).

† **תִּרְצָה** **n.pr.f. et loc.** (*pleasure, beauty*);—**1. f.** daughter of Ṣelophehad of Gilead Nu 26^{33} 27^1 36^{11} Jos 17^3; Θερσα. **2. loc.** old Can. city Jos 12^{24}, early cap. of N. Isr. (until Omri) 1 K 14^{17} (תִּרְצָתָה), $15^{21.33}$ $16^{6.8.9.15.17.23}$, Θαρσα, usu. Θερσα; Menahem's base of operations 2 K $15^{14.16}$ (Θαρσ(ε)ιλα v[14], Euseb[Onom. 263, 62, ed. Lag] cp. Θαρσιλα, village of Samaritans in Batanea, and Buhl[Geogr. 247] conj. *Tesîl,* 20 m. E. of Lake Gennesaret, but this too remote); in sim. of beauty (om. 𝔊) Ct 6^4 (‖ יְרוּשָׁלָ͏ִם);—site not certain; conj. are: *Tallûza,* just N. of Mt. Ebal (Rob[BR iii. 302 f.]), *Tayaṣir,* c. 10 m. further NE., > *eṭ-Ṭîre,* S. of Gerizim (see, on these, GASm[Geogr. 355] Buhl[Geogr. 203] Aglen[Hast. DB. s. v.]).

† **רָצַח** **vb.** **murder, slay** (NH (rare, also in deriv.) = BH; cf. Ar. رَضَحَ, رَضَخَ *break, bruise, crush*);—**Qal** *Pf.* 3 ms. consec. וְר׳ Nu 35^{27}, וּרְצָחוֹ Dt 22^{26}; 2 ms. (הֲ)רָצַחְתָּ 1 K 21^{19}; *Impf.* 3 ms. יִרְצַח Nu 35^{30} Dt 4^{42}; 2 ms. תִּרְצָח(־צַח) Ex 20^{13} = Dt 5^{17}; *Inf. abs.* רָצֹחַ Ho 4^2 Je 7^9; *Pt. act.* רֹצֵחַ Dt 19^3+, רוֹ׳ 4^{42}+;—*murder, slay,* with premeditation, Ex 20^{13} (E) = Dt 5^{17}, Ho 4^2 Je 7^9 1 K 21^{19} (all abs.); c. acc. pers. Dt 22^{26}, unawares Dt 4^{42}; *slay* as avenger Nu $35^{27.30}$ (P; ‖ הֵמִית v[19.21]); esp. pt. as subst. = *slayer, manslayer,* without intent, Dt 4^{42} $19^{3.4.6}$; also in P: Nu $35^{6.11.12.25.26.27.28}$ Jos $20^{3.5.6}$ $21^{13.21.27.32.38}$ (van d. H., Baer, v[38] Gi; all P); *murderer,* with intent, Nu $35^{16.16.17.17.18.18.19.21.21.30.31}$;

also Jb 24[14]. **Niph.** *Impf.* 1 s. אֵרָצֵחַ Pr 22[13] *I shall be slain; Pt* fs as adj. אִשָּׁה הַנִּרְצָחָה Ju 20[4] *the murdered woman* **Pi.** (intens) *murder, assassinate:* 3 mpl יְרַצֵּחוּ Ho 6[9] (abs.), ψ 94[6] (acc pers, ‖ הָרַג); ψ 62[4] v infr.; *Pt.* מְרַצֵּחַ, as subst 2 K 6[32] *murderer, assassin;* pl מְרַצְּחִים Is 1[21] *assassins.* **Pu.** *Impf*, 2 mpl תְּרָצְּחוּ ψ 62[4], so Baer Gi, van d H תְּרָצְחוּ, but Ben Napht. **Pi.** תְּרַצְּחוּ (Baer[143]), so Vrss Hup-Now De Che Bae al *ye murder* (or *batter, shatter*).

† רֶצַח **n.[m.]** shattering, — בר׳ בעצמותי ψ 42[11] *with a shattering in my bones*, fig. of effect of sneering words (Codd כר׳; Ol Gr Che We כְּרֶקֶב); appar *slaughter* Ez 21[27], but 𝔊 βοῇ (so ‖ תרועה), Co רִנָּה, Houb (in Rosenm) צרח, so Berthol Toy Krae

† רִצְיָא **n.pr.m.** in Asher 1 Ch 7[39], Ρασ(ε)ια.

† רְצִין **n.pr.m.** **1.** king of Aram, Ahaz's time: 2 K 15[37] 16[5.6.9] Is 7[1.4.8] 8[6] 9[10], Ρα(α)σ(σ)ων, Ρασειν **2.** Ezr 2[48] = Ne 7[50], Ρα(α)σων

† [רָצַע] **vb.** bore, pierce (NH = BH; Ar. رَصَعَ *stab violently*), — **Qal** *Pf* 3 ms consec. ורִ׳ Ex 21[6] (E) he *shall pierce* his ear (acc, ב instr.)

† מַרְצֵעַ **n.[m.]** boring-instrument, awl, — abs מ׳ Ex 21[6] (E), Dt 15[17].

† I. [רָצַף] **vb.** fit together, fit out, si vera l (Ecclus 43[8d] id Pi *pave* (fig; si vera l); As. *raṣâpu, join together, build,* Ar رَصَفَ *join together*, cf. DHM[VOJ i 30], Sab רצפם ,רצף Id[ib] Hal [JAS, 1872, Juin 534], Aram רְצַף, رَصِفَ, *arrange in a line;* cf Aram רִצְפְּתָא, ܪܨܦܐ, NH רִצְפָּה, all = *pavement*), — **Qal** *Pt pass* תּוֹכוֹ רָצוּף אַהֲבָה Ct 3[10] *its interior fitted out* (?) *with love* (Gr al הָבְנִי *ebony*)

† רִצְפָה **n. f.** pavement; — abs ר׳ Ez 40[17.17] +, cstr רִצְפַת Est 1[6] (van d. H. רִצְפָּה, פַּת-), — *pavement*, in Ezek's temple, Ez 40[17.17.18.18] 42[3], Sol's temple 2 Ch 7[3], in a palace Est 1[6].

† מַרְצֶפֶת **n.f.** id, — cstr מ׳ אבנים 2 K 16[17].

II רצף (√ of foll, prob. *glow*, cf Ar. رَضْفٌ *heated stone*, رَضَفَ *cauterize, roast;* Syr ܪܨܦܐ *bread baked in ashes* (coals), cf Rob[BR i 485 ii 117 202])

† I. רִצְפָּה **n. f.** glowing stone (or coal) (We[Isr u Jüd Gesch (3) 83]), — ר׳ abs Is 6[6], pl עֻגַת רְצָפִים 1 K 19[6] (cf Syr supr)

† רֶצֶף **n.pr.loc.** conquered by Assyr. (As *Raṣappa*, COT[2 K 19.12] Schr[KGF 167] Dl[Pa 297]; prob. = Ῥησάφα Ptol[v 18]); — 2 K 19[12] = Is 37[12], Ραφε(ι)ς, Ραφεθ, mod *Ruṣâfa*, between Palmyra and the Euphrates Dl[l. c.] Peters[Nippur i 10].

† II רִצְפָּה **n.pr.f.** concubine of Saul, 2 S 3[7] 21[8.10.11], Ρεσφα.

רְצָפִים v. I. רִצְפָּה.

† [רָצַץ] **vb.** crush (NH = BH; Ar. رَضَّ *bruise, bray, crush;* Aram רְעַע, ܪܨ *crush, shatter*), — **Qal** *Pf.* 2 ms sf רַצּוֹתָנוּ 1 S 12[4]; 1 s. רַצּוֹתִי v[3]; *Impf* 3 ms. יָרוּץ (Ges[§ 67 q]) Is 42[4] (Cod. Bab. ירוץ, Niph, so SS here and Ec 12[6a]), 3 fs. תָּרוּץ Ec 12[6a], 1 s. אָרֻץ ψ 18[30] = אָרוּץ 2 S 22[30] (v. infr); *Pt act.* fpl. רצצות Am 4[1]; *pass* רָצוּץ Is 42[3] +, cstr. רְצוּץ Ho 5[11], pl. רְצוּצִים Is 58[6], — *crush:* **1.** lit, **a.** *pt pass* in (הַ)קָּנֶה (הָ)רָצוּץ 2 K 18[21] = Is 36[6], Is 42[3] (all metaph. of weak pers). **b.** impf intrans *get crushed* (rd תרוץ ?), of bowl Ec 12[6a] (in metaph.) **2.** fig *crush, oppress*, acc pers 1 S 12[3.4] Am 4[1]; pt. pass Dt 28[33], as subst *the oppressed* Is 58[6], רצוץ מִשְׁפָּט Ho 5[11] (We Now רֹצֵץ, i e *perverting judgment*, but dub), intrans. *get crushed* (rd. ירוץ ?), of servant of י׳, under fig. of wick, Is 42[4] (+ יכהה) he shall not grow dim or *be crushed out.* **Niph.** *be crushed, broken.* *Pf.* 3 ms consec. וְנָרֹץ (Ges[§ 67 t]) Ec 12[6b] (of wheel at cistern); *Impf.* 2 ms. תרוץ Ez 29[7] (of Pharaoh as reed, cf. **Qal 1 a**), Jb 20[10] rd. perh. יֵרֹצּוּ (for יְרַצּוּ, v רצה Pi), *are crushed* (as) poor men, Bu, cf Hoffm SS Gerber. — Is 42[3] Ec 12[6a] v. **Qal.** **Pi.** *crush in pieces.* **1.** lit (in metaph) *Pf* 2 ms. רִצַּצְתָּ ψ 74[14] c. acc. rei. **2.** fig = *grievously oppress*, 3 ms. רִצַּץ Jb 20[19], *Impf.* 3 ms. וַיְרַצֵּץ מִן הָעָם 2 Ch 16[10]. **Pō'ēl** *Impf* 3 mpl וַיְרֹצְצוּ Ju 10[8], acc pers (= **Pi. 2**; ‖ רָעַץ, רצץ here perh. doublet, so GFM[Hpt], cf. Bu Now). **Hiph.** *Impf.* 3 fs. וַתָּרֶץ (Ko[i 342]; Ba[ZMG xliii (1889), 181] thinks **Qal**) Ju 9[53] *she crushed his skull* **Hithpō'.** recipr., *Impf.* 3 mpl. ויתרצצו הַבָּנִים בקרבה Gn 25[22] (J) *the children crushed* (thrust, struck) *one another within her.*

† [רַץ] **n [m.]** usu piece, bar (?), in phr מִתְרַפֵּס בְּרַצֵּי כָסֶף ψ 68[31], but very obscure and dub, Aq 𝔙 *wheels;* 𝔊 Symm צְרֻפֵי, Che בבצרי כסף, or בְּבֶצַע כ׳, or (JBL[xi (1892) 125]) ברצי כ׳ (i e. mercenaries), Pott We בְּרֹצֵי כָזָב, Du בְּרֹצֵי סֶפֶף.

† II מְרוּצָה **n.f.** crushing, oppression; — Je 22[17] (+ הָעֹשֶׁק)

רַק v. I. רקק; רק v. ריק; רק v. II. רקק.

[רָקַב] **vb.** rot (NH *id.;* Aram. רקב in deriv.);—**Qal** *Impf* 3 ms. יִרְקָב Is 40^{20} (of tree); fig. שֵׁם רְשָׁעִים יִרְקָב Pr 10^{7} (Krochm al. יֻקָּב *be cursed*, √קבב, cf. Toy).

†רָקָב **n.[m.]** rottenness, decay (always fig.);—ר׳ abs; appar. of ravages of worm, in fig Ho 5^{12} (|| עָשׁ) בית יְהוּדָה, cf. Jb 13^{28} (||*id.*), elsewhere of decay of bones, *caries* (in fig.), ר׳ בַּעֲצָמ׳ Hb 3^{16} Pr 12^{4}, cstr רְקַב עֲצָמ׳ 14^{30}.

†רִקָּבוֹן **n.[m.]** id.;—עֵץ ר׳ Jb 41^{19} *wood of rottenness,* =*rotten wood* (in fig.).

†רָקַד **vb. skip about** (NH Pi. Hiph = BH; so Aram. רְקַד Pa., ܪܩܶܕ Pa.; As. *rakâdu, skip, dance;* Ar. رَقَدَ IX. *run with leaps and bounds,* رَقَدَان *leaping up briskly*),—**Qal** *skip about, Pf.* 3 mpl. רָקְדוּ ψ 114^{4} (of mts., כְּאֵילִים); *Impf* 2 mpl. תִּרְקְדוּ v^{6} (id; both of Sinai quaking at law-giving), *Inf. cstr.* עֵת רְקוֹד Ec 3^{4} a time to mourn (סְפוֹד), and *a time to skip about* (gaily). **Pi.** *dance, leap: Impf.* 3 mpl. יְרַקְּדוּ Is 13^{21} (of שְׂעִירִים); יְרַקֵּדוּן Jb 21^{11} (of children, merrily), Jo 2^{5} (of locusts), *Pt* מְרַקֵּד 1 Ch 15^{29} (of David; =מְפַזֵּז, מְכַרְכֵּר, in || 2 S $6^{14.16}$); fs. מְרַקֵּדָה Na 3^{2} (of jolting chariots); in 2 S 6^{21} ins. אֲרַקֵּד *I will dance*, after לִפְנֵי י׳, 𝔊 Th We Dr Bu HPS (מְרַקֵּד). **Hiph.** *Impf.* 3 ms. sf. וַיַּרְקִידֵם ψ 29^{6} *he* (י׳) *made them skip* like calves (trees, by lightning).

רַקָּה v. I. רקק. רַקּוֹן v. II. רקק.

†[רָקַח] **vb. mix,** or compound oil, ointment (perh denom; in this case √ meaning unknown; NH has מִרְקַחַת *ointment,* Ph רקח either *spice-mixer* (Bloch) or *spice-dealer* (Lzb), perh akin to As. *rikku, spice,* Meissn[Suppl 90], cf. *rikkê,* Dl[HWB 630]);—**Qal** *Impf.* 3 ms. יִרְקַח Ex 30^{33}; *Pt* רֹקֵחַ $v^{25.35}$, ר׳ 37^{29} Ec 10^{1}, pl. cstr. רֹקְחֵי 1 Ch 9^{30},—*mix, compound,* Ex 30^{33} (P, כָּמֹהוּ, i e anything like the holy oil), pt. as subst. רֹקְחֵי הַמִּרְקַחַת 1 Ch 9^{30} *compounders of the ointment;* as a professional name, *mixer, perfumer,* Ex $30^{25.35}$ 37^{29} Ec 10^{1}. **Pu.** *Pt* mpl. מְרֻקָּחִים 2 Ch 16^{14} *mixed as ointment* **Hiph.** *Inf abs* הַרְקַח הַמֶּרְקָחָה Ez 24^{10} (|| הָתֵם), as Imv., *spice the spicing* (?), i.e spice (the meat) well, but very dub, Krae prop. הָרֵק הַמָּרָק *empty out the broth*

†רֶקַח **n.[m.]** spice;—יֵין הָר׳ Ct 8^{2} wine, (that is) *spice* (i.e. spiced wine).

†רֹקַח **n.[m.]** spice-mixture, perfume;—of holy oil, ר׳ מִרְקַחַת מַעֲשֵׂה רֹקֵחַ Ex 30^{25}; of incense, ר׳ מַעֲשֵׂה רוֹקֵחַ v^{35}.

†[רַקָּח] **n. m.** ointment-maker, perfumer;—only in phr. בֶּן־הָרַקָּחִים Ne 3^{8}, i.e. one of the perfumers, i e. of that guild.

†[רַקָּחָה] **n.f.** (female) **ointment-maker, perfumer;**—pl. רַקָּחוֹת 1 S 8^{13} (+ טַבָּחוֹת, אֹפוֹת).

†[רִקּוּחַ] **n.[m.]** perfumery;—pl sf רִקֻּחַיִךְ Is 57^{9} *thy perfumeries, unguents.*

†[מֶרְקָח] **n.[m.]** spice, perfume (of cheeks); pl מֶרְקָחִים Ct 5^{13} (v. also מִגְדָּל **3**).

†מֶרְקָחָה **n.f. 1.** ointment-pot, in which ointment is compounded, Jb 41^{23} (fig.). **2.** spice-seasoning (?); as acc. cogn v. √ **Hiph.**

†מִרְקַחַת **n.f. 1.** ointment-mixture. **2.** ointment-pot (?);—**1.** abs רֹקְחֵי הַמּ׳ 1 Ch 9^{30}; ר׳ מ׳ Ex 30^{25}. **2.** בַּמּ׳ 2 Ch 16^{14} *in an ointment-pot* (?), or *as an ointment-mixture.*

†[רָקַם] **vb. variegate** (NH *id;* so Ar. رَقَمَ, Eth. ረቀመ, cf 𝔗 רקם, רִקְמְתָא *variegated cloth* or *skin,* Syr. ܪܘܩܡܐ *freckles*);—**Qal** *Pt. act.* רֹקֵם, as subst. *variegator,* worker (weaver) in colours, c ב mater. Ex 38^{23}, מְלֶאכֶת חָרָשׁ וחשב וְר׳ 35^{35}; esp. מַעֲשֵׂה ר׳ *variegator's work* 26^{36} 27^{16} 28^{39} = 36^{37} 38^{18} 39^{29} (all P; all c mater. exc 28^{39}) **Pu.** *Pf.* 1 s רֻקַּמְתִּי ψ 139^{15} *I was skilfully wrought* (woven, || סכך v^{13})

†רִקְמָה **n.f. variegated stuff** (woven or embroidered),—abs ר׳ Ju 5^{30}+; sf. רִקְמָתֵךְ Ez 16^{18}, ־תָם 26^{16}, du. רִקְמָתַיִם Ju 5^{30}; pl רְקָמוֹת ψ 45^{15};—(piece of) *variegated stuff,* Ju $5^{30.30}$, for garments Ez $16^{10.13}$ $27^{16.24}$ ψ 45^{15}; explicitly, בִּגְדֵי ר׳ Ez 16^{18} 26^{16}, ר׳ appar. = *variegated work* 27^{7}, fig. of variegated plumage 17^{3}; of variegated stone 1 Ch 29^{2}

†רֶקֶם **n.pr. 1 m. a.** a king of Midian Nu 31^{8} (Ροκομ), Jos 13^{21} (Ροβοκ, A Ροκομ, 𝔊 Οροκομ) **b.** a 'son' of Hebron 1 Ch $2^{43.44}$, Ρεκομ, Ροκομ, Ρωκημ. **c.** name in Gilead 1 Ch 7^{16}, 𝔊L Ρακαμ. **2. loc.** in Benj, Jos 18^{27}, Νακαν, A 𝔊L Ρεκεμ[ν].

†[רָקַע] **vb. beat, stamp, beat out, spread out** (NH *id.;* Hiph., Aram. רְקַע Aph, both *spread out,* and deriv, Syr. ܪܩܰܥ *press down* (Lk 6^{38} 𝔖), *spread out,* also *consolidate,* Ar. رَقَعَ *patch, put on a patch, repair,* cf. Chr-Pal. ܡܪܩܥܐ *patch,* ܡܪܩܥܬܐ *swaddling-bands,* Schwally[Idiot 90]; Ph. מרקע *platter,* or *bowl,* of gold CIS[I 90,1]);—**Qal** *Impf.* 1 s. sf. אֶרְקָעֵם 2 S

22[43] *I will stamp them down* (prob. gloss to אֲדִקֵּם preceding, cf. Bae[+ 18, 43]); *Imv* רְקַע בְּרַגְלְךָ Ez 6[11] *beat* (stamp) with thy foot, in token of contemptuous pleasure, cf. Da (|| הַכֵּה בְכַפְּךָ); so *Inf cstr* sf רַקְעֲךָ בְּרֶגֶל 25[6] (|| מַחְאֲךָ יָד); *Pt act* as subst cstr (Ges[§ 65 d]) רֹקַע הָאָרֶץ (i e. י׳) *he that* (beateth out) *spreadeth out the earth* Is 42[5], רֹקַע הָא׳ 44[24], ψ 136[6] רוֹקַע הָא׳ **Pi.** *Impf* 3 ms. sf בַּזָּהָב יְרַקְּעֶנּוּ Is 40[19] a goldsmith *with gold overlayeth it* (lit *beateth it out*), 3 mpl. וַיְרַקְּעוּ אֶת־פַּחֵי הַזָּהָב Ex 39[3] *they beat out the plates of gold*, sf וַיְרַקְּעוּם צִפּוּי Nu 17[4] *they beat them out as plating* **Pu.** *Pt.* כֶּסֶף מְרֻקָּע Je 10[9] *silver beaten out.* **Hiph.** *Impf* 2 ms תַּרְקִיעַ עִמּוֹ לִשְׁחָקִים Jb 37[18] *canst thou make with* (=like) *him a spreading for clouds* (spread out clouds, cf. רָקִיעַ) ?

†רָקִיעַ **n.m.**[Gn 1 6] **extended surface,** (solid) **expanse** (as if *beaten out*; cf Jb 37[18]),—abs. ר׳ Ez 1[22]+, cstr ר׳ Gn 1[14]+;—𝔊 *στερέωμα*, 𝔙 *firmamentum*, cf Syr sub √ supr,—**1.** (flat) *expanse* (as if of ice, cf כְּעֵין הַקֶּרַח), as base, support (Wkl[Altor Forsch iv 347]) Ez 1[22.23.25] (gloss ? cf. CoToy), v[26] (supporting י׳'s throne) Hence (Co[Ez 1 22]) **2.** the vault of heaven, or 'firmament,' regarded by Hebrews as solid, and supporting 'waters' above it, Gn 1[6.7.7.7.8] (called שָׁמַיִם, all P), ψ 19[2] (|| הַשָּׁמַיִם), זֹהַר הָר׳ Dn 12[3]; also ר׳ הַשָּׁמַיִם Gn 1[14 15 17], עַל־פְּנֵי ר׳ הַשׁ׳ v[20] (all P).

†[רִקֻּעַ] **n.[m.] expansion,**— pl cstr. וְעָשׂוּ אֹתָם רִקֻּעֵי פַחִים Nu 17[3] *expansions of plates*, i e they shall be beaten into *broad plates*.

I. **רקק** (√of foll.; Ar. رَقَّ *be thin*, also fig. *be weak, slender, scanty*, etc; Eth. ረቀቀ: *be thin*, ረቂቅ: *thin*; Syr ܪܩ Pa. Aph. *make thin*, ܪܩܝܩܐ *thin*)

רַק †**1 adj. thin**,—fpl. רַקּוֹת, of kine, Gn 41[19 20 27] (|| דַּקּוֹת v[3 4]) **2.**[109] **adv.** with restrictive force, **only, altogether, surely** (syn אַךְ),—**a.** *only*, Gn 14[24] 41[40] רַק הַכִּסֵּא אֶגְדַּל מִמֶּךָּ *only* as regards the throne, etc, 47[22] רַק אַדְמַת הַכֹּהֲנִים לֹא קָנָה, 50[8] Ex 8[5] רַק בַּיְאֹר תִּשָּׁאַרְנָה, 10[17] וְיָסֵר מֵעָלַי רַק הַמָּוֶת הַזֶּה *only* this death, Dt 2[35] (cf. 20[14] Jos 8[2.27]), 3[11] Ju 6[39] (cf אַךְ *ib.* Gn 18[32] Ex 10[17]), 11[34] (circ cl) רַק הִיא יְחִידָה (there being) *only* she, an only one, 1 S 1[13] Am 3[2] רַק אֶתְכֶם יָדַעְתִּי *only* you have I known, etc, Jb 1[15 16 17 19] וָאִמָּלְטָה רַק אֲנִי לְבַדִּי I *only*, ψ 91[8] + oft. Once strengthening אַךְ, †Nu 12[2] הֲרַק אַךְ־בְּמֹשֶׁה דִּבֶּר י׳. And separated (as sts in English) from the word actually emphasized, Pr 13[10] רַק בְּזָדוֹן יִתֵּן מַצָּה by pride there *only* cometh [נָתַן 1 z] contention. **b.** prefixed to *sentences*, to add a limitation on sthg previously expressed (or implied), Gn 19[8] *only* to these men do nothing, 24[8] רַק אֶת־בְּנִי לֹא־תָשֵׁב הֵנָּה, Ex 8[24] I will let you go . . ., *only* go not far, v[25] Nu 20[19] *only*—it is nothing—let me pass through on my feet (cf Dt 2[28]), esp. in Deut. writers, as Dt 10[15] 12[16] 20[16] 1 K 3[2.3] (cf. 2 K 12[4] 14[4] 15[4.35]), 8[19] 11[13] 15[14.23] 2 K 3[2] (cf 14[3] 17[2]), etc, Is 4[1]; emphasizing a command, Dt 4[9] 12[16.23] Jos 1[7 18] 6[18] 13[6] 22[5] (all D[2]) **c.** emphasizing single words, esp adj, *only=nought but, altogether*, Gn 6[5] יֵצֶר מַחְשְׁבוֹת לִבּוֹ רַק רַע is *only* evil, i e *exclusively* evil, *nought but* evil, Gn 26[29] עָשִׂינוּ עִמְּךָ רַק טוֹב *nothing but* good, Dt 28[33] וְהָיִיתָ רַק עָשׁוּק, Is 28[19] רַק זְוָעָה it shall be *nought but* terror to, etc., 1 K 14[8] (cf אַךְ **2 b** β); sq. an adv. Dt 28[13] וְהָיִיתָ רַק לְמַעְלָה above *only*; sq. a vb, Ju 14[16] thou dost *but* hate me. †**d.** after a neg, *save, except* (syn. כִּי אִם **2 a**), 1 K 8[9] אֵין בָּאָרוֹן רַק שְׁנֵי לֻחוֹת הָאֲבָנִים (=2 Ch 5[10]), 15[5] 22[16] (=2 Ch 18[15]), 2 K 17[18]. †**e.** with an affirmative, asseverative force, *only, altogether=surely*, Gn 20[11] רַק אֵין יִרְאַת אֱלֹהִים בַּמָּקוֹם הַזֶּה, Dt 4[6] (so EV, but Ges populus *mere* sapiens, so Di), 1 K 21[25] 2 Ch 28[10] ψ 32[6] רַק לְשֵׁטֶף מַיִם רַבִּים אֵלָיו לֹא יַגִּיעוּ †**f.** רַק אִם (רַק prefixed for emph.) *if only, provided only*, Dt 15[5] רַק אִם שָׁמוֹעַ תִּשְׁמַע וגו׳, 1 K 8[25] (=2 Ch 6[16]) רַק אִם יִשְׁמְרוּ בָנֶיךָ דַרְכָּם לָלֶכֶת וגו׳, 2 K 21[8] (=2 Ch 33[8])

†רָקִיק **n.m. a thin cake,** (RV) **wafer** (cf. Ar. رُقَاقَةٌ *a thin round cake of bread*), always of unleavened bread: Ex 29[23]=Lv 8[26] ר׳ אֶחָד, רְקִיק מַצָּה אֶחָד Nu 6[19], רְקִיקֵי מַצּוֹת Ex 29[2] Lv 2[4] 7[12] Nu 6[15] (all P), 1 Ch 23[29].—𝔊 *λάγανον*.

†רַקָּה **n.f. the temple** (of the head): Ju 4[21] וַתִּתְקַע הַיָּתֵד בְּרַקָּתוֹ, v[22] 5[26] וּמָחֲצָה וְחָלְפָה רַקָּתוֹ, Ct 4[3]=6[7] כְּפֶלַח הָרִמּוֹן רַקָּתֵךְ.

II. [רָקַק] **vb. spit** (NH, Aram רְקַק, ܪܩ, all=BH),—**Qal** *Impf.* 3 ms. יָרֹק Lv 15[8], c. בְּ of pers spit upon.—Cf. יָרַק

†רֹק **n.[m.] spittle**;—abs ר׳ Is 50[6] Jb 30[10] (both of contemptuous spitting); sf רֻקִּי 7[19] while I swallow (בָּלְעִי) *my spittle*, i e for the briefest time.

†רַקּוֹן **n pr.loc.** in Dan, הָר׳ Jos 19[46], prob. doublet of הַיַּרְקוֹן, om 𝔊 Benn Steuern, cf. Di.

†רַקַּת **n.pr.loc.** in Naphtali, Jos 19^{35}; 𝔊 (Ωμαθα) δακεθ, A Ρεκκαθ, 𝔊L Ρακκαθ; a Jewish trad. identified with Tiberias, Talm$^{Jer\ Megilla\ 2b}$ Nbr$^{Geogr\ 208f.}$ Buhl$^{Geogr\ 226}$ GASm$^{Geogr\ 447}$.

רָשׁ v. רושׁ.

רשׁה (√ of foll; cf NH Hiph. *permit*, Hoph Ecclus 3^{22}; JAram רְשָׁא *have power*, Aph. *permit*; OAram. רשי *cause, occasion*, Lzb^{370}, Nab. *allowed*, Id^{ib}; Syr ܪܫܳܐ is usu. *blame*, As. *rašû, possess, râšû, creditor;* Ar. رَسَا(و) *be firm*, iv. *make firm;* Eth. ረሰየ: *set, put in, place over, prepare*, etc; Sab. רשו *servant* of deity JHMordtm$^{ZMG\ xxx\ (1876),\ 31\ f.}$)

†רשׁיון **n.[m.] permission;**—cstr. ר׳ Ezr 3^{7}.

רשׁית v ראשׁית sub ראשׁ.

†[רָשַׁם] **vb. inscribe, note** (NH *id*, so Aram. רְשַׁם, ܪܫܰܡ, Ar. رشم is loan-word No ZMG xxix (1875) 327 Frä$^{137\ 2.0}$),—**Qal** *Pt. pass* c art. as subst. הָרָשׁוּם בכתב אֱמֶת Dn 10^{21} *that which is inscribed in the writing of truth.*

רשׁע (√ of foll.; opp. צדק; cf. Ar. رَسَعَ *be loose* (of limbs) Kam Frey, whence perh. *be (disjointed), ill regulated, abnormal, wicked;* NH רָשָׁע *criminal*, רִשְׁעָה *crime*, vb Hiph. (denom.) *declare guilty;* Aram. רשׁע *be wicked*, ܐܪܫܥ Aph *do wickedly*, and deriv.; Eth. ረሰዐ: usu *forget*, less oft. *err, be wicked*, ረሲዕ: *wicked* (loan-word fr. Syr. ܪܫܝܥܐ Schwally$^{ZMG\ iii\ (1896)\ 13...}$)).

רָשָׁע$_{263}$ **adj. wicked, criminal;**—abs ר׳ Gn 18^{23}+; pl רשׁעים Is 13^{11}+; cstr. רִשְׁעֵי ψ 75^{9} +3 t.; fs רְשָׁעָה Ez 3^{19} (del. Co), v^{19} (רָשָׁע Co);—†**1.** usu. as subst., *one guilty of crime*, deserving punishment, sts. also *wicked;* opp. צַדִּיק; רָשָׁע Ex 2^{13} 23^{1} (E), Dt 25^{2} Pr 17^{23} 18^{5} 25^{5} Jb 9$^{22.24}$, coll. Gn 18$^{23.25.25}$ (J) Mi 6^{10} Pr 3^{33} 28^{4}, רשׁעים 1 S 24^{14} Je 5^{26} Pr 19^{28} 20^{26} 29^{12}, אנשׁים רשׁעים 2 S 4^{11} (murderers), רָשָׁע לָמוּת Nu 35^{31} (P) *guilty of death*, מושׁל ר׳ Pr 28^{15}, cf. 29^{2}, הצדיק ר׳ Ex 23^{7} (E) Is 5^{23} Pr 17^{15}; הִרְשִׁיעַ ר׳ Dt 25^{1} 1 K 8^{32} = השׁיב לְרָשָׁע 2 Ch 6^{23}; אמר לר׳ צדיק Pr 24^{24}. **2.** *guilty of hostility* to God or his people, *wicked enemies*. רשׁע sg ψ 17^{13} + 6 t. ψψ, Is 26^{10}; coll. ψ 9$^{6.17}$ 10^{2} + 6 t. ψψ, Is 11^{4} Hb 3^{13}, רשׁעים ψ 3^{8} 7^{10} 9^{18} + 5 t. ψψ, Is 48^{22} 57$^{20.21}$ Je 25^{31} Ez 21^{34} Mal 3^{21} (+ (poss) other cases; often hard to decide), specif of Pharaoh Ex 9^{27} (J), Babylon Is 13^{11} 14^{5}, Chaldeans Hb 1$^{4.13}$; ‖ שׂנאי יהוה 2 Ch 19^{2}. **3.** *guilty of sin*, against either God or man, *wicked:* האנשׁים הרשׁעים Nu 16^{26} (J, rebellious Korahites), Mal 3^{18} (not serving י׳), opp. צדיק; sg indiv. Ez 3$^{18.18}$ 21^{30} 33$^{8.8}$ ψ 1^{1} 32^{10} Pr 9^{7}+; coll. Is 3^{11} Jb 34^{18} 36$^{6.17}$, pl. רשׁעים Is 53^{9} Je 23^{19} = 30^{23}, Zp 1^{3} ψ 26^{5} Pr 10^{3} Ec 8^{10}+; ‖ חסידים 1 S 2^{9} (poem), ψ 12^{9} 50^{16} 97^{10} 145^{20}, ‖ עֹזְבֵי תוֹרָתֶךָ 119^{53}, cf. v^{61}, +; †אדם ר׳ Pr 11^{7} Jb 20^{29} 27^{13}; איש ר׳ Pr 21^{29}; מלאך ר׳ 13^{17}; זֶרַע רשׁעים ψ 37^{28}; †עֲצַת רשׁעים 1^{1} Jb 10^{3} 21^{16} 22^{18}, †דֶּרֶךְ רשׁעים Je 12^{1} ψ 1^{6} 146^{9} Pr 4^{19} 12^{26}; דֶּרֶךְ רשׁע 15^{9}; מִדַּרְכּוֹ הָרְשָׁעָה Ez 3$^{18.19}$ (but v. Co, supr.); †רִשְׁעֵי (ה)ארץ ψ 75^{9} 101^{8} 119^{119} Ez 7^{21} (𝔊 Co עריצי)—רָשָׁע is rare before exile; chiefly Ez ψψ WisdLit.

†רֶשַׁע **n.m.**$^{1\ 824,\ 14}$ **wickedness**,—abs. ר׳ Mi 6^{10}+, רֶשַׁע Ec 3^{16}; cstr. (perh) רֶשַׁע 7^{25}; sf. רִשְׁעוֹ Dt 9^{27}+, etc;—**1.** *wickedness*, as violence and crime against civil law Ec 3$^{16.16}$; אֶגְרֹף ר׳ Is 58^{4} *fist of wickedness;* חַרְצֻבּוֹת ר׳ v^{6}, לֶחֶם ר׳ Pr 4^{17}; מַטֵּה ר׳ Ez 7^{11}; מֹאזְנֵי ר׳ Mi 6^{11}; אֹצְרוֹת ר׳ v^{10}, cf. Pr 10^{2}, בְּרֶשַׁע ψ 141^{4} Pr 12^{3}; עשׂות ר׳ 16^{12}, מֵרְשָׁעִים יֵצֵא ר׳ 1 S 24^{14} (proverb). **2.** *wickedness* of enemies: of Egypt Ez 31^{11} (dub. Co; gloss Toy); שׁבט הר׳ ψ 125^{3} (𝔊 SS רֶשַׁע). **3.** *wickedness*, in ethical relations. ‖ חטאת Dt 9^{27} (D^{2}); ‖ עָוֹן Je 14^{20}, ‖ עולה Ho 10^{13}; opp. צֶדֶק ψ 45^{8}, אֱמֶת Pr 8^{7}; v. also ψ 5^{5} 10^{15} Jb 34^{10} 35^{8} Ec 7^{25} 8^{8}, אַנְשֵׁי ר׳ Jb 34^{8}, אָהֳלֵי ר׳ ψ 84^{11}; שׁוב מֵרִשְׁעוֹ Ez 3^{19} 33^{12} (v. רִשְׁעָה **3**)

†[רָשַׁע] **vb. denom. be wicked, act wickedly;**—**Qal** *Pf.* 1 s רָשַׁעְתִּי 2 S 22^{22}+, רָשָׁעְנוּ 1 K 8^{47}+; *Impf.* 2 ms תִּרְשַׁע Ec 7^{17}; 1 s. אֶרְשָׁע Jb 9^{29} 10^{7};—**1.** *be wicked, act wickedly*, 1 K 8^{47} = 2 Ch 6^{37}, Dn 9^{15} Ec 7^{17}, + מֵאֱלֹהָי 2 S 22^{22} *(in departing) from my God* = ψ 18^{22}. **2.** *be guilty*, Jb 9^{29} 10$^{7.15}$ **Hiph.** *Pf.* 3 ms. הִרְשִׁיעַ 2 Ch 20^{35}, 3 mpl. הרשׁיעו Dt 25^{1} Dn 12^{10}; 1 pl. הִרְשַׁעְנוּ 9^{5}, etc.: *Impf.* 3 ms. יַרְשִׁיעַ Pr 12^{2}+; יַרְשִׁעֻן Jb 34^{29}; 3 mpl יַרְשִׁיעֻן Ex 22^{8}, etc.; *Inf. cstr* הַרְשִׁיעַ 1 K 8^{32} 2 Ch 22^{3}; *Pt* מַרְשִׁיעַ Pr 17^{15}; pl. cstr. מַרְשִׁיעֵי Dn 11^{32};—**1.** *condemn as guilty*, in civil relations, c. acc. Ex 22^{8} (E) Dt 25^{1} ψ 94^{21} Jb 34^{17} Pr 17^{15}. **2.** *condemn as guilty*, in ethical and religious relations, c acc 1 K 8^{32} Jb 9^{20} 10^{2} 15^{6} 32^{3} 40^{8} ψ 37^{33} Pr 12^{2} Is 50^{9} 54^{17}, abs Jb 34^{29} **3.** *act wickedly* (late), in ethics and religion: Jb 34^{12} (denied of י׳), Ne 9^{33} Dn 12^{10} 2 Ch 22^{3}; ‖ חטא ψ 106^{6} Dn 9^{5}; הרשׁיע לעשׂות 2 Ch 20^{35}, מַרְשִׁיעֵי ברית Dn 11^{32}.—יַרְשִׁיעַ 1 S 14^{47} read יוֹשִׁעַ 𝔊 Capp We Dr Bu HPS.

†רִשְׁעָה **n.f.** wickedness;—abs. ר׳ Is 9^{17}+; cstr רִשְׁעַת Dt 9^{4}+; sf. רִשְׁעָתוֹ Dt 25^{2}+,—**1.** *wickedness* in civil relations, Dt 25^{2} Pr 13^{6} Is 9^{17}, בְּרִשְׁעָתוֹ יִפֹּל רָשָׁע Pr 11^{5}. **2.** *wickedness* of enemies, גְּבוּל ר׳ Mal 1^{4} (Edom), זֹאת הָר׳ Zc 5^{8} (personif); לְרִשְׁעָה Ez 5^{6} (del Co), רִשְׁעַת הַגּוֹיִם Dt $9^{4.5}$. **3.** *wickedness*, ethical and religious, עֹשֵׂה ר׳ Mal $3^{15.19}$, שׁוּב מֵרִשְׁעָתוֹ Ez 18^{27} 33^{19}; רִשְׁעַת (הָ)רָשָׁע 18^{20} 33^{12}.

†מִרְשַׁעַת **n.f.** wickedness,—abs הַמּ׳ 2 Ch 24^{7} Athaliah *the* (embodied) *wickedness*.

רִשְׁעָתַיִם v. כּוּשַׁן ר׳ p. 469.

רשף (√ of foll., Sam. ࠓࠔࠐ *irritavit, incendit*; NH רֶשֶׁף *flame*, Ecclus 43^{17c} רשף *lightning-flame* (? si vera l.), JAram רִשְׁפָּא *flame*, רשף as n. pr. div. in OAram and Ph Lzb[134. 370] Pietschm[Phön 150 ff] EMey[ZMG xxxi (1877). 719] No[ib xlii (1888). 473] Spiegelberg[ZA xiii (1898) 121] Lzb[ib 328] WMM[As. u. Eur. 311 ff] GACooke[Inscr 56 f])

†I. רֶשֶׁף **n.m.**[Hb 3.5] flame, fire-bolt;—abs. ר׳ Dt 32^{24}+, pl רְשָׁפִים ψ 78^{48}, cstr רִשְׁפֵי 76^{4}, רִשְׁפֵי ר׳ אֵשׁ Ct 8^{6}, sf רְשָׁפֶיהָ v.[6],—**1.** *flame*: Ct 8^{6} *its flames* (sc. of אַהֲבָה, קִנְאָה) *are flames of fire*, בְּנֵי ר׳ Jb 5^{7}=*sparks*; ר׳=pointed *flame* of lightning ψ 78^{48} (|| בָּרָד), ר׳ קָשֶׁת 76^{4} sharp *flames of the bow*, fig. for arrows. **2.** *fire-bolt* of י׳, bringing pestilence and death, Dt 32^{24} (cf. Di., || קֶטֶב מְרִירִי), Hb 3^{5} (|| דֶּבֶר).

†II. רֶשֶׁף **n.pr.m.** in Ephr., 1 Ch 7^{25}; Σαραφ, A Ρασεφ, 𝔊L Ρασηφ.

†[רָשַׁשׁ] **vb. Pō̆ēl** beat down, shatter (Syr. ܪܫ *bruise, grind*),—*Impf* 3 ms יְרֹשֵׁשׁ Je 5^{17} one *shall beat down* thy fortified cities. **Pu.** *Pf* 1 pl רֻשַּׁשְׁנוּ Mal 1^{4} *we are beaten down*.

רֶשֶׁת *net*, v. ירשׁ.

†[רָתַח] **vb.** boil (NH *id.*, Ecclus 43^{3} Hiph. *make hot*, Aram רְתַח, ܪܬܚ, *boil*),—**Pi.** *Imv* ms רַתַּח causat. Ez 24^{5} *cause to boil*, bring to boiling, c. acc. rei. **Pu.** *Pf* 3 pl רֻתְּחוּ Jb 30^{27} my bowels *have been made to boil* without quiet (fig. of violent emotion). **Hiph.** *Impf* 3 ms. יַרְתִּיחַ כַּסִּיר מְצוּלָה Jb 41^{23} *he* (the crocod.) *maketh the depth boil like the pot*.

†[רֶתַח] **n.[m.]** boiling;—pl. sf. רְתָחֶיהָ Ez 24^{5}, as acc. cogn. *cause its boilings to boil*, make it boil vigorously; but rd נְתָחֶיהָ Hi-Sm Co Da (poss.) and all mod. (cf. $v^{4.6}$, || עֲצָמִים).

†[רָתַם] **vb. bind, attach** (cf. Ar. رَتِيمَة thread bound to finger as reminder),—**Qal** *Imv* ms. רְתֹם הַמֶּרְכָּבָה לָרֶכֶשׁ Mi 1^{13}.

†רֹתֶם **n.m.**[1 K 19.5] a kind of broom-shrub, **broom-plant, retem** (NH *id.*; Ar. رَتَم (on form Lag[BN 152]); 𝔗 רִיתְמָא, all=BH),—abs. ר׳ אֶחָד 1 K 19^{5}, ר׳ אחת v^{4} Kt (אֶחָד Qr), pl שֹׁרֶשׁ רְתָמִים לַחְמָם Jb 30^{4} (on text v. Bu Che[infr]); גַּחֲלֵי רְתָמִים ψ 120^{4}, Rob[BR i. 84. 203. 205. 300] Löw[No. 313] Post[Hastings DB s. Juniper] Che[Ency Bib Juniper].

†רִתְמָה **n.pr.loc.** station in wilderness, Nu $33^{18.19}$, Ραθαμα, 𝔊L Ραμαθα.

†[רָתַק] **vb. bind** (Ar. رَتَقَ *close up* and *repair, sew up*; Talm רִיתְקָא *fenced enclosure*),—**Pu.** *Pf.* 3 pl רֻתְּקוּ בַזִּקִּים Na 3^{10} her great ones *were bound with fetters*. **Niph.** *Impf* 3 ms יֵרָתֵק Ec 12^{6} Qr (ירחק Kt), from context=*be snapped, broken*; read prob. יִנָּתֵק (Pfannkuche Thes and mod.).

†[רַתֻּקָה] **n.[f.]** chain (?);—pl. cstr. רַתֻּקוֹת כֶּסֶף Is 40^{19}.

†רַתּוֹק **n.[m.]** chain (on form Lag[BN 89]),—abs הָר׳ עֲשֵׂה Ez 7^{23}, i.e. for captives, but very dub.; Co עֲרֵה וּבָקוֹק, Krae עֲשֵׂי הַבַּתּוּק (ב׳=As. *butâku, obstruction*); hence perh. also pl. cstr. רַתִּיקוֹת זָהָב 1 K 6^{21} Qr (Kt רתיקות), *chains of gold* before the דביר in temple.

רַתּוּקוֹת, רַתִּיקוֹת v. foregoing.

רתת (√ of foll.; NH רֶתֶת, Aram רְתַת, ܪܬ, all *tremble*; cf. רטט)

†רְתֵת **n.[m.]** trembling (on form Lag[BN 178] Ba[§7b]),—ר׳ Ho 13^{1} (si vera l.) *when Ephr spoke trembling* (AV Che al.); Ew al. *spoke terror*, Hi Ke RV *spoke, there was trembling*; text dub. (v. Now).

שׂ

שׂ *Sîn*, 21st letter (with שׁ, q.v.).

שׂאר (√of foll.; vb. unknown; cf. NH שְׂאוֹר, סְאוֹר; JAram. סִיאוֹרָא, all *leaven*).

†**שְׂאֹר** n.m.$^{Ex 12,19}$ leaven;—abs. שׂ׳ Ex 13^{7} (J), Dt 16^{4} (D), Ex 12$^{15.19}$ Lv 2^{11} (all P).

שְׂאֵת v. נשׂא. **שָׂב** v. שׂיב.

שׂבך (√of foll.; *interweave;* NH סְבָךְ, der. spec., שְׂבָכָה *hair-net*, etc.; Ar. شَبَكَ *insert, interweave;* Syr. ܣܒܟ *rush in, adhere, embrace, be mixed* with, ܣܒܟܐ *velum reticulatum;* cf. As. *šabikû, headdress,* Dl $^{HWB 638}$).

†**שׂוֹבֶךְ** n.[m.] network of boughs;—cstr. שׂ׳ הָאֵלָה 2 S 18^{9}.

†**שְׂבָכָה** n.f. lattice-work, network;—abs. ר׳ 1 K 7^{18}+, pl. שְׂבָכוֹת v^{41}+, שְׂבָכִים v^{17};—**1.** prob. window-*lattice* 2 K 1^{2}. **2.** net-ornament on pillars, 1 K 7$^{17.17}$ (om. 𝔊 Kit Benz), v$^{18.20}$ (crpt., cf. Kit Benz), v$^{41.42.42}$ 2 Ch 4$^{12.13.13}$ 2 K 25$^{17.17}$ ‖ Je 52$^{22.23}$. **3.** *network, toils,* for catching animals (fig.) Jb 18^{8} (+ רֶשֶׁת, פַּח, צַמִּים).

שְׂבָכִים v. שְׂבָכָה.

†**שְׂבָם** n.pr.loc. Nu 32^{3}, שִׂבְמָה v^{38} Jos 13^{19} Is 16$^{8.9}$ Je 48^{32}; in Moab (Reuben), near Heshbon (cf. also Jerome$^{Is 16,8}$); Σεβαμα.

שָׂבַע, [שָׂבֵעַ]$_{96}$ vb. be sated, satisfied, surfeited (NH (der. spec.)=BH; so As. *šebû*, Ar. شَبِعَ, Aram. סְבַע, ܣܒܥ, Palm. שׂבע; the Eth. vb. of same meaning is ጸግበ);—**Qal**$_{79}$ *Pf.* 3 ms. שָׂבַע 1 Ch 23^{1}, וְשׂ׳ consec. Dt 31^{20}; 3 pl. שָׂבְעוּ Is 9^{19}, וש׳ consec. Dt 14^{29} 26^{12}, etc.; *Impf.* 3 ms. יִשְׂבַּע Pr 12^{11}+, 3 mpl. יִשְׂבְּעוּן ψ 104^{28}, etc.; *Imv.* שְׂבַע־ Pr 20^{13}; *Inf. abs.* שָׂבוֹעַ Jo 2^{26} 2 Ch 31^{10}; cstr. לִשְׂבֹּעַ Ex 16^{8} La 5^{6}, לְשָׂבְעָה Hg 1^{6};—**1.** *be sated* (with food), esp. human subj.: **a.** abs., after אָכַל, Ho 4^{10} Is 9^{19} Dt 8^{10}, Ex 16^{8} (P), + 11 t., cf. Is 44^{16} (‖ אָכַל); exposing men to arrogance Dt 6^{11} 8^{12} 31^{20}, cf. Ho 13$^{6.6}$ (Isr. under fig. of cattle), Je 50^{19} (id.; c. ב loc.; ‖ רָעָה *graze*); =have (or get) enough to eat ψ 37^{19} 59^{16}, enough to drink Am 4^{8}, fig. of sword Je 46^{10}, of wine Hb 2^{5}. **b.** c. acc. of food Je 44^{17} La 5^{16} Ex 16^{12} (P), + 6 t., cf. Ez 39^{20} (of beasts, in fig.), of earth, sated with water (rain) Pr 30^{16}, so of trees (acc. om.) ψ 104^{16}, fig. of requital Pr 18^{20b}. **c.** c. מִן of food Jb 19^{22} (fig.); fig. of earth having its fill (of rain) ψ 104^{13}, and (fig. of requital) Pr 18^{20a}; good sense 12^{14} (del. טוֹב, so Toy), bad sense 1^{31} 14^{14}; c. מִן of source Is 66^{11} (fig.). **2.** more gen., *be sated,* have desire satisfied: **a.** abs. Ez 16$^{28.29}$ (i.e. with harlotry), Je 50^{10} (with plunder), Is 53^{11} (with a given result); of eyes Pr 27^{20}, of Sheʾôl and Abaddôn v^{20}, cf. 30^{15}; =have abundance Pr 30^{9} (exposure to arrogance). **b.** c. acc., *be satisfied with, have one's fill of:* Je 31^{14}, cf. ψ 17^{15} 63^{6}, Pr 5^{10} Ec 5^{9}, cf. (eye subj.) 4^{8}, acc. of sons ψ 17^{14} (si vera l., but text dub., v. Ol Du, cf. Bae We), days of life, i.e. reach the full limit (+ זָקֵן) 1 Ch 23^{1} 2 Ch 24^{15}. **c.** c. ב of goodness ψ 65^{5}, c. מִן id. Ec 6^{3}. **d.** c. ל inf., לֹא־תִשְׂבַּע עַיִן לִרְאוֹת Ec 1^{8} (‖ מָלֵא). **3.** *have in excess, be surfeited with:* **a.** lit., with honey (acc.) Pr 25^{16}. **b.** fig.=*be weary of,* c. acc. of offerings Is 1^{11} (subj. י׳), tossings Jb 7^{4}, poverty Pr 28^{19}, shame Hb 2^{16}, contempt ψ 123$^{3.4}$, c. acc. pers. Pr 28^{17}. **c.** id., c. ב of troubles ψ 88^{4}, of reproach La 3^{30}. †**Niph.** *Pt.* נִשְׂבָּע *sated* Jb 31^{31}. †**Pi.** *satisfy, Impf.* 3 mpl. יְשַׂבֵּעוּ Ez 7^{19} *they shall* not *satisfy* their appetite (נֶפֶשׁ ‖ מִלֵּא); *Imv.* ms. sf., subj. י׳, שַׂבְּעֵנוּ חַסְדֶּךָ ψ 90^{14} (2 acc.). †**Hiph.** *Pf.* 3 ms. הִשְׂבִּיעַ ψ 107^{9}, וְה׳ consec. Is 58^{11}; 2 fs. הִשְׂבַּעַתְּ Ez 27^{33}, etc.; *Impf.* 3 ms. sf. יַשְׂבִּעֵנִי Jb 9^{18}, 2 ms. תַּשְׂבִּיעַ Is 58^{10}, 1 s. וְאַשְׂבִּעַ Je 5^{7}, sf. אַשְׂבִּיעֶךָ ψ 81^{17} van d. H., אַשְׂבִּעֶךָ Baer Gi, etc.; *Inf. cstr.* לְהַשְׂבִּיעַ Jb 38^{27}; *Pt.* מַשְׂבִּיעַ ψ 103^{5} 145^{16};—**1. a.** *satisfy* (esp. with material blessings), subj. י׳, c. acc. pers. Je 5^{7} (exposing men to arrogance), Is 58^{11} (acc. נֶפֶשׁ; of refreshment in drought, ב loc., fig. of help and blessing), ψ 107^{9} (acc. נֶפֶשׁ; ‖ מִלֵּא), cf. 103^{5} (ב instr., on acc. v. עֶדְיֵ׳); c. acc. of ground Jb 38^{27} (i.e. with rain); human subj., c. acc. נֶפֶשׁ Is 58^{10}. **b.** c. acc. of food + pers., י׳ subj., ψ 81^{17} (‖ הֶאֱכִיל), 105^{40} 132^{15} 147^{14}; c. acc. pers. + אֹרֶךְ יָמִים 91^{16}. **c.** י׳ subj., acc. rei + ל pers., מַשׂ׳ לְכָל־חַי רָצוֹן ψ 145^{16}. **d.** י׳ subj., c. acc. of beasts + מִמְּךָ (of Pharaoh, in prophetic fig.) Ez 32^{4}. **2.** *enrich,* subj. Tyre, c. acc. gent. Ez 27^{33} (‖ הֶעֱשִׁיר). **3.** *sate, glut* (with the undesired), subj. י׳, c. acc. pers. + ב rei La 3^{15}, acc. pers. + rei Jb 9^{18}.

†**שָׂבָע** n.[m.] satiety, abundance;—abs. לָשׂ׳ Ex 16^{3}+, cstr. שְׂבַע ψ 16^{11}, לְשׂ׳ Pr 13^{25}; sf. שָׂבְעֲךָ Dt 23^{25}, שָׂבְעָהּ Ru 2^{18};—**1.** *satiety,* as to

food Ru 2^{18}; אָכַל (לֶחֶם) לָשֹׂבַע Ex 16^{3} (P), Lv 25^{19} 26^{5} (both H), cf ψ 78^{25}; אָכַל . . . כְּנַפְשְׁךָ שׂ׳ Dt 23^{25} *eat* grapes *according to thine appetite*, (namely) *thy fill*, cf אָכַל לשׂ׳ נפשׁו Pr 13^{25}. **2.** *satisfying abundance*, שׂ׳ שְׂמָחוֹת ψ 16^{11}

†[שָׂבְעָה] ,[שבעה] **n.f. satiety**,—abs. שׂ׳ Is 56^{11}+, cstr שִׂבְעַת־ Ez 16^{49}, sf שָׂבְעָתֵךְ v^{28},—**1.** as to food, esp אָכַל לשׂ׳ *eat to satiety, one's fill*, Is 23^{18} Ez 39^{19}, לשׂ׳ also Is 55^{2} (fig), שׂ׳ of dogs 56^{11} (fig), שׂ׳־לֶחֶם leading to arrogance, as sin of Sodom Ez 16^{49} (+ גָּאוֹן, etc) **2.** as to carnal desire Ez 16^{28} (fig)

†שָׂבָע **n.m.** $^{Gn\ 41,29}$ **plenty, satiety**,—only abs שׂ׳,—**1** *plenty*, of bread-stuffs Gn $41^{29.30.31\ 34\ 47\ 53}$ (E), Pr 3^{10} **2.** *satiety*, Ec 5^{11}.

†שָׂבֵעַ **adj sated, satisfied, surfeited**;—abs שׂ׳ Gn 25^{8} Pr 19^{23}, cstr. שְׂבַע Dt 33^{23}+, fs שְׂבֵעָה Pr 27^{7}; mpl שְׂבֵעִים 1 S 2^{5},—**1. a** *sated* with food, c בַּלֶּחֶם 1 S 2^{5}, נֶפֶשׁ שׂבעה Pr 27^{7} (opp נ׳ רעבה), *abounding in* י׳'s favour (שְׂבַע רָצוֹן) Dt 33^{23} (‖ מָלֵא), abs *satisfied* Pr 19^{23}. **b.** in phr שְׂבַע יָמִים *satisfied with days*, in a good old age, Gn 35^{29} (P), Jb 42^{17} (both + זָקֵן), 1 Ch 29^{28} (+ בשׂיבה טובה), also abs שָׂבֵעַ Gn 25^{8} (P; + *id* + זָקֵן) **2** bad sense, surfeited with trouble, etc: שְׂבַע רֹגֶז Jb 14^{1}, שׂ׳ קָלוֹן 10^{15}.

†I [שָׂבַר] **vb. inspect, examine** (van d H שבר [so 𝔊 συντρίβων], but Mas שׂ׳ v. Norzi, hence connex with Ar. سَبَرَ *probe* a wound, *try, examine*, improb, and this (acc to Fra^{261}) denom. from Aram loan-word; improb also is connex with Aram סבר *think* (cf foll.), Kau $^{Aram.\ in\ AT,\ 84}$),—**Qal** *Pt* שׂבר, c ב obj, Ne $2^{13\ 15}$ *I examined into* the wall, inspected it closely.

†II [שָׂבַר] **vb. Pi. wait, hope** (Aramaism; cf Aram סְבַר *think*, Pa *hope*, ܣܒܰܪ *believe, hope*, Pa *think*, Aph *hope*),—*Pf* 1 s. שִׂבַּרְתִּי ψ 119^{166}, 3 pl שִׂבְּרוּ Est 9^{1}, *Impf* 3 mpl. יְשַׂבְּרוּ Is 38^{18}, יְשַׂבֵּרוּ ψ 145^{15}, יְשַׂבֵּרוּן ψ 104^{27}, 2 fpl תְּשַׂבֵּרְנָה Ru 1^{13},—**1.** *wait* for, ל pers, Ru 1^{13} **2.** *hope* for, ל rei ψ 119^{166}, אֶל rei Is 38^{18}, אֶל pers. ψ 104^{27} 145^{15}, ל inf Est 9^{1} *hope to rule*.

†[שֵׂבֶר] **n.m. hope**;—sf. שִׂבְרִי ψ 119^{116}, שִׂבְרוֹ עַל־י׳ 146^{5}

[שָׂגָא] **vb. grow, grow great** (√only in Job, Aramaism, cf Aram סְגִי, סְנָא, ܣܓܳܐ, all *increase, grow great*; OAram. BAram. Palm. שׂגי(א) adj *much*),—**Qal** *Impf.* 3 ms. metapl. יִשְׂגֶּא Jb 8^{11} (of plant; metapl form Ges$^{§\ 75\ oo}$; > van d. H יִשְׂגֶּה). **Hiph. 1.** *make great*, pt מַשְׂגִּיא לַגּוֹיִם Jb 12^{23} *he maketh the nations great* (v. ל 3 b) **2.** *magnify, laud*, 2 ms. תַשְׂגִּיא פָעֳלוֹ Jb 36^{24} that *thou magnify his work*.—Vid. שׂגה.

†שַׂגִּיא **adj. great**;—of God, abs. אֵל שַׂגִּיא Jb 36^{26}, cstr שַׂגִּיא־כֹחַ 37^{23}

†[שָׂגַב] **vb. be** (inaccessibly) **high** (cf 𝔗 שַׂגֵּב Pa. [from Heb] *exalt*),—**Qal** *Pf.* **1.** 3 fs. שָׂגְבָה Dt 2^{36}, of city, c מִן, *be* (too) *high* for capture. **2.** 3 mpl. שָׂגְבוּ Jb 5^{11} of pers, *be high* in prosperity. **Niph.** *Pf.* 3 ms. נִשְׂגָּב Is $2^{11\ 17}$, נִשְׂגָּב Pr 18^{10}, 3 fs נִשְׂגְּבָה ψ 139^{6}; *Pt.* נִשְׂגָּב Is 12^{4}+; fs. נִשְׂגָּבָה Is 26^{5}+;—**1.** *be high*, walls Is 30^{13} Pr 18^{11}, city Is 26^{5}; God's knowledge ψ 139^{6} (unattainable) **2.** *be* (safely) *set on high*, Pr 18^{10}. **3.** *be exalted*, of God Is $2^{11\ 17}$ 33^{5}, his name 12^{4} ψ 148^{13}. **Pi.** *Impf.* 3 ms יְשַׂגֵּב Is 9^{10} ψ 107^{41}, sf יְשַׂגֶּבְךָ 20^{2}, etc.,—trans. c. acc.: **1.** *set* (securely) *on high*, ψ 20^{2} 69^{30} 91^{14}, c מִן, of foe 59^{2}, affliction 107^{41}. **2.** *exalt*, in effective hostility, c עַל, Is 9^{10} **Pu.** *Impf.* 3 ms. יְשֻׂגָּב Pr 29^{25} *be set* (securely) *on high*. **Hiph.** *Impf.* 3 ms יַשְׂגִּיב Jb 36^{22} God *acts exaltedly* בְּכֹחוֹ.

†שְׂגוּב **n.pr.m.** (*exalted*),—**1.** son of rebuilder of Jericho (Hiel) 1 K 16^{34} Qr (Kt שְׂגִיב, Ζεγουβ, 𝔊L om. v.). **2.** of Judah 1 Ch $2^{21\ 22}$ (Σερουχ, 𝔊L Σεγουβ).

†I מִשְׂגָּב **n.** [**m.** Albr. $^{ZAW\ xvi\ (1896),\ 60}$] **secure height, retreat**,—מ׳ ψ 9^{10}+, cstr מִשְׂגַּב Is 25^{12}; sf מִשְׂגַּבִּי ψ 18^{3}+, etc;—**1. a.** = stronghold, מִבְצַר מ׳ חוֹמֹתֶיךָ Is 25^{12}. **b.** fig of security Is 33^{16}. **2.** fig of God as refuge ψ $9^{10\ 10}$, 18^{3} = 2 S 22^{3}, ψ $46^{8\ 12}$ 48^{4} $59^{10\ 17\ 18}$ $62^{3\ 7}$ 94^{22} 144^{2}.

†II. מִשְׂגָּב perh. **n.pr.loc.** in Moab,—הַמּ׳ Je 48^{1} (v. Schwally $^{ZAW\ viii\ (1888),\ 198}$ Albr$^{l.\ c.}$), Αμαθ; Gf thinks appell. of Kir Moab (v. II קִיר); most sub I. מ׳ **1.**

†[שָׂגָה] **vb. grow, increase** (late, ‖ form of שׂגא),—**Qal** *Impf.* 3 ms. יִשְׂגֶּה ψ 92^{13} righteous *shall grow great* like cedar (‖ יִפְרָח), cf. Jb 8^{7} (opp מִצְעָר, v^{11} see שׂגא) **Hiph.** *Pf.* 3 pl. הִשְׂגּוּ־חָיִל ψ 73^{12} *they have increased riches*.

שׂגיב v. שְׂגוּב. שׂגשׂג v. II סוג.

† [שָׂדַד] **vb. Pi.** **harrow** (שׂדד *id.* Ecclus 38[25 marg 26]; cf. As. *šadâdu, draw, drag*);—*Impf.* 3 ms. יְשַׂדֵּד Jb 39[10] (of beast), human subj, c. acc. of ground Is 28[24] (+ יְפַתַּח, || יַחֲרֹשׁ); יְשַׂדֶּד־לוֹ Ho 10[11] (|| יַחֲרוֹשׁ; fig. of Jacob)

† שִׂדִּים **n.[m.] pl.** in **n.pr.loc.** עֵמֶק הַשּׂ׳ *vale of Siddim* Gn 14[3] (identif. with Dead Sea), v[8. 10] (= *vale of furrows?* or (Di after Onk Sam) *of fields* (= הַשָּׂדִים); 𝔊 ἡ κοιλὰς [φαραγξ] ἡ ἁλυκή; Renan Hist. Isr i 116; Eng Tr. i 98 We Isr u Jüd. Gesch. (3) 101 prop ע׳ הַשֵּׁדִים *demon-valley*).

שׂדה (√ of foll., meaning unknown; foll. plausibly connected with As. *šadû, mountain*, used by people whose *land* was *mountainous* (cf. Ju 5[18] Dt 32[13]+), by JPPeters JBL xii (1893), 54 f. and (simultan.) Ba ES (1893), 65 f cf. Wkl Altor Forsch ii (1894), 192; Jäger BAS ii. 282 cp. As *šêdtum, pasture-land;* Tel Am (Canaan. gloss) *šatê* Wkl Tel Am. 180, 56; Ph. שד = BH, NH = BH, so Ecclus 40[22]).

† שָׂדַי **n.m.** ψ 96, 12 **field, land** (rare orig form of שָׂדֶה (q v. infr.), only poet);—abs. שׂ׳ Je 4[17], שָׂדָי Ho 10[4]+,—**1.** cultivated *field* 12[12], also 10[4] (si vera l., but v. Now), yielding food Dt 32[13] La 4[9], שֹׁמְרֵי שׂ׳ Je 4[17] *keepers, watchmen, of a field* **2.** home of wild beasts. בהמות שׂ׳ ψ 8[8] Jo 2[22], חַיְתוֹ שׂ׳ Is 56[9] ψ 104[11], זִיז שׂ׳ 50[11] 80[14]. **3.** plain, opp. mt., Je 18[14] (but dub, Co Du שִׁרְיֹן) **4.** *land*, opp. sea, ψ 96[12] (cf שָׂדֶה **3**; || תבל ψ 98[7]).

שָׂדֶה **n.m.** 318 Lv 27 24 id (ordinary contr. form Ges § 84a f).—abs שׂ׳ Gn 2[5.5]+, cstr. שְׂדֵה 14[7]+; sf שָׂדִי Je 32[7.8], שָׂדְךָ Dt 11[15]+, שָׂדְךָ 24[19] Lv 25[3], etc.; pl. שָׂדוֹת 1 S 22[7]+, cstr. שְׂדוֹת Ne 12[29]; also שְׂדֵי 2 S 1[21] Is 32[12] Ru 1[1]+8 t (some might be sg = שְׂדֵה cf Ba ZMG xlii (1888), 341 SS Buhl; note, e.g שְׂדֵי Ru 1[6a], = שדה v[b] 4[3], but v. Ko ii 1, 77); sf שְׂדֹתֶיהָ Ne 11[30], etc.; also שָׂדֶיךָ 1 K 2[26], שָׂדֵינוּ Mi 2[4],—**1.** open *field*, country **a.** pasture-land Gn 29[2] 30[16] Ex 9[3] (all J), Dt 11[15] 1 S 11[5]+10 t. J, JE **b.** unfrequented Gn 24[63.65], exposed to violence 4[8] (J), 2 S 14[6] Dt 21[1] 22[25.27], to wild beasts Ex 22[30] (E), Ez 33[27]. **c.** specif. home of beasts: 2 S 17[8] Je 14[5]; esp. phr חַיַּת הַשּׂ׳ Gn 2[19.20] 3[1.14] (all J) of beasts in gen., and, of wild beasts, Ex 23[11.29] (E), Ho 2[14.20] 4[3] 13[8] Dt 7[22] Lv 26[22] (H), Jb 5[23] (|| חַיַּת הָאָרֶץ), + 16 t.; בְּהֶמַת הַשּׂ׳ 1 S 17[44] cf Jo 1[20]; אַיְלוֹת הַשּׂ׳ Ct 2[7] 3[5], cf. הַצְּבָיִם אֲשֶׁר בַּשּׂ׳ 2 S 2[18]; hunting-ground Gn 25[29] 27[3.5] (all JE), cf. אִישׁ שׂ׳ 25[27] (JE, || אִישׁ יֹדֵעַ צַיִד). **d.** yielding plants and trees: Gn 25[27] (JE), 30[14] (J), Ex 10[5] (JE), 2 K 4[39] Ez 21[2] 39[10]; esp. phr. עֵשֶׂב הַשּׂ׳ Gn 2[5] 3[18] (both J), + 6 t. + עֵ׳ בַּשּׂ׳ Zc 10[1]; שִׂיחַ הַשּׂ׳ Gn 2[5], גֶּפֶן שׂ׳ 2 K 4[39], פַּקֻּעֹת שׂ׳ v[39], צִיץ הַשּׂ׳ Is 40[6] ψ 103[15], צֶמַח הַשּׂ׳ Ez 16[7], עֵץ הַשּׂ׳ (4 t. עֲצֵי׳) Ex 9[25] (JE), Dt 20[19] Lv 26[4] (H) Is 55[12]+8 t; 2 S 1[21] v. תְּרוּמָה, √ רום. **e.** stony, אַבְנֵי הַשּׂ׳ Jb 5[23]. **f.** *open country*, outside of walled city Ju 9[32.42.43.44] 19[16] 1 S 19[3] 20[5.11.11.24.35] 2 K 7[12] Mi 4[10]; as battle-ground Jos 8[24] (J), 2 S 10[8] = 1 Ch 19[9], 2 S 11[23] 18[6], outside of military camp 1 S 4[2] 14[15]; opp. city (in formula) 1 K 14[11] 16[4] 21[24] Je 14[18] Ez 7[15]; שְׂדֵה אֶרֶץ Lv 25[31]; as site of small town, *country*-town 1 S 27[5] (opp. royal city), cf. 1 Ch 27[25], of high places, גְּבָעוֹת בַּשּׂ׳ Je 13[27]; quite gen., 1 S 30[11] Je 40[7.13]; including road Ju 20[31] 1 K 11[29] Je 6[25]; disting from road Nu 22[23] (JE), 2 S 20[12]; outside houses and courtyards Ex 8[9] (P), 1 S 25[15]; בַּשּׂ׳ nearly = *outdoors* Ex 1[14] (P), Ju 13[9]; of surface of country or ground, בַּשּׂ׳ Ex 16[25] (JE, = עַל־פְּנֵי הַמִּדְבָּר v[14]), cf. 1 S 14[25], so עַל־פְּנֵי הַשּׂ׳ (אֶל) 2 K 9[37] Je 9[21] Ez 29[5] (|| הַמִּדְבָּרָה), 32[4] 39[5], same phr. opp house, comfort, etc., 2 S 11[11] Ez 16[5], opp. city Lv 14[7.53], opp tent Nu 19[16] (all P), opp. tent of meeting Lv 17[5] (H). **g.** = expanse of country, opp. mt, in phr. מְרוֹמֵי שׂ׳ Ju 5[18]; הֲרָרִי בַּשּׂ׳ Je 17[3] (of Jerus.) is dub.; cf. לְעִי הַשּׂ׳ Mi 1[6] (Je 18[14] v שָׂדַי). **2.** definite portion of ground, *field, land:* **a.** cultivated ground Gn 37[7] (E), 47[24] (J; זֶרַע הַשָּׂדֶה), Ex 22[4.4.4.5] (E), Lv 27[16.17] (P), Mi 3[12] (in sim.) Ru 2[2]+47 t., + שְׂדֵי תְרוּמוֹת 2 S 1[21], שׂ׳ זֶרַע Ez 17[5], שָׂדֶה טוֹב v[8] *good soil.* **b.** as private property, Mi 2[2.4] Is 5[8.8] Gn 47[20] (J), 23[9.11.13] (P) + 50 t., + 2 Ch 26[23] (as burial-place); also חֶלְקַת (הַ)שּׂ׳, v. חֶלְקָה; and שׂ׳ צֹפִים, v. צפה. **c.** city-land, adjacent to city (town) and subject to its control. Gn 41[48] (E), Lv 25[34] (P), Jos 21[12] (P) = 1 Ch 6[41], Ne 11[25.30] 12[29.44]; specif of Zoan ψ 78[12.43]. **d.** territory of nation, tribe· Gn 32[4] Nu 21[20] (both JE), Ju 5[4] Ru 1[1.2] Gn 14[7]+13 t.+ שְׂדֵה נַחֲלַת יִשׂ׳ Ju 20[6]. **e.** territory of king, 2 S 9[7] 13[30]. **3.** *land*, opp. sea, 1 Ch 16[32] (opp. הַיָּם; = שָׂדַי ψ 96[12]), perhaps also *mainland* Ez 26[6.8] (Co Krae Toy al.; not Sm).

שִׂדִּים v. שׂדד   שְׂדֵרָה v. סדר.

† שֶׂה **n.m.** Gn 30, 32 and (less oft.) **f.** Je 50, 17 **one of a flock, a sheep (or goat)** (As. *šu'u*, Ar. شَاةٌ, pl. شِيَاهٌ, شَوِيٌّ, etc (also *wild ox*), cf Egypt. *sau, sheep* Bondi 65, cf Id Ba NB § 2 b d);—abs. שֶׂה Gn 30[32]+, cstr. שֵׂה Is 43[23]+; sf. שֵׂיוֹ Dt 22[1], שֵׂיהוּ 1 S 14[34]; not in pl.;—**1.** *a sheep*, or *goat*, nom. unit. of צֹאן: as property Gn 32[32.32] (J; + צאן

coll., כְּשָׂבִים ,עִזִּים), Ex 21[37.37] (+ שׁוֹר ,צֹאן coll.), 22[3] (+ חֲמוֹר ,שׁוֹר), v[8] (id), v[9] (id, all E); Dt 22[1] (+ שׁוֹר), 1 S 17[34] (זה Kt van d H erron, v Baer Di), roaming pasture Is 7[25], straying ψ 119[176] (sim.), slaughtered Is 53[7] (in sim), + חֲמוֹר ,שׁוֹר + Ju 6[4] 1 S 22[19] Jos 6[21] (J), + id + גָּמָל 1 S 15[3], as sacrifice Gn 22[7.8] (J), Ex 13[13] Lv 5[12] 12[8] Nu 15[11] (ש׳ בַּכְּבָשִׂים או בָעִזִּים, all P), Dt 18[3] (+ שׁוֹר), Is 43[23] 66[3] (+ שׁוֹר), מִן־הַצֹּאן Ez 45[15]; cf. Ex 34[19] (+ שׁוֹר), v[20] (J). Lv 27[26] (P, + שׁוֹר), fit for sacrifice Lv 22[28] (H), unfit v[23] (H), Dt 17[1] (both ש׳ כשבים וש׳ + שׁוֹר); as food 1 S 14[34] (+ שׁוֹר), ש׳ עִזִּים Dt 14[4] (+ id), for passover Ex 12[3.3.4.4.5] (P), fig. of Isr. Ez 34[17.17] (|| עַתּוּדִים ,אֵילִים), v[20.20.22.22]. **2.** coll *flock* שֶׂה פְזוּרָה Je 50[17] (= צֹאן אֹבְדוֹת v[6])

†[שָׂהֵד] **n.[m.] witness** (Aram loan-word = Heb עֵד, √ סהד, ܣܗܕܐ),—sf שָׂהֲדִי Jb 16[19] (|| עֵדִי)—שָׂהֲדוּתָא Gn 31[47] v BAram Lex

שהר (√ of foll., cf Ar شَهْرٌ *new moon* (شَهَّرَ is *make conspicuous, notorious*), Eth ሠሀር: *id*, 𝔗 סִיהֲרָא, Syr ܣܗܪܐ *moon*, OAram שהר *moon-god* Lzb[373])

†[שַׂהֲרֹן] **n [m.] moon, or crescent**,—only pl הַשַּׂהֲרֹנִים of (non-Israel) ornaments of camels Ju 8[21], kings v[26], women Is 3[18], 𝔊 μηνίσκοι, 𝔙 (Is 3[18]) *lunulae*, on crescent as ornament v. Dozy[II 760] Lane[Egypt II 314] Perles[Anal 79], cf Fra[68]

שׂוא v נשא p 670 a I, II שׂוג v. I, II. סוג

שׂוּחַ Gn 24[63] v. I שׂוּם

†[שׂוּט] **vb. swerve, fall away** (akin to שָׂטָה q v, NH סוּט Hiph. is *shake, move away*; As *šâṭu, rebel*, Meissn[90], Eth ሠየጠ: *bring back, restore*, in 𝔗 *apostatize* is סְטָא),—**Qal** *Pt* pl cstr וְשָׂטֵי כָזָב ψ 40[5] *those falling away to falsehood* (Gunk[Schöpf 40] וְשָׂטָה)

†[שֵׂט, סֵט] **n.[m] swerver, revolter** (?), **deeds that swerve** (fr the right?),—pl וְשַׁחֲטָה שֵׂטִים הֶעְמִיקוּ Ho 5[2] *and revolters have gone deep in slaughter* (or שַׁחַתָה *in corruption*), but dub; We Bae Now GASm, cf. Gu[Kau], וְשַׁחַת הַשִּׁטִּים הע׳ *and the pit of Shittim they have made deep*, עֲשֹׂה סֵטִים ψ 101[3] *to do deeds that swerve* I hate.

†I. [שׂוּךְ] **vb. hedge or fence up, about** (= II סוּךְ, q v),—**Qal** *Pf* 2 ms שַׂכְתָּ בַעֲדוֹ Jb 1[10] *hast fenced him about* (protectingly), *Pt* שָׂךְ Ho 2[8] I *will hedge up* (obstruct) *thy way* (acc)

†[מְשׂוּכָה] **n f. hedge** (= מְסוּכָה),—cstr מְשֻׂכַּת חָדֶק Pr 15[19] (in sim)—מְשׂוּכָתוֹ v III. שׂכך.

II **שׂוֹךְ** (? || II שׂבך · cf. NH סוֹכָה; Aram. סוֹכָא ,סוֹכְתָא, ܣܘܟܐ (ms), ܣܘܟܬܐ,—all *branch*).

†[שׂוֹךְ] **n.[m.] branch or brushwood**,—sf 3 ms שׂוֹכֹה Ju 9[49] (Ges[1910], but v GFM Bu).

†[שׂוֹכָה] **n.f. id.**;—cstr. שׂוֹכַת עֵצִים Ju 9[48]+ perhaps abs. שׂוֹכָה v[49] (so 𝔊 Doorn for MT שׂוֹכֹה).

†שׂוֹכוֹ ,שׂוֹכֹה **n.pr.loc.** in Judah: **1.** in Shephelah, שׂוֹכֹה Jos 15[35] 1 S 17[1] (fr. 𝔊 Σοκχωθ HPS (after We, cf Dr) conj שׂוֹכוֹת), שׂוֹכוֹ 2 Ch 11[7] 28[18], perhaps also שֹׂכֹה 1 K 4[10] (Buhl Benz SS ['perh.'], Th Kit sub **2**), mod *Eš-Šuwêke*, SSE. fr. Beth Shemesh, in Wady-es-Sant Rob[BR I 494] Buhl[Geogr 194], Σωχω, Σοκχωθ, etc **2.** in hill-country, Jos 15[48] (Kt שׂוכה, Qr שׂוכו), prob. also שׂוֹכוֹ 1 Ch 4[18] ('son' of חֶבֶר), mod *Šuwêke*, 4 h S of חֶבְרוֹן Rob[BR II 16 21] Buhl[Geogr 164], Σωχω(ν)

†שׂוּכָתִים **adj. gent. m. pl.** a family of scribes 1 Ch 2[55], Σωχαθιειμ, 𝔊L Σουχαθειμ

I **שׂוּם, שִׂים** 582 **vb. put, place, set** (cf. No[ZMG xxxvii (1883), 532]; NH סוּם Pi *designate, fix*, שׂוּם Ecclus 45[5c] 49[6], Ph. שׂם, As *šâmu, fix, determine*; Sab. שׂים *set, set up*, SabDenkm[No. 7.1 6] CIS[iv 1], Ar شَامَ (ى) is *insert, sheathe*, also *compute*; Eth. ሠየመ: *put, place*, 𝔗 שׂוּם, Syr ܣܳܡ, OAram שׂים),—**Qal** *Pf* 3 ms שָׂם Gn 21[14]+ (2 Ch 1[5] rd. שָׂם 𝔊 𝔙 Gi Be Kau Benz), sf. שָׂמוֹ Ez 17[4]+, שָׂמָהוּ 7[20], 3 fs שָׂמָה 1 S 19[13], sf שָׂמַתְהוּ Ez 19[5] 24[7]; 2 ms שַׂמְתָּ Je 32[20]+, 3 pl שָׂמוּ Gn 40[15]+; 1 pl. שַׂמְנוּ Is 28[15], etc, *Impf* 3 ms יָשִׂים Ex 4[11], יָשֵׂם Gn 30[42]+, יָשֵׂם Jb 23[6]; juss יָשֵׂם 1 S 22[15]+, וַיָּשֶׂם Gn 2[8]+; sf. יְשִׂמֵנִי 2 S 15[4], וַיְשִׂימֵךְ 1 K 10[9], 2 fs וַתָּשִׂימִי Is 51[23], וָאָשִׂים 1 S 28[21]+, וָאָשִׂימָה Ezr 8[17] Ju 12[3] Qr (Kt ואישמה); 2 mpl תְּשִׂימוּ Gn 32[17]+, תְּשִׂימֻן Ex 22[24]+, etc; *Imv* ms. שִׂים Gn 24[2]+, etc; *Inf. abs* שׂוֹם Dt 17[15]+, cstr שׂוּם 45[7]+, שִׂים Jb 20[4]+2 S 14[7] Qr (Kt שׂוּם), שִׂימוֹ Is 10[6] Kt (Qr שׂוּמוֹ), etc.; *Pt* שָׂם Am 7[8]+, fs. הַשָּׂמָה Is 51[10] (so rd for MT הַשָּׂמָה); pl שָׂמִים Mal 2[2]+; *pass.* שִׂים Nu 24[21] (cf Di), Ob[4]; f. acc to most שׂוּמָה 2 S 13[32] (van d H. שׂימה Kt), but v. infr; שִׂימָה ψ 56[9] Bae Buhl, but most Imv. ms;—*put, set* (oft. || נָתַן **2**, q v), c. acc. pers vel rei (expr. or impl): **1. a.** *put, set*, in a place, + שָׁם Gn 2[8] (J), + acc. loc 28[11] (E) + 5 t +, c. 2 acc. + loc., 2 K 10[8] *heads* (in) *heaps* at (acc loc.), cf. Lv 24[6] (עַל), + בְּ 40[15] (E), fig of י׳, *put* his name, בירוש׳ 2 K 21[4.7] = 2 Ch 33[7], cf. c שָׁם 1 K 9[3] Dt 12[5] + 6 t; esp. בְּ

of receptacle Gn 31^{34} (E), Ex 2^{3} (E), Ju 6^{19} + oft.; sackcloth on (ב) loins Gn 37^{34} (J), 1 K 20^{31}, crown on head Zc 6^{11} Est 1^{17}, shoes on feet Ez 24^{17}, hook, etc, in nose 1 K 19^{28} = Is 37^{29} Jb 40^{26}, incense בְּאַפֶּךָ Dt 33^{10}, i.e. cause thee (׳י) to smell it; feet in stocks (fig.) Jb 13^{27} 33^{11}, knife into throat Pr 23^{2} (fig. of self-restraint, Fl in De), words into mouth Ex 4^{15} (J), Nu 22^{38} (E) + 8 t, + Dt 31^{19} teach to say or sing; into heart Jb 22^{22}, ins. also 1 S 29^{10} 𝔊 Th We Dr Kit Bu HPS, trust in God ψ 78^{7}, (guilt of) blood into house Dt 22^{8}, cf. Ju 9^{24} (עַל pers.; so, c. נָתַן Dt 21^{8} Je 26^{15} Jon 1^{14}); something into hand Ex 4^{21} (E), of wonders, i e enable hand to do them, elsewhere = take, of hammer Ju 4^{21}, booty 1 K 20^{6}, so (fig) *take one's life* (נֶפֶשׁ) *into one's palm* (i.e. risk it) Ju 12^{3} 1 S 19^{5} 28^{21} Jb 13^{14}, put eyes בַּפּוּךְ 2 K 9^{30} (v. פּוּךְ, cf. Is 54^{11}); נפשׁ (= *person*), בַּחַיִּים ψ 66^{9} (subj. ׳י); *set* men *at* (the use of) implements 2 S 12^{31} (prob, cf Dr HPS; > וַיָּשַׂר(ם) *sawed them with*, as ‖ 1 Ch 20^{3}, Th We), 1 K 2^{5} (‖ נתן) is dub; 𝔊L Klo Kit rd וַיִּקֹּם, *charge* something *against* (ב pers.; properly *put in*, i.e. attribute, impute, to) 1 S 22^{15} Jb 4^{18}; so, c. ל pers. Dt 22^{14}, cf (ל om) v^{17}; *put* בְּקֶרֶב Am 7^{8} Is 63^{11}, בתוך Ez 26^{12}. **b.** *put* something *upon* (עַל) Nu 21$^{8.9}$ (E) + oft.; jewels, clothes, on person Gn 24^{47} (J), 41^{42} (E), Lv 8^{8} (P), Ru 3^{3}, turban Zc 3$^{5.5}$ Ex 29^{6} (P), Lv 8^{9} (P), cf. (prep. om) Jb 24^{15} 36^{13} (fig), girdle Je 13$^{1.2}$, sackcloth 1 K 21^{27}, שׂ׳ אָדָם עֲלֵי־אָרֶץ Jb 20^{4} (of man's creation), of siege and siege engines, עַל = *against*, Mi 4^{14} Ez 4^{2} 23^{24}; *put, lay, upon* (עַל), 2 K 4^{29} +; hand Gn 48^{18} (J) + 3 t., + *upon mouth*, in silence Ju 18^{19} Jb 21^{5}, and awe Mi 7^{16}, so c ל Jb 29^{9}, לְמוֹ 40$^{4.40}$, upon (עַל) head 2 S 13^{19} (in despair, cf. Je 2^{37}); acc of disease Ex 15^{26} (J), so (ב pers) v^{26} Dt 7^{15}, fig, spirit (עַל) Nu 11^{17} (JE), name 6^{27} (P), duty Jb 37^{15} (?), reproach 1 S 11^{2}, רָעָה תַּחַת טוֹבָה ψ 109^{5} (𝔊 Bae וַיָּשִׁיבוּ, so, or וַיְשַׁלְּמוּ, Hup Che); שׂ׳ עַל לֵב Ct 8^{6} (sim.), so, fig., = remember, treasure up, Is 42^{25} 47^{7} (‖ זָכַר), + 6 t., c. אֶל 2 S 13^{33} 19^{20} (‖ id); c. ב 1 S 21^{13}; cf. שׂ׳ בְּאָזְנֵי Ex 17^{14} (E), impress upon **c.** *put, lay, set*, c. ל, 2 K 11^{16} *lay* (violent) *hands on* = 2 Ch 23^{15}; *put* end *to* Jb 18^{2} 28^{3}; set לְמָרוֹם 5^{11}, *render* glory *to* Jos 7^{19} (JE; ‖ נָתַן), Is 42^{12}; *make* covenant *with* 2 S 23^{5}; *set* food *for* Gn 43^{32} (J), 2 S 12^{20}, prep om Gn 43^{31} (J), so, c לִפְנֵי 1 S 9^{24} 28^{22} 2 K 6^{22}, שׂ׳ לפני elsewhere Ju 18^{21}, of precedence Gn 48^{20b} (E), *set* laws (as authoritative) לִפְנֵי Ex 19^{7} 21^{1} (both E), Dt 4^{44}; God (as moral ruler) לְנֶגְדָּם ψ 54^{5} 86^{14}, שׂ׳ נֶגֶד also Gn 31^{37} (E), נֹכַח Ez 14$^{4.7}$; לְעֵינֵי Gn 30^{41} (J). **d.** *put*, c. בֵּין Jos 24^{7} (E) + 5 t. (Ex 8^{19} v. פדות p. 804), + Gn 30^{36} (J), 32^{17} (E), *put* space *between*; c. תַּחַת Ex 17^{12} (E), + 3 t. (Ob^{7} del. לַחְמְךָ We GASm Now al) + שׂ׳ יָד תַּחַת יְרֵכִי in oath Gn 24$^{2.9}$ 47^{29} (all J); *put*, c אֶל loc. 1 S 6$^{11.15}$ 19$^{13.16}$ Hb 2^{15}, אֶל pers. Jb 5^{8} *commit unto*; c אֵצֶל rei Lv 6^{3} (P), מִצַּד rei Dt 31^{26} (P), שׂ׳ עִמָּךְ 1 S 9^{23} *lay up* something *with thee*, reserve it, *put*, c יַחַד Mi 2^{12} *put together* = collect (‖ קִבֵּץ, אָסַף); without modifier 1 K 18$^{23.23.25}$; Ez 30^{21} *apply* bandage (‖ נָתַן). **2.** *set, direct*: **a.** sword against (ב) Ju 7^{22}; fig *extend* compassion, ל pers. Is 47^{6}. **b.** *direct* לֵב (*mind*) *toward*, pay attention to, c. ל, 1 S 9^{20} Dt 32^{46} Ez 40^{4} 44^{5b}, c. אֶל Ex 9^{21} (J), 1 S 25^{25} 2 S 18$^{3.3}$ Jb 2^{3} 34^{14} (Bu Du del. לב and rd. יָשִׁיב רוחו); c. עַל Hg 1$^{5.7}$ Jb 1^{8}; compl om. Ez 44^{5a} Hg 2$^{15.18.18}$ Is 41^{22}; Ju 19^{30} read perh. לִבְבְכֶם for לָכֶם (or עֵצָה for עֻצוּ), v. esp. GFM$^{Heb. Hpt}$; לֵב om, Is 41^{20} (+ תַּשְׂכִּיל, יָדַע, רָאָה), c. ב pers. Jb 23^{6} (so Bu, who cps. 4^{20} 24^{12} 34^{23}, but all cases dub.); שׂים לב, c. עַל = *intend* Dn 1^{8} (obj cl.) **c.** *set* face (פָּנִים) toward (acc. loc) Gn 31^{21} (E), + לָבוֹא Je 42$^{15.15.17}$ 44^{12}, cf. 2 K 12^{18} Dn 11^{17}, c. אֶל, *toward* or *against* (implying opposition) Ez 6^{2} + 5 t. Ez, c עַל Ez 29^{2} 35^{2}, c. דֶּרֶךְ of direction 21^{2}, c. ב (fig of oppos., subj ׳י, הנני שָׂם פָּנַי בכם לְרָעָה Je 44^{11}, cf. 21^{10} Ez 15^{7} (‖ נתן), Lv 20^{5} (P); c ל rei (human subj.) Dn 11^{18} Qr (< Kt ישׁב); c. עַל pers + לִמְלֹךְ of purpose 1 K 2^{15}, *set* eyes (עֵינַיִם) upon, c. עַל pers = behold Gn 44^{21} (J), = look after, take care of, Je 39^{12} 40^{4}, לְטוֹבָה 24^{6}, but לְרָעָה Am 9^{4}. **3. a.** *set, ordain*, c acc. rei Nu 24^{23} (> acc. pers. Di). **b.** *set, establish* a law, statute, + ל pers Ex 15^{25} Jos 24^{25} (both E), cf Pr 8^{29}; + ב loc. Is 42^{4} ψ 78^{5} (‖ הֵקִים), also 81^{6} Je 33^{25} + 2 S 20^{19} (שָׁמוּ) for שְׁלֻמֵי 𝔊 Ew We Kit Bu HPS, cf. Dr), *establish* something as (ל) law Gn 47^{26} (J), 1 S 30^{25} (+ ל pers); *establish* bazaars (as a right), ב loc, 1 K 20^{34}; *appoint* a set time Ex 9^{5} (J), Jb 34^{23} (rdg. מוֹעֵד for עוֹד GHBWr Bu), ins. (perh) 1 S 13^{8} so Dr Klo HPS (> ins. אמר Th We Bu Kit, after 𝔊 𝔗); a place, + ל pers. Ex 21^{13} 2 S 7^{10} = 1 Ch 17^{9}, ל rei 1 K 8^{21} (+ שָׁם). **c.** *set, found* a nation, Is 44^{7} (si vera l.), *establish* it ψ 89^{30} (לָעַד). **d.** *set, appoint* (as ruler, official) + עַל pers. vel gent., Ex 1^{11} 5^{14} 18^{21} (all E), Dt 17$^{14.15.15.15}$ Ju 11^{11} (+ ל of office), 2 S 17^{25} (+ תַּחַת

instead of) + 6 t. + Gn 47⁶ (J; second acc. = ruler, expressed), 2 S 23²³ (אל), על in ‖ 1 Ch 11²⁵; also 2 acc + ל and ב loc ψ 105²¹, ב loc 2 S 15⁴ 2 Ch 33¹⁴, בראש *at the head of*, Dt 1¹³, 2 acc alone Ct 1⁶, c acc pers. + ל pers Gn 27³⁷ (E), Ho 2² 1 S 8⁵ (+ inf); + ל of title Gn 45⁸·⁹ Ex 2¹⁴ (+ על, all E) + 4 t + Ju 8³³ (+ ל pers), + Ez 44⁸ (perh rd וַתְּשִׂימוּם Hi Sm Co and most), + ל of purpose Hb 1¹², + ב of position, ל pers 1 S 8¹¹, c acc of office alone 1 S 8¹² (+ ל pers), so Co Ez 21²⁷ (שָׂרִים for כָּרִים, v כַּר sub כרר), 1 K 20²⁴ (+ תחת), cf. 2 Ch 23¹⁸, + על, + אל, of task Nu 4¹⁹ (P), Jb 7²⁰ *set me as* (ל) *mark for* (ל) *him* **e.** *set, constitute, make*, c. ב pers vel rei, Gn 13¹⁶ (J) *I will make thy seed as the dust*, 32¹³ (J) 48²⁰ (E), Dt 10²² Ho 11⁸ + 16 t + (bad sense) Ho 2⁵ Na 3⁶ 1 K 19² **f** *set, determine, fix*, bounds Je 5²² (2 acc) Jb 38⁵·³³ ψ 104⁹, pass. *determined, settled*, + על־פה 2 S 13³² (but v. II שום), *appoint, send*, frogs לפרעה Ex 8⁸ (J), c acc pers + על *against* 2 K 18¹⁴. **4. a.** *set, station*, at a post, etc, acc pers Jos 8¹³ (JE), + ב loc 2 K 10²⁴ Je 9⁷ + 5 t, + adv. acc Gn 33² (J), + בין loc Jos 8¹², + ל (against) and אַחֲרֵי loc v² (both JE), + ל against Ju 9²⁵ (+ על loc), + אל against 20²⁹·³⁶, doubtful are 1 S 15² (c ל pers), 1 K 20¹²·¹² (עַל־הָעִיר), where no obj expr (in MT), either an obj has fallen out, or vb (in techn. military sense), here intrans or inwardly trans (Dl ZK ii 397 *forward! take direction toward*, cf also [on Sm] We Dr Lohr), or else שׂ׳ is corrupt (cf HPS Sm) **b** *put* in position, sacred bread, sword, staves, bars, c acc 1 S 21⁷ Ez 21²⁷ Nu 4⁶·⁸·¹¹·¹⁴ + 4 t P, Jb 38¹⁰, + על Ex 32²⁷ (E), 40²⁰ (P), ל מִמַּעַל Je 43¹⁰, מֵעַל Est 3¹, + (various modifiers) 8 t, *set in place*, חבל Jb 34¹³ (De al.), but context favours שָׂכַר Bu, Du שׂ׳ לבו בתבל **c.** *set up* altars 1 K 2¹⁹ Je 11¹³, stone as memorial Gn 18¹⁸ (J), 28²² (E), 1 S 7¹² (cf הקים Gn 31⁴⁵ +), image, etc Ju 18³¹ (‖ הקים), Dt 27¹⁵ 1 K 12²⁹ (ב loc, ‖ נָתַן), 2 K 21⁷ (ב loc.) = 2 Ch 33⁷, cf. ψ 74⁴ Is 57⁸ and, + ב loc, Je 7³⁰ 32³⁴, rods before (לעיני) cattle Gn 30⁴¹ (‖ וַיַּצֵּג v³⁸), cf v⁴², guide-posts Je 31²¹, bed 2 K 4¹⁰ (+ ל pers) **d.** = plant, wheat Is 28²⁵, tree 41¹⁹ (ב loc, ‖ נָתַן), slip Ez 17⁵ (על *by*). **e** *set, fix* (countenance) 2 K 8¹¹, so usu, but acc om, and sense dub, read perh וַיִּשֹּׁם (√ שׁמם, cf e g 1 K 9⁸), so Klo Kmp Kit Benz **5. a.** *make* a thing, or pers. (acc), *for, transform into* (ל), Jos 6¹⁸ (J) make camp לחרם, Mi 1⁶ *make Samaria* לְעִי, Gn 21¹³·¹⁸ (E), Ex 14²¹ (JE), Mi 4⁷ (both good sense), Is 28¹⁷ 42¹⁵·¹⁶ + 12 t. Is. (25² rd עיר for מעיר Vrss Comm), Je 2⁷ + 8 t Je, + 14 t + Ju 1²⁸ *they made the Can. into the corvée*, ψ 85¹⁴ וְיָשֵׂם לְדֶרֶךְ פְּעָמָיו *maketh his steps into a way* (so RV Hup Che Dr, but meaning obscure, De Bae *attend to the way of* (לב om); Schr Hup-Now rd (וישמר ד׳), c 2 acc. Jos 8²⁸ (J), 1 S 11¹¹ Mi 1⁷ 1 K 5²³ (prægn. c. עד loc), + 29 t **b.** *make, constitute*, 2 acc, 1 S 8¹ 18¹³ (+ ל pers) 22⁷ (לְכֻלְּכֶם, ל of acc, or < rd. וְכֻלְּכֶם), Is 3⁷ 60¹⁷ + 6 t, + 1 S 11¹¹ *form people in bands*, cf Jb 1¹⁷ (one acc., *form bands*), + (acc. pers om) Ex 4¹¹ᵇ (J), cf (beast, in fig) Ez 19⁵, 2 acc and acc. + ל in same ver, Is 54¹² *I will make rubies thy pinnacles, and* (transform) *thy gates into carbuncles*, in phr of naming, שָׂם שְׁמוֹ יִשְׂרָאֵל 2 K 17³⁴, cf. Ju 8³¹ Ne 9⁷, c. ל, וַיָּשֶׂם לָהֶם שמות Dn 1⁷, וי׳ לְדָנִיאֵל בֵּלְטְשַׁאצַּר v⁷, *make, fashion*, c. acc rei + ל pers Ex 4¹¹ᵃ (J; י׳ subj); grave Na 1¹⁴ (but on text and mng. v Now Bi SB Wiener Ak 1894, Abh v); c acc דֶּרֶךְ Is 43¹⁹ (ב loc), cf Ez 21²⁴·²⁵ (+ ל inf.), ψ 50²³ is dub, usu. *order* (one's) *way*, De Dr *prepare way* (which), etc, Gr Che תם for שָׂם, *make* name + ל pers. 2 S 7²³ = 1 Ch 17²¹, 2 S 14⁷; *make* for, ל pers (or *give* to), c. acc of posterity Gn 45⁷ (E), 1 S 2²⁰ rd prob. יְשַׁלֵּם 𝔊 We Kit Bu HPS, cf Dr, Ezr 10⁴⁴ᵇ is obscure, Gu-Batten del. וַיָּשִׂימוּ and rd וַיְשַׁלְּחוּ bef נָשִׁים, cf. 3 Esdr 9³⁶ Be-Ry Ryle. **c.** *work, bring to pass*, c acc. rei, of י׳'s signs, etc, + ב loc. Ex 10² (J), Je 32²⁰ Is 66¹⁹ ψ 46⁹ 78⁴³ 105²⁷. **d.** *appoint, give*, acc rei Nu 6²⁶ (P), Is 61³ (‖ נָתַן, both c ל pers); a pledge Jb 17³ (‖ עָרְבֵנִי *go surety for me*, but rd perh עָרְבֹנִי as obj, v p. 786 b), וְשׂוֹם שֶׂכֶל Ne 8⁸ *giving understanding* (making sense clear) †**Hiph.** *Pf* 1 s consec. וַהֲשִׂמֹתִיהוּ Ez 14⁸, acc. pers. + ל, *I will make him for a sign* (< שׁ for שׂ van d. H, √ שׁמם, Co Berthol Toy וַשְׁמֹתִיהוּ (Qal), Krae וְהִשְׁמַדְתִּיהוּ); *Imv*. fs. הָשִׂימִי 21²¹, prob. del as dittogr. Co Krae after 𝔊 𝔖 𝔙 𝔗 No ZMG xxxvii (1883), 530 (> Bo Toy al. הקדימו); *Pt.* מֵשִׂים Jb 4²⁰ = **Qal** (לב) שׂוּם (v²³ᵇ), but phr. dub, and text perh. crpt., v. Me No l.c. †**Hoph.** *Impf* 3 ms וַיּוּשַׂם Gn 24³³ Qr (Kt ויישם Ges § 73 f) *there was set before him* (לְפָנָיו) *to eat*, cf. Ol MB Ak. 1870 389 Ko i 433, who read also וַיּוּשַׂם 50²⁶ *he was laid* in (ב) a mummy-case (for MT וַיִּישֶׂם), Di (ed 4.5.6) allows this.

†[יְשִׂימְאֵל] **n.pr.m.** Simeonite (*Él establisheth*), — ויש׳ 1 Ch 4³⁶ (van d. H. Gi, Baer (וישימאל), 𝔊L Ισμαηλ.

†תְּשׂוּמֶת **n.f.** (deposit, then, cstr. (ת׳ יָד) **pledge, security,** Lv 5^{21} (P; ‖ פִּקָּדוֹן).

II. שׂוּם, שׂים (perh. √ of foll.; cf. Ar. شَأَمَ *be inauspicious,* شُؤْمٌ *ill-luck*).

†שׂוּמָה (van d. H. שימה Kt) perhaps **n.f.** **token of unluckiness, scowl;**—2 S 13^{32}, so Ew$^{G\ iii.\ 234,\ H.\ 172}$ (abbrev. fr. שׂמאל; or emend. שִׂמְחָה) We RS$^{Ency.\ Brit.\ (9)\ David}$ Kit, cf. Dr HPS.

†[שׂוּר] **vb.** saw (‖ form of נָשַׂר; denom. fr. מַשּׂוֹר ?);—**Qal** *Impf.* 3 ms. וַיָּשַׂר 1 Ch 20^{3} (but v. שׂים **1 a**).—Ho 9^{12} v. סור; Ju 9^{22} Ho 8^{4} v. שׂרר; 12^{5} v. שׂרה.

†שׂוֹרָה Is 28^{25} prob. dittogr. for foll. שְׂעֹרָה (Koppe We Che al.; 𝔊 𝔖 om.); > 𝔙 Ges Di al. *in rows* (adv. acc.; but NH שׁוּרָה, Ar. سُورٌ, Lag $^{GGN,\ 1889,\ 298}$; cf. Vogelst$^{Landwirthsch.\ 41}$ who favours שׂ׳ in Is. More plausible would be some grain, as שורה Zinj. Inscr., Lzb^{374} Sachau$^{Panammu\ 23}$).

†שׂוּשׂ, שִׂישׂ **vb. exult, rejoice** (Nö$^{ZMG\ xxxvii\ (1883),\ 536}$ der. ('perh.') fr. interj., as شَأْشَأْ an enticing call, so Gerber^{20});—**Qal** *Pf.* 3 ms. שָׂשׂ Dt 28^{63}+, 1 s. שַׂשְׂתִּי ψ 119^{14}, etc.; *Impf.* 3 ms. יָשִׂישׂ Dt 28^{63}+, 3 mpl. יְשֻׂשׂוּם Is 35^{1} (Ges$^{§\ 47\ n}$ Kö$^{i.\ 510}$, but ם erron. Kenn Ol$^{§\ 244\ a}$, prob. dittogr., so Lo Hi Gr Che^{Hpt} Marti), etc.; *Imv.* fs. שִׂישִׂי La 4^{2}, mpl. שִׂישׂוּ Is 65^{18} 66^{10}; *Inf. abs.* שׂוֹשׂ 61^{10}; *cstr.* לָשׂוּשׂ Dt 30^{9};—*exult, display joy,* c. עַל *over,* Dt $28^{63.63}$ $30^{9.9}$ Je 32^{41} Is 62^{5} Zp 3^{1}(+בְּשִׂמְחָה); ‖ (גִּיל), ψ 119^{162}; c. ב Is 61^{10} (שׂוֹשׂ אָשִׂישׂ), 65^{19} ψ 35^{9} (all ‖ גִּיל); 40^{17} 68^{4} (+בְּשִׂמְחָה ‖ עָלַץ), 70^{5} (all ‖ שָׂמַח); 119^{14} Jb 39^{21} (horse), ψ 19^{6} (sun, as athlete); c. כִּי and cl. La 1^{21}; abs. Is 35^{1} 65^{18} (both ‖ גִּיל), 64^{4} (but del. שָׂשׂ וְ 𝔊 Gr Du Che^{Hpt} Marti), 68^{14}; La 4^{21} (‖ שִׂמְחִי), Jb 3^{22} (‖ שְׂמֵחִים אֱלֵי־גִיל), Is 66^{10} (acc. cogn.; ‖ שִׂמְחוּ, גִּילוּ).—Ez 21^{15} is crpt., Co rds. לְאַנְשֵׁי (for נָשִׂישׂ), Krae לִנְשִׂיאֵי, other conj. in comm.; on cl. vid. esp. Da Toy$^{Heb.\ Hpt.}$.

†שָׂשׂוֹן **n.m.**$^{Is\ 51,\ 3}$ **exultation, rejoicing;**—abs. שׂ׳ ψ 45^{8}+, שָׂשֹׂן Est 8^{16}; cstr. שְׂשׂוֹן (Sta$^{§\ 296\ e}$) ψ 51^{14} 119^{111};—*exultation, joy* (esp. in י׳'s favour), Jo 1^{12} Is 12^{3} ψ 51^{14} 105^{43} 119^{111}; שֶׁמֶן שׂ׳ (i.e. with which guests were anointed; fig.) ψ 45^{8} Is 61^{3} (opp. אֵבֶל); שֵׁם שׂ׳ Je 33^{9} (‖ תְּהִלָּה); on text v. Gie Albr$^{ZAW\ xvi\ (1896),\ 115}$); elsewh. ‖ שִׂמְחָה: Je 7^{34} 15^{16} 16^{9} 25^{10} 33^{11} Is 22^{13} (only here condemned as reckless, wanton), 35^{10} $51^{3.11}$ Zc 8^{19} ψ 51^{10} Est $8^{16.17}$; ‖ שָׂמֵחַ Je 31^{13} (opp. אֵבֶל).

†מָשׂוֹשׂ **n.m.**$^{Is\ 24,\ 8}$ id.;—abs. מ׳ Is 32^{13}+, cstr. מְשׂוֹשׂ Jb 8^{19}+; sf. מְשׂוֹשִׂי Je 49^{25}, מְשׂוֹשָׂהּ Ho 2^{13};—*exultation,* in gen., La 5^{15} (opp. אֵבֶל), Is 24^{11} 66^{10} (acc. cogn.); of bridegroom 62^{5}; מ׳ תֻּפִּים 24^{8}, מ׳ כִּנּוֹר v^{8}; בָּתֵּי מ׳ 33^{13}; of Jerus. (as causing joy) 60^{15} ψ 48^{3} La 2^{15}, cf. Je 49^{25} (מ׳ דּוֹדִי ‖ קִרְיַת מְשׂוֹשִׂי), Is 65^{18} (‖ גִּילָה); (of godless man) Jb 8^{19}; מ׳ פְּרָאִים Is 32^{14}, i.e. desert.—מ׳ Is 8^{6}, si vera l., is cstr. before prep., but (מִפְּנֵי) מָסוֹס, Hi Gie Che Du Kit Marti al.

שִׂחַ v. שׂיח.

†[שָׂחָה] **vb. swim** (NH שָׂחוּ *swimming;* 𝔗 סְחָא, Syr. ܣܚܐ *swim, bathe,* also סַחְיָא, סַחְיָנָא, שַׂחְיָנָא *swimmer;* Aph. *wash*);—**Qal** *Pt.* + *Inf. cstr.* כַּאֲשֶׁר יְפָרֵשׂ הַשֹּׂחֶה לִשְׂחוֹת Is 25^{11}. **Hiph.** *Impf.* 1 s. אַשְׂחֶה ψ 6^{7} *I make* my bed *swim* (with my tears; another view sub שׂיח **Qal 1**).

†שָׂחוּ **n.**[**m.**$^{Sta\ §\ 192\ a}$] **swimming** (on format. (and tone) Ges$^{§\ 84\ a\ c}$ Kö$^{ii.\ 1,\ 60,\ 497}$);—מֵי שׂ׳ Ez 47^{5}.

†[שָׂחַט] **vb. squeeze out** (so NH סָחַט, Aram. סְחַט; Mand. סחט *spread out* Nö$^{M\ 238}$);—**Qal** *Impf.* 1 s. וָאֶשְׂחַט Gn 40^{11} (E; אֶת־הָעֲנָבִים אֶל).

†[שָׂחִיף] **adj.** (?), doubtful (van d. H. שְׂחִיף; √ unknown);—cstr. שְׂחִיף עֵץ Ez 41^{16} usually *panelled, wainscotted, with wood;* or **n.** *a wainscot of wood,* but Co חִפּוּי, Toy חִפּוּי (cstr. חִפּוּי).

†שָׂחַק **vb. laugh** (‖ צחק, q.v.; NH שָׂחַק, סְחַק; Eth. ሠሐቀ:);—**Qal** *Pf.* 3 ms. וְשָׂ׳ consec. Pr 29^{9}; 3 pl. שָׂחֲקוּ La 1^{7} Jb 30^{1}; *Impf.* 3 ms. יִשְׂחַק Jb 39^{7}+, etc.; *Inf. cstr.* שְׂחוֹק Ju 16^{21} Ec 3^{4};—**1. a.** *laugh* at, usu. in contempt, derision, c. עַל pers. Jb 30^{1} ψ 52^{8}; עַל rei La 1^{7}; c. לְ pers. God subj. ψ 37^{13} 59^{9} (‖ לָעַג); c. לְ rei vel pers. = have no fear of, Hb 1^{10} Jb 5^{22} Pr 31^{25}, also, fig., of noble animals Jb $39^{7.18.22}$ 41^{21}; abs., Pr 29^{9} (opp. רָגַז), of י׳ ψ 2^{4} (‖ לָעַג), of wisdom Pr 1^{26} (ב temp.; ‖ *id.*). **b.** c. אֶל pers., appar. of friendly laugh Jb 29^{24}; in gen. Ec 3^{4} (opp. בָּכָה). **2.** *sport, play,* Ju 16^{27}. **Pi.** *Pf.* 1 s. וְשִׂחַקְתִּי 1 S 6^{21}; *Impf.* 3 ms. וַיְשַׂחֵק־ Ju 16^{25}, etc.; *Inf. cstr.* לְשַׂחֶק־ ψ 104^{26}; *Pt.* מְשַׂחֵק Pr 26^{19} 1 Ch 15^{29}, f. מְשַׂחֶקֶת Pr $8^{30.31}$; pl. מְשַׂחֲקִים 2 S 6^{5}+, מְשַׂחֲקוֹת 1 S 18^{7};—**1.** *make sport,* Ju 16^{25} (לְ pers.) 2 S 2^{14} (לִפְנֵי pers.; in tournament), Pr 8^{30} (לְפָנַי), v^{31} (ב loc.). **2.** *jest,* Pr 26^{19}. **3.** *play:* incl. instr. music, singing and dancing 1 S 18^{7}, c. לִפְנֵי י׳

2 S 6⁵ (ב instr), = 1 Ch 13⁸, 2 S 6²¹ 1 Ch 15²⁹ (+ מְרַקֵּד); of merry-making Je 15¹⁷ (|| עָלַז), 30¹⁹ 31⁴; of children's sport Zc 8⁵; of beasts Jb 40²⁰ ψ 104²⁶; of man, *play* with (ב) crocod. Jb 40²⁹. **Hiph.** (declar.) *Pt.* pl. מַשְׂחִיקִים 2 Ch 30¹⁰ they *uttered mockery* עֲלֵיהֶם (|| מַלְעִגִים).

†שְׂחֹק, שְׂחוֹק **n.[m.]** laughter, derision, sport (prop. inf. cstr.);—abs. שְׂחֹק Je 48²⁶ + 5 t.; cstr. Ec 7⁶; abs. שְׂחוֹק Je 20⁷ + 7 t.;—**1.** *laughter* (joyous) Jb 8²¹ (|| תְרוּעָה), ψ 126² (|| רִנָּה), Ec 2² (|| שִׂמְחָה), 10¹⁹ (|| שָׂמַח); as hollow Pr 14¹³ (opp. כְּאֵב), Ec 7³ (opp. כַּעַס), cf. שׂ׳ הַכְּסִיל v⁶. **2.** (object of) *derision*, הָיָה לְשׂ׳, Je 20⁷ 48²⁶·²⁷ (rd. לְשׂ׳ for MT הַשׂ׳ 𝔊 𝔖 𝔙 Gie Du; Co del. vv), v³⁹ La 3¹⁴; elsewh. Jb 12⁴·⁴. **3.** *sport* Pr 10²³.

יִשְׂחָק **n.pr.m.** v. sub צחק.

†מִשְׂחָק **n.[m.]** object of derision, Hb 1¹⁰.

[שֵׂט], שֵׂטִים v. [שׂוט].

†[שָׂטָה] **vb.** turn aside (Aram. סְטָא, ܣܛܐ *id.*; שְׂטָא *stray*; Eth. ሠፈጠ: III. *be seduced*, etc.; cf. Dr J Phil. xi (1882), 205);—**Qal** *Pf.* 2 fs. שָׂטִית Nu 5¹⁹·²⁰; *Impf.* 3 fs. תִּשְׂטֶה v¹²·²⁹, juss. 3 ms. יֵשְׂטְ Pr 7²⁵; *Imv.* ms. שְׂטֵה 4¹⁵;—*turn aside*, of unfaithful wife Nu 5¹² (abs.), + תַּחַת אִישׁ, i.e. while married, v¹⁹ (+ טֻמְאָה adv. acc.), v²⁰·²⁹ (all P); of youth, fr. (מֵעַל) way of evil woman Pr 4¹⁵, toward (אֶל) her ways 7²⁵.

†[שָׂטַם] **vb.** bear a grudge, cherish animosity, against (NH שָׂטַם Niph., 𝔗 Gn 27⁴¹ שְׂטַם; perh. akin to שׂטן q.v.);—**Qal** *Impf.* 3 ms. וַיִּשְׂטֹם Gn 27⁴¹, 3 mpl. sf. יִשְׂטְמוּנִי ψ 55⁴, etc.;—*cherish animosity against*, acc. pers. Gn 27⁴¹ (J), 49²³ (poem in J), 50¹⁵ (E), + בְּאַף ψ 55⁴; of ׳י's persistent assaults on Job, Jb 16⁹ 30²¹.

†מַשְׂטֵמָה **n.f.** animosity;—Ho 9⁷ + v⁸ (del. We, cf. Now).

שׂטן (√of following).

†שָׂטָן **n.m.** ψ 109,6 **1.** adversary. **2.** Satan (NH שָׂטָן, סָטָן; Aram. סָטָנָא, שָׂטָנָא, Syr. ܣܛܢܐ (Hebr.); NH vb. סָטַן, Aram. סְטַן; Ar. شَطَنَ is *be remote*, esp. fr. the truth, and fr. the mercy of God; شَيْطَان *Satan*, Eth. ሰይጣን:);—**1.** *adversary*, in gen., personal or national; הָיָה לְשׂ׳ (ל) Nu 22²² (JE), 1 S 29⁴ (cf. Nes Marg. 15), 2 S 19²³, יָצָא לְשׂ׳ Nu 22³² (JE); שׂ׳ 1 K 5¹⁸ 11²⁵; הֵקִים שׂ׳ ל, subj. God 1 K 11¹⁴·²³, cf. ψ 109⁶ (|| רָשָׁע). **2.** *superhuman adversary*, הַשׂ׳: **a.** of Job, one of בְּנֵי הָאֱלֹהִים Jb 1⁶·⁷·⁷·⁸·⁹·¹²·¹² 2¹·²·²·³·⁴·⁶·⁷. **b.** of h. p. of Isr. bef. ׳י, Zc 3¹·²·²; 𝔊 ὁ διάβολος. **c.** as n.pr. שׂ׳ *Satan* 1 Ch 21¹ (interpr. 2 S 24¹), 𝔊 διάβολος (𝔊 σατάν † 1 K 11¹⁴·²³; Σατανᾶς Mt 4¹⁰ Mk 1¹³ Lk 10¹⁸ + 33 t. NT).

†[שָׂטַן] **vb.denom.** (Gerber³⁰) be or act as adversary;—**Qal** *Impf.* 3 mpl. sf. יִשְׂטְנוּנִי ψ 38²¹ 109⁴; *Inf.cstr.* sf. לְשִׂטְנוֹ Zc 3¹; *Pt.* pl. cstr. שֹׂטְנֵי ψ 71¹³, sf. שֹׂטְנַי 109²⁰, שׂוֹטְנַי v²⁹.

†I. שִׂטְנָה **n.f.** accusation;—Ezr 4⁶.

†II. שִׂטְנָה **n.pr.putei** (*hostility*) Gn 26²¹ (J).

[שִׂיא], שִׂיאֹן v. נשא.

†שׂיב **vb.** be hoary (NH שֵׂיבָה *old age*; As. *šêbu*, *aged man*; Ar. شَابَ (ی) *become hoary*, Eth. ሢበ: (in deriv.); Aram. סִיב *be old*; ܣܳܒ *grow old*, ܣܰܝܒܽܘܬܳܐ *grey hair*);—**Qal** *Pf.* 1 s. וָשַׂבְתִּי 1 S 12²; *Pt.* שָׂב Jb 15¹⁰ (+ יָשִׁישׁ *aged*).

†[שֵׂיב] **n.[m.]** (hoary) age;—sf. שֵׂיבוֹ 1 K 14⁴.

†שֵׂיבָה **n.f.** hoary head, old age;—abs. שׂ׳ Ho 7⁹ +; cstr. שֵׂיבַת Gn 44³¹; sf. שֵׂיבָתִי 42³⁸ 44²⁹, etc.;—**1.** *grey hair, hoary head* Ho 7⁹ (fig.), Gn 42³⁸ 44²⁹·³¹ (all J), 1 K 2⁶·⁹ Pr 16³¹ 20²⁹; אִישׁ שׂ׳ Dt 32²⁵ (opp. יוֹנֵק); || זָקֵן Lv 19³² (H), || זִקְנָה Is 46⁴, + id. ψ 71¹⁸ (in these transition to foll.); fig. of sea Jb 41²⁴. **2.** *old age*, שׂ׳ טוֹבָה Gn 15¹⁵ (JE), 25⁸ (P), Ju 8³² 1 Ch 29²⁸; שׂ׳ also ψ 92¹⁵ (trees, in fig. of righteous), Ru 4¹⁵, + 2 S 19³⁴ (𝔊 Ew Th Bu Kit, cf. We Dr HPS, אֶת־שֵׂיבָתְךָ, for אִתָּךְ).

שִׂיג v. I. [סוג].

שׂיד (√of foll.: NH סִיד *lime*, סַיָּד *white-washer*; Aram. סִידָא, ܣܺܝܕܳܐ *lime*, Ar. شِيدٌ (not loan-word, cf. Frä⁸)).

†שִׂיד **n.[m.]** lime, whitewash;—always שׂ׳;—*lime*, produced by burning bones Am 2¹, in sim. Is 33¹²; as *whitewash* Dt 27²·⁴.

†[שׂוּד, שִׂיד] **vb. denom.** whitewash;—**Qal** *Pf.* 2 ms. וְשַׂדְתָּ אֹתָם בַּשִּׂיד Dt 27²·⁴.

שִׂיו, שְׂיָהוּ v. שֶׂה.

I. שׂיח (√of foll.; NH שִׂיחַ *speak*, שִׂיחָה, סִיחָה *conversation* (oft.); Aram. שִׂיחַ *speak*; Nö ZMG xxxviii (1883), 538 cp. Ar. شَاحَ (ی) *be eager, diligent*, whence (Buhl) *eager occupation* with sthg. as orig. mng. in Heb., but conjectural).

I, II. שׂים, שִׂימָה, שִׂים etc, v. I, II. שׂום.

שׂך, שׂכָּה v. IV. שׂכך. שׂך v. II. שׂכך.

שׂכה (√ of foll., NH סָכָה *look out*, Aram. סְכָא *look out, hope*, סַכְוָאָה *watchman*, סָכוּתָא (for Heb מִצְפָּה) *outlook-point;* ܣܟܐ Pa. *hope for;* Ar شَكَا (و, ى) is *complain* (i.e *disclose grief?*), مِشْكَاة *lamp-niche*, Eth. መስኮት: *window*).

† שֶׂכְוִי **n.[m.]** perh. a celestial appearance, phenomenon (Rabb. Thes *mind*, De (after Talm.) *cock* (cf. NH שֶׂכְוִי *cock*, שֶׂכְוִיָּה *hen*, foreign words acc. Dalm), Di 'Wolkengebilde');—abs. ׳שׂ perh. of clouds (cf. ‖ טֻחוֹת) Jb 38[36] (RV[m] *meteor*).

† [שְׂכִיָּה] **n.f.** very dub, only pl cstr. שְׂכִיּוֹת הַחֶמְדָּה Is 2[16]: perh. gen. term, 𝔙 *quod visu pulchrum est*, Ges[Comm] 'köstliche Anblicke,' cf De, others refer to *imagery* (cf. מַשְׂכִּית; as attracting the gaze) Che[Comm] RV Du; *watchtowers* (v. Aram) Ew Di RV[m], *standards* (as *conspicuous*) Thes; *ships* (*id.*) (Bennett [private letter], and now Gunk[Schöpfung 50] Che[Hpt] Marti, cf. ‖ אֳנִיּוֹת; SS Bu[Jb 40, 31] prop שְׂפִינֹת=׳ס *ships*).

† מַשְׂכִּית **n f.** **show-piece, figure, imagination**;—abs. ׳מ Lv 26[1], sf מַשְׂכִּיתוֹ Ez 8[12], מַשְׂכֻּתוֹ Pr 18[11], pl cstr. מַשְׂכִּיּוֹת Pr 25[11] ψ 73[7], sf. מַשְׂכִּיֹּתָם Nu 33[52],—**1.** *show-piece*, specif. *carved figure*, of idolatrous symbols, Nu 33[52] (P; ‖ צַלְמֵי מַסֵּכֹתָם), אֶבֶן מ׳ Lv 26[1] (‖ מַצֵּבָה etc.), חַדְרֵי מ׳ Ez 8[12] (>del. Co), elsewhere מ׳ כֶסֶף Pr 25[11] *silver carvings.* **2.** *imagination, conceit*, Pr 18[11], מ׳ לֵבָב ψ 73[7].

† שְׂכְיָה (so Baer Gi; var. שָׂכְיָא; van d H. שָׂבְיָה, Kit[Hpt] dub) **n.pr.m.** in Benj 1 Ch 8[10]; Σαβια, Σεβια, 𝔊L Σεχια; 𝔖𝔙 *Sechia.*

† שַׂכִּין **n.[m.]** knife (NH סַכִּין; prob. loanword (Lewy[Fremdw 176]) fr. Aram סַכִּינָא, ܣܟܝܢܐ *id.*, whence also Ar سِكِّين No[M 125] Frä[84]; √dub);—abs. ׳שׂ Pr 23[2].

† שֶׂכוּ **n.pr.loc.** (si vera l.) near Ramah (=*outlook*, Ko[II 1 61]);—1 S 19[22], WMM[As. u. Eur. 165] cp. *T-ku* in Eg. inscr.; but 𝔊 Σεφ(ε)ι, read שְׁפִי Th We Dr Kit Bu HPS.

I. [שָׂכַךְ] **vb. cover, lay over,** so as to screen (cf. ‖ √I סכך);—**Qal** *Pf.* 1 s. וְשַׂכֹּתִי כַפִּי עָלֶיךָ Ex 33[22] (JE).

† שִׂיחַ **n.m.**[ψ 104, 34] **complaint, musing**;—abs. ׳שׂ 1 K 18[27] Pr 23[29]; sf שִׂיחִי 1 S 1[16]+, שִׂחִי Jb 23[2], שִׂיחוֹ 2 K 9[11] ψ 102[1],—**1.** *plaint, complaint.* Jb 7[13] 9[27] 10[1] (‖ מַר נפשׁ), 21[4] 23[2] Pr 23[29] ψ 55[3] 64[2]; קוֹלִי בְשִׂיחִי ; שָׁפַךְ שׂ׳ לִפְנֵי י׳ (‖ אֶהֱמָה) 102[1] 142[3]. Foll are dub.. **2.** *musing*, 1 K 18[27] (E) of a god, ‖ שִׂיג לוֹ, (so RV; SS '*nachdenken*'; Buhl '*beschäftigt sein*', AV *talk*); ψ 104[34] of man (Buhl SS. Bae '*Rede*, oder *Gesang*').—Vid. also [שַׂח] infr. **3.** *anxiety, trouble.* מֵרֹב שִׂיחִי 1 S 1[16] (defined in MT by כַּעַס, cf. HPS; so Buhl SS, but perh =**1**). **4.** *talk:* שִׂיחוֹ 2 K 9[11] (so RV SS, but meaning obscure in context)

† שִׂיחָה **n.f. id**,—abs ׳שׂ ψ 119[99] Jb 15[4], sf. שִׂיחָתִי ψ 119[97],—**1.** *complaint:* שׂ׳ לִפְנֵי־אֵל Jb 15[4] (so Bu al, cf. שִׂיחַ **1** De al. *meditation*, cf. [גֶּרַע]) **2.** (obj. of) *musing, study:* תּוֹרָה ψ 119[97], עֵדוֹת v[99].

† שִׂיחַ **vb. denom. muse, complain, poet. talk (of)**,—**Qal** *Impf* 3 ms. יָשִׂיחַ ψ 119[23]; 3 fs. sf תְּשִׂיחֶךָ Pr 6[22]; 1 s. אָשִׂיחָה ψ 119[78]+, etc., *Imv.* ms. שִׂיחַ Jb 12[8], mpl שִׂיחוּ Ju 5[10]+, *Inf. cstr* שִׂיחַ ψ 119[148],—**1.** *complain* · ψ 55[18] 77[4] (both ‖ הָמָה), Jb 7[11] (בְּמַר נַפְשִׁי), + ψ 6[7] (rd prob אָשִׂיחָה for אַשְׂחֶה) **2.** *muse:* עִם־לְבָבִי ψ 77[7], c. ב, *meditate upon, study*, God's עֲלִילוֹת v[13] (‖ הָגָה); אִמְרָה 119[15.78]; חֻקִּים v[23.48]; נִפְלְאוֹת v[27]; פִּקּוּדִים v[148]; c. acc. דִּבְרֵי נִפְלְאֹתֶיךָ 145[5]. **3. a.** *talk* (about), *sing* (of). abs. Ju 5[10] (ode); c. ב rei, ψ 105[2] =1 Ch 16[9] (‖ זמר, שׁיר; so SS Gerber, but poss. =**2**, so Dr), ψ 69[13] (ב pers *against*; ‖ נגינות, of mocking words) **b.** c. sf. pers *talk* (with) Pr 6[22] (del. Toy), c. לְ *speak to* Jb 12[8] (Di '*sprich sinnend*'; Hi Bu rd. שֶׁרֶץ; Kau חַיַּת (so Bu as altern), Bo al. sub II. שִׂיחַ). **Pôʿlel** *meditate, consider: Impf.* 3 ms. יְשׂוֹחֵחַ Is 53[8] (abs.); 1 s אֲשׂוֹחֵחַ ψ 143[5] (ב rei, ‖ הָגָה)—Gn 24[63] v I שׂוּם

[שַׂח] **n.[m.]** thought;—sf מַגִּיד לְאָדָם מַה־שֵּׂחוֹ Am 4[13], read prob. שִׂחוֹ (against Ba[NB 79, 80]) unless otherwise corrupt.

II. **שׂיח** (√ of foll.; cf perh. As *šâḫu, grow, grow up* (of trees), *šiḫtu*, appar. *a shoot, sprout;* NH=BH; Pun. שח; Syr. ܫܝܚܐ *artemisia Judaica*, cf. Wetzst[Reisebericht 4, 41] Löw[p. 78], so Ar. شِيح Lane[1623] (cf Lag[BN 159])).

† שִׂיחַ **n.[m.]** **bush, shrub, plant**,—׳שׂ abs. coll Jb 30[4], cstr. שׂ׳ הַשָּׂדֶה Gn 2[5] (J), pl. שִׂיחִים Jb 30[7], אַחַד הַשִּׂיחִם Gn 21[15] (E).

†II [שָׂכַךְ] **vb. weave** (cf. ∥ √II סכך), **Po'lel** *Impf.* 2 ms. sf תְּשֹׂכְכֵנִי Jb 10[11] with bones and sinews *thou weavest me together*

†[שַׂךְ] **n [m.] booth, pavilion** (שׂ' perh erron., cf סָךְ, סֻכָּה sub II סכך),—sf. שֻׂכּוֹ La 2[6] *his* [י׳'s] *pavilion* (∥ מֹעֲדוֹ)

III שׂכך (√of foll., cf I. שׂוּךְ, II סוּךְ).

†[מְשׂוּכָה] **n.f hedge**,—sf מְשׂוּכָּתוֹ Is 5[5] (if כ right), perhaps rd מְשֻׂכָּה v sub I שׂוּךְ

IV שׂכך (√of foll., cf Ar شَكَّ *pierce, transfix* (Lane [1582c]), شِكَّةٌ *weapons*, akin also to شَوْكٌ, Eth ሦክ: *thorn, spine*, As *sikkatu, peg*, Syr ܫܟܐ *nail* do not belong here, cf Dl [Prol 196])

†[שֵׂךְ] **n.[m.] thorn**,—pl שִׂכִּים Nu 33[55] (P, ∥ צְנִינִם)

†[שֻׂכָּה] **n.f. barb, spear**,—pl שֻׂכּוֹת Jb 40[31]

†I. שָׂכַל **vb. be prudent** (Gerber[47] denom. fr שֶׂכֶל, but vb early, NH סָכַל, Hithp *shew oneself attentive* (to), *look*, Aram סכל (rare) *understand*, Ithpa *look* (at), *consider*, Aph *instruct*, שְׂכַל only Aph (for Heb. השׂכיל), *understand, make wise*, ܣܟܠ Pa *teach*, Ethpa *understand*, etc., Sam ⵙⵛⵍ Ithpa *look* (for Heb הביט), As *šiklu, clever, šiklûtu, cleverness*, Meissn[Suppl 93]),—**Qal** *Pf.* 3 ms שׂ' 1 S 18[30] *be prudent, circumspect* (SS HPS), Kit Buhl Gerber al *prosper* **Hiph.** *Pf* 3 ms. הִשְׂכִּיל Je 23[5] 1 Ch 28[19], 1 s הִשְׂכַּלְתִּי ψ 119[99], 3 mpl הִשְׂכִּילוּ Jb 34[27]+, *Impf* יַשְׂכִּיל 1 S 18[5]+; 2 ms juss תַּשְׂכֵּל Dn 9[25], etc., *Imv* mpl הַשְׂכִּילוּ ψ 2[10]; *Inf abs* הַשְׂכֵּל Je 9[23]+, הַשְׂכִּיל (Ges[§53k]) Je 3[15] Jb 34[35], *cstr* הַשְׂכִּיל Gn 3[6]+, etc., *Pt* מַשְׂכִּיל 1 S 18[14]+, f מַשְׂכָּלֶת Pr 19[14], pl מַשְׂכִּילִים Dn 11[33]+, etc; meanings hard to classify scholars differ greatly,—**1.** *look at.* נֶחְמָד הָעֵץ לְהַשְׂכִּיל Gn 3[6] (J) *was desirable to look upon* (so 𝔊 Ges De, AV, RV *to make one wise*, Ew Di Buhl SS Dr al sub **3)** **2.** *give attention to, consider, ponder.* Is 41[20] 44[18] Dt 32[29] ψ 64[10] 106[7] Jb 34[27], c לְ Pr 21[12], c אֶל ψ 41[2] Ne 8[13], c עַל Pr 16[20], c בְּ ψ 101[2] Dn 9[13]. **3.** *have insight, comprehension* Je 9[23] (∥יָדֹעַ י׳), ψ 94[8] (∥בִּין), 119[99], Dn 1[4] 9[25] (∥יָדַע), הַשְׂכֵּל(י׳) as subst = *insight, understanding* as י׳'s gift to ruler and teacher, ∥ דֵּעָה Je 3[15], ∥ דַּעַת Jb 34[35], ∥ מַדָּע Dn 1[17], מוּסַר הַשׂ' Pr 1[3], דֶּרֶךְ הַשׂ' 21[16] **4.** *cause to consider, give insight, teach* י׳ subj, acc rei, 1 Ch 28[19], acc pers ψ 32[8] Ne 9[20]; Gabriel subj., 2 acc. Dn 9[22]; לֵב חָכָם subj, acc rei Pr 16[23]; c לְ, Pr 21[11]; הַמַּשְׂכִּילִים שֶׂכֶל טוֹב לי׳ 2 Ch 30[22] (but Bo Ke Benz etc. *who shewed* good *skill*, sc. in music, v[21b]); (הַ)מַּשְׂכִּילִים Dn 11[33.35] 12[3.10] *the teachers* (so Ew Hi Bev; Thes Ke Behrm al. *the wise*) **5.** *act circumspectly, prudently:* abs Am 5[13] ψ 2[10] 36[4], מַשְׂכִּיל as subst ψ 14[2] = 53[3], Pr 10[5.19] 14[35] 15[24] 17[2] Jb 22[2], אִשָּׁה מַשְׂכָּלֶת Pr 19[14].—Je 50[9] has גִּבּוֹר מַשְׁכִּיל acc. to Mas. (van d H Baer Gi), cf 𝔙, i e a child-slaying warrior, but שׂ' Hiph elsewhere only Ho 9[14], of miscarriage; 𝔊 𝔖 Ew and most mod. (Gf Gie Rothst) read מַשְׂכִּיל, either *skilful* or *fortunate* **6.** *prosper, have success* (cf. Dr [1 S 18.5]) abs. 1 S 18[15] Is 52[13] Je 10[21] 20[11] 23[5] Jos 1[8] (D), c בְּ, v[7] (D) 1 S 18[5.14] (rd. בְּכָל־ for לְכָל־ Vrss Th HPS al), cf 2 K 18[7]; c. אֶל, Pr 17[8]. **7.** *cause to prosper:* Dt 29[8] 1 K 2[3] (D).

שֶׂכֶל, שֵׂכֶל **n.m. prudence, insight**;—שׂ' abs. ψ 111[10]+, cstr Pr 19[11]+, שׂ' abs 1 S 25[3]+; שֵׂכֶל Jb 17[4], sf שִׂכְלוֹ Pr 12[8] Dn 8[25],—**1.** *prudence, good sense:* טוֹבַת שׂ' *woman of good sense* 1 S 25[3]. **2.** *insight, understanding.* ∥ בִּינָה 1 Ch 22[12] 2 Ch 2[11], cf Jb 17[4]; שׂ' טוֹב Pr 3[4] 13[15] ψ 111[10] 2 Ch 30[22], אִישׁ שׂ' Ezr 8[18], יוֹעֵץ בְּשׂ' 1 Ch 26[14] מְקוֹר חַיִּים שׂ' בְּעָלָיו Pr 16[22], restrains from anger 19[11], wins praise 12[8], fool despises שׂ' מִלֶּיךָ 23[9], שׂוֹם שׂ' Ne 8[8] (∥הבין) *set forth* (the) *understanding* (i e the meaning) **3.** bad sense, *cunning, craft*, Dn 8[25]

†מַשְׂכִּיל **n.m. contemplative poem** (**Hiph. 2.** De al),—in titles of ψψ 32, 42, 44, 45, 52, 53, 54, 55, 74, 78, 88, 89, 142, also 47[8] זַמְּרוּ מ׳: >Ges al *didactic poem* (**√4**), Ew Ri Pe al. *skilful, artistic song* (**√3**), **√2** alone fits all cases

†II. [שָׂכַל] **vb. Pi. lay crosswise** (so, and not √I שׂ', 𝔊 𝔖 𝔙 𝔗[Jon] and mod., cf. Ar. شَكَلَ *bind* legs of beast, *plait* locks of hair); —*Pf* 3 ms. שִׂכֵּל אֶת־יָדָיו Gn 48[14] (J), Thes Dr, however, *prudentes fecit*, fr √I שׂ'.

שִׂכְלוּת Ec 1[17] v. סכלות.

†שָׂכַר **vb. hire** (NH *id.*; Sab תשכר *hire oneself out* (?), *recompense* (?) DHM[Hofmus. 11]; Eth ሦከረ: *hired*, Ar. شَكَرَ *reward, thank*, mod. Pal شكارة *hired*, of land ploughed by hire, Bergheim[PEQ 1894 196], Palm. שכרא perh *rewarding* Lzb[372]),—**Qal** *Pf.* 3 ms. שׂ' Dt 23[5] 2 K 7[6],

sf. שְׂכָרוֹ Ne 6¹²; 1 s. sf. שְׂכַרְתִּיךָ Gn 30¹⁶; *Impf.* 3 ms. וַיִּשְׂכֹּר Ju 9⁴+, etc.; *Inf. abs.* שָׂכֹר Gn 30¹⁶; *cstr.* לִשְׂכֹּר 1 Ch 19⁶; *Pt. act.* שֹׂכֵר Pr 26¹⁰·¹⁰, pl. שֹׂכְרִים 2 Ch 24¹² (Ezr 4⁵ v. II. סכר); *pass.* שָׂכוּר Ne 6¹³;—*hire*, retainers Ju 9⁴ (ב pret.), soldiers, etc. 2 S 10⁶ = 1 Ch 19⁶·⁷, 2 K 7⁶ 2 Ch 25⁶ (ב pret.), priest Ju 18⁴, artificers Is 46⁶ 2 Ch 24¹², husband's favour שָׂכֹר שְׂכַרְתִּיךָ Gn 30¹⁶ (J; ב pret.); Pr 26¹⁰·¹⁰ obscure, v. De Now Toy; for evil purpose Dt 23⁵ = Ne 13² (עַל *against*), Ne 6¹²·¹³. **Niph.** *hire oneself out, Pf.* נִשְׂכָּרוּ בַּלֶּחֶם 1 S 2⁵. **Hithp.** *earn wages, Pt.* הַמִּשְׂתַּכֵּר Hg 1⁶ (as subst.), מ׳ v⁶ (as vb., + אֶל loc., constr. praegn.).

† **שֶׂכֶר** **n.[m.]** hire, wages;—abs. עֹשֵׂי שׂ׳ Is 19¹⁰ (= שָׂכִיר); cstr. Pr 11¹⁸.

† I. **שָׂכָר** **n.m.**[Ez 29, 18] **hire, wages,** only sg., not c. art.;—abs. שׂ׳ Nu 18³¹+, cstr. שְׂכַר Dt 15¹⁸+, sf. שְׂכָרִי Gn 30¹⁸+, etc.;—**1.** *wages*, of servant, Gn 30²⁸·³²·³³ (J), 31⁸·⁸ Ex 2⁹ (all E), Dt 15¹⁸ (שׂ׳ שָׂכִיר), 24¹⁵ 1 K 5²⁰ Zc 8¹⁰ Mal 3⁵ (שׂ׳ שָׂכִיר); soldiers Ez 29¹⁸·¹⁹; shepherd (symb.) Zc 11¹²·¹²; beast Ex 22¹⁴ (E), Zc 8¹⁰. **2.** = *reward*, for work done, faithfulness, etc., Gn 15¹ (JE), 30¹⁸ (E) in expl. of name יששכר, Nu 18³¹ (P), כִּי יֵשׁ שׂ׳ לִפְעֻלָּתֵךְ Je 31¹⁶ (cf. 2 Ch 15⁷), Is 40¹⁰ = 62¹¹ (fig. of reward of י׳'s labours), ψ 127³ Ec 4⁹ 9⁵. **3.** *passage-money, fare,* Jon 1³.

† II. **שָׂכָר** **n.pr.m. 1.** father of hero of Dvd. 1 Ch 11³⁵, Αχαρ, A Σαχαρ (|| שָׁרָר 2 S 23³³). **2.** doorkeeper 26⁴, Σαχαρ.

† **שָׂכִיר** **adj.** hired;—abs. שׂ׳ Ex 12⁴⁵+, f. שְׂכִירָה Is 7²⁰; cstr. שְׂכִיר Lv 25⁵³; sf. שְׂכִירְךָ v⁶; pl. sf. שְׂכִרֶיהָ Je 46²¹;—**1.** *hired*, of beast Ex 22¹⁴ (E), razor Is 7²⁰ (fig.). **2.** usu. as subst. *hireling, hired labourer* Dt 15¹⁸ 24¹⁴, Lv 19¹³ 22¹⁰ 25⁶·⁴⁰·⁵³ (all H), Ex 12⁴⁵ Lv 25⁵⁰ (both P), Mal 3⁵ Jb 7¹·² 14⁶; כִּשְׁנֵי שׂ׳ Is 16¹⁴ years *like a hireling's years* (reckoned strictly), so 21¹⁶; *mercenaries* Je 46²¹.

יִשָּׂשכָר v. p. 441 supr.

† [**מַשְׂכֹּרֶת**] **n.f.** wages;—sf.: *wages* of servant, מַשְׂכֻּרְתִּי Gn 31⁷·⁴¹, -תֶּךָ 29¹⁵; = *reward* of faithfulness, -תֵּךְ Ru 2¹².

† **שְׂלָו** **n.f.**[Ex 16, 13] quail (prob. foreign word; Ar. سَلْوَى, Syr. ܣܠܘܐ, Sam. [Samaritan]);—*quail*, *coturnix communis* vel *vulgaris* (Tristr[NHB 229 ff.] FFP 124 Post[Hast. DB. Quail], Di[Ex 16, 13]):—abs. coll. Nu 11³² (J), Ex 16¹³ (P), ψ 105⁴⁰ (in all Qr שְׂלָיו); pl. שַׂלְוִים Nu 11³¹ (J; as if from sg. שַׂלְוָה).

שַׂלְמָא, I. **שַׂלְמָה** v. **שַׂלְמוֹן**.

II. **שַׂלְמָה** = שִׂמְלָה v. sub שׂמל.

† **שַׂלְמוֹן** **n.pr.m.** father of Boaz Ru 4²¹ (𝔊 Σαλμαν, A𝔊L -μων), = שַׂלְמָה v²⁰ (𝔊 *id.*; rd. prob. -מוֹן), hence שַׂלְמָא 1 Ch 2¹¹·¹¹ (Σαλμων), also (as father of Bethlehem, on identity v. Be Now[Ruth]) v⁵¹·⁵⁴ (Σαλωμων, 𝔊L Σαμ(α)α)—? rd. שַׂלְמוֹן in all.

† **שַׂלְמַי** **n.pr.m.** head of post-ex. family;—שׂ׳ Ezr 2⁴⁶ Qr (Kt. שמלי [cf. NH n.pr. שַׁמְלַי Dalman, Lihy. שמל DHM[Epigr. Denkm. Ar. No. 13]]; so Baer; van d. H. Gi Qr שַׁלְמַי; Σαμααν, A𝔊L Σελαμ(ε)ι) = שַׂלְמָי Ne 7⁴⁸ (Σελαμει; א Σαμαει).

† [**שָׂלַק**] **vb. kindle, burn** (Ecclus 43⁴ marg. הִשִּׂיק, v²¹·²³ הַסִּיק, *burn;* Aram. (also BA) סְלִק *ascend*, Aph. *cause to go up* (in flame), offer sacrifice; ܣܠܶܩ, Palm. סלק, *ascend*);—**Niph.** *Pf.* 3 fs. אֵשׁ נִשְּׂקָה בְיַעֲקֹב ψ 78²¹ *a fire was kindled against Jacob.* **Hiph.** *make a fire, burn: Pf.* 3 pl. consec. וְהִשִּׂיקוּ, c. ב rei; *Impf.* 3 ms. abs. יַשִּׂיק Is 44¹⁵ (both || בִּעֵר).

שְׂמֹאל, **שְׂמֹאול** (Baer[Jos 1, 7])₅₄ **n.[m.]** the left (NH *id.*; As. *šumêlu;* Ar. شِمَال (also شَمَال and شَأْمَل, شَمْأَل *north wind*); OAram. שמאל, Palm. (sf.) סמלך; Syr. ܣܶܡܳܠܳܐ; √dub., Nö[M 128] Hom[A. u. A. 1. (1892), 21] Kö[ii. 1. 143, 405]; ל + שאם (v. also Thes Dietr[Wortforschung 234]), cf. Ar. شَأَمَ *be unlucky,* شَأْمَةٌ *left,* شَام, شَأْم *north;* Sab. שאם *north, unlucky* DHM[Epigr. Denkm. 29; Epigr. Denkm. Ar. Nos. 6, 7]; other views in Sta[§ 209] Lag[BN 116]);—שְׂמֹאל abs. Gn 13⁹+, cstr. 48¹³ 2 K 23⁸; שְׂמֹאול abs. Nu 20¹⁷+; sf. שְׂמֹאלְךָ 2 S 2²¹, שְׂמֹאלוֹ Gn 48¹³+, etc.;—opp. יָמִין exc. Gn 14¹⁵ Ju 19²⁷ 2 K 23⁸;—**1.** *left*, region on the left, Gn 13⁹ (J); *on the left* is עַל־שׂ׳ 2 K 23⁸ Ez 16⁴⁶ Zc 4³·¹¹, עַל־הַשׂ׳ 1 Ch 6²⁹ cf. 2 Ch 18¹⁸, also מִשׂ׳ (*a sinistra*) Ex 14²²·²⁹ (P), 2 S 16⁶ + 7 t. + מֵהַשׂ׳ 2 Ch 3¹⁷ Ez 1¹⁰, לְשׂ׳ Ec 10², שׂ׳ alone Jb 23⁹; *toward the left* is עַל־שׂ׳ Gn 24⁴⁹ (J), 2 S 2²¹ Zc 12⁶, עַל־הַשׂ׳ 2 S 2¹⁹, שׂ׳ alone 1 S 6¹² Is 9²⁰ + 13 t. †**2.** יַד־שׂ׳ *left hand,* Ju 3²¹ 7²⁰, so שׂ׳ alone Gn 48¹³·¹³·¹⁴ (E), Ju 16²⁹ Ez 39³ Jon 4¹¹ Pr 3¹⁶ Dn 12⁷ Ct 2⁶ 8³. †**3.** = *north* (on *left* of one facing east, cf. אָחוֹר **d,** קֶדֶם **1 b**, יָמִין **4,**) Gn 14¹⁵ Jos 19²⁷ (P); cf. Ez 16⁴⁶.

†[שִׂמְאַל] **vb. denom. Hiph. take the left** (alw. opp. הֵימִין):—*Impf. cohort.* אַשְׂמְאִילָה Gn 13^{9}; 2 mpl. תַּשְׂמְאִילוּ Is 30^{21}; *Imv.* fs. הַשְׂמִילִי (Ges§ 23f Kö I. 276) Ez 21^{21}, cf. *Inf. cstr.* הַשְׂמִיל 2 S 14^{19}; *Pt.* מַשְׂמְאִלִים 1 Ch 12^{2};—**1.** = *go to the left* Gn 13^{9} (J), Ez 21^{21}. **2.** fig. *turn* (aside) *to the left* (fr. true way) 2 S 14^{19} Is 30^{21}. **3.** *use the left hand* 1 Ch 12^{2}.

†שְׂמָאלִי **adj. left, on the left**;—שׂ׳ 1 K 7^{21}+; f. שְׂמָאלִית Lv 14^{15}+;—*left* (usu. opp. יְמָנִי), pillar 1 K 7^{21} = 2 Ch 3^{17}, side of temple 2 K 11^{11} = 2 Ch 23^{10}, side of body Ez 4^{4}, palm Lv 14$^{15.16.26.27}$ (P).

שָׂמַח, שָׂמֵחַ$_{154}$ **vb. rejoice, be glad** (NH *id.*; cf. perh. As. *šamāḫu*, *flourish*, Ar. شَمَخَ *be high, proud*; Pun. n. pr. f. שמחת);—**Qal**$_{126}$ *Pf.* 3 ms. שָׂמַח ψ 16^{9}+; וְשָׂמֵחַ consec. Pr 29^{6}; 3 fs. שָׂמְחָה Est 8^{15}; 2 ms. וְשָׂמַחְתָּ Dt 12^{18}+; 3 mpl. שָׂמְחוּ Ne 12^{43}, etc.; *Impf.* יִשְׂמַח Is 9^{16}+, 3 mpl. יִשְׂמָחוּ 65^{13} ψ 69^{33}, 3 fpl. תִּשְׂמַחְנָה 2 S 1^{20}, etc.; *Imv.* ms. שְׂמַח Dt 33^{18}+, fs. שִׂמְחִי Zp 3^{14}+, שְׂמָחִי Jo 2^{21}, etc.; *Inf. cstr.* שְׂמֹחַ Ez 35^{14}+, etc.; *Pt.* v. שָׂמֵחַ adj.;—24 t. ‖ גִּיל, less oft. ‖ רָנַן, עָלַז, שׂוּשׂ, etc.;—**1.** in common life: **a.** *rejoice*, c. בְּ pers. vel rei *take pleasure in* Ju 9$^{19.19}$ Dt 33^{18} Ec 3^{22} + 7 t. + (prob.) בְּכָל־יָמֵינוּ ψ 90^{14} (others בְּ temp.), cf. Ec 11^{8}; עַל pers. Is 39^{2}+ ‖ 2 K 20^{13} (וישׂמח for MT וישׁמע Vrss mod.), עַל rei Jon 4^{6} 2 Ch 15^{15}; c. cl. temp. Je 41^{13} + 6 t. + (of heart) Pr 23^{15}, in one's heart Ex 4^{14} (J); c. כִּי *because* Is 14^{29} + 3 t.; c. אֵת *with* Is 66^{10}; c. מִן pers. *get pleasure from* Pr 5^{18}; abs. 1 S 11^{9} Ec 3^{12} Pr 13^{9} (fig. of prosperity; subj. אוֹר; opp. דָּעַךְ), + 8 t.; c. לְ rei *at* Jb 21^{12}. **b.** *rejoice* arrogantly, *exult* at, אֶל־ לְ pers., Mi 7^{8} Is 14^{8} Ob^{12} ψ 35$^{19.24}$ 38^{17}, c. לְ rei Ez 25^{6}, בְּ rei Jb 31^{29} ψ 35^{15} Pr 24^{17}; abs. Ho 9^{1} (+ אֶל־גִּיל), 2 S 1^{20} + 3 t., + (said of righteous by Eliphaz) Jb 22^{19}. **2. a.** *rejoice* religiously, c. בְּ rei 1 S 2^{1} Dt 12^{7} ψ 21^{2} + 7 t.; c. בי׳, etc., Jo 2^{23} ψ 32^{11} + 10 t. ψψ + 9^{3} (+ אֶעֶלְצָה בָךְ); c. עַל rei 2 Ch 29^{36}, עַל inf. 1 Ch 29^{9a}; c. לְמַעַן rei ψ 48^{12}; c. כִּי *because* 119^{74}; abs. Zc 2^{14} 4^{10} Jo 2^{21} 1 Ch 29^{9b} (c. acc. cogn.), 16^{31} (of heavens) = ψ 96^{11}, ψ 97^{1} (isles) + 18 t. (12 t. ψψ), + (of heart) Zc 10^{7a} ψ 16^{9} 1 Ch 16^{10}, בְּכָל־לֵב Zp 3^{14} (cf. Ex 4^{14} **1 a** supr.); c. לִפְנֵי י׳ Is 9^{2} and (of joyous feasting etc., at sanctuary) Lv 23^{40} (H), Dt 12$^{12.18}$ 16^{11} 27^{7}, cf. 14^{26} 1 S 11^{15}. **b.** subj. י׳, c. עַל pers. Is 9^{16} (‖ רחם; Perles RÉJ xxxv. 63 *be gentle*, Ar. سَمُحَ), בְּ rei ψ 104^{31}. **Pi.** *Pf.* 3 ms. וְשִׂמַּח consec. Dt 24^{5}, sf. שִׂמְּחָהוּ Je 20^{15}, etc.; *Impf.* 3 ms. יְשַׂמַּח ψ 104^{15}+, etc.; *Imv.* ms. שַׂמַּח ψ 86^{4}, שַׂמַּח Pr 27^{11}, etc.; *Inf. abs.* שַׂמֵּחַ Je 20^{15}; *Pt.* מְשַׂמֵּחַ Ju 9^{13}, pl. cstr. מְשַׂמְּחֵי ψ 19^{9};—*cause to rejoice, gladden*, c. acc. pers. (or equiv.), subj. pers. Dt 24^{5} Je 20^{15} (+ Inf. abs.), Pr 10^{1} 15^{20} 27^{11} 29^{3} (Ho 7^{3} v. משׁח **2**); esp. subj. י׳ (God) Je 31^{13} (c. מִן separ.) Is 56^{7} 2 Ch 20^{27} (c. מִן of source, v. **Qal 1 a**), Ezr 6^{22} Ne 12^{43} (+ acc. cogn.) ψ 86^{4} 90^{15} 92^{5} (בְּ instr.), also, c. לְ pers. *cause to exult at* ψ 30^{2}, *id.* c. עַל pers. La 2^{17}; subj. rei Ju 9^{13} ψ 19^{9} 45^{9} 46^{5} 104^{15} Ec 10^{19} Pr 12^{25} 15^{30} 27^{9}. †**Hiph.** = **Pi.** *Pf.* 2 ms. הִשְׂמַחְתָּ ψ 89^{43} (subj. י׳).

†שָׂמֵחַ **adj. verb. glad, joyful, merry**;—abs. שׂ׳ Dt 16^{15}+, f. שְׂמֵחָה ψ 113^{9}; pl. שְׂמֵחִים 1 K 1^{45}+, cstr. שִׂמְחֵי Is 24^{7}, שְׂמֵחֵי ψ 35^{26};—**1. a.** as adj. *joyful, shewing joy*, 1 K 1^{45} Est 5^{9} (+ טוֹב לֵב), v^{14}; אֵם שְׂמֵחָה ψ 113^{9}; לֵב שׂ׳ Pr 15^{13} 17^{22}; at feast of tab. Dt 16^{15}, in thankfulness to י׳ ψ 126^{3} (both pred. c. הָיָה), 1 K 8^{66} (+ טוֹבֵי לֵב) = 2 Ch 7^{10}. **b.** = pt. 1 K 1^{40} (‖ מְחַלְּלִים *piping*), 4^{20} 2 K 11^{14} (+ תֹּקֵעַ בְּ) = 2 Ch 23^{13}, מִן rei Ec 2^{10}. **2.** as subst. הַשׂ׳ Am 6^{13} (+ לְ rei), Pr 2^{14} (לְ inf.), Jb 3^{22} (+ אֱלֵי־גִיל; ‖ יָשִׂישׂוּ), שִׂמְחֵי־לֵב Is 24^{7}; of malicious joy שׂ׳ Pr 17^{5} (לְ rei), שְׂמֵחֵי רָעָתִי ψ 35^{26}.

שִׂמְחָה$_{93}$ **n.f. joy, gladness, mirth**;—abs. שׂ׳ Gn 31^{27}+, cstr. שִׂמְחַת Is 9^{2}+; sf. שִׂמְחָתִי ψ 137^{6}, etc.; pl. שְׂמָחוֹת ψ 16^{11}, ־ֹת 45^{16};—**1.** *mirth, gladness*, e.g. in festivity, Gn 31^{27} (E), ψ 137$^{3.6}$, 1 K 1^{40} 1 S 18^{6} Is 9$^{2.2}$ 16^{10} ψ 45^{16}; יוֹם מִשְׁתֶּה וְשׂ׳ Est 9$^{17.18.22}$ cf. (יוֹם om.) v^{19} (+ יוֹם טוֹב), v^{22} (‖ יוֹם טוֹב), + 5 t., + קוֹל שׂ׳ Je 7^{34} = 16^{9} = 25^{10} = 33^{11}; *joy* of heart Pr 14$^{10.13}$ Ec 5^{19} Ct 3^{11}, cf. (of inward joy) Jon 4^{6} Pr 15^{23} 21^{15}; = *gaiety, pleasure* Is 22^{13} Ec 2$^{1.2.10}$ 8^{15} 9^{7}, בֵּית שׂ׳ 7^{4}; שׂ׳ חָנֵף Jb 20^{5}, of foolish Pr 15^{21} 21^{17}; malicious joy Ez 35^{15} (לְ rei), so בְּכָל־לֵבָב שׂ׳ 36^{5}. **2.**$_{46}$ (esp. ψψ Chr) religious: 2 S 6^{12} ‖ 1 Ch 15$^{16.25}$ Jo 1^{16}+; יוֹם שׂ׳ Nu 10^{10} (P); עָשָׂה שׂ׳ i.e. make a (sacred) festivity 2 Ch 30^{23} Ne 8^{12} 12^{27}; שִׂמְחַת עוֹלָם Is 35^{10} = 51^{11}, 61^{7}; שׂ׳ c. עַל pers. Ne 12^{44}; *joy* of heart Is 30^{29} Je 15^{16}; as gift of י׳ ψ 4^{8} 21^{7} + 7 t. + (in mockery) Is 66^{5}. †**3.** *joy* of י׳ Zp 3^{17}. †**4.** *glad result, happy issue* ψ 106^{5} (‖ טוֹבָה), Pr 10^{28} 12^{20} (Gr אֱמֻנָה, Toy מִשְׁפָּט; opp. מִרְמָה).

†שְׂמִיכָה **n.f. rug or thick coverlet** (?);—abs. Ju 4^{18} (v. GFM).

שׂמל (√of foll.; Ar. شَمَلَ *enclose, envelope;* شَمْلَةٌ *cloak,* Lane^{1600} Dozy$^{\text{Vêtements, 59 f., 232 f.}}$).

†**שִׂמְלָה** **n.f.** wrapper, mantle;—abs. ׳שׂ Gn 9^{23}+, cstr. שִׂמְלַת Dt 21^{13} 22^{5}; sf. שִׂמְלָֽתְךָ Dt 8^{4}, etc.; pl. שְׂמָלֹת Gn 45$^{22.22}$+, sf. שִׂמְלֹתָם 44^{13}+, etc.;—*wrapper, mantle* (of man or [Ru 3^{3}+] woman), usu. square piece of cloth worn as *outer garment* (v. Mackie$^{\text{Hast. DB. i. 625}}$; Benz$^{\text{Ency. Bib. iii. 2932}}$), Gn 35^{2} Ex 22^{26} (both E), Dt 8^{4} 10^{18} 21^{13} 22^{3} Is 3$^{6.7}$ 9^{4} 2 S 12^{20} Kt, Ru 3^{3} Kt (Qr in both pl.); as *covering* in sleep Gn 9^{23} (J; cf. Ex 22^{26}), bed-covering Dt 22^{17}; covering or receptacle for articles Ex 12^{34} (E), Ju 8^{25} 1 S 21^{10}, cf. Pr 30^{4}; more gen. *garment,* Dt 22^{5}, *clothes* (pl.) Gn 37^{34} 44^{13} (J), 41^{14} Ex 19$^{10.14}$ (all E), Jos 7^{6} (JE); as costly gifts Gn 45$^{22.22}$ Ex 3^{22} 12^{35} (all E).

†**שַׂמְלָה** **n.pr.m.** kg. of Edom Gn 36$^{36.37}$ (P; Σαμ(α)λα) = 1 Ch 1$^{47.48}$ (Σαμαα, Σαβαα).

†**שַׂלְמָה** **n.f.** id. (transp. from שִׂמְלָה);—abs. ׳שׂ Ex 22^{8}+, cstr. שַׂלְמַת v^{25}; sf. שַׂלְמָתוֹ Dt 24^{13}; pl. שְׂלָמוֹת Jos 9^{5}+, sf. שַׂלְמֹתֵיהֶם v^{13}, etc.;—*garment* (of man or [Ct 4^{11}] woman): *outer garment* Ex 22$^{8.25}$ (E), Jos 9$^{5.13}$ (JE), Dt 24^{13} 1 K 11$^{29.30}$ ψ 104^{2} (fig.); in gen. *clothes* (pl.) Dt 29^{4} Ne 9^{21} Jb 9^{31} Ct 4^{11}; as costly gifts 1 K 10^{25} = 2 Ch 9^{24}; as booty Jos 22^{8} (late).—Mi 2^{8} rd. prob. שַׂלְמָה (Roorda, RS$^{\text{Proph. vii. N. 4}}$), or שְׁלֵמִים (We Now GASm), *him* (*those*) *at peace* (*with him*), cf. 𝔊𝔖.

שמלי Kt Ezr 2^{46} v. שַׁלְמַי supr.

[**שָׂמַל**] **Hiph.** v. [שָׂמְאַל] supr.

†**שְׂמָמִית** **n.f.** a kind of lizard (so 𝔊𝔅𝔗 Lv 11, 30 cf. Str^{Pr} (also on ס<שׂ));—abs. ׳שׂ Pr 30^{28} (cf. Shipley-Cook$^{\text{Ency. Bib. Lizard}}$).

שׂמר (appar. √of foll.; meaning dub.).

[**מַשְׂמֵר**], מַשְׂמְרוֹת, Ec 12^{11}, v. [מַסְמֵר], p. 702.

שָׂנֵא$_{145}$ **vb.** hate (NH *id.;* MI^{4} שנאי *my foes;* Sab. שנאם *foe* Sab. Denkm.$^{\text{No. 12, l. 9}}$ cf. Ib.$^{\text{No. 7, l. 9}}$ CIS$^{\text{iv. No. 173, l. 6}}$; Ar. شَنِئَ, شَنَأَ, *hate;* Aram. סְנָא, ܣܢܐ, *id.,* סָנְאָה, ܣܳܢܳܐ *hater,* etc.; Eth. *hate* is ጸልአ:);—**Qal**$_{128}$ *Pf.* 3 ms. ׳שׂ Dt 12^{31}+, sf. שְׂנֵאָהּ 2 S 13^{15}+; 2 ms. שָׂנֵאתָ ψ 5^{6}+, sf. שְׂנֵאתַנִי Ju 14^{16}, etc.; *Impf.* 3 ms. יִשְׂנָא Pr 13^{5} 26^{28}, sf. יִשְׂנָאֶךָּ 9^{8}, etc.; Imv. mpl. שִׂנְאוּ Am 5^{15} ψ 97^{10}; *Inf.* *abs.* שָׂנֹא Ju 15^{2}; *cstr.* שְׂנֹא Gn 37^{5}+, שִׂנְאַת Pr 8^{13}; *Pt. act.* שֹׂנֵא Dt 4^{42}+, שֹׂנַאֲךָ Ex 23^{5} Pr 25^{21}; pl. cstr. שֹׂנְאֵי Ex 18^{21}+, etc.; *pass.* fs. שְׂנוּאָה Gn 29^{31}+; mpl. cstr. שְׂנֻאֵי 2 S 5^{8} Qr (>Kt שְׂנֵאוּ);—*hate* (oft. opp. אָהֵב): **1.** human; **a.** c. acc. pers. Gn 26^{27} (J), 37$^{5.8}$ (E), Ju 11^{7} 2 S 13^{22} Am 5^{10} (‖ תִּעֵב) + 17 t. (evil-doers †ψ 26^{5} 31^{7} 139^{21}), + (obj. wife) Ju 14^{16} 15$^{2.2}$; + pt. pass., of wife, †Gn 29$^{31.31}$ (J), Dt 21$^{15.15.16.17}$, cf. Pr 30^{23}; fig. of Zion Is 60^{15} (+ עֲזוּבָה); specif. of sexual revulsion †2 S 13$^{15.15}$ (+ acc. cogn.), Dt 22$^{13.16}$ 24^{3}; so, obj. man (of Jerus. under fig. of harlot) †Ez 16^{37}; pass. שְׂנֻאֵי נֶפֶשׁ דָּוִד 2 S 5^{8} (but v. obscure); reflex. (acc. נַפְשׁוֹ) †Pr 29^{24}, abs. †Ec 3^{8}. **b.** c. acc. rei, Ez 35^{6} (but rd. בְּדָם אָשַׁמְתָּ 𝔊𝔖 Co Berthol Toy), Ec 2$^{17.18}$, esp. evil Ex 18^{21} (E), Mi 3^{2} ψ 45^{7} + 10 t., virtue, etc. Mi 3^{2} Pr 1^{22} + 4 t. **2.** subj. ׳י; obj. perverse Isr. †Am 6^{8} (its palaces), Ho 9^{15} Je 12^{8}; wickedness ψ 5^{6} 11^{5}; idolatry and evil Am 5^{21} Is 1^{14} 61^{8} Je 44^{4} Mal 2^{16} + 5 t. **3.** *Pt. act.*$_{54}$ as adj. Is 66^{5} (as vb. c. 1 s. pron. 61^{8}, **2** supr.); usu. subst., Pr 13^{24} *one hating his son* (opp. אֹהֵב); elsewhere = *enemy, foe* (usu. cstr. or c. sf.), sg. and pl. (oft. ‖ אֹיֵב, sts. opp. אֹהֵב): foe of man Ex 23^{5} (E), Gn 24^{60} (J), Lv 26^{17} (H) +, nation Ex 1^{10} (E), Est 9$^{1.5.16}$+, abs. Pr 26^{24} 27^{6}, (c. 31 t. in all); + לֹא שֹׂנֵא c. לְ pers., *a no-hater to* one Dt 4^{42} 19$^{4.6}$ Jos 20^{5}, and (without לֹא) Dt 19^{11}; foe of good Mi 3^{2}, cf. Jb 34^{17} + 3 t., of evil †Ex 18^{21} Pr 28^{1}, cf. 15^{27}; of suretyship †11^{15} (i.e. not giving it); foes of ׳י †Ex 20^{5} = Dt 5^{9}, Dt 7$^{10.10}$ 2 Ch 19^{2}. †**Niph.** *Impf.* 3 ms. יִשָּׂנֵא Pr 14^{17} *is hated,* so v^{20} (+ לְ pers. *by,* v. לְ **5 d**). †**Pi.** *Pt.* sf. מְשַׂנְאַי Jb 31^{29} ψ 55^{13}; pl. cstr. מְשַׂנְאֵי 81^{16}; sf. מְשַׂנְאַי 2 S 22^{41}+, etc.;—*enemy* (**Qal 3**) ‖ אֹיֵב, צַר, etc.: **1.** personal and national, Jb 31^{29} Dt 33^{11} (poem), 2 S 22^{41} = ψ 18^{41}, ψ 44$^{8.11}$ 55^{13} 68^{2} 89^{24}. **2.** of ׳י Nu 10^{35} (J), Dt 32^{41} (poem), ψ 81^{16} 83^{3} 139^{21}. **3.** of wisdom Pr 8^{36}.

†[**שָׂנִיא**] **adj.** hated, held in aversion;—fs. הַשְּׂנִיאָה Dt 21$^{15\,b}$ *the hated* (wife; v. √**1 a**); but read probably הַשְּׂנוּאָה (as v$^{15\,a\,bis,\,16}$).

†**שִׂנְאָה** **n.f.** hating, hatred;—abs. ׳שׂ Nu 35^{20}+, cstr. שִׂנְאַת Dt 1^{27} Pr 25^{10}; sf. שִׂנְאָֽתְךָ Ez 35^{11} (pl. ־אֹתֶיךָ prob. meant, Kö$^{\text{ii. 1, § 88}}$ cf. Ol$^{\text{§ 131 k}}$, but <rd. שִׂנְאָֽתְךָ 𝔊 Co Berthol Toy, cf. Ges$^{\text{§ 91 l}}$), etc.;—*hatred* (sts. opp. אַהֲבָה): **1.** human, Nu 35^{20} (P), Ez 23^{29} 35^{11} Pr 10$^{12.18}$ 15^{17} 26^{26} ψ 109^{5} Ec 9$^{1.6}$; דִּבְרֵי ׳שׂ ψ 109^{3}; emphatic, שִׂנְאַת חָמָס 25^{19}, תַּכְלִית ׳שׂ 139^{22} (against ׳י's foes),

also (of sexual revulsion) שׂ׳ גְּדוֹלָה 2 S 13[15] (all acc cogn). **2.** ׳י's *hating*, as vb, c acc pers, Dt 1[27] 9[28]

†**שְׂנִיר n.pr.mont.** Σανειρ. Amorite name of Hermon Dt 3[9], whence came cypress-trees Ez 27[5], prob. northern peak(s) of H 1 Ch 5[23] Ct 4[8] (where + חֶרְמוֹן); so Ar. سنير, Abulf[ed Par 68], Syr ܣܢܝܪ, Ecclus 24[14] *al*, As *Saniru* COT[Dt 3, 9] Dl[Pa 104]. Vid. also Dr[Dt 3, 9] Buhl[Geogr 110 f and reff] [van d H. erron. ׳שׂ Dt Ct]

שׂעף (√of foll, Thes al identif with סעף *divide* (q v), whence foll. as *branching out, involved*, Ba[ES 56] cp شَغَفَ *strike the* (شَغَافُ) *pericardium*, شَعِفَ *be disquieted* by a thing).

†**שְׂעִפִּים n [m.] pl. disquietings, = disquieting or excited thoughts**,—׳שׂ Jb 4[13], sf שְׂעִפַּי (Baer שְׂעִיפַּי) Jb 20[2] (|| חוּשִׁי)

†[**שַׂרְעַפִּים**] **n. [m] pl disquieting thoughts** (cf סְרַעַפָּה sub סעף, Ges[§ 85 w]),—sf שַׂרְעַפַּי ψ 94[19] (appar of anxious doubts), as secrets ׳יָ-, 139[23] (open to ׳י, || לְבָבִי)

I **שׂער** (√of foll, cf Ar شَعِرَ *be hairy*, شَعْرٌ, شَعَرٌ, *hair*, so NH = BH, Eth ሥዕርት: Aram סַעְרָא or (׳שׂ), ܣܥܪܐ, ܣܥܪܬܐ, As *šârtu*, *hairy skin*, on Gk deriv. v Lewy[Fremdw 86], Egypt. v. Bondi[64] WMM[90]).

שֵׂעָר [27] **n.m.**[Lv 13 3] **hair**,—abs ׳שׂ Gn 25[25] +, cstr שְׂעַר Ju 16[22] +, שֵׂעַר Is 7[20] (Ges[§ 93 hh] Ko[ii. 1 78]), sf. שְׂעָרֵךְ Ez 16[7], שַׂעְרֵךְ Ct 4[1] 6[5] (Ko[l c]), שְׂעָרוֹ Lv 14[8] +, שְׂעָרָהּ, v[20], שְׂעָרָה v[4] (Ges[§ 91 e]),—*hair* **1** of animals, as material, ׳אַדֶּרֶת שׂ Gn 25[5] (J), Zc 13[4], prob also ׳אִישׁ בַּעַל שׂ 2 K 1[8] i e a man with a garment of skin **2.** human ׳שׂ׳ ראשׁוֹ Ju 16[22] 2 S 14[26] Nu 6[6] (P), cf v[18] (P), + beard Ezr 9[3], ׳קָדְקֹד שׂ ψ 68[22], incl. head, beard, eyebrows Lv 14[8 9 10] (P), ׳שׂ׳ הָרַגְלַיִם Is 7[20] (i e of genitals, + ראשׁ, זָקָן, in fig.) long *hair* of woman Ez 16[7] Ct 4[1] 6[5], *hair* of skin in (leprosy-)marks Lv 13[3] + 10 t. 13 (P)

†**שַׂעֲרָה n.f.** a hair, nom. unit (Ges[§ 122 t]),—abs. Ju 20[16] cstr in phr מִשַּׂעֲרַת ראשׁוֹ 1 S 14[45] *a single hair of his head*, cf 2 S 14[11] 1 K 1[52] (v. מִן **3 b** (*d*), Dr[1 S 14 45]), ׳שׂ׳ בשׂרי Jb 4[15] (appar. n coll, 𝔊 𝔙 and most, Buhl prop pl), pl cstr. שַׂעֲרוֹת ראשׁי ψ 40[13] 69[5] (both as numerous)

†[**שָׂעַר**] **vb. denom.** bristle, with horror,—**Qal** *Pf* 3 pl שָׂעֲרוּ שַׂעַר Ez 27[35] (|| שָׁמְמוּ, רָעֲמוּ),

Impf. 3 mpl. יִשְׂעֲרוּ עָלֶיךָ שַׂעַר 32[10] (|| שָׁמֵם Hiph.); *Imv* mpl. שַׂעֲרוּ Je 2[12] (|| שֹׁמּוּ עַל־)—Dt 32[17] v. III שׂער

†I. **שַׂעַר n.** [m.] **horror** (prop *bristling*),—׳שׂ abs, as acc cogn Ez 27[35] 32[10] v foregoing, cf ׳אָחֲזוּ שׂ Jb 18[20] (|| נָשַׁמּוּ עַל).

†I **שָׂעִר adj.** hairy,—ms. ׳אִישׁ שׂ Gn 27[11], fpl יָדָיו שְׂעִרֹת v[23] (J)

II. **שָׂעִיר** [53] **n.m.**[Nu 15, 24] **he-goat, buck** (*hairy one*, NH *id*),—abs ׳שׂ Lv 4[24] +, cstr שְׂעִיר Nu 7[16] +; pl. שְׂעִירִם Lv 16[7 8]; cstr. שְׂעִירֵי v[5] Nu 7[87],—*he-goat*, usu שְׂעִיר(־)עִזִּים *buck of goats* (v עֵז p 777). Gn 37[31] (J), Ez 43[22] 45[23] Lv 4[23] 9[3] 23[19] + 20 t. Nu (all P), ׳שְׂעִירֵי ע Lv 16[5] Nu 7[87] (P), ׳שׂ alone = *he-goat* Lv 4[24] + 11 t. Lv 16 (P), שְׂעִיר (הַ)חַטָּאת *he-goat for sin-offering* Ez 43[25] Lv 9[15] + 9 t Lv Nu; שְׂעִירֵי חַ׳ 2 Ch 29[23]; in Dn 8[21] הַשׂ׳ is prob gloss to הַצָּפִיר (cf Dr)

†I [**שְׂעִירָה**] **n.f. she-goat**,—cstr שְׂעִירַת עִזִּים (lit *hairy female of goats*) Lv 4[28] 5[6].

†II [**שְׂעִירָה**] **n. pr. loc.**, prob. in SE Ephraim (= *goat*, Thes),—c ה loc הַשְּׂעִירָתָה Ju 3[26]; Σε(τ)ειρωθα, 𝔊L Σηρωθα.

†III. **שָׂעִיר n.m. satyr, demon** (with *he-goat's* form, or feet, NH *id*, cf Baud[Stud i 136 ff]; *hairy* demons We[Skizzen iii 135, Heid 152] RS[Sem. 113, 423; 2nd ed 120, 441]), abs ׳שׂ Is 34[14] inhabiting desolate ruins, so pl. שְׂעִירִים 13[21], name for idols 2 Ch 11[15] and (שְׂעִירִם) Lv 17[7] (H); prob also בָּמוֹת הַשׂ׳ 2 K 23[8] (MT הַשְּׁעָרִים) Hoffm[ZAW ii (1882). 175] SS Kmp Klo Kit Benz Bur

†**שְׂעֹרָה n f. barley** (*bearded* grain, 𝔊 κριθή, 𝔙 hordeum, NH *id*; Sab שׂערם Glas in Fell[ZMG liv (1900). 256], Ar شَعِيرٌ, OAram שערה, 𝔗 סַעֲרְתָא, Syr. ܣܥܪܬܐ; Dl[260] cp Eth. ሠገም: *wheat, grain*),—abs ׳שׂ Ex 9[31] +; usu pl. שְׂעֹרִים Ho 3[2] +,—*barley*, common grain (oft || חִטָּה, etc) **1.** growing, standing, sg Ex 9[31 31] (J), Dt 8[8] Jb 31[40] Jo 1[11], as sown Is 28[25], standing, pl 2 S 14[30] ׳שְׂעֹר 1 Ch 11[13], reaped קְצִיר (הַ)שְּׂעֹרִים 2 S 21[9] Ru 1[22] 2[23], ׳גֹּרֶן הַשׂ 3[2] **2.** pl, the grains, measured, cooked, etc. Ho 3[2] Ez 4[9] 13[19] 45[13] 2 K 7[1 16 18] Je 41[8] 2 Ch 2[9 14] 27[5] Ru 2[17] 3[15 17], 2 S 17[28] 1 K 5[8] (food for horses); ׳זֶרַע חֹמֶר שׂ Lv 27[16] (P), ׳קֶמַח שׂ Nu 5[15], ׳לֶחֶם שׂ Ju 7[13] 2 K 4[42], ׳עֻגַת שׂ Ez 4[12].

†**שְׂעֹרִים n.pr.m.** priest 1 Ch 24[8], Σεωρειμ.

†שֵׂעִיר **n.pr.** Sē'îr (=שָׂעִיר, *goat?* cf. Gray Prop. N. 94; but note play in שֵׂעָר Gn 25^{25}, שָׂעִר $27^{11.23}$; Nö ZMG xl (1886), 165; Ency. Bib. ii. 1183 cp. n. pr. mont. الاشعر (the 'hairy,' i.e. 'well-wooded,' cf. شَعَارٌ *trees*), n.pr.gent. (orig. n.pr.loc.) الْاَشْعَرُ; Lag BN 92 thinks שׂ׳ orig. n.pr.m., but land much earlier in OT.; perh. = Tel Am. land *Šêri*, Zim ZA vi (1891), 257 Jastr JBL xi (1892), 114 Wkl Tel Am. 181, 26 Buhl Edom. 28 f.);—**1.** Σηειρ: **a. terr.** land of Edom, S. of Dead Sea, אַ֫רְצָה שׂ׳ Gn 32^{4} (J; ‖ שְׂדֵה אֱדוֹם), cf. 36^{30} (P); שׂ׳ alone Ju 5^{4} (poem; ‖ *id.*), Nu 24^{18} (JE; ‖ אֱדוֹם), Dt 1^{44} $2^{4.8.12.22.29}$ 33^{2} Jos 11^{19} (D), Is 21^{11} 2 Ch $20^{23\,b}$; c. ה loc. שֵׂעִ֫ירָה Gn $33^{14.16}$ (J), Jos 12^{7} (D). **b.** specif. **mont.** E. of Arabah, הַר־שׂ׳ Jos 24^{4} (E), Gn $36^{8.9}$ (P), Dt 1^{2} $2^{1.5}$ Ez $35^{2.3.7.15}$ 1 Ch 4^{42} 2 Ch $20^{10.22.23}$; cf. הַרְרָם שׂ׳ Gn 14^{6} (home of הַחֹרִי; on text v. Buhl Edom. 28 Gunk Gn). **c. gent.** Ez 25^{8} = Edom [van d. H. שׂ׳]; but del. 𝔊B Hi Co Berthol Toy Krae. **d.** personif. as **m.** in בְּנֵי־שׂ׳ (v. חֹרִי p. 360; cf. Gn 14^{6}) Gn 36^{20} = 1 Ch 1^{38}, Gn 36^{21} (P; + בְּאֶרֶץ אֱדוֹם); = Edomites 2 Ch $25^{11.14}$ (‖ אֱדוֹמִים). **2. mont.** in Judah, הַר־שׂ׳ Jos 15^{10} (P), Ασσαρ, A Σηειρ, 𝔊L Σιειρ; Di Buhl G 91 al. cp. hill-ruin *Sârîs* c. 9 miles W. of Jerus. (Rob BR iii. 156).

†II. [שָׂעַר] **vb.** sweep or whirl away (of storm-wind) (=סָעַר, q.v.; As. *šâru, wind,* Dl HWB 635; > Thes 1334 cp. I. שׂעַר);—**Qal** *Impf.* 3 ms. sf. יִשְׂעָרֶנּוּ ψ 58^{10} fig. *he* (י׳) *shall sweep it away.* **Niph.** *Pf.* 3 fs. impers. נִשְׂעֲרָה ψ 50^{3} round about him *it is tempestuous* exceedingly. **Pi.** *Impf.* 3 ms. sf. וִישָׂעֲרֵהוּ Jb 27^{21} *and it* [an E. wind] *shall whirl him away* fr. (מִן) his place. **Hithp.** *Impf.* 3 ms. וְיִשְׂתָּעֵר עָלָיו Dn 11^{40} the kg. *shall storm against him.*

†II. שַׂעַר **n.[m.]** storm (=סַעַר);—only cstr. שׂ׳ קֶטֶב Is 28^{2} *a storm of destruction* (in sim.; ‖ זֶרֶם בָּרָד).

†שְׂעָרָה **n.f. id.** (=סְעָרָה);—of way of י׳ בְּסוּפָה וּבִשׂ׳ Na 1^{3}; fig. of י׳'s judgments; אֲשֶׁר־בִּשׂ׳ יְשׁוּפֵנִי Jb 9^{17}.

†III. [שָׂעַר] **vb.** perh. **be acquainted with** (Ar. شَعَرَ *perceive* [Sab. שער *id.?* Hom Chrest. 124]; cf. Aram. סְעַר, ܣܥܰܪ, *visit, inspect,* Ba ES 67 RS in Dr Dt Perles Anal. 79);—**Qal** *Pf.* 3 pl. sf. שְׂעָרוּם Dt 32^{17} new gods, *with whom* your fathers *had* no *acquaintance* (𝔊 εἴδησαν; ‖ יְדָעוּם); usu. *fear,* Thes *revere with awe,* Dr *shudder before,* [שָׂעַר] denom., although not elsewh. c. acc. pers.

IV. שׂער (assumed as √ of foll.).

†שְׂעִירִים **n.[m.]pl.** rain(-drops), si vera l.; (so acc. to Vrss and context; Thes cp. II. שַׂעַר; Lag. prop. רְסִיסִים);—כִּשְׂ׳ עֲלֵי־דֶשֶׁא Dt 32^{2} (‖ רְבִיבִים, טַל, מָטָר).

שְׂפַּדְנָה Je 49^{3} Mas., < mod. edd. ס׳ v. ספד.

שׂפה (√ of foll.; cf. NH = BH; As. *šaptu, lip, edge;* so Syr. ܣܶܦܬܳܐ; Ar. شَفَةٌ *lip,* شَفًا *edge*).

שָׂפָה 176 **n.f.** [**m.** Ex 28^{32}, *edge,* cf. Albr ZAW xvi (1896), 76], **lip, speech, edge**;—abs. שׂ׳ Gn 11^{1} +, cstr. שְׂפַת v^{7} +; sf. שְׂפָתוֹ 1 K 7^{23} +, etc.; oftener du. שְׂפָתַיִם Is 6^{5} +; cstr. שִׂפְתֵי ψ 12^{4} +; sf. שְׂפָתַי Je 17^{16} +, sf. 3 mpl. שִׂפְתֵימוֹ ψ 59^{13} $140^{4.10}$, etc.; pl. (poet. and late) cstr. שִׂפְתוֹת Ec 10^{12}, sf. שִׂפְתוֹתֶיךָ etc. ψ 45^{3} 59^{8} Is 59^{3} Ct $4^{3.11}$ 5^{13};—**1.** *lip:* **a.** usu. (c. 108 t.) human organ of speech (oft. ‖ לָשׁוֹן, פֶּה, rarely [only late poetry] חֵךְ: 10 t. Jb; 25 t. ψψ; 45 t. Pr): (1) Is 29^{13} Lv 5^{4} (P), Jb 13^{6} Mal 2^{6} ψ 12^{5} Pr 5^{3} +; שׂ׳ דַּל ψ 141^{3} (v. דַּל); אִישׁ שׂ׳ Jb 11^{2} = a talker, אֱוִיל שׂ׳ Pr 10^{8} = one talking folly, so v^{10} (MT; but v. Toy); טְמֵא שְׂפָתַיִם Is $6^{5.5}$ cf. v^{7} Dn 10^{16}; עֲרַל שׂ׳ Ex $6^{12.30}$ (P; unskilled in speech); עִקֵּשׁ שׂ׳ 19^{1}; פִּתְחֵה שׂ׳ 20^{19} v. [פָּתָה] p. 834; מוֹצָא שׂ׳ i.e. utterance, Dt 23^{24} Je 17^{16} Nu 30^{13} (P), ψ 89^{35}, רוּחַ שׂ׳ Is 11^{4} (of Mess. kg.), דְּבַר שׂ׳ ψ 59^{13} Pr 14^{23} +, = mere, empty, word 2 K 18^{20} = Is 36^{5}; תְּבוּאַת שׂ׳ Pr 18^{20}, נוּב שׂ׳ Is 57^{19} (thanksgiving), cf. Ho 14^{3} (𝔊𝔖 and most פְּרִי for פָּרִים); of flattery, חֵלֶק שׂ׳ Pr 7^{21}, שְׂפַת חֲלָקוֹת ψ $12^{3.4}$; cf. שְׂפַת אָוֶן, שׂ׳ שֶׁקֶר ψ 31^{19} + 4 t., שִׂפְתֵי מִרְמָה ψ 17^{1} Pr 17^{4}; poison beneath (cf. לָשׁוֹן) ψ 140^{4} (fig.); שׂ׳ יֶתֶר, שׂ׳ אֱמֶת Pr 12^{19}, לְזוּת שׂ׳ 4^{24}; פֶּשַׁע שׂ׳ Pr 12^{13}; 17^{7}, שׂ׳ צֶדֶק 16^{13}, דַּעַת שׂ׳ 14^{7} 20^{15}; חֵן שׂ׳ 22^{11}; שׂ׳ רְנָנוֹת ψ 63^{5} i.e. lips that shout for joy; שָׂפָה בְרוּרָה Zp 3^{9}; c. vbs.: פָּתַח שׂ׳ (to speak) Jb 11^{5} 32^{20} (Gi v^{21}), cf. ψ 51^{17}, מִפְתַּח שׂ׳ Pr 8^{6}; פֹּשֵׂק שׂ׳ 13^{3} i.e. prate; שׂ׳ מָלְאוּ זַעַם Is 30^{27}; שׂ׳ subj. of דִּבֶּר Is 59^{3} Pr 24^{2}; נָשָׂא עַל־שׂ׳ ψ 16^{4}; קֹרֵץ שׂ׳ Pr 16^{30} = backbite; אֹטֵם שׂ׳ 17^{28} = keep silence, so חֹשֵׂךְ שׂ׳ 10^{19}, כָּלָא שׂ׳ ψ 40^{10}. †(2) lips moving in speech, c. נוּעַ 1 S 1^{13}, נִיד Jb 16^{5}. †(3) transition to mng. *speech,* עָלָה עַל־שְׂפַת לָשׁוֹן Ez 36^{3}; = ability to speak Jb 12^{20}. †**b.** organ of laughter Jb 8^{21}. †**c.** of insulting grimace הִפְטִיר בְּשׂ׳ ψ 22^{8}. †**d.** quivering in terror Hb 3^{16}. †**e.** feature of beauty Ct 4^{3} (scarlet). **f.** place of bridle 2 K 19^{28} = Is 37^{29} (v. מֶתֶג).

†g. receiving kiss Pr 24[26] cf Ct 4[11] and (in fig.) 7[10] †h. of divine speech, מִצְוֹת שׂ׳ Jb 23[12], דִּבְרֵי שׂ׳ ψ 17[4]. †2. *language* (v. לָשׁוֹן), Gn 11[1.6.7.7.9] ψ 81[6], עַם עִמְקֵי שׂ׳ Ez 3[5.6] Is 33[19], לַעֲגֵי שׂ׳ 28[11], שְׂפַת כְּנַעַן 19[18] (i e Hebrew). **3.** *edge shore* of sea Gn 22[17] (J) + 7 t, *bank* of river Gn 41[3.17] (E) + 5 t, of wady (נַחַל) Dt 2[36] + 7 t, *lip* (bank) of אָבֵל מְחוֹלָה Ju 7[22] cf. GASm[G 400], *brim* of vessel 1 K 7[23.26] + 7 t., *edge* of altar Ez 43[13], of curtains (in pairs) Ex 26[4.4] (P) + 6 t; of חשֶׁן, toward ephod 28[26] = 39[19] (P), of round opening in robe לְפִיו (יִהְיֶה) שׂ׳ 28[32] = 39[23] (P)

†שָׂפָם **n.[m.] moustache** (cf NSyr ܣܦܡܐ *rete*, on meaning and form v Thes Ol[404] Ko[II 70]);—abs שׂ׳ Mi 3[7] +, sf שְׂפָמוֹ 2 S 19[25],—*moustache* עָשָׂה שׂ׳ 2 S 19[25] (𝔊 μύσταξ) i e trim it; עָטָה עַל־שׂ׳ Mi 3[7] Ez 24[17.22] Lv 13[45] (P, v I עטה 1)

שִׂפְחָה v. III ספח   מִשְׂפָּח v II ספח

שִׂפְמוֹת 1 S 30[28] v שְׂפָ׳.

שָׂפַן v. ספן. I שׂפק, שֶׂפֶק v ספק.

†II [שָׂפַק] **vb suffice** (NH סָפַק *suffice, abound*, so Ecclus 15[18] +, 𝔗 סְפַק, סְפִיק, Syr ܣܦܩ, Ar شَفِقَ is *be niggardly, scanty*, Lane [1571]),—**Qal** *Impf* 3 ms יִשְׂפֹּק 1 K 20[10], subj dust, c לְ rei

†[שֶׂפֶק] **n.[m.] sufficiency, plenty**,—sf שִׂפְקוֹ Jb 20[22] (Baer Gi; ס׳ van d H, opp. צרר).

שַׂק v שקק

†[שָׂקַד] doubtful **vb.**, Ki bind on,—**Niph.** *Pf* 3 ms. נִשְׂקַד עַל La 1[14] (fig), rd perh נִשְׁקַד עַל *watch is kept upon* 𝔊 𝔖 𝔙 Bu, cf Thes (v שקד), other conj in Löhr Bi

שקק (assumed as √ of foll, but nowhere found)

†שַׂק **n m.**[Jos 9 4] **sack, sackcloth** (v. Schwally ZAW xi (1891), 173 who conj Egyptian origin; NH סַק *sackcloth* (rare); As *šakḳu, sack* (Dl[HWB 687 a]), *sackcloth* (Wkl[Altor Forsch vi 44]), Eth ሠቅ፡ = BH, Aram סַקָּא, ܣܩܐ, Gk σάκκος Lewy[Fremdw 87]),—abs שׂ׳ Gn 37[34] +, שָׂק Je 48[37] +, sf. שַׂקִּי ψ 30[12], etc, pl שַׂקִּים Jos 9[4] +, sf. שַׂקֵּיהֶם Gn 42[35];—**1.** *sack*, for grain Gn 42[25.27] (‖ אַמְתַּחַת), v[35.35] (E), Jos 9[4] (JE), perh also Lv 11[32] (P) **2.** *sackcloth* **a.** worn in mourning and humiliation (v. Now[Arch i 192 f] SACook[Ency Bib s v]), either loose garment like sack, or piece of similar material (of rough, dark hair), fastened round body: put (שִׂים) on loins Gn 37[34] (J), 1 K 20[31], on (bare) flesh 21[27] 2 K 6[30], cf Je 48[37] Jb 16[15] (c. תָּפַר); וְהַעֲלֵיתִי עַל־כָּל־מָתְנַיִם שׂ׳ Am 8[10], usu gird on (חָגַר) 2 S 3[31] Is 15[3] 22[12] Je 4[8] 6[26] 49[3] Ez 7[18] 27[31] 1 K 20[32] Jo 1[8], cf Is 3[24], כִּסָּה בַשׂ׳ 2 K 19[1.2] = Is 37[1.2], Jon 3[6.8] 1 Ch 21[16], fig of heavens (cf. קַדְרוּת), שׂ׳ אָשִׂים כְּסוּתָם Is 50[3], late לָבַשׁ שׂ׳ *put on sackcloth* Jon 3[5] Est 4[1], cf v[2] ψ 35[13] 69[12]; בְּצוֹם וְשׂ׳ Ne 9[1], cf Dn 9[3], פִּתַּח שׂ׳ *loosen sackcloth* Is 20[2] (+ מֵעַל), ψ 30[12] (opp שִׂמְחָה), הֵסִיר שׂ׳ מֵעַל Est 4[4]. **b.** same garment (or material) spread out (to lie on), 2 S 21[10] (c הִטָּה), Is 58[5] (c. הִצִּיעַ), cf. Est 4[3], לִינוּ בַשׂ׳ 1 K 21[27], וַיֵּשֶׁב בַּשׂ׳ Jo 1[13].

†[שָׂקַר] **vb. Pi. ogle** (Aram סְקַר *look at* (𝔗 Jb 20[9] 28[7]), סַקְרָנִית *looking about, ogling*; ܣܩܪ *eye* with envy or hatred (e g 1 S 18[9] 𝔖); cf De[11]),—*Pt* fpl מְשַׂקְּרוֹת עֵינַיִם Is 3[16] *ogling of eyes* (women of Jerusalem)

שׂרר v שַׂר

†שַׂרְאֶצֶר **n pr.m.** in Assyr. (Bab.) (van d. H. שׂ׳, but v Baer, and Str[ZMG xxxiii (1879), 302], in As. perhaps [*Ašur, Bêl*, or *Nergal*] *šar-uṣur*, [..] *protect the king!* COT[2 K 19 37], Σαρασα(ρ)),—**1.** son of Sennach, 2 K 19[37] = Is 37[38] (Schr[COT l c] Wkl[KAT 3 84] Stevenson[Hast DB. iv 476]). **2.** a returned exile Zc 7[2] (Stevenson[ib 477]).—Cf. also נֵרְגַל שׂ׳ p 669.

†[שָׂרַג] **vb. Pu. be intertwined** (Talm. סָרַג Pi *enmesh, weave around*; Aram ܣܪܓ *intertwine, involve*, סְרַג *entwine*; Ar شَرَجَ *set in order, join, weave, mix*);—*Impf* 3 mpl יְשֹׂרָגוּ Jb 40[17] *are intertwined* (of sinews of hippopot.). **Hithp.** *Impf* 3 mpl. יִשְׂתָּרְגוּ La 1[14] *they intertwine themselves* (fig of פְּשָׁעַי).

†[שָׂרִיג] **n.m.**[Gn 40. 10] **tendril, twig** (from *interlacing*; cf. Ar. شَرِيجَة palm-leaf *braid*, etc; Eth. ሠረገላት፡ *net* (Prä[BASI 371]); Aram. סְרִיגָא, ܣܪܝܓܐ *network, lattice*);—of vine, pl. שָׂרִיגִם Gn 40[10], שָׂרִגִים v[12], of fig-tree, sf. שָׂרִיגֶיהָ Jo 1[7].

†שְׂרוּג **n.pr.m.** descendant (i e younger branch) of Peleg Gn 11[20.21.22.23] 1 Ch 1[26], Σερουχ (𝔊L Ch Σερουγ)

†I [שָׂרַד] **vb. escape** (Ar شَرَدَ *take fright, shy* (of camel or horse), *run away*; Aram. ܣܪܕ *be terrified*, ܣܪܝܕܐ *survivor*),—**Qal** *Pf.* 3 pl. שָׂרְדוּ Jos 10[20] (JE; c. מִן pers.), Benn del as dittogr.

†I. שָׂרִיד **n.m.** $^{Je\,47.4}$ **survivor** (from a defeat, etc).—abs. ש׳ Is 1^{9}+, sf. שְׂרִידוֹ Jb 27^{15} Kt; pl. שרידִים Jos 10^{20} Jo 3^{5}; cstr. שְׂרִידֵי Je 31^{2}; sf. שְׂרִידָיו Ob^{14} + Jb 27^{15} Qr (van d. H. also Kt);—**1.** *survivor* (oft.‖פְּלִים): esp עַד בִּלְתִּי הִשְׁאִיר לוֹ ש׳ Nu 21^{35} Jos 8^{22} (both JE), Dt 3^{3} Jos 10^{33} 11^{8} 2 K 10^{11} (all D); more simply, לא השׁ׳ ש׳ Dt 2^{34} Jos $10^{28.30.37\,39.40}$ (all D); לֹא יִהְיֶה ... י׳ הוֹתִיר לָנוּ ש׳ Is 1^{9}, ש׳ לְ Je 42^{17} 44^{14} Ob ^{18}, וְהֶאֱבִיד ... אין ש׳ Jb 18^{19}, ש׳ מֵעִיר Nu 24^{19} (JE), עַם שְׂרִידֵי חָרֶב Je 31^{2}, pl. also Jos 10^{20} (subj. of שָׂרְדוּ), Jo 3^{5} Ob ^{14} Jb 27^{15} (v. supra); sg also Ju 5^{13} (obscure, for ש׳ לְ rd. perh. יִשְׂרָאֵל GFM Now cf. Bu), Je 47^{4} La 2^{22}. **2.** of things אין ש׳ לְאָכְלוֹ Jb 20^{21}, i e. nothing has escaped his greed, (אשׁ) יֵרַע ש׳ בְּאָהֳלוֹ v^{26}.

†II. שָׂרִיד **n.pr.loc.** on border of Zebulun;—עד־ש׳ Jos 19^{10} (P; Εσεδεκγωλα, A ἕως Σαρθιδ, 𝔊L Σαρειδ), מש׳ v^{12} (P; ἀπὸ Σεδδουκ, A Σαριδ).

II. שׂרד (√of foll., *plait, braid*? (Lag $^{BN\,175\,ff}$ thinks ש׳ Avestan loan-word))

†שְׂרָד **n.[m.]** perhaps Aram. **plaited** or **braided work** (cf then Aram. סְרָדָא *lattice-work, net-work* (=BH מִכְבָּר), *textile stuff, curtain* (=BH קְלָעִים), סַרְדּוּתָא *plaited* or *braided work*, NH סָרָד *plaiter*, סָרִיד, סָרוּד *woven-work;* Hom $^{ZMG\,xliv\,(1890)\,543}$ cp. Bab *šardu, skin*);—alw. abs (הַ)ש׳ בגדי Ex 31^{10} 35^{19} $39^{1.41}$ (all P; all + הַקֹּדֶשׁ ב׳, and last three + לְשָׁרֵת בַּקֹּדֶשׁ); 𝔊 31^{10} τ. στολὰς τ. λειτουργικάς (cf. 39^{1} [B v^{13}, 𝔊L v^{11}])

†שֶׂרֶד **n.[m.]** from context, a marking-tool for wood, **stylus** (so Thes al., connexion with above √dub., Lewy $^{Fremdw\,57\,f}$ cp. σάρδιον as gem used in gem-cutting),—יְתָאֲרֵהוּ בַשֶּׂרֶד Is 44^{13}.

שָׂרָה **n.f. et pr.** v. sub שׂרר.

†I. שָׂרָה **vb. persist, exert oneself, persevere** (Ar. شَرِيَ *persist, persevere*),—**Qal** *Pf.* 3 ms ש׳ אֶת־א׳ Ho 12^{4} *he persevered with God;* 2 ms. שָׂרִיתָ עִם־א׳ וְעִם אֲנָשִׁים Gn 32^{29} (J)—Ho 12^{5} has *Impf.* וַיָּשַׂר in same meaning, as if from a (non-existent) שׂוּר, < rd. וַיִּשַׂר (apoc. fr. וַיִּשְׂרֶה)—שׂוֹרָה Is 28^{25} v. supra, p 965^{a}

יִשְׂרָאֵל $_{2507}$ **n.pr.m. et gent. Israel** (*Ēl persisteth, persevereth* (or juss *Let Ēl persist*) [usu. *contendeth* (Nes $^{Eg\,60\,ff}$) or *Let Ēl contend* (Gray $^{Prop\,N\,218}$), but v. Dr $^{Hast.\,DB\,JACOB\,530}$]; on vocalization v. Lag $^{BN\,131\,f}$ Kit $^{1\,Ch\,4,16\,(Hpt)}$; MI $^{5,+5\,t.}$ ישראל, in Egypt. *Y-si-r-'l* Steindorff $^{ZAW\,xvi\,(1896),\,331}$, cf. Breasted $^{Bib\,World\,ix\,(1897),\,62\,ff}$ Paton $^{Syr\,and\,Pal\,134}$; As *Sir-'-lai* (=יִשְׂרָאֵלִי) Schr $^{KG\,356\,ff.,\,364;\,COT\,Gn\,36,\,31,\,1\,K\,16\,29}$.—On a poss. relation of יִשׂ׳ to n pr. שָׂרָה, שָׂבִי v. RS $^{K\,257,\,2nd\,ed\,14}$;—cf. (שְׂרָיָה(וּ)),—Ἰσραηλ: **1. n.pr.m.** second name of Jacob Gn 32^{29} + 28 t. Gn (JE), Ex 32^{13} (JE), Ho 12^{13} Ju 18^{29} Ex 6^{14} Nu 1^{20} 26^{5} (all P), 2 K 17^{34} 1 Ch 1^{34} + 8 t. Chr, ψ 105^{23}; בית יִשׂ׳ Ru 4^{11}; בני יִשׂ׳ (lit.) Gn 42^{5} + 3 t E, 2 t. P + Ex 1^{7} (P, transition to wider use), 1 K 18^{31} 1 Ch 2^{1}+; = 12 tribes Ex 28^{9} + 7 t. P; אֱלֹהֵי אַבְרָהָם יִצְחָק וְיִשׂ׳ + 1 K 18^{36} 1 Ch 29^{18} 2 Ch 30^{6}. **2. n.pr.gent.** (usu. **m.** $^{Ju\,11,\,17\,f}$ but **f.** 1 S 17^{21} 2 S 24^{9} [not ‖ 1 Ch 21^{5}], cf. Dr $^{ad\,loc}$ Albr $^{ZAW\,xvi\,(1896),\,57\,f}$) name of Hebrew nation; usu. der. from **1**, but יִשׂ׳ more common in early usage than בְּנֵי יִשׂ׳ (v. בֵּן p. 120^{b}): **a.** (1) undivided kingdom; יִשׂ׳ Gn 47^{27} (J), 49^{7} (poem in J) + 108 t. JE, Dt 1^{1} 18^{6} 33^{10} (poem) + 76 t. D, Gn 34^{7} Ex 12^{15} + 42 t. P, Ju $5^{2.7\,7}$ + 104 t. Ju, oft. 1 and 2 S, 1 K 1–12; כָּל־יִשׂ׳ of whole people 2 S 8^{15}+, of whole army 11^{1}+, opp Judah 2^{9}+ (so also later). (2) יִשׂ׳ = N. tribes, disting fr. Judah, even before disruption, 2 S 2^{9}, cf. v^{10} 3^{10} 4^{1} 5^{5} 12^{7} 20^{1} 1 K 1^{35} 4^{20} 5^{6}+; so at disruption $12^{16\,16.16.18\,19}$; then usu. of N. kingdom, till its fall, v^{28} $24^{7\,10}$ + very oft K, Am 1^{1} 2^{6} 3^{14}+, Ho 1^{5} $4^{15\,15}$ $5^{3.3.5}$+, Mi 1^{13}, etc. (3) יִשׂ׳ of S kingdom, Judah, rarely bef. fall of Samaria Is 1^{3} 8^{18} Mi $1^{14\,15}$, so בני יִשׂ׳ 1 K 12^{17}; after fall of Sam, יִשׂ׳ (less oft. בְּנֵי יִשׂ׳) occurs of entire people, in reference to past or future 2 K 21^{8} 23^{22} Is 17^{9} ψ 103^{7} Je 2^{3} $50^{17\,19}$+; יִשׂ׳ also = Judah Je $2^{14.31}$ 4^{1}+, Ez $13^{2.4.16}$ $14^{1.7\,9}$+, Is 40^{27} 41^{8} 42^{24}+, Ezr 2^{59} = Ne 7^{61}, Ezr 2^{70} 3^{11}+, Ne 10^{34} 10^{3}+, ψ $14^{7\,7}$ = $53^{7\,7}$, 147^{2} 149^{2}+, etc (4) usage in Chr: יִשׂ׳ of whole people 1 Ch 2^{7} + 110 t., of N. kingdom 2 Ch 11^{1} + 16 t., of Judah 12^{6} 19^{8} + 9 t. (5) יִשׂ׳ personif. as עֶבֶד י׳, Is $44^{1\,21}$ 49^{3}. **b.** בְּנֵי יִשׂ׳, (1) of undiv people Ex 1^{12} (J), 3^{9} (E) + 72 t JE, Dt 3^{18} 10^{6} + 25 t D, Gn 32^{33} + 327 t. P; Ju 1^{1} + 60 t. Ju; seld. 1 and 2 Sm, 1 K 1–12; in 13–2 K 25 *pass.* in ref. to older hist. (rarely otherwise) (2) seldom of N. kingdom Am 2^{11} + 9 t. Am Ho, 2 Ch 13^{12} + 7 t Chr. (3) of Judah (late) Ez 2^{3} Ne $1^{6.6}$ Ezr 3^{1} Jo 4^{16}+, 2 Ch 31^{5}. **c.** בית יִשׂ׳ Ex 16^{31} 40^{38} + 142 t. (v. בַּיִת **5 d** (δ), 81 t. Ez, where = Judah; v. esp 37^{16}); שְׁנֵי בָתֵּי יִשׂ׳ Is 8^{14} **d.** other phrases, v. sub אִישׁ, אֶרֶץ, בַּת, (יעד) עֵדָה, (נטה) מַטֶּה, מֶלֶךְ, כִּסֵּא, הַר, גְּבוּל, בְּתוּלָה, שֵׁבֶט, עַם, also (in epith. of י׳) sub אוֹר, אָבִיר, אלהים, I. גֹּאֵל, מֶלֶךְ, מִקְוֶה (I. קוה), 1. צוּר (V. צוּר), קָדוֹשׁ, I. רָעָה **1 d** (3). †**e.** יִשׂ׳ = the laity, opp.

priests, etc. (late) Ezr 10[25] Ne 11[3] 1 Ch 9[2]; כָּל־יִשׂ׳ Ezr 2[70] 10[5]; הָעָם יִשׂ׳ 9[1]; בְּנֵי יִשׂ׳ Ne 10[40], cf שְׁאָר יִשׂ׳ 11[20].

†יִשְׂרְאֵלִי adj. gent. of foregoing;—m. הַיִּשׂ׳ Lv 24[10], f. הַיִּשְׂרְאֵלִית v[10 11], cf. v[10] —2 S 17[25] < הַיִּשְׁמְעֵאלִי, 𝔊[A] Th We Dr al (so ‖ 1 Ch 2[17]).

†שְׂרָיָה(וּ) n.pr.m. (י׳ persisteth Dr [Hast. DB s. Israel]).—usu. Σαραια(ς),—שְׂרָיָה: 1. secretary of David 2 S 8[17], but 𝔊[B] Ασα, ‖ שְׁיָא 20[25] Kt (שְׁוָא Qr), שַׁוְשָׁא 1 Ch 18[16] (in both Ἰησοῦς, 𝔊L Σουσα), שִׁישָׁא 1 K 4[3] (Σαβα, A Σεισα, 𝔊L Σαφατ), orig in all prob שַׁוְשָׁא We Dr Klo (*Sausa*), HPS (שִׁישָׁא), Now (*Šoša*), Bu 2. chief priest 2 K 25[18] = Je 52[24] 3. a captain 2 K 25[23] Je 40[8] 51[59 bis 61] 4. a. son of Kenaz 1 Ch 4[13 14] b. name in Simeon v[35] c. Levite name 5[40 40] 5. a. companion of Zerub Ezr 2[2] b. father of Ezra 7[1] c. one sealed Ne 10[3] d. priest 11[11] 12[1 12] 6. שְׂרָיָהוּ, officer of king Jehoiakim, Je 36[26], τῷ Σαραιᾳ.

II שׂרה (√of foll, = *rule*? cf. שׂרר)

†מִשְׂרָה n f. rule, dominion;—Is 9[5.6].

†שֶׂרַח n pr.f. (cf. Sab n pr m שרח Sab Denkm [No. 3a, l. 1 and p. 72], שרחאל Id [No. 13, l 2. 12], אלשרח DHM [Epigr. Denkm. Arab. (1889)]).—daughter of Asher Gn 46[17] 1 Ch 7[30], שָׂרַח Nu 26[46], Σααρ, Σαρ(ρ)α, etc , 𝔊[B] Nu Καρα

†[שָׂרַט] vb. incise, scratch (NH *id*, so Aram כְּרַט Pa (𝔗 1 S 21[14]), ܣܪܛ, ܣܪܛܐ *scratch*, hence *write* (= χαράσσω), As. *šarâṭu*, *slit up*, *rend*, Ar شَرَطَ *slit* ear of camel, شَرْطٌ, شَرَطٌ *sign*, *mark* (RS[K 248]),—Qal *Impf* 3 mpl c acc cogn וּבִבְשָׂרָם לֹא יִשְׂרְטוּ שָׂרָטֶת Lv 21[5] *shall make no incision*, *Inf abs* c Niph. *Impf* 3 mpl. שָׂרוֹט יִשָּׂרֵטוּ Zc 12[3] those loaded with the stone *shall be severely scratched*, lacerated.

†שֶׂרֶט n [m.] incision,—abs. וְשֶׂ׳ לָנֶפֶשׁ לֹא תִתְּנוּ בִּבְשַׂרְכֶם Lv 19[28]

†[שָׂרֶטֶת] n.f. id (Ba[§ 123 a α]),—שָׂרֶטֶת Lv 21[5], v. vb Qal

שָׂרַי v sub שׂרר

(שְׂרָיָה(וּ v. sub I שׂרה

†שִׂרְיֹן, -ן n.pr.mont (in As *Sirara* COT [in 2 S 1 K 5. 13] Dl [Pa 104f]),—Sidonian name of Hermon Dt 3[9] (Σανιωρ), ה- ψ 29[6] (+ לְבָנוֹן, v an d II al.׳שׁ).

†[שָׂרַךְ] vb. twist (so 𝔗 סְרַךְ (= Heb. עִוָּה, עִוֵּת), perhaps akin to סרג, שׂרג, Talm סָרַךְ is *adhere*, cf Aram. ܣܪܟ, ܣܪܟ; Ar. شَرِكَ is *share*, *participate*, but شِرَاكٌ *sandal-thong*, شَرَكٌ *snare*),—Pi. *Pt* fs מְשָׂרֶכֶת דְּרָכֶיהָ Je 2[23] a swift dromedary *entangling her ways* (galloping aimlessly, fig).

†[שְׂרוֹךְ] n. [m.] (sandal-)thong (? from above √, as *crossed and twisted* over the foot; on vocalization cf. Ar. *supra*, Ges [I Man] Ba [NB § 124 c]),—cstr, שְׂ׳־נַעַל Gn 14[23] Is 5[27].

†שַׂרְסְכִים n.pr.m. a prince of Nebuch. Je 39[3], but read prob. (נבו) שָׁזְבָן, v. Gie Du, cf. p 613[a] supra, 𝔊 Ναβουσαχαρ, etc.

†[שָׂרַע] vb. extend (Ar شَرَعَ *point directly at*, also *enter upon* a path (Fra[213] thinks orig *divide*, then *stretch out*, *make straight*), شُرْعَةٌ *projecting roof*, أَشْرَعُ *long-nosed* (*torto naso* 𝔙 [Lv 21, 18]), Eth. ሠርዐ: *dispose*, *arrange*; Sab. שרע *arrangement*, *security* Hom[Chr 124];—but Aram. ܣܪܥ expl as *mutilated* Lv 21[18] 22[23] PS[2744], cf. 𝔊 ὠτότμητος);—Qal *Pt. pass.* שָׂרוּעַ *extended*, i e too long (in a limb or member), of man Lv 21[18], beast 22[23] (v. II חרם) Hithp. *stretch oneself* *Inf. cstr* הִשְׂתָּרֵעַ Is 28[20] (v מַצָּע p 427[a]).

שַׂרְעַפִּים v. sub שׂעף

שָׂרַף [117] vb. burn (70 t + בָּאֵשׁ, 2 t. + (בְּמוֹרָאשׁ (NH (rare) = BH, As. *šarâpu*, Aram. שְׂרַף (rare), ܣܪܦ is *absorb*, *consume*),—Qal *Pf*. 3 ms. שׂ׳ Jos 11[9] +, 3 fs sf שְׂרָפָתַם Is 47[14], etc; *Impf* 3 ms יִשְׂרֹף Nu 19[5] + 2 t., more oft תִּשְׂרֹף Ex 32[20] +, 2 mpl תשרפון Dt 7[5] + 2 t; *Inf abs*. שָׂרוֹף 2 S 23[7]; cstr שְׂרֹף Je 36[25] +; sf שָׂרְפוֹ Ju 9[52] Am 2[1], *Pt. act* שׂרף Lv 16[28] Nu 19[8], pl שֹׂרְפִים 2 K 17[31]; *pass* mpl. שְׂרֻפִים Nu 17[4]; fs שְׂרוּפָה 1 S 30[3], שְׂרֻפָה ψ 80[17], pl שְׂרוּפוֹת Ne 3[34], cstr. שְׂרֻפוֹת Is 1[7],—*burn* (59 t. + בָּאֵשׁ, 2 t. + (בְּמוֹרָאשׁ 1. in making bricks, + לִשְׂרֵפָה Gn 11[3] (J, obj. om). 2. a. c acc. rei, usu to destroy, e. g. door Ju 9[52], house Ju 12[1] 1 K 16[18] (both c. עַל pers), Je 39[8] + 11 t, cf. pt. pass. Ne 3[34], city Jos 6[24] 1 S 30[1 14] + 16 t, cf. pt pass. 1 S 30[3] Is 1[7], chariots Jos 11[6 9] 2 K 23[11] ψ 46[10] (subj י׳), idols, etc., Ex 32[20] (acc om), Dt 9[21] + 10 t, roll †Je 36[25 27 28. 29. 32], wood †Is 44[16 19] (both + (בְּמוֹרָאשׁ, cf. ψ 80[17] (fig), Je 51[32], hair †Ez 5[4]; bones, to lime (as outrage) †Am 2[1], upon altars (in desecration) †1 K 13[2] 23[16 20] = 2 Ch 34[5]; bodies, as funeral rite †1 S

31[12] (rare custom, RS[Sem. i. 353, 2nd ed 372]; but Klo Bu rd. יִשְׂפְּדוּ [=יס׳]; cf. Benz[Arch. 163. Ency Bib. DEAD] Now[Arch i. 188]); שׂ׳ as funeral rite also (obj. om., prob. spices, cf. 2 Ch 16[14]), †c. לְ pers. mort. Je 34[5], + acc cogn. שְׂרֵפָה 2 Ch 16[14] (cf. שְׂרֵפָה); in ceremonial of P (never of burning sacrif on altar, הִקְטִיר, cf. העלה, but) chiefly (14 t.) of consuming refuse, esp unused portions of victims, etc. (to prevent use), and infected objects, Ex 29[14.34] +, sts. מחוץ לַמַּחֲנֶה Lv 4[12] (+ עַל־עֵצִים), v[21 21] + 4 t., etc., cf. Ez 43[21]; also of burning red heifer (to produce ashes for purification) Nu 19[5.5.8]. †**b.** *burn*, c. acc. pers, (1) as penalty Jos 7[25] (JE), Ju 14[15] 15[6] Lv 20[14], cf. Nu 17[4] (pt. pass.), so, אֵשׁ subj., Is 47[14], c. acc. cogn. שְׂרֵפָה Lv 10[6] (P); (2) as sacrifice, Je 7[31] 19[5]; + לְ dei Dt 12[31] 2 K 17[31]. †**Niph.** *Impf* 3 ms יִשָּׂרֵף Jos 7[15] +, 3 fpl. תִשָּׂרַפְנָה Pr 6[27], etc.;—*be burned* (11 t. + בָּאֵשׁ): of city Je 38[17] + v[23] (read תִּשָּׂרֵף for תשרף 𝔊𝔖𝔗 Hi Ew Gf Gie Du), idols, etc., Mi 1[7] 1 Ch 14[12]; ritually (cf. **Qal 2 a** ad fin) Lv 4[12] 6[23] 7[17 19] 13[52] 19[6]; of pers, as penalty Gn 38[24] (J), Jos 7[15] (JE), 2 S 23[7] (poet.), Lv 21[9] (H). †**Pi.** *Pt.* sf. מְסָרְפוֹ Am 6[10] *his burner*, usu. *one burning him*, but prob. *burning* spices for him, v. Dr and cf **Qal** supra. †**Pu.** *Pf* 3 ms. שֹׂרַף, of goat Lv 10[16] *it was burnt up* (and gone).

†I. שָׂרָף **n.m.**[Is 14, 29] a serpent, usu. venomous (poss from above √, from *burning* effect of poison);—abs. שׂ׳ Nu 21[8] (JE; on Ar parallels v. Jacob[Ar Dichter ii. 93, iv 10 f.]), appos. נָחָשׁ שׂ׳ Dt 8[15], pl הַנְּחָשִׁים הַשְּׂרָפִים Nu 21[6]; a flying serpent, or *dragon*, שָׂרָף מְעוֹפֵף Is 14[29] 30[6].

†II. [שָׂרָף] **n.m.**[Is 6, 2] pl. שְׂרָפִים **seraphim** (prob akin to I. שׂ׳, as beings orig mythically conceived with serpents' bodies (serpent-deities, cf Is 14[29] 30[6]), or (Che[Comm.]) personif. of lightning, cf. arts. SERAPHIM, Strachan[Hast. DB] Che [Encу Bib.]; Di Marti al. cp also Egypt. guardian-griffins, called *Šerref*; v. also כְּרוּב; on As. *Šarrapu* (-*bu*), epith of god Nergal, connected by Dl[WB] with √שָׂרַף, v. שָׂרָב, Zim[KAT 2. 415]);—in OT. majestic beings with six wings, and human hands and voices, attendant upon י׳ Is 6[2.6].

†III. שָׂרָף **n.pr.m.** a Judahite;—1 Ch 4[22]; Σαια, A 𝔊L Σαραφ

†שְׂרֵפָה **n.f.** burning;—abs. שׂ׳ Is 9[4] +, cstr. שְׂרֵפַת Nu 19[6] +;—לִשׂ׳ of brick-burning Gn 11[3] (+ שָׂרַף); destructive Am 4[11] Is 9[4], of land Dt 29[22], of temple, הָיָה לִשְׂרֵפַת אֵשׁ Is 64[10], הַר שׂ׳ Je 51[25] i.e a burnt-out volcano (fig. of Bab.); of heifer Nu 19[6], cf v[17]; of spices (prob.) as funeral rite 2 Ch 16[14] (as acc. cogn.), 21[19] (obj. of עָלָה), v[19]; of pers. (penal) Lv 10[6] (acc. cogn., י׳ subj.), Nu 17[2].

†[מִשְׂרָפָה, מַשְׂרֵפָה] **n.[f.]** a burning;—only pl cstr. מִשְׂרְפוֹת: בְּמ׳ אֲבוֹתֶיךָ Je 34[5] (read כְּמ׳ 𝔊𝔖𝔙 Gie Du al.), *like the burnings* (of spices, cf. √2 a) *for thy fathers;* מ׳ שִׂיד Is 33[12] (fig. of ignominious destruction, cf. Am 2[1]).

†מִשְׂרְפוֹת מַיִם **n.pr.loc.** named with Sidon Jos 11[8] 13[6] (appar. near coast); cp. (dub. Buhl [Geogr 229]) *Musêrfe*, 14 m. S of Tyre, v. Di and reff., Guérin[Gal ii. 168 f] —Μασερων, Μασρεφωθμαειμ, etc.

I. שׂרק (NH סָרַק, Aram. ܣܪܰܩ, סרק, all *comb, card;* Ar. شَرَقَ *slit* sheep's ear, *pluck* fruit)

†[שָׂרִיק] **adj.** carded, combed, of flax;—fpl. פִּשְׁתִּים שְׂרִיקוֹת Is 19[9]

II. שׂרק (cf NH סָרֹק *light red;* הִשְׂרִיק Ecclus[50, 7. 43, 9 marg] *shine brightly* (of sun); As. *šarku, red blood;* Ar. شَرَقَ *rise and shine* (of sun), *shew redness,* شَرِقَ *become red* (like blood); Sab שרק *rise* (of sun), משרק *East,* שרקן epith. dei *the shining* Sab Denkm.[15, 4] Fell[ZMG liv (1900). 253 f.] cf. Hom[Chr 124]).

†I [שָׂרֹק] **adj.** perh. sorrel (? fr. II. שׂ׳, or cf. أَشْقَرُ *having ruddy tinge* over white, of horses *sorrel* Lane[1581]),—pl. אֲדֻמִּים שְׂרֻקִּים וּלְבָנִים Zc 1[8], of horses.

†II. [שָׂרֹק] **n.[m.]** vine-tendrils (or clusters) (from *red* colour?);—pl sf. שְׂרוּקֶּיהָ Is 16[8].

†I שֹׂרֵק **n.[m.]** choice species of vine;—abs. שׂ׳ Is 5[2], שׂו׳ Je 2[21] (both in fig.).

†II. שֹׂרֵק (van d. H. שׂו׳) **n.pr.loc.** in נַחַל שׂ׳ Ju 16[4] (prop. *Wady of choice vines*),—𝔊 Σωρηχ[κ]; prob. *Wady Ṣurâr* (GASm[Geogr 218 f.]), on N. side of which is ruin *Sûrîk*, 3/4 h. W. of *Ṣur'ah* (Ẓor'ah), Survey[iii. 53] GFM[ad loc].

†שֹׂרֵקָה **n.f.** choice vine;—Gn 49[11].

†מַשְׂרֵקָה **n.pr.loc.** in Edom;—מַשׂ׳ Gn 36[36] = 1 Ch 1[47]; 𝔊 ἐκ Μασέκκας (𝔊L[Ch] ἐκ Μασερικα); Euseb[Onom. ed. Lag 277] Μασρηκα.

שׂרר (√of foll.; mng. dub.; Dl[Pr 92] cp. As. *šarâru, rise in splendour* (of sun, etc.), but dub., cf. Hal[REJ xiv (1887), 1-6]).

שַׂר$_{420}$ **n.m. chieftain, chief, ruler, official, captain, prince** (NH esp. of angels; As. *šarru, king*);—abs. שַׂר 2 S 3^{38}+, הַשַּׂר Mi 7^{3}+, שָׂ֑ר Ho 3^{4}+; cstr. שַׂר Ju 4^{2}+; sf. שַׂרְכֶם Dn 10^{21}; pl. שָׂרִים 1 K 4^{2}+; cstr. שָׂרֵי Gn 12^{15}+; sf. שָׂרַי Ju 5^{15} Is 10^{8}, שָׂרֵיכֶם Je 44^{21}, שָׂרֵיהֶם Is 3^{4}+;—**1.** *chieftain, leader:* **a.** pl. of Isr. Nu 21^{18} (poem in JE; ‖ נְדִיבֵי הָעָם), of Issachar Ju 5^{15} (poem); שָׂרֵי גִלְעָד 10^{18} is dub. (we should expect וְשׂ׳, and cf. זִקְנֵי ג׳, instead, 11$^{5-11}$); of Midian 7^{25} 8^{3}; Philistines 1 S 29$^{3.3.4.4.9}$ (appar. = סְרָנִים v$^{2.6.7}$ [We], yet disting. by HPS and [with reserve] Bu; 𝔊 𝔖 𝔙 Th Bu del. in v^{4b}), cf. 18^{30}; poet., of כְּמוֹשׁ (i.e. the leading Moabites) Je 48^{7}, of מלכם (q.v.; i.e. the leading Ammonites) Am 1^{15}= Je 49^{3}. **b.** sg. David as leader of freebooters 1 S 22^{2}; cf. שׂ׳ גְּדוּד 1 K 11^{24}, pl. 2 S 4^{2}. **2.** *vassal, noble, official*, under king (acting, on occasion, as counsellor, commander, etc.): **a.** pl., in Egypt Gn 12^{15} (J) + 3 t. Is + 30^{4} Di Du Skinner (>of foreign embassy [cf. ‖ מַלְאָכָיו] Che al. rdg. [Che$^{Heb. Hpt.}$ Marti] שָׂרִים), ψ 105^{22}; Moab Nu 22^{8} + 8 t. 22, 23 (JE), Am 2^{3}; Edom Is 34^{12} (‖ חֹרִים); As. 10^{8} 31^{9}; Bab. 21^{5} + 7 t. Je + 2 Ch 32^{31} (but here perhaps vaguely = *authorities*); other nations Je 49^{38} + 17 t. Ezr Est; in gen. Is 49^{7}; *officials, official class*, under kings of Israel: David (only Chr) 1 Ch 22^{17} + 5 t. 1 Ch, Ezr 8^{20}; Sol. 1 K 4^{2}; Jehoiachin 2 K 24$^{12.14}$; Zedek. Je 34^{21} 2 Ch 36^{18}; other kings 19 t. 2 Chr; in gen. Ec 10$^{16.17}$; see also (Judah) Je 1^{18} + 31 t. Je (17^{25a} del. שׂ׳ Gf Che Gie Du), 4 t. La, Ez 17^{12}, Zp 1^{8} (where disting. from בְּנֵי הַמֶּלֶךְ, who are never called שׂ׳); so, in gen., Ne 9$^{32.34}$ Dn 9$^{6.8}$; and (N. Isr.) Ho 3^{4} + 6 t. Ho. **b.** as having powers of magistrate (*ḳaḍi*) Ex 2^{14} (E. + שֹׁפֵט); under Moses (over groups of 1000, 100, 50, 10) 18^{21} + 7 t. 18 (E), Dt 1$^{15.15.15.15}$; later in Judah Ho 5^{10} (Now reads שָׂרֵי יִשׂ׳), Is 1^{23}, cf. 3$^{4.14}$ 32^{1} Mi 7^{3} (sg.; ‖ שֹׁפֵט), Zp 3^{3} (‖ *id.*), Ez 22^{27}, cf. Pr 8^{16} (‖ נְדִיבִים); 28^{2} read perhaps צָרָיו, v. Toy. **c.** as ruler or magistrate of a district (מְדִינָה), 1 K 20$^{14.15.17.19}$ (cf. Est 1^{3} 8^{9} 9^{3}, שָׂרֵי עַם וָעָם 3^{12}). **d.** as *commandant* of city, שׂ׳ הָעִיר Ju 9^{30}, cf. 1 K 22^{26}= 2 Ch 18^{25}, 2 K 23^{8} 2 Ch 34^{8}; of citadel, שׂ׳ הַבִּירָה Ne 7^{2}; pl. of city *officials*, שׂ׳ סֻכּוֹת Ju 8$^{6.14}$ (disting. from זְקֵנִים), cf. 2 K 10^{1} 2 Ch 29^{20}. **3.** specif. military, = *captain, general:* **a.** שַׂר־(ה)צבא Gn 21$^{22.32}$ (E), 26^{26} (J), 1 S 12^{9} + 23 t., + שׂ׳־צ׳־י׳ Jos 5$^{14.15}$ (JE; צָבָא **1 b**), angel-captain in vision; v. also **8, 9**; שָׂרֵי הַצ׳ 1 K 1^{25} + 3 t. Chr, שָׂרִים בַּצ׳ 1 Ch 12^{22} (Gi Baer; van d. H. v^{21}); שָׂרֵי צְבָאוֹת Dt 20^{9} 1 K 2^{5} 1 Ch 27^{3}; שַׂר־הַחַיִל 2 S 24^{2} (but read וְאֶל־שָׂרֵי as 𝔊L and ‖ 1 Ch 21^{2} Th We Dr HPS Bu), שָׂרֵי (הַ)ח׳ v$^{4.4}$ 2 K 9^{5} 2 Ch 33^{14} Ne 2^{9}, שָׂרֵי הַחֲיָלִים 1 K 15^{20}= 2 Ch 16^{4}, 2 K 25$^{23.26}$ Je 40$^{7.13}$ + 7 t. Je; שָׂרֵי מִלְחָמוֹת 2 Ch 32^{6}; so (ה)שׂר alone 2 S 18^{5} 19^{7} 1 K 9^{22}= 2 Ch 8^{9} (𝔊^{B} Be Kit שָׂרָיו וְשָׁלִישָׁיו, for MT שׂ׳ שָׂרֵי), 2 K 9$^{5.5}$ 1 Ch 11$^{6.21}$ + 9 t., + Jb 39^{25} Dn 11^{5}; שׂ׳ וְגָדוֹל 2 S 3^{38} (of Abner); poss. military fig. also in שַׂר שָׁלוֹם Is 9^{5} (Mess. name). **b.** leading companies of 50 2 K 1$^{9-14}$ Is 3^{3}, of 100 1 S 22^{7} + 16 t. + 8^{12} (reading מֵאוֹת for חֲמִשִּׁים 𝔊 HPS, cf. We; Bu ins. שָׂרֵי מֵאוֹת), of 1000 1 S 17^{18} + 11 t., + שָׂרֵי הָאֲלָפִים וְהַמֵּאוֹת 1 Ch 13^{1} 26^{26} (disting. from שָׂרֵי הַצָּבָא), 27^{1} 29^{6} 2 Ch 1^{2}; also שׂ׳ הָרֶכֶב *captain of the chariotry* 1 K 22$^{31.32.33}$= 2 Ch 18$^{30.31.32}$ + 3 t. + שָׂרֵי ר׳ וּפָרָשָׁיו 1 K 9^{22}= 2 Ch 8^{9}. **4. a.** *chief, head*, of other official classes: שַׂר הַטַּבָּחִים, Egypt, Gn 37^{36} + 5 t.; שָׂרֵי הָרָצִים 1 K 14^{27}= 2 Ch 12^{10}; שָׂרֵי הַנִּצָּבִים 1 K 5^{30} 9^{23}= 2 Ch 8^{10}; even domestic positions (court of Pharaoh), שַׂר הַמַּשְׁקִים Gn 40^{2} + 5 t., שַׂר הָאוֹפוּת 40^{2} + 4 t. (all E); שָׂרֵי הַמַּחְלְקוֹת 1 Ch 28^{1}, i.e. of the successive courses of royal military officials; cf. הַשַּׂר 27^{28}; שַׂר הַסָּרִיסִים Dn 1$^{7.8.9.10.11.18}$; שַׂר מְנוּחָה Je 51^{59}. **b.** = *overseer:* שַׂר בֵּית הַסֹּהַר Gn 39$^{21.23}$, שָׂרֵי מִקְנֶה 47^{6} (all J; cf. אַבִּיר הָרֹעִים 1 S 21^{8}), שָׂרֵי מִסִּים Ex 1^{11} (J); cf. 1 Ch 15^{27} 29^{6} 27^{31} 28^{1}.—In 1 Ch 15^{22} read prob. סַר הַמַּשָּׂא (= שַׂר) *overseer of the carrying* (for MT בְּמַשָּׂא יָסֹר בַּמַּשָּׂא), so 𝔊 Benz Kit, Be יָשֹׂר = יָסֹר; v. another view יָסַר **Qal**. **5.** of religious office: שָׂרֵי הַכֹּהֲנִים Ezr 8$^{24.29}$ 10^{5} 2 Ch 36^{14}; שׂ׳ הַלְוִיִּם 1 Ch 15$^{16.22}$ 2 Ch 35^{9}, cf. 1 Ch 15$^{5.6.7.8.10.10}$; heads of classes or courses of priests, called שָׂרֵי קֹדֶשׁ 1 Ch 24^{5}, שׂ׳ אֱלֹהִים v^{5};—שָׂרֵי ק׳ Is 43^{28} (usu. *consecrated princes*, whether priests, or kings, or both) is prob. corrupt, read perh. שַׁעֲרֵי (Du) or וַיְחַלְּלוּ שָׂרֶיךָ קָדְשִׁי 𝔊 Houb Klo Che^{Hpt} Gr (substantially). **6.** late, of representative leaders of people, tribal heads, שׂ׳ שִׁבְטֵי יִשׂ׳ 1 Ch 27^{22} 29^{6}, cf. 28^{1}; appar. = elders, שׂ׳ הָעָם Ez 11^{1} 2 Ch 24^{23}; שׂ׳ alone, ψ 68$^{28.28.28}$; in post-exilic Jerus. Ezr 9$^{1.2}$ Ne 4^{10} 10^{1} 11^{1} (שָׂרֵי הָעָם), + elders Ezr 10$^{8.14}$; called שָׂרֵי יְהוּדָה Ne 12$^{31.32}$; of district-rulers 3$^{9.12.14.15.16.17.18.19}$; of heads of families, שָׂרֵי הָאָבוֹת Ezr 8^{29} 1 Ch 29^{6} (= רָאשֵׁי הָא׳ 24^{31} 27^{1} Ne 7^{70}). **7.** late, as term of rank and dignity, Is 23^{8} (cf. 'merchant-*princes*'), Jb 3^{15} 29^{9} (‖ נְגִידִים), 34^{19} ψ 45^{17} 82^{7} 148^{11}, opp. עבד(ים) Pr 19^{10} Ec 10^{7}; formidable foes ψ 119$^{23.161}$. **8.** = *patron-angel*, only Dn: שַׂר (מַלְכוּת) פָּרַס 10$^{13.20}$, שׂ׳ יָוָן v^{20}; specif. of מִיכָאֵל v$^{13.21}$ 12^{1}. **9.**

שַׂר־הַצָּבָא 8[11] = *God* (prob., cf. צָבָא **1 c**; yet v. also צ׳ **1 b**), so שַׂר שָׂרִים v[25].

†[שָׂרַר] **vb. denom.** (Gerber[20]) **be, or act as, prince, rule**;—**Qal** *Impf.* 3 ms. וַיָּשַׂר עַל־יִשְׂרָאֵל Ju 9[22] Abim *ruled over Isr.* three years; 3 mpl. שָׂרִים . . . יָשֹׂרוּ Is 32[1] princes *shall govern* (*prince it*) justly (|| יִמְלָךְ־מֶלֶךְ), cf Pr 8[16], *Pt* לִהְיוֹת . . . שֹׂרֵר Est 1[22] *that* every man *should bear rule* בביתו. **Hithp.** *Impf*, 2 ms + *Inf abs.* כִּי־תִשְׂתָּרֵר עָלֵינוּ גַּם־הִשְׂתָּרֵר Nu 16[13] *that thou shouldst also keep playing the prince over us.*—יָסֹר 1 Ch 15[22] v. יָסַר **Qal** and שַׂר **4 b**. **Hiph.** *Pf.* 3 pl. metapl. השירו (Ges §67 v) Ho 8[4] *they made princes* (abs.; || הִמְלִיכוּ).

†I. [שָׂרָה] **n.f. princess, noble lady**;—cstr. שָׂרָתִי (Ges §90 l) La 1[1]; pl שָׂרוֹת 1 K 11[3], cstr. *id.* Est 1[18]; sf. שָׂרוֹתֶיהָ Ju 5[29], ־תֵיהֶם Is 49[23];—*princesses* attending Sisera's mother Ju 5[29], of Sol.'s wives 1 K 11[3], other queens Is 49[23] (|| מְלָכִים); wives of nobles Est 1[18]; fig of Jerus. La 1[1].

II. שָׂרָה[37] **n.pr.f.** wife of Abraham (*princess*),—Σαρρα Gn 17[15] (where formal change from שָׂרַי), v[17 19 21] 21[1 b.3] 23[1 1 2.2 19] 25[10 12] 49[31] (all P), 18[6] + 9 t. 18, 21[1 a.2 a] 24[36 67] (all J), 20[2 2 14 16.18] 21[6 7 9 12] (all E), as ancestress of Hebrews Is 51[2].

†שָׂרַי **n.pr.f.** wife of Abram (Nö ZMG xlii (1888). 484 Ges § 80 l Ko ii 1. 427 make = foregoing, with old fem. ending ַ י; > Lag BN 82, Anm *, emphasizing diff. in 𝔊, der. fr. a √ شرى, and cp. شراة, name of a barren mt.; cf. RS יִשְׂרָאֵל supr, sub I. שׂרה);—𝔊 Σαρα,—Gn 11[30] (J), v[31] (P), 12[5 11 17] 16[1 2.3.5.6.6.8.8] (all J), 17[15] (P); שָׂרָי 11[29] (J), 16[2] (J), 17[15] (P).

שָׂשׂוֹן, שָׂשׂוֹן v. שׂושׂ.

שׂת v. שְׂאֵת sub נשׂא p. 673[a].

†שָׂתַם **vb.** usu. stop up, in sense of *shut out*, shut ears against (late || form of סָתַם, yet awkward; Ba ES 9 cp. Ar شَمَتَ *frustrate, disappoint*),—**Qal** *Pf* 3 ms. שׂ׳ תְּפִלָּתִי La 3[8] (> van d. H. שָׁתַם) *he* (׳י) *hath shut out my prayer* (Bu שׂ׳ מתּ׳ *shut up* [himself] *from*)

†[שָׂתַר] **vb. Niph. burst or break out,** of tumours (Ar. شَتِرَ *have inverted*, or *cracked, eyelids*, or *lower lips*; Eth. ሠተረ: *lacerate*; As. [*šatâru*] II. *tear down*; Syr. ܣܬܪ *destroy*, so Sab שתר Sab. Denkm. No. 48, 1 2, BAram. סְתַר Ezr 5[12]);—**Niph.** *Impf.* וַיִּשָּׂתְרוּ לָהֶם עפלים 1 S 5[9] and tumours *brake out* to them

שׁ

שׁ *Šin*, 21st letter (with שׂ); = 300 in post B Hebrew.

·שֶׁ, also (†Gn 6[3] [? v. **4 a**], Ju 5[7 7] Ct 1[7] Jb 19[29] [?]) ·שַׁ, ·שְׁ in שְׁאַתָּה †Ju 6[17], and שׁ in שהוא †Ec 2[22], שהם †3[18] (elsewhere before gutt. ·שֶׁ, as שֶׁאֲנִי †Ct 1[6] Ec 2[18], שֶׁאֵין †ψ 146[3], שֶׁהֵם †Ct 6[5] La 4[9], שֶׁעַל †Ju 7[12] 8[26], שֶׁרֹאשִׁי †Ct 5[2]), **rel. part. who, which, that, etc.** (constantly in NH; Aram. of Nerab, Ldzb 171, 445, As. *ša*; Ph. אש (regularly), also sometimes שׁ (Ldzb 227 f)· acc. to Ges Ew § 181 b Ol p 439 Sta § 176 e, abbrev. from אֲשֶׁר; more prob. (Sperling [v. אֲשֶׁר], Ko ii. 323 f) an original demonstr. part), syn. with אֲשֶׁר, but in usage limited to late Heb., and passages with N Palest colouring, viz †Ju 5[7 7] [אֲשֶׁר v[27]], 6[17] 7[12] 8[26] 2 K 6[11] (v. **4 c**), Jon 1[7 12] 4[10] [אֲשֶׁר 11 t], ψ 122[3.4] 123[2] 124[1 2.6] 129[6.7] 133[2.3] 135[2.8 10] 136[23] 137[8.9] 144[15] 146[3.5] La 2[15 16] 4[9] 5[18] Ezr 8[20] 1 Ch 5[20] 27[27], Ct (uniformly, except in title 1[1]), Ec (68 t.; אֲשֶׁר 89 t); also (dub) Gn 6[3] 49[10] (שלה 𝔊 𝔖 𝔗), Jb 19[29]; and in the n.pr. (q.v.) מִישָׁאֵל and מְתוּשָׁאֵל.—In usage, ·שֶׁ is in the main parallel with אֲשֶׁר, viz. **1.** as **pron.** *who, which, whom*, Ju 7[12] כְּחוֹל שֶׁעַל שְׂפַת הַיָּם (cf. חוֹל **c**), ψ 122[3] 124[6] etc, *him whom, that which*, etc, Ct 1[7] 3[1] 1 Ch 27[27] Ec 1[11] 6[3] וְרַב שֶׁיִּהְיוּ יְמֵי חַיָּיו and much (vb.) is *that which* his days amount to (Hi De al.), v[10]; ·שֶׁ הוּא *that which* 1[9.9]; in the genit., ·אַשְׁרֵי שֶׁ †ψ 137[8.9] 146[5].—On ·מַה־שֶּׁ in Ec = *whatever, what*, v. מָה **1 e b**. **2.** as a connecting link; = *where* (cf. אֲשֶׁר p. 81, and **4 b β**), ·מְקוֹם שֶׁ †Ec 1[7] 11[3] (cf. מְקוֹם אֲשֶׁר Gn 39[20] +: Ges § 130 c), *whither* ψ 122[4] (. . . שֶׁשָּׁם), *when* Ct 8[8] Ec 12[3] ·בַּיּוֹם שֶׁ (cf. *ib.* **4 b α**). **3.** as a **conj.** (cf אֲשֶׁר **8**);—**a.** *that*, after רָאָה Ec 2[13] 3[18], יָדַע 1[17] 2[14] 9[5] Jb 19[29] (? v. p. 192[b]), דִּבֶּר Ec 2[15], אָמַר

8^{14}, עָשָׂה אוֹת Ju 6^{17}; as subj. of sentence, Ec 3^{13} 5^{15}; also in the phrases, (*a*) *what is . . . that?* Ct 5^{9} (usu. כִּי; v. מָה **1 d** *b*), מַה הָיָה שֶׁ׳ how comes it *that . . . ?* Ec 7^{10}; (*b*) Ct 3^{4} כִּמְעַט שֶׁעָבַרְתִּי מֵהֶם hardly (was it) *that* (Germ. *kaum dass*) I had passed, etc., Ec 7^{14} עַל דִּבְרַת שֶׁלֹּא יִמְצָא to the intent *that . . .*, 5^{15} כָּל־עֻמַּת שֶׁבָּא exactly *as . . .*, 12^{9} יֹתֵר שֶׁ׳ besides *that*, עַד שֶׁ׳ (עַד שֶׁ׳ †Ju 5^{7}) until *that* ψ 123^{2} Ct 2$^{7.17}$ + (v. III. עַד **II 1 a** *a* and *b*; cf. NH *Yoma* 5^{1}), *while* 1^{12} (ib. **2 d**); עָשָׂה שֶׁ׳ to make or cause *that . . .*, †Ec 3^{14} (cf. Ez 36^{27}). **b.** involving a reason (cf. אֲשֶׁר **8 c**), *because, since*, Ct 1$^{6.6}$ 5^{2} Ec 2^{18b}. Hence שַׁלָּמָה †Ct 1^{7} *since why? =lest* (v. מָה **4 d** *b*). **4.** compounds: **a.** בְּשֶׁ׳, i.q. בַּאֲשֶׁר **c** (p. 84^{a}) *in that, seeing that*, Ec 2^{16}; also (acc. to MT 𝔊 𝔖 Hu De) Gn 6^{3} בְּשַׁגָּם הוּא בָשָׂר *because that* he also is flesh; but v. שָׁגַג. **b.** כְּשֶׁ׳, i.q. כַּאֲשֶׁר p. 455:—(*a*) *according as* Ec 5^{14} 12^{7}; (*b*) *when* (so oft. NH, as *Ab* 1$^{8.8.8.14}$) 9^{12} 10^{3}. **c.** מִשֶּׁ׳, i.q. מֵאֲשֶׁר **a** (p. 84^{a}), 2 K 6^{11} מִי מִשֶּׁלָּנוּ who of *those that* are ours? (but Klo Kamp^{Kau} Benz מְגַלֵּנוּ who *betrays us?* cf. 𝔊); Ec 5^{4} *than that* (cf. מֵאֲשֶׁר 3^{22}), + 2^{24} (read מִשֶּׁיֹּאכַל with Ew De, etc.; cf. 3^{22}). **d.** שֶׁל, like לַאֲשֶׁר (אֲשֶׁר **7 b**), a mark of the genit.: thrice, adding slight emph. to the sf., Ct 1^{6} = 8^{12} כַּרְמִי שֶׁלִּי *my* vineyard (lit. my vineyard, which is mine), 3^{7} מִטָּתוֹ שֶׁלִּשְׁלֹמֹה (so oft. in NH, but without any special emphasis, as *Aboth* 1^{12} הֱוֵי מתלמידיו של־אהרן be of Aaron's disciples, 2^{1} שְׂכָרָן שֶׁל־מִצְוֹת, v^{2} 3^{2} הֱוֵי מתפלל בשלומה של־מלכות; cf. ܕ݁ܝܠ in Syr., as Lk 6^{42} ܡܶܠܰܝ ܕ݁ܺܝܠܝ *my* words, Nö^{§225}). And with בְּ, בְּשֶׁל lit. *through that which belongs to* or *concerns*, pleon. for *on account of* (a late, unidiom. transl. of Aram. בְּדִיל, from בְּ, דִּי, and לְ, as in Onk Gn 12^{13} בדילי *on my account*, 30^{27} 39^{5} בְּדִיל יוֹסֵף, בְּדִיל מָא *on account of* what? Ju 8^{1} 2 S 9^{1} 1 K 11$^{12.39}$, etc.), Jon 1^{7} בְּשֶׁלְּמִי *on account of* whom? (‖ v^{8} בַּאֲשֶׁר לְמִי: v. p. 84; prob. a gloss), v^{12} בְּשֶׁלִּי *on account of* me (𝔗 בְּדִילִי, בְּדִיל מַן); Ec 8^{17} בְּשֶׁל אֲשֶׁר יַעֲמֹל הָאָדָם לְבַקֵּשׁ *on account of* (the fact) *that* (=*seeing that*) man labours, etc. (unidiom. transl. of Aram. בְּדִיל דְּ *because that*, as Gn 6^{3} בְּדִיל דְּאִינוּן בִּסְרָא, 39^{9} בְּדִיל דְּאַתְּ אִיתְּתֵיהּ [for Heb. בַּאֲשֶׁר אַתְּ אִשְׁתּוֹ]; Palm. בדיל די Ldzb^{233},—in Tariff 1^{4} (Cooke$^{N.-Sem. Inscr. 320}$) = ἐπειδή).

[שָׂא] v. [שׂוא].

†[**שָׁאַב**] **vb. draw** (water) (NH *id.*, also *attract*: Aram. שְׁאֵיב, of magnet; Ar. سَأَبَ *be satisfied with drinking*);—**Qal** *Pf.* 2 mpl. consec. וּשְׁאַבְתֶּם Is 12^{3}; *Impf.* 3 fs. וַתִּשְׁאַב Gn 24^{20}, -אָב v^{45}; 1 s. אֶשְׁאָב v$^{19.44}$; 3 mpl. יִשְׁאֲבוּן Ru 2^{9}, וַיִּשְׁאֲבוּ 1 S 7^{6} + 2 t.; *Imv.* fs. שַׁאֲבִי Na 3^{14}; *Pt.* ms. שֹׁאֵב Dt 29^{10}, pl. cstr. שֹׁאֲבֵי Jos 9$^{21.23.27}$; fpl. הַשֹּׁאֲבֹת Gn 24^{11};—*draw* water, c. acc. מַיִם Gn 24^{13} (J), 1 S 7^{6} 9^{11}, + מִן of source 2 S 23^{16} = 1 Ch 11^{18}, Is 12^{3} (fig.); מֵי מָצוֹר שַׁ׳ לָךְ Na 3^{14}; מַיִם om. Gn 24$^{20.43.45}$ and (+ לְ of animals) v$^{19.20.44}$ (all J); c. acc. אֲשֶׁר Ru 2^{9} drink of *that which* the young men *draw*; Pt. fpl. Gn 24^{11} *the water-drawing women*; m. שֹׁאֵב מֵימֶיךָ Dt 29^{10} (servile labour, ‖ חֹטֵב עֵצֶיךָ), so mpl. Jos 9$^{21.23.27}$ (P; all c. לְ, and all ‖ חֹטְבֵי עֵצִים).

†[מַשְׁאָב] **n.** [**m.**] appar. **drawing-place** of water; only pl. מַשְׁאַבִּים Ju 5^{11}.

†**שָׁאַג** **vb. roar** (NH *id.*; Ar. ثَأَجَ *low, bleat*, Frey);—**Qal** *Pf.* 3 ms. וְשׁ׳ Is 5^{29} Kt consec. (>Qr וְיִשְׁאַג), שָׁאַג Am 3^{8}, etc.; *Impf.* 3 ms. יִשְׁאַג Am 3^{4} +, etc.; *Inf. abs.* שָׁאֹג Je 25^{30}; *Pt.* שֹׁאֵג Ju 14^{5} ψ 22^{14}, שׁוֹאֵג Ez 22^{25}, שֹׁאֲגִים Zp 3^{3} ψ 104^{21};—**1.** *roar*, of lion Ju 14^{5} (c. לִקְרָאתוֹ), Am 3$^{4.8}$ ψ 104^{21} (c. לְ of prey), fig. of invaders and foes Je 2^{15} (c. עַל pers.) ψ 22^{14}, cf. 74^{4}, sim. Is 5^{29} Je 51^{38}; fig. of rapacious rulers Zp 3^{3} Ez 22^{25} (read נְשִׂיאֶיהָ for נְבִיאֶיהָ 𝔊 and mod.); of י׳ (like lion) calling scattered Isr. Ho 11$^{10.10}$ (on text of v. see Now); of י׳ roaring in thunder Je 25^{30a} = Am 1^{2} = Jo 3^{16}, also Je 25^{30} (שָׁאֹג יִשְׁאַג, sq. עַל־נָוֵהוּ); cf. יִשְׁאַג־קוֹל Jb 37^{4} (‖ יַרְעֵם). **2.** of human cry in distress ψ 38^{9} (c. מִן causat.).

†**שְׁאָגָה** **n.f. roaring**;—**1.** like lion, abs. שׁ׳ Is 5^{29} (of invaders); of lion, cstr. שַׁאֲגַת Zc 11^{3} Jb 4^{10} (fig. of wicked), sf. קוֹל שַׁאֲגָתוֹ Ez 19^{7} (fig. of conquering king). **2.** human cry in distress, שַׁאֲגָתִי ψ 32^{3}, דִּבְרֵי שׁ׳ 22^{2}, שַׁאֲגֹתָי Jb 3^{24}.

שָׁאָה v. שׁוֹאָה sub שׁוא.

†I. [**שָׁאָה**] **vb. make a din or crash, crash into ruins** (perh. akin to שׁוֹאָה (√שׁוא) *storm, devastation*; >Aram. ܫܘܳܐ *be deserted*, שְׁהָוָא, שַׁהֲוָתָא *desert*);—**Qal** *Pf.* 3 pl. שָׁאוּ Is 6^{11} until cities *have crashed into ruins*; + perh. Na 1^{5} (p. 671^{a}). **Niph.** *Impf.* 3 fs. תִּשָּׁאֶה שְׁמָמָה Is 6^{11}, usu., and the ground *be ruined* into a desolation, but 𝔊 Lo Du Marti תִּשָּׁאֵר *be left* a desol.; 3 mpl. יִשָּׁאוּן Is 17^{12} *they are in uproar* (of nations, ‖ יֶהֱמָיוּן), v^{13} (but del. as doublet Du Che^{Hpt} Marti). **Hiph.** *Inf. cstr.* לְהַשְׁאוֹת Is

37^{26}, = לְהַשְׁוֹת 2 K 19^{25} (Ges §23f Kö 1.570, who follow van d. H. in giving לְהַשְׁאוֹת as Qr, but v. Baer Gi), *to cause ... cities to crash* into ruined heaps.

† שְׁאֵרָה Kt, שׁוֹאָה Qr, **n.f. devastating storm**;—sim. Pr 1^{27} (|| סוּפָה). V. שׁוֹאָה, √II. שׁוא.

† שְׁאִיָּה **n.f. ruin**;—Is 24^{12} (late).

† שָׁאוֹן **n.m.** Ho 10.14 **roar** (of waters, etc.), **din, crash, uproar**;—abs. ש׳ Ho 10^{14}+; cstr. שְׁאוֹן Is 13^{4}+; sf. שְׁאוֹנָהּ 5^{14};— **1.** *roar* of water (waves), Is 17^{12} (|| הָמָה), sim. of noise of invading host, so v^{13}, but del. Du Che Hpt Marti, as doublet; *roar* of this host v^{12} (|| הֲמוֹן), cf. שְׁאוֹן קוֹלָם Je 51^{55}; of waves also ψ $65^{8.8}$; of *din* or *crash* of battle Am 2^{2} Ho 10^{14} ψ 74^{23}; בְּנֵי ש׳ Je 48^{45} (i.e. warriors); of battle in which י׳ beats down his foes Je 25^{31}, cf. Is 66^{6}; of gathering hosts Is 13^{4}; ש׳ זָרִים 25^{5} (Du Marti, plausibly, זֵדִים .גְּאוֹן, as 13^{11}); rd. ש׳ also prob. (for שַׁאֲנָן, q.v.) 2 K 19^{28} = Is 37^{29}; in mocking appell. of Pharaoh (Necho), Je 46^{17} פ׳ (𝔊 𝔖 𝔙) קִרְאוּ שֵׁם call ye the name of Ph. a *Crash*. **2.** *uproar* of revellers Is 5^{14} 24^{8}.—בּוֹר ש׳ ψ 40^{3}, *pit of roaring* (of waters? fig., cf. מַעֲמַקֵּי־מַיִם 69^{3}, where also || יָוֵן); Thes al. *of destruction* (v. √**2**), but against usage of שָׁאוֹן; > Du prop. בּוֹר שָׁוְא (cf. נֶפֶת שָׁוְא Is 30^{28}).

† שְׁאֵת **n.f.** doubtful word; perh. (for *שֵׁאת) din of battle (= שָׁאוֹן); Thes al. **devastation**, cf. שְׁאִיָּה; either meaning suits הַשּׁ׳ La 3^{47} (|| הַשָּׁבֶר); but We Comp. Hex. 2, 351, from II. שׁוא, *desolation*); contr. (acc. to Thes and most) שֵׁת, in בְּנֵי שֵׁת Nu 24^{17} (J) *sons of* (battle-)*din* (warriors, = בְּנֵי שָׁאוֹן in || Je 48^{45}); Vrss take שֵׁת here as n.pr.; Gray prop. שֵׁאֵת = שֵׁת, *pride*, or reading as Je, cf. We Comp. 351.

† II. [שָׁאָה] **vb. Hithp. gaze** (appar. || form of שָׁעָה, q.v.);—*Pt.* ms. הָאִישׁ מִשְׁתָּאֵה לָהּ Gn 24^{21} (J) *the man was gazing at her* (Ges §130a).

[שָׁאַט], שְׁאָט v. II. שׁוט.

שְׁאִיָּה v. I. שׁאה.

שָׁאַל 170 **vb. ask, inquire** (NH *id.*; As. *šaʾâlu*, Ar. سَأَلَ, Eth. ሰአለ: Sab. מסאל *request, petition*, Hom Chrest. 124 Levy-Os ZMG xix (1865), 163; Aram. ܫܐܶܠ, שְׁאֵיל; OAram. Zinj. שאל Ldzb 371, Nab. Hiph. *lend* Id ib.;—on ש׳ cf. Jastr JBL xix (1900), 82 ff.);—**Qal** *Pf.* 3 ms. ש׳ Ju 5^{25}+, שָׁאֵל Ju 8^{26}+2 t.; consec. וְשָׁאַל לוֹ Nu 27^{21}; sf. שְׁאֵלְךָ consec. Gn 32^{18} (Ges §64 f), וּשְׁאֵלֵךְ consec. Ju 4^{20}; 1 s. sf. שְׁאִלְתִּיהוּ 1 S 1^{20}, שְׁאִלְתִּיו Ju 13^{6}; 3 pl. sf. שְׁאֵלוּנוּ ψ 137^{3}; 2 mpl. שְׁאֶלְתֶּם 1 S 12^{13} (del. 𝔊 Th We Dr and most), Jb 21^{29}, וּשְׁאֶלְתֶּם־ consec. 1 S 25^{5}, etc.; *Impf.* 3 ms. יִשְׁאַל Ex 22^{13}+, etc.; *Imv.* שְׁאַל Is 7^{11}+, שְׁאָלוּנִי Is 45^{11} (> תִּשְׁאָלוּנִי We ir Che al.), etc.; *Inf. abs.* שָׁאוֹל Gn 43^{7}+; cstr. לִשְׁאֹל Ju 1^{14}+, etc.; *Pt. act.* שֹׁאֵל 2 S 3^{13}+, fs. שֹׁאֶלֶת 1 K $2^{20.22}$, mpl. הַשֹּׁאֲלִים 1 S 8^{10}; *pass.* שָׁאוּל 1^{28} 2 K 6^{5};— **1. a.** *ask, ask for*, acc. rei (vel pers.) Ju 5^{25} 8^{26} 1 K 3^{10} ψ 122^{6} (= pray for)+; ש׳ אֶת־נַפְשׁוֹ לָמוּת 1 K 19^{4} Jon 4^{8}, i.e. pray for death, but Jb 31^{30} *demand* the life of another בְּאָלָה *by a curse;* c. לְ pers. 1 K $2^{22.22}$+ (לְ pers. reflex.) 1 S $12^{17.19}$+; c. מִן pers. Ju 8^{24} (acc. cogn.), Ezr 8^{22} Zc 10^{1}+; sq. inf. 1 K 3^{11}; sq. cl.: ש׳ מָה אֶתֶּן־לָךְ 1 K 3^{5} = 2 Ch 1^{7}, cf. 2 K 2^{9}; c. acc. + מֵאֵת pers. 1 S 8^{10} ψ 27^{4} (from י׳)+; + מֵעִם pers. Is 7^{11} (from י׳)+; c. acc. pers. (from whom) + rei † ψ 137^{3}; acc. om. Is 7^{12} 1 S 12^{20} 1 K 2^{20}, c. מִן pers. ψ 2^{8}; abs. Mi 7^{3} ψ 105^{40} (of prayer); הִקְשִׁיתָ לִשְׁאוֹל 2 K 2^{10}, i.e. thou hast asked for a difficult thing.—1 S 2^{20} v. **Hiph.** **b.** specif. *ask* as a favour, for temporary use, i.e. *borrow* (cf. לָוָה, as matter of business, v. Bu 1 S 1.28), Ex 22^{13} (E; acc. rei + מֵעִם pers.), 2 K 4^{3} (acc. rei + מִן of source + לְ pers. reflex.), 6^{5} (pt. pass. abs.); so also (acc. to many), c. acc. rei Ex 3^{22} (+ מִן pers.), 11^{2} 12^{35} (both + מֵאֵת pers.; all E),—it is, however, not clear that there was any pretext of mere temporary use; pt. pass. שָׁאוּל לי׳ 1 S 1^{28} (*lent, granted,*) *made over to* י׳ (in effect pass. of Hiph., q.v.). **c.** in weakened sense, *seek, desire* (late), c. acc. 2 Ch 11^{23} Ec 2^{10} (subj. עֵינַי); Pr 20^{4} in harvest he *shall look* [for a crop], וָאָיִן *and there shall be none.* **2. a.** *inquire of*, c. acc. pers. + לֵאמֹר before inquiry Gn 32^{18} (E), 44^{19} (J)+; c. וָאֹמַר Ju 4^{20}, וַיֹּאמֶר, etc., Gn 24^{47} (J), Je 37^{17}; sq. וָאֹמַר without acc. pers. Gn 32^{30} (J), cf. 1 S 19^{22}, sq. לֵאמֹר Jos 4^{6} (JE); c. acc. pers. + עַל rei Ne 1^{2}; עַל rei alone, Ec 7^{10} (+ מֵחָכְמָה, i.e. prompted by wisdom); c. acc. pers. + rei (about which) 2 S 14^{18} Is 45^{11}+4 t.; acc. pers. + indir. quest. Ju 13^{6}; c. acc. pers. only, Ju 8^{14} 1 S 25^{8} Dt 32^{7}+, *inquire of* beasts (acc.) Jb 12^{7}; c. acc. rei only, Je 50^{5}; c. לְ pers. = acc. 2 K 8^{6} (Kö Synt. §289 h); c. לְ rei about which Gn 26^{7} (J), 32^{30} (J), Ju 13^{18} 2 S 11^{7} Je 6^{16} Jb 8^{8}, also (+ לֵאמֹר before the inquiry) Gn 43^{7} (J), and (sq. direct question) Dt 4^{32}; c. לְ pers. about whom, Gn 43^{27} (J), cf. phr. of greeting, ש׳ אִישׁ לְרֵעֵהוּ לְשָׁלוֹם Ex 18^{7} (E)

ask each for (or about) *his fellow as to welfare*, cf †Ju 18[15] 1 S 10[4] 17[22] 25[5] 30[21] [read וַיִּשְׁאֲלוּ לוֹ 𝔊 𝔖 We Dr HPS Bu] 2 S 8[10] Je 15[5] 1 Ch 18[10], sq direct question only, 1 S 17[56] Je 18[13] (c בְּ loc), sq indirect question only (c אִם) Je 30[6], שׁ׳ אֶת־בֵּי׳ Gn 24[57] (J), abs *make inquiry* Dt 13[15] (+ דָּרַשׁ, חָקַר). †**b.** *inquire of, consult*, deity, oracle, etc (Jastr[JBL xix (1900), 88 ff]), sq acc בֵּי׳ Jos 9[14] (JE), Is 30[2], י׳ 65[1] (‖ בקשׁ), elsewhere in Hex only (acc om), Nu 27[21] (P, c. לְ pers for whom, + בְּ instr), cf Jos 19[50], also שׁ׳ אוֹב Dt 18[11] (pt as subst, Jager[BAS ii 292] cp As *maššaku ša šâ'ili*, i e *skin-vessel of the oracle-seeker*, cf Jastr[JBL xix (1900), 96 ff]), c. acc of human agent 1 S 28[16] Je 38[14 27]; usu. (ancient usage, chiefly Ju Sm) שׁ׳ בְּי׳ לֵאמֹר (בְּ perh orig local, so GFM, or instr), Ju 1[1] 20[23] 1 S 23[2] 30[8] 2 S 2[1] 5[19] = 1 Ch 14[10], לאמר om 1 S 10[22] (sq. direct question), 22[10] (לְ pers for whom), 23[4] 28[6] 2 S 5[23] = 1 Ch 14[14] Ju 20[27], שׁ׳ באלהים Ju 18[5] 20[18] 1 S 14[37] (sq direct question), also (לְ pers. for whom), 22[13 15]; שׁ׳ בִּדְבַר הָא׳ 2 S 16[23], likewise שׁ׳ בְּעֵצוֹ Ho 4[12] (i e his idol), בָּאוֹב, בַּתְּרָפִים Ez 21[26], 1 Ch 10[13], perh = *receive as oracle* Dt 18[16] (מֵעִם י׳), Jastr[l c]

†**Niph.** *ask for oneself* (Ges[§ 51 e]), specif *ask leave of absence*, c מִן pers *Pf* 3 ms + *Inf abs* נִשְׁאֹל נִשְׁאַל 1 S 20[6] (sq inf), v[28] (sq עַד; ? ins לְ inf. HPS); *Pf* 1 s נִשְׁאַלְתִּי מִן־הַמֶּלֶךְ Ne 13[6] (abs). †**Pi. 1.** *inquire carefully* *Impf.* 3 mpl. + **Qal** *Inf abs* שָׁאוֹל יְשַׁאֲלוּ 2 S 20[18] (Bu prop **Qal** *Impf* יִשְׁאֲלוּ), c בְּ loc, on foll context v We Dr HPS Bu. **2.** *beg, practise beggary*, *Pf* 3 pl וְשִׁאֲלוּ (consec) ψ 109[10] **Hiph.** (prop. *let* one *ask* [successfully], *give*, or *lend*, *on request*, then) *grant, make over to* (as a favour, with or without request). *Pf* 1 s sf הִשְׁאִלְתִּהוּ לי׳ 1 S 1[28] *I have made him over to* י׳ (cf Dr HPS Bu and **Qal** *Pt pass*, ib), perhaps also read 3 fs הִשְׁאִילָה לי׳ 2[20] (whom) *she hath made over to* י׳ (for שָׁאַל לי׳) Bu HPS (after 𝔊 in part, other conj in Dr), *Impf* 3 mpl sf rei וַיַּשְׁאִלוּם Ex 12[36] (E) *and they handed them over.*

† שְׁאָל **n.pr m** with foreign wife, Ezr 10[29], 𝔊 Σαλουια, 𝔊L Ασαηλ

שָׁאוּל **n.pr.m.** (= *asked* (of י׳), cf שְׁאַלְתִּיאֵל infr; Palm n pr שאילא Lzb[371] Cooke[243]),—Σαουλ **1.** .₉₇ 1st king of Isr, 1 S 9[2.3.5.6] (son of Kish, a Benjamite) + 359 t Sm, 28 t. 1 Chr, ψ 18[1] 52[2] 54[2] 57[1] 59[1] (all in titles), גִּבְעַת שׁ׳ Is 10[29] (and 1 S 11[4] 15[34], 2 S 21[6] v II גבעה). †**2.** a king of Edom Gn 36[37 38] (P) = 1 Ch 1[48 49] †**3.** a son of Simeon Gn 46[10] Ex 6[15] Nu 26[13] (all P) = 1 Ch 4[24]. †**4.** a Levite 1 Ch 6[9]

†שָׁאוּלִי **adj gent.** of **3** supra: c art. = n pr coll. הַשָּׁ׳ Nu 26[13] (P)

שְׁאָלָה Is 7[11] v. שאול **1**

†שְׁאֵלָה [I שֵׁלָה] **n.f.** **request, thing asked for**;—שְׁא׳ Ju 8[24] +, sf שְׁאֵלָתִי 1 S 1[27] +, שְׁאֵלָתִי Jb 6[8], שְׁאֵלָתֵךְ Est 5[6] +, שֵׁלָתֵךְ 1 S 1[17], שְׁאֵלָתָם ψ 106[15],—**1.** *request, petition*, Ju 8[24] 1 K 2[16 20] (both acc cogn c שָׁאַל), Est 5[6 7] (c נָתַן = *grant*), 7[2 3] 9[12]. This passes easily into **2.** *thing asked for*, 1 S 2[20], c. נָתַן 1[17 27] Est 5[8] ψ 106[15], תָּבוֹא שׁ׳ Jb 6[8].—II שֵׁלָה v infr. אֶשְׁתָּאֹל n pr m, v p 84[a].

†[מִשְׁאָלָה] **n.f.** **request, petition**,—pl cstr. מִשְׁאֲלֹת לִבֶּךָ ψ 37[4] (c. נָתַן, of י׳), sf. מִשְׁאֲלוֹתֶיךָ 20[6] (c. מלא, of י׳)

†שְׁאַלְתִּיאֵל **n.pr.m.** (*I have asked* (him) *of God*; on acc. cf. (late) ψ 137[3]),—first son of Jehoiachin and uncle of Zerubbabel acc to 1 Ch 3[17] (cf v[18 19]); but Z's father Hg 1[1] 2[23] Ez 3[2.8] Ne 12[1] (attempts at explan in Be Kit Benz)—Σαλαθιηλ

†שְׁאוֹל, שְׁאֹל **n.f.** [ψ 86, 13] (appar. **m.** Jb 26[6] cf. Is 14[9], v. Albr[ZAW xvi (1896), 51]) **She'ôl, underworld** (√dub.; שׁאל, i.e *place of inquiry* (ref. to necromancy) Jastr[Am JSem. Lang xiv 170, cf JBL xix (1900), 88 ff] (Jerem[Leben n d Tode 109] '*Ort der Entscheidung*'), Thes Bo[De Inf § 133] Di al cp. √ שׁעל, whence שֹׁעַל *hollow hand*, etc.; שׁ׳ then = *hollow place*, '*Holle*,' *hell*; other conj. v Hup[Ps. 6, 6] De[Is 5 14] Beer[Bibl Hades] in Holtzmann[Festgabe, 1902, 1 ff]; most now refrain from positive etymology (e.g Buhl), OAram שׁאול, Syr ܫܝܘܠ, As. *šu-alu* is dub. so read and interpr. Dl[Pa 121 Prol 47 145] Jastr[Am J Sem Lang xiv 165 ff] Ency. Bib[s.v]; opp by Bertin[TSBA viii 269] Jen[Kosmol 223 ff] Zim[KAT 3. 636] al; v. also Muss-Arnolt[JBL xi (1892) 169] and reff),—alw abs., שְׁאוֹל Dt 32[22] + 52 t., שְׁאֹלָה Gn 42[38] ψ 9[18], שְׁאֹל 1 K 2[6] Jb 17[16], שְׁאוֹלָה Gn 37[35] + 7 t; + Is 7[11] (so read for שְׁאָלָה Aq Σ Θ Du Che and now most);—**1.** *the underworld*, שׁ׳ תַּחְתִּית Dt 32[22], מִתַּחַת Is 14[9], מִשּׁ׳ מָטָּה Pr 15[24]; ‖ מָוֶת 5[5] 7[27] Ct 8[6] ψ 89[49]; whither men descend at death, Gn 37[35] (E), 42[38] 44[29.31] (J), 1 S 2[6] 1 K 2[6 9] Jb 7[9] 21[13] Is 14[11.15] ψ 88[4],

and Ḳorah and associates go down alive by י׳'s judgment, Nu $16^{30.33}$ (J), cf. ψ 55^{16}; under mts and sea Jb 26^{5} (cf. v^{5}), בְּטֶן ש׳ Jon 2^{3} (cf. v^{7}); with bars Jb 17^{16} (si vera l.: v. 𝔊 Du); פִּי ש׳ ψ 141^{7}, שַׁעֲרֵי ש׳ Is 38^{10}; personif. Is $28^{15.18}$ (‖ מוֹת) as insatiable monster 5^{14} Hb 2^{5} Pr 1^{12} 27^{20} 30^{16}; as said (fig.) to have snares, חֶבְלֵי ש׳, ψ 18^{6} = 2 S 22^{6}, cf. מְצָרֵי ש׳ ψ 116^{3}; opp. (height of) שָׁמַיִם Am 9^{2} Jb 11^{8} ψ 139^{8} + (opp. לְמַעְלָה) Is 7^{11} (v. supra); dark, gloomy, without return Jb 17^{13} (cf v^{16} 7^{9} 10^{21} 16^{22}; all being alike 3^{17-19} $21^{23.26}$); without work or knowledge or wisdom acc. to Ec $9^{5.6.10}$ (cf. Jb 14^{21}, and v. רְפָאִים sub רפה; yet cf Is 14^{9f}). **2.** condition of righteous and wicked disting. in ש׳ (later than 1 S 28, esp. in WisdLt). **a.** wicked יָשׁוּבוּ לִשְׁאוֹלָה ψ 9^{18}, יִדְּמוּ לִשׁ׳ 31^{18}; death is their shepherd, without power and honour they waste away $49^{14.15}$; ש׳ consumes them as drought water Jb 24^{19}, righteous dread it because no praise or presence of God there (as in temple) ψ 6^{6} (cf. 88^{6}), Is 38^{18}; deliverance from it a blessing ψ 30^{4} 86^{13} Pr 23^{14}. In Ezek. ש׳ is land below, place of reproach, abode of uncircumcised Ez $31^{15.16.17}$ $32^{21.27}$. **b.** righteous shall not be abandoned, לִשׁ׳ ψ 16^{10} (‖ שַׁחַת q v.; opp. אֹרַח חַיִּים, etc, v^{11}, cf 17^{15}), is ransomed from ש׳ 49^{16} (cf. 73^{23-25} Is $57^{1.2}$); cf. Job's expectation and desire Jb 14^{13} 17^{13} (cf. 10^{21} 19^{25f}). **3.** later distinction of places in ש׳: **a.** depths of ש׳ for sensualist Pr 9^{18}. **b.** ש׳ וַאֲבַדּוֹן Pr 25^{11}, v אֲבַדּוֹן. [שַׁחַת and בּוֹר, q v., when ‖ ש׳, are usu. in bad sense (ψ 88^{4}); prob. = pit in ש׳, > ש׳ itself as pit; words at least prepare for local distinctions of postB. Judaism and NT.] **4.** ש׳ fig. of extreme degradation in sin Is 57^{9}; as place of exile for Israel Ho $13^{14.14}$ (cf Is 26^{19}).

†[שָׁאַן] **vb. Pa'l.** (Ges ^{§55d}) **be at ease or at peace, rest securely** (Syr. ܫܝܢ *pacify*, ܫܝܢܐ, Eth ሰላም: *peace*);—*Pf.* 3 ms. שַׁאֲנַן Je 48^{11}, וְשׁ׳ consec 30^{10}+, 3 pl. שַׁאֲנָנוּ Jb 3^{18};—*be at ease, secure*, undisturbed by ill fortune. וְשָׁקַט וְשׁ׳ וְאֵין מַחֲרִיד Je 30^{10} = 46^{27}, 48^{11} (of Moab), ש׳ מִפַּחַד רָעָה Pr 1^{33}, of rest from trouble, etc., in grave Jb 3^{18}.

שְׁאָן v. בֵּית שְׁאָן.

†שַׁאֲנָן **adj. at ease, secure** (Ba $^{NB §143a}$ Ges ^{§84bk});—abs. ש׳ Is 33^{20}; pl שַׁאֲנַנִּים Am 6^{1}+, שַׁאֲנַנּוֹת Is $32^{9.11.18}$;—**1.** *at ease, secure:* נְוֵה ש׳ Is 33^{20} *secure habitation* (of Jerus.), cf מְנוּחֹת ש׳ 32^{18} (‖ מִבְטַחִים). **2.** as subst., *one at ease*, free from misfortune, Jb 12^{5}. **3.** *at ease*, with collat. idea of *careless, wanton, arrogant*, Am 6^{1} Is $32^{9.11}$ Zc 1^{15} ψ 123^{4}. **4** as subst. abstr = *arrogance:* sf. שַׁאֲנַנְךָ 2 K 19^{28} (‖ הִתְרַגֶּזְךָ) = Is 37^{29}, but < שְׁאוֹנְךָ *thine uproar*, Bu $^{ZAW\ xii\ (1892).\ 36}$ Gr Che Marti Kit (perh.), Bur. Cf. שַׁלְאֲנָן.

שֹׁאסַיִךְ Je 30^{16} Kt v. שׁסס, שׁסה.

†I. שָׁאַף **vb. gasp, pant, pant after, long for** (so 𝔗 Jb 7^{2});—**Qal** *Pf.* 3 ms. וְשָׁאַף consec. Jb 5^{5}, 3 fs. שָׁאֲפָה Je 2^{24}, 3 pl. שָׁאֲפוּ 14^{6}; *Impf.* 3 ms. יִשְׁאַף Jb 7^{2}, etc.; *Pt. act.* שׁוֹאֵף Ec 1^{5},—**1.** *gasp*, as a woman in travail, fig of י׳, Is 42^{14} (‖ נָשַׁם); *pant after, snuff up* the wind (acc.), of wild ass Je 2^{24} 14^{6}; constr. praegn. וְאֶל־מְקוֹמוֹ ש׳ Ec 1^{5} *unto his place he panteth* (comes panting), of sun under fig. of racer. **2.** *gasp* or *pant* with desire ψ 119^{131} (‖ יָאַב); *pant after, be eager for*, c. acc. Jb 5^{5} (cf. צַמִּים p 855^{b}), 7^{2} (‖ יְקַוֶּה), 36^{20} (but obscure in context).

†II. [שָׁאַף] **vb. crush, trample upon** (‖ form of שׁוּף (q.v.), if pointing right, cf. Kö $^{I\ 439}$; We Now read שָׁפִים, etc, from שׁוּף, cf Ges ^{§72p}, perh. orig. *pulverize by rubbing*, but also appar by pounding, stamping, treading, Levy ^{ChWB} שׁוּף, Jastr $^{Dict.}$ שׁוּף, שאף;—most make = I שׁאף, but Vrss render as above);—**Qal** *Pf.* 3 ms. sf. שְׁאָפַנִי ψ 56^{2}, 3 pl. שָׁאֲפוּ v^{3}; *Inf abs.* שָׁאֹף Ez 36^{3}; *Pt.* sf. שֹׁאֲפִי ψ 57^{4}; pl שֹׁאֲפִים Am 2^{7} 8^{4};—*trample upon, crush* (the poor, etc.), fig., c. acc. pers. Am 8^{4}; strangely 2^{7} (We Now Marti del. עַל־עֲפַר־אֶרֶץ, which Torrey $^{JBL\ xv\ (1896),\ 152}$ expl. as old doublet, cf 𝔊𝔖; AV RV *pant after the dust*, etc, hyperb. for extreme avarice, cf. Hi Dr; but Dr thinks 𝔙 poss. original: *crush the heads of the poor upon the dust* [cf. Is 3^{15}], in any case del. ב after ש׳ *crush*); שַׁמּוֹת וְשׁ׳ אֶתְכֶם מִסָּבִיב Ez 36^{3}; ψ 56^{2} 57^{4} and (acc. om.) 56^{3}.

I. שָׁאַר $_{133}$ **vb. remain, be left over** (syn. יָתַר) (NH *id;* 𝔗 שְׁאַר; Sab. סאר *remaining* Hom $^{Chr\ 124}$; Ar سَأَرَ, سُؤْر *be left over*, Lane, cf. Lag $^{GGN\ 1889,\ 297}$; OAram. שאר *remainder*, Nab. שארית, v. Lzb ^{371} SAC ^{110});—†**Qal** *Pf.* 3 ms ש׳ 1 S 16^{11} the youngest still *remains.* **Niph.** $_{93}$ *Pf.* 3 ms נִשְׁאַר Gn 47^{18}+; 3 fs. נִשְׁאֲרָה Jos 13^{1} Dn 10^{8}, etc., *Impf.* 3 ms. יִשָּׁאֵר Is $11^{11.16}$, וַיִּשָּׁאֶר Gn 7^{23}, etc, *Pt.* נִשְׁאָר Gn 32^{9}+, וָאִשָּׁאֵר Ez 9^{8} (read ונשאר Hi Toy Krae, וְאֶשָּׁאֵר Sm; del. 𝔊 Hi Co Siegf Berthol); f. נִשְׁאָרָה 2 K 19^{30} = Is 37^{31}, נִשְׁאֶרֶת Ex 10^{5} 2 Ch 30^{6}, נִשְׁאֶרֶת Jos 13^{2}, etc.;—

1. *be left over* (sts ‖ נותר) Ex 8^{27} 10^{19} 14^{28} (all J), Jos 11^{22} (D), Ju 7^3 2 S 14^7 +; in restrictive cl. לא נ׳ זולת 2 K 24^{14} *there were left only*, etc., לא נ׳ לפני אֲדֹני בלתי אם וגו׳ Gn 47^{18} (J), sq acc. adv. (Ges§ 118 q), or appos, Dt 4^{27} Ezr 9^{15}, cf. נ׳ במתי מְעָט Dt 28^{62} (Ges§ 119 i); sts c ב loc Ex $8^{5.7}$ (J), Je 38^{22} +, c. את (prep loc) † Jos $23^{7.12}$ (D), c. מִן = *be left from* (of) † Ex 10^5 (J), Dt 3^{11} Jos 13^{12} (D), Is $11^{11.16}$ Je 8^{3a} (pt; v^b del הנ׳ 𝔊 𝔖 Hi Gf Gie Co), Ne $1^{2.3}$, נ׳ מְעַט מהרבה Je 42^2, c ל *to* or *for*, † 2 K $10^{11.17}$ (pt), Zc 9^7 2 Ch 21^{17}, הַנּ׳ לָכֶם מִן־הַבָּרָד Ex 10^5, cf. 2 Ch 30^6 and (ב loc for ל) Je 21^7; c. ב, *in, among, of*, † 1 S 11^{11} Is 17^6 Je 34^7 37^{10} Lv $26^{36.39}$ (H; pt), 25^{52} (P; of years), even הַנּ׳ בַּדָּם 5^9 (P) *the rest of the blood;* c. עַל † 1 S 5^4, c inf נ׳ לרשתָה † Jos 13^1 (D), = *be left alive, survive*, † Gn 7^{23} (J), Ez 9^8 (but on text v supr), הַנּ׳ = *the survivors*, † Gn 14^{10} 1 S 11^{11} Ez 17^{21}; pt. as term techn. = *the* (purified) *remainder, remnant* (cf שְׁאָר, שארית) Is 4^3 (ב loc.; ‖ הַנּוֹתָר), 2 Ch 34^{21} (ב loc) —הַנּ׳ 1 S 9^{24} is dub, *what is left over*, in polite depreciation, Bu, read הַשְּׁאֵר HPS **2.** *be left behind*, Ex 10^{26} (E), Nu 11^{26} (JE), c לְבַדּוֹ Gn 42^{38} (J), cf. Is 49^{21} Dn 10^8, of widow Ru 1^3, + מִן of the dead v^5. † **Hiph** *Pf.* 3 ms. הִשְׁאִיר Ex 10^{12} +, etc, *Impf* 3 ms. יַשְׁאִיר Dt 28^{51}, 1 pl. נַשְׁאֵר 1 S 14^{36} (Ges§ 48 g. 109 d Ko p. 486 f), etc; *Inf. cstr* הַשְׁאִיר Ezr 9^8, v also infr, —**1.** *leave over, spare*, c. acc. Ex 10^{12} (E), 2 K 25^{22} Je 49^9 = Ob ^{5}, Jos 11^{14} (D), Ju 6^4, אֹכֶל לַאֲשֶׁר אִשׁ׳ Je 50^{20}; esp. לֹא הִשׁ׳ שָׂרִיד *leave no survivor*, Jos 10^{28}, cf $v^{30.33.37.39.40}$ (all D), so עַד־בִּלְתִּי הִשׁ׳ שׂ׳ (sts c. ל pers) Nu 21^{35} (E) = Dt 3^3, cf Dt 2^{34} Jos 8^{22} 11^8 (both JE), 10^{33} (D), 2 K 10^{11}, and מִבְּלִי הִשׁ׳ לוֹ כֹּל Dt 28^{55} (in all these rd. *Inf. cstr.* הַשׁ׳, v. Dr Dt 3. 3. 7 24); c ב, *among, of*, 1 S 14^{36}, ב loc. 1 K 19^{18} Zp 3^{12} (in both of preserving a pious remnant, cf שְׁאָר, שארית), also 2 K 3^{25} (Bur rds אֲבָנֶיהָ for בְּנֵיהָ, Kit אֲנָשִׁים, cf. Klo Benz), c ל pers. Dt 28^{51} 1 K 15^{29} 16^{11} 2 K 13^7 Ezr 9^8, c מִן, *from, of*, 2 K 10^{14}, מִן part 1 S 25^{22} 2 K 25^{12} = Je 52^{16}, Je 39^{10}. **2.** *leave* or *keep over* (מִן part) till morning Nu 9^{12} (P) **3.** תַּשׁ׳ מֵאָה Am 5^3 the city *shall have* 100 *left*, cf. v^3 **4.** *leave* as a gift, וְהִשׁ׳ אַחֲרָיו בְּרָכָה Jo 2^{14}.—We Now read וַיִּשְׁאַר Mal 2^{15}, v. שְׁאָר.

† שְׁאָר **n.m.** Is 16. 14 rest, residue, remnant (= יֶתֶר, esp Is and late, on form Ko ii 1 141 No Beitr z sem. W 30), —שׁ׳ abs Is 14^{22} +, cstr Is 10^{19} +, —*rest, residue, remainder*, of trees Is 10^{19}, silver 2 Ch 24^{14}, city 1 Ch 11^8, territory Est 9^{12}; שׁ׳ דברי שלמה 2 Ch 9^{29} (יֶתֶר in ‖ 1 K 11^{41}, and usu. in like phrase, v. p 451 f.); of men 1 Ch 16^{41} Ezr 3^8 $4^{3.7}$ Ne 10^{29} $11^{1.20}$ Est 9^{16}; of Moab Is 16^{14}, Aram 17^3 (= last remnant), archers of Kedar 21^{17}; ‖ posterity, שֵׁם וּשׁ׳ וְנִין וָנֶכֶד Is 14^{22} (of Babylon), שׁ׳ הַבַּעַל Zp 1^4, i.e *Baal, to the last remnant*, vestige (so We al; 𝔊 שֵׁם, cf Schwally Now GASm); term techn = purified *remnant* of Israel (Gie Beiträge 37 f) Is 10^{20} (‖ פְּלֵיטָה), $v^{21.21.22}$ $11^{11.16}$ 28^5.—וּשׁ׳ רוּחַ לוֹ Mal 2^{15} is obscure; read וַיִּשְׁאַר ר׳ לָנוּ We Now, cf GASm

† שְׁאָר יָשׁוּב **n.pr m.** of Isaiah's son Is 7^3 (= *a remnant shall return*, cf 10^{21}, 𝔊 ὁ καταλειφθεὶς Ἰασουβ).

† שארית **n.f.** rest, residue, remnant, remainder (= שְׁאָר), —שׁ׳ abs 2 S 14^7 +, cstr. Ez 36^3 +, שרית (Ges§ 23 f) 1 Ch 12^{39} (van d H. v^{38}); sf שאריתך Is 14^{30} Ez 5^{10}, -תו Is 44^{17}, -תָם Je 15^9, —**1.** *rest, what is left*, of wood Is 44^{17}, land 15^9 (‖ פְּלֵיטָה), Je $47^{4.5}$ Ez 25^{16}, שׁ׳ חֲמַת ψ 76^{11} is difficult (Gr [cf. Che] prop חֲמָת *Hamath*, Du אֻמֹּת *tribes*), *rest* of princes Je 39^3, of nations (= the other nations, Toy) Ez $36^{3.4.5}$; of Israel 1 Ch 12^{39} (van d H v^{38}), 2 Ch 34^9 Ne 7^{71} (van d. H. v^{72}); = last *remnant* of people, Philistines Am 1^8 (cf. We), Is 14^{30}, Edom Am 9^{12}, Anathoth Je 11^{23}, Ashdod 25^{20}, Babylon 50^{26}, Amalek 1 Ch 4^{43} (+ הַפְּלֵטָה), Isr. 2 K 21^{14} Je 6^9 15^9; *remnant* left after catastrophe Am 5^{15} Je 8^3 24^8 $40^{11.15}$ $41^{10.16}$ $42^{2.15.19}$ 43^5 $44^{12.14.28}$ Ez 5^{10} 9^8 11^{13} Hag $1^{12.14}$ 2^2; even וְשַׂמְתִּי אֶת־הַצֹּלֵעָה לִשׁ׳ Mi 4^7 (as promise, ‖ גּוֹי עָצוּם, cf Gie Beiträge, 42 f); = survivors Je 44^7, הַשׁ׳ מִן־הַחֶרֶב 2 Ch 36^{20}; = faithful *remnant* of Israel or Judah (term techn of proph, cf שְׁאָר ad fin), 2 K 19^4 = Is 37^4, 2 K 19^{31} (‖ פְּלֵיטָה) = Is 37^{32} (‖ *id.*), Mi 2^{12} $5^{6.7}$ 7^{18} Ezr 9^{14} (‖ *id*), Is 46^3 Je 23^3 31^7 Zp $2^{7.9}$ (‖ יֶתֶר), 3^{13} Zc $8^{6.11.12}$ **2.** *remainder* = descendants (= שְׁאָר Is 14^{22})· Gn 45^7, שֵׁם וּשׁ׳ 2 S 14^7.

II. שְׁאֵר (√ of foll; cf As *šêru*, Pun שאר, *flesh*, Ar ثَأْر *blood-revenge*, so Sab תאר, Sab Denkm. No 8. 1 7, perhaps orig. *blood* (cf Je 51^{35}), No ZMG xl (1886), 723 and Id M 101, who cp Mand. תירתא = ثائر *conscience, mind*, etc, perh. prop. *midriff*, cf Hoffm infr)

† שְׁאֵר **n.m.** ψ 73. 26 flesh (perh. orig. the inner flesh, full of blood, next the bones, cf. Hoffm ZAW iii (1883). 107, and בָּשָׂר = (orig.) flesh next the skin), —שׁ׳ abs. ψ $78^{20.27}$, cstr. Mi 3^3 +, sf. שְׁאֵרִי

Je 51^{33} ψ 73^{26}, etc.;—**1.** *flesh*: **a.** as food, Ex 21^{10} (HPS also 1 S 9^{24}, for הַנִּשְׁאָר), ψ 78^{20} (‖ לֶחֶם), v^{27} (‖ עוֹף כָּנָף); fig. Mi 3^{2} (‖ עוֹר), v^{3} (‖ *id.*), Je 51^{35} (‖ דָּם). **b.** fig. for physical power ψ 73^{26} (+ לֵבָב), Pr 5^{11} (+ בָּשָׂר). **2.** in HP=*flesh-* (=blood-) *relation* (i.e. one near of kin): שְׁאֵר אָבִיךָ Lv 18^{12}, cf v^{13} 20^{19}, also 18^{17} (read שְׁאֵרְךָ for שַׁאֲרָה, 𝔊 Ew Dr-Wh; cf. Di Baen); + הַקָּרֹב אֵלָיו 21^{2} Nu 27^{11}; ש׳ בְּשָׂרוֹ Lv 18^{6} 25^{49}. **3.**=*self*, Pr 11^{17} (‖ נֶפֶשׁ).

שַׁאֲרָה Lv 18^{17} v. שְׁאֵר **2.**

†שֶׁאֱרָה **n.pr.f.** 'daughter' of Ephraim;—ש׳ בִּתּוֹ 1 Ch 7^{24} (v. also n.pr loc. אֻזֵּן שׁ׳ p. 25^{a} supr.); $𝔊^{B}$ ἐκείνοις τ. καταλοίποις, but $𝔊^{L}$ (cf. $𝔊^{A}$) ἡ θυγάτηρ αὐτοῦ Σαραα.

מִשְׁאֶרֶת v. p. 602^{a} supr.

שְׂאֵת v. שאה

†שְׁבָא **n.pr.gent. et terr.** Sheba, in SW. Arabia (Sab סבא DHM ZMG xxxvii (1883), 9, סבא vb.= *make campaign* Mordt HI 72 or *expedition* Sab. Denkm. No 12, 1, 3, 14; cf. DSMargoliouth Hast. DB Sheba FB Ency Bib Sheba and reff.);—*Sheba*: מַלְכַּת־שׁ׳ 1 K $10^{1.4.10.13}$=2 Ch $9^{1.3.9.12}$; מַלְכֵי שׁ׳ ψ 72^{10}; famous for trade, רֹכְלֵי שׁ׳ Ez $27^{22.23}$, הֲלִיכֹת שׁ׳ Jb 6^{19} (‖ תֵמָא); yielding costly wares Ez 38^{13}, זְהַב שׁ׳ ψ 72^{15}, לְבוֹנָה מִשׁ׳ Je 6^{20} (‖ מֵאֶרֶץ מֶרְחָק, cf. foll.), paying homage and tribute to Israel in future Is 60^{6}; descended from (Yoktan and) Shem Gn 10^{28} (J)=1 Ch 1^{22}, from (Yokshan and) Abr. and Keṭûrâh Gn 25^{3} (J?)=1 Ch 1^{32} (i.e. a northern branch of Sheba, + דְּדָן, q.v.), but from כּוּשׁ Gn 10^{7} (P)=1 Ch 1^{9}; marauders, N Arabia, Jb 1^{15}.

†[שְׁבָאִי] **adj. gent.** only pl. as subst., לִשְׁבָאִים (Baer Ginsb שְׁבָאִים) Jo 4^{8} (‖ אֶל־גּוֹי רָחוֹק), cf. Je 6^{20} supr.), > 𝔊 Me Now לַשְּׁבִי *into captivity.*

I שׁבב (NH שִׁבֵּב Pi. *hew;* Ar شَبَّ *cut,* Aram (Talm.) שְׁבָא *splinter,* cf. Mand. dim. שאבוניא No M 140).

†שְׁבָבִים **n.** [m.] **pl.** probably **splinters**;—שׁ׳ יִהְיֶה עֵגֶל שֹׁמְרוֹן Ho 8^{6} (cf. We; Vrss appar. conjecture).

II שׁבב (As. *šabâbu, blaze,* cf. Syr. ܫܒ *burn,* ܫܒܫܒܐ *ray, flash* (Lexx., cf. PS); Ar. شَبَّ is *blaze up* (cf Ba ES 60), but ש=ش? (Another etymology in Ber Da 3, 22)).

†[שָׁבִיב] **n.m.** probably **flame** (BAram. שְׁבִיב),—cstr. וְלֹא יִגַּהּ שְׁבִיב אִשּׁוֹ Jb 18^{5} (‖ אוֹר); so Ecclus 8^{10} 45^{19}.

שָׁבָה **vb. take captive** (NH, OAram. *id.*; Ar. سَبَا (سبى); Aram. שְׁבָא, ܫܒܐ);—**Qal** *Pf.* 3 ms ש׳ Je 41^{14}; sf. וְשָׁבָם (consec.) 43^{12} (but rd. וְשָׁבָה Gie; Du conj. וְשָׁמְטוֹ); 2 ms שָׁבִיתָ 2 K 6^{22} ψ 68^{19}, etc.; *Impf.* 3 ms. וַיִּשְׁבְּ Nu 21^{1} Je 41^{10}, etc., *Imv* ms. וּשְׁבֵה Ju 5^{12}, *Inf. cstr.* שְׁבוֹת Ob ^{11}; *Pt act* pl. שֹׁבִים Is 14^{2}, etc., *pass.* mpl. שְׁבוּיִם Is 61^{1}, fpl. cstr. שְׁבֻיוֹת Gn 31^{26};—*take captive*: **1. a.** c. acc pers, Nu 24^{22} (JE), 1 S 30^{2} 2 K 5^{2} 6^{22} (+ בְּ instr.) Je $41^{10.10}$ (but v^{10b} Gie reads וַיִּשְׁבֵּם, cf. 𝔊 Luc), v^{14}, Gn 34^{29} (P), 2 Ch 28^{8} (+ מִן part.), + 6 t.; + Je 43^{12} appar. c acc. idols (but v supra; acc. of land Gie). **b.** acc. חֵילוֹ Ob ^{11}, הָרְכוּשׁ 2 Ch 21^{17}, cattle, etc, 1 Ch 5^{21} 2 Ch 14^{14}. **c.** pt in periphrast. conjug. וְהָיוּ שֹׁבִים (לְשֹׁבֵיהֶם) Is 14^{2}; pt c. sf.=*their captives*, etc, 1 K 8^{46}= 2 Ch 6^{36}, Is 14^{2} Je 50^{33}, + 5 t., pt. pass. Is 61^{1}= *captives;* כִּשְׁבֻיוֹת חָרֶב Gn 31^{26} my daughters *as captives of the sword.* **2.** c. acc. cogn. שְׁבִי Ju 5^{12} *lead captive thy captives,* cf. ψ 68^{19} 2 Ch 28^{17}, so (+ מִן pers.) Nu 21^{1} (JE), and (acc. שִׁבְיָה) 2 Ch $28^{5.11}$; וְשָׁבָה שִׁבְיוֹ Dt 21^{10}=*take him captive.* †**Niph.** *be taken captive*: *Pf.* 3 ms. נִשְׁבָּה, of man Gn 14^{14}, of beast Ex 22^{9} (E), of עֵדֶר י׳ Je 13^{17}; 3 pl. נִשְׁבּוּ, human subj. 1 S $30^{3.5}$ 1 K 8^{47}=2 Ch 6^{17}, Ez 6^{9}.

†שְׁבִי **n.m.** Is 49, 24 **captivity, captives** (coll.);—ש׳ abs. Ex 12^{29} +, cstr. Ezr 2^{1} +; שִׁבְיֵ Nu 21^{1} +, sf שֶׁבְיְךָ Ju 5^{12}, שִׁבְיוֹ Dt 21^{10}, שִׁבְיָם Nu 31^{19}, etc.;—**1.**=state of *captivity,* הָלַךְ בַּשְּׁ׳ Am 9^{4} Dt 28^{41} Na 3^{10} Je 20^{6} 22^{22} 30^{16} Ez 12^{11} (+ בַּגּוֹלָה), $30^{17.18}$ Is 46^{2} La 1^{18}, =הָלַךְ שְׁבִי v^{5}; נָתַן לַשְּׁ׳ ψ 78^{61}, נָתַן בַּשְּׁ׳ Ezr 9^{7}; בַּשְּׁבִי יָבֹא Dn 11^{8}; וַאֲשֶׁר לַשְּׁבִי לַשְּׁבִי Je 15^{2} 43^{11}, לָקַח בַּשְּׁבִי Je 48^{46}; וְנָשֵׁינוּ בַּשְּׁ׳ בַּשְּׁבִי 2 Ch 29^{9}; instr. of judgment Dn 11^{33}; אֶרֶץ שׁ׳ Je 30^{10} 46^{27} 2 Ch $6^{37.38}$; phr. of deliverance (only Ezr Ne): נִשְׁאֲרוּ מִן־הַשּׁ׳ Ne 1^{3}, cf. v^{3}, הָעֹלִים מִשְּׁבִי הַגּוֹלָה, 8^{17} הַשָּׁבִים מִן־הַשְּׁ׳ Ezr 2^{1}=Ne 7^{6}, הַבָּאִים מֵהַשּׁ׳ Ezr 3^{8} 8^{35}. **2.** act of *capture,* עִם שׁ׳ סוּסֵיכֶם Am 4^{10}, שִׂמְלַת שִׁבְיָהּ Dt 21^{13} i.e. garb in which she was captured (> others *captivity* in both: Am 4^{10}=*your captive horses;* Dt 21^{13} *her captive's garb*) **3.** =*captives* (coll.): Ex 12^{29} (J), Nu $31^{12.19.26}$ (man and beast), Is 20^{4} (‖ גָּלוּת), $49^{24.25}$ Hb 1^{9} + Ez 32^{9} 𝔊 al. (v. שֶׁבֶר *ad fin.*); appar fs. Is 52^{2} (but v. שְׁבִי); object of שָׁבָה (q.v.) Ju 5^{12} (> שֹׁבְיְךָ 𝔖 JDMich We Bu Now), Nu 21^{1} (JE), Dt 21^{10} ψ 68^{19} 2 Ch 28^{17}.

†[שְׁבִי **adj.** vel **n.m.** whence] שְׁבִיָּה **n.f. captive** (cf. Rahlfs עני u ענו in Psalm., 63);—שׁ׳ בַּת־צִיּוֹן

Is 52[2b] (Bev[JPhil xvii (1888), p 127] ingeniously, שבי הַבַּת וגו׳, cf ∥ שבי v[4], and, on הַבּ׳, La 2[13]), read also שׁ׳ ירוּשָׁלִָם v[4] (for שבי) Oort Bu Du Che[Hpt] Marti

†**שִׁבְיָה n.f. captivity, captives** (coll.), cf שְׁבִי,—always abs שׁ׳;—**1.** state of *captivity*, Je 48[46] (of בָּנוֹת, ∥ שבי of בָּנִים), אֶרֶץ שׁ׳ Ne 3[36] **2.** body of *captives*, Dt 21[11] 32[42] (∥ חָלָל), 2 Ch 28[14.15], object of שָׁבָה, v[5] (שׁ׳ גדולה), הָשִׁיבוּ הַשּׁ׳ v[11], אֲשֶׁר שביתם.

†**שְׁבִית, שְׁבוּת n.f.** id (√שבה ⅏ Thes SS Preuschen[ZAW xv (1895), 1 ff] Krae[Ez 16.53], > √שׁוּב Ew[JBW v (1852 3), 216 f § 165 b] Ol[§ 412, 417] Bo[§ 464] Kue[TTijdschr viii 519 ff] Oort[Ib xiv 157] Schwally[ZAW viii (1888) 200] al, Kö[ii 1 166 f 474 ii 2 § 329 i] thinks deriv of שבה and שוב are confused, cf. Ew[§ 166 b]),—abs שְׁבִית Nu 21[29], cstr שְׁבוּת Ho 6[11]+, sf שְׁבוּתְךָ Dt 30[3], שְׁבִיתְהֶן Ez 16[53a] (v. infr), שְׁבוּתֵיכֶם Zp 3[20] (rd ־תכם Now GASm), etc. [MT has שבות, etc 16 t, + Kt (שְׁבִית Qr) Zp 2[7] ψ 85[2] 126[4] + Ez 16[53a] (Gi, but Baer שְׁבִיתְהֶן Kt et Qr, v his note), + Qr (Kt שבית) Je 29[14] 49[39] Ez 16[53b.c] + v[d] (but < rd וּשְׁבִתִי for וּשְׁבוּת Vrss Comm.), La 2[14] Jb 42[10]; שבית Kt et Qr Nu 21[29], שביתיך Ez 16[53] (but Co Krae שבותך), שְׁבִית prob earlier Ew[§ 186 b] al ψ 126[1] rd prob שבית for שִׁיבַת],—**1.** in cl נָתַן בִּשְׁבִית Nu 21[29] (JE) *give his daughters into captivity* (or *as captives*, ∥ פְּלִיטִם of sons, cf. Je 48[46]), cf. (perh) La 1[7] (v [מִשְׁבָּת] sub שׁבת) **2.** in phr *restore the captivity of*, acc. after שׁוּב, הֵשִׁיב, subj י׳ [vb **Qal** Dt 30[3] + 15 t., + Ez 16[53d] ψ 126[1] (v infr), **Hiph.** Je 32[44] + 5 t., + **Qal** Kt, **Hiph.** Qr, Je 33[26] + 2 t]: **a.** of Isr (or Judah) Ho 6[11] (⅏ joins to 7[1], so, as gloss, We Now) Zp 2[7] 3[20] Dt 30[3] Je 29[14] 30[3.18] (שׁ׳ אָהֳלֵי יַעֲקֹב), 31[23] 32[44] 33[7.7.11] (שׁ׳ הָאָרֶץ), v[26] La 2[14] (subj. proph.), Ez 16[53a c d] (on text v. supr), 39[25] Am 9[14] Jo 4[1] ψ 14[7] = 53[7], 85[2] 126[1] (v. supr), v[4]. **b.** of other nations Je 48[47] (cf. v[46]), 49[6.39] Ez 29[14] (cf v[13]) **c.** appar in more gen sense, *restore fortunes* of Sodom Ez 16[53b] (Krae, cf foll.) **d.** restore fortunes of individuals, Jb 42[10].

†**שְׁבוֹ n.[f.]** a precious stone (relation to above √dub, = As *šubû*; ⅏𝔙 *agate*),—Ex 28[19] = 39[12] (+ אַחְלָמָה, לֶשֶׁם).

†**שֹׁבִי n.pr.m.** appar Ammonite prince, ושׁ׳ 2 S 17[27], ⅏ Ουεσβει, ⅏L καὶ Ζεφει

†**שֹׁבָי n.pr.m.** in post-ex Israel Ezr 2[42] = Ne 7[45], ⅏[B] Αβαου (Ezr), Σαβει, A (Ezr) ⅏L Σωβαι

†**שְׁבוּאֵל, שְׁבָאֵל n pr.m.** son of Gershom 1 Ch 23[16] 26[24] (שׁב׳), = שׁוּבָאֵל 24[20.20], of Heman 25[4] = שׁוּבָאֵל v[20] (cf Benz on these lists).—⅏ in all usu Σουβαηλ, ⅏L usu. -βιηλ

†**[תִּשְׁבֶּה] n.pr.loc.** (fr above √?),—read prob מתִּשְׁבֵּה גִלְעָד (or תשבי) 1 K 17[1] (for MT מִתֹּשָׁבֵי) ⅏ ἐκ Θεσβῶν (⅏L Θεσσεβῶν) τῆς Γαλααδ, so Jos, Ew Th We Kmp Benz Kit Burney al; home of Elijah, v. Kasteren[ZPV xiii (1890), 207 ff] cp mod *Istib*, in mts. of Ajlûn, so Buhl[G 257].

†**תִּשְׁבִּי adj.gent.**, אֵלִיָּהוּ הַתּ׳ 1 K 17[1] 21[17.28] 2 K 1[3.8] 9[36],—ὁ Θεσβ(ε)ίτης.

†**I [שָׁבַח] vb. Pi. soothe, still** (Ar سَبَحَ *be free from care*, etc, Jen[ZA i (1886), 188, iv (1889), 268], cp As *pašâḫu, grow calm*, so Ba[ES 9] Schulth[Lex]);—**Pi.** *Impf* 3 ms sf. יְשַׁבְּחֶנָּה Pr 29[11] *he stilleth it*, i e רוּחוֹ *his temper* (Bi Toy read חָשַׂךְ אַפּוֹ); 2 ms sf תְּשַׁבְּחֵם ψ 89[10] *thou stillest them*, i.e waves (∥ גֵּאוּת הַיָּם) **Hiph.** *Pt.* (prob. Mass error for **Pi.** מְשַׁבֵּחַ) מַשְׁבִּיחַ שְׁאוֹן יַמִּים ψ 65[8] *stilling the roar of the seas*

†**II [שָׁבַח] vb. Pi. laud, praise** (late Aramaism, cf Aram. (incl OAram.) שבח, ܫܒܰܚ, Pa *praise*, v Schwally[Idiot 91] Schulth[Lex]);—**1.** *laud, praise* God (י׳): *Impf* 3 mpl sf. יְשַׁבְּחוּנְךָ ψ 63[4] (∥ בָּרַךְ), *Imv* fs שַׁבְּחִי 147[12], mpl sf. שַׁבְּחוּהוּ 117[1] (both ∥ הִלֵּל), his works, *Impf.* 3 ms יְשַׁבַּח 145[4] (∥ הִגִּיד) **2.** *commend, congratulate*, the dead, *Inf abs.* שַׁבֵּחַ Ec 4[2] (Ges § 113 gg, c מִן comp), mirth, as best thing, *Pf.* 1 s. שִׁבַּחְתִּי Ec 8[15] **Hithp.** *boast* of (בְּ): *Inf. cstr.* הִשְׁתַּבֵּחַ ψ 106[47] = 1 Ch 16[35], ⅏ (ἐγ)καυχᾶσθαι ἐν.

†**יִשְׁבַּח n.pr.m.** in Judah (?, cf. Lag[BN 131]);— 1 Ch 4[17], Μαρεθ, A Ιεσαβα, ⅏L Ιασαφαι.

שׁבט (√of foll; cf As *šabâṭu, smite, slay, šibṭu, rod, sceptre*; NH שבט = BH, also שָׁבַט *beat* (denom.? so No[ZMG xl (1886), 736], but too sceptical), Sab שבטם *rod, blow*, Sab.Denkm.[No 21.1 5]; Aram שִׁבְטָא, ܫܒܛܳܐ = BH; loan-word in Egypt. demot *šbṭe*, pl hierogl *ša-b-d-y*, WMM[As u Eur 89]; Lewy[Fremdw 122] cp σπάθη)

שֵׁבֶט[189] **n m**[Nu 24 17] (**f.**[Ez 21, 15, 18] but corrupt): **1 rod, staff, club, sceptre 2. tribe**,—שׁ׳ abs Gn 49[10] +, cstr 1 S 10[20] +; שָׁבֶט Dt 1[23] +; sf שִׁבְטוֹ Ju 21[24] +, etc., pl שְׁבָטִים 1 K 11[31] +, cstr. שִׁבְטֵי Gn 49[16] +, sf שְׁבָטֶיךָ Dt 12[14] +, etc.;— †**1. a.** *rod, staff* (evidently common article), for

smiting (esp. הִכָּה בַשּׁ׳) Ex 21[20] (E), Mi 4[14] Is 10[15] (in sim.; ‖ מַטֶּה), Pr 10[13]+; שׁ׳ מוּסָר 22[15], cf. 29[15]; for beating (חָבַט) cummin Is 28[27] (‖ מַטֶּה); as (inferior) weapon (opp. חֲנִית) 2 S 23[21] = 1 Ch 11[23] (cf. מַקֵּל 1 S 17[40.43]); fig. of י׳'s chastisement: national Is 10[24] 30[31] (both ‖ מַטֶּה), 14[29], שׁ׳ אַפִּי 10[5], שׁ׳ עֶבְרָתוֹ La 3[1]; individual Jb 9[34] 21[9] (שׁ׳ אֱלוֹהַּ), 37[13], 2 S 7[14] (שׁ׳ אֲנָשִׁים, i e not *in*-human), ψ 89[33] (both ‖ נְגָעִים). **b.** *shaft*, i e. spear, dart, 2 S 18[14], but < read שְׁלָחִים, 𝔊 βέλη, Th We Kit HPS Bu. **c.** shepherd's implement, *club*, ψ 23[4] (‖ מִשְׁעֶנֶת), רְעֵה בשׁ׳ Mi 7[14] (both fig of י׳); used in mustering or counting sheep Ez 20[37] (fig), Lv 27[32] (cf Je 33[13]), v Mackie[Hast. DB Sod]. **d.** *truncheon, sceptre*, mark of authority, שׁ׳ סֹפֵר Ju 5[14], שׁ׳ מֹשְׁלִים Is 14[5] (‖ מַטֶּה), Gn 49[10] (poem in J; ‖ מְחֹקֵק), Zc 10[11] ψ 45[7 7] Ez 19[11 14] (made from a branch, מַטֶּה); a ruler is תּוֹמֵךְ שׁ׳ Am 1[5.8]; as symbol of conquest Nu 24[17] (JE); שׁ׳ בַּרְזֶל ψ 2[9] (of Mess. king); שׁ׳ הָרֶשַׁע 125[3]; שׁ׳ עֶבְרָתוֹ Pr 22[8] (si vera l, cf Frankenb. Toy).—Vid מַקֵּל, מַטֶּה, מִשְׁעֶנֶת. **2.** ₁₄₅ *tribe* (syn. מַטֶּה, q.v. **3**, p. 641[b]), esp **a.** of (12) tribes of Israel, Gn 49[16.28] (poem in J), Dt 33[5] (poem), Ex 24[4] (E), + oft. [JE 13 t, D 28 t. (מַטֶּה not JED), P 9 t. (cf Gray[Nu 4, 18]; מ׳ 150 t. + in P); Ju 15 t. (never מ׳), S 14 t. (never מ׳), K 13 t. (מ׳ 2 t.), Chr 15 t. (מ׳ 23 t.), ψψ 7 t (never מ׳), proph 16 t. (מ׳ † Hb 3[9], very dub)]; Ju 20[12] 1 S 9[21] rd. שֵׁבֶט (or שִׁבְטֵי Ges[§ 90 l], We Sta[§ 343 a] Dr, for שִׁבְטֵי), Vrss (GFM[Ju]); שִׁבְטֵי נַחֲלָתֶךָ Is 63[17]; שִׁבְטֵי־יָהּ ψ 122[4]. **b.** sg of people (of Judah, late) ψ 74[2], but Je 10[16] = 51[19] del. שׁ׳ נ׳ Gf Gie Du. **c.** of subdivision of tribe, שׁ׳ מִשְׁפְּחוֹת וגו׳ Nu 4[18] (P) —2 S 7[7] rd. שֹׁפְטֵי (cf. v[11], ‖ 1 Ch 17[6], Ew Th We Dr HPS Bu al).

†שַׁרְבִיט **n.m. sceptre** (expanded fr. foreg., Ges[§ 85 w]);—only Est: abs הַשּׁ׳ 5[2]; cstr. שׁ׳ הַזָּהָב 4[11] 5[2]; שַׁרְבִט הַז׳ 8[4].

†שְׁבָט **n.pr. mens.** Sh[e]bāt, 11th month (post-ex.) = Feb.–March; loan-word from Bab *Šabâṭu* (COT[Ne 1, 1] Dl[WB]), Zc 1[7] (der. fr. *šabâtu, strike, kill, destroy* (Dl[Prol. 38, WB]), Lyon[Bib. Sacr Apr 1884, 384] Jen[ZA iv (1889), 273] Muss-Arn[JBL xi (1892), 171 f] al., as month of *destroying* rain; another conjecture in Zim[KAT 3. 504 n]; this month called שבט also in Nab Palm, v. Lzb SAC[111]).

שְׁבִי, שְׁבִיָּה, שְׁבִית v. שׁבה.

שׁבל (√of foll.; cf Ar. سَبَلَ iv. *cause to hang down*, سَبَلَة *flowing dress*; As. *šubultu, šunbultu* (Meissner), Ar. سُنْبُل, سُنْبُلَة (Ba[NB 207]), Eth. ሰብል: Aram. שֻׁבַּלְתָּא, ܫܒܠܬܐ, all *ear* of grain).

†שֹׁבֶל **n.[m.] flowing skirt, train**,—abs. חֶשְׂפִּי־שֹׁ׳ Is 47[2] *strip off* (thy) *train*

†**I.** שִׁבֹּלֶת **n.f. flowing stream**;—שׁ׳ abs. ψ 69[3], as test of dialect Ju 12[6] (cf. סִבֹּלֶת and GFM), cstr. שׁ׳ מַיִם ψ 69[16], שׁ׳ הַנָּהָר Is 27[12].

†**II.** שִׁבֹּלֶת **n.f.** ear of grain;—שׁ׳ abs. Jb 24[24]+; pl. שִׁבֳּלִים Gn 41[5]+, cstr. שִׁבֲּלֵי Zc 4[12],—*ear*, Gn 41[5.6.7 7 22.23.24.24.26.27] Is 17[5.5] Ru 2[2] Jb 24[24]; transf. *spike* (Pusey), end of olive bough Zc 4[12].

†[שְׁבִיל, שְׁבוּל] **n.[m.]** way, path (prop as *flowing along, stretching out*? cf. NH שְׁבִיל, Ar. سَبِيل, Aram. שְׁבִילָא);—pl. sf. וּשְׁבִילְךָ בְּמַיִם רַבִּים [Kt שְׁבִילְךָ, Qr שְׁבִילֶךָ] ψ 77[20] (of י׳; ‖ דַּרְכֶּךָ); cstr. (fig of course of life) שְׁבוּלֵי עוֹלָם Je 18[15] (Kt; Qr שְׁבִילֵי, ‖ דְּרָכִים)

†שׁוֹבָל **n. pr. m. 1.** Edomite name Gn 36[20.23.29] = 1 Ch 1[38.40]. **2. a.** in Caleb 1 Ch 2[50.52]. **b.** in Judah 1 Ch 4[1 2].—Σωβα(λ), Σουβαλ.

שַׁבְלוּל v. בלל.

שׁבן (√of following; meaning dub.).

†שֶׁבְנָא, שֶׁבְנָה **n. pr. m.** secretary and major-domo of Hezekiah; -נָא Is 22[15], 36[22] 37[2] = 2 K 18[37] 19[2]; Is 36[3 11] = -נָה 2 K 18[18.26].—Σομνας.

†שְׁבַנְיָה(וּ) **n. pr. m. 1.** -יָה **a.** Levites, (1) Ne 9[4.5] 10[13], (2) 10[11], Σεβανια, Σαβανια(ς). **b.** priest Ne 10[5], priestly family 12[14] (𝔊L Σεχενια), = שְׁכַנְיָה v[3] (Σεχενια(ς)), and perh. שְׁבַנְיָהוּ 1 Ch 24[11] (Ισχανια, Σεχενια) **2.** -יָהוּ, priest, 1 Ch 15[24] (Σομνια, 𝔊L Σαβανια)

שׁבס (√of following; meaning?).

†[שָׁבִיס] **n.[m.]** front-band (Mishn. *id.*; Levy[NHWB iv 498]; al cp. Ar. شُمَيْس, lit. a *sun*, of small glass *neck-ornament* We[Skizzen iii 145]; Heb. perh. a dimin., v Ges[§ 86 note]),—pl. הַשְּׁבִיסִים Is 3[18], in list of women's finery.

I שֶׁבַע, שִׁבְעָה ₃₉₄ **n.m.** et **f. seven** (NH *id*, MI[16] שבעת; As. *sibi, sibittu* (Dl[Gr § 65, 6]; *s* = שׁ), Ar سَبْعٌ, سَبْعَةٌ, Sab. סבע Hom[Chr 47, 124], Eth. ሰብዐ: ሰብዐቱ: Ph. (Pun) שבע, Nab. שבע, שבעה, Palm. שבעא, שבעה; Aram. שְׁבַע, שִׁבְעָא, ܫܒܥ, ܫܒܥܐ, on etym. cf Lag[BN 37 f]),—**m.** (c. **n.f.**) abs. שֶׁבַע Gn 41[2]+ 115 t.; cstr. שְׁבַע 5[28]+ 47 t., esp P (15 t.) and Chr (20 t.), וּשְׁבַע 1 K

14^{21}. **f.** (c. **n.m.**) abs שבעה Gn 4^{24} + 100 t.; cstr שבעת 7^{10} + 120 t; sf שִׁבְעָתָם 2 S 21^{9} Qr (so Vrss and mod, v. Dr; > Kt שבעתים);—*seven*. **1.** without other num **a.** שֶׁבַע, before n fpl Gn 21^{28} (J), Ju 16^{13} Is 4^{1} + 80 t, esp שׁ׳ שָׁנִים Gn 29^{18} (E) + 32 t. (but read שלוש for שֶׁבַע 2 S 24^{13a}, cf v^{b,c}, also 𝔊 and ‖ 1 Ch 21^{12}, so Th We Dr Bu HPS Now), שׁ׳ פְּעָמִים Gn 33^{3} (J), Lv 4^{6} (P) + 17 t; שׁ׳ בָּאַמָּה רָחְבָּה 1 K 6^{6}; after noun Ez 40$^{22.26}$, n. om Jb 5^{19} Pr 6^{16}, + (=שׁ׳ פְּעָמִים) Lv 26$^{18.21.24.28}$ (H), ψ 119^{64} Pr 24^{16}. **b.** שִׁבְעָה, before n mpl Nu 23$^{1.1.1}$ (E) + 40 t + Jb 42^{13} (read שׁ׳ for שִׁבְעָנָה Ges^{§97c} and most), + (distrib) שׁ׳ וְשׁ׳ Zc 4^{2}, after n. Gn 7^{4} (J), Ex 25^{37} (P) + 12 t. (P Ch Dn Pr), n. om. 1 S 2^{5} + 9 t., incl שׁ׳ as ordinal, v. infr, but read שִׂבְכָה for שבעה 1 K 7$^{17.17}$ 𝔊 Th Kmp Klo Benz Kit Bur; also שׁ׳ שׁ׳ distrib. = 7 *each* Gn 7$^{2.3}$ (J); as pred. Gn 46^{25} (P). **c.** שִׁבְעַת, before n pl Nu 23^{4} (E), 8^{2} (P), Ez 45$^{21.21}$ Jb 2$^{13.13}$ + 97 t, incl שׁ׳ יָמִים Gn 8^{10} (J), + 88 t + Ez 45^{21} (rd. שבעת for שָׁבֻעוֹת, Vrss and mod). **d.** = ordinal, שְׁנַת (הַ)שֶּׁבַע Dt 15^{9} 2 K 12^{2} + 3 t, בְּשִׁבְעָה לַחֹדֶשׁ Ez 30^{20}, cf 45^{20}, לְשִׁבְעַת הַיָּמִים Gn 7^{10} (J), 1 Ch 9^{25}. **2.** †**a.** שְׁבַע עֶשְׂרֵה שָׁנָה 17 *years* Gn 37^{2} + 3 t + 1 K 14^{21} (וּשְׁבַע וגו׳), also as ordin בִּשְׁנַת שׁ׳ עֶשׂ׳ 1 K 22^{52}, בִּשְׁנַת שׁ׳ עֶשׂ׳ שָׁנָה 2 K 16^{1} †**b.** שִׁבְעָה עָשָׂר (sc הַגּוֹרָל *lot*) 1 Ch 24^{15} 25^{24} (cf. also, + other num, 7^{11} Ezr 2^{39} Ne 7^{42}), + יוֹם 17*th day* Gn 7^{11} 8^{4}, unusual is שׁ׳ שְׁקָלִים וַעֲשָׂרָה הַכֶּסֶף Je 32^{9} *7 shekels and 10 the silver* **3.** שְׁבַע מֵאוֹת = 700 Ju 8^{26} + 39 t (but Ne 7^{68} om Mass. Baer Gi q v) **4.** שִׁבְעָה אֶלֶף = 7000 1 K 20^{15} + 2 t., שִׁבְעַת אֲלָפִים = *id.* 1 K 20^{15} + 15 t, 57,000 is 7 + 50 × 1000 Nu 1^{31} 2$^{8.31}$. **5.** שׁ׳ + other num **a** שׁ׳ follows 18 t. (1) n s after שׁ׳ Ju 8^{14}, also (= ord num.) Ez 29^{17} + 2 t, שְׁנַת שְׁלשִׁים וָשׁ׳ שָׁנָה 2 K 13^{10}, cf 15^{1}, (2) n pl. before other num Ezr 8^{35} Ne 7$^{[72].71}$, (3) n.s cstr. precedes שׁ׳ בִּשְׁנַת עֶשְׂרִים וָשׁ׳ 1 K 16$^{10.15}$ (ordin), (4) n. after each num Gn 23^{1} 25^{17} (both P), etc. **b.** שׁ׳ precedes 10 t (P and Est) (1) n.s after other num Gn 8^{14} Ex 6$^{16.20}$ + 3 t Est, (2) n. repeated Gn 5^{7} 11^{21} 47^{28}, cf. 5$^{25.31}$. **c.** 1000 + 17 Ezr 2^{39} = Ne 7^{42} —שׁ׳ oft c. sacred signif.: Gn 21^{28ff} (J), Ex 37^{23} Lv 4$^{6.17}$ 8^{11} 14^{27} + (P), as round number Gn 4^{24} (song in J), 29^{18ff} 31^{23} 41^{2ff} (all E), etc, on bowing 7 t. 33^{3} (J, in great humility), cf. Wkl$^{TelAm\ nos\ 143,230,246}$ Ne$^{Mar\ 11f.}$, all these prob originating with week of seven days, cf esp. Ko$^{Hast\ DB\ Number,\ 562a,\ 563}$

†שִׁבְעָה **n.f pr. putei,** Gn 26^{33} (J), Ὅρκος, (explanation of name בְּאֵר שֶׁבַע)

שִׁבְעִים **n.pl. seventy** (irreg. pl. of שֶׁבַע Ges^{§97e,R1}),—not decl·—*seventy* (oft. as round no, cf Ko$^{Hast.\ DB\ Number\ 563a}$): **1.** without other no: **a.** before n s. year Gn 5^{12} + 12 t, man Ju 9^{2} Nu 11^{25} + 7 t, shekel 7^{13} + 11 t, other n 5 t. **b.** before n pl kings Ju 1^{7}, sons 8^{30} 9^{24} 2 K 10^{1}, brothers Ju 9^{56}, asses 12^{14}, palms Ex 15^{27} Nu 33^{9}, males Ezr 8$^{7.14}$. **c.** after n.coll (בָּקָר) 2 Ch 29^{32}, n.pl. Dn 9^{24} **d.** pred Gn 46^{27} **e.** n om. Ex 24$^{1.9}$ (man), Nu 7^{85} (shekel), cf. Ju 9^{4}. **2.** שׁ׳ אֶלֶף = 70,000 2 S 24^{15} + 6 t **3.** + other num: **a** + unit + n s Ju 8^{14}, n om. 70 + 7 (times) Gn 4^{24}, cf Ezr 2^{40} = Ne 7^{43}, so 2 + 70 Nu 31^{38}; n pl. + 70 + 7 Ezr 8^{35}, 5 years + 70 year Gn 12^{4} **b.** 5 + 70 × 1000 (man) Est 9^{16}, cf. Nu 2^{4} 3^{43} 26^{22}, 2 + 70 × 1000 31^{33} (בָּקָר precedes); 70 man, 50 × 1000 man 1 S 6^{19}; 7 + 70 year + 7 × 100 year Gn 5^{31}; n om. 3 + 70 + 200 Nu 3^{46}. **c.** 70 foll. hundreds · 70 year + 5 years Gn 25^{7}, and (n om) 70 + 2 Ezr 2$^{3.4}$ = Ne 7$^{8.9}$, Ne 11^{19}, + 3 Ezr 2^{36} Ne 7^{39}; 5 + 70 Ezr 2^{5}. **d.** 1000 + 7 × 100 + 5 + 70 shekel Ex 38^{25} and (n. om) v^{28}.

שְׁבִיעִי **m.** שְׁבִיעִית **f.** **adj. num. ord.** seventh,—**m.** שביעי Gn 2^{2} +, שְׁבִעִי Ex 12^{15} +; **f** שביעית Jos 6^{16} +, -עת Ex 23^{11} +, שבעת 21^{2}, -עִית 1 K 18^{44} 2 Ch 23^{1},—*fifth*, esp. P, always c art **1. m.** 7th day Gn 2^{3} + 47 t, month (חֹדֶשׁ) 8^{4} + 23 t + (n om) Ez 45^{25} + 3 t., lot (הַגּוֹרָל) Jos 19^{40} + (n. om) 1 Ch 24^{10} 25^{14}, n. om. also 1 Ch 2^{15} 26$^{3.5}$ (son), 12^{11} (man), 27^{10} (captain). **2. f.** 7th year, 2 K 11^{4} + 7 t + (n. om) Ex 21^{2} 23^{11}, also שְׁנַת הַשְּׁבִיעִית (Ges^{§134p}) Ezr 7^{8}; sabbath Lv 23^{16}, time (פַּעַם) Jos 6^{16} + (n om) 1 K 18^{44}.

שִׁבְעָנָה Jb 42^{13} read שבעה Ges^{§97c} and most.

†שִׁבְעָתַיִם **n.f. du. seven-fold, seven times** (cf Ges^{§§97h,134r}),—**1.** *seven-fold, seven times as much*, Is 30^{26} Pr 6^{31}, as adv Gn 4$^{15.24}$ ψ 79^{12}. **2.** *seven times*, adv. ψ 12^{7}.—2 S 21^{9} read Qr שִׁבְעָתָם, v. 1. שֶׁבַע.

†שָׁבוּעַ **n.m.**$^{Dn\ 9.27}$ **period of seven** (days, years), **heptad, week** (on format. v. Lag$^{BN\ 67}$);—abs. שׁ׳ Dn 9$^{27.27}$, cstr שְׁבֻעַ Gn 29$^{27.28}$; du שְׁבֻעַיִם Lv 12^{5}, pl שָׁבֻעוֹת Ex 34^{22} + 4 t. Dt + (in term. techn.) 2 Ch 8^{13}, late שָׁבֻעִים Dn 9^{24} + 4 t. Dn; cstr שְׁבֻעֹת Je 5^{24} (Ez 45^{21} read שִׁבְעַת with Vrss and all mod, v שֶׁבַע), sf שָׁבֻעֹתֵיכֶם Nu 28^{26},—**1.** *period of seven days* (fr. a given time), *week* Dt 16$^{9.9}$ Lv 12^{5} (P), of marriage feast Gn 29$^{27.28}$ (E; cf. Ju 14^{12} Tob 11^{19}); שָׁבֻעִים יָמִים Dn 10$^{2.3}$ three *weeks, days* (three weeks long);

ש׳ חֻקּוֹת קָצִיר Je 5^{24} *weeks of statutes* (i.e. weeks appointed by י׳) *for harvest;* term. techn. חַג שָׁבֻעֹת Ex 34^{22} (J) *feast of weeks* (ending seven weeks of harvest), Dt 16$^{10.16}$ 2 Ch 8^{13}, so ש׳ alone Nu 28^{26} (P). **2.** *heptad* or *seven* of years, late, Dn 9$^{24.25.26.27.27}$.—שְׁבֻעֵי שְׁבֻעוֹת Ez 21^{28} v. [שָׁבַע].

[שָׁבַע] $_{186}$ **vb. swear** (prob., so to say, *seven oneself*, or *bind oneself by seven things*, cf. Thes (as altern.), Gerb$^{108 ff.}$; NH Niph. = BH; 𝔗 שְׁבַע Ithpe. Aph.; v. also Dr$^{Gn 21.28}$ Kö$^{Hast. DB Numbers, 565}$ RS$^{Sem. i. 166, 2nd ed., 182}$ We$^{Reste Ar. Heid. 2, 186}$);—**Qal** (acc. to Thes Rob Ges) *Pt. pass.* שְׁבֻעֵי שְׁבֻעוֹת Ez 21^{28} *those sworn with* (= who have sworn) *oaths;* both from שְׁבוּעָה, acc. to Krae, *oaths of oaths* (the most sacred); 𝔊 𝔖 Co om.; both from שָׁבוּעַ, Ew Sm ש׳ ש׳ *weeks on weeks* (plenty of time). **Niph.** *Pf.* 3 ms. נִשְׁבַּע Gn 24^{7}+, etc.; *Impf.* 3 ms. יִשָּׁבַע Lv 5^{24}+, וַיִּשָּׁבַע Gn 24^{9}+; 2 ms. תִּשָּׁבַע Dt 6^{13} 10^{20}; 1 s. אִשָּׁבַע Gn 21^{24}, וָאִשָּׁבַע 1 K 2^{8} Ez 16^{8}, etc.; *Imv.* ms. הִשָּׁבְעָה Gn 21^{23}+, etc.; *Inf. abs.* הִשָּׁבֵעַ Nu 30^{3}, הִשָּׁבֹעַ Je 7^{9}; *cstr.* הִשָּׁבַע Je 12$^{16.16}$+ 1 S 20^{17} v. infra; *Pt.* נִשְׁבָּע Zc 5^{3}+, etc.;—*swear, take an oath:* **1.** subj. man: **a.** in asseveration, abs. Gn 21$^{24.31}$ (E), Ju 21$^{1.18}$ 2 S 21^{2}+; also sq. וַיֹּאמֶר 1 S 20^{3} 1 K 1^{29}, sq. לֵאמֹר 2 S 3^{35} Jos 14^{9} (D); c. acc. cogn. Nu 30^{3} (P; ‖ נָדַר); + לַשֶּׁקֶר Je 5^{2} 7^{9} Lv 5^{24} (P; + עַל rei), Mal 3^{5}; + עַל־שׁ׳ Lv 5^{22} (P); + לְמִרְמָה ψ 24^{4}; sq. inf. Lv 5^{4} (P), ψ 15^{4} 119^{106}; + לְ pers. *take an oath to,* Jos 6^{22} (JE), 9^{20} (P; acc. cogn.) Gn 24^{9} (+עַל־הַדָּבָר הַזֶּה)+, so also 1 S 20^{17} (rd. לְהִשָּׁבַע for אֶל־ ,לְהַשְׁבִּיעַ אֶת־, 𝔊 𝔅 Th We Dr al.); oath of allegiance (לי׳) Is 19^{18} 45^{23} Zp 1^{5} 2 Ch 15^{14}, cf. (abs.) v^{15} (Jos 23^{7} v. **Hiph.**); also sq. וַיֹּאמֶר 2 K 25^{24}, sq. לֵאמֹר 2 S 21^{17} 1 K 1^{13} Je 40^{9}; sq. פֶּן = *that not* Ju 15^{12}, sq. אִם = *id.* 1 K 1^{51}; + אֶל pers. sq. לֵאמֹר Je 38^{16}; + בי׳ *by* י׳, sq. inf. Ju 21^{7}; + בְּשֵׁם י׳ 1 S 20^{42} Is 48^{1}, cf. Gn 31^{53} (E), Dt 6^{13} 10^{20} Je 12^{16} (+חַי־י׳), Is 65^{16} Zc 5^{4} (לַשֶּׁקֶר), Lv 19^{12} (*id.*), ψ 63^{12} Dn 12^{7}; + בי׳ sq. אִם 2 S 19^{8}; + לְ pers. c. בי׳ Jos 9$^{18.19}$ (P; pledge faith), sq. לֵאמֹר 1 S 28^{10} 1 K 1^{30} 2$^{8.23}$, sq. כִּי of obj. cl. Jos 2^{12} (JE), 1 K 1^{17}; + לְ pers. c. בא׳, sq. אִם Gn 21^{23} (E), 1 S 30^{15}; as vb. of quotation + obj. חַי־י׳ Ho 4^{15} Je 4^{2} 1 S 19^{6} (+אִם), + אִם in *orat. recta* ψ 132^{2} (‖ נָדַר); also + בְּלֹא אֱלֹהִים Je 5^{7}, בַּבַּעַל 12^{16}, בְּמַלְכָּם Zp 1^{5}, cf. Am 8^{14} (+וְאָמַר). **b.** *imprecate, curse,* בִּי *by me* ψ 102^{9} (cf. שְׁבוּעָה 1 b, קְלָלָה). **2.** subj. י׳: *swear,* c. בִּי *by myself* Gn 22^{16} (JE), Je 22^{5} (cl. כִּי), 49^{13} (*id.*), Is 45^{23} (*id.*), c. בְּקָדְשׁוֹ Am 4^{2} (*id.*), cf. ψ 89^{36} (‖ אִם אֲכַזֵּב), cf. also Am 6^{8} 8^{17} Je 44^{26} 51^{14} Is 62^{8}; *swear,* sq. inf. Dt 1^{35} 4^{21} Jos 21^{41} (van d. H. Baer; v^{43} Gi), sq. מִן inf. = *not to* Is 54$^{9.9}$, sq. אִם ψ 90^{10}, sq. לֵאמֹר Dt 1^{34} Is 14^{24} Nu 32^{10} (P); sq. *orat. recta* ψ 110^{4}; c. לְ pers. *take an oath to,* Gn 24^{7} (J), Ex 13^{11} (J), Dt 2^{14}+7 t. Dt. (acc. cogn. 7^{8} 9^{5}), Ez 16^{8} (‖ בוֹא בִבְרִית), ψ 89^{4} (‖ כָּרַת בְּרִית), v^{50} (בֶּאֱמוּנָתֶךָ), +; לְ pers. + inf. (usu. *to give land*) Ex 13^{5} (J), Dt 1^{8}+9 t. Dt, Jos 1^{6} 5$^{6.6}$ (all R^{D}), Je 11^{5} (+acc. cogn.), 32^{22}; לְ pers. + acc. rei (usu. *land*) = *promise by oath to* Gn 50^{24} Ex 33^{1} Nu 11^{12} (all J), 14$^{16.23}$ (JE), 32^{11} (P), Ju 2^{1} Mi 7^{20} Dt 6^{18}+8 t. Dt (obj. covenant 4^{31} 8^{18}); לְ pers. om. Dt 31^{21}. †**Hiph.** *Perf.* 3 ms. הִשְׁבִּיעַ Ex 13^{19}+, 1 s. הִשְׁבַּעְתִּי Ct 2^{7}+, etc.; *Impf.* 3 ms. וַיַּשְׁבַּע Gn 50^{25}+, sf. וַיַּשְׁבִּעֵנִי Gn 24^{37}, etc.; *Inf. abs.* הַשְׁבֵּעַ Ex 13^{19} 1 S 14^{28}; *cstr.* הַשְׁבִּיעַ 1 S 14^{27} (20^{17} v. **Niph.**); *Pt.* sf. מַשְׁבִּיעֶךָ 1 K 22^{16} = 2 Ch 18^{15};—**1.** *cause to take an oath,* subj. always man: c. acc. pers. Gn 50^{6} (J), 1 S 14^{27} 1 K 18^{10} 2 K 11^{4}, + acc. cogn. Jos 2$^{17.20}$ (J), + לֵאמֹר Gn 24^{37} 50^{5} (both J), v^{25} (E), Jos 6^{26} (J; acc. pers. om.), so (Inf. abs. + Pf.) Ex 13^{19} (JE), 1 S 14^{28}, + וְאָמַר Nu 5^{19} and (c. acc. cogn.) v^{21} (both P), + inf. cl. Ne 5^{12} Ezr 10^{5}; + בי׳ *by* י׳ Gn 24^{3} (J; cl. אֲשֶׁר), 1 K 2^{42} (‖ וָאָעִד בְּךָ + לֵאמֹר), cf. Jos 23^{7} (R^{D}; but read perhaps **Niph.** תִּשָּׁבְעוּ Gr al.; 𝔊 del.), Ne 13^{25} (cl. אִם, *orat. recta*), 2 Ch 36^{13}. **2.** *adjure,* c. acc. pers. 1 K 22^{16} = 2 Ch 18^{15} (both + cl. אֲשֶׁר); elsewhere only Ct: 5^{9}, c. cl. מַה־ interrog. v^{8}, c. cl. אִם *that not* 2^{7} 3^{5} (both + בְּ of oath), = cl. מַה־ 8^{4} (v. מָה **2 a** (*b*)).—1 S 20^{17} v. **Niph.**

†II. שֶׁבַע **n.pr.m.** **1.** in Benj., בֶּן־בִּכְרִי 2 S 20$^{1.2.6.7.10.13.21.22}$; Σαβεε. **2.** in Gad 1 Ch 5^{13}; Σεβεε, A Σωβαθε, 𝔊L Σαβεε.

†III. שֶׁבַע si vera l. **n.pr.loc.** in Simeon, בְּאֵר־שֶׁבַע וְשֶׁבַע Jos 19^{2}; Σαμαα, 𝔊L Σαβε; prob. del. וְשׁ׳ Di al. (om. ‖ 1 Ch 4^{28}).—בְּאֵר שׁ׳ v. p. 92^{a}.

שֶׁבַע v. in cpds. אֱלִישֶׁבַע, (בַּת־שֶׁבַע), יְהוֹשֶׁבַע.

†שְׁבֻעָה, שְׁבוּעָה **n. f.** (Jos 2^{17} read הַזֹּאת Albr$^{ZAW xvi (1896), 116}$) **oath, curse;**—abs. שְׁבֻעָה Jos 9^{20}+, שְׁבֻ׳ Gn 26^{3}+; cstr. שְׁבֻעַת Ex 22^{10}+; sf. שְׁבֻעָתִי Gn 24^{8}, etc.; pl. שְׁבֻעוֹת abs. Ez 21^{28}, cstr. Hb 3^{9} [Je 5^{24} Ez 45^{21} v. שָׁבוּעַ];—*oath* [as acc. cogn. c. הִשְׁבִּיעַ etc. Nu 30^{3}+ (in rel. cl.) 5 t.]: **1.** of man: **a.** attesting innocence Ex 22^{10} (E), friendship 2 S 21^{7}, promise 1 K 2^{43} (after שָׁמַר *keep;* all שְׁבֻעַת י׳ *oath to* י׳); innocence also Nu 5^{21a}; friendship Ne 6^{18} (בַּעֲלֵי שׁ׳ לוֹ), promise Lv 5^{4}; of vow (‖ נדר) Nu 30$^{3.11.14}$ (שְׁבֻעַת אִסָּר), Jos 9^{20} (all P),

Ne 10[30] (|| אָלָה), Ec 9[2], of covenant with י׳ 2 Ch 15[15], שבוּעַת אלהים Ec 8[2] (prob of oath of allegiance to king), שׁבעת שׁקר Zc 8[17], of threat Ju 21[5] 1 S 14[26] (𝔊 שׁבעת י׳), *keep, discharge the oath* is הקים הש׳ Gn 26[3] (J), Je 11[5], נָקָה מש׳ *be free, exempt from an oath* Gn 24[8] (J), cf. Jos 2[17.20]. **b.** = *curse*, Is 65[15] and (|| אָלָה) Nu 5[21] (P), Dn 9[11]. **2.** *oath* of י׳, in promise, Dt 7[8] (שָׁמַר in rel cl), || covenant (ברית), שְׁבוּעָתוֹ ליצחק ψ 105[9] = 1 Ch 16[16].—שבעות מַטּוֹת Hb 3[9] very dub.: AV *oaths of the tribes, oaths, rods* of the word, Hi-St., *sworn* (pt pass שָׁבֻעַ) were *the rods* (= chastisements) of (thy) word, GesHiRVm; *heptads of spears* Ew, cf. Da, text prob corrupt, Now prop (אַשְׁפָּתֶךָ) שִׂבַּעְתָּ מַטּוֹת *thou hast sated with shafts thy quiver*, Marti (after 𝔊[Codd]) *thy bow was satiated with shafts*, GASm *thou gluttest* (?) *thy shafts*.—Ez 21[28] v. √.

†[**שָׁבַץ**] **vb. Pi.** prob **weave in chequer** or **plaited work** (NH שָׁבַץ *ornament* a vessel *with a pattern*, Syr. (lexx) ܫܒܨ *immiscuit*, ܫܒܨܐ *commixtio* v also Lag[BN 143]),—**Pi.** *Pf* 2 ms וְשִׁבַּצְתָּ Ex 28[39] (P), *and thou shalt chequer* (or *plait*) the tunic (in) byssus. **Pu.** *Pt* mpl מְשֻׁבָּצִים זָהָב Ex 28[20] (P), *inwoven* (i e set in a chequered or plaited mounting) *with gold* (-thread) shall they be (of gems).

†**שָׁבָץ** **n.m.** (meaning and connexion with above √ dub),—הַשּׁ׳ 2 S 1[9] אֲחָזַנִי הַשּׁ׳ *hath seized me*, i e perh *cramp* (Ew[G iii 147] Th Ke, cf Dr), al *giddiness* (Thes Klo HPS), as intricacy, confusion, Kit Bu Now leave undecided.

†**מִשְׁבְּצ(וֹ)ת** **n.f.** [Ex 28.25] **pl. chequered** (or **plaited**) **work**, usu of *settings* for gems;—מ׳ זָהָב (i e. plaited with gold-thread) for two gems on high priest's ephod (P) Ex 28[11.13] 39[6.13.16], מ׳ abs 28[14.25.39] 39[18]; ψ 45[14] ממ׳ ז׳ לבושה her clothing is of *chequer work* inwrought with gold, < Krochm Gr Che[Comm] פנינים בְּמִשְׁבְּצוֹת ז׳ לבושה (v. פְּנִימָה p 819 supr) pearls in *plaited settings* of gold(-thread).

†**תַּשְׁבֵּץ** **n.** [**m.**] **chequered** (or **plaited**) **work**,—כתנת ת׳ Ex 28[4].

שבק (√ of foll, cf BAram. 𝔗 שְׁבַק *let go, leave*, so ܫܒܩ, Ar سَبَقَ *outstrip*)

†**שׁוֹבֵק** **n.pr.m.** one of those sealed Ne 10[25], Σωβηκ, 𝔊L Σωβειρ.

†**יִשְׁבָּק** **n.pr.m.** son of Abr. and Ketûrâh, Gn 25[2] 1 Ch 1[32], Ιεσβοκ (B Σοβακ Ch).

שָׁבַר [148] **vb. break, break in pieces** (NH id, Sab תבר *break, destroy* DHM[Hof Mus. no 11 26] Mordtm[HI 74], Ar. ثَبَرَ *restrain, destroy*, Aram תְּבַר, ܬܒܪ, As *šabâru, break, break in pieces*; Eth ሰበረ: *break*);—**Qal** [53] *Pf.* 3 ms. שׁ׳ 1 K 13[28] Is 14[5], etc, *Impf.* 3 ms יִשְׁבֹּר Je 19[11], בּוֹר- Is 42[3]; 3 fs תִּשְׁבָּר־ Pr 25[15], etc, *Imv.* ms שְׁבֹר ψ 10[15], sf שָׁבְרֵם Je 17[18], *Inf cstr* לִשְׁבֹּר Gn 19[9] + 2 t, שְׁבוֹר Je 28[12], *Pt. act* שֹׁבֵר Ez 4[16] + 2 t.; *pass.* שָׁבוּר Lv 22[22], pl. cstr שְׁבוּרֵי ψ 147[3],—*break*, lit, obj earthen vessel Ju 7[20] Lv 11[33] (P), Je 19[11] (in sim), cf v[11] 48[38] Is 30[14], flask Je 19[10], gate-bar Am 1[5] (in metaph.), bow Ho 1[5] Je 49[35], and sword Ho 2[20] (מִן־הָאָרֶץ), bone of lamb Ex 12[46] Nu 9[12] (P), and (in metaph) Pr 25[15], cf שָׁבוּר i e fractured of limb Lv 22[22] (H), yoke Je 28[10.12.13], and, in metaph, of deliverance (י׳ subj) v[2.4.11] 38[8] (c. מֵעַל), + 4 t, of rebellion Je 2[20] 5[5], so staff Is 14[5] + 5 t, reed Is 42[3], arm of Pharaoh Ez 30[21.22.24] cf. ψ 10[15], trees (subj thunder) ψ 29[5], *break in, down*, door Gn 19[9] (J), *rend violently* (of lion), man 1 K 13[26], ass v[28], *wreck* Tyre (as ship) Ez 27[26], fig *break* pride Lv 26[19] (H); *crush* (fig) Is 14[25] (cf Je 48[38] supr), La 1[15] Dn 11[26], מִשְׁנֶה שִׁבָּרוֹן שׁ׳ Je 17[18], *break, rupture*, heart (fig) ψ 69[21] + Ez 6[9] (v. **Niph.** ad fin), שבורי לב ψ 147[3], וָאֶשְׁבֹּר עָלָיו חֻקִּי Jb 38[10] *broke for it my boundary*, of sea, ref to abrupt ending of mainland, = *quench* thirst (*frangere sitim*) ψ 104[11]. **Niph** [57] *Pf* 3 ms. נִשְׁבַּר Ex 22[9] +, etc, *Impf* 3 ms יִשָּׁבֵר Lv 6[21] +, 3 fs וְתִשָּׁבֶר Ec 12[6], 2 ms תִּשָּׁבֵר Ez 29[7], בֵר- 32[28], etc, *Inf cstr.* הִשָּׁבֵר Jon 1[4], *Pt* נִשְׁבָּר ψ 51[19], fs נִשְׁבָּרָה v[19], נִשְׁבֶּרֶת Ez 27[34] +, etc.;—*be broken*, of neck 1 S 4[18], bones ψ 34[21], gate-bars Je 51[30], rod (in fig) Is 14[21] Je 48[17], idols Ez 6[4.6], horn Dn 8[8], cf v[22], arm Jb 31[22] (מִקָּנָה), and (in metaph) Je 48[25] Jb 38[15] ψ 37[17], cf. Ez 30[22], bough Ez 31[12] Is 27[11], cf (fig.) of wickedness, like a tree Jb 24[20], other things ψ 37[15] Je 50[23] Ez 29[7] ψ 124[7]; cisterns Je 2[13] (*id.*), pottery Lv 6[21] 15[12] (P), Ec 12[6] (in fig.); = *be maimed, crippled* (have limb broken), of animal Ex 22[9.13] (E), and (fig) Ez 34[4.16] Zc 11[16], so (fig of men stumbling) Is 8[15] 28[13]; *be wrecked*, of ships 1 K 22[49] (rd Qr נִשְׁבְּרוּ), || 2 Ch 20[37], Jon 1[4], metaph. of Tyre Ez 27[34]; fig. *be crushed*, destroyed (pers, warriors, kingdoms, etc.), Je 14[17] 22[20] 48[4] 51[8] + 10 t.; fig. *be broken*, of heart †Je 23[9] Is 61[1] ψ 34[19] 51[19], cf. רוּחַ נִשׁ׳ v[19].—Ez 6[9] rd. prob וְשִׁבַּרְתִּי (We Sm Berthol Toy Krae); Co בְּשִׁבְרִי **Pi.** [36] *Pf.* 3 ms. שִׁבַּר Is 21[9] +, שִׁבַּר Ex 9[25], etc, *Impf.* 3 ms. יְשַׁבֵּר ψ 46[10] +, 2 mpl. תְּשַׁבֵּרוּן Ex 34[13], etc; *Inf abs* שַׁבֵּר Ex 23[24]; *Pt*

מְשַׁבֵּר 1 K 19^{11};—*shatter, break*, tablets Ex 32^{19} (E), 34^{1} (J), Dt 9^{17} 10^{2}; מַצֵּבוֹת Ex 23^{24} (E; + Inf abs.), 34^{13} (J) + 7 t.; images 2 K 11^{18} + 3 t.; bronze sea, etc., 2 K 25^{13} = Je 52^{17}; horns Dn 8^{7}; jaws Jb 29^{17} (in fig); of hail *shattering* trees Ex 9^{25} (J), cf. 1 K 19^{11}; elsewhere subj ׳י, *shattering* gate-bars, etc., weapons Is 45^{2} 38^{13} La 2^{9} 3^{4} ψ 46^{10} 76^{4} 107^{16}, trees 29^{5} 105^{33}, heads of תַּנִּינִים 74^{13}; *wrecking* ships 48^{8}. †**Hiph.** *cause to break out*, i e. *bring to the birth*, *Impf* 1 s. הַאֲנִי אַשְׁבִּיר וְלֹא אוֹלִיד Is 66^{9} (׳י subj.; cf. מַשְׁבֵּר infr). †**Hoph.** *be broken, shattered* (in heart), *Pf.* 1 s עַל־שֶׁבֶר בַּת־עַמִּי הָשְׁבָּרְתִּי Je 8^{21}.

†I. שֶׁבֶר, שֵׁבֶר **n.m.**$^{Je\ 4.6}$ **breaking, fracture, crushing, breach, crash**;—abs שֶׁבֶר Is 51^{19}+, שֶׁבֶר La 3^{47} Pr 17^{19}, cstr. שֶׁבֶר Is 1^{28}+, שֵׁבֶר Am 6^{6}+; sf שִׁבְרִי Je 10^{19}, etc.; pl שְׁבָרִים Jos 7^{5} Jb 41^{17}(dub, v. infr.), sf. שְׁבָרֶיהָ ψ 60^{4};—**1.** *breaking* of pottery Is 30^{14}, *fracture* of member, limb Lv 21^{19} 24^{20} (H), esp. fig. of people personif. שׁ׳ יוֹסֵף Am 6^{6}, cf Is 30^{26} (מַחַץ מַכָּתוֹ ||), Je 8^{21} 10^{19} 14^{17} 30^{12} (מַכָּה ||), v^{15} (מַכְאוֹב ||), La 2^{11} 3^{48} 4^{10}, also (c. רפא, רפה *heal*) Je 6^{14} 8^{11} La 2^{13} ψ 60^{4}, cf. Na 3^{19}; of sinners Is 1^{28}, *shattering*, crushing, of wall (in fig) Is 30^{13}; (רָעָה || שׁ׳ גָּדוֹל) Je 4^{6} 6^{1}, שׁ׳ עַל־שׁ׳ 4^{20}; שֹׁד וָשׁ׳ Is 59^{7} 60^{18} Je 48^{3}, cf Is 51^{19}; הַשֵּׁאת וְהַשּׁ׳ La 3^{47}, זַעֲקַת שׁ׳ Is 15^{5}, cf. Je 48^{5}, of individ. Pr 16^{18} 17^{19} 18^{12}, fig., שׁ׳ רוּחַ *crushing* of spirit, cf. Pr 15^{4}; so (רוּחַ om.) מִשְּׁבָרִים Jb 41^{17} *from terror*, Di De, cf Bi, but dub.; Buhl Bu conj. מִשְׁבְּרֵי יָם, Gie מִשְּׂאֵיו גִּבּוֹרִים, Du מִשְׁמָרִים **2.** *crashing*, Zp 1^{10} (יְלָלָה, קוֹל צְעָקָה ||), Je 50^{22} (מִלְחָמָה ||), 51^{54} (קוֹל זְעָקָה ||). **3.** *breaking* of a dream, i.e. its interpretation (*solution* of mystery) Ju 7^{15} (cf. GFM). **4.** הַשְּׁבָרִים Jos 7^{5}, perhaps (Di Benn Steuern) *the quarries*, as n pr. loc, 𝔙 Sabarim (> 𝔊 𝔖 𝔗 הַשְּׁבָרִים)— שִׁבְרִי Ez 32^{9}, read שִׁבְיְךָ 𝔊 Co Sta Berthol Krae (not Toy)

†II. שֶׁבֶר **n.pr.m.** a Calebite 1 Ch 2^{48}; Σαβερ, A Σεβερ, 𝔊L Σαβαρ.

שָׁבוּר Lv 22^{22} v. ✓ **Qal.**

†שִׁבָּרוֹן **n.[m.]** **breaking, crushing**;—fig.; cstr. שִׁבְּרוֹן מָתְנַיִם Ez 21^{11} (emotional distress; מְרִירוּת ||), read שׁבָ׳ also (for MT שִׁבָּרוֹן) 23^{33} Co Berthol Krae; *crushing* of opponents Je 17^{18}.

†מַשְׁבֵּר **n.[m.]** **place of breach**, i e. mouth of womb;—בָּאוּ בָנִים עַד־מ׳ וְכֹחַ אַיִן לְלֵדָה 2 K 19^{3} = Is 37^{3} (fig. of helplessness); cstr. מַשְׁבֵּר בָּנִים Ho 13^{13} (fig of opportunity).

†[מִשְׁבָּר] **n.[m.]** **breaker**, of sea;—pl. cstr. מִשְׁבְּרֵי־יָם ψ 93^{4} (קֹלוֹת מַיִם רַבִּים ||); in comp. of ׳י's majesty); fig. of calamities, מִשְׁבְּרֵי־מָוֶת 2 S 22^{5} (חֶבְלֵי־מָוֶת in || ψ 18^{5}); as sent by ׳י, מִשְׁבָּרֶיךָ ψ 88^{8}, מ׳ וְגַלֶּיךָ 42^{8} Jon 2^{4} —Jb 41^{17} v. I. שֶׁבֶר.

†III. שֶׁבֶר **n.[m.]** **corn, grain**, as food stuff (perh. *broken*, i. e. *threshed*, Hoffm$^{ZAW\ iii\ (1883),\ 122}$ SS Siegf$^{Ne\ 10,32}$; > Ko$^{ii\ 1\ 19a}$ *breaking out*, i e. sprouting (as chief fruit of soil); hence NH שִׁבְרוֹן *price of corn*);—שׁ׳ abs Gn 42^{1}+; cstr. v^{19}, sf שִׁבְרָם v^{26}, שִׁבְרוֹ 44^{2},—*corn, grain* $42^{1.2.19.26}$ 43^{2} 44^{2} 47^{14} (acc cogn), Am 8^{5} (*id*); so perh. (for בַּר) Gn 42^{3} Lag$^{BN\ 230}$; כָּל־שׁ׳ Ne 10^{32} *all kinds of grain*.

†[שָׁבַר] **vb. denom.** **buy grain**;—**Qal** *Impf* 2 mpl תִּשְׁבְּרוּ Dt 2^{6}, 1 pl. נִשְׁבְּרָה Gn 43^{4}; *Imv* mpl. שִׁבְרוּ 42^{2}+, *Inf cstr.* לִשְׁבֹּר v^{3}+, לִשְׁבָּר־ v^{7}+; *Pt.* mpl שֹׁבְרִים 47^{14},—*buy grain* for food Gn 41^{57} (v^{56} v. **Hiph.**), 42^{2} (שבר in v^{a}), v^{5}; c. acc אֹכֶל v$^{7.10}$ $43^{2.4.20.22}$ 44^{25} Dt 2^{6} (מִן pers); c acc. בַּר Gn 42^{3}, שֶׁבֶר 47^{14}; fig. Is 55^{1}, c. acc. יַיִן וְחָלָב v^{1}. **Hiph.** *Impf* 1 pl. נַשְׁבִּיר Am 8^{5}, etc.; *Pt.* מַשְׁבִּיר Gn 42^{6} Pr 11^{26},—*sell grain* (prop cause to buy grain), c. לְ pers Gn 42^{6}+ v^{56}(read וַיַּשְׁבֵּר for MT וַיִּשְׁבֹּר Ol Di Gunk), c acc. שֶׁבֶר Am 8^{6}, מַפַּל בַּר v^{6}, cf. Pr 11^{26}; c. sf. pers. + acc. אֹכֶל + בְּ pret. Dt 2^{28}.

שָׁבַת$_{71}$ **vb. cease, desist, rest** (As. *šabâtu*, prob. *cease, be completed* Dl^{WB} Zim$^{KAT\ 3\ 593}$ (Jen$^{ZA\ iv\ (1889)\ 277\ f.}$ is sceptical), Ar. سَبَتَ *cut off, interrupt;* NH has שָׁבַת *neglect*, etc., Aram שִׁבְתָּא *cost of neglect*),—**Qal** $_{27}$ *Pf* 3 ms. שׁ׳ Gn 2^{3}+; 3 pl. שָׁבָתוּ La 5^{14}, etc.; *Impf.* 3 ms. יִשְׁבּוֹת Ho 7^{4}; יִשְׁבֹּת Pr 22^{10}+2 t; 3 fs תִּשְׁבֹּת Lv 26^{35}, תִּשְׁבַּת v^{34} Ne 6^{3}+, etc.;—**1.** *cease:* (abs. 13 t.) of seasons Gn 8^{22} (J), manna Jos 5^{12} (P), etc, Is $14^{4.4}$ Ne 6^{3}+; c מִן Ho 7^{4}+3 t. **2.** *desist* from labour, *rest:* **a.** c מִן (of God) Gn $2^{2.3}$ (P) **b.** מִן om, בְּ temp. Ex 23^{12} (E), 16^{30} 34^{21} (J), 31^{17} (P), בֶּחָרִישׁ וּבַקָּצִיר שׁ׳ 34^{21} (J; i.e, even in these busy seasons). **c.** land in 7th year Lv $26^{34.35.35}$ (H), 2 Ch 36^{21}.—Lv 23^{32} 25^{2} v. [שָׁבַת] vb. denom. infr. †**Niph.** *Pf.* 3 ms. נִשְׁבַּת Is 17^{3}+2 t.; pl. נִשְׁבְּתוּ Ez 6^{6};—*cease*. abs. Ez 6^{6} 30^{18} 33^{28}; c. מִן Is 17^{3}. **Hiph.** $_{40}$ *Pf* 3 ms. הִשְׁבִּית Ru 4^{14}+; 2 ms. הִשְׁבַּתָּ ψ 89^{45} 119^{119}, etc, *Impf.* 3 ms. יַשְׁבִּית Pr 18^{18} Dn 9^{27}; וַיַּשְׁבֵּת 2 K 23^{11} 2 Ch 16^{5}, etc.; *Inf. cstr.* הַשְׁבִּית ψ 8^{3}; לַשְׁבִּית Am 8^{4} (Ges$^{§53\ q}$); *Imv.* mpl. הַשְׁבִּיתוּ Is 30^{11}, *Pt.* מַשְׁבִּית Je 16^{9}

ψ 46^{10};—**1.** *cause to cease, put an end to:* c. acc. mirth Ho 2^{13}, work 2 Ch 16^{5} Ne 4^{5}; sacrifice Dn 9^{27}; war ψ 46^{10}, cf. Is 13^{11} Ez 7^{24} Pr 18^{18} + 6 t., + מִן הִשׁ׳ קוֹל שָׂשׂוֹן Je 7^{34} 16^{9}, cf. 48^{33}. **2.** = *exterminate, destroy:* c. acc. 2 K $23^{5.11}$ Am 8^{4} (Now conj. העשקים), Ho 1^{4} ψ 8^{3} 119^{119}; c. acc. + מִן, Je 36^{29}, מִן הָאָרֶץ Lv 26^{6} (H), Ez 34^{25}; אלילים 30^{13} Dt 32^{26}. **3.** *cause to desist* from: c. מִן Ez 16^{41} 34^{10} Ex 5^{5} (E = give rest from); לְבִלְתִּי inf. Jos 22^{25} (P). **4.** *remove* (= הֵסִיר): c. מִן Ez $23^{27.48}$ ψ 89^{45} (txt. dub.: rd. הִשְׁבַּתָּ מִן) [3] 𝔊 Du; מַטֵּה הוֹדוֹ Herz Che, v. also sub טָהֳר); leaven מבתים Ex 12^{15} (P); הַשׁ׳ אֶח־ק׳ ישׂר׳ מִפָּנֵינוּ Is 30^{11}. **5.** *cause to fail,* let be lacking: salt מֵעַל מִנְחָתֶךָ Lv 2^{12} (P); acc. pers. + לְ pers. Je 48^{35} Ru 4^{14}.

†II. **שֶׁבֶת** **n.f.** cessation (dub.) Pr 20^{3} (c. מֵרִיב, 𝔊 ἀποστρέφεσθαι = שׁוּב); שִׁבְתּוֹ Ex 21^{19} i.e. from work = his loss of time (but Di I. שֶׁבֶת, p. 443 f.).—Is 30^{7} perh. = *a sitting still* (indolently) √ישׁב, but prob. crpt., v. Du Che al.

שַׁבָּת $_{111}$ **n.f.** $^{\text{Ex 31.14+}}$ and **m.** $^{\text{Is 66, 2.6}}$ (under infl. of יוֹם in freq. יוֹם הַשׁ׳, Albr $^{\text{ZAW xvi (1896), 47}}$) **Sabbath** (= שׁבת + ת; NH שַׁבָּת, Aram. שַׁבְּתָא, ܫܰܒܬܳܐ; perh. As. *šabattum* (‖ *um nuḫ libbi, day of rest of heart* (i. e. propitiation) [of deity]: only in lex. tablets); cf. Lotz $^{\text{Quaest. de hist. Sabbati, 1883}}$ Jen $^{\text{ZA iv (1889), 274 ff.}}$ (doubts connexion of As. word with Heb. Sabbath) Id $^{\text{S. S. Times, Jan. 16, 1892, 35 f.}}$ Muss-Arn $^{\text{JBL xi (1892), 93}}$ Schwally $^{\text{Idiot. 127}}$; v. (more recently) Jastr $^{\text{Am. J. Theol. ii (1898), 332 ff.}}$ Toy $^{\text{TBL xviii (1899), 190 ff.}}$ Dr $^{\text{Hast. DB SABBATH (1902)}}$ Zim $^{\text{KAT 3. 592 ff.; ZMG 1904, 199 ff.}}$ [15th day of month so called] $^{\text{458 ff.}}$);—abs. שׁ׳ Ex 16^{25} + 64 t.; cstr. שַׁבַּת v^{23} + 10 t.; sf. שַׁבַּתּוֹ Nu 28^{10} + 3 t. sf.; pl. שַׁבָּתוֹת Lv 23^{15} + 7 t.; cstr. שַׁבְּתֹת v^{38} $25^{8.8}$; sf. שַׁבְּתוֹתַי Is 56^{4} +, etc.;—**1.** *sabbath:* **a.** primitive שׁ׳ ליהוה Ex 16^{25} (J), 20^{10} = Dt 5^{14} (ten words) Lv 23^{3} (P); הַשׁ׳ Ec 16^{29} (J); בְּיוֹם הַשְּׁבִיעִי שׁ׳ Ex 16^{26} (J); on seventh day יוֹם הַשַּׁבָּת $20^{8.11}$ = Dt $5^{12.15}$ (ten words), so throughout; Ex 31^{15} + 3 t. P, Je 17^{21} Ez 46^{4} Ne 10^{32} + 9 t., + (‖ new moon) Is 1^{13} Ez 46^{1} 2 K 4^{23} Am 8^{5}, cf. Is $66^{23.23}$, also חג and מועד Ho 2^{13}; time of change of watch in temple 2 K $11^{5.7.9.9}$ = 2 Ch $23^{4.8.8}$; מיסך הַשׁ׳ (in temple) 2 K 16^{18}; orig. observed simply by *abstinence from labour* Ex $20^{9.10}$ = Dt 5^{12-14}, Ex 23^{12} (E), 34^{21} (J; Br $^{\text{Hex. 181-195}}$). **b.** Deut. reason for day is deliverance fr. Egypt Dt 5^{15}, hence its consecration, לְקַדְּשׁוֹ v^{12} = Ex 20^{8}; קדשׁ יום השׁ׳ Je $17^{22.24.27}$ (esp. no load carried), Ez 20^{20} 44^{24}. **c.** intensified by antith. חלל שׁ׳ Ez 20^{13} + 5 t. Ez, cf. Ne 13^{18}. Phrases in H: שׁמר (ה)שׁ׳ Lv $19^{3.30}$ 26^{2}, then P Ex $31^{13.14.16}$; cf. Is $56^{2.4.6}$; קדושׁ י׳, יוֹם קָדְשִׁי: $58^{13.13}$ (c. כבד). H also שַׁבְּתֹתֵיכֶם Lv 26^{35}; מִמָּחֳרַת הַשׁ׳ $23^{11.15.16}$; שַׁבְּתוֹתַי $19^{3.30}$ 26^{2} Is 56^{4}, Ez 20^{12} 22^{26}, + 8 t. Ez; ‖ מוֹעֵד La 2^{6}. **d.** P gives as basis God's resting Ex 20^{11} 31^{17}; שׁבתות י׳ Lv 23^{38}; שׁ׳ קדשׁ ליהוה Ex 16^{23}, cf. Ne 9^{14}, שׁ׳ שׁבתון Ex 31^{15} 35^{2} Lv 23^{3}; עשׂה השׁ׳ Ex 31^{16}, עֹלַת שׁ׳ בְּשַׁבַּתּוֹ Nu 28^{10}, cf. Is 66^{23}; בְּיוֹם הַשׁ׳ בְּיוֹם הַשׁ׳ Lv 24^{8} *on every sabbath,* abbr. שַׁבַּת שַׁבָּת 1 Ch 9^{32}; לַשַּׁבָּתוֹת, ‖ מועדים + חֳדָשִׁים 23^{31} + 3 t. Chr, Ne 10^{34} (לְ om. by error); work punished by stoning Nu $15^{32.36}$; trade prohib. Ne 10^{32} 13^{15-21}. **2.** *day of atonement* is a שַׁבַּת שַׁבָּתוֹן Lv 16^{31} 23^{32} (P), cf. שַׁבָּת שַׁבַּת v^{32} (P). **3.** *sabbath year,* שַׁבַּת שַׁבָּתוֹן Lv 25^{4} (H); שַׁבָּת ליהוה $v^{2.4}$ (H); רצה (הארץ) שַׁבְּתוֹתֶיהָ $26^{34.34.43}$ (H), 2 Ch 36^{21}. **4.** = *week* (?): שֶׁבַע שַׁבָּתוֹת Lv 23^{15} (H), seven *sabbaths* or *weeks;* שֶׁבַע שַׁבְּתֹת (ה)שָּׁנִים $25^{8.8}$ (H) seven sabbaths or weeks (of years), uncertain (v. Mk $16^{2.9}$ Lk 18^{12} Mt 28^{1}, cf. J Aram. usage); poss. שַׁבָּת Is 66^{23} = *week* (Du). **5.** שַׁבַּת הָאָרֶץ Lv 25^{6} (H) = *produce* in sabbath year (growing of itself).

†[**שָׁבַת**] **vb. denom.** keep, observe (sabbath);—**Qal,** c. acc. cogn.; *Pf.* 3 fs. וְשָׁבְתָה הָאָרֶץ שַׁבָּת לי׳ Lv 25^{2}; 2 mpl. מֵעֶרֶב עַד־עֶרֶב תִּשְׁבְּתוּ שַׁבַּתְּכֶם 23^{32} (P).

†**שַׁבָּתוֹן** **n.m.** sabbath observance, sabbatism;—שׁ׳ Ex 16^{23} + 10 t. P; usu. phrase שַׁבַּת שַׁבָּתוֹן *sabbath of sabbatic observance;*—**1.** of weekly sabbath Ex 31^{15} 35^{2} Lv 23^{3} Ex 16^{23} (שַׁבָּתוֹן שַׁבַּת קֹדֶשׁ, prob. transp.). **2.** day of atonement Lv 16^{31} 23^{32}. **3.** sabbatical year Lv 25^{4}, cf. שְׁנַת שַׁבָּתוֹן v^{5}. **4.** שׁ׳ alone of feast of trumpets Lv 23^{24}, and of first and eighth days of feast of tabernacles $v^{39.39}$.

†**שַׁבְּתַי** **n.pr.** Levite;—Ezr 10^{15} Ne 8^{7} 11^{16}; Σαβ(β)αθαι, etc.

†[**מִשְׁבָּת**] **n.[m.]** cessation, annihilation;—pl. sf. עַל־מִשְׁבַּתֶּהָ La 1^{7} (𝔊 ἐπὶ κατοικεσίᾳ αὐτῆς = עַל־שִׁבְתָּהּ; Marti $^{\text{LCB 1895, Mar. 2. 282}}$ עַל־שְׁבִיתָהּ *her captivity*).

שׁגא v. שָׂגָה.

†[**שָׁגַג**] **vb.** go astray, commit sin or error (‖ שׁוּב, שׁגה);—**Qal** *Pf.* שָׁגַג Lv 5^{18}; *Pt.* שֹׁגֵג Jb 12^{16} ψ 119^{67}; f. שֹׁגֶגֶת Nu 15^{28};—**1.** *err,* mentally Jb 12^{16}. **2.** *sin* ignorantly, inad-

vertently, Lv 5[18] Nu 15[28] (P), cf. ψ 119[67].—בְּשַׁגָּם Gn 6[3] perhaps *Inf. cstr.* sf., *by reason of their going astray*, v. Ges[§67 p] Ew Dr al.; > Vrss *for that he also* is flesh. אֲבִישַׁג, v. p. 4[b].

†שְׁגָגָה **n.f. sin of error, inadvertence**;—abs. שׁ׳ Nu 15[25]+; sf. שִׁגְגָתוֹ Lv 5[18]; שִׁגְגָתָם Nu 15[25];—*error* (opp. sins of intention, or בְּיָד רָמָה) only P Ec: Nu 15[25] = Ec 5[5], cf. Ec 10[5]; עַל שׁ׳ Lv 5[18] Nu 15[25]; חטא בִּשׁ׳ Lv 4[2.22.27] 5[15] Nu 15[27.28]+ (vb. om.) v[26]; עשׂה בִשׁ׳ Lv 4[22] Nu 15[29]+ (לְשׁ׳) v[24]; אכל קֹדֶשׁ בִּשׁ׳ Lv 22[14]; מַכֵּה־נֶפֶשׁ בִּשׁ׳ of unintended killing Nu 35[11.15] = Jos 20[3.9] (‖ in D בִּבְלִי־דַעַת).—1 S 14[24] v. שׁנה.

שִׁגָּיוֹן v. p. 993[b].

†[שָׁגָה] **vb. go astray, err** (Aram. שְׁגָא, ܫܓܐ *id.*);—**Qal** *Pf.* 1 s. שָׁגִיתִי Jb 6[24] 19[4], etc.; *Impf.* 3 ms. יִשְׁגֶּה Pr 5[23], etc.; *Inf. cstr.* שְׁגוֹת 19[27]; *Pt.* שֹׁגֶה Ez 45[20] Pr 20[1], etc.;—**1.** *err, stray,* of flock Ez 34[6] (fig.). **2.** *swerve, meander, reel* or *roll,* in drunkenness, ב of drink Is 28[7.7]; = *be intoxicated,* Pr 20[1]; so with (בּ) love 5[19.20]; שׁ׳ בָּרֹאֶה Is 28[7]. **3.** *go astray,* morally, 1 S 26[21] Pr 5[23] Jb 6[24] 19[4], + 1 S 14[24] (rdg. שׁ׳ שְׁגָגָה) Th We Dr Now (after 𝔊; otherwise Bu HPS); c. מִן, of י׳'s commands ψ 119[21.118], מִן of words of knowledge Pr 19[27]. **4.** specif. *commit sin of ignorance,* inadvertence Lv 4[13] Nu 15[22] (P) Ez 45[20] (cf. שׁגג). **Hiph.** *lead astray:* **1.** lit., *Pt.* מַשְׁגֶּה Dt 27[18] (בַּדָּרֶךְ). **2.** מַשׁ׳ mentally = *mislead* Jb 12[16]. **3.** morally, *Pt.* Pr 28[10] (בְּדֶרֶךְ רָע); *Impf.* 2 ms. sf. תַּשְׁגֵּנִי, c. מִן of God's commands ψ 119[10]; + perhaps Jb 12[23] *leadeth* nations *astray* (𝔊𝔖, i.e. וַיַּשְׁגֵּם for וַיַּנְחֵם).

†[שְׁגִיאָה Kö[ii. 1. 197]] **n.f. error**;—pl. abs. שְׁגִיאוֹת ψ 19[13]; read שְׁגָגוֹת?.

†מִשְׁגֶּה **n.m. mistake** Gn 43[12] (J).

†שָׁגֵה (שָׁגֵא van d. H.) **n.pr.m.** father of a hero of David 1 Ch 11[34].—B Σωλα, A Σαγη, 𝔊L Σαμαια.

†[שָׁגַח] **vb. Hiph. gaze** (NH *id.*, Ecclus 40[29] 50[5]; late Rabb. הַשְׁגָּחָה = *providence* (from ψ 33[14]); JAram. שְׁגַח *gaze, consider*);—c. אֶל־ pers.: *Pf.* 3 ms. הִשְׁגִּיחַ ψ 33[14] (of י׳; מִן loc.); *Impf.* 3 mpl. רֹאֶיךָ אֵלֶיךָ יַשְׁגִּיחוּ Is 14[16] *they that see thee, at thee shall they gaze* (‖ אֵלֶיךָ יִתְבּוֹנָנוּ; cf. משגיח על שלחן Ecclus 40[29]); abs.: *Pt.* מַשְׁגִּיחַ Ct 2[9] (c. מִן *from* (the outside of) *the windows*).

†שִׁגָּיוֹן doubtful word, ψ 7[1] (title), Ew De al. from √שׁגה *go astray, reel,* i.e. wild, passionate song, with rapid changes of rhythm; cf. Lag[BN 201 f.] who cp. שִׁגָּעוֹן, √שׁגע; 𝔊 ψαλμός, rd. prob. מִזְמוֹר; pl. שִׁגְיֹנוֹת Hb 3[1] (title), rd. נְגִינוֹת, so 𝔊.

†[שָׁגֵל] **vb. violate, ravish** (Mass. think verb obscene, and subst. שָׁכַב);—**Qal** *Impf.* 3 ms. sf. יִשְׁגָּלֶנָּה Dt 28[30] Kt (Qr יִשְׁכָּבֶנָּה). **Niph.** *Impf.* 3 fpl. תִּשָּׁגַלְנָה Is 13[16] Zc 14[2] *women shall be ravished* (both Kt; Qr תִּשָּׁכַבְנָה). **Pu.** < **Qal pass.** (Ges[§52 e]) *Pf.* 2 fs. אֵיפֹה לֹא שֻׁגַּלְתְּ Je 3[2] *where hast thou not been ravished?* (Qr שֻׁכַּבְתְּ).

†שֵׁגָל **n.f.** (queen-)**consort** Ne 2[6] ψ 45[10], + perh. Ju 5[30 c] v. שָׁלָל (Palm. n.pr.f. שגל Lzb[372] SAC[111] GACooke[309]; Thes[1363] cp. '*queen,*' orig. '*woman*'; but שׁ׳ loan-word acc. to Lag[BN 51, 153] and not from √[שָׁגֵל]).

†[שָׁגַע] **Pu. be mad** (Ar. سَجَعَ *coo,* of male pigeon, *utter long whinny,* of camel (cf. Hoffm ZAW iii (1883), 89 RS[J Phil. xiv. 119 f.] Goldziher[Arab. Philol. i. 59 ff.] Lag[BN 202]); Eth. ሰገዐ: *be mad* (*n* ins., Di[1055] Ba[ES 50]); As. *šegû, rage, howl;* on meaning in Heb. v. esp. We[Skizzen iii. 130]);—**Pu.** *Pt.* as adj.: pred. וְהָיִיתָ מְשֻׁגָּע Dt 28[34] *thou shalt be maddened* (מִן because of), fig. for driven to despair; מ׳ of proph., contemptuously Ho 9[7], כָּל־אִישׁ מ׳ וּמִתְנַבֵּא Je 29[26], as subst. 2 K 9[11]; pl. מְשֻׁגָּעִים 1 S 21[16] *madmen.* **Hithp.** *shew madness; Pt.* אִישׁ מִשְׁתַּגֵּעַ 1 S 21[15]; *Inf. cstr.* לְהִשְׁתַּגֵּעַ v[16].

†שִׁגָּעוֹן **n.m. madness**;—הִכָּה בְּשׁ׳ Dt 28[28] *smite with madness,* fig. of wild and helpless panic (‖ תִּמְהוֹן לֵבָב, עִוָּרוֹן), Zc 12[4] (‖ תִּמָּהוֹן); בְּשׁ׳ 2 K 9[20] (hyperb.) *madly.*

שׁגר (√of foll.; cf. Aram. שְׁגַר *cast, throw,* Ex 13[12] 𝔗[J] *drop* young, ܫܓܪ *misit, demisit* (rare); cf. Dr[Dt 7. 13]).

†שֶׁגֶר **n.** [**f.** Albr[ZAW xvi (1896), 76]] **offspring, young of beasts** (שגר *id.* Ecclus 40[19]; cf. We[Skizzen iii. 170]);—cstr. שׁ׳;—כָּל־פֶּטֶר שׁ׳ בְּהֵמָה Ex 13[12] (J; כָּל־פ׳ רֶחֶם precedes); also שְׁגַר אֲלָפֶיךָ Dt 7[13] 28[4.18.51] (all ‖ עַשְׁתְּרֹת צֹאנֶךָ).

שַׁד, II. שֹׁד *breast,* v. שׁדה.

†[שֵׁד] **n.** [**m.**] appar. **demon** (loan-word from As. *šêdu,* a protecting spirit, esp. of bull-colossus, Dl[Pa 153 f.; WB 646] COT[Dt 32. 17] Zim[KAT 3. 460 f., 455, 649]; cf. Aram. שֵׁידָא, ܫܐܕܐ *demon,* and (perh.) Ph.

n pr נדשׁר Ne$^{ZMG\ xlii\ (1888),\ 481}$ Lzb^{249}; orig √שׁור (=Ar. سَادَ *rule*) acc to Thes Baud$^{Sem\ Rel\ i\ 130\ ff}$ Dl^{WB} al; >Ar سعد (III, IV *aid*), Hom$^{ZMG\ xlvi\ (1892),\ 529}$, against this Zim$^{l\ c}$);—יזבחו לַשֵּׁדִים לא אֱלֹהַ Dt 32^{17} (cf Dr), ψ 106^{37} (human sacrifice)

I. שֹׁד v. שׁדד

[שָׁדַד]$_{56}$ **vb. deal violently with, despoil, devastate, ruin** (NH *id*, Niph., Ar. سَدَّ *stop up, obstruct, arrest, make firm*, Eth. ሰደደ: *expel*; As *šadâdu* is *draw, drag*),—**Qal** *Pf* 3 pl. consec. וְשָׁדְדוּ Ez 32^{12}, sf. שַׁדּוּנִי ψ 17^{9}; *Impf* 3 ms. יָשׁוּד (metapl, cf. Ges^{§67q} Bae) ψ 91^{6}, sf יְשָׁדֵּם (Ges^{§67n}) Pr 11^{3} Qr (Kt Pf ושׁדם), יְשָׁדְדֵם Je 5^{6}, *Imv* mpl שָׁדְדוּ (Ges^{§67ee}) 49^{28}, *Inf. abs* שָׁדוֹד Mi 2^{4}, cstr. לִשְׁדוֹד Je 47^{4} (Ges^{§45g}), cf. also שֹׁד Ho 10^{14}, *Pt act* שֹׁדֵד Je 6^{26}+, etc., *pass.* שָׁדוּד Ju 5^{27}+, f שְׁדוּדָה ψ 137^{8},—*violently destroy*, pers, =*slay* Ju 5^{27} (pass.), Je 5^{6} (wolf subj, ‖ הִכָּה); acc. Philistines 47^{4} (‖ הכרית), v^{4} (subj 'י), =*devastate*, acc בָּבֶל (subj 'י) Je 51^{55}, cf. ψ 137^{8} (rd. prob הַשּׁוֹדְדָה We Du, cf Ew Hi v הַשְּׁדוּדָה Ko$^{ii\ 194}$), אֶת־גְּאוֹן מִצְרַיִם Ez 32^{12}(‖נשׁמד), cf Ho 10^{14}, אֶת־מַרְעִיתָם Je 25^{36} (subj 'י), abs Is 21^{2} (‖ בָּגַד), 33^{1} (on use of pt v Ges^{§120b}), pass v^{1} (‖ בָּגַד), אֲתִי שָׁדוּד Je 4^{30} (Gf Ba$^{NB\ 179}$, but dub; < Du שׁדוּדָה); =*despoil*, acc. pers. Je 49^{28}, =*bring* pers. *to ruin* Mi 2^{4} (Inf abs. + Niph q v), Pr 11^{3}; weaker, *assail* ψ 17^{9}, elsewhere *Pt. act* as subst *devastator* (*despoiler*?) of national foes Is 16^{4} 21^{2} 33^{1} Je 6^{26}+8 t. Je, שׁוֹדְדֵי לַיְלָה Ob^{5} (‖ גַּנָּבִים) del. Now GASm, personal foe Jb 15^{21}, representing wicked in gen 12^{6} (‖ מַרְגִּיזֵי אֵל) †**Niph.** *Pf* 1 pl שָׁדוֹד נְשַׁדֻּנוּ (Ges^{§67u} Ko$^{i\ 342\ f}$) *we are utterly ruined* †**Pi.** *Impf.* 2 ms אַל־תְּשַׁדֵּד רִבְצוֹ Pr 24^{15} *assault not his dwelling-place* (‖ אַל־תֶּאֱרֹב), *Pt.* as subst מְשַׁדֶּד־אָב Pr 19^{26} *he who assaults, maltreats* (his) father (‖ יַבְרִיחַ אֵם) †**Pu.** *Pf.* 3 ms. שֻׁדַּד Is 15^{1}+, 3 fs. שֻׁדְּדָה Je 4^{20}+, שֻׁדְּדָה Na 3^{7} (Ges^{§52q}), etc,—*be devastated*, of city Is 15$^{1.1}$ 23^{1} Je 48^{1} 49^{3} Na 3^{7}, country or nation Je 4^{20}, cf v^{13} 9^{18} 48$^{15.20}$ 49^{10}, dwellings (אֹהֶל) Je 4^{20} 10^{20}, trees Zc 11^{2} (del. Sta$^{ZAW\ i\ (1881),\ 25}$), cf v^{33}, strength of ships Is 23^{14}, field (by drought) Jo 1^{10}, crop v^{10}. †**Pō'el** *violently destroy*: *Impf* 3 ms. יְשֹׁדֵד מַצֵּבוֹתָם Ho 10^{2} (‖ יַעֲרֹף מִזְבְּחוֹתָם). †**Hoph.** *Impf* (or **Qal** *pass Impf*? cf Ges^{§53u}) *be devastated*: 3 ms. כָּל־מִבְצָרַיִךְ יוּשַּׁד Ho 10^{14} (of Ephr, < We pl. יושׁדו), 2 ms תּוּשַּׁד Is 33^{1} (subj. שׁוֹדֵד, v. **Qal**)

†I. שֹׁד, שׁוֹד (v infr) **n.m. violence, havoc, devastation, ruin**,—'שׁ abs Ho 7^{13}+; cstr Is 22^{4}+,—**1.** *violence, havoc*, as social sin: חָמָס וָשֹׁד Am 3^{10} Je 6^{7} 20^{8} Ez 45^{9}, 'שׁ' וְח Hb 1^{3}, כָּזָב וָשֹׁד Ho 12^{2} (l וָשָׁוְא, 𝔊 We Marti al), שֹׁ' וָשֶׁבֶר Is 59^{7} 60^{18} Pr 24^{2} (‖ עָמָל); שֹׁ' רְשָׁעִים Pr 21^{7}; c genit obj שֹׁ' עֲנִיִּים ψ 12^{6} **2.** *devastation, ruin*, for nation Ho 7^{13}, כשׁד מִשַּׁדַּי יָבוֹא Is 13^{6} (sim of יוֹם 'י)=Jo 1^{15}, Is 16^{4} (Lo Gr Che^{Hpt} Marti שֹׁדֵד, ‖ רמס), 22^{4}, שֹׁ' וָשֶׁבֶר 51^{19} Je 48^{3}, more gen. Am 5$^{9.9}$; for individ Jb 5^{21} (van d. H. שׁוֹד), v^{22}, for beasts Hb 2^{17} (+ חֲמַס לְבָנוֹן).—Ho 10^{14} v. שׁדד *Inf.*—(הָלְכוּ) מִשֹּׁד Ho 9^{6} read אַשּׁוּר We Now Marti —II. שֹׁד, v שׁדה

שַׁדַּי v infr אַשְׁדּוֹד v p 78, > here, Thes al.

שׁדה (√of foll., Ar. ثَدِيَ *moisten*, ثَدْيٌ *breast*, Aram pl תַּדְיָא, ܬܕܝܐ *breasts*, cf Lag$^{BN\ 171}$, Heb n orig *שַׂדְיָה Ba$^{NB\ 9}$, cf Id$^{ZMG\ xli\ (1887),\ 637}$).

†[שַׁד] **n.m.**$^{Ho\ 9\ 14}$ **female breast**,—abs. שַׁד La 4^{3}, elsewhere du. שָׁדַיִם Ho 9^{14}+, cstr שְׁדֵי Ez 23^{21}+, sf שָׁדַי Ct 1^{13} 8^{10}, שָׁדַיִךְ 4^{5}+, etc;—*breast* **1.** of woman Ho 2^{4} Ez 16^{7} 23$^{3.21}$ (שְׁדֵי ‖ דַדֵּיךְ, נְעוּרָיִךְ), v^{34} (> del 𝔊 Codd Co,—all these of personif people), Ct 1^{13} 4^{5} 7$^{4.8.9}$ 8$^{8.10}$, of mother ψ 22^{10}, c. יָנַק *suck* Ct 8^{1} Jb 3^{12} Jo 2^{16}; Ho 9^{14} (v [צָמַק]), עַתִּיקֵי מִשָּׁ' Is 28^{9} i.e. those already weaned, mature (‖ גְּמוּלֵי מֵחָלָב) — Is 32^{12} v. [ספד] **2.** of animal La 4^{3}. **3.** both human and animal, בִּרְכֹת שָׁ' וָרָחַם Gn 49^{25} (poem in J)

†II. שֹׁד **n.m. id.** (cf the rare Arab. ثُدٌّ, Lane^{333} Ba$^{ZMG\ xli\ 637}$),—'שׁ abs, of mother Jb 24^{9}; cstr (fig, c יָנַק · שֹׁ' מְלָכִים Is 60^{16}, שֹׁ' תַּנְחֻמֶיהָ 66^{11}, i.e. the consolations of Jerusalem

†**שְׁדֵיאוּר n.pr.m.** in Reuben (read prob. שַׁדַּי אוּר 'שׁ, is *flame*, v No$^{ZMG\ xv\ (1860),\ 809}$ Ne$^{Eg\ 46}$ Gray$^{Prop.\ N\ 169,\ 197}$),—only in אֱלִיצוּר בֶּן־שׁ' Nu 1^{5} 2^{10} 7$^{30.35}$ 10^{18} (all P), Σεδιουρ.

†**שִׁדָּה n.f.** mng unknown;—only s. et pl. שִׁדָּה וְשִׁדּוֹת Ec 2^{8}, apparently appos. of תַּעֲנֻגוֹת (𝔊 οἰνοχόον καὶ οἰνοχόας, i.e. שָׁדָה וְשָׁדוֹת, from Aram שְׁדָא *pour out* [but not spec. of wine]; Aq κυλίκιον καὶ κυλίκια (cf 𝔙), prob. fr. same √; Dl$^{Prol\ 97}$ Ko$^{ii\ 1.\ 161}$ Wildeb Siegf cp. As *šaddâdu, love* (Siegf 'Haremsperlen'), but this word lacks evidence; poss. שָׂרָה וְשָׂרוֹת, v. I. שָׂרָה).

שַׁדַּי$_{48}$ **n.m. dei** (etym. dub. (1) Aq Sym Theod ἱκανός; Rabb שֶׁ + דַּי (self-)*sufficient*, no moderns. (2)=*almighty*, √שׁדד + י=Thes De

Di Sta, or √שרה=שדד, n. intens. Ew[§155c], but שׁדד (q.v.) is *deal violently* not simply *mightily;* cf. 𝔊 παντοκράτωρ 14 (15) t. (but in Pent. 'אל שׁ is ὁ Θεός μου, σου, etc.), 𝔙 mostly *omnipotens.* (3) < conject. for orig. שַׁדַּי (v. שַׁד) *my sovereign lord,* ‖ בעלי, אֲדֹנָי, Nö [SBA 1880, 775; ZMG xlii (1888), 481]; Hoffm[Ph. Inscr. 53]; used of foreign deities (Dt 32[17]), and so discredited (cf. בַּעַל).—> other conj., e.g. RS[OTJC, 424] √שׁדה *pour forth* (God as rain-giver); Dl[Pr 96 sq.] As. *šadû, high, ilu šâdû'a,* Che[Comm. Is ii. 148], or *šadû, mountain,* also in n. pr.; v. further Dr[Gn 404 ff.]);—**1.** שַׁדַּי Nu 24[4.16] (JE, poem), and so as archaism Ru 1[20.21] ψ 68[15] 91[1] Jo 1[15]=Is 13[6], Ez 1[24] (del. Co); esp. Jb 5[17]+30 t. Jb (+19[29] Ew Di, rdg. 'שׁ for שַׁדִּין). **2.** אֵל שַׁדַּי Gn 49[25] (poem; so read for 'אֵת שׁ, v. Sam 𝔊 𝔖 Saad, Heb. Codd.), and so, as archaism, divine name of patriarchs in P, Gn 17[1] 28[3] 35[11] 48[3] Ex 6[3], Gn 43[14] (R[P]); so Ez 10[5] (del. Co; but 𝔊 Σαδδαι).

שַׁדִּין Jb 19[29] v. דין p. 192[b] supra.

שׁדם (√of following; meaning unknown).

† [שְׁדֵמָה] **n.f.** field;—only pl.: abs. שְׁדֵמוֹת Hb 3[17] Je 31[40] Qr (> Kt השרמות); cstr. שַׁדְמ(וֹ)ת Dt 32[32]+2 t.;—*fields,* as cultivated Dt 32[32], also (c. vb. sg.) Is 16[8] Hb 3[17]; as locality 2 K 23[4], area Je 31[40].—שְׁדֵמָה Is 37[27] v. שְׁדֵפָה.

† [שָׁדַף] **vb.** scorch, blight (NH *id.;* Niph. Hithp. *be blighted;* JAram. שְׁדַף Ithpe. *burn* (up); Ar. سدف iv. *be dark*);—**Qal** *Pt. pass.* cstr., of ears of grain, שְׁדוּפֹת קָדִים Gn 41[6] *scorched by a sirocco,* so 'שְׁדֻפוֹת ק v[23], 'שׁ' הַק v[27] (all E).

† שְׁדֵפָה **n.f.** blighted or blasted thing;—'וּשׁ לִפְנֵי קָמָה 2 K 19[26] *a blasted thing before* (the) *standing grain,* i.e. before maturity (> שְׁדֵמָה *field,* as ‖ Is 37[27], cf. Di), but improb.; Th prop. 'וּשׁ' לִ' קָדִים; Kit שְׁדֵף הַקָּדִים; We (and most since) וּשְׁדֵפָה: לִפְנֵי קָמָה וגו' (Che: וּשְׁפָיִים, for וּשְׁדֵפָה).

† שִׁדָּפוֹן **n.m.** blight, of crops (Lag[BN 202] Vogelst[Landwirthsch. 56]);—'שׁ abs. + יֵרָקוֹן Am 4[9], cf. Hg 2[17], Dt 28[22] 1 K 8[37]=2 Ch 6[28].

† שַׁדְרַךְ **n.pr.m.** Bab. name given to חֲנַנְיָה, one of Daniel's comrades Dn 1[7] (form and mng. dub.; Dl (cf. COT Dr) *Šudur-Aku, command of Aku;* Jen[Th LZ 1895, 329] thinks Pers. [**Khšatraka*]; Kohler[ZA iv (1889), 50] conj. מרדך, so Wkl[Altor. Forsch. iii. 47. 57] Zim[KAT 3. 396]).

שׁדשׁ (√of foll.; Sab. סדת, סת, *six* Sab Denkm[90] Hom[Chrest. 47. 124]; Ar. سَادِسٌ *sixth* (assim. of last cons.), سِتٌّ, سِتَّةٌ *six;* Eth. ሰዱስ፡ ስድስት፡ *six;* As. *sudušu* (*s* !) *six-fold, seššu, sixth;* cf. also Aram. שִׁית, שִׁתָּא, ܫܬܐ, ܫܬ *six,* Nab. שת, Palm. שתא Ldzb[383] SAC[118]).

שֵׁשׁ, שִׁשָּׁה [216] **n.m.** et **f.** six;—**m.** שֵׁשׁ (c. **n.f.**) Gn 31[41]+120 t.; **f.** שִׁשָּׁה (c. **n.m.**) 30[20]+39 t.; cstr. שֵׁשֶׁת Ex 23[12]+30 t. (6+10=16 are additional);—*six* (Hex chiefly P): **1.** no other num.: **a.** bef. n.pl. 75 t.: e.g. שֵׁשׁ שָׁנִים Ex 21[2] (E)+11 t., שֵׁשׁ אַמּוֹת 1 S 17[4]+8 t.; שֵׁשׁ בָּאַמָּה †1 K 6[6]; שִׁשָּׁה בָנִים Gn 30[20] (E)+2 t.; שֵׁשֶׁת יָמִים Ex 23[12] (E)+14 t.; after n. (late) †Ex 28[2] Jos 15[59.62] (all P), 1 Ch 4[27] 26[17] Ne 5[18]; rarely n. om. Lv 24[6] (P)+ (distrib. 2 S 21[20]=1 Ch 20[6]). **b.** =ordin. שְׁנַת שֵׁשׁ לְחִזְקִ' 2 K 18[10] (Ges[§134 o]). **2.** 16, c. **n.f.**: שֵׁשׁ עֶשְׂרֵה, bef. נֶפֶשׁ Gn 46[18] (P), שָׁנָה 2 K 13[10]+9 t., בָּנוֹת 2 Ch 13[21]; after עָרִים Jos 15[41] 19[22] (P); c. **n.m.** שִׁשָּׁה עָשָׂר, bef. אֲדָנִים Ex 26[25] 36[30] (P), also אֶלֶף, 1000, Nu 31[40]+ (P); after בָּנִים 1 Ch 4[27], etc.; =ordin. *16th* 1 Ch 24[14] 25[23]+, 'יוֹם שׁ' ע 2 Ch 29[17]. **3.** 600=שֵׁשׁ מֵאוֹת, Gn 7[6] (P)+63 t.; 6000=שֵׁשֶׁת אֲלָפִים Nu 3[34] (P)+8 t.; 'שׁ' אֶלֶף Ju 20[15]+2 t. **4.** c. tens, 'שׁ foll. Gn 46[26]+13 t., precedes Nu 31[44] (P). **5.** 'שׁ as round no., חָמֵשׁ אוֹ־שׁ' 2 K 13[19], cf. Jb 5[19] Pr 6[16].

שִׁשִּׁי [22] **m.** שִׁשִּׁית [6] **f.** adj. num. ordin. sixth;—(הַ)יּוֹם הַשִּׁשִּׁי Gn 1[31]+5 t., etc.; בַּשָּׁנָה הַשִּׁשִּׁית Lv 25[21] Ez 8[1], etc.; cstr. שִׁשִּׁית הַהִין Ez 4[11] *6th part of the hin,* cf. 45[13] 46[14]; read 'שׁ also 45[13b] (v. [שִׁשָּׁה] infra).

שִׁשִּׁים [59] **n.** indecl. sixty;—bef. n. sg.: city Dt 3[4]+4 t., cubit 1 K 6[2] Ez 40[14], man 2 K 25[19]=Je 52[25], day Lv 12[5], etc.; n.pl. בָּנוֹת 2 Ch 11[21], cf. Ct 3[7]; after n.pl. Nu 7[88.88.88] 2 Ch 3[3] 11[21]+; שִׁשִּׁים אֶלֶף 2 Ch 12[3]+; 'שׁ' foll. units Gn 5[15]+12 t.; 'שׁ precedes unit Is 7[8]+12 t.; 'שׁ' foll. 100 (1000) Ezr 8[10]+11 t.; precedes Gn 5[18]+8 t.

† [שִׁשָּׁה] **vb. Pi. denom.** give sixth part of (si vera l.);—*Pf.* 2 mpl. consec. וְשִׁשִּׁיתֶם הָאֵיפָה Ez 45[13] (+ מִן part.), but < read שִׁשִּׁית Vrss and mod. (‖ שִׁשִּׁית v[a]).—וְשִׁשֵּׁאתִיךָ Ez 39[2] v. שׁשׁא.

† I. שֹׁהַם **n.m.** [Jb 28, 16] a gem, identif. dubious, Vrss vary; *onyx* or *chrysoprasus.* Ri[HWB 2, 336 f.], *onyx* Taylor[Hast. DB iii. 624], *beryl* Ridgeway[Ency. Bib. 545], *malachite* Myres[ib. 4808], etc.; cf. also Dr[Gn 2, 12] (√ unknown; perh. loan-word, cf. As. *sâmtu* Dl[WB 488]);—אֶבֶן הַשֹּׁ' Gn 2[12] (J; + הַבְּדֹלַח), in land

Havilah; אַבְנֵי שׁ׳ Ex 25^{7} 28^{9} $35^{9.27}$ 39^{6} (all P), 1 Ch 29^{2}, אבן om Ez 28^{13}, Ex 28^{20} 39^{13} (both P; all in lists of gems), שׁ׳ יָקָר וְסַפִּיר Jb 28^{16}.

†II. שֹׁהַם **n.pr.m.** Levite;—שׁ׳ 1 Ch 24^{27}; Ισ(σ)οαμ, Ιεσσαμ.

שָׁו Jb 15^{31} Kt, v שָׁוְא

†שְׁוָא **n.pr m.** **1.** Calebite 1 Ch 2^{49}, Σαου, Σουε **2.** secretary, David's time 2 S 20^{25} Qr (Kt שׁיא), Ιησους, A Ισους, 𝔊L Σουσα (v שְׂרָיָה(1) **1**)

I שׁוא (√of foll, cf Ar سَآءَ (med و) *be evil, foul, unseemly*, Eth ሰይአ: *baseness*)

†שָׁוְא **n.[m.]** **emptiness, vanity**,—שׁ׳ abs. Ex 23^{1} + 51 t, שָׁו Jb 15^{31} (Kt),—**1.** *emptiness, nothingness, vanity:* שׁ׳ תְּשׁוּעַת אָדָם ψ 60^{13} *vain* (is) *man's deliverance*, = 108^{13}, שׁ׳ לָכֶם 127^{2} it is *vain* (useless) *for you;* 89^{48} *for* (עַל) *what nothingness* hast thou created man? cf יַרְחֵי שׁ׳ Jb 7^{3}, הַבְלֵי שׁ׳ ψ 31^{7} (idols) = Jon 2^{9}, cf Je 18^{15} + Ho 5^{11} 𝔊 (for צָו), מִנְחַת שׁ׳ Is 1^{13} of ineffective offering to י׳, נשׂא לַשׁ׳ (לא) Ex $20^{7.7}$ *take up* name of God *in vain* (to no good purpose) = Dt $5^{11.11}$, cf ψ 24^{4} 139^{20} [MT *lifted up in vain* are *thy foes*, but rd. שְׁמֶךָ for עָרֶיךָ, cf. נשׂא **1 b** (7), al עָלֶיךָ, v II. עָר], היה שׁ׳ Ho 12^{12} *become nothing* (We עשׂה שׁ׳, and so **3**); ראה שׁ׳ ψ 119^{37}, *adv* לַשׁ׳ *in vain* Je 2^{30} 4^{30} 6^{29} 46^{11}, שׁ׳ ψ $127^{1.1}$ Mal 3^{14} **2.** *emptiness of speech*, ‖ *lying*, שׁ׳ וּדְבַר כָּזָב Pr 30^{8}, דִּבֶּר שׁ׳ ψ 12^{3} 41^{7} $144^{8.11}$ Is 59^{4} Ez 13^{8}, אָלוֹת שׁ׳ Ho 10^{4} + 12^{2} 𝔊 We al. (for שׁד); עֵד שׁ׳ Dt 5^{17} (= עֵד שֶׁקֶר Ex 20^{16}), cf. שֵׁמַע שׁ׳ Ex 23^{1} (E); הָלַךְ עִם־שׁ׳ Jb 31^{5} (‖ מִרְמָה); of false (empty) prophecy חֲזוֹן שׁ׳ Ez 12^{24}, חָזוּ שׁ׳ La 2^{14}, v. also Ez $13^{6.7.9.23}$ 21^{34} 22^{28} Jb 35^{13} (or *empty* complaining, sub **1**), קֶסֶם שׁ׳ Ez 21^{28}, חֲלֹמוֹת הַשׁ׳ Ze 10^{2}. **3.** of conduct, *worthlessness* (Buhl sub **1, 2**); מְתֵי שׁ׳ *worthless men* ψ 26^{4} Jb 11^{11}, *worthless* motives (in fig) חַבְלֵי הַשׁ׳ Is 5^{18}, נָפַת שׁ׳ 30^{28} (i e sifting out the worthless, al *sieve* of (bringing) *disappointment*), play on meanings in Jb $15^{31.31}$, cf Dr $^{Job.\ Psalt\ 464}$

II. שׁוא (√of foll; prob ‖ form of שׁאה).

†[שׁוֹא] **n.[m.]** **ravage** (?),—pl. sf שֹׁאֵיהֶם ψ 35^{17} rescue me from *their ravages* (si vera l.); 𝔊 κακουργία, Ol Dy Gr Che $^{Comm.}$ plausibly שַׁאֲגָם *their roaring*, cf. v $^{16.17c}$, We Du שֹׁאֲנִים.

†שׁוֹאָה, שֹׁאָה **n. f.** **devastation, ruin, waste**;—abs. שׁוֹ׳ Is 10^{3} +, שֹׁאָה 47^{11} Zp 1^{15} Jb 30^{14} (+ 38^{27} van d. H. Gi, but v. Baer's n.); cstr. שׁאת Pr 3^{25},—**1.** *devastation, ruin*, as coming on pers, Is 10^{3} 47^{11} (Babylon personif.), ψ 35^{8a} 63^{10}, שֹׁאַת רְשָׁעִים Pr 3^{25} (obj. genit; ‖ פַּחַד); (יוֹם) שׁ׳ וּמְשׁוֹאָה Zp 1^{15}; prob = *devastating storm*, in sim Ez 38^{9} (‖ עָנָן), Pr 1^{27} (Qr, Kt שׁאוה; ‖ סוּפָה)—ψ 35^{8b} read prob שַׁחְתּוֹ *his pit*, 𝔖 We (cf v ^{7}). **2.** concretely, *ruin, waste*, of the desert, Jb 30^{3} (rdg אֶרֶץ for אמשׁ Ol; otherwise sub **1**), שׁ׳ וּמְשׁוֹאָה 38^{27} (‖ מִדְבָּר v ^{26}); = *ruins* Jb 30^{14}.

†מְשׁוֹאָה, מְשֹׁאָה **n.f.** **desolation**;—**1.** sg. only in שֹׁאָה וּמ׳ Zp 1^{15} Jb 30^{3} 38^{27}, v. foregoing; pl (מְשׁוּאוֹת, rd) מַשּׁוּאוֹת, so Klo Hup-Now Che ^{Comm} Bae Du ψ 74^{3} *ruins* (of temple) and 73^{18} *ruins* (of one's life, fig., but Du here der fr נשׁא: *deceptions*, v. p 674, yet cf. synon. שַׁמָּה v ^{19})

†[תְּשֻׁאָה] **n.f.** **noise** (prop of devastation, storm);—MT only pl. תְּשֻׁאוֹת abs. city noises Is 22^{2} (of עִיר הוֹמִיָּה), adv. acc. = (with) *shoutings* Zc 4^{7}, so cstr. תְּ׳ נוֹגֵשׂ לֹא יִשְׁמָע Jb 39^{7} (subj. wild ass); תְּ׳ סֻכָּתוֹ 36^{29} (of thunder), read perh. sg. תְּשֻׁוָּה (= תְּשֻׁאָה) Jb 30^{22} Kt, dissolvest me *in* (or, *into*) *the roar of the storm* (‖ *make me ride on wind*), so Ew Ol De Di Du Bu al, > תּוּשִׁיָּה Qr AV *my substance* (?), Du מַחֲשׁ׳ 'ohne Halt' (?).

שׁוּב $_{1056}$ **vb.** **turn back, return** (NH *id.*; Hiph in MI $^{8f.12}$; Sab תוב, התב, esp. *requite* Os $^{ZMG\ xix\ (1865),\ 193}$ SabDenkm $^{No\ 20,\ 1\ 1}$ Hom $^{Chrest\ 122}$ CIS $^{iv\ 81\ 1\ 9}$, etc; Ar. ثَابَ *return*, so Aram. תּוּב, ܬܳܒ),—**Qal** $_{683}$ *Pf.* 3 ms. שָׁב Gn 18^{33} +, 3 fs שָׁבָה Ru 1^{15} +, וְשָׁבַת consec. †Ez 46^{17} (Ges ^{§72o}, but Co Toy Krae וְשָׁבָה), 2 ms. שַׁבְתָּ ψ 85^{2}, etc.; *Impf.* 3 ms. יָשׁוּב Ho 11^{5} + oft., יָשֹׁב ψ 146^{4} La 3^{3}, juss יָשֹׁב Ju 7^{3} +, וַיָּשָׁב Gn 26^{18} +; 3 fpl תְּשֻׁבֶן Ez $16^{55.55}$, תְּשׁוּבֶינָה v ^{55}, etc.; *Imv.* ms. שׁוּב Gn 31^{3} +, שֻׁב Ex 4^{19} 1 K 18^{43}, שׁוּבָה Ho 14^{2} +, fpl שֹׁבְנָה Ru $1^{8.11.12}$, etc., *Inf abs.* שׁוֹב Gn 8^{3} +, *cstr.* שׁוּב Ex 4^{21} +, שֻׁב Jos 2^{16} (Ges ^{§72q}), etc.; *Pt.* שָׁב Gn 43^{18} +, fs. שָׁבָה Ru 1^{22} +, etc.; pass cstr. שׁוּבֵי Mi 2^{8},—*turn back, return*: **1.** *turn back*, c. מִן loc Ju 3^{19} 8^{13}, cf 7^{3}, c. מֵאַחֲרֵי pers, i.e from following 2 S 11^{15} 1 K 19^{21} Ru 1^{16}, fr. pursuing 2 S $2^{26.30}$ 1 K 22^{33} = 2 Ch 18^{32}; c מִן of pursuit 1 S 17^{53} 23^{28}, cf 2 Ch 11^{4}; c. אַחֲרֵי pers, i.e. so as to follow 1 S 15^{31} 2 S 23^{10}; *turn back* in fear, מִן rei Jb 39^{22} (of horse), מִפְּנֵי כֹל Pr 30^{30} (of lion), so abs. (of foes) ψ 6^{11} 56^{10} 70^{4}, in shame La 1^{8}; *turn back* and do so and so: Gn 14^{7} Ex 14^{2}, cf. Nu 33^{7} (עַל loc, both P), Jos 8^{21} (E), 11^{10} (J),

1 Ch 21^{20}, sq. inf. 2 Ch 20^{27}; abs. *turn back* (face about) Ct 7$^{1.1.1.1}$ (+ vb.); = be repulsed, defeated ψ 9^{4}, 74^{21}; fig. *turn back*, viz. from a promise or a vow Ju 11^{35}; c. מִן of service Nu 8^{25} (P), i.e. be exempt. **2.** *return, come or go back*, c. מֵעַל pers. 1 S 17^{15} (opp. הלך), 2 S 10^{14} 2 K 18^{14}, מִן pers. Jos 10^{21} (+ בְּשָׁלוֹם), מִן loc., esp. from foreign land 2 K 8^{3} 2 Ch 10^{2} Ru 1$^{6.22}$ 2^{6} 4^{3} Je 31^{16} 40^{12} 43^{5} 44^{28} Ezr 6^{21} Ne 8^{17}, מֵהַכּוֹת Gn 14^{17} (JE?), 1 S 17^{57} 18^{6} 2 S 1^{1} 8^{13}, מֵאַחֲרֵי i.e. from pursuing 1 S 24^{2} (Gi v^{1}); fig., לֹא שׁ׳ מִנִּי חֹשֶׁךְ Jb 15^{22} (v. חֹשֶׁךְ **3 a**); עִבְרוּ וָשׁוּבוּ מִשַּׁעַר לְשַׁעַר Ex 32^{27} (J), i.e. *go back and forth from gate to gate*, cf. (abs.) pt. as subst. עֹבֵר וָשָׁב Zc 7^{14} 9^{8} and (= all persons) Ez 35^{7}; also וַיֵּצֵא יָצוֹא וָשׁוֹב Gn 8^{7} (J), רָצוֹא וָשׁוֹב Ez 1^{14} (del. Hi Co Toy al.; yet v. Krae); Gn 8^{3} (J) v. הלך **4 c** (4). **3.** esp. *return unto*: **a.** *go back*, אֶל pers. Nu 23$^{5.16}$ (JE), 2 K 1^{6} (‖ הָלַךְ, as oft.), Ex 5^{22} (J; אֶל־י׳), 32^{31} (E; *id.*), Nu 17^{15} (P), 2 S 20^{22} (+ acc. loc.), Je 46^{16} (both + אֶל loc.), + 17 t.; אֶל loc. also Gn 21^{32} 28^{21} (both E), 2 S 11^{4} Ho 5^{15} (of י׳), 2 Ch 19^{1} (+ בְּשָׁלוֹם, + לְ pers.), Est 2^{14} (opp. בוא), 7^{8} (+ מִן loc.), + 27 t.; of a dog שׁ׳ עַל־קֵאוֹ Pr 26^{11}; לְ loc. Gn 18^{33} (J), 1 S 26^{25} 29^{4} 1 K 19^{15} (+ ה- loc.), Gn 33^{16} (J; לְדַרְכּוֹ, + *id.*), ψ 7^{8} (of י׳), + 25 t.; לְ pers. †Ru 1^{10} (לְעַמֵּךְ); ה- loc. also Gn 44^{13} (J), Ex 4$^{20.21}$ (R), 13^{17} (E), + 5 t.; שָׁם (= שָׁמָּה) Je 22^{27}; acc. loc. also Ho 8^{13} 9^{3} 1 S 18^{2} 2 S 3^{27} 15^{27} (+ בְּשָׁלוֹם), 2 K 2^{25} (+ מִן loc.), + 15 t.; acc. דֶּרֶךְ Ez 46^{9}; acc. pers. †Nu 10^{36}; אַחֲרֵי pers. Ru 1^{15}; abs. 2 S 3^{16} 19^{16} (+ בוא), 1 K 18^{43} Je 40^{5} (< del. 𝔊 Gie Du), Ez 7^{13b} (del. 𝔊 Co Krae al.) +; sq. vb., *go back* and do so and so, Gn 43^{2} 1 S 1^{19} 29^{7} (שׁוּב וְלֵךְ בְּשָׁלוֹם), 1 K 13^{22} 2 Ch 18^{16} (+ בְּשָׁלוֹם) +, (Je 42^{10} read יָשׁוֹב Vrss and mod.); sq. inf. purpose Ju 14^{8} 2 S 6^{20} + 10 t. **b.** *come back*, אֶל pers. Gn 8^{9} (J; + אֶל loc.), Ex 24^{14} (J), 1 S 23^{23} + 2 S 17^{3} (𝔊 Ew Th We Dr HPS Bu), 1 K 12^{15} (opp. הָלַךְ) + 9 t. + (in hostility) Ju 20^{48}; אֶל loc. also Zc 8^{3} (subj. י׳); Jos 22^{32} (P) has מֵאֵת pers. + מִן loc. + אֶל loc. + אֶל pers.; אֶל rei Ez 7^{13}; עַל pers. †Ne 4^{6} Mi 5^{2} (be reunited to); עַל loc. †1 K 17$^{21.22}$; לְ loc. Jos 1^{15} (R), Zc 1^{16} (subj. י׳), 2 Ch 30^{9} + (from exile) 5 t.; לְ animal., Jb 39^{4}; ה- loc. †Gn 15^{16} (E), 50^{14} (J); acc. loc. †2 Ch 19^{8}; שָׁם Je 20^{11} (opp. יָצָא), שָׁמָּה v^{27}, הֵנָּה 31^{8}; abs. Gn 43^{10} (J), 2 S 10^{5} 2 K 1^{5} Is 21^{12} (‖ אָתָה), Jb 39^{12} (Kt, so Bu Du; of wild ox), + oft.; + בְּשָׁלוֹם Ju 8^{9} 1 K 22^{28} (שׁוּב תָּשׁוּב) = 2 Ch 18^{27}, 2 Ch 18^{26}; + vb., *come back* and do so and so, †Dt 1^{45} 30^{8} Je 37^{8} 1 K 19^{7} 20^{5} 2 K 9^{36} ψ 60^{2} (title), cf. Zc 4^{1} Dn 11^{10}, שׁ׳ לָשֶׁבֶת Nu 35^{32} (P), שׁ׳ לָלֶכֶת Ec 5^{14}. †**4. a.** of dying, עַל־עָפָר Gn 3$^{19.19}$ (J), ψ 104^{29} Ec 3^{20}, שׁ׳ אֶל־(הֶ)עָפָר Jb 34^{15}; שׁ׳ לְאַדְמָתוֹ ψ 146^{4}, cf. אָשׁוּב שָׁמָּה (i.e. בֶּטֶן אִמּוֹ) Jb 1^{21} (v. Di Bu, also Ec 5^{14}); שׁ׳ לִשְׁאוֹלָה ψ 9^{18}; so prob. abs. ψ 90^{3} (> come back to life); of (human) dust, שׁ׳ עַל־הָאָרֶץ Ec 12^{7}; breath, שׁ׳ אֶל־הָאֱלֹהִים v^{7}. **b.** of revival from death, שׁ׳ לְבֵיתוֹ Jb 7^{10}, abs. 10^{21} (opp. הָלַךְ), 16^{22} (*id.*), Pr 2^{19}; also c. אֶל pers. 2 S 12^{23}. †**5.** fig. of human relations: **a.** *return* to leader, king, אֶל pers., Ju 11^{8} 1 K 12$^{27.27}$; to divorced wife Je 3^{1} (opp. הלך). **b.** = change so as to approach (in purpose, desire), אֶל־ pers. Je 15$^{19.19}$. **c.** *turn*, i.e. resort to, לְ pers. ψ 119^{79}. **d.** *return* to a physical condition Jb 33^{25} (לְ rei); to a state or course of life, לְ rei Is 23^{17} Ez 16$^{55.55.55}$ Ne 9^{17} ψ 85^{9} עַל rei Je 11^{10}, הֲלוֹם ψ 73^{10} (but crpt.); בְּ Je 8^{6} (Du rds. שָׁט for שָׁב). **e.** abs. = change course of action; from good to bad, וַיָּשָׁב וַיִּמְרָד־בּוֹ 2 K 24^{1}, Je 34$^{11.16}$; bad to good v^{15}; so שׁ׳ alone Jb 6$^{29.29}$ (prob.; read וְשׁוּבוּ, so Di Da Bu al.; other interpr. De Du al.). **f.** pt. pass. = *averse*, שׁוּבֵי מִלְחָמָה Mi 2^{8} (> We Now שְׁבִי *spoil of war*). **6.** fig., specif. of spiritual relations: **a.** *turn back* from God, = *apostatize*, שׁוּב מֵאַחֲרֵי י׳ Nu 14^{43} (J), 1 S 15^{11} 1 K 9^{6} (תְּשֻׁבוּן), Je 3^{19}, Nu 32^{15} Jos 22$^{16.18.23.29}$ (all P); abs. (usu. + vb.) Ju 2^{19} 8^{33} Jos 23^{12} (R^{D}), Je 8^{4} ψ 78^{41} 2 Ch 7^{19}. **b.** of י׳, *turn away*, מֵאַחֲרֵי pers. Dt 23^{15}. **c.** *turn back* to God (= seek penitently), אֶל־י׳ Ho 6^{1} 7^{10} 14^{3} Je 3^{7} 1 K 8$^{33.48}$ (בְּכָל־לֵבָב), + 18 t.; אֶל־אֱלֹהִים †Ho 5^{4} ψ 51^{15}, cf. Is 10^{21}; עַל־י׳ †2 Ch 15^{4} 30^{9}; עַד־י׳ Am 4$^{6.8.9.10.11}$ Ho 14^{2} Is 9^{12} + 5 t.; עַד־שַׁדַּי †Jb 22^{23}; לִי׳ Is 31^{6}, שׁ׳ נַפְשִׁי לִמְנוּחָיְכִי ψ 116^{7}; cf. לַבַּעַל Ho 7^{16} (for לֹא עָל, Now, cf. Marti); לְתוֹכַחְתִּי Pr 1^{23} (prob. del., v. Toy). **d.** abs. *repent*, Ho 3^{15} 11^{5} Is 6^{10} 10^{22} Je 3$^{7.12.14.22}$ 4^{1} 5^{3} + 14 t., + pt. as subst. Is 1^{27}. **e.** *turn back* from evil, c. מִן (esp. Je Ez) 1 K 8^{35} 13^{33} Je 15^{7} 18^{8} + 8 t. Je, Ez 3^{19} 13^{22} + 12 t. Ez, + 9 t.; cf. שָׁבֵי פֶשַׁע Is 59^{20}; שׁוּבוּ וְהָשִׁיבוּ מִן Ez 18^{30}, so c. מֵעַל 14^{6}; from good, c. מִן, †Ez 3^{20} 18$^{24.26}$ 33^{18}. **f.** of י׳, שׁ׳ מֵחֲרוֹן אַפּוֹ Ex 32^{12} (JE), Dt 13^{18} Jos 7^{26} (J), 2 K 23^{26} Jon 3^{9}; שׁ׳ מִמֶּנּוּ אַף־י׳ Ho 14^{5} Je 2^{35} 4^{8} Nu 25^{4} (P), 2 Ch 12^{12} 29^{10} 30^{8}, so (man's anger) Gn 27^{45} (J) and (abs.) v^{44} (E); abs. of אַף־י׳ Is 5^{25} 9$^{11.16.20}$ 10^{4} 12^{1} Je 23^{20} (opp. יָצָא v^{19}), 30^{24} Jb 14^{13} Dn 9^{16}. **g.** of י׳, *return*

(to shew favour), אֶל pers. + Gn 18[10] (+ inf abs.), v[14] Zc 1[3] Mal 3[7] 2 Ch 30[6], abs. Is 63[17] ψ 80[15] (‖ פָּקַד, הבּיט), 90[13], + vb. Je 12[15] ψ 6[5] Jo 2[14] Jon 3[9], also in hostility, + vb Jos 24[20] (E), c. inf purpose Ho 11[9] **h.** of ׳י, *turn back* from (מן) judgment Je 4[28], מֵאַחֲרֵי אמת ψ 132[11], pers, i e. cease to bless, Je 32[40]. **7.** of inanimate things (sts personified, or treated as things of life): **a.** as perceptibly moving, water Gn 8[3] (J, מעל loc), Jos 4[18] (J, ל loc), Ex 14[26] (P, על pers), v[28] (P, + vb), ψ 104[9] (ל inf), sea Ex 14[27] (J; לְאֵיתָנוֹ); wind ψ 78[39] (opp. הלך), Ec 1[6] (על loc); shadow 2 K 20[9 10] (+ אחרנית), ‖ Is 38[8] (sun on dial), of breath (= revive) Ju 15[19] 1 S 30[12] (אל pers), clouds Ec 12[2] (מן temp); rain and snow Is 55[10] (ה loc), rolling stone Pr 26[27]; sword 2 S 1[22] (מן rei), Ez 21[10], arrow Je 50[9], of plague-spot = *re-appear*, Lv 14[43] (P) **b.** = *be brought back*, Gn 43[18] (J), 1 S 5[11] (ל loc), hence *be restored*, ל pers. Ez 46[17], so of kingdom 1 K 12[26], city 1 S 7[14] (Ez 35[9] v ישב 4), field Lv 27[24] (P), of animal Dt 28[31]. **c.** = *be turned into*, ל rei, Is 29[17], = *be turned back into*, עד rei, Mi 1[7]. **d** *return*, fig of word, (1) Is 45[23], c אֶל pers 55[11] (both opp יָצָא), (2) ψ 35[13] *my prayer turned upon* (על) *my bosom* (was uttered with bowed head, De Bae Du) **e.** *turn away, depart*, of infamy Pr 25[10] **f.** *return* (in recompense), of crime, evil, etc, c בראש 1 K 2[33] Ob[15] ψ 7[17], על־ראשׁ Est 9[25], ל pers. ψ 54[7] (Kt; > Qr Hiph), Pr 12[14] **g.** ψ 94[15] *judgment*(-giving) *shall return to* (עד) *righteousness* (be in accord therewith) **h.** of boundary, = change (sts. reverse) direction (P), ה- loc. Jos 19[12] (+ מן loc), v[34] (+ acc. loc), acc loc. also v[27 29] (+ עד loc), v[29] **i.** *be restored* to healthy condition, of withered hand 1 K 13[6.6] (אל pers), leprous hand Ex 4[7] (J, c כ comp), flesh 2 K 5[10] (ל pers), v[14] Lv 13[16] (‖ נהפך לְלָבָן) †**8.** denoting repetition, etc (Ges[§120d.e]) + vb, *return (and) do* = do again, Gn 26[18] 30[31] Nu 11[4] (all J), Ju 19[7] 1 S 3[5 6] 1 K 13[33] 19[6] 2 K 1[11 13] 19[9] 21[3] = 2 Ch 33[3], Je 18[4] 36[28] Zc 5[1] 6[1] Mal 1[4] Jb 10[16] 17[10] ψ 7[13] Dn 9[25], perh also 2 Ch 19[4]; cf Is 6[13] = *it, in turn, shall be destroyed* (destruction shall be repeated in its case), La 3[3] appar = *do repeatedly*; ׳שׁ + Inf abs Ec 4[1 7] 9[11], in compar. עוד תָּשׁוּב תראה Ez 8[6] *thou shalt see yet* greater abominations, so v[13] and (מן comp.) v[15], ׳שׁ + Inf. cstr. Dt 24[4] 30[9] Jos 5[2] (R[D]), Je 36[28] Ez 8[17] Ezr 9[14] Ne 9[28] Jb 7[7] Ec 1[7]. = *reverse* one's action, + vb. Jos 2[23] (E), Ho 2[11] 2 K 13[25] Dt 30[3] Mi 7[19] Zc 8[15] ψ 71[20.20] 85[7]; = *restore* to original condition by doing, + vb. Dt 23[14] **9.** trans., peculiarly, in phr. ׳שׁ שְׁבוּת *restore captivity* of, etc, c 21 t. (v sub שְׁבָה), ׳שׁ ׳י ציון Is 52[8], ׳שׁ c sf pers ψ 85[2]; elsewhere only שָׁב ׳י אֶת־גאון יַעֲקב וגו׳ Na 2[3], cf. **Hiph. 6.** †**Pōʿl. 1.** *bring back*, *Pf* 1 s. וְשׁבַבְתִּי, c acc. pers + אל loc. Je 50[19] (׳י subj), *Inf cstr* sf. בְּשׁוֹבְבִי, c מן loc. Ez 39[27] and (fig) לְשׁוֹבֵב, c אֶל pers. Is 49[5], *Impf* 2 ms. תְּשׁוֹבֵב לָנוּ ψ 60[3] = *take us back* into power. **2. a.** fig *restore, refresh*, 3 ms נַפְשִׁי יְשׁוֹבֵב ψ 23[3] (׳י subj.), cf. **Hiph. 2 b** **b.** *restore, repair, Pt* מְשׁוֹבֵב נתיבות לָשָׁבֶת Is 58[12]. **3.** *lead away* (enticingly), *Pf.* 1 s sf (of Gog), ׳י subj, וְשֹׁבַבְתִּיךָ Ez 38[4] (del. Co), ׳ושׁ 39[2]; so fig 3 fs. sf. וְדַעְתֵּךְ היא שׁוֹבְבָתֶךְ Is 47[10] (of Bab), — Je 50[6] v. **Qal 4.** *shew turning* = *apostatize* (cf. **Hiph. 8**), *Pf* 3 fs שׁוֹבְבָה Je 8[5] (read שׁובב, and del. ירושלם, c. 𝔊) —Vid. also שׁובב infra †**Puʿl.** *Pt.* f. משׁוֹבֶבֶת Ez 38[8] a land *restored* + מן rei — Vid. also שׁוֹבָב infra **Hiph.**[351] *Pf* 3 ms. Gn 41[13] +, sf והשׁיבך 40[13], וְהֱשִׁיבְךָ Dt 28[68], 2 ms. הֲשֵׁבֹתָ ψ 85[4], הֲשֵׁבֹתָ Dt 4[39] 30[1], sf. וַהֲשֵׁיבוֹתָם 2 Ch 6[25], 1 s consec וַהֲשִׁיבוֹתִי Am 1[8], וַהֲשֵׁבֹתִי Nu 22[8] +, sf וְהוֹשְׁבוֹתִים Zc 10[6] (but rd וַהֲשִׁבוֹתִים, v ישׁב **Hiph.**), etc; *Impf.* 3 ms. יָשִׁיב Ex 21[34] +, (rd יָשֵׁב Dn 11[18 19] > Qr v[18] יָשֵׂם), וַיָּשֶׁב Gn 20[14] +; sf ישׁבני 2 S 15[8] +, וישׁיבם 2 Ch 19[4] + 1 S 12[8] Vrss We Dr al., 3 fpl תְּשִׁבֶנָה Jb 20[10], etc, *Imv* ms הָשֵׁב Gn 20[7] +, הָשִׁיב 2 K 8[6], הָשַׁב Is 42[22], so הָשַׁב Ez 21[35] (v. Ke and still Toy, Ew Sm Krae Inf abs הָשֵׁב), הֲשִׁיבָה Ju 11[13] +, etc, *Inf. abs* הָשֵׁב Ex 23[4] +, cstr הָשִׁיב Gn 42[25] +, etc, *Pt.* מֵשִׁיב 20[7] +, etc.,—*cause to return, bring back:* **1 a.** c acc pers + אל loc. Gn 24[5] (J, הֶהָשֵׁב אָשִׁיב), 28[15] (J), 42[37] (E), 48[21] (E), +, esp. from exile 1 K 8[34] = 2 Ch 6[25], Je 27[22] + 5 t Je, + אֶל pers. 1 K 22[26] = 2 Ch 18[25]; + על loc. Je 16[15] 23[3] 24[6]; + ל loc. 12[15], + acc loc 2 S 15[8] (read הָשֵׁב ישׁבני Vrss Th We Dr al), Dt 28[68] Ez 29[14] 47[6] 2 Ch 33[13], etc., + מן loc Je 41[16] Zc 10[10], מאת pers Je 41[16], מן inf 2 Ch 25[13]; acc pers. only Ju 19[3] 1 K 13[20 23] +, *bring back* into bondage, etc, Je 34[11 16], = *allow to return* 15[19]; acc. pers + rei (= recover, recapture), 28[6] (+ אֶל loc, מן loc), = *recover, rescue*, Gn 14[16] (acc. pers + rei), ψ 35[17] (acc. נַפְשִׁי, מן rei), acc. rei + אֶל pers Gn 44[8] (J), + על pers. Ex 15[9] (song), Pr 20[26], + אֶל loc. 1 K 14[28] = 2 Ch 12[11], Je 28[3] 2 Ch 24[11]; acc. of hand, אֶל־פה 1 S 14[27] Pr 19[24]

26^{15}; esp. of י׳'s hand, in judgment, sq. עַל Am 1^{8} Is 1^{25} Zc 13^{7} ψ 81^{15}, also of man's hand Je 6^{9} Ez 38^{12}; +acc. loc. 2 S $15^{25.29}$; + שָׁם Ne 13^{9}; acc. rei alone Gn $43^{12.21}$ (both בְּיֶדְכֶם), 14^{16} (=recapture), 1 S 6^{21} 30^{19} 1 K 13^{29} (corpse), Lv 26^{26} (H); c. acc. animal. 1 S 6^{7} (מֵאַחֲרֵי), Ez $34^{4.16}$ (fig.); shadow on dial 2 K 20^{11}=Is 38^{8}.—Jb 39^{12} v. **Qal 3 b**. **b.** *put back*: acc. rei, stone, עַל־פִּי הַבְּאֵר Gn 29^{3} (J), veil עַל־פָּנָיו Ex 34^{35} (P), Dagon לִמְקוֹמוֹ 1 S 5^{3}, rod לִפְנֵי הָעֵדוּת Nu 17^{25} (P), sword, + אֶל of sheath, 1 Ch 21^{27} Ez 21^{35} (acc. om.); hand אֶל־חֵיק Ex $4^{7.7}$ (J; opp. הוֹצִיא). **c.** =*draw back*, hand Gn 38^{29} (J), 1 K 13^{4} (opp. שָׁלַח; + אֶל reflex.), Jos 8^{26} (E; opp. נטה), so, fig., י׳ subj. La 2^{3} (אָחוֹר, מִפְּנֵי), ψ 74^{11}; c. מִן=*refrain from* La 2^{8} Ez $18^{8.17}$ (i.e. from oppressing), 20^{22} (מִן om.); foot, c. מִן Is 58^{13} (fig.); *draw in* breath Jb 9^{18}. **d.** =*give back, restore*, acc. pers. vel rei: + לְ pers. Gn 20^{14} (E), v^{7} (E; acc. om.), Ex 23^{4} (E; הָשֵׁב תְּשִׁיב), Dt 22^{1} (*id.*; both acc. animal.), 24^{13} (*id.*), Ex 22^{25} (E), Ju $17^{3.3.4}$ 1 S 12^{3} 2 S 9^{7} Dt 22^{2} (P), Ne 5^{11}, so 2 S 16^{3} 1 K 12^{21}=2 Ch 11^{1} (all acc. of kingdom), c. acc. צְדָקָה Jb 33^{26}; + אֶל pers. Gn 37^{22} (E; acc. pers.); + אֶל loc. 42^{25} (E); acc. rei only, 2 K 8^{6} Ez 18^{7} (read Inf. abs. שׁוּב for חוֹב, Co Toy Krae), 18^{12} 33^{15} Lv 5^{23} (P), Nu 5^{7} (P; + בְּרֹאשׁוֹ=*in full*), ψ 69^{5} (opp. גָּזַל), so of land (or city) Ju 11^{13} 1 K 20^{34} Ne 5^{12}, cf. 2 K 14^{28} (+ בְּיִשְׂרָאֵל), 16^{6} (+ לַאֲרָם); = win back 2 K 13^{25} 14^{22} (+ לְ terr.)= 2 Ch 26^{2}, boundary (i.e. re-establish it) 2 K 14^{25}; *restore* ruined city Dn 9^{25} (+ לִבְנוֹת), conquered nation ψ $80^{4.8.20}$; joy, acc. + לְ pers. ψ 51^{14}.—2 S 8^{3} v. יָד. **2.**—Acc. pers. only, Gn 20^{7} (E), Is 42^{22}; *restore* to office, acc. pers. + עַל Gn $40^{13.21}$ (E), אֶל loc. 2 S 19^{12}, acc. pers. only, 2 S $19^{11.13.44}$, cf. Is 1^{26}; =*pay back* money, Lv 25^{27} (לְ pers.), $v^{51.52}$. **e.** =*relinquish*, c. acc. rei, Jb 20^{10}. **f.**=*give in payment*, requital, c. acc. rei + appos. 1 S 6^{8} (לְ pers.), v^{17} (*id.*; cf. טְחוֹר); also *pay* as tribute (in answer to demand), acc. rei 2 K 17^{3} ψ 72^{10}, + לְ pers. 2 K 3^{4} 2 Ch 27^{5}; *give in exchange* Ez 27^{15}. **g.** *bring* one *back* (from dead) 2 S 12^{23}, so c. מִנִּי מָוֶת Jb 33^{30}; on other hand, אֶל־עָפָר Jb 10^{9}=(acc.) 30^{23}, cf. עַד־דַּכָּא ψ 90^{3}. †**2. a.** *bring back* heart, עַל לֵב pers. Mal 3^{24}; הֲשִׁיבֵנוּ י׳ אֵלֶיךָ La 5^{21} (< Bu *restore*, del. אליך); הֲשִׁיב אֶל־י׳ Ne 9^{26} (cf. v^{29}), 2 Ch 19^{4} 24^{19}, also (מִן of evil) Je 23^{22}, abs. 31^{18}. **b.** acc. נֶפֶשׁ=*refresh* La $1^{11.16.19}$ ψ 19^{8} Pr 25^{13} Ru 4^{15}. **3.** *bring back* words of people, אֶל־י׳ Ex 19^{8} (E); then, in gen., *bring back* word, דָּבָר, *report to*, + acc. pers. Gn 37^{14} Nu 13^{26} 22^{8} (all E), Dt $1^{22.25}$ Jos 14^{7} (R^{D}), 22^{32} (P), + 8 t.; =*answer* 1 S 17^{30} 2 S 3^{11} 1 K 12^{6}=2 Ch 10^{6} + 6 t., + (acc. מִלִּין) Jb 35^{4}; also (דָּבָר om.) Jb 13^{22} 20^{2} $33^{5.32}$ 2 Ch 10^{16} Ne 6^{4} (כַּדָּבָר הַזֶּה); acc. אֲמָרִים + לְ pers. Ju 5^{29} Pr 22^{21}; later c. לְ pers. alone 1 S 12^{3}; c. cl. orat. recta, אֶל pers. Est $4^{13.15}$; similar phrases, Ez 9^{11} Pr 18^{13} 24^{26} 26^{16} Hb 2^{1} Jb 31^{14} 32^{14} (Gi v^{13}), 40^{4}. **4. a.** *bring back* (in retribution, cf. **Qal 7 f**) upon, subj. oft. י׳, acc. of evil, Ju 9^{56}, בְּרֹאשׁ Ju 9^{5} 1 S 25^{39} 1 K 2^{44} Jo $4^{4.7}$, עַל־רֹאשׁ 1 K 2^{32}, אֶל־רֹאשׁ Ne 3^{36}; לְ pers. Gn 50^{15} (E), 1 S 6^{3} (הָשֵׁב תְּשִׁיבוּ), v^{4} 25^{21} (*return evil for good*), +, etc.; abs. = *make requital*, לְ pers. 2 Ch 6^{23} + (כְּ comp.) Ho 12^{3} Pr $24^{12.29}$; †c. acc. of good, לְ pers. 2 S 16^{12} 26^{23} Zc 9^{12}; c. כְּ comp. + לְ pers. ψ $18^{21.25}$=2 S $22^{21.25}$, and (כְּ comp. only) 2 Ch 32^{25}; requite י׳'s benefits, acc. rei + לי׳ ψ 116^{12}, cf. Nu 18^{9} (P). **b.** *pay* as recompense, כֶּסֶף יָשׁ׳ לִבְעָלָיו Ex 21^{34} (E); so (fig.) of י׳, הָשִׁ׳ נָקָם לְ Dt $32^{41.43}$, לְהָשִׁ׳ בְּחֵמָה אַפּוֹ Is 66^{15}. **5.** *turn back, backward*=repel, defeat, c. אֶת־פְּנֵי 2 K 18^{24}=Is 36^{9}, acc. מִלְחָמָה Is 28^{6}, acc. of sword ψ 89^{44}, acc. pers. + אָחוֹר ψ 44^{11} (+ מִנִּי pers.), Is 44^{25} (fig., = refute, confute), fig. of calamity La 1^{13}; = *repulse, hinder* Je 2^{24}, esp. acc. Is 14^{27} (יַד־י׳), cf. 43^{13}, Jb 9^{12} 11^{10} 23^{13}; =*reject, refuse*, (אֶת־)פְּנֵי פ׳ 1 K $2^{16.17.20.20}$ 2 Ch 6^{42} ψ 132^{10}. †**6. a.** *turn away* face, fig., + מֵעַל rei Ez 14^{6}; acc. pers. + מִן rei Mal 2^{6}; anger of י׳ (acc.) + מֵעַל pers. Nu 25^{11} (P), Pr 24^{18}, מִן pers. Je 18^{20} Ezr 10^{14}; acc. only, Jb 9^{13} ψ 78^{38} 106^{23}; acc. of human anger Pr 15^{1} 29^{8}. **b.** late, *turn toward*, acc. face, לְ loc. Dn $11^{18.19}$, acc. foot, אֶל rei ψ 119^{59} (fig.). †**7.** *turn* against, אֶל־אֵל, c. acc. רוּחֶךָ Jb 15^{13}. **8.** הָשִׁ׳ אֶל־לֵבָב *bring back to mind*, take into consideration, c. acc. La 3^{21}, sq. cl. with כִּי Dt 4^{39} (cf. Dr), obj. om. 30^{1} 1 K 8^{47}=2 Ch 6^{37}, Is 44^{19}, + (עַל) 46^{8}. **9.** הֵשִׁיב אֶת־שְׁבוּת פ׳ Je 32^{44} $33^{7.11}$ 49^{6} La 2^{14} Ez 39^{25} + (Qr Hiph., Kt Qal) Je 33^{26} 46^{39} Jo 4^{1} (v. **Qal 9**). †**10.** Hiph. declar., הָשִׁ׳ מֵעַל Ez 14^{6} = *shew a turning away from* your idols (i.e. turn away), cf. (מִן) 18^{30}, abs. הָשִׁ׳ וִחְיוּ v^{32}; of י׳, הָשִׁ׳ מֵחֲרוֹן אַפֶּךָ ψ 85^{4} (but rd. prob. הֲשִׁיבוֹתָ חֲרוֹן א׳ [**6 a** supra]); perhaps in physical sense Jon 1^{13} (אֶל loc.; We Now sc. אֳנִיָּה, etc.). †**11.** *reverse, revoke*, acc. (sf.) rei, i.e. judgment, Am $1^{3.6.9.11.13}$ $2^{1.4.6}$; blessing Nu 23^{20} (poem in E), edict Est $8^{5.8}$. †**Hoph.** *Pf.* 3 ms. הוּשַׁב Gn

42[28] my money *has been returned!* cf *Pt* הַכֶּסֶף הַמּוּשָׁב 43[12] (both J); אָשָׁם הַמּ׳ לי׳ Nu 5[8] (P) the *which is restored to* י׳; pl מוּשָׁבִים Je 27[16] the vessels *are about to be brought back*, c מן loc., *Impf* 3 ms וַיּוּשַׁב אֶת־מֹשֶׁה Ex 10[8] (J; cf. Ges §121 a. b) *Moses was brought back*, c אֶל pers

†שׁוּבָה n.f. retirement, withdrawal (from war, etc, cf. Mi 2[8]),—Is 30[15].

†II [שִׁיבָה] cstr שִׁיבַת *restoration*(?) ψ 126[1], but read שְׁבִית, v sub שָׁבָה I.—שִׁיבָה v. ישׁב.

†I שׁוֹבָב adj. backturning, recusant, apostate (perhaps for מְשׁוֹבָב, Pt Pōʿl Ol §251 b Ges §52 s Ko[1 451]),—שׁ׳ Is 57[17]; pl שׁוֹבָבִים בָּנִים Je 3[14 22]—שׁוֹבָבִים Je 50[6] Kt < Qr שׁוֹבְבִים 𝔊 Comm, cf √Pōʿl

†II. שׁוֹבָב n pr.m. Σωβαβ, etc 1. son of David 2 S 5[14] = 1 Ch 14[4], 1 Ch 3[5]. 2. son of Caleb 1 Ch 2[18]

†שׁוֹבֵב adj. backturning, apostate (perh for מְשׁוֹ׳, v I. שׁוֹבָב),—as subst, לְשׁוֹ׳ Mi 2[4] (but read prob. שֹׁבֵינוּ *our captors*); f. הַבַּת הַשּׁוֹבֵבָה Je 31[22] (of Israel), 49[4] (of Ammon).

†יָשׁוּב n pr.m. usu Ιασουβ,—1. in Issachar Nu 26[24] (P) 1 Ch 7[1] Qr (Kt ישיב) 2. one with foreign wife Ezr 10[29]—Is 7[3] v. שְׁאָר יָשׁוּב.

†יָשֻׁבִי adj.gent. of foregoing 1; c art as subst coll הַיּ׳ Nu 26[24]

†יָשֻׁבִי לֶחֶם n.pr.m. in Judah 1 Ch 4[22], 𝔊L ἐπέστρεψαν ἑαυτοῖς Λεεμ

†יָשָׁבְעָם n.pr.m. a hero of David,—1 Ch 11[11], 12[6], 27[2] (יֹשֵׁב בַּשֶּׁבֶת, q v p 444 supra, in 2 S 23[8], v. Dr), Ιεσεβαδα, Ιεσσεβααλ, Ισβααμ, etc, rd in all אֶשְׁבַּעַל We al

†יוּשַׁב חֶסֶד n.pr.m. son of Zerubbabel, 1 Ch 3[20]; Αροβασουκ, 𝔊L Ιωσαβεε.

†[מְשׁוּבָה], מְשֻׁבָה n.f. turning back, apostasy,—abs מְשֻׁבָה Je 3[6]+, cstr מְשׁוּבַת Pr 1[32], sf מְשׁוּבֹתֵיכֶם, מְשׁוּבָתָם Ho 14[5], pl sf Je 3[22], etc,—*backturning, apostasy*, of Isr, Ho 14[5], מְשׁוּבָתִי 11[7] *apostasy from me* (si vera l), of Judah Je 2[19] 3[22] 5[6] 8[5] 14[7] (all pl) + Ez 37[23] (read מְשׁוּבֹתֵיהֶם for מוֹשׁ׳, 𝔊 Comm), מ׳ נִצַּחַת Je 8[5] *enduring, perpetual apostasy;* also as n concr, appos of foll word, מְשֻׁבָה יִשׂ׳ Je 3[6 8 11 12] *apostate one, Israel* Of individual, מְשׁוּבַת פְּתָיִם Pr 1[32].

†מְשׁוֹבָב n. pr. m. in Simeon, 1 Ch 4[34]; Μοσωβαβ, 𝔊L ἐπιστρέφων.

†[תְּשׁוּבָה] n.f. return, answer;—1. sf. וּתְשֻׁבָתוֹ הָרָמָתָה 1 S 7[17] *and his return was* (= he returned) *to Rama* 2. esp cstr לִתְשׁוּבַת הַשָּׁנָה *at the return of the year*, i. e. of spring, 2 S 11[1] 1 K 20[22 26] 2 Ch 36[10], לְעֵת תְּשׁ׳ הַשׁ׳ 1 Ch 20[1] (‖ 2 S 11[1]) 3. *answer*, pl. abs. תְּשֻׁבֹת Jb 34[36], sf. תְּשׁוּבֹתֵיכֶם 21[34].

שׁוּבָאֵל v שְׁבוּאֵל (cf. Sab n pr חובאל Os ZMG xix (1865) 198 ff Hal[49] DHM ZMG xxxvii (1883) 16)

†שׁוֹבָךְ n. pr. m. Aramaean general, 2 S 10[16 18] (Σωβακ, 𝔊L Σαβεε), = שׁוֹפַךְ 1 Ch 19[16.18] (Σωφαρ, Σαφαθ; A Σωφαχ, Σωβαχ, 𝔊L Σωφακ).

שׁוֹבָל n.pr. v. שׁבל.

שׁוֹבֵק, שׁוֹבֶק n.pr v שׁבק.

שׁוג (√of following, ‖ form of שׁגה, שׁגג).

†[מְשׁוּגָה] n.f. error,—sf מְשׁוּגָתִי Jb 19[4] (? rd. מְשֻׁנָּתִי)

שׁוּד Jb 5[21] van d H, for I. שׁד q v. sub שׁדד.

[שׁוּד] vb, יָשׁוּד ψ 91[6] v. שׁדד

†I שָׁוָה vb. (be even, smooth, v. Pi., hence) agree with, be like, resemble (Ar سوى II *make even, flat, uniform* (with something else); Aram שְׁוָא (der spec) *be like*, ܫܘܐ *be equal, fit, like*, Pa. *lay out smoothly*, Aph *make plain, fit, worthy*),—Qal *Pf* 3 ms. לֹא שׁ׳ לִי Jb 33[27] (si vera l) *it was not equalled to me*, i. e. (v. infra, acc to most) *not requited* (so De Di Da, and Is 16[6] 𝔗); Bu אֵל לֹא שָׁוָה *God did not requite* (or שׁ־ם for שׁוה), Du לֹא שָׁוָה כַּעֲוֹנִי (cf. 𝔊); *Impf* 1 s of י׳, אֶל־מִי . . . אֶשְׁוֶה Is 40[25] *to whom shall I be like?* (‖ תְּדַמְּיוּנִי), implying that he is incomp; 3 mpl לֹא יִשְׁווּ־בָהּ Pr 3[15] *are not comparable with her* (wisdom), so 8[11]; 2 ms פֶּן־תִּשְׁוֶה־לּוֹ Pr 26[4] *lest thou be like him* (a fool); *Pt* שֹׁוֶה ב Est 7[4] *is not an equivalent for*, c לְ, *suitable for* 3[8], so 1[22] Hi Or Ry[Kau] (rdg כָּל שֹׁוֶה עִמּוֹ for כִּלְשׁוֹן עַמּוֹ, but v. Siegf); *adequate for* 5[13] Pi. *Pf* 3 ms שִׁוָּה Is 28[25] *he hath levelled* its (the ground's) surface; 1 s. שִׁוִּיתִי וְדוֹמַמְתִּי נַפְשִׁי ψ 131[2] *I have smoothed* (composed) *and stilled my soul;* so, sc. נַפְשִׁי Is 38[13] 𝔙 Ges De al; Houb Lo Che Du al. read שִׁוַּעְתִּי *I cried*, acc מִשְׁפָּטִים 119[30] *accounted suitable*,

meet (‖דֶּרֶךְ אֱמוּנָה בָחָרְתִּי), Hi, cf. Gr v[123] (v. **Qal** Est 3[8]); We ins. לְנֶגְדִּי (II 'שׁ, cf. ψ 16[8]); Zenner Du אוּיתי. **Hiph.** *make like*· *Impf.* 1 s. מָה לְּמִי תְדַמְּיוּנִי וְתַשְׁווּ.2 mpl.(אֲדַמֶּה‖) La 2[13] אַשְׁוֶה־לָּךְ; Is 46[5] (cf. **Qal** 40[25]). **Nithp.** (appar.) *Pf.* 3 fs. נִשְׁתָּוָה (for נשתוה) Pr 27[15] *are alike*, but read prob. Niph. 3 fs. נִשְׁוָתָה Ges[§75x] Toy al.—חשוה Jb 30[22] Kt v. II. שׁוא.

†I. שָׁוֵה n.[m.] level plain;—in שָׁוֵה קִרְיָתַיִם Gn 14[5] (v. 'ק p. 900[a]; 'ק appos. acc. to Ol[§277e] Lag[BN 43]; ? rd. שָׁוֵה); Σαυη.

†II. שָׁוֵה in n.pr.loc. 'עֵמֶק שׁ Gn 14[17] (v. 'ע); Σαυη.

† יִשְׁוָה n.pr.m. in Asher, Gn 46[17] = 1 Ch 7[30]; Ιεσσαι, Ισουα, Ιεσους, etc.

†I יִשְׁוִי n.pr.m. **1.** in Asher, Gn 46[17] = 1 Ch 7[30], Nu 26[44]; Ιεουλ, Ιουλ, Ισουι, Ιεσου, etc. **2.** a son of Saul 1 S 14[49]; Ιεσσιου(λ), but read אישבעל as 1 Ch 8[33] 9[39] (v. אִישׁ־בֹּשֶׁת p. 36[a]), cf. We Dr al.

†II. יִשְׁוִי adj.gent. of foregoing **1**; c. art. as n. coll. הַיִּ׳, Nu 26[44].

†II. [שָׁוָה] vb. **Pi.** set, place (BAram. Hithpa. 𝔗 שַׁוִּי Pa. *set, make* (oft. 𝔗 = שׂוּם, שִׁית); Thes al. sub I.'שׁ, orig *set, place*, then *set together*, compare, < weakened fr. orig *make even, right*, cf. Vulg. Ar. سَوَّى II. *make* (Wahrm, cf. also Ba[ES 66]));—*Pf.* 1 s. שִׁוִּיתִי ψ 16[8] *I have set* 'י *before me* (לְנֶגְדִּי); 'שׁ עֵזֶר עַל 89[20] *I have placed strength upon* a hero, cf. 21[6]; *Pt.* מְשַׁוֶּה רַגְלַי כָּ 2 S 22[34] *setting my feet like* hinds = ψ 18[34] (cf. 𝔗 שַׁוִּי כְּ Gn 48[20] Je 29[22], for שִׂים כְּ);—Is 38[13] v. I. שׁוה;—*Impf.* = *make, produce*, 3 ms פְּרִי יְשַׁוֶּה לּוֹ Ho 10[1] (Israel as vine), si vera l., v. We Now (‖ עשה פְּרִי Ho 9[16], cf. 8[7]).

†[שׁוּחַ] vb. sink down (Buhl disting. this as II. 'שׁ (Ar. سَاخَ (و) *sink down*, MI[9,23] אשוח prob. *depression, excavation, reservoir*, so אשיח Ecclus 50[3]), and hence שָׁחָה Pr 2[18], si vera l., and foll. deriv, from I. 'שׁ *melt away* (Ar. سَاخَ (ى) *flow and spread, melt away*, Eth ሶሐ: *cause to dwindle*, ሰሐ: *phthisis*, Aram. שְׁחָה, شَخَّ, *flow* or *melt away, vanish*), whence La 3[20] ψ 44[26], but insuff. evidence for I. 'שׁ in Heb);—*sink down*, **Qal** *Pf* 3 fs. שָׁחָה לֶעָפָר נַפְשֵׁנוּ ψ 44[26] (‖דָּבְקָה לָאָרֶץ), אֶל־מָוֶת בֵּיתָהּ 'שׁ Pr 2[18] (‖אֶל־רְפָאִים); but 'ב masc., rd. שָׁחָה, √שׁחה, Albr[ZAW xvi (1896), 82], so Toy); *Impf.* 3 fs. תָּשׁוּחַ עָלַי נַפְשִׁי La 3[20] Qr, **Hiph.** declar. תָּשִׁיחַ Kt, of depression of mind. —ψ 49[15] Gr rds. שָׁחוּ for MT שַׁתּוּ but v. שׁתת.—**Hithp.** ψ 42, 43 v. שׁחח.

† שׁוּחָה n.f. pit;—abs 'שׁ Je 2[6] *land of steppe and pits* (coll); fig, כָּרָה שׁ׳ לִי Je 18[20], so v[22] (Qr); עֲמֻקָּה Pr 23[27] *deep pit* (in fig. of harlot), cf. 22[14].

† שִׁיחָה n.f. id.;—כרה שׁ׳ Je 18[22] Kt (Qr שׁוּחָה), ψ 57[7]; pl. כ׳ שיחות 119[85].

† שַׁחַת n.f. pit;—abs.'שׁ ψ 7[16] +; שָׁחַת 16[10] +; cstr. שַׁחַת Is 38[17] ψ 35[7]; sf. שַׁחְתָּם Ez 19[4.8] (+ שַׁחְתָּה ψ 35[8b] We);—**1.** *pit*, for catching lion (in fig) Ez 19[4.8]; fig. 'פעל שׁ ψ 7[16]; c. עשה 9[16], c. חפר 35[7] (transp 'שׁ to v[8]); c כרה 94[13] Pr 26[27]; + ψ 35[8b] 𝔊 We (for שׁוֹאָה), 'טָבַל בַּשׁ Jb 9[31]. **2.** *pit* of Sh[e]'ôl, 'ירד שׁ Jb 33[24]; 'ראה (ה)שׁ ψ 16[10] (‖שְׁאוֹל), 49[10], 'לשׁ, c הוריד Ez 28[8], and ψ 55[24] (לִבְאֵר שׁ׳); קָרַב Jb 33[22]; יָמוּת Is 51[14]; עָבַר בַּשׁ׳ Jb 33[28]; 'יָרַד אֶל־שׁ ψ 30[10]; 'משׁ, c חשק Is 38[17] (poem), c. חשך Jb 33[18] (מִנִּי); c העלה Jon 2[7]; c. הֵשִׁיב Jb 33[30] (מִנִּי); c. נאל ψ 103[4], personif. Jb 17[14] (‖ רִמָּה)—'שׁ here either = שְׁאוֹל (hollow place, cavern), or < = pit in שְׁאוֹל (cf, from Ezek on, בּוֹר **5**; also אֲבַדּוֹן, p. 2, and עִמְקֵי שְׁאוֹל Pr 9[18]. This distinction of two parts of שְׁאוֹל became important in Jewish and Christian theology).

† שׁוּחַ n.pr.m. son of Abr. and Keturah, Gn 25[2] 1 Ch 1[32]; Σωυε, Σωε, Σουε.—In As *Šuḫi* is named as Aramaean land on Euphr. (left bank Tiele[Gesch 153] < right bank, cf. esp. Schr[KG 142f], it had, however, dependencies on left bank) by TP I. (KB[1 33]), Ašurnasirp. (Id.[Ib 99, 101]).

†II. שׁוּחָה n.pr. 'son' of חוּר, 1 Ch 4[11] (Ασχα, Σουα), = חֻשָׁה v[4] (Ωσαν, Ουσα), v. 'ח.

† שׁוּחִי, שֻׁחִי adj.gent. of שׁוּחַ (Hilpr[Assyriaca 1 (1894), 56] cp. As. ⁼*Su-ḫa-ai*),—בִּלְדַּד הַשֻּׁ׳ Jb 2[11] 8[1] 42[9]; 'הַשּׁ 18[1] 25[1]; ὁ Σαυχ(ε)ιτης, (Σαυχαιων).

† שׁוּחָם n.pr.m. in Dan, Nu 26[42], Σαμ(ε)ι, Σαμε; = II. חֻשִׁים, חוּשִׁים Gn 46[23], Ασομ.

† שׁוּחָמִי adj.gent. of foregoing; c. art. הַשּׁ׳ as n. coll Nu 26[42].

[יְשׁוֹחָיָה] n.pr.m. v. sub שׁחח.

†I. שׁוּט vb. go or rove about (NH Aram. שׁוּט *rove, row* (Jon 1[13]), *swim* (Is 25[11]), *stroke*,

besmear; v. also שׂוּם);—**Qal** *go* or *rove about*. *Pf* 3 pl., abs. שָׁטוּ הָעָם Nu 11[8] (J; gathering manna), so, c ב loc., *Impf* 3 mpl וַיָּשֻׁטוּ 2 S 24[8], *Imv* ms שׁוּט־נָא v[2], *Inf. cstr* שׁוּט Jb 1[7], שׁוּט 2[2] (both ‖ התהלך), perhaps also Gn 24[63] (לָשׂוּם for לָשׂוּחַ, so 𝔖 Thes [1322] cf Dr Gunk Dr), Je 8[6] Du reads שָׁט for שָׁב.—*Pt.* שָׁטִים v שׁוּט denom infr. **Pōl.** *go eagerly, quickly, to and fro*. *Impf* 3 ms ישׁטטו ישׁוטטו לבקשׁ Am 8[12] (‖ וְנָעוּ), abs. Dn 12[4], c ב loc, *Imv* mpl שׁוֹטְטוּ Je 5[1], *Pt.* pl מְשׁוֹטְטִים Zc 4[10], מְשׁוֹטְטוֹת 2 Ch 16[9] (both of עֵינֵי י׳) **Hithpōʿl.** *Imv* fpl., ב loc, הִתְשׁוֹטַטְנָה Je 49[3] *run to and fro*

†שׁוֹט **n.m.** [Is 28,15] **scourge, whip** (NH *id*, so Ar سَوْطٌ, سَاطَ (و) *mix, stir about and beat*, Eth ሰውጥ: Aram שׁוֹטָא, ܫܘܛܐ; from foregoing? cf Germ *streifen;* or onomat., cf *swish, switch?*),—שׁ׳ abs Is 10[26]+, cstr Jb 5[21], pl שׁוֹטִים 1 K 12[11]+,—**1.** *scourge*, for chastisement, 1 K 12[11.14] = 2 Ch 10[11.14] (all c. vb יִסַּר), fig of national scourge (wielded by י׳) Is 10[26] 28[15] (Qr, > Kt שׁיט), v[18] (both שׁ׳ שׁוֹטֵף, v. שׁטף), calamity Jb 9[23], *lash* of (accusing) tongue Jb 5[21] (rd מִשּׁ׳ as 𝔊) **2.** *whip*, for horse, קוֹל שׁ׳ Na 3[2] i.e *crack of whip*, שׁ׳ לַסּוּס Pr 26[3] (‖ שֵׁבֶט לְגֵו כְּסִילִים)

†שֹׁטֵט **n [m.] scourge**,—abs. שׁ׳ בְּצִדֵּיכֶם Jos 23[13] (D; national scourge, < rd שׁוֹטִים)

†שַׁיִט **n.[m.]** rowing (as *whipping, lashing* the water),—only אֳנִי־שׁ׳ Is 33[21] *rowing vessel;*—28[15] Kt v. שׁוט

†[שׁוּט] **vb.denom. row**,—*Pt* pl שָׁטִים *rowers* Ez 27[8.26] (of Tyre as ship)

†מָשׁוֹט **n.[m.]** oar,—תֹּפְשֵׂי מ׳ Ez 27[29].

†[מִשּׁוֹט] **n.[m.]** id, pl. sf. מְשׁוֹטַיִךְ Ez 27[6] (Ko [II 1.3], cf Ges [§72 e]), made of oak-trees.

†II [שׁוּט] **vb. treat with despite**, only Ezek (Aram שׁוּט, ܫܳܛ *despise*, cf perhaps As *šâtu, rebel*, Meissn),—only **Qal** *Pt*, c acc pers · mpl (subst) הַשָּׁאטִים אוֹתָם Ez 28[24.26] (Ko [II 1 108, 146] Ges [§72 p]), fpl. בְּנוֹת פְּלִשְׁתִּים הַשָּׁאטוֹת אוֹתָךְ 16[57] (Ko [ib 189])

†שְׁאָט **n.[m.] despite, contempt** (expanded fr שׁוּט supr, Ko [I 439 II 1.486]),—abs בִּשְׁ׳ בְּנֶפֶשׁ Ez 25[15] *with despite in the soul*, cstr בִּשְׁ׳ נֶפֶשׁ 36[5]; sf בְּכָל־שָׁאטְךָ בִּנ׳ 25[6] (Ges [§23 c] Ko [II 1 67]).

שׁול (√of foll, cf Ar. سَوِلَ *hang down loose*).

†[שׁוּל] **n.m.** [Is 6 1] **skirt**, of robe,—pl. cstr. שׁוּלֵי Ex 28[34]+, sf שׁוּלַיִךְ Na 3[5]+, שׁוּלָיו Is 6[1]+, שׁוּלֶיהָ La 1[9],—*skirts*, of י׳'s train, in vision Is 6[1]; elsewh of city personif. as woman, in phrase of ignominy, גִּלֵּיתִי שׁ׳ עַל־פָּנַיִךְ, חָשַׂפְתִּי שׁוּלַיִךְ Je 13[26], Na 3[5], נִגְלוּ שׁ׳ וגו׳ Je 13[22]; of defilement, טֻמְאָתָהּ בְּשׁ׳ La 1[9]; of high priest's robe Ex 28[33.33.34] = 39[24.25.26] (all P)

שׁוֹלָל v. שׁלל

†שׁוּלַמִּית usually expl. as **adj gent. f. Shulammite**,—c art as n. הַשּׁ׳ heroine of Song of Songs Ct 7[1], = Shunammite (from שׁוּנֵם, mod *Sulem*), B Σουμανεῖτις; but ℵ A Σουλαμιτις; ? cp Nab n pr.f שלימת = سَلِيمَة, سُلَيْمَة Lzb[376].

†[שׁוּם] **n.[m.]** garlic,—pl. שׁוּמִים Nu 11[5] (J) (*allium sativum*, Linn, Thes Low [No 336] Post [Hast DB II 110] Tristr [NHB 443] (or *allium Ascalonicum*, cf Buhl, after Tristr [FFP 430]; v. this and Post [Flora 789] for many kinds of *allium*), Ar. ثُومٌ, Aram תּוּמָא, ܬܘܡܐ, As. *šûmu*)

שָׁמָה v. שׁוּמָתִי infra

†שׁוּנִי **1. n.pr.m.** in Gad, Gn 46[16] Nu 26[15]; Σαυν(ε)ις, Σουνει, Σωυνι **2. adj.gent.** of **1**, c art = n. coll Nu 26[15].

†שׁוּנֵם **n.pr.loc.** in Issachar,—Jos 19[18] (P), 1 S 28[4] 2 K 4[8]; Σουναν[μ], Σωμαν, Σουμαν, 𝔊L Jos Συνημ; in Egypt *Ša-n-m-â, Ša-na-mą* WMM [As u Eur 170]; mod. *Sûlem*, N. of *Zerʿîn* (*Jezreel*), Buhl [G 217], cf GASm [G 400 ff].

†שׁוּנַמִּית **adj. gent. f.** of foregoing **1.** אֲבִישַׁג הַשּׁ׳ 1 K 1[3.15] 2[17.21] (הַשּׁ׳), v[22] (*id.*) **2.** הַשּׁ׳ 2 K 4[12.25.36]

†[שָׁוַע] **vb. Pi. cry out for help** (Gerb [33] thinks denom from שַׁוְעָה, and this from √akin to ישׁע *deliver*),—*Pf.* 1 s שִׁוַּעְתִּי ψ 30[3] + 3 t., *Impf.* 3 fs תְּשַׁוֵּעַ Jb 24[12], 2 ms. תְּשַׁוַּע Is 58[9], etc., *Inf cstr* sf שַׁוְּעִי ψ 28[2] 31[23]; שַׁוְעִי 5[3] (Ol [§182 d]), etc; *Pt.* מְשַׁוֵּעַ 72[12] Jb 29[12],—*cry for help:* abs ψ 72[12] Jb 19[7] 24[12] 29[12] 30[28] 35[9], + Is 38[13] Houb Lo Che Du al (for שׁויתי); specif. to God ψ 5[3] 18[42] 119[147] Jb 36[13] Is 58[9] Jon 2[3] Hb 1[2] La 3[8]; c. אֶל ψ 18[7] 22[25] 28[2] = 31[23], 30[3] 88[14] + v[2] (rd. with Weir אֱלֹהֵי שִׁוַּעְתִּי יוֹם צָעַקְתִּי), Jb 30[20] 38[41].

†I שׁוּעַ, [?שֶׁוַע] **n m. cry for help**,—לָהֵן שׁ׳ Jb 30[24] (Bi Di Bu Du לֹא יְשַׁוֵּעַ); שׁוּעֲךָ 36[19] (Bu Buhl שַׁוְעֲךָ, Du שִׁיחֲךָ).—I. שׁוּעַ v. p. 447[b].

†II. שׁוַע **n.[m.]** cry, perhaps *war-cry*, or *cry for help* in war Is 22^{5}.—I. שׁוע v. ישׁע.

†[שַׁוְעָה] **n.f. cry for help**;—cstr. שַׁוְעַת 1 S 5^{12} Je 8^{19}; sf. שַׁוְעָתִי 2 S 22^{7} = ψ 18^{7}, ψ 39^{13} 40^{2} 102^{2} La 3^{56} (gloss on רוחתי Ew al.); שַׁוְעָתָם Ex 2^{23} (P), ψ 34^{16} 145^{19}.

I. שׁוּעַ, I. II. שׁוַע, שׁוּעָא v. p. 447^{b} supra.

†III. שׁוֹעַ **n.pr.gent.** Ez 23^{23} usu. identified with As. *Sutû*, *Sutî*, nomads of Mesop. and (later) E. of Tigris, Dl$^{Pa\ 234\ ff.}$ COT$^{ad\ loc.}$ Wkl KAT 3. 22 Dr$^{Hast.\ DB\ Koa}$.

†[שׁוּף] **vb. bruise** (NH *id.*, Aram. שׁוּף, שְׁפַף, ܫܦ *rub off, away, grind* (Ex 32^{20} 𝔗𝔓 for טָחַן); v. esp. Dr^{Gn}; > Di al. think ‖ form of I. שׁאף);—**Qal** *Impf.* 3 ms. + 2 ms. הוּא יְשׁוּפְךָ אֲשֶׁר־בִּשְׂעָרָה יְשׁוּפֵנִי ראֹשׁ וְאַתָּה תְּשׁוּפֶנּוּ עָקֵב Gn 3^{15}; Jb 9^{17}; אַךְ חֹשֶׁךְ יְשׁוּפֵנִי ψ 139^{11} mng. unsuitable, read perh. c. Ew al. יְשׂוּכֵּנִי *cover, screen, me*.

שׁוֹפָךְ v. שׁוֹבָךְ. שׁוּפָמִי v. שְׁפוּפָם sub שׁפף.

I. שׁוק (√of foll., meaning dub.; Ar. سَاقَ is *drive* beast, etc., *carry on* affairs; Eth. ሰፍ: *sustain*; cf. Ar. سَاقٌ *leg*, esp. *shank*, Aram. שׁוֹקָא *leg* (rare), ܫܩܐ *leg, thigh*; connexion dub. with As. *suḳu*, *street*, Aram. שׁוּקָא, ܫܘܩܐ, *street, market-place* (whence Ar. سُوقٌ loan-word acc. to Frä^{187}; but then س = שׁ?), Palm. שׁוק *id.*, Lzb^{373}).

שׁוֹק$_{19}$ **n.**[**f.**$^{Lv\ 7,\ 33}$ cf. Albr$^{ZAW\ xvi\ (1896),\ 76\ f.}$, so Ar., v. Lane W$^{AG,\ §290\ (d)}$] **leg**;—שׁ׳ abs. 1 S 9^{24}+, cstr. Ex 29^{27}+; du. שֹׁקַיִם Dt 28^{35} Pr 26^{7}, cstr. שׁוֹקֵי ψ 147^{10}, sf. שׁוֹקָיו Ct 5^{15};—*leg*: **1.** of man, specif. lower leg, calf, disting. from thigh, in וַיַּךְ אוֹתָם שׁ׳ עַל־יָרֵךְ Ju 15^{8} *he smote them, leg upon thigh*, i.e. utterly (cf. GFM), Dt 28^{35} (‖ בִּרְכַּיִם), Pr 26^{7} ψ 147^{10} Ct 5^{15}; of woman (city personif.) Is 47^{2}. **2.** of sacrificial animal, specif. upper *leg*, thigh, *hind leg*, portion eaten 1 S 9^{24} (cf. Klein$^{ZPV\ vi\ (1883),\ 98}$, cited also by Nes$^{Marg.\ 13}$), שׁ׳ הַיָּמִין *right thigh* Ex 29^{22} + 6 t. P (v. יָמִין), שׁ׳ הַתְּרוּמָה Lv 7^{34} + 4 t. P, *thigh of contribution* (v. ת׳ p. 929).—𝔊 βραχίων, 𝔙 *armus*, hence AV al. *shoulder*, but v. Di Baen Dr$^{Dt\ 18,\ 3}$.

†שׁוּק **n.m. street** (Aram.; v. √);—שׁ׳ Pr 7^{8} Ec 12$^{4.5}$; pl. שְׁוָקִים Ct 3^{2}.

†II. [שׁוּק] **vb.** prob. **be abundant** (As. *šûḳu*, *abundance*);—**Pôl.** *Impf.* 3 ms. sf. וַתְּשֹׁקְקֶהָ ψ 65^{10} *thou* (י׳) hast visited the earth *and given it abundance* (Hup Che al.; > Vrss thought of הִשְׁקָה *irrigate*, so Bae EV). **Hiph.** *Pf.* consec. וְהֵשִׁיקוּ הַיְקָבִים תִּירוֹשׁ Jo 2^{24} *the vats overflow with must*, so (acc. om.) 4^{13}.

III. שׁוק (√of foll.; Ba$^{ES\ 46}$ cp. Ar. شَاقَ *attract, impel*, of desire, affection, شَوْقٌ *desire*, but ش = שׁ is doubtful; perhaps therefore (cf. Buhl) cp. سَاقَ *drive*, v. I. שׁוק; or rd. תְּשׁוּקָה; on NH שׁוק, השתוקק, v. Nes$^{ZAW\ xxiv\ (1904),\ 312\ ff.}$).

†[תְּשׁוּקָה] **n.f. longing**;—of woman for man, אֶל־אִישֵׁךְ תְּשׁוּקָתֵךְ Gn 3^{16} (J); of man for woman, אֲנִי לְדוֹדִי וְעָלַי תְּשׁוּקָתוֹ Ct 7^{11}; of beast to devour, fig. אֵלֶיךָ תְּשׁוּקָתוֹ Gn 4^{7} (J). (𝔊 ἀποστροφή Gn, ἐπιστροφή Ct, whence Nes$^{Marg.\ 6}$ prop. תְּשׁוּבָתֵךְ Gn 3^{16}, which Ball^{Hpt} reads in all; but how explain the unusual and striking word in MT?).

†I. [שׁוּר] **vb.** perh. **travel, journey** (As. *šâru*, *pass along, take one's way*, Ar. سَارَ (ى) *go, pass along, journey*, سَيَّارَةٌ *caravan*, Palm. שירתא Lzb^{375} SAC^{113} Cooke^{271}, Syr. ܫܝܪܬܐ (?Ar. loan-wd., Frä^{180}));—**Qal** *Impf.* 2 fs. וַתָּשֻׁרִי לַמֶּלֶךְ בַּשֶּׁמֶן Is 57^{9} *and thou* (the apostate faction) *didst journey to* (the god) *Melek with* (thine) *oil*, i.e. bring, offer it (Che Marti read וַתָּסֹכִּי). *Pt.* fpl. שָׁרוֹתַיִךְ Ez 27^{25} ships of Tarshish were *thy travellers* (i.e. traders), but improbable; Krae שָׁרוֹת לָךְ בְּ *journey for thee* with thy wares; Toy רֹכְלַיִךְ בְּ; Co שֵׁרְתוּךְ *served thee*.

†תְּשׁוּרָה **n.f. gift, present**(?) (fr. above √ = thing brought, offered? very dubious);—ת׳ 1 S 9^{7} (meaning inferred from context).

†II. [שׁוּר] **vb. behold, regard** (esp. Jb);—**Qal** *Impf.* 3 ms. יָשׁוּר Je 5^{26}, sf. יְשׁוּרֶנּוּ Jb 34^{29}, etc.; *Imv.* ms. שׁוּר Jb 35^{5};—**1.** *behold*, c. acc. pers. Nu 23^{9} 24^{17} (poems in JE, ‖ רָאָה), לֹא תְשׁוּרֵנִי, subj. eye, Jb 24^{15}, and (= I shall not exist) 7^{8}, cf. 20^{9} (subj. מְקוֹמוֹ), 17^{15}; God object 34^{29} 35^{14}; *look, gaze*, abs., מִן loc. Ct 4^{8}. **2.** *regard* with watchful care (subj. י׳) Ho 14^{9}; so, = *notice*, Jb 35^{13}; *regard, observe*, acc. rei, God's word Jb 33^{14} (Hi De Da al.), so, (reading 2 ms.), Siegf Bu; Du יְשִׁיבֶנּוּ *he* (God) *retracts it not*. **3.** *watch* stealthily, *lie in wait*, כְּנָמֵר עַל־דֶּרֶךְ אָשׁוּר Ho 13^{7} (subj. י׳; Meinh Marti אַשְׁקֹד; 𝔊𝔖𝔙 We Now al. אַשּׁוּר), Je 5^{26} (subj. wicked).—Jb 33^{27} v. שִׁיר.

†I. [שׁוּר] dub word, only pl. sf. וַתַּבֵּט עֵינִי בְּשׁוּרָי ψ 92[12], read בְּשׁוֹרְרַי (Bae al.) v. foll.

†[שׁוֹרֵר] **n.m.** (insidious) **watcher**, (prop. **Pōʿl.** *Pt*, מְ׳ om, Ges[§52 s]),—pl. sf. שׁוֹרְרַי ψ 56[3], שׁוֹרְרָי 5[9] 27[11], שֹׁרְרָי 54[7] 59[11], 92[12] v. foregoing.

III שׁור (√of foll, Ar. ثَارَ (و) is *become raised, excited, leap, spring;* NH שׁוֹר = BH, = Sab (ן)תור SabDenkm[No. 12. 1. 3] DHM[ZMG xxxvii (1883), 379], Ar ثَوْرٌ, Aram תּוֹרָא, ܬܘܪܐ, Nab תורא as n pr m. Lzb[384] (Gk ταῦρος, Lat *taurus*, Eng. *steer*), As *šûru*, Eth ሰር:)

שׁוֹר[78] **n.m.**[Ne 5 18] **a head of cattle**, bullock, ox, etc (oft + חֲמוֹר, שֶׂה, etc), —שׁ׳ abs Is 1[3]+, cstr. Ex 21[35]+, sf שׁוֹרוֹ 20[17]+, etc, pl. שְׁוָרִים Ho 12[2],—usu a single *head of cattle*, without emphasis on sex (opp בָּקָר coll Ex 21[37] Nu 7[3]) as property, spoil of war, etc Ex 20[17] (E; Gi v[14]) = Dt 5[18], cf. Dt 5[14], Ex 21[33] (E) ‖ Dt 22[4], Ex 21[37 37] (‖ בָּקָר of five head), 22[3 8.9 29] 23[12] (all E), Dt 22[1] Gn 49[6] (poem in J), Dt 28[31] Ju 6[4] 1 S 12[3] Jb 24[3]; as *licking up* (לָחַךְ) grass Nu 22[4] (J), feeding ψ 106[20] (in ref to golden calf), cf. Is 7[25] 32[20]; lowing Jb 6[5], as intelligent Is 1[3], vicious (goring נָגַח) Ex 21[28 28 29] + 11 t. Ex 21 (E), used in ploughing Dt 22[10], threshing 25[4], cf Pr 14[4]; drawing wagon Nu 7[3] (P, opp בָּקָר coll), פְּנֵי שׁ׳ Ez 1[10], specif of male †Jb 21[10] (opp. פָּרָה), of female †Lv 22[28] (H), perhaps also Nu 18[17] (P), appar generic Dt 15[19] 33[17] (poem, fig), rarely coll Gn 32[6] (+ צֹאן), Ex 34[19]—cf Lv 27[26] (P)—Jos 6[21] 7[24] (all J), 1 S 15[3] 22[19], †as slaughtered Pr 7[22], for food 1 S 14[34.34] (but v[b] read אֲשֶׁר (את־) with 𝔊 Th We Dr al), 1 K 1[19 25] Dt 14[4] Lv 17[3] (H), cf Ne 5[18] (שׁ׳ אֶחָד), Pr 15[17], for †sacrifice Ju 6[25] (פַּר־הַשּׁ׳, text strange, cf. GFM), ψ 69[32] (שׁוֹר פָּר, but join פָּר to v[b] Bae), 2 S 6[13] Ho 12[12], Lv 9[4 18] (P), 22[23.27] (H), Nu 15[11] (P), Dt 17[1] 18[3], cf Lv 7[23] 9[19]; זֶבַח מִשּׁוֹר Lv 4[10] (P); illicit sacrifice Is 66[3].

†II שׁוּר **n.[m.] wall** (Aram. שׁוּרָא, ܫܘܪܐ);—Gn 49[22] (poem in J), 2 S 22[30] = ψ 18[30]; pl sf. שׁוּרֹתָם Jb 24[11] *their walls* De Di De, cf Bu, but v שׁוּרָה infra; שָׁרוֹתֶיהָ Je 5[10] = *its walls*, acc to Vrss AV RV Gf Gie, read then שָׁ׳, but v. id

†III. שׁוּר **n.pr.loc.** SW of Palestine, on E. border of Egypt,—Gn 16[7] (J; דֶּרֶךְ שׁ׳), 20[1] (E), towards Egypt 25[18] (J), 1 S 15[7], שׁוּרָה 27[8], מִדְבַּר־שׁ׳ Ex 15[22] (J)—Oft. supposed to denote properly the 'wall' or line of fortresses, built by Egyptian kings across isthmus of Suez; but dub: cf. Dr[Hast DB Shur].

†[שׁוּרָה] **n.f.** prob. **row** of olives or vines (so Du Buhl al.; cf. NH שׁוּרָה, JAram. שׁוּרְתָא *row*, whence mod Ar. شُورَة as loan-word, cf. Vogelst[Landwirthschaft 41 f]),—pl. sf. שׁוּרֹתָם Jb 24[11] (al II. שׁוּר), Bu and Du del. sf; here also Je 5[10] (reading שׁ׳) Du Buhl Dr, *her* (vine-)*rows*, but v. II שׁוּר.

שַׁוְשָׁא **n.pr.m.** 1 Ch 18[16], v. שְׂרָיָה.

†I שׁוּשַׁן, שׁוֹשַׁן **n.m.** שׁוֹשַׁנָּה **n.f.** usually **lily**, prob any lily-like flower (Tristi[NHB 462 ff] Post[Hast DB Lily] Low[No 323]; NH שׁוֹשַׁנָּה, Ar. سَوْسَن (Vulg سُوسَن), esp *iris*, Aram. שׁוֹשַׁנְתָּא, ܫܘܫܢܬܐ (PS[4344]), Gk. σοῦσον Lewy[Fremdw 48], orig loan-word from Egypt. *sššn*, *šošen*, Erman[ZMG xlvi (1892), 117]),—*lily:* in sim., יִפְרַח כַּשּׁוֹשַׁנָּה Ho 14[7] (of Isr), כְּשׁוֹ׳ בֵּין הַחוֹחִים Ct 2[2] (sim. of bride), so cstr. שׁוֹשַׁנַּת הָעֲמָקִים v[1] (cf. חֲבַצֶּלֶת); pl. שׁוֹשַׁנִּים 2[16] 4[5] 6[2.3] 7[3] and (fig of lover's lips) 5[13], of flower-shaped capitals of pillars, מַעֲשֵׂה שׁוּשַׁן 1 K 7[19], מ׳ שׁוֹשָׁן v[22], cf. פֶּרַח שׁוֹשָׁן of brim of molten sea v[26], ‖ פ׳ שׁוֹשַׁנָּה 2 Ch 4[5], elsewh only ψ-titles: אֶל־שֹׁשַׁנִּים ψ 45[1] 69[1], עַל־שׁוּשַׁן עֵדוּת 60[1], עֵדוּת 80[1]; meaning not clear, v Bae et Comm al; yet cf. עֵדוּת, sub עוד.

†II שׁוּשַׁן **n.pr.loc. Susa**, winter residence of Persian kings; Σουσαν, ἐν Σουσοις (cuneif. *Šûšan* Dl[Pa 326] COT[Ne 1, 1] Billerbeck[Susa] Say[Hast. DB Shushan]),—שׁ׳ הַבִּירָה Ne 1[1] (9th month, כִּסְלֵו), Dn 8[2] (in Elam), Est 1[2.5] 2[3.5.8] 3[15a] 8[14] 9[6 11 12] (12th month, אֲדָר, v[1]); הַבִּ׳ om., שׁוּשָׁן Est 4[8 16] and (month אֲדָר) 9[13 14 15 15 18]; הָעִיר שׁ׳ 3[15b] 8[15].

†שׁוּשַׁק **n.pr.m.** 1 K 14[25] Kt, Qr שִׁישַׁק q.v.

שׁוּת v שִׁית.

†שׁוּתֶלַח **n.pr.m.** in Ephraim, Nu 26[35] 1 Ch 7[21], שׁוּתָלַח v[20] Nu 26[36]; Σουταλα, Σωθαλα, etc, 𝔊L Σουθαλα(αμ).

†שֻׁתַלְחִי **adj.gent.** of foregoing; c. art. הַשּׁ׳ as subst. coll Nu 26[35].

†[שָׁזַף] **vb. catch sight of, look on** (of eye),—**Qal** *Pf* 3 fs sf. pers, subj עַיִן, שְׁזָפַתּוּ Jb 20[9], so (rei) 28[7], cf. שֶׁשְּׁזָפַתְנִי הַשָּׁמֶשׁ Ct 1[6] *because the sun hath looked on me.*

[שָׁזַר][21] **vb. Hoph. be twisted** (NH שָׁזַר *twist*, cf Ar. شَزَرَ *look askew at*, also *twist* cord

from the left Ba$^{ES\,49}$ (expl. שׂ, for normal שׁ, as dissim. before ז), Jacob$^{Ar.\ Dichter\ I.\ 52}$);—*Pt.* שֵׁשׁ מָשְׁזָר Ex 26$^{1.31.36}$ + 17 t. Ex (P); שֵׁשׁ om. 39^{24}.

שַׁח v. שחח.

†[שָׁחַד] **vb. give a present, bribe** (Ecclus 35^{14}; Aram. שְׁחַד, ܫܚܕ *bribe;* perh. also As. *šidê, gifts,* Dl$^{WB\,643}$);—**Qal** *Impf.* 2 fs., acc. pers. וַתִּשְׁחֳדִי אוֹתָם Ez 16^{33} *thou didst bribe them* to come (לָבוֹא; ‖ נָתַן נְדָנִים); rd. prob. also *Inf. cstr.* sf. שַׁחְדָהּ Is 47^{11} *to buy it off* (for MT שַׁחְרָהּ, so Kr Gr Buhl Che$^{Hpt\ Heb\ 142}$, cf. Marti; v. Pr 6^{35}); *Imv.* mpl. שִׁחֲדוּ בַּעֲדִי (Ges §64a) Jb 6^{22} *give a bribe for me.*

†שֹׁחַד **n.m. present, specif. bribe**;—שׁ׳ abs. Is 1^{23} + 22 t.;—*bribe,* usu. to pervert justice, obj. of לָקַח Ex 23^{8a} (E), = Dt 16^{19a}, Dt 10^{17} 1 S 8^{3} 2 Ch 19^{7} ψ 15^{5} Pr 17^{23}; + inf., take *bribe* to do something, Dt 27^{25} Ez 22^{12}; אֹהֵב שׁ׳ Is 1^{23}; cf. also 5^{23} 33^{15} Ex 23^{8b} (E) = Dt 16^{19b}, Mi 3^{11} ψ 26^{10} Pr 17^{8} 21^{14}; אָהֳלֵי־שׁ׳ Jb 15^{34}, i.e. abode of bribe-givers; שׁ׳ Pr 6^{35} (‖ כֹּפֶר) is hush-money, or (poss.) legal compensation (cf. Toy); שׁ׳ elsewh. (c. שָׁלַח) of bribing king to take sides 1 K 15^{19} 2 K 16^{8}, cf. Is 45^{13} (‖ מְחִיר).

[שָׁחָה]$_{172}$ **vb. bow down** (NH *id.;* JAram. שְׁחִי (rare); akin to שׁוּחַ, שׁוּחַ, שׁחח);—**Qal** *Imv.* fs. שְׁחִי Is 51^{23} *bow down.* **Hiph.** *Impf.* 3 ms. sf. יַשְׁחֶנָּה Pr 12^{25}, fig., anxiety *depresses it* (sc. לֵב; opp. שִׂמַּח). **Hithpa'lel**$_{170}$ (Ges §75kk) *Pf.* 3 ms. הִשְׁתַּחֲוָה Ez 46^{2}; 2 ms. הִשְׁתַּחֲוִיתָ Dt 4^{19} + 3 t.; 1 s. הִשְׁתַּחֲוֵיתִי 1 S 16^{4} + 2 t.; 3 mpl. הִשְׁתַּחֲווּ Je 8^{2}, etc.; *Impf.* יִשְׁתַּחֲוֶה 2 S 15^{32} + 3 t.; apoc. יִשְׁתָּחוּ Is 44^{17} +; 3 mpl. יִשְׁתַּחֲווּ Gn 49^{8} +; 2 fpl. תִּשְׁתַּחֲוֶיןָ Gn 33^{6} 37^{7}, etc.; *Imv.* fs. הִשְׁתַּחֲוִי ψ 45^{12}; mpl. הִשְׁתַּחֲווּ 29^{2} +; *Inf. cstr.* הִשְׁתַּחֲוֹת Gn 37^{10} +; sf. הִשְׁתַּחֲוָיָתִי 2 K 5^{18} (but 𝔊 𝔙 and mod. -חֲוֹתִי); *Pt.* מִשְׁתַּחֲוֶה 2 K 19^{37}, etc.; מִשְׁתַּחֲוִיתֶם Ez 8^{16}, read -וִים all mod.;—**1.** *bow down, prostrate oneself,* before a monarch or superior, in homage, etc.: **a.** c. לְ, after descriptive cl. (esp. with נפל, קדד **3 b**, q. v.), 1 S 24^{9} Gn 43^{28} (J) 2 S 14$^{4.22}$ Ru 2^{10} 1 K 1^{31} 2 K 4^{37} + 6 t., + (after כָּרַע) Est 3$^{2.2.5}$. **b.** c. לְ, sq. phr. (לפני) על אפים ארצה 2 S 14^{33} 1 K 1^{23}; לאפים Gn 48^{12} (E) 2 S 18^{28}; אפים Gn 42^{6} (E) + 4 t.; om. אפים 33^{3} (J) + 3 t.; על כַּפּוֹת רַגְלַיִךְ Is 60^{14}. **c.** c. לְ pers. only, Gn 23^{7} (P) 27$^{29.29}$ 37^{9} (E), 49^{8} Ex 11^{8} (J) + 8 t.; c. לפני Gn 23^{12} (P); c. אל Is 45^{14} (‖ התפלל); abs. Gn 33$^{6.7.7}$ (J), Ex 18^{7} (E) 2 S 9^{8} 16^{4} Is 49^{7}. **2.** before God, in worship, etc.: **a.** c. לְ, after descriptive phr.: קדד ארצה Ex 34^{8} (J); ארצה om. Gn 24$^{26.48}$ (J) + 4 t.; כרע אפים ארצה 2 Ch 7^{3}; כרע 29^{29}; נפל ארצה Jb 1^{20}; נפל לפני 2 Ch 20^{18}. **b.** sq. phr.: קדד ויש׳ ל׳ אפים ארצה Ne 8^{6}; ארצה ל׳ Gn 24^{52} (J); השׁ׳ ונכרעה ψ 95^{6}; השׁ׳ ל׳ בְּהַדְרַת קֹדֶשׁ 29^{2} 96^{9} = 1 Ch 16^{29}; אֶל־הֵיכַל (looking towards) ψ 5^{8} 138^{2}; לַהֲדֹם רגלים 99^{5} 132^{7}. **c.** c. לְ only: 1 S 1^{28} (but read וַתִּשְׁתַּחוּ 𝔊 and mod.), 15^{25} Je 7^{2} ψ 66^{4} + 9 t.; c. לפני Dt 26^{10} Is 66^{23} + 4 t.; c. בְּ loc. Is 27^{13}; c. לְ loc. ψ 99^{9}; abs. Gn 22^{5} (E) Ju 7^{15} + 5 t.; acc. loc. Ex 33^{10} (E) Je 26^{2} Ez 46^{3}; לפני (ה)מזבח Is 36^{7} = 2 K 18^{22} = 2 Ch 32^{12}; c. על loc. Gn 47^{31} (J) 1 K 1^{47} Ez 46^{2}; מֵרָחֹק *afar off* Ex 24^{1} (E). **d.** before angel in theoph.: after cl. c. קדד, נפל, Jos 5^{14} Nu 22^{31}; sq. אפים ארצה Gn 19^{1}; ארצה 18^{2} (all J). **3.** before other gods: abs. Is 2^{20} 44$^{15.17}$ 46^{6}; acc. loc. 2 K 5$^{18.18.18}$ 19^{37} = Is 37^{38}; c. לְ, Ex 20^{5} = Dt 5^{9} (10 words), Ex 23^{24} (E), Nu 25^{2} (J), Jos 23^{7} (D), Dt 8^{19} 11^{16} 1 K 16^{31} + 34 t.; c. על, Lv 26^{1} (H); לפני 2 Ch 25^{14} (‖ קטר).

†[שְׁחוּת] **n.f. pit** (cf. שַׁחַת from שׁוח);—sf. בִּשְׁחוּתוֹ הוּא יִפּוֹל Pr 28^{10}.

†[שְׁחִית] **n.f.** id.;—pl. sf. נִלְכַּד בִּשְׁחִיתוֹתָם La 4^{20}, וַיְמַלֵּט מִשּׁ׳ ψ 107^{20}.

שִׁיחוֹר v. שִׁחוֹר. שְׁחוֹר v. I. שחר.

†[שָׁחַח] **vb. bow, be bowed down, crouch** (NH *id.;* TelAm. *šaḫâhu* (Wkl$^{TelAm.\ Vocab.}$), *prostrate oneself,* prob. Canaanism; As. *šaḫâḫu* is *oppress, torment*);—**Qal** *Pf.* 3 ms. consec. וְשַׁח Is 2$^{11.17}$, 1 s. שַׁחוֹתִי ψ 38^{7}, שַׁחֹתִי 35^{14}, 3 pl. שָׁחֲחוּ Jb 9^{13}, שַׁחוּ Hb 3^{6} Pr 14^{19}; *Impf.* 3 ms. יָשֹׁחַ ψ 10^{10}, 3 mpl. יָשֹׁחוּ Jb 38^{40}, וַיָּשֹׁחוּ ψ 107^{39}; *Inf. cstr.* (= *abs.*, as adv., Ges §118q Kö$^{II.\ 2,\ §§\ 221,\ 402d}$ cf. also Ba$^{NB\,164}$) שְׁחוֹחַ Is 60^{14};—**1.** *be bowed down, prostrated, humbled,* by י׳, Is 2$^{11.17}$ (both ‖ שָׁפֵל), Hb 3^{6} (of hills), Jb 9^{13} (תַּחְתָּיו שׁ׳), ψ 107^{39} (+ מָעַט); by man 10^{10}. **2.** *bow* in homage, לִפְנֵי pers. Pr 14^{19}; וְהָלְכוּ אֵלַיִךְ שְׁחוֹחַ Is 60^{14} (‖ הִשְׁתַּחֲווּ). **3.** *bow,* of mourner (קֹדֵר), ψ 35^{14} 38^{7}. **4.** *crouch,* of wild beast in lair Jb 38^{40}. **Niph.** *Impf. be prostrated, humbled:* וַיִּשַּׁח אָדָם Is 2^{9} (‖ שָׁפֵל) = 5^{15} (‖ *id.*); *be reduced, weakened,* וְיִשַּׁחוּ כָּל־בְּנוֹת הַשִּׁיר Ec 12^{4}; = *proceed humbly,* of words מֵעָפָר תִּשַּׁח Is 29^{4} (‖ שָׁפֵל). **Hiph.** *prostrate, lay low,* city, walls, etc.; *Pf.* 3 ms. הֵשַׁח Is 25^{12}

26[5] (both ‖ הִשְׁפִּיל). **Hithpō‘.** *be cast down, despairing: Impf.* 3 fs. תִּשְׁתּוֹחֵח ψ 42[7], 2 fs. תִּשְׁתּוֹחֲחִי v[6.12] 43[5] (all c. subj. נַפְשִׁי).

†**שַׁח** **adj.** low, lowly;—cstr. שַׁח־עֵינַיִם Jb 22[29] *lowly of eyes,* humble.

†[**יְשׁוֹחָיָה**] **n.pr.m.** in Simeon (mng.?);—וישׁ׳ 1 Ch 4[36]; Ιασουια, Ιεσουια.

שָׁחַט[84] **vb.** slaughter, beat (orig. *beat, flay*? cf. As. *šaḫâṭu, flay, take off* dress; Ar. سَحَطَ *slay* (but ح=ḥ; is this loan-word in Ar.?); NH=BH, esp. in ritual);—**Qal** *Pf.* 3 ms. שׁ׳ Je 39[6]+, sf. וּשְׁחָטוֹ consec. Lv 3[2], etc.; *Impf.* 3 ms. יִשְׁחַט Lv 4[24]+, 2 fs. וַתִּשְׁחֲטִי Ez 16[21], 3 mpl. sf. וַיִּשְׁחָטוּהוּ Ju 12[6]; *Imv.* mpl. שַׁחֲטוּ Ex 12[21] 2 Ch 35[6]; *Inf. abs.* שָׁחֹט Is 22[13]; cstr. לִשְׁחֹט Gn 22[10], ־וֹט Ez 40[39], sf. שַׁחֲטָם (Ges[§ 64 a]) Ez 23[39]; *Pt. act.* שׁוֹחֵט Is 66[3], etc.; *pass.* שָׁחוּט 1 K 10[16]+, etc.;—*slaughter:* **1.** beast for food 1 S 14[32.34.34] Is 22[13] (‖הָרֹג), cf. Lv 17[3.3], for blood Gn 37[31] (E). **2.** usu. (51 t.; Hex only P, 38 t.) term. techn. of *killing* sacrifice (BJacob[ZAW xvii (1897), 51]), 1 S 1[25] Ex 29[11] Lv 1[5.11] 4[24] 9[3] Nu 19[3] 2 Ch 29[22.22.24]+; abs. Ez 40[41] (אֶל loc.); bird Lv 14[5.6.50.51]; beast in illicit sacrifice Is 66[3]; c. acc. of sacrifice (עוֹלָה, חַטָּאת, אָשָׁם, etc.) Ez 40[39] (אֶל loc.), v[42] 44[11] Lv 4[24] 7[2] 14[13]+; passover lamb †Ex 12[6], acc. הַפֶּסַח †v[21] 2 Ch 30[15] 35[1.6.11] Ezr 6[20]. **3.** *slaughter* pers. Ju 12[6] 1 K 18[40] 2 K 10[7.14] (אֶל loc.), 2 K 25[7]=Je 39[6a]=52[10a], Je 39[6b]=52[10b], 41[7]; ׳ subj. Nu 14[16] (JE); in human sacrifice Gn 22[10] (E), to false gods Ez 16[21] 23[39] Is 57[5]. **4.** pt. pass. =*beaten, hammered,* זָהָב שָׁחוּט 1 K 10[16.17]=2 Ch 9[15a.16], of shekels 2 Ch 9[15b]; so also Je 9[7] Qr חֵץ שָׁחוּט (>Kt שׁוֹחֵט) *hammered* (i.e. sharpened) *arrow.* †**Niph.** *Impf.* 3 ms. יִשָּׁחֵט Nu 11[22] (J) *be slaughtered* for food (subj. beast); 3 fs. תִּשָּׁחֵט Lv 6[18.18] (P) *be slain,* of sacrifice.

†[**שְׁחִיטָה**] **n.f.** act of **slaying**;—cstr. שְׁחִיטַת הַפְּסָחִים 2 Ch 30[17].

†**שַׁחֲטָה** **n.f.** (**Qal** *Inf. cstr.* Kö[i. 263]) doubtful word;—וְשׁ׳ שֵׂטִים הֶעְמִיקוּ Ho 5[2] RV (cf. AV) *the revolters are gone deep in slaughtering* [‘Opferschlächterei’ Kö[ii. 1. 590, n. 1]], Ew Now (formerly), Che *in corrupting* (rd. then שַׁחֲתָה); We Now GASm Marti שַׁחַת הַשִּׁטִּים *have made deep the pit of Shiṭṭim* (as place of idolatry).

שְׁחִין v. שׁחן. **שְׁחִיף** v. [שָׁחִיף].

†**שָׁחִיס** Is 37[30]=סָחִישׁ (in ‖ 2 K 19[29]), q. v.

†**שׁחל** (√of foll.; Dl[Prol. 34] cp. As. *šaḫâlu, call, proclaim;* perh. both onomatop., as Ar. سَحَلَ *bray* (of ass), cf. Nö[ZMG xl (1886), 725]).

שַׁחַל **n.m.** lion (poet.);—abs. שׁ׳ Ho 5[14]+, שָׁחַל Jb 4[10]+;—*lion,* sim. of ^, toward Israel Ho 5[14] (‖ כְּפִיר), 13[7] (‖ נָמֵר); of guilty men Jb 4[10] (‖ אַרְיֵה, כְּפִירִים); fig. of foes ψ 91[13] (‖ כְּפִיר); *lion,* as hunted 10[16] (in sim.); lit. Jb 28[8] Pr 26[13].

†**שְׁחֵלֶת** **n.f.** an ingredient of the holy incense, +נָטָף, חֶלְבְּנָה, Ex 30[34]; 𝔊𝔙 ὄνυξ, *onyx* (whence AV *onycha*), i.e. *unguis odoratus,* the *operculum,* or closing-flap, of certain molluscs, with pungent odour when burnt, v. Thes[1388 f.] Di Shipley-Cook[Ency. Bib. ONYCHA]; so most; KG Jacob[ZMG xliii (1889), 354] prop. *amber.*

שׁחן (√of foll.; cf. Ar. سَخُنَ *be hot,* then *inflamed;* Aram. שְׁחַן, ܫܚܢ *be warm, heat*).

†**שְׁחִין** **n.m.** boil, coll. eruption;—on man 2 K 20[7]=Is 38[21], שׁ׳ רָע Dt 28[35] Jb 2[7]; possibly leprous Lv 13[18.19.20], צָרֶבֶת הַשׁ׳ 13[23] (v. צ׳; all P), in Egypt, on man and beast Ex 9[9.10.11.11] (all P), cstr. שְׁחִין מִצְרַיִם Dt 28[27].

שׁחף (√of שַׁחֶפֶת and poss. of שַׁחַף; Ar. سَحَفَ is *pare, peel off;* also *affect with consumption* of lungs; سُحَافٌ *consumption,* so JAram. שַׁחַפְתָּא [for שַׁחֶפֶת]).

†[**שַׁחַף**] **n.[m.]** prob. **sea-mew, gull** (cf. 𝔊𝔙) (from *attenuated* body, Thes); so Post[Hast. DB Cuckow] Tristr[NHB 210 ff.]; *sterna fluviatilis,* or *tern* Id[FFP 135] M‘Lean-Shipley[Ency. Bib. ID.];—הַשָּׁחַף Dt 14[15]=Lv 11[16] (P), in list of unclean birds.

†**שַׁחֶפֶת** **n.f.** wasting disease, **consumption** Dt 28[22] Lv 26[16] (H).

שׁחץ (√of foll.; cf. NH *act proudly,* and deriv.; Aram. שַׁחְצָא *lion* (†ψ 17[12] edd.); Eth. ሦሐጸ: *be insolent;* Ar. شَخَصَ is *rise, be elevated;* شَخِيصٌ *bulky, man of rank,* but ش=שׁ?).

†[**שַׁחַץ**] **n.[m.]** dignity, pride;—בְּנֵי־הַשָּׁחַץ i.e. majestic wild beasts Jb 28[8] (‖ שָׁחַל), 41[26].

†**שחצומה** Kt, **שַׁחֲצִימָה** Qr (i.e. [שְׁחָצִים] +ה ָ) **n.pr.loc.** in Issachar Jos 19[22]; ἐπὶ Σαλειμ κατὰ θάλασσαν, A𝔊L Σασειμα(θ).

†[**שָׁחַק**] **vb.** rub away, beat fine, pulverize (so Ar. سَحَقَ, سَحْقٌ *worn garment, thin clouds;* Aram. שְׁחַק, ܫܚܩ *pulverize;* Ecclus

שחק 6^{34} is *go often* (wear by treading), Str cp. *iter terere*);—**Qal** *Pf* 3 pl. אֲבָנִים שָׁחֲקוּ מַיִם Jb 14^{19} *waters rub away stones;* 2 ms. וְשָׁחַקְתָּ Ex 30^{36} (P; of pulverizing incense, v. דקק **Hiph.**); fig., acc. of foes, *Impf.* 1 s. sf. וְאֶשְׁחָקֵם 2 S 22^{43} (‖ ארקם)=ψ 18^{43}.

†שַׁחַק **n.m.** $^{Pr 3, 20}$ **dust, cloud** (as fine, thin);—ש׳ abs. ψ 89$^{7.38}$, cstr. Is 40^{15}; pl. שְׁחָקִים Dt 33^{26}+;—**1.** *fine dust,* ש׳ מֹאזְנַיִם Is 40^{15} (sim. of insignif.). **2.** (thin) *cloud,* usu pl (oft. ‖ שָׁמַיִם), Dt 33^{26} (poem), Is 45^{8} Je 51^{9} Jb 35^{5} 36^{28} 37^{21} 38^{37} ψ 36^{6} 57^{11} 68^{35} 77^{18} 78^{23} 108^{5}; opp. תְּהוֹם Pr 3^{20} 8^{28}; עָבֵי ש׳ 2 S 22^{12}=ψ 18^{12}; =heavens, sky Jb 37^{18} (c. הרקיע), and (sg.) ψ 89$^{7.38}$.

שְׁחוֹר v. שִׁיחוֹר.

†I. שָׁחַר **vb. be black** (NH שָׁחוֹר and deriv., *black, blackness,* etc., Ecclus 25^{17} Hiph. *make black;* Aram. שְׁחַר (Jastr Dalm), Aph *grow black,* so ܫܚܪ, ܫܚܘܪܐ *coal;* Jager $^{BAS ii. 293}$ cp. As *šûru, coal, šurinnu, fire-pot*);—ש׳, of skin Jb 30^{30}.

†שְׁחוֹר **n.[m.]** blackness;—חָשַׁךְ מִשּׁ׳ תָּאֳרָם La 4^{8}.

†שָׁחֹר **adj.** black,—ש׳ of hair Lv 13$^{31.37}$(P), so fpl. שְׁחֹרוֹת Ct 5^{11}, of skin, fs. שְׁחוֹרָה 1^{5}; of horses, mpl. שְׁחֹרִים Zc 6$^{2.6}$.

†שַׁחֲרוּת **n.f.** acc. to De^{Comm} Ruetschi^{Kau} **blackness,** viz. of hair (so 𝔗), i.e. (RV) *prime of life* (which Wild allows); usu. **dawn** of youth (II. שחר);—Ec 11^{10} (+ יַלְדוּת).

†[שְׁחַרְחֹר Ges$^{§84b\,n}$] **adj. blackish** (Gann $^{JAS 1864, Fev.-Mars, 156, no. 41}$, cp Isr. n pr. שחרחר on seal =' le brun');—f. שְׁחַרְחֹרֶת Ct 1^{6}.

†אַשְׁחוּר **n.pr.m.** in Judah, called אֲבִי תְקוֹעַ 1 Ch 2^{24} 4^{5}; Ασχω, Σαρα; A Ασδωδ, Ασχουρ; 𝔊L Ασσωρ, Ασωρ.

II. שחר (√ of foll.; MI^{15} שחרת, Ar. سَحَرٌ, As. *šêru*, NH שַׁחַר, Aram. שַׁחְרָא all *dawn*).

†שַׁחַר **n.m.** $^{Gn 19, 15}$ **dawn**;—abs. ש׳ 1 S 9^{26}+, שָׁחַר Ju 19^{25}+; sf. שַׁחְרָהּ Is 47^{11} (but read prob. שַׁחֲרָהּ);—*dawn,* c עָלָה *rise* Gn 19^{15} 32$^{25.27}$ Jos 6^{15} (all J), Ju 19^{25} 1 S 9^{26} Ne 4^{15} Jon 4^{7}; opp. עֵיפָה Am 4^{13}; as adv. *at dawn* ψ 57^{9}=108^{3}; עַפְעַפֵּי־שׁ׳ Jb 3^{9} 41^{10}; כַּנְפֵי־שׁ׳ ψ 139^{9}, 110^{3} rd. prob. רֶחֶם שׁ׳ (v. מִשְׁחָר infr.); ש׳ also Jb 38^{12}, in sim. Ho 6^{3} (but rd. כְּשַׁחֲרֵנוּ כֵּן נִמְצָאֵהוּ as inf., v. following, Gie $^{Beitr 208}$ We Now GASm Marti), Is 58^{8} Ct 6^{10}, Jo 2^{2} (al. *blackness,* ‖ עָנָן וַעֲרָפֶל); בֶּן־שׁ׳ Is 14^{12} (of star, fig. of royal splendour;—lit. as myth RS$^{K 300}$), אין לו ש׳ Is 8^{20} is obscure, so also בַּשּׁ׳ Ho 10^{15} (We *in storm,* i.e. בַּשַּׂעַר).—Is 47^{11} usu., but improbably, *dawn* (origin) of calamity: JHMich Hi Ew Rod (Thes) De Di al. *charm away* (RVm) (Ar سَحَرَ *enchant* (We$^{Heid. 2. 149, 200}$), سِحْرٌ *enchantment* [=Sab. סחר DHM$^{Hofmus. 24\,1}$]); but v. [שָׁחַר].

†[שָׁחַר] **vb denom.** look early, diligently for (late; orig. *look for dawn*),—**Qal** *Pt.* שֹׁחֵר טוֹב Pr 11^{27} (‖ דֹּרֵשׁ, בקש), elsewhere **Pi.** c. acc (sf.) *Pf* 3 ms. sf שִׁחֲרוֹ מוּסָר Pr 13^{24} *seeks him early* (with) *discipline* (chastises him betimes), 2 ms sf. consec וְשִׁחַרְתַּנִי ואינני Jb 7^{21}; lit *Inf* לְשַׁחֵר פָּנֶיךָ Pr 7^{15}, of wild asses, *Pt.* מְשַׁחֲרֵי לַטָּרֶף Jb 24^{5} (Ges$^{§130\,a}$) *seeking eagerly for their food;* usu. of *seeking* God (י׳) earnestly, *Pf* וְשִׁחֲרוּ־אֵל ψ 78^{34} (‖ דָּרַשׁ), *Impf.* 2 ms תְּשַׁחֵר אֶל־אֵל Jb 8^{5} (si vera l.), 3 ms sf. יְשַׁחֲרֻנְנִי (Ges^{§60e}) Ho 5^{15} (‖ בקש), + 6^{3} (v. שַׁחַר), and, acc. wisdom, Pr 1^{28}, *Pt.* sf. מְשַׁחֲרַי Pr 8^{17}; *seek* with longing, long for (י׳), אֲשַׁחֲרֶךָּ Is 26^{9} ψ 63^{2}.

שַׁחֲרוּת v. I שָׁחַר.

†מִשְׁחָר **n.[m.]** dawn;—מֵרֶחֶם מ׳ ψ 110^{3}, but מ prob. dittogr., read שַׁחַר (Du, cf. Buhl).

†שְׁחַרְיָה **n.pr.m.** in Benjamin, 1 Ch 8^{26}; Σα(α)ρ(α)ια.

†שַׁחֲרַיִם **n.pr.m.** in Benjamin, 1 Ch 8^{8}; Σααρηλ[μ], 𝔊L Σεωρειν.

[שָׁחַת] ^{151} **vb.** go to ruin (?), only der spec. (NH Hiph.=BH, Ecclus. שחיתה 30^{11} *corrupt act;* Ar. سَحَتَ *extirpate;* Eth ሰሐጠ: *injure, violate;* TelAm *šaḫâtu* is *fall* (esp. of city), *be prostrate* (? of land), perh. Canaanism (v. Wkl$^{TelAm. Vocab.}$), As. poss *šêtu, flee, escape* (cf. אבד); OAram. (Zinj) שחת *destroy* Lzb^{374}, Aram. שְׁחַת, ܫܚܬ (assim of ܛ), *mutilate;*—very improb. Gerber^{179} denom from שַׁחַת);—†**Niph.** *be marred, spoiled, Pf* 3 ms. נִשְׁחַת, of waistcloth. Je 13^{7}, vessel 18^{4}; *be injured,* or even (hyperb.) *ruined, Impf.* 3 fs. תִּשָּׁחֵת Ex 8^{20} (J) of land (מִפְּנֵי הֶעָרֹב); *be corrupted, corrupt,* in morals and rel., of earth, *Pf* 3 fs. נִשְׁחֲתָה Gn 6^{12} (P), *Impf.* 3 fs. וַתִּשָּׁחֵת לִפְנֵי הָא׳ v^{11} (P); so *Pt* fpl. as adj. נִשְׁחָתוֹת Ez 20^{44}. †**Pi.** *Pf.* 3 ms. שִׁחֵת Ex

32^{7}+, sf שחתך Ho 13^{9}, 2 ms שִׁחֶתְ Is 14^{20}+, etc, *Imv.* mpl שַׁחֲתוּ Je 5^{10}, *Inf. cstr* שחת Gn 13^{10}+, etc;—**1.** *spoil, ruin,* acc. of eye Ex 21^{26} (E), vineyard Je 12^{10} (fig), branches Na 2^{3} (fig.), also = *destroy*, acc pers. 2 S 1^{14} 14^{11} (acc. om), Ez 5^{16} 20^{17}, כָּל־בָּשָׂר Gn 6^{17} 9^{15} (P), city, fortress, etc., Gn 13^{10} 19$^{13.29}$ (all J), 2 S 24^{16} Je 5^{10} (acc om.), 48^{18} Ez 26^{4} 43^{3} La 2^{5}, *ruin* temple v^{6}, nation Ho 11^{9} 13^{9} (read perh. שחתך Oort Now), land 2 K 19^{12} (Hiph in ‖ Is 37^{12}), Ju 6^{5} Jos 22^{33} (P), Ez 22^{30} 30^{11}, earth Gn 9^{11} (P), c. ל obj (ל **3 b**), city 1 S 23^{10}, pers. Nu 32^{15} (P), c acc רַחֲמָיו Am 1^{11}, *destroyed* (stifled) *his compassion* (or, RS$^{K\ 28}$ al, *the bonds of kinship*, v. רַחֲמִים), ושׁ׳ ברית Mal 2^{8}, i e violate it, v. esp ושׁ׳ אַרְצָה (sc. *semen*) Gn 38^{9} (J) *he spoiled* (it) *upon the ground*, made it ineffective, = *waste* words Pr 23^{8} **2.** *pervert, corrupt*, acc wisdom Ez 28^{17}, abs = *deal corruptly*, העמיקו שחתו Ho 9^{9} (cf. [עָמֹק], p 770^{b}, but We Now read שַׁחְתוּ, √שׁוח), Ex 32^{7} (JE), Dt 9^{12}, so שׁ׳ לוֹ 32^{5} **Hiph.**$_{103}$ *Pf.* 3 ms. השחית Gn 6^{12}+; 1 s וְהִשְׁחַתִּי Je 51^{20}, etc, *Impf* 3 ms יַשְׁחִית Dn 8^{24}+, יַשְׁחֵת Mal 3^{11}+, וַיַּשְׁחֵת 1 Ch 20^{1}, 2 fs וַתַּשְׁחִתִי Ez 16^{47}, 2 mpl. תַּשְׁחִתוּן Dt 4^{16} 31^{29}, *Imv.* ms. sf הַשְׁחִיתָהּ 2 K 18^{25} = Is 36^{10}, *Inf. abs.* הַשְׁחֵת Dt 31^{29}, cstr. הַשְׁחִית 1 S 26^{15}+, etc.; *Pt* מַשְׁחִית Gn 19^{14}+, etc,—**1.** *spoil, ruin*, acc crop Ju 6^{4} Mal 3^{11}, trees Dt 20$^{19.20}$ Je 11^{19} (fig), vessels 2 Ch 36^{19}, houses 34^{11}, palaces Je 6^{5}, cf Is 65^{8} Lv 19^{27} (H), Ru 4^{6}, הַשׁ׳ דַּיָּם Je 49^{9} thieves *damage as much as they want*, acc. pers. = *ruin, destroy*, 1 S 26$^{9.15}$ Ju 20$^{21.25}$ (+אַרְצָה), v$^{35.42}$ 2 K 13^{23} 2 Ch 24^{23} (+מִן separ), + 12 t, + (acc pers. om) Is 51^{13}+4 t, acc. בֵּית דָּוִד 2 Ch 21^{7}, abs Is 11^{9} = 65^{25}, also *ruin* one (by words) Pr 11^{9}, acc. עַם 2 S 24^{16} Dt 9^{26}, land 1 S 6^{5} Je 36^{29} Dn 11^{17} (v Dr), city wall 2 S 20^{15} (Ew Th here denom from שַׁחַת *they were making a pit*, < 𝔊 We (?) Klo Dr Bu HPS Now מְחַשְּׁבִים *were devising*), La 2^{8}, cities and nations Gn 18$^{28.28}$ (J, acc om), 19$^{13.14}$ (J), Is 37^{12} (Pi in ‖ 2 K 19^{12}), 36$^{10.10}$ = 2 K 18$^{25.25}$ + 11 t + (Israel personif.) Dt 4^{31} 10^{10} 2 K 8^{19}, pride of Judah Je 13^{9}, earth Je 51^{1}; abs c. adv acc. Dn 8^{24} (v. Dr; Bev conj. יַשְׁחִת or יָשִׂיחַ *utter monstrous things*), cf. 1 Ch 21^{12}, Pt as adj, of lion Je 2^{30}, angel 1 Ch 21^{15}, = *destroyer* Ex 12^{23} (J), Je 22^{7} Is 54^{16}, מַ׳ גּוֹיִם Je 4^{7}, רוּחַ מ׳ 51^{1}, sg. coll. (הַמּ׳ Ges$^{§126\ l}$, *the destroying band*, cf. Dr Bu Now) 1 S 13^{17} 14^{15} (*spoilers, ravagers*), fig for snare, trap, Je 5^{26} †**2.** *pervert, corrupt*, morally, acc. דַּרְכּוֹ Gn 6^{12} (P, v דֶּרֶךְ **6**), נַפְשׁוֹ Pr 6^{32}, cf. Zp 3^{7}, Ez 23^{11} (מִן comp.), הִשׁ׳ הִשְׁחִית הִתְעִיבוּ עֲלִילָה ψ 14^{1} = 53^{2}, הִשְׁחִית תַּשְׁחִ׳ (+vb. of particular act) Dt 4^{16} 31^{29}, declar. = *act corruptly*, Is 1^{4} Dt 4^{25} (+vb. of act), 2 Ch 27^{2}, +מִן comp Ju 2^{19} Ez 16^{47}, *Pt.* as subst. Je 6^{28}, אִישׁ מַשׁ׳ Pr 28^{24} (18^{9} v. infra) — אַל־תַּשְׁחֵת *destroy not* (catchword of old song or melody?) in ψ-titles: †57^{1} 58^{1} 59^{1} 75^{1} †**Hoph.** *Pt* מָשְׁחָת *spoiled, ruined*, of a spring, מָקוֹר Pr 25^{26} (‖ מַעְיָן נִרְפָּשׂ); as subst. Mal 1^{14} sacrificing *a spoiled thing*

†מַשְׁחִית **n.[m.]** *ruin, destruction*,—מ׳ abs Je 5^{26} + 10 t.,—physical *destruction* Ez 5^{16} 9^{6} 21^{36} 25^{15} Ex 12^{13} (P), 2 Ch 20^{23} 22^{4}, בַּעַל מ׳ Pr 18^{9} = *destroyer*, Dn 10^{8} (disfigurement), הַר־מ׳ Je 51^{25} (fig. of Bab. as destroyer), in 2 K 23^{13} = *mt of corruption* (where *bamoth* were, S end of Mt. of Olives, poss adapted from הַר־מִשְׁחָה so Hoffm$^{ZAW\ ii\ (1882),\ 175}$ Benz Kit Bur, 𝔙 *mons offensionis*)

†מַשְׁחֵת **n** [**m.**] id,—כְּלִי מַשְׁחֵתוֹ Ez 9^{1}.

†מִשְׁחַת **n.[m.]** disfigurement of face Is 52^{14}

†מָשְׁחָת **n.[m.]** corruption (ritual), Lv 22^{25} (H)

שַׁחַת v. שׁוח.

שִׁטָּה$_{27}$ **n.f.** acacia, tree and wood (=*שִׁנְטָה, Ar. سَنْط, prob loan-word from Egypt *šndt, šondᵉt*, Thes^{1402} Erman$^{ZMG\ xlvi\ (1892),\ 120}$),—growing in dry places; esp. *acacia* (*mimosa*) *Nilotica;* cf Rob$^{BR\ ii\ 251}$, or *a seyyâl* Post$^{Flora\ 296\ f.\ Hast.\ DB\ SHITTAH\ TREE}$ Tristr$^{NHB\ 390\ ff}$,—שׁ׳ sg Is 41^{19} (to grow in desert), usually pl., עֲצֵי שִׁטִּים *shittîm wood*, material of ark, altars, staves, etc., in tabern, Dt 10^{3} Ex 25$^{5.10.13}$ + 19 t. Ex 25–38 (P); עֲצֵי om, עַמּוּדֵי שׁ׳ *pillars of shittîm* (wood), Ex 26$^{32.37}$ 36^{36} (P).

†שִׁטִּים **n.pr.loc.** alw. הַשּׁ׳; usu Σαττειν: **1.** E. of Jordan, Jos 2^{1} 3^{1} (E), Mi 6^{5} Nu 25^{1} (P); = אָבֵל הַשּׁ׳ 33^{49}; on exact site v. Buhl$^{G\ 116}$ Gray$^{Nu\ 25\ 1}$. **2.** נַחַל הַשּׁ׳ Jo 4^{18} (perh *Wady es-Sant*, W of Jerus., cf. We Buhl$^{Geogr\ 90}$, and views in Dr)

[שָׁטַח] **vb. spread, spread abroad** (NH id, Ar سَطَحَ *spread out;* so Eth ሰጠሐ: Aram. שְׁטַח, ܫܛܰܚ),—**Qal** *Pf* 3 pl sf. consec. וּשְׁטָחוּם לַשֶּׁמֶשׁ Je 8^{2} *they shall spread them abroad*, etc., acc. of many separate things, so *Impf.* 3 fs. וַתִּשְׁטַח 2 S 17^{19} (עַל loc; disting. from פָּרַשׂ *spread*

covering); 3 mpl. + *Inf. abs.* וַיִּשְׁטְחוּ לָהֶם שָׁטוֹחַ Nu 11^{32} (J) *they spread* (sc. the quails) *for themselves all abroad* round about the camp (i.e. to dry them; 𝔙 *siccaverunt;* cf. Di Gray); *Pt.* שֹׁטֵחַ לַגּוֹיִם Jb 12^{23} *expanding the nations* (cf. ל 3 b) **Pi.** *Pf.* 1 s שִׁטַּחְתִּי אֵלֶיךָ כַפָּי ψ 88^{10} *I have spread out unto thee my palms.*

†[מִשְׁטָח] **n.[m.] spreading-place** (NH for drying figs, etc., (ARSKennedy [Ency Bib. Fruit, 1568])); —cstr. מִשְׁטַח חֲרָמִים Ez $26^{5.14}$.

†מִשְׁטוֹחַ **n.[m.]** id.;—מ׳ לַחֲרָמִים Ez 47^{10}

שׁטט v. שׁוט, שֹׁטִים v. supra

†שָׁטַף **vb. overflow, rinse or wash off** (NH id., so JAram. שְׁטַף, As. *šatâpu, overflow,* Ar. سطف id, Cuche),—**Qal** *Pf* 3 ms שׁ׳ Is 8^{8}+, etc., *Impf.* 3 ms וַיִּשְׁטֹף 1 K 22^{38}, etc.; *Pt.* שׁוֹטֵף Is 10^{22}+, pl. שֹׁטְפִים Is 28^{2};—**1.** *overflow,* of river Is 8^{8} Je 47^{2a} (v. נַחַל), Dn $11^{10.40}$, all fig of invading army, cf. Is 28^{15} (qy. by Sta [ThLz. Apr 1891, 235], Du Marti rd. שׁוֹט שֹׁטֵט), v ^{18} (v. שׁוֹט), also (sim. of י׳ in judgment) v ^{2} (מַיִם), 30^{28}, of judicial destruction, שׁוֹטֵף צְדָקָה Is 10^{22}; c. acc. of land Je 47^{2b}, pers. (fig.) Is 43^{2} (נְהָרוֹת), ψ 69^{3} (שִׁבֹּלֶת), v ^{16} (שׁ׳ מַיִם), 124^{4} (מַיִם), cf. Is 28^{17} Ct 8^{7}; גֶּשֶׁם שׁוֹטֵף *flooding rain* (of י׳'s judgment) Ez $11^{11.13}$ 38^{22}; נַחַל שׁוֹטֵף Is 66^{12}, sim., in good sense.—Abs. Dn 11^{26} v. **Niph.**—Fig of *dashing, rushing* horse, כְּסוּס שׁוֹ׳ בַּמִּלְחָמָה Je 8^{6}. **2.** *flow, run,* lit. of נַחַל ψ 78^{20} 2 Ch 32^{4}. **3.** lit., *rinse* or *wash off,* c. acc. of thing washed 1 K 22^{38}, יָדָיו בַּמַּיִם Lv 15^{11} (P); of stain Ez 16^{9} (רָחַץ ‖ מֵעָלַיִךְ), עֲפַר־אֶרֶץ Jb 14^{19}. **Niph.** *Impf* 3 ms. יִשָּׁטֵף בַּמָּיִם Lv 15^{12} *be rinsed out, off* (P, of wooden vessel); 3 mpl. יִשָּׁטְפוּ מִלְּפָנָיו Dn 11^{22} *be swept away* (defeated), read prob. יִשָּׁטֵף (for ישטף), also v ^{26} (cf. Dr). **Pu.** *Pf.* 3 ms. וּמֹרַק וְשֻׁטַּף בַּמָּיִם Lv 6^{21} (P) *it shall be scoured and rinsed.*

†שֶׁטֶף, שֶׁצֶף **n.m.** [Na 1.8] **flood**;—abs. שֶׁטֶף Na 1^{8} + 3 t.; cstr. שֶׁ׳ Pr 27^{4}, שֵׁ׳ ψ 32^{6};—*flood,* fig of י׳'s judgment, שׁ׳ עֹבֵר Na 1^{8}, cf. Dn 9^{26}, זְרֹעוֹת הַשּׁ׳ 11^{22} (cf. Di); of calamity, שׁ׳ מַיִם רַבִּים ψ 32^{6}; שׁ׳ אַף Pr 27^{4} *a flood of anger;* so שֶׁצֶף קֶצֶף Is 54^{8} (צ for ט bef. foll. צ Ew Di; > Du Che Marti del. שׁ׳ as dittogr.), שֶׁטֶף lit. of rainflood, Jb 38^{25}.

שׁטר (√ of foll.; As *šatâru, write,* Sab. סטר Hom [Chr 124] DHM [Ep. Denkm Ar iii 2, iiv 2], Ar. سَطَرَ *rule* (a book), *write,* سَطْرٌ *row, line;* Aram. שְׁטָרָא, ܫܛܪܐ *document,* so Hilpr [Bab. Exp. x. 8] CIS [ii. 67], Nab. Palm. שטר Lzb [374]: Hom [NKZ i 69] all from As).

†שֹׁטֵר **n.m. official, officer** (prop. *scribe, secretary?* or fr. original meaning as *arranger, organizer?*), —abs. שׁ׳ Pr 6^{7}, שׁוֹ׳ 2 Ch 26^{11}; pl. שֹׁטְרִים Dt 1^{15}+, etc.;—appar. subordinate *officer,* judicial, civil or military (cf. Dr [Dt 1 15] Gray [Nu 11, 16]): organizing people for marching Jos 1^{10} 3^{2} (both E), cf. Dt $20^{5.8.9}$; appointed over Isr. by Egypt. overseers Ex 5^{14}, cf. v $^{6.10.15.19}$ (all J); elsewhere + זְקֵנִים Nu 11^{16} (E), Dt 29^{9} 31^{28}; + שֹׁפְטִים 16^{18} 1 Ch 23^{4} 26^{29}, + ז׳ et שֹׁפ׳ Jos 8^{33} (R^{D}), and (+ רָאשִׁים) 23^{2} (R^{D}), 24^{1} (E, or R^{D}), שֹׁט׳ as minor judges also Dt 1^{15}; שֹׁט׳ הַמְשָׁרְתִים אֶת־הַמֶּלֶךְ 1 Ch 27^{1}, chosen from Levites 2 Ch 19^{11} 34^{13} (+ שׁוֹעֲרִים, סוֹפְרִים); as title of individ 26^{11} (‖ הַסּוֹפֵר); of ant, אֵין־לָהּ קָצִין שֹׁטֵר וּמֹשֵׁל Pr 6^{7}.

†שִׁטְרַי **n.pr.m.** an official of David, 1 Ch 27^{29} Kt (> Qr שִׁרְטַי), Ασαρταις, Σατραι

†[מִשְׁטָר] **n.m. rule, authority,**—sf. מִשְׁטָרוֹ Jb 38^{33} (of heavens over earth).

†שַׁי **n.m. gift** offered as homage (√ dub; perh. in spite of ש = ش, Ar. شَيِّ, vb. *wish,* شَيْءٌ *thing* (weakened fr *thing desired*); cf. חֵפֶץ 4),—יוּבַל שׁ׳ Is 18^{7}, יֹבִילוּ שׁ׳ ψ 76^{12}, יוֹבִ׳ שָׁי 68^{30}.

שִׁיא **n.pr.m.** 2 S 20^{25} Kt, v. שְׁוָא.

†שִׁיאֹן **n.pr.loc.** in Issachar, Jos 19^{19}, Σιωνα, Σηω.

I. שִׁיבָה v. ישׁב. II. שִׁיבָה v. שׁוב.

†[שָׁיָה] **vb.** only **Qal** *Impf.* apoc צוּר יְלָדְךָ תֶּשִׁי Dt 32^{18}, but < read תִּשָּׁה (II. נשה) *the Rock which begat thee thou forgattest,* Sam תשא, Di Dr.

†שִׁיזָא **n.pr.m.** in Reuben, 1 Ch 11^{42}, Σαιζα, Σιζαι.

[שִׂיחַ], שִׂיחָה v. שׂוח.

†שִׁיחוֹר **n.pr.flum.** on border of Egypt, prob. E. branch of Nile;—שׁ׳ הַשּׁ׳ מִצְרַיִם Jos 13^{3}, 1 Ch 13^{5}; clearly = Nile, זֶרַע שִׁחֹר Is 23^{3} (‖ קְצִיר יְאוֹר), מֵי שִׁחוֹר Je 2^{18}; cf. Dl [Pa 311] Wilson [Hast DB Shihor] (usu. derived from I. שׁחר, as *black water,* but doubtful)

†שִׁיחוֹר לִבְנָת **n.pr.flum.** in Asher, Jos 19^{26}; τῷ Σειων[ρ] καὶ Λαβαναθ; poss. *Nahr ez-Zerkâ,* S of Carmel, and just N. of Caesarea, Wilson [Hast DB Shihor Libnath], but v. Buhl [G 105].

שַׁיִט v. I שׁוט.

שִׁילוֹ, שִׁלֹה, **n.pr.loc.,** שִׁילֹנִי etc., v. שִׁלֹה.

†שִׁילֹה G 49[10], appar. **n.**, but prob.=שֶׁלּוֹ *he whose it is*, or *that which belongs to him*, v infra, views are: (1) שיל (=שִׁלְיָה, NH *embryo*, + sf ה— =*his son*, 𝔗 Jer Rabb Calv), (2) שִׁלֹה, שִׁלוֹ n pr.loc (q v.) Herder De and most (until recently), (3) n pr. of Messiah, AV RV Munster (1534) on basis of Talm Sanh 98[b], groundless, (4) Jer שִׁלֹה=שִׁלֹּחַ, *qui mittendus est*, (5) שִׁלֹה =שׁ+לוֹ, 𝔗[Onk] *whose is the kingdom*, 𝔖 *whose it is*, so Aphi Ephr 𝔊 ἕως ἂν ἔλθῃ τὰ ἀποκείμενα αὐτῷ (Codd ᾧ ἀπόκειται), so Sam שלה, cf עַד־בֹּא אֲשֶׁר לוֹ הַמִּשְׁפָּט Ez 21[32], Aq Sym Theod Saad, this reading best, but exact transl not certain, v Di [JPhil xiv (1885). 1 ff Gn 418 ff] Br [MP 95 ff. Intr 238 ff] Poznański [Schiloh (1904)]

שִׁילל v שלל

†שִׁימוֹן **n.pr.m.** in Judah, 1 Ch 4[20], Σεμ(ε)ιων, Σαμι

שין (√of foll; cf As *šânu*, Iphte *istin*, *urinate*, *šînâti* (pl), *urine*, vb also Eth. ሸንሀ: Aram ܫܝܢ, ܫܺܝܢ, v Ar مَثَانَةٌ *bladder* (Wabrm))

†[שַׁיִן, שִׁין] **n.**[**m**] *urine*,—pl sf שיניהם 2 K 18[27]=Is 36[12] (both Kt; Qr מֵימֵי רַגְלֵיהֶם)

†[שָׁתַן] **vb. Hiph.** *urinate* (secondary √ from above),—*Pt* מַשְׁתִּין בְּקִיר (i e a male person) 1 S 25[22.34] 1 K 14[10] 16[11] 21[21] 2 K 9[8] (all of exterminating a family)

שִׁיר (√of foll, cf No [ZMG xxxvii (1883) 537])

†שִׁיר[77] **n.m. song** (NH *id*, so Ecclus 40[21]+),—שׁ׳ abs. Ju 5[12]+, cstr 2 Ch 29[27]+, sf. שִׁירִי ψ 28[7], etc, pl שִׁירִים 1 Ch 13[8] Ct 1[1], שִׁרִים Gn 31[27] Pr 25[20], sf שִׁרֶיךָ Am 5[23], etc;—**1.** lyric *song*, +מָשָׁל 1 K 5[12], opp קִינָה Am 8[10]; joyous Gn 31[27] (J) Is 30[29]; שׁ׳ עֲגָבִים Ez 33[32], triumphal Ju 5[12]; love song Ct 1[1] (title שִׁיר הַשִּׁירִים), ψ 45[1] (שִׁיר יְדִידֹת), noisy Am 5[23] Ez 26[13], in drunken revels Is 24[9], cf. 23[16]; שׁ׳ כְּסִילִים Ec 7[5], not for sorrow Pr 25[20] ψ 137[3.3]; בְּנוֹת הַשִּׁיר Ec 12[4] *songstresses* (prob. birds) **2.** religious *song*, in worship, ‖ תפלה ψ 42[9], usu. praise, שִׁיר ψ 28[7], אֲהוֹדֶנּוּ מִשִּׁירִי 69[31]; הלל בשיר שִׁיר י׳ ψ 137[4] 2 Ch 29[27], תְּהִלָּה וְהוֹדוֹת Ne 12[46], שִׁיר חָדָשׁ Is 42[10] (fresh outburst), + 6t, v. חָדָשׁ, in ψ-titles, שִׁיר 46[1], cf Is 26[1]; שִׁיר הַמַּעֲלוֹת *pilgrim songs* ψ 120[1] + 14 t (v. II. מַעֲלָה p 752), c מִזְמוֹר ψ 48[1] + 12 t (v מזמ p. 274), מַשְׂכִּיל שִׁיר 45[1], (שׁ׳ orig. alone in all except 30[1] 92[1] 108[1], v Br [JBL xviii (1899). 138]) **3.** specif song of Levitical choirs, with musical accomp., 1 Ch 6[16.17] 13[8] (so read also ‖ 2 S 6[5] for בְּרוֹשִׁים, 𝔊 Th and mod., cf ׳ב), 25[6.7] 2 Ch 23[13] 29[28] Ne 12[27], כְּלֵי (ה)שִּׁיר instrument to accompany song 1 Ch 15[16] + 6 t. (v כלי **2 b**), cf Am 6[5].

†שִׁירָה **n f. song** (pl [שׁ]ירות Ecclus 39[15]),—abs שׁ׳ Ex 15[1] + 9 t; cstr שִׁירַת Is 5[1] 23[15], pl cstr שירות Am 8[3] (rd שָׁרוֹת 𝔊 Hoffm ZAW iii (1883) We al.),—*song, ode*, Ex 15[1] (E), 2 S 22[1] =ψ 18[1], Dt 31[19.19.21.22.30] 32[44] Nu 21[17] (E) Is 5[1] 23[15].

†[שִׁיר][88] **vb. sing** (denom acc to No [ZMG xxxvii (1883) 537] Gerb[172], but, if so, an old one);—**Qal**[49] *Pf.* 3 ms. שָׁר ψ 7[1], *Impf.* 3 ms יָשִׁיר Ex 15[1] Nu 21[17] (read יָשֻׁר Jb 33[27] for יָשֹׁר, √II. שׁוּר, so SS Bu Gerb, in this sense also Ew De Di RV and all mod); 3 fs. וַתָּשַׁר Ju 5[1], etc.; *Imv.* mpl שִׁירוּ Ex 15[21]+, *Inf. cstr.* לָשׁוּר 1 S 18[6] Kt (<Qr לָשִׁיר, so Bu; 𝔊[B] om, cf Dr Kit[Kau] HPS Now), *Pt.* שָׁר Pr 25[20], pl. שָׁרִים 2 S 19[36]+; f. שָׁרוֹת 2 S 19[36] + 2 t + Am 8[3] (read for שִׁירוֹת, v. שִׁירָה),—*sing*, c acc שִׁיר Is 42[10] ψ 33[3] + 5 t.; שִׁירָה Ex 15[1] Nu 21[17] (E) Is 5[1], שׁ׳ בְּשִׁרִים Pr 25[20]; ψ 137[3] שִׁירוּ לָנוּ מִשִּׁיר צִיּוֹן (𝔊 מזמור), תהלה 106[12]; c acc of theme 59[17] 89[2]; abs. Ju 5[1] 1 S 18[6]; c. לְ ψ 13[6] 96[1.2]=1 Ch 16[23], Ex 15[1.21] Je 20[13], ‖ זמר ψ 68[5.33] 101[1] 104[33] 105[2]=1 Ch 16[9], Ju 5[3], + זמר abs ψ 57[8]=108[2], c. acc theme 21[14]; c לְ pers 27[6], of nature 65[14] (after הִתְרוֹעֲעוּ); עַל אֲנָשִׁים Jb 33[27] (v. supra), pt שָׁרִים *singers* 2 S 19[36] 1 K 10[12] + 6 t (Ez 40[44] read שְׁתַּיִם 𝔊 Hi Co mod); שָׁרוֹת *songstresses* 2 S 19[36] 2 Ch 35[25] Ec 2[8] + Am 8[3] (v. supra)—ψ 138[5] rd. וְיָשִׂיחוּ **Pōl.**[36] *Pf.* 3 mpl. שֹׁרְרוּ Jb 36[24]; *Impf* 3 ms יְשׁוֹרֵר Zp 2[14]; *Pt.* מְשׁוֹרֵר 1 Ch 6[18] 2 Ch 29[28], pl. מְשֹׁרְרִים Ezr 2[65]+, etc,—*sing*. birds Zp 2[14], men Jb 36[24]; elsewh pt. of Levitical singers 1 Ch 6[18] 9[33] + 31 t., + fpl. Ezr 2[65] *songstresses*=Ne 7[67]. †**Hoph.** *be sung*: *Impf* יוּשַׁר הַשִּׁיר הַזֶּה Is 26[1].

†שַׁיִשׁ **n.**[**m**] **alabaster** (foreign word? NH *id.*, Aram שַׁיְשָׁא, ܫܝܫܐ, perhaps As. *šaššu*);—אַבְנֵי־שׁ׳ 1 Ch 29[2] (material of temple); cf. Patrick [Hast DB Marble]

†II שֵׁשׁ **n.m. id**;—עַמּוּדֵי שׁ׳ Ct 5[15] (in fig.), Est 1[6a], material of pavement v[6b] (v. בַּהַט).—I שֵׁשׁ, v. שׁדשׁ.

†שִׁישָׁא **n.pr.m.** Solomon's time, 1 K 4[3], Σαβα, Σεισα, 𝔊L Σαφαρ; cf. שְׁרָיָה.

†שִׁישַׁק **n.pr.m.** king of Egypt, Solomon's time (10th cent. B.C.), 1 K 11^{40} 14^{25} Qr (Kt שושק), = 2 Ch 12^{2}, 2 Ch 12^{9}, שִׁישָׁק $v^{5.5.7}$; = *Šešonk* I, first king of 22nd dynasty, Blau^ZMG xv (1861), 233 ff.^ Steind^BAS i. 351^; = *Sošenk* WMM^As. u. Eur. 166 ff.; Ency. Bib. SHISHAK^; cf. Griffith^Hast. DB SHISHAK^.

†שִׁית **vb. put, set** (Nö^Beitr. z. Sem. Sprachwiss. 39 f.^; cf. Ph. שת שת Lzb^375^; Ecclus שית Pt. pass. 31^{27} (?); v. also (Nö^l. c. 41^) Syr. ܫܘܬܐ *quality, appearance*);—**Qal** *Pf.* 3 ms. שָׁת Gn 4^{25}+, 3 fs. שָׁתָה 1 S 4^{20}+, 2 ms. שַׁתָּה ψ 8^{7}, שַׁתָּ 90^{8}, sf. שַׁתַּנִי $88^{7.9}$, 1 s. שַׁתִּי 73^{28}+; 3 pl. שָׁתוּ Ex 33^{4}+3 t., metapl. שַׁתּוּ ψ 49^{15} 73^{9} (other forms not found); *Impf.* 3 ms. יָשִׁית Ex 21^{22}+, juss. יָשֵׁת Jb 9^{33}, וַיָּשֶׁת Gn 30^{40}+; 3 fs. sf. וַתְּשִׁתֵהוּ Ru 4^{16}, תְּשִׁיתֵמוֹ ψ 21^{10}+, 1 s. sf. אֲשִׁיתֶנּוּ 1 K 11^{34}; *Imv.* ms. שִׁית Pr 27^{23}, שִׁיתָה ψ 9^{21} 141^{3}; fs. שִׁיתִי Je 31^{21}, etc.; *Inf. abs.* שֹׁת Is 22^{7}; *cstr.* שִׁית Jb 30^{1}+; *Pt. pass.* שִׁית (Je 13^{16} Qr, but rd. Kt יָשִׁית); sf. שָׁתִי Ex 10^{1};—**1.** *put, lay* hand upon, עַל, Gn 46^{4} (E), $48^{14.17}$ (J), Jb 9^{33} ψ 139^{5}; c. עִם in evil partnership, Ex 23^{1} (E); *put* ornaments, עַל pers., 33^{4} (J); cf. 1 S 2^{8} Is 15^{9} Jb 22^{24} Ru 3^{15}; *lay* child into (ב) bosom Ru 4^{16}; *put* wisdom, ב loc., Jb 38^{36}, cf. Pr 26^{24}; אָשִׁית עֵצוֹת בְּנַפְשִׁי ψ 13^{3}, i.e. take counsel, plan; מַחְסִי בי׳ ψ 73^{28}; *put* things תַּחַת רַגְלָיו 8^{7}; *lay* (penalty) עַל pers. Ex 21^{22} (E), sin Nu 12^{11} (E), cf. (c. אֲשֶׁר = *where*) ψ 84^{4}; nearly = *give* (נתן), acc. + לְ pers. Gn 4^{25} (J; explan. of name שֵׁת), *appoint* ψ 9^{21}. **2. a.** *set, station*, sheep לְבַדּוֹ Gn 30^{40}, cf. לֹא שָׁתָם עַל v^{40} (J); acc. pers. = *appoint* (עַל *over*) 41^{33} (E); *set* לָמוֹ pers. (ל **3 b**) + ב loc. ψ 73^{18}, so (acc.) 88^{7} and (obj. pers. om.) 12^{6}, *set* crown לְרֹאשׁוֹ 21^{4}, *set* one (מִן partit.) לְכִסֵּא 132^{11}; *set* pers. *among* (ב pers.) 2 S 19^{29} Je 3^{19}, cf. (עִם) Jb 30^{1}; *set* watch לְפִי ψ 141^{3}, snares לִי 140^{6}, enmity, בֵּין pers. Gn 3^{15} (J); iniquities לְנֶגְדֶּךָ ψ 90^{8}, cf. 101^{3}; *set, direct* face, אֶל loc. Nu 24^{1} (J), eyes לִנְטוֹת בָּאָרֶץ ψ 17^{11}. **b.** in phr. שׁ׳ לֵב לְ *set* one's *mind to*, give heed, attention (cf. שׂוּם **2 b**), Ex 7^{23} (E), 2 S 13^{20} Je 31^{21} ψ 48^{14} Pr 22^{17} 27^{23}, c. אֶל Jb 7^{17}, abs. 1 S 4^{20} ψ 62^{11}; Pr 24^{32} *I reflected.* **c.** *set, fix*, גְּבוּל Ex 23^{31} (E; c. מִן ... עַד), תָּשִׁית לִי חֹק Jb 14^{13} wouldst *fix me* a limit, 38^{11} (וּפֹא יָשִׁית בִּגְאוֹן גַּלֶּיךָ) De al. here *shall one fix* it [the boundary, חֹק, v^{10}] = it *shall be fixed* against, etc.: but explan. very forced: Me Kau יִשָּׁבֵר ג׳, Bi Bu יִשְׁבֹּת ג׳). **3.** *constitute, make* one something, 2 acc., 1 K 11^{34} *I will make him prince*, Is 5^{6} 26^{1} Je 22^{6} ψ 21^{7} 84^{7} 88^{9} (+ לָמוֹ ind. obj.), 110^{1} 2 S 22^{12} ‖ ψ 18^{12}; תְּשִׁיתֵמוֹ שֶׁכֶם 21^{13} = *thou wilt make them* (all) *shoulder*, make them turn their back, flee (cf. 18^{41}); acc. + לְ *make* something *into* Je 2^{15} = 50^{3}, 13^{16} ψ 45^{17} (+ ב loc.); acc. + כ comp. *make* one *like* Ho 2^{5} (‖ שׂים), Is 16^{3} ψ 21^{10} $83^{12.14}$; acc. only, *make, prepare*, feast Je 51^{39}, cf. שָׁת קָצִיר לָךְ Ho 6^{11} (rd. poss. שִׁית, pt. pass.), *make* darkness ψ 104^{20}; = *perform* signs, ב loc. Ex 10^{1} (J). **4.** internally trans., = *take one's stand* (cf. שׂים **4 a**) הַפָּרָשִׁים שֹׁת שָׁתוּ הַשָּׁעְרָה Is 22^{7}; c. עַל־ (*against*) ψ 3^{7}.—אָשִׁית מִמֶּנִּי Jb 10^{20} (Kt; > Qr *Imv.* וְשִׁית) is dub., יָשֵׁת = יָשִׁית: De *direct* (attention) *away from me*, cf. Di (ellipsis of יָד, פָּנִים, or לֵב), Du (sc. יָד; reads *Imv.*); Lag (so Bu) prop. יִשְׁבֹּת, Siegf (יָדוֹ) יָשֵׁב, 𝔊 Beer (best) שְׁעֵה (7^{19}), with יְמֵי חֶלְדִּי (𝔊 Bu Be Du) for יָמַי יחדל prob. rightly. **Hoph.** (or **Qal** *pass.* Ges^§ 53 u^), *Impf.* 3 ms. יוּשַׁת Ex 21^{30} (E) if a ransom *be imposed* עָלָיו, v^{30}.

† שִׁית **n.m. garment** (Nö^Beiträge, 41 f.^, cp. Syr. ܫܘܬܐ *appearance*, and qu. שִׁית?);—cstr. שִׁית זוֹנָה Pr 7^{10}; fig. שׁ׳ חָמָס ψ 73^{6} (v. II. עטף).

†I. שֵׁת **n.pr.m.** third son of Adam; Gn 4^{25} (where expl. from √שִׁית), v^{26} $5^{3.4.6.7.8}$ 1 Ch 1^{1}; Σηθ.—In כָּל־בְּנֵי־שֵׁת Nu 24^{17} (poem in J), read prob. שְׁאֵת *tumult* (cf. La 3^{47}), or שְׂאֵת (v. sub נשׂא), cf. Gray.—II. שֵׁת, v. II. שׁתה.

†[שָׁת] **n.m.** (Albr^ZAW xvi (1896), 84^) **foundation, stay** (of society) (√שִׁית Thes Kö^II. 1. 172^);—pl. הַשָּׁתוֹת יֵהָרֵסוּן ψ 11^{3} (prob. fig. of established *usages, laws*, etc., 𝔙 *leges*, Sym. θεσμοί, so Hup-Now Bae Che^(1888)^ al.; > Thes al. of *nobles*); Thes puts here also שָׁתֹתֶיהָ Is 19^{10} (so MT probably intends), which Ew Di Kit then interpret of working-classes, ‖ עֹשֵׂי שֶׂכֶר; but perh. opp. of this, the upper classes, so as to include all ranks of society, Thes De Che^Comm.^; Che^Hpt^ Buhl al. שָׁתֶיהָ *weavers of it* (cf. Du Marti), v. III. שׁתה.

†שַׁיִת **n.[m.] coll. thorn-bushes** (connex. with above √dub.; Dietr^Abh. 73^ cp. (improb.) שׁאה *devastate*, שְׁאִיָּה *ruin*, whence שׁ׳ wild, rough growth);—alw. c. שָׁמִיר: abs. שׁ׳ Is $7^{23.24}$ 9^{17} 27^{4} (cf. Du); שָׁיִת 5^{6} 7^{25}; sf. שֵׁיתוֹ 10^{17} (fig. of Assyr.).

שָׁכַב (Lag^BN 63^) $_{212}$ **vb. lie down** (NH = BH; שכב Ecclus 47^{23} (in death), משכב *bed* 40^{5} 47^{20d}, = *death bed* 46^{19}; Ph. שכב, משכב (v. מ׳ **1** infr.), Lzb^375^; Eth. ሰከበ: *lie*, so Aram. שְׁכַב, ܫܟܒ;

Nab משכבא *couch;* Ar سَكَبَ only *pour out* (water, tears), *be poured out* (cf **Hiph.** infr, and Lag[BN 63])), —**Qal** *Pf.* 3 ms. ׳ש Gn 26[10]+, etc.; *Impf* ישכב Gn 30[16]+, 3 mpl יִשְׁכְּבוּ 1 S 2[22], יִשְׁכָּבוּן Jos 2[8] Jb 30[17], etc, *Imv.* ms. שְׁכַב 2 S 13[5] Ez 4[4], שִׁכְבָה Gn 39[7.12], etc, *Inf abs* שָׁכַב Lv 15[24], *cstr* שְׁכַב 1 K 1[21]+, sf. שָׁכְבוֹ Ru 3[4], שִׁכְבָהּ Gn 19[33.35], שָׁכְבְּךָ Dt 6[7]+2 t., *Pt.* שכב Gn 28[13]+, f. שֹׁכֶבֶת Mi 7[5] Ru 3[8], etc, —**1.** *lie down* (sometimes opp קוּם, הקיץ). **a.** Ju 5[27] (prostrated by blow, +כָּרַע, נפל) **b.** to sleep, Gn 19[4] (J), 28[11] (E), 1 S 3[9] Dt 7[7] Pr 6[22]+oft, read וַיִּשְׁכַּב also (for וַיִּשְׁכְּמוּ) 1 S 9[26] 𝔊 Th We Dr and mod, ׳ש + יָשֵׁן *sleep* 1 K 19[5] ψ 3[6] 4[9], cf. Pr 3[24.24], + נרדם Jon 1[5], *=be lying* 1 S 3[2.3] 26[5] (all ב loc), v[7] 4[5] (acc cogn noon-repose), 2 S 13[8], cf שכב בְּלֶב־יָם Pr 23[34], of two lying (together, for warmth) Ec 4[11], + be sleeping 1 S 26[7], *= keep lying,* c עַד Ju 16[3] 1 S 3[15] Ru 3[13] Pr 6[9], emphasis on *resting,* Lv 26[6] (H), Jb 11[18]; token of mourning, ושכב ארצה (ולן) 2 S 12[16], cf 13[31], ש׳ בשק 1 K 21[27], ש׳ בין שפתים ψ 68[14] (of indolence?); fig of prostration by disease 41[9], among foes 57[5], of humiliation Je 3[25], c על rei land Gn 28[13] (J), usu bed 2 S 13[5] 1 K 21[4] Lv 15[4.20.26], cf v[20], for midday repose 2 S 4[7]. **c** *lie* on (על) one's side Ez 4[4.4.6.9] (symbol) **d** *lie,* על pers 1 K 3[19] (fatally), 2 K 4[34] (to revive) **e.** *lie* בחיק, of lamb (i e. be cherished) 2 S 12[3], of woman Mi 7[5] (intimacy), 1 K 1[2] (vital warmth), *lie down* for copulation Gn 19[33.35] (of woman, v **3** infr, both opp קום) **2.** *= lodge* (for night), (שָׁמָּה) ש׳ Jos 2[1] (E), 2 K 4[11], cf 9[16] (yet perhaps *=lie ill*), Lv 14[47] (ב loc) **3.** of sexual relations, *lie with* subj man, c עם Gn 30[15.16] 39[7.12.14] (J), Ex 22[15] (E), Dt 22[22]+8 t Dt., 2 S 11[4.11] 12[11.24] Lv 15[33], c אֵת fem *with* (MT אֹתָהּ, etc, orig אִתָּהּ, etc, v Dr[28.13.14] and II את, p 85[a] supra), Gn 26[10] 34[2.7] 35[22] (all J), 1 S 2[22] (om 𝔊 and mod), 2 S 13[14] Ez 23[8] (fig), Lv 15[24] (שָׁכֹב יִשְׁכַּב), Nu 5[19], also (c acc cogn. שִׁכְבַת־זֶרַע) v[13] Lv 15[18] 19[20], c acc (sf) fem Dt 28[30] Kt (v. [שָׁגַל]), c אצל fem Gn 39[10] (J), c את vir (sodomy), Lv 18[22] 20[13] (both H; c. acc. cogn משכבי אשה), c עם־בהמה Dt 27[21] Lv 22[13] (H), subj. woman, c עם vir Gn 19[32.34.35] (J) 2 S 13[11], אֵת vir Gn 19[33.34] (cf **1 e** supra) **4. a.** *lie down* in death, Is 14[8] 43[17] (opp קום), Ez 31[18] 32[27.28.29.30] Jb 14[12] (opp הקיץ, קום), ש׳ ואשקוט 3[13], *be lying* (dead) Is 51[20] La 2[21]. **b.** esp. in phr ש׳ עם אבותיו *lie down with his fathers,* of kings 1 K 1[21] 2[10]+35 t. K Ch, cf. Gn 47[30] (J), Dt 31[16], and (c את) 2 S 7[12] **c.** in grave, בביתו Is 14[18] (opp. מקברך), שֹׁכְבֵי קֶבֶר ψ 88[6], עַל־עָפָר Jb 7[21], עַל־ע׳ 20[11] 21[26]; in Sheʾôl Ez 32[21]; in Gehenna(?) Is 50[11]. **5.** fig. = relax Jb 30[17] *my gnawing pains do not sleep,* = have rest, לא ש׳ לבו Ec 2[23] †**Niph. Pu.** *= be lain with* (sexually; subj woman), only as Qr for Kt [שָׁגַל] **Niph. Pu.** q v. †**Hiph.** *lay,* *Pf* 3 fs. השכיבה c. acc. puer. + בחיק 1 K 3[20], so *Impf.* 3 fs sf. וַתַּשְׁכִּיבֵהוּ v[20], cf (על־מטה) 17[19] 2 K 4[21], *Inf abs* הַשְׁכֵּב אוֹתָם אַרְצָה 2 S 8[2] *making them lie down on ground,* *Impf.* also *lay* בְּמִשְׁכָּב 2 Ch 16[14] (of burial), נִבְלֵי שָׁמַיִם מִי יַשְׁכִּיב Jb 38[37] i e tip them so that contents may flow out (cf Ar. سَكَبَ supra). †**Hoph.** *Pt* מֻשְׁכָּב 2 K 4[32] *laid* עַל־מִטָּה; *Pf.* consec. וְהָשְׁכַּב Ez 32[32] *shall be laid* (in death), c. בתוך et את pers (*with*), so *Imv.* ms הָשְׁכְּבָה v[19] (c. אֶת pers. only).

†[שְׁכָבָה] **n f.** **act of lying, layer;**—only cstr שִׁכְבַת, all P, —**1.** act of *lying,* as acc. cogn. c שכב **3**. שִׁכְבַת־זֶרַע Lv 15[18] a man lies with her *a lying of seed* (in copulation), cf 19[20] Nu 5[13]; then (*= semen*), תצא שׁכבת־זרע Lv 15[16.32] 22[4] (+ מִמֶּנּוּ), ש׳ ז׳ alone 15[17]. **2.** *layer* of dew, שִׁכְבַת הַטַּל Ex 16[13.14] (P).

†[שְׁכֹבֶת] Lag[BN 179] Ba[NB 144]] **n. f. copulation,**—sf, all c. נָתַן: וַיִּתֵּן אֶת־שְׁכָבְתּוֹ Nu 5[20] (P; ב fem.), לא תתן שכבתך לְזֶרַע Lv 18[20] (אֶל fem.), בְּכָל־בְּהֵמָה לֹא תִתֵּן ש׳ v[23], cf 20[15] (all H)

מִשְׁכָּב [46] **n.m.** [Lv 15.4] **place of lying, couch; act of lying,**—abs. מ׳ 1 K 1[47]+, cstr. מִשְׁכַּב 2 S 4[5]+, sf. מִשְׁכָּבִי Jb 7[13]+, מִשְׁכַּבְכֶם ψ 4[5], pl. cstr מִשְׁכְּבֵי Gn 49[4]+, sf מִשְׁכְּבוֹתָם Ho 7[14]+, etc, —**1.** *couch, bed* (37 t.), 2 S 4[11] Ho 7[14] Mi 2[1] 1 K 1[47] Ct 3[1]+; וְנָפַל לְמ׳ Ex 21[18] (E) *he takes to his bed;* מ׳ נִדָּתָהּ Lv 15[26] (P, v sub I. נדד); מ׳ as place of copulation Gn 49[4] (poem in J), Is 57[7.8.8] Pr 7[17]; as place of burial Is 57[2] Ez 32[25] 2 Ch 16[14] (v. מ׳ Inscr Tabnit[8] and perh. Jewish inscr Cooke[341]). †**2.** *act of lying.* **a.** in gen., חֲדַר מ׳ chamber of *lying down* = bedchamber, Ex 7[28] (E), 2 S 4[7] 2 K 6[12], בְּחַדְרֵי מִשְׁכָּבְךָ Ec 10[20]; והוא שכב את מ׳ הַצָּהֳרָיִם 2 S 4[5] his noonday *siesta,* 17[23] id. perh. ערשׁ מ׳ couches for *lying down* Klo Bu HPS Now, cf. 𝔊 **b.** (from context) sexually of woman יָדְעַת (איש ל) מִשְׁכָּב Ju 21[11.12] Nu 31[17.35] (P), of man משכבי זָכָר Lv 18[22] 20[13] (+ אֶת־זָכָר sodomy; H); מ׳ דֹּדִים Ez 23[17].

†[שָׁכָה, so most] **vb. Hiph.** *Pt.* as adj. in סוּסִים מוּזָנִים מַשְׁכִּים הָיוּ Je 5^{8} usu., *horses . . . roaming at large* they have become (cf. Eth. ሰከየ:);—but mng. *lustful* needed; Aq Theod ἕλκοντες, Jer *trahentes* (sc. *genitalia*), i.e. מֹשְׁכִים; read with Arnheim Du Dr מַאֲשִׁיכִים, i.e. fed *stallions* (lit. *growing* אֲשָׁכִים, Lv 21^{20}; cf. מַקְרִין, מַפְרִים).

שָׁכַח 102 **vb. forget** (NH *id.*; Ecclus 45^{26c} and (**Pi.**) $11^{25.28}$; Aram. שְׁכַח, ܫܟܚ is *find*);—**Qal** 86 *Pf.* 3 ms. שׁ׳ ψ 9^{13}+, sf. שְׁכֵחַנִי Is 49^{14}; 2 fs. שָׁכַחַתְּ Je 13^{25}; 1 pl. sf. שְׁכַחֲנוּךָ ψ 44^{18}, etc.; *Impf.* יִשְׁכַּח Dt 4^{31}+, etc.; *Imv.* fs. שִׁכְחִי ψ 45^{11}; *Inf. abs.* שָׁכֹחַ; *Pt.* pl. cstr. שֹׁכְחֵי Jb 8^{13} ψ 50^{22};—*forget:* **1.** subj. man, **a.** acc. rei Gn 27^{45} (E), Dt 4^{9} 9^{7} (opp. זָכַר)+, =*forget and leave,* ב loc., 24^{19}; c. obj. cl. c. כִּי Jb 39^{15}; c. מִן inf. ψ 102^{5}. **b.** c. acc. pers., involving *forgetting to mention,* Gn 40^{23} (E; opp. זכר), *ceasing to care for* Je 30^{14} (fig.), Is $49^{15.15}$ (acc. om.), v ^{15} Jb 19^{14} ψ 45^{11}; c. acc. Jerusalem 137^{5a}; יִשְׁכָּחֵהוּ רֶחֶם Jb 24^{20}; abs. ψ 137^{5b} תִּשְׁכַּח יְמִינִי: AE Ki supply הַמַּעֲשֶׂה or הַנִּגּוּן (whence AV *her cunning*), but forced: 𝔊 תִּשָּׁכַח; read prob. (Gr Bu al.) תִּכְחַשׁ *let it grow lean* (109^{24}, cf. Zc 11^{17}), or (Che) תְּכַחֵשׁ *let it disappoint* (me), *fail* (Hb 3^{17}). **c.** esp. c. acc. י׳ (God), Ho 2^{15} 8^{14} 13^{6} Ju 3^{7} 1 S 12^{9} Is 17^{10} Dt 8^{19} (שָׁכֹחַ תִּשׁ׳) + 16 t. (5 t. Dt, 4 t. Je), + ψ 59^{12} (acc. om.); also acc. of divine name Je 23^{27} (בַּבַּעַל), ψ 44^{21}; commands of י׳ Ho 4^{6} Dt 26^{13} (acc. om.) ψ 119^{16} + 7 t. ψ 119, his doings and ways, v ^{139} $78^{7.11}$ 103^{2} 106^{13}, his covenant Dt $4^{23.31}$ 2 K 17^{38} Pr 2^{17}; law of wisdom 3^{1}, sc. acc. בִּינָה 4^{5}. **2.** subj. י׳ (God): **a.** acc. pers. Ho 4^{6} 1 S 1^{11} (opp. זָכַר), La 5^{20} Is 49^{14} (‖ עָזַב), ψ 10^{12} 13^{2} 42^{10}. **b.** acc. of sins Am 8^{7} ψ 10^{11} (acc. om.), cry ψ 9^{13} (opp. זָכַר), cf., of distress, 44^{25}. **c.** voice of foes ψ 74^{23}. **d.** sq. inf. ψ 77^{10}. †**Niph.** *Pf.* 3 ms. נִשְׁכַּח Ec 9^{5}, etc.; *Impf.* יִשָּׁכַח ψ 9^{19}, 3 fs. תִּשָּׁכַח Je 20^{11}, etc.; *Pt.* fs. נִשְׁכָּחָה Is 23^{16}, נִשְׁכַּחַת v ^{15}, pl. נִשְׁכָּחִים Jb 28^{4};—*be forgotten:* subj. rei Gn 41^{30} (E), Dt 31^{21} Je 20^{11} 23^{40} 50^{5} Is 65^{11}; subj. pers. ψ 9^{19} 31^{13} Ec 2^{16}, Tyre Is $23^{15.16}$ (under fig. of harlot), subj. הַנִּשׁ׳ מִנִּי רָגֶל Ec 9^{5}; זִכְרָם Jb 28^{4}. †**Pi.** *Pf.* 3 ms. שִׁכַּח י׳ וגו׳ La 2^{6} י׳ *hath caused to forget* (be forgotten) in Zion assembly and sabbath. †**Hiph.** *Inf.* לְהַשְׁכִּיחַ Je 23^{27} *to make* my people *forget* my name (2 acc.). †**Hithp.** *Impf.* 3 mpl. יִשְׁתַּכְּחוּ Ec 8^{10} *they were forgotten* in the city.

†[שָׁכֵחַ] **adj. forgetting, forgetful**;—pl. הַשְּׁכֵחִים אֶת־הַר ק׳ Is 65^{11} *they who forget the mt.* of my holiness (‖ עֹזְבֵי י׳); cstr. שְׁכֵחֵי א׳ ψ 9^{18} all nations *forgetful of God* (cf. שֹׁכְחֵי pt., Jb 8^{13} ψ 50^{22}).

†[שָׁכַךְ] **vb. decrease, abate** (NH שְׁכִיכָה is *allaying* of anger; שִׁכֵּךְ אֹזֶן *soothe, satisfy* the *ear* (so appar. Dalm), i.e. allow it to hear and understand, cf. Levy[NHWB] (and Ar. سَكَّ *be narrow, have small ears, be deaf,* Frä[90]); Ar. سَكَّ v. *humble oneself,* Wahrm *humiliate*);—**Qal** *Impf.* 3 mpl. וַיָּשֹׁכּוּ Gn 8^{1} the waters *abated; Inf. cstr.* כְּשֹׁךְ Est 2^{1} when *abated* the king's wrath, so *Pf.* 3 fs. שָׁכָכָה 7^{10}.—כְּשַׁךְ יְקוּשִׁים Je 5^{26} usu. *like the bending, crouching, of fowlers* (this meaning for שַׁךְ dub.; Dr כְּשֶׁר; Du del. יָשׁוּר כשׁ, then rds. מוֹקְשִׁים הִצִּיבוּ בַּשַּׁחַת א׳ יִלְכֹּדוּ:). **Hiph.** *Pf.* 1 s. consec. וַהֲשִׁכֹּתִי מֵעָלַי Nu 17^{20} *I will allay from upon me the murmurings* (acc.), etc.

†[שָׁכֹל, שָׁכֵל Lag[BN 26]] **vb. be bereaved** (=Ar. ثَكِلَ, 𝔗 תְּכוֹל, תְּכֵל; cf. Syr. ܬܽܘܟܠܳܐ *loss of children*);—**Qal** *Pf.* 1 s. כַּאֲשֶׁר שָׁכֹלְתִּי שָׁכָלְתִּי Gn 43^{14} (E) *if I am bereaved, I am bereaved* (of father, expr. resignation; on כָּל v. Ges §29 u); *Impf.* 1 s. אֶשְׁכַּל 27^{45} (E), c. acc. pers. *be bereaved* of you both (of mother); 3 fs. תִּשְׁכַּל מִנָּשִׁים אִמֶּךָ 1 S 15^{33} *thy mother shall be bereaved above* (more than) *women.* **Pi.** *Pf.* 3 fs. שִׁכְּלָה 1 S 15^{33}+, sf. וְשִׁכְּלַתְּהוּ Ez 14^{15}, etc.; *Impf.* 3 fs. תְּשַׁכֵּל Dt 32^{25}+, 2 fs. תְּשַׁכְּלִי Ez 36^{14} Qr (v. כָּשַׁל **Pi.**); *Inf. cstr.* sf. לְשַׁכְּלָם v ^{12}; *Pt.* מְשַׁכֵּלָה Ex 23^{26}, -כֶּלֶת Ez 36^{13}, -כָּלֶת 2 K $2^{19.21}$;—**1.** *make childless,* acc. of father Gn 42^{36} (E), of mothers 1 S 15^{33} (subj. חֶרֶב), cf. Ez 5^{17} (subj. famine and beasts), and 14^{15} (*id.*; obj. land); acc. of people Ho 9^{12} (מֵאָדָם), Je 15^{7} (+ אִבַּדְתִּי), Ez 36^{12}, cf. v $^{13.14}$ (v. supra); obj. om. (subj. חֶרֶב) Dt 32^{25} La 1^{20} Ez 21^{19} (Co, for תִּכָּפֵל, v. כָּפַל p. 495^{b}; otherwise Toy Krae). **2. a.** *cause barrenness,* or abortion, הָאָרֶץ מְשַׁכָּ׳ 2 K 2^{19}, cf. v ^{21} (Thes otherwise, v. מְשׁ׳ infra). **b.** *shew barrenness,* or *abortion,* (1) of any female Ex 23^{26} (E; + עֲקָרָה), animals Gn 31^{38} (E) Jb 21^{10}; (2) of vine Mal 3^{11}. **Hiph.** *Pt.* רֶחֶם מַשְׁכִּיל (וְשָׁדַיִם צֹמְקִים) Ho 9^{14} *miscarrying womb.* —Je 50^{9} read מַשְׂכִּיל *successful,* 𝔊 𝔖 Heb Codd. Ew Hi Gf Gie.

†שְׁכוֹל **n. [m.] bereavement, loss of children**;—לֹא אֵדַע שׁ׳ Is 47^{8} (‖ אַלְמָנָה), cf. v ^{9}; fig. ψ 35^{12}.

†[שָׁכוּל] **adj.** childless (through bereavement);—fs. שְׁכוּלָה Is 49[21] (fig. of Zion);—on form v. Ba [NB 47].

†שַׁכּוּל **adj.** bereaved, robbed of offspring (Ba [§ 37 c]);—esp. דֹּב שׁ׳ 2 S 17[8] Ho 13[8] Pr 17[12] (sim. of fierceness); שַׁכֻּלָה נְשֵׁיהֶם שַׁכֻּלוֹת Je 18[21]; וְשַׁכֻּלָה אֵין בָּהֶם Ct 4[2] (of flock, in sim.)=6[6].

†[שִׁכֻּלִים] **n. pl. abstr.** bereavement, childlessness;—בְּנֵי שִׁכֻּלָיִךְ Is 49[20] i.e. *sons of thee, the bereaved.*

†מְשַׁכֶּלֶת acc. to Thes **n.f. abstr.** barrenness, 2 K 2[21] (‖מָוֶת); if so, read <כֹּלֶת- Klo Kit; but probably **Pi.** *Pt.* as v[19], cf. Bur.

שכם (√of foll., meaning unknown; NH Hiph.=BH; Eth. has denom. ሰከመ: *carry on the shoulder;* Ar. سَكَمَ is *take short steps, from weakness* (Kam Frey)).

I. שְׁכֶם **n.m.** [Zp 3, 9] shoulder;—abs. שׁ׳ Gn 48[22]+, שֶׁכֶם 33[19]+, שֶׁכֶם ψ 21[13] (whence orig. **šakm* inferred Ol [§ 147 a ad fin.] Sta [§ 199 a]; but ֶ der. from ְ before ב, Ba [NB 104] Kö [ii. 1. 67, 506]); cstr. שְׁכֶם Gn 9[23]; sf. שִׁכְמוֹ 49[15]+, שִׁכְמָה (for שִׁכְמָהּ Ges [§ 91 e]) Jb 31[22], etc.;—**1.** *shoulder* (sometimes incl. back of neck; כתף=*shoulder-blade*): **a.** as bearing burdens, וַיֵּט שׁ׳ לִסְבֹּל Gn 49[15] (poem in J; Issach. under fig. of ass), cf. 21[14] (E), 24[15.45] Ex 12[34], also Gn 9[23] (all J), Jos 4[5] (E), Ju 9[48] Is 10[27] (‖צַוָּאר), 14[25] (both fig.), ψ 81[7], so, metaph., of responsibility of rule Is 9[5] 22[22] (symbolized by key), of accusation as (easy) burden Jb 31[36]; fig. also לְעָבְדוֹ שׁ׳ אֶחָד Zp 3[9] *to serve him* (with) *one shoulder* (as one man), cf. Syr. ܫܘܼ ܟܬܦܐ. **b.** in statement of Saul's height, מִשִּׁכְמוֹ וָמַעְלָה גָּבֹהַּ מִכָּל־הָעָם 1 S 9[2], cf. 10[23] and (with play on n.pr. loc. שְׁכֶם) נָתַתִּי לְךָ שׁ׳ אַחַד עַל־אַחֶיךָ Gn 48[22] (E; cf. Dr). **2.** in gen. *back:* כְּהַפְנֹתוֹ שִׁכְמוֹ לָלֶכֶת מֵעִם 1 S 10[9]; so תְּשִׁיתֵמוֹ שׁ׳ ψ 21[13], i.e. make them turn (in flight; cf. וְאֹיְבַי נָתַתָּה לִּי עֹרֶף 18[41]); as beaten שׁ׳ מַטֵּה Is 9[3] (‖שֵׁבֶט הַנֹּגֵשׂ בּוֹ); more anatom. כְּתֵפִי מִשּׁ׳ תִפּוֹל Jb 31[22] *let my shoulder-blade fall from its back.*—Ho 6[9] v. II. שְׁכֶם.

שִׁכְמָה v. foregoing.

†II. שְׁכֶם **n.pr.loc.** [48] et **m.** [14] (Συχεμ; 𝔊L oft. Σίκιμα Lag [BN 57]): **1.** district in N. Palestine (prob. *shoulder* (saddle?) of mount.);—מְקוֹם שׁ׳ Gn 12[6], שְׁכֶמָה 37[14]; = city (שְׁכֶם, שְׁכֶמָה, Ho 6[9] שְׁכֶמָה) Jos 24[1]; עִיר שׁ׳ Gn 33[18] Ju 8[31] + 20 t. Ju 9 (בַּעֲלֵי שׁ׳ v[2] + 12 t., מִגְדַּל־שׁ׳ ב׳ v[46.47]), Ho 6[9] + 21 t. (עִיר שׁ׳ Gn 33[18]); city of refuge Jos 20[7] 21[21] 1 Ch 6[52].—WMM [As. u. Eur. 394], cp. Egypt. *Sa-ka-mà* (cf. Jen [ZA x (1895) 356]); mod. *Nablûs* (from Rom. name Neapolis); v. Buhl [G 200 f.] GASm [G 332 ff. 345] Wilson [Hast. DB SHECHEM]. **2. n.pr.m.** (on connexion with **1** cf. Ju 9[28]), 'son' of Ḥamor, also Gn 33[19] 34[2] + 10 t. 34, Jos 24[3].

†שֶׁכֶם **n.pr.m.** in Manasseh (Συχεμ): Nu 26[31] 1 Ch 7[19]; בְּנֵי שׁ׳ Jos 17[2].

†שִׁכְמִי **adj. gent.** of שֶׁכֶם, c. art. as n. coll. הַשּׁ׳ Nu 26[31].

[שָׁכַם] [65] **vb. Hiph. denom.** start, rise, early (prop. *load backs* of beasts for day's journey);—*Pf.* 3 ms. consec. וְהִשְׁכִּים 2 S 15[2] Jb 1[5], etc.; *Impf.* 3 ms. וַיַּשְׁכֵּם Gn 19[27]+, 2 ms. תַּשְׁכִּים Ju 9[33], etc.; *Imv.* הַשְׁכֵּם Ex 8[16]+; *Inf. abs.* הַשְׁכֵּם Je 7[25]+, -כֵּים Je 44[4] Pr 27[14], erron. אַשְׁכִּים Je 25[3] (Ges [§ 53 k]); *Pt.* מַשְׁכִּים Ho 6[4]+, etc.;—*rise early, make an early start,* of journey (Hex only JE); לְדַרְכְּכֶם Ju 19[9] (+מָחָר), cf. Ct 7[13]; +vb. of going Gn 19[2] (J), standing 2 S 15[2], encamping Ju 7[1], etc.; +inf. 1 S 15[12] (cf. Dr), 29[11] 2 K 6[15] (לָקוּם), מַשְׁכִּימֵי קוּם ψ 127[2] (opp. מְאַחֲרֵי שֶׁבֶת); usu. c. בַּבֹּקֶר Gn 19[27] (J; אֶל־הַמָּקוֹם), מַשְׁכִּימֵי בַבּ׳ שֵׁכָר 1 S 29[10.10] + 27 t., + (hyperbol.) יִרְדֹּפוּ Is 5[11] (‖מְאַחֲרֵי בַנֶּשֶׁף); c. מִמָּחֳרָת Ex 32[6] (E), Ju 6[28] + 3 t.; c. בַּעֲלוֹת הַשַּׁחַר Jos 6[15] (J), 1 S 19[26]; וַיְמַהֲרוּ וַיַּשְׁכִּימוּ וַיֵּצְאוּ Jos 8[14] (J) *they made a quick and early start, and went out;* †Inf. abs. (Ges [§ 113 s]) as adv. הַשְׁ׳ וְהַעֲרֵב 1 S 17[16] *at early morning and at evening;* esp. of י׳, in Je: הַשׁ׳ וְדַבֵּר=*speaking early and often* 7[13] 35[14] and (of Je) 25[3], cf. 11[7] 32[33]; oft. הַשׁ׳ וְשָׁלֹחַ=*sending early and often* 7[25] 24[4] 26[5] 29[19] 35[14] 44[4], also 2 Ch 36[15]; so vb. fin. הִשְׁכִּימוּ הִשְׁחִיתוּ Zp 3[7]=*with eagerness they corrupted* (Ges [§ 120 g]); pt. כַּטַּל מַשְׁ׳ הֹלֵךְ Ho 6[4] *like the dew departing early,* 13[3] (Ges [ib.]).—1 S 9[26] read וַיִּשְׁכַּב, v. שׁכב.

שָׁכַן, שָׁכֵן [129] **vb.** settle down, abide, dwell (NH *id.;* Ecclus 43[17 d]+; Ph. שכן Lzb [375]; Aram. שְׁכֵן; Syr. ܫܟܢ, all *dwell;* Ar. سَكَنَ *rest, dwell,* cf. As. *šakânu, set, lay, deposit, set up* (a dwelling), intrans. *be situated* (of city), *maškanu, place, dwelling-place*);—**Qal** *Pf.* 3 ms. שׁ׳ Ex 40[35] + 5 t.; שָׁכֵן Dt 33[12] + 2 t., etc.; *Impf.* 3 ms. יִשְׁכֹּן Gn 16[12]+; יִשְׁכָּן־ Nu 9[17] + 2 t.; 3 mpl. יִשְׁכְּנוּ Je 49[31]; 3 fpl. תִּשְׁכֹּנָּה Ez 17[23], etc.; *Imv.* ms. שְׁכֹן Gn 26[2] ψ 37[27]; שְׁכָן־ v[3]; mpl. שִׁכְנוּ

Je 48^{28}; *Inf. cstr.* לִשְׁכֹּן, בִּשְׁכֹּן (Ges^{§45e}) Gn 35^{22}, 2 Ch 6^{1}, etc.; sf. שָׁכְנִי Ex 29^{46}; שָׁכְנוֹ Dt 12^{5} (but v. **Pi. 1**), etc.; *Pt.* שֹׁכֵן Gn 14^{13}+, שֹׁכְנִי (Ges^{§90lm}) Dt 33^{16}+3 t.; sf. fs. שֹׁכַנְתְּ Je 51^{13}; *Pt. pass.* appar. pl. cstr. c. art. הַשְּׁכוּנֵי Ju 8^{11} (but corrupt, n.pr.loc. needed, v. GFM):—**1.** *settle down to abide:* **a.** of pers.: encamp Nu 24^{2} (E); settle permanently ψ 102^{29} (abs.: ‖ יִכּוֹן); שׁ׳ כמלך Jb 29^{25} (‖ ישׁב); *settle down* (to remain) Ju 5^{17}; תַּחְתָּיו 2 S 7^{10} = 1 Ch 17^{9} (not to be removed); esp. at rest, peace, in security, לבטח Je 23^{6} 33^{16} Dt 33^{12}, cf. בין כתפים v^{12}; ψ 16^{9} (‖ שׂמח) בטח Dt 33^{28} Pr 1^{33}; (ל)בדד Nu 23^{9} (poem) Je 49^{31} Mi 7^{14}; land of Egypt Je 46^{26} (remain undisturbed), so 50^{39} Is 13^{20} (‖ תֵּשֵׁב, cf. ישׁב **4**); c. acc. מרומים 33^{16}; abs. Na 3^{18}, subj. אדירים (We יָשְׁנוּ, Now יִשְׁכְּבוּ ‖ נָמוּ); Pr 7^{11} *her feet tarry not in her house.* **b.** of animals: כְּלָבִיא Dt 33^{20}; ב loc. Is 34^{11} Jb 37^{8}; שָׁם Is 13^{21}; birds שׁ׳ תַּחַת (under) Ez 17^{23}, שׁ׳ בְּצֵל v^{23}; c. עַל = *upon* 31^{13}, = *by* ψ 104^{12}; c. acc. סֶלַע Jb 39^{28}; abs., of man under fig. of bird, אָעוּפָה וְאֶשְׁכֹּנָה ψ 55^{7}. **c.** things: c. עַל of cloud, Jb 3^{5} *settle down over;* cf. Ex 24^{16} 40^{35} Nu 9$^{17.18.22}$ (all P); c. בְּ 10^{12} (P). **2.** *abide, dwell:* **a.** of men: abs. ψ 37^{27} (לְעוֹלָם); שָׁמָּה Is 65^{9}; c. ב loc. ψ 69^{37} Jb 18^{15} 30^{6} Mi 4^{10} Je 48^{28} + 10 t.; לְחוֹף יַמִּים Gn 49^{13}; c. עַל, *by* Ju 5^{17} Je 51^{13}; *upon* ψ 37^{29}; על פני Gn 16^{12} (J); c. עִם *with* ψ 120$^{5.6}$; c. acc. Pr 2^{21} Je 17^{6} + 5 t.; שֹׁכְנֵי אֶרֶץ ‖ ישְׁבֵי Is 18^{3}; מִן ... עַד Gn 25^{18} (J); תֵּבֵל). **b.** of the dead: שֹׁכְנֵי עָפָר Is 26^{19} (‖ רְפָאִים); cf. Jb 26^{5} (‖ *id.*), so mortals, שֹׁכְנֵי בָתֵּי חֹמֶר 4^{19}; שׁ׳ דומה ψ 94^{17} (i.e. שׁאול). **c.** of God: שׁ׳ בָּעֲרָפֶל 1 K 8^{12} = 2 Ch 6^{1} (poem); מָרוֹם Is 33^{5}; שֹׁ׳ עַד 57^{15}; מָרוֹם וְקָדוֹשׁ v^{15}; שׁ׳ סְנֶה Dt 33^{16} (theoph.); בְּאָהֳלֵי־שֵׁם Gn 9^{27} (J, v. Br$^{MP\ 82}$; al. Japheth subj.); בְּתוֹכָם Ex 25^{8} 29^{46} Nu 5^{3} (all P), Ez 43^{9}; c. בְּתוֹךְ elsewh. Ex 29^{45} (P) + 6 t.; ב loc. ψ 85^{10}; later בְּצִיּוֹן Jo 4$^{17.21}$; בְּהַר צִיּוֹן Is 8^{18}; ψ 68$^{17.19}$ (abs.) + 4 t.; שֹׁכֵן יְרוּשָׁלָ͏ִם ψ 135^{21}. **d.** things: אֹהֶל מוֹעֵד, c. את Lv 16^{16} (P); מִשְׁכַּן י׳ שָׁם Jos 22^{19} (P); אור Jb 38^{19}. **e.** abstr. subj.: מִשְׁפָּט Is 32^{16} (בַּמִּדְבָּר); חָכְמָה, c. acc. עָרְמָה Pr 8^{12}. †**Pi.** *Pf.* 3 ms. שִׁכֵּן ψ 78^{60}; 1 s. שִׁכַּנְתִּי Je 7$^{7.12}$; *Impf.* 1 s. אֲשַׁכְּנָה Je 7^{3}; *Inf. cstr.* שַׁכֵּן Nu 14^{30} + 7 t.; sf. שַׁכְּנוֹ Dt 12^{5} (so read for MT לְשִׁכְנוֹ, cf. Kö$^{ii.1.21}$);—**1.** *make settle down, establish:* אֹהֶל שִׁ׳ בָּאָדָם ψ 78^{60}; esp. in Dt, לְשַׁכֵּן שְׁמוֹ שָׁם *establish his name there* (cf. *šakan šuma* as Canaanism Wkl$^{TelAm.\ 133\ Rev.\ 20;\ 181.\ 6}$) Dt 12^{11} 14^{23} 16$^{2.6.11}$ 26^{2}, cf. Je 7^{12} Ne 1^{9}; + לָשׂוּם אֶת־שְׁמוֹ שָׁם לְשִׁכְנוֹ Dt 12^{5} (rd. לְשַׁכְּנוֹ). **2.** *make to dwell:* c. acc. pers., ב loc., Nu 14^{30} (J) Je 7$^{3.7}$. †**Hiph.** *Pf.* 1 s. הִשְׁכַּנְתִּי Ez 32^{4}; *Impf.* 3 ms. juss. יַשְׁכֵּן ψ 7^{6}, וַיַּשְׁכֵּן Gn 3^{24} ψ 78^{55}, etc.;—**1. a.** *lay,* כבודי לעפר ψ 7^{6} *lay my honour in the dust* (of death); *place, set,* Gn 3^{24} (J); *place, establish,* אהל מועד at Shilo Jos 18^{1} (P). **b.** *cause* birds *to settle,* עַל Ez 32^{4}. **2.** *cause to dwell,* c. acc. pers., ב loc., ψ 78^{55}; cf. Jb 11^{14}.

†[שֵׁכֶן?] **n.m. dwelling**;—sf. שִׁכְנוֹ Dt 12^{5} (cf. שכן *dwelling* Ecclus 14^{25}), but v. √ **Pi.**

†שָׁכֵן **adj. inhabitant, neighbour**;—שׁ׳ Is 33^{24}+; cstr. שְׁכַן Ho 10^{5}; sf. שְׁכֵנוֹ Ex 12^{4}; שְׁכֵנַיִךְ 2 K 4^{3}, etc.; f. sf. שְׁכֶנְתָּהּ Ex 3^{22}; fpl. שְׁכֵנוֹת Ru 4^{17};—**1.** *inhabitant,* Is 33^{24} Ho 10^{5}. **2.** *neighbour:* woman Ex 3^{22} (E); pl. Ru 4^{17}; man Ex 12^{4} (P) Je 6^{21} Pr 27^{10}, pl. 2 K 4^{3}; of places Dt 1^{7}; nations, to Judah Ez 16^{26} ψ 79^{12}; מָדוֹן לשׁ׳ 44^{14} 79^{4}, cf. 31^{12}, 89^{42}; חֶרְפָּה לִשְׁכֵנֵי(נוּ) 80^{7}; to Edom Je 49^{10}; to Sodom v^{18} 50^{40}; to י׳ 11^{14} (because to his people).

מִשְׁכָּן$_{139}$ **n.m.**$^{Ex\ 26,6}$ **dwelling-place, 'tabernacle'**;—מ׳ Ex 25^{9}+; cstr. מִשְׁכַּן 38^{21}+, etc.; pl. cstr. מִשְׁכְּנֵי ψ 46^{5} (𝔊 BaeDu מִשְׁכָּנוֹ, מִשְׁכַּן י׳ >); sf. מִשְׁכְּנֹתֵיהֶם Ez 25^{4} (מִירוֹתֵיהֶם ‖ משכנותיהם >), מִשְׁכָּנוֹת Hb 1^{6} ψ 132^{5}; cstr. מִשְׁכְּנוֹת 87^{2}+, etc.;—†**1.** *dwelling-place:* מִשְׁכַּן־קֹרַח דָּתָן וַאֲבִירָם Nu 16$^{24.27}$ (P) [but here orig. מִשְׁכַּן י׳; v. Comm.]; poet. = *tomb,* Is 22^{16}. **2.** elsewhere in sg. always of abode of י׳: †**a.** in gen., of temple, מִשְׁכַּן כְּבוֹדֶךָ 26^{8}; קְדֹשׁ מִ׳ ψ 46^{5}; מ׳ שְׁמֶךָ 74^{7}. **b.** מִשְׁכַּן שִׁלוֹ 78^{60}. **c.** הַמּ׳ in P, of י׳'s 'dwelling' (Ex 25^{9} RVm; rendered conventionally 'tabernacle'), of planks lined with vari-coloured tapestry, with a 'tent' (אֹהֶל) over it, filled with כְּבוֹד י׳ Ex 40$^{34.35}$; over it cloud שכן Nu 9$^{18.22}$ (during the wanderings); its plan given by י׳ Ex 25^{9} 26^{30}; disting. from אֹהֶל מוֹעֵד, the 'tent' over it (cf. אֹהֶל **3**), Ex 26$^{7.12.13}$ 36^{14} 40^{19}; †מִשְׁכַּן י׳ Lv 17^{4} (H), Nu 16^{9} 17^{28} 19^{13} 31$^{30.47}$ Jos 22^{19} (v. also **1**), 1 Ch 16^{39} 21^{29} 2 Ch 1^{5} 29^{6}; †מ׳ הָעֵדֻת Ex 38^{21} Nu 1$^{50.53.53}$ 10^{11}; מ׳ אהל מועד Ex 39^{32} 40$^{2.6.29}$ 1 Ch 6^{17}, מִשְׁכַּן בֵּית הָאֱלֹהִים v^{23}, נָשָׂא אֶת־הַמִּשְׁכָּן 23^{26}; cf. מִשְׁכָּן (prob. gloss on אהל), 2 S 7^{6} ‖ 1 Ch 17^{5}, + 76 t. P. **3.** pl. מִשְׁכָּנוֹת *dwellings* (only poet.): **a.** of Israel, Nu 24^{5} (poem; ‖ אהלים), Je 30^{18} Is 54^{2} + 4 t.; of other nations Je 51^{30} Hb 1^{6}, cf. Ez 25^{4} (v. supra); מ׳ עַוָּל Jb 18^{21}; מ׳ רשׁעים 21^{28}; of wild

ass 39⁶ (|| בית), shepherds Ct 1⁸; = tomb ψ 49¹² (cf **1**) **b.** God's abode in Zion Ez 37²⁷ ψ 132⁵·⁷, cf 43³, 84² (|| חֲצֵרוֹת ^)

†שְׁכַנְיָה(וּ) **n pr.m.** (*" hath taken up his abode*),—שְׁכַנְיָה, Σεχενια(ς), etc · **1.** descendant of Jehoiakin 1 Ch 3²¹·²² (on context v. Kit), Ezr 8³·⁵. **2.** Ezr 10² (diff from **1** ?). **3.** father of a wall-builder Ne 3²⁹ **4** father-in-law of Tobiah Ne 6¹⁸ **5** priestly name **a.** Ne 12³ = שְׁכַנְיָהוּ 1 Ch 24¹¹, cf שְׁכַנְיָה **3** Ne 10⁵ 12¹⁴. **b.** שְׁכַנְיָהוּ 2 Ch 31¹⁵

†I. [שָׁכַר] **vb be, or become, drunk, drunken** (NH *id*, der. spec and deriv, Ecclus 40¹⁸·²⁰ שכר *strong drink*, Ar. سَكِرَ *be drunken*, also *be full*, سَكَّرَ *fill*, As *šikaru*, = שֵׁכָר, *šakkûru*, *drunken*, perhaps also vb *šakâru*; Eth ሰከረ: Aram שִׁכְרָא, ܫܟܪܐ = שֵׁכָר, esp *date-wine* (Low P 12³), cf ܫܟܪ *be drunken*, usu (der. spec) *defile, deform*, etc, from שֵׁכָר, Egypt. *ṯa-k-ṯra* WMM As u Eur 102, Gk. σίκερα Lewy Fremdw 81),—**Qal** *Pf* 3 pl שָׁכְרוּ Is 29⁹, *Impf* 3 ms וַיִּשְׁכָּר Gn 9²¹, 3 mpl יִשְׁכְּרוּן Is 49²⁶, etc; *Imv.* mpl שִׁכְרוּ Je 25²⁷ Ct 5¹, *Inf cstr* לְשָׁכְרָה Hg 1⁶; *Pt pass* שְׁכֻרַת Is 51²¹ (Ges § 130 b Lag BN 60).—*become drunken* Gn 9²¹ (J), of social drinking 43³⁴ (J), Ct 5¹, token of plenty Hg 1⁶; fig. of nations staggering helplessly under calamity Je 25²⁷, 51²¹ (ולא מִיַּיִן), Na 3¹¹, of infatuation Is 29⁹ (ולא יַיִן), of disgrace La 4²¹, self-destruction, כעסים דָּמָם יש׳ Is 49²⁶ **Pi.** *make drunken*. *Impf* 3 ms. sf וַיְשַׁכְּרֵהוּ 2 S 11¹³, lit; fig. 1 s (sf of people) וָאֲשַׁכְּרֵם (read (וְ) Is 63⁶ (subj. ׳י) *I made them drunk* in my wrath (but MSS Ges Hi Ew Che Kit Marti al וָאֲשַׁבְּרֵם *I brake them in pieces*), *Pt.* fs, of Bab, מְשַׁכֶּרֶת כָּל־הָאָרֶץ Je 51⁷, cf *Inf abs* שַׁכֵּר Hb 2¹⁵ (i e. terrorizing nations, read prob. הַשְׁקֵה ואף ש׳ We Now) **Hiph.** *id.* · *Pf* 1 s. והשכרתי Je 51⁵⁷ (subj. ׳י) i.e make princes helpless, והִשְׁכַּרְתִּים v³⁹, *Imv* mpl sf הַשְׁכִּירֻהוּ, obj Moab, i.e. make helpless and disgraced 48²⁶, *Impf* 1 s אַשְׁכִּיר חִצַּי מִדָּם Dt 32⁴².—Ruben JQ xi (1899), 446 prop מַשְׁכִּירוּת Ho 7⁵ for מָשַׁךְ יָדוֹ את **Hithp.** *Impf.* 2 fs. תִּשְׁתַּכָּרִין 1 S 1¹⁴ how long *wilt thou make thyself drunken* [a drunken spectacle]?

†שֵׁכָר **n** [**m.**] **intoxicating drink, strong drink** (Ba NB § 71),—alw ׳ש abs., usu || יַיִן (exc. ψ 69¹³) Is 29⁹; usu condemned, Is 5¹¹·²² 28⁷·⁷ 56¹² (נִסְבְּאָה ש׳), Mi 2¹¹ 1 S 1¹⁵ Pr 20¹; forbidden to priests on duty Lv 10⁹ (P), not for princes Pr 31⁴, nor Nazirite Nu 6³ Ju 13⁴·⁷·¹⁴, cf. חֹמֶץ ש׳ Nu 6³; שׁוֹתֵי ש׳ ψ 69¹³ *drunkards*; but ׳ש as common drink Dt 29⁵ (opp. to miraculous), allowable in sacrif meal 14²⁶, commended for weak and weary Pr 31⁶, נסך ש׳ Nu 28⁷ (P; for יין v¹⁴+); v further Kennedy Ency Bib iv 5309 f.—On form cf Lag BN 37, BN 81.

†שִׁכֹּר, שכור **adj. drunken** (Ba NB § 134 b),—abs שכר 1 S 25³⁶, שכור 1 K 16⁹+, f. שִׁכֹּרָה 1 S 1¹³, pl שכורים Jo 1⁵, cstr. שִׁכֹּרֵי Is 28¹·³,—*drunken*: 1 S 25³⁶, איש ש׳ Je 23⁹, שֹׁתֶה ש׳ 1 K 16⁹ *drinking* (and) *drunken*, 20¹⁶, as subst = *drunken one*, *drunkard* Is 28¹·³ Pr 26⁹, pl. Jo 1⁵ (|| שֹׁתֵי יָיִן), in sim. Is 19¹⁴ Jb 12²⁵ ψ 107²⁷, and (of earth) Is 24²⁰, f. of drunken woman 1 S 1¹³.

†שִׁכָּרוֹן **n.**[**m.**] **drunkenness**,—׳ש only fig. Je 13¹³ Ez 23³³ (Co Berthol Krae שִׁבָּרוֹן, not Toy), both of bewilderment and helplessness under calamity, from drinking blood 39¹⁹.—Vid Lag BN 202 cf 199.

†[שִׁכְּרוֹן] **n.pr.loc** on NW border of Judah, c ה loc שִׁכְּרוֹנָה- Jos 15¹¹, Σοκχωθ, 𝔊L Σαχαρωνα.

II שכר (√of foll., meaning unknown)

†אֶשְׁכָּר **n** [**m.**] gift,—abs ׳אש ψ 72¹⁰ (|| מִנְחָה); sf אשכרך Ez 27¹⁵

†שַׁל in עַל־הַשַּׁל 2 S 6⁷ is disputed; 𝔊 B om.; A𝔊L τῇ προπετείᾳ, *for his hastiness* (prob. from Aram; cf. ܡܢ ܫܠܘ = *suddenly*), 𝔙 *temeritate*; 𝔗 על דאשתלי because he *acted in error* (Aram שְׁלָא, שְׁלִי *err* v. BAram. (שָׁלוּ), hence AV RV *for his error*, <Th We Dr Bu Now fragm. of עַל [אֲשֶׁר] שָׁלַ[ח יָדוֹ ע]ל, || 1 Ch 13¹⁰.

שֶׁל Ct 1⁶ 3⁷ al, בשל Ec 8¹⁷ v. שֶׁ **4 d.**

שַׁלְאֲנָן Jb 21²³ *lapsus cal* for שַׁאֲנָן, q v (cf. Perles Anal 92)

†[שָׁלַב] **vb. Pu. be bound, joined** (NH Pu = BH, שְׁלִיבָה *rung* of ladder, Aram. שְׁלִיבִין appar. only 1 K 7²⁸·²⁹, ܫܠܒܐ *ravine, narrow path between mountains*, Ar. سَلَبَ is *seize, carry off, by force*),—*Pt* fpl מְשֻׁלָּבֹת Ex 26¹⁷ tenons *joined* each to (אֶל) its fellow, 36²² (both P)

שְׁלַבִּים **n.**[**m.**] **pl** joinings of bases (𝔙 *juncturae*),—בֵּין הַשּ׳ 1 K 7²⁸·²⁹, עַל־הַשּ׳ v²⁹; AV RV *ledges*, <*ribs* (Kit) or *frames* (Benz), joining or binding the parts together.

שלג (√of foll., unless loan-word; NH = BH, Ecclus 43[17] שלגו *his snow;* Ar. ثَلْج, Aram. תַּלְגָּא, ܬܠܓܐ, As. *šalgu*).

†**שֶׁלֶג n.m.**[14 53. 10] **snow**;—abs. 'שׁ Is 1[18]+, שָׁלֶג Ex 4[6]+; cstr. שְׁלַג Je 18[14],—*snow,* 2 S 23[20] (יום השׁ') = 1 Ch 11[22], Jb 6[16] 37[6] (|| גֶּשֶׁם מָטָר), ψ 147[16] 148[8] (+ אשׁ, בָּרָד, קִיטוֹר); מימי שׁ' Jb 24[19], cf. 9[30] Qr (בְּמֵי, < Qr במו De Di Bu al., snow as purifying; v. also [מַי]); poet. אֹצְרוֹת שׁ' 38[22] (|| א' בָּרָד); symb. of cold Pr 31[21], as moistening, *fertilizing* Is 55[10] (|| גֶּשֶׁם), on mountains, *fig.* of normal habit, שׁ' לְבָנוֹן Je 18[14]; sim. of whiteness, of leprosy Ex 4[6] (J), Nu 12[10] (E), 2 K 5[27]; c מִן comp., of fair skin La 4[7] (|| חָלָב); sim. of sins, כַּשּׁ' יַלְבִּינוּ Is 1[18], cf. ψ 51[9] (מִן comp.), sim of refreshment Pr 25[13] (drink cooled by snow, v. reff in De Toy), of the unfitting כַּשּׁ' בַּקַּיִץ 26[1] (|| מָטָר)—On snow in Pal. v. Nicol[Hast. DB Snow].

† [שָׁלַג] **vb. denom. Hiph.** snow;—*Impf.* 3 fs. תַּשְׁלֵג (Ges § 109 k), impers. ψ 68[15] *it snows* on Salmon (meaning obscure)

† I. [**שָׁלָה, שָׁלוֹ**] **vb. be quiet, at ease** (Ecclus 47[13] שלוה *prosperity,* 41[1] שליו *prosperous, at ease;* ܫܠܐ *be tranquil, quiet, cease;* ℑ שְׁלָא, שְׁלִי *be at ease,* then *be careless, thoughtless, go astray* [for Heb. שָׁגָה, שָׁגַג], Aph. *neglect* (God, etc), BAram. ℑ שָׁלוּ *error;* Ar. سَلَا (و) *be forgetful, neglectful, content, free* (fr anxiety));— **Qal 1.** *be* (have) *quiet: Pf.* 1 s. שָׁלַוְתִּי Jb 3[26]. **2.** *be at ease, prosper,* of wicked, 3 pl. שָׁלוּ Je 12[1] La 1[5], also *Impf.* 3 mpl. יִשְׁלָיוּ (Ges § 75 u) Jb 12[6], and (of good) ψ 122[6] (יִשְׁל Jb 27[8] v. II. שלה) **Niph.** *Impf.* 2 mpl. תִּשָּׁלוּ juss. 2 Ch 29[11] *be* not *negligent* (easy-going; Germ. 'bequem') **Hiph.** *Impf.* 2 ms. תַּשְׁלֶה juss. 2 K 4[28] *do* not *mislead* me (cf. תַּכְזֵב v[16]), strong Aramaism, whence Klo תַשְׁגֶה.

†[**שָׁלוֹ** Ges § 84 a e Lag[BN 142]] **n.[m.] ease, prosperity** (Perles[Anal 30] *delusion;* cf. Aram שָׁלוּ *error,* sub √, e.g., Gn 43[12]),—sf שַׁלְוִי ψ 30[7] (cf. De Bae); < read שַׁלְוָתִי (or שַׁלְוֹתִי Bi), Ol Hup-Now Du al (> Sta Hup think שַׁלְוִי abbreviated from שלותי).

†[**שֶׁלִי**] **n.[m.] quietness**;—בַּשֶּׁלִי 2 S 3[27], i.e. quietly, privately (cf. ܒܫܠܝܐ often in the same sense PS[4167]).

I. **שֵׁלָה** v. שְׁאֵלָה.

† II. **שֵׁלָה n.pr.m.** son of Judah, Σηλωμ[ν]: Gn 38[5 11 14 26] (J), 46[12] (P), Nu 26[20] (P), 1 Ch 2[3] 4[21].

†**שֵׁלָנִי adj.gent.** of foreg.: c art. as n.coll. השׁ' Nu 26[20] (P). So rd also 1 Ch 9[5] Ne 11[5], v. שִׁילֹנִי.

†**שָׁלֵו** (Lag[BN 43]), **שְׁלֵיו, שָׁלֵיו adj. quiet, at ease**;—**1.** of pers *at ease,* שָׁלֵו Jb 16[12], שְׁלֵיו 21[23] (Kö[II 1 83]); of nation, שָׁלֵיו (poss. diminutive Kö[II 1 144]) Je 49[31] (|| יוֹשֵׁב לָבֶטַח); *prosperous,* of city fs. שְׁלֵוָה Zc 7[7]; of wicked, mpl cstr. וְשַׁלְוֵי עוֹלָם ψ 73[12] (Renan[H. III 131] prop. וְשַׁלְוֵי עֲוִילִים) **2.** of land, *quiet,* שְׁלֵוָה 1 Ch 4[40] (|| שֹׁקֶטֶת). **3.** in לֹא יָדַע שָׁלֵו בְּבִטְנוֹ Jb 20[20] שׁ' is appar n.abstr. *quiet, ease,* so Di De al, read שַׁלְוָה Siegf Bu, Du (after 𝔊) לֹא שָׁלֵו בִּמְטַמּוֹ; שָׁלֵו Ez 23[42] is corrupt, Hi Co Berthol (cf Da) שָׁרוּ *sang,* Toy שָׁרִים, Krae שרים.

†**שַׁלְוָה n.f. quietness, ease**;—abs. 'שׁ ψ 122[7]+; cstr. שַׁלְוַת Ez 16[49] Pr 1[32]; pl sf. שַׁלְוֹתַיִךְ Je 22[21] (< שַׁלְוָתֵךְ Vrss Gie);—*quietness, peace,* Pr 17[1] (opp. רִיב), ψ 122[7] (|| שָׁלוֹם); *ease, careless security,* Ez 16[49] (שַׁלְוַת הַשְׁקֵט), Pr 1[32]; *prosperity,* Je 22[21] Dn 8[25] 11[21 24]; בְּשׁ' *in* (time of) *security* (of sudden attack), if not *unawares* (Thes Ew Hi Ke al); cf. ܡܢ ܫܠܝܐ lit. *out of quiet,* i e. *suddenly, unawares* (e g. 1 Macc 1[30] = ἐξάπινα), ℑ מִן שְׁלִיָא Pr 3[25] 6[15] (= פִּתְאֹם), ψ 30[7] v. [שָׁלוֹ].

† II. [**שָׁלָה**] **vb. draw out, extract** (si vera l; = שָׁלַל; Syr. ܫܠܐ (e g Ex 2[10]), ℑ[Jer] שְׁלִי (e.g. Lv 11[17])),—**Qal** *Impf* 3 ms. apoc (Ges § 109 k) כִּי יֵשֶׁל אֱלוֹהַּ נַפְשׁוֹ Jb 27[8] (De), < read יִשַּׁל, or יֵשֶׁל (√שׁלל) Di, Schnurrer We Siegf Bu Du יִשְׁאַל *demandeth,* Perles[Anal. 48] יִשָּׂא אֶל־אֱלוֹהַּ.

†[**שִׁלְיָה**] **n.f. after-birth** (= Ar سَلًى, Aram. שִׁלְיְתָא, ܫܠܝܬܐ);—sf שִׁלְיָתָהּ Dt 28[57].

†**שִׁלֹה, שִׁילֹה, שִׁלוֹ, שִׁילוֹ n.pr.loc.** (orig שִׁלוֹן, v. adj gent. (otherwise Ba[NB § 224 b]), which also shews that √שׁיל, שׁול, was posited when text of K was fixed, cf. Dr[2 S 15. 12]);—שִׁלֹה Ju 21[19] 1 S 1[24] 3[21] 14[3] Je 7[14] (on destruction of S. v. We[2 S 8. 17]), 26[9] 41[5], מִשְׁכַּן שׁ' ψ 78[60], שִׁילוֹ Ju 21[21.21] Je 7[12]; שִׁלֹה Jos 18[1 8. 9 10] 19[51] 21[2] 22[9 12] (all P or R), Ju 18[31] 21[12] 1 S 1[3. 9] 2[14] 3[21] 4[3. 4 12] 1 K 2[27] 14[2. 4] Je 26[6] (var. שִׁלוֹ

in all these [2 t] given by Gi as Qr) —Σηλωμ, Σηλω(ν) —Mod *Seilûn*, c 9½ m NNE. of Bethel (Beitin), Buhl$^{G 173}$ Di$^{Hast DB Shiloh}$.

†שִׁילֹנִי, שִׁלֹנִי etc, **adj. gent.** of foreg הַשִּׁילֹנִי of Ahijah 1 K 11^{29} 15^{29}, הַשִּׁלֹנִי 12^{15}; הַשִּׁילוֹנִי 2 Ch 9^{29}, הַשִּׁלוֹנִי 10^{15}, also הַשִּׁילוֹנִי (coll) 1 Ch 9^{5}, in ‖ Ne 11^{5} הַשִּׁלֹנִי without n.pr m, but in both these read הַשֵּׁ(י)לָנִי Be Ke Ryle Gu^{Hpt} Siegf^{Ne} Buhl, etc, v II. שֵׁלָה.

שַׁלְהֶבֶת v p 529^{a} supr.

I שָׁלַח$_{814}$ **vb. send** (NH *id*; Ecclus 48^{18}+, Aram שְׁלַח, ܫܠܰܚ, So^{Buhl} Ba$^{ES 41}$ cp Ar. سَرَحَ (*r*=*l*), *send forth, drive* cattle to pasture, *send* messenger, etc., but then diff √ for I. שלח, Ar. سِلَاحٌ, سِلْحٌ *weapon*; As. prob. *šalû* (*send, hurl*?), whence *tešlitu, command*),—**Qal**$_{862}$ *Pf.* 3 ms. שׁ׳ Gn 42^{4}+, 2 ms sf שְׁלַחְתָּנִי Ex 5^{22}, etc, *Impf* 3 ms יִשְׁלַח Gn 3^{22}+, 2 fpl תִּשְׁלַחְנָה Ez 23^{40} (Ju 5^{26} read תִּשְׁלָחֶנָּה? Ob^{3} תִּשְׁלַח יָד? Ges$^{§ 47 k}$); *Imv* ms שְׁלַח 1 S 20^{31}+, mpl שִׁלְחוּ 2 K 2^{17}, *Inf abs* שָׁל(וֹ)חַ Nu 22^{37}+, cstr שְׁלֹחַ v^{15}+, שְׁלֹחַ Is 58^{9}, sf שָׁלְחֲךָ Gn 38^{17}, etc, *Pt act* שֹׁלֵחַ Ex 9^{14}+, etc; שָׁלוּחַ 1 K 14^{6}+, etc,—**1.** *send* human subj, esp **a.** acc pers Gn 42^{4} 43^{8} (both J, c אֵת *with*, pers) Nu 22^{15} (E)+oft, c לְ rei for which Je 14^{3}, sq אֶל pers Gn 37^{13} (J), 2 S 11^{6} Ne 6^{3}+, rarely c לְ pers Gn 32^{19} (J, pass), אֶל loc 2 Ch 16^{4}, בְּ loc 1 S 11^{3}, לְ loc 1 K 5^{28}, acc loc 2 K 22^{3}, ה- loc.+מֵעַל pers. 2 S 13^{17}, מִן loc. Gn 37^{14} (J), Nu 13^{3} (P), etc, sq inf purpose 1 S 25^{14} (+מִן loc.), 2 K 1^{16} Je 40^{14}+, אֶל pers. c inf. purpose 2 S 10^{3} Je 42^{9}+, c וְ subord 2 K 5^{6}, c. vb. fin actionis Ex 2^{5} (E), *sent her maid and took*, +, etc (many combinations), acc. pers alone 24^{5} (E), Jos 7^{22} (E), 2 S 10^{7}+oft **b.** less oft. acc rei (sometimes c בְּיַד of agent), **c.** אֶל pers. 1 S 16^{20} 2 K 5^{5} 20^{12}+, 1 K 5^{21} (=designate by sending unto), לְ pers Ju 3^{15} 1 K 5^{22}+, אֶל loc Est 1^{22}, שָׁמָּה 2 K 6^{14}; +inf purpose 1 Ch 19^{4} Est 4^{4}, +vb fin. action ψ 105^{24}, acc of kid, alone, Gn 38^{23} also (acc. om.) v^{17}, etc **c.** very oft without obj. +vb fin. action, *send and do* so and so, Gn 27^{45} (E), 2 K 11^{4} Jb 1^{5}+, c אֶל pers Ho 5^{13} 2 S 11^{6}+, esp +לֵאמֹר Gn 38^{25} (J), 1 K 20^{5} (oft. SK), Je 29^{28}+; c inf purpose Gn 32^{6} (J), Nu 21^{32} (J), 1 S 22^{11}+, etc (and so 1 S 31^{9}, reading וַיְשַׁלְּחוּ, for **Pi.**, Th We Dr Now, not HPS Bu), abs 2 K 2$^{16\,17}$ 2 S 14^{29}, =*send to inquire* 1 K 20^{17}, etc **2.** *send*: subj. י׳ (God), **a.** acc. pers. Gn 45^{5} (E; לִפְנֵי pers), 1 S 15^{18} (בְּדֶרֶךְ), +אֶל pers 2 S 12^{1}, acc. of angel, לִפְנֵי pers. Gn 24^{7} Ex 33^{2} (both J), אֵת *with* Gn 24^{40} (J), etc; c acc pers =*commission* Ex 3^{12} (E), Ju 6^{14} Is 6^{8} Je 14$^{14\,15}$+oft Je, Zc 2^{13}+, also (c. אֶל pers) Ex 3^{13} (E), Je 25^{4} Ez 3^{6}+, etc.; esp of sending prophet, (שָׁלַח), הַשְׁכֵּם וְשָׁלוֹחַ Je 7^{25}+ (v [שָׁכַם]); acc pers +inf. purpose 1 S 15^{1} Je 19^{14}+; +עַד loc. 2 K 2^{2}, acc loc. v^{4}, ָה loc. v^{6}, etc **b.** c acc rei, plagues Ex 9^{14} (c. אֶל־לֵב, בְּ pers), fig. arrows 2 S 22^{15}=ψ 18^{15} (+vb fin. action), ψ 144^{6}, cf Je 25^{16} al, his word Is 9^{7} (בְּ gent), 55^{11} (אשׁר *to which*), Zc 7^{12} (בְּ agent), ψ 107^{20} (+vb fin. action), 147^{15} (+acc. אֶרֶץ), acc help 20^{3} (מִן loc), light and truth 43^{3} (+vb fin. action.), cf. 57^{4}. **3.** *stretch out*, esp acc. hand: **a.** human subj., c בְּ pers *against*, Gn 37^{22} (E), 1 S 24^{11} Est 2^{21}+; c בְּ rei (property of others) Ex 22$^{7\,10}$ (E), Est 9^{10}+, בַּחַלָּמִישׁ Jb 28^{9}, c. אֶל pers. *against* Gn 22^{12} (E), 2 S 18^{12}, עַל pers. 1 K 13^{4}, etc, אל rei (for good) 2 S 6^{6} (יָד om); from outside, inward, Ct 5^{4} (מִן loc); abs Jb 30^{24} (read טבע for בְּעִי Di Bi Bu) +inf. purpose 1 S 22^{17} 2 S 1^{14} 1 Ch 13^{9}, +vb fin. act Gn 3^{22} (J) Dt 25^{11} Ju 15^{15}+, שׁ׳ אֶצְבַּע Is 58^{9}, in token of scorn; c acc of rod 1 S 14^{27}, שִׁלְחוּ מַגָּל Jo 4^{13} *stretch out* (the) *sickle*. **b.** י׳ subj, acc hand, +אֶל pers. *against* Ex 24^{11} (E), cf (עַל) ψ 138^{7}, +vb fin. act. †Ex 3^{20} (JE), 9^{15} (J), Jb 1^{11} 2^{5}, in favour, Je 1^{9}, abs ψ 144^{7} (מִן loc), also (pass) Ez 2^{9} and (acc תַּבְנִית יָד), 8^{3}. †**c.** acc hand, subj. angel, +acc. loc, inf. purpose 2 S 24^{16}, cherub, אֶל rei, מִן loc Ez 10^{7}; adversary, אל pers. Jb 1^{12}, subj angel, acc. rod Ju 6^{21}. **d.** *stretched out, slender*, of tree Gn 49^{21} (poem in J), v I. אֵלָה supr p 18^{b} **e.** perhaps *extend, direct*, acc rei Ez 8^{17} (v זְמוֹרָה supr. p. 274^{b}, also conj. in Toy Krae) **4.** rarely *send away* (v **Pi.**): human subj, acc. pers Ju 11^{38} (+acc temp), Gn 28^{5} (P) **5.** *let loose* (v **Pi.**), perhaps only ψ 50^{19} (fig.) *thy mouth hast thou let loose in evil*. †**Niph.** *Inf. abs* וְנִשְׁלוֹחַ סְפָרִים=*letters were sent* (Ges$^{§ 113\,z\,ss}$) Est 3^{13} (+אֶל pers., בְּיַד agent., inf. purpose) **Pi.**$_{266}$ *Pf.* 3 ms שִׁלַּח Ex 8^{28}+, sf. שִׁלַּחֲךָ 1 S 20^{22}, etc, *Impf* 3 ms יְשַׁלַּח Je 3^{1}+, יְשַׁלֵּחַ Is 45^{13} Pr 6^{14}, 1 s sf. אֲשַׁלֵּחֲךָ Gn 32^{27}, אֲשַׁלְּחֶךָּ 2 S 11^{12} 1 K 20^{34}, etc, *Imv.* ms. שַׁלַּח Ex 4^{23}+, etc.; *Inf. abs.* Dt 22^{7} 1 K 11^{22}; cstr שַׁלַּח Gn 8^{10}+, שַׁלֵּחַ Ex 7^{27}+, etc; *Pt* מְשַׁלֵּחַ Gn 43^{4}+, etc,—**1.** *send*

off, away, human subj.: **a.** acc. pers. + לְ loc Jos 24^{28} (E), Ju 7^{8} 1 S 10^{25}+; + לְ pers. Je 48^{12}, + ה- loc. Ju 12^{9} and (c. inf. purpose) Gn 28^{6} (P), acc. of goat, לַעֲזָאזֵל Lv 16^{10} (ה- loc.), v^{26}; *send out,* different ways, acc. pers., בְּ loc. Ju 19^{29} 20^{6}; *send* into exile, ׳י subj, c. מִן loc. Je 24^{5}, ה- loc. 29^{20}. **b.** *send away, dismiss,* acc. pers. Gn 21^{14} (E), 25^{6} (J; מֵעַל pers), 2 S 13^{16}+; specif, c acc. of wife (= *divorce*), Dt $22^{19.29}$ $24^{1.3}$ Je 3^{1}+, abs. Mal 2^{16}. **c.** *send away* empty (-handed) רֵיקָם, + acc. pers. Gn 31^{42} (E), Dt 15^{13} Jb 22^{9}. **d.** *send off,* give a 'send-off' (sometimes escort part way), acc. pers., Gn 18^{16} 24^{59} 31^{27} (all J), 1 S 9^{26} 2 K 5^{24} 6^{23}. **e.** acc. rei 1 S 6^{8} Ne 8^{12}+, c. acc. loc. 1 S 5^{10} 6^{3}, אֶל pers. Je 27^{3}, etc. **2. a.** *send away,* subj. ׳י, acc pers. Gn 19^{29} (J; מִתּוֹךְ), 1 K 9^{7} (מֵעַל פְּנֵי) **b.** *give over,* acc. pers. ψ 81^{13} (בְּ of evil) **c.** *cast out,* acc. pers Je 28^{16} (מֵעַל־פְּנֵי), Lv 18^{24} 20^{23} (both מִפְּנֵי) **d.** *send out, forth,* send on a mission, esp of ׳י, c. acc. of hornet Dt 7^{20}, cf 28^{20} 32^{24} (all בְּ pers.), serpents Nu 21^{6} (E, בְּ pers.), lions 2 K $17^{25.26}$ (both *id*), foes 2 K $24^{2.2}$ (+ inf. purpose); pestilence Am 4^{10} Ez 28^{23} (בְּ pers.), etc; also springs into (בְּ) channel ψ 104^{10}. **3.** *let go, set free* (sometimes c. חָפְשִׁי) Ex 4^{23} $5^{2.2}$ (all JE), 2 S $3^{21.23.24}$+, = cease to abuse Ju 19^{25}; + inf purpose Gn 24^{56} (J), Ex 5^{1} (E, + 10 t. Ex), 1 S 5^{11}; c acc. of bird Gn $8^{7.8}$ (+ מֵאִתּוֹ) +; עַל־פְּנֵי הַשָּׂדֶה + Lv 14^{7}, cf. v^{53} (both P); = *let loose,* acc. of beast, Ex 22^{4} (E), Lv 16^{22} (בְּ loc.); acc. of bridle Jb 30^{11} (fig); metaph. of strife Pr $6^{14.19}$ 16^{28}; *let loose* waters, subj. ׳י, Jb 12^{15}. **4.** *shoot forth* branches, Je 17^{8} ψ 80^{12} Ez 31^{5} (but v. I. שֶׁלַח **2**); cf. of locks (פֶּרַע) Ez 44^{20} = *let grow long.* **5.** *let down,* acc. pers. Je 38^{6} (בְּ instr), acc rei v^{11} (*id* + אֶל pers. et loc). **6.** *shoot* (acc. of arrow om), לְשַׁ׳ לִי שִׁלַּח (אֶת־)הָעִיר לְמַטָּרָה 1 S 20^{20}. **7.** phrases: שִׁלַּח (אֶת־)הָעִיר בָּאֵשׁ + Ju 1^{8} 20^{48}, cf. 2 K 8^{12} ψ 74^{7}; but also שִׁ׳ אֵשׁ בְּ + Am $1^{4.7.10.12}$ $2^{2.5}$ Ho 8^{14} Ez 39^{6}; rare expressions are: וַיְשַׁלְּחֵם בְּיַד־פִּשְׁעָם Jb 8^{4} (God subj), *stretch out* hand, בְּ rei (for use) Pr 31^{19}, לְ pers. (charity) v^{20}; חֶבְלֵיהֶם תְּשַׁלַּחְנָה Jb 39^{3} (of hinds, bearing); שַׁלַּח לַחְמְךָ עַל־פְּנֵי הַמָּיִם Ec 11^{1}.—רַגְלַי שִׁלֵּחוּ Jb 30^{12} is corrupt; Theod Ew Di רַגְלָם שִׁלֵּחוּ; Me Bu Be al. dittogr. from v^{11b}.

Pu. *Pf.* 3 ms. שֻׁלַּח Ju 5^{15} Jb 18^{8}, etc; *Impf.* 3 ms יְשֻׁלַּח Pr 17^{11}; *Pt.* מְשֻׁלָּח Is 16^{2}+,—*be sent off* (started on journey) Gn 44^{3} (J); with commission, בְּ pers. Ob^{1} Pr 17^{11}, אֶל pers Dn 10^{11}; *be put away, divorced,* of wife Is 50^{1} (fig.); *be impelled* (?), בְּרַגְלָיו (= *at his heels?*), c. בְּ loc. Ju 5^{15} (vb. dub.), cf. שֻׁלַּח בְּרֶשֶׁת בְּרַגְלָיו Jb 18^{8} *he is hurried into the net with his feet* (? 𝔊 Du שִׁלְּחָה רַגְלוֹ), קֵן מְשֻׁלָּח Is 16^{2} *a driven* (scattered) *nest* (|| עוֹף נוֹדֵד), cf. נָוֶה מְשֻׁ׳ וְנֶעֱזָב כַּמִּדְבָּר 27^{10}; נַעַר מְשֻׁ׳ Pr 29^{15} *a boy let loose* (unrestrained).

†**Hiph.** *Pf.* 1 s. וְהִשְׁלַחְתִּי *and I* (׳י) *will send* famine, בָּאָרֶץ Am 8^{11}, cf. Ez 14^{13}, wild beasts, בְּ pers. Lv 26^{22} (H); *Pt* מַשְׁלִיחַ, acc. of flies, בְּ pers. Ex 8^{17} (J); *Inf. cstr.* לְהַשְׁלִיחַ, acc. of foe, בְּ gent. 2 K 15^{37}.

I. שֶׁלַח **n.[m.] missile, weapon, sprout** (late),—abs. ׳שׁ Jo 2^{8}+, שָׁלַח Ne 4^{11} Jb 33^{18}, sf. שלחו Ne 4^{17}, pl. שְׁלָחִים 2 Ch 23^{10}, etc.;—**1.** *missile, weapon,* Ne 4^{11} and v^{17} (where הַמָּיִם corrupt, read probably בימינו or בְּיָדוֹ; v. Ryle Be-Ry Berthol), 2 Ch 23^{10} (disting. from חֲנִית, מָגֵן); coll. 32^{5} and עָבַר בַּשׁ׳ Jb 33^{18} 36^{12} (*perish by* or < *rush upon* [and perish]), Jo 2^{8} (v. בעד). **2.** *sprout, shoot* (cf. [שְׁלוּחָה], and √ ψ 80^{12} Je 17^{8}), שְׁלָחַיִךְ פַּרְדֵּס Ct 4^{13} (fig; meaning? Perles$^{Anal\ 63}$ prop שְׁנֵי לְחָיַיִךְ *thy two cheeks*); + prob Ez 31^{5} (rd בשלחיו Co Toy al., or בשלחי [with v^{6}] Krae)

†II. שֶׁלַח **n. pr. m.** son of Arphachshad, Σαλα. ׳שׁ Gn 10^{24b} $11^{13.14.15}$ 1 Ch 1^{18b}; שָׁלַח Gn 10^{24a} 11^{12} 1 Ch $1^{18a.24}$.

†III. שֶׁלַח **n.pr.** in בְּרֵכַת הַשׁ׳ Ne 3^{15} = שִׁלֹחַ.

†שִׁלְחִי **n.pr.m.** father of Jehoshaphat's mother;—1 K 22^{42} = 2 Ch 20^{31}; Σεμεει, Σαλαλα, Σαλει, etc.

†שִׁלְחִים **n.pr.loc.** in Negeb of Judah Jos 15^{32}; Σαλη, Σαλειμ, 𝔊L Σελεειμ.

†שִׁלֹחַ **n.pr.font.** at SE. of Jerus. (connex. with above √ not certain (Ba$^{NB\ 66}$), ψ 104^{10} has **Pi.**),—מֵי הַשִּׁ׳ Is 8^{6}; Σ(ε)ιλωαμ; = III. שֶׁלַח; mod. *Birket Silwân*; v. Wilson$^{Hast.\ DB\ Siloam}$ Cond GASm RS$^{Ency\ Bib\ Jerusalem,\ §§\ 2\ 11\ 18}$ Buhl$^{G\ 139}$; on inscription found in adjacent tunnel v. Dr$^{Sm\ xv\ ff.}$ GACooke$^{15\ ff.}$.

†שִׁלּוּחִים **n.[m.] pl. sending away, parting gift**;—**1.** אַחַר שִׁלּוּחֶיהָ Ex 18^{2} (J) *after she had been sent away.* **2.** שִׁלֻּחִים 1 K 9^{16} he gave (city) as *parting gift* (i e dowry) to his daughter; cf. fig. שִׁלּוּחִים Mi 1^{14} thou shalt give *a parting gift* (= say farewell to; lose) Morešeth of Gath.

†[שְׁלוּחָה] **n.f.** shoot, branch (cf 1. שֶׁלַח **2**),—pl sf. שְׁלוּחֹתֶיהָ Is 16[8], of vine of Sibmah (E. of Jordan)

†מִשְׁלָח **n.**[m.] **1.** outstretching; **2.** place of letting loose.—מ׳ only cstr: **1.** בְּכֹל־מ׳ יַד פ׳ *in every outstretching of* one's *hand*, =every undertaking, Dt 12[7. 18] 15[10] 23[21] 28[8. 20] **2.** לְמ׳ שׁוֹר וּלְמִרְמַס שֶׂה Is 7[25] (√**Pi. 3** esp. Is 32[20])

†מִשְׁלוֹחַ **n.**[m.] **1.** outstretching, **2.** sending,—מ׳ only cstr: **1.** מ׳ יָדָם Is 11[14] Edom and Moab are *the outstretching of their hand* (that of which they take possession, cf √**Qal 3**) **2.** מִשְׁלֹחַ מָנוֹת אִישׁ לְרֵעֵהוּ Est 9[19. 22] *the sending of portions to each other.*

†מִשְׁלַחַת **n.f. 1.** discharge, **2.** deputation, sending.—**1.** abs. אֵין מ׳ בַּמִּלְח׳ Ec 8[8] *there is no discharge in war* **2.** cstr. מ׳ מַלְאֲכֵי רָעִים ψ 78[49] *a deputation* (or sending) of angels of evil.

II שׁלח (√of foll., Ar. سَلَخَ *strip off hide*, سَلَاخَة *piece of hide stripped off*; Aram. שְׁלַח, ܫܠܚ *take off* garment, Ar. سَلَخَ, Aram. שִׁלְחָא, ܫܠܚܐ *hide*, perh also Palm שלחא (pl? Lzb, Reckend[ZMG xlii (1888), 41]cp 1 שֶׁלַח), hence שֻׁלְחָן, q v (also NH Ecclus), v GFM[PAOS 1890, lxx, esp Ju 1 7])

שֻׁלְחָן [71] **n.m.**[Ex 25. 23] table (on form of word cf GFM[l c], prop (v supr) *skin* or *leather mat* spread on ground, v also, on early Sem 'table,' Thes[1417] We[Skizzen iv 137] RS[Sem. I 184, 2nd ed 201] Kennedy[Ency Bib iii 2991]),—abs ש׳ 1 S 20[34]+; cstr שֻׁלְחַן 1 K 5[7]+; sf. שֻׁלְחָנִי Ju 1[7]+, etc, pl שֻׁלְחָנוֹת Is 28[8]+, cstr. שֻׁלְחֲנוֹת 1 Ch 28[16. 16],—**1.** *table* for king's repast Ju 1[7] (c תַּחַת), 1 S 20[29. 34] 2 S 9[11] (read ש׳ דָּוִד 𝔊 Th We Dr and mod), v[13] 19[29] 1 K 2[7] 5[1] 18[19] 10[5]=2 Ch 9[4], cf Is 21[5] (c עָרַךְ (q v **1 c**) *arrange*), c עַל 2 S 9[7. 10. 11] Dn 11[27]; for governor Ne 5[17] (c עַל) **2.** for private use 1 K 13[20] (c אֶל), Jb 36[16] ψ 23[5] (fig., c עָרַךְ), cf 78[19] (*id*), 128[3], also (in bedroom) 2 K 4[10], of revellers Is 28[8], cf ψ 69[23] (fig.), of wisdom (fig.) Pr 9[2]. **3.** esp Ez P for sacred uses: in tab Ex 25[23]+ 17 t. 25–40, Nu 3[31], שֻׁלְחַן הַפָּנִים Nu 4[7] (cf 2 Ch 29[18] infr), הַשּׁ׳ הַטָּהֹר Lv 24[26] (cf 2 Ch 13[11] infr), in Sol's temple 1 K 7[48] 2 Ch 29[18], also (10 in no.) 4[8. 19] 13[11], cf 1 Ch 28[16. 16. 16. 16], also Ez 23[41] (c. עָרַךְ), in Ezekiel's temple Ez 40[39. 39]+6 t Ez 40 (8 in no), 40[42] (of stone, 4 in no), like altar 41[22], =altar of burnt-offering 44[16], in second temple, שֻׁלְחַן י׳ Mal 1[7], שׁ׳ אֲדֹנָי v[12], for idolatrous meal Is 65[11], fig of י׳'s sacrif feast Ez 39[20] (eschatol.).

†שָׁלַט **vb.** domineer, be master of (late) (NH *id*, As. *šalâtu, have power;* Ar. سَلُطَ *overcome, prevail;* سَلِيط *strong, hard,* سُلْطَان *dominion,* also *ruler, sultan;* Eth. ሠለጠ: Aram שְׁלֵט, ܫܠܛ (esp der spec.), Nab שלט, (שלטון),—**Qal** *Pf* 3 ms. ש׳ Ec 8[9], etc; *Impf.* 3 ms. יִשְׁלַט Ec 2[19], etc; *Inf. cstr.* שְׁלוֹט Est 9[1];—*domineer, lord it* over, עַל pers, Ne 5[15]; בְּ pers Ec 8[9] (לְרַע לוֹ); בְּ rei 2[19], *become master* of, בְּ pers. Est 9[1]. **Hiph. 1.** *give power of*: *Pf* 3 ms sf pers וְהִשְׁלִיטוֹ לֶאֱכֹל Ec 5[18], so *Impf.* 3 ms sf יַשְׁלִיטֶנּוּ 6[2] (both subj God) **2.** =**Qal**, *get mastery of*. juss 3 fs אַל־תַּשְׁלֶט־בִּי כָל־אָוֶן ψ 119[133]

†שַׁלִּיט **adj.** having mastery, domineering,—**1.** *having mastery*. אֵין אָדָם שׁ׳ בָּרוּחַ Ec 8[8], elsewhere as subst הַשּׁ׳ *the ruler* 10[5], so (c. עַל־הָאָרֶץ) Gn 42[6] (prob late substitution for original word of E), pl. as subst שַׁלִּיטִים Ec 7[19] (specif of Alex's successors Perles[Anal 42]) **2.** *domineering, imperious,* fs (Kö[ii 1 201]) אִשָּׁה זוֹנָה שַׁלָּטֶת Ez 16[30] (Jerusalem personified)

†שִׁלְטוֹן **n.**[m.] mastery (Lag[BN 199]);—Ec 8[8] (c. בְּ)

II. שׁלט (√of foll.; Zehnpf[BAS i 553, No 53] cites As *šaltu, a shield* of leather)

†[שֶׁלֶט] **n.m.**[2 S 8. 7] shield (?),—pl. שְׁלָטִים 2 K 11[10]+, cstr שִׁלְטֵי 2 S 8[7]+; sf. שִׁלְטֵיהֶם Ez 27[11]; —*shields* (so AV RV Thes; al *quivers*, or [v. esp. Barnes[Expos. T x 43 f. (cf. 188)]] *arms, equipment;* Vrss vary; As *šaltu* (v. √) seems to be a specif article), 2 S 8[7]=1 Ch 18[7], 2 K 11[10]=2 Ch 23[9] (where + מָגִנּוֹת, but) Ct 4[4] appos of מָגֵן (q v sub גנן), hung on walls, cf Ez 27[11], מִלְאוּ הַשּׁ׳ Je 51[11] i e., perh, put arms through thongs, ready to use them (but v Barnes[l c], and Gie, cf מלא **Qal 2**).

שַׁלֶּטֶת v שַׁלִּיט supra.

[שָׁלַךְ] [125] **vb. Hiph.** [112] throw, fling, cast (Ph. שלך in cp n pr, meaning dub; Ar. سَلَكَ is *travel* (or *cause to travel*) *along a road, cause to enter*),—*Pf.* 3 ms הִשְׁלִיךְ Am 8[3]+; 2 ms. sf. consec. וְהִשְׁלַכְתּוֹ Je 51[63]; 2 fpl consec וְהִשְׁלַכְתֶּנָה

Am 4[3], etc.; *Impf.* יַשְׁלִיךְ Is 2[20], וַיַּשְׁלֵךְ Ju 9[17]+, etc.; *Imv.* ms. הַשְׁלֵךְ Ex 7[9] ψ 55[23], fs. הַשְׁלִיכִי Je 7[29], etc.; *Inf. abs.* הַשְׁלֵךְ Je 22[19] 36[23]; cstr. הַשְׁלִיךְ Ec 3[5.6], etc.; *Pt.* מַשְׁלִיךְ Mi 2[5] ψ 147[17], etc.;—**1.** usu. human subj., *throw, cast:* **a.** acc. rei, with many prep.: e.g. אֶל loc. 2 K 23[12] Ez 5[4] Zc 5[8.8]+, also (acc. rei om.) Ex 15[25] (J), Nu 19[6] (P)+; ב loc, Ex 32[24] (E), Ez 7[19]+; rarely ל loc. 2 Ch 30[14] and (acc. om.) 24[10]; עַל loc. 2 K 23[6], ־ָה loc. Ex 4[3.3], שָׁמָּה Ju 8[25] 2 K 6[6] (acc. om.), etc.; esp. of casting dead bodies, אֶל loc. Jos 8[29] (J), 10[27] (J), +3 t., ב loc. Am 8[3] 2 K 9[25.26] 13[21], מֵהָלְאָה לְ Je 22[19]; acc. rei + אֶל pers. 1 K 19[19] 2 S 20[22] (acc. om.); acc. rei c. עַל pers. Na 3[6] Ju 9[53] 2 S 11[21] (+מֵעַל), etc.; acc. rei + מִיָּד Ex 32[19] (E), cf. Dt 9[17] (מֵעַל); + ל of animal Ex 22[30] (E), Is 2[20], etc. †**b.** c. acc. pers., אֶל of pit Gn 37[22] (E), Je 38[6.9], ב of pit Gn 37[20] (E), c. ה loc. v[24] (E; pit), Ex 1[22] (J), cf. Am 4[3] (si vera l.); תַּחַת loc. Gn 21[15] (E); acc. 'י, fig., c. אַחֲרֵי גֵוֶךָ 1 K 14[9] (of apostasy), Ez 23[35], so 'י's law Ne 9[26], words (אַחֲרֵי pers. reflex.) ψ 50[17]. †**c.** *throw away,* acc. rei Ju 15[17] (מִיָּדוֹ), 2 K 7[15] Ez 20[7.8] ψ 2[3] (מִן reflex.), Ec 3[5] (opp.=כְּנֹס); acc. om. Je 7[29] Jo 1[7] (of locusts); abs. Ec 3[6] (opp. שָׁמַר); acc. of transgr. Ez 18[31] (fig.; מֵעַל reflex.). †**d.** *cast off, shed,* blossom (like flower) Jb 15[33]. **e.** *cast down* (late), subj. goat, acc. ram, Dn 8[7] (אַרְצָה) little horn, acc. אֱמֶת v[12] (*id.*); acc. pers. (lit.) 2 Ch 25[12] (מִן loc.), Jb 18[7] *his* (own) *counsel felleth him;* so prob. Je 9[18] *they have overthrown* our dwellings (Du reads Hoph.). **f.** fig., ψ 55[23] *cast* עַל־י' *thy lot.* **2.** 'י subj.: **a.** *cast,* acc. rei, + עַל pers. Jos 10[11] (E), Jb 27[22] (acc. rei om.); sandal *upon* Edom ψ 60[10]=108[10] (sign of possession); ice (no prep.) 147[17]. **b.** acc. pers. + ב loc. 2 K 2[16] (subj. רוּחַ י'), Ne 9[11] Jon 2[4] (+acc. loc.); + אַרְצָה Ez 28[17] (fig.); אֶל loc. (of exile) Dt 29[27]; esp. of 'י's rejecting men, acc. pers. + מֵעַל פָּנָיו 2 K 13[23] 24[20], cf. 2 K 17[20] Je 7[15.15] 52[3], also ψ 51[13] and (without מִן) 71[9]; casting sins (acc.) אַחֲרֵי גֵוְךָ Is 38[17], ב loc. Mi 7[19]. **c.** *cast down,* honour of Israel + acc. loc., מִן loc., La 2[1]; acc. pers. ψ 102[11] (opp. נָשָׂא). **3.** phrases: הִשׁ' גּוֹרָל + ל Jos 18[8.10] (R[D]) *cast lots* ל *in behalf of;* מַשׁ' חֶבֶל בְּגוֹרָל Mi 2[5] (v. 2 חֶבֶל, 1. 3 גּוֹרָל); מַשׁ' בַּיְאוֹר חַכָּה Is 19[8] i.e. fishermen; וַיַּשְׁלֵךְ נַפְשׁוֹ מִנֶּגֶד Ju 9[17], v. נֶגֶד 2 c; מִשִּׁנָּיו אַשׁ' טָרֶף Jb 29[17] *out of his teeth I cast the prey.* †**Hoph.** *Pf.* 3 ms. הָשְׁלַךְ Dn 8[11]; 2 ms. הָשְׁלַכְתָּ Is 14[19], etc.; *Impf.* 2 fs. וַתֻּשְׁלְכִי Ez 16[5]; 3 mpl. יֻשְׁלָכוּ Is 34[3]; *Pt.* מֻשְׁלָךְ 2 S 20[21], etc.;—**1.** *be thrown, cast,* acc. of head, אֶל pers. + בְּעַד of wall 2 S 20[21]; carcass, ב loc. 1 K 13[24.25.28] Je 14[16]; לַחֶרֶב 36[30]. **2.** *be cast forth, out,* abs. of dead Is 34[3]; מִן of grave 14[19]; אֶל־פְּנֵי הַשָּׂדֶה Ez 16[5] (Jerus. personified as infant); עַל־הָאָרֶץ Je 22[28] (of exile). **3.** *be cast down,* לָאָרֶץ Ez 19[12] (Isr., fig. of vine); abs. of sanctuary Dn 8[11]. **4.** metaph., *be cast,* עַל of 'י ψ 22[11] (i.e. on his protection).

†שָׁלָךְ **n. [m.]** bird of prey, prob. cormorant (as *hurling* itself from above;—cf. Thes[1419] Di[Lv] Tristr[NHB 252] McLean-Shipley[Ency. Bib. Cormorant]);—Dt 14[17] Lv 11[17] (P).

†I. שַׁלֶּכֶת **n.f.** felling of tree;—Is 6[13].

†II. שַׁלֶּכֶת **n.pr.** of a temple-gate, W. side (? gate of *casting forth;* yet cf. Kit);—1 Ch 26[16].

†I. [שָׁלַל] **vb. draw out** (Ar. سَلَّ *draw,* esp. sword from scabbard, سَلِيلٌ *drawn sword, new-born child* (cf. Frä[75], but also Schulth[Hom. Wurz. 80 f.]); Talm. שָׁלִיל, ת שְׁלִילָא *embryo* or *abortion*);—*Impf.* 2 mpl. + *Inf. abs.* שֹׁל־תָּשֹׁלּוּ לָהּ מִן וגו' Ru 2[16] *ye shall by all means draw out for her* from the sheaves.

†שׁוֹלָל **adj. indecl.** (Ges[§ 118o]) barefoot (appar. *stripped* as to walking; alw. c. הלך);—אֵילְכָה שׁוֹלָל וְעָרוֹם Mi 1[8] Qr *I will go barefoot and naked* (Kt שילל); מוֹלִיךְ יוֹעֲצִים שׁ' Jb 12[17], cf. v[19].

†II. שָׁלַל **vb. spoil, plunder** (usu. identif. with I. שׁ'; NH *id.* (Jastr, cf. Dalm); As. *šalâlu, id.;* Hom[Chr 33] cp. Sab. הלל *plunder,* connecting this with Ar. ثَلَّةٌ *a flock of sheep* (or *goats*); then ת שַׁלְּלָא *booty,* and (rare) Syr. ܫܠܠܐ are loan-words);—**Qal** *Pf.* 3 ms. consec. וְשָׁ' Ez 26[12]; 2 ms. שַׁלּוֹתָ Hb 2[8], etc.; *Impf.* 3 mpl. sf. יְשָׁלּוּךָ v[8]; cstr. לִשְׁלֹל Is 10[6]+; *Pt.* pl. שֹׁלְלִים Zc 2[12], etc.;—*spoil, plunder* (usu. ‖ בָּזַז), c. acc. cogn. שָׁלָל Is 10[6] Ez 29[19] 38[12.13.13], acc. חַיִל *wealth* 26[12]; acc. pers., שֹׁלְלִים Je 50[10] Hb 2[8] Ez 39[10], גּוֹיִם רַבִּים Hb 2[8], cf. Zc 2[12]. **Hithpō'.** *Pf.* 3 pl. אֶשְׁתּוֹלְלוּ (א in אֶשְׁתַּ' is Aram., or scribal error: Ges[§ 54 a n., cf. 53 k]) ψ 76[6] *the stout of heart are spoiled;* *Pt.* מִשְׁתּוֹלֵל Is 59[15] he that departs from evil *is one despoiled.*

†שָׁלָל[75] **n. m.**[1 S 30, 16] prey, spoil, plunder, booty;—abs. 'שׁ Gn 49[27]+; cstr. שְׁלַל Ju 5[30]+,

sf. שְׁלָלֵךְ Zc 14^{1}, שְׁלַלְכֶם Is 33^{4}, etc.;—†**1.** *prey*, of Benj. as wolf Gn 49^{27} (poem in J; c. חֵלֶק). **2.** *booty, spoil* of war, of all kinds (oft. ‖ בַּז): incl. garments, gold and silver Jos 7^{21} (J), ornaments Ju 8$^{24.25}$, fabrics and women 5^{30a,b}, flocks and herds 1 S 30^{20} Je 49^{32} 2 Ch 15^{11}, + persons Dt 20$^{14.14}$, garments, food and drink 2 Ch 28^{15}, etc. (58 t.; among these) שְׁלַל הֶעָרִים Dt 2^{35} 2 S 12^{30} 1 Ch 20^{2} and (+ cattle in addition) Dt 3^{7}, Jos 8^{27} 11^{14} (both R^{D}), cf. (also of city) Is 8^{4} Dt 13$^{17.17}$ Zc 14^{1} and (+ cattle) Jos 8^{2} (R^{D}), but incl. pers. and cattle Dt 20^{14}, cf. v^{14}; fig. of entire nation Je 50^{10} Ez 7^{21} Zc 2^{13}; ש׳ in symbol. n.pr. מַהֵר שָׁלָל וגו׳ Is 8$^{1.3}$, v. supr. p. 555^{a}; ש׳ in metaph. of future majesty of עֶבֶד י׳ Is 53^{12}; וְהָיְתָה־לּוֹ נַפְשׁוֹ לְשׁ׳ i.e. life shall be spared, Je 21^{9} 38^{2} 39^{18}, cf. 45^{5}. †**3.** private *plunder* Is 10^{2} (אַלְמָנוֹת שְׁלָלָם), Pr 1^{13} and (perh. in current saying) 16^{19}. †**4.** = *gain* Pr 31^{11}.—לְצַוְּארֵי ש׳ Ju 5^{30c} is clearly wrong; meaning dub. (v. esp. GFM); plausible conj. are לְצַוָּארַי ש׳ *for my neck as spoil*, Reuss Br al., and לְצַוְּארֵי שֵׁגָל *for the neck of the queen* Ew Be Kit al. (but שֵׁגָל elsewh. late); Now del. שָׁלָל and reads לְצַוָּארָיו.

[שָׁלֵם]$_{103}$ vb. be complete, sound (NH *id.* (Jastr), Ph. שלם Pi. *complete, requite*, esp. in n.pr., Lzb^{376} GACooke$^{99, \text{also } 81, 111, \text{etc.}}$; Ar. سَلِمَ *be safe, secure, free from fault*, II. *make over, resign to*, IV. *resign* or *submit oneself*, esp. to God, whence ptcp. *Muslim*, and inf. *Islām*, prop. *submission* to God; As. *šalâmu*, *be complete, unharmed, be paid;* Aram. שְׁלֵים, ܫܠܡ *be complete, safe*, 𝔗 *peaceful;* OAram. שלם *reward, repay* (Pa; in n.pr.); cf. Sab. סלם *peace* Hom Chr^{124}, Ar. سِلْمٌ, also سَلَامٌ *safety, security;* As. *šulmu*, *welfare;* Eth. ሰላም: Di^{322} *security, peace;* Aram. שְׁלָמָא, ܫܠܳܡܳܐ *security, welfare*, OAram. שלם Lzb^{376}, esp. = *submission*, in n.pr. RS$^{\text{Sem. 79 f.}}$; Bondi^{70} (after Brugsch), cp. *šarmā, greet, do homage*, as loan-word in Egypt.);—**Qal** *Pf.* 3 pl. שָׁלְמוּ Is 60^{20}; *Impf.* 3 ms. וַיִּשְׁלָם Jb 9^{4}; f. תִּשְׁלַם 1 K 7^{51} + 2 t.;—**1.** *be complete, finished, ended:* temple 1 K 7^{51} = 2 Ch 5^{1}; walls of city Ne 6^{15}; of time Is 60^{20}. **2.** *be sound, uninjured*, Jb 9^{4}. **Pi.**$_{89}$ *Pf.* 3 ms. שִׁלַּם Lv 5^{24} +, 1 s. וְשִׁלַּמְתִּי Je 16^{18} +, etc.; *Impf.* 3 ms. יְשַׁלֵּם Ex 21^{34} +; sf. יְשַׁלְּמֶנָּה Lv 24^{18} +, etc.; *Imv.* ms. שַׁלֵּם Ec 5^{3} ψ 50^{14}, etc.; *Inf. abs.* שַׁלֵּם Ex 21^{36} +; cstr. *id.* Pr 22^{27}, etc.; *Pt.* מְשַׁלֵּם Dt 7^{10} +, etc.;—†**1.** *complete, finish*, temple 1 K 9^{25}. †**2.** *make safe*, c. acc. Jb 8^{6}. **3.** *make whole* or *good, restore* thing lost Jo 2^{25}, or stolen Ex 21^{37} (E); pay a debt 2 K 4^{7} ψ 37^{21} Pr 22^{27} Jb 41^{3}; *make compensation*, for injury Lv 24$^{18.21}$ (P); for trespass in sacred things 5^{16} (P). **4.** *make good*, i.e. *pay*, vows, c. acc. נֶדֶר Dt 23^{22} 2 S 15^{7} + 9 t., + (c. לְ to God) ψ 50^{14} 66^{13} 116$^{14.18}$; obj. om. 76^{12}; abs. Is 19^{21}; c. acc. תּוֹדוֹת c. לְ to God ψ 56^{13}; פרים שפתינו Ho 14^{3} (v. p. 830^{b}). **5.** *requite, recompense, reward*, good 1 S 24^{20} Ru 2^{12}; evil Is 65^{6} Je 51^{56}; c. לְ pers. Dt 7^{10} + 4 t., + (c. acc. rei) Je 51^{24}; אֶל pers. Jb 21^{19}; acc. rei Pr 20^{22} Je 16^{18}; שַׁלֵּם גְּמוּל לְ Is 59$^{18.18}$ (but v. 1. שִׁלֻּם), 66^{6} + (v. גְּמוּל); + ש׳ פֹּעַל לְ Jb 34^{11}; ש׳ גְּמוּל עַל Jo 4^{4}; עַל חֵיק Is 65^{6}; אֶל־חֵיק Je 32^{18}; †c. לְ pers. and בְּ of deeds, ש׳ *reward according to one's works* 2 S 3^{39} + 3 t.; acc. pers. ψ 31^{24}; acc. rei †ש׳ רעה תחת טובה Gn 44^{4} (J) ψ 35^{12} 38^{21} (read מְשַׁלְּמֵנִי). **Pu.** *Impf.* 3 ms. יְשֻׁלַּם ψ 65^{2} Je 18^{20}; יְשֻׁלָּם Pr 11^{31} 13^{13};—**1.** *be performed*, of vow ψ 65^{2}. **2.** *be repaid, requited*, Je 18^{20} Pr 11^{31} 13^{13}. **Hiph. 1.** *complete, perform:* *Impf.* 3 ms. יַשְׁלִים Jb 23^{14} Is 44^{26}, יַשְׁלִם v^{28}. **2.** *make an end of*, 2 ms. sf. תַּשְׁלִימֵנִי Is 38$^{12.13}$ (𝔊 Du Marti *deliver up* to pains, as in Aram.).

שָׁלוֹם$_{237}$ n.m.$^{\text{Is. 54, 13}}$ **completeness, soundness, welfare, peace** (Lag$^{\text{BN 174}}$);—ש׳ Gn 29^{6} +; שָׁלֹם (rare) Ez 13^{16} +; cstr. שְׁלוֹם Gn 37^{14} +; sf. שְׁלוֹמִי ψ 41^{10} +, etc.; pl. (all dub.) שְׁלוֹמִים Je 13^{19} ψ 69^{23}; sf. שְׁלֹמָיו 55^{21};—†**1.** *completeness* in no., הָגְלָת שְׁלוֹמִים Je 13^{19} Judah is *wholly carried captive* (but read גָּלוּת שְׁלֵמָה, cf. Am 1^{6}; so 𝔊 We^{Am} SS Buhl). †**2.** *safety, soundness*, in body, אֵין שָׁלוֹם בַּעֲצָמַי ψ 38^{4}; לְשָׁלוֹם Is 38^{17}; שָׁלוֹם אָהֳלֶךָ (Ges$^{\S 141c}$) Jb 5^{24} *is safe, secure*. **3.** *welfare, health, prosperity:* †שָׁאַל לְפ׳ לְשׁ׳ *ask* one *about welfare* Gn 43^{27} (J), Ex 18^{7} (E), Ju 18^{15} + 7 t., cf. 2 S 11$^{7.7.7}$; pregn. ירד לשלום 2 K 10^{13} *descend* (to ask) *about welfare* of, cf. 1 S 17^{18} Je 38^{4}; הלך לשׁ׳ Ex 4^{18} (E) + 5 t.; עלה לשׁ׳ Gn 44^{17} (J), 1 S 25^{35}; דבר לשׁ׳ Gn 37^{4} (JE); שָׁלוֹם לְ *be well with* Gn 29^{6} 43$^{23.28}$ (J), Ju 6^{23} 19^{20} 1 S 20$^{7.21}$ + 10 t., 2 K 4$^{26.26.26}$; שָׁלוֹם בְּ ψ 122$^{7.8}$ *may it be well in;* abs. as obj. of אָמַר *well, be well*, ש׳ Gn 29^{6} (J), 2 S 18^{28} 2 K 9$^{11.17.18.19.22}$ Je 6$^{14.14}$ + 10 t.; הֲשָׁלוֹם אֲבִיכֶם (Ges$^{\S 141c}$) Gn 43^{27} (J); †ש׳ בּוֹאֶךָ 1 S 16^{4} (v. Dr), 1 K 2^{13}; אֵין ש׳ Je 6^{14} + 3 t.; †אין ש׳ לרשעים Is 48^{22} 57^{21}; but ראה

ψ 122^{6}; שׁאל שׁ׳ פ׳ 72^{7} 37^{11} רֹב שׁ׳ † ψ 73^{3} שׁ׳ רשׁעים Pr 3^{2}; שׁ׳ יוֹסִיפוּ לָךְ Dt 23^{7} Ezr 9^{12} (טוב ‖) דרשׁ שׁ׳ בַּשׁ׳ Jb 15^{21} *in time of prosperity.* **4.** *peace, quiet, tranquillity, contentment,* Is 32^{17} (‖ הַשְׁקֵט בַּשׁ׳ (וָבֶטַח); ψ 4^{9} שָׁכַב בשׁ׳ (to sleep); depart life *in tranquillity* Gn 15^{15} (R^{JE}), 1 K 2^{6} + 3 t., יָבוֹא Is 57^{2}; ψ 37^{37} אַחֲרִית לְאִישׁ שׁ׳; Ex 18^{23} (E) בא בשׁ׳ *come in contentment;* Je 12^{5} ארץ שׁ׳; נְוֵה שׁ׳ Is 32^{18}, cf. Je 25^{37} (‖ מבטחים); Jb 21^{9} שׁ׳ מִפָּחַד; ψ 69^{23} ולשׁלומים לְמוֹקֵשׁ *security,* (let it) *become a trap* (but 𝔊 Aq Sym Theod Jer ׳וּלְשִׁלּוּמִים וּלְמ, Du (cf. 𝔗) וּשְׁלָמִים *peace-offerings,* and שֻׁלְחָן v ^{a}).

†**5.** *peace, friendship:* **a.** human relations: Je 20^{10} אֱנוֹשׁ שְׁלֹמִי *man of my friendship,* cf. 38^{22} Ob^{7} ψ 41^{10}; יְעָצֵי שׁ׳ Zc 6^{13}; עֲצַת שׁ׳ בין Pr 12^{20}; ψ 28^{3} 35^{20} Je 9^{7} דבר שׁ׳ (עִם, אֶת); שׁלח ψ 34^{15}; ידע שׁ׳ Is 59^{8}; דֶּרֶךְ שׁ׳ v^{8}; בקשׁ שׁ׳ בשׁ׳ Gn 26^{29} (J); הלך בשׁ׳ v^{31} (J), 1 S 29^{7} + 4 t.; שׁוב בשׁ׳ 2 S 15^{27}; ‖ צדקה in Mess. reign ψ 72^{3}. **b.** *peace* with God, esp. in covt. relation: Is 54^{10} ברית *covt. of my peace,* cf. Nu 25^{12} (P), Ez 34^{25} 37^{26}, also Mal 2^{5}; שׁ׳ י׳ as name of altar Ju 6^{24}; י׳ subj. בֵּרַךְ בשׁ׳ ψ 29^{11}; שׂם שׁ׳ לְ Nu 6^{26} (P); עשׂה שׁ׳ לְ ψ 35^{27}; חפץ שׁ׳; אָסַף שׁ׳ Je 33^{9}; נתן שׁ׳ Je 16^{5} (‖ חסד); ψ 85^{9} דבר שׁ׳ אֶל; מֵאֵת Hg 2^{9}; עשׂה שׁ׳ לְ Je 29^{11} מחשׁבות שׁ׳; man subj. Is 27$^{5.5}$; הלך בשׁ׳ Mal 2^{6}. In this sense ‖ צֶדֶק ψ 85^{11}, ‖ צְדָקָה Is 54^{13} 60^{17}, ‖ שִׂמְחָה 55^{12}, is *like a river* 48^{18} 66^{12}; שׁ׳ עַל־יִשׂראל ψ 125^{5} 128^{6}, שׁ׳ רָב לְאֹהֲבֵי תוֹרָתֶךָ 119^{165}; מוּסַר שׁ׳ Is 53^{5} *chastisement for our peace* (but SS Buhl שְׁלָמֵינוּ). **6.** *peace* from war: (ל) עשׂה שׁ׳ *make peace* (with) Jos 9^{15} Jb 25^{2}; נתן שׁ׳ בארץ Lv 26^{6} (H); † שׁ׳ בין ובין Ju 4^{17} 1 S 7^{14} 1 K 5^{26}; † קרא (ל)שׁ׳ Dt 20^{10} Ju 21^{13} Mi 3^{5}; † שׁוב בשׁ׳ Jos 10^{21} (E), Ju 8^{9} 11^{31}; בא בשׁ׳ 2 S 19$^{25.31}$ + 7 t.; † היה שׁ׳ לְ 1 K 5^{4} + 3 t., cf. 2 S 17^{3} (v. Dr); בקשׁ שׁ׳ Ez 7^{25}; מלאכי שׁ׳ Is 33^{7}; נתן שׁ׳ וָשֶׁקֶט 1 Ch 22^{9}; מוֹצֵאת שׁ׳ Ct 8^{10}; † שׁ׳ (ו)אמת Is 39^{8} = 2 K 20^{19} + 3 t., cf. Zc 8^{19}; עֵת שׁ׳ Ec 3^{8}; בַּשׁ׳ 1 K 2^{5} *in time of peace;* שַׂר שׁ׳ Is 9^{5} (Mess. title), cf. זֶה שׁ׳ Mi 5^{4}. **7.** as adj. ψ 55^{21} שְׁלֹמָיו *those at peace with him* (rd. שְׁלֹמָיו Bae Buhl Du, or שְׁלָמָיו SS; 𝔊 appar. שִׁלּוּמָיו).

שֶׁלֶם $_{87}$ **n. [m.]** **sacrifice for alliance or friendship, 'peace-offering'** (expl. disputed: orig. sacrif. for *alliance* Di; al. *peace-offering* (mark of peace with God), 𝔊$^{Sm. K Pr}$ εἰρηνική, De Sta$^{G I. 496}$ We$^{Held. 71}$ (fellowship between God and worshippers); *welfare-offering,* 𝔊 elsewhere σωτήριον, Ke; *thank-offering* (as due rendered for benefit, or in paying vow, cf. √**Pi. 4,** and Pr 7^{14}) Ges Ew Kn; sacred meal its special feature: v. RS$^{Sem. I. 219; 2nd ed. 237}$; Now$^{Arch. II. 211 f.}$ GFM$^{Ency. Bib. SACRIFICE, §11}$; As. *šulmu* = שֶׁלֶם is cited by JJerem$^{Ency. Bib. RITUAL, §11}$);—cstr. שׁ׳ Am 5^{22}; elsewh. pl. שְׁלָמִים Ex 24^{5} + 69 t.; cstr. שַׁלְמֵי Lv 10^{14}; sf. שְׁלָמֶיךָ Ex 20^{24}, etc.; pl. is abstr. intens. Lv 7^{13} Nu 6^{17} (P) +; pl. of no. Ex 24^{5} (JE), 1 S 11^{15} +; usu. hard to decide; שׁ׳ (in app.) defines זְבָחִים Ex 24^{5} (JE), and so זבח of covt. of Horeb is שׁ׳, as also sacrifice for Saul 1 S 11^{15}; foll. phr. shew שׁ׳ essentially = זבחים in like phr. (v. זבח); שׁ׳ coming to mean ז׳ in all ritual; over against עוֹלוֹת Ex 20^{24} 32^{6} (JE), Lv 6^{5} (P), Dt 27^{7} Jos 8^{31} (D), Ju 20^{26} 21^{4} 1 S 13^{9} 2 S 6$^{17.18}$ 24^{25} 1 K 3^{15} 9^{25} 1 Ch 16$^{1.2}$ 21^{26} 2 Ch 31^{2} Ez 43^{27} 45^{17} 46$^{2.12}$; so in longer lists Lv 9$^{4.22}$ Nu 6^{14} 29^{39} (P), 1 K 8$^{64.64}$ 16^{13} 2 Ch 7^{7} 29^{35} Ez 45$^{15.17}$ 46^{12}; and when שׁ׳ alone Lv 7$^{14.33}$; in P שׁ׳ defines ז׳ in cstr. sg. or pl.: Ex 29^{28} Lv 3^{1} + 34 t. P, Lv 17^{5} 19^{5} 22^{21} 23^{19} (H), so 1 S 10^{8} 1 K 8^{63} 2 Ch 30^{22} 33^{16} Pr 7^{14}; ז׳ שׁ׳ of H and P incl. תודה, נדבה, נדר Lv 7$^{12.16}$, and so זבח תודה שׁ׳ v$^{13.15}$; שׁ׳ disting. from (larger) ז׳ in lists שׁ׳, ז׳, עולות Jos 22^{27} (P); עלה, ז׳, נדר Nu 15^{8} (P); שׁ׳ disting. from נְדָבָה Ez 46^{12} (where may = either of other two); from נדבות, נדרים Nu 29^{39} (P) (and must then ref. to תורות); from נדר Nu 15^{8} (P); appar. then not disting. from תּוֹדָה, תּוֹדוֹת 2 Ch 33^{16} being probably specification.

†**[שָׁלַם]** **vb. denom.** **be in covenant of peace;**—**Qal** *Imv.* שְׁלָם Jb 22^{21} *be at peace* (in covt.); *Pt.* sf. ψ 7^{5} שׁוֹלְמִי i.e. my ally, friend (cf. 41^{10}); *Pt. pass.* cstr. שְׁלֻמֵי 2 S 20^{19}, read שְׁלֹמֵי 𝔊 Ew$^{G III. 264}$ Dr (cf. We) HPS and mod. **Pu.** *Pt.* מְשֻׁלָּם Is 42^{19} *one in covt. of peace* (with י׳; but 𝔊 מֹשְׁלָם *their ruler,* so Che^{Hpt}; Ges Hi Ew al. *one resigned* (to God), read then מֻשְׁלָם, cf. √, Ar. IV.; Kroch Grä Marti מְשֻׁלָּחִי). **Hiph.** *Pf.* 3 fs. הִשְׁלִימָה Jos 10^{4} 11^{19}; 3 mpl. הִשְׁלִימוּ 10^{1}; *Impf.* יַשְׁלִים Is 44^{26} +, יַשְׁלִם Pr 16^{7}; וַיַּשְׁלֵם 1 K 22^{45}, etc.;—**1.** *make peace* with, אֶת, Jos 10$^{1.4}$ 2 S 10^{19} = 1 Ch 19^{19} (עִם); עִם Dt 20^{12} 1 K 22^{45}; c. אֶל pregn. Jos 11^{19} *submitting unto.* **2.** *cause to be at peace,* אֶת, Pr 16^{7}. **Hoph.** *Pf.* 3 fs. הָשְׁלְמָה Jb 5^{23} *live in peace* with, לְ (‖ ברית).

†**I. שָׁלֵם** **adj.** **complete, safe, at peace;**—שׁ׳ Gn 15^{16} +; pl. שְׁלֵמִים Gn 34^{21} Na 1^{12}; f. שְׁלֵמָה Dt 25^{15} +; pl. שְׁלֵמוֹת 27^{6} Jos 8^{31};—**1.** *complete:*

a. *full, perfect*. אֶבֶן שלמה *full weight* Dt 25[15], איפה שׁ׳ v[14] Pr 11[1], of עָוֹן Gn 15[16] (JE), number of captives Am 1[6.9], of army Na 1[12] (text corrupt, 𝔊 משל מַיִם, but ?, v. Comm); of reward Ru 2[12], of stones, *whole* (in natural condition, *unhewn*) Dt 27[6] Jos 8[31] (cf law Ex 20[25]) **b.** *finished*: stones for temple 1 K 6[7], temple 2 Ch 8[16] **2.** *safe, unharmed*, of pers Gn 33[18] (P; Sam שלום, cf בשלום 28[21]; not n pr loc as Vrss). **3.** *in covt of peace*, friendship, c את Gn 34[21] (P); לבב שָׁלֵם עם י׳ *a mind at peace with* י׳, keeping covt relation, hence *complete, perfect*, 1 K 8[61] 11[4] 15[3.14], c אל 2 Ch 16[9], אֶל om 2 K 20[3] = Is 38[3] (לב), 1 Ch 12[38] 2 Ch 15[17] 19[9] 25[2], לב 1 Ch 28[9] 29[9]

†II שָׁלֵם **n.pr.loc.** abbrev fr. יְרוּשָׁלַםִ (q v), and perh (Gunk Dr) intended as archaism Gn 14[18], cf (poet) ψ 76[3] (‖ צִיּוֹן), v. Jos[Ant I 10,2], 𝔊 Σαλημ and (ψ) εἰρήνη.

†I. שלם **n.**[m] recompense (abstr. Ba[NB 73]),—Dt 32[35] (read with 𝔖𝔊 לְיוֹם שׁ׳, ‖ נָקָם), so read also (for יְשַׁלֵּם) Is 59[18.18] Du (otherwise Che[Hpt] Di-Kit Marti)

†II. שלם **n.pr.m.** in Naphtali Gn 46[24] Nu 26[49], Συλλημ, Σελλη(μ).

†שִׁלֵּמִי **adj. gent.** as n coll. הַשּׁ׳ Nu 26[49]

†[שַׁלְמֹן] **n.**[**m.**] reward, bribe,—pl שַׁלְמֹנִים Is 1[23] (‖ שֹׁחַד)

†שִׁלּוּם Mi 7[3], שִׁלֻּם Ho 9[7], **n** [**m.**] requital,—pl שלומים Is 34[8],—**1.** *requital, retribution*, ימי הַשּׁ׳ Ho 9[7] (‖ פְּקֻדָּה); שְׁנַת שׁ׳ Is 34[8] (‖ נָקָם) **2.** *reward, bribe* Mi 7[3] שפט בַּשּׁ׳.

†[שִׁלֻּמָה] **n.f** requital, retribution,—cstr שִׁלֻּמַת ψ 91[8]

†שַׁלּוּם (less oft. שַׁלֻּם) **n.pr.m.** Σελ(λ)ουμ, Σαλ(λ)ουμ, Σελλημ, etc.,—**1.** king of N. Israel 2 K 15[10.13.14.15]. **2.** son of Josiah, and king of Judah Je 22[11] 1 Ch 3[15] = יְהוֹאָחָז **1**, v. p. 219 **3.** husband of Huldah 2 K 22[14] = 2 Ch 34[22], B 𝔊L Σελλημ, A -λουμ **4.** uncle of Jeremiah Je 32[7]. **5.** in Simeon 1 Ch 4[25]. **6.** in Jerahmeel 2[40.41] **7.** in Ephr. 2 Ch 28[12]. **8.** in Napht. 1 Ch 7[13]. **9.** father of a threshold-keeper Je 35[4] **10.** wall-builder Ne 3[12]. **11.** priests 1 Ch 5[38.39] Ezr 7[2] (ancestor of Ezra, perh. = מְשֻׁלָּם **7 a**) **12.** Levites: **a.** 1 Ch 9[17.17], perh. = v[19.31], and Ezr 2[42] ‖ Ne 7[45] (= שֶׁלֶמְיָה **2**, מְשֻׁלָּם **8 c**, (מְשֶׁלֶמְיָה(וּ) **b.** Ezr 10[24] **13.** v[42].

†שַׁלּוּן **n.pr.m.** wall-builder Ne 3[15] = שַׁלּוּם acc. to Thes

†מְשֻׁלָּם **n.pr.m.** Μεσουλαμ, Μοσολλαμ, etc.: **1.** grandfather of Shaphan 2 K 22[3]. **2.** son of Zerub 1 Ch 3[19]. **3.** in Benj.: **a.** 8[17], perh. = **b.** 9[7]. **c.** v[8]. **d.** Ne 11[7]. **4.** in Gad 1 Ch 5[13]. **5.** wall-builders: **a.** Ne 3[4.30]. **b.** 3[6]. **6.** a chief 10[21]. **7.** priests (distinctions in part obscure): **a.** 1 Ch 9[11] Ne 11[11] 12[13] (perh = שַׁלּוּם **11**) **b.** 1 Ch 9[12]. **c.** Ne 10[8]. **d.** Ne 12[6]. **e.** v[33]. **8.** Levites: **a.** 2 Ch 34[12] **b.** Ezr 8[16] 10[15] Ne 8[14] **c.** 12[25] (= שַׁלּוּם **12 a**) **9.** Ezr 10[29].

†מְשִׁלֵּמוֹת **n.pr.m.** Μοσολαμωθ, etc.. **1.** in Ephr. 2 Ch 28[12]. **2.** priest Ne 11[13] = מְשִׁלֵּמִית 1 Ch 9[12] (Μασελμωθ, etc.)

†(מְשֶׁלֶמְיָה(וּ **n.pr.m.** Μεσολλαμια, etc. Levite יָה- 1 Ch 9[21], יָהוּ- (𝔊L Σελεμιας) 26[1.2.9] (= שַׁלּוּם **2**, שֶׁלֶמְיָהוּ **12 a**)

מְשִׁלֵּמִית v. משלמות

†מְשֻׁלֶּמֶת **n.pr.f.** mother of king Amon 2 K 21[19], Μεσολλαμ, A Μασσαλαμειθ.

שְׁלֹמֹה[293] **n.pr.m.** Solomon (Σαλωμων, rarely Σαλομων, 𝔊L mostly Σολομων; cf Lag[BN 63, 96]),—king of Israel, son of David and Bathsheba 2 S 12[24] 1 K 1[11] + [name 2 t S; 162 t. K, 109 t. Ch, 7 t Ezr Ne], born in Jerus 2 S 5[14] 1 Ch 3[5] 14[4], designated by D. as successor, anointed and proclaimed before D.'s death 1 K 1[30.33.34.39] +, king after D's death 1 K 2[12.17] 1 Ch 29[28] 2 Ch 1[1] + [phr. הַמֶּלֶךְ שׁ׳ 1 K 1[34] + 36 t. K, 11 t. Ch, Je 52[20] Ct 3[9.11], הַמּ׳ שׁ׳ 1 K 2[17] 12[2] 1 Ch 29[24] 2 Ch 10[2]; שׁ׳ מֶלֶךְ יהודה 1 K 12[23] 2 Ch 11[3], מ׳ יִשׂ׳ 2 K 23[13] 24[13] 2 Ch 30[26] 35[3] Ne 13[26]]; builder of temple 1 K 5[22] 6[1.2] 1 Ch 5[36] + oft., wise 1 K 3[10] 5[9.10.14] 10[1.2.3.4] 2 Ch 1[7.11] +, author of proverbs (and songs) acc. to Proverbs מִשְׁלֵי שׁ׳ 1[1] 10[1] 25[1] (cf. 1 K 5[12.13]), v. also לשׁ׳ ψ 72[1] 127[1] (titles), Ct 1[1] (title); of written provision for priests, etc. 2 Ch 35[4], cf. 8[14] Ne 12[45]; elsewh. (outside of K Ch) name occurs †Je 52[20] Ct 1[5] (Wkl[Altor Forsch II 196] prop. *Šalmaites*, Nab. שלמו Lzb[376], cf. Levy[TW II 489] Jastr[1587]), 3[7.9.11] 8[11.12], and in phr. בְּנֵי עַבְדֵי שׁ׳ Ezr 2[55.58] = Ne 7[57.60], Ne 11[3].

†שְׁלֹמוֹת, I. שְׁלֹמִית (שְׁלוֹ׳ Ezr 8[10]) **n.pr.m.** **1.** Levites. **a.** מוֹת- 1 Ch 24[22.22] 26[28]; מִית- v[28] 23[18]; מוֹת- 26[25] Kt, מִית- Qr, Σαλωμωθ, 𝔊L Σαλωμιθ **b.** מוֹת- 1 Ch 23[9] Kt, מִית- Qr, Αλωθειμ,

Σαλωμ(ε)ιθ. **2.** ־מִית son (appar.) of Rehob. 2 Ch 11[20], Εμμωθ, A Σαληµωθ, 𝔊L Σαλωμιθ. **3.** ־מִית head of post-ex. family Ezr 8[10], Σαλειμουθ, etc.

†II. **שְׁלֹמִית** **n.pr.f.** Σαλ(ω)μιθ, etc.: **1.** in Israel Lv 24[11]. **2.** daughter of Zerub. 1 Ch 3[19].

†**שְׁלֹמִי** **n.pr.m.** in Asher, Nu 34[27]; Σελεμ(ε)ι.

שׁוּלַמִּית v. p. 1002.

†**שְׁלֻמִיאֵל** **n.pr.m.** in Simeon Nu 1[6] 2[12] 7[36.41] 10[19]; Σαλαμιηλ.

†**שֶׁלֶמְיָה(וּ)** **n.pr.m.** **1.** Jeremiah's time; Σελεμιου (genit.): **a.** ־יָהוּ Je 36[14]. **b.** יָהוּ v[26]. **c.** ־יָה 37[3], ־יָהוּ 38[1]. **d.** ־יָה 37[13]. **2.** Levite, ־יָהוּ 1 Ch 26[14], τῷ Σαλαμεια, etc., = שָׁלוּם **12 a,** q.v. **3.** post-ex. names: **a.** ־יָה Ne 3[30], Τελεμια(ς), 𝔊L Σελ'. **b.** ־יָה Ne 13[13], priest, Σελεμια(ς) (= **c** or **d**?). **c.** ־יָה Ezr 10[39], Σελεμια. **d.** ־יָהוּ v[41], 𝔊 *id.*

†**שַׁלְמַן** (van d. H. ־מָן) **n.pr.m.** vel **loc.** (cf. Palm. n.pr. שלמן GACooke[299]; Ph. n.pr. div. שלמן Lzb[377] GACooke[42]; As. *Salamanu*, of Moabit. prince COT[Ho 10, 14]; n.pr. div. *Šulmanu*, v. foll.);—כְּשֹׁד שׁ׳ בֵּית אַרְבֵאל Ho 10[14], Σαλαμαν (cf. also Field[Hex. ii. 957]);—dub., WeNow think= foll. (and cl. ins. after Hosea's time), cf. also Marti; others cp. Moabitish prince, v. supra; Spiegelberg[ZA xiii (1898), 120 f.] suggests n.pr.loc., cp. *Ša-ra-ma-na* in Egypt.

†**שַׁלְמַנְאֶסֶר** **n.pr.m.** king of Assyria (prop. ־אסרד, = As. *Šulman-ašaridu*, '(God) *Šulman is chief*,' Schr[ZK ii (1885), 197 ff.] Muss-Arnolt[JBL xi (1892), 79]);—2 K 17[3] = 18[9]; Σαλ(α)μανασ(σ)αρ, 𝔅 Salmanasar. This was שׁ׳ IV, B.C. 727–722, Say[Hast. DB s.v.] Johns[Ency. Bib. s.v.].

שַׁלְנִי v. II. .שֶׁלָה **שֵׁלָנִי** v. sub .שָׁלוּ

†**שָׁלַף** **vb.** draw out, off (NH *id., loosen, draw* (nail, sword; Jastr); As. *šalâpu, pluck out, draw* sword; Aram. שְׁלַף *draw* sword, *draw off* shoe, ܫܠܦ *draw* sword, in Lexx. *remove* corselet; Ar. سَلَفَ is *pass, pass away,* سَلَبَ *strip, plunder,* etc.);—**Qal** *Pf.* 3 ms. שׁ׳ Ju 3[22]+; *Impf.* 3 ms. וַיִּשְׁלֹף Ru 4[8], etc.; *Imv.* ms. שְׁלֹף Ju 9[54]+; *Pt. act.* שֹׁלֵף 8[10]+, etc.; *pass.* f. שְׁלוּפָה Nu 22[23]+;—**1.** *draw out* sword from (מִן) wound Ju 3[22], cf. Jb 20[25]; usu. sword from sheath Ju 8[20] 9[54] 1 S 31[4] = 1 Ch 10[4], +מִתַּעְרָהּ 1 S 17[51]; וְחַרְבּוֹ שְׁלוּפָה בְּיָדוֹ Nu 22[23.31] Jos 5[13] (all J), 1 Ch 21[16]; elsewhere אִישׁ שֹׁלֵף ח׳ coll. Ju 8[10] 20[2.15.17.46] 2 S 24[9] 2 K 3[26] 1 Ch 21[5.5], cf. Ju 20[35] and (שֹׁלְפֵי ח׳) v[25]. **2.** *draw off* sandal Ru 4[7.8] (cf. I. חלץ **1**; also RS[K 269] Dr[Dt 25, 9] Bewer[SK lxxvi (1903), 332]). **3.** *shoot up* (?), i.e. *draw out* blade, of grass on roof ψ 129[6] (cf. Ew Bae al.); Che Dr *is unsheathed* (vb. c. subj. indef. = pass.), with same meaning; Hup-Now prop. שָׁלֵם (with ‖ in Syr.); v. Ortenberg[Textkritik d. Ps. (1861), 30] שֶׁחָלַף, We[Hpt] Du חָלַף (as 90[5.6], v. ח׳ **2**).

†[**שֶׁלֶף**] **n.pr.m.** son of Joḳtan;—שָׁלֶף Gn 10[26] = 1 Ch 1[20]; Σαλεφ; identif. by Os[ZMG xi (1857), 153 f.] with S. Ar. tribe سُلَف, cf. Mordtm[ZMG xxxix (1885), 228] Glaser[Skizze ii. 425] Hom[Chr 70], and v. Di Dr.

שלשׁ (√ of following; meaning unknown; conj. in Dietr[Wortforsch. 229 n.]; cf. Lag[BN 173]).

שָׁלשׁ, שָׁלוֹשׁ, שְׁלֹשָׁה, שְׁלֹשָׁה[430] **n.m. et f.** a three, triad (NH *id.*; שלש SI[2]; שלשן 30 MI[2]; Ph. שלש; As. *šalaštu, šalaltu*; Sab. שלת Hom[Chr 47, 124], but also תלת, etc., Id.[47; A. u. A. ii. 175] Sab Denkm[No. 31, 8]; Ar. ثَلَاث, ثَلَاثَة; Eth. ሠለስ: ሠላሳ: Aram. תְּלָתָא, ܬܠܬܐ; Nab. תלת Lzb[377]; Palm. תלת (in תלת מאה) Reckend[ZMG xlii (1888), 408]; v. also Kö[ii. 1. 206]);—**m.** שָׁלשׁ (־שׁ rare, chiefly late), c. **n.f.** Am 4[8]+90 t., also cstr. שְׁלשׁ Gn 18[6]+65 t. (but 38[24] read perh. שְׁלֹשֶׁת Sam., cf. Di al.), שְׁלָשׁ־ Ex 21[11]; **f.** שְׁלֹשָׁה (־שָׁה rare, chiefly late), c. **n.m.** Gn 6[10]+149 t., also cstr. שְׁלֹשֶׁת Am 4[4]+92 t. (3+10=13 are additional; on rare exceptions to rule of gender cf. Ges[§ 97 c]), sf. שְׁלָשְׁתָּם Nu 12[4], שְׁלָשְׁתְּכֶם v[4] Ez 40[10] 41[16];—*three* (Hex chiefly P): **1.** no other num.: **a.** bef. n.pl., שָׁלשׁ 51 t., e.g. שׁ׳ אַמּוֹת Ex 27[1]+, שׁ׳ בָּאַמָּה 1 K 7[27], שְׁלֹשָׁה 90 t., e.g. Gn 18[2]+ (so always שְׁלֹשׁ, שְׁלֹשֶׁת; rd. מִשְּׁלֹשֶׁת Gn 38[24] Sam Di; =מִשׁ׳, from ־מִן); after n. (late: on 1 S 1[24] v. [שְׁלֵשׁ]) 1 Ch 25[5]+17 t.; n. om. 1 S 17[14] 2 S 24[12]=42 t. **b.** =ordin. לִשׁ׳ יָמִים Ex 19[5] *on third day;* הַיּוֹם שׁ׳ הַיָּמִים 1 S 9[20], הַיּוֹם הַשׁ׳ 30[13], both=*three days ago;* esp. בִּשְׁנַת שׁ׳ לְ 1 K 15[28]+7 t. (Ges[§ 134 o]). **2.** 13, c. **n.f.**: שְׁלשׁ עֶשְׂרֵה שָׁנָה Gn 17[25] 1 K 7[1]+ (as ordin.) Gn 14[4] (+שְׁלֹשׁ־), Je 1[2] 25[3]; before עָרִים Jos 21[19]; after, 19[6]+3 t., before עִיר Jos 21[33] 1 Ch 6[45], אַמּוֹת Ez 40[11]; c. **n.m.** שְׁלֹשָׁה עָשָׂר before פָּרִים Nu 29[14]; after, v[13]; ordin. before יוֹם Est 3[12] 9[1]; after, v[17]; יוֹם om. 3[13] 8[12] 9[18]; גּוֹרָל om. 1 Ch 24[13] 25[20] 26[11]. **3.** 300=שְׁלשׁ מֵאוֹת Gn 5[22]+59 t. (1 Ch 11[11] perh. intentional change [HPS[Sm]] from שְׁמֹנֶה ‖ 2 S 23[8], which

certainly orig Vrss Th We Dr and mod.), 3000 = שְׁלֹשֶׁת אֲלָפִים Ex 32[28] + 28 t. **4.** c. tens, שׁ׳ foll. Nu 1[43] + 11 t., precedes Lv 12[4] + 17 t., + (as ordin.) 3 + 20 Je 52[30] + 3 t., 20 + 3 2 K 12[7] + 2 t. **5.** as round, or conventional, no.: 2 (*or*) 3, Am 4[8] Dt 17[6] Jos 7[3] 2 K 9[32] Is 17[6], 3 (*and*) 4, Pr 30[15.18.21.29], *three days' journey* Ex 3[18] 5[3] 8[23], etc.

†I. [שָׁלַשׁ] **Pi. denom.** do a third time, divide into three parts, etc.;—*Pf.* 2 ms וְשִׁלַּשְׁתָּ Dt 19[3] *divide* land *into three parts* (so *Impf* וַיְשַׁלֵּשׁ אֶת־הָעָם [for MT וַיְשַׁלַּח] 2 S 18[2] 𝔊L Bu), 1 S 20[19] *stay three days* (cf. Dr), v[20] We Dr al (cf. 𝔊) read אֲשַׁלֵּשׁ בְּ׳ (for שְׁלֹשֶׁת הַ׳) = *I will shoot on the third day with* the arrows (HPS qu.), *Impf.* 3 mpl. וַיְשַׁלֵּשׁוּ 1 K 18[34], and *Imv* mpl. שַׁלֵּשׁוּ v[34] *do a third time*. **Pu.** *Pt* מְשֻׁלָּשׁ *three years old* Gn 15[9] + 1 S 1[24] (read with 𝔊 Th We etc. בְּפַר מְשֻׁלָּשׁ for בְּפָרִים שְׁלֹשָׁה), f. מְשֻׁלֶּשֶׁת Gn 15[9], הַחוּט הַמְשֻׁלָּשׁ Ec 4[12] *the threefold cord*; fpl מְשֻׁלָּשׁוֹת Ez 42[6] *three-storied* chambers.

שְׁלִישִׁי m. שְׁלִישִׁית f. **adj. num. ord.** 108 **third**,—יוֹם שְׁלִישִׁי Gn 1[13] + 31 t., etc. (64 t., rarely שְׁלִשִׁי), pl שְׁלִשִׁים (*third* 50, set of messengers, etc.) 1 S 19[21] 2 K 1[13] + 4 t., בַּשָּׁנָה הַשְּׁלִישִׁית 1 K 18[1] + 4 t., etc. (33 t.; sometimes שְׁלִשִׁת, שְׁלִשִׁית, etc.), = *third part, a third* 2 S 18[2.2.2] + 13 t., + (cstr.) Nu 15[6] + 4 t., + שְׁלִשִׁתֵךְ (Ges §91 l) Ez 5[12] *third part of thee*; = *third time* 1 S 3[8], also שְׁלִישִׁיָּה Is 19[24] *third* (on par with other two), בַּשְּׁלִישִׁים Ez 42[3] *in the thirds*, i.e. *third story*;—עֶגְלַת שׁ׳ 15[5] Je 48[34], v. ע׳ p. 722.—שְׁלִישִׁתָה Ez 21[19] is corrupt and doubtful; Krae prop וּשְׁלִשָׁה the sword shall be doubled *and trebled*, other conj in Co Toy. 1 S 20[5] del הַשּׁ׳ 𝔊 We Dr al, so v[12] 2 S 23[18] read הַשְּׁלֹשִׁים 𝔖 We Dr al.

†שִׁלְשֹׁם and (less oft.) שִׁלְשׁוֹם 25 **adv.** = **three days ago, specif. day before yesterday** (Ko II.1.255 f. Lag BN 20 Anm Ba NB §216 b),—in phr תְּמוֹל שׁ׳ Ex 5[8] *yesterday* (and) *day before*, idiomat. for *hitherto*, so Ru 2[11], אתמול שׁ׳ 1 S 4[7], כת׳ שׁ׳ Gn 31[2.5] (E), Ex 5[7.14] (J), 2 K 13[5], cf. 1 S 14[21] 19[7]; גַּם־ת׳ גַּם־שׁ׳ Ex 4[10] (J), 2 S 3[17] 1 Ch 11[2], cf. 2 S 5[2]; מת׳ שׁ׳ from *aforetime, previously* Ex 21[29.36] (E), Dt 4[42] 19[4.6] Jos 4[18] (J), 3[4] 20[5] (both R), cf. 1 S 10[11], כת׳ שׁ׳ 1 S 21[6] *as formerly* (but Bu מת׳ שׁ׳ = *for some days*).—שׁ׳ Pr 22[20] Kt is difficult; Qr שָׁלִשִׁים (v. III. שָׁלִישׁ) is imposs.; supply perhaps תְּמוֹל have I not written to thee *heretofore*, etc.?

שְׁלֹשִׁים (very seldom שְׁלוֹשִׁים, שלשם) 174 **n. indecl. thirty**;—**1.** bef. n. sg.: אַמָּה Gn 6[15] + 3 t., +, c. בָּאַמָּה Ex 26[8] + 3 t., שָׁנָה 2 S 5[4] + 12 t. (age of paternity, of Levitical or royal duty, etc.), אִישׁ Ju 14[19] + 3 t., etc., bef. n pl. בָּנִים Ju 10[4] 12[9], אֲנָשִׁים Je 38[10] (read here prob. שְׁלֹשָׁה Ew Hi Gf al.), less common words Ez 40[17] Ezr 1[9.10], etc., after n pl. Gn 32[16], שׁ׳ פְּעָמִים Ez 41[6], שׁ׳ אֶלֶף 1 Ch 23[3] +, שׁ׳ אֲלָפִים Ezr 2[35] Ne 7[38]; שׁ׳ foll. units Gn 11[12] + 14 t., precedes 1 K 22[42] + 29 t., שׁ׳ foll. 100 (1000, etc.) Gn 5[5] + 15 t., precedes 5[3] + 21 t. **2.** as ordin. (בִּ)שְׁנַת שׁ׳ וְאַחַת שָׁנָה לְ 1 K 16[23], cf. v[29] + 4 t.; שָׁנָה om. Ne 5[14] + 4 t., שְׁנַת om. 2 K 25[27] = Je 52[31]; בִּשׁ׳ שָׁנָה alone Ez 1[1].—1 S 13[5] read שְׁלֹשֶׁת 𝔊L We Dr al; 2 S 23[13] read שְׁלֹשָׁה Qr Vrss Th and mod.; 1 Ch 11[11] read הַשְּׁלֹשָׁה, הַשְּׁלֹשֶׁת 𝔊L Kit Benz al. (so ‖ 2 S 23[8] for הַשָּׁלִשִׁי)

†I שָׁלִ(י)שׁ **n.[m.] third** (part, i.e. of ephah? dub.), name of a measure,—for dust Is 40[12], tears ψ 80[6] (in fig.), adv. acc. *measure-wise*.

†II [שָׁלִישׁ] **n.[m.]** pl. שָׁלִשִׁים, a (three-stringed? three-barred? three-cornered?) mus. instr., perhaps a *sistrum* (so 𝔙), or 'triangle' (RVm; cf. Prince EB III 3228), 1 S 18[6] (+ בְּתֻפִּים).

†III. שָׁלִישׁ **n.m.** adjutant or officer (best explained as *third* man (in chariot), v. esp. Hpt BAS iv 586 f. Bender ZAW xxiii (1903), 19 WMM As. u. Eur 329, v. also Kau M N, DPV, 1904, 10; doubted by Dr 1 K 14 7 Baen ib Buhl 14),—abs שׁ׳ of king's personal attendant at court 2 K 7[2.17.19], sf., military officer of king, שָׁלִשׁוֹ 2 K 9[25], שָׁלִשָׁה 15[25] (on abnormal ָ v. Ges §93 xx Ko II L 133, 449, 495); pl שָׁלִישִׁים Ez 23[15] + (sts. שָׁלִשִׁם, etc.) v[23] Ex 14[7] 2 K 10[25.25], + (Qr) 2 S 23[8] (> Kt שָׁלִשִׁי), 1 Ch 11[11] 12[19] (v[18] van d H., Kt in both, שלושים), read in all three רֹאשׁ הַשְּׁלֹשָׁה *chief of the three* 𝔊L We Dr Bu Now.—שָׁלִשִׁים Pr 22[20] Qr v. שִׁלְשֹׁם.

†II [שִׁלֵּשׁ] **adj. pertaining to the third**,—only m.pl. as subst. שִׁלֵּשִׁים *those of third generation* (grandsons), בְּנֵי שׁ׳ Gn 50[23] (E) *sons of those of third generation*, i.e. great-grandsons (v. Ko SK 1898, 533 ff.), עַל־בָּנִים עַל־שִׁ׳ וְעַל־רִבֵּעִים Ex 20[5] (E, v. [רִבֵּעַ]) = Dt 5[9], Nu 14[18], cf. Ex 34[7] (both J).

†שִׁלֵּשׁ (van d H. שִׁלֹּשׁ) **n.pr.m.** in Asher, 1 Ch 7[35], Ζεμη, A Σελλης, 𝔊L Σελεμ.

†**שָׁלִשָׁה n.pr.loc.** doubtful;—אֶרֶץ־שׁ׳ 1 S 9^{4}, B 𝔊L Σελχα, A Σαλισσα; ? cf. בַּעַל שָׁלִשָׁה 2 K 4^{42}.

†**שִׁלְשָׁה n.pr.m.** in Asher, 1 Ch 7^{37}, Σαλεισα, 𝔊L Σελεμσαν.

†**שַׁלְתִּיאֵל n. pr. m.** (= שְׁאַלְתִּיאֵל Thes Buhl);—father of Zerub. Hg $1^{12.14}$ 2^{2}; Σαλαθιηλ.

שָׁם adv. there, thither (Ar. ثَمَّ *there*, cf. ثُمَّ *then;* BAram. תַּמָּה, Eg. Aram. תמה S-C [Pap. A 4, J 6], 𝔗 תַּמָּן (with demonstr. *n*, cf. אֲדַיִן beside אֱדַי), Syr. ܬܡܢ; Zenj [Had. 8] (Cooke [159]) (שם);—**1. a.** *there* Gn $2^{8.12}$ $11^{2.7.31}$ + oft.; placed early in sentence for emph., Mi 4^{10} שָׁם תִּנָּצֵלִי, Na 3^{15} Ez $32^{22.24}$ ψ 104^{26}+, . . . וְשָׁם Gn 41^{12} Ex 15^{27} Nu $13^{22.33}$+, שָׁם . . . וְשָׁם Ex 15^{25} Dt 12^{14} Is 27^{10} Jb 3^{17}+, כִּי שָׁם . . . וְהִנֵּה שָׁם Gn 29^{2}, . . . 11^{9} 21^{31} 35^{7} 2 S 1^{21} 15^{21}+, אַךְ שָׁם . . . Is $34^{14.15}$, גַּם שָׁם . . . 23^{12} 57^{7} ψ 139^{10}; resuming a preceding 'where,' Jb 39^{30} בַּאֲשֶׁר חֲלָלִים שָׁם הוּא, Ju 5^{27} Je 22^{12} Ec 1^{7}, cf. 1^{7}. Repeated, שָׁם . . . שָׁם *here . . . there* Is $28^{10.13}$. In poetry, pointing to a spot in which a scene is localized vividly in the imagination, ψ 14^{5} שם פחדו פחד *there* feared they a fear! 36^{13}, cf. 48^{7} 66^{6} 132^{17}; Hos 6^{7} Zp 1^{14}.—Hb 3^{4} read probably (We Now) שָׂם the flashes at his side *made he* the hiding of his power; Ec 3^{17} שָׁם = *with God,* in the Divine plan or scheme: but read perh. שָׂם Hi De al. **b.** preceded by the rel., אֲשֶׁר שָׁם *where,* Gn 2^{11} Ex 20^{21} 1 S 9^{10}+, usu. with one or more words between, Gn $13^{3.14}$ 19^{27} Ex 29^{42} 2 S 11^{16} 2 K 23^{27} + oft.; after בַּאֲשֶׁר הוּא שָׁם, בַּאֲשֶׁר †Gn 21^{17}. With אשׁר omitted (the rel. being indic. by cstr., Ges [§130 c, d]) Ez 39^{11} מְקוֹם שָׁם קֶבֶר בְּיִשׂ׳ a place *where* a grave (may be) in Isr., but 𝔊 𝔙 Co Or al. read שֵׁם a place *of renown.* **2.** *thither,* after vbs. of motion (= שָׁמָּה, v. **3**), Dt 1^{37} לֹא תָבֹא שָׁם, Ju 19^{15} 21^{10} 1 S 2^{14} 9^{6} al.; אֲשֶׁר . . . שָׁם *whither,* 1 K 18^{10} 21^{18} 2 K $1^{4.6.16}$ Is 20^{6}, more oft. in Je Ez, as Je 8^{3} 22^{27} $23^{3.8}$ 45^{5}+, Ez 4^{13} 12^{16} $36^{20.22}$+; so שֶׁשָּׁם ψ 122^{4}. **3.** with ה loc., שָׁמָּה (shâmmāh): **a.** after vbs. of motion, *thither,* Gn 19^{20} לָנוּס שָׁמָּה to flee *thither,* v^{22} 20^{13} 24^{6} 29^{3} Dt 1^{38} + oft.; = *into it, therein* (of a basket, pit, etc.), Ex 16^{33} וְתֶן־שָׁמָּה מְלֹא הָעֹמֶר, 21^{33} וְנָפַל שָׁמָּה, 30^{18} Ju 8^{25} 2 K 12^{10}; pregnantly, after a verb implying motion, as *to bury,* Gn 23^{13} וְאֶקְבְּרָה אֶת־מֵתִי שָׁמָּה, 25^{10} 49^{31} 50^{5} (all P), נוֹעַד *to meet* Ex $29^{42.43}$ $30^{6.36}$ Nu 17^{19} (all P), Jos 2^{16} 7^{3} Je 13^{7} Jo 4^{7}, perh. Ct 8^{5} (? c). **b.** אֲשֶׁר . . . שָׁמָּה, *whither* Gn 20^{13} Nu 33^{54} Dt $4^{5.14}$ + oft.; *where* 2 K 23^{8} 1 Ch 4^{41}. **c.** more rarely, i.q. שָׁם *there,* Gn 43^{30} וַיֵּבְךְּ שָׁמָּה, Jos 2^{1} Ju 16^{27} 2 K 4^{11} 9^{16} Ho 2^{17} Is 22^{18} 34^{15} 65^{9} Je 18^{2} 27^{22} Ez 23^{3} $32^{29.30}$ ($v^{22.24.26}$ שָׁם), 48^{35} י׳ שָׁמָּה, ψ 76^{4} 122^{5} Ec 3^{16}. **4.** מִשָּׁם *from there, thence:* **a.** oft. after verbs of departing, taking, etc., Gn 2^{10} $11^{8.9}$ 12^{8} 18^{16} 24^{7} 42^{2}, etc., Nu 13^{23} 21^{12} 22^{41} וַיַּרְא מִשָּׁם, Dt 4^{29} וּבִקַּשְׁתֶּם מִשָּׁם, 30^{4} Je 37^{12} Ho 2^{17} Am $9^{2.3.4}$ Jb 39^{29}+. Peculiarly, Gn 49^{24} מִשָּׁם רֹעֶה אֶבֶן יִשְׂר׳ Ges De RVm *from there* [from heaven], (from) the Shepherd (י׳), the Stone (Rock) of Israel, Ew Di Sta *from there* (where is) the Shepherd of (רֹעֵה) the (Bethel-)stone of Israel; but both forced: text dubious; Gunk by the name (מִשֵּׁם; so 𝔖) of the Shepherd, etc. (as Ew Di). **b.** אֲשֶׁר . . . מִשָּׁם *whence* Gn 24^{5} Nu 23^{13}+. **c.** expressing *origin,* Gn 3^{23} the ground אֲשֶׁר לֻקַּח מִשָּׁם, 10^{14} *whence* (= *from whom*) came forth the Phil., Ju 19^{18} מִשָּׁם אָנֹכִי, 1 S 10^{12} אִישׁ מִשָּׁם, Is 65^{20}. **d.** of the mass, *from* which something is taken or made, Gn 27^{9} 30^{32} (of צאן), Lv 2^{2} וְקָמַץ מִשָּׁם וגו׳ (from the meal, etc., of a מנחה), 1 K 17^{13} אַךְ עֲשִׂי לִי מִשָּׁם עֻגָה קְטַנָּה i.e. from the meal and oil, 2 K $7^{2.19}$: וּמִשָּׁם לֹא תֹאכֵל, Ez 5^{3}.

I. **שֵׁם** [864] **n.m.** [237.9] name (√unknown; Thes שׁמה, cf. Ba [ZMG xli (1887), 633]; Lag [BN 160] ושם, Ar. وَسْمٌ *brand, mark,* cf. RS [K 213, 303 ff.] Kö [ii. 1. 104]; NH = BH (esp. הַשֵּׁם = יהוה); Ph. שם Lzb [377]; As. *šumu;* Sab. סם Hom [Chr 124]; Eth. ስም: Ar. اِسْمٌ, أُسْمٌ, سِمٌ, سُمٌ; Aram. שֻׁם, שְׁמָא, also שׁוּם, שֵׁם (Kö [ii. 1. 512]), ܫܡܐ, ܫܡ, OAram., Palm. שם Lzb [377]);—abs. שׁ׳ Gn 6^{4}+; cstr. שֵׁם־ Gn 12^{8}+, rarely שֶׁם־ 1 S 8^{2}+; sf. שְׁמִי Ex 3^{15}+, שִׁמְךָ Gn 32^{9}+, שְׁמֶךָ 1 K 18^{31}+, etc.; pl. שֵׁמוֹת (rarely שְׁמֹת) Gn 2^{20}+; cstr. שְׁמוֹת Ex 6^{16}+, sf. שְׁמוֹתָם Nu 13^{4}+, שְׁמוֹתָן Ez $23^{4.4}$;—*name:* **1.** of river Gn $2^{11.13.14}$, beasts $v^{19.20}$, city 26^{33} (all J)+; שׁ׳ היום †Ez 24^{2}, i.e. exact designation of it (+ אֶת־עֶצֶם הַיּ׳ הַזֶּה). **2. a.** usu. of pers.: Gn $4^{17.19.19}$ (J)+; as signif. 1 S 25^{25}, cf. Pr 21^{24}; esp. in phr. וַיְהִי אִישׁ . . . וּשְׁמוֹ אֶלְקָנָה 1 S 1^{1}, cf. $9^{1.2}$, Je 37^{13} + 28 t.; less oft. as גָּלְיָת שְׁמוֹ 1 S 17^{4}, cf. Zc 6^{12} + 5 t. (cf. in As. Krae [BAS i. 430]); freq. c. קָרָא (q.v. **6**, and **Niph. 2, Pu.**); note here, נִקְרָא שׁ׳ עַל in token of ownership 2 S 12^{28} (v. Dr), Is 4^{1}); rarely, שִׂים אֶת־שְׁמוֹ אֲבִימֶלֶךְ Ju 8^{31}, cf. 2 K 17^{34} Ne 9^{7}; וַיָּשֶׂם לָהֶם שׁ׳ Dn 1^{7}; c. יֵאָמֵר Gn 32^{29} (J); change of name is without vb., as Gn 17^{15} (P), or (usu.) c. יִהְיֶה Gn 35^{10} (P) *Isr. shall be thy name,* cf. 17^{5} 1 K 18^{31} 1 Ch 22^{9}, also

וַיַּסֵּב אֶת־שְׁמוֹ יהו׳ 2 K 23^{34} = 2 Ch 36^{4}, cf. 2 K 24^{17}, and (subj ׳י) ש׳ עוֹלָם אֶתֶּן־לוֹ Is 56^{5}, מַה־שְּׁמֶךָ Gn 32^{28}, cf. Ex 3^{13} Pr 30^{4}, מִי שְׁמֶךָ Ju 13^{17}; *be explicitly mentioned* is: וְכֻלָּם בְּשֵׁמוֹת Ezr 10^{16}, נִקְּבוּ בְשֵׁ׳ Nu 1^{17} 1 Ch 16^{41} 2 Ch 28^{15} 31^{19} Ezr 8^{20}, הַבָּאִים בְּשֵׁ׳ 1 Ch 4^{38}, וַיָּבֹאוּ הַכְּתוּבִים בְּשֵׁ׳ v^{41}, of things, וּבְשֵׁמוֹת תִּפְקְדוּ Nu 4^{32} (P), + v^{27} (read בשמת 𝔊 Di Baen Gray); יְדַעְתִּיךָ בְשֵׁם Ex 33^{12} (subj ׳י), i.e. acknowledge thee, personally (as mine), cf. v^{17} (both J), בְּשֵׁ׳ פ׳ *as the representative of* 1 S 25$^{5.9}$ 1 K 21^{8} Je 29^{25} Est 2^{22} 3^{12} 8$^{8.9.10}$ (cf also **3**) **b.** = *reputation;* (1) וַאֲגַדְּלָה שְׁמֶךָ Gn 12^{2} (J), וְעָשִׂתִי לְךָ שֵׁ׳ גָּדוֹל כְּשֵׁם הַגְּדֹלִים אֲשֶׁר בָּאָרֶץ 2 S 7^{9}, †*make oneself a name* וְנַעֲשֶׂה לָּנוּ שֵׁ׳ Gn 11^{4} (J), וַיַּעַשׂ לוֹ שֵׁ׳ 2 S 8^{13}, of ׳י Je 32^{20}, hence Ne 9^{10} Dn 9^{15}, Is 63$^{12.14}$, so c. שׂוּם 2 S 7^{23} = 1 Ch 17^{21}, וַיֵּצֵא לָךְ שֵׁם בַּ׳ Ez 16^{14} (cf. 1 Ch 14^{17}), וַיֵּלֶךְ שְׁמוֹ עַד־לְמֵרָחוֹק 2 Ch 26^{15} עַד־לְ׳ v^{8}; 2 S 23$^{18.22}$, = *fame, glory,* Zp 3$^{19.20}$ Ez 39^{13} — 34^{29} read perh. שָׁלֹם 𝔊 Siegf Be Toy; Co שָׁלֵם, Krae conj. שָׁמֶן, אַנְשֵׁי הַשֵּׁם Gn 6^{4} (J), Nu 16^{2} (J), אַנְשֵׁי שֵׁמוֹת 1 Ch 5^{24} 12^{31} (van d. H. v^{30}); c. neg בְּנֵי בְלִי־שֵׁם Jb 30^{8}; (2) bad sense, וְהוֹצִא עָלֶיהָ שֵׁם רָע Dt 22^{14}, cf v^{19} Ne 6^{13}, = *byword* Ez 23^{10}, טְמֵאַת הַשֵּׁ׳ 22^{5}. **c.** esp. as giving a man a kind of posthumous life, esp. in his sons, אֵין־לִי בֵן בַּעֲבוּר הַזְכִּיר שְׁמִי 2 S 18^{18}, לְהָקִים לְאָחִיו שֵׁם בְּ׳ Dt 25^{7}, cf. v^{6} Ru 4$^{5.10}$, without whom it is blotted out, etc., Dt 25^{6}, cf Nu 27^{4} (P), Ru 4^{10}, so that to destroy one's name = extirpate family (and שֵׁם sts. is ∥ זֶרַע) 1 S 24^{22} (Gi v^{21}), 2 S 14^{7} (∥ שארית), so of peoples Dt 7^{24} 9^{14} 12^{3} Is 14^{22} +, לֹא יִזָּרַע מִשִּׁמְךָ עוֹד Na 1^{14} (of Nineveh); כֵּן יַעֲמֹד זַרְעֲכֶם וְשִׁמְכֶם Is 66^{22}, more abstr. (∥ זֵכֶר) Jb 18^{17} Pr 10^{7}. **3.** *name,* as designation of God, specif. of ׳י (esp. Je Ez Is$^{2.3}$ ψψ). — first (in Hex) in phr ק׳ בְּשֵׁ׳ ׳י Gn 4^{26} (J), *call with,* i.e. use the name ׳י in worship, so 12^{8} 13^{4} 21^{33} 26^{25} + (v. קרא **2 c**); hence, of place of worship, בְּכָל־הַמָּקוֹם אֲשֶׁר אַזְכִּיר אֶת־שְׁמִי Ex 20^{24} (Gi v^{21}); לָשׂוּם [לְשַׁכֵּן] אֶת־שְׁמוֹ שָׁם Dt 12$^{5.11}$ +; בָּנָה בַיִת לִשְׁמִי 2 S 7^{13} + oft; people come לְשֵׁ׳ ׳י Jos 9^{9} (R^{D}), so לְמַעַן שְׁ׳ 1 K 8^{41} = 2 Ch 6^{32}, Is 60^{9}, seek it ψ 83^{17}; *swear with* בְּשֵׁ׳ ׳י 1 S 20^{42} Dt 6^{13} 10^{20} Lv 19^{12}, cf (לַשָּׁוְא) Ex 20$^{7.7}$ = Dt 5$^{11.11}$; חָפֵשׂ שֵׁ׳ ׳י Pr 30^{9}, נִקְרָא שְׁמִי עַל־, etc., in token of ownership (cf **2 a**), Je 7^{10} + (v. p. 896^{a}); = his reputation, fame, c עָשָׂה לוֹ, v. **1 b** (1), cf. Jos 7^{9}, בְּשֵׁ׳ ׳י, i.e. as his representative Ex 5^{23} (J), 1 S 17^{45} Dt 10^{8} 2 S 6^{18} 2 K 2^{24} + (v. **2 a** ad fin); esp. as embodying the (revealed) character of ׳י: ׳י שְׁמוֹ Am 5^{8} 9^{6} Je 33^{2}, זֶה שְּׁמִי לְעֹלָם Ex 3^{15} (E, ∥ זִכְרִי; fundamental passage), 6^{3} (P), ׳י (א׳) צְבָאוֹת שְׁמוֹ Am 4^{13} 5^{27} Je 10^{16} 46^{18} + 10 t. Je Is^{2}, ׳י קַנָּא שְׁמוֹ Ex 34^{14} (J; cf. 20^{5} Na 1^{2}), שֵׁ׳ קָדוֹשׁ Is 57^{15}, שֵׁ׳ קָדְשִׁי[ו] Am 2^{7} Ez 39^{7} 43^{7} ψ 103^{1} + oft.; hence object of knowledge Is 52^{6} Je 48^{17}, יֹדְעֵי שְׁמֶךָ ψ 9^{11} (∥ דֹּרְשֶׁיךָ), love Is 56^{6}, אֹהֲבֵי שֵׁ׳ ψ 5^{12} 69^{37} 119^{132}, fear 61^{6}, esp. of praise, etc (הִזְכִּיר, הִלֵּל, בֵּרֵךְ, הוֹדָה, etc) לְשִׁמְךָ אֲזַמֵּר 2 S 22^{50} (∥ אוֹדְךָ), and so very oft. ∥ (׳י) = ψ 18^{50}, cf. 1 Ch 16^{10} 29^{13} ψ 45^{18} Is 26^{13} 1 K 8$^{33.35}$ = 2 Ch 6$^{24.26}$ ψ 8$^{2.10}$ +; הָבוּ לי׳ כְּבוֹד שְׁמוֹ 29^{2} 96^{8}, and many combinations; opp נִאֵץ שֵׁ׳, 24^{16} נָקַב שֵׁ׳ ׳י, + חִלֵּל אֶת־שֵׁ׳ א׳ Lv 18^{21} ψ 74$^{10.18}$, etc., הַשֵּׁ׳ הַנִּכְבָּד וְהַנּוֹרָא Dt 28^{58}, cf Ne 1^{11}, לְמַעַן שְׁמֶךָ, in appeals to ׳י to act acc to his character Je 14$^{7.21}$ Ez 20$^{9.14}$ Is 48^{9} 66^{5} ψ 25^{11} 31^{4} +; שֵׁ׳ ׳י is powerful agent, בְּשִׁמְךָ הוֹשִׁיעֵנִי 54^{3} (∥ בִּגְבוּרָתְךָ), cf. 124^{8}; of מַלְאַךְ ׳י, says שְׁמִי בְּקִרְבּוֹ Ex 23^{21} (E); הַשֵּׁם Lv 24^{11} is prob. scribal substitution for word ׳י (already beginning to be thought ineffable, esp c. נָקַב cf. Gei [Urschr 273 f] Di Dr-Wh Baen), on development of this usage, and Jewish use of הַשֵּׁ׳ as personif or hypostasis, v. Levy [NHWB iv] Jastr [s.v.] — קָרוֹב שְׁמֶךָ ψ 75^{2} is striking, but doubtful, < 𝔊 Dy Che Gr Hup-Now קֹרְאֵי שֵׁ׳, Du קָרָאנוּ בְשֵׁ׳ (= קָרְאנוּ). **4.** of false gods, use forbidden Ex 23^{13} (E), Jos 23^{7} (R^{D}), cf. Ho 2^{19} ψ 16^{4}; speak בְּשֵׁם אֱלֹהִים אֲחֵרִים Dt 18^{20}; קָרָא בְשֵׁ׳ א׳ 1 K 18$^{24.25.26}$, יֵלְכוּ בְשֵׁ׳ א׳ Mi 4^{5}. **5.** = *memorial, monument* Is 55^{13} (∥ אוֹת, so Che Du > = *fame* Di-Kit), יָד וָשֵׁם טוֹב מִבָּנִים וגו׳ 56^{5} (with word-play on שֵׁ׳ **1 c**)

†II. שֵׁם **n.pr.m.** first son of Noah; — Gn 5^{32} 6^{10} 7^{13} 10$^{1.22.31}$ 11$^{10.10.11}$ (all P), 9$^{18.23.26.27}$ 10^{21} (all J), 1 Ch 1$^{4.17.24}$, Σημ.

†שֶׁמְאֵבֶר **n.pr.m.** king of Ṣᵉboim; — Gn 14^{2}, Συμοβορ, 𝔊L Συμορ.

שְׁמוּאֵל 140 **n.pr.m.** Samuel (= *name of Ēl* Thes al (or, *his name is Ēl* Hom [Heb Trad. 96 f.] Wkl [KAT 3 225] Now [1 S 1, 20]), cf רְעוּאֵל, פְּנוּאֵל; v Dr [1 S 1, 20]; Prat [ZMG 1903, 777 ff] caritative from יִשְׁמָעֵאל, Palm. שמואל Lzb [377], v. further Gie [AT Schätzung d Gottesn. (1901), 102 ff]), — **1.** great prophet, 11th cent B.C., Σαμουηλ 1 S 1^{20} (name expl as if from שָׁאַל), 1$^{18.21.26}$ + 125 t. 1 S, 1 Ch 6$^{13.18}$ 9^{22} 11^{3} 26^{28} 29^{29} 2 Ch 35^{18} Je 15^{1} ψ 99^{6}. †**2.** in Simeon, Nu 34^{20} (P), Σαλαμιηλ. †**3.** in Issachar 1 Ch 7^{2}, (L)σαμουηλ.

†שְׁמִידָע **n.pr.m.** in Manasseh (*the name knoweth*? cf. Sab. ידעסמהו DHM$^{ZMG\ xxxvii\ (1883),\ 18}$);— Nu 26^{32} (Συμαερ), Jos 17^{2} 1 Ch 7^{19}, Συμαρειμ, etc.; 𝔊L Σαμ(ε)ιδα(ε).

†שְׁמִידָעִי **adj.gent.** as n.coll. הַשׁ׳ Nu 26^{32}.

†שְׁמִירָמוֹת **n.pr.m.** (here acc. to Thes who qu. *nom. altitudinum*, i.e. perhaps of *heavens*): Levites, Σαμε(ι)ραμωθ: **1.** 1 Ch 15$^{18.20}$ 16^{5}. **2.** 2 Ch 17^{8} Qr (Kt שמרימות).

שמא (√of following).

†שִׁמְאָה **n. pr. m.** in Benjamin 1 Ch 8^{32} Σεμαα, Σαμαα, etc., = following.

†שִׁמְאָם **n.pr.m.** = foreg., 1 Ch 9^{38}, Σαμα(α).

שַׁמָּא v. שַׁמָּה, √שמם. שֶׁמְאֵבֶר v. שֵׁם.

†שַׁמְגַּר **n.pr.m.** a 'judge,' son of Anath, Ju 3^{31} 5^{6}, Σαμα[ε]γαρ (on this name (Hittite?) cf. GFM$^{Ju\ 3,\ 31}$; Nö$^{ZMG\ xlii\ (1888),\ 479}$ conj. שמגר).

[שָׁמַד] $_{90}$ **vb. Niph.** **be exterminated, destroyed** (NH der. spec.; Aram. שְׁמַד Pa. *cause to apostatize* (Jastr); Syr. ܫܡܰܕ seems disputed (in Lexx.); Nö$^{Eut.\ Nab.\ 32}$ *curse;* Ba$^{ES\ 10}$ cites As. *ašmud, I destroyed;* Gerber^{112} thinks vb. denom.);—*Pf.* 3 ms. consec. וְנִשְׁמַד Ez 32^{12}+, etc.; *Impf.* 3 ms. יִשָּׁמֵד Is 48^{19} Pr 14^{11}; 2 mpl. תִּשָּׁמֵדוּן Dt 4^{26}; *Inf. abs.* הִשָּׁמֵד v^{26}; cstr. sf. הִשָּׁמֶדְךָ Dt 28^{20}, etc.;—†**1.** of pers. *be annihilated, exterminated*, Gn 34^{30} (J), Ju 21^{16} 2 S 21^{5} (+מֵהִתְיַצֵּב בְּ;—but rd. לְהַשְׁמִידֵנוּ 𝔊 Ew We Dr al.), ψ 37^{38} (|| נִכְרְתָה), 83^{11}; of people Dt 4^{26} (הִשָּׁמֵד תִּשָּׁ׳), 7^{23} 12^{30} (+מִפָּנֶיךָ), 28^{20} (|| אָבַד), v$^{24.45.51.61}$, Je 48^{42} (+מֵעָם), Ez 33^{12} ψ 92^{8} (+עֲדֵי־עַד), cf. also וְלֹא יִשָּׁמֵד שְׁמוֹ מִלְּפָנָי Is 48^{19} (+יִכָּרֵת; וַיְעֵף, etc., in || clause). †**2.** *be destroyed*, of bamoth, Ho 10^{8}, cf. (בֵּית רְשָׁעִים) Pr 14^{11}; *be devastated*, of land, Je 48^{8} (|| אבד).

Hiph. $_{69}$ *Pf.* 3 ms. הִשְׁמִיד Dt 2^{22}+, etc.; *Impf.* 3 ms. יַשְׁמִיד Is 13^{9}+, וַיַּשְׁמֵד 1 K 16^{12} 2 K 10^{28}, etc.; *Imv.* ms. הַשְׁמֵד Dt 33^{27}; *Inf. abs.* הַשְׁמֵד Is 14^{23}, ־יד Am 9^{8}; cstr. לְהַשְׁמִיד Jos 9^{24}+, also †עַד הִשְׁמִידְךָ Dt 7^{24}, ־ךְ 28^{48}, ־ם Jos 11^{14} (but rd. in all הַשׁ׳, as Jos 23^{15}, v. Dr$^{Dt\ 7,\ 24}$), לַשְׁמִד †Is 23^{11}, etc.;—**1.** *annihilate, exterminate:* acc. pers. vel gent., subj. ׳י vel pers. hum., Dt 1^{27} 2^{22} (+מִפְּנֵי pers.), 6^{15} (+מֵעַל־פְּנֵי הָאֲדָמָה), 9^{20}+16 t. Dt, Jos 7^{12} (acc. הַחֵרֶם; +מִקִּרְבְּכֶם), 9^{24}+4 t. Jos (all R^{D}), 2 K 14^{16} 1 K 13^{34} Am 9^{8} Is 13^{9} 26^{14} Est 3$^{6.13}$+23 t.; acc. פִּרְיוֹ וְשָׁרָשָׁיו (fig.) Am 2^{9}, cf. Ez 34^{16} (but Vrss Co Toy al. [not Hi Krae] אֶשְׁמֹר); הַשׁ׳ אֶת־שְׁמִי 1 S 24^{22} (Gi v^{21}), 2 S 22^{38} 1 K 16^{12} ψ 145^{20}; הַשְׁמֵד as subst., Is 14^{23} besom of *extermination;* acc. אֶת־הַבַּעַל 2 K 10^{28}, of extirpating Baal-worship מִיִּשְׂרָאֵל. †**2.** *destroy*, cities Mi 5^{13}, fortresses Is 23^{11}, bamoth Lv 26^{30} (H), Nu 33^{52} (P; || אִבֵּד), חֹזֶק מַמְלְכוֹת הַגּוֹיִם Hg 2^{22}.

שֶׁמֶד **n.pr.m.** 1 Ch 8^{12} Gi Baer, v. שֶׁמֶר.

[שַׁמָּה] **n.pr.m.** whence

†שַׁמָּתִי **adj.gent.** in Caleb, c. art. as n.coll. הַשׁ׳ 1 Ch 2^{53}; Ησαμαθειμ[ν], ὁ Σαμαθι.

שמה (appar. √of foll.; Sta$^{§\ 324\ a}$; so Thes, cp. Ar. سَمَا *be high, lofty* (or is this secondary?); Jen$^{Kosmol.\ (1890),\ 6}$ cp. As. *šamû, id.* (> *šamû* = *sparkle*, Id$^{ZK\ ii\ (1885),\ 53}$); cf. Dl^{WB}).

[שָׁמַי] **n.m.** $^{Dt\ 33,\ 28}$ only pl. שָׁמַיִם $_{421}$ (Sta$^{§\ 324\ a}$) **heavens, sky** (NH *id.;* As. *šamû*, pl. *šamê*, *šamûtu*, also *šamâmu*, cf. Ph. שמם; Sab. סמה Hom$^{Chr\ 46,\ 124}$; Ar. سَمَاءٌ; Eth. ሰማይ: Aram. שְׁמַיָּא, ܫܡܰܝܳܐ; Palm. Nab. שמ(י)ן in n.pr. (cpd. with בעל) Lzb^{153} GACooke^{45}; on pl. form v. Ba$^{ZMG\ xlii\ (1888),\ 341\ f.}$);—abs. שׁ׳ Gn 1^{1}+, ־מַיִם Gn 2^{4}+; הַשָּׁמַיְמָה Ex 9^{8}+; cstr. שְׁמֵי Dt 10^{14}+9 t.; sf. שָׁמֶיךָ ψ 8^{4}+2 t., שָׁמָיו Dt 33^{28}, שְׁמֵיכֶם Lv 26^{19}, c. vb. pl., Ho 2^{23};—**1. a.** *visible heavens, sky*, where stars, etc., are Ju 5^{20} Gn 15^{5} (J), Dt 4^{19} Gn 1$^{14.15.17}$ (P), hence כּוֹכְבֵי הַשׁ׳ 22^{17} (JE)+9 t. (usu. as countless), (כָּל־)צְבָא הַשׁ׳ Dt 4^{19} Je 8^{2}+ (צ׳ **1 c**; rarely of angels, צ׳ **1 b**); before which fowl fly Gn 1^{20} (P), cf. Dt 4^{17} Je 8^{7} Pr 30^{19}, עוֹף הַשׁ׳ Gn 2^{19} (J), 1^{19} (P)+(עוֹף **1**), צִפּוֹר שׁ׳ ψ 8^{9}, נִשְׁרֵי שׁ׳ †La 4^{19}; as רָקִיעַ (q.v.) Gn 1^{8} (P), ψ 19^{2}, with waters beneath and above Gn 1^{9} (P, cf. v^{7}), ψ 148^{4}, darkened with clouds 1 K 18^{45}; cleared by wind Jb 26^{13}; whence comes rain Gn 8^{2} (J), Ju 5^{4} Dt 11^{11}+, and dew Gn 27^{28} (J), v^{39} (E), Dt 33^{28} (poem)+, cf. בִּרְכֹת שׁ׳ †Gn 49^{25} (poem in J), מֶגֶד שׁ׳ †Dt 33^{13} (poem), but also (destructive) fire 2 K 1$^{10.10}$ Jb 1^{16}+ (v. also **2 a** infr.); הֹבְרֵי שׁ׳ Is 47^{13}, i.e. astrologers, cf. אוֹתוֹת הַשׁ׳ Je 10^{2}; as high Gn 11^{4} (J), Am 9^{2} (opp. שְׁאוֹל), v^{6} (opp. אֶרֶץ)+, עַד־לֵב הַשׁ׳ Dt 4^{11}; as over all the earth, תַּחַת (כָּל־)הַשׁ׳ Gn 6^{17} 7^{19} (both P), Dt 2^{25} Ec 1^{13} מִתַּחַת וגו׳ (of extermination) Ex 17^{14} (E), Dt 7^{24} 9^{14}+; specif. of Israel, שָׁמֶיךָ Dt 28^{23}, שְׁמֵיכֶם Lv 26^{19} (H); בֵּין הַשׁ׳ וּבֵין הָאָרֶץ 2 S 18^{9} (hung from tree), 1 Ch 21^{16} (of angel), cf. Ez 8^{3} (Ezekiel in vision), Zc 5^{9} (flying ephah); מִקְצֵה הַשׁ׳ וְעַד־קְצֵה

הַשׁ׳ of limits of horizon Dt 4^{32}, cf. 30^{4} Ne 1^{9} ψ 19^{7}, as made by God Je 51^{15} (opp. תבל), ψ 8^{4} +; enduring Dt 11^{21} Jb 14^{12} ψ 89^{30}, esp (הַ)שׁ׳ וְ(הָ)אָרֶץ = universe (cf. in Sab, SabDenkm No. 41 42, 1 3), Dt 3^{24} Gn 1^{1} (P) + (esp Dt Je Is² ψψ), + הַיָּם Ex 20^{11} Hg 2^{6}, etc, + מַיִם מִתַּחַת לָאָרֶץ Ex 20^{4} = Dt 5^{8}, cf. Pr 30^{4}, etc; opp תְּהוֹם Pr 8^{27} (+ אֶרֶץ v ^{29}); שׁ׳ חֲדָשִׁים וְהָאָרֶץ חֲדָשָׁה as part of future glory †Is 65^{17} 66^{22} **b.** phrases are אֲרֻבּוֹת הַשׁ׳ (letting rain through) †Gn 7^{11} 8^{2} (P), Mal 3^{10} (fig), cf דַּלְתֵי שׁ׳ 2 K $7^{2.19}$, so הַיַעֲשֶׂה י׳ א׳ בַּשׁ׳ לֶחֶם שׁ׳ ψ 78^{23} (for manna), cf. דְּגַן שׁ׳ + v ^{24}, †105^{40}, מוֹסְדוֹת הַשׁ׳ 2 S 22^{8} (‖ הָאָרֶץ, in ‖ ψ 18^{8} (מ׳ הָרִים), עַמּוּדֵי שׁ׳ Jb 26^{11}, חוּג שׁ׳ 22^{14}; *towards the sky* is הַשָּׁמַיְמָה Jos 8^{20} (J), Ex $9^{8.10}$ (P), Jb 2^{12} Ju 13^{20} 20^{40} 2 Ch 6^{13}; עַל־הַשָּׁמַיִם Ex $9^{22.23}$ $10^{21.22}$ (all E), אֶל־שׁ׳ Dt 32^{40} (poem), Dn 12^{7}, שׁ׳ alone 1 K $8^{22.54}$ Jb 35^{5} Pr 23^{5}. **2. a.** as abode of God (י׳) 1 K $8^{30.32}$ + oft, where he sits enthroned ψ 2^{3} Is 66^{1}, etc, cf. רֹכֵב שׁ׳ Dt 33^{26} (poem), ψ 68^{34}, whence he rains brimstone Gn 19^{24} (J), bread Ex 16^{4} (E), cf Ne 9^{15}, casts hailstones Jos 11^{11} (E), talks with Israel Ex 20^{22} (E; Gi v ^{19}) +, cf Gn 21^{17} $22^{11.15}$ (E), looks down Dt 26^{15} +, hears his people ψ 20^{7} + 10 t Chr, etc; he thunders בַּשׁ׳ 1 S 2^{10} ψ 18^{14}, ‖ מִן־שׁ׳ 2 S 22^{14}, he bends (נטה) שׁ׳ to come down v ^{10} = ψ 18^{10}, cf ψ 144^{5} and (*rend*) Is 63^{19}; נִפְתְּחוּ הַשׁ׳ Ez 1^{1} in vision of God, cf שַׁעַר הַשׁ׳ Gn 28^{17} (E, + בית אלהים), though even שְׁמֵי הַשׁ׳ *the highest heavens* cannot hold him †Dt 10^{14} 1 K 8^{27} = 2 Ch 6^{18}, 2 Ch 2^{5} Ne 9^{6} ψ 148^{4}, שְׁמֵי שְׁמֵי־קֶדֶם 68^{34}; he is called אֱלֹהֵי הַשׁ׳ (post-ex title) Ezr 1^{2} = 2 Ch 36^{23}, + 11 t Ezr Ne, Jon 1^{9} (cf. Aram, Dn $2^{18.19.37.44}$, in Gn 24^{7} add c. 𝔊 ואלהי הָאָרֶץ, as v ^{3}), אֵל־הַשׁ׳ ψ 136^{26}, his sword is בַּשׁ׳ Is 34^{5}, but also his חֶסֶד ψ 36^{6}, צֶדֶק 85^{12}, אֱמוּנָה 89^{3}, his word fixed 119^{89} — שׁ׳ are †שָׁמָיו (of Israel) Dt 33^{28} (poem), †שְׁמֵיכֶם Lv 26^{19}; †שָׁמֶיךָ ψ 8^{4} 144^{5}, †שְׁמֵי י׳ La 3^{66}, †שׁ׳ קָדְשׁוֹ ψ 20^{7}. †**b.** Elijah taken up הַשׁ׳ in whirlwind 2 K 2^{1}, cf. v ^{11}. **3.** הַשׁ׳ personified in various relations Is 1^{2} Je 2^{12} Jb 15^{15} ψ 19^{2} 50^{6} = 97^{6}, 89^{6} 148^{4} †**4.** מְלֶכֶת הַשׁ׳ v. מ׳ p 573

I, II. שַׁמָּה v שׁמם שְׁמָה v. שֵׁם.

†**שַׁמְהוּת** **n.pr.m.** captain of Israel 1 Ch 27^{8}, Σαλαωθ, A 𝔊L Σαμαωθ, prob = II. שַׁמָּה **3 b**, q v.

שְׁמוּאֵל v sub שם

שְׁמוֹת v. II שַׁמָּה, √ שׁמם.

שַׁמַּי v. √ שׁמם **שְׁמִידָע, שְׁמִידָעִי** v. -שֵׁם.

שַׁמְלַי Ezr 2^{46}, v. שַׂלְמַי.

†**[שָׁמַט]** **vb.** let drop (NH *id.*, *loosen, detach, draw away*, Niph. *slip off*, Aram. שְׁמַט *loosen, pull away*; ܫܡܛ *draw* sword, *draw* or *pull away*; Ar سَمَطَ is *hang, suspend*, II. *release* debtor (Ḳam), سِمْط *string* of pearls);—**Qal** *let drop, fall*: *Imv.* mpl sf. + *Impf* 3 ms. sf. תִּשְׁמְטוּהָ (final ו dittogr.) שִׁמְטוּהוּ 2 K 9^{33} he said, *Let her fall, and they let her fall*; then fig., of letting land rest in seventh year, 2 ms. sf: תשמטנה Ex 23^{11} (E), *Pf* 2 ms. וְשָׁמַטְתָּה Je 17^{4} *thou shalt let drop* thy hand (read יָדְךָ for וּבְךָ JDMich and mod.) from (מִן) thine inheritance, i e. abandon it, *Inf. abs* שָׁמוֹט Dt 15^{2} *let fall* (a debt in seventh year; v. מַשֶּׁה p. 674^{b}).—Pf 3 pl שָׁמְטוּ הַבָּקָר 2 S 6^{6} = 1 Ch 13^{9} is dub, most naturally either *they let the oxen fall* (slip, stumble), or (as 𝔗) *the oxen let it fall* (reading שְׁמָטוּ, sc. the ark), > Thes *the oxen ran away*; 𝔖 *slipped* (the yoke)? v. further Dr. **Niph.** *Pf.* 3 pl. נִשְׁמְטוּ ψ 141^{6} their judges *have been thrown down*. **Hiph.** 2 ms (?) juss (?) תַּשְׁמֵט Dt 15^{3} *thou shalt cause* thy hand *to let drop*, etc.; Ba NB 147 **Qal**; < read תשמט (cf Dr), יָדְךָ subj

†**שְׁמִטָּה** **n.f.** a letting drop of exactions, a (temporary) remitting תַּעֲשֶׂה שׁ׳ Dt 15^{1} (at end of seven years), v ^{2} כִּי קָרָא שׁ׳ לי׳; whence seventh year is שְׁנַת הַשׁ׳ v ^{9} 31^{10}.

שְׁמִירָמוֹת v. sub שֵׁם.

†**[שָׁמֵם]** **vb.** be desolated, appalled (connex of mngs not clear) (NH *id*, JAram. שְׁמַם Ithp. *be dazed*);—**Qal** *Pf* 3 fs שָׁמֵמָה Ez 35^{15}, etc, *Impf* 3 ms יֵשֹׁם 1 K 9^{8} +, 3 mpl יָשֹׁמּוּ Jb 17^{8} ψ 40^{16}, etc; *Imv.* mpl. שֹׁמּוּ Je 2^{12}; *Inf. cstr.* (?) metapl. שַׁמּוֹת Ez 36^{3} (Ges § 67 r, but v. infra),—תֵּשַׁם, etc. (v [יָשַׁם]) are placed here by most; Ez 6^{6} reads תִּישַׁמְנָה, v. Ges § 67 p dd,—*Pt* שׁוֹמֵם La 3^{11} (v also **Pō.**), f. שֹׁמֵמָה (Ges § 84 a s) 2 S 13^{20} +, pl. שׁוֹמֵמִין La 1^{4}, etc;—**1.** *be desolated*, of Tamar 2 S 13^{20} (i e deflowered, or deserted; others *appalled*), of pers. elsewhere late La 1^{16}; נְתָנַנִי שֹׁמֵמָה v ^{13}, שָׂמַנִי שׁ׳ 3^{11}, pt as n f. בְּנֵי שׁוֹמֵמָה Is 54^{1} (opp. בְּעוּלָה) [Dn 8^{13} + v **Pō.**]; usu of land, etc (sts. = *deserted*), Is 49^{8} Ez 33^{28} (מֵאֵין עוֹבֵר), 35^{12} (read שָׁמֵמוּ Qr Co Toy Krae; > Kt שממה), v ^{15}; הֶעָרִים הַנֶּעֱזָבוֹת ‖ 36^{4} הֶחֳרָבוֹת הַשֹּׁמְמוֹת); שַׁמּוֹת v ^{3} is prob corrupt, Co שָׁאָם as v ^{6}, Hi-Sm

from נשם=שמם, Toy reads נָשַׁם, Krae נָשֹׁם;—pt. fpl as n.=*desolate places* Is 49^{19} 61^{4} (both ‖ חֳרָבוֹת), v^{4} (cf שְׁמָמָה 62^{4}); =*desolations* Dn $9^{18.26}$. **2.** *be appalled, awestruck,* usu at (עַל) judgments on others, Lv 26^{32} (H), Je 2^{12} (v. II. [חרב]), Ez 26^{16} 27^{35} 28^{19} Is 52^{14} Jb 17^{8}, cf. 1 K 9^{8} = 2 Ch 7^{21}, Je 18^{16} 19^{8} 49^{17} 50^{13}; on oneself ψ 40^{16} (עַל־עֵקֶב).—Is 42^{14} v. [נשם]. **Niph.** *Pf.* 3 fs. נָשַׁמָּה Je 12^{11}+, 3 pl. נָשַׁמּוּ Zp 3^{6}+; *Pt.* f נְשַׁמָּה Ez 36^{34}+, etc.;—=**Qal**: **1.** *be desolated,* of roads Lv 26^{22} (H), Is 33^{8}, bamoth Am 7^{9} (‖ יֶחֱרָבוּ), altars Ez 6^{4}; cf. 25^{3} 32^{15} Zp 3^{6} Zc 7^{14} Jo 1^{17} ψ 69^{26}; of lands Ez 29^{12} 30^{7} $36^{34.35}$, cities Is 54^{3} (opp. יוֹשִׁיבוּ), cf. Ez 36^{35} Am 9^{14} Je 33^{10}; הַנְּשַׁמָּה Ez 36^{36} *the desolated* (sc. land, in fig.) **2.** *be appalled* Je 4^{9} La 4^{5} Ez 4^{17} 30^{7}, c. עַל rei Jb 18^{20}. **Pō**. *Pt* **1.** וָאֵשְׁבָה מְשׁוֹמֵם Ezr 9^{3} *I sat appalled,* cf. v^{4}. **2.** transit. *appalling, causing horror* (Dr $^{Dn 150 f}$): (הַ)שִּׁקּוּץ מְשֹׁמֵם Dn 11^{31}, + perh 9^{27a} (v. שִׁקּוּץ), so also שִׁקּ׳ שֹׁמֵם 12^{11} (on ׳שׁ v. Ges $^{§52 s}$), הַפֶּשַׁע שֹׁמֵם 8^{13} *the crime causing horror,* and ׳שׁ as n. *horror-causer, appaller,* 9^{27b}. **Hiph.** *Pf.* 2 ms. הֲשִׁמּוֹתָ Jb 16^{7}, etc.; *Impf.* 3 ms יַשִּׁים (Ges $^{§67 y}$) Je 49^{20} 50^{45}, 3 mpl sf. וַיְשִׁמֵּם 1 S 5^{6}, 1 pl. נַשִּׁים Nu 21^{30}, etc.; *Imv.* mpl. הָשַׁמּוּ (Ges $^{§67 v}$) Jb 21^{5}; *Inf abs* הַשְׁמֵם Mi 6^{13}; *Pt.* מְשִׁמִּים Ez 3^{15};—**1.** *devastate, ravage,* acc. pers. 1 S 5^{6} Ez 20^{26} Ho 2^{14} (fig of vine), Jb 16^{7}; acc. loc. Lv $26^{31.32}$ (H), Je 10^{25} Ez $30^{12.14}$ ψ 79^{7}, so (acc. om.) Nu 21^{30} (poem in JE), Mi 6^{13};—Ez 14^{8} v. שׂים **Hiph.** **2. a.** *appal,* acc. pers, c. עַל *at,* Je 49^{20} 50^{45} Ez 32^{10}. **b.** inwardly trans, וָאֵשֵׁב מַשְׁ׳ 3^{15} *shewing horror,* Jb 21^{5} (Bu Niph. הִשַּׁמּוּ). **Hoph.** *Inf. cstr.* כָּל־יְמֵי הָשַּׁמָּה (sc. הָאָרֶץ) Lv 26^{34} (H) *all the days of* (its) *being desolate,* so v^{35} 2 Ch 36^{21}, Aramaizing, בְּהָשַׁמָּה (Ges $^{§67 y}$) Lv 26^{43}. **Hithpō**. *Impf.* 3 ms. יִשְׁתּוֹמֵם ψ 143^{4}, etc;—**1.** *be appalled, astounded,* כִּי *that, because,* Is 59^{16} 63^{5}; עַל rei Dn 8^{27}, ψ בְּתוֹכִי יִשְׁתּ׳ לִבִּי 143^{4} (cf. 1 pl. נשתומם Ecclus 43^{24}). **2.** *cause oneself desolation, ruin,* Ec 7^{16}.

†שָׁמֵם **adj.** devastated;—׳שׁ of sanctuary Dn 9^{17}; f. שְׁמֵמָה of land Je 12^{11}

שְׁמָמָה $_{56}$ **n.f. a devastation, waste**;—abs ׳שׁ Ex 23^{29}+; pl. cstr שִׁמְמוֹת Je 51^{26}+;—*waste,* usu. of land, city, houses, etc., Ex 23^{29} (E), Is 1^{7} (prob del, with words foll. Stu $^{JPTh. 1877, 714}$ FB $^{JBL (1890), 84}$), Lv 26^{33} (H), Je 4^{27}+14 t. Je (‖ מֵאֵין אָדָם וגו׳ 32^{43}, מֵאֵין ישב 34^{22}), Ez 6^{14}+18 t. Ez (35^{7a} read שְׁמָמָה וּמְשַׁמָּה for MT שִׁמְמָה וּשְׁמָמָה, so Hi Co Toy Krae al)+; of prince, ׳יִלְבַּשׁ שׁ Ez 7^{27}; of idols Mi 1^{7}; כּוֹס שַׁמָּה וּשׁ׳ Ez 23^{33}.—Ez 35^{12} v. שמם **Qal**.

שִׁמְמָה Ez 35^{7} v foregoing.

†שַׁמָּא **n. pr. m.** in Asher, 1 Ch 7^{37}, $\Sigma\epsilon\mu(\mu)a$, etc.

†I. שַׁמָּה **n.f. waste, appalment** (24 t Je);—abs. ׳שׁ Je 5^{30}+; pl. abs. שַׁמּוֹת ψ 46^{9};—**1.** *a waste,* of land, city, etc, Ho 5^{9} Is 5^{9} 13^{9} 24^{12} Zc 7^{14} Je 2^{15} 4^{7} 18^{16} 19^{8} 46^{19} 48^{9} 50^{3} $51^{29.43}$, vine Jo 1^{7}; pers. ψ 73^{19}; כּוֹס שׁ׳ וּשְׁמָמָה Ez 23^{33}. **2.** *appalment, horror,* i.e occasion of it; of people, land, etc., Dt 28^{37} 2 K 22^{19} Mi 6^{16} Zp 2^{15} Je 5^{30} $25^{9.11.18.38}$ 29^{18} $44^{12.22}$ $49^{13.17}$ 50^{23} $51^{37.41}$ 2 Ch 29^{8} 30^{7}; שׁ׳ הַחִזַקְתַּנִי Je 8^{21}.

†II. שַׁמָּה **n.pr.m.** **1.** in Edom Gn $36^{13.17}$ 1 Ch 1^{37}, usu. $\Sigma o\mu\epsilon$. **2.** third son of Jesse 1 S 16^{9} 17^{13}, $\Sigma a\mu(\mu)a$, 𝔊L $\Sigma a\mu a a$; v. שִׁמְעָה, שִׁמְעָא, שִׁמְעִי. **3.** $\Sigma a\mu a\iota a(s)$, etc, heroes of David: **a.** 2 S 23^{11} (om. accid. ‖ 1 Ch 11^{13} Dr), v^{33}. **b.** v^{25} =שַׁמּוֹת 1 Ch 11^{27}, $\Sigma a\mu a\omega\theta$, $\Sigma a\mu(\mu)\omega\theta$; prob. also שַׁמְהוּת 1 Ch 27^{8}.

שַׁמּוֹת **n.pr.m.** v. foregoing.

†שַׁמַּי **n.pr.m.** in Judah: **1.** 1 Ch $2^{28.32}$, $\Sigma a\mu(\mu)a\iota$, etc. **2.** 1 Ch $2^{44.45}$, $\Sigma a\mu a\iota$. **3.** 1 Ch 4^{17}, $\Sigma\epsilon\mu\epsilon\iota$, $\Sigma\epsilon\mu\mu a\iota$, $\Sigma a\mu\iota$.

†שִׁמָּמוֹן **n.** [**m.**] **appalment, horror** (Ba $^{NB 324, 336}$; another view Lag $^{BN 202, 203}$);—abs. Ez 4^{16} *drink water* ׳בְּשׁ, so 12^{19}.

†מְשַׁמָּה **n.f.**=שַׁמָּה;—abs. **1.**=*devastation, waste,* ׳וְנָתַתִּי אֶת־הָאָרֶץ שְׁמָמָה וּמ Ez 6^{14} 33^{28}, cf. v^{29} 35^{3}, + 35^{7a}, v שְׁמָמָה; pl מְשַׁמּוֹת Is 15^{6}=Je 48^{34}. **2.** *horror,* ׳וְהָיְתָה חֶרְפָּה . . . וּמ Ez 5^{15}.

שַׁמָּה v. שָׁם. שְׁמָמִית v שְׂמָמִית.

†I. [שָׁמֵן] **vb. grow fat** (NH Hiph. *id.*, also שָׁמֵן; Ar. سَمِنَ *be fat;* Aram. ܫܡܢ, esp. der. spec. and deriv.; שָׁמֵן adj. *fat:* As. *šamnu, fat,* Ph. (Pun) שמן *oil,* so Palm. שמנא Lzb ^{378}; on relation of meanings Fra ^{147});—**Qal** *Pf.* 2 ms. שָׁמַנְתָּ Dt 32^{15} and *Impf.* 3 ms. וַיִּשְׁמַן v^{15} both of Israel (prosperous and arrogant) under fig. of *fat* beast; so *Pf.* 3 pl. שָׁמְנוּ Je 5^{28} (of wicked). **Hiph.** *Impf.* 3 mpl. וַיַּשְׁמִינוּ Ne 9^{25} were sated *and shewed fatness* (inner causat); *Imv.* ms. הַשְׁמֵן Is 6^{10} *make fat* (dull, unreceptive), לֵב הָעָם הַזֶּה.

†**שָׁמֵן adj. fat, robust**;—ש׳ m. Ju 3^{29}+, f שְׁמֵנָה Gn 49^{20}+,—**1.** *fat, rich*, of food, Gn 49^{20} (poem in J), Is 30^{23} (+דָּשֵׁן), Hb 1^{16} (‖ בְּרִאָה); of land, *fertile* Nu 13^{20} (E), Ne 9$^{25.35}$, pasturage Ez 34^{14} 1 Ch 4^{40}. (1 S 15^{9} v. מִשְׁנֶה **3**) **2.** *stout, robust*, of men Ju 3^{29} (‖ אִישׁ חָיִל; v. GFM); f. coll. (fig of flock) Ez 34^{16} (+הַחֲזָקָה).

†[שָׁמָן] **n.[m.] fat, fertile, place**,—pl cstr. מִשְׁמַנֵּי הָאָרֶץ (Ges §§ 20a. 93ee) Gn 27^{28} (poem in J, מִן partit), v^{39} (poem in E, מִן priv acc to Thes Ew Di Gunk al., < partit here as v^{b}, 𝔙 [𝔊 ἀπὸ in both], AV RV No Ency Bib. 1184, cf. Dr).

שֶׁמֶן$_{192}$ **n.m.** $^{2 K 20, 13}$ (on appar. **f.** Ct 1^{3} cf Albr ZAW xvi (1896), 99, 106) **fat, oil**,—ש׳ abs Gn 28^{18}+, cstr. Lv 8^{2}+, שֶׁ׳ 2 K 4^{6}+, sf. שַׁמְנִי Ho 2^{7}+, etc.; pl שְׁמָנִים Am 6^{6}+; sf שְׁמָנֶיךָ Ct 1^{3}, -נַיִךְ 4^{10},—**1.** *fat, fatness*. קֶרֶן בֶּן־שׁ׳ Is 5^{1} (of fertile slope), pl גֵּיא־שְׁמָנִים 28$^{1.4}$, of food (in fig) 25$^{6.6}$; lit בְּשָׂרִי כָּחַשׁ מִשָּׁמֶן ψ 109^{24} (cf צוֹם v^{a}), cf. מִפְּנֵי שׁ׳ Is 10^{27} (in fig, si vera l., mng. obscure, most now emend by conjecture; RS JPh xiii (1885), 62 עָלָה מִצְּפוֹן שֹׁדֵד [v. also II. חבל], joining to v^{28}, Du Marti *has gone up from P^{e}ne-Rimmon* [??], cf Di-Kit) **2. a.** *oil*, specif olive-oil, as rich product Dt 8^{8}+ (v. זַיִת), hence עֵץ שׁ׳ Is 41^{19} *oil-tree*, usu explained as wild olive, *oleaster*, so Ne 8^{15} (‖ זַיִת), עֲצֵי שׁ׳ *oleaster-wood* 1 K 6$^{23.31.32.33}$, once שׁ׳ הַמֹּר Est 2^{12} (v. מֹר p 600^{b}; מ׳ also in holy anointing oil Ex 30^{23}). **b.** ש׳ as staple (condiment) Nu 11^{8} (J; v. לְשַׁד), of value 1 K 17$^{12.14.16}$ 2 K 2$^{4.6.7}$+4 t, symb of plenty Dt 32^{13} 33^{24} Jb 29^{6}; ascribed (falsely) to gift of Baals Ho 2^{7}, as royal treasure 2 K 20^{13}=Is 39^{2}, cf 1 K 5^{25} (ש׳ כָּתִית, v כ׳)=2 Ch 2$^{9.14}$+3 t; tribute Ho 12^{2}, art of trade Ez 27^{17}, odoriferous Pr 27^{9} Ct 1^{3} 4^{10}, ש׳ רוֹקֵחַ Ec 10^{1}, so (fig.) Ct 1^{3} Ec 7^{1}, Pr 27^{16} is corrupt, v. Toy, sign of luxury Ez 16^{13} Pr 21^{17}, of prosperity Ez 16^{20}. **c.** ש׳ as medicament Is 1^{6}, as unguent, for shield 2 S 1^{21}, person Am 6^{6} Mi 6^{15} Dt 28^{40} Ez 16^{9} Est 2^{12} ψ 92^{11} 104^{15}, not for mourner 2 S 14^{2}; on head, token of happiness Ec 9^{8}, of hospitality, דִּשַּׁנְתָּ בַשֶּׁ׳ רֹאשִׁי ψ 23^{5} (fig), in sim 133^{2} 141^{5} **d.** for anointing king, פַּךְ הַשּׁ׳ 1 S 10^{1} 2 K 9$^{1.3}$, cf. v^{6}, c קֶרֶן 1 S 16$^{1.13}$ 1 K 1^{39}, cf בְּשׁ׳ קָדְשִׁי מְשַׁחְתִּיו ψ 89^{21}. **e.** in various figs., of joy שׁ׳ שָׂשׂוֹן Is 61^{3} ψ 45^{8}; soft words 55^{22} Pr 5^{3}; as penetrating 109^{18}; as clear, transparent Ez 32^{14}. **f.** used in primitive worship, poured on stone Gn 28^{18} (E), 35^{14} (J) **g.** in later ritual · for anointing priests, tabern, altar utensils, etc. (P), made of various ingred., שׁ׳ זַיִת among them, Ex 30^{24}, שׁ׳ הַמִּשְׁחָה 25^{6} Lv 8$^{2.10.12}$+11 t.; שׁ׳ מִשְׁחַת־קֹדֶשׁ Ex 30$^{25.25}$+2 t.; שׁ׳ מ׳ Lv 10^{7}, שׁ׳ מ׳ אֱלֹהָיו 21^{12}; שׁ׳ הַקֹּ׳ Nu 35^{25}; ש׳ alone Lv 14^{10}+12 t. Lv 14; for lighting Ex 25^{6}+6 t.+שׁ׳ זַיִת זָךְ כָּתִית Ex 27^{20} Lv 24^{2} (v. כָּתִית); poured upon מִנְחָה Lv 2^{1}+5 t., cf 5^{11} Nu 5^{15}; smeared (v. מָשַׁח) upon wafers Ex 29^{2} Lv 2^{4}+, and cakes (or mixed in the making? cf. בָּלַל) Ex 29^{2} Lv 2$^{4.5}$+, so סֹלֶת בַּשׁ׳ Lv 2^{7}, etc (c. 45 t. in all), חַלַּת לֶחֶם שׁ׳ Ex 29^{23} Lv 8^{26}. **h.** for use in temple 1 Ch 9^{29}. **i.** for תְּרוּמָה in Ezekiel's temple Ez 45$^{14.14}$+7 t. 45, 46. †**j.** efficacy denied Mi 6^{7}. †**k.** offered to idols Is 57^{9} Ez 16$^{18.19}$ 23^{41}—Vid Macalister Hast. DB Oil, ARSKennedy Ency Bib Oil.

†אַשְׁמַנִּים (elative, Ges §§ 85b, 133a; on נ v. Id. §§ 20a, 93ee) appar. **n.[m.] pl.** בָּא׳ כַּמֵּתִים Is 59^{10} perhaps: (we are) *among the stout* (RV *lusty*) *like dead men*, cf. Di-Kit, or abstr. *in* (actual) *vigour* (Buhl) > AV (after Jos Ki fr. אָשֵׁם Ho 14^{1} '*be desolate*') *in desolate places* (other conj v. Che Hpt Marti).

†[מִשְׁמָן] **n.[m.] fatness**,—cstr. וּמִשְׁמַן בְּשָׂרוֹ יֵרָזֶה Is 17^{4} (fig); pl. concr.: *stout, vigorous, ones*, sf מִשְׁמַנָּיו Is 10^{16} (opp. רָזוֹן, on form v. Ges §93pp), מִשְׁמַנֵּיהֶם ψ 78^{31}, = *fertile spots*, cstr. מִשְׁמַנֵּי מְדִינָה Dn 11^{24}. Cf also 1 S 15^{9}, v. מִשְׁנֶה **3.**

†[מַשְׁמָן] **n.[m.] fat piece, tid bit**;—pl. מַשְׁמַנִּים (Ges l c) Ne 8^{10} (for eating; ‖ מַמְתַקִּים for drinking)

†מַשְׁמַנָּה (Ges l c) **n.pr.m.** a hero of David, 1 Ch 12^{11} (v^{10} van d. H., who reads מִשׁ׳); Μασεμμανη, etc., 𝔊L Μασαμαννη.

II. שמן, שמני (√of following; meaning unknown)

שְׁמֹנֶה (less oft. שְׁמוֹנָה), שְׁמֹנָה$_{109}$ **n.m. et f. eight** (on ◌ֶ cf. Ba NB 20, 200 and (against him) Philippi BAS ii 364, Ar ثَمَانِيَةٌ, ثَمَانٍ, Sab (ת)תמני Hom Chr 47, 122 DHM ZMG xxxvii (1883), 369 f., 373; Aram. תְּמָנֵי, תְּמָנְיָא, ܬܡܢܐ, ܬܡܢܝܐ; Nab. תמונא, Palm. תמניא, Lzb^{386}, NH=BH, Ph שמן; Eth ሰመንቱ: ሰማንቱ: on As. equiv. v. Dl §75);—**m.** (c **n.f.**) alw abs. שמנה Ju 3^{8}+40 t.; **f.** (c **n.m.**) abs. שְׁמֹנָה 1 S 17^{12}+34 t, cstr. שְׁמֹנַת Nu 2^{24}+3 t. (cases of 8+10=18 are additional, v. infr.); pl. שמנים, 80, v. infr.:—**1.** without other num.: **a.** שְׁמֹנָה card, before n.pl. Ju 3^{8} 1 K 7^{10}+8 t.;

before n sg. שָׁנָה 1 K 8[17] (Kt; Qr pl.), 22[1]; after n pl. Ez 40[31]; ordin. בשׁ׳ בִּשְׁנַת שׁ׳ לְ 2 K 24[12], שָׁנִים לְ 2 Ch 34[3]. **b.** שְׁמֹנָה card., before n pl. 1 S 17[12] + 3 t, + (n. om.) Je 14[15] + 2 t., also שׁ׳ אֵלֶּה Gn 22[23] *these* 8, and, as round no, Mi 5[4] 7 *and* 8 (i e. plenty); after n.pl. Nu 29[29] 2 Ch 29[17]; ordin., בְּיוֹם שׁ׳ לְ v[17]. **c.** f. cstr. שְׁמֹנַת יָמִים Gn 17[12] 21[4], שׁ׳ הַבָּקָר Nu 7[8]. **2.** 8 + 10 = 18: **a.** c. **n.f.** שְׁמֹנֶה עֶשְׂרֵה, card.: bef. sg. שָׁנָה Ju 3[14] + 2 t., אַמָּה 1 K 7[15] + 2 t.; after n.pl. 1 Ch 26[9] 2 Ch 11[21], n. om. Ezr 8[18] Ne 7[11]; ordin, בִּשְׁנַת שׁ׳ ע׳ לְ 1 K 15[1] + 4 t; בשׁ׳ ע׳ שָׁנָה לְ 2 K 22[3] + 2 t; הַשָּׁנָה שׁ׳ ע׳ שָׁנָה לְ Je 32[1]. **b.** c. **n.m.** שְׁמֹנָה עָשָׂר card.: bef. sg. אֶלֶף Ju 20[44] + 4 t. + ψ 60[2] (title), so read for שְׁנֵים ע׳, cf. 2 S 8[13] = 1 Ch 18[12]; before pl. Ezr 8[9]; n. om. Gn 14[14], ordin, n. om. 1 Ch 24[15] 25[15]; שְׁמֹנַת עָשָׂר אֶלֶף Ju 20[25]. **3.** c. other numerals: **a.** שְׁמֹנֶה מֵאוֹת 2 S 23[8] (so read also ‖ 1 Ch 11[11] Kit Benz, cf. Th We Dr al), + 16 t. **b.** שְׁמֹנָה אֶלֶף 1 Ch 12[36] (v[35] van d H.), 23[3]; שְׁמֹנַת אֲלָפִים Nu 2[24] + 3 t. **c.** שׁ׳, card., after tens 1 S 4[15] + 20 t.; before ten, only שׁ׳ וְעֶשְׂרִים בָּאַמָּה Ex 26[2] 36[9], ordin, בִּשְׁנַת שְׁלֹשִׁים וּשׁ׳ שָׁנָה לְ 1 K 16[29] 2 K 15[8].

שְׁמִינִי, —ית 31 **adj. num. eighth**;—בַּיּוֹם הַשְּׁמִינִי Ex 22[29] + 16 t; הַחֹדֶשׁ הַשׁ׳ 1 K 6[38] + 4 t.; n.m. om. 1 Ch 24[10] + 4 t; הַשָּׁנָה הַשְּׁמִינִת Lv 25[22]; elsewhere only phr., עַל־הַשְּׁמִינִית 1 Ch 15[21], and titles ψ 6[1] 12[1], usu. *acc. to the eighth key*, or *on the octave*, but wholly dubious.

שְׁמֹנִים 38 **n.pl.indecl. an eighty**;—without other num.: sq. sg. אִישׁ ψ 90[10] + 4 t, שָׁנָה 2 K 10[24] Je 41[5]; sq. n pl. 2 Ch 26[17] Ezr 8[8] Ct 6[8]; n. om 2 K 6[25] 1 Ch 15[9]; c. other num., card.. שׁ׳ אֶלֶף Nu 2[9] + 6 t.; שׁ׳ foll. units Gn 5[25] + 4 t; precedes, Gn 16[16] + 4 t.; foll. 100, etc. 1 Ch 25[7] + 6 t.; precedes, Gn 5[28] + 2 t., ordin., בשׁ׳ שָׁנָה וְאַרְבַּע מֵאוֹת שָׁנָה לְ 1 K 6[1].

[שְׁמֹנִים], שְׁמֹנִי v. שָׁמֵן.

שָׁמַע 1159 **vb. hear** (NH *id.*; Ph. שמע Lzb[378]; As *šemû*; Ar. سَمِعَ, Sab סמע, mostly in deriv., esp. epith. div. סמע *he who hears* Hom Chr 124 Fell ZMG liv (1900), 250, 252 DHM Hofmus. No. 10, l. 1; Eth. ሰምዐ: Aram. שְׁמַע, ܫܡܥ, OAram. שמע Lzb[378], cf. also משמעת MI[28] *obedience*);—**Qal** 1062 *Pf.* 3 ms. שׁ׳ Gn 24[52] +, שָׁמֵעַ Je 36[13] + 3 t; 2 fs. שָׁמַעַתְּ 1 K 1[11] + 2 t; 3 pl. שָׁמְעוּ Ju 2[17] +, etc.; *Impf.* 3 ms. יִשְׁמַע Ex 6[30] +, 1 s. cohort. אֶשְׁמְעָה Nu 9[8], וָאֶשְׁמְעָה (on ־ cf. Ges § 10 h; Ol § 65 e qu. reading) Dn 8[13]; 2 mpl. תִּשְׁמְעוּן Dt 8[20] +, תִּשְׁמָעוּן Dt 1[17], etc.; *Imv.* ms. שְׁמַע Am 7[16] +, שְׁמָעָה Jb 32[10] + (esp. ψψ), שְׁמָעָה Dn 9[19]; fpl. שְׁמַעְנָה Is 32[9] Je 9[19], שְׁמַעַן Gn 4[23] (Ges § 46 f), etc; *Inf. abs* שָׁמוֹעַ Is 6[9] +; cstr. שְׁמֹעַ 1 S 15[22] +, sf. שָׁמְעוֹ Dt 29[18] +, שָׁמְעָתוֹ Is 30[19] (Ges § 45 d), etc.; *Pt* שֹׁמֵעַ Gn 42[23] +; f. שֹׁמַעַת Gn 18[10] +, etc.,—**1.** subj. pers. hum. (vel rei personif): **a.** *hear* (perceive by ear), acc. rei, esp קוֹל Gn 3[10] (J) + 46 t., דבר(ים) Am 8[11] + 50 t., etc.; acc. חָכְמָה i e. wise sayings 1 K 5[14] + 4 t.; so any utterance or sound (c. 150 t. in all) + (obj. om.) Dt 4[33] + 32 t. + (cl. temp.) 1 S 14[27] + 6 t.; very rarely c. ב, שׁ׳ בְּסוֹד י׳ Jb 15[8]; c. obj. cl, כִּי Ex 4[31] + 52 t + Is 39[1b] (rd. כִּי שׁ׳ 𝔊 𝔖 ‖ 2 K 20[12]), אֵת־אֲשֶׁר Jos 2[10] 5[1] (both R[D]),—מַה־ Ju 7[11] + 3 t.; without connect. שׁ׳ אַתָּה עָשִׂיתִי †2 K 19[25] = Is 37[26]; sg. orat. rect. †Is 40[28] Zc 8[23]. †**b.** acc. pers. + מְדַבֵּר *hear one speaking*, Gn 27[6] (J), Je 26[7] Dn 8[13], so בֹּכֶה Nu 11[10] (J), נִבָּא Je 20[1], מְקַלֶּלְךָ Ec 7[21]; occas. pers. om, דְּבָרִים Gn 37[17] (JE), אֶת־מִדַּבֵּר Ez 2[2] 43[6] (v. דבר **Hithp.**); acc pers only Dn 12[7]. †**c.** c. לֵאמֹר only, *hear say* = *hear it said*, 1 S 13[4] 2 S 19[3] Dt 13[13] Jos 22[11] (P), 1 K 16[16]; + עַל pers *concerning* Gn 41[15] (E), Is 37[9]; אֶל pers. *id.* 2 K 19[9]. **d.** *hear of, concerning*: (1) acc rei, את (כָּל־)אֲשֶׁר Ex 18[1] 2 K 19[11] + 5 t, דבר(ים) 1 S 3[11] + 4 t., רָעָה Je 19[3] + 5 t., etc.; כַּאֲשֶׁר 1 S 23[11] ψ 48[9], כָּזֹאת Is 66[8] *hear of anything like this*, כָּאֵלֶּה Je 18[13]; acc, etc, om Ju 9[46] + 43 t., (2) less oft. acc pers. Jb 42[5], אֶל pers. Ez 19[4], pers om. Dt 9[2]; c. ב pers. *hear exultantly* of their fate †ψ 92[12] (prob. imitated from ‖ הַבִּיט בְּ v[a]; v. esp. ראה **8 a** (6)) †**e.** *hear*, abs, = have power to hear, 2 S 19[36] (c. בְּקוֹל), Is 21[3] 32[3] Pr 20[12] Zc 7[11], in sim. ψ 38[14]; c neg. of idols Dt 4[28] ψ 115[6]; fig. (spiritual power) Je 5[21] Dt 29[3] Ez 12[2] Is 42[20].—Pr 21[28] is probably corrupt, v Toy. **f.** *hear with attention, interest, listen to* (sts. ‖ הִקְשִׁיב, הֶאֱזִין), acc. דבר(ים) (54 t.) Am 4[1] +, esp. דבר(י) י׳ Nu 12[6] (JE) + 45 t.; אִמְרָה Is 28[23], קוֹל v[23], זאת Mi 3[9], etc.; oft. abs. Ju 5[3] + 57 t, + (neg.) ψ 38[14] *pay no attention*; abs. לֵב שֹׁמֵעַ 1 K 3[9], אִישׁ שׁוֹמֵעַ Pr 21[28]. †**g.** *understand* (language), שָׂפָה Gn 11[7] (J), Is 33[19], לָשׁוֹן Dt 28[49], דְּבָרִים Ez 3[6], מַה־יְּדַבֵּר Je 5[15], no acc. Gn 42[23] (E), 2 K 18[26] = Is 36[11]. **h.** specif. of *hearing* a (judicial) case, דָּבָר Dt 1[17], cf. v[17]; acc.om. בֵּין pers. v[16], of י׳ Ju 11[10]; c. מִשְׁפָּט 1 K 3[11]; וְשֹׁמֵעַ אֵין לְךָ 2 S 14[17], לִשְׁ׳ הַטּוֹב וְהָרָע 15[3], cf Jb 31[35].

†i. c. acc. pers. in polite address, *hear us* (*me*)! Gn 23$^{6.8.11.13.15}$ (all P), 1 Ch 28^2 2 Ch 13^4 15^2 20^{20}. **j.** *listen, give heed* (sts. ‖ הִקְשִׁיב), abs., Gn 42^{21} (E) + 18 t., + (usu. ‖ הִטָּה אֹזֶן), Je 7^{13} + 14 t. Je, + (opp. חָדַל) Ez 2^5 + 3 t. Ez; + שִׂים עַל־לֵב Mal 2^2; *hear + do* Dt 5^{24} 2 K 18^{12}, etc.; *=consent, agree,* Gn 37^{27} (J), *grant request* Ju 11^{17}; c. לְ pers. (mostly late) Ju 19^{25} 1 S 30^{24} Jb 15^{17} + 16 t., לִי Ho 9^{17} Lv 26$^{14.18.21.27}$; לְדִבְרֵי י׳ 1 S 15^1, לְעֵצָה Pr 12^{15}. **k.** c. אֶל pers. + *listen to, yield to* Gn 49^2 Ju 2^{17} + 69 t. (אֶל־י׳ 15 t., esp. Je 7^{26} + 10 t. Je), עַל pers. 2 K 20^{13}; אֶל־דִּבְרֵי etc., Dt 18^{19} Je 29^{19} + 14 t., עַל־דִּבְרֵי etc., 2 K 22^{13} + 3 t.; very rarely acc. rei 1 S 24^{10} (Gi v^9). **l.** שׁ׳ לְקוֹל *=id., obey,* Gn 3^{17} (J) + 11 t. + (לְקוֹל י׳) Ju 2^{20} Ex 15^{26} (JE). **m.** very oft., שׁ׳ בְּקוֹל *=obey* 1 S 8^7 + 25 t., + שׁ׳ בְּקוֹל י׳ (י׳'s word, etc.) Dt 4^{30} Je 3^{13} + 65 t. (Dt 18 t., Je 18 t.). **n.** *obey,* c. acc. (דבר(ים Jos 1^{18} + 2 t. + (ד׳ י׳) Je 11^3 + 5 t. Je, 1 K 12^{24} = 2 Ch 11^4, etc.; acc. pers. Ex 6^{12} (P), 2 Ch 28^{11}. **o.** abs. *be obedient* (esp. to י׳) Is 1^{19} Mi 5^{14} Je 12^{17} + 4 t. Je + 7 t. **2.** י׳ (God) subj.: **a.** acc. קוֹל, דברים, etc., Gn 21^{17} (E), 2 K 19$^{4.4.16}$, usually with favour implied Nu 20^{16} Dt 33^7 +, so esp. acc. תְּחִנָּה, תְּפִלָּה, etc., 1 K 8^{45} ψ 6^{10} +. **b.** obj. cl. כִּי Gn 29^{33} (J). **c.** no obj. (32 t.) Is 59^2 Je 22^{21}, usu. *hear and forgive, help,* etc., 1 K 8$^{30.32}$ Is 30^{19} +; *hear and be angry* ψ 78^{59}, cf. 55^{20}. **d.** *= be able to hear* Is 59^1 ψ 94^9. **e.** שׁ׳ בְּקוֹל = *hear* (*and grant*) Gn 30^6 (J) + 6 t. **f.** *hear and answer,* c. אֶל of cry, etc., Gn 21^7 16^{11} 1 K 8^{28} + 8 t.; c. אֶל pers. Dt 3^{26} + 12 t. **g.** c. לְ of utterance Je 18^{19} ψ 61^6; לְ pers. Jos 24^{10} (E). **h.** *hear,* acc. pers. + מִתְנוֹדֵד Je 31^{18}; favourably, c. acc. pers. Mi 7^7 + 3 t., so, + לְ *concerning,* Gn 17^{20} (P); obj. om. 2 K 22^{19} ψ 22^{25} + 3 t. + ψ 34$^{7.18}$ (hear and deliver); c. cl. temp. Je 11^{14}.

Niph. $_{42}$ *Pf.* 3 ms. נִשְׁמַע Gn 45^{16} +, etc.; *Impf.* 3 ms. יִשָּׁמַע Ex 23^{13} +, יִשָּׁמֵעַ 1 S 1^{13}, etc.; *Inf. cstr.* הִשָּׁמַע Est 2^8; *Pt.* f. נִשְׁמַעַת Je 51^{46}, etc.;— **1.** *be heard,* of voice, sound, etc., 1 S 1^{13} 1 K 6^7 Jb 26^{14} (or 1 pl. **Qal** *Impf.*?); of a report, נִשׁ׳ . . . לֵאמֹר Gn 45^{16} (E); subj. cl., כִּי, Ne 6^1 (לְ pers.), cf. cl. וְהַיְּהוּדִים חֹשְׁבִים Ne 6^6; v^7 *be reported,* (לַמֶּלֶךְ) כַּדְּבָרִים הָאֵלֶּה; *be heard,* לִפְנֵי אֱלֹהֶיךָ Dn 10^{12}. **2.** *be heard of,* כָּמֹהוּ Dt 4^{32}. **3.** *be regarded, obeyed,* Ec 9^{17}; in 2 S 22^{45} = ψ 18^{45} it is *be obedient* (לִי), si vera l. (read perh. **Qal,** cf. Now). **4.** וַיִּשׁ׳ בְּקוֹלָם 2 Ch 30^{27} = (favourable) *hearing was granted to their voice.* †**Pi.** *Impf.* 3 ms. וַיְשַׁמַּע 1 S 15^4 *he caused* the people (acc.) *to hear* (and respond, i.e. he assembled them), so 23^8 (v. **Hiph. 1 c**). **Hiph.** $_{63}$ *Pf.* 3 ms. הִשְׁמִיעַ 1 K 15^{22} +, etc.; *Impf.* 3 ms. sf. יַשְׁמִעֵנִי Dt 30$^{12.13}$; 2 ms. juss. תַּשְׁמַע Ju 18^{25}, etc.; *Imv.* ms. sf. הַשְׁמִיעֵנִי ψ 143^8; fs. sf. הַשְׁמִיעִנִי Ct 2^{14} 8^{13}, etc.; *Inf. cstr.* לַשְׁמִעַ ψ 26^7 (Ges$^{§ 53 q}$); *Pt.* מַשְׁמִיעַ Je 4^{15} +, etc.;—**1.** of man: **a.** *cause to hear,* acc. pers. + rei Dt 30$^{12.13}$ Ct 2^{14} 8^{13} + 4 t.; obj. rei om. (*=make proclamation to*) 1 K 15^{22}; obj. pers. om. Je 5^{20} +; acc. שָׁלוֹם † Is 52^7 Na 2^1 i.e. *proclaim* peace; אָוֶן † Je 4^{15} (מִן loc.); הַשׁ׳ קוֹל *utter a sound* Jos 6^{10} (J; ‖ הֵרִיעַ), cf. Ju 18^{25} (עִמָּנוּ + ,קוֹלֶךָ), Is 42^2 58^4; הַשׁ׳ קוֹל תְּהִלָּתוֹ + ψ 66^8, בְּקוֹל תּוֹדָה + 26^7. **b.** abs. as musical term, *sound aloud,* בִּמְצִלְתַּיִם לְהַשְׁמִיעַ 1 Ch 15^{19} (perhaps to mark the time, Gr$^{\psi 67}$ De: cf. 16^5; also ψ 150^5 לְהַשׁ׳ קוֹל אֶחָד, בְּצִלְצְלֵי שָׁמַע), מַשְׁמִיעִים 15$^{16.28}$ 16^{42}, 2 Ch 5^{13} i.e. prob. in unison (Prince$^{EB\ iii.\ 3241}$), Ne 12^{42}. **c.** abs. *make proclamation* (oft. ‖ הִגִּיד), Am 3^9 4^5 Is 41^{26} Je 4^5 + 6 t. Je. †**d.** הַשְׁמִיעוּ, acc. pers. + אֶל loc. *= summon* Je 50^{29}, עַל loc. 51^{27} (cf. **Pi.**). **2.** י׳ subj.: **a.** *cause to hear,* acc. pers. et rei Dt 4$^{10.36}$ (מִן loc.), 2 K 7^6 + 4 t.; acc. pers. om. Is 30^{30} + 3 t.; acc. rei om. 44^8 48^5. †**b.** *=tell,* acc. pers. + כָּזֹאת Ju 13^{23}; acc. pers. only, Is 42^9; acc. rei only, 48^3 Ez 36^{15} (אֵלַיִךְ). †**c.** abs., *make proclamation* Is 43^{12} 62^{11} (אֶל loc.).

†I. [שֶׁמַע] **n.** [**m.**] sound;—הַלְלוּהוּ בְּצִלְצְלֵי־שָׁמַע ψ 150^5 (‖ תְּרוּעָה).

†II. שֶׁמַע **n.pr.m.** usu. Σαμα(α), Σεμαα (cf. Sab. n.pr. סמע Hal^{509});—**1.** in Judah 1 Ch 2^{44}, שָׁמַע v^{43}. **2.** in Reuben 5^8. **3.** in Benj. 8^{13} (= שִׁמְעִי v^{21}). **4.** post-ex. Ne 8^4, Σαμαιας.

†שֵׁמַע **n.** [**m.**] hearing, report (on form cf. Lag$^{BN\ 143}$);—שׁ׳ abs. Is 23^5; cstr. v^5 +; sf. שִׁמְעִי 66^{19}, etc.;—*report,* usu. c. genit. obj.: acc. with שֵׁמַע Gn 29^{13} (J) *the tidings about Jacob,* Is 23^5 + (c. sf.) Nu 14^{15} (JE), Dt 2^{25} 1 K 10^1 = 2 Ch 9^1, Na 3^{19} Hb 3^2 Je 37^5 50^{43} Is 66^9; c. לְ genit. Is 23^5; לַעֲדָתָם Ho 7^{12} usu. *according to the report* (*heard by*) *their congregation* (!), but inexpl. and prob. corrupt, We Now; Marti (cf. Oettli) (כְּשֵׁמַע) עַל־רָעָתָם as gloss) *according to their wickedness;* נָשָׂא שׁ׳ שָׁוְא Ex 23^1 (E) *take up* (utter) *a false report;* לְשׁ׳ אֹזֶן ψ 18^{45} i.e. as soon as heard of, *=mere report* Jb 42^5 (opp. personal knowledge), cf. שְׁמֻעָה 28^{22}.

†[שֵׁמַע] **n. m.**$^{Ex 8.4}$ report;—sf. שָׁמְעוֹ: וַיְהִי שׁ׳ שָׁמְעוֹ Jos 6^{27}, *the report of him went*, etc.; שׁ׳ שָׁמְעוֹ 9^{9} (both R^{D}), Je 6^{24}; וְשׁ׳ הוֹלֵךְ בְּכָל־הַמְּדִינוֹת Est 9^{4}.

†שֶׁמַע **n. pr. loc.** in S Judah, Jos 15^{26}, Σα(λ)μα(α).

†שָׁמָע **n.pr.m.** a hero of David 1 Ch 11^{44}, Σαμαθα, Σαμμα (cf. OSem. שמע on scarab Cl Gann JAs 1883 Fev.-Mars, 135, No 9; also on seal from Megiddo (1904), cf. Kau$^{Mitth u Nachr DPV, 1904 2ff}$)

שִׁמְעָא **n.pr.m. 1.** brother of David 2 S 21^{21} Qr (cf. Dr; Kt שמעי) Σεμεει, 𝔊L Σαμαα, = 1 Ch 20^{7}, third son of Jesse 1 Ch 2^{13}; = שִׁמְעָה 1 S 13$^{3.32}$, Σαμα(α), etc., שַׁמָּה (q.v.) 1 S 16^{9} 17^{13} **2.** son of David 1 Ch 3^{5} (= שַׁמּוּעַ **1**), Σαμαν, Σαμαα. **3.** Levites, Σομεα, Σαμα(α): **a.** 1 Ch 6^{15}. **b.** v^{24}.

שִׁמְעָה **n.pr.m.** v. שִׁמְעָא **1.**

†שְׁמָעָה **n.pr.m.** c. art. הַשׁ׳ הַגִּבְעָתִי 1 Ch 12^{3}, Αμα, Σαμαα, 𝔊L Ασμα.

†שִׁמְעָת **n. pr. f.**$^{2 Ch 24\ 26}$ mother of one of Joash's murderers, 2 K 12^{22} (Ιεμουαθ), called Ammonitess 2 Ch 24^{26} (Σαμα(αθ)).

†שִׁמְעָתִים **adj. gent. pl.** as **subst.**, family of scribes 1 Ch 2^{55}, Σαμαθ(ι)ειμ[ν].

†שְׁמוּעָה **n.f.** report;—abs. שׁ׳ 1 S 4^{19}+, שְׁמֻעָה 2^{24}+; cstr. שְׁמֻעַת 2 S 4^{4}; sf. שְׁמֻעָתֵנוּ Is 53^{1}; pl. abs. שְׁמֻעוֹת Dn 11^{44},—**1.** *report*, sts. after שָׁמַע 1 S 2^{24} 4^{19} (= *news*), 1 K 10^{7} = 2 Ch 9^{6}, 2 K 19^{7} = Is 37^{7}, Je 51^{46}; שׁ׳ רָעָה Je 49^{23}, cf. ψ 112^{7}, and שׁ׳ טוֹבָה Pr 15^{30} 25^{25}; *tidings about* Saul 2 S 4^{4}; c. בָּאָה 13^{30} (+ לֵאמֹר), 1 K 2^{28} Ez 21^{12} Je 10^{22}, cf. 51^{46} + (בָּאָה om.) v^{46}; תָּבוֹא שׁ׳ אֶל־שׁ׳ Ez 7^{26}; שׁ׳ יְבַהֲלֻהוּ Dn 11^{44}; שְׁמֻעָתֵנוּ Is 53^{1} *the report that reached us*, cf. also Is 28$^{9.19}$ Je 49^{14} Ob^{1} (De Du al. specif. of prophetic message, but v. Gie$^{Beiträge 135 f}$ We Now$^{Ob 1}$). **2.** = *mention*, לֹא הָיְתָה סְדֹם לִשְׁ׳ בְּפִיךְ Ez 16^{56}.

†שַׁמּוּעַ **n.pr.m. 1.** son of David 2 S 5^{14} = 1 Ch 14^{4}, Σαμμους[ε], Σαμαα (= שִׁמְעָא **2**). **2.** Reubenite, Nu 13^{4}, Σαμουηλ, Σαλαμιηλ, etc. **3.** Levite, Ne 11^{17} (= שְׁמַעְיָה 1 Ch 9^{16}), Σαμουει, etc.; 12^{18} (? same person), 𝔊L Σαμουε.

שִׁמְעוֹן$_{44}$ **n.pr.m.** (cf. n pr. שמעון in Palm. Lzb^{378}; meaning doubtful; RS al cp. سِمْعٌ, said to mean *offspring of hyena and wolf*; v. Hogg$^{EB iv 4531}$);—**1.** second son of Jacob and Leah, Συμεων: Gn 29^{33} (name expl. from שָׁמַע), 35^{23} Ex 1^{2} + 14 t. (assoc. esp. with Levi Gn 34$^{25.30}$ 49^{5}). **2.** tribal name Ju 1$^{3.3.17}$ Nu 1^{6}+, so בְּנֵי שׁ׳ Nu 1^{22} + 7 t, מַטֵּה שׁ׳ Nu 1^{23} 2^{12} 13^{5}, מַטֵּה בְנֵי שׁ׳ 10^{19} 34^{20} Jos 19$^{1.8}$ 21^{9} 1 Ch 6^{50}. †**3.** post-ex. Jew with foreign wife Ezr 10^{31}.

†שִׁמְעֹנִי **adj. gent.** c. art. as n. coll., Nu 25^{14} 26^{14} 1 Ch 27^{16}; מַטֵּה הַשׁ׳ Jos 21^{4}.

I. שִׁמְעִי$_{43}$ **n.pr.m.** usu. Σεμεει · **1.** in Benj: **a.** 2 S 16$^{5.7.13}$ 19$^{17.19.22.24}$, 1 K 2^{8} + 10 t. 1 K 2. †**b.** 1 K 1^{8}, perh. = 4^{18}. **2.** a Ramathite 1 Ch 27^{27}. †**3.** Levites: **a.** 'son' of Gershon Ex 6^{17} Nu 3^{18} 1 Ch 6^{2} 23$^{7.9.10.10}$. **b.** 6^{14}. **c.** v^{27}. **d.** 25^{17}. **e.** 2 Ch 29^{14} **f.** 31$^{12.13}$. **g.** Ezr 10^{23}. †**4.** brother of Zerub. 1 Ch 3^{19}. †**5.** in Simeon 4$^{26.27}$. †**6.** in Reuben 5^{4}. †**7.** 1 Ch 8^{13} = (II) שֶׁמַע v^{13}. †**8.** post-ex. names: **a.** Ezr 10^{33}. **b.** v^{38} (cf **3 g** supr.). †**9.** grandfather of Mordecai Est 2^{5}. **10.** 2 S 21^{21} Kt (Qr שִׁמְעָא q. v. **1**).

†II. שִׁמְעִי **adj. gent.** of **3 a**;—c. art. as **n. coll.** הַשׁ׳ Nu 3^{21}; cf. Zc 12^{13}.

†שְׁמַעְיָה(וּ) **n.pr.m.** Σαμαιας, etc.: שְׁמַעְיָה, **1.** prophet, Rehob.'s time 1 K 12^{22} 2 Ch 12$^{5.7.15}$; = ־יָהוּ 11^{2}. **2.** Jer.'s time: **a.** false proph. Je 29$^{31.31.32}$ = ־יָהוּ v^{24}. **b.** ־יָהוּ 36^{12}. **3.** ־יָהוּ a prophet's father 26^{20}. **4.** descendant of Zerub 1 Ch 3$^{22.22}$. **5.** in Simeon 4^{37}. **6.** in Reuben 5^{4}. **7.** Levites: **a.** 1 Ch 9^{14}. **b.** v^{16} = שַׁמּוּעַ **3**. **c.** 15$^{8.11}$. **d.** 24^{6}. **e.** 26$^{4.6.7}$. **f.** 2 Ch 29^{14}. **g.** Ezr 8^{16} **h.** Ne 11^{15}. Also ־יָהוּ **i.** 2 Ch 17^{8}. **j.** 31^{15}. **k.** 35^{9}. **8.** companions of Ezra: **a.** Ezr 8^{13}. **b.** 10^{21}. **c.** v^{31}. **9.** of Neh.: **a.** Ne 3^{29}. **b.** 6^{10}. **10.** priests: **a.** Ne 10^{9} 12^{42}. **b.** v$^{6.18}$ **c.** v^{35}. **d.** v^{36}. **11.** a prince v^{34}.

אֶשְׁתְּמוֹעַ v. p. 84.

יִשְׁמָעֵאל$_{48}$ **n. pr. m.** (*Ēl heareth*; Sab. יסמעאל Hal^{187}; on form cf Lag$^{BN 131}$);—**1.** son of Abraham and Hagar Gn 16^{11} (name expl. כִּי שָׁמַע י׳ וגו׳), v$^{15.16}$ + 11 t. Gn 17. 25, 28$^{9.9}$ 36^{3} 1 Ch 1$^{28.29.31}$; Ισμαηλ. **2.** usu. Ισμαηλ: murderer of Gedaliah Je 40$^{8.14.15.16}$ + 17 t. Je 41, 2 K 25$^{23.25}$ (𝔊L Ισραηλ!). **3.** in Benj 1 Ch 8^{38} 9^{44}. **4.** in Judah: **a.** 2 Ch 19^{11}. **b.** 23^{1}. **5.** Jew with foreign wife Ezr 10^{22}, Σαμαηλ, A 𝔊L Ισμαηλ.

†יִשְׁמְעֵאלִי **adj. gent.** of יִשׁ׳ **1**;—sg c. art. הַיִּשׁ׳ 1 Ch 2^{17} + ∥ 2 S 17^{25} (so read for הַיִּשְׂרְאֵלִי, v. Comm); הַיִּשְׁמְעֵלִי 1 Ch 27^{30}, pl. (הַ)יִּשְׁמְעֵאלִים *Ishmaelites* Gn 37$^{25.27.28}$ 39^{1} Ju 8^{24} ψ 83^{7}.

† יִשְׁמַעְיָה(וּ) **n.pr.m.** (**'י** *heareth*);—Σαμαιας: **1.** ־יָה, Gibeonite, one of David's heroes 1 Ch 12^{4}. **2.** ־יָהוּ in Zebulun 27^{19}.

† הַשְׁמָעוּת **n.f. a causing to hear** (prop. Aramaizing Inf. Hiph.; Ges$^{§ 53.1}$ Sta$^{§ 304a}$);—לְהַשׁ׳ אָזְנָיִם Ez 24^{26} *to cause ears to hear*, i.e. bring tidings in person (? rd. ־מַּעַת Nö$^{ZMG\ lviii\ (1903),\ 416}$).

† I. [מִשְׁמָע] **n.[m.] thing heard**;—cstr. לֹא־לְמִשְׁמַע אָזְנָיו Is 11^{3} *not according to what his ears hear*, not superficially (‖ לְמַרְאֵה עֵינָיו).

† II. מִשְׁמָע **n. pr. m.** Μασ(α)μα(ν): **1.** in Ishmael Gn 25^{14} 1 Ch 1^{30}. **2.** in Simeon 4$^{25.26}$.

† [מִשְׁמַעַת] **n.f. obedient band, body of subjects**;—only sf.: **1.** prob. = *body-guard*, as esp. bound to obedience, מִשְׁמַעְתֶּךָ 1 S 22^{14} captain over *thy guard* (Ew Be^{Ch} Dr Bu Now), cf. ־תּוֹ 2 S 23^{23} = 1 Ch 11^{25}. **2.** ־תָּם Is 11^{14} the sons of Ammon (shall be) *their subjects* (‖ מוֹאָב מִשְׁלוֹחַ יָדָם; cf. משמעת MI^{28}).

שׁמץ (√ of foll.; cf. NH שֶׁמֶץ *accusation* (or *suspicion*); Thes cp. Ar. شَمَصَ *speak rapidly (and indistinctly)* (Ḳam Frey), but dub.; *rapidity* seems main idea;—and ש = ش ?).

† שֶׁמֶץ **n.[m.] whisper**;—ש׳ abs. Jb 4^{12}; cstr. ש׳ דָּבָר 26^{14} *a* (mere) *whisper of a word*, something wholly inadequate.

† שִׁמְצָה **n. f.** (derisive) **whisper, derision**;—ש׳ Ex 32^{25} (J).

I. **שָׁמַר** $_{465}$ **vb. keep, watch, preserve** (NH *id.*; Ph. שמר in n.pr. and (Pun.) = *watchman*; Tel Am. *šimiru* is perhaps *overseer* (Canaanism), Wkl$^{No.\ 80,\ l.\ 23}$; Mand. סמירא *preserved* Nö$^{M\ 46}$; cf. Ar. سَمَرَ *converse by night, stay awake* (v. Lag$^{BN\ 105}$); Ba$^{NB\ 175\ f.;\ ES\ 43}$ infers from ܫܡܪܐ *eyelid* (cf. [שְׁמֻרָה] infr.), and Ar. تَمَلَ *support, aid, protect* (*l*=*r*), that two √√ are combined in Heb.; but proof insuff.);—**Qal** $_{425}$ *Pf.* 3 ms. ש׳ Gn 37^{11}+, etc.; *Impf.* 3 ms. יִשְׁמֹר 1 S 2^{9}+, ־יִשְׁמָר Je 5^{24}+, sf. 3 ms. יִשְׁמְרֶנּוּ Ex 21$^{29.36}$; 3 fs. sf. תִּשְׁמוּרֶם Pr 14^{3} (rd. תִּשְׁמְרוּם, v. Ges$^{§ 47g}$ Toy), etc.; *Imv.* ms. שְׁמֹר Jb 2^{6}+, שָׁמְרָה 1 Ch 29^{18}+; mpl. שִׁמְרוּ Jos 6^{18}+, etc.; *Inf. abs.* שָׁמוֹר Dt 5^{12}+; cstr. שְׁמֹר Gn 3^{24}+, sf. שָׁמְרָהּ 2^{15}, etc.; *Pt. act.* שֹׁמֵר 1 S 1^{12}+, etc.; *pass.* שָׁמוּר Ec 5^{12} (1 S 9^{24} v. infr.), etc.;—[Synon. I. נָטַר, נָצַר, q.v.]: **1. a.** *keep, have charge of*, garden Gn 2^{15} (J), ark 1 S 7^{1}, property in trust Ex 22$^{6.9}$ (E), cf. 1 S 25^{21}; *tend* flock Gn 30^{31} (E), cf. Zc 3^{7} Nu 3^{8} (P); so perh. (obj. om.) Ho 12^{13} (where ש׳ chosen for parallelism Now Marti al.); Pt. הֲשֹׁמֵר אָחִי אָנֹכִי Gn 4^{9} (J), ש׳ of sheep 1 S 17^{20}, ש׳ הַכֵּלִים v^{22}, ש׳ הַבְּגָדִים 2 K 22^{14} 2 Ch 34^{22}, ש׳ הַנָּשִׁים Est 2$^{3.8.15}$, cf. v^{14}, etc. **b.** *keep, guard*, captives Jos 10^{18} (J), 1 K 20^{39}, דֶּרֶךְ Gn 3^{24} (J); *keep watch and ward*, אֶל pers. for whom 1 S 26^{15} (ψ 59^{10} v. **3** end), עַל pers. v^{16} Pr 6^{22}; בַּנַּעַר 2 S 18^{12} *have a care of* (read לִי for מִי ⅏ and mod.); in hostile sense, אֶל הָעִיר (in siege) 2 S 11^{16}, עַל חַטָּאתִי Jb 14^{16} (but rd. תַּעֲבֹר c. ⅏ Ew Di Du al. [not Hi Bu]); abs. c. מֵעַל Ec 5^{7} *watcheth above*, etc. (v. p. 759^{a} **d**); *keep* one's mouth, be prudent of speech †Pr 21^{23}, cf. Mi 7^{5}; *keep* = protect, save, one's life, נֶפֶשׁ †Pr 13^{3} 16^{17} 19^{16} 22^{5}, another's Jb 2^{6}; in Pr, acc. pers., subj. wisdom, 4^{6} *she shall preserve thee*, cf. (+ מִן of evil) 6^{24} 7^{5}; esp. Pt. *watch, watchman*, of city Is 21$^{11.11.12}$ 62^{6} (fig.), Ct 3^{3} 5$^{7.7}$ ψ 127^{1}; ש׳ הַסַּף (in temple) Je 35^{4}+ (v. סַף), הַשֹּׁ׳ פֶּתַח בֵּית הַמֶּלֶךְ 1 K 14^{27} = 2 Ch 12^{10}, ש׳ הַשְּׁעָרִים Ne 13^{22}, שֹׁמְרֵי הַבַּיִת (fig.) Ec 12^{3}; ש׳ הַבַּיִת *keep the house* (of David's concubines) †2 S 15^{16} 16^{21} 20^{3}; שֹׁמֵר הַכֵּלִים 1 S 17^{22}, ש׳ הַבְּגָדִים 2 K 22^{14}, ש׳ הַפַּרְדֵּס Ne 2^{8}, ש׳ הַנָּשִׁים Est 2$^{3.14.15}$, שֹׁמְרִים abs. Ju 7^{19} Je 51^{12}. **c.** hence *watch for, wait for*, acc. pers. 1 S 19^{11} (to kill him), cf. ψ 59^{1} (title; acc. הַבַּיִת); c. עֲקֵבַי ψ 56^{7} = dog my steps, 71^{10} Je 20^{10}; = watch (suspiciously) Jb 10^{14} 13^{27} 33^{11}; abs. הַשֹּׁמְרִים Ju 1^{24}; *wait for*, נֶשֶׁף Jb 24^{15}, לַבֹּקֶר ψ 130$^{6.6}$. **d.** *watch, observe*, acc. rei 1 S 1^{12} Ec 11^{4} Jb 39^{1} Je 8^{7} (of birds), with intelligence Is 42^{20} ψ 107^{43}; acc. pers. 37^{37} (‖ ראה), Zc 11^{11}; acc. of sin ψ 31^{7} 130^{3}; acc. rei, for the purpose of avoiding, 17^{4}. **2. a.** *keep, retain*, of storing up (food) Gn 41^{35} (E); abs. Ec 3^{6} (opp. הַשְׁלִיךְ); *treasure up* (in memory) Gn 37^{11} (E), cf. Mal 2^{7} 1 Ch 29^{18} Pr 4^{21} (בְּתוֹךְ לְבָבֶךָ), 22^{18} (בְּבִטְנֶךָ); *retain* wrath Am 1^{11} (read שָׁמַר לָנֶצַח We Now GASm Marti; v. also נָטַר **1**) + (anger om.) Je 3^{5} (‖ נטר). **b.** *keep* within bounds, *restrain*, obj. שׁוֹר Ex 21$^{29.36}$ (E); c. acc. hand, מִן of evil Is 56^{2}; fig. *keep thy foot*, c. cl. temp. Ec. 4^{17}; אֶשׁ־לְפִי מַחְסוֹם ψ 39^{2} (⅏ Du al. אָשִׂימָה); appar. reflex. (= **Niph.**), †Jos 6^{18} (+ מִן־הַחֵרֶם), poss. sc. נַפְשְׁכֶם Di. **3. a.** *observe, celebrate*, acc. of festival, etc., Ex 23^{15} (E), 34^{18} (J), 12^{17}, of day v^{17} (P), of month Dt 16^{1}. **b.** *keep* sabbath †Dt 5^{12} Lv 19$^{3.30}$ 26^{2} (all H), Ex 31$^{13.14.16}$ (P), Is 56^{4}, also (+ מֵחַלְּלוֹ) v$^{2.6}$. **c.** of other obligations: *keep* covenant Ez 17^{14}, esp.

covenant of 'י Dt 29⁸ 1 K 11¹¹ + 5 t., 'שְׁבֻעַת י 1 K 2⁴³, *perform* vow Dt 23²⁴; *keep* commands Je 35¹⁸ Ez 20¹⁸; esp. מִצְוֹת, חֻקִּים, עֵדֹת, etc., of 'י (sts. ‖נצר), Ex 20⁶ = Dt 5¹⁰, Am 2⁴ 1 K 2³ ψ 119⁸·¹⁷·³¹ + very oft. (c. 120 t.), 'ש׳ דֶּרֶךְ י Gn 18¹⁹ (J) + 4 t., 'דַּרְכֵי י 2 S 22²² = ψ 18²², 'ד׳ י om. Ju 2²²ᵇ; ש׳ (תֵּלֵךְ בְּדֶרֶךְ טוֹבִים ‖) Pr 2²⁰ ש׳ אָרְחוֹת צַדִּיקִים דְּרָכַי (ways of wisdom) 8³² (ψ 17⁴ v. **1 d**); *keep, discharge* an office, כְּהֻנָּה Nu 3¹⁰ 18⁷ (both P), abs. 2 Ch 5¹¹; a function or duty, esp. ש׳ מִשְׁמֶרֶת Lv 8³⁵ Nu 1⁵³ + c. 32 t. (v. 'מ infr); acc. of obligation oft. om., esp. D (and R^D) *keep and do* Dt 4⁶ 7¹² + 8 t.; *to do* 5¹·²⁹ + 16 t D + 3 t., etc. **d.** *observe* = follow dictates of (prudence, justice, kindness, wisdom) Ho 12⁷ (חֶסֶד וּמִשְׁפָּט), Is 56¹ Pr 4⁴ 5² 7¹·²; bad sense, *observe* vanities ψ 31⁷.—Doubtful are: לִשְׁמֹר abs. Ho 4¹⁰, very strange (conj. in We Now Marti); שָׁמוּר 1 S 9²⁴, HPS עֻזִּי אֵלֶיךָ אֲזַמֵּרָה, cf. Now Bu^Comm; ψ 59¹⁰ read אַחֲרָיו (as v¹⁸, 𝔖 Che Bae). **4.** sts. 'י subj.: **a.** *keep, preserve, protect*, acc. pers., + בְּ of way, etc., Gn 28¹⁵·²⁰ (J), Ex 23²⁰ (E; of מַלְאָךְ), ψ 91¹¹ (מ׳), Jos 24¹⁷ (E); acc. pers (or נפש) only · 1 S 30²³ Je 31⁹ Nu 6²⁴ (P), Jb 29² ψ 16¹ + 10 t. ψψ; + מִן ψ 121⁷ + 2 t.; acc. רַגְלֵי 1 S 2⁹, cf. Pr 3²⁶ (מִן); *Pt* שֹׁמְרֶךָ ψ 121³·⁵, cf. v⁴, etc; acc. of city 127¹. **b.** c. acc. בְּרִית, לְ pers. Dt 7¹², + חֶסֶד v⁷ + 5 t., הַשְּׁבֻעָה Dt 7⁸, etc; הַשֹּׁ׳ אֱמֶת לְעוֹלָם ψ 146⁶, pass. of covenant ('י agent) עֲרוּכָה בַכֹּל וּשְׁמֻרָה 2 S 23⁵ (legal terminology, Di) **5.** *keep, reserve*, weeks of harvest Je 5²⁴ (לְ pers.)

Niph. ₃₆ *Pf.* 3 ms. נִשְׁמַר 2 S 20¹⁰, etc.; *Impf.* 3 fs תִּשָּׁמֵר Ju 13¹³; 2 mpl תִּשָּׁמְרוּ Ex 23¹³; *Imv.* ms. הִשָּׁמֵר Is 7⁴ (לְךָ) הִשָּׁמֶר Gn 24⁶ +; fs. הִשָּׁמְרִי Ju 13⁴, etc.;—**1.** *be on one's guard*, c. בַּחֶרֶב 2 S 20¹⁰ *by reason of the sword*, i e. against it; c. בְּ temp. 1 S 19², שָׁם 2 K 6¹⁰; *take heed* Ex 23¹³ (E) Dt 2⁴; c. מִן pers. Ex 23²¹ (E), Je 9³; מִן rei Ju 13¹³ Dt 23¹⁰; מִן inf. *take care not to*, etc. Gn 31²⁹ (E), 2 K 6⁹; inf. without מִן Ex 19¹² (J), but rd prob. מֵעֲלוֹת; sq. פֶּן *lest* Gn 24⁶ (J) + 11 t. (esp Dt); c. (וְ)אַל juss. Ex 10²⁸ (J), Ju 13⁴ Jb 36²¹, c. Imv. coord. Is 7⁴.—Very oft Imv (24 t.), esp. in phr. הִשָּׁמֶר־לְךָ (12 t.), הִשָּׁמְרוּ לָכֶם (3 t); בְּנַפְ׳ + לְנַפְשֹׁתֵיכֶם + Dt 4¹⁵ Jos 23¹¹ (R^D; + inf); + Je 17²¹ appar. בְּ pret. *on peril of your life* (cf. בְּ **III. 3 a**), so perhaps also בְּרוּחֲכֶם Mal 2¹⁵·¹⁶ (We Now). †**2.** *keep oneself, refrain, abstain*, מֵאִשָּׁה 1 S 21⁵. †**3.** *be kept, guarded*, Ho 12¹⁴ (cf. 'ש of Jacob v¹³): be preserved (by 'י) ψ 37²⁸ עַוָּלִים (לְעוֹלָם) נִשְׁמָדוּ, but rd. prob. (לְעוֹלָם) Hup- Ri (Now) Che Bae Du Dr. †**Pi.** *Pt.* pl. מְשַׁמְּרִים הַבְלֵי־שָׁוְא Jon 2⁹ *those paying regard to false vanities* (cf. Qal ψ 31⁷). †**Hithp.** *Impf.* 1 s. וָאֶשְׁתַּמֵּר מֵעֲוֹנִי ψ 18²⁴ *I kept myself from*, etc. = 2 S 22²⁴ (vb. cohort.); 3 ms. וְיִשְׁתַּמֵּר חֻקּוֹת עָמְרִי Mi 6¹⁶, but read וַתִּשְׁמֹר *thou keepest, observest*, We Now GASm.

†**I. שֶׁמֶר n.pr.m.** (prop clan-name, cf. Sta^ZAW v (1885) 166f, cf. Sab שמר Os¹³, but NAram. شِمْر DHM ^ZMG xxxvii (1883). 14 Sab Denkm ³⁰);—Σεμ(μ)ηρ, etc.: **1.** 'שׁ orig. owner of hill where Sam. was built 1 K 16²⁴·²⁴ **2.** שָׁמֶר: **a.** Levite 1 Ch 6³¹. **b.** in Asher 7³⁴, A 𝔊L Σωμηρ; = שׁמר v³² **c.** in Benj. 8¹² van d. H.; > שֶׁמֶד q v.

†**שָׁמְרָה n.f.** guard, watch;—'שִׁיתָה י׳ שׁ׳ לְפִי ψ 141³ (‖ נִצְּרָה עַל־דַּל שְׂפָתָי).

†**שֹׁמֵר n.pr.m. 1.** father of one of Joash's murderers 2 K 12²², Σωμηρ, 𝔊L Σεμμηρ (called שִׁמְרִית q.v., a Moabitess, ‖ 2 Ch 24²⁶) **2.** Asherite 1 Ch 7³², Σαμηρ, Σωμηρ; = שָׁמֶר **2 b.**

†**שִׁמְרִי n.pr.m.** usu. Σαμαρει, etc.: **1.** in Simeon, 1 Ch 4³⁷. **2.** father of a hero of David 1 Ch 11⁴⁵. **3.** Levites · **a.** 1 Ch 26¹⁰. **b.** 2 Ch 29¹³, Ζαμβρει, Σαμβρι.

†**שִׁמְרָת n.pr.m.** in Benj. 1 Ch 8²¹, Σαμαραθ, -ρει.

†**שִׁמְרִית n.pr.f.** Moabitish mother of one of Joash's murderers 2 Ch 24²⁶ (**m.** Σομαιωθ, A Σαμαριθ; **f.** 𝔊L Σαμιραμωθ), ‖ שֹׁמֵר n.pr m. 2 K 12²².

†**[שְׁמֻרָה] n.f.** eye-lid (from its *guarding* the eye),—pl. cstr. שְׁמֻרוֹת עֵינָי ψ 77⁵

†**[שִׁמֻּר] n.[m.]** watching, vigil (so Di; > *observance*);—pl לֵיל שִׁמֻּרִים לַי׳ Ex 12⁴² *a night of vigils to* 'י, שׁ׳ לְכָל־בְּנֵי יִשׂ׳ v⁴².

†**שְׁמַרְיָה(וּ) n. pr. m.** ('י *has kept, preserved*);—Σαμαρ(ε)ια(ς): **1.** ־יָהוּ a hero of David 1 Ch 12⁶ (van d. H. v⁵). Elsewhere ־יָה: **2.** son of Rehoboam 2 Ch 11¹⁹. **3.** contemporaries of Ezra: **a.** Ezr 10³². **b.** v⁴¹.

שֹׁמְרוֹן ₁₀₉ **n.pr.loc.** capital of N. Isr. from Omri's time (*belonging to clan* שֶׁמֶר, Sta^ZAW v (1885), 165–170; originally שָׁמְרוֹן or שַׁמְרַיִן, As. *Samerina* COT^1 K 16, 24);—'שׁ 1 K 16²⁴ (name expl. as from שֶׁמֶר, orig. owner of site), v²⁸·²⁹·³² 20¹·¹⁰ +; שֹׁמְרוֹנָה 1 K 20⁴³ 2 K 6¹⁹ 14¹⁴; personified as woman Ez 16⁴⁶·⁵¹·⁵³·⁵⁵ 23⁴·³³; king of N. Israel is מֶלֶךְ שׁ׳

1 K 21[1] 2 K 1[3]; מ׳ יִשׁ׳ אֲשֶׁר בְּשֹׁ׳ 1 K 21[18], cf. מֶלֶךְ עַל־יִשׁ׳ בְּשֹׁ׳ 22[52] + 9 t.; thence name of territory, שְׂדֵה שֹׁ׳ Ob[19], עָרֵי שֹׁ׳ 1 K 13[32] (point of view of later editor), 2 K 17[24.26] 23[19]; הָרֵי שֹׁ׳ Am 3[9] Je 31[5],—cf. הַר־שֹׁ׳ Am 4[1] 6[1] 1 K 16[24]; perh. שֹׁ׳ alone Je 23[13] 1 K 18[2] 2 K 7[24.28] 2 Ch 25[13]; חֵיל שֹׁ׳ Ne 3[34].—𝔊 usu. Σαμαρεια, but 1 K 16[24] Σεμερω, Σαεμερων, Σομορων; = mod. *Sebastieh*; vid. GASm[G 346 ff.] Buhl[G 207 f.] Cowley[Ency. Bib. s. v.] Wilson[Hast. DB s. v.].

†[שֹׁמְרֹנִי] **adj. gent.** Samaritan, only as n.pl. הַשֹּׁמְרֹנִים 2 K 17[29] *the Samaritans*.

†I. שִׁמְרוֹן **n.pr.loc.** Canaanite city, with king: Jos 11[1], in Zebulun 19[15], Συμοων, Σομερων, etc., = שׁ׳ מְראוֹן 12[20].

†II. שִׁמְרוֹן **n.pr.m.** son of Issachar, Gn 46[13] Nu 24[64] 1 Ch 7[1]; Ζαμβραμ, Σαμβρα, Σεμερων, etc.

†שִׁמְרֹנִי **adj. gent.** of foregoing; c. art. as n.coll. הַשִּׁ׳ Nu 26[24].

†אַשְׁמֹרֶת, אַשְׁמוּרָה† **n.f.** watch (division of time);—abs. אַשְׁמוּרָה בַלָּיְלָה ψ 90[4]; ראשׁ הָאַשְׁמֹרֶת הַתִּיכוֹנָה Ju 7[19]; cstr. אַשְׁמֹרֶת הַבֹּקֶר Ex 14[24] (J), 1 S 11[11]; pl.abs. אַשְׁמֻרוֹת La 2[19] ψ 63[7] 119[148].

†יִשְׁמְרַי **n.pr.m.** in Benj., 1 Ch 8[18], Σαμαρει; A Ιεσαμαρι, 𝔊L Ιασσημαρι.

†מִשְׁמָר **n.[m.]** place of confinement, gaol, prison; late, guard, watch, observance;—abs. מ׳ Gn 42[17] +; cstr. מִשְׁמַר 40[3] +; sf. מִשְׁמָרוֹ Ne 7[3], etc.; pl. sf. ־רָיו 13[14];—**1.** *gaol, prison*, מ׳ בֵּית שַׂר הַטַּבָּחִים Gn 40[3], cf. v[4] (abs.), v[7] 41[10]; 42[17] (abs.), + v[30] (𝔊), בֵּית מִשְׁמַרְכֶם v[19] (all E); *guard-house* in camp Lv 24[12] (H), Nu 15[34] (P). **2.** *guard*, Je 51[12] Ne 4[3.16], אַנְשֵׁי הַמּ׳ v[17]; *guard-post* 7[3]; fig. of י׳ setting a *guard*, כִּי תָשִׂים עָלַי מ׳ Jb 7[12]; *band of* (Levit.) *guards* or functionaries 1 Ch 26[16] Ne 12[24] (cf. מִשְׁמֶרֶת); *act of guarding*, מִכָּל־מ׳ Pr 4[23] *above all guarding* watch thy heart.—לְמ׳ Ez 38[7] is doubtful, Hi Co Toy al. *reserve*; Krae לְמֹשֵׁל. **3.** pl. *observances*, services, of temple Ne 13[14].

מִשְׁמֶרֶת[78] **n.f.** guard, watch, also charge, function;—מ׳ abs. 2 S 20[3] +, cstr. 2 K 11[5] +; abs. מִשְׁמָרֶת Ex 16[34]; sf. מִשְׁמַרְתִּי Gn 26[5] +, etc.; pl. מִשְׁמָרוֹת 1 Ch 9[23] +; cstr. מִשְׁמְרוֹת Ne 7[3]; sf. ־רוֹתָם 2 Ch 7[6] +, ־תֵיהֶם 2 Ch 31[17];—†**1.** *guard, watch*: בֵּית מ׳ 2 S 20[3] = *house of detention, confinement*; מ׳ אַתָּה עִמָּדִי 1 S 22[23] i.e. protected, secure; c. שָׁמַר *keep the watch* 2 K 11[5.6.7] 1 Ch 12[30] (van d. H. v[29]); = *post of watch* (fig.) Is 21[8] (|| מִצְפֶּה), Hb 2[1] (|| מָצוֹר); pl. = *guards* Ne 7[3] 1 Ch 9[23]. †**2.** *keeping, preserving*, וְהָיָה לָכֶם לְמ׳ Ex 12[6] i.e. ye shall keep it; הַנִּיחוּ לָכֶם לְמ׳ 16[23], cf. v[32.33.34] Nu 19[9] (all P). †**3.** *charge, injunction* of י׳, c. שָׁמַר, in gen. Dt 11[1] (+ חֻקּוֹת, מִצְוֹת, מִשְׁפָּטִים), cf. Gn 26[5] 1 K 2[3], and (מ׳ מִצְוַת י׳) Jos 22[3] (all R[D]), Mal 3[14]; of specif. injunctions Lv 18[30] Nu 9[19.23]. †**4. a.** ceremonial *office* or *function* (AV RV usu. *charge*) of priest or Levite (P [esp. Nu], Ez 40, 44, 48, Chr Zc), mostly c. שָׁמַר: מ׳ מִשְׁכַּן הָעֵדוּת Nu 1[53], מ׳ מִשְׁכַּן י׳ 31[30.47], מ׳ אֹהֶל מוֹעֵד Ez 44[15] Nu 3[38], מ׳ הַמִּקְדָּשׁ 18[4] cf. v[3], 1 Ch 23[32], מ׳ הַקֹּדֶשׁ Nu 3[28.32] 18[5] 1 Ch 23[32], מ׳ קָדָשַׁי (of Isr. in gen.) Ez 44[8], מ׳ הַמִּזְבֵּחַ Nu 18[5] Ez 40[46], תְּרוּמֹתָי Nu 18[8], מ׳ הַבַּיִת Ez 40[45] 44[14], מ׳ הַטָּהֳרָה Ne 12[45]; c. genit. (sf.) שׁ׳ מ׳ = *perform the service imposed by, due to*, Lv 8[35] 22[9] Ez 44[8.16] 48[11] Zc 3[7], מ׳ אֱלֹהֵיהֶם Ne 12[45] (of Judah in gen.); מ׳ הָעֵדָה Nu 3[7], מ׳ בְּנֵי יִשׂ׳ 3[8.38], מ׳ בְּנֵי גֵרְשׁוֹן 3[25], cf. v[7 a.31.36] 4[27.28.31.32] 18[3] 1 Ch 23[32]; also, in secular sense, מ׳ בֵּית שָׁאוּל 1 Ch 12[30]; מ׳ מַשָּׂאָם Nu 4[31], כְּלֵי מ׳ מַשָּׂאָם v[32] (v[27] read c. 𝔊 Di Gr Gray, etc. בְּשֵׁמוֹת for במ׳, and perhaps מִשְׁמֶרֶת after אֵת, cf. v[32]); עֲלֵיהֶם מ׳ 1 Ch 9[27] i.e. the duty rested upon them;—25[8] 26[12] v. I. עִמָּה c, d (p. 769 supr.); עַל־מ׳ עֹמְדִים 2 Ch 7[6] were standing *according to* (or *in*) *their offices*, הֶעֱמִיד עַל מ׳ appoint *to their offices* 8[14] 35[2]. **b.** pl. of Levitical *divisions* for service Ne 12[9].

II. שמר (√ of foll.; cf. NH שְׁמָרִים = BH, also vb. denom.; 𝔗 שְׁמְרָא; meaning of √ and relation (if any) to I. שׁ׳ obscure; cf. poss. Ar. شَمِرَ *be tawny, dark*, in colour, Lane[1425 a]).

†II. [שֶׁמֶר] **n.m.** [Is 25, 6] only **pl.** lees, dregs (fig.);—abs. שְׁמָרִים Is 25[6.6] (in both = *wine* matured by resting undisturbed *on the lees*); sf. שֹׁקֵט הוּא אֶל־שְׁמָרָיו Je 48[11] (of Moab's undisturbed life), cf. (of careless men) הַקֹּפְאִים עַל־שִׁמְרֵיהֶם Zp 1[12]; שְׁמָרֶיהָ ψ 75[9] (of י׳'s cup of judgment).

III. שמר (√ of foll.; mng. dub.; NH שָׁמִיר *diamond*, so Aram. שְׁמִירָא (also *flint*), ܫܡܝܪܐ; Ar. سَمُرٌ = *mimosa gummifera*, Lane[1425 b]).

שמור v. III. שָׁמִיר.

†I. שָׁמִיר **n.m.** [Ez 3, 9] thorn(s), adamant, flint;—abs. שׁ׳ Is 5[6] +; sf. שְׁמִירוֹ 10[17];—**1.** coll.

thorns, thorn-bushes, token of waste-land, only Is, + שַׁיִת Is 5^{6} 7$^{23.24.25}$ 27^{4}; fig. 9^{17} 10^{17}; קוֹץ שׁ׳ 32^{13}. **2.** *adamant,* as sharp, כְּתוּבָה . . . בְּצִפֹּרֶן שׁ׳ Je 17^{1} (|| בְּעֵט בַּרְזֶל); as hard, fig. of prophet's firmness Ez 3^{9}; Zc 7^{12} fig. of hard heart.

†II. שָׁמִיר **n.pr.loc. 1.** in הַר אֶפְרָיִם Ju 10$^{1.2}$, Σαμειρ; A 𝔊L Σαμαρεια. **2.** in הַר (יְהוּדָה) Jos 15^{48}, Σαμειρ; A 𝔊L Σαφειρ.

†III. שָׁמִיר **n.pr.m.** Levite, 1 Ch 24^{24} Qr, Σαμηρ, Σεμμηρ (Kt שׁמוּר).

שׁמשׁ (√of foll.; mng. unknown; NH = BH; Ph. שמש, As. *šamšu;* Aram. שִׁמְשָׁא, ܫܡܫܐ, OAram., Palm. שמש Lzb[379]; Ar. شَمْسٌ, Sab. שמסם *goddess,* SabDenkm[20 56 ff] DHM[B.u.S 1032] Wkl[ZMG liv (1900) 408 ff] RS[K 299] No[ZMG xli (1887), 712]).

שֶׁמֶשׁ 133 **n.f.** [Ju 19,14] **et m.** [Gn 19,23] (Albr[ZAW xv (1895), 324]) **sun**,—abs. שׁ׳ Jos 10^{12} +, שָׁמֶשׁ Ju 20^{43} +; sf. שִׁמְשֵׁךְ Is 60^{20}, שִׁמְשָׁהּ Je 15^{9}; pl. sf. שִׁמְשֹׁתַיִךְ Is 54^{12};—**1.** *sun,* Gn 37^{9} (E; + moon, stars); marking time: as rising (vb. זָרַח q.v.) Ex 22^{2} (E) + 8 t + Mal 3^{20} (fig. שׁ׳ צְדָקָה, of reward of the faithful, with wings, i.e rays? NowGASm; or winged sun-disc [cf. We]?); vb יָצָא Gn 19^{23} (J), Is 13^{10} Ju 5^{31} (sim. of splendour; v. יָצָא **1 f**); setting (vb. בּוֹא) Gn 15^{17} (J), Am 8^{9} + 19 t., + וַיְהִי הַשּׁ׳ לָבוֹא Gn 15^{12} (JE), שׁ׳ יָדַע מְבוֹאוֹ ψ 104^{19} (v. בּוֹא **1 i**, מָבוֹא **2**); as giving daylight Is 60^{19}; hot 1 S 11^{9} Ne 7^{3} Ex 16^{21} (P), cf Is 49^{10} Jon 4^{8} ψ 121^{6}, as ripening crops Dt 33^{14} (poem), cf (fig) Jb 8^{16}, tanning the face Ct 1^{6}; standing still at Joshua's word Jos 10$^{12.13a}$ (poem in J; || יָרֵחַ), v^{13b} (J), cf. Hb 3^{11} (+ יָרֵחַ); casting shadow (on dial), יָרְדָה בְּמַעֲלוֹת אָחָז בַּשּׁ׳ Is 38^{8}, וַתָּשָׁב הַשּׁ׳ v^{8}, set in sky by י׳ Je 31^{35} ψ 19^{5} 74^{16} 136^{8}, enduring 72$^{5.17}$ (cf. עִם **1 g**, p. 768; [פָּנֶה] **II. 4 a** (*e*), p. 817), also 89^{37}; personif., called to praise י׳ 148^{3} (+ יָרֵחַ); to be darkened by י׳'s judgment, Ez 32^{7} Jo 2^{10} 3^{4} 4^{15} (cf. Am 8^{9} supr., Mi 3^{6}). **2.** of direction: מִמִּזְרַח הַשּׁ׳ Nu 21^{11} (E) *toward sun-rise,* = *East,* cf. Dt 4$^{41.47}$ + 16 t. (v. מִזְרָח p. 280); מְבוֹא הַשּׁ׳ Dt 11^{30} + 3 t. (v. מָבוֹא **2**, p. 99) **3.** obj of worship (usu. + moon, stars, etc) 2 K 23^{5} Je 8^{2} Ez 8^{16} Dt 4^{19}; horses given to שׁ׳ 2 K 23^{11}, מַרְכְּבוֹת הַשּׁ׳ v^{11}.—Vid. also בֵּית שׁ׳ p. 112^{b}. **4.** other phr: †**a.** נֶגֶד הַשּׁ׳, i e. *openly, publicly,* 2 S 12^{12} Nu 25^{4} (P), so לְעֵינֵי הַשּׁ׳ 2 S 12^{11}. †**b.** fig of living, חָזָה שׁ׳ ψ 58^{9}, רָאָה שׁ׳ Ec 6^{5} 7^{11} 11^{7}, opp. תֶּחְשַׁךְ הַשּׁ׳ 12^{2}. **c.** תַּחַת הַשּׁ׳, i e. on the earth, Ec 1^{3} + 28 t. Ec (cf. Gk. ὑφ' ἡλίῳ, Kue[Od. iii. 196; Ezid. iii. 197]). **5.** *pinnacle,* as *glittering, shining,* pl. Is 54^{12} *thy pinnacles, battlements* (of Zion), so perhaps sg. ψ 84^{12} שׁ׳ וּמָגֵן י׳ אֱלֹהִים *battlement and shield is* י׳ א׳ (Gr Bae Du Buhl; most *sun,* and so Thes De Che SS; Hup-Now hesitates).

שִׁמְשׁוֹן 38 **n. pr. m.** Samson (As n.pr. *Šamšânu,* Hilpr[Murashu 27 70]; on שמש in Ar. n pr. trib. cf. No[ZMG xl (1886), 166]),—Σαμψων: Ju 13^{24} 14$^{1.3}$ + 35 t. Ju 14, 15, 16

†שַׁמְשְׁרַי **n.pr.m.** in Benj. 1 Ch 8^{26}, Ισμασαρια, A Σαμσαρια, 𝔊L Σαμψαια.

שְׁמָתִי v [שָׁמָה]

שַׁן, שֵׁן v. בֵּית שְׁאָן. שֵׁן v. שׁנן.

שְׁנָא v. I [שָׁנָה]. שֵׁנָא v. ישׁן √ שׁנה.

†שִׁנְאָב **n.pr.m.** king of Admah Gn 14^{2}, Σενναααρ (v. שִׁנְעָר v^{1}, 𝔊 *id.*).

שִׁנְאָן v. sub II. שׁנה.

†שֶׁנְאַצַּר **n.pr.m.** uncle of Zerub. 1 Ch 3^{18}, Σανεσαρ, 𝔊L Σανασαρ (EMey[Entstehung 77] cp. שֵׁשְׁבַּצַּר, but v. Now[Hx 1, 1]).

שׁנב (√of following; meaning dub).

†אֶשְׁנָב **n.[m.] window-lattice** (אשנב Ecclus 42^{11});—abs. א׳ Ju 5^{28}; sf. אֶשְׁנַבִּי Pr 7^{6} (both || חַלּוֹן).

†I. [שָׁנָה] **vb. change** (NH Pi, etc.; Ecclus 42^{24}, etc.; As *šanû, change,* Aram. שְׁנָא, Nab. Ethpa. Lzb[379]; Syr. ܫܢܐ, esp. mentally = *grow insane;* cf. (prob) NH שָׁנָה *year,* = Ph שנת, שת; MI[2.8] שת, As. *šattu* (cf. Muss-Arnolt JBL xi (1892), 73 n.); Ar. سَنَةٌ; Aram. שַׁתָּא, שְׁנָא, ܫܢܐ, ܫܢܬܐ; OAram, Nab., Palm. שנן, שת, שנת, שנתא Lzb[379 f]; on *year* from *changing* seasons, v. Philippi[ZMG xxxii (1878), 79 f.] Ba[ZMG xli (1887), 612, 621, 636] (esp. against DHM[VIme Orient. Congr ii. 1, 452] who proposes bilit √), cf. Thes; a daring suggestion by Jen ZA vii (1892), 177);—**Qal** *Pf* 1 s לֹא שָׁנִיתִי Mal 3^{6} I am י׳, *I do not change; Impf* 3 ms. יִשְׁנֶא (Ges[§ 77 rr]) La 4^{1} how *is* the fine gold *changed* (si vera l; Lohr[Now] יִשָּׂנֵא; gloss on יעם Bu Lohr); *Inf. cstr.* שְׁנוֹת יְמִין עֶלְיוֹן ψ 77^{11} *the right hand of the Highest is changed* (𝔖 𝔙 𝔗 Aq Sym Theod Hup-Now RVm Bae Du We Buhl; AV RV Ew De Che al. *years,* usu ins. *I will remember*); *Pt.* שׁוֹנִים Est 1^{7} *differing, different,* c. מִן, cf. 3^{8} (so Ecclus 42^{24});

Pr 24[21] *those who change* (but dub., v. Toy). **Pi.** transit., *change, alter*. *Pf.* 3 ms. שִׁנָּה Je 52[33] c acc garments, =שִׁנָּא (Ges[§ c]) 2 K 25[29], *Impf* 3 ms. יְשַׁנֶּה דִין Pr 31[5] *lest he pervert the judgment;* וַיְשַׁנּוֹ 1 S 21[14] (read וַיְשַׁן Ges[§ 75 bb], וַיְשַׁנֶּה We Dr (and reff), cf Bu HPS Now), c. acc טַעְמוֹ (v. טַעַם, and As *šanê têmi, madness*); וַיְשַׁנֶּהָ Est 2[9], i e *changed her* place לְטוֹב בֵּית הַנָּשִׁים; 1 s. ψ 89[35] the utterance of my lips *I will not change* (לֹא אֲחַלֵּל בְּרִיתִי ‖); *Inf. cstr* לְשַׁנּוֹת אֶת־דַּרְכֵּךְ Je 2[36] i e change thy political course; בְּשַׁנּוֹתוֹ אֶת־טַעְמוֹ ψ 34[1] (title, cf 1 S 21[14] supr), *Pt* מְשַׁנֶּה פָנָיו Jb 14[20] *altering his face,* i e. in death (subj. God) **Pu.** *Impf.* 3 ms וְעֹז פָּנָיו יְשֻׁנֶּא (Ges[§ 75 rr]) Ec 8[1], usu *is changed*, mollified, Siegf יְשֻׂנָּא *is hated* (on עֹז פ׳ v. עֹז **4**, √ עזז) **Hithp.** *Pf* 2 fs consec. קוּמִי נָא וְהִשְׁתַּנִּית 1 K 14[2] *arise, pray, and disguise thyself*

שָׁנָה [877] **n.f.** (on appar exc v Albr[ZAW xvi (1896), 46]) **year** (etym v √),—abs. ש׳ Am 2[10]+; cstr שְׁנַת Gn 41[50]+; sf שְׁנָתוֹ Ez 46[13]+, שְׁנָתָהּ Lv 14[10] +2 t, du. שְׁנָתַיִם Am 1[1]+, -תָיִם 1 K 15[25]+; pl. שָׁנִים Ex 21[2]+, cstr. שְׁנֵי Gn 23[1]+24 t, שְׁנוֹת Dt 32[7]+8 t (poet and late); sf שָׁנָיו Lv 25[52]+ 4 t sf; שְׁנוֹתַי Is 38[15] ψ 31[11], שְׁנוֹתָם 78[33]+8 t sf,—*year*, as division of time, Ex 23[14 17] 3 t. רֵשִׁית הַשּׁ׳ Dt 11[12], opp אַחֲרִית הַשּׁ׳, +בַּשָּׁנָה, etc.; צֵאת הַשּׁ׳ v[12], תְּקוּפַת הַשּׁ׳ Ex 23[16], 34[22] 2 Ch 24[23], תְּשׁוּבַת הַשּׁ׳ 2 S 11[1]+, etc.; בָּא שָׁנָה 2 K 13[20], rd כְּבֹא ש׳ 𝔊 Bur, בארץ ש׳ בש׳ Kit, cf ש׳ בש׳= *year by year* 1 S 1[7]+, בְּשָׁנָה Benz, cf. Ne 10[31], so ש׳ ש׳ Dt 14[22], ש׳ אַחֲרֵי ש׳ 2 S 21[1], בְּכָל־ש׳ וש׳ Est 9[21 27], esp of duration of life, (יְמֵי) שְׁנֵי חַיֵּי פ׳ Gn 23[1] 25[7]+(P), שְׁנֵיהֶם Jb 36[11]+, שְׁנוֹתַי ψ 31[11] (חַיַּי ‖), etc, of God Jb 10[5] ψ 102[25 28], in phr of age, v בֵּן **9**, בַּת **9**; indef. שָׁנִים Ez 38[17]=*for years,* לְקֵץ ש׳ Dn 11[6], זֶה־יָמִים אוֹ זֶה שָׁנִים 1 S 29[3], specif. בִּשְׁנַת מוֹת הַמֶּלֶךְ Is 6[1] 14[28], בִּשְׁנַת בֹּא תַרְתָּן 20[1], שְׁנַת הַשְּׁמִטָּה Dt 15[9] 31[10], שְׁנַת הַיּוֹבֵל Lv 25[13]+, etc; שְׁנֵי שָׂכִיר Is 16[14] 21[16] (v שָׂכִיר); ש׳ רָצוֹן לי׳ Is 61[2], שְׁנַת פְּקֻדָּתָם Je 11[23]+2 t., etc; שְׁנוֹת דֹּר־וָדֹר Dt 32[7], cf. Jo 2[2]; most oft. c. num. card.: pl after units, appos, Ex 21[2]+, so also שְׁתַּיִם שָׁנִים 2 S 2[10]+, but du שְׁנָתַיִם Am 1[1] +4 t., שְׁנָתַיִם יָמִים Gn 41[1]+4 t.; very rarely c num (certainly) cstr שְׁתֵּי שָׁנִים 1 S 13[1] (corrupt), שָׁלֹשׁ ש׳ Lv 25[21], 8+שָׁנָה+2 K 22[1], before unit (rare, late) 2 Ch 11[17 17] Dn 1[5]; sg. after 11–19, tens, and hundreds Gn 5[3.9] 14[4]+oft; so 90+9 *years* 17[24]+, rarely 30+3 *years* 1 K 2[11], etc, but אֶלֶף שָׁנִים ψ 90[4] 1000 *years*, so (+פַּעֲמַיִם) Ec 6[6] 1000 *years twice over;* with cp. num. oft. repeated, 900 *year*+30 *year* Gn 5[5], etc.; 100 *year*+70 *year*+5 *years* 25[7], etc.; c. num. card.=ord, בִּשְׁנַת אַרְבַּע לְ 1 K 22[41] *in the fourth year of*, etc., also בִּשְׁנַת חֲמִשִּׁים שָׁנָה לְ 2 K 15[23], etc; but בְּאַרְבַּע עֶשְׂרֵה ש׳ לְ 2 K 18[13], etc. (oft.), and בִּשְׁנָה הָאַחַת עֶשְׂרֵה 1 K 6[38], etc; also (c units), בַּשָּׁנָה הָרְבִיעִת Lv 19[24]+, etc, +לְ 2 K 17[6] *the ninth year of*, etc, and even (Ges[§ 134 p]) בִּשְׁנַת הַתְּשִׁיעִית לְ 2 K 25[1], cf Ezr 7[8] Je 46[2] 51[59]+(Kt) 28[1] 32[1] (Qr בַּשָּׁנָה)

II. שׁנה (√ of foll, meaning dub; Thes cp Ar. سَنَا *shine*, Eth ሰነየ:=ሠናይ: *be beautiful,* Dl[Pr 72], cf. Philippi[ZAW xxxii (1878), 79], but As *šinîtu* is *dyed cloth*)

שָׁנִי [42] **n.[m.]** scarlet (prop. *coccus ilicis*, which attaches itself to leaves and twigs of *quercus coccifera;* the dried body of female yields colouring matter, cf. Tristr[NHB 319] Post[Hast. DB Scarlet] M'Lean[Ency Bib. id]);—usu תִּקְוַת ש׳ חוּט הַשּׁ׳ הַזֶּה Jos 2[18] *this cord of thread of scarlet*, חוּט הַשּׁ׳ v[21], ת׳ הַשּׁ׳ Ct 4[3] (sim. of lips), so (הַ)שּׁ׳ alone Gn 38[28.30] (J), and as material of clothing 2 S 1[24] Je 4[30] Pr 31[21] (pl שָׁנִים, on order of ll. v. Toy); pl also in sim Is 1[18] if your sins are like *scarlet* (robes), elsewh. (P) תּוֹלַעַת (הַ)שּׁ׳ (v. ת׳) of material for curtain, veil, ephod, etc, Ex 25[4] 26[1] +24 t. Ex; בֶּגֶד ת׳ ש׳ Nu 4[8] (v II. ב׳ **2**); cstr. שְׁנִי (הַ)ת׳ used in purif, †Lv 14[4.6 19.51 52] Nu 19[6]

†III שָׁנָה vb. repeat, do again (NH *id.;* Ecclus 42[1]; Ar ثَنَى *bend, fold, double;* Aram. תְּנָא *repeat*, also *teach*, ܬܢܐ, As. *šanû*, esp. Pi. *repeat, relate*, cf. Scheil[ZA v (1890), 409] (Dl thinks denom); on ש׳ as √ of שְׁנַיִם *two*, v. Philippi[ZMG xxxii (1878), 77] Ba[ib. xli (1887), 603]),—**Qal** *Pf.* 3 ms. ש׳ 2 S 20[10]; *Impf* 1 s. אֶשְׁנֶה 1 S 26[8], etc.; *Imv.* mpl שְׁנוּ 1 K 18[34], *Pt.* שׁוֹנֶה Pr 17[9] 26[11],—*do again:* וַיַּכֵּהוּ... וְלֹא שָׁ׳ לוֹ 2 S 20[10], cf 1 S 26[8]; abs 1 K 18[34.34] Ne 13[21]; =*speak again* Jb 29[22] +40[5] acc to many moderns (אשנה for MT אענה), שׁ׳ בְּדָבָר Pr 17[9] *repeat with a thing*, keep talking about it (שנות דבר Ecclus 42[1]); 26[11] a dullard *repeats with* (ב) his folly, does it over again (learns nothing by experience) **Niph.** *Inf cstr.* וְעַל הִשָּׁנוֹת הַחֲלוֹם אֶל־פַּרְעֹה פַּעֲמָיִם Gn 41[32] (E) *concerning the dream's being repeated*, etc.

שְׁנַיִם, שְׁתַּיִם (Philippi[ZMG xlix (1895), 202] Ges[§ 97 b note]) [768] **n.m. et f. du. two** (NH *id.;* Ph. אשנם (and שני *second*), Pun שנם Lzb[380]; Ar.

اِثْنَانِ; Sab. תני Hom[Chr 47], Aram. תְּרֵין, ܬܪܝܢ, (תִּנְיָנָא, ܬܢܝܢܐ second); Nab. תרין, Palm. f. תרתן, תרתיא, Lzb[388]; As. *šinâ*; on etym. v. √, and esp. Philippi[ZMG xxxii (1878), 21-98]); — **m.** (c. **n.m.**) שְׁנַיִם Am 3[3]+; cstr. שְׁנֵי Is 7[16]+, sf. שְׁנֵיהֶם Gn 2[25]+, etc.; **f.** (c. **n.f.**) שְׁתַּיִם Am 4[8]+; cstr. שְׁתֵּי Gn 4[19], וּשְׁתֵּי Is 7[21]+, etc., מִשְּׁתֵּי Ju 16[28] (v. GFM); sfs. v. infr. (2 + 10 = 12, v. infr.); Hex chiefly P:—*two:* **1.** no other num.: **a.** usu. cstr. before n.pl. (שְׁנֵי (צְמִידִים Gn 24[22] + 194 t. + 2 S 23[20] ‖ 1 Ch 11[22] (ins. בְּנֵי 𝔊 Th mod., otherwise RS Sem. i. 469, 2nd ed., 488); (שְׁתֵּי (נָשִׁים Gn 4[19] + 132 t., 1 S 10[4] ins. כִּכְּרוֹת Klo HPS Bu Now; Lv 16[21] read du. יָדָיו Qr, + Ju 16[28] (v. supr.) + שְׁתֵּי־אֵלֶּה Is 47[9] *both these things;* before n.sg., שְׁנֵי Ex 16[22] (Ges[§ 134 e]); sf. שְׁנֵיהֶם *the two of them* Gn 2[25] + 62 t., + Pr 24[22] (> *their years* 𝔊 𝔗 De al.; prob. crpt., v. Toy), שְׁנֵינוּ Gn 31[37] + 2 t., שְׁנֵיכֶם †Gn 27[45]; שְׁתֵּיהֶם (msf.! Ges[§ 135 o]) †Ru 1[19] 4[11], שְׁתֵּיהֶן †1 S 25[43] Ez 23[13]. **b.** abs. (1) שְׁנַיִם (90 t.), before n.pl. Ju 11[37] + 26 t.; after n.pl. 2 S 1[1] Ex 29[1] + 21 t. (usu. P Chr), n.sg. (coll.) Gn 46[27] Nu 7[17] + 11 t. Nu 17; n. om. Gn 7[2] 44[27] + 26 t.; שׁ׳ שׁ׳ distrib. Gn 7[9]+; לִשׁ׳ cut *in two* †2 K 3[25] Je 34[18]; = *double amount* †Ex 22[3.6.8] (E); פִּי שׁ׳ †Dt 21[17] *double portion,* + בְּרוּחֲךָ †2 K 2[9] *in* (of) *thy spirit,* + בָּהּ †Zc 3[18]; (2) שְׁתַּיִם (55 t.), bef. n.pl. 1 K 3[16] + 16 t.; after n.pl. (usu. P and late) 2 Ch 24[3] + 9 t.; n. om., = *two things* †Is 51[19] Jb 13[20] Pr 30[7]; שְׁתַּיִם = *twice* †2 K 6[10] Jb 40[5] ψ 62[12] (or as Pr 30[7]), בִּשׁ׳ Jb 33[14] either so, or *in two ways* RVm (v. De); as ordin. בִּשְׁנַת שְׁתַּיִם לְ 1 K 15[25] + 9 t., etc.; (3) as round number, שְׁנַיִם עֵצִים 1 K 17[12] *a few sticks* (Germ. 'ein paar'), cf. 2 K 9[32] Is 17[6]; שְׁתַּיִם שָׁלֹשׁ Am 4[8], פַּעַם וּשְׁתַּיִם Ne 13[20], cf. Je 3[14] אֶחָד מֵעִיר וּשְׁנַיִם מִמִּשְׁפָּחָה = a small no.; Ezr 10[13] *not for one or two days* (but for many), 2 K 6[10]. **2.** *twelve:* c. **n.m.** שְׁנֵים עָשָׂר Gn 42[13] + 87 t., לִשְׁנֵי עָשָׂר Ex 28[21] + 4 t.; c. **n.f.** שְׁתֵּים עֶשְׂרֵה, שְׁתֵּי עֶשְׂרֵה Ex 24[4] + 34 t., †Ez 32[1.17] 33[21]; before n.pl. Gn 17[20] Ex 15[27]+; after n.pl. Nu 7[84.84]+; before n.sg. Ex 28[21]+, Gn 14[4] (12 *year*)+, etc.; as ord., בְּיוֹם שְׁנֵים עָשָׂר יוֹם Nu 7[78], בִּשְׁתֵּי עֶשְׂרֵה שָׁנָה Ez 32[1]+, etc. **3.** with larger num.: 10 (etc.) + 2, 2 S 8[5] Ju 10[3] + 56 t.; 2 + 10 (etc.) Nu 1[35] (P), 2 Ch 22[2] + 18 t. (Kö[ii. 1. 215 ff.] Ges[§ 97 f.]); 200 + 2 + 30, 1 K 20[15]; 50 + 2 as ord. 2 K 15[27] + 2 t.; cf. 2 + 20, 1 Ch 24[17].

שֵׁנִי **m.** שֵׁנִית **f.**,[157] **adj. num. ord. second;**—בַּיּוֹם הַשֵּׁנִי Ex 2[13]+, etc. (שֵׁנִי 82 t. + Ne 3[30], read שֵׁנִית; read וְהַשֵּׁנִי also 1 Ch 6[13] for (ושני); בַּשָּׁנָה הַשֵּׁנִית Gn 47[18]+, etc. (שֵׁנִית 72 t. + Ne 3[30] v. supr.), שִׁבְעַת יָמִים שׁ׳ Lv 13[5.33.54] *a second heptad of days;* שֵׁנִית = *a second time* Gn 22[15] + 16 t. + (= *again,* of similar—not identical—act, or another point in a series) Ez 4[6] Mal 2[13], וְהַשֵּׁנִית 2 S 16[19]; †mpl. שְׁנִיִּם Nu 2[16] they shall set out *as second,* but Gn 6[16] *second stories* (in ark).

†מִשְׁנֶה **n.[m.]** **double, copy, second;**—abs. מ׳ Gn 41[43]+; cstr. מִשְׁנֵה Je 16[18] + 3 t., so read also Dt 15[18] (van d. H., > ־נֶה Gi), Je 17[18] (Gie Buhl al.); sf. מִשְׁנֵהוּ 1 S 8[2]+; pl. מִשְׁנִים 1 Ch 15[18] (1 S 15[9] Ezr 1[10] v. infr.);—**1.** (the) *double:* כֶּסֶף מ׳ Gn 43[12] (J) *money of double amount,* cf. מ׳ כֶּסֶף v[15] (J), *a double amount* (in) *money* (Ges[§ 131 q]); לֶחֶם מ׳ Ex 16[22] (P); מ׳ עַל אֲשֶׁר וגו׳ v[5] (P) *the double above what* they gathered daily; מִשְׁנֵה שְׂכַר שָׂכִיר Dt 15[18] (v. Dr); מ׳ עֲוֹנָם Je 16[18] *the double of their guilt,* 17[18] (v. supr.); *a double portion* Is 61[7.7] Zc 9[12], Jb 42[10]. **2.** written *copy* of law Dt 17[18] Jos 8[32] (D). **3.** *second* in order: **a.** *second rank,* מִרְכֶּבֶת הַמּ׳ Gn 41[43] (J), רֶכֶב הַמּ׳ 2 Ch 35[24]; of pers. *one second in rank,* priest next to high-priest, (הַ)מ׳ 2 K 23[4] 25[18] = Je 52[24]; אֶהְיֶה־לְּךָ לְמ׳ 1 S 23[17], מ׳ לַמֶּלֶךְ Est 10[3]; 2 Ch 28[7], מִשְׁנֵה הַמֶּלֶךְ 1 Ch 15[18] 16[5] 2 Ch 31[12]; מ׳ מֵאֶחָיו Ne 11[17].—1 S 15[9] read (cf. 𝔊 𝔗) הַמַּשְׁמַנִּים (Ne 8[10]) Th, הַשְּׁמֵנִים or הַשְּׁמֻנִים We Dr Bu, etc. (Ez 34[16]); מִשׁ׳ Ezr 1[10] is appar. corruption of a numeral. **b.** *second in age,* 1 S 8[2] 17[13] 2 S 3[3] 1 Ch 5[12]. **3.** *second quarter, district,* of city, הַמִּשְׁנֶה 2 K 22[14] = 2 Ch 34[22], Zp 1[10], cf. הָעִיר מִשְׁנֶה Ne 11[9] over *the city,* viz. the *second quarter.*

†שִׁנְאָן **n.[m.]** repetition (?);—אַלְפֵי שִׁנְאָן ψ 68[18] *thousands of repetition,* i.e. *thousands twice-told,* Che; *redoubled,* Dr, i.e. thousands on thousands (Du, reading אֶלֶף, as שִׁנְאָם c. sf. *removed them,* treating שנאן אדני מסיני בק׳ as gloss).

שֵׁנָה v. √ יָשֵׁן. שֶׁנְהַבִּים v. √ שנן.

†[שָׁנַן] **vb. whet, sharpen** (cf. Ar. سَنَّ *id.;* Aram. שְׁנִינָא, ܫܢܝܢܐ *sharp,* etc.; Eth. [ሰነነ] III, 2, ተሰነነ: *contend, litigate;* hence שֵׁן *tooth,* NH *id.,* As. *šinnu,* Ar. سِنّ, Eth. ስን: Aram. שִׁנָּא, ܫܢܐ);—**Qal** *whet, sharpen: Pf.* 1 s. אִם שַׁנּוֹתִי בְּרַק חַרְבִּי (Ges[§ 67 ee]) Dt 32[41], of י׳'s preparation for judgment; 3 pl. (כַחֶרֶב) שָׁנְנוּ לְשׁוֹנָם ψ 64[4] 140[4] of uttering sharp words; *Pt. pass.* שְׁנוּנִים *sharpened,* of arrows, Is 5[28] ψ 45[6], fig. of tongue 120[4], of false witness Pr 25[18].

Pi. *Pf.* consec. וְשִׁנַּנְתָּם לְבָנֶיךָ Dt 6^{7} i.e. teach the words *incisively*, Germ. 'einschärfen.' **Hithpo'.** *Impf* 1 s ψ 73^{21} in my kidneys אֶשְׁתּוֹנָן *I was pierced* (of poignant envy).

†I שֵׁן **n.f.**$^{1\,8\,2.13}$ (yet **m.** 1 S 14^{5} cf Dr) **tooth, ivory**,—שׁ׳ abs Ex 21^{24}+, cstr v^{27}+, שֶׁן־ Dt 32^{24}, sf שִׁנּוֹ Ex 21^{27}; du שִׁנַּיִם Pr 10^{26}, cstr שִׁנֵּי Je 31^{29}+, sf. שִׁנֵּיהֶם ψ 124^{6}, שִׁנֵּימוֹ 58^{7}, etc,—**1.** *tooth*: **a.** of man, Ex $21^{27.27.27}$ (E), Nu 11^{33} (J), Gn 49^{12} (poem in J), Am 4^{6} Ct 4^{2} 6^{6}, שׁ׳ רָעָה Pr 25^{19}, v II רעע **2**, of *lex talionis*, שׁ׳ תַּחַת שׁ׳ Ex 21^{24}(E), Lv 24^{20}(H), שֵׁן בְּשׁ׳ Dt 19^{21}; irritated by acid Pr 10^{26}, dulled by it (in proverb of inherited guilt) Je $31^{29.30}$ Ez 18^{2}, חָרַק שׁ׳ La 2^{16} Jb 16^{9} ψ 35^{16} 112^{10}, v חָרַק; אֶשָּׂא בְשָׂרִי בְשִׁנָּי Jb 13^{14} = *risk my life* (del עַל־מָה, dittogr.; ‖ נַפְשִׁי אָשִׂים בְּכַפִּי); בְּעוֹר שִׁנָּי 19^{20}, v. מלט **Hithp.** (other conj v Di Bi Bu Du) **b.** of beasts Dt 32^{24}, crocodile Jb 41^{6}, locusts Jo 1^{6} (teeth of lions); esp fig of false prophets Mi 3^{5}, of foes Zc 9^{7}, oppressors Jb 29^{17}, wicked 4^{10} ψ 3^{8} 58^{7} 124^{6}, of their weapons Pr 30^{14} ψ 57^{5}; of Isr. shattered by י׳ **c.** *tooth* of a fork, *tine*, 1 S 2^{13} (cf Dr$^{Sm\ 29}$), of cliff, הַשֵּׁן הַסֶּלַע $14^{4.4}$, cf Jb 39^{28}, הַשֵּׁן 1 S 14^{4}. **2.** *ivory*, of commerce, קַרְנוֹת שֵׁן Ez 27^{15} (i.e. *tusks*?), as material, מִטּוֹת שׁ׳ Am 6^{4}, כִּסֵּא־שׁ׳ 1 K 10^{18} = 2 Ch 9^{17}, בֵּית הַשׁ׳ 1 K 22^{39}, cf Am 3^{15}, הֵיכְלֵי שׁ׳ ψ 45^{9}, also Ez 27^{6} Ct 5^{14} 7^{5}.

II שֵׁן **n.pr.loc.** הַשׁ׳ 1 S 7^{12}, v. יְשָׁנָה p 446^{a}.

†שְׁנִינָה **n.f. sharp (cutting) word, taunt**,—Dt 28^{37} 1 K 9^{7} = 2 Ch 7^{20}, Je 24^{9} (cf ψ 64^{4} 140^{4}).

†שֶׁנְהַבִּים appar. **n.m. [pl.]**, in list of Solomon's imports, 1 K 10^{22} = 2 Ch 9^{21}, AV RV **ivory** (elsewh. שֵׁן alone), hence הַבִּים = *elephants* acc to Ges (in Thes) Ew Hi Schr$^{ZMG\ xxvii\ (1873),\ 709}$ COT$^{1\ K}$, cf 𝔊 (2 Ch, and A in 1 K) ὀδόντων ἐλεφαντίνων, 𝔙 (in 1 K) *dentes elephantorum*, 𝔗; but this very dub, < id. Rod^{Thes} Th Be Che$^{EB\ 1154}$ שֵׁן (וְ)הָבְנִים *ivory* (and) *ebony* (Ez 27^{15})

†[שָׁנַס] **vb. Pi. gird up** (si vera l, in Tulm (Aram) שְׁנַץ = *bind* sandals; NH שְׁנָץ *thong*),—*Impf* 3 ms וַיְשַׁנֵּס מָתְנָיו וַיָּרָץ 1 K 18^{46}.

שְׁנָת ψ 132^{4} v שֵׁנָה p 446^{a}.

†שִׁנְעָר **n. pr loc. Shinar** = **Babylonia** (= Bab *Šumêr* acc to COT$^{Gn\ 11,1}$ al, > denied by Hal$^{Rev\ Crit\ 1893,\ 44}$ Jen$^{ZK\ ii\ (1885)\ 419}$, Egypt. *Sangar* (WMM$^{As\ u\ Eur\ 279}$), TelAm. *Šanḫar* (Wkl$^{TelAm\ 25}$) identif. with שׁ׳ by Mey$^{Aegyptiaca\ 63}$; cf., further, Pinches$^{Hast.\ DB\ Shinar}$),—אֶרֶץ שׁ׳ Gn 10^{10} 11^{2} Zc 5^{11} Dn 1^{2}; מֶלֶךְ־שׁ׳ (Amraphel) Gn $14^{1.9}$; שׁ׳ alone Is 11^{11} (as place of diaspora), אַדֶּרֶת שׁ׳ Jos 7^{21}; 𝔊 usu Σεν(ν)ααρ; Zc 5^{11} (ἐν γῇ) Βαβυλῶνος.

שְׁנָת *sleep*, v. שֵׁנָה sub יָשֵׁן.

†[שָׁסָה] **vb. spoil, plunder** (rarer syn. of בזז, שׁלל, with this √ WMM$^{As\ u\ Eur\ 131}$ connects Egypt name of Beduin plunderers *Šôs* [*ša-su, ša-sa*]; connex. doubted by Jen$^{ZA\ x\ (1895),\ 331}$),—**Qal** *Pf.* 3 pl. שָׁסוּ לָמוֹ ψ 44^{11} *they plunder for themselves*, *Impf.* 3 ms יִשְׁסֶה אוֹצַר וגו׳ Ho 13^{15}, elsewh. *Pt* שֹׁסִים *plunderers* Ju 2^{14} 2 K 17^{20}; c acc. loc 1 S 23^{1}; c sf. (as obj) שֹׁסֵהוּ 1 S 14^{48} (prob pl = שֹׁסָיו, so Sta$^{p.345}$ Dr Bu, cf Ges^{§91k}), שׁוֹסֵינוּ Is 17^{14} (‖ בּוֹזֵינוּ), שֹׁסֵיהֶם Ju 2^{16}; שֹׁסַיִךְ Je 30^{16} Qr (Kt v. שׁסס; ‖ בֹּזְזַיִךְ); cstr. שֹׁסֵי נַחֲלָתִי 50^{11}, *pass* עַם־בָּזוּז וְשָׁסוּי Is 42^{22}. **Po'.** = **Qal** *Pf* 1 s. שׁוֹשֵׂתִי (Ges^{§6k}) Is 10^{13}, c. acc rei; read also prob. *Pt* מְשׁוֹסָה Is 42^{24} (‖ בֹּזְזִים), for מְשׁוּסָּה Kt, מְשִׁסָּה Qr; so Du Klo Che^{Hpt} Marti.

†[שָׁסַס] **vb. id.** (‖ form of שׁסה);—**Qal** *Pf* 3 pl שַׁסֻּהוּ ψ 89^{42} they *have plundered him*; *Impf.* 3 mpl וַיָּשֹׁסּוּ Ju 2^{14} (acc. pers); 1 S 17^{53} (acc. loc.), *Pt.* sf. שֹׁאסַיִךְ Je 30^{16} Kt (Qr v שׁסה), Aram form, Ges^{§67s} **Niph.** *be plundered, rifled*, of houses: *Pf.* 3 pl consec. וְנָשַׁסּוּ Zc 14^{2}; *Impf.* 3 mpl יִשַּׁסּוּ Is 13^{16}.

†מְשִׁסָּה **n.f. booty, plunder**;—abs. מ׳ 2 K 21^{14}+, so Is 42^{24} Qr (מְשִׁסָּה Gi, מְשִׁיסָּה Baer; Kt מְשׁוּסָה, usu. read מְשׁוֹסָה, < read מְשֹׁסָּה, v. שׁסה **Po'.**); pl abs מְשִׁסּוֹת Hb 2^{7},—*plunder, spoil, prey*, usu הָיָה לִמְ׳ (and ‖ בַּז) 2 K 21^{14} Je 30^{16} Hb 2^{7} Zp 1^{13} (‖ שְׁמָמָה), cf Is 42^{22} (v^{24} see above).

†[שָׁסַע] **vb. divide, cleave** (NH Pi. *tear apart*; 𝔗^{Jer} Pa. La 3^{11} *tear in pieces* (for 𝔐 פִּשְּׁחַ));—**Qal** *Pt* (c acc cogn שֶׁסַע): ms. וְשֹׁסַע שֶׁסַע פַּרְסָה Lv 11^{7} (P, on שׁ׳ cf Lag$^{BN\ 84}$) *cleaving the cleft of the hoof*, i e having cloven hoof, so fs שֹׁסַעַת v^{7}, cf Dt 14^{6}; שֹׁסַע אֵינֶנָּה שֹׁסַעַת Lv 11^{26} (P); *pass* הַפַּרְסָה הַשְּׁסוּעָה Dt 14^{7} **Pi.** *tear in two*, a lion, kid, *Impf.*, *Inf cstr.* וַיְשַׁסְּעֵהוּ כְּשַׁסַּע הַגְּדִי Ju 14^{6}; a bird (by, or at, its wings), *Pf.* 3 ms. consec וְשִׁסַּע אֹתוֹ Lv 1^{17} (P); *Impf* 3 ms. וַיְשַׁסַּע (אֶת־אֲנָשָׁיו בַּדְּבָרִים) 1 S 24^{8} gives too violent a meaning, prob. crpt for word = *restrain*, or the like Dr HPS, cf. Bu Now (hesitantly).

†שֶׁ֫סַע **n.[m.]** cleft;—as acc. cogn. c [שָׁסַע], q v.; abs Lv 11[26], cstr. v[3.7] Dt 14[6].

†[שִׁסַּף] **vb.** dub.: **Pi.** hew in pieces (Vrss and context);—*Impf.* 3 ms וַיְשַׁסֵּף 1 S 15[33], acc. pers;—Gr Dr HPS qy. וַיְשַׁסַּע, but improb.

†שָׁעָה **vb.** gaze (steadily, with interest, etc.) (As. *šeʾû, behold, look for, aim at*);—**Qal** *Pf.* 3 ms. שׁ׳ Gn 4[5], etc.; *Impf* 3 ms. יִשְׁעֶה Is 17[7.8], apoc. וַיִּשַׁע Gn 4[4], 1 s אֶשְׁעָה (Ges[§75 l]) ψ 119[117], etc.; *Imv.* ms. שְׁעֵה Jb 14[6]; mpl. שְׁעוּ Is 22[4];—*gaze* at, *regard* (with favour), ׳י subj, c. אֶל Gn 4[4.5] (J); c. מִן pers. = *turn gaze away* Is 22[4] Jb 7[19] Thes Ew Che, + prob. 10[20] (for יָשִׁית), c. מֵעַל pers 14[6]; man subj, *regard* God (with trust, devotion), c. עַל Is 17[7] 31[1]; c. אֶל rei 17[8]; c. בְּ of words, statutes, Ex 5[9] (J) ψ 119[117]; abs. 3 fpl. תִּשְׁעֶינָה Is 32[3] *shall* not *behold* makes no sense, read prob תְּשֻׁעֶינָה (√I. שׁעע, Ew and most), 3 mpl. יִשְׁעוּ 2 S 22[42] *they look* (about) for help, < as ‖ ψ 18[42] יְשַׁוְּעוּ. **Hiph.** *Imv.* ms. הָשַׁע מִמֶּנִּי ψ 39[14] *cause thy gaze to turn away from me* (see also √I. שׁעע), < **Qal** שְׁעֵה as Jb 14[6] (cf. 7[19] Is 22[4]) Hup Bae Du Ges[§75 gg]. **Hithp.** *Impf.* 2 ms. apoc. אַל־תִּשְׁתָּע Is 41[10] *gaze not about* (in anxiety, ‖ אַל־תִּירָא); 1 pl. וְנִשְׁתָּעָה (Ges[§75 l]) v[23] *let us look at each other* (in rivalry, v. ראה **Hithp.**).

שׁעט (√of following; Ar. شَعَطَ II. *pound to pieces*)

†[שַׁעֲטָה] **n.f. stamping** (of hoofs);—cstr. שַׁעֲטַת פַּרְסוֹת אַבִּירָיו Je 47[3].

†שַׁעַטְנֵז **n m. mixed stuff** (perh. of Egypt. origin; Kn der. from Copt. *saht, woven, + nudj, false* (Peyron[Lex 254 133]), and thinks orig שַׁעַטְנוּז; 𝔊 has *κίβδηλος, spurious*),—a kind of cloth forbidden for garments; defined Dt 22[11] by צֶמֶר וּפִשְׁתִּים יַחְדָּו, and Lv 19[19] (H) by כִּלְאַיִם.

שְׂעִיר v. שׂעיר.

I. שׁעל (√of following; NH שַׁעַל *deep, depth,* of sea, Aram. שְׁעָלָא, שְׁעוֹלָא, ܡܫܥܠܐ = BH [שֹׁעַל])

†[שֹׁ֫עַל] **n.[m.]** hollow hand, handful;— **1.** *hollow hand*. sf. בְּשָׁעֳלוֹ Is 40[12] (fig. of ׳י holding waters) **2.** *handful:* pl שְׁעָלִים 1 K 20[10] (dust, in hyperb.); cstr. שַׁעֲלֵי שְׂעֹרִים (as if fr. [שַׁ֫עַל] Ko[II 1 35]) Ez 13[19] *handfuls of barley.*

†מִשְׁעוֹל **n.m. hollow way,** road shut in;—cstr. מ׳ הַכְּרָמִים Nu 22[24] (JE) i.e. road shut in between vineyards.

II. שׁעל (√of foll.; NH שׁוּעָל, שֻׁעָל; Ar. ثُعَالَةُ, ثُعَلٌ; Aram. תַּעֲלָא, ܬܥܠܐ, all = BH שׁוּעָל).

†I שׁוּעָל **n.m.** [Ct 2, 15] fox, perhaps also jackal;—abs. שׁ׳ Ne 3[35]; pl. שׁוּעָלִים Ju 15[4] +, שֻׁ׳ Ez 13[4] Ct 2[15 b];—*fox* (prob.) Ne 3[35] Ct 2[15.15]; perh. (fr. large no) *jackal* Ju 15[4]; as haunting ruins Ez 13[4] La 5[18], eating offal ψ 63[11].

†II. שׁוּעָל **n.pr loc.** district in Israel;—אֶרֶץ שׁ׳ 1 S 13[17] (דֶּרֶךְ עָפְרָה); not identified.—Vid. also חֲצַר שׁ׳ p. 347[b] supr.

†III שׁוּעָל **n.pr.m.** in Asher;—1 Ch 7[36], Σουλα, A Σουαλ, 𝔊L Σουαν.

†שַׁעַלְבִים **n.pr.loc.** (perh. haunt of *foxes;* Ar. ثَعْلَب, As. *šêlibu, fox*);—in (orig) territory of Dan, Ju 1[35] (cf. GFM, on etym. and site), 1 K 4[9], Θαλαβειν, Σαλαβειμ, Ju also αἱ ἀλώπεκες, as doublet, or (A 𝔊L) alone, = שַׁעֲלַבִּין Jos 19[42], Σα(α)λαβειν.

שַׁעֲלַבִּין v. foregoing.

†שַׁעַלְבֹנִי **adj.gent.** (of foregoing?);—2 S 23[32] = 1 Ch 11[33]; ὁ Σαλβωνείτης, Σαλαβωνι, etc

†שַׁעֲלִים **n.pr.loc.** district in Israel;—אֶרֶץ שׁ׳ 1 S 9[4], Εασακεμ, A Σααλειμ, 𝔊L Σεγαλειμ; near Michmash Schick[ZPV iv 248]; not identified; = שַׁעַלְבִים We Dr Now; cf. II שׁוּעָל Th HPS Bu.

שׁעם √assumed by Thes for מִשְׁעָם n.pr. q.v.

†[שָׁעַן] **vb. Niph.** lean, support oneself,—*Pf.* 3 ms consec וְנִשְׁעַן Nu 21[15] Is 10[20]; 1 pl נִשְׁעַנּוּ 2 Ch 14[10], etc., *Impf* 3 ms. יִשָּׁעֵן Jb 8[15] +, etc.; *Imv.* mpl הִשָּׁעֲנוּ Gn 18[4]; *Inf. cstr.* הִשָּׁעֵן Is 10[20], sf. הִשָּׁעֶנְךָ 2 Ch 16[7.8], etc.; *Pt.* נִשְׁעָן 2 S 1[6] +;—*lean*, c. עַל *upon*, 2 S 1[6] 2 K 5[18] 7[2.17], *against* pillars Ju 16[26], house Jb 8[15] (fig.); תַּחַת הָעֵץ Gn 18[4] (J), poet. of cliff, וְנִשׁ׳ לִגְבוּל Nu 21[15] *leans to* (upon) *the border* of Moab; *lean* (fig. = trust) upon, עַל pers. king Is 10[20] Ez 29[7] 2 Ch 16[7]; עַל־׳י Mi 3[11] Is 10[20] 2 Ch 13[18] 14[10] 16[7.8], בֵּאלֹהָיו Is 50[10]; abs. Jb 24[23]; עַל־סוּסִים Is 31[1], עַל c. n. abstr. 30[12] Pr 3[5].

†אֶשְׁעָן **n.pr.loc.** in hills of Judah Jos 15[52], Σομα, 𝔊L Εσαν.

†מִשְׁעָן n.[m.] support, staff,—abs. מ׳, fig. of י׳, 2 S 22[19] = ψ 18[19], cstr כל מִשְׁעַן־לֶחֶם וכל מִשְׁעַן־מָיִם Is 3[1] (gloss, v. Comm.)

†מַשְׁעֵן n.m. id.,—abs מ׳ וּמַשְׁעֵנָה Is 3[1] fig support and staff

†מַשְׁעֵנָה n.f. id., v. foregoing (m. et f. to exhaust the category = support of every kind).

†מִשְׁעֶנֶת n.f. staff,—abs Ju 6[21] 2 K 4[31], cstr 2 K 18[21]+, sf משענתו Ex 21[19] Zc 8[4], etc., pl sf משעֲנֹתָם Nu 21[18],—staff, Ex 21[19] (E) Nu 21[18] (J) Ju 6[21] 2 K 4[29.29.31] Zc 8[4], fig of political support, מִשְׁעֶנֶת הַקָּנֶה הָרָצוּץ 2 K 18[21] = Is 36[6], cf Ez 29[6], of י׳ as shepherd ψ 23[4] (+ שֵׁבֶט)

†I [שָׁעַע] vb. be smeared over, blinded (Aram שׁעע smear (akin to שׁוע id.), ܫܥܐ to smooth, שָׁעִיעַ smooth (of words), flattering, ܡܫܥܝܐ smooth (cf also ܫܥܐ, ܫܥܥ smear over, close up)),—Qal Imv + Hithpalp. Imv mpl השתעשעו שֹׁעוּ Is 29[9] blind yourselves and be blind! (|| התמהמהו ותמהו), > Buhl הִשְׁתָּעוּ וְשֹׁעוּ, √שׁעה look about (2 S 22[42]), Is 32[3] rd. prob 3 fpl. תִשְׁעֶינָה, of eyes, be blinded (v. שׁעה) Hiph. Imv ms וְעֵינָיו הָשַׁע Is 6[10] and its eyes besmear!—So perhaps עֵינֶיךָ) הָשַׁע ψ 39[14] om) was intended by Mas. (but wrongly, v. Ol al), see שָׁעָה

†II. [שָׁעַע] vb. Pilp., etc., sport, take delight in, delight (usu. made = I ש׳ smooth over, please; Buhl cp Aram. ܫܥܫܥ, Ithpe sport, trifle, Vulg Ar. مشعشع (loan-word?) Vollers ZMG xlv (1891) 86, l. 8),—Pilp. Pf. 3 ms consec. וְשִׁעֲשַׁע Is 29[9] the suckling shall sport on (עַל) the cobra's hole, 1 s שִׁעֲשָׁעְתִּי ψ 119[70] I take delight in thy law (acc.; but? rd שַׁעֲשֻׁעַי, v[77]), Impf transit 3 mpl. יְשַׁעַשְׁעוּ ψ 94[19] thy consolations delight my soul (acc.) Palp. Impf 2 mpl תְּשָׁעֳשָׁעוּ Is 66[12] upon (עַל) the knees shall ye be fondled Hithpalp. Impf 1 s אֶשְׁתַּעֲשָׁע ψ 119[16] in (בּ) thy statutes will I delight myself, cf v[47]

†[שַׁעֲשֻׁעִים], שׁוּעִים- n.[m.]pl. intens. delight (Ba[NB 206]),—abs שׁוּעִים- Je 31[20] Pr 8[30], sf. שׁוּעָיו- Is 5[7], usu שֻׁעַי- Pr 8[31] ψ 119[24], שֻׁעָי- v[77] + 3 t;—delight, in phr נְטַע ש׳ Is 5[7] the planting of his delight (in which he took delight), so יֶלֶד ש׳ Je 31[20] (|| בֵּן יַקִּיר), ש׳ אֶת־ Pr 8[31] my delight (was) with the sons of men, elsewhere = object of delight, of wisdom v[30]; God's law, etc., ψ 119[24.77.92.143.174].

†שַׁעַף n.pr.m. in clan of Caleb, Σαγαε, A Σαγαφ, 𝔊L Σααφ;—1. ש׳ 1 Ch 2[49]. 2. שָׁעַף v[47].

I. שׁער (√of foll.; Ar. ثَغَرَ break, break off, through, ثُغْرٌ gap, opening; Eth. ሰበረ: tear in two, dissolve; Aram ܬܪܥ (transp.) split, divide, תְּרַע tear down; NH שַׁעַר gate, so MI[22] שעריה (pl. sf), Ph שער Lzb[381]; Tel Am. šaḫri, as Canaanism, Wkl[19b, 1.16]; Aram תַּרְעָא, ܬܪܥܐ; Nab תרעא Lzb[358],—Egypt šaār is loan-word Bondi[70]).

שַׁעַר[373] n.m.[2 8 18 24] (f.[Is 14 31] in personif., Albr ZAW xvi (1896) 86) gate,—ש׳ abs Ju 9[40]+, cstr. Gn 22[17]+; c. ה loc, שַׁעְרָה Is 28[6]+, pl. שְׁעָרִים 2 S 18[24]+, cstr שַׁעֲרֵי 1 S 17[52]+; sf. שְׁעָרֶיךָ Dt 12[15]+, שַׁעֲרֵיהֶם Ez 21[20] 48[31], etc;—1. a. gate, entrance to city, shut (סָגַר) by night Jos 2[5.7] (JE), cf. Is 45[1], opened (פָּתַח) by day Ne 7[3], cf. Is 60[11]; for entrance (בּוֹא), and exit (יָצָא) Je 17[19.20.21.24.25.27] La 4[12] Ez 26[10]+; עָבַר ש׳ Mi 2[13] pass out through (disreg accents), ע׳ בַּשׁ׳ Is 62[10], with bars ψ 147[13]; attacked Ez 21[20.27], cf. Is 28[6] Mi 1[9.12] 1 S 17[52]; on Ju 5[8.11] v. Comm., burned (by foe) Je 19[27] 51[58] Ne 1[3] 2[3.13.17], as giving control, possession, of city, יָרַשׁ את ש׳ איביו Gn 22[17] 24[60] (J); פֶּתַח הַשּׁ׳ Ju 9[40]+ (v. פ׳), דַּלְתוֹת הַשּׁ׳ 1 S 21[14]+ (v. ד׳ 3); פֶּתַח־הַשּׁ׳ Ju 18[16.17] of farm or village; so of camp Ex 32[26.27] (J) In cities, elaborate structure, with roof 2 S 18[24], upper chamber 19[1]; cf שְׂאוּ שְׁעָרִים רָאשֵׁיכֶם ψ 24[7.9]; write laws בַּשׁ׳ Dt 6[9] (+ עַל־מְזוּזוֹת בֵּיתֶךָ), 11[20] (+id), אֶל־תּוֹךְ הַשּׁ׳ 1 S 9[18] בְּתוֹךְ הַשּׁ׳ 2 S 3[27], לְ)יַד ש׳) as public, 1 S 4[18], + v[13] 𝔊 Th We Dr al, cf 2 S 15[2] 18[4] Pr 8[3] (|| מְבוֹא פְתָחִים) b. particular gates of Jerusalem are. (1) ש׳ אֶפְרַיִם 2 K 14[13] || 2 Ch 25[23], Ne 8[16] 12[39], (2) ש׳ הָאַשְׁפֹּת Ne 2[13] 3[14] 12[31] = ש׳ הַשְׁפוֹת 3[13]; (3) ש׳ בִּנְיָמִן Je 37[13] 38[7] Zc 14[10]; (4) ש׳ הַגַּיְא Ne 2[13.15] 3[13] 2 Ch 26[9], (5) ש׳ הַדָּגִים Zp 1[10] Ne 3[3] 12[39] 2 Ch 33[14]; (6) ש׳ בֵּין הַחֹמֹתַיִם 2 K 25[4] = Je 52[7], cf. Je 39[4], (7) ש׳ הַיְשָׁנָה Ne 3[6] 12[39]; (8) ש׳ החרסות Je 19[2]; (9) ש׳ הַמִּזְרָח 3[29]; (10) ש׳ הַמַּטָּרָה 12[39]; (11) ש׳ הַמַּיִם 8[1.3.16]; (12) ש׳ הַמַּיִם לַמִּזְרָח 3[26], cf 12[37]; (13) ש׳ הַמִּפְקָד 3[31]; (14) ש׳ הָעַיִן 2[14] 3[15] 12[37]; (15) ש׳ הַסּוּסִים Je 31[40] Ne 3[28] (cf. 3 b); (16) ש׳ הַפִּנָּה 2 K 14[13] || 2 Ch 25[23] (rd. הַפִּנָּה for הַפּוֹנֶה), Je 31[38] 2 Ch 26[9], prob. = ש׳ הַפִּנִּים Zc 14[10]; (17) ש׳ הָרִאשׁוֹן Zc 14[10], (18) ש׳ הַצֹּאן Ne 3[1.32] 12[39],—on sites and rel. to each other v RS-GASm Encý Bib Jerusalem Conder Hast DB id Buhl G 132 ff Bd Pal s v. Murray Hd. Bk s v Be-Ry Ne p. 182 ff Gu ZPV. esp. v (1882), 7 ff.,

viii (1885), 245 ff Comm.$^{ad\ loc.\ var}$. **c.** of Ezekiel's holy city, שַׁעֲרֵי הָעִיר Ez 48^{31}, three on each side, named for tribes, v$^{31\ 31.31\ 31}$ + 12 t. Ez 48. **2. a.** *gate*=space inside gate, as public meeting-place, market 2 K 7$^{1\ 18}$, place of public well 2 S 23$^{15\ 16}$=1 Ch 11$^{17\ 18}$, where elders, judges, king, sat officially Dt 21^{19} 22^{15} Am 5$^{12.15}$ Is 29^{21} 2 S 18^{24} 19^{9} 1 K 22^{10}=2 Ch 18^{9}, Gn 19^{1} (J) Pr 24^{7} Jb 5^{4} 31^{21} Ru 4$^{1\ 11}$ Pr 31$^{23.31}$, etc.; of conqueror Je 1^{15}; appar.=רְחוֹב שׁ׳ Gn 19^{2} (J) Ne 8^{16} 1 Ch 9^{18}+ (v. I. ר׳); Gn 34^{20} (P) one *came unto* gate (בָּא אֶל־), so בָּאֵי שׁ׳ 23$^{10.18}$ (P) *those entering the gate*, i.e. having citizens' rights; also *went out* (to), יָצָא שׁ׳ Jb 29^{7} (i.e., in this case, from his own house, outside the city), hence כָּל־יֹצְאֵי שׁ׳ Gn 34$^{24.24}$ (P; cf. also הוֹצִיא אֶל־ Dt 21^{19} 22$^{15\ 24}$); hence=body of citizens, כָּל־שׁ׳ עַמִּי Ru 3^{11}. **b.** hence also=city Is 14^{31} (‖ עִיר), ψ 87^{2}, etc. **c.** specif. in Dt, בִּשְׁעָרֶיךָ *in thy gates*, i.e. thy cities, towns, etc., Dt 5^{14}=Ex 20^{10}, Dt 12$^{12\ 15\ 17\ 21}$ + 22 t. Dt + 1 K 8^{37} (read בְּאַחַד שׁ׳, cf. Dt 18^{6} 23^{17}, so 𝔊 𝔖 mod.), so ‖ 2 Ch 6^{28}, + (perh.) Je 14^{2} (but 15^{7} Na 3^{13} fig. of *gates* as entrance to land); of private house, שַׁעֲרֵי צַדִּיק Pr 14^{19} (perh. cf. Ju 18^{16} **1 a** supr.). **3. a.** *gate* of royal castle or palace 2 K 9^{31} Je 22$^{2.4}$ Ne 2^{8} Est 2^{19} + 10 t. Est; specif. (of king of Judah), שׁ׳ סוּר 2 K 11^{6}=שׁ׳ הַיְסוֹד 2 Ch 23^{5} (v. ס׳, ים׳), שׁ׳ הָרָצִים 2 K 11^{19}, שׁ׳ הַסּוּסִים בֵּית הַמּ׳ 2 Ch 23^{15}; הַשַּׁ׳ אַחַר הָר׳ v^{6} (=מְבוֹא הַס׳ ‖ 2 K 11^{16}); appar. of official residence, פֶּתַח שׁ׳ יְהוֹשֻׁעַ 2 K 23^{8}. **b.** of temple Je 7$^{2.2}$ 1 Ch 9^{23} 16^{42} + 12 t. Ch, incl. שַׁעֲרֵי מַחֲנוֹת י׳ 2 Ch 31^{2} (v. מַחֲנֶה **1**, p. 334), cf. ψ 100^{4} 118^{20}, שַׁעֲרֵי צֶדֶק v^{19}; specif. שׁ׳ בִּנְיָמִן הָעֶלְיוֹן Je 20^{2}, and (om. בני׳) 2 K 15^{35}=2 Ch 27^{3}, Ez 9^{2}, 2 Ch 23^{20}, שׁ׳ (בית) י׳ הֶחָדָשׁ Je 26^{10} 36^{10}, שׁ׳ הַפְּנִימִית הַפּוֹנָה צָפוֹנָה Ez 8^{3} cf. v^{14}, 8^{5} שׁ׳ הַמִּזְבֵּחַ, שַׁעַר בֵּית י׳ הַקַּדְמֹנִי 10^{19} 11^{1}; שׁ׳ שַׁלֶּכֶת 1 Ch 26^{16}; שַׁעַר הַמֶּלֶךְ 1 Ch 9^{18}. **c.** of Ezekiel's temple and courts Ez 40$^{3.6}$ 44$^{11\ 17}$ + 67 t. Ez 40–47. **d.** of court of tabern. (P), שׁ׳ הֶחָצֵר Ex 27^{16} 35^{17} + 6 t. Ex + Nu 4^{26}. **4.** fig. זֶה שׁ׳ הַשָּׁמָיִם Gn 28^{17} (E; ‖ בֵּית אֱלֹהִים); pl. שַׁעֲרֵי שְׁאוֹל Is 38^{10}; שׁ׳־מָוֶת Jb 38^{17} ψ 9^{14} 107^{18}; שׁ׳ צַלְמָוֶת Jb 38^{17}.

שֹׁעֵר $_{37}$ **n.m.** porter (denom. from I. שַׁעַר);—abs. שׁוֹ׳ 2 Ch 31^{14}, cstr. שׁ׳ 2 K 7^{10} 1 Ch 9^{21}, + f. שׁוֹעֶרֶת 2 S 4^{6} (for MT [בָּאוּ עַד תּ[וֹך) We Dr HPS Bu Now after 𝔊 (Th פְּקִידַת דֶּלֶת); pl. שֹׁעֲרִים 2 K 7^{11}+; cstr. שֹׁעֲרֵי 2 Ch 23^{4},—*porter* of city gate 2 K 7$^{10\ 11}$ (2 S 18^{26} rd הַשַּׁעַר 𝔊 𝔖 𝔙 Th We Dr and most); *portress* of house 2 S 4^{6} (v. supr.); elsewhere (34 t. Ch Ezr Ne) of gate-keepers in sanctuary 1 Ch 9$^{17\ 18.24}$+; 4,000 in no., 23^{5}; שׁ׳ פֶּתַח לְאֹהֶל מוֹעֵד 9^{21}; שֹׁעֲרִים בַּסִּפִּים v^{22}; שׁ׳ לָאָרוֹן 15$^{23\ 24}$; שֹׁעֲרֵי הַסִּפִּים 2 Ch 23^{4}, בְּנֵי הַשֹּׁעֲרִים Ezr 2^{42}.

†שְׁעַרְיָה **n.pr.m.** in Benjamin, 1 Ch 8^{38}=9^{44}, Σαρ(α)ια, Σααρια.

†שַׁעֲרַיִם **n.pr.loc.** **1.** in the Shephelah of Judah (Buhl$^{Geogr\ 194}$) Jos 15^{36}, Σακαρειμ, 𝔊L Σεβωρειμ; דֶּרֶךְ שׁ׳ 1 S 17^{52} (𝔊 τῶν πυλῶν) **2.** in the Negeb (Simeon), וּבְשַׁעֲרָיִם 1 Ch 4^{31}, Σεωρειμ, 𝔊L Σααριμ, =שָׁרוּחֶן (q.v.) Jos 19^{6}, and perhaps שִׁלְחִים (in Negeb of Judah) 15^{32}; Buhl$^{Geogr\ 185}$.

†II. שָׁעַר **vb.** calculate, reckon (NH Pi. J Aram. Pa. *put a valuation on, estimate;* J Aram. שַׁעֲרָא *interest, market-price;* Ar. سِعْر *market-price* is loan-word Fra^{189});—**Qal** *Pf.* 3 ms. כְּמוֹ־שָׁ׳ בְּנַפְשׁוֹ כֶּן־הוּא Pr 23^{7} *as he has calculated in his soul, so is he*, but dub.: De שֹׁעֵר *as one who calculates;* more radical conj. in Bi Toy.

†II. [שַׁעַר] **n.[m.]** measure (prop. *reckoning*);—pl. מֵאָה שְׁעָרִים Gn 26^{12} (J) 100 *measures*, i.e. 100 for one=100-fold.

III. שׁער (√ of following).

†[שֹׁעָר] **adj.** horrid, disgusting (Ba$^{NB\ 167}$);—pl. כַּתְּאֵנִים הַשֹּׁעָרִים Je 29^{17} (uneatable).

†שַׁעֲרוּרָה **n.f.** horror=horrible thing;—שַׁמָּה וְשׁ׳ Je 5^{30} *an astounding and horrible thing* has occurred; בִּנְבִאֵי ירו׳ רָאִיתִי שׁ׳ 23^{14}.

†שַׁעֲרוּרִיָּה, שַׁעֲרֻרִית **n.f.** id.;—abs. רָאִיתִי שַׁעֲרוּרִיָּה Ho 6^{10} Qr (> Kt שערירית); שַׁעֲרֻרִת עָשְׂתָה בְּתוּלַת יִשׂ׳ Je 18^{13}.

†שַׁעַשְׁגַז **n.m. pers.** Est 2^{14}, Γαι.

†I. [שָׁפָה] **vb.** sweep bare (Ar. سَفَا (ى), of wind, *raise and carry off* dust, أَسْفَى of horse, *scanty* in hair of forelock; NH Pi. *plane off;* Aram. ܫܦܐ Pt. pass. *level* (Is 40^{4}=מישור), *smooth, limpid*, ܫܦܦ *make level, smooth* (and deriv.));—**Niph.** *be wind-swept, bare; Pt.* הַר־נִשְׁפֶּה Is 13^{2} *a bare mt*; **Pu.** *Pf.* consec. וְשֻׁפּוּ עַצְמֹתָיו Jb 33^{21} Qr *his bones are laid bare* (so lean is he; Kt וּשְׁפִי *bareness* are his bones).

†שְׁפוֹת (Ko$^{II\ 1\ 136}$) **n.f.** dub., perhaps cream (as *skimmed off*? cf. Wetzst$^{ZAW\ III\ (1883),\ 276\ f.}$, who connects with Ar. شُفَافَة *cream*, and this with √ شف *take off the top* (but ש=ش?); EV *cheese*

(after 𝔖𝔗, cf. ARSK[ZB 3091)]); —cstr שְׁפוֹת בָּקָר 2 S 17[29] *cream of the herd* (+דְּבַשׁ וְחֶמְאָה וְצֹאן), cf. Now Bu, 𝔊L HPS *calves*.

†שְׁפוֹ **n.pr.m.** in Edom, Gn 36[23], Σωφ, 𝔊L Σωφαν; =II. שְׁפִי 1 Ch 1[40], Σωβ, 𝔊L Σαπφει.

†I. שְׁפִי **n m.** bareness, smooth or bare (treeless) height;—**1.** *bareness*, Jb 33[21] Kt (v √). **2.** *bare place, height:* שֶׁפִי Nu 23[3] (E), i e an outlook-point; pl. שְׁפָיִים Is 41[18] 49[9] Je 3[21], שְׁפָיִם 3[2] 4[11] (‖מִדְבָּר), 7[29], 12[12] (בַּמִּדְבָּר), 14[6].

אַשְׁפָּה *quiver*, vid. s. v.

†יִשְׁפָּה **n.pr m.** in Benjamin 1 Ch 8[16], Σαφαν, 𝔊L Ιεσφα —יָשְׁפֵה v p 448[b] supr.

II. שׁפה (cf Ar. أُثْفِيَّةٌ *stone* (one of three) supporting kettle, Aram أثفيا *tripod*, also תַּפְיָא *fire-jar;* hence perhaps as denom. Heb. [שָׁפַת] q.v, Fra[63]; cf ثفى II, Aram أثفا, תְּפִי *set on a kettle or pot;* v. also GFM[Ju 5, 16] RS[Sem 1 357, 2nd ed 377]).

†[שָׁפַת] **vb denom.** set (on the fire) (NH; v √; Sab. שפת = *bestow*, SabDenkm[No 8, 1 15]);— **Qal 1.** *Imv* ms שְׁפֹת הַסִּיר 2 K 4[38] *set on the pot*, so Ez 24[3], cf. v[3] (del Co, not Krae, Toy allows); later more gen (subj 'י): *Impf* 2 ms. sf תִּשְׁפְּתֵנִי ψ 22[16] in the dust of death *thou settest me.* **2.** *ordain, establish*, 2 ms. תִּשְׁפֹּת שָׁלוֹם לָנוּ Is 26[12].

†אַשְׁפֹּת **n.** [m.] **ash-heap** (?), **refuse-heap, dung-hill** (prob orig *fire-place stones*, cf. Ar sub √),—'א abs as beggars' resting-place 1 S 2[8] = ψ 113[7] (both ‖ עָפָר; cf Jb 2[8] Wetzst ap. De), so pl. אַשְׁפַּתּוֹת La 4[5]; שַׁעַר הָאַשְׁפֹּת Ne 2[13] 3[14] 12[31] = שׁ׳ הָשְׁפוֹת 3[13] (Ges[§ 35 d]).

†I. שְׁפַתַּיִם **n.** [m.] **du.** prob. = מִשְׁפְּתַיִם, infr, q.v,—בֵּין שׁ׳ ψ 68[14] (based on Ju 5[16]?).

II שְׂפָתַיִם v. p. 1052 infr.

מִשְׁפְּתַיִם **n.** [m.] **du.** prob. **fire-places** or **ash-heaps** (viz. of the villages or encampments of the tribe) (>Ki Thes and most *sheepfolds*, v. Stu[Ju]),—בֵּין הַמִּשְׁפְּתַיִם Ju 5[16] (poem; cf. GFM), so (-תַּיִם) Gn 49[14] (poem in J).

שׁפח (√ of foll, cf. Sab. ספח *pour*, also n מספחת *effusion* (?) DHM[VOJ ii (1888) 189] Hom[Chr 124], Ar. سَفَحَ *pour out* water, *shed* blood; note (with ref. to etym. of foll. words) phr. سَافَحَهَا *commit fornication with her* (Lane), i e *effudit* *cum ea* (sc *semen*) Fl in De[Jes 3, 78 Anm.]; on Ph. שפח *servant* (?) cf. Hoffm[Ph Inscr 18] Lzb[381]).

†שִׁפְחָה **n.f.** **maid, maid-servant** (syn. אָמָה, q. v.; orig. = *concubine*? cf. √);—abs. 'שׁ Gn 16[1]+; cstr. שִׁפְחַת v[2]+; sf. שִׁפְחָתִי v[2]+, etc, pl. abs. שְׁפָחוֹת 12[16]+, sf. שִׁפְחָתֶךָ Ru 2[13], etc;—**1.** lit., *maid, maid-servant*, as belonging to a mistress Gn 16[1.3.6.8] (PJ) 29[24.29] (P) ψ 123[2], Pr 30[23] Is 24[2]; even where concubine of master (cf. אָמָה) Gn 16[2.5] (PJ) 25[12] 35[25.26] (P) 30[4.7.9.10.12.18] (all JE); less oft. ref. to master 29[24.29] (J), Ru 2[13], of concubine Gn 32[23], cf 33[1.2.6] (all J); marriageable Lv 19[20] (H, cf. Ex 11[5]; not elsewhere in legisl.), in gen., esp. of menial service (never אָמָה) Ex 11[5] (J) 1 S 25[41] (opp. אָמָה) 2 S 17[17] (‖ עֶבֶד) Gn 12[16] 24[35] (J) 20[14] (E) 30[43] (P) 32[6] (J; coll) Dt 28[68] 1 S 8[16] 2 K 5[26] Is 14[2] Je 34[9.10.11.11.16.16] Jo 3[2] Ec 2[7] 2 Ch 28[10] Est 7[4]. **2.** fig. in address, שִׁפְחָתְךָ, etc, of speaker, in token of humility (v אָמָה) Ru 2[13] (‖ אָמָה 3[9]), 1 S 1[18] (‖ *id.* v[16]), 25[27] (‖ v[24 f]), 28[21.22] 2 S 14[6.7.12.15.17.19] (‖ אָמָה v[15.16]), 2 K 4[2.16], not toward God; but v. אָמָה.

מִשְׁפָּחָה **n.f.** **clan** (RS[Sem 1 256 2nd ed. 276, K 149, 2nd ed 175] Ba[NB § 161 a]);—abs. 'מ Am 3[1]+; cstr מִשְׁפַּחַת Ju 9[1]+, sf. מִשְׁפַּחְתִּי Gn 24[38]+, etc; pl מִשְׁפָּחוֹת Na 3[4]+; cstr. מִשְׁפְּחוֹת Am 3[2]+; sf. מִשְׁפְּחֹתֵיהֶם Gn 8[19]+2 t., usu. -תָם Nu 1[18]+84 t., etc.,—**1.** *clan* · **a.** family connexion of individ. Gn 24[38] (+בֵּית־אָבִי), v[40] (+*id*), v[41] (all J, = מוֹלַדְתִּי v[4]), 2 S 14[7], united in sacrifice 1 S 20[6.29], in passover Ex 12[21] (JE; cf. Benz[Ency. Bib Passover §§ 9, 12]), cf Lv 20[5] (H), 25[10.41] (P), v[49] (P; defined as מִשְּׁאֵר בְּשָׂרוֹ), non-Heb. v[47] (H), v[45] (P), Ju 1[25], מִשְׁפְּחוֹתֶיהָ Jos 6[23] (E or R) is unintelligible, probably del (cf. Steuern Holz; בֵּית אָבִיהָ in v[25] [J]), cf Nu 27[4.11] (P); מ׳ בֵּית אֲבִי אִמּוֹ Ju 9[1] *clan of his mother's father-house;* incl. individuals, and included by שֵׁבֶט 1 S 9[21.21] 10[21]: with specif name, in series שֵׁבֶט, מ׳, בַּיִת, גֶּבֶר Jos 7[14.14.17 b, c] (all J; v[17 a] read pl Di Benn, or <שֵׁבֶט GFM[Ju 13, 2]; Steuern allows either), cf. Dt 29[17] Ju 21[24], מ׳ אֲבִי בֵיתִשׁ 1 S 1[18] (+חַיַּי, v II [חַי]), אִישׁ . . . מִמּ׳ בֵּית־שָׁאוּל 2 S 16[5], with name also Ru 2[1.3] and (non-Isr) Jb 32[2]. **b.** in loose, popular sense = tribe, Ju 13[2] 17[7] 18[19], cf. v[2] (‖ שֵׁבֶט v[1]), v[11] (yet in these two rd. poss. pl, v GFM). **c.** techn divisions of people of Isr. Nu 11[10] (J) Je 2[4] 31[1], cf. 3[14]; Nu 1[2.18] 2[34] 33[54] (all P), so (post-ex) Ne 4[7]: Est 9[28] (מְדִינָה, מ׳, דּוֹר). **d.** usu. (P) techn. divisions of tribes of

Israel, Ex $6^{14.15.19.25}$ Nu 3^{15} + 112 t. Nu (93 t. Nu 26, incl. v^{43} where הַשּׁוּתַלְחִי appar. = Dan), 34 t. Jos 13–21; also 1 Ch $6^{4.45}$ 7^{5} Zc 12^{13}; divisions of Gershom, etc. (in Levi) Nu $3^{18.19.20}$ + 41 t. Ex Nu Jos Ch; subdivisions of these divisions (in Levi) Nu $3^{21.21}$ + 6 t. Nu 3 + 4^{18}; cf. (in other tribes) 1 Ch 2^{53} $4^{2.8.21.27.38}$ 5^{7}; also Zc $12^{12b,c\ 13b\ 14a}$, and (distrib.) $v^{12a\ 14b}$, pleonast. מ׳ מַטֵּה אֲבֹתָם Nu 36^{6} cf. v^{8}, and (מַטֵּה מ׳ א׳) v^{12}. **e.** late, div. of other peoples 1 Ch 16^{28} = ψ 96^{7}, ψ 22^{28}; in Edom Gn 36^{40} (P). **f.** in wider sense = people, nation; כֹּל מִשְׁפְּחוֹת הָאֲדָמָה Am 3^{2} Gn 12^{3} 28^{14} (both J), cf. Je 10^{25} Ez 20^{32} Na 3^{4} (all ‖ גּוֹיִם), Zc 14^{17} Je 1^{15} 25^{9}; as one's posterity Gn $10^{30.31.32}$ (all P), so prob. v^{5} (P; Di Dr); = all Isr. Am 3^{1}, Judah Mi 2^{3} Je 8^{3} (הַמִּ׳ הָרָעָה הַזֹּאת), Isr. + Judah, שְׁתֵּי הַמִּ׳ 33^{24}; מִשְׁפַּחַת מִצְרַיִם Zc 14^{18}; cf. ψ 107^{41}. †**2.** = *guild* 1 Ch 2^{55} (of scribes; orig. hereditary in families). †**3.** = *species, kind:* **a.** of judgments Je 15^{3}. **b.** animals Gn 8^{19} (P). †**4.** pl. = *aristocrats* Jb 31^{34} (cf. Eng. 'the classes').

שֻׁפִּים **n.pr.m.** v. √שׁפף.

שָׁפַט 185 **vb. judge, govern** (NH in deriv.; Ph. שפט = שֹׁפֵט, also in n.pr.; Pun. *sufet* Lzb[381]; BAram. שָׁפְטִין; As. *šapâtu* (*t* = ת), syn. *dânu* (דִּין), *judge* Dl[WB 684], *šipṭu* (ט), prob. *judgment* [and *šapiṭu, captain* ?] Jen[ZA iv (1889), 278 f.]; on poss. connexion with Ar. سفط v. Nö[ZMG xl (1886), 724]; on usage of vb. see Ferguson[JBL viii (1888), 130 ff.]);—**Qal** *Pf.* 3 ms. שׁ׳ Ju 16^{31} +, etc.; *Impf.* 3 ms. יִשְׁפֹּט Gn 16^{5}, יִשְׁפּוֹט Is 11^{3}; 3 mpl. יִשְׁפְּטוּ Gn 31^{53} +, יִשְׁפּוּטוּ Ex 18^{26} (Ki יִשְׁפֹּטוּ; cf. Ges[§ 47 r]), etc.; *Inf. abs.* שָׁפוֹט Gn 19^{9}; cstr. שְׁפֹט Ru 1^{1}, לִשְׁפֹּט Ex 8^{13} +, etc.; *Imv.* שְׁפָט־ Pr 31^{9}, שָׁפְטָה ψ 82^{8} La 3^{59}, שִׁפְטוּ Is 1^{17} +, שְׁפֹטוּ Zc 7^{9}, etc.; *Pt.* שֹׁפֵט 1 S 3^{13} +, etc.;—**1.** *act as law-giver, judge, governor* (giving law, deciding controversies and executing law, civil, religious, political, social; both early and late): **a.** of God only, שֹׁפֵט כל הארץ Gn 18^{25} (J), ‖ מְחֹקֵק, מֶלֶךְ Is 33^{22}. **b.** of man, Gn $19^{9.9}$ (J), Moses deciding cases Ex 18^{13} (E), making known statutes v^{16} (E); so his assistants $v^{22.22.26.26}$ (E), ‖ Dt 1^{16}; of שֹׁפְטֵי ישׂראל Nu 25^{5} (executioners); י׳ set שֹׁפְטִים over Isr. Ju $2^{16.18}$ 2 S 7^{11} = 1 Ch 17^{10}, to deliver Isr., שֹׁפֵט ישׂראל Ju 3^{10} 4^{4} $10^{2.3}$ + 9 t. Ju, 1 S 4^{18} $7^{15.16.17}$ 2 K 23^{22}, cf. 1 S 7^{6}; Pt. שֹׁפֵט as subst. also Ju $2^{17.18.19}$ 1 S $8^{1.2}$ 2 K 23^{22}; שֹׁפְטֵי יִשׂ׳ 1 Ch 17^{6} (‖ 2 S 7^{7} שִׁבְטֵי), בִּימֵי שְׁפֹט הַשֹּׁפְטִים Ru 1^{1} (cf. מוֹשִׁיעִים Ob[21]); שֹׁפֵט, ‖ מֶלֶךְ 1 S $8^{5.6.20}$ Ho 7^{7} 13^{10}; שֹׁפֵט ישׂראל Mi 4^{14} (= king); king *judges* people 1 K $3^{9.9}$ = 2 Ch 1^{10}, 1 K 15^{5} = 2 Ch 26^{21}, 2 Ch 1^{11}; abs. 1 K 7^{7} Is 16^{5}; ‖ שׂרים Ex 2^{14} (E) Am 2^{3} Zp 3^{3}; ‖ יוֹעֵץ Is 1^{26} Jb 12^{17}, cf. Is 3^{2}; שֹׁפְטֵי אֶרֶץ Is 40^{23} (‖ רוֹזְנִים), Pr 8^{16} (‖ שׂרים), ψ 2^{10} 148^{11} (‖ מלכים); שֹׁפְטֵינוּ אשׁר שְׁפָטוּנוּ Dn $9^{12.12}$. **2.** specif. *decide controversy*, discriminate betw. persons, in civil, political, domestic and religious questions: **a.** of God ψ 82^{1}: שׁ׳ בֵּין . . . וּבֵין Gn 16^{5} (J; domestic), Ju $11^{27.27}$ 1 S $24^{13.16}$ (all of war), Ez 34^{20} (relig.); c. בֵּין . . . לְ Ez $34^{17.22}$ (relig.); c. בֵּינֵינוּ Gn 31^{53} (E; domestic), Is 2^{4} = Mi 4^{3} (of war); c. בְּ 2 Ch 20^{12} (war); c. acc. 1 K 8^{32} = 2 Ch 6^{23}, Ec 3^{17}, condemning wicked and justifying righteous Jb 21^{22} (‖ ידע), 23^{7}; abs. Ex 5^{21} (J) Jb 22^{13}; שׁ׳ צֶדֶק Je 11^{20} ψ 9^{5}; י׳ is שׁוֹפֵט צַדִּיק 7^{12}. **b.** of man, שׁ׳ בֵּין . . . וּבֵין Ex 18^{16} (E) Nu 35^{24} (P) Dt 1^{16} (all civil), Is 5^{3} (relig.); c. acc. Lv 19^{15} (H) Dt 25^{1} (all civil), Ez $20^{4.4}$ $22^{2.2}$ 23^{36}; שׁ׳ מִשְׁפָּט Dt 16^{18} 1 K 3^{28} (Sol.); במשׁפטים Ez 44^{24}, c. לְ 2 Ch 19^{6}; abs. Ez 44^{24} Is 11^{3} (king); influenced by bribes Mi 3^{11} 7^{3} Jb 9^{24}; Absalom desires to decide cases as שֹׁפֵט 2 S 15^{4} (implying lack of such in his time); acc. to 2 Ch $19^{5.6}$ Jehoshaphat set up שֹׁפְטִים, appar. for the first as judges in this specific sense; code of Dt recognizes them: הַשֹּׁפֵט declares דְּבַר הַמִּשְׁפָּט Dt $17^{9.12}$ 25^{2}; שׁפטים + שֹׁטְרִים 16^{18} 1 Ch 23^{4} 26^{29} Jos 8^{33} (+ זְקֵנִים), 23^{2} 24^{1} (D; both + רָאשִׁים, זקנים), + זקנים only Dt 21^{2} Ezr 10^{14}, + כֹּהֲנִים Dt $19^{17.18}$, שׂרים 2 Ch 1^{2}. **3.** *execute judgment:* **a.** *discriminating*, of man only, משׁפט אמת Zc 7^{9}, מֵישָׁרִים שׁ׳ ψ 58^{2} *judge uprightly;* משׁפט שׁלום Zc 8^{16}, צֶדֶק Pr 31^{9}, עָוֶל ψ 82^{2}. **b.** *vindicating*, c. acc.: (1) subj. God, יתום ψ 10^{18}, acc. pers. 26^{1} 43^{1} 58^{12} (rd. שֹׁפְטִים for שׁפטים), שׁ׳ משׁפט La 3^{59}; מִיַּד *vindicate by delivering from hand of* 1 S 24^{16} 2 S $18^{19.31}$; שָׁפְטֵנִי כְצִדְקִי ψ 7^{9}; שָׁפְטֵנִי כְצִדְקְךָ 35^{24}. (2) subj. man, c. acc. יתום Is $1^{17.23}$; (דל(ים 11^{4} Pr 29^{14} ψ 82^{3}; עניי עם 72^{4}; משׁפט אביונים Je 5^{28}. **c.** *condemning and punishing*, (1) God פ׳ כְּדַרְכֵי *acc. to ways of* Ez $7^{3.8}$ 18^{30} 24^{14} 33^{20} 36^{19}; במשׁפטים 7^{27} 23^{24}; משׁפטי נאפות 16^{38} (= 23^{45} of human judges); c. acc. 1 S 3^{13} ψ 51^{6} Is 51^{5} Ez $11^{10.11}$ 21^{35} 35^{11}. (2) of man, only שֹׁפְטֵי נַפְשׁוֹ ψ 109^{31} and Ez 23^{45} supr., prob. also ψ 141^{6} (corrupt). **d.** *at theophanic advent for final judgment:* God is שֹׁפֵט ψ 50^{6} 75^{8}; שׁפט הארץ 94^{2}, c. acc. בא לשׁפט הארץ 96^{13} = 1 Ch 16^{33}, ψ 98^{9}; שׁ׳ הארץ 82^{8}; כל הגוים Jo 4^{12}; עמים ψ 67^{5}; תבל 9^{9} 96^{13} = 98^{9}; שׁ׳ מישׁרים

75^{3}. **Niph.** *Pf.* 1 s. נִשְׁפַּטְתִּי Ez 20^{36} + 4 t.; *Impf.* 1 s. אִשָּׁפֵט Ez 20^{36}; אִשָּׁפְטָה 1 S 12^{7}, etc.; *Inf. cstr.* הִשָּׁפֵט 2 Ch 22^{8}; sf. הִשָּׁפְטוֹ ψ 37^{33} 109^{7}; *Pt.* נִשְׁפָּט Is 59^{4} + 4 t.;—**1.** recipr., (Ges$^{§ 51 d}$), *enter into controversy, plead:* c. אֵת *with*, of God Je 2^{35} Ez 17^{20} 20$^{35.36.36}$ 38^{22}; of man 1 S 12^{7} (+ וְאַגִּידָה לָכֶם 𝔊 We Dr Bu^{Hpt} Now), Pr 29^{9}; c. עִם, of God Jo 4^{2}, of man 2 Ch 22^{8}; c. לְ, of God Je 25^{31}; נשׁ׳ יחד Is 43^{26} *have controversy together;* באשׁ *by fire* (of God) 66^{16}; באמונה 59^{4}. **2.** pass. *be judged*, ψ 9^{20} 37^{33} 109^{7}. **Pô'el** *Pt.* sf. מְשֹׁפְטִי (dub.; Hi Bu מִשְׁפָּטִי), = *my opponent-at-law* (Ges$^{§ 55 b}$) Jb 9^{15}; + Zf 3^{15} ψ 109^{31} We al.

†[שֶׁפֶט] **n.m.**$^{Ex 6, 6}$ judgment;—pl. שְׁפָטִים Ex 6^{6} +, sf. שְׁפָטַי Ez 14^{21};—*acts of judgment* (cf. משׁפטים), בשׁפטים גדלים *by great acts of judgment* Ex 6^{6} 7^{4} (P); c. בְּ, עשׂה שׁפטים 12^{12} Nu 33^{4} (P), Ez 5$^{10.15}$ 11^{9} 16^{41} 25^{11} 28$^{22.26}$ 30$^{14.19}$ (all of God); men Ez 16^{41}; c. את, 2 Ch 24^{24} (Syrians against Joash); שׁפטים of God (four: sword, famine, wild beasts, pestilence) Ez 14^{21}; נכונו שׁ׳ ללצים Pr 19^{29} *judgments are prepared for scorners* (𝔊 שְׁבָטִים *rods*, so Perles$^{Anal. 69}$ [or שׁוֹטִים], Toy).

†שְׁפוֹט **n.m.** si vera l. **judgment, act of judgment**;—abs. שׁ׳ 2 Ch 20^{9} (so 𝔊 𝔖, but dub.); pl. שְׁפוּטִים Ez 23^{10} (Toy שְׁפָטִים, Co del.).

†שָׁפָט **n.pr.m.** (*he hath judged*);—usually Σαφατ[θ]: **1.** father of Elisha 1 K 19$^{16.19}$ 2 K 3^{11} 6^{31}. **2.** prince of Simeon Nu 13^{5}. **3.** grandson of Zerub. 1 Ch 3^{22}. **4.** Gaddite chief 5^{12} (Σαβατ, Σαφαμ [ν]). **5.** herdsman of David 27^{29} (Σωφαν, A Σωφατ, 𝔊L Σαφατ).

מִשְׁפָּט$_{422}$ **n. m.** $^{Gn 40, 13}$ **judgment**; — abs. מִשְׁפָּט Ex 21^{31} + 203 t., + לְמִשְׁפָּט Ez 44^{24} (but read Kt לְשְׁפֹּט with 𝔊𝔗𝔖 Co al.); cstr. מִשְׁפַּט Ex 23^{6} + 50 t.; sf. מִשְׁפָּטִי Is 40^{27} +; מִשְׁפָּטָם Je 49^{12} +; מִשְׁפָּטָן Nu 27^{5}; pl. מִשְׁפָּטִים Je 4^{12} + 34 t.; sf. מִשְׁפָּטֶיךָ Dt 33^{10} +, etc.;—**1.** *judgment*: **a.** *act of deciding a case:* מ׳ belongeth to God Dt 1^{17}, is from him Pr 16^{33} 29^{26}; אֱלֹהֵי הַמּ׳ Mal 2^{17}; חֹשֶׁן מ׳ Ex 28^{15} *the pouch of judgment*, so v$^{29.30}$ (P); worn on heart of Aaron v^{30} (P); מ׳ צֶדֶק Dt 16^{18}; הֵבִין מ׳ Jb 32^{9}; שׁפט מ׳ 1 K 3^{28}; עשׂה מ׳ 1 K 3^{28}; דְּבַר (ה)מ׳ Dt 17^{9} 2 Ch 19^{6}; רוח מ׳ Is 28^{6}; במשׁפט Lv 19$^{15.35}$ (H) Dt 1^{17} Pr 16^{10} 24^{23}; במ׳ האורים Nu 27^{21} (P); למשׁפט 35^{12} Jos 20^{6} (P) Dt 17^{8} Ju 4^{5} 2 S 15$^{2.6}$ 2 Ch 19^{8} Is 34^{5} 41^{1} 54^{17} 59^{11} Hb 1^{12} Mal 3^{5} ψ 9^{8} 35^{23} 76^{10} 122^{5} Jb 9^{19} (Ez 44^{24} v. supr.). †**b.** *place, court, seat of judgment* Dt 25^{1} 1 K 7^{7} Is 28^{6} Ec 3^{16}. †**c.** *process, procedure, litigation* before judges: הֵבִיא במ׳ Jb 14^{3} Ec 11^{9} 12^{14}; בא במ׳, c. עם Is 3^{14} Jb 22^{4}, c. את ψ 143^{2}, c. יחדו Jb 9^{32}, הלך במ׳ Jb 34^{23}, cf. Ez 34^{16} ψ 112^{5}; pl. דבר משׁפטים, c. את *litigate with* Je 1^{16} 4^{12} 12^{1} 39^{5} = 52^{9}, sg. מִשְׁפָּט in ‖ 2 K 25^{6}, by error. †**d.** *case* or *cause* presented for judgment: בעל מ׳ Is 50^{8}; ערך מ׳ Jb 13^{18} 23^{4}; שׁמע מ׳ 1 K 3^{11}; שׁפט מ׳ La 3^{59}, cf. Nu 27^{5} (P) 2 S 15^{4}. †**e.** *sentence, decision* of judgment: כן משׁפטך 1 K 20^{40} *thus is thy sentence;* עת ומ׳ Ec 8$^{5.6}$ *time and sentence;* על מ׳ Dt 17^{11} *according to the sentence;* מ׳ מָוֶת 19^{6} 21^{22} Je 26$^{11.16}$; מ׳ דמים Ez 7^{23}, cf. Hb 1$^{4.4}$ ψ 7^{7} 17^{2} Ez 23^{45}; pl. only Ez 16^{68} משׁפטֵי נאפות; Ho 6^{5} rd. sg. מִשְׁפָּטִי כָאוֹר for מִשְׁפָּטֶיךָ אור after 𝔊 𝔖 𝔗 Ew Hi Che and most mod. †**f.** *execution* of judgment, in gen., עשׂה מ׳, c. בֵּין Je 7^{5} Ez 18^{8}, cf. Dt 32^{41} Zp 3^{8}; c. בְּ *against* ψ 119^{84} 149^{9}; ב om. 9^{17} Ez 39^{21}, מ׳ בא אל Je 48^{21}, ברוח מ׳ Is 4^{4}, מ׳ מואב Je 48^{47}, cf. Is 53^{8} Je 51^{9} Ho 5$^{1.11}$ 10^{4} Jb 36^{17}; pl. Is 26$^{8.9}$ Ez 5^{8} Zp 3^{15} ψ 10^{5}; *in favour of*, עשׂה משׁפטי Mi 7^{9} ψ 9^{5}; מ׳ לעשׁוקים 146^{7}; דין מ׳ והציל Je 21^{12}, cf. Zc 7^{9} 8^{16}; pl. ψ 48^{12} = 97^{8}, 103^{6} 105$^{5.7}$ = 1 Ch 16$^{12.14}$. †**g.** *time of judgment*, לא יקומו במ׳ ψ 1^{5} (late; prob. judgment of the resurrection). **2.** attribute of the שֹׁפֵט, *justice, right, rectitude:* **a.** of God, הֲשֹׁפֵט כָּל־הָאָרֶץ לֹא יַעֲשֶׂה מ׳ Gn 18^{25} (J), cf. Jb 40^{8} Dt 32^{4} ψ 111^{7}; אלהי מ׳ Is 30^{18}; he loves it 33^{5} 37^{28} 99^{4}; צדק ומ׳ Ho 2^{21} ψ 89^{15} = 97^{2}; will not pervert it Jb 8^{3} 34^{12}, cf. 37^{23}; כמשׁפטך ψ 119^{149} (‖חסדך); מִשְׁפָּטְךָ תְּהוֹם רַבָּה 36^{7} (read sg.). **b.** of man: אַשְׁרֵי שֹׁמְרֵי מ׳ ψ 106^{3} (‖צדקה); the tongue of the wise speaketh מ׳ 37^{30}; so of thoughts מ׳ Pr 12^{5}; put on מ׳ as robe Jb 29^{14}, chosen 34^{4}; עשׂה מ׳: God requires that man should do it Mi 6^{8} Is 1^{17} 56^{1}, cf. 61^{8}; it is the joy of the righteous Pr 21^{15}; rulers should know it Mi 3^{1}, cf. Pr 29^{4}; wicked ruler שׂוֹנֵא מ׳ Jb 34^{17}; abhors it Mi 3^{9}, cf. Pr 19^{28} 21^{7} 28^{5}. **3.** *ordinance* promulgated by שֹׁפֵט: 1 S 8$^{9.11}$ 10^{25} (law of king); Levit. ordinances Lv 5^{10} 9^{16} + 13 t. P, 1 Ch 15^{13} 24^{19} 2 Ch 4$^{7.20}$ 8^{14} 35^{13} Ne 8^{18}; חק ומ׳ Ex 15^{25} Jos 24^{25} (E) 1 S 30^{25}, cf. ψ 81^{5}; חקת מ׳ Nu 27^{11} 35^{29} (P); divine law in gen. מ׳ יהוה Je 8^{7}; מ׳ אלהים Is 58^{2} Je 5$^{4.5}$ (‖ דֶּרֶךְ), cf. ψ 25^{9}; ‖ תורה Is 42^{4} 51^{4} Ezr 7^{10}; cf. Zp 2^{3} ψ 119$^{43.160}$; pl. of particular ordinances Dt 33$^{10.21}$ (poem), Is 58^{2} Ez 44^{24} ψ 19^{10} 119^{7} + 16 t., 147^{20}. **4.** *decision* of the שֹׁפֵט in a case of law (v. Br$^{Hex 252 sq.}$): sg. of particular decision of a case Ex 21^{31} (E); pl.

of series of decisions 21^{1} 24^{3} (JE) Dt 7^{12} (D^{2}); in covt. code and D, collection of pentades in conditional or temp. cl., c. כי or אם in D, and subj. in combination, חקים ומשפטים 4$^{1.5.8.14.45}$+; in code of H and after, in combin. חקות ומשפטים, Lv 18$^{4.5.26}$ 19^{37}+; (the specific type of these laws in H is אִישׁ כִּי, over against אדם כי נפש כי or in code of P, v. Br$^{Hex\ 254\ f.}$); other combin., redactional and later, Lv 26^{46} Nu 36^{13} Dt 30^{16} 2 K 17^{37} 2 Ch 33^{8} Ne 9^{13} ψ 18^{23} 89^{31} 147^{19}. **5.** one's (legal) *right, privilege, due:* מ׳ הַכֹּהֲנִים Dt 18^{3} *due of the priests,* מ׳ הַבְּכֹרָה 21^{17}; מ׳ הַיְרֻשָּׁה הַגְּאֻלָּה Je 32^{7} *right of redemption;* מ׳ הַיְרֻשָּׁה v^{8}; הִטָּה מ׳ Ex 23^{6} (E) *wrest right,* so Dt 16^{19} 23^{6} 24^{17} 27^{19} 1 S 8^{3} La 3^{35}, cf. Pr 18^{5}; מ׳ יָתוֹם Dt 10^{18}; מ׳ אביון Ex 23^{6} (E) Je 5^{28} ψ 140^{13}; מ׳ עניים Is 10^{2} Jb 36^{6}; הסיר מ׳ 27^{2} 34^{5}, cf. Is 40^{27} 49^{4}. **6. a.** *proper, fitting, measure* 1 K 5^{8}; *fitness* Is 28^{26}, 40^{14} (of fitness in the order of nature; cf. Di). **b.** *custom, manner:* מ׳ הכהנים 1 S 2^{13} *custom of the priests* (*rightful due,* acc. to ThWe Dr and most); מִשְׁפָּטוֹ 27^{11} *his* (David's) *custom;* מ׳ הגוים 2 K 17^{33} *manner of the nations,* cf. 2 K 17$^{26.27}$ (RS$^{Sem.\ 1,\ 24,\ 2nd\ ed.\ 23}$); כמ׳ *after the manner, custom, fashion* (of) Gn 40^{13} Ex 21^{9} (E) Ju 18^{7} 1 K 18^{28} 2 K 11^{14} 17^{34} 1 Ch 6^{17} Ez 42^{11} ψ 119^{132}. †**c.** מה משפט Ju 13^{12} *what manner of* a boy, cf. 2 K 1^{7}. †**d.** *plan . . .* of the tabernacle Ex 26^{30} (P); temple 1 K 6^{38}; palace Je 30^{18}.

†שְׁפַטְיָה(וּ) **n.pr.m.** (י׳ *hath judged, vindicated*);—usu. Σαφατια(ς): **1.** -יָה: **a.** fifth son of David 2 S 3^{4} = 1 Ch 3^{3} (Σαβατεια, A Σαφαθια, 𝔊L Σαφατιας). **b.** contemp. of Jerem. Je 38^{1} (B Σαφανιας). **c.** man of Judah Ne 11^{4}. **d.** chiefs of families of restoration: (1) Ezr 2^{4} = Ne 7^{9}, Ezr 8^{8}; (2) 2^{57} = Ne 7^{59}. **e.** Benjamite 1 Ch 9^{8}. **2.** -יָהוּ: **a.** son of Jehosh. 2 Ch 21^{2}. **b.** hero of David 1 Ch 12^{5}. **c.** Simeonite 27^{16}.

†שִׁפְטָן **n.pr.m.** (*judgment*);—prince of Ephraim Nu 34^{24}; Σαβαθα(ν), 𝔊L Σαφαταν.

I. שְׁפִי v. I. שׁפה. II. שְׁפִי v. שְׁפוֹ sub I. שׁפה.

שְׁפִּים v. שׁפף.

שָׁפַךְ 113 **vb.** pour out, pour (NH *id.;* As. *šapâku, pour out,* esp. (Dl^{WB} Jen$^{Kosmol.\ 41}$) earth, to form mound; Ar. سَفَكَ *pour out,* cf. سَبَكَ *melt and pour into mould;* Eth. ሰበከ: Aram. שְׁפַךְ, ܫܦܟ (rare) = BH);—**Qal** *Pf.* 3 ms. שׁ׳ 1 K 2^{31}+; 3 fs. sf. שְׁפָכַתְהוּ Ez 24^{7}, etc.; *Impf.* 3 ms. יִשְׁפֹּךְ 2 K 19^{32}+; 2 ms. sf. 3 ms. תִּשְׁפְּכֶנּוּ Dt 12^{16}+, etc.; *Imv.* ms. שְׁפוֹךְ Ju 6^{20}+, שְׁפָךְ־ ψ 69^{25}; fs. שִׁפְכִי La 2^{19}, etc.; *Inf. cstr.* שְׁפָךְ־ 1 K 18^{28}+, לִשְׁפֹּךְ Is 59^{7}+, etc.; *Pt. act.* שֹׁפֵךְ Gn 9^{6}+, f. שֹׁפֶכֶת Ez 22^{3}, etc.; *pass.* שָׁפוּךְ ψ 79^{10}, שְׁפוּכָה Ez 20$^{33.34}$;—**1.** lit.: **a.** *pour out, pour* water Ex 4^{9} (J; acc. loc.), 1 S 7^{6} (+ לִפְנֵי י׳, unique, symb. of contrition), עַל־פְּנֵי הָאָרֶץ (subj. י׳) Am 5^{8} 9^{6}; blood like water (to flow away and be absorbed), עַל־הָאָרֶץ Dt 12$^{16.24}$ 15^{23}, cf. Lv 17^{13} (H) Ez 24^{7}; also + אֶל loc. Ex 29^{12} Lv 4$^{7.18.25.30.34}$; + עַל pers. reflex. 1 K 18^{28}; *pour out* broth Ju 6^{20}, libation (נֶסֶךְ, to (ל) false gods) Is 57^{6}; dust Lv 14^{41} (P; אֶל loc.); c. acc. סֹלְלָה *mound* (in siege), = *make by pouring* (earth, orig. from baskets, see esp. As. *šapâku* Dl$^{WB\ 679\ b}$ Jen$^{Kosmol.\ 41}$), + עַל־ of city 2 K 19^{32} = Is 37^{33}, Je 6^{6} Ez 4^{2} 26^{8}, אֶל־ 2 S 20^{15}; abs. Ez 17^{17} 21^{27} Dn 11^{15}; וַיִּשׁ׳ מֵעָיו אַרְצָה 2 S 20^{10} (by a sword-thrust in the belly), cf. יִשׁ׳ לָאָרֶץ מְרֵרָתִי Jb 16^{13} (metaph., י׳ subj.). **b.** techn., acc. דָּם *shed blood* Gn 37^{22} (E) 9^{6} (P) 1 S 25^{31} Ez 22^{4} + 9 t. Ez, + 15 t. (pass. ψ 79^{10}) + Ez 36^{18} (c. עַל־הָאָרֶץ), 1 Ch 22^{8} (c. אַרְצָה); acc. דָּמִים + 1 K 2^{31} 1 Ch 28^{3} ψ 79^{3} (כַּמַּיִם). **2.** fig.: **a.** י׳ subj., *pour out* anger, etc.: עֲלֵיהֶם אֶשׁ׳ כַּמַּיִם עֶבְרָתִי Ho 5^{10}; שׁ׳ חֲמָתִי עַל Ez 14^{19} + 8 t. Ez, Je 10^{25} Is 42^{25} ψ 79^{6} (אֶל et עַל); acc. ח׳ om. Je 6^{11}; c. ב loc. La 2^{4}; ח׳ שְׁפוּכָה Ez 20$^{33.34}$; acc. חֲרוֹן אַפּוֹ La 4^{11}; acc. זַעַם (עַל pers.) Ez 21^{36} + 3 t.; acc. בּוּז *contempt,* עַל pers., Jb 12^{21} = ψ 107^{40}; *pour* their own wickedness עֲלֵיהֶם Je 14^{16} (i.e. requite it); *pour out* רוּחִי עַל Ez 39^{29}, cf. Zc 12^{10} Jo 3$^{1.2}$. **b.** hum. subj. *pour out* one's heart, etc., כַּמַּיִם לִבֵּךְ La 2^{19}, לְפָנָיו לְבַבְכֶם ψ 62^{9} (i.e. bef. י׳), אֶת־נַפְשִׁי לִפְנֵי י׳ 1 S 1^{15}, עָלַי (reflex.; v. עַל **1 d**) ψ 42^{5}; אֶת־שִׂיחוֹ לִפְנֵי י׳ ψ 102^{1} (title), cf. 142^{3}; in bad sense, וַתִּשְׁפְּכִי אֶת־תַּזְנוּתַיִךְ עַל־ Ez 16^{15}, cf. 23^{8}. †**Niph.** *Pf.* 3 ms. נִשְׁפַּךְ La 2^{11}, etc.; *Impf.* 3 ms. יִשָּׁפֵךְ Gn 9^{6}+, etc.; *Inf. cstr.* הִשָּׁפֵךְ Ez 16^{36};—*be poured out:* of ashes 1 K 13$^{3.5}$, blood (עַל loc.) Dt 12^{27}; *be shed,* of blood Gn 9^{6} (P) Dt 19^{10}; in fig. La 2^{11} *my liver is poured* לָאָרֶץ (cf. **Qal 1 a** *ad fin.*); ψ 22^{15} *I am poured out like water* (nerveless, helpless); subj. נְחֻשְׁתֵּךְ Ez 16^{36} (v. II. [נְחֹשֶׁת]; cf. v^{15} **Qal 2 b**). †**Pu.** *Pf.* 3 ms. consec. וְשֻׁפַּךְ Zp 1^{17} *be poured out* כֶּעָפָר, of blood; שֻׁפָּךְ Nu 35^{33} (P) *be shed,* of blood; 3 fs. שֻׁפְּכָה ψ 73^{2} Kt my steps *were caused to slip* (Qr שֻׁפְּכוּ). †**Hithp.** *Impf.* 3 fs. עָלַי תִּשְׁתַּפֵּךְ נַפְשִׁי Jb 30^{16} *my soul pours itself out upon me* (v. **Qal 2 b**); 3 fpl. תִּשְׁתַּפֵּכְנָה אַבְנֵי־קֹדֶשׁ

La 4[1] fig of slaughter, *Inf. cstr.* בהשתפך נפשם אל־חיק אמתם 2[12], i.e they expire.

†**שֶׁפֶךְ** **n.[m.]** place of pouring;—cstr. ש׳ הַדֶּשֶׁן Lv 4[12 12] (P)

†**שָׁפְכָה** **n.f.** male organ (as fluid-duct),—abs כְּרוּת ש׳ Dt 23[2] (|| פְּצוּעַ־דַּכָּה)

†**שָׁפֵל** **vb.** be or become low, be abased (NH, der spec, As *šapâlu*, der. spec and deriv., Sab ספל n *humility* or *lowland* DHM xxix (1875), 604, Ar سَفَلَ, سَفِلَ, سَفُلَ *be low* (Lag BN 48), Aram שְׁפֵל, ܫܦܠ (der spec)),—**Qal** *Pf.* 3 ms ש׳ Is 2[11], 2 fs וְשָׁפַלְתְּ 29[4], etc, *Impf.* 3 ms וַיִּשְׁפַּל 2[9] 5[15], 3 fpl. תִּשְׁפַּלְנָה 5[15], etc; *Inf. cstr.* שְׁפַל Ec 12[4] Pr 16[19], v. infr;—**1.** all Is: *become* (be brought, laid) *low*, of trees Is 10[33] (|| נִגְדָּעִים), mts. 40[4] (opp. נִשָּׂא), of כָּל־נִשָּׂא 2[12] (but read, for ש׳, וְגָבֹהַּ [Kohler], or נִשְׂגָּב [Lag], so Du Che Hpt Di-Kit Marti); fig *be humiliated*, of man 2[9] 5[15], his loftiness 2[17], haughty eyes v[11] (all || שָׁחַח), 5[15], of city 32[19]; as helping vb (=adv) וּשְׁ׳ מֵאֶרֶץ תְּדַבֵּרִי 29[4] *thou shalt speak low out of the ground* (Ges § 120 g, || מֵעָפָר תִּשַּׁח אִמְרָתֵךְ). **2.** שְׁפַל־רוּחַ Pr 16[19] *to be lowly of spirit*, so Buhl SS Toy al., Thes Rob Ges al sub שָׁפָל. **3.** of sound Ec 12[4]

Hiph. *Pf* 3 ms הִשְׁפִּיל Is 25[12], etc, *Impf* 3 ms יַשְׁפִּיל ψ 75[8], sf יַשְׁפִּילָהּ יַשְׁפִּילֶנָּה Is 26[5] (but 2nd vb. prob doublet), etc., *Imv* mpl (sf) הַשְׁפִּילוּ Jb 40[11] Je 13[18], *Inf. cstr* sf הַשְׁפִּילְךָ Pr 25[7] (Ez 21[31] read *abs* הַשְׁפִּיל, || הַגְבֵּהַּ, so Co Krae Ges § 113 bb R 3), *Pt* מַשְׁפִּיל 1 S 2[7] ψ 147[6], מַשְׁפִּילִי (Ges § 90 l) ψ 113[6],—**1.** usu. fig, י׳ subj, *lay low*, tree Ez 17[24] (opp הִגְבַּהְתִּי); city Is 26[5] (|| הֵשַׁח), fortress 25[12] (+ הֵשַׁח; Du thinks doublet of 26[5]); *humiliate* pride v[11] 13[11], cf Jb 40[11], obj. עֵינַיִם רָמוֹת ψ 18[28], so read also || 2 S 22[28], י׳ מַשְׁ׳ אַף־מְרוֹמֵם 1 S 2[7], רְשָׁעִים ψ 147[6], זֶה יַשְׁ׳ וְזֶה יָרִים 75[8], cf. Ez 21[31]. **2.** hum. subj *set* one *in a lower place* Pr 25[7], subj hum. pride Pr 29[23], declar. Is 57[9] *thou didst shew abasement* עַד־שְׁאוֹל. **3.** as helping vb. + vb. coord., הַשְׁ׳ שֵׁבוּ Je 13[18] *make low, sit down*=take a low seat (Ges § 120 g), + inf. מַשְׁ׳ לִרְאוֹת ψ 113[6] *he who maketh low to look* upon heaven and earth (i e י׳; || הַמַּגְבִּיהִי לָשָׁבֶת v[5], Ges § 114 m)—הִשְׁפִּילוּ וַתֹּאמֶר גֵּוָה Jb 22[29] is dub; || יוֹשִׁעַ favours אֱלוֹהַּ as subj, which Bu conj for וַתֹּא׳, read then הִשְׁפִּיל א׳ *hath abased pride*, so (in part) Du, > *they cast* (thee) *down* (RV); *men are cast down* (הִשׁ׳ intrans; AV, cf Lag BN 121); (thy ways) *are brought low* (Ew De Di).

†**שֵׁפֶל** **n.[m.]** low estate, condition;—abs. ש׳ Ec 10[6] (opp. מְרוֹמִים), sf. שֶׁבְּשִׁפְלֵנוּ ψ 136[23].

†**שִׁפְלָה** **n.f.** humiliation,—Is 32[19] (of city).

שָׁפָל **adj.** low,—abs. ש׳ 2 S 6[22] +, cstr. שְׁפַל ψ 29[23] +, fs שְׁפָלָה Ez 17[14] +, cstr. שִׁפְלַת v[6]; pl. שְׁפָלִים Jb 5[11],—**1.** *low*, in height, of vine Ez 17[6], tree v[24] (opp. גָּבֹהַּ); ש׳ מִן־הָעוֹר Lv 13[20] *lower* (deeper) *than the skin* (around it), so v[21 26], cf. 14[37]. **2.** of a modest, unambitious kingdom Ez 17[14] 29[14 15], *low* in station Jb 5[11] (opp. שְׂגָבוּ), Ez 21[31] (Ges § 90 f, rd הַשְׁפִּלָה). **3.** *humiliated*, ש׳ בְּעֵינַי 2 S 6[22], pl. Mal 2[9] (|| נִבְזִים). **4.** *lowly*, as subst ψ 138[6] (opp. גָּבֹהַּ), רוּחַ שְׁפָלִים Is 57[15] (|| נִדְכָּאִים), שְׁפַל רוּחַ v[15], Pr 29[23] (opp. גַּאֲוַת אָדָם), + 16[19] Thes al. (but v. ✓**Qal 2**).

†**שְׁפֵלָה** **n.f.** lowland;—alw. abs ש׳ c. art., exc sf. שְׁפֵלָתָהּ Jos 11[16],—*lowland*: **1.** usually term. techn. of strip W. of Judaean mts. (on exact limits v GASm Geogr 201 ff., Expos Dec. 1896, 404 f. Buhl Geogr 104 Dr Hast DB iii. 892 f) almost alw. disting. from הָהָר and הַנֶּגֶב, sts from הָעֲרָבָה, in Dt 1[7] Jos 9[1] (R^D) also from חוֹף הַיָּם, cf Jos 10[40] 12[8] (both R^D), Ju 1[9] (perh. R^D, cf. Bu GFM), Jos 15[33] (P), Je 17[26] 32[44] 33[13] Ob[19] Zc 7[7] 2 Ch 26[10] (disting. from הַמִּישׁוֹר, table-land E. of Jordan); region of sycomores 1 K 10[27] = 2 Ch 1[15] 9[27], 1 Ch 27[28]. **2.** of lowland (near coast) N. of Carmel Jos 11[2]; W. of mts. of Ephr. v[16] (both R^D).

†**שִׁפְלוּת** **n.f.** sinking;—cstr. ש׳ יָדַיִם Ec 10[18] *sinking of hands*, negligence (|| עֲצַלְתַּיִם).

†**שָׁפָם** **n.pr.m.** in Gad 1 Ch 5[12]; 𝔊B Σαβατ, A Σαφαμ, 𝔊L Σαφαν.

†**שְׁפָם** **n.pr.loc.** on E border of Israel; ש׳ Nu 34[10], שְׁפָמָה v[11]; 𝔊 Σεπφαμαρ, site unknown.

שְׁפָם v. שָׂפָם sub שׂפה.

†**שִׁפְמוֹת** (so Baer with codd. and edd.; Thes שִׂפ׳; van d. H. Gi שְׂפ׳);—**n.pr.loc.** in Negeb 1 S 30[28], Σαφει, A Σαφαμως, 𝔊L Σεφειμωθ.

†**שִׁפְמִי** **adj gent.** (of foreg.?);—1 Ch 27[27].

שׁוּפָמִי **adj. gent.** v. שְׁפוּפָם sub שׁפף.

שׁפן (✓of foll; cf Ar. ثُفْن Fresnel JAs 1838, 514 Thes 1467 [usu called وَبْر or طُنْشُن])

†**I. שָׁפָן** **n. m.** Lv 11,5 rock-badger, *hyrax syriacus*, AV RV *coney*;—abs. ש׳ Dt 14[7] = Lv

11[5] (P; unclean animal); living in rocks, pl. שְׁפַנִּים ψ 104[18] Pr 30[26].—Vid. Rob[BR III 66,387] Tr[NHB 75; FFP 1, and Pl 1] Dr[Dt] Post[Hast DB CONEY] McLean-Shipley[Ency Bib. ib].

†II. שָׁפָן n.pr.m. Σαφ(φ)αν: **1.** secretary (הַסֹּפֵר) under Josiah 2 K 22[3.8.8.9 10 10.12 14] 2 Ch 34[8 15 16.16 18.18.20]. **2.** father of אֲחִיקָם, contemp. of **1** (improb.=**1**): 2 K 22[12] 25[22] Je 26[24] 39[14] 40[5.9 11] 41[2] 43[6] 2 Ch 34[20]. **3.** father of אֶלְעָשָׂה Je 29[3], perh.=**2.** **4.** father of גְּמַרְיָהוּ 36[10] (called הַסֹּפֵר), v[11 12], perh.=**1.** **5.** father of יַאֲזַנְיָהוּ Ez 8[11], possibly=**1.**

שׁוּפָן v. עַטְרוֹת p. 743[a] supr.

† יִשְׁפָּן n.pr.m. in Benjamin 1 Ch 8[22]; Ισφαν, A Εσφαν, 𝔊L Ιεσφαν.

שׁפע (√ of foll.; NH שָׁפַע *flow abundantly, be abundant;* 𝔗 שְׁפַע, Syr. ܫܦܥ, *overflow, abound*)

† שֶׁפַע n.[m.] abundance,—cstr. ׳שׁ Dt 33[19]

† [שִׁפְעָה], שִׁפְעַת n.f. abundance, quantity;—appar. abs. שִׁפְעַת 2 K 9[17], *a multitude* (of men), (Bur שִׁפְעָה, or שִׁפְעַת אֲנָשִׁים as Klo Benz al.; > 𝔊[B] Kit עָפָר); cstr. שִׁפְעַת יֵהוּא v[17] *Jehu's multitude;* cstr, of horses Ez 26[10], camels Is 60[6]; of waters Jb 22[11] 38[34].

† שִׁפְעִי n.pr.m. in Simeon 1 Ch 4[37]; Σεφει, 𝔊L Σωφει.

שׁפף (√ of following).

† שְׁפִיפֹן n.[m.] horned snake, 𝔊 κεράστης (Ar. سُفٌّ, سِفٌّ Frey);—abs. ׳שׁ Gn 49[17] (‖ נָחָשׁ); =*cerastes cornutus* or *Hasselquistii*, cf. Tr[NHB 273] Post[Hast. DB iv 457 f.] McLean-Shipley[Ency Bib. iv 4393] Dr[ad loc]—שְׁפוּפָם, שְׁפוּפָן vid. s.v.

† שְׁפוּפָם n.pr.m. in Benjamin,—Nu 26[39], Σουταλα, 𝔊L Σοφαν (=שֻׁפִּים מֻפִּים וְחֻפִּים Gn 46[21], שֻׁפִּם וְחֻפִּם 1 Ch 7[12]).

† שׁוּפָמִי adj. gent. of foregoing, c. art. as n.coll. Nu 26[39].

† שְׁפוּפָן n.pr.m. in Benj. 1 Ch 8[5], Σωφαρφακ, A Σωφαν, 𝔊L Σεπφαμ.

† שֻׁפִּים n.pr.m. **1.** ׳שׁ 1 Ch 7[15], Μαμφειν, A Σεφφειμ, 𝔊L Σαφιν, appar.=שֻׁפִּם v[12], Σαπφειν, 𝔊L Σαφαν (cf. שְׁפוּפָם, מֻפִּים). **2.** שֻׁפִּים doorkeeper, 1 Ch 26[16].

† [שָׁפַר] vb. be beautiful, fair, comely (Ar. سَفَرَ *remove veil* (of women), *shine*, Aram. שְׁפַר *be pleasing* (v. Dn 6[2]), ܫܦܪ *be beautiful, bright, pleasing*, ܫܦܝܪ *beautiful*);—**Qal** *Pf* 3 fs. שָׁפְרָה עָלָי (Aram) ψ 16[6] (the) heritage *is beautiful for* (pleasing to) *me* (v. עַל **II. 8**).

† I. [שֶׁפֶר] n.m. beauty, goodliness;—abs. אִמְרֵי־שָׁפֶר Gn 49[21] (v. אָמִיר, אֵמֶר).

† II. [שֶׁפֶר] n.pr.mont. as a station in wilderness;—הַר־שָׁפֶר Nu 33[23.24] (P); Σαφαρ.

† I. שִׁפְרָה n.f. fairness, clearness, of sky;—abs. ׳שׁ Jb 26[13] by his breath the sky becomes *fair(ness)*, v. esp. De Di Bu Du; > Che[JQ 1897, 578] (after 𝔊) בְּרִיחַי שָׁמַיִם סגר הוּא.

† II. שִׁפְרָה n.pr.f. Hebrew midwife, Ex 1[15] (E); Σεπφωρα (cf. Lag[BN 90]).

† שָׁפִיר n.pr.loc. in Philist. plain, Mi 1[11] (=שָׁמִיר Jos 15[48]?), 𝔊 καλῶς (!).

אֶשְׁפָּר vid s.v.

שׁוֹפָר, שֹׁפָר[72] n.m.[Is 27,13] horn, for blowing (Aram. שִׁיפוּרָא √ dub; CAdler[PAOS 1889, clxxi ff] cp. As. *šappar(u)* a species of wild goat; in any case the ׳שׁ is a curved horn, as of cow or ram, cf. Dr[Am 2.2] (with illustr.));—abs. ׳שׁוֹ 2 S 6[15]+, ׳שׁ Ex 19[16]+; cstr. שׁוֹפַר Lv 25[9]; pl שׁוֹפָרוֹת Ju 7[22]+, cstr. שׁוֹפְרוֹת Jos 6[4]+; sf שׁוֹפְרֹתֵיהֶם Ju 7[8],—*horn*, mostly as used in war, rarely, and chiefly late, as sacred instr.: Ho 8[1] Ju 7[8.16] Is 58[1] (sim.) Jb 39[25] (׳בְּדֵי שׁ, v. דַּי **2 a**); ׳שׁ (הַ)יּוֹבְלִים Jos 6[4] *rams' horns* (v. יבל), so v[6.8.13] (all E); קוֹל (הַ)שׁ׳ Ex 19[16 19] 20[18] (Gi v[15]), Jos 6[5.20] (all E), Am 2[2] + 13 t.; ׳תָּקַע בַּשׁ = *give a blast with the horn*, Ju 3[27] 6[34] Jos 6[4] + 9 t. Jos, 1 S 13[3] 1 K 1[34.39] + 9 t., + (׳י subj.) Zc 9[14]; ׳תָּקַע שׁ Ho 5[8] Am 3[6] (vb Niph), Je 4[5] + 7 t, + תִּקְעוּ הַשׁ׳ Jos 6[9] Qr (Kt תָּקְעוּ); cf. הַשׁ׳ לִתְקוֹעַ Ju 7[20], ׳בתקע שׁ ψ 150[3]; also הֶעֱבִיר שׁ׳ תְּרוּעָה Lv 25[9a] (H), cf v[9b] (P), יוֹם שׁ׳ וּתְרוּעָה Zp 1[16]; used on religious occasions, Jos 6[4ff.] Lv 25[9] Jo 2[1 15] ψ 47[6] 81[4] 98[6] 150[3] 2 Ch 15[14].—On ׳שׁ v. Adler[The Shophar (1894)] Dr[Am 2.2] Hpt[We ψ Transl. 221 f.] Abrahams[Hast DB TRUMPET].

† [שַׁפְרוּר Kt, שַׁפְרִיר Qr] n.[m.] doubtful, Thes *splendour* (√ שׁפר; Dl[Prol. 126] cp. As. vb. *šuparruru, spread out* (Id[HWB 684])); appar. of (*brightly-coloured?*) royal *pavilion, canopy*, or poss. *carpet*, sf. נָטָה שפרורו Je 43[10] (Qr שַׁפְרִירוֹ).

[שָׁפָה], אַשְׁפֹּת, מִשְׁפְּתַיִם v. II. שׁפה

†II שְׁפַתַּיִם n.[m.] du. doubtful word: usu hook-shaped pegs, hooks, so 𝔗 Thes AV RV, abs 'וְהַשׁ Ez 40[43], < 𝔊 𝔙 Co וּשְׂפָתָם and their edge, so Aq Theod Symm and prob 𝔊, cf. Hi-Sm, and Krae (וּשׂפת).—I 'שׁ v. √שׁפה.

שֶׁצֶף v. שֶׁטֶף sub שׁטף

†שָׁקַד vb. watch, wake (Ph שקד be circumspect, NH שָׁקַד be insistent; 𝔗 שְׁקַד = BH),—**Qal** *Pf* 3 ms 'שׁ ψ 127[1], שָׁקַדְתִּי Je 31[28] ψ 102[8], *Impf* 3 ms יִשְׁקוֹד Jb 21[32] (Me Bu יִשְׁקְדוּ), וַיִּשְׁקֹד Dn 9[14], 1 s. אֶשְׁקֹד Je 31[28], *Imv* mpl שִׁקְדוּ Ezr 8[29], *Inf cstr.* לִשְׁקֹד Pr 8[34]; *Pt. act* שֹׁקֵד Je 1[12]+; pl cstr שֹׁקְדֵי Is 29[20],—**1.** *keep watch of, be wakeful over*, 'י subj, עַל pers, to benefit or injure Je 31[28.28] 44[27], עַל rei, to perform it 1[12] Dn 9[14], so (men subj) שֹׁקְדֵי אָוֶן Is 29[20], of leopard *watching* עַל־עָרֵיהֶם Je 5[6] (to seize prey, fig), of man *watching* (for admission) at (עַל) wisdom's doors Pr 8[34] (‖ שָׁמַר), = *keep guard* over (עַל) Jb 21[32], cf (abs) 'שׁ וְשִׁמְרוּ Ezr 8[29], and (of watchman, ‖ שׁמר) ψ 127[1]. **2.** *be wakeful, wake*, as mourner, sufferer ψ 102[8] — La 1[14] rd. perh **Niph.** *Pf.* נִשְׁקַד עַל־פְּשָׁעַי (𝔊 Bu) *watch has been kept over my transgressions* (cf. **1** supra), for MT 'נִשְׂקַד עֹל פ.—**Pu.** denom v. infra

†שָׁקֵד n.[m.] almond(-tree) (NH *id.*; so called from its early *waking* out of winter's sleep, acc to Ki Thes Lag[BN 45] al; Aram שִׁגְדָּא, شُغْدٌ, شُغْدانٌ, whence Eth. ሰገድ: cf No[M 39], cf Löw[No 319]),—**1.** *almond*, i e the nut, pl שְׁקֵדִים Gn 43[11] (J, + בָּטְנִים, etc.), Nu 17[23] (P) **2.** *almond-tree* Je 1[11] and (prob) Ec 12[5].

†[שָׁקַד] vb **Pu. denom.**—only *Pt.* pl in גְּבִעִים מְשֻׁקָּדִים *cups shaped like almond* (blossoms) Ex 25[33.33.34] 37[19.19.20] (all P).

†[שָׁקָה] vb. **Hiph.** cause to drink water, give to drink (NH Hiph *id*, Ar سَقَى *give to drink*, Sab סקי *be irrigated* Fell[ZMG liv (1900) 246], מסקי *drinks* Hom[Chr 121], מסתקין *id* DHM[Holmus, No 117], Eth ሰቀየ: *water, irrigate*; As *šakû* I. = Heb. Hiph, Aram אַשְׁקֵי, ܐܫܩܝ Aph),—for **Qal** v II שָׁתָה,—*Pf* 3 ms consec. וְהִשְׁקָה Gn 2[6]+, sf. וְהִשְׁקָהּ Nu 5[27], 2 ms consec. וְהִשְׁקִיתָ Nu 20[8]+, 1 s. consec. וְהִשְׁקֵיתִי Ez 32[6], etc.; *Impf.* 3 ms יַשְׁקֶה Nu 5[26], וַיַּשְׁקְ Gn 29[10]+, etc, *Imv.* ms. sf. הַשְׁקֵהוּ Pr 25[21]; fs. sf. הַשְׁקִינִי Gn 24[43]+; *Inf. cstr.* הַשְׁקוֹת Gn 2[10]+, sf. הַשְׁקֹתוֹ 24[19], *Pt* מַשְׁקֶה ψ 104[13], cstr. Hb 2[15] (v. also I., II. מַשְׁקֶה),—**1.** *water, irrigate*, ground: subj. mist Gn 2[6], river v[10] (both J), spring Jo 4[18]; subj 'י Is 27[3] (כֶּרֶם), Ez 17[7] (גֶּפֶן), both in fig, fig. also 32[6] *water land* מִדָּם, lit. c. מִן of source ψ 104[13] (הָרִים) and (subj man) Ec 2[6] (יַעַר) **2.** *water, give drink to*, usu. human subj, acc of beast, Gn 24[14.46.46] 29[2] (מִן of source), v[3.7.8.10] Ex 2[16.17.19] (all J), ψ 104[11] (subj springs); acc. pers. Gn 21[19] (E), 24[18.19.45] (J), Hb 2[15] (fig), Is 43[20] ('י subj.), ψ 78[15] (*id*), 2 Ch 28[15], c ב of vessel Est 1[7], c acc. pers et animal. Nu 20[8] (P); *give* one something *to drink*, acc pers. + rei (water, wine, etc), Am 2[12] Gn 19[32.33.34.35] 24[43] (all J), Ju 4[19] 1 S 30[11] 2 S 23[15] = 1 Ch 11[18], Jb 22[7], cf. Ct 8[2] (מִיַּיִן), fig Je 8[14] 9[14] 16[7] 23[15] 25[15] ψ 69[22], cf וְנַחַל עֲדָנֶיךָ תַשְׁקֵם 36[9], and וַתַּשְׁקֵמוֹ בִּדְמָעוֹת 80[6]; acc. rei om, lit. Ju 4[19] Ex 32[20] (E), fig Je 25[17].—Vid. also I מַשְׁקֶה infra **Pu.** *Impf* 3 ms וּמֹחַ עַצְמוֹתָיו יְשֻׁקֶּה Jb 21[24] *the marrow of his bones is watered*, (refreshed, invigorated)—נשקה Am 8[8] v. שׁקע.

†שִׁקּוּי n.[m.] drink (Ba[§ 102 d]),—'שׁ לְעַצְמוֹתֶיךָ Pr 3[8] *drink* (fig for refreshment) *to thy bones* (cf. vb **Pu.**), pl sf. שִׁקּוּיַי (Ol[§ 186 b]) ψ 102[10] (+ לֶחֶם v[5]), שִׁקּוּיָי Ho 2[7].

†שֹׁקֶת, [שֶׁקֶת] n. f. watering-trough (Ges[§ 95 f] Ba[ZMG xli (1887), 605], Ar. سَاقِيَةٌ *irrigating canal*, سِقَايَةٌ *watering-place, drinking vessel*);—abs. 'הַשֹּׁ Gn 24[20] (J), pl cstr. שִׁקֲתוֹת הַמָּיִם 30[38] (J)

†I מַשְׁקֶה n.m. butler, cup-bearer (prop. *Pt* **Hiph.** = *one giving drink*),—abs 'מ Gn 40[5] (E), Ne 1[11], cstr. מַשְׁקֵה Gn 40[1], sf מַשְׁקֵהוּ v[13], pl. מַשְׁקִים v[2.9.20.21.23] 41[9] (all E), sf מַשְׁקָיו 1 K 10[5] = 2 Ch 9[4] (> II. 'מ).

†II מַשְׁקֶה n.m.[Lv 11 34] irrigation, drink,—abs 'מ Gn 13[10] Lv 11[34], cstr מַשְׁקֵה 1 K 10[21] + 3 t, sf מַשְׁקֵהוּ Gn 40[21],—**1.** *irrigation* Gn 13[10] (J, abstr. for concrete, =) *well-irrigated*, of land; Ez 45[15] (< 𝔊 Co Siegf Berthol Toy Krae מִשְׁפְּחוֹת, Gr מקנה) **2.** *drink* Is 32[6] Lv 11[34]; 'כְּלֵי מ *drinking-vessels* 1 K 10[21] = 2 Ch 9[20]. **3.** = office of butler, *butlership* Gn 40[21] (E).

†שָׁקַט vb. be quiet, undisturbed (𝔗 שקט (rare), NH שׁקט is *sink down*; Ar. سَقَطَ is *drop down*);—**Qal** *Pf* 3 ms. consec. 'וְשׁ

Je 30[10] 46[27], 3 fs. שָׁקְטָה Jos 11[23]+, 2 K 11[20]+; 1 s. שָׁקַטְתִּי Jb 3[26], וְשָׁקַטְתִּי Ez 16[42]; *Impf.* 3 ms. יִשְׁקֹט Ru 3[18]; 2 fs. תִּשְׁקֳטִי Je 47[6.7]; 1 s. אֶשְׁקוֹט Is 62[1] Jb 3[13], אשקוטה Is 18[4] Kt, Qr אֶשְׁקֳטָה (Ges[§ 10 h, 48 c]), *Pt.* שֹׁקֵט Ju 18[7]+, fs. שֹׁקֶטֶת 1 Ch 4[40], שֹׁקָטֶת Zc 1[11]; pl. הַשֹּׁקְטִים Ez 38[11];—*be quiet, undisturbed:* **1.** of land, *at peace*, abs. Ju 3[11.30] 5[31] 8[28] Is 14[7] (+נָחָה), 2 Ch 13[23]; +מִמִּלְחָמָה Jos 11[23] 14[15] (D?), cf. v[8] (P); ושׁ׳ ושׁלֵוָה 1 Ch 4[40]; of earth, ישֶׁבֶת ושׁ׳ Zc 1[11]; abs. of city 2 K 11[20]=2 Ch 23[21], kingdom 2 Ch 20[30], +לִפְנֵי pers. 14[4], of people, שׁ׳ ובטח *in peace and security* Ju 18[7.27], הַשֹּׁקְטִים ישְׁבֵי לָבֶטַח Ez 38[11]; שַׁאֲנַן ... וְשָׁקַט+ Je 30[10]=46[27], of Moab, אֶל־שְׁמָרָיו 48[11] *undisturbed upon its lees* (fig. of wine); of Job, *quiet* in death Jb 3[13], *be at rest* (from apprehensions of evil) v[26] (+שָׁלַוְתִּי, נַחְתִּי) **2.** *be quiet, inactive:* of י׳+וְאַבִּיטָה Is 18[4] *I will be quiet and gaze*, i.e. gaze as an inactive spectator, ψ 83[2] (‖ חרשׁ, דמה *be silent*); =be pacified Ez 16[42]; of sword of י׳ Je 47[6.7]; of Boaz Ru 3[18] *he will not be quiet* until he has finished the matter; of prophet Is 62[1] (‖ חָשָׁה *be silent*). **Hiph.** *Impf.* 3 ms. יַשְׁקִיט Pr 15[18], יַשְׁקִט Jb 34[29]; *Imv.* ms הַשְׁקֵט Is 7[4], *Inf abs* הַשְׁקֵט Is 32[17]+; cstr. הַשְׁקִיט ψ 94[13], -קֵט Jb 37[17], -קֵט Is 57[20] Je 49[23];—**1.** *shew quietness* (inner causat.), of men Is 7[4] (+אַל־תִּירָא), of sea Is 57[20]=Je 49[23], earth Jb 37[17] (+מִדָּרוֹם); hence *Inf. abs* =subst., *quietness, display of quietness* Is 30[15], עֲבֹדַת הַצְּדָקָה הַשְׁקֵט וָבֶטַח 32[17] *the product of righteousness is quietness and security* (Du Che[Hpt] Marti del הַשׁ׳ as dittogr. from v[a], read הַמִּשְׁפָּט for הַשְׁקֵט, and del. וְ: *the product of justice is security*); (*presumptuous*) *security*, שַׁלְוַת הַשְׁקֵט Ez 16[49] (of Sodom). **2.** *cause quietness:* subj. י׳ Jb 34[29], לְהַשְׁקִיט לוֹ מִימֵי רָע ψ 94[13]; *pacify, allay*, obj. רִיב Pr 15[18].

†שֶׁקֶט n.[m.] quietness;—1 Ch 22[9] (+שָׁלוֹם).

†שָׁקַל vb. weigh (NH *id.*; Ar. ثَقُلَ *be heavy*, ثِقْل *heaviness, weight*, ثَقَل *load*, OAram. תקל *weigh*, Aram. תְּקַל, ܬܩܠ (*weigh*), *pay*, תִּקְלָא *shekel*, but also (OAram. Zinj.) שׁקל, שְׁקַל Lzb[372]; ܫܩܠ *lift up;* As. *šakâlu, weigh, šiklu* (appar.) =שֶׁקֶל; Eth. ሰቀለ: *hang up, weigh;* Ph. משקל *weight;* cf. Fra[202], also Gk. σίγλος (𝔊 σίκλος), Lag[M ii 357] Lewy[Fremdw 118 f];—on connex. of mngs. cf. *weigh* trans and intrans. = Germ. *wagen, wiegen*, also *heave, heavy, heft* (=*weight*, obs. or colloq.));—**Qal** *Pf* 3 ms. שׁ׳ 2 S 14[26] Is 40[12]; *Impf.* 3 ms. יִשְׁקֹל Ex 22[16], sf. יִשְׁקְלֵנִי Jb 31[6], etc.; *Inf abs.* שָׁקוֹל Jb 6[2]; cstr. לִשְׁקוֹל Est 4[7]; *Pt. act.* שֹׁקֵל Is 33[18], 2 S 18[12] read perhaps *pass* שָׁקֻל, v. infra;—**1.** *weigh*, human subj, acc. rei 2 S 14[26] Is 46[6] (בְּ of scale); fig., י׳ subj. Is 40[12], also (acc. pers) Jb 31[6] (both c בְּ of scale); cf Inf abs. sub **Niph.**; *weigh* precious metals intrusted to one, לְ pers. Ezr 8[25], עַל־יָדָם v[26], acc. rei om. v[29] (לִפְנֵי of superior) **2.** *weigh out* a price (i e. pay)· acc of silver Ex 22[16] (E), 1 K 20[39] Zc 11[12] Je 32[10] (בְּ of scale), Is 55[2] (c. בְּ, *in exchange for*); +לְ pers. Je 32[9] Gn 23[16] (P), +עַל־כַּפִּי 2 S 18[12] (read perhaps שָׁקֻל, so We Kit[Kau] Bu Buhl), עַל־יְדֵי פ׳ Est 3[9], עַל־גִּנְזֵי הַמֶּלֶךְ 4[7] **Niph.** *be weighed:* **1.** *Pf.* 3 ms. נִשְׁקַל, subj. rei Ezr 8[33] (pass. of Qal v[25 f]); *Impf.* 3 ms. fig (+**Qal** *Inf. abs*), לוּ שָׁקוֹל יִשָּׁקֵל כַּעְשִׂי Jb 6[2]. **2.** *be weighed out*, as price, 28[15]

שֶׁקֶל[87] n.m. [Lv 27 6] a weight, shekel (orig.=*weight;* late Heb =*coin* GACooke[Inscr 356]);—abs שׁ׳ Am 8[5]+, שָׁקֶל Ex 38[29]+; pl. שְׁקָלִים Jos 7[21]+; cstr. שִׁקְלֵי 1 Ch 21[25];—*shekel*, as standard weight Am 8[5]; of weight of bronze armour 1 S 17[5], iron spear-head v[7], +2 S 21[16b] (v. מִשְׁקָל), hair 2 S 14[26], food Ez 4[10], implying value, of wedge of gold Jos 7[21] (JE); of nails in temple (gold) 2 Ch 3[9], usu. a definite weight of silver (used in payment or valuation) Ex 21[32] (E), Jos 7[21] (JE), 1 S 9[8] 2 S 24[24] 2 K 7[1.1.16.16.18.18] 15[20] Je 32[9] Ez 45[12.12] (v. infra), and (=coin, fr time of Darius I) Ne 5[15] 10[33] Lv 5[15] 27[3.4.5.6] (all P), +53 t. P; also מַחֲצִית הַשׁ׳ Ex 30[13.13.15] 38[26] (=בֶּקַע), all *half-shekel*, atonement-money; cf. שְׁלִישִׁית הַשׁ׳ Ne 10[33] *one-third;* also רֶבַע שׁ׳ 1 S 9[8] *one-fourth of shekel;* שׁ׳=20 גֵּרָה (ג׳ otherwise unknown) Ez 45[12] Ex 30[13] Lv 27[25] Nu 3[47]; 50 שׁ׳ =one maneh Ez 45[12] (read וַחֲמִשִּׁים for וחמשׁה [and עֲשָׂרָה for עֶשְׂרִים preceding], 𝔊[A] Boeckh Hi-Sm Co Toy Da Krae Berthol); שׁ׳ הַקֹּדֶשׁ Ex 30[13.24] Lv 5[15] Nu 3[47.50] 7[13]+21 t. P; land estimated in שׁ׳ of gold 1 Ch 21[25], שׁ׳ also often om. after num.—שׁ׳ was of two standards, one one-half the other; actual weights (and values) varied, but most persistent were: (1) gold, 252$\frac{2}{3}$ gr. Troy (or 126$\frac{1}{3}$), mod. equiv. c. £2 1s, or $10; (2) silver, 224$\frac{1}{2}$ gr. (nearly $\frac{1}{2}$ oz.)=שׁ׳ הַקֹּדֶשׁ (v. supra), or 112$\frac{1}{4}$, mod. equiv. c. 2s 9d., or 67 c.; שׁ׳ בְּאֶבֶן הַמֶּלֶךְ 2 S 14[26] is dub.; if late (Bu HPS Lohr Now) it prob. ref. to a Bab. or Pers. scale

(cf. S-C [Pap] באבני מלכא oft.), 60 (or 50) ש׳=1 mina, 60 minas=1 talent (v כִּכָּר, מָנֶה) Vid esp. ARSKennedy [Hast DB WEIGHTS AND MEASURES, and MONEY].

†מִשְׁקוֹל n.[m.] heaviness, weight,—במ׳ Ez 4[10] *by weight*.

מִשְׁקָל, מִשְׁקָל n.m. id,—abs מ׳ 1 K 25[16]+, cstr. מִשְׁקַל Ju 8[26]+; sf מִשְׁקָלוֹ Gn 24[22]+, etc,—*weight* Gn 24[22.22] (J), Jos 7[21] (JE), Ju 8[26] 1 S 17[5] 2 S 12[30] 21[16a] (v[16b] read שֶׁקֶל with 𝔊 [v. esp 𝔊L] We Dr and mod), 1 K 7[47] 10[14] Nu 7[13]+11 t Nu 7 (P), 7 t Chr, of wind Jb 28[25], במשקלו Gn 43[21] (J) *in its* (full) *weight*, cf מאוני מ׳ Ez 5[1]; בַּמ׳ *by weight* Lv 26[26] 1 Ch 28[14a.15], בּמ׳ *id*. Ez 4[16] (of bread), Ezr 8[34] 1 Ch 28[14b.15.15.17.17], בַּמ׳ Lv 19[35] *in respect to weight*, cf. מ׳ 1 Ch 28[16] *as to weight, in weight*; לֹא־הָיָה מ׳ (i e there was too much to be weighed) 2 K 25[16]=Je 52[20], אין מ׳ 1 Ch 22[3.14].

†[מִשְׁקֹלֶת], מִשְׁקֶלֶת n.f. levelling instrument, level (for horizontal accuracy);—abs מִשְׁקָלֶת Is 28[17] (fig of צְדָקָה, ‖ קַו); cstr -קֶלֶת, fig, מ׳ בית אַחְאָב 2 K 21[13].

†[שִׁקְמָה] n.f. sycomore tree (NH *id*, Aram. שִׁקְמָא, ܫܩܡܬܐ, Low [No 356], hence Gk. συκάμινος, *mulberry* Lewy [Fremdw 23]),—pl abs. שִׁקְמִים Am 7[14]+, sf שִׁקְמוֹתָם ψ 78[47],—*sycomore, ficus sycomorus* Linn (Tristr [NHB 397 ff] Post [Flora of Syria 730] Hast DB s.v.) a common tree Is 9[9], growing in the Shephela 1 K 10[27]=2 Ch 1[15]=9[27], 1 Ch 27[28], as property ψ 78[47] (‖ גֶּפֶן), בּוֹלֵס שִׁקְמִים Am 7[14] *a tender of sycomores* (v. [בָּלַס])

[שָׁקַע] vb. sink, sink down (so NH שָׁקַע, Aram שְׁקַע, Ar has سُقِعَ *be smitten, prostrated, collapse*),—**Qal** *Pf.* 3 fs consec. וְשָׁקְעָה Am 9[5] *it shall sink* like the Nile (of land, opp עָלָה), 3 fs ותִּשְׁקַע Nu 11[2] (JE), of fire, *it sank down*, died out, תִּשְׁקַע Je 51[64], of Babylon (like stone in water, opp קוּם) **Niph.** 3 fs. נִשְׁקְעָה Am 8[8] Qr, of land, *sink* (opp עָלָה, =**Qal** 9[5]; Kt erron נשקה, cf. W [SG 257]) **Hiph.** *Impf.* 1 s. אַשְׁקִיעַ מֵימֵיהֶם Ez 32[14] *I will make their waters sink* (settle, grow clear); 2 ms וּבְחֶבֶל תַּשְׁקִיעַ לְשֹׁנוֹ Jb 40[25] *with a cord wilt thou make* his tongue *sink* (? pull or press it down, of crocodile; Mich [Suppl 2349], cited Thes [1477], cp. Sam. ▽Pw= חבש *bind*)

[מִשְׁקָע] n.[m.] what is settled, clarified (cf √ **Hiph.**),—cstr מִשְׁקַע־מַיִם תשתו Ez 34[18] *the clear* (of) *water* ye drink (cf. 32[14] supra)

[שְׁקַעֲרוּרָה] v. קער.

†I. [שָׁקַף] vb. Niph. Hiph. overhang, look out and down (NH Niph. Hiph =BH; cf. Aram שְׁקִיפָא, ܡܫܩܦܐ *rocky pinnacle, rock*, Ar سَقْف *ceiling, roof, sky* (on connex. of mngs. cf. Ar. أَشْرَفَ *overtop, overlook*, from شَرُفَ *be high*, اِطَّلَعَ *look down upon*, from طَلَعَ *rise*));—**Niph.** *Pf* 3 fs. נִשְׁקָפָה Ju 5[28]+, וְנִשְׁקָפָה Nu 21[20] (read prob pt הַנִּשְׁקָפָה, cf 23[28], GBG), 1 s. נשקפתי Pr 7[6]; *Pt* נִשְׁקָף Nu 23[28] 1 S 13[18] ψ 85[12]; f. נִשְׁקָפָה Ct 6[10],—*lean over* (and look), *look down*, c בְּעַד of window, *through* Ju 5[28] 1 S 2[16]=1 Ch 15[29], Pr 7[6]; abs. *look down, forth* Ct 6[10]; c. מִן of direction whence Je 6[1] ψ 85[12] (both fig); of mt. *lean over upon* (עַל־פְּנֵי), *overhang* Nu 21[20] 23[28] 1 S 13[18] (read הַגֶּבַע for הגבול We Dr HPS al) **Hiph.** *Pf.* 3 ms. הִשְׁקִיף ψ 14[2]+, *Impf.* 3 ms. יַשְׁקִיף La 3[50], וַיַּשְׁקֵף Gn 19[28]+, etc; *Imv.* ms. cohort. הַשְׁקִיפָה Dt 26[15];—*look down* (=**Niph.**): c. בְּעַד of window Gn 26[8] (J), 2 K 9[30], c אֶל pers v[32]; *look down* upon, עַל־פְּנֵי, subj pers Gn 18[16] 19[28] (both J), abs וַיַּשְׁ׳ וַיַּרְא 2 S 24[20] (וַיַּבֵּט in ‖ 1 Ch 21[21]), esp subj י׳, c. אֶל loc Ex 14[24] (J), c מִן loc Dt 26[15] ψ 102[20], +עַל pers 14[2]=53[3], +וְיֵרֶא La 3[50].

II. שׁקף (√of foll., cf Aram. שְׁקַף, ܫܩܦ *strike*, whence foll as that against which the door *strikes*, v Fra [20], Ar سَقَفَ *to ceil* or *roof*, سَقْف *ceiling, roof*)

†[שֶׁקֶף] n.[m.] frame-work, casing of doors (cf. NH שָׁקוֹף *lintel*, Aram שְׁקָפָא, שְׁקוֹף *threshold*);—שָׁקֶף 1 K 7[5].

†[שְׁקוּף, שָׁקוּף] n.m. [1 K 6.4] frame, casing of windows,—pl חַלּוֹנֵי שְׁקֻפִים 1 K 6[4] *windows of narrowing frames*, so read also, inserting ש׳, Ez 41[16] (Co Toy; > Krae Berthol read ש׳ for שחיף v[b]), ש׳ alone 1 K 7[4].

†מַשְׁקוֹף n.[m.] prob. lintel of door;—הַמ׳ Ex 12[7] (P), v[22.23] (J)

שׁקץ (√of foll., cf. As *šiksu*, appar. a (skin-?) disease, NH Pi שִׁקֵּץ, Aram Pa שַׁקֵּץ *detest*, are denom.; RS [J Phil. xvi 71 ff] conj original meaning *let fall, throw away*, cf. Ar. سَقَطَ *fall, drop down*, but very dubious)

†שֶׁקֶץ n. m. [Lv 7.21] detestation, detestable thing,—ש׳ of the ceremonially unclean Lv 7[21];

creatures forbidden as food: water animals without fins or scales 11[10 11 12], birds of prey, etc., v[13], winged creeping things v[20.23], creeping vermin v[41 42] (all P), cf. Is 66[17] (+ בְּשַׂר הַחֲזִיר, הָעַכְבָּר); v. RS[Sem. i. 275, 2nd ed. 293, K 309 f 2nd ed. 311 f.].—Ez 8[10] read prob. שקוצים, v. שִׁקּוּץ.

†[שִׁקֵּץ] **vb. Pi. denom.** detest, make detestable;—*Pf.* 3 ms. שִׁקַּץ ψ 22[25], *Impf.* 2 mpl. תְּשַׁקְּצוּ Lv 11[13]+, etc.; *Inf. abs* שַׁקֵּץ Dt 7[26];— **1.** *detest*, c. acc. rei Dt 7[26] (Impf. + Inf. abs.; ‖ תַּעֵב תְּתַעֲבֶנּוּ), Lv 11[11 13] (P), ‖ בָּזָה ψ 22[25]. **2.** *make detestable*, obj. נַפְשֹׁתֵיכֶם (= reflex) Lv 11[43] (P), 20[25] (H).

†שִׁקּוּץ, שִׁקֻּץ **n.m.**[Dn 11. 31] detested thing;— abs שִׁקּוּץ Dn 11[31] 12[11], cstr. שִׁקֻּץ 1 K 11[5]+; pl. שִׁקּוּצִים 2 Ch 15[8], שִׁקֻּצִים 2 K 23[24]; cstr. שִׁקּוּצֵי Ez 20[7.8], sf. שִׁקּוּצֵיהֶם Je 16[18]+, etc.;—*detested thing*, epith. of Isr. Ho 9[10] (si vera l.; not elsewhere bef. Dt); of filth Na 3[6], appar. of unclean food Zc 9[7] (as שֶׁקֶץ); of idols (so usu; oft. ‖ תּוֹעֵבָה, גִּלּוּל, etc.), Dt 29[16] 2 K 23[24] Je 4[1] 7[30] = 32[34], 13[27] 16[18] Ez 5[11] 7[20] 11[18.21] 20[7.8.30] 37[23], of idolatrous practices Dn 9[27], but rd. prob. as 11[31] (so 𝔊 Θ), and כַּנּוֹ for כנף (v. Dr); שׁ׳ (מְ)שֹׁמֵם 11[31] 12[11] *detested thing causing horror* is the heathen altar erected in temple by Ant. Epiph., with (prob.) a statue of Zeus Olympios = (Ph.) בעלשמם *lord of heaven;* the prophet puts שקוץ for בעל, and (מְ)שֹׁמֵם for שָׁמַיִם; cf. Nes[ZAW iv (1884), 248] Che[OP 105] Dr[Dn].

†[שָׁקַק] **vb.** run, run about, rush (appar. akin to √I. שׁוּק, whence שׁוֹק),—**Qal** *Impf.* 3 mpl. בָּעִיר יָשֹׁקּוּ Jo 2[9], of locusts (‖ יְרֻצוּן; > Gr prop. יָסֹקּוּ from סלק); *Pt* שֹׁקֵק Is 33[4], c. בּ rei *rush at, upon* (like locusts), of *roving, ranging* bear Pr 28[15] (unless we read שֹׁקֵל, Toy), fig. of נֶפֶשׁ *longing* for water Is 29[8] (‖ עָיֵף and, v[8], רֵקָה), ψ 107[9] (‖ רְעֵבָה). **Hithpalp.** *Impf.* 3 mpl. יִשְׁתַּקְשְׁקוּן Na 2[5], of chariots, *they rush to and fro.*

†[מַשָּׁק] **n.[m.]** running, rushing;—cstr. מַשַּׁק Is 33[4], of locusts.

שקר (√of following; *deceive;* Aram. שְׁקַר *deceive*, also n. *deceit*, ܫܩܪ Pa. *deceive*, and deriv.; As *taškirtu* [Dl -*gir*-] *a lie*, so NH שֶׁקֶר, Ar سَقَرَ and شَقَرَ (loan-word?))

שֶׁקֶר[113] **n.m.** deception, disappointment, falsehood;—שׁ׳ Ex 23[7] + 64 t.; שָׁקֶר Ex 5[9] + 42 t.; pl. שְׁקָרִים ψ 101[7] + 3 t; sf שִׁקְרֵיהֶם Je 23[32];—**1.** *deception*, what deceives, disappoints, and betrays one: a molten image Je 10[14] = 51[17]; gift Pr 25[14]; grace of person 31[30], etc; אֹרַח שׁ׳ ψ 119[104 128], דֶּרֶךְ שׁ׳ v[29]; בטח בשׁ׳ Je 13[25]; נחל שׁ׳ 16[19], cf. also ψ 7[15] 33[17] 119[118] Is 28[15]; לַשֶּׁקֶר *for disappointment, in vain* 1 S 25[21] Je 3[23]. **2.** *deceit, fraud, wrong:* עשה (ל)שׁ׳ *do* or *practise fraud, wrong* Ho 7[1] Je 6[13] 8[8.10]; c. בְּ, 2 S 18[13]; פְּעֻלַּת שׁ׳ Pr 11[18], לֶחֶם שׁ׳ Pr 20[17] *food got by fraud;* זֶרַע שׁ׳ Is 57[4]; עַם שׁ׳ Je 8[5]; ילד שׁ׳ ψ 7[15] (‖ עמל); דרך לשׁן קשׁת שׁ׳ Je 9[2]; בְּשׁ׳ 3[10] (‖ בגד), adv. שקר *fraudulently, wrongfully* ψ 35[19] 38[20] 69[5] 119[78.86]. **3.** injurious *falsehood*, in testimony, esp. in courts: עֵד שֶׁקֶר Ex 20[16] (E) Dt 19[18] ψ 27[12] Pr 6[19] 14[5] 25[18]; עד שקרים 12[17] 19[5.9]; ענה שׁ׳ Dt 19[18] *testify falsehood;* שְׁבֻעַת שׁ׳ Zc 8[17] *false oath;* נשׁבע לשׁ׳ *swear falsely* Je 5[2] + 5 t; נשׁבע על שׁ׳ Lv 5[22]; דבר שׁ׳ Mi 6[12] + (v. [דָּבַר], דָּבָר); אִמְרֵי שׁ׳ Is 32[7]; שפת(י) שׁ׳ ψ 31[19] 120[2] Pr 10[18] 17[7], מַטְפֵל שׁ׳ Jb 13[4] ψ 119[69], cf. v[163], abs. *false!* 2 K 9[12] Je 37[14]. **4.** *falsity*, of false or self-deceived *prophets:* נבא שׁ׳ *prophesy falsely* Je 14[14] 23[25.26] 29[21], + לְ pers 27[10 14 16]; נ׳ לשׁ׳ v[15]; נ׳ בשׁ׳ 5[31] 20[6] 29[9]; מוֹרֶה שׁ׳ Is 9[14] Hb 2[18]; חזה שׁ׳ Zc 10[2]; חֲזוֹן שׁ׳ Je 14[14], etc., (+ 12 t.); רוּחַ שׁ׳ v. p. 925[b]. **5.** *lie, falsehood*, in gen: דבר שׁ׳ ψ 101[7] (‖ רְמִיָּה), דְּבַר שׁ׳ Pr 13[5], of מלים Jb 36[4]; לשׁון שׁ׳ *false tongue* Pr 6[17] 12[19] 21[6] 26[28] ψ 109[2]; of lips Pr 12[22]; אישׁ שׁ׳ 17[4] *liar.*

†[שָׁקַר] **vb. denom.** do or deal falsely;— **Qal** *Impf.* 2 ms. תִּשְׁקֹר Gn 21[23] *thou wilt not do falsely* to me (לִי). **Pi.** *Pf* 1 pl. שִׁקַּרְנוּ ψ 44[18]; *Impf* 3 ms. יְשַׁקֵּר 1 S 15[29]; 3 mpl. יְשַׁקְּרוּ Is 63[8], etc;—*deal falsely* 1 S 15[29] Is 63[8], c. בּ pers. Lv 19[11] (‖ כחשׁ); c. בּ rei ψ 44[18] 89[34].

שִׁקְּתוֹת, שֹׁקֶת v. שׁקה. שֹׁר v שׁרר.

שַׁרְאֶצֶר **n.pr.m.** v. שַׂרְאֶצֶר.

שרב (√of foll., *parch;* NH שָׁרַב *be scorched* (by sun), שָׁרָב *parching heat* (of sun); Ecclus 43[22] דשׁן שרב *parched grass;* Aram. שָׁרִיב, שְׁרַב, ܫܪܒ, *be parched,* שָׁרָב *heat, drought:* cf. prob also As. n.pr. div. *Šarrabu* (-*pu*) Zim[KAT 3. 412]; > cp. Ar. سَرَابٌ *mirage* [Rob[BR i 42]] Ges[Is 35. 7] al, see against this esp. Che[Introd. Is. 269])

†שָׁרָב **n.m.** **1.** burning heat; **2.** parched ground,—only abs.: וְלֹא יַכֵּם שׁ׳ וָשָׁמֶשׁ Is 49[10]; of ground, הַשּׁ׳ Is 35[7] (‖ צִמָּאוֹן).

†שֵׁרֵבְיָה **n.pr.m.** a Levite with Ezra (י׳

hath sent burning heat, or cp Syr ܫܪܒ Pa. *propagavit*),—Σαραβια(ς). Ezr 8[18.24] Ne 8[7] 9[4.5] 10[13] 12[8.24]

שַׁרְבִּיט v. שׁבט.

I [שָׁרָה] **vb. let loose** (NH *id*, *dissolve*, As *šarû*, Pi *open* (building, for use), *dedicate it*; *tašrîtu*, *dedication*; OAram שרה *loose*, so Aram. שְׁרָא, ܫܪܐ, Eth ሰረየ: *remit, condone*),—**Qal** *Impf.* 3 ms sf. יִשְׁרֵהוּ Jb 37[3] *he* (God) *lets it loose* (i e the thunder) **Pi.** *Pf* 1 s. sf שֵׁרִיתִךָ Je 15[11] Qr *I will set thee free* (cf. 40[4] 𝔗 𝔖), but dub, Kt שרותך (i e. שֵׁרוֹתִךָ, √שׁרר), Thes Gie *I vex thee* [שָׁרַר=צָרַר, very dub], Ew al RV *strengthen thee*, this yields best sense, but as Aram. שׁרר is intrans, read then שֵׁרַרְתִּךָ or הִשְׁרוֹתִךָ, Di, Jerome Rabb rd. שׁאריתך=שריתך *thy remnant* (AV)

II שׁרה (√of foll.; cf Ar. ثَرِىَ *be moist*, Aram שְׁרָא, תְּרָא, ܬܪܐ *id*; ܡܫܪܬܐ *grape-juice*, NH שָׁרָא *soften, dissolve*; whence foll. prop.=*moisture* (Di[Nu] Dr[§178] Paterson[Nu Hpt] Gray[Nu]), and so As *mešru, succulence* (Hpt[Paterson Nu])).

†[מִשְׁרָה] **n.f.** juice,—cstr. מִשְׁרַת עֲנָבִים Nu 6[3] (P) *the juice of grapes* (+ יַיִן, שֵׁכָר).

III. שׁרה (√of following, cf Ar سِرْوَةٌ, سِرْيَةٌ *short dart*).

†שִׁרְיָה **n.f** a weapon, perhaps lance, javelin;—ש׳ Jb 41[18] (+ חֶרֶב, חֲנִית, מַסָּע),—yet 𝔊 θώρακα, 𝔙 *thorax*, i.e שִׁרְיוֹן.

IV שׁרה (√of foll; meaning dub.; cf As *siriyâm*, *body-armour* (Inscr of Sennach), Aram. ܫܪܝܢܐ *id*; Ecclus 43[20] *id*; also Egypt. *tu-ṛa-na*, *ta-ra-y-na*, WMM[As u Eur 102])

†שִׁרְיוֹן, שִׁרְיֹן **n.[m.] body-armour**,—abs שִׁרְיוֹן 1 S 17[5.38], שִׁרְיָן (Ges[§29u]) 1 K 22[34]=2 Ch 18[33], שִׁרְיָן Is 59[17], pl שִׁרְיֹנִים Ne 4[10], שִׁרְיֹנוֹת 2 Ch 26[14],—*body-armour*, perh. more exactly *breast-armour*, Ne 4[10]; with appendages (הַדְּבָקִים) 1 K 22[34]=2 Ch 18[33]; c vb לבשׁ 1 S 17[5], made of scale-like plates (קַשְׂקַשִּׂים) of bronze v[5], named with helmet here, so v[38] 2 Ch 26[14] and (fig) Is 59[17].—ש׳ n pr v שִׂרְיוֹן

[שֵׁרָה] *bracelet*, v. שׁרר.

†שָׁרוּחֶן **n.pr.loc.** in Simeon;—Jos 19[6] (𝔊 οἱ ἀγροὶ αὐτῶν, ? rdg שְׂדֵיהֶן), WMM[As u Eur 161.166] identif. with Egypt. *Ša-r(a)-ḥa-na*

שָׁרוֹן **n.pr.loc.** שָׁרוֹנִי **adj.gent.** (†1 Ch 27[29]) v. ישׁר

שׁרות Je 15[11] v. I. שׁרה, שָׁרוֹתֶיהָ Je 5[10] v. II. שׁוּר, שׁוּרָה

שִׁרְטַי 1 Ch 27[29] Qr, v שִׁטְרַי.

†שָׁרַי **n.pr.m.** one with foreign wife Ezr 10[40], Σαριου, ℵ Σαρουε, 𝔊L Σαρουα.

שִׁרְיָה v. III. שׁרה שִׁרְיוֹן v. IV שׁרה

שְׁרִית v. שׁארית שריתך Je 15[11] v. I. שׁרה.

שְׁרֵמוֹת v [שְׁדֵמָה] sub שׁדם.

שִׁרְיָן v שִׁרְיוֹן sub IV. שׁרה

†שָׁרַץ **vb. swarm, teem** (NH *id*; Aram. ܫܪܨ *crawl*, ܫܪܨ=שְׁרַץ, so שִׁרְצָא (rare); Eth. ሠረጸ: *germinate, sprout*),—**Qal** *Pf.* 3 ms. ש׳ ψ 105[30], שָׁרְצוּ Gn 1[21], etc, *Impf* 3 ms. יִשְׁרֹץ Ez 47[9], etc, *Imv* mpl. שִׁרְצוּ Gn 9[7], *Pt* הַשֹּׁרֵץ 7[21]+, f הַשֹּׁרֶצֶת Lv 11[46], Hex only P·—**1.** *swarm, teem* with (acc. animal), subj. water Gn 1[20.21], cf Ex 7[28], land ψ 105[30]. **2.** *swarm*, subj animal. Gn 8[17] (+ רָבָה, פָּרָה), Ez 47[9], הַשֹּׁרֵץ Gn 7[21] Lv 11[29.41.42.46] (all עַל־הָאָרֶץ), v[43]; subj. men Gn 9[7] (+ רָבָה, פָּרָה), Ex 1[7] (*id*, + עָצַם)

†שֶׁרֶץ **n.m.**[Gn 7.21] **coll. swarmers, swarming things**,—ש׳ abs. Lv 11[20]+, שָׁרֶץ v[31], cstr. v[20]+,—*swarming things* (H D and P), aquatic Gn 1[20] Lv 11[10], small reptiles and quadrupeds Gn 7[21] (+ חַיָּה, בהמה, עוֹף), Lv 5[2] (+ בְּהֵמָה, חַיָּה), 11[29] (weasel, mouse, lizard), v[31 41 42 43] (c. cogn. שָׁרַץ), v[44], cf. 22[5]; insects, ש׳ הָעוֹף Dt 14[19], + הֹלֵךְ עַל־אַרְבַּע Lv 11[20.21], cf v[23]. Cf. Dr[DB i 518]

†שָׁרַק **vb. hiss, perh. also whistle, pipe** (NH *id*, *hiss* (dub), Aram. שְׁרִיק *id*. 𝔗 Lv 2[15.16], ܫܪܩ *id*,—from ש׳ comes Gk σῦριγξ acc. to Lag[Abh GGW xxvi 19] Lewy[Fremdw 163]),—**Qal** *Pf* 3 ms. consec וש׳ Is 5[26], etc, *Impf.* 3 ms יִשְׁרֹק Is 7[18]+ (Jb 27[23] read יִשְׁרְקוּ Me Bi Siegf Bu); 1 s אֶשְׁרְקָה Zc 10[8],—*hiss*, as signal, לְ pers., fig., י׳ subj· Is 5[26] 7[18] Zc 10[1]; in derision, עַל civitat., etc (oft. + שָׁמֵם *be astounded*), Je 19[8] 49[17] 50[13] La 2[15] (+ הֵנִיעַ ראשׁ), Ez 27[36], abs. Zp 2[15] La 2[16] 1 K 9[8] (+ חָרַק שֵׁן), עַל pers. Jb 27[23] (c. מִן loc).

†שְׁרֵקָה **n.f** (object of derisive) **hissing**;—always abs ש׳, and always + שַׁמָּה: Je 19[8] 25[9.18]

(חֶרְבָּה, חֲרָפָה, קְלָלָה +), 29[18] (חֶרְפָּה, אָלָה +), 51[37] Mi 6[16] (חֶרְפָּה +), 2 Ch 29[8].

†[שְׁרִיקָה] **n.[f.] hissing,** perhaps also **whistling, piping**;—pl. abs. (intens.) שְׁרִיקֹת Je 18[16] Qr *hissing*, in derision, + שַׁמָּה (v. שְׁרֵקָה), Kt שרוקת; cstr. שְׁרִקוֹת עֲדָרִים Ju 5[16] as signal *hissings* (or whistlings, pipings) *for flocks.*

שרר (√of [שָׁרִיר], שְׁרִירוּת, and perhaps of other words following; OAram. שרר *be firm, sound*, Aram. שְׁרַר *be firm, hard*, [Syr.] *be firm, consistent, substantial, truthful*, [Syr.] *strengthen, confirm*; Aram. and NH שָׁרִיר *firm, hard*; [Syr.] *firmness, strength, constancy*).

†[שֹׁר] **n.[m.] navel-string** (cf. Aram. שׁוּרָא Ez 16[4] 𝔗, [Syr.], Ar. سُرٌّ, all *id.*);—sf. לֹא כָרַּת שָׁרֵּךְ Ez 16[4] (Ges[§ 22 s] Kö[ii. 1. 45]) *thy navel-string was not cut*; questioned are: שָׁרֶּךָ Pr 3[8] (De al. *navel*, synechd. for body, ‖ עַצְמוֹתֶיךָ; 𝔊 τῷ σώματί σου, cf. 𝔖, Clericus Bi Frankenberg בְּשָׂרֶךָ, Ew Hi Kmp al. שְׁאֵרֶךָ, Toy either); שָׁרְרֵךְ Ct 7[3] (𝔊 ὀμφαλός σου; ‖ בִּטְנֵךְ), = שָׁרֵּךְ Thes al.; now oft. interpreted as = *vulva*, cf. Ar. سِرٌّ *secret part*, Hi Stickel Buhl Öttli, noticed also by Thes, but Arabism dub., v. Bu.

†[שֵׁרָה] **n.[f.] bracelet** (Aram. שֵׁירָא *id.*, [Syr.] *chain*, Gn 24[22] 𝔖 𝔗: Ar. سِوَارٌ *bracelet*, Qor 18[30] [Frä[56]] is said by Lane[1465] to be from the Persian, and, if Sem., would be fr. √سور);—pl. abs. הַשֵּׁרוֹת Is 3[19] (in list of finery).

†שָׁרָר **n.pr.m.** 2 S 23[33] = 11. שָׂכָר, q.v.

†[שָׁרִיר] **n.[m.] sinew, muscle** (so context suggests);—pl. cstr. אוֹנוֹ בִּשְׁרִירֵי בִטְנוֹ Jb 40[16] (‖ כֹּחוֹ בְמָתְנָיו).

†שְׁרִירוּת, usu. **שְׁרִרוּת n. f. firmness,** always = **stubbornness**; only cstr. 'שׁ, sq. לֵב: שׁ' לִבָּם הָרָע Je 9[13] 13[10] 23[17] Dt 29[18] ψ 81[13] (שְׁרִירוּת); Je 3[17] 7[24] 11[8] (שְׁרִ'), so (לִבּוֹ) 16[12] 18[12].

[שַׁרְשָׁה] Ex 28[22] v. following.

†[שַׁרְשְׁרָה] **n.f.** (in spite of foll. sf. masc. Ex 28[14], Ges[§ 135 o] Albr[ZAW xv (1895), 316, xvi (1896), 96]) **chain** (As. *šaršarratu, chain, fetter*; Mishn. שַׁרְשְׁרוֹת, Talm. שַׁרְשׁוּרָא, Syr. [Syr.], *chain* or *rope* of palm-leaves, etc., but also NH שַׁלְשֶׁלֶת *chain*, 𝔗 שֵׁישְׁלָא, Syr. [Syr.] [whence Ar. سِلْسِلَةٌ, v. Eth. [Eth.]], (connex. with שַׁר' denied by Nö[BSSW 56 Anm. 9]));—pl. שַׁרְשְׁרוֹת, abs. 1 K 7[17] +, -רֹת abs. 2 Ch 3[16], cstr. Ex 28[14] +, שַׁרְשֹׁת v[22] (either abbrev. or textual error);—*chains* of gold, like wreaths, attached to ephod Ex 28[14.14.22] 39[15]; ornaments on pillars at porch of temple 1 K 7[17] (גְּדִלִים מַעֲשֵׂה שׁ'), ‖ 2 Ch 3[15.16.16].

שרשׁ (appar. √of foll.; Di[Jb 40.16] Buhl al. think = שׁרשׁר, √שׁרר, cf. שֹׁר, etc., Eth. [Eth.] *nerve, muscle*, whence שֹׁרֶשׁ as root-*fibre*, but word very ancient, and this der. quite unproven; <Schwally[ZMG lii (1898), 140 f.] cp. Ar. شَرْسٌ (ش by dissimilation), *thorn-bush*, شَرْسٌ *hard, rough, rugged* (of ground), شَرِسٌ *ill-natured, cross*; hence שֹׁרֶשׁ, from *tough, gnarled* root-fibres; NH and Ph. שרש, As. *šuršu*, all *root*, Sab. שרס (v. Ar. supr.) *root, foundation* Hom[Chr 124], אשרם *foundation* DHM[ZMG xxix (1875), 606; xxxvii (1883), 415]; Aram. שׁוּרְשָׁא, [Syr.] *root*).

†שֹׁרֶשׁ **n.m.**[Dt 29, 17] **root**;—'שׁ abs. Dt 29[17] +, cstr. Is 11[10] +; sf. שָׁרְשִׁי Jb 29[19], etc.; pl. cstr. שָׁרְשֵׁי 13[27] (v. infr.) 36[30], sf. שָׁרָשָׁיו Am 2[9] +, שָׁרָשֶׁיהָ Ez 17[7] +;—**1.** *root* of people under fig. of tree, involving firmness, permanence, Am 2[9] Ho 9[16] 14[6] Is 14[30] 2 K 19[30] = Is 37[31];—שָׁרְשָׁם Ju 5[14] is prob. corrupt, v. GFM;—so of pers. (cf. Ph, Eshmunazar[11] GACooke[pp. 30, 36]) Is 5[24] Mal 3[19] Jb 8[17] 18[16] 29[19] Pr 12[3.12]; = stock, family Is 11[1.10] Dn 11[7], cf. (of serpent) Is 14[29]; = source or cause Dt 29[17], שׁ' דָּבָר Jb 19[28]. **2.** lit. *root* of tree or shrub Je 17[8] (sim.), Ez 31[7] (metaph. of people), Is 53[2] (sim.), Jb 14[8] 30[4]; of vine (metaph. of people) Ez 17[6.7.9.9] ψ 80[10] (acc. cogn. c. שׁרשׁ **Hiph.**). **3.** *root*, fig. = lowest stratum, of mt. Jb 28[9], of sea 36[30] = bottom (text strange and dub.: Du רָאשֵׁי הָרִים, with אֵדוֹ in v[4]); of feet, שָׁרְשֵׁי רַגְלֶי 13[27], i.e. soles Ew Di De Da al. (elsewhere כַּף), Bu place of treading, *footholds*; Du (arbitrarily) שָׁרְשֵׁי, del. רגלי.

†[שֵׁרֵשׁ] **vb. denom. Pi.** = **deal with the roots**;—**1.** *root up, out*: *Pf.* 3 ms. sf. consec. וְשֵׁרֶשְׁךָ ψ 52[7] *he shall root thee up* from (מִן) the land of the living; of fire (*burn*) *roots, root*: *Impf.* 3 fs. תְּשָׁרֵשׁ בְּ Jb 31[12] fire (fig.) *roots at* all my increase. **Pu.** *Impf.* 3 mpl. יְשֹׁרָשׁוּ 31[8] *be rooted up* (of produce). **2. Po'ēl** *take root*, establish oneself firmly: *Pf.* 3 ms. שֹׁרֵשׁ בָּאָרֶץ גִּזְעָם Is 40[24] (fig. of princes, etc.). **Po'al** *id.*: *Pf.* 3 mpl. שֹׁרָשׁוּ Je 12[2] (fig. of wicked). **Hiph.** *id.*: *Impf.* 3 ms. יַשְׁרֵשׁ Is 27[6] (fig. of Isr.); 3 fs. וַתַּשְׁרֵשׁ ψ 80[10] (*id.*; c. acc. cogn.); *Pt.* מַשְׁרִישׁ Jb 5[3] (fig. of pers.).

†שֶׁרֶשׁ n.pr.m. in Manasseh (cf OAram. n pr שרש Lzb^{384}),—1 Ch 7^{16}, Σο[υ]ρος, ϬL Φορος

[שַׁרְשָׁה], [שַׁרְשְׁרָה] v. שרר.

[שָׁרַת]$_{97}$ vb. Pi. minister, serve (cf. NH שרות (temple-)ministry, Ph. משרת ministry, and perhaps ✓b שרת minister),—**Pi.** *Pf.* 3 ms. שֵׁרֵת Nu 8^{26} Dt 18^{7}, 3 mpl שֵׁרְתוּ Nu 3^{6}; *Impf.* 3 ms וַיְשָׁרֶת Gn 39^{4}, 3 mpl יְשָׁרְתוּ Nu 3^{31} +, etc; *Inf. cstr* לְשָׁרֵת Ex 28^{35} +, לְשָׁרֶת שָׁם Dt 17^{12}, etc, *Pt* מְשָׁרֵת Nu 11^{28} + (2 S 13^{9} v מְשָׁרֵת, p 602^{a}), *f* מְשָׁרַתְ 1 K 1^{15}, etc,—*serve* **1.** of ministerial service (opp menial, עבד) **a.** higher domestic service Joseph Gn 39^{4} 40^{4} (JE), Elisha's chief servant 2 K 4^{43} 6^{15}, royal domestics 2 S 13$^{17.18}$ 1 K 10^{5} 2 Ch 9^{4} Est 2^{2} 6^{3}, Abishag 1 K 1$^{4.15}$. **b.** of royal *officers* (late) 1 Ch 27^{1} 28^{1} 2 Ch 17^{19} 22^{8} Est 1^{10} Pr 29^{12}. **c.** Joshua as chief assistant to Moses Ex 24^{13} 33^{11} (E), Nu 11^{28} (J), Jos 1^{1} (D), Elisha to Elijah 1 K 19^{21}. **d.** of angels to ׳י ψ 103^{21}, cf 104^{4} **e.** of kings of nations in proph Is 60^{10} **2.** usu of special service in worship. **a.** of Levit priests, abs 1 K 8^{11} = 2 Ch 5^{14}, c acc. ׳י Dt 10^{8} 17^{12} 21^{5} Je 33^{21} + (strangely) מְשָׁרְתֵי אֹתִי v^{22}; also Is 60^{7} of animals put fig for those sacrificing them; of foreigners admitted to priesthood Is 61^{6}, cf 56^{6}; so prob Samuel conceived as priest 1 S 2^{11} 3^{1}, ׳את פני י 2^{18} (פני prob. acc, cf Ϭ τῷ προσώπῳ v^{11}), ׳ש׳ בשם י Dt 18$^{5.7}$ **b.** Levites (P, and late), c acc of Aaronic priests Nu 3^{6} 8^{26} 18^{2}, c acc of ׳י 1 Ch 15^{2} 2 Ch 29^{11}, prob. also in ref to Lev. singer ψ 101^{6}, c. acc. tabern. Nu 1^{50} (P), congregation 16^{9} (P), people Ez 44^{11} + v^{12} (of idolatry), abs. 1 Ch 16^{4} 2 Ch 23^{6} 29^{11b} 31^{2} Ezr 8^{17} (pt as subst., *ministers*), ש׳ לִפְנֵי ׳אֲרוֹן בְּרִית י ש׳ נגד הַכֹּהֲנִים 1 Ch 16^{37}, 2 Ch 8^{14}, ש׳ c. בּ loc 1 Ch 26^{12}, esp c בּ, of sacred vessels Nu 3^{31} 4$^{9.12.14}$ 2 K 25^{14} = Je 52^{18}, בְּשִׁיר 1 Ch 6^{17}. **c.** Zadokite priests (Ez), abs. Ez 42^{14} + 3 t, c acc ׳י 40^{46} + 4 t, cstr מְשָׁרְתֵי before sacred place 45$^{4.5}$ 46^{24} **d.** Aaronic priests, abs Ex 28^{35} + 4 t P, c acc ׳י 1 Ch 23^{13}, ׳לִי 2 Ch 13^{10}, ׳מְשָׁרְתֵי י Jo 1$^{9.13}$ 2^{17}, מְשָׁרְתֵי מִזְבֵּחַ Jo 1^{13}, c. בַּקֹּדֶשׁ Ex 28^{43} + 4 t P. **e.** of idolatry, c acc עֵץ וָאֶבֶן Ez 20^{32}

†שָׁרֵת n.m. religious ministry;—כְּלֵי הַשּׁ׳ *vessels of m* in tabern Nu 4^{12}, temple 2 Ch 24^{14}

[שָׁשָׂה] v. [שסה] Pō.

I. שֵׁשׁ *six*, v. שׁדשׁ. II שֵׁשׁ v. שַׁיִשׁ.

†III שֵׁשׁ n.m.$^{Ez\ 26.1}$ byssus (loan-wd. prob. fr. Eg *šen-suten* Reinisch ap. DHM$^{VOJ\ viii\ (1894).7}$ Copt. *šens*, cf. Copt. *šent*, *weave*; v. M'Lean$^{Ency\ Bib,\ Linen}$; on spinning, weaving, and wearing of linen in Egypt Erman$^{Aegypten\ 594\ ff\quad Eng\ Trans.\ 448\ f}$),—always abs ש׳ (שֶׁשִׁי Ez 16^{13} is error).—*byssus*, fine Egyptian linen (בּוּץ, q v, is later synon), i.e. the linen thread (spun by women Ex 35^{25}), and the material woven from it. used for garments Gn 41^{42} (E), Ez 16$^{10.13}$ (שֶׁשִׁי, read שֵׁשׁ), Pr 31^{22}; for sail (in fig. of Tyre as ship) Ez 27^{7} (brought from Egypt), elsewhere P, of priestly vestments Ex 28$^{5.39.39}$ 39$^{3.27.28.28}$, also ש׳ מָשְׁזָר *twisted linen* 28$^{6.8.15}$ 39$^{2.5.8.28.29}$ + v^{24} (read ׳ושש מ Sam Ϭ Bae), ש׳ of hangings, etc, in tabern 25^{4} 35$^{6.23.25.35}$ 38^{23}, and so ש׳ מָשְׁזָר 26$^{1.31.36}$ 27$^{9.16.18}$ 36$^{8.35.37}$ 38$^{9.16.18}$.

†[שָׁשָׁא] vb. intens. appar. lead on, so Vrss and context, *Pf* 1 s sf. וְשִׁשֵּׁאתִיךָ Ez 39^{2} consec, *I* (׳י) *will lead thee on* (acc. of Gog) (form **Pilp.** fr assumed ✓שׁאא Ol^{§253} Sta$^{§112\ a\ Anm.\ 2,\ 464}$ Hi-Sm Krae Berthol)

†שֵׁשְׁבַּצַּר (Baer Gi; ׳שֵׁשׁ van d H) **n.pr.m.** prince of Judah, leader of returning exiles Ezr 1$^{8.11}$ (cf. BAram. 5$^{14.16}$), Σαβανασαρ, A Σασαβασσαρος, ϬL Σαβασαρης, in 1 Esdr Σαναμασσαρος, etc (prob = *Šamaš-bal-uṣur* or *Sin-bal-uṣur* Mey$^{Entstehung\ d\ Jud\ 75\ ff.,\ 193}$ Selbie$^{Hast\ DB\ s\ v}$ Che$^{Ency.\ Bib\ s.\ v}$ Berthol$^{Ezr\ 1,\ 8}$ and reff.),—long identified with Zerub., so Be-Ry Ryle, but improbable, v. Sm$^{Listen\ 19}$ Kosters$^{Herstel\ 32\ f}$ Mey$^{Entstehung\ l\ c}$; Mey^{77} al identify with שֶׁנְאַצַּר 1 Ch 3^{18} (against this Now$^{Hg\ l\ l}$, yet v. Berthol$^{l\ c}$).

[שֵׁשָׁה] v. I שֵׁשׁ sub שׁדשׁ

†שָׁשַׁי n pr. m. Jew with foreign wife Ezr 10^{40}, Σεσ(ε)ει

†שֵׁשַׁי n.pr.m. a son of Anak (Aram. form, cf. GFM^{Ju}),—Nu 13^{22} Jos 15^{14} (both JE), Ju 1^{10}, Σεσ(σ)ει, Σουσαι, Σουσει.

שִׁשִּׁי, שִׁשִּׁים, שִׁשִּׁית v. I שֵׁשׁ sub שׁדשׁ.

†שֵׁשַׁךְ n. pr. terr. = בָּבֶל (Jer Rabb and mod., by *Atbaš* (׳את׳בש), i e. disguising name by substituting last letter of alphabet for first, next last for second, etc, cf. Thes);—Je 51^{41} and hence (perhaps gloss) 25^{26} (v. Gie).

†שֵׁשָׁן n. pr. m. in Judah, 1 Ch 2$^{31.31}$ (with one son), v$^{34.34.35}$ (no sons, but daughters, cf. Benz Kit); Σωσαν[μ], ϬL Σισαν.

†שָׁשַׁק (Baer Gi; van d. H. שָׁשָׁק, שָׁשֵׁק) **n.pr.m.** in Benjamin, 1 Ch 8[14.25]; Σωκηλ, Σωιηκ, A Σωσηκ, 𝔊L Σισαχ (acc. to Simon. (Thes) = שְׁקַשְׁק *one longed for* (√שקק)).

†[שָׁשַׁר] **n.[m.] red colour, vermilion** (etym unknown),—*vermilion*, formerly gained from *kermes* insect (*vermiculus*): מָשׁוֹחַ בַּשָּׁשַׁר Je 22[14] (𝔊 μίλτος, *red ochre;* 𝔙 *sinopis* [from city Sinopis, whence the colour came Plin [NH xxxv. (6) 13]], cf. Thatcher [DB Colours] Canney [EB 1b]); חֲקֻקִים בַּשָּׁשַׁר Ez 23[14].

[שָׁת], I. שת v. שית

II. שֵׁת v. שאת sub I. [שאה].

III. שֵׁת v. II שתה

I. שָׁתָה [217] **vb. drink** (NH *id.;* As. *šatû*, Eth. ሰተየ: OAram. שתה, Aram. אִשְׁתִּי, שְׁתָא, [ܐܫܬܝ], ܫܬܐ; Sab. שתי DHM [ZMG xxxvii (1883) 403] Hom [Chr 124]);—**Qal**[216] *Pf* 3 ms. ש׳ Ex 34[28]+, 1 s. שָׁתִיתִי 1 S 1[15]+, etc; *Impf.* 3 ms. יִשְׁתֶּה Gn 44[5]+, וַיֵּשְׁתְּ 1 K 19[8], usu. וַיֵּשְׁתְּ Gn 9[21]+; juss. וַיֵּשְׁתְּ 1 K 13[18]; 3 fs. וַתֵּשְׁתְּ Nu 20[11]; 2 ms. apoc תֵּשְׁתְּ Ju 13[14]+, וַתֵּשְׁתְּ 1 K 13[22]; 1 s וָאֵשְׁתְּ Gn 24[46], 3 mpl יִשְׁתָּיוּן ψ 78[44], etc, *Imv.* ms שְׁתֵה Gn 24[14]+, etc; *Inf. abs.* שָׁתֹה Is 21[5] Je 49[12] (in 1 S 1[9] after prep, anom., Ges [§ 113 e], om. 𝔊 Th We Dr and mod), שָׁתוֹ Je 25[28]+, שָׁתוֹת Is 22[13] (Ges [§ 75 n]), cstr. שְׁתוֹ †Pr 31[4], שְׁתוֹת Je 35[8.14], לִשְׁתֹּת Gn 24[19]+, sf. שְׁתוֹתוֹ 1 K 13[23], לִשְׁתוֹתָהּ Is 51[22] etc; *Pt act.* שֹׁתֶה Is 29[8]+, f. שֹׁתָה Jb 6[4], etc;—**1. a.** of man: *drink*, water, wine, etc., Ex 34[28] (JE), cf. 15[24] (J), 1 S 30[12] Am 2[8] 4[8] 5[11] Is 5[22] 62[8.9] Pr 31[4], Ju 13[4.7.14]+oft. (2 t. JE; 6 t. D); by measure (short allowance) Ez 4[11.16]; milk †Ez 25[4], cf Ct 5[1], blood 1 Ch 11[19] (fig. of water gained by hazard); fig. חֲמָתָם שֹׁתָה רוּחִי Jb 6[4] *whose venom* [of arrows of י׳] *my spirit drinks up*, acc.+מִן of source †Ex 7[18] (J), v[21] (E), 15[23] (J), Pr 5[15] (fig); acc. (of wine, water, etc) om. Gn 24[11.14] 27[25] 43[34] (all J)+11 t. J, Ex 7[24] 17[6] (E), Nu 20[5] (JE), v[11] 33[14] (P), Ju 15[19]+oft., acc שִׁין †2 K 18[27]=Is 36[12]; מַמְתַּקִּים Ne 8[10]; abs Ec 2[24]+; +מִן of source 1 K 17[4.6] ψ 110[7], מלכו 2 S 12[3]; ש׳ בְּמִזְרְקֵי יַיִן †Am 6[6], cf. Gn 44[5]; ש׳ בְּיֵין +Pr 9[5]; c. מִן partit. Gn 9[21] Ex 7[24] Ru 2[9], also (fig.) Je 51[7] (and Jb 21[20] infra). †**b.** pt. as subst. שֹׁתֵי מַיִם Ez 31[14.16], שֹׁתֵי יַיִן Jo 1[5]; שׁוֹתֵי שֵׁכָר ψ 69[13]. **c.** *drink* wine in sacrificial feast Dt 32[38] (poem), blood of sacrificial victim ψ 50[13] (fig. of י׳). **d.** subj. animals Nu 20[19] Jon 3[7] (both+men), also (fig.) Ez 34[18.19], acc. (water) om. Gn 24[19.22] 30[38.38]. **e.** fig. of drinking cup of י׳'s wrath, ש׳ אֶת־כּוֹס חֲמָתוֹ Is 51[17] (+מִיַּד י׳), cf. v[17], v[22], v. also Ez 23[32.34] and (acc. om.) Je 25[16.26.27]+8 t. Je, Hb 2[16]; abs. Ob[16.16.16]; acc. שְׁמָרִים ψ 75[9]; ש׳ מֵחֲמַת שַׁדַּי Jb 21[20]. †**f.** *drink* blood, fig. of slaughter, Nu 23[24] (JE; of lion, metaph. of Isr.), Zc 9[15] (read דָּמָם for הָמוּ 𝔊 [Codd] Sta Now Marti); so (blood of י׳'s sacrifice) Ez 39[17.18.19]. **g.** fig. of wicked deeds: יֵין חֲמָסִים יִשְׁתּוּ Pr 4[17] (‖ לָחֲמוּ לֶחֶם רֶשַׁע; these are their food and drink), cf Jb 15[16] 34[7], but Pr 26[6] appar = *suffers* violence (cf. De Toy). †**2.** late, =*feast* Est 3[15] 7[1] (cf. מִשְׁתֶּה). †**Niph.** *Impf.* 3 ms. יִשָּׁתֶה Lv 11[34] (P) all which *is* (may be) *drunk*, c. בְּ of vessel.—נשתוה Pr 27[15] v. I שוה *ad fin.* For *cause, give, to drink* v. שׁקה.

†I. שְׁתִי **n.[m.] drinking, drinking-bout**;—Ec 10[17].

†שְׁתִיָּה **n.f. drinking** (mode or amount) Est 1[8].

מִשְׁתֶּה [45] **n.m.** [Gn 21, 8] **1. feast; 2. drink**;—abs. מ׳ Gn 19[3]+; cstr. מִשְׁתֵּה 1 S 25[36]+; sf. משתיו Dn 1[5]+(Ges [§ 93 ss]), etc.;—**1.** *feast, banquet* (occasion for drinking, drinking-bout), 1 S 25[36.36] Is 5[12] Je 51[39] (fig), Jb 1[5] Est 2[18] 5[14] 8[17] 9[19], lasting seven days Ju 14[12.17] (wedding-feast, cf Gn 29[27], and v. Benz [Arch. 143] [Ency Bib 2949] Now [Arch 1 163]); עָשָׂה מ׳ *give* or *make a feast* (sts +לְ pers) Gn 19[3] 26[30] (both J), 21[8] 40[20] (both E), Ju 14[10] 2 S 3[20] 1 K 3[15] Est 1[3]+8 t. Est, Jb 1[4]+2 S 13[27.27] 𝔊 Th We Dr and mod; מִשְׁתֵּה הַיַּיִן Est 5[6] 7[2.7], בית משתה Je 16[8] Ec 7[2], בית משתה היין Est 7[8]; יוֹם מ׳ וְשִׂמְחָה Est 9[17.18], cf v[22], of י׳'s banquet for all peoples Is 25[6] (fig. of Messianic blessings); fig. also in טוֹב־לֵב מ׳ תָּמִיד Pr 15[15]. †**2.** *drink* (late): מַאֲכָל וּמ׳ וָשֶׁמֶן Ezr 3[7]; sf. יֵין מִשְׁתָּיו Dn 1[5.8]; מִשְׁתֵּיכֶם v[16]; משתיהם v[10].

II. שתה (√of foll.; ‖ √of שית; =*set, sit*)

†III. שֵׁת **n.[m.] seat** (of body), **buttocks** (cf. NH שֵׁית, Aram. ܫܬܐ *foundation;* cf. [שָׁת] p. 1011; No [M 98]);—abs. ש׳ Is 20[4]; pl. sf. שְׁתוֹתֵיהֶם 2 S 10[4].

III. שתה (√of foll.; Aram. שְׁתִי, ܫܬܐ *weave* (Ju 16[13] 𝔗 𝔖); ܫܬܝܐ *textura;* cf. Ar. سَدَّى, أَسْدَى, أَسْتَى, *set the warp*).

II. שְׁתִי [9] **n.m. warp** (NH *id.;* Ar. سَتًى, سَدًى *id.*);—always ש׳ abs.;—*warp*, the set of

threads drawn lengthwise in loom, through which the shuttle bearing the woof (II עֵרֶב p 786) is thrown crosswise; Lv 13[48] + 7 t. Lv 13; cf. GFM [PAOS, Oct. 1880 clxxviii] ARSK [EB Weaving]

שָׁתוֹת v [שָׁת] sub שִׁית.

שְׁתַיִם v שְׁנַיִם sub II. שנה

†[שָׁתַל] **vb. transplant** (NH *id*; Aram. שְׁתַל, ܫܬܠ; Vulg Ar. شَتْل *plant*, شَتْلَة *slip, cutting*, Dozy (loan-words ?) Thes[1488], As *šitlu* appar = *shoot, slip*),—**Qal** *Pf* 1 s שָׁתַלְתִּי Ez 17[22]; *Impf* 1 s sf אֶשְׁתָּלֶנּוּ v[23], *Pt pass* שָׁתוּל Je 17[8] = ψ 1[3], etc. (8 t.);—*transplant* (poet) tree or vine, c בְּ loc, Ez 17[10 23] 19[13] ψ 92[14], עַל־מַיִם Ez 19[10] Je 17[8], ‖ עַל־פַּלְגֵי מַיִם ψ 1[3], עַל־הַר Ez 17[22], אֶל־מַיִם v[8], לְצוֹר שְׁתוּלָה בְנָוֶה Ho 9[13] is corrupt 𝔊 Che We Now (both in transl) GASm Harper לְצַיִד שָׁתוּ בָנָיו (or the like; somewhat differently Marti) Ephraim . *for a prey have they set his sons*

†[שָׁתִיל] **n. [m.] transplanted shoot, slip**,—pl cstr. שְׁתִלֵי זֵיתִים ψ 128[3] *slips of olive* (in simile).

†[שָׁתַם] **vb.** dub, if text correct, **open** (NH Aram שתם *open* [vessel]);—only **Qal** *Pt. pass.* cstr. הַגֶּבֶר שְׁתֻם הָעָיִן Nu 24[3 15] (poems in JE) the man *opened of* [mental] *eye*, so 𝔖 Ki Ew al. RVm; 𝔙 Rod Ke Di al render *closed of* [bodily] *eye*, reading then implicitly שְׂתֻם (cf. שָׂתַם סָתַם La 3[8]), v further Gray

[הִשְׁתִּין, שתן] v שִׁין.

†[שָׁתַק] **vb. be quiet** (late) (NH *id.*, *be silent*; Aram. שְׁתַק, שְׁתִיק, ܫܬܩ *be quiet, silent* (cf also שׁקט)),—**Qal** *Impf.* 3 ms., of sea יִשְׁתֹּק הַיָּם Jon 1[11 12] (sq מֵעַל), of quarrel, strife Pr 26[20]; 3 mpl. of persons at sea, וַיִּשְׁתֹּקוּ ψ 107[30].

†שֵׁתָר **n pr.m.** a prince of Persia Est 1[14]; Σαρσαθαιος

†[שָׁתַת] **vb. set, appoint** (poet.) (‖ form of שׁית Ges[§ 67 ee]),—**Qal** *Pf* 3 pl. כַּצֹּאן לִשְׁאוֹל שַׁתּוּ ψ 49[15] *they have been appointed* (lit. they have appointed them, indef. subj) *like a flock for Sh'ôl*, but Gr rds שָׁחוּ (שׁוח), Bae[3] נַחֲתוּ (נחת); (וּלְשׁוֹנָם תִּהֲלַךְ בָּאָרֶץ ‖) 73[9] שַׁתּוּ בַשָּׁמַיִם פִּיהֶם

ת

ת, ת Tāw, 22nd letter; = 400 in postB Heb

†תָּא **n.m.**[Ez 40, 21] **chamber** (NH *id*, perhaps Aramaism, cf. Ar ثَوَى *dwell*, مَثْوًى *abode* (? akin to أَوَى *turn aside to lodge*, אֻונָא, ܘܘܢܐ *lodging-place*), Aram. תָּא (in Ez 40 תָּוָא, תְּוָא), ܬܘܐ *room, chamber*),—ת׳ abs. Ez 40[7] +, cstr 1 K 4[28], sf. תָּאוֹ Ez 40[21] Kt (Qr תָּאָיו), so v[29.33.36], pl תָּאִים v[7] +, תָּאוֹת v[12]; cstr תָּאֵי v[10],—*chamber*. תָּא הָרָצִים 1 K 4[28] *chamber of the guards* = 2 Ch 12[11], in Ezekiel's temple Ez 40[7 7 10.12 12 13 16.21 29.33.36].

†I. [תָּאַב, תָּאֵב] **vb long for** (NH *id*, תֵּאָבוֹן *desire*; Aram תְּאֵב, תאיב *long for*; ? secondary √ from אָבָה, or denom from תַּאֲבָה, and this from אבה, cf Buhl; but v. Ol[§ 137]),—**Qal** *Pf.* 1 s תָּאַבְתִּי, c לְ rei, ψ 119[40 174].

†תַּאֲבָה **n.f. longing**;—ψ 119[20].

II [תָּאַב] **vb. Pi.** loathe, abhor, v. תעב

†[תָּאָה] **vb. Pi** *Impf* 3 mpl תְּתָאוּ Nu 34[7.8] appar. *ye shall mark out* (the boundary), but this (and הִתְאַוִּיתֶם v[10], √אוה q v) very dub., v. Gray, and [תָּאַר]

†תְּאוֹ **n.m. antelope** (whether *antilope leucoryx* Tr [NHB 59; FFP 5], or *oryx beatrix* Post [Hast DB Ox], on form v. Ol[§ 173 e]),—abs. ת׳ Dt 14[5] (clean animal, cf. Dr), cstr. תּוֹא Is 51[20].

תַּאֲוָה v. I תוה, I אוה. תַּאֲלָה v. II. אלה.

תאם (Buhl after Ba[NB § 182 b] prop. وأم, III. *agree* as √ of following, but dub, v As *tu'âmu*, Ar. تَوْأَم, Syr. ܬܐܡܐ, all *twin*).

†[תְּאוֹם] (Ko[II. 1 69] (תאם)) **n.m. twin** (NH *id.*; cf Ph n pr m תאם, Gk. Θωμᾶς = δίδυμος John 20[24]);—pl abs of two boys תוֹמִם Gn 25[24] (Ges[§ 23 f]) (תְּאוֹמִים) 38[27] (both J); of animals, cstr. תְּאוֹמֵי צְבִיָּה Ct 4[5], תָּאֳמֵי צ׳ 7[4].

†[תָּאַם] **vb. denom. be double**;—**Qal**

Pt. pl. תאֹמִם Ex 26[24] ‖ תּוֹאֲמִים 36[29]; so rd. also (for תַּמִּים) 26[24] 36[29] (both P), cf. Sam Di Baen ARSK [Hast DB iv 661]. **Hiph.** *bear twins: Pt* f. pl. מַתְאִימוֹת Ct 5[2] 6[6].

תְּאֻנָה, תַּאֲנָה v. III. אנה.

†תְּאֵנָה **n.f.** fig-tree, (then) fig (✓dub.; Ar. تِين, Aram. תְּאֵנָא, ܬܐܢܐ; perhaps Pun. תין (v. Lzb[383]; i.e. תְּיֵן Eut, v. DHM [VOJ i 28]), As. *tittu, a tree;* Lag [M i 58 ff] combines ת׳ (precariously) with ✓(III) אנה *meet opportunely,* with ref to fructifying of fig by another tree, cf. Hom [Aufsätze u Abh i (1892), 100]);—abs ת׳ Ju 9[10]+; sf. תְּאֵנָתִי 1 K 5[5]+, etc.; pl. תְּאֵנִים Nu 13[23]+; cstr. תְּאֵנֵי Je 24[2]; sf. תְּאֵנֵיכֶם Am 4[9];—**1.** *fig-tree* (*ficus carica* Post [Flora 730, Hast. DB, s.v.] Tr [NHB 350] M'Lean-Th-Dyer [Ency Bib., s v]; cf. Low [§ 335]; oft. + גֶּפֶן): Ju 9[10 11] (in allegory), Am 4[9] Ho 9[10] Na 3[12] 1 K 5[5] 2 K 18[31] = Is 36[16], Mi 4[4] Is 34[4] Pr 27[18], עֲלֵה ת׳ Gn 3[7] (J) *fig-leaves,* הַתּ׳ חָנְטָה פַגֶּיהָ Ct 2[13]; coll. Nu 20[5] (JE), Ho 2[14] Je 5[17] 8[13] Dt 8[8] Hb 3[17] Hg 2[19] Zc 3[10] Jo 1[7 12] 2[22] ψ 105[33]. **2.** *fig,* alw. pl.: Nu 13[23] (JE), Je 24[1.2.2.3.3.5.8] 29[17] (all symbolic of Judæans), Je 8[13] (אֵין ת׳ בַּתְּאֵנָה), Ne 8[13]; as medicament, דְּבֶלֶת ת׳ 2 K 20[7] = Is 38[21]; תְּאֵנֵי הַבַּכֻּרוֹת Je 24[2] *the figs of early ripeness* (cf. Du).

תַּאֲנִיָּה v. I. [אנה] תְּאֻנִים v. I. און.

†תַּאֲנַת שִׁלֹה **n.pr.loc.** on border of Ephr. Jos 16[6]; Θηνασα καὶ Σελλησα, A Τηναθσηλω, 𝔊L Θηναθασηλω; acc. to Survey [WP ii. 232, 245] Wilson [Hast DB Taanath Shiloh] Buhl [Geogr 202] = mod. *Ta'na,* c 7 miles ESE. from Nablûs.

†[תָּאַר] **vb.** appar. **incline** (perh. akin to תור Thes; > Buhl denom. from תֹּאַר, q. v.),—**Qal** *Pf.* 3 ms. ת׳, subj. *boundary:* Jos 18[14], c. ה loc 15[9b.11]; c. עַל ... מִן v[9a]; c. מִן only, 18[17]; prob. also c. acc. loc. 19[13] (read רִמּוֹנָה וְתָאַר הַנֵּעָה *to Rimmon, and it inclined to Ne'a* Di Steuern Benn al.). Vid. also [תָּאַר] **Pi.** infr.

†תֹּאַר **n.m.** [La 4. 8] **outline, form** (Ph. תאר; acc. to Schwally [Idiot 100] prop. *something gazed at,* from ✓תאר = ChrPal Aram. ܬܐܪ *gaze at*),—ת׳ abs. Gn 29[17]+; cstr Ju 8[18]; sf. תָּאֳרוֹ (Ges [§ 93 q]) Is 52[14], תָּאֳרוֹ 1 S 28[14];—*form,* of woman, יְפַת ת׳ Gn 29[17] (E; + מַרְאֶה, ‖ later צֶלֶם וּדְמוּת 1[26], Lag [Or. ii 62, BN 149]), Est 2[7] (+ *id*), 1 S 25[3] Dt 21[11]; of man, יְפֵה־ת׳ Gn 39[11] (J; + מַרְאֶה), cf. Is 52[14] (+ *id.*), 53[2] (+ *id.*, הָדָר), Ju 8[18], so also 1 Ch 17[17] (for MT תור) Klo Perles [Anal 68]; אִישׁ ת׳ 1 S 16[18], טוֹב־ת׳ 1 K 1[6]; מַה־תָּאֳרוֹ 1 S 28[14]; v. La 4[8] (where by metonymy = *aspect, visage*); of cattle, יְפוֹת ת׳ Gn 41[18] (E), רָעוֹת ת׳ v[19] (E); tree, זַיִת רַעֲנָן יְפֵה פְרִי־ת׳ Je 11[16] (Du יְפִיפֵה ת׳, v. 46[20]).

†[תָּאַר] **vb. Pi. denom. draw in outline, trace out;**—*Impf.* 3 ms. sf. יְתָאֲרֵהוּ Is 44[13.13] (both c. בּ instr.), of shaping idols; for MT 2 mpl. תְּתָאוּ Nu 34[7.8] Che [Ency Bib 2109] prop. תְּתָאֲרוּ *ye shall trace out* (the boundary; with וְתֵאַרְתֶּם for וְהִתְאַוִּיתֶם v[10]); v. also תאה, תוה.

תַּאֲרֻעַ v. תַּחְרֵעַ sub חרע p. 357.

תְּאַשּׁוּר v. sub [אָשַׁר] p. 81.

†תֵּבָה **n.f.** ark (prop *chest, box* (cf. NH תֵּבָה); prob. Egypt. loan-word from *T-b-t, chest, coffin* (Brugsch, Erman [ZMG xlvi (1892), 123]); > Bab word Jen [ZA iv (1889), 272 f.] Hal [JAs., 1888 (Nov.-Dec.), 517]),—abs. ת׳ Gn 7[1]+; cstr. תֵּבַת 6[14] Ex 2[3];—vessel in which infant Moses was laid among reeds v[3] (made of papyrus, גֹּמֶא), v[5] (both E; 𝔊 θῖβις, θήβη, cf. Lewy [Fremdw 100]); vessel which saved Noah and his family, with animals, during flood (𝔊 κιβωτός). Gn 7[1 7 9 17 23] 8[6.9 9 10 13] 9[18] (all J), 6[14] (made of עֲצֵי גֹפֶר), v[14 15.16 16.18.19] 7[13.15 18] 8[1 4 16.19] 9[10] (all P).

תְּבוּאָה v. בוא. תְּבוּנָה, תְּבוּנָם v. בין.

תֻּבְנִתוֹ v. בין. תְּבוּסָה v. בוס.

†תָּבוֹר **n.pr. 1. mont.** NE. edge of Great Plain, SW. of Sea of Galilee, on border of Issachar, Zeb. and Napht, mod. *Jebel et-Ṭûr;* cf. Rel [Pal. 331 ff] Burckhardt [Travels, 332 ff] Rob [BR iii 340 f.] Bad [Pal. Index, s.v.] Buhl [Geogr 108] GACooke [Ency Bib., s.v.];—הַר(־)ת׳ Ju 4[6 12.14]; ת׳ alone Ho 5[1] Je 46[18] Jos 19[22.34] (P), ψ 89[13] (+ חֶרְמוֹן); 𝔊 Θαβωρ (so Euseb [Onom.]), but Ho Je Ιταβυριον, and so Jos [Ant v. 1. 22 [84], BJ iv 1. 8 [54], etc] (other Gk. forms v. Cooke [l.c.]). **2. loc.** Ju 8[18] (too far away to be = **1** Be al.), GFM conj. טַבּוּר (9[37]), Bu תבץ (9[50]); 𝔊 Θαβωρ. **3. loc.** Levit. city in Zebulun 1 Ch 6[62]; appar. = כִּסְלֹת ת׳ Jos 19[12], and perh. ת׳ v[22] (in Issachar), 𝔊 Θαχχεια, A 𝔊L Θαβωρ **4. arbor.** in אֵלוֹן ת׳ 1 S 10[3], near Bethel; 𝔊 Θαβωρ.

תֵּבֵל v. יבל. תֶּבֶל v. בלל. תֻּבַל v. תוּבַל.

תַּבְלִית v. [בלה] תְּבַלֻּל v. בלל.

†תֶּבֶן **n.m.** [Ex 5. 16] **straw** (✓unknown; Ges al. cp בנה (cf. Thes [1492]), but v Lag [BN 138]; NH = BH; As. *tibnu;* Aram. תִּבְנָא, ܬܒܢܐ, whence Ar. تِبْن as loan-wd. Fra [124]),—abs. ת׳ Gn 24[25]+,

תֶּבֶן Ex 5[10]+;—*straw*, i.e. straw threshed fine: chaff Je 23[28] (opp. בַּר), blown by wind Jb 21[18] (in sim.; ‖ מֹץ), yielding 41[19] (sim.); food for camels Gn 24[25.32] (J), asses Ju 19[19] (all + מִסְפּוֹא), בָּקָר Is 11[7] 65[25], horses 1 K 5[8] (+ שְׂעֹרִים); mixed with clay in brick-making Ex 5[7.7.10.11.12] (opp. קַשׁ), v[13.16.18] (J);—v. further Vogelstein[Landwirthsch. 67].

† מַתְבֵּן **n.[m.]** straw-heap;—מ׳ Is 25[10].

† תִּבְנִי **n.pr.m.** rival of Omri (We[Isr. u. Jüd. Gesch., 3rd ed., 70], cp. Sidon. *Thabnit*);—1 K 16[21.22.22]; Θαμνει, 𝔊L Θαβεννει.

תַּבְנִית v. בנה. תַּבְעֵרָה v. בער.

† תֵּבֵץ **n.pr.loc.** near Shechem: Ju 9[50.50] (תֵּבֵץ; also 8[18] Bu for תָּבוֹר q.v.), 2 S 11[21]; mod. *Ṭûbâs*, 4 h. N. of Shechem Rob[BR iii. 305] Guérin[Sam. i. 357 ff.] Buhl[G 204]; Θηβης, Θαιβαις (in Ju), Θαμασ(ε)ι, 𝔊L Θαμεσσει (in S).

† תִּגְלַת פִּלְאֶסֶר **n.pr.m.** Tiglathpileser (III), king of Assyria (Zinj. תגלתפליסר, תגלתפלסר, GACooke[Inscr. 178. 183. 188]; = As. *Tukulti-apil-êšarra* Rost[Keilinschr. TP III (1893), 42] COT[2 K 15, 29]; v. also Pinches[Ency. Bib. TP] Say[Hast. DB. TP]);—2 K 15[29] 16[10] = ת׳ פִּלְסֶר v[7]; corrupt תִּלְּגַת פִּלְנְאֶסֶר 1 Ch 5[6] 2 Ch 28[20], ת׳ פִּלְנֶסֶר 1 Ch 5[26]; v. also פּוּל;—Αλγαθφελλασαρ, Θαλγαθ[λ]φελλασαρ, Θαλγαβανασαρ, etc., 𝔊L (Kings) Θεγλαφαλασαρ.

[תַּגְמוּל] v. גמל. [תִּגְרָה] v. [גרה].

† תֹּגַרְמָה, תּוֹ׳ **n.pr.terr.** Gn 10[3] = תּוֹ׳ 1 Ch 1[6]; בֵּית תּוֹ׳ Ez 27[14] 38[6]; Θοργαμα, Θεργ., etc.; it lay in (SW.) Armenia acc. to Di[Gn 10, 2] (and reff.), Dl[Pa 246] (*Til-garimmu*); > NW. Asia Minor (Gk. Τευθρανία) Lag[Ges. Abh. 257; Armen. Stud. § 865; Abh. GGW. xxxv (1888), 142].

תִּדְהָר v. p. 187.

† תַּדְמֹר **n.pr.loc.** built by Solomon, acc. to 1 K 9[18] Qr = 2 Ch 8[4]; *Tadmor* = Palmyra (RS[Ency. Brit. (9) PALMYRA] Mommsen[Röm. Gesch. v. 423], cf. Lag[BN 125]); but read in both places תָּמָר Th RS[l. c.] Mommsen[l. c.] Kmp Benz Kit Bur Reckend[ZMG xlii (1888), 402] Lag[l. c.] GASm[Geogr. 270, N. 2; 580, N. 2]; v. II. תָּמָר.

† תִּדְעָל **n.pr.m.** king allied with Chedorlaomer, called מֶלֶךְ גּוֹיִם Gn 14[1.9]; Θαλγα[λ], 𝔊L Θαργαλ (n.pr. *Tudḫula* occurs on late Bab. tablet, Pinches[Trans. Vict. Inst., xxix (1897), 47, 73], Say[Acad. Mar. 21, 1896, 242; Hast. DB TIDAL]; but ident. of pers. unproven, LW King[Hammurabi i (1898), lii] Hpt[Ball Gn 14, 1] Che[Ency. Bib. TIDAL]).

תהה (√ of foll.; mng. dub.: Aram. תְּהָא is *rage, roar* (of earth, with ref. to Gn 1[2]), of man, *bluster*; al. cf. Ar. تَاهَ (ى) *go astray*, تِيهٌ *desert waste*, but this very doubtful).

† תֹּהוּ **n.m.**[1 S 12, 21] (Albr[ZAW xvi (1896), 112]) **formlessness, confusion, unreality, emptiness** (primary meaning difficult to seize; Vrss usu. κενόν, οὐδέν, μάταιον, *inane, vacuum, vanum*; cf. Lag[Or. ii. 60; BN 144]);—**1.** *formlessness*, of primaeval earth Gn 1[2] (P), of land reduced to primaeval chaos Je 4[23] (both + וָבֹהוּ *and voidness*), Is 34[11] (אַבְנֵי בֹהוּ ‖ קַו־ת׳), 45[18] (לֹא ת׳ בְרָאָהּ ‖ לָשֶׁבֶת יְצָרָהּ); 24[10] קִרְיַת־ת׳ *city of chaos* (of ruined city); = *nothingness, empty space*, Jb 26[7] תֹּלֶה אֶרֶץ עַל־ת׳; of empty, trackless *waste* Dt 32[10] (‖ מִדְבָּר), Jb 6[18] 12[24] = ψ 107[40]. **2.** fig. of what is *empty, unreal*, as idols 1 S 12[21] (coll.: אַחֲרֵי הַתּ׳ אֲשֶׁר לֹא יוֹעִילוּ), v[21] Is 41[29] רוּחַ וָת׳ נִסְכֵּיהֶם, 44[9] (of idol-makers), groundless arguments or considerations, Is 29[21] וַיַּטּוּ בַתּ׳ צַדִּיק, 59[4] moral unreality or falsehood (בָּטוֹחַ עַל־תּ׳ ‖ וְדַבֶּר־שָׁוְא); = *a thing of nought* (cf. Ecclus 41[10] מתהו אל תהו), Is 40[17] (אֶפֶס ‖ אַיִן), v[23] (שֹׁפְטֵי אֶרֶץ כַּתּ׳ עָשָׂה ‖ לְאַיִן), *worthlessness* 49[4] (לָרִיק יָגַעְתִּי ‖ לְת׳ וְהֶבֶל כֹּחִי כִלֵּיתִי); as adv. acc. 45[19] I said not, תֹּהוּ בַקְּשׁוּנִי seek me *emptily, to no purpose*. Cf. 29[13] 𝔊 וְתֹהוּ for וַתְּהִי.

תָּהֳלָה **n.f.** error (? si vera l.; √ תהל acc. to Di[Lex. Æth. 522], who cp. Eth. ተሀለ: III. *rove, wander*; Ar. وَهِلَ is *commit error*, cf. Ba[NB § 179, Anm. 3]);—וּבְמַלְאָכָיו יָשִׂים תּ׳ Jb 4[18], < rd. תִּפְלָה q.v.

תְּהִלָּה v. II. הלל. [תַּהֲלוּכָה] v. הלך.

תהם (prob. √ of following, in view of As. *tiâmtu, tâmtu* (= תְּהוֹם) Dl[HWB 698] Jen[Kosmol. 542] Barton[JAOS xv, 1 ff.], Syr. ܬܗܘܡܐ; all from √ הום Thes Ew[§ 161] Ol[§ 213d] Sta[§ 264] al.).

† תְּהוֹם **n.f.**[Gn 7, 11 + 7 t.] **et m.**[Jb. 28, 14 + 5 t.] (Albr[ZAW xvi (1896), 62] Kö[ii. 2. 167] Ency. Bib.[DEEP]) **deep, sea, abyss** (almost alw. poet.);—abs. ת׳ Gn 1[2]+; pl. abs. תְּהֹמוֹת ψ 77[17]+, etc., בַּתּ׳ Is 63[13] ψ 106[9] (only here c. art.); cstr. תְּהוֹמוֹת 71[20] (but v. **5** infra);—**1.** *deep*, of subterranean waters, Gn 49[25] (poem in J; opp. שָׁמַיִם), Dt 33[13] (opp. *id.*); מַעְיְנוֹת ת׳ רַבָּה Gn 7[11] 8[2] (P; ‖ אֲרֻבֹּת הַשָּׁמַיִם), עינות ת׳ Pr 8[28] (‖ שְׁחָקִים), Jb 28[14] 38[16] (both ‖ יָם); תְּהוֹם רַבָּה Am 7[4] (prob.), ψ 36[7] מִשְׁפָּטֶיךָ ת׳ רַבָּה (opp. צִדְקָתְךָ כְּהַרְרֵי אֵל), Is 51[10] (perh.); so pl. תְּהֹמוֹת, Pr 8[24] (‖ מַעְיָנוֹת), 3[20] (opp. שְׁחָקִים), and prob. ψ 33[7] (‖ מֵי הַיָּם), 135[6] (+ יַמִּים). **2.** (deep) *sea*, overwhelming Tyre

Ez 26^{19} (‖ הַמַּיִם הָרַבִּים), roaring at theoph. Hb 3^{10}; in gen., ‖ יָם, Jb 38^{30} (פְּנֵי ת׳); ‖ מַיִם Jon 2^{6}; alone Jb 41^{24}; fig., ψ 42^{8} (‖ מִשְׁבָּרִים, גַּלִּים; ת׳ אֶל־ת׳ קוֹרֵא; but poss. here of Jordan, cf. **4**); in pl. = *abysses* of sea, Ex 15$^{5.8}$ (of Red Sea, so) Is 63^{13} ‖ ψ 106^{9}, ψ 77^{17}; also 78^{15} (in sim.), 107^{26} (poet. of hollows of great waves, opp. שָׁמַיִם); vaguely, כָּל־תְּהֹמוֹת ψ 135^{6} 148^{7}. **3.** *primaeval ocean, deep,* in Heb. cosmogony, פְּנֵי ת׳ Gn 1^{2} (P; ‖ פְּנֵי הַמַּיִם), Pr 8^{27} (‖ שָׁמַיִם), ψ 104^{6}.—(Cf., further, Gunk Schöpfung u. Chaos 21 ff. OC Whitehouse Hast. DB Cosmogony Zim KAT^{3}. 492 f., 509 f., 585). **4.** *deep, depth,* of river Ez 31^{4} (Nile; ‖ מַיִם, + נַהֲרֹתֶיהָ), v^{15} (‖ *id.*); pl. of *bursts* of water fertilizing Canaan, יוצאים בבקעה ובהר Dt 8^{7} (+ נַחֲלֵי מַיִם, עֲיָנֹת).—On ψ 42^{8} v. **2.** **5.** *abyss* (si vera l.): תְּהוֹמוֹת הָאָרֶץ = *Sheʾôl,* ψ 71^{20}, but Ol We תַּחְתִּיּוֹת.

[תַּהְפֻּכָה] v. הפך. **תָּו** v. I. תוה.

תוֹא v. תְּאוֹ. **[תוֹאָם]** v. תאם.

†**תּוּבַל** **n.pr.terr. et gent.** in E. Asia Minor, perh. nearly = Cappadocia (= As. *Tabalu* Dl Pa 250 f. COT Gn 10.2, cf. Di Gn 10.2);—ת׳ Is 66^{19} Ez 27^{13}, תֻּבַל 32^{26}, תֻּבָל Gn 10^{2} = 1 Ch 1^{5}, Ez 38$^{2.3}$ 39^{1}; Θοβελ.

†**תּוּבַל (-) קַיִן** **n.pr.m.** first worker in metal, acc. to Gn 4$^{22.22}$ (J); Θοβελ.

תּוּבַנְתַר v. תְּבוּנָה sub בין. **תּוּגָה** v. ינה.

תּוֹדָה v. ידה.

I. **תוה** (√ of foll.; cf. NH תָּאוֹ = BH תָּו, תְּוָה vb. denom. Pi.; 𝔗 תָּוָא Ez 9^{4}; Levy NHWB iv. 622 derives following from √אוה).

†**תָּו** **n.m.** mark;—abs. ת׳, *mark* on forehead, sign of exemption fr. judgment Ez 9$^{4.6}$; sf. תָּוִי Jb 31^{35} = *my* (written) *mark* (in attestation).

†**[תַּאֲוָה]** **n.f.** boundary (as described by a *mark*?);—cstr. תַּאֲוַת גִּבְעֹת עוֹלָם Gn 49^{26} (this mng. AV RV Ew §186 b [√תָּאָה] De Gn √אוה, תאה, תוה), but < *desire* = *desirable things,* so most.

[תָּוָה] **vb.denom.** make or set a mark;—**Pi.** *Impf.* 3 ms. ויתו Kt, וַיְתָיו Qr 1 S 21^{14} (Ges §75bb) and *he made marks* on (עַל) the doors, but < 𝔊 𝔙 Th We Dr Ges l.c. and most וַיָּתָף *he drummed* (v. תפף). **Hiph.** וְהִתְוִיתָ תָו עַל־ Ez 9^{4} *set a mark* (acc. cogn.) *upon.*

†II. **[תָּוָה]** **vb. Hiph.** prob. pain, wound (fig.) (Aram. ܬܘܳܐ (oft.), תְּוָא (rare) תְּהָא 𝔗^{J}, all *repent*);—*Pf.* 3 pl. וּקְדוֹשׁ יִשׂ׳ הִתְווּ ψ 78^{41} (‖ וַיְנַסּוּ) *the Holy One of Isr. they pained* (𝔊 παρώξυναν).

†**תּוֹחַ** **n.pr.m.** ancestor of Samuel 1 Ch 6^{19} [Levite?]; Θειε, Θοουε, 𝔊L Ναωθ; ‖ תֹּחוּ 1 S 1^{1}; Θοκε, Θοου, 𝔊L Θωε.

תּוֹחֶלֶת v. יחל.

תּוֹךְ *injury,* v. תֹּךְ sub תכך.

תָּוֶךְ 418 **subst.** midst (NH *id.*, also denom. תָּוֵוךְ; √unknown; not apparently in cognate languages);—abs. תָּוֶךְ Gn 15^{10} +; cstr. תּוֹךְ 1^{6} +; תּוֹכֵכִי ψ 116^{19} 135^{9}, etc., 2 fs. תּוֹכוֹ, תּוֹכִי, תּוֹלה † Ez 48$^{15.21}$, תּוֹכֲכֶם Gn 23^{9} +, תּוֹכֶהְנָה † Ez 16^{53} (Ges §91 f);—*midst,* whether of a space or place, a number of people or things, or of a line: abs. † Ju 16^{29} עַמּוּדֵי הַתָּוֶךְ = the *middle* columns, Je 39^{3} שַׁעַר הַתּ׳, בַּתָּוֶךְ Gn 15^{10} וַיְבַתֵּר, אֹתָם בַּתּ׳, Nu 35^{5} וְהָעִיר בַּתָּוֶךְ, Jos 8^{22} Ju 15^{4} Is 66^{17} אַחַר אֶחָד בַּתָּוֶךְ; cstr. 1 K 8^{64} קִדַּשׁ הַמֶּלֶךְ אֶת־ תּוֹךְ הֶחָצֵר, Ez 15^{4} וְתוֹכוֹ נָחָר; usu. c. prep., as בְּ (oft. = an emph. *in,* in the very heart and midst of), Gn 1^{6} בְּתוֹךְ הַמַּיִם, 2^{9} בְּת׳ הַגָּן, 9^{21} בְּת׳ אָהֳלֹה, 18^{24} בְּת׳ הָעִיר, 37^{7} בְּת׳ הַשָּׂדֶה, Ex 11^{4} אני יוצא בת׳ מצרים, 39^{3}, Jos 8^{9} בְּת׳ הָעָם, Ju 7^{16} בת׳ הַכַּדִּים, 1 K 3^{20} בְּת׳ הַלָּיְלָה; בְּתוֹכָהּ (of land or city) Nu 13^{32} Is 7^{6}, etc.; in Ez בְּתוֹכֵךְ, בְּתוֹכָהּ, etc., of sins done, or judgment to be wrought, *in the very midst* of Jerusalem, Ez 5$^{8.10}$ 9^{4} 22$^{3.7.9.13}$ +; בְּת׳ מֵעַי ψ 22^{15}, 40^{9} תּוֹרָתְךָ בְּת׳ מֵעָי, v^{11} בְּת׳ לִבִּי, cf. Pr 4^{21}; after verbs of motion, = *into* Ex 14^{27} 1 S 9^{14}, = *through* Ex 14^{29} Nu 33^{8} Ez 9^{4} Ne 9^{11}; of a number of persons = *among* (not necess. of the actual *middle*), Gn 40^{20} בְּת׳ עֲבָדָיו, 23^{6} בְּתוֹכֵנוּ, 1 S 10^{10} Jb 1^{6}, etc., הַגֵּר בְּתוֹכְכֶם Lv 17$^{8.10.13}$ +; = *between* (of things arranged by twos) Ex 39^{25}; in P oft. (12 t.) of the divine presence, or dwelling, *in the midst of* Isr., Ex 25^{8} 29$^{45.46}$ Lv 15^{31} 16^{16} + (Carpenter Hex. i. 209, ed. 2, 410; JED in such cases have alw. קֶרֶב), so Ez 37$^{26.28}$ 43$^{7.9}$, cf. Hg 2^{5}; מִן, as Gn 19^{29} מִתּוֹךְ הַהֲפֵכָה, Ex 3^{2} מִתּ׳ הַסְּנֶה, 33^{11} לֹא יָמִישׁ מִתּ׳ הָאֹהֶל, Dt 4^{12} + מִתּ׳ הָאֵשׁ, 1 S 15^{6} רְדוּ מִתּ׳ עֲמָלֵק; = *from among,* as to take, separate, etc., מִתּ׳ הָעָם, מִתּוֹכָם, etc., Ex 7^{5} 28^{1} Nu 3^{12} 4$^{2.18}$ 16$^{21.33}$ 17^{10} 19^{20} (all P) +; אֶל, as Ex 14^{23} ויבאו . . . אֶל־תּוֹךְ הַיָּם, Lv 11^{33}, Nu 17^{12} וַיָּרָץ אֶל־תּ׳ הַקָּהָל, 19^{6} Dt 21^{12} וַהֲבֵאתָהּ אֶל־תּ׳ בֵּיתֶךָ, 22^{2} 23^{11} 2 S 3^{27} 4^{6} Je 21^{4} +; מֵעַל † Ez 11^{23}.—תּוֹךְ is used by most writers, occurring c. 8–10 times in many books, but is esp. frequent in P (c. 106 t.) and Ez (116 t.). Syn. קֶרֶב, q.v.

†תִּיכֹן, תִּיכוֹן **adj.** middle;—abs. תּ׳ Ex 26^{28}+, fs תִּי(וֹ)כוֹנָה Ju 7^{19}+, fpl ־נוֹת Ez 42$^{5.6}$ (on form, v. הִיצוֹן p 300, Ges^{§27s});—Ex 26^{28} = 36^{33} (P) הַבְּרִיחַ הַתִּיכֹן בְּתוֹךְ הַקְּרָשִׁים the *middle* bar (holding the 'boards' in their place); Ju 7^{19} הָאַשְׁמֹרֶת הַתּ׳ the *middle* watch (of the night); of the *middle* story of side-chambers to Temple 1 K 6$^{8.8b}$ (v^{8a} rd c. 𝔊 𝔗 הַתַּחְתֹּנָה for הַתִּי׳), Ez 41^{7b} (read c 𝔊 𝔖 וּמִן־התחתונה יַעֲלוּ לַתִּיכוֹנָה וּמִן־הַתִּיכוֹנָה עַל־העליונה), 42$^{5.6}$, 2 K 20^{4} הָעִיר הַתִּיכֹנָה (but rd c Qr Vrss חָצֵר הַתּ׳, i e. the חָצֵר הָאַחֶרֶת, v. I. חָצֵר **2**) — חָצֵר הַתִּיכוֹן Ez 47^{16}, v. p 347^{b}

תּוֹכֵחָה, תּוֹכַחַת v יכח   תֻּכִּיִּים v. תֻּכ׳.

תּוֹלֵד, [תּוֹלְדוֹת] v. ילד   תּוֹלוֹן v. תילן.

†[תּוֹלָל] **n.m.** doubtful word, only pl sf. וְתוֹלָלֵינוּ ψ 137^{3}, AV RV *they that wasted us*, cf 𝔗, but rd then וְשׁוֹלָלֵינוּ Bae al; >Thes^{596} Hup De al *made us wail* (√ילל)

תּוֹמִיךְ v תמך   תּוֹמִים v [תּוֹאָם], תאם.

תּוֹמָן v II תֵּימָן sub ימן.   תּוֹעָה v תעה.

[תּוֹעָפָה] v II. יעף   [תּוֹצָאָה] v. יצא

תוקהת Kt, תָּקְהַת Qr, v III תִּקְוָה p 876.

תוף (√of foll [Levy$^{NHWB\ iv\ 661}$, s. v. תופת, assumes √תפף]; akin to Eth ቶፍአ: *spit*, Aram (Talm) תְּפַף *id*, Ar تُفًّا *fie! for shame!* Syr ܐܬܦ Aph (and deriv) also = *spew out* (Ba$^{ES\ 28}$), but prob. simply *return*).

†I. תֹּפֶת **n.f.** act of **spitting**,—abs וְתֹ׳ לְפָנִים Jb 17^{6} *a spitting in the face* do I become, i.e men spit in my face (‖ לְמָשָׁל עַמִּים; Perles Baer Bu מֹפֵת לפניהם)   II. תֹּפֶת v. תפת

†**תּוּר** **vb. seek out, spy out, explore** (NH *id* (rare), perh orig *turn* (to or about), As. *târu*, *turn about, back*, *tairûru* adj *turning back*, also *merciful*, and subst *mercy*, Ar. تَارَ (و) IV *go about* (rare), تُرْجُمَان *a go-between*),—**Qal** *Pf* 1 s תַּרְתִּי Ez 20^{6} Ec 2^{3}, 3 pl תָּרוּ Nu 13^{32}, 2 mpl תַּרְתֶּם 14^{34}, *Impf* 3 mpl יָתֻרוּ 13^{2}, וַיָּתֻרוּ v^{21}; rd also 3 ms. יָתוּר Jb 39^{8} 𝔙 𝔗 Ew Di Bu Du and most (for יְתוּר), 2 mpl. תָתוּרוּ Nu 15^{39}, *Inf cstr.* תּוּר 10^{33}+, *Pt.* pl תָּרִים 14^{6}, on 1 K 10^{15} 2 Ch 9^{14} v infra,—**1.** *seek out, select* לָתוּר לָהֶם מְנוּחָה Nu 10^{33} (J, subj ark of י׳), cf Dt 1^{33} (subj י׳), Ez 20^{6} (*id*, acc land), sq. inf. = *find out how* to do something, תּ׳ בְלִבִּי ל Ec 2^{3}. **2** *spy out, explore*, acc. of land Nu 13$^{2.16.17.21.25.32.32}$ 14$^{7.34.36.38}$, acc of mts. Jb 39^{8} (v. supr), cf. Pt. as subj. *explorers, spies* Nu 14^{6} (all P); *explore* mentally, לָדַעַת וְלָתוּר וּבַקֵּשׁ חָכְמָה Ec 7^{25}, cf. 9^{1} Gr (ת׳ for בוּר q v), 1^{13} לָת׳ בְּחָכְמָה עַל־ (Kue$^{Ond\ 2,\ iii\ 196}$). **3.** *go about*, fig אַחֲרֵי לְבַבְכֶם Nu 15^{39} (P); *Pt.* אַנְשֵׁי הַתָּרִים 1 K 10^{15} 2 Ch 9^{14}, usually *merchants* (‖ סֹחֲרִים רֹכְלִים), Kit, after 𝔖 2 Ch, prop. הָעָרִים for הַתָּרִים. **Hiph.** *Impf* 3 mpl. וַיָּתִירוּ בְבֵית־אֵל Ju 1^{23} *they made a reconnoisance at Bethel* (Vrss disagree, Gie וַיִּחֲנוּ, cf GFM); 3 ms. יָתֵר מֵרֵעֵהוּ צַדִּיק Pr 12^{26} *the righteous searches out* (RV *is a guide to*) *his friend*, 𝔗 AV *is more excellent than* (reading יָתֵר), Hi Ew De al. *spies out his pasture* (מִרְעֵהוּ, in spiritual sense), all dubious; Toy conjectures יָסֵר מֵרָעָה

†I תֹּר, תּוֹר **n.m. plait, turn** (Ar. تَارَةٌ *period, succession* (περίοδος)),—pl. תּוֹרִים *plaits* (of hair?) Ct 1^{10}, cstr. תּוֹרֵי זָהָב v^{11} *plaits, circlets of gold*; sg. *turn*, opportunity, cstr. תֹּר נַעֲרָה Est 2^{12}, cf v^{15}.—תּוֹר אדם 1 Ch 17^{17} is corrupt, ‖ 2 S 7^{19} תּוֹרַת הָאָדָם, also difficult, v. תּוֹרָה **3**, p. 436; Klo Perles$^{Anal\ 63}$ תֹּאַר, q.v.

יתור Jb 39^{8} appar **n.m.** a *searching*, but v. √.

II תּוֹר v. II תֹּר.

תּוֹרָה v. ירה.   תּוֹשָׁב v. ישב.

תּוּשִׁיָּה v. ישה.   תּוֹתָח Jb 41^{21} v. יתח.

†[הִתַּז] **vb. Hiph. strike away** (𝔗 נְתַז (rare) *spring forth*; NH נִתַּז *spring, spurt, out*; Hiph., Aph. *cut off* (head, etc)),—*Pf* 3 ms אֶת־הַנְּטִישׁוֹת הֵסִיר הֵתַז Is 18^{5}.

תַּזְנוּת v. זנה   [תַּחְבֻּלָה] v I חבל.

תחו v. תּוֹחַ.   תַּחְכְּמֹנִי v. p. 315^{b}.

תַּחֲלֻאִים v I חלא.   תְּחִלָּה v. II חלל p 321.

תֹּחֶלֶת v. תּוֹחֶלֶת sub יחל.   תַּחְמָס v. חמס.

תַּחַן v חנה.   I, II תְּחִנָּה v. I. חנן.

תַּחֲנוּן v. חנן.   [תַּחֲנָה], תַּחֲנִי v חנה.

†**תַּחְפַּנְחֵס** **n. pr. loc.** Egyptian city Je 43$^{7.8.9}$ 44^{1} 46^{14}, so Je 2^{16} Qr (Kt תחפנס); = תְּחַפְנְחֵס Ez 30^{18}, Ταφνα(ι)ς [Ταφναι]; identif. with Gk *Daphnae*, mod. *Tel Defenneh*, c. 18 m. ESE from Tanis, c. 9 m. W. of *El-Kantara*, Bad$^{Egypt.\ 5th\ ed.\ (1902),\ 189}$ Petrie$^{Defenneh\ (Tanis\ II),\ 1888}$.

†תַּחְפְּנֵיס **n.pr.f.** Egyptian queen;—1 K 11[19.20], -נֵס v[20]; Θεκ[χ]εμεινα.

†תַּחְרָא **n.[m.]** prob. (linen) corselet (𝔗[Onk] שריון);—abs. ת׳ Ex 28[32], ‖39[23] (P), in sim.

[תַּחֲרָה] v. חרה. תַּחֲרֻעַ v. חרע.

†I. תַּחַשׁ **n.m.** taḥaš, a kind of leather or skin, and perh. the animal yielding it (prob. the *dugong*, cf. Ar. تُخَس *dolphin*, Thes[1500] Di-Ry[Ex 25.5] Post[Hast. DB Badger]; As. *taḫšu* (Dl Baer Ezech. xvi), for which Dl[Prol. 77 ff.; HWB 705] conj. meaning *sheep(skin)*; Bondi[Egyptiaca 1 ff.] cp. Egypt. *tḥś*, *leather;* v. summary of views M'Lean-Shipley[Ency. Bib. Badgers' Skins]);—abs. ת׳ Nu 4[6]+, תָּחַשׁ v[8]+; pl. תְּחָשִׁים Ex 25[5]+;—leather used for (woman's) sandals Ez 16[10]; elsewhere for cover of tabernacle Nu 4[25], עוֹר ת׳ v[6.8.10.11.12.14], עֹרֹת (הַ)תְּחָשִׁים Ex 25[5] 26[14] 35[7.23] 36[19] 39[34] (all P).

†II. תַּחַשׁ **n.pr.m.** 'son' of Nahor Gn 22[24]; Τοχος; identif. by Wkl[Mitth. d. Vorderas. Gesellsch. 1896, 207] with *Tiḫeši* (Egypt.), which WMM[As. u. Eur. 258] puts N. of Kadesh on Orontes.

תַּחַת **n.[m.]** the under part (Ar. تَحْتُ *id.*), hence as **adv. accus.** and **prep. underneath, below, instead of** (so Ar. تَحْتَ, Sab. תחת, Eth. ታሕተ: Ph. תחת (Lzb[385]); BAram. 𝔗 תְּחוֹת, Palm. in מן לתחת Tariff 1[4] (Cooke[320]), Syr. ܬܚܘܬ);—**I.** as **adv. accus.** †Gn 49[25] (=Dt 33[13]) the deep רֹבֶצֶת תָּ֑חַת that coucheth *beneath;* more usu. with מִן, מִתַּחַת lit. *off* (מִן **1 c**) *the under part=beneath,* †Ex 20[4] (=Dt 5[8]) בָּאָרֶץ מִתָּ֑חַת (so Dt 4[39] Jos 2[11] 1 K 8[23] [both D[2]], Is 51[6]), Dt 33[27] Ju 7[8] Am 2[9] Is 14[9] Jb 18[16] Ez 47[1b]. **II.** as **prep.**; so cstr., and with sf. (usu. in the pl., and so lit. *in the parts underneath*) תַּחְתַּי Hb 3[16]+, תַּחְתֵּנִי (cf. עוֹדֶנִּי, בַּעֲדֵנִי: Ges[§103d]) †2 S 22[37.40.48] (ψ 18[37.40.48] תַּחְתָּ֑י); תַּחְתֶּיךָ; תַּחְתָּיו (Kt תחתו †2 S 2[23] 3[12] 16[8] Jb 9[13]), תַּחְתֶּיהָ Lv 13[23]+16 t., תַּחְתֶּ֫נָּה (cf. עוֹדֶנָּה, אֵינֶנָּה) †Gn 2[21]; תַּחְתֵּינוּ †1 S 14[9] ψ 47[4]; תַּחְתֵּיכֶם †Jos 2[14] Am 2[13]; תַּחְתֵּיהֶם †Nu 16[31] 1 K 20[24] 1 Ch 4[41] 5[22] 2 Ch 12[10] (for תַּחְתָּם 1 K 14[27]), תַּחְתָּם Dt 2[12]+10 t., תַּחְתֵּיהֶן †Je 28[13];—**1.** *under, beneath,* Gn 7[19] תַּחַת כָּל־הַשָּׁמַיִם *under* the whole heaven (so †Dt 2[25] 4[19] Jb 28[24] 37[3] 41[3] Dn 9[12]), 18[4] ת׳ הָעֵץ, 21[15] 24[2]+ oft.; Jb 30[14] ת׳ שֹׁאָה *under* the crash they roll themselves against me; ת׳ הַשֶּׁמֶשׁ Ec 1[3.9.13]+oft. Ec. (so in Ph., Cooke[4.7; 5.12]). With לְ, †2 Ch 4[3] תַּחַת לוֹ, Ct 2[6]=8[3] ת׳ לְרֹאשִׁי. Idiom. **a.** תַּחַת הָהָר *at the foot of* the mt., Ex 24[4] Dt 4[11], so 3[17] ת׳ אַשְׁדֹּת הַפִּסְגָּה, Jos 11[3.17]+; fig. ψ 18[37] תַּרְחִיב צַעֲדִי תַחְתָּי thou broadenest my steps *under me,* Jb 36[16] רַחַב לֹא מוּצָק תַּחְתֶּיךָ (so read for תחתיה, Di Bu) breadth unstraitened is *beneath thee.* **b.** ת׳ הַלָּשׁוֹן, of something held there as a dainty morsel, and ready, when needed, to be brought out, fig. of sweetness Ct 4[11], of evil ψ 10[7] ת׳ לְשׁוֹנוֹ עָמָל וָאָוֶן, Jb 20[12] (so ת׳ שְׂפָתֵימוֹ ψ 140[4]), of praise ψ 66[17] וְרוֹמַם ת׳ לְשׁוֹנִי (syn. בִּגְרוֹנָם 149[6]). **c.** תַּחַת פ׳: (*a*) of subjection, ψ 18[40] תַּכְרִיעַ קָמַי תַּחְתָּ֑י, v[48] (cf. 47[4] 144[2]), 45[6] Jb 9[13]. (*b*) of a woman, ת׳ אִישָׁהּ, i.e. under his authority, Nu 5[19.20.29], so Ez 23[5] תַּחְתָּ֑י being *under me*=being *mine* (fig. of Israel as י׳'s spouse), cf. ὕπανδρος Rom 7[2], and تَحْتَ Kor 66[10]. (*c*) of being burdened or oppressed under, Is 24[5] the earth חָנְפָה ת׳ יֹשְׁבֶיהָ, Pr 30[21] ת׳ שָׁלוֹשׁ רָגְזָה אֶרֶץ, v[22.23]; Hb 3[7] ת׳ אָוֶן i.e. (si vera l.) suffering *under* calamity. **d.** ת׳ יַד פ׳, of authority or control, Gn 41[35] וְיִצְבְּרוּ בָר ת׳ יַד פַּרְעֹה; Ju 3[30] (cf. ψ 106[42]), 1 S 21[4.5] (del. אֶל; dittogr. חל), v[9] Is 3[6]. **e.** ת׳ רַגְלֵי פ׳, of subjection or conquest, ψ 8[7] כֹּל שַׁתָּה ת׳ רַגְלָיו, 18[39] 47[4] La 3[34], cf. Mal 3[21]. **2.** *what is under* one, *the place in which* one stands: hence as accus., **a.** with reflex. pron., idiom., *in one's place, where one stands,* Ex 16[29] שְׁבוּ אִישׁ תַּחְתָּיו abide every one *in his place,* Lv 13[23.28] Jos 5[8] 6[5.20] Ju 7[21] 1 S 14[9] וְעָמַדְנוּ תַחְתֵּינוּ we will *remain where we are,* 2 S 2[23] וַיָּמָת תַּחְתָּו he died *where he was* (cf. Je 38[9] [read וּמֵת]), 7[10] Is 25[10] 46[7] Am 2[13] Hb 3[16] וְתַחְתַּי אֶרְגָּז I tremble *where I stand,* Zc 12[6] 14[10] Jb 36[20] 40[12] וַהֲדֹךְ רְשָׁעִים תַּחְתָּם. **b.** in transferred sense, *in place of, instead of:* (*a*) Gn 2[18] 4[25] ת׳ הֶבֶל *instead of* Abel, 22[13] ת׳ בְּנוֹ, 30[2] הֲתַ֫חַת אלהים אנכי (cf. 50[19]), 44[33] 2 S 19[1]+oft.; Jb 16[4] Is 3[24] 55[13] 61[3.7]; of one succeeding to the place of another, וַיִּמְלֹךְ תַּחְתָּיו Gn 36[33–39] 1 K 8[20] 11[43] 14[20]+oft., Dt 2[12.21] וַיֵּשְׁבוּ תַחְתָּם, Lv 16[32] 1 K 2[35]+; ψ 45[17] *in place of* thy fathers (whom thou mayest therefore forget) will be thy children. Cf. in Ph. CIS[1.3.9] (Cooke[30]). Sq. inf. Is 60[15] ת׳ הֱיוֹתֵךְ *instead of thy being ...* Peculiarly Jb 34[26] (si vera l.)= *as if they were, like;* but text very dubious; Bi Bu תַּחַת חֲמָתוֹ רְשָׁעִים his wrath breaketh in pieces the wicked. (*b*) in partic., of things mutually interchanged, *in place of, in exchange* or *return for:* Gn 30[15] ת׳ דּוּדָאֵי בְנֵךְ *in return for* thy son's love-apples, Ex 21[23] נֶפֶשׁ ת׳ נָפֶשׁ life *for* life, v[24.25.26.27.36.37], Jos 2[14] נַפְשֵׁנוּ תַחְתֵּיכֶם

לָמוּת, 1 S 2^{20} 1 K 20^{39} נפשך ת׳ נפשו, v^{42} (cf. 2 K 10^{24}), 21^{2} Is $43^{3.4}$; often with vbs. of requiting, Gn 44^{4} לָמָּה שִׁלַּמְתֶּם רָעָה ת׳ טוֹבָה why have ye rewarded evil *in exchange for* good? 1 S 25^{21} 2 S 16^{12} 19^{22} ψ 35^{12} יְשַׁלְּמוּנִי רָעָה ת׳ טוֹבָה, 38^{21a} $109^{4.5}$ Pr 17^{13}+; Je 5^{19} תַּחַת מֶה *in return for what?* (cf. עַל־מֶה 22^{8} Dt 29^{23} 1 K 9^{8}). So sq. inf. ψ 38^{21b}. †**3.** as **conj.**: **a.** תַּחַת אֲשֶׁר: (*a*) *instead of that* (Germ. *anstatt dass*), Dt 28^{62} ת׳ א׳ הֱיִיתֶם *instead of that* ye were ..., *instead of* your being ..., Ez 36^{34}. (*b*) *in return for* (the fact) *that, because that* (𝔊 ἀνθ᾽ ὧν Am 1^{3}+ oft.), Nu 25^{13} ת׳ אֲשֶׁר קִנֵּא לא׳, Dt 21^{14} 22^{29} 28^{47} 1 S 26^{21} 2 K 22^{17}=2 Ch 34^{25}, Is 53^{12} Je 29^{19} 50^{7} 2 Ch 21^{12}. **b.** תַּחַת כִּי Dt 4^{37} (but? read וַתְּחִי as end of v^{36}), Pr 1^{29}. Cf. עֵקֶב אֲשֶׁר (כִּי). **III.** compounds:—†**1.** אֶל־תַּחַת, after a vb. of motion: **a.** (*in*) *under*, Ju 6^{19} וַיּוֹצֵא אֶל־ ת׳ הָאֵלָה, 1 K 8^{6} (‖ 2 Ch 5^{7}), Je 3^{6} 38^{11} (on 1 S 21^{5} v. **II. 1 d**); after קָרָא Zc 3^{10}: so אֶל־ת׳ ל׳ Ez 10^{2}. **b.** *into the place of*, Lv 14^{42}. **2.** מִתַּחַת (=ὑπ᾽ ἐκ): **a.** alone, *from under, from beneath*, as מִתַּחַת הַשָּׁמַיִם †Gn 1^{7}, and esp. after such vbs. as שַׁחֵת 6^{17}, מָחָה Ex 17^{14} Dt 9^{14} 25^{19} 29^{19} 2 K 14^{27}, הָאֱבִיד Dt 7^{24}, cf. La 3^{66}; Ez 47^{1a} מִת׳ מִפְתַּן הַבַּיִת, Pr 22^{27} לָמָּה יִקַּח מִשְׁכָּבְךָ מִתַּחְתֶּיךָ; Ex $6^{6.7}$ מִת׳ סִבְלֹת מִצְרַיִם, Ho 4^{12} וַיִּזְנוּ מִת׳ אֱלֹהֵיהֶם (cf. **II. 1 c** *a, b*); מִת׳ יַד פ׳ (cf. **II. 1 d**) *from under the hand* (power) *of* ... Ex 18^{10} 2 K $8^{20.22}$ 13^{5} 17^{7}+; מִתַּחְתָּיו (cf. **II. 2 a**) *from his place* Ex 10^{23} Zc 6^{12}. Rarely=תַּחַת or מִתַּחַת לְ׳, Gn 1^{9} (P) Ez 1^{8} 42^{9} 46^{23} Jb 26^{5}. **b.** מִתַּחַת לְ׳ (opp. מִמַּעַל לְ׳) *under, beneath*: Gn 1^{17} הַמַּיִם אֲשֶׁר מִת׳ לָרָקִיעַ, Ex 20^{4} הַמַּיִם מִתַּחַת לָאָרֶץ (so Dt 4^{18} 5^{8}), Ju 3^{16} מִת׳ לְמַדָּיו, Je 38^{12}+; of locality, †Gn 35^{8} מִת׳ לְבֵית־אֵל, 1 S 7^{11} 1 K 4^{12}. **c.** † לְמִתַּחַת לְ׳ (cf. מִן **9 b**), i. q. מִתַּחַת לְ׳ 1 K 7^{32}.

†תַּחְתּוֹן **adj.** lower, lowest;—abs. ת׳ Jos 16^{3}+, fs. ־תֹּנָה Is 22^{9}+, fpl. ־תֹּנֹת Ez $42^{5.6}$;—*lower*, Is 22^{9} הַבְּרֵכָה הַתּ׳ the *lower* pool (in Jerus.), of pavement and gate of outer (lower) temple-court Ez $40^{18.19}$ (l. הַשּׁ׳ הַתַּחְתּוֹן), of *lower* ledge (עֲזָרָה) of altar, 43^{14}; of the *lowest* of the three stories of side-chambers surrounding the temple, 1 K 6^{6} הַיָּצִועַ הַתּ׳, +v^{8a} (v. תִּיכוֹן), Ez 41^{7} (read וּמִן for וְכֵן), $42^{5.6}$; in place-name, בֵּית־חוֹרֹן תּ׳ Jos 16^{3} 18^{13} 1 K 9^{17} (‖ 2 Ch 8^{5} הַתּ׳), בֵּית־חוֹרֹן הַתּ׳ 1 Ch 7^{24} 2 Ch 8^{5}.

†תַּחְתִּי **adj.** and **subst.** lower, lowest (places):—fs. תַּחְתִּיָּה †ψ 86^{13}, תַּחְתִּית Ex 19^{17}+; mpl. תַּחְתִּיִּם †Gn 6^{16}; fpl. תַּחְתִּיּוֹת ψ 63^{10}+;—Ex 19^{17} ויתיצבו בְּתַחְתִּית הָהָר in the *lower part* of the mt., Ju 1^{15}=Jos 15^{19} (so read here with 𝔊^MSS 𝔖 𝔗 𝔙 for גֻּלֹּת תַּחְתִּיּוֹת) אֵת גֻּלַּת תַּחְתִּית the *lower* spring, Jb 41^{16} כְּפֶלַח תַּחְתִּית like the *lower* mill-stone, Gn 6^{16} (P) תַּחְתִּיִּם=*lower stories;* of Sheʾôl, Dt 32^{22} עַד שְׁאוֹל תַּחְתִּית to the *lowest* Sheʾôl, ψ 86^{13} מִשְּׁ׳ תַּחְתִּיָּה, so אֶרֶץ תַּחְתִּית the *lowest* earth (or land), i.e. Sh., Ez $31^{14.16.18}$, אֶרֶץ תַּחְתִּיּוֹת the land of *lowest places* 26^{20} $32^{18.24}$, בּוֹר תַּחְתִּיּוֹת the pit of *lowest places* Lam 3^{55} ψ 88^{7}, תַּחְתִּיּוֹת הָאָרֶץ 63^{10} (+perh. 71^{20}) the *lowest places* of the earth, ת׳ אֶרֶץ Is 44^{23}, and fig. of the dark and hidden interior of the womb ψ 139^{15}.—Ne 4^{7} וָאַעֲמִיד מִתַּחְתִּיּוֹת לַמָּקוֹם and I set (𝔊^L *and they stood*) *at parts below* (מִן as in מִתַּחַת לְ׳) the place (where they were to work), so Ke Gu, but text perhaps corrupt (Berthol Sgf).

†II. תַּחַת **n.pr. 1. m. a.** Levite 1 Ch $6^{9.22}$. **b.** Ephraimite $7^{20.20}$.—Θααθ, Καaθ, etc. **2. loc.** station in wilderness Nu $33^{26.27}$; Καταaθ.

תַּחְתִּים חָדְשִׁי v. II. קָדֵשׁ **2.** תִּיכוֹן v. תָּוֶךְ.

†תִּילוֹן **n.pr.m.** in Judah, 1 Ch 4^{20} Qr (Kt תולון); Ιωνων, A Θιλων, 𝔊L Θωλειμ.

†תֵּימָא **n.pr.terr.** et **gent.** (OAram. תימא Lzb[385]; in As. *Têma* Dl[Pa 301 f.] Schr[KGF 261 ff.];=*south country*, √ימא (cf. תֵּימָן, √ימן) acc. to Nö[Ency. Bib. Ishmael]);—ישְׁבֵי אֶרֶץ ת׳ Is 21^{14}, people Je 25^{23}; ת׳ 'son' of Ishmael Gn 25^{15} ‖ 1 Ch 1^{30}; אָרְחוֹת תֵּמָא (l. אֹרְ׳) Jb 6^{19}; Θαιμαν. Mod. *Teyma*, NW. Arabia, Doughty[Arab. Des. i. pass., esp. 284–299] Wilson[Hast. DB Tema], and on inscr. found there Eut[Nab. Inschr. 35] CIS[ii, No. 113.114] Nö[SBAk. 1884, 813 f.] Hal[RÉJ xii, 111 ff.] Cooke[195 ff.]

I. II. תֵּימָן, תֵּימָנִי, תֵּימְנִי v. ימן.

[תִּימָרָה] v. תמר.

†תִּיצִי **adj.gent.** (?): הַתּ׳ 1 Ch 11^{45}, unknown.

תִּירוֹשׁ תִּירשׁ v. ירשׁ.

†תִּירְיָא **n.pr.m.** in Judah, 1 Ch 4^{16}; Ζαιρα, A Θηρια, 𝔊L Εθρια.

†תִּירָס **n.pr.terr.** et **gent.** 'son' of Japhet Gn 10^{2} 1 Ch 1^{5}; Θειρας; identified by Mey[Gesch. d. Alt. i. 260] Di Holz Gunk al. with Gk. Τυρσηνοί, Egypt. *Turuša*, on coast of Ægean.

†[תַּיִשׁ] **n.m.** he-goat (NH *id.*; Ar. تَيْس, Aram. תֵּישָׁא, תַּיְשָׁא, ܬܝܫܐ *id.*; √unknown);—

abs. תַּיִשׁ Pr 30[31]; pl. תְּיָשִׁים Gn 30[35] (J), 32[15] (E; + עִזִּים *she-goats*), 2 Ch 17[11].

תֹּךְ v. תכך.

† [תָּכָה] **vb.** meaning wholly dub.;—**Pu.** *Pf.* 3 pl. וְהֵם תֻּכּוּ לְרַגְלֶךָ Dt 33[3]; *were led* or *assembled* would suit context; v. esp. Dr Berthol.

תְּכוּנָה v. כון.

† תֻּכִּיִּים **n.m.** peacocks (acc. to 𝔗 𝔖 Jerome Rabb.; perh. = Malabar *tôgai, tôghai, peacock* Thes[1502]);—1 K 10[22] = תּוּכִּיִּים 2 Ch 9[21] + ivory, apes.

תכך (√ of foll., cf. pl.; Ar. تَكَّ *overcome* (of wine), *tread under foot;* akin to Aram. ܬܵܟ, 𝔗 תּוּךְ (rare) *injure*, ܬܘܟܐ, תּוּכָא (rare) *injury*).

† תֹּךְ, II. תּוֹךְ **n.m.** injury, oppression;—abs. תֹּךְ, + מִרְמָה ψ 10[7] 55[12] (so Gi; Baer תּוֹךְ); תּוֹךְ, + חָמָס (gloss) 72[14]; pl. אִישׁ תְּכָכִים Pr 29[13] *oppressor* (𝔙 *creditor;* cf. איש חמסים 2 S 22[49] ψ 140[2.5]).—I. תּוֹךְ v. תָּוֶךְ.

תְּכָכִים v. תֹּךְ. תַּכְלִית, תִּכְלָה v. כלה.

תְּכֵלֶת [48] **n.f.** violet, i.e. violet thread and stuff; 𝔊 usu. ὑάκινθος, ὑακίνθινος; v. Thatcher Hast. DB Colours (NH = BH; 𝔗 תִּכְלָא, תַּכְלָא, תִּכְלְתָא);—**1.** *violet thread* (spun, Ex 35[25]; woven, 39[3]): **a.** in Ex (P) of hangings of tabern., ephod, etc., + ת׳ + אַרְגָּמָן, תּוֹלַעַת שָׁנִי (q. v.; oft. also שֵׁשׁ, זהב), Ex 25[4] 26[1] 28[5.6] 28[33] 35[25] + 20 t.; of temple hangings (+ אַרְגָּוָן, אַרְגָּמָן, כַּרְמִיל, בוּץ) 2 Ch 2[6.13.14]; loops or cords of ת׳ (alone) Ex 26[4] 28[28.31.37] 36[11] 39[21.22.31] Nu 15[38] (all P). **b.** palace hangings in Shushan, + חוּר Est 1[6]. †**2.** *violet stuff, fabric;* גְּלוֹמֵי ת׳ לְבוּשֵׁי ת׳ Ez 23[6], 27[24]; ת׳ וְאַרְגָּמָן לְבוּשָׁם Je 10[9]; also in trade Ez 27[7] (+ שֵׁשׁ בְּרִקְמָה, אַרְגָּמָן), cf. בֶּגֶד ת׳ for covering sacred utensils Nu 4[6.7.9.11.12] (P).

† [תָּכַן] **vb.** regulate, measure, estimate (cf. Aram. Pa. תַּכֵּן (rare) *prepare* (= כּוֹנֵן, הֵכִין); acc. to Ry[Syn. d. Wahren u. Guten 33] a secondary √ from כון);—**Qal** *Pt. estimate*, fig.: וְתֹכֵן רוּחוֹת ׳ Pr 16[2], so (לִבּוֹת) 21[2] 24[12]. **Niph. 1.** *Pf.* 3 pl. וְלֹא [לוֹ] נִתְכְּנוּ עֲלִלוֹת 1 S 2[3] *by him* (׳) *are actions estimated.* **2.** *Impf., be adjusted to the standard*, i.e. right, equitable: subj. דֶּרֶךְ (of ׳ and of Israel), 3 ms. יִתָּכֵן Ez 18[25.25.29.29] 33[17.17.20]; 3 mpl. יִתָּכְנוּ 18[29], יִתָּכְנוּ v[25]. **Pi.** *Pf.* 3 ms.: *mete out*, מַיִם תִּכֵּן בְּמִדָּה Jb 28[25]; וְשָׁמַיִם בַּזֶּרֶת ת׳ Is 40[12] (‖ כול, מדד); מִי ת׳ אֶת־רוּחַ ׳ v[13] (v. **Qal**; read poss. הֵבִין or הֵכִין); 1 s. ψ 75[4] תִּכַּנְתִּי עַמּוּדֶיהָ I *regulate* (or *adjust*) her pillars (i.e. of earth). **Pu.** *Pt.* הַכֶּסֶף הַמְתֻכָּן 2 K 12[12] the silver which was *measured out.*

† I. תֹּכֶן **n.m.** [Ez 45,11] measurement;—cstr. ת׳ לְבֵנִים Ex 5[18] (J) *the measurement*, tale, *of bricks;* abs. Ez 45[11] *capacity* (of ephah and bath).

† II. תֹּכֶן **n.pr.loc.** in Simeon, 1 Ch 4[32]; Θοκκα, A Θοχχαν, 𝔊L Ενθεκεμ.

† תָּכְנִית **n.f.** measurement, proportion;—abs. Ez 43[10] (< read תַּבְנִיתוֹ 𝔊 Ew Hi Co Toy al.); 28[12] חוֹתֵם ת׳ thou wert *one sealing up* (the) *measure* (RVm), i.e. exhibiting perfect proportion; Codd Sm al. חוֹתַם ת׳ *the seal of* (perfect) *proportion;* but dub., v. Comm.

† מַתְכֹּנֶת **n.f.** measurement, tale, proportion;—**1.** cstr. מ׳ הַלְּבֵנִים Ex 5[8] (J) *the tale of bricks* (cf. I. תֹּכֶן). **2.** sf. -כֻּנְתּוֹ *measurement, proportion*, of ephah and bath Ez 45[11]; of composition of sacred oil Ex 30[32], -תָּהּ v[37] (P); of temple, *its measurement, proportion* -תּוֹ 2 Ch 24[13].

תַּכְרִיךְ v. כרך. תֵּל and cpds. v. תלל.

† תָּלָא **vb.** hang (‖ form of תלה, Ges[§ 75 rr]);—**Qal** *Pf.* 3 pl. sf. תְּלָאוּם 2 S 21[12] Qr the Philistines *had hanged them* (Kt תלום; v. Dr); *Pt. pass.* תְּלֻאִים Dt 28[66] thy life shall be *hung up* before thee, i.e. be in suspense, each moment uncertain.—וְעַמִּי תְלוּאִים לִמְשׁוּבָתִי Ho 11[7] *my people is hung up to my backsliding* is certainly corrupt (AV *bent to backsliding from me*, i.e. hung or swung toward turning from me, cf. GASm, but very dub.); Marti conj. נִלְאִים; Oettli Now[2] Harper נִלְאָה or הֶלְאָנִי אֶל־עֲצַבִּים; *has wearied itself* [*me*] in backsliding.

[תַּלְאֻבָה] v. לאב. תְּלָאָה v. לאה.

† תְּלַאשָּׂר **n.pr.loc.** appar. in Mesopot.;—ת׳ 2 K 19[12] = תְּלַשָּׂר Is 37[12] (abode of בְּנֵי־עֶדֶן); cf. As. *Til-ašuri* (Esarhaddon) Dl[Par. 264 f.]; near Edessa Wkl[Gesch. Bab. u. As. 269, 335 f.]; v. Schr[KGF 199 f.]; identification not certain, cf. Johns[Ency. Bib. Telassar].

תְּלֻנֹּת v. תְּלֻנֹּת פִּל׳. לבשׁ v. תִּלְבֹּשֶׁת.

† תָּלָה **vb.** hang (NH *id.;* As. Pi. *tullû*, *hang up;* Ar. تَلَّ *let down, dangle* (a rope, etc.); Aram. תְּלָא, ܬܠܐ *hang;* perh. OAram. תלה *id.*,

Lzb[386]; Eth ተለወ: in derived sense, *be devoted, addicted, to*),—**Qal** *Pf.* 3 ms ת׳ Gn 40[22]+; 2 ms וְתָלִיתָ Dt 21[22] consec; 3 pl. תָּלוּ Est 8[7] 9[14], sf. תלום 2 S 21[12] Kt (Qr v תלא), etc.; *Impf.* 3 ms sf וַיִּתלֵם Jos 10[26], etc, *Imv.* mpl sf. תְּלֻהוּ Est 7[9], *Inf. cstr* לתלות Ez 15[3] Est 6[4], *Pt act* תֹּלֶה Jb 26[7]; *pass* תָּלוּי Dt 31[23]+2 t., pl. תלוים Jos 10[26];—*hang* **1.** *hang up* any object: acc of hands and feet of slain, +עַל־הַבְּרֵכָה 2 S 4[12], תָּלוּי of Absalom בָּאֵלָה *in the terebinth* 18[10], ת׳ c acc rei, +עַל Is 22[24] Ez 15[3] Ct 4[4] ψ 137[2], subj י׳, ת׳ אֶרֶץ עַל־בְּלִימָה Jb 26[7]. **2.** specif *put to death by hanging*, c acc. pers. Gn 40[22] 41[13] (both E), 2 S 21[12] (cf. תלא), Est 9[14], abs תָּלוּי Dt 21[23] *one hanged*, acc pers +עַל־עֵץ Gn 40[19] (E), Dt 21[22] Jos 8[29] 10[26.26] (all JE), Est 5[14] 6[4] 7[9.10] 8[7] 9[13.25] **Niph.** *Pf* 3 pl. שָׂרִים בְּיָדָם נִתְלוּ La 5[12] *princes have been hung up by their hands; Impf.* 3 mpl. וַיִּתָּלוּ עַל־עֵץ Est 2[23] *they were hanged on a tree*; +3 ms apoc. וַיִּתַּל 2 S 18[9] (for וַיִּתֵּן v. נתן **Hoph.**) **Pi.** *hang up* for display, c acc. rei *Pf.* 3 pl. תלו Ez 27[10] (ב loc), v[11] (עַל־חוֹמוֹתַיִךְ).

†[תְּלִי] **n.[m.]** quiver (with its arrows) (as *hanging* from shoulder),—sf. תֶּלְיְךָ וְקַשְׁתֶּךָ Gn 27[3] (J, 𝔊 φαρετρα, 𝔙 *pharetra*)

תְּלָה v. תל infra.

†יִתְלָה **n pr. loc.** in (Southern) Dan Jos 19[42], Σιλαθα, 𝔊L Ιθλα.

†תֶּלַח **n. pr m.** in Ephraim;—1 Ch 7[25], Θαλε(ες), Θαλα

I. תלל (appar √of foll; NH תל *heap*, תלולית *hill*, 𝔗[J] תְּלִיל *lofty*; Ar. تَلّ, Syr. ܬܠܐ *mound*, =(perhaps) OAram תלי CIS[II No III] Lzb[386] SAC[120], Jen in Brock[Syr. Lex] thinks תל As loan-word from *tîlu, ruin-heap, mound*).

†תֵּל **n.[m.]** mound,—**1.** *mound*, ruin-heap (of city). cstr תֵּל(־)עוֹלָם Jos 8[28] (JE), Dt 13[17], תֵּל שְׁמָמָה Je 49[2] **2.** *mound* or hill on which city stood sf תִּלָּם Jos 11[13] (D), תִּלָּהּ Je 30[18]

†תֵּל אָבִיב **n.pr loc.** in Babylonia, on the 'river Chebar,' Ez 3[15]

†תֵּל חַרְשָׁא **n. pr. loc.** in Babylonia;—Ezr 2[59]=Ne 7[61], Θααρησα, (Θελ)αρησα, etc., 𝔊L Ezr Θαλαα καὶ Ρησα.

†תֵּל מֶלַח **n. pr. loc.** in Babylonia;—Ezr 2[59]=Ne 7[61], Θερμελεθ, Θελμελεθ[χ]

†תָּלוּל **adj.** exalted, lofty (prop **Qal** *Pt. pass*),—הַר־גָּבֹהַּ ות׳ Ez 17[22] *a high and lofty mt.*

†תַּלְתַּלִּים **n.f.**(?) **pl.** as fig. of woman's locks, mng. dub. קְוֻצּוֹתָיו ת׳ שְׁחֹרוֹת כָּעוֹרֵב Ct 5[11]; Thes (from above √) *waving palm-branches*, 𝔊 ἐλάται; NH once, fig., Levy[NHWB iv 649] *high hills* cf. Jastr[Dict 1674] *heaps, piles*; but Magnus[Hohes Lied] and Jacob[Stud Arab. Dichter iv 21] *envelope* or sheath of spadix of date-palm (with which hair oft cp in Ar poetry Jacob[ib. iii 46f], cf. Ar. تَلْتَلَة *drinking vessel* made of this envelope Lane); so perhaps As *taltallu* Dl[HWB 708].

†II [תָּלַל] **vb. Hiph.** mock, deceive, trifle with (perhaps akin to Ar. دَلّ *act coquettishly*; cf. secondary √[הָתַל] p 251);—*mock, trifle with*, c בְּ pers. *Pf.* 3 ms הֵתֶל (בי) Gn 31[7] (E), 2 ms. הַתַּלְתָּ Ju 16[10.13.15], *Impf* 3 mpl. יְהָתֵלּוּ Je 9[4], 2 mpl תְּהָתֵלּוּ Jb 13[9] (on both v. Ges[§ 53 q] Baer[ad loc]), *Inf. cstr* Jb 13[19] and (abs.) Ex 8[25] (J) **Hoph.** *Pf* 3 ms הוּתַל Is 44[20] a heart (which) *is deceived*.—Vid [הָתַל], הֲתֻלִּים p 251.

תלם (√of foll, cf. NH תֶּלֶם=BH; Ar. تَلَمٌ, mod Pal. تِلْم Bergheim[PEF 1894, 195]; Eth. ትልም: Aram. תַּלְמָא; the nearest verbal √ is Ar. ثَلَمَ *break edge of, make a breach, gap*, but ث=ت? cf. Fra[131])

†תֶּלֶם **n.m.**[Jb 31,38] **furrow**,—abs. ת׳ Jb 39[10] (other conj Du Perles[Anal 53]); pl cstr. תַּלְמֵי שָׂדָי Ho 10[4] 12[12]; sf. תְּלָמֶיהָ Jb 31[38] ψ 65[11]—On ploughing in Pal. v. Hogg[Ency Bib Agriculture] Vogelstein[Landwirthsch 25 ff], on depth of furrow (not more than 8–10 centim.) Id[ib 36] Anderlind[ZPV ix 26, 29], also Benz Arch. s.v—תֶּלֶם v. תל supr.

†תַּלְמַי **n.pr.m.** **1.** king of Geshur, father-in-law of David, 2 S 3[3] 13[37] 1 Ch 3[2]. **2.** a son of 'Anak Nu 13[22] Jos 15[14], תַּלְמַי Ju 1[10]; Θομμει, Θολμει, Θαλαμειν, etc

תַּלְמִיד v. למד. [תְּלָנָּה] v II לון.

תלע (√of foll., perhaps *gnaw*, v. מְתַלְּעוֹת infra, and Dl[Pr 113], cf. As. *tultu, worm*).

†I. תּוֹלָע **n.[m.]** worm, scarlet stuff (dyed with the *coccus ilicis*, v שָׁנִי, Thatcher[Hast DB Colours]),—**1.** *worm*, only pl. תּוֹלָעִים, in stale manna Ex 16[20] (P). **2.** *scarlet stuff*, abs. sg תּוֹלָע Is 1[18] (in sim. ‖ שָׁנִים; opp. צֶמֶר); token of luxury La 4[5].

†II. תּוֹלָע **n.pr.m.** in Issachar; a judge of Israel Ju 10[1]; assigned to earlier time by Gn 46[13] Nu 26[23] (both P), 1 Ch 7[1.2.2].

†תּוֹלָעִי **adj. gent.** of foregoing; c. art. as n. coll. Nu 26[23].

תּוֹלַעַת, תּוֹלֵעָה[40] **n.f.** worm;—abs. תּוֹלֵעָה Is 14[11] Jb 25[6]; תּוֹלַעַת Is 41[14]+, תּוֹלַעַת Dt 28[39] Nu 19[6]; cstr. תּוֹלַעַת Ex 25[4]+; sf. תּוֹלַעְתָּם Is 66[24];—**1.** *worm, grub,* vine-weevil Jon 4[7] Dt 28[39] (coll.); devouring the dead Is 14[11] (coll.: ‖ רִמָּה), 66[24] (coll.); symbol of insignificance 41[14] Jb 25[6] (‖ רִמָּה), ψ 22[7]. **2.** elsewh. (P) specif., + שָׁנִי (q.v.), of the *coccus ilicis* yielding *scarlet* colour: (הַ)ת׳ שָׁנִי Lv 14[4.6.49.51.52] Nu 19[6]; of crimson stuff, תְּכֵלֶת וְאַרְגָּמָן בֶּגֶד ת׳ שָׁנִי 4[8]; usu. וְת׳ (הַ)שָּׁנִי וגו׳ Ex 25[4] 26[1]+24 t. Ex.

†[תָּלַע] **vb. Pu. denom.** clad in scarlet (v. I. תּוֹלָע **2**; תּוֹלֵעָה **2.**—NH Hiph. denom. is *breed worms,* etc.);—*Pt.* pl. מְתֻלָּעִים Na 2[4] (‖ מְאָדָּם).

†מְתַלְּעוֹת **n.f.pl.** teeth (AV RV *jaw-teeth*) (perhaps *gnawers,* v. √);—*teeth, incisors,* late (always ‖ שִׁנַּיִם): cstr. מ׳ Jb 29[17] and (of lion) Jo 1[6]; sf. מְתַלְּעֹתָיו Pr 30[14].

†תַּלְפִּיּוֹת **n.f.pl.** Ges (in Thes) *exitialia, fatal things* (√ תלף = Ar. تَلِفَ *perish*);—poet. for *weapons;* many other conj. in Comm.: כְּמִגְדַּל דָּוִיד צַוָּארֵךְ בָּנוּי לְת׳ Ct 4[4], doubtful; Che Expos. Times, ix. 423; JQ, July 1899, 562 שְׁלָטִים *shields,* cf. v[b].

תְּלַשַּׂר v. תְּלַאשַּׂר. תַּלְתַּלִּים v. I. תלל.

תֹּם, תָּם, תָּמָה, תַּם v. תמם. תֵּמָא v. תֵּימָא.

†[תָּמַהּ] **vb.** be astounded, dumbfounded (NH *id.;* so Aram. תְּמַהּ, ܬܡܗ);—**Qal** *Pf.* 3 pl. תָּמָהוּ ψ 48[6]; *Impf.* 2 ms. תִּתְמַהּ Ec 5[7]; 3 mpl. יִתְמָהוּ Jb 26[11], etc.; *Imv.* mpl. תְּמָהוּ Is 29[9] Hb 1[5];—*be astounded,* Is 29[9] Hb 1[5] (v. Hithp.), Je 4[9] (‖ שׁמם, Niph.), ψ 48[6]; + מִן caus. Jb 26[11]; + עַל rei at which Ec 5[7]; *look in astonishment* at ת׳ אִישׁ אֶל־רֵעֵהוּ Gn 43[33] (J), Is 13[8]. **Hithp.** *Imv.* mpl. + **Qal** *Imv.* וְהִתַּמְּהוּ תְּמָהוּ Hb 1[5] (v. supr.), lit. *astonish yourselves, be astounded,* but We **Hithpalp.** הִתְמַהְמְהוּ; Gr rds. inf. abs. תָּמֹהַּ (Marti al. וּתְמָהוּ) for תמהו.

†תִּמָּהוֹן **n.[m.]** bewilderment;—abs. ת׳ Zc 12[4]; cstr. תִּמְהוֹן Dt 28[28];—*bewilderment, stupefaction;* ת׳ לֵבָב v[28], of those infatuated (v. Dr.); ת׳ alone of bewildered horses Zc 12[4].

†תַּמּוּז **n.pr.div.** Tammuz (Bab. *Dûzu* (also *Dumuzi*) COT[Ez 8.14] Zim[KAT3, 397 f.] Jastr[Rel. Bab. 482 et pass.]; on the phonetic change Hpt[ZA ii. 270], but also Jäger[BAS i. 591]);—מְבַכּוֹת אֶת־הַתּ׳ Ez 8[14]; ת׳ = Gk. Adonis (אדון); cf. Baud[Rel. Sem. i. 35. 300 f.] Dr[Dn 11. 37] Che[Ency. Bib. TAMMUZ] Say[Hast. DB ib.].

תְּמוּנָה v. מין. תְּמוּרָה v. מור.

תְּמוּתָה v. מות.

†תֶּמַח **n.pr.m.** head of a Jewish family, Ezr 2[53] = Ne 7[55]; 𝔊 Θεμα (Ne Ημαθ), 𝔊L Θεμαα.

תָּמִיד v. מוד p. 556.

תָּמִים Ex 26[24]·36[29] v. [תָּאַם].

†[תָּמַךְ] **vb.** grasp, support, attain (Aram. תְּמַךְ Pa. *hold fast;* cf. Ph. and OAram. תמכאל *Ēl hath sustained* Lzb[386] SAC[121] Cooke[361]);—**Qal** *Pf.* 3 fs. תָּמְכָה ψ 63[9], etc.; *Impf.* 3 ms. יִתְמֹךְ Pr 29[23], 3 mpl. יִתְמְכוּ Jb 36[17] Pr 5[5], etc.; *Inf. abs.* תָּמוֹךְ ψ 17[5]; cstr. תְּמֹךְ Is 33[15]; *Pt.* תּוֹמֵךְ Am 1[5.8], תּוֹמִיךְ ψ 16[5] (? rd. ־מִיךָ Ges[§ 50 e], or תֹּמֵךְ, cf. Vrss Du; > Ol תּוֹסִיף, Bi Che תָּמִיד), etc.;—**1.** *grasp, lay hold of,* c. acc. rei Gn 48[17] (E), Pr 31[19] (‖ שִׁלַּח יד בְּ); acc. pers. (wisdom) Pr 3[18] (‖ מַחֲזִיק); acc. rei (grasp and) *wield* Am 1[5.8]; ψ 16[5] (v. supr.) *thou dost grasp my lot* (i.e. take and cast it for me, cf. mod. Pal. الله يَقُوم بَخْتِي *may Allah uphold my lot,* Bergheim[PEF 1894, 194]); fig., Jb 36[17] judgment and justice *seize* (thee; but v. obscure and doubtful); Pr 5[5] her steps *lay hold of* Sheʾôl (keep the path to it); lit., c. בְּ rei Is 33[15], בְּ pers. Pr 28[17] (or sub **3**; mng. dub.); *lay hold of, attain,* honour, wealth (acc.) Pr 11[16.16]. **2.** *hold up, support,* c. בְּיָדָיו Ex 17[2] (E); fig., בְּ pers. Is 42[1] ψ 41[13] 63[9]; acc. pers. Is 41[10] (בְּ instr.), Pr 29[23] (opp. הִשְׁפִּיל). **3.** *hold, keep,* c. acc. rei Pr 4[4] let thy heart *keep* my words (‖ שְׁמֹר); *hold firmly* ψ 17[5] (בְּ loc.; opp. נָמֹטּוּ). **Niph.** *Impf.* וּבְחַבְלֵי חַטָּאתוֹ יִתָּמֵךְ Pr 5[22] *in the cords of his sin is he seized* (‖ לָכַד).

†תְּמוֹל (תְּמֹל)[23], אֶתְמוֹל[5], †אִתְּמוֹל 1 S 10[11], †אֶתְמוּל Is 30[33] Mi 2[8] (v. inf.), **subst.,** used sts. as **adv. acc.,** yesterday, fig. recently, formerly (Aram. תְּמָלֵי, אִתְמָלֵי, sts. אִתְמוֹל, ܐܬܡܠܝ, ܐܬܡܠ, ܬܡܠ; Mand. עתמאל Nö[M 202]; Eth. ትማልም: As. *timâli, itimâli, ina timâli* (Dl[158, 721]); der. dub.; acc. to Me[Gr. Syr. 118] Kö[ii. 264 f.] from Ar. مَلَّ II. *prolongavit,* IV. *longam vitam*

concessit, تَلَّ *tempus*, الْمَلَوَانِ *the two times*, i e night and day, in form an inf of vi تَمَالُ, hence prop *long time*, (past) *time*, specialized to *yesterday*),—*yesterday*, but usually fig = *recently* or *formerly* **1.** 2 S 15^{20} תְּמוֹל בּוֹאֶךָ *yesterday* (=*only lately*) was thy coming, Jb 8^{9} תמול אנחנו (of) yesterday (Ges^{§141d}) are we, ψ 90^{4} (genit.) כְּיוֹם אֶתְמוֹל. **2.** usu in combin with שלשם *yesterday* (and) *the third day*, to express the idea of *formerly*: thus **a.** as *adv acc.* (*a*) גַּם תמול גַּם הַיּוֹם 1 S 20^{27} (lit.), cf Ex 5^{14} (sub **b**), (*b*) תמול שלשם Ex 5^{8} Ru 2^{11}, so אתמ׳ 1 S 4^{7}, (*c*) גַּם ת׳ גַּם שׁ׳ 2 S 3^{17} 1 Ch 11^{2} (∥ 2 S 5^{2} with אתמ׳) **b.** כתמול שלשם *as formerly* Gn $31^{2.5}$ Ex 5^{7} Jos 4^{18} 1 S 21^{6} (but Bu מת׳, as **c**) 2 K 13^{5}, כִּאֶתְמ׳ שׁ׳ 1 S 14^{21} 19^{7}; Ex 5^{14} כְּת׳ שׁ׳ גַּם תמול גַּם הַיּוֹם *as yesterday* (and) *the third day* (=*as formerly*), both yesterday and to-day (=*so more recently*) **c.** מתמול שׁ׳ = (*from*) *aforetime*, Ex $21^{29.36}$ Jos 3^{4}, והוא לא שנא לו מת׳ שׁ׳ Dt 4^{42} $19^{4.6}$ Jos 20^{5}, so מאתמול שׁ׳ 1 S 10^{11}; גַּם מת׳ גַּם מִשׁ׳ Ex 4^{10}. **3.** מֵאֶתְמוֹל (alone) Is 30^{33} *from yesterday* = *already*; ואתמול עמי Mi 2^{8} corrupt, read ואתם לעמי (WRS, with עַל ,יָקוּם), and v. שַׂלְמָה עמי We Now, with תָּקוּמוּ), and v. שַׂלְמָה.

†[תָּמַם, תַּם] **vb. be complete, finished** (Ar تَمَّ *id*, Ph תם, Syr. ܬܡ der spec and deriv, cf NH = BH (rare), Aram תְּמִימָא, ܡܫܡܠܝܐ *perfect*),—**Qal** *Pf* 3 ms תַּם Gn 47^{18} + 3 t (+ Qr מאשׁ תם Je 6^{29}), 3 pl תַּמּוּ Dt 2^{16} +, תָּמּוּ 2 K 7^{13}, 1 pl תַּמְנוּ (Ges^{§67dd}) Nu 17^{28} ψ 64^{7}, תָּמְנוּ Je 44^{18}, (La 3^{22} rd תַּמּוּ 𝔗 𝔖 Ew Lohr Bu), *Impf* 3 ms יִתֹּם (Ges^{§67g}) Gn 47^{18} Ez 47^{12}, 3 fs תִּתֹּם Ez 24^{11} (Ges^{§67q}, del Co), תתם Gn 47^{18} 1 K 7^{22}, 1 s אִיתָּם ψ 19^{14}, 3 mpl. יִתַּמּוּ Nu 14^{35} +, וַיִּתְּמוּ Dt 34^{8}, *Inf cstr* תֹּם Lv 25^{29} + 10 t, תֹּם־ Is 18^{5}, sf תֻּמִּי Je 27^{8} + 7 t sf.,—**1.** *be finished, completed*; the writing of words Dt $31^{24.30}$ (v Dr, J), Jb 31^{40}, building of temple 1 K 6^{22}, cf 7^{22}; *fulfilled*, י׳'s command (by obedience) Jos 4^{10} (E), as auxil + vb fin = *completely, wholly, entirely*, תַּמּוּ נִכְרָתוּ Jos 3^{16} (E) *were wholly cut off*, סָפוּ תַּמּוּ ψ 73^{19} *entirely consumed*; sq. לְ inf תַּמּוּ לַעֲבוֹר *were finished in regard to*, etc, i e. *were entirely passed over* Jos 3^{17} $4^{1.11}$ (JE) 2 S 15^{24}, תַּמּוּ לְהִמּוֹל Jos 5^{8} (E) *entirely circumcised*, Nu 17^{28} **2.** *be finished, come to an end, cease*. the year, Gn 47^{18} (J), Lv 25^{29} (P), Je 1^{3}; the years of י׳ have no end ψ 102^{28}; days of weeping Dt 34^{8} (P), cf La 4^{22}; also Is 18^{5} La 3^{22}. **3.** *be complete*, of number, 1 S 16^{11}. **4.** *be consumed, exhausted, spent*: silver Gn $47^{15.18}$ (J); strength Lv 26^{20} (H), lead Je 6^{29} (Qr), bread 37^{21}, fruit Ez 47^{12}; rust 24^{11}. **5.** *be finished, consumed, destroyed* people Nu 14^{35} (J), v^{33} 17^{28} (P, ∥ מות), 32^{13} (J), Jos 8^{24} 10^{20} (JE), Dt $2^{14.15.16}$ Jos 5^{6} (D), 1 K 14^{10} 2 K 7^{13} Is 16^{4} Je 14^{15} 24^{10} 27^{8} 36^{23} $44^{12.12.18.27}$ ψ 9^{7} (but read דָּמוּ), 104^{35}. **6.** *be complete, sound, unimpaired*, ethically, ψ 19^{14} (∥ נקה; late) **7.** twice, very strangely, si vera l., trans · ψ 64^{7} תמנו *we have completed* (rd prob. הֲתִמֹּנוּ); Je 27^{8} עַד־תֻּמִּי אֹתָם בְּיָדוֹ (read with Gr תִּתִּי). **Hiph.** *Pf* 1 s. הַתִמֹּתִי Ez 22^{15}; 3 mpl. הֵתַמּוּ 2 S 20^{18}; *Impf.* יַתֵּם 2 K 22^{4}, 2 ms תָּתֵם Jb 22^{3} (Ges^{§67y}), *Inf. abs* הָתֵם Ez 24^{10}; *cstr*, *id*, Dn 8^{23} + 9^{24} Qr (v Dr); sf. הֲתִמְּךָ (Ges^{§67v}) Is 33^{1},—**1** *finish, complete, perfect*, a matter 2 S 20^{18} (but **Qal**, *come to an end*, c. ה interrog., We Dr al); flesh in cooking Ez 24^{10}. **2.** *finish, cease doing* a thing, sq pt (Ges^{§120b}), שׁוֹדֵד Is 33^{1}. **3.** *complete, sum up*, c. acc. money 2 K 22^{4} (other conj Klo Gr Gi), transgressions Dn 8^{23}, sin 9^{24} (Qr, Kt חתם). **4.** *destroy* uncleanness, c מִן *from*, Ez 22^{15}. **5.** causative (of **Qal 6**) acc. דרכיך Jb 22^{3} *make sound thy ways* **Hithp.** *Impf.* 2 ms תִּתַּמָּם 2 S 22^{26}, c. עִם *deal in integrity with* = ψ 18^{26} (late, v. **Qal 6**)

†תֹּם **n.[m.] completeness, integrity**,—תֹּם abs Pr 10^{29} +, cstr. Jb 4^{6} ψ 78^{72}, cstr. also תָּם־ Pr 13^{6} + 4 t, sf. תֻּמִּי ψ 26^{1} + 11 t sf; pl. תֻּמִּים Ex 28^{30} + 3 t, sf תֻּמֶּיךָ Dt 33^{8},—**1.** *completeness, fulness* כְּתֻמָּם Is 47^{9} *acc to their full measure*, בְּעֶצֶם תֻּמּוֹ Jb 21^{23} *in his very completeness*. **2.** *innocence, simplicity*: הלכים לְתֻמָּם 2 S 15^{11}, מָשַׁךְ בַּקֶּשֶׁת לְתֻמּוֹ 1 K 22^{34} = 2 Ch 18^{33}, i e without definite aim **3.** *integrity*: תם לבב *integrity of mind* Gn $20^{5.6}$ (E), 1 K 9^{4} ψ 78^{72} 101^{2}; תָּם־דָּרֶךְ Pr 13^{6} Jb 4^{6}, (הת)הלך בְּתֻם Pr 10^{9}, 19^{1} 20^{7} 28^{6}, בְּתֻמִּי ψ $26^{1.11}$; הֹלְכֵי תֹם Pr 2^{7}, 7^{9} כְּתֻמִּי, 41^{11} בְּתֻמִּי, תֹּם וָיֹשֶׁר ψ 25^{21} מָעוֹז לַתֹּם Pr 10^{29} **4.** תֻּמִּים in אוּרִים וְתֻמִּים (mng dub, v., אוּרִים) Dt 33^{8}, Ex 28^{30} (P) Lv 8^{8} (P), Ezr 2^{63} = Ne 7^{65}, + 1 S 14^{41} (for תָּמִים) We Dr Bu HPS; also Ho 3^{4} (for תרפים) Che$^{JQ. July 1899, 564}$ and 4^{6} (תֻּמֶּיךָ for אִמֶּךָ) Ruben$^{JQ. April 1899, 44}$ Che$^{l.c.}$.

[תֻּמָּה] **n.f. integrity** (late);—cstr תֻּמַּת Pr 11^{3}, sf. תֻּמָּתִי Jb 27^{5} 31^{6}; תֻּמָּתֶךָ 2^{9}, תֻּמָּתוֹ v^{3}.

†תָּם **adj. complete**,—ת׳ Gn 25^{27} + 10 t.;

sf. תַּמָּתִי Ct 5² 6⁹ (late, exc. Gn 25²⁷);—**1.** *complete, perfect*. in beauty Ct 5² 6⁹; of physical strength ψ 73⁴ (rd לָמוֹ תָּם Ew De Dr[Sam. xxxi] Che Bae al.) **2.** *sound, wholesome:* אִישׁ תָּם, of Jacob as tent-dweller, opp. Esau, hunter, Gn 25²⁷ (J; De *leutseliger Mann*, Di *ruhig, still*, AV RV *plain man;* ת׳ here poss. redactional, =3) **3.** *complete, morally innocent, having integrity:* אִישׁ תָּם Jb 1¹ 2³, ת׳ alone 1¹ 8²⁰ 9²⁰·²¹·²² Pr 29¹⁰ ψ 37³⁷ 64⁵.—תַּמִּים v. [תְּאֹם].

תָּמִים[91] **adj.** complete, sound;—ת׳ Gn 6⁹+; f. תְּמִימָה Lv 3⁹+; cstr. תְּמִים Jb 36⁴ 37¹⁶; pl. תמימים Ez 43²⁵+, תְּמִימֹת Lv 23¹⁵; cstr. תְּמִימֵי ψ 119¹ Pr 11²⁰;—†**1.** *complete, whole, entire,* Jb 36⁴ תְּמִים דֵּעוֹת, 37¹⁶. **2.** *whole, sound, healthful,* of men Pr 1¹² (‖ חַיִּים), vine Ez 15⁵; usu. of sacrif. animals, P; Ex 12⁵+40 t., so Ez 43²²+10 t †**3.** *complete, entire,* of time: day Jos 10¹³; year Lv 25³⁰, sabbaths 23¹⁵. †**4.** *sound, wholesome, unimpaired, innocent, having integrity:* of God's way ψ 18³¹ = 2 S 22³¹, work Dt 32⁴; law ψ 19⁸; elsewh. of man Gn 6⁹ 17¹ (P; both ‖ הִתְהַלֵּךְ אֶת (לִפְנֵי) אלהים; ת׳ עם י׳ Dt 18¹³ ψ 18²¹, c. לְ in ‖ 2 S 22²¹, oft. c. דֶּרֶךְ *way*. תְּמִימֵי דָרֶךְ ψ 101²; ת׳ בדרכֶיךָ Ez 28¹⁵; דֶּרֶךְ ת׳ Pr 11²⁰ ψ 119¹, ויתן ת׳ ‖ וַיִּתֵּר ת׳ דרכו 2 S 22³³ ψ 18³³; הלך בדרך ת׳ 101⁶, הֹלֵךְ תמים, om דֶּרֶךְ Pr 28¹⁸ ψ 15²; לב ת׳ 119⁸⁰; =noun (late), man of *integrity* Pr 11⁵ Jb 12⁴; pl. Pr 2²¹ 28¹⁰ ψ 37¹⁸. †**5.** as neuter adj.=subst *what is complete, entirely in accord with truth and fact:* דִּבֶּר ת׳ Am 5¹⁰, עֲבַדְתֶּם אִם־בֶּאֱמֶת וּבת׳ עֲשִׂיתֶם Ju 9¹⁶·¹⁹, עִבְדוּ י׳ בת׳ וּבֶאֱמֶת Jos 24¹⁴ (E); *integrity* גְּבַר ת׳ ψ 18²⁶ (cstr. Ges[§93s], ‖ 2 S 22²⁶ גִּבּוֹר), 84¹², הֹלְכִים בת׳.—1 S 14⁴¹ v. תם **4.**

†**מְתֹם n.[m.]** soundness, in phr. אין מתם ב׳ Is 1⁶ ψ 38⁴·⁸, מֵעִיר מְתֹם Ju 20⁴⁸ *from entire city* (Codd. De Rossi Bu GFM מְתִם, v. מַת and cf. עיר מת(י)ם Dt 2³⁴ 3⁶ Jb 24¹²).

תֵּמָן, תֵּמָנִי v. תֵּימָן sub ימן.

תְּמוּנָה, תִּמְנָתָה, תִּמְנִי, תִּמְנַת v. מנה.

תִּמְנָע v. מָנַע. **תֶּמֶס** v. מסס.

תמר (√of foll.; cf perh Ar. إِتْمَأَرَّ *be erect, stiff* (e g. of lance), so Buhl¹³, who derives thence תמר *palm-tree*, and also תִּימָרָה, NH תִּמְרָה *column* of smoke, NH תמור *rising motion*, etc, but these denom. from תָּמָר Levy[NHWB] Buhl¹⁴; cf. Ar. تَمْرٌ *date*, Eth ተምር: *id.*, ተመርት: *date-palm*, Aram. תַּמְרָא, ܬܡܪܐ *date-palm*, NH תָּמָר *date(-palm)*).

†**תֹּמֶר n.m.** palm-tree, post;—cstr. ת׳ דְּבוֹרָה Ju 4⁵ *palm-tree* of Deborah, כת׳ מִקְשָׁה Je 10⁵ *like a post* (i.e. a *scare-crow*, cf. Bar 6⁷⁰) *in a cucumber field* (sim. of idol).

†I. **תָּמָר n.m.** palm-tree, date-palm, *Phoenix dactylifera;*—ת׳ Jo 1¹², in sim of prosperity ψ 92¹³, of (graceful) stature Ct 7⁸, cf. (fig.) v⁹, pl. תְּמָרִים in oasis Ex 15²⁷ (J), ‖ Nu 33⁹ (P); כַּפֹּת ת׳ Lv 23⁴⁰ (H) *palm-branches,* cf עֲלֵי ת׳ Ne 8¹⁵, עיר הַתְּמָרִים = Jericho Dt 34³ (JE), 2 Ch 28¹⁵ Ju 1¹⁶ 3¹³ —Vid. Post[Hast. DB Palm-tree] M'Lean[Ency Bib. ID] Tr[NHB 378 ff] Theob. Fischer [Dattelpalme, 1881].

II **תָּמָר**[23] **n.pr. 1. f.** †**a.** daughter-in-law of Judah Gn 38⁶·¹¹ ¹¹ ¹³·²⁴ 1 Ch 2⁴ Ru 4¹². **b.** daughter of David, sister of Absalom 2 S 13¹ ² +11 t. 13, 2 Ch 3⁹. †**c.** daughter of Absalom 2 S 14²⁷. †**2. loc.** Ez 47¹⁹ 48²⁸, 1 K 9¹⁸ Kt (> Qr תַּדְמֹר q v), so read also ‖ 2 Ch 8⁴ (for MT תַּדְמֹר); site not certain, cf. Buhl[G 184].—בַּעַל תָּמָר v. בַּעַל.

תִּמֹרָה[19] **n.f.** palm(-tree) figure, as ornament,—ת׳ Ez 41¹⁸+(van d H. תִּמ׳, so throughout); pl. תִּמֹרִת 1 K 6²⁹+ (Gi תִּמ׳), תִּמֹרִים Ez 40¹⁶+; sf. תִּמֹרָיו v²² Qr (Kt תימרו);—*palm-figure* in Sol.'s temple 1 K 6²⁹·³²·³²·³⁵ 7³⁶ 2 Ch 3⁵; in Ezekiel's temple Ez 40¹⁶·²²·²⁶+10 t. 40, 41

†[**תִּימָרָה**] **n.f.** (palm-like) column (spreading at top; cf. Ol[§184b]);—pl. cstr. תִּימֲרוֹת עָשָׁן Jo 3³ Ct 3⁶ (cf. עַמּוּד עָשָׁן in prose Ju 20⁴⁰).

†II. [**תַּמְרוּר**] **n.m.** pl. תַּמְרוּרִים Je 31²¹, doubtful word; sense, and ‖ צִיֻּנִים, require mng. *sign-posts* (= תאמ׳, cf Ar. تُؤْمُورٌ *sign-post,* √أمر, v. أَمَارٌ *sign*, أَمَرَةٌ *stones* (heaped up) as way-mark; Eth. አመረ: *shew, point out, give sign or signal*);—Gie rejects strange form, reading תמרים *palm-trees,* as posts —I. ת׳ v. מרר.

תַּמְרוּק, תַּמְרִיק, v מרק. I. **תַּמְרוּר** v. מרר.

תַּן v. תנן.

I. [**תָּנָה**] **vb.** hire (si vera l., akin to נתן);—**Qal** *Impf.* 3 mpl. יִתְנוּ בַגּוֹיִם Ho 8¹⁰ *hire* (allies) among the nations; **Hiph.** *Pf.* 3 pl. הִתְנוּ v⁹ *have hired* lovers —We in both יִתְּנוּ *give:* v⁹ *give* amorous favours, v¹⁰ *give* (these), cp. Now Marti Harper.—תְּנָה ψ 8² v. נתן **Qal 2 b.**

†**אֶתְנָה n.f.** hire of a harlot;—א׳ abs., Ho 2¹⁴ (in fig of Israel as adulteress);—on אֶתְנַן (which We Now Marti read here also) v. II. תנן.

†יַתְנִיאֵל **n.pr.m.** a Levite (*Ēl hireth*);—1 Ch 26²; Ιενουηλ, 𝔊L Ναθαναηλ

†II [תָּנָה] **vb.** recount, rehearse (?) (𝔗 תְּנֵי, Syr ܬܢܳܐ, is *recount*, Ar ثَنَّى II, IV is *celebrate*, but Heb ת = Aram ת = Ar. ث is very dub),—**Pi.** *Impf* 3 mpl יְתַנּוּ Ju 5¹¹ *let them recount* (Vrss) the victories of י׳, *Inf. cstr.* לְתַנּוֹת 11⁴⁰ *to celebrate* (mod), or *mourn* (Vrss), c ל pers

[תְּנוּאָה] v [נוא]. תְּנוּבָה v. [נוב].

תנך (√of following)

†תְּנוּךְ **n.[m.]** tip, i e. lobe of ear (𝔊 λοβὸς τοῦ ὠτός, 𝔙 *extremum auriculae*, and so most ancient authorities, cf. Thes¹⁵¹¹),—cstr in phr. ת׳ אֹזֶן פ׳ Ex 29²⁰·²⁰ Lv 8²³·²⁴ 14¹⁴·¹⁷·²⁵·²⁸ (all P).

תְּנוּמָה v. נום. תְּנוּפָה v I נוף

†תַּנּוּר **n.m.**^Lv 26 26^ portable stove or fire-pot (loan-word from As *tinûru*, *id*, acc. to DHM ^Voj i. 23^ (otherwise Dvořák ^ZK i 155 ff^); ת׳, a large earthen jar, still in Syria, Wetzst ^Verhandl d Berl Anthrop. Gesell., 1882, 467^ Whitehouse ^Heb. Antiq 7. 3^ ARSK ^EB i 606^, Ar. تَنُّور is loan-word from Aram. תַּנּוּרָא, ܬܢܘܪܐ, and this from Pers. *tanûra*, acc. to Fra²⁶),—ת׳ abs Ho 7⁴+, cstr Gn 15¹⁷ ψ 21¹⁰; pl תַּנּוּרִים Ne 3¹¹ 12³⁸,—*fire-pot*, for baking (אָפָה) Ho 7⁴ (read ת׳ בֹּעֵר הֵם אַפֵּהוּ וגו׳, Oort ^Th Tijdschr. 1890, 480 ff^ Albi ^ZAW xvi (1896) 88^), cf v⁶·⁷ (all in sim), Ex 7²⁸ (J), Lv 2⁴ 7⁹ 26²⁶ (P), also (breakable) 11³⁵, ת׳ עָשָׁן Gn 15¹⁷ (JE) in vision, symbol of י׳'s presence, cf Is 31⁹ (‖ אוּר); sim. of heat La 5¹⁰, of judgment Mal 3¹⁹, and so ת׳ אֵשׁ ψ 21¹⁰, מִגְדַּל הַתַּנּוּרִים Ne 3¹¹ 12³⁸ a tower on wall of Jerus.

[תַּנְחוּם], תַּנְחוּמוֹת, תַּנְחֻמֶת v. [נחם].

I **תנן** (√of following, ? akin to II. תנה in sense *lament*, i e *howl*).

†[תַּן] **n.[m. et] f.**^La 4 3^ jackal (so most; Tr ^NHB 109 ff, 263 f^ Shipley-Cook ^Ency Bib. Jackal^; but *wolf* Post ^Hast DB Dragon^, cf Che ^Is 13, 22^ and (rare) Ar ثُعْبَان),—pl. תַּנִּים Mi 1⁸+, תַּנִּין La 4³ (Ges ^§ 87 e^), לְתַנּוֹת Mal 1³ (si vera l., 𝔊 Thes al interpret = *dwellings*, Sta Now conjecture נְאוֹת, Marti נְתַתִּי ל),—*jackal*, howling mournfully in waste places, Mi 1⁸ Jb 30²⁹ (both ‖ בְּנוֹת יַעֲנָה), Is 13²² (‖ אִיִּים), in desert also 43²⁰ (‖ בְּנוֹת יַעֲנָה), deserted sites called נְוֵה ת׳ מְעוֹן ת׳ Je 9¹⁰ 10²² 49³³ 51³⁷, ת׳ נוה Is 34¹³ 35⁷, מְקוֹם ת׳ ψ 44²⁰, ת׳ מִדְבַּר Mal 1³ (si vera l., but v supra), ת׳ as snuffing up wind Je 14⁶, giving suck La 4³.

†תַּנִּין (erron. תַּנִּים) **n.m.**^Ez 29, 3^ serpent, dragon, sea-monster (NH *id.* (rare); Ar. تِنِّين, loan-word from Aram תַּנִּינָא, ܬܢܝܢܐ, Fra¹²³, Eth ተመን:),—abs. ת׳ Ex 7⁹+, ־ים Ez 29³ 32² (by confusion with pl. of [תַּן]), pl. תַּנִּינִם Gn 1²¹, etc.;—**1.** *serpent*, Dt 32³³ (venomous), ψ 91¹³ (‖ פֶּתֶן), Ex 7⁹·¹⁰·¹² (P) **2.** *dragon*, as devourer (sim) Je 51³⁴; עֵין הַת׳ Ne 2¹³, near Jerus. **3.** *sea- (or river-) monster*, Gn 1²¹ (P); fig Jb 7¹² ψ 74¹³ (i e. Egyptians), Is 27¹ 51⁹ (‖ רַהַב, mythol personif. of chaos), in summons to praise י׳ ψ 148⁷ (‖ תְּהֹמוֹת)—Vid. Che ^Ency Bib. Dragon^ Gunk ^Schöpfung 69 ff^ Barton ^JAOS xv 1 (1891) 23 f^; personif of water-spout RS ^Sem i 161; 2nd ed 176^; cf. Gk. fish-name θύννος Lewy ^Fremdw 15^.

II **תנן** (√of following; apparently ‖ נתן; cf also I. תנה)

†אֶתְנַן **n.m.**^Ez 16 34^ hire of harlot (= אֶתְנָה);—abs. א׳ Ez 16³⁴·⁴¹, אֶתְנָן Ho 9¹+; cstr אֶתְנַן Dt 23¹⁹+, sf. אֶתְנַנָּהּ Is 23¹⁸, ־נָהּ v¹⁷; pl. sf. אֶתְנַנֶּיהָ Mi 1⁷ᵃ (We proposes אֲשֵׁרֶיהָ, cf Now Marti);—harlot's *hire*, Dt 23¹⁹ (א׳ זוֹנָה); elsewhere in fig.: of idolatrous Israel Ho 9¹, Jerus. Ez 16³¹·³⁴·³⁴·⁴¹, Tyre Is 23¹⁷·¹⁸; of costly idols of Samaria Mi 1⁷ᵇ·⁷ᶜ, cf v⁷ᵃ (v. supra)

תַּנְשֶׁמֶת v. [נשם].

תעב (√of foll.; cf. תאב (v [תָּעַב] Am 6⁸) is erroneous; cf. NH תּוֹעֵבָה, תעב Pi; Ph תעבת, Aram תּוֹעֲבָא).

תּוֹעֵבָה₁₁₇ **n.f.** abomination;—abs. ת׳ Gn 43³²+21 t.; תֹּעֵבָה Je 44⁴; cstr. תּוֹעֲבַת Gn 46³⁴+; pl. תּוֹעֵבוֹת Ez 8⁶+, cstr. תּוֹעֲבוֹת 6¹¹+, etc.; sf. תֹּעֲבֹתָיו 2 Ch 36⁸, etc.,—**1.** ritual sense · **a.** Isr.'s sacrifices, ת׳ מִצְרַיִם (gen. obj.) Ex 8²²·²² (E), cf. Gn 46³⁴ (J), ת׳ לְמִצְרַיִם 43³² (J); ת׳ ל of physical repugnance ψ 88⁹. **b.** to God and his people. ת׳ of unclean food Dt 14³, worshipper of idols Is 41²⁴, cf Je 2⁷, various objectionable acts: ת׳ לִפְנֵי י׳ Dt 24⁴, ת׳ י׳ 7²⁵ (חֵרֶם, cf. v²⁶), 17¹ 18¹² 22⁵ 23¹⁹ 27¹⁵; offering of children (עשה) 12³¹, cf. Je 32³⁵, also pl. 2 K 16³ = 2 Ch 28³, Dt 18⁹·¹² (+ witchcraft); idolatrous practices (sts with other illegal acts) עשה (כ)ת׳ Dt 13¹⁵ 17⁴ Ez 16⁵⁰ 18¹² Mal 2¹¹ (intermarriage with idolaters), cf. Je 44⁴; usu c pl noun Dt 20¹⁸ 1 K 14²⁴ 2 K 21²·¹¹ 2 Ch 33² 36⁸ Je 7¹⁰ 44²² Ez 8⁶+12 t. Ez., cf. תועבות 2 Ch 36¹⁴ Ezr 9¹·¹¹·¹⁴ Ez 5⁹+18 t. Ez.;

of idols Dt 32^{16}; (תועבה) 2 K 23^{13} Is 44^{19} (cf. Dt 27^{15}), idolatrous objects 2 Ch 34^{33}; || שקוצים Je 16^{18} (R^{JE}) Ez 5^{11} 11$^{18.21}$, (צַלְמֵי ת׳) 7^{20}; || גלולים 14^{6}, cf. 6^{9}, גִּלּוּלֵי ת׳ 16^{36}. **2.** ethical sense: **a.** c. gen obj. of man, ת׳ שְׂפָתַי Pr 8^{7}, ת׳ מלכים 16^{12}, ת׳ צדיקים 29^{27}, ת׳ כסילים 13^{19}, ת׳ רָשָׁע 29^{27}, ת׳ לְאָדָם 24^{9}. **b.** to God and his people: ת׳ of sacrifice of wicked Pr 21^{27} (cf 15^{8}), his prayers 28^{9} cf. Is 1^{13} (ת׳ לִי), prob. also Je 6^{15}=8^{12} (of various kinds of wickedness); unchastity Lv 18^{22}; c. עשה 20^{13} (H) Ez 22^{11} 33^{26}; cf. תועבות Lv 18$^{26.27.29}$ (cf. v^{30}; H), also Pr 26^{25}; ת׳ י׳ Dt 25^{16} Pr 3^{32} + 10 t Pr., cf. 6^{16}.

†[תָּעַב] **vb. denom. Niph. Pi.. Niph.** *Pf.* 3 ms. נִתְעַב 1 Ch 21^{6}; *Pt.* נתעב Is 14^{19} Jb 15^{16};—*be abhorred:* **1.** ritual sense: נֵצֶר נתעב Is 14^{19} *an abhorred* (rejected) *branch* (< נֵץ *vulture*, the unclean scavenger bird), נִתְעָב וְנֶאֱלָח Jb 15^{16} *abhorred and corrupt*, fr. disease (נאלח elsewhere †ψ 14^{3}=53^{4} || התעיב) **2.** ethically· David's census, acc. to 1 Ch 21^{6}. **Pi.** *Pf* 3 pl. sf. תעבוני Jb 9^{31} + 2 t; *Impf* יְתָעֵב ψ 106^{40} 5^{7} (read 2 ms. תְּתַעֵב); 3 fs. תְּתַעֵב ψ 107^{18}; 2 ms. תְּתַעֵב Dt 23$^{8.8}$, etc.; *Inf. abs.* תַּעֵב Dt 7^{26}, *Pt.* מְתָעֵב Is 49^{7} (but v. infra), + Am 6^{8} (so read for מתאב Gei$^{Urschrift\ 349}$ We Now Marti Harper); pl. מְתַעֲבִים Mi 3^{9};—**1.** *regard as an abomination, abhor:* **a.** ritual sense: (1) of God; c. acc. of Israel, because of idols ψ 106^{40}. (2) of man· c. acc., of abomination Dt 7$^{26.26}$, cf. 23$^{8.8}$; Job Jb 19^{19} 30^{10}. **b.** ethically: (1) of God; || שׂנא, c acc.: איש דמים ומרמה ψ 5^{7} (Am 6^{8} v. II. תאב). (2) of man; c. acc. משפט Mi 3^{9}, דֹּבֵר תָּמִים Am 5^{10} (|| שׂנא), שֶׁקֶר ψ 119^{163} (|| שׂנא). **c.** physically: c. acc. כָּל־אֹכֶל ψ 107^{18}. **2.** *cause to be an abomination:* c. acc., ritual sense Ez 16^{25}; Job, from filthy garments Jb 9^{31}; מְתָעֵב גּוֹי Is 49^{7} (|| בְּזֹה נֶפֶשׁ) (read prob. **Pu.** מְתֹעָב, as Oort SS BuDu). **Hiph.** *Pf.* 2 fs. הִתְעַבְתְּ Ez 16^{52}; 3 mpl. הִתְעִיבוּ ψ 14^{1}=53^{2}; *Impf.* וַיַּתְעֵב 1 K 21^{26},—*make abominable, do abominably*· **1.** ritual sense: c acc. rei, Ez 16^{52}, לְ c. inf. 1 K 21^{26}. **2.** ethically: c acc עלילה ψ 14^{1}=53^{2} (עול).

†תָּעָה **vb.** err (|| form of טָעָה, q.v.; Aram. (sts.) תְּעָא, תְּעֵי *id.;* NH = BH (rare));—**Qal** *Pf.* 3 ms. ת׳ Is 21^{4}; 1 s. תָּעִיתִי ψ 119$^{110.176}$, etc.; *Impf.* 3 fs תתע Gn 21^{14} Pr 7^{25}; 3 mpl. יִתְעוּ Is 35^{8}+; *Inf. cstr.* תְּעוֹת Ez 44^{10}+, *Pt.* תֹּעֶה Gn 37^{15}+, etc;—**1.** physically, *wander about*, abs. Ex 23^{4} (E) Is 35^{8} 53^{6} Jb 38^{41} ψ 119^{176}; c. בְּ loc. Gn 21^{14} 37^{15} (JE), Pr 7^{25} ψ 107^{4}; c. לְ loc Is 47^{15}; acc loc. 16^{8}. **2.** of intoxication, c. בְּ of wine Is 28^{7}; מִן of wine v^{7}; fig. of perplexity, subj. לבב 21^{4}. **3.** ethically, abs Ez 44^{10} 48$^{11.11.11}$ ψ 58^{4}, prob. Pr 14^{22} (cf. חוטא v^{21}, but Bu Toy *go astray to ruin*), תעי רוח Is 29^{24}, תעי לבב ψ 95^{10}, c מִן 119^{110} Pr 21^{16}, מֵאַחֲרֵי Ez 14^{11}, מֵעָלַי Ez 44$^{10.15}$. **Niph. 1.** *be made to wander about*, as a drunkard: *Inf. cstr.* הִתָּעוֹת Is 19^{14}. **2.** ethically: *Pf.* 3 ms. נִתְעָה *be led astray* Jb 15^{31} (c. בשוא). **Hiph.** *Pf.* 3 ms. הִתְעָה Ho 4^{12} (We הִתְעָם); *Impf.* וַיֶּתַע 2 Ch 33^{9}; sf. וַיַּתְעֵם Jb 12^{24}+; *Pt.* מַתְעָה Is 30^{28}+;—**1.** physically: *cause to wander about:* abs Is 30^{28} (of bridle, in fig), Pr 10^{17}; Je 50^{6} (acc. of people as sheep); acc. pers. Pr 12^{26}; c. מִן loc Gn 20^{13} (E), בְּ loc. Jb 12^{24}=ψ 107^{40}. **2.** of intoxication, Is 19$^{13.14}$ Jb 12^{25}. **3.** mentally and morally. *cause to err, mislead.* abs. Is 3^{12} 9^{15} Ho 4^{12}; c. acc. pers Am 2^{4} Mi 3^{5} 2 K 21^{9}=2 Ch 33^{9}, Je 23$^{13.32}$; c בְּ obj. Je 42^{20} (so Gf; Ke al (so Pr 10^{17}) intr *err at cost of*, 𝔊 Ew Du Co הֲרֵעֹתֶם), c. מִן of י׳ Is 63^{17}.

†תּוֹעָה **n.f.** wandering, error;—**1.** *error* in morals and religion, c דִּבֶּר, Is 32^{6}. **2.** *confusion, disturbance*, c. עָשָׂה, Ne 4^{2}.

תֹּעִי v. תעי. תְּעוּדָה v. [עוד] p. 730.

†תֹּעִי **n.pr.m.** king of Hamath, 2 S 8$^{9.10.10}$= תֹּעוּ (which We Dr al. prefer) 1 Ch 18$^{9.10}$

I, II. תְּעָלָה v. עלה p. 752

תַּעֲלוּלִים v. I. עלל

תַּעֲלֻמָה v. I. [עלם]. תַּעֲנוּג v. [ענג].

תַּעֲנִית v. III. [ענה] p. 777.

†תַּעְנַךְ **n.pr.loc.** in Great Plain, [ת׳ Baer Gi, van d H. תַּעֲנָךְ, exc. Jos 21^{25} 1 Ch 7^{29}]; usu named with Megiddo· old Can. city, Ju 5^{19} Jos 12^{21} (=Egypt. *Ta-'-n-k-â, Ta-'a-na-k*, WMM$^{As\ u\ Eur\ 170,\ 195}$); assigned to Manasseh 17^{11} 21^{25} Ju 1^{27} 1 Ch 7^{29} (yet within territory of Issachar Jos 17^{11} 19^{15} 𝔊); named also 1 K 4^{12}; 𝔊 Θανααχ, Θααναχ, Ταναχ, etc.; =mod. *Ta'annuk*, c. 4½ m. SSE. from *Lejjun* (Megiddo), Rob$^{BR\ III.\ 117}$ Guérin$^{Sam.\ II.\ 226\ ff}$ Buhl$^{G\ 208\ f.}$ Wilson$^{Hast.\ DB\ Taanach}$.

†[תָּעַע] **vb. Pilp. Hithp.** mock (cf. Ar. تَعْتَعَ *stammer*, also *shake violently;* onomatop);—**Pilp.** *Pt.* מְתַעְתֵּעַ Gn 27^{12}=subst. *a mocker*. **Hithp.** *Pt.* pl. מִתַּעְתְּעִים 2 Ch 36^{16}, c בְּ pers., *mocking at* his prophets (+ בּוֹזִים, מַלְעִבִים).

†תַּעְתֻּעִים **n.[m.] pl. abstr. mockery**;—מַעֲשֵׂה ת׳, epith. of idols, Je 10[15] 51[18] (both + הֶבֶל).

[תַּעֲצֻמָה] v. I. [עצם]. תְּעֻפָה v. II. עוף.

תַּעַר v. [ערה]. [תַּעֲרֻבָה] v. II. ערב p. 787.

תַּעְתֻּעִים v. [תעע]. תֹּף v. [תפף].

תִּפְאָרָה v. I. [פאר]. I, II, III. תַּפּוּחַ v. [נפח].

[תְּפוּצָה] v. I. [פוץ].

†[תֻּפִינִים] **n.[m.] pl.** doubtful word; AV RV *baken pieces* (Thes from √אפה *bake*);—only cstr. תֻּפִינֵי מִנְחַת פִּתִּים Lv 6[14]; text prob. crpt.; rd. תְּפַתֶּנָּה (√פתת), *thou shalt break it* into a meal-offering of pieces, Me[ZWTh vi. 60 f.] (𝔖), Di[ad loc.]

I. **תפל** (√of foll.; NH תָּפֵל, 𝔗 אִיתַּפֵּל, in Midr. expl. of Dt 1[1]; on 2 S 22[27] תִּתַּפָּל v. פָּתַל; NH תָּפֵל *unsalted*, of fish, תִּפְלָה = BH; Ar. تَفَلَ is *spit*, تُفْل *spittle*).

†I. תָּפֵל **adj. tasteless, unseasoned**;—abs. ת׳, as subst. Jb 6[6]; fig. of unsatisfying prophecies La 2[14] (+ שָׁוְא).

†תִּפְלָה **n.f.** (moral) **unsavouriness, unseemliness**;—abs. ת׳; *unseemliness*, of men Je 23[13] Jb 24[12]; לֹא נָתַן ת׳ לֵא׳ 1[21] *he did not ascribe unseemliness to God;* so read also 4[18] (for MT תָּהֳלָה) Hup Me Bu.

II. **תפל** (√of following; akin to טָפַל).

†II. תָּפֵל **n.[m.] whitewash**;—applied to wall, in Ezekiel's vision Ez 13[10.11.14.15]; fig. of false prophet 22[28].

†תֹּפֶל **n.pr.loc.** in, or near, the *ʿArabah*;—Dt 1[1]; = mod. *Ṭafîleh*, 15 m. SE. of Dead Sea Rob[BR ii. 167] v. Burckhardt[Travels 402 f.], but *Ṭ* = ת improb. v. Di Dr; 𝔊 Τοφολ (cf. Lag[BN 54]).

תְּפִלָּה v. [פלל]. [תִּפְלֶצֶת] v. [פלץ].

תִּפְסַח v. I. פסח.

תפף (√of following; cf. 𝔗 תּוּפָא Ex 15[20] *timbrel*, Ar. دُفّ *drum*).

†תֹּף **n.m. timbrel, tambourine**;—abs. ת׳ Gn 31[27] +; pl. תֻּפִּים Ju 11[34] +; sf. תֻּפֶּיךָ Ez 28[13], תֻּפַּיִךְ Je 31[4];—*timbrel*, held and struck with hand, esp. by dancing women, oft. with other musical instr.:—sign of merriment, gladness Gn 31[27] (E) Jb 21[12], revelry Is 5[12]; מְשׂוֹשׂ ת׳ 24[8], cf. Je 31[4] Ez 28[13]; exultation, triumph Ex 15[20.20] (E) Ju 11[34] 1 S 18[6] Is 30[32]; used by prophets in ecstasy 1 S 10[5]; in praise of י׳ 2 S 6[5] ‖ 1 Ch 13[8], ψ 81[3] 149[3] 150[4].—Vid. Prince[EB Music, § 3].

†[תָּפַף] **vb. denom. sound the timbrel, beat**;—**Qal** *Pt.* עֲלָמוֹת תּוֹפֵפוֹת ψ 68[26]; rd. *Impf.* וַיְּתֹף 1 S 21[14] 𝔊 (v. תוה). **Po'ēl** *Pt.* כְּקוֹל יוֹנִים מְתֹפְפֹת עַל־לִבְבֵהֶן Na 2[8]; > Sta (after 𝔊) מְצַפְצְפוֹת *twittering*.

†[**תָּפַר**] **vb. sew together** (NH *id.*; Aram. תְּפַר);—**Qal** *Impf.* 3 mpl. וַיִּתְפְּרוּ Gn 3[7] (J) *they sewed together* fig-leaves (acc.); *Pf.* 1 s. תָּפַרְתִּי Jb 16[15], c. acc. + עֲלֵי, *sackcloth I have sewed upon* my skin; *Inf. cstr.* עֵת לִתְפּוֹר Ec 3[6] *a time to sew together* (opp. קְרֹעַ). **Pi.** *Pt.* as subst. f.pl. מְתַפְּרוֹת Ez 13[18] *those who keep sewing*, c. acc. + עַל.

†**תָּפַשׂ** **vb. lay hold of, wield** (= NH תָּפַשׂ, תָּפַס, Aram. תְּפַשׂ, תְּפַס);—**Qal** *Pf.* 3 ms. ת׳ 2 K 14[13] +, sf. consec. וּתְפָשָׂהּ Dt 22[28], etc.; *Impf.* 3 ms. יִתְפֹּשׂ Is 3[6], 1 pl. נִתְפְּשֵׂם 2 K 7[12], etc.; *Imv.* mpl. תִּפְשׂוּ 1 K 18[40], etc.; *Inf. abs.* תָּפֹשׂ Je 34[3]; cstr. תְּפֹשׂ Ez 14[5], לְתָפְשׂ 21[16] 30[21], sf. לְתָפְשָׂהּ Dt 20[19], etc.; *Pt.* תֹּפֵשׂ Gn 4[21] +, cstr. תֹּפְשֵׂי Je 49[16] (Ges[§ 90 l]), etc.;—**1.** *lay hold of, seize* (with the hand), acc. pers., Gn 39[12] (J; + בְּבִגְדוֹ), also (ב pers.) Is 3[6] Dt 21[19] Je 37[14] Ez 29[7] (in fig.; + ב instr.); c. ב rei 1 K 11[30] Dt 9[17]; *arrest, catch,* acc. pers. 1 S 23[26] 1 K 13[4] 18[40.40] Je 26[8] 37[13], 2 K 14[13] = 2 Ch 25[23], 2 K 25[6] = Je 52[9], ψ 71[11]; in phrase *catch, capture alive* (חַי), acc. pers. Jos 8[23] (JE), 1 S 15[8] 1 K 20[18.18] 2 K 7[12] 10[14.14]; *seize* city (acc.) Jos 8[8] (JE), 2 K 14[7] 16[9] 18[13] = Is 36[1], Dt 20[9] Je 40[10]; fig. Ez 14[5] *seize* Isr. (acc.) by (ב) their heart (terrorize them); Pr 30[9] *seize* (do violence to) the name (acc.) of my God; תָּפוּשׂ זָהָב Hb 2[19] *grasped* (sheathed) *in gold;* ת׳ מְרוֹם גִּבְעָה Je 49[16] *holding* (occupying) *the height of the hill.* **2.** *grasp* in order to *wield, wield, use skilfully: grasp* sword בַּכַּף Ez 21[16] (acc. om.), cf. 30[21] (ב of sword), and esp. pt.: תֹּפֵשׂ הַקֶּשֶׁת Am 2[15], תֹּפֵשׂ כִּנּוֹר Gn 4[21] (J), ת׳ מָגֵל Je 50[16], תֹּפְשֵׂי מָגֵן 46[9a] (del. ת׳ v[9b] 𝔊 Gie Co Du), ת׳ מָשׁוֹט Ez 27[29], ת׳ חֲרָבוֹת 38[4]; even ת׳ הַתּוֹרָה Je 2[8] *they that handle* (deal with, are expert in) *the law*, ת׳ הַמִּלְחָמָה Nu 31[27] (P) *those skilled in war*.—Je 34[3] v. infr. **Niph.** *Pf.* 3 ms. נִתְפַּשׂ Ez 19[4], 2 fs. נִתְפַּשְׂתְּ Je 50[24], etc.; *Impf.* 3 fs. וַתִּתָּפֵשׂ 51[41], 2 ms. תִּתָּפֵשׂ Je 34[3] 38[23], etc.;

Inf. cstr. לְהִתָּפֵשׂ Ez 21[25];—*be seized, arrested, caught* (sts. ‖ נִלְכַּד), subj pers, Je 38[23] (ב instr.), 50[24] (fig. of Bab.), also (c. ב instr) Ez 12[13] 17[20] 19[4.8] (both fig of Israel), 21[29], and (without ב) v[23] Nu 5[13]; + *Inf. abs* **Qal** תָּפֹשׂ תִּתָּפֵשׂ Je 34[3]; *be seized,* of fortress, city Je 48[41] 51[41] (both ‖ נִלְכַּד), 50[46], cf. 51[32]; fig. ψ 10[2] *may they be caught in* (ב) *the devices* which they have planned. **Pi.** *Impf.* 2 ms. תְּתַפֵּשׂ Pr 30[28] a lizard *thou mayest grasp* with the hands (ב);—or rd. תִּתָּפֵשׂ Niph. Impf. 3 fs., v. De Toy.

I. תֹּפֶת v. תוף.

†II. **תֹּפֶת n.pr.loc.** in valley of בֶּן־הִנֹּם, S of Jerusalem (etym. doubtful, v. GFM[Ency Bib Molech], RS[Sem 1.357, 2nd ed 372,377] al. think Aram., = *fire-place*, cf. שׁפת);—c. art. הַתֹּ׳ 2 K 23[10] + 5 t, art. om. Je 7[32] 19[11.12];—place of sacrificing children Je 7[31], cf. v[32a] 19[6] (cf. v[5]), 2 K 23[10], to become burial-place Je 7[32b] 19[11]; in sim of desecrated city v[12.13] (מְקוֹם הַתֹּ׳); scene of a prophecy of Jerem, v[14];—Ταφέθ, Ταφεθ (cf. Lag[BN 73]), 𝔊L[2 K 23.10] Θαφφεθ.—Vid GFM[l.c.] Salmond[Hast. DB Tophet].

†תָּפְתֶּה **n.pr.loc.** (si vera l.) **id.**;—as a place of burning, in fig. of י׳'s judgment on Assyria Is 30[33] (Klo Che Buhl Marti al תֹּפֶת, joining ה to following as interrogative)

תָּקְהַת Qr, תוקהת Kt, v. III. תִּקְוָה p. 876.

I, II, III. תִּקְוָה v. I [קוה]. תְּקוּמָה v. קום.

[תְּקוּמָם], מְיֹדָ- v. p. 879. [תְּקוּפָה] v. קוף.

†[תָּקַן] **vb. become straight** (NH תִּקֵּן *arrange, put right,* Ecclus 47[9] תיקן *set in order;* As. *takânu, be well ordered,* esp Pi. as NH; Aram تقن *be established, firm,* Pa. تقّن, תַּקֵּן, *fix, arrange, prepare,* etc., Palm. Pa. *erect*),—**Qal** *Inf cstr.* לתקן Ec 1[15] (opp. מְעֻוָּת *bent*) **Pi.** *Inf. cstr.* לתקן 7[13] *make straight* (opp. עִוָּה); *Pf.* 3 ms. תִּקֵּן 12[9] *put straight, arrange in order* (proverbs)

תָּקַע 67 **vb. thrust, clap, give a blow, blast** (NH *id*; JAram. תְּקַע *strike, blow horn;* Eth. ጠቀዐ: *blow* trumpet);—**Qal** *Pf.* 3 ms ת׳ Gn 31[25] +, 1 s. וְתָקַעְתִּי Ju 7[18], etc.; *Impf.* 3 ms וַיִּתְקַע 3[27] +, sf וַיִּתְקָעֵהוּ Ex 10[19], etc, *Imv* mpl. תִּקְעוּ Ho 5[8] +; *Inf abs.* תָּקוֹעַ Jos 6[9.13]; cstr. לִתְקֹעַ Ju 7[20], כת׳ Is 18[3]; *Pt. act.* תקע Pr 17[18] +, etc; *pass.* f. תְּקוּעָה Is 22[25],—**1.** *thrust, drive,* weapon (acc) into (ב) a person Ju 3[21] 4[21] 2 S 18[14], peg into (ב) sthg Is 22[23.25] (cf. Ju 4[21]); hence *pitch* a tent (acc.), i.e drive its pegs: Gn 31[25a] Je 6[3] (+ עַל against, in fig.), acc om. Gn 31[25b]; *thrust, drive, beat* (strands of hair together) בַּיָּתֵד Ju 16[14], ins. also v[13] (so 𝔊, cf. GFM[Comm and PAOS Oct. 1889 176 ff]), *thrust, drive* locusts seaward (ה loc.), Ex 10[19] (J);—cf. ת׳ בְּ 1 S 31[10] of fastening bodies to wall, and similarly 1 Ch 10[10] (but rd in both הוקיעו, √יקע Lag We Dr and mod.). **2.** *give a blast, blow* (Germ. 'stossen'), c. ב of instr. (usu. horn or clarion) Jos 6[4.8.9.13.13.16.20] (JE), Ju 3[27] 6[34] 7[18.18.19.20] + 14 t., + Nu 10[3.4.8.10] (P; v. חֲצֹצְרָה), also Ez 7[14] (v. תָּקוֹעַ infr.), ת׳ alone Ju 7[20] Nu 10[7] (P; opp. הֵרִיעַ *sound an alarm*), c. acc. תְּרוּעָה v[5.6] (P; v. חֲצֹצְרָה); c. acc. of instrument Ju 7[22] Ho 5[8] Is 18[3] Je 4[5] 6[1] 51[27] Jo 2[1.15] ψ 81[4], + תקעו Jos 6[9] (Kt; Qr תֹּקְעֵי). **3.** *strike, clap* hands; in triumph, ת׳ כַּף עָלֶיךָ Na 3[19], ת׳ כָף ψ 47[2]; also (late) of gesture ratifying a bargain, specif pledging oneself to become surety, only Pr. (all ‖ עָרַב): ת׳ כַּף, ת׳ לְזָר כַּפֶּיךָ 17[18] 22[26]; abs. 11[15] †**Niph.** *Impf.* 3 ms. **1.** יִתָּקַע שׁוֹפָר Am 3[6] if *a horn be blown,* cf יִת׳ בְּשׁ׳ Is 27[13] *it shall be blown* (a blast shall be given) on a horn. **2.** מִי־הוּא לְיָדִי יִתָּקֵעַ: Jb 17[3] *who is there that will strike himself* (i e. pledge himself) *into my hand?*

†תֵּקַע **n.** [**m.**] blast of horn;—cstr. בְּתֵ׳ שׁוֹפָר ψ 150[3] *with horn-blast.*

†תָּקוֹעַ **n.** [**m.**] **a blast-(wind-)instrument** (si vera l),—abs. תָּקְעוּ בַתּ׳ Ez 7[14] (but del ב, and treat תָּקוֹעַ as inf. abs., so Co and mod).

†תְּקוֹעַ **n.pr.loc.** in S Judah (connex. with above √ dub),—Am 1[1] Je 6[1] 2 Ch 11[6], as 'son' of Ashḥur 1 Ch 2[24] 4[5]; תְּקוֹעָה 2 S 14[2]; מִדְבַּר תְּ׳ 2 Ch 20[20]; 𝔊 Θεκωε (also -ουε); mod. *Teḳû'a,* c. 5 m. S. of Bethlehem, v. Rob[BR i 486 f] Buhl[G 157 f.] Taylor[Hast DB Tekoa] GASm[Twelve Proph 1.74 f] Dr[Am 1.1].

†תְּקוֹעִי, תקעי **adj.gent.** of foregoing: הַתּ׳ 2 S 23[26] = 1 Ch 11[28] 27[9]; f. הָאִשָּׁה הַתְּקֹעִית 2 S 14[4.9], pl as subst. הַתְּקוֹעִים Ne 3[5.27].

†[תָּקַף] **vb. prevail over, overpower** (late; NH *id.*; Aramaism; Aram. תְּקֵיף, تقف *be strong,* Nab תקף *authority;* cf. No[ZMG xlvii (1893), 102], Sab. תקף *overpower* SabDenkm[No. 9, l 13]; Ar ثَقِفَ *attain to, overtake, overpower*),—**Qal** *Impf.*: 3 ms sf יִתְקְפוֹ Ec 4[12] (Ges[§ 60 d]) if *one overpower him,* so 3 fs. sf. תִּתְקְפֵהוּ Jb 14[20]; 3 fs. sf. *id* 15[24].

†תֹּקֶף **n. m.** power, strength, energy (Aram תְּקֹף, תקוף, ܬܘܩܦܐ),—ת׳ abs Est 9[29], cstr. Dn 11[17] *the strength of his whole kingdom*, sf תָּקְפּוֹ Est 10[2] the deeds *of his power* (+ גְּבוּרָתוֹ, etc)

†תַּקִּיף **adj.** mighty (Aram תַּקִּיף, ܬܩܝܦ),—c מִן comp Ec 6[10]

†II תֹּר, תּוֹר, תֹר **n.f.**[Lv 5.7] (**m.**[Lv 14.30]) turtle-dove (onomatop),—abs. תר Gn 15[9] (J; + גוזל), Je 8[7] (as migratory), as sacrif offering (RS[Sem I 202, 2nd ed 219, 294]) [usu (בְּנֵי) יוֹנָה [בן] Lv 1[14] 5[7. 11] 12[6. 8] 14[22. 30] 15[14. 29] Nu 6[10] (all P; cf also Gn 15[9]), קוֹל הַתּוֹר Ct 2[12], sf תּוֹרֶךָ ψ 74[19] (fig of י׳'s people)—Vid Tristr[NHB 201 ff] Shipley-Cook[Ency Bib Dove] Post[Hast DB Turtle-Dove]—I תר v. I תור.

†תַּרְאֲלָה **n.pr.loc.** in Benjamin Jos 18[27], Θαρεηλα, 𝔊L Θεραλα

תַּרְבּוּת, תַּרְבִּית v. I [רבה]

תִּרְגַּל v. רָגַל Tiph.

†[תִּרְגֵּם] **vb.quadril.** interpret, translate (As. *targumânu*, *interpreter* (so also TelAm), perh. from √רגם, cf رَجَمَ *conjecture, opine* We[Reste Arab Heid 207], v also Dl[HWB 713] Vollers[ZA xii 138]; NH = BH; Aram. תַּרְגֵּם, ܬܪܓܡ, Ar تَرْجَمَ),—*Pt pass* מְתֻרְגָּם Ez 4[7].—On *Targum* v Walker[Hast. DB s v].

תַּרְדֵּמָה v [רדם].

†תִּרְהָקָה **n.pr.m** king of Egypt, of Ethiop dynasty 2 K 19[9] = Is 37[9], Θαρακα, 𝔊L Θαρθακ, = Egypt *T-h-r-k*, As *Tarku*, Steindorff[BAS i 342 f] COT[2 K 19. 9] Wiedemann[Äg Gesch 590 ff] Brugsch[Egypt under Pharaohs (new ed 1891), 4.0 ff] WMM[Ency Bib Tirhakah] Griffith[Hast DB ib]

תְּרוּמָה, תְּרוּמִיָּה v. רום. תְּרוּעָה v [רוע]

תְּרוּפָה v. רוף.

†תִּרְזָה **n.f.** a tree, AV *cypress*, RV *holm-tree*, but very dub.: Tr[NHB 378] Post[Hast DB Cypress], 𝔙 *ilex*, and so M'Lean[Ency Bib Cypress],—abs ת׳ Is 44[14] (+ אַלּוֹן, ‖ אֲרָזִים).

†תֶּרַח **n.pr.** **1. m.** father of Abraham: (a kind of *ibex* RS[K (1st ed) 220] (cf As *turâḫu*, Ar تَأْرَخ No[ZMG xxxiii (1879) 331], Syr ܬܪܚܐ *capra caucasica*), but against this No[ZMG xl (1886), 167], n pr div. Jen[ZA vi 70]),—ת׳ Gn 11[24. 26. 27. 27. 28. 31. 32. 32] Jos 24[2], תָּרַח Gn 11[24] 1 Ch 1[26], Θαρρα, 𝔊L Θαρα.—Vid Selbie[Hast DB Terah]. **2. loc.** station on Exodus journey Nu 33[27. 28], Ταραθ.

תַּרְחֲנָה v רחן.

תְּרָמָה, תַּרְמִית, תרמות, תרמה v. II. [רמה].

†תֹּרֶן **n.m.** mast (NH *id*; √unknown; Hoffm[Ph Inschr 27 f] conj. תארן, from ארן, v אֹרֶן),—abs ת׳, of Tyre as ship Ez 27[5], ת׳ עַל־רֹאשׁ הָהָר Is 30[17] (‖ נֵס), i e. a (solitary) standard-pole, flag-staff, sf. תָּרְנָם 33[23] (‖ נֵס, חֲבָלִים)

תַּרְעֵלָה v [רעל].

†תִּרְעָתִים **n.pr.m.pl.** a Kenite family, 1 Ch 2[55]; Θαργαθιιμ

†תְּרָפִים **n.m.**[Zc 10.2] **pl.** (= pl majest. No[ZMG xlii (1888), 476]) a kind of idol, obj of reverence, and means of divination (√and etymol.-mng. dub, cf. GFM[Hast DB Teraphim] Say[ZA ii 195] (citing Neubauer, and As *tarpû*, *spectre*), al √רפא, cf רְפָאִים),—alw. ת׳:—portable and sts. small Gn 31[19. 34. 35] (called אֱלֹהִים v[30], all E), but in size and shape like a man 1 S 19[13. 16], in household shrine (v. also l c) Ju 17[5] (+ אפוד, cf. GFM[Ju]), 18[14. 17] (both + אפוד, פֶּסֶל, מַסֵּכָה), cf v[20] (om. מַסֵּכָה), Ho 3[4] (+ א׳, זֶבַח, מַצֵּבָה); condemned 1 S 15[23] 2 K 23[24] (+ גִּלֻּלִים), used in divining (by king of Bab.) שָׁאַל בַּת׳ Ez 21[26] (+ קִלְקַל בַּחִצִּים, רָאָה בַּכָּבֵד); as giving empty oracles Zc 10[2] (‖ הַקּוֹסְמִים)—Vid GFM[l c] Now[Arch ii 23] Sta[Bib Theol d A T s v].

תִּרְצָה v. רצה

†תֶּרֶשׁ **n.pr.m.** eunuch at court of Ahasuerus (Scheft[53] cp OIran *tarša*, '*Begierde*,' used as n pr. in NPers);—Est 2[21] 6[2], Θαρ(ρ)ας.

†I תַּרְשִׁישׁ **n.m.** a precious stone, perhaps *yellow jasper*, or other gold-coloured stone (𝔊 Ex 28[20] 39[13] χρυσόλιθος, so Jos[Ant. iii 7. 5 (168)], v Petrie[Hast. DB Stones, Precious] Myres[Ency Bib Id § 17] Dr[Dn 10.6]);—כְּעֵין ת׳ Ez 1[6], כְּעֵין אבן ת׳ 10[9], in list of gems 28[13] Ex 28[20] 39[13]; in sim. of resplendent body Dn 10[6], cf Ct 5[14]

†II תַּרְשִׁישׁ **n.pr.** **1. loc.** a distant port, site not certainly known (Wkl[Altor Forsch v 445]); most *Tartessus* in Spain Thes (after older authorities) Ges[Is i 719] Mey[Gesch d Alt i § 281], other views are · *Tyrseni* (Etruscans) in Italy, WMM[Hast DB Tarshish], *Phoenicia* Renouf[PSBA xvi. 134 ff], *Sardinia* Hal[RÉJ xiii 14]; v. also Ency. Bib.[Tarshish];—

Tarshish, 𝔊 usu. Θαρσ(ε)ις (Is 23^{1.14} Καρχηδων = *Carthage*);—esp. in phr. אֳנִיּוֹת ת׳ *Tarshish-ships* (large, sea-going vessels, *fit* to ply to Tarshish) Is 2^{16} (𝔊 πλοῖον θαλάσσης), 23^{1.14} 60^{9} Ez 27^{25} 1 K 22^{49}, ‖ 2 Ch 20^{36.37} (where the ships *go to* ת׳); אֳנִי ת׳ 1 K 10^{22.22} ‖ 2 Ch 9^{21} (אֳנִיּוֹת), + v^{21} (ships *go to* ת׳); ת׳ alone Is 23^{6} Jon 1^{3.3} 4^{2} (all c. ה loc.), Gn 10^{4} ‖ 1 Ch 1^{7} (erron. ה loc.), Is 66^{19} ψ 72^{10} Jon 1^{3}; בַּת־ת׳ Is 23^{10}; trading-port Ez 27^{12} 38^{13}, whence comes silver Je 10^{9}. **2. m. a.** in Benjamin 1 Ch 7^{10}. **b.** Persian noble Est 1^{14}; expl. by Scheft^{53} as OIran. *tṛšus*, '*der Gierige*.'

†**תִּרְשָׁתָא** **n.m. Tirshathâ**, title of Persian governor in Judaea, acc. to Mey ^{Entstehung d. Jud. 194} al. = *His Excellency* (read *Tarshathâ*) otherwise Lag^{Symm. i. 60 (cf. Arm. Stud. §§ 280, 1680)}.—As Mey^{l.c.}, Scheft ^{93 f.} (*taršta, the feared, revered*) Moss^{Hast. DB Tirshatha} Che^{Ency. Bib. id.};—הַתּ׳ Ezr 2^{63} = Ne 7^{65}, Ne 7^{69} (Baer Gi; v^{70} van d. H.); of Nehemiah Ne 8^{9} 10^{1}.

†**תַּרְתָּן** **n.m.** title of As. general = **field-marshal** (loan-word from As. *tartânu, turtânu* Dl^{WB 716} Tiele^{Gesch. 495 f.} Pinches^{Hast. DB Tartan} Johns ^{Ency. Bib. id.});—Is 20^{1} 2 K 18^{17} (+ רַב־שָׁקֵה, רַב־סָרִיס); only this last in ‖ Is 36^{2}).

†**תַּרְתָּק** **n.pr.div.** of הָעַוִּים, 2 K 17^{31}; Θαρθακ; not identified, cf. Pinches^{Hast. DB Tartak}.

תְּשׂוּמֶת v. I. שׂום. [**תְּשֻׁאָה**] v. II. שׁוא.

תֹּשָׁב v. תּוֹשָׁב sub ישׁב. **תִּשְׁבִּי** v. שׁבה.

תַּשְׁבֵּץ v. [שׁבץ]. [**תְּשׁוּבָה**] v. שׁוב.

תשוה Jb 30^{22} v. [תְּשֻׁאָה] sub II. שׁוא.

תְּשׁוּעָה, תְּשֻׁעָה v. ישׁע.

תְּשׁוּקָה v. III. שׁוק.

תְּשׁוּרָה v. I. שׁור. **תּוּשִׁיָּה** v. תּוּשִׁיָּה sub ישׁה.

תֵּשַׁע, תִּשְׁעָה ₅₈ **n.m. et. f. a nine, nonad** (NH = BH; As. *tišit* (fem.), *nine, tešû, ninth;* Sab. תסעת *nine,* תסעי *ninety* Hom^{Chr 48}; Liḥy. תסע DHM^{Ep. Denkm. Ar. 52}, Ar. تِسْعٌ, Eth. ተስዐ; Aram. תְּשַׁע, ܬܫܥ, Nab. Palm. תשע Lzb^{388}, Mand. (א for ע; sts. ע pref.) תשא, עשתא Nö^{M 188}, all *nine*);—**m.c.n.f.** abs. תֵּשַׁע Dt 3^{11} + 20 t., cstr. תְּשַׁע Ju 4^{3} + 18 t.; **f. c. n.m.** abs. תִּשְׁעָה 2 S 14^{8} + 13 t., cstr. תִּשְׁעַת Jos 13^{7} + 2 t. (these include 9 + 10 = 19);—*nine* (Hex chiefly P); **1.** no other num.: **a.** before n.pl. תְּשַׁע אַמּוֹת Dt 3^{11}, ת׳ שָׁנִים 2 K 17^{1} Gn 11^{19}, ת׳ הַיָּדוֹת Ne 11^{1}, תִּשְׁעַת הַשְּׁבָטִים Jos 13^{7}(JE?), 2 S 24^{8}, תִּשְׁעָה חֳדָשִׁים cf. 14^{2} Nu 34^{13} (both P); after n.pl. עָרִים תֵּשַׁע Jos 15^{44.51} 21^{16} (all P), פָּרִים תִּשְׁעָה Nu 29^{26} (P); n. om. 1 Ch 3^{8}. **b.** = ordin. בְּתִשְׁעָה לַחֹדֶשׁ 2 K 25^{3} + 3 t. *on the ninth* (day) *of the month;* שְׁנַת־תְּשַׁע לְ 18^{10} *the ninth year of.* **2.** 9 + 10 = 19, c. **n.f.** תְּשַׁע־עֶשְׂרֵה שָׁנָה Gn 11^{25}, עָרִים תְּשַׁע־ שְׁנַת תְּשַׁע־עֶשְׂרֵה Jos 19^{38} (both P), as ordinal עֶשְׂרֵה תִּשְׁעָה עֶשְׂרִים שָׁנָה לְ 2 K 25^{8} ‖ Je 52^{12}; **c. n.m.** תִּשְׁעָה עָשָׂר אִישׁ 2 S 2^{30}, cf. (as ordin., גּוֹרָל om.) 1 Ch 24^{16} 25^{26}. **3.** 900 = תְּשַׁע מֵאוֹת Ju 4^{3} + 14 t. **4.** c. tens (20, 30, etc.): ת׳ foll. 2 K 14^{2} + 10 t., precedes Gn 11^{24} + 6 t., cf. Kö^{ii. 1. 215 ff.}

תְּשִׁיעִי, תְּשִׁעִי m. **תְּשִׁיעִית** f. **adj. num. ord.**₁₈ **ninth**;—בַּיּוֹם הַתְּשִׁיעִי Nu 7^{60}, הַתּ׳ of series of men 1 Ch 12^{12} 27^{12}, of lot 24^{11} 25^{16}; הַחֹדֶשׁ הַתּ׳ Je 36^{9.22} Zc 7^{1} 1 Ch 27^{12} Ezr 10^{9}, ת׳ om. Hg 2^{10.18}; הַשָּׁנָה הַתְּשִׁיעִית Lv 25^{22} + 3 t., בִּשְׁנַת הַתּ׳ (Ges^{§ 134 p}) 2 K 17^{6} 25^{1}.

תִּשְׁעִים ₂₀ **n. indecl. ninety** (archaic pl., DHM^{ZMG xxxvii (1883), 9 f.} Prät^{BAS i. 376}, but cf. Ges^{§ 97 f.});—before n. sg.: שָׁנָה Gn 5^{9} 17^{17} +, אַמָּה Ez 41^{12}, יוֹם Ez 4^{5.9}; less oft. after n.pl. אֵילִים Ezr 8^{35}, cf. Dn 12^{11}; in combination, ת׳ precedes units 1 S 4^{15} + 7 t.; foll. Gn 5^{17.30}; ת׳ foll. 100 Ez 4^{5.9} + 4 t.

BIBLICAL ARAMAIC

[Dn 2[4b]–7[28], Ezr 4[8]–6[18], 7[12–26], Je 10[11], Gn 31[47 bis].]

NOTE.—In the case of words common to Biblical Aramaic and Biblical Hebrew the etymological matter already given with the Hebrew words is not repeated here. The sign ‡ is prefixed to all words peculiar to the Biblical Aramaic. In other cases, except where 𝔗 or Syr is mentioned alone, it may be understood that the words occur also in the Aramaic of the Targums and in Syriac, even when this is not expressly stated.

א

[אָב] v. אבה.

†[אֵב K[§ 55, 5 a) 2]] **n.m. fruit** (BH, √אנב),—sf. 3 ms. אִנְבֵּהּ (K[§ 11, 4 b)]) Dn 4[9.11.18].

†[אֲבַד] **vb. perish** (BH),—**Pe.** *Impf.* 3 mpl. יֵאבַדוּ (not ־ן, v. K[§ 26, 1]) Je 10[11] *they shall perish*, pass away. **Haph.** (OAram האבד Lzb[205], Cooke[189]) *destroy*. *Impf.* 2 ms. אַל־תְּהוֹבֵד (K[§ 41 c]) Dn 2[24] (c. ל pers.), 3 mpl. יְהוֹבְדוּן v.[18] (indef. subj., acc. pers.), *Inf.* לְהוֹבָדָא v.[12.24] (both c. ל pers.), ־דָה 7[26] (abs.). **Hoph.** (K[§ 41 c], W[CG 224]) *be destroyed*. *Pf.* 3 ms. הוּבַד 7[11].

אבה (assumed as √ of foll., v. p. 3).

†[אַב D[§ 40, 4], אַבָא Id[1b] Me[Chr 16]] **n.m. father** (BH אָב),—**1.** lit. *father*, sf. אֲבִי Dn 5[13] (v. Behrm. Marti), אֲבוּהִי v.[2.11.11.11.18] אֲבוּךְ (K[§ 53, 2 a]) v.[2]. **2.** pl. *fathers, ancestors* [אֲבָהָן D[l.c.]], sf. אֲבָהָתִי 2[23] (Baer ־תָי, but v. K[§ 53, 1]), אֲבָהָתָךְ Ezr 4[15], ־תָנָא (Str ־תַנָא) 5[12].

†אֶבֶן **n.f.** [Dn 2 34] **stone** (BH *id.*),—abs. א׳ Dn 2[34]+, emph. אַבְנָא v.[35],—**1.** *a (the) stone* Dn 2[34.35.45] 6[18]. **2.** *stone*, material of idols 5[4.23], of buildings Ezr 5[8] 6[4].

†אִגְּרָה (K[§ 60, 1]) **n.f. letter-missive** (late BH אִגֶּרֶת, OAram אגרת, Palm אגרתא Lzb[207]),—abs. א׳ Ezr 4[8] (v.[11] and H ־רָא), emph. אִגַּרְתָּא 4[11] 5[6].

†אֱדַיִן [87] **adv. then, thereupon** (so Eg. Aram. (S-C[Pap H 1, J 1]), not 𝔗. the usu. Aram. forms are הידין, ܗܝܕܝܢ, Mand האידין (No[M 207]), from [אֱדַי] = BH אֲזַי (v. אָז) + determ. affix *n* (as in דִּכֵּן, תַּמָּן, in Sab = post-pos. art., Hom[Chr 117]; cf. W[CG 115]), No[GGA 1884, 1020]. אֲזַי, [אֱדַי], prob. from same demonstr. √ as זֶה, דָּא, דִּי, etc., إِذْ, إِذَا *lo*, إِذًا *well then, in that case*, Eth ሚዓዜ: *when?* ይእዜ: *now* (Di[Lex 157, 1072]), Syr. ܐܝܕܝܢ (enclitic) *but*),—*then, thereupon*, Dn 2[14.17.19.25.48] 3[24]+, Ezr 4[9.23] 5[4.9]+ (alw., exc. Ezr 5[4], at beg. of sentence, introducing new stage of narrative with some emph.), so c. ב, בֵּאדַיִן (3 t. Ezr., 26 t. Dn) Dn 2[14.35.46] 3[3.13.19.21.26], etc., Ezr 4[24] 5[2] 6[1], מִן־אֱדַיִן *from that time* †Ezr 5[16].

†אֲדָר (K[§ 57 a]) **n.pr.** 12th month (BH *id.*),—Ezr 6[15].

†[אִדַּר K[§ 59 c)]] **n.m. threshing-floor** (𝔗 *id.*, Syr. ܐܕܪܐ, cf. Chr-Pal Schulth[Lex 3], hence Ar. أَنْدَرٌ as loan-word Frä[136], conj. on etym. Lag[Ges. Abh. 10] Hoffm[ZCB 1892, 8.9] Jen[ZA vii (1892) 216]);—pl. cstr. אִדְּרֵי־קַיִט Dn 2[35].

‡†[אֲדַרְגָּזַר] **n.m. counsellor** (Pers. loan-word = *andarzaghar* No[COT Dn 3 2, Tabari 462] Andr[M M] Str[42] Dr Scheft[11 57], Mey[Entst. J. 25] questions, and thinks military title),—pl. emph. אֲדַרְגָּזְרַיָּא Dn 3[2.3].

†אַדְרַזְדָּא **adv. correctly, exactly** (acc. to Haug[JBW 1853, 192 f.] Scheft[68 f.] from Zend *derez, make firm*, whence Skr. ptcp. pass. *dṛḍha, firm, sure, suitable*, Zend *dereśta, holding firm*, Pers. *durust, whole, complete, correct*; > Nö[KAT² 617] from אַזְדָּא, q.v.);—Ezr 7[23] יִתְעֲבֵד א׳.

אֶדְרַע v. דרע.

אוה (✓of foll.; v. BH אוֹת, II. אוה).

†[אָת] **n.m.**[Dn 3, 33] **sign** (alw. as wrought by God, and alw. c. תמהין *wonders*);—pl. abs. אָתִין Dn 6[28]; emph. אָתַיָּא 3[32]; sf. אָתוֹהִי v[33].

אול (✓of following, BH II. אול, איל).

†אִילָן (D[138]) **n.m.**[Dn 4, 7] **tree** (𝔗 אִילָן, Syr. ܐܝܠܢܐ; cf. BH אֵלָה, אַלּוֹן, p. 18);—abs. א׳ Dn 4[7]; emph. ־נָא v[8.11.17.20.23].

†[אזא] **vb. make hot, heat** (𝔗 *id.* [rare]; cf. Ar. أَزَّ *kindle, burn*);—**Pe.** *Inf.* לְמֵזֵא (K[§ 11, 3 b)]) Dn 3[19] (ל acc.), sf. לְמֵזְיֵהּ v[19]; *Pt. pass.* אֲזֵה (K[§ 15 e)]) v[22].

†אַזְדָּא (so Gi, with most MSS.; Baer אַזְדָּא) **adj. sure, assured** (Pers. *azda*, Skr. *addhâ*, 'certain' (Kern[ZDMG 1869, 220]); so first Nö[KAT² 617]; confirmed now by Eg. Aram. (RÉS[361, B3]) הן אזד יתעבד מן if it is made certain (certified) by, etc.; > 𝔊 Ki AV al. (v. Thes) as vb. *is gone*, or (אַזְדָּא) *is going*, from Talm. אֲזַד (= אֲזַל) *go away* (Levy NHWB I. 50)); so Scheft[MGWJ 1903, 310] from Zend **azda* 'gone,' ptcp. pass. of *azaiti* 'go');—Dn 2[5] מִלְּתָה דִּי־אַזְדָּא מִנִּי מִלְּתָא v[8], מִנִּי אַזְדָּא the word is *assured* on my part (the thing is fully resolved upon by me: cf. 𝔊 ܡܫܪܪܐ; IE קִיָּמָא וֶאֱמֶת); + 3[14] (v. צְדָא).

†אֲזַל **vb. go, go off** (BH [rare]);—**Pe.** *Pf.* 3 ms. א׳ Dn 2[24] + (אֲזַל v[17] 6[20]); 3 pl. אֲזַלוּ Ezr 4[23]; 1 pl. אֲזַלְנָא 5[8]; *Imv.* ms. (אֱזַל־אַחֵת) v[15] (for אֱזַל K[§§ 15 e); 38, 1 c)]);—**1.** *go, go off*, c. ל loc. Dn 2[17] 6[19.20] Ezr 4[23] (+ על pers.), 5[8]; *go* and say Dn 2[24], *go* (and) put Ezr 5[15].

און (✓of following; BH II. און, מֹאזְנַיִם).

†מֹאזַנְיָא (Baer Gi Str) **n.m.emph. scale, balance** (cf. also Mand. מוזאניא Nö[M 148], Eg. Aram. מוזנא S-C[G24], Chr-Pal. ܡܘܙܢܐ Schulth Lex. 5 Nö[BSW 56] Jacob[ZAW xxii (1902), 90]);—Dn 5[27] (van d. H. du. emph. מֹאזַנְיָא, v. K[§ 51, 1, Anm.] M[33 *]).

אחד (✓of following; v. BH אֶחָד).

†חַד **adj. one, a**;—ms. ח׳ Dn 2[31] +; fs. חֲדָה Ezr 4[8] +;—**1.** *one* side Dn 7[5]; n. om. 6[3]; חֲדָה 2[9] = *one and invariable (inevitable)*; כַּחֲדָה v[35] *as one, altogether* (so S-C[K3] 𝔗, and late BH כְּאֶחָד Ezr 2[64] +); = ordinal, שְׁנַת חֲדָה *first year* 7[1] Ezr 5[13] 6[3]; ח׳ = *a certain one* (τινὰ) Dn 7[16] (c. מִן partit.). **2.** *a* (indef. art.) c. subst. Dn 2[31] 6[18] 4[16] (v. שָׁעָה), Ezr 4[8] 6[2], חַד שִׁבְעָה Dn 3[19] = *seven-fold* (as Syr.: Nö[§ 241] PS[1194]; cf. Ex 16[5] 𝔖), v. K[§ 66, 2].

אחה (assumed as ✓of foll.; cf. BH אָח p. 26).

†[אַח] **n. m. brother**;—pl. sf. אחיך Kt (? ־ָיךְ K[§ 53, 2, Anm. b)]), אַחָךְ Qr (K[§ 63]) Ezr 7[18] *thy brethren*, i.e. fellows, associates.

[אַחֲוָיָה] v. [חוה]. [אַחִידָה] v. חוד.

†אַחְמְתָא (orig. ־תָן or ־תָנָא Nö in Streck ZA 15, 368) **n.pr.loc. Ecbatana**, Ezr 6[2]; capital of Media, captured by Cyrus (B.C. 550), and then summer residence of Pers. kings; mod. همدان *Ḥamadân*, Spieg[244] Margoliouth[Hast. DB ACHMETHA], esp. Brugsch[Reise n. Persien (1862), I. 360-392] (OMed. *Agmatana* Dl[Calwer Bib. Lex.]; OPers. *Hañgmatâna* (= *place of assembling*) Spieg[l.c.], Bab. *Agam(a)tanu* Beh[60], Bez[p. 26], etc.; Ἀγβάτανα Herod[1. 98]; 𝔊 Ἐκβάτανα 2 Macc 9[3] +; Mey[Gesch. d. Alt. I. § 485] Streck l. c. 367 f.).

†[אחר] pl. c. אַחֲרֵי, **prep. after** (Cappad. and Eg. Aram. אחר *afterwards* (Lzb[Eph. I. 361] S-C[Pap. C 8]), prob. Nab. אחר *after* (Lzb[212] SAC[16]); Eg. Aram. אחריכם (S-C[Pap. C 8+]); 𝔗 (sts.) אֲחוֹרֵי; BH אַחַר);—אַחֲרֵי דְנָה *after this* Dn 2[29.45]; c. sf. אַחֲרֵיהֹן 7[24]. Usu. Aram. syn. בָּאתַר, q. v.

†אָחֳרִי **adj. f. another**: v. אָחֳרָן.

†אחרין Dn 4[5] Kt, וְעַד אחרין עַל קָדָמַי דָּנִיֵּאל; very dub. (v. Comm.); usu. *and unto the last* (= *at last*) came in, etc.; but word in this sense unknown: Qr אָחֳרֵין; read perh. (Bev) וְעַד אָחֳרָן (or ? Kt אָחֳרִין; cf. ܘܥܕܡܐ) and yet *another* came in before me.

†אַחֲרִית **n.f. cstr. end** (Hebraism; so (cf. Jacob[ZAW, 1902, 84-6]) Chr-Pal., Schulth[6]);—Dn 2[28] בְּאַ׳ יוֹמַיָּא (from BH בְּאַ׳ הַיָּמִים p. 31 a).

†אָחֳרָן **adj. m. another** (Eg. Aram. אחרן S-C[D11+]; Nab. Palm. *id.* (Lzb[212]); 𝔗 אוֹחֲרָן; cf.

Syr ܐܚܪܝܢ (?),—Dn 2[11.44] 3[29] 4[5] Kt 5[17] 7[24]. The **f.** in use is אָחֳרִי (Eg Aram אחרה, RÉS[246], 𝔗 Talm אוחרי (D[§20.5]), cf K[§61.5] M[§87d] No[Beitr 51]), Dn 2[39] מַלְכוּ א׳, v[39] 7[5.6.8.20].

†[אֲחַשְׁדַּרְפְּנִין] **n.m.pl. satraps** (BH ־נִים; cf M[52*]),—emph. ־נַיָּא Dn 3[2.3.27] 6[2.3.4.5.7.8].

אול v. אִילָן

†[אֵימְתָן D[§30.1*]] **adj. terrible** (𝔗 אֵימְתָן, fr. אימתא=BH אֵימָה, q.v., √אים),—fs abs אימתני (K[§61.5]) Dn 7[7] (on form v Prat[ZMG lvi (1902) 156] No[BSSW 51 Anm 1])

†אִיתַי (Baer אִתַי, exc. bef sf, v. Baer[Dn 2, 10]) **part. there is, are** (prop a **subst.** foll by a gen., v BH יֵשׁ. Eg Aram איתי RÉS[361], S-C[Pap], Nab איתי, Palm. אית, 𝔗 Talm אית (Dalm[§44,4]), Syr ܐܝܬ, Sam ࠀࠉࠕ, Mand. אית, עית (No[M §213. 272]). v further BH יֵשׁ),—אִיתַי Dn 2[10], sf אִיתָיךְ 2[26] Kt (Qr אִיתָךְ K[§63, 2 b]), אִיתוֹהִי 2[11], איתינא Kt (i.e. prob. אִיתַיְנָא · K[l c]), Qr אִיתַנָא 3[18], אִיתֵיכוֹן v[14.15],—*there is (are)* . . , abs. Dn 2[28] אִיתַי אֱלָהּ בִּשְׁמַיָּא *there is* a God in heaven, v[30] not by wisdom דִּי־אִיתַי בִּי that *is* in me, 3[12] 5[11], sq ptcp or adj 2[26] הַאִיתָיךְ כָּהֵל *art* thou able . . ? 3[15.17]; sq דִּי, Ezr 5[17] הֵן אִיתַי דִּי if *it is that* . . With neg לָא אִיתַי (so S-C[D 10+], 𝔗 Syr Mand לית, ܠܝܬ, Zenj sf לישה (Cooke[184]), cf. sub BH יֵשׁ) Dn 2[10] . . . לָא אִיתַי אֱנָשׁ דִּי, 3[29] 4[32], after the subj 2[11]. 3[25] וְחֲבָל לָא א׳ בְּהוֹן, Ezr 4[16], sq. ptcp. or adj Dn 3[14.18], with pleon. sf, 2[11] דִּי מְדָרְהוֹן עִם־בִּשְׂרָא לָא אִיתוֹהִי.

†[אֲכַל] **vb. eat, devour** (BH),—**Pe.** *Pf* 3 mpl אֲכַלוּ Dn 3[8] 6[25], *Impf.* 3 ms. יֵאכֻל 4[30], 3 fs תֵּאכֻל 7[23], *Imv* fs אֲכֻלִי v[5], *Pt.* fs אָכְלָה v[7.19],—**1.** *eat*, of beast, Dn 4[30] (acc rei). **2.** *devour*, of beast in vision, 7[5] (acc rei), abs v[7.19], hence fig. of kingdom, *devour, devastate*, v[23] (acc. of earth) **3.** in phr. אֲ׳ קַרְצֵיהוֹן 3[8] *eat their pieces*, i.e. slander them, cf. 6[25] (v. קְרַץ).

†אַל **adv.** of prohibition, **do not** . . , **let not** , sq impf (=BH I אַל, Zenj. אל (Had[22 23.29]) Cooke[p. 161 f]; cf. Pehlevi (No[GGA 1884, 1016]); not 𝔗 Syr);—Dn 2[24] אַל־תְּהוֹבֵד, 4[16] 5[10].

†אֵל **demonstr.pron. pl. these** (v אֵלֶּה infr.), Ezr 5[15] Qr (Kt אלה)

אֱלָהּ [94] **n.m. god, God** (=BH אֱלֹהַּ (p. 43), v also √I. אלה p. 41),—א׳ abs. Dn 2[28]+, cstr. v[18]+; emph אֱלָהָא v[20]+; sf. אֱלָהִי 6[23], ־הָךְ Ezr 9[14]+, ־הּה Dn 6[6]+, ־הֲהֹם Ezr 5[5] 7[16], ־הֲהוֹן Dn 3[28.28.29], ־הֲכֹם Ezr 7[17], etc; pl. abs. אֱלָהִין Dn 2[11]+, emph. ־הַיָּא Je 10[11], cstr. ־הֵי Dn 5[4.23], sf. ־הַי 3[14], etc. [c pref לֵאלָהָא Dn 5[23], לֵאלָהָיךְ 3[14], etc.; but not in sg. abs. or cstr., e g לֶאֱלָהּ Ezr 5[12], etc.];— **1.** *god*, in gen Dn 6[8.13], heathen deities Je 10[11] Dn 2[11] 3[15]+15 t. Dn (made of gold, etc. 5[4.23]), +בַּר־אֱלָהִין 3[25] (v בַּר) **2.** [73] *God* (of Isr.), Dn 2[23] Ezr 5[2]+; phr. אֱלָהּ יִשׂ׳ Ezr 5[1] 6[14] 7[15]; א׳ ירושלם 7[19], א׳ אֲבָהָתִי Dn 2[23], א׳ שְׁמַיָּא Ezr 5[11] (+וְאַרְעָא), v[12] 6[9.10] Dn 2[18.19]+6 t. (v. שְׁמַיִם **2 a**); א׳ רַב Dn 2[45]; א׳ אֱלָהִין v[47], אֱלָהָא עִלָּיָא 3[26.32] 5[18.21]; א׳ חַיָּא 6[21.27]; also בֵּית אֱלָהָא 5[3] Ezr 4[24] 5[2]+16 t. Ezr, עֲבִידַת א׳ Ezr 6[18].

†אֵלֶּה **demonstr. pron. pl. these** (Nab. אלה (Lzb[264] Cooke[241]), Cappad. and Eg Aram. אלה (Lzb[Eph i 323] RÉS[361 A 3] S-C[Pap E 13. K 13]). prob. therefore not, as used to be supposed, a Hebraism, but a peculiarity of the dialects of Je 10[11] and of Ezr (in which the usu. Aram. form אִלֵּין does not occur): v. further אִלֵּין),—*these*, Je 10[11] Ezr 5[15] Kt

†אֲלוּ **interj. lo!** (der. uncertain: usu. regarded as by-form of אֲרוּ, q v; cf. Eg. Aram. הלו, Cooke[No 73], RÉS[492 B]=S-C[M 6]),—וַאֲלוּ Dn 2[31], וַחֲזֵה הֲוֵית וַאֲלוּ 4[7.10] 7[8], always in description of a vision.

†אִלֵּין (אלן Dn 2[44] 6[7]) **demonstr.pron.pl. these** (pl of דְּנָה, q.v.: Palm. אלן (Lzb[264] Eph i 343. 344] Cooke[26]), 𝔗 אִילֵין, Mand עלין (No[M 81]); Talm (with emph *hā* prefixed, W[CG 109]) הָאלֵין: v further sub BH אֵלֶּה, and add Eg Aram. אלו Cooke[26]),—*these*, only Dn: Dn 2[40] דִּי מְרָעַע כָּל־אִלֵּין, 6[3] אֲחַשְׁדַּרְפְּנַיָּא אִלֵּין, כָּל־אִלֵּין מַלְכְוָתָא [44] (so v[7]), אִלֵּין חֵיוָתָא 7[17].

†אִלֵּךְ **demonstr. pron. pl. these** (pl. of דֵּךְ, q v: Eg Aram אלך (Cooke[207] RÉS[361 B] S-C[Pap. K 6+]). with *hā* prefixed, OSyr. ܗܠܝܢ, f ܗܠܝܢ, No[§67 M §82] Burkitt[Evang da Mepharreshe ii 42], Chr-Pal ܗܠܝܢ (m and f) Schw[Idiot 24], cf. Ar أُولَاكَ, Eth. አልክቱ: Di[Lex 1057]: the demonst affix ךְ as in דֵּךְ, ذَاكَ, etc, W[CG 110]);—*these*, אִלֵּךְ גֻּבְרַיָּא *these men*, Dn 3[12.13.21.22.23.27] 6[6.12.16.25] Ezr 4[21] 6[8b]; also Ezr 5[9] 6[8a]

†אֲלַף n.m. 1,000 (=BH II. אֶלֶף);—abs. 'א (n. pers. precedes) Dn 5[1]; n. om., emph. אַלְפָּא v[1] *the thousand* (just mentioned); cstr.+pl. abs. אֶלֶף אַלְפִּים Dn 7[10] *a thousand thousands* (< Qr אַלְפִין K[§51, 2]).

†[אַמָּה] K[§51, 2, Anm. 2] n.f.[Dn 3, 1] cubit (=BH *id.*; v. p. 52; Eg. Aram. (pl.) אמן RÉS[246] S-C[C 44]);—pl. אַמִּין (so 𝔗 Syr.) Dn 3[1.1] Ezr 6[3.3].

†אֻמָּה n.f. nation (BH *id.*, late);—abs. 'א Dn 3[29]; pl. emph. אֻמַּיָּא 3[4.7.31] 5[19] 6[26] 7[14] Ezr 4[10].

†[אֲמַן] vb. Haph. trust (BH);—*Pf.* 3 ms. הֵימִן בֵּאלָהֵהּ Dn 6[24]; *Pt. pass.* מְהֵימַן *trusty, trustworthy*, of pers. 6[5], interpretation 2[45].

אמר vb. say, tell, command (BH אָמַר);—Pe. *Pf.* 3 ms. 'א Dn 2[12]+, אֲמַר 7[1]; 3 fs. אֲמַרַת 5[10] (K[§38, 1a]); 1 s. אַמְרֵת 4[5]; 1 pl. אֲמַרְנָא 5[4.9], etc.; *Impf.* 3 ms. יֵאמַר (K[§41]) 2[7]+; 2 mpl. תֵּאמְרוּן Je 10[11], etc.; *Imv.* ms. אֱמַר 2[4]+; mpl. אֱמַרוּ 2[9]; *Inf.* לְמֵאמַר v[9], לְמֵמַר Ezr 5[11] (K[§41a]); *Pt.* אָמַר Dn 2[5]+oft., pl. אָמְרִין 3[4] Ezr 5[3]+;—**1.** *say* (oft. in phr. *answer and say*): sq. orat. rect. (only), Dn 2[7.10]+13 t. Dn, Ezr 5[11]; +לְ pers. Dn 2[5] 3[14]+14 t. Dn [pl. c. indef. subj. for pass. 4[23]], Ezr 5[15]; +קֳדָם pers. Dn 2[9] 5[17] 6[13.14]; +כֵּן 4[11] 7[23], כֵּן c. לְ pers. Ezr 5[3] Dn 2[24.25] 6[7], cf. 7[5]; +כְּנֵמָא c. לְ pers. Ezr 5[4.9]; +כִּדְנָה c. לְ pers. Je 10[11]; sq. acc. rei+עַל pers. against whom Dn 3[29]. **2.** *relate, tell*: sq. acc. rei Dn 4[6.15] 7[1], +לְ pers. 2[4.9.7] 7[16] (acc. rei om.), +קֳדָם pers. 2[36] 4[4.5]. **3.** *command*: sq. inf. 2[12.46]+6 t. Dn; sq. vb. fin. 5[29] 6[17.25]; sq. לְ pers.+or. rect. 3[4] [pl. c. indef. subj., for pass., K[§76e], so 4[23]].

†מֵאמַר n.[m.] word;—cstr. Dn 4[14] Ezr 6[9].

†[אִמַּר] n.m. lamb (As. *immeru* (also=*child*; *immertu*, *girl*; conj. as to etym. Dl [Prol. 28] Jen [ZMG xliii (1889), 203; ZA vii. 216] Schwally[Idiot. 114]), 𝔗 אִמְּרָא; Syr. ܐܶܡܪܳܐ, Pun. אמר, Palm. pl. emph. אמריא Lzb[220] Cooke[Inscr. 120.337]; Ar. أُمَّرٌ (loan-word? cf. Frä[107], but also DHM[VOJ i. 24]));—pl. אִמְּרִין, *lambs*, as sacrif. victims Ezr 6[9.17] 7[17].

אִנְבֵּהּ v. אֵב.

†אֲנָא Dn 2[8] Ezr 6[12] 7[21] in common edd.: v. אֲנָה.

†אֲנָה pr. 1 s. I (=Heb. אֲנִי, q.v.: Zenj. Cilic. Eg. Aram. אנה (Cooke[182.194.202]; S-C[oft.]), Nab ···נה (Lzb[221]); 𝔗 אנא, Syr. ܐܶܢܳܐ);—*I*, Dn 2[30] 4[6.27] 5[16], before a ptcp. 3[25] 4[34], after a ptcp. (K[§76, 2b]) 2[8] מִן־יַצִּיב יָדַע אֲנָה, v[23] 4[4]; sq. a n.pr. 4[1] אֲנָה נבוכדנצר שְׁלֵה הֲוֵית, v[15.34] 7[15] Ezr 6[12] 7[21], as nom. pendens, Dn 4[31] 7[28]; emphasizing a sf. (K[§87, 3]) 7[15] Ezr 7[21] (cf. S-C[B 8, J 12, K 3.5]).

†אִנּוּן pr. 3 mpl. they, those (pl. of הוּא: 𝔗 אִינּוּן, f. אִינִּין, e.g. Gn 3[7] 6[2]; Syr. ܗܶܢܽܘܢ, ܐܶܢܽܘܢ, f. ܗܶܢܶܝܢ, ܐܶܢܶܝܢ; Talm. אִינְהִי, אִינְהוּ (for אִינְהוֹן, אִינְהִין); Mand. הינון, היניך;—all from הֵן, הֵן, with demonstr. syll. אן, הן 'lo,' prefixed, W[CG 98, 106] Nö[M 86]);—*they, those*, Dn 2[44] מַלְכַיָּא אִנּוּן *those kings*, 6[25] as accus. רְמוֹ אִנּוּן, 7[17] Kt דִּי אִנּוּן אַרְבַּע (Qr f. אִנִּין) which are four (Dr[1810.19] K[§87, 3]), Ezr 5[4]... מָה אִנּוּן שְׁמָהָת: *what are the names*...? (Dr[§201, 3, Obs.], K[l. c.]). Cf. הוּא.

†אֲנַחְנָא (Ezr 4[16] אֲנַחְנָה) pr. 1 pl. we (Eg. Aram. RÉS[361] S-C[Pap.] אנחנה; BH אֲנַחְנוּ; W[CG 100 f]), Dn 3[16.17] Ezr 4[16] (after ptcp.), 5[11].

†אִנִּין they (f.) Dn 7[17] Qr: Kt אִנּוּן, q.v.

†[אֲנַס] vb. oppress (BH [late] *constrain*);—Pe. *Pt.* אָנֵס לָךְ Dn 4[6].

†[אַנַּף, אַף K[§55, 4]] n.m. only du. (Schulth ZAW xxii (1902), 164) face (BH אַף, √אנף; Aram. of Têma אנפי SAC[23] Lzb[222] Cooke[69, l. 14], so S-C[G 19] and (usu.) 𝔗[J]; 𝔗[Onk Jon] אפין, ܐܰܦܶܐ Syr. Chr-Pal. (Schulth[Lex. 13]); also אפי Palm. Lzb[222] Cooke[p. 329], Chr-Pal. c. prep. ܠܩܒܠ Schulth[Lex. 14], etc.);—pl. sf. 3 ms. אַנְפּוֹהִי Dn 2[46] 3[19].

I. אנשׁ (√of foll.; cf. BH II. אנשׁ, II. אֱנוֹשׁ).

†אֱנָשׁ n.m. man, mankind;—abs. 'א Dn 2[10]+; emph. אֲנָשָׁא v[38]+, so Qr 4[13.14] (>Kt אנושא K[§57 f]); so Nab. אנוש oft. Lzb[222] Cooke[219] SAC[22]): pl. אֲנָשִׁים 4[14] (Hebraism, M[53*] prop. אֲנָשָׁא);—**1.** *man*, human being, Dn 2[10] 3[10] 4[13] 5[5.7.7] 6[13.13] 7[4.4.8] Ezr 6[11]; so בַּר־אֱנָשׁ Dn 7[13] *a son of man*, human being (v. esp. Dr[Dn 102; DB Son of Man]). **2.** coll. *men, people*, Ezr 4[11] Dn 4[14a.22.22.29.29.30] 5[21], cf. pl. 4[14]; זְרַע א' 2[43] i.e. human offspring; בְּנֵי אֲנָשָׁא *sons of men*,=men, 2[38] 5[21].

II. אנשׁ (√of foll.; BH III. אנשׁ, אִשָּׁה).

†[נְשִׁין] n.f. pl. wives (so Zinj. (Cooke[62, 8]) cstr. נשי, 𝔗 נְשִׁין, Syr. ܢܶܫ̈ܐ, Heb. נָשִׁים, Ar. نِسَاءٌ: on sing. v. BH אִשָּׁה, and add Aram. of Nineveh cstr. אשת (CIS[1.16]), and Eg. Aram. אנתה S-C[Pap. D 10+]);—pl. sf. נְשֵׁיהוֹן Dn 6[25].

‡**אנתה** Kt$_{14}$ (i.e. אַנְתָּה, peculiar to BAram.; Qr אַנְתְּ) **pr. 2 ms. thou** (BH אַתָּה p. 61 b; Cappad. and Eg. Aram. אנת (Lzb [Eph. i. 67]; S-C [A 11+], f. אנתי *ib.* [D 9. 11. 26+]), Nerab את (Cooke [186. 190]), Palm. אנת (*ib.* [308]); 𝔗⁰ את, 𝔗ᴶ אנת (D [§16. 1]); Syr. ܐܢܬ);—*thou*, Dn 2[29.31.37.38] etc., Ezr 7[25].

†**אַנְתּוּן** **pr. 2 mpl. ye, you** (BH אַתֶּם p. 61 b), Dn 2[8].

†**אָסְנַפַּר** **n.pr.m.** Asnappar, who transported peoples to Samaria Ezr 4[10]; Ασενναφαρ, 𝔊L Σαλμανασσάρης; prob.=As.kg. *Ašurbanipal* (B.C. 668–626), i.e. אס(רב)נפל, Gelzer [Äg. Zeitsch. 1875. 78] COT [ad loc.] Mey [E Jud. 29 f.] Zim [KAT 3. 351] Berthol [ad loc.] Ency. Bib.[342].

†**אָסְפַּרְנָא** **adv.** thoroughly, RV. with (all) diligence (Zend *aspĕre, asperenō*, Pers. *siparī, asperī*, all *complete*, Castell [1669], Thes Haug [JBW 1853, 154] Lag [Sem. i. 48] Andr [Marti, Gl. 53*] Scheft [MGWJ 1903, 415 (correcting Arisches im AT. 73 f.)]);—Ezr 5[8] א׳ מִתְעַבְדָא, 6[8.12.13] 7[17.21.26] (cf. OAram. אספרן, on a weight, *complete, correct:* Lzb[223], Cooke[193]).

אסר (√of foll.; BH [אָסַר] *bind*, אֱסוּר *bond*, אִסָּר *binding obligation*).

†**אֱסוּר** **n.[m.] band, bond** (𝔗 אֱסוּר, אִיסוּר, Syr. ܐܣܘܪܐ, ܐܣܘܪ);—abs. א׳ Dn 4[12.20] (of iron and bronze, for stump, in Neb.'s vision); pl. abs. אֱסוּרִין Ezr 7[26] *bonds*=imprisonment.

†**אֱסָר** **n.m.** interdict (as *binding*);—א׳ abs. Dn 6[8.13.16]; cstr. v[13]; emph. אֱסָרָא v[9.10.14].

†**אָע** **n.m.** [Ezr 5, 8] wood (so 𝔗, for עֵץ; Eg. Aram. עק S-C [H 5]; BH עֵץ, √II. עצה);—**1.** abs. א׳ *timber*, for building Ezr 5[8] 6[4]; *beam* v[11]. **2.** emph. אָעָא *wood*, material of idols Dn 5[4.23].

†**אַף** **conj. also** (BH אַף; Eg. Aram., Palm. אף (S-C [Pap.] Lzb[224]); 𝔗 אַף, 𝔗ᴶ also אוּף; Syr. ܐܦ);—*also*, always וְאַף Dn 6[23] Ezr 5[10.14] 6[5].

‡†**אֲפָרְסָיֵא** (K [§52. 2 d)]) **n.pr.pl. gent.** Ezr 4[9], 𝔊 Ἀφρασαῖοι, A Ἀφαρσαῖοι; Ges [Lex. Man.] Röd [Thes. Add. 107] Hoffm [ZA ii. 55] Mey [Enst. J. 38] *Persians;* Dl [Baer Ezr ix] Scheft[75] *Parsua* (in Media [v. Streck ZA xv. 308 ff.]; yet v. COT [ad loc.]); Marquart[64] (א)סָפְרַיָּא *secretaries* (א dittogr. of preceding); oft. identif. with following, so Andr [M 53*].

‡†**אֲפַרְסְכָיֵא** Ezr 5[6] 6[6]=(acc. to most) ‡†**אֲפַרְסַתְכָיֵא** 4[9], **n.pr.pl. gent.**, so most hitherto, and still Mey [Enst. J. 38 ff.] (*Persians*), but many moderns think official title (Hoffm [ZA ii. 54] Marquart[64] Jen [ThLZ. 1895, 509] Ency. Bib. [190 f.]; plausible explanations are: Andr [M 53*]=As. *šuparšak* (v. Muss-Arnolt [As. Dict. 1098] *šāqû* **3**, *general*, Id [AJ Sem. Lang. xx (1904), 186 ff.]); Scheft[76]=OIran. *aparasaraka, lesser ruler;* Id [MGWJ 47 (1903), 315 f.] expl. -תְכָיֵא as OPers. **aparaθrāka, lesser governor*).

†**אַפְּתֹם** or **אַפְּתוֹם** (so edd.: > Gi Baer [v. p. 102 f.] from MSS, אַפְּתֹם) Ezr 4[13] וְא׳ מַלְכִים תְּהַנְזִק; of uncertain mng.: Thes Haug [JBW 1853, 156] *in the end* (from Pehlevi *afdom*, Pers. فدام *end*); Scheft[79] *treasuries* (from Zend *pathmā*, pl. of *pathma, treasury,* √ *path, to fill up*), will endamage *the treasuries* of kings.

[**אֶצְבַּע**] v. צבע. **אַרְבַּע** v. רבע.

†[**אַרְגְּוָן**] **n.m. purple, red-purple** (BH *id.*, אַרְגָּמָן);—emph. אַרְגְּוָנָא Dn 5[7.16.29].

ארה (√of foll.; BH I. ארה, אַרְיֵה).

†**אַרְיֵה** **n.m.** [Dn 6, 25 b] lion;—abs. א׳ Dn 7[4] (sim.); pl. emph. אַרְיָוָתָא (D[153]) 6[8.13.17.20.21.23.25.25.28].

†**אֲרוּ** **interj.** lo (of uncertain der.: only BAram. (? Nab., v. CIS [ii. 186]); אֲלוּ, p. 1080, and NH הֲרֵי *see! here!* Ab 3[4] al., are perh. allied), Dn 7[2] וַאֲרוּ . . . חָזֵה הֲוֵית, v[5.6.7.13], always in description of a vision (cf. אֲלוּ).

†[**אֹרַח**] ? as 𝔗 Syr.] **n.[m.?] way** (fig.) (BH);—pl. sf. אָרְחָתָךְ (cf. K [§51. 2. Anm. 3]) Dn 5[23] *thy ways* (the progress and outcome of thine affairs); -תֵהּ 4[34] *his ways* (i.e. the course of God's dealings, ‖ מַעֲבָדוֹהִי).

אַרְיֵה v. ארה.

†**אַרְיוֹךְ** **n.pr.m.** in Bab. (BH *id.*, cf. Dl [Baer Dn ix]);—Dn 2[14.15.15.24.25]; Αριωχ(ης).

†I. **ארך** (√of foll.; BH [אָרֵךְ, אָרַךְ]).

†**אַרְכָה** (Baer [Dn 4, 24] K [§54. 3. 2]) **n.f. a lengthening, prolonging** (𝔗);—of time Dn 4[24] 7[12].

II. **ארך** (√of foll.; acc. to most, weakened fr. ערך (cf. BH) Be-Ry [Ezr 4, 14]; but אַרִיךְ loan-word fr. Pers. (OIranian) *āryaka, worthy of an Aryan*, Scheft[79]).

†**אֲרִיךְ** **adj.vb. fitting, proper** (א׳ Baer K [§16, 5] M [§82, Anm. 2]; van d. H. Gi Str אָרִיךְ, cf. D [WB 39]; 𝔗 *id.;* orig. *Pt. pass.* K [§57 b) γ)]);—Ezr 4[14].

אַרְכֻבָּתֵהּ Dn 5[6], v. ברך.

†אַרְכְּוָי **n.pr.gent.** people of Erech (BH אֶרֶךְ; so also Mey[EJud 40]);—pl emph Ezr 4[9] (Qr אַרְכְּוָיֵא; cf. K[§61,6]).

[אֲרַע][21] **n.[f.] earth** (so 𝔗 Syr, =BH אֶרֶץ, q v.),—emph אַרְעָא Dn 2[35.39] + 16 t. Dn, Ezr 5[11] Je 10[11b]; אַרְעָא (D[§§9 5a, 44 1a]) = אֲרַע + א—ָ of direction, *earthward*, i.e. *downward*, אַרְעָא מִנָּךְ Dn 2[39] Kt *lower than thou*, i e. inferior to thee Qr אֲרַע (cf. 𝔗 אֲרַע מִן Ru 4[4]),—Je 10[11a] v. [אֲרַק].

†[אַרְעִי] **n.f.denom. bottom** (so 𝔗; cf. also 𝔗 אַרְעָאָה *lower*),—cstr. אַרְעִית Dn 6[25].

†[אֲרַק] **n.[f.] earth** (=[אֲרַע], ארקא Eg. Aram. S-C[Pap. B 15+oft] (sts. also ארעא, as ib.[16]), Ninev. and Bab Aram Cooke[192], also Mand. No[M §66], Zinj, Lzb[227] Cooke[166 (cf.183)], ק=ע, as Zinj מוקא=מוצא, רקי=רצה, Cooke[166.155], cf. K[§7,2 and Anm 1] and reff. Cooke[185] No[ZMG xlvii (1893), 100, M §66] Gunk[Schöpf 18] Lzb[Eph i 223] SAC[JQ 1903-4 273]);—emph. אַרְקָא Je 10[11a].

†אַרְתַּחְשַׁשְׂתְּא **n.pr.m.** of king, Ezr 4[8 11 23] 6[14] = -שַׁסְתְּא 7[12.21] (BH -שַׁשְׂתָּא; Eg. Aram. ארתחשסש RÉS[433], S-C[B2+], v. also Andr[M 84*] Scheft[1 79]);—Αρσαρθα, Α(ρ)σαθαθα, Αρθασαθα; 𝔊L Αρταξερξης.

†[אשׁ K[§55,5c]] **n.m.**[Ezr 6,3] **foundation** (prob. loan-word fr. As. *uššu*, *id*, √אשׁשׁ (v BH), so Zim[KAT 3,649]; 𝔗 f. אוּשָׁא, NH אוֹשָׁה, Chr-Pal. ܐܫܐ, ܐܫܬܐ, Schulth[Lex 19]; Ar. أُسّ. No[M 99]);—pl. emph. אֻשַּׁיָּא Ezr 4[12] 5[16]; sf אֻשּׁוֹהִי 6[3].

†אֶשָּׁא **n.[f.] fire** (BH אֵשׁ; K[§55,5.2b] thinks emph. fr. onomatop √אשׁשׁ; D[161] Buhl √אשׁא, cf. 𝔗 אִישָׁא, אִישָׁתָא, Syr. ܐܫܬܐ),—Dn 7[11].

אֻשַּׁיָּא, אֻשּׁוֹהִי v. [אשׁ].

†אָשַׁף (K[§58a]) **n.m.** conjurer, enchanter (prob Bab loan-word, so BH אַשָּׁף),—abs. א׳ Dn 2[10]; pl abs אָשְׁפִין v[27] 5[11], emph אָשְׁפַיָּא 4[4] 5[7 15].

‡†אֻשַּׁרְנָא **n.m.** meaning and √dub (K[§62] Buhl[14]);—‖בַּיְתָא Ezr 5[3 9], most *wall* (𝔖𝔙 *walls*), M[3a*] cp As *ašurrû*, *wall*, but ?, Hpt in Gu[Ezr pp 34.63] thinks=[*ašrâna*] fr As *ašru*, *sanctuary*; pointed by Mas. as if=אֻשַּׁיָּא (4[12] 5[16]); other conj. Marquart[44] Scheft[79f].

אֶשְׁתַּדּוּר v. שדר. אִשְׁתִּיו v. [שְׁתָה].

†אֲתָה, אֲתָא **vb.** come (BH poet. אָתָה; Palm אתי Haph. Lzb[230], Chr-Pal. ܐܬܐ Schulth[Lex]),—**Pe.** *Pf.* 3 ms אֲתָה Ezr 5[3] Dn 7[22]; א—ָ Ezr 5[16]; 3 mpl אֲתוֹ 4[12]; *Imv.* mpl. אֱתוֹ(ו) Dn 3[26]; *Inf.* מֵאתֵא (K[§41c]) v[2]; *Pt.* אָתֵה 7[13],—*come*, c. עַל pers. Ezr 4[12] (+ לְ loc.), 5[3]; c. לְ rei Dn 3[2]; abs v[26] 7[13.22], sq. vb. fin. act Ezr 5[16]. **Haph.** *bring:* *Pf* 3 ms הַיְתִי (K[1 c]), Dn 5[13] (acc. pers + מִן loc), 3 mpl. הַיְתִיו, acc. rei 5[3], so (לְ acc.) v[23] (+ קֳדָם pers), 6[17] (לְ acc. pers.), v[25] (acc. pers); *Inf.* לְהַיְתָיָה (so Eg. Aram RÉS[361C]) 3[13] (לְ acc. pers), 5[2] (לְ acc. rei) **Hêphal** (pass, K[1 e]) *be brought*: *Pf.* 3 fs הֵיתָיִת (K[§47 Beisp 6], W[CG 225]) subj. rei Dn 6[18], 3 mpl. הֵיתָיוּ subj. pers 3[13] (+ קֳדָם pers)

אָת v. אוה.

†אַתּוּן **n. m.**[Dn 3,19] (prob **f.** [v 26]) **furnace** (prob loan-word from As. *utûnu*, *atûnu*, *id.* [also TelAm.], DHM[VOJ i 23] Buhl; Syr. ܐܬܘܢܐ, hence Ar. أَتُّون as loan-word Fra[26]; Eth. አቶን፡ Di[763]; conj on etym. in K[§59 Anm] Lag[BN 111]);—cstr א׳ Dn 3[6 11 15 17 20.21 23.26], emph. אַתּוּנָא 3[19.22].

אִתַי v. איתי.

†אֲתַר **n.m.** place (so Eg. Aram., Nab., Palm; 𝔗, Syr. ܐܬܪܐ *place;* Zinj אשר Lzb[229f], Ar. إِثْر *footstep;* cf. Heb. אֲשׁוּר, and sub אֲשֶׁר);—*place:* **a.** Dn 2[35] וְכָל־אֲתַר לָא־הִשְׁתְּכַח לְהוֹן, Ezr 5[15] וּבֵית אֱלָהָא יִתְבְּנֵא עַל־אַתְרֵהּ, 6[3.7]. Hence **b.** בָּאתַר (Dn 7[6] Baer בָּתַר) *after* (lit. *in the track of:* so Zinj. באשר. (Cooke[160 f., 170]), Palm. 𝔗 בָּתַר, Syr. ܒܬܪ), בָּאתַר דְּנָה *after this*, Dn 7[6.7], sf. Dn 2[39] וּבָתְרָךְ and *after* thee.

אַתְרוּ v. נתר.

ב

ב **prep. in, with, through, etc** (BH בְּ),—sf בִּי, בָּךְ Dn 4[6] +, 3 ms. בֵּהּ 3[7] +, f בַּהּ 2[4] 3[16] +, 3 pl. בְּהוֹן 3[23] +;—**1.** *in*, of place, 2[38] 3[1] 4[12] +בְּאֱסוּר+; *at* Ezr 5[10], of time Dn 2[28] 3[5] (*at*), 5[2] +; 4[12] Ezr 4[16] חֲלָק ב׳ a share *in* (BH **I. 2**). **2.** *into*, Dn 2[38] יְהַב בִּידָךְ, Ezr 5[12]; עֲדָה ב׳ pass *over* or *upon* Dn 3[27]. **3.** of the instrument, *by*, *with* Dn 2[30.34] 3[4] 4[12b 24 27] +; 5[2.3] (Am 6[6]: BH **III. 2**). **4.** of the price (*ib* **III. 3**), *with*, Ezr 7[17 18]. **5.** יוֹם בְּיוֹם Ezr 6[9] = *day by day* (*ib.* **III. 3**, *end;* so Syr. PS[1577], cf. ירח בירח S-C[L4], ܝܘܡܐ ܒܝܘܡܐ

PS[4240]) **6.** *through, on account of* (*ib.* **III. 5**), Ezr 6^{14} **7.** *in the matter of,* Dn $6^{6.13}$. **8.** after vbs. of *ruling,* Dn 2^{38}+, *trusting* 6^{24}, *looking at* 7^{8}, עֲבַד בּ to do *with* 4^{32} Ezr 7^{18}. Cf Lzb[232] K § 68

†**באשׁ** **vb. be evil, bad** (so 𝔗, Syr. ܒܐܫ, OAram באשׁ Lzb[233] SAC[27] Cooke[191]; cf BH);—**Pe.** *Pf.* 3 ms impers בְּ׳ עֲלוֹהִי Dn 6^{15} i.e. *it was evil (displeasing) to him* (cf BH [רעע] **1**)

†[**בְּאִישׁ** K § 11 3b)] **adj. bad** (so Eg Aram. ובאישתא Cooke[75.2], 𝔗 בִּישׁ, Syr. ܒܝܫ),—fs. emph. בִּאִישְׁתָּא Ezr 4^{12} rebellious *and bad* city (not בָּאוּשְׁתָּא, v. Baer[n])

אֲתַר ,בָּתַר ,בָּאתַר v אֲתַר

בָּבֶל **n pr.loc. Babylon** (BH *id*);—Dn 2^{12}+15 t. Dn, 9 t Ezr

†[**בָּבְלָי**] **adj. gent.** pl. emph as subst. בָּבְלָיֵא Ezr 4^{9} *the Babylonians*

†[**בדר**] **vb. Pa. scatter** (so 𝔗 Syr, BH [בָּזַר]),—*Imv* mpl וּבַדַּרוּ Dn 4^{11} (acc rei)

†[**בהל**] **vb. Pa. alarm, dismay** (so usu 𝔗 (not Syr), BH [בָּהַל]),—*Impf* 3 ms sf. יְבַהֲלָךְ Dn 4^{16} and 3 mpl sf -לְנַנִי 4^{2} $7^{15.28}$ (both juss Str § 13 c M § 52 a); -לוּךְ 5^{10}, -לְנֵהּ 4^{16}, -לוּנֵהּ 5^{6}. **Hithpe.** *hasten* (so Pi in late BH, 𝔗 Ithpe (rare)); *Inf.* בְּהִתְבְּהָלָה = *in haste* (orig 'in alarm') Dn 2^{25} 3^{24} 6^{20} **Hithpa.** *Pt pass.* מִתְבָּהַל Dn 5^{9} was greatly *alarmed*

†**בְּהִילוּ** **n.f. haste** (𝔗),—בִּב׳ Ezr 4^{23} (K § 61.4)).

בול (assumed as prob. √ of foll, Brock Schulth, Lane[277]).

†**בָּל** **n.[m.] mind** (Syr ܒܠܐ *id* PS[529], Ar. بَالٌ *heart*),—abs שָׂם בָּ׳ Dn 6^{15} (sq Inf, cf Syr. ܣܡ ܒܠܐ PS[1 c] Schulth[Lex 80]).

†[**בטל**] **vb. cease** (late BH),—**Pe.** *Pf.* 3 fs בְּטֵלַת Ezr 4^{24}, *Pt* fs בָּטְלָא v[24] (both of work) **Pa.** *make to cease,* acc pers: *Pf* 3 mpl בַּטִּלוּ 4^{23} 5^{5}; *Inf* לְבַטָּלָא 4^{21}, acc pers. om. 6^{8}.

†**בֵּין** **prep. between** (BH [בַּיִן] ,בֵּין, 𝔗 ,בֵּין ,בֵּינֵי, Syr ܒܝܢ ,ܒܝܬ), Dn 7^{5}, c. sf 3 pl. m בֵּינֵיהוֹן v[7] Kt (Qr 3 pl. f. בֵּינֵיהֵן)

‡†**בִּינָה** **n.f. understanding** (BH; √ בין; 𝔗 בִּיוּנָא, Syr ܒܝܘܢܐ);—abs. בּ׳ Dn 2^{21}.

†**בִּירְתָא** (Baer -תָא) **n.f.** emph **castle** (so Egypt. Aram RES[361.A5.B12] S-C[Pap B3.C16]+; Nab. = *temple* CIS[II 164 3], BH בִּירָה);—Ezr 6^{2}.

[**בַּיִת**][44] **n.m.**[Ezr 6.7] **house** (BH בַּיִת);—emph. בַּיְתָא Ezr 5^{3}+, -תָה 5^{12} 6^{15}, cstr. (בֵּית(־ 4^{24} 5^{2}+; sf בַּיְתִי Dn 4^{1} (Baer[n], cf. M § 76 c; van d. H. Gi (בֵּיתִי), בַּיְתֵהּ 2^{17}+; pl. sf. בָּתֵּיכוֹן Dn 2^{5};—†**1.** *house,* of men: Ezr 6^{11} Dn $2^{5.17}$ 3^{29} 6^{11}; of king Ezr 6^{4} Dn 4^{4}, בּ׳ מִשְׁתְּיָא 5^{10}, בּ׳ נִנְזַיָּא דִּי מַלְכָּא Ezr 5^{17}, cf 7^{20} = בּ׳ סִפְרַיָּא וגו׳ 6^{1}, בּ׳ מַלְכוּ 4^{30} *royal residence* (of Bab). **2.** *house* of God, temple at Jerusalem Dn $5^{3.23}$ Ezr 4^{24}+28 t. Ezr.

†[**בית** D[WB 62]] **vb denom.** (lodge,) **pass the night** (𝔗 *id*),—**Pe.** *Pf* 3 ms בָּת Dn 6^{19}.

בָּל v. בול

†[**בְּלָא**] **vb. Pa. wear away, out** (BH בלה),—*Impf.* 3 ms יְבַלֵּא Dn 7^{25}, fig. for *harass continually* (acc pers).

†**בְּלוֹ** **n.[m.] tribute** (loan-word from As. *biltu,* √ ובל, acc. to most mod.; but Scheft[80] cp OIran *bali, tribute,* OPers **bari, payment in kind,* so (in Bab. *bara*) Mey[G d Altert. III 88] Scheft[MGWJ 47 (1903). 316] Buhl[14] 'vielleicht');—abs. מִנְדָּה בּ׳ וַהֲלָךְ Ezr $4^{13.20}$ 7^{24}.

בֵּלְטְשַׁאצַּר[8] **n.pr.m.** Bab. name of Daniel (BH *id.*, p 117),—Dn 2^{26} 4^{5}+6 t. Dn, Βαλτασαρ.

†**בֵּלְשַׁאצַּר** **n.pr.m.** king of Bab, acc. to Dn $5^{1.2.9.22.29}$ (BH *id*, p 128) = בֵּלְאשַׁצַּר v[30] 7^{1}; Βαλτασαρ; vid Bev[Ency Bib. BELSHAZZAR] Dr[Dn xxviii f].

†[**בְּנָא ,בְּנָה**] **vb. build** (BH בָּנָה);—**Pe.** *Pf.* 3 ms sf. 3 ms בְּנָהִי Ezr 5^{11}; 1 s sf. בְּנַיְתַהּ Dn 4^{27}; *Impf.* 3 mpl יִבְנוֹן Ezr 6^{7}, *Inf* לְמִבְנֵא 5^{2}+, לְמִבְנְיָה v[9] (rd לְמִבְנֵא M § 44 a or < לְמִבְנֵה, so S-C[AS 64]), לִבְנֵא (rd לְמִבְנֵא Str § 23 M § 1 e) v[3.13]; *Pt. act* pl בָּנַיִן 4^{12}+, *pass* בְּנֵה 5^{11} (v. on forms K § 47, Beisp pass),—*build*. c acc. of temple Ezr $5^{2.3.9.11.13.17}$ $6^{7.8}$, so 5^{4} (acc. cogn), pass of temple v[11]; c acc of city 4^{12} Dn 4^{27}, abs. Ezr $6^{14.14}$. **Hithpe.** *be built*. *Impf* 3 ms יִתְבְּנֵא of temple Ezr 5^{15} 6^{3}, 3 fs. תִּתְבְּנֵא of city v[13.16.21]; *Pt.* מִתְבְּנֵא of temple 5^{8} (c. acc. mater.), v[16].

†[**בִּנְיָן**] **n.[m.] a building** (so 𝔗 Syr),—emph בִּנְיָנָא Ezr 5^{4}.

†**בנס** **vb. be angry** (𝔗[J] *id*; Sam. ࠁࠍࠎ),—**Pe** *Pf* 3 ms בּ׳ וּקְצַף שַׂגִּיא Dn 2^{12}.

†**בְּעָא vb. ask, seek,** only Dn (BH בעה (rare));—**Pe.** *Pf.* 3 ms. ב׳ $2^{16.49}$; 3 mpl בְּעוֹ v^{13}; 1 pl. בְּעֵינָא v^{23}; *Impf.* 3 ms. יִבְעֵא $6^{8.13}$; 1 s אֶבְעֵא־ 7^{16}; *Inf* לְמִבְעֵא 2^{18}; *Pt.* בָּעֵא $6^{12.14}$, pl. בָּעַיִן v^{5};—**1.** *ask, request,* c. מִן pers. 2^{16} (obj. cl. c. דִּי), v^{49} 7^{16} (+acc rei); *ask* of God 2^{23} (+*id.*), of God or man 6^{8} (+acc. cogn.), v^{13}; c מִן־קֳדָם of God 2^{18} (acc. rei); =*pray,* ב׳ וּמִתְחַנַּן קֳדָם א׳ 6^{12}, ב׳ בָּעוּתֵהּ v^{14}. **2.** *seek,* acc pers 2^{13}, acc. rei 6^{5}. **Pa.** *Impf.* 3 mpl. יְבַעוֹן (K §47 3); M ad loc conj יבעון) 4^{33} *resort* (for favours) to, לְ pers

†בָּעוּ (K §61.4) **n.f. petition** (𝔗 Syr);—abs. ב׳ Dn 6^{8}; sf. בָּעוּתֵהּ v^{14} (both acc. cogn. c. בְּעָא).

†בְּעֵל (K §54.3) **n.m. owner, lord** (Syr. ܒܥܠܐ, used similarly; cf. BH בַּעַל, √בָּעַל; also 𝔗 בְּעֵיל);—cstr. ב׳־טְעֵם Ezr $4^{8.9.17}$ i.e *commander* (Andı M 56* as translation of Persian *framātār, commander*)

†[בִּקְעָא] **n.f. plain** (𝔗, BH בִּקְעָה, √בקע; cf. Syr. ܦܩܥܬܐ, √ܦܩܥ);—cstr. בְּבִקְעַת דּוּרָא Dn 3^{1}.

†[בַּקַּר] **vb. Pa. inquire, seek** (only Ezr) (𝔗 Syr.; v. BH),—*Pf.* 3 mpl. בַּקַּרוּ 4^{19} 6^{1}, *Impf.* 3 ms. יְבַקַּר 4^{15}; *Inf.* לְבַקָּרָה 7^{14};—**1.** *inquire,* c עַל (rei) *concerning* 7^{14}; c. subj indef, =pass, 4^{19} *search was made,* so 6^{1}, 4^{15}. **Hithpa.** *Impf* 3 ms. יִתְבַּקַּר 5^{17}, impers, *let search be made*

†I. **בַּר n.m. son** (𝔗 *id* ; Syr. ܒܪܐ, Mand. ברא No M §148, OAram. Nab. Palm. בר (and בן) Lzb 242 f, Sab בר acc to Mordtm VOJ x 154 f; =בן, ן becoming ר, Philippi ZMG xxxii (1878), 36 ff Brock Syr Gr §78 al, √diff. fr. בן acc. to JHMich Thes K §63 al.; BH בַּר Aramaism for בן),—cstr. ב׳ Dn 3^{25}+; sf. בְּרֵהּ 5^{22}; pl. cstr. בני Ezr 6^{9}+; sf. בְּנוֹהִי 6^{10} 7^{23}, בְּנֵיהוֹן Dn 6^{25};—**1.** *son(s)* Ezr $5^{1.2}$ 6^{14} Dn 5^{22} 6^{25} Ezr 6^{10} 7^{23}; בְּנֵי יִשְׂרָאֵל 6^{16}=*Israelites,* בְּנֵי גָלוּתָא =*captives* v^{16} Dn 2^{25} 5^{13} 6^{14}; בַּר־אֱנָשׁ 7^{13} i e *one of human kind,* בני אֲנָשָׁא *men* 2^{38} 5^{21}, בַּר־אֱלָהִין 3^{25} *a divine* (or angelic) *being* (v. Dr, and cf. BH Gn 6^{2} Jb 1^{6}), בַּר שְׁנִין וגו׳ 6^{1} *a son of* 62 *years* =62 *years old* (BH בן 9). **2.** of bullocks, בְּנֵי תוֹרִין Ezr 6^{9}.

II. בַּר v. ברר.

†[בְּרַךְ] **vb. kneel, bless** (so BH),—**Pe.** *Pt.* **1.** *act.* בָּרֵךְ עַל־בִּרְכוֹהִי Dn 6^{11} *kneeling on his knees* (in prayer). **2.** *pass.* בְּרִיךְ Dn 3^{28} *blessed* (be) the God, etc. **Pa.** *bless, praise : Pf.* 3 ms. בָּרִךְ 2^{19}, 1 s. בָּרְכֵת (K §39.3) 4^{31}, both c. לְ of God; *Pt. pass* מְבָרַךְ 2^{20} the name of God (be) *blessed.*

†[בְּרֵךְ] **n.[f.] knee,**—pl. sf בִּרְכוֹהִי Dn 6^{11}.

†[אַרְכֻבָּה] **n.f. id** (by transp; cf. 𝔗 רְכוּבָא, 𝔗 J אַרְכּוּבְתָא; Chr-Pal. ܐܪܟܘܒܬܐ Schwally Idiot. 89 (who > expl. from √רכב, cf. Schulth Lex. 194); Ar. رُكْبَة *id.*),—pl. sf. אַרְכֻבָּתֵהּ Dn 5^{6} *his knees*

†**בְּרַם adv.** with adversative force, **only, nevertheless** (der uncertain: No M 202 =מָא+בַּר, lit *except what.* 𝔗 בְּרַם oft. for אַךְ, אוּלָם; Syr. ܒܪܡ Ex 9^{16} 21^{21}, and in NT for πλήν, Chr-Pal. (ܒܪܡ, ܒܪܝ);—Dn 2^{28} 4^{12} hew down the tree, etc, בְּרַם . . . שְׁבֻקוּ *only* leave the stump, etc., v^{20} 5^{17} Ezr 5^{13}.

ברר (√of foll.; BH ברר, בַּר †Jb 39^{4})

†II. [בַּר] **n.[m.] open field**;—emph בָּרָא, in חֵיוַת בּ׳ (=BH חַיַּת הַשָּׂדֶה), Dn 2^{38} $4^{9.18.20.22.29}$, דִּתְאָא דִי ב׳ $v^{12.20}$.

†**בְּשַׂר n.m. flesh** (𝔗 בְּסַר, Syr. ܒܣܪܐ, BH בָּשָׂר, √בשר);—abs ב׳ Dn 7^{5} *flesh* (as devoured by beast); emph בִּשְׂרָא 2^{11} *flesh*=mankind, כָּל־ב׳ 4^{9}=all creatures

†[בַּת] **n.[m.] bath, liquid measure** (𝔗; perh loan-word from BH II בַּת, √בתת),—pl abs. בַּתִּין Ezr $7^{22.22}$.

בָּתַר v. sub אֲתַר.

ג

גאה (prob. √of foll.; BH גָּאָה *rise up*).

†**גֵּוָה n.f. pride** (𝔗 גֵּיוָה; BH גֵּאָה; cf. K §60 1 (but also 6 a));—abs. ב׳ Dn 4^{34} *in pride*

†[גַּב] **n.[m.]** either **back** (𝔗 גַּב *back, top;* BH גַּב, √גבב), or < **side** (√נגב, cf Ar. جَنْبٌ *side,* Syr. ܓܢܒܐ *side,* √ܓܢܒ,—v. also D WB 63),—pl. sf. Dn 7^{6} Kt wings עַל־גַּבַּיהּ on *its sides* (Bev Behrm Dr; Qr גַּבַּהּ perh. *its back,* so most).

†[גֹּב] **n.m. pit, den of lions** (𝔗 גּוּב, Syr. ܓܘܒܐ *pit;* ? cf BH גֹּב n pr loc., √נקב);—cstr. ג׳ Dn $6^{8.25}$, גוב v^{13}, emph. גֻּבָּא $v^{17.18.20.21.24.24.25}$.

גבר (√of foll.; *be strong,* so 𝔗; BH גָּבַר).

גְּבַר$_{21}$ **n.m.** man (BH);—abs. ג׳ Dn 2[25] 5[11]; pl. abs. גֻּבְרִין (K § 54. 3 c) 3[24.25], also, = *certain* ones, v[8.12.20]; emph. גֻּבְרַיָּא Ezr 4[21] 5[4.10] 6[8] Dn 3[12] + 9 t. Dn.

† [גְּבוּרָה] **n.f. might**;—emph. גְּבוּרְתָא (K §§ 9 c); 57 b) a) but M § 72 c) Dn 2[20.23].

† [גִּבָּר] **n.m. mighty one**;—pl. cstr. גִּבָּרֵי־ חַיִל Dn 3[20] (= BH גִּבּוֹרֵי חַיִל).

‡ † גְּדָבְרַיָּא **n.m.pl.emph.** Dn 3[2.3], dub.: most think ‖ form of [גִּזְבָּר] *treasurer* (or, Mey Entst. J.[23], text. err. for גז׳); Gr Bev al. rd. הַדָּבְרַיָּא *ministers* (3[24]); poss. (v. Lag Dr al.) dittogr. for following דְּתָבְרַיָּא.

† [גְּדַד] **vb. hew down** (𝔗[J]; Syr. (rare); BH *cut*);—**Pe.** *Imv.* mpl. גֹּדּוּ אִילָנָא (K § 46, Beisp. a) Dn 4[11.20].

† [גַּו] **n.m. midst** (Eg. Aram. Nab. Palm. גו; 𝔗 גַּוִּי; esp. cstr. מִגּוֹ, לְגוֹ, בְּגוֹ; so Syr. [illegible]; cf. BH גֵּו, p. 156);—cstr. גּוֹא (so Nab. Cooke[No. 94]) Dn 3[26] +, 7[15] edd., Gi גּוֹ (Baer גּוֹא, v. on 3[6]); sf. 3 ms. גַּוֵּהּ † Ezr 5[7], 3 fs. גַּוַּהּ † 4[15] 6[2];—*midst*, alw. c. preps.: **a.** בְּגוֹא (= Heb. בְּתוֹךְ), Dn 3[25] בְּגוֹא נוּרָא, 4[7] 7[15] Ezr 4[15]; 5[7] וְכִדְנָה כְּתִיב בְּגַוֵּהּ, 6[2]. **b.** לְגוֹא Dn 3[6.11.15.21.23.24]. **c.** מִן־גּוֹא Dn 3[26].

גֵּוָה v. גאה.

† [גִּזְבָּר] **n.m. treasurer** (Pers. loan-word (Scheft[81]); 𝔗 Syr. BH; K § 64. 3; in Bab. *ganzabaru* Peiser ZAW xvii (1897). 347);—pl. emph. גִּזַבְרַיָּא Ezr 7[21].—Vid. גְּדָבְרַיָּא.

† [גְּזַר] **vb. cut, (divide,) determine** (so 𝔗 Syr., in both mngs.; BH usu. *divide*, † Jb Est *decree*);—**Pe.** *Pt. act.* as subst., pl. abs. גָּזְרִין *determiners* (of fate; astrologers or soothsayers) Dn 2[27] 5[11]; emph. גָּזְרַיָּא 4[4] 5[7] (cf. Dr.; Ar. جزّار, RS J Phil. xiii (1885). 781). **Hithpe.** *Pf.* 3 fs. הִתְגְּזֶרֶת 2[34] a stone *was cut out*, so אִתְגְּ׳ (K §§ 23. 1; 30. 2) v[45] (c. מִן of source).

† [גְּזֵרָה] **n.f. decree** (𝔗 גְּזֵירָא, Syr. [illegible]);—cstr. גְּזֵרַת Dn 4[14.21].

† [גִּין] c. בְּ, בְּגִין **prep. on account of** (so Galil. Aram., D § 47. 3), read perh. in 7[15]: v. נִדְנֶה.

† [גִּיר] **n.[m.] chalk, plaster** (so 𝔗; BH once, p. 162);—emph. גִּירָא Dn 5[5].

[גַּלְגַּל] v. גלל.

† [גְּלָה, גְּלָא] **vb. reveal** (BH גָּלָה *uncover, reveal*);—**Pe.** *reveal* secrets, human agent: *Inf.* לְמִגְלֵא Dn 2[47]; of God, *Pt. act.* גָּלֵא v[22.28.29.47]. **Peʿîl** *Pf.* גְּלִי v[19], גֱּלִי v[30], *revealed* (W[CG 225] Nö LCB. 1896. 703);—of secret, c. לְ pers. **Haph.** *take into exile* (BH **Hiph.**), *Pf.* 3 ms. הַגְלִי, c. acc. pers. Ezr 4[10] 5[12] (לְ loc.).

† [גָּלוּ K § 61. 4] **n.f. exile**;—emph. בְּנֵי גָלוּתָא i.e. exiles, Ezr 6[16] Dn 2[25] 5[13] 6[14] (cf. BH גּוֹלָה).

גלל (√ of following; BH II. גלל; Palm. גללא Lzb[250] SAC[36] Cooke[334], = στήλη λιθίνη).

† גְּלָל **n.[m.] rolling**;—abs. אֶבֶן גּ׳ Ezr 5[8] 6[4] *stones of rolling*, too heavy for carrying.

† [גַּלְגַּל] **n.m. wheel** (𝔗 BH; Syr. [illegible]);—pl. sf. גַּלְגִּלּוֹהִי Dn 7[9] of throne-chariot of God.

† מְגִלָּה **n.f.** (book-)**roll** (𝔗 BH);—Ezr 6[2].

† [גְּמַר] **vb. complete** (oft. 𝔗 Syr.; rare BH);—**Pe.** *Pt. pass.* גְּמִיר Ezr 7[12] as adj. *perfect* (read perh. שְׁלָם ג׳, Torrey Berthol; cf. 5[7]).

† [גְּנַז] **n.m.** Ezr 6. 1 **treasure** (𝔗; v. BH [גְּנָזִים], sub גנז);—pl. emph. גִּנְזַיָּא *treasures* Ezr 6[1], בֵּית ג׳ דִּי מַלְכָּא 5[17], cstr. בֵּית גִּנְזֵי מַלְכָּא 7[20].

† [גַּף] **n.f.** Dn 7. 4 **wing** of bird (𝔗 גַּף, גַּפָּא, גַּדְפָּא (? D[WB79]), Syr. [illegible]; akin to BH אֲגַף, As. *agappu*? acc. to Nö[M77] (cf. Mand. גאדפא, 𝔗 גַּדְפָּא), Id GGA. 1884. 1019, √ נדף, Ar. جَدَفَ, جَذَفَ *fly, row* (but this loan-word Frä[227]));—pl. abs. *wings*, גַּפִּין Dn 7[4.6]; sf. גַּפֵּיהּ v[4] Kt (Qr sg. גַּפַּהּ).

† [גְּרַם] **n.[m.] bone** (BH גֶּרֶם; Chr-Pal. [illegible] Schulth Lex. 46);—pl. sf. גַּרְמֵיהוֹן Dn 6[25].

† [גְּשֵׁם] **n.m.** Dn 4. 30 **body** (v. √ גשם in BH; 𝔗[J] גִּשְׁמָא, גּוּשְׁמָא (D[WB 83]), Syr. [illegible], *body, self*);—*body* of man, sf. גִּשְׁמֵהּ Dn 4[30] 5[21], so pl. sf. גִּשְׁמֵיהוֹן (K § 15 a) 3[27.28], both Kt, Qr sg. גֶּשְׁמְהוֹן (K § 54. 3 b)).

ד

† דָּא **demonstr. pr. f. this** (= BH זֹה; Zinj. Têma, Cappad. Eg. Aram. זא, Nab. דא, Palm. דה (Lzb[264]; Eph. 1. 323 Cooke[26]), 𝔗 דָּא: v. further sub BH זֶה. The corresp. masc. is דְּנָה);—*this*, Dn 4[27] הֲלָא דָא הִיא בָּבֶל רַבְּתָא, 5[6] דָּא לְדָא נָקְשָׁן *one* striking against *another*, similarly 7[3] (cf. זֶה **1 b**), v[8] בְּקַרְנָא־דָא.

†דֹּב n.[m.] bear (so 𝔗 BH √דבב; Syr. ܕܒܐ);—abs. ד׳ Dn 7⁵.

†[דְּבַח] vb. sacrifice (BH זָבַח);—Pe. *Pt. act.* pl. דָּבְחִין Ezr 6³, c. acc. דָּבְחִין, v. foll.

†[דְּבַח] n.[m.] sacrifice;—pl. abs. דִּבְחִין Ezr 6³.

†[מַדְבַּח] n.[m.] altar;—emph. מַדְבְּחָא Ezr 7¹⁷.

†[דְּבַק] vb. cling (BH);—Pe. *Pt.* pl. דָּבְקִין דְּנָה עִם־דְּנָה Dn 2⁴³.

†[דִּבְרָה] n.f. cause, reason (BH *id.*, √דבר, cf. על דבר Eg. Aram. S-C Pap. B 5.6.8.16);—cstr. in adv. phr. עַל־דִּבְרַת דִּי Dn 2³⁰ *for the cause* (to the intent) *that*, 4¹⁴ (rd. עַל for עַד K § 11.2 Bev).

דְּהַב n.m. Dn 2.32 23 gold (so 𝔗 Syr.; BH זָהָב);—abs. ד׳ Dn 2³²+, דְּהַב Ezr 7¹⁵; emph. דַּהֲבָה 5¹⁴ 6⁵ 7¹⁸, בָא- Dn 2³⁵+15 t. Dn.

‡†דהוא Kt, דֶּהָיֵא Qr, acc. to Thes and most n. pr. gent. Ezr 4⁹, v. conj. identif. by Dl Baer Dn x Scheft 31 f.; < read דֶּהוּא *that is*, Hoffm ZA ii. 54 Marquart 64 Mey Entst. J. 36, 𝔊 οἵ εἰσιν.

†[דּוּר] vb. dwell (v. BH);—Pe. *Impf.* 3 fs. of beasts תְּדוּר Dn 4¹⁴; 3 mpl. birds יְדֻרוּן v⁹ (Qr f. יְדוּרָן, f. subj., צִפֲּרֵי, follows, cf. v¹⁸ and K § 98, 2 c, Anm. 3); *Pt.* pl. of men, דָּארִין Kt 2³⁸ 3³¹ 6²⁶ (Qr דָּיְרִין); as subst., cstr. דָּאְרֵי Kt 4³²·³² (Qr דָּיְרֵי) *dwellers*.

דָּר n.[m.] generation (BH דּוֹר);—abs. in phr. עִם־דָּר וְדָר Dn 3³³ 4³¹ (is) *with generation and generation*, i.e. endures gen. after gen.

†[מְדוֹר] n.[m.] dwelling-place;—sf. מְדֹרָךְ Dn 4²²·²⁹, מְדוֹרֵהּ, 5²¹.

†[מְדָר] n.m. id.;—sf. מְדָרְהוֹן Dn 2¹¹.

†תְּדִירָא n.f. continuance (𝔗 *id.*; v. BH דור);—abs. in phr. בִּת׳ *continually* Dn 6¹⁷·²¹.

†דּוּרָא n.pr.loc. near Bab., only בִּקְעַת ד׳ Dn 3¹, 𝔊 τοῦ περιβόλου (Syro-Hex. περίβολον), Θ Δεειρα; *Dûru* is name of several places in Babylonia Dl Par. 216; Baer Dn. p. x, cf. Andr M 58*; Hoffm Pers. Märtyrer 164 f.; name of small river and mounds Opp Expéd. i. 238 f. (v. Dr); improb. expl. as =زور *zôr, depression* (name actually used of lower Euphr. and Tigris valleys) by Wetzst De Jes³ 701 f.; Bab. *dûru*=*wall*.

†[דּוּשׁ] vb. tread down (BH);—Pe. *Impf.* 3 fs. (sf. of earth) תְּדוּשִׁנַּהּ Dn 7²³, subj. beast.

‡†[דַּחֲוָה] n.f. dub.;—pl. abs. דַּחֲוָן Dn 6¹⁹, Vrss conject.; AV RV *instr. of music* (so AE, assuming meaning *strike* [strings] for דְּחָא [BH דָּחָה] *thrust;* Saad RVm *dancing-girls;* Bertholdt al. *concubines* (fr. sens. obsc. of Ar. دَحَى), but then read prob. לְחֵנָן (5²·³·²³) Marti Prince Dr.

†[דְּחַל] vb. fear (so 𝔗 Syr.; BH II. [זָחַל]);—Pe. *Pt. act.* pl. דָּחֲלִין Dn 5¹⁹, c. מִן־קֳדָם of king, 6²⁷, *id.* of God; *pass.* דְּחִיל *terrible* 2³¹, f. דְּחִילָה 7⁷·¹⁹. Pa. *Impf.* 3 ms. sf. וִידַחֲלִנַּנִי 4² the dream *made me afraid*.

דִּי part. of relation, who, which, that, used also as mark of gen. and conj. that, because (Aram. of Nineveh, Bab. Zinj. Nerab, Cilicia, Têma, Egypt, זי (Lzb 267. 446 RÉS 361 S-C Pap. A 2+); Nab. Palm. די; 𝔗 דְּ (exc. in cpds., as דִּילִי *mine,* דִּילֵיהּ *his*); Sam. ࠃ; Syr. ܕ; Eth. **H:** *za:* of same origin as Ar. ذُو *possessor of* [cf. sub BH זֶה]. Properly a demonstr. *that* [cf. זֶה; in Eth. *ze* is 'this,' *za* 'which']; but this being referred by usage to something preceding becomes equiv. to the relative *who, which,* used, however, more widely than Heb. אֲשֶׁר);—**1.** as **rel.** *who, which* (construed like אֲשֶׁר): **a.** Je 10¹¹ Dn 2¹¹ דִּי מְדָרְהוֹן *whose* dwelling, v²⁴ דִּי מַנִּי מַלְכָּא *whom* the king had appointed, v²⁶ דִּי שְׁמֵהּ ב׳ *whose* name was B., 4⁵ 5¹²·²³, etc.; =*that which* 2²³; =*him that* Ezr 7²⁵; 6¹⁵ Dn 7¹⁷ דִּי אִנּוּן אַרְבַּע *which* are four (v. אִנּוּן). Sq. pron. of 2 ps. (cf. אֲשֶׁר **3**), Dn 2³⁷ thou, O king . . . , דִּי . . . יְהַב לָךְ *to whom* . . . hath given, 4¹⁹; 4⁶ *as to whom* I know, etc. (cf. אֲשֶׁר **4 d** *end*). Sq. תַּמָּה=*where* Ezr 6¹, so דִּי alone 6³ Dn 2³⁸; of time, בְּעִדָּנָא דִּי at the time *when*, etc., 3⁵·¹⁵. With the pred. an inf. c. לְ, Dn 6⁹ כְּתָבָא דִּי לָא לְהַשְׁנָיָה *which* is not to be changed, Ezr 6⁸; a place- or other determination, Dn 3²⁰ valiant men דִּי בְחֵילֵהּ *that* were in his army, 5² הֵיכְלָא דִּי בִירוּשְׁלֶם, 7²⁰ Ezr 4²⁴ 5⁶ 6²·⁶; cf. Dn 2²⁵ 5¹³ 7⁷ Ezr 7²³. דִּי לָא=*without*, Ezr 6⁹ 7²² (so דְּלָא 𝔗 Gn 15² Ex 21¹¹); cf. Dn 2³⁴·⁴⁵. **b.** מַה דִּי, מַן דִּי (cf. in late Heb. מַה־שֶׁ׳, מָה **1 e** *b*) *whoever, whatever*, so †Dn 3⁶·¹¹ מַן־דִּי־לָא *whoever* does not fall down, 4¹⁴ לְמַן דִּי יִצְבֵּא יִפֵּל to *whomsoever* he willeth, v²²·²⁹ 5²¹; מָה דִּי *whatever* (or simply *what*), †Dn 2²⁸ מָה דִּי לֶהֱוֵא what will be, v²⁹·²⁹·⁴⁵ Ezr 6⁸ 7¹⁸.—Cf. K § 103. **2.** as

mark of the gen., Dn 2[14] שליטא די מלכא prop the captain, *that of* the king = *the king's captain* (a genuine Aram idiom: so 𝔗 ד, Syr ܕ constantly), v[19.25.49] + oft the subst. in such cases may be either in the emph state (determined), as ll cc. Ezr 4[14] 5[2], etc, or in the abs state (undetermined), Dn 5[5] 7[4.9.10] נְהַר דִּי נוּר, or it may have a pleon sf, 2[20] שְׁמֵהּ דִּי אֱלָהָא lit his name, *that of* God = *God's name*, v[41] 3[8.25.26] 4[23], etc (so also 𝔗 Syr) To circumscribe an adj, esp in specif of the *material*. Dn 2[38] thou art רֵאשָׁה דִּי דַהֲבָא the head of gold, v[39] 3[1] 5[7.16] Ezr 5[14] 6[4] +, as predic Dn 2[32] רֵאשֵׁהּ דִּי־דְהַב טָב his head (was) *of* fine gold, v[33] 7[19], with a pron. Dn 2[20] wisdom and might דִּי־לֵהּ הִיא are *his*; cf 6[27] וּמַלְכוּתֵהּ דִּי־לָא תִתְחַבַּל his kingdom (is one) which shall not be destroyed, 7[14] —Vid further K[§91]. **3.** as **conj.** (cf. אֲשֶׁר **8**) **a** *that* (*quod*), after vbs. of knowing, Dn 2[8.9], seeing 2[45] 3[27], hearing 5[14], etc; introducing the subject of a sentence, ... יְדִיעַ ... דִּי 3[18] Ezr 4[13]; Dn 2[47] ... אֻמְנָם כִּי) True is it *that* ... (cf. מִן־קְשֹׁט דִּי Jb 12[2]) **b.** = *in that, inasmuch as, whereas*. Dn 2[41] and *whereas* (דִּי) thou sawest, etc ... it shall be a divided kingdom, v[43] 4[20.23], as a connecting link = *seeing that, because, for* (cf אֲשֶׁר **8 c**) 2[9.20 b.23 b.47 b] 4[15] 6[24 b]. **c.** *that* (*ut*), after vbs. of asking Dn 2[16], commanding 3[10.29], expressing a purpose 4[3] 5[15] Ezr 4[15] 6[10] +, דִּי לָא *that not* (*ne*) Dn 2[18] 3[28] 6[18] (on דִּי לְמָה *lest* Ezr 7[23], see מה) **d.** prefixed to direct narr (like כִּי **1 b**, and sts. אֲשֶׁר **8 a** γ, and ὅτι *recitativum*), Dn 2[25] and said thus unto him דִּי־הַשְׁכַּחַת (that) I have found, etc, 5[7] 6[6.14] **4.** with preps. and other prefixes · **a.** כְּדִי (like Heb כַּאֲשֶׁר; so Eg Aram. כזי, Palm Nab כדי, Lzb[293] SAC[G1 62,61] Cooke[369 b] RES[361]; 𝔗 כַּד, Syr ܟܕ), *a according as*, Dn 2[43], *b so soon as, when*, 3[7] 5[20] 6[11.15]. **b.** מִן־דִּי. *a. because that*, Dn 3[22] Ezr 5[12] (cf מֵאֲשֶׁר Is 43[4]), *b from* (the time) *that, after* (*ex quo*), Dn 4[23] Ezr 4[23] **c.** עַד דִּי *until*, Dn 2[9.34] 4[30] 7[22]; = *ere that* 6[25]. **d.** עַל דִּי Dn 3[19] is not a conj, but means *above that which* . **e.** for עַל דִּבְרַת דִּי and כָּל־קֳבֵל דִּי see [דִּבְרָה] and קֳבֵל.

†[דִּין] **vb** judge (BH),—**Pe.** *Pt* pl דָּאְנִין Ezr 7[25] Kt (Qr דָּיְנִין), sq. לְ pers

†דִּין **n.m.** [Ezr 7.26] **judgment**,—abs ד׳ Dn 4[34] = *justice* (of ways of God); emph. דִּינָה מִתְעֲבֵד מִנֵּהּ Ezr 7[26] *judgment be executed upon him*, דִּינָא = *judges, court* Dn 7[10.26] + perhaps v[22] (reading וְדִ׳ יָתִב וְשָׁלְטָנָא יְהִב], Ew Bev Kmp Dr), MT however = *judgment was given in favour of* (v. Dr)

†[דַּיָּן] **n.m. judge**,—pl דַּיָּנִין Ezr 7[25].

†[מְדִינָה] **n. f.** (judicial) **district, province** (K[§60, 3) d)]; also BH),—emph מְדִינְתָּא (M[§72 c]) Ezr 5[8] 6[2], cstr. מְדִינַת Dn 2[48.49] 3[1.12.30] Ezr 7[16], pl abs מְדִנָן 4[15], emph מְדִינָתָא Dn 3[2.3].

דָּנִיֵּאל **n.pr.m. Daniel** (BH *id.*),—Dn 2[13.14] + 50 t Dn

דִּינָיֵא **n.pr.gent.** (?) Ezr 4[9] (so most, but Hoffm [ZA 1.55] Marquart[64] Andr [M 59*] Mey [Entst. 39] Str[46*] read דַּיָּנַיָּא *judges* (as transl. of Pers. *dâtabara*), while Scheft[81] (improb) cp. OIran. **denya*, (the) *orthodox*, i e Persians)

†דֵּךְ **demonstr. pr. m. this, f.** דָּךְ; only Ezr, Dn uses דִּכֵּן (Eg and Cappad. Aram. זך (CIS [II 1.1] RES [361 B] S-C [Pap] (f דכא, דכי ib. [F 6, 9]), Lzb [Eph 1 67]); 𝔗 דִּיכִי, f דָּךְ, Ar. ذَاكَ, Eth ዝኩ፡ From ذَا, זֶה, דָּא (f), with the affix ךְ (W [CG 110]), thus lit. = Germ *dieser da* The pl. is אִלֵּךְ, q v),—*this* (always after its subst), Ezr 5[16] בֵּית־אֱלָהָא דֵךְ, v[17] שְׁשַׁבַּצַּר דֵּךְ, 6[7.8.12], f 4[13.15.16.19.21] קִרְיְתָא דָךְ, 5[8].

†דִּכֵּן **demonstr. pr. comm. this, that**; only Dn, Ezr uses דֵּךְ (דך + demonstr. affix *n*, W [CG 111]),—Dn 2[31] צַלְמָא דִ׳, 7[20.21] קַרְנָא דִ׳.

†[דְּכַר] **n.m. ram** (𝔗 דִּכְרָא, Syr. ܕܶܟܪܳܐ *id.*, also (and primarily) *male*, v BH זָכָר);—pl. דִּכְרִין for sacrifice Ezr 6[9.17] 7[17].

†[דִּכְרוֹן] **n.[m.] memorandum, record** (BH זִכָּרוֹן, √זכר, cf. Nab Palm. דכר(ו)ן Lzb[263] SAC[40] Cooke[214+]),—emph. דִּכְרוֹנָה Ezr 6[2].

†[דָּכְרָן] **n.[m.]** id.;—pl. emph. סְפַר דָּכְרָנַיָּא Ezr 4[15.15]

†[דְּלַק] **vb. burn** (BH);—**Pe.** *Pt. act.* דָּלִק (K[§29, 1]) Dn 7[9] *burning* fire

†[דְּמָה] **vb. be like** (BH I. דָּמָה),—**Pe.** *Pt. act* דָּמֵה Dn 3[25] (לְ pers), f דָּמְיָה לְ (לְדֹב)

57 דְּנָה **demonstr. pr. comm. this** (Zinj. זן, זנה, Eg. Aram. זנה (S-C [Pap. B 17+]); זנך (ib [C 6, D 8]), Nab. Palm דנה (Lzb[264] Cooke[26]); 𝔗 דֵּין (e g. 1 S 10[27]) and (with הָ, i e. הָא, ܗܳܐ *ecce*) הָדֵין; Aram of Têma הא זא (Cooke[195.199]); Syr ܗܳܢܳܐ (contr for הָדְנָא); Mand. האזין, Sab. ذن (Hom [Chrest 13]); Eth. ዝንቱ፡ all from [זָה, דָּה], זה, + demonstr. *n* (W [CG 108 f]); fem. BAram. דָּא, 𝔗 דָּא, הָדָא, Syr. ܗܳܕܶܐ, Mand האזא, Eth ዛቲ፡ without the *n*; the pl. is אִלֵּין, q v.),—*this*:

a. Dn 2^{18} רָזָא דְנָה *this* secret, $v^{28.29.30}$+, Ezr 4^{11} $5^{3.4.8}$+, כָּל־דְּנָה Dn 5^{22}. **b.** אַחֲרֵי דְנָה *after this* †Dn $2^{29.45}$; so בָּאתַר דְּנָה †$7^{6.7}$. **c.** כִּדְנָה *like this, thus,* †Je 10^{10} (=Heb. כֹּה), Dn 2^{10} מִלְּתָא כִדְנָה a word *like this* (cf. כָּזֹאת Est 4^{11}), 3^{29} Ezr 5^{7}. **d.** עַל־דְּנָה *on account of this* †Dn 3^{16} Ezr 4^{22} $5^{5.17}$ 6^{11}; as conj.=*therefore* (cf. Heb. עַל־זאת) Ezr $4^{14.15}$.—Vid also קֳבֵל and קֳדָמָה.

†[דְּקַק] **vb. be shattered, fall to pieces** (BH),—**Pe.** *Pf.* 3 mpl. דָּקוּ Dn 2^{35}. **Haph.** *break in pieces: Pf.* 3 fs. הַדֶּקֶת $2^{34.45}$, 3 mpl הַדִּקוּ 6^{25} (all sq. acc.); *Impf.* 3 fs. תַּדִּק 2^{40} (abs.), v^{44} (acc.); sf תַּדִּקִנַּהּ 7^{23}; *Pt. act.* מְהַדֵּק 2^{40} (acc), f. מַדְּקָה (K $^{§46.3b}$) abs $7^{7.19}$.

דָּר v. דּוּר.

דָּרְיָוֶשׁ n.pr.m. (BH *id.*; Eg.Aram. דריוהוש RES^{361} S-C^{H1+});—**1.** Darius Hystaspis Ezr 4^{24} +8t Ezr. **2.** 'Darius the Mede' Dn $6^{1.2.7.10.26.29}$.

דרע (√of following; BH II. זרע, זְרוֹעַ).

†[דְּרָע] **n.[f.] arm** (so ℑ Syr.);—pl. sf. דְּרָעוֹהִי Dn 2^{32}.

†אֶדְרָע (K$^{§60.1}$) **n.[f.] force** (prop. *arm*, ℑ (rare), BH אֶזְרוֹעַ);—abs בְּאֶ׳ וְחָיִל Ezr 4^{23} *by force and power*, forcibly

†דָּת **n.f.**$^{Dn 6,9}$ **decree, law** (Syr.; Pers. loan-word, v. BH);—ד׳ abs. Dn 6^{16} 7^{25}, cstr. Ezr 7^{14}+; emph. דָּתָא Ezr 7^{12}+; sf. דָּתְכוֹן Dn 2^{9};—**1.** *decree* of king Dn $2^{13.15}$ Ezr 7^{26}; c. sf. Dn 2^{9} *decree against you.* **2.** unchangeable *law* of Medes and Pers. Dn $6^{9.13.16}$. **3.** *law* of God (in mouth of non-Jews): Dn 6^{6} Ezr $7^{12.14.21.26}$, so (abs.) Dn 7^{25}; *laws* of God Ezr 7^{25}.

†[דֶּתֶא] **n.[m.] grass** (so ℑ Syr.; BH דֶּשֶׁא),—emph. דִּתְאָא Dn $4^{12.20}$.

‡†[דְּתָבַר] **n.m. judge** (loan-word fr. Pers *dâtabara, law-bearer, judge* (cf דִּינַיֵּא), Andr$^{M 49*}$ Mey$^{Entst. J. 23}$ Dr^{Dn}; in Bab. as *dâtabar(r)i* Hilpr$^{Bab. Exp. IX 29}$);—pl. emph. דְּתָבְרַיָּא Dn $3^{2.3}$.

ה

הֲ **interrog. part.** (BH הֲ, q.v: ℑ הֲ; not Syr.: on the vocal., v. K^{§87,2});—Dn 2^{26} הַאִיתָךְ *art thou ... ?* 3^{14} הַצְדָּא (Baer Gi; edd. הַצְּדָא), 6^{21} הֲיִכֻל *can he ... ?* הֲלָא *nonne?* †3^{24} 4^{27} 6^{13}.

†הָא **demonstr. part. lo! behold!** (BH הָא (twice); Eg. Aram. and Têma הא (Cooke$^{195.199}$); ℑ הָא; Syr. ܗܐ; Mand. הא (No$^{M 81}$); Ar. هَا: in Aram. also oft. prefixed to pr. 3 ps. for greater definiteness, as ℑ הָהוּא, ܗܘ (for *hā-hū*), v. No$^{M 89f}$ W$^{CG 106f}$), Dn 3^{25}.

†הָא **demonstr. part.,** prefixed idiom. to כְּ for greater definiteness, lit. *behold like* (BH הָא, v. הָא supr), only in הָא־כְדִי Dn 2^{43} הָא־כְדִי פַּרְזְלָא לָא מִתְעָרַב *like as* iron doth not mingle with clay (cf. **a.** ℑ^{O} הָא כְמַיָּא Gn 49^{4}, so ℑ^{Jon} הא כ׳ Is 5^{28} 9^{4}+oft; ℑ^{Jer} הי כ׳ Gn $26^{4.13.22}$+oft.; היך ψ 2^{9} $5^{10.13}$+, also pleon. הֵיךְ כְּ׳ ψ $22^{14.15.17}$+ oft. **b.** Palm. הֵיךְ *as* (Lzb^{259}), as היך בנמוסא *as* (is) in the law (Cooke^{321}; so ℑ^{Jer} ψ 2^{9}, etc), הֵיךְ דִי conj. (like Dn הָא כְדִי: =Heb. כַּאֲשֶׁר), as היך די נבא *like as* he levied, Cooke$^{Tariff II. b 12. 18, c 14. 17. 21. 26}$ [ℑ$^{O Jon}$ for כַּאֲשֶׁר have כְּמָא ד׳, ℑ^{Jer} הֵיכְמָא ד׳, 𝔖 ܐܝܟ ܕ]. It is dub whether הא כדי belongs to **a** (notice esp. ℑ^{Jon}) or **b**· Schulth$^{ZAW 1902, 164 f.}$ to **b**, reading הֵאךְ דִי (but א rare and late D$^{(2) § 43. 1}$); Nes$^{OLtz 1892, 488}$ from הֵיךְ (v. BH) *how?*)

‡†[הַדָּבַר] **n.m. counsellor, minister** (Pers. loan-word; orig. form and mng dub., cf. Andr$^{M 60*}$ Mey$^{Entst. J. 23}$ Dr$^{Dn 3. 24}$),—pl. emph. הַדָּבְרַיָּא Dn 6^{8}; cstr הַדָּבְרֵי 3^{27}, sf. הַדָּבְרַי 4^{33}, -רוֹהִי 3^{24}—Vid. נְדָבְרַיָּא

†[הַדָּם] **n.[m.] member, limb** (loan-word from Pers. اندام, هندام *id.* Lag$^{Ges. Abh 28}$ Fl$^{Levy ChWB I 423b}$); pl. abs. הַדָּמִין תִּתְעַבְדוּן Dn 2^{5} *ye shall be made members,* i.e. *dismembered,* so 3^{29}.

†[הַדַּר] **vb. Pa. glorify God** (ℑ Syr. BH *honour* man);—*Impf* 2 ms. הַדַּרְתָּ Dn 5^{23}, 1 s. הַדְּרֵת 4^{31}, *Pt. act.* מְהַדַּר v^{34} (all c. ל pers.)

†[הֲדַר] **n.[m.] honour, majesty,** of kg.,— emph. הַדְרָא Dn 5^{18}; sf. הַדְרִי $4^{27.33}$ (where Behrm plausibly (after Theod) הַדְרֵת [ℑ הֲדַר *return*]).

הֲוָא, הֲוָה **vb. come to pass, become, be** (BH הָיָה);—**Pe** *Pf.* 3 ms. הֲוָה Dn 4^{26}+, הֲוָא Dn 5^{19}+; 2 ms. הֲוַיְתָ Dn $2^{31.34}$, 1 s. הֲוֵית 4^{1}+; 3 mpl. הֲווֹ Dn 2^{35}+; *Impf.* 3 ms. לֶהֱוֵא (K$^{§47. 1) b)}$ Dr$^{§204 Obs.}$ No$^{M 215 ff}$; in JAram as jussive D$^{§61.1 e)}$) Dn 2^{20}+; 3 fs. תֶּהֱוֵה Dn 4^{24}+, ־א Ezr 6^{8}+, 3 mpl. לֶהֱוֺן Ezr 6^{10}+6 t., 3 fpl. לֶהֶוְיָן Dn 5^{17}; *Imv.* mpl. הֱווֹ Ezr 4^{22}, הֱווֹ 6^{6};—**1.** *come to pass* Dn $2^{28.29.29.45}$. **2.** *come into being, arise* Ezr 7^{23}; *become, come to be,* c. n pred. Dn 4^{24} 5^{29} and (=*represent*) 7^{23}; c. כְּ *like* 2^{35a}, c. ל pred.

v^{35b}, c. adj. pred. Ezr 6^{6}, c. adv. phr. 5^{5} Dn 4^{22}; oft. periphrast., c. pt.: יְדִיעַ לֶהֱ׳ *let it become known* 3^{18} Ezr $4^{12.13}$ 5^{8}; so *let it be given* $6^{8.9}$, also 7^{26} Dn 2^{20}. **3.** *be*, as copula, c. adj. pred. Dn $2^{40.42}$ 7^{19}; so very often in periphrast. conj. c. pt., ה׳ צָבֵא *wish* $5^{19.19.19.19}$, חָזֵה ה׳ *behold* $2^{31.34}$ $7^{2.4.6}$+, etc.

†**הוּא** m. **הִיא** f. **pron. of 3 s.** he, she, it (=BH הוּא, הִיא; Zinj. and Palm. (once) הא, Palm. (usually) Nab. Eg. Aram. הו, f. הי, Lzb^{257}, S-C$^{Pap. A 1, 12+; A 4, C 9+}$. The pl. is אִנּוּן, q.v.);—*he, she, it*, Dn 2^{21} . . . וְהוּא מְהַשְׁנֵא and *he* will change, etc., v$^{22.44}$ 6^{5} $7^{7.24}$ Ezr 5^{8}; Dn 2^{32} הוּא צַלְמָא *that* image (nom. pend.); 4^{19} אַנְתְּה הוּא thou art *it*. Resuming the subj. with emph. (BH **2 b**) 2^{47} 6^{17}; resuming the subj. in predication (*ib.* **3 b**) 2^{20} חָכְמְתָא וּגְבוּרְתָא דִּי־לֵהּ הִיא *it* is his, v^{28}. Anticipating the subj. (*ib.* **4 a**) 2^{9} חֲדָה הִיא דָתְכוֹן; with a pron. (*ib.* **4 b**) 2^{38} . . . אַנְתְּה הוּא *thou art* the head of gold 5^{13}; 3^{15} . . . אֱלָהּ . . . מַן הוּא *who is* the god . . . ? (so pl. אִנּוּן Ezr 5^{4}); 4^{27} . . . הֲלָא דָא הִיא (*ib.* **4 b** γ); 6^{27} . . . דִּי הוּא *who is* . . . (*ib.* **2 c**), Ezr 6^{15} (so . . . דִּי אִנּוּן Dn 7^{17}). [Cf. in 𝔗 Ex 14^{25} 15^{11} 2 S 20^{19} 24^{17} ψ 43^{2} 63^{4} 66^{3}+.] Affirming existence (BH **6 b**) Dn 4^{21}. Cf. Dr$^{§§ 198-201}$, K$^{§ 87, 3}$.

†[**הֵיכַל**] **n.m. palace, temple** (As. loanword; BH; also Palm. היכלא and הכלא Lzb^{259} SAC^{45});—emph. הֵיכְלָא Ezr 4^{14}+; cstr. הֵיכַל Dn 4^{26}; sf. הֵיכְלִי 4^{1}, ־לֵהּ 6^{19};—**1.** *palace* of king Dn $4^{1.26}$ 5^{5} 6^{19} Ezr 4^{14} (v. מְלַח). **2.** *temple*: **a.** in Jerusalem Dn $5^{2.3}$ Ezr $5^{14a.15}$ $6^{5.5}$. **b.** in Babylon $5^{14b.c}$.

†[**הֲלַךְ**] **vb.** go (BH; 𝔗; Syr. only Pa.);—**Pe.** syncop. (so 𝔗 D$^{§ 70, 9}$, Eg. Aram. Cooke^{209}, Impf. S-C$^{D 22, G 25, 28}$) *go*, of men: *Impf.* 3 ms. יְהָךְ (K$^{§ 44a}$; al. יִהָךְ) Ezr 6^{5}, יְהָךְ 5^{5}; of inanimate things = be brought, 7^{13}; *Inf.* לִמְהָךְ (K$^{l.c.}$; al. ־ֵךְ) v^{13}. **Pa.** *Pt.* מְהַלֵּךְ *walking about* Dn 4^{26} (עַל loc.). **Haph.** *id.*: *Pt.* pl. מַהְלְכִין 3^{25} (בְּגוֹא); fig. 4^{34} *walk* in pride (? rd. **Pa.** in these).

†**הֲלָךְ** (K$^{§ 57 a)}$) **n.[m.]** toll;—Ezr $4^{13.20}$ 7^{24}.

†**הִמּוֹ** (Ezr), **הִמּוֹן** (Dn), **pron. 3 pl.** they, them (=BH הֵם, הֵמָּה, q.v., but the more original forms. Eg. Aram. המו CIS$^{145 B 4}$ (Cooke^{207}), $^{149 A 1}$, S-C$^{Pap. C 7, 10+}$; not 𝔗 Syr., which use אִנּוּן, ܐܶܢܽܘܢ, ܗܶܢܽܘܢ, instead; Ar. هُمْ. The *n* in הִמּוֹן, as in דִּין, אִלֵּין, by the side of אֵלֶּה ,זֶה, ܐܠܶܐ; Nö$^{M 86}$ W$^{CG 106}$);—*they, them*: **a.** as nom. Ezr 5^{11} אֲנַחְנָא הִמּוֹ עַבְדוֹהִי *we are* his servants (constr. as in Syr., Nö$^{§ 312 D}$ Mt 5^{13}, K$^{§ 87, 3}$). **b.** as accus. (in BAram., as in Syr., there being no verbal sf. of 3 pl.; so Eg. Aram. Cooke$^{76 B 4}$, S-C$^{Pap. E 5+}$), Dn 2^{34} והדקת הִמּוֹ and crushed *them*, v^{35} 3^{22} Ezr $4^{10.23}$ $5^{5.12.14.14.15}$ 7^{17}.—Comp. אִנּוּן.

†**הַמְנִיכָא** Qr (Kt המינכא, also [Gi] המוניכא, etc.) **n.[m.] chain, necklace** (Talm. הַמְנְקָא D$^{WB 108}$; Syr. ܗܡܝܢܟܐ; loan-word from Gk. μανιάκης K$^{§ 64, 4}$; or < Pers. *hämyān, girdle* [dimin. would be *hamyānak*] (whence also Gk. μαν., Bev Dr$^{Dn 5, 7}$) Andr$^{M 60*}$ (rdg. הַמְיָנְכָא); v. also Behrm^{1x} Lag$^{Ges. Abh. 40; Arm. Stud. 1420}$; v. Krauss$^{5 f.}$ (who cp. also Talm. מוניק, מָנְיָיק *necklace, bracelet*, Levy$^{NHWB III, 62b, 168b}$ D^{230}));—of gold, Dn $5^{7.16.29}$.

†**הֵן** **conj.** if, whether (BH הֵן, q.v.: Zenj. Eg. Aram. (S-C$^{Pap. A 7+}$), Palm. Nab. הן, Mand. הין *if* [𝔗^{OJon} use אם, 𝔗^{Jer} אין, Syr. ܐܶܢ]);—**1.** *if*, Dn 2^{6} $3^{15.17}$ 4^{24} 5^{16} Ezr $4^{13.16}$ 5^{17}, . . . הֵן לָא Dn $2^{5.9}$ 3^{15}; v^{18} הֵן לָא *if not*. **2.** repeated, הֵן . . . הֵן *sive . . . sive, whether . . . or* (cf. BH אִם, **1 b** 1), Ezr 7^{26} (so Palm.$^{Tariff II. c. 19}$). **3.** in indirect question, *whether* (cf. אִם, **2 b**), Ezr 5^{17b} . . . הֵן אִיתַי . . . יִתְבַּקַּר.—Vid. also לָהֵן.

הַסִּק etc., v. סלק Haph.

הרהר (√of foll., 𝔗 הַרְהֵר, NH הִרְהֵר *reflect, brood impurely* D$^{WB 112}$; Syr. ܗܰܪܗܰܪ is *injure, irritate, quarrel* PS).

†[**הַרְהֹר**] **n.[m.] fancy, imagining**;—pl. abs. הַרְהֹרִין Dn 4^{2} *fancies* (in dream).

ו

וְ, וּ conj. and (BH וְ), used mostly as in Heb., except that there is no ו 'consecutive';—*and*, connecting both words (Dn 2^{5}) and sentences (*ib.*). When three or more words are connected together, וְ may connect them all (Dn $2^{6.10}$ 4^{34} 5^{18}), or only the two last (2^{17} 3^{4} 4^{4} Ezr 6^{9}), or the three last (Dn 2^{37} 3^{21}), or be omitted altogether (2^{27} 5^{11}, cf. 3^{2} Ezr 4^{9}). וְ also connects vbs., in cases where BH would use וַ, as Dn 4^{2} 5^{29} $6^{17.25}$; in such cases a *pf.* is oft. followed by a *ptcp.*, as Dn 2^{7} עֲנוֹ וְאָמְרִין, so v^{10} $3^{9.16.24}$+,

hence in 2[5.8.15.20] and often read prob. with No [GGA 1884, 1021] עָנֵה וְאָמַר (for עָנֵה). Special senses:— **a.** *and that* Dn 4[10.12.20] Ezr 6[8.9] (cf. Dn 2[16.18]); *and also* Dn 6[29]; =*with*, 7[1]. **b.** connecting *contrasted* ideas, *but* Dn 2[6] 3[6.15] 4[4]. **c.** =*and so*, Dn 2[49] 6[3], esp. after imv. 2[4.9.24], or impf. 2[7]. **d.** to express an intention Dn 5[2] וְיִשְׁתּוֹן *that* they might drink: after a command, etc., even with ptcp. or perf., nearly=*that*, 2[13] 6[2] (cf. K[§102]). **e.** introducing the pred. (cf. BH **5 c**), Dn 7[20] וְקַרְנָא דִכֵּן וְעַיְנִין לַהּ and this horn, *it had* eyes, but the case is isolated, and del. prob. ו with Marti.

ז

†[זְבַן] **vb.** buy, gain (𝔗 *id*, *buy*, Syr. ܙܒܢ, OAram. Nab. Palm זבן (oft.) Lzb[264] SAC[47], cf. As. *zibânîtu, scales*),—**Pe.** *Pt act.* pl. זָבְנִין Dn 2[8] time ye (are seeking to) *gain*

†[זְהַר] **vb. Pe.** *Pt. pass.* pl. זְהִירִין Ezr 4[22] be *warned* (𝔗 Syr., cf. BH II. [זָהַר] **Hiph.** *warn*).

†[זוּד] **vb.** be presumptuous (𝔗[J], v. BH [זוד, זיד]);—**Haph.** *Inf.* לַהֲזָדָה Dn 5[20] *act presumptuously*.

†[זוּן] **vb.** feed (𝔗 זוּן; Syr. ܙܢ; cf. BH);—**Hithpe.** *be fed*: *Impf.* יִתְּזִין (K[§45.1d]; so in Syr. W[CG 234] No[LCB, 1896, 703]) Dn 4[9], מִן of source.

†מָזוֹן (K[§15a]) **n.[m.]** food (𝔗 Syr.),—abs. מ׳ Dn 4[9.18].

†[זוּעַ] **vb.** tremble (𝔗 Syr: cf. BH);—**Pe.** *Pt.* pl. זָאֲעִין Kt, Qr זָיְעִין; מִן־קֳדָם pers, Dn 5[19] 6[27].

†[זִיו] **n.m.** brightness, splendour (𝔗 *id*, Syr. ܙܝܘܐ, perhaps loan-word from As *zîmu*, chiefly of *countenance*, Dl[WB 252] Pr[152] No[ZMG xl (1886). 732] Jen[ZK II 43] Brock[Lex Syr 91]),—sf זִיוִי Dn 4[33] *splendour* of royalty; זִיוֵהּ 2[31] (of image); pl. *brightness* of countenance: sf. זִיוָךְ 7[28], זיויך Kt, זִיוָךְ Qr, 5[10], זִיוֹהִי 5[6.9].

†זָכוּ (K[§61.4]) **n.f.** purity, innocence (cf. BH זָכָה, also 𝔗 דְּכָא, Syr. ܙܟܐ *be clean* (Ar زَكَا is *be bright* (of fire), *acute* (of mind), etc.), or Ar. زَكَا *be pure, good*, 𝔗 זְכָא, Syr. ܙܟܐ *be pure, innocent*; are these forms with ז secondary? or ancient ‖ ?);—abs. ז׳ Dn 6[13] *innocence* in God's sight.

†זְכַרְיָה **n.pr.m.** prophet (BH *id.*), Ezr 5[1] 6[14].

†זְמַן **n.m.**[Dn 3,7] time (prob loan-word from OPers. *zrvan, zarvâna, time, age*, No[M 132] Scheft[45]; cf BH (late); and (on change of *v* [*b*] to *m*) Fra[ZA III 52]; Nab. זמן, Palm. (Nab) זבן Lzb[266 263] SAC[45 49]);—abs. ז׳ Dn 2[16] 7[12], emph. זִמְנָא Ezr 5[3]+; pl. abs. Dn 6[11]+, emph. זִמְנַיָּא Dn 2[21];—*time*: *specified time* Dn 2[16]; *appointed time* 7[12.22], cf 2[21]; בהּ זִמְנָא *at that time* Ezr 5[3] Dn 3[7.8] 4[33]; (festival) *seasons* 7[25]; *time, occurrence*, 6[11.14] *three times in the day*.

†[זְמַן] **vb. denom. Hithpa.** agree together (𝔗);—*Pf* 3 mpl Dn 2[9] Qr הִזְדְּמִנְתּוּן (D[211, 2nd ed 263] M[§12a], Kt **Haph.** הַזְמִנְתּוּן, v. 𝔗[Onk] Ex 5[14] D[(2) 263, 403]), sq Inf. לְמֵאמַר.

†[זְמָר] **n.[m.]** music (cf. BH I. [זֶמֶר]);—emph זְמָרָא Dn 3[5.7.10.15]

†[זַמָּר K[§59d]] **n.m.** singer;—pl. emph. זַמָּרַיָּא Ezr 7[24].

†[זַן] **n.[m.]** kind, sort (𝔗 Syr.; cf BH),—pl cstr. זְנֵי זְמָרָא Dn 3[5.7.10.15]

†זְעִק **vb.** cry, call (𝔗 Syr.; cf. BH),—**Pe.** *Pf.* 3 ms ז׳ Dn 6[21] (ב of voice).

זער (𝔗 Syr., *be small*; BH צָעִיר √זער, Eg. Aram. זער Cooke[213], Nab. זעירא, Palm. זערא Lzb[268] SAC[49])

†[זְעֵיר] **adj.** little, small;—fs. קֶרֶן זְעֵירָה Dn 7[8].

†[זְקַף] **vb.** raise, lift up (𝔗 Syr.; cf BH (late; rare));—**Pe.** *Pt pass.* וּזְקִיף יִתְמְחֵא עֲלוֹהִי Ezr 6[11] *and, lifted up, he be fastened upon it* (sc. the timber erected; ref. prob. to impalement, v. Ryle Berthol)

†זְרֻבָּבֶל **n.pr.m.** (BH *id*);—Ezr 5[2].

†זְרַע **n.[m.]** seed (cf. BH I. זרע),—cstr. ז׳ אֲנָשָׁא Dn 2[43] *seed* (offspring) of men.

ח

†[חֲבַל] **vb. Pa.** destroy, hurt (v. BH II. חבל),—*Pf.* 3 mpl. sf חַבְּלוּנִי Dn 6[23] (of lions); *Imv.* mpl sf. חַבְּלוּהִי 4[20] (sf. of tree); *Inf.* לְחַבָּלָה Ezr 6[12] (acc. of temple). **Hithpa.** *be destroyed*: *Impf* 3 fs. לָא תִתְחַבַּל Dn 2[44] 6[27] 7[14] (-בַּל); all of kingdom of God).

†חֲבָל n. m. [Dn 6 24] hurt, injury;—abs. ח׳ Dn 3[25] 6[24], cf RES[362 A 2], emph חֲבָלָא Ezr 4[22].

†חֲבוּלָא n.f. hurtful act, crime;—abs. ח׳ Dn 6[23]

†[חֲבַר] n. m. fellow, comrade (𝔗 Syr., v BH),—pl sf חַבְרוֹהִי Dn 2[13 17 18].

†[חַבְרָה] n.f. fellow,—pl sf. חַבְרָתַהּ Dn 7[20] its fellows (in vision of horns)

†חַגַּי n.pr m. prophet (BH id),—Ezr 5[1] 6[14].

חַד ,הֲדָה v אחד

†חֶדְוָה n.f. joy (𝔗 Syr.; v. BH II. חדה),—abs בח׳ Ezr 6[16] with joy

†[חֲדִי], or (K[§ 55, 6 a)]) [חַד] n m. breast (𝔗 Syr, v BH II חזה),—du. (Schulth[ZAW xxii (1902), 164]) sf. חֲדוֹהִי Dn 2[32]

†חֲדַת adj. new (𝔗 Syr., BH חדש),—ח׳ Ezr 6[4].

חוד (✓of following; 𝔗 חִוָּר, חוּדִיתָא, riddle, v BH and K[§ 57 b) α)])

†[אֲחִידָה] n. f. riddle,—fpl abs אֲחִידָן Dn 5[12].

†[חֲוָה] vb. Pa. Haph. (M[§ 63c]) declare (𝔗 Syr, BH III. [חָוָה] (late)),—**Pa.** c acc פִּשְׁרָא (or equiv) *Impf.* 3 ms sf יְחַוִּנַּנִי (sf pers indir. obj) Dn 5[7], יְחַוִּנַּהּ 2[11] (קֳדָם pers), 1 s אֲחַוֵּה 2[24] (ל pers), 1 pl נְחַוֵּה v[4] **Haph.** usu. c. acc פִּשְׁרָא (or equiv) *Impf.* 3 ms. יְהַחֲוֵה Dn 5[12], 2 mpl תְּהַחֲוֻן 2[6], sf. (of indir. obj) תְּהַחֲוֻנַּנִי v[9], 1 pl נְהַחֲוֵה v[7], *Imv.* mpl sf. (of indir. obj) הַחֲוֹנִי v[6], *Inf* לְהַחֲוָיָה v[10] 5[15]; + ל pers 2[16 27]; c acc of signs and wonders 3[32]

†[אַחֲוָיָה] n f a declaring (prop Inf Aph, K[§ 60 1)]);—cstr אַחֲוָיַת אֲחִידָן Dn 5[12] the declaring of riddles (cf. לְהַגִּיד הַחִידָה Ju 14[14 f], Bev).

†[חוּט or חִיט] vb. repair (foundations);—**Haph.** *Impf* 3 mpl יַחִיטוּ Ezr 4[12] (si vera l. [No[GGA 1884 1018] Str[§ 13b]]), rare form for יחיטון K[§§ 16, 5 26, 1] M[§ 63g Anm], but perh read this, and regard as **Qal** (orig. meaning dub., Ar خَاطَ is sew, = 𝔗 חוּט, Syr ܚܳܛ, cf BH חוּט thread; Syr Pa. also *join together* (so here Schulth[ZAW xxii (1902) 162 Anm.]), cf. Ar. حَطَّ *conjunxit* trabes (de Goeje Bibl Geogr Arab., Pt. iv (1879) Gloss 231 cf Pt viii (1894), Gloss. p xx); Fra[ZAW xix (1899) 180] conj *pull down* and clear away (for rebuilding), cf *ḫaiaṭu* Dl[WB 274]; Jen [KB vi. 314] cp As. *ḫâṭu*, *observe, learn* (Dl[WB] I. חיט), i e *examine, test*, Hpt[Gu Ezr-Ne 62] conj. ✓ חטט *excavate*, cf. Ar احتط *secure* site *by a mark*, *found* a town; Str[Gr (1905) 40] יַחִיטוּ (after Seybold), cf Ezr 5[16]; al. conj *build wall*, denom., cf. Ar حَائِط *wall* (✓ حوط *guard, surround*))

†חִוָּר adj. white (𝔗 Syr., BH I. [חָוָר]),—Dn 7[9] (robe).

†חֲזָה vb. see, behold (v. BH),—**Pe.** *Pf.* 3 ms ח׳ Dn 4[20] 5[1], 2 ms חֲזַיְתָ 2[43]+, -תָה 2[41.41]; 1 s. חֲזֵית v[46]+, 2 mpl חֲזֵיתוּן 2[8]; **Pe.** *Inf.* לְמֶחֱזֵא Ezr 4[14], *Pt. act* חָזֵה Dn 2[31]+ 14 t.; pl חָזַיִן 3[27] 5[23]; *pass* חֲזֵה 3[19];—**1.** *see*, have sense of sight Dn 5[23]. **2.** *see, behold*: **a.** acc pers. 3[25], c. ל v[27], acc rei 5[5]. **b.** *see, witness* dishonour of king (acc) Ezr 4[14]. **3.** usu *behold* in dream or vision (oft. pt in periphrast. conj), acc pers, 4[20], acc rei 2[41 41 43] 4[17], abs 2[34] 7[4 7 9 11 11.21], + אֲלוּ 2[31] 4[7 10], אֲרוּ 7[2 6 13], c obj cl. 2[8 45]; *behold* a dream, acc. חֵלֶם, 2[26] 4[2 6 15] 7[1]. **4.** pass. = *customary* (*seemly*) Dn 3[19] (so 𝔗 Lv 5[10] al, v Dr).

†[חֱזוּ] n.m. vision, appearance,—emph. חֶזְוָא (K[§ 55 6 b)]) Dn 2[19], sf -וָךְ 7[2], -וֵהּ v[20], pl. cstr. חֶזְוֵי 2[28]+,—**1.** *vision* (as mode of revelation) 2[19] (ח׳ די לֵילְיָא), 7[2], so 7[7 13], ח׳ רֵישָׁא 2[28] 4[2 7 10] 7[1 15], ח׳ חֶלְמָא 4[6] (Gie[GGA 1895. 598] reads אַחֲוֵא *I will relate*). **2.** *appearance* 7[20].

†[חָזוּת K[§ 55 6 b)] rd. perh -וֹת K[§ 61 4 b), Anm]] n. f. sight, visibility (v. Schulth[ZAW xxii (1902), 160 f]),—sf חֲזוֹתֵהּ Dn 4[8.17]

†[חֲטָי] n. [m.] sin (v. BH חטא),—sf חֲטָיָךְ Dn 4[24] (Qr חֲטָאָךְ K[§ 57 a) β)]), < pl. (for חֲטָיָיךְ) Hi Bev Kmp Behrm, cf. ‖ עֲוָיָתָךְ.

†חַטָּיָא n.f. sin-offering (BH חַטָּאת **4**, Nab. חטיאת *penalty*, acc to SAC[51]),—abs. ח׳ Ezr 6[17] Kt, Qr חַטָּאָה.

†[חֲיָא] vb. live (v. BH חָיָה);—**Pe.** *Imv.* חֱיִי לְעָלְמִין *live for ever!* Dn 2[4] 3[9] 5[10] 6[7 22]. **Haph.** *Pt.* מַחֵא (K[§§ 11, 3 b) γ)] Hpt[Kmp Dn 23]) Dn 5[19] *let live.*

†חַי adj living (BH *id.*),—**1.** of God: abs ח׳ Dn 4[31], emph. חַיָּא 6[21 27]; men, pl emph. חַיַּיָּא *the living* 2[30] 4[14]. **2.** pl. as n. abstr. *life* (BH חַיִּים) חַיִּין 7[12], cstr. חַיֵּי Ezr 6[10].

†חֵיוָה ,חֵיוָא n.f. beast (BH II. חַיָּה);—abs. א— Dn 4[13], ה— 7[5 7]; emph. חֵיוְתָא 7[6 11 19 23], and (coll) 4[11 12] 5[21]; cstr. (coll.) חֵיוַת בָּרָא 2[38] 4[9 18 20 22.29], pl abs חֵיוָן 7[3], emph. חֵיוָתָא 7[7 12.17].

†חַיִל n.m. power, strength, army (v. BH II. חיל, חול);—**1.** *power:* abs. בְּאֶדְרָע וְחָיִל Ezr 4^{23} *by force and power;* קרא בְחַ׳ i.e. *call loudly* Dn 3^{4}, בְּחַיִל 4^{11} 5^{7}; גִּבָּרֵי־חַ׳ 3^{20} *mighty men of power.* **2.** *force, army,* sf. חֵילֵהּ 3^{20}; cstr. חֵיל שְׁמַיָּא 4^{32} (=BH צְבָא הַשָּׁמַיִם).

[חַכִּים] 14 n.m. wise man (v. BH חכם);—pl. abs. חַכִּימִין Dn 2^{21}; elsewhere of the class possessed of occult learning in Bab. v^{27}, emph. -מַיָּא v^{13} 5^{15}; cstr. -מֵי $2^{12.14}$+7 t. Dn.

†חָכְמָה n.f. wisdom;—חָ׳ abs. Dn 2^{30}+, emph. חָכְמְתָא Dn 2^{20}+, cstr. חָכְמַת 5^{11} Ezr 7^{25};—*wisdom,* attrib of God Dn 2^{20}; of gods 5^{11}; of man 2^{30}; of God imparted to man Ezr 7^{25} (practical wisdom), Dn 2^{21}; =occult knowledge (v. foregoing) imparted to men v^{23} $5^{11.14}$.

חֵ֫לֶם 22 n.m. ^Dn 4 2^ dream (𝔗 Syr.; v. BH חֲלוֹם, √ II. חלם);—abs. חֵ׳ Dn 4^{2} 7^{1}; emph. חֶלְמָא 2^{4}+; sf. חֶלְמִי 4^{6}, -מָךְ 2^{28}; pl. חֶלְמִין 5^{12},—*dream,* as vehicle of revelation Dn 2^{4}+10 t., 4^{3}+6 t., 5^{12}; to prophet 7^{1}.

†[חֲלַף] vb. pass (over) (v. BH);—**Pe.** c. עַל pers *pass over* one (of time): *Impf.* 3 mpl. יַחְלְפוּן Dn $4^{13.20.22.29}$.

†חֲלָק n.[m.] portion, possession, lot (v. BH),—abs. חֲ׳ *possession* in land Ezr 4^{16}; sf. חֲלָקֵהּ Dn $4^{12.20}$, i.e. his appointed lot

†[מַחְלְקָה] n.f. class, division, of priests and Levites (BH מַחֲלֹקֶת);—pl sf. מַחְלְקָתְהוֹן Ezr 6^{18}.

חֱמָא v. יחם.

†חֲמַר n.m. wine (𝔗 Syr.; BH חֶמֶר (poet and late), √I. חמר);—abs. חֲ׳ Ezr 6^{9} 7^{22}; emph. חַמְרָא Dn $5^{1.2.4.23}$.

†[חִנְטָה] n.f. wheat (v. BH חִטָּה, √ חָנַט; No^LCB, 1896, 703^ cp. Eg. *chnt;* OAram has חטה, pl. חטי, Palm. חטא Lzb^{279} SAC^{61});—pl. חִנְטִין Ezr 6^{9} 7^{22}.

†[חֲנֻכָּה] n.f. dedication (𝔗; BH *id,* √חנך),—cstr. חֲנֻכַּת, of image Dn $3^{2.3}$; temple Ezr $6^{16.17}$.

†[חֲנַן] vb. shew favour (v. BH);—**Pa.** *Inf.* c. acc. pers. מִחַן (K § 46, 3 a) Dn 4^{24} (cf. BH **Pō`.** Pr 14^{21}). **Hithpa.** *implore favour* (of God; so BH Hithp.), *Pt.* מִתְחַנַּן Dn 6^{12}.

†חֲנַנְיָה n.pr.m. (=BH *id.* **5**);—Dn 2^{17}.

†[חֲסַן] vb. **Haph.** take possession of (Syr. *be strong, overcome;* 𝔗 *be strong, take possession of;* Eg. Aram. Haph. החסן *hold property* S-C^D 2+^, cf BH חסן),—*Pf.* 3 mpl. הֶחֱסִנוּ (K § 38 3 Kmp^ad loc.^) Dn 7^{22}; *Impf.* 3 mpl. יַחְסְנוּן (K § 38, 1 b) v^{18} (perhaps point -סְנוּן).

†[חֱסֶן] n.m. (royal) power;—emph. חִסְנָא Dn 2^{37}; sf. חִסְנִי 4^{27}.

†חֲסַף n.[m.] clay, potsherd (𝔗 *id.;* Chr-Pal. ܚܨܦܐ *clay vessel,* ܚܪܣܐ pl. *potsherds* Schulth^{68}, Syr. ܚܶܨܦܳܐ *potsherd;* 𝔗 חַצְבָּא, NH חָצָב *clay vessel;* As *ḫasbu, id.;* ܚܨܒܐ *jar* (PS^{1238}), whence Ar. خَزَف *pottery* Fra^{169}, but Sab. חסף *jar,* acc. to Hom^ZMG xlvi (1892), 532^; cf. Eth ጸሕብ: *jar* (transp; Di^{1265}); v. BH [חַסְפַּס]);—חֲ׳ abs Dn 2^{41} (חֲ׳ דִּי פֶחָר), חֲסַף $v^{33.42}$; cstr. חֲ׳ טִינָא $v^{41.43}$; emph. חַסְפָּא $v^{34.35.43.45}$.

†חַסִּיר adj. lacking, wanting, deficient (cf. BH חָסֵר),—חַ׳ Dn 5^{27}.

†[חֲצַף] vb. **Haph.** shew insolence, harshness (NH חצף **Hiph.** *act insolently,* so 𝔗 Aph.; Syr. ܚܨܦ be audacious);—*Pt.* f. מְהַחְצְפָה (K § 33, 2 a) Dn 3^{22} *overbearing* (of command), מְהַחְצְפָה 2^{15} *harsh* (*id*).

†[חֲרַב] vb. be waste (v. BH II. חרב);—**Hoph.** *Pf.* הָחָרְבַת Ezr 4^{15} city *was laid waste*

‡†חַרְטֹם n.m. magician (BH *id.,* √I. חרט);—abs. Dn 2^{10}, pl abs. חַרְטֻמִּין 2^{27} 5^{11}, -מַיָּא $4^{4.6}$.

†[חֲרַךְ] vb. singe (𝔗 Syr.; NH חָרַךְ);—**Hithpa.** *Pf.* 3 ms. הִתְחָרַךְ Dn 3^{27} (of hair)

†[חֲרַץ] n.[m.] loin (v. BH חָלָץ, √ II. [חָלַץ]);—sf. חַרְצֵהּ Dn 5^{6} the joints of *his loin* (v. קְטַר).

†[חֲשַׁב] vb. think, account (v. BH);—**Pe.** *Pt. pass.* pl. כְּלָה חֲשִׁיבִין Dn 4^{32} *like those not accounted of,* of no account, Bev Dr.

†[חֲשַׁח] vb. need (As. *ḫašâḫu, crave;* Syr. ܚܫܚ *in need of;* not 𝔗);—**Pe.** *Pt* pl. חָשְׁחִין Dn 3^{16}, sg. Inf. (van d. H., wrongly, חָשׁ׳).

†[חַשְׁחָה] n.f. thing needed (Syr. ܚܫܚܬܐ; No in K^p. 173^);—pl. חַשְׁחָן Ezr 6^{9}.

†[חַשְׁחוּ] n.f.coll. things needed, requirement (Syr. *id.*);—cstr. חַשְׁחוּת בֵּית אֱלָהָךְ Ezr 7^{20}.

†[יְדָא] **vb. Haph.** **praise** (v. BH ידה);—*Pt. act.* מְהוֹדֵא Dn 2^{23} (לְ dei), מוֹדֵא (K$^{§§ 53, 2; 43, 1. c)}$) 6^{11} (קֳדָם dei).

†יְדַע **vb. know** (v. BH);—**Pe.** *Pf.* 3 ms. ׳י Dn 5^{21} 6^{11}, 2 ms. יְדַ֫עְתְּ 5^{22}, 1 s. יִדְעֵת 4^{6}; *Impf.* 2 ms. תִּנְדַּע (K$^{§ 11, 4. b) δ)}$) Ezr 4^{15}+, etc.; *Imv.* דַּע ms. (K$^{§ 11, 3 a)}$) Dn 6^{16}; *Pt. act.* יָדַע 2^{8}+; pl. יָדְעִין 5^{23}, etc.; *pass.* יְדִיעַ 4^{12}+;—*know*, c. acc. rei Dn 2^{30} 5^{22}, acc. rei om. Ezr 7^{25}; יָדְעֵי דָּתֵי א׳ v^{25}, יָדְעֵי בִינָה Dn 2^{21}; c. obj. cl. v$^{8.9.22}$ 4$^{6.14.23.29}$ 5^{21} 6$^{11.16}$ Ezr 4^{15}, so (of God) Dn 4^{22}; *pt. act.* abs. 5^{23} *having capacity of knowledge*; *pass.* in periphr. conjug., subj. cl. + לְ pers. 3^{18} Ezr 4$^{12.13}$ 5^{8}. **Haph.** *Pf.* 3 ms. הוֹדַע Dn 2^{15}+, sf. הוֹדְעָךְ v^{29}, 2 ms. sf. הוֹדַעְתַּ֫נִי v^{23}, ־תֶּ֫נָה v^{23}, 1 pl. הוֹדַ֫עְנָא Ezr 4^{14}; *Impf.* 3 ms. יְהוֹדַע Dn 2^{25}, sf. יְהוֹדְעִנַּנִי 7^{16}, etc. (v. K$^{§ 43 c)}$); *Inf.* לְהוֹדָעָה 5^{8}, sf. לְהוֹדָעֻתַ֫נִי 4^{15} 5^{16}, etc.; *Pt. act.* pl. מְהוֹדְעִין 4^{4}+;—*cause to know, inform*: לְ pers. Ezr 4^{14}, +acc. rei Dn 2$^{15.17.25.30}$ 4^{4} 5$^{8.17}$, so (sf. pers.) 2$^{5.9.26}$ 4$^{3.15}$ 5$^{15.16}$ 7^{16}, and (subj. God) 2^{23}; לְ pers. + obj. cl. Ezr 4^{16} 7^{24}, so (of God) Dn 2$^{28.29.45}$, and (sf. pers.) v^{23}; acc. pers. only Ezr 5^{10} 7^{25}.

†מַנְדַּע **n.** [**m.**] **knowledge, power of knowing** (𝔗^{J} *id.*; Syr. ܡܕܥܐ, ܡܰܕܥܳܐ; BH מַדָּע (late); cf. 'Mandâ' = γνῶσις, Nö$^{M\ xx}$);—abs. Dn 5^{12}; emph. ־דְּעָא 2^{21}; sf. ־דְּעִי 4$^{31.33}$.

†יְהַב **vb. give** (𝔗 Syr.; cf. BH);—**Pe.** *Pf.* 3 ms. ׳י Ezr 5^{12}+; 2 ms. יְהַבְתְּ Dn 2^{23}; 3 mpl. יְהַ֫בוּ וִיהַ֫בוּ 3^{28}; *Imv.* ms. הַב (K$^{§ 11, 3. a)}$) 5^{17}; *Pt. act.* יָהֵב 2^{21}, pl. יָהֲבִין 6^{3};—**1.** *give*, acc. rei + לְ pers. Dn 2^{48} 5^{17}, also (subj. God) 2$^{21.23.37.38}$ 5$^{18.19}$; *give* report 6^{3} (לְ pers.); *give over*, acc. pers. + בְּיַד (יַד **2**) Ezr 5^{12} (subj. God); *give up, surrender* Dn 3^{28} (one's body, acc.). **2.** *place, lay* foundations Ezr 5^{16} (Nab. also *place* Cooke$^{102, 1. 6}$ SAC$^{JQ\ 1904, 274}$; v. ܝܗܒ **2** Schulth$^{Lex;\ and\ ZAW\ xxii\ (1902),\ 162}$; cf. D^{WB} ^{171}). **Pe'îl** (W$^{CG\ 224}$), *be given*, subj. rei, c. לְ pers.: 3 ms. יְהִיב Dn 7$^{4.6}$, יְהַב v$^{14.22}$, 3 fs. יְהִיבַת 5^{28} 7$^{12.27}$; 3 mpl. וִיהִיבוּ Ezr 5^{14}; *be given up* (לְ of flame) Dn 7^{11}. **Hithpe.** *Impf.* 3 ms. יִתְיְהֵב Dn 4^{13}, 3 fs. תִּתְיְהִב Ezr 6^{4}; 3 mpl. יִתְיַהֲבוּן Dn 7^{25}; *Pt.* מִתְיְהֵב Ezr 4^{20} 6^{9}, fs. מִתְיַהֲבָא v^{8}, pl. ־בִין 7^{19};—**1.** *be given*, subj. rei, לְ pers., Dn 4^{13} Ezr 6^{9} 7^{19}; *be given over*, subj. pers. בִּידֵהּ (יַד **2**) Dn 7^{25}. **2.** *be paid*, of cost Ezr 6^{4} (מִן of source), v^{8} (לְ pers.), toll 4^{20} (לְ pers.).

†יְהוּד **n.pr.terr. Judah** (secondary format. from foll. acc. to M$^{§ 68. b}$ Buhl; cf. BH יְהוּדָה);—Dn 5^{13b} Ezr 5$^{1.8}$ 7^{14}; בְּנֵי גָלוּתָא דִּי י׳ Dn 2^{25} 5^{13a} 6^{14}.

†[יְהוּדָי] **n.gent. Jew** (BH יְהוּדִי);—pl. abs. יְהוּדָאִין (K$^{§ 61, 6)}$) Dn 3^{12}; emph. יְהוּדָיֵא (Ib.$^{ib.}$) v^{8} Ezr 4$^{12.23}$ 5$^{1.5}$ 6$^{7.7.8.14}$.

†יוֹם **n.m.** $^{Ezr\ 6,\ 15}$ **day** (v. BH);—abs. ׳י Ezr 6$^{9.9.15}$, emph. יוֹמָא Dn 6$^{11.14}$; pl. abs. יוֹמִין v^{8}+, emph. יוֹמַיָּא 2^{28}+; cstr. יוֹמֵי 5^{11}, and יוֹמָת (K $^{§ 51, 2, Anm. 3)}$) Ezr 4$^{15.19}$; sf. יוֹמֵיהוֹן Dn 2^{44};—*day*, as division of time Dn 6$^{11.14}$, *day* of month Ezr 6^{15}; thirty days Dn 6$^{8.13}$; יוֹם בְּיוֹם Ezr 6^{9} *day by day*; pl. esp. of duration: עַתִּיק י׳ *one aged of days*, aged man Dn 7$^{9.13.22}$; י׳ עָלְמָא *days of old* Ezr 4$^{15.19}$: of a period: life-time, or reign, of king Dn 2^{44} 5^{11}; לִקְצָת י׳ 4^{31} *at the end of the days* (appointed time), בְּאַחֲרִית י׳ 2^{28} *in the latter part of the* (future) *days*.

†יוֹצָדָק **n.pr.m.** Ezr 5^{2} (BH *id.*, √הָיָה).

יוב v. שֵׁיזִב.

יחם (√of foll.; v. BH יָחַם, whence חֵמָה).

†חֱמָא **n.f. rage**;—abs. Dn 3^{19}, חֱ׳ v^{13}.

†[יְטַב] **vb. be** (**good,**) **pleasing** (𝔗; Eg. Aram. Haf. הוטב S-C$^{B\ 11+}$; v. BH יטב);—**Pe.** *Impf.* יֵיטַב (K$^{§ 43, 2}$) Ezr 7^{18} (עַל pers., +inf.).

†יְכִל (K$^{§ 25. a) β)}$) **vb. be able** (Dn) (𝔗; Nab. (rare) SAC^{60}; Eg. Aram. S-C$^{E\ 8,\ 11+}$; Chr-Pal. Schulth^{83}; BH יָכֹל);—**Pe. 1.** c. Inf. *be able* to do: *Pf.* 3 ms. יְכִל Dn 6^{21} (subj. God), 2 ms. יְכֵלְתָּ 2^{47}; *Impf.* 3 ms. יוּכַל (Hebraism, K$^{§ 43, 1. Beisp. b)}$) v^{10}, יִכֻּל 3^{29} (subj. a god), 2 ms. תוכל 5$^{16.16}$ (<both Qr תִּכּוּל, K$^{l.\ c.}$); *Pt.* יָכִל 3^{17} 4^{34} (both subj. God); pl. יָכְלִין 2^{27} 4^{15} 6^{5}. **2.** *prevail* (BH **2**) *against* (לְ), *Pt.* fs. יָכְלָה 7^{21}.

†[יָם] **n.m. sea** (𝔗 Syr.; v. BH יָם, √ימם);—emph. יַמָּא Dn 7$^{2.3}$.

†[יְסַף] **vb. add** (v. BH);—**Hoph.** (W$^{CG\ 225}$) *Pf.* 3 fs. הוּסְפַת (K$^{§§ 15\ d);\ 17,\ 1;\ 43,\ 1.\ Beisp.\ c)}$) Dn 4^{33} *was added*, לְ pers.

†[יְעַט] **vb. advise** (so JAram.; BH יעץ);—**Ithpa.** *Pf.* 3 mpl. אִתְיָעַטוּ (K$^{§§ 23, 1. Anm.; 39, 5)}$) Dn 6^{8} recipr. *took counsel with each other*, sq. inf.

†[יָעַט] **n.m.** counsellor (prop. Pt. act.),—pl sf יָעֲטֹהִי Ezr 7[14], יָעֲטוֹהִי v[15].

†עֵטָא **n.f.** counsel,—abs. Dn 2[14] (v. טעם 2)

יצא v. שיצא

†[יְצַב] **vb. Pa.** make certain, gain certainty (𝔗; cf BH);—**Pa.** *Inf.* לְיַצָּבָא Dn 7[19], c עַל *concerning*

†יַצִּיב **adj.** certain, true (𝔗 *id.*, *firm, native* (=אֶזְרָח));—abs י׳ Dn 2[8.45], emph ־בָא 3[24] (K§ 59.2), fs ־בָא 6[13] 7[16],—**1.** *certain, sure* Dn 2[45], in exclam. 3[24] *undoubtedly!* מִן־יַצִּיב v[8] *of a surety*. **2.** *true* 6[13]; f. as subst 7[16] *the truth* concerning, עַל rei.

†[יְקַד] **vb.** burn (v. BH),—**Pe.** *Pt act.* f. יָקִדְתָּא Dn 3[6 11 15 17 20.21 23.26]

†[יְקֵדָה] **n.f.** burning,—cstr לִיקֵדַת אֶשָּׁה Dn 7[11].

†[יְקָר] **n.m.** [Dn 2 6] honour (v BH),—abs וִיקָר Dn 2[6] 7[14], cstr. *id* 4[27], לִיקָר v[33] (K§ 57 Anm Str ־קָר), emph וִיקָרָא 2[37] 5[18], ־ה v[20]

†[יַקִּיר] **adj.** honourable, difficult,—**1.** *honourable*, emph יַקִּירָא Ezr 4[10]. **2.** *difficult* (cf. BH כָּבֵד **adj. 1 d**), fs יַקִּירָה Dn 2[11]

ירושלם [25] **n. pr. loc.** Jerusalem (BH יְרוּשָׁלַםִ);—Dn 5[2.3] 6[11] Ezr 4[8 12] + 20 t. Ezr.

†[יְרַח] **n.m.** month (v. BH),—abs לִירַח אֲדָר Ezr 6[15], pl. abs יַרְחִין Dn 4[26]

†[יַרְכָה] **n.f.** thigh, or loin (𝔗; v. BH יָרֵךְ),—pl sf. יַרְכָתֵהּ Dn 2[32].

†יִשְׂרָאֵל **n pr. gent.** Israel (BH *id*, √I שָׂרָה),—אֱלָהּ יִשׂ׳ Ezr 5[1] 6[14] 7[15], מֶלֶךְ לְיִשׂ׳ 5[11], בְּנֵי יִשׂ׳ 6[16], עַמָּא יִשׂ׳ 7[13].

†יֵשׁוּעַ **n.pr.m.** (BH *id* **3**, p 221),—Ezr 5[2]

ישן (√of following, BH יָשֵׁן, שֵׁנָה)

†II. [שְׁנָה] **n.f.** sleep (𝔗 Syr),—sf שִׁנְתֵהּ (K§ 12 d) Dn 6[19]—I. [שְׁנָה] v [שְׁנָא]

†יָת **mark of accus.** (=BH I אֵת, Palm. ית, Zinj [Had 28] c sf. ותה, Nab Palm c sf יתה (Lzb[283] Cooke[170], cf. RES[468]), 𝔗 Sam יָת, Syr. ܝܬ (rare), v. further p 84b);—Dn 3[12] דִּי מַנִּיתָ יָתְהוֹן whom thou hast appointed.

†יְתִב (K§ 25 a) β)) **vb.** sit, dwell (𝔗 Syr; v. BH יָשַׁב),—**Pe. 1.** *sit, be seated*. *Pf* 3 ms. יְתִב Dn 7[9] and (of judgment=the judge) v[10], so *Impf.* 3 ms יִתִּב (K§ 43.1 Beisp. b), cf. BH יֵשֵׁב) 7[26]. **2.** *dwell*, *Pt* pl abs יָתְבִין Ezr 4[17] (בְּ loc.). **Haph.** *cause to dwell*. *Pf.* 3 ms. הוֹתֵב 4[10] (acc + בְּ loc.).

†יַתִּיר **adj.** pre-eminent, surpassing (v. BH יֶתֶר),—ms abs. י׳ Dn 2[31]; fs. יַתִּירָא 6[4], usu. ־ה 4[33] 5[12 14], as adv. *exceedingly* 3[22] 7[7 19] (cf. יתיר מתבריך Eut [8a 493] wh. Lzb[401] reads יתירית בריך).

כ

כְּ **part.** like, as, about (BH כְּ, q v.);—*like, as*, Dn 2[40] כְּפַרְזְלָא תַּקִּיפָא, 4[5.32] 5[1] +; *according to* 4[32] וּכְמִצְבְּיֵהּ עָבֵד and *according to* his will he doeth, Ezr 6[9 18]+, *about* (as BH **1 a**. cf. Zinj. Lzb[444] [כשלשן מלכ[ן), Dn 4[16] כְּשָׁעָה חֲדָה, 6[1], with inf. (BH **3 b**), 6[21] וּכְמִקְרְבֵהּ לְגֻבָּא and *as* he drew near, etc. Cpds:—כְּדִי and כִּדְנָה, v. דִּי and דְּנָה, כַּחֲדָה *together*, v חַד (sub אחד).

†[כְּדַב] **adj.** false (𝔗 Syr., v. BH כזב),—fs abs. מִלָּה כִדְבָה Dn 2[9] (> n. appos. K[170] M[66*]).

כדי v. די.

†כָּה **adv.** here (BH כה, 𝔗 Mand. כָּא; Chr-Pal ܟܐ, Syr. with prefixes, as ܠܟܐ *hither*, ܠܐܟܐ *whither?*),—Dn 7[28] עַד־כָּה סוֹפָא דִי־מִלְּתָא *hitherto* (cf Je 48[47] 51[64]) is the end of the matter.

†[כְּהַל] **vb.** be able (𝔗 *id*, Eg. Aram., S-C [Pap. A 6, 8 11]+; Eth. ከሀለ: cf syn. יְכִל),—**Pe.** *Pt act.*, usu sq. inf.: abs כָּהֵל Dn 2[26] 4[15] (inf. om); pl abs. כָּהֲלִין 5[8 15].

†[כָּהֵן] **n m.** priest (v. BH כהן);—emph. כָּהֲנָא Ezr 7[12 21], pl. emph. ־נַיָּא 6[9 16.18] 7[16.24], sf. (of Isr.) ־נוֹהִי v[13].

[כַּוָּה] No[GGA 1884, 1019] **n.f.** window (𝔗 כַּוְּתָא, Syr ܟܘܬܐ, cf. Schulth[Lex 91] (sub *ܟܘ), hence Ar. كَوَّة, كُوَّة *id*, as loan-word Fra[13]),—pl. abs כַּוִּין פְּתִיחָן Dn 6[11] (cf. S-C[J6]).

†[כֹּר] **n.[m.]** kôr, a measure of wheat (BH כֹּר p. 499),—pl abs. כֹּרִין Ezr 7[22].

כּוֹרֶשׁ, **n.pr.m.** Cyrus (BH *id*);—Dn 6[29] Ezr 5[13] + 6 t. Ezr.

[כַּכַּר], כַּכְּרִין v. כרר. כֹּל v. כלל.

† [כְּלַל] **vb.** complete (v. BH I. [כָּלַל]; but שַׁכ׳ perhaps loan-word from As. *šuklulu, ušaklil, uštaklil*, Dl[WB 331], cf. שֵׁיזִב, שֵׁיצִא and Buhl[14]);—**Shaph.** of building: *Pf.* 3 ms. sf. שַׁכְלְלֵהּ Ezr 5[11] *he finished it;* 3 mpl. שַׁכְלִלוּ 6[14], also (c. acc. rei) 4[12] (Kt. שורי אשכללו, read Qr) שׁוּרַיָּא שׁ׳; *Inf.* לְהַשְׁכְלָלָה, acc. rei 5[3.9]. **Ishtaph.** *be completed*, of walls; *Impf.* 3 mpl. יִשְׁתַּכְלְלוּן 4[13.16].

כֹּל, כָּל־ **n.m.** the whole, all (BH כֹּל);—emph. כֹּלָּא Dn 2[40]+, cstr. כֹּל 2[12] 3[2]+, כָּל־ 2[8]+, sf. 3 mpl. כָּלְּהוֹן (so Palm. Lzb[296] Cooke[No. 117. Tariff II b, 18]) †2[38] 7[19] (Qr f. כָּלְּהֵן);—**1.** כֹּל חַכִּימֵי בָבֶל *the whole of* (=*all*) the wise men of B. 3[2.3.5], etc.; 6[2] כל־מלכותא *the whole of* the kingdom, v[4]; c. sf. *the whole of* them, 2[38] 7[19]. **2.** with a sg. noun, understood collectively, *every, any*, or with a neg. *none* (BH **1 b**): 3[29] דִּי כָל־עַם אֻמָּה וְלִשָּׁן that *every* people, nation, and language, etc., 6[8] מִן־כָּל־אֱלָהּ of *any* god, Ezr 6[12] כָּל־מֶלֶךְ וְעַם; כל אנש די *every man who*=*whoever*, Dn 3[10] 5[7] 6[13] Ezr 6[11]; Dn 2[10] כל מלך . . . לא שְׁאֵל *no* king hath asked . . . , v[35] 4[6] 6[5.24]; so כָּל־דִּי (=Heb. כָּל־אֲשֶׁר) *whoever* 6[8] Ezr 7[26], *whatever* v[23], בְּכָל־דִּי *wherever* Dn 2[38] (cf. אֲשֶׁר **4 b** γ). †**3.** emph. כֹּלָּא, used absolutely, as Heb. הַכֹּל (BH **2 b**): Dn 2[40] חָשֵׁל כֹּלָּא crushing *all things*, 4[9.18] וּמָזוֹן לְכֹלָּא־בֵהּ and food *for all* was in it, v[25] כֹּלָּא מְטָא *all* came upon N. (cf. הַכֹּל בָּא Jos 21[43]), Ezr 5[7] שְׁלָמָא כֹלָּא *all* peace (K § 83 d; cf. in Heb. כֻּלּוֹ etc., *after* their noun: BH **1 d** *a*).—For כָּל־קֳבֵל v. קֳבֵל.

† **כֵּן** **adv.** thus, as follows (BH כֵּן; 𝔗 כֵּן, Syr. ܟܢ);—usu. c. אֲמַר (אֲמַר, etc.; cf. Eg. Aram. CIS[ii. 149 A 1, B-C 3] RÉS[492 B 5]), Dn 2[24] וְכֵן אֲמַר־לֵהּ, v[25] 4[11] 6[7] 7[5.23] Ezr 5[3]; 6[2] וְכֵן־כְּתִיב בְּגַוַּהּ.

† **כְּנֵמָא** **adv.** accordingly, as follows (der. uncertain: Nö[GGA, 1884, 1021] Marti al. from כֵּן + indef. מָא, *so somewhat, ungefähr so:* v. older improb. view (*as we should say*, from כְּ and נֵאמַר=נֵימָא, cf. Talm. נֵימָא for נֵימַר) in Thes[652]): referring backwards, Ezr 6[13] כְּנֵמָא . . . עֲבַדוּ did *accordingly;* referring forwards, 4[8] . . . כְּתַבוּ כְנֵמָא wrote a letter . . . *as follows*, 5[4] (rd. c. 𝔊 אֲמַרוּ; אֲמַרְנָא from v[9], Mey[Entst. 25]), v[9.11].

† [כְּנַשׁ] **vb.** gather (𝔗 *id.;* OAram. Palm. כנש Lzb[298]; Syr. ܟܢܫ; v. also BH [כָּנַס]);—**Pe.** *Inf.* לְמִכְנַשׁ, sq. לְ acc. pers. Dn 3[2]. **Hithpa.** *Pt.* pl. מִתְכַּנְּשִׁין (were) *assembled* 3[3.27].

† [כְּנָת] **n.m.** associate (OAram. *id.*, Lzb[298] SAC[65]; S-C[86]; Syr. ܟܢܬܐ; Chr-Pal. [ܟܢܬܐ, ܟܢܬ] Schwally[Idiot. 46] Schulth[Lex. 95]; √ appar. כנה K § 56, a) β 2 M § 74 c; Buhl makes loan-wd. from As. *kinâtu, 'Genosse,'* but v. Dl[WB 338] Zim[M. p. 66*]);—*associate*, pl. sf. כְּנָוָתֵהּ Ezr 5[6], -תְהוֹן 4[9.17.23] 5[3] 6[6.13].

כסא (v. BH כִּסֵּא *throne*).

† **כָּרְסֵא** (K § 11. 4 b) α); 62) **n.m.**[Dn 7, 9 a] throne;—cstr. כ׳ Dn 5[20]; sf. כָּרְסְיֵהּ 7[9 b]; pl. abs. כָּרְסָוָן 7[9 a].

כַּשְׂדָּי v. **כסדי**.

† **כְּסַף** **n.m.**[Ezr 7, 17] silver (v. BH);—abs. כ׳ Ezr 7[15]+, כְּסַף Dn 2[32]; emph. כַּסְפָּא v[35]+;—**1.** as material Dn 2[32.35.45] 5[2.4.23] Ezr 5[14] 6[5]. **2.** as money or its equivalent Ezr 7[17], v[15.16.18.22].

כְּעַן, כְּעֶנֶת, כְּעֶת v. sub ענה.

† **כְּפַת** **vb.** bind (𝔗 *id.;* NH כָּפַת; Syr. ܟܦܬ *form knots*, ܟܦܬ *twist into a knot*, Ar. كَفَتَ *draw together*, As. [*kapâtu*] II. *bring together*);—**Peʿîl** *Pf.* 3 mpl. כְּפִתוּ (W[CG 224]) Dn 3[21] *they were bound.* **Pa.** *bind: Inf.* לְכַפָּתָה Dn 3[20] (לְ acc. pers.); *Pt. pass.* pl. מְכַפְּתִין *bound* v[23.24].

† [כְּרָא] **vb. Ithpe.** be distressed (cf. 𝔗 כְּרָא III. adj. *suffering*, כְּרִיוּתָא n. *id.* D[WB 197]; Syr. ܟܪܐ *be short, abridged*, ܟܪܝܐ ܠܝ *it grieved me;* ܟܘܪܗܢܐ *pain, grief;* cf. As. *kûru, pain;* also ܟܪܗ (der. spec.) *be ill*, Ar. كَرِهَ *dislike, shrink from*);—*Pf.* 3 ms. אֶתְכְּרִיַּת רוּחִי (K § 47. Beisp. 2) Dn 7[15].

† [כַּרְבְּלָא] **n.f.** prob. helmet, cap (> al. *mantle*, e.g. K § 62; v. Dr) (NH כַּרְבֹּלֶת *comb* of cock; so JAram. כַּרְבַּלְתָּא, Syr. ܟܪܒܠܬܐ; As. *karballatu, cap* Andr[M 67*], Muss-Arn[As. Dict. 436 a]; so SAC[JPhil. xxvi. 310 f.], cf. BH [כרבל]);—pl. sf. כַּרְבְּלָתְהוֹן Dn 3[21].

† [כָּרוֹז] **n.m.** herald (loan-word from Gk. κῆρυξ, κηρύσσειν (K § 64, 4 Krauss[ii. 296 f.]; Nö[GGA 1884, 1019] doubts); 𝔗 *id.*, Syr. ܟܪܘܙܐ (v. Brock), Chr-Pal. [ܟܪܘܙ] Schulth[Lex. 97]; cf. D § 37 ad fin., also K § 64, 4 Bev[Dn 3, 29] M § 89);—emph. כָּרוֹזָא Dn 3[4].

† [כְּרַז] **vb. denom. Haph.** make proclamation (poss. directly dependent on κηρύξ (D § 37, p. 146 (2nd ed. 183) K l. c. M 67*), but even then formed as denom.; cf. 𝔗 כְּרַז, NH כָּרַז, Syr. ܟܪܙ Af. Ethpe., so Chr-Pal. Schwally[Idiot. 46] Schulth[Lex. 97]);—*Pf.* 3 mpl. הַכְרִזוּ Dn 5[29], c. עַל pers. *concerning.*

כָּרְסֵא v. כּסא.

כרר (√of foll.; cf. BH כָּרַר, כִּכָּר **3**).

†[כַּכַּר] **n.** [**f.**] talent;—pl. abs. כַּכְּרִין Ezr 7^{22}.

†כַּשְׂדָּי **n. pr. gent. Chaldean** (v. BH כַּשְׂדִּים);—abs. כ׳ Dn 2^{10}; emph. כשדיא Dn 5^{30} Kt (Qr כַּשְׂדָּאָה), כסדיא Ezr 5^{12} Kt (Qr כַּסְדָּאָה); pl. abs. כַּשְׂדָּאִין 3^{8} 5^{11}, emph. כשדיא Kt, כַּשְׂדָּאֵי Qr, Dn 2$^{5.10}$ 4^{4} 5^{7};—**1.** *Chaldean* by race Dn 3^{8} 5^{30} Ezr 5^{12}. **2.** as learned, of the class of Magi (BH כ׳ **1 c**), Dn 2$^{5.10.10}$ 4^{4} 5$^{7.11}$.

†**כתב** **vb.** write (v. BH);—**Pe.** *Pf.* 3 ms. כ׳ Dn 6^{26} ל pers. + orat. rect., 7^{1} acc. rei; 3 mpl. כְּתַבוּ Ezr 4^{8} acc. אִגְּרָה; 1 pl. נִכְתּוּב 5^{10}, acc. rei; *Pt. act.* abs. fs. כָּתְבָה Dn 5^{5}, subj. יְדָא, fpl. כָּתְבָן v^{5}, subj. אֶצְבְּעָן. **Pe'îl** (W$^{CG\ 224}$) *Pf.* 3 ms. כְּדְנָה כְּתִיב Ezr 5^{7} *thus (it) was written*, so כֵּן כ׳ 6^{2}.

†כְּתָב **n.m.**$^{Dn\ 5,7}$ **writing**;—abs. כְּתָב Ezr 7^{22} (Baer כְּתָב, but v. K$^{§57\ ad\ fin.}$ Str); cstr. כ׳ 6^{18}; emph. כְּתָבָא Dn 5^{8}+, כְּתָבָה 5$^{7.15}$;—**1.** *writing, inscription* (on wall) Dn 5$^{7.8.15.16.17.24.25}$. **2. a.** *written decree* 6$^{9.10.11}$. **b.** *written requirement* Ezr 6^{18} 7^{22}.

†כְּתַל (K$^{§54,3\ a)\ c)\ and\ c)}$) **n.** [**m.**] **wall** (BH כֹּתֶל, √כתל);—cstr. כ׳ Dn 5^{5}; pl. emph. כֻּתְלַיָּא Ezr 5^{8}.

ל

ל **prep. to, for, in regard to, at, mark of accus.** (BA לְ, and general Aram.);—sf. לִי, לָךְ, לֵהּ לַהּ Dn 7$^{4.5}$ +; לַנָא †Ezr 4^{14}; לְכֹם †5$^{3.9}$ 7^{24} (so Eg. Aram. S-C$^{Pap.\ H\ 12,\ 14+}$), לְכוֹן †Dn 3^{4}; לְהוֹם †Je 10^{11}, לְהֹם †Ezr 5$^{3.4.9.10}$ 6^{9} (so Zinj., Cooke^{184}; Nab., ib.$^{Nos.\ 85,\ 91}$), לְהוֹן †Dn 2^{35} 3^{14} 6^{3} 7^{12} (v^{21} לְהֹן), Ezr 4^{20} 5^{2} (so Palm., Cooke$^{No.\ 110,\ Tariff\ ii.\ c.15\ (p.329)}$);—**1.** *to*, after vbs. of *saying, declaring, writing*, etc., Dn 2$^{4.5.7.19}$ 6$^{21.26}$, etc., *giving* 2$^{16.21}$ +, *offering* Ezr 6^{10}; of *going* (Aram. does not use אֶל), usu. to a *place*, 2^{17} לְבַיְתֵהּ אֲזַל, 3^{26} 4^{8} 6^{20} + oft., rarely to a *person* Ezr 5^{5}; = *towards* Dn 4^{31}; *into* 3$^{6.11}$ 6^{17} +; in address of decree or letter 3^{31} Ezr 5^{7} 7^{12}; to fall or come *to* Dn 4$^{16.18}$ 5^{17} Ezr 5^{7} 7^{20}, be confirmed *to* Dn 4^{23}. **2.** as mark of *accus.* (as oft. in Aram.; cf. in late Heb., BH **3**), Dn 2$^{10.12.14.24}$ + oft., Ezr 7^{25} . . . לכל (cf. אֵת Ju 3^{15} Is 8^{2}). **3.** to become or make *into* (BH **4**) Dn 2^{35} 4^{27}. **4. a.** *with reference to* Ezr 6^{8} לְמָא דִּי, 7^{14} (but rd. prob. וְעַל יְרוּשׁ׳). **b.** *belonging to* Dn 5^{23} לֵהּ, 7$^{4.6.7}$, and in דִּי לֵהּ = *his* 2^{20} +; c. אִיתַי Ezr 4^{16}; הַשְׁכַּח לְ to find (belonging) *to* 2^{35} 6$^{5.6.23}$ (cf. BH מָצָא לְ Dt 22^{14} +). **c.** as periphr. for the *genitive* (BH **5 c**) Dn 7^{1} בִּשְׁנַת חֲדָה לְ, Ezr 5^{13} 6$^{3.15.15}$; 5$^{8.11}$. **d.** of the *object* or *purpose, for* (BH **5 g**) Dn 4^{9} וּמָזוֹן לְכֹלָּא־בֵהּ v$^{27.27.33}$ 7^{22} Ezr 6$^{9.17}$ 7$^{19.23}$; *on behalf of* Ezr 6^{10b}. **e.** *according to* (BH **5 i**) Ezr 6^{17} לְמִנְיָן . . . *according to* the number of . . . **5.** of *time, at* Dn 4^{26} לִקְצָת . . . *at the end of* . . ., v^{31}; *to* Dn 2$^{4.44}$ + לְעָלְמִין. **6.** with an *inf.* (BH **7**), after such vbs. as *be able, think, need, agree, command, decree*, Dn 2$^{9.10.12.24}$ 3$^{13.16.19.32}$ 6$^{4.5.8.24}$ Ezr 4$^{21.22}$ 5^{3} + oft.; = *in order to* Dn 2$^{13.14}$ 3$^{2.20}$, *so as to* 5^{20}. With לָא = *not to be* . . . 6$^{9.16\ end}$ Ezr 6^{8}, v. לָא. Cf. the synopsis Lzb$^{300\ f.}$

לָא (לָה †Dn 4^{32}) **adv. not** (BH לֹא; Aram. of Têma, Eg., etc., לא; Nerab ל (Lzb^{301} Cook$^{Gl.\ 67}$); 𝔗 לָא; Syr. ܠܐ);—*not* Je 10^{11} Dn 2$^{5.9.10}$, etc.; before a ptcp. (so rarely in BH, **1 b** *c*), 2$^{27.43}$ 3^{16} 4$^{4.6.15}$ +, so v^{32} וְכָל־דָּאְרֵי אַרְעָא כְּלָה חֲשִׁיבִין are *as men not accounted of* (so Bev Behrm Marti, cf. Is 53^{3} 𝔗 בסירין ולא חשיבין; > most 'accounted *as nothing*,' for which no analogy, yet cf. ψ 39^{6} 𝔗); sq. אִיתַי, v. אִיתַי. With inf. and לְ Dn 6^{9} דִּי לָא לְהַשְׁנָיָה which *it is not* to alter = which *is not to be* altered (cf. v^{16}), Ezr 6^{8} (K^{§67,1} Dr^{§202,2}; cf. Is 35^{6} 𝔗, D$^{Aram.\ Dialektproben,\ p.1}$). With interr. הֲלָא †Dn 3^{24} 4^{27} 6^{13}.

לאך (√of foll.; BH מַלְאָךְ, לאך).

†[מַלְאַךְ] **n.m. angel** (𝔗 Syr.);—sf. מַלְאֲכֵהּ Dn 3^{28} 6^{23}.

†לְבַב **n.m.**$^{Dn\ 4,\ 13}$ **heart** (v. BH; so Eg. Aram. S-C$^{B\ 12+}$);—cstr. ל׳ Dn 4^{13} 7^{4}; sf. לִבְבָךְ 2^{30} 5^{22}, -בֵהּ 4^{13} 5$^{20.21}$.

†[לֵב] **n.** [**m.**] **id.** (BH *id.*; so 𝔗 Syr.; Eg. Aram., Lzb^{301} = Cooke$^{76\ A\ 6}$);—sf. לִבִּי Dn 7^{28}.

†[לְבִשׁ] **vb. be clothed** (v. BH);—**Pe.** *Impf.* acc. אַרְגְּוָנָא: 3 ms. יִלְבַּשׁ Dn 5^{7}, 2 ms. תִּלְבַּשׁ v^{16}. **Haph.** *Pf.* 3 mpl. הַלְבִּשׁוּ v^{29} *clothe* one (ל) with (acc.).

†[לְבוּשׁ] **n.m. garment** (BH *id.*);—sf. לְבוּשֵׁהּ Dn 7^{9}; pl. sf. לְבוּשֵׁיהוֹן 3^{21}.

לָה v. לָא.

†I. [לָהֵן] **conj.** therefore (BH לָהֵן †Ru $1^{13.13}$, Aram. of Têma להן CIS$^{\text{ii. 113}}$ = Cooke^{195}), Dn $2^{6.9}4^{24}$(Lambert$^{\text{RÉJ. 1904. 273}}$ denies I. לָהֵן, taking BAram. always as = לָהֵן).

†II. לָהֵן **conj.** **except, but** (from לָא and הֵן 'not if' (cf. Heb. אם לא Gn 24^{38}); so Nab. and Eg. Aram. להן Cooke$^{217. 219. 241}$ S-C$^{\text{Pap. C 6, 7+}}$; *lâinnî, however* Socin$^{\text{Arab. Dial. v. Marokko 44, Anm. 103}}$; 𝔗 אֱלָהֵין Gn $32^{29}43^{3}$ al.);—**1.** after a neg. (= BH כִּי אִם, q.v.): **a.** *except* Dn 2^{11} 3^{28} $6^{6.8}$. **b.** *but* (Germ. *sondern*) Dn 2^{30}. **2.** without a neg.: *however, but* Ezr 5^{12}.

†[לֵוָי] **n. gent.** **Levite** (BH לֵוִי);—pl. emph. לויא Kt, לֵוָיֵא Qr (K §§ 61. 6); 52. d), Ezr $6^{16.18}$ $7^{13.24}$ (all + priests).

†לְוָת **prep.** **to, at, beside** (der. uncertain; v. K$^{128\text{ n.}}$; perhaps akin to לָוָה ,לְוִי, ܠܘܐ *join;* 𝔗 לְוָת, Syr. ܠܘܬ *to*), c. מִן, Ezr 4^{12} the Jews which came up מִן־לְוָתָךְ *from thee* (*de chez toi;* cf. ܡܢ ܠܘܬ, מִלְּוָת, e.g. Ex $8^{8}9^{33}$ 𝔖𝔗 = Heb. מֵעִם).

†לְחֶם (K§ 54. 3. 7) **n.m.** **feast** (𝔗 Syr. *bread,* so BH, q.v. √ II. לחם);—abs. עֲבַד לְ׳ Dn 5^{1} *made a feast.*

†[לְחֵנָה] **n.f.** **concubine** (𝔗 לְחֵינְתָא; Fl Levy NHWB ii. 534 f. cp. Ar. لَخْنَاءُ, indelicate epithet for woman; Batten$^{\text{Ezr 2. 65}}$ cp. Ar. لَحْن *note, tune, song;* still otherwise Wetzst$^{\text{De. HL u. Koh. 454}}$);—pl. sf. לְחֵנָתָךְ Dn 5^{23}, ־הּ v$^{2.3}$.

†[לֵילְיָא] **n.[m.]** **night** (v. BH לַיְלָה);—emph. לֵילְיָא Dn 2^{19} 5^{30} $7^{2.7.13}$.

†לִשָּׁן **n.m.**$^{\text{Dn 3, 7}}$ **tongue** (𝔗 Syr.; v. BH לָשׁוֹן, √לשן);—*tongue = language,* fig. for *people:* abs. עַם אֻמָּה וְלִ׳ Dn 3^{29}; pl. emph. עַ׳ אֻ׳ וְלִשָּׁנַיָּא v$^{4.7.31}$ 5^{19} 6^{26} 7^{14} (cf. BH לָשׁוֹן **2,** Is 66^{18}).

מ

מָא v. מָה.

†מְאָה **n.f.** **hundred** (v. BH);—abs. מ׳ after noun enum., Ezr 6^{17} $7^{22.22.22.22}$, so אַרְבַּע מ׳ 6^{17}, מ׳ וְעֶשְׂרִין Dn 6^{1}, and du. מָאתַיִן Ezr 6^{17}.

מֹאזַנְיָא v. אזן. מֵאמַר v. אמר.

†[מָאן] **n.m.**$^{\text{Ezr 7, 19}}$ **vessel, utensil** (𝔗 מָ(א)ן, Syr. ܡܐܢܐ, so Chr-Pal., Schulth$^{\text{Lex. 106}}$; OAram. מאן, Ph. מנם; poss. √אנה, v. BH II. אנה, cf. Lag$^{\text{BN 183}}$ Buhl);—pl., *vessels* of temple at Jerus.: emph. מָאנַיָּא Ezr $5^{14.15}$ 7^{19} Dn 5^{23}; cstr. מָאנֵי v$^{2.3}$ Ezr 6^{5}.

מְגִלָּה v. גלל.

†[מְגַר] **vb.** **Pa.** **overthrow** (𝔗, Syr. (Lexx.); v. BH (late, rare));—*Impf.* 3 ms. יְמַגַּר כָּל־מֶלֶךְ Ezr 6^{12} (of God).

[מַדְבַּח] v. דבח. מִדָּה v. מנ׳.

[מְדוֹר] v. דור.

†מָדַי **n.pr. gent. et terr.** **Medes, Media** (BH *id.*);—**1.** **gent.** Dn 5^{28} $6^{9.13.16}$. **2.** **terr.** Ezr 6^{2}.

מדיא Kt, מָדָאָה Qr (K § 61. 6) **n. gent.** **Mede**;—Dn 6^{1}.

[מְדִינָה] v. דין. [מְדָר] v. דור.

†מָה (מָא †Ezr 6^{8}) **pron. interr.** and **indef.** **what?** (BH מָה; Nab. מה; Zinj. מ; 𝔗 מא; Syr. ܡܢܐ; Ar. مَا: cf. W$^{\text{CG 124 f.}}$);—**1.** *what?* Dn 4^{32} מה עבדת. **2.** *whatever, what* (cf. BH **1 b** end) Dn 2^{22} ידע מה בחשוכא knoweth *what* is in darkness, Ezr 6^{9}: so מָה דִּי (cf. דִּי **1 b**: so Nab.; Palm. מא די, מדי, Lzb^{306} Cooke$^{320, 332}$) Dn $2^{28.29.29.45}$ Ezr 6^{8} למא די תעבדון with regard to *what* ye shall do, 7^{18} (= *whatsoever*). **3.** with prefixes: **a.** כְּמָה *how!* Dn $3^{33.33}$. **b.** לְמָה *why?* (cf. BH לָמָּה) Ezr 4^{22} be not slack herein: *why* should damage grow, etc., virtually = *lest* damage grow (𝔊 μή ποτε), 7^{23} די למה להוא קצף *for why should there be* wrath? = *lest* [𝔊 μή ποτε] *there be* wrath (cf. 𝔗 דִּילְמָא, Syr. ܕܠܡܐ *lest:* and v. מָה **4 d** *b,* p. 554^{a}). **c.** על־מה *wherefore?* Dn 2^{15}.

†מוֹת **n.[m.]** **death** (𝔗 Syr.; v. BH);—abs. Ezr 7^{26}.

מָזוֹן v. זון.

†[מְחָא] **vb.** **smite** (v. BH II. מָחָה);—**Pe.** *Pf.* 3 fs. מְחָת, לְ rei, Dn $2^{34.35}$ (+ עַל). **Pa.** *Impf.* 3 ms. יְמַחֵא בִידֵהּ 4^{32}, i.e. hinder him (cf. Ec 8^{4} 𝔗; D$^{\text{Aram. Dialektproben. p. 5}}$; Talm.: Levy$^{\text{NHWB s.v.}}$). **Hithpa.** *Impf.* 3 ms. יִתְמְחֵא Ezr 6^{11} *let him be smitten* (nailed) עֲלֹהִי.

[מַחְלְקָה] v. חלק.

†מְטָא, מְטָה **vb. reach, attain** (𝔗 *id*, Syr. ܡܛܐ, cf Chr-Pal. Schulth[Lex 108], Eth መጠወ: Ar أَنْطَى (for أَمْطَى) No[ZMG xl (1886) 736], distinct from BH מָצָא, etc, q v),—**Pe.** *Pf* 3 ms. מְטָא Dn 4[25], ־ָה 7[13.22], 3 fs. מְטָת 4[19], מְטָת v[21] Qr (Kt, erron, מטית K § 47 Beisp. 1) a)), 3 mpl מטו 6[25], *Impf* 3 ms. יִמְטֵא 4[8 17],—**1. a.** *reach, come to* Dn 6[25] (ל loc), *come* unto, as far as 7[13] (עַד pers); abs. *arrive* 7[22] (of time; 𝔊 ἐδόθη, v. Nes[MM 41] who cp Ar عَطَى IV *give*) **b.** *reach, extend*, ל loc. 4[8 17 19] **2.** c. עַל pers. *come upon, befall* 4[21 25]

†מִישָׁאֵל **n pr.m.** (=BH *id*, **2**, sub מִי);—Dn 2[17].

מֵישַׁךְ **n.pr.m.** (BH *id*),—Dn 2[49] 3[12] + 11 t 3

†[מְלָא] **vb** fill (v. BH);—**Pe.** *Pf* 3 fs מלאת Dn 2[35] (c acc) **Hithpe.** *Pf* 3 ms התמלי חֱמָא 3[19] *was filled with rage.*

[מַלְאַךְ] v לאך   מִלָּה v. מלל

†מְלַח **n.m.** salt (v BH);—מ׳ abs Ezr 6[9] 7[22] (both for sacrifices), cstr. 4[14].

†[מְלַח] **vb. denom.** c acc. cogn, eat salt,—**Pe.** *Pf* 1 pl מְלַחְנָא Ezr 4[14] *we have eaten the salt of the palace* (so most), i.e have assumed obligations of loyalty, cf. M[69 *] K[§ 71 2] (and Syr ܐܬܡܠܚ *be intimate with* PS[2134]), Str (after Nes[MM 30 f]) thinks n c. sf: *our salt is the salt of the palace.*

I מלך (√of following, v. BH)

מֶלֶךְ[178] **n.m. king** (general Sem., v. BH),—מ׳ abs Dn 2[10] + 2 t., cstr 4[34] + 6 t; usu. emph מַלְכָּא Ezr 4[8] + 154 t, ־ָה Dn 2[11]; pl. מַלְכִין Ezr 4[13] + 9 t, ־ִים— 4[17] (Hebraism, Be-Ry M[41 *]); emph. מַלְכַיָּא Dn 2[44] + 2 t.,—*king* Dn 2[4.5] + 132 t Dn, Ezr 4[8 11] + 42 t Ezr (מֶלֶךְ מַלְכַיָּא of Neb. Dn 2[37], of Artax Ezr 7[12] [cf. Cooke[71 3], of Xerxes], מַלְכִין Dn 7[17] = kingdoms, cf מַלְכוּ v[23])

†[מַלְכָּה] **n.f** queen, — emph. מַלְכְּתָא Dn 5[10 10]

†מַלְכוּ **n.f. royalty, reign, kingdom**;—abs מ׳ Dn 2[39] +, cstr מַלְכוּת Ezr 4[24] +; emph ־תָא Dn 2[37] +, ־תָה 2[44], sf ־תִי 4[15] +, ־תֵהּ 3[33] +, ־תָךְ 4[23] +; pl cstr מַלְכְוָת 7[27], emph ־וָתָא 2[44] 7[23];—**1.** *royalty, kingship, kingly authority* Dn 4[23.28.33]; כָּרְסֵא מ׳ 5[20]. בֵּית מ׳ v[27], הֵיכַל מ׳ v[26], **2.** organized (world-) kingdom. 2[39 39.40.41 42 44] 7[23 23.24 27], מ׳ אֲנָשָׁא 4[14 22.29] 5[21]; of specif. kings 2[37] 5[18 28] 6[1]; of God 3[33] 7[27] (both מ׳ עָלַם), 2[44.44] 3[33] 4[31] 6[27] 7[27], of Mess. 7[14 14], of saints 7[18.18.22.27]. **3.** *realm* (territorial) 4[15.33 b] 5[7 11 16.29] 6[2.2.4 8.27] Ezr 7[13.23], meton 6[4] = administration of realm. **4.** *reign*, time of reigning Dn 5[26] 6[29 29] Ezr 4[24] 6[15].

II מלך (√of foll.; As. *malâku, counsel, advise*; 𝔗 מְלַךְ, Syr ܡܠܟ, Chr-Pal. ܡܠܟ Schulth[112], BH II. [מָלַךְ] †Ne 5[7] as loan-word).

†[מְלַךְ] **n.m. counsel, advice**;—sf. מלכי Dn 4[24] let *my counsel* be acceptable to thee.

†[מַלִּל] **vb. Pa. speak, say** (so 𝔗 Syr.; cf BH מלל **Pi.** (rare)),—*Pf* 3 ms. מַלִּל Dn 6[22] *he spoke* with (עִם pers); acc. of words, *Impf.* 3 ms יְמַלִּל 7[25] (c. לְצַד of God), so *Pt. act.* מְמַלִּל v[8] (van d. H. here מְמַלֵּל), v[20], f. מְמַלְּלָא (K § 15 d) v[11].

†מִלָּה **n.f. word, thing**,—abs מ׳ Dn 2[5] +, cstr מִלַּת v[10] +; emph. מִלְּתָא v[5] +, ־ָא v[8] +; pl. abs. מִלִּין 7[1 25], cstr. מִלֵּי 5[10], emph מִלַּיָּא 7[11 16],—**1.** *word, utterance* Dn 4[28] 6[15], pl 5[10] 7[11 28]; in bad sense, מ׳ כדבה ושחיתה 2[9], מִלַּיָּא רַבְרְבָתָא 7[11] (cf רַבְרְבָן alone v[8 20]), *word* of God's judgment 4[30]; = *command* 2[5.8] 3[22.28] 6[13]. **2.** *thing, affair, matter*. 2[10 10.11 15 17 23] 5[15.26] 7[24.28], pl. v[1 16].

†מַן (so Gi, with most MSS., supported by Syr. ܡܰܢ, Ar. مَنْ; v K § 22.1), מָן (Baer v. on Dn 3[6]), **interr pron. who?** (OAram. Nab Palm. מן (Lzb[312] Cooke[138]), 𝔗 מַן, Syr. ܡܰܢ, Eth. መኑ: Ar. مَنْ W[CG 123]: BH מִי);—**1.** *who?* Ezr 5[3 9]; strengthened by הוּא, Dn 3[15] וּמַן־הוּא אֱלָהּ דִּי *who is* the God who...? (cf. Syr ܡܰܢܘ contr. from ܡܰܢ ܗܘ, and מַנּוּ in the Syriacizing 𝔗 to Pr: also BH מִי הוּא, הוּא **4 b β**), so in the pl Ezr 5[4] מַן־אִנּוּן שְׁמָהָת *what* (lit. *who* · cf מִי **1 a**, and Gn 32[28] Ex 3[13] 𝔗) are the names of...? **2.** מַן־דִּי *whosoever* (lit *who is there that*...? v. BH מִי **g**) Dn 3[6 11] מַן־דִּי לָא יִפֵּל, 4[14] וּלְמַן דִּי יִצְבֵּא יִתְּנִנַּהּ to *whomsoever* he willeth, he giveth it, v[22.29] 5[21] (so Nab מן די, Cooke[241 323 ff]; 𝔗 מַן דְּ; Syr. ܡܰܢ ܕ; cf Eg. Aram. S-C[Pap K 7.12] ולמן זי צבית תנתן).

מִן **prep. from, out of, by, by reason of, at, more than** (BH and general Aram. *id*),—rarely assimilated, as in Heb, v. Dn 6[5] מִצַּד, Ezr 5[11] 6[14], sf. מִנִּי, מִנָּךְ, 3 m מִנֵּהּ, f מִנַּהּ †Dn

2^{42} 7^{24}; 3 mpl. מִנְּהוֹן (so Palm.[Tariff II. a 34]; Nab. Eg. Aram. מנהם, Cooke[No. 89. 6], S-C[Pap. A 10]) †Dn $2^{33.33.41.41.42.42}$ Kt (Qr each time f. מִנְּהֵן), $6^{3.3}$;—**1.** of place: **a.** *from*, Dn $4^{10.11.23}$ 7^{4}+, מִן תַּמָּה †Ezr 6^{6}; fig. *on the side* or *part of* (cf. BH **1 c**) Dn 6^{5} מִצַּד מַלְכוּתָא. **b.** *out of*, Dn $3^{15.26}$ 5^{2} 7^{3}, etc. **c.** (coming) *from* 2^{35}, *away from*, 2^{45} $4^{11.22.28}$ Je 10^{11}. **d.** to ask or exact *of* a person, Dn $2^{16.49}$+; Ezr 7^{26}; to deliver *from* Dn 6^{21}. **2. a.** of the *source* (BH **2 b**), as to be fed *from* Dn 4^{9}; or *author* (*ib.* **d**), מִנִּי שִׂים טְעֵם = *by* me is a decree made, Dn 3^{29} 4^{3} (6^{27} מִן־קֳדָמַי), Ezr 4^{19}+, cf. 5^{17}; מִנִּי = *on my part* Dn $2^{5.8}$ (v. אַזְדָּא). **b.** of the *immediate cause, as a result of, by*, Dn 4^{22} (= ב $v^{12.20}$), v^{30} 5^{21}: so with a vb. of *fearing* 5^{19}. **c.** of the *remoter cause, by reason of* (BH **2 f**), Dn 5^{19} מִן־רְבוּתָא, 7^{11}; so מִן־דִּי, v. דִּי **3.** **d.** of the *norm* (cf. BH **2 g**) = *at, according to*, Ezr 6^{14} מִן־טַעַם אֱלָהּ יִשׂ׳ *at the decree* of, etc., 7^{23}; Dn 2^{8} מִן־יַצִּיב *according to* certainty, v^{47} מִן־קְשֹׁט. **3.** partitively (BH **3**), Dn 6^{3} חַד מִנְּהוֹן, $7^{8.16}$; 2^{25} 5^{13}; (some) *of* 2^{41} מִנְּהוֹן . . . מִנְּהוֹן; מִן־נִצְבְּתָא *some . . . others* of them $2^{33.41.42a}$; so v^{42b} מִנַּהּ . . . מִן־קְצָת. **4.** of time, *from*, Dn 2^{20} (מִן . . . וְעַד), Ezr $4^{15.19}$; v. also אֱדַיִן and דִּי **4.** **5.** in *comparisons*, different *from* Dn $7^{3.7.19.23.24}$, *beyond, more than* $2^{30.39}$ 6^{30} $7^{20\ end}$; 4^{13} לִבְבֵהּ מִן־אֲנָשָׁא יְשַׁנּוֹן let his heart be changed *away from* man's (BH **7 b** *b*; Is 52^{14}). **6.** cpds.:—v. תְּחוֹת, [קַדְמָה], קֳדָם, לְוָת.

מְנֵא v. מנה.

†מִדָּה, מִנְדָּה (?) **n.f.** tribute (As. loan-word, cf. BH II. [מִדָּה]);—abs. מִנ׳ Ezr 4^{13} 7^{24}+ 4^{20} Baer (van d. H. Gi Str מִדָּה); cstr. מִדַּת 6^{8}.

מַנְדַּע v. ידע.

†מְנָה **vb.** number, reckon (v. BH);—**Pe.** *Pf.* 3 ms. מ׳ Dn 5^{26} God *has numbered* (the days of) thy kingdom (acc.; i.e. put an end to it);—מְנֵא v. infr. **Pa.** *appoint*, acc. pers.: *Pf.* 3 ms. מַנִּי Dn 2^{24} (+Inf.), v^{49} (ל pers. + עַל rei); 2 ms. מַנִּיתָ 3^{12} (עַל rei); *Imv.* ms. מַנִּי (K[§ 47, 3. c]) Ezr 7^{25}.

†מְנֵא **n.[m.]** maneh, mina, a weight (v. BH; OAram. מנה SAC[75] Lzb[313]);—abs. Dn $5^{25.25.26}$, v. ClGann[JAs Juillet-Août, 1886, 36 ff.] Nö[ZA i. 414 f.] Dr al.; its connexion in Dn with מְנָה is due to word-play; v. also תְּקֵל, פְּרֵס.

†מִנְיָן **n.[m.]** number;—cstr. מ׳ Ezr 6^{17}.

†מִנְחָה **n.f.** gift, offering (BH *id.*, √מנח);—**1.** *oblation*, to God's representative, abs. מ׳ Dn 2^{46}. **2.** techn. *meal-offering*, pl. sf. מִנְחָתְהוֹן Ezr 7^{17}.

מִנְיָן v. מנה.

†[מְעָא] **n.[m.]** **pl.** external belly (v. BH [מֵעָה] **6**);—sf. מְעוֹהִי Dn 2^{32} (of image in vision).

מַעֲבַד v. עבד. מְעוֹהִי v. [מְעָא].

מֵעָל v. II. עלל.

†מָרֵא **n.m.** lord (𝔗 מָר, c. מָרֵי; Syr. ܡܳܪܳܐ, e. ܡܳܪܝ, ܡܳܪܰܢ, Eg. Aram. מרא (RÉS[1. 361]); Chr-Pal. ܡܪܐ, etc., Schulth[Lex. 115]; OAram. Nab. Palm. מר(א) (Lzb[316]); cf. n.pr. dei מרנא (μαρνα), god of Gaza, SAC[77]; also Ar. مَرْءٌ *man*, Sab. מרא *man, lord* Hom[Chr 127; AA 293] RÉS[1. 454, 2]);—*lord*: of God, cstr. מ׳ שְׁמַיָּא Dn 5^{23}, מָרֵא מַלְכִין 2^{47}; of king, sf. מָרְאִי Kt (as Nab., SAC[l. c.]; K[§ 58, 1]), Qr מָרִי (as Palm., SAC[l. c.]) $4^{16.21}$.

†מְרַד **n.[m.]** rebellion (v. BH);—abs. מ׳ Ezr 4^{19}.

†[מָרָד K[§ 59 d]] **adj.** rebellious;—of city, f. abs. מָרָדָא Ezr 4^{15}, emph. מָרָדְתָּא (K[ib.]) v^{12}.

מָרֵה v. מָרֵא.

†[מְרַט] **vb.** pluck (v. BH);—**Pe'il** *Pf.* 3 mpl. מְרִיטוּ Dn 7^{4} *were plucked off* (wings).

†מֹשֶׁה **n.pr.m.** Moses (BH *id.*);—סְפַר מ׳ Ezr 6^{18}.

†מְשַׁח **n.[m.]** oil (v. BH);—abs. Ezr 6^{9} 7^{22}.

[מִשְׁכַּב] v. שכב. [מִשְׁכַּן] v. שכן.

[מַשְׁרוֹקִית] v. שרק. [מִשְׁתֵּה] v. שתה.

[מַתְּנָא] v. נתן.

נ

נבא (√of foll.; v. BH *id.*, but esp. Bewer[Am. J. Sem. Lang., Jan. 1902] who cp. As. *nabû, tear away, lead forcibly*, hence proph. as (fig.) *carried away* by divine frenzy, ecstasy, cf. 1 S $10^{6.10}$ $19^{20.24}$).

†[נְבִיא] **n.m.** prophet (Hebraism? also 𝔗 Syr.; v. BH);—emph. נְבִיאָה Kt, נְבִיָּא Ezr 5^{1} 6^{14}; pl. emph. נְבִיאַיָּא $5^{1.2}$.

†[נְבוּאָה] **n.f.** **prophesying**;—cstr. נְבוּאַת Ezr 6^{14}.

נְבוּכַדְנֶצַּר $_{31}$ **n.pr.m.** (=BH נְבוּכַדְרֶאצַּר-, etc.);—Dn 2^{28}+23 t. Dn, Ezr $5^{12.14}$ 6^{5}; נְבֻכַ׳ Dn 3^{3}+3 t. Dn.

†נְבִזְבָּה **n.f.** **reward** (so 𝔗 (rare); prob. Pers. loan-word, Haug[Ew. Jahrb. 1853, 160] prop. OP *nibağrâ, presentation; but perh. crpt., v. M[71*]);—abs. נ׳ Dn 2^{6}; pl. sf. נְבִזְבְּיָתָךְ (al. נְבָזְ׳, נְבִזְ׳) 5^{17}.

†נֶבְרַשְׁתָּא **n.f. emph.** **the candlestick** (𝔗 *id.*, Syr. ܢܒܪܫܬܐ, NH נִבְרֶשֶׁת; Ar. نِبْرَاس is loan-word from Aram. Frä[95]; prob. foreign word K[§62] Fra[95] Bev al.; ? As., cf. Ba[ZA ii. 117]);—Dn 5^{5}.

†[נְגַד] **vb.** **stream, flow** (𝔗 נְגַד, Syr. ܢܓܕ *draw along, lead*, 𝔗 also intrans. *move along* Is 30^{24}, *flow* Dt $33^{13.22}$, נַגְדִּין *streams* Is 44^{4}+);—**Pe.** *Pt.* Dn 7^{10} נְהַר דִּי נוּר נָגֵד וְנָפֵק מִן־קֳדָמוֹהִי.

‡†נֶגֶד **prep.** **in front of, facing** (=BH, v. √ p. 616ᵇ; not elsewhere known in Aram.), Dn 6^{11} נגד ירושלם.

†[נְגַהּ] **n.[f.]** **brightness, daylight** (𝔗 Syr.; BH *id.*);—emph. נָגְהָא (K[§54 c), 1]) Dn 6^{20}.

†[נְדַב] **vb. Hithpa.** **volunteer, offer freely** (𝔗; BH נָדַב);—*Pf.* 3 mpl. הִתְנַדַּבוּ Ezr 7^{15}; *Inf.* הִתְנַדָּבוּת v[16]; *Pt.* מִתְנַדַּב v[13]; pl. מִתְנַדְּבִין v[16];—**1.** *volunteer*, sq. inf., Ezr 7^{13}. **2.** *give*, or *offer freely*, v[15], acc. rei + לְ of God; v[16], c. לְ of temple; *freewill gift* (inf., prop. *freewill giving*) v[16].

†נִדְבָּךְ **n.m.** **row or layer, course** (𝔗 NH *id.*; NH also מִדְבָּךְ *id.* (Levy[NHWB iii. 23]), cf. مِدْمَاك as loan-word Frä[12]; borrowed from As. *nadbaku, mountain-slope* acc. to Dl[Pr 150] (cf. Ba[ZA ii. 116 f.] Hpt[GN 1883, 96; BAS i. 8. 15]), but mng. not very suitable Nö[ZMG xl (1886), 733] Mey[Entst. 46]);—abs. נ׳ Ezr 6^{4}, pl. נִדְבָּכִין v[4].

†[נְדַד] **vb.** **flee** (v. BH I. נדד);—**Pe.** *Pf.* 3 fs. שִׁנְתֵּהּ נַדַּת עֲלוֹהִי (K[§46. Beisp. a)]) Dn 6^{19}.

†נִדְנֶה (Mas Baer) **n.[m.]** **sheath** (𝔗 נִדְנָא, לְדַן; v. BH (late) נָדָן, Pers. loan-word);—רוּחִי . . . בְּנ׳ Dn 7^{15} *my spirit in* (its) *sheath*, i.e. my body; < נִדְנָה emph., or sf. נִדְנַהּ (K[§54. 3. 8)]); or (Nö[GGA. 1884, 1022] Bev) נִדְנַהּ; but expression at best strange; rd. prob. בְּגִין דְּנָה *on account of this* (בְּגִין as 𝔗[J]; D[§47. 3 (2nd ed. 47. 10)]), M[72*] cf. Buhl Dr.

†נְהַר $_{14}$ **n.m.**[Dn 7, 10] **river** (v. BH I. נהר);—abs. נ׳ Dn 7^{10}; emph. נַהֲרָה Ezr 4^{10}+, ־ָא 4^{16};—*river*, usu. of Euphr., in phr. עֲבַר נ׳ Ezr $4^{10.11.16}$+ 10 t. Ezr; נ׳ דִּי־נוּר Dn 7^{10} *a river of fire*, in vision.

†[נְהוֹר, נְהִיר] **n.m.** **light** (𝔗 נְהוֹרָא, Syr. ܢܘܗܪܐ; v. BH II. נהר);—emph. נהירא Kt, < נְהוֹרָא Qr (cf. 𝔗 Syr.; Nö[LCB 1896, 703]) Dn 2^{22}.

†נַהִירוּ (K[§§ 16, 5; 61, 4]) **n.f.** **illumination, insight** (Syr. *id.*);—abs. Dn $5^{11.14}$ (both + שָׂכְלְתָנוּ, חָכְמָה).

†[נוּד] **vb.** **flee** (𝔗 Syr.; cf. [נְדַד] supra and BH נוּד **1 a**);—**Pe.** *Impf.* 3 fs. תְּנֻד מִן Dn 4^{11}.

†נְוָלִי, נְוָלוּ (K[§61. 4. 5]) **n.f.** **refuse-heap** (𝔗 נְוָלִי *dung-heap*; perh. loan-word fr. As. *namâlu* (*nawâlu*), *ruin*, Jen[KB vi. 363]);—נְוָלוּ Ezr 6^{11}, נְוָלִי Dn 2^{5} 3^{29}.

נוּר $_{17}$ **n.f.**[Dn 3, 6] **et m.**[7, 9] **fire** (𝔗 Syr.; v. √ נור BH);—abs. נ׳ Dn 3^{27} $7^{9.9.10}$; emph. נוּרָא 3^{6}+12 t. 3.

†[נְזִק] **vb.** **suffer injury** (𝔗 *id.*; As. *nazâḳu*, *injure*; on combin. with Ar. نقص *impair*, v. Ba[ES 51] Frä[BAS iii. 81]);—**Pe.** *Pt.* נָזִק Dn 6^{3}. **Haph.** *injure*: *Impf.* 3 fs. תְּהַנְזִק (K[§33. 2]) Ezr 4^{13} (acc. pers.). *Pt. act.* f. cstr. מְהַנְזְקַת מַלְכִין v[15]; *Inf. cstr.* לְהַנְזָקַת מ׳ v[22] (K[ib. d)]; M[§48 c] ־קָת).

†נְחָשׁ **n.m.** **copper, bronze** (𝔗 Syr.; BH נְחֹשֶׁת, נְחוּשָׁה, √ III. נחשׁ);—as material: abs. נ׳ Dn 2^{32} $4^{12.20}$ 7^{19}; emph. נְחָשָׁא $2^{35.39.45}$ $5^{4.23}$.

†[נְחִת] **vb.** **descend** (𝔗 Syr.; v. BH (poet., and late));—**Pe.** *Pt.* נָחִת Dn $4^{10.20}$ (both מִן־שְׁמַיָּא). **Haph.** *deposit*, ב loc.: *Impf.* 2 ms. תַּחֵת (K[§42, b)]) Ezr 6^{5} (Gu[Hpt] reads 3 mpl.); *Imv.* ms. אֲחֵת (K[§15 d)]) 5^{15} (acc. rei); *Pt. pass.* pl. מְהַחֲתִין 6^{1} (were) *deposited*. **Hoph.** (W[CG 225]) *be deposed*: *Pf.* 3 ms. הָנְחַת Dn 5^{20} (מִן־כָּרְסֵא).

†[נְטַל] **vb.** **lift** (𝔗 Syr.; BH (rare));—**Pe.** *Pf.* 1 s. עַיְנַי לִשְׁמַיָּא נִטְלֵת Dn 4^{31} (As. *naṭâlu* = *look*). **Pe'îl** (W[CG 224]) *be lifted*: *Pf.* 3 fs. נְטִילַת מִן־אַרְעָא 7^{4}.

†[נְטַר] **vb.** **keep** (𝔗 Syr.; v. BH I. נצר, and (rarely) נָטַר);—**Pe.** *Pf.* 1 s. מִלְּתָא בְּלִבִּי נִטְרֵת Dn 7^{28}.

†[נִיחוֹחַ] **n.[m.]** **soothing, tranquillizing** (prob. Hebraism, v. BH *id.*, √ נוּחַ (√ also 𝔗 Syr.));—pl. נִיח(ו)חִין Ezr 6^{10} Dn 2^{46} i.e. *soothing* offerings.

†[נְכַס] **n.[m.]**, pl. נִכְסִין riches, property (𝔗 Syr.; Eg. Aram. S-C[E4+]; BH (late));—עֲנָשׁ נ׳ Ezr 7[26] *confiscation of property;* cstr. נִכְסֵי 6[8].

†נְמַר **n.** [m.] leopard (v. BH);—abs. Dn 7[6].

†[נְסַח] **vb.** pull away (𝔗; v. BH);—**Hithpe.** *be pulled away: Impf.* 3 ms. יִתְנְסַח Ezr 6[11] (מִן).

†נְסַךְ **vb.** pour out (v. BH I. נָסַךְ);—**Pa.** (more gen.): *Inf.* לְנַסָּכָה לֵהּ Dn 2[46] *to offer in sacrifice to him,* c. acc. מִנְחָה וְנִיחֹחִין.

†[נְסַךְ] **n.** [m.] drink-offering (𝔗 Syr.; cf. BH);—pl. sf. נִסְכֵּיהוֹן Ezr 7[17] (+ מִנְחָתְהוֹן, etc.).

נסק v. סלק.

†נְפַל **vb.** fall (v. BH);—**Pe.** *Pf.* 3 ms. נ׳ Dn 2[46]; נְפַל 4[28]; 3 mpl. נְפַלוּ 3[23] + 7[20] Kt (Qr 3 fpl. נְפַלָה, K[§ 23, 2]); *Impf.* 3 ms. יִפֵּל (K[§ 42]) Dn 3[6]+; 2 mpl. תִּפְּלוּן 3[5.15]; *Pt.* pl. נָפְלִין 3[7];—**1.** *fall,* עַל־אַנְפּוֹהִי Dn 2[46]; *fall down* and do homage 3[5.6.7.10.11.15]; לְ loc. 3[23]; of voice, מִן־שְׁמַיָּא 4[28]. **2.** *fall* by violence 7[20] (c. קֳדָם). **3.** יִפֵּל לָךְ Ezr 7[20] *it shall fall to thee* (thou shalt need) to give (cf. Chr-Pal. Schulth[Lex. 126 and ZAW xxii (1902), 163]).

נְפַק **vb.** go, or come, out, forth (𝔗 *id.*, NH נָפַק, Syr. ܢܦܩ, so Chr-Pal. Schulth[Lex. 126], OAram. Nab. Palm. נפק Lzb[324], cf. Ar. نَافِقَاءُ *hole* of field mouse; v. also Aram. נִפְקוּתָא, ܢܦܩܬܐ *outlay,* Eg. Aram. נפקתה Cooke[Inscr. 212], Ar. نَفَقَة *household outlay* (Aram. loan-word Schwally[ZMG lii (1898), 133]));—**Pe.** *Pf.* 3 ms. נ׳ Dn 2[14] *he went out,* c. inf.; 3 fs. נֶפְקַת v[13] decree *went forth* (cf. Lu 2[1]); 3 mpl. נפקו 5[5] Kt (Qr 3 fpl. נְפַקָה, K[§ 23, 2]) 'fingers *came forth;* c. מִן loc.: *Imv.* mpl. פֻּקוּ (K[§ 42]) 3[26] *come forth! Pt.* pl. נָפְקִין v[26] (both of men); sg. נָפֵק 7[10] (=*flow out*). **Haph.** *bring forth,* acc. rei + מִן loc.: *Pf.* 3 ms. הַנְפֵּק Ezr 5[14.14] 6[5] Dn 5[2]; 3 mpl. הַנְפִּקוּ v[3] (so Eg. Aram. S-C[Pap. D 15, 17+]).

†[נִפְקָה] **n.f.** outlay;—emph. נִפְקְתָא Ezr 6[4.8].

†[נִצְבָּה] **n.f.** firmness (v. BH נצב);—emph. נִצְבְּתָא Dn 2[41].

†[נְצַח] **vb. Hithpa.** distinguish oneself (v. BH I. נצח);—*Pt.* מִתְנַצַּח Dn 6[4], עַל pers.

†[נְצַל] **vb. Haph.** rescue, deliver (v. BH Eg. Aram. הנצל *take away,* S-C[C 10, D 18]);—of God, abs.: *Pt. act.* מַצִּל 6[28], *Inf.* לְהַצָּלָה Dn 3[29]; of man, sf. pers. לְהַצָּלוּתֵהּ 6[15].

†נְקֵא **adj.** clean, pure (v. BH נקה);—כַּעֲמַר נ׳ Dn 7[9] *like pure wool.*

†[נְקַשׁ] **vb.** knock (v. BH (rare));—**Pe.** *Pt. act.* fpl. נָקְשָׁן Dn 5[6] of knees *knocking* דָּא לְדָא.

†נְשָׂא **vb.** lift, take, carry (cf. BH; rare in Aram.; v. נְסֵי, נְסָא ChWB, NHWB);—**Pe.** *Pf.* 3 ms. נ׳ Dn 2[35] *carry away* (of wind, c. acc. rei); *Imv.* ms. שֵׂא Ezr 5[15] *take* (acc. vessels). **Hithpa.** *make a rising, an insurrection: Pt.* fs. מִתְנַשְּׂאָה Ezr 4[19], עַל pers.

נְשֵׁיהוֹן v. [נְשִׁין] sub II. אנשׁ.

†[נִשְׁמָה] **n.f.** breath (v. BH, √נשׁם);—sf. נִשְׁמְתָךְ Dn 5[23], i.e. breath of life.

†נְשַׁר **n.m.** griffon-vulture or eagle (v. BH);—abs. נ׳ Dn 7[4]; pl. abs. נִשְׁרִין 4[30].

†[נִשְׁתְּוָן] **n.m.** [Ezr 4, 18] letter (prob. Pers.; v. BH);—emph. נִשְׁתְּוָנָא Ezr 4[18.23] 5[5].

†[נְתִינִין] **n.m.pl.** Nethinîn (prob. loan-word from BH נְתִינִים, √נָתַן);—servants of sanctuary, emph. נְתִינַיָּא Ezr 7[24].

†[נְתַן] **vb.** give (v. BH; 𝔗 rare; OAram. נתן, Impf. ינתן, so Nab.; Zinj. Palm. יתן; Eg. Aram. Impf. ינתן, אנתן, etc., S-C[Pap. A 7+], pl. sf. תנתנונה ib.[J 9], Inf. למנתן S-C[C 6, 9+]);—**Pe.** *Impf.* 3 ms. יִנְתֵּן־ (K[§ 42]) Dn 2[16], sf. יִתְּנִנַּהּ 4[15]+; 2 ms. תִּנְתֵּן Ezr 7[20]; 3 mpl. יִנְתְּנוּן 4[13]; *Inf.* לְמִנְתַּן 7[20];—**1.** *give,* subj. God, c. sf. rei + לְ pers., Dn 4[14.22.29]. **2.** of man, *give, allow,* acc. time, 2[16]. **3.** *give, pay,* acc. rei, Ezr 4[13] 7[20] (+ מִן of source), abs. v[20].

†[מַתְּנָא] **n.f.** gift;—pl. abs. מַתְּנָן Dn 2[6.48]; sf. מַתְּנָתָךְ 5[17].

†[נְתַר] **vb. Haph.** strip off (𝔗 נְתַר *fall off;* Syr. ܢܬܪ; Ar. نَثَرَ *scatter;* As. *našâru, diminish, shorten,* NH נָשַׁר *fall off*);—*Imv.* mpl. אַתַּרוּ (K[§ 42 b)]) Dn 4[11] (acc. of leaves).

ס

שַׂבְּכָא v. סַבְּכָא.

‡†[סְבַל] **vb.** si vera l. bear, carry a load (v. BH);—**Pō.** *Pt. pass.* אֻשּׁוֹהִי מְסוֹבְלִים (K[§ 36] Nö[GGA, 1884, 1016]) Ezr 6[3] *its foundations* (be) *raised* (Thes al.; W[CG 203, 225]), very dub.; Hpt[Gu ad loc.]

conj. אֶשָּׁהִי מְס׳ *his* (God's) *fire-offerings they bring* (As. *zabâlu*), so (hesitantly) Berthol.

†[סְבַר] **vb. think, intend** (𝔗 Syr.; v. BH II. שׂבר (late));—**Pe.** *Impf.* 3 ms. יִסְבַּר Dn 7^{25}, sq. inf.

†סְגִד **vb. do homage** (by prostration) (𝔗 Syr.; BH (late));—**Pe.** *Pf.* 3 ms. ס׳ Dn 2^{46}; *Impf.* 3 ms. יִסְגֻּד Dn 3^{6}+, 3 mpl. יִסְגְּדוּן 3^{28}, etc.; *Pt. act.* pl. סָגְדִין 3^{7}+;—*do homage* לְצֶלֶם Dn $3^{5.7.10.12.14.15.18}$, לְ of false god v^{28}; לְצ׳ om., $v^{6.11.15}$; ס׳ לְדָנִיֵּאל 2^{46} (perh. as representing God, cf. v^{b}, yet v. Dr).

†[סְגַן] **n.m. prefect** (𝔗 (rare), Eg. Aram. S-C^{D13}; v. BH (late), As. loan-word);—pl. abs. סִגְנִין Dn 2^{48}; emph. סִגְנַיָּא $3^{2.3.27}$ 6^{8}.

†סְגַר **vb. shut** (v. BH);—**Pe.** *Pf.* 3 ms. ס׳ Dn 6^{23} *shut* the lions' mouth (acc.).

†סוּמְפֹּנְיָה **n.f. bag-pipe, or < double pipe or Pan's pipe** (v. GFM$^{JBL. 1905, 166 ff.}$) (NH Levy $^{NHWB\ iii. 492}$; NH Aram. סִימְפּוֹן is *tube*, esp. *vein, artery* Id$^{ib. 513}$; loan-word fr. (late) Gk. *συμφωνία*, Krauss$^{ii. 376, 390}$ Bev^{41} Dr$^{Dn\ 3, 5}$ Nes$^{MM\ 37}$ (hence also later Lat. *symphonia*, Ital. *zampogna*), Prince$^{EB\ 3230}$);—abs. ס׳ Dn $3^{5.15}$, = סיפניה Kt, סוּפֹּנְיָה Qr v^{10} (Syr. ܨܘܦܢܝܐ *id.*; cf. Palm. ספון = *σύμφωνος, in agreement*, Lzb^{330} GACooke$^{Inscr. 338}$).

†[סוּף] **vb. be fulfilled** (prop. ended) (𝔗 Syr. (oft.); v. BH);—**Pe.** *Pf.* 3 fs. מִלְּתָא סָפַת Dn 4^{30} (cf. BH I. כָּלָה **Qal 1 c**). **Haph.** *put an end to*: *Impf.* 3 fs. תָּסֵף Dn 2^{44} (acc. rei).

†סוֹף **n.[m.]** end;—cstr. ס׳ *end* of the earth Dn $4^{8.19}$; emph. סוֹפָא 7^{28} *end, conclusion* of the matter; עַד־ס׳ = *for ever* 6^{27} 7^{26}.

סוּפֹּנְיָה, סִיפֹנְיָה, סִיפֹּנְיָה v. סוּמְפֹּנְיָה.

†[סְלִק] **vb. come up** (Aram. loan-word in BH, q.v.);—**Pe.** *Pf.* 3 fs. סִלְקַת Dn 7^{20}, ־ת (!) v^{8} (K$^{§ 25 b)}$); 3 mpl. סְלִקוּ 2^{29} Ezr 4^{12}; *Pt.* fpl. סָלְקָן Dn 7^{3};—*come up*, מִן pers. Ezr 4^{12}, מִן־יַמָּא Dn 7^{3}; abs. of horn in vision $7^{8.20}$; fig. of thoughts 2^{29}. **Haph.** *lift, take up*: *Pf.* 3 mpl. הַסִּקוּ (as if from נסק; K$^{§ 44 b)}$) Dn 3^{22}; *Inf.* לְהַנְסָקָה (K$^{l. c.}$ Str$^{§ 3 h)}$) 6^{24} (מִן loc.), both c. לְ acc. pers. **Hoph.** (W$^{CG\ 225}$) *be taken up*: *Pf.* 3 ms. הֻסַּק 6^{24} (מִן loc.).

†[סְעַד] **vb. Pa. support, sustain** (𝔗 Zinj.; v. BH);—*Pt. act.* pl. מְסַעֲדִין לְהוֹן Ezr 5^{2}.

†סְפַר **n.m.** $^{Dn\ 7, 10}$ **book** (v. BH סֵפֶר);—cstr. ס׳ דָּכְרָנַיָּא Ezr $4^{15.15}$, ס׳ מֹשֶׁה 6^{18}; pl. abs. סִפְרִין Dn 7^{10} *books* (of records, v. Dr); emph. בֵּית סִפְרַיָּא Ezr 6^{1} *house of records*.

†[סָפַר] **n.m. secretary, scribe** (𝔗 Syr.; BH סֹפֵר);—emph. סָפְרָא *the secretary*, Persian official, Ezr $4^{8.9.17.23}$; cstr. סָפַר *the scribe* $7^{12.21}$, of Ezra as learned in God's law.

†[סַרְבָּל] **n.[m.]** prob. mantle (v. esp. SAC $^{JPhil.\ xxvi\ (1899),\ 307\ f.}$, cf. Andr$^{M\ 74*}$, with conj. as to orig. Pers. form; > *trousers*; NH; JAram. *id.*, with both mngs., also *shoes*; Ar. سِرْبَال *mantle* is loan-word Frä^{47}; Egypt. Ar. زربول *shoe* is Gk. loan-word acc. to Vollers$^{ZMG\ li\ (1897),\ 298}$, cf. Krauss $^{ii. 412}$);—pl. sf. סַרְבָּלֵיהוֹן Dn $3^{21.27}$.

†[סָרַךְ] **n.m. chief, overseer** (𝔗 *id.* (= BH שֹׁטֵר); etym. dub.; prob. with Bev^{Dn} Dr^{Dn} Andr $^{M\ 75*}$, loan-word fr. Pers. *sār* (and **sarak*?), *head, chief*);—pl. abs. סָרְכִין Dn 6^{3}, emph. סָרְכַיָּא $v^{4.5.7}$, cstr. סָרְכֵי v^{8}.

†I. [סְתַר] **vb. Pa. hide** (v. BH);—*Pt. pass.* fpl. emph. מְסַתְּרָתָא Dn 2^{22} *the hidden things*.

†II. [סְתַר] **vb. destroy** (Syr. ܣܬܪ; v. BH שׁתר);—**Pe.** *Pf.* 3 ms. sf. סַתְרֵהּ Ezr 5^{12} (acc. of temple).

ע

עֲבַד **vb. make, do** (𝔗 Syr. OAram. Nab. Palm. Eg. Aram. (S-C$^{Pap.}$; cf. אֲוָדָא); = BH עָבַד, q.v., but in mng. ‖ עשׂה);—**Pe.** *Pf.* 3 ms. ע׳ Dn 3^{1}+, 2 ms. עֲבַדְתְּ (K$^{§ 13, 2)}$) 4^{32}; 1 s. עַבְדֵת 3^{15} 6^{23}, 3 mpl. עֲבַדוּ Ezr 6^{13}+; *Impf.* 2 mpl. תַּעַבְדוּן (Baer K$^{§ 38, 1. b)}$; תֶּעֶבְדוּן Gi Str) Ezr 6^{8} 7^{18}; *Inf.* מֶעְבַּד (K$^{§ 15, a) 2)}$) 4^{22} 7^{19} (מֶעְבַּד); *Pt. act.* עָבֵד 7^{26}+, fs. עָבְדָא Dn 7^{21}; mpl. עָבְדִין Ezr 4^{15};—**1.** *make*, acc. rei Dn $3^{1.15}$ and (of creation) Je 10^{11}; *make* a feast Dn 5^{1}, war 7^{21} (עִם pers.), ded. of temple Ezr 6^{16}. **2.** *do*, acc. of deed, Dn 4^{32} (of God), 6^{23} Ezr $4^{15.22}$; *do, act*, כְּנֵמָא, *thus*, Ezr 6^{13}, כְּ, *according to*, Dn 7^{18} and (of God) 4^{32}, abs. 6^{11}; acc. + בְּ rei Ezr 7^{18} *do* something *with*, + עִם pers. 6^{8}; *do, perform*, acc. of God's law 7^{26}, acc. of signs, etc. (subj. God) Dn 6^{28} and (+ עִם pers.) 3^{32}. **Hithpe.** *Impf.* 3 ms. יִתְעֲבֵד Ezr 6^{11}+, ־ד 6^{12} 7^{21}; 2 mpl. תִּתְעַבְדוּן Dn 2^{5}; *Pt.* מִתְעֲבֵד Ezr 7^{26}, ־בֶד־ 4^{19}, fs. ־עַבְדָא 5^{8};—

1. *be made into,* c. n. pred., Dn 2[5] 3[29] Ezr 6[11]. **2.** *be done, wrought,* 4[19], 5[8] (subj. עֲבִידְתָא); *be performed, executed,* of command Ezr 6[12] 7[21 23], judgment 7[26].

†[עֲבַד] D[p 105], or עבד K[§ 54, 2, γ)] **n.m. slave, servant** (BH עֶבֶד);—cstr. עֲבַד Dn 6[21] *servant* of God; pl. sf. of king, עבדיך Kt (K[§ 53 Anm. b)]), עַבְדָךְ Qr Ezr 4[11], עַבְדָךְ Qr Dn 2[4]; sf. of God, עַבְדוֹהִי, Dn 3[26.28] Ezr 5[11], of king Dn 2[7].

†עֲבֵד נְגוֹ **n. pr. m.** comrade of Daniel (BH *id.*);—Dn 2[49] 3[12]+ 10 t. 3, + עֲבֵד נְגוֹא 3[29], = עֲזַרְיָה 2[17].

†[עֲבִידָה] **n.f. work, service** (BH עֲבֹדָה);—emph. עֲבִידְתָא Ezr 5[8] Dn 2[49], cstr. עֲבִידַת Ezr 4[24]+,—**1.** *work,* of building temple, Ezr 4[24] 5[8] 6[7]; =*administration* Dn 2[49] 3[12]. **2.** *ritual, service,* of God Ezr 6[18].

†[מַעֲבַד K[§ 60 3) b)]] **n. [m.] work** (BH [מַעְבָּד] +Jb 34[25]; +𝔗[1b]; Syr. ܡܥܒܕܐ of magic *works*);—pl. sf. מַעֲבָדוֹהִי Dn 4[34] (sf. of God).

†עֲבַר **n.m. region across, beyond** (v. BH I. עֵבֶר, √עבר);—cstr. in phr. עֲבַר(־)נַהֲרָה, i e. Syria (Scheft[87]): Ezr 4[10.11 17 20] 5[3 6.6] 6[6.6.8.13] 7[21.25], ע׳ נהרא 4[16]. Cf. in Cilic Aram, Cooke[346].

עַד v עדה.

†[עֲדָה] **vb. pass on, away** (𝔗 (oft. for Heb. עָבַר, Syr.; v. BH I. עָדָה (rare, late));—**Pe.** *Pf.* 3 fs. עֲדָת Dn 3[27] 4[28], *Impf.* 3 ms. יֶעְדֵּה 7[14], 3 fs. תֶּעְדֵּא 6[9];—**1.** *pass on, over,* c. ב pers Dn 3[27]. **2.** *pass away,* of kingdom 4[28] (מִן pers.), 7[14]; of law 6[9]. **Haph.** *take away* (so Eg. Aram. S-C[G 35]). *Pf.* 3 mpl. הֶעְדִּיו, acc. rei, Dn 5[20] (מן pers.), 7[12], *Impf.* 3 mpl. יְהַעְדּוֹן v[26]; *Pt* מְהַעְדֵּה 2[21] *remove, depose* kings, of God.

†עַד [35] **prep. and conj. even to, until** (BH III. עַד; so 𝔗 Syr. OAram. Nab. Palm Eg Aram. (Lzb[336] S-C[A 5+]));—**1.** *prep.:* **a.** of space, *even to* Dn 7[13]; עַד־כָּא v[28]. **b.** of amount, *up to* Ezr 7[22 (4 t.)]. **c.** of time, *until* Dn 2[20] 6[15 27] 7[13 18 26] Ezr 4[24]; 5[16] [וְעַד־כְּעַן]; =our *against* 6[15] (cf. BH, p. 724[a] top); *to* (the end of) = *during* Dn 6[8] עַד יוֹמִין תְּלָתִין, v[13] 7[12.25]. On עַד־אָחֳרֵין Dn 4[5] v. אָחֳרֵין; and on עַד־דִּבְרַת דִּי 4[14] v. [דִּבְרָה]. **2.** *conj.:* **a.** עַד־דִּי *until,* sq. pf. (of past time) Dn 2[34] 4[30] 5[21] 7[4.9 11 22]; sq. impf. (of fut.) 2[9] 4[20.22.29].—Dn 6[25] לָא מְטוֹ . . . עַד דִּי שְׁלִטוּ וגו׳ *up to the time that . . .,* i. e. *ere that.* **b.** עַד alone, Ezr 4[21] 5[5].

†עִדָּן **n.m.**[Dn 2, 9] **time** (𝔗 *id.*, Syr. ܥܶܕܳܢܳܐ, perh. loan-word from As. *adannu, fixed, appointed,* or *definite, time;* [Ar. عدّان prob. Aram. loan-wd., Schwally[ZMG liii (1899), 197]]);—abs. ע׳ Dn 7[12]+; emph. עִדָּנָא 2[8]+; pl. abs. עִדָּנִין 4[13]+, emph. עִדָּנַיָּא 2[21],—**1.** in gen., *time,* as duration Dn 2[8] 7[12], involving specif. conditions 2[9 21]; (point of) *time* 3[5 15]. **2.** definite time, =*year* (as mod. Gk. χρόνος, v. EASophocles[1173]): שִׁבְעָה ע׳ = *seven years,* 4[13.20.22.29]; עִדָּן וְעִדָּנִין וּפְלַג עִדָּן 7[25] (i.e. 3½ years, v. Dr; perhaps read du. for pl., cf. Bev Gunk[Schöpf 201]).

†עוֹד **adv. still** (BH; S-C[K 13]; 𝔗[O Jon]; Chr-Pal. Schulth[143 f.]), Dn 4[28] עוֹד מִלְּתָא בְּפֻם מַלְכָּא (cf BH **1 a** *a*).

†[עֲוָיָה] **n.f. iniquity** (BH II. עוה, עָוֹן; cf. 𝔗 עֲוָיָא),—pl. sf. עֲוָיָתָךְ (K[§ 54 a) β) 2]) Dn 4[24].

†עוֹף **n. [m.] fowl** (v. BH, √ I. עוף);—ע׳ abs. Dn 7[6] wings of *a fowl;* cstr. 2[38] coll.

†עוּר **n. [m.] chaff** (JAram. (Talm., rare), Syr. ܥܘܪܐ; Ar. غَائِرٌ, عُوَّارٌ *mote* (in eye, tending to cause *blindness* [עִוֵּר]) acc. to Ar. Lexx., Lane[2195]);—abs. ע׳ Dn 2[35] (in sim).

[עז], עִזִּין v. ענז.

†[עִזְקָה] **n.f. signet-ring** (𝔗 Syr.; √עזק = *surround,* v. BH);—sf עִזְקְתֵהּ Dn 6[18]; pl. cstr. ־קָת v[18].

†עֶזְרָא **n.pr.m. Ezra** (BH *id.*);—Ezr 7[12.21 25].

†עֲזַרְיָה **n.pr.m.** comrade of Daniel (BH *id.;* Dn 1[6]+);—Dn 2[17], = עֲבֵד נְגוֹ v[49]+.

עֵטָא v. יעט.

†[עַיִן] **n.f.**[Ezr 5, 5] **eye** (v. BH I. ע׳),—cstr. עֵין Ezr 5[5] (of God); pl. (K[§ 51, 1]) of horn, עַיְנִין Dn 7[8.20]; of man, du. cstr. עַיְנֵי v[8], sf. עַיְנַי 4[31].

†עִיר **n.m. waking, or wakeful, one, i.e. angel** (√עיר, cf. Syr. ܥܳܪ *wake,* ܥܺܝܪܳܐ *waking* (PS[2843]), JAram. עִיר, NH עֵר adj *awake*);—abs. ע׳ Dn 4[10.20]; pl. abs עִירִין v[14]; Aq Symm. ἐγρήγορος; cf. Charles[Enoch 1 5, xxxix 12, also p. 358] Dr[ad loc.]; doubtful is the connex with Ph. *Zophesemim* (Euseb. [Praep. Evang 10]), i.e. צפי שמים *watchers of heaven,* as *keeping watch over* or *spying out* (Zim[KAT 3. 629] Jerem[AT im Licht d. AO 83]).

עַל, עֵלָּא v. עלה. עִלָּה v. I. עלל.

עלה (√of foll.; v. BH עָלָה).

†[עֲלָת K $^{§56,a)\beta)2}$] **n.f. burnt-offering** (BH עֹלָה; cf. Palm. עלתא *altar*, SAC^{92} Lzb^{341});—pl. abs. עֲלָוָן Ezr 6^{9}.

†[עִלַּי K $^{§59\,1)\,c)}$] **adj. highest**;—alw. emph. עליא Kt, עִלָּאָה Qr, *the Most High* God: אֱלָהָא ע׳ Dn $3^{26.32}$ $5^{18.21}$; ע׳ alone, *the Most High*, $4^{14.21.22.29.31}$ 7^{25} (cf. Nab. n.pr. עליאל Lzb^{341} SAC^{91}).

‡†[עֶלְיוֹן] **adj. id.** (BH *id.*);—pl. of God, קַדִּישֵׁי עֶלְיוֹנִין (double pl., Buhl, as sts. BH, Ges ^{§124q} Kö$^{ii.1.438f}$) Dn $7^{18.22.25.27}$.

†[עִלִּי] **n.f. roof-chamber** (cf. Dr; BH עֲלִיָּה);—sf. עִלִּיתֵהּ Dn 6^{11}.

עַל prep. upon, over, on account of, above, to, against (BH and general Aram. *id.*);—sf. 1 s. עֲלַי; 2 ms. עליך Kt (so Eg. Aram., Cooke$^{No.\,77,\,A\,5,6,\,B\,8}$, S-C $^{Pap.\,A\,3,\,B\,5+}$), עֲלָךְ, Qr (𝔗 עֲלָךְ, Dalm ^{§47,2}) Dn 3^{12} + 6 t. Dn, Ezr 7^{18}; 3 ms. עֲלוֹהִי (so Nab. Palm.; Eg. Aram. עלוי S-C $^{A\,6+}$) Dn 3^{28}+, עֲלֹהִי †Ezr 6^{11}; 3 fs. עליה Kt (so Eg. Aram., S-C $^{D\,24}$), עֲלַהּ Qr (so 𝔗) †Dn 4^{14} 5^{21}; 1 pl. עֲלֶינָא †Ezr 4^{12}, עֲלָנָא 4^{18} 5^{17} Baer (Gi עֲלֶינָא); 3 mpl. עֲלֵיהֹם (so Nab., CIS$^{ii.226}$; Eg. Aram., S-C $^{Pap.\,F\,5,\,8+}$) †7^{24}, עֲלֵיהוֹן †$5^{1.3}$;—**1. a.** *upon*, Dn $2^{10.28.46}$ $5^{5.7}$ 6^{11} + oft., 4^{26} עַל־הֵיכַל מַלְכוּתָא (2 S 11^{2}); to be established עַל מַלְכוּתִי 4^{33} (cf. 2 Ch 1^{1}; BH **II. 1**) to lay an impost *upon*, Ezr 7^{24}; to trust *on*, Dn 3^{28}; after a vb. of motion, מְטָא עַל to come *upon*, Dn $4^{21.25}$; of times, to pass *over*, $4^{13.20.22.29}$; Ezr 5^{1} בְּשֻׁם אֱלָהּ יִשְׂרָאֵל עֲלֵיהוֹן i.e. (named) *over* them. **b.** idiom. (as in BH; v. **II. 1 d**) of the pers. who is the *subj.* of an emotion or experience, Dn 5^{9} וְזִיוֹהִי שָׁנַיִן עֲלוֹהִי were changed *upon* him, 7^{28}; 6^{19} וְשִׁנְתֵּהּ נַדַּת עֲלוֹהִי (cf. 2^{1}). **c.** *on acc. of* (BH **1 f** *b*), Dn 3^{16} עַל־דְּנָה פִּתְגָם. So in עַל־דְּנָה *on this acc.* †Ezr $4^{15.22}$ 5^{17}, עַל־מָה wherefore? †Dn 2^{15}; and עַל דִּבְרַת דִּי (v. דִּי). **d.** *on behalf of* (*ib.* **1 f** *c*), Ezr 6^{17}. **e.** *regarding, concerning* (*ib.* **1 f** *g*), Dn 2^{18} $5^{14.29}$ $6^{6.13}$ Ezr 7^{14} + oft. **2.** *over*, with vbs. of ruling, appointing, etc., Dn $2^{48.49}$ 3^{12} 4^{14}+, Ezr 4^{20} 6^{18}. **3.** in a compar. sense, *above, beyond*, Dn 3^{19} 6^{4}. **4.** expressing *direction*: **a.** *to*, of a person, after a vb. of motion (cf. BH **7 c** *a* *a*), Dn 2^{24} $4^{31.33}$ $6^{7.16}$ Ezr $4^{12.23}$ + oft.; after to *send* (a letter, etc.) Ezr $4^{11.17.18}$ 5^{6}+, *write* 4^{7}, *prophesy* 5^{1}; of the direction of the mind (*ib.* **7 c** *c*), Dn 3^{12} $6^{14.14.15}$; cf. Ezr 5^{5} עַל וְעֵין אֱלָהֲהֹם הֲוָת עַל (cf. Je 40^{4} and אֶל ψ 34^{16}). **b.** *against*, Dn $3^{19.29}$ 5^{23} $6^{5.6}$+; Ezr 4^{8} 7^{23}. **5.** in such phrases as טְאֵב עַל, שְׁפַר עַל (to be) good or acceptable *to* (as in Syr. and *late* Heb.: v. BH **8**), Ezr 5^{17} אִם עַל מַלְכָּא טָב, $7^{18.18}$ Dn 4^{24} (יִשְׁפַּר), 6^{15} (בְּאֵשׁ), v^{24} (טְאֵב).—Comp. the synopsis of meanings in Lzb^{340}.

†עֵלָּא **adv. above** (from **n.** עַל, with א- of direction, D$^{§44.1\,n.}$; Nab., Eg. Aram., *id.*, Lzb^{341} S-C$^{A\,5+}$; 𝔗 עֵיל, עֵילָא; Syr. ܥܠ in ܠܥܶܠ *above*);—Dn 6^{3} עֵלָּא מִנְּהוֹן *above* (*over*) them (cf. Cooke^{96,2}, Dt 28^{43} 𝔗).

†עִלָּה **n.f. matter, affair, occasion** (Syr. ܥܶܠܬܳܐ, v. BH I. עלל);—abs. ע׳ Dn $6^{5.5.6}$ (= ground of accusation).

†[עֲלַל] **vb. go or come in** (𝔗 Syr.; v. BH III. עלל);—**Pe.** *Pf.* 3 ms. עַל Dn 2^{16}; c. עַל pers. v^{24}; c. לְבַיְתֵהּ 6^{11}, so 3 fs. עללת Kt, עַלַּת Qr 5^{10}; *Pt.* עללין Kt, עָלִּין Qr, abs. 4^{4} 5^{8}. **Haph.** *bring in*, c. קֳדָם pers.: *Pf.* 3 ms. הַנְעֵל (K $^{§11.4.b}$; so Eg. Aram., S-C $^{G\,6,7,24,27}$ הנעלת; cf. D$^{§71.7;\,Dial.-Proben,\,p.4}$); Dn 2^{25} (לְ acc. pers.), 6^{19} (acc. rei); *Imv.* ms. sf. pers., הַעֵלְנִי 2^{24}; *Inf.* לְהַנְעָלָה 4^{3} (לְ acc. pers.); no קֳדָם pers., לְהַעָלָה 5^{7} (*id.*). **Hoph.** (W$^{CG\,225}$) *be brought*, subj. pers. + קֳדָם pers.: *Pf.* 3 ms. הֻעַל Dn 5^{13}, 3 mpl. הֻעַלּוּ v^{15}.

†[מֶעָל] **n.[m.] going in** (Syr., 𝔗^{J}; 𝔗^{Onk}, etc., מַעֲלָנָא);—pl. cstr. מֶעָלֵי שִׁמְשָׁא Dn 6^{15} i.e. *sunset* (so read Nö $^{GGA,\,1884,\,1020}$ Str M Bev, cf. Syr. ܡܰܥܠܳܢܳܐ, ܡܶܥܠܰܝ; > van d. H. Gi מֶעָלֵי, Baer מֵעָלֵי; cf. K $^{§60,\,Beisp.\,b)}$).

†עָלַם **n.[m.] perpetuity, antiquity** (v. BH III. עלם, עוֹלָם);—ע׳ abs. Dn 3^{33}+, cstr. 7^{18}; emph. עָלְמָא 2^{20}+; pl. עָלְמִין 2^{4}+, emph. עָלְמַיָּא 2^{44} 7^{18};—*perpetuity* in the future: מַלְכוּת ע׳ Dn 3^{33} 7^{27}, cf. 4^{31} 7^{14}; ע׳ as adv. *for ever* 4^{31}; עַד־עָלְמָא 7^{18} וְעַד־עָלַם עָלְמַיָּא; pl. לְע׳ *for ever* $2^{4.44.44}$ 3^{9} 5^{10} $6^{7.22.27}$; *antiquity*, מִן־יוֹמָת עָלְמָא Ezr $4^{15.19}$; of limitless time both past and future: מִן־ע׳ וְעַד־ע׳ Dn 2^{20}.

†עֵלְמָיֵא **n.gent. pl. Elamites** (cf. BH עֵילָם);—Ezr 4^{9}.

†[עֲלַע] **n.f. rib** (𝔗 Syr.; v. BH I. צלע, צֶלַע);—pl. abs. עִלְעִין Dn 7^{5}.

[עִלַּת] v. עלה.

†עַם **n.m.** $^{Ezr\ 6.12}$ people (v. BH I. עַם, עמם),—ע׳ abs. Dn 2^{41} 3^{29} Ezr 6^{12}, cstr. Dn 7^{27}; emph. עַמָּה Ezr 5^{12}, עַמָּא $7^{13\ 16\ 25}$; pl. emph. עַמְמַיָּא (K $^{§\ 15\ d)\ 55,\ 5\ a)}$) Dn $3^{4\ 7\ 7\ 31}$ 5^{19} 6^{26} 7^{14}.

עִם $_{22}$ **prep.** with (BH עִם: so 𝔗 Syr. (ܥܡ) and general Aram.);—sf. עִמִּי +Dn 3^{32}, עִמָּךְ +Ezr 7^{13}, עִמֵּהּ +Dn 2^{22}, עִמְּהוֹן +Ezr 5^{2};—**1. a.** *together with*, Dn $2^{18.43}$ 7^{13} עִם־עֲנָנֵי שְׁמַיָּא, Ezr 5^{2}+; whose dwelling, portion, etc., is *with* Dn $2^{11\ 22}$ 4^{12} 5^{21}. **b.** to speak *with* Dn 6^{22}, to make war *with* 7^{21}; to do *with* (= *towards*) 3^{32} דִּי עֲבַד עִמִּי (cf. ψ86^{17}), cf. Ezr 6^{8}; שַׁוִּי עִם to make like *to* Dn 6^{21}. †**2.** of time, Dn 3^{33} = 4^{31} עִם־דָּר וְדָר (co-exists) *with* all generations (cf. BH **1 g**); 7^{2} עִם־לֵילְיָא *during* the night.

†[עֲמִיק] **adj.** deep (v. BH עמק);—fpl emph, as n., עֲמִיקָתָא Dn 2^{22} *the deep things.*

†עֲמַר **n.m.** wool (𝔗 Syr., Eg. Aram. עמר S-C ^{G7,10}, קמר Id. ^{H8}; cf. Mand. אקאמרא, No $^{M\ 72}$; v. BH צמר),—abs. Dn 7^{9}.

†I. [עֲנָה] **vb.** answer (v. BH I. עָנָה),—**Pe.** *Pf.* 3 fs. עֲנָת Dn 5^{10}; 3 mpl. עֲנוֹ 2^{7}+; *Pt. act.* (עָנֵה No $^{GGA.\ 1884,\ 1021}$) עָנֵה 2^{5}+, pl. עָנַיִן (K $^{§\ 47\ Beisp.\ *)}$) 3^{24},—alw + אמר Pt, *answered and said* (ל [or קֳדָם] pers usu foll אמר, foll ע׳ $2^{10\ 27.47}$).—**1.** *answer, make reply*, to something said: Dn $2^{5\ 7\ 8\ 10\ 27}$ $3^{16\ 24\ 25}$ 4^{16b} 5^{17} $6^{13\ 14}$. **2.** *respond* to occasion, speak in view of a situation: $2^{10\ 20.26}$ $3^{9.14\ 19.24\ 26\ 28}$ $4^{16a\ 27}$ 5^{10}.

†כְּעַן **adv.** now (so Eg. Aram. (CIS $^{II\ 137}$ = Cooke $^{No\ 73}$ RES $^{361\ B}$ S-C $^{Pap.\ C\ 8}$); 𝔗, e g Nu 22^{4}. עַן prob. a subst. fr. [עֲנָה] the √of עֵת (p. 773^{a}), *time*; so כְּעַן lit. *at* (this) *time* = Heb. עַתָּה: K $^{§\ 67,\ 4}$);—Dn 2^{23} וּכְעַן הוֹדַעְתַּנִי, 3^{15} 4^{34} $5^{12\ 15\ 16}$ 6^{9} Ezr $4^{13\ 14\ 21}$ 5^{17} 6^{6}; עַד־כְּעַן *until now* Ezr 5^{16} (so 𝔗 Gn 18^{22}+).

†כְּעֶנֶת and (Ezr 4^{17}) contr. כְּעֶת **adv.** now (f. of כְּעַן; so first SS Torrey $^{JBL\ 16\ (1897),\ 166\ ff}$; now confirmed by Eg Aram. כענת Cowley $^{PSBA\ xxv\ 264,\ 311,\ 312}$ (= RES $^{492-4}$ = S-C $^{M\ N,\ O}$); וכ׳ formerly taken to mean *and so forth*);—alw. וכ׳, and alw. in a letter, introducing the business of the letter, and to be connected with what follows, not, as MT, with what precedes: Ezr 4^{10} (del., as introduced by error from end of v^{11}), v^{11} (joining to v^{12}) *and now*, let it be known, etc, v^{17f} *and now*, the letter which, etc., 7^{12f} *and now*, I make a decree, etc. (cf. וְעַתָּה similarly in letters 2 K 5^{6} 10^{2}, and καὶ νῦν 2 Macc. 1^{6}).

II. **עָנָה** (√of foll.; v. BH III. ענה, עָנָו, עָנִי).

†[עֲנֵי K $^{§\ 57\ a)\ \beta)}$ Str, or עָנֵה cf. Buhl, M] **adj.** poor, needy;—pl. abs. עֲנָיִן (Baer Gi K $^{1\ a)}$), or עֲנַיִן (van d. H. Buhl M ^{77*}; cf. D $^{§\ 39.1}$) as n. Dn 4^{24} *the poor.*

ענז (√of following; v. BH עזז, עֵז).

†[עֵז] **n.[f.]** (she-)goat;—pl. עִזִּין Ezr 6^{17}.

†[עֲנָן K $^{§\ 57\ a)\ \alpha)}$] **n.[m.]** cloud (v. BH I. ענן);—pl cstr. עֲנָנֵי שְׁמַיָּא Dn 7^{13}.

†[עֲנַף] **n.[m.]** bough (v. BH ענף);—pl. sf. עַנְפוֹהִי Dn $4^{9.11\ 11\ 18}$.

†עֲנָשׁ (K $^{§\ 57\ a)\ \alpha)}$) **n.[m.]** amercing, confiscation (not 𝔗 Syr., v. BH);—cstr. ע׳ נִכְסִין Ezr 7^{26}

עֶנֶת v. כְּעֶנֶת sub I. [עֲנָה].

עפא (√of foll., 𝔗 עַפָּא Pa., Syr. ܥܦܐ Pa., *enwrap*, עֲפִי *foliage*, ܥܘܦܝܐ *flower*, etc., BH עֳפִים as loan-word; cf. perh. As. *upû, cloud*(-mass))

†[עֳפִי] **n.m.** $^{Dn\ 4.9}$ leafage, foliage;—sf. עָפְיֵהּ Dn $4^{9\ 11\ 18}$

†[עֲצַב] **vb.** pain, grieve (𝔗 (rare), v. BH I. עצב);—**Pe.** *Pt pass*, as adj · בְּקָל עֲצִיב Dn 6^{21} *a pained voice* (cf 𝔗 Est 4^{1}, $𝔗^{J}$ Ex 12^{31}).

†עִקַּר (<ـַר־ K $^{§\ 59\ c)}$) **n.[m.]** root, stock (√עקר, v BH, and, on meaning of √, Schwally $^{ZMG\ III\ (1898),\ 140}$),—cstr. ע׳ שָׁרְשׁוֹהִי Dn $4^{12\ 20\ 23}$.

†[עֲקַר] **vb. denom. Hithpe.** be rooted up,—*Pf.* 3 pl. (m.? v. K $^{§\ 23,\ 2}$) אֶתְעֲקַרוּ Kt, fpl. ־רָה Qr, Dn 7^{8}.

[עָר], עָרִיךְ v. עור.

†[עֲרַב] **vb.** mix (𝔗 (oft.); Syr. (rare); v. BH I. ערב);—**Pa.** *Pt. pass.* מְעָרַב *mixed* with (ב) Dn $2^{41\ 43}$. **Hithpa.** *Pt. id.*: מִתְעָרַב v^{43} (עִם), pl. ־רְבִין v^{43} (ב).

†[עֲרָד K $^{§\ 57\ a)\ \alpha)}$] **n. m.** wild ass (𝔗 Syr.; √ערד, perh. = Ar. غرد *give a cry* No $^{SBWAk\ cxlii.\ v.\ ii\ 1900}$, v. BH עָרוֹד as loan-word (K $^{Aramaismen\ 72}$, but dub. No $^{ZMG\ lviii\ (1903),\ 413}$));—pl. emph. עֲרָדַיָּא Dn 5^{21}.

‡†[עַרְוָה] **n.f.** dishonour (√ערה, BH *be naked* (q.v.), עֶרְוָה *nakedness*);—cstr. עַרְוַת Ezr 4^{14}.

ערר (√ of foll., cf BH II צָרַר, III. צַר)

‡†[עָר M^77*] **n. m. foe** (cf. JAram. עָרָר *objection*, on dub. BH עָר v. p. 786);—pl sf. עריך Kt (K § 53 Anm. b)), עָרָךְ Qr Dn 4^16.

†עֲשַׂב **n. [m.] herbage, grass** (v BH עשב),—emph עִשְׂבָּא, as fodder · Dn 4^22 29.30 5^21.

†עֲשַׂר, עַשְׂרָה **n. m. et f. a ten** (v. BH),—**m.** (foll **n.f.**) Dn 7^7 20 24, **f.** (before **n m.**) v^24, תְּרֵי עֲשַׂר=*twelve* (foll **n m.**) 4^26 Ezr 6^17.

†עשרין **n pl. indecl. twenty**,—מְאָה וע׳ Dn 6^2 (follows **n.m.**).

†[עֲשִׁת], עֲשִׁית (K § 36 1 a) 17 2, Anm 2) **vb. think, plan** (BH II עשת (q v.) as Aramaism; 𝔗 אתעשׁת, not Syr), —*Pf* 3 ms (strictly *Pt. pass* No^GGA 1884, 1019 Syr Gr § 280 M^78*) ע׳ Dn 6^4, sq inf, *plan* to do so and so.

כְּעַת v יְעַת

†[עֲתִיד] **adj. ready** (v BH I. עתד),—pl עתידין Dn 3^15, sq cl c די.

†עַתִּיק **adj. advanced, aged** (BH (as Aramaism), √עתק, q v);—cstr. ע׳ יומין (-מַיָּא) *one advanced, aged, in days* Dn 7^9 13 22 (cf. Syr. ܥܬܝܩ ܝܘܡܬܐ Ecclus 25^4 al, PS^3011).

פ

†פֶּחָה **n m.** (Bab or Pers) **governor** (As. loan-word, BH *id*),—abs. פ׳ Ezr 5^14; cstr. פַּחַת Ezr 5^3.6 6^6.7 13; pl. emph. פַּחֲוָתָא Dn 3^2.3.27 6^1

†פֶּחָר **n.m. potter** (=*paḫḫâr*, 𝔗 פַּחָר (also *clay*), Syr. ܦܚܪܐ, prob. loan-word fr As *paḫaru, potter*, cf. Brock Zim^Buhl),—abs. פ׳ Dn 2^41

†[פַּטִּשׁ] **n. [m] a garment**, meaning dub, *tunic* (Thes) or *leggings* SAC^JPhil xxvi (1899) 309, (prob. later insertion in text Id.^ib 311ff) (Talm. (rare); √פטשׁ *spread out* acc. to K § 57 b) a));—pl. sf פטשׁיהון Kt (prob. פטי׳ K §§ 54, 3 a) a) 57, b) a)), Kmp ad loc M^78* al. (פַּטִּי׳), פַּטְּשֵׁיהוֹן Qr, Dn 3^21; conj. on meaning v. in Behrm Bev Dr M^78*.

†[פְּלַג] **vb. divide** (𝔗 Syr.; cf. BH (chiefly late));—**Pe.** *Pt. pass.* fs. פְּלִיגָה תֶּהֱוֵה Dn 2^41 *shall be divided.*

†פְּלַג **n. [m.] half**,—cstr. פ׳ Dn 7^25.

†פְּלֻגָּה **n.f. division**;—sf. פְּלֻגָּתְהוֹן Ezr 6^18.

†[פְּלַח] **vb. pay reverence to, serve** (deity) (cf As *palâḫu, fear, revere* (and BH יָרֵא, פָּחַד etc), Eg. Aram. פלח *worship* Lzb^361, 𝔗 פְּלַח *serve*, Syr. ܦܠܚ, Palm. פלחא *soldier*);—**Pe. 1.** *pay reverence to* deity (usu. ל acc): *Impf.* 3 mpl. יִפְלְחוּן Dn 3^28 7^14 27, so *Pt act* פָּלַח 6^17 21, pl. פָּלְחִין 3^12 14 18, and (acc. dei) v^17. **2.** pl. cstr. as n פָּלְחֵי בֵּית אֱלָהָא Ezr 7^24 *servants of the house of God* (+ priests, Nethinim, etc)

†פָּלְחָן **n. [m.] service, worship**;—cstr. פ׳ בֵּית אֱלָהָךְ Ezr 7^19.

†פֻּם **n.m.**^Dn 7, 8 **mouth** (cf BH פֶּה; on form v. K § 61 2) M § 76f.);—פ׳ abs. Dn 7^8.20, cstr. 4^28+, sf. פֻּמַהּ (on form v K l c No^Zur Gram d Class. Ar 15 (1896) (expansion of biliteral √), Ba^ZMG xli (1887), 633 f.) 7^5,—*mouth* of king Dn 4^28, lions 6^23, beast (in vision) 7^5, horn (ib.) v^8.20; *mouth* of pit 6^18.

פַּס v. פסס.

†פְּסַנְטֵרִין **n. [m.] a (triangular) stringed instrument** (Gk ψαλτήριον, Krauss^i 12, 99, 101, ii 473 Prince^EB 3232 Dr^Dn lviii, and on 3, 5),—פ׳ Dn 3^7, פְּסַנְתֵּרִין v^5 10 15.

פסס (√ of foll.; v. BH I. פסס, [פַּס]).

†פַּס **n.m. palm of hand**;—cstr. Dn 5^5, emph. פַּסָּא v^24.

†פַּרְזֶל n.m.^Dn 2, 40 19 **iron** (𝔗 Syr., v. BH בַּרְזֶל),—abs. Dn 2^33 (-זְל‎), 4^12+; emph. פַּרְזְלָא 2^34+,—Dn 2^33.34 + 11 t. 2; 4^12.20 5^4.23 7^7 19.

†[פְּרַס] **vb. break in two** (v. BH פרס),—**Pe'il** (W^CG 224) *Pf* 3 fs. פְּרִיסַת מַלְכוּתָךְ Dn 5^28.

†פְּרֵס (rd. פְּרַס? M^78*f) prob. **n. [m.] half-mina** (NH פְּרָס, OAram פרס, פרשׁ Lzb^354 SAC^99 Cooke^176, 408; v. מנא and reff),—abs. פ׳ Dn 5^25; pl. פַּרְסִין(?) [read פְּרָסִין? v. M l c] v^28.

†פָּרַס **n.pr. terr. et gent. Persia** (as kingdom), **Persians** (v. BH *id.*),—פ׳ Dn 6^9 13.16; פָּרָס 5^28 Ezr 4^24 6^14.

†[פַּרְסִי] **adj. gent. Persian**;—emph. פרסיא Kt, פָּרְסָאָה Qr (K § 61, 6) Dn 6^29 *the Persian.*

†[פְּרַק] **vb. tear away, break off** (v, BH [פָּרַק]);—**Pe.** *Imv* ms פְּרֻק Dn 4^24 (cf. Dr), acc. of sins + ב instr

†[פָּרַשׁ] **vb. make distinct** (cf. BH (chiefly late));—**Pa.** *Pt. pass.* Ezr 4[18] *made distinct* (BH Ne 8[8]; 𝔗 NH).

†פַּרְשֶׁגֶן **n.m.**[Ezr 4.23] **copy** (𝔗 -שַׁנָּא, Syr. ܦܪܫܓܢܐ; Aram. loan-word in BH, where also פַּתְשֶׁגֶן *id.*; loan-word from Pers. (Thes[1133; Add 106]), cf. Armen. *patčên, copy*, Gildemeister[ZKM iv 210] Lag[Ges. Abh. 79, Armen Stud. § 1838] Mey[Entst. J 22] Hoffm[ZA ii 52], OIran. **paticayan, id*, acc. to Andr[M 79*], not clear whether פר׳ is text. err. for פת׳ (Hoffm[l.c.]), or from diff. orig. (Andr[l.c.] *paračayan? paricayan?*), or from same √ in diff. stage (so appar. Scheft[52], citing, for both, OBaktr. *fra-sĕnhana, announcement*, OIran. *praśamsana, praśāsana, command*, Ar. *frasasti, command, patisêñhana, answer*, OP. **patithañhana, announcement, answer*));—cstr. פ׳ Ezr 4[11.23] 5[6].

†[פְּשַׁר] **vb. interpret** (a dream) (𝔗 *id.*, Syr. ܦܫܪ, perh. Eg Aram. פשר Lzb[355] SAC[100] (Ar. فسّر loan-word, v. Fra[263]); As. *pašâru*);—**Pe.** *Inf* לְמִפְשַׁר Dn 5[16], acc. cogn. פִּשְׁרִין. **Pa.** *Pt act.* מְפַשַּׁר Dn 5[12], acc. חֶלְמִין.

פְּשַׁר[31] **n.m.**[Dn 2.45] **interpretation** (of dream) (cf. BH as loan-word);—cstr. פ׳ Dn 4[3] 5[15.26] 7[16], emph. פִּשְׁרָא 2[4] + 7 t. Dn, + 4[15 16] Kt (Qr ה—); ה—ָ 2[7] 5[12]; sf. ה— 2[5.6.6] + 11 t. Dn, + Qr 4[15 16] (Kt א—ָ); pl פִּשְׁרִין 5[16].

†פִּתְגָם **n.m.**[Ezr 6.11] **command, word, affair** (Pers.: v. BH);—abs. פ׳ Dn 3[16]; emph. -מָא Ezr 4[17] +,—*command* Ezr 6[11], *word*, by missive 5[7], from king 4[17] (both c. שְׁלַח), in answer 5[11] (c. התיב); weakened, *thing, affair* Dn 3[16] 4[14].

†[פְּתַח] **vb. open** (v. BH);—**Pe.** *Pt. pass.* fpl. פְּתִיחָן Dn 6[11] *opened* (windows). **Pe'îl** (W[CG 224]) *Pf.* 3 mpl. פְּתִיחוּ 7[10] books *were opened.*

פתא (√of foll; 𝔗 Syr; BH פתה (rare)).

†[פְּתָי] **n.[m.] breadth** (𝔗 Syr.; Eg Aram RÉS[246] S-C[D4]);—sf. פְּתָיֵהּ Dn 3[1] Ezr 6[3].

צ

†[צְבָא] **vb. be inclined, desire, be pleased** (𝔗 Syr.; cf. BH II. צבה);—**Pe. 1.** *desire: Pf.* 1 s צְבִית (K[§ 47 Beilage 1) a)] No[GGA, 1884, 1019] pf. intrans.) Dn 7[19] (c. inf.). **2.** *be pleased, will* (without hindrance), abs., of God: *Impf.* 3 ms. יִצְבֵּא 4[14.22 29]; *Inf.* sf. מִצְבְּיֵהּ v[32] acc. to *his willing*; of Neb: *Pt. act.* צָבֵא 5[19 19 19 19].

†צְבוּ **n.f. thing, anything** (orig. *purpose*) (Palm. צבו Lzb[357] SAC[100] Cooke[266], Syr. ܨܶܒܘܬܳܐ, all *thing*; cf. NH חֵפֶץ *thing*, from חָפֵץ *delight in, crave*);—Dn 6[18].

I. [צְבַע] **vb. dip, wet** (𝔗 Syr; cf. BH I צבע);—**Pa.** *Pt.act.* pl. מְצַבְּעִין Dn 4[22] *wet* thee (ל), + מְטַל. **Hithpa.** *Impf.* יִצְטַבַּע (also -בַּע), *be wet*, c. בְּטַל 4[12.20], מִטַּל v[30] 5[21].

II. **צבע** (√of foll.; cf. BH II. צבע)

†[אֶצְבַּע] **n.f. 1. finger; 2. toe** (𝔗 Syr.; BH *id.*);—pl. **1.** abs. אֶצְבְּעָן Dn 5[5]. **2.** emph. —ָתָא 2[41]; cstr. —ָע v[42].

†צַד **n.[m.] side** (very rare in Aram.; perh. Hebr., v. BH *id*, √ צדד);—cstr., c. prep.: לְצַ׳ עליא Dn 7[25], i. e. *against*; מִצַּ׳ מַלְכוּתָא 6[5], i. e. *arising from, touching.*

‡†צְדָא **n.[m.]** usu. (malicious) **purpose** (Hebraism from BH צְדִיָּה, √ I צדה);—c. ה interrog. הַצְדָא Dn 3[14]; < read הַאֻמְנָא Bev Dr Kmp.

†צִדְקָה **n.f. right doing** (Talm., OAram.; v. BH צְדָקָה, √ צדק),—צ׳ Dn 4[24].

†[צַוַּאר] **n.m. neck** (𝔗 Syr.; v. BH sub I. צור);—sf. צַוְּארָךְ Dn 5[16], צַוְּארֵהּ v[7 29].

†[צְלָא] **vb. Pa. pray** (orig *bow* in prayer) (𝔗 *id., bow*, Pa, *pray*, so Syr. ܨܠܐ and Pa.; As. *sullû, entreat* (appar. not of prayer to gods Zim[KAT 3. 610 f]); Ar. صَلًا *middle of the back*, صلى II. *pray*, Eth. ጸለወ: *bow*, ጸለየ: *pray*; Sab צלות *shrine* Hom[Chr 125; AA 155]);—*Pt.* מְצַלֵּא Dn 6[11] (abs.); pl. מְצַלַּיִן (K[§ 47 a)]) Ezr 6[10] (c. ל *in behalf of*).

†[צְלַח] **vb. prosper** (v. BH II. צלח);—**Haph.** *Pf.* 3 ms. הַצְלַח Dn 3[30] 6[29]; *Pt.* מַצְלַח Ezr 5[8], pl. -לְחִין 6[14];—**1.** *cause to prosper* Dn 3[30] (c. ל pers.). **2.** *shew prosperity, be prosperous* 6[29] (of pers.); *have success* (in building) Ezr 6[14], *be successful* (of work) 5[8] (בִּידְהֹם).

†צְלֵם[17] **n.m.**[Dn 2.31] **image** (v. BH צלם);—abs. צ׳ Dn 2[31] 3[1]; cstr. צ׳ 3[19], צְלֵם v[5] +; emph. צַלְמָא 2[31] +;—*image* Dn 2[31 31.32.34.35] 3[1] + 10 t. 3; צ׳ אַנְפּוֹהִי 3[19] i.e. his expression.

†[צְפַר] **n.f.** Dn 4,18 (cf. K. p. 165, Anm. 3) **bird** (v. BH II. צפר);—pl. abs. צִפְּרִין Dn 4^{30}, emph. צִפְּרַיָּא v^{11}, cstr. צִפֲּרֵי $v^{9.18}$.

†[צְפִיר] **n.m. he-goat** (v. BH V. צפר);—pl. cstr. צְפִירֵי עִזִּין Ezr 6^{17}.

ק

קבל (√of following, *be in front of*).

קֳבֵל $_{29}$ **subst.** front, as **prep.** in front of, before, because of; sq. דִּי as **conj.** because that (perh. in form a dimin., Bev Dn 2,8; 𝔗 קְבֵיל, c. לְ, לְקֳבֵיל, sf. לְקִבְלִי, etc., *in front of* (Dalm. § 47,7); Syr. ܩܘܒܠܐ, ܩܘܒܠ̈ܐ *aspect*, ܡܢ ܩܘܒܠܐ *in front*, ܠܩܘܒܠܐ, sf. ܠܩܘܒܠܗ *in front (of)*, *opposite (to)*, cf. Gn 15^{10} 𝔗 𝔖; Palm. לקבל *before* (Cooke 321, cf. 193));—cstr. לָקֳבֵל Dn 2^{8}+, sf. לָקָבְלָךְ †2^{31};—†**1.** c. לְ: **a.** Dn 3^{3} לק׳ צַלְמָא *before* the image, 2^{31} $5^{1.5}$; *in view of, by reason of*, 5^{10} לק׳ מִלֵּי מַלְכָּא *by reason of* the words, etc., Ezr 4^{16} לָקֳבֵל דְּנָה (cf. Eg. Aram. לקבל זנה זי, RÉS 361 B 5). **b.** sq. דִּי as **conj.** *because that* Ezr 6^{13} (so Palm. CIS ii. 164). **2.** c. כֹּל, כָּל־קֳבֵל *in view of, because of* (but read probably כְּלָקֳבֵל *according to the front of*, i.e. *having regard to, because of*: Luzz Chald. Gr. § 123 Lambert RÉJ, 1895, 47 f. Marti § 95 d Nö LCB, 1896, 703 Nes OLZ, 1902, 487 Strack 56 al.; cf. BH I. עֻמָּה **d**): **a.** as **prep.** כָּל־קֳבֵל דְּנָה *because of this, therefore*, †Dn $2^{12.24}$ $3^{7.8}$ 6^{10} Ezr 7^{17}; Dn 3^{22} pointing forwards, כָּל־קֳבֵל דְּנָה מִן־דִּי וגו׳ *on this account*, (viz.) because that, etc. **b.** sq. דִּי as **conj.** *because that, inasmuch as*, Dn 2^{8} כָּל־קֳבֵל (כְּלָקֳבֵל) דִּי חֲזֵיתוּן *because* ye see, $v^{10.41.45}$+, Ezr 4^{14} 7^{14}; Dn 5^{22} = *although*. In Dn 2^{40} 6^{11} taken by 𝔊 (ὃν τρόπον, καθώς), Ges (Thes, not Lex), Ew Hi as = *according as* (as Ec 5^{15} 𝔗 כל קבל דאתא *according as* he came), but not Bev Behrm Marti. [Occas. in 𝔗, usu. = *before*; cf. in 𝔗^{J} Gn 28^{17} 31^{32}, D §§ 47.7; 50].

†קַבֵּל **vb. denom. Pa.** receive (BH (late), q.v.; 𝔗 Syr.: prop. *come in front of, come to meet*, cf. Germ. *entgegennehmen*);—*Pf.* 3 ms. קַבֵּל Dn 6^{1}; *Impf.* 2 mpl. תְּקַבְּלוּן *ye shall receive* 2^{6}, 3 mpl. וִיקַבְּלוּן 7^{18}; all c. acc. rei.

קֳדָם $_{42}$ **prep.** before (so OAram. Nab. Palm. etc. (Lzb 360 f.), 𝔗 קֳדָם, Syr. ܩܕܡ; prop. a subst. *the front*, cf. Ar. قُدَّام *the front*; for √ v. BH קדם);—sf. קֳדָמַי Dn 2^{9}+, -מָךְ v^{6}; קדמיך Kt, קֳדָמָךְ Qr, †5^{23} 6^{23}; קֳדָמוֹהִי 4^{5}+ (cf. Nerab קדמוה, Cooke 189); 3 fs. קדמיה Kt, קֳדָמַהּ Qr, †$7^{7.8.20}$; קֳדָמֵיהוֹן †4^{4};—**1.** *before* (= Heb. לִפְנֵי), esp. in the phrases *to answer, pray, say*, etc., *before* a superior (as more respectful than *to*), Dn 2^{9} לְמֵאמַר קֳדָמַי, $v^{10.11.27}$ 6^{11} (v. Dr), $v^{12.13.14}$; קְרִי ק׳ Ezr $4^{18.23}$; $5^{23.28}$; with שְׁפַר to *seem fair* Dn 3^{32} 6^{2}; after vbs. of motion, *in before*, Dn $2^{24.25}$ 3^{13} 4^{3}+; of time 7^{7}. †**2.** מִן־קֳדָם *from before* (= מִלִּפְנֵי, but as used in *late* Heb., Est 1^{19} 4^{8}: p. 818ᵃ), c. קַבֵּל Dn 2^{6}, בְּעָא v^{18}; of a decree, 6^{27} מִן־קֳדָמַי שִׂים טְעֵם (‖ מִנִּי 3^{29}+), cf. 2^{15} Ezr 7^{14}; of God, Dn 5^{24} מִן־קֳדָמוֹהִי שְׁלִיחַ פַּסָּא דִי־יְדָא, 7^{10} (so very oft. in 𝔗, Dr Sm lxx f., lxxiii). Also = Heb. מִפְּנֵי, with to *fear* Dn 5^{19} 6^{27}, be *rooted up* 7^{8}, *fall* v^{20}.

†[קַדְמָה] **n.f. former time** (cf. BH קַדְמָה, Zinj. קדמה (Cooke 177), *former state*);—cstr. Dn 6^{11} מִן־קַדְמַת דְּנָה = *before this, formerly*; so Ezr 5^{11} מִקַּדְמַת דְּ׳. Cf. Gn 28^{19} 𝔗^{J}, Ez 38^{17} 𝔗.

†[קַדְמָי] **adj. former, first** (so Nab. Palm. 𝔗 Syr.);—fs. emph. קַדְמָיְתָא *the first* Dn 7^{4}, fpl. emph. קַרְנַיָּא קַדְמָיָתָא *the former* horns v^{8}, mpl. emph. קַדְמָיֵא v^{24}.

קדשׁ (√of foll.; 𝔗 Syr.; v. BH *id.*, קָדוֹשׁ).

†קַדִּישׁ **adj. holy**;—abs. ק׳ Dn $4^{10.20}$; pl. -שִׁין 4^{5}+, cstr. -שֵׁי 7^{18}+;—gods Dn $4^{5.6.15}$ 5^{11}; as subst., of angels $4^{10.14.20}$; of Isr. (as holy ones, saints) $7^{21.22}$, קַדִּישֵׁי עֶלְיוֹנִין *saints of the Most High* $v^{18.22.25.27}$.

קול (√of following; BH קוֹל, קֹל).

†קָל **n.m.** Dn 4,28 **voice** (𝔗 Syr.);—ק׳ abs. Dn 4^{28} 6^{21}; cstr. *sound* of words 7^{11}, instr. $3^{5.7.10.15}$.

[קוּם] **vb. arise, stand** (v. BH);—**Pe.** *Pf.* 3 ms. קָם Dn 3^{24}, 3 mpl. קָמוּ Ezr 5^{2}; *Impf.* 3 ms. יְקוּם Dn 6^{20} 7^{24}, 3 fs. תְּקוּם $2^{39.44}$; 3 mpl. יְקוּמוּן $7^{10.17.24}$ (יְקֻ׳); *Pt.* קָאֵם 2^{31}, pl. קאמין Kt, קָיְמִין Qr, 3^{3}, emph. קָאֲמַיָּא 7^{16};—**1.** lit. *arise* Dn 3^{24} (i.e. from throne), 6^{20} (from bed). **2.** fig. = come on the scene of history: of kingdom 2^{39}, king $7^{17.24}$ (both מִן of source), v^{24}. **3.** *arise* (out of inaction), and build Ezr 5^{2}, devour Dn 7^{5b}. **4.** *stand*, lit., לָקֳבֵל pers. 2^{31}, cf. 3^{3}, קֳדָם pers. 7^{10}; pt. as n., *those standing* (there) v^{16}. **5.** *endure*, of kingdom 2^{44}. **Pa.** *set up, establish* an ordinance (קְיָם): *Inf.* לְקַיָּמָה 6^{8}. **Haph.** (K § 45,4)

Pf. 3 ms. הֲקִים Dn 3[2]+, וַהֲקִים 6[2], sf. הֲקִימֵהּ 5[11], אֲקִימֵהּ 3[1]; 3 fs. הֲקִמַת 7[5]; 2 ms. הֲקֵימְתָּ 3[12 18]; 1 s הֲקֵימֶת לָא 3[14]; *Impf.* 3 ms. יְהָקֵים (K § 45, b)) 5[21] 6[16], יְקִים 2[44] 4[14]; *Inf.* sf. לַהֲקָמוּתֵהּ 6[4]; *Pt. act.* מְהָקֵים 2[21],—**1.** *set up*, lit. image 3[1 2.3.5.5.7 12 14 18]; fig. kings 2[21], kingdom v[44]. **2.** *lift up* one side 7[5a] (Dr) **3.** *establish*, c. acc. קְיָם 6[16] (=**Pa.**), אֱסָרָא v[9]. **4.** *appoint* Ezr 6[18], 2 acc. Dn 5[11]; sf pers + עַל 6[4], לְ acc. pers. + עַל 4[14] 5[21] 6[2] **Hoph.** *Pf.* 3 fs. הֳקִימַת (variants in Str; cf K § 45, 5; not Hebraism No[GGA 1867, 1784]; W[CG 225, 253]) 7[4] *be made to stand* עַל־רַגְלַיִן.

†**קְיָם** **n.[m.] statute** (Eg. Aram קימיהם Cooke[209]),—abs. Dn 6[16], cstr. v[8].

†**קַיָּם** **adj. enduring** (cf. Nab. קים (Cooke[217] Lzb קַיָּם, SAC, privately, prob. קַיָּם));—abs. ק׳ Dn 6[27] (of God, so oft. 𝔗 NH, cf. Dr); fs. קַיָּמָה 4[23] (of kingdom).

†**[קְטַל]** **vb. slay** (𝔗 Syr. (oft.); v. BH (late, rare)),—**Pe.** *Pt act* קָטֵל Dn 5[19], acc. pers **Pe'il** *be slain*: *Pf.* 3 ms קְטִיל 5[30], 3 fs קְטִילַת 7[11]. **Pa.** *slay*: *Pf.* 3 ms. קַטֵּל 3[22] (acc. pers), *Inf.* לְקַטָּלָה 2[14] (לְ acc. pers.) **Hithpe.** *be slain*: *Inf.* לְהִתְקְטָלָה 2[13]; *Pt.* (=gerundive, K § 76 3) pl מִתְקַטְּלִין v[13] were *to be slain.*

קטר (✓of foll.; 𝔗 קְטַר, Syr. ܩܛܰܪ *bind*, whence קִטְרָא, ܩܶܛܪܳܐ *knot*, etc; cf. BH II. [קטר])

†**[קְטַר]** **n.m.**[Dn 5, 6] **joint, knot**,—lit. pl. cstr. קִטְרֵי Dn 5[6] *joints* of his loin; fig. abs. קִטְרִין v[12 16], usu. *knotty things*, difficulties (Syr. PS[1591]); but prob. of magic *spells, banns* (also Syr PS[l. c.], cf. Brock[319 b]), so Bev, v also Dr.

†**קַיִט** **n.[m.] summer** (𝔗 Syr., v. BH II. קיץ),—abs. ק׳ Dn 2[35]

קָיָם, קַיָּם v. קום.

†**קיתרס** Kt, **קַתְרֹס** Qr, **n.[m.] lyre, zither** (also 𝔗; loan-word from Gk. κίθαρις Krauss[ii 193, ii, 573]);—Dn 3[5.7 10 15]; Kmp קִיתָרֹס.

קָל v. קול.

†**[קְנָא]** **vb. acquire, buy** (v. BH I. קנה),—**Pe.** *Impf.* 2 ms. תִּקְנֵא Ezr 7[17] c. acc. rei, +בְּכַסְפָּא.

קצא (✓of following; BH I. קָצָה, קצה).

†**קְצָת** **n.f. end** (so BH (late); 𝔗 (Gn 47[2]); not Syr.; cf. Eg. Aram. RÉS[361 A 4]);—cstr. לִקְ׳ *at the end of* (months, days) 4[26.31]; מִן־קְ׳ מַלְכוּתָא 2[42]=*part of* (‖ מִנַּהּ v[4], cf. BH קָצָת **2**).

†**קְצַף** **vb. be wroth** (Syr., v. BH I. קצף);—**Pe.** *Pf.* 3 ms. ק׳ Dn 2[12]

‡†**קְצַף** **n.[m.] wrath** (of God) (only Syr. ܩܶܨܦܳܐ *sadness, anxiety*, in Lexx.);—abs ק׳ Ezr 7[23].

קְצָת v. קצא.

†**[קְרָא]** **vb. call, read out, aloud** (v. BH I. קרא);—**Pe.** *Impf.* 3 ms. יִקְרֵא Dn 5[7], 1 s. אֶקְרֵא v[17]; 3 mpl. יִקְרוֹן v[15]; *Inf.* לְמִקְרָא v[8 15]; *Pt. act.* קָרֵא 3[4]+;—**1.** *call, proclaim*, בְּחַיִל: Dn 3[4] 4[11] 5[7]. **2.** *read out, aloud*, acc. כְּתָבָא 5[7.8.15 16], v[17] (לְ pers.). **Pe'il** (W[CG 225]) *Pf.* 3 ms קְרִי Ezr 4[18.23] *it was read*, קֳדָם pers **Hithpe.** *be summoned*, *Impf.* 3 ms יִתְקְרֵי Dn 5[12].

†**קְרֵב** **vb. approach** (v. BH I קרב);—**Pe.** *Pf.* 3 ms. ק׳ Dn 3[26] (לְ loc.); 1 s קִרְבֵת 7[16] (עַל pers); abs., 3 mpl. קְרִבוּ Dn 3[8] 6[13], *Inf.* sf. בְּמִקְרְבֵהּ 6[21] *when he approached*, לְ loc. **Pa.** *offer* sacrifice: *Impf.* 2 ms תְּקָרֵב Ezr 7[17], c. acc. +עַל of altar. **Haph. 1.**=**Pa.**: c. acc. *Pf.* 3 mpl. הַקְרִבוּ Ezr 6[17], *Pt. act.* מְהַקְרְבִין v[10] (לְ dei) **2.** *bring near*: *Pf* sf. הַקְרְבוּהִי Dn 7[13] (קֳדָם dei).

†**קְרָב** (K § 57 a)) **n.[m.] war** (𝔗 Syr. NH *id.*; BH as Aramaism),—abs Dn 7[21].

†**קִרְיָה**, **־ָא**, **n.f. city** (𝔗 Syr.; S-C[A 9+] קריה; v. BH, ✓קרה; also No[Beitr 62]);—abs. ־ָה Ezr 4[10], ־ָא v[15]; emph. קִרְיְתָא v[12 13.15 15 16.19 21]

†**קֶרֶן** **n.f.**[Dn 7, 8] **horn** (v. BH קרן);—abs. ק׳ Dn 7[8]; emph. קַרְנָא 3[5]+, du. (often!) קַרְנַיִן 7[7]; emph ־נַיָּא 7[8]+,—**1.** instr. of music, Dn 3[5.7 10 15]. **2.** symbolic, in vision, 7[7 8.8.8.11 20 20.21 24].

[קְרַץ] **n.[m.] piece** (𝔗, v. BH קרץ);—pl. sf. קַרְצוֹהִי Dn 6[25], ־צֵיהוֹן 3[8], both in phr. אֲכַלוּ ק׳, i e *accuse maliciously* (so 𝔗 Syr. PS[3756] (cf. OAram אמר כרצי פ׳ Lzb[299] SAC[56] Cooke[205 f.]; כרץ also Mand.), prob. borrowed from As. *karṣe akâlu*, *malign*, *slander* (oft.; also TelAm.); cf. also *uktarriṣu* Hamm[Law 161]; further Ar أَكَلَ لَحْمَهُ *id.*, and kindred phr.; Eth. በልዐ: ሥጋ: Di[499]).

†קְשֹׁט **n.[m.]** truth (𝔗 Syr.; v. BH קֹשֶׁט (once, Aramaism));—abs. Dn 4^{34}, מִן־ק׳ 2^{47} *of a truth.*

קַתְרֹס v. קיתרס.

ר

ראה (✓of foll.; not Aram.; BH רָאָה *see*).

†[רֵו] **n.m.** appearance (𝔗, rare),—sf רֵוֵהּ Dn 2^{31} 3^{25}.

†רֵאשׁ **n.m.** $^{Dn\,7\,6}$ head (Eg. Aram., S-C^{Pap}, Palm. רש; 𝔗 רֵישׁ, Syr. ܪܺܫܳܐ; BH רֹאשׁ),—cstr. ר׳ Dn 7^{1}, emph. ־ָה 2^{38}, sf. רֵאשִׁי 4^{2}+, ־ָךְ 2^{28}, ־ֵהּ v^{32}+, ־ַהּ 7^{20}, ־הוֹן 3^{27}, pl. abs רֵאשִׁין 7^{6}, sf. רָאשֵׁיהֹם (K$^{\S\,53,\ Anm\ b)}$. ^{63} Gu$^{Hpt\ ad\ loc.}$) Ezr 5^{10},—**1.** *head* of man Dn 3^{27}, cf 7^{9}; in vision: of image 2$^{32.38}$, beast 7$^{6\,20}$ **2.** *head* as seat of visions, חֶזְוֵי רֵאשָׁךְ, etc., 2^{28} 4$^{2\,7\,10}$ 7$^{1\,15}$. **3.** =*chief,* בר׳ Ezr 5^{10} *in the capacity of their chiefs* **4.** *sum,* essential content, of matters Dn 7^{1} (Nes$^{MM\,40}$ *beginning*)

רבב (✓of foll.; v. BH I. רבב, רַב, רִבּוֹ)

רַב **adj.** great (𝔗 Syr.),—abs Dn 2^{31}+, cstr. v^{14}+, emph m. רַבָּא Ezr 4^{10}+; f. רַבְּתָא Dn 4^{27}, mpl redupl רַבְרְבִין (K$^{\S\,59,4}$) 3^{33}, fpl. ־ָן 2^{48}+, emph ־ָתָא 7$^{11\,17}$,—**1.** *great,* lit, of image Dn 2^{31}, rock v^{35}, city 4^{27}, sea 7^{2}, beast v$^{3.17}$, teeth v^{7}, gifts 2^{48}, *great,* imposing, feast 5^{1}, signs 3^{33}, words 7$^{8.11\,20}$, c מִן comp 7^{20}. **2.** fig of power, influence, etc.: *great* king 2^{10} Ezr 4^{10} 5^{11} (cf Zinj. מלכן רברבן Cooke^{183}), God 5^{8} Dn 2^{45}. **3.** as n =*captain, chief.* רַב טַבָּחַיָּא Dn 2^{14}, ר׳ סִגְנִין v^{48}, ר׳ חַרְטֻמַּיָּא 4^{6} 5^{11}.

†רִבּוֹ (K$^{\S\,65,4}$) **n.f. myriad** (𝔗 Syr.),—abs ר׳+pl. רבון Kt (rd רִבְּוָן K$^{l\,c}$), רִבְבָן Qr Dn 7^{10} *a myriad myriads.*

†[רַבְרְבָן] **n.m.** lord, noble (cf. 𝔗 Syr.);—pl. sf רַבְרְבָנַי Dn 4^{33} *my lords* (of Neb); ־נוֹהִי (of Belshazzar) 5$^{1\,2.3.9\,10}$, of Darius 6^{18}; ־ניך Kt, ־ָנָךְ Qr (K$^{\S\,53,\ Anm\ b)}$) of Belshazzar v^{23}.

†רְבָה **vb.** grow great (𝔗 Syr; v. BH I. רבה);—**Pe.** *Pf* 3 ms. ר׳ Dn 4^{8}+, 3 fs רְבַת v^{19}; 2 ms רְבַיְתָ Kt (>רבת Qr K$^{\S\,47\ Beisp\ 1)\,a)}$) v^{19},—*grow tall and large,* of tree Dn 4$^{8\,17}$, *grow long,* of hair v^{30}; fig *grow great,* of king v^{19}, *increase,* of greatness v^{19}. **Pa.** *make great. Pf* 3 ms רַבִּי 2^{48} c. לְ acc. pers.

†רְבוּ **n.f.** greatness (𝔗 Syr.);—abs. ר׳ Dn 4^{33}, emph. רְבוּתָא 5^{18}+, sf. ־ָךְ 4^{19};—*greatness* of king Dn 4$^{19.33}$ 5$^{18\,19}$, of kingdom 7^{27}.

רבע (v BH אַרְבַּע, רביעי, ✓רבע).

†אַרְבַּע, אַרְבְּעָה **n.m. et f.** four,—**1. m.**: bef. **n.fpl.** Dn 7$^{2.3}$; **n.fs.** א׳ מְאָה Ezr 6^{17}; after **n.fpl.** Dn 7^{6}; as pred. אַרְבַּע v^{17}. **2. f.**: bef. **n.mpl.** Dn 7$^{6.17}$; after **n.mpl.** 3^{25}.

†[רְבִיעָי] **adj. num. ord.** fourth,—f. abs. רביעיא Kt, רְבִיעָאָה Qr (K$^{\S\,66,1}$) Dn 2^{40} 3^{25} 7$^{7.23}$; emph. רְבִיעָיְתָא v$^{19.23}$.

רַבְרְבִין etc. v. רַב supr. רַבְרְבָן v. רבב.

†[רְגַז] **vb. Haph.** enrage (cf. BH);—*Pf.* 3 mpl. הַרְגִּזוּ Ezr 5^{12}, c. acc לֶאֱלָהּ שְׁמַיָּא

†רְגַז **n.m.** rage;—abs. Dn 3^{13} (of king).

†[רְגַל] **n.[f.]** foot (v. BH);—*du.* abs. רַגְלַיִן Dn 7^{4}, emph. ־לַיָּא 2$^{41\,42}$; sf. ־לוֹהִי v$^{33.34}$, רגליה Kt, רַגְלַהּ Qr (K$^{\S\,53,2,\ Anm\ b)}$) 7$^{7\,19}$;—*feet;* in vision, of image Dn 2$^{33.34.41\,42}$, of beast 7$^{4.7\,19}$.

†[רְגַשׁ] **vb.** be in tumult (𝔗; Syr. (rare; usu *feel, perceive*); v BH (late, rare));—**Haph.** *shew tumultuousness, come thronging: Pf.* 3 mpl הַרְגִּשׁוּ, c. עַל pers. Dn 6$^{7\,16}$, abs v^{12}.

רֵוֵהּ v. [רֵו] sub ראה.

רוח (✓of foll.; v. BH *id.*, רוּחַ, רֵיחַ).

†רוּחַ **n.f.** $^{Dn\,5,12}$ wind, spirit,—ר׳ abs. Dn 5^{12} 6^{4}, cstr. 4^{5}+, emph. רוּחָא 2^{35}, sf. רוּחִי 7^{15}, ־ֵהּ 5^{20}; pl cstr. רוּחֵי 7^{2},—**1.** *wind* Dn 2^{35} 7^{2}. **2.** *spirit:* **a.** of man, 5^{20} 7^{15}; as faculty of knowledge, ר׳ יַתִּירָא 5^{12} 6^{4}. **b.** ר׳ אֱלָהִין קַדִּישִׁין 4$^{5.6\,15}$ 5^{11}, ר׳ א׳ v^{14}

†רֵיחַ **n.f.** smell,—cstr ר׳ נוּר Dn 3^{27}.

†[רוּם] **vb.** rise (v BH);—**Pe.** *Pt pass.* רם Dn 5^{20} *lifted up,* of heart, i.e presumptuous. **Pōʿl.** *extol Pt.* מְרוֹמֵם 4^{34} (לְ dei) **Haph.** *exalt: Pt.* מָרִים 5^{19} (acc. pers.). **Hithpōʿl.** *lift oneself up* against, 5^{23} (עַל dei).

†[רוּם] **n.m.** $^{Dn\,4\,7}$ height;—sf. רוּמֵהּ, of temple Ezr 6^{3}, image Dn 3^{1}, tree in vision 4$^{7\,8\,17}$.

†רָז **n.m** $^{Dn\,2,\,18}$ secret (𝔗 *id*, Syr. ܐܪܙ, ܐܪ̈ܙܐ, ܐܪܙܐ; Pers loan-word; =Phlv. *rāž*, NPers. *rāz* Andr$^{M\,83\,*}$),—abs. ר׳ Dn 4^{6}, emph רָזָא 2$^{18\,19\,27\,30.47}$; pl. abs. רָזִין v$^{28.47}$, emph. רָזַיָּא v^{29}.

רחוּם **n.pr.m.** Persian official Ezr 4^{8} (usu. expl. from √רחם, v. BH, p. 933; Scheft[92] thinks poss. orig. רוּחם, OIran. n pr. *rukma*, =*splendour*).

רַחֲמִין **n. [m.] pl. intens.** compassion (BH רַחֲמִים, √I. רחם);—abs. ר׳ Dn 2^{18}.

†**[רְחַץ]** **vb.** trust (𝔗 *id.*, Chr-Pal. ܪܚܨ Schwally[Idiot 126] Schulth[Lex 193], As. *raḫâṣu*; Ar. رَخَّصَ II. *have indulgence, permission*);—**Hithpe.** *set one's trust* upon (עַל dei) *Pf.* 3 mpl. הִתְרְחִצוּ Dn 3^{28}.

רחק (√of following; v BH רחק, רָחוֹק).

†**[רַחִיק]** **adj.** far;—pl. abs. רַחִיקִין הֲווֹ מִן־תַּמָּה Ezr 6^{6}, i. e. keep aloof.

רֵיחַ v. רוח.

†**[רְמָא]** **vb.** cast, throw (v. BH I. רמה (rare));—**Pe.** *Pf.* 3 mpl. רְמוֹ Dn $6^{17.25}$; 1 pl. רְמֵינָא 3^{24}; *Inf.* לְמִרְמֵא v^{20} Ezr 7^{24},—**1.** *cast*, acc. pers + לְ loc. Dn 3^{24} 6^{25}; acc. pers. om. v^{17} 3^{20}. **2.** fig. *throw* (burden of) tribute, עַל pers., Ezr 7^{24}. **Pe'îl** *Pf.* 3 mpl. רְמִיו (W[CG 225]): **1.** *were cast*, subj pers. c. לְ loc, Dn 3^{21}. **2.** *were placed, set*, 7^{9} (cf. 𝔗 Je 1^{15} Dr, and BH ירה **2**) **Hithpe.** *be cast*, subj. pers. c. לְ loc.: *Impf.* 3 ms. יִתְרְמֵא Dn $3^{6.11}$ $6^{8.13}$; 2 mpl. תִּתְרְמוֹן 3^{15}.

רעה (√of following; cf BH III. רעה).

[רְעוּ] **n.f.** good pleasure, will,—cstr. רְעוּת of king Ezr 5^{17}, of God 7^{18}.

†**[רַעְיוֹן]** **n.m.** [Dn 4.16] thought;—pl. cstr. רַעְיוֹנֵי לִבְבָךְ Dn 2^{30}; sf. ־נַי 7^{28}, ־נִיךְ Kt, ־נָךְ Qr (K[§ 53 Anm. b)]) 2^{29} 5^{10}, רַעְיֹנֹהִי 4^{16} 5^{6}.

†**רַעְנַן** **adj.** flourishing (perh. loan-word from BH רַעֲנָן *luxuriant*, √רען);—fig. of pers. Dn 4^{1} (cf. BH ψ 92^{15}).

†**[רְעַע]** **vb.** crush, shatter (𝔗 Syr; v. BH רצץ);—**Pe.** *Impf.* 3 fs. (ו)תֵּרֹעַ Dn 2^{40} (obj. om). **Pa.** *Pt. act* מְרָעַע 2^{40} (acc. rei).

†**[רְפַס]** **vb.** tread, trample (cf. BH (late)),—**Pe.** *Pt. act.* fs. בְּרַגְלַיהּ רָפְסָה, c. acc. rei Dn $7^{7.19}$.

†**רְשַׁם** **vb.** inscribe, sign (𝔗 Syr.; v. BH (once, late)),—**Pe.** *Pf.* 3 ms ר׳ Dn 6^{10}; 2 ms. רְשַׁמְתָּ v^{13}, רְשַׁמְתָּ v^{14}; *Impf.* 2 ms. (וְ)תִרְשֻׁם v^{9};—*inscribe* (prob. with one's name, i.e.) *sign*, acc. כְּתָבָא Dn $6^{9.10}$, אֱסָר $v^{13.14}$. **Pe'îl** *Pf.* 3 ms. רְשִׁים, subj. כְּתָבָא: **1.** *be inscribed, written*, Dn $5^{24.25}$. **2.** *be signed* 6^{11}.

שׂ

†**שַׂבְּכָא** (>van d. H. ס׳, v. Baer) **n. [f.]** trigon, mus instr. (whence prob. Gk. σαμβύκη, triang instr. with four strings, v. Thes Lewy [Fremdw 161 f] Prince [EB 3235] Dr [Dn 3. 5]; also BH שְׂבָכָה *lattice-work*, √שבך, cf. Syr. ܣܒܟܐ),—Dn $3^{5.7.10.15}$.

†**[שְׂגָא]** **vb.** grow great (𝔗 ס׳, Syr. ܣ׳; v. BH שׂגא (Aramaism in Job)),—**Pe.** *Impf.* 3 ms. יִשְׂגֵּא, of injury Ezr 4^{22}; יִשְׂ׳ שְׁלָמְכוֹן Dn 3^{31} 6^{26}.

שַׂגִּיא **adj.** great, much;—abs. שׂ׳ Dn 2^{6}+, fpl. שַׂגִּיאָן 2^{48} Ezr 5^{11};—**1.** *great*, of image Dn 2^{31} (in vision), height of tree 4^{7} (*id.*); of honour 2^{6}. **2.** *much*, fruit $4^{9.18}$, flesh 7^{5}; pl. *many*, years Ezr 5^{11}, gifts Dn 2^{48}. **3.** as adv. *exceedingly*, 2^{12} 5^{9} $6^{15.24}$ 7^{28}.

†**[שָׂהֲדוּ]** **n.f.** testimony (√שׂהד = 𝔗 סְהַד *testify*, Syr. ܣܗܕ, Ar شَهِدَ *testify*, cf BH [שָׂהֵד] (once, as loan-wd.) K[Aram 86]; Eg. Aram. pl. שהדיא *witnesses*, Cooke[404] S-C[A 15+oft]);—emph. שָׂהֲדוּתָא Gn 31^{47} (‖ BH עֵד).

[שׂוּם], שִׂים **vb.** set, make (v. BH; for Pers. infl. on usage cf. Scheft[63]),—**Pe.** *Pf.* 3 ms. שָׂם Ezr 5^{3}+, sf. שָׂמֵהּ 5^{14}; 2 ms. שַׂמְתָּ Dn 3^{10}; 1 s. שָׂמֶת טְעֵם Ezr 6^{12}; 3 mpl. שָׂמוּ Dn 3^{12}; *Imv.* mpl. שִׂימוּ Ezr 4^{21},—**1.** *make*, acc. טעם = *make decree* Dn 3^{10} Ezr $6^{1.12}$, + vb. fin v^{3}, + inf. 4^{21} 5^{13} and (c. לְ pers.) $v^{3.9}$. **2.** *make, appoint*, one's name Dn 5^{12} (2 acc.), one to office Ezr 5^{14} (2 acc). **3.** *set, fix*, acc. בָּל *mind*, Dn 6^{15} (c. inf.); acc. טעם 3^{12} 6^{14} *pay* due regard (טְעֵם) to (עַל pers.). **Pe'îl** 3 ms. מִנִּי שִׂים טעם Ezr 4^{19} *from me a decree is made*, so 5^{17} $6^{8.11}$ $7^{13.21}$ Dn 3^{29} 4^{3} 6^{27}; lit 3 fs. שָׂמַת (rd. prob. שִׂימַת K[§ 45, Beisp. 1 d)]) 6^{18} (of stone, עַל loc). **Hithpe.** *be made*: *Impf.* 3 ms. יִתְּשָׂם Ezr 4^{21} (of decree, טְעֵם c. מִן agent.); 3 mpl. יִתְּשָׂמוּן Dn 2^{5} subj. rei + n. pred. *be made into*; *Pt.* מִתְּשָׂם Ezr 5^{8} lit. *be set, laid*, of wood, בְּ of wall.

†**שְׂטַר** **n.m.** side (Eg. Aram. S-C[A 4]; 𝔗 סְטַר, סִטְרָא, Syr. ܣܛܪܐ, Chr-Pal. ܣܛܪ Schulth[Lex 134], cf. Schwally[Idiot. 62, 122]; Ar. شَطْرٌ *half*),—abs. שׂ׳ Dn 7^{5} (of beast in vision).

†[שִׂיב] **vb.** be hoary (v. BH);—**Pe.** *Pt* pl as subst. = *elders*, term. techn, abs. שָׂבֵי יְהוּדָיֵא Ezr 5[5] 6[7 8 14], so emph שָׂבַיָּא 5[9]

†[שׂכל] **vb. Hithpe.** consider, contemplate (v. BH I. שׂכל),—*Pt.* משׂתַּכַּל Dn 7[8] (ב rei)

†שָׂכְלְתָנוּ (K[§61 4)]) **n.f.** insight,—Dn 5[11 12 14].

†[שְׂנָא] **vb.** hate (𝔗 סְנָא, Syr. ܣܢܐ; v BH שָׂנֵא),—**Pe.** *Pt* pl sf שׂנאיך Kt, שָׂנְאָךְ Qr (K[§ 53, 2, Anm b)]) Dn 4[16] = *thy foes* (BH **3**, MI'Sab).

†שְׂעַר **n m** [Dn 3, 27] hair, of head (𝔗 ס׳, Syr. ܣ׳, v BH I שֵׂעָר),—cstr. Dn 3[27] 7[9]; sf שַׂעְרֵהּ 4[30]

שׁ

שׁאל **vb** ask (v. BH),—**Pe.** *Pf.* 3 ms. שׁ׳ Dn 2[10], pl. שְׁאֵלְנָא Ezr 5[9 10], *Impf* 3 ms sf יִשְׁאֲלִנְּכוֹן Ezr 7[21], *Pt act* שָׁאֵל Dn 2[11 27],—**1.** *ask for, request*, acc rei Dn 2[10] (לְ pers.), v[11 27] Ezr 7[21] (sf pers.). **2.** *inquire about, for*, acc rei Ezr 5[9] (לְ pers), sq orat. rect. v[10] (*id.*)

†[שְׁאֵלָה] **n.f.** affair (weakened fr. *question, inquiry*, cf Dr),—emph שְׁאֵלְתָא Dn 4[14]

†שְׁאָר **n.m.** [Ezr 7 20] rest, remainder (v BH I שְׁאָר, Eg Aram n. שאר Cooke[203], vb ישתאר *be left* (outstanding) Cooke[404] = S-C[L 9], Chr-Pal ܫܐܪ),—שׁ׳ abs Ezr 4[10] +, cstr. v[9] +; emph שְׁאָרָא Dn 7[7 19],—of a thing, *remainder* Ezr 7[18 20], of cities 4[10 17], of persons v[9 10 17] 6[16] Dn 2[18], of beasts 7[7 12 19]

†שׁבב (√of foll., cf. BH II. שׁבב)

[שְׁבִיב] **n.[m.]** flame,—emph שְׁבִיבָא דִי נוּרָא Dn 3[22], pl abs שְׁבִבִין דִי נוּר 7[9].

†[שַׁבַּח] **vb. Pa** laud, praise (𝔗 Syr., v BH II שׁבח (Aramaism)),—*Pf* 2 ms. שַׁבַּחְתְּ Dn 5[23], 1 s שַׁבְּחֵת 4[31], 3 mpl שַׁבַּחוּ 5[4]; *Pt. act* מְשַׁבַּח 2[23] 4[34];—*praise*, c לְ dei Dn 2[23] 4[31 34]; לְ of idols 5[4 23]

†[שְׁבַט] **n.m.** tribe (BH שֵׁבֶט, √שׁבט);—pl cstr שִׁבְטֵי יִשְׂרָאֵל Ezr 6[17].

†[שְׁבַע], only שִׁבְעָה **n.f.** seven (BH I שֶׁבַע);—abs שׁ׳ bef **n.m** pl Dn 4[13 20 22 29], cstr שִׁבְעַת bef **n.m.** pl Ezr 7[14], חַד שִׁבְעָה עַל־דִּי Dn 3[19] *seven times above what* (more than), v. חַד, √אחד.

†[שְׁבַק] **vb.** leave, let alone (𝔗 שְׁבַק, Syr. ܫܒܩ, cf BH, p. 990);—**Pe.** *Inf.* לְמִשְׁבַּק Dn 4[23] *leave* roots, so *Imv.* mpl. שְׁבֻקוּ v[12 20] (both c ב loc), Ezr 6[7] *let alone*, c. לְ acc rei. **Hithpe.** *Impf.* 3 fs. תִשְׁתְּבִק Dn 2[44] *be left* (of kingdom, + לְ gent).

†[שְׁבַשׁ] **vb. Hithp.** be perplexed (𝔗 *id*, *entangle, beguile*, NH שִׁבֵּשׁ *confuse, disarrange;* cf As *šabâšu* (*šabasu*), *turn about;* Syr. ܫܒܫ *flatter, allure*, Schulth[Hom. Wurz 90]; so Mand Pa שׁבּשׁ No[M 49], cf Ar. شَوَّشَ (as loan-word No[l c]) *confuse*),—*Pt.* pl. מִשְׁתַּבְּשִׁין Dn 5[9].

†[שֵׁגַל] **n.f.** (royal) consort (cf. BH *id.*; √unknown Hpt[Gu Ezr Ne, p 66] conj. As. *šigrêti, harem-women*),—pl. sf. שֵׁגְלָתָךְ Dn 5[23], שֵׁגְלָתֵהּ v[2 3].

†[שְׁדַר] **vb. Hithpa.** struggle, strive (𝔗 *id.* Pa *wrestle*, Ithpa *be recalcitrant*, also שְׁדַל Ithpa. *strive*, and so NH שִׁדֵּל (ל for ר), Syr. ܫܕܠ *beguile*, esp Pa, v. No[ZMG xl (1886), 734]);—*Pt.* מִשְׁתַּדַּר Dn 6[15] *he was striving*, sq Inf

‡†אֶשְׁתַּדּוּר **n.m.** revolt;—abs. Ezr 4[15 19].

שַׁדְרַךְ **n.pr.m.** (cf BH *id*);—Dn 2[49] 3[12 13] + 11 t 3.

שׁדת (√of foll; BH שׁרשׁ, שׁשׁ).

†שֵׁת, שִׁת **n.m.** six,—abs. שִׁת after **n.f.** Dn 3[1], שְׁנַת־שֵׁת Ezr 6[15] *year six = sixth year.*

†שִׁתִּין **n. indecl.** sixty,—אַמִּין שׁ׳ Ezr 6[3 3] Dn 3[1]; שְׁנִין שׁ׳ וְתַרְתֵּין 6[1].

†I [שְׁוָה] **vb.** become like (BH I שָׁוָה),—**Pa.** *Pf.* 3 mpl. שַׁוִּיו Qr (v ו foll, > **Peʿîl** שׁוי Kt, v K[§ 47 Beisp 3, and p 170]) Dn 5[21], acc. rei, c עִם

†II. [שְׁוָה] **vb. Hithpa.** be set, made (Pa שַׁוִּי *make*, Cappadoc Aram Lzb[Eph i 67]; cf. BH II. [שָׁוָה]),—*Impf* 3 ms יִשְׁתַּוֵּה Dn 3[29], subj rei + acc. *be made into* something (K[§ 84 3]).

שׁוק (√of following; BH I שׁוק, שׁוק).

†[שָׁק] **n.[m.]** lower leg,—pl sf. שָׁקוֹהִי Dn 2[33].

†[שׁוּר] **n m.** wall (cf BH II. שׁוּר *id.*; Eg. Aram. שׁור RÉS [361 A 5, B 1]),—pl emph שׁוּרַיָּה Ezr 4[16], ־ָא v[13], v[12] rd. שׁוּרַיָּא שׁ׳ Qr, for שׁורי אשׁ׳ Kt.

שׁוּשַׁנְכָיֵא **n. pr. gent. pl.** the Susians, people of Susa Ezr 4[9], v. דהוא (Dl[Pa 327]; sg. [שׁוּשַׁנָךְ] acc to Scheft[92], = OP **šušana-ka, from Susa*, so (as altern) Andr[M 85*]; cf. (on Elam. god *Šušinak*) Weissbach[Anzanische Inschr 136] Jen[VOJ

$^{vi\ 54}$ Zim$^{KAT\ 2.485}$, and (on *Šušunka* in Elam. inscr., appar. n pr. terr.) v. Weissb$^{l\ c}$ Jen$^{ZMG\ lv\ (1901),\ 229}$)

†[שְׁחַת] **vb. corrupt** (𝔗^{J} (once), Syr. ܫܚܬ; BH [שָׁחַת]);—**Pe.** *Pt. pass* fs. שְׁחִיתָה Dn 2^{9} *corrupt* word; as n. = *fault* 6$^{5.5}$ (cf. 𝔗 ψ 17^{3} Ru 4^{22}).

†שֵׁיזִב **vb. deliver** (prob. **Shaph.** as loan-word from As. *šûzub(u), ušêzib, deliver*, √*ezêbu* (א$_4$ = עזב), Dl$^{Pr\ 140}$ Hpt$^{GGN\ 1883,\ 91;\ BAS\ i\ 13}$ K$^{§\ 43.\ 1,\ Anm}$; 𝔗 שֵׁיזֵב, Syr. ܫܘܙܒ, Chr-Pal. ܫܘܙܒ Schulth$^{Lex\ 203}$, also Nab. שיזב Cooke^{255}; cf. n pr. מְשֵׁיזַבְאֵל BH; OAram. צלמשזב SAC^{102}; v. also foll. art.);—*Pf.* 3 ms. שֵׁיזִב Dn 3^{28} 6^{28}; *Impf.* 3 ms יְשֵׁיזִב 3^{17}; sf. יְשֵׁיזְבִנָּךְ 6^{17}, -ִנְכוֹן 3^{15}; *Inf.* sf לְשֵׁיזָבוּתָךְ 6^{21}, -תֵה v^{15}, -תַנָא 3^{17};—*deliver* (usu. c. מִן): Dn 3^{17b}, לְ acc. pers. v^{28} 6^{28b}, sf. pers 3$^{15.17a}$ 6$^{15.17.21}$, abs. v^{28a}.

†שֵׁיצִיא Kt, שֵׁיצִי Qr **vb. bring out** (to an end), **finish** (prob. **Shaph.** as loan-word fr. As. *šû-ṣû, û-še-ṣû, bring out*, √*aṣû* (יצא, BH יצא, = Aram. יְעָא, cf. No$^{GGA\ 1884,\ 1019}$), Dl$^{l\ c}$ Hpt$^{l\ c}$ K$^{l\ c}$; 𝔗 שֵׁיצִי *complete, put an end to*, also *come to an end*, pass. *be finished*, Chr-Pal. ܫܝܨܝ Schulth$^{Lex\ 205}$);—*finish* temple: *Pf.* 3 ms. 'שׁ Ezr 6^{15}, but read prob. 3 mpl. שֵׁיצִיו K$^{§\ 43,\ 1\ ad\ fin}$ Berthol Gu^{Hpt} (so 𝔊 𝔙); > *Pf.* pass. Be-Ry.

שכב (√of foll.; BH מִשְׁכָּב, שָׁכַב)

†[מִשְׁכַּב] **n.[m.] couch, bed**,—sf. מִשְׁכְּבִי Dn 4$^{2.7.10}$; -ָךְ 2$^{28.29}$; -ֵהּ 7^{1}.

†[שְׁכַח] **vb. Haph.** (K$^{§\ 40,\ 4}$ No$^{GGA\ 1884,\ 1019}$) **find** (𝔗 שְׁכַח *find*, Syr. ܐܫܟܚ, Chr-Pal ܫܟܚ Schulth$^{Lex\ 206}$, Eg Aram השכח S-C$^{E\ 5}$, pass. אשתכח RÉS$^{361\ A\ 2}$).—*Pf.* 1 s. הַשְׁכַּחַת Dn 2^{25}; 3 mpl. הַשְׁכַּחוּ Ezr 4^{19} Dn 6^{12}; *Impf.* 2 ms. תְּהַשְׁכַּח Ezr 4^{15} 7^{16}; *Inf.* לְהַשְׁכָּחָה Dn 6$^{5.5}$;—*find*, acc. rei, 6^{5} (לְ pers.), v$^{5.6}$ (לְ pers.), v^{6} (עַל pers., acc. rei om.), Ezr 7^{16} (בְּ loc.), sq. cl. דִּי 4^{15} (בְּ loc.), v^{19}; acc. pers. Dn 2^{25}; לְ pers. 6^{12} (+ pt. action.). **Hithpe.** *Pf.* 3 ms. הִשְׁתְּכַח Dn 2^{35} +, 2 ms. -כַּחַתְּ 5^{27}, 3 fs -כַּחַת 5^{11} +;—*be found*, subj. rei, בְּ loc, Ezr 6^{2}, בְּ pers. Dn 5$^{11.12.14}$ 6^{24}; עַל pers. v^{5}; לְ pers. + קֳדָם pers. v^{23}; לְ rei 2^{35} (v. אֲתַר); subj pers. 5^{27} + חַסִּיר *thou hast been found wanting* (K$^{§\ 85,\ 3}$).

שַׁכְלֱלָה etc, v. כלל.

†[שְׁכַן cf. 𝔗] **vb. dwell** (BH מִשְׁכָּן, שָׁכַן);—**Pe.** *Impf.* 3 fpl. יִשְׁכְּנָן Dn 4^{18} *dwell*, of birds, בְּ loc. **Pa.** causat.: *Pf.* 3 ms. שַׁכִּן שְׁמֵהּ תַּמָּה Ezr 6^{12}, of God, *cause his name to dwell there*.

†[מִשְׁכַּן] **n.[m.] abode, of God**;—sf. מִשְׁכְּנֵהּ Ezr 7^{15}, of Jerusalem.

שלה, שלו (√of foll; BH I. שלה (late)).

†שְׁלֵה **adj. at ease** (Eg. Aram. Cooke^{210}),—'שׁ הֲוֵית בְּ Dn 4^{1} *I was at ease in* my house — 3^{29} v. following.

†שָׁלוּ **n.f. neglect, remissness** (𝔗 *id*);—abs. 'שׁ Ezr 4^{22} 6^{9} Dn 6^{5} + 3^{29} Qr; Kt שלה usu. thought an error for שלו; Hi Bev M (perhaps) expl. as שָׁלָה = שְׁאֵלָה = *thing, affair* (4^{14})

†[שְׁלֵוָה] **n.f. ease, prosperity**;—sf. שְׁלֵוְתָךְ Dn 4^{24}.

†שְׁלַח **vb. send** (BH I. שָׁלַח);—**Pe.** *Pf.* 3 ms. 'שׁ Ezr 4^{17} +; 3 mpl. שְׁלַחוּ 4^{11} +; 2 mpl. שְׁלַחְתּוּן 4^{18}; 1 pl. שְׁלַחְנָא 4^{14}; *Impf.* 3 ms. יִשְׁלַח 5^{17} 6^{12}; *Pt. pass.* שְׁלִיחַ 7^{14} Dn 5^{24};—*send*, acc. of letter, etc, c. עַל pers. Ezr 4$^{11.17.18}$ 5$^{6.7.17}$; abs. 6^{13}, sq. vb. fin 4^{14}, + acc. pers. Dn 3^{28} 6^{23}, sq. Inf. Dn 3^{2}; *send out* hand (acc.) to harm (Inf); *pass, be sent*, c. מִן־קֳדָם pers.: subj pers. Ezr 7^{14}, subj כַּפָּא Dn 5^{24}.

†שְׁלֵט **vb. have power, rule** (𝔗 Syr.; BH (q.v.) late),—**Pe.** *Pf.* 3 ms 'שׁ Dn 3^{27}, 3 mpl שְׁלִטוּ 6^{25}; *Impf.* 3 ms. יִשְׁלַט 5^{7}, 3 fs. תִּשְׁלַט 2^{39}, 2 ms. תִּשְׁלַט 5^{16};—*have power* upon, בְּ rei, Dn 3^{27} (of fire); *fall upon, assault* (𝔗 = פְּגַע בְּ), בְּ pers. 6^{25} (of lions); subj pers. *rule, be ruler*, abs, 5$^{7.16}$, subj. kingdom, בְּ of earth, 2^{39}. **Haph.** *make ruler*: *Pf.* 3 ms. sf. הַשְׁלְטָךְ 2^{38} (בְּ pers, etc.); הַשְׁלְטֵהּ v^{48} (עַל of province).

†שָׁלְטָן (K$^{§\ 61\ 3,\ Beisp.\ a)}$) **n.m.**$^{Dn\ 7\ 6}$ **dominion**;—'שׁ abs. Dn 7$^{6.14}$, cstr. 6^{27} +; emph שָׁלְטָנָא 7^{27}; sf. שָׁלְטָנָךְ 4^{19}, -נֵהּ 3^{33} +, -נְהוֹן 7^{12}; pl. emph. שָׁלְטָנַיָּא 7^{27};—**1.** *dominion, sovereignty* (usu. of God): Dn 3^{33} 4$^{19.31.31}$ 6^{27b} 7$^{6.12.14.14.14.26.27.27}$. **2.** *realm* 6^{27a}.

†שַׁלִּיט **adj. having mastery, ruling**;—abs. 'שׁ Ezr 7^{24} +, emph -ָא Dn 2^{15}; mpl. שַׁלִּיטִין Ezr 4^{20}, -ן Dn 4^{23};—**1.** *having, exercising, mastery*: **a.** of God, sq בְּ, Dn 4$^{14.22.29}$ 5^{21}, abs., of heavens 4^{23}. **b.** of kings Ezr 4^{20} (בְּ). **2.** as n. = *ruler* Dn 2^{10}, *captain* v^{15}. **3.** *having authority* to do a thing (Inf.), hence impers. = *it is authorized*, Ezr 7^{24} (so oft. in Syr.; cf. S-C$^{A\ 11\ +}$ אנת שליט למבנה).

†[שְׁלֵם] **vb. be complete** (v. BH; Eg. Aram. שלם *pay in full* Cooke^{404} = S-C$^{L\ 5.\ 7}$);—**Pe.** *Pt. pass.* שְׁלִם Ezr 5^{16} *finished*, of temple. **Haph.**

Pf. 3 ms. sf. הַשְׁלְמַהּ Dn 5^{26} God *has finished it* (the kingdom; brought it to an end), *Imv* ms. הַשְׁלֵם Ezr 7^{19} *render in full*, acc. rei (cf. Syr. Aph., Be-Ry Berthol), sq קֳדָם dei.

†שְׁלָם **n.m.** $^{Dn\ 3.31}$ **welfare, prosperity**;—in greetings abs Ezr 4^{17} *prosperity!* emph שְׁלָמָא 5^{7}, sf שְׁלָמְכוֹן יִשְׂגֵּא Dn 3^{31} 6^{26}.

†שֻׁם **n.m. name** (v. BH שֵׁם);—cstr. שׁ׳ Ezr 5^{1}+; sf שְׁמֵהּ Dn 2^{20}+, pl. cstr. שְׁמָהָת Ezr 5^{4}, sf שְׁמָהָתְהֹם v^{10},—*name*, dei: Dn 2^{20} 4^{5} Ezr 5^{1} 6^{12}; vir. Dn 2^{26} $4^{13.16}$ 5^{12} (all Dan.), Ezr $5^{4.10.10}$ also v^{14}, with which cf S-C$^{K\ 4,5,8\ f.,\ 12f}$

†[שְׁמַד] **vb Haph. destroy** (𝔗 Pa *make apostatize*, cf. BH),—*Inf* לְהַשְׁמָדָה Dn 7^{26} (obj om., = dominion).

†[שְׁמַיִן] **n.m. pl. heavens** (BH [שָׁמַי], שָׁמַיִם, √ שמה),—alw emph שְׁמַיָּא **1.** visible *sky* Je 10^{11} Dn $4^{8.10.17.19.20.22.28}$; צִפְּרֵי שׁ׳ עוֹף שׁ׳ 2^{38}, שׁ׳ $4^{9.18}$, טַל שׁ׳ v$^{12.20.22.30}$ 5^{21}, רוּחֵי שׁ׳ 7^{2} *winds of the sky*, עֲנָנֵי שׁ׳ v^{13}, *heavens* + earth = universe Je 10^{11}, where God shews signs Dn 6^{28} **2.** *heavens* as abode of God Dn 2^{28} 4^{11}, hence, fig., as ruling v^{23} (שׁ׳ sometimes = *God* in NH J Aram., D$^{Worte\ Jesu\ 179;\ Eng\ Tr\ 218f.}$); as abode of angels v^{32} (Di), elsewh. in phr אֱלָהּ שׁ׳ $2^{18.19.37.44}$ Ezr $5^{11.12}$ $6^{9.10}$ $7^{12.21.23.23}$, מֶלֶךְ שׁ׳ Dn 4^{34}, מָרֵא שׁ׳ 5^{23}.

†[שְׁמַם] **vb. Ethpōʿl. be appalled** (𝔗 (rare), v BH, Chr-Pal. ܫܡ, Schulth^{209}),—*Pf.* 3 ms אֶשְׁתּוֹמַם (K^{§36}) Dn 4^{16}.

†שְׁמַע **vb. hear** (v BH),—**Pe.** *Pf* 3 ms שׁ׳ Dn 6^{15}, 1 s. שִׁמְעֵת $5^{14.16}$, *Impf.* 3 ms יִשְׁמַע 3^{10}, 2 mpl. תִּשְׁמְעוּן $3^{5.15}$, *Pt. act* שָׁמְעִין 3^{7} 5^{23},—*hear* = *have sense of hearing* Dn 5^{23}; c. acc of sound $3^{5.7.10.15}$, word 6^{15}, c cl. דִּי + עַל pers. *concerning*, $5^{14.16}$ **Hithpe** *shew oneself obedient*. *Impf.* 3 mpl יִשְׁתַּמְעוּן Dn 7^{27}, c לְ pers (prob).

†שָׁמְרַיִן **n.pr.loc.** (BH שֹׁמְרוֹן, I. שָׁמַר),—Ezr 4^{17} ^{10}

I. שמשׁ (√of following, BH שֶׁמֶשׁ, שמשׁ).

†[שְׁמַשׁ] **n.[m.** so D^{WB}**] sun**,—emph. שִׁמְשָׁא Dn 6^{15}

†II [שְׁמַשׁ] **vb. Pa. minister** (𝔗 **Pa.** *id*, תַּשְׁמִישׁ *use*, Palm. שמשׁ, תשמישׁ, SAC$^{114.\ cf.\ 122}$ Lzb^{379}, Syr ܫܰܡܶܫ, ܬܫܡܫܬܐ, Chr-Pal ܫܡܫ Pa, ܫܡܫܐ; NH שִׁמֵּשׁ, תַּשְׁמִישׁ, Egypt *šms, servant*, Kopt. *šemše*, cf WMM in Buhl^{14}),—*Impf* 3 mpl sf. יְשַׁמְּשׁוּנֵּהּ Dn 7^{10} *were ministering to him*.

†שֵׁמְשַׁי **n.pr.m.**;—always שׁ׳ סָפְרָא. Ezr $4^{8.9.17.23}$ (Andr$^{M\ 86*}$ conj. OIran. caritative שְׁשְׁמַי, conformed to שמשׁ, cf Scheft^{92}, who, however, prefers OBaktr *simēzhi* = *simaēzhi*, n.pr).

שן v. שׁנן.

[שְׁנָא] **vb. change** (v. BH I שׁנה);—**Pe.** *Pf.* 3 mpl. שְׁנוֹ Dn 3^{27}, sf. שְׁנוֹהִי 5^{6} (rd. prob. שְׁנוֹ עֲלוֹהִי); *Impf* 3 ms. יִשְׁנֵא 7^{24}, 3 fs. תִּשְׁנֵא 6^{18} 7^{23}; *Pt act.* fs. שָׁנְיָא 7^{19}, mpl. שָׁנַיִן 5^{9}, fpl שָׁנְיָן 7^{3},—intrans *change, be changed*. of garment, by fire Dn 3^{27}, brightness (זִיו) of face $5^{6.9}$, purpose 6^{18}, *be different* from (מִן) $7^{3.19.23.24}$. **Pa.** *Pf.* 3 mpl. שַׁנִּיו (K$^{§47\ e).\ and\ Beisp.\ 3}$) Dn 3^{28}; *Impf* 3 mpl. יְשַׁנּוֹן 4^{13}, *Pt. pass* fs מְשַׁנְּיָא (Baer) 7^{7};—trans *change* Dn 4^{13} (לִבְבֵהּ מִן־אֲנָשָׁא); = *frustrate* word of king 3^{28}, pt pass. intrans. *different* 7^{7} (מִן) **Ithpa.** *Pf.* 3 mpl. אֶשְׁתַּנּוֹ Dn 3^{19} Kt (K$^{§47,\ Beisp.\ 4}$; נוֹ_ No$^{GGA\ 1884,\ 1019}$ Str$^{§23\ d}$ M^{24*}), > 3 ms. אֶשְׁתַּנִּי Qr; *Impf.* 3 ms יִשְׁתַּנֵּא 2^{9}, 3 mpl -נּוֹ (ן om. in pause, K$^{§26,\ 1}$, but *modus apocop* No$^{GGA\ 1884,\ 1015}$, as יֵאבַדוּ Je 10^{11}, יְבַהֲלוּךְ Dn 5^{10}; v. also Cooke^{166}) 5^{10}, -נּוֹן 7^{28},—*be changed* of זִיו Dn 5^{10} 7^{28} (v. **Pe.**; עַל pers.), צְלֵם אַנְפּוֹהִי 3^{19} (*id.*); of time, conditions 2^{9}. **Haph** *Impf.* 3 ms יְהַשְׁנֵא Ezr 6^{11}; *Inf.* לְהַשְׁנָיָה v^{12}+, *Pt. act* מְהַשְׁנֵא Dn 2^{21};—trans. *change, alter*, times, etc. (v **Ithpa.**) Dn 2^{21} 7^{25}; acc. om $6^{9.16}$ Ezr 6^{12}, *frustrate* edict (v. **Pa.**) 6^{11}.

†I. [שְׁנָה] **n.f. year** (v. BH שָׁנָה, √ I. [שָׁנָה]),—cstr. שְׁנַת · שׁ׳ חֲדָה = *first year* Ezr 5^{13} 6^{3} Dn 7^{1}; שׁ׳ תַּרְתֵּין Ezr 4^{24} *second year*, שׁ׳ שֵׁת 6^{15}, pl. שְׁנִין שִׁתִּין וּת׳ Dn 6^{1} *62 years*, שׁ׳ שְׂגִיאָן Ezr 5^{11} —II. [שְׁנָה] v. ישׁן.

שׁנן (√of following, v. BH [שָׁנַן], שֵׁן).

†[שֵׁן] **n.[f.] tooth**;—du. (of rows of teeth) abs שִׁנַּיִן Dn 7^{7};—sf. שניה Kt (K$^{§53.\ 2.\ b)}$), שִׁנַּהּ Qr, v$^{5.19}$ (all of beasts in vision).

†שָׁעָה **n.f. brief time, moment** (𝔗 *id*, שַׁעְתָּא, NH שָׁעָה *time, hour;* Syr. ܫܥܬܐ *moment*, then *hour* Brock^{369}, but Chr-Pal ܫܥܐ *moment, hour* Schwally$^{Idiot\ 97}$ Schulth$^{Lex\ 211}$, perh = As. *šattu, duration;* Tel Am$^{91,\ 77}$ *še-ti, time, hour* (as Canaanism) Wkl$^{KAT\ 3,\ 33}$, Ar. سِعْوٌ, سَاعَةٌ *portion* of time, Eth. ሰዐ: *time*, ሰዓት: *hour, time* (Buhl calls Ar. Eth. loan-words, but v. Wkl$^{l.c.}$); √unknown: poss. As. loan-word (v. Wkl$^{l.c.}$); Dl$^{Pr\ 39f}$ conj * שִׁיעַ = שָׁעָה *look*, hence *moment* = '*Augenblick*,' but vb. שׁ׳ rather of steady gaze);—*moment:* usu. emph. בַּהּ־שַׁעֲתָא (rd. poss. שָׁ׳ as

𝔗 Syr., M[86 f.] Buhl[14] cf. var. in Str) *in the same moment, forthwith* Dn 3[6.15] 4[16] 5[5]; abs. שָׁעָה חֲדָה 4[16] *for a moment.*

‡† [שְׁפַט] **vb. judge** (BH שָׁפַט);—*Pt.* as n pl. abs. שָׁפְטִין Ezr 7[25] *judges*

שַׁפִּיר v. שפר.

† [שְׁפֵל] **vb. be low** (v. BH);—**Haph.** *bring low, humble*: *Pf.* 2 ms. הַשְׁפֵּלְתְּ לִבְבָךְ Dn 5[22] *thou hast* not *humbled thine heart*; *Impf* 3 ms. יְהַשְׁפֵּל 7[24], *Inf.* לְהַשְׁפָּלָה 4[34], *Pt.* מַשְׁפִּל 5[19], all c. acc. pers. *bring low, put down.*

† שְׁפַל **adj.** low in station;—cstr. 'שׁ Dn 4[14]

† שְׁפַר **vb. be fair, seemly** (𝔗 Syr.; cf. BH (rare and mostly late); Palm ל שפר *merit well of,* SAC[117]; Cappad. Aram. שפירא Lzb Eph 160);—**Pe.** *Pf.* 3 ms. 'שׁ, c. קֳדָם pers *it seemed good to* Dn 3[32] 6[2]; *Impf.* 3 ms. יִשְׁפַּר עַל 4[24] *let* my counsel *be acceptable to* thee.

† שַׁפִּיר **adj. fair, beautiful**;—of foliage Dn 4[9 18].

† [שְׁפַרְפָּר] **n.[m.] dawn** (𝔗 *id.*; redupl. (K § 59, 5) fr. above √ ?);—emph שְׁפַרְפָּרָא Dn 6[20].

שָׁק v. שוק.

† [שְׁרָא] **vb. 1. loosen. 2. abide** (v. BH I. שרה);—**Pe.** *Inf.* לְמִשְׁרֵא Dn 5[16]; rd. 'משׁ also v[12], for 'מְשָׁ (K § 40 a M[87]* al.),—*Pt. pass.* שְׁרֵא (K § 47, Beisp. f) 2[22]; pl. שְׁרַיִן 3[25];—**1.** *loosen*: lit. pt. pass. *loosed* Dn 3[25] (opp. bound); fig *loosen* knots, i.e. solve difficulties, 5[12 16]. **2.** *abide* (from *loosening* girths, loads, at encampment; cf. 𝔗 NH [also on pt. pass]), fig. 2[22] (עִם pers.). **Pa.** *Pf.* 3 mpl שָׁרִיו Ezr 5[2] *begin* (v. BH III. [חָלַל] **Hiph. 2**), sq inf. **Hithpa.** *Pt.* mpl. מִשְׁתָּרַיִן Dn 5[6] joints *were loosened* (in fear).

שרק (𝔗 שְׁרִיק, Syr. ܫܪܩ, BH שָׁרַק *hiss, whistle* (onomatop.))

† [מַשְׁרוֹקִי] **n.f. pipe** (cf. Syr. (rare));—emph. מַשְׁרוֹקִיתָא Dn 3[5 7 15] מַשְׁרֹקִי, 3[10]

† [שֹׁרֶשׁ] **n.m.** [Dn 4 12] **root** (v. BH);—pl. sf. שָׁרְשׁוֹהִי of tree Dn 4[12.20.23].

‡† שרשו Kt (i.e. שְׁרֹשׁוּ K § 61, 4, 5), Qr שְׁרֹשִׁי **n.f. uprooting, fig. banishment**;—abs. Ezr 7[26].

שֵׁת, שִׁת *six*, v. שדת.

† [שְׁתָה] **vb. drink** (𝔗 אִשְׁתִּי, שְׁתָא, Syr. ܐܫܬܝ*; v. BH I. שָׁתָה);—**Pe.** *Pf.* 3 mpl. אִשְׁתִּיו (K § 11, 4, a) Dn 5[3.4]; *Impf.* 3 mpl. יִשְׁתּוֹן v[2]; *Pt. act.* שָׁתֵה v[1], pl. שָׁתַיִן v[23];—*drink*, acc. wine Dn 5[1 4], + בּ of vessel v[23] and (acc. om) v[2.3].

† [מִשְׁתֵּי so 𝔗] **n.m. feast** (as BH מִשְׁתֶּה),—emph. בֵּית מִשְׁתְּיָא Dn 5[10].

שִׁתִּין *sixty*, v. שדת.

† שְׁתַר בּוֹזְנַי **n.pr.m.** Pers official Ezr 5[3.6] 6[6 13]; Σαθαρβουζανα (αι, ε, ηι); 𝔊L Σαθραβωζανης (Andr[M 87]* prop. 'מתרב, Gk. Μιθροβουζάνης, = OIran. **Mithrabauzana, Mithra is deliverer* (or the like), so Mey[Entst. J 32]; Scheft[92 f] OIran. *Šēthrabûzana, empire-delivering;* Wkl[MVAG 1897, 291 f] conj. a title)

ת

† [תְּבַר] **vb. break** (𝔗 Syr.; BH שָׁבַר);—**Pe.** *Pt. pass.* fs. תְּבִירָה Dn 2[42] *broken in pieces* (kingdom).

תְּדִירָא v. דור.

† [תּוּב] **vb. return** (𝔗 Syr.; BH שׁוּב);—**Pe.** *Impf.* 3 ms. יְתוּב, c. עַל pers., of brightness (זִיו) of face Dn 4[33 b], of knowledge v[31 33 a]. **Haph.** *Pf.* 3 ms. הֲתִיב Dn 2[14]; 3 mpl. sf. הֲתִיבוּנָא Ezr 5[11], *Impf* 3 mpl. יַהֲתִיבוּן 6[5], יְתִיבוּן (K § 33, 3) 5[5]; *Inf.* sf. לַהֲתָבוּתָךְ Dn 3[16];—**1.** *restore,* acc. rei Ezr 6[5]. **2.** *return* (acc. of answer, etc.) 5[5 11] Dn 3[16] (sf. pers.), 'הֲתִ עֵטָא וּטְעֵם 2[14].

† תְּוַהּ **vb. be startled, alarmed** (𝔗 *id.*, Syr. ܬܘܗ);—**Pe.** *Pf.* 3 ms. 'ת Dn 3[24].

† [תּוֹר] **n.m. bullock** (𝔗 Syr.; BH שׁוֹר, √ III. שור);—pl. abs. תּוֹרִין, for sacrifice Ezr 6[9 17] 7[17]; as eating grass Dn 4[22 29.30] 5[21].

† תְּחוֹת **prep. under** (BH תַּחַת; 𝔗 תְּחוֹת, Syr. ܬܚܝܬ, ܬܚܘܬ, adv. ܠܬܚܬ; Palm. מן לתחת Cooke[320]);—Dn 7[27] תְּחוֹת כָּל־שְׁמַיָּא (cf. BH **II. 1**); in pl. c sf. (as BH Syr. 𝔗) 4[9] תְּחֹתוֹהִי (so 𝔗O Lv 15[10]: Dalm § 47, 2), v[18]. With מִן, Je 10[11] מִן תְּחוֹת שְׁמַיָּא (cf. BH **III. 2**); sf. Dn 4[11] מִן־תַּחְתּוֹהִי (the form as Syr. adv. supr., unless a Hebraizing punct.).

† תְּלַג **n.[m.] snow** (𝔗 Syr.; BH שֶׁלֶג);—abs. 'ת Dn 7[9] (sim.).

†תְּלָת n.m., תְּלָתָה f., three (𝔗 Syr.; BH שָׁלשׁ ,שְׁלשָׁה);—**m.** תְּלָת bef. **n.f.** pl. Dn 7[5]; n.f. om. v[8.20]; **f.** תְּלָתָה bef. **n.m.** pl. 7[24]; after, 3[24] 6[3.11.14], so א‍ָ‍— Ezr 6[4]; יוֹם תְּלָתָה 6[15] *third day;* sf. תְּלָתֵּהוֹן (K[§65, Anm.1]) Dn 3[23] *the three of them.*

†[תְּלָת] **n.[m.] a third part** (so 𝔗 תְּלָתָא, תִּלְתָּא, Syr. ܬܘܠܬܐ, Nab. תלת SAC[121], Ar. ثُلْث, ثُلُث, As. *šulultu* (=*šuluštu*) Meissn Suppl. 93, cf. Dl[WB]; v. also M[88*] Dr[Dn 5,7]);—emph. תַּלְתָּא adv. *as one of three* Dn 5[16.29] (Bev *the third day*, every three days, v. So in M[88*]).

‡†תַּלְתִּי **adj. denom.** (only BAram.) as subst. **third** (ruler), i.e. *triumvir* (M[89*]), cf. foregoing, which possibly is abnormal form of same (K[§65.1. Anm.3]), Dn 5[7].

†[תְּלִיתָי] **adj. third** (𝔗 תְּלִיתַי, Syr. ܬܠܝܬܝܐ);—f. תְּלִיתָיָא Kt, תָאָה- Qr (K[§11,1b]) Dn 2[39] *the third kingdom.*

†תְּלָתִין **n.indecl. thirty**;—יוֹמִין ת׳ Dn 6[8.13].

†תַּמָּה **adv. there** (so Eg. Aram. (RÉS 361 B5 [also תנה A4, so Cilic., Cooke[68, 5], cf. Palm. תנן ib.[121, 3], Syr. ܬܢܢ] S-C[A4, J6]); 𝔗 תַּמָּן, Syr. ܬܡܢ, v. BH שָׁם);—Ezr 5[17] 6[1.12]; מִן־ת׳ *thence* 6[6].

†[תְּמַהּ] **n.m. wonder,** as wrought by God (𝔗 Syr.; cf. BH [תָּמַהּ]);—pl. abs. תִּמְהִין Dn 6[28]; emph. תִּמְהַיָּא 3[32], pl. sf. תִּמְהוֹהִי v[33].

תנא (𝔗 Syr.; =BH II. שְׁנַיִם ,שָׁנָה ,שֵׁנִי).

†[תִּנְיָן] **adj. second**;—fs. תִּנְיָנָה (K[§66,1]) Dn 7[5].

†תִּנְיָנוּת (K[§66,2]) **adv. the second time**;—Dn 2[7].

†[תְּרֵין] **n.m.,** תַּרְתֵּין (K[§65, Anm.1]) **f., two** (so in Aram. dialects generally (note Nab. f. תרתין over ag. Palm. תרתן Lzb[398]); v. Philippi ZMG xxxii (1878), 21 ff.; **adj.** acc. to M[§89b]);—**m.** only cstr. in תְּרֵי עֲשַׂר *twelve,* after **n.m.** pl. Dn 4[26] Ezr 6[17]; **f.** after **n.f.** pl. שְׁנִין שִׁתִּין וְת׳ Dn 6[1] *years sixty and two;* =ord., שְׁנַת תַּרְתֵּין 4[24] *second year.*

†תִּפְתָּיֵא Kt, תָּאֵי- Qr, **n.m.pl.** name of official Dn 3[2.3] (so Eg. Aram. RÉS 361 B4 דיניא תיפתיא ונרשכיא; meaning unknown, conj. in Bev, Behrm, cf. Dr).

[תַּקִּיף] v. תְּקֵף.

†[תְּקַל] **vb. weigh** (𝔗 Syr.; BH שָׁקַל, שֶׁקֶל);—**Peʿîl** *Pf.* 2 ms. תְּקִילְתָּא (W[CG 224]) Dn 5[27] *thou hast been weighed,* בְּ of scales.

†תְּקֵל **n.[m.] shekel** (v. BH שֶׁקֶל; 𝔗 תִּקְלָא);—abs. ת׳ Dn 5[25.27]; v. מְנֵא and reff.

†[תְּקַן] **vb. be in order** (𝔗 Syr.; BH (late));—**Hoph.** *Pf.* 1 s. הָתְקְנֵת (W[CG 225]) Dn 4[33] *I was established,* עַל of kingdom.

†[תְּקֵף] **vb. grow strong** (𝔗 Syr.; BH, q.v., (late));—**Pe.** *Pf.* 3 ms. תְּקֵף, of tree, Dn 4[8.17]; 2 ms. תְּקֵפְתְּ 4[19], of king; 3 fs. תִּקְפַת 5[20] fig. *grow arrogant,* of spirit of man. **Pa.** *make strong, stringent: Inf.* לְתַקָּפָה Dn 6[8] acc. of interdict.

†תְּקֹף **n.[m.] might**;—cstr. בֵּית ת׳ חִסְנִי Dn 4[27], of king.

†[תְּקֹף] **n.[m.]** id.;—emph. תָּקְפָּא Dn 2[37].

†[תַּקִּיף] **adj. strong, mighty**;—fs. abs. תַּקִּיפָה, of kingdom, Dn 2[40] (like iron), v[42]; א‍ָ‍— 7[7], of beast; mpl. abs. תַּקִּיפִין, of kings Ezr 4[20], God's wonders Dn 3[33].

[תְּרֵין], תַּרְתֵּין *two,* v. תנא.

†תְּרַע **n.[m.] gate, door** (𝔗 Syr.; BH שַׁעַר, √I. שׁער);—cstr. ת׳: **1.** *door* of furnace Dn 3[26]. **2.** *gate* of king, i.e. palace, court, Dn 2[49] (cf. Est 2[19], v. שַׁעַר **3 a**; also Ar. بَاب *gate,* then الباب *the court* of a sovereign; pl. الأبواب *Sublime Porte,* of Turkish court, v. esp. Dozy[I. 124]).

†[תָּרָע i.e. *tarrāʿ* K[§59 d)]] **n.m. porter, doorkeeper,** in temple: pl. emph. תָּרָעַיָּא Ezr 7[24].

†תַּתְּנַי **n.pr.m.** Pers. perfect in Syria;—Ezr 5[3.6] 6[6.13]; Θανθανας, Ταναθαναι, A Θαθθαναι; 𝔊L Ταναθαναιος, Σισιννης; Σισιννης also 3 Esdr 6[3] 7[26] Jos Ant. xi. 12, 89, etc. (Lag Psalt. Hieron. 162 n.; AS § 1335 n.; Mey Entst. J.32 assumes OP **Thithnaya*, or **Thathnaia*); but *Uštanni, Uštanu,* was prefect in Syria under Darius, acc. to contr. tablets, v. Strassm Darius 27. 82; names prob. identical; Meissn ZAW xvii (1897), 191 f. reads therefore ושתני (וְשְׁתָּנַי Hpt), cf. Buhl Gu Ezr-Neh. 63; Scheft[94], however, thinks תתני= תסני=OP *thāsna*, Av. *sāsna* (*teaching*), and this transp. in NBab. *Uštanu.*

ADDENDA ET CORRIGENDA

Page 3b. אָב אב **9**: see also Ew[Gesch. i. 524. H i. 365]. On the force of אָב in proper names (in many prob. a divine title), v. Che[Ency. Bib., Abi, Names with] Nö[ib., Names, §§ 44, 45].

4b. אַבְרָם: Spiegelberg[Randglossen 14] cp. Pal. n.pr. geogr. *ḥkr'ȝ 'ȝbrru* = חקל אברם (c. Eg. art. masc.), in Sheshonk list. As regards etym., Nö[l.c.] al. expl. as 'the father [a divine title] is exalted' (cf. [אֲ]חִירָם, מַלְכִּירָם, יְהוֹרָם).

5b. II. אבל: etym. conject. very dub.; connex. (Lag.) of أَبَلَ *withstand*, with أَبْلٌ *herbage, forage* (sts. *dry*) improb., and of latter with إِبِلٌ *herd of camels* obscure; √ mng. *grow green* unattested; Syr. ܬܰܒܠܳܐ, ܐܰܒܠܳܐ, Talm. יַבְלָא, Pun. ιεβαλ, '*grass*,' appar. = a specific kind of fodder, ἄγρωστις, v. Löw[No. 141] (GFM, privately).

6a. III. אבל, אוֹבִיל: on this etym., form או׳ needs explanation; GFM (privately) queries whether, if genuine, name may not be theophoric (*x* + *īl*), poss. err. for אַרְבְּאֵל; or Aram. Aph. from יבל (which in any case may have influenced pronunciation).

7a. [אֹבֶן] **2**: Spiegelberg[ZA xiv (1900), 269 ff.; Randglossen 19 ff.] expl. as *the two stones* [rd. אֲבָנַיִם], i.e. bearing-stool of 'stones' = bricks, tiles.

7b. אַבִּיר **1**: transfer Ju 5[22] Je 46[15] to **3** end (but Je 46[15] many MSS. 𝔊 Aq Symm Theod 𝔙 many moderns read אַבִּירֶךָ *thy bull*, i.e. Apis).

— אַבְרֵךְ: Spiegelberg[Randglossen 14 ff.] expl. as Eg. *'brk* = *give attention!*

8a. אגא: authority for Ar. vb. أَجَأَ *flee* is slender, but word occurs as n.pr.mont., and elsewhere (GFM, privately).

— אגר: Aram. א׳ (Talm., once, Levy) prob. Hebraism.

— אגם: Ar. أَجِمَ also = *spoil* (of water); cf. أَجَمَةٌ (أُجُمٌ) = *pool, reed-bed* (also *tangled thicket*, etc.) Lane, and *marsh* Dozy[i. 11].

10a. אֱדוֹם **2, 3**: v. now FBuhl[Gesch. d. Edomiter (1893)].

11b. אֲדֹנִי־בֶזֶק: rd. prob. א׳־צֶדֶק, v. GFM[Ju 1. 5].

13b. I. אהל: Nö[ZMG xl (1886), 154, 720] doubts אֹהֶל = أَهْلٌ = *ālu*; but أَهْلٌ = *dwelling* actually in vulg. Ar. acc. to So[Buhl].

15a. Before אוּאֵל ins. 'או Pr 31[4] Kt, v. [אֵי].'

— אוב: after *return* add 'whence Kö[Off.-begr. ii. 150] Sta[G. i. 504; Bibl. Theol. i. 186] Now[Arch. ii. 273] as *rediens*, "revenant"; but doubtful.'

15b. אֵיד: Bev[J Phil. xxvi. 302] der. from Ar. آدَ *be strong* [also *oppress, burden*], whence مُؤْيِدٌ (or مُؤْيَدٌ) *calamity*.

— אֵד: Ar. derivation very dub.; Dl[W 125, cf. WB 22] KS[2. 4] Hpt[JAOS 1896, 158 ff.] Gunk[Gn 2, 6] Holz[Gn 2, 5] Buhl cp. As. *edû, flood, mass of waters* (√ אדה), *editu, overflow* (for irrigation); 𝔊𝔖𝔙 Aq in Gn 2[6] have *spring*, 𝔗 *cloud*, so 𝔊 𝔗 Jb 36[27]; add perh. Jb 36[30] אֵדוֹ for אוֹרוֹ (Du Dr).

16b. תַּאֲוָה **2**: add Gn 49[26] (v. p. 1063a).

— II. [אָוָה] end: v. also [תָּאַר], p. 1061b.

17b. II. אול, איל: Ar. آَوَّلَ, etc., from وَآلَ, v. Lane.

19a. אַיָּל: Ar. إِيَّلٌ = *ibex* (i.q. وَعْلٌ, وَعِلٌ).

19b. אָוֶן: on etym., cf. also Bev[J Phil. xxvi. 300–2].

20b. אוּפָז: crpt., v. Siegf[ThLz, Nov. 7, 1885, 530]; he expl. מֵא׳ Je 10[9] as err. for מוּפָז 1 K 10[18], and א׳ Dn 10[5] as borrowed from Je 10[9]; in Je 10[9] Gie reads מֵאוֹפִיר, Du either this or מוּפָז (v. פזז); read מֵאוֹפִיר perhaps also Dn 10[5] (Dr).

— אוֹפִיר: WMM[As. u. Eur. 111] identifies with Egypt. *Pvnt*, on W. coast of Red Sea.

23b. אֵזוֹב: prob. a kind of wild marjoram (*origanum Maru*) Post[Hast. DB Hyssop].

24b. [מאזן], l. 5: after שַׁחַק ins. 'Is 40[15].'

25a. III. אָח: Ez 18[10] אָח is a *vox nihili* (dittogr. from foll. אחד: v. Comm.): in 21[10] also dub. (𝔊 εἰ); read אַךְ Ew Hi Sm Toy, חַדָּה Co Berthol, אַתְּ Oort Krae.

25b. אחד **5**· Nu 10^{4} בְּאַחַת is rather '*in one* (of the trumpets)', Jb 33^{14} it = *in one way;* Pr 28^{18} read prob. with 𝔖 Lag Dys Bi בְּשַׁחַת; Ju 16^{28} is rather 'vengeance for *one* of my two eyes' (v. GFM) Je 10^{8} בְּאַחַת prob = *in one, altogether.* אחד **7** transpose 'abs. Jb 42^{14}' (l 5) to precede 'Ez 10^{14}' (l 2)

26b. On pr. names compounded with אָח, v reff given under אָב supr.

— אַחְאָב, ll 4, 5· read 'Bar Hebraeus[Chron Ecclesiast II 23],' and del 'in Euseb'

— אֲחִיָּהוּ **3**, l 1: ins. '15^{29}' after '$14^{2.4}$,' and in **4**, l. 1, del '^{29}'.

27a אֲחִיסָן · אֲחִיסָן <, v Norzi[Nu 13, 22] GFM[Ju 1 10] (after Ven [1] Mich)

28b אֲחוּיָהוּ cf Ar احد viii, + וַיְּלִּדוּ = *adopt,* hence perhaps '' *hath adopted*

— אָח *fire-pot* is loan-word fr Eg *'aḥ* acc. to WMM[OLZ 3. 51], Je 36^{22} rd. וְאֵשׁ הָאָח

32b איך **2** end. add Ho 11^{8} acc. to Hi Ke We Marti al.

33a IV. אי Jb 22^{30} read perhaps אֵל (Me), or אֱלֹהַּ (Ley), with ונמלט in v^{b}.

35b. איש, l 5 from bottom. אֲנָשִׁים Ez $24^{17.22}$ is textual error, We (ap Sm) אֲנָשִׁים; Toy[Hpt] אונים (Ho 9^{4})

38b מְכֹלֶת so read also ‖ 2 Ch 2^{9} (MT מַכּוֹת)

— אַלְמוֹדָד add Glas[Skizze ii 425, 445].

41b אֵלֶּה **c** in Jos 17^{9} עָרִים הָאֵלֶּה rd. הֶעָרִים, cf 17^{12} $19^{8.16.31.48}$, etc

43a אֵל **7** v. also Brock[ZAW xxvi (1906). 29 ff] (mng 'might' very dub · renders *belongs to the god of (my) hand,* supposing phrase a survival, with orig mng forgotten, of ancient idea, found also among other nations, of spirits conferring powers upon particular members of body).

45b. אֱלִיעָם. < = *Ēl is kinsman* (v. Gray[Ency Bib Ammi Names with] No[Ib. Names, § 46])

48b I. [אָלַף], l. 5: after 'pers' ins. 'Jb 15^{5}.'

49a At end of II. אֶלֶף ins. '[אָלַף] **vb. denom. Hiph.** ψ 144^{13} מַאֲלִיפוֹת *producing thousands* (subj. צֹאן).'

— אֶלְקֹשִׁי: on etymol., and site of place, v. Da[Nahum, etc., 9 ff] GASm[Twelve Proph II. 79 f].

— At bottom, insert 'אַלְתּוֹלַד v. sub I אֵל.'

49b. אם etym.: add '𝔗[Onk Jon] אם, 𝔗[Hag] אין'

51a. 1 אָמוֹן. Je 46^{25} Spiegelberg[Randglossen 43 ff] reads נֹא אָמֹן (as Na 3^{8}) for אָמוֹן נֹא, and finds in both a Thebes in the Delta.

54a, l 17: ins. 'Jos' bef. '24^{14}.'

55b, l. 9: Is 40^{26} read probably אֹמֶן (𝔊).

57a. אֱמֹרִי: meaning *mountain-dwellers* very dub, on 'א = Eg *'A-ma-ra* v. WMM[As. u. Eur 229 ff], = TelAm. and As *Amurru,* v. Wkl[TelAm 36*] Jastr[EB Canaan § 10] Say[Hast DB Amorites] al; cf. also GFM[Ju 4, 5] Dr[Dt 1 7] Gray[Nu 13, 29].

58b. III [אָנָה] **Pu.**. after תְאֻנֶּה ins. 'ψ 91^{10}.'

60a [אָנַף, אָנֵף]. in Heb, vb. denom. fr. אַף.

61b. אָסָא: perhaps apoc. theophoric name, cf רְפָאֵל.

62b אָסַף **Niph. 1** end add 'so יֵאָסֵף Jb 27^{19}; but read prob. יאסף = יוסף (Ex 5^{7}), 𝔊 𝔖 Ew De Di Du'

66a. [אַפֶּדֶן]: Dieulafoy[RÉJ xvi (1888) p cclxxv f] makes *apadâna,* more precisely, *throne-room,* cf. Dr[Dn 11. 45].

67a אֲפֵנָה: Ar. أفن in fact = *milk* (camel, etc.) *dry, empty;* مأفون = *empty-headed man;* this does not support *be confused, helpless* (GFM, privately)

67b. אפק· now prob. that **1** should include Jos 12^{18} 1 S 4^{1} 29^{1} and 2 K 13^{22} 𝔊L; town not near Jezreel, but at N. end of Philistine plain; cf. 𝔊L[1 c] We[Comp 254] Dr[1 S 29. 11] RS[OTJC 2. 435] GASm[Geogr 400 f] Buhl[Geogr 212 (and N.)] Bu[RS 235 f.], more doubtful are 1 K $20^{26.30}$ 2 K 13^{17} (Kit[1 K 20 26]); these, with Jos 19^{30} Ju 1^{31}, might denote an Aphek near Jezreel.

— l. 8 from below: Jb 12^{21} rd perh. אַבִּירִים Du (v also Bu)

68a. אַפִּרְיוֹן read 'Syr.' for '𝔖,' and 'Talm.' for '𝔗,' thus: 'Syr. ܦܘܪܝܐ (and ܦܘܪܝܘܢ) PS[3073]; Sota 9^{14} and Talm אַפִּרְיוֹן, Talm. also פּוּרְיָא and פוריון, Levy[NHWB i. 150, iv 17 f]'

68b. אפת· but Thes[612. Add 72] del אפת, and der. מוֹפֵת from √ו״פ, so Ba[NB § 172 e]; v. also, on افت as late by-form of أفك, DBMacdonald[JBL xiv (1895). 58 ff].

70a. אָרַב: del. 'also أَرَبَ *tie* (a knot) Frey.'

71b. [אֻרְוָה]· Vulg. Ar. آرِيّ = *manger* Moḥiṭ[19. 15] (GFM, privately), cf. Lane[51 c].

— At the end: add 'also pl אורות 2 Ch 32^{28b} (read prob. וְאֻרוֹת לַעֲדָרִים 𝔊 𝔙 Kit Benz al.).'

72a. אֲרִיאֵל: Du[Is 29. 1] (q.v.) makes **1** = אֲרִיאֵל, from אָרָה + ל afform., *hearth* (not + אֵל *hearth of Ēl*)

73a. אֹרַח, ll. 3, 19: אָרְחִי ψ 139^{3} < *Inf. cstr.,* and ‖ רִבְעִי (*Inf. cstr.* of II. רבע), *not* דַּרְכִּי, cf. Bae.

73b. אַרְיוֹךְ: on *Rim-Aku* (=*Eri-Aku*?), v. now also Dr[Comm. Gn. 156 ff.]; Zim[KAT 3. 367] thinks identification very dubious.

— After אַרְיוֹךְ insert: '†אֲרִיסַי n.pr.m. son of Haman Est 9[9]; Αρσαιος.'

74b. אֲרָם end: add No[Ency Bib. Aram].

77a, l. 13 fr. below: אשׁ 'm.' is dub.· Nu 16[13] rd עָלֶיהָ for 2nd עֲלֵיהֶם (𝔊[B]); Je 20[9] v. Ges[§ 132d]; 48[45] rd. (many MSS, Nu 21[28]) יצאה; ψ 104[4] rd. perh. (Ol Du) לַהֲטָה:, or וְלֹהֵט:; Jb 20[26] v. Ges[§ 145 n (or 121 b)]: cf. Albr[ZAW xvi (1896), 63].

78b. אשׁה, [אֲשִׁיָּה]: read 'אשׁה (√of foll.).'

Also '†[אֲשִׁיָּה] n.f. wall, bulwark (Talm. אֲשִׁיתָא (Levy No); Mand. אשׁיתא *wall* No[M 113]; 𝔗 pl. sf. אֻשְׁיָתְהָא (Dalm[WB] אֻשְׁיָתְהָא) Je 50[15], אשׁיתנא Ct 2[9]; Ar. آسِيَة *column, support* is loan-word acc. to Fra[11]);—only pl sf *bulwarks* of city of Babylon,' etc.

79b. אָשָׁם, l. 2· for 'أَثِمَ *reum judicavit*,' read 'إِثْمٌ *sin, offence*,' and before 'fault' insert 'requital.' — **Niph.**: after Jo 1[18] add '(si vera l.; Me We al. נָשַׁמּוּ, √שׁמם, cf Dr[ad loc.]).'

81a. אֲשֵׁרָה: see now also GFM[EB Asherah] Dr[Dt 16, 21] Allen[DB Asherah], all doubtful as to Can. goddess Asherah; question left open by Zim[KAT 3. 436 ff] (on Sem. goddess *Aširtu-Ašratu* Id[ib. 432 ff.]); but v. Jeremias[AT im Licht d Alten Orients 207] (name of goddess *Aširat* in letter found at Taanach by Sellin (1902–3) and Id[ib. 37 237]) (Oppenheim's find at Ras el-'Ain in Mesop., stone shaft with veiled head as top, supposed to identify *post* with *goddess*; if 2 K 23[7] refers to draped Asherim [v. on text Benz Bur], this even more plausible), Id.[ib. 23, 208 f., 236]. On pictorial representations of *Asherah*-symbol v. WHWard[AJSL xix. 1 (Oct. 1902)].

83b. אֲשֶׁר: **4 b** (γ) transfer Ec 8[4] to בַּאֲשֶׁר **c** (p. 84a); and **8 e** add 'In Dt 15[14] also read כַּאֲשֶׁר. note ברכך before.'

85a. For ll. 20, 21, substitute: '(J) וַיּוֹלֶד לַחֲנוֹךְ, 17[5] (P) לֹא יִקָּרֵא עוֹד אֶת־שִׁמְךָ אַבְרָם אֶת־עִירָד *there shall not be called* (=one shall not call) *thy name Abram*, 21[3] (E).'

91b. בְּאֵר לַחַי רֹאִי: לְחִי perhaps orig. 1. לְחִי *jaw(-bone)*, on n pr.loc. cpd. with לחי, γνάθος, v. 𝔊[Ju 15, 9] We[Prol 344] Nes[AJSem Lang xiii (1897), 176].

92a. בְּאֵרִי: < *the man from Beer*? Nes[l. c.].

94b, l. 8 fr. bottom: Jb 17[16] rd. הַעִמָּדִי (for בַּדֵּי) 𝔊 Du Dr, with נָחַת in v[b] (for נַחַת).

96a. Before בִּדְקֵךְ, ins.: '†[בָּדַק] vb. denom. mend fissures (of),—**Qal** *Inf. cstr.* לִבְדּוֹק 2 Ch 34[10] (+וּלְחַזֵּק; acc. הַבַּיִת).'

101b. בוֹשׁ: add ref. to עַד־בּוֹשׁ *to the point of confusion* †Ju 3[25] (cf. GFM), 2 K 2[17] 8[11].

103a. בּוּק: Nes[AJSL xiii (1897), 176] conj. mng. *gravel*, cf. mod. *Ramle*=*sand*.

— בָּזַק: err. in Ju 1[4.5] (v. GFM).

— I. [בָּחַל]: No[ZAW xvii (1897), 188] disproves Syr. ܒܚܠ, and adopts the view of Gei[Urschrift 270] (בחל euphem. for a √II. בעל = *loathe*, c. בְּ, assumed (Thes Buhl) for Je 3[14] 31[32]; v. infr. on p. 127a).

103b, l. 2 (exc. '—**Qal**') belongs in l. 5.

110b. בית ad fin.: on בְּ as abbrev. בית v. Wetzst[Hauran 110] Kampffmeyer[ZPV xv (1892), 111].

111a. בֵּית־דָּגוֹן. Jerome[Opp. (ed. Vallarsi), iii, 38] defines as *domus tritici*, and says (Id.[ib. 174]): 'sed et usque hodie grandis vicus Capherdago inter Diospolim et Jamniam demonstratur.' [Elsewhere he defines דגון (Id.[ib. 43]) as 'piscis tristitiae'] (HPS, privately).

114b. בכורה. בַּכֻּרוֹת Je 24[2] prob. a diff. word, pl abstr.=*early ripeness*, cf. Du.

126a. אבנט described Jos[Ant. iii. 7, 2] as a sash wound round breast several times, and falling to the feet; in 𝔗𝔖 הֶמְיָן (Pers) a money-bag wound round body Sta[ThLz, 1894, 236].

— בסר: l. 2 read ܚܨܪܐ (PS; syllable ܨ uncertain [Nes, privately]; Polyglotts and Castell have ܚܨܪܐ).

127a. בָּעַל: Je 3[14] 31[32] AW JosKi Thes, comparing Ar. بَعِلَ *be disgusted*, derive from II. בָּעַל loathe (sq. בְּ); so Buhl: Gie Du Co in 31[32] read גָּעַלְתִּי (treating 3[14] as I. בָּעַל)

129b. II. [בָּעַר]: **Niph.** Je 10[14]=51[17] rather *stupefied* (by spectacle 10[13]=51[16]).

132b, last line and foll., read: 'in lat. of Shiloh; N. border of Amorites, Nu 21[24] (v. Di), Ju 11[22]; in its upper course it runs S. to N., hence (W.) border of Ammon, Dt 3[16] (cf. 2[37]), Jos 12[2]; mod. *Wady Zerqa* Bd[Pal 151].'

135a. I. בָּרָא: Ar. بَرَأَ prob. loan-word.

137b. בַּרְזִלַּי: no adj. fr. names of metals; perh. Aram, and בַּר=*son*, Nes[ZPV xv 257; AJSL, Apr 1897, 173].

141a. 1. בר: Is 1[25] read prob. כַּבֹּר *as in a furnace* (Is 48[10]), there seems no evidence that

'lye' (i e water mixed with the burnt ashes of plants containing potash, used formerly for washing) was ever used in refining gold or silver. cf J. Napier$^{\text{Anc Workers in Metal (1856) 15 20 25}}$ WAW in Smith$^{\text{DB II 368 Amer Rev Ed (1871 vol III). 1939}}$.

151^a. [נָדַד] **Hithpo. 1** ad fin, for 'or perh (cf גוּר) sub' rd 'We Now Marti Harper (cf I, II. גור)'

— **2** ad fin, Je 5^7 rd prob. יִתְגֹּרָרוּ 𝔊 Gie Du al.

152^b, l 13 after 'ψ 18^{51}' ins 'so ‖ 2 S 22^{51} (Kt מַגְדִּיל, > Qr מִגְדּל)'

— l 6 from below cstr גדל Ex 15^{16} belongs rather sub גֹּדֶל, l 3, after 'ψ 79^{11}.'

154^b, l. 21 bef 'sq. two' ins 'Ez 20^{27}'

156^a. I גו: del 'abs Jb 30^5'

161^b [גִּיחַ] **2 b** rather '*break forth* (with that which is to be born),' but text dub At end, also, add Ju 20^{33}.

163^b גָּלוּת Am $1^{6.9}$ cf Ob$^{20.20}$ and Je 13^{19} (𝔊 Du Co al) belong sub **2** = *body of exiles*

165^a II. גָּלִיל **2** for '—See also גְּלִילָה *ad fin*,' rd ', הַגָּלִילָה Galilee, 2 K 15^{29} (‖ אֶרֶץ נַפְתָּלִי) Ew$^{§ 173 h n}$ Sta$^{§ 308 a 2}$ Ges$^{§ 90 f}$'

165^b, l 1 del '2 K 15^{29},' and ll 5^b, 6

— [גלגל] Vid Baud$^{\text{ZMG 1904 395 ff}}$ (cps. BAram גלל (אבן), Palm גללא$^{\text{Tarif I 9}}$ = στήλη λιθίνη, and concludes that it was orig a designation of the primitive stone menhir or מַצֵּבָה)

168^b גַּם, l 2 also Zinj. (Lzb^{250} Cooke^{166})

175^a I גָּרַם l 1, rd. 'mng. dub; ? cut off, hence **reserve**.'

178^b גְּשׁוּרִי **2**: Jos 13^2 read prob הַגְּזוּרִי We and Dr (on 1 S 27^8), Mey$^{\text{ZAW I 126 n}}$ GFM$^{\text{Ju 1 29 n}}$

184^a עַל־דְּבַר ,עַל־דִּבְרִי *for the sake of*, *in reference to*, v Ko$^{\text{Expositor Aug 1902 142-148}}$, and add for עַל־דְּבַר Nu $25^{18\ 18\ 18}$ 31^{16} 2 S 18^5, and for עַל־דִּבְרֵי Je 7^{22} 2 K 22^{13a} = 2 Ch 34^{21a}, and perh ψ 7^1

186^a דָּגוֹן oldest tradition (Jerome) seems to waver between דָּג *fish* and דָּגָן *grain*, as explan of דָּגוֹן, v בית ד׳

187^a דָּדָן **1** Je 25^{23}, transfer to **2**.

189^a דּוּכִיפַת, name of bird poss of Egypt origin, Bondi$^{\text{ZMG 1 (1896) 292}}$ (Arabic, Ol$^{§ 221}$ cf. Ko$^{\text{ET ix (1898) 476}}$)

189^b דּוּר *circle, ball* — **1** *circle* Du$^{\text{Is 29 3}}$ thinks noun here also is כַּדּוּר (or כִּדּוֹר = כידור) *onset* of combatants, Marti כַּדּוּר as 𝔊 Lo Brd al.

192^b, l. 6. on יָדוֹן Gn 6^3 cp perh دان *continue, do* something *continually*, in mod. Eg Ar (So$^{\text{SK lxvii (1894) 211 f}}$)

193^b מְדִינָה cf also OAram מדינתא *city*, Palm מדיתא *city*, sf מדיתהון, pl. מדינתא SAC^{79} Lzb^{106} Cooke^{266}

218^a יהוה: theories of non-Heb. or non-Sem. origin, opposed (in their older forms) by Bau$^{\text{Rel I 181 ff (v esp 230)}}$, Dl$^{\text{Pa 162 ff}}$ claimed Bab origin for יהו, against this Kue$^{\text{National Religions, etc., Note iv (Eng Trans. 329 ff)}}$ Jastr$^{\text{JBL xiii (1894) 103 f}}$ cf. Hpt$^{\text{BAS I 170 N}}$; Dl$^{\text{Babel u Bibel, 46 f., 73 f}}$ makes same claim for יהוה, agst this v esp Hirsch$^{\text{ZAW xxiii (1903) 355 ff}}$ Zim$^{\text{KAT3, 465 ff}}$, Spiegelberg$^{\text{ZMG liii (1899), 633 ff}}$ prop (improb) Egyptian etymol for יהוה, further discussions see in Ko$^{\text{EB Names § 112 and n 3}}$ 'Jehovah' found in Jacob (? Johann.) Wessel (†1480), acc. to Schwally$^{\text{ThLz. 1905 col 612}}$.

228^b, l 14 fr below, rd. אמן for ימן.

229^b [הָלָא] Mi 4^7 We prop הַנַּחֲלָה (√חלה) *her that is diseased* (note ‖ הַצֹּלֵעָה, and cf. Ez 34^{21}), so Now; Gr הַנִּלְאָה *her that is exhausted;* Marti allows either of these.

231^b הָלַךְ (5) *e* ה׳ לפני also (less oft.) = *go* (and present oneself) *before* a deity or shrine 1 K 12^{30} 1 Ch 21^{30} (cf בוא לפני Ex 28^{30}, קדם פני ψ 95^2).

239^b. מַהֲלַלְאֵל rd. מְהַלַּלְאֵל Gray$^{\text{Prop N 201}}$.

— l 6 fr. below. on תהלתיך ψ 9^{15} as error for ־לָּתֶךָ or ־לָּתֶיךָ, v. Ol$^{§ 131 k, 39 e}$ Sta$^{§ 354 b}$ Hup-Now al *ad loc.*

241^b הֵמָּה **2** ad fin. add '—הֵמָּה כִּדְוֵי לַחְמִי Jb 6^7 rd perh. וְהֵמָּה וגו׳ (or וְזָהֲמָה) it is *loathesome* (√זהם)

242^b הָמוֹן **4**: 2 Ch 11^{23} for וַיִּשְׁאַל הֲמוֹן נָשִׁים Perles$^{\text{Anal 47}}$ prop וישאו לָהֶם נ׳ (cf. נשׂא **3 d**)

246^b. הרג, l. 5. for '1 S 14^7' rd. '2 S 14^7'

248^a II הָרָה, l 5. for '1 S 11^5' rd '2 S 11^5.'

251^b. Bef התת ins '† מַהֲתַלּוֹת **n.f.pl.** deceptions,—Is 30^{10}.'

256^a. זבי on Palm. זבי (prob abbrev. from ... זבד), v Lzb^{263} Cooke$^{273, 291}$.

257^a I זֶבַח. Ph זבח of an offering of bread and oil CIS$^{\text{I 165 12 167 8}}$, cf. RS$^{\text{Sem 205 (2nd ed 222)}}$.

262^b זָהָב **1**. Jb 37^{22} rd. perh. זֹהַר Du and Dr.

265^a. I זיז on As *zîzê, teats*, v. RFHarper AJSL$^{\text{xiv (1897 1898) 174}}$.

269a. זַבַּי: Nes (privately) suggests that this might be abbrev. fr. זכריה.

271a, l. 17: *recorder*. Rather, probably, *the* (king's) *reminder*, who brought important business to his notice: cf. Ew[Gesch iii 365, ii iii. 267] Ke[2 S 8, 16] Benz[Arch 310] Now[Arch i. 308] Kit[1 K 4 3].

271a. זָכָר: against Schwally's view see JPeritz[Woman in the Ancient Hebrew Cult, JBL xvii (1898) 111 ff].

272a. זִכָּרוֹן. cite also (sub **1**) זִכְרֹנֵיכֶם מִשְׁלֵי־אֵפֶר Jb 13[12] *your memorial words are ashen sayings* (i.e. worthless), cf. Bu Du, Margolis (privately) suggests that 𝔊 seems to have read רִנְּכֶם [רְנָנְכֶם > ?] יִמָּשֵׁל לְאֵפֶר *your exultation shall be like ashes.*

273a. זָמַם ad fin: the text of Pr 30[32] is questioned by Frankenberg Toy al.; v. on II. נבל, 614b infr.

273b. מְזִמָּה, l. 3. rd in Je 11[15] altogether עֲשֹׂתָהּ מְזִמָּת הָֽנְּדָרִים וּבְשַׂר קֹדֶשׁ יַעַבְרוּ מֵעָלַיִךְ רָעָתֵךְ.

— זְמָן; Mand. זבאן, v. No[M 1,2]; on OPers. origin v. BAram.

275a. III. זמר: Ar. دمر is *urge with chiding, reproof*, دِمَارٌ *thing involving blame* (if not protected, defended); this hardly supports meaning *choice products* for III. זִמְרָה.

276b זָעַם **2** is prob. denom. fr. זַעַם (v. Buhl).

277b. זָעַק **Niph.**: = *be called out* for military service, pass. of **Hiph. 1**; cf GFM[Ju 18 23]

279a. I [זָקַק]: perh prop. *strain* or *filter through*, cf. Jb 36[27] Is 25[6].

279b. זְרֻבָּבֶל; prob. = Bab. *Zêr-Bâbili* = *offspring of Babylon*, oft in Inscr. (Mey[E Jud 7]).

284b. [זָרַר]: וַיְזוֹרֵר 2 K 4[35] om. 𝔊, Gr Bur think MT arose (by dittogr.) fr. וַיִּנְהַר עַל־הַנַּעַר

288a, l. 11 fr. below: rd. 'הַחַיִּים Ec 9[4]'

293a חָדַל **2**, l 2 from end add 'Jb 10[20] (but rd. here prob יְמֵי חֶלְדִּי 𝔊 𝔖 Bi Bu Du)'

293b. [חָדַר]. Ph. is only חדר, חדרת (temple- or sepulchral) *chamber* (Lzb[271] Cooke[126]), Ez 21[19] is best explained from Syr ܚܕܰܪ *go about, surround*, ܚܕܳܪ *around*. It seems uncertain whether חֶדֶר, Ph חדר *chamber*, Ar. خِدْرٌ *curtain, chamber, tent*, etc, are (ultimately) fr. this √ (as something *surrounding*), or (Buhl) from II. חדר = خَدِرَ II. *conceal behind curtain, conceal, confine*, IV *conceal oneself*, also *abide, stay, remain behind* (Lane[707 c]), Eth ኀደረ: *abide, dwell* (Dr, privately, Nov. 1905)

293b. חֶדֶר, l. 3. ማኅደር: is not 'chamber,' but (fr. √ ኀደረ: *dwell*) *dwelling-place, abode, tent.*

297a, l 11 fr. below: omit 'מְחוֹלָלֶת Is 51[9]' (which belongs to I. חָלַל)

310b. חֲמוּשׁ. cf. Nab. חמישו, Cooke[245].

314a. חֲכִילָה n pr loc, alw c. art.

321b. חַלָּמוּת, l. 6: the ref is to Job's sufferings (from which as little joy comes as from eating unsavoury food, so now Comm generally), rather than to the unpalatable words of his friends It is doubtful whether Di's reason for preferring *purslain* to 𝔗 חֶלְמוֹנָא *yolk* of egg (רִיר ח׳ *slime of yolk*, i e. the white of the egg) is convincing, viz. that ancient Hebrews did not keep hens, or that of De, viz that white of egg is not *slime*, and is not unpalatable; mng. *yolk* preferred also by Da Bu Du.

325a, l. 12: rd '+ 25 t in Ch, + (of royal officials) 1 Ch 28[1]'

326a. חֶמְאָה: on mode of making *lebben*, by shaking milk in sour milk-skin, v. Doughty[Arab. Des. i. 221, 263, ii. 304, etc] Thomson[Land and Book ii 418]. See also ARSK[Ency Bib. MILK].

— After חֶמְאָה ins. as new article: '† מַחֲמָאֹת **n.f.pl. curd-like things** = smooth, hypocritical, words, only cstr. חָלְקוּ מ׳ פִיו ψ 55[22] *smooth are the butter-words of his mouth* (Ew De Hup), but read prob. חלק(ו) מֵחֶמְאַת פִּיו (פניו) *his mouth* (*face*) *is smoother than curds* (Vrss Ki Thes Ol Che Bae We Du [מַחֲמָאֹה])'

— l. 2 fr. below: add 'ψ 39[12]' after חֲמוּדוֹ.

329a, l. 5: after Vog[No. 123a] ins. '= Cooke[N Sem. Inscr, No. 136]; Lzb[Ephem ii (1906), 290].'

339a, l. 28: after 'Dr)' ins. ', c. אֶת־ Gn 24[49].'

340b. Bef חָסֹן ins '† [חָסַן] **vb.** only **Niph. denom.** *Impf.* 3 ms יֵחָסֵן Is 23[18] *be treasured up, hoarded* (‖ יֵאָצֵר)'

342b. II. חפף cf. No[ZMG lvii (1903), 416].

345b. חֲצִי, l 16, for מנח rd נוח, and so seven lines below.

346b. חֵץ **2** Here also חֲצָצֶיךָ ψ 77[18]

347a. I חָצֵר end: add '42[6] הַחִיצֹנוֹת for הַחֲצֵרוֹת.'

351a, ll. 1, 2: rd '1. חֹר, v. II. חור; II, III. חֹר, חָר, v. II, III. חרר.'

— Before I [חָרֵב] ins. '† [מַחֲרָאָה] **n.f.** only pl. **cloaca, cess-pool**; — מחראות 2 K 10[27] Kt (Qr מוֹצָאוֹת).'

351^b. II. חָרֵב, l. 3: after Zp 2^{14} add '(but rd. ערב, 𝔊 We al).'

354^a. [חַרְטֹם] the fact that the word is alw. applied to Egypt. magicians, exc. Dn 2^2 (late), suggests Egypt. origin, but no agreement among Egyptologists. Harkavy JAs., 1870, Mars-Avril, 169 prop *χar, speak + tum, hidden = teller of hidden things;* Wied Samml 44 thinks Heb word perh imitating an Egypt *cher-tem-t, he who holds the book;* FCCook 'Speaker's Comm i 279 prop *cher-tum = bearer of sacred words*

359^a I. [חָרַר]: **Niph. 1.** נִחַר Je 6^{29} from √נחר *snort, puff,* acc to Mich Ew Gf Gie al.,—not Du.

359^b. II. [חר], l 2 cf. No ZMG lvii (1903) 416, and l 5. del '6^{17} 13^{17}' before 'Je 27^{20}.'

360^a חַרְסִית, חרסות Je 19^2. v Baldensperger PEF 1904, 136 on the crushing of potsherds in the Valley of Hinnom

361^a II [חָרַשׁ] add '**Hithp.** *Impf* 3 mpl וַיִּתְחָרְשׁוּ Ju 16^2 *and they kept quiet*'

369^a [חָתַת]. יֵחַת Je 21^{13} v נָחַת.

— ll 6, 5 fr below: in Je 14^4 rd prob. with Du (after 𝔊) Co Dr ועבדי הא׳ חַתּוּ.

371^a. I. טָבַל add '**Niph.** *Pf.* 3 mpl נטבלו Jos 3^{15} *be dipped,* ב of water'

382^a טַף note that the word includes (or implies) *women* as well as children, in foll. Gn 47^{12} Ex 12^{37} (E), $10^{10\,24}$ (J), Nu $32^{16\,17}$ (JE; cf. Di on v^{26})

385^b תבל, l. 12. before '89^{12}' ins. 'ψ.'

391^b יָד end add, for מִתַּחַת יַד, 2 K $8^{20\,22}$ (= 2 Ch $21^{8\,10}$), 13^5 17^7.

392^a [יָדָה], l. 12: Palm ידחא *pious,* read (נה)ירחא SAC^{90}, also Id JQ 1904, 593.

396^b. [יָהַב], l. 1: ? cf 𝔗 יְהַבַת ψ 11^6, יְהָבִית Ec 5^{10}

402^a Before יוֹרֶה ins 'יוֹעֵשׁ v. sub יהוה; יוֹעָם v. II עמם **Hoph.**'

402^b Bef יַיִן ins. יזן, √of **Pu.** *Pt* pl מְיֻזָּנִים Je 5^8 Qr, v [זוּן], p. 266^a.

403^a. יַחַד **2** (4) Jb 17^{16} rd נַחַת for נָחַת (v. Addenda, on pp 94^b, 629^a), יַחַד here will then belong to (1).

404^a. [יָחַל] **Pi.** add '**3.** caus *make to hope* ψ 119^{49} (of pers),' and, under **2**, l 2, del. '^{49}' and ins. 'ψ 147^{11}'

405^b, l 2 fr below ins 'ψ 33^3.'

410^a. Bef [יָלַל] ins 'יָלוֹן **n.pr.m.** in Judah 1 Ch 4^{17}; 𝔊 Αμων, A 𝔊L Ιαλων.'

410^b. יָם: of Mediterr. in pl Dn 11^{45} [cf **8 d**] Hi Ke Meinh Bev Dr (world-encircling seas Behrm).

418^a. יָעָה cf also Ar. وِعَاءٌ *vessel* Gn 42^{25} Saad, cf. Baldensperger PEF 1904 53, who cp. Mod. Ar. *wa'â* (وَعَا)

419^a. Bef. I [יָעַף] ins 'יְעֹעֵרוּ Is 15^5 v I. [עור] **Pilp.**'

430^a יָקָר end: Zc 14^6 '*but*' is very dub.; rd prob חֹם וְקָרוֹת *there shall be neither heat nor cold,* etc (We al.).

438^a יְרֵמוֹת ad fin.: add 'see רָ(א)מוֹת **1 c,** p 928^b.'

440^b. תירוש: on mng, v. ARSK Ency Bib. Wine (iv 5307 f.).

446^a. Bef. [יָשַׁע] ins 'ישׁנו v. יֵשׁ'

450^a. Bef. ישׁשׁ ins. 'שָׁרוֹנִי **adj. gent.** of foregoing, 1 Ch 27^{29}'

452^b. יֹתֶרֶת· GFM (Dec. 28, 1899, privately) points out that fat parts are alw disting. from this; cf now on יתרת Id Sacrifice EB 4208 and esp. Id Oriental Stud für Th Nöldeke (1906), 761, where it is shewn to be the *caudate lobe* of the liver.

458^b. I [כָּבוֹד]: ψ 45^{14} belongs to II. כָּבוֹד **2**; cstr. as Ges § 141 d; v. also כל **1 a** end.

461^b. כידור and 462^a. כַּדּוּר: v. note on דור, 189^b.

467^b ad fin. [כַּוָּן], prob Bab. loan-word, fr. *kamânu,* cake used in worship of Ištar, Zim KAT3 441.

468^a. I. כור, l. 4. كُورٌ means also a camel's saddle (or 'howdah') with its apparatus, v. Frey Lane

— 1 [כַּר]: for *basket-saddle* read < *camel-palankeen,* the palankeen, or tent-like erection, on the saddle (Burckh Bedouins and Wahábys 266 Doughty Arab Des i 437 ii 304 Lane Mod Egyptians (5) ii 153 al.), which seems intended here, is distinct from the basket or pannier (in which some women also travelled, Porter Travels ii 212)

489^a. II. כְּנַעֲנִי· add 'pl. sf כִּנְעָנֶיהָ (si vera l) Is 23^8 (‖ סֹחֲרֶיהָ)'

497^a I כפר, on orig. mng cf now Dr Hast DB Propitiation, also As *kuppuru, purify* (and deriv. *takpirtu*) Zim KAT3 601 f Morgenstern Sin in Bab Rel. (MVG, 1905, 3) 44, 122.

498a, l. 14: others understand מִן as=*away from;* cf. Di[Lv 4. 26], Ri[Sühne 50 f.].

521a. [לָאָה] end: transpose 'Mi 6[3]' to follow 'Je 12[5].'

523a. לֵבָב, l. 7: bef. לְבַבְהֶן ins. 'pl. c. sf.'

525a, l. 10: after נתן לב לְ rd. 'Ec 1[13.17] 7[21]. 8[9.16] Pr 23[26] Dn 10[12].'

— l. 11: Ne 2[12] 7[5] differ from Ec 7[2] 9[1] (the 'heart' here not being the subject's).

527a. לִבְנֶה: named fr. exuding milky (white) gum De Ges al.

546b. לָשׁוֹן **5**: so As. *lišânu;* v. Meissner [ZAW xxiii (1903), 151 f.] Johns [As. Deeds 2, 281].

555b, l. 5 fr. below: ins. '22[1]' after '†Nu'.

556a. מוּג: in view of prevailing fig. use, and of Ar. مَاجَ (موج) *be in tumult, commotion,* of sea, people, *be agitated, perplexed,* it is perh. dub. whether *melt* is orig. meaning; *be moved, agitated* is usu. poss., and even Am 9[13] ψ 65[11] (both late), where (esp. Am) *moistening* is suggested, this may be perh. derived fr. *agitating, loosening, dissolving.*

557b. II. [מוּל], l. 2: after 'cut off' add 'but only seemingly in the dub. passages (v. III. [מָלַל] and Comm.) Jb 14[2] 18[16] 24[24] [MS Levy], ψ 37[2] 90[6].'

560b. Bef. מוֹתָר ins. '(לְ)מוֹתָם) ψ 73[4] v. [חַרְצֻבָּה] and תֹּם **1**.'

568a. [מִין], del. 'so Syr. (Edessa) ܡܝܢܐ,' ref. due to early text. err. (GFM, privately, Dec. 28, 1899).

571b. מְלוֹא: Schwally [ZMG lii (1898), 137] cp. As. *mulu=earthwork, mound, terrace,* Dl[411] M-A[544].

583b. מִן **9**, l. 2: for מִלְּ in Mish. see e.g. Bab. Mez 7[10] Kil 8[1] Ter 8[11] Pes 1[6] Taan 2[7] Yeb 8[2]; Ec 4[17] מִלַּעֲשׂוֹת (have no knowledge *so as not* to do evil) is read by Siegfr Wild.

610b. [נָאַף] **Pi. 1 a**: transpose 'Ez 23[37]' to foll. 'Ez 16[32]' sub **b**.

611a. נבא, v. in BAram. Appendix.

614b, l. 16: II. [נָבֵל]: **Qal**=*be foolish* †Pr 30[32] is doubted by Frankenberg Toy (where see various renderings), al., who think text crpt.

617b. נֶגֶד **2 a**: note that in NH כְּנֶגֶד=*in front of,* Ber 4[5], 9[5] Ab 2[10], מכנגד פני Git 7[7] al.

629a, l. 16: on Ju 16[25] (rd. '16[26]') v. GFM.

629a. 1. נַחַת **2**: Jb 17[16] rd. נֵחָת (𝔊 Du Dr), √נחת=*descend* (cf. 21[13]).

635a, l. 9: Jb 12[23] rd. prob. וַיַּנְחֵם *and leaves them* (Je 14[9]).

637a, l. 5 from below: נִחוּם <=*comforting, full of comfort* (sc. *is* י״י cf. ARSK [DB Nahum] Dr[Na 1. 1, Century Bible]).

638a. I. נחשׁ, l. 2: after 'Thes' ins. 'on assumption that it is i. q. לחשׁ.'

643b. מַטָּרָה **1**: add Ne 3[25].

646b. מַכָּה, l. 3: after 'etc.;' rd. 'pl. מַכִּים 2 K 8[29]=9[15]=2 Ch 22[6]; מַכּוֹת abs. Zc 13[6]+, cstr.,' etc.

648a, l. 1: Ar. نَكِرَ *be shrewd,* appar. rare, cf. نُكْرٌ *cunning* Lane[2850a].

648b. II. נכר, ll. 5 f.: for 'نَكِرَ in sense *be bad, evil,*' etc., rd. 'نَكِرَ *be ignorant of,* Qor 11[73]; II. *change, alter,* so as not to be known, *disguise* Qor 27[41]; IV=I, also *deny,* Qor 16[85] *repudiate.*'

— l. 9: Syr. ܢܟܪ *reject* is rare (twice), and PS prop. ܢܟܪ *alienavit* each time.

— נֵכָר, l. 1: after 'foreign' ins. '(prop. *unknown,* cf. Ar. √).'

650b. III. מַסָּה: v. Gall [Kultstätten 32] interprets as *place of trial* (ancient judgment-place) and identif. with Ḳadesh, called also (מֵי) מְרִיבָה and עֵין מִשְׁפָּט.

656a. 1. תַּפּוּחַ, v. also Hom [A. u. A. 100, 106, 107]; Tristr [NHB 334 f.] thinks ת׳=*apricot* (so Id.[Smith DB (2) Apple]); M'Lean-Dyer [EB Apple] makes ת׳=*quince.*

658b, l. 7 fr. below: after 'v. Qal' ins. ';=*break up* rafts 1 K 5[23].'

663a. מַצֵּבָה: on this v. also Lagrange [Études Bibl. 197 ff.] and review by Bau [ZMG lvii (1903), 830]; also GFM [EB Massebah] Sta [Bib. Theol. I. § 55] OCWhitehouse [Hast. DB Pillar].

667a. [נָקָה]: 𝔗 נְקָא Pa.=*cleanse* (with lye) Is 1[25]; adj. נְקָא *clean* of bread or fruit Gn 40[16] 𝔗[J1], Dt 6[3] 𝔗[J II], =*exempt* (BH נָקִי) 1 K 15[22].

671a. נָשָׂא **2 b**, l. 8: after 'cf. v[23];' ins. '*incur guilt* Ex 28[43].'

677b. נָתַח: rd. נְתָחֶיהָ also Ez 24[5] for MT רתחיה Hi-Sm Co Berthol Toy Siegf[Kau] Krae Da ('poss.').

691a. שִׂיג 1 K 18[27]: om. 𝔊L, dittogr. for שִׂיחַ Klo Bur.

693a. 1. סוּף **2**: cf. also Che [EB Red Sea].

695ª. [סָחַר], l 3 · add ‘𝔗 סחר, אַסחַר *go about*, סחו̇ר = Heb. סָבִיב’

697ᵇ. סכך . transfer to I. [סָכַךְ]

700ᵇ II סלל, l 3 add ‘cf *sull*, a round wicker basket used by women in Palestine for carrying fruit on their heads to market, Baldensperger PEF 1904, 135.’

703ᵇ. סַרְעַפָּה cf. Syr ܣܘܟܣܟܐ *branches*, Ez 31^{8} al (PS 3946), from √ܣܘܟ *propagavit, germinavit*

711ª סָתַם cf As *bit sutummu, storehouse, treasury*, Zehnpf BAS I. 511

713ª. עָבַד **2** end add Je 25^{14} 27^{7} 30^{8}

717ᵇ עָבַר **3**, l 7: Jb 14^{5} is *pass over, beyond* (cf **1 i**)

718ᵇ עָבַר **Pi 1** after NH ins. ‘מְעֻבֶּרֶת *pregnant*, Yeb 4^{12} 7^{3} Keth 1^{9}’, but note also that in 𝔗ᴶ and Talm (both Aram and Heb.) עבר = *conceive*, עִבּוּר *conception*, עוּבָּר *embryo*

719ᵇ I עֵבֶר **1 B** ad fin cf late As *ebir nari* Schr KB iv 304 l 7 fr below, KAT3 184, 437.

721ª II [עָבוּר] **1 a**: Je 14^{4} < rd ועבדי הָאֲדָמָה חַתּוּ Du, cf. 𝔊.

723ᵇ I עַד, l 4 add ‘so Gn 49^{26} (rd. הַרְרֵי עַד for הוֹרַי עַד)’

— II עַד cf 𝔗 עדי *booty*, Is 10^{2} 33^{23} +

735ª, l 2 fr. below ins ‘עָיִר כָּל־חֹמָתוֹ ψ 78^{34}’

741ª עֲזַרְיָה occurs also Je 43^{2} = (ו)יְזַנְיָה 42^{1} (v p 24^{b} supra), and as friend of Daniel †Dn $1^{6.7.11.19}$

744ª. I עַיִן **1 j**, l 8 after ‘Jb 14^{3}’ ins. ‘שים ע׳ על Gn 44^{21} (J) Je 39^{12} 40^{4}, + לטובה 24^{6}, + לרעה Am 9^{4}’, and in l 9 for ‘v^{40}’ rd. ‘2 Ch 6^{40}’

751ᵇ מֵעַל **2 b** (*b*) (γ) · Hg $2^{15.18}$ *and onwards* (as β) is more prob. v Now We kl Proph ed 3 (1898) Marti Dr

759ᵇ עֲלָטָה · for ‘**thick darkness**’ rd. < **darkness, dusk**, which suits both passages (Bev, privately)

762ª, l 7 Is 57^{11} 𝔊 𝔙 Che Hpt Du Marti rd מַעְלִם for מעולם, cf I. [עָלַם] **Hiph.** ψ 10^{1}.

769ª II [עַם] *kinsman*, later development of I עַם RS K. 88, 2nd ed 72

769ᵇ. I [עִמָּה] **c** ins ‘Ec 7^{14} *side by side with, as well as*’

770ᵇ [עָמַס etc] ad fin add ‘**Hiph.** *Pf* 3 ms הֶעְמִיס 1 K 12^{11} *load* upon (acc rei + על pers) = 2 Ch 10^{11}

776ᵇ, l. 10 fr below: bef. ‘29^{18}’ ins ‘Jb’

777ª, l. 3: rd ‘ψ 9^{13} (Kt), v^{19} (Qr)’

783ᵇ. עָצַר cf As. *usurtu, taboo* SAC JA. 1904, 754.

785ᵇ עַקְרָב : < [**f.**] as in NH Syr Mand. Ar. (Levy gives Talm [Aram] as **m.**, but are rdgs correct ?), No (privately).

789ª. עָרוֹד perh √عَرَدَ [*run away*?], < √‘عرد *schreien* [DHM zu Asma'i, Farq p 43] das auch vom Wildesel vorkommt Amra alqais 4. 21, Zuhair 1 25’—No Fünf Mo all II 75 (SB Wiener Ak cxlii).

790ª מַעֲרָכָה ad fin · add ‘**3.** *order, arrangement*. ’בַּמ Ju 6^{26} *in the* (proper or usual) *arrangement* of an altar, cf. עָרַךְ **1 a** Nu 23^{4} of altar.’

792ª [עָרַק] = Syr. in Lexx, and Pa; but Syr usu *flee*, as 𝔗.

795ª עָשָׂה **Niph. 2 f** transpose ‘+ לְ rei’ to follow ‘*be used*’

799ᵇ [עָשַׁשׁ]: acc to Jacob ZMG 1901 342, ZAW 1902, 107 *be dark*, cf. עששא *darkness*, in Chr-Pal.

— [עַשְׁתֻּנָה] · < [עָשַׁת] Margolis (privately)

806ª. [פּוּג], l. 2 f.: rd ‘Syr ܦܳܓ *become cold* (Mt 24^{12}), *fail, become weak, inefficient;* 𝔗 פוג *become cold, fail, be* or (Pa.) *make ineffectual;* NH *id, fail, vanish.*’

807ᵇ פּוּר Scheft 49f cp. OIran. *fravi*, etc., *progress, fortune, fate, lot*

809ª I פַּח: cf also Baldensperger PEF 1905, 38 (*pah* used now of a trap with a net).

809ᵇ פָּטַר **Hiph.** cf. in Syr. PS 3053.

814ᵇ פֶּן, l. 1 · after ‘Makkeph’ ins. ‘exc. Gn 38^{23} 44^{34} Dt 7^{25} 32^{27} [not Gi], Is 27^{3} Pr 25^{8}: Mandelkern Conc s.v.’

823ª, l. 2 bef. ‘**Pilp.**’ ins. ‘**Hithpō̆**. *Impf.* 3 mpl יִתְפֹּצְצוּ Hb 3^{6} *and* the eternal mts. *were shattered* (al. √פוץ *were scattered*).’

823ᵇ, l. 1. del ‘ψ 8^{6} (|| זָכַר)’—already given (correctly) sub **1 a**

— פָּקַד **Pu.**: Is 38^{10} sense dub, Ges *am* (shall be) *missed for;* Hi Di De Che Comm *am punished, mulcted of*

828ª. פַּרְנֵךְ cf. Palm. פרנך Lzb 354 Cooke 293.

834ᵇ [פָּתָה] **Niph., Pi.** · Je 20^{7} rather *be persuaded, persuade*, **Pu.** Je 20^{10} *be beguiled.*

841ª. צַד, l. 12. tr ‘Dt 31^{26}’ to follow ‘*at the side of*’

— [צָדַד, צְדָד] del. ‘צְדָד,’.

845^{b}, l. 2: for '*erect*' rd. '*heap up* (stones).'

851^{b}. II. ציץ: Aram. צִיץ *wing* dub. Levy^{322b}; Aram. נתִיץ very rare; but note NH צִיץ *filament, small hair.*

852^{a}. II. ציר: cf. Ar. صار (med. *a*) = *turn* or *incline* one's face or neck, or a bough, etc. Lane^{1744}.

853^{b}. צַלְמָוֶת: cf ظُلْمَة *darkness;* We$^{Kl\ Proph\ ed\ 3,\ 81}$ would read fpl. צַלְמוּת, like ظُلُمَات Qor $2^{16\ 18}$, and frequently.

864^{a}. צָרַף, ll. 3, 4: cf. صَرِيف *pure silver*, etc., Schulth$^{GGA,\ 1902,\ 673}$; also Zim$^{GGA\ 1899,\ 250;\ KAT\ 3.\ 650}$ (Heb., etc, borrowed from As).

865^{a}. II. צַר: add Jb 36^{19}.

866^{a}. II. צֹר, l. 7: after 'חֶלְקַת הצ' ins. '2 S 2^{16}.'

879^{a}. קָמָה. 2 K 19^{26} = Is 37^{27} dub, < rd. לְפָנַי . . . קֻמְךָ and join to v^{28}: *before me is thy rising up* and thy sitting down We Bur Du Che^{Hpt} al.; cf. sub שְׁדֵפָה.

904^{a}. קָשַׁב: 2 K 4^{31} (so rd) Baer has קֶשֶׁב

914^{b}. Bef. † רִבִּית ins. art: '† [רָבַב] **Pu. denom.** fr. preceding:—*Pt.* fpl. מְרֻבָּבוֹת ψ 144^{13} *multiplied ten thousand-fold*'

927^{b}. רום **Hiph. 1 d**, l. 2: bef. '49^{22}' ins 'Is.'

931^{a}. מִרְזַח, l. 4: add 'Lzb$^{Ephem\ II\ 281}$ ברבנות מרזחותה די כמרי בל.'

935^{b}. רָחֵק **2 a**: 'ψ 139^{2}' transfer to **b**.

939^{a}. רָכַב **4**: 2 K 7^{14} rd perh. רַכָּבֵי, cf. 𝔊 and 2 K 9^{16} Bur.

945^{a}. I. רָעָה **1 d** (2), l. 3: Je 17^{16} fig. of prophet (but Aq Symm 𝔖 Gie Du Co מֵרָעָה).

950^{b}. רַעַשׁ **1** ad fin: del. 'by warhorse('s hoofs) Jb 39^{24} (+רֹגֶז)', and **3** after '*quivering*' add 'of horse eager to start Jb 39^{24} (+רֹגֶז);'.

954^{a}. רָצִין · As has *Raṣunnu*, hence rd. perh. רצֹן, cf. Wkl$^{KAT\ 3.\ 133}$.

956^{a}. רָקִיעַ **2**: add 'ψ רקיע עֻזּוֹ 150^{1} (sf. ref. to 'י).'

959^{a}. שְׁבָבָה **2**: rd. also 1 K $7^{17\ 17}$ (for שבעה) Bo Th Sta Klo Kmp Benz Kit Bur.

959^{b}. [שָׂבַע] **Pi.**: Now (after 𝔖 and 𝔊 Codd.) reads שִׂבַּעְתָּ Hb 3^{9}, for שְׁבֻעוֹת, cf. GASm; Gr Marti שְׂבֵעַת (adj f. cstr.) thy bow is *sated* with shafts. We thinks hopeless.

967^{b}. מַשְׂכִּית **1**: Lv 26^{1}: on ancient rock-carvings in Canaan cf. Ghosn-el-Howie$^{JBL\ xxiii\ (1904),\ 211\ ff}$.

968^{a}. For 'IV. שׂכך,' etc, substitute: 'IV [שָׂכַךְ] **Pilp.** prick or spur on (cf. Ar. شَاكَ *pierce* (perh denom. from) شَوْك *thorn*, شَوْكَة *point* of spear, etc; Eth. ሦክ: *thorn*);—*prick* or *spur on*, acc pers: *Pf* 1 s. וְסִכְסַכְתִּי Is 19^{2} (+ ב against); *Impf.* 3 ms יְסַכְסֵךְ 9^{10}.'

1076^{a}. תֶּרַח, ll 2, 4: the deriv. was withdrawn afterwards by RS himself, v. RS$^{K\ (2nd\ ed.)\ vii}$.

PRINTED IN
GREAT BRITAIN
AT THE
UNIVERSITY PRESS
OXFORD
BY
JOHN JOHNSON
PRINTER
TO THE
UNIVERSITY

CPSIA information can be obtained
at www.ICGtesting.com
Printed in the USA
LVHW012113270821
696291LV00006B/395

9 781362 854876